SCOTT

2009
Specialized Catalogue of United States Stamps & Covers

EIGHTY-SEVENTH EDITION

CONFEDERATE STATES • CANAL ZONE • DANISH WEST INDIES
GUAM • HAWAII • UNITED NATIONS

UNITED STATES ADMINISTRATION:
Cuba • Puerto Rico • Philippines • Ryukyu Islands

Released October 2008
Includes New Stamp Listings through the October 2008 *Scott Stamp Monthly* Catalogue Update

Scott Publishing Co.

911 Vandemark Road, Sidney, OH 45365-0828
A division of AMOS PRESS, INC., publishers of *Linn's Stamp News, Coin World* and *Scott Stamp Monthly* magazine.

Copyright Notice

Trademark Notice

Please Note

Effective as of 1978, designs of all United States stamps are copyrighted.

Scott Catalogue accepts all advertisements in good faith, but does not endorse or assume any responsibility for the contents of advertisements.

ISBN 0-89487-426-8

Library of Congress Card No. 2-3301

Scott Publishing Mission Statement

The Scott Publishing Team exists to serve the recreational, educational and commercial hobby needs of stamp collectors and dealers.

We strive to set the industry standard for philatelic information and products by developing and providing goods that help collectors identify, value, organize and present their collections.

Quality customer service is, and will continue to be, our highest priority. We aspire toward achieving total customer satisfaction.

Scott Publishing Co.

SCOTT 911 VANDEMARK ROAD, SIDNEY, OHIO 45365 937-498-0802

Dear Scott Catalogue User:

***Noteworthy editorial changes in the* 2009 Scott Specialized Catalogue of United States Stamps and Covers.**

Quite a number of significant editorial changes and enhancements have been made in this year's U.S. Specialized catalogue, and it is possible only to touch on some of the most important topics in this brief letter.

No doubt one of the most important changes is the raising to full major-number status of the perforated 12¢ black Washington stamp from plate 3 issued in 1860. This stamp was minor-number Scott 36b until this year, but it is now major-number 36B. The reasoning behind this change appears in the first of two Special Feature articles in this year's U.S. Specialized. The creation of the 12¢ perforated stamps from plate 3 parallels the creation of the 3¢ 1851-57 varieties that were made major numbers in last year's U.S. Specialized. In fact, the case for the plate 3 12¢ stamp being made a major number is, if anything, even more compelling. The Special Feature article spells out the history of these stamps in some detail, but the basic fact of the matter is that virtually all of the 12¢ stamps from plate 1 had all four of their outer frame lines and often their inner lines at left and right recut on the plate, stamp by stamp. Because the frame lines on the original die were very faint, they were also faint on the transfer roll, and the frame lines that were transferred to the somewhat uneven plates were faint, uneven and often broken in places. When plate 3 was created, the same die and transfer process was used, but a decision was made by the printer not to recut any of the frame lines or inner lines. As a result, the issued stamps from plate 3 retained their uneven, often broken frame lines. The different plate-making techniques created significantly different stamps visually, and these differences are at least as important as the long-accepted differences among many of the 1¢, 3¢ and 10¢ stamps of the same series. The new listings bring the treatment of the 12¢ stamps more closely into line with these other denominations.

A second Special Feature article, this one by collector and respected philatelic researcher Edward (Ted) Liston, explains the editorial decision to delete from the Scott catalogue the so-called "China Clay" Washington/Franklin stamps, formerly accorded minor-number status as Scott 331b-332b and 333a-340a. A great deal of research and testing has led to the inescapable conclusions that the stamps formerly listed as "China Clay" varieties have nothing to do with China clay, were not a paper experiment similar to the Blue Paper experimentation that created Scott 357-366 and 369, and were not a paper-making error (except to the degree that the paper was somewhat to quite a bit under Bureau of Engraving and Printing specifications). Liston's article spells out all the details, and it is essential reading for specialists and generalists alike.

Collectors and dealers will be happy to learn that the Booklet Panes and Covers section has been revamped totally to make it far clearer and easier to use. Three main factors help to explain the enhancement. First, illustrations of complete booklet panes are now shown, rather than the small portions of the panes shown previously. Second, the listings for each booklet immediately follow the illustration of the booklet pane(s) involved, making it easy to match a pane or booklet to the illustration and go directly to the appropriate listing. Third, the booklet covers have been integrated into listings and pane illustrations, so it is no longer necessary to page back to a separate booklet cover section. The Looney Tunes panes and the Wright Brothers Centenary pane previously included within the Booklet Pane section have been removed, because it is felt that these items more closely fit the souvenir sheet definition than the booklet definition. The Booklet Pane section is now somewhat longer than it was before (due to the full pane illustrations), but the editors feel that the enhancement in user-friendliness make this very worthwhile. Take a look, and let us know how you feel.

Many other editorial changes have been made in the 2009 U.S. Specialized catalogue, but there is room here only to mention them without going into detail. New earliest-documented-use dates appear, but only a handful this year (there are still more out there to be discovered, no doubt!). There are new varieties listed in the 1943-44 Overrun Countries issue, Scott 909-921, following an exhaustive review of a major philatelic holding by the editor. There are new, major numbers in the R.F overprints section following the Air Post listings, in the Local stamps section, in the Stamped Envelopes, in the Revenues, in the Essays and Proofs, in the Post Office Seals, in the Test stamps, and in the Confederate States Postmasters' Provisionals. And these additions do not address the more voluminous new minor listings, including a significant number of newly discovered major errors.

Observant collectors might remember that last year a number of listings and footnotes concerning imperforate or part-perforate items from 1979 to 1993 were either deleted or had their footnotes changed, indicating that the stamps were actually proofs on stamp paper from the American Bank Note Co. archives that had been sold into the marketplace. This year a new group of listings appears in the Die and Plate Proof section chronicling in detail these interesting items.

Where are values changing?

More than 14,600 values have been changed in this year's U.S. Specialized catalogue, with more than 4,800 of those changes being in the Postage section and more than 4,600 being in the Revenue section. Other changes are spread rather evenly throughout the remainder of the many sections of the catalogue.

The value increases that we have seen for stamps in grades above very fine in recent years have not translated into higher values for stamps in the grade of very fine or below. In fact, there are numerous small decreases in values in the earlier issues, especially for stamps without gum.

On the other hand, there are some very large value increases among the rarer stamps in the Classic period, including rare 1867 Grills, later Special Printings, Inverted Centers including Scott 121b, Scott 296a and once again Scott C3a, some of the early and rare Coils, and the 1914 Compound Perforations (Scott 423A-423D). A few lower-value Classic stamps did increase in value, including the 3¢ perforated type II, Scott 25A, which climbs to $450 used from $375 used last year.

A bit of softness exists in the modern error market and also in the market for common plate-number coils, and this is reflected in a lowering of many values.

On the upside, some modern stamps show an increase in value, such as the 1995 32¢ Santa Christmas self-adhesive coils, Scott 3014-3017, which jump to $2.50 per mint stamp from $1.50 each last year. Another stamp showing an increase is the 1999 20¢ Pheasant booklet pane of five with one stamp turned sideways, Scott 3051Ab and BK242A. The pane of five moves to $9 this year, and the booklet of two panes moves to $19. The 2004 24¢ Butterfly plate block with water-activated gum, Scott 4000, has made a quick move upward, to $8 mint never hinged from just $2 last year. A number of other sheet, booklet and coil issues show upward movement.

All in all, it has been an interesting philatelic year, and this year's U.S. Specialized catalogue reflects the research, new discoveries, and the ups and downs in the marketplace.

A hobby is a great gift. Enjoy.

James E Kloetzel

James E. Kloetzel/Catalogue Editor

Table of contents

Acknowledgments

Our appreciation and gratitude go to the following individuals and organizations who have assisted us in preparing information included in this year's edition of the Scott Specialized Catalogue of U.S. Stamps and Covers. Some helpers prefer anonymity. Those individuals have generously shared their stamp knowledge with others through the medium of the Scott Catalogue.

Those who follow provided information that is in addition to the hundreds of dealer price lists and advertisements and scores of auction catalogues and realizations which were used in producing the Catalogue Values provided herein. It is from those noted here that we have been able to obtain information on items not normally seen in published lists and advertisements. Support from these people of course goes beyond data leading to Catalogue Values, for they also are key to editorial changes.

Michael E. Aldrich
(Michael E. Aldrich, Inc.)
Roland Austin
Steven R. Belasco
Alan Berkun
John Birkinbine II
Charles R. Biro
Victor Bove (AVB Stamps)
John D. Bowman
(Carriers and Locals Society)
Roger S. Brody
Randall Brooksbank
Lawrence A. Bustillo
(Suburban Stamp Inc.)
James R. Callis, Jr.
(Precancel Stamp Society)
Alan C. Campbell
Gil Celli (Gold Mine Cover Co.)
Richard A. Champagne (Richard A. Champagne, Ltd.)
Leroy P. Collins III (United Postal Stationery Society)
Harry Corrigan
Francis J. Crown, Jr.
Tony L. Crumbley (Carolina Coin & Stamp, Inc.)
Stephen R. Datz
Charles Deaton
Kenneth E. Diehl
Bob Dumaine (Sam Houston Philatelics)
Mark Eastzer (Markest Stamp Co.)
Jeremiah Farrington
Henry Fisher
Jeffrey M. Forster
Robert S. Freeman
Richard Friedberg
Melvin Getlan
Stan Goldfarb
Marty Graff
Harry Hagendorf
Bruce Hecht (Bruce L. Hecht Co.)
Steven Hines
Peter Hoffman
Doug Iams
Tom Jacks (Mountainside Stamps)
Eric Jackson
Michael Jaffe (Michael Jaffe Stamps, Inc.)
Allan Katz (Ventura Stamp Co.)
Lewis Kaufman (The Philatelic Foundation)
Patricia A. Kaufmann (Confederate Stamp Alliance)
Jim Kotanchik
Maurice J. Landry (Maurice J. Landry Covers)
Lester C. Lanphear III
John L. Larson
Richard L. Lazorow
(The Plate Block Stamp Co.)
James E. Lee
Ronald E. Lesher, Sr.
William A. Litle
Larry Lyons
Robert L. Markovits
(Quality Investors, Ltd.)
Frank Marrelli (F & M Stamps)
Peter Martin
William K. McDaniel
Timothy M. McRee
Allen Mintz
William E. Mooz
Gary M. Morris
(Pacific Midwest Co.)
Peter Mosiondz, Jr.
Bruce M. Moyer
(Moyer Stamps & Collectibles)
James Natale
Gerald Nylander
Michael O. Perry
Stanley M. Piller
(Stanley M. Piller & Associates)
Peter W. W. Powell
Louis E. Repeta
Martin D. Richardson
Peter A. Robertson
Peter Robin
Robert G. Rufe
Richard H. Salz
Byron Sandfield
(Park Cities Stamps)
Jacques C. Schiff, Jr.
(Jacques C. Schiff, Jr., Inc.)
Craig Selig
J. Randall Shoemaker (Professional Stamp Experts, Inc.)
Merle Spencer
(The Stamp Gallery)
Frank J. Stanley, III
Alfred E. Staubus
Philip & Henry Stevens (postalstationery.com)
Gordon Stimmell
Jerry Summers
Alan Thomson (Plate Number Coil Collectors' Club)
David R. Torre
Scott R. Trepel (Robert A. Siegel Auction Galleries, Inc.)
Steven R. Unkrich
George P. Wagner
Philip T. Wall
William R. Weiss, Jr.
(Weiss Auctions)
Alan B. Whitman
Kirk Wolford
(Kirk's Stamp Company)
Robert Wurdeman
Robert F. Yacano
(K-Line Philippines)
John P. Zuckerman (Robert A. Siegel Auction Galleries, Inc.)

Expertizing Services

The following organizations will, for a fee, provide expert opinions about stamps submitted to them. Collectors should contact these organizations to find out about their fees and requirements before submitting philatelic material to them. The listing of these groups here is not intended as an endorsement by Scott Publishing Co.

General Expertizing Services

American Philatelic Expertizing Service (a service of the American Philatelic Society)
100 Match Factory Place
Bellefonte PA 16823-1367
Ph: (814) 933-3803
Fax: (814) 933-6128
www.stamps.org
E-mail: apsinfo@stamps.org

Philatelic Foundation
70 West 40th St., 15th Floor
New York NY 10018
Ph: (212) 221-6555
Fax: (212) 221-6208
www.philatelicfoundation.org
E-mail: philatelicfoundation@verizon.net

Professional Stamp Experts
PO Box 6170
Newport Beach CA 92658
Ph: (877) STAMP-88
Fax: (949) 833-7955
www.collectors.com/pse
E-mail: pseinfo@collectors.com

Expertizing Services Covering Specific Fields Or Countries

American First Day Cover Society Expertizing Committee
P.O. Box 141379
Columbus, OH 43214

Confederate Stamp Alliance Authentication Service
c/o Patricia A. Kaufmann
10194 N. Old State Road
Lincoln, DE 19960-9797
Ph: (302) 422-2656
Fax: (302) 424-1990
www.webuystamps.com/csaauth.htm
E-mail: trishkauf@comcast.net

Errors, Freaks and Oddities Collectors Club Expertizing Service
138 East Lakemont Dr.
Kingsland GA 31548
Ph: (912) 729-1573

Hawaiian Philatelic Society Expertizing Service
PO Box 10115
Honolulu HI 96816-0115

Addresses, Telephone Numbers & E-Mail Addresses of General & Specialized Philatelic Societies

Collectors can contact the following groups for information about the philately of the areas within the scope of these societies, or inquire about membership in these groups. Many more specialized philatelic societies exist than those listed below. Aside from the general societies, we limit this list to groups which specialize in areas covered by the Scott U.S. Specialized Catalogue. These addresses were compiled two months prior to publication, and are, to the best of our knowledge, correct and current. Groups should inform the editors of address changes whenever they occur. The editors also want to hear from other such specialized groups not listed.

American Air Mail Society
Stephen Reinhard
P.O. Box 110
Mineola NY 11501
www.americanairmailsociety.org
E-mail: sr1501@aol.com

American First Day Cover Society
Douglas Kelsey
P.O. Box 65960
Tucson AZ 85728-5960
Ph: (520) 321-0880
http://www.afdcs.org
E-mail: afdcs@aol.com

American Philatelic Society
100 Match Factory Place
Bellefonte PA 16823-1367
Ph: (814) 933-3803
http://www.stamps.org
E-mail: apsinfo@stamps.org

American Revenue Association
Eric Jackson
P.O. Box 728
Leesport PA 19533-0728
Ph: (610) 926-6200
http://www.revenuer.org
E-mail: eric@revenuer.com

American Society for Philatelic Pages and Panels
Gerald N. Blankenship
539 North Gum Gully
Crosby TX 77532
Ph: (281) 324-2709
www.asppp.org
E-mail: membership@asppp.org

American Stamp Dealers Association
Matthew Hansen
3 School St.
Glen Cove NY 11542
Ph: (516) 759-7000
http://www.asdaonline.com
E-mail: asda@erols.com

American Topical Association
Ray E. Cartier
P.O. Box 57
Arlington TX 76004-0057
Ph: (817) 274-1181
http://americantopicalassn.org
E-mail: americantopical@msn.com

Canal Zone Study Group
Richard H. Salz
60 27th Ave.
San Francisco CA 94121

Carriers and Locals Society
John D. Bowman
232 Leaf Lane
Alabaster AL 35007
Ph: (205) 621-8449
http://www.pennypost.org
E-mail: johndbowman@charter.net

Christmas Seal & Charity Stamp Society
John Denune
234 East Broadway
Granville OH 43023
Ph: (740) 587-0276
http://cscss.home.att.net
E-mail: webmaster@christmas-seals.net

Confederate Stamp Alliance
Patricia A. Kaufmann
10194 N. Old State Road
Lincoln, DE 19960-9797
www.csalliance.org
E-mail: trishkauf@comcast.net

Errors, Freaks, and Oddities Collectors Club
Stan Raugh
4217 8th Avenue
Temple, PA 19560
Ph: (610) 921-5717
www.efocc.org
E-mail: trex@bigplanet.com

Hawaiian Philatelic Society
Kay H. Hoke
P.O. Box 10115
Honolulu HI 96816-0115
Ph: (808) 521-5721
E-mail: bannan@pixi.com

International Philippine Philatelic Society
Robert F. Yacano
P.O. Box 100
Toast NC 27049
Ph: (336) 783-0768
E-mail: ryacano@triad.rr.com

International Society of Reply Coupon Collectors
Dr. Allan Hauck
P.O. Box 165
Somers WI 53171-0165

National Duck Stamp Collectors Society
Anthony J. Monico
P.O. Box 43
Harleysville PA 19438-0043
http://www.ndscs.org
E-mail: ndscs@hwcn.org

Perfins Club
Kurt Ottenheimer
462 West Walnut St.
Long Beach NY 11561
Ph: (516) 431-3412
E-mail: oak462@juno.com

Plate Number Coil Collectors Club
Ronald E. Maifeld
P.O. Box 54622
Cincinnati OH 45254-0622
http://www.pnc3.org
E-mail: ron.maifeld@pnc3.org

Post Mark Collectors Club
Dave Proulx
7629 Homestead Dr.
Baldwinsville NY 13207
E-mail: stampdance@baldcom.net

Postal History Society
Kalman V. Illyefalvi
8207 Daren Court
Pikesville MD 21208-2211
Ph: (410) 653-0665

Precancel Stamp Society
Arthur Damm
176 Bent Pine Hill
North Wales PA 19454
Ph: (215) 368-6082
E-mail: sandadamm@enter.net

Ryukyu Philatelic Specialists Society
Laura Edmonds, Sec'y
P.O. Box 240177
Charlotte NC 28224-0177

Souvenir Card Collectors Society
Dana Marr
P.O. Box 4155
Tulsa OK 74159-0155
Ph: (918) 664-6724
E-mail: dmarr5569@aol.com

State Revenue Society
Harold Effner, Jr.
27 Pine St.
Lincroft NJ 07738
www.staterevenue.org

United Nations Philatelists
Blanton Clement, Jr.
P. O. Box 146
Morrisville PA 19067-0146
http://www.unpi.com
E-mail: bclemjr@yahoo.com

United Postal Stationery Society
Cora Collins
P.O. Box 1792
Norfolk VA 23501-1792
http://www.upss.org
E-mail: poststat@juno.com

U.S. Cancellation Club
Roger Rhoads
6160 Brownstone Ct.
Mentor OH 44060
http://www/geocities.com/athens/2088/uscchome.html
E-mail: rrrhoads@aol.com

U.S. Philatelic Classics Society
Rob Lund
2913 Fulton
Everett WA 98201-3733
http://www.uspcs.org
E-mail: membershipchairman@uspcs.org

U.S. Possessions Philatelic Society
Geoffrey Brewster
6453 East Stallion Rd.
Paradise Valley AZ 85253-3151
Ph: (480) 607-7184

United States Stamp Society
P.O. Box 6634
Katy TX 77491-6634
http://www.usstamps.org
E-mail: webmaster@usstamps.org

Information on Catalogue Values, Grade and Condition

Catalogue Value

The Scott Catalogue value is a retail value; that is, an amount you could expect to pay for a stamp in the grade of Very Fine with no faults. Any exceptions to the grade valued will be noted in the text. The general introduction on the following pages and the individual section introductions further explain the type of material that is valued. The value listed for any given stamp is a reference that reflects recent actual dealer selling prices for that item.

Dealer retail price lists, public auction results, published prices in advertising and individual solicitation of retail prices from dealers, collectors and specialty organizations have been used in establishing the values found in this catalogue. Scott Publishing Co. values stamps, but Scott is not a company engaged in the business of buying and selling stamps as a dealer.

Use this catalogue as a guide for buying and selling. The actual price you pay for a stamp may be higher or lower than the catalogue value because of many different factors, including the amount of personal service a dealer offers, or increased or decreased interest in the country or topic represented by a stamp or set. An item may occasionally be offered at a lower price as a "loss leader," or as part of a special sale. You also may obtain an item inexpensively at public auction because of little interest at that time or as part of a large lot.

Stamps that are of a lesser grade than Very Fine, or those with condition problems, generally trade at lower prices than the values shown in this catalogue. Stamps of exceptional quality in both grade and condition often command higher prices than the values listed.

Values for pre-1900 unused issues are for stamps with approximately half or more of their original gum. Stamps with most or all of their original gum may be expected to sell for more, and stamps with less than half of their original gum may be expected to sell for somewhat less than the values listed. On rarer stamps, it may be expected that the original gum will be somewhat more disturbed than it will be on more common issues. Post-1900 unused issues are assumed to have full original gum. From breakpoints in most countries' listings, stamps are valued as never hinged, due to the wide availability of stamps in that condition. These notations are prominently placed in the listings and in the country information preceding the listings. Some countries also feature listings with dual values for hinged and never-hinged stamps.

Grade

A stamp's grade and condition are crucial to its value. The accompanying illustrations show examples of Very Fine stamps from different time periods, along with examples of stamps in Fine to Very Fine and Extremely Fine grades as points of reference. When a stamp seller offers a stamp in any grade from fine to superb without further qualifying statements, that stamp should not only have the centering grade as defined, but it also should be free of faults or other condition problems.

FINE stamps (illustrations not shown) have designs that are noticeably off center on two sides. Imperforate stamps may have small margins, and earlier issues may show the design touching one edge of the stamp design. For perforated stamps, perfs may barely clear the design on one side, and very early issues normally will have the perforations slightly cutting into the design. Used stamps may have heavier than usual cancellations.

FINE-VERY FINE stamps may be somewhat off center on one side, or slightly off center on two sides. Imperforate stamps will have two margins of at least normal size, and the design will not touch any edge. For perforated stamps, the perfs are well clear of the design, but are still noticeably off center. *However, early issues of a country may be printed in such a way that the design naturally is very close to the edges. In these cases, the perforations may cut into the design very slightly.* Used stamps will not have a cancellation that detracts from the design.

VERY FINE stamps may be slightly off center on one or two sides, but the design will be well clear of the edge. The stamp will present a nice, balanced appearance. Imperforate stamps will have three normal-sized margins. *However, early issues of many countries may be printed in such a way that the perforations may touch the design on one or more sides. Where this is the case, a boxed note will be found defining the centering and margins of the stamps being valued.* Used stamps will have light or otherwise neat cancellations. This is the grade used to establish Scott Catalogue values.

EXTREMELY FINE stamps are close to being perfectly centered. Imperforate stamps will have even margins that are larger than normal. Even the earliest perforated issues will have perforations clear of the design on all sides.

Scott Publishing Co. recognizes that there is no formally enforced grading scheme for postage stamps, and that the final price you pay or obtain for a stamp will be determined by individual agreement at the time of transaction.

Condition

Grade addresses only centering and (for used stamps) cancellation. *Condition* refers to factors other than grade that affect a stamp's desirability.

Factors that can increase the value of a stamp include exceptionally wide margins, particularly fresh color, the presence of selvage, and plate or die varieties. Unusual cancels on used stamps (particularly those of the 19th century) can greatly enhance their value as well.

Factors other than faults that decrease the value of a stamp include loss of original gum, regumming, a hinge remnant or foreign object adhering to the gum, natural inclusions, straight edges, and markings or notations applied by collectors or dealers.

Faults include missing pieces, tears, pin or other holes, surface scuffs, thin spots, creases, toning, short or pulled perforations, clipped perforations, oxidation or other forms of color changelings, soiling, stains, and such man-made changes as reperforations or the chemical removal or lightening of a cancellation.

Grading Illustrations

On the following page are illustrations of 11 different representative stamps from various time periods, 1847 to the modern era. Beginning with the 1847 10¢ Washington, examples are shown from the 1851-57 imperforates, two examples from the difficult 1857-61 perforated issues, a Black Jack representative of the 1861-67 issues, a Franklin stamp from the 1869 issue, a Bank Note stamp representative of the 1870-88 issues, an 1898 commemorative, a stamp from the 1902-03 issue, a representative 1908-22 Washington-Franklin design, and a 20th century definitive from the 1922 issue.

The editors believe these illustrations will prove useful in showing the margin size and centering that will be seen in the different time periods of U.S. stamp production.

In addition to the matters of margin size and centering, collectors are reminded that the very fine stamps valued in the Scott catalogues also will possess fresh color and intact perforations, and they will be free from defects.

Examples shown are computer-manipulated images made from single digitized master illustrations.

Stamp Illustrations Used in the Catalogue

It is important to note that the stamp images used for identification purposes in this catlaogue may not be indicative of the grade of stamp being valued. Refer to the written discussion of grades on this page and to the grading illustrations on the following two pages for grading information.

1847 ISSUE | 1851-57 ISSUES | 1857-61 ISSUES | 1857-61 ISSUES | 1861-67 ISSUES | 1869 ISSUE

Fine-Very Fine →

SCOTT CATALOGUES VALUE STAMPS IN THIS GRADE

Very Fine →

Extremely Fine →

1870-88 ISSUES | 1898 TRANS-MISSISSIPPIS | 1902-03 ISSUES | 1908-20 WASHINGTON-FRANKLIN ISSUES | 1922-25 ISSUES

Fine-Very Fine →

SCOTT CATALOGUES VALUE STAMPS IN THIS GRADE

Very Fine →

Extremely Fine →

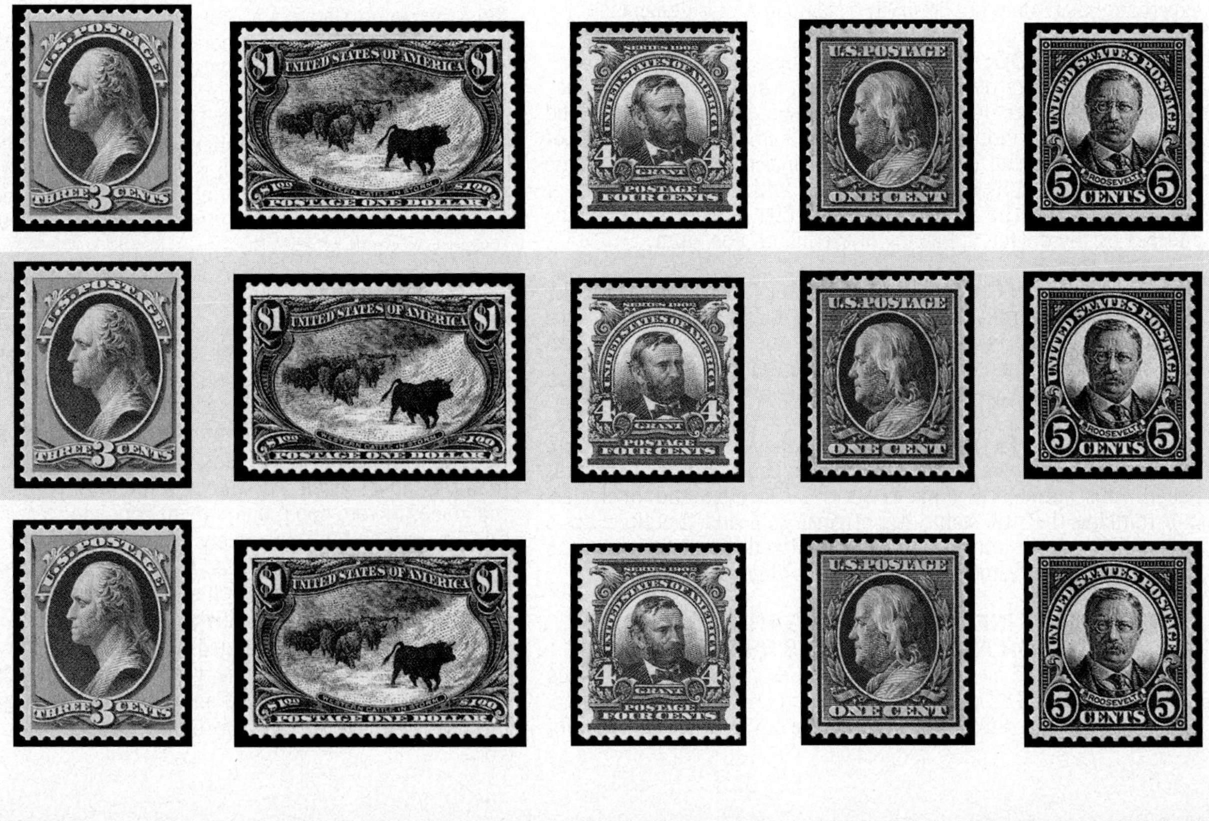

For purposes of helping to determine the gum condition and value of an unused stamp, Scott Publishing Co. presents the following chart which details different gum conditions and indicates how the conditions correlate with the Scott values for unused stamps. Used together, the Illustrated Grading Chart on the previous page and this Illustrated Gum Chart should allow catalogue users to better understand the grade and gum condition of stamps valued in the *Scott U.S. Specialized Catalogue.*

Gum Categories:	MINT N.H.	ORIGINAL GUM (O.G.)				NO GUM

	Mint Never Hinged *Free from any disturbance*	**Lightly Hinged** *Faint impression of a removed hinge over a small area*	**Hinge Mark or Remnant** *Prominent hinged spot with part or all of the hinge remaining*	**Large part o.g.** *Approximately half or more of the gum intact*	**Small part o.g.** *Approximately less than half of the gum intact*	**No gum** *Only if issued with gum*
Commonly Used Symbol:	★★	★	★	★	★	(★)
PRE-1879 ISSUES	*Very fine pre-1890 stamps in these categories trade at a premium over Scott value*			Scott Value for "Unused"		Scott "No Gum" Values thru No. 218
1879-1935 ISSUES	Scott "Never Hinged" Values for Nos. 182-771	Scott Value for "Unused" (Actual value will be affected by the degree of hinging of the full o.g.)				
1935 TO DATE	Scott Value for "Unused"					

Never Hinged (NH; ★★): A never-hinged stamp will have full original gum that will have no hinge mark or disturbance. The presence of an expertizer's mark does not disqualify a stamp from this designation.

Original Gum (OG; ★): Pre-1890 stamps should have approximately half or more of their original gum. On rarer stamps, it may be expected that the original gum will be somewhat more disturbed than it will be on more common issues. Stamps issued in 1890 or later should have full original gum. Original gum will show some disturbance caused by a previous hinge(s) which may be present or entirely removed. The actual value of an 1890 or later stamp will be affected by the degree of hinging of the full original gum.

Disturbed Original Gum: Gum showing noticeable effects of humidity, climate or hinging over more than half of the gum. The significance of gum disturbance in valuing a stamp in any of the Original Gum categories depends on the degree of disturbance, the rarity and normal gum condition of the issue and other variables affecting quality.

Regummed (RG; (★)): A regummed stamp is a stamp without gum that has had some type of gum privately applied at a time after it was issued. This normally is done to deceive collectors and/or dealers into thinking that the stamp has original gum and therefore has a higher value. A regummed stamp is considered the same as a stamp with none of its original gum for purposes of grading.

IMPORTANT INFORMATION REGARDING VALUES FOR NEVER-HINGED STAMPS

Collectors should be aware that the values given for never-hinged stamps from No. 182 on are for stamps in the grade of very fine. The never-hinged premium as a percentage of value will be larger for stamps in extremely fine or superb grades, and the premium will be smaller for fine-very-fine, fine or poor examples. This is particulary true of the issues of the late-19th and early 20th centuries. For example, in the grade of very fine, an unused stamp from this time period may be valued at $100 hinged and $200 never hinged. The never-hinged premium is thus 100%. But in a grade of extremely fine, this same stamp will not only sell for more hinged, but the never-hinged premium will increase, perhaps to 200%-400% or more over the higher extremely fine value. In a grade of superb, a hinged copy will sell for much more than a very fine copy, and additionally the never-hinged premium will be much larger, perhaps as large as 500%-1,000%. On the other hand, the same stamp in a grade of fine or fine-very fine not only will sell for less than a very fine stamp in hinged condition, but additionally the never-hinged premium will be smaller than the never-hinged premium on a very fine stamp, perhaps as small as 15%-30%.

Please note that the above statements and percentages are NOT a formula for arriving at the values of stamps in hinged or never-hinged condition in the grades of very good, fine, fine to very fine, extremely fine or superb. The percentages given apply only to the size of the premium for never-hinged condition that might be added to the stamp value for hinged condition. Further, the percentages given are only generalized estimates. Some stamps or grades may have percentages for never-hinged condition that are higher or lower than the ranges given. For values of the most popular U.S. stamps in the grades of very good, fine, fine to very fine, very fine to extremely fine, extremely fine, extremely fine to superb and superb, see the *Scott United States Specialized Valuing Supplement*, updated and issued twice each year in April and October.

Never-Hinged Plate Blocks

Values given for never-hinged plate blocks are for blocks in which all stamps have original gum that has never been hinged and has no disturbances, and all selvage, whether gummed or ungummed, has never been hinged.

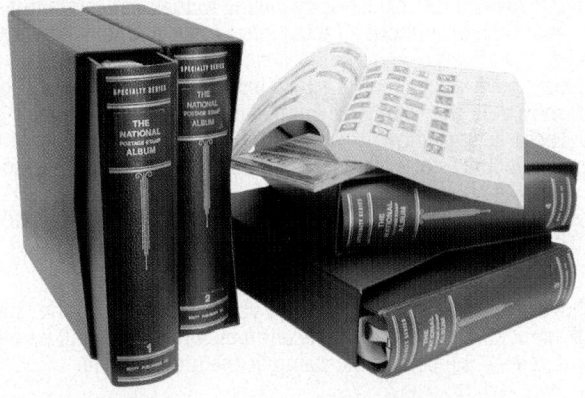

Understanding the Listings

On the opposite page is an enlarged "typical" listing from this catalogue. Following are detailed explanations of each of the highlighted parts of the listing.

1 Scott number — Stamp collectors use Scott numbers to identify specific stamps when buying, selling, or trading stamps, and for ease in organizing their collections. Each stamp issued by a country has a unique number. Therefore, U.S. Scott 219 can only refer to a single stamp. Although the Scott Catalogue usually lists stamps in chronological order by date of issue, when a country issues a set of stamps over a period of time the stamps within that set are kept together without regard to date of issue. This follows the normal collecting approach of keeping stamps in their natural sets.

When a country is known to be issuing a set of stamps over a period of time, a group of consecutive catalogue numbers is reserved for the stamps in that set, as issued. If that group of numbers proves to be too few, capital-letter suffixes are added to numbers to create enough catalogue numbers to cover all items in the set. Scott uses a suffix letter, e.g., "A," "b," etc., only once. If there is a Scott 296B in a set, there will not be a Scott 296b also.

There are times when the block of numbers is too large for the set, leaving some numbers unused. Such gaps in the sequence also occur when the editors move an item elsewhere in the catalogue or remove it from the listings entirely. Scott does not attempt to account for every possible number, but rather it does attempt to assure that each stamp is assigned its own number.

Scott numbers designating regular postage normally are only numerals. Scott numbers for other types of stamps, e.g., air post, special delivery, and so on, will have a prefix of either a capital letter or a combination of numerals and capital letters.

2 Illustration number — used to identify each illustration. Where more than one stamp in a set uses the same illustration number, that number needs to be used with the description line (noted below) to be certain of the exact variety of the stamp within the set. Illustrations normally are 75, 100, or 150 percent of the original size of the stamp. An effort has been made to note all illustrations not at those percentages. Overprints are shown at 100 percent of the original, unless otherwise noted. Letters *in parentheses* which follow an illustration number refer to illustrations of overprints or surcharges.

3 Listing styles — there are two principal types of catalogue listings: major and minor.

Majors may be distinguished by having as their catalogue number a numeral with or without a capital-letter suffix and with or without a prefix.

Minors have a small-letter suffix (or, only have the small letter itself shown if the listing is immediately beneath its major listing). These listings show a variety of the "normal," or major item. Examples include color variation or a different watermark used for that stamp only.

Examples of major numbers are 9X1, 16, 28A, 6LB1, C13, RW1, and TS1. Examples of minor numbers are 22b, 279Bc and C3a.

4 Denomination — normally value printed on the stamp (generally known as the *face value*), which is — unless otherwise stated — the cost of the stamp at the time of issue.

5 Basic information on stamp or set — introducing each stamp issue, this section normally includes the date of issue, method of printing, perforation, watermark, and sometimes additional information. New information on method of printing, watermark or perforation measurement may appear when that information changes. Dates of issue are as precise as Scott is able to confirm, either year only, month and year, or month, day and year.

In stamp sets issued over more than one date, the year or span of years will be in bold type above the first catalogue number. Individual stamps in the set will have a date-of-issue appearing in italics. Stamps without a year listed appeared during the first year of the span. Dates are not always given for minor varieties.

6 Color or other description — this line provides information to solidify identification of the stamp. Historically, when stamps normally were printed in a single color, only the color appeared here. With modern printing techniques, which include multicolor presses which mix inks on the paper, earlier methods of color identification are no longer applicable. When space permits, a description of the stamp design will replace the terms "multi" or "multicolored." The color of the paper is noted in italic type when the paper used is not white.

7 Date of issue — As precisely as Scott is able to confirm, either year only; month and year, or month, day and year. In some cases, the earliest known use (eku) is given. All dates, especially where no official date of issue has been given, are subject to change as new information is obtained. Many cases are known of inadvertent sale and use of stamps prior to dates of issue announced by postal officials. These are not listed here.

8 Value unused and **Value used** — the catalogue values are in U. S. dollars and are based on stamps that are in a grade of Very Fine unless stated otherwise. Unused values refer to items that have not seen postal or other duty for which they were intended. For pre-1890 issues, unused stamps must have at least most of their original gum; for later issues, complete gum is expected. Stamps issued without gum are noted. Unused values are for never-hinged stamps beginning at the point immediately following a prominent notice in the actual listing. Scott values for used self-adhesive stamps are for examples either on piece or off piece.

Some sections in this book have more than two columns for values. Check section introductions and watch for value column headers. See the sections "Catalogue Values" and "Understanding Valuing Notations" for an explanation of the meaning of these values.

9 Changes in basic set information — bold or other type is used to show any change in the basic data between stamps within a set of stamps, e.g., perforation from one stamp to the next or a different paper or printing method or watermark.

10 Other varieties — these include additional shades, plate varieties, multiples, used on cover, plate number blocks. coil line pairs, coil plate number strips of three or five, ZIP blocks, etc.

On early issues, there may be a "Cancellation" section. Values in this section refer to single stamps off cover, unless otherwise noted. Values with a "+" are added to the basic used value. See "Basic Stamp Information" for more details on stamp and cancellation varieties.

11 Footnote — Where other important details about the stamps can be found.

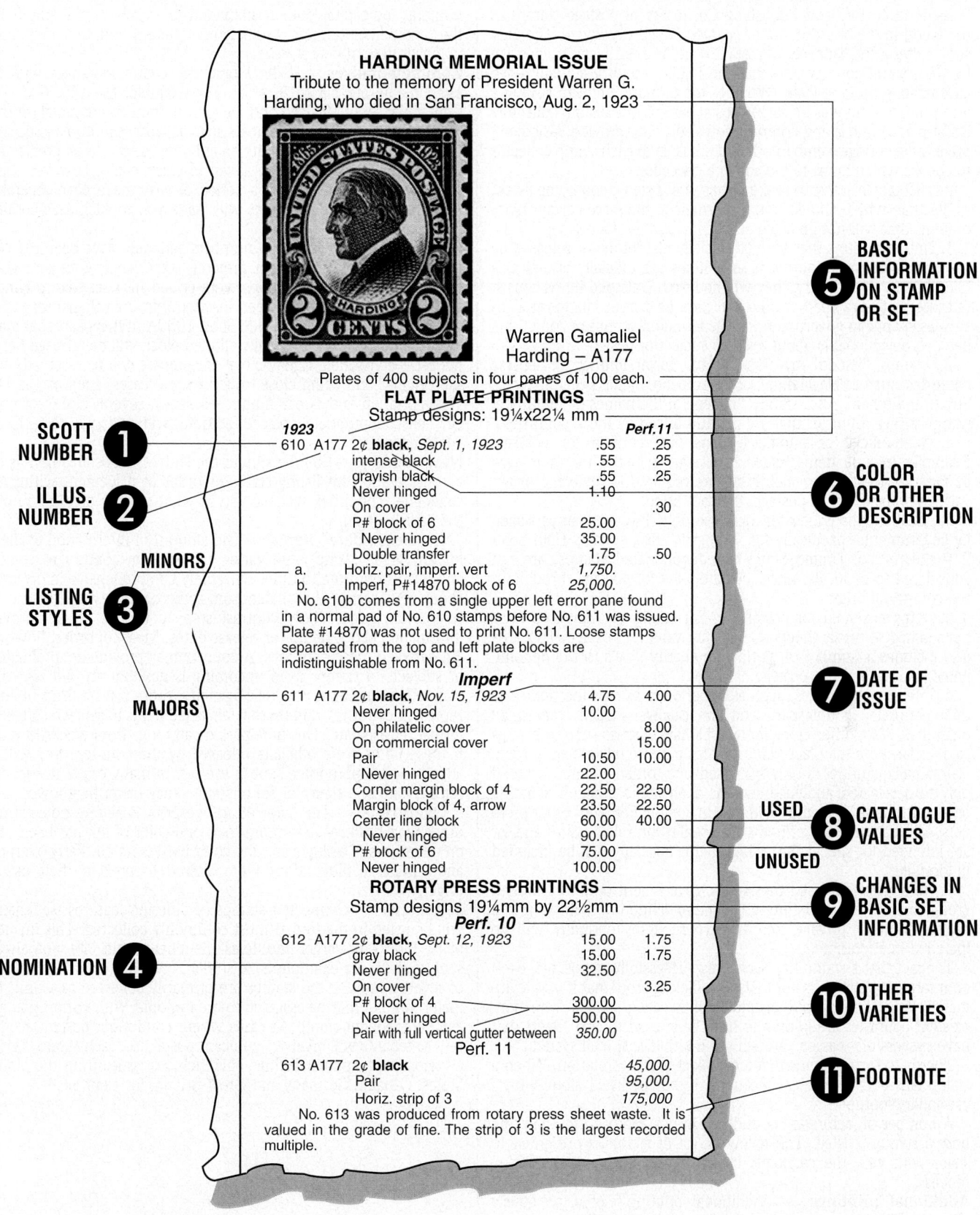

HARDING MEMORIAL ISSUE

Tribute to the memory of President Warren G. Harding, who died in San Francisco, Aug. 2, 1923

Warren Gamaliel Harding – A177

Plates of 400 subjects in four panes of 100 each.

FLAT PLATE PRINTINGS

Stamp designs: 19¼x22¼ mm

1923			***Perf.11***
610 A177	2¢ **black,** *Sept. 1, 1923*	.55	.25
	intense black	.55	.25
	grayish black	.55	.25
	Never hinged	1.10	
	On cover		.30
	P# block of 6	25.00	—
	Never hinged	35.00	
	Double transfer	1.75	.50
a.	Horiz. pair, imperf. vert	*1,750.*	
b.	Imperf, P#14870 block of 6	*25,000.*	

No. 610b comes from a single upper left error pane found in a normal pad of No. 610 stamps before No. 611 was issued. Plate #14870 was not used to print No. 611. Loose stamps separated from the top and left plate blocks are indistinguishable from No. 611.

Imperf

611 A177	2¢ **black,** *Nov. 15, 1923*	4.75	4.00
	Never hinged	10.00	
	On philatelic cover		8.00
	On commercial cover		15.00
	Pair	10.50	10.00
	Never hinged	22.00	
	Corner margin block of 4	22.50	22.50
	Margin block of 4, arrow	23.50	22.50
	Center line block	60.00	40.00
	Never hinged	90.00	
	P# block of 6	75.00	—
	Never hinged	100.00	

ROTARY PRESS PRINTINGS

Stamp designs 19¼mm by 22½mm

Perf. 10

612 A177	2¢ **black,** *Sept. 12, 1923*	15.00	1.75
	gray black	15.00	1.75
	Never hinged	32.50	
	On cover		3.25
	P# block of 4	300.00	
	Never hinged	500.00	
	Pair with full vertical gutter between	*350.00*	

Perf. 11

613 A177	2¢ **black**		*45,000.*
	Pair		*95,000.*
	Horiz. strip of 3		*175,000*

No. 613 was produced from rotary press sheet waste. It is valued in the grade of fine. The strip of 3 is the largest recorded multiple.

1 SCOTT NUMBER

2 ILLUS. NUMBER

3 LISTING STYLES — MINORS / MAJORS

4 DENOMINATION

5 BASIC INFORMATION ON STAMP OR SET

6 COLOR OR OTHER DESCRIPTION

7 DATE OF ISSUE

8 CATALOGUE VALUES — USED / UNUSED

9 CHANGES IN BASIC SET INFORMATION

10 OTHER VARIETIES

11 FOOTNOTE

Catalogue Listing Policy

It is the intent of Scott Publishing Co. to list all postage stamps of the world in the *Scott Standard Postage Stamp Catalogue.* The only strict criteria for listing is that stamps be decreed legal for postage by the issuing country and that the issuing country actually have an operating postal system. Whether the primary intent of issuing a given stamp or set was for sale to postal patrons or to stamp collectors is not part of our listing criteria. Scott's role is to provide basic comprehensive postage stamp information. It is up to each stamp collector to choose which items to include in a collection.

It is Scott's objective to seek reasons why a stamp should be listed, rather than why it should not. Nevertheless, there are certain types of items that will not be listed. These include the following:

1. Unissued items that are not officially distributed or released by the issuing postal authority. If such items are officially issued at a later date by the country, they will be listed. Unissued items consist of those that have been printed and then held from sale for reasons such as change in government, errors found on stamps or something deemed objectionable about a stamp subject or design.

2. Stamps "issued" by non-existent postal entities or fantasy countries, such as Nagaland, Occusi-Ambeno, Staffa, Sedang, Torres Straits and others. Also, stamps "issued" in the names of legitimate, stamp-issuing countries that are not authorized by those countries.

3. Semi-official or unofficial items not required for postage. Examples include items issued by private agencies for their own express services. When such items are required for delivery, or are valid as prepayment of postage, they are listed.

4. Local stamps issued for local use only. Postage stamps issued by governments specifically for "domestic" use, such as Haiti Scott 219-228, or the United States non-denominated stamps, are not considered to be locals, since they are valid for postage throughout the country of origin.

5. Items not valid for postal use. For example, a few countries have issued souvenir sheets that are not valid for postage. This area also includes a number of worldwide charity labels (some denominated) that do not pay postage.

6. Intentional varieties, such as imperforate stamps that look like their perforated counterparts and are usually issued in very small quantities. Also, other egregiously exploitative issues such as stamps sold for far more than face value, stamps purposefully issued in artificially small quantities or only against advance orders, stamps awarded only to a selected audience such as a philatelic bureau's standing order customers, or stamps sold only in conjunction with other products. All of these kinds of items are usually controlled issues and/or are intended for speculation. These items normally will be included in footnotes.

7. Items distributed by the issuing government only to a limited group, such as a stamp club, philatelic exhibition or a single stamp dealer, or other private company. These items normally will be included in a footnote.

The fact that a stamp has been used successfully as postage, even on international mail, is not in itself sufficient proof that it was legitimately issued. Numerous examples of so-called stamps from non-existent countries are known to have been used to post letters that have successfully passed through the international mail system.

There are certain items that are subject to interpretation. When a stamp falls outside our specifications, it may be listed along with a cautionary footnote.

A number of factors are considered in our approach to analyzing how a stamp is listed. The following list of factors is presented to share with you, the catalogue user, the complexity of the listing process.

Additional printings — "Additional printings" of a previously issued stamp may range from an item that is totally different to cases where it is impossible to differentiate from the original. At least a minor number (a small-letter suffix) is assigned if there is a distinct change in stamp shade, noticeably redrawn design, or a significantly different perforation measurement. A major number (numeral or numeral and capital-letter combination) is assigned if the editors feel the "additional printing" is sufficiently different from the original that it constitutes a different issue.

Commemoratives — Where practical, commemoratives with the same theme are placed in a set. For example, the U.S. Civil War Centennial set of 1961-65 and the Constitution Bicentennial series of 1989-90 appear as sets. Countries such as Japan and Korea issue such material on a regular basis, with an announced, or at least predictable, number of stamps known in advance. Occasionally, however, stamp sets that were released over a period of years have been separated. Appropriately placed footnotes will guide you to each set's continuation.

Definitive sets — Blocks of numbers generally have been reserved for definitive sets, based on previous experience with any given country. If a few more stamps were issued in a set than originally expected, they often have been inserted into the original set with a capital-letter suffix, such as U.S. Scott 1059A. If it appears that many more stamps than the originally allotted block will be released before the set is completed, a new block of numbers will be reserved, with the original one being closed off. In some cases, such as the U.S. Transportation and Great Americans series, several blocks of numbers exist. Appropriately placed footnotes will guide you to each set's continuation.

New country — Membership in the Universal Postal Union is not a consideration for listing status or order of placement within the catalogue. The index will tell you in what volume or page number the listings begin.

"No release date" items — The amount of information available for any given stamp issue varies greatly from country to country and even from time to time. Extremely comprehensive information about new stamps is available from some countries well before the stamps are released. By contrast some countries do not provide information about stamps or release dates. Most countries, however, fall between these extremes. A country may provide denominations or subjects of stamps from upcoming issues that are not issued as planned. Sometimes, philatelic agencies, those private firms hired to represent countries, add these later-issued items to sets well after the formal release date. This time period can range from weeks to years. If these items were officially released by the country, they will be added to the appropriate spot in the set. In many cases, the specific release date of a stamp or set of stamps may never be known.

Overprints — The color of an overprint is always noted if it is other than black. Where more than one color of ink has been used on overprints of a single set, the color used is noted. Early overprint and surcharge illustrations were altered to prevent their use by forgers.

Se-tenants — Connected stamps of differing features (se-tenants) will be listed in the format most commonly collected. This includes pairs, blocks or larger multiples. Se-tenant units are not always symmetrical. An example is Australia Scott 508, which is a block of seven stamps. If the stamps are primarily collected as a unit, the major number may be assigned to the multiple, with minors going to each component stamp. In cases where continuous-design or other unit se-tenants will receive significant postal use, each stamp is given a major Scott number listing. This includes issues from the United States, Canada, Germany and Great Britain, for example.

Scott Numbering Practices and Special Notices

Classification of stamps

The *Scott Specialized Catalogue of United States Stamps* lists the stamps of the United States and its possessions and territories and the stamps of the United Nations. The next level is a listing by section on the basis of the function of the stamps or postal stationery. In each case, the items are listed in specialized detail. The principal sections cover regular postage stamps; air post stamps; postage due stamps, special delivery, and so on. Except for regular postage, catalogue numbers for most sections include a prefix letter (or number-letter combination) denoting the class to which the stamp belongs.

The Table of Contents, on page 4A, notes each section and, where pertinent, the prefix used. Some, such as souvenir cards and encased postage, do not have prefixes. Some sections, such as specimens and private perforations, have suffixes only.

New issue listings

Updates to this catalogue appear each month in the *Scott Stamp Monthly.* Included are corrections and updates to the current edition of this catalogue.

From time to time there will be changes in the listings from the *Scott Stamp Monthly* to the next edition of the catalogue, as additional information becomes available.

The catalogue update section of the *Scott Stamp Monthly* is the most timely presentation of this material available. For current subscription rates, see advertisements in this catalogue or write Scott Publishing Co., P.O. Box 828, Sidney, OH 45365-0828.

Additions, deletions & number changes

A list of catalogue additions, deletions, and number changes from the previous edition of the catalogue appears in each volume. See Catalogue Additions, Deletions & Number Changes in the Table of Contents for the location of this list.

Understanding valuing notations

The *absence of a value* does not necessarily suggest that a stamp is scarce or rare. In the U.S. listings, a dash in the value column means that the stamp is known in a stated form or variety, but information is lacking or insufficient for purposes of establishing a usable catalogue value. These could include rarities, such as Scott 3X4 on cover, or items that have a limited market, such as used plate blocks of Scott 1097.

Stamp values in *italics* generally refer to items which are difficult to value accurately. For expensive items, e.g., value at $1,000 or more, a value in italics represents an item which trades very seldom, such as a unique item. For inexpensive items, a value in italics represents a warning.

The Scott Catalogue values for used stamps reflect canceled-to-order material when such are found to predominate in the marketplace for the issue involved. Frequently notes appear in the stamp listings to specify items which are valued as canceled-to-order (Canal Zone Scott O1-O8) or if there is a premium for postally used examples.

Scott values for used stamps are not for precanceled examples, unless so stated. Precanceled copies must not have additional postal cancellations.

An example of a warning to collectors is a stamp that used has a value considerably higher than the unused version. Here, the collector is cautioned to be certain the used version has a readable, contemporaneous cancellation.

The *minimum catalogue value* of a stamp is 20 cents, to cover a dealer's costs of purchase and preparation for resale. The minimum catalogue value of a first day cover is one dollar. As noted, the sum of these values does not properly represent the "value" of a packet of unsorted or unmounted stamps sold in bulk. Such large collections, mixtures or packets generally consist of the lower-valued stamps. There are examples where the catalogue value of a block of stamps is less than the sum of the values of the individual stamps. This situation is caused by the overhead involved in handling single stamps, and should not be considered a suggestion that all blocks be separated into individual stamps to achieve a higher market value.

Values in the "unused" column are for stamps with original gum, if issued with gum. The stamp is valued as hinged if the listing appears *before* the point at which stamps are valued as never hinged. This point is marked by prominent notes in many sections. A similar note will appear at the beginning of the section's listing, noting exactly where the dividing point between hinged and never hinged is for each section of the listings. Where a value for a used stamp is considerably higher than for the unused stamp, the value applies to a stamp showing a distinct contemporaneous cancellation.

Covers

Prices paid for stamps on original covers vary greatly according to condition, appearance, cancellation or postmark and usage. Values given in this volume are for the commonest form with stamps in a grade of very fine "tied on" by the cancellation. A stamp is said to be "tied" to an envelope or card when the cancellation or postmark falls on both the stamp and envelope or card. Letters addressed to foreign countries showing unusual rates and transit markings normally are much in demand and often command large premiums.

Values are for covers bearing a single copy of the stamp referenced and used during the period when the stamp was on sale at post offices unless stated otherwise. If the postage rate was higher than the denomination of the stamp, then the stamp must represent the highest denomination possible to use in making up this rate. In this case, the value is the on-cover value of the stamp plus the used values of the additional stamps. As a general rule, the stamp must be tied to the cover.

Values for patriotic covers of the Civil War period (bearing pictorial designs of a patriotic nature) are for the commonest designs. Approximately 10,000 varieties of designs are known.

Cancellations

A complete treatment of this subject is impossible in a catalogue of this limited size. Only postal markings of meaning — those which were necessary to the proper function of the postal service — are recorded here, while those of value owing to their fanciness only are disregarded. The latter are the results of the whim of some postal official. Many of these odd designs, however, command high prices, based on their popularity, scarcity and clearness of impression.

Although there are many types of most of the cancellations listed, only one of each is illustrated. The values quoted are for the most common type of each.

Values for cancellation varieties are for stamp specimens off cover. Some cancellation varieties (e.g., pen, precancel, cut) are valued individually. Other varieties on pre-1900 stamps (e.g., less common colors, specific dates, foreign usages) are valued using premiums (denoted by "+") which are added to the stated value for the used stamp. When listed on cover, the distinctive cancellation must be on the stamp in order to merit catalogue valuation. Postal markings that denote origin or a service (as distinguished from canceling a stamp) merit catalogue valuation when on a cover apart from the stamp, provided the stamp is otherwise tied to the cover by a cancellation.

One type of "Paid" cancellation used in Boston, and shown in this introduction under "Postal Markings," is common and values given are for types other than this.

Examination

Scott Publishing Co. will not pass upon the genuineness, grade or condition of stamps, because of the time and responsibility involved. Rather, there are several expertizing groups which undertake this work for both collectors and dealers. Neither will Scott Publishing Co. appraise or identify philatelic material. The Company cannot take responsibility for unsolicited stamps or covers sent by individuals.

All letters, E-mails, etc. are read attentively, but they are not always answered due to time considerations

How to order from your dealer

It is not necessary to write the full description of a stamp as listed in this catalogue. All that you need is the name of the country or *U.S. Specialized* section, the Scott Catalogue number and whether the item is unused or used. For example, "U.S. Scott 833" is sufficient to identify the stamp of the United States listed as the 2-dollar value of a set of stamps issued between 1938-43. This stamp was issued September 29, 1938. It is yellow green and black in color, has a perforation of 11, and is printed on paper without a watermark by a flat plate press. Sections without a prefix or suffix must be mentioned by name.

Abbreviations

Scott Publishing Co. uses a consistent set of abbreviations throughout this catalogue and the *Standard Postage Stamp Catalogue* to conserve space while still providing necessary information. The first block shown here refers to color names only:

COLOR ABBREVIATIONS

amb	amber	ind	indigo
anil	aniline	int	intense
ap	apple	lav	lavender
aqua	aquamarine	lem	lemon
az	azure	lil	lilac
bis	bister	lt	light
bl	blue	mag	magenta
bld	blood	man	manila
blk	black	mar	maroon
bril	brilliant	mv	mauve
brn	brown	multi	multicolored
brnsh	brownish	mlky	milky
brnz	bronze	myr	myrtle
brt	bright	ol	olive
brnt	burnt	olvn	olivine
car	carmine	org	orange
cer	cerise	pck	peacock
chlky	chalky	pnksh	pinkish
cham	chamois	Prus	Prussian
chnt	chestnut	pur	purple
choc	chocolate	redsh	reddish
chr	chrome	res	reseda
cit	citron	ros	rosine
cl	claret	ryl	royal
cob	cobalt	sal	salmon
cop	copper	saph	sapphire
crim	crimson	scar	scarlet
cr	cream	sep	sepia
dk	dark	sien	sienna
dl	dull	sil	silver
dp	deep	sl	slate
db	drab	stl	steel
emer	emerald	turq	turquoise
gldn	golden	ultra	ultramarine
grysh	grayish	ven	venetian
grn	green	ver	vermilion
grnsh	greenish	vio	violet
hel	heliotrope	yel	yellow
hn	henna	yelsh	yellowish

When no color is given for an overprint or surcharge, black is the color used. Abbreviations for colors used for overprints and surcharges

Additional abbreviations used in this catalogue are shown below:

Adm. .... Administration
AFL .... American Federation of Labor
Anniv. .... Anniversary
APU .... Arab Postal Union
APS .... American Philatelic Society
ASEAN .... Association of South East Asian Nations
ASPCA .... American Society for the Prevention of Cruelty to Animals
Assoc. .... Association

b. .... Born
BEP .... Bureau of Engraving and Printing
Bicent. .... Bicentennial
Bklt. .... Booklet
Brit. .... British
btwn. .... Between
Bur. .... Bureau

c. or ca. .... Circa
CAR .... Central African Republic
Cat. .... Catalogue
Cent. .... Centennial, century, centenary
CEPT .... Conference Europeenne des Administrations des Postes et des Telecommunications
CIO .... Congress of Industrial Organizations
Conf. .... Conference
Cong. .... Congress
Cpl. .... Corporal
CTO .... Canceled to order

d. .... Died
Dbl. .... Double
DDR .... German Democratic Republic (East Germany)

EC .... European Community
ECU .... European currency unit
EEC .... European Economic Community
EKU .... Earliest known use
Engr. .... Engraved
Exhib. .... Exhibition
Expo. .... Exposition

FAO .... Food and Agricultural Organization of the United Nations
Fed. .... Federation
FIP .... Federation International de Philatelie

GB .... Great Britain
Gen. .... General
GPO .... General post office

Horiz. .... Horizontal

ICAO .... International Civil Aviation Organization
ICY .... International Cooperation Year
ILO .... International Labor Organization
Imperf. .... Imperforate
Impt. .... Imprint
Intl. .... International
Invtd. .... Inverted
IQSY .... International Quiet Sun Year
ITU .... International Telecommunications Union
ITY .... International Tourism Year
IWY .... International Women's Year
IYC .... International Year of the Child
IYD .... International Year of the Disabled
IYSH .... International Year of Shelter for the Homeless
IYY .... International Youth Year

L. .... Left
Lieut. .... Lieutenant
Litho. .... Lithographed

LL............Lower left
LR ....Lower right

mm............Millimeter
Ms.............Manuscript

NASA ....National Aeronautics and Space Administration
Natl. ....National
NATO.........North Atlantic Treaty Organization
No. ....Number
NY.............New York
NYC ....New York City

OAU..........Organization of African Unity
OPEC ....Organization of Petroleum Exporting Countries
Ovpt. ....Overprint
Ovptd. ....Overprinted

P#..............Plate number
Perf............Perforated, perforation
Phil............Philatelic
Photo.........Photogravure
PO ....Post office
Pr...............Pair
P.R. ....Puerto Rico
PRC...........People's Republic of China (Mainland China)
Prec. ....Precancel, precanceled
Pres. ....President

R ....Right
Rio.............Rio de Janeiro
ROC ....Republic of China (Taiwan)

SEATO........South East Asia Treaty Organization
Sgt. ....Sergeant
Soc. ....Society
Souv. ....Souvenir
SSR............Soviet Socialist Republic
St................Saint, street
Surch...........Surcharge

Typo. ....Typographed

UAE...........United Arab Emirate
UAMPT ......Union of African and Malagasy Posts and Telecommunications
UL ....Upper left
UN ....United Nations
UNESCO ....United Nations Educational, Scientific and Cultural Organization
UNICEF......United Nations Children's Fund
Univ ....University
UNPA ....United Nations Postal Administration
Unwmkd ....Unwatermarked
UPU ....Universal Postal Union
UR.............Upper Right
US ....United States
USPO ....United States Post Office Department
USPS ....United States Postal Service (also "U.S. Postage Stamp" when referring to the watermark)
USSR ....Union of Soviet Socialist Republics

Vert ....Vertical
VP ....Vice president

WCY ....World Communications Year
WFUNA......World Federation of United Nations Associations
WHO.........World Health Organization
Wmk ....Watermark
Wmkd ....Watermarked
WMO ....World Meteorological Organization
WRY.........World Refugee Year
WWF.........World Wildlife Fund
WWI ....World War I
WWII ....World War II

YAR ....Yemen Arab Republic
Yemen PDR. Yemen People's Democratic Republic

Postmasters General of the United States

1775 Benjamin Franklin, July 26.
1776 Richard Bache, Nov. 7.
1782 Ebenezer Hazard, Jan. 28.
1789 Samuel Osgood, Sept. 26.
1791 Timothy Pickering, Aug. 12.
1795 Joseph Habersham, Feb. 25.
1801 Gideon Granger, Nov. 28.
1814 Return J. Meigs, Jr., Apr. 11.
1823 John McLean, July 1.
1829 William T. Barry, Apr. 6.
1835 Amos Kendall, May 1.
1840 John M. Niles, May 26.
1841 Francis Granger, Mar. 8.
1841 Charles A. Wickliffe, Oct. 13.
1845 Cave Johnson, Mar. 7.
1849 Jacob Collamer, Mar. 8.
1850 Nathan K. Hall, July 23.
1852 Samuel D. Hubbard, Sept. 14.
1853 James Campbell, Mar. 8.
1857 Aaron V. Brown, Mar. 7.
1859 Joseph Holt, Mar. 14.
1861 Horatio King, Feb. 12.
1861 Montgomery Blair, Mar. 9.
1864 William Dennison, Oct. 1.
1866 Alexander W. Randall, July 25.
1869 John A.J. Creswell, Mar. 6.
1874 Jas. W. Marshall, July 7.
1874 Marshall Jewell, Sept. 1.
1876 James N. Tyner, July 13.
1877 David McK. Key, Mar. 13.
1880 Horace Maynard, Aug. 25.
1881 Thomas L. James, Mar. 8.
1882 Timothy O. Howe, Jan. 5.
1883 Walter Q. Gresham, Apr. 11.
1884 Frank Hatton, Oct. 14.
1885 Wm. F. Vilas, Mar. 7.
1888 Don M. Dickinson, Jan. 17.
1889 John Wanamaker, Mar. 6.
1893 Wilson S. Bissell, Mar. 7.
1895 William L. Wilson, Apr. 4.
1897 James A. Gary, Mar. 6.
1898 Charles Emory Smith, Apr. 22.
1902 Henry C. Payne, Jan. 15.
1904 Robert J. Wynne, Oct. 10.
1905 Geo. B. Cortelyou, Mar. 7.
1907 Geo. von L. Meyer, Mar. 4.
1909 Frank H. Hitchcock, Mar. 6.
1913 Albert S. Burleson, Mar. 5.
1921 Will H. Hays, Mar. 5.
1922 Hubert Work, Mar. 4.
1923 Harry S. New, Mar. 4.
1929 Walter F. Brown, Mar. 6.
1933 James A. Farley, Mar. 4.
1940 Frank C. Walker, Sept. 11.
1945 Robert E. Hannegan, July 1.
1947 Jesse M. Donaldson, Dec. 16.
1953 Arthur E. Summerfield, Jan. 21.
1961 J. Edward Day, Jan. 21.
1963 John A. Gronouski, Sept. 30.
1965 Lawrence F. O'Brien, Nov. 3.
1968 W. Marvin Watson, Apr. 26.
1969 Winton M. Blount, Jan. 22.

U.S. POSTAL SERVICE

1971 Elmer T. Klassen, Dec. 7.
1975 Benjamin Bailar, Feb. 15.
1978 William F. Bolger, Mar. 1.
1985 Paul N. Carlin, Jan. 1.
1986 Albert V. Casey, Jan. 6.
1986 Preston R. Tisch, Aug. 17.
1988 Anthony M. Frank, Mar. 1.
1992 Marvin T. Runyon, Jr., July 6.
1998 William J. Henderson, May 16.
2001 John E. Potter, June 1

Basic Stamp Information

A stamp collector's knowledge of the combined elements that make a given issue of a stamp unique determines his or her ability to identify stamps. These elements include paper, watermark, method of separation, printing, design and gum. On the following pages these important areas are described in detail.*

The guide below will direct you to those philatelic terms which are not major headings in the following introductory material. The major headings are:

Plate	Paper	Gum	Postal Markings
Printing	Perforations	Luminescence	General Glossary

Guide to Subjects

Tete Beche .... See General Glossary
Tied On .... See Postal Markings
Transfer .... See Plate
Transfer Roll .... See Plate
Triple Transfer .... See Plate
Type .... See General Glossary
Typeset .... See Printing
Typeset Stamps .... See Printing
Typography .... See Printing
Vertical Half .... See General Glossary (Bisect)
Watermarks .... See Paper
Wet Printings .... See Note after Scott 1029
Wove Paper .... See Paper

Plate

Die

Transfer Roll

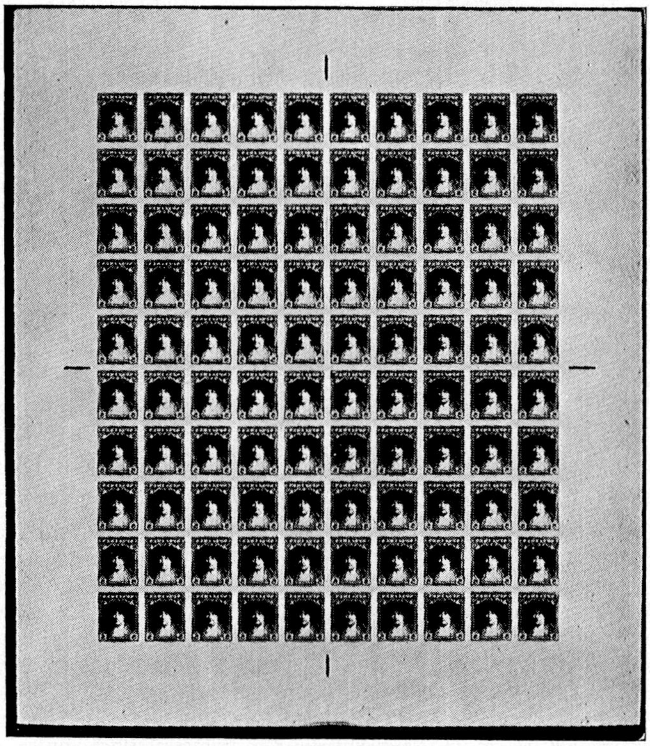

Plate

LINE ENGRAVING (INTAGLIO)

Die — Making the die is the initial operation in developing the intaglio plate. The die is a small flat piece of soft steel on which the subject (design) is recess-engraved in reverse. Dies are usually of a single-subject type, but dies exist with multiple subjects of the same design, or even different designs. After the engraving is completed, the die is hardened to withstand the stress of subsequent operations.

Transfer Roll — The next operation is making the transfer roll, which is the medium used to transfer the subject from the die to the plate. A blank roll of soft steel, mounted on a mandrel, is placed under the bearers of a transfer press. The hardened die is placed on the bed of the press and the face of the roll is brought to bear on the die. The bed is then rocked backed and forth under increasing pressure until the soft steel of the roll is forced into every line of the die. The resulting impression on the roll is known as a "relief" or "relief transfer." Several reliefs usually are rocked in on each roll. After the required reliefs are completed, the roll is hardened.

Relief — A relief is the normal reproduction of the design on the die, in reverse. A defective relief, caused by a minute piece of foreign material lodging on the die, may occur during the rocking-in process, or from other causes. Imperfections in the steel of the transfer roll may also result in a breaking away of parts of the design. If the damaged relief is continued in use, it will transfer a repeating defect to the plate. Also reliefs sometime are deliberately altered. "Broken relief" and "altered relief" are terms used to designate these changed conditions.

Plate — A flat piece of soft steel replaces the die on the bed of the transfer press and one of the reliefs on the transfer roll is brought to bear on this soft steel. The position of the plate is determined by position dots, which have been lightly marked on the plate in advance. After the position of the relief is determined, pressure is brought to bear and, by following the same method used in the making of the transfer roll, a transfer is entered. This transfer reproduces, in reverse, every detail of the design of the relief. As many transfers are entered on the plate as there are to be subjects printed at one time.

After the required transfers have been entered, the positions dots, layouts and lines, scratches, etc., are burnished out. Also, any required guide lines, plate numbers, or other marginal markings are added. A proof impression is then taken and if certified (approved), the plate is machined for fitting to the press, hardened and sent to the plate vault until used.

Rotary press plates, after being certified, require additional machining. They are curved to fit the press cylinder and gripper slots are cut into the back of each plate to receive the grippers, which hold the plate securely to the press. The rotary press plate is not hardened until these additional processes are completed.

Transfer — An impression entered on the plate by the transfer roll. A relief transfer is made when entering the design of the die onto the transfer roll.

Double Transfer — The condition of a transfer on a plate that shows evidences of a duplication of all or a portion of the design. A double transfer usually is the result of the changing of the registration between the relief and the plate during the rolling of the original entry.

Occasionally it is necessary to remove the original transfer from a plate and enter the relief a second time. When the finished re-transfer shows indications of the original transfer, because of incomplete erasure, the result is known as a double transfer.

Triple Transfer — Similar to a double transfer, this situation shows evidences of a third entry or two duplications.

Foreign Entry — When original transfers are erased incompletely from a plate, they can appear with new transfers of a different design which are entered subsequently on the plate.

Re-entry — When executing a re-entry, the transfer roll is reapplied to the plate at some time after the latter has been put to press. Thus, worn-out designs may be resharpened by carefully re-entering the transfer roll. If the transfer roll is not carefully entered, the registration will not be true and a double transfer will result. With the protective qualities of chromium plating, it is no longer necessary to resharpen the plate. In fact, after a plate has been curved for the rotary press, it is impossible to make a re-entry.

Shifted Transfer (Shift) — In transferring, the metal displaced on the plate by the entry of the ridges, constituting the design on the transfer roll, is forced ahead of the roll as well as pressed out at the sides. The amount of displaced metal increases with the depth of the entry. When the depth is increased evenly, the design will be uniformly entered. Most of the displaced metal is pressed ahead of the roll. If too much pressure is exerted on any pass (rocking), the impression on the previous partial entry may be floated (pushed) ahead of the roll and cause a duplication of the final design. The duplication appears as an increased width of frame lines or a doubling of the lines.

The ridges of the displaced metal are flattened out by the hammering or rolling back of the plate along the space occupied by the subject margins.

Short Transfer — Occasionally the transfer roll is not rocked its entire length in the entering of a transfer onto a plate, with the result that the finished transfer fails to show the complete design. This is known as a short transfer.

Short transfers are known to have been made deliberately, as in the Type III of the 1-cent issue of 1851-60 (Scott 8, 21), or accidentally, as in the 10-cent 1847 (Scott 2).

Re-engraved — Either the die that has been used to make a plate or the plate itself may have its temper drawn (softened) and be recut. The resulting impressions for such re-engraved die or plate may differ very slightly from the original issue and are given the label "re-engraved."

Re-cut — A re-cut is the strengthening or altering of a line by use of an engraving tool on unhardened plates.

Retouching — A retouch is the strengthening or altering of a line by means of etching.

PLATE ARRANGEMENT

Arrangement — The first engraved plates used to produce U.S. postage stamps in 1847 contained 200 subjects. The number of subjects to a plate varied between 100 and 300 until the issue of 1890, when the 400-subject plate was first laid down. Since that time, this size of plate has been used for a majority of the regular postal issues (those other than commemoratives). Exceptions to this practice exist, particularly among the more recent issues, and are listed under the headings of the appropriate issues in the catalogue.

Sheet — In single-color printings, the complete impression from a plate is termed a sheet. A sheet of multicolored stamps (two or more colors) may come from a single impression of a plate, i.e., many Giori-type press printings from 1957, or from as many impressions from separate plates as there are inks used for the particular stamp. Combination process printings may use both methods of multicolor production: Giori-type intaglio with offset lithography or with photogravure.

The Huck multicolor press used plates of different format (40, 72 or 80 subjects). The sheet it produced had 200 subjects for normal-sized commemoratives or 400 subjects for regular-issue stamps, similar to the regular products of other presses.

See the note on the Combination Press following the listing for Scott 1703.

In casual usage, a "pane" often is referred to as a "sheet."

Pane — A pane is the part of the original sheet that is issued for sale at post offices. A pane may be the same as an entire sheet, where the plate is small, or it may be a half, quarter, or some other fraction of a sheet where the plate is large.

The illustration shown later under the subtopic "Plate Markings" shows the layout of a 400-subject sheet from a flat plate, which for issuance would have been divided along the intersecting guide lines into four panes of 100.

Panes are classified into normal reading position according to their location on the printed sheet: U.L., upper left; U.R., upper right; L.L., lower left; and L.R., lower right. Where only two panes appear on a sheet, they are designed "R" (right) and "L" (left) or "T" (top) and "B" (bottom), on the basis of the division of the sheet vertically or horizontally.

To fix the location of a particular stamp on any pane, except for those printed on the Combination press, the pane is held with the subjects in the normal position, and a position number is given to each stamp starting with the first stamp in the upper left corner and proceeding horizontally to the right, then staring on the second row at the left and counting across to the right, and so on to the last stamp in the lower right corner.

In describing the location of a stamp on a sheet of stamps issued prior to 1894, the practice is to give the stamp position number first, then the pane position and finally the plate number, i.e., "1R22." Beginning with the 1894 issue and on all later issues the method used is to give the plate number first, then the position of the pane, and finally the position number of the stamp, i.e., "16807LL48" to identify an example of Scott 619 or "2138L2" to refer to an example of Scott 323.

BOOKLET STAMPS

Plates for Stamp Booklets — These are illustrated and described preceding the listing of booklet panes and covers in this catalogue.

Booklet Panes — Panes especially printed and cut to be sold in booklets which are a convenient way to purchase and store stamps. U.S. Booklet panes are straight-edged on three sides, but perforated between the stamps. Die cut, ATM and other panes will vary from this. Except for BK64 and BK65, the A.E.F. booklets, booklets were sold by the Post Office Department for a one-cent premium until 1962. Other sections of this catalogue with listings for booklet panes include Savings, Telegraphs and Canal Zone.

A.E.F. Booklets — These were special booklets prepared principally for use by the U.S. Army Post Office in France during World War I. They were issued in 1-cent and 2-cent denominations with 30 stamps to a pane (10 x 3), bound at right or left. As soon as Gen. John J. Pershing's organization reached France, soldiers' mail was sent free by means of franked envelopes.

Stamps were required during the war for the civilian personnel, as well as for registered mail, parcel post and other types of postal service. See the individual listings for Scott 498f and 499f and booklets BK64 and BK65.

COIL STAMPS

First issued in 1908-09, coils (rolls) originally were produced in two sizes, 500 and 1,000 stamps, with the individual stamps arranged endways or sideways and with and without perforations between.

Rolls of stamps for use in affixing or vending machines were first constructed by private companies and later by the Bureau of Engraving and Printing. Originally, it was customary for the Post Office Department to sell to the private vending companies and others imperforate sheets of stamps printed from the ordinary 400-subject flat plates. These sheets were then pasted together end-to-end or side-to-side by the purchaser and cut into rolls as desired, with the perforations being applied to suit the requirements of the individual machines. Such stamps with private perforations are listed in this catalogue under "Vending and Affixing Machine Perforations."

Later the Bureau produced coils by the same method, also in rolls of 500 and 1,000. These coils were arranged endways or sideways and were issued with or without perforation.

With the introduction of the Stickney rotary press, curved plates made for use on these presses were put into use at the Bureau of Engraving and Printing, and the sale of imperforate sheets was discontinued. This move marked the end of the private perforation. Rotary press coils have been printed on a number of presses over the years and have been made in sizes of 100, 500, 1,000, 3,000 and 10,000 stamps, etc.

Paste-up — the junction of two flat-plate printings joined by pasting the edge of one sheet onto the edge of another sheet to make coils. A two-stamp example of this joining is a "paste-up pair." See Splice.

Guide Line Pair — attached pair of flat-plate-printed coil stamps with printed line between. This line is identical with the guide line (See listing under "Plate Markings") found in sheets.

Joint Line — The edges of two curved plates do not meet exactly on the press and the small space between the plates takes ink and prints a line. A pair of rotary-press-printed stamps with such a line is called a "joint line pair."

Coil stamps printed on the Multicolor Huck Press do not consistently produce such lines. Occasionally accumulated ink will print partial lines in one or more colors, and very occasionally complete lines will be printed. Stamps resulting from such situations are not listed in this Catalogue. The "B" and "C" presses do not print joint lines at all.

Splice — the junction of two rotary-press printings by butting the ends of the web (roll) of paper together and pasting a strip of perforated translucent paper on the back of the junction. The two-stamp specimen to show this situation is a "spliced pair."

Splices occur when a web breaks and is repaired or when one web is finished and another begins.

Plate Number — for U.S. coil stamps prior to Scott 1891, Scott 1947, War Savings Coils and Canal Zone:

On a rotary-press horizontal coil the top or bottom part of a plate number may show. On a vertical coil, the left or right part of a plate number may show. The number was entered on the plate to be cut off when the web was sliced into coils and is found only when the web was sliced off center. Every rotary press coil plate number was adjacent to a joint line, so both features could occur together in one strip.

For U.S. stamps from Scott 1891 onward (excluding Scott 1947) and Official coils:

The plate number is placed in the design area of the stamp, so it will not be trimmed off. Such items are normally collected unused with the stamp containing the plate number in the center of a strip of three or five stamps. They normally are collected used as singles. The line, if any, will be at the right of the plate-number stamp. On the Cottrell press, the number occurs every 24th stamp, on the "B" press every 52nd stamp, on the "C," "D" and "F" presses every 48th stamp.

Unused plate number strips of three and five are valued in this catalogue.

Hidden Plate Number — A plate number may be found entirely on a coil made from flat plates, but usually is hidden by a part of the next sheet which has been lapped over it.

Coil Waste — an occurrence brought about by stamps issued in perforated sheets from a printing intended for coils. These stamps came from short lengths of paper at the end of the coil run. Sometimes the salvaged sections were those which had been laid aside for mutilation because of some defect. Because the paper had been moistened during printing, it sometimes stretched slightly and provided added printing area. Sheets of 70, 100, and 170 are known. See Scott 538-541, 545-546, 578-579, and 594-595.

"T" — Letter which appears in the lower design area of Scott 2115b, which was printed on a experimental pre-phosphored paper. The stamp with the plate number is inscribed "T1."

SHEET STAMPS

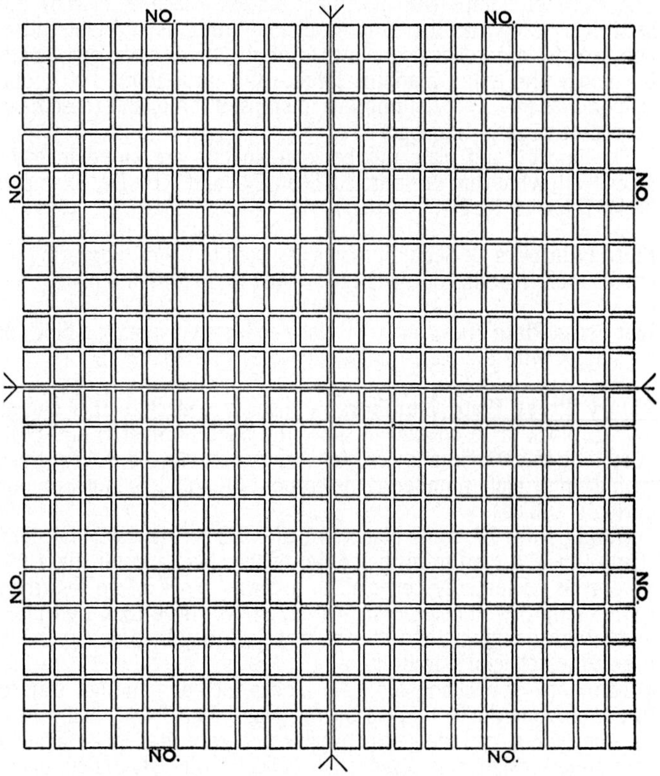

A typical 400-subject plate of 1922

Plate Markings — The illustration above shows a typical 400-subject plate of the 1922 issue with markings as found on this type of plate. Other layouts and markings are found further in the Catalogue text.

Guide Lines — Horizontal or vertical colored lines between the stamps, extending wholly or partially across the sheet. They serve as guides for the operators of perforating machines or to indicate the point of separation of the sheet into panes.

A block of stamps divided by any of the guide lines is known as a "line block" or "guide line block." The block of stamps from the exact center of the sheet, showing the crossed guide lines, is a "center line block."

Gutters — When guide lines are used to mark the division of the sheet into panes, the space between the stamps at the edge of the pane is no different than the space between any other stamps on the sheet. Some plates provide a wide space, or gutter, between the panes. These plates do not produce guide lines.

A pair of stamps with the wide space between is known as a "gutter pair", and blocks with that situation are "gutter blocks." A block of stamps from the exact center of the sheet, showing the two wide spaces crossing, is a "center gutter block" or "cross gutter block."

Gutter pairs or gutter blocks must contain complete stamps on both sides of the gutter, intact including perforation teeth unless imperforate. The stamps on either side of the gutter may or may not be creased; either way they qualify as the listed variety.

Arrows — arrow-shaped markings were used in the margins of stamp sheets, in place of guide lines, on the issues of 1870 through 1894. Since 1894, guide lines with arrows at both ends have been the standard practice on flat-plate printings.

A margin block of at least four stamps, showing the arrow centered at one edge, is known as a "margin block with arrow."

Color Registration Markings — marks of different sizes and shapes used as an aid in properly registering the colors in producing a bicolored or multicolored stamp.

Imprint — design containing the name of the producer of the stamps which appears on the sheet margin usually near the plate number.

A block of stamps with the sheet margin attached, bearing the imprint, is known as the "imprint block." Imprints and plate numbers usually are collected in blocks of six, or of sufficient length to include the entire marking. From 1894 until about 1907, one fashion was to collect the imprints in strips of three, and these have been noted in this Catalogue.

The imprint and plate number combination are found in eight types I-VII, which are illustrated at Scott 245 and Scott E3. Example: "T V" refers to Type V.

Plate Numbers — Serial numbers assigned to plates, appearing on one or more margins of the sheet or pane to identify the plate.

Flat Press Plate Numbers — usually collected in a margin block of six stamps with the plate number centered in the margin.

Rotary Press Plate Numbers — usually collected in a corner margin block large enough to show the plate number(s) and position along the margin and complete selvage on two sides. For issues with a single plate number at the corner of the pane a block of four normally suffices.

During 1933-39, some plates had the number opposite the third stamp (up or down) from the corner of the sheet and for these the number is customarily collected in a corner block of no less than eight stamps. Multicolored stamps may have more than one plate number in the margin and the "plate block" may then be expanded to suit the collector's desire.

The Catalogue listing for plate blocks includes enough stamps to accommodate all numbers on the plate. Plate block listings for se-tenant issues include all the designs as part of the block. When a continuous design is involved, such as Scott 1629-31, the complete design will be included in the plate number block. The entire pane constitutes the plate number block for issues such as the State Birds and Flowers (Scott 1953-2002).

Plate numbers take a further designation from the position on the sheet on which they appear, e.g. U.L. refers to upper left pane, etc.

See note following Scott 1703 for description of combination press markings.

Private Contractor Marks — On rotary plates from Scott 1789 onward: "A" denotes issues produced by private contractor American Bank Note Co., "B" by Banknote Corp of America, "D" by Dittler Brothers, "G" by Guilford Gravure, "K" by KCS Industries, "M" by 3M Corp., "P" by Ashton-Potter (USA) Ltd., "S" by Stamp Venturers, Inc. (now Sennett Security Products), "U" by U.S. Bank Note Co., "V" by Avery Dennison.

Stars — used on the flat plates to indicate a change from the previous spacing of the stamps. They also were used as a check on the assignment of the printed sheets to a perforating machine of the proper setting. Stars appear on certain rotary plates used for printing stamps for coils, appearing adjacent to the plate joint line and above stamp No. 1 on the 170-subject plates, and to the left of stamp No. 141 on the 150-subject plates.

"A" — On flat plates; used on plates having uniform vertical spacing between rows of subjects, but wider than those with the star marking.

"C.S." and "C" — plate has been chromium plated.

"E.I." — abbreviation for Electrolytic Iron. The designation is for plates made by the electrolytic process.

"F" — used to indicate the plate is ready for hardening. This appears only on flat plates and generally precedes the upper right plate number.

"O" — Plate has undergone an experimental oil-hardening process during manufacture.

"Top" — marking on the top sheet margin of printings from both plates of some bicolored issues. This marking is used to check printings for "inverts." Beginning with the 6-cent bicolored airpost issue of 1938 (Scott C23), bicolored crosses also were used as an additional check.

"Coil Stamps" — appearing on the side sheet margins, designates plates used in the production of endwise coils.

"S 20," "S 30," "S 40" — marginal markings appearing on certain 150- and 170-subject rotary press plates to designate experimental variations in the depth and character of the frame line to over-come excess inking. "S 30" was adopted as the standard. Blocks showing these markings are listed as "Margin Block with S 20," etc., in this Catalogue.

Initials — used in sheet margins to identify individuals in the Bureau of Engraving and Printing who participated in the production or use of the plates.

Gutter Dashes — on the first 400-subject rotary plates, 3⁄16-inch horizontal dashes appear in the gutter between the 10th and 11th vertical rows of stamps. This arrangement was superseded by dashes 3⁄16-inch at the extreme ends of the vertical and horizontal gutters, and a ¼-inch cross at the central gutter intersection. This latter arrangement continued until replaced by the scanning marks on the Electric Eye plates. See Electric Eye.

Margin — border outside the printed design or perforated area of a stamp, also known as selvage, or the similar border of a sheet of stamps. A block of stamps from the top, side or bottom of a sheet or pane to which is attached the selvage (margin) is known as a "margin block." A block of stamps from the corner of a sheet with full selvage attached to two adjoining sides is known as a "corner block."

NOTE — The descriptions and definitions above indicate that a certain number of stamps make up an arrow or plate number block. Any block of stamps, no matter how large or small, which had an arrow or plate number on its margin would be considered by that name. The usual practice is to collect flat-plate numbers in margin blocks of six and arrow blocks in margin blocks of four. Plate number blocks from rotary press printings generally are collected in blocks of 4 when the plate number appears beside the stamp at any of the four corners of the sheet. Particularly relative to bi-colored stamps, an arrow block is now separated from a plate number block. Thus, in those situations, the two individual types of blocks might form a block of eight or 10, as the situation dictates.

PRINTING

Methods Used — all four basic forms of printing have been used in producing U.S. stamps, engraved, photogravure, lithography, and typography. Holography has been used on some envelopes.

Engraved (Recess or Intaglio) — process where ink is received and held in lines depressed below the surface of the plate. Initially, in printing from such plate damp paper was forced into the depressed lines and therefore picked up ink. Consequently, ink lines on the stamp are slightly raised. This also is noted from the back of the stamp, where depressions mark where ink is placed on the front.

When the ornamental work for a stamp is engraved by a machine, the process is called "engine turned" or lathe-work engraving. An example of such lathe-work background is the 3-cent stamp of 1861 (Scott Illustration No. A25).

Engraved stamps were printed only with flat plates until 1914, when rotary press printing was introduced. "Wet" and "dry" printings are explained in the note in the text of the Catalogue following Scott 1029. The Giori press, used to print some U.S. stamps from 1957 (see Scott 1094, 4-cent Flag issue), applied two or three different colored inks simultaneously.

The Huck Multicolor press, put into service at the Bureau of

Engraving and Printing in 1968, was used first to produce the 1969 Christmas stamp (Scott 1363) and the 6-cent flag coil of 1969 (Scott 1338A). Developed by the Bureau's technical staff and the firm of graphic arts engineers whose name it bears, the Huck press printed, tagged with phosphor ink, gummed and perforated stamps in a continuous operation. Printing was accomplished in as many as nine colors. Fed by paper from a roll, the Huck Multicolor used many recess-engraved plates of smaller size than any used previously for U.S. stamp printing. Its product has certain characteristics which other U.S. stamps do not have. Post office panes of the 1969 Christmas stamp, for example, show seven or eight plate numbers in the margins. Joint lines appear after every two or four stamps. Other presses providing multiple plate numbers are the Andreotti, Champlain, Combination, Miller Offset, A Press, D Press and more.

Photogravure — the design of a stamp to be printed by photogravure usually is photographed through an extremely fine screen, lined in minute quadrille. The screen breaks up the reproduction into tiny dots, which are etched onto the plate and the depressions formed hold the ink. Somewhat similarly to engraved printing, the ink is lifted out of the lines by the paper, which is pressed against the plate. Unlike engraved printing, however, the ink does not appear to be raised relative to the surface of the paper.

Gravure is most often used for multicolored stamps, generally using the three primary colors (red, yellow and blue) and black. By varying the dot matrix pattern and density of these colors, virtually any color can be reproduced. A typical full-color gravure stamp will be created from four printing cylinders (one for each color). The original multicolored image will have been photographically separated into its component colors.

For U.S. stamps, photogravure first appeared in 1967 with the Thomas Eakins issue (Scott 1335). The early photogravure stamps were printed by outside contractors until the Bureau obtained the multicolor Andreotti press in 1971. The earliest stamp printed on that press was the 8-cent Missouri Statehood issue of 1971 (Scott 1426).

Color control bars, dashes or dots are printed in the margin of one pane in each "Andreotti" sheet of 200, 160 or 128 stamps. These markings generally are collected in blocks of 20 or 16 (two full rows of one pane), which include the full complement of plate numbers, Mr. Zip and the Zip and Mail Early slogans.

Details on the Combination Press follow the listing for Scott 1703.

Modern gravure printing may use computer-generated dot-matrix screens, and modern plates may be of various types including metal-coated plastic. The catalogue designation of Photogravure (or "Photo") covers any of these older and more modern gravure methods of printing.

Lithography — this is the most common and least expensive process for printing stamps. In this method, the design is drawn by hand or transferred in greasy ink from an original engraving to the surface of a lithographic stone or metal plate. The stone or plate is wet with an acid fluid, which causes it to repel the printing ink except at the greasy lines of the design. A fine lithographic print closely resembles an engraving, but the lines are not raised on the face or depressed on the back. Thus there usually is a more dull appearance to the lithograph than to the engraving.

Offset Printing or Offset Lithography — a modern development of the lithographic process. Anything that will print — type, woodcuts, photoengravings, plates engraved or etched in intaglio, halftone plates, linoleum blocks, lithographic stones or plates, photogravure plates, rubber stamps, etc. — may be used. Greasy ink is applied to the dampened plate or form and an impression made on a rubber blanket. Paper immediately is pressed against the blanket, which transfers the ink. Because of its greater flexibility, offset printing has largely displaced lithography.

Because the processes and results obtained are similar, stamps printed by either of these two methods normally are considered to be "lithographed."

The first application of lithographic printing for any U.S. items listed in this Catalogue was for Post Office seals, probably using stone printing bases. See also some Confederates States general issues. Offset lithography was used for the 1914 documentary revenues (Scott R195-R216). Postage stamps followed in 1918-20 (Scott 525-536) because of war-time shortages of ink, plates, and manpower relative to the regular intaglio production.

The next use of offset lithography for postage stamps was in 1964 with the Homemakers issue (Scott 1253), in combination with intaglio printing. Many similar issues followed, including the U.S. Bicentennial souvenir sheets of 1976 (Scott 1686-1689), all of which were produced by the combination of the two printing methods. The combination process serves best for soft backgrounds and tonal effects.

Typography — an exact reverse of engraved-plate printing, this process provides for the parts of the design which are to show in color to be left at the original level of the plate and the spaces between cut away. Ink is applied to the raised lines and the pressure of the printing forces these lines, more or less into the paper. The process impresses the lines on the face of the stamp and slightly raises them on the back. Normally, a large number of electrotypes of the original are made and assembled into a plate with the requisite number of designs for printing a sheet of stamps. Stamps printed by this process show greater uniformity, and the stamps are less expensive to print than with intaglio printing.

The first U.S. postal usage of an item printed by typography, or letterpress, under national authority was the 1846 "2" surcharge on the United States City Despatch Post 3-cent carrier stamp (Scott 6LB7). The next usage was the 1865 newspaper and periodical stamp issue, which for security reasons combined the techniques of machine engraving, colorless embossing and typography. This created an unusual first.

Most U.S. stamp typography consists of overprints, such as those for the Canal Zone, the Molly Pitcher and Hawaii Sesquicentennial stamps of 1928 (Scott 646-648), the Kansas-Nebraska control markings (Scott 658-679), Bureau-printed precancels, and "specimen" markings.

Embossed (relief) Printing — method in which the design is sunk in the metal of the die and the printing is done against a platen that is forced into the depression, thus forming the design on the paper in relief. Embossing may be done without ink (blind embossing), totally with ink, or a combination thereof. The U.S. stamped envelopes are an example of this form of printing.

Typeset — made from movable type.

Typeset Stamps — printed from ordinary printer's type. Sometimes electrotype or stereotype plates are made, but because such stamps usually are printed only in small quantities for temporary use, movable type often is used for the purpose. This method of printing is apt to show broken type and lack of uniformity. See Hawaii Scott 1-4 and 12-26.

Holograms — for objects to appear as holograms on stamps, a model exactly the same size as it is too appear on the hologram must be created. Rather than using photographic film to capture the image, holography records an image on a photoresist material. in processing, chemicals eat away at certain exposed areas, leaving a pattern of constructive and destructive interference. When the photoresist is developed, the result is a pattern of uneven ridges that acts as a mold. This mold is then coated with metal, and the resulting form is used to press copies in much the same way phonograph records are produced.

A typical reflective hologram used for stamps consists of a reproduction of the uneven patterns on a plastic film that is applied to a reflective background, ususally a silver or gold foil. Light is reflected off the background through the film, making the pattern present on the film visible. Because of the uneven pattern of the film, the viewer will perceive the objects in their proper three-dimensional relationships with appropriate brightness.

The first hologram on a stamp was produced by Austria in 1988 (Scott 1441).

Foil Application — A modern tecnique of applying color to stamps involves the application of metallic foil to the stamp paper. A pattern of foil is applied to the stamp paper by use of a stamping die. The foil usually is flat, but it may be textured. Canada Scott 1735 has three different foil applications in pearl, bronze, and gold. The gold foil was texured using a chemical-etch copper embossing die. The printing of this stamp also involved two-colored offset lithography plus embossing.

ADDITIONAL TERMS

Multicolored Stamps — until 1957 when the Giori press was introduced, bicolored stamps were printed on a flat-bed press in two runs, one for each color (example: Norse-American Issue of 1925, Scott 620-621). In the flat-press bicolors, if the sheet were fed to the press on the second run in reversed position, the part printed in the second color would be upside down, producing an "invert" such as the famed Scott C3a.

With the Giori press and subsequent presses, stamps could be printed in more than one color at the same time.

Many bicolored and multicolored stamps show varying degrees of poor color registration (alignment). Such varieties are not listed in this Catalogue.

Color Changeling — a stamp which, because of exposure to the environment, has naturally undergone a change of ink colors. Orange U.S. stamps of the early 1900's are notorious for turning brown as the ink reacts with oxygen. Exposure to light can cause some inks to fade. These are not considered color omitted errors. Exposure to other chemicals can cause ink colors to change. These stamps are merely altered stamps, and their value to collectors is greatly diminished.

Color Trials — printings in various colors, made to facilitate selection of color for the issued stamp.

Double Impression — a second impression of a stamp over the original impression.

This is not to be confused with a "double transfer," which is a plate imperfection and does not show a doubling of the entire design. A double impression shows every line clearly doubled. See also "Printed on Both Sides."

Essay — A proposed design, a designer's model or an incomplete engraving. Its design differs in some way — great or small — from the issued item.

Inverted Center — bicolored or multicolored stamp with the center printed upside down relative to the remainder of the design. A stamp may be described as having an inverted center even if the center is printed first. See "Multicolored Stamps."

Flat Plate Printing — stamp printed on a flat-bed press, rather than on a rotary press. See "Plate."

Overprint — any word, inscription or device printed across the face of a stamp to alter its use or locality or otherwise to serve a special purpose. An example is U.S. Scott 646, the "Molly Pitcher" overprint, which is Scott 634 with a black overprinted inscription as a memorial to the Revolutionary War heroine. See "Surcharge."

Printed on Both Sides — Occasionally a sheet of stamps already printed will, through error, be turned over and passed through the press a second time, creating the rare "printed on both sides" variety. On one side the impression is almost always poor or incomplete. This often is confused with an "offset," which occurs when sheets of stamps are stacked while the ink is still wet.

The "printed on both sides" variety will show the design as a positive (all inscriptions reading correctly) and the offset shows a reverse impression. See "Double Impression."

Progressive Proof — a type of essay that is an incomplete engraving of the finished accepted die.

Proofs — trial printings of a stamp made from the original die or the finished plate.

Reprints and Reissues — are impressions of stamps (usually obsolete) made from the original plates or stones. If they are valid for postage and reproduce obsolete issues (such as U.S. Scott 102-111), the stamps are *reissues.* If they are from current issues, they are designated as *second, third,* etc., *printing.* If designated for a particular purpose, they are called *special printings.*

When special printings are not valid for postage, but are made from original dies and plates by authorized persons, they are *official reprints. Private reprints* are made from the original plates and dies by private hands. An example of a private reprint is that of the 1871-1932 reprints made from the original die of the 1845 New Haven, Conn., postmaster's provisional. *Official reproductions* or imitations are made from new dies and plates by government authorization. Scott will list those reissues that are valid for postage if they differ significantly from the original printing.

The U.S. government made special printings of its first postage stamps in 1875. Produced were official imitations of the first two stamps (listed as Scott 3-4), reprints of the demonetized pre-1861 issues (Scott 40-47) and reissues of the 1861 stamps, the 1869 stamps and the then-current 1875 denominations. Even though the official imitations and the reprints were not valid for postage, Scott lists all of these U.S. special printings.

Most reprints or reissues differ slightly from the original stamp in some characteristic, such as gum, paper, perforation, color or watermark. Sometimes the details are followed so meticulously that only a student of that specific stamp is able to distinguish the reprint or reissue from the original.

Rotary Press Printings — stamps which have been printed on a rotary-type press from curved plates. Rotary press-printed stamps are longer or wider than stamps of the same design printed from flat plates. All rotary press printings through 1953, except coil waste (such as Scott 538), exist with horizontal "gum breaker ridges" varying from one to four per stamp. See: "Plate."

Surcharge — overprint which alters or restates the face value or denomination of the stamp to which it was applied. An example is Scott K1, where U.S. stamps were surcharged for use by U.S. Offices in China. Many surcharges are typeset. See: "Overprint" and "Typeset."

COMMON FLAWS

Cracked Plate — A term to describe stamps which show evidences that the plate from which they were printed was cracked.

Plate cracks have various causes, each which may result in a different formation and intensity of the crack. Cracks similar to the above illustration are quite common in older issues and are largely due to the plate being too-quickly immersed in the cooling bath when being tempered. These cracks are known as crystallization cracks. A jagged line running generally in one direction and most often in the gutter between stamps is due to the stress of the steel during the rolling in or transferring process.

In curved (rotary) plates, there are two types of cracks. Once is the bending or curving crack, which is quite marked and always runs in the direction in which the plate is curved.

The accompanying illustration shows the second type, the gripper crack. This type is caused by the cracking of the plate over the slots cut in the underside of the plate, which receive the "grippers" that fasten the plate to the press. These occur only on curved plates and are to be found in the row of stamps adjoining the plate joint. These appear on the printed impression as light irregularly colored lines, usually parallel to the plate joint line.

Rosette Crack — cluster of fine cracks radiating from a central point in irregular lines. These usually are caused by the plate receiving a blow.

Scratched Plate — caused by foreign matter scratching the plate, these usually are too minor to mention. See: "Gouge."

Gouge — exceptionally heavy and usually short scratches, these may be caused by a tool falling onto the plate.

Surface Stains — irregular surface marks resembling the outline of a point on a map. Experts differ on the cause. These are too minor to list.

PAPER

Paper falls broadly into two types: wove and laid. The difference in the appearance is caused by the wire cloth upon which the pulp is first formed.

Paper also is distinguished as thick or thin, hard or soft, and by its color (such as bluish, yellowish, greenish, etc.).

Wove — where the wire cloth is of even and closely woven nature, producing a sheet of uniform texture throughout. This type shows no light or dark figures when held to the light.

Laid — where the wire cloth is formed of closely spaced parallel wires crossed at much wider intervals by cross wires. The resultant paper shows alternate light and dark lines. The distances between the widely spaced lines and the thickness of these lines may vary, but on any one piece of paper they will be the same.

Pelure — type of paper which is very thin and semi-transparent. It may be either wove or laid.

Bluish — The 1909 so-called "bluish" paper was made with 35 percent rag stock instead of all wood pulp. The bluish (actually grayish-blue) color goes through the paper, showing clearly on back and face. See the note with Scott 331.

Manila — a coarse paper formerly made of Manila hemp fiber. Since about 1890, so-called "manila" paper has been manufactured entirely from wood fiber. It is used for cheaper grades of envelopes and newspaper wrappers and normally is a natural light brown. Sometimes color is added, such as in the U.S. "amber manila" envelopes. It may be either wove or laid.

Silk — refers to two kinds of paper found by stamp collectors.

One type has one or more threads of silk embedded in the substance of the paper, extending across the stamp. In the catalogues, this type of paper usually is designated as "with silk threads."

The other type, used to print many U.S. revenue stamps, has shortsilk fibers strewn over it and impressed into it during manufacture. This is simply called "silk paper."

Ribbed — paper which shows fine parallel ridges on one or both sides of a stamp.

India — a soft, silky appearing wove paper, usually used for proof impressions.

Double Paper — as patented by Charles F. Steel, this style of paper consists of two layers, a thin surface paper and a thicker backing paper. Double paper was supposed to be an absolute safeguard against cleaning cancellations off stamps to permit reuse, for any attempt to remove the cancellation would result in the destruction of the upper layer. The Continental Bank Note Co. experimented with this paper in the course of printing Scott 156-165. See "Rotary Press Double Paper."

China Clay Paper — See note preceding Scott 331.

Fluorescent or Bright Paper — See "Luminescence."

Rotary Press Double Paper — Rotary press printings occasionally are found on a double sheet of paper. The web (roll) of paper used on these press must be continuous. Therefore, any break in the web during the process of manufacture must be lapped and pasted. The overlapping portion, when printed upon, is known as a "double paper" variety. More recently, the lapped ends are joined with colored or transparent adhesive tape.

Such results of splicing normally are removed from the final printed material, although some slip through quality control efforts.

In one instance known, two splices have been made, thus leaving three thicknesses of paper. All rotary press stamps may exist on double paper.

Watermarks — Closely allied to the study of paper, watermarks normally are formed in the process of paper manufacture. Watermarks used on U.S. items consist of the letters "USPS" (found on postage stamps). "USPOD" (found on postal cards), the Seal of the United States (found on official seals), "USIR" (found on revenue items), and various monograms of letters, numbers, and so on, found on stamped envelopes.

The letters may be single- or double-lined and are formed from dies made of wire or cut from metal and soldered to the frame on which the pulp is caught or to a roll under which it is passed. The action of these dies is similar to the wires causing the prominent lines of laid paper, with the designs making thin places in the paper which show by more easily transmitting light.

The best method of detecting watermarks is to lay the stamp face down on a dark tray and immerse the stamp in a commercial brand of watermark fluid, which brings up the watermark in dark lines against a lighter background. When collectors discuss watermarks, they refer to their appearance as viewed from the back of the stamp.

Note: This method of detecting watermarks may damage certain stamps printed with inks that run when immersed (such as U.S. Scott 1260 and 1832). It is advisable to first test a damaged stamp of the same type, if possible.

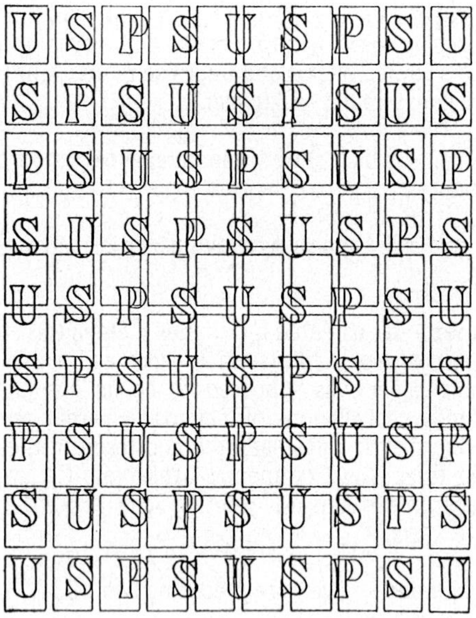

Wmk. 191
PERIOD OF USE
Postage: 1895-1910 Revenue: none

In the 1895-1903 U.S. issues, the paper was fed through the press so that the watermark letter read horizontally on 400 subject sheets and vertically on 200 subject sheets.

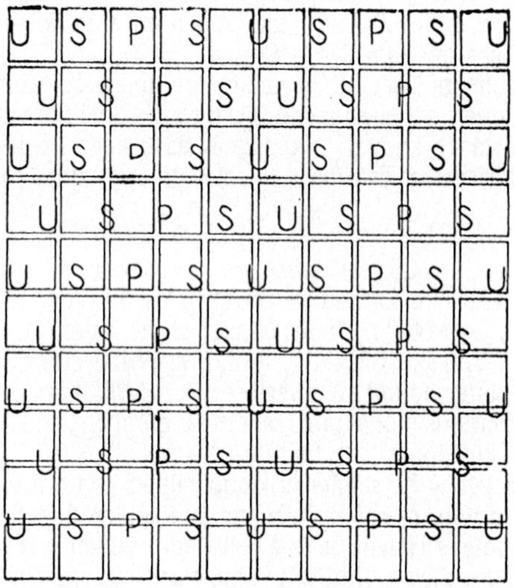

Wmk. 190
PERIOD OF USE
Postage: 1910-1916 Revenue: 1914

Wmk. 191R
PERIOD OF USE
Postage (unintentionally): 1895 (Scott 271a, 272a), 1951 (832b) Revenue: 1878-1958

Paper watermarked "USPOD" was used for postal cards from 1873 to 1875. For watermarks used on stamped envelopes, see Envelope Section in the text.

Watermarks may be found normal, reversed, inverted, inverted reversed and sideways, as seen from the back of the stamp.

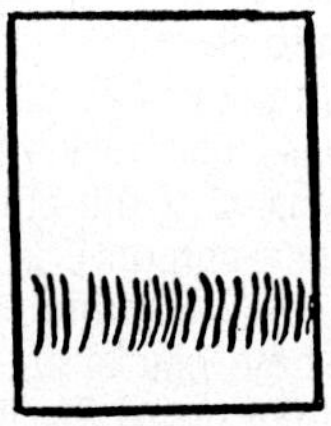

Stitch Watermark — a type of watermark consisting of a row of short parallel lines. This is caused by the stitches which join the ends of the band on which the paper pulp is first formed. Stitch watermarks have been found on a great many issues, and may exist on all.

GRILLS

The grill consists of small square pyramids in parallel rows, impressed or embossed on the stamp. The object of the process is to break the fibers of the paper so that the ink from the cancellation would soak into the paper and make washing for reuse impossible. Grill impressions, when viewed from the face of the stamp, may be either "points up" or "points down." This process was used on U.S. Scott 79-101, 112-122 and 134-144 as well as some examples of 156-165 and 178-179.

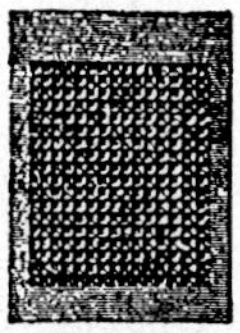

Regular Grill

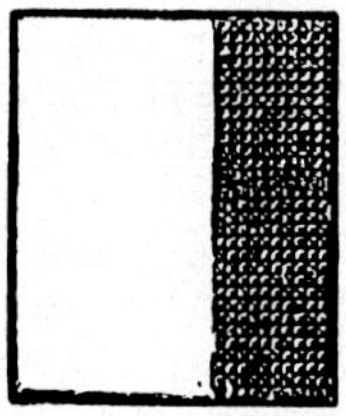

Continuous Marginal Grill

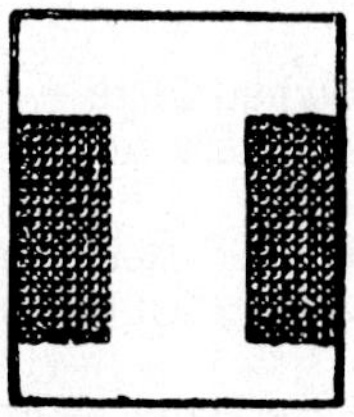

Split Grill

Continuous Marginal Grill — includes continuous rows of grill points impressed by the untrimmed parts of the ends of the grill rollers, noted as "end roller grill" on the 1870 and 1873 issues, and those grills which came from a continuous band lengthwise of the roller.

Split Grill — situation on a stamp showing portions of two or more grills, caused by a sheet being fed under the grill roller off center.

Double (or Triple) Grill — stamp showing two or more separate grill impressions. This is not to be confused with a split grill, which shows two or four partial impressions from a single grill impression.

Rotary Grills — grilled appearance occasionally found on rotary press printings that was produced unintentionally by a knurled roller during the perforating process.

Similarly, grill-like impressions can be left on stamps dispensed from vending machines.

SEPARATION

"Separation" is the general term used to describe methods used to separate stamps. The standard forms currently in use in the United States are perforating and die-cutting. These methods are done during the stamp production process, after printing. Sometimes these methods are done on-press or sometimes as a separate step. The earliest issues, such as the 1847 5¢ Franklin (Scott 1), did not have any means provided for separation. It was expected the stamps would be cut apart with scissors or folded and torn. These are examples of imperforate stamps. Many stamps were first issued in imperforate formats and were later issued with perforations. Therefore, care must be observed in buying single imperforate stamps to be certain they were issued imperforate and are not perforated copies that have been altered by having the perforations trimmed away. Stamps issued imperforate usually are valued as singles. However, imperforate varieties of normally perforated stamps should be collected in pairs or larger pieces as indisputable evidence of their imperforate character.

PERFORATIONS

The chief style of separation of U.S. stamps has been perforating. This is produced by cutting away the paper between the stamps in a line of holes (usually round) and leaving little bridges of paper between the stamps. These little bridges are the "teeth" of the perforation and, of course, project from the stamp when it is torn from the pane.

As the gauge of the perforation often is the distinguishing difference among stamps, it is necessary to measure and describe them by a gauge number. The standard for this measurement is the number of such teeth within two centimeters. Thus, we say that a stamp is perforated 12 or 10½ to note that there are either 12 or 10½ teeth counted within two centimeters.

Some later U.S. stamps are "stroke" perforated rather than "line" perforated. While it is difficult to tell the difference on a single stamp, with a block of four or more stamps the difference is more easily seen where the horizontal and vertical perforations cross. On the "stroke"-perforated items, the crossing point is clean and no holes are out of line. On the "line"-perforated stamps, the crossing point only rarely is perfect and generally there is a roughness.

Perforation Gauge — tool for measuring perforation, as described above.

Fine Perforation — perforation with small holes and teeth close together.

Coarse Perforation — perforation with large holes and teeth far apart, frequently irregularly spaced.

Rough Perforation — holes not clean cut, but jagged.

Compound Perforation — normally where perforations at the top and bottom differ from the perforations at the sides of the stamp. In describing compound perforations, the gauge of the top is given first, then the sides.

Some stamps are found where one side will differ from the other three, and in this case the reading will be the top first, then the right side, then the bottom, then the left side.

Double Perforations — often found on early U.S. revenue stamps and occasionally on postage issues, double perforations are applied in error. They do not generally command a premium over catalogue values of properly perforated stamps and are not to be confused with a variety found on occasional rotary press printings where stamps adjacent to the center gutters will show the entire width of the gutter and a line of perforations on the far end of the gutter. These are caused by the sheet having been cut off center and are called "gutter snipes." They command a small premium.

Many double perforations were privately made to increase the value of the stamp, and are to be considered damaged stamps.

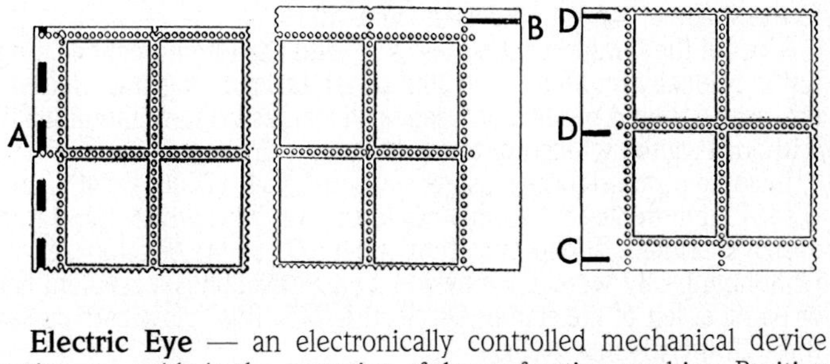

Electric Eye — an electronically controlled mechanical device acting as a guide in the operation of the perforating machine. Positive identification of stamps perforated by the electric eye process may be made by means of the distinctive marks in the gutters and margins of the full sheets on the printed web of paper. The original marks consisted of a series of heavy dashes dividing the vertical sheet gutter between the left and right panes (illustration A), together with a single line (margin line, illustration B), in the right sheet margin at the end of the horizontal sheet gutter between the upper and lower panes.

They first were used in 1933 on 400-subject plates for Scott 634, which was distributed to post offices in 1935 (used were plates 21149-50 and 21367-68). On these plates the plate numbers were placed opposite the ends of the third row of stamps from the top or bottom of the full sheet.

In later experiments, the margin line was broken into closely spaced thin vertical lines. Then it was again returned to its original form, but somewhat narrower.

In 1939, the Bureau of Engraving and Printing installed a new perforating machine which required a different layout to operate the centering mechanism. The vertical dashes remained the same, but the margin line was removed from the right sheet margin and a corresponding line ("gutter bar," illustration C) was placed in the left sheet margin at the end of the horizontal sheet gutter. Additional horizontal lines ("frame bars," illustration D) were added in the left sheet margin opposite the top frame line of the adjacent stamp design of all horizontal rows except the upper horizontal row of each left pane, where the frame bar is omitted. The plate numbers were moved back to their normal positions adjoining the corner stamps. Plates for the two types of machines could not be interchanged.

Later in 1939 a "convertible" plate was employed, consisting of a combination of the two previous layouts, the current one with the addition of a margin line (B) in its former position in the right sheet margin, thus making the perforation possible on either machine.

Originally laid out as 400-subject plates, electric eye plates were later used for 200-subject horizontal or vertical format (commemorative, special delivery and airpost issues), 280-subject (Famous Americans and those with similar formats) and 180- and 360-subject plates (booklet panes of definitives, airpost, postal savings and war savings issues).

In laying out the plates for the 400-subject and 200-subject horizontal format issues, the marks retained the same relative position to the stamp designs. This was changed, however, in entering the design for the stamps of the 200-subject vertical format and 280-subject issues because the stamp designs were turned 90 degrees. That is, the designs were entered on the plates with the longer dimension horizontal. Although the electric eye marks were entered on the plates in the usual positions, on the printed sheet they appear as though shifted 90 degrees when the stamps are held in the customary upright position.

Thus a "horizontal" mark on a 400-subject or 200-subject horizontal format sheet would become a "vertical" mark on a 200-subject vertical format or 280-subject sheet. This situation has caused confusion among collectors and dealers in determining a definite description of the various marks. The designation of the position of the plate numbers also has not been uniform for the "turned" designs.

To solve this confusion, the United States Stamp Society (formerly the Bureau Issues Association) adopted a standard terminology for all the marks appearing on the electric eye sheets. Dashes (A), Margin Line (B), Gutter Bar (C) and Frame Bars (D), whereby each type of mark may be identified readily without referring to its plate number position. The plate number designation of the panes will continue to be established by holding the pane of stamps with the designs in an upright position; the corner of the pane on which the plate number appears will determine the pane is upper left, upper right, lower left, or lower right.

DIE CUTTING

The other major form of U.S. stamp separation is die-cutting. This is a method where a die in the pattern of separation is created that later cuts the stamp paper in a stroke motion. This process is used for self-adhesive postage stamps. Die-cutting can appear in straight lines, such as U.S. Scott 2522; shapes, such as U.S. Scott 1552; or imitating the appearance of perforations, such as U.S. Scott 2920.

On stamps where the die cutting is unintentionally omitted, the terms "die cutting omitted" or "imperforate" may be used interchangeably.

ROULETTING

A third type of separation is seen on a few revenue stamps. In rouletting, the stamp paper is cut partly or wholly through in a series of short consecutive cuts, with no paper removed. The number of cuts made in a two-centimeter space determines the gauge of the roulette just as the number of perforations in two centimeters determines the gauge of the perforation.

GUM

The Illustrated Gum Chart in the first part of this introduction shows and defines various types of gum condition. Because gum condition has an important impact on the value of unused stamps, we recommend studying this chart and the accompanying text carefully.

The gum on the back of a stamp may be shiny, dull, smooth, rough, dark, white, colored or tinted. Most stamp gumming adhesives use gum arabic or dextrine as a base. Certain polymers such as polyvinyl alcohol (PVA) have been used extensively since World War II.

The *Scott Standard Postage Stamp Catalogue* does not list items by types of gum. The *Scott Specialized Catalogue of United States Stamps* does differentiate among some types of gum for certain issues.

As collectors generally prefer unused stamps with original gum, many unused stamps with no gum have been regummed to make them more desirable (and costly) to collectors who want stamps with full original gum. Some used stamps with faint cancels have had these cancels chemically removed and have been regummed. Skillful regumming can be difficult to detect, particularly on imperforate stamps. Certification of such stamps by competent authorities is suggested.

Reprints of stamps may have gum differing from the original issues. In addition, some countries have used different gum formulas for different seasons. These adhesives have different properties that may become more apparent over time.

Many stamps have been issued without gum, and the catalogue will note this fact. See United States Scott PR33-PR56.

LUMINESCENCE

Kinds of Luminescence — Fluorescence and phosphorescence, two different luminescent qualities, are found in U.S. postage stamps and postal stationery. While all luminescent stamps glow when exposed to short-wave ultraviolet (UV) light, only those with phosphorescent properties display brief afterglow when the UV light source is extinguished.

Fluorescent or "Hi-Bright" Papers — The Bureau of Engraving and Printing, at one point accepting paper for the printing of stamps without regard to fluorescent properties, unknowingly used a mix of paper with infinitely varying amounts of fluorescent optical brighteners added during the papermaking process. In March 1964, to preserve uniformity of product and as a safeguard for an emerging but still incomplete plan for nationwide use of luminescent stamps, BEP purchasing specifications were amended to limit the use of fluorescent paper brighteners. The amended specification permitted paper with some brightener content, but excluded brilliantly glowing papers known in the printing trade as "hi-bright."

Stamps printed on such papers emit a distinctive, intense whitish-violet glow when viewed with either long or short-wave UV. In following years, stamps were produced on papers with lower levels of fluorescence permitted by amended specifications.

Tagged Stamps — The Post Office Department (now the U.S. Postal Service) field-tested automated mail-handling equipment to face, cancel and sort mail at rates up to 30,000 pieces an hour, by sensing UV-light-activated afterglow from phosphorescent substances. For the first tests at Dayton, Ohio, started after August 1, 1963, the 8-cent carmine airpost stamp (Scott C64a) was over-printed (tagged) with a so-called "nearly-invisible" calcium silicate compound which phosphoresces orange-red when exposed to short-wave UV. A facer-canceler, with modifications that included a rapidly cycling on-off UV light, activated the phosphor-tagged airpost stamps and extracted envelopes bearing them from the regular flow of mail.

While the airpost extraction test was still in progress, the entire printing of the City Mail Delivery commemorative (Scott 1238) was ordered tagged with a yellow-green glowing zinc orthosilicate compound intended for use with the automated recognition circuits to be tested with surface transported letter mail.

After the first-day ceremonies October 26, 1963, at Washington, D.C., it was learned the stamps had been tagged to publicize the innovative test by coupling tagging with stamps memorializing "100 years of postal progress" and to provide the first national distribution of tagged stamps for collectors. Between October 28 and November 2, to broaden the scope of the test in the Dayton area, the 4-cent and 5-cent denominations of the regular issue then in use were issued with the same green glowing compound applied in an experimental tagging format (Scott 1036b, 1213b, 1213c, and 1229a).

By June 1964, testing had proven sufficiently effective for the Post Office Department to order all 8-cent airpost adhesive stamps phosphor-tagged for general distribution. By January 1966, all airpost stamps, regardless of denomination, were ordered tagged. Meanwhile, from 1963 through 1965, limited quantities of the Christmas issues were tagged for use in the continuing test in the Dayton area on the use of tagging to automatically position (face) and cancel mail. (Scott 1240a, 1254a-1257a, and 1276a).

On May 19, 1966, the use of phosphor-tagged stamps was expanded to the Cincinnati Postal Region, which then included offices in Ohio, Kentucky and Indiana. During the last half of 1966, primarily to meet postal needs of that region, phosphor-tagged issues were authorized to include additional denominations of regular issues, some postal stationery, and about 12 percent of each commemorative issue starting with the National Park Service 5-cent issue (Scott 1314a) and continuing through the Mary Cassatt 5-cent commemorative (Scott 1322a). After January 1, 1967, most regular values through the 16-cent, all commemoratives, and additional items of postal stationery were ordered tagged.

Adhesive stamps precanceled by the Bureau of Engraving and Printing (Bureau precancels), however, were not tagged, with the exception of Scott 1394, 1596, 1608, and 1610. Because there was no need to cancel mail with these stamps and since precancel permit holders post such mail already faced, postal officials bypassed facer-canceler operations and avoided the cost of tagging.

Overall phosphorescent overprints, when newly issued, are practically invisible in ordinary light. After aging three to five years, the tagging can discolor and become more easily visible. When viewed with UV light, there is little change in the hue of either orange-red or yellow-green emitted light. Even though observable discoloration exists, the presence or absence of tagging is best determined by examination with UV light.

Bar, or block, tagging, instead of the usual overall phosphorescent overprint, was used for some stamps beginning with the Andreotti-printed Mail Order Business commemorative (Scott 1468). These are much easier to identify than the overall overprint, often without need for a UV light.

Band tagging, a bar extending across two or more stamps, was first used with Scott 1489-1498.

Beginning in the 1990s, many stamps are printed on prephosphored paper. Unlike overall tagging, in which the tagging substance is applied to the entire stamp after it is printed, prephosphored paper has the tagging substance added to the surface of the paper during the paper-making process, before printing occurs.

In the late 1990s, some stamps appeared with the tagging formed in the shape of the stamp design elements.

Most of the luminescent issues exist with the luminescent coating unintentionally omitted. Such stamps are termed "tagging omitted" errors and should not be confused with stamps printed intentionally without tagging, which are termed "untagged."

In some postal stationery, such as Scott U551, UC40, UX48a, and UX55, the luminescent element is in the ink with which the stamp design is printed. The luminescent varieties of stamp envelopes Scott U550 and UC37 were made by adding a vertical phosphorescent bar or panel at left of the stamp. On Scott UC42, this "glow-bar" passes through the tri-globe design.

The *Scott Specialized Catalogue of U.S. Stamps and Covers* lists different tagging types when more than one type is known on a stamp. Currently, these types can be large or small block tagging, overall tagging and prephosphored paper. Prephosphored paper is further broken down into two types, each listed separately. It can have a "mottled tagging" appearance, which results from the application of the tagging substance to uncoated paper, or it can have a "solid tagging" appearance, either absolutely uniform or just slightly "grainy." The solid tagging appearance results from the application of the tagging substance to coated paper. Information in the catalogue reflects the most recent findings. Research on tagging is ongoing.

NOTE: Users of UV light should avoid prolonged exposure, which can burn the eyes. Sunglasses (particularly those that feature a "UV block") or prescription eyeglasses, tinted or plain, screen the rays and provide protection.

POSTAL MARKINGS

Postal markings are those marks placed by postal employees of this and other countries on the stamp or cover or both. These marks may indicate the mailing place of a letter, date, rate, route, accounting between post offices, and so on.

In addition to the basis town designations, there are many varieties of supplemental markings. Among these are rate marks, route marks, obliterators, special dating markings usually found on advertised or dead letter covers, transportation markings (rail, steam, ship, airpost, etc.), and service markings (advertised, forwarded, missent, second delivery, mail route, too late, charged, paid box, due, returned for postage, soldier's letter, held for postage, short paid, unpaid, not paid, paid, free, dead letter office, etc.).

These markings originated, for material mailed in what is now the United States, in the Colonial period when manuscript postal markings were first introduced under the Ordinance of December 10, 1672, of New York, which established an inland postal system between the colonies. A "Post Payd" is found on the first letter ever sent under the system, on January 22, 1673. Manuscript postal markings continued in use right through the pre-stamp period and even can be found on some letters today.

The earliest handstamp associated with the American service is a "NEW/YORK" blank handstamp found on letters conveyed via the Bristol Packet line in 1710-12 between New York and England. Following the demise of this operation, the first regular handstamp postal markings were introduced at New York in 1756, when a post office packet service was established between Falmouth, England, and New York. The marking merely was "NEW YORK" on two lines of type. The marking (see illustration), with each word of the city name on a separate line, is represented in presentations such as this as "NEW/YORK." Similar markings were later introduced at other towns, such as ANNA/POLIS, by 1766; CHARLES/TOWN, by 1770; PHILA/DELPHIA, by 1766; HART/FORD, by 1766; while other offices received a single line marking: BOSTON, by 1769; ALBANY, by 1773; PENSACOLA, by 1772; SAVANNA, by 1765, BALTIMORE, by 1772, and WMSBURG, by 1770.

Some of these early letters also bear a circular date stamp containing the month in abbreviated form, i.e., "IV" for June and "IY" for July, and the date in a 14-17mm circle. Known from at least nine towns, these are called "Franklin marks" after Benjamin Franklin, then deputy postmaster general for the English crown. The marks also are known as "American Bishopmarks" to distinguish them from the Bishopmark used in England, which has a center line.

First U.S. Handstamp

Franklin Mark

During 1774-1775, an American provisional postal system was established in opposition to that of the English crown. Both manuscript and handstamp markings have been attributed to it. This system was taken over by Congress on July 26, 1775, and the same markings were continued in use. The earliest reported Congressional marks are a manuscript "Camb Au 8" and a blue-green straightline "NEW*YORK*AU*24." Postal markings are known throughout the

Congressional marks are a manuscript "Camb Au 8" and a blue-green straightline "NEW*YORK*AU*24." Postal markings are known throughout the Revolution, including English occupation markings. Most are manuscript.

In the post-war Confederation period, handstamped circular markings were introduced at Charleston, South Carolina, in 1778-1780, and later at New London, Connecticut. Straightlines and manuscripts continued to dominate until the use of oval markings became widespread about 1800, with circles becoming the predominant markings shortly thereafter.

Handstamp rate markings are known as early as the 1789 pennyweight markings of Albany. Such types of markings became more common in the 1830's and almost the standard by the "5" and "10"-cent rate period which began on July 1, 1845. This period also is when envelopes began to replace folded letter sheets. Before that date, envelopes were charged with an extra rate of postage. These "5," "10," and succeeding "3," "6," "5," and "10" rates of 1851-56 were common on domestic mail until prepayment became compulsory April 1, 1855, on all but drop or local letters domestically. The markings were common on foreign mail through about 1875.

Only 1.3 percent of all letters posted between 1847 and 1852 bore stamps. This proportion increased to 25 percent in 1852, 32 percent in 1853, 34 percent in 1854, 40 percent in 1855, and 64 percent in 1856. Stampless covers are commonplace, although there are some which are highly prized on the basis of their markings. Most are more common than stamped covers of the same period.

While the government began issuing handstamps as early as 1799 and obliterators in 1847, many postmasters were required, or at least permitted, to purchase their own canceling devices or to use pen strokes. Pen cancellations continued to be common in the smaller offices into the 1880's. Because of collector prejudice against pen-canceled stamps, many have ended up being "cleaned" (having the pen cancel removed). These are sold either as unused or with a different, faked cancellation to cover the evidence of cleaning. Ultraviolet light (long-wave) usually will reveal traces of the original pen markings.

From around 1850 until 1900, many postmasters used obliterators cut from wood or cork. Many bear fanciful designs, such as bees, bears, chickens, locks, eagles, Masonic symbols, flags, numerals and so on. Some of the designs symbolized the town of origin. These are not listed in this Catalogue, for they owe their origin to the whim of some individual rather than a requirement of the postal regulations. Many command high prices and are eagerly sought by collectors. This has led to extensive forgery of such markings so that collectors are advised to check them carefully.

Rapid machine cancellations were introduced at Boston in 1880-90 and later spread across the country. Each of the various canceling machine types had identifiable characteristics and collectors form collections based on type. One sub-specialty is that of flag cancellations. While handstamp flag designs are known earlier, the first machine flag cancellation was that of Boston in November-December 1894.

Specialists have noted that different canceling inks are used at different times, depending partly on the type of canceling device used. Rubber handstamps, prohibited in 1893 although used for parcel post and precanceling after that date, require a different type of ink from the boxwood or type-metal cancelers of the classic period, while a still different ink is used for the steel devices of the machine cancels.

Registry of letters was first authorized in this country in the Dutch colony of New Netherlands on overseas mail. Records of valuable letters were kept by postmasters throughout the stampless period while an "R" marking was introduced at Philadelphia in 1845 for registered mail. Cincinnati also had such a registry system. The first appearance of the word "registered" appears on mail in November 1847, in manuscript, and in handstamp in May 1850. The official registration for U.S. mail, however, did not begin until July 1, 1855.

In recent years, the handstamped and machine types of cancellations have been standardized by the Post Office Department and its successor and supplied to the various post offices.

Postmarks — markings to indicate the office of origin or manner of postal conveyance. In general terms, the postmark refers to the post office of origin, but sometimes there also are receiving postmarks of the post office of destination or of transit. Other post office markings include: advertised, forwarded, mail route, missent, paid, not paid, second delivery, too late, etc. Postmarks often serve to cancel postage stamps with or without additional obliterating cancels.

Cancellations — postal markings which make further use of the postage stamps impossible. As used in the listings in this Catalogue, cancellations include both postmarks used as cancellations and obliterations intended primarily to cancel (or "kill") the stamp.

Carrier Postmarks — usually show the words "Carrier" "City Delivery," or "U.S.P.O. Dispatch." They were applied to letters to indicate the delivery of mail by U.S. Government carriers. These markings should not be confused with those of local posts or other private mail services which used postmarks of their own. Free delivery of city mail by carriers was begun on July 1, 1863.

Free — handstamp generally used on free, franked mail. The marking occasionally is seen on early adhesives of the United States used as a canceling device.

Railroad Postmarks — usually handstamps, the markings were used to postmark unpouched mail received by route agents of the Post Office Department traveling on trains on railway mail route. The route name in an agent's postmark often was similar to the name of the railroad or included the terminals of the route. The earliest known use of the word "Railroad" as a postmark is 1838. Route agents gradually became R.P.O. clerks and some continued to use their handstamps after the route agent service ceased June 30, 1882. The railroad postmarks of the 1850 period and later usually carried the name of the railroad.

A sub-group of railroad postmarks is made up of those applied in the early days by railroad station agents, using the railroad's ticket dating handstamp as a postmark. Sometimes the station agent was also the postmaster.

In 1864, the Post Office Department equipped cars for the general distribution of mails between Chicago and Clinton, Iowa.

Modern railroad marks, such as "R.P.O." (Railway Mail Service) is a mark indicating transportation by railroad, and includes Railway Post Office, Terminal Railway Post Office, Transfer Office, Closed Mail Service, Air Mail Field, and Highway Post Office.

Effective November 1, 1949, the Railway Mail Service was merged with others of like nature under the consolidated title Postal Transportation Service (PTS). The service was discontinued June 30, 1977.

The modern "railway marks" are quite common and are not the types referred to under cancellations as listed in the Catalogue.

Way Markings — Way letters are those received by a mail carrier on his way between post offices and delivered at the first post office he reached. The postmaster ascertained where the carrier received them and charged, in his postbills, the postage from those places to destination. He wrote "Way" against those charges in his bills and also wrote or stamped "Way" on each letter. If the letter was exempt from postage, it should have been marked "Free."

The term "mail carrier" above refers to any carrier under contract to carry U.S. mail: a stage line, a horseback rider, or a steamboat or railroad that did not have a route agent on board. Only unpouched mail (not previously placed in a post office) was eligible for a Way fee of one cent. The postmaster paid this fee to the carrier, if demanded, for the carrier's extra work of bringing the letter individually to the post office. For a limited time at certain post offices, the Way fee was added to the regular postage. This explains the use of a numeral with the "Way" marking.

Packet Markings — Packet markings listed in this Catalogue are those applied on a boat traveling on inland or coastal waterways. This group does not include mail to foreign countries that contains the words "British Packet," "American Packet," etc, or their abbreviations. These are U.S. foreign-mail exchange-office markings.

Listed packet markings are in two groups: 1) waterways route-agent markings which denote service exactly the same as that of the railroad route-agent markings, except that the route agent traveled on a boat instead of a train; 2) name-of-boat markings placed on the cover to advertise the boat or, as some believe, to expedite payment of Way and Steam fees at the post office where such letters entered the U.S. mails.

Occasionally waterways route-agent markings included the name of a boat, or "S.B.," "STEAMBOAT," or merely a route number. Such supplemental designations do not alter the character of the markings as those of a route-agent.

19th Century U.S. Express Mail Postmarks — In pre-stamp days these represented either an extra-fast mail service or mail under the care of an express-mail messenger who also carried out-of-mail-express packages. The service was permitted as a practical means of competing with package express companies that also carried mail in competition with the U.S. Mail. Several of these early postmarks were later used by U.S. Mail route agents on the New York-Boston and New York-Albany runs, or by U.S. steamboat letter carriers on the coastal run between Boston and St. John, New Brunswick.

Steamboat or **Steam Markings** — Except for the circular markings "Maysville Ky. Steam" and "Terre Haute Stb." and the rectangular "Troy & New York Steam Boat," these markings contain only the word "STEAMBOAT" or "STEAM," with or without a rating numeral. They represent service the same as that of Way markings, except that the carrier was an inland or coastal steamer that had no contract to carry U.S. mails. Such boats, however, were required by law to carry to the nearest post office any mail given them at landings. The boat owner was paid a two-cent fee for each letter so delivered, except on Lake Erie where the fee was one-cent. At some post offices, the Steamboat fee was added to regular postage. In 1861, the two-cent fee was again added to the postage, and in 1863 double postage was charged.

Ship Postmarks — postal markings indicating arrival on a private ship (one not under contract to carry mail). This marking was applied to letters delivered by such ships to the post office at their port of entry as required by law, for which they received a fee and the letter were taxed with a specified fee for the service in place of the ordinary open postage.

The use of U.S. postage stamps on ship letters is unusual, except for letters from Hawaii, because the U.S. inland postage on ship letters from a foreign point did not need to be prepaid. "U.S. SHIP" is a special marking applied to mail posted on naval vessels, especially during the Civil War period.

Steamship Postmarks — akin to Ship postmarks, but they appear to have been used mostly on mail from Caribbean or Pacific ports to New Orleans or Atlantic ports carried on steamships having a U.S. mail contract. An associated numeral usually designates the through rate from where the letter was received by the ship to its inland destination.

Receiving Mark — impression placed on the back of envelopes by the receiving post office to indicate the name of the office and date of arrival. It also is known as a "backstamp." Generally discontinued about 1913, the marking was employed for a time on air mail service until it was found the practice slowed the service. The markings now are used on registry and special delivery mail.

Miscellaneous Route Markings — wordings associated with the previously described markings include Bay Route, River Mail, Steamer, Mail Route, etc. Classification of the marking ordinarily is evident from the usage, or it can be identified from publications on postal markings.

U.S. Foreign-Mail Exchange-Office Markings — These served to meet the accounting requirements of the various mail treaties before the Universal Postal Union was established. The markings usually designate the exchange office or the carrier (British Packet, Bremen Packet, American Packet, etc.). Sometimes these markings are a restatement of the through rate, or a numeral designating the amount credited or debited to the foreign country as a means of allocating the respective parts of the total postage, according to conditions of route, method of transit, weight, etc.

Gridiron Cancellation — commonest types of cancellations on early U.S. stamps. The markings consist of circles enclosing parallel lines. There are, however, many varieties of grid cancellations.

Paid Markings — generally consist of the word "PAID," sometimes within a frame, indicating regular postage prepaid by the sender of a letter. They are found as separate handstamps, within town or city postmarks, and as a part of obliterating cancels. In each case, the "paid" marking may be used with or without an accompany or combined rate numeral indication.

Precancels — stamps having the cancellation applied before the article is presented for mailing. The purpose is to reduce handling and speed up the mails. A permit is required for use by the public, except for special cases, such as the experiments using Scott 1384a, 1414a-1418a, or 1552 for Christmas mail. Normally the precanceling is done with devices not used for ordinary postal service. Most precancellations consist of the city and state names between two lines or bars.

Precancels are divided into two groups: locals and Bureaus. Locals were printed, usually from 100-subject plates, or handstamped, usually by means of a 10- or 25-subject device having a rubber, metal or vinyl surface, at the town using the stamps. Most locals were made with devices furnished by the Postal Service, but a number were made with devices created in the city using them. Early locals include the printed "PAID" or "paid" on Scott 7 and 9, "CUMBERLAND, ME." on Scott 24-26 and the Glen Allen, Virginia stars. The U.S. Postal Service discontinued the practice of local precanceling as of July 5, 2007.

Many styles of precancellation are known. More than 600,000 different precancels exist from more than 20,000 post offices in the United States.

The Bureaus, or Bureau Prints, are precancels furnished to the post offices by the Post Office Department in Washington. For 75 years these were printed by the Bureau of Engraving and Printing, hence the name "Bureaus." In late 1991, the American Bank Note Co. and J.W. Fergusson and Sons for Stamp Venturers also began producing precanceled stamps under contract with the Postal Service. Other companies have followed. Since the stamps go to the local post office from the same source, the Postal Service, and the method of production is essentially the same as used by the BEP, the term "Bureau precancel" has been retained in this catologue. The cancellations consist of the name of the city and state where the stamps are to be used, lines or the class of mail. They originated in 1916 when postal officials were seeking ways to reduce costs as well as increase the legibility of the overprint. The BEP was low bidder in three cities, which resulted in the "experimentals." These 16 denominations, including two postage dues, were issued for Augusta, Maine (one value); Springfield, Massachusetts (14 values); and New Orleans (six values) in quanities ranging from 4,000,000 down to 10,000. Electrotype plates mounted on a flat bed press were used to print the precancellations.

Regular production of Bureau Prints began on May 2, 1923, with Scott 581 precanceled "New York, N.Y." All regular Bureaus until 1954 were produced by the Stickney rotary press, whereby the stamps, immediately after printing, pass under the precanceling plates. Then the roll is gummed, perforated and cut into sheets or coils. Since 1954, a variety of printing methods have been used.

Precancels are listed in the Catalogue only if the precanceled stamp is different from the nonprecanceled version (untagged stamps such as Scott 1582a); or, if the stamp only exists precanceled (Scott 2265). Classic locals and experimental bureaus are also included as cancellations. See Service Indicators.

Service Indicators — inscription included in the design of the stamp to indicate the category of postal service to be rendered. The first regular postage stamp to include a service indicator was the 7.9-cent Drum stamp of the Americana series, which was for bulk rate mailings. This stamp was issued with Bureau precancels for proper usage from 107 cities. Copies without the Bureau precancellation were for philatelic purposes.

A second category of service indicators came about when the USPS began to include the postal service between the lines of the Bureau precancellation. Examples of this group are "Bulk Rate" and "Nonprofit Organization."

Finally, with the 16.7-cent Transportation coil (Scott 2261), issued July 7, 1988, the USPS went back to including the service indicator in the design with the indicator serving as the cancellation. With the precancellation now part of the design, the USPS stopped offering tagged versions of the stamps for collectors. The only "precancels" currently in use are the service class/rate inscribed coils, and mailers' postmarks. This change was announced in Postal Bulletin 22210, dated July 5, 2007.

In all cases, the "service indicator" stamp does not normally receive an additional cancellation when used for the indicated service. For examples see Postal Markings - Bureau Precancels.

Tied On — when the cancellation (or postmark) extends from the stamp to the envelope.

Postal Markings, Cancellations Examples

Numerals
Values are for rating marks such as those illustrated. Later types of numerals in grids targets, etc., are common.

The common Boston Paid cancellation
(Values are for types other than this)

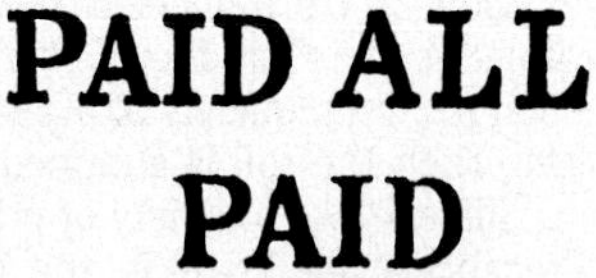

Steamship

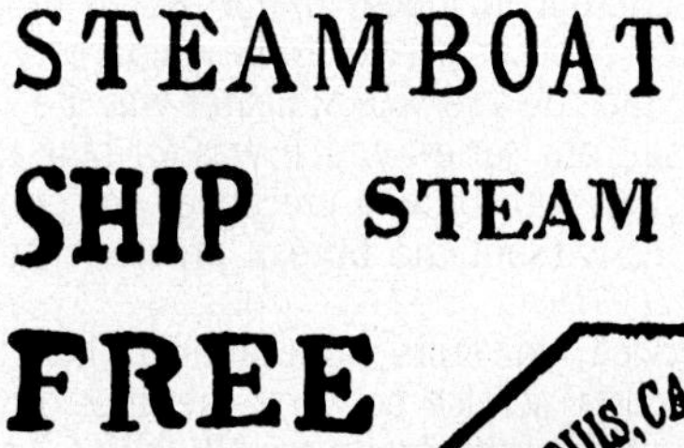

Steamboat
(Route agent marking)

Packet Boat
(Name-of-boat marking)

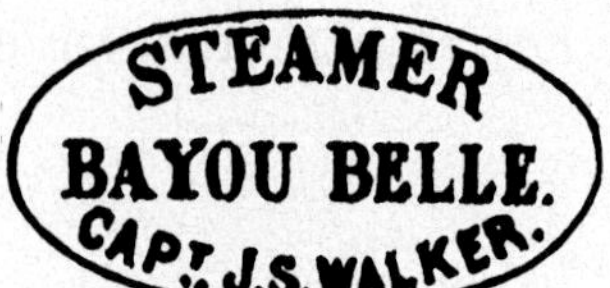

Packet Boat
(Name-of-boat marking)

Packet Boat
(Name-of-boat marking)

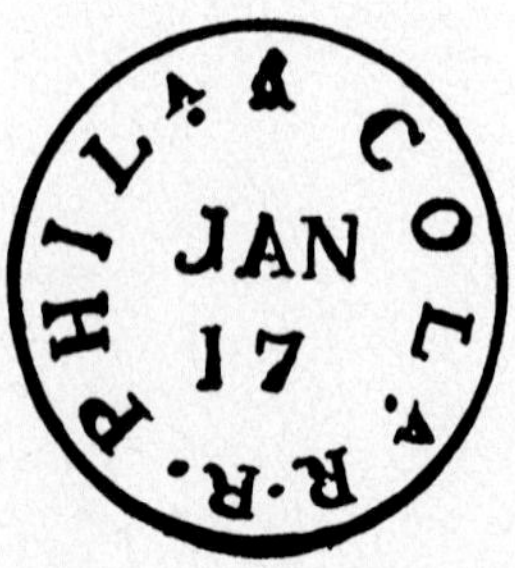

Railroad
(Route agent marking)

U.S. Express Mail
(Route agent marking)

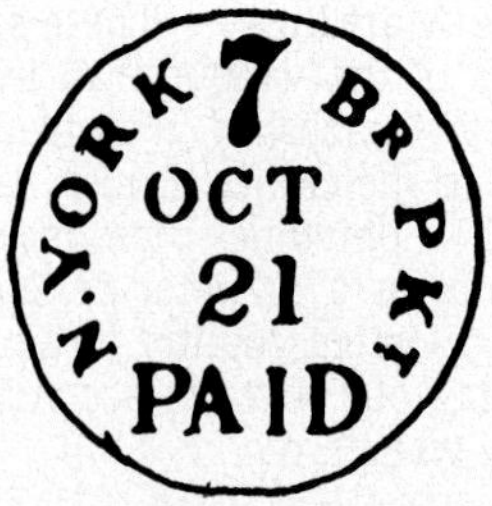

(In red on letter to Germany via Prussian Closed Mail, via British Packet. Credits 7 cent to Prussia.)

Express Company

Army Field Post

Carrier

Canadian

Town

Fort

Year dated

Vera Cruz, Mexico 1914

U.S. Postmark used in China

Exposition Station
Used while exposition is open. Many styles.

U.S. Postmark
used in Japan

Exposition advertising.
Used before exposition opens. Many styles.

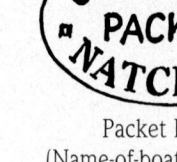

New York City Foreign Mail — A group of design cancellations used between 1871 and 1877 in New York City on outgoing foreign mail only. This group of handstamps totals about 200 different fancy stars, geometric designs, wheels conventionalized flowers, etc., the majority within a circle 26-29 mm in diameter.

Patent Defacing Cancellations — When adhesive stamps came into general use, the Post Office Department made constant efforts to find a type of cancellation which would make the re-use of the stamp impossible. Many patents were granted to inventors and some of the cancellations (killers) came into more or less general use. Some of them appear in combination with the town postmarks.

About 125 different types are known on the stamps issues up to about 1887. Their principal use and greatest variety occur on Scott 65, 147, 158, 183 and 184.

Patent cancellations generally fall into three groups:

1) Small pins or punches which pierce the paper or depress it sufficiently to break the fiber.

2) Sharp blades or other devices for cutting the paper.

3) Rotation of a portion of the canceler so that part of the paper is scraped away.

1. Dot punches through paper

2. Blades cut the paper

2. Small circle cuts the paper

3. Scraped in the shaded circle

Supplementary Mail — markings which designate the special post office service of dispatching mail after the regular mail closed. Two kinds of supplementary mail were available:

1. Foreign mail. For New York, the postmaster general established in 1853 a fee of double the regular rate. This paid to get the mail aboard ship after the regular mail closing and before sailing time. The service continued until 1939. Postmark Types A, D, E, F, and G were used.

2. Domestic mail. For Chicago, at no extra fee, supplementary mail entitled a letter to catch the last eastbound train. Postmark Types B and C were used. No foreign destination was implied.

Similar service with "Supplementary" in the postmark apparently available in Philadelphia and possibly elsewhere.

Type A

Type D

Type E

Type F
Combination Handstamp
(Also comes with numeral "1")
(Stamps with numeral cancel alone do not qualify for Supplementary Mail cancel premiums.)

Type G (also with other numerals)

Type B

Type C

Military Postmarks – Although mail from soldiers and sailors exists for all of the wars back to the American Revolution, such early letters were ordinarily sent through nearby civilian post offices. In fact, the first postal stations specifically for the handling of military mail were opened during the Spanish-American War in 1898. They were initially set up at training camps in the U.S. However, as the actual conflict took place in the Spanish colonies in the Caribbean and the Pacific, 77 special post offices were opened to handle military mail in Cuba, Puerto Rico, Guam and the Philippines. Most of these offices were issued cancels inscribed "Military Postal Station No. __" with the name of the town and territory in which they were located.

For many years, the warships of the U.S. Navy did not have post offices, so sailors' mail was simply deposited at the next convenient port. However, in 1908 the creation of on-board postal facilities was authorized, resulting in new postmarks showing the name of each vessel, thus creating a vast new collecting field. During both World Wars, these were replaced with generic cancels reading simply "U.S. Navy" so that they would not provide any information about ships' names or locations to enemy agents.

When the United States entered World War I on April 6, 1917, a vast expansion of U.S. military forces was required. This had to be met with an equally large expansion of postal facilities. Many post offices were opened at training camps in the U.S. In addition, an entirely new system of Army Post Offices (APOs) was created overseas, with the first being opened at St. Nazaire, France on July 10, 1917. This system eventually involved about 200 different military stations. Most were located in France, but some were in Italy. Following the Armistice on November 11, 1918, other offices were opened in Belgium, Germany, Luxembourg and The Netherlands.

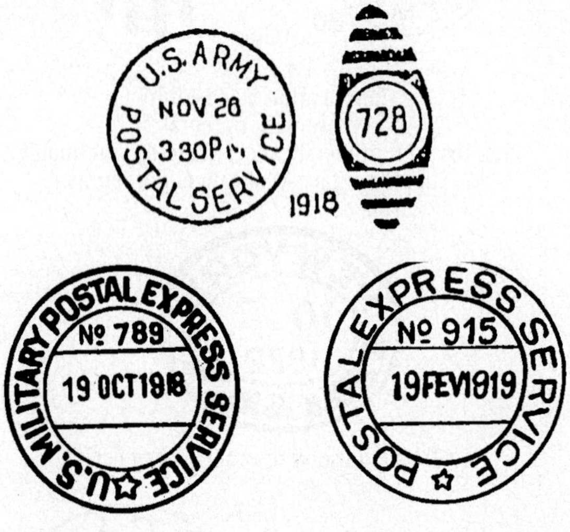

At first, members of the AEF were allowed to send mail from the APOs to the U.S., its territories and possessions at domestic postage rates, which were 1¢ for postcards and 2¢ for letters. However, from October 4, 1917, the troops were granted free postage for such items, although they were still required to pay at domestic rates for special services such as registration, special delivery and parcel post.

Civilians serving with the army, war correspondents and workers with welfare organizations, including the American Red Cross, YMCA, Knights of Columbus and Salvation Army, were permitted to use the APOs but had to pay domestic postage, including the war tax of 1¢ per piece that was in effect from November 2, 1917, until June 30, 1919.

Some American units participated in the Allied intervention in Russia in 1918-1920, including Siberia and North Russia. A U.S. postal agency was opened in Vladivostok, Siberia to handle mail from the AEF-Siberia, but the troops in North Russia used the British postal facilities (with their so-called "Polar Bear" markings).

Elsewhere, American forces were involved in military interventions in China, the Caribbean and Latin America (Cuba, Dominican Republic, Haiti, Mexico and Nicaragua). In each case, U.S. military postal facilities were opened to serve the troops, thus creating new postal markings that are collected by specialists.

During World War II the first new U.S. military post offices were opened in connection with the bases acquired from Great Britain in exchange for a fleet of old destroyers. The first of these offices was opened on January 15, 1941, using a postmark inscribed "American Forces in Newfoundland." As other offices opened, the inscription was changed to "American Base Forces" and an APO number added. After the U.S. entered the war on December 7, 1941, there was a vast expansion of the system, and the postmarks were changed to "U.S. Army Postal Service" with an APO number.

During the course of the war and its aftermath, more than 1,000 APOs were created, serving Army and Air Force personnel around the world. Some of these were open for very short periods and are scarce. As in World War I, the troops were granted free franking for surface cards and letters from April 1, 1942, to December 31, 1947, but postage was required for special services, including airmail, at normal domestic rates.

More recently, of course, there is military mail from the conflicts in Korea, Vietnam, Kuwait and Iraq, not to mention smaller events in places like Grenada, Panama and Kosovo. It should be noted that the APO numbering system was switched over to five digits in 1965 to bring it in line with the civilian zip code designations.

In looking at covers, collectors will find that most military mail from World War I on bears evidence of military and/or civilian censorship, after which the letters were permitted to be forwarded.

Readers desiring more information on military postal markings, censorship and the handling of military mail, or for a list of available publications on these and related subjects, are invited to visit www.MilitaryPHS.org, the website of the Military Postal History Society.

Bureau Precancels

AUGUSTA
MAINE

NEW
ORLEANS
LA.

SPRINGFIELD
MASS.

Experimentals

PERU
IND.

LANSING
MICH.

SAINT LOUIS
MO.

New Orleans
La.

San Francisco
Calif.

PORTLAND
ME.

LAKEWOOD
N. J.

KANSAS
CITY
MO.

POUGHKEEPSIE
N. Y.

LONG ISLAND
CITY, N. Y.

CORPUS
CHRISTI
TEXAS

ATLANTA
GEORGIA

ATLANTA
GA.

PEORIA
IL

CINCINNATI
OH

Service Indicators

Blk. Rt.
CAR-RT
SORT

Bulk Rate

Nonprofit
Org.

Nonprofit
Org.

PRESORTED
FIRST-CLASS

ZIP+4

Local Precancels

QUINCY
ILLINOIS

FITCHBURG
MASS.

LOS ANGELES
CALIF.

Fergus Falls
Minn.

COVINGTON
KY.

REDWOOD CITY
CALIF.

BELMONT
CALIF.

ELGIN
ILLINOIS

Electroplates

Ashland
Wis.

PALMYRA
N. Y.

Northhampton
MASS.

DES PLAINES
ILL.

RICHMOND
VA.

BROOKFIELD
ILLINOIS

PAONIA
COLO.

GOSHEN
IND

TOWER CITY
N. DAK.

NEW BRUNSWICK
N. J.

ORLANDO,
FLA.

RICHTON PARK
ILL.

M U L I N O,
OREG.

PINE HILL
N.Y.

FARRELL,
PA

SACRAMENTO
CA

Handstamps

General Glossary

Scott Publishing Co. uses the following terms in its Catalogues, as appropriate. Definitions follow each term.

Imperforate — stamps without perforations, rouletting, or other form of separation. Self-adhesive stamps are die cut, though they look imperforate.

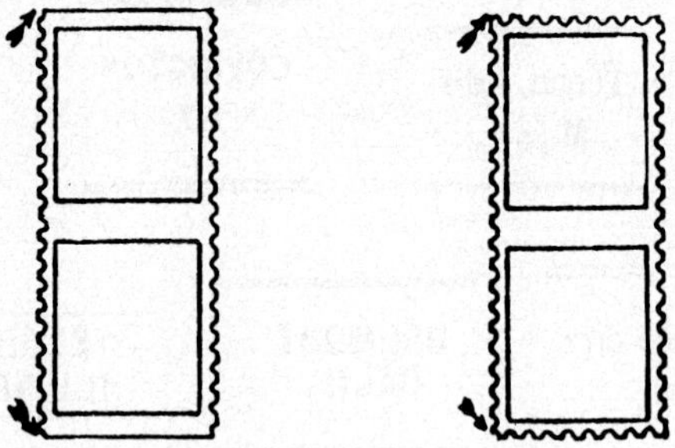

Type A Type B

Part-Perforate — Stamps with perforations on the two opposite sides, the other two sides remaining imperforate. See coils.

Vertical Pair, Imperforate Horizontally — (Type A illustrated) indicating that a pair of stamps is fully perforated vertically, but has no horizontal perforations.

Horizontal Pair, Imperforate Vertically — (Type A) indicating that a pair of stamps is fully perforated horizontally but has no vertical perforations.

Vertical Pair, Imperforate Between — (Type B illustrated) indicating that the vertical pair is fully perforated at the top, side and bottom, but has no perforations between the stamps.

Horizontal Pair, Imperforate Between — (Type B) indicating that the horizontal pair is fully perforated at the top, sides, and bottom, but has no perforations between the stamps.

Note: Of the above two types (A and B), Type A is the more common.

Blind Perforations — the slight impressions left by the perforating pins if they fail to puncture the paper. While multiples of stamps showing blind perforations may command a slight premium over normally perforated stamps, they are not imperforate errors. Fakers have removed gum from stamps to make blind perforations less evident.

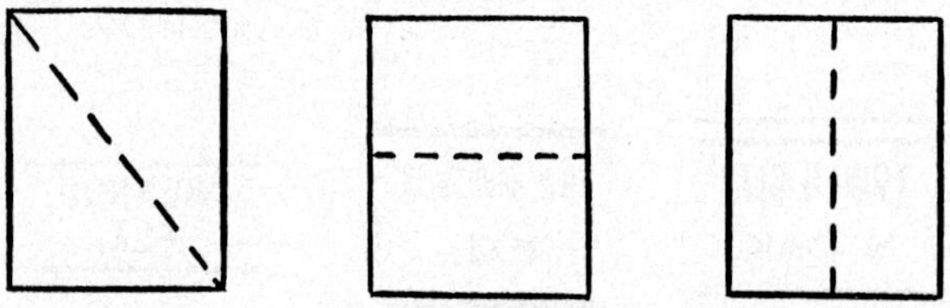

Diagonal *Horizontal* *Vertical*

Bisect — Stamps cut in half so that each portion prepaid postage. These items were used in emergencies where no stamps of the lower denomination were available. These may be diagonal, horizontal or vertical. Listings are for bisects on full covers with the bisected stamp tied to the cover on the cut side. Those on piece or part of a cover sell for considerably less. "Half-stamps" that receive a surcharge or overprint are not considered bisects.

This catalogue does not list unofficial bisects after the 1880's.

Block of Four, Imperforate Within — Examples exist of blocks of four stamps that are perforated on all four outside edges, but lack both horizontal and vertical perforations within the block. Scott 2096c, the Smokey the Bear commemorative, is an accidental example of this phenomenon. Scott RS173j and RS174j are examples of a situation where internal perforations were omitted intentionally to create 4-cent "stamps" from four 1-cent stamps.

Rouletting — short consecutive cuts in the paper to facilitate separation of the stamps, made with a toothed wheel or disc.

Booklets — Many countries have issued stamps in booklets for the convenience of users. This idea is becoming increasingly popular today in many countries. Booklets have been issued in all sizes and forms, often with advertising on the covers, on the panes of stamps or on the interleaving.

The panes may be printed from special plates or made from regular sheets. All panes from booklets issued by the United States and many from those of other countries are imperforate on three sides, but perforated between the stamps. Any stamplike unit in the pane, either printed or blank, which is not a postage stamp, is considered a *label* in the Catalogue listings. The part of the pane through which stitches or staples bind the booklet together, or which affixes the pane to the booklet cover, is considered to be a *binding stub* or *tab.*

Scott lists and values booklets in this volume. Except for panes from Canal Zone, handmade booklet panes are not listed when they are fashioned from existing sheet stamps and, therefore, are not distinguishable from the sheet-stamp foreign counterparts.

Panes usually do not have a "used" value because there is little market activity in used panes, even though many exist used.

Cancellations — the marks or obliterations put on a stamp by the authorities to show that it has done service and is no longer valid for use. If made with a pen, it is a "pen cancellation." When the location of the post office appears in the cancellation, it is a "town cancellation." When calling attention to a cause or celebration, it is a "slogan cancellation." Many other types and styles of cancellations exist, such as duplex, numerals, targets, etc.

Coil Stamps — stamps issued in rolls for use in dispensers, affixing and vending machines. Those of the United States, and its territories are perforated horizontally or vertically only, with the outer edges imperforate. Coil stamps of some countries, such as Great Britain, are perforated on all four sides.

Commemorative Stamps — Special issues which commemorate some anniversary or event or person. Usually such stamps are used for a limited period concurrently with the regular issue of stamps. Examples of commemorative issues are Scott 230-245, 620-621, 946, 1266, C68, and U218-U221.

Covers — envelopes, with or without adhesive postage stamps, which have passed through the mail and bear postal or other markings of philatelic interest. Before the introduction of envelopes in about 1840, people folded letters and wrote the address on the outside. Many people covered their letters with an extra sheet of paper on the outside for the address, producing the term "cover." Used air letter sheets and stamped envelopes also are considered covers. Stamps on paper used to cover parcels are said to be "on wrapper." ("Wrapper" also is the term used for postal stationery items which were open at both sides and wrapped around newspapers or pamphlets.) Often stamps with high face values are rare on cover, but more common on wrapper. Some stamps and postal stationery items are difficult to find used in the manner for which they were intended, but quite common when used to make philatelic items such as flight or first day covers. High face-value stamps also may be more common on package address tags. See postal cards.

Earliest Documented Use (EDU) — For stamps that do not have a designated first day of issue, the earliest documented use is the date when a stamp was first used in the U.S. mails. These dates are listed in the U.S. Specialized catalog, and new dates must be documented with recognized certificates from leading expertizing committees.

Error — stamps having some unintentional major deviation from the normal. Errors include, but are not limited to, mistakes in color, paper, or watermark, inverted centers or frames on multicolor printing, missing color, inverted or double surcharges or overprints, imperforates and part-perforates, unintentionally omitted tagging, and double impressions. A factually wrong or misspelled inscription, if it appears on all examples of a stamp, even if corrected later, is not classified as a philatelic error.

Color-Omitted Errors — This term refers to stamps where a missing color is caused by the complete failure of the printing plate to deliver ink to the stamp paper or any other paper. Generally, this is caused by the printing plate not being engaged on the press or the ink station running dry of ink during printing.

Color-Missing Errors — This term refers to stamps where a color or colors were printed somewhere but do not appear on the finished stamp. There are four different classes of color-missing errors, and the catalog indicates with a two-letter code appended to each such listing what caused the color to be missing:

FO = A *foldover* of the stamp sheet during printing may block ink from appearing on a stamp. Instead, the color will appear on the back of the foldover (where it might fall on the back of the selvage or perhaps on the back of another stamp). FO also will be used in the case of foldunders, where the paper may fold underneath the other stamp paper and the color will print on the platen.

EP = A piece of *extraneous paper* falling across the plate or stamp paper will receive the printed ink. When the extraneous paper is removed, an unprinted portion of stamp paper remains and shows partially or totally missing colors.

CM = A misregistration of the printing plates during printing will result in a *color misregistration*, and such a misregistration may result in a color not appearing on the finished stamp.

PS = A *perforation shift* after printing may remove a color from the finished stamp. Normally, this will occur on a row of stamps at the edge of the stamp pane.

First Day Cover — A philatelic term to designate the use of a certain stamp (on cover) or postal stationery item on the first day of sale at a place officially designated for such sale or so postmarked. Current U.S. stamps may have such a postal marking applied considerably after the actual issue date.

Gum Breaker Ridges — Colorless marks across the backs of some rotary press stamps, impressed during manufacture to prevent curling. Many varieties of "gum breaks" exist.

Original Gum — A stamp is described as "O.G." if it has the original gum as applied when printed. Some are issued without gum, such as Scott 730, 731, 735, 752, etc; government reproductions, such as Scott 3 and 4; and official reprints.

Overprinted and Surcharged Stamps — Overprinting is a wording or design placed on stamps to alter the place of use (e.g., "Canal Zone" on U.S. stamps), to adapt them for a special purpose ("I.R." on 1-cent and 2-cent U.S. stamps of the 1897-1903 regular issue for use as revenue stamps. Scott R153-R155A) or for a special occasion (U.S. Scott 646-648).

Surcharge is an overprint which changes or restates the face value of the item.

Surcharges and overprints may be handstamped, typeset or, occasionally, lithographed or engraved. A few hand-written overprints and surcharges are known. The world's first surcharge was a handstamped "2" on the United States City Despatch Post stamps of 1846.

Postal Cards — cards that have postage printed on them. Ones without printed stamps are referred to as "postcards."

Proofs and Essays — Proofs are impressions taken from an approved die, plate or stone in which the design and color are the same as the stamp issued to the public. Trial color proofs are impressions taken from approved dies, plates or stones in varying colors. An essay is the impression of a design that differs in some way from the stamp as issued.

Provisionals — stamps issued on short notice and intended for temporary use pending the arrival of regular (definitive) issues. They usually are issued to meet such contingencies as changes in government or currency, shortage of necessary values, or military occupation.

In the 1840's, postmasters in certain American cities issued stamps that were valid only at specific post offices. Postmasters of the Confederate States also issued stamps with limited validity. These are known as "postmaster's provisionals." See U.S. Scott 9X1-9X3 and Confederate States Scott 51X1.

Se-Tenant — joined, referring to an unsevered pair, strip or block of stamps differing in design, denomination or overprint. See U.S. Scott 2158a. Unless the se-tenant item has a continuous design (see U.S. Scott 1451a, 1694a) the stamps do not have to be in the same order as shown in the catalogue (see U.S. Scott 2158a).

Tete Beche — A pair of stamps in which one is upside down in relation to the other. Some of these are the result of intentional sheet arrangements, i.e. Morocco Scott B10-B11. Others occurred when one or more electrotypes accidentally were placed upside down on the plate. See Hawaii Scott 21a and 22a. Separation of the stamps, of course, destroys the tete beche variety.

Specimens — One of the regulations of the Universal Postal Union requires member nations to send samples of all stamps they put into service to the International Bureau in Switzerland. Member nations, of the UPU receive these specimens as samples of what stamps are valid for postage. Many are overprinted, handstamped or initial-perforated "Specimen," "Canceled" or "Muestra."Stamps distributed to government officials or for publicity purposes, and stamps submitted by private security printers for official approval also may receive such defacements.

These markings prevent postal use, and all such items generally are known as "specimens." There is a section in this volume devoted to this type of material. U.S. officials with "specimen" overprints and printings are listed in the Special Printings section.

Territorial and Statehood Dates

	Territorial Date	Statehood Date	
Alabama	Sept. 25, 1817	Dec. 14, 1819	Territory by enabling act of March 3, 1817, effective Sept. 25, 1817. Created out of part of existing Mississippi Territory.
Alaska	Oct. 18, 1867	Jan. 3, 1959	A district from Oct. 18, 1867, until it became an organized territory Aug. 24, 1912.
Arizona	Feb. 24, 1863	Feb. 14, 1912	This region was sometimes called Arizona before 1863 though still in the Territory of New Mexico.
Arkansas	July 5, 1819*	June 15, 1836	The territory was larger than the state. After statehood, the left-over area to the west had post offices that continued for some years to use an Arkansas abbreviation in the postmarks although really they were in the "Indian Country."
California		Sept. 9, 1850	Ceded by Mexico by the Treaty of Guadalupe-Hidalgo, concluded Feb. 2, 1848, and proclaimed July 4, 1848. From then until statehood, California had first a military government until Dec. 20, 1849, and then a local civil government. It never had a territorial form of government.
Colorado	Feb. 28, 1861	Aug. 1, 1876	
Connecticut		Jan. 9, 1788	The fifth of the original 13 colonies.
Delaware		Dec. 7, 1787	The first of the original 13 colonies.
Dakota	March 2, 1861	Nov. 2, 1889	Became two states: North and South Dakota.
Deseret	March 5, 1849		Brigham Young created the unofficial territory of Deseret. In spite of the fact that Utah Territory was created Sept. 9, 1850, Deseret continued to exist unofficially, in what is now Utah, at least as late as 1862.
Frankland or Franklin			This unofficial state was formed in Aug. 1784, in the northeast corner of what is now Tennessee, and the government existed until 1788. In reality it was part of North Carolina.
Florida	March 30, 1822	March 3, 1845	
Georgia		Jan. 2, 1788	The fourth of the original 13 colonies.
Hawaii	Aug. 12, 1898	Aug. 21, 1959	The territorial date given is that of the formal transfer to the United States, with Sanford B. Dole as first Governor.
Idaho	March 3, 1863	July 3, 1890	
Illinois	March 2, 1809*	Dec. 3, 1818	
Indiana	July 5, 1800*	Dec. 11, 1816	There was a residue of Indiana Territory which continued to exist under that name from Dec. 11, 1816 until Dec. 3, 1818, when it was attached to Michigan Territory.
Indian Territory		Nov. 16, 1907	In the region first called the "Indian Country," established June 30, 1834. It never had a territorial form of government. Finally, with Oklahoma Territory, it became the State of Oklahoma on Nov. 16, 1907.
Iowa	July 4, 1838	Dec. 28, 1846	
Jefferson	Oct. 24, 1859		An unofficial territory from Oct. 24, 1859, to Feb. 28, 1861. In reality it included parts of Kansas, Nebraska, Utah and New Mexico Territories, about 30% being in each of the first three and 10% in New Mexico. The settled portion was mostly in Kansas Territory until Jan. 29, 1861, when the State of Kansas was formed from the eastern part of Kansas Territory. From this date the heart of "Jefferson" was in unorganized territory until Feb. 28, 1861, when it became the Territory of Colorado.
Kansas	May 30, 1854	Jan. 29, 1861	
Kentucky		June 1, 1792	Never a territory, it was part of Virginia until statehood.
District of Louisiana	Oct. 1, 1804		An enormous region, it encompassed all of the Louisiana Purchase except the Territory of Orleans. Created by Act of March 26, 1804, effective Oct. 1, 1804, and attached for administrative purposes to the Territory of Indiana.
Territory of Louisiana	July 4, 1805		By Act of March 3, 1805, effective July 4, 1805, the District of Louisiana became the Territory of Louisiana.
Louisiana		April 30, 1812	With certain boundary changes, had been the Territory of Orleans.
District of Maine		March 16, 1820	Before statehood, what is now the State of Maine was called the District of Maine and belonged to Massachusetts.
Maryland		April 28, 1788	The seventh of the original 13 colonies.

	Territorial Date	Statehood Date	
Massachusetts		Feb. 6, 1788	The sixth of the original 13 colonies.
Michigan	July 1, 1805	Jan. 26, 1837	
Minnesota	March 3, 1849	May 11, 1858	
Mississippi	May 7, 1798	Dec. 10, 1817	Territory by Act of April 7, 1798, effective May 7, 1798.
Missouri	Dec. 7, 1812	Aug. 10, 1821	The state was much smaller than the territory. The area to the west and northwest of the state, which had been in the territory, was commonly known as the "Missouri Country" until May 30, 1854, and certain of the post offices in this area show a Missouri abbreviation in the postmark.
Montana	May 26, 1864	Nov. 8, 1889	
Nebraska	May 30, 1854	March 1, 1867	
Nevada	March 2, 1861	Oct. 31, 1864	
New Hampshire		June 21, 1788	The ninth of the original 13 colonies.
New Jersey		Dec. 18, 1787	The third of the original 13 colonies.
New Mexico	Dec. 13, 1850	Jan. 6, 1912	
New York		July 26, 1788	The 11th of the original 13 colonies.
North Carolina		Nov. 21, 1789	The 12th of the original 13 colonies.
North Dakota		Nov. 2, 1889	Had been part of the Territory of Dakota.
Northwest Territory	July 13, 1787		Ceased to exist March 1, 1803, when Ohio became a state. The date given is in dispute, Nov. 29, 1802 often being accepted.
Ohio		March 1, 1803	Had been part of Northwest Territory until statehood.
Oklahoma	May 2, 1890	Nov. 16, 1907	The state was formed from Oklahoma Territory and Indian Territory.
Oregon	Aug. 14, 1848	Feb. 14, 1859	
Orleans	Oct. 1, 1804		A territory by Act of March 26, 1804, effective Oct. 1, 1804. With certain boundary changes, it became the State of Louisiana, April 30, 1812.
Pennsylvania		Dec. 12, 1787	The second of the original 13 colonies.
Rhode Island		May 29, 1790	The 13th of the original 13 colonies.
South Carloina		May 23, 1788	The eighth of the original 13 colonies.
South Dakota		Nov. 2, 1889	Had been part of Dakota Territory.
Southwest Territory			Became the State of Tennessee, with minor boundary changes, June
Tennessee		June 1, 1796	Had been Southwest Territory before statehood.
Texas		Dec. 29, 1845	Had been an independent Republic before statehood
Utah	Sept. 9, 1850	Jan. 4, 1896	
Vermont		March 4, 1791	Until statehood, had been a region
Virginia		June 25, 1788	The 10th of the original 13
Washington	March 2, 1853	Nov. 11, 1889	
West Virginia		June 20, 1863	Had been par
Wisconsin	July 4, 1836	May 29, 1848	The state was s the Territory of W
Wyoming	July 29, 1868	July 10, 1890	

* The dates followed by an asterisk are one day later than those generally accepted. T and after July 4." While it was undoubtedly the intention of Congress to create Arkansas as and after July 4," for instance, meant "July 5."

Territorial and statehood data compiled by Dr. Carroll Chase and Richard McP. Cabeen.

Domestic Letter Rates

Effective Date	Prepaid	Collect
1845, July 1		
Reduction from 6¢ to 25¢ range on single-sheet letters		
Under 300 miles, per ½ oz	5¢	5¢
Over 300 miles, per ½ oz	10¢	10¢
Drop letters	2¢	
1847-1848		
East, to or from Havana (Cuba) per ½ oz	12½¢	12½¢
East, to or from Chagres (Panama) per ½ oz	20¢	20¢
East, to or from Panama, across Isthmus, per ½ oz.	30¢	30¢
To or from Astoria (Ore.) or Pacific Coast, per ½ oz	40¢	40¢
Along Pacific Coast, per ½ oz	12½¢	12½¢
1847, July 1		
Unsealed circulars		
1 oz. or less	3¢	
1851, July 1		
Elimination of rates of 1847-1848 listed above		
Up to 3,000 miles, per ½ oz.	3¢	5¢
Over 3,000 miles, per ½ oz	6¢	10¢
Drop letters	1¢	
Unsealed circular		
1 oz. or less up to 500 miles	1¢	
Over 500 miles to 1,500 miles	2¢	
Over 1,500 miles to 2,500 miles	3¢	
Over 2,500 miles to 3,500 miles	4¢	
Over 3,500 miles	5¢	
1852, September 30		
Unsealed circulars		
3 oz. or less anywhere in U.S.	1¢	
Each additional ounce	1¢	
(Double charge if collect)		
1855, April 1		
Prepayment made compulsory		
Not over 3,000 miles, per ½ oz.	3¢	
Over 3,000 miles, per ½ oz.	10¢	
Drop letters	1¢	
1863, July 1		
Distance differential eliminated		
All parts of United States, per ½ oz.	3¢	
...83, October 1		
...r rate reduced one-third		
...rts of United States, per ½ oz.	2¢	
...ly 1		
...reased to 1 oz.		
...United States, per 1 oz.	2¢	
...r 1		
...ry started		

Effective Date	Prepaid
1917, November 2	
War emergency	
All parts of United States, per 1 oz.	3¢
1919, July 1	
Restoration of pre-war rate	
All parts of United States, per 1 oz.	2¢
1932, July 6	
Rise due to depression	
All parts of United States, per 1 oz.	3¢
1958, August 1	
All parts of United States, per 1 oz.	4¢
1963, January 7	
All parts of United States, per 1 oz.	5¢
1968, January 7	
All parts of United States, per 1 oz.	6¢
1971, May 16	
All parts of United States, per 1 oz.	8¢
1974, March 2	
All parts of United States, per 1 oz.	10¢
1975, December 31	
All parts of United States, 1st oz.	13¢
1978, May 29	
All parts of United States, 1st oz.	15¢
1981, March 22	
All parts of United States, 1st oz.	18¢
1981, November 1	
All parts of United States, 1st oz.	20¢
1985, February 17	
All parts of United States, 1st oz.	22¢
1988, April 3	
All parts of United States, 1st oz.	25¢
1991, February 3	
All parts of United States, 1st oz.	29¢
1995, January 1	
All parts of United States, 1st oz.	32¢
1999, January 10	
All parts of United States, 1st oz.	33¢
2001, January 7	
All parts of United States, 1st oz.	34¢
2002, June 30	
All parts of United States, 1st oz.	37¢
2006, January 8	
All parts of United States, 1st oz.	39¢
2007, May 14	
All parts of United States, 1st oz.	41¢
2008, May 12	
All parts of United States, 1st oz.	42¢

Domestic Air Mail Rates

Effective Date	Prepaid
1911-1916 – The Pioneer Period	
Special official Post Office Flights at Fairs, aviation meets, etc., per 1 oz.	2¢
Postal cards and postcards	1¢
(Regulations prohibited an additional charge for air service on Post Office authorized flights.)	
1918, May 15 - July 13, 1918	
Service between Washington, DC, New York and Philadelphia (including 10¢ special delivery fee), per 1 oz.	24¢
1918, July 15-Dec. 14, 1918	
Service between Washington, DC, New York and Philadelphia (including 10¢ special delivery fee), per 1 oz.	16¢
Additional ounces	6¢
1918, Dec. 15-July 17, 1919	
Service between selected cities (other cities added later, special delivery no longer included), per 1 oz.	6¢
1919, July 18-June 29, 1924	
No specific airmail rate: mail carried by airplane on space available basis but airmail service not guaranteed, per 1 oz.	2¢
Postal cards and postcards, per 1 oz.	1¢
1924, June 30-Jan. 31, 1927	
Airmail service per zone (New York-Chicago; Chicago-Cheyenne, Wyo.; Cheyenne-San Francisco), per 1 oz. (each zone or portion thereof)	8¢
1925, July 1-Jan. 31, 1927	
Special overnight service New York-Chicago (with three intermediate stops), per 1 oz.	10¢
1926, Feb. 15-Jan. 31, 1927	
Contract routes not exceeding 1,000 miles (first flight Feb. 15) per 1 oz. (each route or portion thereof)	10¢
Contract routes between 1,000 and 1,500 miles (Seattle-Los Angeles, first flight Sept. 15) per 1 oz.	15¢
Mail traveling less than entire Seattle-Los Angeles route per 1 oz.	10¢
Contract routes exceeding 1,500 miles (none established during this rate period) per 1 oz.	20¢
Additional service on govt. route, per 1 oz. (each route or portion thereof)	5¢
1927, Feb. 1-July 31, 1928	
All contract routes or govt. zones, or combinations thereof, per ½ oz.	10¢
1928, Aug. 1-July 5, 1932	
All routes, 1st oz.	5¢
Each additional ounce or fraction thereof	10¢

Effective Date	Prepaid
1932, July 6-June 30, 1934	
All routes, 1st oz.	8¢
Each additional ounce or fraction thereof	13¢
1934, July 1-Mar. 25, 1944	
All routes, per oz.	6¢
1944, Mar. 26-Sept. 30, 1946	
All routes, per oz.	8¢
1946, Oct. 1-Dec. 31, 1948	
All routes, per oz.	5¢
1949, Jan. 1-July 31, 1958	
All routes, per oz.	6¢
Postal cards and postcards, per oz.	4¢
1958, Aug. 1-Jan. 6, 1963	
All routes, per oz.	7¢
Postal cards and postcards, per oz.	5¢
1963, Jan. 7-Jan. 6, 1968	
All routes, per oz.	8¢
Postal cards and postcards, per oz.	6¢
1968, Jan. 7-May 15, 1971	
All routes, per oz.	10¢
Postal cards and postcards, per oz.	8¢
1971, May 16-Mar. 1, 1974	
All routes, per oz.	11¢
Postal cards and postcards, per oz.	9¢
1974, Mar. 2-Oct. 10, 1975	
All routes, per oz.	13¢
Postal cards and postcards, per oz.	11¢

As of Oct. 11, 1975, separate domestic airmail service was abolished, although at least one more airmail rate was published; effective Dec. 28, 1975, 17¢ per 1st oz., 15¢ each additional oz., 14¢ for postal cards and postcards. It lasted until May 1, 1977.

Many thanks to the American Air Mail Society for sharing information on airmail rates. For further study, we highly recommend the society's book, *Via Airmail, An Aerophilatelic Survey of Events, Routes, and Rates;* Simine Short, editor; James R. Adams, author (available from the American Airmail Society, P.O. Box 110, Mineola, NY 11501. Price: $20, plus $2.50 postage to U.S. addresses; $3.50 to addresses outside the U.S.).

IDENTIFIER OF DEFINITIVE ISSUES — ARRANGED BY TYPE NUMBERS

This section covers only listed postage stamps. See the Proofs section for imperforate items in the stamp colors mentioned which are not listed here and the Trial Color Proofs section for items in other colors.

ISSUES OF 1847-75

Benjamin Franklin — A1

Reproduction — A3

5¢ On the originals the left side of the white shirt frill touches the oval on a level with the top of the "F" of "Five." On the reproductions it touches the oval about on a level with the top of the figure "5."

George Washington — A2

Reproduction — A4

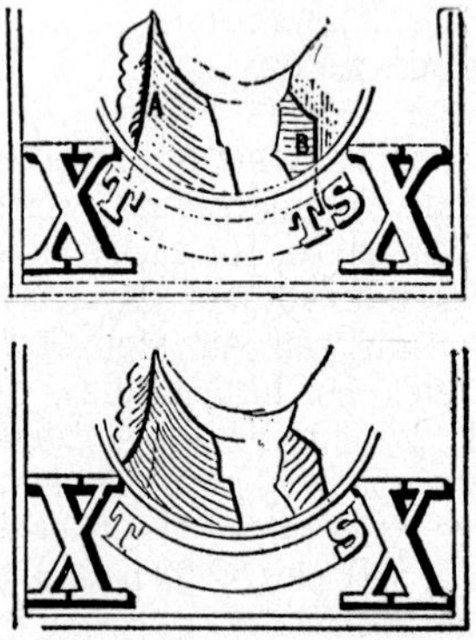

Top image original, bottom image reproduction

10¢ On the originals line of coat (A) points to "T" of TEN and (B) it points between "T" and "S" of CENTS.

On the reproductions line of coat (A) points to right tip of "X" and line of coat (B) points to center of "S."

On the reproductions the eyes have a sleepy look, the line of the mouth is straighter, and in the curl of the hair near the left cheek is a strong black dot, while the originals have only a faint one.

Imperforate and Unwatermarked

Design Number		*Scott Number*
A1	5¢ red brown	1
A1	5¢ blue (reproduction)	948a
A3	5¢ red brown (reproduction, Special Printing)	3
A2	10¢ black	2
A2	10¢ brown orange (reproduction)	948b
A4	10¢ black (reproduction, Special Printing)	4

ISSUE OF 1851-75

Franklin — A5

A5

Type I Has a curved line outside the labels with "U.S. Postage" and "One Cent." The scrolls below the lower label are turned under, forming little balls. The scrolls and outer line at top are complete.

A6

Type Ia Same as I at bottom but top ornaments and outer line at top are partly cut away.

Type Ib Same as I but balls below the bottom label are not so clear. The plume-like scrolls at bottom are not complete.

Type Ic Same as type Ia, but bottom right plume and ball ornament is incomplete. The bottom left plume is complete or almost complete.

A7

Type II The little balls of the bottom scrolls and the bottoms of the lower plume ornaments are missing. The side ornaments are complete.

A8

Type III The top and bottom curved lines outside the labels are broken in the middle. The side ornaments are complete.

Type IIIa Similar to III with the outer line broken at top or bottom but not both. Type IIIa from Plate IV generally shows signs of plate erasure between the horizontal rows. Those from Plate IE show only a slight break in the line at top or bottom.

A9 Type IV

A20 Type V

Type IV Similar to II, but with the curved lines outside the labels recut at top or bottom or both.

The seven types listed account for most of the varieties of recutting.

Type V Similar to type III of 1851-56 but with side ornaments partly cut away.

A5	1¢ blue, type I, imperf.	5
A5	1¢ blue, type Ib, imperf.	5A
A5	1¢ blue, type I, perf. 15½	18
A5	1¢ bright blue, perf. 12 (Special Printing)	40
A6	1¢ blue, type Ia, imperf.	6
A6	1¢ blue, type Ic, imperf.	6b
A6	1¢ blue, type Ia, perf. 15½	19
A6	1¢ blue, type Ic, perf. 15½	19b
A7	1¢ blue, type II, imperf.	7
A7	1¢ blue, type II, perf. 15½	20
A8	1¢ blue, type III, imperf.	8
A8	1¢ blue, type IIIa, imperf.	8A
A8	1¢ blue, type III, perf. 15½	21
A8	1¢ blue, type IIIa, perf. 15½	22
A9	1¢ blue, type IV, imperf.	9
A9	1¢ blue, type IV, perf. 15½	23
A20	1¢ blue, type V, perf. 15½	24
A20	1¢ blue, type V, perf. 15½, laid paper	24b

Washington, Type I — A10

Type I

Type I. There is an outer frame line on all four sides. The outer frame lines at the sides are always recut, but the inner lines at the sides are not.

Type II

Type II. As type I, but with the inner lines at the sides also recut.

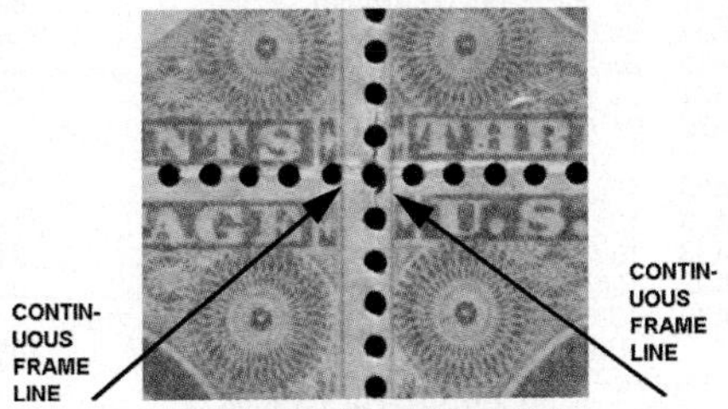

Washington (Type III) — A21

Type III. There are no outer frame lines at top and bottom. The side frame lines were recut so as to be continuous from the top to the bottom of the plate.

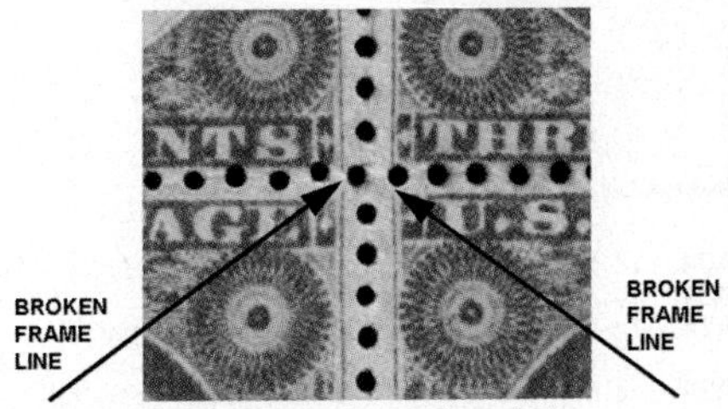

Washington (Type IV) — A21a

Type IV — As type III, but the side frame lines extend only to the top and bottom of the stamp design. All Type IV stamps are from plates 10 and 11 (each of which exists in three states), and these plates produced only Type IV. The side frame lines were recut individually for each stamp, thus being broken between the stamps vertically.

Beware of type III stamps with frame lines that stop at the top of the design (from top row of plate) or bottom of the design (from bottom row of plate). These are often mistakenly offered as No. 26A.

Jefferson, Type I There are projections on all four sides. — A11

Type II, The projections at top and bottom are partly cut away. Several minor types could be made according to the extent of cutting of the projections. — A22

Nos. 40-47 are reprints produced by the Continental Bank Note Co. The stamps are on white paper without gum, perf. 12. They were not good for postal use. They also exist imperforate.

A10 3¢ orange brown, type I, imperf. **10**
A10 3¢ orange brown, type II, imperf. **10A**
A10 3¢ dull red, type I, imperf. **11**
A10 3¢ dull red, type II, imperf. **11A**
A10 3¢ rose, type I, perf. 15½ **25**
A10 3¢ rose, type II, perf. 15½ **25A**
A10 3¢ scarlet, perf. 12 (Special Printing) **41**
A10 3¢ dull red, type III, perf. 15½ **26**
A10 3¢ dull red, type IV, perf. 15½ **26A**
A11 5¢ red brown, type I, imperf. **12**
A11 5¢ brick red, type I, perf. 15½ **27**
A11 5¢ red brown, type I, perf. 15½ **28**
A11 5¢ Indian red, type I, perf. 15½ **28A**
A11 5¢ brown, type I, perf. 15½ **29**
A22 5¢ orange brown, type II, perf. 15½ **30**
A22 5¢ brown, type II, perf. 15½ **30A**
A22 5¢ orange brown, type II, perf. 12 (Special Printing) **42**

Washington, Type I — A12

Washington — A16

A12 Type I The shells at the lower corners are practically complete. The outer line below the label is very nearly complete. The outer lines are broken above the middle of the top label and the "X" in each upper corner.

A13 Type II The design is complete at the top. The outer line at the bottom is broken in the middle. The shells are partly cut away.

A14 Type III The outer lines are broken above the top label and the "X" numerals. The outer line at the bottom and the shells are partly cut away as in Type II.

A15 Type IV The outer lines have been recut at top or bottom or both.

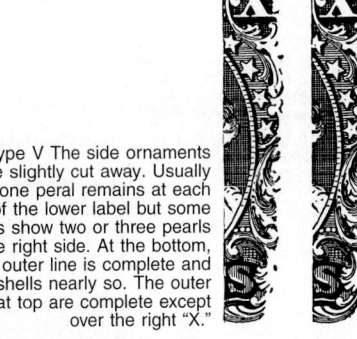

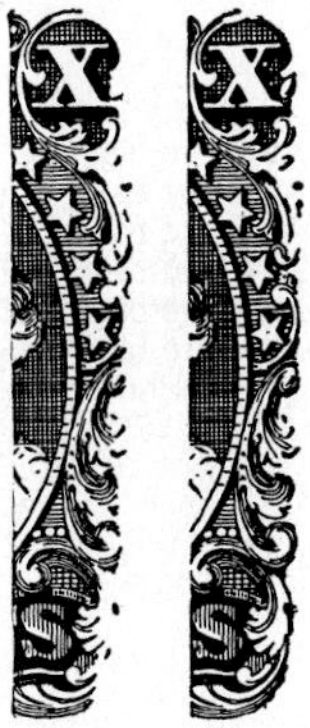

A23 Type V The side ornaments are slightly cut away. Usually only one peral remains at each end of the lower label but some copies show two or three pearls at the right side. At the bottom, the outer line is complete and the shells nearly so. The outer lines at top are complete except over the right "X."

A16 Plate 1 Outer frame lines recut on plate and complete.

Plate 3 Outer frame lines not recut and light, uneven and/or broken.

A12 10¢ green, type I, imperf. **13**
A12 10¢ green, type I, perf. 15½ **31**
A12 10¢ blue green, perf. 12 (Special Printing) ... **43**
A13 10¢ green, type II, imperf. **14**
A13 10¢ green, type II, perf. 15½ **32**
A14 10¢ green, type III, imperf. **15**
A14 10¢ green, type III, perf. 15½ **33**
A15 10¢ green, type IV, imperf. **16**
A15 10¢ green, type IV, perf. 15½ **34**
A23 10¢ green, type V, perf. 15½ **35**
A16 12¢ black, imperf. **17**
A16 12¢ black, plate 1, perf. 15½ **36**
A16 12¢ black, plate 3 .... **36B**
A16 12¢ greenish black, perf. 12 .... **44**

Washington — A17

Franklin — A18

Washington — A19

A17 24¢ gray lilac, perf. 15½ **37**
A17 24¢ blackish violet, perf. 12 (Special Printing) **45**
A18 30¢ orange, perf. 15½ **38**
A18 30¢ yellow orange, perf. 12 (Special Printing) **46**
A19 90¢ blue, perf. 15½ **39**
A19 90¢ deep blue, perf. 12 (Special Printing) **47**

ISSUES OF 1861-75

Franklin — A24

A24 See the essay section for type A24 in indigo on perf. 12 thin, semi-transparent paper without the dash under the tip of the ornament at the right of the numeral in the upper left corner.

A24 1¢ blue, perf. 12 63
A24 1¢ blue, same, laid paper 63c
A24 1¢ blue, grill 11x14mm 85A
A24 1¢ blue, grill 11x13mm 86
A24 1¢ blue, grill 9x13mm 92
A24 1¢ blue, no grill, hard white paper (Special Printing) 102

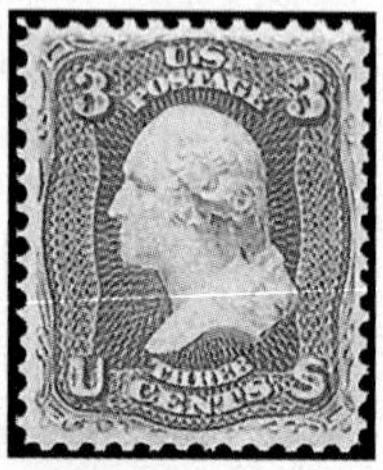

Washington — A25

A25 See the essay section for type A25 in brown rose on perf. 12 thin, semi-transparent paper with smaller ornaments in the corners which do not end in a small ball.

A25 3¢ pink, no grill, perf. 12 64
A25 3¢ lake, same (Special Printing) 66
A25 3¢ scarlet, same (Special Printing) 74
A25 3¢ rose, same 65
A25 3¢ rose, same, laid paper 65b
A25 3¢ rose, grilled all over 79
A25 3¢ rose, grill 18x15mm 82
A25 3¢ rose, grill 13x16mm 83
A25 3¢ rose, grill 12x14mm 85
A25 3¢ rose, grill 11x14mm 85C
A25 3¢ rose, grill 11x13mm 88
A25 3¢ red, grill 9x13mm 94
A25 3¢ brown red, no grill, hard white paper (Special Printing) 104

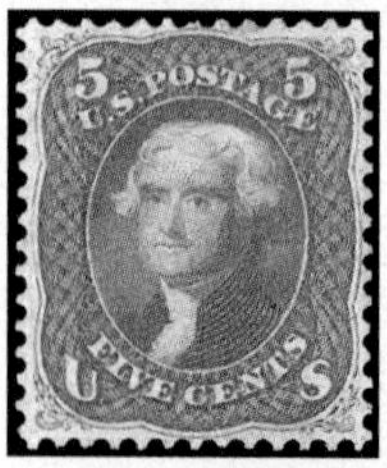

Jefferson — A26

A26 See the essay section for type A26 in brown on perf. 12 thin, semi-transparent paper without the leaflet in the foliated ornament at each corner.

A26 5¢ buff, no grill 67
A26 5¢ red brown, no grill 75
A26 5¢ brown, no grill 76
A26 5¢ brown, laid paper 76b
A26 5¢ brown, grilled all over 80
A26 5¢ brown, grill 9x13mm 95
A26 5¢ brown, no grill, hard white paper 105

A27a

Washington — A27

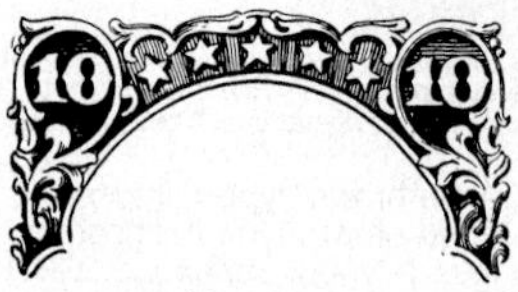

A27 A heavy curved line has been cut below the stars and an outer line added to the ornaments above them.

A27a 10¢ dark green, thin paper 62B
A27 10¢ green, see illustration A27 68
A27 10¢ green, grill 11x14mm 85D
A27 10¢ green, grill 11x13mm 89
A27 10¢ yellow green, grill 9x13mm 96
A27 10¢ green, no grill, hard white paper (Special Printing) 106

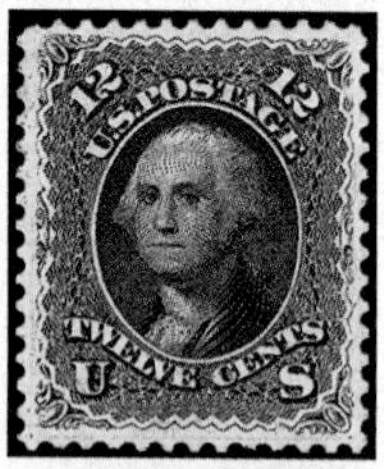

Washington — A28

A28 See the essay section for type A28 in black on perf. 12 thin, semi-transparent paper without corner ornaments.

A28 12¢ black, no grill 69
A28 12¢ black, grill 11x14mm 85E
A28 12¢ black, grill 11x13mm 90
A28 12¢ black, grill 9x13mm 97
A28 12¢ black, no grill, hard white paper, (Special Printing) 107

Washington — A29

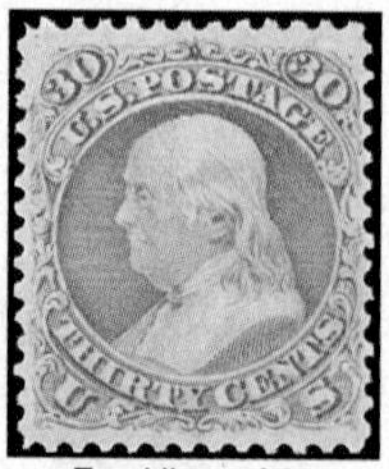

Franklin — A30

See the Trial Color proof section for type A29 in dark violet on perf. 12 thin paper without grill and type A30 in red orange on perf. 12 thin paper without grill.

A29 24¢ red lilac, no grill 70
A29 24¢ violet, no grill, thin, transparent paper 70c
A29 24¢ lilac, no grill 78
A29 24¢ gray lilac, grill 9x13mm 99
A29 24¢ deep violet, no grill, hard white paper, (Special Printing) 109
A30 30¢ orange, no grill 71
A30 30¢ orange, grilled all over 81
A30 30¢ orange, grill 9x13mm 100
A30 30¢ brownish orange, no grill, hard white paper, (Special Printing) 110

Washington — A31

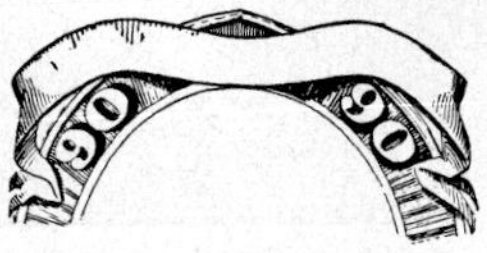

A31 See the essay section for type A31 in dull blue on perf. 12 thin semi-transparent paper without dashes between the parallel lines which form the angle above the ribbon with "U.S. Postage," and without the point of color at the apex of the lower line.

A31 90¢ blue, no grill 72
A31 90¢ blue, grill 9x13mm 101
A31 90¢ blue, no grill, hard white paper, (Special Printing) 111

ISSUES OF 1861-75

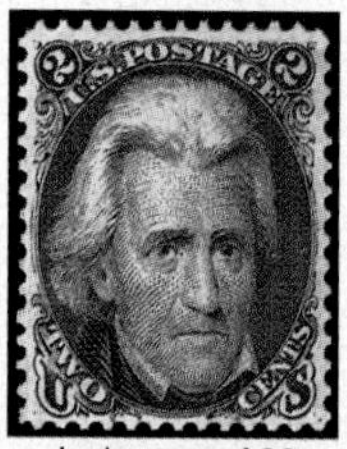

Jackson — A32

Lincoln — A33

Perf. 12, Unwmkd.

A32 2¢ black, no grill 73
A32 2¢ black, laid paper 73d
A32 2¢ black, grill 12x14mm 84
A32 2¢ black, grill 11x14mm 85B
A32 2¢ black, grill 11x13mm 87
A32 2¢ black, grill 9x13mm 93
A32 2¢ black, no grill, hard white paper, (Special Printing) 103
A33 15¢ black, no grill 77
A33 15¢ black, grill 11x14mm 85F
A33 15¢ black, grill 11x13mm 91
A33 15¢ black, grill 9x13mm 98
A33 15¢ black, no grill, hard white paper, (Special Printing) 108

ISSUES OF 1869-80

Franklin — A34

A34 1¢ buff, grill 9½x9mm 112
A34 1¢ buff, no grill 112b
A34 1¢ buff, no grill, hard white paper (Special Printing) 123
A34 1¢ buff, no grill, soft porous paper (Special Printing) 133
A34 1¢ brown orange, same without gum (Special Printing) 133a

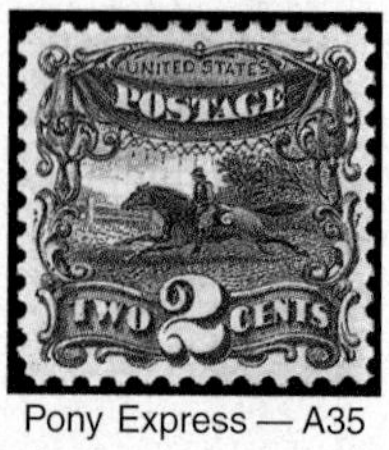

Pony Express — A35

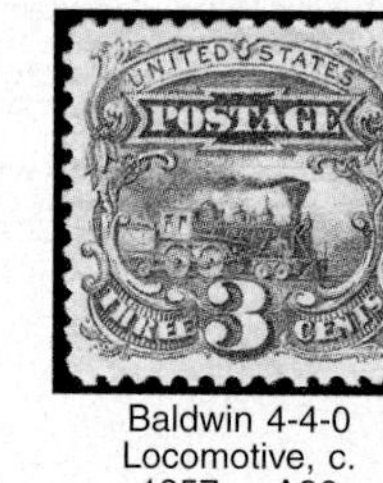

Baldwin 4-4-0 Locomotive, c. 1857 — A36

A35 2¢ brown, grill 9½x9mm **113**
A35 2¢ brown, no grill **113b**
A35 2¢ brown, no grill, hard white paper (Special Printing) **124**
A36 3¢ ultramarine, grill 9½x9mm **114**
A36 3¢ ultramarine, no grill **114a**
A36 3¢ blue, no grill, hard white paper (Special Printing) **125**

Washington — A37

Shield and Eagle — A38

S.S. Adriatic — A39

A37 6¢ ultramarine, grill 9½x9mm **115**
A37 6¢ blue, no grill, hard white paper (Special Printing) **126**
A38 10¢ yellow, grill 9½x9mm **116**
A38 10¢ yellow, no grill, hard white paper (Special Printing) **127**
A39 12¢ green, grill 9½x9mm **117**
A39 12¢ green, no grill, hard white paper (Special Printing) **128**

Landing of Columbus — A40

A40 Type I Picture unframed

A40a Type II Picture framed

Type III same as Type I but without the fringe of brown shading lines around central vignette.

A40 15¢ brown & blue, type I, grill 9½x9mm **118**
A40 15¢ brown & blue, type I, no grill **118a**
A40 15¢ brown & blue, type III, no grill, hard white paper (Special Printing) **129**
A40a 15¢ brown & blue, type II, grill 9½x9mm **119**

The Declaration of Independence — A41

Shield, Eagle and Flags — A42

Lincoln — A43

A41 24¢ green & violet, grill 9½x9mm **120**
A41 24¢ green & violet, no grill **120a**
A41 24¢ green & violet, no grill, hard white paper (Special Printing) **130**
A42 30¢ ultramarine & carmine, grill 9½x9mm **121**
A42 30¢ ultramarine & carmine, no grill **121a**
A42 30¢ ultramarine & carmine, no grill, hard white paper (Special Printing) **131**
A43 90¢ carmine & black, grill 9½x9mm **122**
A43 90¢ carmine & black, no grill **122a**
A43 90¢ carmine & black, no grill, hard white paper (Special Printing) **132**
A43 90¢ carmine & black, 28x28mm, imperf., litho. & engraved **2433a**
A43 90¢ blue & brown, 28x28mm, imperf., litho. & engraved **2433b**
A43 90¢ green & blue, 28x28mm, imperf., litho. & engraved **2433c**
A43 90¢ scarlet & blue, 28x28mm, imperf., litho. & engraved **2433d**

ISSUES OF 1870-88

The secret mark shown in the detail of A45a is seldom found on the actual stamps. Stamps Nos. 146 and 157 are best identified by color which is red brown for No. 146 and brown for No. 157.

Note I: Special printings of 1880-83 — All denominations of this series were printed on special order from the Post Office Department during the period the stamps were current. The paper being the same as used on current issue, the special printings are extremely difficult to identify. The 2¢ brown, 7¢ scarlet vermilion, 12¢ blackish purple and 24¢ dark violet are easily distinguished by the soft porous paper as these denominations were never previously printed on soft paper. The other denominations can be distinguished by shades only, those of the special printings being slightly deeper and richer than the regular issue. The special printings except No. 211B were issued without gum. The only certain way to identify them is by comparison with stamps previously established as special printings.

Franklin — A44

A44

A44a With secret mark. In the pearl at the left of the numeral "1" there is a small dash.

A44b Re-engraved. The vertical lines in the upper part of the stamp have been so deepened that the background often appears to be solid. Lines of shading have been added to the upper arabesques.

A44 1¢ ultramarine, with grill **134**
A44 1¢ ultramarine, no grill **145**
A44a 1¢ ultramarine, white wove paper no grill **156**
A44a 1¢ ultramarine, with grill **156e**
A44a 1¢ ultramarine, hard white paper, without gum (Special Printing) **167**
A44a 1¢ dark ultra, soft porous paper **182**
A44a 1¢ dark ultra, soft porous paper, without gum (Special Printing, see note I) **192**
A44b 1¢ gray blue **206**

Jackson — A45

A45

A45a Under the scroll at the left of "U.S." there is a small diagonal line.

A45 2¢ red brown, with grill **135**
A45 2¢ red brown, no grill **146**
A45a 2¢ brown, white wove paper no grill **157**
A45a 2¢ brown, with grill **157c**
A45a 2¢ dark brown, hard white paper, without gum (Special Printing) **168**
A45a 2¢ black brown, soft porous paper, without gum (Special Printing) **193**
A45a 2¢ vermilion, yellowish paper **178**
A45a 2¢ vermilion, same, with grill **178c**
A45a 2¢ vermilion, soft porous paper **183**
A45a 2¢ carmine vermilion, hard white paper, without gum (Special Printing) **180**
A45a 2¢ scarlet vermilion, soft porous paper, without gum (Special Printing, see note I) **203**

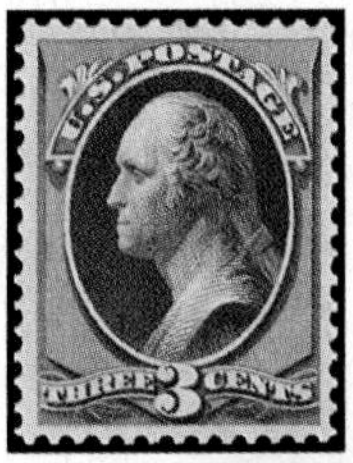

Washington — A46

A46

A46a With secret mark. The under part of the tail of the left ribbon is heavily shaded.

A46b Re-engraved. The shading at the sides of the central oval appears only about one half the previous width. A short horizontal dash has been cut about 1mm. below the "TS" of "CENTS."

A46 3¢ green, with grill **136**
A46 3¢ green, no grill **147**
A46a 3¢ green, white wove paper, no grill **158**
A46a 3¢ green, same, with grill **158e**
A46a 3¢ blue green, hard white paper, without gum (Special Printing) **169**
A46a 3¢ green, soft porous paper **184**
A46a 3¢ blue green, soft porous paper, without gum (Special Printing see note I) **194**
A46b 3¢ blue green, re-engraved **207**
A46b 3¢ vermilion re-engraved **214**

Lincoln — A47

A47

A47a With secret mark. The first four vertical lines of the shading in the lower part of the left ribbon have been strengthened.

A47b Re-engraved. On the original stamps four vertical lines can be counted from the edge of the panel to the outside of the stamp. On the re-engraved stamps there are three lines in the same place.

A47	6¢ carmine, with grill	**137**
A47	6¢ carmine, no grill	**148**
A47a	6¢ dull pink, no grill, white wove paper	**159**
A47a	6¢ dull pink, with grill	**159b**
A47a	6¢ dull rose, hard white paper, without gum (Special Printing)	**170**
A47a	6¢ pink, soft porous paper	**186**
A47a	6¢ dull rose, soft porous paper, without gum (Special Printing see note I)	**195**
A47b	6¢ rose, re-engraved	**208**

Edwin McMasters Stanton — A48

Thomas Jefferson — A49

A48

A48a With secret mark. Two small semi-circles are drawn around the ends of the lines which outline the ball in the lower right hand corner.

A49

A49a With secret mark. A small semi-circle in the scroll at the right end of the upper label.

A49b Re-engraved. On the original stamps there are five vertical lines between the left side of the oval and the edge of the shield. There are only four lines on the re-engraved stamps. In the lower part of the re-engraved stamps the horizontal lines of the background have been strengthened.

Henry Clay — A50

A50

A50a With secret mark. The balls of the figure "2" are crescent shaped.

A48	7¢ vermilion, with grill	**138**
A48	7¢ vermilion, no grill	**149**
A48a	7¢ orange verm., white wove paper no grill	**160**
A48a	7¢ orange verm., same, with grill	**160a**
A48a	7¢ reddish verm., hard white paper, without gum (Special Printing)	**171**
A48a	7¢ scarlet verm., soft porous paper, without gum (Special Printing)	**196**
A49	10¢ brown, with grill	**139**
A49	10¢ brown, no grill	**150**
A49	10¢ brown, soft porous paper	**187**
A49a	10¢ brown, white wove paper no grill	**161**
A49a	10¢ brown, with grill	**161c**
A49a	10¢ pale brown, hard white paper, without gum (Special Printing)	**172**
A49a	10¢ brown, soft porous paper	**188**
A49a	10¢ deep brown, soft porous paper, without gum (Special Printing, see note I)	**197**
A49b	10¢ brown, re-engraved	**209**
A50	12¢ dull violet, with grill	**140**
A50	12¢ dull violet, no grill	**151**
A50a	12¢ blackish violet, white wove paper, no grill	**162**
A50a	12¢ blackish violet, with grill	**162a**
A50a	12¢ dark violet, hard white paper, without gum (Special Printing)	**173**
A50a	12¢ blackish purple, soft porous paper, without gum (Special Printing)	**198**

Webster — A51

A51

A51a With secret mark. In the lower part of the triangle in the upper left corner two lines have been made heavier forming a "V." This mark can be found on some of the Continental and American (1879) printings, but not all stamps show it.

A51	15¢ orange, with grill	**141**
A51	15¢ bright orange, no grill	**152**
A51a	15¢ yellow orange, white wove paper, no grill	**163**
A51a	15¢ yellow orange, with grill	**163a**
A51a	15¢ bright orange, hard white paper, without gum (Special Printing)	**174**
A51a	15¢ red orange, soft porous paper	**189**
A51a	15¢ orange, soft porous paper, without gum (Special Printing, see note I)	**199**

General Winfield Scott — A52

Hamilton — A53

Perry — A54

Secret marks were added to the dies of the 24¢, 30¢ and 90¢ but new plates were not made from them. The various printings of these stamps can be distinguished only by the shades and paper.

A52	24¢ purple, with grill	**142**
A52	24¢ purple, no grill	**153**
A52	24¢ purple, vertically ribbed white wove paper, no grill	**164**
A52	24¢ dull purple, hard white paper, without gum (Special Printing)	**175**
A52	24¢ dark violet, soft porous paper, without gum (Special Printing)	**200**
A53	30¢ black, with grill	**143**
A53	30¢ black, no grill	**154**
A53	30¢ full black, soft porous paper	**190**
A53	30¢ gray black, white wove paper, no grill	**165**
A53	30¢ greenish black, with grill	**165c**
A53	30¢ greenish black, hard white paper, without gum (Special Printing)	**176**
A53	30¢ greenish black, soft porous paper, without gum (Special Printing, see note I)	**201**
A53	30¢ orange brown	**217**
A54	90¢ carmine, with grill	**144**
A54	90¢ carmine, no grill	**155**
A54	90¢ carmine, soft porous paper	**191**
A54	90¢ rose carmine, white wove paper	**166**
A54	90¢ violet carmine, hard white paper, without gum (Special Printing)	**177**
A54	90¢ dull carmine, soft porous paper, without gum (Special Printing, see note I)	**202**
A54	90¢ purple	**218**

ISSUES OF 1875-88

Taylor — A55

Garfield — A56

Perf. 12, Unwmkd.

A55	5¢ blue, yellowish wove paper, no grill	**179**
A55	5¢ blue, with grill	**179c**
A55	5¢ bright blue, hard, white wove paper, without gum (Special Printing)	**181**
A55	5¢ blue, soft porous paper	**185**
A55	5¢ deep blue, soft porous paper, without gum (Special Printing, see note I)	**204**
A56	5¢ yellow brown	**205**
A56	5¢ gray brown, soft porous paper, without gum (Special Printing, see note I)	**205C**
A56	5¢ indigo	**216**

Washington — A57

Jackson — A58

A57 2¢ red brown **210**
A57 2¢ pale red brown, soft porous paper (Special Printing, see note I) **211B**
A57 2¢ green **213**
A58 4¢ blue green **211**
A58 4¢ deep blue green, soft porous paper, without gum (Special Printing, see note I)...... .... **211D**
A58 4¢ carmine.. **215**

Franklin — A59

A59 1¢ ultramarine.. **212**

ISSUES OF 1890-93

Franklin — A60

Washington — A61

Jackson — A62

Lincoln — A63

Grant — A64

Garfield — A65

William T. Sherman — A66

Daniel Webster — A67

Henry Clay — A68

Jefferson — A69

Perry — A70

A60 1¢ dull blue.. **219**
A61 2¢ lake.. **219D**
A61 2¢ carmine.. **220**
A62 3¢ purple.. **221**
A63 4¢ dark brown.. **222**
A64 5¢ chocolate.. **223**
A65 6¢ brown red.. **224**
A66 8¢ lilac.. **225**
A67 10¢ green.. **226**
A68 15¢ indigo.. **227**
A69 30¢ black.. **228**
A70 90¢ orange.. **229**

ISSUES OF 1894-1903

This series, the first to be printed by the Bureau of Engraving and Printing, closely resembles the 1890 series but is identified by the triangles which have been added to the upper corners of the designs.

The Catalogue divides this group into three separate series, the first of which was issued in 1894 and is unwatermarked. In 1895 the paper used was watermarked with the double line letters USPS (United States Postage Stamp). The stamps show one complete letter of the watermark or parts of two or more letters.

This watermark appears on all United States stamps issued from 1895 until 1910.

In 1898 the colors of some of the denominations were changed, which created the third series noted in the Catalogue.

Other than the watermark, or lack of it, there are three styles of the corner triangles used on the 2 cent stamps and two variations of designs are noted on the 10 cent and $1 denomination. In the following list all of these variations are illustrated and described immediately preceding the denominations on which they appear.

USPS Wmkd. (191) Horizontally

or Vertically USPS

(Actual size of letter)

Franklin — A87

Washington — A88

Jackson — A89

Lincoln — A90

Grant — A91

Garfield — A92

Sherman — A93

Webster — A94

Clay — A95

Jefferson — A96

Perry — A97

James Madison — A98

John Marshall — A99

A87 1¢ ultramarine, unwmkd.. **246**
A87 1¢ blue, unwmkd.. **247**
A87 1¢ blue, wmkd.. **264**
A87 1¢ deep green, wmkd.. **279**
A87 1¢ on 1¢ yellow green, "CUBA"........ **Cuba 221**
A87 1¢ deep green, "GUAM"........................ **Guam 1**
A87 1¢ yellow green, "PHILIPPINES"....... **Phil. 213**
A87 1¢ yellow green, "PORTO RICO"........ **P.R. 210**
A87 1¢ yellow green, "PUERTO RICO"...... **P.R. 215**

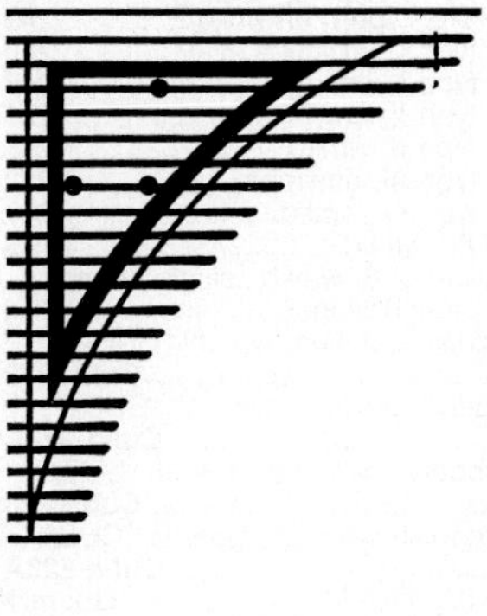
Triangle A (Type I) The horizontal lines of the ground work run across the triangle and are of the same thickness within it as without.

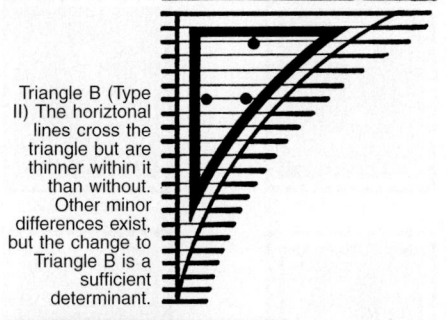

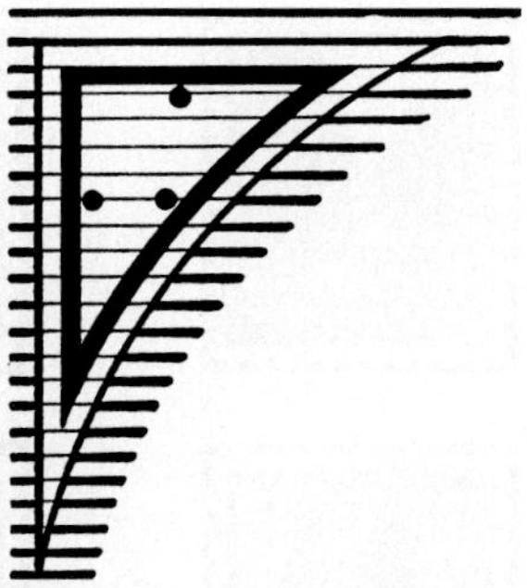

Triangle B (Type II) The horiztonal lines cross the triangle but are thinner within it than without. Other minor differences exist, but the change to Triangle B is a sufficient determinant.

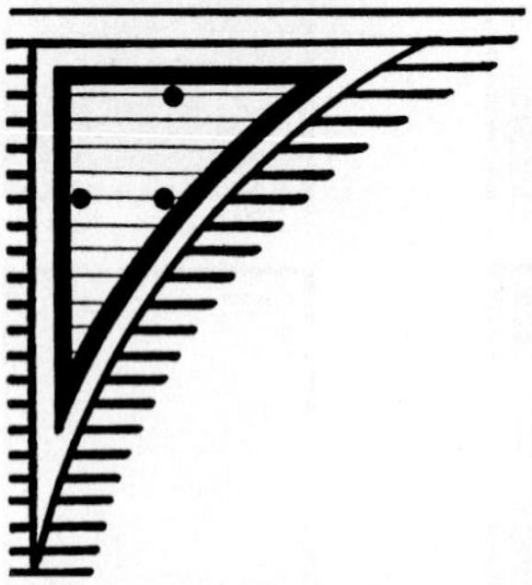

Triangle C (Types III & IV) Type III: The horizontal lines do not cross the double lines of the triangle. The lines within the triangle are thin, as in Triangle B.

The rest of the design is the same as Type II, except that most of the designs had the dot in the "S" of "CENTS" removed. Stamps with this dot are listed; some specialists refer to them as "Type IIIa" varieties.

Type IV: Same triangle C as type III, but other design differences including (1) recutting and lengthening of hairline, (2) shaded toga button, (3) strengthening of lines on sleeve, (4) additional dots on ear, (5) "T" of "TWO" straight at right, (6) background lines extend into white oval opposite "U" of "UNITED." Many other differences exist.

A88	2¢ pink, type I, unwmkd.	**248**
A88	2¢ carmine lake, type I, unwmkd.	**249**
A88	2¢ carmine, type I, unwmkd.	**250**
A88	2¢ carmine, type I, wmkd.	**265**
A88	2¢ carmine, type II, unwmkd.	**251**
A88	2¢ carmine, type II, wmkd.	**266**
A88	2¢ carmine, type III, unwmkd.	**252**
A88	2¢ carmine, type III, wmkd.	**267**
A88	2¢ red, type IV, wmkd.	**279B**
A88	2¢ booklet pane of 6, wmkd., single stamps with 1 or 2 straight edges	**279Bj**
A88	2c on 2¢ reddish carmine, type III "CUBA"	**Cuba 222**
A88	2c on 2¢ reddish carmine, type IV, "CUBA"	**Cuba 222A**
A88	2 ½c on 2¢ reddish carmine, type III, "CUBA"	**Cuba 223**
A88	2 ½c on 2¢ reddish carmine, type IV, "CUBA"	**Cuba 223A**
A88	2¢ red, type IV, "GUAM"	**Guam 2**
A88	2¢ red, type IV, "PHILIPPINES"	**Phil. 214**
A88	Same, booklet pane of 6	**Phil. 214b**
A88	2¢ reddish carmine, type IV, "PORTO RICO"	**P.R. 211**
A88	Same, "PUERTO RICO"	**P.R. 216**
A89	3¢ purple, unwmkd.	**253**
A89	3¢ purple, wmkd.	**268**
A89	3¢ on 3¢ purple, "CUBA"	**Cuba 224**
A89	3¢ purple, "GUAM"	**Guam 3**
A89	3¢ purple "PHILIPPINES"	**Phil. 215**
A90	4¢ dark brown, unwmkd.	**254**
A90	4¢ dark brown, wmkd.	**269**
A90	4¢ rose brown, wmkd.	**280**
A90	4¢ lilac brown, "GUAM"	**Guam 4**
A90	4¢ orange brown, "PHILIPPINES"	**Phil. 220**
A91	5¢ chocolate, unwmkd.	**255**
A91	5¢ chocolate, wmkd.	**270**
A91	5¢ dark blue, wmkd.	**281**
A91	5¢ on 5¢ blue, "CUBA"	**Cuba 225**
A91	5¢ blue, "GUAM"	**Guam 5**
A91	5¢ blue, "PHILIPPINES"	**Phil. 216**
A91	5¢ blue, "PORTO RICO"	**P.R. 212**
A92	6¢ dull brown, unwmkd.	**256**
A92	6¢ dull brown, wmkd. USPS	**271**
A92	6¢ dull brown, wmkd. USIR	**271a**
A92	6¢ lake, wmkd.	**282**
A92	6¢ lake, "GUAM"	**Guam 6**
A92	6¢ lake, "PHILIPPINES"	**Phil. 221**
A93	8¢ violet brown, unwmkd.	**257**
A93	8¢ violet brown, wmkd. USPS	**272**
A93	8¢ violet brown, wmkd. USIR	**272a**
A93	8¢ violet brown, "GUAM"	**Guam 7**
A93	8¢ violet brown, "PHILIPPINES"	**Phil. 222**
A93	8¢ violet brown, "PORTO RICO"	**P.R. 213**

Type I The tips of the foliate ornaments do not impinge on the white curved line below "ten cents."

Type II The tips of the ornaments break the curved line below the "e" of "ten" and the "t" of "cents."

A94	10¢ dark green, unwmkd.	**258**
A94	10¢ dark green, wmkd.	**273**
A94	10¢ brown, type I, wmkd.	**282C**
A94	10¢ orange brown, type II, wmkd.	**283**
A94	10¢ on 10¢ brown, type I, "CUBA"	**Cuba 226**
A94	Same, type II, "CUBA"	**Cuba 226A**
A94	10¢ brown, type I, "GUAM"	**Guam 8**
A94	10¢ brown, type II, "GUAM"	**Guam 9**
A94	10¢ brown, type I, "PHILIPPINES"	**Phil. 217**
A94	10¢ orange brown, type II, "PHILIPPINES"	**Phil. 217A**
A94	10¢ brown, type I, "PORTO RICO"	**P.R. 214**
A95	15¢ dark blue, unwmkd.	**259**
A95	15¢ dark blue, wmkd.	**274**
A95	15¢ olive green, wmkd.	**284**
A95	15¢ olive green, "GUAM"	**Guam 10**
A95	15¢ olive green, "PHILIPPINES"	**Phil. 218**
A96	50¢ orange, unwmkd.	**260**
A96	50¢ orange, wmkd.	**275**
A96	50¢ orange, "GUAM"	**Guam 11**
A96	50¢ orange, unwmkd., "PHILIPPINES"	**Phil. 212**
A96	50¢ orange, wmkd., "PHILIPPINES"	**Phil. 219**

A97 Type I The circles enclosing "$1" are broken where they meet the curved line below "One Dollar."

A97 Type II The circles are complete.

A97	$1 black, type I, unwmkd.	**261**
A97	$1 black, type I, wmkd.	**276**
A97	$1 black, type II, unwmkd.	**261A**
A97	$1 black, type II, wmkd.	**276A**
A97	$1 black, type I, "GUAM"	**Guam 12**
A97	$1 black, type II, "GUAM"	**Guam 13**
A97	$1 black, type I, "PHILIPPINES"	**Phil. 223**
A97	$1 black, type II, "PHILIPPINES"	**Phil. 223A**
A98	$2 bright blue, unwmkd.	**262**
A98	$2 blue, perf. 11, tagged	**2875a**
A98	$2 bright blue, wmkd.	**277**
A98	$2 dark blue, "PHILIPPINES"	**Phil. 224**
A99	$5 dark green, unwmkd.	**263**
A99	$5 dark green, wmkd.	**278**
A99	$5 dark green, "PHILIPPINES"	**Phil. 225**

ISSUES OF 1902-17

Franklin — A115

Washington — A116

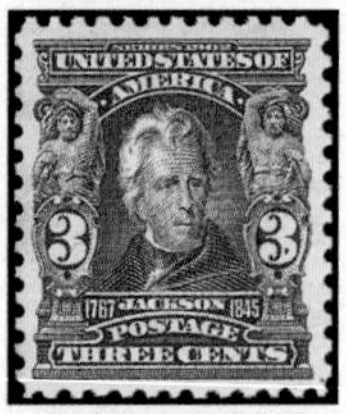

Jackson — A117

Grant — A118

Lincoln — A119

Garfield — A120

Martha Washington — A121

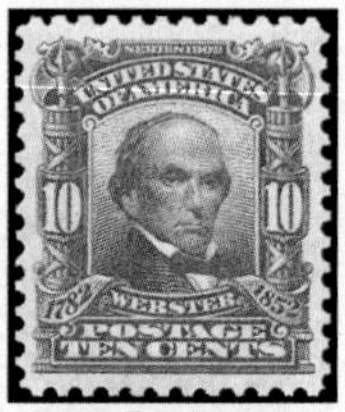

Daniel Webster — A122

Benjamin Harrison — A123

Henry Clay — A124

Jefferson — A125

David G. Farragut — A126

Madison — A127

Marshall — A128

Unless otherwise noted all stamps are Perf. 12 and Wmkd. (191)

Single stamps from booklet panes show 1 or 2 straight edges.

A115	1¢ blue green	**300**
A115	1¢ booklet pane of 6	**300b**
A115	1¢ blue green, imperf.	**314**
A115	1¢ blue green, perf. 12 horiz., pair	**316**
A115	1¢ blue green, perf. 12 vert., pair	**318**
A115	1¢ blue green, "CANAL ZONE PANAMA"	**C.Z. 4**

Type	Description	No.
A115	1¢ blue green, "PHILIPPINES"	**Phil. 226**
A116	2¢ carmine	**301**
A116	2¢ booklet pane of 6	**301c**
A116	2¢ carmine, "PHILIPPINES"	**Phil. 227**
A117	3¢ bright violet	**302**
A117	3¢ bright violet, "PHILIPPINES"	**Phil. 228**
A118	4¢ brown	**303**
A118	4¢ brown, imperf.	**314A**
A118	4¢ brown, "PHILIPPINES"	**Phil. 229**
A119	5¢ blue	**304**
A119	5¢ blue, imperf.	**315**
A119	5¢ blue, perf. 12 horiz. pair	**317**
A119	5¢ blue, "CANAL ZONE PANAMA"	**C.Z. 6**
A119	5¢ blue, "PHILIPPINES"	**Phil. 230**
A120	6¢ claret	**305**
A120	6¢ brownish lake, "PHILIPPINES"	**Phil. 231**
A121	8¢ violet black	**306**
A121	8¢ violet black, "CANAL ZONE PANAMA"	**C.Z. 7**
A121	8¢ violet black, "PHILIPPINES"	**Phil. 232**
A122	10¢ pale red brown	**307**
A122	10¢ pale red brown, "CANAL ZONE PANAMA"	**C.Z. 8**
A122	10¢ pale red brown, "PHILIPPINES"	**Phil. 233**
A123	13¢ purple black	**308**
A123	13¢ purple black, "PHILIPPINES"	**Phil. 234**
A124	15¢ olive green	**309**
A124	15¢ olive green, "PHILIPPINES"	**Phil. 235**
A125	50¢ orange	**310**
A125	50¢ orange, "PHILIPPINES"	**Phil. 236**
A126	$1 black	**311**
A126	$1 black, "PHILIPPINES"	**Phil. 237**
A127	$2 dark blue	**312**
A127	$2 dark blue, unwmkd., perf. 10	**479**
A127	$2 dark blue, "PHILIPPINES"	**Phil. 238**
A128	$5 dark green	**313**
A128	$5 light green, unwmkd., perf. 10	**480**
A128	$5 dark green, "PHILIPPINES"	**Phil. 239**

ISSUES OF 1903

Washington — A129

Type I

Type II

Specialists recognize over a hundred shades of this stamp in various hues of vermilion, red, carmine and lake. The Scott Catalogue lists only the most striking differences.

The Government coil stamp, No. 322 should not be confused with the scarlet vermilion coil of the International Vending Machine Co., which is perforated 12½ to 13.

Type	Description	No.
A129	2¢ carmine, type I, wmkd.	**319**
A129	2¢ lake, type II	**319f**
A129	2¢ carmine, type I, booklet pane of 6	**319g**
A129	Same, type II	**319h**
A129	2¢ carmine, type I, imperf.	**320**
A129	2¢ lake, type II, imperf.	**320a**
A129	2¢ carmine, perf. 12 horiz. pair	**321**
A129	2¢ carmine, perf. 12 vert. pair	**322**
A129	2¢ carmine, "CANAL ZONE PANAMA"	**C.Z. 5**
A129	2¢ carmine, "PHILIPPINES"	**Phil. 240**
A129	2¢ carmine, same, booklet pane of 6	**Phil. 240a**

ISSUES OF 1908-09

This series introduces for the first time the single line watermark USPS. Only a small portion of several letters is often all that can be seen on a single stamp.

Franklin — A138

Washington — A139

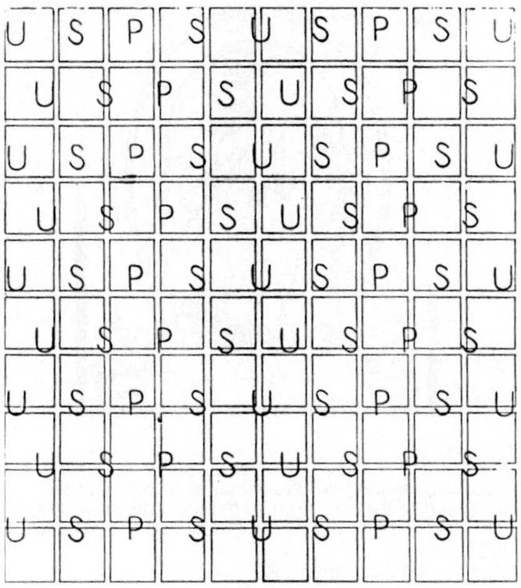

Wmk. 190

Type	Description	No.
A138	1¢ green, perf. 12, double line wmk.	**331**
A138	1¢ green, perf. 12, single line wmk.	**374**
A138	1¢ green, perf. 12, bluish paper	**357**
A138	1¢ green, imperf., double line wmk.	**343**
A138	1¢ green, imperf., single line wmk.	**383**
A138	1¢ green, perf. 12 horiz., double line wmk.	**348**
A138	1¢ green, perf. 12 horiz., single line wmk.	**385**
A138	1¢ green, perf. 12 vert., double line wmk.	**352**
A138	1¢ green, perf. 12 vert., single line wmk.	**387**
A138	1¢ green, perf. 8½ horiz., single line wmk.	**390**
A138	1¢ green, perf. 8½ vert., single line wmk.	**392**
A139	2¢ carmine, perf. 12, double line wmk.	**332**
A139	2¢ carmine, perf. 12, single line wmk.	**375**
A139	2¢ carmine, perf. 12, bluish paper	**358**
A139	2¢ carmine, perf. 11, double line wmk.	**519**
A139	2¢ carmine, imperf., double line wmk.	**344**
A139	2¢ carmine, imperf., single line wmk.	**384**
A139	2¢ carmine, perf. 12 horiz., double line wmk.	**349**
A139	2¢ carmine, perf. 12 horiz., single line wmk.	**386**
A139	2¢ carmine, perf. 12 vert., double line wmk.	**353**
A139	2¢ carmine, perf. 12 vert., single line wmk.	**388**
A139	2¢ carmine, perf. 8½ horiz. single line wmk.	**391**
A139	2¢ carmine, perf. 8½ vert., single line wmk.	**393**

Single stamps from booklet panes show 1 or 2 straight edges.

Type	Description	No.
A138	1¢ green, perf. 12, double line wmk., booklet pane of 6	**331a**
A138	1¢ green, perf.12, single line wmk., booklet pane of 6	**374a**
A139	2¢ carmine, perf. 12, double line wmk., booklet pane of 6	**332a**
A139	2¢ carmine, perf. 12, single line wmk., booklet pane of 6	**375a**

ISSUES OF 1908-21
FLAT BED AND ROTARY PRESS STAMPS

The Rotary Press Stamps are printed from plates that are curved to fit around a cylinder. This curvature produces stamps that are slightly larger, either horizontally or vertically, than those printed from flat plates. Designs of stamps from flat plates measure about 18½-19mm. wide by 22mm. high. When the impressions are placed sidewise on the curved plates the designs are 19½-20mm. wide; when they are placed vertically the designs are 22½ to 22¾mm. high. A line of color (not a guide line) shows where the curved plates meet or join on the press.

Rotary Press Coil Stamps were printed from plates of 170 subjects for stamps coiled sidewise, and from plates of 150 subjects for stamps coiled endwise.

Washington — A140

1¢ A138 Portrait of Franklin, value in words.
2¢ A139 Portrait of Washington, value in words.
A140 Portrait of Washington, value in numerals.

Type	Description	No.
A140	1¢ green, perf. 12, single line wmk.	**405**
A140	1¢ green, same, booklet pane of 6	**405b**
A140	1¢ green, perf. 11, flat plate, unwmkd.	**498**
A140	1¢ green, same, booklet pane of 6	**498e**
A140	1¢ green, same, booklet pane of 30	**498f**
A140	1¢ green, perf. 11, rotary press measuring 19mmx22½mm, unwmkd.	**544**
A140	1¢ green, same, measuring 19½ to 20mmx22mm	**545**
A140	1¢ gray green, perf. 11, offset, unwmkd.	**525**
A140	1¢ gray green, perf. 12½	**536**
A140	1¢ green, perf. 11x10	**538**
A140	1¢ green, perf. 10x11	**542**
A140	1¢ green, perf. 10, single line wmk.	**424**
A140	1¢ green, same, perf. 12x10	**423A**
A140	1¢ green, same, perf. 10x12	**423D**
A140	1¢ green, perf.10, single line wmk., booklet pane of 6	**424d**
A140	1¢ green, perf. 10, flat plate, unwmkd.	**462**
A140	1¢ green, same, booklet pane of 6	**462a**
A140	1¢ green, perf. 10, rotary press, unwmkd.	**543**
A140	1¢ green, imperf., single line wmk.	**408**
A140	1¢ green, imperf., unwmkd.	**481**
A140	1¢ green, imperf., offset	**531**
A140	1¢ green, perf. 10 horiz., flat plate, single line wmk.	**441**
A140	1¢ green, same, rotary press	**448**
A140	1¢ green, perf. 10 horiz., rotary press, unwmkd.	**486**
A140	1¢ green, perf. 10 vert., flat plate, single line wmk.	**443**
A140	1¢ green, same, rotary press	**452**
A140	1¢ green, perf. 10 vert., rotary press, unwmkd.	**490**
A140	1¢ green, perf. 8½ horiz. single line wmk.	**410**
A140	1¢ green, perf. 8½ vert., same	**412**

TYPES OF TWO CENTS

TYPE I

TYPE IA

Type Ia *The design characteristics are similar to type I except that all of the lines of the design are stronger.*

The toga button, toga rope and rope shading lines are heavy. The latter characteristics are those of type II, which, however, occur only on impressions from rotary plates.

Used only on flat plates 10208 and 10209.

Type II *Shading lines in ribbons as on type I.*
The toga button, rope and rope shading lines are heavy.
The shading lines of the face at the lock of hair end in a strong, vertical curved line.
Used on rotary press printings only.

Type III

Type III *Two lines of shading in the curves of the ribbons.*
Other characteristics similar to type II.
Used on rotary press printings only.

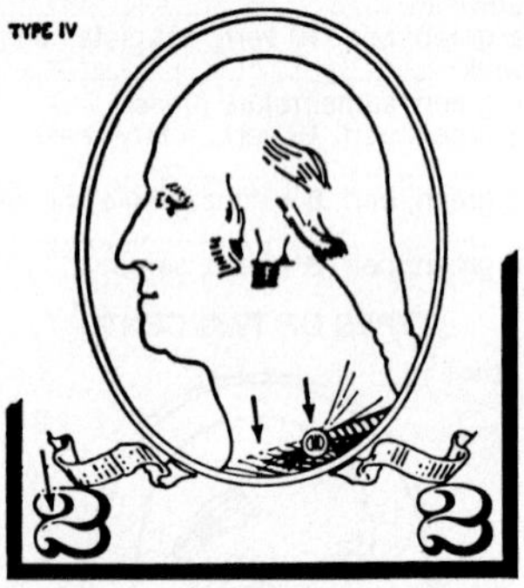

Type IV *Top line of the toga rope is broken.*
The shading lines in the toga button are so arranged that the curving of the first and last form "ID."
The line of color in the left "2" is very thin and usually broken.
Used on offset printings only.

Type V *Top line of the toga is complete.*
There are five vertical shading lines in the toga button.
The line of color in the left "2" is very thin and usually broken.
The shading dots on the nose are as shown on the diagram.
Used on offset printings only.

Type Va *Characteristics are the same as type V except in the shading dots of the nose. The third row of dots from the bottom has four dots instead of six. The overall height is ⅓mm shorter than type V.*
Used on offset printings only.

Type VI *General characteristics the same as type V except that the line of color in the left "2" is very heavy. Used on offset printings only.*

Type VII *The line of color in the left "2" is invariably continuous, clearly defined and heavier than in type V or Va but not as heavy as type VI.*
An additional vertical row of dots has been added to the upper lip.
Numerous additional dots have been added to the hair on top of the head.
Used on offset printings only.

A140 2¢ carmine, perf. 12, type I, single line wmk. **406**
A140 2¢ carmine, same, booklet pane of 6 .... **406a**
A140 2¢ pale car. red, perf. 11, single line wmk., type I **461**
A140 2¢ rose, perf. 11, flat plate, unwmkd., type I **499**
A140 2¢ rose, same, booklet pane of 6 .... **499e**
A140 2¢ rose, same, booklet pane of 30 .... **499f**
A140 2¢ deep rose, perf. 11, unwmkd., type Ia **500**
A140 2¢ carmine rose, perf. 11, rotary press, unwmkd., type III **546**
A140 2¢ carmine, perf. 11, offset, unwmkd., type IV **526**
A140 2¢ carmine, same, type V **527**
A140 2¢ carmine, same, type Va **528**
A140 2¢ carmine, same, type VI **528A**
A140 2¢ carmine, same, type VII **528B**
A140 2¢ carmine rose, perf. 11x10, type II **539**
A140 2¢ carmine rose, same, type III **540**
A140 2¢ rose red, perf. 10x12, single line wmk., type I **423B**
A140 2¢ rose red, perf. 12x10, single line wmk., type I **423E**
A140 2¢ rose red, perf. 10, single line wmk., type I **425**
A140 2¢ rose red, same, perf. 10, booklet pane of 6 .... **425e**
A140 2¢ carmine, perf. 10, unwmkd., type I **463**
A140 2¢ carmine, same, booklet pane of 6 .... **463a**
A140 2¢ carmine, imperf., flat plate, single line wmk., type I **409**
A140 2¢ carmine, imperf., rotary press, single line wmk., type I **459**
A140 2¢ carmine, imperf., flat plate, unwmkd., type I **482**
A140 2¢ deep rose, same, type Ia **482A**
A140 2¢ carmine rose, imperf., offset, unwmkd., type IV **532**
A140 2¢ carmine rose, same, type V **533**
A140 2¢ carmine, same, type Va **534**
A140 2¢ carmine, same, type VI **534A**
A140 2¢ carmine, same, type VII **534B**
A140 2¢ carmine, perf. 10 horiz., flat plate, single line wmk., type I **442**
A140 2¢ red, same, rotary press **449**
A140 2¢ carmine, same, type III **450**
A140 2¢ carmine, perf. 10 horiz., rotary press unwmkd., type II **487**
A140 2¢ carmine, same, type III **488**
A140 2¢ carmine, perf. 10 vert., flat plate, single line wmk., type I **444**
A140 2¢ carmine rose, same, rotary press **453**
A140 2¢ red, same, type II **454**
A140 2¢ carmine, same, type III **455**
A140 2¢ carmine, perf. 10 vert., rotary press, unwmkd., type II **491**
A140 2¢ carmine, same, type III **492**
A140 2¢ carmine, perf. 8½ horiz., type I **411**
A140 2¢ carmine, perf. 8½ vert., type I **413**

TYPES OF THREE CENTS

Type I *The top line of the toga rope is weak and the rope shading lines are thin. The 5th line from the left is missing. The line between the lips is thin.*

Type II *The top line of the toga rope is strong and the rope shading lines are heavy and complete.*
The line between the lips is heavy.
Used on both flat plate and rotary press printings.

Type III The top line of the toga rope is strong but the 5th shading line is missing as in type I.
Center shading line of the toga button consists of two dashes with a central dot.
The "P" and "O" of "POSTAGE" are separated by a line of color.
The frame line at the bottom of the vignette is complete.
Used on offset printings only.

Type IV *The shading lines of the toga rope are complete.*
The second and fourth shading lines in the toga button are broken in the middle and the third line is continuous with a dot in the center.
The "P" and "O" of "POSTAGE" are joined.
The frame line at the bottom of the vignette is broken.
Used on offset printings only.

A140 3¢ deep violet, perf. 12, double line wmk., type I ... 333
A140 3¢ deep violet, perf. 12, single line wmk., type I ... 376
A140 3¢ deep violet, perf. 12, bluish paper, type I ... 359
A140 3¢ light violet, perf. 11, unwmkd., type I ... 501
A140 3¢ light violet, same, booklet pane of 6 ... 501b
A140 3¢ dark violet, perf. 11, unwmkd., type II ... 502
A140 3¢ dark violet, same, booklet pane of 6 ... 502b
A140 3¢ violet, perf. 11, offset, type III ... 529
A140 3¢ purple, same, type IV ... 530
A140 3¢ violet, perf. 11x10, type II ... 541
A140 3¢ deep violet, perf. 10, single line wmk., type I ... 426
A140 3¢ violet, perf. 10, unwmkd., type I ... 464
A140 3¢ deep violet, imperf., double line wmk., type I ... 345
A140 3¢ violet, imperf., unwmkd., type I ... 483
A140 3¢ violet, same, type II ... 484
A140 3¢ violet, imperf., offset, type IV ... 535
A140 3¢ deep violet, perf. 12 vert., single line wmk., type I ... 389
A140 3¢ violet, perf. 10 vert., flat plate, single line wmk., type I ... 445
A140 3¢ violet, perf. 10 vert., rotary press, single line wmk., type I ... 456
A140 3¢ violet, perf. 10 vert., rotary press, unwmkd., type I ... 493
A140 3¢ violet, same, type II ... 494
A140 3¢ violet, perf. 10 horiz., type I ... 489
A140 3¢ deep violet, perf. 8½ vert., type I ... 394
A140 4¢ orange brown, perf. 12, double line wmk. ... 334
A140 4¢ orange brown, perf. 12, bluish paper ... 360
A140 4¢ brown, perf. 12, single line wmk. ... 377
A140 4¢ brown, perf. 11, unwmkd. ... 503
A140 4¢ brown, perf. 10, single line wmk. ... 427
A140 4¢ orange brown, perf. 10, unwmkd. ... 465
A140 4¢ orange brown, imperf. ... 346
A140 4¢ orange brown, perf. 12 horiz. ... 350
A140 4¢ orange brown, perf. 12 vert. ... 354
A140 4¢ brown, perf. 10 vert., flat plate, single line wmk. ... 446
A140 4¢ brown, same, rotary press ... 457
A140 4¢ orange brown, perf. 10 vert., rotary press, unwmkd. ... 495
A140 4¢ brown, perf. 8½ vert., single line wmk. ... 395
A140 5¢ blue, perf. 12, double line wmk. ... 335
A140 5¢ blue, perf. 12 bluish paper ... 361
A140 5¢ blue, perf. 12, single line wmk. ... 378
A140 5¢ blue, perf. 11, unwmkd. ... 504
A140 5¢ rose (error), same ... 505
A140 5¢ carmine (error), perf. 10, unwmkd. ... 467
A140 5¢ blue, perf. 10, single line wmk. ... 428
A140 5¢ blue, perf. 12x10 ... 423C
A140 5¢ blue, perf. 10, unwmkd. ... 466
A140 5¢ blue, imperf. ... 347
A140 5¢ carmine (error), imperf. ... 485
A140 5¢ blue, perf. 12 horiz. ... 351
A140 5¢ blue, perf. 12 vert. ... 355
A140 5¢ blue, perf. 10 vert., flat plate, single line wmk. ... 447
A140 5¢ blue, same, rotary press ... 458
A140 5¢ blue, perf. 10 vert., rotary press, unwmkd. ... 496
A140 5¢ blue, perf. 8½ vert. ... 396
A140 6¢ red orange, perf. 12, double line wmk. ... 336
A140 6¢ red orange, perf. 12, bluish paper ... 362
A140 6¢ red orange, perf. 12, single line wmk. ... 379
A140 6¢ red orange, perf. 11, unwmkd. ... 506
A140 6¢ red orange, perf. 10, single line wmk. ... 429
A140 6¢ red orange, perf. 10, unwmkd. ... 468
A140 7¢ black, perf. 12, single line wmk. ... 407
A140 7¢ black, perf. 11, unwmkd. ... 507
A140 7¢ black, perf. 10, single line wmk. ... 430
A140 7¢ black, perf. 10, unwmkd. ... 469
A140 8¢ olive green, perf. 12, double line wmk. ... 337
A140 8¢ olive green, perf. 12, bluish paper ... 363
A140 8¢ olive green, perf. 12, single line wmk. ... 380
A140 10¢ yellow, perf. 12, double line wmk. ... 338
A140 10¢ yellow, perf. 12, bluish paper ... 364
A140 10¢ yellow, perf. 12, single line wmk. ... 381
A140 10¢ yellow, perf. 12 vert. ... 356
A140 13¢ blue green, perf. 12, double line wmk. ... 339
A140 13¢ blue green, perf. 12, bluish paper ... 365
A140 15¢ pale ultra, perf. 12, double line wmk. 340
A140 15¢ pale ultra, perf. 12, bluish paper ... 366
A140 15¢ pale ultra, perf. 12, single line wmk. ... 382
A140 50¢ violet ... 341
A140 $1 violet brown ... 342

ISSUES OF 1912-19

A148

Franklin — A149

Designs of 8¢ to $1 denominations differ only in figures of value.

A148 8¢ pale olive green, perf. 12, single line wmk. ... 414
A148 8¢ olive bister, perf. 11, unwmkd. ... 508
A148 8¢ pale olive grn., perf. 10, single line wmk. ... 431
A148 8¢ olive green, perf. 10, unwmkd. ... 470
A148 9¢ salmon red, perf. 12, single line wmk. ... 415
A148 9¢ salmon red, perf. 11, unwmkd. ... 509
A148 9¢ salmon red, perf. 10, single line wmk. ... 432
A148 9¢ salmon red, perf. 10, unwmkd. ... 471
A148 10¢ orange yellow, perf. 12, single line wmk. ... 416
A148 10¢ orange yellow, perf. 11, unwmkd. ... 510
A148 10¢ orange yellow, perf. 10, single line wmk. ... 433
A148 10¢ orange yellow, perf. 10, unwmkd. ... 472
A148 10¢ orange yellow, perf. 10 vert., same ... 497
A148 11¢ light green, perf. 11, unwmkd. ... 511
A148 11¢ dark green, perf. 10, single line wmk. ... 434
A148 11¢ dark green, perf. 10, unwmkd. ... 473
A148 12¢ claret brown, perf. 12, single line wmk. ... 417
A148 12¢ claret brown, perf. 11, unwmkd. ... 512
A148 12¢ claret brown, perf. 10, single line wmk. ... 435
A148 12¢ claret brown, perf. 10, unwmkd. ... 474
A148 13¢ apple green, perf. 11, unwmkd. ... 513
A148 15¢ gray, perf. 12, single line wmk. ... 418
A148 15¢ gray, perf. 11, unwmkd. ... 514
A148 15¢ gray, perf. 10, single line wmk. ... 437
A148 15¢ gray, perf. 10, unwmkd. ... 475
A148 20¢ ultramarine, perf. 12, single line wmk. ... 419
A148 20¢ light ultra., perf. 11, unwmkd. ... 515
A148 20¢ ultramarine, perf. 10, single line wmk. ... 438
A148 20¢ light ultra, perf. 10, unwmkd. ... 476
A148 30¢ orange red, perf. 12, single line wmk. ... 420
A148 30¢ orange red, perf. 11, unwmkd. ... 516
A148 30¢ orange red, perf. 10, single line wmk. ... 439
A148 30¢ orange red, perf. 10, unwmkd. ... 476A
A148 50¢ violet, perf. 12, single line wmk. ... 421
A148 50¢ violet, perf. 12, double line wmk. ... 422
A148 50¢ red violet, perf. 11, unwmkd. ... 517
A148 50¢ violet, perf. 10, single line wmk. ... 440
A148 50¢ light violet, perf. 10, unwmkd. ... 477
A148 $1 violet brown, perf. 12, double line wmk. ... 423
A148 $1 violet brown, perf. 11, unwmkd. ... 518
A148 $1 violet black, perf. 10, double line wmk. ... 460
A148 $1 violet black, perf. 10, unwmkd. ... 478

ISSUES OF 1918-20
Perf. 11 Unwmkd.

A149 $2 orange red & black ... 523
A149 $2 carmine & black ... 547
A149 $5 deep green & black ... 524

ISSUES OF 1922-32

Nathan Hale — A154

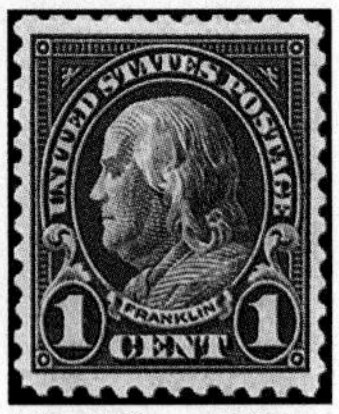

Franklin — A155

Warren G. Harding — A156

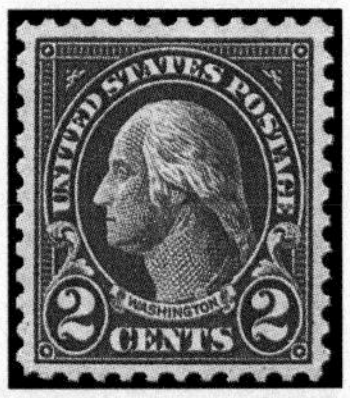

Washington — A157

Lincoln — A158

Martha Washington — A159

Theodore Roosevelt — A160

Garfield — A161

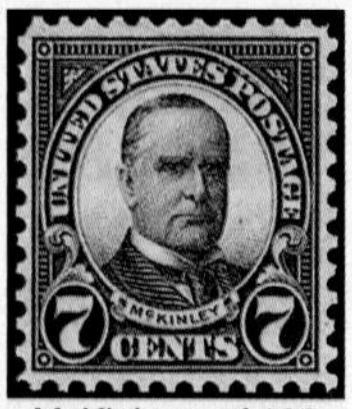
McKinley — A162

Grant — A163

Jefferson — A164

Monroe — A165

Hayes — A166

Cleveland — A167

American Indian — A168

Statue of Liberty — A169

Golden Gate — A170

Niagara Falls — A171

Buffalo — A172

Arlington Amphitheater and Tomb of the Unknown Soldier — A173

Lincoln Memorial — A174

United States Capitol — A175

"America" — A176

Canal Zone Overprints:
Type A has flat-topped "A's" in "CANAL."

Type B has sharp-pointed "A's" in "CANAL."

Unwmkd.

Type	Description	No.
A154	½¢ olive brown, perf. 11	**551**
A154	½¢ olive brown, perf. 11x10½	**653**
A154	½¢ olive brown, "CANAL ZONE"	**C.Z. 70**
A155	1¢ deep green, perf. 11, flat plate	**552**
A155	1¢ deep green, booklet pane of 6	**552a**
A155	1¢ green, perf. 11, rotary press 19¾x22¼mm	**594**
A155	1¢ green, same, 191/4x22½mm (used)	**596**
A155	1¢ green, perf. 11x10, rotary press	**578**
A155	1¢ green, perf. 10	**581**
A155	1¢ green, perf. 11x10½	**632**
A155	1¢ green, same, booklet pane of 6	**632a**
A155	1¢ green, ovpt. Kans.	**658**
A155	1¢ green, ovpt. Nebr.	**669**
A155	1¢ green, imperf.	**575**
A155	1¢ green, perf. 10 vert.	**597**
A155	1¢ yellow green, perf. 10 horiz.	**604**
A155	1¢ deep green, "CANAL ZONE" type A, perf. 11	**C.Z. 71**
A155	1¢ deep green, same, booklet pane of 6	**C.Z. 71e**
A155	1¢ green, "CANAL ZONE" type B, perf. 11x10½	**C.Z. 100**
A156	1½¢ yellow brown, perf. 11	**553**
A156	1½¢ yellow brown, perf. 11x10½	**633**
A156	1½¢ brown, ovpt. Kans	**659**
A156	1½¢ brown, ovpt. Nebr	**670**
A156	1½¢ brown, perf. 10	**582**
A156	1½¢ brown, perf. 10 vert.	**598**
A156	1½¢ yellow brown, perf. 10 horiz.	**605**
A156	1½¢ yellow brown, imperf., flat plate	**576**
A156	1½¢ yellow brown, imperf., rotary press, 19¼x22½mm	**631**
A156	1½¢ yellow brown "CANAL ZONE"	**C.Z. 72**

Type I

No heavy hair lines at top center of head. Outline of left acanthus scroll generally faint at top and toward base at left side.

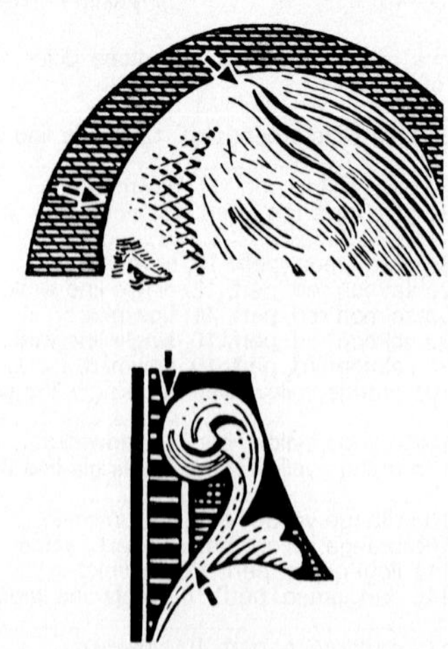
Type II

Three heavy hair lines at top center of head; two being outstanding in the white area. Outline of left acanthus scroll very strong and clearly defined at top (under left edge of lettered panel) and at lower curve (above and to left of numeral oval).

Type	Description	No.
A157	2¢ carmine, perf. 11, flat plate	**554**
A157	2¢ carmine, same, booklet pane of 6	**554c**
A157	2¢ carmine, perf. 11, rotary press, 19¾x22¼mm	**595**
A157	2¢ carmine, perf. 11x10	**579**
A157	2¢ carmine, perf. 11x10½, type I	**634**
A157	2¢ carmine, perf. 11x10½, type II	**634A**
A157	2¢ carmine lake, same, type I	**634b**
A157	2¢ carmine lake, same, booklet pane of 6	**634d**
A157	2¢ carmine, overprt. Molly Pitcher	**646**
A157	2¢ carmine, overprt. Hawaii 1778-1928	**647**
A157	2¢ carmine, overprt. Kans.	**660**
A157	2¢ carmine, overprt. Nebr.	**671**
A157	2¢ carmine, perf. 10	**583**
A157	2¢ carmine, same, booklet pane of 6	**583a**
A157	2¢ carmine, imperf.	**577**
A157	2¢ carmine, perf. 10 vert., type I	**599**
A157	2¢ carmine, same, type II	**599A**
A157	2¢ carmine, perf. 10 horiz.	**606**
A157	2¢ carmine, "CANAL ZONE" type A, perf. 11	**C.Z. 73**
A157	2¢ carmine, same, booklet pane of 6	**C.Z. 73a**
A157	2¢ carmine, "CANAL ZONE" type B, perf. 11	**C.Z. 84**
A157	2¢ carmine, same, booklet pane of 6	**C.Z. 84d**
A157	2¢ carmine, "CANAL ZONE" type B, perf. 10	**C.Z. 97**
A157	2¢ carmine, same, booklet pane of 6	**C.Z. 97b**
A157	2¢ carmine, "CANAL ZONE" type B, perf. 11x10½	**C.Z. 101**
A157	2¢ carmine, same, booklet pane of 6	**C.Z. 101a**
A158	3¢ violet, perf. 11	**555**
A158	3¢ violet, perf. 11x10½	**635**
A158	3¢ violet, overprt. Kans.	**661**
A158	3¢ violet, overprt. Nebr.	**672**
A158	3¢ violet, perf. 10	**584**
A158	3¢violet, perf. 10 vert.	**600**
A158	3¢ violet, "CANAL ZONE" perf. 11	**C.Z. 85**
A158	3¢ violet, "CANAL ZONE" perf. 10	**C.Z. 98**
A158	3¢ violet, "CANAL ZONE" perf. 11x10½	**C.Z. 102**
A159	4¢ yellow brown, perf. 11	**556**
A159	4¢ yellow brown, perf. 11x10½	**636**
A159	4¢ yellow brown, ovrpt. Kans.	**662**
A159	4¢ yellow brown, ovrpt. Nebr.	**673**
A159	4¢ yellow brown, perf. 10	**585**
A159	4¢ yellow brown, perf. 10 vert.	**601**
A160	5¢ dark blue, perf. 11	**557**
A160	5¢ dark blue, perf. 11x10½	**637**
A160	5¢ dark blue, ovpt. Hawaii 1778-1928	**648**
A160	5¢ deep blue, ovpt. Kans.	**663**
A160	5¢ deep blue, ovpt. Nebr.	**674**
A160	5¢ blue, perf. 10	**586**
A160	5¢ dark blue, perf. 10 vert.	**602**
A160	5¢ dark blue, "CANAL ZONE" type A, perf. 11	**C.Z. 74**
A160	5¢ dark blue, same, type B	**C.Z. 86**
A160	5¢ dark blue, same, perf. 11x10½	**C.Z. 103**
A161	6¢ red orange, perf. 11	**558**
A161	6¢ red orange, perf. 11x10½	**638**
A161	6¢ red orange, ovrpt. Kans.	**664**
A161	6¢ red orange, ovrpt. Nebr.	**675**
A161	6¢ red orange, perf. 10	**587**
A161	6¢ deep orange, perf. 10 vert.	**723**
A162	7¢ black, perf. 11	**559**
A162	7¢ black, perf. 11x10½	**639**
A162	7¢ black, ovrpt. Kans.	**665**
A162	7¢ black, ovrpt. Nebr.	**676**
A162	7¢ black, perf. 10	**588**
A163	8¢ olive green, perf. 11	**560**
A163	8¢ olive green, perf. 11x10½	**640**
A163	8¢ olive green, ovrpt. Kans.	**666**
A163	8¢ olive green, ovrpt. Nebr.	**677**
A163	8¢ olive green, perf. 10	**589**
A164	9¢ rose, perf. 11	**561**
A164	9¢ orange red, perf. 11x10½	**641**
A164	9¢ light rose, ovrpt. Kans.	**667**
A164	9¢ light rose, ovrpt. Nebr.	**678**
A164	9¢ rose, perf. 10	**590**
A165	10¢ orange, perf. 11	**562**
A165	10¢ orange, perf. 11x10½	**642**
A165	10¢ orange yellow, ovrpt. Kans.	**668**
A165	10¢ orange yellow, ovrpt. Nebr.	**679**
A165	10¢ orange, perf. 10	**591**
A165	10¢ orange, perf. 10 vert.	**603**
A165	10¢ orange, "CANAL ZONE" type A, perf. 11	**C.Z. 75**
A165	10¢ orange, same, type B	**C.Z. 87**
A165	10¢ orange, same, perf. 10	**C.Z. 99**
A165	10¢ orange, same, perf. 11x10½	**C.Z. 104**
A166	11¢ light blue, perf. 11	**563**
A166	11¢ light blue, perf. 11x10½	**692**
A167	12¢ brown violet, perf. 11	**564**
A167	12¢ brown violet, perf. 11x10½	**693**
A167	12¢ brown violet, "CANAL ZONE" type A	**C.Z. 76**
A167	12¢ brown violet, same, type B	**C.Z. 88**
A168	14¢ blue, perf. 11	**565**

A168 14¢ dark blue, perf. 11x10½........................ **695**
A168 14¢ dark blue, "CANAL ZONE" type A, perf. 11........................ **C.Z. 77**
A168 14¢ dark blue, same, type B................ **C.Z. 89**
A168 14¢ dark blue, same, perf. 11x10½.... **C.Z. 116**
A169 15¢ gray, perf. 11........................ **566**
A169 15¢ gray, perf. 11x10½........................ **696**
A169 15¢ gray, "CANAL ZONE" type A......... **C.Z. 78**
A169 15¢ gray, "CANAL ZONE" type B......... **C.Z. 90**
A170 20¢ carmine rose, perf. 11........................ **567**
A170 20¢ carmine rose, perf. 10½x11................ **698**
A170 20¢ carmine rose, "CANAL ZONE"...... **C.Z. 92**
A171 25¢ yellow green, perf. 11........................ **568**
A171 25¢ blue green, perf. 10½x11.................... **699**
A172 30¢ olive brown, perf. 11........................ **569**
A172 30¢ brown, perf. 10½x11........................ **700**
A172 30¢ olive brown, "CANAL ZONE" type A........................ **C.Z. 79**
A172 30¢ olive brown, "CANAL ZONE" type B........................ **C.Z. 93**
A173 50¢ lilac, perf. 11........................ **570**
A173 50¢ lilac, perf. 10½x11........................ **701**
A173 50¢ lilac, "CANAL ZONE" type A.......... **C.Z. 80**
A173 50¢ lilac, "CANAL ZONE" type B.......... **C.Z. 94**
A174 $1 violet brown, perf. 11........................ **571**
A174 $1 violet brown, perf. 10¾x10½............. **4075a**
A174 $1 violet brown, "CANAL ZONE" type A........................ **C.Z. 81**
A174 $1 violet brown, "CANAL ZONE" type B........................ **C.Z. 95**
A175 $2 deep blue, perf. 11........................ **572**
A175 $2 deep blue, perf. 10¾x10½................ **4075b**
A176 $5 carmine & blue, perf. 11........................ **573**
A176 $5 carmine & blue, perf. 10¾x10½........ **4075c**

REGULAR ISSUES OF 1925-26, 1930 and 1932

Harrison — A186

Wilson — A187

A186 13¢ green, perf. 11........................ **622**
A186 13¢ yellow green, perf. 11x10½................ **694**
A187 17¢ black, perf. 11........................ **623**
A187 17¢ black, perf. 10½x11........................ **697**
A187 17¢ black, "CANAL ZONE".................. **C.Z. 91**

Harding — A203

Taft — A204

A203 1½¢ brown, perf. 11x10½........................ **684**
A203 1½¢ brown, perf. 10 vert........................ **686**
A204 4¢ brown, perf. 11x10½........................ **685**
A204 4¢ brown, perf. 10 vert........................ **687**

Washington — A226

A226 3¢ deep violet, perf. 11x10½........................ **720**
A226 3¢ deep violet, same, booklet pane of 6 **720b**
A226 3¢ deep violet, perf. 10 vert........................ **721**
A226 3¢ deep violet, perf. 10 horiz........................ **722**
A226 3¢ deep violet, "CANAL ZONE".......... **C.Z. 115**

PRESIDENTIAL ISSUE OF 1938

Benjamin Franklin — A275

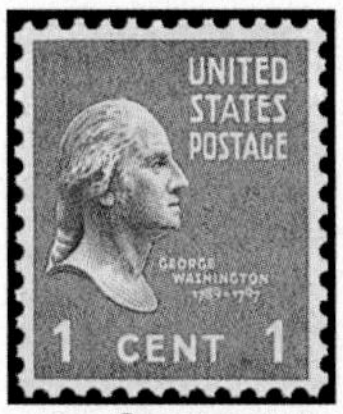

George Washington — A276

Zachary Taylor — A289

Millard Fillmore — A290

Martha Washington A277

John Adams A278

Franklin Pierce — A291

James Buchanan — A292

Thomas Jefferson — A279

James Madison — A280

Abraham Lincoln — A293

Andrew Johnson — A294

The White House — A281

James Monroe — A282

Ulysses S. Grant — A295

Rutherford B. Hayes — A296

John Quincy Adams — A283

Andrew Jackson — A284

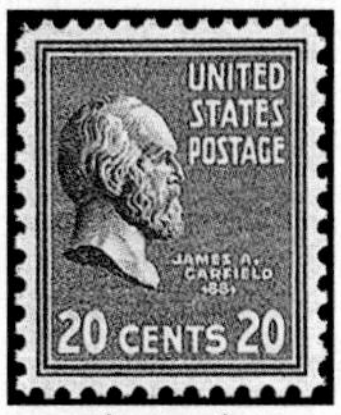

James A. Garfield — A297

Chester A. Arthur — A298

Martin Van Buren — A285

William H. Harrison — A286

Grover Cleveland — A299

Benjamin Harrison — A300

John Tyler — A287

James K. Polk — A288

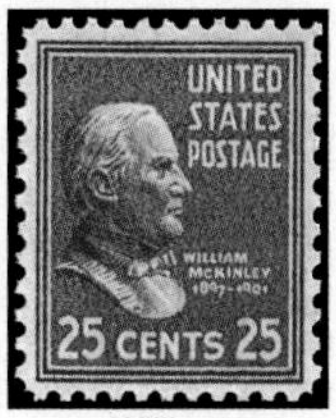

William McKinley — A301

Theodore Roosevelt — A302

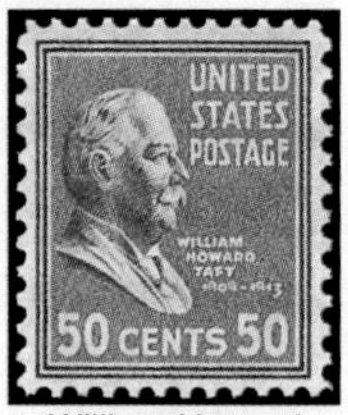

William Howard Taft — A303

Woodrow Wilson — A304

Warren G. Harding — A305

Calvin Coolidge — A306

Rotary Press Printing
Unwmkd.

A275 ½¢ deep orange, perf. 11x10½ **803**
A275 ½¢ red orange, "CANAL ZONE" .... **C.Z. 118**
A276 1¢ green, perf. 11x10½ **804**
A276 1¢ green, booklet pane of 6 .... **804b**
A276 1¢ green, perf. 10 vert. **839**
A276 1¢ green, perf. 10 horiz. **848**
A277 1½¢ bister brown, perf. 11x10½ **805**
A277 1½¢ bister brown, perf. 10 vert. **840**
A277 1½¢ bister brown, perf. 10 horiz. **849**
A277 1½¢ bister brown, "CANAL ZONE" .... **C.Z. 119**
A278 2¢ rose carmine, perf. 11x10½ **806**
A278 2¢ booklet pane of 6 .... **806b**
A278 2¢ rose carmine, perf. 10 vert. **841**
A278 2¢ rose carmine, perf. 10 horiz. **850**
A279 3¢ deep violet, perf. 11x10½ **807**
A279 3¢ deep violet, booklet pane of 6 .... **807a**
A279 3¢ deep violet, perf. 10 vert. **842**
A279 3¢ deep violet, perf. 10 horiz. **851**
A280 4¢ red violet, perf. 11x10½ **808**
A280 4¢ red violet, perf. 10 vert. **843**
A281 4½¢ dark gray, perf. 11x10½ **809**
A281 4½¢ dark gray, perf. 10 vert. **844**
A282 5¢ bright blue, perf. 11x10½ **810**
A282 5¢ bright blue, perf. 10 vert. **845**
A283 6¢ red orange, perf. 11x10½ **811**
A283 6¢ red orange, perf. 10 vert. **846**
A284 7¢ sepia, perf. 11x10½ **812**
A285 8¢ olive green, perf. 11x10½ **813**
A286 9¢ rose pink, perf. 11x10½ **814**
A287 10¢ brown red, perf. 11x10½ **815**
A287 10¢ brown red, perf. 10 vert. **847**
A288 11¢ ultramarine, perf. 11x10½ **816**
A289 12¢ bright violet, perf. 11x10½ **817**
A290 13¢ blue green, perf. 11x10½ **818**
A291 14¢ blue, perf. 11x10½ **819**
A292 15¢ blue gray, perf. 11x10½ **820**
A293 16¢ black, perf. 11x10½ **821**
A294 17¢ rose red, perf. 11x10½ **822**
A295 18¢ brn. carmine, perf. 11x10½ **823**
A296 19¢ bright violet, perf. 11x10½ **824**
A297 20¢ bright blue green, perf. 11x10½ **825**
A298 21¢ dull blue, perf. 11x10½ **826**
A299 22¢ vermilion, perf. 11x10½ **827**
A300 24¢ gray black, perf. 11x10½ **828**
A301 25¢ dp. red lilac, perf. 11x10½ **829**
A302 30¢ deep ultra, perf. 11x10½ **830**
A303 50¢ lt. red violet, perf. 11x10½ **831**

Flat Plate Printing
Perf. 11

A304 $1 pur. & blk., unwmkd. **832**
A304 $1 pur. & blk., wmkd. USIR **832b**
A304 $1 red vio. & blk., thick white paper, smooth colorless gum **832c**
A305 $2 yellow green & black **833**
A306 $5 carmine & black **834**

LIBERTY ISSUE 1954-73

Benjamin Franklin A477

George Washington A478

Palace of the Governors, Santa Fe — A478a

Mount Vernon — A479

Thomas Jefferson — A480

Bunker Hill Monument and Massachusetts Flag 1776 — A481

Statue of Liberty — A482

Abraham Lincoln — A483

The Hermitage — A484

James Monroe — A485

Theodore Roosevelt — A486

Woodrow Wilson — A487

Statue of Liberty (Rotary and flat plate printing) — A488

Design slightly altered; see position of torch (Giorgi press printing) — A489

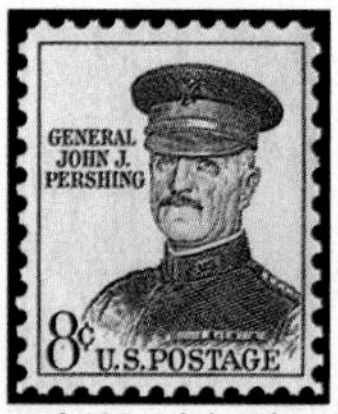

A489a John J. Pershing — 1042A

The Alamo — A490

Independence Hall — A491

A491a Statue of Liberty

Benjamin Harrison — A492

John Jay — A493

Monticello — A494

Paul Revere — A495

Robert E. Lee — A496

John Marshall — A497

Susan B. Anthony — A498

Patrick Henry — A499

Alexander Hamilton — A500

Unwmkd.

A477 ½¢ red orange, perf. 11x10½ **1030**
A478 1¢ dark green, perf. 11x10½ **1031**
A478 1¢ dark green, perf. 10 vert. **1054**
A478a 1¼¢ turquoise, perf. 10½x11 .... **1031A**
A478a 1¼¢ turquoise, perf. 10 horiz. **1054A**
A479 1½¢ brown carmine, perf. 10½x11 .... **1032**

A480	2¢ carmine rose, perf. 11x10	1033
A480	2¢ carmine rose, perf. 10 vert.	1055
A481	2½¢ gray blue, perf. 11x10½	1034
A481	2½¢ gray blue, perf. 10 vert.	1056
A482	3¢ deep violet, perf. 11x10½	1035
A482	3¢ deep violet, perf. 10 vert.	1057
A482	3¢ deep violet, imperf., size: 24x28mm	1075a
A483	4¢ red violet, perf. 11x10½	1036
A483	4¢ red violet, perf. 10 vert.	1058
A484	4½¢ blue green, perf. 10½x11	1037
A484	4½¢ blue green, perf. 10 horiz.	1059
A485	5¢ deep blue, perf. 11x10½	1038
A486	6¢ carmine, perf. 11x10½	1039
A487	7¢ rose carmine, same	1040
A488	8¢ dark violet blue & carmine, flat plate printing, perf. 11, mapprox. 22.7mm high	1041
A488	8¢ dark violet blue & carmine, rotary press printing, perf. 11, appprox. 22.9mm high	1041B
A488	8¢ dark violet blue & carmine, imperf., size: 24x28mm	1075b
A489	8¢ dark violet blue & carmine, perf. 11	1042
A489a	8¢ brown, perf. 11x10½	1042A
A490	9¢ rose lilac, perf. 10½x11	1043
A491	10¢ rose lake, same	1044
A491a	11¢ carmine & dark violet blue, perf. 11	1044A
A492	12¢ red, perf. 11x10½	1045
A493	15¢ rose lake, perf. 11x10½	1046
A494	20¢ ultramarine, perf. 10½x11	1047
A495	25¢ green, perf. 11x10½	1048
A495	25¢ green, perf. 10 vert.	1059A
A496	30¢ black, perf. 11x10½	1049
A497	40¢ brown red, perf. 11x10½	1050
A498	50¢ bright purple, perf. 11x10½	1051
A499	$1 purple, perf. 11x10½	1052
A500	$5 black, perf. 11	1053

ISSUE OF 1962-66

Andrew Jackson — A646

George Washington — A650

A646	1¢ green, perf. 11x10½	1209
A646	1¢ green, perf. 10 vert.	1225
A650	5¢ dk. bl. gray, perf. 11x10½	1213
A650	5¢ dk. bl. gray, perf. 10 vert.	1229

PROMINENT AMERICANS ISSUE 1965-81

Thomas Jefferson — A710

Albert Gallatin — A711

Frank Lloyd Wright and Guggenheim Museum, New York — A712

Francis Parkman — A713

Abraham Lincoln A714

George Washington A715

Re-engraved — A715a

Franklin D. Roosevelt — A716

Franklin D. Roosevelt (vertical coil)

Benjamin Franklin and his signature — A727a — A816

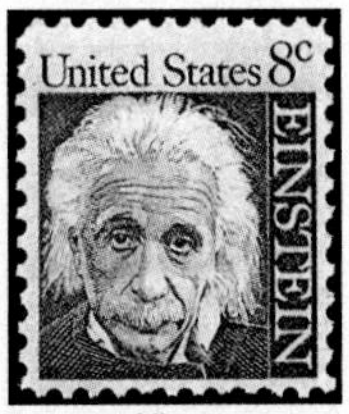

Albert Einstein — A717

Andrew Jackson — A718

Henry Ford and 1909 Model I — A718a

John F. Kennedy — A719

Fiorello H. LaGuardia and New York skyline — A817a

Oliver Wendell Holmes — A720

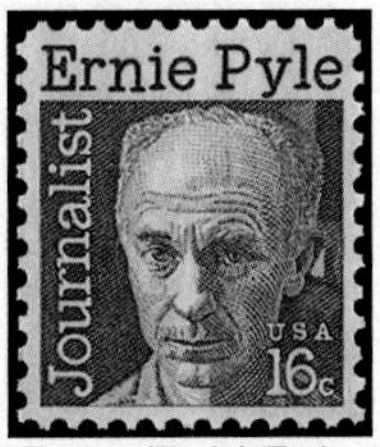

Ernest (Ernie) Taylor Pyle — A818

Dr. Elizabeth Blackwell — A818a

George C. Marshall — A721

Amadeo P. Giannini — A818b

Frederick Douglass — A722

John Dewey — A723

Thomas Paine — A724

Lucy Stone — A725

Eugene O'Neill — A726

John Bassett Moore — A727

Types of 15¢:

I — Necktie barely touches coat at bottom; crosshatching of tie strong and complete. Flag of "5" is true horizontal. Crosshatching of "15" is colorless when visible.

II — Necktie does not touch coat at bottom; LL to UR crosshatching lines strong, UL to LR lines very faint. Flag of "5" slants down slightly at right. Crosshatching of "15" is colored and visible when magnified.

A third type, used only for No. 1288B, is smaller in overall size, and "15¢" is ¾mm closer to head.

Unwmkd.

Rotary Press Printing

A710	1¢ green, perf. 11x10½	1278
A710	1¢ green, perf. 10, vert., tagged	1299
A711	1¼¢ light green, perf. 11x10½	1279
A712	2¢ dk. bl. gray, perf. 11x10½	1280
A713	3¢ violet, perf. 10½x11	1281
A713	3¢ violet, perf. 10 horiz.	1297
A714	4¢ black, perf. 11x10½	1282
A714	4¢ black, perf. 10, vert.	1303
A715	5¢ blue, perf. 11x10½	1283
A715	5¢ blue, perf. 10 vert.	1304
A715a	5¢ blue, perf. 11x10½	1283B
A715a	5¢ blue, perf. 10 vert.	1304C
A716	6¢ gray brown, perf. 10½x11	1284
A716	6¢ gray brown, perf. 10 horiz., tagged	1298
A727a	6¢ gray brown, perf. 10 vert., tagged	1305
A816	7¢ bright blue, perf. 10½x11	1393D
A717	8¢ violet, perf. 11x10½	1285
A718	10¢ lilac, perf. 11x10½	1286
A718a	12¢ black, perf. 10½x11	1286A
A719	13¢ brown, perf. 11x10½	1287
A817a	14¢ gray brown, perf. 11x10½	1397
A720	15¢ magenta, perf. 11x10½	1288
A720	15¢ magenta, perf. 10 (booklet panes only)	1288B
A720	15¢ magenta, perf. 10 vert.	1305E
A818	16¢ brown	1398
A818a	18¢ violet, perf. 11x10½	1399
A721	20¢ deep olive, perf. 11x10½	1289
A818b	21¢ green, perf. 11x10½	1400
A722	25¢ rose lake, perf. 11x10½	1290
A723	30¢ red lilac, perf. 10½x11	1291
A724	40¢ blue black, perf. 11x10½	1292

A725 50¢ rose magenta, perf. 11x10½ **1293**
A726 $1 dull purple, perf 11x10½..................... **1294**
A726 $1 dull purple, perf. 10 vert, tagged..... **1305C**
A727 $5 gray black, perf 11x10½ **1295**

Dwight D. Eisenhower — A815

A815a

A815 6¢ dark blue gray, perf. 11x10½............. **1393**
A815 6¢ dk. bl. gray, perf. 10, vert. **1401**
A815 8¢ deep claret, perf. 11x10½ (Booklet panes only).. **1395**
A815 8¢ deep claret, perf. 10 vert **1402**
A815a 8¢ blk., red & bl. gray, perf. 11............... **1394**

FLAG ISSUE 1968-71

Flag and White House — A760

A760 6¢ dark blue, red & green, perf. 11, size: 19x22mm.. **1338**
A760 6¢ dark blue, red & green, perf. 11x10½, size: 18¼x21mm **1338D**
A760 6¢ dark blue, red & green, perf. 10 vert., size: 18¼x21mm **1338A**
A760 8¢ multicolored, perf. 11x10½ **1338F**
A760 8¢ multicolored, perf. 10 vert............... **1338G**

REGULAR ISSUE 1971-74

U.S. Postal Service Emblem — A817

50-Star and 13-Star Flags — A923

Jefferson Memorial and quotation from Declaration of Independence A924

Mail Transport and "Zip Code" A925

Liberty Bell — A926

A817 8¢ multicolored, perf. 11x10½ **1396**
A923 10¢ red & blue, perf 11x10½................... **1509**
A923 10¢ red & blue, perf. 10 vert. **1519**
A924 10¢ blue, perf. 11x10½............................ **1510**
A924 10¢ blue, perf. 10 vert. **1520**
A925 10¢ multicolored, perf. 11x10½ **1511**
A926 6.3¢ brick red, perf. 10 vert. **1518**

AMERICANA ISSUE 1975-81

Inkwell and Quill — A984

Speaker's Stand — A985

Early Ballot Box — A987

Books, Bookmark, Eyeglasses — A988

Dome of Capitol — A994

Contemplation of Justice — A995

Early American Printing Press — A996

Torch Statue of Liberty — A997

Liberty Bell — A998

Eagle and Shield — A999

Ft. McHenry Flag — A1001

Head Statue of Liberty — A1002

Old North Church — A1003

Ft. Nisqually — A1004

Sandy Hook Lighthouse A1005

Morris Township School No. 2, Devil's Lake A1006

Iron "Betty" Lamp Plymouth Colony, 17th-18th Centuries — A1007

Rush Lamp and Candle Holder — A1008

Kerosene Table Lamp — A1009

Railroad Conductors Lantern, c. 1850 — A1010

COIL STAMPS

Six-string guitar — A1011

Weaver violins — A1199

Saxhorns — A1012

Drum — A1013

Steinway Grand Piano, 1857 — A1014

A984 1¢ dark blue, greenish, perf. 11x10½...... **1581**
A984 1¢ dark blue, greenish, perf. 10 vert. **1811**
A985 2¢ red brown, greenish, perf. 11x10½ **1582**
A987 3¢ olive, greenish, perf 11x10½ **1584**
A988 4¢ rose magenta, cream, perf. 11x10½ **1585**
A994 9¢ slate green, gray, perf. 11x10½ (booklet panes only)... **1590**
A994 9¢ slate green, gray, perf. 10x9¾ (booklet panes only).. **1590A**
A994 9¢ slate green, gray, perf. 11x10½........ **1591**
A994 9¢ slate green, gray, perf. 10 vert. **1616**
A995 10¢ violet, gray, perf. 10 vert.................. **1617**
A995 10¢ violet, gray, perf. 11x10½ **1592**
A996 11¢ orange, gray, perf. 11x10½ **1593**
A997 12¢ red brown, beige, perf. 11x10½ **1594**
A997 12¢ red brown, beige, perf. 10 vert......... **1816**

A998 13¢ brown, perf. 11x10½ **1595**
A998 13¢ brown, perf. 10 vert. **1618**
A999 13¢ multicolored **1596**
A1001 15¢ gray, dark blue & red, perf. 11 .... **1597**
A1001 15¢ gray, dark blue & red, perf. 11x10½ (booklet panes only) **1598**
A1001 15¢ gray, dark blue & red, perf. 10 vert. **1618C**
A1002 16¢ blue, perf. 11x10½ **1599**
A1002 16¢ blue, perf. 10 vert. **1619**
A1003 24¢ red, blue, perf. 11x10½ **1603**
A1004 28¢ brown, blue, perf. 11x10½ **1604**
A1005 29¢ blue, blue, perf. 11x10½ **1605**
A1006 30¢ green, perf. 11x10½ **1606**
A1007 50¢ black & orange, perf. 11 .... **1608**
A1008 $1 brown, orange & yellow, tan, perf. 11 .... **1610**
A1009 $2 dark green & red, tan, perf. 11 .... **1611**
A1010 $5 red brown, yellow & orange, tan, perf. 11 .... **1612**
A1011 3.1¢ brown, yellow, perf. 10 vert. **1613**
A1199 3.5¢ purple, yellow, perf. 10 vert. **1813**
A1012 7.7¢ brown, bright yellow, perf. 10 vert. **1614**
A1013 7.9¢ carmine, yellow, perf. 10 vert. **1615**
A1014 8.4¢ dark blue, yellow, perf. 10 vert. **1615C**

FLAG ISSUE 1975-77

13-star Flag over Independence Hall — A1015

Flag over Capitol — A1016

A1015 13¢ dark blue & red, perf. 11x10¾ **1622**
A1015 13¢ dark blue & red, perf. 11¼ **1622C**
A1015 13¢ dark blue & red, perf. 10 vert. **1625**
A1016 13¢ blue & red, perf. 11x10½ (booklet panes only) **1623**
A1016 13¢ blue & red, perf. 10x9¾ (booklet panes only) **1623B**

REGULAR ISSUE 1978

Indian Head, Penny, 1877 A1123

Dolley Madison A1209

Red Masterpiece and Medallion Roses — A1126

A1123 13¢ brown & blue, green, bister, perf. 11 .... **1734**
A1126 15¢ multicolored, perf 10 (booklet panes only) **1737**
A1209 15¢ red brown & sepia, perf. 11 .... **1822**

REGULAR ISSUE 1978-85

"A" Eagle — A1124

"B" Eagle — A1207

"C" Eagle — A1332

"C" Eagle (Booklet) — A1333

"D" Eagle A1496

"D" Eagle (Booklet) A1497

A1124 (15¢) orange, perf. 11 .... **1735**
A1124 (15¢) orange, perf. 11x10½ (booklet panes only) **1736**
A1124 (15¢) orange, perf. 10 vert. **1743**
A1207 (18¢) violet, perf. 11x10½ **1818**
A1207 (18¢) violet, perf. 10 (booklet panes only) **1819**
A1207 (18¢) violet, perf. 10 vert. **1820**
A1332 (20¢) brown, perf. 11x10½ **1946**
A1332 (20¢) brown, perf. 10 vert. **1947**
A1333 (20¢) brown, perf. 11x10½ (booklet panes only) **1948**
A1496 (22¢) green, perf. 11 .... **2111**
A1496 (22¢) green, perf. 10 vert. **2112**
A1497 (22¢) green, perf. 11 (booklet panes only) **2113**

GREAT AMERICANS ISSUE 1980-99

A1231

A1551

A1232

A1552

A1233

A1553

A1234

A1554

A1235

A1555

A1556

A1236

A1237

A1238

A1239

A1240

A1557

A1241

A1242

A1243

A1558

A1559

A1244

A1560

A1245

A1246

A1247

A1248

A1249

A1561

A1562

A1250

A1563

A1564

A1565

A1566

A1567

A1251

A2248

A2249

A2250

A2251

A1252

A1568

A1253

A1254

A1255

A1569

A1570

A2253

A1256

A1571

A2255

A2256

A1572

A1573

A1574

A2257

A2258

A1575

A1576

A1577

A1578

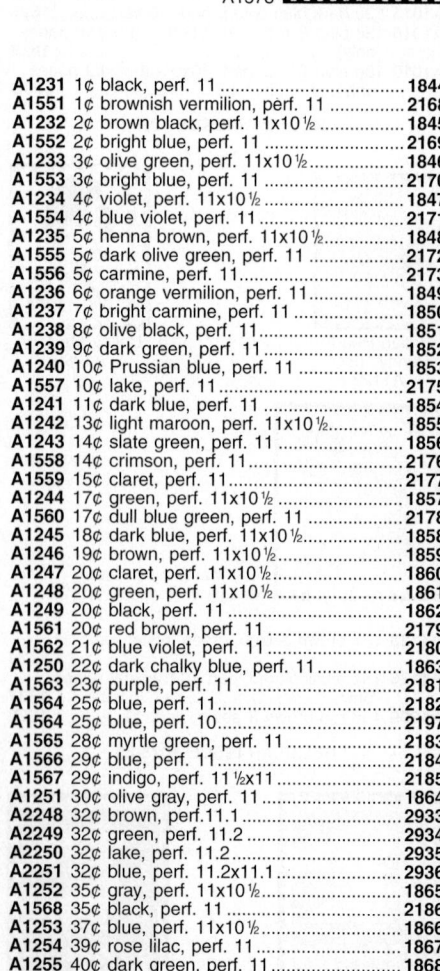

A1231	1¢ black, perf. 11	**1844**
A1551	1¢ brownish vermilion, perf. 11	**2168**
A1232	2¢ brown black, perf. 11x10½	**1845**
A1552	2¢ bright blue, perf. 11	**2169**
A1233	3¢ olive green, perf. 11x10½	**1846**
A1553	3¢ bright blue, perf. 11	**2170**
A1234	4¢ violet, perf. 11x10½	**1847**
A1554	4¢ blue violet, perf. 11	**2171**
A1235	5¢ henna brown, perf. 11x10½	**1848**
A1555	5¢ dark olive green, perf. 11	**2172**
A1556	5¢ carmine, perf. 11	**2173**
A1236	6¢ orange vermilion, perf. 11	**1849**
A1237	7¢ bright carmine, perf. 11	**1850**
A1238	8¢ olive black, perf. 11	**1851**
A1239	9¢ dark green, perf. 11	**1852**
A1240	10¢ Prussian blue, perf. 11	**1853**
A1557	10¢ lake, perf. 11	**2175**
A1241	11¢ dark blue, perf. 11	**1854**
A1242	13¢ light maroon, perf. 11x10½	**1855**
A1243	14¢ slate green, perf. 11	**1856**
A1558	14¢ crimson, perf. 11	**2176**
A1559	15¢ claret, perf. 11	**2177**
A1244	17¢ green, perf. 11x10½	**1857**
A1560	17¢ dull blue green, perf. 11	**2178**
A1245	18¢ dark blue, perf. 11x10½	**1858**
A1246	19¢ brown, perf. 11x10½	**1859**
A1247	20¢ claret, perf. 11x10½	**1860**
A1248	20¢ green, perf. 11x10½	**1861**
A1249	20¢ black, perf. 11	**1862**
A1561	20¢ red brown, perf. 11	**2179**
A1562	21¢ blue violet, perf. 11	**2180**
A1250	22¢ dark chalky blue, perf. 11	**1863**
A1563	23¢ purple, perf. 11	**2181**
A1564	25¢ blue, perf. 11	**2182**
A1564	25¢ blue, perf. 10	**2197**
A1565	28¢ myrtle green, perf. 11	**2183**
A1566	29¢ blue, perf. 11	**2184**
A1567	29¢ indigo, perf. 11½x11	**2185**
A1251	30¢ olive gray, perf. 11	**1864**
A2248	32¢ brown, perf.11.1	**2933**
A2249	32¢ green, perf. 11.2	**2934**
A2250	32¢ lake, perf. 11.2	**2935**
A2251	32¢ blue, perf. 11.2x11.1	**2936**
A1252	35¢ gray, perf. 11x10½	**1865**
A1568	35¢ black, perf. 11	**2186**
A1253	37¢ blue, perf. 11x10½	**1866**
A1254	39¢ rose lilac, perf. 11	**1867**
A1255	40¢ dark green, perf. 11	**1868**
A1569	40¢ dark blue, perf. 11	**2187**
A1570	45¢ bright blue, perf. 11	**2188**

A2253 46¢ carmine, perf. 11.1 2938
A1256 50¢ brown, perf. 11 1869
A1571 52¢ purple, perf. 11 2189
A2255 55¢ green, perf. 11 2940
A2256 55¢ black, serpentine die cut 11½, self-adhesive 2941
A1572 56¢ scarlet, perf. 11 2190
A1573 65¢ dark blue, perf. 11 2191
A1574 75¢ deep magenta, perf. 11 2192
A2257 77¢ blue, perf.11.8x11.6 2942
A2258 78¢ purple, perf. 11.2 2943
A1575 $1 dark Prussian green, perf. 11 2193
A1576 $1 dark blue, perf. 11 2194
A1577 $2 bright violet, perf. 11 2195
A1578 $5 copper red, perf. 11 2196

WILDLIFE ISSUES 1981-82

Bighorn — A1267

Puma — A1268

Harbor Seal — A1269

Bison — A1270

Brown bear — A1271

Polar bear — A1272

Elk (wapiti) — A1273

Moose — A1274

White-tailed deer A1275

Pronghorn A1276

Rocky Mountain Bighorn — A1334

FROM BOOKLET PANES

A1267 18¢ dark brown, perf. 11 1880
A1268 18¢ dark brown, perf. 11 1881
A1269 18¢ dark brown, perf. 11 1882
A1270 18¢ dark brown, perf. 11 1883
A1271 18¢ dark brown, perf. 11 1884
A1272 18¢ dark brown, perf. 11 1885
A1273 18¢ dark brown, perf. 11 1886
A1274 18¢ dark brown, perf. 11 1887
A1275 18¢ dark brown, perf. 11 1888
A1276 18¢ dark brown, perf. 11 1889
A1334 20¢ dark blue, perf. 11 1949

FLAG ISSUES 1981-85

A1277

A1278

Field of 1777 flag — A1279

A1280

A1281

A1498

Of the People, By the People, For the People A1499

A1277 18¢ multicolored, perf. 11 1890
A1278 18¢ multicolored, perf. 10 vert. 1891
A1279 6¢ perf. 11 (booklet panes only) 1892
A1280 18¢ perf. 11 (booklet panes only) 1893
A1281 20¢ black, dark blue & red, perf. 11 1894
A1281 20¢ black, dark blue & red, perf. 10 vert. 1895
A1281 20¢ black, dark blue & red, perf. 11x10½ (booklet panes only) 1896
A1498 22¢ blue, red & black, perf. 11 2114
A1498 22¢ blue, red & black, perf. 10 vert. 2115
A1499 22¢ blue, red & black, perf. 10 horiz. (booklet panes only) 2116

TRANSPORTATION ISSUE 1981-95

A1283

A1604a

A1284

A1604b

A1284a

A1622

A1506

A1285

A1810

A1507

A1286

A1623

A1811

A1811a

A1812

A1287

A1624

A1508

A1288

A1509

A1510

A1289

A1629

A1517

A1625

A1511

A1630

A1631

A1626

A1512

A1293

A1518

A1290

A1627

A1632

A1294

A1816

A1513

A1295

A1633

A1291

A1292

A1822

A1634

A1514

A1515

A1635

A1823

A1516

A1628

A1636

A1519

A1825

A1827

A1283	1¢ violet	**1897**
A1604a	1¢ violet	**2225**
A1284	2¢ black	**1897A**
A1604b	2¢ black	**2226**
A1284a	3¢ dark green	**1898**
A1622	3¢ claret	**2252**
A1506	3.4¢ dark bluish green	**2123**
A1285	4¢ reddish brown, inscription 19½mm long	**1898A**
A1285	4¢ reddish brown, inscription 17mm long	**2228**
A1810	4¢ claret	**2451**
A1507	4.9¢ brown black	**2124**
A1286	5¢ gray green	**1899**
A1623	5¢ black	**2253**
A1811	5¢ carmine, engraved	**2452**
A1811	5¢ carmine, photogravure	**2452B**
A1811a	5¢ carmine	**2452D**
A1812	5¢ brown, engraved (Bureau precanceled)	**2453**
A1812	5¢ red, photogravure (Bureau precanceled)	**2454**
A1287	5.2¢ carmine	**1900**
A1624	5.3¢ black (Bureau precanceled)	**2254**
A1508	5.5¢ deep magenta	**2125**
A1288	5.9¢ blue	**1901**
A1509	6¢ red brown	**2126**
A1510	7.1¢ lake	**2127**
A1289	7.4¢ brown	**1902**
A1625	7.6¢ brown (Bureau precanceled)	**2255**
A1511	8.3¢ green, inscription 18½mm long	**2128**
A1511	8.3¢ green, same, untagged (Bureau precanceled)	**2128a**
A1511	8.3¢ green, inscription 18mm long, untagged (Bureau precanceled)	**2231**
A1626	8.4¢ deep claret, (Bureau precanceled)	**2256**
A1512	8.5¢ dark Prussian green	**2129**
A1290	9.3¢ carmine rose	**1903**
A1627	10¢ sky blue	**2257**
A1816	10¢ green, engraved (Bureau precanceled)	**2457**
A1816	10¢ green, photogravure (Bureau precanceled	**2458**
A1513	10.1¢ slate blue	**2130**
A1291	10.9¢ purple	**1904**
A1292	11¢ red	**1905**
A1514	11¢ dark green	**2131**
A1515	12¢ dark blue	**2132**
A1516	12.5¢ olive green	**2133**
A1628	13¢ black, (Bureau precanceled)	**2258**
A1629	13.2¢ slate green, (Bureau precanceled)	**2259**
A1517	14¢ sky blue	**2134**
A1630	15¢ violet	**2260**
A1631	16.7¢ rose, (Bureau precanceled)	**2261**
A1293	17¢ ultramarine	**1906**
A1518	17¢ sky blue	**2135**
A1632	17.5¢ dark violet	**2262**
A1294	18¢ dark brown	**1907**
A1295	20¢ vermilion	**1908**
A1633	20¢ blue violet	**2263**
A1822	20¢ green	**2463**
A1634	20.5¢ rose, (Bureau precanceled)	**2264**
A1635	21¢ olive green, (Bureau precanceled)	**2265**
A1823	23¢ dark blue	**2464**
A1636	24.1¢ deep ultramarine, (Bureau precanceled)	**2266**
A1519	25¢ orange brown	**2136**
A1825	32¢ blue	**2466**
A1827	$1 dark blue & scarlet	**2468**

REGULAR ISSUE 1983-99

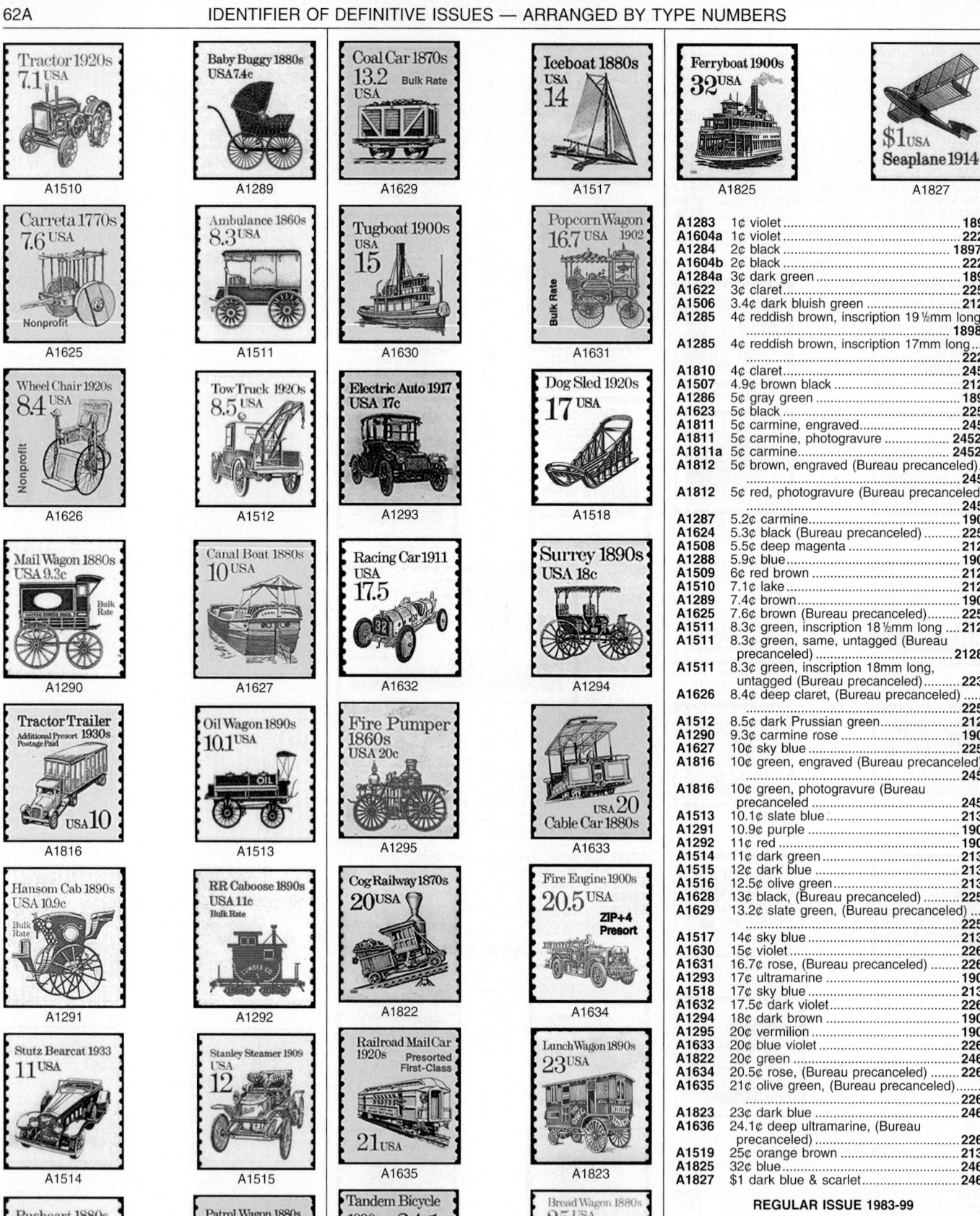

A1894

A1897

A1898

A2532

A1758

Eagle and Moon — A1296

A1895

Eagle and Half Moon — A1505

A1898a

A2533

A1896

A1894 $2.90 multicolored, perf. 11 .... **2540**
A1897 $2.90 multicolored, perf. 11x10½.......... **2543**
A1898 $3 multicolored, perf. 11 .... **2544**
A2532 $3.20 multicolored, serpentine die cut 11.5 .... **3261**
A1758 $8.75 multicolored, perf. 11 .... **2394**
A1296 $9.35 multicolored, perf. 10 vert. (booklet panes only) **1909**
A1296 $9.35 multicolored, booklet pane of 3 .... **1909a**
A1895 $9.95 multicolored, perf. 11 .... **2541**
A1505 $10.75 multicolored, perf. 10 vert. (booklet panes only) **2122**
A1898a $10.75 multicolored, perf. 11 .... **2544A**
A2533 $11.75 multicolored, serpentine die cut 11.5 .... **3262**
A1896 $14 multicolored, perf. 11 .... **2542**

REGULAR ISSUE 1982-85

George Washington Washington Monument — A1532

Consumer Education — A1390

Sealed Envelopes — A1533

A1532 18¢ multicolored, perf. 10 vert. **2149**
A1532 18¢ multicolored, same, untagged (Bureau precanceled) **2149a**
A1390 20¢ sky blue, perf. 10 vert. **2005**
A1533 21.1¢ multicolored, perf. 10 vert. **2150**
A1533 21.1¢ multicolored, same, untagged (Bureau precanceled) **2150a**

REGULAR ISSUE 1987-88

A1646

A1647

A1648

A1649

A1646 22¢ multicolored, perf. 11....................... **2276**
A1647 (25¢) multicolored, perf. 11 .... **2277**
A1647 (25¢) multicolored, perf. 10 .... **2282**
A1647 (25¢) multicolored, perf. 10 vert. **2279**
A1648 25¢ multicolored, perf. 11....................... **2278**
A1648 25¢ multicolored, perf. 10.................... **2285A**
A1649 25¢ multicolored, perf. 10 vert. **2280**

FLORA & FAUNA ISSUE 1988-2001

A1840

A1841

A2335

A1842

A2336

A1847

A1649a

A1649c

A1848

A1852

A1854

A1879

A1843

A2350

A1649b

A1649d

A1849

A1853

A1875

A1844

A1850

A2351

A2551

A2553

A2635

A2637

A2695

A2339

A1851

A2550

A2552

A2634

A2636

A2694

A1845

A1846

A1840	1¢ multicolored, perf. 11	**2476**
A1841	1¢ multicolored, perf. 11	**2477**
A1841	1¢ multicolored, serpentine die cut 10½, self-adhesive	**3031**
A1841	1¢ multicolored, blue inscriptions, serpentine die cut 11¼, self-adhesive	**3031A**
A1841	1¢ multicolored, perf. 9.8 vert.	**3044**
A2335	2¢ multicolored, perf. 11.1	**3032**
A2335	2¢ multicolored, perf. 9¾ vert.	**3045**
A1842	3¢ multicolored, perf. 11	**2478**
A2336	3¢ multicolored, perf. 11.1	**3033**
A1843	19¢ multicolored, perf. 11½x11	**2479**
A1847	20¢ multicolored, perf. 11x10 (booklet panes only)	**2483**
A1847	20¢ multicolored, serpentine die cut 10½x11, self-adhesive	**3048**
A1847	20¢ multicolored, serpentine die cut 11½ vert, self-adhesive	**3053**
A2350	20¢ multicolored, serpentine die cut 11¼, self-adhesive	**3050**
A2350	20¢ multicolored, serpentine die cut 10.6 on top and 10.6 on bottom or 10.6 on top and 10.4 on bottom, self-adhesive (booklet panes only)	**3051**
A2350	20¢ multicolored, serpentine die cut 10.6x10.4 on 3 sides, self-adhesive (booklet panes only)	**3051A**
A2350	20¢ multicolored, serpentine die cut 9¾ vert., self-adhesive	**3055**
A1649a	25¢ multicolored, perf. 11 (booklet panes only)	**2283**
A1649b	25¢ multicolored, perf. 10 (booklet panes only)	**2284**
A1649c	25¢ multicolored, perf. 10	**2285**
A1649d	25¢ multicolored, perf. 10 vert.	**2281**
A1848	29¢ black & multicolored, perf. 10 (booklet panes only)	**2484**
A1848	29¢ red & multicolored, perf. 11 (booklet panes only)	**2485**
A1849	29¢ multicolored, perf. 10x11 (booklet panes only)	**2486**
A1852	29¢ multicolored, die cut, self-adhesive	**2489**
A1853	29¢ red, green & black, die cut, self-adhesive	**2490**
A1854	29¢ multicolored, die cut, self-adhesive	**2491**
A1875	(29¢) yellow, black, red & yellow green, perf. 13	**2517**
A1875	(29¢) yellow, black, dull red & dark yellow green, perf. 10 vert.	**2518**
A1875	(29¢) yellow, black, dull red & dark green, bullseye perf. 11.2 (booklet panes only)	**2519**
A1875	(29¢) pale yellow, black, red & brightgreen, perf. 11 (booklet panes only)	**2520**
A1879	29¢ dull yellow, black, red & yellow green, perf. 11	**2524**
A1879	29¢ dull yellow, black, red & yellow green, perf. 13x12¾	**2524A**
A1879	29¢ pale yellow, black, red & yellow green, roulette 10 vert.	**2525**
A1879	29¢ pale yellow, black, red & yellow green, perf. 10 vert.	**2526**
A1879	29¢ pale yellow, black, red & bright green, perf. 11 (booklet panes only)	**2527**
A1844	30¢ multicolored, perf. 11½x11	**2480**
A1850	32¢ multicolored, perf. 11x10 (booklet panes only)	**2487**
A1850	32¢ multicolored, serpentine die cut, self-adhesive	**2493**
A1850	32¢ multicolored, serpentine die cut vert., self-adhesive	**2495**
A1851	32¢ multicolored, perf. 11x10 (booklet panes only)	**2488**
A1851	32¢ multicolored, serpentine die cut, self-adhesive	**2494**
A1851	32¢ multicolored, serpentine die cut vert., self-adhesive	**2495A**
A1853	32¢ pink, green & black, serpentine die cut, self-adhesive	**2492**
A1853	32¢ yellow, orange, green & black, serpentine die cut 11.3x11.7, self-adhesive	**3049**
A1853	32¢ yellow, orange, green & black, serpentine die cut 9.8 vert., self-adhesive	**3054**

A2351 33¢ multicolored, serpentine die cut 11½x11¼ on 2, 3, or 4 sides, self-adhesive (booklet panes only) **3052**
A2351 33¢ multicolored, serpentine die cut 10¾x10½ on 2 or 3 sides, self-adhesive (booklet panes only) **3052E**
A2550 33¢ multicolored, serpentine die cut 11.2x11.7, self-adhesive (booklet panes only) **3294**
A2550 33¢ multicolored, serpentine die cut 9.5x10, self-adhesive (booklet panes only)...... **3298**
A2550 33¢ multicolored, serpentine die cut 8.5 vert., self-adhesive.............................. **3302**
A2551 33¢ multicolored, serpentine die cut 11.2x11.7, self-adhesive (booklet panes only) **3295**
A2551 33¢ multicolored, serpentine die cut 9.5x10, self-adhesive (booklet panes only)...... **3300**
A2551 33¢ multicolored, serpentine die cut 8.5 vert., self-adhesive.............................. **3303**
A2552 33¢ multicolored, serpentine die cut 11.2x11.7, self-adhesive (booklet panes only) **3296**
A2552 33¢ multicolored, serpentine die cut 9.5x10, self-adhesive (booklet panes only)...... **3299**
A2552 33¢ multicolored, serpentine die cut 8.5 vert., self-adhesive.............................. **3305**
A2553 33¢ multicolored, serpentine die cut 11.2x11.7, self-adhesive (booklet panes only) **3297**
A2553 33¢ multicolored, serpentine die cut 9.5x10, self-adhesive (booklet panes only)...... **3301**
A2553 33¢ multicolored, serpentine die cut 8.5 vert., self-adhesive.............................. **3304**
A2634 33¢ multicolored, serpentine die cut 8½ horiz., self-adhesive............................ **3404**
A2635 33¢ multicolored, serpentine die cut 8½ horiz., self-adhesive............................ **3405**
A2636 33¢ multicolored, serpentine die cut 8½ horiz., self-adhesive............................ **3406**
A2637 33¢ multicolored, serpentine die cut 8½ horiz., self-adhesive............................ **3407**
A2694 34¢ multicolored, serpentine die cut 11¼ on 2, 3 or 4 sides (booklet panes only), self-adhesive.. **3491**
A2694 34¢ multicolored, serpentine die cut 11½x10¾ on 2 or 3 sides (booklet panes only), self-adhesive............................. **3493**
A2695 34¢ multicolored, serpentine die cut 11¼ on 2, 3 or 4 sides (booklet panes only), self-adhesive.. **3492**
A2695 34¢ multicolored, serpentine die cut 11½x10¾ on 2 or 3 sides (booklet panes only), self-adhesive............................. **3494**
A1845 45¢ multicolored, perf. 11 .... **2481**
A2339 $1 multicolored, serpentine die cut 11½x11¼, self-adhesive...................... **3036**
A1846 $2 multicolored, perf. 11 .... **2482**

REGULAR ISSUE 1989-98

A1793

A1834

A1877

A1884

A1947

A1950

A1951

A1793 25¢ multicolored, die cut, self-adhesive......... .... **2431**
A1834 25¢ dark red & dark blue, die cut, self-adhesive **2475**
A1877 (29¢) black, blue & dark red, die cut, self-adhesive **2522**
A1884 29¢ black, gold & green, die cut, self-adhesive **2531A**
A1947 29¢ brown & multicolored, die cut, self-adhesive **2595**
A1947 29¢ green & multicolored, die cut, self-adhesive **2596**
A1947 29¢ red & multicolored, die cut, self-adhesive **2597**
A1950 29¢ red, cream & blue, die cut, self-adhesive **2598**
A1951 29¢ multicolored, die cut, self-adhesive......... .... **2599**
A1951 32¢ red, light blue, dark blue & yellow, serpentine die cut 11, self-adhesive..... **3122**
A1951 32¢ red, light blue, dark blue & yellow, serpentine die cut 11.5x11.8, self-adhesive **3122E**

REGULAR ISSUE 1991-94

A1876

A1881

A1882

A1878

A1880

A1883

A1876 (4¢) bister & carmine, perf. 11 .... **2521**
A1881 19¢ multicolored, perf. 10 vert. **2529**
A1881 19¢ multicolored, perf. 10 vert., two rope loops on piling...................................... **2529**
A1881 19¢ multicolored, perf. 10 vert., one rope loop on piling..................................... **2529C**
A1882 19¢ multicolored, perf. 10 (booklet panes only) **2530**
A1878 29¢ multicolored, engraved, perf. 10 vert. **2523**
A1878 29¢ multicolored, photogravure, perf. 10 vert. **2523A**
A1880 29¢ multicolored, perf. 11 (booklet panes only) **2528**

A1883 29¢ multicolored, perf. 11........................ **2531**

REGULAR ISSUE 1991-98

A1956

A1957

A2534

A1959

A1960

A1946

A1961

A1939

A1942

A1944

A1956 (10¢) multicolored, perf. 10 vert. (Bureau precanceled) **2602**
A1957 (10¢) orange yellow & multicolored, perf. 10 vert. (Bureau precanceled) **2603**
A1957 (10¢) gold & multicolored, perf. 10 vert. (Bureau precanceled) **2604**
A1957 (10¢) gold & multicolored, serpentine die cut 11.5 vert, self-adhesive......................... **2907**
A2534 (10¢) multicolored, perf. 9.9 vert. (Bureau precanceled) **3270**
A2534 (10¢) multicolored, serpentine die cut 9.9 vert., self-adhesive (Bureau precanceled).... .... **3271**
A1959 (23¢) multicolored, perf. 10 vert. (Bureau precanceled) **2605**
A1960 23¢ multicolored, perf. 10 vert. (Bureau precanceled) **2606**
A1960 23¢ multicolored, perf. 10 vert., "23" 7mm long (Bureau precanceled) **2607**

A1960 23¢ violet blue, red & black, perf. 10 vert., “First Class” 8½mm long (Bureau precanceled) **2608**
A1946 29¢ black & multicolored, perf. 10 (booklet panes only) **2593**
A1946 29¢ black & multicolored, perf. 11x10 (booklet panes only) **2593B**
A1946 29¢ red & multicolored, perf. 11x10 (booklet panes only) **2594**
A1961 29¢ blue & red, perf. 10 vert. **2609**
A1939 32¢ red brown, perf. 11.2 .... **2587**
A1942 $1 blue, perf. 11½ **2590**
A1944 $5 slate green, perf. 11½ **2592**

G RATE ISSUE 1994-95

A2206

A2210

A2207

A2209

A2208

A2206 (3¢) tan, bright blue & red, perf. 11x10.8 .... **2877**
A2206 (3¢) tan, dark blue & red, perf. 10.8x10.9 .... **2878**
A2210 (5¢) green & multicolored, perf. 9.8 vert. (Bureau precanceled) **2893**
A2207 (20¢) black “G,” yellow & multicolored, perf. 11.2x11.1 .... **2879**
A2207 (20¢) red “G,” yellow & multicolored, perf. 11x10.9 .... **2880**
A2209 (25¢) black “G,” blue & multicolored, perf. 9.8 vert.(Bureau precanceled) **2888**
A2208 (32¢) black “G” & multicolored, perf. 11.2x11.1 .... **2881**
A2208 (32¢) black “G” & multicolored, perf. 10x9.9 (booklet panes only) **2883**
A2208 (32¢) black “G” & multicolored, die cut, self-adhesive, small number of blue shading dots in white stripes below blue field ... **2886**
A2208 (32¢) black “G” & multicolored, die cut, self-adhesive, thin translucent paper, more blue shading dots in white stripes below blue field **2887**
A2208 (32¢) black “G” & multicolored, perf. 9.8 vert. **2889**
A2208 (32¢) red “G” & multicolored, perf. 11x10.9, distance from bottom of “G” to top of flag is 13¾mm **2882**
A2208 (32¢) red “G” & multicolored, perf. 11x10.9 on 2 or 3 sides (booklet panes only), distance from bottom of “G” to top of flag is 13½mm **2885**
A2208 (32¢) red “G” & multicolored, perf. 9.8 vert. **2891**
A2208 (32¢) red “G” & multicolored, rouletted. 9.8 vert. **2892**
A2208 (32¢) blue “G” & multicolored, perf. 10.9 (booklet panes only) **2884**
A2208 (32¢) blue “G” & multicolored, perf. 9.8 vert. **2890**

REGULAR ISSUE 1995-2004

A2217

A2218

A2489

A2853

A2220

A2509

A2223

A2724

A2225

A2490

A2212

A2230

A2217 (5¢) yellow, red & blue, perf. 9.8 vert. (Bureau precanceled) **2902**
A2217 (5¢) yellow, red & blue, serpentine die cut 11.5 vert, self-adhesive (Bureau precanceled) **2902B**
A2218 (5¢) purple & multicolored, perf. 9.9 vert. (Bureau precanceled) **2903**
A2218 (5¢) purple & multicolored, serpentine die cut 11.2 vert., self-adhesive (Bureau precanceled) **2904A**
A2218 (5¢) purple & multicolored, serpentine die cut 9.8 vert., self-adhesive (Bureau precanceled) **2904B**
A2218 (5¢) blue & multicolored, perf. 9.9 vert. (Bureau precanceled) **2904**
A2489 (5¢) multicolored, perf. 10 vert. (Bureau precanceled) **3207**
A2489 (5¢) multicolored, serpentine die cut 9.7 vert., self-adhesive (Bureau precanceled) **3207A**
A2853 (5¢) multicolored, serpentine die cut 8½ vert., self-adhesive (Bureau precanceled) **3693**
A2853 (5¢) multicolored, perf. 9¾ vert., “2003” date in blue, unclear dots in surf (Bureau precanceled) **3775**
A2853 (5¢) multicolored, serpentine die cut 9½x10 (coil stamp), self-adhesive (Bureau precanceled) **3785**
A2853 (5¢) multicolored, perf. 9¾ vert., “2004” date in black, rows of dots in surf (Bureau precanceled) **3864**
A2853 (5¢) multicolored, serpentine die cut 10 vert., “2003” date in black, self-adhesive (Bureau precanceled) **3874**
A2853 (5¢) multicolored, serpentine die cut 11½ vert., “2004” date in black, self-adhesive (Bureau precanceled) **3875**
A2220 (10¢) black, red brown & brown, perf. 9.8 vert. (Bureau precanceled) **2905**
A2220 (10¢) black, red brown & brown, serpentine die cut 11.5 vert., self-adhesive (Bureau precanceled) **2906**
A2509 (10¢) multicolored, serpentine die cut 9.8 vert., self-adhesive (Bureau precanceled) **3228**
A2509 (10¢) multicolored, perf 9.9 vert. (Bureau precanceled) **3229**
A2223 (15¢) dark orange, yellow & multicolored (dark, bold colors, heavy shading lines, heavily shaded chrome), perf. 9.8 vert. **2908**
A2223 (15¢) buff & multicolored (more subdued colors, finer details, shinier chrome), perf. 9.8 vert. **2909**
A2223 (15¢) buff & multicolored, serpentine die cut 11.5 vert., self-adhesive **2910**
A2724 (15¢) multicolored, serpentine die cut 11½ vert., self-adhesive (Bureau precanceled **3522**
A2225 (25¢) dark red, dark yellow green & multicolored (dark, saturated colors, dark blue lines in music selection board), perf.9.8 vert. **2911**
A2225 (25¢) dark red, yellow green & multicolored, serpentine die cut 9.8 vert, self-adhesive **2912B**
A2225 (25¢) bright orange red, bright yellow green & multicolored (bright colors, less shading and light blue lines in music selection board), perf. 9.8 vert. **2912**
A2225 (25¢) bright orange red, bright yellow green & multicolored, serpentine die cut 11.5 vert., self-adhesive **2912A**
A2225 (25¢) bright orange red, bright yellow green & multicolored, imperf, with simulated perforations, self-adhesive **3132**
A2490 (25¢) multicolored, perf. 10 vert. **3208**
A2490 (25¢) multicolored, serpentine die cut 9.7 vert., self-adhesive (Bureau precanceled) **3208A**
A2212 32¢ multicolored, perf. 10.4 .... **2897**
A2212 32¢ blue, tan, brown, red & light blue, perf. 10.8x9.8 (booklet panes only) **2916**
A2212 32¢ blue, tan, brown, red & light blue (pronounced blue shading in flag and red “1995”), perf. 9.8 vert. **2913**
A2212 32¢ blue, yellow brown, red & gray (gray shading in flag and blue “1995”), perf. 9.8 vert. **2914**
A2212 32¢ multicolored, serpentine die cut 8.7 vert., self-adhesive **2915**
A2212 32¢ dark blue, tan, brown, red & light blue, red “1996,” serpentine die cut 9.8 vert., self-adhesive **2915A**
A2212 32¢ dark blue, tan, brown, red & light blue, red “1997,” serpentine die cut 9.8 vert., straight cut at bottom and top with 9 teeth between, self-adhesive **2915D**
A2212 32¢ dark blue, tan, brown, red & light blue (sky shows color graduation at lower right, blue “1996”), serpentine die cut 9.9 vert., self-adhesive **3133**
A2212 32¢ dark blue, tan, brown, red & light blue, serpentine die cut 10.9 vert, self-adhesive **2915C**
A2212 32¢ dark blue, tan, brown, red & light blue, serpentine die cut 11.5 vert, self-adhesive **2915B**
A2212 32¢ multicolored, serpentine die cut 8.8 on 2, 3 or 4 adjacent sides, dated “1995” in blue, self-adhesive (booklet panes only) **2920**
A2212 32¢ multicolored, serpentine die cut 11.3 on 2, 3 or 4 adjacent sides, dated “1996” in blue, self-adhesive (booklet panes only) **2920D**
A2212 32¢ dark blue, tan, brown, red & light blue, serpentine die cut 9.8 on 2 or 3 adjacent sides, dated “1996” in red, self-adhesive (booklet panes only) **2921**
A2212 32¢ dark blue, tan, brown, red & light blue, serpentine die cut 9.8 on 2 or 3 adjacent sides, dated “1997” in red, self-adhesive (booklet panes only) **2921b**
A2230 32¢ multicolored, die cut, self-adhesive **2919**

H RATE ISSUE 1999

A2529

A2530

A2531

A2529 (1¢) multicolored, white USA, black "1998," perf. 11.2 .... **3257**
A2529 (1¢) multicolored, pale blue USA, blue "1998," perf. 11.2 .... **3258**
A2530 22¢ multicolored, serpentine die cut 10.8, self-adhesive **3259**
A2530 22¢ multicolored, serpentine die cut 9.9 vert, self-adhesive **3263**
A2530 22¢ multicolored, perf. 9¾ vert. **3353**
A2531 (33¢) multicolored, perf. 11.2 .... **3260**
A2531 (33¢) multicolored, perf. 9.8 vert. **3264**
A2531 (33¢) multicolored, serpentine die cut 9.9 vert., stamp corners at right angles, backing paper same size as stamp, self-adhesive **3265**
A2531 (33¢) multicolored, serpentine die cut 9.9 vert., stamp corners rounded, backing paper larger than stamp, self-adhesive **3266**
A2531 (33¢) multicolored, serpentine die cut 9.9, (booklet panes only), self-adhesive **3267**
A2531 (33¢) multicolored, serpentine die cut 11.2x11.1 (booklet panes only), self-adhesive **3268**
A2531 (33¢) multicolored, die cut 8 (booklet panes only), self-adhesive **3269**

REGULAR ISSUE 1999

A2540

A2541

A2540 33¢ multicolored, perf. 11.2 .... **3277**
A2540 33¢ multicolored, serpentine die cut 11.1, self-adhesive **3278**
A2540 33¢ multicolored, serpentine die cut 11½x11¾, self-adhesive **3278F**
A2540 33¢ multicolored, serpentine die cut 9.8 (booklet panes only), self-adhesive **3279**
A2540 33¢ multicolored, perf. 9.9 vert. **3280**
A2540 33¢ multicolored, serpentine die cut 9.8 vert., stamp corners at right angles, backing paper same size as stamp, self-adhesive **3281**
A2540 33¢ multicolored, serpentine die cut 9.8 vert., stamp corners rounded, backing paper same larger than stamp, self-adhesive **3282**
A2541 33¢ multicolored, serpentine die cut 7.9 (booklet panes only), self-adhesive **3283**

DISTINGUISHED AMERICANS ISSUE 2000-08

A2650

A2652

A2656

A2657

A2657a

A2658

A2660

A2661

A2661a

A2662

A2663

A2664

A2650 10¢ red & black, perf 11 .... **3420**
A2652 23¢ red & black, litho. & engr., serpentine die cut 11¼x10¾, self-adhesive **3422**
A2652 23¢ red & black, litho., serpentine die cut 11¼x10¾ on 3 sides, self-adhesive (booklet panes only) **3436**
A2656 33¢ red & black, perf 11 .... **3426**
A2657 58¢ red & black, serpentine die cut 11, self-adhesive **3427**
A2657a 59¢ multicolored, serpentine die cut 11¼x10¾, self-adhesive **3427A**
A2658 63¢ red & black, serpentine die cut 11¼x11, self-adhesive **3428**
A2660 75¢ red & black, serpentine die cut 11¼x10¾, self-adhesive **3430**
A2661 76¢ red & black, serpentine die cut 11, self-adhesive **3431**
A2661 76¢ red & black, serpentine die cut 11½x11, self-adhesive **3432**
A2661a 59¢ multicolored, serpentine die cut 11¼x10¾, self-adhesive **3432A**
A2662 83¢ red & black, serpentine die cut 11x11¾, self-adhesive **3433**
A2663 83¢ red & black, serpentine die cut 11¼, self-adhesive **3434**
A2664 87¢ red & black, serpentine die cut 11¼x11, self-adhesive **3435**

AMERICAN CULTURE ISSUE 2000-03

A2677

A2722

A2875

A2677 (10¢) multicolored, serpentine die cut 11½ vert., self adhesive (Bureau precanceled) **3447**
A2677 (10¢) multicolored, perf. 10 vert. (Bureau precanceled) **3769**
A2722 (10¢) multicolored, serpentine die cut 8½ vert., self-adhesive (Bureau precanceled) **3520**
A2722 (10¢) multicolored, serpentine die cut 11 vert., self-adhesive (Bureau precanceled) **3770**
A2875 $1 multicolored, serpentine die cut 11¼x11 vert., self-adhesive **3766**

REGULAR ISSUE 2000-03

A2686

A2687

A2678

A2679

A2680

A2681

A2682

A2683

A2684

A2685

A2688

A2689

A2690

A2691

A2692

A2693

A2696

A2686 20¢ dark carmine, serpentine die cut 11¼x11 on 3 sides (booklet panes only), self-adhesive **3482**
A2686 20¢ dark carmine, serpentine die cut 10½x11 on 3 sides (booklet panes only), self-adhesive **3483**
A2687 21¢ multicolored, perf. 11¼ **3467**
A2687 21¢ multicolored, serpentine die cut 11¼ on 3 sides, self-adhesive (booklet panes only) **3484**
A2687 21¢ multicolored, serpentine die cut 10½x11¼ on 3 sides, self-adhesive (booklet panes only **3484A**
A2687 21¢ multicolored, serpentine die cut 11, self-adhesive **3468**
A2687 21¢ multicolored, serpentine die cut 8½ vert., self-adhesive **3475**
A2686 23¢ green, perf. 11¼ **3616**
A2686 23¢ green, serpentine die cut 11¼x11¾, self-adhesive **3468A**
A2686 23¢ green, serpentine die cut 8½ vert., self-adhesive (Banknote Corp. Printing) **3475A**
A2686 23¢ gray green, serpentine die cut 8½ vert., self-adhesive (Avery Printing) **3617**
A2686 23¢ green, serpentine die cut 11¼ on 3 sides, self-adhesive (booklet panes only **3618**
A2686 23¢ green, serpentine die cut 10½x11¼ on 3 sides, self-adhesive (booklet panes only) **3619**
A2686 23¢ gray green, serpentine die cut 11, self-adhesive (Avery Printing) **3819**
A2678 (34¢) multicolored, perf. 111/4 .... **3448**
A2678 (34¢) multicolored, serpentine die cut 11¼, self-adhesive **3449**
A2678 (34¢) multicolored, serpentine die cut 8 on 2, 3 or 4 sides (booklet panes only), self-adhesive **3450**
A2679 (34¢) multicolored, serpentine die cut 11 on 2, 3 or 4 sides (booklet panes only), self-adhesive **3451**
A2680 (34¢) multicolored, perf. 9¾ vert. **3452**
A2680 (34¢) multicolored, serpentine die cut 10 vert., self-adhesive **3453**
A2681 (34¢) purple & multicolored, serpentine die cut 10½x10¾ on 2 or 3 sides (booklet panes only), self-adhesive **3454**
A2681 (34¢) purple & multicolored, serpentine die cut 11½x11¾ on 2 or 3 sides (booklet panes only), self-adhesive **3458**
A2681 (34¢) purple & multicolored, serpentine die cut 8½ vert., self-adhesive **3465**
A2682 (34¢) tan & multicolored, serpentine die cut 10½x10¾ on 2 or 3 sides (booklet panes only), self-adhesive **3455**
A2682 (34¢) tan & multicolored, serpentine die cut 11½x11¾ on 2 or 3 sides (booklet panes only), self-adhesive **3459**
A2682 (34¢) tan & multicolored, serpentine die cut 8½ vert., self-adhesive **3464**
A2683 (34¢) green & multicolored, serpentine die cut 10½x10¾ on 2 or 3 sides (booklet panes only), self-adhesive **3456**
A2683 (34¢) green & multicolored, serpentine die cut 11½x11¾ on 2 or 3 sides (booklet panes only), self-adhesive **3460**
A2683 (34¢) green & multicolored, serpentine die cut 8½ vert., self-adhesive **3462**
A2684 (34¢) red & multicolored, serpentine die cut 10½x10¾ on 2 or 3 sides (booklet panes only), self-adhesive **3457**
A2684 (34¢) red & multicolored, serpentine die cut 11½x11¾ on 2 or 3 sides (booklet panes only), self-adhesive **3461**
A2684 (34¢) red & multicolored, serpentine die cut 8½ vert., self-adhesive **3463**
A2685 34¢ multicolored, serpentine die cut 9¾ vert., stamp corners rounded, backing paper larger than stamp, self-adhesive **3466**
A2685 34¢ multicolored, perf. 9¾ vert. **3476**
A2685 34¢ multicolored, serpentine die cut 9¾ vert., stamp corners at right angles, backing paper same size as stamp, self-adhesive **3477**
A2688 34¢ multicolored, perf. 11¼ **3469**
A2688 34¢ multicolored, serpentine die cut 11¼, self-adhesive **3470**
A2688 34¢ multicolored, serpentine die cut 8 on 2, 3 or 4 sides, self-adhesive (booklet panes only **3495**
A2689 34¢ multicolored, serpentine die cut 11 on 2, 3 or 4 sides (booklet panes only), self-adhesive **3485**
A2690 34¢ green & multicolored, serpentine die cut 8½ vert., self-adhesive **3478**
A2690 34¢ green & multicolored, serpentine die cut 10½x10¾ on 2 or 3 sides (booklet panes only), self-adhesive **3489**
A2691 34¢ red & multicolored, serpentine die cut 8½ vert., self-adhesive **3479**
A2691 34¢ red & multicolored, serpentine die cut 10½x10¾ on 2 or 3 sides (booklet panes only), self-adhesive **3490**
A2692 34¢ tan & multicolored, serpentine die cut 8½ vert., self-adhesive **3480**
A2692 34¢ tan & multicolored, serpentine die cut 10½x10¾ on 2 or 3 sides (booklet panes only), self-adhesive **3488**
A2693 34¢ purple & multicolored, serpentine die cut 8½ vert., self-adhesive **3481**
A2693 34¢ purple & multicolored, serpentine die cut 10½x10¾ on 2 or 3 sides (booklet panes only), self-adhesive **3487**
A2696 55¢ multicolored, serpentine die cut 10¾, self-adhesive **3471**
A2696 57¢ multicolored, serpentine die cut 10¾, self-adhesive **3471A**

WASHINGTON VIEWS ISSUE 2001-03

A2697

A2818

A2698

A2819

A2697 $3.50 multicolored, serpentine die cut 11¼x11½, self-adhesive **3472**
A2818 $3.85 multicolored, serpentine die cut 11¼, self-adhesive **3647**
A2818 $3.85 multicolored, serpentine die cut 11x10¾, self-adhesive **3647A**
A2698 $12.25 multicolored, serpentine die cut 11¼x11½, self-adhesive **3473**
A2819 $13.65 multicolored, serpentine die cut 11¼, self-adhesive **3648**

UNITED WE STAND ISSUE 2001-02

A2744

A2744 34¢ multicolored, serpentine die cut 11¼ on 2, 3 or 4 sides, self-adhesive (booklet panes only) **3549**
A2744 34¢ multicolored, serpentine die cut 10½x10¾ on 2 or 3 sides, self-adhesive (booklet panes only) **3549B**
A2744 34¢ multicolored, serpentine die cut 9¾ vert., stamp corners at right angles, backing paper same size as stamp, self-adhesive **3550**
A2744 34¢ multicolored, serpentine die cut 9¾ vert., stamp corners rounded, backing paper larger than stamp, self-adhesive **3550A**

AMERICAN DESIGN ISSUE 2002-08

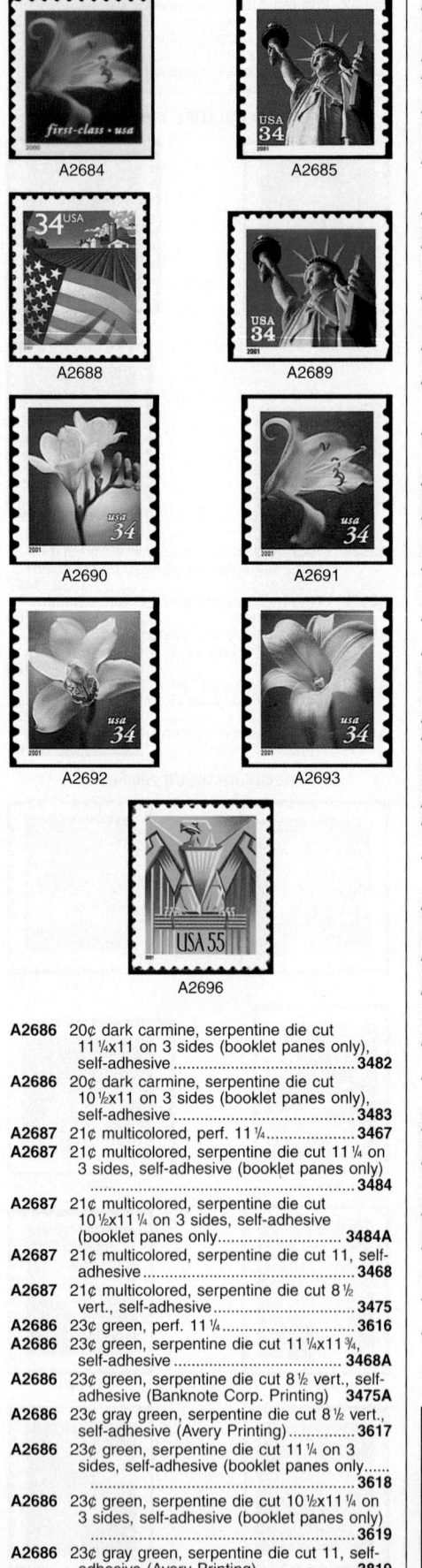

A2866

A2858

A2868

A2859

A2805

A2860

A2866 1¢ multicolored, serpentine die cut 11¼x11, self-adhesive 3749
A2866 1¢ multicolored, serpentine die cut 11, self-adhesive 3749A
A2866 1¢ multicolored, perf. 9¾ vert., photo., without microprinting, dated "2003" 3758
A2866 1¢ multicolored, perf. 9¾ vert., litho., with microprinting, dated "2008" 3758A
A2858 2¢ multicolored, serpentine die cut 11, without microprinting,self-adhesive, dated "2004" 3750
A2858 2¢ multicolored, without microprinting, serpentine die cut 11¼x11½, self-adhesive, dated "2006" 3751
A2858 2¢ multicolored, with microprinting at right, serpentine die cut 11¼x11, self-adhesive, dated "2006" 3752
A2858 2¢ multicolored, with microprinting at left, serpentine die cut 11¼x10¾, self-adhesive, date "2007" 3753
A2868 3¢ multicolored, serpentine die cut 11¼x11, self-adhesive 3754
A2868 3¢ multicolored, perf. 9¾ vert. 3759
A2859 4¢ multicolored, serpentine die cut 10¾x10¼, self-adhesive 3755
A2859 4¢ multicolored, perf. 9¾ vert. 3761
A2805 5¢ multicolored, serpentine die cut 11¼x11¾, self-adhesive 3756
A2805 5¢ multicolored, perf. 9¾ vert. 3612
A2860 10¢ multicolored, serpentine die cut 11¼x11½, self-adhesive 3757
A2860 10¢ multicolored, perf. 9¾ vert. 3762

REGULAR ISSUE 2002-05

A2806

A2807

A2808

A2809

A2810

A2811

A2813

A2814

A2815

A2816

A2812

A2817

A2806 3¢ red, blue & black, serpentine die cut 11, self-adhesive, lithographed, year at lower left 3613
A2806 3¢ red, blue & black, serpentine die cut 10, self-adhesive, photogravure, year at lower right 3614
A2806 3¢ red, blue & black, perf. 10 vert., photogravure, year at lower left 3615
A2807 (37¢) multicolored, perf. 11¼x11 3620
A2807 (37¢) multicolored, serpentine die cut 11¼x11, self-adhesive 3621
A2807 (37¢) multicolored, serpentine die cut 10 vert., self-adhesive 3622
A2807 (37¢) multicolored, serpentine die cut 11¼ on 2, 3 or 4 sides, self-adhesive (booklet panes only) 3623
A2807 (37¢) multicolored, serpentine die cut 10½x10¾ on 2 or 3 sides, self-adhesive (booklet panes only) 3624
A2807 (37¢) multicolored, serpentine die cut 8 on 2, 3 or 4 sides, self-adhesive (booklet panes only) 3625
A2808 (37¢) multicolored, serpentine die cut 11 on 2, 3 or 4 sides, self-adhesive (booklet panes only) 3626
A2809 (37¢) multicolored, serpentine die cut 11 on 2, 3 or 4 sides, self-adhesive (booklet panes only) 3627
A2810 (37¢) multicolored, serpentine die cut 11 on 2, 3 or 4 sides, self-adhesive (booklet panes only) 3628
A2811 (37¢) multicolored, serpentine die cut 11 on 2, 3 or 4 sides, self-adhesive (booklet panes only) 3629
A2812 37¢ multicolored, perf. 11¼ 3629F
A2812 37¢ multicolored, serpentine die cut 11¼x11, self-adhesive 3630
A2812 37¢ multicolored, perf. 10 vert. 3631
A2812 37¢ multicolored, serpentine die cut 9¾ vert., self-adhesive 3632
A2812 37¢ multicolored, serpentine die cut 10¼ vert., self-adhesive, lacking points of stars at upper left 3632A
A2812 37¢ multicolored, serpentine die cut 11¾ vert., self-adhesive 3632C
A2812 37¢ multicolored, serpentine die cut 8½ vert., rounded corners, self-adhesive ... 3633
A2812 37¢ multicolored, serpentine die cut 8½ vert., right angle corners, self-adhesive 3633A
A2812 37¢ multicolored, serpentine die cut 9½ vert., with microprinted "USA" in top red stripe, self-adhesive 3633B
A2812 37¢ multicolored, serpentine die cut 11 on 3 sides, self-adhesive (booklet panes only) 3634
A2812 37¢ multicolored, serpentine die cut 11¼ on 2 or 3 sides, self-adhesive (booklet panes only) 3635
A2812 37¢ multicolored, serpentine die cut 10½x10¾ on 2 or 3 sides, self-adhesive (booklet panes only) 3636
A2812 37¢ multicolored, serpentine die cut 11¼x11 on 2 or 3 sides, self-adhesive (booklet panes only) 3636D
A2812 37¢ multicolored, serpentine die cut 8 on 2, 3 or 4 sides, self-adhesive (booklet panes only) 3637
A2813 37¢ multicolored, serpentine die cut 8½ horiz., self-adhesive 3638
A2813 37¢ multicolored, serpentine die cut 11 on 2, 3 or 4 sides, self-adhesive (booklet panes only) 3643
A2814 37¢ multicolored, serpentine die cut 8½ horiz., self-adhesive 3639
A2814 37¢ multicolored, serpentine die cut 11 on 2, 3 or 4 sides, self-adhesive (booklet panes only) 3642
A2815 37¢ multicolored, serpentine die cut 8½ horiz., self-adhesive 3640
A2815 37¢ multicolored, serpentine die cut 11 on 2, 3 or 4 sides, self-adhesive (booklet panes only) 3645
A2816 37¢ multicolored, serpentine die cut 8½ horiz., self-adhesive 3641
A2816 37¢ multicolored, serpentine die cut 11 on 2, 3 or 4 sides, self-adhesive (booklet panes only) 3644
A2817 60¢ multicolored, serpentine die cut 11x11¼ self-adhesive 3646

PURPLE HEART ISSUE 2003-08

A2891

A2891 37¢ multicolored, serpentine die cut 11¼x10¾, self-adhesive 3784
A2891 37¢ multicolored, serpentine die cut 10¾x10¼, self-adhesive 3784A
A2891 39¢ multicolored, serpentine die cut 11¼x11, self-adhesive 4032
A2891 41¢ multicolored, serpentine die cut 11¼x10¾, self-adhesive 4164
A2891 42¢ multicolored, perf. 11¼ 4263
A2891 42¢ multicolored, serpentine die cut 11¼x10¾, self-adhesive 4264

EAGLE ISSUE 2003-04

A2898

A2899

A2898 (25¢) gray & gold, serpentine die 11¾ vert. 3792
A2898 (25¢) gray & gold, perf. 9¾ vert. 3844
A2898 (25¢) dull blue & gold, serpentine die 11¾ vert. 3794
A2898 (25¢) dull blue & gold, perf. 9¾ vert. 3852
A2898 (25¢) green & gold, serpentine die 11¾ vert. 3796
A2898 (25¢) green & gold, perf. 9¾ vert. 3850
A2898 (25¢) Prussian blue & gold, serpentine die 11¾ vert. 3798
A2898 (25¢) Prussian blue & gold, perf. 9¾ vert. 3848
A2898 (25¢) red & gold, serpentine die cut 11¾ vert. 3800
A2898 (25¢) red & gold, perf. 9¾ vert. 3846
A2899 (25¢) gold & red, serpentine die cut 11¾ vert. 3793
A2899 (25¢) gold & red, perf. 9¾ vert. 3853
A2899 (25¢) gold & Prussian blue, serpentine die cut 11¾ vert. 3795

A2899 (25¢) gold & Prussian blue, perf. 9¾ vert. **3851**
A2899 (25¢) gold & gray, serpentine die cut 11¾ vert. **3797**
A2899 (25¢) gold & gray, perf. 9¾ vert. **3849**
A2899 (25¢) gold & dull blue, serpentine die cut 11¾ vert. **3799**
A2899 (25¢) gold & dull blue, perf. 9¾ vert. **3847**
A2899 (25¢) gold & green, serpentine die cut 11¾ vert. **3801**
A2899 (25¢) gold & green, perf. 9¾ vert. **3845**

WILDLIFE ISSUE 2003-08

A3151

A3152

A2925

A3230

A3151 17¢ multicolored, without microprinting, serpentine die cut 11, self-adhesive **4138**
A3151 17¢ multicolored, without microprinting, serpentine die cut 11 vert., self-adhesive **4140**
A3152 26¢ multicolored, with microprinting, perf. 11¼x11 ...... **4137**
A3152 26¢ multicolored, with microprinting, serpentine die cut 11¼x11 ...... **4139**
A3152 26¢ multicolored, with microprinting, serpentine die cut 11 vert. **4141**
A3152 26¢ multicolored, without microprinting, serpentine die cut 11¼x11 on 3 sides (booklet panes only) **4142**
A2925 37¢ multicolored, serpentine die cut 8½ vert., self-adhesive **3829**
A2925 37¢ multicolored, serpentine die cut 9½ vert., self-adhesive **3829A**
A2925 37¢ multicolored, without microprinting, serpentine die cut 11½x11 on 2, 3 or 4 sides, self-adhesive (booklet panes only) **3830**
A2925 37¢ multicolored, with microprinting, serpentine die cut 11½x11 on 2, 3 or 4 sides, self-adhesive (booklet panes only) **3830D**
A3230 62¢ multicolored, serpentine die cut 11¼x11, self-adhesive **4267**

FLAG AND STATUE OF LIBERTY ISSUE 2005-06

A3038

A3040

A3038 (39¢) multicolored, with microprinting, perf. 11¼ **3965**
A3038 (39¢) multicolored, with microprinting, serpentine die cut 11¼x11, self-adhesive **3966**
A3038 (39¢) multicolored, without microprinting, perf. 9¾ vert. **3967**
A3038 (39¢) multicolored, without microprinting, serpentine die cut 8½ vert., self-adhesive **3968**
A3038 (39¢) multicolored, without microprinting, serpentine die cut 10¼ vert., self-adhesive **3969**
A3038 (39¢) multicolored, with microprinting, serpentine die cut 9½ vert., self-adhesive **3970**
A3038 (39¢) multicolored, lithographed, without microprinting, serpentine die cut 11¼x10¾ on 2 or 3 sides, self-adhesive (booklet panes only) **3972**
A3038 (39¢) multicolored, without microprinting, serpentine die cut 10¼x10¾ on 2 or 3 sides, self-adhesive (booklet panes only) **3973**
A3038 (39¢) multicolored, photogravure, without microprinting, serpentine die cut 11¼x11 on 2 or 3 sides, self-adhesive (booklet panes only) **3974**
A3038 (39¢) multicolored, without microprinting, serpentine die cut 8 on 2, 3 or 4 sides, self-adhesive (booklet panes only) **3975**
A3040 39¢ multicolored, with microprinting, serpentine die cut 11¼x10¾, self-adhesive **3978**
A3040 39¢ multicolored, without microprinting, perf. 10 vert. **3979**
A3040 39¢ multicolored, without microprinting, serpentine die cut 11 vert., self-adhesive **3980**
A3040 39¢ multicolored, with microprinting, serpentine die cut 9½ vert., self-adhesive **3981**
A3040 39¢ multicolored, without microprinting, serpentine die cut 10¼ vert., self-adhesive **3982**
A3040 39¢ multicolored, without microprinting, serpentine die cut 8½ vert., self-adhesive **3983**
A3040 39¢ multicolored, without microprinting, serpentine die cut 11¼x10¾ on 2 or 3 sides, self-adhesive (booklet panes only) **3985**

REGULAR ISSUE 2006

A3053

A3054

A3055

A3056

A3057

A3058

A3053 24¢ multicolored, perf. 11¼ **4000**
A3053 24¢ multicolored, serpentine die cut 11, self-adhesive **4001**
A3053 24¢ multicolored, serpentine die cut 8½ horiz., self-adhesive **4002**
A3054 39¢ multicolored, serpentine die cut 10¼ horiz., self-adhesive **4003**
A3054 39¢ multicolored, serpentine die cut 10¾x10½ on 2 or 3 sides, self-adhesive (booklet panes only) **4012**
A3054 39¢ multicolored, serpentine die cut 10¾x11¼ on 2 or 3 sides, self-adhesive (booklet panes only) **4013**
A3055 39¢ multicolored, serpentine die cut 10¼ horiz., self-adhesive **4004**
A3055 39¢ multicolored, serpentine die cut 10¾x10½ on 2 or 3 sides, self-adhesive (booklet panes only) **4011**
A3055 39¢ multicolored, serpentine die cut 10¾x11¼ on 2 or 3 sides, self-adhesive (booklet panes only) **4017**
A3056 39¢ multicolored, serpentine die cut 10¼ horiz., self-adhesive **4005**
A3056 39¢ multicolored, serpentine die cut 10¾x10½ on 2 or 3 sides, self-adhesive (booklet panes only) **4010**
A3056 39¢ multicolored, serpentine die cut 10¾x11¼ on 2 or 3 sides, self-adhesive (booklet panes only) **4016**
A3057 39¢ multicolored, serpentine die cut 10¼ horiz., self-adhesive **4006**
A3057 39¢ multicolored, serpentine die cut 10¾x10½ on 2 or 3 sides, self-adhesive (booklet panes only) **4009**
A3057 39¢ multicolored, serpentine die cut 10¾x11¼ on 2 or 3 sides, self-adhesive (booklet panes only) **4015**
A3058 39¢ multicolored, serpentine die cut 10¼ horiz., self-adhesive **4007**
A3058 39¢ multicolored, serpentine die cut 10¾x10½ on 2 or 3 sides, self-adhesive (booklet panes only) **4008**
A3058 39¢ multicolored, serpentine die cut 10¾x11¼ on 2 or 3 sides, self-adhesive (booklet panes only) **4014**

X-PLANES ISSUE 2006

A3059

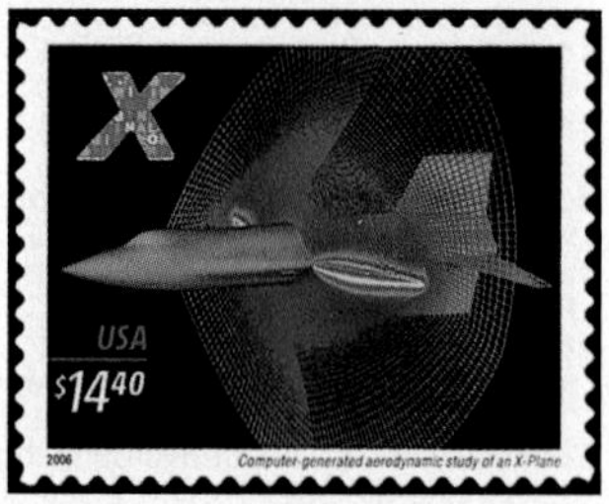

A3060

A3059 $4.05 multicolored, serpentine die cut 10¾x10½, self-adhesive **4018**
A3060 $14.40 multicolored, serpentine die cut 10¾x10½, self-adhesive **4019**

LIBERTY BELL (FOREVER) ISSUE 2007

A3148

Large

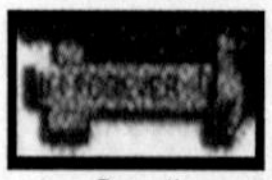
Small

Medium

A3148 (41¢) multicolored, large microprinting, bell 16mm wide, serpentine die cut 11¼x10¾ on 2 or 3 sides, self-adhesive (booklet panes only) **4125**
A3148 (41¢) multicolored, large microprinting, bell 16mm wide, serpentine die cut 8 on 2, 3 or 4 sides, self-adhesive (booklet panes only) **4128**
A3148 (41¢) multicolored, small microprinting, bell 16mm wide, serpentine die cut 11¼x10¾ on 2 or 3 sides, self-adhesive (booklet panes only) **4126**
A3148 (41¢) multicolored, medium microprinting, bell 15mm wide, serpentine die cut 11¼x10¾ on 2 or 3 sides, self-adhesive (booklet panes only) **4127**

FLAG ISSUE 2007

A3149

A3184

A3149 (41¢) multicolored, perf. 11¼ **4129**
A3149 (41¢) multicolored, serpentine die cut 11¼x10¾, self-adhesive **4130**
A3149 (41¢) multicolored, perf. 9¾ vert. **4131**
A3149 (41¢) multicolored, serpentine die cut 9½ vert., with perpendicular corners, self-adhesive **4132**
A3149 (41¢) multicolored, serpentine die cut 11 vert., with perpendicular corners, self-adhesive **4133**
A3149 (41¢) multicolored, serpentine die cut 8½ vert., with perpendicular corners, self-adhesive **4134**
A3149 (41¢) multicolored, serpentine die cut 11 vert., with rounded corners, self-adhesive **4135**
A3184 41¢ multicolored, serpentine die cut 9½ vert., with "USPS" microprinted on right side of flagpole, self-adhesive **4186**
A3184 41¢ multicolored, serpentine die cut 11 vert., with "USPS" microprinted on left side of flagpole, self-adhesive, with perpendicular corners **4187**
A3184 41¢ multicolored, serpentine die cut 8½ vert., with "USPS" microprinted on flagpole, self-adhesive, with perpendicular corners **4188**
A3184 41¢ multicolored, serpentine die cut 11 vert., with "USPS" microprinted on flagpole, self-adhesive, with rounded corners **4189**
A3184 41¢ multicolored, serpentine die cut 11¼x10¾ on 3 sides, with "USPS" microprinted on right side of flagpole, self-adhesive (booklet panes only).............**4190**
A3184 41¢ multicolored, serpentine die cut 11¼x10¾ on 2 or 3 sides, with "USPS" microprinted on leftt side of flagpole, self-adhesive (booklet panes only).............**4191**

PRESIDENTIAL AIRCRAFT ISSUE 2007

A3154

A3155

A3154 $4.60 multicolored, serpentine die cut 10¾, self-adhesive **4144**
A3155 $16.25 multicolored, serpentine die cut 10¾, self-adhesive **4145**

PATRIOTIC BANNER ISSUE 2007

Patriotic Banner — A3167

A3167 (10¢) multicolored, serpentine die cut 11 vert., photo., self-adhesive...................**4157**
A3167 (10¢) multicolored, serpentine die cut 11¾ vert., litho., self-adhesive **4158**

FLOWERS ISSUE 2007

Iris — A3174

Dahlia — A3175

Magnolia — A3176

Red Gerbera Daisy — A3177

Coneflower — A3178

Tulip — A3179

Water Lily — A3180

Poppy — A3181

Chrysanthemum A3182

Orange Gerbera Daisy A3183

A3174 41¢ multicolored, serpentine die cut 9½ vert., self-adhesive..............................**4166**
A3174 41¢ multicolored, serpentine die cut 11¼x11½ on 2 or 3 sides, self-adhesive (booklet pane only) **4178**
A3175 41¢ multicolored, serpentine die cut 9½ vert., self-adhesive **4167**
A3174 41¢ multicolored, serpentine die cut 11¼x11½ on 2 or 3 sides, self-adhesive (booklet pane only) **4179**
A3176 41¢ multicolored, serpentine die cut 9½ vert., self-adhesive **4168**
A3176 41¢ multicolored, serpentine die cut 11¼x11½ on 2 or 3 sides, self-adhesive (booklet pane only) **4180**
A3177 41¢ multicolored, serpentine die cut 9½ vert., self-adhesive **4169**
A3177 41¢ multicolored, serpentine die cut 11¼x11½ on 2 or 3 sides, self-adhesive (booklet pane only) **4181**
A3178 41¢ multicolored, serpentine die cut 9½ vert., self-adhesive **4170**
A3178 41¢ multicolored, serpentine die cut 11¼x11½ on 2 or 3 sides, self-adhesive (booklet pane only) **4184**
A3179 41¢ multicolored, serpentine die cut 9½ vert., self-adhesive **4171**
A3179 41¢ multicolored, serpentine die cut 11¼x11½ on 2 or 3 sides, self-adhesive (booklet pane only) **4185**
A3180 41¢ multicolored, serpentine die cut 9½ vert., self-adhesive **4172**
A3180 41¢ multicolored, serpentine die cut 11¼x11½ on 2 or 3 sides, self-adhesive (booklet pane only) **4182**
A3181 41¢ multicolored, serpentine die cut 9½ vert., self-adhesive **4173**
A3181 41¢ multicolored, serpentine die cut 11¼x11½ on 2 or 3 sides, self-adhesive (booklet pane only) **4183**
A3182 41¢ multicolored, serpentine die cut 9½ vert., self-adhesive **4174**
A3182 41¢ multicolored, serpentine die cut 11¼x11½ on 2 or 3 sides, self-adhesive (booklet pane only) **4176**
A3183 41¢ multicolored, serpentine die cut 9½ vert., self-adhesive **4175**
A3183 41¢ multicolored, serpentine die cut 11¼x11½ on 2 or 3 sides, self-adhesive (booklet pane only) **4177**

FLAG ISSUE 2008

Flag at Dusk — A3214

Flag at Night — A3215

Flag at Dawn — A3216

Flag at Midday — A3217

A3214 42¢ multicolored, perf. 10 vert., without microprinting...**4228**
A3214 42¢ multicolored, serpentine die cut 9½ vert., with microprinting, self-adhesive, with perpendicular corners..........................**4232**
A3214 42¢ multicolored, perf. 11 vert., without microprinting, self-adhesive, with perpendicular corners..........................**4236**
A3214 42¢ multicolored, serpentine die cut 8½ vert., without microprinting, self-adhesive, with perpendicular corners **4240**
A3214 42¢ multicolored, serpentine die cut 11 vert., without microprinting, self-adhesive, with rounded corners..................................**4244**
A3215 42¢ multicolored, perf. 10 vert., without microprinting...**4229**
A3215 42¢ multicolored, serpentine die cut 9½ vert., with microprinting, self-adhesive, with perpendicular corners..........................**4233**
A3215 42¢ multicolored, perf. 11 vert., without microprinting, self-adhesive, with perpendicular corners..........................**4237**
A3215 42¢ multicolored, serpentine die cut 8½ vert., without microprinting, self-adhesive, with perpendicular corners **4241**
A3215 42¢ multicolored, serpentine die cut 11 vert., without microprinting, self-adhesive, with rounded corners..................................**4245**
A3216 42¢ multicolored, perf. 10 vert., without microprinting...**4230**
A3216 42¢ multicolored, serpentine die cut 9½ vert., with microprinting, self-adhesive, with perpendicular corners..........................**4234**
A3216 42¢ multicolored, perf. 11 vert., without microprinting, self-adhesive, with perpendicular corners..........................**4238**
A3216 42¢ multicolored, serpentine die cut 8½ vert., without microprinting, self-adhesive, with perpendicular corners **4242**
A3216 42¢ multicolored, serpentine die cut 11 vert., without microprinting, self-adhesive, with rounded corners..................................**4246**
A3217 42¢ multicolored, perf. 10 vert., without microprinting...**4231**
A3217 42¢ multicolored, serpentine die cut 9½ vert., with microprinting, self-adhesive, with perpendicular corners..........................**4235**
A3217 42¢ multicolored, perf. 11 vert., without microprinting, self-adhesive, with perpendicular corners..........................**4239**

A3217 42¢ multicolored, serpentine die cut 8½ vert., without microprinting, self-adhesive, with perpendicular corners **4243**

A3217 42¢ multicolored, serpentine die cut 11 vert., without microprinting, self-adhesive, with rounded corners **4247**

TROPICAL FRUIT ISSUE 2008

Pomegranate
A3223

Star Fruit
A3224

Kiwi — A3225

Papaya — A3226

Guava — A3227

A3223 27¢ multicolored, serpentine die cut 11¼x10¾, self-adhesive **4253**

A3223 42¢ multicolored, serpentine die cut 8½ vert., self-adhesive **4260**

A3224 27¢ multicolored, serpentine die cut 11¼x10¾, self-adhesive **4254**

A3224 42¢ multicolored, serpentine die cut 8½ vert., self-adhesive **4261**

A3225 27¢ multicolored, serpentine die cut 11¼x10¾, self-adhesive **4255**

A3225 42¢ multicolored, serpentine die cut 8½ vert., self-adhesive **4262**

A3226 27¢ multicolored, serpentine die cut 11¼x10¾, self-adhesive **4256**

A3226 42¢ multicolored, serpentine die cut 8½ vert., self-adhesive **4258**

A3227 27¢ multicolored, serpentine die cut 11¼x10¾, self-adhesive **4257**

A3227 42¢ multicolored, serpentine die cut 8½ vert., self-adhesive **4259**

AMERICAN LANDMARKS ISSUE 2008

Mount Rushmore
A3231

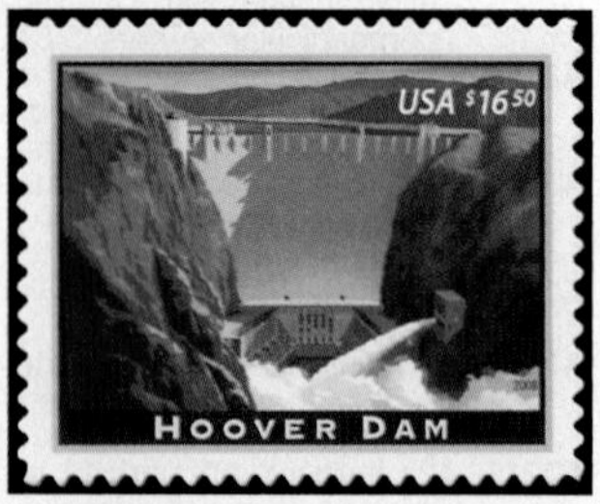

Hoover Dam — A3232

A3231 $4.80 multicolored, serpentine die cut 10¾x10½, self-adhesive **4268**

A3232 $16.50 multicolored, serpentine die cut 10¾x10½, self-adhesive **4269**

SUBJECT INDEX OF REGULAR, COMMEMORATIVE & AIR POST ISSUES

Additions, Deletions & Number Changes

Number in 2008 Catalogue	Number in 2008 Catalogue
36b	36B
331b	deleted
332b	deleted
333a	deleted
334a	deleted
335a	deleted
336a	deleted
337a	deleted
338a	deleted
339a	deleted
340a	deleted
new	910c
new	912c
new	913b
new	917c
new	920b
new	920c
new	1430d
new	1463a
new	1477a
new	1501c
new	1555b
new	1565a
new	1617c
new	1623g
new	1704b
new	2012a
new	2060a
new	2061a
new	2127c
new	2393b
new	2422a
new	2452Df
new	2492i
new	2492j
new	2511c
new	2545b
new	2905b
new	2920k
new	2975z
new	2980c
new	3264a
new	3265e
new	3450b
new	3636d
new	3770a
new	3784d
new	3830Df
new	3879b
new	4127d
new	4127e
new	4133a
new	4144a

Air Post Stamps

new	C26a
new	C63d
new	C100a

R.F. Overprints

new	CM11
new	CM12
new	UCM8

Postage Due Stamps

new	J66b

Booklets: Panes and Covers

BK295	deleted

Local Stamps

new	163L1a
15LU6Ab	deleted
new	75L6
new	117L2A
new	117L2B
new	117L2C
new	117L2Ca
117L7	deleted

Number in 2008 Catalogue	Number in 2008 Catalogue

Local Stamps

new	117L7
new	117L8
new	117L9

Stamped Envelopes and Wrappers

new	U447A
U447A	U447C
U447B	U447D
new	U458n
new	U506a
new	U520E
new	U590a
new	U659a
new	UC50a

Postal Cards

new	UX38d
new	UX39g
new	UX47a
new	UX48b
new	UX67b
new	UX47a
new	UX82a
new	UX124e
new	UY17b

Air Post Postal Cards

new	UXC14b

Revenue Stamps

new	R32e
new	R288a-R294a
new	RB13ec
new	RC3b
new	RF26A
new	RF27A
new	RF28a
new	RF28B
RG47A	RG57A
RG51A	RG57B
RG53A	RG57C
RG54A	RG57D
RG57A	RG57E
new	RJA94C
new	RN-H6

Junior Duck Stamps

new	JDS3a

Telegraph Stamps

new	2T4a
new	16T16a

Essays

new	17-E3
new	112-E4a
new	113-E3g
new	145-E1
145E1	145-E1C
145-E2	145-E2C
new	J4-E2
new	LO1-E3e

Proofs

new	295Pb
new	319iPb
new	1789P-2788aP
new	RS3P
new	RS12P
RS1TC	RS3P1
RS10TC	RS12P1

Post Office Seals

new	LOX13a
new	LOX45

Number in 2008 Catalogue	Number in 2008 Catalogue

Test Stamps

new	TD14b
new	TD14C
new	TD50A
new	TD101a

Test Booklets

new	TDB40B

Confederate Postmasters' Provisionals

1XU2	1UX1a
3XU3	3XU2a
6XU3	6XU2a
6XU7	6XU5a
7XU1	deleted
14XU2	14XU1a
103XU1	deleted
20XU3	20XU1b
new	21X2
21XU5	deleted
new	28XU2
34XU3	34XU2a
40XU6	40XU1a
43XU3	43XU1a
47XU6	47XU5a
new	121X2
54XU2	54XU1a
57XU3	57XU1b
59XU6	59XU1a
106XU2	106XU1a
70XU3	70XU1a
70XU4	70XU2a
73XU4	73XU3a
101XU5	101XU1a
101XU6	101XU2a
77XU3	77XU1a
79XU2	79XU1a
80XU3	80XU1a
80XU4	80XU2a
94XU3	94XU2a
89XU2	89XU1a

Confederate States General Issues

new	13c
13c	13d
13d	13e

POSTMASTERS' PROVISIONALS

The Act of Congress of March 3, 1845, effective July 1, 1845, established rates of postage as follows:

"For every single letter in manuscript or paper of any kind by or upon which information shall be asked or communicated in writing or by marks designs, conveyed in the mail, for any distance under 300 miles, five cents; and for any distance over 300 miles, ten cents; and for a double letter there shall be charged double these rates; and for a treble letter, treble these rates; and for a quadruple letter, quadruple these rates; and every letter or parcel not exceeding half an ounce in weight shall be deemed a single letter, and every additional weight of half an ounce, shall be charged with an additional single postage. All drop letters, or letters placed in any post office, not for transmission through the mail but for delivery only, shall be charged with postage at the rate of two cents each."

Circulars were charged 2 cents, magazines and pamphlets 2½ cents; newspapers according to size.

Between the time of the Act of 1845, effecting uniform postage rates, and the Act of Congress of March 3, 1847, authorizing the postmaster-general to issue stamps, postmasters in various cities issued provisional stamps.

Before adhesive stamps were introduced, prepaid mail was marked "Paid" either with pen and ink or handstamps of various designs. Unpaid mail occasionally was marked "Due." Most often, however, unpaid mail did not have a "Due" marking, only the amount of postage to be collected from the recipient, e.g. "5," "10," "18¾," etc. Thus, if a letter was not marked "Paid," it was assumed to be unpaid. These "stampless covers" are found in numerous types and usually carry the town postmark.

New York Postmaster Robert H. Morris issued the first postmaster provisional in July 1845. Other postmasters soon followed. The provisionals served until superseded by the federal government's 5c and 10c stamps issued July 1, 1847.

Postmasters recognized the provisionals as indicating postage prepaid. On several provisionals, the signature of initials of the postmaster vouched for their legitimate use.

On July 12, 1845, Postmaster Morris sent examples of his new stamp to the postmasters of Boston, Philadelphia, Albany and Washington, asking that they be treated as unpaid until they reached the New York office. Starting in that year, the New York stamps were distributed to other offices. Postmaster General Cave Johnson reportedly authorized this practice with the understanding that these stamps were to be sold for letters directed to or passing through New York. This was an experiment to test the practicality of the use of adhesive postage stamps.

ALEXANDRIA, VA.

Daniel Bryan, Postmaster

A1

All known examples cut to shape.
Type I — 40 asterisks in circle.
Type II — 39 asterisks in circle.

1846	Typeset		Imperf.
1X1 A1 5c **black,** *buff,* type I			—
a. 5c black, *buff,* type II		100,000.	
On cover (I or II)			200,000.
1X2 A1 5c **black,** *blue,* type I, on cover			—

Cancellations

Red circular town
Black "PAID"
Black ms. accounting number ("No. 45," "No. 70")

The approximately 6 examples of Nos. 1X1 and 1X1a known on cover or cover front are generally not tied by postmark and some are uncanceled. The value for "on cover" is for a stamp obviously belonging on a cover which bears the proper circular dated town, boxed "5" and straight line "PAID" markings.

No. 1X2 is unique. It is canceled with a black straight line "PAID" marking which is repeated on the cover. The cover also bears a black circular "Alexandria Nov. 25" postmark.

ANNAPOLIS, MD.

Martin F. Revell, Postmaster
ENVELOPE

E1

1846	Printed in upper right corner of envelope
2XU1 E1 5c **carmine red,** *white*	300,000.

No. 2XU1 exists in two sizes of envelope.

Envelopes and letter sheets are known showing the circular design and figure "2" handstamped in blue or red. They were used locally. Value, blue $7,500., red $11,000.

Letter sheets are known showing the circular design and figure "5" handstamped in blue or red. Value, blue $3,500, red $5,000.

Similar circular design in blue without numeral or "PAID" is known to have been used as a postmark.

BALTIMORE, MD.

James Madison Buchanan, Postmaster

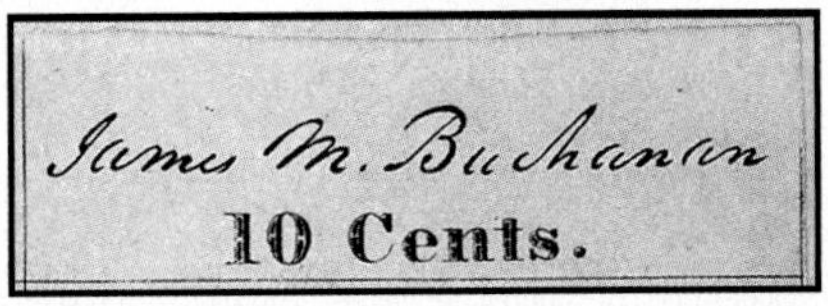

Signature of Postmaster — A1

Printed from a plate of 12 (2x6) containing nine 5c stamps (Pos. 1-6, 8, 10, 12) and three 10c (Pos. 7, 9, 11).

1845	Engr.		Imperf.
3X1 A1 5c **black**			6,000.
On cover			13,500.
Vertical pair on cover			35,000.
3X2 A1 10c **black,** on cover			70,000.
3X3 A1 5c **black,** *bluish*		65,000.	6,000.
On cover			13,500.
3X4 A1 10c **black,** *bluish*			60,000.
On cover			—

Nos. 3X3-3X4 preceded Nos. 3X1-3X2 in use.

No. 3X3 unused is unique. Value is based on 1997 auction sale.

Cancellations

Blue circular town
Blue straight line
"PAID"
Blue "5" in oval
Blue "10" in oval
Black pen

Off cover values are for stamps canceled by either pen or handstamp. Stamps on cover tied by handstamps command premiums.

BALTIMORE, MD. Envelopes

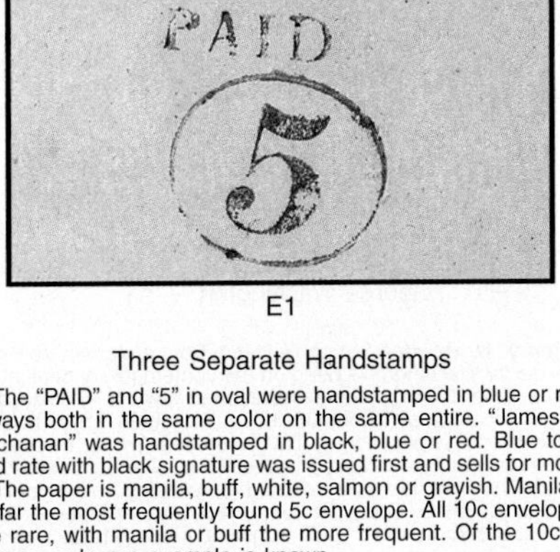

E1

Three Separate Handstamps

The "PAID" and "5" in oval were handstamped in blue or red, always both in the same color on the same entire. "James M. Buchanan" was handstamped in black, blue or red. Blue town and rate with black signature was issued first and sells for more.

The paper is manila, buff, white, salmon or grayish. Manila is by far the most frequently found 5c envelope. All 10c envelopes are rare, with manila or buff the more frequent. Of the 10c on salmon, only one example is known.

The general attractiveness of the envelope and the clarity of the handstamps primarily determine the value.

The color listed is that of the "PAID" and "5" in oval.

1845	Various Papers	Handstamped
3XU1 E1 5c **blue**		6,500.
3XU2 E1 5c **red**		10,000.
3XU3 E1 10c **blue**		16,000.
3XU4 E1 10c **red**		20,000.

Earliest documented uses: Sept. 7, 1845 (No. 3UX1); Apr. 27, 1846 (No. 3XU2); Nov. 16, 1845 (No. 3XU3); June 12, 1846 (No. 3XU4).

Cancellations

Blue circular town
Blue "5" in oval

The second "5" in oval on the unlisted "5 + 5" envelopes is believed not to be part of the basic prepaid marking, but envelopes bearing this marking merit a premium over the values for Nos. 3XU1-3XU2.

BOSCAWEN, NH.

Worcester Webster, Postmaster

A1

1846 (?) **Typeset** ***Imperf.***

4X1 A1 5c **dull blue,** *yellowish,* on cover *300,000.*

One example known, uncanceled on cover with ms. postal markings.

BRATTLEBORO, VT.

Frederick N. Palmer, Postmaster

Initials of Postmaster (FNP) — A1

Printed from plate of 10 (5x2) separately engraved subjects with imprint "Eng'd by Thos. Chubbuck, Bratto." below the middle stamp of the lower row (Pos. 8).

1846 ***Imperf.***

Thick Softwove Paper Colored Through

5X1 A1 5c **black,** *buff*		*11,000.*
On cover		*35,000.*
Two singles on cover		*230,000.*

Earliest documented use: Aug. 28, 1846.

Cancellations

Red straight line "PAID"
Red pen
Blue "5"

The red pen-marks are small and lightly applied. They were used to invalidate a single sample sheet. One example of each plate position is known so canceled.

The No. 5X1 cover with two singles is unique. Value represents 2007 auction sale price.

LOCKPORT, N.Y.

Hezekiah W. Scovell, Postmaster

A1

"Lockport, N.Y." oval and "PAID" separately handstamped in red, "5" in black ms.

1846 ***Imperf.***

6X1 A1 5c **red,** *buff,* on cover *300,000.*

Cancellation

Black ms. "X"

One example of No. 6X1 is known. Small fragments of two other copies adhering to one cover also exist.

MILLBURY, MASS.

Asa H. Waters, Postmaster

George Washington — A1

Printed from a woodcut, singly, on a hand press.

1846 ***Imperf.***

7X1 A1 5c **black,** *bluish*	*130,000.*	*50,000.*
On cover		*125,000.*

Earliest documented use: Aug. 21, 1846.

Cancellations

Red straight line "PAID"
Red circular "MILBURY, MS.," date in center

NEW HAVEN, CONN.

Edward A. Mitchell, Postmaster
ENVELOPES

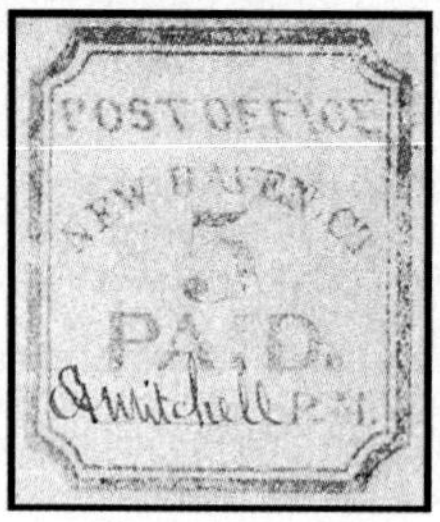

E1

Impressed from a brass handstamp at upper right of envelope.

Signed in blue, black or magenta ms., as indicated in parenthesis.

1845

8XU1 E1 5c **red** (Bl or M)	*100,000.*
Cut square	*40,000.*
Cut to shape	*15,000.*
8XU2 E1 5c **red,** *light bluish* (Bk)	*125,000.*
8XU3 E1 5c **dull blue,** *buff* (Bl)	*125,000.*
Cut to shape (Bk)	*55,000.*
8XU4 E1 5c **dull blue** (Bl)	*125,000.*

Values of Nos. 8XU1-8XU4 are a guide to value. They are based on auction realizations and take condition into consideration. All New Haven envelopes are of almost equal rarity. An entire of No. 8XU2 is the finest example known. The other envelopes and cut squares are valued according to condition as much as rarity.

REPRINTS

Twenty reprints in dull blue on white paper, signed by E. A. Mitchell in lilac rose ink, were made in 1871 for W. P. Brown and others, value $1,250. Thirty reprints in carmine on hard white paper, signed in dark blue or red, were made in 1874 for Cyrus B. Peets, Chief Clerk for Mitchell, value $1,000. Unsigned reprints were made for N. F. Seebeck and others about 1872, value $300.

Edward A. Mitchell, grandson of the Postmaster, in 1923 delivered reprints in lilac on soft white wove paper, dated "1923" in place of the signature, value $300.

In 1932, the New Haven Philatelic Society bought the original handstamp and gave it to the New Haven Colony Historical Society. To make the purchase possible (at the $1000 price) it was decided to print 260 stamps from the original handstamp. Of these, 130 were in red and 130 in dull blue, all on hard, white wove paper, value approximately $200 each.

According to Carroll Alton Means' booklet on the New Haven Provisional Envelope, after this last reprinting the brass handstamp was so treated that further reprints cannot be made. The reprints were sold originally at $5 each. A facsimile signature of the postmaster, "E. A. Mitchell," (blue on the red reprints, black on the blue) was applied with a rubber handstamp. These 260 reprints are all numbered to correspond with the number of the booklet issued then.

NEW YORK, N.Y.

Robert H. Morris, Postmaster

George Washington — A1

Printed by Rawdon, Wright & Hatch from a plate of 40 (5x8). The die for Washington's head on the contemporary bank notes was used for the vignette. It had a small flaw—a line extending from the corner of the mouth down the chin—which is quite visible on the paper money. This was corrected for the stamp.

The stamps were usually initialed "ACM" (Alonzo Castle Monson) in magenta ink as a control before being sold or passed through the mails. There are four or five styles of these initials. The most common is "ACM" without periods. The scarcest is "A.C.M.", believed written by Marcena Monson. The rare initials "RHM" (Robert H. Morris, the postmaster) and "MMJr" (Marcena Monson) are listed separately.

The stamps were printed on a variety of wove papers varying in thickness from pelure to thick, and in color from gray to bluish and blue. A thick brown gum was used first, succeeded by a thin whitish transparent gum. Some stamps appear to have a slight ribbing or mesh effect. A few also show letters of a double-line papermaker's watermark, a scarce variety. All used true blue copies carry "ACM" without periods; of the three unused copies, two lack initials.

Nos. 9X1-9X3 and varieties unused are valued without gum. Examples with original gum are extremely scarce and will command higher prices.

Earliest documented use: July 15, 1845 (No. 9X1e).

1845-46 **Engr.** **Bluish Wove Paper** ***Imperf.***

9X1 A1 5c **black,** signed ACM, connected, *1846*	1,500.	525.
On cover		650.
On cover to France or England		*2,250.*
On cover to other European countries		*5,500.*
Pair	5,750.	1,350.
Pair on cover		2,100.
Pair on cover to England		*4,500.*
Pair on cover to Canada		*5,500.*
Strip of 3		*5,000.*
Strip of 3 on cover		*9,000.*
Strip of 4	*12,500.*	
Strip of 4 on cover		*20,000.*
Block of 4		*50,000.*
Double transfer at bottom (Pos. 2)	1,700.	600.
Double transfer at top (Pos. 7)	1,700.	600.
Bottom frame line double (Pos. 31)	1,700.	600.
Top frame line double (Pos. 36)	1,700.	600.

The only blocks currently known are a used block of 4 off cover (faulty) and a block of 9 on cover.

Cancellations

Blue pen	525.
Black pen	+25.
Magenta pen	+100.
Red square grid (New York)	+50.
Black circular date stamp	—
Red round grid (Boston)	+350.
Blue numeral (Philadelphia)	+750.
Red "U.S" in octagon frame (carrier)	+1,200.
Red "PAID"	+50.
Red N.Y. circular date stamp	+100.
Large red N.Y. circular date stamp containing "5"	+125.
Small red "5"	—

a. Signed ACM, AC connected	1,750.	575.
On cover		725.
On cover to France or England		*2,250.*
On cover to other European countries		*6,000.*
Pair	5,750.	1,600.
Pair, Nos. 9X1, 9X1a	—	4,500.
Pair on cover		*2,100.*
Double transfer at bottom (Pos. 2)	1,800.	700.
Double transfer at top (Pos. 7)	1,800.	700.
Bottom frame line double (Pos. 31)	1,800.	700.
Top frame line double (Pos. 36)	1,800.	700.

Cancellations

Blue pen	575.
Black pen	+25.
Magenta pen	+100.
Red N.Y. circular date stamp	+125.
Large red N.Y. circular date stamp with "5"	+150.
Red square grid	+100.
Red "PAID"	+50.

b. Signed A.C.M.	*3,750.*	*700.*
On cover		*850.*
On cover to France or England		*2,750.*
On cover to other European countries		*6,000.*
Pair		*2,400.*
Pair on cover		*3,250.*
Double transfer at bottom (Pos. 2)	—	*950.*
Double transfer at top (Pos. 7)	—	*950.*
Bottom frame line double (Pos. 31)		*950.*
Top frame line double (Pos. 36)		*950.*

Cancellations

Blue pen	*700.*
Black pen	+25.
Red square grid	+100.
Red N.Y. circular date stamp	+100.
Large red N.Y. circular date stamp containing "5"	+150.
Red "PAID"	+50.

c. Signed MMJr		*10,000.*
On cover		—
Pair on cover front		*26,500.*
d. Signed RHM	*13,000.*	*3,500.*
Pair		*12,000.*
On cover		*5,500.*
On cover from New Hamburgh, N.Y.		*12,500.*

Cancellations

Blue pen	*3,250.*
Black pen	+150.
Red square grid	+250.
Red N.Y. circular date stamp	+400.
Red "PAID"	+300.

Earliest documented use: July 17, 1845.

e.	Without signature	4,000.	900.
	On cover		1,350.
	On cover to France or England		*2,400.*
	On cover to other European countries		*6,000.*
	On cover, July 15, 1845		*30,000.*
	Pair		*2,500.*
	Pair on cover		*2,750.*
	Double transfer at bottom (Pos. 2)	4,250.	1,000.
	Double transfer at top (Pos. 7)	4,250.	1,000.
	Bottom frame line double (Pos. 31)	4,250.	1,000.
	Top frame line double (Pos. 36)	4,250.	1,000.
	Ribbed paper	—	—

Cancellations

Blue pen	900.
Black pen	+25.
Red square grid	+100.
Red N.Y. circular date stamp	+100.
Large red N.Y. circular date stamp containing "5"	+150.
Red "PAID"	+100.

Known used from Albany, Boston, Jersey City, N.J., New Hamburgh, N.Y., Philadelphia, Sing Sing, N.Y., Washington, D.C., and Hamilton, Canada, as well as by route agents on the Baltimore R.R. Covers originating in New Hamburgh are known only with No. 9X1d (one also bearing the U.S. City Despatch Post carrier); one also known used to Holland.

1847 Engr. Blue Wove Paper *Imperf.*

9X2	A1	5c	**black,** signed ACM connected	*6,500.*	3,500.
			On cover		*5,750.*
			Pair		*13,000.*
			Pair on cover		—
			Double transfer at bottom (Pos. 2)		4,000.
			Double transfer at top (Pos. 7)		4,000.
			Bottom frame line double (Pos. 31)		4,000.
			Top frame line double (Pos. 36)		4,000.
a.			Signed RHM		—
b.			Signed ACM, AC connected		*5,000.*
d.			Without signature	*11,000.*	*7,250.*

Earliest documented use: Mar. 4, 1847.

Cancellations

Red square grid	3,500.
Red "PAID"	+100.
Red N.Y. circular date stamp	+650.

On the only example known of No. 9X2a the "R" is illegible and does not match those of the other "RHM" signatures.

1847 Engr. Gray Wove Paper *Imperf.*

9X3	A1	5c	**black,** signed ACM connected	5,250.	2,250.
			On cover		*5,250.*
			On cover to Europe		*8,500.*
			Pair		*7,750.*
			Pair on cover		*8,750.*
			Double transfer at bottom (Pos. 2)		2,600.
			Double transfer at top (Pos. 7)		2,600.
			Bottom frame line double (Pos. 31)		2,600.
			Top frame line double (Pos. 36)		2,600.
a.			Signed RHM		*7,000.*
b.			Without signature		*13,000.*

Earliest documented use: Feb. 8, 1847.

Cancellations

Red square grid	2,250.
Red N.Y. circular date stamp	2,250.
Red "PAID"	+100.

All known used examples of No. 9X3a have red square grid or red "PAID" in arc cancel.

The first plate was of nine subjects (3x3). Each subject differs slightly from the others, with Position 8 showing the white stock shaded by crossed diagonal lines. At some point prints were struck from this plate in black on deep blue and white bond paper, as well as in blue, green, scarlet and brown on white bond paper. These are listed in the Proof and Trial Color Proof sections. Stamps from this plate were not issued, and it is possible that it is an essay, as the design differs slightly from the issued stamps from the sheet of 40. No examples from the plate of nine are known used.

ENVELOPES

Postmaster Morris, according to newspaper reports of July 2 and 7, 1845, issued envelopes. The design was not stated and no example has been seen. It is possible that these items were envelopes to which stamps had been affixed.

PROVIDENCE, R.I.

Welcome B. Sayles, Postmaster

A1 & A2

Engraved on copper plate containing 12 stamps (3x4). Upper right corner stamp (Pos. 3) "TEN"; all others "FIVE." The stamps were engraved directly on the plate, each differing from the other. The "TEN" and Pos. 4, 5, 6, 9, 11 and 12 have no period after "CENTS."

Yellowish White Handmade Paper

Earliest documented use: Aug. 25, 1846 (No. 10X1).

1846, Aug. 24 *Imperf.*

10X1	A1	5c	**gray black**	350.	*1,750.*
			On cover, tied by postmark		*20,000.*
			On cover, pen canceled		*4,500.*
			Two on cover		—
			Pair	725.	
			Block of four	1,450.	
10X2	A2	10c	**gray black**	1,150.	*15,000.*
			On cover, pen canceled		*35,000.*
a.			Se-tenant with 5c	*2,000.*	
			Complete sheet	*5,500.*	

Cancellations

Black pen check mark
Red circular town
Red straight line "PAID" (2 types)
Red "5"

All canceled examples of Nos. 10X1-10X2, whether or not bearing an additional handstamped cancellation, are obliterated with a black pen check mark. There is only one known certified used example off cover of No. 10X2, and it has a minor fault. Value represents a 1997 sale. All genuine covers must bear the red straight line "PAID," the red circular town postmark, and the red numeral "5" or "10" rating mark.

Reprints were made in 1898. In general, each stamp bears one of the following letters on the back: B. O. G. E. R. T. D. U. R. B. I. N. However, some reprint sheets received no such printing on the reverse. All reprints are without gum. Value for 5c, $50; for 10c, $125; for sheet, $725. Reprints without the printing on the reverse sell for more.

ST. LOUIS, MO.

John M. Wimer, Postmaster

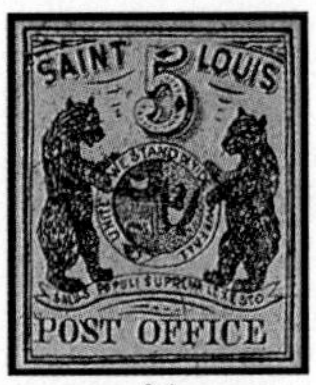

A1

A2

A3

Missouri Coat of Arms

Printed from a copper plate of 6 (2x3) subjects separately engraved by J. M. Kershaw.

The plate in its first state, referred to as Plate 1, comprised: three 5c stamps in the left vertical row and three 10c in the right vertical row. The stamps vary slightly in size, measuring from 17¾ to 18¼ by 22 to 22½mm.

Later a 20c denomination was believed necessary. So two of the 5c stamps, types I (pos. 1) and II (pos. 3) were changed to 20c by placing the plate face down on a hard surface and hammering on the back of the parts to be altered until the face was driven flush at those points. The new numerals were then engraved. Both 20c stamps show broken frame lines and the paw of the right bear on type II is missing. The 20c type II (pos. 3) also shows retouching in the dashes under "SAINT" and "LOUIS." The characteristics of types I and II of the 5c also serve to distinguish the two types of the 20c. This altered, second state of the plate is referred to as Plate 2. It is the only state to contain the 20c.

The demand for the 20c apparently proved inadequate, and the plate was altered again. The "20" was erased and "5" engraved in its place, resulting in noticeable differences from the 5c stamps from Plate 1. In type I (pos. 1) reengraved, the "5" is twice as far from the top frame line as in the original state, and the four dashes under "SAINT" and "LOUIS" have disappeared except for about half of the upper dash under each word. In type II (pos. 3) reengraved, the ornament in the flag of the "5" is a diamond instead of a triangle; the diamond in the bow is much longer than in the first state, and the ball of the "5," originally blank, contains a large dot. At right of the shading of the "5" is a short curved line which is evidently a remnant of the "0" of "20." Type III (pos. 5) of the 5c was slightly retouched. This second alteration of the plate is referred to as Plate 3.

Type characteristics common to Plates 1, 2 and 3:

5 Cent. Type I (pos. 1). Haunches of both bears almost touch frame lines.

Type II (pos. 3). Bear at right almost touches frame line, but left bear is about ¼mm from it.

Type III (pos. 5). Haunches of both bears about ½mm from frame lines. Small spur on "S" of "POST."

10 Cent. Type I (pos. 2). Three dashes below "POST OFFICE."

Type II (pos. 4). Three pairs of dashes.

Type III (pos. 6). Pairs of dashes (with rows of dots between) at left and right. Dash in center with row of dots above it.

20 Cent. Type I. See 5c Type I.

Type II. See 5c Type II.

Nos. 11X1-11X8 unused are valued without gum.

Wove Paper Colored Through

1845, Nov.-1846 *Imperf.*

11X1	A1	5c	**black,** *greenish*	*50,000.*	*8,000.*
			On cover		*17,500.*
			Pair	—	*18,000.*
			Two on cover		*25,000.*
			Strip of 3		*35,000.*
			Strip of 3 plus single on cover		*45,000.*
11X2	A2	10c	**black,** *greenish*	*50,000.*	*8,000.*
			On cover		*14,000.*
			Pair		*18,000.*
			Pair on cover		*22,500.*
			Strip of 3		*32,500.*
			Strip of 3 on cover		*40,000.*
			Five on cover		*225,000.*
			On cover, #11X2, 11X6		*75,000.*
11X3	A3	20c	**black,** *greenish*		*160,000.*
			On cover, #11X5, two #11X3		*325,000.*

Printed from Plate 1 (3 varieties each of the 5c and 10c) and Plate 2 (1 variety of the 5c, 3 of the 10c, 2 of the 20c).

1846

11X4	A1	5c	**black,** (III), *gray lilac*	—	*55,000.*
			On cover		—
11X5	A2	10c	**black,** *gray lilac*	*50,000.*	*8,000.*
			On cover		*12,000.*
			Pair		*19,000.*
			Pair, 10c (III), 5c (III)		*90,000.*
			Strip of 3		*40,000.*
			Strip of 3 on cover		*160,000.*
			Pair 10c (II), 10c (III) se-tenant with 5c (III)		*70,000.*
			Strip of 3 10c (I, II, III) se-tenant with 5c (III)		*300,000.*
11X6	A3	20c	**black,** *gray lilac*	*100,000.*	*50,000.*
			On cover		*60,000.*
			Pair		*110,000.*
			Pair on cover		*125,000.*
			On cover, #11X6 and #11X5		*62,500.*
			Pair, #11X6 and #11X5		*125,000.*
			Pair, #11X6 and #11X5, on cover		*210,000.*
			Strip of 3, 2#11X6 and #11X4		*175,000.*

Printed from Plate 2 (1 variety of the 5c, 3 of the 10c, 2 of the 20c).

No. 11X6 unused is unique. It is in the grade of fine and is valued thus.

The used pair of No. 11X6 is unique. The left margin cuts into the frameline, and it is valued thus.

1846 Pelure Paper

11X7	A1	5c	**black,** *bluish*	—	*11,000.*
			On cover		*16,000.*
			Pair		*40,000.*
			Two on cover		*37,500.*
11X8	A2	10c	**black,** *bluish*		*13,000.*
			On cover		*18,500.*
a.			Impression of 5c on back		—

Printed from Plate 3 (3 varieties each of the 5c, 10c).

Earliest documented use: Nov. 25, 1846 (#11X8).

Cancellations, Nos. 11X1-11X8

Black pen
Ms. initials of postmaster (#11X2, type I)
Red circular town
Red straight line "PAID"
Red grid (#11X7)

Values of Nos. 11X7-11X8, on and off cover, reflect the usual poor condition of these stamps, which were printed on fragile pelure paper. Attractive examples with minor defects sell for considerably more.

Values for used off-cover stamps are for pen-canceled examples. Handstamp-canceled stamps sell for much more. Values for stamps on cover are for examples with pen cancels. Covers with the stamps tied by handstamp sell at considerable premiums depending upon the condition of the stamps and the general attractiveness of the cover. In general, covers with multiple frankings (unless separately valued) are valued at the "on cover" value of the highest item, plus the "off cover" value of the other stamps.

POSTAGE

GENERAL ISSUES

Please Note:
Stamps are valued in the grade of very fine unless otherwise indicated.
Values for early and valuable stamps are for examples with certificates of authenticity from acknowledged expert committees, or examples sold with the buyer having the right of certification. This applies to examples with original gum as well as examples without gum. Beware of stamps offered "as is," as the gum on some unused stamps offered with "original gum" may be fraudulent, and stamps offered as unused without gum may in some cases be altered or faintly canceled used stamps.

Issues from 1847 through 1894 are unwatermarked.

Benjamin Franklin — A1

Double transfer of top frame line — (A) position 80R1

Double transfer of top and bottom frame lines — (B) position 90R1

Double transfer of bottom frame line and lower part of left frame line — (C)

Double transfer of top, bottom and left frame lines, also numerals — (D)

Double transfer of "U," "POST OFFICE" and left numeral — (E)

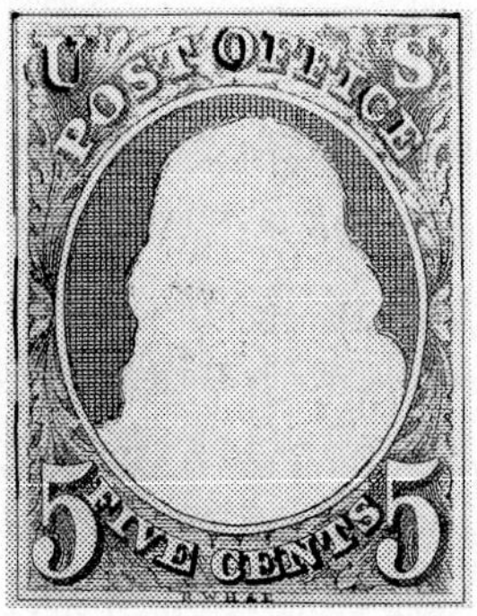
Double transfer of top frame line, upper part of side frame lines, "U," and "POST OFFICE" — (F)

This issue was authorized by an Act of Congress, approved March 3, 1847, to take effect July 1, 1847, from which date the use of Postmasters' Stamps or any which were not authorized by the Postmaster General became illegal.
This issue was declared invalid as of July 1, 1851.

Produced by Rawdon, Wright, Hatch & Edson.
o panes of 100 each.

1847, July 1 Engr. *Imperf.*

Thin Bluish Wove Paper

1	A1	5c **red brown**	6,750.	600.
		pale brown	6,750.	600.
		brown	7,000.	625.
		No gum	2,400.	
		On cover		675.
		On cover to England or France		2,750.
		On cover to other European countries		3,250.
		Pair	16,000.	1,300.
		Pair on cover		1,500.
		Strip of 3	*26,000.*	2,500.
		Strip of 4		5,000.
		Block of 4	*42,500.*	*27,500.*
		Block of 4 on cover		*240,000.*
		Dot in "S" in upper right corner	7,000.	650.
		Cracked plate (69R1)		—
a.		5c **dark brown**	8,750.	800.
		No gum	3,250.	
		Pair	*21,000.*	2,100.
		Block of 4	*55,000.*	
		grayish brown	9,000.	875.
		No gum	3,500.	
		Pair		2,250.
		blackish brown	10,000.	1,100.
		No gum	3,750.	
		Pair	*25,000.*	2,750.
b.		5c **orange brown**	9,000.	900.
		No gum	3,500.	
		Pair		2,250.
		Block of 4 on cover		—
c.		5c **red orange**	*25,000.*	*9,500.*
		No gum	*9,500.*	
		Pair		*35,000.*
d.		5c **brown orange**	—	1,600.
		No gum	*4,500.*	
		Pair on cover		—
e.		Double impression		—
(A)		Double transfer of top frame line (80R1)		725.
(B)		Double transfer of top and bottom frame lines (90R1)	—	725.
(C)		Double transfer of bottom frame line and lower part of left frame line		3,250.
(D)		Double transfer of top, bottom and left frame lines, also numerals		3,250.
(E)		Double transfer of "U," "POST OFFICE" and left numeral		1,500.
(F)		Double transfer of top frame line, upper part of side frame lines, "U," and "POST OFFICE"		—

The only known double impression shows part of the design doubled.
Some students believe that the "E double transfer" actually shows plate scratches instead.

Earliest documented use: July 7, 1847.

Cancellations

Red	600.
Red town	+200.
Orange red	+15.
Orange red town	+220.
Blue	+35.
Blue town	+125.
Black	+100.
Black town	+400.
Magenta	+250.
Orange	+750.
Ultramarine	+1,000.
Violet	+900.
Violet town	—
Green	+1,250.
"Paid"	+50.
"Paid" in grid (demonetized usage)	+300.
"Free"	+400.

Railroad	+200.
U. S. Express Mail (on the cover)	+100.
U. S. Express Mail (on stamp)	—
U. S. Express Mail in black (on stamp) (demonetized usage)	+12,500.
"Way"	+250.
"Way" with numeral	+500.
"Steamboat"	+350.
"Steam"	+200.
"Steamship"	+300.
Philadelphia RR	—
Hotel (on the cover)	*+2,000.*
Numeral	+100.
Canada	+3,000.
Wheeling, Va., grid	+6,000.
Pen	300.

George Washington — A2

Double transfer in "X" at lower right

Double transfer in "Post Office"

Double transfer in "X" at lower right

Double transfer of left and bottom frame line

2	A2	10c	**black**	*35,000.*	1,400.
			gray black	*35,000.*	1,400.
			No gum	*15,000.*	
			greenish black	—	—
			On cover		1,700.
			On cover to Canada		2,100.
			On cover to Great Britain		3,250.
			On cover to France		*5,250.*
			On cover with 5c No. 1		*45,000.*
			Pair	*80,000.*	*3,350.*
			Pair on cover		*3,850.*
			Strip of 3	*125,000.*	*11,000.*
			Block of 4	*200,000.*	*75,000.*
			Short transfer at top	*37,500.*	1,500.
			Vertical line through second "F" of "OFFICE" (68R1)	—	2,000.
			With "Stick Pin" in tie (52L1)	—	3,000.
			With "harelip" (57L1)	—	3,000.
a.			Diagonal half used as 5c on cover		*13,000.*
b.			Vertical half used as 5c on cover		*35,000.*
c.			Horizontal half used as 5c on cover		—
(A)			Double transfer in "X" at lower right (1R1)	*70,000.*	2,400.
(B)			Double transfer in "Post Office" (31R1)	—	3,500.
(C)			Double transfer in "X" at lower right (2R1)	—	3,000.
(D)			Double transfer of left and bottom frame line (41R1)	—	2,400.

Earliest documented use: July 2, 1847.

Two examples of the unused block are recorded, only one of which is available to collectors.

The value for the used block of 4 represents a block with manuscript cancel. One block is recorded with a handstamp cancellation and it is worth significantly more.

Cancellations

Red	1,400.
Orange red	+25.
Blue	+50.
Orange	+500.
Black	+350.
Magenta	+650.
Violet	+850.
Green	+2,000.
Ultramarine	+900.
"Paid"	+100.
"Free"	+800.
Railroad	+1,000.
Philadelphia RR straightline	+500.
U.S. Express Mail (on the cover)	+500.
"Way"	+550.
Numeral	+250.
"Steam"	+350.
"Steamship"	+400.
"Steamboat"	+650.
"Steamer 10"	+1,000.
Canada	+3,000.
Panama	—
Wheeling, Va., grid	+5,500.
Pen	750.

A3

A4

REPRODUCTIONS of 1847 ISSUE

Actually, official imitations made from new plates of 50 subjects made by the Bureau of Engraving and Printing by order of the Post Office Department. These were not valid for postal use.

Reproductions. The letters R. W. H. & E. at the bottom of each stamp are less distinct on the reproductions than on the originals.

5c. On the originals the left side of the white shirt frill touches the oval on a level with the top of the "F" of "Five." On the reproductions it touches the oval about on a level with the top of the figure "5." On the originals, the bottom of the right leg of the "N" in "CENTS" is blunt. On the reproductions, the "N" comes to a point at the bottom.

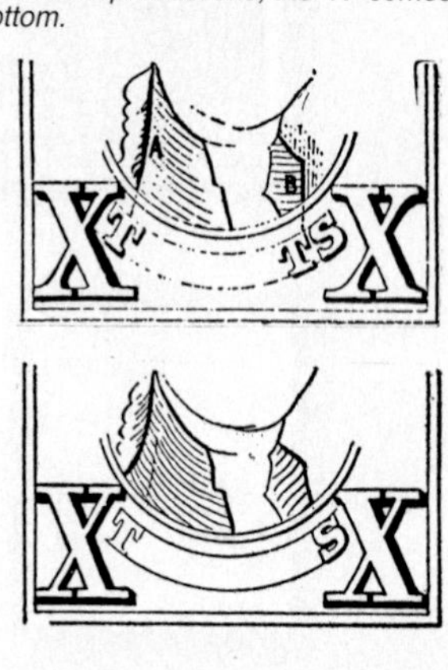

10c. On the originals line of coat (A) points to "T" of TEN and (B) it points between "T" and "S" of "CENTS."

On the reproductions line of coat (A) points to right tip of "X" and line of coat (B) points to center of "S."

The bottom of the right leg of the "N" of "CENTS" shows the same difference as on the 5c originals and reproductions.

On the reproductions the eyes have a sleepy look, the line of the mouth is straighter, and in the curl of the hair near the left cheek is a strong black dot, while the originals have only a faint one.

(See Nos. 948a and 948b for 1947 reproductions — 5c blue and 10c brown orange in larger size.)

1875			**Bluish paper, without gum**	***Imperf.***
3	A3	5c	**red brown** *(4779)*	800.
			brown	800.
			dark brown	800.
			Pair	1,750.
			Block of 4	*5,250.*
4	A4	10c	**black** *(3883)*	975.
			gray black	975.
			Pair	2,100.
			Block of 4	*6,500.*

Numbers in parentheses are quantities sold.

Produced by Toppan, Carpenter, Casilear & Co.

Stamps of the 1851-57 series were printed from plates consisting of 200 subjects and the sheets were divided into two panes of 100 each. Stamps printed from different positions on the plate often have characteristics which make them more valuable than the basic listing. It is, therefore, necessary to be able to clearly identify each position on the plates used to print these stamps. In order that each stamp in the sheet and within each pane could be identified easily in regard to its relative position it was devised that the stamps in each pane be numbered from one to one hundred, starting with the top horizontal row and numbering consecutively from left to right. Thus the first stamp at the upper left corner would be 1 and the last stamp at the bottom right corner, would be 100. The left and right panes are indicated by the letters "L" or "R." The number of the plate is given last. As an example, the best-known of the scarce type III, one cent 1851 being the 99th stamp in the right pane of Plate No. 2 is listed as (99R2), *i.e.* 99th stamp, right pane, Plate No. 2.

One plate of the one cent and several plates of the three cents were reentered after they had been in use. The original state of the plate is called "Early" and the reentered state is termed "Late." If the plate was reentered twice, the inbetween state is called "Intermediate." Identification of "Early," "Intermediate" or "Late" state is explained by the addition of the letters "E," "I" or "L" after the plate numbers. The sixth stamp of the right pane of Plate No. 1 from the "Early" state would be 6R1E. The same plate position from the "Late" state would be 6R1L.

One plate of the three cent stamp never had a plate number and is referred to by specialists as "Plate O."

The position of the stamp in the sheet is placed within parentheses, for example: (99R2).

The different values of this issue were intended primarily for the payment of specific rates, though any value might be used in making up a rate. The one cent stamp was to pay the postage on newspapers, drop letters and circulars, and the one cent carrier fee in some cities from 1856. The three cent stamp represented the rate on ordinary letters and two of them made up the rate for distances over 3000 miles prior to Apr. 1, 1855. The five cent stamp was originally for the registration fee but the fee was usually paid in cash. Occasionally two of them were used to pay the rate over 3000 miles, after it was changed in April, 1855. Singles paid the "Shore to ship" rate to certain foreign countries and, from 1857, triples paid the fifteen-cent rate to France. Ten cents was the rate to California and points distant more than 3000 miles. The twelve cent stamp was for quadruple the ordinary rate. Twenty-four cents represented the single letter rate to Great Britain. Thirty cents was the rate to Germany. The ninety cent stamp was apparently intended to facilitate the payment of large amounts of postage.

Act of Congress, March 3, 1851. "From and after June 30, 1851, there shall be charged the following rates: Every single letter not exceeding 3000 miles, prepaid postage, 3 cents; not prepaid, 5 cents; for any greater distance, double these rates. Every single letter or paper conveyed wholly or in part by sea, and to or from a foreign country over 2500 miles, 20 cents; under 2500 miles, 10 cents. Drop or local letters, 1 cent each. Letters uncalled for and advertised, to be charged 1 cent in addition to the regular postage."

Act of Congress, March 3, 1855. "For every single letter, in manuscript or paper of any kind, in writing, marks or signs, conveyed in the mail between places in the United States not exceeding 3000 miles, 3 cents; and for any greater distance, 10 cents. Drop or local letters, 1 cent."

The Act of March 3, 1855, made the prepayment of postage on domestic letters compulsory April 1, 1855, and prepayment of postage on domestic letters compulsory by stamps effective Jan. 1, 1856.

The Act authorized the Postmaster to establish a system for the registration of valuable letters, and to require prepayment of postage on such letters as well as registration fee of five cents. Stamps to prepay the registry fee were not required until June 1, 1867.

In Nos. 5-17 the 1c, 3c and 12c have very small margins between the stamps. The 5c and 10c have moderate size margins. The values of these stamps take the margin size into consideration.

Franklin — A5

ONE CENT. Issued July 1, 1851.

Type I. Has complete curved lines outside the labels with "U. S. Postage" and "One Cent." The scrolls below the lower label are turned under, forming little balls. The ornaments at top are substantially complete.

Type Ib. As type I, but balls below bottom label are not so clear. Plume-like scrolls at bottom are incomplete.

1851-57 ***Imperf.***

5	A5 1c **blue,** type I (7R1E)	*225,000.*	*85,000.*
	dark blue		—
	On cover		*95,000.*
	Pair, types I, Ib		*115,000.*
	On cover, pair, one stamp type I		—
	Strip of 3, one stamp type I		*210,000.*
	On cover, strip of 3, one stamp type I		*220,000.*

Only one example of No. 5 in the dark blue shade is recorded.

Earliest documented use: July 5, 1851.

Cancellations

Blue	+1,000.
Blue town	—
Red grid	+3,000.
Red town	—
Red "Paid"	—

Values for No. 5 are for examples with margins touching or cutting slightly into the design, or for examples with four margins and minor faults. Very few sound example with the design untouched exist, and these sell for much more than the values shown.

Value for No. 5 unused is for a stamp with no gum. Only one example unused with original gum is recorded. It is in a larger multiple and is creased.

5A	A5 1c **blue,** type Ib, *July 1, 1851* (Less distinct examples 3-5, 9R1E)	*22,500.*	*9,500.*
	No gum	*8,500.*	
	Pair	*47,500.*	*20,000.*
	On cover		*10,000.*
	blue, type Ib (Best examples 6, 8R1E)	*35,000.*	*16,000.*
	No gum	*14,000.*	
	On cover		*19,000.*
	Pair, type Ib, II		*14,000.*
	Block of 4, pair type Ib, pair type IIIa (8-9, 18-19R1E)		—

Earliest documented use: July 1, 1851 (FDC).

Cancellations

Blue town	+300.
Red town	—
Red Carrier	—
Red "Paid"	+550.

Pen (3, 4, 5 or 9R1E)	*4,500.*
Pen (6 or 8R1E)	*7,500.*

A6

Type Ia. Same as type I at bottom, but top ornaments and outer line at top are partly cut away. Type Ia comes only from the bottom row of both panes of Plate 4. All type Ia stamps have the flaw below "U" of "U.S.," but this flaw also appears on some stamps of types Ic, III and IIIa of Plate 4.

Type Ic. Same as type Ia, but bottom right plume and ball ornament incomplete. Bottom left plume complete or nearly complete. Best examples are from bottom row, "F" relief, positions 91 and 96R4. Less distinct examples are "E" reliefs from 5th and 9th rows, positions 47L, 49L, 83L, 49R, 81R, 82R, and 89R, Plate 4, and early impressions of 41R4.

6	A6 1c **blue,** type Ia, *1857*	*45,000.*	*13,000.*
	No gum	*20,000.*	
	On cover		*17,500.*
	Pair	—	*30,000.*
	Strip of 3 on cover		*75,000.*
	Pair, types Ia, Ic		*26,000.*
	Horizontal strip of 3, (95-97R4) types Ia, Ic, Ia		*37,500.*
	Vertical pair, types Ia, III	*75,000.*	*18,000.*
	Vertical pair, types Ia, IIIa	*55,000.*	*17,000.*
	Block of 4, types Ia, IIIa	*110,000.*	
	"Curl on shoulder" (97L4)	*47,500.*	*14,000.*
	"Curl in C" (97R4)	*47,500.*	*14,000.*

The horizontal strip of 3 represents positions 95-97R4, position 96R4 being type 1c.

Earliest documented use: Apr. 19, 1857.

Cancellations

Blue	+100.
Black Carrier	+350.
Red Carrier	+350.
Pen	*6,250.*

6b	A6 1c **blue,** type Ic ("E" relief, less distinct examples)	*7,000.*	*2,750.*
	No gum	*3,000.*	
	On cover		*4,250.*
	Horizontal pair (81-82R4)		—
	Pair, types Ic, III		—
	Pair, types Ic, IIIa		—
	blue, type Ic ("F" relief, best examples, 91, 96R4)	*27,500.*	*10,000.*
	No gum	*12,500.*	
	On cover		*11,000.*
	Vertical pair (81-91R4)		—

Earliest documented use: May 20, 1857 (dated cancel on off-cover stamp); June 6, 1857 (on cover).

Cancellations

Blue ("E" relief)	—
Red ("E" relief)	—
Blue town ("F" relief)	—
Red("F" relief)	—
Pen ("E" relief)	*1,500.*
Pen ("F" relief)	*5,000.*

A7

Type II — Same as Type I at top, but the little balls of the bottom scrolls and the bottoms of the lower plume ornaments are missing. The side ornaments are substantially complete.

7	A7 1c **blue,** type II, (Plates 1E, 2); *July 1, 1851* (Plate 1E)	1,150.	170.
	No gum	450.	
	On cover		200.
	Pair	2,650.	375.
	Strip of 3	4,000.	575.
	Block of 4 (Plate 1E)	—	—
	Block of 4 (Plate 2)	*5,500.*	1,150.
	P# block of 8, Impt. (Plate 2)	*37,500.*	
	Design complete at top (10R1E only)	—	*2,000.*
	Pair, types II, IIIa (Plate 1E)	7,500.	1,350.
	Double transfer (Plate 1E or 2)	1,250.	180.
	Double transfer (89R2)	1,300.	220.
	Double transfer, one inverted (71L1E)	1,600.	390.
	Triple transfer, one inverted (91L1E)	1,600.	410.
	Cracked Plate (2L, 12L, 13L, 23L and 33L, Plate 2)	1,450.	390.
	Plate 1L (4R1L only, double transfer), *June 1852*	2,000.	360.
	Pair, types II (4R1L), IV	*3,900.*	*650.*
	Plate 3, *May, 1856*	*9,000.*	600.
	On cover		850.

Visualize selling.

Lilly 1967

Kapiloff 1992

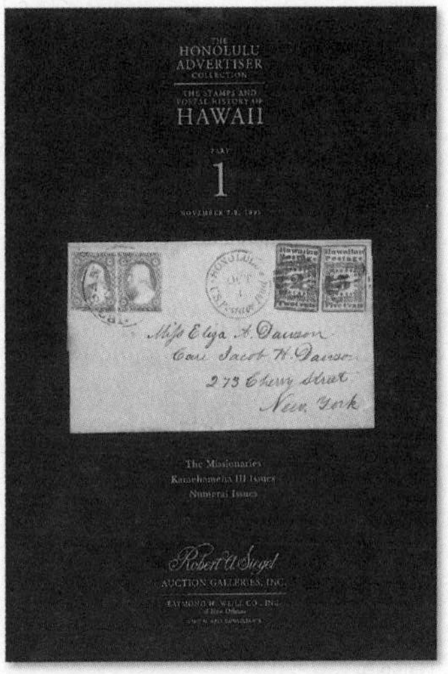

Honolulu Advertiser 1995

Zoellner 1998

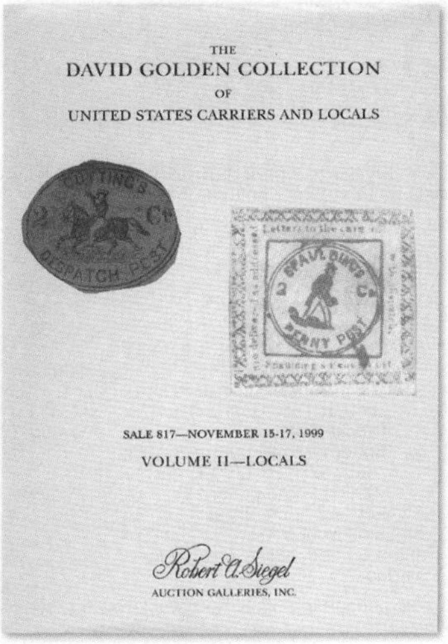

Golden 1999

Hall 2001

LeBow 2004

Scarsdale 2006

The next great Siegel sale could have your name on it.

Robert A. Siegel

AUCTION GALLERIES, INC.

60 EAST 56th STREET, 4th FLOOR
NEW YORK, N.Y. 10022
Ph. (212) 753-6421 Fax (212) 753-6429
E-mail: stamps@siegelauctions.com

www.siegelauctions.com

Pair	—	1,500.
Block of 4	—	—
Double transfer		700.
Major plate crack (22L, 24L, 31L, 33L, 34L, 8R, Plate 3)		950.
Plate 4, *April, 1857*	3,500.	*1,100.*
On cover		*1,350.*
Pair	—	*2,300.*
Pair (vert.), types II, IIIa	—	—
Vertical strip of 3 (9L, 19L, 29F; Plate 4), types II, III, III, on cover		—
Block of 4, type II and types III, IIIa	—	
"Curl in hair" (3R, 4R4)	—	*1,200.*
Double transfer (10R4)	—	—
Perf. 12½, unofficial	22,500.	*8,500.*
On cover		*35,000.*

See note concerning unofficial perfs following listings for No. 11.

Earliest documented uses: July 1, 1851 (Plate 1E) (FDC); Dec. 5, 1855 (Plate 2); May 6, 1856 (Plate 3).

Cancellations

Blue	+7.50
Red	+20.00
Magenta	+80.00
Ultramarine	+150.00
Green	+350.00
Orange	—
1855 year date	+10.00
1856 year date	+5.00
1857 year date	+2.50
1858 year date	—
"Paid"	+5.00
"Way"	+35.00
Red "Too Late"	+200.00
Numeral	+15.00
Railroad	+50.00
"Steam"	+50.00
"Steamboat"	+70.00
Red Carrier	+35.00
Black Carrier	+25.00
U. S. Express Mail	+25.00
Territorial	+200.00
Printed precancel "PAID"	+2,500.
Printed precancel "paid"	+2,500.
Pen	80.00

A8

Type III — The top and bottom curved lines outside the labels are broken in the middle. The side ornaments are substantially complete.

The most desirable examples of type III are those showing the widest breaks in the top and bottom framelines.

A special example is 99R2. All other stamps come from plate 4 and almost all show the breaks in the lines less clearly defined. Some of these breaks, especially of the bottom line, are very small.

Type IIIa — Similar to III with the outer line broken at top or, rarely, at bottom but not both. The side ornaments are substantially complete.

8 A8 1c **blue,** type III (Plate 4) see below for 99R2	*25,000.*	3,500.
No gum	*9,500.*	
On cover		3,750.
Pair	*55,000.*	7,250.
Pair, types III, IIIa	*35,000.*	*5,250.*
Strip of 3		*11,500.*
Block of 4, types III, IIIa	—	—

Earliest documented use: July 7, 1857 (on off-cover stamp); July 9, 1857 (on cover).

Cancellations

Blue	+60.
Red	+150.
Red Carrier	+200.
Black Carrier	+250.
Pen	1,750.

Values for type III are for at least a 2mm break in each outer line. Examples of type III with wider breaks in outer lines command higher prices; those with smaller breaks sell for much less.

(8) A8 1c **blue,** type III (99R2)	*35,000.*	*12,500.*
No gum	*13,000.*	
Pair, types III (99R2), II	—	*13,500.*
Pair, types III (99R2), IIIa	*45,000.*	—
Block of 4, type III (99R2), 3 type II	*47,500.*	
On cover (99R2)		*18,000.*

Cancellations

Blue	+150.00
Green	—
"Paid"	—
Red Carrier	+500.00

8A A8 1c **blue,** type IIIa (Plate 1E) *July 1, 1851*	6,000.	1,200.
No gum	2,250.	
On cover		1,300.
Pair	*12,500.*	2,900.
Double transfer, one inverted (81L1E)	*6,500.*	1,450.
Plate 1E (100R), break in lower line	—	—
Plate 2 (100R), break in lower line	—	—
Plate 4, *April, 1857*	*6,250.*	1,250.
No gum	2,350.	
On cover		1,400.
Pair	*13,500.*	2,600.
Block of 4	—	*9,500.*

Earliest documented uses: July 3, 1851 (Plate 1E); Apr. 4, 1857 (Plate 4).

Cancellations

Blue	+50.00
Red	+100.00
"Paid"	+90.00
Black Carrier	+160.00
Red Carrier	+150.00
Pen	600.00

Values are for stamps with at least a 2mm break in the top outer line. Examples with a wider break or a break in the lower line command higher prices, those with a smaller break sell for less.

"Paid" Cancellations

Values for "Paid" cancellations are for those OTHER than the common Boston type. See Postal Markings in the Introduction for illustrations.

A9

Type IV. Similar to type II, but with the curved lines outside the labels recut at top or bottom or both.

9 A9 1c **blue,** type IV, *1852*	850.00	130.00
No gum	300.00	
On cover		150.00
Pair	1,850.	275.00
Strip of 3	2,800.	450.00
Block of 4	4,000.	*2,000.*
P# block of 8, Impt. (Plate 1)	—	
Double transfer	950.00	140.00
Triple transfer, one inverted (71L1L, 81L1L and 91L1L)	1,000.	180.00
Cracked plate	1,000.	180.00
Bottom frameline broken (30L, 50L, 67R, 89R, 90R, 99R1L), late printings	—	275.00
Perf. 12½, unofficial		*12,500.*
Strip of 3		—
a. Printed on both sides, reverse inverted		—

See note concerning unofficial perfs following listings for No. 11.

VARIETIES OF RECUTTING

Stamps of this type were printed from Plate 1 after it had been reentered and recut in 1852. All but one stamp (4R, see No. 7 for listings) were recut and all varieties of recutting are listed below:

Recut once at top and once at bottom, (113 on plate)	850.00	130.00
Recut once at top, (40 on plate)	875.00	135.00
Recut once at top and twice at bottom, (21 on plate)	900.00	140.00
Recut twice at bottom, (11 on plate)	925.00	150.00
Recut once at bottom, (8 on plate)	950.00	160.00
Recut once at bottom and twice at top, (4 on plate)	1,000.	170.00
Recut twice at bottom and twice at top, (2 on plate)	1,050.	225.00

Earliest documented use: June 5, 1852.

Cancellations

Blue	+5.00
Red	+30.00
Ultramarine	+150.00
Brown	+150.00
Green	+350.00
Violet	+300.00
1853 year date	+250.00
1855 year date	+10.00
1856 year date	+7.50
1857 year date	+10.00
"Paid"	+10.00
"U. S. PAID"	+50.00
"Way"	+50.00
"Free"	+75.00
Railroad	+75.00
"Steam"	+60.00
Numeral	+10.00
"Steamboat"	+90.00
"Steamship"	+60.00
Red Carrier	+15.00
Black Carrier	+25.00
U. S. Express Mail	+60.00
Express Company	—
Packet boat	—
Printed precancel "PAID"	+2,500.
Printed precancel "paid"	+2,500.
Pen	65.00

These 1c stamps were often cut apart carelessly, destroying part or all of the top and bottom lines. When this is so, it makes it difficult to determine whether a stamp is type II, III, IIIa or IV without identifying the position. Such mutilated examples sell for much less.

PLEASE NOTE:

Stamps are valued in the grade of very fine unless otherwise indicated.

Values for early and valuable stamps are for examples with certificates of authenticity from acknowledged expert committees, or examples sold with the buyer having the right of certification. This applies to examples with original gum as well as examples without gum. Beware of stamps offered "as is," as the gum on some unused stamps offered with "original gum" may be fraudulent, and stamps offered as unused without gum may in some cases be altered or faintly canceled used stamps.

VALUES FOR NEVER-HINGED STAMPS PRIOR TO SCOTT No. 182

This catalogue does not value pre-1879 stamps in never-hinged condition. Premiums for never-hinged condition in the classic era invariably are even larger than those premiums listed for the 1879 and later issues. Generally speaking, the earlier the stamp is listed in the catalogue, the larger will be the never-hinged premium. On some early classics, the premium will be several multiples of the unused, hinged values given in the catalogue.

Washington — A10

All of the 3c stamps of the 1851 and 1857 issues were recut at least to the extent of the outer frame lines and often other lines in triangles, diamond blocks, label blocks and/or top/bottom frame lines. Some of the most prominent varieties are listed below each major listing (others are described in "The 3c Stamp of U.S. 1851-57 Issue," by Carroll Chase).

Type I

THREE CENTS. Issued July 1, 1851 (Plate 1E).

Type I — There is an outer frame line on all four sides. The outer frame lines at the sides are always recut, but the inner lines at the sides are not recut.

10 A10 3c **orange brown,** type I (Plates 1E, 1i)	4,000.	160.00
No gum	1,500.	
deep orange brown	4,250.	200.00
No gum	1,600.	
On cover, orange brown		250.00
On cover (3c circular rate - 1000-1500 miles)		1,000.
Pair	9,000.	575.00
Pair on cover (double rate)		675.00
Pair on cover (6c West Coast rate)		750.00
Strip of 3	*14,500.*	1,300.
Block of 4	*22,000.*	—
Pair, types I, II	*12,500.*	*900.00*
Double transfer		190.00

Gash on shoulder		180.00

VARIETIES OF RECUTTING

1 line recut in upper left triangle	4,250.	180.00
2 lines recut at top of upper right diamond block		225.00

Earliest documented uses: July 1, 1851 (Plate 1E) (FDC); July 12, 1851 (Plate 1i).

Cancellations

Blue	+3.00
Red	+5.00
Orange red	+10.00
Brown	+40.00
Ultramarine	+25.00
Green	+225.00
Violet	+250.00
1851 year date	*+1,500.*
1852 year date	+750.00
"Paid"	+5.00
"Way"	+40.00
"Way" with numeral	+150.00
"Free"	+50.00
Numeral	+15.00
Railroad	+50.00
U. S. Express Mail	+20.00
"Steam"	+35.00
"Steamship"	+60.00
"Steamboat"	+70.00
Packet Boat	+300.00
Black Carrier (circular)	+400.00
Blue Carrier (circular)	+600.00
Blue Carrier (New Orleans "snowshovel")	+400.00
Green Carrier (New Orleans "snowshovel")	+500.00
Canadian	—
Territorial	+200.00
Pen	60.00

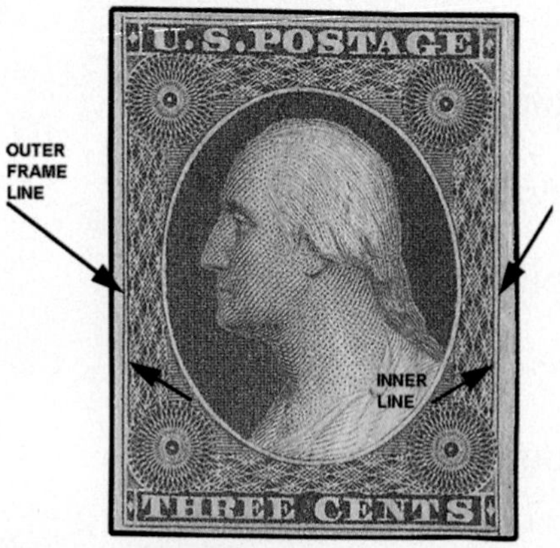

Type II

Type II — As type I, but with the inner lines at the sides also recut.

10A A10 3c	**orange brown,** type II (Plates 1E, 1i, 2E, 5E, 0)	3,750.	150.00
	No gum	1,400.	
	deep orange brown	4,000.	190.00
	No gum	1,500.	
	copper brown	*4,750.*	1,250.
	No gum	*1,800.*	
	On cover, orange brown		210.00
	On cover (3c circular rate - 1000-1500 miles)		1,000.
	Pair	8,500.	550.00
	Pair on cover (double rate)		600.00
	Pair on cover (6c West Coast rate)		700.00
	Strip of 3	*14,000.*	1,250.
	Block of 4	*20,000.*	—
	Double transfer		180.00
	Triple transfer		450.00
	Gash on shoulder		170.00
	Dot in lower right diamond block (69L5E)		325.00
	On part-India paper		*1,250.*
b.	Printed on both sides		*12,000.*

Only one example of No. 10Ab is recorded.

VARIETIES OF RECUTTING

All of these stamps also were recut at least to the extent of the outer frame lines at the sides and the inner lines at the sides (the basic type II criteria).

Left inner line only recut		200.00
Right inner line only recut		160.00
1 line recut in upper left triangle	4,250.	160.00
2 lines recut in upper left triangle		160.00
3 lines recut in upper left triangle		180.00
5 lines recut in upper left triangle (47L0)		1,000.
1 line recut in lower left triangle		160.00
1 line recut in lower right triangle		160.00
2 lines recut in lower right triangle (57L0)		1,000.
2 lines recut in upper left triangle and 1 line recut in lower right triangle		225.00
1 line recut in upper right triangle		170.00
Upper part of top label and diamond block recut	4,000.	150.00
Top label and right diamond block joined		160.00
Top label and left diamond block joined at top (6R2E, 100R2E)		300.00
Lower label and right diamond block joined		210.00
1 line recut at bottom of lower left diamond block (34R2E)		1,000.
Vertical line ties upper left corner of upper left diamond block to top frame line (45R2E)		1,000.

Earliest documented uses: July 1, 1851 (Plate 1E) (FDC); July 12, 1851 (Plate 1i); July 23, 1851 (Plate 2E); July 19, 1851 (Plate 5E); Sept. 6, 1851 (Plate 0).

Cancellations

Blue	+3.00
Red	+5.00
Orange red	+10.00
Orange	—
Brown	+40.00
Ultramarine	+25.00
Green	+225.00
Violet	+250.00
1851 year date	*+1,000.*
1852 year date	+750.00
"Paid"	+5.00
"Way"	+40.00
"Way" with numeral	+150.00
"Free"	+50.00
Numeral	+15.00
Railroad	+50.00
U. S. Express Mail	+20.00
"Steam"	+35.00
"Steamship"	+60.00
"Steamboat"	+70.00
Packet Boat	+300.00
Black Carrier (circular)	+400.00
Blue Carrier (circular)	+600.00
Blue Carrier (New Orleans "snowshovel")	+400.00
Green Carrier (New Orleans "snowshovel")	+500.00
Canadian	—
Territorial	+200.00
Pen	70.00

11 A10 3c	**dull red** (1855), type I (Plates 4, 6, 7, 8)	300.00	15.00
	orange red (1855)	300.00	15.00
	rose red (1855)	300.00	15.00
	No gum	90.00	
	brownish carmine (1856)	325.00	18.00
	No gum	100.00	
	claret (1857)	350.00	21.00
	No gum	125.00	
	deep claret (1857)	375.00	25.00
	No gum	135.00	
	plum (1857)	—	*2,000.*
	No gum	—	
	pinkish		—
	On cover, dull red		17.50
	On cover, orange red		19.00
	On cover, brownish carmine		24.00
	On cover, claret		26.00
	On cover, plum		—
	On propaganda cover, dull red		400.00
	Pair	700.00	62.50
	Pair on cover (double rate)		70.00
	Pair on cover (6c West Coast rate)		—
	Pair, types I, II	—	
	Strip of 3	1,150.	140.00
	Block of 4	2,100.	1,000.
	P# block of 8, Impt.	*4,500.*	
	Double transfer	325.00	18.00
	Gash on shoulder	325.00	17.00
	Worn plate	300.00	13.00
	Perf. 12½, unofficial		*6,000.*
	On cover		*9,000.*

The unofficial perf varieties listed under Nos. 7, 11 and 11A represent the first perforated stamps in the U. S. made using a true perforating machine. Known as the "Chicago perfs," both the perf. 11 and perf. 12½ stamps were made by Dr. Elijah W. Hadley, using a machine of his construction. None of the perf 11 stamps are believed to have been used.

VARIETIES OF RECUTTING

All of these stamps were recut at least to the extent of three outer frame lines (including both sides) and often other lines in triangles, diamond blocks, label blocks and/or top/bottom frame lines. Some of the most prominent varieties are listed below.

Lines on bust and bottom of medallion circle recut (47R6)	*1,200.*	500.00
Top label and right diamond block joined	325.00	16.00
Top label and right diamond block joined at top and bottom (68R4)	350.00	17.50
Lower label and right diamond block joined	350.00	17.50
Extra line at right	350.00	17.50

Earliest documented uses: Mar. 28, 1855 (Plate 4); Feb. 18, 1856 (Plate 6); Feb. 9, 1856 (Plate 7); Apr. 14, 1856 (Plate 8).

Cancellations

Blue	+1.00
Red	+7.50
Orange red	+5.00
Orange	+250.00
Brown	+75.00
Magenta	+50.00
Ultramarine	+40.00
Green	+125.00
Violet	+250.00
Purple	+250.00
Olive	+200.00
1855 year date	+50.00
1856 year date	+12.50
1857 year date	+12.50
1858 year date	+1.00
1859 year date	+25.00
"Paid"	+1.50
"Way"	+10.00
"Free"	+25.00
Numeral	+25.00
Railroad	+20.00
Supplemental Mail Type A	*+2,500.*
"Steam"	+25.00
"Ship"	+25.00
"New York Ship"	+35.00
"Steamboat"	+45.00
"Steamship"	+45.00
Packet boat	+120.00
Express Company	+120.00
Black Carrier	+60.00
Red Carrier (New York)	+100.00
Blue Carrier (New Orleans)	+300.00
Green Carrier (New Orleans)	+500.00
Canada	—
Territorial	+200.00
Pen	8.00

11A A10 3c	**dull red** (1853-54-55), type II (Plates 1L, 2L, 3, 5L)	300.00	15.00
	orange red (1855)	300.00	15.00
	rose red (1854-55)	300.00	15.00
	No gum	90.00	
	brownish carmine (1851-52)	325.00	18.00
	No gum	100.00	
	claret (1852)	350.00	21.00
	No gum	125.00	
	experimental orange brown (1851-52, Plate 1L))	—	400.00
	On cover, dull red		17.50
	On cover, orange red		19.00
	On cover, brownish carmine		24.00
	On cover, claret		26.00
	On cover, experimental orange brown (Plate 1L)		900.00
	On propaganda cover, dull red		400.00
	On cover (3c circular rate - 1000-1500 miles)		850.00
	Pair	700.00	62.50
	Pair on cover (double rate)		70.00
	Pair on cover (6c West Coast rate)		100.00
	Strip of 3	1,150.	140.00
	Block of 4	2,100.	1,000.
	P# block of 8, Impt.	*4,500.*	
	Double transfer in "Three Cents"	325.00	18.00
	Double transfer line through "Three Cents" and rosettes double (92L1L)	450.00	70.00
	Double transfer, "Gents" instead of "Cents" (66R2L)	450.00	55.00
	Triple transfer (92L2L)	450.00	55.00
	Gash on shoulder (2L5L)	325.00	17.00
	Dot in lower right diamond block (69L5L)	400.00	45.00
	Major cracked plate (84L, 94L, 9R, Plate 5L)	*825.00*	160.00
	Intermediate cracked plate (80L, 96L, 71R, Plate 5L)	*550.00*	80.00
	Minor cracked plate (8L, 27L, 31L, 44L, 45L, 51L, 55L, 65L, 71L, 72L, 74L, 78L, 79L, 7R, Plate 5L)	*425.00*	60.00
	Worn plate	300.00	13.00
	Perf. about 11, unofficial	*6,500.*	
	Block of 4	*27,500.*	
	Perf. 12½, unofficial		*6,000.*
	On cover		*9,000.*
	Pair on cover		—
c.	Vertical half used as 1c on cover		*5,000.*
	Strip of 4 No. 11Ac used as 6c on cover		*15,000.*
d.	Diagonal half used as 1c on cover		*5,000.*
e.	Double impression		*5,000.*

The unofficial perf varieties listed represent the first perforated stamps in the U. S. made using a true perforating machine. Known as the "Chicago perfs," both were made by Dr. Elijah W. Hadley, using a machine of his construction. None of the perf 11 stamps are believed to have been used.

The strip of 4 No. 11Ac on cover is the only recorded multiple of a bisected stamp in United States philately.

VARIETIES OF RECUTTING

All of these stamps also were recut at least to the extent of the outer lines at the sides and the inner frame lines at the sides (the basic type II criteria).

Right inner line only recut	325.00	17.50
1 line recut in upper left triangle	325.00	16.00
2 lines recut in upper left triangle	325.00	16.00
3 lines recut in upper left triangle	350.00	16.00
5 lines recut in upper left triangle (95L1L)	675.00	200.00
1 line recut in lower left triangle	350.00	16.00
1 line recut in lower right triangle	325.00	16.00

1 line recut in upper right triangle	450.00	18.00
1 line recut in UL, LL and LR triangles (49L1L, 95R3)	500.00	32.50
2 lines recut in UL triangle, 1 line recut in LL triangle (9L1L)	500.00	32.50
Recut button on shoulder (10R2L)	500.00	100.00
Upper part of top label and diamond block recut	300.00	16.00
Top label and right diamond block joined	325.00	16.00
Top label and left diamond block joined	350.00	17.50
Lower label and right diamond block joined	350.00	17.50
1 extra vertical line outside of left frame line (29L, 39L, 49L, 59L, 69L, 79L, Plate 3)	325.00	17.50
2 extra vertical lines outside of left frame line (89L, 99L, Plate 3)	400.00	32.50
1 extra vertical line outside of right frame line (58L, 68L, 78L, 88L, 98L, Plate 3)	450.00	20.00
No inner line and frame line close to design at right (9L, 19L, Plate 3)	400.00	32.50
No inner line and frame line close to design at left (70, 80, 90, 100L, Plate 3)	350.00	19.00

Earliest documented uses: Oct. 6, 1851 (Plate 1L); Jan. 7, 1852 (Plate 2L); Jan. 15, 1852 (Plate 3); July 13, 1855 (Plate 5L).

Cancellations

Blue	+1.00
Red	+7.50
Orange red	+5.00
Orange	+250.00
Brown	+75.00
Magenta	+50.00
Ultramarine	+40.00
Green	+175.00
Violet	+250.00
Purple	+250.00
Olive	+200.00
Yellow	*+5,000.*
Yellow, on cover	*10,000.*
1852 year date	*+300.00*
1852 year date, on cover	1,000.
1853 year date	+100.00
1854 year date	—
1855 year date	+50.00
1856 year date	+12.50
"Paid"	+1.50
"Way"	+10.00
"Way" with numeral	+60.00
"Free"	+25.00
Numeral	+7.50
Railroad	+20.00
U. S. Express Mail	+5.00
Supplemental Mail Type A	*+2,500.*
"Steam"	+15.00
"Ship"	+20.00
"New York Ship"	+35.00
"Steamboat"	+45.00
"Steamship"	+45.00
Packet boat	+120.00
Express Company	+120.00
Black Carrier	+60.00
Red Carrier (New York)	+50.00
Blue Carrier (New Orleans)	+200.00
Green Carrier (New Orleans)	+350.00
Canada	—
Territorial	+100.00
Pen	8.00

Thomas Jefferson — A11

FIVE CENTS.
Type I — Projections on all four sides.

12 A11 5c **red brown,** type I, *1856*	*30,000.*	900.
dark red brown	*30,000.*	900.
No gum	*11,500.*	
On domestic cover		1,400.
Single on cover to France		1,750.
Strip of 3 on cover to France		5,750.
Pair	*67,500.*	2,100.
Strip of 3	*100,000.*	4,750.
Block of 4	*200,000.*	*45,000.*
Double transfer (40R1)		*1,200.*
Defective transfer (23R1)		*1,400.*

Earliest documented use: Mar. 24, 1856.

Cancellations

Red	+150.
Magenta	+200.
Blue	+125.
Green	+900.
1856 year date	+25.
1857 year date	+25.
1858 year date	—
"Paid"	+200.
"Steamship"	+200.
U.S. Express Mail	+200.
Express Company	+400.
"Steamboat"	+350.
Railroad	+400.
Numeral	+1,000.
Pen	450.

Washington — A12

TEN CENTS
Type I — The "shells" at the lower corners are practically complete. The outer line below the label is very nearly complete. The outer lines are broken above the middle of the top label and the "X" in each upper corner. Beware of type V perforated (No. 35) trimmed to resemble type I imperforate (No. 13). Note that the pearls on No. 35 normally will be missing from each end of the lower label.

Types I, II, III and IV have complete ornaments at the sides of the stamps, and three pearls at each outer edge of the bottom panel.

Type I comes only from the bottom row of both panes of Plate 1.

13 A12 10c **green,** type I, *1855*	*18,000.*	950.
dark green	*18,000.*	950.
yellowish green	*18,000.*	950.
No gum	*7,000.*	
On domestic cover		1,050.
Pair	*40,000.*	2,200.
Strip of 3		3,250.
Vert. pair, types III, I	*25,000.*	1,550.
Vert. pair, types IV, I (86, 96L1)		*5,250.*
Vertical strip of 3, types II, III, I		4,250.
Block of 4, types III, I	*55,000.*	*10,500.*
Block of 4, types III, IV, I		*16,000.*
Double transfer (100R1)	*19,000.*	1,050.
"Curl" in left "X" (99R1)	*19,000.*	1,050.

Earliest documented use: July 11, 1855.

Cancellations

Blue	+40.
Red	+75.
Magenta	+200.
Orange	—
1855 year date	+25.
1856 year date	+25.
1857 year date	+25.
"Paid"	+50.
"Steamship"	+150.
Railroad	+175.
Territorial	+400.
Numeral	+50.
U.S. Express Mail	—
Pen	500.

A13

Type II — The design is complete at the top. The outer line at the bottom is broken in the middle. The shells are partly cut away.

14 A13 10c **green,** type II, *1855*	5,000.	200.
dark green	5,000.	200.
yellowish green	5,000.	200.
No gum	1,800.	
On domestic cover		260.
Pair	11,000.	450.
Strip of 3	17,000.	775.
Block of 4	*25,000.*	*4,000.*
Pair, types II, III	11,000.	450.
Pair, types II, IV	*42,500.*	*2,200.*
Vertical strip of 3, types II, III, IV		*2,600.*
Block of 4, types II, III	—	*3,500.*
Block of 4, types II, IV		—
Block of 4, types II, III, IV		*10,000.*
Double transfer (31L, 51L, and 20R, Plate 1)	5,500.	280.
"Curl" opposite "X" (10R1)	5,500.	300.

Earliest documented use: May 12, 1855.

Cancellations

Blue	+10.
Red	+25.
Brown	+75.
Ultramarine	+100.
Magenta	+100.
Green	+200.
Violet	+150.
1855 year date	+100.
1856 year date	+50.
1857 year date	+10.
1858 year date	+10.
"Paid"	+25.
"Way"	+75.
"Free"	+75.
Railroad	+75.
Steamship	+75.
Steamboat	+100.
Numeral	+50.
Territorial	+150.
Express Company	+200.
U. S. Express Mail	+75.
Pen	90.

A14

Type III — The outer lines are broken above the top label and the "X" numerals. The outer line at the bottom and the shells are partly cut away similar to type II.

15 A14 10c **green,** type III, *1855*	5,000.	200.
dark green	5,000.	200.
yellowish green	5,000.	200.
No gum	1,800.	
On domestic cover		260.
Pair	11,000.	450.
Strip of 3	17,000.	775.
Pair, types III, IV	*40,000.*	*2,200.*
Double transfer at top and at bottom		—
"Curl" on forehead (85L1)	550.	300.
"Curl" to right of left "X" (87R1)	550.	300.

Earliest documented use: May 19, 1855.

Cancellations

Blue	+10.
Red	+25.
Orange red	+35.
Magenta	+100.
Violet	+150.
Brown	+75.
Orange	+100.
Green	+200.
1855 year date	—
1856 year date	+50.
1857 year date	+10.
1858 year date	+10.
"Paid"	+25.
Steamship	+75.
U. S. Express Mail	+75.
Express Company	+200.
Packet boat	—
Canada (on cover)	+1000.
Territorial	+150.
Railroad	+75.
Numeral	+50.
Pen	90.

A15

Type IV — The outer lines have been recut at top or bottom or both.

16 A15 10c **green,** type IV, *1855*	*35,000.*	1,700.
dark green	*35,000.*	1,700.
yellowish green	*35,000.*	1,700.

No gum	*15,000.*	
On domestic cover		2,000.
Pair	—	4,500.
Block of 4 (54-55, 64-65L)		—

VARIETIES OF RECUTTING

Eight stamps on Plate 1 were recut. All are listed below.

Outer line recut at top (65L, 74L, 86L, and 3R, Plate 1)	*35,000.*	1,700.
Outer line recut at bottom (54L, 55L, 76L, Plate 1)	*36,500.*	1,800.
Outer line recut at top and bottom (64L1)	*40,000.*	2,100.

Positions 65L1 and 86L1 have both "X" ovals recut at top, as well as the outer line.

Earliest documented use: June 4, 1855.

Cancellations

Blue	+75.
Red	+150.
Brown	+250.
1857 year date	—
1859 year date	—
"Paid"	+150.
Steamship	+300.
Territorial	+500.
Express Company	+750.
Numeral	+150.
Pen	900.

Types I, II, III and IV occur on the same sheet, so it is possible to obtain pairs and blocks showing combinations of types. For listings of type combinations in pairs and blocks, see Nos. 13-15.

Washington — A16

17	A16 12c	**black,** *July 1, 1851*	6,500.	350.
		gray black	6,500.	350.
		intense black	6,500.	350.
		No gum	2,250.	
		Single, on cover		1,500.
		Single on cover with No. 11 to France		1,150.
		Pair	*15,000.*	750.
		Pair, on cover to England		850.
		Block of 4	*35,000.*	*5,500.*
		Double transfer	6,750.	375.
		Triple transfer (5R1 & 49R1)	7,000.	500.
		Not recut in lower right corner	6,750.	375.
		Recut in lower left corner (43L, 53L, 63L, 73L and 100L, Plate 1)	6,750.	425.
		Cracked plate (32R1)		—
		On part-India paper	—	1,100.
		No gum	*5,000.*	
a.		Diagonal half used as 6c on cover		*2,750.*
		Diagonal half used as 6c on "Via Nicaragua" cover		*5,750.*
b.		Vertical half used as 6c on cover		*8,500.*
c.		Printed on both sides		*25,000.*

Earliest documented use: Aug. 4, 1851.

Cancellations

Red	+20.
Orange red	+45.
Blue	+10.
Brown	+60.
Magenta	+75.
Orange	+150.
Green	+600.
"Paid"	+25.
"Way"	+75.
Steamship	+100.
Steamboat	+125.
Supplementary Mail Type A	+125.
Railroad	+100.
"Honolulu" in red (on cover)	+400.
U. S. Express Mail	+125.
Pen	175.

Please Note:

Stamps are valued in the grade of very fine unless otherwise indicated.

Values for early and valuable stamps are for examples with certificates of authenticity from acknowledged expert committees, or examples sold with the buyer having the right of certification. This applies to examples with original gum as well as examples without gum. Beware of stamps offered "as is," as the gum on some unused stamps offered with "original gum" may be fraudulent, and stamps offered as unused without gum may in some cases be altered or faintly canceled used stamps.

SAME DESIGNS AS 1851-57 ISSUES

Printed by Toppan, Carpenter & Co.

Nos. 18-39 have small or very small margins. The values take into account the margin size.

1857-61 *Perf. 15½*

18	A5 1c	**blue,** type I (Plate 12), *1861*	2,400.	700.
		No gum	900.	
		On cover		850.
		On patriotic cover		1,400.
		Pair	5,250.	1,500.
		Strip of 3	8,250.	2,600.
		Block of 4	*14,000.*	
		Pair, types I, II	4,000.	1,100.
		Pair, types I, IIIa	5,500.	1,350.
		Block of 4, types I, II	*9,500.*	5,250.
		Block of 4, types I, II, IIIa	*11,000.*	6,500.
		Double transfer	2,900.	750.
		Cracked plate (91R12)		950.

Plate 12 consists of types I & II. A few positions are type IIIa. Late printings of position 46L12 are type III.

Earliest documented use: Jan. 25, 1861.

Cancellations

Blue	+10.
Red	+35.
Violet	+100.
Steamboat	+100.
"Paid"	+25.
"Free"	+750.
Black Carrier	+85.
Red Carrier	+85.
Pen	350.

19	A6 1c	**blue,** type Ia (Plate 4)	*40,000.*	*11,000.*
		No gum	*18,000.*	
		On cover		*13,500.*
		Pair	*90,000.*	*25,000.*
		Strip of 3	*135,000.*	*40,000.*
		Vertical pair, types Ia, III	*62,500.*	*15,000.*
		Vertical pair, types Ia, IIIa	*47,500.*	*12,500.*
		Pair, types Ia, Ic	—	—
		Strip of 3, types Ia, Ia, Ic		—
		Block of 4, types Ia, Ic, and IIIa	*100,000.*	
		Block of 4, pair type Ia and types III or IIIa	—	—
		"Curl on shoulder" (97L4)	*42,500.*	*11,500.*

Examples of this stamp exist with perforations not touching the design at any point. Such examples command very high prices.

Type Ia comes only from the bottom row of both panes of Plate 4.

Earliest documented use: Sept. 9, 1857. No. 19 is known on a folded circular with Aug. 1 postmark, but the year of use has not been certified.

Cancellations

Red Carrier	+200.
Green	+1,750.
Pen	4,750.

19b	A6 1c	**blue,** type Ic ("E" relief, less distinct examples)	*4,500.*	*2,250.*
		No gum	*1,900.*	
		On cover		*3,000.*
		Horizontal pair (81-82R4)	—	—
		Pair, types Ic, III		—
		Pair, types Ic, IIIa		—
		blue, type Ic ("F" relief, best examples, 91, 96R4)	*20,000.*	*7,000.*
		No gum	*9,000.*	
		On cover		*8,000.*

Type Ic — Same as Ia, but bottom right plume and ball ornament incomplete. Bottom left plume complete or nearly complete. Best examples are from bottom row, "F" relief, positions 91 and 96R4. Less distinct examples are "E" reliefs from 5th and 9th rows, positions 47L, 49L, 83L, 49R, 81R, 82R, and 89R, Plate 4, and early impressions of 41R4. Several combination type multiples can be found in the unused complete left pane of 100 from Plate 4.

Examples of the "F" relief type Ic stamps exist with perforations not touching the design at any point. Such examples command a substantial premium.

Cancellations

Pen ("E" relief)	*1,000.*
Blue ("F" relief)	—
Red ("F" relief)	—
Pen ("F" relief)	*3,000.*

20	A7 1c	**blue,** type II (Plate 2)	1,200.	300.
		No gum	450.	
		On cover		350.
		Pair	2,500.	675.
		Strip of 3	3,900.	1,050.
		Block of 4	*6,000.*	2,500.
		Double transfer (Plate 2)	1,250.	325.
		Double transfer (89R2)	*2,500.*	*1,000.*
		Cracked plate (2L, 12L, 13L, 23L & 33L, Plate 2)	3,000.	800.
		Plate 1L (4R1L only, double transfer), *July 1857*		1,000.
		Pair, types II (4R1L), IV		*2,500.*
		Plate 4	3,500.	*1,250.*
		On cover		*1,500.*
		Pair	7,500.	*2,750.*
		Strip of 3	—	—
		Double transfer (10R4)	3,750.	*1,800.*
		"Curl in hair" (3R, 4R4)	—	*1,350.*
		Plate 11	1,750.	750.
		On cover		1,000.
		On patriotic cover		—
		Pair	3,000.	1,650.
		Strip of 3		—
		Double transfer	—	—
		Plate 12	1,200.	300.
		On cover		350.
		On patriotic cover		700.
		Pair	2,500.	650.
		Strip of 3	4,000.	1,050.
		Block of 4	*6,000.*	*2,500.*
		Double transfer	—	—

Earliest documented uses: July 26, 1857 (Plate 2), July 26, 1857 (Plate 4), Jan. 12, 1861 (Plate 11), Jan. 21, 1861 (Plate 12).

No. 20, plate 2, is also known on two folded circulars dated July 24 and July 25, respectively, but no postal year date or docketing verifies the actual day of mailing.

Cancellations

Blue	+5.
Red	+20.
Green	+200.
1857 year date	+10.
1858 year date	+5.
1861 year date	+5.
"FREE"	—
1863 year date	+200.
"Paid"	+15.
Railroad	+60.
"Way"	+75.
Steamboat	+75.
Red Carrier	+35.
Black Carrier	+50.
Pen	150.

21	A8 1c	**blue,** type III (Plate 4), see below for 99R2	*17,500.*	2,750.
		No gum	*7,000.*	
		On cover		3,250.
		Pair	*40,000.*	6,250.
		Strip of 3		9,500.
		Block of 4	—	
		Pair, types III, IIIa	*22,500.*	3,500.
		Vertical pair, types III, II	—	—
		Block of 4, types III, IIIa	—	
		Plate 12 (46L12)	—	—
a.		Horiz. pair, imperf between		*23,000.*

Earliest documented use: Sept. 18, 1857.

Cancellations

Blue	+35.
Red	+60.
Green	+750.
1858 year date	+35.
"Paid"	+60.
Black Carrier	+175.
Red Carrier	+150.
Pen	1,350.

Values for type III are for at least a 2mm break in each outer line. Examples of type III with wider breaks in outer lines command higher prices; those with smaller breaks sell for less.

No. 21a is unique and is contained in a strip of three. Value reflects auction sale in 1999.

(21)	A8 1c **blue,** type III (99R2)	—	*20,000.*
	On cover		—
	Pair, types III (99R2), II		—
	Pair, types III (99R2), IIIa		—
	Strip of 3, types III (99R2), II, IIIa		—
	Block of 9, one type III (99R2), others type II	*110,000.*	

The only recorded unused example is the one in the block of 9. Only two covers are recorded bearing No. 21 (99R2).

Earliest documented use: Oct. 27, 1857.

22	A8 1c **blue,** type IIIa (Plate 4)	2,600.	550.
	No gum	1,000.	
	On cover		600.
	On patriotic cover		900.
	Pair	5,750.	1,200.
	Vertical pair, types IIIa, II	—	*1,900.*
	Strip of 3	8,500.	1,900.
	Block of 4	*13,000.*	*5,500.*
	Block of 4, types IIIa, II	—	—
	Double transfer	2,750.	600.
	Plate 2 (100R)	—	—
	Plate 11 and Plate 12	2,750.	575.
	On cover		625.
	On patriotic cover		1,050.
	Pair	*6,000.*	1,250.
	Vert. pair, types IIIa, II (Plate 11)	*5,250.*	1,250.
	Strip of 3	*9,000.*	1,800.
	Strip of 3, types IIIa, II, I (46-48L12)		—
	Block of 4	*13,000.*	
	Block of 4, types IIIa, II (Plate 11)	*12,500.*	*4,250.*
	Double transfer	2,900.	600.
	Triple transfer (Plate 11)	—	—
	Bottom line broken (46L12)	—	*2,000.*
b.	Horizontal pair, imperf. between		*5,000.*

One pair of No. 22b is reported. Beware of numerous pairs that have blind perforations. These are not to be confused with No. 22b.

Earliest documented uses: July 26, 1857 (Plate 4), Dec. 1860 (day unknown) (dated cancel on off-cover stamp) (Plate 11), Dec. 31, 1860, (on cover) (Plate 11), Jan. 25, 1861 (Plate 12).

Cancellations

Blue	+5.
Red	+30.
Green	+250.
1857 year date	—
1858 year date	—
1861 year date	—
1863 year date	—
"Paid"	+25.
"Steamboat"	—
Red Carrier	+35.
Black Carrier	+50.
Blue Carrier	+100.
Pen	325.

23	A9 1c **blue,** type IV	10,000.	850.
	No gum	4,000.	
	On cover		1,050.
	Pair	*22,500.*	1,900.
	Strip of 3	*35,000.*	2,900.
	Block of 4		*25,000.*
	Double transfer	*11,000.*	900.
	Triple transfer, one inverted (71L1L, 81L1L and 91L1L)	*17,500.*	4,000.
	Cracked plate	*10,500.*	*975.*
	Bottom line broken (89R1L)	—	*2,000.*

Three or four used blocks of No. 23 are presently known. Value of used block of four is based on 1998 auction sale of the well-centered block of 5 sold at auction in 1998. Other blocks are poorly centered and will sell for much less.

VARIETIES OF RECUTTING

Recut once at top and once at bottom, (113 on plate)	10,000.	850.
Recut once at top, (40 on plate)	10,250.	875.
Recut once at top and twice at bottom, (21 on plate)	10,500.	875.
Recut twice at bottom, (11 on plate)	10,250.	900.
Recut once at bottom, (8 on plate)	10,500.	925.
Recut twice at top and once at bottom, (4 on plate)	11,000.	950.
Recut twice at top and twice at bottom, (2 on plate)	11,500.	950.

One example of the "recut twice at top and once at bottom" variety is pos. 71L1L, valued separately under the main listing.

Earliest documented use: July 25, 1857.

Cancellations

Blue	+15.
Red	+60.
1857 year date	+50.
"Paid"	+25.
Red Carrier	+80.
Black Carrier	+80.
Railroad	+100.
"Way"	+120.
"Steamboat"	+135.
"Steam"	+100.
Pen	425.

Franklin — A20

Type V — Similar to type III of 1851-57 but with side ornaments partly cut away. About one-half of all positions have side scratches. Wide breaks in top and bottom framelines.

Type Va — Stamps from Plate 5 with almost complete ornaments at right side and no side scratches. Many, but not all, stamps from Plate 5 are Type Va, the remainder being Type V.

24	A20 1c **blue,** type V (Plates 5, 7, 8, 9, 10) *1857*	170.00	45.00
	No gum	65.00	
	On cover		52.50
	On patriotic cover		300.00
	Pair	375.00	97.50
	Strip of 3	575.00	160.00
	Block of 4	800.00	425.00
	P# strip of 4, Impt.	1,400.	
	P# block of 8, Impt.	3,500.	—
	Double transfer at top (8R and 10R, Plate 8)	230.00	90.00
	Double transfer at bottom (52R9)	290.00	100.00
	Curl on shoulder, (57R, 58R, 59R, 98R, 99R, Plate 7)	230.00	72.50
	With "Earring" below ear (10L9)	600.00	100.00
	"Curl" over "C" of "Cent"	240.00	72.50
	"Curl" over "E" of "Cent" (41R and 81R8)	260.00	87.50
	"Curl in hair," 23L7; 39, 69L8; 34, 74R9	230.00	62.50
	"Curl" in "O" of "ONE" (62L5)	—	—
	Horizontal dash in hair (24L7)	350.00	90.00
	Horizontal dash in hair (36L8)	350.00	90.00
	Long double "curl" in hair (52, 92R8)	290.00	85.00
	Type Va	500.00	250.00
	On cover (Type Va)		350.00
	Pair (Type Va)	—	—
	Strip of 3 (Type Va)	—	—
	Block of 4 (Type Va)	—	—
	"Curl" on shoulder (48L5)	—	—
b.	Laid paper		*1,750.*

Earliest documented uses: Dec. 2, 1857 (Plate 5); Dec. 31, 1857 (Plate 7); Nov. 17, 1857 (Plate 8); Aug. 2, 1859 (Plate 9); June 14, 1860 (Plate 10).

Cancellations

Blue	+2.50
Red	+15.00
Green	+250.00
Brown	+150.00
Magenta	+150.00
Ultramarine	+100.00
1857 year date	+70.00
1858 year date	+2.50
1859 year date	+2.50
1860 year date	+2.50
1861 year date	+2.50
1862 year date	—
1863 year date	+250.00
Printed Precancel "CUMBERLAND, ME." (on cover)	—
"Paid"	+5.00
"Free"	+25.00
Railroad	+50.00
Numeral	+12.50
Express Company	+90.00
Steamboat	+55.00
"Steam"	+30.00
Steamship	+40.00
Packet boat	—
Supp. Mail Type A, B, or C	+55.00
"Way"	+30.00
Red Carrier	+20.00
Black Carrier	+12.50
Blue Carrier	+50.00
"Old Stamps-Not Recognized"	+1,500.
Territorial	+80.00
Pen	20.00

25	A10 3c **rose,** type I (Plates 4, 6, 7, 8)	3,000.	125.00
	rose red	3,000.	125.00
	dull red	3,000.	125.00
	No gum	1,150.	
	On cover		140.00
	claret	3,250.	140.00
	No gum	1,200.	
	On patriotic cover		500.00
	Pair	*6,500.*	300.00
	Strip of 3	*10,000.*	475.00
	Block of 4	*16,000.*	7,000.
	Double transfer	3,300.	160.00
	Worn plate	3,000.	125.00
	Major cracked plate (47R, 48R, Plate 7)	*5,000.*	750.00
	Gash on shoulder	3,250.	140.00
b.	Vert. pair, imperf. horizontally		*10,000.*

All type I perforated stamps were printed from 4 of the plates used for the imperfs., so many varieties exist both imperf. and perf.

VARIETIES OF RECUTTING

Lines on bust and bottom of medallion circle recut (47R6)	—	1,500.
Top label and right diamond block joined	—	600.00
Top label and right diamond block joined at top and bottom (68R4)	—	600.00
Lower label and right diamond block joined	—	600.00
Extra line at right	—	750.00

All varieties of recutting listed under No. 11 are found on No. 25.

Earliest documented use: May 9, 1857 (Plate 4); April 30, 1857 (Plate 6); Feb. 28, 1857 (Plate 7); April 15, 1857 (Plate 8).

Cancellations

Blue	+5.00
Red	+12.50
Orange red	+25.00
Orange	+150.00
Brown	+100.00
Ultramarine	+100.00
Green	+200.00
1857 year date	+10.00
1858 year date	+10.00
1859 year date	+10.00
"Paid"	+5.00
"Way"	+20.00
Numeral	+10.00
Railroad	+25.00
"Steam"	+20.00
Steamship	+35.00
Steamboat	+45.00
Packet Boat	+50.00
Supplementary Mail Type A	+40.00
U. S. Express Mail	+7.50
Express Company	+65.00
Black Carrier	+30.00
"Old Stamps-Not Recognized"	+1,000.
Territorial	+50.00
Printed precancel "Cumberland, Me." (on cover)	—
Pen	55.00

25A	A10 3c **rose,** type II, (Plates 2L, 3, 5L)	4,750.	450.00
	rose red	4,750.	450.00
	dull red	4,750.	450.00
	No gum	1,900.	
	On cover		525.00
	claret	5,000.	525.00
	No gum	2,250.	
	Pair	*10,500.*	1,100.
	Strip of 3	*17,000.*	1,800.
	Block of 4	*24,000.*	*10,000.*
	Double transfer "Gents" instead of "Cents" (66R2L)	—	1,250.
	Triple transfer	—	1,250.
	Dot in lower right diamond block (69L5L)	—	*525.00*
	Major cracked plate (84L, 94L, 9R, Plate 5L)	*5,750.*	1,000.
	Intermediate cracked plate (80L, 96L, 71R, Plate 5L)	*5,250.*	750.00
	Minor cracked plate (8L, 27L, 31L, 44L, 45L, 51L, 55L, 65L, 71L and 72L, 74L, 78L, 79L, 7R, Plate 5L)	*5,000.*	500.00
	Gash on shoulder	5,000.	500.00
	Worn plate	4,750.	450.00

All type II perforated stamps were printed from 3 of the plates used for the imperfs., so many varieties exist both imperf. and perf.

VARIETIES OF RECUTTING

Recut inner line only at right		575.00
1 extra vertical line outside of left frame line (29L, 39L, 49L, 59L, 69L, 79L, Plate 3)	—	600.00
2 extra vertical lines outside of left frame line (89L, 99L, Plate 3)	—	625.00
1 extra vertical line outside of right frame line (58L, 68L, 78L, 88L, 98L, Plate 3)	—	600.00
No inner line and frame line close to design at right (9L, 19L, Plate 3)	—	625.00
No inner line and frame line close to design at left (70L, 80L, 90L, 100L, Plate 3)	—	600.00
Recut button (10R2L)		1,750.

Except for "5 lines recut in upper left triangle," all varieties of recutting listed under No. 11A are found on No. 25A.

Earliest documented use: July 16, 1857 (Plate 2L); July 16, 1857 (Plate 3); April 15, 1857 (Plate 5L).

Cancellations

Blue	+5.00
Red	+10.00
Orange red	+25.00
Orange	+150.00
Brown	+100.00
Ultramarine	+100.00
Green	+200.00
1857 year date	+5.00

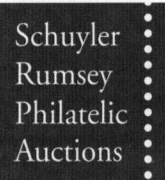

1858 year date	+5.00
1859 year date	+5.00
"Paid"	+5.00
"Way"	+20.00
Numeral	+10.00
Railroad	+25.00
"Steam"	+20.00
Steamship	+35.00
Steamboat	+45.00
Packet Boat	+50.00
Supplementary Mail Type A	+40.00
Express Company	+65.00
Black Carrier	+30.00
Green Carrier (New Orleans "snow shovel")	—
Territorial	+50.00
Pen	250.00

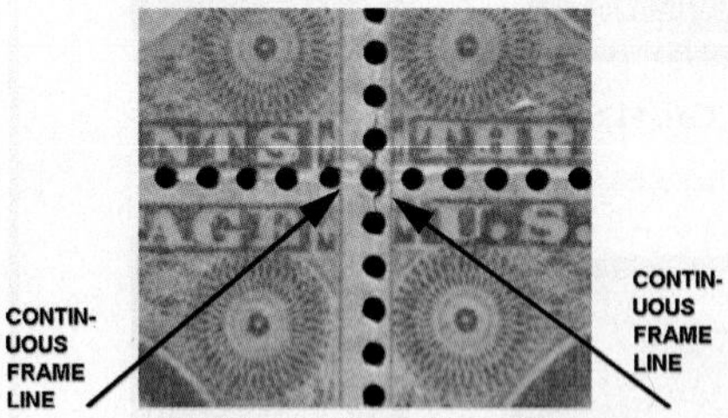

Washington (Type III) — A21

Type III — There are no outer frame lines at top and bottom. The side frame lines were recut so as to be continuous from the top to the bottom of the plate. Stamps from the top or bottom rows show the ends of the side frame lines and may be mistaken for Type IV.

Beware of type III stamps with frame lines that stop at the top of the design (from top row of plate) or bottom of the design (from bottom row of plate). These are often mistakenly offered as No. 26A.

No.	Design	Denom.	Description	Unused	Used
26	A21	3c	**dull red,** type III (Plates 9, 12-28)	75.00	9.00
			red	75.00	9.00
			rose	75.00	9.00
			No gum	25.00	
			brownish carmine	150.00	20.00
			No gum	50.00	
			claret	170.00	25.00
			No gum	60.00	
			orange brown	—	—
			plum		—
			On cover, dull red		10.50
			On cover, orange brown		*950.00*
			On patriotic cover		125.00
			On Confederate patriotic cover		2,000.
			On Pony express cover		—
			Pair	170.00	21.00
			Strip of 3	250.00	42.50
			Block of 4	375.00	175.00
			P# block of 8, Impt.	3,250.	
			Double transfer	110.00	20.00
			Double transfer, rosettes double and line through "Postage" and "Three Cents" (87R15)	—	*2,500.*
			Left frame line double	110.00	20.00
			Right frame line double	110.00	20.00
			Cracked plate (71L18)	*1,000.*	*400.00*
			Cracked plate (62L, 72L, Plate 18)	*750.00*	*250.00*
			Damaged transfer above lower left rosette	85.00	11.00
			Same, retouched	105.00	12.00
			Same, retouched with 2 vertical lines	140.00	13.00
			Same, both damaged areas retouched	325.00	100.00
			"Quadruple" plate flaw (18L28)	—	*1,750.*
			1 line recut in upper left triangle	—	30.00
			5 lines recut in upper left triangle (52L25)		500.00
			Inner line recut at left		*500.00*
			Inner line recut at right	—	350.00
			Worn plate	75.00	8.50
b.			Horiz. pair, imperf. vertically	*4,000.*	—
c.			Vert. pair, imperf. horizontally		*12,000.*
d.			Horizontal pair, imperf. between		—
e.			Double impression		*2,500.*

Frame line double varieties are separate and distinct for virtually the entire length of the stamp. Examples with partly split lines are worth considerably less.

Earliest documented use: Sept. 14, 1857.

Cancellations

Blue	+.25
Red	+1.50
Orange red	+2.50
Orange	+150.00
Brown	+100.00
Ultramarine	+100.00
Violet	+100.00
Green	+150.00
1857 year date	+3.00
1858-1861 year date	+1.00
Printed Circular Precancel "Cumberland, Me." (on cover)	—
"Paid"	+.50
"Paid All"	+15.00
"Free"	+20.00
"Collect"	+40.00
Numeral	+2.50
"Steam"	+12.50
Steamer	—
Steamboat	+22.50
Steamship	+22.50
"Way"	+12.50
Railroad	+15.00
U. S. Express Mail	+20.00
Express Company	+65.00
Packet boat	+65.00
Supp. Mail Type A, B or C	+500.00
Black Carrier	+30.00
Red Carrier	+25.00
"Southn. Letter Unpaid"	+750.00
Territorial	+20.00
"Old Stamps-Not Recognized"	+500.00
On cover	7,500.
Pen	3.25

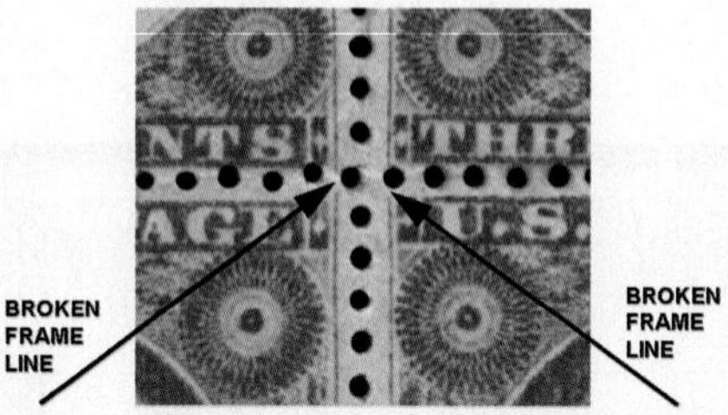

Washington (Type IV) — A21a

Type IV — As type III, but the side frame lines extend only to the top and bottom of the stamp design. All Type IV stamps are from plates 10 and 11 (each of which exists in three states), and these plates produced only Type IV. The side frame lines were recut individually for each stamp, thus being broken between the stamps vertically.

Beware of type III stamps with frame lines that stop at the top of the design (from top row of plate) or bottom of the design (from bottom row of plate). These are often mistakenly offered as No. 26A.

No.	Design	Denom.	Description	Unused	Used
26A	A21a	3c	**dull red,** type IV (Plates 10-11)	500.00	110.00
			brownish carmine	500.00	110.00
			rose	500.00	110.00
			No gum	170.00	
			claret	525.00	120.00
			No gum	180.00	
			On cover		150.00
			On patriotic cover		400.00
			Pair	1,050.	275.00
			Strip of 3	1,600.	450.00
			Block of 4	*5,000.*	*2,250.*
			P# block of 8, Impt.	*12,500.*	
			Double transfer	575.00	180.00
			Double transfer, line through rosettes (61R10i, 61R10L, 98R10i, 98R10L)	—	900.00
			Double transfer of rosettes and lower part of stamp (91R11L)	—	250.00
			Triple transfer	—	450.00
			Damaged transfer above lower left rosette	550.00	130.00
			Same, retouched	525.00	125.00
			Same, both damaged areas retouched (10R11)		300.00
			Inner line recut at right	—	300.00
			Inner line recut at left (79L10)	—	500.00
			Left frame line double (70, 80, 90, 100R11)	—	210.00
			Worn plate	500.00	110.00
f.			Horiz. strip of 3, imperf. vert., on cover		*14,500.*

No. 26Af is unique.

Earliest documented use: July 11, 1857.

Cancellations

Blue	+2.50
Red	+10.00
Orange red	+15.00
Orange	+150.00
Brown	+100.00
Ultramarine	+100.00
Violet	+150.00
Green	+175.00
1857 year date	+2.50
1858 or 1859 year date	+1.50
"Paid"	+2.50
"Paid All"	+15.00
"Free"	+20.00
"Collect"	+40.00
Numeral	+2.50
"Steam"	+15.00
Steamer	—
Steamboat	+25.00
Steamship	+25.00
"Way"	+15.00
Railroad	+17.50
U. S. Express Mail	+17.50
Express Company	+65.00
Packet boat	+65.00
Black Carrier	+30.00
Red Carrier	+20.00
Territorial	+30.00
Pen	27.50

No.	Design	Denom.	Description	Unused	Used
27	A11	5c	**brick red,** type I, *1858*	*80,000.*	1,800.
			No gum	*20,000.*	
			On cover		2,200.
			On patriotic cover		5,000.
			Pair	*175,000.*	4,250.
			Strip of 3		*6,500.*
			Block of 4	*375,000.*	*40,000.*
			Defective transfer (23R1)	—	—

The unused block of 4 is unique.

Earliest documented use: Oct. 6, 1858.

Cancellations

Blue	+150.
Red	+175.
Ultramarine	+450.
1859 year date	+50.
1860 year date	+50.
"Paid"	+50.
Supplementary Mail Type A	+150.
"Steamship"	+150.
Pen	950.

No.	Design	Denom.	Description	Unused	Used
28	A11	5c	**red brown,** type I	10,000.	1,200.
			pale red brown	10,000.	1,200.
			No gum	3,500.	
			On cover		1,400.
			Pair	*22,500.*	2,750.
			Strip of 3		4,250.
			Block of 4	*75,000.*	*8,000.*
			Defective transfer (23R1)		—
b.			**Bright red brown**	12,500.	1,750.
			No gum	4,500.	

Earliest documented use: Aug. 23, 1857 (No. 28).

Cancellations

Blue	+25.
Ultramarine	—
Red	+45.
1857 year date	+20.
1858 year date	+15.
"Paid"	+35.
Railroad	+75.
"Short Paid"	—
Pen	575.

No.	Design	Denom.	Description	Unused	Used
28A	A11	5c	**Indian red,** type I, *1858*	*175,000.*	3,750.
			No gum	*40,000.*	
			On cover		5,250.
			Pair		*8,000.*
			Strip of 3		*13,500.*
			Block of 4		—

There are only four recorded examples of No. 28A with any amount of original gum. Value is for a fine stamp, the highest recorded grade (two thus).

Earliest documented use: Mar. 31, 1858.

Cancellations

Red	+100.
Blue	+150.
1858 year date	+50.
1859 year date	+25.
Pen	1,800.

No.	Design	Denom.	Description	Unused	Used
29	A11	5c	**brown,** type I, *1859*	3,500.	450.
			pale brown	3,500.	450.
			deep brown	3,500.	450.
			yellowish brown	3,500.	450.
			No gum	1,350.	
			On cover		575.
			Pair	*7,500.*	950.
			Strip of 3	*12,500.*	1,550.
			Block of 4	*42,500.*	*5,000.*
			Defective transfer (23R1)	—	—

Earliest documented use: Mar. 21, 1859.

Cancellations

Blue	+10.
Ultramarine	—
Red	+25.
Brown	+75.
Magenta	+125.
Green	+350.
1859 year date	+10.
1860 year date	+10.
"Paid"	+15.
"Steam"	+75.
Steamship	+100.
Numeral	+80.
Pen	185.

Jefferson — A22

FIVE CENTS.
Type II — The projections at top and bottom are partly cut away. Several minor types could be made according to the extent of cutting of the projections.

30 A22 5c **orange brown,** Type II, *1861*	1,250.	1,300.
deep orange brown	1,250.	1,300.
No gum	475.	
On cover		*2,400.*
On patriotic cover		—
Pair	2,600.	*3,250.*
Strip of 3	4,100.	—
Block of 4	*6,500.*	—

Earliest documented use: May 8, 1861.

Cancellations

Blue	+30.
Red	+75.
Green	—
"Paid"	+75.
Steamship	+110.
Supplementary Mail Type A	+150.
Railroad	—
Pen	700.

30A A22 5c **brown,** type II, *1860*	2,400.	325.
dark brown	2,400.	325.
yellowish brown	2,400.	325.
No gum	900.	
On cover		375.
On patriotic cover		—
Pair	5,250.	675.
Strip of 3	*8,000.*	1,050.
Block of 4	*12,000.*	*3,250.*
Cracked plate	—	
b. Printed on both sides		*40,000.*

Earliest documented use: May 4, 1860.

Cancellations

Blue	+5.
Red	+20.
Magenta	+75.
Green	+350.
"Paid"	+20.
Supplementary Mail Type A	+50.
"Steamship"	+50.
"Steam"	+40.
Express Company	+250.
Railroad	—
Packet boat	—
Pen	160.

31 A12 10c **green,** type I	*30,000.*	1,300.
dark green	*30,000.*	1,300.
bluish green	*30,000.*	1,300.
yellowish green	*30,000.*	1,300.
No gum	*10,000.*	
On domestic cover		1,500.
On patriotic cover		3,500.
Pair	*65,000.*	2,800.
Vertical pair, types III, I	*40,000.*	1,700.
Vertical pair, types IV, I (86, 96 L 1)		—
Strip of 3		—
Vertical strip of 3, types II, III, I		—
Block of 4, types III, I	*75,000.*	—
Block of 4, types III, IV, I		*9,750.*
Vertical block of 6, 2 each types II, III, I	*90,000.*	
Double transfer (100R1)	*32,500.*	1,400.
"Curl" in left "X" (99R1)	*32,500.*	1,400.

Type I comes only from the bottom row of both panes of Plate 1.

Earliest documented use: Aug. 25, 1857.

Cancellations

Blue	+15.
Red	+50.
Green	+600.
Supplementary Mail Type A	—
"Steamship"	+100.
Canadian	—
Pen	650.

Act of February 27, 1861. Ten cent rate of postage to be prepaid on letters conveyed in the mail from any point in the United States east of the Rocky Mountains to any State or Territory on the Pacific Coast and vice versa, for each half-ounce.

32 A13 10c **green,** type II	6,250.	300.
dark green	6,250.	300.
bluish green	6,250.	300.
yellowish green	6,250.	300.
No gum	2,250.	
On domestic cover		350.
On pony express cover		8,500.
Pair	*13,000.*	625.
Strip of 3	—	950.
Block of 4	*30,000.*	*4,500.*
Pair, types II, III	*13,000.*	700.
Pair, types II, IV	*60,000.*	2,700.
Vertical strip of 3, types II, III, IV		—
Block of 4, types II, III	*30,000.*	*3,500.*
Block of 4, types II, IV		—
Block of 4, types II, III, IV	*95,000.*	*18,000.*
Double transfer (31L, 51L and 20R, Plate 1)	6,500.	325.
"Curl opposite left X" (10R1)		375.

Earliest documented use: July 27, 1857 (dated cancel on off-cover stamp), Aug. 8, 1857 (on cover).

Cancellations

Blue	+10.
Red	+30.
Brown	+125.
Green	+300.
"Paid"	+20.
1857 year date	+10.
Supplementary Mail Type A	—
Steamship	+50.
Packet boat	—
Railroad	—
Express Company	—
Pen	150.

33 A14 10c **green,** type III	6,250.	300.
dark green	6,250.	300.
bluish green	6,250.	300.
yellowish green	6,250.	300.
No gum	2,250.	
On domestic cover		350.
Pair	*13,000.*	625.
Strip of 3	—	950.
Pair, types III, IV		2,700.
"Curl" on forehead (85L1)	—	375.
"Curl in left X" (87R1)		375.

Earliest documented use: Aug. 8, 1857.

Cancellations

Blue	+10.
Red	+30.
Brown	+125.
Ultramarine	+100.
1857 year date	+10.
"Paid"	+20.
"Steam"	+45.
Steamboat	—
Steamship	+50.
Numeral	+15.
Packet boat	—
Pen	150.

34 A15 10c **green,** type IV	*50,000.*	2,500.
dark green	*50,000.*	2,500.
bluish green	*50,000.*	2,500.
yellowish green	*50,000.*	2,500.
No gum	*20,000.*	
On domestic cover		2,900.
Pair		*6,250.*
Block of 4 (54-55, 64-65L)		—

VARIETIES OF RECUTTING

Eight stamps on Plate I were recut. All are listed below.

Outer line recut at top (65L, 74L, 86L and 3R, Plate I)	*50,000.*	2,500.
Outer line recut at bottom (54L, 55L, 76L, Plate 1)	*52,500.*	2,600.
Outer line recut at top and bottom (64L1)	*55,000.*	2,750.

Earliest documented use: Oct. 5, 1857.

Cancellations

Blue	+75.
Red	+125.
Steamship	+200.
Packet boat	—
Pen	1,250.

Types I, II, III and IV occur on the same sheet, so it is possible to obtain pairs and blocks showing combinations of types. For listings of type combinations in pairs and blocks, see Nos. 31-33.

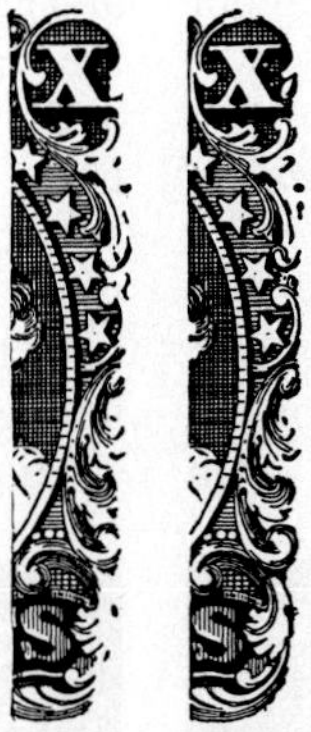

Washington (Two typical examples) — A23

Type V — The side ornaments are slightly cut away. Usually only one pearl remains at each end of the lower label, but some copies show two or three pearls at the right side. At the bottom the outer line is complete and the shells nearly so. The outer lines at top are complete except over the right "X."

35 A23 10c **green,** type V, (Plate 2), *1859*	260.00	65.00
dark green	260.00	65.00
yellowish green	260.00	65.00
No gum	100.00	
On domestic cover		77.50
On patriotic cover		625.00
On pony express cover		—
On cover to Canada		125.00
Pair	550.00	140.00
Block of 4	1,200.	650.00
P# block of 8, Impt.	*17,500.*	
Double transfer at bottom (47R2)	340.00	90.00
Small "Curl" on forehead (37, 78L2)	310.00	77.50
Curl in "e" of "cents" (93L2)	340.00	90.00
Curl in "t" of "cents" (73R2)	340.00	90.00
Cracked plate		—

Earliest documented use: Apr. 29, 1859.

Cancellations

Red	+7.50
Orange red	+12.50
Brown	+100.00
Blue	+5.00
Orange	+150.00
Magenta	+100.00
Green	+250.00
1859 year date	+5.00
"Paid"	+5.00
"Paid All"	—
Red carrier	—
Railroad	+40.00
Steamship	+35.00
"Steam"	+30.00
Numerals	+15.00
Supp. Mail Type A or C	+60.00
Express Company	+135.00
"Southn Letter Unpaid"	—
Territorial	—
Pen	30.00

TWELVE CENTS. Printed from two plates.
Plate 1 (No. 36) — Outer frame lines were recut on the plate and are complete. Very narrow spacing of stamps on the plate.

No. 36 outer frame lines recut on plate

36 A16 12c **black** (Plate 1)	1,900.	325.
gray black	1,900.	325.
No gum	600.	
Single on cover		750.
Single on cover with No. 26 to France		425.
Pair on cover to England		850.
Pair on patriotic cover		—
Pair	4,250.	700.
Block of 4	*10,500.*	2,600.
Not recut in lower right corner	2,100.	350.
Recut in lower left corner (43, 53, 63, 73, 100L)	2,100.	350.
Double transfer	2,100.	350.
Triple transfer	2,300.	—
a. Diagonal half used as 6c on cover		*17,500.*
c. Horizontal pair, imperf. between		*12,500.*

Earliest documented use: July 30, 1857.

Cancellations

Blue	+5.
Red	+10.
Brown	+75.
Magenta	+55.
Green	+250.
1857 year date	+100.
"Paid"	+10.
Supplementary Mail Type A	+60.
Express Company	—
Railroad	+60.
Numeral	+20.
"Southn Letter Unpaid"	—
Pen	150.

Typical No. 36B, outer frame lines not recut

Plate 3 (No. 36B) — Weak outer frame lines from the die were not recut and are noticeably uneven or broken, sometimes partly missing. Somewhat wider spacing of stamps on the plate.

36B A16 12c **black** (Plate 3)	825.	375.
intense black	825.	375.
No gum	400.	
Single on cover		1,250.
Single on cover with No. 26 to France		475.
Pair on cover to England		850.
Pair	1,700.	825.
Block of 4	5,000.	3,500.
Double frame line at right	875.	400.

The Two Types of the 12-Cent 1857 Stamps Now Recognized as Major Numbers in the Scott Catalogue

James E. Kloetzel
Scott Catalogue Editor

It has long been recognized that two major types exist of the perforated 12¢ black Washington stamp of 1857. For many years, the Scott catalogue explained the difference between stamps from plate 1 and plate 3 in a footnote. Then, in 1965, the second type from plate 3 was given a lettered minor listing as No. 36b. In the *2009 Scott Specialized Catalogue of United States Stamps and Covers*, this minor number has been elevated to the major number 36B. The reason parallels the reason why major numbers were created for the 3¢ issues of 1851-57.

The 2008 U.S. Specialized catalogue recognized the major recutting varieties of the 3¢ 1851-57 stamps by adding major Nos. 10A, 11A, 25A and 26A after Nos. 10, 11, 25 and 26. Collectors who specialize in these issues usually discuss them not only in terms of their color and perforations but also in terms of the manner in which their frame lines and inner lines have been recut. The Scott editors recognized the importance of this distinction, and now list the stamps with no recut inner lines (type I) as Nos. 10, 11 and 25, while the stamps with recut inner lines also (now termed type II stamps) have been given the major numbers 10A, 11A and 25A.

At the same time, the perforated 3¢ stamps listed as No. 26 (old type II, now type III) and No. 26a (old type IIa, now type IV), were designated Nos. 26 and 26A., thus giving each of the significantly different types major number status, rather than one major with a minor listing attached.

We will review these changes again below, but first a discussion of this year's change of another lettered minor listing to a full major listing is in order.

The types of the 12¢ 1857 stamp parallel the 3¢ stamps' production history

Proofs from the original die of the 12¢ black show that the frame lines were not cut very deep. As a result, these lines transferred fairly lightly to the plate. Due to unevenness on the plate, the lines at times transferred as weak or broken. As a result (just as with the 3¢ issue), a decision was made to recut the frame lines of stamps on plate 1 more deeply on the plate itself. All four of the outer frame lines on virtually every stamp on the plate, and often the inner lines at left and right as well, were recut carefully, stamp by stamp, on plate 1.

A new 12¢ plate was made late in 1859 or early in 1860. It is believed that the same transfer roll used in making the first plate was also used to make the second plate. Actually, this "second" plate seems to have been the third plate made, for examples are known with imprint and plate 3. Records indicate an actual second plate was made in 1857, but it appears that some damage made this plate unserviceable, and no stamps from such a plate have ever been identified. Plate 3 is the only plate from which a plate number in the selvage has been seen, and thus it is only out of convenience of identification that philatelists call the first plate used number 1.

With the creation of plate 3, a pattern of plate making very similar to that seen on the 3¢ plates of the same period ensued. That is, the same light and often broken frame lines appeared on the images that had been rocked into the plate by the transfer roll, but on this plate a decision was made not to recut the frame lines or inner lines on the plate. This decision tends to mirror the decision made on some later 3¢ plates not to recut the inner lines on those plates. Perhaps a business decision was made in both cases to cut back on the time and labor that would be required to do this work.

The recut 12¢ stamps from plate 1 have consistently even and complete frame lines (Figure 1). The decision not to recut the frame lines and inner lines on plate 3 resulted in stamps with frame lines that are easily identifiable by their light, uneven and often broken appearance (Figure 2).

Collectors have always desired examples of both major types of the 12¢ perforated stamp, and even collectors who form their collections on the basis of major Scott numbers tend strongly to add both types to their collections.

Based on clear design differences resulting from significantly different production techniques, the Scott catalogue treatment of

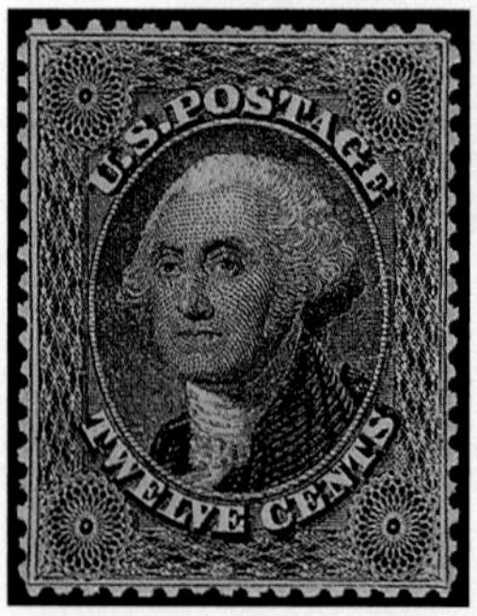

Figure 1. 12¢ stamps from plate 1 are easily identified by their complete frame lines, which were recut on the plate.

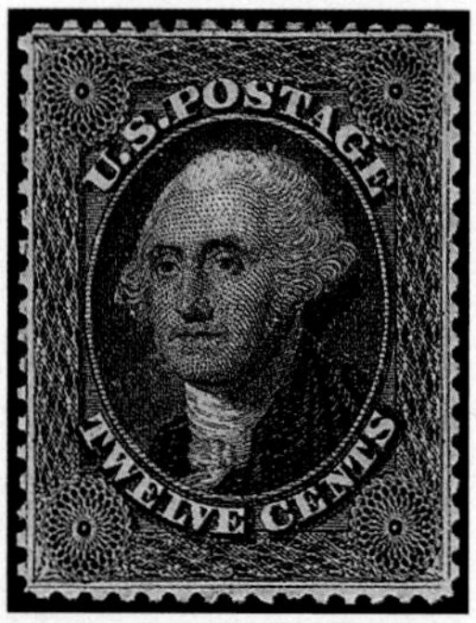

Figure 2. 12¢ stamps from plate 3 are characterized by light, uneven and often broken frame lines. These frame lines were not recut.

Figure 3. At the left is a type I 3¢ stamp showing outer frame lines only recut. At right is a type II 3¢ stamp showing recut outer frame lines and recut inner lines.

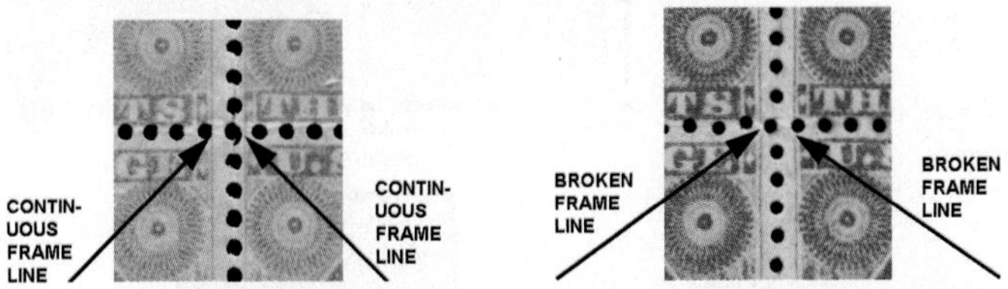

Figure 4. At left is a cropped block of four of Scott 26, showing continuous frame lines at the sides from the top to the bottom of the plate. At right is Scott 26A, showing broken frame lines at the sides recut individually for each stamp.

similar stamps of this period, plus the known desire of collectors to place both major types of this stamp in their collections, the decision to raise the catalogue number of the plate 3 12¢ stamp from minor-number status as No. 36b to major-number status as No. 36B was an easy one.

A brief history of the 3¢ 1851-57 listings in the Scott catalogue

The Scott editors know that not all collectors purchase a new Scott U.S. Specialized catalogue every year (though they should, of course, in order to keep abreast of all the latest value and editorial changes and enhancements). Many collectors may have missed the Special Feature article in the 2008 edition concerning the creation of major numbers 10A, 11A, 25A and 26A. Thus, a brief review of that article seems appropriate in order to round out the story of the creation of new major number Scott 36B.

Dr. Carroll Chase wrote the definitive book on the 3¢ stamp (*The 3¢ Stamp of the United States 1851-1857 Issue*, published by the American Philatelic Society, 1929 [revised in 1942]). Chase writes (on pages 80-82 of the 1942 edition): "According to Scott's Catalogue there are two types of the 3¢ 1851-1857 stamps, the first, Type I, showing a frame line all around the design, existing both imperforate and perforated [Scott 10, 11 and 25]; the second, Type II, showing no frame line at top or bottom, existing only perforated [Scott 26]. . . . If desired, both of these main types may be divided into two sub-types, the Type I stamps existing with, and those existing without 'inner lines' (Figure 3) . . . The perforated, Type II, stamps may also be divided into two sub-types. All the plates, excepting 10 and 11, show that the side frame lines were recut by drawing a continuous line from the top to the bottom of the plate. . . . But on plates 10 and 11, the side frame lines were drawn separately for each stamp, these lines being broken between the stamps vertically." (Figure 4)

The two sub-types of type I noted by Chase were not originally incorporated into the Scott catalogue listings, and the two sub-types of Chase's type II stamps were first differentiated by Scott as Nos. 26 and 26a in the 1955 U.S. Specialized catalogue. Interestingly, for the years 1958 through 1961, the listing was changed to the major number 26A, but in 1962 it reverted once again to the minor number 26a.

The overall result of the Scott listings for the 3¢ stamps was that they showed far less specialization than the listings of the 1¢ and 10¢ denominations. The changes announced in the 2008 U.S. Specialized catalogue go a long way toward evening out the listing treatment of all these stamps. Now, the new treatment of the 12¢ perforated stamp of 1857 in the 2009 edition completes the more consistent treatment of the stamps of these issues.

The production of the 3¢ stamps of 1851-57

Reviewing the production methods for the 3¢ stamps that were further differentiated as major numbers in the 2008 Scott U.S. Specialized catalogue will fill in some information for those who did not see the Special Feature article in that edition, and it will put the new catalogue-number change for the plate 3 12¢ perforated stamp into a larger context.

Just as only one die of the 12¢ Washington stamp was created and used, the original die for the 3¢ Washington stamp was never changed during the life of preparing these plates. To make the plates for the 3¢ stamps, the original die was used to create a transfer roll with three images of the original die. That transfer roll was then used to make several plates of 200 images divided into two panes of 100 each. The original die of the 12¢ stamp was used to make a transfer roll with just a single image, and that transfer roll also was used to make plates of 200 images.

Every single 3¢ stamp design on every plate used to print these stamps was recut to some extent on the plate itself. All stamps had their outer frame lines recut at the sides (and often at the top and bottom) for the imperforate stamps Nos. 10 and 11 and the perforated No. 25, now termed type I. Other stamps had the outer frame lines recut *and* their inner lines also recut. These are the stamps now termed type II (Nos. 10A, 11A and 25A). When the 3¢ stamp was perforated beginning in 1857 (Scott 25 and 25A), the perforations usually impinged on the design both vertically and horizontally. A decision was made that new plates should be made allowing for larger margins (Scott 26 and 26A). Part of the larger margins was created by eliminating the horizontal frame lines from the top and bottom of the designs. This was accomplished by removing these lines from the transfer rolls.

Plates 9 through 28 were then made using the modified transfer rolls. Plates numbered 9 and 12-28 all show designs with vertical frame lines that run continuously from the top to the bottom of the plate on both the left and right sides of each stamp. Plates 10 and 11, however were made with the vertical frame line at left and right running only from the top to the bottom of each individual stamp design, being broken between stamps. There is no known documentation explaining why these two different styles were adopted for adding the side frame lines.

Both of these types were combined in a single Scott listing until 1955, at which time the more common stamps with continuous vertical frames lines were made the major Scott number 26, while the less common stamps from plates 10 and 11 were listed as No. 26a (26A from 1958-61). Beginning in the 2008 U.S. Specialized catalogue, Scott once again raised the 3¢ perforated stamps with no top or bottom frame lines and non-continuous side frame lines to major-number status as No. 26A.

For a more detailed description of the plates used to produce the 3¢ stamps, we direct the interested reader to the Special Feature article in last year's edition of the U.S. Specialized catalogue.

Double frame line at left	875.	400.
Vertical line through rosette (95R3)	1,000.	450.

Earliest documented use: June 1, 1860. (The previously listed Dec. 3, 1859, cover requires expertization in order to be considered.)

Cancellations

Blue	+7.
Red	+12.
Brown	+85.
Magenta	+60.
Green	+250.
1860 year date	+100.
1861 year date	+50.
"Paid"	+12.
Supplementary Mail Type A	+300.
Express Company	—
Railroad	+65.
Numeral	+25.
"Southn Letter Unpaid"	—
Pen	175.

Washington — A17

Franklin — A18

37	A17	24c	**gray lilac**, *1860*	1,600.	400.
a.		24c	**gray**	1,600.	400.
			No gum	600.	
			On cover to England		1,050.
			On patriotic cover		*4,000.*
			Pair	3,600.	875.
			Block of 4, gray lilac	*9,500.*	*6,500.*
			P# block of 12, Impt.	*32,500.*	

The technical configuration of a No. 37 plate block is eight stamps. The unique plate block currently is contained in the listed block of twelve stamps.

Earliest documented use: July 7, 1860.

Cancellations

Blue	+10.
Red	+40.
Magenta	+80.
Violet	+150.
Green	+450.
1860 year date	+15.
"Paid"	+25.
"Paid All"	+50.
"Free"	+150.
Supplementary Mail Type A	+150.
Railroad	+150.
Packet Boat	+200.
Red Carrier	—
Numeral	+40.
"Southn Letter Unpaid"	—
Pen	190.

See Trial Color Proofs for the 24c red lilac.

38	A18	30c	**orange**, *1860*	2,400.	500.
			yellow orange	2,400.	500.
			reddish orange	2,400.	500.
			No gum	900.	
			On cover to Germany or France		*1,350.*
			On patriotic cover		*9,000.*
			Pair	*5,250.*	1,100.
			Block of 4	*14,000.*	*6,750.*
			Double transfer (89L1 and 99L1)	2,650.	575.
			Recut at bottom (52L1)	2,900.	625.
			Cracked plate	—	—

Earliest documented use: Aug. 8, 1860.

Cancellations

Blue	+20.
Red	+40.
Magenta	+90.
Violet	+200.
Green	+1000.
1860 year date	+30.
"Paid"	+35.
"Free"	—
Black town	+30.
Supplementary Mail Type A	+125.
Steamship	—
Express Company	—
Pen	250.

Washington — A19

39	A19	90c	**blue**, *1860*	3,500.	*9,500.*
			deep blue	3,500.	*9,500.*
			No gum	1,250.	
			On cover		*225,000.*
			Pair	*7,000.*	—
			Block of 4	*30,000.*	*45,000.*
			Double transfer at bottom	3,750.	—
			Double transfer at top	3,750.	—
			Short transfer at bottom right and left (13L1 and 68R1)	3,750.	

The used block of 4 is believed to be unique and has perfs trimmed off at left and bottom clear of design. Value is based on 1993 auction sale.

Earliest documented use: Sept. 11, 1860.

Cancellations

Red	9,500.
Black	+200.
Blue	+300.
Red town	+1,000.
Black town	+1,000.
1861 year date	+1,000.
Boston "Paid"	+750.
Red Carrier	—
N.Y. Ocean Mail	+1,000.
Pen	2,900.

Genuine cancellations on the 90c are very scarce.
All used examples of No. 39 must be accompanied by certificates of authenticity issued by recognized expertizing committees.

See Die and Plate Proofs for imperfs. on stamp paper.

REPRINTS OF 1857-60 ISSUE

These were not valid for postal use, though one example each of Nos. 43 and 45 are known with contemporaneous cancels.
Produced by the Continental Bank Note Co.

White paper, without gum.

The 1, 3, 10 and 12c were printed from new plates of 100 subjects each differing from those used for the regular issue.

1875 ***Perf. 12***

40	A5	1c	**bright blue** *(3846)*	*625.*	
			Pair	*1,350.*	
			Block of 4	*3,500.*	
			Cracked plate, pos. 91	*775.*	
			Double transfer, pos. 94	*775.*	
41	A10	3c	**scarlet** *(479)*	*3,250.*	
42	A22	5c	**orange brown** *(878)*	*1,400.*	
			Pair	*3,250.*	
			Vertical margin strip of 4, Impt. & P#	*11,500.*	
43	A12	10c	**blue green** *(516)*	*3,000.*	—
			Pair	*7,000.*	
44	A16	12c	**greenish black** *(489)*	*3,250.*	
			Pair	*7,500.*	
45	A17	24c	**blackish violet** *(479)*	*3,250.*	—
46	A18	30c	**yellow orange** *(480)*	*3,250.*	
47	A19	90c	**deep blue** *(454)*	*4,750.*	

Nos. 41-46 are valued in the grade of fine.
Nos. 40-47 exist imperforate. Very infrequent sales preclude establishing a value at this time. One set of imperforate pairs is recorded. An imperforate horizontal strip of 3 of No. 44 also is recorded.
Numbers in parentheses are quantities sold.

Produced by the National Bank Note Co.

Franklin — A24

Washington — A25

Jefferson — A26

Washington — A27

A27a

A27

Washington — A28

A29
Washington

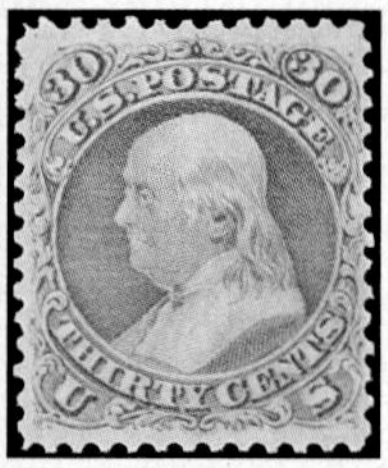
A30
Franklin

Washington — A31

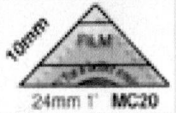

1c — There is a dash under the tip of the ornament at right of the numeral in upper left corner.
3c — Ornaments at corners end in a small ball.
5c — There is a leaflet in the foliated ornaments at each corner.
10c (A27) — A heavy curved line has been cut below the stars and an outer line added to the ornaments above them.
12c — There are corner ornaments consisting of ovals and scrolls.
90c — Parallel lines form an angle above the ribbon with "U. S. Postage"; between these lines there is a row of dashes and a point of color at the apex of the lower line.

Patriotic Covers covering a wide range of historical interest were used during the Civil War period, in the North as well as the South, and are collected by manufacturer and topic as well as generally, both used and unused. There are believed to be as many as 12,000 varieties.

During the war, these stamps were used as small change until Postage Currency was issued.

The Act of Congress of March 3, 1863, effective July 1, 1863, created a rate of three cents for each half ounce, first class domestic mail. This Act was the first law which established uniform rate of postage regardless of the distance. This rate remained in effect until Oct. 1, 1883.

Plates of 200 subjects in two panes of 100 each.

The following items, formerly listed here as Nos. 55-62, are considered to be essays or trial color proofs. They will be found in their respective sections as follows. Previous No. 58 has been combined with No. 62B.

Formerly	Currently	Formerly	Currently
55	63-E11e	59	69-E6e
56	65-E15h	60	70eTC
57	67-E9e	61	71bTC
58	62B	62	72-E7h

The paper of Nos. 62B-72 is thicker and more opaque than the essays and trial color proofs, except Nos. 62B, 70c, and 70d.

1861 ***Perf. 12***

62B A27a	10c **dark green**		*8,000.*	1,500.
	dark yellow green		*8,000.*	1,500.
	No gum		*3,250.*	
	On cover			2,000.
	On patriotic cover			3,000.
	Pair		*17,500.*	3,500.
	Block of 4		*37,500.*	*13,000.*
	Foreign entry 94R4		*9,250.*	—
	Block of 4, one stamp 94R4		—	

The foreign entry is of the 90c 1861.

Earliest documented use: Sept. 17, 1861.

Cancellations

Red	+80.
Blue	+50.
"Paid"	+60.
Steamship	+100.
Express Company	+200.
Supplementary Mail Type A	+125.

1861-62 ***Perf. 12***

63 A24	1c **blue,** *Aug. 17, 1861*	350.00	50.00
	pale blue	350.00	50.00
	bright blue	350.00	50.00
	No gum	125.00	
	On cover (single)		57.50
	On prisoner's letter		—
	On patriotic cover		225.00
	Pair	750.00	105.00
	Block of 4	1,750.	500.00
	P# block of 8, Impt.	*6,500.*	
	Double transfer	—	62.50
	Dot in "U"	375.00	55.00
a.	1c **ultramarine**	*2,500.*	*650.00*
	No gum	*1,000.*	
	dark ultramarine	*5,000.*	*1,500.*
	No gum	*2,250.*	
b.	1c **dark blue**	800.00	400.00
	No gum	300.00	
c.	Laid paper, horiz. or vert.	*11,000.*	*9,000.*
d.	Vertical pair, imperf. horiz.		—
e.	Printed on both sides	—	*4,000.*

Earliest documented use: Aug. 17, 1861 (dated cancel on off-cover stamp); Aug. 21, 1861 (on cover).

Cancellations

Blue	+2.00
Red	+7.50
Magenta	+50.00
Green	+250.00
Violet	+50.00
1861 year date	+7.50
1865 year date	+2.00
1866 year date	+2.00
"Free"	+40.00
"Paid"	+2.50
"Paid All"	+15.00
Supp. Mail Type A or B	+30.00
Steamship	+35.00
Steam	+30.00
Express Company	+175.00
Red Carrier	+10.00
Black Carrier	+10.00
Railroad	+30.00
Numeral	+10.00
"Steamboat"	+50.00
Printed Precancel "CUMBERLAND, ME."	—

64 A25	3c **pink,** *Aug. 17, 1861*	*14,000.*	1,000.
	No gum	*5,000.*	
	On cover		1,100.
	On patriotic cover		1,300.
	Pair	*30,000.*	*2,500.*
	Block of 4	*65,000.*	—

Earliest documented use: Aug. 17, 1861 (FDC).

Cancellations

Blue	+50.00
Red	+150.00
Green	+500.00
1861 date	—
"Paid"	+25.00
"Free"	+175.00
"Ship"	+85.00
Supplementary Mail Type B	+150.00
Railroad	+125.00
Steamboat	+175.00

a.	3c **pigeon blood pink**	*45,000.*	*4,000.*
	No gum	*12,500.*	
	On cover		*4,750.*
	On patriotic cover		*7,000.*

Earliest documented use: Aug. 21, 1861.

b.	3c **rose pink,** *Aug. 17, 1861*	600.00	160.00
	No gum	230.00	
	On cover		190.00
	On patriotic cover		250.00
	Pair	1,350.	350.00
	Block of 4	3,250.	875.00

Earliest documented use: Aug. 17, 1861 (FDC).

Cancellations

Blue	+10.00
Red	+20.00
Orange red	+25.00
Green	+150.00
Orange	—
"Paid"	+10.00
"Free"	+75.00
Supplementary Mail Type C	—
"Ship"	+30.00
Railroad	+60.00
Steamboat	+90.00

65 A25	3c **rose**	140.00	3.00
	bright rose	140.00	3.00
	dull red	140.00	3.00
	rose red	140.00	3.00
	No gum	50.00	
	On cover		3.50
	On patriotic cover		40.00
	On prisoner's letter		150.00
	On pony express cover		—
	Pair	300.00	6.75
	Block of 4	700.00	42.50
	P# block of 8, Impt.	4,250.	
	Double transfer	170.00	6.00
	Cracked plate	—	—
	brown red	*290.00*	5.50
	No gum	110.00	
	pale brown red	*225.00*	5.50
	No gum	80.00	
	dull brown red	*260.00*	5.50
	No gum	100.00	
	Block of 4	*1,300.*	
	deep pinkish rose	*290.00*	25.00
	On cover		—
b.	Laid paper, horiz. or vert.	—	500.00
d.	Vertical pair, imperf. horiz.	*6,000.*	*750.00*
e.	Printed on both sides	*22,500.*	*5,000.*
	Pair	*47,500.*	
f.	Double impression		*7,500.*

See Die and Plate Proofs for imperfs. on stamp paper.

Earliest documented use: Aug. 19, 1861.

Cancellations

Blue	+.25
Ultramarine	+2.75
Brown	+50.00
Red	+3.00
Orange red	+3.50
Violet	+35.00
Magenta	+8.00
Green	+100.00
Olive	+100.00
Orange	+150.00
Yellow	*+3,500.*
1861 year date	+.50
1867 or 1868 year date	+.50
"Paid"	+.35
"Paid All"	+7.50
"Mails Suspended"	—
Railroad	+12.50
"Way"	+20.00
"Free"	+20.00
"Collect"	+35.00
"Ship"	+15.00
"U. S. Ship"	+35.00
"Steam"	+12.00
Steamship	+15.00
Steamboat	+20.00
"Ship Letter"	+35.00
Red Carrier	+15.00
Blue Carrier	+25.00
Black Carrier	+20.00
Supplementary Mail Type A, B or C	+15.00
Numeral	+3.00
Express Company	+90.00
Army Field Post	+60.00
Packet Boat	+40.00
"Registered"	+30.00
"Postage Due"	+25.00
"Advertised"	+15.00
"U.STATES"	+300.00
Territorial	+25.00
St. Thomas	—
China	—

The 3c lake can be found under No. 66 in the Trial Color Proofs section.

67 A26	5c **buff**	*27,500.*	1,100.
	No gum	*10,500.*	
	On cover		1,350.
	On patriotic cover		*4,000.*
	Pair	*60,000.*	2,500.
	Block of 4	*11,500.*	*12,500.*
a.	5c **brown yellow**	*30,000.*	1,300.
	No gum	*11,500.*	
b.	5c **olive yellow**	—	3,000.

The unused block of 4 is unique but very faulty. Value is based on actual 1993 sale.

Earliest documented uses: Aug. 19, 1861 (No. 67); Aug. 21, 1861 (No. 67a).

Cancellations

Red	+40.00
Blue	+20.00
Magenta	+125.00
Green	+750.00
1861 year date	+10.00
"Paid"	+25.00
Supplementary Mail Type A	+100.00
Express Company	+250.00
Numeral	+50.00
"Steamship"	+100.00

Values of Nos. 67, 67a, 67b reflect the normal small margins.

68 A27	10c **green**	1,200.	62.50
	yellow green	1,150.	62.50
	No gum	450.	
	On cover		75.00
	On patriotic cover		375.00
	On cover to Canada		100.00
	Pair	2,500.	130.00
	Block of 4	*5,750.*	650.00
	P# block of 8, Impt.	*13,000.*	
	Double transfer	1,300.	65.00
	deep yellow green on thin paper	1,400.	70.00
a.	10c **dark green**	1,450.	85.00
	blue green	1,450.	85.00
	No gum	550.	
b.	Vertical pair, imperf. horiz.		*3,500.*

Earliest documented use: Aug. 20, 1861.

Cancellations

Blue	+2.00
Red	+5.00
Purple	+50.00
Magenta	+50.00
Brown	+50.00
Green	+250.00
1865 year date	+3.50
"Paid"	+2.50
"Collect"	+32.50
"Short Paid"	+50.00
"P.D." in circle	+30.00
"Free"	+25.00
Numeral	+7.50
Red Carrier	+45.00
Railroad	+20.00
Steamship	+15.00
"Steamboat"	+35.00
Supplementary Mail Type A	+30.00
Red Supp. Mail Type D	—
Express Company	+70.00
China	—
Japan	+200.00
St. Thomas	—

Stamps are valued in the grade of very fine unless otherwise indicated.

Please Note:

Values for early and valuable stamps are for examples with certificates of authenticity from acknowledged expert committees, or examples sold with the buyer having the right of certification.

This applies to examples with original gum as well as examples without gum.

Beware of stamps offered "as is," as the gum on some unused stamps offered with "original gum" may be fraudulent, and stamps offered as unused without gum may in some cases be altered or faintly canceled used stamps.

69 A28	12c **black**	2,000.	120.00
	gray black	2,000.	130.00
	No gum	800.	
	intense black	2,100.	135.00
	No gum	825.	
	On domestic cover		160.00
	On patriotic cover		900.00
	On cover to France or Germany with #65		180.00
	Pair	4,500.	280.00
	Block of 4	*10,500.*	1,150.
	Double transfer of top frame line	2,100.	150.00
	Double transfer of bottom frame line	2,100.	150.00
	Double transfer of top and bottom frame lines	2,200.	155.00

Earliest documented use: Aug. 30, 1861.

Cancellations

Blue		+2.50
Ultramarine		—
Red		+20.00
Purple		+50.00
Magenta		+100.00
Green		+550.00
1861 year date		+5.00
"Paid"		+5.00
"Registered"		+35.00
Supp. Mail Type A, B or C		+45.00
Express Company		+175.00
Railroad		+50.00
Numeral		+15.00
70 A29 24c **red lilac**	3,000.	300.00
No gum	1,150.	
On cover		350.00
On patriotic cover		*3,000.*
Pair	6,500.	625.00
Block of 4	*15,000.*	*3,000.*
Scratch under "A" of "Postage"		—
a. 24c **brown lilac**	3,250.	225.00
No gum	1,250.	
Block of 4	*17,000.*	*3,500.*
b. 24c **steel blue** ('61)	*16,500.*	900.00
No gum	*6,250.*	
On cover		1,350.
Block of 4	*75,000.*	
c. 24c **violet,** thin paper, *Aug. 20, 1861*	*35,000.*	2,100.
No gum	*13,500.*	
d. 24c **pale gray violet,** thin paper	17,500.	2,600.
No gum	6,000.	

There are numerous shades of the 24c stamp in this and the following issue.

Color changelings, especially of No. 78, are frequently offered as No. 70b. Obtaining a certificate from an acknowledged expert committee is strongly advised.

Nos. 70c and 70d are on a thinner, harder and more transparent paper than Nos. 70, 70a, 70b or the latter Nos. 78, 78a, 78b and 78c. No. 70eTC (formerly No. 60, see Trial Color Proofs section) is distinguished by its distinctive dark color.

Earliest documented uses: Jan. 7, 1862 (No. 70); Feb. 5, 1862 (No. 70a); Sept. 21, 1861 (No. 70b); Aug. 20, 1861 (No. 70c); Sept. 10, 1861 (No. 70d).

Cancellations, No. 70

Blue		+5.00
Red		+15.00
Magenta		+200.00
Brown		+125.00
Green		+300.00
1865 year date		+5.00
"Paid"		+15.00
Supp. Mail Types A or B		+75.00
Express Company		+350.00
71 A30 30c **orange**	2,400.	200.
deep orange	2,400.	200.
No gum	950.	
On cover to France or Germany		400.
On patriotic cover		*3,500.*
Pair	5,000.	450.
Block of 4	*16,000.*	*2,500.*
P# strip of 4, Impt.	—	
a. Printed on both sides		—

Values for No. 71 are for examples with small margins, especially at sides. Large-margined examples sell for much more.

Earliest documented use: Aug. 20, 1861.

Cancellations

Blue		+10.00
Magenta		+100.00
Brown		+100.00
Red		+25.00
"Paid"		+15.00
"Paid All"		+35.00
"Registered"		—
Railroad		—
Packet Boat		—
"Steamship"		+75.00
Supplementary Mail Type A		+75.00
Red Supp. Mail Type D		—
Express Company		+350.00
Japan		—
72 A31 90c **blue**	3,500.	600.
dull blue	3,500.	600.
No gum	1,400.	
On cover		*25,000.*
Pair	*7,500.*	1,300.
Block of 4	*28,000.*	*5,000.*
P# strip of 4, Impt.	*25,000.*	
a. 90c **pale blue**	3,500.	600.
No gum	1,400.	
b. 90c **dark blue**	4,250.	750.
No gum	1,700.	

The unique plate number and imprint strip of 4 of No. 72 has no gum and is valued thus.

Earliest documented use: Nov. 27, 1861.

Cancellations

Blue	+25.
Red	+75.
Green	+750.
1865 year date	+35.
"Paid"	+25.
"Registered"	+75.
Express Company	+500.
Supplementary Mail Type A	+100.

Nos. 68a, 69, 71 and 72 exist as imperforate sheet-margin singles with pen cancel. They were not regularly issued.

The 90c was distributed to several post offices in the last two weeks of August, 1861.

Owing to the Civil War, stamps and stamped envelopes in current use or available for postage in 1860, were demonetized by various post office orders, beginning in August, 1861, and extending to early January, 1862.

P. O. Department Bulletin.

"A reasonable time after hostilities began in 1861 was given for the return to the Department of all these (1851-56) stamps in the hands of postmasters, and as early as 1863 the Department issued an order declining to longer redeem them."

The Act of Congress, approved March 3, 1863, abolished carriers' fees and established a prepaid rate of two cents for drop letters, making necessary the 2-cent Jackson (No. 73).

Free City Delivery was authorized by the Act of Congress of March 3, 1863, effective in 49 cities with 449 carriers, beginning July 1, 1863.

Produced by the National Bank Note Co.
DESIGNS AS 1861 ISSUE

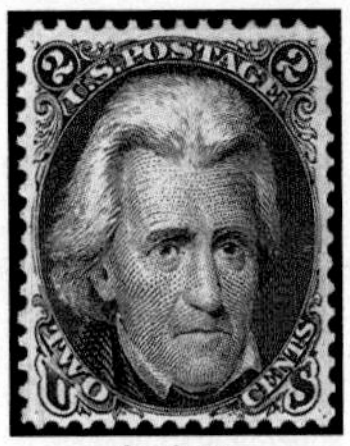

Andrew Jackson — A32

Abraham Lincoln — A33

1861-66 *Perf. 12*

73 A32 2c **black,** *1863*	375.00	70.00
gray black	375.00	70.00
intense black	375.00	75.00
No gum	140.00	
On cover		90.00
On prisoner's letter		—
On patriotic cover		*2,000.*
Pair	800.00	150.00
Block of 4	*4,000.*	*1,350.*
P# strip of 4, Impt.	*4,500.*	
P# block of 8, Impt.	*15,000.*	
Double transfer	425.00	75.00
Major double transfer of top left corner and "Postage" ("Atherton shift")		*15,000.*
Major double transfer of right side, pos. 81, right pane ("Preston shift")	*5,000.*	*4,500.*
Major double transfer of frame in all corners plus hair and chin ("Metzger shift")		—
Triple transfer		—
Short transfer	400.00	75.00
Cracked plate	—	—
a. Diagonal half used as 1c as part of 3c rate on cover		1,750.
b. Diagonal half used alone as 1c on cover		*3,000.*
c. Horiz. half used as 1c as part of 3c rate on cover		*3,500.*
d. Vert. half used as 1c as part of 3c rate on cover		2,000.
e. Vert. half used alone as 1c on cover		*4,000.*
f. Printed on both sides	—	*15,000.*
g. Laid paper	—	*12,500.*

Earliest documented use: July 1, 1863 (dated cancel on off-cover stamp); July 6, 1863 (on cover).

Cancellations

Blue	+5.00
Brown	+75.00
Red	+50.00
Orange red	+60.00
Magenta	+200.00
Ultramarine	+150.00
Orange	+200.00
Green	+1,000.
1863 year date	+5.00
Printed Precancel "Jefferson, Ohio"	—
"PAID ALL"	+40.00
"Paid"	+10.00
Numeral	+15.00
"Way"	+150.00
Railroad	+300.00
"Steam"	+40.00
Steamship	+100.00
"Steamboat"	+65.00
"Ship Letter"	+150.00
Black Carrier	+20.00
Blue Carrier	+35.00
Supp. Mail Type A or B	+100.00
Express Company	+300.00
"Short Paid"	+250.00
Territorial	+100.00
China	—

The 3c scarlet, design A25, can be found under No. 74 in the Trial Color Proofs section.

75 A26 5c **red brown**	5,750.	600.
dark red brown	5,750.	600.
No gum	2,200.	
On cover		900.
On patriotic cover		*4,000.*
Pair	*12,000.*	1,500.
Block of 4	*62,500.*	*7,750.*
Double transfer	*6,000.*	650.

Values for No. 75 reflect the normal small margins.

Earliest documented use: Jan. 2, 1862.

Cancellations

Blue	+10.
Red	+35.
Magenta	+65.
"Paid"	+25.
Supplementary Mail Type A	+50.
Express Company	+300.

76 A26 5c **brown**, *1863*	1,750.	150.
pale brown	1,750.	150.
dark brown	1,750.	150.
No gum	650.	
On cover		200.
On patriotic cover		2,000.
Pair	3,900.	325.
Block of 4	*8,750.*	1,200.
P# strip of 4, Impt.	*15,000.*	
Double transfer of top frame line	1,850.	160.
Double transfer of bottom frame line	1,850.	160.
Double transfer of top and bottom frame lines	1,900.	175.
a. 5c **black brown**	2,250.	300.
No gum	850.	
Block of 4	*9,000.*	*2,000.*
b. Laid paper		—

Values of Nos. 76, 76a reflect the normal small margins.
The plate no. strip of 4 with imprint of No. 76 is unique.

Earliest documented use: Feb. 3, 1863.

Cancellations

Blue	+5.00
Magenta	+75.00
Red	+25.00
Brown	+150.00
Green	+650.00
1865 year date	+10.00
"Paid"	+15.00
"Short Paid"	+75.00
Supp. Mail Type A or F	+55.00
Express Company	+175.00
"Steamship"	+65.00
Packet boat	—

77 A33 15c **black**, *April 1866*	4,500.	225.
full black	4,500.	225.
No gum	1,750.	
On cover to France or Germany		300.
Pair	9,500.	500.
Block of 4	*32,500.*	*1,150.*
P# block of 8, Impt.	—	
Double transfer	4,750.	250.
Cracked plate	—	—

Earliest documented use: April 21, 1866.

Cancellations

Blue	+5.
Indigo	+10.
Purple	+60.
Lavender	+150.
Violet	+75.
Magenta	+100.
Red	+35.
Brown	+125.
Green	+375.
Ultramarine	+75.
"Paid"	+15.
"Short Paid"	+85.
"Insufficiently Paid" or "Insufficiently Prepaid"	+150.
"Ship"	+50.
Steamship	+50.
Supplementary Mail Type A	+70.

78 A29 24c **lilac**, *1862*	2,600.	250.
dark lilac	2,600.	250.
a. 24c **grayish lilac**	2,600.	300.
b. 24c **gray**	2,600.	300.
No gum	950.	
On cover		325.
Pair	5,500.	525.
Block of 4	*17,500.*	1,850.
Scratch under "A" of "Postage"	—	—
c. 24c **blackish violet**	*60,000.*	*15,000.*
No gum	*22,500.*	
On cover		*20,000.*

Only three examples are recorded of No. 78c unused with original gum. No. 78c unused with and without gum are valued in the grade of fine-very fine.

d. Printed on both sides		*25,000.*
On cover		*32,500.*

Earliest documented uses: Oct. 23, 1862 (No. 78a); May 1, 1863 (No. 78c).

Cancellations

Blue	+7.50
Red	+15.00
Magenta	+90.00
Green	+400.00
"Paid"	+15.00
Numeral	+20.00
Supplementary Mail Type A	+50.00
"Free"	+100.00

Nos. 73, 76-78 exist as imperforate sheet-margin singles, all with pen cancel except No. 76 which is uncanceled. They were not regularly issued.

SAME DESIGNS AS 1861-66 ISSUES
Printed by the National Bank Note Co.

Grill

Embossed with grills of various sizes. Some authorities believe that more than one size of grill probably existed on one of the grill rolls.

A peculiarity of the United States issues from 1867 to 1870 is the grill or embossing. The object was to break the fiber of the paper so that the ink of the canceling stamp would soak in and make washing for a second using impossible. The exact date at which grilled stamps came into use is unsettled. Luff's "Postage Stamps of the United States" places the date as probably August 8, 1867.

Horizontal measurements are given first.

GRILL WITH POINTS UP

Grills A and C were made by a roller covered with ridges shaped like an inverted V. Pressing the ridges into the stamp paper forced the paper into the pyramidal pits between the ridges, causing irregular breaks in the paper. Grill B was made by a roller with raised bosses.

A. GRILL COVERING THE ENTIRE STAMP.

1867 ***Perf. 12***

79 A25 3c **rose**	8,500.	1,750.
No gum	2,750.	
On cover		2,250.
Pair	*18,000.*	4,000.
Block of 4	*55,000.*	
b. Printed on both sides		—

Earliest documented use: Aug. 13, 1867.

Cancellations

Blue	+75.
Ultramarine	+250.
Railroad	—

Values for No. 79 are for fine-very fine examples with minor perf. faults.

An essay (#79-E15) which is often mistaken for No. 79 shows the points of the grill as small squares faintly impressed in the paper but not cutting through it. On the issued stamp the grill generally breaks through the paper. Examples without defects are rare.

See Die and Plate Proofs for imperf. on stamp paper.

80 A26 5c **brown**	—	*130,000.*
a. 5c **dark brown**		*130,000.*
81 A30 30c **orange**		*100,000.*

Eight examples of Nos. 80 and 80a (four unused and four used), and eight examples of No. 81 (one in a museum and not available to collectors) are known. All are more or less faulty and/or off center. Values are for off-center examples with small perforation faults.

B. GRILL ABOUT 18x15mm (22x18 POINTS)

82 A25 3c **rose**		*240,000.*

The four known examples of No. 82 are valued in the grade of fine.

Earliest documented use: Feb. 1?, 1869 (dated cancel on off-cover stamp).

C. GRILL ABOUT 13x16mm (16 TO 17 BY 18 TO 21 POINTS)

The grilled area on each of four C grills in the sheet may total about 18x15mm when a normal C grill adjoins a fainter grill extending to the right or left edge of the stamp. This is caused by a partial erasure on the grill roller when it was changed to produce C grills instead of the all-over A grill. Do not mistake these for the B grill. Unused exists and is very rare, value unused $7,500; value used $2,750; on cover $4,500.

83 A25 3c **rose**	6,500.	1,100.
No gum	2,400.	
On cover		1,300.
Pair	*14,000.*	3,250.
Block of 4	*30,000.*	—
Double grill	*7,750.*	2,400.
Grill with points down	*7,250.*	1,350.

Earliest documented use: Nov. 16, 1867.

Cancellation

Blue	+25.

See Die and Plate Proofs for imperf. on stamp paper.
The 1c, 3c, 5c, 10c, 12c, 30c of 1861 are known with experimental C grills. They are listed in the Essays section. The 3c differs slightly from No. 83.

GRILL WITH POINTS DOWN

The grills were produced by rollers with the surface covered, or partly covered, by pyramidal bosses. On the D, E and F grills the tips of the pyramids are vertical ridges. On the Z grill the ridges are horizontal.

D. GRILL ABOUT 12x14mm (15 BY 17 TO 18 POINTS)

84 A32 2c **black**	*16,000.*	4,500.
No gum	*6,500.*	
On cover		5,000.
Pair	35,000.	9,250.
Block of 4	*80,000.*	—
Double transfer	—	—
Split grill		4,750.

No. 84 is valued in the grade of fine.

Earliest documented use: Feb. 15, 1868.

Cancellations

Red	+100.
Blue	+500.
"Paid All"	+100.

85 A25 3c **rose**	6,750.	1,250.
No gum	2,750.	
On cover		1,400.
Pair	*14,000.*	2,850.
Block of 4	*35,000.*	—
Double grill	—	
Split grill		1,350.

Earliest documented use: Feb. 2, 1868.

Cancellations

Blue	+20.
Green	+400.
"Paid"	+50.

Z. GRILL ABOUT11x14mm (13 TO 14 BY 18 POINTS)

85A A24 1c **blue**		*3,000,000.*

Two examples of No. 85A are known. One is contained in the New York Public Library collection.

85B A32 2c **black**	15,000.	1,500.
No gum	5,750.	
On cover		1,650.
Pair	*32,500.*	3,400.
Block of 4	*75,000.*	—
Double transfer	*16,000.*	1,600.
Double grill		—
Split grill		—

Earliest documented use: Jan. 17, 1868 (on piece); Feb. 11, 1868 (on cover).

Cancellations

Blue	+50.
Red	+100.
Black Carrier	+75.
"Paid All"	+75.

85C A25 3c **rose**	*25,000.*	3,750.
No gum	*9,000.*	
On cover		4,250.
Pair		—
Block of 4	*120,000.*	
Double grill	*27,000.*	

Earliest documented use: Feb. 12, 1868.

Cancellations

Green	+250.
Blue	+25.
Red	+75.
"Paid"	+50.

85D A27 10c **green**		*225,000.*

Six examples of No. 85D are known. One is contained in the New York Public Library collection. Value is for a well-centered example with small faults.

85E A28 12c **intense black**	*14,000.*	2,500.
black	*14,000.*	2,500.
No gum	*5,750.*	
On cover		3,000.
Strip of 3		—

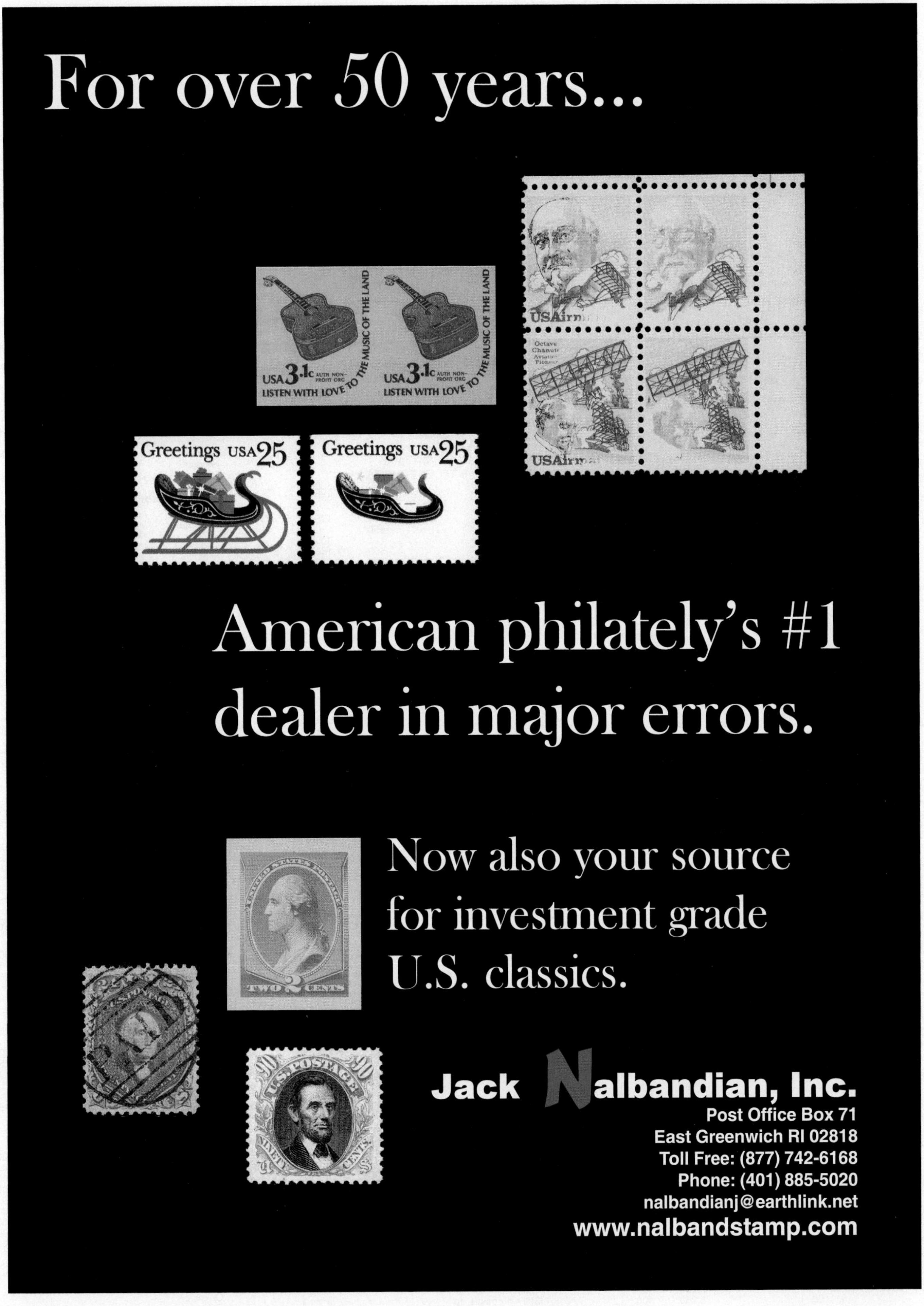
For over 50 years...
American philately's #1 dealer in major errors.
Now also your source for investment grade U.S. classics.
Jack Nalbandian, Inc.
Post Office Box 71
East Greenwich RI 02818
Toll Free: (877) 742-6168
Phone: (401) 885-5020
nalbandianj@earthlink.net
www.nalbandstamp.com

	Block of 4	—	—
	Double transfer of top frame line		2,600.

Earliest documented use: Feb. 12, 1868.

85F A33 15c	**black**		*1,000,000.*

Two examples of No. 85F are documented, one in the grade of very good, the other extremely fine. Value is for the extremely fine example.

E. GRILL ABOUT 11x13mm (14 BY 15 TO 17 POINTS)

86 A24 1c	**blue**	3,750.	550.
	No gum	1,500.	
a. 1c	**dull blue**	3,750.	525.
	No gum	1,500.	
	On cover		650.
	Pair	*8,000.*	1,150.
	Block of 4	*20,000.*	*3,300.*
	Double grill	—	675.
	Split grill	4,000.	600.
	Very thin paper		—

Earliest documented use: Mar. 9, 1868.

Cancellations

Blue	+10.
Red	+60.
Green	+400.
"Paid"	+25.
Steamboat	+90.
Red Carrier	+80.

87 A32 2c	**black**	1,850.	200.
	gray black	1,850.	200.
	No gum	725.	
	intense black	1,950.	225.
	No gum	750.	
	On cover		300.
	Pair	4,000.	425.
	Block of 4	*8,750.*	6,250.
	P# strip of 4, Impt.	*9,750.*	
	Double grill	—	—
	Double grill, one split	—	
	Triple grill		—
	Split grill	2,100.	210.
	Grill with points up	—	
	Double transfer	2,000.	210.
a.	Diagonal half used as 1c on cover		*2,000.*
b.	Vertical half used as 1c on cover		*2,000.*

Earliest documented use: Mar. 7, 1868.

Cancellations

Blue	+7.50
Purple	+40.00
Brown	+40.00
Red	+50.00
Green	+1,000.
"Paid"	+10.00
Steamship	+60.00
Black Carrier	+35.00
"Paid All"	+20.00
"Short Paid"	+65.00
Japan	—

88 A25 3c	**rose**	1,100.	27.50
	pale rose	1,100.	27.50
	rose red	1,100.	27.50
	No gum	425.	
	On cover		32.50
	Pair	2,300.	57.50
	Block of 4	*6,000.*	360.
	P# block of 8, Impt.	*13,000.*	
	Double grill	—	—
	Double grill, one split	—	—
	Triple grill	—	—
	Split grill	1,200.	32.50
	Very thin paper	1,150.	32.50
a. 3c	**lake red**	1,300.	50.
	No gum	500.	
b.	Two diagonal halves from different stamps used as 3c stamp (fraudulent use), one half having grill with points up, on cover		—

Earliest documented use: Feb. 12, 1868.

Cancellations

Blue	+2.50
Red	+5.00
Ultramarine	+3.00
Green	+80.00
"Paid"	+3.00
"Way"	+20.00
Numeral	+2.00
Steamboat	+35.00
Railroad	+25.00
Express Company	+80.00

89 A27 10c	**green**	5,500.	325.
	dark green	5,500.	325.
	blue green	5,500.	325.
	No gum	2,200.	
	On cover		425.
	Pair	*11,500.*	700.
	Block of 4	*26,000.*	*3,500.*
	Double grill	7,000.	525.
	Split grill	5,750.	350.
	Double transfer	—	350.
	Very thin paper	5,750.	350.

Earliest documented use: Feb. 21, 1868.

Cancellations

Blue	+20.
Red	+60.
"Paid"	+15.
Steamship	+50.
Japan	+225.

90 A28 12c	**black**	5,250.	400.
	gray black	5,250.	400.
	intense black	5,250.	400.
	No gum	2,100.	
	On cover		550.
	Pair	*11,000.*	850.
	Block of 4	*32,500.*	*2,750.*
	Double transfer of top frame line	5,500.	425.
	Double transfer of bottom frame line	5,500.	425.
	Double transfer of top and bottom frame lines	5,750.	475.
	Double grill	6,000.	750.
	Split grill	5,500.	425.

Earliest documented use: Mar. 3, 1868.

Cancellations

Blue	+20.
Red	+65.
Purple	—
Green	+225.
Railroad	+60.
"Paid"	+20.

91 A33 15c	**black**	13,500.	700.
	gray black	13,500.	700.
	No gum	5,250.	
	On cover		925.
	Pair	*30,000.*	1,450.
	Block of 4	*72,500.*	*12,500.*
	Double grill	—	1,000.
	Split grill	—	725.

Earliest documented use: May 2, 1868.

Cancellations

Blue	+15.
Magenta	+100.
Red	+100.
"Paid"	+30.
Supplementary Mail Type A	+100.

F. GRILL ABOUT 9x13mm (11 TO 12 BY 15 TO 17 POINTS)

92 A24 1c	**blue**	3,500.	550.
	dark blue	3,500.	550.
	No gum	1,200.	
a. 1c	**pale blue**	3,000.	475.
	No gum	950.	
	On cover		600.
	Pair	7,500.	1,150.
	Block of 4	*16,500.*	3,100.
	Double transfer	3,750.	600.
	Double grill	—	925.
	Split grill	3,750.	600.
	Double grill, one split		—
	Very thin paper	3,750.	575.

Earliest documented use: Aug. 11 1868.

Cancellations

Blue	+5.00
Red	+20.00
Green	+250.00
"Paid"	+10.00
Red Carrier	+25.00
"Paid All"	+15.00

93 A32 2c	**black**	525.	60.00
	gray black	525.	60.00
	No gum	200.	
	On cover		75.00
	Pair	1,100.	130.00
	Block of 4	2,750.	525.00
	P# strip of 4, Impt.	*6,500.*	
	P# block of 8, Impt.	—	
	Double transfer	575.	67.50
	Double grill	—	180.00
	Split grill	575.	65.00
	Double grill, one split		—
	Double grill, one quadruple split	*1,100.*	—
	Very thin paper	575.	65.00
a.	Vertical half used as 1c as part of 3c rate on cover		*1,250.*
b.	Diagonal half used as 1c as part of 3c rate on cover		*1,250.*
c.	Horizontal half used alone as 1c on cover		*2,500.*
d.	Diagonal half used alone as 1c on cover		*2,500.*

Earliest documented use: Mar. 27, 1868.

Cancellations

Blue	+5.00
Red	+15.00
Green	+200.00
"Paid"	+5.00
"Paid All"	+15.00
Black Carrier	+20.00
Red Carrier	+30.00
Japan	+350.00

94 A25 3c	**red**	400.	10.00
	rose red	400.	10.00
a. 3c	**rose**	400.	10.00
	No gum	140.	
	On cover		11.00
	Pair	850.	21.00
	Block of 4	*3,000.*	135.00
	P# block of 8, Impt.	*8,750.*	
	Double transfer	450.	12.50
	Double grill		—
	Double grill, one normal, one partial with points up		—
	Triple grill	—	160.00
	End roller grill		350.00
	Split grill	425.	10.50
	Quadruple split grill	725.	130.00
	Double grill, one quadruple split		—
	Grill with points up		—
	Very thin paper	425.	10.50
c.	Vertical pair, imperf. horiz.	*1,500.*	
	Block of 4	*10,000.*	
d.	Printed on both sides	*7,500.*	

Seven examples of No. 94d are recorded. Six are in the top row of an unused top margin imprint block of 18 (6x3).

Earliest documented use: Mar. 21, 1868.

Cancellations

Blue	+.25
Ultramarine	+3.00
Red	+3.50
Violet	+5.50
Green	+70.00
Numeral	+3.00
"Paid"	+2.25
"Paid All"	+12.50
"Free"	+20.00
Railroad	+30.00
Steamboat	+40.00
Packet boat	+80.00
Express Company	+50.00

See Die and Plate Proofs for imperf. on stamp paper.

95 A26 5c	**brown**	3,750.	900.
	No gum	1,400.	
	dark brown	3,900.	1,000.
	No gum	1,450.	
	On cover		950.
	Pair	7,750.	1,900.
	Block of 4	*17,500.*	*8,500.*
	Double transfer of top frame line	—	—
	Double transfer of bottom frame line	—	
	Double grill	—	—
	Split grill	4,250.	925.
	Very thin paper	4,000.	900.
a. 5c	**black brown**	4,500.	1,200.
	No gum	1,700.	

Earliest documented use: Aug. 19, 1868.

Cancellations

Blue	+10.
Magenta	+55.
Violet	+60.
Red	+50.
Green	+200.
"Paid"	+25.
"Free"	+50.
"Steamship"	+100.

Values of Nos. 95, 95a reflect the normal small margins.

96 A27 10c	**yellow green**	3,250.	275.
	green	3,250.	275.
	blue green	3,250.	275.
	dark green	3,250.	350.
	No gum	1,150.	
	On cover		325.
	Pair	6,750.	575.
	Block of 4	*26,500.*	*3,500.*
	P# strip of 4, Impt.	*29,000.*	
	Double transfer	—	—
	Double grill	—	450.
	Split grill	3,500.	300.
	Quadruple split grill		725.
	Very thin paper	3,500.	300.

Earliest documented use: May 28, 1868.

Cancellations

Blue	+5.00
Red	+25.00
Magenta	+30.00
Green	+200.00
"Paid"	+10.00
"Free"	+50.00
Supplementary Mail Type A	—
Steamship	+75.00
Japan	+200.00
China	—

97 A28 12c	**black**	3,500.	300.
	gray black	3,500.	300.
	No gum	1,300.	
	On cover		350.
	Pair	7,250.	625.
	Block of 4	*30,000.*	*2,500.*
	P# strip of 4, Impt.	*32,500.*	
	Double transfer of top frame line	3,900.	325.
	Double transfer of bottom frame line	3,900.	325.
	Double transfer of top and bottom frame lines	—	350.
	Double grill	—	525.
	Triple grill		—
	Split grill	3,900.	325.
	End roller grill		—
	Very thin paper	3,900.	325.

Earliest documented use: May 27, 1868.

Cancellations

Blue	+5.00
Red	+50.00
Magenta	+50.00
Brown	+50.00
Green	+250.00
Purple	+150.00
"Paid"	+15.00
"Insufficiently Prepaid"	+100.00
"Paid All"	+25.00
Supplementary Mail Type A	+50.00

98 A33 15c	**black**	4,500.	375.
	gray black	4,500.	375.
	No gum	1,700.	
	On cover		425.
	Pair	*9,500.*	775.

Block of 4 35,000. 6,000.
P# block of 8, Impt. 47,500.
Double transfer of upper right corner — —
Double grill — 525.
Split grill 4,750. 400.
Quadruple split grill 5,250. 700.
Very thin paper 4,750. 400.

Value for the plate block is for an example in fine condition.
Earliest documented use: May 4, 1868.

Cancellations

Blue +2.50
Magenta +75.00
Red +150.00
Orange red +40.00
Green +275.00
Orange +175.00
Purple +100.00
Lavender +150.00
"Paid" +20.00
"Insufficiently Prepaid" +135.00
"Insufficiently Paid" +135.00
Japan +300.00
Supplementary Mail Type A +80.00

99 A29 24c **gray lilac** 8,500. 1,300.
gray 8,500. 1,300.
No gum 3,500.
On cover 2,250.
Pair *18,000.* 2,750.
Block of 4 *42,500.* *9,500.*
P# block of 8, Impt. *85,000.*
Double grill 9,500. 2,200.
Split grill 8,750. 1,400.
Scratch under "A" of "Postage" —

Earliest documented use: Jan. 5, 1869.

Cancellations

Blue +15.
Red +100.
"Paid" +50.

100 A30 30c **orange** 8,500. 900.
deep orange 8,500. 900.
No gum 3,250.
On cover 2,000.
Pair *18,000.* 1,900.
Block of 4 *42,500.* *10,000.*
Double grill 11,000. 1,800.
Split grill 8,750. 950.
Double grill, one split —
Triple grill, two split —

Values for No. 100 are for examples with small margins, especially at sides. Large-margined examples sell for much more.

Earliest documented use: Nov. 10, 1868.

Cancellations

Blue +10.
Red +65.
Magenta +75.
Green +500.
"Paid" +50.
Supplementary Mail Type A +100.
Japan +400.

101 A31 90c **blue** 14,500. 2,200.
dark blue 14,500. 2,200.
No gum 5,500.
On cover *100,000.*
Pair *31,500.* 4,750.
Block of 4 *75,000.* *25,000.*
Double grill *19,000.*
Split grill 15,000. 2,300.

Two usages on cover are recorded (one being a cover front). Value is for use on full cover to Peru.

Earliest documented use: May 8, 1869.

Cancellations

Blue +70.
Red +150.
Japan +600.
"Paid" +50.

RE-ISSUE OF 1861-66 ISSUES
Produced by the National Bank Note Co.
Without grill, hard white paper, with white crackly gum.
The 1, 2, 5, 10 and 12c were printed from new plates of 100 subjects each.

1875 ***Perf. 12***

102 A24 1c **blue** *(3195)* *900.* *1,250.*
No gum *400.*
On cover —
Block of 4 *7,500.* —
103 A32 2c **black** *(979)* *4,250.* *7,000.*
No gum *2,000.*
Block of 4 *30,000.*
104 A25 3c **brown red** *(465)* *4,750.* *12,500.*
No gum *2,250.*
Block of 4 *37,500.*
105 A26 5c **brown** *(672)* *3,250.* *6,000.*
No gum *1,600.*
Block of 4 *26,500.*
106 A27 10c **green** *(451)* *4,000.* *20,000.*
No gum *1,900.*
Block of 4 *30,000.*
107 A28 12c **black** *(389)* *4,750.* *9,500.*
No gum *2,350.*
Block of 4 *32,500.*
108 A33 15c **black** *(397)* *5,250.* *16,000.*
No gum *2,600.*
Block of 4 *40,000.*
109 A29 24c **deep violet** *(346)* *6,500.* *17,500.*
No gum *3,000.*
Block of 4 *55,000.*
110 A30 30c **brownish orange** *(346)* *6,750.* *17,500.*
No gum *3,250.*
Pair *16,500.*
Block of 4 *57,500.*
111 A31 90c **blue** *(317)* *7,250.* *110,000.*
No gum *3,500.*

Earliest documented uses: No. 102, July 25, 1881; No. 104, July ?, 1883 (dated cancel on off-cover stamp); No. 111, Nov. 30, 1888 (dated cancel on off-cover stamp).

These stamps can be distinguished from the 1861-66 issue by the brighter colors, the sharper proof-like impressions and the paper which is very white instead of yellowish. The gum is almost always somewhat yellowed with age, and unused stamps with original gum are valued with such gum.

Numbers in parentheses are quantities sold.

Five examples are recorded of No. 111 used, one of which has a non-contemporaneous cancel. Value is for centered and sound example (two are known thus).

PLEASE NOTE:

Stamps are valued in the grade of very fine unless otherwise indicated.

Values for early and valuable stamps are for examples with certificates of authenticity from acknowledged expert committees, or examples sold with the buyer having the right of certification. This applies to examples with original gum as well as examples without gum. Beware of stamps offered "as is," as the gum on some unused stamps offered with "original gum" may be fraudulent, and unused stamps offered without may in some cases be altered or faintly canceled used stamps.

VALUES FOR NEVER-HINGED STAMPS PRIOR TO SCOTT No. 182

This catalogue does not value pre-1879 stamps in never-hinged condition. Premiums for never-hinged condition in the classic era invariably are even larger than those premiums listed for the 1879 and later issues. Generally speaking, the earlier the stamp is listed in the catalogue, the larger will be the never-hinged premium. On some early classics, the premium will be several multiples of the unused, hinged values given in the catalogue.

Produced by the National Bank Note Co.
Plates for the 1c, 2c, 3c, 6c, 10c and 12c consisted of 300 subjects in two panes of 150 each. For the 15c, 24c, 30c and 90c plates of 100 subjects each.

NOTE: Stamps of the 1869 issue without grill cannot be guaranteed except when unused and with the original gum or traces of the original gum. This does not apply to No. 114 on gray paper.

Franklin — A34

Post Horse and Rider — A35

G. Grill measuring 9½x9mm
(12 by 11 to 11½ points)

1869 **Hard Wove Paper** ***Perf. 12***

112 A34 1c **buff** 800. 175.
brown orange 800. 175.
dark brown orange 850. 200.
No gum 300.
On cover, single 300.
Pair 1,650. 400.
Block of 4 *6,000.* *2,250.*
Margin block of 4, arrow *6,250.*
P# block of 10, Impt. —
Double transfer — —
Double grill 1,200. 350.
Split grill 900. 225.
Double grill, one split —
Double grill, one quadruple split —
b. Without grill, original gum *10,000.*

Earliest documented use: Apr. 1, 1869.

Cancellations

Blue +15.
Ultramarine +1,000.
Magenta +55.
Purple +75.
Red +50.
Green +1,000.
"Paid" +50.
Numeral +100.
Steamship +110.
Black town +30.
Blue town +30.
Red town +80.
Black Carrier +80.
Blue Carrier +100.
Japan +600.

113 A35 2c **brown** 750. 100.
pale brown 750. 100.
dark brown 750. 100.
yellow brown 750. 100.
No gum 275.
On cover, single 140.
Pair 1,600. 250.
Block of 4 3,750. 1,350.
Margin block of 4, arrow 3,850.
P# block of 10, Impt. —
Double grill — 325.
Split grill 900. 125.
Quadruple split grill — 450.
End roller grill 1,200.
Double transfer 120.
b. Without grill, original gum *4,500.*
c. Half used as 1c on cover, diagonal, vertical or horizontal *6,000.*
d. Printed on both sides *9,000.*

Earliest documented use: Mar. 20, 1869.

Cancellations

Blue +15.
Red +30.
Orange red +35.
Orange +100.
Magenta +35.
Purple +40.
Ultramarine +60.
Green +500.
Brown +150.
"Paid" +15.
"Paid All" +25.
Steamship +75.
Black town +10.
Blue town +30.
Japan +250.
Blue Carrier +90.
Black Carrier +80.
China —
Printed Precancellation "Jefferson, Ohio" +6,500.

Locomotive — A36

Washington — A37

114 A36 3c	**ultramarine**	325.	20.00
	pale ultramarine	325.	20.00
	dark ultramarine	325.	20.00
	No gum	115.	
	blue	625.	100.00
	No gum	225.	
	violet blue		—
	On cover		25.00
	Pair	700.	45.00
	Block of 4	1,700.	450.00
	Margin block of 4, arrow	1,850.	
	P# block of 10, Impt.	*7,500.*	
	Double transfer	400.	37.50
	Double grill	625.	110.00
	Triple grill	—	—
	Sextuple grill	—	*7,000.*
	Split grill	375.	40.00
	Quadruple split grill	675.	150.00
	Double grill, one split		—
	Double grill, one quadruple split		—
	End roller grill	—	—
	Grill with points up		—
	Gray paper	—	100.00
	On cover		850.00
	Without grill		—
	Cracked plate	—	160.00
a.	Without grill, original gum	*12,500.*	
b.	Vert. one-third used as 1c on cover		—
c.	Vert. two-thirds used as 2c on cover		*5,000.*
e.	Printed on both sides		—

The grill-with-points-up variety is found on a unique margin "pair" of stamps where the paper was folded over prior to perforating and grilling. The stamps have drastic freak perfs.

The existence of the violet blue shade has been questioned by specialists. The editors would like to receive authenticated evidence of its existence.

Earliest documented use: Mar. 27, 1869.

Cancellations

Blue	+5.
Ultramarine	+25.
Magenta	+35.
Purple	+75.
Violet	+65.
Red	+15.
Orange red	+20.
Brown	+200.
Green	+500.
Orange	—
Yellow	—
Black town	+3.
Blue town	+7.
Red town	+30.
Numeral	+15.
"Paid"	+20.
"Paid All"	+15.
"Steamboat"	—
"Steamship"	+50.
Ship	+35.
"U. S. Ship"	+450.
Railroad	+30.
Packet Boat	+100.
Black Carrier	+30.
Blue Carrier	+40.
Express Company	+250.
"Way"	—
"Free"	+150.
Alaska	—
Japan	+600.

The authenticity of the yellow cancel has been questioned by some specialists. The editors would like to see an expertizing certificate for this stamp and cancel.

115 A37 6c	**ultramarine**	3,000.	250.
	pale ultramarine	3,000.	250.
	No gum	1,150.	
	On cover		450.
	Pair	6,250.	600.
	Block of 4	*16,500.*	*9,000.*
	Margin block of 4, arrow	*17,500.*	
	Double grill	—	675.
	Split grill	3,250.	325.
	Quadruple split grill	—	850.
	Double transfer		290.
b.	Vertical half used as 3c on cover		*50,000.*

Earliest documented use: Apr. 26, 1869.

No. 115b is unique.

Cancellations

Blue	+5.
Brown	+125.
Magenta	+40.
Purple	+75.
Red	+50.
Green	+1,000.
"Paid"	+15.
"Paid All"	+25.
Black town	+30.
"Short Paid"	+75.
"Insufficiently Paid"	+75.
Steamship	+45.
Railroad	+50.
Japan	+1,500.

Shield and Eagle — A38

S.S. "Adriatic" — A39

116 A38 10c	**yellow**	2,500.	150.
	yellowish orange	2,500.	150.
	No gum	950.	
	On cover		425.
	Pair	5,250.	350.
	Block of 4	*14,000.*	*8,000.*
	Margin block of 4, arrow	*14,000.*	
	Double grill	—	425.
	Split grill	2,750.	175.
	End roller grill	—	—

Earliest documented use: Apr. 1, 1869.

Cancellations

Blue	+35.
Magenta	+60.
Purple	+250.
Red	+40.
Ultramarine	+200.
Green	+5,000.
Black town	+20.
Numeral	—
Steamship	+35.
Railroad	+45.
"Paid"	+15.
"Paid All"	+30.
"Insufficiently Paid"	+50.
Supplementary Mail Type A	+150.
Express Company	—
Alaska	+5,000.
St. Thomas	—
Hawaii	—
Japan	+150.
China	—

117 A39 12c	**green**	2,500.	160.
	yellowish green	2,500.	160.
	bluish green	2,750.	200.
	No gum	950.	
	On cover		500.
	Pair	5,250.	340.
	Block of 4	*14,000.*	*1,800.*
	Margin block of 4, arrow	*14,500.*	
	Double grill	—	425.
	Split grill	3,000.	190.
	Double grill, one quadruple split		—
	End roller grill		600.

Earliest documented use: Apr. 1, 1869.

Cancellations

Blue	+150.
Magenta	+125.
Purple	+250.
Brown	+200.
Red	+150.
Green	+4,000.
Numeral	+125.
"Paid"	+25.
"Paid All"	+40.
"Too Late"	+100.
"Insufficiently Paid"	+125.
Black town	+35.
Red town	+200.
Japan	+500.

Landing of Columbus — A40

No. 118 has horizontal shading lines at the left and right sides of the vignette.

118 A40 15c	**brown & blue,** type I, Picture unframed	10,000.	750.
	dark brown & blue	10,000.	750.
	No gum	3,750.	
	On cover		1,900.
	Pair	*22,500.*	1,750.
	Block of 4	*60,000.*	*30,000.*
	Double grill	*18,000.*	950.
	Split grill	10,500.	800.
a.	Without grill, original gum	*15,000.*	

Earliest documented use: Mar. 31, 1869 (dated cancel on off-cover stamp); Apr. 2, 1869 (on cover).

Cancellations

Blue	+65.
Red	+90.
Brown	+150.
"Paid"	+50.
"Paid All"	+100.
"Insufficiently Paid"	+150.
Black town	+50.
Blue town	+120.
Steamship	+100.

A40a

No. 119 has diagonal shading lines at the left and right sides of the vignette.

119 A40a 15c	**brown & blue,** type II, Picture framed	3,750.	275.
	dark brown & blue	3,750.	275.
	No gum	1,450.	
	On cover		900.
	Pair	8,000.	600.
	Block of 4	*18,500.*	*9,000.*
	P# block of 8, Impt.	*45,000.*	
	Double transfer	—	—
	Double grill	6,000.	525.
	Split grill	4,000.	350.
b.	Center inverted	*1,250,000.*	*17,500.*
	No gum	750,000.	
c.	Center double, one inverted		*80,000.*

Earliest documented use: Apr. 5, 1869.

Cancellations

Blue	+60.
Purple	+110.
Magenta	+110.
Red	+150.
Brown	+200.
Green	+1,500.
Numeral	+75.
"Paid"	+20.
"Paid All"	+35.
Black town	+30.
Blue town	+75.
Red town	+110.
"Steamship"	+75.
Supp. Mail Type A or F	+40.
Japan	+500.

Most examples of No. 119b are faulty. Values are for fine centered examples with only minimal faults. Three examples of No. 119b unused are recorded; only one has original gum.

Three examples of No. 119c are recorded. Value is for the finer of the two sound examples.

The Declaration of Independence — A41

120 A41 24c	**green & violet**	9,500.	775.
	bluish green & violet	9,500.	775.
	No gum	3,750.	
	On cover, domestic usage		*12,500.*
	On cover, foreign usage		*24,000.*
	Pair	*21,000.*	1,650.
	Block of 4	*52,500.*	*25,000.*
	Double grill	—	2,250.
	Split grill	9,750.	900.
a.	Without grill, original gum	*13,500.*	
b.	Center inverted	*750,000.*	*22,500.*
	On cover		*105,000.*
	Pair		*57,500.*
	Block of 4		*600,000.*

Earliest documented use: Apr. 7, 1869 (No. 120); Mar. 1874 (No. 120b).

Cancellations

Blue	+250.
Red	+300.
Black town	+100.
Red town	+400.
"Paid All"	+150.
"Steamship"	+250.
Supp. Mail Type A	+200.
China	+750.

Most examples of No. 120b are faulty. Values are for fine centered examples with only minimal faults. No. 120b unused is valued without gum, as all of the three examples available to collectors are without gum.

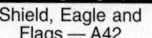

Shield, Eagle and Flags — A42

Lincoln — A43

121 A42 30c	**ultramarine & carmine**	7,500.	550.
	ultramarine & dark carmine	7,500.	550.
	No gum	3,000.	
	On cover, domestic usage		*17,500.*
	On cover, foreign usage		*32,500.*
	Pair	*16,500.*	1,250.
	Block of 4	*40,000.*	*3,750.*
	Double grill	—	1,250.
	Split grill	8,000.	600.
	Double paper (without grill), original gum	*8,250.*	
a.	Without grill, original gum	*12,000.*	
	Block of 4	*50,000.*	
	P# block of 8, Impt.	—	
b.	Flags inverted	*1,000,000.*	*100,000.*
	No gum	*250,000.*	

Seven examples of No. 121b unused are recorded. Only one has part of its original gum.

Earliest documented use: May 22, 1869.

Cancellations

Blue	+200.
Red	+250.
Brown	+600.
Purple	+1,000.
Green	+7,500.
"Paid"	+50.
"Paid All"	+250.
Black town	+100.
Steamship	+85.
"Steam"	+70.
Supp. Mail Type A	+75.
Japan	+600.
China	—

122 A43 90c	**carmine & black**	13,000.	2,500.
	carmine rose & black	13,000.	2,500.
	No gum	5,000.	
	On cover		—
	Pair	*32,500.*	*6,000.*
	Block of 4	*115,000.*	*50,000.*
	Split grill	—	—
a.	Without grill, original gum	*25,000.*	

Cancellations

Blue	+1,500.
Red	+500.
Orange red	+600.
Brown	+2,000.
Purple	+3,000.
Ultramarine	+1,200.
Black town	+1,500.
Red town	+1,750.
Magenta town	+2,500.
"Paid"	—
"Paid All"	—
N.Y. steamship	+1,000.

Nos. 112, 114, 117, 118, 120b, 121, 122 exist as imperf. singles. They were not regularly issued.

CANCELLATIONS

The common type of cancellation on the 1869 issue is the block or cork similar to illustrations above. Japanese cancellations seen on this issue (not illustrated) resulted from the sale of U.S. stamps in Japanese cities where post offices were maintained for mail going from Japan to the United States.

RE-ISSUE OF 1869 ISSUE

Produced by the National Bank Note Co.

Without grill, hard white paper, with white crackly gum.

The gum is almost always somewhat yellowed with age, and unused stamps with original gum are valued with such gum.

A new plate of 150 subjects was made for the 1c and for the frame of the 15c. The frame on the 15c is the same as type I but without the fringe of brown shading lines around central vignette.

1875 ***Perf. 12***

123 A34 1c	**buff** *(10,000)*	650.	400.
	No gum	275.	
	Block of 4	*3,500.*	
	On cover		*3,000.*
124 A35 2c	**brown** *(4755)*	750.	875.
	No gum	300.	
	Block of 4	*4,500.*	
	On cover		*12,500.*
125 A36 3c	**blue** *(1406)*	*5,500.*	*27,500.*
	No gum	2,750.	
	On cover		—

Cancellation

Supplementary Mail Type F	—

Very few authenticated sound used examples of No. 125 are recorded. The used value is for an attractive fine to very fine example with minimal faults. Examples of No. 114 with faint or pressed-out grill are frequently offered as No. 125. Expertization by competent authorities is required.

126 A37 6c	**blue** *(2226)*	2,000.	*2,750.*
	No gum	900.	
	Block of 4	*24,000.*	
	On cover		—
127 A38 10c	**yellow** *(1947)*	2,000.	2,000.
	No gum	900.	
	Block of 4	*19,000.*	
	On cover		*22,500.*
128 A39 12c	**green** *(1584)*	2,750.	*3,250.*
	No gum	1,250.	
	Block of 4	*30,000.*	
	On cover		—
129 A40 15c	**brown & blue,** Type III, *(1981)*	1,750.	1,300.
	No gum	800.	
	Pair		*6,000.*
	Block of 4	*29,000.*	
	On cover		*22,500.*
a.	Imperf. horizontally, single	*6,250.*	*7,000.*
	No gum	4,000.	
130 A41 24c	**green & violet** *(2091)*	2,500.	1,750.
	No gum	1,100.	
	Pair		*10,000.*
	On cover		*27,500.*
131 A42 30c	**ultra & carmine** *(1535)*	3,000.	3,000.
	No gum	1,450.	
	Pair		*28,000.*
132 A43 90c	**carmine & black** *(1356)*	4,500.	*6,500.*
	No gum	1,900.	
	Pair		*32,500.*
	Block of 4	*35,000.*	
	P# block of 10, Impt.	*325,000.*	

Numbers in parentheses are quantities sold.

Two used examples of No. 129a are recorded. Both are faulty and are valued thus.

Earliest documented uses:
No. 123, Dec. 9, 1877;
No. 124, Mar. 20, 1880;
No. 127, Nov. 11, 1880;
No. 128, Mar. 20, 1880.
No. 129, Mar. 20, 1880;
No. 130, Mar. 27, 1880.

RE-ISSUE OF 1869 ISSUE

Produced by the American Bank Note Co.

Without grill, soft porous paper.

1880-82

133 A34 1c	**buff,** issued with gum (5,000)	350.	350.
	No gum	150.	
	Block of 4, with gum	1,750.	
	Margin block of 10, Impt. & P#	*22,500.*	
	On cover		1,900.
a.	1c **brown orange,** issued without gum, *1881-82* (18,252)	225.	300.
	Block of 4, without gum	1,050.	
	Margin block of 10, Impt. & P#, without gum	*22,500.*	

Earliest documented use: Oct. 5, 1880 (No. 133).

PRODUCED BY THE NATIONAL BANK NOTE COMPANY

Plates of 200 subjects in two panes of 100 each.

Franklin — A44

Jackson — A45

Washington — A46

Lincoln — A47

Edwin M. Stanton — A48

Jefferson — A49

Henry Clay — A50

Daniel Webster — A51

Two varieties of grill are known on this issue.

H. Grill about 10x12mm (11 to 13 by 14 to 16 points.) On all values 1c to 90c.

I. Grill about 8½x10mm (10 to 11 by 10 to 13 points.) On 1, 2, 3, 6, 7, 10 and 15c.

On the 1870-71 stamps the grill impressions are usually faint or incomplete. This is especially true of the H grill, which often shows only a few points.

Values for 1c-7c are for stamps showing well-defined grills.

Killer cancellation of the oval grid type with letters or numeral centers was first used in 1876 Bank Note issues. By order of the Postmaster-General (July 23, 1860) it was prohibited to use the town mark as a canceling instrument, and a joined town and killer cancellation was developed.

Numeral cancellations-see "Postal Markings-Examples."

White Wove Paper, Thin to Medium Thick.

1870-71 ***Perf. 12***

134 A44	1c **ultramarine,** *Apr. 1870*	2,500.	200.00
	pale ultramarine	2,500.	200.00
	dark ultramarine	2,500.	200.00
	No gum	950.	
	On cover		230.00
	Pair	*5,250.*	425.00
	Block of 4	*12,500.*	1,100.
	Double transfer	2,750.	220.00
	Double grill	—	350.00
	Split grill	3,000.	220.00
	Quadruple split grill	—	550.00
	End roller grill		725.00

Earliest documented use: Apr. 9, 1870.

Cancellations

Blue	+5.00
Red	+15.00
Green	+100.00
"Paid"	+10.00
"Paid All"	+20.00
"Steamship"	+45.00

135 A45	2c **red brown,** *Apr. 1870*	1,250.	80.00
	pale red brown	1,250.	80.00
	dark red brown	1,250.	80.00
	No gum	475.	
	On cover		105.00
	Pair	2,600.	170.00
	Block of 4	6,000.	475.00
	Double grill	1,650.	150.00
	Split grill	1,300.	95.00
	Quadruple split grill	*2,500.*	240.00
	End roller grill	*2,000.*	*400.00*
	Grill with points up		*500.00*
a.	Diagonal half used as 1c on cover		—
b.	Vertical half used as 1c on cover		—

Earliest documented use: July 14, 1870.

Cancellations

Blue	+3.00
Red	+10.00
Brown	+8.00
Green	+100.00
"Paid"	+5.00
"Paid All"	+10.00
Numeral	+5.00
China	—

136 A46	3c **green,** *Mar. 1870*	750.	27.50
	pale green	750.	27.50
	yellow green	750.	27.50
	deep green	750.	27.50
	No gum	275.	
	On cover		32.50
	Pair	1,550.	57.50
	Block of 4	3,500.	220.00
	P# block of 10, Impt.	*9,000.*	
	P# block of 12, Impt.	*11,000.*	
	Printed on both sides	—	
	Double transfer	—	32.50
	Double grill	1,150.	85.00
	Split grill	800.	32.50
	Quadruple split grill	—	150.00
	End roller grill		275.00
	Cracked plate	—	100.00
a.	Pair, one without grill, on cover		—

Earliest documented use: Mar. 24, 1870.

Cancellations

Blue	+1.00
Purple	+2.50
Magenta	+5.00
Red	+5.00
Orange red	+6.00
Orange	+10.00
Brown	+2.50
Green	+45.00
"Paid"	+2.50
Railroad	+10.00
"Steamship"	+20.00
"Paid All"	+15.00
Numeral	+4.00
"Free"	+25.00

See Die and Plate Proofs for imperf. on stamp paper.

137 A47	6c **carmine,** *Apr. 1870*	6,000.	525.00
	pale carmine	6,000.	525.00
	carmine rose	6,000.	525.00
	No gum	2,250.	
	On cover		750.00
	Pair	*12,500.*	1,100.
	Block of 4	*28,500.*	
	Double grill	—	900.00
	Split grill	*6,250.*	550.00
	Quadruple split grill	—	950.00
	End roller grill	*7,500.*	*1,100.*
a.	Pair, one without grill		—
	Strip of 4 + single, one in strip without grill, on cover		—

Earliest documented use: Apr. 11, 1870.

Cancellations

Blue	+10.
Red	+35.
"Paid"	+35.

138 A48	7c **vermilion,** *1871*	5,000.	525.
	deep vermilion	5,000.	525.
	No gum	1,900.	
	On cover		700.
	Pair	10,500.	1,100.
	Block of 4	*25,000.*	
	Double grill		825.
	Split grill	5,250.	550.
	Quadruple split grill		950.
	End roller grill		*1,000.*

Earliest documented use: Feb. 12, 1871.

Cancellations

Blue	+10.00
Purple	+20.00
Red	+35.00
Green	+200.00
"Paid"	+25.00

The 7c stamps, Nos. 138 and 149, were issued for a 7c rate of July 1, 1870, to Prussia, German States and Austria, including Hungary, via Hamburg (on the Hamburg-American Line steamers), or Bremen (on North German Lloyd ships), but issue was delayed by the Franco-Prussian War.

The rate for this service was reduced to 6c in 1871.

For several months there was no 7c rate, but late in 1871 the Prussian closed mail rate via England was reduced to 7c which revived an important use for the 7c stamps.

The rate to Denmark direct via Baltic Lloyd ships, or via Bremen and Hamburg as above, was 7c from Jan. 1, 1872.

139 A49	10c **brown,** *Apr. 1870*	7,500.	800.
	yellow brown	7,500.	800.
	dark brown	7,500.	800.
	No gum	2,800.	
	On cover		1,000.
	Pair	*15,500.*	1,600.
	Block of 4	*35,000.*	—
	Double grill	—	1,350.
	Split grill	7,750.	825.
	End roller grill		*1,700.*

Earliest documented use: May 6, 1870.

Cancellations

Blue	+15.
Red	+50.
"Steamship"	+50.
"Honolulu Paid All"	—

140 A50	12c **dull violet,** *Apr. 1870*	*27,500.*	3,500.
	No gum	*13,000.*	
	On cover		*6,750.*
	Pair	*60,000.*	*8,000.*
	Strip of 3		*16,000.*
	Strip of 4		*20,000.*
	Block of 4	*130,000.*	
	Split grill	—	3,750.
	End roller grill		*7,000.*

Earliest documented use: June 17, 1870.

Cancellations

Blue	+50.
Red	+100.
"Paid all"	—

141 A51	15c **orange,** *Apr. 1870*	9,000.	1,400.
	bright orange	9,000.	1,400.
	deep orange	9,000.	1,400.
	No gum	3,250.	
	On cover		2,100.
	Pair	19,000.	3,000.
	Block of 4	*45,000.*	—
	Double grill		*4,000.*
	Split grill	9,250.	1,500.
	Quadruple split grill		—

Earliest documented use: June 2, 1870.

Cancellations

Blue	+20.
Purple	+50.
Red	+90.
Green	+300.

General Winfield Scott — A52

Alexander Hamilton — A53

142 A52	24c **purple**	—	7,500.
	On cover		—
	Pair, double grill		—
	Split grill		—
	End roller grill		—
	Grill with points up		—

Earliest documented use: July 11, 1872.

Cancellations

Red	+500.
Blue	+500.
Purple	—

The pair of No. 142 is the unique multiple of this stamp.

143 A53	30c **black,** *Apr. 1870*	20,000.	3,750.
	full black	20,000.	3,750.
	No gum	7,500.	
	On cover		4,750.
	Pair	*42,500.*	8,000.
	Block of 4	*100,000.*	—
	Double grill		—
	End roller grill		*5,000.*

Earliest documented use: Aug. 18, 1870.

Cancellations

Blue	+65.
Red	+125.

Commodore Oliver Hazard Perry — A54

144 A54	90c **carmine,** *Apr. 12, 1870*	25,000.	2,500.
	dark carmine	25,000.	2,500.
	No gum	10,000.	
	On cover		—
	Pair	*55,000.*	5,500.
	Block of 4	*125,000.*	*12,500.*
	Double grill		—
	Split grill		2,600.

Cancellations

Blue	+80.
Red	+140.

PRODUCED BY THE NATIONAL BANK NOTE COMPANY.

White Wove Paper, Thin to Medium Thick.

Issued (except 3c, 6c and 7c) in April, 1870.

Without Grill.

1870-71 ***Perf. 12***

145 A44	1c **ultramarine**	675.	20.00
	pale ultramarine	675.	20.00
	dark ultramarine	675.	20.00
	gray blue	675.	20.00
	No gum	250.	
	On cover		22.50
	Pair	1,400.	42.50
	Block of 4	3,250.	125.00
	P# block of 12, Impt.	*4,500.*	
	Double transfer	—	25.00
	Worn plate	675.	20.00

Only one plate block of No. 145 is known in private hands. It is of average condition and is without gum. Value is based on 1998 auction sale.

Earliest documented use: May 7, 1870.

Cancellations

Blue	+.1.00
Ultramarine	+2.50
Magenta	+2.00
Purple	+2.00
Brown	+2.00
Red	+5.00
Green	+55.00
"Paid"	+3.00
"Paid All"	+15.00
"Steamship"	+25.00
Railroad	+20.00
Numeral	+2.00

146 A45	2c **red brown**	375.	17.50
	pale red brown	375.	17.50
	dark red brown	375.	17.50
	No gum	140.	
	orange brown	400.	19.00
	No gum	150.	
	On cover		20.00
	Pair	775.	37.50
	Block of 4	1,750.	120.00
	P# block of 10, Impt.	*7,000.*	
	Double transfer	—	20.00
a.	Diagonal half used as 1c on cover		*700.00*
b.	Vertical half used as 1c on cover		*800.00*
c.	Horiz. half used as 1c on cover		*800.00*
d.	Double impression	*6,500.*	

The No. 146 plate block is unique. Value is 1998 auction realization. No. 146d is also unique. It has VG-Fine centering and faults and is valued thus.

Earliest documented use: May 7, 1870.

Cancellations

Blue	+.50
Purple	+.75
Red	+3.00
Green	+55.00
Brown	+1.00
"Paid"	+2.00
"Paid All"	+10.00
Numeral	+2.00

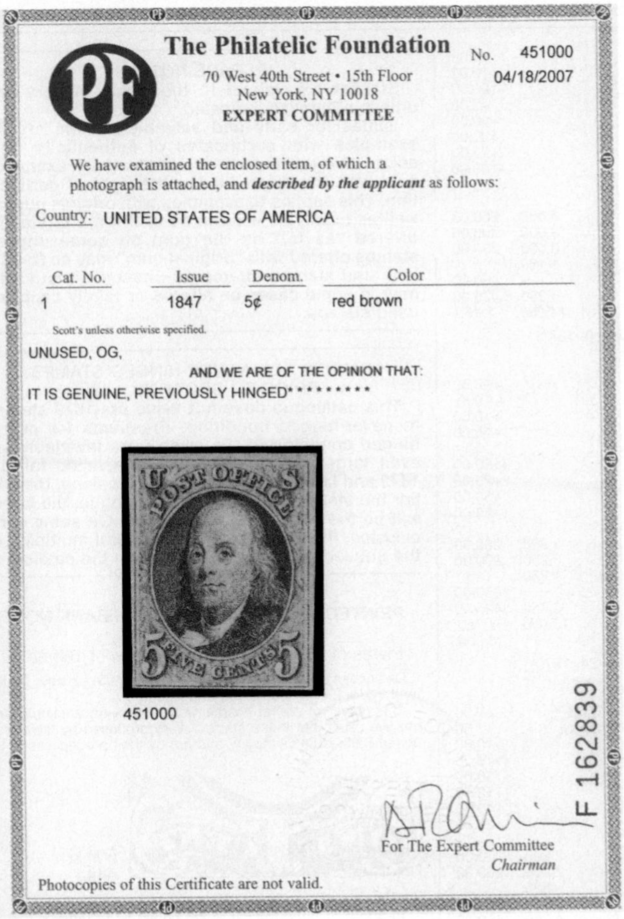

The Philatelic Foundation
70 West 40th Street • 15th Floor
New York, NY 10018
EXPERT COMMITTEE

No. 451000
04/18/2007

We have examined the enclosed item, of which a photograph is attached, and *described by the applicant* as follows:

Country: UNITED STATES OF AMERICA

Cat. No.	Issue	Denom.	Color
1	1847	5¢	red brown

Scott's unless otherwise specified.

UNUSED, OG,

AND WE ARE OF THE OPINION THAT:

IT IS GENUINE, PREVIOUSLY HINGED*********

451000

F 162839

For The Expert Committee
Chairman

Photocopies of this Certificate are not valid.

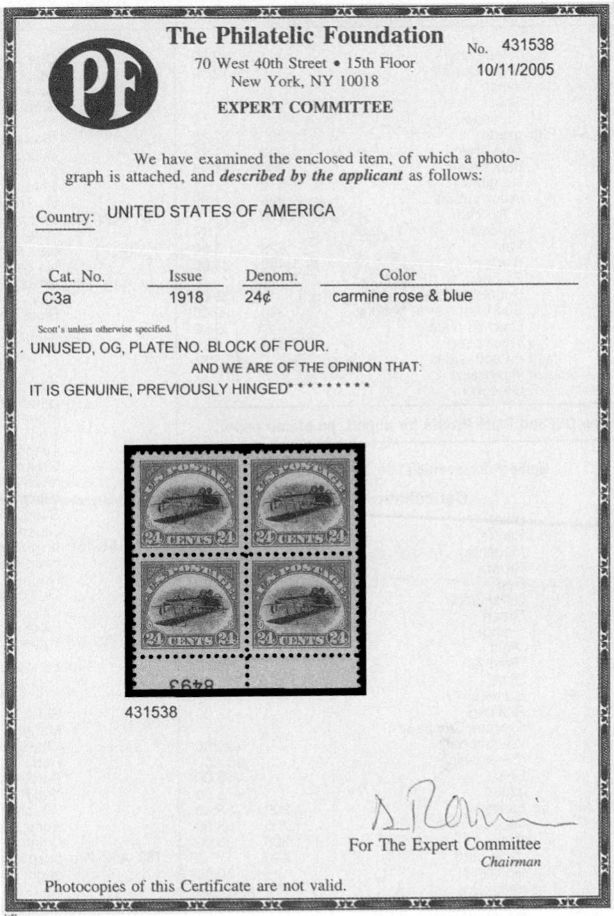

The Philatelic Foundation
70 West 40th Street • 15th Floor
New York, NY 10018
EXPERT COMMITTEE

No. 431538
10/11/2005

We have examined the enclosed item, of which a photograph is attached, and *described by the applicant* as follows:

Country: UNITED STATES OF AMERICA

Cat. No.	Issue	Denom.	Color
C3a	1918	24¢	carmine rose & blue

Scott's unless otherwise specified.

UNUSED, OG, PLATE NO. BLOCK OF FOUR.

AND WE ARE OF THE OPINION THAT:

IT IS GENUINE, PREVIOUSLY HINGED*********

431538

For The Expert Committee
Chairman

Photocopies of this Certificate are not valid.

Stamp Certificates You Trust

And Now – Faster Service

Philatelic Foundation certificates are valued by collectors and dealers alike. Backed by a multimillion-dollar reference collection and a staff of professional experts, a Philatelic Foundation Certificate is the standard of excellence for our hobby. Plus the PF offers you the option of numerical grading at no extra cost and...

Faster Service!

Call 1-212-221-6555 or visit www.PhilatelicFoundation.org today to download a submission form for single or multiple items. Fill out the one-page form and send it to us with your stamps or covers. Request Priority or Express Service and your stamp or cover will be returned in 20 business days or less.

Reward yourself with the security of a Philatelic Foundation Certificate, the "gold standard" of certificates for over 60 years.

The Philatelic Foundation
70 West 40th Street, 15th Floor
New York, NY 10018
(212) 221-6555
www.PhilatelicFoundation.org

"Steamship"	+22.50
Black Carrier	+12.50
Japan	—
China	—
Curacao	—

No.	Design	Denom.	Description	Unused	Used
147	A46	3c	**green**	300.	1.75
			pale green	300.	1.75
			dark green	300.	1.75
			No gum	110.	
			yellow green	325.	1.85
			No gum	120.	
			On cover		2.25
			Pair	625.	3.60
			Block of 4	1,400.	24.00
			P# block of 10, Impt.	*3,750.*	
			Double transfer	—	12.00
			Short transfer at bottom	325.	20.00
			Cracked plate	—	55.00
			Worn plate	300.	1.75
a.			Printed on both sides		*12,500.*
b.			Double impression		*40,000.*
			On cover		—

See Die and Plate Proofs for imperf. on stamp paper.

Earliest documented use: Mar. 1, 1870.

Cancellations

Blue	+.10
Purple	+.35
Magenta	+.35
Brown	+1.50
Red	+2.50
Ultramarine	+2.00
Green	+55.00
Orange	+750.00
"Paid"	+2.00
"Paid All"	+10.00
"Free"	+15.00
Numeral	+2.00
Railroad	+10.00
Express Company	—
"Steamboat"	+20.00
"Steamship"	+17.50
Ship	+15.00
Japan	+75.00

No.	Design	Denom.	Description	Unused	Used
148	A47	6c	**carmine**	1,200.	35.00
			dark carmine	1,200.	35.00
			rose	1,200.	35.00
			No gum	400.	
			On cover		50.00
			Pair	2,500.	75.00
			Block of 4	5,500.	350.00
			Double transfer		45.00
			Double paper	—	*100.00*
			brown carmine	1,250.	65.00
			No gum	480.	
			violet carmine	1,400.	90.00
			No gum	550.	
a.			Vertical half used as 3c on cover		*3,500.*
b.			Double impression		*1,500.*
			On cover		*3,000.*

Earliest documented use: Mar. 28, 1870.

Cancellations

Blue	+1.00
Purple	+1.50
Violet	+1.50
Ultramarine	+3.00
Brown	+1.50
Red	+5.00
Claret	+10.00
Orange red	+7.00
Orange	+10.00
Green	+115.00
"Paid"	+3.00
"Steamship"	+25.00
"Paid All"	+15.00
Numeral	—
Supp. Mail Type A or D	+25.00
China	+75.00
Japan	+150.00

No.	Design	Denom.	Description	Unused	Used
149	A48	7c	**vermilion,** *Mar. 1871*	1,250.	95.00
			deep vermilion	1,250.	95.00
			No gum	450.	
			On cover		160.00
			Pair	2,600.	210.00
			Block of 4	6,250.	*750.00*
			Cracked plate		—

Earliest documented use: May 11, 1871.

Cancellations

Blue	+2.50
Purple	+7.50
Ultramarine	+12.50
Red	+10.00
Green	+450.00
Japan	+150.00

No.	Design	Denom.	Description	Unused	Used
150	A49	10c	**brown**	1,750.	30.00
			dark brown	1,750.	30.00
			yellow brown	1,750.	30.00
			No gum	650.	
			On cover		45.00
			Pair	3,750.	62.50
			Block of 4	8,000.	*275.00*
			P# block of 10, Impt.	—	
			Double transfer	—	85.00

Earliest documented use: May 14, 1870 (stamp on piece); May 19, 1870 (on cover).

Cancellations

Blue	+.50
Purple	+2.00
Magenta	+2.00
Ultramarine	+4.00
Red	+4.00
Orange red	+5.00
Orange	+10.00
Green	+120.00
Brown	+3.00
"Paid All"	+20.00
"Steamship"	+20.00
Supp. Mail Type A or D	+25.00
Japan	+120.00
China	—
St. Thomas	—

No.	Design	Denom.	Description	Unused	Used
151	A50	12c	**dull violet**	3,000.	200.00
			violet	3,000.	200.00
			dark violet	3,000.	200.00
			No gum	1,150.	
			On cover		450.00
			Pair	6,250.	425.00
			Block of 4	*14,000.*	*2,150.*

Earliest documented use: July 9, 1870.

Cancellations

Blue	+25.00
Ultramarine	+1,000.
Magenta	+10.00
Red	+15.00
Orange	—
Green	+150.00
"Paid All"	+25.00
"Steamship"	+50.00
Supp. Mail Type A or D	+40.00
Japan	—

No.	Design	Denom.	Description	Unused	Used
152	A51	15c	**bright orange**	3,250.	200.00
			deep orange	3,250.	200.00
			No gum	1,250.	
			On cover		350.00
			Pair	6,750.	425.00
			Block of 4	*15,000.*	*1,750.*
a.			Double impression		*6,000.*

Earliest documented use: June 24, 1870.

Cancellations

Blue	+7.50
Magenta	+7.50
Ultramarine	+10.00
Red	+15.00
Purple	+750.00
"Paid"	+12.50
"Steamship"	+40.00
Supp. Mail Type A or F	+30.00
China	—

No.	Design	Denom.	Description	Unused	Used
153	A52	24c	**purple**	2,200.	200.00
			bright purple	2,200.	200.00
			No gum	825.	
			On cover		*1,500.*
			Pair	4,750.	450.00
			Block of 4	*14,000.*	*3,500.*
			Double paper	—	—

Earliest documented use: Nov. 18, 1870.

Cancellations

Red	+15.00
Blue	+5.00
Purple	+7.50
China	—
"Paid"	+25.00
Town	+15.00
"Steamship"	—
Supp. Mail Type A, D or F	+30.00

No.	Design	Denom.	Description	Unused	Used
154	A53	30c	**black**	7,500.	275.00
			full black	7,500.	275.00
			No gum	2,750.	
			On cover		825.00
			Pair	*16,000.*	575.00
			Block of 4	*38,500.*	

Earliest documented use: July 13, 1870.

Cancellations

Blue	+5.00
Brown	+50.00
Magenta	+15.00
Red	+50.00
"Steamship"	+55.00
Supplementary Mail Type A	+40.00

No.	Design	Denom.	Description	Unused	Used
155	A54	90c	**carmine**	5,500.	350.00
			dark carmine	5,500.	350.00
			No gum	2,100.	
			On cover		—
			Pair	*11,500.*	725.00
			Block of 4	*26,000.*	2,250.
			P# strip of 5, Impt.	*36,000.*	

Earliest documented use: Sept. 1, 1872.

Cancellations

Blue	+10.00
Purple	+15.00
Magenta	+15.00
Green	+275.00
Red	+50.00
Town	+20.00
Supp. Mail Type A or F	+40.00
Japan	—

PLEASE NOTE:

Stamps are valued in the grade of very fine unless otherwise indicated.

Values for early and valuable stamps are for examples with certificates of authenticity from acknowledged expert committees, or examples sold with the buyer having the right of certification. This applies to examples with original gum as well as examples without gum. Beware of stamps offered "as is," as the gum on some unused stamps offered with "original gum" may be fraudulent, and stamps offered as unused without gum may in some cases be altered or faintly canceled used stamps.

VALUES FOR NEVER-HINGED STAMPS PRIOR TO SCOTT No. 182

This catalogue does not value pre-1879 stamps in never-hinged condition. Premiums for never-hinged condition in the classic era invariably are even larger than those premiums listed for the 1879 and later issues. Generally speaking, the earlier the stamp is listed in the catalogue, the larger will be the never-hinged premium. On some early classics, the premium will be several multiples of the unused, hinged values given in the catalogue.

PRINTED BY THE CONTINENTAL BANK NOTE COMPANY

Plates of 200 subjects in two panes of 100 each.

Designs of the 1870-71 Issue with secret marks on the values from 1c to 15c, as described and illustrated:

The object of secret marks was to provide a simple and positive proof that these stamps were produced by the Continental Bank Note Company and not by their predecessors.

Franklin — A44a

1c. In the pearl at the left of the numeral "1" there is a small crescent.

Jackson — A45a

2c. Under the scroll at the left of "U. S." there is a small diagonal line. This mark seldom shows clearly. The stamp, No. 157, can be distinguished by its color.

Washington — A46a

3c. The under part of the upper tail of the left ribbon is heavily shaded.

Lincoln — A47a

6c. The first four vertical lines of the shading in the lower part of the left ribbon have been strengthened.

Stanton — A48a

7c. Two small semi-circles are drawn around the ends of the lines that outline the ball in the lower right hand corner.

Jefferson — A49a

10c. There is a small semi-circle in the scroll at the right end of the upper label.

Clay — A50a

12c. The balls of the figure "2" are crescent shaped.

Webster — A51a

15c. In the lower part of the triangle in the upper left corner two lines have been made heavier forming a "V." This mark can be found on some of the Continental and American (1879) printings, but not all stamps show it.

Secret marks were added to the dies of the 24c, 30c and 90c but new plates were not made from them. The various printings of the 30c and 90c can be distinguished only by the shades and paper.

J. Grill about 7x9 ½mm exists on all values except 24c and 90c. Grill was composed of truncated pyramids and was so strongly impressed that some points often broke through the paper.

White Wove Paper, Thin to Thick

1873, July (?) *Perf. 12*

156 A44a 1c **ultramarine** 275. 5.00
pale ultramarine 275. 5.00
gray blue 275. 5.00
blue 275. 5.00
No gum 95.
dark ultramarine 300. 5.00
No gum 105.
On cover 6.50
Pair 575. 10.50
Block of 4 1,250. 47.50
P# block of 12, Impt. *6,250.*
Double transfer 350. 9.00
Double paper *1,000.* 200.00
Ribbed paper 400. 16.00
Paper with silk fibers — 27.50
Cracked plate —
Paper cut with "cogwheel" punch *450.*
e. With grill *2,000.*
f. Imperf., pair — *1,500.*

The No. 156 plate block is unique. Value is 1998 auction sale.
No. 156f may not have been regularly issued.

Earliest documented use: Aug. 22, 1873.

Cancellations

Blue +.25
Purple +.35
Magenta +.35
Ultramarine +1.00
Red +3.50
Orange red +4.00
Orange +5.00
Brown +20.00
Green +60.00
"Paid All" +7.00
"Paid" +1.00
Railroad +12.00
"Free" +12.00
Black carrier +15.00
Numeral +2.50
Alaska —
Japan —
Printed "G." Precancel (Glastonbury, Conn.) +200.00
Printed Star Precancel (Glen Allen, Va.) +100.00

157 A45a 2c **brown** 425. 22.50
dark brown 425. 22.50
dark reddish brown 425. 22.50
yellowish brown 425. 22.50
No gum 160.
With secret mark 450. 25.00
No gum 170.
On cover 27.50
Pair 875. 47.50
Block of 4 1,900. 175.00
P# block of 12, Impt. *6,250.*
P# block of 14, Impt. *10,000.*
Double paper 1,050. 105.00
Ribbed paper 550. 45.00
Double transfer — 27.50
Cracked plate —
c. With grill *1,850.* *750.00*
d. Double impression — *5,000.*
e. Vertical half used as 1c on cover —

Earliest documented use: July 12, 1873.

Cancellations

Blue +.75
Magenta +1.00
Purple +1.00
Red +5.00
Orange red +5.50
Orange +7.50
Green +100.00
"Paid" +2.50
"Insufficiently Paid" —
"Paid All" +13.50
"P. D." in circle +15.00
Town +2.00
Numeral +1.50
Black Carrier +8.50
"Steamship" +15.00
Supplementary Mail Type F +5.00
China —
Japan +100.00
Printed Star Precancellation (Glen Allen, Va.) —

158 A46a 3c **green** 140. 1.00
bluish green 140. 1.00
yellow green 140. 1.00
dark yellow green 140. 1.00
dark green 140. 1.00
No gum 45.
olive green, ribbed paper *375.* 15.00
No gum 150.
On cover 1.20
Pair 290. 2.10
Block of 4 625. 14.50
P# strip of 5, Impt. 825.
P# strip of 6, Impt. 975.
P# block of 10, Impt. 2,800.
P# block of 12, Impt. *3,750.*
P# block of 14, Impt. *4,750.*
Double paper 425. 50.00
Paper cut with "cogwheel" punch 280. 225.
Ribbed paper 310. 5.25
Paper with silk fibers — 5.25
Cracked plate — 32.50
Major plate crack at bottom *350.00*
Double transfer — 6.00
Short transfer at bottom 15.00
e. With grill *500.*
End roller grill *950.* *425.*
h. Horizontal pair, imperf. vert. —
i. Horizontal pair, imperf. between *1,300.*
j. Double impression *10,000.*
k. Printed on both sides *12,000.*

See Die and Plate Proofs for imperfs. on stamp paper, with and without grill.

Earliest documented use: July 17, 1873.

Cancellations

Blue +.10
Magenta +.20
Purple +.20
Ultramarine +1.25
Red +2.50
Orange red +2.75
Orange +3.50
Green +25.00
Town +.05
"Paid" +2.50
"Paid All" +20.00
"Free" +15.00
Numeral +1.00
China —
Railroad +7.00
"R. P. O." +1.50
"P. D." in circle —
"Steamboat" —
"Steamship" —
Supplementary Mail Type D +11.00
Supplementary Mail Type F +8.50
Express Company —
Black Carrier +8.00
Red Carrier +25.00
Japan +65.00
Alaska —

159 A47a 6c **dull pink** 475. 20.00
brown rose 475. 20.00
No gum 170.
On cover 47.50
Pair 1,000. 42.50
Block of 4 2,250. *150.00*
P# block of 12, Impt. *16,000.*
Double paper — —
Ribbed paper — 42.50
Paper with silk fibers — 42.50
a. Diagonal half used as 3c on cover *4,000.*
b. With grill *1,800.*
End roller grill *2,400.*

Earliest documented use: June 8, 1873.
No. 159a is unique.
No. 159b is valued in the grade of fine.

Cancellations

Blue +1.00
Indigo +2.50
Magenta +1.50
Purple +1.50
Violet +3.00
Ultramarine +2.50
Red +7.50
Orange red +9.00
Green +100.00
Numeral +1.50
"Paid" +10.00
"Paid All" +15.00
Supp. Mail Type D, E or F +15.00
Japan +100.00
China +125.00
Railroad +6.00
"R. P. O." +3.00

160 A48a 7c **orange vermilion** 1,500. 90.00
vermilion 1,500. 90.00
No gum 525.
On cover 175.00
Pair 3,150. 190.00
Block of 4 6,500.
P# block of 12, Impt. *14,500.*
Double transfer of "7 cents" (1R22) — 210.00
Double transfer in lower left corner — 160.00
Double paper —
Ribbed paper — 105.00
Paper with silk fibers 2,000. 140.00
a. With grill *3,500.*

The plate block of 12 is in fine condition. It is unique.

Earliest documented use: Sept. 10, 1873.

Cancellations

Blue +4.00
Red +10.00
Purple +10.00
Brown +5.00
"Paid" +15.00

161 A49a 10c **brown** 1,300. 25.00
dark brown 1,300. 25.00
yellow brown 1,300. 25.00
No gum 450.
On cover 40.00
Pair 2,750. 52.50
Block of 4 6,250. *200.00*
P# block of 10, Impt. *16,500.*
P# block of 12, Impt. *21,500.*
Double paper —
Ribbed paper — 55.00
Paper with silk fibers 1,800. 55.00
Double transfer — 55.00
c. With grill *3,750.*
d. Horizontal pair, imperf. between *2,750.*

Earliest documented use: Aug. 2, 1873.

Cancellations

Blue +1.50
Ultramarine —
Purple +2.00
Red +6.00
Orange red +7.00
Orange +10.00
Magenta +2.00
Brown +20.00
Green +100.00
"Paid" +4.00
"P. D." in circle +20.00
"Steamship" +15.00
Supplementary Mail Type E +7.00
Supplementary Mail Type F +2.50
Japan +100.00
China —
Alaska —

162 A50a 12c **blackish violet** 2,750. 125.00
No gum 1,000.
On cover 325.00
Pair 5,750. 260.00
Block of 4 *12,500.* *950.00*
Ribbed paper — 210.00
a. With grill *5,500.*

Earliest documented use: Jan. 3, 1874.

Cancellations

Blue +2.50
Ultramarine +15.00
Brown +5.00
Red +15.00
Purple +500.00
Supplementary Mail Type D +15.00
Japan +200.00

163 A51a 15c **yellow orange** 3,000. 140.00
pale orange 3,000. 140.00
reddish orange 3,000. 140.00
No gum 1,050.
On cover 325.00
Pair 6,250. 300.00
Block of 4 *14,000.* *1,150.*
Double paper —
Paper with silk fibers 3,250. 190.00
Vertical ribbed paper 3,150. 190.00
a. With grill *5,750.*

Earliest documented use: July 22, 1873.

Cancellations

Blue +5.00
Purple +10.00
Red +20.00
Green +350.00
Brown —
Supplementary Mail Type E —
Supplementary Mail Type F +10.00
"Steamship" —
Numeral +7.50
Puerto Rico —
China —

164 A52 24c **purple** *357,500.*

The Philatelic Foundation has certified as genuine a 24c on vertically ribbed paper, and that is the unique stamp listed as No. 164. Specialists believe that only Continental used ribbed paper. It is not known for sure whether or not Continental also printed the 24c value on regular paper; if it did, specialists currently are not able to distinguish these from No. 153. The catalogue value represents a 2004 auction sale price realized.

165 A53 30c **gray black** 3,500. 130.
greenish black 3,500. 130.
No gum 1,250.
On cover *725.*
Pair 7,500. 275.
Block of 4 *17,500.* *1,200.*
Double transfer — 160.
Double paper —

			Ribbed paper	3,750.	150.
			Paper with silk fibers	—	—
c.			With grill	*22,500.*	

Earliest documented use: Oct. 14, 1874.

Cancellations

Purple	+10.00
Blue	+5.00
Red	+25.00
Brown	+30.00
Magenta	+10.00
"Steamship"	—
Supplementary Mail Type E	+10.00
Supplementary Mail Type F	+5.00
Japan	+200.00

166	A54	90c	**rose carmine**	2,750.	275.00
			pale rose carmine	2,750.	275.00
			No gum	1,000.	
			On cover		*7,500.*
			Pair	*5,750.*	575.00
			Block of 4	*12,000.*	*2,500.*
			P# strip of 5, Impt.	*15,000.*	

Earliest documented use: June 25, 1875.

Cancellations

Blue	+10.
Purple	+40.
Red	+40.
Supplementary Mail Type F	+30.

SPECIAL PRINTING OF 1873 ISSUE
Produced by the Continental Bank Note Co.

1875 *Perf. 12*

Hard, white wove paper, without gum

167	A44a	1c	**ultramarine**	*20,000.*	
168	A45a	2c	**dark brown**	*10,000.*	
169	A46a	3c	**blue green**	*25,000.*	—
			On cover		—
170	A47a	6c	**dull rose**	*24,000.*	
171	A48a	7c	**reddish vermilion**	*6,250.*	
172	A49a	10c	**pale brown**	*23,000.*	
173	A50a	12c	**dark violet**	*8,000.*	
			Horizontal pair	—	
174	A51a	15c	**bright orange**	*23,000.*	
175	A52	24c	**dull purple**	*5,500.*	*17,500.*
			Horizontal pair	—	
176	A53	30c	**greenish black**	*19,000.*	
177	A54	90c	**violet carmine**	*30,000.*	

Although perforated, these stamps were usually cut apart with scissors. As a result, the perforations are often much mutilated and the design is frequently damaged.

These can be distinguished from the 1873 issue by the shades; also by the paper, which is very white instead of yellowish.

These and the subsequent issues listed under the heading of "Special Printings" are special printings of stamps then in current use which, together with the reprints and re-issues, were made for sale to collectors. They were available for postage except for the Officials, Newspaper and Periodical, and demonetized issues.

Only No. 169 is documented on cover (unique; postmarked Mar. 5, 1876).

Only one example of No. 175 used has been certified. It is off-center and creased, and it is valued thus.

PRINTED BY THE CONTINENTAL BANK NOTE COMPANY

REGULAR ISSUE

Yellowish Wove Paper

1875 *Perf. 12*

178	A45a	2c	**vermilion,** *June 1875*	425.	12.50
			No gum	140.	
			On cover		15.00
			Pair	900.	26.00
			Block of 4	2,000.	130.00
			P# strip of 6, Impt.	*3,250.*	
			P# block of 12, Impt.	—	
			P# block of 14, Impt.	*7,500.*	
			Double transfer		—
			Double paper	—	—
			Ribbed paper	—	—
			Paper with silk fibers	450.	17.50
b.			Half used as 1c on cover		*750.00*
c.			With grill	900.	*2,750.*

See Die and Plate Proofs for imperf. on stamp paper.

Earliest documented use: July 15, 1875.

Cancellations

Blue	+.25
Purple	+.50
Magenta	+.50
Red	+6.00
"Paid"	+8.00
"Steamship"	—
Supplementary Mail Type F	+5.50
Black Carrier	+15.00
Railroad	+12.50

Zachary Taylor — A55

179	A55	5c	**blue,** *June 1875*	800.	25.00
			dark blue	800.	25.00
			bright blue	800.	25.00
			light blue	800.	25.00
			No gum	275.	
			greenish blue	825.	30.00
			No gum	290.	
			On cover		37.50
			Pair	1,700.	52.50
			Block of 4	4,000.	375.00
			Cracked plate	—	*170.00*
			Double transfer	—	37.50
			Double paper	*950.*	
			Ribbed paper	—	—
			Paper with silk fibers	—	37.50
c.			With grill	4,500.	
			End roller grill	—	

Earliest documented use: July 10, 1875.

Cancellations

Blue	+1.00
Ultramarine	+3.00
Purple	+2.00
Magenta	+2.00
Red	+10.00
Green	+70.00
Numeral	+5.00
Railroad	+17.50
"Steamship"	+12.50
Ship	+12.50
Supplementary Mail Type E	+5.00
Supplementary Mail Type F	+2.00
China	—
Japan	+100.00
Peru	—

The five cent rate to foreign countries in the Universal Postal Union began on July 1, 1875. No. 179 was issued for that purpose.

SPECIAL PRINTING OF 1875 ISSUE
Produced by the Continental Bank Note Co.

Hard, White Wove Paper, without gum

1875

180	A45a	2c	**carmine vermilion**	*80,000.*
181	A55	5c	**bright blue**	*450,000.*

Unlike Nos. 167-177, Nos. 180-181 were not cut apart with scissors.

Numbers sold: No. 180, 917; No. 181, 317. However, fewer than 25 No. 180 and fewer than 10 No. 181 have been expertized and are available to collectors.

IMPORTANT INFORMATION REGARDING VALUES FOR NEVER-HINGED STAMPS

Collectors should be aware that the values given for never-hinged stamps from No. 182 on are for stamps in the grade of very fine, just as the values for all stamps in the catalogue are for very fine stamps unless indicated otherwise. The never-hinged premium as a percentage of value will be larger for stamps in extremely fine or superb grades, and the premium will be smaller for fine-very fine, fine or poor examples. This is particularly true of the issues of the late-19th and early-20th centuries. For example, in the grade of very fine, an unused stamp from this time period may be valued at $100 hinged and $200 never hinged. The never-hinged premium is thus 100%. But in a grade of extremely fine, this same stamp will not only sell for more hinged, but the never-hinged premium will increase, perhaps to 200%-400% or more over the higher extremely fine value. In a grade of superb, a hinged stamp will sell for much more than a very fine stamp, and additionally the never-hinged premium will be much larger, perhaps as large as 500%-1,000%. On the other hand, the same stamp in a grade of fine or fine-very fine not only will sell for less than a very fine stamp in hinged condition, but additionally the never-hinged premium will be smaller than the never-hinged premium on a very fine stamp, perhaps as small as 15%-30%.

Please note that the above statements and percentages are NOT a formula for arriving at the values of stamps in hinged or never-hinged condition in the grades of very good, fine, fine to very fine, extremely fine or superb. The percentages given apply only to the size of the premium for never-hinged condition that might be added to the stamp value for hinged condition. Further, the percentages given are only generalized estimates. Some stamps or grades may have percentages for never-hinged condition that are higher or lower than the ranges given. For values of the most popular U.S. stamps in the grades of very good, fine, fine to very fine, very fine, very fine to extremely fine, extremely fine and superb, see the *Scott United States Specialized Valuing Supplement*, updated and issued twice each year in April and October.

VALUES FOR NEVER-HINGED STAMPS PRIOR TO SCOTT 182

This catalogue does not value pre-1879 stamps in never-hinged condition. Premiums for never-hinged condition in the classic era invariably are even larger than those premiums listed for the 1879 and later issues. Generally speaking, the earlier the stamp is listed in the catalogue, the larger will be the never-hinged premium. On some early classics, the premium will be several multiples of the unused, hinged values given in the catalogue.

NEVER-HINGED PLATE BLOCKS

Values given for never-hinged plate blocks are for blocks in which all stamps have original gum that has never been hinged and has no disturbances, and all selvage, whether gummed or ungummed, has never been hinged.

PRINTED BY THE AMERICAN BANK NOTE COMPANY

The Continental Bank Note Co. was consolidated with the American Bank Note Co. on February 4, 1879. The American Bank Note Company used many plates of the Continental Bank Note Company to print the ordinary postage, Departmental and Newspaper stamps. Therefore, stamps bearing the Continental Company's imprint were not always its product.

The A. B. N. Co. also used the 30c and 90c plates of the N. B. N. Co. Some of No. 190 and all of No. 217 were from A. B. N. Co. plate 405.

Early printings of No. 188 were from Continental plates 302 and 303 which contained the normal secret mark of 1873. After those plates were re-entered by the A. B. N. Co. in 1880, pairs or multiple pieces contained combinations of normal, hairline or missing marks. The pairs or other multiples usually found contain at least one hairline mark which tended to disappear as the plate wore.

A. B. N. Co. plates 377 and 378 were made in 1881 from the National transfer roll of 1870. No. 187 from these plates has no secret mark.

Identification by Paper Type:

Collectors traditionally have identified American Bank Note Co. issues by the soft, porous paper on which they were printed. However, the Continental Bank Note Co. used a soft paper from August 1878 through early 1879, before the consolidation of the companies. When the consolidation occurred in the late afternoon of Feb. 4, 1879, American Bank Note Co. took over the presses, plates, paper, ink, and the employees of Continental. Undoubtedly they also acquired panes of finished stamps and sheets of printed stamps that had not yet been gummed and/or perforated. Since the soft paper that was in use at the time of the consolidation and after is approximately the same texture and thickness as the soft paper that American Bank Note Co. began using regularly in June or July of 1879, all undated soft paper stamps have traditionally been classified as American Bank Note Co. printings.

However, if a stamp bears a dated cancellation or is on a dated cover from Feb. 4, 1879 or earlier, collectors (especially specialist collectors) must consider the stamp to be a Continental Bank Note printing. Undated stamps off cover, and stamps and covers dated Feb. 5 or later, traditionally have been considered to be American Bank Note Co. printings since that company held the contract to print U.S. postage stamps beginning on that date. The most dedicated and serious specialist students sometimes attempt to determine the stamp printer of the issues on soft, porous paper in an absolute manner (by scientifically testing the paper and/or comparing printing records).

Earliest documented uses for American Bank Note Co. issues are given for stamps on the soft, porous paper that has been traditionally associated with that company. But, for reasons given above, sometimes that date will precede the Feb. 4, 1879 consolidation date.

SAME AS 1870-75 ISSUES

Soft Porous Paper

1879 *Perf. 12*

182	A44a	1c	**dark ultramarine**	325.	4.50
			blue	325.	4.50
			gray blue	325.	4.50
			Never hinged	1,100.	
			No gum	110.	
			On cover		4.75
			Pair	675.	9.00
			Block of 4	1,550.	62.50
			P# block of 10, Impt.	*4,750.*	
			Double transfer	—	11.50

Earliest documented use: Jan. 3, 1879.

Cancellations

Blue	+.05
Magenta	+.10
Purple	+.10
Red	+7.00
Printed Star Precancellation (Glen Allen, Va.)	+75.00
Green	+35.00
"Paid"	+4.00
Supplementary Mail Type F	+10.00
Railroad	+12.50
Printed "G." Precancellation (Glastonbury, Conn.)	+100.00

183	A45a	2c	**vermilion**	130.	3.25
			orange vermilion	130.	3.25
			Never hinged	500.	
			No gum	45.	
			On cover		3.75
			Pair	275.	6.75
			Block of 4	650.	50.00
			P# block of 10, Impt.	2,000.	
			P# block of 12, Impt.	*2,500.*	
			Double transfer	—	—
a.			Double impression	—	*5,500.*
b.			Half used as 1c on cover		*750.00*

Earliest documented use: Aug. 19, 1878.

Cancellations

Blue	+.25
Purple	+.40
Magenta	+.40
Red	+6.00
Green	+175.00
"Paid"	+5.00
"Paid All"	—
"Ship"	—
Numeral	+4.00
Railroad	+15.00
Supplementary Mail Type F	+8.00
China	—
Printed Star Precancellation in black (Glen Allen, Va.)	+350.00
Printed Star Precancellation in red (Glen Allen, Va.)	+1,750.

184	A46a	3c	**green**	110.	.80
			light green	110.	.80
			dark green	110.	.80
			Never hinged	400.	
			No gum	35.	
			On cover		.90
			Pair	230.	1.70
			Block of 4	500.	11.50
			P# block of 10, Impt.	1,450.	
			P# block of 12, Impt.	1,750.	
			P# block of 14, Impt.	2,150.	
			Double transfer	—	—
			Short transfer	—	6.25
b.			Double impression		*5,500.*

See Die and Plate Proofs for imperf. on stamp paper.

Earliest documented use: July 2, 1878.

Cancellations

Blue	+.10
Magenta	+.15
Purple	+.15
Violet	+.15
Brown	+1.00
Red	+7.50
Green	+25.00
"Paid"	+3.00
"Free"	+15.00
Numeral	+2.00
Railroad	+12.50
"Steamboat"	—
Supplementary Mail Type F	+8.00
Printed Star Precancel (Glen Allen, Va.)	—
China	+60.00
Alaska	—

185	A55	5c	**blue**	525.	15.00
			light blue	525.	15.00
			bright blue	525.	15.00
			dark blue	525.	15.00
			Never hinged	*1,850.*	
			No gum	180.	
			On cover		25.00
			Pair	1,100.	32.50
			Block of 4	2,400.	180.00
			P# block of 12, Impt.	*12,500.*	
			Double transfer	—	

Earliest documented use: Jan. 16, 1879.

Cancellations

Blue	+.25
Purple	+1.00
Magenta	+1.00
Ultramarine	+3.50
Red	+7.50
Railroad	+20.00
Numeral	+2.00
Supplementary Mail Type F	+1.50
"Steamship"	+35.00
China	+60.00
Peru	—
Panama	—

186	A47a	6c	**pink**	1,050.	27.50
			dull pink	1,050.	27.50
			brown rose	1,050.	27.50
			Never hinged	*3,750.*	
			No gum	375.	
			On cover		47.50
			Pair	2,300.	57.50
			Block of 4	5,000.	*625.00*

Earliest documented use: April 18, 1879.

Cancellations

Blue	+.50
Ultramarine	+3.00
Purple	+1.00
Magenta	+1.00
Red	+12.00
Supplementary Mail Type F	+4.00
Railroad	+22.50
Numeral	+4.00
China	+70.00

187	A49	10c	**brown,** without secret mark	3,500.	32.50
			yellow brown	3,500.	32.50
			Never hinged	*12,000.*	
			No gum	1,200.	
			On cover		50.00
			Pair	7,250.	70.00
			Block of 4	*16,000.*	—
			Double transfer	—	52.50
			Double paper	*6,000.*	—

Earliest documented use: Sept. 5, 1879.

Cancellations

Blue	+.50
Magenta	+1.50
Red	+10.00
"Paid"	+3.50
Supplementary Mail Type F	+3.00
China	+70.00

188	A49a	10c	**brown,** with secret mark	2,250.	27.50
			yellow brown	2,250.	27.50
			Never hinged	*8,250.*	
			No gum	850.	
			black brown	2,500.	40.00
			Never hinged	*8,750.*	
			No gum	950.	
			On cover		42.50
			Pair	4,750.	57.50
			Block of 4	*11,000.*	300.00
			Pair, one stamp No. 187	*10,000.*	725.00
			Double transfer		47.50
			Cracked plate	—	—

Earliest documented use: Oct. 5, 1878.

Cancellations

Blue	+.50
Ultramarine	+3.00
Purple	+2.00
Magenta	+2.00
Red	+10.00
Green	+70.00
"Paid"	+7.50
Supplementary Mail Type F	+5.00
Numeral	+3.00
Printed Star Precancel (Glen Allen, Va.)	-

189	A51a	15c	**red orange**	325.	25.00
			orange	325.	25.00
			yellow orange	325.	25.00
			Never hinged	1,000.	
			No gum	120.	
			On cover		87.50
			Pair	675.	52.50

Block of 4	1,750.	230.00
P# block of 12, Impt.	*7,250.*	
Double transfer		—

Earliest documented use: Jan. 20, 1879.

Cancellations

Blue	+1.50
Purple	+3.00
Magenta	+3.00
Ultramarine	+5.00
Red	+12.00
"Steamship"	+22.50
Supplementary Mail Type E	—
Supplementary Mail Type F	+5.00
Japan	+120.00
China	—

190 A53 30c **full black**	1,100.	80.00
greenish black	1,100.	80.00
Never hinged	*4,000.*	
No gum	450.	
On cover		425.00
Pair	2,300.	175.00
Block of 4	5,000.	500.00
P# block of 10, Impt.	*15,000.*	

Earliest documented use: April 5, 1881.

Cancellations

Blue	+1.50
Purple	+3.00
Magenta	+3.00
Red	+20.00
Supplementary Mail Type F	+6.00
"Steamship"	+35.00
Tahiti	—
Samoa	—

191 A54 90c **carmine**	2,500.	325.00
rose	2,500.	325.00
carmine rose	2,500.	325.00
Never hinged	*8,500.*	
No gum	1,000.	
On cover		*5,000.*
Pair	5,500.	675.00
Block of 4	*13,000.*	1,750.
Double paper	—	

See Die and Plate Proofs for imperf. on stamp paper.

Earliest documented use: May 27, 1882 (dated cancel on off-cover stamp), June 24, 1882 (on cover).

Cancellations

Blue	+15.00
Purple	+20.00
Red	+45.00
Supplementary Mail Type F	+20.00

SPECIAL PRINTING OF 1879 ISSUE

Produced by the American Bank Note Co.

1880 *Perf. 12*

Soft porous paper, without gum

192 A44a 1c **dark ultramarine**	*75,000.*
193 A45a 2c **black brown**	*27,500.*
194 A46a 3c **blue green**	*110,000.*
195 A47a 6c **dull rose**	*100,000.*
196 A48a 7c **scarlet vermilion**	*9,000.*
197 A49a 10c **deep brown**	*55,000.*
198 A50a 12c **blackish purple**	*15,000.*
199 A51a 15c **orange**	*50,000.*
200 A52 24c **dark violet**	*14,000.*
201 A53 30c **greenish black**	*35,000.*
202 A54 90c **dull carmine**	*45,000.*
203 A45a 2c **scarlet vermilion**	*150,000.*
204 A55 5c **deep blue**	*350,000.*

Nos. 192 and 194 are valued in the grade of fine.

No. 197 was printed from Continental plate 302 (or 303) after plate was re-entered. Therefore, the stamp may show normal, hairline or missing secret mark.

The Post Office Department did not keep separate records of the 1875 and 1880 Special Printings of the 1873 and 1879 issues, but the total quantity sold of both is recorded.

Unlike the 1875 hard-paper Special Printings (Nos. 167-177), the 1880 soft-paper Special Printings were never cut apart with scissors.

Numbers Sold of 1875 and 1880 Special Printings.

1c ultramarine & dark ultramarine *(388)*
2c dark brown & black brown *(416)*
2c carmine vermilion & scarlet vermilion *(917)*
3c blue green *(267)*
5c bright blue & deep blue *(317)*
6c dull rose *(185)*
7c reddish vermilion & scarlet vermilion *(473)*
10c pale brown & deep brown *(180)*
12c dark violet & blackish purple *(282)*
15c bright orange & orange *(169)*
24c dull purple & dark violet *(286)*
30c greenish black *(179)*
90c violet carmine & dull carmine *(170)*

IMPORTANT INFORMATION REGARDING VALUES FOR NEVER-HINGED STAMPS

Collectors should be aware that the values given for never-hinged stamps from No. 182 on are for stamps in the grade of very fine, just as the values for all stamps in the catalogue are for very fine stamps unless indicated otherwise. The never-hinged premium as a percentage of value will be larger for stamps in extremely fine or superb grades, and the premium will be smaller for fine-very fine, fine or poor examples. This is particularly true of the issues of the late-19th and early-20th centuries. For example, in the grade of very fine, an unused stamp from this time period may be valued at $100 hinged and $200 never hinged. The never-hinged premium is thus 100%. But in a grade of extremely fine, this same stamp will not only sell for more hinged, but the never-hinged premium will increase, perhaps to 200%-400% or more over the higher extremely fine value. In a grade of superb, a hinged stamp will sell for much more than a very fine stamp, and additionally the never-hinged premium will be much larger, perhaps as large as 500%-1,000%. On the other hand, the same stamp in a grade of fine or fine-very fine not only will sell for less than a very fine stamp in hinged condition, but additionally the never-hinged premium will be smaller than the never-hinged premium on a very fine stamp, perhaps as small as 15%-30%.

Please note that the above statements and percentages are NOT a formula for arriving at the values of stamps in hinged or never-hinged condition in the grades of very good, fine, fine to very fine, very fine to extremely fine, extremely fine or superb. The percentages given apply only to the size of the premium for never-hinged condition that might be added to the stamp value for hinged condition. Further, the percentages given are only generalized estimates. Some stamps or grades may have percentages for never-hinged condition that are higher or lower than the ranges given. For values of the most popular U.S. stamps in the grades of very good, fine, fine to very fine, very fine, very fine to extremely fine, extremely fine and superb, see the *Scott United States Specialized Valuing Supplement*, updated and issued twice each year in April and October.

VALUES FOR NEVER-HINGED STAMPS PRIOR TO SCOTT 182

This catalogue does not value pre-1879 stamps in never-hinged condition. Premiums for never-hinged condition in the classic era invariably are even larger than those premiums listed for the 1879 and later issues. Generally speaking, the earlier the stamp is listed in the catalogue, the larger will be the never-hinged premium. On some early classics, the premium will be several multiples of the unused, hinged values given in the catalogue.

NEVER-HINGED PLATE BLOCKS

Values given for never-hinged plate blocks are for blocks in which all stamps have original gum that has never been hinged and has no disturbances, and all selvage, whether gummed or ungummed, has never been hinged.

REGULAR ISSUE

Printed by the American Bank Note Co.

James A. Garfield — A56

1882, Apr. 10 *Perf. 12*

205 A56 5c **yellow brown**	300.	10.00
brown	300.	10.00
gray brown	300.	10.00
Never hinged	1,000.	
No gum	100.	
On cover		18.50
Pair	625.	22.50
Block of 4	1,300.	120.00
P# strip of 5, Impt.	1,900.	
P# strip of 6, Impt.	2,250.	
P# block of 10, Impt.	*5,750.*	
P# block of 12, Impt.	*6,500.*	

Earliest documented use: Feb. 18, 1882.

Cancellations

Blue	+.50
Purple	+.75
Magenta	+.75
Red	+7.00
"Ship"	—
Numeral	+2.00
Supplementary Mail Type F	+2.50
Red Express Co.	—
China	+125.00
Japan	+125.00
Samoa	+150.00
Puerto Rico	—

SPECIAL PRINTING

Printed by the American Bank Note Co.

1882 *Perf. 12*

Soft porous paper, without gum

205C A56 5c **gray brown** *85,000.*

Although Post Office records indicate that 2,463 examples of the 5c Garfield Special Printing were sold, almost all of these stamps appear to have been from supplies of the regular issue No. 205. The actual Special Printings, No. 205C, came from a small supply sent to the Third Assistant Post Master General before the regular issue was available. Only 22 examples have been certified as genuine Special Printings.

DESIGNS OF 1873 RE-ENGRAVED

Franklin — A44b

1c — The vertical lines in the upper part of the stamp have been so deepened that the background often appears to be solid. Lines of shading have been added to the upper arabesques.

1881-82

206 A44b 1c **gray blue,** *Aug. 1881*	90.00	1.00
ultramarine	90.00	1.00
dull blue	90.00	1.00
slate blue	90.00	1.00
Never hinged	300.00	
No gum	25.00	
On cover		1.50
Pair	190.00	2.10
Block of 4	425.00	16.00
P# strip of 5, Impt.	550.00	
P# strip of 6, Impt.	650.00	
P# block of 10, Impt.	*1,900.*	
P# block of 12, Impt.	*2,100.*	
Double transfer	115.00	6.00
Punched with 8 small holes in a circle	*200.00*	
P# block of 10, Impt. (8-hole punch)	*2,750.*	

Earliest documented use: Nov. 2, 1881.

Cancellations

Purple	+.10
Magenta	+.10
Blue	+.20
Red	+3.00
Orange red	+3.50
Orange	+5.00
Green	+50.00
"Paid"	+4.75
"Paid All"	+12.00
Numeral	+3.50
Supplementary Mail Type F	+5.00
Railroad	+10.00
Printed Star Precancel (Glen Allen, Va.)	+55.00
China	—

Washington — A46b

3c. The shading at the sides of the central oval appears only about one-half the previous width. A short horizontal dash has been cut about 1mm below the "TS" of "CENTS."

207 A46b 3c **blue green,** *July 16, 1881*	95.00	.55
green	95.00	.55
yellow green	95.00	.55
Never hinged	310.00	
No gum	27.50	
On cover		.70
Pair	200.00	1.15
Block of 4	425.00	30.00
P# strip of 5, Impt.	575.00	
P# block of 10, Impt.	*1,900.*	
Double transfer	—	12.00
Cracked plate	—	
Punched with 8 small holes in a circle	*220.00*	
P# block of 10, Impt. (8-hole punch)	*3,000.*	
c. Double impression		—

Earliest documented use: Aug. 7, 1881.

Cancellations

Purple	+.10
Magenta	+.10
Blue	+.25
Brown	+1.50
Red	+2.50
"Paid"	+3.00
"Paid All"	—
Numeral	+2.50
"Ship"	—
Railroad	+5.00

Supplementary Mail Type F	+8.00
Printed Star Precancellation (Glen Allen, Va.)	—

Lincoln — A47b

6c. On the original stamps four vertical lines can be counted from the edge of the panel to the outside of the stamp. On the re-engraved stamps there are but three lines in the same place.

208	A47b 6c **rose**	850.	100.00
	dull rose	850.	100.00
	Never hinged	3,000.	
	No gum	260.	
	On cover (rose)		180.00
	Pair (rose)	1,800.	210.00
	Block of 4 (rose)	4,250.	850.00
	P# block of 10, Impt.	*11,500.*	
	Double transfer	950.	120.00
a.	6c **deep brown red**	650.	160.00
	Never hinged	2,100.	
	No gum	200.	
	pale brown red	575.	110.00
	Never hinged	1,850.	
	No gum	175.	
	On cover (deep brown red)		*425.00*
	Pair (deep brown red)	1,350.	330.00
	Block of 4 (deep brown red)	3,000.	1,200.
	P# strip of 5, Impt.	3,750.	
	P# strip of 6, Impt.	*4,500.*	
	P# block of 10, Impt.	*9,500.*	
	P# block of 12, Impt.	—	

Earliest documented use: June 1, 1882.

Cancellations

Magenta	+3.00
Purple	+3.00
Blue	+5.00
Red	+15.00
Supplementary Mail Type F	+10.00

Jefferson — A49b

10c. On the original stamps there are five vertical lines between the left side of the oval and the edge of the shield. There are only four lines on the re-engraved stamps. In the lower part of the latter, also, the horizontal lines of the background have been strengthened.

209	A49b 10c **brown,** *Apr. 1882*	190.	6.00
	yellow brown	190.	6.00
	orange brown	190.	6.00
	Never hinged	600.	
	No gum	60.	
	dark brown	200.	6.50
	purple brown	220.	6.50
	olive brown	220.	6.50
	Never hinged	625.	
	No gum	65.	
	On cover		11.00
	Pair	425.	12.50
	Block of 4	975.	40.00
	P# strip of 5, Impt.	1,350.	
	P# strip of 6, Impt.	1,575.	
	P# block of 10, Impt.	*3,900.*	
	P# block of 12, Impt.	*4,600.*	
	Never hinged	*8,750.*	
b.	10c **black brown**	2,500.	325.00
	Never hinged	5,000.	
	No gum	800.	
	On cover		*525.00*
	Pair	—	675.00
	Block of 4	—	—
c.	Double impression		—

Specimen stamps (usually overprinted "Sample") without overprint exist in a brown shade that differs from No. 209. The unoverprinted brown specimen is cheaper than No. 209. Expertization is recommended.

Earliest documented use: May 4, 1882.

Cancellations

Purple	+.50
Magenta	+.50
Blue	+1.00
Red	+4.00
Green	+35.00
Numeral	+2.00
"Paid"	+2.50
Supplementary Mail Type F	+3.00
Express Company	—
Japan	+75.00
China	—
Samoa	—

Printed by the American Bank Note Company.

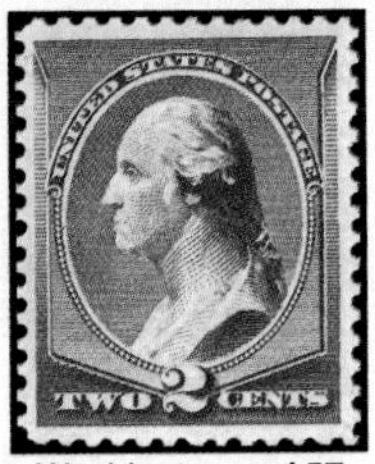
Washington — A57

Jackson — A58

Nos. 210-211 were issued to meet the reduced first class rate of 2 cents for each half ounce, and the double rate, which Congress approved Mar. 3, 1883, effective Oct. 1, 1883.

1883, Oct. 1 ***Perf. 12***

210	A57 2c **red brown**	47.50	.60
	dark red brown	47.50	.60
	orange brown	47.50	.60
	Never hinged	150.00	
	No gum	15.00	
	On cover		.70
	Pair	100.00	1.25
	Block of 4	220.00	12.00
	P# strip of 5, Impt.	280.00	
	P# strip of 6, Impt.	350.00	
	P# block of 10, Impt.	*1,100.*	
	P# block of 12, Impt.	*1,300.*	
	Double transfer	52.50	2.25

See Die and Plate Proofs for imperf. on stamp paper.

Earliest documented use: Oct. 1, 1883 (FDC).

Cancellations

Purple	+.10
Margenta	+.10
Blue	+.20
Violet	+.30
Brown	+.30
Red	+3.50
Green	+25.00
Numeral	+2.50
"Paid"	+3.00
Railroad	+5.00
Express Company	—
Supplementary Mail Type F	+5.00
"Ship"	—
"Steamboat"	—
China	—

211	A58 4c **blue green**	325.	22.50
	deep blue green	325.	22.50
	Never hinged	1,100.	
	No gum	110.	
	On cover		50.00
	Pair	675.	47.50
	Block of 4	1,400.	120.00
	P# strip of 5, Impt.	2,000.	
	P# strip of 6, Impt.	2,400.	
	P# block of 10, Impt.	*5,500.*	
	P# block of 12, Impt.	*6,400.*	
	Never hinged	*9,000.*	
	Double transfer	—	—
	Cracked plate	—	

See Die and Plate Proofs for imperf. on stamp paper.

Earliest documented use: Oct. 1, 1883 (FDC).

Cancellations

Purple	+1.00
Magenta	+1.00
Green	+50.00
Blue	+1.00
Numeral	+2.00
Supplementary Mail Type F	+5.00

SPECIAL PRINTING

Printed by the American Bank Note Company.

1883-85 **Soft porous paper** ***Perf. 12***

211B	A57 2c **pale red brown,** with gum ('85)	400.	—
	Never hinged	950.	
	No gum	150.	
	Block of 4	1,750.	
c.	Horizontal pair, imperf. between	*2,000.*	
	Never hinged	*3,000.*	
	Top margin strip of 6, "Steamer-American Bank Note Co." imprint	*5,000.*	
	Never hinged	*7,000.*	

Earliest documented use: May 23, 1885 (dated cancel on off-cover stamp).

211D A58 4c **deep blue green,** without gum *80,000.*

Postal records indicate that 26 examples of No. 211D were sold. Records also indicate an 1883 delivery and sales of 55 examples of the 2c red brown stamp, but there is no clear evidence that these can be differentiated from no gum examples of No. 210.

No. 211B is from a special trial printing by a new steam-powered American Bank Note Company press. Approximately 1,000 of these stamps (in sheets of 200 with an imperf gutter between the panes of 100) were delivered as samples to the Third Assistant Postmaster General and subsequently made their way to the public market.

REGULAR ISSUE

Printed by the American Bank Note Company.

Franklin — A59

1887 ***Perf. 12***

212	A59 1c **ultramarine,** *June*	110.00	2.25
	bright ultramarine	110.00	2.25
	Never hinged	375.00	
	No gum	35.00	
	On cover		3.00
	Pair	230.00	4.75
	Block of 4	500.00	35.00
	P# strip of 5, Impt.	650.00	
	P# strip of 6, Impt.	800.00	
	P# block of 10, Impt.	*1,675.*	
	P# block of 12, Impt.	*2,000.*	
	Double transfer		—

See Die and Plate Proofs for imperf. on stamp paper.

Earliest documented use: July 15, 1887. The previously listed July 7, 1887, cover has not been adequately documented. The editors would like to see authenticated evidence of its existence.

Cancellations

Purple	+.10
Magenta	+.10
Blue	+.10
Red	+5.50
Numeral	+2.00
Railroad	+10.00
Supplementary Mail Type F	+5.00
China	—

213	A57 2c **green,** *Sept. 10*	47.50	.50
	bright green	47.50	.50
	dark green	47.50	.50
	Never hinged	140.00	
	No gum	15.00	
	On cover		.65
	Pair	100.00	1.10
	Block of 4	220.00	10.00
	P# strip of 5, Impt.	290.00	
	P# strip of 6, Impt.	350.00	
	P# block of 10, Impt.	*1,250.*	
	Never hinged	*2,250.*	
	P# block of 12, Impt.	*1,500.*	
	Double transfer	—	3.25
b.	Printed on both sides		—

See Die and Plate Proofs for imperf. on stamp paper.

Earliest documented use: Sept. 20, 1887 (dated cancel on off-cover stamp); Sept. 21, 1887 (on cover).

Cancellations

Purple	+.10
Magenta	+.10
Blue	+.90
Red	+5.00
Green	+25.00
"Paid"	+5.00
Railroad	+12.00
Numeral	+2.00
"Steam"	—
"Steamboat"	—
Supplementary Mail Type F	+7.50
China	—
Japan	—

214	A46b 3c **vermilion,** *Sept.*	75.00	62.50
	Never hinged	230.00	
	No gum	22.50	
	On cover (single)		105.00
	Pair	160.00	130.00
	Block of 4	350.00	350.00
	P# strip of 5, Impt.	450.00	
	P# strip of 6, Impt.	525.00	
	P# block of 10, Impt.	*1,400.*	
	Never hinged	*3,250.*	
	P# block of 12, Impt.	*1,600.*	

Earliest documented use: Sept. 23, 1887.

Cancellations

Purple	+5.00
Magenta	+5.00
Green	+150.00
Blue	+10.00
Supplementary Mail Type F	+15.00
Railroad	+30.00

Printed by the American Bank Note Company.
SAME AS 1870-83 ISSUES

1888 ***Perf. 12***

215	A58 4c **carmine,** *Nov.*	240.	22.50
	rose carmine	240.	22.50
	pale rose	240.	22.50
	Never hinged	725.	
	No gum	80.	
	On cover		45.00
	Pair	500.	47.50

Block of 4	1,050.	150.00
P# strip of 5, Impt.	1,600.	
Never hinged	*4,250.*	
P# strip of 6, Impt.	1,850.	
P# block of 10, Impt.	*4,750.*	
P# block of 12, Impt.	*5,500.*	

Earliest documented use: Jan. 18, 1889.

Cancellations

Blue	+1.00
Red	+5.00
Purple	+2.00
Magenta	+2.00
Supplementary Mail Type F	+5.00

216 A56 5c **indigo,** *Feb.*	275.	15.00
deep blue	275.	15.00
Never hinged	900.	
No gum	90.	
On cover		27.50
Pair	575.	32.50
Block of 4	1,200.	130.00
P# strip of 5, Impt.	1,600.	
P# strip of 6, Impt.	2,000.	
P# block of 10, Impt.	*7,500.*	
P# block of 12, Impt.	*9,000.*	

Earliest documented use: Mar. 15, 1888.

Cancellations

Purple	+1.00
Magenta	+1.00
Blue	+1.00
Supplementary Mail Type F	+3.00
China	+85.00
Japan	+85.00
Puerto Rico	+75.00
Samoa	—

217 A53 30c **orange brown,** *Jan.*	425.	120.00
deep orange brown	425.	120.00
Never hinged	1,350.	
No gum	145.	
On cover		*1,400.*
Pair	950.	260.00
Block of 4	2,000.	675.00
P# strip of 5, Impt.	*2,750.*	
P# block of 10, Impt.	*7,250.*	
P# block of 12, Impt.	—	

Earliest documented use: Aug. 18, 1888 (dated cancel on off-cover stamp); Sept. 7, 1888 (on cover).

Cancellations

Blue	+5.00
Magenta	+10.00
Supplementary Mail Type F	+10.00
"Paid All"	+25.00
"Paid"	+15.00

218 A54 90c **purple,** *Feb.*	1,100.	260.00
bright purple	1,100.	260.00
Never hinged	3,500.	
No gum	400.	
On cover		*10,000.*
Pair	2,300.	575.00
Block of 4	*5,500.*	1,450.
P# strip of 5, Impt.	*6,750.*	
P# block of 10, Impt.	*23,500.*	
P# block of 12, Impt.	—	

Earliest documented use: Sept. (day ?), 1888 (dated cancel on off-cover stamp); Oct. 29, 1888 (on cover).

Cancellations

Blue	+10.00
Purple	+15.00
Supplementary Mail Type F	+25.00

See Die and Plate Proofs for imperfs. on stamp paper.

Printed by the American Bank Note Company. Plates for the 1c and 2c were of 400 subjects in 4 panes of 100 each. All other values were from plates of 200 subjects in two panes of 100 each.

Franklin — A60

Washington — A61

Jackson — A62

Lincoln — A63

Ulysses S. Grant — A64

Garfield — A65

William T. Sherman — A66

Daniel Webster — A67

Henry Clay — A68

Jefferson — A69

Perry — A70

1890-93 ***Perf. 12***

219 A60 1c **dull blue,** *Feb. 22, 1890*	28.	.60
deep blue	28.	.60
ultramarine	28.	.60
Never hinged	90.	
On cover		.65
Block of 4	120.	4.75
P# strip of 5, Impt. & letter	165.	
P# strip of 6, Impt. & letter	225.	
P# strip of 7, Impt. & letter	260.	
P# block of 10, Impt. & letter	800.	
P# block of 12, Impt. & letter	1,100.	
P# block of 14, Impt. & letter	1,500.	
Never hinged	*3,500.*	
Double transfer	—	—

Earliest documented use: Feb 27, 1890.

Cancellations

Samoa	—
China	—

219D A61 2c **lake,** *Feb. 22, 1890*	240.	5.00
Never hinged	800.	
On cover		7.00
Block of 4	1,000.	45.00
P# strip of 5, Impt.	1,300.	
P# block of 10, Impt.	4,000.	
Double transfer	—	—

Earliest documented use: Feb. 22, 1890 (FDC).

Cancellation

Supplementary Mail Type F	+3.00

220 A61 2c **carmine,** *1890*	25.00	.55
dark carmine	25.00	.55
carmine rose	25.00	.55
rose	25.00	.75
Never hinged	75.00	
On cover		.60
Block of 4	110.00	2.25
P# strip of 5, Impt. & letter	160.00	
P# strip of 6, Impt. & letter	210.00	
Never hinged	400.00	
P# strip of 7, Impt. & letter	250.00	
P# block of 10, Impt. & letter	600.00	
P# block of 12, Impt. & letter	850.00	
P# block of 14, Impt. & letter	1,100.	
Never hinged	—	
Double transfer	—	3.25
a. Cap on left "2" (Plates 235-236, 246-247-248)	140.00	10.00
Never hinged	425.00	
Block of 4	625.00	*150.00*
Pair, Nos. 220, 220a	—	—
Never hinged	—	
c. Cap on both "2's" (Plates 245, 246)	675.00	30.00
Never hinged	2,000.	
Pair, Nos. 220a, 220c	—	—
Never hinged	—	

Earliest documented uses: Mar. 11, 1890 (No. 220); Sept. 9, 1892 (No. 220a); July 7, 1892 (No. 220c).

Cancellations

Blue	+.05
Purple	+.05
Supp. Mail Types F or G	+3.00
China	+20.00

221 A62 3c **purple,** *Feb. 22, 1890*	85.00	7.50
bright purple	85.00	7.50
dark purple	85.00	7.50
Never hinged	260.00	
On cover		16.00
Block of 4	375.00	50.00
P# strip of 5, Impt.	525.00	
P# block of 10, Impt.	2,900.	
Never hinged	—	

Earliest documented use: Feb. 28, 1890.

Cancellation

Samoa	—

222 A63 4c **dark brown,** *June 2, 1890*	110.00	4.00
blackish brown	110.00	4.00
Never hinged	340.00	
On cover		15.00
Block of 4	475.00	30.00
P# strip of 5, Impt.	675.00	
P# block of 10, Impt.	3,500.	
Never hinged	*5,500.*	
Double transfer	125.00	—

Earliest documented use: July 16, 1890.

Cancellation

China	+40.00

223 A64 5c **chocolate,** *June 2, 1890*	90.00	4.00
yellow brown	90.00	4.00
Never hinged	280.00	
On cover		14.00
Block of 4	390.00	26.50
P# strip of 5, Impt.	500.00	
P# block of 10, Impt.	3,000.	
Never hinged	—	
Double transfer	105.00	3.75

Earliest documented use: June 14, 1890.

Cancellations

China	+35.00
Samoa	—
Supp. Mail Types F or G	+3.00

224 A65 6c **brown red,** *Feb. 22, 1890*	80.00	22.50
dark brown red	80.00	22.50
Never hinged	250.00	
On cover		37.50
Block of 4	350.00	120.00
P# strip of 5, Impt.	475.00	
P# block of 10, Impt.	2,900.	
Never hinged	*4,500.*	

Earliest documented use: May 8, 1890.

Cancellation

Supplementary Mail Type F	+3.00

225 A66 8c **lilac,** *Mar. 21, 1893*	65.00	15.00
grayish lilac	65.00	15.00
magenta	65.00	15.00
Never hinged	200.00	
On cover		30.00
Block of 4	275.00	95.00
P# strip of 5, Impt.	375.00	
P# block of 10, Impt.	1,950.	
Never hinged	3,750.	

The 8c was issued because the registry fee was reduced from 10 to 8 cents effective Jan. 1, 1893.

Earliest documented use: May 4, 1893.

226 A67 10c **green,** *Feb. 22, 1890*	210.00	3.75
bluish green	210.00	3.75
dark green	210.00	3.75
Never hinged	650.00	
On cover		10.00
Block of 4	900.00	37.50
P# strip of 5, Impt.	1,150.	
P# block of 10, Impt.	4,250.	
Never hinged	*7,000.*	
Double transfer	—	—

Earliest documented use: Mar. 5, 1890.

Cancellations

Samoa	—
Supp. Mail Type F or G	+2.50

227 A68 15c **indigo,** *Feb. 22, 1890*	275.00	25.00
deep indigo	275.00	25.00
Never hinged	850.00	
On cover		65.00
Block of 4	1,200.	135.00
P# strip of 5, Impt.	1,750.	
P# block of 10, Impt.	*9,500.*	
Never hinged	—	
Double transfer	—	—
Triple transfer		—

Earliest documented use: May 16, 1890.

Cancellation

Supplementary Mail Type F	+3.00

228 A69 30c **black,** *Feb. 22, 1890*	425.00	37.50
gray black	425.00	37.50
full black	425.00	37.50
Never hinged	1,300.	
On cover		*600.00*
Block of 4	1,800.	210.00
P# strip of 5, Impt.	2,500.	
P# block of 10, Impt.	*13,500.*	
Never hinged	—	
Double transfer	—	—

Earliest documented use: April 14, 1890.

Cancellation

			Supplementary Mail Type F		+5.00
229	A70	90c	**orange,** *Feb. 22, 1890*	650.00	140.00
			yellow orange	650.00	140.00
			red orange	650.00	140.00
			Never hinged	2,000.	
			On cover		—
			Block of 4	2,750.	725.00
			P# strip of 5, Impt.	3,750.	
			P# block of 10, Impt.	*27,500.*	
			Never hinged	*42,500.*	
			Short transfer at bottom	—	—

Earliest documented use: (?) 16, 1890 (dated cancel on off-cover stamp); Feb. 7, 1892 (on cover).

Cancellation

Supp. Mail Type F or G		+10.00
Nos. 219-229 (12)	2,283.	265.40

VALUES FOR VERY FINE STAMPS
Please note: Stamps are valued in the grade of Very Fine unless otherwise indicated.

COLUMBIAN EXPOSITION ISSUE

World's Columbian Exposition, Chicago, Ill., May 1 - Oct. 30, 1893, celebrating the 400th anniv. of the discovery of America by Christopher Columbus.

See Nos. 2624-2629 for souvenir sheets containing stamps of designs A71-A86 but with "1992" at upper right.

Columbus in Sight of Land — A71

Landing of Columbus — A72

"Santa Maria," Flagship of Columbus — A73

Fleet of Columbus — A74

Columbus Soliciting Aid from Queen Isabella — A75

Columbus Welcomed at Barcelona — A76

Columbus Restored to Favor — A77

Columbus Presenting Natives — A78

Columbus Announcing His Discovery — A79

Columbus at La Rábida — A80

Recall of Columbus — A81

Queen Isabella Pledging Her Jewels — A82

Columbus in Chains — A83

Columbus Describing His Third Voyage — A84

Queen Isabella and Columbus — A85

Columbus — A86

Type of imprint and plate number

Exposition Station Handstamp Postmark

Printed by the American Bank Note Company.
Plates of 200 subjects in two panes of 100 each (1c, 2c).
Plates of 100 subjects in two panes of 50 each (2c-$5).
Issued (except 8c) Jan. 1 (a Sunday) and Jan. 2 (Monday), 1893. Jan. 1 and Jan. 2 first day covers are documented for the 1c, 2c, 3c, 4c, 5c and 10c. Jan. 2-only first day covers exist for the 6c and $2. See the First Day Cover section for values.

1893 ***Perf. 12***

230	A71	1c	**deep blue**	20.00	.40
			blue	20.00	.40
			pale blue	20.00	.40
			Never hinged	60.00	
			On cover		.90
			Pair on cover, Expo. station machine canc.		100.00
			Pair on cover, Expo. station duplex handstamp canc.		175.00
			Block of 4	85.00	7.00
			P# strip of 3, Impt.	80.00	
			P# strip of 4, Impt. & letter	120.00	
			P# block of 6, Impt.	500.00	
			Never hinged	700.00	
			P# block of 8, Impt. & letter	750.00	
			Never hinged	1,100.	
			Double transfer	25.00	.75
			Cracked plate	90.00	

Earliest documented use: Jan. 1, 1893 (FDC).

Cancellation

China	—
Philippines	—

"Broken hat" variety
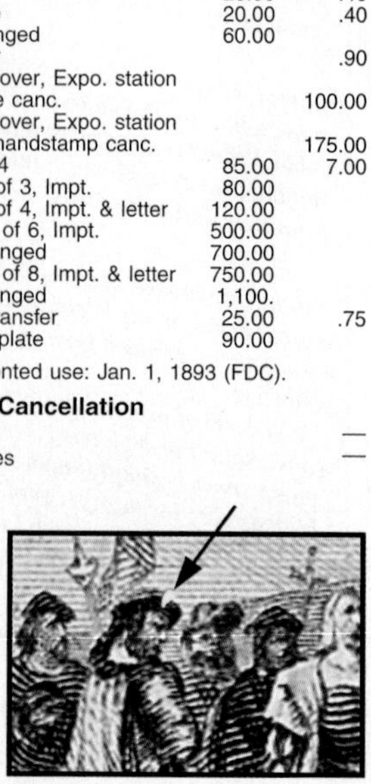

231	A72	2c	**brown violet**	20.00	.30
			deep brown violet	20.00	.30
			gray violet	20.00	.30

Never hinged	60.00	
On cover		.35
On cover or card, Expo. station machine cancel		55.00
On cover or card, Expo. station duplex handstamp cancel		110.00
Block of 4	85.00	4.50
P# strip of 3, Impt.	80.00	
P# strip of 4, Impt. & letter	120.00	
Never Hinged	300.00	
P# block of 6, Impt.	500.00	
Never hinged	700.00	
P# block of 8, Impt. & letter	750.00	
Never hinged	1,100.	
Double transfer	25.00	.35
Triple transfer	60.00	—
Quadruple transfer	95.00	
Broken hat on third figure to left of Columbus	60.00	3.50
Never hinged	175.00	
Broken frame line	22.50	.45
Recut frame lines	22.50	—
Cracked plate	85.00	—

There are a number of different versions of the broken hat variety, some of which may be progressive.

Earliest documented use: Jan. 1, 1893 (FDC).

Cancellations

China		—
Supplementary Mail Type G		+3.50

See Die and Plate Proofs for the 2c, imperf. on stamp paper.

232 A73 3c **green**	55.00	15.00
dull green	55.00	15.00
dark green	55.00	15.00
Never hinged	160.00	
On cover		32.50
On cover, Expo. station machine canc.		225.00
On cover, Expo. station duplex handstamp cancel		325.00
Block of 4	240.00	125.00
P# strip of 3, Impt.	220.00	
Never hinged	450.00	
P# strip of 4, Impt. & letter	325.00	
Never hinged	675.00	
P# block of 6, Impt.	800.00	
Never hinged	1,400.	
P# block of 8, Impt. & letter	1,250.	
Never hinged	2,250.	
Double transfer	75.00	—

Earliest documented use: Jan. 1, 1893 (FDC).

Cancellations

China		—
Supp. Mail Type F or G		+7.50
233 A74 4c **ultramarine**	80.00	7.50
dull ultramarine	80.00	7.50
deep ultramarine	80.00	7.50
Never hinged	240.00	
On cover		22.50
On cover, Expo. station machine canc.		275.00
On cover, Expo. station duplex handstamp cancel		400.00
Block of 4	350.00	70.00
P# strip of 3, Impt.	325.00	
P# strip of 4, Impt. & letter	475.00	—
P# block of 6, Impt.	1,100.	
Never hinged	1,800.	
P# block of 8, Impt. & letter	2,250.	
Never hinged	3,750.	
Double transfer	115.00	—
a. 4c **blue** (error)	*19,000.*	*16,500.*
Never hinged	*35,000.*	
Block of 4	*95,000.*	—
Never hinged	*160,000.*	
P# strip of 4, Impt., letter	*200,000.*	

No. 233a exists in two shades. No. 233a used is valued with small faults, as almost all examples come thus.

Earliest documented use: Jan. 1, 1893 (FDC).

Cancellation

Supplementary Mail Type G		+3.00
234 A75 5c **chocolate**	85.00	8.00
pale brown	85.00	8.00
yellow brown	85.00	8.00
dark chocolate	85.00	8.00
Never hinged	260.00	
On cover		22.50
On cover, Expo. station machine canc.		275.00
On cover, Expo. station duplex handstamp cancel		400.00
Block of 4	360.00	80.00
P# strip of 3, Impt.	350.00	
P# strip of 4, Impt. & letter	550.00	
P# block of 6, Impt.	1,400.	
Never hinged	2,400.	
P# block of 8, Impt. & letter	2,750.	
Never hinged	4,700.	
Double transfer	145.00	—

Earliest documented use: Jan. 1, 1893 (FDC).

Cancellations

China		—
Philippines		—
Supplementary Mail Type F		+3.00
235 A76 6c **purple**	80.00	22.50
dull purple	80.00	22.50
Never hinged	240.00	
a. 6c **red violet**	80.00	22.50
Never hinged	240.00	
On cover		50.00
On cover, Expo. station machine canc.		300.00
On cover, Expo. station duplex handstamp cancel		450.00
Block of 4	350.00	160.00
P# strip of 3, Impt.	310.00	
P# strip of 4, Impt. & letter	475.00	
P# block of 6, Impt.	1,200.	
Never hinged	2,100.	
P# block of 8, Impt. & letter	2,250.	
Never hinged	3,750.	
Double transfer	105.00	30.00

Earliest documented use: Jan. 2, 1893 (FDC).

Cancellations

China		—
Supplementary Mail Type F		+5.00
236 A77 8c **magenta,** *Mar. 1893*	72.50	11.00
light magenta	72.50	11.00
dark magenta	72.50	11.00
Never hinged	215.00	
On cover		22.50
On cover, Expo. station machine canc.		300.00
On cover, Expo. station duplex handstamp cancel		475.00
Block of 4	320.00	90.00
P# strip of 3, Impt.	275.00	
P# strip of 4, Impt. & letter	425.00	
P# block of 6, Impt.	1,100.	
Never hinged	1,800.	
P# block of 8, Impt. & letter	1,650.	
Never hinged	2,800.	
Double transfer	80.00	—

Earliest documented use: Mar. 18, 1893.

Cancellations

China		—
Supplementary Mail Type F		+4.50
237 A78 10c **black brown**	135.00	8.00
dark brown	135.00	8.00
gray black	135.00	8.00
Never hinged	400.00	
On cover		32.50
On cover, Expo. station machine canc.		400.00
On cover, Expo. station duplex handstamp cancel		550.00
Block of 4	575.00	80.00
P# strip of 3, Impt.	550.00	
P# strip of 4, Impt. & letter	775.00	
Never hinged	1,700.	
P# block of 6, Impt.	3,750.	
Never hinged	*6,500.*	
P# block of 8, Impt. & letter	6,500.	
Never hinged	*11,000.*	
Double transfer	160.00	12.50
Triple transfer	—	

Earliest documented use: Jan. 1, 1893 (FDC).

Cancellations

Philippines		—
Supp. Mail Types F or G		+4.00
238 A79 15c **dark green**	240.00	75.00
green	240.00	75.00
dull green	240.00	75.00
Never hinged	750.00	
On cover		225.00
On cover, Expo. station machine canc.		700.00
On cover, Expo. station duplex handstamp cancel		*1,000.*
Block of 4	1,025.	600.00
P# strip of 3, Impt.	975.	
P# strip of 4, Impt. & letter	1,500.	
P# block of 6, Impt.	*4,250.*	
Never hinged	*7,250.*	
P# block of 8, Impt. & letter	*7,500.*	
Never hinged	*13,000.*	
Double transfer	—	—

Earliest documented use: Jan. 26, 1893.

Cancellations

China		+75.00
Supp. Mail Type F or G		+10.00
239 A80 30c **orange brown**	275.00	90.00
bright orange brown	275.00	90.00
Never hinged	850.00	
On cover		400.00
On cover, Expo. station machine canc.		*1,250.*
On cover, Expo. station duplex handstamp cancel		*1,750.*
Block of 4	1,300.	800.00
P# strip of 3, Impt.	1,150.	
P# strip of 4, Impt. & letter	1,700.	—
P# block of 6, Impt.	*9,000.*	
Never hinged	*15,000.*	
P# block of 8, Impt. & letter	*16,000.*	
Never hinged	*25,000.*	

Earliest documented use: Jan. 10, 1893 (dated cancel on off-cover stamp); Feb. 8, 1893 (cover).

Cancellations

Supp. Mail Types F or G		+25.00
240 A81 50c **slate blue**	600.00	180.00
dull state blue	600.00	180.00
Never hinged	1,800.	
On cover		625.00
On cover, Expo. station machine canc.		*1,750.*
On cover, Expo. station duplex handstamp cancel		2,250.
Block of 4	2,750.	2,000.
P# strip of 3, Impt.	2,500.	
P# strip of 4, Impt. & letter	*4,000.*	—
Never hinged	8,250.	
P# block of 6, Impt.	*15,000.*	
Never hinged	*25,000.*	
P# block of 8, Impt. & letter	*30,000.*	
Never hinged	*50,000.*	
Double transfer	—	—
Triple transfer	—	—

Earliest documented use: Feb. 8, 1893.

Cancellation

Supp. Mail Types F or G		+30.00
241 A82 $1 **salmon**	1,200.	650.
dark salmon	1,200.	650.
Never hinged	4,250.	
No gum	600.	
On cover		*2,000.*
On cover, Expo. station machine canc.		*3,500.*
On cover, Expo. station duplex handstamp cancel		4,500.
Block of 4	5,250.	*5,000.*
P# strip of 3, Impt.	5,500.	
P# strip of 4, Impt. & letter	8,500.	
P# block of 6, Impt.	*52,500.*	
P# block of 8, Impt. & letter	*90,000.*	
Never hinged	*140,000.*	
Double transfer	—	—

Earliest documented use: Jan. 11, 1893 (dated cancel on off-cover stamp); Jan. 21, 1893 (on cover).

Cancellations

Supp. Mail Types F or G		+50.
242 A83 $2 **brown red**	1,250.	650.
deep brown red	1,250.	650.
Never hinged	4,250.	
No gum	625.	
On cover		*2,100.*
On cover, Expo. station machine canc.		*3,500.*
On cover, Expo. station duplex handstamp cancel		*4,500.*
Block of 4	5,500.	*5,500.*
P# strip of 3, Impt.	5,750.	
P# strip of 4, Impt. & letter	9,000.	
P# block of 6, Impt.	*75,000.*	
P# block of 8, Impt. & letter	*95,000.*	

Earliest documented use: Jan. 2, 1893 (FDC).

Cancellations

Supplementary Mail Type G		+50.

The No. 242 plate block of 8 is believed to be unique.

243 A84 $3 **yellow green**	1,900.	1,000.
pale yellow green	1,900.	1,000.
Never hinged	6,500.	
No gum	950.	
a. $3 **olive green**	1,900.	1,000.
Never hinged	6,500.	
No gum	950.	
On cover		*2,600.*
On cover, Expo. station machine canc.		*5,000.*
On cover, Expo. station duplex handstamp cancel		*7,000.*
Block of 4	*10,000.*	*10,000.*
P# strip of 3, Impt.	*8,500.*	
P# strip of 4, Impt. & letter	*12,000.*	
P# block of 6, Impt.	*95,000.*	

Earliest documented use: Mar. 24, 1893.

244 A85 $4 **crimson lake**	2,600.	1,300.
Never hinged	8,750.	
No gum	1,300.	
a. $4 **rose carmine**	2,600.	1,300.
pale aniline rose	2,600.	1,300.
Never hinged	8,750.	
No gum	1,300.	
On cover		*4,000.*
On cover, Expo. station machine canc.		*6,500.*
On cover, Expo. station duplex handstamp cancel		*9,000.*
Block of 4	*13,000.*	*15,000.*
P# strip of 3, Impt.	*11,500.*	
P# strip of 4, Impt. & letter	*16,500.*	
P# block of 6, Impt.	*300,000.*	
P# block of 8, Impt. & letter	*400,000.*	

The No. 244 plate block of 8 is unique; it has full original gum with light hinge marks.

Earliest documented use: Mar. 24, 1893.

245 A86 $5 **black**	3,000.	1,500.
grayish black	3,000.	1,500.
Never hinged	10,500.	
No gum	1,500.	
On cover		*4,750.*
On cover, Expo. station machine canc.		*15,000.*
On cover, Expo. station duplex handstamp cancel		*17,500.*
Block of 4	*15,000.*	*15,000.*
P# strip of 3, Impt.	*16,000.*	
P# strip of 4, Impt. & letter	*65,000.*	
Never hinged	*195,000.*	

P# block of 6, Impt.	*250,000.*
Never hinged	*325,000.*
P# block of 8, Impt. & letter	*300,000.*

Earliest documented use: Jan. 6, 1893.

The No. 245 plate block of 8 is unique; it has traces of original gum.

See Nos. 2624-2629 for souvenir sheets containing stamps of designs A71-A86 but with "1992" at upper right.

Nos. 230-245 exist imperforate; not issued. See Die and Plate proofs for the 2c.

Never-Hinged Stamps

See note before No. 182 regarding premiums for never-hinged stamps.

BUREAU ISSUES

In the following listings of postal issues mostly printed by the Bureau of Engraving and Printing at Washington, D.C., the editors acknowledge with thanks the use of material prepared by the Catalogue Listing Committee of the Bureau Issues Association.

The Bureau-printed stamps until 1965 were engraved except the Offset Issues of 1918-19 (Nos. 525-536). Engraving and lithography were combined for the first time for the Homemakers 5c (No. 1253). The Bureau used photogravure first in 1971 on the Missouri 8c (No. 1426).

Stamps in this section that were not printed by the Bureau begin with Nos. 909-921 and are so noted.

"*On cover*" listings carry through No. 701. Beyond this point a few covers of special significance are listed. Many Bureau Issue stamps are undoubtedly scarce properly used on cover. Most higher denominations exist almost exclusively on pieces of package wrapping and usually in combination with other values. Collector interest in covers is generally limited to fancy cancellations, attractive corner cards, uses abroad and other special usages.

Plate number blocks are valued unused. Although many exist used, and are scarcer in that condition, they tend to sell for less than the value of the unused examples because they are less sought after.

IMPRINTS AND PLATE NUMBERS

In listing the Bureau of Engraving & Printing Imprints, the editors have followed the classification of types adopted by the Bureau Issues Association. Types I, II, IV, V and VIII occur on postage issues and are illustrated below. Types III, VI and VII occur only on Special Delivery plates, so are illustrated with the listings of those stamps; other types are illustrated with the listings of the issues on which they occur.

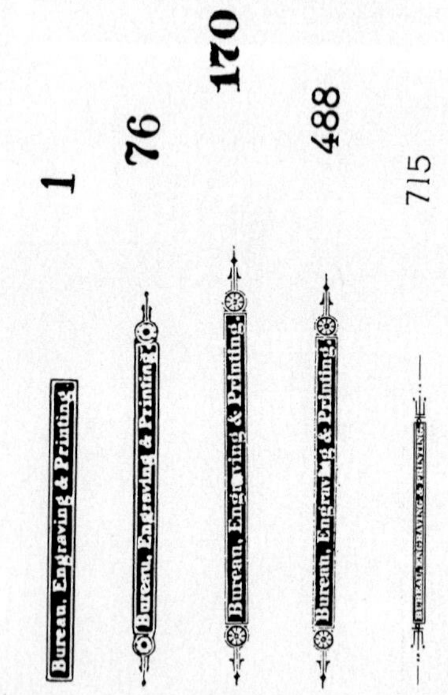

Type I II IV V VIII

In listing Imprint blocks and strips, the editors have designated for each stamp the various types known to exist. If, however, the Catalogue listing sufficiently describes the Imprint, no type number is given. Thus a listing reading: "P# block of 6, Impt. (Imprint) & A" in the 1912-14 series would not be followed by a type number as the description is self-explanatory. Values are for the commonest types.

PLATE POSITIONS

At the suggestion of the Catalogue Listing Committee of the Bureau Issues Association (now the United States Stamp Society), all plate positions of these issues are indicated by giving the plate number first, next the pane position, and finally the stamp position. For example: 20234 L.L. 58.

Franklin — A87

Washington — A88

Jackson — A89

Lincoln — A90

Grant — A91

Garfield — A92

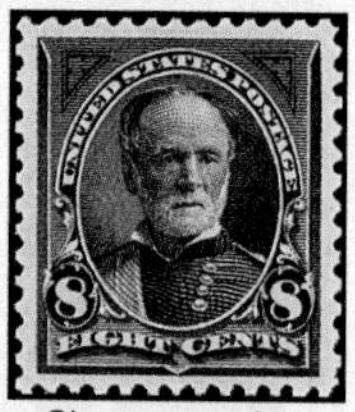

Sherman — A93

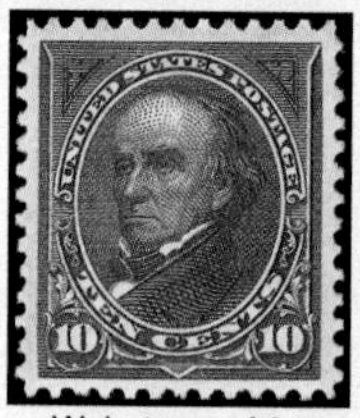

Webster — A94

Clay — A95

Jefferson — A96

Perry — A97

James Madison — A98

John Marshall — A99

Designed by Thomas F. Morris.

REGULAR ISSUE

Plates for the issue of 1894 were of two sizes: 400 subjects for all 1c, 2c and 10c denominations; 200 subjects for all 6c, 8c, 15c, 50c, $1.00, $2.00 and $5.00, and both 400 and 200 subjects for the 3c, 4c and 5c denominations; all issued in panes of 100 each.

1894 **Unwmk.** ***Perf. 12***

246 A87 1c **ultramarine,** *Oct. 1894*	32.50	5.00
bright ultramarine	32.50	5.00
dark ultramarine	32.50	5.00
Never hinged	97.50	
On cover		20.00
Block of 4	140.00	35.00
P# strip of 3, Impt., T I	145.00	
Never hinged	325.00	
P# block of 6, Impt., T I	450.00	
Never hinged	900.00	
Double transfer	40.00	6.00

Earliest documented use: Oct. 17, 1894.

Cancellation

China		—
247 A87 1c **blue**	75.00	3.00
bright blue	75.00	3.00
dark blue	75.00	3.00
Never hinged	225.00	
On cover		17.50
Block of 4	325.00	22.50
P# strip of 3, Impt., T I or II	325.00	
Never hinged	675.00	
P# block of 6, Impt., T I or II	900.00	
Never hinged	1,700.	
Double transfer	—	4.50

Earliest documented use: Nov. 5, 1894.

TWO CENTS:

Triangle A (Type I)

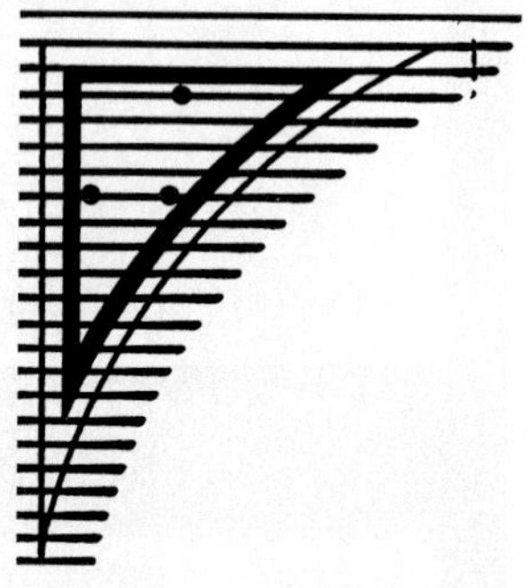

Type I (Triangle A). The horizontal lines of the ground work run across the triangle and are of the same thickness within it as without.

Triangle B (Type II)

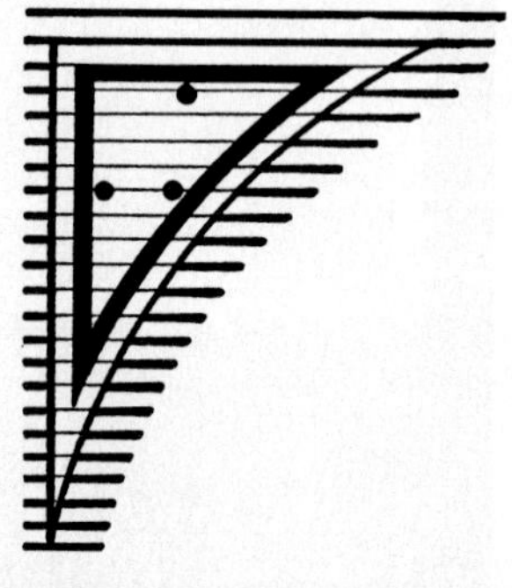

Type II (Triangle B). The horizontal lines cross the triangle but are thinner within it than without. Other minor design differences exist, but the change to Triangle B is a sufficient determinant.

Triangle C (Types III and IV)

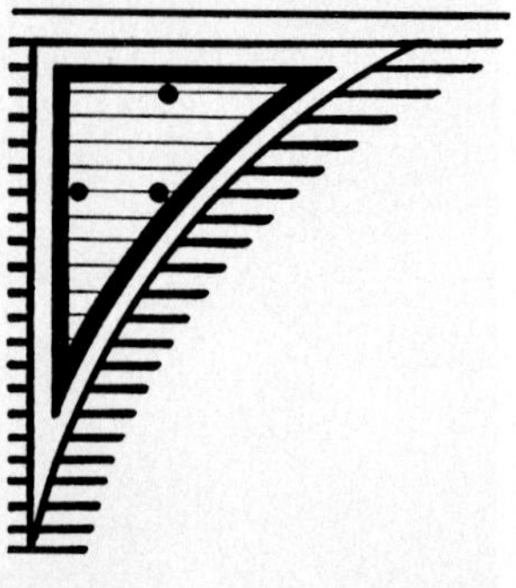

Type III (Triangle C). The horizontal lines do not cross the double lines of the triangle. The lines within the triangle are thin, as in Type II. The rest of the design is the same as Type II, except that most of the designs had the dot in the "S" of "CENTS" removed. Stamps with this dot present are listed; some specialists refer to them as "Type IIIa" varieties.

Type IV (Triangle C). See No. 279B and its varieties. Type IV is from a new die with many major and minor design variations including, (1) re-cutting and lengthening of hairline, (2) shaded toga button, (3) strengthening of lines on sleeve, (4) additional dots on ear, (5) "T" of "TWO" straight at right, (6) background lines extend into white oval opposite "U" of "UNITED." Many other differences exist.

For further information concerning type IV, see also George Brett's article in the Sept. 1993 issue of the "The United States Specialist" and the 23-part article by Kenneth Diehl in the Dec. 1994 through Aug. 1997 issues of the "The United States Specialist."

248	A88	2c **pink,** type I, *Oct. 1894*	30.00	7.50
		pale pink	30.00	7.50
		Never hinged	90.00	
		On cover		15.00
		Block of 4	130.00	42.50
		P# strip of 3, Impt., T I or II	120.00	
		Never hinged	275.00	
		P# block of 6, Impt., T I or II	300.00	
		Never hinged	675.00	
		Double transfer	—	—
a.		Vert. pair, imperf horiz.	*5,500.*	

Earliest documented use: Oct. 16, 1894.

249	A88	2c **carmine lake,** type I, *Oct. 1894*	175.00	5.50
		dark carmine lake	175.00	5.50
		Never hinged	550.00	
		On cover		11.50
		Block of 4	750.00	40.00
		P# strip of 3, Impt., T I or II	700.00	
		Never hinged	1,650.	
		P# block of 6, Impt., T I or II	2,500.	
		Never hinged	5,000.	
		Double transfer	—	6.50
a.		Double impression		—

Earliest documented use: Oct. 11, 1894.

250	A88	2c **carmine,** type I, *Oct. 1894*	30.00	2.50
		dark carmine	30.00	4.50
		Never hinged	90.00	
		On cover		3.50
		Block of 4	130.00	18.00
a.		2c **rose,** type I, *Oct. 1894*	30.00	4.50
		Never hinged	90.00	
		On cover		5.50
		Block of 4	130.00	20.00
b.		2c **scarlet,** type I, *Jan. 1895*	30.00	2.50
		Never hinged	90.00	
		On cover		3.50
		Block of 4	130.00	18.00
		P# strip of 3, Impt., T I or II	120.00	
		Never hinged	300.00	
		P# block of 6, Impt., T I or II	375.00	
		Never hinged	750.00	
		Double transfer	—	5.00
d.		Horizontal pair, imperf. between	*2,000.*	

Earliest documented uses: Oct. 15, 1894 (No. 250), Oct. 13, 1894 (No. 250a), Jan. 17, 1895 (No. 250b).

251	A88	2c **carmine,** type II, *Feb. 1895*	350.00	12.00
		dark carmine	350.00	12.00
		Never hinged	1,100.	
		On cover		20.00
		Block of 4	1,250.	100.00
a.		2c **scarlet,** type II, *Feb. 1895*	350.00	9.00
		Never hinged	1,100.	
		On cover		15.00
		Block of 4	1,250.	70.00
		P# strip of 3, Impt., T II	1,200.	
		Never hinged	3,500.	
		P# block of 6, Impt., T II	3,250.	
		Never hinged	7,000.	

Earliest documented uses: Feb. 12, 1895 (No. 251, dated cancel on off-cover stamp); Feb. 16, 1895 (No. 251, on cover); Feb. 19, 1895 (No. 251a).

252	A88	2c **carmine,** type III, *Mar. 1895*	130.00	12.00
		pale carmine	130.00	12.00
		Never hinged	400.00	
a.		2c **scarlet,** type III, *Mar. 1895*	130.00	12.00
		Never hinged	400.00	
		On cover		16.00
		Block of 4	550.00	100.00
		P# strip of 3, Impt., T II or IV	525.00	
		Never hinged	1,400.	
		P# block of 6, Impt., T II or IV	1,900.	
		Never hinged	4,000.	
		Dot in "S" of "CENTS" (carmine)	150.00	5.75
		Never hinged	390.00	
b.		Horiz. pair, imperf. vert.	*5,000.*	
c.		Horiz. pair, imperf. between	*5,500.*	

Former Nos. 252a, 252b are now Nos. 252b, 252c.

Earliest documented uses: Apr. 2, 1895 (dated cancel tying No. 252 dot in "S" variety on piece); Apr. 5, 1895 (No. 252); Apr. 17, 1895 (No. 252a).

253	A89	3c **purple,** *Sept. 1894*	125.00	11.00
		dark purple	125.00	11.00
		Never hinged	400.00	
		On cover		25.00
		Block of 4	550.00	80.00
		Margin block of 4, arrow, R or L	575.00	
		P# strip of 3, Impt., T I or II	500.00	
		Never hinged	1,350.	
		P# block of 6, Impt., T I or II	1,500.	
		Never hinged	3,500.	

Earliest documented use: Oct. 20, 1894 (dated cancel on off-cover stamp); Nov. 15, 1894 (on cover).

See Die and Plate Proofs for imperf. on stamp paper.

254	A90	4c **dark brown,** *Sept. 1894*	175.00	7.50
		brown	175.00	7.50
		Never hinged	525.00	
		On cover		21.00
		Block of 4	750.00	42.50
		Margin block of 4, arrow, R or L	775.00	
		P# strip of 3, Impt., T I or II	725.00	
		Never hinged	1,750.	

			P# block of 6, Impt., T I or II	2,000.	
			Never hinged	4,250.	

Earliest documented use: Oct. 16, 1894 (dated cancel on off-cover stamp); Nov. 21, 1894 (on cover).

See Die and Plate Proofs for imperf. on stamp paper.

Cancellations

			Supplementary Mail Type F		+2.00
255	A91	5c	**chocolate,** *Sept. 1894*	125.00	7.00
			deep chocolate	125.00	7.00
			yellow brown	125.00	7.00
			Never hinged	375.00	
			On cover		20.00
			Block of 4	550.00	50.00
			Margin block of 4, arrow, R or L	575.00	
			P# strip of 3, Impt., T I, II or IV	550.00	
			Never hinged	1,275.	
			P# block of 6, Impt., T I, II or IV	1,350.	
			Never hinged	2,750.	
			Double transfer	150.00	6.50
			Worn plate, diagonal lines missing in oval background	125.00	5.00
c.			Vert. pair, imperf. horiz.	*4,000.*	
			P# block of 6, Impt., T IV	—	

See Die and Plate Proofs for imperf. on stamp paper.

Earliest documented use: Oct. 23, 1894.

Cancellations

			Supplementary Mail Type G		+2.00
			China		—
256	A92	6c	**dull brown,** *July 1894*	175.00	25.00
			Never hinged	525.00	
			On cover		47.50
			Block of 4	750.00	175.00
			Margin block of 4, arrow, R or L	775.00	
			P# strip of 3, Impt., T I	725.00	
			Never hinged	1,750.	
			P# block of 6, Impt., T I	2,750.	—
			Never hinged	*5,750.*	
a.			Vert. pair, imperf. horiz.	*3,000.*	
			P# block of 6, Impt., T I	*21,500.*	

Earliest documented use: Aug. 11, 1894.

257	A93	8c	**violet brown,** *Mar. 1895*	175.00	18.50
			bright violet brown	175.00	18.50
			Never hinged	525.00	
			On cover		45.00
			Block of 4	750.00	130.00
			Margin block of 4, arrow, R or L	775.00	
			P# strip of 3, Impt., T I	725.00	
			Never hinged	1,750.	
			P# block of 6, Impt., T I	2,500.	
			Never hinged	*5,500.*	

Earliest documented use: May 8, 1895.

258	A94	10c	**dark green,** *Sept. 1894*	325.00	16.00
			green	325.00	16.00
			dull green	325.00	16.00
			Never hinged	1,000.	
			On cover		35.00
			Block of 4	1,350.	90.00
			P# strip of 3, Impt., T I	1,450.	
			Never hinged	3,250.	
			P# block of 6, Impt., T I	3,500.	
			Never hinged	*7,250.*	
			Double transfer	375.00	15.00

See Die and Plate Proofs for imperf. on stamp paper.

Earliest documented use: Nov. 2, 1894.

Cancellations

			China		—
			Supp. Mail Types F, G		+2.00
259	A95	15c	**dark blue,** *Oct. 1894*	325.00	60.00
			indigo	325.00	60.00
			Never hinged	1,000.	
			On cover		115.00
			Block of 4	1,350.	400.00
			Margin block of 4, arrow, R or L	1,400.	
			P# strip of 3, Impt., T I	1,500.	
			Never hinged	3,250.	
			P# block of 6, Impt., T I	5,000.	
			Never hinged	*10,000.*	

Earliest documented use: Dec. 6, 1894.

Cancellation

			China		—
260	A96	50c	**orange,** *Nov. 1894*	600.	140.
			deep orange	600.	140.
			Never hinged	1,900.	
			On cover		1,000.
			Block of 4	2,750.	1,150.
			Margin block of 4, arrow, R or L	2,850.	
			P# strip of 3, Impt., T I	2,600.	
			Never hinged	*5,750.*	
			P# block of 6, Impt., T I	20,000.	
			Never hinged	*32,500.*	

Earliest documented use: Dec. 12, 1894 (dated cancel on off-cover stamp); Jan. 15, 1895 (on cover).

Cancellations

Supp. Mail Type F or G	—
China	—

Type I

Type II

ONE DOLLAR
Type I. The circles enclosing "$1" are broken where they meet the curved line below "One Dollar."
Type II. The circles are complete.
The fifteen left vertical rows of impressions from plate 76 are Type I, the balance being Type II.

261	A97	$1	**black,** type I, *Nov. 1894*	1,200.	350.
			grayish black	1,200.	350.
			Never hinged	3,750.	
			No gum	375.	
			On cover		*2,750.*
			Block of 4	5,500.	*2,100.*
			Margin block of 4, arrow, L	5,750.	
			P# strip of 3, Impt., T V	4,750.	
			P# block of 6, Impt., T V	*20,000.*	

Earliest documented use: Jan. 18, 1895.

261A	A97	$1	**black,** type II, *Nov. 1894*	2,400.	800.
			Never hinged	7,500.	
			No gum	750.	
			On cover		*4,500.*
			Block of 4	*10,000.*	*5,000.*
			Margin block of 4, arrow, R	*10,500.*	
			Horizontal pair, types I and II	*4,250.*	*1,400.*
			Block of 4, two each of types I and II	*9,500.*	—
			P# strip of 3, Impt., T V, one stamp No. 261	7,000.	
			P# block of 6, Impt., T V, two stamps No. 261	*40,000.*	

Earliest documented use: Mar. 22, 1895. A Mar. 11, 1895, cover has been reported. The editors would like to see evidence of certification of this date.

262	A98	$2	**bright blue,** *Dec. 1894*	3,250.	1,250.
			Never hinged	10,000.	
			No gum	1,100.	
			dark blue	3,400.	1,300.
			Never hinged	10,500.	
			On cover		*5,000.*
			Block of 4	*14,500.*	*9,000.*
			Margin block of 4, arrow, R or L	*15,000.*	
			P# strip of 3, Impt., T V	*15,000.*	
			P# block of 6, Impt., T V	*45,000.*	

Earliest documented use: July 6, 1895 (dated cancel on off-cover stamp); July 15, 1895 (on cover).

263	A99	$5	**dark green,** *Dec. 1894*	5,000.	2,750.
			Never hinged	16,500.	
			No gum	2,500.	
			On cover		—
			Block of 4	*24,000.*	*15,000.*
			Margin block of 4, arrow, R or L	*24,500.*	
			P# strip of 3, Impt., T V	*25,000.*	

Earliest documented use: July 6, 1896 (dated cancel on off-cover stamp).

REGULAR ISSUE

Designed by Thomas F. Morris.

(Actual size of letter)

repeated in rows, thus

HORIZONTAL WATERMARK ORIENTATIONS

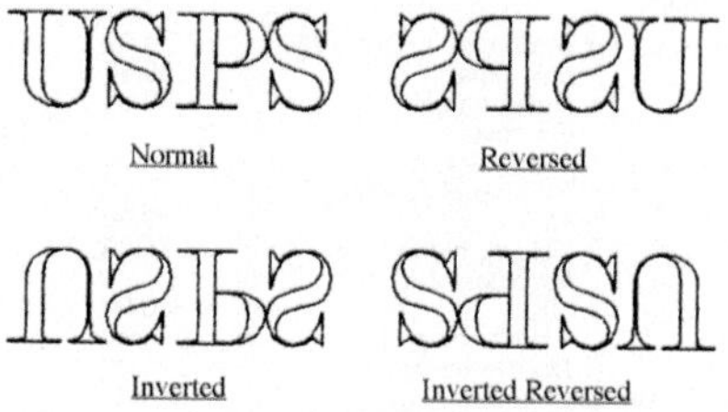

VERTICAL WATERMARK ORIENTATIONS

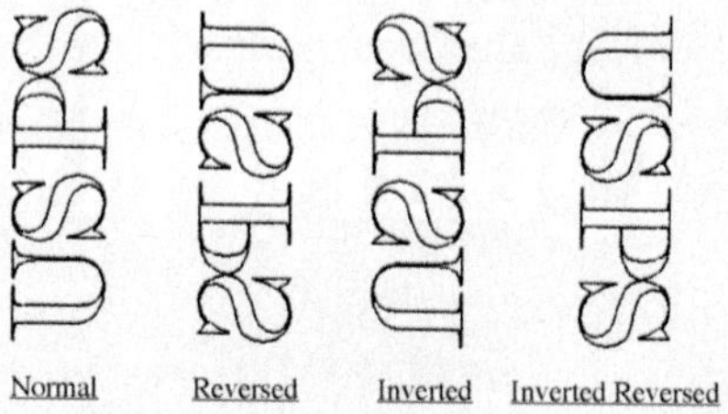

Watermark 191

The letters stand for "United States Postage Stamp."

Plates for the 1895 issue were of two sizes:
400 subjects for all 1c, 2c and 10c denominations; 200 subjects for all 3c, 4c, 5c, 6c, 8c, 15c, 50c, $1, $2 and $5; all issued in panes of 100 each.
Printings from the 400 subject plates show the watermark reading horizontally, on the 200 subject printings the watermark reads vertically. Watermarks are viewed from the back of the stamp.

Wmk. 191 Horizontally or Vertically

1895 ***Perf. 12***

264	A87	1c	**blue,** *Apr. 1895*	6.50	.50
			dark blue	6.50	.50
			pale blue	6.50	.50
			Never hinged	19.00	
			On cover		1.25
			Block of 4	27.50	5.00
			P# strip of 3, Impt., T I, II, IV or V	27.50	
			Never hinged	70.00	
			P# block of 6, Impt., T I, II, IV or V	250.00	
			Never hinged	450.00	
			Double transfer	—	1.00

Earliest documented use: May 16, 1895.

Cancellations

			China		—
			Philippines		—
			Samoa		—
265	A88	2c	**carmine,** type I, *May 1895*	30.00	3.00
			deep carmine	30.00	3.00
			Never hinged	90.00	
			On cover		5.00
			Block of 4	130.00	16.00

		Unused	Used
	P# strip of 3, Impt., T II	120.00	
	Never hinged	325.00	
	P# block of 6, Impt., T II	400.00	
	Never hinged	800.00	
	Double transfer	45.00	6.75

Earliest documented use: May 2, 1895.

		Unused	Used
266 A88 2c	**carmine,** type II, *May 1895*	35.00	5.00
	Never hinged	110.00	
	On cover		8.50
	Block of 4	200.00	40.00
	Horizontal pair, types II and III	150.00	17.50
	Never hinged	425.00	
	P# strip of 3, Impt., T II or IV	140.00	
	Never hinged	375.00	
	P# block of 6, Impt., T II or IV	500.00	
	Never hinged	1,000.	

Earliest documented use: May 27, 1895.

		Unused	Used
267 A88 2c	**carmine,** type III *May 1895*	5.50	.40
	deep carmine	5.50	.40
	reddish carmine	5.50	.40
	Never hinged	16.00	
	On cover		.55
	Block of 4	24.00	3.25
	P# strip of 3, Impt., T II, IV or V	22.50	
	Never hinged	57.50	
	P# block of 6, Impt., T II, IV or V	190.00	
	Never hinged	325.00	
	Dot in "S" of "CENTS"	7.50	.50
	Never hinged	22.50	
	Double transfer	16.50	1.25
a.	2c **pink,** type III, *Nov. 1897*	20.00	2.00
	Never hinged	60.00	
	bright pink	25.00	5.00
	Never hinged	75.00	
	On cover		1.50
	Block of 4	90.00	14.00
	P# strip of 3, Impt., T II, IV or V	75.00	
	Never hinged	200.00	
	P# block of 6, Impt., T II, IV or V	425.00	
	Never hinged	825.00	
	Dot in "S" of "CENTS"	35.00	2.50
	Never hinged	110.00	
b.	2c **vermilion,** type III, *early 1899*	*50.00*	9.00
c.	2c **rose carmine,** type III, *Mar. 1899*	—	—

Earliest documented uses:
No. 267, May 28, 1895;
No. 267 with dot in "S", July 15, 1895;
No. 267a, Dec. 8, 1897;
No. 267a with dot in "S", Mar. 18, 1898.

Cancellations

Green	—
China	—
Hawaii	—
Philippines	—
Samoa	—

The three left vertical rows of impressions from plate 170 are Type II, the balance being Type III.

		Unused	Used
268 A89 3c	**purple,** *Oct. 1895*	37.50	2.00
	dark purple	37.50	2.00
	Never hinged	115.00	
	On cover		8.00
	Block of 4	160.00	20.00
	Margin block of 4, arrow, R or L	175.00	
	P# strip of 3, Impt., T II or V	150.00	
	Never hinged	400.00	
	P# block of 6, Impt., T II or IV	725.00	
	Never hinged	1,300.	
	Double transfer	45.00	4.50

Earliest documented use: Dec. 1, 1895.

Cancellations

Guam	—
China	—
Philippines	—

		Unused	Used
269 A90 4c	**dark brown,** *June, 1895*	50.00	3.00
	dark yellow brown	50.00	3.00
	Never hinged	150.00	
	On cover		11.00
	Block of 4	210.00	27.50
	Margin block of 4, arrow, R or L	225.00	
	P# strip of 3, Impt., T I, II, IV or V	200.00	
	Never hinged	500.00	
	P# block of 6, Impt., T I, II, IV or V	825.00	
	Never hinged	1,650.	
	Double transfer	55.00	5.00

Earliest documented use: July 22, 1895.

Cancellations

Philippines	—
China	—
Samoa	—

		Unused	Used
270 A91 5c	**chocolate,** *June, 1895*	37.50	3.00
	deep brown	37.50	3.00
	chestnut	37.50	3.00
	Never hinged	115.00	
	On cover		7.50
	Block of 4	160.00	27.50
	Margin block of 4, arrow, R or L	170.00	
	P# strip of 3, Impt., T I, II, IV or V	150.00	
	Never hinged	400.00	
	P# block of 6, Impt., T I, II, IV or V	700.00	
	Never hinged	1,300.	
	Double transfer	45.00	4.50
	Worn plate, diagonal lines missing in oval background	40.00	3.25

Earliest documented use: Sept. 12, 1895.

Cancellations

China	—
Supplementary Mail G	+2.50

		Unused	Used
271 A92 6c	**dull brown,** *Aug. 1895*	130.00	7.50
	claret brown	130.00	7.50
	Never hinged	400.00	
	On cover		27.50
	Block of 4	600.00	65.00
	Margin block of 4, arrow, R or L	625.00	
	P# strip of 3, Impt., T I, IV or V	525.00	
	Never hinged	1,300.	
	P# block of 6, Impt., T I, IV or V	3,000.	
	Never hinged	5,500.	
	Very thin paper	150.00	7.50
a.	Wmkd. USIR	*12,500.*	*10,000.*
	Pair	—	—
	P# strip of 3, Impt.	—	

Earliest documented use: Sept. 14, 1895.

Cancellation

Philippines	—

Nos. 271a, 272a must have an identifiable portion of the letters "I" or "R." Single stamps from the same sheets, but showing the "U" or "S" are considered to be Nos. 271 and 272.

		Unused	Used
272 A93 8c	**violet brown,** *July 1895*	75.00	2.50
	dark violet brown	75.00	2.50
	Never hinged	225.00	
	On cover		14.00
	Block of 4	325.00	17.50
	Margin block of 4, arrow, R or L	340.00	
	P# strip of 3, Impt., T I, IV or V	310.00	
	Never hinged	800.00	
	P# block of 6, Impt., T I, IV or V	1,000.	
	Never hinged	2,100.	
	Double transfer	90.00	4.00
a.	Wmkd. USIR	*6,000.*	1,000.
	Block of 4		*5,500.*
	P# strip of 3 Impt., T I	*20,000.*	

Earliest documented use: Sept. 11, 1895.

Cancellations

China	—
Guam	—
Philippines	—
Puerto Rico, 1898	—
Samoa	—
Supplementary Mail Type G	+2.50

		Unused	Used
273 A94 10c	**dark green,** *June 1895*	100.00	2.00
	green	100.00	2.00
	Never hinged	300.00	
	On cover		15.00
	Block of 4	425.00	20.00
	P# strip of 3, Impt., T I or IV	425.00	
	Never hinged	1,000.	
	P# block of 6, Impt., T I or IV	1,750.	
	Never hinged	3,500.	
	Double transfer	125.00	4.50

Earliest documented use: July 25, 1895.

Cancellations

Green	—
China	—
Cuba	—
Philippines	—
Supp. Mail Types F, G	+2.00

		Unused	Used
274 A95 15c	**dark blue,** *Sept. 1895*	250.00	16.00
	indigo	250.00	16.00
	Never hinged	750.00	
	On cover		55.00
	Block of 4	1,050.	100.00
	Margin block of 4, arrow, R or L	1,075.	
	P# strip of 3, Impt., T I or IV	1,000.	
	Never hinged	2,500.	
	P# block of 6, Impt., T I or IV	3,750.	
	Never hinged	*10,000.*	

Earliest documented use: May 5, 1896.

Cancellations

China	—
Philippines	—
Supplementary Mail Type G	+3.00

		Unused	Used
275 A96 50c	**orange,** *Nov. 1895*	300.	35.00
	Never hinged	950.	
	On cover		400.00
	Block of 4	1,300.	200.00
	Margin block of 4, arrow, R or L	1,350.	
	P# strip of 3, Impt., T I	1,200.	
	P# block of 6, Impt., T I	6,000.	
	Never hinged	*12,500.*	
a.	50c **red orange**	360.	42.50
	Never hinged	1,100.	
	On cover		400.00
	Block of 4	1,550.	250.00
	Margin block of 4, arrow, R or L	1,600.	
	P# strip of 3, Impt., T I	1,450.	
	P# block of 6, Impt., T I	6,500.	

Earliest documented use: May 5, 1896.

Cancellations

China	—
Philippines	—
Supp. Mail Types F, G	+5.

		Unused	Used
276 A97 $1	**black,** type I, *Aug. 1895*	700.	100.
	greenish black	700.	100.
	Never hinged	2,200.	
	No gum	200.	
	On cover		*2,250.*
	Block of 4	3,000.	750.
	Margin block of 4, arrow, L	3,100.	
	P# strip of 3, Impt., T V	2,900.	
	Never hinged	*7,000.*	
	P# block of 6, Impt., T V	*40,000.*	

Earliest documented use: Mar. 1, 1898.

Cancellation

Philippines	—

		Unused	Used
276A A97 $1	**black,** type II, *Aug. 1895*	1,500.	225.
	greenish black	1,500.	225.
	Never hinged	4,750.	
	No gum	475.	
	On cover		*3,750.*
	Block of 4	6,750.	1,550.
	Margin block of 4, arrow, R	7,000.	
	Horizontal pair, types I and II	*2,600.*	*2,600.*
	Block of 4, two each of types I and II	*6,500.*	*6,500.*
	P# strip of 3, Impt., T V, one stamp No. 276	*5,250.*	
	P# block of 6, Impt., T V, two stamps No. 276	*125,000.*	

Earliest documented use: Apr. 6, 1896.

Cancellation

China	—
Philippines	—

The fifteen left vertical rows of impressions from plate 76 are Type I, the balance being Type II.

		Unused	Used
277 A98 $2	**bright blue**	1,100.	450.
	Never hinged	3,500.	
	No gum	350.	
a.	$2 **dark blue**	1,100.	450.

	Never hinged	3,500.	
	No gum	350.	
	On cover		3,500.
	Block of 4	5,000.	3,000.
	Margin block of 4, arrow, R or L	5,250.	
	P# strip of 3, Impt., T V	4,500.	—
	P# block of 6, Impt., T V	75,000.	

Earliest documented use: July 18, 1895.

Cancellation

	Supplementary Mail Type G		—
278 A99 $5	**dark green,** *Aug. 1895*	2,400.	650.
	Never hinged	7,500.	
	No gum	800.	
	On cover		12,500.
	Block of 4	10,500.	4,000.
	Margin block of 4, arrow, R or L	11,000.	
	P# strip of 3, Impt., T V	10,000.	
	P# block of 6, Impt., T V	200,000.	

Earliest documented use: Nov. 3, 1896.

See Die and Plate Proofs for imperf. or horiz. pair, imperf. vert. (1c) on stamp paper.

REGULAR ISSUE

Designed by Thomas F. Morris.

Wmk. 191 Horizontally or Vertically

1897-1903 ***Perf. 12***

Plates for the sheet stamps for the 1897-1903 issue were of two sizes:

400 subjects for the 1c and 2c denominations; 200 subjects for all 4c, 5c, 6c and 15c denominations; and both 400 and 200 for the 10c denomination; all issued in panes of 100 each.

Printings from the 400 subject plates show the watermark reading horizontally. On the 200 subject plate printings the watermark reads vertically.

Plates for booklet panes for the 1897-1903 issue were of two sizes: 360 subjects and 180 subjects. Printings from the 360-subject plates show the watermark reading horizontally, while printings from the 180-subject plates show the watermark reading vertically.

In January, 1898, the color of the 1-cent stamp was changed to green and in March, 1898, that of the 5-cents to dark blue in order to conform to the colors assigned these values by the Universal Postal Union. These changes necessitated changing the colors of the 10c and 15c denominations in order to avoid confusion.

279 A87 1c	**deep green,** horizontal watermark, *Jan. 1898*	9.00	.50
	green	9.00	.50
	yellow green	9.00	.50
	dark yellow green	9.00	.50
	Never hinged	25.00	
	On cover		.60
	Block of 4	37.50	5.00
	P# strip of 3, Impt., T V	37.50	—
	Never hinged	85.00	
	P# block of 6, Impt., T V	185.00	
	Never hinged	350.00	
	Double transfer	12.00	1.10
a. 1c	**deep green,** vertical watermark (error), *May 1902*	40.00	7.50
	Never hinged	120.00	
	On cover		22.50
	Block of 4	200.00	
	P# strip of 3, Impt., T V	250.00	
	Never hinged	650.00	

Earliest documented use: Jan. 31, 1898

Cancellations

	China		—
	Guam		—
	Puerto Rico, 1898		—
	Philippines		—
279B A88 2c	**red,** type IV *May 1899*	9.00	.40
	light red, *May 1899*	9.00	.40
	Never hinged	25.00	
	deep red, *Sept. 1901*	13.50	1.25
	Never hinged	32.50	
	On cover		.50
	Block of 4	37.50	3.00
	P# strip of 3, Impt., T V	37.50	
	Never hinged	85.00	
	P# block of 6, Impt., T V	200.00	
	Never hinged	360.00	
	P# strip of 4, Impt., T V (plate 802, UR position)	250.00	
	P# block of 8, Impt., T V (plate 802, UR position)	750.00	
	Double transfer	18.00	.75
	Triple transfer	—	
	Triangle at upper right without shading	22.50	6.00
c. 2c	**rose carmine,** type IV, *Mar. 1899*	300.00	200.00
	bright carmine rose, *Mar. 1899*	300.00	200.00
	Never hinged	850.00	
	Block of 4	1,250.	—
	P# strip of 3, Impt., T V	1,200.	
	Never hinged	2,500.	
	P# block of 6, Impt., T V	3,250.	
d. 2c	**orange red,** type IV, horizontal watermark, *June 1900*	11.50	.55
	pale orange red	11.50	.55
	dark orange red, *Sept. 1902*	11.50	.55
	deep orange red, *Jan. 1903*	11.50	.55
	Never hinged	32.50	
	On cover		.70
	Block of 4	50.00	4.00
	P# strip of 3, Impt., T V	42.50	
	Never hinged	115.00	
	P# block of 6, Impt., T V	220.00	
	Never hinged	400.00	
e. 2c	**orange red,** type IV, vertical watermark (error), *May 1902*	35.00	5.00
	Never hinged	110.00	
	On cover		17.50
	Block of 4	175.00	
	P# strip of 3, Impt., T V	300.00	
	Never hinged	750.00	
	P# block of 6, Impt., T V, never hinged	2,750.	
f. 2c	**carmine,** type IV, *Nov. 1897*	10.00	.50
	reddish carmine, *Dec. 1898*	10.00	.50
	Never hinged	27.50	
	On cover		.65
	Block of 4	42.50	3.00
	P# strip of 3, Impt., T V	40.00	
	Never hinged	95.00	
	P# block of 6, Impt., T V	220.00	
	Never hinged	385.00	
g. 2c	**pink,** type IV, *Nov. 1897*	50.00	1.75
	Never hinged	150.00	
	bright pink	60.00	2.00
	Never hinged	180.00	
	On cover		2.00
	Block of 4	225.00	12.50
	P# strip of 3, Impt., T V	175.00	
	Never hinged	525.00	
	P# block of 6, Impt., T V	600.00	
	Never hinged	1,200.	
h. 2c	**vermilion,** type IV, *Jan. 1899*	11.00	.55
	pale vermilion	11.00	.55
	Never hinged	30.00	
	On cover		.75
	Block of 4	47.50	4.00
	P# strip of 3, Impt., T V	45.00	
	Never hinged	120.00	
	P# block of 6, Impt., T V	235.00	
	Never hinged	425.00	
i. 2c	**brown orange,** type IV, *Jan. 1899*	150.00	15.00
	Never hinged	425.00	
	P# strip of 3, Impt., T V	650.00	
j.	Booklet pane of 6, **red,** type IV, horizontal watermark, *Apr. 18, 1900*	500.00	1,250.
	light red	500.00	1,250.
	orange red, *1901*	500.00	1,250.
	Never hinged	1,000.	
k.	Booklet pane of 6, **red,** type IV, vertical watermark ('02)	500.00	1,250.
	Never hinged	1,000.	

Earliest documented uses:

No. 279B, July 6, 1899;
No. 279Bc, Mar 30, 1899;
No. 279Bc in bright rose carmine, July 16, 1899;
No. 279Bd, June 8, 1900;
No. 279Bf, Nov. 18, 1897;
No. 279Bg, Dec. 1, 1897;
No. 279Bh, Feb. 27, 1899.
No. 279Bj booklet single (red), May 4, 1900;
No. 279Bj booklet single (orange red), May 7, 1902;

Cancellations

	Puerto Rico, 1898		—
	Philippines, 1898		—
	Guam, 1899 or 1900		—
	Supplementary Mail Type G		+4.00
	Cuba, 1898		—
	China		—
	Samoa		—
280 A90 4c	**rose brown,** *Oct. 1898*	30.00	3.00
	Never hinged	90.00	
a. 4c	**lilac brown**	30.00	3.00
	brownish claret	30.00	3.00
	Never hinged	90.00	
b. 4c	**orange brown**	30.00	3.00
	Never hinged	90.00	
	On cover		11.00
	Block of 4	130.00	25.00
	Margin block of 4, arrow, R or L	140.00	
	P# strip of 3, Impt., T V	120.00	
	Never hinged	300.00	
	P# block of 6, Impt., T V	700.00	
	Never hinged	1,250.	
	Double transfer	35.00	4.50
	Extra frame line at top (Plate 793 R 62)	50.00	9.00

Earliest documented use: Nov. 13, 1898.

Cancellations

	Supplementary Mail Type G		+3.00
	China		—
	Philippines		—
281 A91 5c	**dark blue,** *Mar. 1898*	35.00	2.00
	blue	35.00	2.00
	bright blue	35.00	2.00
	Never hinged	110.00	
	On cover		10.00
	Block of 4	150.00	13.00
	Margin block of 4, arrow, R or L	160.00	
	P# strip of 3, Impt., T V	140.00	
	Never hinged	375.00	
	P# block of 6, Impt., T V	650.00	
	Never hinged	1,250.	
	Double transfer	45.00	4.00
	Worn plate (diagonal lines missing in oval background)	40.00	2.25

Earliest documented use: Mar. 19, 1898.

Cancellations

	Puerto Rico, 1898		—
	Supplementary Mail Type G		+4.00
	China		—
	Cuba		—
	Guam		—
	Philippines		—
282 A92 6c	**lake,** *Dec. 1898*	50.00	6.00
	claret	50.00	6.00
	Never hinged	160.00	
	On cover		17.50
	Block of 4	210.00	47.50
	Margin block of 4, arrow, R or L	220.00	
	P# strip of 3, Impt., T V	200.00	
	Never hinged	550.00	
	P# block of 6, Impt., T V	900.00	
	Never hinged	1,650.	
	Double transfer	60.00	8.50
a. 6c	**purple lake**	75.00	14.00
	Never hinged	225.00	
	Block of 4	325.00	85.00
	Margin block of 4, arrow	340.00	
	P# strip of 3, Impt., T V	300.00	
	Never hinged	775.00	
	P# block of 6, Impt., T V	1,250.	
	Never hinged	2,200.	

Earliest documented use: Mar. 13, 1899.

Cancellations

	Supplementary Mail Type G		+4.00
	China		—
	Philippines		—

Type I. The tips of the foliate ornaments do not impinge on the white curved line below "ten cents."

282C A94 10c	**brown,** type I, *Nov. 1898*	210.00	6.00
	dark brown	210.00	6.00
	Never hinged	650.00	
	On cover		17.50
	Block of 4	900.00	55.00
	P# strip of 3, Impt., T IV or V	825.00	
	Never hinged	2,000.	
	P# block of 6, Impt., T IV or V	2,600.	
	Never hinged	4,500.	
	Double transfer	240.00	10.00

Earliest documented use: Dec. 10, 1898.

Cancellation

	Supplementary Mail Type G		+2.50

Type II. The tips of the ornaments break the curved line below the "e" of "ten" and the "t" of "cents."

283 A94 10c	**orange brown,** type II, horizontal watermark	160.00	5.00
	brown	160.00	5.00
	yellow brown	160.00	5.00
	Never hinged	500.00	
	On cover		17.50
	Block of 4	700.00	47.50
	P# strip of 3, Impt., T V	575.00	
	Never hinged	1,650.	
	P# block of 6, Impt., T V	1,900.	
	Never hinged	3,750.	
	Pair, type I and type II	15,000.	—
a. 10c	**orange brown,** type II, vertical watermark, *early 1900*	225.00	10.00
	Never hinged	700.00	
	On cover		35.00
	Block of 4	950.00	
	Margin block of 4, arrow, R or L	1,000.	—
	P# strip of 3, Impt., T V	1,000.	
	Never hinged	2,500.	
	P# block of 6, Impt., T V	2,850.	
	Never hinged	5,250.	

Earliest documented use: Mar. 13, 1899.

Cancellations

	Supplementary Mail Type G		+2.50
	China		—
	Puerto Rico		—

On the 400 subject plate 932, all are Type I except the following: UL 20; UR 11, 12, 13; LL 61, 71, 86, these 7 being Type II.

284 A95 15c	**olive green,** *Nov. 1898*	175.00	12.00
	dark olive green	175.00	12.00

Never hinged	550.00	
On cover		32.50
Block of 4	750.00	85.00
Margin block of 4, arrow, R or L	800.00	
P# strip of 3, Impt., T IV	700.00	
Never hinged	1,800.	
P# block of 6, Impt., T IV	2,250.	
Never hinged	4,250.	

Earliest documented use: Mar. 3, 1899.

Cancellations

Supp. Mail Type F or G	+2.50
China	—
Samoa	—

Nos. 279-284 (8)	678.00	34.90

VALUES FOR VERY FINE STAMPS
Please note: Stamps are valued in the grade of Very Fine unless otherwise indicated.

TRANS-MISSISSIPPI EXPOSITION ISSUE

Omaha, Nebr., June 1 - Nov. 1, 1898.

Jacques Marquette on the Mississippi A100

Farming in the West — A101

Indian Hunting Buffalo — A102

John Charles Frémont on the Rocky Mountains A103

Troops Guarding Wagon Train — A104

Hardships of Emigration A105

Western Mining Prospector A106

Western Cattle in Storm — A107

Mississippi River Bridge, St. Louis — A108

Exposition Station Handstamp Postmark

Designed by Raymond Ostrander Smith.

Plates of 100 (10x10) subjects, divided vertically into 2 panes of 50.

See Nos. 3209-3210 for bi-colored reproductions of Nos. 285-293.

1898, June 17 **Wmk. 191** ***Perf. 12***

285	A100	1c	**dark yellow green**	27.50	6.50
			yellow green	27.50	6.50
			green	27.50	6.50
			Never hinged	80.00	
			On cover		9.75
			On card, Expo. station canc.		200.00
			Pair, on cover, Expo. station canc.		300.00
			Block of 4	120.00	45.00
			Margin block of 4, arrow, R or L	130.00	—
			P# pair, Impt., T VIII	65.00	
			Never hinged	180.00	
			P# strip of 3, Impt., T VIII	110.00	
			Never hinged	280.00	
			P# block of 4, Impt., T VIII	250.00	
			Never hinged	425.00	
			P# block of 6, Impt., T VIII	450.00	
			Never hinged	750.00	
			Double transfer	37.50	7.50

Earliest documented use: June 17, 1898 (FDC).

Cancellations

Supp. Mail Type F or G	+1.50
China	—
Philippines	—
Puerto Rico, 1898	—

286	A101	2c	**copper red**	27.50	2.50
			brown red	27.50	2.50
			light brown red	27.50	2.50
			Never hinged	80.00	
			On cover		3.50
			On cover, Expo. station canc.		175.00
			Block of 4	120.00	15.00
			Margin block of 4, arrow, R or L	130.00	—
			P# pair, Impt., T VIII	65.00	
			Never hinged	180.00	
			P# strip of 3, Impt., T VIII	110.00	
			Never hinged	280.00	
			P# block of 4, Impt., T VIII	250.00	
			Never hinged	425.00	
			P# block of 6, Impt., T VIII	450.00	
			Never hinged	750.00	
			Double transfer	42.50	3.75
			Worn plate	30.00	3.00

Earliest documented use: June 17, 1898 (FDC).

Cancellations

China	—
Hawaii	—
Puerto Rico, 1898	—
Philippines	—

287	A102	4c	**orange**	130.00	24.00
			deep orange	130.00	24.00
			Never hinged	400.00	
			On cover		57.50
			On cover, Expo. station canc.		750.00
			Block of 4	550.00	185.00
			Margin block of 4, arrow, R or L	575.00	—
			P# pair, Impt., T VIII	325.00	

Never hinged	850.00	
P# strip of 3, Impt., T VIII	550.00	
Never hinged	1,350.	
P# block of 4, Impt., T VIII	1,000.	
Never hinged	1,800.	
P# block of 6, Impt., T VIII	1,750.	
Never hinged	3,250.	

Earliest documented use: June 17, 1898 (FDC).

Cancellations

Supp. Mail Type F or G		+5.00
China		—
Philippines		—
288 A103 5c **dull blue**	130.00	22.50
bright blue	130.00	22.50
Never hinged	400.00	
On cover		50.00
On cover, Expo. station canc.		500.00
Block of 4	550.00	150.00
Margin block of 4, arrow, R or L	575.00	—
P# pair, Impt., T VIII	325.00	—
Never hinged	875.00	
P# strip of 3, Impt., T VIII	575.00	
Never hinged	1,350.	
P# block of 4, Impt., T VIII	900.00	
Never hinged	1,800.	
P# block of 6, Impt., T VIII	1,600.	
Never hinged	3,250.	

Earliest documented use: June 17, 1898 (FDC).

Cancellations

Supp. Mail Type F or G		+5.00
China		—
Philippines		—
Puerto Rico, 1898		—
289 A104 8c **violet brown**	190.00	45.00
dark violet brown	190.00	45.00
Never hinged	600.00	
On cover		115.00
On cover, Expo. station canc.		1,000.
Block of 4	800.00	275.00
Margin block of 4, arrow, R or L	825.00	—
P# pair, Impt., T VIII	450.00	
P# strip of 3, Impt., T VIII	800.00	
P# block of 4, Impt., T VIII	2,000.	
Never hinged	3,500.	
P# block of 6, Impt., T VIII	3,250.	
Never hinged	5,500.	
a. Vert. pair, imperf. horiz.	*27,500.*	
P# block of 4, Impt., T VIII	*125,000.*	

Earliest documented use: June 17, 1898 (FDC).

Cancellations

Philippines		—
Samoa		—
290 A105 10c **gray violet**	175.00	32.50
blackish violet	175.00	32.50
Never hinged	550.00	
On cover		90.00
On cover, Expo. station canc.		750.00
Block of 4	750.00	200.00
Margin block of 4, arrow, R or L	775.00	—
P# pair, Impt., T VIII	450.00	
Never hinged	1,250.	
P# strip of 3, Impt., T VIII	650.00	
Never hinged	1,800.	
P# block of 4, Impt., T VIII	2,100.	
Never hinged	3,600.	
P# block of 6, Impt., T VIII	3,500.	
Never hinged	6,000.	

Earliest documented use: June 17, 1898 (FDC).

Cancellations

Supplementary Mail Type G		+5.00
China		—
Philippines		—
291 A106 50c **sage green**	700.00	190.00
dark sage green	700.00	190.00
Never hinged	2,200.	
On cover		1,750.
Block of 4	3,250.	1,250.
Margin block of 4, arrow, R or L	3,400.	—
P# pair, Impt., T VIII	1,950.	
Never hinged	4,750.	
P# strip of 3, Impt., T VIII	*2,900.*	
Never hinged	*7,000.*	
P# block of 4, Impt., T VIII	*15,000.*	
Never hinged	*25,000.*	
P# block of 6, Impt., T VIII	*27,500.*	

Earliest documented use: June 17, 1898 (FDC).

Cancellations

Supp. Mail Type F or G		+25.
Cuba		—
Philippines		—
292 A107 $1 **black**	1,250.	650.
Never hinged	3,900.	
No gum	600.	
On cover		*4,000.*
Block of 4	*6,000.*	*4,000.*
Margin block of 4, arrow, R or L	*6,250.*	
P# pair, Impt., T VIII	*3,250.*	
Never hinged	*8,500.*	
P# strip of 3, Impt., T VIII	*5,500.*	
Never hinged	*12,500.*	
P# block of 4, Impt., T VIII	*35,000.*	
Never hinged	*50,000.*	
P# block of 6, Impt., T VIII	*50,000.*	
Never hinged	*70,000.*	

Earliest documented use: June 17, 1898 (FDC).

Cancellation

Philippines		—
293 A108 $2 **orange brown**	2,100.	1,050.
dark orange brown	2,100.	1,050.
Never hinged	6,500.	
No gum	1,000.	
On cover		*12,500.*
Block of 4	*9,000.*	*6,250.*
Margin block of 4, arrow, R or L	*9,500.*	
P# pair, Impt., T VIII	*5,000.*	
P# strip of 3, Impt., T VIII	*9,000.*	
P# block of 4, Impt., T VIII	*80,000.*	
Never hinged	—	
P# block of 6, Impt., T VIII	*150,000.*	

Earliest documented use: June 24, 1898.

Nos. 285-293 (9)	4,730.	2,023.

Never-Hinged Stamps

See note before No. 205 regarding premiums for never-hinged stamps.

PAN-AMERICAN EXPOSITION ISSUE

Buffalo, N.Y., May 1 - Nov. 1, 1901.
On sale May 1-Oct. 31, 1901.

Fast Lake Navigation (Steamship "City of Alpena") — A109

Empire State Express — A110

Electric Automobile in Washington — A111

Bridge at Niagara Falls — A112

Canal Locks at Sault Ste. Marie — A113

Fast Ocean Navigation (Steamship "St. Paul") — A114

Exposition Station Machine Cancellation

Designed by Raymond Ostrander Smith.

Plates of 200 subjects in two panes of 100 each.

1901, May 1 **Wmk. 191** ***Perf. 12***

294 A109 1c **green & black**	17.50	3.00
dark blue green & black	17.50	3.00
Never hinged	45.00	
On cover		4.50
On Expo. cover or card, Expo. station machine canc.		50.00
On Expo. cover or card, Expo. station duplex handstamp canc.		150.00
Block of 4	75.00	25.00
Margin block of 4, top arrow & markers	77.50	
Margin block of 4, bottom arrow & markers & black P#	80.00	
P# strip of 3, Impt., T V	80.00	
Never hinged	160.00	
P# block of 6, Impt., T V	300.00	
Never hinged	475.00	
Margin strip of 5, bottom Impt. T V, two P#, arrow & markers	115.00	
Never hinged	260.00	
Margin block of 10, bottom Impt., T V, two P#, arrow & markers	700.00	
Never hinged	1,100.	
Double transfer	25.00	5.25
a. Center inverted	*12,500.*	*14,000.*
Never hinged	*22,500.*	
On cover		—
Block of 4	*75,000.*	
P# strip of 4, Impt.	*150,000.*	

Earliest documented uses: May 1, 1901 (No. 294 FDC); Aug. 2, 1901 (No. 294a). The No. 294a cover sold at auction in 1999 for $121,000. Two other uses on cover are recorded.

295 A110 2c **carmine & black**	16.50	1.00
carmine & gray black	16.50	1.00
dark carmine & black	16.50	1.00
rose carmine & black	16.50	1.00
scarlet & black	16.50	1.00
Never hinged	42.50	
On cover		1.50
On Expo. cover or card, Expo. sta. machine cancel		60.00
On Expo. cover or card, Expo. sta. duplex handstamp canc.		200.00
Block of 4	70.00	8.00
Margin block of 4, top arrow & markers	72.50	
P# block of 4, bottom arrow & markers and black P#	75.00	
P# strip of 3, Impt., T V	70.00	
Never hinged	150.00	
P# block of 6, Impt., T V	300.00	
Never hinged	475.00	
P# strip of 5, bottom Impt., T V, two P#, arrow & markers	130.00	
Never hinged	250.00	
P# block of 10, bottom Impt., T V, two P#, arrow & markers	700.00	
Never hinged	1,100.	
Double transfer	24.00	2.25
a. Center inverted	*55,000.*	*60,000.*
Block of 4	*425,000.*	

Almost all unused examples of No. 295a have partial or disturbed gum. Values are for examples with full original gum that is slightly disturbed. Value for No. 295a used is for a well-centered example with faults, as there are no known fault-free examples.

Earliest documented use: May 1, 1901 (No. 295 FDC); Feb. 26, (1902?) (No. 295a, dated cancel on off-cover stamp). The dated No. 295a stamp is the only used example showing a date of any kind. Sold at auction in 2001 for $66,000.

296 A111 4c **deep red brown & black**	80.00	17.50
chocolate & black	80.00	17.50
Never hinged	200.00	
On cover		40.00
On cover, Expo. station machine cancel		350.00
On cover, Expo. station duplex handstamp canc.		*750.00*
Block of 4	340.00	135.00

Margin block of 4, top arrow & markers	360.00	
P# block of 4, bottom arrow & markers & black P#	375.00	
P# strip of 3, Impt., T V	325.00	
Never hinged	700.00	
P# block of 6, Impt., T V	2,100.	
Never hinged	*3,500.*	
P# strip of 5, bottom Impt., T V, two P#, arrow & markers	600.00	
Never hinged	1,200.	
P# block of 10, bottom Impt., T V, two P#, arrow & markers	*4,250.*	
Never hinged	*6,000.*	
a. Center inverted	*70,000.*	—
Block of 4	*500,000.*	
P# strip of 4, Impt.	*550,000.*	

No. 296a was a Special Printing and not regularly issued.

Almost all unused examples of No. 296a have partial or disturbed gum. Values are for examples with full orginal gum that is slightly disturbed.

See No. 296a-S, "Specimen" Stamps.

Earliest documented use: May 1, 1901 (FDC).

297 A112 5c **ultramarine & black**	90.00	16.00
dark ultramarine & black	90.00	16.00
Never hinged	225.00	
On cover		42.50
On cover, Expo. station machine cancel		350.00
On cover, Expo. station duplex handstamp canc.		*750.00*
Block of 4	400.00	120.00
Margin block of 4, top arrow & markers	425.00	
P# block of 4, bottom arrow & markers & black P#	440.00	
P# strip of 3, Impt., T V	360.00	
Never hinged	725.00	
P# block of 6, Impt., T V	2,250.	
Never hinged	*3,750.*	
P# strip of 5, bottom Impt., T V, two P#, arrow & markers	700.00	
Never hinged	1,350.	
P# block of 10, bottom Impt., T V, two P#, arrow & markers	*4,250.*	
Never hinged	*6,000.*	

Earliest documented use: May 1, 1901 (FDC).

298 A113 8c **brown violet & black**	110.00	50.00
purplish brown & black	110.00	50.00
Never hinged	275.00	
On cover		110.00
On cover, Expo. station machine cancel		*750.00*
On cover, Expo. station duplex handstamp canc.		*1,250.*
Block of 4	475.00	400.00
Margin block of 4, top arrow & markers	500.00	
P# block of 4, bottom arrow & markers & black P#	525.00	
P# strip of 3, Impt., T V	450.00	
Never hinged	975.00	
P# block of 6, Impt., T V	*4,000.*	
Never hinged	*6,250.*	
P# strip of 5, bottom Impt., T V, two P#, arrow & markers	875.00	
Never hinged	1,750.	
P# block of 10, bottom Impt., T V, two P#, arrow & markers	*7,000.*	
Never hinged	*9,500.*	

Earliest documented use: May 1, 1901 (FDC).

299 A114 10c **yellow brown & black**	145.00	27.50
dark yellow brown & black	145.00	32.50
Never hinged	360.00	
On cover		125.00
On cover, Expo. station machine cancel		*1,000.*
On cover, Expo. station duplex handstamp canc.		*1,500.*
Block of 4	625.00	260.00
Margin block of 4, top arrow & markers	650.00	
P# block of 4, bottom arrow & markers & black P#	700.00	
P# strip of 3, Impt., T V	600.00	
Never hinged	1,400.	
P# block of 6, Impt., T V	6,750.	
Never hinged	*9,000.*	
P# strip of 5, bottom Impt., T V, two P#, arrow & markers	1,175.	
Never hinged	2,350.	
P# block of 10, bottom Impt., T V, two P#, arrow & markers	10,000.	
Never hinged	*14,000.*	
Nos. 294-299 (6)	459.00	115.00
Nos. 294-299, never hinged	1,148.	

Earliest documented use: May 1, 1901 (FDC).

VALUES FOR VERY FINE STAMPS
Please note: Stamps are valued in the grade of Very Fine unless otherwise indicated.

Franklin — A115

Washington — A116

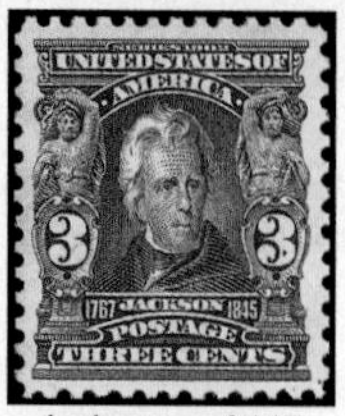
Jackson — A117

Grant — A118

Lincoln — A119

Garfield — A120

Martha Washington — A121

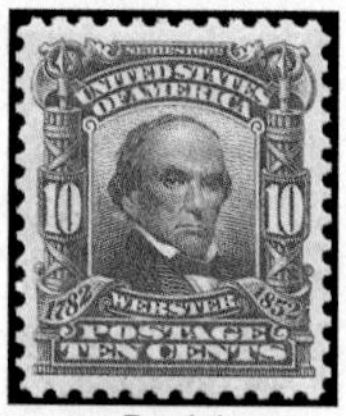
Daniel Webster — A122

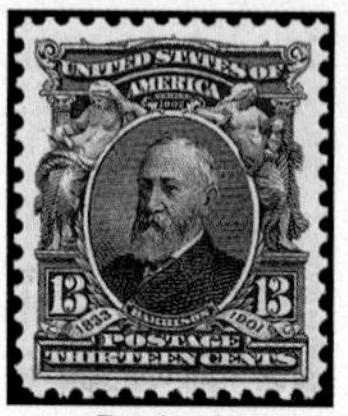
Benjamin Harrison — A123

Henry Clay — A124

Jefferson — A125

David G. Farragut — A126

Madison — A127

Marshall — A128

REGULAR ISSUE

Designed by Raymond Ostrander Smith and/or Clair Aubrey Huston.

Plates of 400 subjects in four panes of 100 each for all values from 1c to 15c inclusive. Certain plates of 1c, 2c type A129, 3c and 5c show a round marker in margin opposite the horizontal guide line at right or left.

Plates of 200 subjects in two panes of 100 each for 15c, 50c, $1, $2 and $5.

1902-03 Wmk. 191 *Perf. 12*

Many stamps of this issue are known with blurred printing due to having been printed on dry paper.

300 A115 1c **blue green,** *Feb. 1903*	12.00	.25
green	12.00	.25
deep green	12.00	.25
gray green	12.00	.25
yellow green	12.00	.25
Never hinged	30.00	
On cover		.30
Block of 4	50.00	3.50
P# strip of 3, Impt., T V	47.50	
Never hinged	95.00	
P# block of 6, Impt., T V	225.00	
Never hinged	350.00	
Double transfer	17.50	1.00
Worn plate	13.00	.35
Cracked plate	14.00	.30
b. Booklet pane of 6, *Mar. 6, 1907*	600.00	*12,500.*
Never hinged	1,150.	

Earliest documented uses: Feb. 3, 1903 (No. 300); Mar. 22, 1907 (No. 300b single).

301 A116 2c **carmine,** *Jan. 22, 1903*	16.00	.40
bright carmine	16.00	.40
deep carmine	16.00	.40
carmine rose	16.00	.40
Never hinged	40.00	
On cover		.45
Block of 4	67.50	5.00
P# strip of 3, Impt., T V	65.00	
Never hinged	130.00	
P# block of 6, Impt., T V	275.00	
Never hinged	425.00	
Double transfer	27.50	1.25
Cracked plate	—	1.25
c. Booklet pane of 6, *Jan. 24, 1903*	500.00	*2,250.*
Never hinged	950.00	

Earliest documented use: Feb. 2, 1903 (No. 301); Mar. 28, 1903 (No. 301c single); Apr. 4, 1903 (No. 301c pane).

Four unused single imperforate sheet margin examples of No. 301 are recorded. These are considered printer's waste.

302 A117 3c **bright violet,** *Feb. 1903*	55.00	3.50
violet	55.00	3.50
deep violet	55.00	3.50
Never hinged	140.00	
On cover		11.00
Block of 4	230.00	30.00
P# strip of 3, Impt., T V	220.00	
Never hinged	450.00	
P# block of 6, Impt., T V	800.00	
Never hinged	1,350.	
Double transfer	77.50	4.75
Cracked plate	—	—

Earliest documented use: Mar. 19, 1903.

303 A118 4c **brown,** *Feb. 1903*	60.00	2.30
dark brown	60.00	2.30
yellow brown	60.00	2.30
orange brown	60.00	2.30
red brown	60.00	2.30
Never hinged	150.00	
On cover		12.50
Block of 4	250.00	25.00
P# strip of 3, Impt., T V	240.00	
Never hinged	500.00	
P# block of 6, Impt., T V	825.00	
Never hinged	1,425.	
Double transfer	77.50	2.75

Earliest documented use: Mar. 10, 1903 (on cover front).

304 A119 5c **blue,** *Jan. 1903*	60.00	2.00
pale blue	60.00	2.00
bright blue	60.00	2.00
dark blue	60.00	2.00
Never hinged	150.00	
On cover		7.50
Block of 4	250.00	15.00
P# strip of 3, Impt., T V	240.00	
Never hinged	500.00	
P# block of 6, Impt., T V	825.00	—
Never hinged	1,375.	
Double transfer	82.50	3.75
Cracked plate	70.00	4.75

Earliest documented use: Feb. 9, 1903.

305 A120 6c **claret,** *Feb. 1903*	67.50	5.00
deep claret	67.50	5.00
brownish lake	67.50	5.00
dull brownish lake	67.50	5.00
Never hinged	170.00	
On cover		15.00
Block of 4	290.00	45.00
P# strip of 3, Impt., T V	280.00	
Never hinged	600.00	
P# block of 6, Impt., T V	925.00	
Never hinged	1,600.	
Double transfer	72.50	4.50

Earliest documented use: May 8, 1903.

306 A121 8c **violet black,** *Dec. 1902*	42.50	3.00
black	42.50	3.00
slate black	42.50	3.00
gray lilac	42.50	3.00
Never hinged	105.00	
lavender	52.50	3.75
Never hinged	130.00	
On cover		8.00
Block of 4	185.00	27.50
P# strip of 3, Impt., T V	170.00	
Never hinged	350.00	

	P# block of 6, Impt., T V	750.00	
	Never hinged	1,250.	
	Double transfer	47.50	3.75

Earliest documented use: Dec. 27, 1902.

307 A122 10c	**pale red brown,** *Feb. 1903*	70.00	2.80
	red brown	70.00	2.80
	dark red brown	70.00	2.80
	Never hinged	175.00	
	On cover		9.00
	Block of 4	280.00	17.50
	P# strip of 3, Impt., T V	275.00	
	Never hinged	575.00	
	P# block of 6, Impt., T V	1,100.	
	Never hinged	1,850.	
	Double transfer	80.00	10.00

Earliest documented use: Mar. 12, 1903.

308 A123 13c	**purple black,** *Nov. 1902*	45.00	9.00
	brown violet	45.00	9.00
	Never hinged	115.00	
	On cover		37.50
	Block of 4	190.00	95.00
	P# strip of 3, Impt., T V	180.00	
	Never hinged	375.00	
	P# block of 6, Impt., T V	700.00	
	Never hinged	1,150.	

Earliest documented use: Nov. 18, 1902.

309 A124 15c	**olive green,** *May 27, 1903*	200.00	12.00
	dark olive green	200.00	12.00
	Never hinged	500.00	
	On cover		80.00
	Block of 4	800.00	100.00
	Margin block of 4, arrow	825.00	
	P# strip of 3, Impt., T V	750.00	
	Never hinged	1,650.	
	P# block of 6, Impt., T V	3,400.	
	Never hinged	5,750.	
	Double transfer	230.00	14.00

Earliest documented use: July 1903 (on registry tag); Sept. 11, 1903 (on cover).

310 A125 50c	**orange,** *Mar. 23, 1903*	475.	30.00
	deep orange	475.	30.00
	Never hinged	1,400.	
	On cover		700.00
	Block of 4	2,000.	240.00
	Margin block of 4, arrow	2,100.	
	P# strip of 3, Impt., T V	1,900.	
	Never hinged	4,500.	
	P# block of 6, Impt., T V	*7,500.*	

Earliest documented use: Oct. 6, 1903 (on cover front).

311 A126 $1	**black,** *June 5, 1903*	700.00	80.00
	grayish black	700.00	80.00
	Never hinged	2,100.	
	No gum	165.00	
	On cover		1,500.
	Block of 4	3,000.	550.00
	Margin block of 4, arrow	3,250.	
	P# strip of 3, Impt., T V	3,000.	
	P# block of 6, Impt., T V	*20,000.*	

Earliest documented use: Sept. 30, 1903.

312 A127 $2	**dark blue,** *June 5, 1903*	1,100.	225.00
	blue	1,100.	225.00
	Never hinged	3,500.	
	No gum	275.00	
	On cover		2,500.
	Block of 4	4,750.	1,850.
	Margin block of 4, arrow	5,250.	
	P# strip of 3, Impt., T V	4,750.	
	P# block of 6, Impt., T V	*32,500.*	

Earliest documented use: Feb. 17, 1904.

313 A128 $5	**dark green,** *June 5, 1903*	2,800.	750.00
	Never hinged	*8,500.*	
	No gum	700.00	
	On cover		*5,000.*
	Block of 4	*13,000.*	*6,000.*
	Margin block of 4, arrow	*13,500.*	
	P# strip of 3, Impt., T V	*11,500.*	
	P# block of 6, Impt., T V	*180,000.*	

Earliest documented use: Feb. 17, 1904.

	Nos. 300-313 (14)	5,703.	1,125.

For listings of designs A127 and A128 with Perf. 10 see Nos. 479 and 480.

Earliest documented use dates for imperforates are for the imperforate sheet stamps, not for imperforate stamps with vending and affixing machine perforations or for flat plate imperforate coil stamps. EDU dates for VAMP and flat plate imperf coil stamps are shown in their respective sections later in the catalogue.

1906-08 ***Imperf.***

314 A115 1c	**blue green,** *Oct. 2, 1906*	16.00	16.50
	green	16.00	16.50
	deep green	16.00	16.50
	Never hinged	35.00	
	On cover		27.50
	Pair	35.00	35.00
	Never hinged	70.00	
	Block of 4	70.00	*80.00*
	Never hinged	140.00	
	Corner margin block of 4	77.50	*82.50*
	Margin block of 4, arrow	80.00	*85.00*
	Margin block of 4, arrow & round marker	175.00	130.00
	Center line block	135.00	110.00
	Never hinged	260.00	
	P# block of 6, Impt.	200.00	—
	Never hinged	325.00	
	Double transfer	30.00	19.00

Earliest documented use: Dec. 20, 1906.

314A A118 4c	**brown,** *Apr. 1908*	*90,000.*	*50,000.*
	Never hinged	*140,000.*	
	On cover		*140,000.*
	Pair	*225,000.*	
	Guide line pair	*375,000.*	

This stamp was issued imperforate but all examples were privately perforated with large oblong perforations at the sides (Schermack type III).

Beware of examples of No. 303 with trimmed perforations and fake private perfs. added.

Used and on-cover values are for contemporaneous usage.

Earliest documented use: May 27, 1908.

315 A119 5c	**blue,** *May 12, 1908*	220.	*1,250.*
	Never hinged	390.	
	On cover, pair		*45,000.*
	Pair	475.	*10,000.*
	Never hinged	825.	
	Block of 4	925.	*25,000.*
	Never hinged	1,600.	
	Corner margin block of 4	1,025.	
	Margin block of 4, arrow	1,500.	
	Margin block of 4, arrow & round marker	2,400.	
	Center line block	*10,000.*	
	P# block of 6, Impt.	2,750.	—
	Never hinged	4,000.	

Earliest documented use: Sept. 15, 1908.

Beware of examples of No. 304 with perforations removed.

Used examples of No. 315 must have contemporaneous cancels. Single examples of No. 315 on cover are not known to exist.

COIL STAMPS

Warning! Imperforate stamps are known fraudulently perforated to resemble coil stamps and part-perforate varieties. Fully perforated stamps and booklet stamps also are known with perforations fraudulently trimmed off to resemble coil stamps.

1908 ***Perf. 12 Horizontally***

316 A115 1c	**blue green,** *Feb. 18*	*70,000.*	
	Pair	*200,000.*	
	Guide line pair	*325,000.*	
317 A119 5c	**blue,** *Feb. 24*	*6,000.*	—
	Never hinged	*17,500.*	
	Pair	*17,500.*	
	Never hinged	*50,000.*	
	Guide line pair	*70,000.*	
	Never hinged	*160,000.*	

Earliest documented use: Sept. 18, 1908.

Perf. 12 Vertically

318 A115 1c	**blue green,** *July 31*	*6,000.*	
	Never hinged	*11,500.*	
	Pair	*16,500.*	
	Guide line pair	*35,000.*	
	Double transfer	—	

The No. 318 mint never hinged single is valued in the grade of fine.

Coil stamps for use in vending and affixing machines are perforated on two sides only, either horizontally or vertically. They were first issued in 1908, using perf. 12. This was changed to 8½ in 1910, and to 10 in 1914.

Imperforate sheets of certain denominations were sold to the vending machine companies which applied a variety of private perforations and separations (see Vending and Affixing Machine Perforations section of this catalogue).

Several values of the 1902 and later issues are found on an apparently coarse-ribbed paper. This is caused by worn blankets on the printing presses and is not a true paper variety.

All examples of Nos. 316-318 must be accompanied by certificates of authenticity issued by recognized expertizing committees.

Washington — A129

Plate of 400 subjects in four panes of 100 each.

Type I

Type II

Designed by Clair Aubrey Huston.

1903 **Wmk. 191** ***Perf. 12***

319 A129 2c	**carmine,** type I, *Nov. 12, 1903*	6.00	.25
	bright carmine	6.00	.25
	red	6.00	.25
	Never hinged	15.00	
	On cover		.30
	Block of 4	25.00	2.50
	P# strip of 3, Impt., T V	24.00	
	Never hinged	45.00	
	P# block of 6, Impt., T V	180.00	
	Never hinged	310.00	
	Double transfer	12.50	2.00
a.	2c **lake,** type I	—	—
	carmine lake	—	
b.	2c **carmine rose,** type I	10.00	.40
	Never hinged	25.00	
	On cover		.60
	Block of 4	42.50	9.00
	P# strip of 3, Impt., T V	40.00	
	Never hinged	75.00	
	P# block of 6, Impt., T V	250.00	
	Never hinged	375.00	
c.	2c **scarlet,** type I	10.00	.30
	Never hinged	25.00	
	On cover		.40
	Block of 4	42.50	6.00
	P# strip of 3, Impt., T V	40.00	
	Never hinged	75.00	
	P# block of 6, Impt., T V	250.00	
	Never hinged	375.00	
d.	Vert. pair, imperf. horiz., No. 319	*7,500.*	
	Never hinged	*15,000.*	
e.	Vertical pair, imperf. between, No. 319	2,500.	
	As "e," rouletted between	*3,250.*	

No. 319e comes from a single pane of stamps on which a line of horizontal perfs were omitted between rows 9 and 10. Additionally, during the use of this stamp, the Postmaster at San Francisco discovered in his stock sheets of No. 319, each of which had the horizontal perforations missing between the two top rows of stamps. To facilitate their separation, the imperf. rows were rouletted, and the stamps sold over the counter. So vertical pairs are found from this source with regular perforations all around and rouletted between.

"Gash on Face" Variety

The gash may appear as double lines due to different plate wiping techniques.

f. 2c **lake,** type II 10.00 .30
carmine lake 10.00 .30
Never hinged 25.00
On cover .35
Block of 4 42.50 5.50
P# strip of 3, Impt., T V 45.00
Never hinged 95.00
P# block of 6, Impt., T V 325.00
Never hinged 475.00
"Gash on face" plate flaw (carmine lake, 4671 LL 16) —
g. Booklet pane of 6, **car.**, type I 125.00 *550.00*
Never hinged 240.00
Wmk. horizontal *4,000.*
Never hinged *6,500.*
h. Booklet pane of 6, **car.**, type II 900.00
Never hinged 1,500.
i. 2c **carmine,** type II 75.00 *50.00*
red 75.00 *50.00*
Never hinged 175.00
On cover *150.00*
j. 2c **carmine rose,** type II 70.00 1.75
Never hinged 160.00
Block of 4 300.00 20.00
P# block of 6, Impt., T V *1,100.*
k. 2c **scarlet,** type II 70.00 .65
Never hinged 160.00
Block of 4 300.00 5.00
P# block of 6, Impt., T V *1,100.*
n. Booklet pane of 6, **car. rose** (I) 250.00 *650.00*
Never hinged 450.00
p. Booklet pane of 6, **scarlet** (I) 185.00 *575.00*
Never hinged 350.00
q. Booklet pane of 6, **lake** (II) 300.00 *750.00*
Never hinged 575.00

Earliest documented uses:
No. 319, Nov. 19, 1903;
No. 319a, Sept. 23, 1904;
No. 319b. Nov. 3, 1903;
No. 319c, Dec. 16, 1903;
No. 319f, Sept. 25, 1908;
No. 319g single, Dec. 7, 1903;
No. 319h single, June 8, 1908;
No. 319i, June 5, 1908;
No. 319j, June 30, 1908;
No. 319k, June 11, 1908
No. 319p single, Apr. 12, 1904.

1906 ***Imperf.***

320 A129 2c **carmine,** type I *Oct. 2* 16.00 *17.50*
Never hinged 35.00
On cover 22.50
Pair 35.00 *37.50*
Never hinged 72.50
Block of 4 70.00 75.00
Corner margin block of 4 72.50 100.00
Margin block of 4, arrow 75.00 110.00
Margin block of 4, arrow & round marker —
Center line block 150.00 200.00
Never hinged 250.00
P# block of 6, Impt., T V, carmine 200.00 —
Never hinged 325.00
Double transfer 24.00 21.50

Earliest documented use: Oct. 26, 1906.

a. 2c **lake,** type II 45.00 *50.00*
carmine lake 45.00 *50.00*
Never hinged 100.00
On cover —
Pair 100.00 *120.00*
Never hinged 225.00
Block of 4 200.00 *275.00*
Corner margin block of 4 205.00
Margin block of 4, arrow 210.00
Center line block 425.00 —
Never hinged 700.00
P# block of 6, Impt., T V 725.00 —
Never hinged 1,150.
"Gash on face" plate flaw (see No. 319f) —
b. 2c **scarlet,** type I 18.50 15.00
Never hinged 40.00
On cover 22.50
Pair 39.00
Never hinged 85.00
Block of 4 77.50
Corner margin block of 4 80.00
Margin block of 4, arrow 82.50 —
Center line block 205.00 —
Never hinged 325.00
P# block of 6, Impt., T V 225.00
Never hinged 350.00
c. 2c **carmine rose,** type I 60.00 42.50
Never hinged 130.00
d. 2c **carmine,** type II *120.00* *250.00*
Never hinged *175.00*
On cover *600.00*

Pair *225.00*
Never hinged *425.00*
Guide line pair *450.00*

No. 320d was issued imperforate, but all examples were privately perforated with large oblong perforations at the sides (Schermack type III).

COIL STAMPS

1908 ***Perf. 12 Horizontally***

321 A129 2c **carmine,** type I, pair, *Feb. 18* *450,000.*
On cover, single *250,000.*
Guide line pair —

Four authenticated unused pairs of No. 321 are known and available to collectors. A fifth, unauthenticated pair is in the New York Public Library Miller collection. The value for an unused pair is for a fine-very fine example. Two fine pairs are recorded and one very fine pair. There are no authenticated unused single stamps recorded. There are 2 authenticated examples of the single used on cover, both used from Indianapolis in 1908. Numerous counterfeits exist.

Earliest documented use: Oct. 2, 1908.

Perf. 12 Vertically

322 A129 2c **carmine,** type II, *July 31* *7,000.* —
Never hinged *13,500.*
Pair *18,000.*
Guide line pair *35,000.*
Double transfer —

This Government Coil Stamp should not be confused with those of the International Vending Machine Co., which are perforated 12½.

All examples of Nos. 321-322 must be accompanied by certificates of authenticity issued by recognized expertizing committees.

VALUES FOR VERY FINE STAMPS
Please note: Stamps are valued in the grade of Very Fine unless otherwise indicated.

LOUISIANA PURCHASE EXPOSITION ISSUE
St. Louis, Mo., Apr. 30 - Dec. 1, 1904

Robert R. Livingston — A130

Thomas Jefferson — A131

James Monroe — A132

William McKinley — A133

Map of Louisiana Purchase — A134

Designed by Clair Aubrey Huston.

Plates of 100 (10x10) subjects, divided vertically into 2 panes of 50.

Exposition Station Machine Cancellation

1904, Apr. 30 **Wmk. 191** ***Perf. 12***

323 A130 1c **green** 27.50 5.00
dark green 27.50 5.00
Never hinged 75.00
On cover 7.00
On Expo. card, Expo. station machine canc. 40.00
On Expo. card, Expo. station duplex handstamp canc. 100.00
Block of 4 120.00 35.00
Margin block of 4, arrow, R or L 125.00 —
P# pair, Impt., T V 80.00
Never hinged 190.00
P# strip of 3, Impt., T V 120.00
Never hinged 275.00
P# block of 4, Impt., T V 200.00
Never hinged 350.00
P# block of 6, Impt., T V 350.00
Never hinged 550.00
Diagonal line through left "1" (2138 L 2) 50.00 12.50
Double transfer —

Earliest documented use: Apr. 30, 1904 (FDC).

324 A131 2c **carmine** 27.50 2.00
bright carmine 27.50 2.00
Never hinged 75.00
On cover 3.00
On Expo. cover, Expo. station machine canc. 60.00
On Expo. cover, Expo. station duplex handstamp canc. 150.00
Block of 4 120.00 17.50
Margin block of 4, arrow, R or L 130.00 —
P# pair, Impt., T V 75.00
Never hinged 170.00
P# strip of 3, Impt., T V 110.00
Never hinged 240.00
P# block of 4, Impt., T V 200.00
Never hinged 350.00
P# block of 6, Impt., T V 350.00
Never hinged 550.00
a. Vertical pair, imperf. horiz. *17,500.*
Block of 4 *40,000.*
P# block of 4, Impt., T V *55,000.*

Earliest documented use: Apr. 30, 1904 (FDC).

325 A132 3c **violet** 85.00 30.00
Never hinged 220.00
On cover 65.00
On cover, Expo. station machine canc. 200.00
On cover, Expo. station duplex handstamp canc. *400.00*
Block of 4 360.00 225.00
Margin block of 4, arrow, R or L 380.00 —
P# pair, Impt., T V 220.00
Never hinged 500.00
P# strip of 3, Impt., T V 350.00
Never hinged 750.00
P# block of 4, Impt., T V 625.00
Never hinged 1,100.
P# block of 6, Impt., T V 950.00
Never hinged 1,750.
Double transfer —

Earliest documented use: Apr. 30, 1904 (FDC).

326 A133 5c **dark blue** 87.50 25.00
Never hinged 225.00
On cover 50.00
On cover, Expo. station machine canc. 400.00
On cover, Expo. station duplex handstamp canc. *500.00*
Block of 4 375.00 200.00
Margin block of 4, arrow, R or L 400.00 —
P# pair, Impt., T V 220.00
Never hinged 500.00
P# strip of 3, Impt., T V 375.00
Never hinged 825.00
P# block of 4, Impt., T V 675.00
Never hinged 1,200.
P# block of 6, Impt., T V 1,000.
Never hinged 1,850.

Earliest documented use: Apr. 30, 1904 (FDC).

327 A134 10c **red brown** 160.00 30.00
dark red brown 160.00 30.00
Never hinged 425.00
On cover 125.00
On cover, Expo. station machine canc. 450.00
On cover, Expo. station duplex handstamp canc. *750.00*
Block of 4 675.00 225.00
Margin block of 4, arrow, R or L 725.00 —
P# pair, Impt., T V 400.00
Never hinged 950.00
P# strip of 3, Impt., T V 700.00
Never hinged 1,400.
P# block of 4, Impt., T V 1,325.

Never hinged	2,250.	
P# block of 6, Impt., T V	2,250.	
Never hinged	4,000.	

Earliest documented use: Apr. 30, 1904 (FDC).

Nos. 323-327 (5)	387.50	92.00
Nos. 323-327, never hinged	1,020.	

JAMESTOWN EXPOSITION ISSUE

Hampton Roads, Va., Apr. 26 - Dec. 1, 1907

Captain John Smith — A135

Founding of Jamestown — A136

Pocahontas — A137

Plates of 200 subjects in two panes of 100 each.

Exposition Station Machine Cancellation

Designed by Clair Aubrey Huston.

1907 **Wmk. 191** ***Perf. 12***

328	A135	1c **green,** *Apr. 26*	27.50	5.00
		dark green	27.50	5.00
		Never hinged	75.00	
		On cover		8.00
		On Expo. card, Expo. station machine canc.		25.00
		On Expo. card, Expo. station duplex handstamp canc.		125.00
		Block of 4	115.00	50.00
		Margin block of 4, arrow	120.00	—
		P# strip of 3, Impt., T V	105.00	
		Never hinged	240.00	
		P# block of 6, Impt., T V	500.00	
		Never hinged	725.00	
		Double transfer	35.00	6.00

Earliest documented use: Apr. 26, 1907 (FDC).

329	A136	2c **carmine,** *Apr. 26*	32.50	4.50
		bright carmine	32.50	4.50
		Never hinged	85.00	
		On cover		6.00
		On Expo. cover, Expo. station machine canc.		100.00
		On Expo. cover, Expo. station duplex handstamp canc.		150.00
		Block of 4	140.00	35.00
		Margin block of 4, arrow	150.00	—
		P# strip of 3, Impt., T V	120.00	
		Never hinged	290.00	
		P# block of 6, Impt., T V	550.00	
		Never hinged	800.00	
		Double transfer	40.00	6.00

Earliest documented use: Apr. 26, 1907 (FDC).

330	A137	5c **blue**	140.00	32.50
		deep blue	140.00	32.50
		Never hinged	350.00	
		On cover		85.00
		On cover, Expo. station machine canc.		350.00
		On cover, Expo. station duplex handstamp canc.		*500.00*
		Block of 4	600.00	225.00
		Margin block of 4, arrow	625.00	—
		P# strip of 3, Impt., T V	500.00	
		Never hinged	1,250.	
		P# block of 6, Impt., T V	2,750.	
		Never hinged	5,250.	
		Double transfer	150.00	37.50

Earliest documented use: May 8, 1907.

Nos. 328-330 (3)	200.00	42.00
Nos. 328-330, never hinged	510.00	

REGULAR ISSUE

Plates of 400 subjects in four panes of 100 each for all values 1c to 15c inclusive.

Plates of 200 subjects in two panes of 100 each for 50c and $1 denominations.

In 1909 the Bureau prepared certain plates with horizontal spacings of 3mm between the outer seven vertical stamp rows and 2mm between the others. This was done to try to counteract the effect of unequal shrinkage of the paper. *However, some unequal shrinkage still did occur and intermediate spacings are frequently found.* The listings of 2mm and 3mm spacings are for exact measurements. Intermediate spacings sell for approximately the same as the cheaper of the two listed spacings.

All such plates were marked with an open star added to the imprint and exist on the 1c, 2c, 3c, 4c, and 5c denominations only. A small solid star was added to the imprint and plate number for 1c plate No. 4980, 2c plate No. 4988 and for the 2c Lincoln. All other plates for this issue are spaced 2mm throughout.

There are several types of some of the 2c and 3c stamps of this and succeeding issues. These types are described under the dates at which they first appeared. Illustrations of Types I-VII of the 2c (A140) and Types I-IV of the 3c (A140) are reproduced by permission of H. L. Lindquist.

Imprint, plate number and open star

Imprint, plate number and small solid star

Imprint, plate number and "A"

(Illustrations reduced in size)

"A" and number only **A 5805**

Number only **988**

The above illustrations are several of the styles used on plates of issues from 1908 to date.

The previously listed "China Clay Paper" stamps, formerly Scott 331b-332b and 333a-340a, have been removed from the catalogue. Research has shown that the "experimental paper" explanation for the existence of these stamps was incorrect. The only paper experiment during this time period was the 35 percent rag stock paper (Blue Paper, Scott 357-366, 369) of 1909. The stamps previously known as "China Clay Paper" stamps were, in fact, normal stamps printed on paper that was defective to varying degrees. These interesting varieties, which have nothing to do with China clay, can appear to be thin, thick, translucent, opaque, somewhat dark or very dark, but they are not the kind of items that the Scott catalogue or other catalogues normally list. This is not to say that these various paper varieties are of no value or are not of great interest to specialists of the stamps from this period. It is only to say that these various types and degrees of paper varieties are subjects which are beyond the scope of stamp catalogues. Specialist collectors will no doubt continue to study and treasure these varieties.

Franklin — A138

Washington — A139

1908-09 **Wmk. 191** ***Perf. 12***

331	A138	1c **green,** *Dec. 1908*	7.25	.40
		bright green	7.25	.40
		dark green	7.25	.40
		yellow green	7.25	.40
		Never hinged	18.00	
		On cover		.55
		Block of 4 (2mm spacing)	32.50	2.50
		Block of 4 (3mm spacing)	35.00	3.00
		P# block of 6, Impt., T V	100.00	
		Never hinged	175.00	
		P# block of 6, Impt. & star	95.00	
		Never hinged	160.00	
		P# block of 6, Impt. & small solid star (plate 4980)	*1,500.*	
		Never hinged	*2,250.*	
		Double transfer	9.50	.75
		Cracked plate	—	—
	a.	Booklet pane of 6, *Dec. 1908*	160.00	*450.00*
		Never hinged	285.00	

No. 331 exists in horizontal pair, imperforate between, a variety resulting from booklet experiments. Not regularly issued. Value, $2,500.

No. 331a used is valued with a contemporaneous cancel. A certificate of authenticity is advised.

Earliest documented uses: Dec. 1, 1908 (No. 331); Dec. 2, 1908 (No. 331a single) (FDC).

332	A139	2c **carmine,** *Nov. 1908*	6.75	.35
		light carmine	6.75	.35
		dark carmine	6.75	.35
		Never hinged	16.00	
		On cover		.40
		Block of 4 (2mm spacing)	30.00	2.00
		Block of 4 (3mm spacing)	32.50	2.50
		P# block of 6, Impt., T V	90.00	

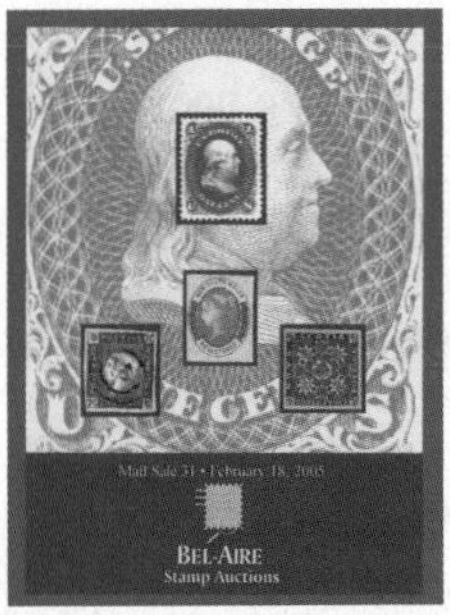

2009 EDITION SPECIAL FEATURE

The So-Called "China Clay" Paper Varieties are Deleted from the Scott U.S. Specialized Catalogue

Edward (Ted) Liston

Starting about 1910, collectors began noticing stamps that looked different than the normal Washington-Franklin stamps of the series, Scott Nos. 331-342, 367, 357-366, and 369. In the older literature, these were called "experimental papers" because philatelists did not know what they were and there was no information from the United States Bureau of Engraving and Printing (BEP) saying why they looked different. They were variously described as: thin, thick, uneven in texture, even in texture, dense, opaque, translucent, white, cream, slightly grayish, gray, dark, hard, soft, and "China Clay."

The most probable reason for the belief in the presence of China clay in these stamp papers is the following sentence from the Annual Report (published February 1910) from the Third Assistant Postmaster General for fiscal year 1908-1909:

> *As the part-rag paper [the 'Bluish Paper,' acknowledged to be an experiment in paper production, Scott Nos. 357-366, 369] did not reduce the waste [from poor placement of perforations], the chemical wood fiber stock will be continued for the present, 2 per cent of china clay being added to improve the color and surface of the paper.*

I believe that this statement was meant to indicate that the addition of China clay would be done in the future, not that it had already been done. This belief is based on the next sentence in the same Report, which begins:

> *The bureau has accomplished the desired result [getting better centering], however, by the use of printing plates having longitudinal margins of varying widths between the stamps.*

These would be what we now call the "star" plates. Therefore, the Bureau officials may have entertained the use of China clay, but it was not a priority because they believed they had already solved the problem of poor centering of perforations. However, the statement about China clay was picked up two months later (in April 1910) by philatelic writer Charles R. Morris, who wrote:

". . . since the experiments tried with the rag paper last Spring were not considered a success, the Bureau has been using a paper with china clay in it which gives a different look from the old pulp paper, there have been several disappointed collectors who thought they had the rag paper stamps."

This assumption, that the BEP was already using China clay in their paper, led to the belief that, in 1910, the Bureau of Engraving and Printing ordered some "experimental paper" that was to contain 2 percent China clay and, that, mistakenly, some paper containing 20 percent China clay was delivered and used to print a few stamps. I believe that this second assumption concerning 20 percent China clay paper was accepted by philatelists to explain the existence of the darker stamps. I have not been able to determine exactly who first suggested "20% China clay." My earliest reference to that is in *Philadelphia Stamp News*, Vol. 2 (19), Aug. 5, 1911, p.162, in an article by William Webb, where he states that there are "20% china clay" stamps in the collection of Philip Ward. Regardless of who actually coined the term, this was the time when the legend of "China Clay Stamps" was born.

In fact, a careful reading of 390 letters by the BEP to the paper manufacturers in 1908-10 shows no evidence that the BEP ordered, or would have used, an "experimental paper" containing more than trace levels of China clay. If it had, there certainly would have been an extensive paper trail, such as is found for the experimental "Bluish Paper" stamps of 1909. Both the manufacture and release to the public of the experimental "Bluish Paper" stamps is well documented in these letters and required the specific permission of the Secretary of the Treasury, so it is extremely unlikely that any other watermarked "experimental paper" could have been made, tested and released without leaving some record in the letters of the BEP. Nowhere in all the BEP correspondence and records is there any mention of any paper containing China clay, either 2 percent or 20 percent.

Since 1975 I have performed several scientific studies of stamps that were certified by expertizing bodies to be (and others that were thought to be) "China Clay" stamps. All of these studies have proven that, to a scientific certainty, there is no detectable China clay, or any other filler, in any of those stamps. However, those stamps are somewhat darker than the "normal stamps" of that series. The question became, "if these stamps are not 'China clay,' what are they?"

The beginning of the answer came from some letters in the National Archives from the director of The Bureau of Engraving and Printing to two of the paper companies that had the contracts to furnish paper to the Bureau from 1908 to 1910.

In letters from the Eastern Paper Manufacturing Co. in 1908 and 1909, the firm stated that they were having problems making good paper "because of low water level at the mill." I have had discussions with the current operators of that mill, and they agree that, at those times, a low water level in the river, where they got their water, would have resulted in significant silt in the

Figure 1. Typical "clean" paper as seen under high magnification.

Figure 2. "Dirty" paper, containing significant levels of river silt.

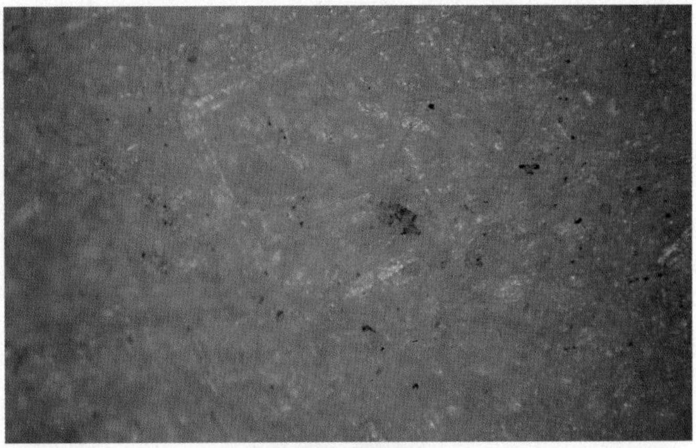

Figure 3. The Bureau of Engraving and Printing sometimes had to use paper that was not up to its specifications when its paper supply was low, such as this paper containing unacceptable black specks.

paper which would have made darker looking paper.

Other letters, in 1909 and 1910, to the Champion Coated Paper Co. (CCPC), showed that Champion was having problems making paper that simultaneously met the BEP specifications for both the thickness and weight of the paper. At various times the BEP called the paper "thin," "thick," "off color," "translucent" or "containing black specks." These are the same terms that were used to describe the so-called "experimental papers" or "China Clay paper" in the literature after 1910 and that were used to describe these papers in the Scott catalogue before 1984.

Also, there were comments, in the letters from the BEP, that the CCPC "must eliminate in the greatest degree practicable the black specks that are somewhat noticeable in the present paper" and "we [the BEP] are short on paper so we will use your paper that contains translucent spots and black specs but you must make every attempt to get rid of them." These visible black specks were very small, but they would have made the paper appear darker than normal, depending on how much dirt was in each batch of paper. There is also one letter in which the BEP complains that the paper is "too thin or off color." Thus, the BEP, which at times was down to only three days of paper on hand, was forced to use defective paper that would normally have been rejected. At times the BEP was using as much as 100,000 sheets a day from carload lots of one million sheets (enough paper for 400,000,000 stamps).

I made a series of photographs through my microscope to confirm that the darker color was caused by dirt in the stamp paper. Typical "clean" paper is shown in Figure 1.

Typical silty paper is shown in Figure 2. Notice how the silt stacks up against the edge of the paper fibers.

Typical black specks are shown in Figure 3. I have seen specks as large as 1 mm in the stamps that I have examined.

I also measured the color (the reflectivity) of 266 used stamps and six "China Clay" stamps, and I found that there was a wide variation in color, with the "China Clay" stamps being the darkest of that group of stamps.

My conclusion from these studies is that the stamps called "China Clay" stamps are only normal stamps that were printed on defective paper that was either structurally deficient (too thin, too thick, or too weak) or just the dirtiest of that series of stamps, and in no way were they printed on "experimental paper." They are not rare because they are just the dirtiest of very large runs of printings. I do not believe that they deserve a special "variety" listing, any more than stamps with varying shades of gum deserve a "variety" listing.

For a much more detailed discussion of my findings, please see *The United States Specialist*, vol. 77, nos. 1 and 2, January and February 2006. The *Specialist* is the Journal of the United States Stamp Society (formerly the Bureau Issues Association). These two articles were first published in slightly different form in the March-April 2005 and May-June 2005 issues of the *Collectors Club Philatelist*, the journal of The Collectors Club (New York).

Edward (Ted) Liston has a Ph.D. in chemical engineering (with a specialty in instrumental analysis) from the University of Southern California. He is a Fellow of the Royal Philatelic Society of London, a life member of the American Philatelic Society, an expert for the APS Expert Committee, and a member of the International Association of Philatelic Experts.

Ted started collecting at age 8 (in a Scott International Album, of course) and, after a 15- year break for college and military, resumed collecting in 1960. His specialist collections have been United States Washington/Franklins, U.S. officials overprinted "Specimen" and world wide forgeries. He is now collecting world wide classics in the reprint of the Scott "Brown Albums," and he is also performing studies in several philatelic areas using scientific techniques.

Editor's note:

It has been more than three years since Ted Liston's ground-breaking research was published, and his conclusions were known to many philatelic students prior to that time. In this period since publication, there has been no research and no rebuttal that would challenge his conclusions. Philatelic specialists have accepted the fact that there was no special paper experimentation done during the 1908-10 period other than the well-known and well-documented 35-percent-rag-content "Bluish paper" experimentation in 1909.

Thus, the Scott catalogue editors have accepted the conclusions presented here, and we have concluded that it is appropriate to delete the numbered listings for "China Clay" paper stamps that have appeared in the Scott Specialized Catalogue of United States Stamps and Covers for many years. These interesting paper varieties, which have nothing to do with China clay, can appear to be thin, thick, translucent, opaque, somewhat dark or very dark, but they are not the kind of items that the Scott catalogue or other catalogues normally list. This is not to say that these various paper varieties are of no value or are not of great interest to specialists of the stamps from this time period. It is only to say that these various types and degrees of paper varieties are subjects which are beyond the scope of stamp catalogues. Specialist collectors will no doubt continue to study and treasure these varieties.

Never hinged 150.00
P# block of 6, Impt. & star 85.00
Never hinged 140.00
P# block of 6, Impt. & small solid star (plate 4988) *1,750.*
Never hinged *2,750.*
Double transfer 12.50 —
Foreign entry, design of 1c (plate 5299) *2,250.* *2,750.*
On cover *5,000.*
Rosette crack —
Cracked plate — —

a. Booklet pane of 6 135.00 *400.00*
Never hinged 230.00

No. 332a used is valued with a contemporaneous cancel. A certificate of authenticity is advised.

No. 332 with foreign entry, used, is valued in the grade of fine.

Earliest documented uses: Dec. 3, 1908 (No. 332), Nov. 16, 1908 (No. 332a single).

Washington — A140

TYPE I

THREE CENTS.

Type I. The top line of the toga rope is weak and the rope shading lines are thin. The 5th line from the left is missing. The line between the lips is thin. (For descriptions of 3c types II, III and IV, see notes and illustrations preceding Nos. 484, 529-530.)

Used on both flat plate and rotary press printings.

333 A140 3c **deep violet,** type I, *Dec. 1908* 35.00 3.00
violet 35.00 3.00
light violet 35.00 3.00
Never hinged 85.00
On cover 8.50
Block of 4 (2mm spacing) 145.00 26.50
Block of 4 (3mm spacing) 150.00 29.00
P# block of 6, Impt., T V 375.00
Never hinged 600.00
P# block of 6, Impt. & star 400.00
Never hinged 650.00
Double transfer 37.50 5.75

Earliest documented use: Jan. 12, 1909.

334 A140 4c **orange brown,** *Dec. 1908* 42.50 1.50
brown 42.50 1.50
light brown 42.50 1.50
dark brown 42.50 1.50
Never hinged 100.00
On cover 7.00
Block of 4 (2mm spacing) 180.00 12.50
Block of 4 (3mm spacing) 190.00 14.00
P# block of 6, Impt., T V 450.00
Never hinged 725.00
P# block of 6, Impt. & star 450.00
Never hinged 725.00
Double transfer 55.00 —

Earliest documented use: Jan. 12, 1909.

335 A140 5c **blue,** *Dec. 1908* 55.00 2.50
bright blue 55.00 2.50
dark blue 55.00 2.50
Never hinged 125.00
On cover 8.50
Block of 4 (2mm spacing) 230.00 20.00
Block of 4 (3mm spacing) 240.00 17.50
P# block of 6, Impt., T V 525.00
Never hinged 1,000.
P# block of 6, Impt. & star 550.00
Never hinged 1,050.
Double transfer 60.00 —

Earliest documented use: Jan. 12, 1909.

336 A140 6c **red orange,** *Jan. 1909* 70.00 6.50
pale red orange 70.00 6.50
orange 70.00 6.50
Never hinged 175.00
On cover 22.50
Block of 4 275.00 50.00
P# block of 6, Impt., T V 750.00
Never hinged 1,400.
Never hinged —

Earliest documented use: Jan. 6, 1909.

337 A140 8c **olive green,** *Dec. 1908* 50.00 3.00
deep olive green 50.00 3.00
Never hinged 115.00
On cover 18.00
Block of 4 210.00 25.00
P# block of 6, Impt., T V 525.00
Never hinged 875.00
Double transfer 57.50 —

Earliest documented use: Jan. 8, 1909.

338 A140 10c **yellow,** *Jan. 1909* 75.00 2.00
Never hinged 190.00
On cover 10.00
Block of 4 300.00 15.00
P# block of 6, Impt., T V 800.00
Never hinged 1,500.
Double transfer — —
Very thin paper —

Earliest documented use: Jan. 18, 1909.

339 A140 13c **blue green,** *Jan. 1909* 42.50 19.00
deep blue green 42.50 19.00
Never hinged 100.00
On cover 110.00
Block of 4 190.00 175.00
P# block of 6, Impt., T V 500.00
Never hinged 875.00
Line through "TAG" of "POSTAGE" (4948 LR 96) 70.00 —

Earliest documented use: Mar. 5, 1909.

340 A140 15c **pale ultramarine,** *Jan. 1909* 70.00 6.50
ultramarine 70.00 6.50
Never hinged 175.00
On cover 125.00
Block of 4 290.00 65.00
P# block of 6, Impt., T V 650.00
Never hinged 1,175.

Earliest documented use: Mar. 12, 1909.

341 A140 50c **violet,** *Jan. 13, 1909* 350.00 20.00
dull violet 350.00 20.00
Never hinged 800.00
On cover *5,000.*
Block of 4 1,500. 150.00
Margin block of 4, arrow, right or left 1,550.
P# block of 6, Impt., T V *7,000.* —
Never hinged *15,000.*

Earliest documented use: Oct. 23, 1909 (on registry tag); June 2, 1916 (on cover).

342 A140 $1 **violet brown,** *Jan. 29, 1909* 550.00 100.00
light violet brown 550.00 100.00
Never hinged 1,250.
On cover *6,000.*
Block of 4 2,400. 700.00
Margin block of 4, arrow, right or left 2,500. 725.00
P# block of 6, Impt., T V *20,000.*
Double transfer — —

Earliest documented use: July 26, 1909.

Nos. 331-342 (12) 1,354. 164.75

For listings of other perforated sheet stamps of A138, A139 and A140 see:
Nos. 357-366 Bluish paper
Nos. 374-382, 405-407 Single line wmk. Perf. 12
Nos. 423A-423C Single line wmk. Perf 12x10
Nos. 423D-423E Single line wmk. Perf 10x12
Nos. 424-430 Single line wmk. Perf. 10
Nos. 461 Single line wmk. Perf. 11
Nos. 462-469 unwmk. Perf. 10
Nos. 498-507 unwmk. Perf. 11
Nos. 519 Double line wmk. Perf. 11
Nos. 525-530 and 536 Offset printing
Nos. 538-546 Rotary press printing

Plate Blocks

Scott values for plate blocks printed from flat plates are for very fine side and bottom positions. Top position plate blocks with full wide selvage sell for more.

Earliest documented use dates for imperforates are for the imperforate sheet stamps, not for imperforate stamps with vending and affixing machine perforations or for flat plate imperforate coil stamps. EDU dates for VAMP and flat plate imperf coil stamps are shown in their respective sections later in the catalogue.

Imperf

343 A138 1c **green,** *Dec. 1908* 4.25 *5.00*
dark green 4.25 *5.00*
yellowish green 4.25 *5.00*
Never hinged 9.00
On cover 11.00
Pair 9.00 *11.00*
Never hinged 19.00
Block of 4 (2mm or 3mm spacing) 19.00 22.50
Corner margin block of 4, 2mm or 3mm 20.00 25.00
Margin block of 4, arrow, 2mm or 3mm 22.50 *25.00*
Center line block 30.00 *35.00*
Never hinged 55.00
P# block of 6, Impt., T V 47.50 —
Never hinged 75.00
P# block of 6, Impt. & star 57.50 —
Never hinged 90.00
P# block of 6, Impt. & small solid star (plate 4980) *675.00*
Never hinged *1,050.*
Double transfer 11.00 7.75

Earliest documented use: Jan. 4, 1909.

344 A139 2c **carmine,** *Dec. 1908* 5.25 3.25
light carmine 5.25 3.25
dark carmine 5.25 3.25
Never hinged 11.00
On cover 8.25
Pair 11.00 8.00
Never hinged 23.00
Block of 4 (2mm or 3mm spacing) 23.00 16.00
Corner margin block of 4, 2mm or 3mm 25.00 22.50
Margin block of 4, arrow, 2mm or 3mm 27.50 22.50
Center line block 37.50 *40.00*
Never hinged 67.50
P# block of 6, Impt., T V 77.50 —
Never hinged 120.00
P# block of 6, Impt. & star 70.00 —
Never hinged 110.00
Double transfer 12.50 4.00
Foreign entry, design of 1c (plate 5299) *1,250.* —

Earliest documented use: Dec. 7, 1908.

The existence of the foreign entry on the imperforate sheet stamp No. 344 has been questioned by specialists. The editors would like to see evidence of the existence of the item, either unused or used.

345 A140 3c **deep violet,** type I, *1909* 10.00 *22.50*
violet 10.00 *22.50*
Never hinged 21.00
On cover 65.00
Pair 21.00 *55.00*
Never hinged 44.00
Block of 4 42.50 *110.00*
Corner margin block of 4 45.00 *115.00*
Margin block of 4, arrow 50.00 *115.00*
Center line block 75.00 *140.00*
Never hinged 135.00
P# block of 6, Impt., T V 155.00 —
Never hinged 240.00
Double transfer 22.50 —

Earliest documented use: Feb. 13, 1909.

346 A140 4c **orange brown,** *Feb. 25, 1909* 15.00 *25.00*
brown 15.00 *25.00*
Never hinged 32.50
On cover 100.00
Pair 32.50 *62.50*
Never hinged 70.00
Block of 4 (2 or 3mm spacing) 65.00 *125.00*
Corner margin block of 4 (2 or 3mm spacing) 70.00 *130.00*
Margin block of 4, arrow, (2 or 3mm spacing) 75.00 *130.00*
Center line block 120.00 *220.00*
Never hinged 220.00
P# block of 6, Impt., T V 175.00 —
Never hinged 275.00
P# block of 6, Impt. & star 210.00 —
Never hinged 325.00
Double transfer 35.00 —

Earliest documented use: Mar. 13, 1909.

347 A140 5c **blue,** *Feb. 25, 1909* 30.00 *37.50*
dark blue 30.00 *37.50*
Never hinged 65.00
On cover 140.00
Pair 65.00 *110.00*
Never hinged 140.00
Block of 4 135.00 *220.00*
Corner margin block of 4 145.00 *235.00*
Margin block of 4, arrow 155.00 *245.00*
Center line block 220.00 *325.00*
Never hinged 400.00
P# block of 6, Impt., T V 275.00 —
Never hinged 500.00
Cracked plate —

Earliest documented use: Mar. 4, 1909.

Nos. 343-347 (5) 64.50 *93.25*
Nos. 343-347, never hinged 138.50

For listings of other imperforate stamps of designs A138, A139 and A140 see Nos. 383, 384, 408, 409 and 459 Single line wmk.
Nos. 481-485 unwmk.
Nos. 531-535 Offset printing

Used values for coil singles, pairs and line pairs reflect examples with contemporaneous cancels.

COIL STAMPS

1908-10 ***Perf. 12 Horizontally***

348 A138 1c **green,** *Dec. 29, 1908* 37.50 *50.00*
dark green 37.50 *50.00*
Never hinged 80.00
On cover 70.00
Pair 95.00 *140.00*
Never hinged 210.00
Guide line pair 275.00 *625.00*
Never hinged 600.00

Earliest documented use: Jan. 25, 1909.

349 A139 2c **carmine,** *Jan. 1909* 80.00 *100.00*
dark carmine 80.00 *100.00*
Never hinged 180.00
On cover 125.00

			Pair	210.00	*300.00*
			Never hinged	500.00	
			Guide line pair	550.00	*1,100.*
			Never hinged	1,300.	
			Foreign entry, design of 1c (plate 5299)	—	*3,000.*

Earliest documented use: May 14, 1909.

350	A140	4c	**orange brown,** *Aug. 15, 1910*	150.00	*210.00*
			Never hinged	350.00	
			On cover		275.00
			Pair	370.00	*625.00*
			Never hinged	825.00	
			Guide line pair	1,250.	*2,750.*
			Never hinged	2,750.	

Earliest documented use: Mar. 22, 1912.

351	A140	5c	**blue,** *Jan. 1909*	160.00	*275.00*
			dark blue	160.00	*275.00*
			Never hinged	375.00	
			On cover		625.00
			Pair	425.00	*825.00*
			Never hinged	950.	
			Guide line pair	1,150.	*3,000.*
			Never hinged	2,500.	

Earliest documented use: Sept. 21, 1909.

1909 ***Perf. 12 Vertically***

352	A138	1c	**green,** *Jan. 1909*	95.00	*190.00*
			dark green	95.00	*190.00*
			Never hinged	210.00	
			On cover		225.00
			Pair (2mm spacing)	250.00	*600.00*
			Never hinged	550.00	
			Pair (3mm spacing)	235.00	*575.00*
			Never hinged	525.00	
			Guide line pair	825.00	*1,650.*
			Never hinged	1,800.	
			Double transfer	—	—
353	A139	2c	**carmine,** *Jan. 12, 1909*	95.00	*220.00*
			dark carmine	95.00	*220.00*
			Never hinged	215.00	
			On cover		275.00
			Pair (2mm spacing)	250.00	*575.00*
			Never hinged	550.00	
			Pair (3mm spacing)	235.00	*550.00*
			Never hinged	525.00	
			Guide line pair	750.00	*1,300.*
			Never hinged	1,750.	

Earliest documented use: June 14, 1909.

354	A140	4c	**orange brown,** *Feb. 23, 1909*	220.00	*275.00*
			Never hinged	475.00	
			On cover		325.00
			Pair (2mm spacing)	550.00	*825.00*
			Never hinged	1,200.	
			Pair (3mm spacing)	525.00	*825.00*
			Never hinged	1,150.	
			Guide line pair	1,500.	*1,550.*
			Never hinged	3,250.	

Earliest documented use: June 9, 1909.

355	A140	5c	**blue,** *Feb. 23, 1909*	225.00	*300.00*
			Never hinged	500.00	
			On cover		375.00
			Pair	575.00	*875.00*
			Never hinged	1,250.	
			Guide line pair	1,500.	*2,050.*
			Never hinged	3,250.	

Earliest documented use: Oct. 25, 1909.

These Government Coil Stamps, Nos. 352-355, should not be confused with those of the International Vending Machine Co., which are perf. 12½-13.

356	A140	10c	**yellow,** *Jan. 7, 1909*	3,250.	*4,500.*
			Never hinged	7,000.	
			On cover		*10,000.*
			Pair	*7,000.*	*10,500.*
			Never hinged	*15,000.*	
			Guide line pair	*17,500.*	*29,000.*
			Never hinged	*55,000.*	

Earliest documented use: Mar. 9, 1909 (dated cancel on off-cover stamp).

The used guide line pair of No. 356 is unique. Value reflects price realized at auction in 2002.

For listings of other coil stamps of designs A138 A139 and A140 see:

Nos. 385-396, 410-413, 441-459, single line watermark.

Nos. 486-496, unwatermarked.

Beware of stamps offered as No. 356 which may be examples of No. 338 with perfs. trimmed at top and/or bottom. Beware also of plentiful fakes in the marketplace of Nos. 348-355, made by fraudulently perforating imperforate stamps or by fraudulently trimming perforations off fully perforated stamps. Authentication of all these coils is advised.

BLUISH PAPER

This was made with 35 percent rag stock instead of all wood pulp. The "bluish" color (actually grayish blue) goes through the paper showing clearly on the back as well as on the face.

1909 ***Perf. 12***

357	A138	1c	**green,** *Feb. 16, 1909*	100.00	100.00
			Never hinged	210.00	
			On postcard		120.00
			On cover		220.00
			Block of 4 (2mm spacing)	425.00	*600.00*
			Block of 4 (3mm spacing)	*800.00*	
			P# block of 6, Impt., T V	1,100.	
			Never hinged	1,850.	
			P# block of 6, Impt. & star	*3,100.*	
			Never hinged	*5,200.*	

Earliest documented use: Feb. 21, 1909.

358	A139	2c	**carmine,** *Feb. 16, 1909*	90.00	*100.00*
			Never hinged	190.00	
			On cover		190.00
			Block of 4 (2mm spacing)	375.00	*650.00*
			Block of 4 (3mm spacing)	475.00	
			P# block of 6, Impt., T V	1,000.	
			Never hinged	1,800.	
			P# block of 6, Impt. & star	1,650.	
			Never hinged	2,750.	
			Double transfer	—	

Earliest documented use: Feb. 23, 1909.

359	A140	3c	**deep violet,** type I	2,000.	*5,000.*
			Never hinged	4,500.	
			On cover		—
			Block of 4	*8,500.*	
			P# block of 6, Impt., T V	*22,500.*	
			Never hinged	*31,000.*	

Earliest documented use: Dec. 27, 1910.

360	A140	4c	**orange brown**	*27,500.*	
			Never hinged	*80,000.*	
			Block of 4	*140,000.*	
			P# strip of 3, Impt., T V	*140,000.*	

The No. 360 plate number strip of three is unique.

361	A140	5c	**blue**	6,000.	*15,000.*
			Never hinged	*15,000.*	
			On cover		27,500.
			Block of 4	*26,000.*	—
			P# block of 6, Impt., T V	*90,000.*	

The No. 361 plate block is unique.

Earliest documented use: May 18, 1910.

362	A140	6c	**red orange**	1,500.	*15,000.*
			Never hinged	3,750.	
			On cover		*22,500.*
			Block of 4	*6,250.*	
			P# block of 6, Impt., T V	*16,000.*	
			Never hinged	*30,000.*	

Earliest documented use: Sept. 14, 1911.

363	A140	8c	**olive green**	*30,000.*	
			Never hinged	*85,000.*	
			Block of 4	*135,000.*	
			P# strip of 3, Impt., T V	*150,000.*	

The No. 363 plate number strip of three is unique.

364	A140	10c	**yellow**	1,900.	*7,000.*
			Never hinged	5,000.	
			On cover		—
			Block of 4	8,000.	
			P# block of 6, Impt., T V	*33,500.*	

Earliest documented use: Feb. 3, 1910.

365	A140	13c	**blue green**	3,000.	*2,250.*
			Never hinged	7,000.	
			On cover		—
			Block of 4	*13,000.*	*10,000.*
			P# block of 6, Impt., T V	*30,000.*	
366	A140	15c	**pale ultramarine**	1,500.	*11,000.*
			Never hinged	3,500.	
			On cover		—
			Block of 4	*6,250.*	
			P# block of 6, Impt., T V	*11,500.*	
			Never hinged	*20,000.*	

Earliest documented use: Jan. 15, 1911.

Nos. 360 and 363 were not regularly issued.

Used examples of Nos. 357-366 must bear contemporaneous cancels, and Nos. 359-366 used must be accompanied by certificates of authenticity issued by recognized expertizing committees.

IMPORTANT INFORMATION REGARDING VALUES FOR NEVER-HINGED STAMPS

Collectors should be aware that the values given for never-hinged stamps from No. 182 on are for stamps in the grade of very fine, just as the values for all stamps in the catalogue are for very fine stamps unless indicated otherwise. The never-hinged premium as a percentage of value will be larger for stamps in extremely fine or superb grades, and the premium will be smaller for fine-very fine, fine or poor examples. This is particularly true of the issues of the late-19th and early-20th centuries. For example, in the grade of very fine, an unused stamp from this time period may be valued at $100 hinged and $200 never hinged. The never-hinged premium is thus 100%. But in a grade of extremely fine, this same stamp will not only sell for more hinged, but the never-hinged premium will increase, perhaps to 200%-400% or more over the higher extremely fine value. In a grade of superb, a hinged stamp will sell for much more than a very fine stamp, and additionally the never-hinged premium will be much larger, perhaps as large as 500%-1,000%. On the other hand, the same stamp in a grade of fine or fine-very fine not only will sell for less than a very fine stamp in hinged condition, but additionally the never-hinged premium will be smaller than the never-hinged premium on a very fine stamp, perhaps as small as 15%-30%.

Please note that the above statements and percentages are NOT a formula for arriving at the values of stamps in hinged or never-hinged condition in the grades of very good, fine, fine to very fine, very fine, very fine to extremely fine, extremely fine or superb. The percentages given apply only to the size of the premium for never-hinged condition that might be added to the stamp value for hinged condition. Further, the percentages given are only generalized estimates. Some stamps or grades may have percentages for never-hinged condition that are higher or lower than the ranges given. For values of the most popular U.S. stamps in the grades of very good, fine, fine to very fine, very fine, very fine to extremely fine, extremely fine and superb, see the *Scott United States Specialized Valuing Supplement*, updated and issued twice each year in April and October.

VALUES FOR NEVER-HINGED STAMPS PRIOR TO SCOTT 182

This catalogue does not value pre-1879 stamps in never-hinged condition. Premiums for never-hinged condition in the classic era invariably are even larger than those premiums listed for the 1879 and later issues. Generally speaking, the earlier the stamp is listed in the catalogue, the larger will be the never-hinged premium. On some early classics, the premium will be several multiples of the unused, hinged values given in the catalogue.

NEVER-HINGED PLATE BLOCKS

Values given for never-hinged plate blocks are for blocks in which all stamps have original gum that has never been hinged and has no disturbances, and all selvage, whether gummed or ungummed, has never been hinged.

Lincoln — A141

William H. Seward — A142

LINCOLN CENTENARY OF BIRTH ISSUE

Designed by Clair Aubrey Huston.

Plates of 400 subjects in four panes of 100 each

1909 **Wmk. 191** ***Perf. 12***

367	A141	2c	**carmine,** *Feb. 12*	5.25	2.00
			bright carmine	5.25	2.00
			Never hinged	11.00	
			On cover		4.00
			Block of 4 (2mm spacing)	22.00	16.00
			Block of 4 (3mm spacing)	22.00	15.00
			P# block of 6, Impt. & small sol-id star	200.00	
			Never hinged	275.00	
			Double transfer	7.25	2.75

Earliest documented use: Feb. 12, 1909 (FDC).

Imperf

368	A141	2c	**carmine,** *Feb. 12*	17.00	22.50
			Never hinged	35.00	
			On cover		35.00
			Pair	37.00	50.00
			Never hinged	80.00	
			Block of 4 (2mm or 3mm spacing)	77.50	95.00
			Corner margin block of 4	82.50	95.00
			Margin block of 4, arrow	85.00	100.00
			Center line block	145.00	125.00
			Never hinged	260.00	
			P# block of 6, Impt. & small solid star	200.00	—
			Never hinged	390.00	
			Double transfer	42.50	30.00

Earliest documented use: Feb. 12, 1909 (FDC).

BLUISH PAPER

Perf. 12

369	A141	2c	**carmine,** *Feb.*	200.00	*275.00*
			Never hinged	425.00	
			On cover		425.00
			Block of 4 (2mm or 3mm spacing)	900.	*1,250.*
			P# block of 6, Impt. & small solid star	*3,000.*	
			Never hinged	*4,500.*	

Earliest documented use: Feb. 27, 1909 (dated cancel on off-cover stamp); Mar. 27, 1909 (on cover).

ALASKA-YUKON-PACIFIC EXPOSITION ISSUE

Seattle, Wash., June 1 - Oct. 16, 1909

Designed by Clair Aubrey Huston.

Plates of 280 subjects in four panes of 70 each

1909 **Wmk. 191** ***Perf. 12***

370	A142	2c	**carmine,** *June 1*	8.00	2.25
			bright carmine	8.00	2.25
			Never hinged	17.50	
			On cover		5.00
			On Expo. card or cover, Expo. station machine canc.		65.00
			On Expo. card or cover, Expo. station duplex handstamp canc.		250.00
			Block of 4	35.00	19.00
			P# block of 6, Impt., T V	200.00	
			Never hinged	320.00	
			Double transfer (5249 UL 8)	10.50	5.00

Earliest documented use: June 1, 1909 (FDC).

Imperf

371	A142	2c	**carmine,** *June*	19.00	24.00
			Never hinged	40.00	
			On cover		42.50
			On cover, Expo. station machine canc.		*450.00*
			Pair	40.00	52.50
			Never hinged	82.50	
			Block of 4	90.00	130.00
			Corner margin block of 4	95.00	—
			Margin block of 4, arrow	97.50	140.00
			Center line block	175.00	175.00
			Never hinged	300.00	
			P# block of 6, Impt., T V	225.00	—
			Never hinged	350.00	
			Double transfer	32.50	30.00

Earliest documented use: June 7, 1909.

HUDSON-FULTON CELEBRATION ISSUE

Tercentenary of the discovery of the Hudson River and the centenary of Robert Fulton's steamship, the "Clermont."

Henry Hudson's "Half Moon" and Fulton's Steamship "Clermont" A143

Designed by Clair Aubrey Huston.

Plates of 240 subjects in four panes of 60 each

1909, Sept. 25 **Wmk. 191** ***Perf. 12***

372	A143	2c	**carmine**	11.50	4.75
			Never hinged	24.00	
			On cover		8.50
			Block of 4	47.50	30.00
			P# block of 6, Impt., T V	280.00	
			Never hinged	425.00	
			Double transfer (5393 and 5394)	16.00	5.00

Earliest documented use: Sept. 25, 1909 (FDC).

Imperf

373	A143	2c	**carmine**	22.50	27.50
			Never hinged	47.50	
			On cover		40.00
			Pair	47.50	60.00
			Never hinged	100.00	
			Block of 4	100.00	130.00
			Corner margin block of 4	105.00	—
			Margin block of 4, arrow	110.00	135.00
			Center line block	210.00	160.00
			Never hinged	360.00	
			P# block of 6, Impt., T V	240.00	—
			Never hinged	375.00	
			Double transfer (5393 and 5394)	45.00	32.50

Earliest documented use: Sept. 25, 1909 (FDC).

Earliest documented use dates for imperforates are for the imperforate sheet stamps, not for imperforate stamps with vending and affixing machine perforations or for flat plate imperforate coil stamps. EDU dates for VAMP and flat plate imperf coil stamps are shown in their respective sections later in the catalogue.

REGULAR ISSUE

DESIGNS OF 1908-09 ISSUES

In this issue the Bureau used three groups of plates:

(1) The old standard plates with uniform 2mm spacing throughout (6c, 8c, 10c and 15c values);

(2) Those having an open star in the margin and showing spacings of 2mm and 3mm between stamps (for all values 1c to 10c); and

(3) A third set of plates with uniform spacing of approximately 2¾mm between all stamps. These plates have imprints showing

a. "Bureau of Engraving & Printing," "A" and number.
b. "A" and number only.
c. Number only.
(See above No. 331)

These were used for the 1c, 2c, 3c, 4c and 5c values.

On or about Oct. 1, 1910 the Bureau began using paper watermarked with single-lined letters:

(Actual size of letter)

repeated in rows, this way:

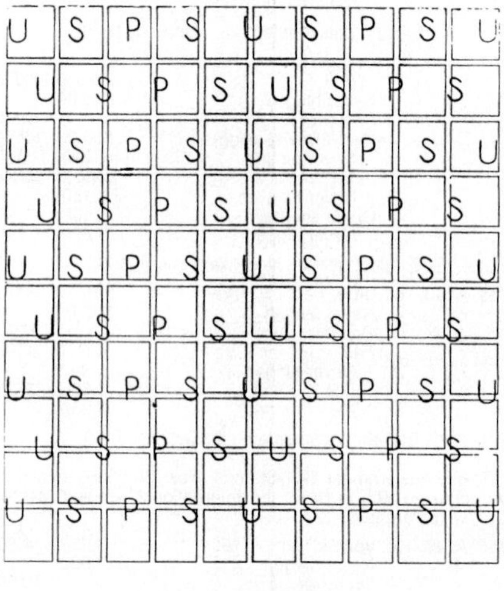

Watermark 190

Plates of 400 subjects in four panes of 100 each

1910-11 **Wmk. 190** ***Perf. 12***

374	A138	1c	**green,** *Nov. 23, 1910*	7.00	.25
			light green	7.00	.25
			dark green	7.00	.25
			Never hinged	16.00	
			On cover		.30
			Block of 4 (2mm spacing)	30.00	3.25
			Block of 4 (3mm spacing)	32.50	3.00
			P# block of 6, Impt., & star	100.00	
			Never hinged	160.00	
			P# block of 6, Impt. & "A"	125.00	—
			Never hinged	175.00	
			Double transfer	14.00	—
			Cracked plate	—	—
			Pane of 60	*1,750.*	—
a.			Booklet pane of 6, *Oct. 7, 1910*	225.00	*300.00*
			Never hinged	375.00	

Earliest documented uses: Feb. 7, 1911 (No. 374); Feb. 28, 1911 (No. 374a single).

Panes of 60 of No. 374 were regularly issued in Washington, D.C. during Sept. and Oct., 1912. They were made from the six outer vertical rows of imperforate "Star Plate" sheets that had been rejected for use in vending machines on account of the 3mm spacing.

These panes have sheet margins on two adjoining sides and are imperforate along the other two sides. Upper and lower right panes show plate number, star and imprint on both margins; upper and lower left panes show plate number, star and imprint on side margins, but only the imprint on top or bottom margins.

375	A139	2c	**carmine,** *Nov. 23, 1910*	7.00	.25
			bright carmine	7.00	.25

dark carmine	7.00	.25
Never hinged	16.00	
On cover		.30
Block of 4 (2mm spacing)	30.00	2.00
Block of 4 (3mm spacing)	29.00	1.75
P# block of 6, Impt. & star	125.00	
Never hinged	185.00	
P# block of 6, Impt. & "A"	135.00	
Never hinged	200.00	
Cracked plate	—	—
Double transfer	12.00	—
Foreign entry, design of 1c (plate 5299)	—	*1,450.*
a. Booklet pane of 6, *Nov. 30, 1910*	125.00	*200.00*
Never hinged	200.00	
b. 2c **lake**	*900.00*	
Never hinged	*1,900.*	
c. Double impression	*600.00*	
Never hinged	*1,200.*	

Earliest documented use: Dec. 29, 1910 (No. 375); May 10, 1911 (No. 375a single).

376 A140 3c **deep violet,** type I, *Jan. 16, 1911*	21.50	2.00
violet	21.50	2.00
Never hinged	47.50	
lilac	26.00	2.25
Never hinged	55.00	
On cover		8.00
Block of 4 (2mm spacing)	90.00	15.00
Block of 4 (3mm spacing)	92.50	14.00
P# block of 6, Impt. & star	300.00	
Never hinged	450.00	
P# block of 6	325.00	
Never hinged	475.00	

Earliest documented use: June 9, 1911.

377 A140 4c **brown,** *Jan. 20, 1911*	32.50	1.00
dark brown	32.50	1.00
orange brown	32.50	1.00
Never hinged	75.00	
On cover		7.50
Block of 4 (2mm spacing)	145.00	6.50
Block of 4 (3mm spacing)	140.00	6.00
P# block of 6, Impt. & star	325.00	
Never hinged	475.00	
P# block of 6	350.00	
Never hinged	550.00	
Double transfer	—	—

Earliest documented use: Mar. 7, 1911.

378 A140 5c **blue,** *Jan. 25, 1911*	32.50	.75
light blue	32.50	.75
dark blue	32.50	.75
bright blue	32.50	.75
Never hinged	75.00	
On cover		5.25
Block of 4 (2mm spacing)	145.00	6.00
Block of 4 (3mm spacing)	140.00	5.00
P# block of 6, Impt., T V	350.00	
Never hinged	550.00	
P# block of 6, Impt. & star	350.00	
Never hinged	550.00	
P# block of 6, "A"	400.00	
Never hinged	625.00	
P# block of 6	400.00	
Never hinged	625.00	
Double transfer	—	—

Earliest documented use: Feb. 14, 1911.

379 A140 6c **red orange,** *Jan. 1911*	37.50	1.00
light red orange	37.50	1.00
Never hinged	85.00	
On cover		13.00
Block of 4 (2mm spacing)	160.00	12.50
Block of 4 (3mm spacing)	155.00	11.00
P# block of 6, Impt., T V	500.00	
Never hinged	800.00	
P# block of 6, Impt. & star	440.00	
Never hinged	700.00	

Earliest documented use: Jan. 12, 1911.

380 A140 8c **olive green,** *Feb. 8, 1911*	115.00	15.00
dark olive green	115.00	15.00
Never hinged	260.00	
On cover		45.00
Block of 4 (2mm spacing)	475.00	100.00
Block of 4 (3mm spacing)	475.00	95.00
P# block of 6, Impt., T V	1,100.	
Never hinged	1,900.	
P# block of 6, Impt., & star	*1,300.*	
Never hinged	*2,200.*	

Earliest documented use: May 27, 1911.

381 A140 10c **yellow,** *Jan. 24, 1911*	110.00	6.00
Never hinged	250.00	
On cover		22.50
Block of 4 (2mm spacing)	460.00	50.00
Block of 4 (3mm spacing)	460.00	47.50
P# block of 6, Impt., T V	1,150.	
Never hinged	2,000.	
P# block of 6, Impt. & star	1,250.	
Never hinged	2,250.	

Earliest documented use: Feb. 17, 1911.

382 A140 15c **pale ultramarine,** *Mar. 1, 1911*	275.00	19.00
Never hinged	625.00	
On cover		100.00
Block of 4	1,150.	130.00
P# block of 6, Impt., T V	2,500.	
Never hinged	4,500.	

Earliest documented use: April 25, 1911.

Nos. 374-382 (9)	638.00	45.25

Earliest documented use dates for imperforates are for the imperforate sheet stamps, not for imperforate stamps with vending and affixing machine perforations or for flat plate imperforate coil stamps. EDU dates for VAMP and flat plate imperf coil stamps are shown in their respective sections later in the catalogue.

1910, Dec. ***Imperf.***

383 A138 1c **green**	2.10	2.00
dark green	2.10	2.00
yellowish green	2.10	2.00
bright green	2.10	2.00
Never hinged	4.50	
On cover		5.00
Pair	4.50	4.50
Never hinged	10.00	
Block of 4 (2mm or 3mm spacing)	9.50	14.00
Corner margin block of 4	10.50	
Margin block of 4, arrow	11.00	13.50
Center line block	24.00	16.00
Never hinged	40.00	
P# block of 6, Impt., & star	45.00	—
Never hinged	72.50	
P# block of 6, Impt. & "A"	82.50	—
Never hinged	125.00	
Double transfer	6.50	—

Earliest documented use: Jan. 28, 1911.

Rosette plate crack on head

384 A139 2c **carmine**	3.50	2.50
light carmine	3.50	2.50
Never hinged	7.50	
dark carmine	55.00	12.50
On cover		3.50
Horizontal pair	11.00	7.50
Never hinged	24.00	
Vertical pair	8.00	6.00
Never hinged	18.00	
Block of 4 (2mm or 3mm spacing)	24.00	16.00
Corner margin block of 4	27.00	20.00
Margin block of 4, arrow	27.50	21.00
Center line block	50.00	50.00
Never hinged	85.00	
P# block of 6, Impt. & star	130.00	—
Never hinged	200.00	
P# block of 6, Impt. & "A"	170.00	—
Never hinged	260.00	
Double transfer	7.50	—
Rosette plate crack on head	*150.00*	—

Earliest documented use: Dec. 8, 1910.

COIL STAMPS

1910, Nov. 1 ***Perf. 12 Horizontally***

385 A138 1c **green**	45.00	45.00
dark green	45.00	45.00
Never hinged	100.00	
On cover		70.00
Pair	110.00	*135.00*
Never hinged	240.00	
Guide line pair	450.00	*675.00*
Never hinged	1,000.	
386 A139 2c **carmine**	110.00	100.00
light carmine	110.00	100.00
Never hinged	250.00	
On cover		125.00
Pair	300.00	280.00
Never hinged	650.00	
Guide line pair	1,400.	*1,150.*
Never hinged	3,250.	

Earliest documented use: Dec. 9, 1910.

1910-11 ***Perf. 12 Vertically***

387 A138 1c **green,** *Nov. 1, 1910*	200.00	140.00
Never hinged	425.00	
On cover		175.00
Pair (2mm spacing)	475.00	425.00
Never hinged	1,050.	
Pair (3mm spacing)	500.00	410.00
Never hinged	1,100.	
Guide line pair	1,200.	*1,150.*
Never hinged	2,600.	

Earliest documented use: Nov. 5, 1910.

388 A139 2c **carmine,** *Nov. 1, 1910*	1,500.	*2,250.*
Never hinged	3,500.	
On cover		*2,500.*
Pair (2mm spacing)	3,500.	*7,500.*
Never hinged	8,000.	
Pair (3mm spacing)	3,750.	*8,000.*
Never hinged	8,250.	
Guide line pair	*8,750.*	*23,000.*
Never hinged	*25,000.*	

The used guide line pair of No. 388 is unique. It is the center pair in a strip of four, is fine-very fine and is valued thus.

Stamps offered as No. 388 frequently are privately perforated examples of No. 384, or copies of No. 375 with top and/or bottom perfs trimmed.

Earliest documented use: Jan. 4, 1911.

389 A140 3c **deep vio.,** type I, *Jan. 24, 1911*	*110,000.*	*11,000.*
Never hinged	*225,000.*	
On cover		*27,500.*
Pair	*250,000.*	*37,500.*

No. 389 is valued in the grade of fine.

Only a small supply of this coil was used at Orangeburg, N.Y. The used pair listed is part of a strip of 3 (three such strips exist). Each strip is in average grade or condition, and the pairs are valued thus. No other used multiples are recorded. There is only one mint, never-hinged example recorded.

Stamps offered as No. 389 sometimes are examples of No. 376 with top and/or bottom perfs trimmed. Expertization by competent authorities is recommended.

Earliest documented use: Mar. 8, 1911.

Beware of plentiful fakes in the marketplace of Nos. 385-389, made by fraudulently perforating the 1c and 2c imperforate stamps or by fraudulently trimming perforations off fully perforated stamps.

1910 ***Perf. 8½ Horizontally***

390 A138 1c **green,** *Dec. 12, 1910*	5.00	*14.00*
dark green	5.00	*14.00*
Never hinged	11.00	
On cover		17.50
Pair	11.50	*45.00*
Never hinged	24.00	
Guide line pair	37.50	*125.00*
Never hinged	80.00	
Double transfer	—	—

Earliest documented use: Oct. 5, 1911.

391 A139 2c **carmine,** *Dec. 23, 1910*	42.50	*50.00*
light carmine	42.50	*50.00*
Never hinged	90.00	
On cover		70.00
Pair	110.00	170.00
Never hinged	240.00	
Guide line pair	260.00	*1,350.*
Never hinged	575.00	

Earliest documented use: May 3, 1911.

1910-13 ***Perf. 8½ Vertically***

No.	Design	Description	Unused	Used
392	A138	1c **green,** *Dec. 12, 1910*	30.00	*55.00*
		dark green	30.00	*55.00*
		Never hinged	65.00	
		On cover		75.00
		Pair	75.00	*155.00*
		Never hinged	160.00	
		Guide line pair	200.00	*500.00*
		Never hinged	425.00	
		Double transfer	—	—

Earliest documented use: Dec. 16, 1910.

No.	Design	Description	Unused	Used
393	A139	2c **carmine,** *Dec. 16, 1910*	47.50	45.00
		dark carmine	47.50	45.00
		Never hinged	110.00	
		On cover		65.00
		Pair	125.00	130.00
		Never hinged	275.00	
		Guide line pair	300.00	275.00
		Never hinged	650.00	

Earliest documented use: Dec. 27, 1910.

No.	Design	Description	Unused	Used
394	A140	3c **deep violet,** type I, *Sept. 1911*	60.00	67.50
		violet	60.00	67.50
		red violet	60.00	67.50
		Never hinged	135.00	
		On cover		115.00
		Pair (2mm spacing)	150.00	*220.00*
		Never hinged	350.00	
		Pair (3mm spacing)	145.00	*210.00*
		Never hinged	325.00	
		Guide line pair	425.00	*650.00*
		Never hinged	925.00	

Earliest documented use: Sept. 18, 1911.

No.	Design	Description	Unused	Used
395	A140	4c **brown,** *Apr. 15, 1912*	62.50	*70.00*
		dark brown	62.50	*70.00*
		Never hinged	140.00	
		On cover		115.00
		Pair (2mm spacing)	160.00	200.00
		Never hinged	375.00	
		Pair (3mm spacing)	150.00	200.00
		Never hinged	350.00	
		Guide line pair	475.00	*650.00*
		Never hinged	1,100.	

Earliest documented use: June 21, 1912.

No.	Design	Description	Unused	Used
396	A140	5c **blue,** *Mar. 1913*	60.00	67.50
		dark blue	60.00	67.50
		Never hinged	135.00	
		On cover		115.00
		Pair	160.00	190.00
		Never hinged	375.00	
		Guide line pair	425.00	*825.00*
		Never hinged	975.00	

Earliest documented use: April 5, 1913.

Beware of plentiful fakes in the marketplace of Nos. 390-393, made by fraudulently perforating imperforate stamps.

PANAMA-PACIFIC EXPOSITION ISSUE

San Francisco, Cal., Feb. 20 - Dec. 4, 1915

Vasco Nunez de Balboa — A144

Pedro Miguel Locks, Panama Canal — A145

Golden Gate — A146

Discovery of San Francisco Bay — A147

Exposition Station Cancellation.

Designed by Clair Aubrey Huston.

Plates of 280 subjects in four panes of 70 each.

1913 **Wmk. 190** ***Perf. 12***

No.	Design	Description	Unused	Used
397	A144	1c **green,** *Jan. 1, 1913*	17.50	2.00
		deep green	17.50	2.00
		yellowish green	17.50	2.00
		Never hinged	42.50	
		On cover		3.50
		On Expo. card, Expo. station 1915 machine cancel		*30.00*
		Pair on cover, Expo. station 1915 duplex handstamp cancel		*150.00*
		Block of 4	72.50	14.00
		P# block of 6	300.00	
		Never hinged	450.00	
		Double transfer	22.50	3.25

Earliest documented use: Jan. 1, 1913 (FDC).

No.	Design	Description	Unused	Used
398	A145	2c **carmine,** *Jan. 1913*	20.00	1.00
		deep carmine	20.00	1.00
		Never hinged	45.00	
		On cover		1.75
		On cover, Expo. station 1915 machine cancel		75.00
		On cover, Expo. station 1915 duplex handstamp cancel		*250.00*
		Block of 4	82.50	10.00
		P# block of 6	400.00	
		Never hinged	625.00	
		Double transfer	40.00	3.50
a.		2c **carmine lake**	*1,500.*	
		Never hinged	*2,500.*	
b.		2c **lake**	*5,000.*	

Earliest documented use: Jan. 17, 1913.

No.	Design	Description	Unused	Used
399	A146	5c **blue,** *Jan. 1, 1913*	80.00	10.00
		dark blue	80.00	10.00
		Never hinged	180.00	
		On cover		27.50
		On cover, Expo. station 1915 machine cancel		300.00
		Block of 4	325.00	70.00
		P# block of 6	1,900.	
		Never hinged	3,200.	

Earliest documented use: Jan. 1, 1913 (FDC).

No.	Design	Description	Unused	Used
400	A147	10c **orange yellow,** *Jan. 1, 1913*	135.00	22.50
		Never hinged	300.00	
		On cover		57.50
		On cover, Expo. station 1915 machine cancel		500.00
		Block of 4	575.00	150.00
		P# block of 6	2,350.	
		Never hinged	3,850.	

Earliest documented use: Jan. 1, 1913 (FDC).

No.	Design	Description	Unused	Used
400A	A147	10c **orange,** *Aug. 1913*	225.00	20.00
		Never hinged	500.00	
		On cover		75.00
		On cover, Expo. station 1915 machine cancel		550.00
		Block of 4	950.00	110.00
		P# block of 6	*12,000.*	
		Never hinged	*20,000.*	

Earliest documented use: Nov. 12, 1913.

	Unused	Used
Nos. 397-400A (5)	477.50	55.50
Nos. 397-400A, never hinged	1,068.	

1914-15 ***Perf. 10***

No.	Design	Description	Unused	Used
401	A144	1c **green,** *Dec. 1914*	27.50	7.00
		dark green	27.50	7.00
		Never hinged	65.00	
		On cover		16.00
		On Expo. card, Expo. station 1915 machine cancel		75.00
		Block of 4	120.00	47.50
		P# block of 6	400.00	
		Never hinged	650.00	

Earliest documented use: Dec. 21, 1914.

No.	Design	Description	Unused	Used
402	A145	2c **carmine,** *Jan. 1915*	75.00	2.75
		deep carmine	75.00	2.75
		red	75.00	2.75
		Never hinged	180.00	
		On cover		6.50
		On cover, Expo. station 1915 machine cancel		150.00
		On cover, Expo. station 1915 duplex handstamp cancel		450.00
		Block of 4	325.00	19.00
		P# block of 6	1,950.	
		Never hinged	3,250.	

Earliest documented use: Jan. 13, 1915.

No.	Design	Description	Unused	Used
403	A146	5c **blue,** *Feb. 1915*	175.00	20.00
		dark blue	175.00	20.00
		Never hinged	425.00	
		On cover		55.00
		On cover, Expo. station 1915 machine cancel		450.00
		Block of 4	750.00	130.00
		P# block of 6	4,000.	
		Never hinged	6,750.	

Earliest documented use: Feb. 6, 1915.

No.	Design	Description	Unused	Used
404	A147	10c **orange,** *July 1915*	850.00	70.00
		Never hinged	2,000.	
		On cover		175.00
		On cover, Expo. station 1915 machine cancel		600.00
		Block of 4	*3,800.*	500.00
		P# block of 6	*14,000.*	
		Never hinged	22,000.	

Earliest documented use: Aug. 27, 1915.

	Unused	Used
Nos. 401-404 (4)	1,127.	99.75
Nos. 401-404, never hinged	2,670.	

VALUES FOR VERY FINE STAMPS

Please note: Stamps are valued in the grade of Very Fine unless otherwise indicated.

REGULAR ISSUE

Washington — A140

The plates for this and later issues were the so-called "A" plates with uniform spacing of 2¾mm between stamps.

Plates of 400 subjects in four panes of 100 each for all values 1c to 50c inclusive.

Plates of 200 subjects in two panes of 100 each for $1 and some of the 50c (No. 422) denomination.

1912-14 **Wmk. 190** ***Perf. 12***

No.	Design	Description	Unused	Used
405	A140	1c **green,** *Feb. 1912*	7.00	.25
		light green	7.00	.25
		dark green	7.00	.25
		yellowish green	7.00	.25
		Never hinged	16.00	
		On cover		.30
		Block of 4	30.00	2.50
		P# block of 6, Impt. & "A"	125.00	
		Never hinged	200.00	
		P# block of 6, "A"	115.00	
		Never hinged	185.00	
		P# block of 6	110.00	
		Never hinged	170.00	
		Cracked plate	14.50	—
		Double transfer	8.50	—
a.		Vert. pair, imperf. horiz.	*2,000.*	—
b.		Booklet pane of 6, *1912*	65.00	*75.00*
		Never hinged	110.00	
c.		Double impression		*1,250.*

Earliest documented uses: Feb. 2, 1912 (No. 405); Jan. 16, 1912 (No. 405b single).

TYPE I

TYPE I

TWO CENTS

Type I. There is one shading line in the first curve of the ribbon above the left "2" and one in the second curve of the ribbon above the right "2."

The button of the toga has only a faint outline.

The top line of the toga rope, from the button to the front of the throat, is also very faint.

The shading lines of the face terminate in front of the ear with little or no joining, to form a lock of hair.

Used on both flat plate and rotary press printings.

No.	Design	Description	Unused	Used
406	A140	2c **carmine,** type I, *Feb. 1912*	7.00	.25
		bright carmine	7.00	.25
		Never hinged	16.00	
		dark carmine	7.50	.25
		Never hinged	17.00	
		On cover		.30
		Block of 4	30.00	2.50
		P# block of 6, Impt. & "A"	150.00	
		Never hinged	240.00	
		P# block of 6, "A"	140.00	
		Never hinged	230.00	
		P# block of 6	125.00	
		Never hinged	200.00	
		P# single, Electrolytic, (Pl. 6023)	*650.00*	

	Never hinged	*1,100.*	
	Double transfer	9.00	—
a.	Booklet pane of 6, *Feb. 8, 1912*	65.00	*90.00*
	Never hinged	110.00	
b.	Double impression	—	
c.	2c **lake,** type I	*2,000.*	*2,750.*
	Never hinged	*4,500.*	

Earliest documented uses: Feb. 15, 1912 (No. 406); May 2, 1912 (No. 406a single).

407 A140 7c	**black,** *Apr. 1914*	80.00	14.00
	grayish black	80.00	14.00
	intense black	80.00	14.00
	Never hinged	180.00	
	On cover		75.00
	Block of 4	350.00	100.00
	P# block of 6	1,200.	
	Never hinged	2,000.	

Earliest documented use: May 1, 1914.

Earliest documented use dates for imperforates are for the imperforate sheet stamps, not for imperforate stamps with vending and affixing machine perforations or for flat plate imperforate coil stamps. EDU dates for VAMP and flat plate imperf coil stamps are shown in their respective sections later in the catalogue.

Plate Blocks

Scott values for plate blocks printed from flat plates are for very fine side and bottom positions. Top position plate blocks with full wide selvage sell for more.

1912 ***Imperf.***

408 A140 1c	**green,** *Mar. 1912*	1.00	1.00
	yellowish green	1.00	1.00
	dark green	1.00	1.00
	Never hinged	2.00	
	On cover		1.75
	Pair	2.10	2.10
	Never hinged	4.20	
	Block of 4	4.20	4.20
	Corner margin block of 4	4.30	4.30
	Margin block of 4, arrow	4.40	4.40
	Center line block	10.00	10.00
	Never hinged	17.50	
	P# block of 6, Impt. & "A," T, B or L	45.00	—
	Never hinged	75.00	
	P# block of 6, Impt. & "A," at right	*550.00*	—
	Never hinged	*850.00*	
	P# block of 6, "A"	26.00	—
	Never hinged	45.00	
	P# block of 6	18.00	—
	Never hinged	29.00	
	Double transfer	2.40	2.40
	Cracked plate	—	—

Earliest documented use: April 26, 1912.

409 A140 2c	**carmine,** type I, *Feb. 1912*	1.20	1.20
	deep carmine	1.20	1.20
	scarlet	1.20	1.20
	Never hinged	2.40	
	On cover		2.00
	Pair	2.50	2.50
	Never hinged	5.00	
	Block of 4	5.00	5.00
	Corner margin block of 4	5.25	
	Margin block of 4, arrow	5.50	5.50
	Center line block	11.00	11.00
	Never hinged	19.00	
	P# block of 6, Impt. & "A"	47.50	—
	Never hinged	80.00	
	P# block of 6, "A"	45.00	—
	Never hinged	75.00	
	P# block of 6	35.00	—
	Never hinged	57.50	
	Cracked plate (Plates 7580, 7582)	14.00	—

Earliest documented use: Apr. 15, 1912.

In late 1914, the Post Office at Kansas City, Missouri, had on hand a stock of imperforate sheets of 400 of stamps Nos. 408 and 409, formerly sold for use in vending machines, but not then in demand. In order to make them salable, they were rouletted with ordinary tracing wheels and were sold over the counter with official approval of the Post Office Department given January 5, 1915.

These stamps were sold until the supply was exhausted. Except for one full sheet of 400 of each value, all were cut into panes of 100 before being rouletted and sold. They are known as "Kansas City Roulettes". Value, authenticated blocks of 4, 1c *$100,* 2c *$200.*

Earliest documented uses of "Kansas City Roulettes": Oct. 22, 1914 (No. 408); Nov. 25, 1914 (No. 409).

COIL STAMPS

1912 ***Perf. 8½ Horizontally***

410 A140 1c	**green,** *Mar. 1912*	6.00	*12.50*
	dark green	6.00	*12.50*
	Never hinged	13.00	
	On cover		17.50
	Pair	15.00	*42.50*
	Never hinged	32.50	
	Guide line pair	30.00	*90.00*
	Never hinged	65.00	
	Double transfer	—	—

Earliest documented use: Apr. 17, 1912.

411 A140 2c	**carmine,** type I, *Mar. 1912*	10.00	*15.00*
	deep carmine	10.00	*15.00*
	Never hinged	22.50	
	On cover		20.00
	Pair	25.00	*45.00*
	Never hinged	55.00	
	Guide line pair	55.00	*90.00*
	Never hinged	125.00	
	Double transfer	12.50	—

Earliest documented use: June 12, 1912.

Perf. 8½ Vertically

412 A140 1c	**green,** *Mar. 18, 1912*	25.00	25.00
	deep green	25.00	25.00
	Never hinged	55.00	
	On cover		35.00
	Pair	60.00	75.00
	Never hinged	130.00	
	Guide line pair	120.00	175.00
	Never hinged	260.00	

Earliest documented use: May 21, 1912.

413 A140 2c	**carmine,** type I, *Mar. 1912*	55.00	25.00
	dark carmine	55.00	25.00
	Never hinged	120.00	
	On cover		32.50
	Pair	115.00	75.00
	Never hinged	250.00	
	Guide line pair	300.00	175.00
	Never hinged	625.00	
	Double transfer	52.50	—

Earliest documented use: April 16, 1912.

Beware of plentiful fakes in the marketplace of Nos. 410-413, made by fraudulently perforating imperforate stamps.

Franklin — A148

1912-14 **Wmk. 190** ***Perf. 12***

414 A148 8c	**pale olive green,** *Feb. 1912*	45.00	2.00
	olive green	45.00	2.00
	Never hinged	110.00	
	On cover		15.00
	Block of 4	200.00	15.00
	P# block of 6, Impt. & "A"	475.00	
	Never hinged	800.00	
415 A148 9c	**salmon red,** *Apr. 1914*	55.00	14.00
	rose red	55.00	14.00
	Never hinged	130.00	
	On cover		50.00
	Block of 4	240.00	125.00
	P# block of 6	650.00	
	Never hinged	1,100.	

Earliest documented use: May 1, 1914.

416 A148 10c	**orange yellow,** *Jan. 1912*	45.00	.80
	yellow	45.00	.80
	Never hinged	110.00	
	On cover		2.75
	Block of 4	200.00	5.25
	P# block of 6, Impt. & "A"	500.00	
	Never hinged	825.00	
	P# block of 6, "A"	550.00	
	Never hinged	900.00	
	Double transfer	—	—
a.	10c **brown yellow**	*1,250.*	
	Never hinged	*2,750.*	

Earliest documented use: Feb. 12, 1912.

417 A148 12c	**claret brown,** *Apr. 1914*	50.00	5.00
	deep claret brown	50.00	5.00
	Never hinged	120.00	
	On cover		25.00
	Block of 4	225.00	37.50
	P# block of 6	625.00	
	Never hinged	1,050.	
	Double transfer	55.00	—
	Triple transfer	72.50	—

Earliest documented use: May 5, 1914.

418 A148 15c	**gray,** *Feb. 1912*	85.00	4.50
	dark gray	85.00	4.50
	Never hinged	200.00	
	On cover		17.50
	Block of 4	350.00	35.00
	P# block of 6, Impt. & "A"	675.00	
	Never hinged	1,400.	
	P# block of 6, "A"	850.00	
	Never hinged	1,550.	
	P# block of 6	1,000.	
	Never hinged	1,700.	
	Double transfer	—	—

Earliest documented use: Apr. 26, 1912.

419 A148 20c	**ultramarine,** *Apr. 1914*	200.00	19.00
	dark ultramarine	200.00	19.00
	Never hinged	450.00	
	On cover		*150.00*
	Block of 4	825.00	135.00
	P# block of 6	2,000.	
	Never hinged	3,500.	

Earliest documented use: May 1, 1914.

420 A148 30c	**orange red,** *Apr. 1914*	125.00	19.00
	dark orange red	125.00	19.00
	Never hinged	280.00	
	On cover		*250.00*
	Block of 4	525.00	140.00
	P# block of 6	1,450.	
	Never hinged	2,400.	

Earliest documented use: May 1, 1914.

421 A148 50c	**violet,** *1914*	450.00	30.00
	bright violet	450.00	30.00
	Never hinged	1,000.	
	On cover		*2,000.*
	Block of 4	1,900.	200.00
	P# block of 6	*10,000.*	
	Never hinged	*16,000.*	

Earliest documented use: May 1, 1914.

No. 421 almost always has an offset of the frame lines on the back under the gum. No. 422 does not have this offset.

1912, Feb. 12 **Wmk. 191**

422 A148 50c	**violet**	260.00	22.50
	Never hinged	600.00	
	On cover		*2,000.*
	Block of 4	1,050.	150.00
	Margin block of 4, arrow, R or L	1,100.	
	P# block of 6, Impt. & "A"	*4,750.*	
	Never hinged	*7,500.*	

Earliest documented use: Oct. 31, 1914.

423 A148 $1	**violet brown**	550.00	75.00
	Never hinged	1,200.	
	On cover		*7,000.*
	Block of 4	2,300.	1,000.
	Margin block of 4, arrow, R or L	2,350.	
	P# block of 6, Impt. & "A"	*13,500.*	
	Never hinged	*20,000.*	
	Double transfer (5782 L 66)	550.00	—

Earliest documented use: July 15, 1915.

During the United States occupation of Vera Cruz, Mexico, from April to November, 1914, letters sent from there show Provisional Postmarks.

For other listings of perforated sheet stamps of design A148, see:

Nos. 431-440 — Single line wmk. Perf. 10
Nos. 460 — Double line wmk. Perf. 10
Nos. 470-478 — Unwmkd. Perf. 10
Nos. 508-518 — Unwmkd. Perf. 11

1914 Compound Perforations

As the Bureau of Engraving and Printing made the changeover to perf 10 from perf 12, in the normal course of their stamp production they perforated limited quantities of 1c, 2c and 5c stamps with the old 12-gauge perforations in one direction and the new 10-gauge perforations in the other direction. These were not production errors. These compound-perforation stamps previously were listed as Nos. 424a, 424b, 425c, 425d and 428a.

All examples of Nos. 423A-423E must be accompanied by certificates of authenticity issued by a recognized expertizing committee. Fakes made from perf 12, perf 10 and imperfs exist.

1914 Wmk. 190 *Perf. 12x10*

423A A140 1c **green** *20,000.* *10,000.*
Never hinged —
Pair — *22,500.*
Block of 4 — *45,000.*
On postcard *15,000.*
On cover, pair *20,000.*

Formerly No. 424a. Seventeen unused and 54 used examples are recorded. Value for unused is for a sound stamp with perfs touching or just cutting the design. Value for used is for a sound stamp in the grade of fine-very fine. Of the used examples, 23 are precanceled Quincy IL (very scarce) or Chicago (usually inverted). The unused block of four, used block of four and pair on cover are each unique (top stamp of pair on cover with small piece missing and valued thus). The block of 4 has perfs slightly cutting at top and is valued thus.

423B A140 2c **rose red,** type I *175,000.* *32,500.*

Formerly No. 425d. One unused (a plate #7082 single) and 30 used examples are recorded. Value for used is for a sound stamp in the grade of fine-very fine. There are no precancels known on this issue.

423C A140 5c **blue** *37,500.*
Pair —

Formerly No. 428a. 24 used examples are recorded. No unused examples are recorded. Three examples are precanceled: Tampa FL (2) and Rahway NJ (1). Value is for a sound stamp in the grade of fine-very fine. The pair is unique (one stamp creased, the other with a small tear).

Earliest documented use: April 14, 1915 (dated cancel on off-cover stamp).

1914 Wmk. 190 *Perf. 10x12*

423D A140 1c **green** *20,000.*

Formerly No. 424b. 40 used examples are recorded. No unused examples are recorded. 36 examples are precanceled: Dayton OH (33), Buffalo NY (2) and Elkhart IN (1). Value is for a sound stamp in the grade of fine-very fine.

423E A140 2c **rose red,** type I —

Formerly No. 425c. Only one used example has been certified (by the Philatelic Foundation). It is well centered, has a machine cancel, and has small thinning and a crease.

Plates of 400 subjects in four panes of 100 each.

Type of plate number and imprint used for the 12 special 1c and 2c plates designed for the production of coil stamps.

1913-15 Wmk. 190 *Perf. 10*

424 A140 1c **green,** *Sept. 5, 1914* 2.50 .20
bright green 2.50 .20
deep green 2.50 .20
yellowish green 2.50 .20
Never hinged 5.25
On cover .25
Block of 4 10.50 1.50
P# block of 6 60.00
Never hinged 90.00
Block of ten with imprint "COIL STAMPS" and number (6581-82, 85, 89) 150.00
Never hinged 250.00
Cracked plate — —
Double transfer 4.75 —
c. Vert. pair, imperf. horiz. *2,800.* *2,500.*
Never hinged *4,250.*
d. Booklet pane of 6 5.25 *7.50*
Never hinged 8.75
e. As "d," imperf. *2,000.*
f. Vert. pair, imperf. between and with straight edge at top *9,000.*

For former Nos. 424a and 424b, see Nos. 423A and 423D.
All known examples of No. 424e are without gum.
The unique example of No. 424f is never hinged, and it is valued thus.

Earliest documented uses: Oct. 21, 1914 (No. 424); Dec. 18, 1913 (No. 424d single).

425 A140 2c **rose red,** type I, *Sept. 5, 1914* 2.30 .20
dark rose red 2.30 .20
carmine rose 2.30 .20
carmine 2.30 .20
dark carmine 2.30 .20
scarlet 2.30 .20
red 2.30 .20
Never hinged 4.75
On cover .25
Block of 4 9.50 1.50
P# block of 6 40.00
Never hinged 75.00
Block of 10 with imprint "COIL STAMPS" and number (6568, 70-72) 160.00
Never hinged 250.00
Cracked plate 9.50 —
Double transfer — —
e. Booklet pane of 6, *Jan. 1914* 17.50 *25.00*
Never hinged 30.00

For former Nos. 425c and 425d, see Nos. 423E and 423B.

The aniline inks used on some printings of Nos. 425, 426 and 435a caused a pink tinge to permeate the paper and appear on the back. These are called "pink backs."

Earliest documented uses: Oct. 27, 1914 (No. 425); Jan. 6, 1914 (No. 425e single).

426 A140 3c **deep violet,** type I, *Sept. 18, 1914* 15.00 1.50
violet 16.00 1.50
bright violet 16.00 1.50
reddish violet 16.00 1.50
Never hinged 35.00
On cover 3.50
Block of 4 62.50 12.50
P# block of 6 250.00
Never hinged 400.00

See "pink backs" note after No. 425.

Earliest documented use: Oct. 11, 1914.

427 A140 4c **brown,** *Sept. 7, 1914* 35.00 1.00
dark brown 35.00 1.00
orange brown 35.00 1.00
yellowish brown 35.00 1.00
Never hinged 80.00
On cover 5.25
Block of 4 145.00 9.00
P# block of 6 475.00
Never hinged 775.00
Double transfer 45.00 —

Earliest documented use: Jan. 2, 1915.

428 A140 5c **blue,** *Sept. 14, 1914* 35.00 1.00
bright blue 35.00 1.00
dark blue 35.00 1.00
indigo blue 35.00 1.00
Never hinged 80.00
On cover 3.00
Block of 4 145.00 8.00
P# block of 6 425.00
Never hinged 650.00

For former No. 428a, see No. 423C.

Earliest documented use: Dec. 2, 1914.

429 A140 6c **red orange,** *Sept. 28, 1914* 50.00 2.00
deep red orange 50.00 2.00
pale red orange 50.00 2.00
Never hinged 115.00
On cover 9.00
Block of 4 (2mm spacing) 215.00 16.00
Block of 4 (3mm spacing) 210.00 15.00
P# block of 6, Impt. & star 425.00
Never hinged 725.00
P# block of 6 525.00
Never hinged 875.00

430 A140 7c **black,** *Sept. 10, 1914* 100.00 5.00
gray black 100.00 5.00
intense black 100.00 5.00
Never hinged 225.00
On cover 37.50
Block of 4 425.00 40.00
P# block of 6 1,000.
Never hinged 1,650.

Earliest documented use: April 14, 1915.

431 A148 8c **pale olive green,** *Sept. 26, 1914* 37.50 3.00
olive green 37.50 3.00
Never hinged 87.50
On cover 8.00
Block of 4 160.00 25.00
P# block of 6, Impt. & "A" 450.00
Never hinged 725.00
P# block of 6, "A" 550.00
Never hinged 900.00
Double transfer — —
a. Double impression —

Earliest documented use: Jan. 20, 1915.

432 A148 9c **salmon red,** *Oct. 6, 1914* 50.00 9.00
dark salmon red 50.00 9.00
Never hinged 115.00
On cover 27.50
Block of 4 210.00 70.00
P# block of 6 725.00
Never hinged 1,150.

Earliest documented use: Oct. 7, 1915 (dated cancel on off-cover block of 4); Feb. 25, 1916 (on cover).

433 A148 10c **orange yellow,** *Sept. 9, 1914* 50.00 1.00
golden yellow 50.00 1.00
Never hinged 115.00
On cover 7.75
Block of 4 210.00 6.50
P# block of 6, Impt. & "A" 650.00
Never hinged 1,100.
P# block of 6, "A" 950.00
Never hinged 1,600.
P# block of 6 825.00
Never hinged 1,400.

Earliest documented use: Nov. 13, 1914.

434 A148 11c **dark green,** *Aug. 11, 1915* 25.00 8.50
bluish green 25.00 8.50
Never hinged 60.00
On cover 25.00
Block of 4 105.00 65.00
P# block of 6 300.00
Never hinged 475.00

435 A148 12c **claret brown,** *Sept. 10, 1914* 27.50 6.00
deep claret brown 27.50 6.00
Never hinged 65.00
On cover 17.50
Block of 4 115.00 45.00
P# block of 6 350.00
Never hinged 525.00
Double transfer 35.00 —
Triple transfer 40.00 —
a. 12c **copper red** 32.50 7.00
Never hinged 75.00
On cover 20.00
Block of 4 125.00 50.00
P# block of 6 350.00
Never hinged 550.00

All so-called vertical pairs, imperf. between, have at least one perf. hole or "blind perfs" between the stamps.
See "pink backs" note after No. 425.

Earliest documented use: Feb. 22, 1915.

437 A148 15c **gray,** *Sept. 16, 1914* 135.00 7.25
dark gray 135.00 7.25
Never hinged 300.00
On cover 52.50
Block of 4 575.00 70.00
P# block of 6, Impt. & "A" 1,050.
Never hinged 2,100.
P# block of 6, "A" 1,225.
Never hinged 2,250.
P# block of 6 1,125.
Never hinged 2,150.

Earliest documented use: Sept. 21, 1915.

438 A148 20c **ultramarine,** *Sept. 19, 1914* 220.00 6.00
dark ultramarine 220.00 6.00
Never hinged 500.00
On cover *150.00*
Block of 4 900.00 45.00
P# block of 6 3,250.
Never hinged *5,500.*

Earliest documented use: Nov. 28, 1914.

439 A148 30c **orange red,** *Sept. 19, 1914* 260.00 17.50
dark orange red 260.00 17.50
Never hinged 600.00
On cover *250.00*
Block of 4 1,050. 135.00
P# block of 6 *4,100.*
Never hinged *6,750.*

Earliest documented use: Feb. 13, 1915.

440 A148 50c **violet,** *Dec. 10, 1915* 575.00 17.50
Never hinged 1,300.
On cover *1,750.*
Block of 4 2,250. 135.00
P# block of 6 *15,000.*
Never hinged —
Nos. 424-440 (16) 1,619. 86.65

COIL STAMPS

1914 *Perf. 10 Horizontally*

441 A140 1c **green,** *Nov. 14, 1914* 1.00 *1.50*
deep green 1.00 *1.50*
Never hinged 2.00
On cover 2.75
Pair 2.75 *7.00*
Never hinged 5.75
Guide line pair 8.00 *27.50*
Never hinged 17.50

442 A140 2c carmine, type I, *July 22, 1914* 10.00 *45.00*
deep carmine 10.00 *45.00*
Never hinged 22.50
On cover 60.00
Pair 25.00 *130.00*
Never hinged 55.00
Guide line pair 60.00 *180.00*
Never hinged 130.00

1914 *Perf. 10 Vertically*

443 A140 1c **green,** *May 29, 1914* 30.00 *45.00*
deep green 30.00 *45.00*
Never hinged 65.00
On cover 60.00
Pair 75.00 *135.00*
Never hinged 160.00
Guide line pair 155.00 *225.00*
Never hinged 325.00

Earliest documented use: June. 19, 1914.

444 A140 2c **carmine,** type I, *Apr. 25, 1914* 50.00 40.00
deep carmine 50.00 40.00
red 50.00 40.00
Never hinged 125.00
On cover 52.50
Pair 130.00 125.00
Never hinged 275.00
Guide line pair 325.00 190.00
Never hinged 700.00
a. 2c **lake** *1,250.*

Earliest documented use: May 19, 1914.

445 A140 3c **violet,** type I, *Dec. 18, 1914* 250.00 250.00
deep violet 250.00 250.00
Never hinged 575.00
On cover *325.00*
Pair 575.00 *750.00*

	Never hinged	1,250.	
	Guide line pair	1,300.	*3,000.*
	Never hinged	2,800.	

Earliest documented use: August 13, 1915.

446 A140 4c	**brown,** *Oct. 2, 1914*	140.00	*150.00*
	Never hinged	325.00	
	On cover		200.00
	Pair	325.00	*425.00*
	Never hinged	700.00	
	Guide line pair	750.00	*1,150.*
	Never hinged	1,650.	

Earliest documented use: Aug. 4, 1915.

447 A140 5c	**blue,** *July 30, 1914*	50.00	*115.00*
	Never hinged	110.00	
	On cover		125.00
	Pair	115.00	*375.00*
	Never hinged	240.00	
	Guide line pair	260.00	*950.00*
	Never hinged	550.00	

Earliest documented use: May 9, 1916.

Beware of plentiful fakes in the marketplace of Nos. 441-447, made by fraudulently perforating imperforate stamps or by fraudulently trimming perforations off fully perforated stamps.

ROTARY PRESS STAMPS

The Rotary Press Stamps are printed from plates that are curved to fit around a cylinder. This curvature produces stamps that are slightly larger, either horizontally or vertically, than those printed from flat plates. Designs of stamps from flat plates measure about 18½-19mm wide by 22mm high.

When the impressions are placed sidewise on the curved plates the designs are 19½-20mm wide; when they are placed vertically the designs are 22½ to 23mm high. A line of color (not a guide line) shows where the curved plates meet or join on the press.

Rotary Press Coil Stamps were printed from plates of 170 subjects for stamps coiled sidewise, and from plates of 150 subjects for stamps coiled endwise.

Double paper varieties of Rotary Press stamps are not listed in this catalogue. Collectors are referred to the note on "Rotary Press Double Paper" in the "Information for Collectors" in the front of the catalogue.

ROTARY PRESS COIL STAMPS

Stamp designs: 18½-19x22½mm

1915 ***Perf. 10 Horizontally***

448 A140 1c	**green,** *Dec., 1915*	7.50	*17.50*
	light green	7.50	*17.50*
	Never hinged	16.00	
	On cover		22.50
	Pair	17.50	*50.00*
	Never hinged	40.00	
	Joint line pair	60.00	*115.00*
	Never hinged	125.00	

Earliest documented use: Dec. 11, 1915.

TYPE II

TWO CENTS.
Type II. Shading lines in ribbons as on type I.
The toga button, rope and rope shading lines are heavy.
The shading lines of the face at the lock of hair end in a strong vertical curved line.
Used on rotary press printings only.

TYPE III

Type III. Two lines of shading in the curves of the ribbons.
Other characteristics similar to type II.
Used on rotary press printings only.

449 A140 2c	**red,** type I, *1915*	3,000.	650.00
	Never hinged	6,500.	
	carmine rose, type I	3,250.	
	On cover, type I		1,350.
	Pair, type I	7,000.	*5,250.*
	Never hinged	*14,500.*	
	Joint line pair, type I	*16,000.*	*25,000.*
	Never hinged	*32,500.*	

Earliest documented uses: Oct. 29, 1915 (on cover front or dated cancel on off-cover stamp); Nov. 4, 1915 (on cover).

450 A140 2c	**carmine,** type III, *1915*	12.50	*22.50*
	carmine rose, type III	12.50	*22.50*
	red, type III	12.50	*22.50*
	Never hinged	27.50	
	On cover, type III		32.50
	Pair, type III	30.00	*67.50*
	Never hinged	65.00	
	Joint line pair, type III	230.00	*190.00*
	Never hinged	550.00	

Earliest documented use: Dec. 21, 1915.

1914-16 ***Perf. 10 Vertically***

Stamp designs: 19½-20x22mm

452 A140 1c	**green,** *Nov. 11, 1914*	10.00	*17.50*
	Never hinged	21.00	
	On cover		22.50
	Pair	25.00	*55.00*
	Never hinged	55.00	
	Joint line pair	75.00	*100.00*
	Never hinged	160.00	

Earliest documented use: Nov. 25, 1914.

453 A140 2c	**carmine rose,** type I, *July 3, 1914*	150.00	17.50
	Never hinged	325.00	
	On cover, type I		22.50
	Pair, type I	325.00	55.00
	Never hinged	675.00	
	Joint line pair, type I	725.00	500.00
	Never hinged	1,550.	
	Cracked plate, type I	—	—

Earliest documented use: Sept. 26, 1914.

454 A140 2c	**red,** type II, *June, 1915*	75.00	22.50
	carmine, type II	75.00	22.50
	Never hinged	170.00	
	On cover, type II		40.00
	Pair, type II	175.00	70.00
	Never hinged	375.00	
	Joint line pair, type II	425.00	400.00
	Never hinged	900.00	

Earliest documented use: July 7, 1915.

455 A140 2c **carmine,** type III, *Dec. 1915* 8.50 3.50
carmine rose, type III 8.50 3.50
Never hinged 19.00
On cover, type III 5.00
Pair, type III 21.00 *27.50*
Never hinged 45.00
Joint line pair, type III 50.00 *100.00*
Never hinged 110.00

Earliest documented use: Dec. 15, 1915.

Fraudulently altered examples of Type III (Nos. 455, 488, 492 and 540) have had one line of shading scraped off to make them resemble Type II (Nos. 454, 487, 491 and 539).

456 A140 3c **violet,** type I, *Feb. 2, 1916* 250.00 170.00
deep violet 250.00 170.00
red violet 250.00 170.00
Never hinged 525.00
On cover 250.00
Pair 600.00 650.00
Never hinged 1,250.
Joint line pair 1,250. *1,800.*
Never hinged 2,600.

Earliest documented use: Apr. 13, 1916.

457 A140 4c **brown,** *1915* 25.00 30.00
light brown 25.00 30.00
Never hinged 55.00
On cover 50.00
Pair 60.00 95.00
Never hinged 130.00
Joint line pair 150.00 *230.00*
Never hinged 325.00
Cracked plate 35.00 —

Earliest documented use: Nov. 5, 1915.

458 A140 5c **blue,** *Mar. 9, 1916* 30.00 30.00
Never hinged 65.00
On cover 50.00
Pair 72.50 95.00
Never hinged 160.00
Joint line pair 175.00 230.00
Never hinged 375.00
Double transfer — —

Earliest documented use: Apr. 6, 1916.

Horizontal Coil

1914, June 30 ***Imperf.***

459 A140 2c **carmine,** type I 200. *1,300.*
Never hinged 320.
Pair 410. *3,500.*
Never hinged 650.
Joint line pair, with crease 650.
Never hinged 1,100.
Joint line pair, without crease 1,000. *21,000.*
Never hinged 1,900.

Most line pairs of No. 459 are creased. The value for joint line pair with crease is for a pair creased vertically between the stamps, but not touching the design.

When the value for a used stamp is higher than the unused value, the stamp must have a contemporaneous cancel. Valuable stamps of this type should be accompanied by certificates of authenticity issued by recognized expertizing committees. The used value for No. 459 is for an example with such a certificate.

Beware of examples of No. 453 with perforations fraudulently trimmed to resemble single examples of No. 459.

Earliest documented use: Dec. 1914 (dated cancel on a used joint line pair, off cover).

FLAT PLATE PRINTINGS

1915 **Wmk. 191** ***Perf. 10***

460 A148 $1 **violet black,** *Feb. 8* 850. 150.
Never hinged 1,900.
On cover *12,000.*
Block of 4 3,750. 750.
Margin block of 4, arrow, R or L 3,850.
P# block of 6, Impt. & "A" *13,500.*
Never hinged *20,000.*
Double transfer (5782 L. 66) 900. 175.

Earliest documented uses: May 25, 1916 (dated cancel on stamp on mailing tag); June 2, 1916 (unique usage on cover is from Shanghai, China).

Wmk. 190 ***Perf. 11***

461 A140 2c **pale car. red,** type I, *June 17* 150. *360.*
Never hinged 350.
On cover *1,200.*
Block of 4 625. *3,000.*
P# block of 6 *1,500.*
Never hinged *2,600.*

Beware of fraudulently perforated examples of No. 409 being offered as No. 461.

See note on used stamps following No. 459.

Earliest documented use: June 24, 1915.

VALUES FOR VERY FINE STAMPS

Please note: Stamps are valued in the grade of Very Fine unless otherwise indicated.

FLAT PLATE PRINTINGS

Plates of 400 subjects in four panes of 100 each for all values 1c to 50c inclusive.

Plates of 200 subjects in two panes of 100 each for $1, $2 and $5 denominations.

The Act of Oct. 3, 1917, effective Nov. 2, 1917, created a 3 cent rate. Local rate, 2 cents.

1916-17 **Unwmk.** ***Perf. 10***

462 A140 1c **green,** *Sept. 27, 1916* 7.00 .35
light green 7.00 .35
dark green 7.00 .35
bluish green 7.00 .35
Never hinged 16.00
On cover .50
Block of 4 30.00 3.25
P# block of 6 160.00
Never hinged 275.00
Experimental bureau precancel, New Orleans 10.00
Experimental bureau precancel, Springfield, Mass. 10.00
Experimental bureau precancel, Augusta, Me. 25.00
a. Booklet pane of 6, *Oct. 15, 1916* 9.50 *12.50*
Never hinged 16.00

Earliest documented use: Apr. 5, 1917 (No. 462a single).

463 A140 2c **carmine,** type I, *Sept. 1916* 4.50 .40
dark carmine 4.50 .40
rose red 4.50 .40
Never hinged 10.00
On cover .45
Block of 4 20.00 3.50
P# block of 6 150.00
Never hinged 250.00
Double transfer 6.50 —
Experimental bureau precancel, New Orleans *500.00*
Experimental bureau precancel, Springfield, Mass. 22.50
a. Booklet pane of 6, *Oct. 8, 1916* 110.00 *110.00*
Never hinged 180.00

See No. 467 for P# block of 6 from plate 7942.

Earliest documented uses: Sept. 12, 1916 (No. 463).

464 A140 3c **violet,** type I, *Nov. 11, 1916* 75.00 19.00
deep violet 75.00 19.00
Never hinged 170.00
On cover 42.50
Block of 4 325.00 150.00
P# block of 6 1,350.
Never hinged 2,250.
Double transfer in "CENTS" *90.00* —
Experimental bureau precancel, New Orleans *1,000.*
Experimental bureau precancel, Springfield, Mass. 200.00

Beware of fraudulently perforated examples of No. 483 being offered as No. 464.

Earliest documented use: Mar. 9, 1917.

465 A140 4c **orange brown,** *Oct. 7, 1916* 45.00 2.50
deep brown 45.00 2.50
brown 45.00 2.50
Never hinged 100.00
On cover 11.00
Block of 4 190.00 25.00
P# block of 6 650.00
Never hinged 1,100.
Double transfer — —
Experimental bureau precancel, Springfield, Mass. 175.00

466 A140 5c **blue,** *Oct. 17, 1916* 75.00 2.50
dark blue 75.00 2.50
Never hinged 170.00
On cover 13.00
Block of 4 310.00 22.50
P# block of 6 950.00
Never hinged 1,600.
Experimental bureau precancel, Springfield, Mass. 175.00

Earliest documented use: Dec. 7, 1916.

467 A140 5c **carmine** (error in plate of 2c) 525.00 *850.00*
Never hinged 1,050.
On cover *5,000.*
Block of 9, #467 in middle 1,150. *1,600.*
Never hinged 1,900.
Block of 12, two middle stamps #467 2,150. *3,000.*
Never hinged 3,400.
P# block of 6 2c stamps (#463), P#7942 140.00
Never hinged 250.00

No. 467 is an error caused by using a 5c transfer roll in re-entering three subjects: 7942 UL 74, 7942 UL 84, 7942 LR 18; the balance of the subjects on the plate being normal 2c entries. No. 467 imperf. is listed as No. 485. The error perf 11 on unwatermarked paper is No. 505.

The first value given for the error in blocks of 9 and 12 is for blocks with the error stamp(s) never hinged. The second value given is for blocks in which all stamps are never hinged. See note on used stamps following No. 459.

Earliest documented use: May 22, 1917.

468 A140 6c **red orange,** *Oct. 10, 1916* 95.00 9.00
Never hinged 210.00
On cover 37.50
Block of 4 400.00 70.00
P# block of 6 1,350.
Never hinged 2,500.
Double transfer — —
Experimental bureau precancel, New Orleans *2,500.*
Experimental bureau precancel, Springfield, Mass. 175.00

Earliest documented use: April 19, 1917.

469 A140 7c **black,** *Oct. 10, 1916* 130.00 15.00
gray black 130.00 15.00
Never hinged 290.00
On cover 45.00
Block of 4 550.00 125.00
P# block of 6 1,350.
Never hinged 2,500.
Experimental bureau precancel, Springfield, Mass. 175.00

Earliest documented use: Feb. 19, 1917.

470 A148 8c **olive green,** *Nov. 13, 1916* 60.00 8.00
dark olive green 60.00 8.00
Never hinged 135.00
On cover 27.50
Block of 4 250.00 65.00
P# block of 6, Impt. & "A" 550.00
Never hinged 900.00
P# block of 6, "A" 600.00
Never hinged 1,050.
Experimental bureau precancel, Springfield, Mass. 165.00

Earliest documented use: Jan. 26, 1917 (dated cancel on off-cover stamp); Feb. 13, 1917 (on cover).

471 A148 9c **salmon red,** *Nov. 16, 1916* 60.00 18.50
Never hinged 135.00
On cover 42.50
Block of 4 250.00 135.00
P# block of 6 750.00
Never hinged 1,250.
Experimental bureau precancel, Springfield, Mass. 150.00

Earliest documented use: Dec. 27, 1917.

472 A148 10c **orange yellow,** *Oct. 17, 1916* 110.00 2.50
Never hinged 250.00
On cover 8.50
Block of 4 460.00 16.50
P# block of 6 1,350.
Never hinged 2,250.
Experimental bureau precancel, Springfield, Mass. 160.00

Earliest documented use: Oct. 24, 1916.

473 A148 11c **dark green,** *Nov. 16, 1916* 45.00 18.50
Never hinged 100.00
On cover 47.50
Block of 4 175.00 140.00
P# block of 6 360.00
Never hinged 625.00
Experimental bureau precancel, Springfield, Mass. *575.00*

Earliest documented use: Apr. 13, 1917.

474 A148 12c **claret brown,** *Oct. 1916* 60.00 7.50
Never hinged 135.00
On cover 22.50
Block of 4 230.00 55.00
P# block of 6 625.00
Never hinged 1,050.
Double transfer 65.00 8.50
Triple transfer 77.50 11.00
Experimental bureau precancel, Springfield, Mass. 200.00

Earliest documented uses: Oct. 6, 1916 (dated cancel on off-cover pair); Oct. 13, 1916 (on cover).

475 A148 15c **gray,** *Nov. 16, 1916* 200.00 16.00
dark gray 200.00 16.00
Never hinged 440.00
On cover 87.50
Block of 4 850.00 125.00
P# block of 6 3,000.
Never hinged 5,250.
P# block of 6, Impt. & "A" —
Experimental bureau precancel, Springfield, Mass. 150.00

Earliest documented use: Mar. 2, 1917.

476 A148 20c **light ultramarine,** *Dec. 5, 1916* 250.00 17.50
ultramarine 250.00 17.50
Never hinged 575.00
On cover *725.00*
Block of 4 1,050. 135.00
P# block of 6 3,600.
Never hinged *6,000.*
Experimental bureau precancel, Springfield, Mass. 125.00

476A A148 30c **orange red** *3,750.*
Never hinged *7,500.*
Block of 4 *17,000.*
Never hinged *37,500.*
P# block of 6, never hinged *67,500.*

No. 476A is valued in the grade of fine.

477 A148 50c **light violet,** *Mar. 2, 1917* 1,100. 80.00
Never hinged 2,400.
On cover *2,250.*
Block of 4 4,750. 575.00
P# block of 6 *57,500.*
Never hinged —

Earliest documented use: Aug. 31, 1917.

478 A148 $1 **violet black,** *Dec. 22, 1916* 800.00 25.00
Never hinged 1,800.
On cover *3,000.*
Block of 4 3,500. 175.00
Margin block of 4, arrow, R or L 3,650.
P# block of 6, Impt. & "A" *13,500.*
Never hinged *21,000.*
Double transfer (5782 L 66) 825.00 32.50

Earliest documented use: May 24, 1917 (on large part of parcel label).

TYPES OF 1902-03 ISSUE

1917, Mar. 22 Unwmk. *Perf. 10*

479 A127 $2 **dark blue**	250.00	42.50
Never hinged	550.00	
On cover (other than first flight or Zeppelin)		*1,250.*
On first flight cover		*350.00*
On Zeppelin flight cover		*750.00*
Block of 4	1,100.	325.00
Margin block of 4, arrow, R or L	1,250.	
P# block of 6	4,250.	
Never hinged	*6,750.*	
Double transfer	—	

Earliest documented use (on large piece of reg'd parcel wrapper): Apr. 6, 1917.

480 A128 $5 **light green**	200.00	40.00
Never hinged	430.00	
On cover		*1,250.*
Block of 4	875.00	300.00
Margin block of 4, arrow, R or L	975.00	
P# block of 6	3,300.	—
Never hinged	*5,500.*	

Earliest documented use: Apr. 6, 1917 (on large piece of reg'd parcel wrapper).

Earliest documented use dates for imperforates are for the imperforate sheet stamps, not for imperforate stamps with vending and affixing machine perforations or for flat plate imperforate coil stamps. EDU dates for VAMP and flat plate imperf coil stamps are shown in their respective sections later in the catalogue.

1916-17 *Imperf.*

481 A140 1c **green,** *Nov. 1916*	.95	.95
bluish green	.95	.95
deep green	.95	.95
Never hinged	1.90	
On cover		1.50
Pair	2.00	2.00
Never hinged	4.00	
Block of 4	4.00	4.00
Corner margin block of 4	4.25	4.25
Margin block of 4, arrow	4.40	4.40
Center line block	8.50	8.50
Never hinged	14.00	
P# block of 6	30.00	—
Never hinged	45.00	
Margin block of 6, Electrolytic (Pl. 13376)	450.00	
Never hinged	800.00	
Margin block of 6, Electrolytic (Pl. 13377)	750.00	
Never hinged	1,250.	
Double transfer	2.50	2.50

Earliest documented use: Nov. 17, 1916.

During September, 1921, the Bureau of Engraving and Printing issued a 1c stamp printed from experimental electrolytic plates made in accordance with patent granted to George U. Rose. Tests at that time did not prove satisfactory and the method was discontinued. Four plates were made, viz., 13376, 13377, 13389 and 13390 from which stamps were issued. They are difficult to distinguish from the normal varieties. (See No. 498).

TYPE Ia

TWO CENTS
Type Ia. The design characteristics are similar to type I except that all of the lines of the design are stronger.
The toga button, toga rope and rope and rope shading lines are heavy.
The latter characteristics are those of type II, which, however, occur only on impressions from rotary plates.
Used only on flat plates 10208 and 10209.

482 A140 2c **carmine,** type I, *Dec. 8, 1916*	1.30	1.30
deep carmine	1.30	1.30
carmine rose	1.30	1.30
deep rose	1.30	1.30
Never hinged	2.60	
On cover		2.50
Pair	2.75	2.75
Never hinged	5.50	
Block of 4	5.50	6.50
Corner margin block of 4	5.75	*6.75*
Margin block of 4, arrow	6.00	*7.00*
Center line block	8.50	*10.00*
Never hinged	14.00	
P# block of 6	30.00	—
Never hinged	45.00	
Cracked plate	—	—

Earliest documented use: Dec. 16, 1916.

See No. 485 for P# block of 6 from plate 7942.

482A A140 2c **deep rose,** type Ia		*65,000.*
On cover		*70,000.*
Pair		*140,000.*

Earliest documented use: Feb. 17, 1920.

The imperforate, type Ia, was issued but all known examples were privately perforated with large oblong perforations at the sides (Schermack type III).
The No. 482A pair is unique.

TYPE II

THREE CENTS
Type II. The top line of the toga rope is strong and the rope shading lines are heavy and complete.
The line between the lips is heavy.
Used on both flat plate and rotary press printings.

483 A140 3c **violet,** type I, *Oct. 13, 1917*	10.00	10.00
light violet	10.00	10.00
Never hinged	22.00	
On cover		22.50
Pair	22.00	22.50
Never hinged	47.50	
Block of 4	45.00	45.00
Corner margin block of 4	47.50	47.50
Margin block of 4, arrow	50.00	50.00
Center line block	75.00	75.00
Never hinged	135.00	
P# block of 6	115.00	—
Never hinged	190.00	
Double transfer	17.50	—
Triple transfer		—

Earliest documented use: Nov. 8, 1917.

484 A140 3c **violet,** type II	8.00	8.00
deep violet	8.00	8.00
Never hinged	18.00	
On cover		13.00
Pair	17.00	17.00
Never hinged	36.00	
Block of 4	35.00	35.00
Corner margin block of 4	37.50	37.50
Margin block of 4, arrow	40.00	40.00
Center line block	67.50	67.50
Never hinged	120.00	
P# block of 6	87.50	—
Never hinged	150.00	
Double transfer	12.50	—

Earliest documented use: Apr. 30, 1918.

485 A140 5c **carmine** (error), *Mar. 1917*	*12,000.*	
Never hinged	*20,000.*	
Block of 9, #485 in middle	*22,500.*	
Never hinged	*32,500.*	
Block of 12, two middle stamps #485	*42,500.*	
Never hinged	*52,500.*	
P# block of six 2c stamps (#482), P#7942	130.00	
Never hinged	220.00	

No. 485 is usually seen either as the center stamp in a block of 9 with 8 No. 482 (the first value given being with No. 485 never hinged) or as two center stamps in a block of 12 (the first value given being with both examples of No. 485 never hinged). A second value is given for each block with all stamps in the block never hinged.
See note under No. 467.

ROTARY PRESS COIL STAMPS
(See note over No. 448)

1916-19 *Perf. 10 Horizontally*
Stamp designs: 18½-19x22½mm

486 A140 1c **green,** *Jan. 1918*	.85	.85
yellowish green	.85	.85
Never hinged	1.75	
On cover		1.15
Pair	2.00	*2.50*
Never hinged	4.25	
Joint line pair	4.50	*12.50*
Never hinged	9.50	
Cracked plate	—	—
Double transfer	2.25	—

Earliest documented use: June 30, 1918.

487 A140 2c **carmine,** type II, *Nov. 15, 1916*	12.50	14.00
Never hinged	26.00	
On cover		19.00
Pair	30.00	37.50
Never hinged	65.00	
Joint line pair	110.00	125.00
Never hinged	250.00	
Cracked plate		—

Earliest documented use: Sept. 21, 1917.

(See note after No. 455)

488 A140 2c **carmine,** type III, *1916*	3.00	*5.00*
carmine rose	3.00	*5.00*
Never hinged	6.50	
On cover		7.00
Pair	8.00	*17.50*
Never hinged	17.50	
Joint line pair	40.00	*95.00*
Never hinged	90.00	
Cracked plate	12.50	10.00

Earliest documented use: Apr. 25, 1917.

489 A140 3c **violet,** type I, *Oct. 10, 1917*	4.50	2.25
dull violet	4.50	2.25
bluish violet	4.50	2.25
Never hinged	10.00	
On cover		3.50
Pair	10.50	9.00
Never hinged	22.50	
Joint line pair	32.50	27.50
Never hinged	70.00	

Earliest documented use: Dec. 29, 1917.

Rosette plate crack on head

1916-22 *Perf. 10 Vertically*
Stamp designs: 19½-20x22mm

490 A140 1c **green,** *Nov. 17, 1916*	.50	*.60*
yellowish green	.50	*.60*
Never hinged	1.05	
On cover		.80
Pair	1.25	*2.25*
Never hinged	2.60	
Joint line pair	3.25	*9.00*
Never hinged	7.00	
Double transfer	—	—
Cracked plate (horizontal)	7.50	—
Cracked plate (vertical) retouched	9.00	—
Rosette plate crack on head	*60.00*	—

Earliest documented use: Jan. 3, 1917 (dated cancel on off-cover pair); March 6, 1917 (on cover).

491 A140 2c **carmine,** type II, *Nov. 17, 1916*	2,600.	750.00
Never hinged	5,500.	
On cover, type II		1,100.
Pair, type II	6,000.	3,750.
Never hinged	*13,000.*	
Joint line pair, type II	*14,000.*	*15,000.*
Never hinged	*27,500.*	

Earliest documented use: Jan. 2, 1917.
See note after No. 455.

492 A140 2c **carmine,** type III	9.00	1.00
carmine rose, type III	9.00	1.00
Never hinged	19.00	
On cover, type III		1.40
Pair, type III	21.50	5.00
Never hinged	45.00	
Joint line pair, type III	55.00	25.00
Never hinged	115.00	
Double transfer, type III	—	—
Cracked plate	—	—

Earliest documented use: April 1, 1917.

493 A140 3c **violet,** type I, *July 23, 1917*	14.00	4.50
reddish violet, type I	14.00	4.50
Never hinged	30.00	
On cover, type I		8.00
Pair, type I	35.00	12.50
Never hinged	75.00	
Joint line pair, type I	110.00	75.00
Never hinged	230.00	

Earliest documented use: Nov. 2, 1917.

494 A140 3c **violet,** type II, *Feb. 4, 1918*	10.00	2.50
dull violet, type II	10.00	2.50
gray violet, type II	10.00	2.50
Never hinged	21.50	
On cover, type II		2.40
Pair, type II	24.00	9.00
Never hinged	50.00	
Joint line pair, type II	75.00	17.50
Never hinged	160.00	

Earliest documented use: Apr. 16, 1918.

495 A140 4c **orange brown,** *Apr. 15, 1917*	10.00	7.00
Never hinged	21.50	
On cover		10.00
Pair	24.00	20.00
Never hinged	50.00	

Joint line pair	75.00	35.00
Never hinged	160.00	
Cracked plate	25.00	—

Earliest documented use: June 20, 1917.

496 A140 5c **blue,** *Jan. 15, 1919*	3.25	2.50
Never hinged	7.00	
On cover		3.00
Pair	8.00	10.00
Never hinged	17.50	
Joint line pair	30.00	17.50
Never hinged	65.00	

Earliest documented use: April 15, 1919.

497 A148 10c **orange yellow,** *Jan. 31, 1922*	19.00	17.50
Never hinged	40.00	
On cover		22.50
Pair	45.00	*57.50*
Never hinged	95.00	
Joint line pair	130.00	*180.00*
Never hinged	280.00	

Earliest documented use: Jan. 31, 1922 (FDC).

Blind Perfs

Listings of imperforate-between varieties are for examples which show no trace of "blind perfs," traces of impressions from the perforating pins which do not cut into the paper.

Some unused stamps have had the gum removed to eliminate the impressions from the perforating pins. These stamps do not qualify as the listed varieties.

FLAT PLATE PRINTINGS

Plates of 400 subjects in four panes of 100.

TYPES OF 1913-15 ISSUE

1917-19 Unwmk. *Perf. 11*

498 A140 1c **green,** *Mar. 1917*	.35	.25
light green	.35	.25
dark green	.35	.25
yellowish green	.35	.25
Never hinged	.75	
On cover		.30
Block of 4	1.40	1.50
P# block of 6	22.50	
Never hinged	35.00	
Margin block of 6, Electrolytic (Pl, 13376-7, 13389-90) *See note after No. 481*	*1,000.*	
Never hinged	*1,750.*	
Cracked plate (10656 UL and 10645 LR)	7.50	—
Double transfer	5.50	2.00
a. Vertical pair, imperf. horiz.	900.00	
Never hinged	*1,750.*	
b. Horizontal pair, imperf. between	575.00	
Never hinged	*1,250.*	
c. Vertical pair, imperf. between	*700.00*	—
d. Double impression	250.00	*4,000.*
e. Booklet pane of 6, March 1917	2.50	*2.00*
Never hinged	4.25	
f. Booklet pane of 30, *Aug. 1917*	*1,150.*	
Never hinged	*1,800.*	
g. Perf. 10 at top or bottom	*15,000.*	*45,000.*
Never hinged	*22,500.*	

Earliest documented use: March 30, 1917 (No. 498e booklet pair); Aug. 8, 1917 (No. 498f single).

No. 498g also known as a transitional stamp gauging 10 at left bottom and 11 at right bottom (bottom center stamp in a plate block of 6).

499 A140 2c **rose,** type I, *Mar. 1917*	.35	.25
dark rose, type I	.35	.25
carmine rose, type I	.35	.25
deep rose, type I	.35	.25
Never hinged	.75	
On cover, type I		.30
Block of 4, type I	1.40	1.50
P# block of 6, type I	22.50	
Never hinged	35.00	
Cracked plate, type I	—	—
Recut in hair, type I	*1,500.*	*2,300.*
Never hinged	*3,000.*	
Double transfer, type I	6.00	—
a. Vertical pair, imperf. horiz., type I	600.00	
Never hinged	1,200.	
b. Horiz. pair, imperf. vert., type I	*375.00*	*225.00*
Never hinged	*750.00*	
c. Vert. pair, imperf. btwn., type I	*1,000.*	*300.00*
e. Booklet pane of 6, type I, *Mar. 31, 1917*	4.00	*2.50*
Never hinged	6.75	
f. Booklet pane of 30, type I, *Aug. 1917*	*28,000.*	—
Never hinged	*38,000.*	
g. Double impression, type I	200.00	—
Never hinged	*400.00*	
On cover		*750.00*
As "g," second impression displaced 15mm		—
h. 2c **lake,** type I	500.00	350.00
Never hinged	*1,000.*	
On cover		—

No. 499b is valued in the grade of fine.

See No. 505 for P# block of 6 from plate 7942.

No. 499h occurs in two different lake shades. The true lake is similar to the lake on other lake shades noted elsewhere in this catalogue. A somewhat more common lake shade is known as "Boston lake," and it is a very distinctive and duller lake shade. Certificates of authenticity recommended for these and all listed lake shades.

Earliest documented uses: Mar. 27, 1917 (No. 499); July 19, 1917 (No. 499e single); Aug. 7, 1917 (No. 499f single).

500 A140 2c **deep rose,** type Ia	275.00	240.00
Never hinged	600.00	
On cover, type Ia		*650.00*
Block of 4, type Ia	1,200.	*1,500.*
P# block of 6, type Ia	2,150.	
Never hinged	3,750.	—
P# block of 6, two stamps type I (P# 10208 LL)	*15,000.*	
Never hinged	*22,500.*	
Pair, types I and Ia (10208 LL 95 or 96)	*1,275.*	

Earliest documented use: Dec. 15, 1919.

No. 500 exists with imperforate top sheet margin. Examples have been altered by trimming perforations. Some also have faked Schermack perfs.

501 A140 3c **light violet,** type I, *Mar. 1917*	11.00	.40
violet, type I	11.00	.40
dark violet, type I	11.00	.40
reddish violet, type I	11.00	.40
Never hinged	25.00	
On cover, type I		.50
Block of 4, type I	45.00	4.00
P# block of 6, type I	140.00	
Never hinged	240.00	
Double transfer, type I	12.00	
b. Bklt. pane of 6, type I, *Oct. 17, 1917*	75.00	*60.00*
Never hinged	125.00	
c. Vert. pair, imper. horiz., type I	*2,500.*	
Never hinged	*3,500.*	
d. Double impression	*3,500.*	*2,750.*
Never hinged	*5,500.*	

Earliest documented uses: June 5, 1917 (No. 501); Feb. 8, 1918 (No. 501b single).

502 A140 3c **dark violet,** type II	14.00	.75
violet, type II	14.00	.75
Never hinged	32.50	
On cover, type II		1.00
Block of 4, type II	57.50	5.50
P# block of 6, type II	160.00	
Never hinged	275.00	
b. Bklt. pane of 6, type II, *Feb. 25, 1918*	60.00	*55.00*
Never hinged	100.00	
c. Vert. pair, imperf. horiz., type II	*1,400.*	*750.00*
Never hinged	*2,750.*	
On cover		*1,500.*
d. Double impression	750.00	750.00
Never hinged	1,500.	
e. Perf. 10 at top or bottom	*15,000.*	*12,500.*
Never hinged	*21,500.*	

Earliest documented uses: Jan. 30, 1918 (No. 502); June 12, 1918 (No. 502b single).

503 A140 4c **brown,** *Mar. 1917*	10.00	.40
dark brown	10.00	.40
orange brown	10.00	.40
yellow brown	10.00	.40
Never hinged	22.50	
On cover		2.10
Block of 4	40.00	3.50
P# block of 6	150.00	
Never hinged	250.00	
Double transfer	15.00	—
b. Double impression	—	
504 A140 5c **blue,** *Mar. 1917*	9.00	.35
light blue	9.00	.35
dark blue	9.00	.35
Never hinged	20.00	
On cover		.45
Block of 4	37.50	3.00
P# block of 6	140.00	
Never hinged	225.00	
Double transfer	11.00	—
a. Horizontal pair, imperf. between	*20,000.*	—
b. Double impression	*2,000.*	*900.00*

Earliest documented use: June 5, 1917.

505 A140 5c **rose** (error)	325.00	*550.00*
Never hinged	675.00	
On cover		2,250.
Block of 9, middle stamp #505	700.00	*1,100.*
Never hinged	1,100.	
Block of 12, two middle stamps #505	1,400.	*2,100.*
Never hinged	2,150.	
Margin block of six 2c stamps (#499), P# 7942	40.00	
Never hinged	70.00	

Earliest documented use: Mar. 27, 1917.

Value notes under No. 467 also apply to No. 505.

506 A140 6c **red orange,** *Mar. 1917*	12.00	.40
orange	12.00	.40
Never hinged	27.50	
On cover		2.50
Block of 4	52.50	4.00
P# block of 6	180.00	
Never hinged	300.00	
Double transfer	—	—
a. Perf. 10 at top or bottom	*5,000.*	*9,000.*

No. 506a also exists as a transitional stamp gauging partly perf 10 and partly perf 11 at top. Value thus the same as normal 506a.

507 A140 7c **black,** *Mar. 1917*	27.50	1.25
gray black	27.50	1.25
intense black	27.50	1.25
Never hinged	65.00	
On cover		7.75
Block of 4	115.00	12.50
P# block of 6	250.00	
Never hinged	450.00	
Double transfer	—	—
a. Perf. 10 at top	*20,000.*	—

Only two unused and one used example of No. 507a are recorded. The two unused stamps are the top two stamps in a block of four with two normal No. 507.

508 A148 8c **olive bister,** *Mar. 1917*	12.00	.65
dark olive green	12.00	.65
olive green	12.00	.65
Never hinged	27.50	
On cover		2.75
Block of 4	50.00	6.50
P# block of 6, Impt. & "A"	170.00	
Never hinged	285.00	
P# block of 6, "A"	220.00	
Never hinged	370.00	
P# block of 6	140.00	
Never hinged	240.00	
b. Vertical pair, imperf. between	—	—
c. Perf. 10 at top or bottom		*16,000.*
509 A148 9c **salmon red,** *Mar. 1917*	13.00	1.75
salmon	13.00	1.75
Never hinged	30.00	
On cover		13.00
Block of 4	57.50	19.00
P# block of 6	150.00	
Never hinged	250.00	
Double transfer	20.00	4.50
a. Perf. 10 at top or bottom	*4,250.*	*7,000.*
Never hinged	*6,750.*	

No. 509a also exists as a transitional stamp gauging partly perf 10 and partly perf 11 at top or bottom. Value thus the same as normal 509a.

510 A148 10c **orange yellow,** *Mar. 1917*	17.50	.25
golden yellow	17.50	.25
Never hinged	40.00	
On cover		2.00
Block of 4	70.00	2.00
P# block of 6, "A"	290.00	
Never hinged	475.00	
P# block of 6	200.00	
Never hinged	325.00	
a. 10c **brown yellow**	*1,500.*	
Never hinged	*2,500.*	

Earliest documented use: Mar. 27, 1917.

511 A148 11c **light green,** *May 1917*	9.00	2.50
green	9.00	2.50
Never hinged	20.00	
dark green	10.00	2.50
Never hinged	20.00	
On cover		8.50
Block of 4	37.50	22.50
P# block of 6	150.00	
Never hinged	260.00	
Double transfer	12.50	3.25
a. Perf. 10 at top or bottom	*5,000.*	*4,500.*
Never hinged	*7,500.*	

No. 511a also exists as a transitional stamp gauging partly perf 10 and partly perf 11 at top or bottom. Value thus the same as normal 511a.

512 A148 12c **claret brown,** *May 1917*	9.00	.40
Never hinged	20.00	
On cover		4.00
Block of 4	37.50	3.75
P# block of 6	150.00	
Never hinged	260.00	
Double transfer	12.50	—
Triple transfer	20.00	—
a. 12c **brown carmine**	10.00	.50
Never hinged	22.50	
On cover		4.50
Block of 4	40.00	4.50
P# block of 6	150.00	
Never hinged	260.00	
b. Perf. 10 at top or bottom	*17,500.*	*6,000.*
On cover		—

Earliest documented use: Aug. 15, 1917 (No. 512a); Aug. 26, 1924 (No. 512b).

513 A148 13c **apple green,** *Jan. 10, 1919*	11.00	6.00
pale apple green	11.00	6.00
Never hinged	25.00	
deep apple green	12.50	6.50
Never hinged	30.00	
On cover		19.00
Block of 4	45.00	45.00
P# block of 6	140.00	
Never hinged	240.00	

Earliest documented use: Jan. 25, 1919.

514 A148 15c **gray,** *May 1917*	37.50	1.50
dark gray	37.50	1.50
Never hinged	85.00	
On cover		25.00
Block of 4	160.00	12.50
P# block of 6	550.00	—
Never hinged	900.00	
Double transfer	—	—
a. Perf. 10 at bottom		*10,000.*

Earliest documented use: Nov. 15, 1917.

515 A148 20c **light ultramarine,** *May 1917*	45.00	.45
gray blue	45.00	.45
Never hinged	95.00	
deep ultramarine	50.00	.55
Never hinged	105.00	
On cover		75.00
Block of 4	200.00	3.50
P# block of 6	600.00	
Never hinged	1,000.	

			Double transfer	—	—
b.			Vertical pair, imperf. between	*2,000.*	*1,750.*
c.			Double impression	*1,250.*	
d.			Perf. 10 at top or bottom	—	*15,000.*

No. 515b is valued in the grade of fine.

Beware of pairs with blind perforations inside the design of the top stamp that are offered as No. 515b.

Earliest documented use: May 4, 1918.

516	A148	30c	**orange red,** *May 1917*	37.50	1.50
			dark orange red	37.50	1.50
			Never hinged	85.00	
			On cover		150.00
			Block of 4	160.00	12.50
			P# block of 6	600.00	
			Never hinged	925.00	
			Double transfer	—	
a.			Perf. 10 at top or bottom	*20,000.*	*7,500.*
			Never hinged	*40,000.*	
b.			Double impression		—

Earliest documented use: Jan. 12, 1918.

517	A148	50c	**red violet,** *May 1917*	65.00	.75
			Never hinged	150.00	
			violet	75.00	.75
			Never hinged	150.00	
			light violet	80.00	.75
			Never hinged	180.00	
			On cover		*400.00*
			Block of 4	290.00	5.00
			P# block of 6	1,600.	
			Never hinged	2,550.	
			Double transfer	100.00	1.75
b.			Vertical pair, imperf. between & at bottom	—	*10,000.*
c.			Perf. 10 at top or bottom		*10,000.*

No. 517b is valued in average condition and may be a unique used pair (precanceled). The editors would like to see authenticated evidence of an unused pair.

Earliest documented use: Dec. 28, 1917 (on registry tag).

518	A148	$1	**violet brown,** *May 1917*	50.00	1.50
			violet black	50.00	1.50
			Never hinged	120.00	
			On cover		*550.00*
			Block of 4	210.00	12.50
			Margin block of 4, arrow right or left	230.00	
			P# block of 6, Impt. & "A"	1,300.	—
			Never hinged	2,100.	
			Double transfer (5782 L. 66)	70.00	2.00
b.		$1	**deep brown**	*1,800.*	*1,250.*
			Never hinged	*3,750.*	
			Block of 4		*5,500.*
			P# block of 6, Impt. & "A," never hinged	*32,500.*	

Earliest documented use: May 19, 1917.

No. 518b is valued in the grade of fine to very fine.

Nos. 498-504,506-518 (20) 665.70 261.30

TYPE OF 1908-09 ISSUE

1917, Oct. 10 Wmk. 191 *Perf. 11*

This is the result of an old stock of No. 344 which was returned to the Bureau in 1917 and perforated with the then current gauge 11. Only lower left panes of No. 344 were perforated 11, and therefore only left and bottom plate blocks exist.

519	A139	2c	**carmine**	425.00	*1,400.*
			Never hinged	900.00	
			On cover		*3,250.*
			Block of 4	1,900.	—
			P# block of 6, T V, Impt.	3,500.	—
			Never hinged	*6,500.*	

Beware of examples of No. 344 fraudulently perforated and offered as No. 519. Obtaining a certificate from a recognized expertizing committee is strongly recommended.

Warning: See note following No. 459 regarding used stamps.

Earliest documented use: Oct. 10, 1917.

Franklin — A149

Plates of 100 subjects.

1918, Aug. Unwmk. *Perf. 11*

523	A149	$2	**orange red & black**	600.	250.
			red orange & black	600.	250.
			Never hinged	1,300.	
			On cover		*2,000.*
			Block of 4	2,500.	1,300.
			Margin block of 4, arrow	2,600.	
			Center line block	2,800.	1,400.
			P# block of 8, 2# & arrow	*12,000.*	—
			Never hinged	*18,000.*	

Earliest documented use: Dec. 17, 1918.

524	A149	$5	**deep green & black**	190.	35.
			Never hinged	425.	
			On cover		*2,500.*
			Block of 4	800.	200.
			Margin block of 4, arrow	850.	210.
			Center line block	1,050.	225.
			P# block of 8, 2# & arrow	4,500.	
			Never hinged	*7,000.*	

Earliest documented use: Mar. 20, 1920.

For other listing of design A149 see No. 547.

OFFSET PRINTING

Plates of 400, 800 or 1600 subjects in panes of 100 each, as follows:

No. 525 — 400 and 1600 subjects
No. 526 — 400, 800 and 1600 subjects
No. 529 — 400 subjects
No. 531 — 400 subjects
No. 532 — 400, 800 and 1600 subjects
No. 535 — 400 subjects
No. 536 — 400 and 1600 subjects

TYPES OF 1917-19 ISSUE

1918-20 Unwmk. *Perf. 11*

525	A140	1c	**gray green,** *Dec. 1918*	2.50	.90
			Never hinged	6.00	
			emerald	3.50	1.25
			Never hinged	8.25	
			On cover		1.75
			Block of 4	10.50	6.00
			P# block of 6	30.00	
			Never hinged	50.00	
			"Flat nose"	—	
a.		1c	**dark green**	7.00	1.75
			Never hinged	17.50	
c.			Horizontal pair, imperf. between	100.00	*700.00*
d.			Double impression	40.00	—
			Never hinged	90.00	

Earliest documented use: Dec. 24, 1918.

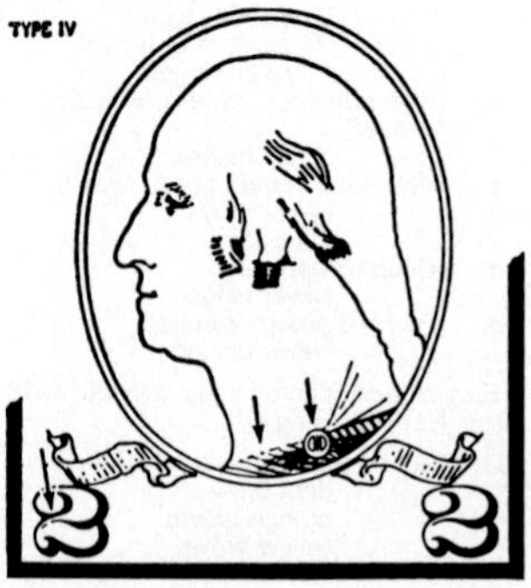

TYPE IV

TWO CENTS

Type IV — Top line of the toga rope is broken.

The shading lines in the toga button are so arranged that the curving of the first and last form "D (reversed) ID."

The line of color in the left "2" is very thin and usually broken.

Used on offset printings only.

TYPE V

Type V — Top line of the toga is complete.

There are five vertical shading lines in the toga button.

The line of color in the left "2" is very thin and usually broken.

The shading dots on the nose are as shown on the diagram.

Used on offset printings only.

TYPE Va

Type Va — Characteristics are the same as type V except in the shading dots of the nose. The third row of dots from the bottom has four dots instead of six. The overall height is ⅓mm shorter than type V.

Used on offset printings only.

TYPE VI

Type VI — General characteristics the same as type V except that the line of color in the left "2" is very heavy.

Used on offset printings only.

TYPE VII

Type VII — The line of color in the left "2" is invariably continuous, clearly defined and heavier than in type V or Va but not as heavy as type VI.

An additional vertical row of dots has been added to the upper lip.

Numerous additional dots have been added to the hair on top of the head.

Used on offset printings only.

Dates of issue of types after type IV are not known but official records show the first plate of each type to have been certified as follows:

Type IV, Mar. 6, 1920
Type V, Mar. 20, 1920
Type Va, May 4, 1920
Type VI, June 24, 1920
Type VII, Nov. 3, 1920

526	A140	2c	**carmine,** type IV, *1920*	27.50	4.00
			rose carmine, type IV	27.50	4.00
			Never hinged	62.50	
			On cover, type IV		11.00
			Block of 4, type IV	120.00	30.00
			P# block of 6, type IV	240.00	
			Never hinged	450.00	
			Gash on forehead, type IV	60.00	—
			Never hinged	125.00	
			Malformed "2" at left, type IV (10823 LR 93)	40.00	6.00

Earliest documented use: Mar. 15, 1920 (FDC).

527	A140	2c	**carmine,** type V, *1920*	20.00	1.25
			bright carmine, type V	20.00	1.25
			rose carmine, type V	20.00	1.25
			Never hinged	45.00	
			On cover		2.75
			Block of 4, type V	85.00	10.00
			Block of 6, P# only, type V	185.00	
			Never hinged	350.00	
			Line through "2" & "EN," type V	35.00	—
			Never hinged	75.00	
a.			Double impression, type V	75.00	—
			Never hinged	160.00	
b.			Vert. pair, imperf. horiz., type V	*850.00*	
c.			Horiz. pair, imperf. vert., type V	*1,000.*	—

Earliest documented use: Apr. 16, 1920.

528	A140	2c	**carmine,** type Va, *1920*	9.50	.40
			Never hinged	22.50	
			On cover, type Va		.75
			Block of 4, type Va	40.00	3.50
			Block of 6, P# only, type Va	100.00	
			Never hinged	175.00	
			Block of 6, monogram over P#	200.00	
			Never hinged	300.00	
			Retouches in "P" of Postage type Va	*52.50*	—
			Retouched on toga, type Va	—	—
			Variety C"R"NTS, type Va	*37.50*	
			Never hinged	85.00	

Top margin P# block of 6 containing the C"R"NTS variety, type Va 450.00
c. Double impression, type Va 55.00
Never hinged 125.00
g. Vert. pair, imperf. between *3,500.*

Earliest documented use: June 18, 1920.

528A A140 2c **carmine,** type VI, *1920* 52.50 2.00
bright carmine, type VI 52.50 2.00
Never hinged 125.00
On cover, type VI 3.75
Block of 4, type VI 225.00 15.00
P# block of 6, type VI 425.00
Never hinged 800.00
Block of 6, monogram over P# 525.00
Never hinged 900.00
d. Double impression, type VI 180.00 —
Never hinged 400.00
f. Vert. pair, imperf. horiz., type VI —
h. Vert. pair, imperf. between *1,000.*

Earliest documented use: July 30, 1920.

528B A140 2c **carmine,** type VII, *1920* 22.50 .75
Never hinged 55.00
On cover, type VII 1.00
Block of 4, type VII 95.00 6.00
P# block of 6, type VII 200.00
Never hinged 375.00
Gash on cheek, type VII *300.00* —
Retouched on cheek, type VII *750.00* —
Vertical plate scratch through face, type VII *200.00*
e. Double impression, type VII 80.00 *400.00*

Earliest documented use: Nov. 10, 1920.

TYPE III

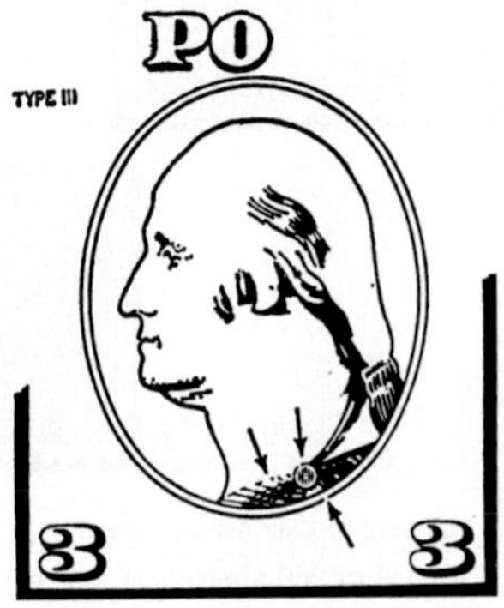

THREE CENTS

Type III — The top line of the toga rope is strong but the 5th shading line is missing as in type I.

Center shading line of the toga button consists of two dashes with a central dot.

The "P" and "O" of "POSTAGE" are separated by a line of color.

The frame line at the bottom of the vignette is complete.

Used on offset printings only.

TYPE IV

Type IV — The shading lines of the toga rope are complete.

The second and fourth shading lines in the toga button are broken in the middle and the third line is continuous with a dot in the center.

The "P" and "O" of "POSTAGE" are joined.

The frame line at the bottom of the vignette is broken.

Used on offset printings only.

529 A140 3c **violet,** type III, *Mar. 1918* 3.60 .50
light violet, type III 3.60 .50
dark violet, type III 3.60 .50
Never hinged 8.00
On cover, type III .60
Block of 4, type III 15.00 4.00
P# block of 6, type III 75.00
Never hinged 125.00
a. Double impression, type III 45.00 —
Never hinged 100.00
b. Printed on both sides, type III *2,500.*

Earliest documented use: Apr. 8, 1918 (No. 529); June 24, 1918 (No. 529a).

530 A140 3c **purple,** *June 1918* type IV 2.00 .30
light purple, type IV 2.00 .30
deep purple, type IV 2.00 .30
violet, type IV 2.00 .30
Never hinged 4.50
On cover, type IV .35
Block of 4, type IV 8.50 2.00
P# block of 6, type IV 32.50
Never hinged 55.00
"Blister" under "U.S.," type IV 5.00 —
Recut under "U.S.," type IV 5.00 —
a. Double impression, type IV 35.00 —
On cover *2,250.*
b. Printed on both sides, type IV *350.00*
Never hinged *650.00*
c. Triple impression, type IV *1,750.* —
Nos. 525-530 (8) 140.10 10.10

Earliest documented use: June 30, 1918.

Earliest documented use dates for imperforates are for the imperforate sheet stamps, not for imperforate stamps with vending and affixing machine perforations or for flat plate imperforate coil stamps. EDU dates for VAMP and flat plate imperf coil stamps are shown in their respective sections later in the catalogue.

1918-20 ***Imperf.***

Dates of issue of 2c types are not known, but official records show that the first plate of each type known to have been issued imperforate was certified as follows:

Type IV, Mar. 1920
Type V, May 4, 1920
Type Va, May 25, 1920
Type VI, July 26, 1920
Type VII, Dec. 2, 1920

531 A140 1c **green,** *Jan. 1919* 11.00 12.00
gray green 11.00 12.00
Never hinged 23.00
On cover 17.50
Pair 23.00 52.50
Never hinged 52.50
Block of 4 47.50 75.00
Corner margin block of 4 50.00 —
Margin block of 4, arrow 52.50 80.00
Center line block 75.00 *90.00*
Never hinged 135.00
P# block of 6 110.00 —
Never hinged 190.00

Earliest documented use: Mar. 17, 1919 (dated cancel on off-cover plate block); April 7, 1919 (cover).

532 A140 2c **carmine rose,** type IV, *1920* 37.50 35.00
Never hinged 80.00
On cover 70.00
Pair 80.00 *110.00*
Never hinged 175.00
Block of 4 160.00 *225.00*
Corner margin block of 4 170.00
Margin block of 4, arrow 175.00
Center line block 230.00
Never hinged 400.00
P# block of 6 370.00 —
Never hinged 625.00

Earliest documented use: April 12, 1923.

533 A140 2c **carmine,** type V, *1920* 100.00 95.00
Never hinged 210.00
On cover 210.00
Pair 220.00 250.00
Never hinged 450.00
Block of 4 450.00 *550.00*
Corner margin block of 4 475.00 *675.00*
Margin block of 4, arrow 500.00 *675.00*
Center line block 750.00 *700.00*
Never hinged 1,300.
P# block of 6 1,100. —
Never hinged 1,800.
Line through "2" and "EN," type V 225.00
Never hinged 450.00

Earliest documented use: Sept. 29, 1920 (dated cancel on off-cover center line block of 4).

534 A140 2c **carmine,** type Va, *1920* 12.50 9.00
carmine rose 12.50 9.00
Never hinged 27.50
On cover 16.00
Pair 27.50 22.50
Never hinged 60.00
Block of 4 55.00 57.50
Corner margin block of 4 57.50
Margin block of 4, arrow 60.00 60.00
Center line block 70.00 *90.00*
Never hinged 130.00
P# block of 6 130.00 —
Never hinged 200.00
Block of 6, monogram over P# 225.00
Never hinged 360.00

Earliest documented use: June 24, 1920.

534A A140 2c **carmine,** type VI, *1920* 42.50 32.50
Never hinged 90.00
On cover 45.00
Pair 90.00 85.00
Never hinged 190.00
Block of 4 180.00 230.00
Corner block of 4 200.00 250.00
Block of 4, arrow 210.00 —
Center line block 260.00 *300.00*
Never hinged 475.00
Block of 6, P# only 400.00 —
Never hinged 650.00

Earliest documented use: Aug. 31, 1920.

534B A140 2c **carmine,** type VII, *1920* 1,900. 1,250.
Never hinged 3,500.
On cover *5,000.*
Pair 4,000. *4,500.*
Never hinged 6,750.
Block of 4 8,250. *7,000.*
Corner margin block of 4 8,500.
Margin block of 4, arrow 8,750.
Center line block *10,500.*
Never hinged 16,000.
P# block of 6 *17,000.*
Never hinged *25,000.*

Earliest documented use: Oct. 1, 1921 (dated cancel on on-piece pair); Mar. 22, 1923 (on cover). A cover purported to be an Oct. 20, 1920, usage is believed to exist. The editors would like to see authenticated evidence of its genuineness.

Beware of perforated 2c offset stamps that may have been fraudulently trimmed to resemble Nos. 532-534B.

Examples of the 2c type VII with Schermack type III vending machine perforations have been cut down at sides to simulate the rarer No. 534B imperforate. The No. 534B with Schermack type III perforations is much less expensive than the fully imperforate No. 534B listed here.

535 A140 3c **violet,** type IV, *1918* 9.00 5.00
Never hinged 20.00
On cover 11.00
Pair 20.00 15.00
Never hinged 42.50
Block of 4 40.00 32.50
Corner margin block of 4 42.50 35.00
Margin block of 4, arrow 45.00 35.00
Center line block 60.00 *50.00*
Never hinged 105.00
P# block of 6 80.00 —
Never hinged 125.00
a. Double impression 95.00 —
Never hinged 200.00
Nos. 531-534A,535 (6) 212.50 188.50

Earliest documented use: Sept. 30, 1918.

Cancellation

Haiti —

1919, Aug. 15 ***Perf. 12½***

536 A140 1c **gray green** 22.50 *27.50*
Never hinged 50.00
On cover 150.00
Block of 4 95.00 *150.00*
P# block of 6 225.00
Never hinged 375.00
a. Horiz. pair, imperf. vert. *1,250.*

Earliest documented use: Aug. 21, 1919.

VICTORY ISSUE

Victory of the Allies in World War I

"Victory" and Flags of Allies — A150

Designed by Clair Aubrey Huston

FLAT PLATE PRINTING

Plates of 400 subjects in four panes of 100 each

1919, Mar. 3 Unwmk. *Perf. 11*

537	A150 3c **violet**	10.00	3.25
	Never hinged	20.00	
	On cover		9.00
	Block of 4	42.50	17.50
	P# block of 6	275.00	
	Never hinged	400.00	
	Double transfer	—	—
a.	3c **deep red violet**	*1,250.*	*2,250.*
	Never hinged	*2,100.*	
	On cover		—
	Block of 4	*5,250.*	*8,750.*
	P# block of 6	*10,000.*	
	Never hinged	*16,000.*	
b.	3c **light reddish violet**	125.00	45.00
	Never hinged	250.00	
	On cover		200.00
	Block of 4	550.00	180.00
	P# block of 6	1,150.	
	Never hinged	1,750.	
c.	3c **red violet**	150.00	55.00
	Never hinged	300.00	
	On cover		225.00
	Block of 4	650.00	
	P# block of 6	1,250.	
	Never hinged	1,900.	

No. 537a is valued in the grade of fine.

Earliest documented date: Mar. 3, 1919 (FDC).

REGULAR ISSUE

ROTARY PRESS PRINTINGS

(See note over No. 448)

1919 Unwmk. *Perf. 11x10*

Issued in panes of 170 stamps (coil waste), later in panes of 70 and 100 (#538, 540)

Stamp designs: 19½-20x22-22¼mm

538	A140 1c **green,** *June*	11.00	9.00
	yellowish green	11.00	9.00
	bluish green	11.00	9.00
	Never hinged	25.00	
	On cover		22.50
	Block of 4	47.50	*55.00*
	P# block of 4 & "S 30"	95.00	
	Never hinged	160.00	
	P# block of 4	110.00	
	Never hinged	180.00	
	P# block of 4, star	140.00	
	Never hinged	225.00	
	Double transfer	17.50	—
a.	Vert. pair, imperf. horiz.	50.00	*100.00*
	Never hinged	90.00	
	Block of 4	110.00	*250.00*
	Never hinged	200.00	
	P# block of 4	900.00	
	Never hinged	1,375.	

No. 538a used is valued with a contemporaneous cancel. A certificate of authenticity is advised.

Earliest documented use: June 28, 1919 (No. 538); Sept. 5, 1927 (No. 538a).

539	A140 2c **carmine rose,** type II	2,850.	*5,500.*
	Never hinged	4,250.	
	On cover, type II		*60,000.*
	Block of 4, type II	*11,000.*	*35,000.*
	P# block of 4, type II, & "S 20"	*17,500.*	
	Never hinged	*25,000.*	

No. 539 is valued in the grade of fine.

(See note after No. 455.)

Earliest documented use: June 30, 1919. This is the unique usage on cover. The used block of four also is unique.

540	A140 2c **carmine rose,** type III, *June 14*	13.00	9.50
	carmine	13.00	9.50
	Never hinged	30.00	
	On cover, type III		25.00
	Block of 4, type III	55.00	*60.00*
	Never hinged	125.00	
	P# block of 4, type III, & "S 30"	105.00	
	Never hinged	175.00	
	P# block of 4, type III, & "S 30" inverted	450.00	
	Never hinged	725.00	
	P# block of 4, type III	105.00	
	Never hinged	175.00	
	P# block of 4, type III, star	160.00	
	Never hinged	275.00	
	Double transfer, type III	22.50	—

Earliest documented use: June 17, 1919.

a.	Vert. pair, imperf. horiz., type III	50.00	*100.00*
	Never hinged	100.00	
	Block of 4	110.00	*250.00*
	Never hinged	220.00	
	P# block of 4, type III	1,000.	
	Never hinged	1,500.	
	P# block of 4, type III, Star	1,050.	
	Never hinged	1,600.	
b.	Horiz. pair, imperf. vert., type III	*1,750.*	

No. 540a used is valued with a contemporaneous cancel. A certificate of authenticity is advised.

Earliest documented use: June 17, 1919 (No. 540); Nov. 4, 1922 (No. 540a).

541	A140 3c **violet,** type II, *June 14, 1919*	45.00	32.50
	gray violet, type II	45.00	32.50
	Never hinged	110.00	
	On cover		100.00
	Block of 4	190.00	*260.00*
	P# block of 4	360.00	
	Never hinged	625.00	

Earliest documented use: June 14, 1919 (FDC).

1920, May 26 *Perf. 10x11*

Plates of 400 subjects in four panes of 100.

Stamp design: 19x22½-22¾mm

542	A140 1c **green**	14.00	1.50
	bluish green	14.00	1.50
	Never hinged	35.00	
	On cover		5.50
	Block of 4	60.00	12.50
	Vertical margin block of 6, P# opposite center horizontal row	165.00	
	Never hinged	300.00	

Earliest documented use: May 26, 1920 (FDC).

1921, May *Perf. 10*

Plates of 400 subjects in four panes of 100 each

Stamp design: 19x22½mm

543	A140 1c **green**	.70	.40
	deep green	.70	.40
	Never hinged	1.75	
	On cover		.45
	Block of 4	2.80	2.00
	Vertical margin block of 6, P# opposite center horizontal row	32.50	
	Never hinged	57.50	
	Corner margin block of 4, P# only	17.50	
	Never hinged	30.00	
	Double transfer		—
	Triple transfer	—	—
a.	Horizontal pair, imperf. between	*2,750.*	

Earliest documented use: May 21, 1921.

1922 *Perf. 11*

Rotary press sheet waste

Stamp design: 19x22½mm

544	A140 1c **green**	*22,500.*	*3,750.*
	Never hinged	*37,500.*	
	On cover		*7,500.*

No. 544 is valued in the grade of fine.

Earliest documented use: Dec. 21, 1922.

1921, May

Issued in panes of 170 stamps (coil waste), later in panes of 70 and 100

Stamp designs: 19½-20x22mm

545	A140 1c **green**	200.00	210.00
	yellowish green	200.00	210.00
	Never hinged	475.00	
	On cover		*1,800.*
	Block of 4	825.00	*1,050.*
	P# block of 4, "S 30"	1,100.	
	Never hinged	2,150.	
	P# block of 4	1,150.	
	Never hinged	2,200.	
	P# block of 4, star	1,200.	
	Never hinged	2,300.	

Earliest documented use: June 25, 1921.

546	A140 2c **carmine rose,** type III	125.00	*190.00*
	deep carmine rose	125.00	*190.00*
	Never hinged	280.00	
	On cover		*800.00*
	Block of 4	525.00	*925.00*
	P# block of 4, "S 30"	750.00	
	Never hinged	1,400.	
	P# block of 4	775.00	
	Never hinged	1,450.	
	P# block of 4, star	800.00	
	Never hinged	1,500.	
	Recut in hair	140.00	*210.00*
a.	Perf. 10 on left side	*7,500.*	*10,000.*

Earliest documented use: May 5, 1921.

FLAT PLATE PRINTING

Plates of 100 subjects

1920, Nov. 1 *Perf. 11*

547	A149 $2 **carmine & black**	150.	40.
	Never hinged	330.	
	On cover (commercial)		1,000.
	On flown cover (philatelic)		250.
	Block of 4	650.	200.
	Margin block of 4, arrow	675.	
	Center line block	800.	—
	Margin block of 8, two P#, & arrow	4,500.	
	Never hinged	7,000.	
a.	$2 **lake & black**	210.	40.
	Never hinged	450.	

Earliest documented use: Dec. 6, 1920 (on piece).

From No. 548 forward, almost all U.S. stamps have had officially designated first days of sale and use. Therefore, from this point, earliest documented uses are given only for those stamps for which there were not designated first days of sale. For first day covers, see the First Day Cover section later in the catalogue.

PILGRIM TERCENTENARY ISSUE

Landing of the Pilgrims at Plymouth, Mass.

The "Mayflower" — A151

Landing of the Pilgrims — A152

Signing of the Compact — A153

Designed by Clair Aubrey Huston

Plates of 280 subjects in four panes of 70 each

1920, Dec. 21 Unwmk. *Perf. 11*

548	A151 1c **green**	4.75	2.25
	dark green	4.75	2.25
	Never hinged	12.00	
	On cover		3.50
	Block of 4	20.00	14.00
	P# block of 6	70.00	
	Never hinged	100.00	
	Double transfer	—	—
549	A152 2c **carmine rose**	6.25	1.60
	carmine	6.25	1.60
	rose	6.25	1.60
	Never hinged	16.00	
	On cover		2.50
	Block of 4	26.50	9.00
	P# block of 6	85.00	
	Never hinged	125.00	
	Cancellation		
	China		—
550	A153 5c **deep blue**	42.50	14.00
	dark blue	42.50	14.00
	Never hinged	105.00	
	On cover		22.50
	Block of 4	190.00	75.00
	P# block of 6	475.00	
	Never hinged	750.00	
	Nos. 548-550 (3)	53.50	17.85
	Nos. 548-550, never hinged	133.00	

IMPORTANT INFORMATION
REGARDING VALUES FOR
NEVER-HINGED STAMPS

Collectors should be aware that the values given for never-hinged stamps from No. 182 on are for stamps in the grade of very fine, just as the values for all stamps in the catalogue are for very fine stamps unless indicated otherwise. The never-hinged premium as a percentage of value will be larger for stamps in extremely fine or superb grades, and the premium will be smaller for fine-very fine, fine or poor examples. This is particularly true of the issues of the late-19th and early-20th centuries. For example, in the grade of very fine, an unused stamp from this time period may be valued at $100 hinged and $200 never hinged. The never-hinged premium is thus 100%. But in a grade of extremely fine, this same stamp will not only sell for more hinged, but the never-hinged premium will increase, perhaps to 200%-400% or more over the higher extremely fine value. In a grade of superb, a hinged stamp will sell for much more than a very fine stamp, and additionally the never-hinged premium will be much larger, perhaps as large as 500%-1,000%. On the other hand, the same stamp in a grade of fine or fine-very fine not only will sell for less than a very fine stamp in hinged condition, but additionally the never-hinged premium will be smaller than the never-hinged premium on a very fine stamp, perhaps as small as 15%-30%.

Please note that the above statements and percentages are NOT a formula for arriving at the values of stamps in hinged or never-hinged condition in the grades of very good, fine, fine to very fine, very fine, very fine to extremely fine, extremely fine or superb. The percentages given apply only to the size of the premium for never-hinged condition that might be added to the stamp value for hinged condition. Further, the percentages given are only generalized estimates. Some stamps or grades may have percentages for never-hinged condition that are higher or lower than the ranges given. For values of the most popular U.S. stamps in the grades of very good, fine, fine to very fine, very fine, very fine to extremely fine, extremely fine and superb, see the *Scott United States Specialized Valuing Supplement*, updated and issued twice each year in April and October.

VALUES FOR NEVER-HINGED STAMPS
PRIOR TO SCOTT 182

This catalogue does not value pre-1879 stamps in never-hinged condition. Premiums for never-hinged condition in the classic era invariably are even larger than those premiums listed for the 1879 and later issues. Generally speaking, the earlier the stamp is listed in the catalogue, the larger will be the never-hinged premium. On some early classics, the premium will be several multiples of the unused, hinged values given in the catalogue.

NEVER-HINGED PLATE BLOCKS

Values given for never-hinged plate blocks are for blocks in which all stamps have original gum that has never been hinged and has no disturbances, and all selvage, whether gummed or ungummed, has never been hinged.

REGULAR ISSUE

Nathan Hale — A154

Franklin — A155

Warren G. Harding — A156

Washington — A157

Lincoln — A158

Martha Washington — A159

Theodore Roosevelt — A160

Garfield — A161

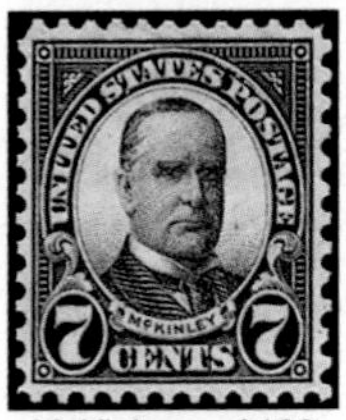

McKinley — A162

Grant — A163

Jefferson — A164

Monroe — A165

Rutherford B. Hayes — A166

Grover Cleveland — A167

American Indian — A168

Statue of Liberty — A169

Golden Gate — A170

Niagara Falls — A171

American Buffalo — A172

Arlington Amphitheater — A173

Lincoln Memorial — A174

United States Capitol — A175

Head of Freedom Statue, Capitol Dome — A176

Plates of 400 subjects in four panes of 100 each for all values ½c to 50c inclusive.

Plates of 200 subjects for $1 and $2. The sheets were cut along the horizontal guide line into two panes, upper and lower, of 100 subjects each.

Plates of 100 subjects for the $5 denomination, and sheets of 100 subjects were issued intact.

The Bureau of Engraving and Printing in 1925 in experimenting to overcome the loss due to uneven perforations, produced what is known as the "Star Plate." The vertical rows of designs on these plates are spaced 3mm apart in place of 2¾mm as on the regular plates. Most of these plates were identified with a star added to the plate number.

Designed by Clair Aubrey Huston.

FLAT PLATE PRINTINGS

1922-25			**Unwmk.**		***Perf. 11***
551	A154	½c	**olive brown,** *Apr. 4, 1925*	.25	.20
			pale olive brown	.25	.20
			deep olive brown	.25	.20
			Never hinged	.50	
			On 1c stamped envelope (3rd class)		2.50
			Block of 4	1.00	.50
			P# block of 6	15.00	
			Never hinged	25.00	
			"Cap" on fraction bar (Pl. 17041)	.75	.20
552	A155	1c	**deep green,** *Jan. 17, 1923*	1.30	.20
			green	1.30	.20
			pale green	1.30	.20
			Never hinged	2.75	
			On postcard		.25
			Block of 4	5.25	.40
			P# block of 6	37.50	
			Never hinged	55.00	
			Double transfer	3.50	—
a.			Booklet pane of 6, *Aug. 11, 1923*	7.50	*4.00*
			Never hinged	12.50	

Earliest documented use: Dec. 21, 1923 (No. 552a pair).

553	A156	1½c	**yellow brown,** *Mar. 19, 1925*	2.30	.20
			pale yellow brown	2.30	.20
			brown	2.30	.20
			Never hinged	4.75	
			On 3rd class cover		2.25
			Block of 4	9.50	1.10
			P# block of 6	67.50	—
			Never hinged	95.00	
			Double transfer	—	—
554	A157	2c	**carmine,** *Jan. 15, 1923*	1.20	.20

light carmine 1.20 .20
deep claret —
Never hinged 2.75
On cover .25
Block of 4 5.00 .30
P# block of 6 42.50
Never hinged 60.00
P# block of 6 & small 5 point star, top only 550.00
Never hinged 775.00
P# block of 6 & large 5 point star, side only 65.00
Never hinged 97.50
Same, large 5-pt. star, top 600.00
Never hinged 1,000.
Same, large 6-pt. star, top 750.00
Never hinged 1,200.
Same, large 6-pt. star, side only (Pl. 17196) 1,000.
Never hinged 1,500.
Double transfer 2.50 .80

a. Horiz. pair, imperf. vert. *275.00*
b. Vert. pair, imperf. horiz. *4,000.*
Never hinged —
c. Booklet pane of 6, *Feb. 10, 1923* 7.00 *3.00*
Never hinged 12.00
d. Perf. 10 at top or bottom *7,000.* *5,500.*
On cover *9,000.*

No. 554d unused is unique. It is never hinged and has a natural straight edge at left. Value represents the sale price at 2001 auction.

Earliest documented use: Feb. 10, 1923 (No. 554c single); Nov. 23, 1923 (No. 554d).

555 A158 3c **violet,** *Feb. 12, 1923* 17.50 1.25
deep violet 17.50 1.25
dark violet 17.50 1.25
red violet 17.50 1.25
bright violet 17.50 1.25
Never hinged 37.50
On 2c stamped envelope (single UPU rate) 8.00
Block of 4 72.50 9.00
P# block of 6 225.00
Never hinged 375.00

556 A159 4c **yellow brown,** *Jan. 15, 1923* 20.00 .50
brown 20.00 .50
Never hinged 45.00
On cover 9.00
Block of 4 82.50 3.00
P# block of 6 250.00
Never hinged 400.00
Double transfer — —
a. Vert. pair, imperf. horiz. *10,500.*
b. Perf. 10 at top or bottom *3,500.* *25,000.*

No. 556a is unique. It resulted from a sheet that was damaged and patched during production.

No. 556b used also exists as a transitional stamp gauging 10 at left top and 11 at right top. Value the same.

557 A160 5c **dark blue,** *Oct. 27, 1922* 20.00 .30
deep blue 20.00 .30
Never hinged 45.00
On UPU-rate cover 6.00
Block of 4 82.50 2.00
P# block of 6 250.00
Never hinged 400.00
Double transfer (15571 UL 86) — *350.00*
a. Imperf., pair *2,000.*
Never hinged *3,500.*
P# block of 6 *27,500.*
b. Horiz. pair, imperf. vert. —
c. Perf. 10 at top or bottom — *11,000.*
On cover *17,500.*

Earliest documented use: Nov. 12, 1923 (No. 557c).

558 A161 6c **red orange,** *Nov. 20, 1922* 37.50 1.00
pale red orange 37.50 1.00
Never hinged 80.00
Pair on special delivery cover 17.50
Block of 4 155.00 7.50
P# block of 6 400.00
Never hinged 650.00
Double transfer (Plate 14169 LR 60 and 70) 57.50 2.00
Same, recut 57.50 2.00

559 A162 7c **black,** *May 1, 1923* 8.50 .75
gray black 8.50 .75
Never hinged 18.00
On registered cover with other values 27.50
Block of 4 37.50 6.00
P# block of 6 125.00
Never hinged 200.00
Double transfer — —

560 A163 8c **olive green,** *May 1, 1923* 50.00 1.00
pale olive green 50.00 1.00
Never hinged 110.00
Pair on airmail cover 12.50
Block of 4 210.00 7.50
P# block of 6 575.00
Never hinged 900.00
Double transfer — —

561 A164 9c **rose,** *Jan. 15, 1923* 14.00 1.25
pale rose 14.00 1.25
Never hinged 30.00
On registered cover with other values 22.50
Block of 4 57.50 9.00
P# block of 6 250.00
Never hinged 400.00
Double transfer — —

562 A165 10c **orange,** *Jan. 15, 1923* 17.50 .35
pale orange 17.50 .35
Never hinged 37.50
On special delivery cover with 2c 6.00
Block of 4 72.50 2.00
P# block of 6 275.00
Never hinged 425.00
a. Vert. pair, imperf. horiz. *2,250.*
Never hinged *3,500.*
b. Imperf., pair *2,500.*
P# block of 6 *25,000.*
c. Perf. 10 at top or bottom — *20,000.*
Pair *42,500.*

No. 562b is valued without gum and without blue pencil defacing lines. No. 562c is valued in the grade of fine.

563 A166 11c **greenish blue,** *Oct. 4, 1922* 1.40 .60
Never hinged 3.10
light blue 1.75 .60
Never hinged 3.50
On registered cover with other values 12.50
Block of 4 5.75 3.50
P# block of 6 55.00
Never hinged 80.00
a. 11c **light bluish green** 1.40 .60
light yellow green 1.40 .60
Never hinged 2.90
On registered cover with other values 14.00
Block of 4 5.75 4.00
P# block of 6 40.00
Never hinged 60.00
d. Imperf., pair *20,000.*

Many other intermediate shades exist for Nos. 563 and 563a, all falling within the blue or green color families.

564 A167 12c **brown violet,** *Mar. 20, 1923* 6.00 .35
deep brown violet 6.00 .35
Never hinged 13.00
On special delivery cover 12.50
Block of 4 25.00 3.00
P# block of 6 115.00
Never hinged 175.00
P# block of 6 & large 5 point star, side only 150.00
Never hinged 230.00
P# block of 6 & large 6 point star, side only 250.00
Never hinged 400.00
Double transfer, (14404 UL 73 & 74) 12.50 1.10
a. Horiz. pair, imperf. vert. *1,750.*

565 A168 14c **blue,** *May 1, 1923* 4.00 .90
deep blue 4.00 .90
Never hinged 8.75
On registered cover with other values 15.00
Block of 4 16.50 7.50
P# block of 6 80.00
Never hinged 130.00
Double transfer — —

Horizontal pairs of No. 565 are known with spacings up to 3mm instead of 2mm between. These are from the 5th and 6th vertical rows of the right panes of Plate 14515 and also between stamps Nos. 3 and 4 of the same pane. A plate block of Pl. 14512 is known with 3mm spacing.

566 A169 15c **gray,** *Nov. 11, 1922* 20.00 .30
light gray 20.00 .30
Never hinged 45.00
On registered cover with 2c 3.50
Block of 4 85.00 2.00
P# block of 6 275.00
Never hinged 425.00
P# block of 6 & large 5 point star, side only 550.00
Never hinged 825.00

567 A170 20c **carmine rose,** *May 1, 1923* 20.00 .30
deep carmine rose 20.00 .30
Never hinged 45.00
On registered UPU-rate cover 12.50
Block of 4 85.00 2.00
P# block of 6 300.00
Never hinged 450.00
P# block of 6 & large 5 point star, side only 575.00
Never hinged 850.00
a. Horiz. pair, imperf. vert. *2,000.*
Never hinged *3,500.*

"Bridge over Falls" plate scratches

568 A171 25c **yellow green,** *Nov. 11, 1922* 18.00 .75
green 18.00 .75
deep green 18.00 .75
Never hinged 40.00
On contract airmail cover 27.50
Block of 4 75.00 6.00
P# block of 6 300.00
Never hinged 425.00
Double transfer — —
Plate scratches ("Bridge over Falls") (17445 LL 26) *500.00* —
b. Vert. pair, imperf. horiz. *2,500.*
c. Perf. 10 at one side *5,000.* *11,000.*
Never hinged *7,500.*

No. 568b is valued in the grade of fine.

Double Transfer

569 A172 30c **olive brown,** *Mar. 20, 1923* 30.00 .60
Never hinged 65.00
On registered cover with other values 20.00
Block of 4 140.00 5.00
P# block of 6 325.00
Never hinged 475.00
Double transfer (16065 UR 52) 55.00 —

570 A173 50c **lilac,** *Nov. 11, 1922* 45.00 .40
dull lilac 45.00 .40
Never hinged 100.00
On Federal airmail cover 27.50
Block of 4 190.00 2.00
P# block of 6 575.00
Never hinged 900.00

571 A174 $1 **violet brown,** *Feb. 12, 1923* 42.50 .65
violet black 42.50 .65
Never hinged 95.00
On post-1932 registered cover with other values 22.50
Block of 4 180.00 4.50
Margin block of 4, arrow, top or bottom 190.00
P# block of 6 350.00
Never hinged 650.00
Double transfers, Pl. 18642 L 30 and Pl. 18682 95.00 1.60

572 A175 $2 **deep blue,** *Mar. 20, 1923* 75.00 9.00
Never hinged 165.00
On post-1932 registered cover with other values 55.00
Block of 4 325.00 65.00
Margin block of 4, arrow, top or bottom 340.00
P# block of 6 750.00
Never hinged 1,200.

573 A176 $5 **carmine & blue,** *Mar. 20, 1923* 100.00 15.00
Never hinged 220.00
On post-1932 registered cover with other values 175.00
Block of 4 425.00 95.00
Margin block of 4, arrow 450.00
Center line block 550.00 *105.00*
Never hinged 975.00
P# block of 8, two P# & arrow 2,250. —
Never hinged 3,500.
a. $5 **carmine lake & dark blue** 190.00 20.00
Never hinged 350.00
On post-1932 registered cover with other values 190.00
Block of 4 850.00 140.00
Margin block of 4, arrow 875.00
Center line block 950.00 *175.00*
Never hinged 1,600.
P# block of 8, two P# & arrow 3,000.
Never hinged 4,500.
Nos. 551-573 (23) 551.95 36.05
Nos. 551-573, never hinged 1,222.

For other listings of perforated stamps of designs A154 to A176 see:
Nos. 578 & 579, Perf. 11x10
Nos. 581-591, Perf. 10
Nos. 594-596, Perf. 11
Nos. 632-642, 653, 692-696, Perf. 11x10½
Nos. 697-701, Perf. 10½x11
This series also includes #622-623 (perf. 11), 684-687 & 720-723.

Plate Blocks

Scott values for plate blocks printed from flat plates are for very fine side and bottom positions. Top position plate blocks with full wide selvage sell for more.

Earliest documented use dates for imperforates are for the imperforate sheet stamps, not for imperforate stamps with vending and affixing machine perforations or for flat plate imperforate coil stamps. EDU dates for VAMP and flat plate imperf coil stamps are shown in their respective sections later in the catalogue.

1923-25 ***Imperf.***

Stamp design 19¼x22¼mm

575 A155 1c **green,** *Mar. 1923* 5.00 5.00
deep green 5.00 5.00
Never hinged 11.00
On commercial cover *100.00*
On philatelic cover 8.50

	Unused	Used
Pair	11.00	12.50
Never hinged	24.00	
Block of 4	22.00	27.50
Corner margin block of 4	25.00	*27.50*
Corner margin block of 4 (UR), "O" in selvage	—	
Margin block of 4, arrow	27.00	*30.00*
Center line block	40.00	40.00
Never hinged	70.00	
P# block of 6	80.00	—
Never hinged	115.00	

Earliest documented use: Mar. 16, 1923.

	Unused	Used
576 A156 1½c **yellow brown,** *Apr. 4, 1925*	1.25	*1.50*
pale yellow brown	1.25	*1.50*
brown	1.25	*1.50*
Never hinged	2.70	
On commercial cover		*25.00*
On philatelic cover		6.00
Pair	2.75	*3.75*
Never hinged	6.00	
Block of 4	5.75	*8.50*
Corner margin block of 4	6.00	*9.00*
Margin block of 4, arrow	6.25	*10.00*
Center line block	11.00	*20.00*
Never hinged	20.00	
P# block of 6	30.00	—
Never hinged	45.00	
Double transfer	—	—

The 1½c A156 Rotary press imperforate is listed as No. 631.

	Unused	Used
577 A157 2c **carmine**	1.30	1.25
light carmine	1.30	1.25
Never hinged	2.90	
On commercial cover		*20.00*
On philatelic cover		6.00
Pair	2.80	3.00
Never hinged	6.00	
Block of 4	5.75	7.00
Corner margin block of 4	6.00	*8.00*
Margin block of 4, arrow	6.25	*10.00*
Center line block	13.00	*15.00*
Never hinged	22.50	
P# block of 6	30.00	—
Never hinged	45.00	
P# block of 6, large 5 point star	75.00	—
Never hinged	110.00	
Nos. 575-577 (3)	7.55	7.75
Nos. 575-577, never hinged	16.60	

ROTARY PRESS PRINTINGS
(See note over No. 448)
Issued in sheets of 70, 100 or 170 stamps, coil waste of Nos. 597, 599
Stamp designs: 19¾x22¼mm

1923 ***Perf. 11x10***

	Unused	Used
578 A155 1c **green**	85.00	*160.00*
Never hinged	190.00	
On cover		*700.00*
Block of 4	360.00	*1,000.*
P# block of 4, star	925.00	
Never hinged	1,450.	

Earliest documented use: Nov. 7, 1923.

	Unused	Used
579 A157 2c **carmine**	80.00	*140.00*
deep carmine	80.00	*140.00*
Never hinged	175.00	
Block of 4	340.00	*1,750.*
On cover		*400.00*
P# block of 4, star	600.00	
Never hinged	1,000.	
Recut in eye, plate 14731	*110.00*	*150.00*

Earliest documented use: Feb. 20, 1923.

Warning: See note following No. 459 regarding used stamps.

Plates of 400 subjects in four panes of 100 each
Stamp designs: 19¼x22½mm

1923-26 ***Perf. 10***

	Unused	Used
581 A155 1c **green,** *Apr. 21, 1923*	10.00	.75
yellow green	10.00	.75
pale green	10.00	.75
Never hinged	22.50	
On postcard		.85
On 3rd class cover		1.35
Block of 4	42.50	4.50
P# block of 4	175.00	
Never hinged	250.00	

Earliest documented use: May 18, 1923.

	Unused	Used
582 A156 1½c **brown,** *Mar. 19, 1925*	5.50	.65
dark brown	5.50	.65
Never hinged	12.50	
On 3rd class cover		6.00
Block of 4	24.00	4.00
P# block of 4	85.00	
Never hinged	125.00	
Pair with full horiz. gutter btwn.	*160.00*	
Pair with full vert. gutter btwn.	*210.00*	

No. 582 was available in full sheets of 400 subjects but was not regularly issued in that form.

	Unused	Used
583 A157 2c **carmine,** *Apr. 14, 1924*	2.75	.30
deep carmine	2.75	.30
Never hinged	6.00	
On cover		2.50
Block of 4	13.00	2.00
P# block of 4	70.00	
Never hinged	110.00	
a. Booklet pane of 6, *Aug. 27, 1926*	95.00	*150.00*
Never hinged	175.00	

Earliest documented use (unprecanceled): May 15, 1924.

	Unused	Used
584 A158 3c **violet,** *Aug. 1, 1925*	27.50	3.00
Never hinged	62.50	
On postcard (UPU rate)		12.50
Block of 4	130.00	17.50
P# block of 4	275.00	
Never hinged	425.00	
585 A159 4c **yellow brown,** *Mar. 1925*	18.00	.65
deep yellow brown	18.00	.65
Never hinged	40.00	
On cover		15.00
Block of 4	80.00	4.00
P# block of 4	275.00	
Never hinged	425.00	
586 A160 5c **blue,** *Dec. 1924*	18.00	.40
deep blue	18.00	.40
Never hinged	40.00	
On UPU-rate cover		6.00
Block of 4	80.00	3.00
P# block of 4	275.00	
Never hinged	425.00	
Double transfer	—	—
a. Horizontal pair, imperf. vertically		*8,000.*

No. 586a is unique, precanceled, with average centering and small faults, and it is valued as such.

	Unused	Used
587 A161 6c **red orange,** *Mar. 1925*	9.25	.60
pale red orange	9.25	.60
Never hinged	21.00	
On registered cover with other values		15.00
Block of 4	40.00	4.00
P# block of 4	225.00	
Never hinged	325.00	
588 A162 7c **black,** *May 29, 1926*	12.50	6.25
Never hinged	27.50	
On registered cover with other values		30.00
Block of 4	57.50	45.00
P# block of 4	200.00	
Never hinged	300.00	
589 A163 8c **olive green,** *May 29, 1926*	27.50	4.50
pale olive green	27.50	4.50
Never hinged	60.00	
On airmail cover		22.50
Block of 4	125.00	25.00
P# block of 4	300.00	
Never hinged	450.00	
590 A164 9c **rose,** *May 29, 1926*	6.00	2.50
Never hinged	13.50	
On registered cover with other values		22.50
Block of 4	26.00	17.50
P# block of 4	150.00	
Never hinged	225.00	
591 A165 10c **orange,** *June 8, 1925*	55.00	.50
Never hinged	125.00	
On airmail cover		17.50
Block of 4	275.00	3.00
P# block of 4	475.00	
Never hinged	750.00	
Nos. 581-591 (11)	192.00	20.10
Nos. 581-591, never hinged	430.50	

Bureau Precancels: 1c, 64 diff., 1½c, 76 diff., 2c, 58 diff., 3c, 41 diff., 4c, 36 diff., 5c, 38 diff., 6c, 36 diff., 7c, 18 diff., 8c, 18 diff., 9c, 13 diff., 10c, 39 diff.

Issued in sheets of 70 or 100 stamps, coil waste of Nos. 597, 599
Stamp designs approximately 19¾x22¼mm

1923 ***Perf. 11***

	Unused	Used
594 A155 1c **green**	*27,500.*	12,500.
On cover		*20,000.*
Pair		*27,500.*

No. 594 unused is valued without gum; both unused and used are valued with perforations just touching frameline on one side.

Earliest documented use: Mar. 25, 1924.

	Unused	Used
595 A157 2c **carmine**	275.00	*375.00*
deep carmine	275.00	*375.00*
Never hinged	550.00	
On cover		550.00
Block of 4	1,200.	*1,750.*
P# block of 4, star	2,150.	—
Never hinged	3,100.	
Recut in eye, plate 14731	—	

Earliest documented uses: Mar. 31, 1923 (dated cancel on off-cover pair of stamps); June 29, 1923 (on cover).

Rotary press sheet waste
Stamp design approximately 19¼x22½mm

	Unused	Used
596 A155 1c **green,** machine cancel		*130,000.*
With Bureau precancel		*110,000.*

A majority of examples of No. 596 carry the Bureau precancel "Kansas City, Mo."
No. 596 is valued in the grade of fine.

COIL STAMPS
ROTARY PRESS

1923-29 ***Perf. 10 Vertically***
Stamp designs aproximately 19¾x22¼mm

	Unused	Used
597 A155 1c **green,** *July 18, 1923*	.25	.20
yellow green	.25	.20
grayish green	—	—
Never hinged	.50	
Three on cover		2.25
Pair	.55	.25
Never hinged	1.20	
Joint line pair	2.00	.75
Never hinged	4.00	
Gripper cracks	2.60	1.00
Double transfer	2.60	1.00
598 A156 1½c **brown,** *Mar. 19, 1925*	.90	.20
deep brown	.90	.20
Never hinged	1.80	
On 3rd class cover		6.00
Pair	1.90	.25
Never hinged	3.80	
Joint line pair	4.50	.75
Never hinged	9.00	

TYPE I

TYPE II

TYPE I

TYPE II

TYPE I. No heavy hair lines at top center of head. Outline of left acanthus scroll generally faint at top and toward base at left side.

TYPE II. Three heavy hair lines at top center of head; two being outstanding in the white area. Outline of left acanthus scroll very strong and clearly defined at top (under left edge of lettered panel) and at lower curve (above and to left of numeral oval). This type appears only on Nos. 599A and 634A.

	Unused	Used
599 A157 2c **carmine,** type I, *Jan. 1923*	.35	.20
deep carmine, type I	.35	.20
Never hinged	.70	
On cover		1.10
Pair, type I	.75	.20
Never hinged	1.50	
Joint line pair, type I	2.25	.50
Never hinged	4.50	
Double transfer, type I	1.90	1.00
Gripper cracks, type I	2.30	2.00
b. 2c **carmine lake,** type I, never hinged	*750.00*	
Pair, never hinged	*1,500.*	
Joint line pair, never hinged	*3,750.*	

Earliest documented use: Jan. 10, 1923 (precanceled version).

	Unused	Used
599A A157 2c **carmine,** type II, *Mar. 1929*	120.00	17.50
Never hinged	225.00	
On cover		32.50
Pair, type II	240.00	60.00
Never hinged	475.00	
Joint line pair, type II	650.00	350.00
Never hinged	1,300.	
Joint line pair, types I & II	750.00	*1,000.*
Never hinged	1,400.	

Earliest documented use: Mar. 29, 1929.

	Unused	Used
600 A158 3c **violet,** *May 10, 1924*	6.25	.20
deep violet	6.25	.20
Never hinged	12.50	
On cover		6.00
Pair	13.00	.35
Never hinged	25.00	
Joint line pair	22.50	2.50
Never hinged	45.00	
Cracked plate	—	
601 A159 4c **yellow brown,** *Aug. 5, 1923*	3.75	.35
brown	3.75	.35
Never hinged	7.50	
On cover		14.00
Pair	8.25	.95
Never hinged	16.50	
Joint line pair	27.50	6.00
Never hinged	55.00	

Earliest documented use: Sept. 14, 1923.

	Unused	Used
602 A160 5c **dark blue,** *Mar. 5, 1924*	1.50	.20
Never hinged	3.00	
On UPU-rate cover		6.00
Pair	3.25	.35
Never hinged	6.50	
Joint line pair	10.00	1.50
Never hinged	21.00	
603 A165 10c **orange,** *Dec. 1, 1924*	3.50	.20
Never hinged	7.00	
On special delivery cover with 2c		22.50

Pair	8.00	.25
Never hinged	16.00	
Joint line pair	25.00	2.00
Never hinged	50.00	

The 6c design A161 coil stamp is listed as No. 723.
Bureau Precancels: 1c, 296 diff., 1½c, 188 diff., 2c, type I, 113 diff., 2c, type II, Boston, Detroit, 3c, 62 diff., 4c, 34 diff., 5c, 36 diff., 10c, 32 diff.

1923-25 ***Perf. 10 Horizontally***

Stamp designs: 19¼x22½mm

604	A155	1c	**green,** *July 19, 1924*	.30	.20
			yellow green	.30	.20
			Never hinged	.60	
			Three on cover		6.00
			Pair	.70	.20
			Never hinged	1.40	
			Joint line pair	3.50	.55
			Never hinged	7.00	
605	A156	1½c	**yellow brown,** *May 9, 1925*	.30	.20
			brown	.30	.20
			Never hinged	.60	
			On 3rd class cover		17.50
			Pair	.70	.35
			Never hinged	1.40	
			Joint line pair	3.00	.75
			Never hinged	6.00	
606	A157	2c	**carmine,** *Dec. 31, 1923*	.30	.20
			Never hinged	.60	
			On cover		3.50
			Pair	.65	.45
			Never hinged	1.40	
			Joint line pair	2.25	1.00
			Never hinged	4.50	
			Cracked plate	5.25	2.00
a.		2c	**carmine lake**	*150.00*	
			Never hinged	*300.00*	
			Pair, never hinged	*650.00*	
			Joint line pair, never hinged	*1,750.*	
			Nos. 597-599,600-606 (10)	17.40	2.15
			Nos. 597-599, 600-606, never hinged	34.80	

HARDING MEMORIAL ISSUE

Tribute to the memory of President Warren G. Harding, who died in San Francisco, Aug. 2, 1923.

Warren Gamaliel Harding — A177

Plates of 400 subjects in four panes of 100 each

FLAT PLATE PRINTINGS

Stamp designs: 19¼x22¼mm

1923 ***Perf. 11***

610	A177	2c	**black,** *Sept. 1, 1923*	.55	.25
			intense black	.55	.25
			grayish black	.55	.25
			Never hinged	1.10	
			On cover		.30
			P# block of 6	25.00	—
			Never hinged	35.00	
			Double transfer	1.75	.50
a.			Horiz. pair, imperf. vert.	*1,750.*	
b.			Imperf, P#14870 block of 6	*25,000.*	

No. 610b comes from a single upper left error pane found in a normal pad of No. 610 stamps before No. 611 was issued. Plate #14870 was not used to print No. 611. Loose stamps separated from the top and left plate blocks are indistinguishable from No. 611.

Imperf

611	A177	2c	**black,** *Nov. 15, 1923*	4.75	4.00
			Never hinged	10.00	
			On philatelic cover		8.00
			On commercial cover		15.00
			Pair	10.50	10.00
			Never hinged	22.00	
			Corner margin block of 4	22.50	22.50
			Margin block of 4, arrow	23.50	22.50
			Center line block	60.00	40.00
			Never hinged	90.00	
			P# block of 6	75.00	—
			Never hinged	100.00	

ROTARY PRESS PRINTINGS

Stamp designs: 19¼x22½mm

Perf. 10

612	A177	2c	**black,** *Sept. 12, 1923*	15.00	1.75
			gray black	15.00	1.75
			Never hinged	32.50	
			On cover		3.25
			P# block of 4	300.00	
			Never hinged	500.00	
			Pair with full vertical gutter between	*350.00*	

Perf. 11

613	A177	2c	**black**	*45,000.*	
			Pair	*95,000.*	
			Horiz. strip of 3	*175,000.*	

No. 613 was produced from rotary press sheet waste. It is valued in the grade of fine. The strip of three is the largest recorded multiple.

HUGUENOT-WALLOON TERCENTENARY ISSUE

300th anniversary of the settling of the Walloons, and in honor of the Huguenots.

Ship "Nieu Nederland" A178

Walloons Landing at Fort Orange (Albany) — A179

Jan Ribault Monument at Duval County, Fla. — A180

"Broken Circle" flaw

Designed by Clair Aubrey Huston

FLAT PLATE PRINTINGS

Plates of 200 subjects in four panes of 50 each

1924, May 1 ***Perf. 11***

614	A178	1c	**dark green**	2.00	*3.25*
			green	2.00	*3.25*
			Never hinged	4.25	
			On cover		4.50
			P# block of 6	40.00	—
			Never hinged	70.00	
			Double transfer	6.50	6.50
615	A179	2c	**carmine rose**	4.25	2.25
			dark carmine rose	4.25	2.25
			Never hinged	8.75	
			On cover		3.50
			P# block of 6	60.00	—
			Never hinged	90.00	
			Double transfer	12.00	3.50
616	A180	5c	**dark blue**	18.00	13.00
			deep blue	18.00	13.00
			Never hinged	37.50	
			On UPU-rate cover		20.00
			P# block of 6	250.00	—
			Never hinged	375.00	
			Added line at bottom of white circle around right numeral, "broken circle" plate flaw (15754 UR 2, 3, 4, 5)	50.00	15.00
			Nos. 614-616 (3)	24.25	18.50
			Nos. 614-616, never hinged	50.50	

LEXINGTON-CONCORD ISSUE

150th anniv. of the Battle of Lexington-Concord.

Washington at Cambridge A181

"Birth of Liberty," by Henry Sandham A182

The Minute Man, by Daniel Chester French — A183

Plates of 200 subjects in four panes of 50 each

1925, Apr. 4 ***Perf. 11***

617	A181	1c	**deep green**	1.90	2.50
			green	1.90	2.50
			Never hinged	4.00	
			On cover		3.75
			P# block of 6	40.00	—
			Never hinged	65.00	
618	A182	2c	**carmine rose**	3.90	4.00
			pale carmine rose	3.90	4.00
			Never hinged	8.00	
			On cover		5.50
			P# block of 6	60.00	—
			Never hinged	90.00	
619	A183	5c	**dark blue**	17.00	13.00
			blue	17.00	13.00
			Never hinged	35.00	
			On UPU-rate cover		20.00
			P# block of 6	200.00	—
			Never hinged	310.00	
			Line over head (16807 LL 48)	42.50	19.00
			Nos. 617-619 (3)	22.80	19.50
			Nos. 617-619, never hinged	47.00	

NORSE-AMERICAN ISSUE

Arrival in New York, on Oct. 9, 1825, of the sloop "Restaurationen" with the first group of immigrants from Norway.

Sloop "Restaurationen" A184

Viking Ship A185

Designed by Clair Aubrey Huston.

Plates of 100 subjects.

1925, May 18 ***Perf. 11***

620	A184	2c	**carmine & black**	3.50	3.00
			deep carmine & black	3.50	3.00
			Never hinged	7.00	
			On cover		4.50
			Margin block of 4, arrow	17.50	
			Center line block	24.00	
			Never hinged	40.00	
			P# block of 8, two P# & arrow	200.00	—
			Never hinged	300.00	
			P# block of 8, carmine & arrow; black P# omitted	*3,250.*	—
621	A185	5c	**dark blue & black**	11.00	11.00
			Never hinged	24.00	
			On UPU-rate cover		17.50
			Margin block of 4, arrow	62.50	
			Center line block	75.00	
			Never hinged	135.00	
			P# block of 8, two P# & arrow	500.00	—
			Never hinged	750.00	

REGULAR ISSUE

Benjamin Harrison — A186

Woodrow Wilson — A187

Plates of 400 subjects in four panes of 100.

1925-26 *Perf. 11*

622	A186	13c	**green,** *Jan. 11, 1926*	11.00	.75
			light green	11.00	.75
			Never hinged	22.50	
			On registered cover with other values		17.50
			P# block of 6	215.00	—
			Never hinged	325.00	
			P# block of 6, large 5 point star, right side only	*2,100.*	—
			Never hinged	*3,000.*	
623	A187	17c	**black,** *Dec. 28, 1925*	12.00	.30
			gray black	12.00	.30
			Never hinged	25.00	
			On registered cover		6.00
			P# block of 6	250.00	—
			Never hinged	350.00	

Plate Blocks

Scott values for plate blocks printed from flat plates are for very fine side and bottom positions. Top position plate blocks with full wide selvage sell for more.

SESQUICENTENNIAL EXPOSITION ISSUE

Sesquicentennial Exposition, Philadelphia, Pa., June 1 - Dec. 1, 1926, and 150th anniv. of the Declaration of Independence.

Liberty Bell — A188

Designed by Clair Aubrey Huston.

Plates of 200 subjects in four panes of 50.

1926, May 10 *Perf. 11*

627	A188	2c	**carmine rose**	2.50	.50
			Never hinged	4.50	
			On cover		1.00
			On cover, Expo. station machine canc.		7.50
			On cover, Expo. station duplex handstamp canc.		35.00
			P# block of 6	37.50	—
			Never hinged	50.00	
			Double transfer	—	—

ERICSSON MEMORIAL ISSUE

Unveiling of the statue of John Ericsson, builder of the "Monitor," by the Crown Prince of Sweden, Washington, D.C., May 29, 1926.

Statue of John Ericsson — A189

Designed by Clair Aubrey Huston.

Plates of 200 subjects in four panes of 50.

1926, May 29 *Perf. 11*

628	A189	5c	**gray lilac**	5.50	3.25
			Never hinged	9.50	
			On UPU-rate cover		8.00
			P# block of 6	60.00	—
			Never hinged	95.00	

BATTLE OF WHITE PLAINS ISSUE

150th anniv. of the Battle of White Plains, N. Y.

Alexander Hamilton's Battery — A190

Designed by Clair Aubrey Huston.

Plates of 400 subjects in four panes of 100.

1926, Oct. 18 *Perf. 11*

629	A190	2c	**carmine rose**	1.90	1.70
			Never hinged	3.25	
			On cover		2.25
			P# block of 6	37.50	—
			Never hinged	60.00	

INTERNATIONAL PHILATELIC EXHIBITION ISSUE

Souvenir Sheet

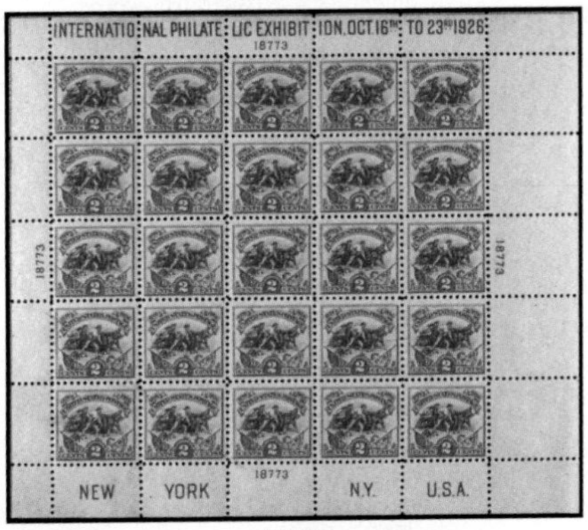

A190a

Illustration reduced.

Plates of 100 subjects in four panes of 25 each, separated by one inch wide gutters with central guide lines.

Condition valued:

Centering: Overall centering will average very fine, but individual stamps may be better or worse.

Perforations: No folds along rows of perforations.

Gum: There may be some light gum bends but no gum creases.

Hinging: There may be hinge marks in the selvage and on up to two or three stamps, but no heavy hinging or hinge remnants (except in the ungummed portion of the wide selvage.

Margins: Top panes should have about ½ inch bottom margin and 1 inch top margin.

Bottom panes should have about ½ inch top margin and just under ¾ inch bottom margin. Both will have one wide side (usually 1 inch plus) and one narrow (½ inch) side margin. The wide margin corner will have a small diagonal notch on top panes.

1926, Oct. 18 *Perf. 11*

630	A190a	2c	**carmine rose,** sheet of 25	375.00	450.00
			Never hinged	600.00	
			On cover		—
			Dot over first "S" of "States" 18774 LL 9 or 18773 LL 11, sheet	400.00	475.00

Issued in sheets measuring 158-160¼x136-146½mm containing 25 stamps with inscription "International Philatelic Exhibition, Oct. 16th to 23rd, 1926" in top margin.

VALUES FOR VERY FINE STAMPS

Please note: Stamps are valued in the grade of Very Fine unless otherwise indicated.

REGULAR ISSUE

ROTARY PRESS PRINTINGS

(See note over No. 448.)

Plates of 400 subjects in four panes of 100 each

Stamp designs 19¼x22½mm

1926, Aug. 27 *Imperf.*

631	A156	1½c	**yellow brown**	1.80	1.70
			light brown	1.80	1.70
			Never hinged	2.75	
			On philatelic cover		12.50
			Pair	4.00	4.00
			Never hinged	5.75	
			Pair, vert. gutter between	4.50	5.00
			Pair, horiz. gutter between	4.50	5.00
			Margin block with dash (left, right, top or bottom)	10.00	*14.00*
			Center block with crossed gutters and dashes	25.00	*27.50*
			Never hinged	37.50	
			P# block of 4	57.50	—
			Never hinged	85.00	
			Without gum breaker ridges	50.00	
			Pair, vert. gutter between	*125.00*	
			Pair, horiz. gutter btwn.	*125.00*	
			Margin block with dash (left, right, top or bottom)	*350.00*	
			Center block with crossed gutters and dashes	*700.00*	
			Never hinged	*1,050.*	
			P# block of 4	450.00	
			Never hinged	700.00	

1926-34 *Perf. 11x10½*

632	A155	1c	**green,** *June 10, 1927*	.20	.20
			yellow green	.20	.20
			Never hinged	.20	
			Three on cover		1.25
			P# block of 4	2.00	—
			Never hinged	3.25	

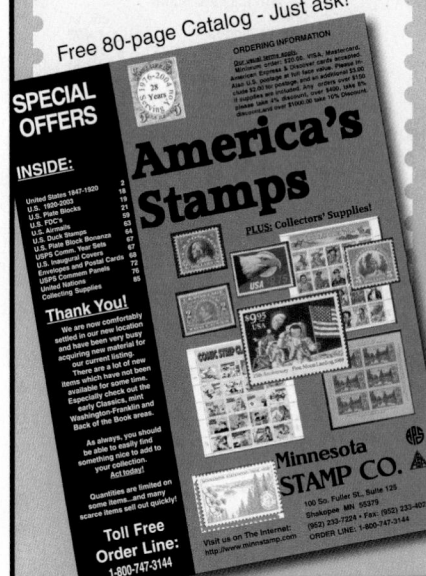

Pair with full vertical gutter btwn. 150.00 —
Cracked plate — —
a. Booklet pane of 6, *Nov. 2, 1927* 5.00 *4.00*
Never hinged 8.00
b. Vertical pair, imperf. between *4,500.* —
Never hinged *7,000.*
c. Horiz. pair, imperf. between *5,000.*

No. 632c is valued in the grade of fine and never hinged. It is possibly unique.

633 A156 1½c **yellow brown,** *May 17, 1927* 1.70 .20
deep brown 1.70 .20
Never hinged 2.60
On 3rd class cover 2.50
P# block of 4 70.00 —
Never hinged 120.00

Normal

Recut ("long ear")

634 A157 2c **carmine,** type I, *Dec. 10, 1926* .20 .20
Never hinged .20
On cover .20
P# block of 4, type I, # opposite corner stamp 3.75 —
Never hinged 6.50
Vertical P# block of 10, # opposite 3rd horizontal row from top or bottom (Experimental Electric Eye plates) 5.00 —
Never hinged 8.50
Margin block of 4, Electric Eye marking .45 .25
Pair with full vertical gutter between 200.00
Recut ("long ear"), type I, 20342 UR 34 *400.00* —
Recut face, type I, 20234 LL 58 —
b. 2c **carmine lake**, type I *225.00* —
Never hinged *425.00*
P# block of 4 *1,500.*
Never hinged 2,750.
c. Horizontal pair, type I, imperf. between *7,000.*
d. Booklet pane of 6, type I, *Feb. 25, 1927* 1.50 *1.50*
Never hinged 2.50
e. As "d," carmine lake *2,000.*
Never hinged *4,000.*

Shades of the carmine exist.
No. 634, Type I, exists on a thin, tough experimental paper.
No. 634c is valued in the grade of fine.

Earliest documented use: FDC (No. 634); Dec. 20, 1929 (No. 634b).

634A A157 2c **carmine,** type II, *Dec. 1928* 325.00 13.50
Never hinged 650.00
On cover 21.00
P# block of 4, type II 2,200. —
Never hinged 3,000.
Pair with full horiz. gutter btwn. 850.00 —
Never hinged *1,400.*
Pair with full vert. gutter btwn. 850.00 —
Never hinged *1,400.*
Center block with crossed gutters 2,750.
Never hinged *4,250.*

Earliest documented use: Dec. 15, 1928.

No. 634A, Type II, was available in full sheet of 400 subjects but was not regularly issued in that form.

635 A158 3c **violet,** *Feb. 3, 1927* .40 .20
Never hinged .60
On cover 2.00
P# block of 4 17.50 —
Never hinged 35.00
a. 3c **bright violet,** *Feb. 7, 1934* re-issue, Plates 21185 & 21186 .20 .20
Never hinged .30
On cover .25
P# block of 4 11.00 —
Never hinged 20.00
Gripper cracks 3.25 2.00

636 A159 4c **yellow brown,** *May 17, 1927* 1.90 .20
Never hinged 3.00
On cover 8.00
P# block of 4 75.00 —
Never hinged 120.00
Pair with full vert. gutter btwn. *200.00*

637 A160 5c **dark blue,** *Mar. 24, 1927* 1.90 .20
Never hinged 3.00
On UPU-rate cover 4.50
P# block of 4 15.00 —
Never hinged 22.50
Pair with full vert. gutter btwn. *275.00*
Double transfer — —

638 A161 6c **red orange,** *July 27, 1927* 1.90 .20
Never hinged 3.00
On airmail cover 6.00
P# block of 4 15.00 —
Never hinged 22.50
Pair with full horiz. gutter btwn. —
Pair with full vert. gutter btwn. *200.00*

639 A162 7c **black,** *Mar. 24, 1927* 1.90 .20
Never hinged 3.00
On registered cover with other values 15.00
P# block of 4 15.00 —
Never hinged 22.50
a. Vertical pair, imperf. between *325.00 250.00*
Never hinged *500.00*

640 A163 8c **olive green,** *June 10, 1927* 1.90 .20
olive bister 1.90 .20
Never hinged 3.00
On airmail cover 8.00
P# block of 4 15.00 —
Never hinged 22.50

641 A164 9c **rose,** *May 17, 1927* 1.90 .20
salmon rose 1.90 .20
orange red, *1931* 1.90 .20
Never hinged 3.00
On registered cover with other values 8.00
P# block of 4 15.00 —
Never hinged 22.50
Pair with full vert. gutter btwn. —

642 A165 10c **orange,** *Feb. 3, 1927* 3.10 .20
Never hinged 5.00
On special delivery cover with 2c 6.00
P# block of 4 20.00 —
Never hinged 30.00
Double transfer — —
Nos. 632-634,635-642 (11) 17.00 2.20
Nos. 632-634, 635-642 never hinged 26.60

The 1½c, 2c, 4c, 5c, 6c, 8c imperf. (dry print) are printer's waste.

See No. 653.

Bureau Precancels: 1c, 292 diff., 1½c, 147 diff., 2c, type I, 99 diff., 2c, type II, 4 diff., 3c, 101 diff., 4c, 60 diff., 5c, 91 diff., 6c, 78 diff., 7c, 66 diff., 8c, 78 diff., 9c, 60 diff., 10c, 97 diff.

VERMONT SESQUICENTENNIAL ISSUE

Battle of Bennington, 150th anniv. and State independence.

Green Mountain Boy — A191

FLAT PLATE PRINTING

Plates of 400 subjects in four panes of 100.

1927, Aug. 3 *Perf. 11*
643 A191 2c **carmine rose** 1.20 .80
Never hinged 2.00
On cover 1.50
P# block of 6 35.00 —
Never hinged 55.00

BURGOYNE CAMPAIGN ISSUE

Battles of Bennington, Oriskany, Fort Stanwix and Saratoga.

"The Surrender of General Burgoyne at Saratoga," by John Trumbull A192

Plates of 200 subjects in four panes of 50.

1927, Aug. 3 *Perf. 11*
644 A192 2c **carmine rose** 3.10 2.10
Never hinged 5.50
On cover 3.00
P# block of 6 32.50 —
Never hinged 45.00

VALLEY FORGE ISSUE

150th anniversary of Washington's encampment at Valley Forge, Pa.

Washington at Prayer — A193

Plates of 400 subjects in four panes of 100.

1928, May 26 *Perf. 11*
645 A193 2c **carmine rose** .95 .50
Never hinged 1.50
On cover .75
P# block of 6 25.00 —
Never hinged 40.00
a. 2c **lake** —
Never hinged —

BATTLE OF MONMOUTH ISSUE

150th anniv. of the Battle of Monmouth, N.J., and "Molly Pitcher" (Mary Ludwig Hayes), the heroine of the battle.

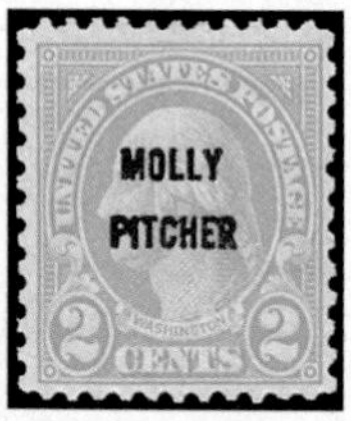

No. 634 Overprinted

ROTARY PRESS PRINTING

1928, Oct. 20 *Perf. 11x10½*
646 A157 2c **carmine** 1.00 1.00
Never hinged 1.60
On cover 1.60
P# block of 4 37.50 —
Never hinged 55.00
Wide spacing, vert. pair 50.00 —
a. "Pitcher" only *500.00*

No. 646a is valued in the grade of fine.
Normally the overprints were placed 18mm apart vertically, but pairs exist with a space of 28mm between the overprints.

HAWAII SESQUICENTENNIAL ISSUE

Sesquicentennial Celebration of the discovery of the Hawaiian Islands.

Nos. 634 and 637 Overprinted

ROTARY PRESS PRINTING

1928, Aug. 13 *Perf. 11x10½*
647 A157 2c **carmine** 4.00 4.00
Never hinged 7.25
On cover 5.75
P# block of 4 125.00 —
Never hinged 225.00
Wide spacing, vert. pair 125.00
648 A160 5c **dark blue** 11.00 12.50
Never hinged 21.50
On cover 20.00
P# block of 4 275.00 —
Never hinged 425.00

Nos. 647-648 were sold at post offices in Hawaii and at the Postal Agency in Washington, D.C. They were valid throughout the nation.
Normally the overprints were placed 18mm apart vertically, but pairs exist with a space of 28mm between the overprints.

AERONAUTICS CONFERENCE ISSUE

Intl. Civil Aeronautics Conf., Washington, D.C., Dec. 12 - 14, 1928, and 25th anniv. of the 1st airplane flight by the Wright Brothers, Dec. 17, 1903.

Wright Airplane A194

Globe and Airplane A195

"Prairie Dog" plate flaw

FLAT PLATE PRINTING

Plates of 200 subjects in four panes of 50.

1928, Dec. 12 *Perf. 11*

No.	Type	Denom.	Description	Unused	Used
649	A194	2c	**carmine rose**	1.10	.80
			Never hinged	1.75	
			On cover		1.50
			P# block of 6	12.00	—
			Never hinged	20.00	
650	A195	5c	**blue**	4.50	3.25
			Never hinged	7.25	
			On UPU-rate cover		5.00
			P# block of 6	45.00	—
			Never hinged	70.00	
			Plate flaw "prairie dog" (19658 LL 50)	27.50	12.50

GEORGE ROGERS CLARK ISSUE

150th anniv. of the surrender of Fort Sackville, the present site of Vincennes, Ind., to Clark.

Surrender of Fort Sackville A196

Plates of 100 subjects in two panes of 50.

1929, Feb. 25 *Perf. 11*

No.	Type	Denom.	Description	Unused	Used
651	A196	2c	**carmine & black**	.70	.50
			deep carmine & black	.70	.50
			Never hinged	1.10	
			On cover		1.00
			Margin block of 4, arrow (line only) right or left	3.25	
			P# block of 6, two P# & "Top"	12.00	—
			Never hinged	20.00	
			P# block of 10, red P# only	—	—
			Double transfer (19721 R 14, 29 & 44)	4.25	2.25

REGULAR ISSUE

Type of 1922-26 Issue

ROTARY PRESS PRINTING

Plates of 400 subjects in four panes of 100.

1929, May 25 *Perf. 11x10½*

No.	Type	Denom.	Description	Unused	Used
653	A154	½c	**olive brown**	.20	.20
			Never hinged	.25	
			On 1c stamped envelope (3rd class)		1.00
			P# block of 4	2.00	—
			Never hinged	3.00	
			Damaged plate, (19652 LL 72)	1.50	.75
			Retouched plate, (19652 LL 72)	1.50	.75
			Pair with full horiz. gutter btwn.	*150.00*	

Bureau Precancels: 99 diff.

Edison's First Lamp — A197

Major General John Sullivan — A198

ELECTRIC LIGHT'S GOLDEN JUBILEE ISSUE

Invention of the 1st incandescent electric lamp by Thomas Alva Edison, Oct. 21, 1879, 50th anniv.

Designed by Alvin R. Meissner.

FLAT PLATE PRINTING

Plates of 400 subjects in four panes of 100.

1929 *Perf. 11*

No.	Type	Denom.	Description	Unused	Used
654	A197	2c	**carmine rose,** *June 5*	.60	.65
			Never hinged	1.00	
			On cover		1.10
			P# block of 6	25.00	—
			Never hinged	45.00	

ROTARY PRESS PRINTING

Perf. 11x10½

No.	Type	Denom.	Description	Unused	Used
655	A197	2c	**carmine rose,** *June 11*	.55	.20
			Never hinged	.90	
			On cover		.25
			P# block of 4	35.00	—
			Never hinged	55.00	

ROTARY PRESS COIL STAMP

Perf. 10 Vertically

No.	Type	Denom.	Description	Unused	Used
656	A197	2c	**carmine rose,** *June 11*	11.00	1.75
			Never hinged	21.00	
			On cover		2.75
			Pair	25.00	4.00
			Never hinged	45.00	
			Joint line pair	60.00	27.50
			Never hinged	110.00	

SULLIVAN EXPEDITION ISSUE

150th anniversary of the Sullivan Expedition in New York State during the Revolutionary War.

PLAT PLATE PRINTING

Plates of 400 subjects in four panes of 100.

1929, June 17 *Perf. 11*

No.	Type	Denom.	Description	Unused	Used
657	A198	2c	**carmine rose**	.60	.60
			Never hinged	1.00	
			On cover		1.00
			P# block of 6	22.50	—
			Never hinged	37.50	
a.		2c	**lake**	325.00	300.00
			Never hinged	575.00	
			P# block of 6	*2,750.*	
			Never hinged	*3,750.*	

REGULAR ISSUE

Nos. 632 to 642 Overprinted

Officially issued May 1, 1929.

Some values known canceled as early as Apr. 15.

This special issue was authorized as a measure of preventing losses from post office burglaries. Approximately a year's supply was printed and issued to postmasters. The P.O. Dept. found it desirable to discontinue the State overprinted stamps after the initial supply was used.

ROTARY PRESS PRINTING

1929, May 1 *Perf. 11x10½*

No.	Type	Denom.	Description	Unused	Used
658	A155	1c	**green**	2.00	2.00
			Never hinged	4.00	
			P# block of 4	50.00	—
			Never hinged	75.00	
			Wide spacing, pair	32.50	
a.			Vertical pair, one without ovpt.	*375.00*	
659	A156	1½c	**brown**	3.10	2.90
			Never hinged	6.25	
			P# block of 4	60.00	—
			Never hinged	85.00	
			Wide spacing, pair	70.00	
a.			Vertical pair, one without ovpt.	*425.00*	
660	A157	2c	**carmine**	3.75	1.00
			Never hinged	7.00	
			P# block of 4	60.00	—
			Never hinged	85.00	
			Wide spacing, pair	55.00	
661	A158	3c	**violet**	18.50	15.00
			Never hinged	37.50	
			P# block of 4	225.00	—
			Never hinged	325.00	
a.			Vertical pair, one without ovpt.	*525.00*	
			Never hinged	*675.00*	
662	A159	4c	**yellow brown**	18.50	9.00
			Never hinged	37.50	
			P# block of 4	225.00	—
			Never hinged	325.00	
a.			Vertical pair, one without ovpt.	*500.00*	
663	A160	5c	**deep blue**	12.00	9.75
			Never hinged	24.00	
			P# block of 4	200.00	—
			Never hinged	300.00	
664	A161	6c	**red orange**	27.50	18.00
			Never hinged	55.00	
			P# block of 4	450.00	—
			Never hinged	650.00	
665	A162	7c	**black**	27.50	27.50
			Never hinged	55.00	
			P# block of 4	500.00	—
			Never hinged	725.00	
666	A163	8c	**olive green**	90.00	70.00
			Never hinged	180.00	
			P# block of 4	700.00	—
			Never hinged	1,000.	
667	A164	9c	**light rose**	13.00	11.50
			Never hinged	26.00	
			P# block of 4	275.00	—
			Never hinged	400.00	
668	A165	10c	**orange yellow**	22.50	12.50
			Never hinged	45.00	
			P# block of 4	375.00	—
			Never hinged	575.00	
			Pair with full horizontal gutter between	*4,750.*	
			Nos. 658-668 (11)	238.35	179.15
			Nos. 658-668, never hinged	477.25	

See notes following No. 679.

Overprinted

1929, May 1

No.	Type	Denom.	Description	Unused	Used
669	A155	1c	**green**	3.10	2.25
			Never hinged	6.25	
			P# block of 4	60.00	—
			Never hinged	90.00	
			Wide spacing, pair	40.00	—
b.			No period after "Nebr." (19338, 19339 UR 26, 36)	50.00	
670	A156	1½c	**brown**	2.90	2.50
			Never hinged	5.75	
			P# block of 4	65.00	—
			Never hinged	95.00	
			Wide spacing, pair	37.50	
671	A157	2c	**carmine**	2.90	1.30
			Never hinged	5.75	
			P# block of 4	50.00	—
			Never hinged	75.00	
			Wide spacing, pair	57.50	
672	A158	3c	**violet**	12.00	12.00
			Never hinged	24.00	
			P# block of 4	200.00	—
			Never hinged	300.00	
			Wide spacing, pair	80.00	
a.			Vertical pair, one without ovpt.	*500.00*	
673	A159	4c	**yellow brown**	17.50	15.00
			Never hinged	35.00	
			P# block of 4	275.00	—
			Never hinged	400.00	

			Wide spacing, pair	120.00	
674	A160	5c	**deep blue**	16.00	15.00
			Never hinged	32.50	
			P# block of 4	300.00	—
			Never hinged	425.00	
675	A161	6c	**red orange**	37.50	24.00
			Never hinged	75.00	
			P# block of 4	525.00	—
			Never hinged	750.00	
676	A162	7c	**black**	21.00	18.00
			Never hinged	42.50	
			P# block of 4	325.00	—
			Never hinged	525.00	
677	A163	8c	**olive green**	32.50	25.00
			Never hinged	65.00	
			P# block of 4	400.00	—
			Never hinged	600.00	
			Wide spacing, pair	175.00	
678	A164	9c	**light rose**	35.00	27.50
			Never hinged	70.00	
			P# block of 4	525.00	—
			Never hinged	750.00	
			Wide spacing, pair	160.00	
a.			Vertical pair, one without ovpt.	*750.00*	
679	A165	10c	**orange yellow**	115.00	22.50
			Never hinged	230.00	
			P# block of 4	925.	—
			Never hinged	1,300.	
			Nos. 669-679 (11)	295.40	165.05
			Nos. 669-679, never hinged	591.75	

Nos. 658-661, 669-673, 677-678 are known with the overprints on vertical pairs spaced 32mm apart instead of the normal 22mm.

Important: Nos. 658-679 with original gum have either one horizontal gum breaker ridge per stamp or portions of two at the extreme top and bottom of the stamps, 21mm apart. Multiple complete gum breaker ridges indicate a fake overprint. Absence of the gum breaker ridge indicates either regumming or regumming and a fake overprint.

General Wayne Memorial — A199

Lock No. 5, Monongahela River — A200

BATTLE OF FALLEN TIMBERS ISSUE

Memorial to Gen. Anthony Wayne and for 135th anniv. of the Battle of Fallen Timbers, Ohio.

FLAT PLATE PRINTING

Plates of 400 subjects in four panes of 100.

1929, Sept. 14 — ***Perf. 11***

680	A199	2c	**carmine rose**	.70	.70
			deep carmine rose	.70	.70
			Never hinged	1.10	
			On cover		1.10
			P# block of 6	20.00	—
			Never hinged	32.50	

OHIO RIVER CANALIZATION ISSUE

Completion of the Ohio River Canalization Project, between Cairo, Ill. and Pittsburgh, Pa.

Plates of 400 subjects in four panes of 100.

1929, Oct. 19 — ***Perf. 11***

681	A200	2c	**carmine rose**	.60	.60
			Never hinged	.95	
			On cover		1.10
			P# block of 6	14.00	—
			Never hinged	25.00	
a.		2c	**lake**		—

Massachusetts Bay Colony Seal — A201

Gov. Joseph West and Chief Shadoo, a Kiowa — A202

MASSACHUSETTS BAY COLONY ISSUE

300th anniversary of the founding of the Massachusetts Bay Colony.

Plates of 400 subjects in four panes of 100.

1930, Apr. 8 — ***Perf. 11***

682	A201	2c	**carmine rose**	.50	.50
			Never hinged	.85	
			On cover		1.00
			P# block of 6	22.50	—
			Never hinged	35.00	

CAROLINA-CHARLESTON ISSUE

260th anniv. of the founding of the Province of Carolina and the 250th anniv. of the city of Charleston, S.C.

Plates of 400 subjects in four panes of 100.

1930, Apr. 10 — ***Perf. 11***

683	A202	2c	**carmine rose**	1.05	1.05
			Never hinged	1.65	
			On cover		1.40
			P# block of 6	40.00	—
			Never hinged	57.50	

REGULAR ISSUE

Harding — A203

Taft — A204

Type of 1922-26 Issue

ROTARY PRESS PRINTING

1930 — ***Perf. 11x10½***

684	A203	1½c	**brown,** *Dec.1*	.35	.20
			yellow brown	.35	.20
			Never hinged	.50	
			On 3rd class cover		2.00
			P# block of 4	2.00	—
			Never hinged	3.00	
			Pair with full horiz. gutter btwn.	*175.00*	
			Pair with full vert. gutter btwn.	—	
685	A204	4c	**brown,** *June 4*	.80	.25
			deep brown	.80	.25
			Never hinged	1.25	
			On cover		5.00
			P# block of 4	15.00	—
			Never hinged	25.00	
			Gouge on right "4" (20141 UL 24)	2.10	.60
			Recut right "4" (20141 UL 24)	2.10	.65
			Pair with full horiz. gutter btwn.	—	

Bureau Precancels: 1½c, 96 diff., 4c, 46 diff.

ROTARY PRESS COIL STAMPS

Perf. 10 Vertically

686	A203	1½c	**brown,** *Dec. 1*	1.65	.20
			Never hinged	2.50	
			On 3rd class cover		5.00
			Pair	3.50	.20
			Never hinged	5.25	
			Joint line pair	7.00	.75
			Never hinged	10.50	
687	A204	4c	**brown,** *Sept. 18*	3.00	.45
			Never hinged	4.50	
			On cover		10.00
			Pair	6.25	1.00
			Never hinged	9.50	
			Joint line pair	11.00	2.50
			Never hinged	22.00	

Bureau Precancels: 1½c, 107 diff., 4c, 23 diff.

Statue of George Washington — A205

General von Steuben — A206

BRADDOCK'S FIELD ISSUE

175th anniversary of the Battle of Braddock's Field, otherwise the Battle of Monongahela.

Designed by Alvin R. Meissner.

FLAT PLATE PRINTING

Plates of 400 subjects in four panes of 100.

1930, July 9 — ***Perf. 11***

688	A205	2c	**carmine rose**	.90	.85
			Never hinged	1.40	
			On cover		1.00
			P# block of 6	32.50	—
			Never hinged	45.00	

VON STEUBEN ISSUE

Baron Friedrich Wilhelm von Steuben (1730-1794), participant in the American Revolution.

FLAT PLATE PRINTING

Plates of 400 subjects in four panes of 100.

1930, Sept. 17 — ***Perf. 11***

689	A206	2c	**carmine rose**	.50	.50
			Never hinged	.75	
			On cover		1.05
			P# block of 6	17.50	—
			Never hinged	30.00	
a.			Imperf., pair	*2,750.*	
			Never hinged	*3,500.*	
			P# block of 6	*12,500.*	

The No. 689a plate block is unique but damaged. The value is for the item in its damaged condition.

General Casimir Pulaski — A207

"The Greatest Mother" — A208

PULASKI ISSUE

150th anniversary (in 1929) of the death of Gen. Casimir Pulaski, Polish patriot and hero of the American Revolutionary War.

Plates of 400 subjects in four panes of 100.

1931, Jan. 16 — ***Perf. 11***

690	A207	2c	**carmine rose**	.30	.25
			deep carmine rose	.30	.25
			Never hinged	.40	
			On cover		.50
			P# block of 6	10.00	—
			Never hinged	17.50	

REGULAR ISSUE

TYPE OF 1922-26 ISSUES

ROTARY PRESS PRINTING

1931 — ***Perf. 11x10½***

692	A166	11c	**light blue,** *Sept. 4*	2.50	.25
			Never hinged	3.75	
			On registered cover with other values		10.00
			P# block of 4	15.00	—
			Never hinged	27.50	
			Retouched forehead (20617 LL 2, 3)	20.00	1.00
693	A167	12c	**brown violet,** *Aug. 25*	5.00	.20
			violet brown	5.00	.20
			Never hinged	8.00	
			Pair on registered cover		8.00
			P# block of 4	22.50	—
			Never hinged	40.00	
694	A186	13c	**yellow green,** *Sept. 4*	1.90	.25
			light yellow green	1.90	.25
			blue green	1.90	.25
			Never hinged	3.00	
			On special delivery cover		27.50
			P# block of 4	15.00	
			Never hinged	27.50	
			Pair with full vert. gutter btwn.	150.00	
695	A168	14c	**dark blue,** *Sept. 8*	3.50	.60
			Never hinged	5.50	
			On registered cover with other values		20.00
			P# block of 4	26.00	—
			Never hinged	40.00	
696	A169	15c	**gray,** *Aug. 27*	7.75	.25
			dark gray	8.00	.25
			Never hinged	12.00	
			On registered cover with 3c		5.00
			P# block of 4	37.50	—
			Never hinged	52.50	

Perf. 10½x11

697	A187	17c	**black,** *July 25*	4.25	.25
			Never hinged	6.50	
			On registered cover		5.00
			P# block of 4	37.50	—
			Never hinged	52.50	
698	A170	20c	**carmine rose,** *Sept. 8*	7.75	.25
			Never hinged	12.50	
			On registered UPU-rate cover		12.50
			P# block of 4	37.50	—
			Never hinged	60.00	
			Double transfer (20538 LR 26)	20.00	—
699	A171	25c	**blue green,** *July 25*	8.00	.25
			Never hinged	13.00	
			On Federal airmail cover		20.00
			P# block of 4	42.50	—
			Never hinged	75.00	
700	A172	30c	**brown,** *Sept. 8*	13.00	.25
			Never hinged	22.50	
			On Federal airmail cover		17.50
			P# block of 4	72.50	—
			Never hinged	110.00	
			Retouched in head (20552 UL 83)	27.50	.85
			Cracked plate (20552 UR 30)	26.00	.85

701 A173 50c **lilac,** *Sept. 4*	30.00	.25
red lilac	30.00	.25
Never hinged	52.50	
On Federal airmail cover		25.00
P# block of 4	175.00	—
Never hinged	250.00	
Nos. 692-701 (10)	83.65	2.80
Nos. 692-701, never hinged	138.50	

Bureau Precancels: 11c, 33 diff., 12c, 33 diff., 13c, 28 diff., 14c, 27 diff., 15c, 33 diff., 17c, 29 diff., 20c, 37 diff., 25c, 29 diff., 30c, 31 diff., 50c, 28 diff.

RED CROSS ISSUE

50th anniversary of the founding of the American Red Cross Society.

FLAT PLATE PRINTING

Plates of 200 subjects in two panes of 100.

1931, May 21 ***Perf. 11***

702 A208 2c **black & red**	.20	.20
Never hinged	.30	
Margin block of 4, arrow right or left	1.05	
P# block of 4, two P#	2.25	—
Never hinged	3.00	
Double transfer	1.50	.50
a. Red cross missing (FO)	*40,000.*	

The cross tends to shift, appearing in many slightly varied positions.

One example of No. 702a is documented; believed to be unique. Value reflects most recent sale price at auction in 1994.

YORKTOWN ISSUE

Surrender of Cornwallis at Yorktown, 1781.

Rochambeau, Washington, de Grasse A209

First Plate Layout — Border and vignette plates of 100 subjects in two panes of 50 subjects each. Plate numbers between 20461 and 20602.

Second Plate Layout — Border plates of 100 subjects in two panes of 50 each, separated by a 1 inch wide vertical gutter with central guide line and vignette plates of 50 subjects. Plate numbers between 20646 and 20671.

Issued in panes of 50 subjects.

1931, Oct. 19 ***Perf. 11***

703 A209 2c **carmine rose & black**	.35	.25
Never hinged	.50	
Margin block of 4, arrow marker, right or left	1.70	
Center line block	1.80	
P# block of 4, 2#	3.00	—
Never hinged	4.00	
P# block of 4, 2# & arrow & marker block	3.00	—
Never hinged	4.00	
P# block of 6, 2# & "TOP," arrow & marker	3.50	—
Never hinged	4.50	
P# block of 8, 2# & "TOP"	3.75	—
Never hinged	5.00	
Double transfer	1.75	.75
a. 2c **lake & black**	4.50	.75
Never hinged	6.25	
b. 2c **dark lake & black**	*400.00*	
Never hinged	*750.00*	
P# block of 4, 2#	*2,250.*	
Never hinged	*3,000.*	
c. Horiz. pair, imperf. vertically	*5,000.*	
Never hinged	*6,250.*	
Center line block of 10	*17,000.*	
P# block of 10, top, 2#, arrow, marker and "TOP," block	*28,500.*	
P# block of 10, bottom, 2#, arrow and marker	*23,000.*	

WASHINGTON BICENTENNIAL ISSUE

200th anniversary of the birth of George Washington. Various Portraits of George Washington.

By Charles Willson Peale, 1777 — A210

From Houdon Bust, 1785 — A211

By Charles Willson Peale, 1772 — A212

By Gilbert Stuart, 1796 — A213

By Charles Willson Peale, 1777 — A214

By Charles Peale Polk — A215

By Charles Willson Peale, 1795 — A216

By John Trumbull, 1792 — A217

By John Trumbull, 1780 — A218

By Charles B. J. F. Saint Memin, 1798 — A219

By W. Williams, 1794 — A220

By Gilbert Stuart, 1795 — A221

Broken Circle

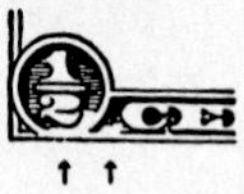

ROTARY PRESS PRINTINGS

Plates of 400 subjects in four panes of 100 each

1932, Jan. 1 ***Perf. 11x10½***

704 A210 ½c **olive brown**	.20	.20
Never hinged	.20	
P# block of 4	6.50	—
Never hinged	10.00	
Broken circle (20560 U.R. 8)	.75	.20
705 A211 1c **green**	.20	.20
Never hinged	.30	
P# block of 4	4.00	—
Never hinged	6.00	
Gripper cracks (20742 UL and UR)	2.75	1.75
706 A212 1½c **brown**	.45	.20
Never hinged	.60	
P# block of 4	15.00	—
Never hinged	30.00	
707 A213 2c **carmine rose**	.20	.20
Never hinged	.30	
P# block of 4	1.25	—
Never hinged	2.25	
Pair with full vert. gutter between	—	
Gripper cracks (20752 LR, 20755 LL & LR, 20756 LL, 20774 LR, 20792 LL & LR, 20796 LL & LR)	1.75	.65

Double Transfer

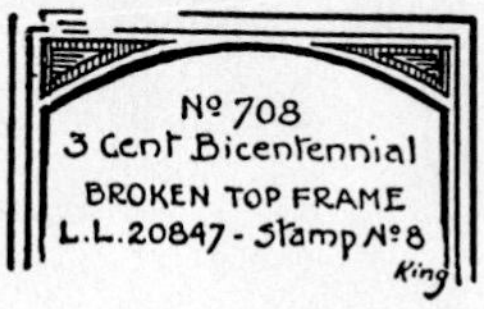

708 A214 3c **deep violet**	.55	.20
Never hinged	.80	
P# block of 4	17.50	—
Never hinged	25.00	
Double transfer	1.75	.65
Broken top frame line (20847 LL 8)	4.00	.90

Retouch in Eyes — 4c

Cracked Plate — 5c

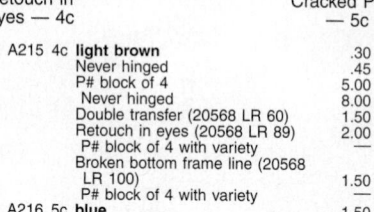

709 A215 4c **light brown**	.30	.20
Never hinged	.45	
P# block of 4	5.00	—
Never hinged	8.00	
Double transfer (20568 LR 60)	1.50	.25
Retouch in eyes (20568 LR 89)	2.00	.35
P# block of 4 with variety	—	
Broken bottom frame line (20568 LR 100)	1.50	.50
P# block of 4 with variety	—	
710 A216 5c **blue**	1.50	.20
Never hinged	2.25	
P# block of 4	15.00	—
Never hinged	25.00	
Cracked plate (20637 UR 80)	5.25	1.10
711 A217 6c **red orange**	3.00	.20
Never hinged	4.50	
P# block of 4	52.50	—
Never hinged	72.50	

Double Transfer

712 A218 7c **black**	.40	.20
Never hinged	.60	
P# block of 4	9.00	—
Never hinged	14.00	
Double transfer (20563 UL 1 or 20564 LL 91)	1.25	.25
P# block of 4 with variety	—	
713 A219 8c **olive bister**	2.75	.50
Never hinged	4.00	
P# block of 4	50.00	—
Never hinged	70.00	
Pair with full vert. gutter between	—	
714 A220 9c **pale red**	2.25	.20
orange red	2.25	.20
Never hinged	3.25	
P# block of 4	35.00	—
Never hinged	50.00	
715 A221 10c **orange yellow**	10.00	.20
Never hinged	15.00	
P# block of 4	90.00	—
Never hinged	130.00	
Nos. 704-715 (12)	21.80	2.70
Nos. 704-715, never hinged	31.65	

Skier — A222

Boy and Girl Planting Tree — A223

OLYMPIC WINTER GAMES ISSUE

3rd Olympic Winter Games, held at Lake Placid, N.Y., Feb. 4-13, 1932.

FLAT PLATE PRINTING

Plates of 400 subjects in four panes of 100.

1932, Jan. 25 ***Perf. 11***

716 A222 2c **carmine rose**	.40	.20
carmine	.40	.20
Never hinged	.55	
P# block of 6	10.00	—
Never hinged	14.00	

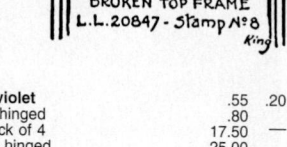

Cracked plate (20823 UR 41, 42; UL 48, 49, 50) 5.00 1.65
Recut (20823 UR 61) 3.50 1.50
Colored "snowball" (20815 UR 64) 25.00 5.00
a. 2c **lake** —
Never hinged —
carmine lake —
Never hinged —

ARBOR DAY ISSUE

1st observance of Arbor Day in the state of Nebraska, Apr. 1872, 60th anniv., and cent. of the birth of Julius Sterling Morton, who conceived the plan and the name "Arbor Day," while he was a member of the Nebraska State Board of Agriculture.

ROTARY PRESS PRINTING

Plates of 400 subjects in four panes of 100.

1932, Apr. 22 ***Perf. 11x10½***

717 A223 2c **carmine rose** .20 .20
Never hinged .30
P# block of 4 5.50 —
Never hinged 7.50

OLYMPIC GAMES ISSUE

Issued in honor of the 10th Olympic Games, held at Los Angeles, Calif., July 30 to Aug. 14, 1932.

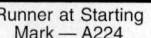

Runner at Starting Mark — A224

Myron's Discobolus — A225

Designed by Victor S. McCloskey, Jr.

ROTARY PRESS PRINTING

Plates of 400 subjects in four panes of 100.

1932, June 15 ***Perf. 11x10½***

718 A224 3c **violet** 1.40 .20
deep violet 1.40 .20
Never hinged 1.75
P# block of 4 12.00 —
Never hinged 18.50
Gripper cracks (20906 UL 1) 4.25 .75
P# block of 4 with variety —
719 A225 5c **blue** 2.20 .20
deep blue 2.20 .20
Never hinged 2.75
P# block of 4 20.00 —
Never hinged 27.50
Gripper cracks (20868 UL & UR) 4.25 1.00

Washington, by Gilbert Stuart — A226

REGULAR ISSUE

ROTARY PRESS PRINTING

Plates of 400 subjects in four panes of 100.

1932 ***Perf. 11x10½***

720 A226 3c **deep violet,** *June 16* .20 .20
light violet .20 .20
Never hinged .25
P# block of 4 1.60 —
Never hinged 2.00
Double transfer 1.00 .30
Recut face (20986 UR 15) 2.00 .75
Gripper cracks 1.25 .30
Pair with full vert. gutter btwn. *200.00*
Pair with full horiz. gutter btwn. *200.00*
b. Booklet pane of 6, *July 25* 35.00 *12.50*
Never hinged 60.00
c. Vertical pair, imperf. between *700.00* *1,350.*
Never hinged *1,400.*

Bureau Precancels: 64 diff.

ROTARY PRESS COIL STAMPS

1932 ***Perf. 10 Vertically***

721 A226 3c **deep violet,** *June 24* 2.75 .20
light violet 2.75 .20
Never hinged 3.50
Pair 5.75 .25
Never hinged 7.00
Joint line pair 10.00 1.50
Never hinged 12.50
Gripper cracks — —
Recut face (20995, pos. 29) — —
Recut lines around eyes — —

Perf. 10 Horizontally

722 A226 3c **deep violet,** *Oct. 12* 1.50 .35
light violet 1.50 .35
Never hinged 2.00
Pair 3.25 .80
Never hinged 4.25
Joint line pair 6.25 2.75
Never hinged 8.00

Bureau Precancels: No. 721, 46 diff.

TYPE OF 1922-26 ISSUES

1932, Aug. 18 ***Perf. 10 Vertically***

723 A161 6c **deep orange** 11.00 .30
Never hinged 15.00
Pair 24.00 .70
Never hinged 32.50
Joint line pair 60.00 5.00
Never hinged 82.50

Bureau Precancels: 5 diff.

William Penn — A227

Daniel Webster (1782-1852), Statesman — A228

WILLIAM PENN ISSUE

250th anniv. of the arrival in America of Penn (1644-1718), English Quaker and founder of Pennsylvania.

FLAT PLATE PRINTING

Plates of 400 subjects in four panes of 100 each

1932, Oct. 24 ***Perf. 11***

724 A227 3c **violet** .45 .20
Never hinged .60
P# block of 6 8.50 —
Never hinged 12.50
a. Vert. pair, imperf. horiz. —

DANIEL WEBSTER ISSUE

FLAT PLATE PRINTING

Plates of 400 subjects in four panes of 100.

1932, Oct. 24 ***Perf. 11***

725 A228 3c **violet** .45 .25
light violet .45 .25
Never hinged .60
P# block of 6 16.00 —
Never hinged 22.50

Gen. James Edward Oglethorpe — A229

Washington's Headquarters at Newburgh, N.Y. — A230

GEORGIA BICENTENNIAL ISSUE

200th anniv. of the founding of the Colony of Georgia, and honoring Oglethorpe, who landed from England, Feb. 12, 1733, and personally supervised the establishing of the colony.

FLAT PLATE PRINTING

Plates of 400 subjects in four panes of 100.

1933, Feb. 12 ***Perf. 11***

726 A229 3c **violet** .45 .20
Never hinged .60
P# block of 6 10.00 —
Never hinged 15.00
P# block of 10, "CS" in selvage 11.00
Never hinged 16.00
Bottom margin block of 20, no P# —

PEACE OF 1783 ISSUE

150th anniv. of the issuance by George Washington of the official order containing the Proclamation of Peace marking officially the ending of hostilities in the War for Independence.

ROTARY PRESS PRINTING

Plates of 400 subjects in four panes of 100 each

1933, Apr. 19 ***Perf. 10½x11***

727 A230 3c **violet** .20 .20
Never hinged .20
P# block of 4 3.00 —
Never hinged 5.50
Pair with horiz. gutter between 100.00 —
Pair with vert. gutter between 100.00 —
Center block with crossed gutters and dashes —

No. 727 was available in full sheets of 400 subjects with gum, but was not regularly issued in that form. All examples of No. 727 must have original gum, including the gutter pairs and blocks, which are from the full sheets of 400. These should not be confused with similar blocks without gum, which are from the No. 752 Special Printing.

See No. 752 in the Special Printings following No. 751.

CENTURY OF PROGRESS ISSUES

"Century of Progress" Intl. Exhibition, Chicago, which opened June 1, 1933, and centenary of the incorporation of Chicago as a city.

Restoration of Fort Dearborn — A231

Federal Building — A232

ROTARY PRESS PRINTING

Plates of 400 subjects in four panes of 100.

1933, May 25 ***Perf. 10½x11***

728 A231 1c **yellow green** .20 .20
Never hinged .25
On card, Expo. station machine canc. 1.00
On card, Expo. station duplex handstamp canc. 3.00
P# block of 4 1.75 —
Never hinged 3.00
Pair with horizontal gutter between 200.00
Pair with vertical gutter between 200.00
Center block with crossed gutters and dashes *5,000.*
Gripper cracks (21133 UR & LR) 2.00 —
729 A232 3c **violet** .25 .20
Never hinged .35
On cover, Expo. station machine canc. 2.00
On cover, Expo. station duplex handstamp canc. 6.00
P# block of 4 2.40 —
Never hinged 4.00
Pair with horiz. gutter between 200.00
Pair with vert. gutter between 200.00
Center block with crossed gutters and dashes *5,000.*

Nos. 728 and 729 were not regularly issued in full sheets of 400 with gum. The gutter pairs and blocks come from a very few non-issued sheets that were retained by Postmaster James A. Farley.

AMERICAN PHILATELIC SOCIETY ISSUE

SOUVENIR SHEETS

A231a

A232a

Illustrations reduced.

FLAT PLATE PRINTING

Plates of 225 subjects in nine panes of 25 each.

1933, Aug. 25 ***Imperf.***

Without Gum

730 A231a 1c **deep yellow green,** sheet of 25 27.50 27.50
  a. Single stamp .75 .50
    Single on card, Expo. station machine canc. 1.50
    Single on card, Expo. station duplex handstamp canc. 5.00
731 A232a 3c **deep violet,** sheet of 25 25.00 25.00
  a. Single stamp .65 .50
    Single on cover, Expo. station machine canc. 3.00
    Single on cover, Expo. station duplex handstamp canc. 7.50

Issued in sheets measuring 134x120mm containing twenty-five stamps, inscribed in the margins:
PRINTED BY THE TREASURY DEPARTMENT, BUREAU OF ENGRAVING AND PRINTING, — UNDER AUTHORITY OF JAMES A. FARLEY, POSTMASTER-GENERAL, AT CENTURY OF PROGRESS, — IN COMPLIMENT TO THE AMERICAN PHILATELIC SOCIETY FOR ITS CONVENTION AND EXHIBITION — CHICAGO, ILLINOIS, AUGUST, 1933. PLATE NO. 21145.
Also used were plates 21159 (1c), 21146 and 21160 (3c).

See Nos. 766-767 in the Special Printings following No. 751.

NATIONAL RECOVERY ACT ISSUE

Issued to direct attention to and arouse the support of the nation for the National Recovery Act.

Group of Workers — A233

ROTARY PRESS PRINTING

Plates of 400 subjects in four panes of 100.

1933, Aug. 15 ***Perf. 10½x11***

732 A233 3c **violet** .20 .20
  Never hinged .20
  P# block of 4 1.50 —
  Never hinged 2.00
  Gripper cracks (21151 UL & UR, 21153 UR & LR) 1.50 —
  Recut at right (21151 UR 47) 4.00

BYRD ANTARCTIC ISSUE

Issued in connection with the Byrd Antarctic Expedition of 1933 and for use on letters mailed through the Little America Post Office established at the Base Camp of the Expedition in the territory of the South Pole.

A Map of the World (on van der Grinten's Projection) — A234

Designed by Victor S. McCloskey, Jr.

FLAT PLATE PRINTING

Plates of 200 subjects in four panes of 50 each

1933, Oct. 9 ***Perf. 11***

733 A234 3c **dark blue** .50 .50
  Never hinged .60
  P# block of 6 12.00 —
  Never hinged 15.00
  Double transfer (21167 LR 2) 2.75 1.00

In addition to the postage charge of 3 cents, letters sent by the ships of the expedition to be canceled in Little America were subject to a service charge of 50 cents each.

See No. 753 in the Special Printings following No. 751.

KOSCIUSZKO ISSUE

Kosciuszko (1746-1807), Polish soldier and statesman served in the American Revolution, on the 150th anniv. of the granting to him of American citizenship.

Statue of General Tadeusz Kosciuszko — A235

Designed by Victor S. McCloskey, Jr.

FLAT PLATE PRINTING

Plates of 400 subjects in four panes of 100 each

1933, Oct. 13 ***Perf. 11***

734 A235 5c **blue** .55 .25
  Never hinged .65
  P# block of 6 27.50 —
  Never hinged 35.00
  Cracked plate —
  a. Horizontal pair, imperf. vertically *2,250.*
    Never hinged *2,800.*
    P# block of 8 *35,000.*

The No. 734a plate block is unique but damaged.

NATIONAL STAMP EXHIBITION ISSUE

SOUVENIR SHEET

A235a

Illustration reduced.

TYPE OF BYRD ISSUE

Plates of 150 subjects in 25 panes of six each.

1934, Feb. 10 ***Imperf.***

Without Gum

735 A235a 3c **dark blue,** sheet of 6 11.00 10.00
  a. Single stamp 1.85 1.65

Issued in sheets measuring 87x93mm containing six stamps, inscribed in the margins: "Printed by the Treasury Department, Bureau of Engraving and Printing, under authority of James A. Farley, Postmaster General, in the National Stamp Exhibition of 1934. New York, N. Y., February 10-18, 1934. Plate No. 21184." Plate No. 21187 was used for sheets printed at the Exhibition, but all these were destroyed.

See No. 768 in the Special Printings following No. 751.

MARYLAND TERCENTENARY ISSUE

300th anniversary of the founding of Maryland.

"The Ark" and "The Dove" — A236

Designed by Alvin R. Meissner.

FLAT PLATE PRINTING

Plates of 400 subjects in four panes of 100.

1934, Mar. 23 ***Perf. 11***

736 A236 3c **carmine rose** .25 .20
  Never hinged .35
  P# block of 6 6.25 —
  Never hinged 9.50
  Double transfer (21190 UL 1) — —
  a. Horizontal pair, imperf between *7,000.*

MOTHERS OF AMERICA ISSUE

Issued to commemorate Mother's Day.

Adaptation of Whistler's Portrait of his Mother — A237

Designed by Victor S. McCloskey, Jr.

Plates of 200 subjects in four panes of 50.

ROTARY PRESS PRINTING

1934, May 2 ***Perf. 11x10½***

737 A237 3c **deep violet** .20 .20
  Never hinged .25
  P# block of 4 1.00 —
  Never hinged 1.50

FLAT PLATE PRINTING

Perf. 11

738 A237 3c **deep violet** .20 .20
  Never hinged .20
  P# block of 6 4.25 —
  Never hinged 6.00

See No. 754 in the Special Printings following No. 751.

WISCONSIN TERCENTENARY ISSUE

Arrival of Jean Nicolet, French explorer, on the shores of Green Bay, 300th anniv. According to historical records, Nicolet was the 1st white man to reach the territory now comprising the State of Wisconsin.

Nicolet's Landing A238

Designed by Victor S. McCloskey, Jr.

FLAT PLATE PRINTING

Plates of 200 subjects in four panes of 50.

1934. July 7 ***Perf. 11***

739 A238 3c **deep violet** .25 .20
  violet .25 .20
  Never hinged .40
  P# block of 6 2.90 —
  Never hinged 4.25
  a. Vert. pair, imperf. horiz. *350.00*
    Never hinged *600.00*
  b. Horiz. pair, imperf. vert. *500.00*
    Never hinged *850.00*
    P# block of 6 *2,250.*

See No. 755 in the Special Printings following No. 751.

NATIONAL PARKS YEAR ISSUE

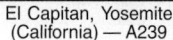

El Capitan, Yosemite (California) — A239

Old Faithful, Yellowstone (Wyoming) — A243

View of Grand Canyon (Arizona) A240

Mt. Rainier and Mirror Lake (Washington) A241

Cliff Palace, Mesa Verde Park (Colorado) A242

Crater Lake (Oregon) A244

Great Head, Acadia Park (Maine) A245

Great White Throne, Zion Park (Utah) — A246

Great Smoky Mountains (North Carolina) — A248

Mt. Rockwell (Mt. Sinopah) and Two Medicine Lake, Glacier National Park (Montana) A247

FLAT PLATE PRINTING

Plates of 200 subjects in four panes of 50.

1934		Unwmk.	*Perf. 11*	
740	A239	1c **green,** *July 16*	.20	.20
		light green	.20	.20
		Never hinged	.25	
		P# block of 6	1.00	—
		Never hinged	1.75	
		Recut	1.50	.50
a.		Vert. pair, imperf. horiz., with gum	*1,500.*	
		Never hinged	*2,200.*	
741	A240	2c **red,** *July 24*	.20	.20
		orange red	.20	.20
		Never hinged	.25	
		P# block of 6	1.50	—
		Never hinged	2.00	
		Double transfer	1.25	—
a.		Vert. pair, imperf. horiz., with gum	*575.00*	
		Never hinged	*1,000.*	
		P# block of 6	—	
b.		Horiz. pair, imperf. vert., with gum	*600.00*	
		Never hinged	*1,000.*	
		P# block of 6	*2,000.*	
		Never hinged	*3,250.*	
742	A241	3c **deep violet,** *Aug. 3*	.20	.20
		Never hinged	.25	
		P# block of 6	1.80	—
		Never hinged	2.25	
		Recut	1.50	—
a.		Vert. pair, imperf. horiz., with gum	*700.00*	
		Never hinged	*1,200.*	
		P# block of 6	—	
743	A242	4c **brown,** *Sept. 25*	.40	.40
		light brown	.40	.40
		Never hinged	.60	
		P# block of 6	7.00	—
		Never hinged	9.00	
a.		Vert. pair, imperf. horiz., with gum	*1,000.*	
		Never hinged	*1,700.*	
744	A243	5c **blue,** *July 30*	.70	.65
		light blue	.70	.65
		Never hinged	1.00	
		P# block of 6	9.00	—
		Never hinged	12.00	
a.		Horiz. pair, imperf. vert., with gum	*600.00*	
		Never hinged	*1,050.*	
		P# block of 6	—	
745	A244	6c **dark blue,** *Sept. 5*	1.10	.85
		Never hinged	1.60	
		P# block of 6	17.50	—
		Never hinged	25.00	
746	A245	7c **black,** *Oct. 2*	.60	.75
		Never hinged	.90	
		P# block of 6	9.00	—
		Never hinged	12.00	
		Double transfer	3.00	1.25
a.		Horiz. pair, imperf. vert., with gum	*600.00*	
		Never hinged	*1,050.*	
		P# block of 6, never hinged	*6,000.*	
747	A246	8c **sage green,** *Sept. 18*	1.60	1.50
		Never hinged	2.40	
		P# block of 6	17.50	—
		Never hinged	25.00	
748	A247	9c **red orange,** *Aug. 27*	1.50	.65
		orange	1.50	.65
		Never hinged	2.25	
		P# block of 6	15.00	—
		Never hinged	22.50	
749	A248	10c **gray black,** *Oct. 8*	3.00	1.25
		gray	3.00	1.25
		Never hinged	4.50	
		P# block of 6	22.50	—
		Never hinged	32.50	
		Nos. 740-749 (10)	9.50	6.65
		Nos. 740-749, never hinged	14.00	

Imperforate varieties of the 2c and 5c exist as errors of the perforated Parks set, but are virtually impossible to distinguish from gummed examples from the imperforate sheets of 200.

Also, beware of fakes of the part-perforate errors of Nos. 740-749, including those with gum (see "without gum" note before No. 752.

AMERICAN PHILATELIC SOCIETY ISSUE

SOUVENIR SHEET

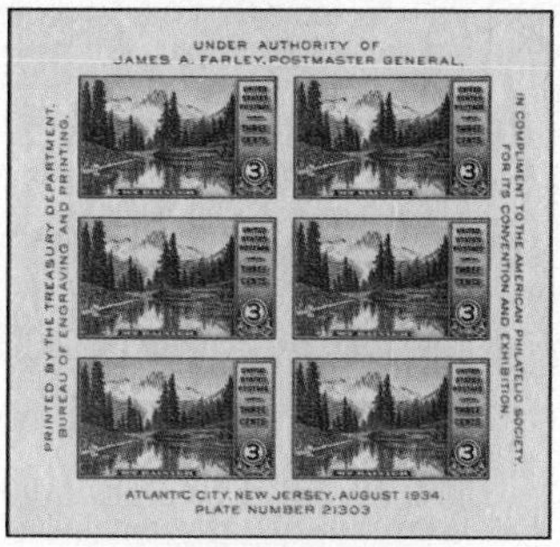

A248a

Illustration reduced.

Plates of 120 subjects in 20 panes of 6 stamps each.

1934, Aug. 28			*Imperf.*	
750	A248a	3c **deep violet,** sheet of 6	30.00	27.50
		Never hinged	37.50	
a.		Single stamp	3.50	3.25
		Never hinged	4.50	

Issued in sheets measuring approximately 98x93mm containing six stamps, inscribed in the margins: PRINTED BY THE TREASURY DEPARTMENT, BUREAU OF ENGRAVING AND PRINTING, — UNDER AUTHORITY OF JAMES A. FARLEY, POSTMASTER GENERAL, — IN COMPLIMENT TO THE AMERICAN PHILATELIC SOCIETY FOR ITS CONVENTION AND EXHIBITION, — ATLANTIC CITY, NEW JERSEY, AUGUST, 1934. PLATE NO. 21303.

See No. 770 in the Special Printings following No. 751.

TRANS-MISSISSIPPI PHILATELIC EXPOSITION ISSUE

SOUVENIR SHEET

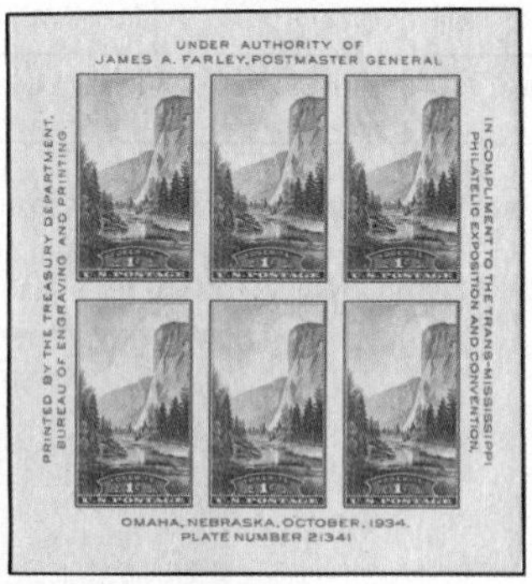

A248b

Illustration reduced.

Plates of 120 subjects in 20 panes of 6 stamps each.

1934, Oct. 10			*Imperf.*	
751	A248b	1c **green,** sheet of 6	12.50	12.50
		Never hinged	16.00	
a.		Single stamp	1.40	1.60
		Never hinged	1.85	

Issued in sheets measuring approximately 92x99mm containing six stamps, inscribed in the margins: PRINTED BY THE TREASURY DEPARTMENT, BUREAU OF ENGRAVING AND PRINTING, — UNDER AUTHORITY OF JAMES A. FARLEY, POSTMASTER GENERAL, — IN COMPLIMENT TO THE TRANS-MISSISSIPPI PHILATELIC EXPOSITION AND CONVENTION, OMAHA, NEBRASKA, — OCTOBER, 1934. PLATE NO. 21341.

See No. 769 in the Special Printings that follow.

SPECIAL PRINTING

(Nos. 752-771 inclusive)

"Issued for a limited time in full sheets as printed, and in blocks thereof, to meet the requirements of collectors and others who may be interested." — From Postal Bulletin No. 16614.

Issuance of the following 20 stamps in complete sheets resulted from the protest of collectors and others at the practice of presenting, to certain government officials, complete sheets of unsevered panes, imperforate (except Nos. 752 and 753) and generally ungummed.

Designs of Commemorative Issues
Without Gum

NOTE: In 1940 the P.O. Department offered to and did gum full sheets of Nos. 756-765 and 769-770 sent in by owners. No other Special Printings were accepted for gumming.

TYPE OF PEACE ISSUE

Issued in sheets of 400, consisting of four panes of 100 each, with vertical and horizontal gutters between and plate numbers at outside corners at sides.

ROTARY PRESS PRINTING

1935, Mar. 15 Unwmk. *Perf. 10½x11*

752	A230	3c	**violet**	.25	.20
			Pair with horiz. gutter between	5.75	—
			Pair with vert. gutter between	9.50	—
			Gutter block of 4 with dash (left or right)	17.50	—
			Gutter block of 4 with dash (top or bottom)	22.50	—
			Center block with crossed gutters and dashes	60.00	—
			P# block of 4	30.00	—

TYPE OF BYRD ISSUE

Issued in sheets of 200, consisting of four panes of 50 each, with vertical and horizontal guide lines in gutters between panes, and plate numbers centered at top and bottom of each pane. This applies to Nos. 753-765 and 771.

FLAT PLATE PRINTING
Perf. 11

753	A234	3c	**dark blue**	.50	.45
			Pair with horiz. line between	2.25	—
			Pair with vert. line between	30.00	—
			Margin block of 4, arrow & guide line (left or right)	4.75	—
			Margin block of 4, arrow & guide-line (top or bottom)	62.50	—
			Center line block	75.00	15.00
			P# block of 6, number at top or bottom	20.00	—

No. 753 is similar to No. 733. Positive identification is by blocks or pairs showing guide line between stamps. These lines between stamps are found only on No. 753.

TYPE OF MOTHERS OF AMERICA ISSUE
Issued in sheets of 200
FLAT PLATE PRINTING
Imperf

754	A237	3c	**deep violet**	.60	.60
			Pair with horiz. line between	1.75	—
			Pair with vert. line between	1.50	—
			Margin block of 4, arrow & guide-line (left or right)	3.75	—
			Margin block of 4, arrow & guide-line (top or bottom)	3.25	—
			Center line block	7.25	—
			P# block of 6, number at top or bottom	12.00	—

TYPE OF WISCONSIN ISSUE
Issued in sheets of 200
FLAT PLATE PRINTING
Imperf

755	A238	3c	**deep violet**	.60	.60
			Pair with horiz. line between	1.75	—
			Pair with vert. line between	1.50	—
			Margin block of 4, arrow & guide-line (left or right)	3.75	—
			Margin block of 4, arrow & guide-line (top or bottom)	3.25	—
			Center line block	7.25	—
			P# block of 6, number at top or bottom	12.00	—

TYPES OF NATIONAL PARKS ISSUE
Issued in sheets of 200
FLAT PLATE PRINTING
Imperf

756	A239	1c	**green**	.20	.20
			Pair with horiz. line between	.45	—
			Pair with vert. line between	.55	—
			Margin block of 4, arrow & guide-line (left or right)	1.00	—
			Margin block of 4, arrow & guide-line (top or bottom)	1.25	—
			Center line block	3.00	—
			P# block of 6, number at top or bottom	4.50	—

See note above No. 766.

757	A240	2c	**red**	.25	.25
			Pair with horiz. line between	.70	—
			Pair with vert. line between	.55	—
			Margin block of 4, arrow & guide-line (left or right)	1.60	—
			Margin block of 4, arrow & guide-line (top or bottom)	1.25	—
			Center line block	4.00	—
			P# block of 6, number at top or bottom	5.75	—
			Double transfer	—	
758	A241	3c	**deep violet**	.50	.45
			Pair with horiz. line between	1.40	—
			Pair with vert. line between	1.25	—
			Margin block of 4, arrow & guide-line (left or right)	3.10	—
			Margin block of 4, arrow & guide-line (top or bottom)	2.75	—
			Center line block	5.25	—
			P# block of 6, number at top or bottom	14.00	—
759	A242	4c	**brown**	.95	.95
			Pair with horiz. line between	2.75	—
			Pair with vert. line between	2.25	—
			Margin block of 4, arrow & guide-line (left or right)	5.75	—
			Margin block of 4, arrow & guide-line (top or bottom)	4.75	—
			Center line block	8.50	—
			P# block of 6, number at top or bottom	22.50	—
760	A243	5c	**blue**	1.50	1.40
			Pair with horiz. line between	3.50	—
			Pair with vert. line between	4.25	—
			Margin block of 4, arrow & guide-line (left or right)	7.50	—
			Margin block of 4, arrow & guide-line (top or bottom)	9.00	—
			Center line block	15.00	—
			P# block of 6, number at top or bottom	27.50	—
			Double transfer	—	
761	A244	6c	**dark blue**	2.25	2.25
			Pair with horiz. line between	6.00	—
			Pair with vert. line between	5.00	—
			Margin block of 4, arrow & guide-line (left or right)	12.00	—
			Margin block of 4, arrow & guide-line (top or bottom)	11.00	—
			Center line block	17.50	—
			P# block of 6, number at top or bottom)	37.50	—
762	A245	7c	**black**	1.50	1.40
			Pair with horiz. line between	4.25	—
			Pair with vert. line between	3.75	—
			Margin block of 4, arrow & guide-line (left or right)	9.25	—
			Margin block of 4, arrow & guide-line (top or bottom)	8.25	—
			Center line block	14.00	—
			P# block of 6, number at top or bottom	30.00	—
			Double transfer	—	
763	A246	8c	**sage green**	1.80	1.50
			Pair with horiz. line between	4.25	—
			Pair with vert. line between	5.25	—
			Margin block of 4, arrow & guide-line (left or right)	12.50	—
			Margin block of 4, arrow & guide-line (top or bottom)	15.00	—
			Center line block	20.00	—
			P# block of 6, number at top or bottom	37.50	—
764	A247	9c	**red orange**	1.90	1.75
			Pair with horiz. line between	5.00	—
			Pair with vert. line between	4.50	—
			Margin block of 4, arrow & guide-line (left or right)	11.50	—
			Margin block of 4, arrow & guide-line (top or bottom)	10.50	—
			Center line block	22.50	—
			P# block of 6, number at top or bottom	42.50	—
765	A248	10c	**gray black**	3.75	3.50
			Pair with horiz. line between	9.00	—
			Pair with vert. line between	10.50	—
			Margin block of 4, arrow & guide-line (left or right)	20.00	—
			Margin block of 4, arrow & guide-line (top or bottom)	24.00	—
			Center line block	30.00	—
			P# block of 6, number at top or bottom	50.00	—
			Nos. 756-765 (10)	14.60	13.65

SOUVENIR SHEETS

Note: Single items from these sheets are identical with other varieties, 766 and 730, 766a and 730a, 767 and 731, 767a and 731a, 768 and 735, 768a and 735a, 769 and 756, 770 and 758.

Positive identification is by blocks or pairs showing wide gutters between stamps. These wide gutters occur only on Nos. 766-770 and measure, horizontally, 13mm on Nos. 766-767; 16mm on No. 768, and 23mm on Nos. 769-770.

TYPE OF CENTURY OF PROGRESS ISSUE

Issued in sheets of 9 panes of 25 stamps each, with vertical and horizontal gutters between panes.

FLAT PLATE PRINTING
Imperf

766	A231a	1c	**yellow green,** pane of 25	25.00	25.00
a.			Single stamp	.70	.50
			Block of 4	2.80	1.70
			Pair with horiz. gutter between	5.00	—
			Pair with vert. gutter between	7.00	—
			Block with crossed gutters	16.00	
			Block of 50 stamps (two panes)	70.00	
767	A232a	3c	**violet,** pane of 25	23.50	23.50
a.			Single stamp	.60	.50
			Pair with horiz. gutter between	5.00	—
			Pair with vert. gutter between	6.50	—
			Block with crossed gutters	17.50	—
			Block of 50 stamps (two panes)	65.00	

NATIONAL EXHIBITION ISSUE
TYPE OF BYRD ISSUE

Issued in sheets of 25 panes of 6 stamps each, with vertical and horizontal gutters between panes.

FLAT PLATE PRINTING
Imperf

768	A235a	3c	**dark blue,** pane of six	20.00	15.00
a.			Single stamp	2.80	2.40
			Pair with horiz. gutter between	7.00	—
			Pair with vert. gutter between	8.00	—
			Block of 4 with crossed gutters	20.00	—
			Block of 12 stamps (two panes)	47.50	

TYPES OF NATIONAL PARKS ISSUE

Issued in sheets of 20 panes of 6 stamps each, with vertical and horizontal gutters between panes.

FLAT PLATE PRINTING
Imperf

769	A248b	1c	**green,** pane of six	12.50	11.00
a.			Single stamp	1.85	1.80
			Pair with horiz. gutter between	5.50	—
			Pair with vert. gutter between	7.50	—
			Block of 4 with crossed gutters	15.00	—
			Block of 12 stamps (two panes)	30.00	
770	A248a	3c	**deep violet,** pane of six	30.00	24.00
a.			Single stamp	3.25	3.10
			Pair with horiz. gutter between	12.00	—
			Pair with vert. gutter between	10.50	—
			Block of 4 with crossed gutters	27.50	—
			Block of 12 stamps (two panes)	70.00	

TYPE OF AIR POST SPECIAL DELIVERY

Issued in sheets of 200, with vertical and horizontal guide lines between panes.

FLAT PLATE PRINTING
Imperf

771	APSD1	16c	**dark blue**	2.60	2.60
			Pair with horiz. line between	7.75	—
			Pair with vert. line between	6.50	—
			Margin block of 4, arrow & guideline (left or right)	17.50	—
			Margin block of 4, arrow & guideline (top or bottom)	15.00	—
			Center line block	65.00	—
			P# block of 6, number at top or bottom	55.00	—

Catalogue values for unused stamps in this section, from this point to the end, are for Never Hinged items.

VALUES FOR HINGED STAMPS AFTER NO. 771
This catalogue does not value unused stamps after No. 771 in hinged condition. Hinged unused stamps from No. 772 to the present are worth considerably less than the values given for unused stamps, which are for never-hinged examples.

CONNECTICUT TERCENTENARY ISSUE

300th anniv. of the settlement of Connecticut.

The Charter Oak — A249

ROTARY PRESS PRINTING

Plates of 200 subjects in four panes of 50.

1935, Apr. 26 Unwmk. *Perf. 11x10½*

772	A249	3c	**violet**	.30	.20
			rose violet	.30	.20
			P# block of 4	2.00	—
			Defect in cent sign (21395 UR 4)	5.00	4.00

CALIFORNIA PACIFIC EXPOSITION ISSUE

California Pacific Exposition at San Diego.

View of San Diego Exposition A250

ROTARY PRESS PRINTING
Plates of 200 subjects in four panes of 50.

1935, May 29 **Unwmk.** ***Perf. 11x10½***

773 A250 3c **purple** .30 .20
On cover, Expo. station machine canc. (non-first day) *2.50*
On cover, Expo. station duplex handstamp canc. (non-first day) *20.00*
P# block of 4 1.30 —
Pair with full vertical gutter between —

BOULDER DAM ISSUE

Dedication of Boulder Dam.

Boulder Dam (Hoover Dam) — A251

FLAT PLATE PRINTING
Plates of 200 subjects in four panes of 50.

1935, Sept. 30 **Unwmk.** ***Perf. 11***

774 A251 3c **purple** .30 .20
deep purple .30 .20
P# block of 6 1.65 —

MICHIGAN CENTENARY ISSUE

Advance celebration of Michigan Statehood centenary.

Michigan State Seal — A252

Designed by Alvin R. Meissner.

ROTARY PRESS PRINTING
Plates of 200 subjects in 4 panes of 50.

1935, Nov. 1 **Unwmk.** ***Perf. 11x10½***

775 A252 3c **purple** .30 .20
P# block of 4 1.75 —

TEXAS CENTENNIAL ISSUE

Centennial of Texas independence.

Sam Houston, Stephen F. Austin and the Alamo — A253

Designed by Alvin R. Meissner.

ROTARY PRESS PRINTING
Plates of 200 subjects in four panes of 50.

1936, Mar. 2 **Unwmk.** ***Perf. 11x10½***

776 A253 3c **purple** .30 .20
On cover, Expo. station machine canc. 2.00
On cover, Expo. station duplex handstamp canc. *40.00*
P# block of 4 1.50 —

RHODE ISLAND TERCENTENARY ISSUE

300th anniv. of the settlement of Rhode Island.

Statue of Roger Williams — A254

ROTARY PRESS PRINTING
Plates of 200 subjects in four panes of 50.

1936, May 4 **Unwmk.** ***Perf. 10½x11***

777 A254 3c **purple** .35 .20
rose violet .35 .20
P# block of 4 1.25 —
Pair with full gutter between *200.00*

THIRD INTERNATIONAL PHILATELIC EXHIBITION ISSUE

SOUVENIR SHEET

A254a

Illustration reduced.

Plates of 120 subjects in thirty panes of 4 each.
FLAT PLATE PRINTING

1936, May 9 **Unwmk.** ***Imperf.***

778 A254a **violet,** sheet of 4 1.75 1.25
a. 3c Type A249 .40 .30
b. 3c Type A250 .40 .30
c. 3c Type A252 .40 .30
d. 3c Type A253 .40 .30

Issued in sheets measuring 98x66mm containing four stamps, inscribed in the margins: "Printed by the Treasury Department, Bureau of Engraving and Printing, under authority of James A. Farley, Postmaster General, in compliment to the third International Philatelic Exhibition of 1936. New York, N. Y., May 9-17, 1936. Plate No. 21557 (or 21558)."

ARKANSAS CENTENNIAL ISSUE

100th anniv. of the State of Arkansas.

Arkansas Post, Old and New State Houses A255

ROTARY PRESS PRINTING
Plates of 200 subjects in four panes of 50.

1936, June 15 **Unwmk.** ***Perf. 11x10½***

782 A255 3c **purple** .30 .20
P# block of 4 1.40 —

OREGON TERRITORY ISSUE

Opening of the Oregon Territory, 1836, 100th anniv.

Map of Oregon Territory A256

ROTARY PRESS PRINTING
Plates of 200 subjects in four panes of 50.

1936, July 14 **Unwmk.** ***Perf. 11x10½***

783 A256 3c **purple** .25 .20
P# block of 4 1.10 —
Double transfer (21579 UL 3) 4.00 2.50

SUSAN B. ANTHONY ISSUE

Susan Brownell Anthony (1820-1906), woman-suffrage advocate, and 16th anniv. of the ratification of the 19th Amendment which grants American women the right to vote.

Susan B. Anthony — A257

ROTARY PRESS PRINTING
Plates of 400 subjects in four panes of 100.

1936, Aug. 26 **Unwmk.** ***Perf. 11x10½***

784 A257 3c **violet** .25 .20
rose violet .25 .20
P# block of 4 1.10 —
Period missing after "B" (21590 LR 100) 4.00 2.00

ARMY ISSUE

Issued in honor of the United States Army.

Generals George Washington, Nathanael Greene and Mt. Vernon A258

Maj. Gen. Andrew Jackson, Gen. Winfield Scott and the Hermitage A259

Generals William T. Sherman, Ulysses S. Grant and Philip H. Sheridan A260

Generals Robert E. Lee, "Stonewall" Jackson and Stratford Hall — A261

U. S. Military Academy, West Point — A262

ROTARY PRESS PRINTING
Plates of 200 subjects in four panes of 50.

1936-37 **Unwmk.** ***Perf. 11x10½***

785 A258 1c **green,** *Dec. 15, 1936* .25 .20
yellow green .25 .20
P# block of 4 1.10 —

			Pair with full vertical gutter between	—	
786	A259	2c	**carmine,** *Jan. 15, 1937*	.25	.20
			P# block of 4	1.10	—
787	A260	3c	**purple,** *Feb. 18, 1937*	.35	.20
			P# block of 4	1.75	—
788	A261	4c	**gray,** *Mar. 23, 1937*	.55	.20
			P# block of 4	8.50	—
789	A262	5c	**ultramarine,** *May 26, 1937*	.65	.25
			P# block of 4	8.00	—
			Nos. 785-789 (5)	2.05	1.05

NAVY ISSUE

Issued in honor of the United States Navy.

John Paul Jones and John Barry — A263

Stephen Decatur and Thomas MacDonough A264

Admirals David G. Farragut and David D. Porter — A265

Admirals William T. Sampson, George Dewey and Winfield S. Schley A266

Seal of US Naval Academy and Naval Midshipmen A267

ROTARY PRESS PRINTING

Plates of 200 subjects in four panes of 50.

1936-37 **Unwmk.** ***Perf. 11x10½***

790	A263	1c	**green,** *Dec. 15, 1936*	.25	.20
			yellow green	.25	.20
			P# block of 4	1.10	—
791	A264	2c	**carmine,** *Jan. 15, 1937*	.25	.20
			P# block of 4	1.10	—
792	A265	3c	**purple,** *Feb. 18, 1937*	.35	.20
			P# block of 4	1.10	—
793	A266	4c	**gray,** *Mar. 23, 1937*	.55	.20
			P# block of 4	9.00	—
794	A267	5c	**ultramarine,** *May 26, 1937*	.65	.25
			P# block of 4	8.75	—
			Pair with full vert. gutter btwn.	—	
			Nos. 790-794 (5)	2.05	1.05

ORDINANCE OF 1787 SESQUICENTENNIAL ISSUE

150th anniv. of the adoption of the Ordinance of 1787 and the creation of the Northwest Territory.

Manasseh Cutler, Rufus Putnam and Map of Northwest Territory A268

ROTARY PRESS PRINTING

Plates of 200 subjects in four panes of 50.

1937, July 13 **Unwmk.** ***Perf. 11x10½***

795	A268	3c	**red violet**	.30	.20
			P# block of 4	1.40	—

VIRGINIA DARE ISSUE

350th anniv. of the birth of Virginia Dare, 1st child born in America of English parents (Aug. 18, 1587), and the settlement at Roanoke Island.

Virginia Dare and Parents — A269

FLAT PLATE PRINTING

Plates of 192 subjects in four panes of 48 each, separated by 1 ¼ inch wide gutters with central guide lines.

1937, Aug. 18 **Unwmk.** ***Perf. 11***

796	A269	5c	**gray blue**	.35	.20
			P# block of 6	6.50	—

SOCIETY OF PHILATELIC AMERICANS ISSUE

SOUVENIR SHEET

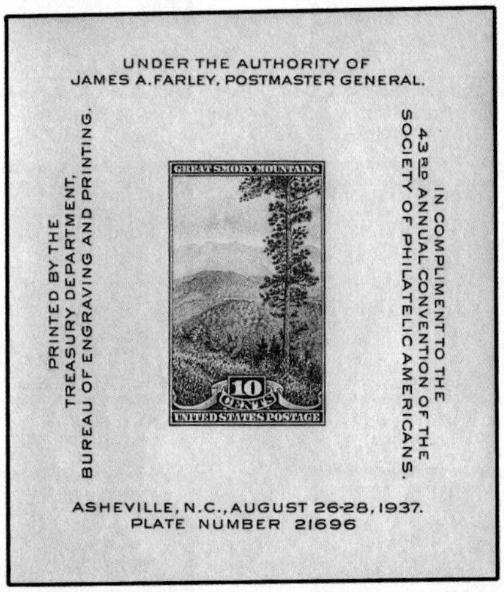

A269a

Illustration reduced.

TYPE OF NATIONAL PARKS ISSUE

Plates of 36 subjects

FLAT PLATE PRINTING

1937, Aug. 26 **Unwmk.** ***Imperf.***

797	A269a	10c	**blue green**	.60	.40

Issued in sheets measuring 67x78mm, inscribed in margins: "Printed by the Treasury Department, Bureau of Engraving and Printing — Under the Authority of James A. Farley, Postmaster General — In Compliment to the 43rd Annual Convention of the Society of Philatelic Americans - Asheville, N.C., August 26-28, 1937. Plate Number 21695 (6)."

CONSTITUTION SESQUICENTENNIAL ISSUE

150th anniversary of the signing of the Constitution on September 17, 1787.

"Adoption of the Constitution" A270

ROTARY PRESS PRINTING

Plates of 200 subjects in four panes of 50.

1937, Sept. 17 **Unwmk.** ***Perf. 11x10½***

798	A270	3c	**bright red violet**	.35	.20
			P# block of 4	1.60	—

TERRITORIAL ISSUES

Hawaii

Statue of Kamehameha I, Honolulu — A271

Alaska

Mt. McKinley A272

Puerto Rico

La Fortaleza, San Juan — A273

Virgin Islands

Charlotte Amalie Harbor, St. Thomas A274

ROTARY PRESS PRINTING

Plates of 200 subjects in panes of 50.

1937 **Unwmk.** ***Perf. 10½x11***

799	A271	3c	**violet,** *Oct. 18*	.30	.20
			P# block of 4	1.40	—
			Perf. 11x10½		
800	A272	3c	**violet,** *Nov. 12*	.30	.20
			P# block of 4	1.40	—
			Pair with full gutter between	—	
801	A273	3c	**bright violet,** *Nov. 25*	.30	.20
			P# block of 4	1.40	—
802	A274	3c	**light violet,** *Dec. 15*	.30	.20
			P# block of 4	1.40	—
			Pair with full vertical gutter between	*275.00*	
			Nos. 799-802 (4)	1.20	.80

PRESIDENTIAL ISSUE

Benjamin Franklin — A275

George Washington — A276

Martha Washington — A277

John Adams — A278

Thomas Jefferson — A279

James Madison — A280

The White House — A281

James Monroe — A282

John Quincy Adams — A283

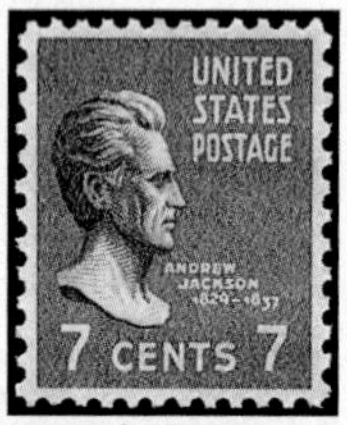

Andrew Jackson — A284

Martin Van Buren — A285

William H. Harrison — A286

John Tyler — A287

James K. Polk — A288

Zachary Taylor — A289

Millard Fillmore — A290

Franklin Pierce — A291

James Buchanan — A292

Abraham Lincoln — A293

Andrew Johnson — A294

Ulysses S. Grant — A295

Rutherford B. Hayes — A296

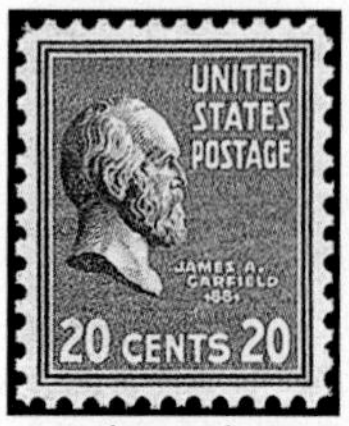

James A. Garfield — A297

Chester A. Arthur — A298

Grover Cleveland — A299

Benjamin Harrison — A300

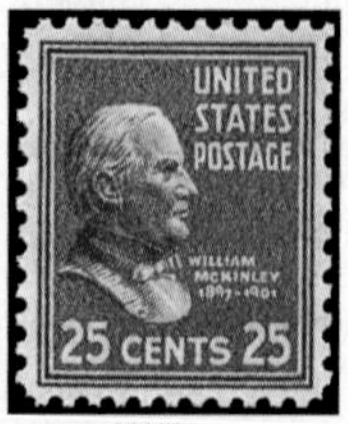

William McKinley — A301

Theodore Roosevelt — A302

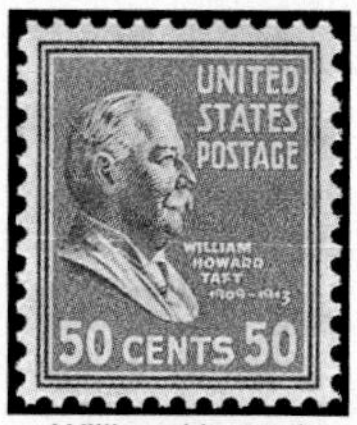

William Howard Taft — A303

Woodrow Wilson — A304

Warren G. Harding — A305

Calvin Coolidge — A306

ROTARY PRESS PRINTING

Ordinary and Electric Eye (EE) Plates of 400 subjects in four panes of 100. (For details of EE Markings, see Information for Collectors in first part of this Catalogue.)

1938			Unwmk.	*Perf. 11x10½*	
803	A275	½c	**deep orange,** *May 19*	.20	.20
			P# block of 4	.50	—
804	A276	1c	**green,** *Apr. 25*	.20	.20
			light green	.20	.20
			P# block of 4	.50	—
			Pair with full vert. gutter btwn.	*160.00*	—
b.			Booklet pane of 6	2.00	*.50*
c.			Horiz. pair, imperf between (from booklet pane)		—
805	A277	1½c	**bister brown,** *May 5*	.20	.20
			buff ('43)	.20	.20
			P# block of 4	.30	—
			Pair with full horiz. gutter btwn.	*175.00*	
			Pair with full vert. gutter btwn.	—	
b.			Horiz. pair, imperf. between	150.00	20.00

No. 805b used is always Bureau precanceled St. Louis, Mo., and is generally with gum. Value is for gummed pair.

806	A278	2c	**rose carmine,** *June 3*	.20	.20
			rose pink ('43)	.20	.20
			P# block of 4, # opposite corner stamp	.40	—
			Vertical margin block of 10, P# opposite 3rd horizontal row (Experimental EE plates)	7.00	
			Recut at top of head, Pl. 22156 U.L. 3	3.00	1.50
			Pair with full horiz. gutter btwn.	*125.00*	
			Pair with full vert. gutter btwn.	—	
b.			Booklet pane of 6	5.50	*1.00*
807	A279	3c	**deep violet,** *June 16*	.20	.20
			P# block of 4, # opposite corner stamp	.35	.25
			Vertical margin block of 10, P# opposite 3rd horizontal row (Experimental EE plates)	95.00	
			Pair with full vert. gutter btwn.	*150.00*	
			Pair with full horiz. gutter btwn.	*200.00*	
a.			Booklet pane of 6	8.50	*2.00*
			Horiz. booklet pair with full vert. gutter between	—	
b.			Horiz. pair, imperf. between	*2,000.*	—
c.			Imperf., pair	*2,750.*	
d.			As "a," imperf between vert.	—	
808	A280	4c	**red violet,** *July 1*	.75	.20
			rose violet ('43)	.75	.20
			P# block of 4	3.25	—
809	A281	4½c	**dark gray,** *July 11*	.25	.20
			gray ('43)	.25	.20
			P# block of 4	1.50	—
810	A282	5c	**bright blue,** *July 21*	.30	.20
			light blue	.30	.20
			P# block of 4	1.25	—
			Pair with full vert. gutter btwn.	—	
811	A283	6c	**red orange,** *July 28*	.35	.20
			P# block of 4	1.50	—
812	A284	7c	**sepia,** *Aug. 4*	.40	.20
			violet brown	.40	.20
			P# block of 4	1.75	—
813	A285	8c	**olive green,** *Aug. 11*	.40	.20
			light olive green ('43)	.40	.20
			olive ('42)	.40	.20
			P# block of 4	1.75	—
814	A286	9c	**rose pink,** *Aug. 18*	.35	.20
			pink ('43)	.35	.20
			P# block of 4	1.60	—
			Pair with full vert. gutter btwn.	—	
815	A287	10c	**brown red,** *Sept. 2*	.40	.20
			pale brown red ('43)	.40	.20
			P# block of 4	1.80	—
816	A288	11c	**ultramarine,** *Sept. 8*	.75	.20
			bright ultramarine	.75	.20
			P# block of 4	3.25	—
817	A289	12c	**bright violet,** *Sept. 14*	1.00	.20
			P# block of 4	5.00	—
818	A290	13c	**blue green,** *Sept. 22*	1.30	.20
			deep blue green	1.30	.20
			P# block of 4	7.00	—

819	A291	14c	**blue,** *Oct. 6*	1.00	.20
			P# block of 4	4.50	—
820	A292	15c	**blue gray,** *Oct. 13*	.55	.20
			P# block of 4	2.40	—
821	A293	16c	**black,** *Oct. 20*	1.25	.25
			P# block of 4	7.00	—
822	A294	17c	**rose red,** *Oct. 27*	1.00	.20
			deep rose red	1.10	.20
			P# block of 4	4.75	—
823	A295	18c	**brown carmine,** *Nov. 3*	2.25	.20
			rose brown ('43)	2.25	.20
			P# block of 4	12.50	—
824	A296	19c	**bright violet,** *Nov. 10*	1.30	.35
			P# block of 4	6.50	—
825	A297	20c	**bright blue green,** *Nov. 10*	1.00	.20
			deep blue green ('43)	1.00	.20
			P# block of 4	4.50	—
826	A298	21c	**dull blue,** *Nov. 22*	1.30	.20
			P# block of 4	7.50	—
827	A299	22c	**vermilion,** *Nov. 22*	1.20	.40
			P# block of 4	9.00	—
828	A300	24c	**gray black,** *Dec. 2*	3.50	.20
			P# block of 4	15.00	—
829	A301	25c	**deep red lilac,** *Dec. 2*	1.00	.20
			rose lilac ('43)	1.00	.20
			P# block of 4	4.50	—
			Pair with full vert. gutter btwn.	*900.00*	
830	A302	30c	**deep ultramarine,** *Dec. 8*	4.00	.20
			P# block of 4	17.00	—
a.		30c	**blue**	17.00	—
b.		30c	**deep blue**	*260.00*	—
831	A303	50c	**light red violet,** *Dec. 8*	5.00	.20
			P# block of 4	22.50	—

Bureau Precancels: ½c, 199 diff., 1c, 701 diff., 1½c, 404 diff., 2c, 161 diff., 3c, 87 diff., 4c, 30 diff., 4½c, 27 diff., 5c, 44 diff., 6c, 45 diff., 7c, 44 diff., 8c, 44 diff., 9c, 38 diff., 10c, 43 diff.

Also, 11c, 41 diff., 12c, 33 diff., 13c, 28 diff., 14c, 23 diff., 15c, 38 diff., 16c, 6 diff., 17c, 27 diff., 18c, 5 diff., 19c, 8 diff., 20c, 39 diff., 21c, 5 diff., 22c, 4 diff., 24c, 8 diff., 25c, 23 diff., 30c, 27 diff., 50c, 24 diff.

FLAT PLATE PRINTING
Plates of 100 subjects

1938 *Perf. 11*

832	A304	$1	**purple & black,** *Aug. 29*	7.00	.20
			Margin block of 4, bottom or side arrow	30.00	—
			Center line block	32.50	*4.00*
			Top P# block of 4, 2#	35.00	—
			Top P# block of 20, 2#, arrow, 2 TOP, 2 registration markers and denomination	145.00	—
a.			Vert. pair, imperf. horiz.	*1,500.*	
			Top P# blk of 8, imperf horiz.	*8,500.*	
b.			Watermarked USIR ('51)	150.00	65.00
			Hinged	90.00	
			Center line block	*1,500.*	
			P# block of 4, 2#	*1,800.*	
			Top P# block of 20, 2#, arrow, 2 TOP, 2 registration markers and denomination	3,250.	
c.		$1	**red violet & black,** *Aug. 31, 1954*	6.00	.20
			Top or bottom P# block of 4, 2#	30.00	—
d.			As "c," vert. pair, imperf. horiz.	*1,500.*	
e.			Vertical pair, imperf. between	*2,750.*	
f.			As "c," vert. pair, imperf. btwn.	*8,500.*	

No. 832c is dry printed from 400-subject flat plates on thick white paper with smooth, colorless gum.

833	A305	$2	**yellow green & black,** *Sept. 29*	18.00	3.75
			green & black ('43)	18.00	3.75
			Margin block of 4, bottom or side arrow	77.50	—
			Center line block	82.50	35.00
			Top P# block of 4, 2#	95.00	—
			Top P# block of 20, 2#, arrow, 2 TOP, 2 registration markers and denominations	450.00	—
			Top P# block of 20, 2#, black # and marginal markings only (yellow green # and markings omitted)	*3,000.*	
834	A306	$5	**carmine & black,** *Nov. 17*	90.00	3.00
			Hinged	50.00	
			dark red & black	—	—
			Margin block of 4, bottom or side arrow	375.00	—
			Center line block	400.00	*25.00*
			Top P# block of 4, 2#	400.00	—
			Top P# block of 20, 2#, arrow, 2 TOP, 2 registration markers and denominations	2,200.	
a.		$5	**red brown & black**	*3,000.*	*7,000.*
			Hinged	*2,000.*	
			Top P# block of 4, 2#	*15,000.*	
			Hinged	*9,500.*	
			Nos. 803-834 (32)	146.60	13.15
			Nos. 803-834, P# blocks of 4	674.95	

Top plate number blocks of Nos. 832, 833 and 834 are found both with and without top arrow or registration markers.

No. 834 can be chemically altered to resemble Scott 834a. No. 834a should be purchased only with competent expert certification.

Watermarks

All stamps from No. 835 on are unwatermarked.

CONSTITUTION RATIFICATION ISSUE

150th anniversary of the ratification of the United States Constitution.

Old Courthouse, Williamsburg, Va. — A307

ROTARY PRESS PRINTING
Plates of 200 subjects in four panes of 50.

1938, June 21 *Perf. 11x10½*

835	A307	3c	**deep violet**	.45	.20
			P# block of 4	3.50	—

SWEDISH-FINNISH TERCENTENARY ISSUE

Tercentenary of the founding of the Swedish and Finnish Settlement at Wilmington, Delaware.

"Landing of the First Swedish and Finnish Settlers in America," by Stanley M. Arthurs — A308

FLAT PLATE PRINTING
Plates of 192 subjects in four panes of 48 each, separated by 1¼ inch wide gutters with central guide lines.

1938, June 27 *Perf. 11*

836	A308	3c	**red violet**	.35	.20
			P# block of 6	2.25	—

NORTHWEST TERRITORY SESQUICENTENNIAL

"Colonization of the West," by Gutzon Borglum — A309

ROTARY PRESS PRINTING
Plates of 400 subjects in four panes of 100.

1938, July 15 *Perf. 11x10½*

837	A309	3c	**bright violet**	.30	.20
			rose violet	.30	.20
			P# block of 4	6.00	—

IOWA TERRITORY CENTENNIAL ISSUE

Old Capitol, Iowa City — A310

ROTARY PRESS PRINTING
Plates of 200 subjects in four panes of 50.

1938, Aug. 24 *Perf. 11x10½*

838	A310	3c	**violet**	.35	.20
			P# block of 4	6.00	—
			Pair with full vertical gutter between	—	

REGULAR ISSUE
ROTARY PRESS COIL STAMPS
Types of 1938

1939, Jan. 20 *Perf. 10 Vertically*

839	A276	1c	**green**	.30	.20
			light green	.30	.20
			Pair	.60	.20
			Joint line pair	1.40	.35
840	A277	1½c	**bister brown**	.30	.20
			buff	.30	.20
			Pair	.60	.20
			Joint line pair	1.50	.75
841	A278	2c	**rose carmine**	.40	.20
			Pair	.80	.20
			Joint line pair	1.75	.35
842	A279	3c	**deep violet**	.50	.20
			violet	.50	.20
			Pair	1.00	.20
			Joint line pair	2.00	.35
			Gripper cracks	—	
			Thin translucent paper	2.50	—
843	A280	4c	**red violet**	7.50	.40
			Pair	16.50	.90
			Joint line pair	27.50	5.00
844	A281	4½c	**dark gray**	.70	.40
			Pair	1.50	.90
			Joint line pair	5.00	2.25
845	A282	5c	**bright blue**	5.00	.35
			Pair	10.50	.75
			Joint line pair	27.50	5.00
846	A283	6c	**red orange**	1.10	.20
			Pair	2.25	.40
			Joint line pair	7.50	1.50
847	A287	10c	**brown red**	11.00	1.00
			Pair	24.00	2.50
			Joint line pair	42.50	4.50

Bureau Precancels: 1c, 269 diff., 1½c, 179 diff., 2c, 101 diff., 3c, 46 diff., 4c, 13 diff., 4½c, 3 diff., 5c, 6 diff., 6c, 8 diff., 10c, 4 diff.

1939, Jan. 27 *Perf. 10 Horizontally*

848	A276	1c	**green**	.85	.20
			Pair	1.75	.30
			Joint line pair	2.75	.75
849	A277	1½c	**bister brown**	1.25	.30
			Pair	2.50	.65
			Joint line pair	4.50	2.00
850	A278	2c	**rose carmine**	2.50	.40
			Pair	5.00	.90
			Joint line pair	7.50	3.50
851	A279	3c	**deep violet**	2.50	.40
			Pair	5.00	.90
			Joint line pair	8.50	3.75
			Thin translucent paper	—	
			Nos. 839-851 (13)	33.90	4.45

"Tower of the Sun" — A311

Trylon and Perisphere — A312

GOLDEN GATE INTL. EXPOSITION, SAN FRANCISCO

ROTARY PRESS PRINTING
Plates of 200 subjects in four panes of 50.

1939, Feb. 18 *Perf. 10½x11*

852	A311	3c	**bright purple**	.30	.20
			On cover, Expo. station machine canc. (non-first day)		3.00
			On cover, Expo. station duplex handstamp canc. (non-first day)		15.00
			P# block of 4	1.40	—

NEW YORK WORLD'S FAIR ISSUE

ROTARY PRESS PRINTING
Plates of 200 subjects in four panes of 50.

1939, Apr. 1 *Perf. 10½x11*

853	A312	3c	**deep purple**	.30	.20
			On cover, Expo. station machine canc. (non-first day)		3.00
			On cover, Expo. station duplex handstamp canc.		10.00
			P# block of 4	1.75	—

WASHINGTON INAUGURATION ISSUE

Sesquicentennial of the inauguration of George Washington as First President.

Washington Taking Oath of Office, Federal Building, New York City — A313

FLAT PLATE PRINTING
Plates of 200 subjects in four panes of 50.

1939, Apr. 30 *Perf. 11*

854	A313	3c	**bright red violet**	.55	.20
			P# block of 6	3.50	—

BASEBALL CENTENNIAL ISSUE

Sandlot Baseball Game — A314

Designed by William A. Roach.

ROTARY PRESS PRINTING
Plates of 200 subjects in four panes of 50.

1939, June 12 *Perf. 11x10½*

855	A314	3c	**violet**	1.75	.20
			P# block of 4	7.50	—

PANAMA CANAL ISSUE

25th anniv. of the opening of the Panama Canal.

Theodore Roosevelt, Gen. George W. Goethals and Ship in Gaillard Cut — A315

Designed by William A. Roach.

FLAT PLATE PRINTING
Plates of 200 subjects in four panes of 50.

1939, Aug. 15 *Perf. 11*

856	A315	3c	**deep red violet**	.35	.20
			P# block of 6	3.50	—

PRINTING TERCENTENARY ISSUE

Issued in commemoration of the 300th anniversary of printing in Colonial America. The Stephen Daye press is in the Harvard University Museum.

Stephen Daye Press — A316

Designed by William K. Schrage.

ROTARY PRESS PRINTING
E.E. Plates of 200 subjects in four panes of 50.

1939, Sept. 25 *Perf. 10½x11*

857	A316	3c	**violet**	.25	.20
			P# block of 4	1.10	—

50th ANNIVERSARY OF STATEHOOD ISSUE

Map of North and South Dakota, Montana and Washington A317

ROTARY PRESS PRINTING
E.E. Plates of 200 subjects in four panes of 50.

1939, Nov. 2 *Perf. 11x10½*

858	A317	3c	**rose violet**	.35	.20
			P# block of 4	2.00	—

FAMOUS AMERICANS ISSUES

ROTARY PRESS PRINTING
E.E. Plates of 280 subjects in four panes of 70.

AMERICAN AUTHORS

Washington Irving — A318

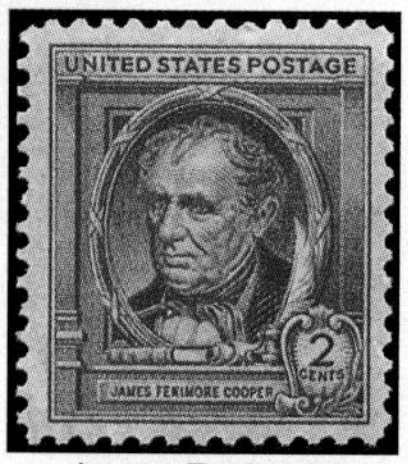

James Fenimore Cooper — A319

Ralph Waldo Emerson — A320

Louisa May Alcott — A321

Samuel L. Clemens (Mark Twain) — A322

1940 *Perf. 10½x11*

859	A318	1c	**bright blue green,** *Jan. 29*	.20	.20
			P# block of 4	.95	—
860	A319	2c	**rose carmine,** *Jan. 29*	.20	.20
			P# block of 4	.95	—
861	A320	3c	**bright red violet,** *Feb. 5*	.25	.20
			P# block of 4	1.25	—
862	A321	5c	**ultramarine,** *Feb. 5*	.35	.20
			P# block of 4	8.25	—
863	A322	10c	**dark brown,** *Feb. 13*	1.75	1.20
			P# block of 4	32.50	—
			Nos. 859-863 (5)	2.75	2.00

AMERICAN POETS

Henry Wadsworth Longfellow — A323

John Greenleaf Whittier — A324

James Russell Lowell — A325

Walt Whitman — A326

James Whitcomb Riley — A327

864	A323	1c	**bright blue green,** *Feb. 16*	.20	.20
			P# block of 4	1.75	—
865	A324	2c	**rose carmine,** *Feb. 16*	.20	.20
			P# block of 4	1.75	—
866	A325	3c	**bright red violet,** *Feb. 20*	.25	.20
			P# block of 4	2.25	—
867	A326	5c	**ultramarine,** *Feb. 20*	.50	.20
			P# block of 4	9.50	—
868	A327	10c	**dark brown,** *Feb. 24*	1.75	1.25
			P# block of 4	32.50	—
			Nos. 864-868 (5)	2.90	2.05

AMERICAN EDUCATORS

Horace Mann — A328

Mark Hopkins — A329

Charles W. Eliot — A330

Frances E. Willard — A331

Booker T. Washington — A332

869	A328	1c	**bright blue green,** *Mar. 14*	.20	.20
			P# block of 4	2.25	—
870	A329	2c	**rose carmine,** *Mar. 14*	.20	.20
			P# block of 4	1.50	—
871	A330	3c	**bright red violet,** *Mar. 28*	.25	.20
			P# block of 4	2.00	—
872	A331	5c	**ultramarine,** *Mar. 28*	.50	.20
			P# block of 4	9.00	—
873	A332	10c	**dark brown,** *Apr. 7*	2.00	1.10
			P# block of 4	27.50	—
			Nos. 869-873 (5)	3.15	1.90

AMERICAN SCIENTISTS

John James Audubon — A333

Dr. Crawford W. Long — A334

Luther Burbank — A335

Dr. Walter Reed — A336

Jane Addams — A337

874	A333	1c	**bright blue green,** *Apr. 8*	.20	.20
			P# block of 4	.90	—
875	A334	2c	**rose carmine,** *Apr. 8*	.20	.20
			P# block of 4	.95	—
876	A335	3c	**bright red violet,** *Apr. 17*	.25	.20
			P# block of 4	1.10	—
877	A336	5c	**ultramarine,** *Apr. 17*	.50	.20
			P# block of 4	5.50	—
878	A337	10c	**dark brown,** *Apr. 26*	1.50	.85
			P# block of 4	16.00	—
			Nos. 874-878 (5)	2.65	1.65

AMERICAN COMPOSERS

Stephen Collins Foster — A338

John Philip Sousa — A339

Victor Herbert — A340

Edward A. MacDowell — A341

Ethelbert Nevin — A342

879	A338	1c	**bright blue green,** *May 3*	.20	.20
			P# block of 4	.95	—
880	A339	2c	**rose carmine,** *May 3*	.20	.20
			P# block of 4	1.00	—
881	A340	3c	**bright red violet,** *May 13*	.25	.20
			P# block of 4	1.10	—
882	A341	5c	**ultramarine,** *May 13*	.50	.20
			P# block of 4	9.25	—
883	A342	10c	**dark brown,** *June 10*	3.75	1.35
			P# block of 4	32.50	—
			Nos. 879-883 (5)	4.90	2.15

AMERICAN ARTISTS

Gilbert Charles Stuart — A343

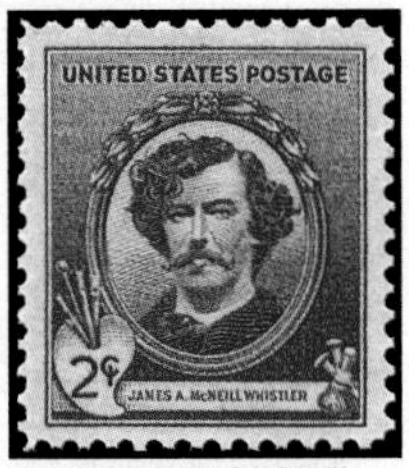

James A. McNeill Whistler — A344

Augustus Saint-Gaudens — A345

Daniel Chester French — A346

Frederic Remington — A347

884	A343	1c	**bright blue green,** *Sept. 5*	.20	.20
			P# block of 4	1.00	—
885	A344	2c	**rose carmine,** *Sept. 5*	.20	.20
			P# block of 4	.95	—
886	A345	3c	**bright red violet,** *Sept. 16*	.30	.20
			P# block of 4	1.50	—
887	A346	5c	**ultramarine,** *Sept. 16*	.50	.20
			P# block of 4	8.00	—
888	A347	10c	**dark brown,** *Sept. 30*	1.75	1.25
			P# block of 4	20.00	—
			Nos. 884-888 (5)	2.95	2.05

AMERICAN INVENTORS

Eli Whitney — A348

Samuel F. B. Morse — A349

Cyrus Hall McCormick — A350

Elias Howe — A351

Alexander Graham Bell — A352

889	A348	1c	**bright blue green,** *Oct. 7*	.25	.20
			P# block of 4	2.25	—
890	A349	2c	**rose carmine,** *Oct. 7*	.30	.20
			P# block of 4	2.00	—
891	A350	3c	**bright red violet,** *Oct. 14*	.30	.20
			P# block of 4	1.50	—
892	A351	5c	**ultramarine,** *Oct. 14*	1.10	.30
			P# block of 4	12.50	—
893	A352	10c	**dark brown,** *Oct. 28*	11.00	2.00
			P# block of 4	50.00	—
			Nos. 889-893 (5)	12.95	2.90
			Nos. 859-893 (35)	32.25	14.70
			Nos. 859-893, P# blocks of 4	305.36	

PONY EXPRESS, 80th ANNIV. ISSUE

Pony Express Rider — A353

ROTARY PRESS PRINTING

E.E. Plates of 200 subjects in four panes of 50.

1940, Apr. 3			***Perf. 11x10½***		
894	A353	3c	**henna brown**	.40	.20
			P# block of 4	3.25	—

PAN AMERICAN UNION ISSUE

Founding of the Pan American Union, 50th anniv.

The Three Graces (Botticelli) — A354

ROTARY PRESS PRINTING

E.E. Plates of 200 subjects in four panes of 50.

1940, Apr. 14			***Perf. 10½x11***		
895	A354	3c	**light violet**	.30	.20
			P# block of 4	2.75	—

IDAHO STATEHOOD, 50th ANNIV.

Idaho State Capitol A355

ROTARY PRESS PRINTING

E.E. Plates of 200 subjects in four panes of 50.

1940, July 3			***Perf. 11x10½***		
896	A355	3c	**bright violet**	.35	.20
			P# block of 4	2.00	—

WYOMING STATEHOOD, 50th ANNIV.

Wyoming State Seal — A356

ROTARY PRESS PRINTING

E.E. Plates of 200 subjects in four panes of 50.

1940, July 10			***Perf. 10½x11***		
897	A356	3c	**brown violet**	.30	.20
			P# block of 4	1.75	—

CORONADO EXPEDITION, 400th ANNIV.

"Coronado and His Captains" Painted by Gerald Cassidy A357

ROTARY PRESS PRINTING

E.E. Plates of 200 subjects in four panes of 50.

1940, Sept. 7 *Perf. 11x10½*

898 A357 3c **violet** .25 .20
P# block of 4 1.60 —

NATIONAL DEFENSE ISSUE

Statue of Liberty — A358

90-millimeter Anti-aircraft Gun — A359

Torch of Enlightenment — A360

ROTARY PRESS PRINTING

E.E. Plates of 400 subjects in four panes of 100

1940, Oct. 16 *Perf. 11x10½*

899 A358 1c **bright blue green** .20 .20
P# block of 4 .45 —
Cracked plate (22684 UR 10) 3.00
Gripper cracks 3.00
Pair with full vert. gutter between *200.00*
a. Vertical pair, imperf. between *625.00* —
b. Horizontal pair, imperf. between 32.50 —
900 A359 2c **rose carmine** .20 .20
P# block of 4 .45 —
Pair with full vert. gutter between *275.00*
a. Horizontal pair, imperf. between 37.50 —
901 A360 3c **bright violet** .20 .20
P# block of 4 .60 —
Pair with full vert. gutter between —
a. Horizontal pair, imperf. between 25.00 —
Nos. 899-901 (3) .60 .60

Bureau Precancels: 1c, 316 diff., 2c, 25 diff., 3c, 22 diff.

THIRTEENTH AMENDMENT ISSUE

75th anniv. of the 13th Amendment to the Constitution abolishing slavery.

Emancipation Monument; Lincoln and Kneeling Slave, by Thomas Ball — A361

Designed by William A. Roach.

ROTARY PRESS PRINTING

E.E. Plates of 200 subjects in four panes of 50.

1940, Oct. 20 *Perf. 10½x11*

902 A361 3c **deep violet** .30 .20
dark violet .30 .20
P# block of 4 3.00 —

VERMONT STATEHOOD, 150th ANNIV.

State Capitol, Montpelier A362

Designed by Alvin R. Meissner.

ROTARY PRESS PRINTING

E.E. Plates of 200 subjects in four panes of 50.

1941, Mar. 4 *Perf. 11x10½*

903 A362 3c **light violet** .45 .20
P# block of 4 3.00 —

KENTUCKY STATEHOOD, 150th ANNIV.

Daniel Boone and Three Frontiersmen, from Mural by Gilbert White — A363

Designed by William A. Roach.

ROTARY PRESS PRINTING

E.E. Plates of 200 subjects in four panes of 50.

1942, June 1 *Perf. 11x10½*

904 A363 3c **violet** .30 .20
P# block of 4 1.50 —

WIN THE WAR ISSUE

American Eagle — A364

ROTARY PRESS PRINTING

E.E. Plates of 400 subjects in four panes of 100.

1942, July 4 *Perf. 11x10½*

905 A364 3c **violet** .20 .20
light violet .20 .20
P# block of 4 .55 —
Pair with full vert. or horiz. gutter between *175.00*
b. 3c **reddish violet** *750.00 500.00*

Bureau Precancels: 26 diff.

All examples of No. 905b are precanceled either Los Angeles, Calif., or Fremont, Ohio. Value is for Los Angeles, which is the more common.

CHINESE RESISTANCE ISSUE

Issued to commemorate the Chinese people's five years of resistance to Japanese aggression.

Map of China, Abraham Lincoln and Sun Yat-sen, Founder of the Chinese Republic A365

ROTARY PRESS PRINTING

E.E. Plates of 200 subjects in four panes of 50.

1942, July 7 *Perf. 11x10½*

906 A365 5c **bright blue** 1.25 .20
P# block of 4 8.25 —

ALLIED NATIONS ISSUE

Allegory of Victory — A366

Designed by Leon Helguera.

ROTARY PRESS PRINTING

E.E. Plates of 400 subjects in four panes of 100.

1943, Jan. 14 *Perf. 11x10½*

907 A366 2c **rose carmine** .20 .20
P# block of 4 .30 —
Pair with full vert. or horiz. gutter between *225.00*

Bureau Precancels: Denver, Baltimore.

FOUR FREEDOMS ISSUE

Liberty Holding the Torch of Freedom and Enlightenment — A367

Designed by Paul Manship.

ROTARY PRESS PRINTING

E.E. Plates of 400 subjects in four panes of 100.

1943, Feb. 12 *Perf. 11x10½*

908 A367 1c **bright blue green** .20 .20
P# block of 4 .70 —

Bureau Precancels: 20 diff.

OVERRUN COUNTRIES ISSUE

Printed by the American Bank Note Co.

FRAMES ENGRAVED, CENTERS OFFSET LETTERPRESS

ROTARY PRESS PRINTING

Plates of 200 subjects in four panes of 50.

Due to the failure of the printers to divulge detailed information as to printing processes used, the editors omit listings of irregularities, flaws and blemishes which are numerous in this issue. Exceptions are made for certified double impressions, the widely recognized "KORPA" variety, and "reverse" vs. "normal" printings of the flag colors.

Flag of Poland A368

1943-44 *Perf. 12*

909 A368 5c **blue violet, bright red & black,** *June 22, 1943* .25 .20
Margin block of 4, Inscribed "Poland" 3.50 —
Top margin block of 6, with red & blue violet guide markings and "Poland" 4.75 —
Bottom margin block of 6, with red & black guide markings 1.65 —
a. Double impression of "Poland" —
b. Double impression of black flag color and red "Poland" —
c. Reverse printing of flag colors (bright red over black) — —

Flag of Czechoslovakia — A368a

910 A368a 5c **blue violet, blue, bright red & black,** *July 12, 1943* .25 .20
Margin block of 4, inscribed "Czechoslovakia" 2.75 —
Top margin block of 6, with red & blue violet guide markings and "Czechoslovakia" 3.25 —
a. Double impression of "Czechoslovakia" —
b. Reverse printing of flag colors (blue and bright red over black) —
c. Partial reverse printing of flag colors (bright red over black and black over blue) —

Flag of Norway A368b

911 A368b 5c **blue violet, dark rose, deep blue & black,** *July 27, 1943* .25 .20
Margin block of 4, inscribed "Norway" 1.30 —
Bottom margin block of 6 with dark rose & blue violet guide markings 1.65 —
a. Double impression of "Norway" —
b. Reverse printing of flag colors (dark rose and deep blue over black) —

Flag of Luxembourg A368c

912 A368c 5c **blue violet, dark rose, light blue & black,** *Aug. 10, 1943* .25 .20
Margin block of 4, inscribed "Luxembourg" 1.30 —
Top margin block of 6 with light blue & blue violet guide markings & "Luxembourg" 1.65 —
a. Double impression of "Luxembourg" —
b. Reverse printing of flag colors (dark rose and light blue over black) —
c. Partial reverse printing of flag colors (dark rose over black and black over light blue) —

Flag of Netherlands A368d

913 A368d 5c **blue violet, dark rose, blue & black,** *Aug. 24, 1943* .25 .20
Margin block of 4, inscribed "Netherlands" 1.25 —
Bottom margin block of 6 with blue & blue violet guide markings 1.65 —
a. Reverse printing of flag colors (dark rose and blue over black) — —
b. Partial reverse printing of flag colors (blue over black and black over dark rose) .25 .20

Flag of Belgium A368e

914 A368e 5c **blue violet, dark rose, yellow & black,** *Sept. 14, 1943* .25 .20
Margin block of 4, inscribed "Belgium" 1.25 —
Top margin block of 6, with yellow & blue violet guide markings and "Belgium" 1.65 —
a. Double impression of "Belgium" —

Flag of France A368f

915 A368f 5c **blue violet, deep blue, dark rose & black,** *Sept. 28, 1943* .25 .20
Margin block of 4, inscribed "France" 1.25 —
Bottom margin block of 6 with dark rose & blue violet guide markings 1.65 —
a. Reverse printing of flag colors (deep blue and dark rose over black) —
b. Partial reverse printing of flag colors (dark rose over black and black over deep blue) —

Flag of Greece A368g

916 A368g 5c **blue violet, pale blue, greenish blue & black,** reverse printing of flag colors (pale blue flag stripes over pale blue shading), *Oct. 12, 1943* .50 .25
Margin block of 4, inscribed "Greece" 11.00 —
Top margin block of 6 with pale blue & blue violet guide markings & "Greece" 11.50 —
a. "Normal" printing of flag colors (dark blue shading over pale blue flag stripes) —

Flag of Yugoslavia A368h

Normal

Reverse Printing of Flag Colors

917 A368h 5c **blue violet, blue, dark rose & black,** *Oct. 26, 1943* .40 .20
Margin block of 4, inscribed "Yugoslavia" 4.25 —
Bottom margin block of 6 with dark rose & blue violet guide markings 2.60 —
a. Reverse printing of flag colors (blue and dark rose over black) — —
b. Double impression of black —
c. Partial reverse printing of flag colors (dark rose over black and black over blue) —

Flag of Albania A368i

918 A368i 5c **blue violet, dark red & black,** *Nov. 9, 1943* .25 .20
Margin block of 4, inscribed "Albania" 4.25 —
Top margin block of 6, with dark red & blue violet guide markings & "Albania" 6.50 —
a. Double impression of "Albania" —

Flag of Austria A368j

919 A368j 5c **blue violet, red & black,** *Nov. 23, 1943* .30 .20
Margin block of 4, inscribed "Austria" 3.50 —
Bottom margin block of 6, with red & blue violet guide markings 2.00 —
a. Double impression of "Austria" —
b. Reverse printing of flag colors (red over black) —

Flag of Denmark A368k

920 A368k 5c **blue violet, red & black,** *Dec. 7, 1943* .30 .20
Margin block of 4, inscribed "Denmark" 5.25 —
Top margin block of 6, with red & blue violet guide markings & "Denmark" 6.00 —
a. Reverse printing of flag colors (red over black) —
b. 5c **blue violet, red & gray** .30 .20
c. As "b," reverse printing of flag colors (red over gray) — —

Flag of Korea A368m

"KORPA" plate flaw

921 A368m 5c **blue violet, red, light blue & gray,** reverse printing of flag colors (light blue over gray), *Nov. 2, 1944* .25 .20

Margin block of 4, inscribed "Korea" 4.50 —

Top margin block of 6 with blue & black guide markings and "Korea" 5.25 —

"KORPA" plate flaw 19.00 12.50

a. Double impression of "Korea" —

b. "Normal" printing of flag colors (gray over light blue) .25 .20

The "P" of "KORPA" is actually a mangled "E." Occurs only on some panes, position 26.

Nos. 909-921 (13) 3.75 2.65

Nos. 909-921, Name blocks of 4 47.10

TRANSCONTINENTAL RAILROAD ISSUE

Completion of the 1st transcontinental railroad, 75th anniv.

"Golden Spike Ceremony" Painted by John McQuarrie A369

ENGRAVED

ROTARY PRESS PRINTING

E.E. Plates of 200 subjects in four panes of 50.

1944, May 10 ***Perf. 11x10½***

922 A369 3c **violet** .25 .20

P# block of 4 1.75 —

STEAMSHIP ISSUE

1st steamship to cross the Atlantic, 125th anniv.

"Savannah" A370

ROTARY PRESS PRINTING

E.E. Plates of 200 subjects in four panes of 50.

1944, May 22 ***Perf. 11x10½***

923 A370 3c **violet** .20 .20

P# block of 4 1.25 —

TELEGRAPH ISSUE

1st message transmitted by telegraph, cent.

Telegraph Wires and Morse's First Transmitted Words "What Hath God Wrought" A371

ROTARY PRESS PRINTING

E.E. Plates of 200 subjects in four panes of 50.

1944, May 24 ***Perf. 11x10½***

924 A371 3c **bright red violet** .20 .20

P# block of 4 1.00 —

PHILIPPINE ISSUE

Final resistance of the US and Philippine defenders on Corregidor to the Japanese invaders in 1942.

Aerial View of Corregidor, Manila Bay — A372

ROTARY PRESS PRINTING

E.E. Plates of 200 subjects in four panes of 50.

1944, Sept. 27 ***Perf. 11x10½***

925 A372 3c **deep violet** .20 .20

P# block of 4 1.25 —

MOTION PICTURE, 50th ANNIV.

Motion Picture Showing for Armed Forces in South Pacific — A373

ROTARY PRESS PRINTING

E.E. Plates of 200 subjects in four panes of 50.

1944, Oct. 31 ***Perf. 11x10½***

926 A373 3c **deep violet** .20 .20

P# block of 4 1.10 —

FLORIDA STATEHOOD, CENTENARY

State Seal, Gates of St. Augustine and Capitol at Tallahassee A374

ROTARY PRESS PRINTING

E.E. Plates of 200 subjects in four panes of 50.

1945, Mar. 3 ***Perf. 11x10½***

927 A374 3c **bright red violet** .20 .20

P# block of 4 1.10 —

UNITED NATIONS CONFERENCE ISSUE

United Nations Conference, San Francisco, Calif.

"Toward United Nations, April 25, 1945" — A375

ROTARY PRESS PRINTING

E.E. Plates of 200 subjects in four panes of 50.

1945, Apr. 25 ***Perf. 11x10½***

928 A375 5c **ultramarine** .20 .20

P# block of 4 .45 —

IWO JIMA (MARINES) ISSUE

Battle of Iwo Jima and honoring the achievements of the US Marines.

Marines Raising American Flag on Mount Suribachi, Iwo Jima, from a photograph by Joe Rosenthal — A376

ROTARY PRESS PRINTING

E.E. Plates of 200 subjects in four panes of 50.

1945, July 11 ***Perf. 10½x11***

929 A376 3c **yellow green** .30 .20

P# block of 4 2.00 —

FRANKLIN D. ROOSEVELT ISSUE

Franklin Delano Roosevelt (1882-1945).

Roosevelt and Hyde Park Residence A377

Roosevelt and the "Little White House" at Warm Springs, Ga. — A378

Roosevelt and White House — A379

Roosevelt, Map of Western Hemisphere and Four Freedoms A380

ROTARY PRESS PRINTING

E.E. Plates of 200 subjects in four panes of 50.

1945-46 ***Perf. 11x10½***

930 A377 1c **blue green,** *July 26, 1945* .20 .20

P# block of 4 .35 —

931 A378 2c **carmine rose,** *Aug. 24, 1945* .20 .20

P# block of 4 .45 —

932 A379 3c **purple,** *June 27, 1945* .20 .20

P# block of 4 .60 —

933 A380 5c **bright blue,** *Jan. 30, 1946* .20 .20

P# block of 4 .45 —

Nos. 930-933 (4) .80 .80

ARMY ISSUE

Achievements of the US Army in World War II.

United States Troops Passing Arch of Triumph, Paris — A381

ROTARY PRESS PRINTING

E.E. Plates of 200 subjects in four panes of 50.

1945, Sept. 28 ***Perf. 11x10½***

934 A381 3c **olive** .20 .20

P# block of 4 .60 —

NAVY ISSUE

Achievements of the U.S. Navy in World War II.

United States Sailors — A382

ROTARY PRESS PRINTING

E.E. Plates of 200 subjects in four panes of 50.

1945, Oct. 27 *Perf. 11x10½*

935 A382 3c **blue** .20 .20
P# block of 4 .60 —

COAST GUARD ISSUE

Achievements of the US Coast Guard in World War II.

Coast Guard Landing Craft and Supply Ship — A383

ROTARY PRESS PRINTING

E.E. Plates of 200 subjects in four panes of 50.

1945, Nov. 10 *Perf. 11x10½*

936 A383 3c **bright blue green** .20 .20
P# block of 4 .70 —

ALFRED E. SMITH ISSUE

Alfred E. Smith, Governor of New York — A384

ROTARY PRESS PRINTING

E.E. Plates of 400 subjects in four panes of 100.

1945, Nov. 26 *Perf. 11x10½*

937 A384 3c **purple** .20 .20
P# block of 4 .45
Pair with full vert. gutter btwn. —
Pair with full horiz. gutter btwn. *300.00*

TEXAS STATEHOOD, 100th ANNIV.

Flags of the United States and the State of Texas — A385

ROTARY PRESS PRINTING

E.E. Plates of 200 subjects in four panes of 50.

1945, Dec. 29 *Perf. 11x10½*

938 A385 3c **dark blue** .20 .20
P# block of 4 .50 —

MERCHANT MARINE ISSUE

Achievements of the US Merchant Marine in World War II.

Liberty Ship Unloading Cargo — A386

ROTARY PRESS PRINTING

E.E. Plates of 200 subjects in four panes of 50.

1946, Feb. 26 *Perf. 11x10½*

939 A386 3c **blue green** .20 .20
P# block of 4 .50 —

VETERANS OF WORLD WAR II ISSUE

Issued to honor all veterans of World War II.

Honorable Discharge Emblem — A387

ROTARY PRESS PRINTING

E.E. Plates of 400 subjects in four panes of 100.

1946, May 9 *Perf. 11x10½*

940 A387 3c **dark violet** .20 .20
P# block of 4 .50 —
Pair with full vert. gutter btwn. *225.00*

TENNESSEE STATEHOOD, 150th ANNIV.

Andrew Jackson, John Sevier and State Capitol, Nashville A388

ROTARY PRESS PRINTING

E.E. Plates of 200 subjects in four panes of 50.

1946, June 1 *Perf. 11x10½*

941 A388 3c **dark violet** .20 .20
P# block of 4 .50 —

IOWA STATEHOOD, 100th ANNIV.

Iowa State Flag and Map — A389

ROTARY PRESS PRINTING

E.E. Plates of 200 subjects in four panes of 50.

1946, Aug. 3 *Perf. 11x10½*

942 A389 3c **deep blue** .20 .20
P# block of 4 .45 —

SMITHSONIAN INSTITUTION ISSUE

100th anniversary of the establishment of the Smithsonian Institution, Washington, D.C.

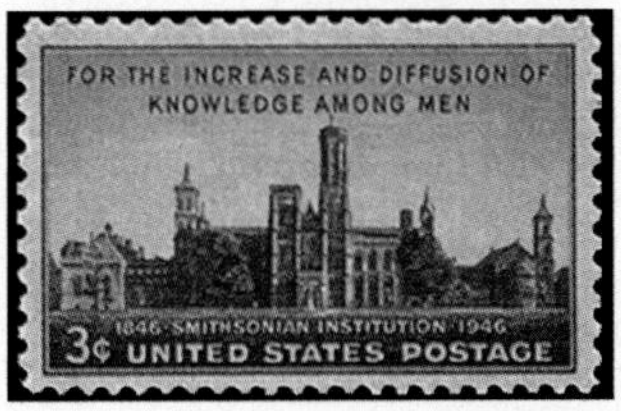

Smithsonian Institution A390

ROTARY PRESS PRINTING

E.E. Plates of 200 subjects in four panes of 50.

1946, Aug. 10 *Perf. 11x10½*

943 A390 3c **violet brown** .20 .20
P# block of 4 .40 —

KEARNY EXPEDITION ISSUE

100th anniversary of the entry of General Stephen Watts Kearny into Santa Fe.

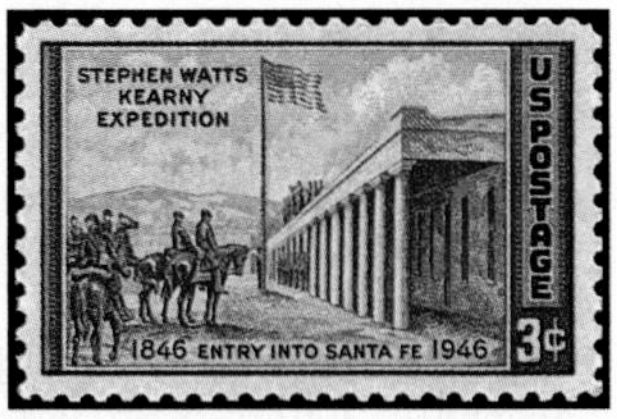

"Capture of Santa Fe" by Kenneth M. Chapman A391

ROTARY PRESS PRINTING

E.E. Plates of 200 subjects in four panes of 50.

1946, Oct. 16 *Perf. 11x10½*

944 A391 3c **brown violet** .20 .20
P# block of 4 .40 —

THOMAS A. EDISON ISSUE

Thomas A. Edison (1847-1931), Inventor — A392

ROTARY PRESS PRINTING

E.E. Plates of 280 subjects in four panes of 70.

1947, Feb. 11 *Perf. 10½x11*

945 A392 3c **bright red violet** .20 .20
P# block of 4 .40 —

JOSEPH PULITZER ISSUE

Joseph Pulitzer (1847-1911), Journalist, and Statue of Liberty A393

Designed by Victor S. McCloskey, Jr.

ROTARY PRESS PRINTING

E.E. Plates of 200 subjects in four panes of 50.

1947, Apr. 10 *Perf. 11x10½*

946 A393 3c **purple** .20 .20
P# block of 4 .40 —

POSTAGE STAMP CENTENARY ISSUE

Centenary of the first postage stamps issued by the United States Government

Washington and Franklin, Early and Modern Mail-carrying Vehicles A394

Designed by Leon Helguera.

ROTARY PRESS PRINTING

E.E. Plates of 200 subjects in four panes of 50.

1947, May 17 *Perf. 11x10½*

947 A394 3c **deep blue** .20 .20
P# block of 4 .40 —

CENTENARY INTERNATIONAL PHILATELIC EXHIBITION ISSUE

SOUVENIR SHEET

A395

Illustration reduced.

FLAT PLATE PRINTING
Plates of 30 subjects

1947, May 19 ***Imperf.***

948 A395	Sheet of 2	.55	.45
a.	5c **blue**, type A1	.20	.20
b.	10c **brown orange**, type A2	.25	.25

Sheet inscribed below stamps: "100th Anniversary United States Postage Stamps" and in the margins:
"PRINTED BY THE TREASURY DEPARTMENT, BUREAU OF ENGRAVING AND PRINTING. — UNDER AUTHORITY OF ROBERT E. HANNEGAN, POSTMASTER GENERAL. — IN COMPLIMENT TO THE CENTENARY INTERNATIONAL PHILATELIC EXHIBITION. — NEW YORK, N.Y., MAY 17-25, 1947."
Sheet size varies: 96-98x66-68mm.

DOCTORS ISSUE

Issued to honor the physicians of America.

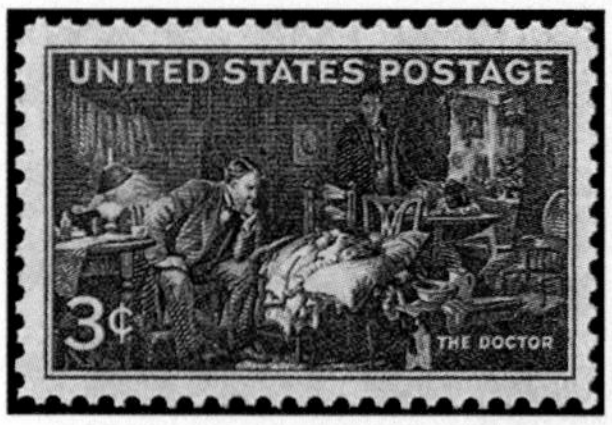

"The Doctor" by Sir Luke Fildes — A396

Designed by Charles R. Chickering.

ROTARY PRESS PRINTING
E.E. Plates of 200 subjects in four panes of 50.

1947, June 9 ***Perf. 11x10½***

949 A396 3c **brown violet**		.20	.20
	P# block of 4	.40	—

UTAH ISSUE

Centenary of the settlement of Utah.

Pioneers Entering the Valley of Great Salt Lake — A397

Designed by Charles R. Chickering.

ROTARY PRESS PRINTING
E.E. Plates of 200 subjects in four panes of 50.

1947, July 24 ***Perf. 11x10½***

950 A397 3c **dark violet**		.20	.20
	P# block of 4	.60	—

U.S. FRIGATE CONSTITUTION ISSUE

150th anniversary of the launching of the U.S. frigate Constitution ("Old Ironsides").

Naval Architect's Drawing of Frigate Constitution A398

Designed by Andrew H. Hepburn.

ROTARY PRESS PRINTING
E.E. Plates of 200 subjects in four panes of 50.

1947, Oct. 21 ***Perf. 11x10½***

951 A398 3c **blue green**		.20	.20
	P# block of 4	.40	—

Great White Heron and Map of Florida — A399

Dr. George Washington Carver — A400

EVERGLADES NATIONAL PARK ISSUE

Dedication of the Everglades National Park, Florida, Dec. 6, 1947.

Designed by Robert I. Miller, Jr.

ROTARY PRESS PRINTING
E.E. Plates of 200 subjects in four panes of 50.

1947, Dec. 5 ***Perf. 10½x11***

952 A399 3c **bright green**		.20	.20
	P# block of 4	.40	—

GEORGE WASHINGTON CARVER ISSUE

5th anniversary of the death of Dr. George Washington Carver, (1864-1943), botanist.

ROTARY PRESS PRINTING
E.E. Plates of 280 subjects in four panes of 70.

1948, Jan. 5 ***Perf. 10½x11***

953 A400 3c **bright red violet**		.20	.20
	P# block of 4	.45	—

CALIFORNIA GOLD CENTENNIAL ISSUE

Sutter's Mill, Coloma, California A401

Designed by Charles R. Chickering.

ROTARY PRESS PRINTING
E.E. Plates of 200 subjects in four panes of 50.

1948, Jan. 24 ***Perf. 11x10½***

954 A401 3c **dark violet**		.20	.20
	P# block of 4	.40	—

MISSISSIPPI TERRITORY ISSUE

Mississippi Territory establishment, 150th anniv.

Map, Seal of Mississippi Territory and Gov. Winthrop Sargent A402

Designed by William K. Schrage.

ROTARY PRESS PRINTING
E.E. Plates of 200 subjects in four panes of 50.

1948, Apr. 7 ***Perf. 11x10½***

955 A402 3c **brown violet**		.20	.20
	P# block of 4	.50	—

FOUR CHAPLAINS ISSUE

George L. Fox, Clark V. Poling, John P. Washington and Alexander D. Goode, the 4 chaplains who sacrificed their lives in the sinking of the S.S. Dorchester, Feb. 3, 1943.

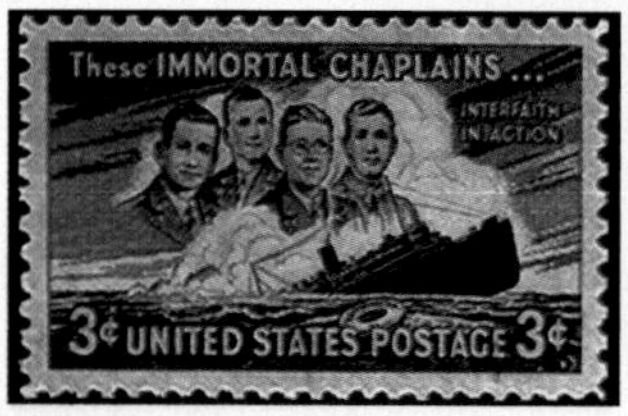

Four Chaplains and Sinking S.S. Dorchester A403

Designed by Charles R. Chickering.

ROTARY PRESS PRINTING
E.E. Plates of 200 subjects in four panes of 50.

1948, May 28 ***Perf. 11x10½***

956 A403 3c **gray black**		.20	.20
	P# block of 4	.50	—

WISCONSIN STATEHOOD, 100th ANNIV.

Map on Scroll and State Capitol A404

Designed by Victor S. McCloskey, Jr.

ROTARY PRESS PRINTING
E.E. Plates of 200 subjects in four panes of 50.

1948, May 29 ***Perf. 11x10½***

957 A404 3c **dark violet**		.20	.20
	P# block of 4	.50	—

SWEDISH PIONEER ISSUE

Centenary of the coming of the Swedish pioneers to the Middle West.

Swedish Pioneer with Covered Wagon Moving Westward A405

Designed by Charles R. Chickering.

ROTARY PRESS PRINTING
E.E. Plates of 200 subjects in four panes of 50.

1948, June 4 ***Perf. 11x10½***

958 A405 5c **deep blue**		.20	.20
	P# block of 4	.45	—

PROGRESS OF WOMEN ISSUE

Century of progress of American Women.

Elizabeth Stanton, Carrie Chapman Catt and Lucretia Mott — A406

Designed by Victor S. McCloskey, Jr.

ROTARY PRESS PRINTING
E.E. Plates of 200 subjects in four panes of 50.

1948, July 19 ***Perf. 11x10½***

959 A406 3c **dark violet**		.20	.20
	P# block of 4	.55	—

WILLIAM ALLEN WHITE ISSUE

William Allen White (1868-1944), Writer and Journalist — A407

ROTARY PRESS PRINTING

E.E. Plates of 280 subjects in four panes of 70.

1948, July 31 *Perf. 10½x11*

960 A407 3c **bright red violet** .20 .20
P# block of 4 .40 —

UNITED STATES-CANADA FRIENDSHIP ISSUE

Century of friendship between the US and Canada.

Niagara Railway Suspension Bridge — A408

Designed by Leon Helguera, modeled by V. S. McCloskey, Jr.

ROTARY PRESS PRINTING

E.E. Plates of 200 subjects in four panes of 50.

1948, Aug. 2 *Perf. 11x10½*

961 A408 3c **blue** .20 .20
P# block of 4 .40 —

FRANCIS SCOTT KEY ISSUE

Francis Scott Key (1779-1843), Maryland lawyer and author of "The Star-Spangled Banner" (1813).

Francis Scott Key and American Flags of 1814 and 1948 — A409

Designed by Victor S. McCloskey, Jr.

ROTARY PRESS PRINTING

E.E. Plates of 200 subjects in four panes of 50.

1948, Aug. 9 *Perf. 11x10½*

962 A409 3c **rose pink** .20 .20
P# block of 4 .40 —

SALUTE TO YOUTH ISSUE

Issued to honor the Youth of America and to publicize "Youth Month," September, 1948.

Girl and Boy Carrying Books — A410

ROTARY PRESS PRINTING

E.E. Plates of 200 subjects in four panes of 50.

1948, Aug. 11 *Perf. 11x10½*

963 A410 3c **deep blue** .20 .20
P# block of 4 .40 —

OREGON TERRITORY ISSUE

Centenary of the establishment of Oregon Territory.

John McLoughlin, Jason Lee and Wagon on Oregon Trail — A411

ROTARY PRESS PRINTING

E.E. Plates of 200 subjects in four panes of 50.

1948, Aug. 14 *Perf. 11x10½*

964 A411 3c **brown red** .20 .20
P# block of 4 .50 —

HARLAN F. STONE ISSUE

Harlan Fiske Stone (1872-1946) of New York, Associate Justice of the Supreme Court, 1925-1941, and Chief Justice, 1941-1946 — A412

ROTARY PRESS PRINTING

E.E. Plates of 280 subjects in four panes of 70.

1948, Aug. 25 *Perf. 10½x11*

965 A412 3c **bright violet** .20 .20
P# block of 4 .60 —

PALOMAR MOUNTAIN OBSERVATORY ISSUE

Dedication, August 30, 1948.

Observatory, Palomar Mountain, California — A413

Designed by Victor S. McCloskey, Jr.

ROTARY PRESS PRINTING

E.E. Plates of 280 subjects in four panes of 70.

1948, Aug. 30 *Perf. 10½x11*

966 A413 3c **blue** .20 .20
P# block of 4 .95 —
a. Vert. pair, imperf. between *350.*

CLARA BARTON ISSUE

Clara Barton (1821-1912), Founder of the American Red Cross in 1882 — A414

Designed by Charles R. Chickering.

ROTARY PRESS PRINTING

E.E. Plates of 200 subjects in four panes of 50.

1948, Sept. 7 *Perf. 11x10½*

967 A414 3c **rose pink** .20 .20
P# block of 4 .50 —

POULTRY INDUSTRY CENTENNIAL ISSUE

Light Brahma Rooster A415

Designed by Charles R. Chickering.

ROTARY PRESS PRINTING

E.E. Plates of 200 subjects in four panes of 50.

1948, Sept. 9 *Perf. 11x10½*

968 A415 3c **sepia** .20 .20
P# block of 4 .50 —

GOLD STAR MOTHERS ISSUE

Issued to honor the mothers of deceased members of the United States armed forces.

Star and Palm Frond — A416

Designed by Charles R. Chickering.

ROTARY PRESS PRINTING

E.E. Plates of 200 subjects in four panes of 50.

1948, Sept. 21 *Perf. 10½x11*

969 A416 3c **orange yellow** .20 .20
P# block of 4 .40 —

FORT KEARNY ISSUE

Establishment of Fort Kearny, Neb., centenary.

Fort Kearny and Pioneer Group — A417

ROTARY PRESS PRINTING

E.E. Plates of 200 subjects in four panes of 50.

1948, Sept. 22 *Perf. 11x10½*

970 A417 3c **violet** .20 .20
P# block of 4 .60 —

VOLUNTEER FIREMEN ISSUE

300th anniv. of the organization of the 1st volunteer firemen in America by Peter Stuyvesant.

Peter Stuyvesant, Early and Modern Fire Engines A418

ROTARY PRESS PRINTING

E.E. Plates of 200 subjects in four panes of 50.

1948, Oct. 4 *Perf. 11x10½*

971 A418 3c **bright rose carmine** .20 .20
P# block of 4 .60 —

INDIAN CENTENNIAL ISSUE

Centenary of the arrival in Indian Territory, later Oklahoma, of the Five Civilized Indian Tribes: Cherokee, Chickasaw, Choctaw, Muscogee and Seminole.

Map of Indian Territory and Seals of Five Tribes — A419

ROTARY PRESS PRINTING

E.E. Plates of 200 subjects in four panes of 50.

1948, Oct. 15 *Perf. 11x10½*

972 A419 3c **dark brown** .20 .20
P# block of 4 .60 —

ROUGH RIDERS ISSUE

50th anniversary of the organization of the Rough Riders of the Spanish-American War.

Statue of Capt. William O. (Bucky) O'Neill by Solon H. Borglum A420

Designed by Victor S. McCloskey, Jr.

ROTARY PRESS PRINTING
E.E. Plates of 200 subjects in four panes of 50.

1948, Oct. 27 ***Perf. 11x10½***
973 A420 3c **violet brown** .20 .20
P# block of 4 .50 —

JULIETTE LOW ISSUE

Low (1860-1927), founder of the Girl Scouts of America. Mrs. Low organized the 1st Girl Guides troop in 1912 at Savannah. The name was changed to Girl Scouts in 1913 and headquarters moved to New York.

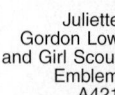

Juliette Gordon Low and Girl Scout Emblem A421

Designed by William K. Schrage.

ROTARY PRESS PRINTING
E.E. Plates of 200 subjects in four panes of 50.

1948, Oct. 29 ***Perf. 11x10½***
974 A421 3c **blue green** .20 .20
P# block of 4 .50 —

Will Rogers, (1879-1935), Humorist and Political Commentator. — A422

Fort Bliss, El Paso, Texas, and Rocket Firing — A423

WILL ROGERS ISSUE

ROTARY PRESS PRINTING
E.E. Plates of 280 subjects in four panes of 70.

1948, Nov. 4 ***Perf. 10½x11***
975 A422 3c **bright red violet** .20 .20
P# block of 4 .45 —

FORT BLISS CENTENNIAL ISSUE

Designed by Charles R. Chickering.

ROTARY PRESS PRINTING
E.E. Plates of 280 subjects in four panes of 70.

1948, Nov. 5 ***Perf. 10½x11***
976 A423 3c **henna brown** .20 .20
P# block of 4 1.00 —

MOINA MICHAEL ISSUE

Moina Michael (1870-1944), educator who originated (1918) the Flanders Field Poppy Day idea as a memorial to the war dead.

Moina Michael and Poppy Plant — A424

ROTARY PRESS PRINTING
E.E. Plates of 200 subjects in four panes of 50.

1948, Nov. 9 ***Perf. 11x10½***
977 A424 3c **rose pink** .20 .20
P# block of 4 .50 —

GETTYSBURG ADDRESS ISSUE

85th anniversary of Abraham Lincoln's address at Gettysburg, Pennsylvania.

Abraham Lincoln and Quotation from Gettysburg Address A425

Designed by Charles R. Chickering.

ROTARY PRESS PRINTING
E.E. Plates of 200 subjects in four panes of 50.

1948, Nov. 19 ***Perf. 11x10½***
978 A425 3c **bright blue** .20 .20
P# block of 4 .60 —

Torch and Emblem of American Turners A426

Joel Chandler Harris (1848-1908), Georgia Writer, Creator of "Uncle Remus" and newspaperman. A427

AMERICAN TURNERS ISSUE

Formation of the American Turners Soc., cent.

Designed by Alvin R. Meissner.

ROTARY PRESS PRINTING
E.E. Plates of 200 subjects in four panes of 50.

1948, Nov. 20 ***Perf. 10½x11***
979 A426 3c **carmine** .20 .20
P# block of 4 .40 —

JOEL CHANDLER HARRIS ISSUE

ROTARY PRESS PRINTING
E.E. Plates of 280 subjects in four panes of 70.

1948, Dec. 9 ***Perf. 10½x11***
980 A427 3c **bright red violet** .20 .20
P# block of 4 .55 —

MINNESOTA TERRITORY ISSUE

Establishment of Minnesota Territory, cent.

Pioneer and Red River Oxcart — A428

ROTARY PRESS PRINTING
E.E. Plates of 200 subjects in four panes of 50.

1949, Mar. 3 ***Perf. 11x10½***
981 A428 3c **blue green** .20 .20
P# block of 4 .45 —

WASHINGTON AND LEE UNIVERSITY ISSUE

Bicentenary of Washington and Lee University.

George Washington, Robert E. Lee and University Building, Lexington, Va. — A429

ROTARY PRESS PRINTING
E.E. Plates of 200 subjects in four panes of 50.

1949, Apr. 12 ***Perf. 11x10½***
982 A429 3c **ultramarine** .20 .20
P# block of 4 .40 —

PUERTO RICO ELECTION ISSUE

First gubernatorial election in the Territory of Puerto Rico, Nov. 2, 1948.

Puerto Rican Farmer Holding Cogwheel and Ballot Box — A430

ROTARY PRESS PRINTING
E.E. Plates of 200 subjects in four panes of 50.

1949, Apr. 27 ***Perf. 11x10½***
983 A430 3c **green** .20 .20
P# block of 4 .40 —

ANNAPOLIS TERCENTENARY ISSUE

Founding of Annapolis, Maryland, 300th anniv.

James Stoddert's 1718 Map of Regions about Annapolis, Redrawn A431

ROTARY PRESS PRINTING
E.E. Plates of 200 subjects in four panes of 50.

1949, May 23 ***Perf. 11x10½***
984 A431 3c **aquamarine** .20 .20
P# block of 4 .40 —

G.A.R. ISSUE

Final encampment of the Grand Army of the Republic, Indianapolis, Aug. 28 - Sept. 1, 1949.

Union Soldier and G.A.R. Veteran of 1949 — A432

Designed by Charles R. Chickering.

ROTARY PRESS PRINTING
E.E. Plates of 200 subjects in four panes of 50.

1949, Aug. 29 ***Perf. 11x10½***
985 A432 3c **bright rose carmine** .20 .20
P# block of 4 .40 —

EDGAR ALLAN POE ISSUE

Edgar Allan Poe (1809-1849), Boston-born Poet, Story Writer and Editor — A433

ROTARY PRESS PRINTING

E.E. Plates of 280 subjects in four panes of 70.

1949, Oct. 7 *Perf. 10½x11*

986 A433 3c **bright red violet** .20 .20
P# block of 4 .45 —
Thin outer frame line at top, inner line missing (24143 LL 42) 6.00

AMERICAN BANKERS ASSOCIATION ISSUE

75th anniv. of the formation of the Association.

Coin, Symbolizing Fields of Banking Service A434

Designed by Charles R. Chickering.

ROTARY PRESS PRINTING

E.E. Plates of 200 subjects in four panes of 50.

1950, Jan. 3 *Perf. 11x10½*

987 A434 3c **yellow green** .20 .20
P# block of 4 .40 —

SAMUEL GOMPERS ISSUE

Samuel Gompers (1850-1924), British-born American Labor Leader — A435

ROTARY PRESS PRINTING

E.E. Plates of 280 subjects in four panes of 70.

1950, Jan. 27 *Perf. 10½x11*

988 A435 3c **bright red violet** .20 .20
P# block of 4 .40 —

NATIONAL CAPITAL SESQUICENTENNIAL ISSUE

150th anniversary of the establishment of the National Capital, Washington, D.C.

Statue of Freedom on Capitol Dome — A436

Executive Mansion A437

Supreme Court Building A438

United States Capitol — A439

ROTARY PRESS PRINTING

E.E. Plates of 200 subjects in four panes of 50.

1950 *Perf. 10½x11, 11x10½*

989 A436 3c **bright blue,** *Apr. 20* .20 .20
P# block of 4 .40 —
990 A437 3c **deep green,** *June 12* .20 .20
P# block of 4 .50 —
991 A438 3c **light violet,** *Aug. 2* .20 .20
P# block of 4 .30 —
992 A439 3c **bright red violet,** *Nov. 22* .20 .20
P# block of 4 .55 —
Gripper cracks (24285 UL 11) 4.50 3.00
Nos. 989-992 (4) .80 .80

RAILROAD ENGINEERS ISSUE

Issued to honor the Railroad Engineers of America. Stamp portrays John Luther (Casey) Jones (1864-1900), locomotive engineer killed in train wreck near Vaughn, Miss.

"Casey" Jones and Locomotives of 1900 and 1950 — A440

ROTARY PRESS PRINTING

E.E. Plates of 200 subjects in four panes of 50.

1950, Apr. 29 *Perf. 11x10½*

993 A440 3c **violet brown** .20 .20
P# block of 4 .50 —

KANSAS CITY, MISSOURI, CENTENARY ISSUE

Kansas City, Missouri, incorporation.

Kansas City Skyline, 1950 and Westport Landing, 1850 — A441

ROTARY PRESS PRINTING

E.E. Plates of 200 subjects in four panes of 50.

1950, June 3 *Perf. 11x10½*

994 A441 3c **violet** .20 .20
P# block of 4 .40 —

BOY SCOUTS ISSUE

Honoring the Boy Scouts of America on the occasion of the 2nd National Jamboree, Valley Forge, Pa.

Three Boys, Statue of Liberty and Scout Badge A442

ROTARY PRESS PRINTING

E.E. Plates of 200 subjects in four panes of 50.

1950, June 30 *Perf. 11x10½*

995 A442 3c **sepia** .20 .20
P# block of 4 .50 —

INDIANA TERRITORY ISSUE

Establishment of Indiana Territory, 150th anniv.

Gov. William Henry Harrison and First Indiana Capitol, Vincennes A443

ROTARY PRESS PRINTING

E.E. Plates of 200 subjects in four panes of 50.

1950, July 4 *Perf. 11x10½*

996 A443 3c **bright blue** .20 .20
P# block of 4 .50 —

CALIFORNIA STATEHOOD ISSUE

Gold Miner, Pioneers and S.S. Oregon A444

ROTARY PRESS PRINTING

E.E. Plates of 200 subjects in four panes of 50.

1950, Sept. 9 *Perf. 11x10½*

997 A444 3c **yellow orange** .20 .20
P# block of 4 .50 —

UNITED CONFEDERATE VETERANS FINAL REUNION ISSUE

Final reunion of the United Confederate Veterans, Norfolk, Virginia, May 30, 1951.

Confederate Soldier and United Confederate Veteran A445

ROTARY PRESS PRINTING

E.E. Plates of 200 subjects in four panes of 50.

1951, May 30 *Perf. 11x10½*

998 A445 3c **gray** .20 .20
P# block of 4 .45 —

NEVADA CENTENNIAL ISSUE

Centenary of the settlement of Nevada.

Carson Valley, c. 1851 — A446

Designed by Charles R. Chickering.

ROTARY PRESS PRINTING

E.E. Plates of 200 subjects in four panes of 50.

1951, July 14 *Perf. 11x10½*

999 A446 3c **light olive green** .20 .20
P# block of 4 .50 —

LANDING OF CADILLAC ISSUE

250th anniversary of the landing of Antoine de la Mothe Cadillac at Detroit.

Detroit Skyline and Cadillac Landing A447

ROTARY PRESS PRINTING

E.E. Plates of 200 subjects in four panes of 50.

1951, July 24 ***Perf. 11x10½***

1000 A447 3c **blue** .20 .20
P# block of 4 .30 —

COLORADO STATEHOOD, 75th ANNIV.

Colorado Capitol, Mount of the Holy Cross, Columbine and Bronco Buster by Proctor A448

ROTARY PRESS PRINTING

E.E. Plates of 200 subjects in four panes of 50.

1951, Aug. 1 ***Perf. 11x10½***

1001 A448 3c **blue violet** .20 .20
P# block of 4 .40 —

AMERICAN CHEMICAL SOCIETY ISSUE

75th anniv. of the formation of the Society.

A.C.S. Emblem and Symbols of Chemistry A449

ROTARY PRESS PRINTING

E.E. Plates of 200 subjects in four panes of 50.

1951, Sept. 4 ***Perf. 11x10½***

1002 A449 3c **violet brown** .20 .20
P# block of 4 .50 —

BATTLE OF BROOKLYN, 175th ANNIV.

Gen. George Washington Evacuating Army; Fulton Ferry House at Right — A450

ROTARY PRESS PRINTING

E.E. Plates of 200 subjects in four panes of 50.

1951, Dec. 10 ***Perf. 11x10½***

1003 A450 3c **violet** .20 .20
P# block of 4 .40 —

BETSY ROSS ISSUE

200th anniv. of the birth of Betsy Ross, maker of the first American flag.

"Birth of Our Nation's Flag," by Charles H. Weisgerber — Betsy Ross Showing Flag to Gen. George Washington, Robert Morris and George Ross — A451

ROTARY PRESS PRINTING

E.E. Plates of 200 subjects in four panes of 50.

1952, Jan. 2 ***Perf. 11x10½***

1004 A451 3c **carmine rose** .20 .20
P# block of 4 .40 —

4-H CLUB ISSUE

Farm, Club Emblem, Boy and Girl — A452

ROTARY PRESS PRINTING

E.E. Plates of 200 subjects in four panes of 50.

1952, Jan. 15 ***Perf. 11x10½***

1005 A452 3c **blue green** .20 .20
P# block of 4 .50 —

B. & O. RAILROAD ISSUE

125th anniv. of the granting of a charter to the Baltimore and Ohio Railroad Company by the Maryland Legislature.

Charter and Three Stages of Rail Transportation A453

ROTARY PRESS PRINTING

E.E. Plates of 200 subjects in four panes of 50.

1952, Feb. 28 ***Perf. 11x10½***

1006 A453 3c **bright blue** .20 .20
P# block of 4 .45 —

A. A. A. ISSUE

50th anniversary of the formation of the American Automobile Association.

School Girls and Safety Patrolman Automobiles of 1902 and 1952 — A454

ROTARY PRESS PRINTING

E.E. Plates of 200 subjects in four panes of 50.

1952, Mar. 4 ***Perf. 11x10½***

1007 A454 3c **deep blue** .20 .20
P# block of 4 .40 —

NATO ISSUE

Signing of the North Atlantic Treaty, 3rd anniv.

Torch of Liberty and Globe — A455

ROTARY PRESS PRINTING

E.E. Plates of 400 subjects in four panes of 100.

1952, Apr. 4 ***Perf. 11x10½***

1008 A455 3c **deep violet** .20 .20
P# block of 4 .40 —

GRAND COULEE DAM ISSUE

50 years of Federal cooperation in developing the resources of rivers and streams in the West.

Spillway, Grand Coulee Dam — A456

ROTARY PRESS PRINTING

E.E. Plates of 200 subjects in four panes of 50.

1952, May 15 ***Perf. 11x10½***

1009 A456 3c **blue green** .20 .20
P# block of 4 .40 —

LAFAYETTE ISSUE

175th anniversary of the arrival of Marquis de Lafayette in America.

Marquis de Lafayette, Flags, Cannon and Landing Party — A457

Designed by Victor S. McCloskey, Jr.

ROTARY PRESS PRINTING

E.E. Plates of 200 subjects in four panes of 50.

1952, June 13 ***Perf. 11x10½***

1010 A457 3c **bright blue** .20 .20
P# block of 4 .45 —

MT. RUSHMORE MEMORIAL ISSUE

Dedication of the Mt. Rushmore National Memorial in the Black Hills of South Dakota, 25th anniv.

Sculptured Heads on Mt. Rushmore — A458

Designed by William K. Schrage.

ROTARY PRESS PRINTING

E.E. Plates of 200 subjects in four panes of 50.

1952, Aug. 11 ***Perf. 10½x11***

1011 A458 3c **blue green** .20 .20
P# block of 4 .75 —

ENGINEERING CENTENNIAL ISSUE

American Society of Civil Engineers founding.

George Washington Bridge and Covered Bridge of 1850's A459

ROTARY PRESS PRINTING

E.E. Plates of 200 subjects in four panes of 50.

1952, Sept. 6 ***Perf. 11x10½***

1012 A459 3c **violet blue** .20 .20
P# block of 4 .45 —

SERVICE WOMEN ISSUE

Women in the United States Armed Services.

Women of the Marine Corps, Army, Navy and Air Force — A460

ROTARY PRESS PRINTING

E.E. Plates of 200 subjects in four panes of 50.

1952, Sept. 11 ***Perf. 11x10½***

1013 A460 3c **deep blue** .20 .20
P# block of 4 .40 —

GUTENBERG BIBLE ISSUE

Printing of the 1st book, the Holy Bible, from movable type, by Johann Gutenberg, 500th anniv.

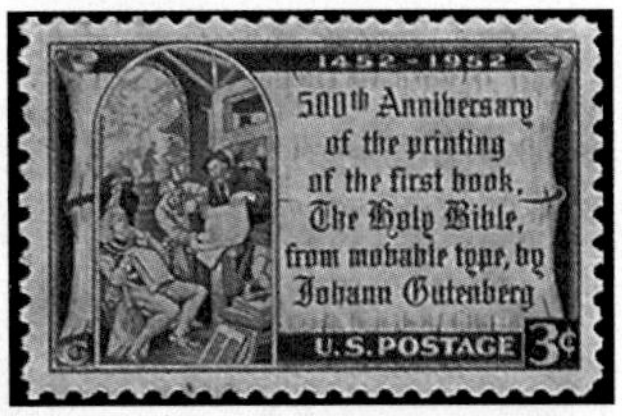

Gutenberg Showing Proof to the Elector of Mainz — A461

ROTARY PRESS PRINTING

E.E. Plates of 200 subjects in four panes of 50.

1952, Sept. 30 ***Perf. 11x10½***

1014 A461 3c **violet** .20 .20
P# block of 4 .40 —

NEWSPAPER BOYS ISSUE

Newspaper Boy, Torch and Group of Homes A462

ROTARY PRESS PRINTING

E.E. Plates of 200 subjects in four panes of 50.

1952, Oct. 4 ***Perf. 11x10½***

1015 A462 3c **violet** .20 .20
P# block of 4 .40 —

RED CROSS ISSUE

Globe, Sun and Cross — A463

ROTARY PRESS PRINTING

Cross Typographed

E.E. Plates of 200 subjects in four panes of 50.

1952, Nov. 21 ***Perf. 11x10½***

1016 A463 3c **deep blue & carmine** .20 .20
P# block of 4 .40 —

NATIONAL GUARD ISSUE

National Guardsman, Amphibious Landing and Disaster Service A464

ROTARY PRESS PRINTING

E.E. Plates of 200 subjects in four panes of 50.

1953, Feb. 23 ***Perf. 11x10½***

1017 A464 3c **bright blue** .20 .20
P# block of 4 .40 —

OHIO STATEHOOD, 150th ANNIV.

Ohio Map, State Seal, Buckeye Leaf — A465

ROTARY PRESS PRINTING

E.E. Plates of 280 subjects in four panes of 70.

1953, Mar. 2 ***Perf. 11x10½***

1018 A465 3c **chocolate** .20 .20
P# block of 4 .45 —

WASHINGTON TERRITORY ISSUE

Organization of Washington Territory, cent.

Medallion, Pioneers and Washington Scene — A466

ROTARY PRESS PRINTING

E.E. Plates of 200 subjects in four panes of 50.

1953, Mar. 2 ***Perf. 11x10½***

1019 A466 3c **green** .20 .20
P# block of 4 .45 —

LOUISIANA PURCHASE, 150th ANNIV.

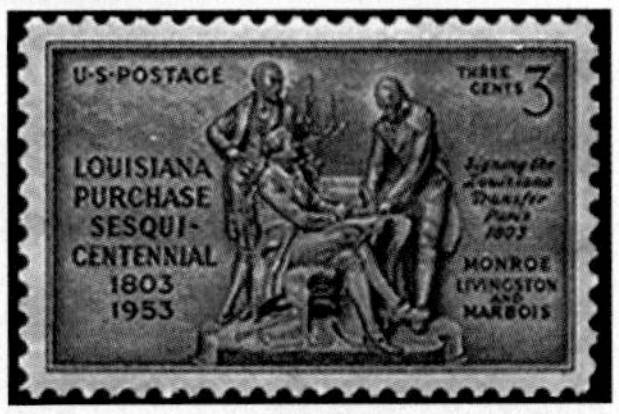

James Monroe, Robert R. Livingston and Marquis Francois de Barbé-Marbois A467

ROTARY PRESS PRINTING

E.E. Plates of 200 subjects in four panes of 50.

1953, Apr. 30 ***Perf. 11x10½***

1020 A467 3c **violet brown** .20 .20
P# block of 4 .90 —

OPENING OF JAPAN CENTENNIAL ISSUE

Centenary of Commodore Matthew Calbraith Perry's negotiations with Japan, which opened her doors to foreign trade.

Commodore Matthew C. Perry and First Anchorage off Tokyo Bay — A468

ROTARY PRESS PRINTING

E.E. Plates of 200 subjects in four panes of 50.

1953, July 14 ***Perf. 11x10½***

1021 A468 5c **green** .20 .20
P# block of 4 .65 —

AMERICAN BAR ASSOCIATION, 75th ANNIV.

Section of Frieze, Supreme Court Room — A469

ROTARY PRESS PRINTING

E.E. Plates of 200 subjects in four panes of 50.

1953, Aug. 24 ***Perf. 11x10½***

1022 A469 3c **rose violet** .20 .20
P# block of 4 .40 —

SAGAMORE HILL ISSUE

Opening of Sagamore Hill, Theodore Roosevelt's home, as a national shrine.

Home of Theodore Roosevelt A470

ROTARY PRESS PRINTING

E.E. Plates of 200 subjects in four panes of 50.

1953, Sept. 14 ***Perf. 11x10½***

1023 A470 3c **yellow green** .20 .20
P# block of 4 .40 —

FUTURE FARMERS ISSUE

25th anniversary of the organization of Future Farmers of America.

Agricultural Scene and Future Farmer A471

ROTARY PRESS PRINTING

E.E. Plates of 200 subjects in four panes of 50.

1953, Oct. 13 ***Perf. 11x10½***

1024 A471 3c **deep blue** .20 .20
P# block of 4 .40 —

TRUCKING INDUSTRY ISSUE

50th anniv. of the Trucking Industry in the US.

Truck, Farm and Distant City — A472

ROTARY PRESS PRINTING

E.E. Plates of 200 subjects in four panes of 50.

1953, Oct. 27 ***Perf. 11x10½***

1025	A472	3c	**violet**	.20	.20
			P# block of 4	.40	—

GENERAL PATTON ISSUE

Honoring Gen. George S. Patton, Jr. (1885-1945), and the armored forces of the US Army.

Gen. George S. Patton, Jr., and Tanks in Action — A473

ROTARY PRESS PRINTING

E.E. Plates of 200 subjects in four panes of 50.

1953, Nov. 11 ***Perf. 11x10½***

1026	A473	3c	**blue violet**	.20	.20
			P# block of 4	.45	—

NEW YORK CITY, 300th ANNIV.

Dutch Ship in New Amsterdam Harbor A474

ROTARY PRESS PRINTING

E.E. Plates of 200 subjects in four panes of 50.

1953, Nov. 20 ***Perf. 11x10½***

1027	A474	3c	**bright red violet**	.20	.20
			P# block of 4	.40	—

GADSDEN PURCHASE ISSUE

Centenary of James Gadsden's purchase of territory from Mexico to adjust the US-Mexico boundary.

Map and Pioneer Group — A475

ROTARY PRESS PRINTING

E.E. Plates of 200 subjects in four panes of 50.

1953, Dec. 30 ***Perf. 11x10½***

1028	A475	3c	**copper brown**	.20	.20
			P# block of 4	.40	—

COLUMBIA UNIVERSITY, 200th ANNIV.

Low Memorial Library A476

ROTARY PRESS PRINTING

E.E. Plates of 200 subjects in four panes of 50.

1954, Jan. 4 ***Perf. 11x10½***

1029	A476	3c	**blue**	.20	.20
			P# block of 4	.40	—

Wet and Dry Printings

In 1953 the Bureau of Engraving and Printing began experiments in printing on "dry" paper (moisture content 5-10 per cent). In previous "wet" printings the paper had a moisture content of 15-35 per cent.

The new process required a thicker, stiffer paper, special types of inks and greater pressure to force the paper into the recessed plates. The "dry" printings show whiter paper, a higher sheen on the surface, feel thicker and stiffer, and the designs stand out more clearly than on the "wet" printings.

Nos. 832c and 1041 (flat plate) were the first "dry" printings to be issued of flat-plate, regular-issue stamps. No. 1063 was the first rotary press stamp to be produced entirely by "dry" printing.

Stamps printed by both the "wet" and "dry" process are Nos. 1030, 1031, 1035, 1035a, 1036, 1039, 1049, 1050-1052, 1054, 1055, 1057, 1058, C34-C36, C39, C39a, J78, J80-J84, QE1-QE3, RF26-RF28, S1, S1a, S2, S2a, S3. The "wet" printed 4c coil, No. 1058, exists only Bureau precanceled.

In the Liberty Issue listings that follow, wet printings are listed first, followed by dry printings. Where only one type of printing of a stamp is indicated, it is "dry."

All postage stamps have been printed by the "dry" process since the late 1950s.

LIBERTY ISSUE

Benjamin Franklin — A477

George Washington — A478

Palace of the Governors, Santa Fe — A478a

Mount Vernon — A479

Thomas Jefferson — A480

Bunker Hill Monument and Massachusetts Flag, 1776 — A481

Statue of Liberty — A482

Abraham Lincoln — A483

The Hermitage, Home of Andrew Jackson, near Nashville — A484

James Monroe — A485

Theodore Roosevelt — A486

Woodrow Wilson — A487

Statue of Liberty — A488

Statue of Liberty — A489

John J. Pershing — A489a

The Alamo, San Antonio — A490

Independence Hall — A491

Statue of Liberty — A491a

Benjamin Harrison — A492

John Jay — A493

Monticello, Home of Thomas Jefferson, near Charlottesville, Va. — A494

Paul Revere — A495

Robert E. Lee — A496

John Marshall — A497

Susan B. Anthony — A498

Patrick Henry — A499

Alexander Hamilton — A500

ROTARY PRESS PRINTING

E.E. Plates of 400 subjects in four panes of 100

1954-68 ***Perf. 11x10½***

1030a A477 ½c **red orange,** wet printing, *Oct. 20, 1955* .20 .20
P# block of 4 .35 —
1030 A477 ½c **red orange,** dry printing, *May 1958* .20 .20
P# block of 4 (#25980 and up) .25 —

1031b A478 1c **dark green,** wet printing, *Aug. 26, 1954* .20 .20
P# block of 4 .25 —
1031 A478 1c **dark green,** dry printing, *Mar. 1956* .20 .20
P# block of 4 (#25326 and up) .25 —
Pair with full vert. gutter between *150.00*
Pair with full horiz. gutter between *150.00*

Perf. 10½x11

1031A A478a 1¼c **turquoise,** *June 17, 1960* .20 .20
P# block of 4 .45 —
1032 A479 1½c **brown carmine,** *Feb. 22, 1956* .20 .20
P# block of 4 1.75 —

Perf. 11x10½

1033 A480 2c **carmine rose,** *Sept. 15, 1954* .20 .20
P# block of 4 .25 —
Pair with full vert. gutter between —
Pair with full horiz. gutter between —
a. Silkote paper *350.*
P# block of 4 *2,250.*
On cover —

Silkote paper was used in 1954 for an experimental printing of 50,000 stamps. The stamps were put on sale at the Westbrook, Maine post office in Dec. 1954. Only plates 25061 and 25062 were used to print No. 1033a (these plates also used to print No. 1033 on normal paper). Competent expertization is required for No. 1033a.

1034 A481 2½c **gray blue,** *June 17, 1959* .20 .20
P# block of 4 .50 —
1035e A482 3c **deep violet,** wet printing, *June 24, 1954* .20 .20
P# block of 4 .40 —
a. Booklet pane of 6, *June 30, 1954* 4.00 *1.25*
g. As "a," vert. imperf. between *5,000.*
1035 A482 3c **deep violet,** dry printing .20 .20
P# block of 4 (#25235 and up) .30 —
Pair with full vert. gutter between *150.00*
Pair with full horiz. gutter between *150.00*
b. Tagged, *July 6, 1966* .35 .25
P# block of 4 5.75 —
c. Imperf., pair *2,000.*
d. Horiz. pair, imperf. between —
f. Booklet pane of 6, dry printing 5.00 *1.50*

No. 1057a measures about 19½x22mm; No. 1035c, about 18¾x22½mm.

1036c A483 4c **red violet,** wet printing, *Nov. 19, 1954* .20 .20
P# block of 4 .50 —
1036 A483 4c **red violet,** dry printing .20 .20
P# block of 4 (#25445 and up) .35 —
Pair with full vert. gutter between *675.00*
Pair with full horiz. gutter between *900.00*
a. Booklet pane of 6, *July 31, 1958* 2.75 *1.25*
b. Tagged, *Nov. 2, 1963* .65 .40

P# block of 4 9.00 —
d. As "a," imperf. horiz. —
e. Horiz. pair, imperf between *3,500.*

No. 1036e resulted from a booklet pane foldover after perforating and before cutting into panes.

Perf. 10½x11

1037 A484 4½c **blue green,** *Mar. 16, 1959* .20 .20
P# block of 4 .65 —

Perf. 11x10½

1038 A485 5c **deep blue,** *Dec. 2, 1954* .20 .20
P# block of 4 .60 —
Pair with full vert. gutter btwn. *200.00*

1039a A486 6c **carmine,** wet printing, *Nov. 18, 1955* .40 .20
P# block of 4 2.00 —
1039 A486 6c **carmine,** dry printing .25 .20
P# block of 4 (#25427 and up) 1.25 —
b. Imperf, block of 4 (unique) *23,000.*

1040 A487 7c **rose carmine,** *Jan. 10, 1956* .20 .20
P# block of 4 1.00 —
a. 7c **dark rose carmine** .20 .20
P# block of 4 1.00 —

FLAT PLATE PRINTING

Plates of 400 subjects in four panes of 100 each

Size: 22.7mm high

Perf. 11

1041 A488 8c **dark violet blue & carmine,** *Apr. 9, 1954* .25 .20
P# block of 4, 2# 2.00 —
Corner P# block of 4, blue # only —
Corner P# block of 4, red # only —
a. Double impression of carmine *575.00*

FLAT PRINTING PLATES
Frame: 24912-13-14-15, 24926, 24929-30, 24932-33.
Vignette: 24916-17-18-19-20, 24935-36-37, 24939.
See note following No. 1041B.

ROTARY PRESS PRINTING

Plates of 400 subjects in four panes of 100 each

Size: 22.9mm high

Perf. 11

1041B A488 8c **dark violet blue & carmine,** *Apr. 9, 1954* .40 .20
P# block of 4, 2# 3.50 —

ROTARY PRINTING PLATES
Frame: 24923-24, 24928, 24940, 24942.
Vignette: 24927, 24938.

No. 1041B is slightly taller than No. 1041, about the thickness of one line of engraving.

GIORI PRESS PRINTING

Plates of 400 subjects in four panes of 100 each

Redrawn design

Perf. 11

1042 A489 8c **dark violet blue & carmine rose,** *Mar. 22, 1958* .20 .20
P# block of 4 .90 —

ROTARY PRESS PRINTING

E.E. Plates of 400 subjects in four panes of 100 each

Perf. 11x10½

1042A A489a 8c **brown,** *Nov. 17, 1961* .20 .20
P# block of 4 .90 —

Many collectors do not consider No. 1042A to be part of the Liberty issue. Instead, they prefer to group it with Nos.1209 and 1213.

Perf. 10½x11

1043 A490 9c **rose lilac,** *June 14, 1956* .30 .20
P# block of 4 1.30 —
a. 9c **dark rose lilac** .30 .20
P# block of 4 1.30 —

1044 A491 10c **rose lake,** *July 4, 1956* .30 .20
P# block of 4 1.40 —
b. 10c **dark rose lake** .25 .20
P# block of 4 1.10 —
d. Tagged, *July 6, 1966* 2.00 1.00
P# block of 4 *35.00* —

No. 1044b is from later printings and is on a harder, whiter paper than No. 1044.

GIORI PRESS PRINTING

Plates of 400 subjects in four panes of 100.

Perf. 11

1044A A491a 11c **carmine & dark violet blue,** *June 15, 1961* .30 .20
P# block of 4 1.50 —
c. Tagged, *Jan. 11, 1967* 2.50 1.60
P# block of 4 *45.00* -

ROTARY PRESS PRINTING

E.E. Plates of 400 subjects in four panes of 100 each

Perf. 11x10½

1045 A492 12c **red,** *June 6, 1959* .35 .20
P# block of 4 1.50 —
a. Tagged, *1968* .35 .20
P# block of 4 4.00 —

1046 A493 15c **rose lake,** *Dec. 12, 1958* .60 .20
P# block of 4 3.00 —
a. Tagged, *July 6, 1966* 1.10 .80
P# block of 4 13.00

Perf. 10½x11

1047 A494 20c **ultramarine,** *Apr. 13, 1956* .50 .20
P# block of 4 2.25 —
a. 20c **deep bright ultramarine** .50 .20
P# block of 4 2.25 —

No. 1047a is from later printings and is on a harder, whiter paper than No. 1047.

Perf. 11x10½

1048 A495 25c **green,** *Apr. 18, 1958* 1.10 .75
P# block of 4 4.75 —

1049a A496 30c **black,** wet printing, *Sept. 21, 1955* 1.20 .75
P# block of 4 5.25 —
1049 A496 30c **black,** dry printing, *June 1957* 1.00 .20
P# block of 4 (#25487 and up) 4.50 —
b. 30c **intense black** .80 .20
P# block of 4 3.75 —

No. 1049b is from later printings and is on a harder, whiter paper than No. 1049.

1050a A497 40c **brown red,** wet printing, *Sept. 24, 1955* 1.75 .25
P# block of 4 9.00 —
1050 A497 40c **brown red,** dry printing, *Apr. 1958* 1.50 .20
P# block of 4 (#25571 and up) 7.50 —

1051a A498 50c **bright purple,** wet printing, *Aug. 25, 1955* 1.75 .20
P# block of 4 11.00 —
Cracked plate (25231 UL 1) — —
1051 A498 50c **bright purple,** dry printing, *Apr. 1958* 1.50 .20
P# block of 4 (#25897 and up) 8.00 —

1052a A499 $1 **purple,** wet printing, *Oct. 7, 1955* 5.25 1.00
P# block of 4 22.50 —
1052 A499 $1 **purple,** dry printing, *Oct. 1958* 4.50 .20
P# block of 4 (#25541 and up) 19.00 —

FLAT PLATE PRINTING

Plates of 400 subjects in four panes of 100.

Perf. 11

1053 A500 $5 **black,** *Mar. 19, 1956* 60.00 6.75
P# block of 4 275.00 —

Bureau Precancels: ½c, 37 diff., 1c, 113 diff., 1¼c, 142 diff., 1½c, 45 diff.
2c, 86 diff., 2½c, 123 diff., 3c, 106 diff., 4c, 95 diff., 4½c, 23 diff., 5c, 20 diff., 6c, 23 diff., 7c, 16 diff.

Also, No. 1041, 12 diff., No. 1042, 12 diff., No. 1042A, 16 diff., 9c, 15 diff., 10c, 16 diff., 11c, New York, 12c, 6 diff. 15c, 12 diff., 20c, 20 diff., 25c, 11 diff., 30c, 17 diff., 40c, 10 diff., 50c, 19 diff., $1, 5 diff.

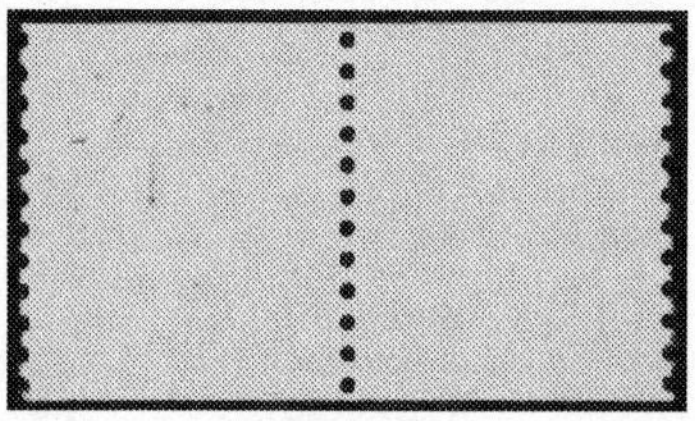

Large Holes

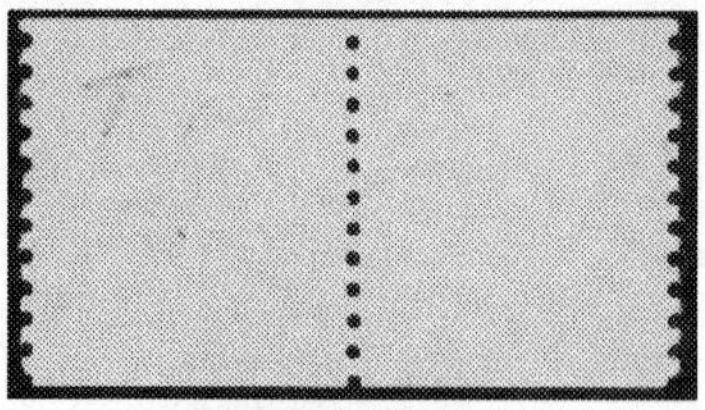

Small Holes

With the change from 384-subject plates to 432-subject plates the size of the perforation holes was reduced. While both are perf. 10 the later holes are smaller than the paper between them. The difference is most noticible on pairs.

ROTARY PRESS COIL STAMPS

1954-80 ***Perf. 10 Vertically***

1054c	A478	1c **dark green,** large holes, wet printing, *Oct. 8, 1954*	.35	.20
		Pair	.70	.40
		Joint line pair	1.75	.90
1054	A478	1c **dark green,** small holes, *Feb. 1960*	.20	.20
		Pair	.40	.25
		Joint line pair	1.00	.65
		Large holes, dry printing, *Aug. 1957*	1.00	.20
		Pair	2.00	.25
		Joint line pair	4.00	.65
b.		Imperf., pair	*2,500.*	—

Perf. 10 Horizontally

1054A	A478a	1¼c **turquoise,** *June 17, 1960,* small holes	.20	.20
		Pair	.25	.25
		Joint line pair	2.25	1.00
		Large holes	*6.00*	.20
		Pair	*15.00*	.25
		Joint line pair	*150.00*	1.25

Perf. 10 Vertically

1055d	A480	2c **carmine rose,** large holes, wet printing, *Oct. 22, 1954*	.40	.20
		Pair	.80	.20
		Joint line pair	3.50	.40
		Small holes	—	
		Pair	—	
		Joint line pair	—	
1055	A480	2c **carmine rose,** large holes, dry printing, *May 1957*	.35	.20
		Pair	.80	.20
		Joint line pair	1.50	.25
		Small holes, *Aug. 1961*	7.00	.20
		Pair	17.50	.25
		Joint line pair	50.00	.40
a.		Tagged, small holes, shiny gum, *May 6, 1968*	.20	.20
		Pair	.20	.20
		Joint line pair	.75	.20
		Dull gum, tagged, small holes	.75	
		Pair	1.50	
		Joint line pair	6.00	
b.		Imperf., pair, untagged, shiny gum (Bureau precanceled, Riverdale, MD)		*450.00*
		Joint line pair		*1,200.*
c.		Imperf. pair, tagged, shiny gum	*550.00*	
		Joint line pair	*1,200.*	
1056	A481	2½c **gray blue,** large holes *Sept. 9, 1959*	.30	.25
		Pair	.60	.50
		Joint line pair	3.50	1.75
		Small holes, *Jan. 1961*	*400.00*	*100.00*
		Pair	*850.00*	*200.00*
		Joint line pair	*3,000.*	*400.00*

No. 1056 with small holes only known with Bureau precancels. It was against postal regulations to make mint precanceled stamps available other than to permit holders for their use. Resale was prohibited. Since some mint examples do exist in the marketplace, values are furnished here.

1057c	A482	3c **deep violet,** large holes, wet printing, *July 20, 1954*	.35	.20
		Pair	.80	.25
		Joint line pair	2.75	.60
		Small holes, *Jan. 1961*	—	
		Pair	—	
		Joint line pair	—	
1057	A482	3c **deep violet,** large holes, dry printing, *Oct. 1956*	.35	.20
		Pair	.80	.20
		Joint line pair	2.75	.25
		Gripper cracks	—	—
		Small holes, *Mar. 1958*	.20	.20
		Pair	.20	.20
		Joint line pair	.55	.20
a.		Imperf., pair	*1,500.*	*800.00*
		Joint line pair	*2,750.*	—
b.		Tagged, small holes, philatelic printing, *June 26, 1967*	1.00	.50
		Pair	3.00	1.00
		Joint line pair	25.00	—
d.		Tagged, small holes, Look magazine printing, *Oct. 1966*	5.00	4.00
		On cover		—
		Pair	11.00	8.00
		Joint line pair	*300.00*	

Earliest known use No. 1057d: Dec. 29, 1966.

No. 1057a measures about 19½x22mm; No. 1035c, about 18¾x22½mm.

The second tagged printing (No. 1057b) was a "philatelic reprint" made when the original stock of tagged stamps was exhausted. The original tagged printing (No. 1057d, specially printed for "Look" magazine) has a less intense color, the impression is less sharp and the tagging is brighter.

The reprint was printed on a slightly fluorescent paper, while the original paper is dead under longwave UV light.

1058b	A483	4c **red violet,** large holes, wet printing (Bureau precanceled)	*22.50*	.50
		Pair	*47.50*	—
		Joint line pair	*325.00*	

It was against postal regulations to make mint precanceled examples of No. 1058b available other than to permit holders for their use. Resale was prohibited. Since some mint examples do exist in the marketplace, values are furnished here.

1058	A483	4c **red violet,** large holes, dry printing, *July 31, 1958*	.50	.20
		Pair	1.50	.30
		Joint line pair	2.50	.40
		Small holes	.20	.20
		Pair	.35	.20
		Joint line pair	.70	.25
a.		Imperf., pair	85.00	70.00
		Joint line pair	200.00	

Perf. 10 Horizontally

1059	A484	4½c **blue green,** large holes, *May 1, 1959*	1.50	1.00
		Pair	3.00	2.25
		Joint line pair	14.00	3.00
		Small holes	12.00	—
		Pair	35.00	—
		Joint line pair	*450.00*	—

Perf. 10 Vertically

1059A	A495	25c **green,** *Feb. 25, 1965*	.50	.30
		Pair	1.00	.60
		Joint line pair	2.00	1.20
b.		Tagged, shiny gum, *Apr. 3, 1973*	.80	.20
		Pair	1.60	.40
		Joint line pair	3.25	1.25
		Tagged, dull gum, *1980*	4.00	
		Pair	8.00	
		Joint line pair	12.00	
c.		Imperf., pair	40.00	
		Joint line pair	90.00	

Value for No. 1059Ac is for fine centering.

Bureau Precancels: 1c, 118 diff., 1¼c, 105 diff., 2c, 191 diff., 2½c, 94 diff., 3c, 142 diff., 4c, 83 diff., 4½c, 23 diff.

NEBRASKA TERRITORY ISSUE

Establishment of the Nebraska Territory, centenary.

"The Sower," Mitchell Pass and Scotts Bluff — A507

ROTARY PRESS PRINTING

E.E. Plates of 200 subjects in four panes of 50.

1954, May 7 ***Perf. 11x10½***

1060 A507 3c **violet**	.20	.20
P# block of 4	.45	—

KANSAS TERRITORY ISSUE

Establishment of the Kansas Territory, centenary

Wheat Field and Pioneer Wagon Train — A508

ROTARY PRESS PRINTING

E.E. Plates of 200 subjects in four panes of 50.

1954, May 31 ***Perf. 11x10½***

1061 A508 3c **brown orange**	.20	.20
P# block of 4	.55	—

GEORGE EASTMAN ISSUE

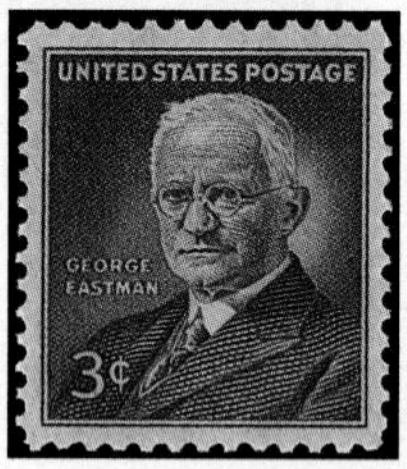

Eastman (1854-1932), inventor of photographic dry plates, flexible film and the Kodak camera; Rochester, N.Y., industrialist. — A509

ROTARY PRESS PRINTING

E.E. Plates of 280 subjects in four panes of 70.

1954, July 12 ***Perf. 10½x11***

1062 A509 3c **violet brown**	.20	.20
P# block of 4	.40	—

LEWIS AND CLARK EXPEDITION

150th anniv. of the Lewis and Clark expedition.

Meriwether Lewis, William Clark and Sacagawea Landing on Missouri Riverbank A510

ROTARY PRESS PRINTING

E.E. Plates of 200 subjects in four panes of 50.

1954, July 28 ***Perf. 11x10½***

1063 A510 3c **violet brown**	.20	.20
P# block of 4	.75	—

PENNSYLVANIA ACADEMY OF THE FINE ARTS ISSUE

150th anniversary of the founding of the Pennsylvania Academy of the Fine Arts, Philadelphia.

Charles Willson Peale in his Museum, Self-portrait — A511

ROTARY PRESS PRINTING

E.E. Plates of 200 subjects in four panes of 50.

1955, Jan. 15 ***Perf. 10½x11***

1064 A511 3c **rose brown**	.20	.20
P# block of 4	.45	—

LAND GRANT COLLEGES ISSUE

Centenary of the founding of Michigan State College and Pennsylvania State University, first of the land grant institutions.

Open Book and Symbols of Subjects Taught
A512

ROTARY PRESS PRINTING

E.E. Plates of 200 subjects in four panes of 50.

1955, Feb. 12 ***Perf. 11x10½***

1065	A512	3c	**green**	.20	.20
			P# block of 4	.45	—

ROTARY INTERNATIONAL, 50th ANNIV.

Torch, Globe and Rotary Emblem
A513

ROTARY PRESS PRINTING

E.E. Plates of 200 subjects in four panes of 50.

1955, Feb. 23 ***Perf. 11x10½***

1066	A513	8c	**deep blue**	.25	.20
			P# block of 4	1.25	—

ARMED FORCES RESERVE ISSUE

Marine, Coast Guard, Army, Navy and Air Force Personnel
A514

ROTARY PRESS PRINTING

E.E. Plates of 200 subjects in four panes of 50.

1955, May 21 ***Perf. 11x10½***

1067	A514	3c	**purple**	.20	.20
			P# block of 4	.40	—

NEW HAMPSHIRE ISSUE

Sesquicentennial of the discovery of the "Old Man of the Mountains."

Great Stone Face — A515

ROTARY PRESS PRINTING

E.E. Plates of 200 subjects in four panes of 50.

1955, June 21 ***Perf. 10½x11***

1068	A515	3c	**green**	.20	.20
			P# block of 4	.70	—

SOO LOCKS ISSUE

Centenary of the opening of the Soo Locks.

Map of Great Lakes and Two Steamers
A516

ROTARY PRESS PRINTING

E.E. Plates of 200 subjects in four panes of 50.

1955, June 28 ***Perf. 11x10½***

1069	A516	3c	**blue**	.20	.20
			P# block of 4	.40	—

ATOMS FOR PEACE ISSUE

Issued to promote an Atoms for Peace policy.

Atomic Energy Encircling the Hemispheres
A517

Designed by George R. Cox.

ROTARY PRESS PRINTING

E.E. Plates of 200 subjects in four panes of 50.

1955, July 28 ***Perf. 11x10½***

1070	A517	3c	**deep blue**	.20	.20
			P# block of 4	.40	—

FORT TICONDEROGA ISSUE

Bicentenary of Fort Ticonderoga, New York.

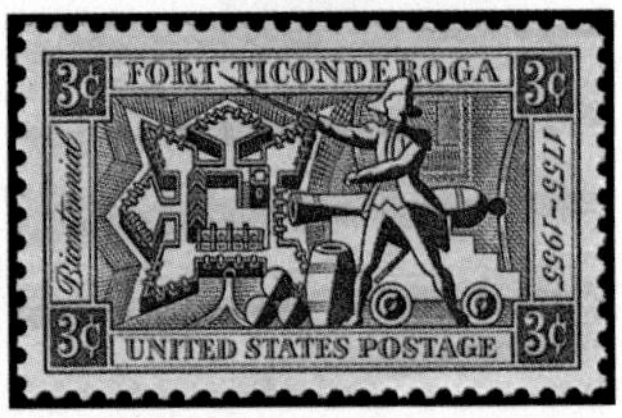

Map of the Fort, Ethan Allen and Artillery
A518

Designed by Enrico Arno.

ROTARY PRESS PRINTING

E.E. Plates of 200 subjects in four panes of 50.

1955, Sept. 18 ***Perf. 11x10½***

1071	A518	3c	**light brown**	.20	.20
			P# block of 4	.40	—

Andrew W. Mellon (1855-1937), US Secretary of the Treasury (1921-32), Financier and Art Collector — A519

"Franklin Taking Electricity from the Sky," by Benjamin West — A520

ANDREW W. MELLON ISSUE

Designed by Victor S. McCloskey, Jr.

ROTARY PRESS PRINTING

E.E. Plates of 280 subjects in four panes of 70.

1955, Dec. 20 ***Perf. 10½x11***

1072	A519	3c	**rose carmine**	.20	.20
			P# block of 4	.40	—

BENJAMIN FRANKLIN ISSUE

250th anniv. of the birth of Benjamin Franklin.

Designed by Charles R. Chickering.

ROTARY PRESS PRINTING

E.E. Plates of 200 subjects in four panes of 50.

1956, Jan. 17 ***Perf. 10½x11***

1073	A520	3c	**bright carmine**	.20	.20
			P# block of 4	.40	—

BOOKER T. WASHINGTON ISSUE

Washington (1856-1915), black educator, founder and head of Tuskegee Institute in Alabama.

Log Cabin — A521

Designed by Charles R. Chickering.

ROTARY PRESS PRINTING

E.E. Plates of 200 subjects in four panes of 50.

1956, Apr. 5 ***Perf. 11x10½***

1074	A521	3c	**deep blue**	.20	.20
			P# block of 4	.40	—

FIFTH INTERNATIONAL PHILATELIC EXHIBITION ISSUES

FIPEX, New York City, Apr. 28 - May 6, 1956.

SOUVENIR SHEET

A522

Illustration reduced.

FLAT PLATE PRINTING

Plates of 24 subjects

1956, Apr. 28 ***Imperf.***

1075	A522	Sheet of 2	2.00	1.50
a.		A482 3c deep violet	.80	.60
b.		A488 8c dark violet blue & carmine	1.00	.75

No. 1075 measures 108x73mm. Nos. 1075a and 1075b measure 24x28mm.

Inscriptions printed in dark violet blue; scrolls and stars in carmine.

New York Coliseum and Columbus Monument A523

Designed by William K. Schrage.

ROTARY PRESS PRINTING

E.E. Plates of 200 subjects in four panes of 50.

1956, Apr. 30 ***Perf. 11x10½***

1076 A523 3c **deep violet** .20 .20
P# block of 4 .30 —

WILDLIFE CONSERVATION ISSUE

Issued to emphasize the importance of Wildlife Conservation in America.

Wild Turkey A524

Pronghorn Antelope A525

King Salmon A526

Designed by Robert W. (Bob) Hines.

ROTARY PRESS PRINTING

E.E. Plates of 200 subjects in four panes of 50.

1956 ***Perf. 11x10½***

1077 A524 3c **rose lake,** *May 5* .20 .20
P# block of 4 .35 —
1078 A525 3c **brown,** *June 22* .20 .20
P# block of 4 .35 —
1079 A526 3c **blue green,** *Nov. 9* .20 .20
P# block of 4 .35 —
Nos. 1077-1079 (3) .60 .60

PURE FOOD AND DRUG LAWS, 50th ANNIV.

Harvey Washington Wiley — A527

Designed by Robert L. Miller

ROTARY PRESS PRINTING

E.E. Plates of 200 subjects in four panes of 50.

1956, June 27 ***Perf. 10½x11***

1080 A527 3c **dark blue green** .20 .20
P# block of 4 .50 —

WHEATLAND ISSUE

Pres. Buchanan's Home, Lancaster, Pa. — A528

ROTARY PRESS PRINTING

E.E. Plates of 200 subjects in four panes of 50.

1956, Aug. 5 ***Perf. 11x10½***

1081 A528 3c **black brown** .20 .20
P# block of 4 .40 —

LABOR DAY ISSUE

Mosaic, AFL-CIO Headquarters — A529

Designed by Victor S. McCloskey, Jr.

ROTARY PRESS PRINTING

E.E. Plates of 200 subjects in four panes of 50.

1956, Sept. 3 ***Perf. 10½x11***

1082 A529 3c **deep blue** .20 .20
P# block of 4 .40 —

NASSAU HALL ISSUE

200th anniv. of Nassau Hall, Princeton University.

Nassau Hall, Princeton, N.J. — A530

ROTARY PRESS PRINTING

E.E. Plates of 200 subjects in four panes of 50.

1956, Sept. 22 ***Perf. 11x10½***

1083 A530 3c **black,** *orange* .20 .20
P# block of 4 .50 —

DEVILS TOWER ISSUE

Issued to commemorate the 50th anniversary of the Federal law providing for protection of American natural antiquities. Devils Tower National Monument, Wyoming, is an example.

Devils Tower — A531

Designed by Charles R. Chickering.

ROTARY PRESS PRINTING

E.E. Plates of 200 subjects in four panes of 50.

1956, Sept. 24 ***Perf. 10½x11***

1084 A531 3c **violet** .20 .20
P# block of 4 .45 —
Pair with full horiz. gutter btwn. —

CHILDREN'S ISSUE

Issued to promote friendship among the children of the world.

Children of the World — A532

Designed by Ronald Dias.

ROTARY PRESS PRINTING

E.E. Plates of 200 subjects in four panes of 50.

1956, Dec. 15 ***Perf. 11x10½***

1085 A532 3c **dark blue** .20 .20
P# block of 4 .40 —

ALEXANDER HAMILTON (1755-1804)

Alexander Hamilton and Federal Hall — A533

Designed by William K. Schrage.

ROTARY PRESS PRINTING

E.E. Plates of 200 subjects in four panes of 50.

1957, Jan. 11 ***Perf. 11x10½***

1086 A533 3c **rose red** .20 .20
P# block of 4 .40 —

POLIO ISSUE

Honoring "those who helped fight polio," and on for 20th anniv. of the Natl. Foundation for Infantile Paralysis and the March of Dimes.

Allegory — A534

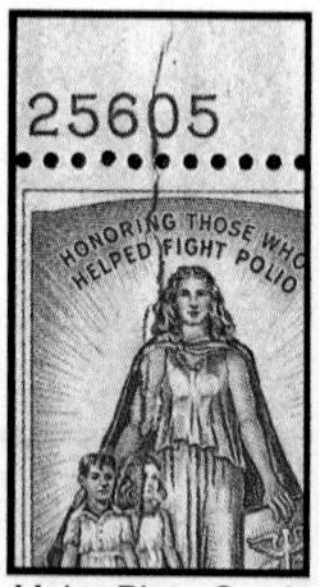

Major Plate Crack

Designed by Charles R. Chickering.

ROTARY PRESS PRINTING

E.E. Plates of 200 subjects in four panes of 50.

1957, Jan. 15 ***Perf. 10½x11***

1087 A534 3c **red lilac** .20 .20
P# block of 4 .40 —
Major plate crack (25605 UL 1) —

COAST AND GEODETIC SURVEY ISSUE

150th anniversary of the establishment of the Coast and Geodetic Survey.

Flag of Coast and Geodetic Survey and Ships at Sea — A535

Designed by Harold E. MacEwen.

ROTARY PRESS PRINTING

E.E. Plates of 200 subjects in four panes of 50.

1957, Feb. 11 ***Perf. 11x10½***

1088 A535 3c **dark blue** .20 .20
P# block of 4 .40 —

ARCHITECTS ISSUE

American Institute of Architects, centenary.

Corinthian Capital and Mushroom Type Head and Shaft — A536

Designed by Robert J. Schultz.

ROTARY PRESS PRINTING
E.E. Plates of 200 subjects in four panes of 50.

1957, Feb. 23 *Perf. 11x10½*

1089 A536 3c **red lilac** .20 .20
P# block of 4 .40 —

STEEL INDUSTRY ISSUE

Centenary of the steel industry in America.

American Eagle and Pouring Ladle — A537

Designed by Anthonio Petruccelli.

ROTARY PRESS PRINTING
E.E. Plates of 200 subjects in four panes of 50.

1957, May 22 *Perf. 10½x11*

1090 A537 3c **bright ultramarine** .20 .20
P# block of 4 .40 —

INTERNATIONAL NAVAL REVIEW ISSUE

Issued to commemorate the International Naval Review and the Jamestown Festival.

Aircraft Carrier and Jamestown Festival Emblem A538

Designed by Richard A. Genders.

ROTARY PRESS PRINTING
E.E. Plates of 200 subjects in four panes of 50.

1957, June 10 *Perf. 11x10½*

1091 A538 3c **blue green** .20 .20
P# block of 4 .40 —

OKLAHOMA STATEHOOD, 50th ANNIV.

Map of Oklahoma, Arrow and Atom Diagram A539

Designed by William K. Schrage.

ROTARY PRESS PRINTING
E.E. Plates of 200 subjects in four panes of 50.

1957, June 14 *Perf. 11x10½*

1092 A539 3c **dark blue** .20 .20
P# block of 4 .50 —

SCHOOL TEACHERS ISSUE

Teacher and Pupils — A540

ROTARY PRESS PRINTING
E.E. Plates of 200 subjects in four panes of 50.

1957, July 1 *Perf. 11x10½*

1093 A540 3c **rose lake** .20 .20
P# block of 4 .40 —

FLAG ISSUE

"Old Glory" (48 Stars) — A541

Designed by Victor S. McCloskey, Jr.

GIORI PRESS PRINTING
Plates of 200 subjects in four panes of 50.

1957, July 4 *Perf. 11*

1094 A541 4c **dark blue & deep carmine** .20 .20
P# block of 4 .45 —

"Virginia of Sagadahock" and Seal of Maine — A542

Ramon Magsaysay — A543

SHIPBUILDING ISSUE

350th anniversary of shipbuilding in America.

Designed by Ervine Metzel, Mrs. William Zorach, A. M. Main, Jr., and George F. Cary II.

ROTARY PRESS PRINTING
E.E. Plates of 280 subjects in four panes of 70.

1957, Aug. 15 *Perf. 10½x11*

1095 A542 3c **deep violet** .20 .20
P# block of 4 .45 —

CHAMPION OF LIBERTY ISSUE

Magsaysay (1907-57), Pres. of the Philippines.

Designed by Arnold Copeland, Ervine Metzl and William H. Buckley.

GIORI PRESS PRINTING
Plates of 192 subjects in four panes of 48 each.

1957, Aug. 31 *Perf. 11*

1096 A543 8c **carmine, ultramarine & ocher** .20 .20
P# block of 4, 2# .85 —
P# block of 4, ultra. # omitted —

Marquis de Lafayette (1757-1834) — A544

Whooping Cranes — A545

LAFAYETTE BICENTENARY ISSUE

Designed by Ervine Metzl.

ROTARY PRESS PRINTING
E.E. Plates of 200 subjects in four panes of 50.

1957. Sept. 6 *Perf. 10½x11*

1097 A544 3c **rose lake** .20 .20
P# block of 4 .40 —

WILDLIFE CONSERVATION ISSUE

Issued to emphasize the importance of Wildlife Conservation in America.

Designed by Bob Hines and C.R. Chickering.

GIORI PRESS PRINTING
Plates of 200 subjects in four panes of 50.

1957, Nov. 22 *Perf. 11*

1098 A545 3c **blue, ocher & green** .20 .20
P# block of 4 .40 —

Bible, Hat and Quill Pen — A546

"Bountiful Earth" — A547

RELIGIOUS FREEDOM ISSUE

300th anniv. of the Flushing Remonstrance.

Designed by Robert Geissmann.

ROTARY PRESS PRINTING
E.E. Plates of 200 subjects in four panes of 50.

1957, Dec. 27 *Perf. 10½x11*

1099 A546 3c **black** .20 .20
P# block of 4 .40 —

GARDENING HORTICULTURE ISSUE

Issued to honor the garden clubs of America and in connection with the centenary of the birth of Liberty Hyde Bailey, horticulturist.

Designed by Denver Gillen.

ROTARY PRESS PRINTING
E.E. Plates of 200 subjects in four panes of 50.

1958, Mar. 15 *Perf. 10½x11*

1100 A547 3c **green** .20 .20
P# block of 4 .40 —

BRUSSELS EXHIBITION ISSUE

Issued in honor of the opening of the Universal and International Exhibition at Brussels, April 17.

US Pavilion at Brussels A551

Designed by Bradbury Thompson.

ROTARY PRESS PRINTING
E.E. Plates of 200 subjects in four panes of 50.

1958, Apr. 17 *Perf. 11x10½*

1104 A551 3c **deep claret**	.20	.20
On cover, Expo. station ("U.S. Pavilion") canc.		3.00
P# block of 4	.40	—

JAMES MONROE ISSUE

James Monroe (1758-1831), 5th President of the US — A552

Designed by Frank P. Conley.

ROTARY PRESS PRINTING
E.E. Plates of 280 subjects in four panes of 70.

1958, Apr. 28 *Perf. 11x10½*

1105 A552 3c **purple**	.20	.20
P# block of 4	.45	—

MINNESOTA STATEHOOD, 100th ANNIV.

Minnesota Lakes and Pines — A553

Designed by Homer Hill.

ROTARY PRESS PRINTING
E.E. Plates of 200 subjects in four panes of 50.

1958, May 11 *Perf. 11x10½*

1106 A553 3c **green**	.20	.20
P# block of 4	.45	—

GEOPHYSICAL YEAR ISSUE

International Geophysical Year, 1957-58.

Solar Disc and Hands from Michelangelo's "Creation of Adam" — A554

Designed by Ervine Metzl.

GIORI PRESS PRINTING
Plates of 200 subjects in four panes of 50.

1958, May 31 *Perf. 11*

1107 A554 3c **black & red orange**	.20	.20
P# block of 4	.40	—

GUNSTON HALL ISSUE

Issued for the bicentenary of Gunston Hall and to honor George Mason, author of the Constitution of Virginia and the Virginia Bill of Rights.

Gunston Hall, Virginia A555

Designed by Rene Clarke.

ROTARY PRESS PRINTING
E.E. Plates of 200 subjects in four panes of 50.

1958, June 12 *Perf. 11x10½*

1108 A555 3c **light green**	.20	.20
P# block of 4	.40	—

Mackinac Bridge — A556

Simon Bolívar — A557

MACKINAC BRIDGE ISSUE

Dedication of Mackinac Bridge, Michigan.

Designed by Arnold J. Copeland.

ROTARY PRESS PRINTING
E.E. Plates of 200 subjects in four panes of 50.

1958, June 25 *Perf. 10½x11*

1109 A556 3c **bright greenish blue**	.20	.20
P# block of 4	.50	—

CHAMPION OF LIBERTY ISSUE

Simon Bolívar, South American freedom fighter.

ROTARY PRESS PRINTING
E.E. Plates of 280 subjects in four panes of 70.

1958, July 24 *Perf. 10½x11*

1110 A557 4c **olive bister**	.20	.20
P# block of 4	.40	—

GIORI PRESS PRINTING
Plates of 288 subjects in four panes of 72 each.
Perf. 11

1111 A557 8c **carmine, ultramarine & ocher**	.20	.20
P# block of 4, 2#	1.25	—
P# block of 4, ocher # only		—

ATLANTIC CABLE CENTENNIAL ISSUE

Centenary of the Atlantic Cable, linking the Eastern and Western hemispheres.

Neptune, Globe and Mermaid A558

Designed by George Giusti.

ROTARY PRESS PRINTING
E.E. Plates of 200 subjects in four panes of 50.

1958, Aug. 15 *Perf. 11x10½*

1112 A558 4c **reddish purple**	.20	.20
P# block of 4	.40	—

LINCOLN SESQUICENTENNIAL ISSUE

Sesquicentennial of the birth of Abraham Lincoln. No. 1114 also for the centenary of the founding of Cooper Union, New York City. No. 1115 marks the centenary of the Lincoln-Douglas Debates.

Lincoln by George Healy — A559

Lincoln by Gutzon Borglum — A560

Lincoln and Stephen A. Douglas Debating, from Painting by Joseph Boggs Beale — A561

Daniel Chester French Statue of Lincoln as Drawn by Fritz Busse — A562

Designed by Ervine Metzl.

ROTARY PRESS PRINTING
E.E. Plates of 200 subjects in four panes of 50.

1958-59 *Perf. 10½x11*

1113 A559 1c **green**, *Feb. 12, 1959*	.20	.20
P# block of 4	.25	—
1114 A560 3c **purple**, *Feb. 27, 1959*	.20	.20
P# block of 4	.40	—

Perf. 11x10½

1115 A561 4c **sepia**, *Aug. 27, 1958*	.20	.20
P# block of 4	.60	—
1116 A562 4c **dark blue**, *May 30, 1959*	.20	.20
P# block of 4	.40	—
Nos. 1113-1116 (4)	.80	.80

Lajos Kossuth — A563

Early Press and Hand Holding Quill — A564

CHAMPION OF LIBERTY ISSUE

Lajos Kossuth, Hungarian freedom fighter.

ROTARY PRESS PRINTING
E.E. Plates of 280 subjects in four panes of 70.

1958, Sept. 19 *Perf. 10½x11*

1117 A563 4c **green**	.20	.20
P# block of 4	.40	—

GIORI PRESS PRINTING
Plates of 288 subjects in four panes of 72 each.
Perf. 11

1118 A563 8c **carmine, ultramarine & ocher**	.20	.20
P# block of 4, 2#	1.10	—

FREEDOM OF PRESS ISSUE

Honoring Journalism and freedom of the press in connection with the 50th anniv. of the 1st School of Journalism at the University of Missouri.

Designed by Lester Beall and Charles Goslin.

ROTARY PRESS PRINTING
E.E. Plates of 200 subjects in four panes of 50.

1958, Sept. 22 *Perf. 10½x11*

1119 A564 4c **black**	.20	.20
P# block of 4	.40	—

OVERLAND MAIL ISSUE

Centenary of Overland Mail Service.

Mail Coach and Map of Southwest US — A565

Designed by William H. Buckley.

ROTARY PRESS PRINTING

E.E. Plates of 200 subjects in four panes of 50.

1958, Oct. 10 *Perf. 11x10½*

1120 A565 4c **crimson rose** .20 .20
P# block of 4 .40 —

Noah Webster — A566

Forest Scene — A567

NOAH WEBSTER ISSUE

Webster (1758-1843), lexicographer and author.

Designed by Charles R. Chickering.

ROTARY PRESS PRINTING

E.E. Plates of 280 subjects in four panes of 70.

1958, Oct. 16 *Perf. 10½x11*

1121 A566 4c **dark carmine rose** .20 .20
P# block of 4 .40 —

FOREST CONSERVATION ISSUE

Issued to publicize forest conservation and the protection of natural resources and to honor Theodore Roosevelt, a leading forest conservationist, on the centenary of his birth.

Designed by Rudolph Wendelin.

GIORI PRESS PRINTING

Plates of 200 subjects in four panes of 50.

1958, Oct. 27 *Perf. 11*

1122 A567 4c **green, yellow & brown** .20 .20
P# block of 4 .40 —

FORT DUQUESNE ISSUE

Bicentennial of Fort Duquesne (Fort Pitt) at future site of Pittsburgh.

British Capture of Fort Duquesne, 1758; Brig. Gen. John Forbes on Litter, Colonel Washington Mounted A568

Designed by William H. Buckley and Douglas Gorsline.

ROTARY PRESS PRINTING

E.E. Plates of 200 subjects in four panes of 50.

1958, Nov. 25 *Perf. 11x10½*

1123 A568 4c **blue** .20 .20
P# block of 4 .40 —

OREGON STATEHOOD, 100th ANNIV.

Covered Wagon and Mt. Hood — A569

Designed by Robert Hallock.

ROTARY PRESS PRINTING

E.E. Plates of 200 subjects in four panes of 50.

1959, Feb. 14 *Perf. 11x10½*

1124 A569 4c **blue green** .25 .20
P# block of 4 1.10 —

José de San Martin — A570

NATO Emblem — A571

CHAMPION OF LIBERTY ISSUE

San Martin, So. American soldier and statesman.

ROTARY PRESS PRINTING

E.E. Plates of 280 subjects in four panes of 70.

1959, Feb. 25 *Perf. 10½x11*

1125 A570 4c **blue** .20 .20
P# block of 4 .40 —
a. Horiz. pair, imperf. between *1,250.*

GIORI PRESS PRINTING

Plates of 288 subjects in four panes of 72 each.

Perf. 11

1126 A570 8c **carmine, ultramarine & ocher** .20 .20
P# block of 4 .90 —

NATO ISSUE

North Atlantic Treaty Organization, 10th anniv.

Designed by Stevan Dohanos.

ROTARY PRESS PRINTING

E.E. Plates of 280 subjects in four panes of 70.

1959, Apr. 1 *Perf. 10½x11*

1127 A571 4c **blue** .20 .20
P# block of 4 .40 —

ARCTIC EXPLORATIONS ISSUE

Conquest of the Arctic by land by Rear Admiral Robert Edwin Peary in 1909 and by sea by the submarine "Nautilus" in 1958.

North Pole, Dog Sled and "Nautilus" A572

Designed by George Samerjan.

ROTARY PRESS PRINTING

E.E. Plates of 200 subjects in four panes of 50.

1959, Apr. 6 *Perf. 11x10½*

1128 A572 4c **bright greenish blue** .20 .20
P# block of 4 .40 —

WORLD PEACE THROUGH WORLD TRADE ISSUE

Issued in conjunction with the 17th Congress of the International Chamber of Commerce, Washington, D.C., April 19-25.

Globe and Laurel — A573

Designed by Robert Baker.

ROTARY PRESS PRINTING

E.E. Plates of 200 subjects in four panes of 50.

1959, Apr. 20 *Perf. 11x10½*

1129 A573 8c **rose lake** .20 .20
P# block of 4 .85 —

SILVER CENTENNIAL ISSUE

Discovery of silver at the Comstock Lode, Nevada.

Henry Comstock at Mount Davidson Site — A574

Designed by Robert L. Miller and W.K. Schrage.

ROTARY PRESS PRINTING

E.E. Plates of 200 subjects in four panes of 50.

1959, June 8 *Perf. 11x10½*

1130 A574 4c **black** .20 .20
P# block of 4 .40 —

ST. LAWRENCE SEAWAY ISSUE

Opening of the St. Lawrence Seaway.

Great Lakes, Maple Leaf and Eagle Emblems A575

Designed by Arnold Copeland, Ervine Metzl, William H. Buckley and Gerald Trottier.

GIORI PRESS PRINTING

Plates of 200 subjects in four panes of 50.

1959, June 26 *Perf. 11*

1131 A575 4c **red & dark blue** .20 .20
P# block of 4 .40 —
Pair with full horiz. gutter btwn. —

See Canada No. 387.

49-STAR FLAG ISSUE

U.S. Flag, 1959 — A576

Designed by Stevan Dohanos.

GIORI PRESS PRINTING

Plates of 200 subjects in four panes of 50.

1959, July 4 *Perf. 11*

1132 A576 4c **ocher, dark blue & deep carmine** .20 .20
P# block of 4 .40 —

SOIL CONSERVATION ISSUE

Issued as a tribute to farmers and ranchers who use soil and water conservation measures.

Modern Farm — A577

Designed by Walter Hortens.

GIORI PRESS PRINTING

Plates of 200 subjects in four panes of 50.

1959, Aug. 26 *Perf. 11*

1133 A577 4c **blue, green & ocher** .20 .20
P# block of 4 .40 —

PETROLEUM INDUSTRY ISSUE

Centenary of the completion of the nation's first oil well at Titusville, Pa.

Oil Derrick — A578

Designed by Robert Foster.

ROTARY PRESS PRINTING

E.E. Plates of 200 subjects in four panes of 50.

1959, Aug. 27 ***Perf. 10½x11***

1134 A578 4c **brown**	.20	.20
P# block of 4	.40	—

DENTAL HEALTH ISSUE

Issued to publicize Dental Health and for the centenary of the American Dental Association.

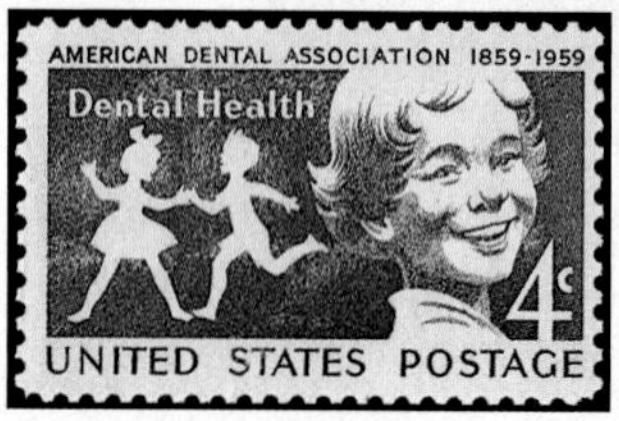

Children A579

Designed by Charles Henry Carter.

ROTARY PRESS PRINTING

E.E. Plates of 200 subjects in four panes of 50.

1959, Sept. 14 ***Perf. 11x10½***

1135 A579 4c **green**	.20	.20
P# block of 4	.40	—

Ernst Reuter — A580

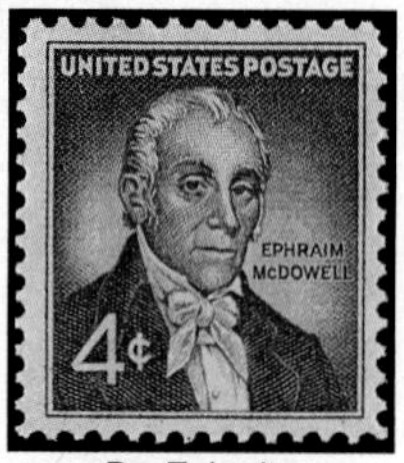

Dr. Ephraim McDowell — A581

CHAMPION OF LIBERTY ISSUE

Ernst Reuter, Mayor of Berlin, 1948-53.

ROTARY PRESS PRINTING

E.E. Plates of 280 subjects in four panes of 70.

1959, Sept. 29 ***Perf. 10½x11***

1136 A580 4c **gray**	.20	.20
P# block of 4	.40	—

GIORI PRESS PRINTING

Plates of 288 subjects in four panes of 72 each.

Perf. 11

1137 A580 8c **carmine, ultramarine & ocher**	.20	.20
P# block of 4	.90	—
a. Ocher missing (EP)	*4,250.*	
b. Ultramarine missing (EP)	*4,250.*	
c. Ocher & ultramarine missing (EP)	*4,500.*	
d. All colors missing (EP)	*2,500.*	

DR. EPHRAIM McDOWELL ISSUE

Honoring McDowell (1771-1830) on the 150th anniv. of the 1st successful ovarian operation in the US, performed at Danville, Ky., 1809.

Designed by Charles R. Chickering.

ROTARY PRESS PRINTING

E.E. Plates of 280 subjects in four panes of 70.

1959, Dec. 3 ***Perf. 10½x11***

1138 A581 4c **rose lake**	.20	.20
P# block of 4	.40	—
a. Vert. pair, imperf. btwn.	*400.00*	
b. Vert. pair, imperf. horiz.	*275.00*	

VALUES FOR HINGED STAMPS AFTER NO. 771

This catalogue does not value unused stamps after No. 771 in hinged condition. Hinged unused stamps from No. 772 to the present are worth considerably less than the values given for unused stamps, which are for never-hinged examples.

AMERICAN CREDO ISSUE

Issued to re-emphasize the ideals upon which America was founded and to honor those great Americans who wrote or uttered the credos.

Quotation from Washington's Farewell Address, 1796 — A582

Benjamin Franklin Quotation A583

Thomas Jefferson Quotation A584

Francis Scott Key Quotation A585

Abraham Lincoln Quotation A586

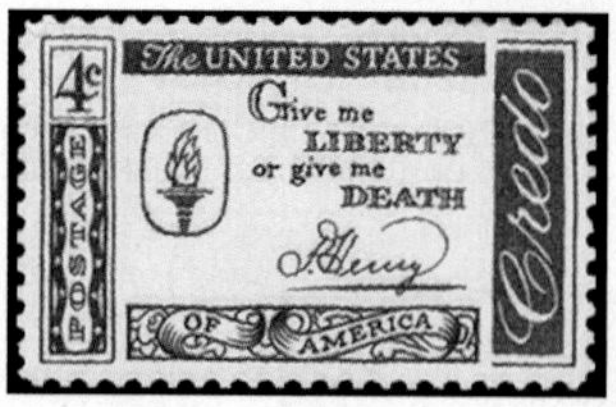

Patrick Henry Quotation A587

Designed by Frank Conley.

GIORI PRESS PRINTING

Plates of 200 subjects in four panes of 50.

1960-61 ***Perf. 11***

1139 A582 4c **dark violet blue, & carmine,** *Jan. 20, 1960*	.20	.20
P# block of 4	.40	—
1140 A583 4c **olive bister & green,** *Mar. 31, 1960*	.20	.20
P# block of 4	.40	—
1141 A584 4c **gray & vermilion,** *May 18, 1960*	.20	.20
P# block of 4	.60	—
1142 A585 4c **carmine & dark blue,** *Sept. 14, 1960*	.20	.20
P# block of 4	.50	—
1143 A586 4c **magenta & green,** *Nov. 19, 1960*	.20	.20
P# block of 4	.50	—
Pair with full horiz. gutter between	525.	
1144 A587 4c **green & brown,** *Jan. 11, 1961*	.20	.20
P# block of 4	.65	—
Nos. 1139-1144 (6)	1.20	1.20

BOY SCOUT JUBILEE ISSUE

50th anniv. of the Boy Scouts of America.

Boy Scout Giving Scout Sign — A588

Designed by Norman Rockwell.

GIORI PRESS PRINTING

Plates of 200 subjects in four panes of 50.

1960, Feb. 8 ***Perf. 11***

1145 A588 4c **red, dark blue & dark bister**	.20	.20
P# block of 4	.55	—

Olympic Rings and Snowflake — A589

Thomas G. Masaryk — A590

OLYMPIC WINTER GAMES ISSUE

Opening of the 8th Olympic Winter Games, Squaw Valley, Feb. 18-29, 1960.

Designed by Ervine Metzl.

ROTARY PRESS PRINTING

E.E. Plates of 200 subjects in four panes of 50.

1960, Feb. 18 ***Perf. 10½x11***

1146 A589 4c **dull blue**	.20	.20
P# block of 4	.40	—

CHAMPION OF LIBERTY ISSUE

Issued to honor Thomas G. Masaryk, founder and president of Czechoslovakia (1918-35), on the 110th anniversary of his birth.

ROTARY PRESS PRINTING

E.E. Plates of 280 subjects in four panes of 70.

1960, Mar. 7 ***Perf. 10½x11***

1147 A590 4c **blue**	.20	.20
P# block of 4	.40	—
a. Vert. pair, imperf. between	*2,750.*	

GIORI PRESS PRINTING

Plates of 288 subjects in four panes of 72 each.

Perf. 11

1148 A590 8c **carmine, ultramarine & ocher**	.20	.20
P# block of 4	.95	—
a. Horiz. pair, imperf. between	—	

WORLD REFUGEE YEAR ISSUE

World Refugee Year, July 1, 1959-June 30, 1960.

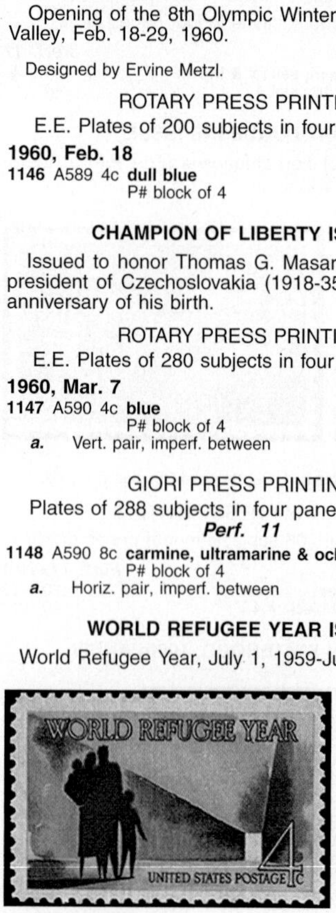

Family Walking Toward New Life — A591

Designed by Ervine Metzl.

ROTARY PRESS PRINTING

E.E. Plates of 200 subjects in four panes of 50.

1960, Apr. 7 ***Perf. 11x10½***

1149 A591 4c **gray black**	.20	.20
P# block of 4	.40	—

WATER CONSERVATION ISSUE

Issued to stress the importance of water conservation and to commemorate the 7th Watershed Congress, Washington, D.C.

Water: From Watershed to Consumer A592

Designed by Elmo White.

GIORI PRESS PRINTING

Plates of 200 subjects in four panes of 50.

1960, Apr. 18 *Perf. 11*

1150 A592 4c **dark blue, brown orange & green** .20 .20
P# block of 4 .40 —
a. Brown orange missing (EP) *2,400.*

SEATO ISSUE

South-East Asia Treaty Organization and for the SEATO Conf., Washington, D.C., May 31-June 3.

SEATO Emblem — A593

Designed by John Maass.

ROTARY PRESS PRINTING

E.E. plates of 280 subjects in four panes of 70.

1960, May 31 *Perf. 10½x11*

1151 A593 4c **blue** .20 .20
P# block of 4 .40 —
a. Vertical pair, imperf. between *140.00*

AMERICAN WOMAN ISSUE

Issued to pay tribute to American women and their accomplishments in civic affairs, education, arts and industry.

Mother and Daughter A594

Designed by Robert Sivard.

ROTARY PRESS PRINTING

E.E. Plates of 200 subjects in four panes of 50.

1960, June 2 *Perf. 11x10½*

1152 A594 4c **deep violet** .20 .20
P# block of 4 .40 —

50-STAR FLAG ISSUE

US Flag, 1960 — A595

Designed by Stevan Dohanos.

GIORI PRESS PRINTING

Plates of 200 subjects in four panes of 50.

1960, July 4 *Perf. 11*

1153 A595 4c **dark blue & red** .20 .20
P# block of 4 .40 —

PONY EXPRESS CENTENNIAL ISSUE

Pony Express Rider — A596

Designed by Harold von Schmidt.

ROTARY PRESS PRINTING

E.E. Plates of 200 subjects in four panes of 50.

1960, July 19 *Perf. 11x10½*

1154 A596 4c **sepia** .20 .20
P# block of 4 .65 —

Man in Wheelchair Operating Drill Press — A597

World Forestry Congress Seal — A598

EMPLOY THE HANDICAPPED ISSUE

Promoting the employment of the physically handicapped and publicizing the 8th World Congress of the Intl. Soc. for the Welfare of Cripples, New York City.

Designed by Carl Bobertz.

ROTARY PRESS PRINTING

E.E. Plates of 200 subjects in four panes of 50.

1960, Aug. 28 *Perf. 10½x11*

1155 A597 4c **dark blue** .20 .20
P# block of 4 .40 —

WORLD FORESTRY CONGRESS ISSUE

5th World Forestry Cong., Seattle, Wash., Aug. 29-Sept. 10.

ROTARY PRESS PRINTING

E.E. Plates of 200 subjects in four panes of 50.

1960, Aug. 29 *Perf. 10½x11*

1156 A598 4c **green** .20 .20
P# block of 4 .40 —

Independence Bell — A599

Washington Monument and Cherry Blossoms — A600

MEXICAN INDEPENDENCE, 150th ANNIV.

Designed by Leon Helguera and Charles R. Chickering.

GIORI PRESS PRINTING

Plates of 200 subjects in four panes of 50.

1960, Sept. 16 *Perf. 11*

1157 A599 4c **green & rose red** .20 .20
P# block of 4 .40 —

See Mexico No. 910.

US-JAPAN TREATY ISSUE

Centenary of the United States-Japan Treaty of Amity and Commerce.

Designed by Gyo Fujikawa.

GIORI PRESS PRINTING

Plates of 200 subjects in four panes of 50.

1960, Sept. 28 *Perf. 11*

1158 A600 4c **blue & pink** .20 .20
P# block of 4 .40 —

Ignacy Jan Paderewski — A601

Robert A. Taft — A602

CHAMPION OF LIBERTY ISSUE

Jan Paderewski, Polish statesman and musician.

ROTARY PRESS PRINTING

E.E. Plates of 280 subjects in four panes of 70.

1960, Oct. 8 *Perf. 10½x11*

1159 A601 4c **blue** .20 .20
P# block of 4 .40 —

GIORI PRESS PRINTING

Plates of 288 subjects in four panes of 72 each.

Perf. 11

1160 A601 8c **carmine, ultramarine & ocher** .20 .20
P# block of 4 .90 —

SENATOR TAFT MEMORIAL ISSUE

Senator Robert A. Taft (1889-1953) of Ohio.

Designed by William K. Schrage.

ROTARY PRESS PRINTING

E.E. Plates of 280 subjects in four panes of 70.

1960, Oct. 10 *Perf. 10½x11*

1161 A602 4c **dull violet** .20 .20
P# block of 4 .45 —

WHEELS OF FREEDOM ISSUE

Issued to honor the automotive industry and in connection with the National Automobile Show, Detroit, Oct. 15-23.

Globe and Steering Wheel with Tractor, Car and Truck — A603

Designed by Arnold J. Copeland.

ROTARY PRESS PRINTING

E.E. Plates of 200 subjects in four panes of 50.

1960, Oct. 15 *Perf. 11x10½*

1162 A603 4c **dark blue** .20 .20
P# block of 4 .40 —

BOYS' CLUBS OF AMERICA ISSUE

Boys' Clubs of America movement, centenary.

Profile of Boy — A604

Designed by Charles T. Coiner.

GIORI PRESS PRINTING

Plates of 200 subjects in four panes of 50.

1960, Oct. 18 ***Perf. 11***

1163 A604 4c **indigo, slate & rose red** .20 .20
P# block of 4 .40 —

FIRST AUTOMATED POST OFFICE IN THE US ISSUE

Publicizing the opening of the 1st automated post office in the US at Providence, R.I.

Architect's Sketch of New Post Office, Providence, R.I. — A605

Designed by Arnold J. Copeland and Victor S. McCloskey, Jr.

GIORI PRESS PRINTING

Plates of 200 subjects in four panes of 50.

1960, Oct. 20 ***Perf. 11***

1164 A605 4c **dark blue & carmine** .20 .20
P# block of 4 .40 —

Baron Gustaf Mannerheim — A606

Camp Fire Girls Emblem — A607

CHAMPION OF LIBERTY ISSUE

Baron Karl Gustaf Emil Mannerheim (1867-1951), Marshal and President of Finland.

ROTARY PRESS PRINTING

E.E. Plates of 280 subjects in four panes of 70.

1960, Oct. 26 ***Perf. 10½x11***

1165 A606 4c **blue** .20 .20
P# block of 4 .40 —

GIORI PRESS PRINTING

Plates of 288 subjects in four panes of 72 each.
Perf. 11

1166 A606 8c **carmine, ultramarine & ocher** .20 .20
P# block of 4 .80 —

CAMP FIRE GIRLS ISSUE

50th anniv. of the Camp Fire Girls' movement and in connection with the Golden Jubilee Convention celebration of the Camp Fire Girls.

Designed by H. Edward Oliver.

GIORI PRESS PRINTING

Plates of 200 subjects in four panes of 50.

1960, Nov. 1 ***Perf. 11***

1167 A607 4c **dark blue & bright red** .20 .20
P# block of 4 .65 —

Giuseppe Garibaldi — A608

Walter F. George — A609

CHAMPION OF LIBERTY ISSUE

Giuseppe Garibaldi (1807-1882), Italian patriot and freedom fighter.

ROTARY PRESS PRINTING

E.E. Plates of 280 subjects in four panes of 70.

1960, Nov. 2 ***Perf. 10½x11***

1168 A608 4c **green** .20 .20
P# block of 4 .40 —

GIORI PRESS PRINTING

Plates of 288 subjects in four panes of 72 each.
Perf. 11

1169 A608 8c **carmine, ultramarine & ocher** .20 .20
P# block of 4 .85 —

SENATOR GEORGE MEMORIAL ISSUE

Walter F. George (1878-1957) of Georgia.

Designed by William K. Schrage.

ROTARY PRESS PRINTING

E.E. Plates of 280 subjects in four panes of 70.

1960, Nov. 5 ***Perf. 10½x11***

1170 A609 4c **dull violet** .20 .20
P# block of 4 .45 —

Andrew Carnegie — A610

John Foster Dulles — A611

ANDREW CARNEGIE ISSUE

Carnegie (1835-1919), industrialist & philanthropist.

Designed by Charles R. Chickering.

ROTARY PRESS PRINTING

E.E. Plates of 280 subjects in four panes of 70.

1960, Nov. 25 ***Perf. 10½x11***

1171 A610 4c **deep claret** .20 .20
P# block of 4 .40 —

JOHN FOSTER DULLES MEMORIAL ISSUE

Dulles (1888-1959), Secretary of State (1953-59).

Designed by William K. Schrage.

ROTARY PRESS PRINTING

E.E. Plates of 280 subjects in four panes of 70.

1960, Dec. 6 ***Perf. 10½x11***

1172 A611 4c **dull violet** .20 .20
P# block of 4 .40 —

ECHO I — COMMUNICATIONS FOR PEACE ISSUE

World's 1st communications satellite, Echo I, placed in orbit by the Natl. Aeronautics and Space Admin., Aug. 12, 1960.

Radio Waves Connecting Echo I and Earth — A612

Designed by Ervine Metzl.

ROTARY PRESS PRINTING

E.E. Plates of 200 subjects in four panes of 50.

1960, Dec. 15 ***Perf. 11x10½***

1173 A612 4c **deep violet** .20 .20
P# block of 4 .65 —

CHAMPION OF LIBERTY ISSUE

Mohandas K. Gandhi, leader in India's struggle for independence.

Mahatma Gandhi — A613

ROTARY PRESS PRINTING

E.E. Plates of 280 subjects in four panes of 70.

1961, Jan. 26 ***Perf. 10½x11***

1174 A613 4c **red orange** .20 .20
P# block of 4 .40 —

GIORI PRESS PRINTING

Plates of 288 subjects in four panes of 72 each.
Perf. 11

1175 A613 8c **carmine, ultramarine & ocher** .20 .20
P# block of 4 1.00 —

RANGE CONSERVATION ISSUE

Issued to stress the importance of range conservation and to commemorate the meeting of the American Society of Range Management. "The Trail Boss" from a drawing by Charles M. Russell is the Society's emblem.

The Trail Boss and Modern Range — A614

Designed by Rudolph Wendelin.

GIORI PRESS PRINTING

Plates of 200 subjects in four panes of 50.

1961, Feb. 2 ***Perf. 11***

1176 A614 4c **blue, slate & brown orange** .20 .20
P# block of 4 .60 —

HORACE GREELEY ISSUE

Horace Greeley (1811-1872), Publisher and Editor — A615

Designed by Charles R. Chickering.

ROTARY PRESS PRINTING

E.E. Plates of 280 subjects in four panes of 70.

1961, Feb. 3 ***Perf. 10½x11***

1177 A615 4c **dull violet** .20 .20
P# block of 4 .45 —

CIVIL WAR CENTENNIAL ISSUE

Centenaries of the firing on Fort Sumter (No. 1178), the Battle of Shiloh (No. 1179), the Battle of Gettysburg (No. 1180), the Battle of the Wilderness (No. 1181) and the surrender at Appomattox (No. 1182).

Sea Coast Gun of 1861 — A616

Rifleman at Battle of Shiloh, 1862 — A617

Blue and Gray at Gettysburg, 1863 — A618

Battle of the Wilderness, 1864 — A619

Appomattox, 1865 — A620

Designed by Charles R. Chickering (Sumter), Noel Sickles (Shiloh), Roy Gjertson (Gettysburg), B. Harold Christenson (Wilderness), Leonard Fellman (Appomattox).

ROTARY PRESS PRINTING

E.E. Plates of 200 subjects in four panes of 50.

1961-65 ***Perf. 11x10½***

1178 A616 4c **light green,** *Apr. 12, 1961* .30 .20
P# block of 4 1.25 —
1179 A617 4c **black,** *peach blossom, Apr. 7, 1962* .20 .20
P# block of 4 .75 —

GIORI PRESS PRINTING

Plates of 200 subjects in four panes of 50.

Perf. 11

1180 A618 5c **gray & blue,** *July 1, 1963* .20 .20
P# block of 4 .85 —
1181 A619 5c **dark red & black,** *May 5, 1964* .20 .20
P# block of 4 .60 —
Margin block of 4, Mr. Zip and "Use Zip Code" .55 —
1182 A620 5c **Prus. blue & black,** *Apr. 9, 1965* .35 .20
P# block of 4 1.50 —
Margin block of 4, Mr. Zip and "Use Zip Code" 1.30 —
a. Horiz. pair, imperf. vert. *4,500.*
Nos. 1178-1182 (5) 1.25 1.00

KANSAS STATEHOOD, 100th ANNIV.

Sunflower, Pioneer Couple and Stockade A621

GIORI PRESS PRINTING

Plates of 200 subjects in four panes of 50.

1961, May 10 ***Perf. 11***

1183 A621 4c **brown, dark red & green,** *yellow* .20 .20
P# block of 4 .55 —

SENATOR NORRIS ISSUE

Senator George W. Norris of Nebraska, and Norris Dam — A622

Designed by Charles R. Chickering.

ROTARY PRESS PRINTING

E.E. Plates of 200 subjects in four panes of 50.

1961, July 11 ***Perf. 11x10½***

1184 A622 4c **blue green** .20 .20
P# block of 4 .40 —

NAVAL AVIATION, 50th ANNIV.

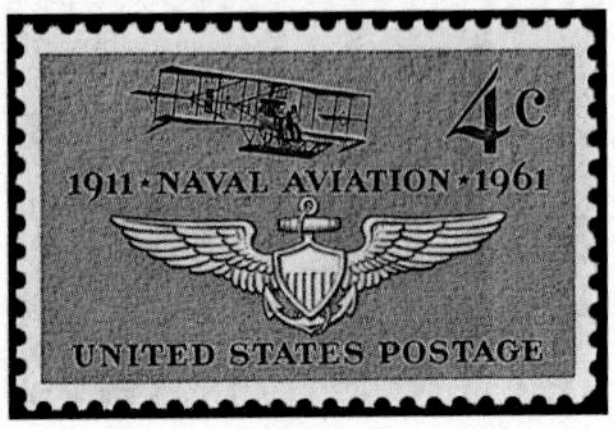

Navy's First Plane (Curtiss A-1 of 1911) and Naval Air Wings — A623

Designed by John Maass.

ROTARY PRESS PRINTING

E.E. Plates of 200 subjects in four panes of 50.

1961, Aug. 20 ***Perf. 11x10½***

1185 A623 4c **blue** .20 .20
P# block of 4 .40 —
Pair with full vert. gutter btwn. *150.00*

WORKMEN'S COMPENSATION ISSUE

50th anniv. of the 1st successful Workmen's Compensation Law, enacted by the Wisconsin legislature.

Scales of Justice, Factory, Worker and Family — A624

Designed by Norman Todhunter.

ROTARY PRESS PRINTING

E.E. Plates of 200 subjects in four panes of 50.

1961, Sept. 4 ***Perf. 10½x11***

1186 A624 4c **ultramarine,** *grayish* .20 .20
P# block of 4 .40 —
P# block of 4 inverted .60 —

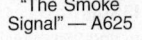

"The Smoke Signal" — A625

Sun Yat-sen — A626

FREDERIC REMINGTON ISSUE

Remington (1861-1909), artist of the West. The design is from an oil painting, Amon Carter Museum of Western Art, Fort Worth, Texas.

Designed by Charles R. Chickering.

GIORI PRESS PRINTING

Panes of 200 subjects in four panes of 50.

1961, Oct. 4 ***Perf. 11***

1187 A625 4c **multicolored** .20 .20
P# block of 4 .40 —

REPUBLIC OF CHINA ISSUE

50th anniversary of the Republic of China.

ROTARY PRESS PRINTING

E.E. Plates of 200 subjects in four panes of 50.

1961, Oct. 10 ***Perf. 10½x11***

1188 A626 4c **blue** .20 .20
P# block of 4 .45 —

Basketball — A627

Student Nurse Lighting Candle — A628

NAISMITH — BASKETBALL ISSUE

Honoring basketball and James Naismith (1861-1939), Canada-born director of physical education, who invented the game in 1891 at Y.M.C.A. College, Springfield, Mass.

Designed by Charles R. Chickering.

ROTARY PRESS PRINTING

E.E. Plates of 200 subjects in four panes of 50.

1961, Nov. 6 ***Perf. 10½x11***

1189 A627 4c **brown** .20 .20
P# block of 4 .50 —

NURSING ISSUE

Issued to honor the nursing profession.

Designed by Alfred Charles Parker.

GIORI PRESS PRINTING

Plates of 200 subjects in four panes of 50.

1961, Dec. 28 ***Perf. 11***

1190 A628 4c **blue, green, orange & black** .20 .20
P# block of 4, 2# .50 —

NEW MEXICO STATEHOOD, 50th ANNIV.

Shiprock A629

Designed by Robert J. Jones.

GIORI PRESS PRINTING

Plates of 200 subjects in four panes of 50.

1962, Jan. 6 ***Perf. 11***

1191 A629 4c **lt. blue, maroon & bister** .20 .20
P# block of 4 .50 —

ARIZONA STATEHOOD, 50th ANNIV.

Giant Saguaro Cactus — A630

Designed by Jimmie E. Ihms and James M. Chemi.

GIORI PRESS PRINTING

Plates of 200 subjects in four panes of 50.

1962, Feb. 14 *Perf. 11*
1192 A630 4c **carmine, violet blue & green** .20 .20
P# block of 4 .50 —

PROJECT MERCURY ISSUE

1st orbital flight of a US astronaut, Lt. Col. John H. Glenn, Jr., Feb. 20, 1962.

"Friendship 7" Capsule and Globe — A631

GIORI PRESS PRINTING

Plates of 200 subjects in four panes of 50.

1962, Feb. 20 *Perf. 11*
1193 A631 4c **dark blue & yellow** .20 .20
P# block of 4 .40 —

Imperfs. are printers waste.

MALARIA ERADICATION ISSUE

World Health Organization's drive to eradicate malaria.

Great Seal of US and WHO Symbol A632

Designed by Charles R. Chickering.

GIORI PRESS PRINTING

Plates of 200 subjects in four panes of 50.

1962, Mar. 30 *Perf. 11*
1194 A632 4c **blue & bister** .20 .20
P# block of 4 .40 —

Charles Evans Hughes — A633

"Space Needle" and Monorail — A634

CHARLES EVANS HUGHES ISSUE

Hughes (1862-1948), Governor of New York, Chief Justice of the US.

Designed by Charles R. Chickering.

ROTARY PRESS PRINTING

E.E. Plates of 200 subjects in four panes of 50.

1962, Apr. 11 *Perf. 10½x11*
1195 A633 4c **black,** *buff* .20 .20
P# block of 4 .40 —

SEATTLE WORLD'S FAIR ISSUE

"Century 21" International Exposition, Seattle, Wash., Apr. 21-Oct. 21.

Designed by John Maass.

GIORI PRESS PRINTING

Plates of 200 subjects in four panes of 50.

1962, Apr. 25 *Perf. 11*
1196 A634 4c **red & dark blue** .20 .20
On cover, "Century 21" Expo. cancel 5.00
On cover, "Space Needle" Expo. cancel 2.00
P# block of 4 .40 —

LOUISIANA STATEHOOD, 150th ANNIV.

Riverboat on the Mississippi A635

Designed by Norman Todhunter.

GIORI PRESS PRINTING

Plates of 200 subjects in four panes of 50.

1962, Apr. 30 *Perf. 11*
1197 A635 4c **blue, dark slate green & red** .20 .20
P# block of 4 .50 —

HOMESTEAD ACT, CENTENARY

Sod Hut and Settlers A636

Designed by Charles R. Chickering.

ROTARY PRESS PRINTING

E.E. Plates of 200 subjects in four panes of 50.

1962, May 20 *Perf. 11x10½*
1198 A636 4c **slate** .20 .20
P# block of 4 .40 —

GIRL SCOUTS ISSUE

50th anniversary of the Girl Scouts of America.

Senior Girl Scout and Flag — A637

Designed by Ward Brackett.

ROTARY PRESS PRINTING

E.E. Plates of 200 subjects in four panes of 50.

1962, July 24 *Perf. 11x10½*
1199 A637 4c **rose red** .20 .20
P# block of 4 .40 —
Pair with full vertical gutter between 250.00

SENATOR BRIEN McMAHON ISSUE

McMahon (1903-52) of Connecticut had a role in opening the way to peaceful uses of atomic energy through the Atomic Energy Act establishing the Atomic Energy Commission.

Brien McMahon and Atomic Symbol A638

Designed by V. S. McCloskey, Jr.

ROTARY PRESS PRINTING

E.E. Plates of 200 subjects in four panes of 50.

1962, July 28 *Perf. 11x10½*
1200 A638 4c **purple** .20 .20
P# block of 4 .40 —

APPRENTICESHIP ISSUE

National Apprenticeship Program and 25th anniv. of the National Apprenticeship Act.

Machinist Handing Micrometer to Apprentice A639

Designed by Robert Geissmann.

ROTARY PRESS PRINTING

E.E. Plates of 200 subjects in four panes of 50.

1962, Aug. 31 *Perf. 11x10½*
1201 A639 4c **black,** *yellow bister* .20 .20
P# block of 4 .40 —

SAM RAYBURN ISSUE

Rayburn (1882-1961), Speaker of the House of Representatives.

Sam Rayburn and Capitol — A640

Designed by Robert L. Miller.

GIORI PRESS PRINTING

Plates of 200 subjects in four panes of 50.

1962, Sept. 16 *Perf. 11*
1202 A640 4c **dark blue & red brown** .20 .20
P# block of 4 .45 —

DAG HAMMARSKJOLD ISSUE

Hammarskjold, UN Sec. General, 1953-61.

UN Headquarters and Dag Hammarskjold, UN Sec. Gen., 1953-61 A641

Designed by Herbert M. Sanborn.

GIORI PRESS PRINTING

Plates of 200 subjects in four panes of 50.

1962, Oct. 23 *Perf. 11*
1203 A641 4c **black, brown & yellow** .20 .20
P# block of 4, 2# .40 —
a. Yellow inverted, on cover, see note —

No. 1203a can only be collected on a cover postmarked before Nov. 16, 1962 (the date the Hammarskjold Special Printing, No. 1204, was issued). Covers are known machine postmarked Cuyahoga Falls, Ohio, Nov. 14, 1962, and notarized in the lower left corner by George W. Schwartz, Notary Public. Other covers are reported postmarked Oct. 26, 1962, Brooklyn, NY, Vanderveer Station. Unaddressed, uncacheted first day covers also exist. Other covers may exist. All covers must be accompanied by certificates from recognized expertizing committees.

An unused pane of 50 was signed in the selvage by ten well-known philatelists attesting to its genuineness. This pane was donated to the American Philatelic Society in 1987.

An unknown number of "first day covers" exist bearing Artmaster cachets. These were contrived using examples of No. 1204.

Hammarskjold Special Printing

No. 1204 was issued following discovery of No. 1203 with yellow background inverted.

GIORI PRESS PRINTING

Plates of 200 subjects in four panes of 50.

1962, Nov. 16 *Perf. 11*
1204 A641 4c **black, brown & yel** (yellow inverted) .20 .20
P# block of 4, 2#, yellow # inverted 1.25 —

The inverted yellow impression is shifted to the right in relation to the black and brown impression. Stamps of first vertical row of UL and LL panes show no yellow at left side for a space of 11-11½mm in from the perforations.

Stamps of first vertical row of UR and LR panes show vertical no-yellow strip 9¾mm wide, covering UN Building. On all others, the vertical no-yellow strip is 3½mm wide, and touches UN Building.

CHRISTMAS ISSUE

Wreath and Candles — A642

Designed by Jim Crawford.

GIORI PRESS PRINTING

Plates of 400 subjects in four panes of 100.
Panes of 90 and 100 exist without plate numbers due to provisional use of smaller paper.
Value per pane thus $50.

1962, Nov. 1		*Perf. 11*	
1205 A642 4c **green & red**		.20	.20
	P# block of 4	.40	—

HIGHER EDUCATION ISSUE

Higher education's role in American cultural and industrial development and the centenary celebrations of the signing of the law creating land-grant colleges and universities.

Map of U.S. and Lamp — A643

Designed by Henry K. Bencsath.

GIORI PRESS PRINTING

Plates of 200 subjects in panes of 50.

1962, Nov. 14		*Perf. 11*	
1206 A643 4c **blue green & black**		.20	.20
	P# block of 4, 2#	.40	—

WINSLOW HOMER ISSUE

Homer (1836-1910), painter, showing his oil, "Breezing Up," which hangs in the National Gallery, Washington, D.C.

"Breezing Up" — A644

Designed by Victor S. McCloskey, Jr.

GIORI PRESS PRINTING

Plates of 200 subjects in four panes of 50.

1962, Dec. 15		*Perf. 11*	
1207 A644 4c **multicolored**		.20	.20
	P# block of 4	.45	—
a.	Horiz. pair, imperf. btwn. and at right	*6,750.*	

FLAG ISSUE

Flag over White House — A645

Designed by Robert J. Jones.

GIORI PRESS PRINTING

Plates of 400 subjects in four panes of 100.

1963-66		*Perf. 11*	
1208 A645 5c **blue & red,** *Jan. 9, 1963*		.20	.20
	P# block of 4	.40	—
	Pair with full horiz. gutter between	—	
a.	Tagged, *Aug. 25, 1966*	.20	.20
	P# block of 4	2.00	—
b.	Horiz. pair, imperf. between, tagged	*1,500.*	

Beware of pairs with faint blind perfs between offered as No. 1208b.

REGULAR ISSUE

Andrew Jackson — A646

George Washington — A650

Designed by William K. Schrage.

ROTARY PRESS PRINTING

E.E. Plates of 400 subjects in four panes of 100.

1962-66		*Perf. 11x10½*	
1209 A646 1c **green,** *Mar. 22, 1963*		.20	.20
	P# block of 4	.20	—
	Pair with full vert. gutter btwn.	—	
a.	Tagged, *July 6, 1966*	.20	.20
	P# block of 4	.40	—
1213 A650 5c **dark blue gray,** *Nov. 23, 1962*		.20	.20
	P# block of 4	.40	—
	Pair with full vert. gutter btwn.	—	
	Pair with full horiz. gutter btwn.	*425.00*	
a.	Booklet pane of 5 + label	3.00	*2.00*
b.	Tagged, *Oct. 28, 1963*	.50	.20
	P# block of 4	4.50	—
c.	As "a," tagged, *Oct. 28, 1963*	2.00	*1.50*
d.	Horiz. pair, imperf between	*2,750.*	

Bureau Precancels: 1c, 10 diff., 5c, 18 diff.

No. 1213d resulted from a paper foldover after perforating and before cutting into panes. At least six individually unique panes exist, including at least one that contains two error pairs. Recent auction prices for panes have ranged between $1,400 and $4,000.

COIL STAMPS
(Rotary Press)

1962-66		*Perf. 10 Vertically*	
1225 A646 1c **green,** *May 31, 1963*		.20	.20
	Pair	.30	.20
	Joint line pair	2.25	.20
a.	Tagged, *July 6, 1966*	.20	.20
	Joint line pair	.75	.20
1229 A650 5c **dark blue gray,** *Nov. 23, 1962*		1.50	.20
	Pair	3.00	.20
	Joint line pair	4.00	.35
a.	Tagged, *Oct. 28, 1963*	1.80	.20
	Joint line pair	12.00	.20
b.	Imperf., pair	*350.00*	
	Joint line pair	*900.00*	

Bureau Precancels: 1c, 5 diff., 5c, 14 diff.

See Luminescence note in "Basic Stamp Information" in the introduction.

CAROLINA CHARTER ISSUE

Tercentenary of the Carolina Charter granting to 8 Englishmen lands extending coast-to-coast roughly along the present border of Virginia to the north and Florida to the south. Original charter on display at Raleigh.

First Page of Carolina Charter A662

Designed by Robert L. Miller.

GIORI PRESS PRINTING

Plates of 200 subjects in four panes of 50.

1963, Apr. 6		*Perf. 11*	
1230 A662 5c **dark carmine & brown**		.20	.20
	P# block of 4	.45	—

FOOD FOR PEACE-FREEDOM FROM HUNGER ISSUE

American "Food for Peace" program and the "Freedom from Hunger" campaign of the FAO.

Wheat — A663

Designed by Stevan Dohanos.

GIORI PRESS PRINTING

Plates of 200 subjects in four panes of 50.

1963, June 4		*Perf. 11*	
1231 A663 5c **green, buff & red**		.20	.20
	P# block of 4	.40	—

WEST VIRGINIA STATEHOOD, 100th ANNIV.

Map of West Virginia and State Capitol A664

Designed by Dr. Dwight Mutchler.

GIORI PRESS PRINTING

Plates of 200 subjects in four panes of 50.

1963, June 20		*Perf. 11*	
1232 A664 5c **green, red & black**		.20	.20
	P# block of 4	.50	—

EMANCIPATION PROCLAMATION ISSUE

Centenary of Lincoln's Emancipation Proclamation freeing about 3,000,000 slaves in 10 southern states.

Severed Chain — A665

Designed by Georg Olden.

GIORI PRESS PRINTING

Plates of 200 subjects in four panes of 50.

1963, Aug. 16		*Perf. 11*	
1233 A665 5c **dark blue, black & red**		.20	.20
	P# block of 4	.50	—

ALLIANCE FOR PROGRESS ISSUE

2nd anniv. of the Alliance for Progress, which aims to stimulate economic growth and raise living standards in Latin America.

Alliance Emblem A666

Designed by William K. Schrage.

GIORI PRESS PRINTING

Plates of 200 subjects in four panes of 50.

1963, Aug. 17		*Perf. 11*	
1234 A666 5c **ultramarine & green**		.20	.20
	P# block of 4	.40	—

CORDELL HULL ISSUE

Hull (1871-1955), Secretary of State (1933-44).

Cordell Hull — A667

Designed by Robert J. Jones.

ROTARY PRESS PRINTING
E.E. Plates of 200 subjects in four panes of 50.

1963, Oct. 5 *Perf. 10½x11*

1235 A667 5c **blue green** .20 .20
P# block of 4 .50 —

ELEANOR ROOSEVELT ISSUE

Mrs. Franklin D. Roosevelt (1884-1962).

Eleanor Roosevelt A668

Designed by Robert L. Miller.

ROTARY PRESS PRINTING
E.E. Plates of 200 subjects in four panes of 50.

1963, Oct. 11 *Perf. 11x10½*

1236 A668 5c **bright purple** .20 .20
P# block of 4 .45 —

SCIENCE ISSUE

Honoring the sciences and in connection with the centenary of the Natl. Academy of Science.

"The Universe" A669

Designed by Antonio Frasconi.

GIORI PRESS PRINTING
Plates of 200 subjects in four panes of 50.

1963, Oct. 14 *Perf. 11*

1237 A669 5c **Prussian blue & black** .20 .20
P# block of 4 .40 —

CITY MAIL DELIVERY ISSUE

Centenary of free city mail delivery.

Letter Carrier, 1863 — A670

Designed by Norman Rockwell.

GIORI PRESS PRINTING
Plates of 200 subjects in four panes of 50.

1963, Oct. 26 **Tagged** *Perf. 11*

1238 A670 5c **gray, dark blue & red** .20 .20
P# block of 4 .50 —
a. Tagging omitted 9.50

RED CROSS CENTENARY ISSUE

Cuban Refugees on S.S. Morning Light and Red Cross Flag — A671

Designed by Victor S. McCloskey, Jr.

GIORI PRESS PRINTING
Plates of 200 subjects in four panes of 50.

1963, Oct. 29 *Perf. 11*

1239 A671 5c **bluish black & red** .20 .20
P# block of 4 .50 —

CHRISTMAS ISSUE

National Christmas Tree and White House — A672

Designed by Lily Spandorf; modified by Norman Todhunter.

GIORI PRESS PRINTING
Plates of 400 subjects in four panes of 100.

1963, Nov. 1 *Perf. 11*

1240 A672 5c **dark blue, bluish black & red** .20 .20
P# block of 4 .50 —
a. Tagged, *Nov. 2, 1963* .65 .50
P# block of 4 5.00 —
Pair with full horiz. gutter between —
b. Horiz. pair, imperf between *7,750.*

"Columbia Jays" by Audubon — A673

Sam Houston — A674

JOHN JAMES AUDUBON ISSUE

Audubon (1785-1851), ornithologist and artist. The birds pictured are actually Collie's magpie jays. See No. C71.

Designed by Robert L. Miller.

GIORI PRESS PRINTING
Plates of 200 subjects in four panes of 50.

1963, Dec. 7 *Perf. 11*

1241 A673 5c **dark blue & multicolored** .20 .20
P# block of 4 .45 —

SAM HOUSTON ISSUE

Houston (1793-1863), soldier, president of Texas, US senator.

Designed by Tom Lea.

ROTARY PRESS PRINTING
E.E. Plates of 200 subjects in four panes of 50.

1964, Jan. 10 *Perf. 10½x11*

1242 A674 5c **black** .25 .20
P# block of 4 1.05 —
Margin block of 4, Mr. Zip and "Use Zip Code" 1.00 —

CHARLES M. RUSSELL ISSUE

Russell (1864-1926), painter. The design is from a painting, Thomas Gilcrease Institute of American History and Art, Tulsa, Okla.

"Jerked Down" — A675

Designed by William K. Schrage.

GIORI PRESS PRINTING
Plates of 200 subjects in four panes of 50.

1964, Mar. 19 *Perf. 11*

1243 A675 5c **multicolored** .20 .20
P# block of 4 .40 —
Margin block of 4, Mr. Zip and "Use Zip Code" .35 —

NEW YORK WORLD'S FAIR ISSUE

New York World's Fair, 1964-65.

Mall with Unisphere and "Rocket Thrower" by Donald De Lue — A676

Designed by Robert J. Jones.

ROTARY PRESS PRINTING
E.E. Plates of 200 subjects in four panes of 50.

1964, Apr. 22 *Perf. 11x10½*

1244 A676 5c **blue green** .20 .20
On cover, Expo. station machine cancel (non-first day) 2.00
On cover, Expo. station handstamp cancel (non-first day) 10.00
P# block of 4 .45 —
Margin block of 4, Mr. Zip and "Use Zip Code" .40 —

JOHN MUIR ISSUE

Muir (1838-1914), naturalist and conservationist.

John Muir and Redwood Forest — A677

Designed by Rudolph Wendelin.

GIORI PRESS PRINTING
Plates of 200 subjects in four panes of 50.

1964, Apr. 29 *Perf. 11*

1245 A677 5c **brown, green, yellow green & olive** .20 .20
P# block of 4 .45 —

KENNEDY MEMORIAL ISSUE

President John Fitzgerald Kennedy, (1917-1963).

John F. Kennedy and Eternal Flame — A678

Designed by Raymond Loewy/William Snaith, Inc.

Photograph by William S. Murphy.

ROTARY PRESS PRINTING

E.E. Plates of 200 subjects in four panes of 50.

1964, May 29 *Perf. 11x10½*

1246 A678 5c **blue gray** .20 .20
P# block of 4 .60 —

NEW JERSEY TERCENTENARY ISSUE

300th anniv. of English colonization of New Jersey. The design is from a mural by Howard Pyle in the Essex County Courthouse, Newark, N.J.

Philip Carteret Landing at Elizabethtown, and Map of New Jersey — A679

Designed by Douglas Allen.

ROTARY PRESS PRINTING

E.E. Plates of 200 subjects in four panes of 50.

1964, June 15 *Perf. 10½x11*

1247 A679 5c **brt. ultramarine** .20 .20
P# block of 4 .50 —
Margin block of 4, Mr. Zip and "Use Zip Code" .40 —

NEVADA STATEHOOD, 100th ANNIV.

Virginia City and Map of Nevada A680

Designed by William K. Schrage.

GIORI PRESS PRINTING

Plates of 200 subjects in four panes of 50.

1964, July 22 *Perf. 11*

1248 A680 5c **red, yellow & blue** .25 .20
P# block of 4 1.05 —
Margin block of 4, Mr. Zip and "Use Zip Code" 1.00 —

Flag — A681

William Shakespeare — A682

REGISTER AND VOTE ISSUE

Campaign to draw more voters to the polls.

Designed by Victor S. McCloskey, Jr.

GIORI PRESS PRINTING

Plates of 200 subjects in four panes of 50.

1964, Aug. 1 *Perf. 11*

1249 A681 5c **dark blue & red** .20 .20
P# block of 4 .45 —
Margin block of 4, Mr. Zip and "Use Zip Code" .40 —

SHAKESPEARE ISSUE

William Shakespeare (1564-1616).

Designed by Douglas Gorsline.

ROTARY PRESS PRINTING

E.E. Plates of 200 subjects in four panes of 50.

1964, Aug. 14 *Perf. 10½x11*

1250 A682 5c **black brown,** *tan* .20 .20
P# block of 4 .40 —
Margin block of 4, Mr. Zip and "Use Zip Code" .35 —

DOCTORS MAYO ISSUE

Dr. William James Mayo (1861-1939) and his brother, Dr. Charles Horace Mayo (1865-1939), surgeons who founded the Mayo Foundation for Medical Education and Research in affiliation with the Univ. of Minnesota at Rochester. Heads on stamp are from a sculpture by James Earle Fraser.

Drs. William and Charles Mayo — A683

ROTARY PRESS PRINTING

E.E. Plates of 200 subjects in four panes of 50.

1964, Sept. 11 *Perf. 10½x11*

1251 A683 5c **green** .20 .20
P# block of 4 .70 —
Margin block of 4, Mr. Zip and "Use Zip Code" .40 —

AMERICAN MUSIC ISSUE

50th anniv. of the founding of the American Society of Composers, Authors and Publishers (ASCAP).

Lute, Horn, Laurel, Oak and Music Score — A684

Designed by Bradbury Thompson.

GIORI PRESS PRINTING

Plates of 200 subjects in four panes of 50.

1964, Oct. 15 *Perf. 11*

Gray Paper with Blue Threads

1252 A684 5c **red, black & blue** .20 .20
P# block of 4 .40 —
Margin block of 4, Mr. Zip and "Use Zip Code" .35 —
a. Blue omitted *850.00*
b. Blue missing (PS) —

Beware of copies offered as No. 1252a which have traces of blue.

HOMEMAKERS ISSUE

Honoring American women as homemakers and for the 50th anniv. of the passage of the Smith-Lever Act. By providing economic experts under an extension service of the U.S. Dept. of Agriculture, this legislation helped to improve homelife.

Farm Scene Sampler A685

Designed by Norman Todhunter.

Plates of 200 subjects in four panes of 50.

Engraved (Giori Press); Background Lithographed

1964, Oct. 26 *Perf. 11*

1253 A685 5c **multicolored** .20 .20
P# block of 4 .40 —
Margin block of 4, Mr. Zip and "Use Zip Code" .35 —

CHRISTMAS ISSUE

Holly — A686

Mistletoe — A687

Poinsettia — A688

Sprig of Conifer — A689

Designed by Thomas F. Naegele.

GIORI PRESS PRINTING

Plates of 400 subjects in four panes of 100.

Panes contain 25 subjects each of Nos. 1254-1257

1964, Nov. 9 *Perf. 11*

1254 A686 5c **green, carmine & black** .25 .20
a. Tagged, *Nov. 10* .75 .50
b. Printed on gummed side —
1255 A687 5c **carmine, green & black** .25 .20
a. Tagged, *Nov. 10* .75 .50
1256 A688 5c **carmine, green & black** .25 .20
a. Tagged, *Nov. 10* .75 .50
1257 A689 5c **black, green & carmine** .25 .20
a. Tagged, *Nov. 10* .75 .50
b. Block of 4, #1254-1257 1.00 1.00
P# block of 4 1.10 —
Margin block of 4, Zip and "Use Zip Code" 1.00 —
c. Block of 4, tagged 3.00 2.25
P# block of 4 6.00 —
Zip block of 4 3.25 —

No. 1254b resulted from a paper foldover before printing and perforating.

VERRAZANO-NARROWS BRIDGE ISSUE

Opening of the Verrazano-Narrows Bridge connecting Staten Island and Brooklyn.

Verrazano-Narrows Bridge and Map of New York Bay — A690

ROTARY PRESS PRINTING

E.E. Plates of 200 subjects in four panes of 50.

1964, Nov. 21 *Perf. 10½x11*

1258 A690 5c **blue green** .20 .20
P# block of 4 .45 —
Margin block of 4, Mr. Zip and "Use Zip Code" .40 —

FINE ARTS ISSUE

Abstract Design by Stuart Davis — A691

GIORI PRESS PRINTING

Plates of 200 subjects in four panes of 50.

1964, Dec. 2 *Perf. 11*

1259 A691 5c **ultra., black & dull red** .20 .20
P# block of 4, 2# .45 —
Margin block of 4, Mr. Zip and "Use Zip Code" .40 —

AMATEUR RADIO ISSUE

Issued to honor the radio amateurs on the 50th anniversary of the American Radio Relay League.

Radio Waves and Dial — A692

Designed by Emil J. Willett.

ROTARY PRESS PRINTING

E.E. Plates of 200 subjects in four panes of 50.

1964, Dec. 15 *Perf. 10½x11*

1260 A692 5c **red lilac** .20 .20
P# block of 4 .70 —
Margin block of 4, Mr. Zip and "Use Zip Code" .40 —

BATTLE OF NEW ORLEANS ISSUE

Battle of New Orleans, Chalmette Plantation, Jan. 8-18, 1815, established 150 years of peace and friendship between the US and Great Britain.

General Andrew Jackson and Sesquicentennial Medal — A693

Designed by Robert J. Jones.

GIORI PRESS PRINTING

Plates of 200 subjects in four panes of 50.

1965, Jan. 8 *Perf. 11*

1261 A693 5c **deep carmine, violet blue & gray** .20 .20
P# block of 4 .60 —
Margin block of 4, Mr. Zip and "Use Zip Code" .50 —

Discus Thrower — A694

Microscope and Stethoscope — A695

PHYSICAL FITNESS-SOKOL ISSUE

Publicizing the importance of physical fitness and for the centenary of the founding of the Sokol (athletic) organization in America.

Designed by Norman Todhunter.

GIORI PRESS PRINTING

Plates of 200 subjects in four panes of 50.

1965, Feb. 15 *Perf. 11*

1262 A694 5c **maroon & black** .20 .20
P# block of 4 .50 —
Margin block of 4, Mr. Zip and "Use Zip Code" .40 —

CRUSADE AGAINST CANCER ISSUE

Issued to publicize the "Crusade Against Cancer" and to stress the importance of early diagnosis.

Designed by Stevan Dohanos.

GIORI PRESS PRINTING

Plates of 200 subjects in four panes of 50.

1965, Apr. 1 *Perf. 11*

1263 A695 5c **black, purple & red orange** .20 .20
P# block of 4, 2# .40 —
Margin block of 4, Mr. Zip and "Use Zip Code" .35 —

CHURCHILL MEMORIAL ISSUE

Sir Winston Spencer Churchill (1874-1965), British statesman and World War II leader.

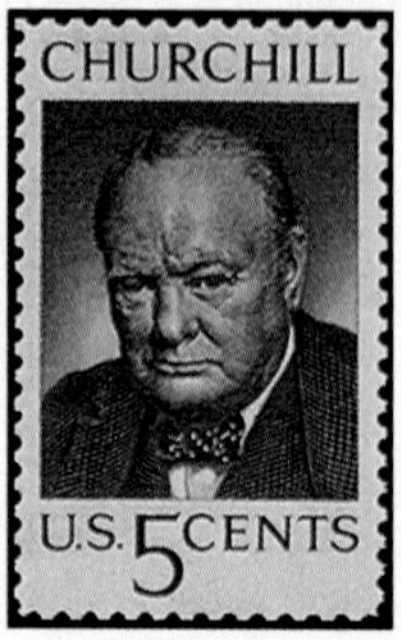

Winston Churchill — A696

Designed by Richard Hurd.

ROTARY PRESS PRINTING

E.E. Plates of 200 subjects in four panes of 50.

1965, May 13 *Perf. 10½x11*

1264 A696 5c **black** .20 .20
P# block of 4 .40 —
Margin block of 4, Mr. Zip and "Use Zip Code" .35 —

MAGNA CARTA ISSUE

750th anniversary of the Magna Carta, the basis of English and American common law.

Procession of Barons and King John's Crown — A697

Designed by Brook Temple.

GIORI PRESS PRINTING

Plates of 200 subjects in four panes of 50.

1965, June 15 *Perf. 11*

1265 A697 5c **black, yellow ocher & red lilac** .20 .20
P# block of 4, 2# .40 —
Margin block of 4, Mr. Zip and "Use Zip Code" .35 —
Corner block of 4, black # omitted —

INTERNATIONAL COOPERATION YEAR

ICY, 1965, and 20th anniv. of the UN.

International Cooperation Year Emblem A698

Designed by Herbert M. Sanborn and Olav S. Mathiesen.

GIORI PRESS PRINTING

Plates of 200 subjects in four panes of 50.

1965, June 26 *Perf. 11*

1266 A698 5c **dull blue & black** .20 .20
P# block of 4 .40 —
Margin block of 4, Mr. Zip and "Use Zip Code" .35 —

SALVATION ARMY ISSUE

Centenary of the founding of the Salvation Army by William Booth in London.

A699

Designed by Sam Marsh.

GIORI PRESS PRINTING

Plates of 200 subjects in four panes of 50.

1965, July 2 *Perf. 11*

1267 A699 5c **red, black & dark blue** .20 .20
P# block of 4 .40 —
Margin block of 4, Mr. Zip and "Use Zip Code" .35 —

Dante after a 16th Century Painting — A700

Herbert Hoover — A701

DANTE ISSUE

Dante Alighieri (1265-1321), Italian poet.

Designed by Douglas Gorsline.

ROTARY PRESS PRINTING

E.E. Plates of 200 subjects in four panes of 50.

1965, July 17 *Perf. 10½x11*

1268 A700 5c **maroon,** *tan* .20 .20
P# block of 4 .40 —
Margin block of 4, Mr. Zip and "Use Zip Code" .35 —

HERBERT HOOVER ISSUE

President Herbert Clark Hoover, (1874-1964).

Designed by Norman Todhunter; photograph by Fabian Bachrach, Sr.

ROTARY PRESS PRINTING

E.E. Plates of 200 subjects in four panes of 50.

1965, Aug. 10 *Perf. 10½x11*

1269 A701 5c **rose red** .20 .20
P# block of 4 .55 —
Margin block of 4, Mr. Zip and "Use Zip Code" .40 —

ROBERT FULTON ISSUE

Fulton (1765-1815), inventor of the 1st commercial steamship.

Robert Fulton and the Clermont A702

Designed by John Maass; bust by Jean Antoine Houdon.

GIORI PRESS PRINTING

Plates of 200 subjects in four panes of 50.

1965, Aug. 19 *Perf. 11*

1270 A702 5c **black & blue** .20 .20
P# block of 4 .40 —
Margin block of 4, Mr. Zip and "Use Zip Code" .35 —

FLORIDA SETTLEMENT ISSUE

400th anniv. of the settlement of Florida, and the 1st permanent European settlement in the continental US, St. Augustine, Fla.

Spanish Explorer, Royal Flag of Spain and Ships — A703

Designed by Brook Temple.

GIORI PRESS PRINTING

Plates of 200 subjects with four panes of 50.

1965, Aug. 28 *Perf. 11*

1271 A703 5c	**red, yellow & black**	.20	.20
	P# block of 4, 3#	.50	—
	Margin block of 4, Mr. Zip and "Use Zip Code"	.40	—
a.	Yellow omitted	*250.00*	

See Spain No. 1312.

TRAFFIC SAFETY ISSUE

Issued to publicize traffic safety and the prevention of traffic accidents.

Traffic Signal — A704

Designed by Richard F. Hurd.

GIORI PRESS PRINTING

Plates of 200 subjects in four panes of 50.

1965, Sept. 3 *Perf. 11*

1272 A704 5c	**emerald, black & red**	.20	.20
	P# block of 4, 2#	.45	—
	Margin block of 4, Mr. Zip and "Use Zip Code"	.40	—

JOHN SINGLETON COPLEY ISSUE

Copley (1738-1815), painter. The portrait of the artist's daughter is from the oil painting "The Copley Family," which hangs in the National Gallery of Art, Washington, D.C.

Elizabeth Clarke Copley — A705

Designed by John Carter Brown.

GIORI PRESS PRINTING

Plates of 200 subjects in four panes of 50.

1965, Sept. 17 *Perf. 11*

1273 A705 5c	**black, brown & olive**	.20	.20
	P# block of 4	.50	—
	Margin block of 4, Mr. Zip and "Use Zip Code"	.40	—

INTERNATIONAL TELECOMMUNICATION UNION, 100th ANNIV.

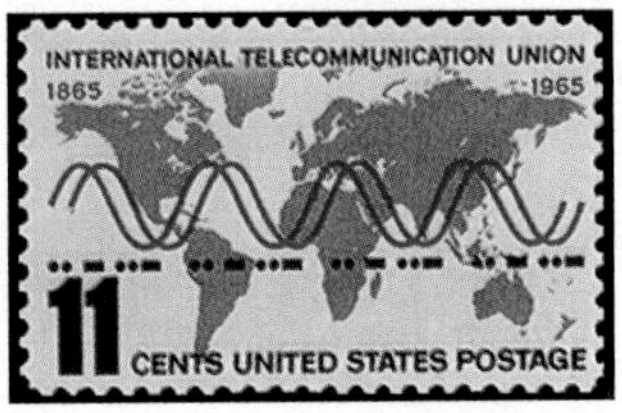

Galt Projection World Map and Radio Sine Wave — A706

Designed by Thomas F. Naegele.

GIORI PRESS PRINTING

Plates of 200 subjects with four panes of 50.

1965, Oct. 6 *Perf. 11*

1274 A706 11c	**black, carmine & bister**	.35	.20
	P# block of 4, 2#	2.00	—
	Margin block of 4, Mr. Zip and "Use Zip Code"	1.50	—

ADLAI STEVENSON ISSUE

Adlai Ewing Stevenson (1900-65), governor of Illinois, US ambassador to the UN.

Adlai E. Stevenson — A707

Designed by George Samerjan; photograph by Philippe Halsman.

LITHOGRAPHED, ENGRAVED (Giori)

Plates of 200 subjects in four panes of 50.

1965, Oct. 23 *Perf. 11*

1275 A707 5c	**pale blue, black, carmine & violet blue**	.20	.20
	P# block of 4	.40	—

CHRISTMAS ISSUE

Angel with Trumpet, 1840 Weather Vane — A708

Designed by Robert Jones.

After a watercolor by Lucille Gloria Chabot of the 1840 weather vane from the People's Methodist Church, Newburyport, Mass.

GIORI PRESS PRINTING

Plates of 400 subjects in four panes of 100.

1965, Nov. 2 *Perf. 11*

1276 A708 5c	**carmine, dark olive green & bister**	.20	.20
	P# block of 4	.40	—
	Margin block of 4, Mr. Zip and "Use Zip Code"	.35	—
	Pair with full vert. gutter btwn.	—	
a.	Tagged, *Nov. 15*	.75	.25
	P# block of 4	5.50	—
	Zip block of 4	3.50	—

PROMINENT AMERICANS ISSUE

Thomas Jefferson — A710

Albert Gallatin — A711

Frank Lloyd Wright and Guggenheim Museum, New York — A712

Francis Parkman — A713

Abraham Lincoln A714

George Washington A715

George Washington (redrawn) — A715a

Franklin D. Roosevelt — A716

Albert Einstein — A717

Andrew Jackson — A718

Henry Ford and 1909 Model T — A718a

John F. Kennedy — A719

Oliver Wendell Holmes — A720

George Catlett Marshall — A721

Frederick Douglass — A722

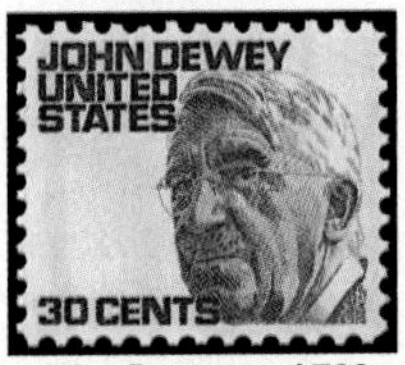

John Dewey — A723

Thomas Paine — A724

Lucy Stone — A725

Eugene O'Neill — A726

John Bassett Moore — A727

Designers: 1c, Robert Geissmann, after portrait by Rembrandt Peale. 1 ¼c, Robert Gallatin. 2c, Patricia Amarantides; photograph by Blackstone-Shelburne. 3c, Bill Hyde. 4c, Bill Hyde; photograph by Mathew Brady. 5c, Bill Hyde, after portrait by Rembrandt Peale. 5c, No. 1283B, Redrawn by Stevan Dohanos. 6c, 30c, Richard L. Clark. 8c, Frank Sebastiano; photograph by Philippe Halsman. 10c, Lester Beall. 12c, Norman Todhunter. 13c, Stevan Dohanos; photograph by Jacques Lowe. 15c, Richard F. Hurd. 20c, Robert Geissmann. 25c, Walter DuBois Richards. 40c, Robert Geissmann, after portrait by John Wesley Jarvis. 50c, Mark English. $1, Norman Todhunter. $5, Tom Laufer.

ROTARY PRESS PRINTING

E.E. Plates of 400 subjects in four panes of 100

1965-78 ***Perf. 11x10½, 10½x11***

Types of 15c:

I. Necktie barely touches coat at bottom; crosshatching of tie strong and complete. Flag of "5" is true horizontal. Crosshatching of "15" is colorless when visible.

II. Necktie does not touch coat at bottom; LL to UR crosshatching lines strong, UL to LR lines very faint. Flag of "5" slants down slightly at right. Crosshatching of "15" is colored and visible when magnified.

A third type, used only for No. 1288B, is smaller in overall size and "15¢" is ¾mm closer to head.

1278 A710 1c **green,** tagged, shiny gum, *Jan. 12, 1968* .20 .20
P# block of 4 .20 —
Margin block of 4, "Use Zip Codes" .20 —
Dull gum (from bklt. pane) .20
a. Booklet pane of 8, shiny gum, *Jan. 12, 1968* 1.00 .75
Dull gum 2.00
b. Bklt. pane of 4+2 labels, *May 10, 1971* .80 .60
c. Untagged (Bureau precanceled) 6.25 1.25
P# block of 4 175.00
Margin block of 4, "Use Zip Codes" 30.00
d. Tagging omitted (not Bureau precanceled) 3.50 —
e. As "a," dull gum, tagging omitted *75.00*

1279 A711 1 ¼c **light green,** *Jan. 30, 1967* .20 .20
P# block of 4 4.50 —

1280 A712 2c **dark blue gray,** tagged, shiny gum, *June 8, 1966* .20 .20
P# block of 4 .25 —
Margin block of 4, "Use Zip Codes" .20 —
Pair with full vert. gutter between —
Dull gum (from bklt. pane) .20
a. Bklt. pane of 5 + label, *Jan. 8, 1968* 1.25 .80
b. Untagged (Bureau precanceled) 1.35 .40
P# block of 4 27.50
Margin block of 4, "Use Zip Codes" 7.50
c. Bklt. pane of 6, shiny gum, *May 7, 1971* 1.00 .75
Dull gum 1.10
d. Tagging omitted (not Bureau precanceled) 4.00 —

1281 A713 3c **violet,** tagged, *Sept. 16, 1967* .20 .20
P# block of 4 .25 —
Margin block of 4, "Use Zip Codes" .20 —
Pair with full horiz. gutter between —
a. Untagged (Bureau precanceled) 3.00 .75
P# block of 4 —
Margin block of 4, "Use Zip Codes" 30.00
b. Tagging omitted (not Bureau precanceled) 5.00 —

1282 A714 4c **black,** *Nov. 19, 1965* .20 .20
P# block of 4 .40 —
a. Tagged, *Dec. 1, 1965* .20 .20
P# block of 4 .55 —
Pair with full horiz. gutter between *700.00*

1283 A715 5c **blue,** *Feb. 22, 1966* .20 .20
P# block of 4 .50 —
a. Tagged, *Feb. 23, 1966* .20 .20
P# block of 4 .60 —
Pair with full vert. gutter between —

1283B A715a 5c **blue,** tagged, shiny gum, *Nov. 17, 1967* .20 .20
P# block of 4 .50 —
Pair with full horiz. gutter between *175.00*
Dull gum .20
P# block of 4 1.40
d. Untagged (Bureau precanceled) 12.50 1.00
P# block of 4 —
e. Tagging omitted (not Bureau precanceled), shiny gum 4.00
Dull gum 5.50

No. 1283B is redrawn; highlights, shadows softened.

1284 A716 6c **gray brown,** *Jan. 29, 1966* .20 .20
P# block of 4 .60 —
Margin block of 4, "Use Zip Codes" (Bureau precanceled) 3.00
Pair with full horiz. gutter between *150.00*
Pair with full vert. gutter between *150.00*
a. Tagged, *Dec. 29, 1966* .20 .20
P# block of 4 .80 —
Margin block of 4, "Use Zip Codes" .65 —
b. Booklet pane of 8, *Dec. 28, 1967* 1.50 1.00
c. Bklt. pane of 5+ label, *Jan. 9, 1968* 1.50 1.00
d. Horiz. pair, imperf. between *1,500.*
e. As "b," tagging omitted *50.00* —

For untagged sheet stamps, "Use Zip Codes" and "Mail Early in the Day" marginal markings are found only on panes with Bureau precancels.

1285 A717 8c **violet,** *Mar. 14, 1966* .20 .20
P# block of 4 .85 —
a. Tagged, *July 6, 1966* .20 .20
P# block of 4 .95 —
Margin block of 4, "Use Zip Codes" .85 —

1286 A718 10c **lilac,** tagged, *Mar. 15, 1967* .20 .20
P# block of 4 1.00 —
Margin block of 4, "Use Zip Codes" .85 —
b. Untagged (Bureau precanceled) 57.50 1.75
P# block of 4 —
Margin block of 4, "Use Zip Codes" 275.00
e. Tagging omitted (not Bureau precanceled) 10.00

1286A 718a 12c **black,** tagged, *July 30, 1968* .25 .20
P# block of 4 1.20
Margin block of 4, "Use Zip Codes" 1.00 —
c. Untagged (Bureau precanceled) 4.75 1.00
P# block of 4 145.00
Margin block of 4, "Use Zip Codes" 27.50
d. Tagging omitted (not Bureau precanceled) 35.00

1287 A719 13c **brown,** tagged, *May 29, 1967* .30 .20
P# block of 4 1.50 —
Pair with full horiz. gutter between —
a. Untagged (Bureau precanceled) 6.00 1.00
P# block of 4 100.00
b. Tagging omitted (not Bureau precanceled) *15.00* —

1288 A720 15c **magenta,** type I, tagged, *Mar. 8, 1968* .30 .20
P# block of 4 1.25 —
Margin block of 4, "Use Zip Codes" 1.25 —
Pair with full horiz. gutter between *200.00*
Pair with full vert. gutter between *325.00*
a. Untagged (Bureau precanceled) .75 .75
P# block of 4 29.50
Margin block of 4, "Use Zip Codes" 7.50
d. Type II .55 .20
P# block of 4 8.00 —
Zip block of 4 3.50 —
Pair with full vert. gutter between —
f. As "d," tagging omitted (not Bureau precanceled) 7.50 —
h. As No. 1288, tagging omitted (not Bureau precanceled) 20.00

Imperforates exist from printer's waste.

Values for No. 1288a are for the bars-only precancel. Also exists with city precancels, and worth more thus.

The existence of the No. 1288d pair with vert. gutter between has been questioned by specialists. The editors would like to see evidence of its existence.

1288B A720 15c **magenta,** tagged, perf. 10 (from blkt. pane) .35 .20
c. Booklet pane of 8, *June 14, 1978* 2.80 1.75
e. As "c," vert. imperf. between *1,750.*
g. Tagging omitted *10.00* —
i. As "c," tagging omitted *85.00 50.00*

No. 1288B issued in booklets only. All stamps have one or two straight edges. Plates made from redrawn die.

1289 A721 20c **deep olive,** shiny gum, *Oct. 24, 1967* .40 .20
P# block of 4 1.75 —
Margin block of 4, "Use Zip Codes" 1.65 —
Dull gum .45
P# block of 4 2.10
Zip block of 4 1.90
a. Tagged, shiny gum, *Apr. 3, 1973* .40 .20
P# block of 4 1.75 —
Zip block of 4 1.65 —
b. 20c **black olive,** tagged, shiny gum .50 .20
P# block of 4 3.50 —
Zip block of 4 2.25 —
Dull gum .50
P# block of 4 3.50
Zip block of 4 2.25

1290 A722 25c **rose lake,** *Feb. 14, 1967* .55 .20
P# block of 4 2.25 —
Margin block of 4, "Use Zip Codes" 2.20 —
a. Tagged, shiny gum, *Apr. 3, 1973* .45 .20
P# block of 4 2.00 —
Zip block of 4 1.90 —
Dull gum .45
P# block of 4 2.00
Zip block of 4 1.90
b. 25c **magenta** *25.00* —
On cover —
P# block of 4 *150.00*

1291 A723 30c **red lilac,** *Oct. 21, 1968* .65 .20
P# block of 4 2.90 —
Margin block of 4, "Use Zip Codes" 2.70 —
a. Tagged, *Apr. 3, 1973* .50 .20
P# block of 4 2.25 —
Zip block of 4 2.10 —

1292 A724 40c **blue black,** *Jan. 29, 1968* .80 .20
P# block of 4 3.25 —
Margin block of 4, "Use Zip Codes" 3.25 —
a. Tagged, shiny gum, *Apr. 3, 1973* .65 .20
P# block of 4 2.75 —
Zip block of 4 2.65 —
Dull gum .70
P# block of 4 3.00
Zip block of 4 2.90

1293 A725 50c **rose magenta,** *Aug. 13, 1968* 1.00 .20
P# block of 4 4.25 —
Margin block of 4, "Use Zip Codes" 4.00 —
Pair with full vert. gutter btwn. —
a. Tagged, *Apr. 3, 1973* .80 .20
P# block of 4 3.50 —
Zip block of 4 3.25 —

1294 A726 $1 **dull purple,** *Oct. 16, 1967* 2.25 .20
P# block of 4 10.00 —
Margin block of 4, "Use Zip Codes" 9.25 —
a. Tagged, *Apr. 3, 1973* 1.65 .20
P# block of 4 6.75 —
Zip block of 4 6.65 —

1295 A727 $5 **gray black,** *Dec. 3, 1966* 10.00 2.25
P# block of 4 42.50 —
a. Tagged, *Apr. 3, 1973* 8.50 2.00
P# block of 4 35.00 —
Nos. 1278-1295 (21) 18.85 6.25
Nos. 1278-1288, 1289-1295, P# blocks of 4 (20) 78.65

Bureau Precancels: 1c, 19 diff., 1 ¼c, 14 diff., 2c, 41 diff., 3c, 11 diff., 4c, 49 diff., No. 1283, 7 diff., No. 1283B, 29 diff., 6c, 35 diff., 8c, 18 diff., 10c, 12 diff., 12c, 3 diff., 13c, 3 diff., No. 1288a, 9 diff., 20c, 14 diff., 25c, 9 diff., 30c, 14 diff., 40c, 7 diff., 50c, 14 diff., $1, 8 diff.

See Luminescence note in "Information for Collectors" at front of book.

COIL STAMPS

1967-75 **Tagged** ***Perf. 10 Horizontally***

1297 A713 3c **violet,** shiny gum, *Nov. 4, 1975* .20 .20
Pair .20 .20
Joint line pair .45 .20
Dull gum .75
Joint line pair 3.00
a. Imperf., pair, shiny gum *22.50*
Imperf., joint line pair *45.00*
Imperf, pair, dull gum 22.50
Imperf, joint line pair 45.00
b. Untagged (Bureau precanceled), shiny gum .40 .25
Pair .80 .50
Joint line pair 62.50 3.75
Dull gum .25
Pair .50
Joint line pair 3.75
c. As "b," imperf. pair *6.00* —
Joint line pair 22.50

No. 1297c is precanceled "Nonprofit Org. / CAR RT SORT."

1298 A716 6c **gray brown,** *Dec. 28, 1967* .20 .20
Pair .30 .20
Joint line pair 1.10 .25
a. Imperf., pair *1,900.*
Imperf., joint line pair *4,750.*
b. Tagging omitted 3.50

Bureau Precancels: 3c, 9 diff.

Franklin D. Roosevelt — A727a

Revised design by Robert J. Jones and Howard C. Mildner.

COIL STAMPS

1966-81 Tagged ***Perf. 10 Vertically***

1299 A710 1c **green,** *Jan. 12, 1968* .20 .20
Pair .20 .20
Joint line pair .25 .20
a. Untagged (Bureau precanceled) 8.00 1.75
Pair 17.50 4.00
Joint line pair *295.00* —
b. Imperf., pair *25.00* —
Imperf., joint line pair *52.50*
1303 A714 4c **black,** *May 28, 1966* .20 .20
Pair .30 .20
Joint line pair .75 .20
a. Untagged (Bureau precanceled) 8.75 .75
Pair 19.00 1.75
Joint line pair *250.00* —
b. Imperf., pair *700.00*
Imperf., joint line pair *1,650.*
c. Tagging omitted (not Bureau precanceled) *15.00* —
1304 A715 5c **blue,** shiny gum, *Sept. 8, 1966* .20 .20
Pair .25 .20
Joint line pair .40 .20
Dull gum .75
Joint line pair 5.00
a. Untagged (Bureau precanceled) 6.50 .65
Pair 14.00 1.40
Joint line pair *175.00* —
b. Imperf., pair *140.00*
Joint line pair *250.00*
e. As "a," imperf., pair 275.00
Joint line pair 850.00
f. Tagging omitted (not Bureau precanceled) — —

No. 1304b is valued in the grade of fine.
No. 1304e is precanceled Mount Pleasant, Iowa. Also exists from Chicago, Illinois; value $1,500 for pair.

1304C A715a 5c **blue,** *Jan., 1981* .20 .20
Pair .30 .20
Joint line pair 1.25 —
d. Imperf., pair *575.00*
Joint line pair *1,850.*
1305 A727a 6c **gray brown,** *Feb. 28, 1968* .20 .20
Pair .30 .20
Joint line pair .55 .20
a. Imperf., pair *60.00*
Joint line pair *115.00*
b. Untagged (Bureau precanceled) 20.00 1.00
Pair 42.50 2.25
Joint line pair *675.00* —
k. Tagging omitted (not Bureau precanceled) 3.50 —
1305E A720 15c **magenta,** type I, shiny gum, *June 14, 1978* .25 .20
Pair .50 .20
Joint line pair 1.10 .30
Dull gum .75
Joint line pair 4.25
f. Untagged (Bureau precanceled, Chicago, IL) 32.50 —
Pair 75.00 —
Joint line pair *1,250.* —
g. Imperf., pair, shiny gum 25.00
Joint line pair 55.00
Imperf., pair, dull gum 30.00
Joint line pair 70.00
h. Pair, imperf. between 150.00
Joint line pair *450.00*
i Type II, dull gum 1.50 .20
Joint line pair 5.00 —
j. Type II, dull gum, Imperf., pair *70.00*
Joint line pair *165.00*
l Tagging omitted —
1305C A726 $1 **dull purple,** shiny gum, *Jan. 12, 1973* 2.75 .40
Pair 5.50 .80
Joint line pair 9.00 1.50
Dull gum 4.00
Joint line pair 14.00
d. Imperf., pair *1,850.*
Joint line pair *4,000.*
Nos. 1297-1305C (9) 4.40 2.00

Bureau Precancels: 1c, 5 diff., 4c, 35 diff., No. 1304a, 45 diff., 6c, 30 diff.

MIGRATORY BIRD TREATY ISSUE

Migratory Birds over Canada-US Border A728

Designed by Burt E. Pringle.

GIORI PRESS PRINTING
Plates of 200 subjects in four panes of 50.

1966, Mar. 16 ***Perf. 11***
1306 A728 5c **black, crimson & dark blue** .20 .20
P# block of 4, 2# .40 —
Margin block of 4, Mr. Zip and "Use Zip Code" .35 —

HUMANE TREATMENT OF ANIMALS ISSUE

Issued to promote humane treatment of all animals and for the centenary of the American Society for the Prevention of Cruelty to Animals.

Mongrel A729

Designed by Norman Todhunter.

LITHOGRAPHED, ENGRAVED (Giori)
Plates of 200 subjects in four panes of 50.

1966, Apr. 9 ***Perf. 11***
1307 A729 5c **orange brown & black** .20 .20
P# block of 4 .40 —
Margin block of 4, Mr. Zip and "Use Zip Code" .35 —

Sesquicentennial Seal; Map of Indiana with 19 Stars and old Capitol at Corydon — A730

Clown — A731

INDIANA STATEHOOD, 150th ANNIV.

Designed by Paul A. Wehr.

GIORI PRESS PRINTING
Plates of 200 subjects in four panes of 50.

1966, Apr. 16 ***Perf. 11***
1308 A730 5c **ocher, brown & violet blue** .20 .20
P# block of 4, 2# .50 —
Margin block of 4, Mr. Zip and "Use Zip Code" .40 —

AMERICAN CIRCUS ISSUE

Issued to honor the American Circus on the centenary of the birth of John Ringling.

Designed by Edward Klauck.

GIORI PRESS PRINTING
Plates of 200 subjects in four panes of 50.

1966, May 2 ***Perf. 11***
1309 A731 5c **multicolored** .20 .20
P# block of 4, 2# .50 —
Margin block of 4, Mr. Zip and "Use Zip Code" .40 —

SIXTH INTERNATIONAL PHILATELIC EXHIBITION ISSUES

Sixth International Philatelic Exhibition (SIPEX), Washington, D.C., May 21-30.

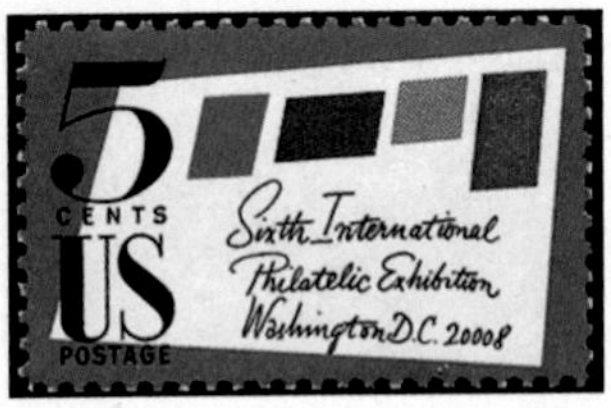

Stamped Cover — A732

Designed by Thomas F. Naegele.

LITHOGRAPHED, ENGRAVED (Giori)
Plates of 200 subjects in four panes of 50.

1966 ***Perf. 11***
1310 A732 5c **multicolored,** *May 21* .20 .20
P# block of 4 .40 —
Margin block of 4, Mr. Zip and "Use Zip Code" .35 —

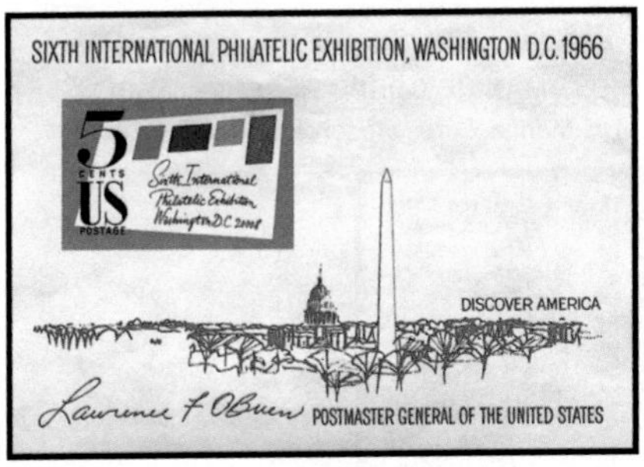

A733

Illustration reduced.

Designed by Brook Temple.

SOUVENIR SHEET
Plates of 24 subjects
Imperf

1311 A733 5c **multicolored,** *May 23* .20 .20

No. 1311 measures 108x74mm. Below the stamp appears a line drawing of the Capitol and Washington Monument. Marginal inscriptions and drawing are green.

"Freedom" Checking "Tyranny" — A734

Polish Eagle and Cross — A735

BILL OF RIGHTS, 175th ANNIV.

Designed by Herbert L. Block (Herblock).

GIORI PRESS PRINTING
Plates of 200 subjects in four panes of 50.

1966, July 1 ***Perf. 11***
1312 A734 5c **carmine, dark & light blue** .20 .20
P# block of 4, 2# .45 —
Margin block of 4, Mr. Zip and "Use Zip Code" .40 —

POLISH MILLENNIUM ISSUE

Adoption of Christianity in Poland, 1000th anniv.

Designed by Edmund D. Lewandowski.

ROTARY PRESS PRINTING
E.E. Plates of 200 subjects in four panes of 50.

1966, July 30 ***Perf. 10½x11***
1313 A735 5c **red** .20 .20
P# block of 4 .45 —
Margin block of 4, Mr. Zip and "Use Zip Code" .40 —

NATIONAL PARK SERVICE ISSUE

50th anniv. of the Natl. Park Service of the Interior Dept. The design "Parkscape U.S.A." identifies Natl. Park Service facilities.

National Park Service Emblem A736

Designed by Thomas H. Geismar.

LITHOGRAPHED, ENGRAVED (Giori)
Plates of 200 subjects in four panes of 50.

1966, Aug. 25 ***Perf. 11***

1314 A736 5c **yellow, black & green** .20 .20
P# block of 4 .50 —
Margin block of 4, Mr. Zip and "Use Zip Code" .40 —
a. Tagged, *Aug. 26* .35 .35
P# block of 4 2.25 —
Zip block of 4 1.50 —

MARINE CORPS RESERVE ISSUE

US Marine Corps Reserve founding, 50th anniv.

Combat Marine, 1966; Frogman; World War II Flier; World War I "Devil Dog" and Marine, 1775 — A737

Designed by Stella Grafakos.

LITHOGRAPHED, ENGRAVED (Giori)
Plates of 200 subjects in four panes of 50.

1966, Aug. 29 ***Perf. 11***

1315 A737 5c **black, bister, red & ultra.** .20 .20
P# block of 4 .45 —
Margin block of 4, Mr. Zip and "Use Zip Code" .40 —
a. Tagged .40 .20
P# block of 4 2.25 —
Zip block of 4 1.70 —
b. Black & bister (engraved) missing (EP) *16,000.*

GENERAL FEDERATION OF WOMEN'S CLUBS ISSUE

75 years of service by the General Federation of Women's Clubs.

Women of 1890 and 1966 — A738

Designed by Charles Henry Carter.

GIORI PRESS PRINTING
Plates of 200 subjects in four panes of 50.

1966, Sept. 12 ***Perf. 11***

1316 A738 5c **black, pink & blue** .20 .20
P# block of 4, 2# .45 —
Margin block of 4, Mr. Zip and "Use Zip Code" .40 —
a. Tagged, *Sept. 13* .40 .20
P# block of 4, 2# 2.25 —
Zip block of 4 1.70 —

AMERICAN FOLKLORE ISSUE
Johnny Appleseed

Issued to honor Johnny Appleseed (John Chapman 1774-1845), who wandered over 100,000 square miles planting apple trees, and who gave away and sold seedlings to Midwest pioneers.

Johnny Appleseed — A739

Designed by Robert Bode.

GIORI PRESS PRINTING
Plates of 200 subjects in four panes of 50.

1966, Sept. 24 ***Perf. 11***

1317 A739 5c **green, red & black** .20 .20
P# block of 4, 2# .45 —
Margin block of 4, Mr. Zip and "Use Zip Code" .40 —
a. Tagged, *Sept. 26* .40 .20
P# block of 4, 2# 2.25 —
Zip block of 4 1.70 —

BEAUTIFICATION OF AMERICA ISSUE

Issued to publicize President Johnson's "Plant for a more beautiful America" campaign.

Jefferson Memorial, Tidal Basin and Cherry Blossoms A740

Designed by Miss Gyo Fujikawa.

GIORI PRESS PRINTING
Plates of 200 subjects in four panes of 50.

1966, Oct. 5 ***Perf. 11***

1318 A740 5c **emerald, pink & black** .20 .20
P# block of 4, 2# .45 —
Margin block of 4, Mr. Zip and "Use Zip Code" .40 —
a. Tagged .40 .20
P# block of 4, 2# 2.25 —
Zip block of 4 1.70 —

Map of Central United States with Great River Road — A741

Statue of Liberty and "Old Glory" — A742

GREAT RIVER ROAD ISSUE

Issued to publicize the 5,600-mile Great River Road connecting New Orleans with Kenora, Ontario, and following the Mississippi most of the way.

Designed by Herbert Bayer.

LITHOGRAPHED, ENGRAVED (Giori)
Plates of 200 subjects in four panes of 50.

1966, Oct. 21

1319 A741 5c **vermilion, yellow, blue & green** .20 .20
P# block of 4 .60 —
Margin block of 4, Mr. Zip and "Use Zip Code" .40 —
a. Tagged, *Oct. 22* .40 .20
P# block of 4 2.50 —
Zip block of 4 1.70 —

SAVINGS BOND-SERVICEMEN ISSUE

25th anniv. of US Savings Bonds, and honoring American servicemen.

Designed by Stevan Dohanos, photo by Bob Noble.

LITHOGRAPHED, ENGRAVED (Giori)
Plates of 200 subjects in four panes of 50.

1966, Oct. 26 ***Perf. 11***

1320 A742 5c **red, dark blue, light blue & black** .20 .20
P# block of 4 .45 —
Margin block of 4, Mr. Zip and "Use Zip Code" .40 —
a. Tagged, *Oct. 27* .40 .20
P# block of 4 2.00 —
Zip block of 4 1.70 —
b. Red, dark blue & black missing (EP) *4,250.*
c. Dark blue (engr.) missing (EP) *5,500.*

CHRISTMAS ISSUE

Madonna and Child, by Hans Memling — A743

Designed by Howard C. Mildner.

Modeled after "Madonna and Child with Angels," by the Flemish artist Hans Memling (c.1430-1494), Mellon Collection, National Gallery of Art, Washington, D.C.

LITHOGRAPHED, ENGRAVED (Giori)
Plates of 400 subjects in four panes of 100.

1966, Nov. 1 ***Perf. 11***

1321 A743 5c **multicolored** .20 .20
P# block of 4 .40 —
Margin block of 4, Mr. Zip and "Use Zip Code" .35 —
a. Tagged, *Nov. 2* .40 .20
P# block of 4 2.00 —
Zip block of 4 1.70 —

MARY CASSATT ISSUE

Cassatt (1844-1926), painter. The painting "The Boating Party" is in the Natl. Gallery of Art, Washington, D.C.

"The Boating Party" — A744

Designed by Robert J. Jones.

GIORI PRESS PRINTING
Plates of 200 subjects in four panes of 50.

1966, Nov. 17 ***Perf. 11***

1322 A744 5c **multicolored** .20 .20
P# block of 4, 2# .60 —
Margin block of 4, Mr. Zip and "Use Zip Code" .50 —
a. Tagged .40 .25
P# block of 4, 2# 2.00 —
Zip block of 4 1.70 —

NATIONAL GRANGE ISSUE

Centenary of the founding of the National Grange, American farmers' organization.

Grange Poster, 1870 — A745

Designed by Lee Pavao.

GIORI PRESS PRINTING
Plates of 200 subjects in four panes of 50.

1967, Apr. 17 **Tagged** ***Perf. 11***

1323 A745 5c **orange, yellow, brown, green & black** .20 .20
P# block of 4, 2# .40 —

Margin block of 4, Mr. Zip and "Use Zip Code" .35 —
a. Tagging omitted *6.00* —

CANADA CENTENARY ISSUE

Centenary of Canada's emergence as a nation.

Canadian Landscape A746

Designed by Ivan Chermayeff.

GIORI PRESS PRINTING
Plates of 200 subjects in four panes of 50.

1967, May 25 **Tagged** ***Perf. 11***

1324 A746 5c **lt. blue, dp. green, ultra., olive & black** .20 .20
On cover, Expo. station ("U.S. Pavilion") machine canc. 1.00
On cover, Expo. station handstamp canc. 2.50
P# block of 4, 2# .40 —
Margin block of 4, Mr. Zip and "Use Zip Code" .35 —
a. Tagging omitted *7.50* —

ERIE CANAL ISSUE

150th anniversary of the Erie Canal ground-breaking ceremony at Rome, N.Y. The canal links Lake Erie and New York City.

Stern of Early Canal Boat — A747

Designed by George Samerjan.

LITHOGRAPHED, ENGRAVED (Giori)
Plates of 200 subjects in four panes of 50.

1967, July 4 **Tagged** ***Perf. 11***

1325 A747 5c **ultra., greenish blue, black & crimson** .20 .20
P# block of 4 .40 —
Margin block of 4, Mr. Zip and "Use Zip Code" .35 —
a. Tagging omitted *22.50* —

"SEARCH FOR PEACE" — LIONS ISSUE

Issued to publicize the search for peace. "Search for Peace" was the theme of an essay contest for young men and women sponsored by Lions International on its 50th anniversary.

Peace Dove — A748

Designed by Bradbury Thompson.

GIORI PRESS PRINTING
Plates of 200 subjects in four panes of 50.

1967, July 5 **Tagged** ***Perf. 11***

Gray Paper with Blue Threads

1326 A748 5c **blue, red & black** .20 .20
P# block of 4 .40 —
Margin block of 4, Mr. Zip and "Use Zip Code" .35 —
a. Tagging omitted *7.50* —

HENRY DAVID THOREAU ISSUE

Henry David Thoreau (1817-1862), writer.

Henry David Thoreau — A749

Designed by Leonard Baskin.

GIORI PRESS PRINTING
Plates of 200 subjects in four panes of 50.

1967, July 12 **Tagged** ***Perf. 11***

1327 A749 5c **carmine, black & blue green** .20 .20
P# block of 4 .50 —
Margin block of 4, Mr. Zip and "Use Zip Code" .40 —
a. Tagging omitted *200.00*

NEBRASKA STATEHOOD, 100th ANNIV.

Hereford Steer and Ear of Corn — A750

Designed by Julian K. Billings.

LITHOGRAPHED, ENGRAVED (Giori)
Plates of 200 subjects in four panes of 50.

1967, July 29 **Tagged** ***Perf. 11***

1328 A750 5c **dark red brown, lemon & yellow** .20 .20
P# block of 4 .70 —
Margin block of 4, Mr. Zip and "Use Zip Code" .40 —
a. Tagging omitted *7.50* —

VOICE OF AMERICA ISSUE

25th anniv. of the radio branch of the United States Information Agency (USIA).

Radio Transmission Tower and Waves — A751

Designed by Georg Olden.

LITHOGRAPHED, ENGRAVED (Giori)
Plates of 200 subjects in four panes of 50.

1967, Aug. 1 **Tagged** ***Perf. 11***

1329 A751 5c **red, blue, black & carmine** .20 .20
P# block of 4 .40 —
Margin block of 4, Mr. Zip and "Use Zip Code" .35 —
a. Tagging omitted *20.00* —

AMERICAN FOLKLORE ISSUE

Davy Crockett (1786-1836), frontiersman, hunter, and congressman from Tennessee who died at the Alamo.

Davy Crockett and Scrub Pine — A752

Designed by Robert Bode.

LITHOGRAPHED, ENGRAVED (Giori)
Plates of 200 subjects in four panes of 50.

1967, Aug. 17 **Tagged** ***Perf. 11***

1330 A752 5c **green, black, & yellow** .20 .20
P# block of 4 .60 —
Margin block of 4, Mr. Zip and "Use Zip Code" .40 —
a. Vertical pair, imperf. between *7,000.*
b. Green (engr.) missing (FO) —
c. Black & green (engr.) missing (FO) —
e. Tagging omitted *9.00* —

A foldover on a pane of No. 1330 resulted in one example each of Nos. 1330b-1330c. Part of the colors appear on the back of the selvage and one freak stamp. An engraved black-and-green-only impression appears on the gummed side of one almost-complete "stamp."

ACCOMPLISHMENTS IN SPACE ISSUE

US accomplishments in space. Printed with continuous design in horizontal rows of 5. In the left panes the astronaut stamp is 1st, 3rd and 5th, the spaceship 2nd and 4th. This arrangement is reversed in the right panes.

Space-Walking Astronaut A753

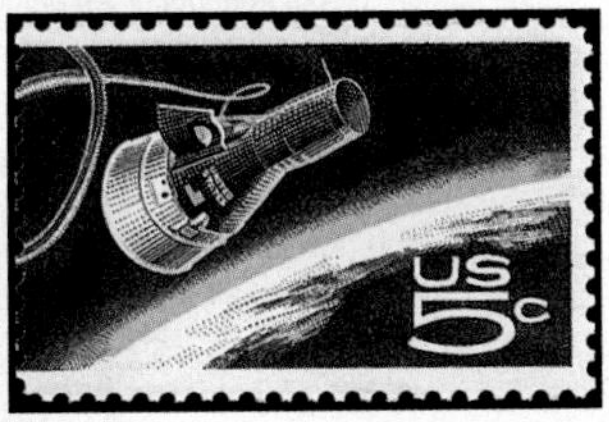

Gemini 4 Capsule A754

Designed by Paul Calle.

LITHOGRAPHED, ENGRAVED (Giori)
Plates of 200 subjects in four panes of 50.

1967, Sept. 29 **Tagged** ***Perf. 11***

1331 A753 5c **multicolored** .50 .20
a. Tagging omitted *25.00* —
1332 A754 5c **multicolored** .50 .20
P# block of 4 2.25 —
Margin block of 4, Mr. Zip and "Use Zip Code" 2.10 —
Plate flaw (red stripes of flag on capsule omitted; 29322, 29325 UL 19) 210.00
a. Tagging omitted *25.00* —
b. Pair, #1331-1332 1.10 *1.25*
c. As "b," tagging omitted *60.00* —

View of Model City — A755

Finnish Coat of Arms — A756

URBAN PLANNING ISSUE

Publicizing the importance of Urban Planning in connection with the Intl. Conf. of the American Institute of Planners, Washington, D.C., Oct. 1-6.

Designed by Francis Ferguson.

LITHOGRAPHED, ENGRAVED (Giori)
Plates of 200 subjects in four panes of 50.

1967, Oct. 2 **Tagged** ***Perf. 11***

1333 A755 5c **dark blue, light blue & black** .20 .20
P# block of 4 .50 —
Margin block of 4, Mr. Zip and "Use Zip Code" .40 —
a. Tagging omitted *50.00*

FINNISH INDEPENDENCE, 50th ANNIV.

Designed by Bradbury Thompson.

ENGRAVED (Giori)
Plates of 200 subjects in four panes of 50.

1967, Oct. 6 **Tagged** ***Perf. 11***

1334 A756 5c **blue** .20 .20
P# block of 4 .50 —
Margin block of 4, Mr. Zip and "Use Zip Code" .40 —
a. Tagging omitted *100.00*

THOMAS EAKINS ISSUE

Eakins (1844-1916), painter and sculptor. The painting is in the Natl. Gallery of Art, Washington, D.C.

"The Biglin Brothers Racing" (Sculling on Schuylkill River, Philadelphia) A757

Printed by Photogravure & Color Co., Moonachie, N.J.

PHOTOGRAVURE
Plates of 200 subjects in four panes of 50.

1967, Nov. 2 **Tagged** ***Perf. 12***

1335 A757 5c **gold & multicolored** .20 .20
P# block of 4, 6# .50 —
a. Tagging omitted *40.00* —

Plate number blocks from upper left or lower left panes show clipped corner of margin.

CHRISTMAS ISSUE

Madonna and Child, by Hans Memling — A758

LITHOGRAPHED, ENGRAVED (Giori)
Plates of 200 subjects in four panes of 50.

1967, Nov. 6 **Tagged** ***Perf. 11***

1336 A758 5c **multicolored** .20 .20
P# block of 4 .40 —
Margin block of 4, Mr. Zip and "Use Zip Code" .35 —
a. Tagging omitted *5.50* —

See note on painting above No. 1321.

MISSISSIPPI STATEHOOD, 150th ANNIV.

Magnolia A759

Designed by Andrew Bucci.

GIORI PRESS PRINTING
Plates of 200 subjects in four panes of 50.

1967, Dec. 11 **Tagged** ***Perf. 11***

1337 A759 5c **brt. greenish blue, green & red brown** .20 .20
P# block of 4, 2# .60 —
Margin block of 4, Mr. Zip and "Use Zip Code" .40 —
a. Tagging omitted *10.00* —

FLAG ISSUE

Flag and White House — A760

Designed by Stevan Dohanos.

GIORI PRESS PRINTING
Plates of 400 subjects in four panes of 100.

1968, Jan. 24 **Tagged** ***Perf. 11***
Size: 19x22mm

1338 A760 6c **dark blue, red & green** .20 .20
P# block of 4 .45 —
Margin block of 4, "Use Zip Code" .40 —
Pair with full vert. gutter btwn. —
k. Vert. pair, imperf. btwn. *400.00 175.00*
m. Tagging omitted *4.50* —
s. Red missing (FO) —
u. Vert. pair, imperf horiz. *475.00*

Beware of regumming on No. 1338u. Most examples have had the gum washed off to make it difficult or impossible to detect blind perfs. Check carefully for blind perfs. Value is for pair with original gum.

No. 1338s is unique.

COIL STAMP

MULTICOLOR HUCK PRESS

1969, May 30 **Tagged** ***Perf. 10 Vertically***
Size: 18¼x21mm

1338A A760 6c **dark blue, red & green** .20 .20
Pair .30 .20
b. Imperf., pair *475.00*
q. Tagging omitted *10.00* —

MULTICOLOR HUCK PRESS
Panes of 100 (10x10) each

1970-71 **Tagged** ***Perf. 11x10½***
Size: 18¼x21mm

1338D A760 6c **dark blue, red & green,** *Aug. 7, 1970* .20 .20
Margin block of 20+ 2.60 —
e. Horiz. pair, imperf. between *125.00*
n. Tagging omitted *4.00* —

1338F A760 8c **dark blue, red & slate green,** *May 10, 1971* .20 .20
Margin block of 20+ 3.00 —
i. Imperf., vert. pair 37.50
j. Horiz. pair, imperf. between 45.00
o. Tagging omitted *4.00* —
p. Slate green omitted *325.00*
t. Horiz. pair, imperf. vertically —

+ Margin blocks of 20 come in four versions: (1) 2 P#, 3 ME, 3 zip; (2) 3 P#, 2 ME, 2 zip; (3) 2 P#, 3 ME, 2 zip; (4) 3 P#, 2 ME, 3 zip.

COIL STAMP

MULTICOLOR HUCK PRESS

1971, May 10 **Tagged** ***Perf. 10 Vertically***
Size: 18¼x21mm

1338G A760 8c **dk blue, red & slate green** .30 .20
Pair .60 .20
h. Imperf., pair *50.00*
r. Tagging omitted *5.00* —

Farm Buildings and Fields of Ripening Grain — A761

Map of North and South America and Lines Converging on San Antonio — A762

ILLINOIS STATEHOOD, 150th ANNIV.

Designed by George Barford.

LITHOGRAPHED, ENGRAVED (Giori)
Plates of 200 subjects in four panes of 50.

1968, Feb. 12 **Tagged** ***Perf. 11***

1339 A761 6c **dk blue, blue, red & ocher** .20 .20
P# block of 4 .60 —
Margin block of 4, Mr. Zip and "Use Zip Code" .45 —
a. Tagging omitted —

HEMISFAIR '68 ISSUE

HemisFair '68 exhibition, San Antonio, Texas, Apr. 6-Oct. 6, for the 250th anniv. of San Antonio.

Designed by Louis Macouillard.

LITHOGRAPHED, ENGRAVED (Giori)
Plates of 200 subjects in four panes of 50.

1968, Mar. 30 **Tagged** ***Perf. 11***

1340 A762 6c **blue, rose red & white** .20 .20
On cover, Expo. station machine canc. 10.00
On cover, Expo. roller canc. 25.00
P# block of 4 .50 —
Margin block of 4, Mr. Zip and "Use Zip Code" .45 —
a. White omitted *1,100.*

AIRLIFT ISSUE

Issued to pay for airlift of parcels from and to US ports to servicemen overseas and in Alaska, Hawaii and Puerto Rico. Valid for all regular postage. On Apr. 26, 1969, the Post Office Department ruled that henceforth No. 1341 "may be used toward paying the postage or fees for special services on *airmail* articles."

Eagle Holding Pennant A763

Designed by Stevan Dohanos.

After a late 19th century wood carving, part of the Index of American Design, National Gallery of Art.

LITHOGRAPHED, ENGRAVED (Giori)
Plates of 200 subjects in four panes of 50.

1968, Apr. 4 **Untagged** ***Perf. 11***

1341 A763 $1 **sepia, dk. blue, ocher & brown red** 2.00 1.25
P# block of 4 8.50 —
Margin block of 4, Mr. Zip and "Use Zip Code" 8.25 —
Pair with full horiz. gutter btwn. —

"SUPPORT OUR YOUTH" — ELKS ISSUE

Support Our Youth program, and honoring the Benevolent and Protective Order of Elks, which extended its youth service program in observance of its centennial year.

Girls and Boys — A764

Designed by Edward Vebell.

LITHOGRAPHED, ENGRAVED (Giori)
Plates of 200 subjects in four panes of 50.

1968, May 1 **Tagged** ***Perf. 11***

1342 A764 6c **ultramarine & orange red** .20 .20
P# block of 4 .55 —
Margin block of 4, Mr. Zip and "Use Zip Code" .45 —
a. Tagging omitted *9.50* —

Policeman and Boy — A765

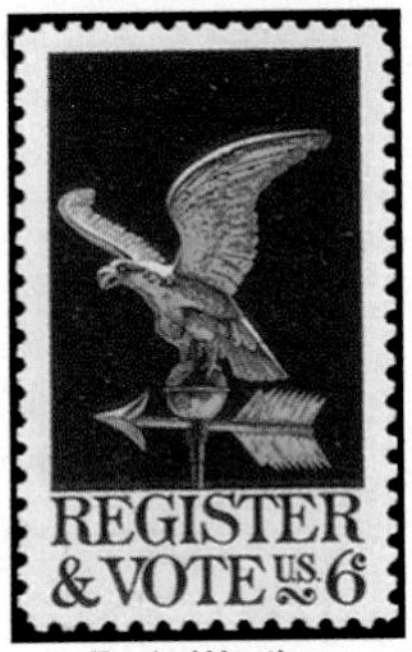

Eagle Weather Vane — A766

LAW AND ORDER ISSUE

Publicizing the policeman as protector and friend and to encourage respect for law and order.

Designed by Ward Brackett.

GIORI PRESS PRINTING

Plates of 200 subjects in four panes of 50 each

1968, May 17	**Tagged**	***Perf. 11***	
1343 A765 6c **chalky blue, black & red**		.20	.20
P# block of 4		.55	—
Margin block of 4, Mr. Zip and "Use Zip Code"		.45	—
a. Tagging omitted		*175.00*	*90.00*

REGISTER AND VOTE ISSUE

Campaign to draw more voters to the polls. The weather vane is from an old house in the Russian Hill section of San Francisco, Cal.

Designed by Norman Todhunter and Bill Hyde; photograph by M. Halberstadt.

LITHOGRAPHED, ENGRAVED (Giori)

Plates of 200 subjects in four panes of 50.

1968, June 27	**Tagged**	***Perf. 11***	
1344 A766 6c **black, yellow & orange**		.20	.20
P# block of 4		.50	—
Margin block of 4, Mr. Zip and "Use Zip Code"		.45	—
a. Tagging omitted		—	

HISTORIC FLAG SERIES

Flags carried by American colonists and by citizens of the new United States. Printed se-tenant in vertical rows of 10. The flag sequence on the 2 upper panes is as listed. On the 2 lower panes the sequence is reversed with the Navy Jack in the 1st row and the Fort Moultrie flag in the 10th.

Ft. Moultrie, 1776 — A767

Ft. McHenry, 1795-1818 A768

Washington's Cruisers, 1775 — A769

Bennington, 1777 — A770

Rhode Island, 1775 — A771

First Stars and Stripes, 1777 — A772

Bunker Hill, 1775 — A773

Grand Union, 1776 — A774

Philadelphia Light Horse, 1775 — A775

First Navy Jack, 1775 — A776

ENGR. (Giori) (#1345-1348, 1350);
ENGR. & LITHO. (#1349, 1351-1354)

Plates of 200 subjects in four panes of 50.

1968, July 4	**Tagged**	***Perf. 11***	
1345 A767 6c **dark blue**		.40	.25
1346 A768 6c **dark blue & red**		.40	.25
1347 A769 6c **dark blue & olive green**		.30	.25
1348 A770 6c **dark blue & red**		.30	.25
1349 A771 6c **dark blue, yellow & red**		.30	.25
1350 A772 6c **dark blue & red**		.30	.25
1351 A773 6c **dark blue, olive green & red**		.30	.25
1352 A774 6c **dark blue & red**		.30	.25
1353 A775 6c **dark blue, yellow & red**		.30	.25
1354 A776 6c **dark blue, red & yellow**		.30	.25
a. Strip of ten, #1345-1354		3.25	*3.25*
P# block of 20, inscriptions, #1345-1354		6.75	—
b. #1345b-1354b, any single, tagging omitted		—	
c. As "a," imperf		—	

WALT DISNEY ISSUE

Walt Disney (1901-1966), cartoonist, film producer and creator of Mickey Mouse.

Walt Disney and Children of the World — A777

Designed by C. Robert Moore.

Designed after portrait by Paul E. Wenzel.
Printed by Achrovure Division of Union-Camp Corp., Englewood, N.J.

PHOTOGRAVURE

Plates of 400 subjects in eight panes of 50.

1968, Sept. 11	**Tagged**	***Perf. 12***	
1355 A777 6c **multicolored**		.40	.20
P# block of 4, 5#		1.75	—
P# block of 4, 5#, 5 dashes		1.75	—
Margin block of 4, Mr. Zip and "Use Zip Code"		1.60	—
a. Ocher omitted ("Walt Disney," "6c," etc.)		*500.00*	—
b. Vert. pair, imperf. horiz.		*600.00*	
c. Imperf., pair		*500.00*	
d. Black omitted		*1,850.*	
e. Horiz. pair, imperf. between		*4,500.*	
f. Blue omitted		*1,850.*	
g. Tagging omitted		*18.00*	—

FATHER MARQUETTE ISSUE

Father Jacques Marquette (1637-1675), French Jesuit missionary, who together with Louis Jolliet explored the Mississippi River and its tributaries.

Father Marquette and Louis Jolliet Exploring the Mississippi A778

Designed by Stanley W. Galli.

GIORI PRESS PRINTING

Plates of 200 subjects in four panes of 50.

1968, Sept. 20	**Tagged**	***Perf. 11***	
1356 A778 6c **black, apple green & orange brown**		.20	.20
P# block of 4		.60	—
Margin block of 4, Mr. Zip and "Use Zip Code"		.65	—
a. Tagging omitted		*6.00*	—

AMERICAN FOLKLORE ISSUE

Daniel Boone (1734-1820), frontiersman and trapper.

Pennsylvania Rifle, Powder Horn, Tomahawk Pipe and Knife — A779

Designed by Louis Macouillard.

LITHOGRAPHED, ENGRAVED (Giori)

Plates of 200 subjects in four panes of 50.

1968, Sept. 26	**Tagged**	***Perf. 11***	
1357 A779 6c **yellow, deep yellow, maroon & black**		.20	.20
P# block of 4		.50	—
Margin block of 4, Mr. Zip and "Use Zip Code"		.45	—
a. Tagging omitted		—	

ARKANSAS RIVER NAVIGATION ISSUE

Opening of the Arkansas River to commercial navigation.

Ship's Wheel, Power Transmission Tower and Barge — A780

Designed by Dean Ellis.

LITHOGRAPHED, ENGRAVED (Giori)

Plates of 200 subjects in four panes of 50.

1968, Oct. 1 **Tagged** ***Perf. 11***

1358 A780 6c	**bright blue, dark blue & black**	.20	.20
	P# block of 4	.50	—
	Margin block of 4, Mr. Zip and "Use Zip Code"	.45	—
a.	Tagging omitted		—

LEIF ERIKSON ISSUE

Leif Erikson, 11th century Norse explorer, called the 1st European to set foot on the American continent, at a place he called Vinland. The statue by the American sculptor A. Stirling Calder is in Reykjavik, Iceland.

Leif Erikson by A. Stirling Calder — A781

Designed by Kurt Weiner.

LITHOGRAPHED & ENGRAVED

Plates of 200 subjects in four panes of 50.

1968, Oct. 9 **Tagged** ***Perf. 11***

1359 A781 6c	**light gray brown & black brown**	.20	.20
	P# block of 4	.50	—
	Margin block of 4, Mr. Zip and "Use Zip Code"	.45	—

The luminescent element is in the light gray brown ink of the background. The engraved parts were printed on a rotary currency press.

CHEROKEE STRIP ISSUE

75th anniversary of the opening of the Cherokee Strip to settlers, Sept. 16, 1893.

Racing for Homesteads in Cherokee Strip, 1893 — A782

Designed by Norman Todhunter.

ROTARY PRESS PRINTING

E.E. Plates of 200 subjects in four panes of 50.

1968, Oct. 15 **Tagged** ***Perf. 11x10½***

1360 A782 6c	**brown**	.20	.20
	P# block of 4	.80	—
	Margin block of 4, Mr. Zip and "Use Zip Code"	.50	—
a.	Tagging omitted	*7.50*	—

JOHN TRUMBULL ISSUE

Trumbull (1756-1843), painter. The stamp shows Lt. Thomas Grosvenor and his attendant Peter Salem. The painting hangs at Yale University.

Detail from "The Battle of Bunker's Hill" — A783

Modeled by Robert J. Jones.

LITHOGRAPHED, ENGRAVED (Giori)

Plates of 200 subjects in four panes of 50.

1968, Oct. 18 **Tagged** ***Perf. 11***

1361 A783 6c	**multicolored**	.20	.20
	P# block of 4	.60	—
	Margin block of 4, Mr. Zip and "Use Zip Code"	.50	—
a.	Tagging omitted	*125.00*	—
b.	Black (engr.) missing (FO)	*11,000.*	—

WATERFOWL CONSERVATION ISSUE

Wood Ducks — A784

Designed by Stanley W. Galli.

LITHOGRAPHED, ENGRAVED (Giori)

Plates of 200 subjects in four panes of 50.

1968, Oct. 24 **Tagged** ***Perf. 11***

1362 A784 6c	**black & multicolored**	.20	.20
	P# block of 4	.75	—
	Margin block of 4, Mr. Zip and "Use Zip Code"	.60	—
a.	Vertical pair, imperf. between	*275.00*	—
b.	Red & dark blue omitted	*750.00*	
c.	Red omitted		*1,750.*

Dangerous fakes exist of Nos. 1362b and 1362c. Authentication by experts is required.

Angel Gabriel, from "The Annunciation" by Jan van Eyck — A785

Chief Joseph, by Cyrenius Hall — A786

CHRISTMAS ISSUE

"The Annunciation" by the 15th century Flemish painter Jan van Eyck is in the National Gallery of Art, Washington, D.C.

Designed by Robert J. Jones.

ENGRAVED (Multicolor Huck press)

Panes of 50 (10x5)

1968, Nov. 1 **Tagged** ***Perf. 11***

1363 A785 6c	**multicolored**	.20	.20
	P# block of 10 +	2.00	—
a.	Untagged, *Nov. 2*	.20	.20
	P# block of 10 +	2.00	—
b.	Imperf., pair, tagged	*175.00*	
c.	Light yellow omitted	*50.00*	—
d.	Imperf., pair, untagged	*250.00*	

+ P# blocks come in two versions: (1) 7 P#, 3 ME; (2) 8 P#, 2 ME.

AMERICAN INDIAN ISSUE

Honoring the American Indian and to celebrate the opening of the Natl. Portrait Gallery, Washington, D.C. Chief Joseph (Indian name, Thunder Traveling over the Mountains), a leader of the Nez Percé, was born in eastern Oregon about 1840 and died at the Colesville Reservation in Washington State in 1904.

Designed by Robert J. Jones; lettering by Crimilda Pontes.

LITHOGRAPHED, ENGRAVED (Giori)

Plates of 200 subjects in four panes of 50.

1968, Nov. 4 **Tagged** ***Perf. 11***

1364 A786 6c	**black & multicolored**	.20	.20
	P# block of 4	.75	—
	Margin block of 4, Mr. Zip and "Use Zip Code"	.60	—
a.	Tagging omitted	—	—

BEAUTIFICATION OF AMERICA ISSUE

Publicizing the Natural Beauty Campaign for more beautiful cities, parks, highways and streets. In the left panes Nos. 1365 and 1367 appear in 1st, 3rd and 5th place, Nos. 1366 and 1368 in 2nd and 4th place. This arrangement is reversed in the right panes.

Capitol, Azaleas and Tulips — A787

Washington Monument, Potomac River and Daffodils A788

Poppies and Lupines along Highway A789

Blooming Crabapples Lining Avenue A790

Designed by Walter DuBois Richards.

LITHOGRAPHED, ENGRAVED (Giori)

Plates of 200 subjects in four panes of 50.

1969, Jan. 16 **Tagged** ***Perf. 11***

1365 A787 6c	**multicolored**	.25	.20
1366 A788 6c	**multicolored**	.25	.20
1367 A789 6c	**multicolored**	.25	.20
1368 A790 6c	**multicolored**	.25	.20
a.	Block of 4, #1365-1368	1.00	*1.25*
	P# block of 4	1.25	—
	Margin block of 4, Mr. Zip and "Use Zip Code"	1.10	—
b.	#1365b-1368b, tagging omitted, any single	—	

Eagle from Great Seal — A791

July Fourth, by Grandma Moses — A792

AMERICAN LEGION, 50th ANNIV.

Designed by Robert Hallock.

LITHOGRAPHED, ENGRAVED (Giori)
Plates of 200 subjects in four panes of 50.

1969, Mar. 15 **Tagged** ***Perf. 11***

1369 A791 6c **red, blue & black**	.20	.20
P# block of 4	.45	—
Margin block of 4, Mr. Zip and "Use Zip Code"	.40	—
a. Tagging omitted	—	

AMERICAN FOLKLORE ISSUE

Grandma Moses (Anna Mary Robertson Moses, 1860-1961), primitive painter of American life.

Designed by Robert J. Jones.

LITHOGRAPHED, ENGRAVED (Giori)
Plates of 200 subjects in four panes of 50.

1969, May 1 **Tagged** ***Perf. 11***

1370 A792 6c **multicolored**	.20	.20
P# block of 4	.50	—
Margin block of 4, Mr. Zip and "Use Zip Code"	.45	—
a. Horizontal pair, imperf. between	*175.00*	—
b. Engraved black ("6c U.S. Postage") & Prus. blue ("Grandma Moses") omitted	*700.00*	
c. Tagging omitted	7.50	—

Beware of pairs with blind perfs. being offered as No. 1370a.
No. 1370b often comes with mottled or disturbed gum. Such stamps sell for about two-thirds as much as copies with perfect gum.

APOLLO 8 ISSUE

Apollo 8 mission, which 1st put men into orbit around the moon, Dec. 21-27, 1968. The astronauts were: Col. Frank Borman, Capt. James Lovell and Maj. William Anders.

Moon Surface and Earth — A793

Designed by Leonard E. Buckley after a photograph by the Apollo 8 astronauts.

GIORI PRESS PRINTING
Plates of 200 subjects in four panes of 50.

1969, May 5 **Tagged** ***Perf. 11***

1371 A793 6c **black, blue & ocher**	.20	.20
P# block of 4	1.00	—
Margin block of 4, Mr. Zip and "Use Zip Code"	.60	—

Imperfs. exist from printer's waste.

W.C. HANDY ISSUE

Handy (1873-1958), jazz musician and composer.

William Christopher Handy — A794

Designed by Bernice Kochan.

LITHOGRAPHED, ENGRAVED (Giori)
Plates of 200 subjects in four panes of 50.

1969, May 17 **Tagged** ***Perf. 11***

1372 A794 6c **violet, deep lilac & blue**	.20	.20
P# block of 4	.65	—
Margin block of 4, Mr. Zip and "Use Zip Code"	.45	—
a. Tagging omitted	9.00	—

CALIFORNIA SETTLEMENT, 200th ANNIV.

Carmel Mission Belfry — A795

Designed by Leonard Buckley and Howard C. Mildner.

LITHOGRAPHED, ENGRAVED (Giori)
Plates of 200 subjects in four panes of 50.

1969, July 16 **Tagged** ***Perf. 11***

1373 A795 6c **orange, red, black & light blue**	.20	.20
P# block of 4	.60	—
Margin block of 4, Mr. Zip and "Use Zip Code"	.45	—
a. Tagging omitted	10.00	—
b. Red (engr.) missing (CM)	—	

JOHN WESLEY POWELL ISSUE

Powell (1834-1902), geologist who explored the Green and Colorado Rivers 1869-75, and ethnologist.

Major Powell Exploring Colorado River, 1869 — A796

Designed by Rudolph Wendelin.

LITHOGRAPHED, ENGRAVED (Giori)
Plates of 200 subjects in four panes of 50.

1969, Aug. 1 **Tagged** ***Perf. 11***

1374 A796 6c **black, ocher & light blue**	.20	.20
P# block of 4	.60	—
Margin block of 4, Mr. Zip and "Use Zip Code"	.45	—
a. Tagging omitted	10.00	—

ALABAMA STATEHOOD, 150th ANNIV.

Camellia and Yellow-shafted Flicker — A797

Designed by Bernice Kochan

LITHOGRAPHED, ENGRAVED (Giori)
Plates of 200 subjects in four panes of 50.

1969, Aug. 2 **Tagged** ***Perf. 11***

1375 A797 6c **magenta, rose red, yellow, dark green & brown**	.20	.20
P# block of 4	.75	—
Margin block of 4, Mr. Zip and "Use Zip Code"	.45	—
a. Tagging omitted	*140.00*	—

BOTANICAL CONGRESS ISSUE

11th Intl. Botanical Cong., Seattle, Wash., Aug. 24-Sept. 2. In left panes Nos. 1376 and 1378 appear in 1st, 3rd and 5th place; Nos. 1377 and 1379 in 2nd and 4th place. This arrangement is reversed in right panes.

Douglas Fir (Northwest) A798

Lady's-slipper (Northeast) A799

Ocotillo (Southwest) A800

Franklinia (Southeast) A801

Designed by Stanley Galli.

LITHOGRAPHED, ENGRAVED (Giori)
Plates of 200 subjects in four panes of 50.

1969, Aug. 23 **Tagged** ***Perf. 11***

1376 A798 6c **multicolored**	.35	.20
1377 A799 6c **multicolored**	.35	.20
1378 A800 6c **multicolored**	.35	.20
1379 A801 6c **multicolored**	.35	.20
a. Block of 4, #1376-1379	1.50	*1.75*
P# block of 4	1.75	—
Margin block of 4, Mr. Zip and "Use Zip Code"	1.60	—

DARTMOUTH COLLEGE CASE ISSUE

150th anniv. of the Dartmouth College Case, which Daniel Webster argued before the Supreme Court, reasserting the sanctity of contracts.

Daniel Webster and Dartmouth Hall — A802

Designed by John R. Scotford, Jr.

ROTARY PRESS PRINTING
E.E. Plates of 200 subjects in four panes of 50.

1969, Sept. 22 **Tagged** ***Perf. 10½x11***

1380 A802 6c **green**	.20	.20
P# block of 4	.50	—
Margin block of 4, Mr. Zip and "Use Zip Code"	.45	—

PROFESSIONAL BASEBALL, 100th ANNIV.

Batter — A803

Designed by Alex Ross.

LITHOGRAPHED, ENGRAVED (Giori)
Plates of 200 subjects in four panes of 50.

1969, Sept. 24	**Tagged**	***Perf. 11***	
1381 A803 6c **yellow, red, black & green**		.55	.20
P# block of 4		2.50	—
Margin block of 4, Mr. Zip and "Use Zip Code"		2.25	—
a. Black omitted ("1869-1969, United States, 6c, Professional Baseball")		*800.00*	
b. Tagging omitted		—	

INTERCOLLEGIATE FOOTBALL, 100th ANNIV.

Football Player and Coach — A804

Designed by Robert Peak.

LITHOGRAPHED, ENGRAVED (Giori)
Plates of 200 subjects in four panes of 50.

1969, Sept. 26	**Tagged**	***Perf. 11***	
1382 A804 6c **red & green**		.20	.20
P# block of 4		1.00	—
Margin block of 4, Mr. Zip and "Use Zip Code"		.60	—
a. Tagging omitted			—
b. Vert. pair, imperf between		—	

The engraved parts were printed on a rotary currency press.

DWIGHT D. EISENHOWER ISSUE

Dwight D. Eisenhower, 34th President (1890-1969) — A805

Designed by Robert J. Jones; photograph by Bernie Noble.

GIORI PRESS PRINTING
Plates of 128 subjects in 4 panes of 32 each.

1969, Oct. 14	**Tagged**	***Perf. 11***	
1383 A805 6c **blue, black & red**		.20	.20
P# block of 4		.55	—
Margin block of 4, Mr. Zip and "Use Zip Code"		.45	—
a. Tagging omitted			—
b. Blue ("U.S. 6c Postage") missing (PS)		—	

CHRISTMAS ISSUE

The painting, painted about 1870 by an unknown primitive artist, is the property of the N.Y. State Historical Association, Cooperstown, N.Y.

Winter Sunday in Norway, Maine A806

Designed by Stevan Dohanos.

ENGRAVED (Multicolor Huck)
Panes of 50 (5x10)

1969, Nov. 3	**Tagged**	***Perf. 11x10½***	
1384 A806 6c **dark green & multicolored**		.20	.20
P# block of 10, 5#, 2-3 zip, 2-3 Mail Early		1.40	—
Precancel		.50	.20
b. Imperf., pair		*800.00*	
c. Light green omitted		30.00	
d. Light green, red & yellow omitted		*700.00*	—
e. Yellow omitted		*2,000.*	
f. Tagging omitted		*5.00*	—
g. Red & yellow omitted		*2,750.*	
h. Light green and yellow omitted		—	
i. Light green and red omitted		—	

The precancel value applies to the least expensive of experimental precancels printed locally in four cities, on tagged stamps, with the names between lines 4½mm apart: in black or green, "ATLANTA, GA" and in green only "BALTIMORE, MD," "MEMPHIS, TN" and "NEW HAVEN, CT." They were sold freely to the public and could be used on any class of mail at all post offices during the experimental program and thereafter. The Baltimore precancel is known with tagging omitted; value, unused $50.

Most copies of No. 1384c show orange where the offset green was. Value is for this variety. Copies without orange sell for more.

On No. 1384i, almost all of the yellow is also omitted. Do not confuse with No. 1384d.

Cured Child — A807

HOPE FOR CRIPPLED ISSUE

Issued to encourage the rehabilitation of crippled children and adults and to honor the National Society for Crippled Children and Adults (Easter Seal Society) on its 50th anniversary.

Designed by Mark English.

LITHOGRAPHED, ENGRAVED (Giori)
Plates of 200 subjects in four panes of 50.

1969, Nov. 20	**Tagged**	***Perf. 11***	
1385 A807 6c **multicolored**		.20	.20
P# block of 4		.50	—
Margin block of 4, Mr. Zip and "Use Zip Code"		.45	—
a. Tagging omitted		—	

WILLIAM M. HARNETT ISSUE

"Old Models" — A808

Harnett (1848-1892), painter. The painting hangs in the Museum of Fine Arts, Boston.

Designed by Robert J. Jones.

LITHOGRAPHED, ENGRAVED (Giori)
Plates of 128 subjects in 4 panes of 32 each.

1969, Dec. 3	**Tagged**	***Perf. 11***	
1386 A808 6c **multicolored**		.20	.20
P# block of 4		.55	—
Margin block of 4, Mr. Zip and "Use Zip Code"		.45	—

NATURAL HISTORY ISSUE

Centenary of the American Museum of Natural History, New York City. Nos. 1387-1388 alternate in 1st row, Nos. 1389-1390 in 2nd row. This arrangement is repeated throughout the pane.

American Bald Eagle — A809

African Elephant Herd — A810

Tlingit Chief in Haida Ceremonial Canoe — A811

Brontosaurus, Stegosaurus and Allosaurus from Jurassic Period — A812

Designers: No. 1387, Walter Richards; No. 1388, Dean Ellis; No. 1389, Paul Rabut; No. 1390, detail from mural by Rudolph Zallinger in Yal Peabody Museum, adapted by Robert J. Jones.

LITHOGRAPHED, ENGRAVED (Giori)
Plates of 128 subjects in 4 panes of 32 each (4x8).

1970, May 6	**Tagged**	***Perf. 11***	
1387 A809 6c **multicolored**		.20	.20
1388 A810 6c **multicolored**		.20	.20
1389 A811 6c **multicolored**		.20	.20
1390 A812 6c **multicolored**		.20	.20
a. Block of 4, #1387-1390		.55	*.60*
P# block of 4		.70	—
Margin block of 4, Mr. Zip and "Use Zip Code"		.60	—
b. As "a," tagging omitted			—

MAINE STATEHOOD, 150th ANNIV.

The painting hangs in the Metropolitan Museum of Art, New York City.

The Lighthouse at Two Lights, Maine, by Edward Hopper A813

Designed by Stevan Dohanos.

LITHOGRAPHED, ENGRAVED (Giori)
Plates of 200 subjects in four panes of 50.

1970, July 9 Tagged *Perf. 11*

1391 A813 6c **black & multicolored** .20 .20
P# block of 4 .60 —
Margin block of 4, Mr. Zip and "Use Zip Code" .45 —
a. Tagging omitted — —

WILDLIFE CONSERVATION ISSUE

American Buffalo — A814

Designed by Robert Lougheed.

ROTARY PRESS PRINTING
E.E. Plates of 200 subjects in four panes of 50.

1970, July 20 Tagged *Perf. 11x10½*

1392 A814 6c **black,** *light brown* .20 .20
P# block of 4 .75 —
Margin block of 4, Mr. Zip and "Use Zip Code" .45 —

REGULAR ISSUE
Dwight David Eisenhower

Dot between "R" and "U" — A815

No Dot between "R" and "U" — A815a

Benjamin Franklin — A816

U.S. Postal Service Emblem — A817

Fiorello H. LaGuardia A817a

Ernest Taylor Pyle — A818

Dr. Elizabeth Blackwell — A818a

Amadeo P. Giannini A818b

Designers: Nos. 1393-1395, 1401-1402, Robert Geissman; photograph by George Tames. 7c, Bill Hyde. No. 1396, Raymond Loewy/William Smith, Inc. 14c, Robert Geissman; photograph by George Fayer. 16c, Robert Geissman; photograph by Alfred Eisenstadt. 18c, Robert Geissman; painting by Joseph Kozlowski. 21c, Robert Geissman.

ROTARY PRESS PRINTING
E.E. Plates of 400 subjects in four panes of 100.

1970-74 Tagged *Perf. 11x10½*

1393 A815 6c **dark blue gray,** shiny gum, *Aug. 6, 1970* .20 .20
P# block of 4 .50 —
Margin block of 4, "Use Zip Codes" .45 —
Dull gum .20
P# block of 4 1.00
Zip block of 4 .55
a. Booklet pane of 8, shiny gum 1.50 .75
Dull gum 1.90
b. Booklet pane of 5 + label 1.50 .75
c. Untagged (Bureau precanceled) 12.75 3.00
P# block of 4 *175.00*
Margin block of 4, "Use Zip Codes" 75.00
g. Tagging omitted (not Bureau precanceled) *150.00* —
h. As "a," tagging omitted, shiny gum *250.00* —
Dull gum —

Perf. 10½x11

1393D A816 7c **bright blue,** shiny gum, *Oct. 20, 1972* .20 .20
P# block of 4 .60 —
Margin block of 4, "Use Zip Codes" .55 —
Dull gum .20
P# block of 4 1.25
Zip block of 4 .90
e. Untagged (Bureau precanceled) 4.25 1.00
P# block of 4 52.50
Margin block of 4, "Use Zip Codes" 22.50
f. Tagging omitted (not Bureau precanceled) 4.00 —

GIORI PRESS PRINTING
Plates of 400 subjects in four panes of 100.
Perf. 11

1394 A815a 8c **black, red & blue gray,** *May 10, 1971* .20 .20
P# block of 4 .60 —
Margin block of 4, "Use Zip Codes" .55 —
Pair with full vert. gutter btwn. —
a. Tagging omitted 4.50 —
b. Red missing (PS) *175.00*
c. Red and blue missing (PS) —

ROTARY PRESS PRINTING
Perf. 11x10½ on 2 or 3 sides

1395 A815 8c **deep claret,** shiny gum (from blkt. pane) .20 .20
Dull gum .20
a. Booklet pane of 8, shiny gum, *May 10, 1971* 1.80 1.25
b. Booklet pane of 6, shiny gum, *May 10, 1971* 1.25 1.10
c. Booklet pane of 4 + 2 labels, dull gum, *Jan. 28, 1972* 1.65 1.00
d. Booklet pane of 7 + label, dull gum, *Jan. 28, 1972* 1.90 1.10
e. Vert. pair, imperf between *800.00*
f. As "a," tagging omitted — —
g. As "b," tagging omitted *40.00* —
h. As "c," tagging omitted *40.00* —
i. As "d," tagging omitted —

No. 1395 was issued only in booklets.

1395e resulted from a paper foldover after perforating and before cutting into panes. At least 4 pairs are recorded from 3 panes (one No. 1395a and two 1395d) with different foldover patterns. A pane of No. 1395d also is known with a foldover resulting in a vertical pair of stamp and label, imperf between.

PHOTOGRAVURE (Andreotti)
Plates of 400 subjects in four panes of 100.
Perf. 11x10½

1396 A817 8c **multicolored,** *July 1, 1971* .20 .20
P# block of 12, 6# 2.00
P# block of 20, 6#, "Mail Early in the Day," "Use Zip Codes" and rectangular color contents (UL pane) 3.25
Margin block of 4, "Use Zip Codes" .65 —

ROTARY PRESS PRINTING
E.E. Plates of 400 subjects in four panes of 100.

1397 A817a 14c **gray brown,** *Apr. 24, 1972* .25 .20
P# block of 4 1.15 —
Margin block of 4, "Use Zip Codes" —
a. Untagged (Bureau precanceled) *140.00* 17.50
P# block of 4 —
Margin block of 4, "Use Zip Codes" —

1398 A818 16c **brown,** *May 7, 1971* .35 .20
P# block of 4 2.50 —
Margin block of 4, "Use Zip Codes" 1.50 —
a. Untagged (Bureau precanceled) 22.50 5.00
P# block of 4 —
Margin block of 4, "Use Zip Codes" 175.00
b. Tagging omitted (not Bureau precanceled) — —

1399 A818a 18c **violet,** *Jan. 23, 1974* .35 .20
P# block of 4 1.50 —
Margin block of 4, "Use Zip Codes" 1.40 —

1400 A818b 21c **green,** *June 27, 1973* .40 .20
P# block of 4 1.65 —
Margin block of 4, "Use Zip Codes" 1.60 —
Nos. 1393-1400 (9) 2.35 1.80

Bureau Precancels: 6c, 6 diff., 7c, 13 diff., No. 1394, 24 diff., 14c, 3 diff., 16c, NYC, 3 diff. Greensboro, NC.

COIL STAMPS
ROTARY PRESS PRINTING

1970-71 Tagged *Perf. 10 Vert.*

1401 A815 6c **dark blue gray,** shiny gum, *Aug. 6, 1970* .20 .20
Pair .30 .20
Joint line pair .50 .20
Dull gum .85
Joint line pair 7.00
a. Untagged (Bureau precanceled) 19.50 3.00
Pair 42.50 6.50
Joint line pair *525.00* —
b. Imperf., pair *1,900.*
Joint line pair —

1402 A815 8c **deep claret,** *May 10, 1971* .20 .20
Pair .30 .20
Joint line pair .60 .20
a. Imperf., pair 37.50
Joint line pair 65.00
b. Untagged (Bureau precanceled) 6.75 .75
Pair 15.00 1.60
Joint line pair *185.00* —
c. Pair, imperf. between *6,250.*

Bureau Precancels: 6c, 4 diff., 8c, 34 diff.

EDGAR LEE MASTERS ISSUE

Edgar Lee Masters (1869-1950), Poet — A819

Designed by Fred Otnes.

LITHOGRAPHED, ENGRAVED (Giori)
E.E. Plates of 200 subjects in four panes of 50.

1970, Aug. 22 Tagged *Perf. 11*

1405 A819 6c **black & olive bister** .20 .20
P# block of 4 .50 —
Margin block of 4, Mr. Zip and "Use Zip Code" .45 —
a. Tagging omitted 125.00 —

WOMAN SUFFRAGE ISSUE

50th anniversary of the 19th Amendment, which gave the vote to women.

Suffragettes, 1920, and Woman Voter, 1970 — A820

Designed by Ward Brackett.

GIORI PRESS PRINTING
Plates of 200 subjects in four panes of 50.

1970, Aug. 26 Tagged *Perf. 11*

1406 A820 6c **blue** .20 .20
P# block of 4 .50 —
Margin block of 4, Mr. Zip and "Use Zip Code" .45 —

SOUTH CAROLINA ISSUE

300th anniv. of the founding of Charles Town (Charleston), the 1st permanent settlement of South Carolina. Against a background of pine wood the line drawings of the design represent the economic and historic development of South Carolina: the spire of St. Phillip's Church, Capitol, state flag, a ship, 17th century man and woman, a Fort Sumter cannon, barrels, cotton, tobacco and yellow jasmine.

Symbols of South Carolina
A821

Designed by George Samerjan.

LITHOGRAPHED, ENGRAVED (Giori)

Plates of 200 subjects in four panes of 50.

1970, Sept. 12	Tagged	Perf. 11	
1407 A821 6c **bister, black & red**		.20	.20
P# block of 4		.55	—
Margin block of 4, Mr. Zip and "Use Zip Code"		.45	—

STONE MOUNTAIN MEMORIAL ISSUE

Dedication of the Stone Mountain Confederate Memorial, Georgia, May 9, 1970.

Robert E. Lee, Jefferson Davis and "Stonewall" Jackson
A822

Designed by Robert Hallock.

GIORI PRESS PRINTING

Plates of 200 subjects in four panes of 50.

1970, Sept. 19	Tagged	Perf. 11	
1408 A822 6c **gray**		.20	.20
P# block of 4		.50	—
Margin block of 4, Mr. Zip and "Use Zip Code"		.45	—

FORT SNELLING ISSUE

150th anniv. of Fort Snelling, Minnesota, an important outpost for the opening of the Northwest.

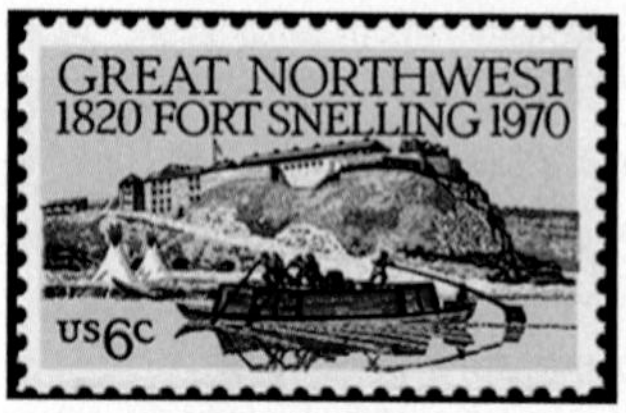

Fort Snelling, Keelboat and Tepees
A823

Designed by David K. Stone.

LITHOGRAPHED, ENGRAVED (Giori)

Plates of 200 in four panes of 50.

1970, Oct. 17	Tagged	Perf. 11	
1409 A823 6c **yellow & multicolored**		.20	.20
P# block of 4		.55	—
Margin block of 4, Mr. Zip and "Use Zip Code"		.45	—
a. Tagging omitted			—

ANTI-POLLUTION ISSUE

Issued to focus attention on the problems of pollution.

In left panes Nos. 1410 and 1412 appear in 1st, 3rd and 5th place; Nos. 1411 and 1413 in 2nd and 4th place. This arrangement is reversed in right panes.

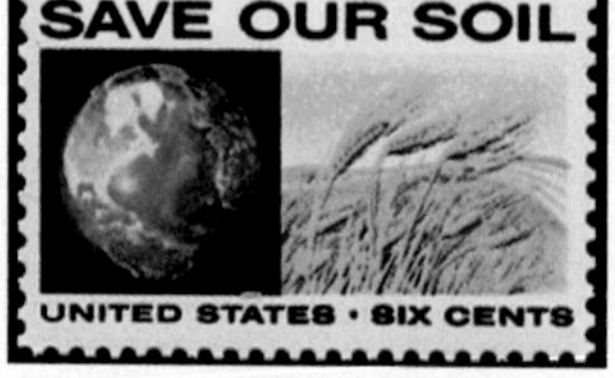

Globe and Wheat — A824

Globe and City — A825

Globe and Bluegill
A826

Globe and Seagull
A827

Designed by Arnold Copeland and Walter DuBois Richards.

Printed by Bureau of Engraving and Printing at Guilford Gravure, Inc., Guilford, Conn.

PHOTOGRAVURE

Plates of 200 subjects in four panes of 50.

1970, Oct. 28	Tagged	Perf. 11x10½	
1410 A824 6c **multicolored**		.25	.20
1411 A825 6c **multicolored**		.25	.20
1412 A826 6c **multicolored**		.25	.20
1413 A827 6c **multicolored**		.25	.20
a. Block of 4, #1410-1413		1.10	*1.25*
P# block of 10, 5#		2.25	—
Margin block of 4, Mr. Zip and "Use Zip Code"		1.25	—

CHRISTMAS ISSUE

In left panes Nos. 1415 and 1417 appear in 1st, 3rd and 5th place; Nos. 1416 and 1418 in 2nd and 4th place. This arrangement is reversed in right panes.

Nativity, by Lorenzo Lotto — A828

Tin and Cast-iron Locomotive
A829

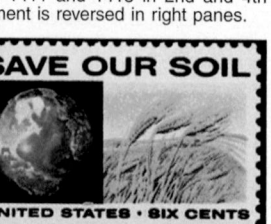

Toy Horse on Wheels
A830

Mechanical Tricycle
A831

Doll Carriage
A832

Designers: No. 1414, Howard C. Mildner, from a painting by Lorenzo Lotto (1480-1556) in the National Gallery of Art, Washington, D.C. Nos. 1415-1418, Stevan Dohanos, from a drawing (locomotive) by Charles Hemming and from "Golden Age of Toys" by Fondin and Remise.

Printed by Guilford Gravure, Inc., Guilford, Conn.

PHOTOGRAVURE

Plates of 200 subjects in four panes of 50.

1970, Nov. 5	Tagged	Perf. 10½x11	
1414 A828 6c **multicolored**		.20	.20
P# block of 8, 4#		1.10	—
Margin block of 4, Mr. Zip and "Use Zip Code"		.50	—
a. Precanceled		.20	.20
P# block of 8, 4#		1.90	—
Margin block of 4, Mr. Zip and "Use Zip Code"		.70	—
b. Black omitted		*450.00*	
c. As "a," blue omitted		*1,450.*	
d. Type II		.20	.20
P# block of 8, 4#		2.75	—
Zip block of 4		.85	—
e. Type II, precanceled		.25	.20
P# block of 8, 4#		4.00	—
Zip block of 4		1.25	—

No. 1414 has pregummed paper, a slightly blurry impression, snowflaking in the sky and no gum breaker ridges. No. 1414d has shiny surfaced paper, sharper impression, no snowflaking and vertical and horizontal gum breaker ridges.

No. 1414a has a slightly blurry impression, snowflaking in the sky, no gum breaker ridges and the precancel is grayish black. No. 1414e has sharper impression, no snowflaking, gum breaker ridges and the precancel is intense black.

Perf. 11x10½

1415 A829 6c **multicolored**		.30	.20
a. Precanceled		.75	.20
b. Black omitted		*2,500.*	
c. Tagging omitted			—
1416 A830 6c **multicolored**		.30	.20
a. Precanceled		.75	.20
b. Black omitted		*2,500.*	
c. Imperf., pair (#1416, 1418)			*2,500.*
1417 A831 6c **multicolored**		.30	.20
a. Precanceled		.75	.20
b. Black omitted		*2,500.*	
c. Tagging omitted			—
1418 A832 6c **multicolored**		.30	.20
a. Precanceled		.75	.20
b. Block of 4, #1415-1418		1.25	*1.40*
P# block of 8, 4#		3.00	—
Margin block of 4, Mr. Zip and "Use Zip Code"		1.25	—
c. As "b," precanceled		3.25	*3.50*
P# block of 8, 4P#		6.25	—
Margin block of 4, Mr. Zip and "Use Zip Code"		3.50	—
d. Black omitted		*2,500.*	
e. As "b," black omitted		*10,000.*	
f. As "b," black omitted on #1417 & 1418		*5,000.*	
g. P# block of 8, black omitted on #1415 & 1416		*5,000.*	

Nos. 1415-1418 and 1415a-1418a are known both without gum breaker ridges (common) and with gum breaker ridges (scarce).

The precanceled stamps, Nos. 1414a-1418a, were furnished to 68 cities. The plates include two straight (No. 1414a) or two wavy (Nos. 1415a-1418a) black lines that make up the precancellation. Unused values are for stamps with gum and used values are for stamps with an additional cancellation or without gum.

UNITED NATIONS, 25th ANNIV.

"UN" and UN Emblem
A833

Designed by Arnold Copeland.

LITHOGRAPHED, ENGRAVED (Giori)
Plates of 200 subjects in four panes of 50.

1970, Nov. 20 Tagged *Perf. 11*

1419 A833 6c	**black, verm. & ultra.**	.20	.20
	P# block of 4	.50	—
	Margin block of 4, Mr. Zip and "Use Zip Code"	.45	—
	Pair with full horiz. gutter btwn.	—	
a.	Tagging omitted	*85.00*	—

LANDING OF THE PILGRIMS ISSUE

350th anniv. of the landing of the Mayflower.

Mayflower and Pilgrims — A834

Designed by Mark English.

LITHOGRAPHED, ENGRAVED (Giori)
Plates of 200 subjects in four panes of 50.

1970, Nov. 21 Tagged *Perf. 11*

1420 A834 6c	**blk., org., yel., magenta, bl. & brn.**	.20	.20
	P# block of 4	.50	—
	Margin block of 4, Mr. Zip and "Use Zip Code"	.45	—
a.	Orange & yellow omitted	*700.00*	
b.	Tagging omitted		—

DISABLED AMERICAN VETERANS AND SERVICEMEN ISSUE

No. 1421 for the 50th anniv. of the Disabled Veterans of America Organization; No. 1422 honors the contribution of servicemen, particularly those who were prisoners of war, missing or killed in action. Nos. 1421-1422 are printed se-tenant in horizontal rows of 10.

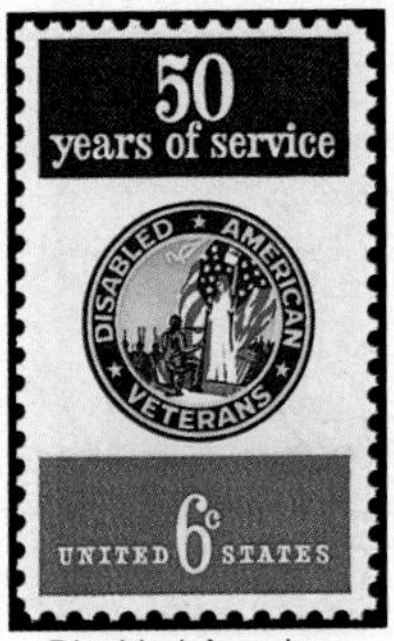

Disabled American Veterans Emblem — A835

A836

Designed by Stevan Dohanos.

LITHOGRAPHED, ENGRAVED (Giori)
Plates of 200 subjects in four panes of 50.

1970, Nov. 24 Tagged *Perf. 11*

1421 A835 6c	**dark blue, red & multicolored**	.20	.20

ENGRAVED

1422 A836 6c	**dark blue, black & red**	.20	.20
a.	Pair, #1421-1422	.30	.30
	P# block of 4	1.00	—
	Margin block of 4, Mr. Zip and "Use Zip Code"	.65	—
b.	As "a," tagging omitted	75.00	—

Ewe and Lamb — A837

Gen. Douglas MacArthur — A838

AMERICAN WOOL INDUSTRY ISSUE

450th anniv. of the introduction of sheep to the North American continent and the beginning of the American wool industry.

Designed by Dean Ellis.

LITHOGRAPHED, ENGRAVED (Giori)
Plates of 200 subjects in four panes of 50.

1971, Jan. 19 Tagged *Perf. 11*

1423 A837 6c	**multicolored**	.20	.20
	P# block of 4	.55	—
	Margin block of 4, Mr. Zip and "Use Zip Code"	.45	—
a.	Tagging omitted	11.00	—
b.	Teal blue ("United States") missing (CM)	*575.00*	

GEN. DOUGLAS MacARTHUR ISSUE

MacArthur (1880-1964), Chief of Staff, Supreme Commander for the Allied Powers in the Pacific Area during World War II and Supreme Commander in Japan after the war.

Designed by Paul Calle; Wide World photograph.

GIORI PRESS PRINTING
Plates of 200 subjects in four panes of 50.

1971, Jan. 26 Tagged *Perf. 11*

1424 A838 6c	**black, red & dark blue**	.20	.20
	P# block of 4	.60	—
	Margin block of 4, Mr. Zip and "Use Zip Code"	.45	—
a.	Red missing (PS)	—	
b.	Tagging omitted	125.00	—
c.	Blue missing (PS)	—	

BLOOD DONOR ISSUE

Salute to blood donors and spur to increased participation in the blood donor program.

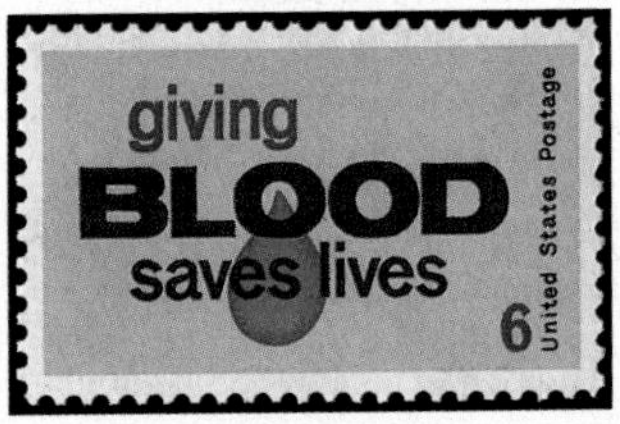

"Giving Blood Saves Lives" — A839

Designed by Howard Munce.

LITHOGRAPHED, ENGRAVED (Giori)
Plates of 200 subjects in four panes of 50.

1971, Mar. 12 Tagged *Perf. 11*

1425 A839 6c	**blue, scarlet & indigo**	.20	.20
	P# block of 4	.50	—
	Margin block of 4, Mr. Zip and "Use Zip Code"	.45	—
a.	Tagging omitted	10.00	—

MISSOURI STATEHOOD, 150th ANNIV.

The stamp design shows a Pawnee facing a hunter-trapper and a group of settlers. It is from a mural by Thomas Hart Benton in the Harry S Truman Library, Independence, Mo.

"Independence and the Opening of the West," Detail, by Thomas Hart Benton A840

Designed by Bradbury Thompson.

PHOTOGRAVURE (Andreotti)
Plates of 200 subjects in four panes of 50.

1971, May 8 Tagged *Perf. 11x10½*

1426 A840 8c	**multicolored**	.20	.20
	P# block of 12, 6#	3.00	—
	Margin block of 4, Mr. Zip and "Use Zip Code"	.65	—
a.	Tagging omitted		—

See note on Andreotti printings and their color control markings in Information for Collectors under Printing, Photogravure.

WILDLIFE CONSERVATION ISSUE

Nos. 1427-1428 alternate in first row, Nos. 1429-1430 in second row. This arrangement repeated throughout pane.

Trout A841

Alligator — A842

Polar Bear and Cubs A843

California Condor — A844

Designed by Stanley W. Galli.

LITHOGRAPHED, ENGRAVED (Giori)
Plates of 128 subjects in 4 panes of 32 each (4x8).

1971, June 12 Tagged *Perf. 11*

1427 A841 8c	**multicolored**	.20	.20
a.	Red omitted		*1,250.*
b.	Green (engr.) omitted		—
1428 A842 8c	**multicolored**	.20	.20
1429 A843 8c	**multicolored**	.20	.20
1430 A844 8c	**multicolored**	.20	.20
a.	Block of 4, #1427-1430	.80	*.90*
	P# block of 4	.90	—
	Margin block of 4, Mr. Zip and "Use Zip Code"	.85	—
b.	As "a," light green & dark green omitted from #1427-1428	*4,500.*	
c.	As "a," red omitted from #1427, 1429-1430	*7,000.*	
d.	As "a," tagging omitted	—	

ANTARCTIC TREATY ISSUE

Map of Antarctica A845

Designed by Howard Koslow.

Adapted from emblem on official documents of Consultative Meetings.

GIORI PRESS PRINTING

Plates of 200 subjects in four panes of 50.

1971, June 23 **Tagged** ***Perf. 11***

1431 A845 8c **red & dark blue** .20 .20
P# block of 4 .65 —
Margin block of 4, Mr. Zip and "Use Zip Code" .60 —
a. Tagging omitted *10.00*
b. Both colors missing (EP) *500.00*

No. 1431b should be collected se-tenant with a normal stamp and/or a partially printed stamp.

AMERICAN REVOLUTION BICENTENNIAL

Bicentennial Commission Emblem — A846

Designed by Chermayeff & Geismar.

LITHOGRAPHED, ENGRAVED (Giori)

Plates of 200 subjects in four panes of 50.

1971, July 4 **Tagged** ***Perf. 11***

1432 A846 8c **gray, red, blue & black** .20 .20
P# block of 4 .85 —
Margin block of 4, Mr. Zip and "Use Zip Code" .80 —
a. Gray & black missing (EP) *550.00*
b. Gray ("U.S. Postage 8c") missing (EP) *950.00*
c. Tagging omitted 125.00

JOHN SLOAN ISSUE

John Sloan (1871-1951), painter. The painting hangs in the Phillips Gallery, Washington, D.C.

The Wake of the Ferry — A847

Designed by Bradbury Thompson.

LITHOGRAPHED, ENGRAVED (Giori)

Plates of 200 subjects in four panes of 50.

1971, Aug. 2 **Tagged** ***Perf. 11***

1433 A847 8c **multicolored** .20 .20
P# block of 4 .70 —
Margin block of 4, Mr. Zip and "Use Zip Code" .65 —
a. Tagging omitted —
b. Red engr. ("John Sloan" and "8") missing (CM) *950.00*

SPACE ACHIEVEMENT DECADE ISSUE

Decade of space achievements and the Apollo 15 moon exploration mission, July 26-Aug. 7. In the left panes the earth and sun stamp is 1st, 3rd and 5th, the rover 2nd and 4th. This arrangement is reversed in the right panes.

Earth, Sun and Landing Craft on Moon — A848

Lunar Rover and Astronauts A849

Designed by Robert McCall.

LITHOGRAPHED, ENGRAVED (Giori)

Plates of 200 subjects in four panes of 50.

1971, Aug. 2 **Tagged** ***Perf. 11***

1434 A848 8c **black, blue, gray, yellow & red** .20 .20
a. Tagging omitted *45.00*
1435 A849 8c **black, blue, gray, yellow & red** .20 .20
a. Tagging omitted *45.00*
b. Pair, #1434-1435 .40 .45
P# block of 4 .65 —
Margin block of 4, Mr. Zip and "Use Zip Code" .60 —
c. As "b," tagging omitted *125.00*
d. As "b," blue & red (litho.) omitted *1,250.*

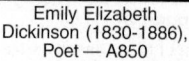

Emily Elizabeth Dickinson (1830-1886), Poet — A850

Sentry Box, Morro Castle, San Juan — A851

EMILY DICKINSON ISSUE

Designed by Bernard Fuchs after a photograph.

LITHOGRAPHED, ENGRAVED (Giori)

Plates of 200 subjects in four panes of 50.

1971, Aug. 28 **Tagged** ***Perf. 11***

1436 A850 8c **multicolored,** *greenish* .20 .20
P# block of 4 .65 —
Margin block of 4, Mr. Zip and "Use Zip Code" .60 —
a. Black & olive (engr.) omitted *600.00*
b. Pale rose missing (EP) *6,250.*
c. Red omitted —
d. Tagging omitted 150.00 —

SAN JUAN ISSUE

450th anniversary of San Juan, Puerto Rico.

Designed as a woodcut by Walter Brooks.

LITHOGRAPHED, ENGRAVED (Giori)

Plates of 200 subjects in four panes of 50.

1971, Sept. 12 **Tagged** ***Perf. 11***

1437 A851 8c **pale brown, black, yellow & dark brown** .20 .20
P# block of 4 .65 —
Margin block of 4, Mr. Zip and "Use Zip Code" .60 —
a. Tagging omitted *9.00*

VALUES FOR HINGED STAMPS AFTER NO. 771
This catalogue does not value unused stamps after No. 771 in hinged condition. Hinged unused stamps from No. 772 to the present are worth considerably less than the values given for unused stamps, which are for never-hinged examples.

Young Woman Drug Addict — A852

Hands Reaching for CARE — A853

PREVENT DRUG ABUSE ISSUE

Drug Abuse Prevention Week, Oct. 3-9.

Designed by Miggs Burroughs.

PHOTOGRAVURE (Andreotti)

Plates of 200 subjects in four panes of 50.

1971, Oct. 4 **Tagged** ***Perf. 10½x11***

1438 A852 8c **blue, deep blue & black** .20 .20
P# block of 6, 3# 1.00 —
Margin block of 4, "Use Zip Code" .65 —

CARE ISSUE

25th anniversary of CARE, a US-Canadian Cooperative for American Relief Everywhere.

Designed by Soren Noring

PHOTOGRAVURE (Andreotti)

Plates of 200 subjects in four panes of 50.

1971, Oct. 27 **Tagged** ***Perf. 10½x11***

1439 A853 8c **blue, blk., vio. & red lilac** .20 .20
P# block of 8, 4# 1.25 —
Margin block of 4, Mr. Zip and "Use Zip Code" .65 —
a. Black omitted *2,500.*
b. Tagging omitted 5.00

HISTORIC PRESERVATION ISSUE

Nos. 1440-1441 alternate in 1st row, Nos. 1442-1443 in 2nd row. This arrangement is repeated throughout the pane.

Decatur House, Washington, D.C. — A854

Whaling Ship Charles W. Morgan, Mystic, Conn. — A855

Cable Car, San Francisco — A856

San Xavier del Bac Mission, Tucson, Ariz. — A857

Designed by Melbourne Brindle.

LITHOGRAPHED, ENGRAVED (Giori)

1971, Oct. 29 **Tagged** ***Perf. 11***

1440 A854 8c **black brown & ocher,** *buff* .20 .20
1441 A855 8c **black brown & ocher,** *buff* .20 .20
1442 A856 8c **black brown & ocher,** *buff* .20 .20
1443 A857 8c **black brown & ocher,** *buff* .20 .20
a. Block of 4, #1440-1443 .75 *.85*
P# block of 4 .90 —
Margin block of 4, Mr. Zip and "Use Zip Code" .80 —
b. As "a," black brown omitted *1,650.*
c. As "a," ocher omitted —
d. As "a," tagging omitted *75.00*

CHRISTMAS ISSUE

Adoration of the Shepherds, by Giorgione — A858

"Partridge in a Pear Tree" — A859

Designers: No. 1444, Bradbury Thompson, using a painting by Giorgione in the National Gallery of Art, Washington, D.C. No. 1445, Jamie Wyeth.

PHOTOGRAVURE (Andreotti)

Plates of 200 subjects in four panes of 50.

1971, Nov. 10 **Tagged** ***Perf. 10½x11***

1444 A858 8c **gold & multicolored** .20 .20
P# block of 12, 6# 1.80 —
Margin block of 4, Mr. Zip and "Use Zip Code" .60 —
a. Gold omitted *400.00*
b. Tagging omitted —
1445 A859 8c **dark green, red & multicolored** .20 .20
P# block of 12, 6# 1.80
Margin block of 4, Mr. Zip and "Use Zip Code" .60 —

Sidney Lanier — A860

Peace Corps Poster, by David Battle — A861

SIDNEY LANIER ISSUE

Lanier (1842-81), poet, musician, lawyer, educator.

Designed by William A. Smith.

GIORI PRESS PRINTING

Plates of 200 subjects in four panes of 50.

1972, Feb. 3 **Tagged** ***Perf. 11***

1446 A860 8c **black, brown & light blue** .20 .20
P# block of 4 .65 —
Margin block of 4, Mr. Zip and "Use Zip Code" .60 —
a. Tagging omitted 55.00

PEACE CORPS ISSUE

Designed by Bradbury Thompson.

PHOTOGRAVURE (Andreotti)

Plates of 200 subjects in four panes of 50.

1972, Feb. 11 **Tagged** ***Perf. 10½x11***

1447 A861 8c **dark blue, light blue & red** .20 .20
P# block of 6, 3# 1.00 —
Margin block of 4, Mr. Zip and "Use Zip Code" .65 —
a. Tagging omitted 5.00

NATIONAL PARKS CENTENNIAL ISSUE

Centenary of Yellowstone National Park, the 1st National Park, and of the entire National Park System. See No. C84.

A862 A863

A864 A865

Cape Hatteras National Seashore

Wolf Trap Farm, Va. — A866

Old Faithful, Yellowstone — A867

Mt. McKinley, Alaska — A868

Designers: 2c, Walter D. Richards; 6c, Howard Koslow; 8c, Robert Handville; 15c, James Barkley.

LITHOGRAPHED, ENGRAVED (Giori)

1972 **Tagged** ***Perf. 11***

Plates of 400 subjects in 4 panes of 100 each

1448 A862 2c **black & multi.,** *Apr. 5* .20 .20
1449 A863 2c **black & multi.,** *Apr. 5* .20 .20
1450 A864 2c **black & multi.,** *Apr. 5* .20 .20
1451 A865 2c **black & multi.,** *Apr. 5* .20 .20
a. Block of 4, #1448-1451 .25 *.30*
P# block of 4 .50 —
Margin block of 4, "Use Zip Codes" .30 —
b. As "a," black (litho.) omitted *1,400.*

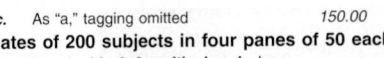

c. As "a," tagging omitted *150.00*

Plates of 200 subjects in four panes of 50 each

1452 A866 6c **black & multicolored,** *June 26* .20 .20
P# block of 4 .55 —
Margin block of 4, Mr. Zip and "Use Zip Code" .50 —
a. Tagging omitted *10.00*

Plates of 128 subjects in four panes of 32 (8x4)

1453 A867 8c **blk., blue, brn. & multi.,** *Mar. 1* .20 .20
P# block of 4 .70 —
Margin block of 4, Mr. Zip and "Use Zip Code" .65 —
a. Tagging omitted 140.00

Plates of 200 subjects in four panes of 50 each

1454 A868 15c **black & multi.,** *July 28* .30 .20
P# block of 4 1.30 —
Margin block of 4, Mr. Zip 1.25 —
a. Tagging omitted 125.00
b. Yellow omitted *5,750.*

FAMILY PLANNING ISSUE

Family — A869

LITHOGRAPHED, ENGRAVED (Giori)

Plates of 200 subjects in four panes of 50.

1972, Mar. 18 **Tagged** ***Perf. 11***

1455 A869 8c **black & multicolored** .20 .20
P# block of 4 .65 —
Margin block of 4, Mr. Zip and "Use Zip Code" .60 —
a. Yellow omitted *400.00*
c. Dark brown missing (FO) *9,000.*
d. Tagging omitted —

AMERICAN BICENTENNIAL ISSUE
Colonial American Craftsmen

In left panes Nos. 1456 and 1458 appear in 1st, 3rd and 5th place; Nos. 1457 and 1459 in 2nd and 4th place. This arrangement is reversed in right panes.

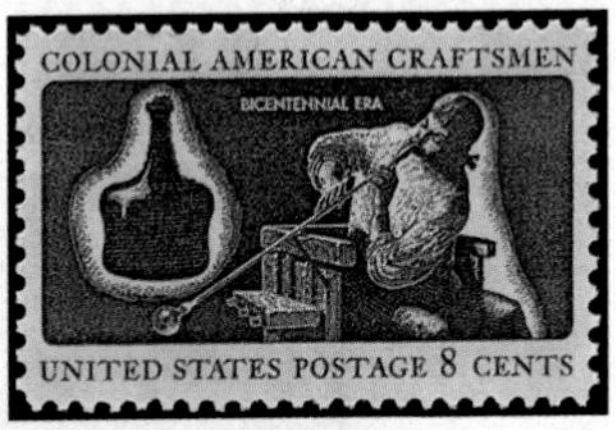

Glass Blower A870

Silversmith A871

Wigmaker A872

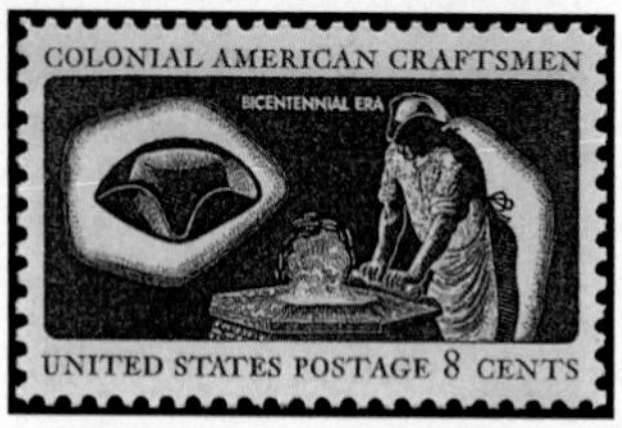

Hatter — A873

Designed by Leonard Everett Fisher.

ENGRAVED

E.E. Plates of 200 subjects in four panes of 50.

1972, July 4 Tagged *Perf. 11x10½*

1456	A870	8c	**deep brown,** *dull yellow*	.20	.20
1457	A871	8c	**deep brown,** *dull yellow*	.20	.20
1458	A872	8c	**deep brown,** *dull yellow*	.20	.20
1459	A873	8c	**deep brown,** *dull yellow*	.20	.20
a.			Block of 4, #1456-1459	.65	*.75*
			P# block of 4	.80	—
			Margin block of 4, Mr. Zip and "Use Zip Code"	.70	—
b.			As "a," tagging omitted	*150.00*	

Margin includes Bicentennial Commission emblem and inscription: USA BICENTENNIAL / HONORS COLONIAL / AMERICAN CRAFTSMEN.

OLYMPIC GAMES ISSUE

11th Winter Olympic Games, Sapporo, Japan, Feb. 3-13 and 20th Summer Olympic Games, Munich, Germany, Aug. 26-Sept. 11. See No. C85.

Bicycling and Olympic Rings — A874

Bobsledding and Olympic Rings — A875

Running and Olympic Rings — A876

"Broken red ring" Cylinder Flaw

Designed by Lance Wyman.

PHOTOGRAVURE (Andreotti)

Plates of 200 subjects in four panes of 50.

1972, Aug. 17 Tagged *Perf. 11x10½*

1460	A874	6c	**black, blue, red, emerald & yellow**	.20	.20
			P# block of 10, 5#	1.25	—
			Margin block of 4, Mr. Zip and "Use Zip Code"	.50	—
			Cylinder flaw (broken red ring) (33313 UL 43)	10.00	
1461	A875	8c	**black, blue, red, emerald & yellow**	.20	.20
			P# block of 10, 5#	1.60	—
			Margin block of 4, Mr. Zip and "Use Zip Code"	.65	—
a.			Tagging omitted	7.50	
1462	A876	15c	**black, blue, red, emerald & yel**	.30	.20
			P# block of 10, 5#	3.00	—
			Margin block of 4, Mr. Zip and "Use Zip Code"	1.15	—
			Nos. 1460-1462 (3)	.70	.60

PARENT TEACHER ASSN., 75th ANNIV.

Blackboard A877

Designed by Arthur S. Congdon III.

PHOTOGRAVURE (Andreotti)

Plates of 200 subjects in four panes of 50.

1972, Sept. 15 Tagged *Perf. 11x10½*

1463	A877	8c	**yellow & black**	.20	.20
			P# block of 4, 2#	.65	—
			P# block of 4, yellow # reversed	.75	—
			Margin block of 4, Mr. Zip and "Use Zip Code"	.60	—
a.			Tagging omitted	—	

WILDLIFE CONSERVATION ISSUE

Nos. 1464-1465 alternate in 1st row, Nos. 1468-1469 in 2nd row. This arrangement repeated throughout pane.

Fur Seals A878

Cardinal — A879

Brown Pelican — A880

Bighorn Sheep — A881

Designed by Stanley W. Galli.

LITHOGRAPHED, ENGRAVED (Giori)

Plates of 128 subjects in 4 panes of 32 (4x8).

1972, Sept. 20 Tagged *Perf. 11*

1464	A878	8c	**multicolored**	.20	.20
1465	A879	8c	**multicolored**	.20	.20
1466	A880	8c	**multicolored**	.20	.20
1467	A881	8c	**multicolored**	.20	.20
a.			Block of 4, #1464-1467	.65	*.75*
			P# block of 4	.90	—
			Margin block of 4, Mr. Zip and "Use Zip Code"	.70	—
b.			As "a," brown omitted	*3,750.*	
c.			As "a," green & blue omitted	*3,750.*	
d.			As "a," red & brown omitted	*3,750.*	
e.			As "a," tagging omitted	—	

MAIL ORDER BUSINESS ISSUE

Centenary of mail order business, originated by Aaron Montgomery Ward, Chicago. Design based on Headsville, W.Va., post office in Smithsonian Institution, Washington, D.C.

Rural Post Office Store — A882

Designed by Robert Lambdin.

PHOTOGRAVURE (Andreotti)

Plates of 200 subjects in four panes of 50.

1972, Sept, 27 Tagged *Perf. 11x10½*

1468	A882	8c	**multicolored**	.20	.20
			P# block of 12, 6#	1.75	—
			Margin block of 4, Mr. Zip and "Use Zip Code"	.60	—

The tagging on No. 1468 consists of a vertical bar of phosphor 10mm wide.

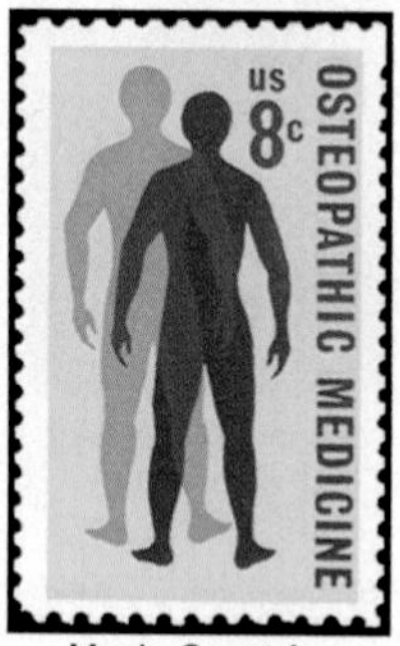

Man's Quest for Health — A883

Tom Sawyer, by Norman Rockwell — A884

OSTEOPATHIC MEDICINE ISSUE

75th anniv. of the American Osteopathic Assoc., founded by Dr. Andrew T. Still (1828-1917), who developed the principles of osteopathy in 1874.

Designed by V. Jack Ruther.

PHOTOGRAVURE (Andreotti)

Plates of 200 subjects in four panes of 50.

1972, Oct. 9 Tagged *Perf. 10½x11*

1469	A883	8c	**multicolored**	.20	.20
			P# block of 6, 3#	1.10	—
			Margin block of 4, Mr. Zip and "Use Zip Code"	.65	—

AMERICAN FOLKLORE ISSUE
Tom Sawyer

Designed by Bradbury Thompson.

LITHOGRAPHED, ENGRAVED (Giori)

Plates of 200 subjects in four panes of 50.

1972, Oct. 13 Tagged *Perf. 11*

1470	A884	8c	**black, red, yellow, tan, blue & rose red**	.20	.20
			P# block of 4	.65	—
			Margin block of 4, Mr. Zip and "Use Zip Code"	.60	—
a.			Horiz. pair, imperf. between	*4,250.*	
b.			Red & black (engr.) omitted	*1,350.*	
c.			Yellow & tan (litho.) omitted	*2,000.*	
d.			Tagging omitted	*125.*	

CHRISTMAS ISSUE

Angels from "Mary, Queen of Heaven" — A885

Santa Claus — A886

Designers: No. 1471, Bradbury Thompson, using detail from a painting by the Master of the St. Lucy legend, in the National Gallery of Art, Washington, D.C. No. 1472, Stevan Dohanos.

PHOTOGRAVURE (Andreotti)

Plates of 200 subjects in four panes of 50.

1972, Nov. 9 Tagged *Perf. 10½x11*

1471 A885 8c **multicolored**		.20	.20
	P# block of 12, 6#	1.75	—
	Margin block of 4, Mr. Zip and "Use Zip Code"	.60	—
a.	Pink omitted	*120.00*	
b.	Black omitted	*3,250.*	
1472 A886 8c **multicolored**		.20	.20
	P# block of 12, 6#	1.75	—
	Margin block of 4, Mr. Zip and "Use Zip Code"	.60	—

PHARMACY ISSUE

Honoring American druggists in connection with the 120th anniversary of the American Pharmaceutical Association.

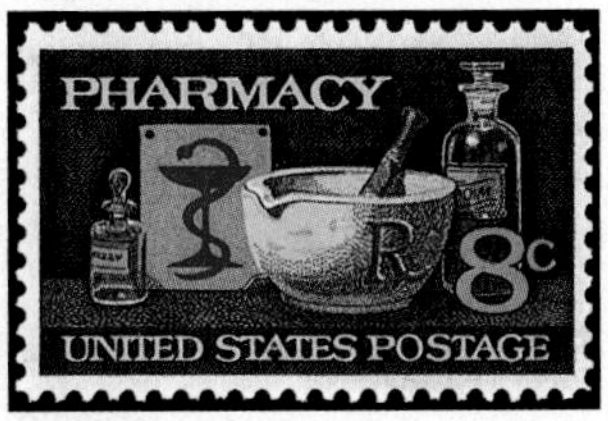

Mortar and Pestle, Bowl of Hygeia, 19th Century Medicine Bottles — A887

Designed by Ken Davies.

LITHOGRAPHED, ENGRAVED (Giori)

Plates of 200 subjects in four panes of 50.

1972, Nov. 10 Tagged *Perf. 11*

1473 A887 8c **black & multicolored**		.20	.20
	P# block of 4	.65	—
	Margin block of 4, Mr. Zip and "Use Zip Code"	.60	—
a.	Blue & orange omitted	*700.00*	
b.	Blue omitted	*1,750.*	
c.	Orange omitted	*1,750.*	
d.	Tagging omitted	120.00	—
e.	Vertical pair, imperf horiz.	*2,100.*	

STAMP COLLECTING ISSUE

Issued to publicize stamp collecting.

U.S. No. 1 under Magnifying Glass — A888

Designed by Frank E. Livia.

LITHOGRAPHED, ENGRAVED (Giori)

Plates of 160 subjects in four panes of 40.

1972, Nov. 17 Tagged *Perf. 11*

1474 A888 8c **multicolored**		.20	.20
	P# block of 4	.65	—
	Margin block of 4, Mr. Zip and "Use Zip Code"	.60	—
a.	Black (litho.) omitted	*500.00*	
b.	Tagging omitted	4.50	

LOVE ISSUE

"Love," by Robert Indiana A889

Designed by Robert Indiana.

PHOTOGRAVURE (Andreotti)

Plates of 200 subjects in four panes of 50.

1973, Jan. 26 Tagged *Perf. 11x10½*

1475 A889 8c **red, emerald & violet blue**		.20	.20
	P# block of 6, 3#	1.00	—
	Margin block of 4, Mr. Zip and "Use Zip Code"	.65	—

AMERICAN BICENTENNIAL ISSUE
Communications in Colonial Times

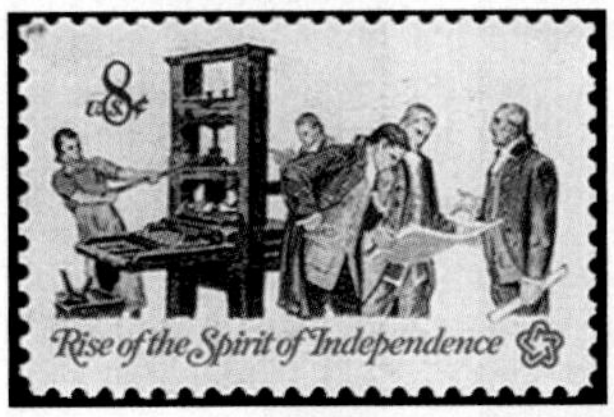

Printer and Patriots Examining Pamphlet A890

Posting a Broadside A891

Postrider A892

Drummer A893

Designed by William A. Smith.

GIORI PRESS PRINTING

Plates of 200 subjects in four panes of 50.

1973 Tagged *Perf. 11*

1476 A890 8c **ultra., greenish blk. & red,** *Feb. 16*		.20	.20
	P# block of 4	.65	—
	Margin block of 4, Mr. Zip and "Use Zip Code"	.60	—
a.	Tagging omitted	50.00	
1477 A891 8c **black, vermilion & ultra.,** *Apr. 13*		.20	.20
	P# block of 4	.65	—
	Margin block of 4, Mr. Zip and "Use Zip Code"	.60	—
	Pair with full horiz. gutter btwn.	—	
a.	Tagging omitted	—	

LITHOGRAPHED, ENGRAVED (Giori)

1478 A892 8c **blue, black, red & green,** *June 22*		.20	.20
	P# block of 4	.65	—
	Margin block of 4, Mr. Zip and "Use Zip Code"	.60	—
a.	Red missing (CM)	—	
1479 A893 8c **blue, black, yellow & red,** *Sept. 28*		.20	.20
	P# block of 4	.65	—
	Margin block of 4, Mr. Zip and "Use Zip Code"	.60	—
	Nos. 1476-1479 (4)	.80	.80

Margin of Nos. 1477-1479 includes Bicentennial Commission emblem and inscription.

AMERICAN BICENTENNIAL ISSUE
Boston Tea Party

In left panes Nos. 1480 and 1482 appear in 1st, 3rd and 5th place, Nos. 1481 and 1483 appear in 2nd and 4th place. This arrangement is reversed in right panes.

British Merchantman A894

British Three-master A895

Boats and Ship's Hull — A896

Boat and Dock — A897

Designed by William A. Smith.

LITHOGRAPHED, ENGRAVED (Giori)

Plates of 200 subjects in four panes of 50.

1973, July 4 Tagged *Perf. 11*

1480 A894 8c **black & multicolored**		.20	.20
1481 A895 8c **black & multicolored**		.20	.20
1482 A896 8c **black & multicolored**		.20	.20
1483 A897 8c **black & multicolored**		.20	.20
a.	Block of 4, #1480-1483	.65	*.75*
	P# block of 4	.75	—
	Margin block of 4, Mr. Zip and "Use Zip Code"	.70	—
b.	As "a," black (engraved) omitted	*1,100.*	
c.	As "a," black (litho.) omitted	*1,100.*	
d.	As "a," tagging omitted	—	—

Margin includes Bicentennial Commission emblem and inscription.

AMERICAN ARTS ISSUE

George Gershwin (1898-1937), composer (No. 1484); Robinson Jeffers (1887-1962), poet (No. 1485); Henry Ossawa Tanner (1859-1937), black painter (No. 1486); Willa Cather (1873-1947), novelist (No. 1487).

Gershwin, Sportin' Life, Porgy and Bess — A898

Robinson Jeffers, Man and Children of Carmel with Burro — A899

Henry Ossawa Tanner, Palette and Rainbow A900

Willa Cather, Pioneer Family and Covered Wagon A901

Designed by Mark English.

PHOTOGRAVURE (Andreotti)
Plates of 160 subjects in four panes of 40.

1973	Tagged	Perf. 11	
1484 A898 8c **dp. green & multi.**, *Feb. 28*		.20	.20
	P# block of 12, 6#	1.75	—
	Margin block of 4, Mr. Zip, "Use Zip Code" and "Mail Early in the Day"	.60	—
	P# block of 16, 6#, Mr. Zip and slogans	2.50	—
a.	Vertical pair, imperf. horiz.	*175.00*	
1485 A899 8c **Prussian blue & multi.**, *Aug. 13*		.20	.20
	P# block of 12, 6#	1.75	—
	Margin block of 4, Mr. Zip, "Use Zip Code" "Mail Early in the Day"	.60	—
	P# block of 16, 6#, Mr. Zip and slogans	2.50	—
a.	Vertical pair, imperf. horiz.	*225.00*	
1486 A900 8c **yellow brown & multi.**, *Sept. 10*		.20	.20
	P# block of 12, 6#	1.75	—
	Margin block of 4, Mr. Zip, "Use Zip Code" "Mail Early in the Day"	.60	—
	P# block of 16, 6#, Mr. Zip and slogans	2.50	—
1487 A901 8c **deep brown & multi.**, *Sept. 20*		.20	.20
	P# block of 12, 6#	1.75	—
	Margin block of 4, Mr. Zip, "Use Zip Code" "Mail Early in the Day"	.60	—
	P# block of 16, 6#, Mr. Zip and slogans	2.50	—
a.	Vertical pair, imperf. horiz.	*225.00*	
	Nos. 1484-1487 (4)	.80	.80

COPERNICUS ISSUE

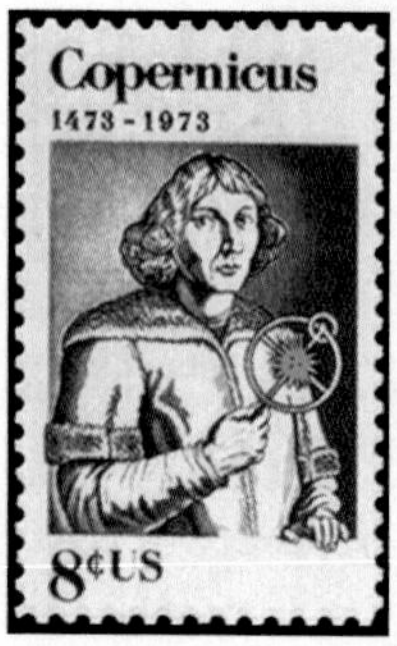

Nicolaus Copernicus (1473-1543), Polish Astronomer — A902

Designed by Alvin Eisenman after 18th century engraving.

LITHOGRAPHED, ENGRAVED (Giori)
Plates of 200 subjects in four panes of 50.

1973, Apr. 23	Tagged	Perf. 11	
1488 A902 8c **black & orange**		.20	.20
	P# block of 4	.65	—
	Margin block of 4, Mr. Zip and "Use Zip Code"	.60	—
a.	Orange omitted	*850.00*	
b.	Black (engraved) omitted	*875.00*	
c.	Tagging omitted	*125.00*	

The orange can be chemically removed. Expertization of No. 1488a is required.

POSTAL SERVICE EMPLOYEES ISSUE

A tribute to US Postal Service employees. Nos. 1489-1498 are printed se-tenant in horizontal rows of 10. Emerald inscription on back, printed beneath gum in water-soluble ink, includes Postal Service emblem, "People Serving You" and a statement, differing for each of the 10 stamps, about some aspect of postal service.

Each stamp in top or bottom row has a tab with blue inscription enumerating various jobs in postal service.

Stamp Counter — A903

Mail Collection — A904

Letter Facing on Conveyor Belt — A905

Parcel Post Sorting — A906

Mail Canceling — A907

Manual Letter Routing — A908

Electronic Letter Routing — A909

Loading Mail on Truck — A910

Mailman — A911

Rural Mail Delivery — A912

Designed by Edward Vebell.

PHOTOGRAVURE (Andreotti)
Plates of 200 subjects in four panes of 50.

1973, Apr. 30	Tagged	Perf. 10½x11	
1489 A903 8c **multicolored**		.20	.20
1490 A904 8c **multicolored**		.20	.20
1491 A905 8c **multicolored**		.20	.20
1492 A906 8c **multicolored**		.20	.20
1493 A907 8c **multicolored**		.20	.20
1494 A908 8c **multicolored**		.20	.20
1495 A909 8c **multicolored**		.20	.20
1496 A910 8c **multicolored**		.20	.20
1497 A911 8c **multicolored**		.20	.20
1498 A912 8c **multicolored**		.20	.20
a.	Strip of 10, #1489-1498	1.75	*1.90*
	P# block of 20, 5# and 10 tabs	3.75	—
b.	As "a," tagging omitted	*300.00*	—

The tagging on Nos. 1489-1498 consists of a ½-inch horizontal band of phosphor.

HARRY S. TRUMAN ISSUE

Harry S Truman, 33rd President, (1884-1972) — A913

Designed by Bradbury Thompson; photograph by Leo Stern.

GIORI PRESS PRINTING
Plates of 128 subjects in four panes of 32 each.

1973, May 8	Tagged	Perf. 11	
1499 A913 8c **carmine rose, black & blue**		.20	.20
	P# block of 4	.75	—
a.	Tagging omitted	7.50	

ELECTRONICS PROGRESS ISSUE

See No. C86.

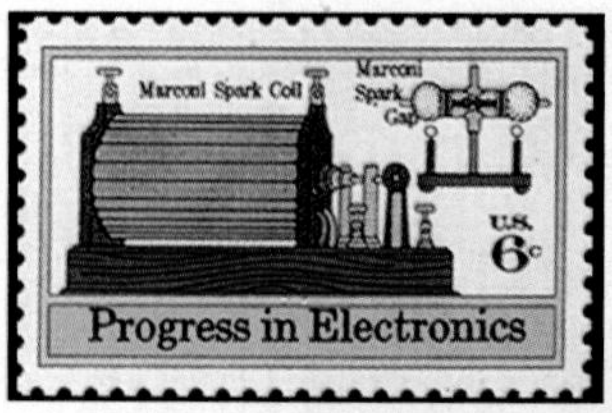

Marconi's Spark Coil and Spark Gap — A914

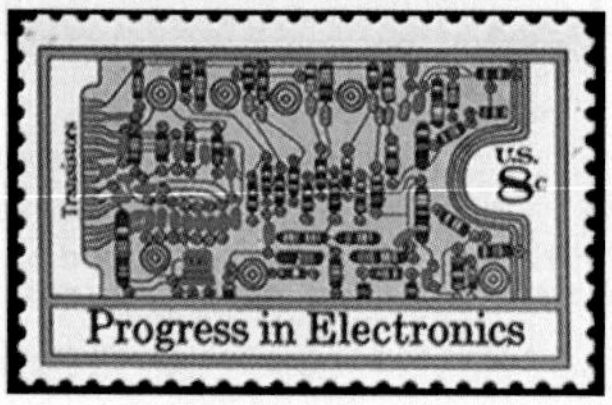

Transistors and Printed Circuit Board — A915

Microphone, Speaker, Vacuum Tube and TV Camera Tube — A916

Designed by Walter and Naiad Einsel.

LITHOGRAPHED, ENGRAVED (Giori)

Plates of 200 subjects in four panes of 50.

1973, July 10 Tagged *Perf. 11*

1500 A914 6c **lilac & multicolored** .20 .20
P# block of 4 .55 —
Margin block of 4, Mr. Zip and "Use Zip Code" .50 —
a. Tagging omitted 100.00

1501 A915 8c **tan & multicolored** .20 .20
P# block of 4 .70 —
Margin block of 4, Mr. Zip and "Use Zip Code" .65 —
a. Black (inscriptions & "U.S. 8c") omitted *375.00*
b. Tan (background) & lilac omitted *1,000.*
c. Tagging omitted —

Many examples of No. 1501b are hinged. Value about one-half never hinged value.

1502 A916 15c **gray green & multicolored** .30 .20
P# block of 4 1.30 —
Margin block of 4, Mr. Zip and "Use Zip Code" 1.20 —
a. Black (inscriptions & "U.S. 15c") omitted *1,250.*
Nos. 1500-1502 (3) .70 .60

LYNDON B. JOHNSON ISSUE

Lyndon B. Johnson, 36th President (1908-1973) — A917

Designed by Bradbury Thompson, portrait by Elizabeth Shoumatoff.

PHOTOGRAVURE (Andreotti)

Plates of 128 subjects in four panes of 32 each.

1973, Aug. 27 Tagged *Perf. 11*

1503 A917 8c **black & multicolored,** *Aug. 27* .20 .20
P# block of 12, 6# 2.20 —
a. Horiz. pair, imperf. vert. *275.00*

RURAL AMERICA ISSUE

Centenary of the introduction of Aberdeen Angus cattle into the US (#1504); of the Chautauqua Institution (#1505); and of the introduction of hard winter wheat into Kansas by Mennonite immigrants (#1506).

Angus and Longhorn Cattle — A918

Chautauqua Tent and Buggies A919

Wheat Fields and Train — A920

No. 1504 modeled by Frank Waslick after painting by F. C. "Frank" Murphy. Nos. 1505-1506 designed by John Falter.

LITHOGRAPHED, ENGRAVED (Giori)

Plates of 200 subjects in four panes of 50.

1973-74 Tagged *Perf. 11*

1504 A918 8c **multicolored,** *Oct. 5, 1973* .20 .20
P# block of 4 .65 —
Margin block of 4, Mr. Zip and "Use Zip Code" .60 —
a. Green & red brown omitted *800.00*
b. Vert. pair, imperf. between *5,000.*
c. Tagging omitted 80.00

1505 A919 10c **multicolored,** *Aug. 6, 1974* .20 .20
P# block of 4 .85 —
Margin block of 4, Mr. Zip and "Use Zip Code" .80 —
a. Black (litho.) omitted *1,750.*
b. Tagging omitted —

1506 A920 10c **multicolored,** *Aug. 16, 1974* .20 .20
P# block of 4 .85 —
Margin block of 4, Mr. Zip and "Use Zip Code" .80 —
a. Black and blue (engr.) omitted *650.00*
b. Tagging omitted 100.00
Nos. 1504-1506 (3) .60 .60

CHRISTMAS ISSUE

Small Cowper Madonna, by Raphael — A921

Christmas Tree in Needlepoint — A922

Designers: No. 1507, Bradbury Thompson, using a painting in the National Gallery of Art, Washington, D.C. No. 1508, Dolli Tingle.

PHOTOGRAVURE (Andreotti)

Plates of 200 subjects in four panes of 50.

1973, Nov. 7 Tagged *Perf. 10½x11*

1507 A921 8c **multicolored** .20 .20
P# block of 12, 6# 1.75 —
Margin block of 4, Mr. Zip and "Use Zip Code" .60 —
Pair with full vert. gutter btwn. —

1508 A922 8c **multicolored** .20 .20
P# block of 12, 6# 1.75 —
Margin block of 4, Mr. Zip and "Use Zip Code" .60 —
Pair with full horiz. gutter btwn. —
a. Vertical pair, imperf. between *250.00*

The tagging on Nos. 1507-1508 consists of a 20x12mm horizontal bar of phosphor.

50-Star and 13-Star Flags — A923

Jefferson Memorial and Signature — A924

Mail Transport — A925

Liberty Bell — A926

Designers: No. 1509, Ren Wicks. No. 1510, Dean Ellis. No. 1511, Randall McDougall. 6.3c, Frank Lionetti.

MULTICOLOR HUCK PRESS

Panes of 100 (10x10)

1973-74 Tagged *Perf. 11x10½*

1509 A923 10c **red & blue,** *Dec. 8, 1973* .20 .20
P# block of 20, 4-6#, 2-3 "Mail Early" and 2-3 "Use Zip Code" 4.25 —
a. Horizontal pair, imperf. between *45.00* —
b. Blue omitted *165.00* —
c. Imperf., vert. pair *850.00*
d. Horiz. pair, imperf. vert. *900.00*
e. Tagging omitted *9.00*
f. Vert. pair, imperf between —

No. 1509 exists imperf and with red omitted from printer's waste.

ROTARY PRESS PRINTING

E.E. Plates of 400 subjects in four panes of 100.

1510 A924 10c **blue,** *Dec. 14, 1973* .20 .20
P# block of 4 .85 —
Margin block of 4, "Use Zip Codes" .80 —
a. Untagged (Bureau precanceled) 4.00 1.00
P# block of 4 50.00
Margin block of 4, "Use Zip Codes" 25.00
b. Booklet pane of 5 + label 1.65 .90
c. Booklet pane of 8 1.65 1.00
Pair with full vert.. gutter btwn. 225.00
d. Booklet pane of 6, *Aug. 5, 1974* 5.25 1.75
e. Vert. pair, imperf. horiz. *425.00*
f. Vert. pair, imperf. between *475.00*
g. As No. 1510, tagging omitted (not Bureau precanceled) 5.00
h. As "c," tagging omitted —

Bureau Precancels: 10 different.

No. 1510f resulted from a paper foldover after perforating and before cutting into booklet panes.

PHOTOGRAVURE (Andreotti)

Plates of 400 subjects in four panes of 100.

1511 A925 10c **multicolored,** *Jan. 4, 1974* .20 .20
P# block of 8, 4# 1.75 —
Margin block of 4, "Use Zip Codes" .80 —
Pair with full horiz. gutter btwn. —
a. Yellow omitted *45.00*

Beware of copies with yellow chemically removed offered as No. 1511a.

COIL STAMPS

ROTARY PRESS PRINTING

1973-74 Tagged *Perf. 10 Vert.*

1518 A926 6.3c **brick red,** *Oct. 1, 1974* .20 .20
Pair .25 .20
Joint line pair .80 —
a. Untagged (Bureau precanceled) .35 .20
Pair .70 .30
Joint line pair 1.65 1.65
b. Imperf., pair *165.00*
Joint line pair *425.00*
c. As "a," imperf., pair *85.00*
Joint line pair *175.00*

A total of 129 different Bureau precancels were used by 117 cities.

No. 1518c is precanceled Washington, DC. Columbus, Ohio and Garden City, N.Y. Values for Columbus pair $550, for Garden City pair $850.

MULTICOLOR HUCK PRESS

1519 A923 10c **red & blue,** *Dec. 8, 1973* .20 .20
Pair .40 .20
a. Imperf., pair 37.50
b. Tagging omitted *9.00*

ROTARY PRESS PRINTING

1520 A924 10c **blue,** *Dec. 14, 1973* .25 .20
Pair .50 .20
Joint line pair .75 —
a. Untagged (Bureau precanceled) 5.50 1.25
Pair 12.00 2.75
Joint line pair *185.00* —
b. Imperf., pair 32.50
Joint line pair 62.50

Bureau Precancels: No. 1520a, 14 diff.

VETERANS OF FOREIGN WARS ISSUE

75th anniversary of Veterans of Spanish-American and Other Foreign Wars.

Emblem and Initials of Veterans of Foreign Wars — A928

Designed by Robert Hallock.

GIORI PRESS PRINTING
Plates of 200 subjects in 4 plates of 50.

1974, Mar. 11 **Tagged** ***Perf. 11***

1525 A928 10c **red & dark blue** .20 .20
P# block of 4 .85 —
Margin block of 4, Mr. Zip and "Use Zip Code" .80 —
a. Tagging omitted *90.00*
b. Blue missing (PS) —

ROBERT FROST ISSUE

Robert Frost (1873-1963), Poet — A929

Designed by Paul Calle; photograph by David Rhinelander.

ROTARY PRESS PRINTING
E.E. Plates of 200 subjects in four panes of 50.

1974, Mar. 26 **Tagged** ***Perf. 10½x11***

1526 A929 10c **black** .20 .20
P# block of 4 .85 —
Margin block of 4, Mr. Zip and "Use Zip Code" .80 —

EXPO '74 WORLD'S FAIR ISSUE

EXPO '74 World's Fair "Preserve the Environment," Spokane, Wash., May 4-Nov. 4.

"Cosmic Jumper" and "Smiling Sage" — A930

Designed by Peter Max.

PHOTOGRAVURE (Andreotti)
Plates of 160 subjects in four panes of 40.

1974, Apr. 18 **Tagged** ***Perf. 11***

1527 A930 10c **multicolored** .20 .20
On cover, Expo. station hand-stamp canc. 12.50
P# block of 12, 6# 2.50 —
Margin block of 4, Mr. Zip, "Use Zip Code" and "Mail Early in the Day" .80 —
P# block of 16, 6#, Mr. Zip and slogans 3.40 —

HORSE RACING ISSUE

Kentucky Derby, Churchill Downs, centenary.

Horses Rounding Turn — A931

Designed by Henry Koehler.

PHOTOGRAVURE (Andreotti)
Plates of 200 subjects in four panes of 50.

1974, May 4 **Tagged** ***Perf. 11x10½***

1528 A931 10c **yellow & multicolored** .25 .20
P# block of 12, 6# 3.50 —
Margin block of 4, Mr. Zip and "Use Zip Code" 1.10 —
a. Blue ("Horse Racing") omitted *800.00*
b. Red ("U.S. postage 10 cents") omitted *2,250.*
c. Tagging omitted 150.00

Beware of stamps offered as No. 1528b that have traces of red.

SKYLAB ISSUE

First anniversary of the launching of Skylab I, honoring all who participated in the Skylab project.

Skylab — A932

Designed by Robert T. McCall.

LITHOGRAPHED, ENGRAVED (Giori)
Plates of 200 subjects in four panes of 50.

1974, May 14 **Tagged** ***Perf. 11***

1529 A932 10c **multicolored** .20 .20
P# block of 4 .85 —
Margin block of 4, Mr. Zip and "Use Zip Code" .80 —
a. Vert. pair, imperf. between —
b. Tagging omitted *10.00*

UNIVERSAL POSTAL UNION ISSUE

UPU cent. In the 1st row Nos. 1530-1537 are in sequence as listed. In the 2nd row Nos. 1534-1537 are followed by Nos. 1530-1533. Every row of 8 and every horizontal block of 8 contains all 8 designs. The letter writing designs are from famous works of art; some are details. The quotation on every second stamp, "Letters mingle souls," is from a letter by poet John Donne.

Michelangelo, from "School of Athens," by Raphael, 1509 — A933

"Five Feminine Virtues," by Hokusai, c. 1811 — A934

"Old Scraps," by John Fredrick Peto, 1894 — A935

"The Lovely Reader," by Jean Etienne Liotard, 1746 — A936

"Lady Writing Letter," by Gerard Terborch, 1654 — A937

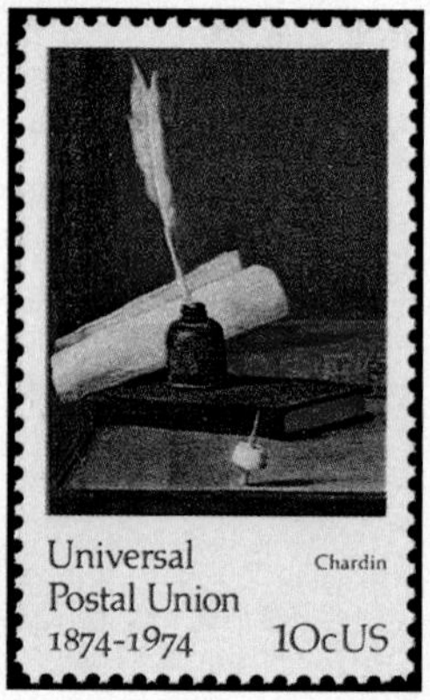

Inkwell and Quill, from "Boy with a Top," by Jean-Baptiste Simeon Chardin, 1738 — A938

Mrs. John Douglas, by Thomas Gainsborough, 1784 — A939

Don Antonio Noriega, by Francisco de Goya, 1801 — A940

Designed by Bradbury Thompson.

PHOTOGRAVURE (Andreotti)

Plates of 128 subjects in four panes of 32 each.

1974, June 6		**Tagged**	***Perf. 11***	
1530	A933	10c **multicolored**	.20	.20
1531	A934	10c **multicolored**	.20	.20
1532	A935	10c **multicolored**	.20	.20
1533	A936	10c **multicolored**	.20	.20
1534	A937	10c **multicolored**	.20	.20
1535	A938	10c **multicolored**	.20	.20
1536	A939	10c **multicolored**	.20	.20
1537	A940	10c **multicolored**	.20	.20
a.		Block or strip of 8 (#1530-1537)	1.75	1.75
		P# block of 16, 5#, "Mail Early in the Day," Mr. Zip and "Use Zip Code"	3.50	—
		P# block of 10, 5#; no slogans	2.25	—
b.		As "a," (block), imperf. vert.	*7,500.*	

MINERAL HERITAGE ISSUE

The sequence of stamps in 1st horizontal row is Nos. 1538-1541, 1538-1539. In 2nd row Nos. 1540-1541 are followed by Nos. 1538-1541.

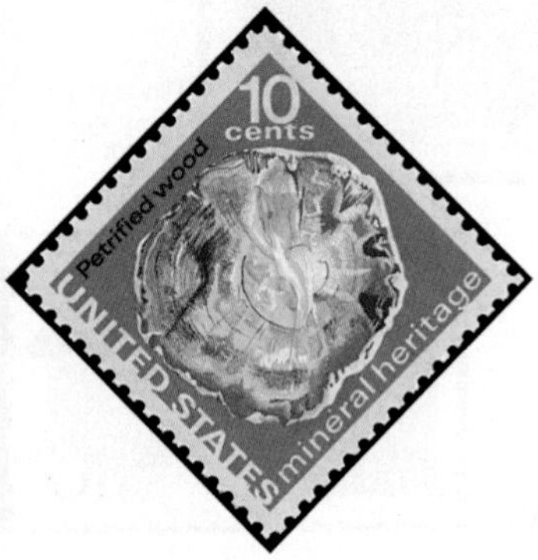

Petrified Wood A941

Tourmaline — A942

Amethyst A943

Rhodochrosite — A944

Designed by Leonard F. Buckley.

LITHOGRAPHED, ENGRAVED (Giori)

Plates of 192 subjects in four panes of 48 (6x8).

1974, June 13		**Tagged**	***Perf. 11***	
1538	A941	10c **blue & multicolored**	.20	.20
a.		Light blue & yellow (litho.) omitted	—	
1539	A942	10c **blue & multicolored**	.20	.20
a.		Light blue (litho.) omitted	—	
b.		Black & purple (engr.) omitted	—	
1540	A943	10c **blue & multicolored**	.20	.20
a.		Light blue & yellow (litho.) omitted	—	
1541	A944	10c **blue & multicolored**	.20	.20
a.		Block or strip of 4, #1538-1541	.80	.90
		P# block of 4	.90	—
		Margin block of 4, Mr. Zip and "Use Zip Code"	.85	—
b.		As "a," light blue & yellow (litho.) omitted	*1,700.*	—
c.		Light blue (litho.) omitted	—	
d.		Black & red (engr.) omitted	—	
e.		Block of 4, two right stamps being Nos. 1539b and 1541d	*4,500.*	
f.		As "a," tagging omitted	*225.00*	

No. 1541e is usually collected as a transition block of six or larger.

KENTUCKY SETTLEMENT, 150th ANNIV.
Fort Harrod, first settlement in Kentucky.

Covered Wagons at Fort Harrod — A945

Designed by David K. Stone.

LITHOGRAPHED, ENGRAVED (Giori)

Plates of 200 subjects in four panes of 50.

1974, June 15		**Tagged**	***Perf. 11***	
1542	A945	10c **green & multicolored**	.20	.20
		P# block of 4	.85	—
		Margin block of 4, Mr. Zip and "Use Zip Code"	.80	—
a.		Dull black (litho.) omitted	*650.00*	
b.		Green (engr. & litho.), black (engr. & litho.) & blue missing (EP)	*3,000.*	
c.		Green (engr.) missing (EP)	*3,000.*	
d.		Green (engr.) & black (litho.) missing (EP)	*3,000.*	
e.		Tagging omitted	150.00	
f.		Blue (litho.) omitted	—	

No. 1542f was caused by an occurrence that seems to be unique for U.S. total color omitted/missing errors. According to the BEP, oil on the printing blanket made a small area unreceptive to the blue ink. No blue at all was printed on one unique error stamp.

AMERICAN REVOLUTION BICENTENNIAL ISSUE
First Continental Congress

Nos. 1543-1544 alternate in 1st row, Nos. 1545-1546 in 2nd row. This arrangement is repeated throughout the pane.

Carpenters' Hall, Philadelphia A946

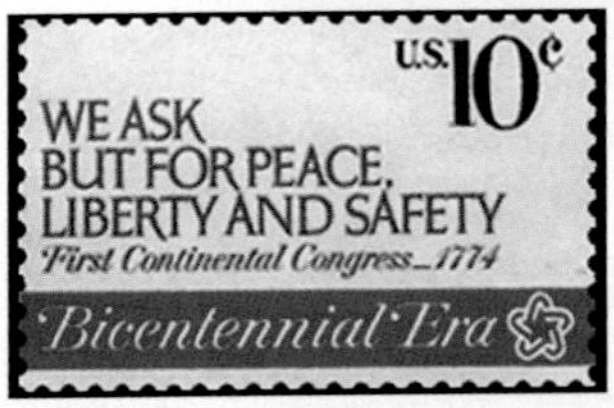

"We ask but for peace . . ." A947

"Deriving their just powers . . ." A948

Independence Hall — A949

Designed by Frank P. Conley

GIORI PRESS PRINTING

Plates of 200 subjects in four panes of 50.

1974, July 4		**Tagged**	***Perf. 11***	
1543	A946	10c **dark blue & red**	.20	.20
1544	A947	10c **gray, dark blue & red**	.20	.20
1545	A948	10c **gray, dark blue & red**	.20	.20

1546 A949 10c **red & dark blue** .20 .20
a. Block of 4, #1543-1546 .80 .90
P# block of 4 .90 —
Margin block of 4, Mr. Zip and "Use Zip Code" .85 —
b. As "a," tagging omitted *65.00*

Margin includes Bicentennial Commission emblem and inscription.

ENERGY CONSERVATION ISSUE

Publicizing the importance of conserving all forms of energy.

Molecules and Drops of Gasoline and Oil — A950

Designed by Robert W. Bode.

LITHOGRAPHED, ENGRAVED (Giori)
Plates of 200 subjects in four panes of 50.

1974, Sept. 23 **Tagged** ***Perf. 11***
1547 A950 10c **multicolored** .20 .20
P# block of 4 .85 —
Margin block of 4, Mr. Zip and "Use Zip Code" .80 —
a. Blue & orange omitted *800.00*
b. Orange & green omitted *500.00*
c. Green omitted *800.00*
d. Tagging omitted 7.00

AMERICAN FOLKLORE ISSUE
Legend of Sleepy Hollow

The Headless Horseman in pursuit of Ichabod Crane from "Legend of Sleepy Hollow," by Washington Irving.

Headless Horseman and Ichabod A951

Designed by Leonard Everett Fisher.

LITHOGRAPHED, ENGRAVED (Giori)
Plates of 200 subjects in four panes of 50.

1974, Oct. 12 **Tagged** ***Perf. 11***
1548 A951 10c **dk. bl., blk., org. & yel.** .20 .20
P# block of 4 .85 —
Margin block of 4, Mr. Zip and "Use Zip Code" .80 —
a. Tagging omitted *200.00* —

RETARDED CHILDREN ISSUE

Retarded Children Can Be Helped, theme of annual convention of the National Association of Retarded Citizens.

Retarded Child — A952

Designed by Paul Calle.

GIORI PRESS PRINTING
Plates of 200 subjects in four panes of 50.

1974, Oct. 12 **Tagged** ***Perf. 11***
1549 A952 10c **brown red & dark brown** .20 .20
P# block of 4 .85 —
Margin block of 4, Mr. Zip and "Use Zip Code" .80 —
a. Tagging omitted 9.00

CHRISTMAS ISSUE

Angel — A953

"The Road-Winter," by Currier and Ives — A954

Dove Weather Vane atop Mount Vernon — A955

Designers: No. 1550, Bradbury Thompson, using detail from the Pérussis altarpiece painted by anonymous French artist, 1480, in Metropolitan Museum of Art, New York City. No. 1551, Stevan Dohanos, using Currier and Ives print from drawing by Otto Knirsch. No. 1552, Don Hedin and Robert Geissman.

PHOTOGRAVURE (Andreotti)
Plates of 200 subjects in four panes of 50.

1974, Oct. 23 **Tagged** ***Perf. 10½x11***
1550 A953 10c **multicolored** .20 .20
P# block of 10, 5# 2.10 —
Margin block of 4, Mr. Zip and "Use Zip Code" .80 —

Perf. 11x10½

1551 A954 10c **multicolored** .20 .20
P# block of 12, 6# 2.50 —
Margin block of 4, Mr. Zip and "Use Zip Code" .80 —
a. Buff omitted 12.50
b. Tagging omitted —

No. 1551a is difficult to identify. Competent expertization is necessary.

Die Cut, Paper Backing Rouletted

1974, Nov. 15 **Untagged**
Self-adhesive; Inscribed "Precanceled"

1552 A955 10c **multicolored** .20 .20
P# block of 20, 6#, 5 slogans 4.25
P# block of 12, 6#, 5 different slogans 2.60
Nos. 1550-1552 (3) .60 .60

Unused value of No. 1552 is for stamp on rouletted paper backing as issued. Used value is for stamp on piece, with or without postmark. **Most examples are becoming discolored, probably from the adhesive. The Catalogue value is for discolored examples.**

Die cutting includes crossed slashes through dove, applied to prevent removal and re-use of the stamp. The stamp will separate into layers if soaked.

Two different machines were used to roulette the sheet.

AMERICAN ARTS ISSUE

Benjamin West (1738-1820), painter (No. 1553); Paul Laurence Dunbar (1872-1906), poet (No. 1554); David (Lewelyn) Wark Griffith (1875-1948), motion picture producer (No. 1555).

Self-portrait — A956

A957

A958

Designers: No. 1553, Bradbury Thompson; No. 1554, Walter D. Richards; No. 1555, Fred Otnes.

PHOTOGRAVURE (Andreotti)
Plates of 200 subjects in four panes of 50.

1975 **Tagged** ***Perf. 10½x11***
1553 A956 10c **multicolored,** *Feb. 10* .20 .20
P# block of 10, 5# 2.10 —
Margin block of 4, Mr. Zip and "Use Zip Code" .80 —

Perf. 11

1554 A957 10c **multicolored,** *May 1* .20 .20
P# block of 10, 5# 2.10 —
Margin block of 4, Mr. Zip and "Use Zip Code" .80 —
a. Imperf., pair *1,000.*

LITHOGRAPHED, ENGRAVED (Giori)
Perf. 11

1555 A958 10c **brown & multicolored,** *May 27* .20 .20
P# block of 4 .85 —
Margin block of 4, Mr. Zip and "Use Zip Code" .80 —
a. Brown (engr.) omitted *625.00*
b. Tagging omitted *160.00*
Nos. 1553-1555 (3) .60 .60

SPACE ISSUES

US space accomplishments with unmanned craft. Pioneer 10 passed within 81,000 miles of Jupiter, Dec. 10, 1973. Mariner 10 explored Venus and Mercury in 1974 and Mercury again in 1975.

Pioneer 10 Passing Jupiter A959

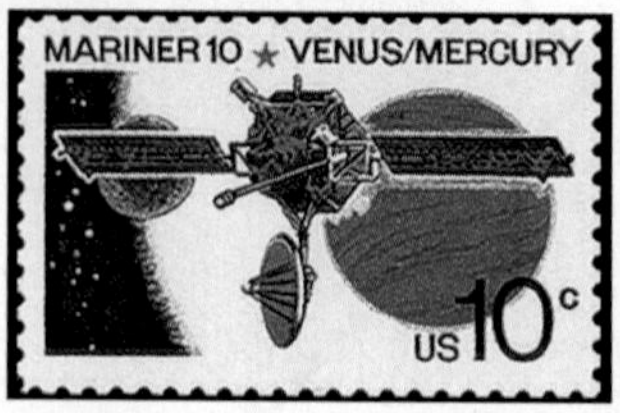

Mariner 10, Venus and Mercury A960

Designed by Robert McCall (No. 1556); Roy Gjertson (No. 1557).

LITHOGRAPHED, ENGRAVED (Giori)
Plates of 200 subjects in four panes of 50.

1975 **Tagged** ***Perf. 11***
1556 A959 10c **light yellow, dark yellow, red, blue & 2 dark blues** *Feb. 28* .20 .20
P# block of 4 .85 —
Margin block of 4, Mr. Zip and "Use Zip Code" .80 —
a. Red & dark yellow omitted *1,100.*
b. Dark blues (engr.) omitted *750.00*
c. Tagging omitted *11.00*
d. Dark yellow omitted —

Imperfs. exist from printer's waste.

1557 A960 10c **black, red, ultra. & bister,** *Apr. 4* .20 .20
P# block of 4 .85 —
Margin block of 4, Mr. Zip and "Use Zip Code" .80 —
a. Red omitted *375.00* —
b. Ultramarine & bister omitted *1,650.*
c. Tagging omitted *11.00*
d. Red missing (PS) —

COLLECTIVE BARGAINING ISSUE

Collective Bargaining law, enacted 1935, in Wagner Act.

"Labor and Management" A961

Designed by Robert Hallock.

PHOTOGRAVURE (Andreotti)
Plates of 200 subjects in four panes of 50.

1975, Mar. 13 **Tagged** ***Perf. 11***
1558 A961 10c **multicolored** .20 .20
P# block of 8, 4# 1.75 —
Margin block of 4, Mr. Zip and "Use Zip Code" .80 —

Imperforates exist from printer's waste.

AMERICAN BICENTENNIAL ISSUE
Contributors to the Cause

Sybil Ludington, age 16, rallied militia, Apr. 26, 1777; Salem Poor, black freeman, fought in Battle of Bunker Hill; Haym Salomon, Jewish immigrant, raised money to finance Revolutionary War; Peter Francisco, Portuguese-French immigrant, joined Continental Army at 15. Emerald inscription on back, printed beneath gum in water-soluble ink, gives thumbnail sketch of portrayed contributor.

Sybil Ludington A962

Salem Poor — A963

Haym Salomon A964

Peter Francisco A965

Designed by Neil Boyle.

PHOTOGRAVURE (Andreotti)
Plates of 200 subjects in four panes of 50.

1975, Mar. 25 **Tagged** ***Perf. 11x10½***
1559 A962 8c **multicolored** .20 .20
P# block of 10, 5# 1.50 —
Margin block of 4, Mr. Zip and "Use Zip Code" .65 —
a. Back inscriptions omitted *200.00*
1560 A963 10c **multicolored** .20 .20
P# block of 10, 5# 2.10 —
Margin block of 4, Mr. Zip and "Use Zip Code" .80 —
a. Back inscription omitted *175.00*
1561 A964 10c **multicolored** .20 .20
P# block of 10, 5# 2.10 —
Margin block of 4, Mr. Zip and "Use Zip Code" .80 —
a. Back inscription omitted *175.00*
b. Red omitted *225.00*
1562 A965 18c **multicolored** .35 .20
P# block of 10, 5# 3.60 —
Margin block of 4, Mr. Zip and "Use Zip Code" 1.45 —
Nos. 1559-1562 (4) .95 .80

Lexington-Concord Battle, 200th Anniv.

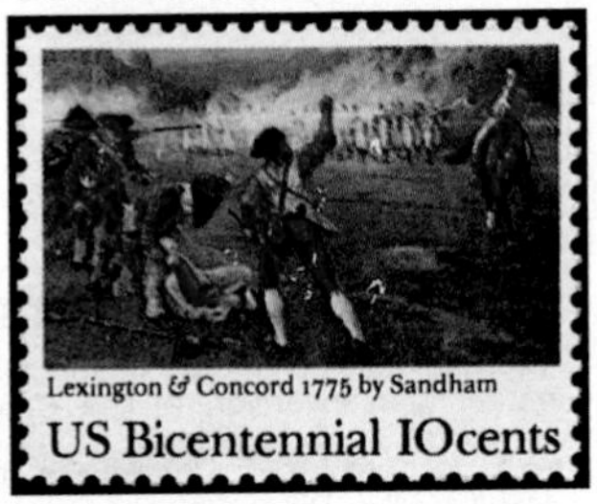

"Birth of Liberty," by Henry Sandham A966

Designed by Bradbury Thompson.

PHOTOGRAVURE (Andreotti)
Plates of 160 subjects in four panes of 40.

1975, Apr. 19 **Tagged** ***Perf. 11***
1563 A966 10c **multicolored** .20 .20
P# block of 12, 6# 2.50 —
Margin block of 4, Mr. Zip, "Use Zip Code" and "Mail Early in the Day" .80 —
P# block of 16, 6 P#, Mr. Zip and slogans 3.40 —
a. Vert. pair, imperf. horiz. *400.00*

Bunker Hill Battle, 200th Anniv.

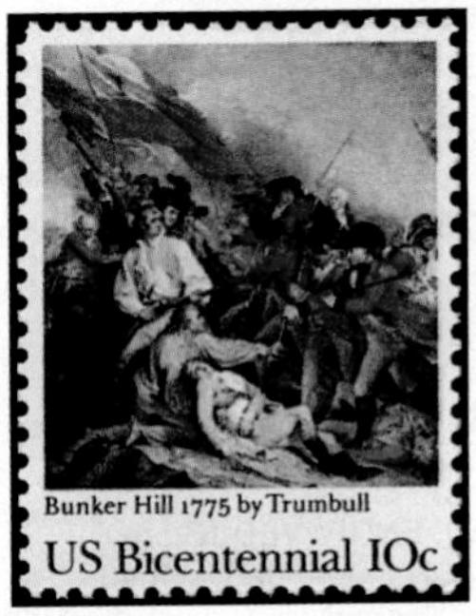

Battle of Bunker Hill, by John Trumbull — A967

Designed by Bradbury Thompson.

PHOTOGRAVURE (Andreotti)
Plates of 160 subjects in four panes of 40.

1975, June 17 **Tagged** ***Perf. 11***
1564 A967 10c **multicolored** .20 .20
P# block of 12, 6# 2.50 —
Margin block of 4, Mr. Zip, "Use Zip Code" and "Mail Early in the Day" .80 —
P# block of 16, 6#, Mr. Zip and slogans 3.40 —

Military Uniforms

Bicentenary of US Military Services. Nos. 1565-1566 alternate in one row, Nos. 1567-1568 in next row.

Soldier with Flintlock Musket, Uniform Button — A968

Sailor with Grappling Hook, First Navy Jack, 1775 — A969

Marine with Musket, Fullrigged Ship — A970

Militiaman with Musket and Powder Horn — A971

Designed by Edward Vebell.

PHOTOGRAVURE (Andreotti)
Plates of 200 subjects in four panes of 50.

1975, July 4 **Tagged** ***Perf. 11***
1565 A968 10c **multicolored** .20 .20
a. Tagging omitted —
1566 A969 10c **multicolored** .20 .20
1567 A970 10c **multicolored** .20 .20
1568 A971 10c **multicolored** .20 .20
a. Block of 4, #1565-1568 .85 .90
P# block of 12, 6# 2.50 —
P# block of 20, 6#, Mr. Zip and slogans 4.50 —
Margin block of 4, Mr. Zip and "Use Zip Code" 1.00 —

APOLLO SOYUZ SPACE ISSUE

Apollo Soyuz space test project, Russo-American cooperation, launched July 15; link-up, July 17. Nos. In the 1st row, No. 1569 is in 1st and 3rd space, No. 1570 is 2nd space; in the 2nd row No. 1570 is in 1st and 3rd space, No. 1569 in 2nd space, etc.

Participating US and USSR crews: Thomas P. Stafford, Donald K. Slayton, Vance D. Brand, Aleksei A. Leonov, Valery N. Kubasov.

Apollo and Soyuz after Link-up, and Earth — A972

Spacecraft before Link-up, Earth and Project Emblem — A973

Illustrations reduced.

Designed by Robert McCall (No. 1569) and Anatoly M. Aksamit of USSR (No. 1570).

PHOTOGRAVURE (Andreotti)
Plates of 96 subjects in four panes of 24 each.

1975, July 15 **Tagged** ***Perf. 11***
1569 A972 10c **multicolored** .20 .20
Pair with full horiz. gutter btwn. —
1570 A973 10c **multicolored** .20 .20
a. Pair, #1569-1570 .45 .40
P# block of 12, 6# 2.50 —
Margin block of 4, Mr. Zip, "Use Zip Code" .85 —
P# block of 16, 6#, Mr. Zip, "Use Zip Code" 3.40 —
Pair with full horiz. gutter btwn. —
b. As "a," tagging omitted *30.00* —
c. As "a," vert. pair imperf. horiz. *2,100.*
d. As "a," yellow omitted —

Nos. 1569-1570 totally imperforate are printer's waste.
See Russia Nos. 4339-4340.

INTERNATIONAL WOMEN'S YEAR ISSUE

International Women's Year 1975.

Worldwide Equality for Women A974

Designed by Miriam Schottland.

PHOTOGRAVURE (Andreotti)

Plates of 200 subjects in four panes of 50.

1975, Aug. 26		Tagged	Perf. 11x10½	
1571 A974 10c		**blue, orange & dark blue**	.20	.20
		P# block of 6, 3#	1.30	—
		Margin block of 4, Mr. Zip and "Use Zip Code"	.80	—
a.		Tagging omitted		10.00

US POSTAL SERVICE BICENTENNIAL ISSUE

Nos. 1572-1573 alternate in 1st row, Nos. 1574-1575 in 2nd row. This arrangement is repeated throughout the pane.

Stagecoach and Trailer Truck — A975

Old and New Locomotives A976

Early Mail Plane and Jet — A977

Satellite for Transmission of Mailgrams A978

Designed by James L. Womer.

PHOTOGRAVURE (Andreotti)

Plates of 200 subjects in four panes of 50.

1975, Sept. 3		Tagged	Perf. 11x10½	
1572 A975 10c		**multicolored**	.20	.20
1573 A976 10c		**multicolored**	.20	.20
1574 A977 10c		**multicolored**	.20	.20
1575 A978 10c		**multicolored**	.20	.20
a.		Block of 4, #1572-1575	.85	.90
		P# block of 12, 6#	2.50	—
		P# block of 20, 6#, Mr. Zip and slogans	4.50	—
		Margin block of 4, Mr. Zip and "Use Zip Code"	1.00	—
b.		As "a," red "10c" omitted	*7,500.*	

WORLD PEACE THROUGH LAW ISSUE

A prelude to 7th World Law Conference of the World Peace Through Law Center at Washington, D.C., Oct. 12-17.

Law Book, Gavel, Olive Branch and Globe — A979

Designed by Melbourne Brindle.

GIORI PRESS PRINTING

Plates of 200 subjects in four panes of 50.

1975, Sept. 29		Tagged	Perf. 11	
1576 A979 10c		**green, Prussian blue & rose brown**	.20	.20
		P# block of 4	.85	—
		Margin block of 4, Mr. Zip and "Use Zip Code"	.80	—
a.		Tagging omitted	7.50	
b.		Horiz. pair, imperf vert.	*7,500.*	

BANKING AND COMMERCE ISSUE

Banking and commerce in the U.S., and for the Centennial Convention of the American Bankers Association.

Designed by V. Jack Ruther.

Engine Turning, Indian Head Penny, Morgan-type Silver Dollar — A980

Seated Liberty Quarter, $20 Gold Double Eagle and Engine Turning A981

LITHOGRAPHED, ENGRAVED (Giori)

Plates of 160 subjects in four panes of 40.

1975, Oct. 6		Tagged	Perf. 11	
1577 A980 10c		**multicolored**	.25	.20
1578 A981 10c		**multicolored**	.25	.20
a.		Pair, #1577-1578	.50	.40
		P# block of 4	1.20	—
		Margin block of 4, Mr. Zip and "Use Zip Code"	1.00	—
b.		As "a," brown & blue (litho) omitted	*2,000.*	
c.		As "a," brown, blue & yellow (litho) omitted	*2,500.*	
d.		As No. 1578, tagging omitted		—

CHRISTMAS ISSUE

Madonna and Child, by Domenico Ghirlandaio — A982

Christmas Card, by Louis Prang, 1878 — A983

Designed by Stevan Dohanos.

PHOTOGRAVURE (Andreotti)

Plates of 200 subjects in four panes of 50.

1975, Oct. 14		Tagged	Perf. 11	
1579	A982 (10c)	**multicolored**	.20	.20
		P# block of 12, 6#	2.50	—
		Margin block of 4, Mr. Zip and "Use Zip Code"	.80	—
		Plate flaw ("d" damaged) (36741-36746 LL 47)	5.00	—
a.		Imperf., pair	*90.00*	
		Perf. 11.2		
1580	A983 (10c)	**multicolored**	.20	.20
		P# block of 12, 6#	2.50	—
		Margin block of 4, Mr. Zip and "Use Zip Code"	.80	—
a.		Imperf., pair	*90.00*	
c.		Perf. 10.9	.25	.20
		P# block of 12, 6#	3.50	—
		Margin block of 4, Mr. Zip and "Use Zip Code"	1.00	—
		Perf. 10.5x11.3		
1580B	A983 (10c)	**multicolored,**	.65	.20
		P# block of 12, 6#	15.00	—
		Margin block of 4, Mr. Zip and "Use Zip Code"	2.75	—

AMERICANA ISSUE

Inkwell and Quill — A984

Speaker's Stand — A985

Early Ballot Box — A987

Books, Bookmark, Eyeglasses — A988

Dome of Capitol — A994

Contemplation of Justice, by J. E. Fraser — A995

Early American Printing Press — A996

Torch, Statue of Liberty — A997

Liberty Bell — A998

Eagle and Shield — A999

Fort McHenry Flag (15 Stars) — A1001

Head, Statue of Liberty — A1002

Old North Church, Boston — A1003

Fort Nisqually, Wash. — A1004

Sandy Hook Lighthouse, NJ — A1005

Morris Township School No. 2, Devils Lake, ND — A1006

Iron "Betty" Lamp, Plymouth Colony, 17th-18th Centuries — A1007

Rush Lamp and Candle Holder — A1008

Kerosene Table Lamp — A1009

Railroad Conductor's Lantern, c. 1850 — A1010

Designed by: 2c, 4c, 15c, V. Jack Ruther Robert Hallock. 3c, Clarence Holbert. 9c, 10c, 11c, Walter Brooks. 12c, George Mercer. No. 1595, Bernard Glassman. No. 1596, James L. Womer.

ROTARY PRESS PRINTING

E.E. Plates of 400 subjects in four panes of 100.

1975-81 **Tagged** *Perf. 11x10½*

Size: 18½x22½mm

1581 A984 1c **dark blue,** *greenish,* shiny gum, *Dec. 8, 1977* .20 .20
P# block of 4 .25 —
Margin block of 4, "Use Zip Code" .20 —
Dull gum .20
P# block of 4 .50
Zip block of 4 .20
Pair with full vert. gutter btwn. —
a. Untagged (Bureau precanceled) 4.50 1.50
P# block of 4 22.50
Margin block of 4, "Use Zip Codes" 18.50
c. White paper, dull gum — —
d. Tagging omitted (not Bureau precanceled), shiny gum 4.50
Dull gum 4.00

1582 A985 2c **red brown,** *greenish,* shiny gum, *Dec. 8, 1977* .20 .20
P# block of 4 .25 —
Margin block of 4, "Use Zip Code" .20 —
Dull gum .20
P# block of 4 2.50
Zip block of 4 .50
a. Untagged (Bureau precanceled) 4.50 1.50
P# block of 4 22.50
Zip block of 4 18.50
b. Cream paper, dull gum, *1981* .20 .20
P# block of 4 .25
Zip block of 4 .20
c. Tagging omitted (not Bureau precanceled) 4.50

1584 A987 3c **olive,** *greenish,* shiny gum, *Dec. 8, 1977* .20 .20
P# block of 4 .30 —
Margin block of 4, "Use Zip Code" .25 —
Dull gum .20
P# block of 4 .50
Zip block of 4 .30
Pair with full horiz. gutter btwn. —
a. Untagged (Bureau precanceled) .75 .50
P# block of 4 9.50
Zip block of 4 5.00
b. Tagging omitted (not Bureau precanceled) 7.50

Values for No. 1584a are for the lines-only precancel. Also known with city precancels, and valued at $100 thus.

1585 A988 4c **rose magenta,** *cream,* shiny gum, *Dec. 8, 1977* .20 .20
P# block of 4 .40 —
Margin block of 4, "Use Zip Code" .35 —
Dull gum .20
P# block of 4 1.10
Zip block of 4 .65
a. Untagged (Bureau precanceled) 1.00 .75
P# block of 4 13.50
Zip block of 4 6.00
b. Tagging omitted (not Bureau precanceled), dull gum *65.00*
Shiny gum *35.00*

Values for No. 1585a are for the lines-only precancel. Also known with city precancels, and worth more thus.

Size: 17½x20½mm

1590 A994 9c **slate green** (from bklt. pane #1623a), *Mar. 11, 1977* .45 .20
Pair with full horiz. gutter between —

Perf. 10x9¾

1590A A994 9c **slate green** (from bklt. pane #1623Bc), *Mar. 11, 1977* 17.50 15.00

Size: 18½x22½mm

Perf. 11x10½

1591 A994 9c **slate green,** *gray,* shiny gum, *Nov. 24, 1975* .20 .20
P# block of 4 .85 —
Margin block of 4, "Use Zip Code" .80 —
Dull gum 1.00
P# block of 4 5.00
Zip block of 4 4.25
a. Untagged (Bureau precanceled) 1.75 1.00
P# block of 4 50.00
Zip block of 4 11.50
b. Tagging omitted (not Bureau precanceled) 5.00

Values for No. 1591a are for the lines-only precancel. Also known with city precancels, and valued at $32.50 thus.

1592 A995 10c **violet,** *gray,* shiny gum, *Nov. 17, 1977* .20 .20
P# block of 4 .90 —
Margin block of 4, "Use Zip Code" .80 —
Dull gum .20
P# block of 4 .90
Zip block of 4 .80
a. Untagged (Bureau precanceled, Chicago) 9.50 5.00
P# block of 4 95.00
Zip block of 4 42.50
b. Tagging omitted (not Bureau precanceled) 7.50

1593 A996 11c **orange,** *gray, Nov. 13, 1975* .20 .20
P# block of 4 .90 —
Margin block of 4, "Use Zip Code" .85 —
Pair with full horiz. gutter between —
a. Tagging omitted 4.00

1594 A997 12c **red brown,** *beige, Apr. 8, 1981* .25 .20
P# block of 4 1.60 —
Zip block of 4 1.10 —
a. Tagging omitted 5.00

1595 A998 13c **brown** (from bklt. pane), *Oct. 31, 1975* .30 .20
a. Booklet pane of 6 2.25 1.00
b. Booklet pane of 7 + label 2.25 1.00
c. Booklet pane of 8 2.25 1.00
d. Booklet pane of 5 + label, *Apr. 2, 1976* 1.75 1.00
e. Vert. pair, imperf. btwn. *1,250.*
f. Tagging omitted — —
g. Horiz. pair, imperf. btwn. —

Nos. 1595e and 1595g resulted from paper foldovers after perforating and before cutting into panes. Beware of printer's waste consisting of complete panes with perfs around all outside edges.

PHOTOGRAVURE (Andreotti)

Plates of 400 subjects in four panes of 100.

Perf. 11.2

1596 A999 13c **multicolored,** *Dec. 1, 1975* .25 .20
P# block of 12, 6# 3.25 —
P# block of 20, 6# and slogans 5.50 —
Margin block of 4, "Use Zip Code" 1.00 —
Pair with full horiz. gutter btwn. *150.00*
a. Imperf., pair *40.00* —
b. Yellow omitted *115.00* —
d. Line perforated *27.50* —
P# block of 12, 6# *375.00* —

On No. 1596 the entire sheet is perforated at one time so the perforations meet perfectly at the corners of the stamp. On No. 1596d the perforations do not line up perfectly and are perf. 11.

ENGRAVED (Combination Press)

Plates of 460 subjects (20x23) in panes of 100 (10x10)

1597 A1001 15c **gray, dark blue & red,** large block tagging, *June 30, 1978* .30 .20
P# block of 6 1.90 —
P# block of 20, 1-2# 6.50 —
a. Small block tagging .30 .20
P# block of 6 1.90 —
P# block of 20, 1-2# 6.50 —
b. Gray omitted *425.00*
c. Vert. strip of 3, imperf. btwn. and at top or bottom *450.00*
d. Tagging omitted 3.00
e. Imperf., vert. pair *15.00*

Plate number appears 3 times on each plate of 23 rows. With no separating gutters, each pane has only left or right sheet margin. Plate numbers appear on both margins; there are no slogans.

ENGRAVED

Perf. 11x10½

1598 A1001 15c **gray, dark blue & red** (from bklt. pane), *June 30, 1978* .40 .20
a. Booklet pane of 8 4.25 .80

1599 A1002 16c **blue,** *Mar. 31, 1978* .35 .20
P# block of 4 1.90 —
Margin block of 4, "Use Correct Zip Code" 1.40 —

1603 A1003 24c **red,** *blue, Nov. 14, 1975* .50 .20
P# block of 4 2.25 —
Margin block of 4, "Use Zip Code" 2.00 —
a. Tagging omitted 7.50

1604 A1004 28c **brown,** *blue,* shiny gum, *Aug. 11, 1978* .55 .20
P# block of 4 2.40 —
Margin block of 4, "Use Correct Zip Code" 2.25 —
Dull gum 1.10
P# block of 4 10.00
Zip block of 4 5.00

1605 A1005 29c **blue,** *light blue,* shiny gum, *Apr. 14, 1978* .60 .20
P# block of 4 3.00 —
Margin block of 4, "Use Correct Zip Code" 2.40 —
Dull gum 2.00
P# block of 4 15.00
Zip block of 4 9.00

1606 A1006 30c **green,** *blue, Aug. 27, 1979* .55 .20
P# block of 4 2.40 —
Margin block of 4, "Use Correct Zip Code" 2.25 —
a. Tagging omitted 65.00

LITHOGRAPHED AND ENGRAVED

Perf. 11

1608 A1007 50c **tan, black & orange,** *Sept. 11, 1979* .85 .20
P# block of 4 3.75 —
Margin block of 4, "Use Correct Zip Code" 3.50 —
a. Black omitted *250.00*
b. Vert. pair, imperf. horiz. *1,500.*
c. Tagging omitted 16.00

Beware of examples offered as No. 1608b that have blind perfs.

1610 A1008 $1 **tan, brown, orange & yellow,** *July 2, 1979* 2.00 .20
P# block of 4 8.50 —
Margin block of 4, "Use Correct Zip Code" 8.00 —
Pair with full vert. gutter btwn. —
a. Brown (engraved) omitted *225.00*
b. Tan, orange & yellow omitted *250.00*
c. Brown inverted *21,000.*
d. Tagging omitted *12.50*

1611 A1009 $2 **tan, dark green, orange & yellow,** *Nov. 16, 1978* 3.75 .75
P# block of 4 16.00 —
Margin block of 4, "Use Correct Zip Code" 15.00 —
a. Tagging omitted —

1612 A1010 $5 **tan, red brown, yellow & orange,** *Aug. 23, 1979* 8.50 1.75
P# block of 4 36.00 —
Margin block of 4, "Use Correct Zip Code" 34.00 —
Nos. 1581-1612 (23) 38.50 21.50

Nos. 1590, 1590A, 1595, 1598, 1623 and 1623b were issued only in booklets. All stamps have one or two straight edges.

Bureau Precancels: 1c, 3 diff., 2c, Chicago, Greensboro, NC, 3c, 6 diff., 4c, Chicago, lines only, No. 1591a, 4 diff., No. 1596, 5 diff., 30c, lines only, 50c, 2 spacings, lines only, $1, 2 spacings, lines only. The 30c, 50c, $1 and No. 1596 are precanceled on tagged stamps.

Six-string Guitar — A1011

Saxhorns — A1012

Drum — A1013

Steinway Grand Piano, 1857 — A1014

Designers: 3.1c, George Mercer. 7.7c, Susan Robb. 7.9c, Bernard Glassman. 10c, Walter Brooks. 15c, V. Jack Ruther.

COIL STAMPS
ENGRAVED

1975-79 *Perf. 10 Vertically*

1613	A1011	3.1c **brown**, *yellow, Oct. 25, 1979*	.20	.20
		Pair	.25	.20
		Joint line pair	1.25	—
a.		Untagged (Bureau precanceled, lines only)	.35	.35
		Pair	.70	.70
		Joint line pair	7.00	—
b.		Imperf., pair	*1,250.*	
		Joint line pair	*2,750.*	
1614	A1012	7.7c **brown**, *bright yellow, Nov. 20, 1976*	.20	.20
		Pair	.40	.20
		Joint line pair	.90	—
a.		Untagged (Bureau precanceled)	.40	.30
		Pair	.80	.60
		Joint line pair	3.25	—
b.		As "a," imperf., pair	1,500.	
		Joint line pair	*2,750.*	

A total of 160 different Bureau precancels were used by 153 cities.

No. 1614b is precanceled Washington, DC. Also exists with Marion, OH precancel; value $1,950 for pair.

1615	A1013	7.9c **carmine**, *yellow*, shiny gum, *Apr. 23, 1976*	.20	.20
		Pair	.40	.20
		Joint line pair	.75	—
		Dull gum	1.00	
		Pair	2.00	
		Joint line pair	6.00	
a.		Untagged (Bureau precanceled), shiny gum	.40	.40
		Pair	.80	.80
		Joint line pair	2.75	—
		Dull gum	.45	
		Pair	.90	
		Joint line pair	4.50	
b.		Imperf., pair	*550.00*	

A total of 109 different Bureau precancels were used by 107 cities plus two types of CAR. RT./SORT.

1615C	A1014	8.4c **dark blue**, *yellow*, shiny gum, *July 13, 1978*	.20	.20
		Pair	.40	.20
		Joint line pair	3.25	.30
d.		Untagged (Bureau precanceled), shiny gum	.50	.40
		Pair	1.00	.80
		Joint line pair	4.25	—
		Dull gum	.40	
		Pair	.80	
		Joint line pair	3.25	
e.		As "d," pair, imperf. between	45.00	
		Joint line pair	*110.00*	
f.		As "d," imperf., pair	15.00	
		Joint line pair	*25.00*	

A total of 145 different Bureau precancels were used by 144 cities.

No. 1615Ce is precanceled with lines only. No. 1615Cf is precanceled with lines only (value shown) and also exists in pairs precanceled Newark, N.J. ($27.50), Brownstown, Ind. ($1,000.), Oklahoma City, Okla. ($1,500.) and Washington, DC ($1,500).

1616	A994	9c **slate green**, *gray, Mar. 5, 1976*	.20	.20
		Pair	.40	.20
		Joint line pair	.90	—
a.		Imperf., pair	*135.00*	
		Joint line pair	*300.00*	
b.		Untagged (Bureau precanceled), shiny gum	1.15	.75
		Pair	2.30	1.50
		Joint line pair	42.50	—
		Dull gum	.75	
		Pair	1.50	
		Joint line pair	19.50	
c.		As "b," imperf., pair	*650.00*	
		Joint line pair	—	

Values for No. 1616b with shiny gum are for the lines-only precancel. Also known with city precancels, and worth more thus.

No. 1616c is precanceled Pleasantville, NY.

1617	A995	10c **violet**, *gray*, shiny gum, *Nov. 4, 1977*	.20	.20
		Pair	.40	.20
		Joint line pair	1.00	—
		Dull gum	.30	
		Pair	.60	
		Joint line pair	2.50	
a.		Untagged (Bureau precanceled, shiny gum)	42.50	1.35
		Pair	90.00	2.75
		Joint line pair	*1,150.*	—
		Dull gum	1.35	
		Pair	2.75	
		Joint line pair	47.50	
b.		Imperf., pair, shiny gum	55.00	
		Joint line pair, shiny gum	*115.00*	
		Imperf., pair, dull gum	55.00	
		Joint line pair, dull gum	115.00	
c.		As "a," imperf pair, dull gum	—	
		Joint line pair, dull gum	—	
1618	A998	13c **brown**, shiny gum, *Nov. 25, 1975*	.25	.20
		Pair	.50	.20
		Joint line pair	.75	—
		Dull gum	1.50	
		Pair	3.00	
		Joint line pair	9.00	
a.		Untagged (Bureau precanceled), shiny gum	5.75	.75
		Pair	12.00	1.50
		Joint line pair	90.00	—
		Dull gum	.75	
		Pair	1.50	
		Joint line pair	35.00	
b.		Imperf., pair	22.50	
		Joint line pair	45.00	
g.		Vertical pair, imperf. between	—	
h.		As "a," imperf., pair	—	

Values for No. 1618a with shiny gum are for the lines-only precancel. Also known with city precancels, and worth more thus.

1618C	A1001	15c **gray, dark blue & red**, *June 30, 1978*	.75	.20
		Pair	1.50	.20
d.		Imperf., pair	20.00	
e.		Pair, imperf. between	*135.00*	
f.		Gray omitted	30.00	
i.		Tagging omitted	50.00	
1619	A1002	16c **ultramarine**, overall tagging, *Mar. 31, 1978*	.35	.20
		Pair	.70	.20
		Joint line pair	1.50	—
a.		Block tagging	.50	.20
		Pair	1.00	.25
		Nos. 1613-1619 (9)	2.55	1.80

No. 1619a (the Huck press printing) has a white background without bluish tinge, is a fraction of a millimeter smaller than No. 1619 (the Cottrell press printing) and has no joint lines.

Nos. 1615a, 1615d, 1616b, 1617a, 1618a, issued also with dull gum.

Bureau Precancels: 9c, 7 diff., 10c, 3 diff., 13c, 12 diff. See Nos. 1811, 1813, 1816.

13-Star Flag over Independence Hall — A1015

Flag over Capitol — A1016

Designers: No. 1622, Melbourne Brindle. No. 1623, Esther Porter.

Panes of 100 (10x10) each.

1975-81 *Perf. 11x10¾*

1622	A1015	13c **dk blue, red & brown red**, *Nov. 15, 1975*	.25	.20
		P# block of 20, 2-3#, 2-3 Zip, 2-3 Mail Early	5.75	—
a.		Horiz. pair, imperf. between	45.00	
b.		Vertical pair, imperf.	*425.00*	
e.		Horiz. pair, imperf. vert.	—	
f.		Tagging omitted	4.00	

No. 1622 was printed on the Multicolored Huck Press. Plate markings are at top or bottom of pane. It has large block tagging and nearly vertical multiple gum ridges.

See note after No. 1338F for marginal markings.

Perf. 11¼

1622C	A1015	13c **dk blue, red & brown red**, *1981*	1.00	.25
		P# block of 20, 1-2#, 1-2 Zip	32.50	—
		P# block of 6	20.00	—
d.		Vertical pair, imperf	125.00	

No. 1622C was printed on the Combination Press. Plate markings are at sides of pane. It has small block tagging and shiny flat gum.

See note after No. 1703.

BOOKLET STAMPS

1977, Mar. 11 **Engr.** *Perf. 11x10½*

1623	A1016	13c **blue & red**	.25	.20
a.		Booklet pane, 1 #1590 + 7 #1623	2.25	1.25
d.		Pair, #1590 & #1623	.70	*1.00*
f.		Tagging omitted		—
g.		As "a," tagging omitted	—	

Perf. 10x9¾

1623B	A1016	13c **blue & red**	.80	.80
c.		Booklet pane, 1 #1590A + 7 #1623B	22.50	—
e.		Pair, #1590A & #1623B	18.50	18.50

COIL STAMP

1975, Nov. 15 *Perf. 10 Vertically*

1625	A1015	13c **dk blue, red & brown red**	.35	.20
		Pair	.70	.20
a.		Imperf., pair	20.00	
b.		Tagging omitted		—

No. 1625 was printed on both the Huck and "B" presses. Huck press printings have pebbled gum (gummed on press), while "B" press printings have smooth gum (pregummed paper). Huck press printings often show portions of a joint line, but this feature is not consistent. Values for coils and imperf coils the same for both varieties.

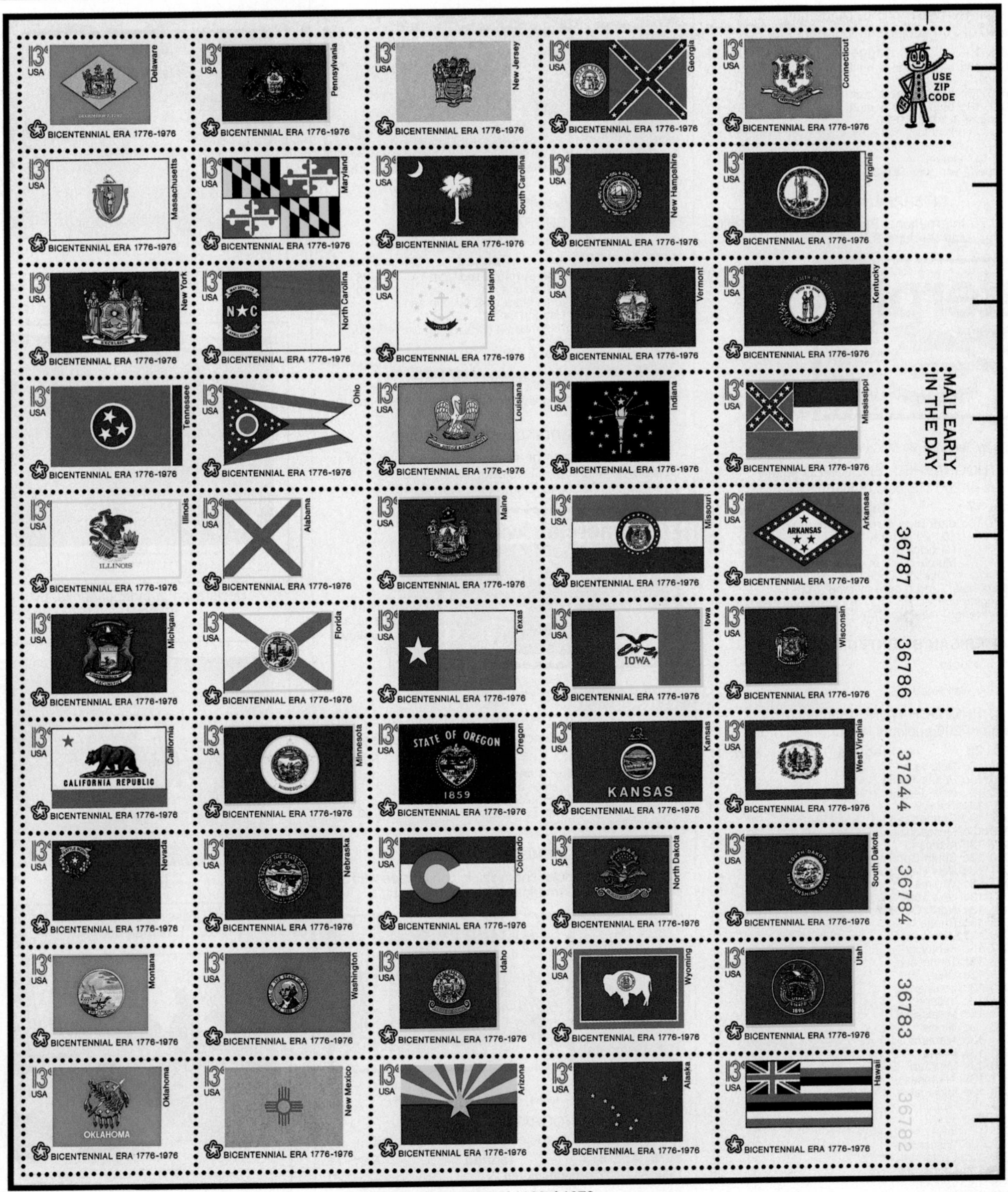

State Flags A1023-A1072

AMERICAN BICENTENNIAL ISSUE
The Spirit of '76

Designed after painting by Archibald M. Willard in Abbot Hall, Marblehead, Massachusetts. Nos. 1629-1631 printed in continuous design.

Left panes contain 3 No. 1631a and one No. 1629; right panes contain one No. 1631 and 3 No. 1631a.

Drummer Boy — A1019

Old Drummer — A1020

Fifer — A1021

Designed by Vincent E. Hoffman.

PHOTOGRAVURE (Andreotti)

Plates of 200 subjects in four panes of 50.

1976, Jan. 1 Tagged *Perf. 11*

1629	A1019	13c **blue violet & multi**	.25	.20
a.		Imperf., vert. pair	—	
1630	A1020	13c **blue violet & multi**	.25	.20
1631	A1021	13c **blue violet & multi**	.25	.20
a.		Strip of 3, #1629-1631	.75	.75
		P# block of 12, 5#	3.50	—
		P# block of 20, 5#, slogans	5.75	—
b.		As "a," imperf.	*850.00*	
c.		Imperf., vert. pair, #1631	*700.00*	

INTERPHIL ISSUE

Interphil 76 International Philatelic Exhibition, Philadelphia, Pa., May 29-June 6.

"Interphil 76" A1022

Designed by Terrence W. McCaffrey.

LITHOGRAPHED, ENGRAVED (Giori)

Plates of 200 subjects of four panes of 50.

1976, Jan. 17 Tagged *Perf. 11*

1632	A1022	13c **dark blue & red (engr.), ultra. & red (litho.)**	.20	.20
		P# block of 4	1.00	—
		Margin block of 4, Mr. Zip and "Use Zip Code"	1.00	—
a.		Dark blue & red (engr.) missing (CM)	—	
b.		Tagging omitted	85.00	—
c.		Red (engr,) missing (CM)	—	

AMERICAN BICENTENNIAL ISSUE

Illustration reduced.

Designed by Walt Reed.

PHOTOGRAVURE (Andreotti)

Plates of 200 subjects in four panes of 50.

1976, Feb. 23 Tagged *Perf. 11*

1633	A1023	13c Delaware	.30	.25
1634	A1024	13c Pennsylvania	.30	.25
1635	A1025	13c New Jersey	.30	.25
1636	A1026	13c Georgia	.30	.25
1637	A1027	13c Connecticut	.30	.25
1638	A1028	13c Massachusetts	.30	.25
1639	A1029	13c Maryland	.30	.25
1640	A1030	13c South Carolina	.30	.25
1641	A1031	13c New Hampshire	.30	.25
1642	A1032	13c Virginia	.30	.25
1643	A1033	13c New York	.30	.25
1644	A1034	13c North Carolina	.30	.25
1645	A1035	13c Rhode Island	.30	.25
1646	A1036	13c Vermont	.30	.25
1647	A1037	13c Kentucky	.30	.25
1648	A1038	13c Tennessee	.30	.25
1649	A1039	13c Ohio	.30	.25
1650	A1040	13c Louisiana	.30	.25
1651	A1041	13c Indiana	.30	.25
1652	A1042	13c Mississippi	.30	.25
1653	A1043	13c Illinois	.30	.25
1654	A1044	13c Alabama	.30	.25
1655	A1045	13c Maine	.30	.25
1656	A1046	13c Missouri	.30	.25
1657	A1047	13c Arkansas	.30	.25
1658	A1048	13c Michigan	.30	.25
1659	A1049	13c Florida	.30	.25
1660	A1050	13c Texas	.30	.25
1661	A1051	13c Iowa	.30	.25
1662	A1052	13c Wisconsin	.30	.25
1663	A1053	13c California	.30	.25
1664	A1054	13c Minnesota	.30	.25
1665	A1055	13c Oregon	.30	.25
1666	A1056	13c Kansas	.30	.25
1667	A1057	13c West Virginia	.30	.25
a.		Tagging omitted		.25
1668	A1058	13c Nevada	.30	.25
1669	A1059	13c Nebraska	.30	.25
1670	A1060	13c Colorado	.30	.25
1671	A1061	13c North Dakota	.30	.25
1672	A1062	13c South Dakota	.30	.25
1673	A1063	13c Montana	.30	.25
1674	A1064	13c Washington	.30	.25
1675	A1065	13c Idaho	.30	.25
1676	A1066	13c Wyoming	.30	.25
1677	A1067	13c Utah	.30	.25
1678	A1068	13c Oklahoma	.30	.25
1679	A1069	13c New Mexico	.30	.25
1680	A1070	13c Arizona	.30	.25
1681	A1071	13c Alaska	.30	.25
1682	A1072	13c Hawaii	.30	.25
a.		Pane of 50	17.50	15.00

TELEPHONE CENTENNIAL ISSUE

Centenary of first telephone call by Alexander Graham Bell, March 10, 1876.

Bell's Telephone Patent Application, 1876 — A1073

Designed by George Tscherny.

ENGRAVED (Giori)

Plates of 200 subjects in four panes of 50.

1976, Mar. 10 Tagged *Perf. 11*

1683	A1073	13c **black, purple & red,** *tan*	.25	.20
		P# block of 4	1.10	—
		Margin block of 4, Mr. Zip and "Use Zip Code"	1.00	—
a.		Black & purple missing (EP)	*450.00*	
b.		Red missing (EP)	—	
c.		All colors missing (EP)	—	

On No. 1683a, the errors have only tiny traces of red present, so are best collected as a horiz. strip of 5 with 2 or 3 error stamps. No. 1683c also must be collected as a transitional strip.

COMMERCIAL AVIATION ISSUE

50th anniversary of first contract airmail flights: Dearborn, Mich. to Cleveland, Ohio, Feb. 15, 1926; and Pasco, Wash. to Elko, Nev., Apr. 6, 1926.

Ford-Pullman Monoplane and Laird Swallow Biplane A1074

Designed by Robert E. Cunningham.

PHOTOGRAVURE (Andreotti)

Plates of 200 subjects in four panes of 50 each

1976, Mar. 19 Tagged *Perf. 11*

1684	A1074	13c **blue & multicolored**	.25	.20
		P# block of 10, 5#	2.75	—
		Margin block of 4, Mr. Zip and "Use Zip Code"	1.00	—
a.		Tagging omitted		—

CHEMISTRY ISSUE

Honoring American chemists, in conjunction with the centenary of the American Chemical Society.

Various Flasks, Separatory Funnel, Computer Tape — A1075

Designed by Ken Davies.

PHOTOGRAVURE (Andreotti)

Plates of 200 subjects in four panes of 50.

1976, Apr. 6 Tagged *Perf. 11*

1685	A1075	13c **multicolored**	.25	.20
		P# block of 12, 6#	3.25	—
		Margin block of 4, Mr. Zip and "Use Zip Code"	1.00	—
		Pair with full vert. gutter btwn.	—	

AMERICAN BICENTENNIAL ISSUES

SOUVENIR SHEETS

Designs, from Left to Right, No. 1686: a, Two British officers. b, Gen. Benjamin Lincoln. c, George Washington. d, John Trumbull, Col. Cobb, von Steuben, Lafayette, Thomas Nelson. e, Alexander Hamilton, John Laurens, Walter Stewart (all vert.).

No. 1687: a, John Adams, Roger Sherman, Robert R. Livingston. b, Jefferson, Franklin. c, Thomas Nelson, Jr., Francis Lewis, John Witherspoon, Samuel Huntington. d, John Hancock, Charles Thomson. e, George Read, John Dickinson, Edward Rutledge (a, d, vert., b, c, e, horiz.).

No. 1688: a, Boatsman. b, Washington. c, Flag bearer. d, Men in boat. e, Men on shore (a, d, horiz., b, c, e, vert.).

No. 1689: a, Two officers. b, Washington. c, Officer, black horse. d, Officer, white horse. e, Three soldiers (a, c, e, horiz., b, d, vert.).

Surrender of Cornwallis at Yorktown, by John Trumbull — A1076

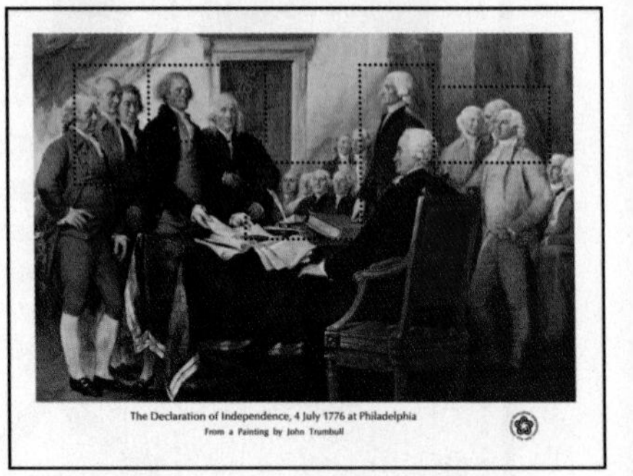

Declaration of Independence, by John Trumbull — A1077

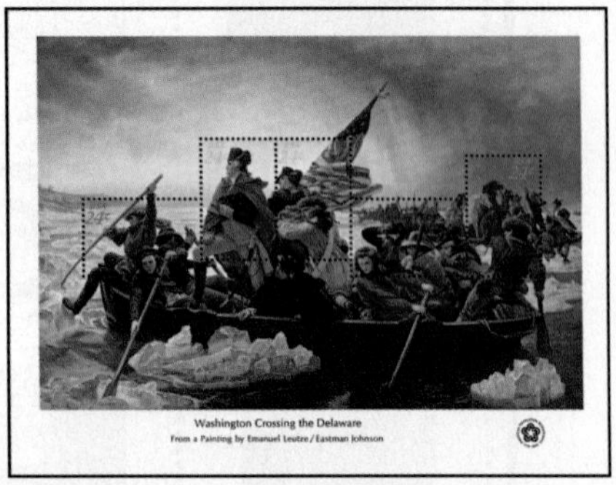

Washington Crossing the Delaware, by Emmanuel Leutze / Eastman Johnson — A1078

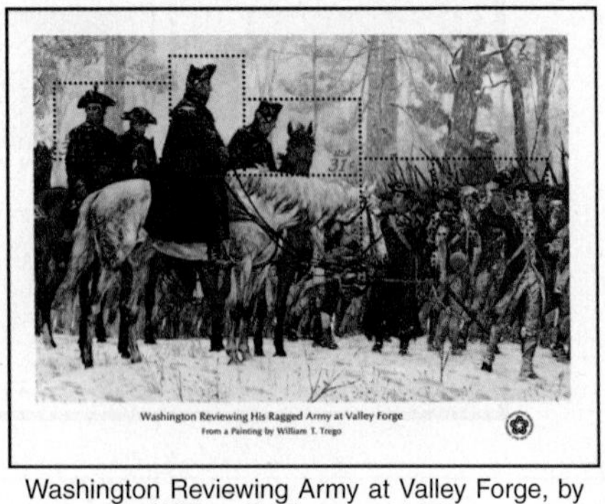

Washington Reviewing Army at Valley Forge, by William T. Trego — A1079

Illustrations reduced.

Designed by Vincent E. Hoffman.

LITHOGRAPHED

Plates of 30 subjects in six panes of 5 each.

1976, May 29 Tagged *Perf. 11*

1686	A1076	Sheet of 5	3.25	2.25
a.-e.		13c **multicolored**	.45	.40
f.		"USA/13c" omitted on "b," "c" & "d," imperf, tagging omitted	—	*2,000.*
g.		"USA/13c" omitted on "a" & "e"	*450.00*	—
h.		Imperf., tagging omitted		*2,250.*
i.		"USA/13c" omitted on "b," "c" & "d"	*450.00*	
j.		"USA/13c" double on "b"	—	
k.		"USA/13c" omitted on "c" & "d"	*750.00*	
l.		"USA/13c" omitted on "e"	*550.00*	
m.		"USA/13c" omitted, imperf., tagging omitted		—
n.		As "g," imperf., tagging omitted		—
o.		"USA/13c" missing on "a" (PS)	—	

p.		As No. 1686, tagging omitted		—
q.		"USA/13c" omitted on "a"	—	
1687	A1077	Sheet of 5	4.25	3.25
a.-e.		18c **multicolored**	.55	.55
f.		Design & marginal inscriptions omitted	*3,250.*	
g.		"USA/18c" omitted on "a" & "c"	*600.00*	
h.		"USA/18c" omitted on "b," "d" & "e"	*450.00*	
i.		"USA/18c" omitted on "d"	*475.00*	*475.00*
j.		Black omitted in design	*2,000.*	
k.		"USA/18c" omitted, imperf., tagging omitted	*2,000.*	
m.		"USA/18c" omitted on "b" & "e"	*500.00*	
n.		"USA/18c" omitted on "b" & "d"	*1,000.*	
p.		Imperf. (tagged)	*1,000.*	
q.		"USA/18c" omitted on "c"	—	
r.		Yellow omitted	—	
s.		"USA/18c" missing on "a," "c" and "d" (PS)	—	
t.		"USA/18c" missing on "a" and "d" (PS)	—	
1688	A1078	Sheet of 5	5.25	4.25
a.-e.		24c **multicolored**	.70	.70
f.		"USA/24c" omitted, imperf., tagging omitted	*1,500.*	
g.		"USA/24c" omitted on "d" & "e"	*450.00*	*450.00*
h.		Design & marginal inscriptions omitted	*2,750.*	
i.		"USA/24c" omitted on "a," "b" & "c"	*500.00*	*500.00*
j.		Imperf., tagging omitted	*1,750.*	
k.		"USA/24c" of "d" & "e" inverted	—	
l.		As "i," imperf, tagging omitted	*3,250.*	—
m.		Tagging omitted on "e" and "f"	—	
n.		As No. 1688, perfs inverted and reversed	*450.00*	
o.		As No. 1688, tagging omitted	—	
1689	A1079	Sheet of 5	6.25	5.25
a.-e.		31c **multicolored**	.85	.85
f.		"USA/31c" omitted, imperf.	*1,500.*	
g.		"USA/31c" omitted on "a" & "c"	*400.00*	
h.		"USA/31c" omitted on "b," "d" & "e"	*500.00*	—
i.		"USA/31c" omitted on "e"	*450.00*	
j.		Black omitted in design	*1,500.*	
k.		Imperf., tagging omitted		*2,000.*
l.		"USA/31c" omitted on "b" & "d"	*600.00*	
m.		"USA/31c" omitted on "a," "c" & "e"	—	
n.		As "m," imperf., tagging omitted	—	
p.		As "h," imperf., tagging omitted		*2,000.*
q.		As "g," imperf., tagging omitted	*2,750.*	
r.		"USA/31c" omitted on "d" & "e"	*600.00*	
s.		As "f," tagging omitted	*2,250.*	
t.		"USA/31c" omitted on "d"	*750.00*	
u.		As No. 1689, tagging omitted	—	
v.		As No. 1689, perfs inverted	—	
w.		"USA/31c" missing on "a," "b," "c" and "d" (PS)	—	
x.		As No. 1689, tagging omitted	—	
		Nos. 1686-1689 (4)	19.00	

Issued in connection with Interphil 76 International Philatelic Exhibition, Philadelphia, Pa., May 29-June 6. Size of sheets: 153x204mm; size of stamps: 25x39½mm, 39½x25mm.

Benjamin Franklin

American Bicentennial: Benjamin Franklin (1706-1790), deputy postmaster general for the colonies (1753-1774) and statesman. Design based on marble bust by anonymous Italian sculptor after terra cotta bust by Jean Jacques Caffieri, 1777. Map published by R. Sayer and J. Bennett in London.

Franklin and Map of North America, 1776 — A1080

Designed by Bernard Reilander (Canada).

LITHOGRAPHED, ENGRAVED (Giori)

Plates of 200 subjects in four panes of 50.

1976, June 1		**Tagged**		*Perf. 11*
1690	A1080 13c	**ultramarine & multicolored**	.25	.20
		P# block of 4	1.10	—
		Margin block of 4, Mr. Zip and "Use Zip Code"	1.00	—
a.		Light blue omitted	*200.00*	
b.		Tagging omitted	7.50	

See Canada No. 691.

Declaration of Independence

Designed after painting of Declaration of Independence, by John Trumbull, in the Rotunda of the Capitol, Washington, D.C. Nos. 1691-1694 printed in continuous design. Left panes contain 10 No. 1694a and 5 each of Nos. 1691-1692; right panes contain 5 each of Nos. 1693-1694 and 10 No. 1694a.

A1081

A1082

A1083

A1084

Designed by Vincent E. Hoffman.

PHOTOGRAVURE (Andreotti)

Plates of 200 subjects in four panes of 50.

1976, July 4		**Tagged**		*Perf. 11*
1691	A1081 13c	**blue & multicolored**	.30	.20
1692	A1082 13c	**blue & multicolored**	.30	.20
1693	A1083 13c	**blue & multicolored**	.30	.20
1694	A1084 13c	**blue & multicolored**	.30	.20
a.		Strip of 4, #1691-1694	1.20	1.10
		P# block of 20, 5#, "Mail Early in the Day," Mr. Zip and "Use Zip Code"	7.25	—
		P# block of 16, 5#, "Mail Early in the Day"	6.00	—
		Margin block of 4, Mr. Zip and "Use Zip Code"	1.25	—

OLYMPIC GAMES ISSUE

12th Winter Olympic Games, Innsbruck, Austria, Feb. 4-15, and 21st Summer Olympic Games, Montreal, Canada, July 17-Aug. 1. Nos. 1695-1696 alternate in one row, Nos. 1697-1698 in other row.

Diving — A1085

Skiing — A1086

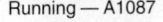

Running — A1087

Skating — A1088

Designed by Donald Moss.

PHOTOGRAVURE (Andreotti)

Plates of 200 subjects in four panes of 50.

1976, July 16		**Tagged**		*Perf. 11*
1695	A1085 13c	**multicolored**	.30	.20
1696	A1086 13c	**multicolored**	.30	.20
1697	A1087 13c	**multicolored**	.30	.20
1698	A1088 13c	**multicolored**	.30	.20
a.		Block of 4, #1695-1698	1.20	1.20
		P# block of 12, 6#	4.00	—
		P# block of 20, 6#, Mr. Zip and slogans	8.75	—
		Margin block of 4, Mr. Zip and "Use Zip Code"	1.40	—
b.		As "a," imperf.	*575.00*	

CLARA MAASS ISSUE

Clara Louise Maass (1876-1901), volunteer in fight against yellow fever, birth centenary.

Clara Maass and Newark German Hospital Pin — A1089

Designed by Paul Calle.

PHOTOGRAVURE (Andreotti)

Plates of 160 subjects in four panes of 40.

1976, Aug. 18		**Tagged**		*Perf. 11*
1699	A1089 13c	**multicolored**	.25	.20
		P# block of 12, 6#	4.00	—
		Margin block of 4, Mr. Zip, "Use Zip Code" and "Mail Early in the Day"	1.00	—
a.		Horiz. pair, imperf. vert.	*400.00*	

ADOLPH S. OCHS ISSUE

Adolph S. Ochs (1858-1935), publisher of the New York Times, 1896-1935.

Adolph S. Ochs — A1090

Designed by Bradbury Thompson; photograph by S. J. Woolf.

GIORI PRESS PRINTING

Plates of 128 subjects in four panes of 32 (8x4).

1976, Sept. 18		**Tagged**		*Perf. 11*
1700	A1090 13c	**black & gray**	.25	.20
		P# block of 4	1.10	
		Margin block of 4, Mr. Zip and "Use Zip Code"	.90	—
a.		Tagging omitted	*50.00*	—

CHRISTMAS ISSUE

Nativity, by John Singleton Copley A1091

"Winter Pastime," by Nathaniel Currier A1092

Designers: No. 1701, Bradbury Thompson after 1776 painting in Museum of Fine Arts, Boston. No. 1702, Stevan Dohanos after 1855 lithograph in Museum of the City of New York.

PHOTOGRAVURE (Andreotti)

Plates of 200 subjects in four panes of 50.

1976, Oct. 27		**Tagged**	***Perf. 11***	
1701	A1091 13c	**multicolored**	.25	.20
		P# block of 12, 6#	3.25	—
		Margin block of 4, Mr. Zip and "Use Zip Code"	1.00	—
a.		Imperf., pair	*85.00*	
1702	A1092 13c	**multi,** overall tagging	.25	.20
		P# block of 10, 5#	2.75	—
		Margin block of 4, Mr. Zip and "Use Zip Code"	1.00	—
a.		Imperf., pair	*90.00*	

Plates of 230 (10x23) subjects in panes of 50 (5x10)

Tagged, Block

1703	A1092 13c	**multicolored**	.25	.20
		P# block of 20, 5-8#	6.00	—
a.		Imperf., pair	*90.00*	
b.		Vert. pair, imperf. between	*325.00*	
c.		Tagging omitted	12.50	
d.		Red omitted	—	
e.		Yellow omitted	—	

No. 1702 has overall tagging. Lettering at base is black and usually ½mm below design. As a rule, no "snowflaking" in sky or pond. Pane of 50 has margins on 4 sides with slogans. Plate Nos. 37465-37478.

No. 1703 has block tagging the size of printed area. Lettering at base is gray black and usually ¾mm below design. "Snowflaking" generally in sky and pond. Plate Nos. 37617-37621 or 37634-37638.

Examples of No. 1703 are known with various amounts of red or yellow missing. Nos. 1703d-1703e are stamps with the colors totally omitted. Expertization is recommended.

COMBINATION PRESS

Cylindrical plates consist of 23 rows of subjects, 10 across for commemoratives (230 subjects), 20 across for definitives (460 subjects), with selvage on the two outer edges only. Guillotining through the perforations creates individual panes of 50 or 100 with selvage on one side only.

Failure of the guillotine to separate through the perforations resulted in straight edges on some stamps. Perforating teeth along the center column and the tenth rows were removed for issues released on or after May 31, 1984 (the 10c Richard Russell, for definitives; the 20c Horace Moses, for commemoratives), creating panes with straight edged stamps on three sides.

Three sets of plate numbers, copyright notices (starting with No. 1787), and zip insignia (starting with No. 1927) are arranged identically on the left and right sides of the plate so that each pane has at least one of each marking. The markings adjacent to any particular row are repeated either seven or eight rows away on the cylinder.

Fifteen combinations of the three marginal markings and blank rows are possible on panes.

AMERICAN BICENTENNIAL ISSUE

Washington at Princeton

Washington's Victory over Lord Cornwallis at Princeton, N.J., bicentenary.

Washington, Nassau Hall, Hessian Prisoners and 13-star Flag, by Charles Willson Peale — A1093

Designed by Bradbury Thompson.

PHOTOGRAVURE (Andreotti)

Plates of 160 subjects in four panes of 40.

1977, Jan. 3		**Tagged**	***Perf. 11***	
1704	A1093 13c	**multicolored**	.25	.20
		P# block of 10, 5#	2.75	—
		Margin block of 4, Mr. Zip and "Use Zip Code", "Mail Early in the Day"	1.00	—
a.		Horiz. pair, imperf. vert.	*500.00*	
b.		Black (inscriptions) missing (PS)	—	

SOUND RECORDING ISSUE

Centenary of the invention of the phonograph by Thomas Alva Edison and development of sophisticated recording industry.

Tin Foil Phonograph A1094

Designed by Walter and Naiad Einsel.

LITHOGRAPHED, ENGRAVED (Giori)

Plates of 200 subjects in four panes of 50.

1977, Mar. 23		**Tagged**	***Perf. 11***	
1705	A1094 13c	**black & multicolored**	.25	.20
		P# block of 4	1.10	—
		Margin block of 4, Mr. Zip and "Use Zip Code"	1.00	—

AMERICAN FOLK ART SERIES

Pueblo Pottery

Pueblo art, 1880-1920, from Museums in New Mexico, Arizona and Colorado.

Nos. 1706-1709 are printed in blocks and strips of 4 in panes of 40. In the 1st row Nos. 1706-1709 are in sequence as listed. In the 2nd row Nos. 1708-1709 are followed by Nos. 1706-1709, 1708-1709.

Zia Pot — A1095

San Ildefonso Pot — A1096

Hopi Pot — A1097

Acoma Pot — A1098

Designed by Ford Ruthling.

PHOTOGRAVURE (Andreotti)

Plates of 160 subjects in four panes of 40.

1977, Apr. 13		**Tagged**	***Perf. 11***	
1706	A1095 13c	**multicolored**	.25	.20
1707	A1096 13c	**multicolored**	.25	.20
1708	A1097 13c	**multicolored**	.25	.20
1709	A1098 13c	**multicolored**	.25	.20
a.		Block or strip of 4, #1706-1709	1.00	1.00
		P# block of 10, 5#	2.75	—
		P# block of 16, 5#; Mr. Zip and slogans	4.25	—
		Margin block of 6, Mr. Zip and "Use Zip Code" "Mail Early in the Day"	1.50	—
b.		As "a," imperf. vert.	*2,000.*	

LINDBERGH FLIGHT ISSUE

Charles A. Lindbergh's solo transatlantic flight from New York to Paris, 50th anniversary.

Spirit of St. Louis A1099

Designed by Robert E. Cunningham.

PHOTOGRAVURE (Andreotti)

Plates of 200 subjects in four panes of 50.

1977, May 20		**Tagged**	***Perf. 11***	
1710	A1099 13c	**multicolored**	.25	.20
		P# block of 12, 6#	3.25	—
		Margin block of 4, Mr. Zip and "Use Zip Code"	1.00	—
a.		Imperf., pair	*850.00*	

Beware of private overprints on No. 1710.

COLORADO STATEHOOD ISSUE

Issued to honor Colorado as the "Centennial State." It achieved statehood in 1876.

Columbine and Rocky Mountains — A1100

Designed by V. Jack Ruther.

PHOTOGRAVURE (Andreotti)

Plates of 200 subjects in four panes of 50.

1977, May 21		**Tagged**	***Perf. 11***	
1711	A1100 13c	**multicolored**	.25	.20
		P# block of 12, 6#	3.25	—
		Margin block of 4, Mr. Zip and "Use Zip Code"	1.00	—
a.		Horiz. pair, imperf. between	—	
b.		Horiz. pair, imperf. vertically	*750.00*	
c.		Perf. 11.2	.35	.25
		P# block of 12, 6#	20.00	

Perforations do not run through the sheet margin on about 10 percent of the sheets of No. 1711.

BUTTERFLY ISSUE

Nos. 1712-1713 alternate in 1st row, Nos. 1714-1715 in 2nd row. This arrangement is repeated throughout the pane. Butterflies represent different geographic US areas.

Swallowtail A1101

Checkerspot A1102

Dogface A1103

Orange-Tip A1104

Designed by Stanley Galli.

PHOTOGRAVURE (Andreotti)

Plates of 200 subjects in four panes of 50.

1977, June 6	**Tagged**	***Perf. 11***	
1712 A1101 13c	**tan & multicolored**	.25	.20
1713 A1102 13c	**tan & multicolored**	.25	.20
1714 A1103 13c	**tan & multicolored**	.25	.20
1715 A1104 13c	**tan & multicolored**	.25	.20
a.	Block of 4, #1712-1715	1.00	1.00
	P# block of 12, 6#	3.25	—
	P# block of 20, 6#, Mr. Zip and slogans	5.50	—
	Margin block of 4, Mr. Zip and "Use Zip Code"	1.05	—
b.	As "a," imperf. horiz.	*15,000.*	

AMERICAN BICENTENNIAL ISSUES
Marquis de Lafayette

200th anniversary of Lafayette's Landing on the coast of South Carolina, north of Charleston.

Marquis de Lafayette — A1105

Designed by Bradbury Thompson.

GIORI PRESS PRINTING

Plates of 160 subjects in four panes of 40.

1977, June 13	**Tagged**	***Perf. 11***	
1716 A1105 13c	**blue, black & red**	.25	.20
	P# block of 4	1.10	—
	Margin block of 4, Mr. Zip and "Use Zip Code"	1.00	—
a.	Red missing (PS)		—

Skilled Hands for Independence

Nos. 1717-1718 alternate in 1st row, Nos. 1719-1720 in 2nd row. This arrangement is repeated throughout the pane.

Seamstress A1106

Blacksmith A1107

Wheelwright A1108

Leatherworker A1109

Designed by Leonard Everett Fisher.

PHOTOGRAVURE (Andreotti)

Plates of 200 subjects in four panes of 50.

1977, July 4	**Tagged**	***Perf. 11***	
1717 A1106 13c	**multicolored**	.25	.20
1718 A1107 13c	**multicolored**	.25	.20
1719 A1108 13c	**multicolored**	.25	.20
1720 A1109 13c	**multicolored**	.25	.20
a.	Block of 4, #1717-1720	1.00	1.00
	P# block of 12, 6#	3.25	
	P# block of 20, 6#, Mr. Zip and slogans	5.50	—
	Margin block of 4, Mr. Zip and "Use Zip Code"	1.05	—

PEACE BRIDGE ISSUE

50th anniversary of the Peace Bridge, connecting Buffalo (Fort Porter), N.Y. and Fort Erie, Ontario.

Peace Bridge and Dove — A1110

Designed by Bernard Brussel-Smith (wood-cut).

ENGRAVED

Plates of 200 subjects in four panes of 50.

1977, Aug. 4	**Tagged**	***Perf. 11x10½***	
1721 A1110 13c	**blue**	.25	.20
	P# block of 4	1.10	—
	Margin block of 4, Mr. Zip and "Use Zip Code"	1.00	—

AMERICAN BICENTENNIAL ISSUE
Battle of Oriskany

200th anniv. of the Battle of Oriskany, American Militia led by Brig. Gen. Nicholas Herkimer (1728-77).

Herkimer at Oriskany, by Frederick Yohn A1111

Designed by Bradbury Thompson after painting in Utica, N.Y. Public Library.

PHOTOGRAVURE (Andreotti)

Plates of 160 subjects in four panes of 40.

1977, Aug. 6	**Tagged**	***Perf. 11***	
1722 A1111 13c	**multicolored**	.25	.20
	P# block of 10, 5#	2.75	—
	Margin block of 6, Mr. Zip and "Use Zip Code" and "Mail Early in the Day"	1.50	—

ENERGY ISSUE

Conservation and development of nation}s energy resources. Nos. 1723-1724 se-tenant vertically.

"Conservation" A1112

"Development" A1113

Designed by Terrance W. McCaffrey.

PHOTOGRAVURE (Andreotti)

Plates of 160 subjects in four panes of 40.

1977, Oct. 20	**Tagged**	***Perf. 11***	
1723 A1112 13c	**multicolored**	.25	.20
1724 A1113 13c	**multicolored**	.25	.20
a.	Pair, #1723-1724	.50	.50
	P# block of 12, 6#	3.25	—
	Margin block of 4, Mr. Zip, "Use Zip Code" and "Mail Early in the Day"	1.00	—

ALTA CALIFORNIA ISSUE

Founding of El Pueblo de San José de Guadalupe, first civil settlement in Alta California, 200th anniversary.

Farm Houses A1114

Designed by Earl Thollander.

LITHOGRAPHED, ENGRAVED (Giori)

Plates of 200 subjects in four panes of 50.

1977, Sept. 9	**Tagged**	***Perf. 11***	
1725 A1114 13c	**black & multicolored**	.25	.20
	P# block of 4	1.10	—
	Margin block of 4, Mr. Zip and "Use Zip Code"	1.00	—
a.	Tagging omitted	—	—

AMERICAN BICENTENNIAL ISSUE
Articles of Confederation

200th anniversary of drafting the Articles of Confederation, York Town, Pa.

Members of Continental Congress in Conference
A1115

Designed by David Blossom.

ENGRAVED (Giori)
Plates of 200 subjects in four panes of 50.

1977, Sept. 30 **Tagged** ***Perf. 11***
1726 A1115 13c **red & brown,** *cream* .25 .20
P# block of 4 1.10 —
Margin block of 4, Mr. Zip and "Use Zip Code" 1.00 —
a. Tagging omitted 125.00
b. Red omitted *600.00*
c. Red & brown omitted *400.00*

No. 1726b also has most of the brown omitted. No. 1726c must be collected as a transition multiple, certainly with No. 1726b and preferably also with No. 1726.

TALKING PICTURES, 50th ANNIV.

Movie Projector and Phonograph
A1116

Designed by Walter Einsel.

LITHOGRAPHED, ENGRAVED (Giori)
Plates of 200 subjects in four panes of 50.

1977, Oct. 6 **Tagged** ***Perf. 11***
1727 A1116 13c **multicolored** .25 .20
P# block of 4 1.10 —
Margin block of 4, Mr. Zip and "Use Zip Code" 1.00 —

AMERICAN BICENTENNIAL ISSUE
Surrender at Saratoga

200th anniversary of Gen. John Burgoyne's surrender at Saratoga.

Surrender of Burgoyne, by John Trumbull
A1117

Designed by Bradbury Thompson.

PHOTOGRAVURE (Andreotti)
Plates of 160 subjects in four panes of 40.

1977, Oct. 7 **Tagged** ***Perf. 11***
1728 A1117 13c **multicolored** .25 .20
P# block of 10, 5# 2.75 —
Margin block of 6, Mr. Zip, "Use Zip Code" and "Mail Early in the Day" 1.50 —

CHRISTMAS ISSUE

Washington at Valley Forge — A1118

Rural Mailbox — A1119

Designers: No. 1729, Stevan Dohanos, after painting by J. C. Leyendecker. No. 1730, Dolli Tingle.

PHOTOGRAVURE (Combination Press)
Plates of 460 subjects (20x23) in panes of 100 (10x10).

1977, Oct. 21 **Tagged** ***Perf. 11***
1729 A1118 13c **multicolored** .25 .20
P# block of 20, 5-8# 5.75 —
a. Imperf., pair *65.00*

See Combination Press note after No. 1703.

PHOTOGRAVURE (Andreotti)
Plates of 400 subjects in 4 panes of 100.

1730 A1119 13c **multicolored** .25 .20
P# block of 10, 5# 2.75 —
Margin block of 4, Mr. Zip and "Use Zip Code" 1.00 —
Pair with full vert. gutter btwn. —
a. Imperf., pair *225.00*

CARL SANDBURG ISSUE

Carl Sandburg (1878-1967), poet, biographer and collector of American folk songs, birth centenary.

Carl Sandburg, by William A. Smith, 1952 — A1120

Designed by William A. Smith.

GIORI PRESS PRINTING
Plates of 200 subjects in four panes of 50.

1978, Jan. 6 **Tagged** ***Perf. 11***
1731 A1120 13c **black & brown** .25 .20
P# block of 4 1.25 —
Margin block of 4, Mr. Zip 1.05 —
a. Brown omitted *2,250.*
b. Tagging omitted —

CAPTAIN COOK ISSUE

Capt. James Cook, 200th anniversary of his arrival in Hawaii, at Waimea, Kauai, Jan. 20, 1778, and of his anchorage in Cook Inlet, near Anchorage, Alaska, June 1, 1778. Nos. 1732-1733 printed in panes of 50, containing 25 each of Nos. 1732-1733 including 5 No. 1733b.

Capt. Cook, by Nathaniel Dance — A1121

"Resolution" and "Discovery," by John Webber
A1122

Designed by Robert F. Szabo (No. 1732; Jak Katalan (No. 1733.

GIORI PRESS PRINTING
Plates of 200 subjects in four panes of 50.

1978, Jan. 20 **Tagged** ***Perf. 11***
1732 A1121 13c **dark blue** .25 .20
1733 A1122 13c **green** .25 .20
a. Vert. pair, imperf. horiz. —
b. Pair, #1732-1733 .50 .50
P# block of 4, #1732 or 1733 1.10 —
Margin block of 4, Mr. Zip, #1732 or 1733 1.05 —
P# block of 20, 10 each #1732-1733, P# and slogans 5.25 —
c. As "b," imperf. between *4,250.*
d. As "b," tagging omitted *25.00*

Indian Head Penny, 1877 — A1123

Eagle — A1124

Red Masterpiece and Medallion Roses — A1126

ENGRAVED (Giori)
Plates of 600 subjects in four panes of 150.

1978 **Tagged** ***Perf. 11***
1734 A1123 13c **brown & blue green,** *bister, Jan. 11, 1978* .25 .20
P# block of 4 1.25 —
Margin block of 4, "Use Correct Zip Code" 1.00 —
Vert. pair with full horiz. gutter between —
a. Horiz. pair, imperf. vert. *250.00*
b. Tagging omitted —

PHOTOGRAVURE (Andreotti)
Plates of 400 subjects in four panes of 100.

1735 A1124 (15c) **orange,** *May 22, 1978* .30 .20
P# block of 4 1.40 —
Margin block of 4, "Use Zip Code" 1.25 —
Vert. pair with full horiz. gutter between —
a. Imperf., pair *85.00*
b. Vert. pair, imperf. horiz. *600.00*
c. Perf. 11.2 .35 .20
P# block of 4 1.80 —
Zip block of 4 1.50 —

BOOKLET STAMPS
ENGRAVED
Perf. 11x10½ on 2 or 3 sides

1736 A1124 (15c) **orange** .30 .20
a. Booklet pane of 8, *May 22, 1978* 2.50 1.50
b. As "a," tagging omitted —
c. Vert. pair, imperf between *850.00*

Perf. 10

1737 A1126 15c **multicolored** .30 .20
a. Booklet pane of 8, *July 11, 1978* 2.50 1.50
b. Imperf, pair *450.00*
c. As "a," imperf *2,200.*
d. As "a," tagging omitted *50.00*

A1127

A1128

A1129

A1130

A1131

Designed by Ronald Sharpe.

BOOKLET STAMPS
ENGRAVED

1980, Feb. 7 **Tagged** ***Perf. 11 on 2 or 3 sides***
1738 A1127 15c **sepia,** *yellow* .30 .20
1739 A1128 15c **sepia,** *yellow* .30 .20
1740 A1129 15c **sepia,** *yellow* .30 .20
1741 A1130 15c **sepia,** *yellow* .30 .20

1742 A1131 15c **sepia,** *yellow* .30 .20
a. Booklet pane of 10, 2 each #1738-1742 3.50 3.00
b. Strip of 5, #1738-1742 1.50 1.40

COIL STAMP

1978, May 22 ***Perf. 10 Vert.***
1743 A1124 (15c) **orange** .30 .20
Pair .60 .20
Joint line pair .75 —
a. Imperf., pair 80.00
Joint line pair —

No. 1743a is valued in the grade of fine.

BLACK HERITAGE SERIES

Harriet Tubman (1820-1913), born a slave, helped more than 300 slaves escape to freedom.

Harriet Tubman and Cart Carrying Slaves — A1133

Designed by Jerry Pinkney after photograph.

PHOTOGRAVURE (Andreotti)

Plates of 200 subjects in four panes of 50.

1978, Feb. 1 **Tagged** ***Perf. 10½x11***
1744 A1133 13c **multicolored** .25 .20
P# block of 12, 6# 3.25 —
Margin block of 4, Mr. Zip 1.00 —

AMERICAN FOLK ART SERIES
Quilts

Nos. 1745-1746 alternate in 1st row, Nos. 1747-1748 in 2nd.

Basket Design

A1134 A1135

A1136 A1137

Designed by Christopher Pullman after 1875 quilt made in New York City. Illustration reduced.

PHOTOGRAVURE (Andreotti)

Plates of 192 subjects in four panes of 48 (6x8).

1978, Mar. 8 ***Perf. 11***
1745 A1134 13c **multicolored** .25 .20
1746 A1135 13c **multicolored** .25 .20
1747 A1136 13c **multicolored** .25 .20
1748 A1137 13c **multicolored** .25 .20
a. Block of 4, #1745-1748 1.00 1.00
P# block of 12, 6# 3.25 —
P# block of 16, 6#, Mr. Zip and copyright 4.50 —
Margin block of 4, Mr. Zip, copyright 1.05 —

AMERICAN DANCE ISSUE

Nos. 1749-1750 alternate in 1st row, Nos. 1751-1752 in 2nd.

Ballet
A1138

Theater
A1139

Folk Dance
A1140

Modern Dance
A1141

Designed by John Hill.

PHOTOGRAVURE (Andreotti)

Plates of 192 subjects in four panes of 48 (6x8).

1978, Apr. 26 **Tagged** ***Perf. 11***
1749 A1138 13c **multicolored** .25 .20
1750 A1139 13c **multicolored** .25 .20
1751 A1140 13c **multicolored** .25 .20
1752 A1141 13c **multicolored** .25 .20
a. Block of 4, #1749-1752 1.00 1.00
P# block of 12, 6# 3.25 —
P# block of 16, 6#, Mr. Zip and copyright 4.50 —
Margin block of 4, Mr. Zip, copyright 1.05 —

AMERICAN BICENTENNIAL ISSUE

French Alliance, signed in Paris, Feb. 6, 1778 and ratified by Continental Congress, May 4, 1778.

King Louis XVI and Benjamin Franklin, by Charles Gabriel Sauvage — A1142

Designed by Bradbury Thompson after 1785 porcelain sculpture in Du Pont Winterthur Museum, Delaware.

GIORI PRESS PRINTING

Plates of 160 subjects in four panes of 40.

1978, May 4 **Tagged** ***Perf. 11***
1753 A1142 13c **blue, black & red** .25 .20
P# block of 4 1.10 —
Margin block of 4, Mr. Zip 1.00 —
a. Red missing (PS) —

EARLY CANCER DETECTION ISSUE

George Papanicolaou, M.D. (1883-1962), cytologist and developer of Pap Test, early cancer detection in women.

Dr. Papanicolaou and Microscope — A1143

Designed by Paul Calle.

ENGRAVED

Plates of 200 subjects in four panes of 50.

1978, May 18 **Tagged** ***Perf. 10½x11***
1754 A1143 13c **brown** .25 .20
P# block of 4 1.10 —
Margin block of 4, Mr. Zip 1.00 —

PERFORMING ARTS SERIES

Jimmie Rodgers (1897-1933), the "Singing Brakeman, Father of Country Music" (No. 1755); George M. Cohan (1878-1942), actor and playwright (No. 1756).

Jimmie Rodgers with Guitar and Brakeman's Cap, Locomotive — A1144

George M. Cohan, "Yankee Doodle Dandy" and Stars — A1145

Designed by Jim Sharpe.

PHOTOGRAVURE (Andreotti)

Plates of 200 subjects in four panes of 50.

1978 **Tagged** ***Perf. 11***
1755 A1144 13c **multicolored,** *May 24* .25 .20
P# block of 12, 6# 4.00 —
Margin block of 4, Mr. Zip 1.25 —
1756 A1145 15c **multicolored,** *July 3* .30 .20
P# block of 12, 6# 4.00 —
Margin block of 4, Mr. Zip 1.25 —

CAPEX ISSUE

CAPEX '78, Canadian International Philatelic Exhibition, Toronto, Ont., June 9-18.

Wildlife from Canadian-United States Border — A1146

Illustration reduced.

Designed by Stanley Galli.

LITHOGRAPHED, ENGRAVED (Giori)
Plates of 24 subjects in four panes of 6 each.

1978, June 10	Tagged		*Perf. 11*	
1757	A1146	Block of 8, **multicolored**	2.00	1.75
a.		13c Cardinal	.25	.20
b.		13c Mallard	.25	.20
c.		13c Canada goose	.25	.20
d.		13c Blue jay	.25	.20
e.		13c Moose	.25	.20
f.		13c Chipmunk	.25	.20
g.		13c Red fox	.25	.20
h.		13c Raccoon	.25	.20
		P# block of 8	2.25	—
		Margin block of 8, Mr. Zip and copyright	2.10	—
		Pane of 6 No. 1757, P#, Mr. Zip and copyright	13.00	—
i.		As No. 1757, yellow, green, red, brown, blue, black (litho) omitted	*7,000.*	
j.		Strip of 4 (a-d), imperf. vert.	*5,000.*	
k.		Strip of 4 (e-h), imperf. vert.	*3,000.*	
l.		As No. 1757, "d" and "h" with black (engr.) omitted	—	
m.		As No. 1757, "b" with blue missing (PS)	—	

No. 1757k is worth more when contained in the sheet of 8. Value is for strip only.

PHOTOGRAPHY ISSUE

Photography's contribution to communications and understanding.

Camera, Lens, Color Filters, Adapter Ring, Studio Light Bulb and Album — A1147

Designed by Ben Somoroff.

PHOTOGRAVURE (Andreotti)
Plates of 160 subjects in four panes of 40.

1978, June 26	Tagged		*Perf. 11*	
1758	A1147	15c **multicolored**	.30	.20
		P# block of 12, 6#	4.00	—
		Margin block of 4, Mr. Zip and copyright	1.25	—
		P# block of 16, 6#, Mr. Zip and copyright	5.00	—

VIKING MISSIONS TO MARS ISSUE

Second anniv. of landing of Viking 1 on Mars.

Viking 1 Lander Scooping up Soil on Mars — A1148

Designed by Robert McCall.

LITHOGRAPHED, ENGRAVED (Giori)
Plates of 200 subjects in four panes of 50.

1978, July 20	Tagged		*Perf. 11*	
1759	A1148	15c **multicolored**	.30	.20
		P# block of 4	1.35	—
		Margin block of 4, Mr. Zip	1.25	—
a.		Tagging omitted	*60.00*	

WILDLIFE CONSERVATION

Nos. 1760-1761 alternate in one horizontal row. Nos. 1762-1763 in the next.

Great Gray Owl — A1149

Saw-whet Owl — A1150

Barred Owl — A1151

Great Horned Owl — A1152

Designed by Frank J. Waslick.

LITHOGRAPHED, ENGRAVED (Giori)
Plates of 200 subjects in four panes of 50.

1978, Aug. 26	Tagged		*Perf. 11*	
1760	A1149	15c **multicolored**	.30	.20
1761	A1150	15c **multicolored**	.30	.20
1762	A1151	15c **multicolored**	.30	.20
1763	A1152	15c **multicolored**	.30	.20
a.		Block of 4, #1760-1763	1.25	1.25
		P# block of 4	1.40	—
		Margin block of 4, Mr. Zip	1.25	—
b.		As "a," tagging omitted		—

AMERICAN TREES ISSUE

Nos. 1764-1765 alternate in 1st row, Nos. 1766-1767 in 2nd.

Giant Sequoia A1153

White Pine — A1154

White Oak — A1155

Gray Birch — A1156

Designed by Walter D. Richards.

PHOTOGRAVURE (Andreotti)
Plates of 160 subjects in four panes of 40.

1978, Oct. 9	Tagged		*Perf. 11*	
1764	A1153	15c **multicolored**	.30	.20
1765	A1154	15c **multicolored**	.30	.20
1766	A1155	15c **multicolored**	.30	.20
1767	A1156	15c **multicolored**	.30	.20
a.		Block of 4, #1764-1767	1.25	1.25
		P# block of 12, 6#	4.00	—
		P# block of 16, 6#, Mr. Zip and copyright	5.25	—
		Margin block of 4, Mr. Zip, copyright	1.30	—
b.		As "a," imperf. horiz.	*17,500.*	

No. 1767b is unique.

CHRISTMAS ISSUE

Madonna and Child with Cherubim, by Andrea della Robbia — A1157

Child on Hobby Horse and Christmas Trees — A1158

Designed by Bradbury Thompson (No. 1768) after terra cotta sculpture in National Gallery, Washington, D.C. by Dolli Tingle (No. 1769).

PHOTOGRAVURE (Andreotti)
Plates of 400 subjects in four panes of 100.

1978, Oct. 18			*Perf. 11*	
1768	A1157	15c **blue & multicolored**	.30	.20
		P# block of 12, 6#	4.00	—
		Margin block of 4, "Use Correct Zip Code"	1.25	—
a.		Imperf., pair	*85.00*	

Value for No. 1768a is for an uncreased pair.

1769	A1158	15c **red & multicolored**	.30	.20
		P# block of 12, 6#	4.00	—
		Margin block of 4, "Use Correct Zip Code"	1.25	—
		Pair with full horiz. gutter btwn.	—	
a.		Imperf., pair	*85.00*	
b.		Vert. pair, imperf. horiz.	*1,600.*	

Robert F. Kennedy — A1159

Martin Luther King, Jr. and Civil Rights Marchers — A1160

ROBERT F. KENNEDY ISSUE

Designed by Bradbury Thompson after photograph by Stanley Tretick.

ENGRAVED

Plates of 192 subjects in four panes of 48 (8x6).

1979, Jan. 12	**Tagged**	***Perf. 11***	
1770 A1159 15c **blue**		.35	.20
P# block of 4		1.75	—
Margin block of 4, Mr. Zip		1.50	—
a. Tagging omitted		*60.00*	

BLACK HERITAGE SERIES

Dr. Martin Luther King, Jr. (1929-1968), Civil Rights leader.

Designed by Jerry Pinkney.

PHOTOGRAVURE (Andreotti)

Plates of 200 subjects in four panes of 50.

1979, Jan. 13	**Tagged**	***Perf. 11***	
1771 A1160 15c **multicolored**		.40	.20
P# block of 12, 6#		5.75	—
Margin block of 4, Mr. Zip		1.75	—
a. Imperf., pair		*1,400.*	

INTERNATIONAL YEAR OF THE CHILD ISSUE

Children of Different Races A1161

Designed by Paul Calle.

ENGRAVED

Plates of 200 subjects in four panes of 50.

1979, Feb. 15	**Tagged**	***Perf. 11***	
1772 A1161 15c **orange red**		.30	.20
P# block of 4		1.40	—
Margin block of 4, Mr. Zip		1.25	—

John Steinbeck (1902-1968), Novelist — A1162

Albert Einstein (1879-1955), Theoretical Physicist — A1163

LITERARY ARTS SERIES

Designed by Bradbury Thompson after photograph by Philippe Halsman.

ENGRAVED

Plates of 200 subjects in four panes of 50.

1979, Feb. 27	**Tagged**	***Perf. 10½x11***	
1773 A1162 15c **dark blue**		.30	.20
P# block of 4		1.40	—
Margin block of 4, Mr. Zip		1.25	—

ALBERT EINSTEIN ISSUE

Designed by Bradbury Thompson after photograph by Hermann Landshoff.

ENGRAVED

Plates of 200 subjects in four panes of 50.

1979, Mar. 4	**Tagged**	***Perf. 10½x11***	
1774 A1163 15c **chocolate**		.35	.20
P# block of 4		1.75	—
Margin block of 4, Mr. Zip		1.50	—
Pair, horiz. gutter btwn.		—	

AMERICAN FOLK ART SERIES

Pennsylvania Toleware, c. 1800

Coffeepot — A1164

Tea Caddy — A1165

Sugar Bowl — A1166

Coffeepot — A1167

Designed by Bradbury Thompson.

PHOTOGRAVURE (Andreotti)

Plates of 160 subjects in four panes of 40.

1979, Apr. 19	**Tagged**	***Perf. 11***	
1775 A1164 15c **multicolored**		.30	.20
1776 A1165 15c **multicolored**		.30	.20
1777 A1166 15c **multicolored**		.30	.20
1778 A1167 15c **multicolored**		.30	.20
a. Block of 4, #1775-1778		1.25	1.25
P# block of 10, 5#		3.25	—
P# block of 16, 5#; Mr. Zip and copyright		5.25	—
Margin block of 6, Mr. Zip and copyright		2.00	—
b. As "a," imperf. horiz.		*3,750.*	

AMERICAN ARCHITECTURE SERIES

Nos. 1779-1780 alternate in 1st row, Nos. 1781-1782 in 2nd.

Virginia Rotunda, by Thomas Jefferson — A1168

Baltimore Cathedral, by Benjamin Latrobe — A1169

Boston State House, by Charles Bulfinch — A1170

Philadelphia Exchange, by William Strickland — A1171

Designed by Walter D. Richards.

ENGRAVED (Giori)

Plates of 192 subjects in four panes of 48 (6x8).

1979, June 4	**Tagged**	***Perf. 11***	
1779 A1168 15c **black & brick red**		.30	.20
1780 A1169 15c **black & brick red**		.30	.20
1781 A1170 15c **black & brick red**		.30	.20
1782 A1171 15c **black & brick red**		.30	.20
a. Block of 4, #1779-1782		1.25	1.25
P# block of 4		1.45	—
Margin block of 4, Mr. Zip		1.30	—
b. As "a," tagging omitted		—	

ENDANGERED FLORA ISSUE

Nos. 1783-1784 alternate in one horizontal row. Nos. 1785-1786 in the next.

Persistent Trillium — A1172

Hawaiian Wild Broadbean — A1173

Contra Costa Wallflower — A1174

Antioch Dunes Evening Primrose — A1175

Designed by Frank J. Waslick.

PHOTOGRAVURE (Andreotti)
Plates of 200 subjects in four panes of 50.

1979, June 7		Tagged		*Perf. 11*	
1783	A1172	15c	**multicolored**	.30	.20
1784	A1173	15c	**multicolored**	.30	.20
1785	A1174	15c	**multicolored**	.30	.20
1786	A1175	15c	**multicolored**	.30	.20
a.			Block of 4, #1783-1786	1.25	1.25
			P# block of 12, 6#	4.00	—
			P# block of 20, 6#, Mr. Zip and copyright	6.50	—
			Margin block of 4, Mr. Zip	1.30	—
			As "a," full vert. gutter btwn.		—
b.			As "a," imperf.	*275.00*	

SEEING EYE DOGS ISSUE

1st guide dog program in the US, 50th anniv.

German Shepherd Leading Man — A1176

Designed by Joseph Csatari.

PHOTOGRAVURE (Combination Press)
Plates of 230 (10x23) subjects in panes of 50 (10x5).

1979, June 15		Tagged		*Perf. 11*	
1787	A1176	15c	**multicolored**	.30	.20
			P# block of 20, 5-8#, 1-2 copyright	6.50	—
a.			Imperf., pair	*400.00*	
b.			Tagging omitted	12.00	

See Combination Press note after No. 1703.

Child Holding Winner's Medal — A1177

John Paul Jones, by Charles Willson Peale — A1178

SPECIAL OLYMPICS ISSUE

Special Olympics for special children, Brockport, N.Y., Aug. 8-13.

Designed by Jeff Cornell.

PHOTOGRAVURE (Andreotti)
Plates of 200 subjects in four panes of 50.

1979, Aug. 9		Tagged		*Perf. 11*	
1788	A1177	15c	**multicolored**	.30	.20
			P# block of 10, 5#	3.25	—
			Zip block of 4	1.25	—

JOHN PAUL JONES ISSUE

John Paul Jones (1747-1792), Naval Commander, American Revolution.

Designed after painting in Independence National Historical Park, Philadelphia.

Printed by American Bank Note Co. and J. W. Fergusson and Sons.

Designed by Bradbury Thompson.

PHOTOGRAVURE (Champlain)
Plates of 200 subjects in four panes of 50.

1979, Sept. 23		Tagged		*Perf. 11x12*	
1789	A1178	15c	**multicolored**	.30	.20
			P# block of 10, 5#+A	3.25	—
			Zip block of 4	1.25	—
c.			Vert. pair, imperf. horiz.	*150.00*	

Imperforates on gummed stamp paper, including gutter pairs and blocks, are proofs from the ABNCo. archives.

Perf. 11

1789A	A1178	15c	**multicolored**	.55	.20
			P# block of 10, 5#+A	4.00	—
			Zip block of 4	3.25	—
d.			Vertical pair, imperf. horiz.	*125.00*	

Perf. 12

1789B	A1178	15c	**multicolored**	*3,500.*	*3,500.*
			P# block of 10, 5#+A	*40,000.*	
			Zip block of 4	*15,000.*	—

OLYMPIC GAMES ISSUE

22nd Summer Olympic Games, Moscow, July 19-Aug. 3, 1980. Nos. 1791-1792 alternate in one horizontal row, Nos. 1793-1794 in next.

Javelin — A1179

Running
A1180

Swimming
A1181

Rowing
A1182

Equestrian
A1183

Designed by Robert M. Cunningham.

PHOTOGRAVURE
Plates of 200 subjects in four panes of 50.

1979, Sept. 5		Tagged		*Perf. 11*	
1790	A1179	10c	**multicolored**	.20	.20
			P# block of 12, 6#	3.00	—
			Zip block of 4	.85	—

1979, Sept. 28					
1791	A1180	15c	**multicolored**	.30	.20
1792	A1181	15c	**multicolored**	.30	.20
1793	A1182	15c	**multicolored**	.30	.20
1794	A1183	15c	**multicolored**	.30	.20
a.			Block of 4, #1791-1794	1.25	1.25
			P# block of 12, 6#	4.00	—
			Zip block of 4	1.30	—
			P# block of 20, 6#, zip, copyright	6.50	—
b.			As "a," imperf.	*1,400.*	

OLYMPIC GAMES ISSUE

13th Winter Olympic Games, Lake Placid, N.Y., Feb. 12-24. Nos. 1795-1796 alternate in one horizontal row, Nos. 1797-1798 in next.

Speed Skating
A1184

Downhill Skiing
A1185

Ski Jump
A1186

Ice Hockey
A1187

Designed by Robert M. Cunningham

PHOTOGRAVURE
Plates of 200 subject in four panes of 50.

1980, Feb. 1		Tagged		*Perf. 11¼x10½*	
1795	A1184	15c	**multicolored**	.35	.20
1796	A1185	15c	**multicolored**	.35	.20
1797	A1186	15c	**multicolored**	.35	.20
1798	A1187	15c	**multicolored**	.35	.20
b.			Block of 4, #1795-1798	1.50	1.40
			P# block of 12, 6#	4.50	—
			Zip block of 4	1.55	—
			P# block of 20, 6#, zip and copyright	7.50	—

Perf. 11

1795A	A1184	15c	**multicolored**	1.10	.60
1796A	A1185	15c	**multicolored**	1.10	.60
1797A	A1186	15c	**multicolored**	1.10	.60
1798A	A1187	15c	**multicolored**	1.10	.60
c.			Block of 4, #1795A-1798A	4.50	3.50
			P# block of 12, 6#	15.00	—
			Zip block of 4	4.75	—
			P# block of 20, 6#, zip and copyright	27.50	—

CHRISTMAS ISSUE

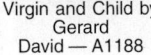

Virgin and Child by Gerard David — A1188

Santa Claus, Christmas Tree Ornament — A1189

Designed by Bradbury Thompson (No. 1799) and by Eskil Ohlsson (No. 1800).

No. 1799 is designed after a painting in National Gallery of Art, Washington, D.C.

PHOTOGRAVURE (Andreotti)

Plates of 400 subjects in four panes of 100.

1979, Oct. 18 **Tagged** ***Perf. 11***

1799 A1188 15c	**multicolored**	.30	.20
	P# block of 12, 6#	4.00	—
	Zip block of 4	1.25	—
	P# block of 20, 6#, zip, copyright	6.50	—
a.	Imperf., pair	*85.00*	
b.	Vert. pair, imperf. horiz.	*600.00*	
c.	Vert. pair, imperf. between	*1,100.*	
d.	Tagging omitted	—	
1800 A1189 15c	**multicolored**	.30	.20
	P# block of 12, 6#	4.00	—
	Zip block of 4	1.25	—
	P# block of 20, 6#, zip, copyright	6.50	—
a.	Green & yellow omitted	*500.00*	
b.	Green, yellow & tan omitted	*500.00*	
c.	Vert. se-tenant pair, #1800a & 1800b	*1,350.*	

Nos. 1800a and 1800b always have the remaining colors misaligned.

Nos. 1800a, 1800b and 1800c are valued in the grade of fine.

VALUES FOR HINGED STAMPS AFTER NO. 771

This catalogue does not value unused stamps after No. 771 in hinged condition. Hinged unused stamps from No. 772 to the present are worth considerably less than the values given for unused stamps, which are for never-hinged examples.

PERFORMING ARTS SERIES

Will Rogers (1879-1935), actor and humorist.

Will Rogers — A1190

Designed by Jim Sharpe.

PHOTOGRAVURE (Andreotti)

Plates of 200 subjects in four panes of 50.

1979, Nov. 4 **Tagged** ***Perf. 11***

1801 A1190 15c	**multicolored**	.30	.20
	P# block of 12, 6#	4.00	—
	Zip block of 4	1.25	—
	P# block of 20, 6#, zip, copyright	6.50	—
a.	Imperf., pair	*175.00*	

VIETNAM VETERANS ISSUE

A tribute to veterans of the Vietnam War.

Ribbon for Vietnam Service Medal A1191

Designed by Stevan Dohanos.

PHOTOGRAVURE (Andreotti)

Plates of 200 subjects in four panes of 50.

1979, Nov. 11 **Tagged** ***Perf. 11***

1802 A1191 15c	**multicolored**	.30	.20
	P# block of 10, 5#	3.25	—
	Zip block of 4	1.25	—

W.C. Fields — A1192

Benjamin Banneker — A1193

PERFORMING ARTS SERIES

W.C. Fields (1880-1946), actor and comedian.

Designed by Jim Sharpe.

PHOTOGRAVURE

Plates of 200 subjects in four panes of 50.

1980, Jan. 29 **Tagged** ***Perf. 11***

1803 A1192 15c	**multicolored**	.30	.20
	P# block of 12, 6#	4.00	—
	Zip block of 4	1.25	—
	P# block of 20, 6#, zip, copyright	6.50	—
a.	Imperf., pair	—	

BLACK HERITAGE SERIES

Benjamin Banneker (1731-1806), astronomer and mathematician.

Designed by Jerry Pinkney.

Printed by American Bank Note Co. and J. W. Fergusson and Sons.

PHOTOGRAVURE

Plates of 200 subjects in four panes of 50.

1980, Feb. 15 **Tagged** ***Perf. 11***

1804 A1193 15c	**multicolored**	.35	.20
	P# block of 12, 6#+A	4.50	—
	Zip block of 4	1.50	—
	Plate block of 20, 6#+A, zip, copyright	6.50	—
a.	Horiz. pair, imperf. vert.	*450.00*	

Imperfs, including gutter pairs and blocks, exist from printer's waste. These have been fraudulently perforated to simulate No. 1804a. Genuine examples of No. 1804a do not have colors misregistered.

NATIONAL LETTER WRITING WEEK ISSUE

National Letter Writing Week, Feb. 24-Mar. 1. Nos. 1805-1810 are printed vertically se-tenant.

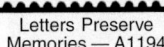

Letters Preserve Memories — A1194

P.S. Write Soon — A1195

Letters Lift Spirits — A1196

Letters Shape Opinions — A1197

Designed by Randall McDougall.

Plates of 240 subjects in four panes of 60 (10x6) each.

PHOTOGRAVURE

1980, Feb. 25 **Tagged** ***Perf. 11***

1805 A1194 15c	**multicolored**	.30	.20
1806 A1195 15c	**purple & multi**	.30	.20
1807 A1196 15c	**multicolored**	.30	.20
1808 A1195 15c	**green & multi**	.30	.20
1809 A1197 15c	**multicolored**	.30	.20
1810 A1195 15c	**red & multi**	.30	.20
a.	Vertical strip of 6, #1805-1810	1.85	*2.00*
	P# block of 36, 6#	13.00	—
	Zip block of 12	3.75	—
	Nos. 1805-1810 (6)	1.80	1.20

AMERICANA TYPE

Weaver Violins — A1199

Designer: 3.5c, George Mercer.

COIL STAMPS

1980-81 **Engr.** ***Perf. 10 Vertically***

1811 A984 1c	**dark blue,** *greenish,* shiny gum, *Mar. 6, 1980*	.20	.20
	Pair	.20	.20
	Joint line pair	.40	—
	Dull gum	.35	
	Joint line pair	1.75	
a.	Imperf., pair	*165.00*	
	Joint line pair	*260.00*	
b.	Tagging omitted	—	
1813 A1199 3.5c	**purple,** *yellow, June 23, 1980*	.20	.20
	Pair	.20	.20
	Joint line pair	1.00	—
a.	Untagged (Bureau precanceled, lines only)	.20	.20
	Pair	.35	.35
	Joint line pair	1.95	—
b.	Imperf., pair	*165.00*	
	Joint line pair	*425.00*	
1816 A997 12c	**red brown,** *beige, Apr. 8, 1981*	.25	.20
	Pair	.50	.20
	Joint line pair	2.00	—
a.	Untagged (Bureau precanceled), **red brown,** *beige*	1.15	1.15
	Pair	2.40	2.40
	Joint line pair	47.50	—
b.	Imperf., pair	165.00	
	Joint line pair	300.00	
c.	As "a," **brownish red,** *reddish beige*	1.65	1.65
	Pair	3.50	3.50
	Joint line pair	67.50	—
	Nos. 1811-1816 (3)	.65	.60

Bureau Precancels: No. 1816a, lines only, (valued) PRESORTED/FIRST CLASS (value unused $135); No. 1816c, PRESORTED/FIRST CLASS.

Eagle — A1207

PHOTOGRAVURE
Plates of 400 subjects in four panes of 100.

1981, Mar. 15	Tagged	Perf. 11x10½	
1818 A1207 (18c) **violet**		.35	.20
	P# block of 4	1.60	—
	Zip block of 4	1.50	—
	Pair with full vert. gutter between	—	

BOOKLET STAMP
ENGRAVED
Perf. 10

1819 A1207 (18c) **violet**		.40	.20
a.	Booklet pane of 8	3.75	2.25

COIL STAMP
Perf. 10 Vert.

1820 A1207 (18c) **violet**		.40	.20
	Pair	.80	.20
	Joint line pair	1.60	—
a.	Imperf., pair	*85.00*	
	Joint line pair	*150.00*	

Frances Perkins A1208

Dolley Madison A1209

FRANCES PERKINS ISSUE

Frances Perkins (1882-1965), Secretary of Labor, 1933-1945 (first woman cabinet member).

Designed by F.R. Petrie.

ENGRAVED
Plates of 200 subjects in four panes of 50.

1980, Apr. 10	Tagged	Perf. 10½x11	
1821 A1208 15c **Prussian blue**		.30	.20
	P# block of 4	1.30	—
	Zip block of 4	1.25	—

DOLLEY MADISON ISSUE

Dolley Madison (1768-1849), First Lady, 1809-1817.

Designed by Esther Porter.

ENGRAVED
Plates of 600 subjects in four panes of 150.

1980, May 20	Tagged	Perf. 11	
1822 A1209 15c **red brown & sepia**		.30	.20
	P# block of 4	1.40	—
	Zip block of 4	1.25	—
a.	Red brown missing (PS)	—	

Emily Bissell — A1210

Helen Keller and Anne Sullivan — A1211

EMILY BISSELL ISSUE

Emily Bissell (1861-1948), social worker; introduced Christmas seals in United States.

Designed by Stevan Dohanos.

ENGRAVED
Plates of 200 subjects in four panes of 50.

1980, May 31	Tagged	Perf. 11	
1823 A1210 15c **black & red**		.35	.20
	P# block of 4	1.75	—
	Zip block of 4	1.50	—
a.	Vert. pair, imperf. horiz.	*350.00*	
b.	All colors missing (EP)	—	
c.	Red missing (FO)	—	

HELEN KELLER ISSUE

Helen Keller (1880-1968), blind and deaf writer and lecturer taught by Anne Sullivan (1867-1936).

Designed by Paul Calle.

LITHOGRAPHED AND ENGRAVED
Plates of 200 subjects in four panes of 50.

1980, June 27	Tagged	Perf. 11	
1824 A1211 15c **multicolored**		.30	.20
	P# block of 4	1.30	—
	Zip block of 4	1.25	—

Veterans Administration Emblem — A1212

Gen. Bernardo de Galvez — A1213

VETERANS ADMINISTRATION, 50th ANNIV.

Designed by Malcolm Grear.

Printed by American Bank Note Co. and J. W. Fergusson and Sons.

PHOTOGRAVURE
Plates of 200 subjects in four panes of 50.

1980, July 21	Tagged	Perf. 11	
1825 A1212 15c **carmine & violet blue**		.30	.20
	P# block of 4, 2#+A	1.30	—
	Zip block of 4	1.25	—
a.	Horiz. pair, imperf. vert.	*425.00*	

BERNARDO DE GALVEZ ISSUE

Gen. Bernardo de Galvez (1746-1786), helped defeat British in Battle of Mobile, 1780.

Designed by Roy H. Andersen.

LITHOGRAPHED & ENGRAVED
Plates of 200 subjects in four panes of 50.

1980, July 23	Tagged	Perf. 11	
1826 A1213 15c **multicolored**		.30	.20
	P# block of 4	1.30	—
	Zip block of 4	1.25	—
a.	Red, brown & blue (engr.) omitted	*650.00*	
b.	Blue, brown, red (engr.) & yellow (litho.) omitted	*1,150.*	

CORAL REEFS ISSUE

Nos. 1827-1828 alternate in one horizontal row, Nos. 1829-1830 in the next.

Brain Coral, Beaugregory Fish — A1214

Elkhorn Coral, Porkfish — A1215

Chalice Coral, Moorish Idol — A1216

Finger Coral, Sabertooth Blenny — A1217

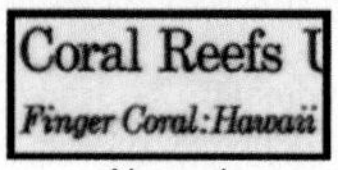

Normal

Cylinder Flaw

Designed by Chuck Ripper.

PHOTOGRAVURE
Plates of 200 subjects in four panes of 50.

1980, Aug. 26	Tagged	Perf. 11	
1827 A1214 15c **multi**		.30	.20
1828 A1215 15c **multi**		.30	.20
1829 A1216 15c **multi**		.30	.20
1830 A1217 15c **multi**		.30	.20
	Cylinder flaw (period between "Finger coral" and "Hawaii" instead of colon) (39390 LR 48)	—	—
a.	Block of 4, #1827-1830	1.25	1.10
	P# block of 12, 6#	4.00	—
	Zip block of 4	1.30	—
b.	As "a," imperf.	*450.00*	
c.	As "a," vert. imperf. between	—	
d.	As "a," imperf. vert.	*3,250.*	

American Bald Eagle — A1218

Edith Wharton — A1219

ORGANIZED LABOR ISSUE

Designed by Peter Cocci.

PHOTOGRAVURE
Plates of 200 subjects in four panes of 50.

1980, Sept. 1	Tagged	Perf. 11	
1831 A1218 15c **multi**		.30	.20
	P# block of 12, 6#	3.50	—
	Zip block of 4	1.25	—
a.	Imperf., pair	*300.00*	

LITERARY ARTS SERIES

Edith Wharton (1862-1937), novelist.

Designed by Bradbury Thompson after 1905 photograph.

ENGRAVED
Plates of 200 subjects in four panes of 50.

1980, Sept. 5	Tagged	Perf. 10½x11	
1832 A1219 15c **purple**		.30	.20
	P# block of 4	1.30	—
	Zip block of 4	1.25	—

EDUCATION ISSUE

"Homage to the Square: Glow" by Josef Albers — A1220

Designed by Bradbury Thompson

Printed by American Bank Note Co. and J. W. Fergusson and Sons.

PHOTOGRAVURE
Plates of 200 subjects in four panes of 50.

1980, Sept. 12	Tagged	Perf. 11	
1833 A1220 15c **multi**		.30	.20
	P# block of 6, 3#+A	1.90	—
	Zip block of 4	1.25	—
a.	Horiz. pair, imperf. vert.	*200.00*	

AMERICAN FOLK ART SERIES

Pacific Northwest Indian Masks

Heiltsuk, Bella Bella Tribe — A1221

Chilkat Tlingit Tribe — A1222

Tlingit Tribe — A1223

Bella Coola Tribe — A1224

Designed by Bradury Thompson after photographs.

PHOTOGRAVURE
Plates of 160 subjects in four panes of 40.

1980, Sept. 25	Tagged	Perf. 11	
1834 A1221 15c **multi**		.35	.20
1835 A1222 15c **multi**		.35	.20
1836 A1223 15c **multi**		.35	.20
1837 A1224 15c **multi**		.35	.20
a.	Block of 4, #1834-1837	1.50	1.25
	P# block of 10, 5#	5.00	—
	Zip, copyright block of 6	2.25	—

AMERICAN ARCHITECTURE SERIES

Smithsonian A1225

Trinity Church A1226

Penn Academy A1227

Lyndhurst A1228

Designed by Walter D. Richards.

ENGRAVED (Giori)
Plates of 160 subjects in four panes of 40.

1980, Oct. 9	Tagged	Perf. 11	
1838 A1225 15c **black & red**		.30	.20
1839 A1226 15c **black & red**		.30	.20
1840 A1227 15c **black & red**		.30	.20
1841 A1228 15c **black & red**		.30	.20
a.	Block of 4, #1838-1841	1.25	1.25
	P# block of 4	1.50	—
	Zip block of 4	1.30	—
b.	As "a," red missing on Nos. 1838, 1839 (PS)	*375.00*	
c.	As "a," tagging omitted	—	

CHRISTMAS ISSUE

Madonna and Child — A1229

Wreath and Toys — A1230

Designed by Esther Porter (No. 1842) after Epiphany Window, Washington Cathedral, and by Bob Timberlake (No. 1843).

PHOTOGRAVURE
Plate of 200 subjects in four panes of 50.

1980, Oct. 31	Tagged	Perf. 11	
1842 A1229 15c **multi**		.30	.20
	P# block of 12, 6#	4.00	—
	Zip block of 4	1.25	—
	Pair with full vert. gutter btwn.	—	
a.	Imperf., pair	*50.00*	

PHOTOGRAVURE (Combination Press)
Plates of 230 subjects (10x23) in panes of 50 (10x5).

1843 A1230 15c **multi**		.30	.20
	P# block of 20, 5-8 #, 1-2 copyright	6.50	—
a.	Imperf., pair	*65.00*	
b.	Buff omitted	*22.50*	
c.	Vert. pair, imperf. horiz.	—	
d.	Horiz. pair, imperf. between	*3,750.*	
e.	Tagging omitted	125.00	—

No. 1843b is difficult to identify and should have a competent certificate.

See Combination Press note after No. 1703.

GREAT AMERICANS ISSUE

A1231

A1232

A1233

A1234

A1235

A1236

A1237

A1238

A1239

A1240

A1241

A1242

A1243

A1244

A1245

A1246

A1247

A1248

A1249

A1250

A1251

A1252

A1253

A1254

A1255

A1256

Designers: 1c, Bernie Fuchs. 2c, Burt Silverman, 3c, 17c, 40c, Ward Brackett. 4c, 7c, 10c, 18c, 30c, Richard Sparks. 5c, Paul Calle. 6c, No. 1861, Dennis Lyall. 8c, Arthur Lidov. 9c, 11c, Robert Alexander Anderson. 13c, Brad Holland. 14c, Bradbury Thompson. 19c, 39c, Roy H. Andersen. No. 1860, Jim Sharpe. No. 1862, 22c, 50c, 37c, Christopher Calle. 35c, Nathan Jones.

ENGRAVED

1980-85 Tagged ***Perf. 11x10½***
Perf. 11 (1c, 6c-11c, 14c, No. 1862, 22c, 30c, 39c, 40c, 50c)

1844 A1231 1c **black,** perf. 11.2, small block tagging, *Sept. 23, 1983* .20 .20
P# block of 6 .35 —
P# block of 20, 1-2 #, 1-2 copyright 2.00 —
a. Imperf., pair *350.00*
b. Vert. pair, imperf. btwn. and at bottom *1,900.*
c. Perf. 10.9, small block tagging .20 .20
P# block of 6 .35 —
P# block of 20, 1-2 #, 1-2 copyright 2.00 —
d. Perf. 10.9, large block tagging, *1985* .20 .20
P# block of 6 .35 —
P# block of 20, 1-2 #, 1-2 copyright 2.00 —
e. Vert. pair, imperf. horiz. —
1845 A1232 2c **brn blk,** overall tagging, *Nov. 18, 1982* .20 .20
P# block of 4 .35 —
Zip block of 4 .25 —
Vert. pair, full gutter between —
a. Tagging omitted 150.00
1846 A1233 3c **olive green,** overall tagging, *July 13, 1983* .20 .20
P# block of 4 .55 —
Zip block of 4 .30 —
a. Tagging omitted 5.00
1847 A1234 4c **violet,** overall tagging, *June 3, 1983* .20 .20
P# block of 4 .65 —
Zip block of 4 .35 —
a. Tagging omitted 5.00
1848 A1235 5c **henna brown,** overall tagging, *June 25, 1983* .30 .20
P# block of 4 1.50 —
Zip block of 4 1.25 —
1849 A1236 6c **orange vermilion,** large block tagging, *Sept. 19, 1985* .20 .20
P# block of 6 .85 —
P# block of 20, 1-2 #, 1-2 zip, 1-2 copyright 5.00 —
a. Vert. pair, imperf. between and at bottom *1,900.*
1850 A1237 7c **bright carmine,** small block tagging, *Jan. 25, 1985* .20 .20
P# block of 6 .95 —
P# block of 20, 1-2 #, 1-2 zip, 1-2 copyright 4.00 —
1851 A1238 8c **olive black,** overall tagging, *July 25, 1985* .20 .20
P# block of 4 .85 —
Zip block of 4 .60 —
a. Tagging omitted —
1852 A1239 9c **dark green,** small block tagging, *June 7, 1985* .20 .20
P# block of 6 1.30 —
P# block of 20, 1-2 #. 1-2 zip, 1-2 copyright 5.00 —
1853 A1240 10c **Prus. blue,** small block tagging, *May 31, 1984* .25 .20
P# block of 6 2.00 —
P# block of 20, 1-2 #, 1-2 copyright, 1-2 zip 9.00 —
a. Large block tagging .30 .20
P# block of 6 2.25 —
P# block of 20, 1-2 #, 1-2 copyright, 1-2 zip 9.00 —
b. Vert. pair, imperf. between *750.00*
c. Horiz. pair, imperf. between *1,850.*
d. Vert. pair, imperf horiz. —

Completely imperforate tagged or untagged stamps are from printer's waste.

1854 A1241 11c **dark blue,** overall tagging, *Feb. 12, 1985* .40 .20
P# block of 4 2.00 —
Zip block of 4 1.60 —
a. Tagging omitted 35.00
1855 A1242 13c **light maroon,** overall tagging, *Jan. 15, 1982* .40 .20
P# block of 4 2.25 —
Zip block of 4 1.60 —
a. Tagging omitted 7.50
1856 A1243 14c **slate green,** small block tagging, *Mar. 21, 1985* .30 .20
P# block of 6 2.25 —
P# block of 20, 1-2 #, 1-2 zip, 1-2 copyright 9.00 —
a. Large block tagging .30 .20
P# block of 6 2.25 —
P# block of 20, 1-2 #, 1-2 zip, 1-2 copyright 9.00 —
b. Vert. pair, imperf. horiz. *110.00*
c. Horiz. pair, imperf. between 9.00
d. Vert. pair, imperf. between *1,650.*
e. All color omitted —

No. 1856e comes from a partially printed pane and should be collected as a vertical strip of 10, one stamp normal, one stamp transitional and 8 stamps with color omitted.

1857 A1244 17c **green,** overall tagging, *May 28, 1981* .35 .20
P# block of 4 2.00 —
Zip block of 4 1.40 —
a. Tagging omitted 17.50
1858 A1245 18c **dark blue,** overall tagging, *May 7, 1981* .35 .20
P# block of 4 3.00 —
Zip block of 4 1.40 —
Pair with full horiz. gutter between —
a. Tagging omitted 6.50
1859 A1246 19c **brown,** overall tagging, *Dec. 27, 1980* .45 .20
P# block of 4 2.75 —
Zip block of 4 1.90 —
1860 A1247 20c **claret,** overall tagging, *Jan. 12, 1982* .40 .20
P# block of 4 3.75 —
Zip block of 4 1.65 —
a. Tagging omitted 7.50
1861 A1248 20c **green,** overall tagging, *June 10, 1983* .50 .20
P# block of 4 4.00 —
Zip block of 4 2.00 —
a. Tagging omitted —
1862 A1249 20c **black,** perf 10.9, small block tagging, dull gum, *Jan. 26, 1984* .40 .20
P# block of 6 4.50 —
P# block of 20, 1-2 #, 1-2 copyright, 1-2 zip 12.00 —
a. Perf. 11.2, large block tagging, dull gum .40 .20
Corner P# block of 4 3.00 —
Zip block of 4 1.60 —
b. Perf. 11.2, overall tagging, dull gum, *1990* .40 —
Corner P# block of 4 3.75 —
Zip block of 4 1.60 —
c. Tagging omitted, perf. 11.2 11.50
d. Prephosphored uncoated paper (mottled tagging), shiny gum, perf. 11.2, *1993* .40 .20
Corner P# block of 4 2.50
Zip block of 4 1.60
1863 A1250 22c **dark chalky blue,** small block tagging, *Apr. 23, 1985* .75 .20
P# block of 6 9.00 —
P# block of 20, 1-2 #, 1-2 zip, 1-2 copyright 17.50 —
a. Large block tagging 1.00 .20
P# block of 6 12.50 —
P# block of 20, 1-2 #, 1-2 zip, 1-2 copyright 22.50 —
b. Perf. 11.2, large block tagging, *1987* .65 .20
Corner P# block of 4 7.00 —
Zip block of 4 2.75 —
c. Tagging omitted 7.50
d. Vert. pair, imperf. horiz. *1,900.*
e. Vert. pair, imperf. between —
f. Horiz. pair, imperf. between *1,900.*
1864 A1251 30c **olive gray,** small block tagging, *Sept. 2, 1984* .60 .20
P# block of 6 3.50 —
P# block of 20, 1-2 #, 1-2 copyright, 1-2 zip 17.50 —
a. Perf. 11.2, large block tagging .55 .20
Corner P# block of 4 3.25 —
Zip block of 4 2.50 —
b. Perf. 11.2, overall tagging 2.00 .20
Corner P# block of 4 25.00 —
Zip block of 4 8.50 —
c. Tagging omitted —
1865 A1252 35c **gray,** overall tagging, *June 3, 1981* .75 .20
P# block of 4 4.25 —
Zip block of 4 3.25 —
a. Tagging omitted 85.00
1866 A1253 37c **blue,** overall tagging, *Jan. 26, 1982* .80 .20
P# block of 4 3.75 —
Zip block of 4 3.25 —
a. Tagging omitted 12.50
1867 A1254 39c **rose lilac,** perf 10.9, small block tagging, *Mar. 20, 1985* .90 .20
P# block of 6 5.75 —
P# block of 20, 1-2 #, 1-2 zip, 1-2 copyright 22.50 —
a. Vert. pair, imperf. horiz. *500.00*
b. Vert. pair, imperf. between *1,850.*
c. Large block tagging, perf 10.9 .90 .20
P# block of 6 5.75 —
P# block of 20, 1-2 #, 1-2 zip, 1-2 copyright 20.00 —
d. Perf. 11.2, large block tagging .90 .20
Corner P# block of 4 7.00 —
Zip block of 4 3.75 —
1868 A1255 40c **dark green,** perf 10.9, small block tagging, *Feb. 24, 1984* .90 .20
P# block of 6 6.50 —
P# block of 20, 1-2 #, 1-2 copyright, 1-2 zip 20.00 —
a. Perf. 11.2, large block tagging .90 .20
Corner P# block of 4 6.50 —
Zip block of 4 3.75 —

1869	A1256	50c	**brown,** perf 10.9, overall tagging, shiny gum, *Feb. 22, 1985*	.95	.20
			P# block of 4	7.50	—
			Zip block of 4	4.00	—
a.			Perf. 11.2, large block tagging, dull gum	.95	.20
			P# block of 4	6.25	—
			Zip block of 4	4.00	—
b.			Tagging omitted	11.00	
c.			Tagging omitted, perf. 11.2, dull gum	9.00	
d.			Perf. 11.2, overall tagging, dull gum	2.50	.20
			P# block of 4	35.00	—
			Zip block of 4	11.00	—
e.			Perf. 11.2, prephosphored uncoated paper (mottled tagging), shiny gum, *1992*	.90	.20
			P# block of 4	5.00	—
			Zip block of 4	4.00	—
			Nos. 1844-1869 (26)	11.35	5.20

A1261

A1262

EVERETT DIRKSEN (1896-1969)

Senate minority leader, 1960-1969.

Designed by Ron Adair.

ENGRAVED

Plates of 200 subjects in four panes of 50.

1981, Jan. 4 **Tagged** ***Perf. 11***

1874	A1261	15c	**gray**	.30	.20
			P# block of 4	1.40	—
			Zip block of 4	1.25	—
a.			All color omitted	*500.00*	

No. 1874a comes from a partially printed pane and may be collected as a vertical strip of 3 or 5 (1 or 3 stamps normal, one stamp transitional and one stamp with color omitted) or as a pair with one partially printed stamp.

BLACK HERITAGE SERIES

Whitney Moore Young, Jr. (1921-1971), civil rights leader.

Designed by Jerry Pinkney.

PHOTOGRAVURE

Plates of 200 subjects in four panes of 50.

1981, Jan. 30 **Tagged** ***Perf. 11***

1875	A1262	15c	**multi**	.35	.20
			P# block of 4, 6#	1.75	—
			Zip block of 4	1.50	—

FLOWER ISSUE

A1263

A1264

A1265

A1266

Illustration reduced.

Designed by Lowell Nesbitt.

PHOTOGRAVURE

Plates of 192 subjects in four panes of 48 (8x6).

1981, Apr. 23 **Tagged** ***Perf. 11***

1876	A1263	18c	**multicolored**	.35	.20
1877	A1264	18c	**multicolored**	.35	.20
1878	A1265	18c	**multicolored**	.35	.20
1879	A1266	18c	**multicolored**	.35	.20
a.			Block of 4, #1876-1879	1.40	1.25
			P# block of 4, 6#	1.75	—
			Zip block of 4	1.45	—

AMERICAN WILDLIFE

A1267

A1268

A1269

A1270

A1271

A1272

A1273

A1274

A1275

A1276

Designs from photographs by Jim Brandenburg.

ENGRAVED

1981, May 14 **Tagged** ***Perf. 11***

Dark brown

1880	A1267	18c	Bighorn	.80	.20
a.			Tagging omitted		—
1881	A1268	18c	Puma	.80	.20
1882	A1269	18c	Harbor seal	.80	.20
1883	A1270	18c	American Buffalo	.80	.20
1884	A1271	18c	Brown bear	.80	.20
1885	A1272	18c	Polar bear	.80	.20
1886	A1273	18c	Elk (wapiti)	.80	.20
a.			Tagging omitted		—
1887	A1274	18c	Moose	.80	.20
a.			Tagging omitted		—
1888	A1275	18c	White-tailed deer	.80	.20
1889	A1276	18c	Pronghorn	.80	.20
a.			Booklet pane of 10, #1880-1889	8.50	6.00
b.			Tagging omitted		—

Nos. 1880-1889 issued in booklet only. All stamps have one or two straight edges.

Imperfs are from printer's waste.

FLAG AND ANTHEM ISSUE

A1277

A1278

A1279

A1280

Designed by Peter Cocci.

ENGRAVED

Plates of 460 subjects (20x23) in panes of 100 (10x10).

1981, Apr. 24 **Tagged** ***Perf. 11***

1890	A1277	18c	**multicolored**	.35	.20
			P# block of 6	2.25	—
			P# block of 20, 1-2 #	10.00	—
a.			Imperf., pair	*90.00*	
b.			Vert. pair, imperf. horiz.	*700.00*	

See Combination Press note after No. 1703.

Coil Stamp

Perf. 10 Vert.

1891	A1278	18c	**multicolored**	.35	.20
			Pair	.70	.20
			P# strip of 3, #1	50.00	
			P# strip of 3, #2	12.50	
			P# strip of 3, #3	50.00	
			P# strip of 3, #4	3.00	
			P# strip of 3, #5	3.00	
			P# strip of 3, #6	*800.00*	
			P# strip of 3, #7	9.00	
			P# strip of 5, #1	300.00	
			P# strip of 5, #2	60.00	
			P# strip of 5, #3	625.00	
			P# strip of 5, #4	6.00	
			P# strip of 5, #5	4.75	
			P# strip of 5, #6	*3,250.*	
			P# strip of 5, #7	24.00	
			P# single, #1	—	2.50
			P# single, #2	—	1.00
			P# single, #3	—	9.00
			P# single, #4	—	1.00
			P# single, #5	—	1.00
			P# single, #6	—	*675.00*
			P# single, #7	—	25.00
a.			Imperf., pair	20.00	—
b.			Pair, imperf. between	*1,150.*	
c.			Tagging omitted		—

Beware of pairs offered as No. 1891b that have faint blind perfs.

Vertical pairs and blocks exist from printer's waste.

Booklet Stamps

Perf. 11

1892	A1279	6c	**multicolored**	.50	.20
1893	A1280	18c	**multicolored**	.30	.20
a.			Booklet pane of 8 (2 #1892, 6 #1893)	3.00	2.50
b.			As "a," vert. imperf. between	*70.00*	
c.			Se-tenant pair, #1892 & #1893	.90	1.00
d.			As "a," tagging omitted	—	

Bureau Precanceled Coils

Starting with No. 1895b, Bureau precanceled coil stamps are valued unused as well as used. The coils issued with dull gum may be difficult to distinguish.

When used normally these stamps do not receive any postal markings so that used stamps with an additional postal cancellation of any kind are worth considerably less than the values shown here.

FLAG OVER SUPREME COURT ISSUE

A1281

Designed by Dean Ellis

ENGRAVED

Plates of 460 subjects (20x23) in panes of 100 (10x10)

1981, Dec. 17 **Tagged** ***Perf. 11***

1894	A1281	20c	**black, dark blue & red,** dull gum	.40	.20
			P# block of 6	2.75	—
			P# block of 20, 1-2 #	9.00	—
a.			Vert. pair, imperf.	32.50	
b.			Vert. pair, imperf. horiz.	*450.00*	
c.			Dark blue omitted	*70.00*	
d.			Black omitted	*275.00*	
e.			Perf. 11.2, shiny gum	.35	.20

P# block of 6 2.50 —
P# block of 20, 1-2 # 8.50 —
f. Tagging omitted —

Coil Stamp

Perf. 10 Vert.

1895 A1281 20c **black, dark blue & red,** wide block tagging .40 .20
Pair .80 .20
P# strip of 3, #1 2.00
P# strip of 3, #2 3.50
P# strip of 3, #3 3.50
P# strip of 3, #5 3.50
P# strip of 3, #11 3.50
P# strip of 3, #13, 14 2.75
P# strip of 5, #1 60.00
P# strip of 5, #2 6.00
P# strip of 5, #3 4.00
P# strip of 5, #5 4.00
P# strip of 5, #11 7.00
P# strip of 5, #13, 14 4.00
P# single, #1 — .75
P# single, #2-3 — .50
P# single, #5 — .50
P# single, #11 — 3.00
P# single, #13, 14 — .50
a. Narrow block tagging .40 .20
Pair .80 .20
P# strip of 3, #4 6.00
P# strip of 3, #6 9.00
P# strip of 3, #8 3.00
P# strip of 3, #9-10 2.75
P# strip of 3, #12 4.25
P# strip of 5, #4 *425.00*
P# strip of 5, #6 175.00
P# strip of 5, #8 11.00
P# strip of 5, #9 3.75
P# strip of 5, #10 4.00
P# strip of 5, #12 7.25
P# single, #4 — .80
P# single, #6 — 2.25
P# single, #8 — .40
P# single, #9 — .40
P# single, #10 — .60
P# single, #12 — .75
b. Untagged (Bureau precanceled, lines only) .50 .50
P# strip of 3, #14 32.50
P# strip of 5, #14 37.50
P# single, #14 40.00
c. Tagging omitted (not Bureau precanceled *15.00*
P# strip of 3, #4 —
P# strip of 3, #3, 5, 8, 10, 11, 14 —
P# strip of 5, #5, 10, 11, 14 —
P# single, #5, 8-11, 14 — —
d. Imperf., pair 8.50 —
e. Pair, imperf. between *800.00*
f. Black omitted *45.00*
g. Dark blue omitted *1,350.*
h. Black field of stars instead of blue —

The wide block tagging on No. 1895 and narrow block tagging on No. 1895a differentiate stamps printed on two different presses. The wide blocks are approximately 20-21mm high by 18mm wide with a 4mm untagged gutter between tagging blocks.

The narrow blocks are approximately 21-22mm high and approximately 16-16½mm wide with a 5½-6½ untagged gutter between tagging blocks.

BOOKLET STAMP

Perf. 11x10½

1896 A1281 20c **black, dark blue & red,** small block tagging .40 .20
a. Booklet pane of 6 3.00 2.25
Scored perforations 3.00 2.25
b. Booklet pane of 10, *June 1, 1982* 5.25 3.25
c. Tagging omitted 100.00 —
d. Large block tagging ('83) .40 .20
e. As "d," booklet pane of 10 5.25 3.25
Scored perforations 5.25 3.25
f. As "a," tagging omitted — —

Booklets containing two panes of ten of No. 1896e were issued Nov. 17, 1983.

The small block tagging is 16x18mm (Nos. 1896-1896b). The large block tagging is 18x21mm (Nos. 1896d-1896e).

TRANSPORTATION ISSUE

A1283

A1284

Designer: 1c, 2c, David Stone.

COIL STAMPS
ENGRAVED

1981-84 **Tagged** ***Perf. 10 Vert.***

1897 A1283 1c **violet,** *Aug. 19, 1983* .20 .20
Pair .20 .20
P# strip of 3, line, #1, 2 .30
P# strip of 3, line, #3, 4 .30
P# strip of 3, line, #5, 6 .30
P# strip of 5, line, #1, 2 .40
P# strip of 5, line, #3, 4 .50
P# strip of 5, line, #5, 6 .40
P# single, #1, 2 — .25
P# single, #3, 4 — .65
P# single, #5, 6 — .30
b. Imperf., pair *550.00*
Joint line pair —
e. Tagging omitted —

1897A A1284 2c **black,** *May 20, 1982* .20 .20
Pair .20 .20
P# strip of 3, line, #2-4, 6, 8, 10 .45
P# strip of 5, line, #2-4, 6, 8, 10 .50
P# single, #2-4, 6, 8, 10 — .40
c. Imperf., pair 45.00
Joint line pair —
d. Tagging omitted 27.50

A1284a

A1285

Designers: 3c, Walter Brooks. 4c, Jim Schleyer.

1898 A1284a 3c **dark green,** *Mar. 25, 1983* .20 .20
Pair .20 .20
P# strip of 3, line, #1-4 .50
P# strip of 5, line, #1-4 .60
P# single, #1-4 — .55

1898A A1285 4c **reddish brown,** *Aug. 19, 1982* .20 .20
Pair .20 .20
P# strip of 3, line, #1-4 .50
P# strip of 3, line, #5-6 1.50
P# strip of 5, line, #1-4 .90
P# strip of 5, line, #5-6 2.00
P# single, #1-4 — .75
P# single, #5-6 — 2.00
b. Untagged (Bureau precanceled, Nonprofit Org.) .20 .20
P# strip of 3, line, #3-6 3.25
P# strip of 5, line, #3-6 4.50
P# single, #3, 4 — 4.00
P# single, #5, 6 — 4.25
c. As "b," imperf., pair *700.00*
d. As No. 1898A, imperf. pair *750.00* —
e. Tagging omitted (not Bureau precanceled) *35.00* 15.00

See also No. 2228.

A1286

A1287

Designers: 5c, 5.2c, Walter Brooks.

1899 A1286 5c **gray green,** *Oct. 10, 1983* .20 .20
Pair .25 .20
P# strip of 3, line, #1-4 .50
P# strip of 5, line, #1-4 .90
P# single, #1-4 — .75
a. Imperf., pair *2,500.*
b. Tagging omitted 22.50 —

1900 A1287 5.2c **carmine,** *Mar. 21, 1983* .20 .20
Pair .25 .20
P# strip of 3, line, #1-2 2.00
P# strip of 3, line, #3 90.00
P# strip of 3, line, #5 60.00
P# strip of 5, line, #1-2 6.75
P# strip of 5, line, #3 225.00
P# strip of 5, line, #5 160.00
P# single, #1-2 — 5.50
P# single, #3 — *170.00*
P# single, #5 — *140.00*
a. Untagged (Bureau precanceled, lines only) .20 .20
P# strip of 3, line, #1-3 6.50
P# strip of 3, line, #4 7.50
P# strip of 3, line, #5 6.50
P# strip of 3, line, #6 7.50
P# strip of 5, line, #1-3 9.00
P# strip of 5, line, #4, 6 11.00
P# strip of 5, line, #5 9.00
P# single, #1, 2 — 2.50
P# single, #3 — 1.50
P# single, #4 — 10.00
P# single, #5 — 1.75
P# single, #6 — 10.00
b. Tagging omitted —

A1288

A1289

Designers: 5.9c, David Stone. 7.4c, Jim Schleyer.

1901 A1288 5.9c **blue,** *Feb. 17, 1982* .25 .20
Pair .50 .20
P# strip of 3, line, #3-4 2.50
P# strip of 5, line, #3-4 10.00
P# single, #3-4 — 5.00
a. Untagged (Bureau precanceled, lines only) .20 .20
P# strip of 3, line, #3-4 15.00
P# strip of 3, line, #5-6 80.00
P# strip of 5, line, #3-4 25.00
P# strip of 5, line, #5-6 100.00
P# single, #3-4 — 5.00
P# single, #5-6 — 60.00
b. As "a," imperf., pair *150.00*
Joint line pair —

1902 A1289 7.4c **brown,** *Apr. 7, 1984* .20 .20
Pair .40 .20
P# strip of 3, #2 3.50
P# strip of 5, #2 7.25
P# single, #2 — 5.75
a. Untagged (Bureau precanceled, Blk. Rt. CAR-RT SORT) .20 .20
P# strip of 3, #2 3.50
P# strip of 5, #2 4.00
P# single, #2 — 3.75

A1290

A1291

Designers: 9.3c, Jim Schleyer. 10.9c, David Stone.

1903 A1290 9.3c **carmine rose,** *Dec. 15* .30 .20
Pair .60 .20
P# strip of 3, line, #1-2 2.50
P# strip of 3, line, #3-4 5.00
P# strip of 3, line, #5-6 75.00
P# strip of 5, line, #1-2 11.00
P# strip of 5, line, #3-4 25.00
P# strip of 5, line, #5-6 325.00
P# single, #1-2 — 7.00
P# single, #3-4 — 15.00
P# single, #5-6 — 175.00
a. Untagged (Bureau precanceled, lines only) .25 .25
P# strip of 3, line, #1 8.50
P# strip of 3, line, #2 7.50
P# strip of 3, line, #3 14.00
P# strip of 3, line, #4 10.00
P# strip of 3, line, #5-6 1.75
P# strip of 3, line, #8 190.00
P# strip of 5, line, #1 12.00
P# strip of 5, line, #2 11.00
P# strip of 5, line, #3 22.50
P# strip of 5, line, #4 15.00
P# strip of 5, line, #5-6 2.25
P# strip of 5, line, #8 225.00
P# single, #1-2 — 9.00
P# single, #3 — 10.00
P# single, #4 — 9.50
P# single, #5-6 — 1.75
P# single, #8 — 200.00
b. As "a," imperf., pair 100.00
Joint line pair 175.00

1904 A1291 10.9c **purple,** *Mar. 26, 1982* .30 .20
Pair .60 .20
P# strip of 3, line, #1-2 6.00
P# strip of 5, line, #1-2 27.50
P# single, #1-2 — 12.00
a. Untagged (Bureau precanceled, lines only) .30 .25
P# strip of 3, line, #1-2 11.00
P# strip of 3, line, #3-4 110.00
P# strip of 5, line, #1-2 25.00
P# strip of 5, line, #3-4 200.00
P# single, #1-2 — 7.50
P# single, #3-4 — 65.00
b. As "a," imperf., pair 140.00
Joint line pair —

A1292

A1293

Designers: 11c, Jim Schleyer. 17c Chuck Jaquays.

1905 A1292 11c **red,** *Feb. 3, 1984* .30 .20
Pair .60 .20
P# strip of 3, #1 1.60
P# strip of 5, #1 3.25
P# single, #1 — 3.00
a. Untagged *Sept. 1991* .25 .20
Pair .50 .20
P# strip of 3, #1 1.60
P# strip of 3, #2, precanceled 1.90
P# strip of 5, #1 3.00
P# strip of 5, #2, precanceled 2.75
P# single, #1 — 2.75
P# single, #2, precanceled — 2.00

Untagged stamps from plate 1 come only Bureau precanceled with lines. Untagged stamps from plate 2 come both without and with Bureau precancel lines.

1906 A1293 17c **ultramarine,** *June 25* .35 .20
Pair .70 .20
P# strip of 3, line, #1-5 1.40
P# strip of 3, line, #6 6.00
P# strip of 3, line, #7 2.25
P# strip of 5, line, #1-5 2.25
P# strip of 5, line, #6 12.00
P# strip of 5, line, #7 5.00
P# single, #1-5 — 1.50
P# single, #6 — 12.00
P# single, #7 — 4.75
a. Untagged (Bureau precanceled, Presorted First Class) .35 .35
P# strip of 3, line, #1, 2 6.00
P# strip of 3, line, #3-5 2.50
P# strip of 3, line, #6, 7 7.00
P# strip of 5, line, #1, 2 8.75
P# strip of 5, line, #3-5 3.75
P# strip of 5, line, #6-7 10.50
P# single, #1, 2 — 7.25
P# single, #3-5 — 3.00
P# single, #6, 7 — 9.00

Three different precancel styles exist in four different lengths: "PRESORTED" measuring 11.3mm, 12.8mm, 13.4mm and 14.1mm. These measurements can vary slightly. The most common is the 11.3mm. Combination pairs exist of the 11.3mm and 12.8mm varieties. The 13.4mm and 14.1mm lengths have the same "type" style and vary in length, and as a result many coil collectors prefer to refer to, and collect, only the three different "type" styles.

b. Imperf., pair 140.00
Joint line pair —
c. As "a," imperf., pair *550.00*
Joint line pair —

A1294

A1295

Designers: 18c, David Stone. 20c, Jim Schleyer.

1907 A1294 18c **dark brown,** *May 18* .35 .20
Pair .70 .20
P# strip of 3, line, #1 17.00
P# strip of 3, line, #2 2.25
P# strip of 3, line, #3, 4 17.00
P# strip of 3, line, #5, 6 2.25
P# strip of 3, line, #7 8.00
P# strip of 3, line, #8 2.25
P# strip of 3, line, #9-12 6.00
P# strip of 3, line, #13, 14 2.25
P# strip of 3, line, #15, 16 8.00
P# strip of 3, line, #17, 18 2.25
P# strip of 5, line, #1 80.00
P# strip of 5, line, #2 3.00
P# strip of 5, line, #3-4 80.00
P# strip of 5, line, #5, 6 3.00
P# strip of 5, line, #7 22.50
P# strip of 5, line, #8 3.00
P# strip of 5, line, #9-12 13.00
P# strip of 5, line, #13, 14 3.00
P# strip of 5, line, #15, 16 22.50
P# strip of 5, line, #17, 18 3.00
P# single, #1 — 8.00
P# single, #2 — .75
P# single, #3, 4 — 9.25
P# single, #5, 6 — .75
P# single, #7 — 8.00
P# single, #8 — .75
P# single, #9-14 — 3.50
P# single, #15, 16 — 19.00
P# single, #17, 18 — 3.50
a. Imperf., pair 110.00
Joint line pair —
b. Tagging omitted —

1908 A1295 20c **vermilion,** *Dec. 10* .35 .20
Pair .70 .20
P# strip of 3, line, #1 20.00
P# strip of 3, line, #2 40.00
P# strip of 3, line, #3, 4 2.00
P# strip of 3, line, #5 2.00
P# strip of 3, line, #6 16.00
P# strip of 3, line, #7, 8 40.00
P# strip of 3, line, #9, 10 1.75
P# strip of 3, line, #11 7.50
P# strip of 3, line, #12 2.00
P# strip of 3, line, #13 2.25
P# strip of 3, line, #14 2.00
P# strip of 3, line, #15, 16 2.00
P# strip of 5, line, #1 125.00
P# strip of 5, line, #2 625.00
P# strip of 5, line, #3, 4 4.25
P# strip of 5, line, #5 2.75
P# strip of 5, line, #6 35.00
P# strip of 5, line, #7-8 200.00
P# strip of 5, line, #9-10 2.75
P# strip of 5, line, #11 100.00
P# strip of 5, line, #12 7.25
P# strip of 5, line, #13 4.25
P# strip of 5, line, #14 7.25
P# strip of 5, line, #15-16 4.25
P# single, #1 — .75
P# single, #2 — 7.50
P# single, #3, 4 — .65
P# single, #5 — .75
P# single, #6 — 1.25
P# single, #7, 8 — 1.00
P# single, #9, 10 — .75
P# single, #11 — .75
P# single, #12 — 6.25
P# single, #13 — .65
P# single, #14 — 6.25
P# single, #15, 16 — 2.00
a. Imperf., pair 90.00
Joint line pair *275.00* —
b. Tagging omitted —
Nos. 1897-1908 (14) 3.60 2.80

See Nos. 2225-2228.

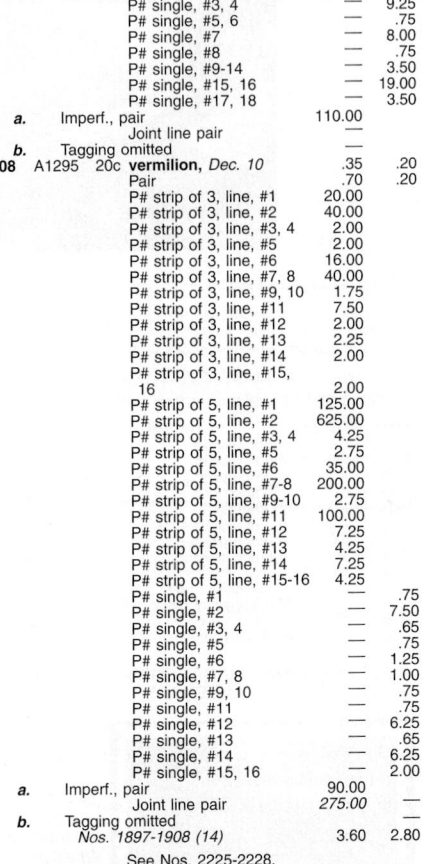

Eagle and Moon — A1296

Booklet Stamp
PHOTOGRAVURE

1983, Aug. 12 **Untagged** ***Perf. 10 Vert.***
1909 A1296 $9.35 **multicolored** 20.00 15.00
a. Booklet pane of 3 60.00 —

A1297

A1298

AMERICAN RED CROSS CENTENNIAL

Designed by Joseph Csatari.

PHOTOGRAVURE

Plates of 200 subjects in four panes of 50.

1981, May 1	Tagged	*Perf. 10½x11*	
1910 A1297 18c **multicolored**		.35	.20
P# block of 4, 6#		1.50	—
Zip block of 4		1.40	—

SAVINGS & LOAN SESQUICENTENNIAL

Designed by Don Hedin.

PHOTOGRAVURE

Plates of 200 subjects in four panes of 50.

1981, May 8	Tagged	*Perf. 11*	
1911 A1298 18c **multicolored**		.35	.20
P# block of 4, 6#		1.50	—
Zip block of 4		1.40	—

SPACE ACHIEVEMENT ISSUE

A1299

A1302

A1300

A1301

A1303

A1306

A1304

A1305

Designed by Robert McCall.

Designs: A1299, Moon walk. A1300-A1301, A1304-A1305, Columbia space shuttle. A1302, Skylab. A1303, Pioneer 11. A1306, Telescope. Se-tenant in blocks of 8.

PHOTOGRAVURE

Plates of 192 subjects in four panes of 48 each.

1981, May 21	Tagged	*Perf. 11*	
1912 A1299 18c **multicolored**		.40	.20
1913 A1300 18c **multicolored**		.40	.20
1914 A1301 18c **multicolored**		.40	.20
1915 A1302 18c **multicolored**		.40	.20
1916 A1303 18c **multicolored**		.40	.20
1917 A1304 18c **multicolored**		.40	.20
1918 A1305 18c **multicolored**		.40	.20
1919 A1306 18c **multicolored**		.40	.20
a. Block of 8, #1912-1919		3.25	3.00
P# block of 8, 6#		3.75	—
Zip, copyright block of 8		3.25	—
b. As "a," imperf.		*7,500.*	
c. As "a," tagging omitted		—	

PROFESSIONAL MANAGEMENT EDUCATION CENTENARY

Joseph Wharton (Founder of Wharton School of Business) A1307

Designed by Rudolph de Harak.

PHOTOGRAVURE

Plates of 200 subject in four panes of 50.

1981, June 18	Tagged	*Perf. 11*	
1920 A1307 18c **blue & black**		.35	.20
P# block of 4, 2#		1.50	—
Zip block of 4		1.40	—

PRESERVATION OF WILDLIFE HABITATS

Great Blue Heron — A1308

Badger — A1309

Grizzly Bear — A1310

Ruffed Grouse — A1311

Designed by Chuck Ripper

PHOTOGRAVURE

Plates of 200 subjects in four panes of 50.

1981, June 26	Tagged	*Perf. 11*	
1921 A1308 18c **multicolored**		.35	.20
1922 A1309 18c **multicolored**		.35	.20
1923 A1310 18c **multicolored**		.35	.20
1924 A1311 18c **multicolored**		.35	.20
a. Block of 4, #1921-1924		1.50	1.25
P# block of 4, 5#		2.00	—
Zip block of 4		1.55	—

INTERNATIONAL YEAR OF THE DISABLED

Man Using Microscope A1312

Designed by Martha Perske

PHOTOGRAVURE

Plates of 200 subjects in four panes of 50.

1981, June 29	Tagged	*Perf. 11*	
1925 A1312 18c **multicolored**		.35	.20
P# block of 4, 6#		1.50	—
Zip block of 4		1.40	—
a. Vert. pair, imperf. horiz.		*2,500.*	

EDNA ST. VINCENT MILLAY ISSUE

A1313

Designed by Glenora Case Richards

LITHOGRAPHED AND ENGRAVED

Plates of 200 subjects in four panes of 50.

1981, July 10	Tagged	*Perf. 11*	
1926 A1313 18c **multicolored**		.35	.20
P# block of 4, 7#		1.50	—
Zip block of 4		1.40	—
a. Black (engr., inscriptions) omitted		*275.00*	—

ALCOHOLISM

A1314

Designed by John Boyd

ENGRAVED

Plates of 230 (10x23) subjects in panes of 50 (5x10)

1981, Aug. 19	Tagged	*Perf. 11*	
1927 A1314 18c **blue & black**		.45	.20
P# block of 6		10.00	—
P# block of 20, 1-2 #, 1-2 copyright, 1-2 Zip		20.00	—
a. Imperf., pair		*375.00*	
b. Vert. pair, imperf. horiz.		*2,400.*	

See Combination Press note after No. 1703.

AMERICAN ARCHITECTURE SERIES

New York University Library by Stanford White A1315

Biltmore House By Richard Morris Hunt — A1316

Palace of the Arts by Bernard Maybeck A1317

National Farmer's Bank by Louis Sullivan A1318

Designed by Walter D. Richards

ENGRAVED

Plates of 160 subjects in four panes of 40.

1981, Aug. 28	Tagged	Perf. 11	
1928 A1315 18c **black & red**		.40	.20
a. Tagging omitted			—
1929 A1316 18c **black & red**		.40	.20
1930 A1317 18c **black & red**		.40	.20
a. Tagging omitted			—
1931 A1318 18c **black & red**		.40	.20
a. Block of 4, #1928-1931		1.65	1.65
P# block of 4		2.10	—
Zip block of 4		1.80	—
b. As "a," tagging omitted			—

SPORTS PERSONALITIES

Mildred Didrikson Zaharias — A1319

Robert Tyre Jones — A1320

Designed by Richard Gangel

ENGRAVED

Plates of 200 subjects in four panes of 50.

1981, Sept. 22	Tagged	Perf. 10½x11	
1932 A1319 18c **purple**		.40	.20
P# block of 4		3.00	—
Zip block of 4		1.75	—
1933 A1320 18c **green**		.60	.20
P# block of 4		3.25	—
Zip block of 4		2.50	—

FREDERIC REMINGTON

Coming Through the Rye — A1321

Designed by Paul Calle

LITHOGRAPHED AND ENGRAVED

Plates of 200 in four panes of 50.

1981, Oct. 9	Tagged	Perf. 11	
1934 A1321 18c **gray, olive green & brown**		.35	.20
P# block of 4, 3#		1.60	—
Zip block of 4		1.50	—
a. Vert. pair, imperf. between		*225.00*	
b. Brown omitted		*375.00*	

JAMES HOBAN

Irish-American Architect of the White House A1322

Designed by Ron Mercer and Walter D. Richards.

PHOTOGRAVURE

Plates of 200 in four panes of 50.

1981, Oct. 13	Tagged	Perf. 11	
1935 A1322 18c **multicolored**		.35	.20
P# block of 4, 6#		1.60	—
Zip block of 4		1.50	—
1936 A1322 20c **multicolored**		.35	.20
P# block of 4, 6#		1.65	—
Zip block of 4		1.50	—

See Ireland No. 504.

AMERICAN BICENTENNIAL

Battle of Yorktown A1323

Battle of the Virginia Capes A1324

Designed by Cal Sacks.

LITHOGRAPHED AND ENGRAVED

Plates of 200 in four panes of 50.

1981, Oct. 16	Tagged	Perf. 11	
1937 A1323 18c **multicolored**		.35	.20
1938 A1324 18c **multicolored**		.35	.20
a. Pair, #1937-1938		.90	.75
P# block of 4, 7#		2.00	—
Zip block of 4		1.65	—
b. As "a," black (engr., inscriptions) omitted		*350.00*	
c. As "a," tagging omitted		*100.00*	

CHRISTMAS

Madonna and Child, Botticelli — A1325

Felt Bear on Sleigh A1326

Designed by Bradbury Thompson (No. 1939) and by Naiad Einsel (No. 1940).

PHOTOGRAVURE

Plates of 400 in four panes of 100 (No. 1939)

Plates of 200 in four panes of 50 (No. 1940)

1981, Oct. 28	Tagged	Perf. 11	
1939 A1325 (20c) **multicolored**		.40	.20
P# block of 4, 6#		1.75	—
Zip block of 4		1.65	—
a. Imperf., pair		*100.00*	
b. Vert. pair, imperf. horiz.		*1,150.*	
c. Tagging omitted		*17.50*	
1940 A1326 (20c) **multicolored**		.40	.20
P# block of 4, 5#		1.75	—
Zip block of 4		1.65	—
a. Imperf., pair		*200.00*	
b. Vert. pair, imperf. horiz.		*2,750.*	

JOHN HANSON

First President of the Continental Congress — A1327

Designed by Ron Adair.

PHOTOGRAVURE

Plates of 200 in panes of 50

1981, Nov. 5	Tagged	Perf. 11	
1941 A1327 20c **multicolored**		.40	.20
P# block of 4, 5#		1.75	—
Zip block of 4		1.65	—

DESERT PLANTS

Barrel Cactus — A1328

Saguaro — A1331

Agave — A1329

Beavertail Cactus — A1330

Designed by Frank J. Waslick.

LITHOGRAPHED AND ENGRAVED
Plates of 160 in four panes of 40

1981 Dec. 11	Tagged		Perf. 11	
1942 A1328 20c **multicolored**			.35	.20
1943 A1329 20c **multicolored**			.35	.20
1944 A1330 20c **multicolored**			.35	.20
1945 A1331 20c **multicolored**			.35	.20
a.	Block of 4, #1942-1945		1.50	1.25
		P# block of 4, 7#	1.90	—
		Zip block of 4	1.55	—
b.	As "a," deep brown (litho.) omitted		*4,250.*	
c.	No. 1945 imperf., vert. pair		*3,500.*	
d.	As "a," dark green & dark blue (engr.) missing (EP)			—
e.	As "a," dark green (engr.) missing on left stamp (EP)			—
f.	As "a," tagging omitted			—

A1332

A1333

Designed by Bradbury Thompson.

PHOTOGRAVURE
Plates of 400 in panes of 100.

1981, Oct. 11	Tagged		Perf. 11x10½	
1946 A1332 (20c) **brown**			.40	.20
		P# block of 4	2.00	—
		Zip block of 4	1.65	—
a.	Tagging omitted		7.00	
b.	All color omitted			—

No. 1946b comes from a partially printed pane with most stamps normal. It must be collected as a vertical pair or strip with normal or partially printed stamps attached.

ENGRAVED
COIL STAMP
Perf. 10 Vert.

1947 A1332 (20c) **brown**			.60	.20
		Pair	1.20	.20
		Joint line pair	1.50	—
a.	Imperf. pair		*950.00*	
		Joint line pair		—

BOOKLET STAMPS
Perf. 11

1948 A1333 (20c) **brown**		.40	.20
a.	Booklet pane of 10	4.50	3.25

Rocky Mountain Bighorn — A1334

BOOKLET STAMP
ENGRAVED

1982, Jan. 8	Tagged	Perf. 11	
1949 A1334 20c **dark blue**		.55	.20
a.	Booklet pane of 10	5.50	2.50
b.	As "a," imperf. between	*95.00*	
c.	Type II	1.40	.20
d.	Type II, booklet pane of 10	14.00	—
e.	As #1949, tagging omitted	5.00	—
f.	As "e," booklet pane of 10	*50.00*	—

No. 1949 is 18¾mm wide and has overall tagging. No. 1949c is 18½mm wide and has block tagging.

FRANKLIN DELANO ROOSEVELT

A1335

Designed by Clarence Holbert.

ENGRAVED
Plates of 192 in four panes of 48

1982, Jan. 30	Tagged	Perf. 11	
1950 A1335 20c **blue**		.40	.20
	P# block of 4	1.75	—
	Zip block of 4	1.65	—

LOVE ISSUE

A1336

Designed by Mary Faulconer.

PHOTOGRAVURE
Plates of 200 in four panes of 50.

1982, Feb. 1	Tagged		Perf. 11¼	
1951 A1336 20c **multicolored**			.40	.20
		P# block of 4, 5#	1.75	—
		Zip block of 4	1.65	—
b.	Imperf., pair		*225.00*	
c.	Blue omitted		*200.00*	
d.	Yellow omitted		*950.00*	
e.	Purple omitted			—
f.	Tagging omitted		100.00	—

No. 1951c is valued in the grade of fine.

Perf. 11¼x10½

1951A A1336 20c **multicolored**		.75	.25
	P# block of 4, 5#	3.50	—
	Zip block of 4	3.00	—

GEORGE WASHINGTON

A1337

Designed by Mark English.

PHOTOGRAVURE
Plates of 200 in four panes of 50.

1982, Feb. 22	Tagged	Perf. 11	
1952 A1337 20c **multicolored**		.40	.20
	P# block of 4, 6#	1.75	—
	Zip block of 4	1.65	—

STATE BIRDS AND FLOWERS ISSUE

Illustration reduced.

Designed by Arthur and Alan Singer.

PHOTOGRAVURE (Andreotti)
Plates of 200 subjects in four panes of 50.

1982, Apr. 14	Tagged	Perf. 10½x11¼	
1953 A1338 20c Alabama		.55	.30
1954 A1339 20c Alaska		.55	.30
1955 A1340 20c Arizona		.55	.30
1956 A1341 20c Arkansas		.55	.30
1957 A1342 20c California		.55	.30
1958 A1343 20c Colorado		.55	.30
1959 A1344 20c Connecticut		.55	.30
1960 A1345 20c Delaware		.55	.30
1961 A1346 20c Florida		.55	.30
1962 A1347 20c Georgia		.55	.30
1963 A1348 20c Hawaii		.55	.30
1964 A1349 20c Idaho		.55	.30
1965 A1350 20c Illinois		.55	.30
1966 A1351 20c Indiana		.55	.30
1967 A1352 20c Iowa		.55	.30
1968 A1353 20c Kansas		.55	.30
1969 A1354 20c Kentucky		.55	.30
1970 A1355 20c Louisiana		.55	.30
1971 A1356 20c Maine		.55	.30
1972 A1357 20c Maryland		.55	.30
1973 A1358 20c Massachusetts		.55	.30
1974 A1359 20c Michigan		.55	.30
1975 A1360 20c Minnesota		.55	.30
1976 A1361 20c Mississippi		.55	.30
1977 A1362 20c Missouri		.55	.30
1978 A1363 20c Montana		.55	.30
1979 A1364 20c Nebraska		.55	.30
1980 A1365 20c Nevada		.55	.30
1981 A1366 20c New Hampshire		.55	.30
b.	Black missing (EP)	*6,000.*	
1982 A1367 20c New Jersey		.55	.30
1983 A1368 20c New Mexico		.55	.30
1984 A1369 20c New York		.55	.30
1985 A1370 20c North Carolina		.55	.30
1986 A1371 20c North Dakota		.55	.30
1987 A1372 20c Ohio		.55	.30
1988 A1373 20c Oklahoma		.55	.30
1989 A1374 20c Oregon		.55	.30
1990 A1375 20c Pennsylvania		.55	.30
1991 A1376 20c Rhode Island		.55	.30
b.	Black missing (EP)	*6,000.*	
1992 A1377 20c South Carolina		.55	.30
1993 A1378 20c South Dakota		.55	.30
1994 A1379 20c Tennessee		.55	.30
1995 A1380 20c Texas		.55	.30
1996 A1381 20c Utah		.55	.30
1997 A1382 20c Vermont		.55	.30
1998 A1383 20c Virginia		.55	.30
1999 A1384 20c Washington		.55	.30
2000 A1385 20c West Virginia		.55	.30
2001 A1386 20c Wisconsin		.55	.30
b.	Black missing (EP)	*6,000.*	
2002 A1387 20c Wyoming		.55	.30
b.	A1338-A1387 Pane of 50, Nos. 1953-2002	27.50	20.00
d.	Pane of 50, imperf.	*27,500.*	

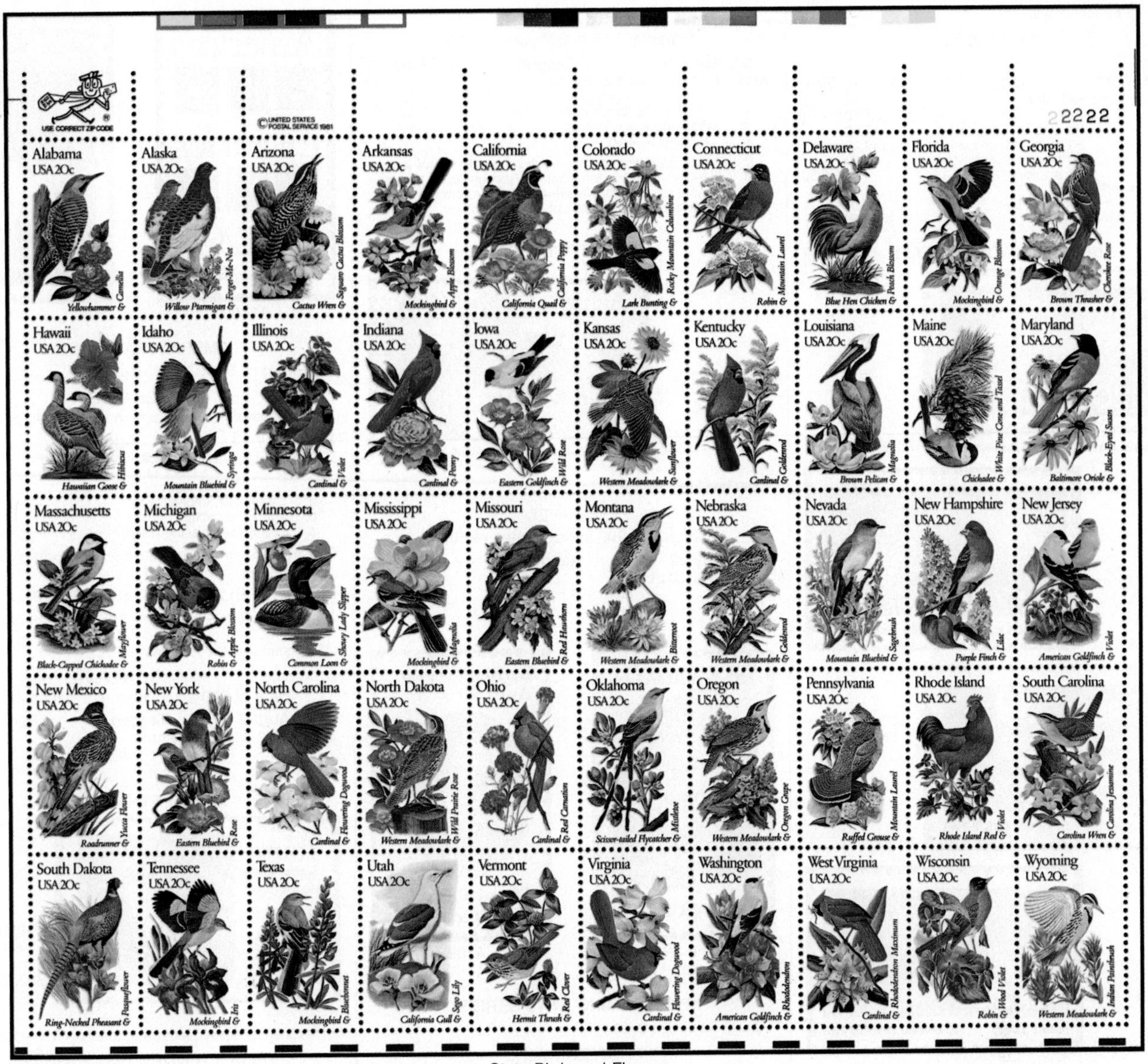

State Birds and Flowers
A1338-A1387

Perf. 11¼x11

1953A	A1338	20c	Alabama	.65	.30
1954A	A1339	20c	Alaska	.65	.30
1955A	A1340	20c	Arizona	.65	.30
1956A	A1341	20c	Arkansas	.65	.30
1957A	A1342	20c	California	.65	.30
1958A	A1343	20c	Colorado	.65	.30
1959A	A1344	20c	Connecticut	.65	.30
1960A	A1345	20c	Delaware	.65	.30
1961A	A1346	20c	Florida	.65	.30
1962A	A1347	20c	Georgia	.65	.30
1963A	A1348	20c	Hawaii	.65	.30
1964A	A1349	20c	Idaho	.65	.30
1965A	A1350	20c	Illinois	.65	.30
1966A	A1351	20c	Indiana	.65	.30
1967A	A1352	20c	Iowa	.65	.30
1968A	A1353	20c	Kansas	.65	.30
1969A	A1354	20c	Kentucky	.65	.30
1970A	A1355	20c	Louisiana	.65	.30
1971A	A1356	20c	Maine	.65	.30
1972A	A1357	20c	Maryland	.65	.30
1973A	A1358	20c	Massachusetts	.65	.30
1974A	A1359	20c	Michigan	.65	.30
1975A	A1360	20c	Minnesota	.65	.30
1976A	A1361	20c	Mississippi	.65	.30
1977A	A1362	20c	Missouri	.65	.30
1978A	A1363	20c	Montana	.65	.30
1979A	A1364	20c	Nebraska	.65	.30
1980A	A1365	20c	Nevada	.65	.30
1981A	A1366	20c	New Hampshire	.65	.30
1982A	A1367	20c	New Jersey	.65	.30
1983A	A1368	20c	New Mexico	.65	.30
1984A	A1369	20c	New York	.65	.30
1985A	A1370	20c	North Carolina	.65	.30
1986A	A1371	20c	North Dakota	.65	.30
1987A	A1372	20c	Ohio	.65	.30
1988A	A1373	20c	Oklahoma	.65	.30
1989A	A1374	20c	Oregon	.65	.30
1990A	A1375	20c	Pennsylvania	.65	.30
1991A	A1376	20c	Rhode Island	.65	.30
1992A	A1377	20c	South Carolina	.65	.30
1993A	A1378	20c	South Dakota	.65	.30
1994A	A1379	20c	Tennessee	.65	.30
1995A	A1380	20c	Texas	.65	.30
1996A	A1381	20c	Utah	.65	.30
1997A	A1382	20c	Vermont	.65	.30
1998A	A1383	20c	Virginia	.65	.30
1999A	A1384	20c	Washington	.65	.30
2000A	A1385	20c	West Virginia	.65	.30
2001A	A1386	20c	Wisconsin	.65	.30
2002A	A1387	20c	Wyoming	.65	.30
c.			A1338-A1387 Pane of 50, Nos. 1953A-2002A	32.50	22.50

US-NETHERLANDS

200th Anniv. of Diplomatic Recognition by The Netherlands
A1388

Designed by Heleen Tigler Wybrandi-Raue.

PHOTOGRAVURE

Plates of 230 (10x23) subjects in panes of 50 (5x10).

1982, Apr. 20 **Tagged** ***Perf. 11***

2003	A1388	20c	**verm., brt. blue & gray blk.**	.40	.20
			P# block of 6	3.50	—
			P# block of 20, 1-2 #, 1-2 copyright, 1-2 zip	10.00	—
a.			Imperf., pair	*275.00*	

See Combination Press note after No. 1703.
See Netherlands Nos. 640-641.

LIBRARY OF CONGRESS

A1389

Designed by Bradbury Thompson.

ENGRAVED

Plates of 200 subjects in four panes of 50.

1982, Apr. 21 **Tagged** ***Perf. 11***

2004	A1389	20c	**red & black**	.40	.20
			P# block of 4	1.75	—
			Zip block of 4	1.65	—
a.			All color missing		—

No. 2004a must be collected as a right margin horiz. strip of 5 or 3 with 3 (or 1) normal, one transitional and one with color omitted.

A1390

Designed by John Boyd.

ENGRAVED
Coil Stamp

1982, Apr. 27 — Tagged — *Perf. 10 Vert.*

2005	A1390 20c **sky blue**	.55	.20
	Pair	1.10	.20
	P# strip of 3, line, #1-4	10.00	
	P# strip of 5, line, #1-2	140.00	
	P# strip of 5, line, #3-4	80.00	
	P# single, #1-4	—	1.50
a.	Imperf., pair	95.00	
	Joint line pair	*375.00*	
b.	Tagging omitted	*7.50*	

KNOXVILLE WORLD'S FAIR

A1391

A1392

A1393

A1394

Illustration reduced.

Designed by Charles Harper.

PHOTOGRAVURE
Plates of 200 in four panes of 50.

1982, Apr. 29 — Tagged — *Perf. 11*

2006	A1391 20c **multicolored**	.45	.20
2007	A1392 20c **multicolored**	.45	.20
2008	A1393 20c **multicolored**	.45	.20
2009	A1394 20c **multicolored**	.45	.20
	Any single on cover, Expo. station handstamp cancel		10.00
a.	Block of 4, #2006-2009	1.80	1.50
	P# block of 4, 6#	2.40	—
	Zip block of 4	1.90	—

HORATIO ALGER

A1395

Designed by Robert Hallock.

ENGRAVED
Plates of 200 in four panes of 50.

1982, Apr. 30 — Tagged — *Perf. 11*

2010	A1395 20c **red & black,** *tan*	.40	.20
	P# block of 4	1.75	—
	Zip block of 4	1.65	—
a.	Red and black omitted	—	
b.	Tagging omitted		—

The Philatelic Foundation has issued a certificate for a pane of 50 with red and black colors omitted. Recognition of this error is by the paper and by a tiny residue of red ink from the tagging roller. The engraved plates did not strike the paper.

AGING TOGETHER

A1396

Designed by Paul Calle.

ENGRAVED
Plates of 200 in four panes of 50.

1982, May 21 — Tagged — *Perf. 11*

2011	A1396 20c **brown**	.40	.20
	P# block of 4	1.75	—
	Zip block of 4	1.65	—

John, Ethel and Lionel Barrymore — A1397

A1398

PERFORMING ARTS SERIES

Designed by Jim Sharpe.

PHOTOGRAVURE
Plates of 200 in four panes of 50.

1982, June 8 — Tagged — *Perf. 11*

2012	A1397 20c **multicolored**	.40	.20
	P# block of 4, 6#	1.75	—
	Zip block of 4	1.65	—
a.	Black missing (EP)	—	

DR. MARY WALKER

Designed by Glenora Richards.

PHOTOGRAVURE
Plate of 200 in four panes of 50.

1982, June 10 — Tagged — *Perf. 11*

2013	A1398 20c **multicolored**	.40	.20
	P# block of 4, 6#	1.75	—
	Zip block of 4	1.65	—

INTERNATIONAL PEACE GARDEN

Dunseith, ND-Boissevain, Manitoba — A1399

Designed by Gyo Fujikawa.

LITHOGRAPHED AND ENGRAVED
Plate of 200 in four panes of 50.

1982, June 30 — Tagged — *Perf. 11*

2014	A1399 20c **multicolored**	.50	.20
	P# block of 4, 5#	2.25	—
	Zip block of 4	2.00	—
a.	Black (engr.) omitted	*225.00*	

A1400

A1401

AMERICA'S LIBRARIES

Designed by Bradbury Thompson.

ENGRAVED
Plate of 200 subjects in four panes of 50.

1982, July 13 — Tagged — *Perf. 11*

2015	A1400 20c **red & black**	.40	.20
	P# block of 4	1.75	—
	Zip block of 4	1.65	—
a.	Vert. pair, imperf. horiz.	*250.00*	
b.	Tagging omitted	*9.00*	
c.	All colors missing (EP)	*175.00*	

On No. 2015c, an albino impression of the design is present.

BLACK HERITAGE SERIES

Jackie Robinson (1919-72), baseball player.

Designed by Jerry Pinkney.

PHOTOGRAVURE
Plate of 200 subjects in four panes of 50.

1982, Aug. 2 — Tagged — *Perf. 10½x11*

2016	A1401 20c **multicolored**	1.10	.20
	P# block of 4, 5#	6.00	—
	Zip block of 4	4.75	—

TOURO SYNAGOGUE

Oldest Existing Synagogue Building in the U.S. — A1402

Designed by Donald Moss and Bradbury Thompson.

PHOTOGRAVURE AND ENGRAVED
Plates of 230 (10x23) subjects in panes of 50 (5x10).

1982, Aug. 22 — Tagged — *Perf. 11*

2017	A1402 20c **multicolored**	.45	.20
	P# block of 20, 6-12 #, 1-2 copyright, 1-2 zip	12.50	—
a.	Imperf., pair	*2,350.*	

See Combination Press note after No. 1703.

WOLF TRAP FARM PARK

A1403

Designed by Richard Schlecht.

PHOTOGRAVURE
Plates of 200 in four panes of 50.

1982, Sept. 1 — Tagged — *Perf. 11*

2018	A1403 20c **multicolored**	.40	.20
	P# block of 4, 5#	1.75	—
	Zip block of 4	1.65	—

AMERICAN ARCHITECTURE SERIES

A1404

A1405

A1406

A1407

Designed by Walter D. Richards.

ENGRAVED
Plates of 160 subjects in four panes of 40.

1982, Sept. 30 **Tagged** ***Perf. 11***

2019	A1404 20c **black & brown**		.45	.20
a.	Tagging omitted			—
b.	Red missing (PS)		—	
2020	A1405 20c **black & brown**		.45	.20
a.	Red missing (PS)		—	
2021	A1406 20c **black & brown**		.45	.20
2022	A1407 20c **black & brown**		.45	.20
a.	Block of 4, #2019-2022		2.00	1.75
		P# block of 4	2.50	—
		Zip block of 4	2.10	—

FRANCIS OF ASSISI

A1408

Designed by Ned Seidler.

Printed by American Bank Note Co. and J.W. Fergusson and Sons.

PHOTOGRAVURE
Plates of 200 subjects in four panes of 50.

1982, Oct. 7 **Tagged** ***Perf. 11***

2023	A1408 20c **multicolored**		.40	.20
		P# block of 4, 6#+A	1.75	—
		Zip block of 4	1.65	—

PONCE DE LEON

A1409

Designed by Richard Schlecht.

PHOTOGRAVURE (Combination press)
Plates of 230 subjects (10x23) in panes of 50 (5x10).

1982, Oct. 12 **Tagged** ***Perf. 11***

2024	A1409 20c **multicolored**		.50	.20
		P# block of 6, 5#	3.50	—
		P# block of 20, 5 or 10 #, 1-2 zip, 1-2 copyright	12.00	—
a.	Imperf., pair		*425.00*	
b.	Vert. pair, imperf. between and at top		—	

See Combination Press note after No. 1703.

CHRISTMAS ISSUES

A1410

A1411

A1412

A1413

A1414

A1415

PHOTOGRAVURE
Plates of 200 subjects in four panes of 50

Designed by Chuck Ripper.

1982, Nov. 3 **Tagged**

2025	A1410 13c **multicolored**		.25	.20
		P# block of 4	1.40	—
		Zip block of 4	1.10	—
a.	Imperf., pair		*475.00*	

PHOTOGRAVURE (Combination Press)
Plates of 230 subjects (10x23) in panes of 50 (5x10).

Designed by Bradbury Thompson.

1982, Oct. 28 **Tagged**

2026	A1411 20c **multicolored**		.40	.20
		P# block of 20, 5 or 10 #, 1-2 copyright, 1-2 zip	11.00	—
a.	Imperf. pair		135.00	
b.	Horiz. pair, imperf. vert.		—	
c.	Vert. pair, imperf. horiz.		—	

See Combination Press note after No. 1703.

PHOTOGRAVURE
Plates of 200 in four panes of 50.

Designed by Dolli Tingle.

2027	A1412 20c **multicolored**		.60	.20
2028	A1413 20c **multicolored**		.60	.20
2029	A1414 20c **multicolored**		.60	.20
2030	A1415 20c **multicolored**		.60	.20
a.	Block of 4, #2027-2030		2.40	1.50
		P# block of 4, 4#	2.75	—
		Zip block of 4	2.50	—
b.	As "a," imperf.		*1,800.*	
c.	As "a," imperf. horiz.		*800.00*	

SCIENCE & INDUSTRY

A1416

Designed by Saul Bass.

LITHOGRAPHED AND ENGRAVED
Plates of 200 in four panes of 50.

1983, Jan. 19 **Tagged** ***Perf. 11***

2031	A1416 20c **multicolored**		.40	.20
		P# block of 4, 4#	1.75	—
		Zip block of 4	1.65	—
a.	Black (engr.) omitted		*1,250.*	
b.	Tagging omitted			—

BALLOONS

Intrepid — A1417

Explorer II — A1420

A1418

A1419

Designed by Davis Meltzer.

PHOTOGRAVURE
Plates of 160 in four panes of 40.

1983, Mar. 31 **Tagged** ***Perf. 11***
2032 A1417 20c **multicolored** .50 .20
2033 A1418 20c **multicolored** .50 .20
2034 A1419 20c **multicolored** .50 .20
2035 A1420 20c **multicolored** .50 .20
a. Block of 4, #2032-2035 2.00 1.50
P# block of 4, 5# 2.25 —
Zip block of 4 2.10 —
b. As "a," imperf. *3,750.*
c. As "a," right stamp perf., otherwise imperf. *4,250.*

US-SWEDEN

Benjamin Franklin A1421

Designed by Czeslaw Slania, court engraver of Sweden.

ENGRAVED
Plates of 200 in four panes of 50.

1983, Mar. 24 **Tagged** ***Perf. 11***
2036 A1421 20c **blue, blk & red brn** .40 .20
P# block of 4 1.75 —
Zip block of 4 1.65 —

See Sweden No. 1453.

CCC, 50th ANNIV.

A1422

Designed by David K. Stone.

PHOTOGRAVURE
Plates of 200 in four panes of 50.

1983, Apr. 5 **Tagged** ***Perf. 11***
2037 A1422 20c **multicolored** .40 .20
P# block of 4, 6# 1.75 —
Zip block of 4 1.65 —
a. Imperf., pair *3,000.*
b. Vert. pair, imperf. horiz. —

JOSEPH PRIESTLEY

Discoverer of Oxygen — A1423

Designed by Dennis Lyall.

Printed by American Bank Note Company and J.W. Ferguson and Sons.

PHOTOGRAVURE
Plates of 200 in four panes of 50.

1983, Apr. 13 **Tagged** ***Perf. 11***
2038 A1423 20c **multicolored** .40 .20
P# block of 4, 6#+A 1.75 —
Zip block of 4 1.65 —

VOLUNTARISM

A1424

Designed by Paul Calle.

ENGRAVED (Combination Press)
Plates of 230 subjects (10x23) in panes of 50 (5x10).

1983, Apr. 20 **Tagged** ***Perf. 11***
2039 A1424 20c **red & black** .40 .20
P# block of 6 3.00 —
P# block of 20, 1-2 #, 1-2 copyright, 1-2 zip 10.00 —
a. Imperf., pair *325.00*

See Combination Press note after No. 1703.

US-GERMANY

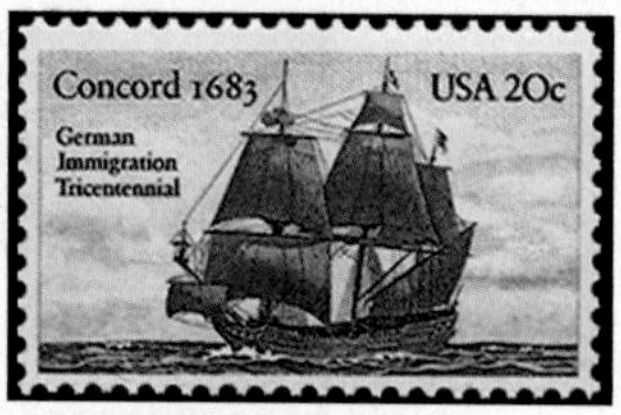

A1425

Designed by Richard Schlecht.

ENGRAVED
Plates of 200 in four panes of 50.

1983, Apr. 29 **Tagged** ***Perf. 11***
2040 A1425 20c **brown** .40 .20
P# block of 4 1.75 —
Zip block of 4 1.65 —
a. Tagging omitted —

See Germany No. 1397.

BROOKLYN BRIDGE

A1426

Normal

"Unfinished Bridge" Short Transfer

Designed by Howard Koslow.

ENGRAVED
Plates of 200 in four panes of 50.

1983, May 17 **Tagged** ***Perf. 11***
2041 A1426 20c **blue** .40 .20
P# block of 4 1.75 —
Zip block of 4 1.65 —
Short transfer (unfinished bridge) (UL 2) 9.00 .75
P# block of 4 15.00
a. Tagging omitted *150.00*
b. All color missing (EP) *75.00*

On No. 2041b, an albino impression of the stamp is evident.

TVA

Norris Hydroelectric Dam — A1427

Designed by Howard Koslow.

PHOTOGRAVURE AND ENGRAVED (Combination Press)
Plates of 230 in panes of 50

1983, May 18 **Tagged** ***Perf. 11***
2042 A1427 20c **multicolored** .40 .20
P# block of 20, 5-10 #, 1-2 copyright, 1-2 zip 10.00 —

Runners, Electrocardiograph Tracing — A1428

Designed by Donald Moss.

PHOTOGRAVURE (Combination Press)
Plates of 230 in panes of 50.

1983, May 14 **Tagged** ***Perf. 11***
2043 A1428 20c **multicolored** .40 .20
P# block of 6, 4# 3.00 —
P# block of 20, 4-8 #, 1-2 copyright, 1-2 zip 10.00 —

BLACK HERITAGE SERIES

Scott Joplin (1868-1917), Ragtime composer.

A1429

Designed by Jerry Pinkney.

PHOTOGRAVURE

Plates of 200 in four panes of 50.

1983, June 9 **Tagged** ***Perf. 11***

2044	A1429	20c	**multicolored**	.50	.20
			P# block of 4, 6#	2.40	—
			Zip block of 4	2.10	—
a.			Imperf., pair	*425.00*	
b.			Tagging omitted	—	—

MEDAL OF HONOR

A1430

Designed by Dennis J. Hom.

LITHOGRAPHED AND ENGRAVED

Plates of 160 in four panes of 40.

1983, June 7 **Tagged** ***Perf. 11***

2045	A1430	20c	**multicolored**	.55	.20
			P# block of 4, 5#	2.50	—
			Zip block of 4	2.25	—
a.			Red omitted	*225.00*	

A1431

A1432

GEORGE HERMAN RUTH (1895-1948)

Designed by Richard Gangel.

ENGRAVED

Plates of 200 in four panes of 50.

1983, July 6 **Tagged** ***Perf. 10½x11***

2046	A1431	20c	**blue**	1.40	.20
			P# block of 4	6.25	—
			Zip block of 4	5.75	—

LITERARY ARTS SERIES

Nathaniel Hawthorne (1804-1864), novelist.

Designed by Bradbury Thompson after 1851 painting by Cephus Giovanni Thompson.

PHOTOGRAVURE

Plates of 200 in four panes of 50.

1983, July 8 **Tagged** ***Perf. 11***

2047	A1432	20c	**multicolored**	.45	.20
			P# block of 4, 4#	2.10	—
			Zip block of 4	1.90	—

1984 SUMMER OLYMPICS
Los Angeles, July 28-August 12

Discus
A1433

High Jump — A1434

Archery
A1435

Boxing
A1436

Designed by Bob Peak.

PHOTOGRAVURE

Plates of 200 in four panes of 50.

1983, July 28 **Tagged** ***Perf. 11***

2048	A1433	13c	**multicolored**	.35	.20
2049	A1434	13c	**multicolored**	.35	.20
2050	A1435	13c	**multicolored**	.35	.20
2051	A1436	13c	**multicolored**	.35	.20
a.			Block of 4, #2048-2051	1.50	1.25
			P# block of 4, 4#	1.75	—
			Zip block of 4	1.65	—

SIGNING OF TREATY OF PARIS

John Adams, B. Franklin, John Jay, David Hartley
A1437

Designed by David Blossom after an unfinished painting by Benjamin West in Winterthur Museum.

PHOTOGRAVURE

Plates of 160 in four panes of 40.

1983, Sept. 2 **Tagged** ***Perf. 11***

2052	A1437	20c	**multicolored**	.40	.20
			P# block of 4, 4#	1.75	—
			Zip block of 4	1.65	—
a.			Tagging omitted		—

CIVIL SERVICE

A1438

Designed by MDB Communications, Inc.

PHOTOGRAVURE AND ENGRAVED

Plates of 230 in four panes of 50.

1983, Sept. 9 **Tagged** ***Perf. 11***

2053	A1438	20c	**buff, blue & red**	.40	.20
			P# block of 6	3.00	—
			P# block of 20, 1-2P#, 1-2 Zip, 1-2 Copyright	10.00	—
a.			Tagging omitted		—

METROPOLITAN OPERA

Original State Arch and Current 5-arch Entrance
A1439

Designed by Ken Davies.

LITHOGRAPHED AND ENGRAVED

Plates of 200 in four panes of 50.

1983, Sept. 14 **Tagged** ***Perf. 11***

2054	A1439	20c	**yellow & maroon**	.40	.20
			P# block of 4, 2#	1.75	—
			Zip block of 4	1.65	—
a.			Tagging omitted	*8.50*	

AMERICAN INVENTORS

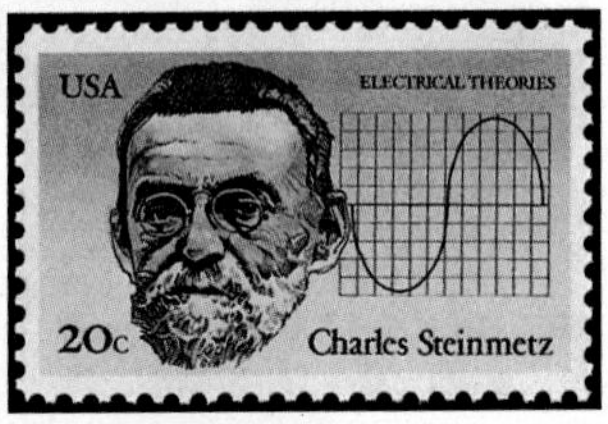

Charles Steinmetz and Curve on Graph
A1440

Edwin Armstrong and Frequency Modulator
A1441

Nikola Tesla and Induction Motor — A1442

Philo T. Farnsworth and First Television Camera
A1443

Designed by Dennis Lyall.

LITHOGRAPHED AND ENGRAVED
Plates of 200 in four panes of 50.

1983, Sept. 21 Tagged *Perf. 11*

2055 A1440 20c **multicolored**	.50	.20
2056 A1441 20c **multicolored**	.50	.20
2057 A1442 20c **multicolored**	.50	.20
2058 A1443 20c **multicolored**	.50	.20
a. Block of 4, #2055-2058	2.00	1.50
P# block of 4, 2#	2.75	—
Zip block of 4	2.10	—
b. As "a," black omitted	*325.00*	

STREETCARS

A1444

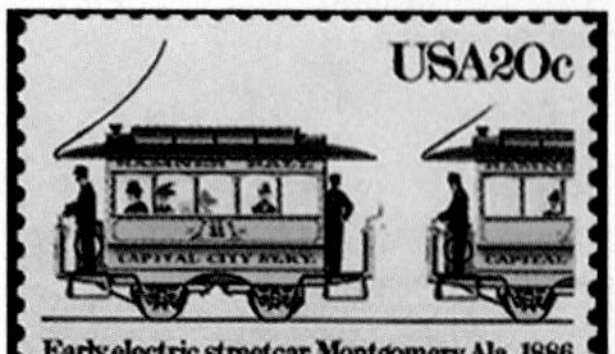

A1445

A1446

A1447

Designed by Richard Leech.

PHOTOGRAVURE AND ENGRAVED
Plates of 200 in four panes of 50.

1983, Oct. 8 Tagged *Perf. 11*

2059 A1444 20c **multicolored**	.50	.20
2060 A1445 20c **multicolored**	.50	.20
a. Horiz. pair, black (engr.) missing on Nos. 2059, 2060 (EP)	—	
2061 A1446 20c **multicolored**	.50	.20
a. Vert. pair, black (engr.) missing on Nos. 2059, 2061 (EP)	—	
2062 A1447 20c **multicolored**	.50	.20
a. Block of 4, #2059-2062	2.00	1.50
P# block of 4, 5#	2.60	—
Zip block of 4	2.10	—
b. As "a," black (engr.) omitted	*325.00*	
c. As "a," black (engr.) omitted on #2059, 2061	—	

CHRISTMAS

Niccolini-Cowper Madonna, by Raphael — A1448

Santa Claus A1449

Designed by Bradbury Thompson (No. 2063), and John Berkey (No. 2064).

PHOTOGRAVURE
Plates of 200 in four panes of 50 (No. 2063),
Plates of 230 in panes of 50 (Combination Press, No. 2064)

1983, Oct. 28 Tagged *Perf. 11*

2063 A1448 20c **multicolored**	.40	.20
P# block of 4, 5#	1.75	—
Zip block of 4	1.65	—
2064 A1449 20c **multicolored**	.40	.20
P# block of 6, 5#	3.00	—
P# block of 20, 5-10 P#, 1-2 copyright, 1-2 zip	11.50	—
a. Imperf., pair	*125.00*	
b. Tagging omitted	—	

See Combination Press note after No. 1703.

German Religious Leader, Founder of Lutheran Church (1483-1546) — A1450

Caribou and Alaska Pipeline — A1451

MARTIN LUTHER

Designed by Bradbury Thompson.

Printed by American Bank Note Company.

PHOTOGRAVURE
Plates of 200 in four panes of 50.

1983, Nov. 11 Tagged *Perf. 11*

2065 A1450 20c **multicolored**	.40	.20
P# block of 4, 5#+A	1.75	—
Zip block of 4	1.65	—

ALASKA STATEHOOD, 25th ANNIV.

Designed by Bill Bond.

Printed by American Bank Note Company and J.W. Ferguson and Sons.

PHOTOGRAVURE
Plates of 200 in four panes of 50.

1984, Jan. 3 Tagged *Perf. 11*

2066 A1451 20c **multicolored**	.40	.20
P# block of 4, 5#+A	1.75	—
Zip block of 4	1.65	—

14th WINTER OLYMPIC GAMES, Sarajevo, Yugoslavia, Feb. 8-19

Ice Dancing — A1452

Downhill Skiing — A1453

Cross-country Skiing — A1454

Hockey — A1455

Designed by Bob Peak.

PHOTOGRAVURE
Plates of 200 in four panes of 50.

1984, Jan. 6 Tagged *Perf. 10½x11*

2067 A1452 20c **multicolored**	.55	.20
2068 A1453 20c **multicolored**	.55	.20
2069 A1454 20c **multicolored**	.55	.20
2070 A1455 20c **multicolored**	.55	.20
a. Block of 4, #2067-2070	2.20	1.75
P# block of 4, 4#	3.00	—
Zip block of 4	2.25	—

Pillar, Dollar Sign — A1456

A1457

FEDERAL DEPOSIT INSURANCE CORPORATION, 50TH ANNIV.

Designed by Michael David Brown.

PHOTOGRAVURE
Plates of 200 in four panes of 50
(1 pane each #2071, 2074, 2075 and 2081)

1984, Jan. 12 Tagged *Perf. 11*

2071 A1456 20c **multicolored**	.40	.20
P# block of 4, 6#, UL only	1.75	—
Zip block of 4	1.65	—

LOVE

Designed by Bradbury Thompson.

PHOTOGRAVURE AND ENGRAVED (Combination Press)
Plates of 230 in four panes of 50.

1984, Jan. 31 Tagged *Perf. 11x10½*

2072 A1457 20c **multicolored**	.40	.20
P# block of 20, 6-12#, 1-2 copyright, 1-2 zip	11.50	—
a. Horiz. pair, imperf. vert.	*150.00*	
b. Tagging omitted	*5.00*	

See Combination Press note after No. 1703.

A1458

A1459

BLACK HERITAGE SERIES

Carter G. Woodson (1875-1950), Black Historian.

Designed by Jerry Pinkney.

Printed by American Bank Note Company.

PHOTOGRAVURE
Plates of 200 in four panes of 50.

1984, Feb. 1	Tagged	Perf. 11	
2073 A1458 20c	multicolored	.40	.20
	P# block of 4, 6#+A	2.00	—
	Zip block of 4	1.65	—
a.	Horiz. pair, imperf. vert.	*1,150.*	

SOIL & WATER CONSERVATION

Designed by Michael David Brown.

See No. 2071 for printing information.

1984, Feb. 6	Tagged	Perf. 11	
2074 A1459 20c	multicolored	.40	.20
	P# block of 4, 6#, UR only	1.75	—
	Zip block of 4	1.65	—

50TH ANNIV. OF CREDIT UNION ACT

Dollar Sign, Coin — A1460

Designed by Michael David Brown.

See No. 2071 for printing information.

1984, Feb. 10	Tagged	Perf. 11	
2075 A1460 20c	multicolored	.40	.20
	P# block of 4, 6#, LR only	1.75	—
	Zip block of 4	1.65	—

ORCHIDS

Wild Pink — A1461

Yellow Lady's-slipper A1462

Spreading Pogonia — A1463

Pacific Calypso — A1464

Designed by Manabu Saito.

PHOTOGRAVURE
Plates of 192 in four panes of 48.

1984, Mar. 5	Tagged	Perf. 11	
2076 A1461 20c	multicolored	.50	.20
2077 A1462 20c	multicolored	.50	.20
2078 A1463 20c	multicolored	.50	.20
2079 A1464 20c	multicolored	.50	.20
a.	Block of 4, #2076-2079	2.00	1.50
	P# block of 4, 5#	2.50	—
	Zip block of 4	2.10	—

HAWAII STATEHOOD, 25th ANNIV.

Eastern Polynesian Canoe, Golden Plover, Mauna Loa Volcano A1465

Designed by Herb Kane.

Printed by American Bank Note Company.

PHOTOGRAVURE
Plates of 200 in four panes of 50.

1984, Mar. 12	Tagged	Perf. 11	
2080 A1465 20c	multicolored	.40	.20
	P# block of 4, 5#+A	1.70	—
	Zip block of 4	1.65	—

50TH ANNIV., NATIONAL ARCHIVES

Abraham Lincoln, George Washington — A1466

Designed by Michael David Brown.

See No. 2071 for printing information.

1984, Apr. 16	Tagged	Perf. 11	
2081 A1466 20c	multicolored	.40	.20
	P# block of 4, 6#, LL only	1.70	—
	Zip block of 4	1.65	—

LOS ANGELES SUMMER OLYMPICS
July 28-August 12

Diving — A1467

Long Jump — A1468

Wrestling — A1469

Kayak — A1470

Designed by Bob Peak.

PHOTOGRAVURE
Plates of 200 in four panes of 50.

1984, May 4	Tagged	Perf. 11	
2082 A1467 20c	multicolored	.55	.20
2083 A1468 20c	multicolored	.55	.20
2084 A1469 20c	multicolored	.55	.20
2085 A1470 20c	multicolored	.55	.20
a.	Block of 4, #2082-2085	2.40	1.90
	P# block of 4, 4#	3.50	—
	Zip block of 4	2.50	—
b.	As "a," imperf between vertically	—	

LOUISIANA WORLD EXPOSITION
New Orleans, May 12-Nov. 11

Bayou Wildlife A1471

Designed by Chuck Ripper.

PHOTOGRAVURE
Plates of 160 in four panes of 40.

1984, May 11	Tagged	Perf. 11	
2086 A1471 20c	multicolored	.50	.20
	On cover, Expo. station pictorial handstamp cancel		2.50
	P# block of 4, 5#	2.60	—
	Zip block of 4	2.10	—

HEALTH RESEARCH

Lab Equipment A1472

Designed by Tyler Smith.

Printed by American Bank Note Company.

PHOTOGRAVURE
Plates of 200 in four panes of 50.

1984, May 17	Tagged	Perf. 11	
2087 A1472 20c	multicolored	.40	.20
	P# block of 4, 5#+A	1.75	—
	Zip block of 4	1.65	—

Actor Douglas Fairbanks (1883-1939) — A1473

A1474

PERFORMING ARTS

Designed by Jim Sharpe.

PHOTOGRAVURE AND ENGRAVED (Combination Press)
Plates of 230 in panes of 50.

1984, May 23	Tagged	Perf. 11	
2088 A1473 20c	multicolored	.50	.20
	P# block of 20, 5-10#, 1-2 copyright, 1-2 zip	13.00	—
a.	Tagging omitted	*25.00*	
b.	Horiz. pair, imperf between	—	

See Combination Press note after No. 1703.

JIM THORPE, 1888-1953

Designed by Richard Gangel.

ENGRAVED
Plates of 200 in four panes of 50.

1984, May 24 **Tagged** ***Perf. 11***
2089 A1474 20c **dark brown** .60 .20
P# block of 4 3.00 —
Zip block of 4 1.90 —

PERFORMING ARTS

John McCormack (1884-1945), Operatic Tenor — A1475

Designed by Jim Sharpe (US) and Ron Mercer (Ireland).

PHOTOGRAVURE
Plates of 200 in four panes of 50.

1984, June 6 **Tagged** ***Perf. 11***
2090 A1475 20c **multicolored** .40 .20
P# block of 4, 5# 1.75 —
Zip block of 4 1.65 —

See Ireland No. 594.

ST. LAWRENCE SEAWAY, 25th ANNIV.

Aerial View of Seaway, Freighters A1476

Designed by Ernst Barenscher (Canada).

Printed by American Bank Note Company.

PHOTOGRAVURE
Plates of 200 in four panes of 50.

1984, June 26 **Tagged** ***Perf. 11***
2091 A1476 20c **multicolored** .40 .20
P# block of 4, 4#+A 1.75 —
Zip block of 4 1.65 —

WATERFOWL PRESERVATION ACT, 50th ANNIV.

"Mallards Dropping In" by Jay N. Darling A1477

Design adapted from Darling's work (No. RW1) by Donald M. McDowell.

ENGRAVED
Plates of 200 in four panes of 50.

1984, July 2 **Tagged** ***Perf. 11***
2092 A1477 20c **blue** .50 .20
P# block of 4 2.50 —
Zip block of 4 2.25 —
a. Horiz. pair, imperf. vert. *325.00*

The Elizabeth — A1478

A1479

ROANOKE VOYAGES

Designed by Charles Lundgren.

Printed by American Bank Note Company.

PHOTOGRAVURE
Plates of 200 in four panes of 50.

1984, July 13 **Tagged** ***Perf. 11***
2093 A1478 20c **multicolored** .40 .20
P# block of 4, 5#+A 1.75 —
Zip block of 4 1.65 —
Pair with full horiz. gutter btwn. —

LITERARY ARTS SERIES

Herman Melville (1819-1891), Author

Designed by Bradbury Thompson.

ENGRAVED
Plates of 200 in four panes of 50.

1984, Aug. 1 **Tagged** ***Perf. 11***
2094 A1479 20c **sage green** .40 .20
P# block of 4 1.75 —
Zip block of 4 1.65 —
a. Tagging omitted 60.00 —

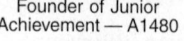

Founder of Junior Achievement — A1480

Smokey Bear — A1481

HORACE MOSES (1862-1947)

Designed by Dennis Lyall.

ENGRAVED (Combination Press)
Plates of 200 in panes of 50.

1984, Aug. 6 **Tagged** ***Perf. 11***
2095 A1480 20c **orange & dark brown** .45 .20
P# block of 6 3.50 —
P# block of 20, 1-2#, 1-2 copyright, 1-2 zip 12.50 —

See Combination Press note after No. 1703.

SMOKEY BEAR

Designed by Rudolph Wendelin.

LITHOGRAPHED AND ENGRAVED
Plates of 200 in panes of 50.

1984, Aug. 13 **Tagged** ***Perf. 11***
2096 A1481 20c **multicolored** .40 .20
P# block of 4, 5# 2.00 —
Zip block of 4 1.65 —
a. Horiz. pair, imperf. btwn. *250.00*
b. Vert. pair, imperf. btwn. *200.00*
c. Block of 4, imperf. btwn. vert. and horiz. *5,000.*
d. Horiz. pair, imperf. vert. *1,250.*
e. Tagging omitted —

ROBERTO CLEMENTE (1934-1972)

Clemente Wearing Pittsburgh Pirates Cap, Puerto Rican Flag — A1482

Designed by Juan Lopez-Bonilla.

PHOTOGRAVURE
Plates of 200 in panes of 50.

1984, Aug. 17 **Tagged** ***Perf. 11***
2097 A1482 20c **multicolored** 1.50 .20
P# block of 4, 6# 6.50 —
Zip block of 4 6.25 —
a. Horiz. pair, imperf. vert. *1,900.*

DOGS

Beagle and Boston Terrier A1483

Chesapeake Bay Retriever and Cocker Spaniel A1484

Alaskan Malamute and Collie A1485

Black and Tan Coonhound and American Foxhound A1486

Designed by Roy Andersen.

PHOTOGRAVURE
Plates of 160 in panes of 40.

1984, Sept. 7 **Tagged** ***Perf. 11***
2098 A1483 20c **multicolored** .50 .20
2099 A1484 20c **multicolored** .50 .20
2100 A1485 20c **multicolored** .50 .20
2101 A1486 20c **multicolored** .50 .20
a. Block of 4, #2098-2101 2.00 1.90
P# block of 4, 4# 3.00 —
Zip block of 4 2.10 —
b. As "a," imperf horiz. —

CRIME PREVENTION

McGruff, the Crime Dog — A1487

Designed by Randall McDougall.

Printed by American Bank Note Company.

PHOTOGRAVURE
Plates of 200 in panes of 50.

1984, Sept. 26	Tagged	*Perf. 11*	
2102 A1487 20c **multicolored**		.40	.20
P# block of 4, 4#+A		1.75	—
Zip block of 4		1.65	—

HISPANIC AMERICANS

A1488

Designed by Robert McCall.

PHOTOGRAVURE
Plates of 160 in four panes of 40.

1984, Oct. 31	Tagged	*Perf. 11*	
2103 A1488 20c **multicolored**		.40	.20
P# block of 4, 6#		1.75	—
Zip block of 4		1.65	—
a. Vert. pair, imperf. horiz.		*2,000.*	

FAMILY UNITY

Stick Figures — A1489

Designed by Molly LaRue.

PHOTOGRAVURE AND ENGRAVED (Combination Press)
Plates of 230 in panes of 50.

1984, Oct. 1	Tagged	*Perf. 11*	
2104 A1489 20c **multicolored**		.40	.20
P# block of 20, 3-6#, 1-2 copyright, 1-2 zip		12.50	—
a. Horiz. pair, imperf. vert.		*450.00*	
b. Tagging omitted		*7.50*	
c. Vert. pair, imperf. btwn. and at bottom		—	
d. Horiz. pair, imperf. between		—	

See Combination Press note after No. 1703.
Used untagged imperfs exist from printer's waste.

A1490

Abraham Lincoln Reading to Son, Tad — A1491

ELEANOR ROOSEVELT (1884-1962)

Designed by Bradbury Thompson.

ENGRAVED
Plates of 192 in panes of 48.

1984, Oct. 11	Tagged	*Perf. 11*	
2105 A1490 20c **deep blue**		.40	.20
P# block of 4		2.00	—
Zip block of 4		1.65	—

NATION OF READERS

Design adapted from Anthony Berger daguerrotype by Bradbury Thompson.

ENGRAVED
Plates of 200 in panes of 50.

1984, Oct. 16	Tagged	*Perf. 11*	
2106 A1491 20c **brown & maroon**		.40	.20
P# block of 4		1.90	—
Zip block of 4		1.65	—

CHRISTMAS

Madonna and Child by Fra Filippo Lippi — A1492

Santa Claus — A1493

Designed by Bradbury Thompson (No. 2107) and Danny La Boccetta (No. 2108).

PHOTOGRAVURE
Plates of 200 in panes of 50.

1984, Oct. 30	Tagged	*Perf. 11*	
2107 A1492 20c **multicolored**		.40	.20
P# block of 4, 5#		1.70	—
Zip block of 4		1.65	—
2108 A1493 20c **multicolored**		.40	.20
P# block of 4, 5#		1.70	—
Zip block of 4		1.65	—
a. Horiz. pair, imperf. vert.		*875.00*	

No. 2108a is valued in the grade of fine.

VIETNAM VETERANS MEMORIAL

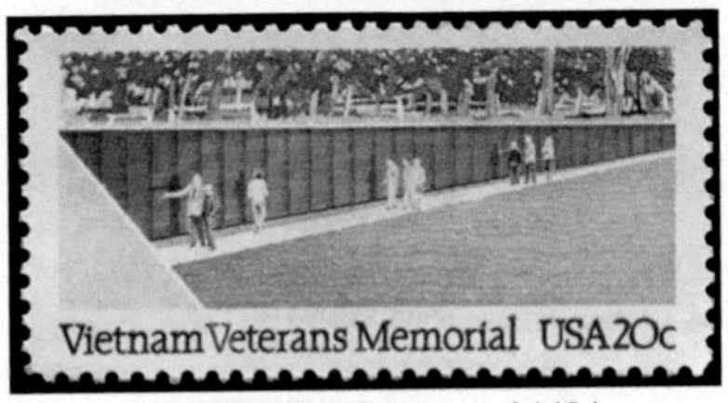

Memorial and Visitors — A1494

Designed by Paul Calle.

ENGRAVED
Plates of 160 in panes of 40.

1984, Nov. 10	Tagged	*Perf. 11*	
2109 A1494 20c **multicolored**		.50	.20
P# block of 4		2.50	—
Zip block of 4		2.10	—
a. Tagging omitted		*75.00*	

PERFORMING ARTS

Jerome Kern (1885-1945), Composer — A1495

Designed by Jim Sharpe.

Printed by the American Bank Note Company.

PHOTOGRAVURE
Plates of 200 in four panes of 50.

1985, Jan. 23	Tagged	*Perf. 11*	
2110 A1495 22c **multicolored**		.40	.20
P# block of 4, 5#+A		1.75	—
Zip block of 4		1.65	—
a. Tagging omitted		*9.00*	

A1496

A1497

Designed by Bradbury Thompson.

PHOTOGRAVURE
Plates of 460 (20x23) in panes of 100.

1985, Feb. 1	Tagged	*Perf. 11*	
2111 A1496 (22c) **green**		.60	.20
P# block of 6		4.50	—
P# block of 20, 1-2 #, 1-2 Zip, 1-2 Copyright		17.50	—
a. Vert. pair, imperf.		35.00	
b. Vert. pair, imperf. horiz.		*1,250.*	
c. Tagging omitted			—

COIL STAMP

Perf. 10 Vert.

2112 A1496 (22c) **green**		.60	.20
Pair		1.20	.20
P# strip of 3, #1, 2		3.50	
P# strip of 5, #1, 2		5.50	
P# single, #1, 2		—	.50
a. Imperf., pair		*45.00*	
b. As "a," tagging omitted		*150.00*	
c. As No. 2112, tagging omitted		—	—

BOOKLET STAMP

ENGRAVED
Perf. 11

2113 A1497 (22c) **green**		.80	.20
a. Booklet pane of 10		8.50	3.00
b. As "a," imperf. btwn. horiz.		—	

A1498

Flag Over Capitol Dome A1499

Designed by Frank Waslick.

ENGRAVED

Plates of 400 subjects in panes of 100.

1985, Mar. 29 Tagged *Perf. 11*

2114	A1498 22c **blue, red & black**	.40	.20
	P# block of 4	1.90	—
	Zip block of 4	1.65	—
	Pair with full horizontal gutter	—	
a.	All color missing (EP)	—	
b.	Tagging omitted		—

No. 2114a should be collected se-tenant with a normal or a partially printed stamp.

COIL STAMP

Perf. 10 Vert.

2115	A1498 22c **blue, red & black,** wide block tagging, 19mmx21.5mm (B press)	.40	.20
	Pair	.80	.20
	P# strip of 3, #2, 4, 6, 10	2.00	
	P# strip of 3, #13	4.50	
	P# strip of 3, #14	12.00	
	P# strip of 3, #15, 16, 21	2.00	
	P# strip of 5, #2, 4, 6, 10	2.50	
	P# strip of 5, #13	6.00	
	P# strip of 5, #14	17.50	
	P# strip of 5, #15, 16, 21	2.50	
	P# single, #2	—	.50
	P# single, #4	—	.50
	P# single, #6	—	6.50
	P# single, #10	—	.65
	P# single, #13	—	9.00
	P# single, #14	—	22.00
	P# single, #15	—	1.50
	P# single, #16	—	2.25
	P# single, #21	—	2.25
a.	Narrow block tagging, 17.5mmx21.5mm (C press)	.40	.20
	P# strip of 3, #1	4.00	
	P# strip of 3, #3	10.00	
	P# strip of 3, #5	2.00	
	P# strip of 3, #7	4.00	
	P# strip of 3, #8, 11-12, 17-20, 22	2.00	
	P# strip of 5, #1	6.00	
	P# strip of 5, #3	30.00	
	P# strip of 5, #5	2.50	
	P# strip of 5, #7	6.00	
	P# strip of 5, #8, 11-12, 17-20, 22	2.50	
	P# single, #1, 3, 5	—	1.00
	P# single, #7-8	—	1.00
	P# single, #11	—	1.00
	P# single, #12	—	1.00
	P# single, #17-18	—	2.00
	P# single, #19	—	1.00
	P# single, #20	—	2.25
	P# single, #22	—	1.00
b.	Wide and tall block tagging, 19.5mmx23mm (D press)	.40	.20
	P# strip of 3, #8	—	
	P# strip of 3, #18	*40.00*	
	P# strip of 3, #20	*40.00*	
	P# strip of 3, #22	*40.00*	
	P# strip of 5, #8	*140.00*	
	P# strip of 5, #18	*55.00*	
	P# strip of 5, #20	*70.00*	
	P# strip of 5, #22	*55.00*	
	P# single, #8	—	*50.00*
	P# single, #18	—	*50.00*
	P# single, #20	—	*50.00*
	P# single, #22	—	*50.00*
c.	Inscribed "T" at bottom, *May 23, 1987*	.50	.40
	P# strip of 3, #1	2.00	
	P# strip of 5, #1	3.00	
	P# single, #1	—	3.00
d.	Black field of stars		—
e.	Tagging omitted	*12.50*	
f.	Imperf., pair	12.50	

No. 2115 is known with capitol in bluish black color, apparently from contaminated ink. Specialists often refer to this as "Erie blue."

BOOKLET STAMP

Perf. 10 Horiz.

2116	A1499 22c **blue, red & black**	.50	.20
a.	Booklet pane of 5	2.50	1.25
	Scored perforations	2.50	

BOOKLET STAMPS

Frilled Dogwinkle — A1500

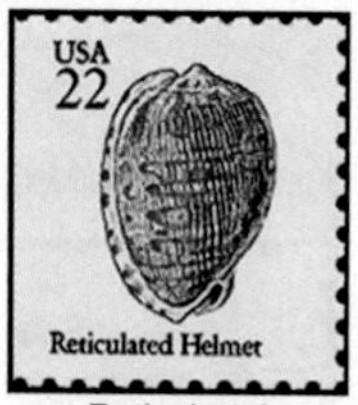

Reticulated Helmet — A1501

New England Neptune — A1502

Calico Scallop — A1503

Lightning Whelk — A1504

Designed by Pete Cocci.

ENGRAVED

1985, Apr. 4 Tagged *Perf. 10*

2117	A1500 22c **black & brown**	.40	.20
a.	Tagging omitted		—
2118	A1501 22c **black & multi**	.40	.20
2119	A1502 22c **black & brown**	.40	.20
a.	Tagging omitted		—
2120	A1503 22c **black & violet**	.40	.20
2121	A1504 22c **black & multi**	.40	.20
a.	Booklet pane of 10, 2 ea #2117-2121	4.00	3.00
b.	As "a," violet omitted on both Nos. 2120	*550.00*	
c.	As "a," vert. imperf. between	*500.00*	
d.	As "a," imperf.	—	
e.	Strip of 5, Nos. 2117-2121	2.00	—

Eagle and Half Moon — A1505

Designed by Young & Rubicam.

TYPE I: washed out, dull appearance most evident in the black of the body of the eagle, and the red in the background between the eagle's shoulder and the moon. "$10.75" appears splotchy or grainy (P# 11111).

TYPE II: brighter, more intense colors most evident in the black on the eagle's body, and red in the background. "$10.75" appears smoother, brighter, and less grainy (P# 22222).

PHOTOGRAVURE

1985, Apr. 29 Untagged *Perf. 10 Vert.*

2122	A1505 $10.75 **multicolored,** type I	19.00	7.50
a.	Booklet pane of 3	60.00	—
b.	Type II, *June 19, 1989*	21.00	10.00
c.	As "b," booklet pane of 3	65.00	—

Coil Plate No. Strips of 3

Beginning with No. 2123, coil plate No. strips of 3 usually sell at the level of strips of 5 minus the face value of two stamps.

TRANSPORTATION ISSUE

A1506

A1507

A1508

A1509

A1510

A1511

A1512

A1513

A1514

A1515

A1516

A1517

A1518

A1519

Designers: 3.4c, 17c, Lou Nolan. 4.9c, 8.5c, 14c, 25c, William H. Bond. 5.5c, David K. Stone. 6c, 8.3c, 10.1c, 12.5c. James Schleyer. 7.1c, 11c, 12c, Ken Dallison.

COIL STAMPS
ENGRAVED

1985-87 Tagged *Perf. 10 Vert.*

2123 A1506 3.4c **dark bluish green,** *June 8* .20 .20
Pair .20 .20
P# strip of 5, line, #1-2 .80
P# single, #1-2 — .75
a. Untagged (Bureau precancel, Non-profit Org. CAR-RT SORT) .20 .20
P# strip of 5, line, #1-2 3.75
P# single, #1-2 — 3.50
2124 A1507 4.9c **brown black,** *June 21* .20 .20
Pair .20 .20
P# strip of 5, line, #3-4 .75
P# single, #3-4 — .75
a. Untagged (Bureau precancel, Non-profit Org.) .20 .20
P# strip of 5, line, #1-6 1.50
P# single, #1-6 — 1.25
2125 A1508 5.5c **deep magenta,** *Nov. 1, 1986* .20 .20
Pair .20 .20
P# strip of 5, #1 1.60
P# single, #1 — 1.25
a. Untagged (Bureau precancel, Non-profit Org. CAR-RT SORT) .20 .20
P# strip of 5, #1 1.50
P# strip of 5, #2 1.75
P# single, #1 — 1.10
P# single, #2 — 1.60

On No. 2125a, both vignette and the precancel inscription were printed from a single printing sleeve.

2126 A1509 6c **red brown,** *May 6* .35 .20
Pair .70 .20
P# strip of 5, #1 2.00
P# single, #1 — 1.00
a. Untagged (Bureau precancel, Non-profit Org.) .20 .20
P# strip of 5, #1 1.75
P# strip of 5, #2 7.00
P# single, #1 — 1.00
P# single, #2 — 2.75
b. As "a," imperf., pair *210.00*
2127 A1510 7.1c **lake,** *Feb. 6, 1987* .20 .20
Pair .30 .20
P# strip of 5, #1 2.00
P# single, #1 — 1.50
a. Untagged (Bureau precancel "Non-profit Org." in black), *Feb. 6, 1987* .20 .20
P# strip of 5, #1 2.50
P# single, #1 — 1.75
b. Untagged (Bureau precancel "Non-profit 5-Digit Zip + 4" in black), *May 26, 1989* .20 .20
P# strip of 5, #1 1.75
P# single, #1 — 1.25
c. As "a," black (precancel) omitted —

On Nos. 2127a and 2127b, both the vignette and the precancel inscription were printed from a single printing sleeve.
On No. 2127c, an albino impression of the precancel is present.

2128 A1511 8.3c **green,** *June 21* .20 .20
Pair .40 .20
P# strip of 5, line, #1-2 1.50
P# single, #1-2 — 1.00
a. Untagged (Bureau precancel, Blk. Rt. CAR-RT SORT) .20 .20
P# strip of 5, line, #1-2 1.50
P# strip of 5, line, #3-4 4.50
P# single, #1-2 — 1.25
P# single, #3-4 — 3.75

On No. 2231 "Ambulance 1860s" is 18mm long; on No. 2128, 18⅛mm long.

2129 A1512 8.5c **dark Prussian green,** *Jan. 24, 1987* .20 .20
Pair .40 .20
P# strip of 5, #1 2.50
P# single, #1 — 2.00
a. Untagged (Bureau precancel, Non-profit Org.) .20 .20
P# strip of 5, #1 2.25
P# strip of 5, #2 9.00
P# single, #1 — 2.00
P# single, #2 — 7.50
2130 A1513 10.1c **slate blue,** *Apr. 18* .55 .20
Pair 1.10 .20
P# strip of 5, #1 3.75
P# single, #1 — 2.00
a. Untagged (Bureau precancel "Bulk Rate Carrier Route Sort" in red) .25 .25
P# strip of 5, #2-3 2.25
P# single, #2-3 — 1.75
Untagged (Bureau precancel "Bulk Rate" and lines in black) .25 .25
P# strip of 5, #1-2 2.25
P# single, #1-2 — 1.75
b. As "a," red precancel, imperf, pair 15.00
As "a," black precancel, imperf, pair 80.00
2131 A1514 11c **dark green,** *June 11* .25 .20
Pair .50 .20
P# strip of 5, line, #1-4 1.40
P# single, #1-4 — 1.00
a. Tagging omitted —
2132 A1515 12c **dark blue,** type I, *Apr. 2* .25 .20
Pair .50 .20
P# strip of 5, line, #1-2 2.00
P# single, #1-2 — 1.25
a. Untagged, type I (Bureau precancel, PRESORTED FIRST-CLASS), *Apr. 2* .25 .25
P# strip of 5, line, #1-2 2.00
P# single, #1-2 — 1.75
b. Untagged, type II, (Bureau precancel, PRESORTED FIRST-CLASS) *1987* .40 .30
P# strip of 5, no line, #1 16.00
P# single, #1 — 15.00
c. Tagging omitted, type I, (not Bureau precanceled), *1987* 15.00

Type II has "Stanley Steamer 1909" ⅓mm shorter (17⅔mm) than No. 2132 (18mm).

2133 A1516 12.5c **olive green,** *Apr. 18* .35 .20
Pair .70 .20
P# strip of 5, #1 2.75
P# strip of 5, #2 3.50
P# single, #1 — 2.25
P# single, #2 — 3.00
a. Untagged (Bureau precancel, Bulk Rate) .25 .25
P# strip of 5, #1 2.75
P# strip of 5, #2 3.00
P# single, #1 — 1.75
P# single, #2 — 3.00
b. As "a," imperf., pair 50.00

All No. 2133 from plate 1 and some No. 2133a from plate 1 were printed with luminescent ink that is orange under long wave UV light.

2134 A1517 14c **sky blue,** type I, *Mar. 23* .30 .20
Pair .60 .20
P# strip of 5, line, #1-4 2.00
P# single, #1-4 — 1.50
a. Imperf., pair 95.00
b. Type II, *Sept. 30, 1986* .30 .20
P# strip of 5, no line, #2 2.50
P# single, #2 — 2.50
c. Tagging omitted, type I 15.00 —

Type II design is ¼mm narrower (17¼mm) than the original stamp (17½mm) and has block tagging. No. 2134 has overall tagging.

2135 A1518 17c **sky blue,** *Aug. 20, 1986* .55 .20
Pair 1.10 .20
P# strip of 5, #2 4.00
P# single, #2 — 1.50
a. Imperf., pair *375.00*
2136 A1519 25c **orange brown,** *Nov. 22, 1986* .45 .20
Pair .90 .20
P# strip of 5, #1-5 3.00
P# single, #1 — 1.00
P# single, #2-4 — .65
P# single, #5 — 2.25
a. Imperf., pair 10.00
b. Pair, imperf. between *600.00*
c. Tagging omitted *27.50*
Nos. 2123-2136 (14) 4.25 2.80

Precancellations on Nos. 2125a, 2127a do not have lines. Precancellation on No. 2129a is in red. See No. 2231.

BLACK HERITAGE SERIES

Mary McLeod Bethune (1875-1955), Educator — A1520

Designed by Jerry Pinkney from a photograph.

Printed by American Bank Note Company.

PHOTOGRAVURE
Plates of 200 in four panes of 50.

1985, Mar. 5 Tagged *Perf. 11*

2137 A1520 22c **multicolored** .60 .20
P# block of 4, 6#+A 3.25 —
Zip block of 4 2.50 —
a. Tagging omitted —

AMERICAN FOLK ART SERIES
Duck Decoys

Broadbill A1521

Mallard A1522

Canvasback A1523

Redhead A1524

Designed by Stevan Dohanos.

Printed by American Bank Note Company.

PHOTOGRAVURE
Plates of 200 in four panes of 50.

1985, Mar. 22 Tagged *Perf. 11*

2138 A1521 22c **multicolored** 1.00 .20
2139 A1522 22c **multicolored** 1.00 .20
2140 A1523 22c **multicolored** 1.00 .20
2141 A1524 22c **multicolored** 1.00 .20
a. Block of 4, #2138-2141 4.00 2.75
P# block of 4, 5#+A 4.50 —
Zip block of 4 4.25 —

WINTER SPECIAL OLYMPICS

Ice Skater, Emblem, Skier — A1525

Designed by Jeff Carnell.

PHOTOGRAVURE
Plates of 160 in four panes of 40.

1985, Mar. 25 Tagged *Perf. 11*

2142 A1525 22c **multicolored** .50 .20
P# block of 4, 6# 2.25 —
Zip block of 4 2.10 —
a. Vert. pair, imperf. horiz. *425.00*

LOVE

A1526

Designed by Corita Kent.

PHOTOGRAVURE
Plates of 200 in four panes of 50.

1985, Apr. 17 Tagged *Perf. 11*

2143 A1526 22c **multicolored** .40 .20
P# block of 4, 6# 1.70 —
Zip block of 4 1.65 —
a. Imperf., pair *1,250.*

RURAL ELECTRIFICATION ADMINISTRATION

REA Power Lines, Farmland
A1527

Designed by Howard Koslow.

PHOTOGRAVURE & ENGRAVED (Combination Press)
Plates of 230 in panes of 50.

1985, May 11 **Tagged** ***Perf. 11***

2144 A1527 22c **multicolored**	.50	.20
P# block of 20, 5-10 #, 1-2 Zip, 1-2 Copyright	17.50	—
a. Vert. pair, imperf between	—	

See Combination Press note after No. 1703.

AMERIPEX '86

US No. 134 — A1528

Designed by Richard Sheaff.

LITHOGRAPHED & ENGRAVED
Plates of 192 in four panes of 48

1985, May 25 **Tagged** ***Perf. 11***

2145 A1528 22c **multicolored**	.40	.20
P# block of 4, 3#	1.75	—
Zip block of 4	1.65	—
a. Red, black & blue (engr.) omitted	*175.00*	
b. Red & black omitted	*1,150.*	
c. Red omitted	*1,650.*	
d. Black missing (PS)	—	

ABIGAIL ADAMS (1744-1818)

A1529

Designed by Bart Forbes.

PHOTOGRAVURE
Plates of 200 in four panes of 50.

1985, June 14 **Tagged** ***Perf. 11***

2146 A1529 22c **multicolored**	.40	.20
P# block of 4, 4#	2.00	—
Zip block of 4	1.65	—
a. Imperf., pair	*225.00*	

FREDERIC AUGUSTE BARTHOLDI (1834-1904)

Architect and Sculptor, Statue of Liberty
A1530

Designed by Howard Paine from paintings by Jose Frappa and James Dean.

LITHOGRAPHED & ENGRAVED
Plates of 200 in four panes of 50.

1985, July 18 **Tagged** ***Perf. 11***

2147 A1530 22c **multicolored**	.40	.20
P# block of 4, 5#	1.90	—
Zip block of 4	1.65	—

Examples of No. 2147 exist with most, but not all, of the engraved black omitted.

George Washington, Washington Monument — A1532

Sealed Envelopes — A1533

Designed by Thomas Szumowski (#2149) based on a portrait by Gilbert Stuart, and Richard Sheaff (#2150).

COIL STAMPS
PHOTOGRAVURE

1985 ***Perf. 10 Vertically***

2149 A1532 18c **multicolored,** low gloss gum, *Nov. 6*	.40	.20
Pair	.80	.20
P# strip of 5, #1112	2.75	
P# strip of 5, #3333	3.50	
P# single, #1112	—	2.00
P# single, #3333	—	3.00
a. Untagged (Bureau precanceled), low gloss gum	.35	.35
P# strip of 5, #11121	6.00	
P# strip of 5, #33333	3.00	
P# single, #11121	—	5.00
P# single, #33333	—	2.00
Dull gum	.35	
P# strip of 5, #33333	4.00	
P# strip of 5, #43444	6.50	
P# single, #43444	—	5.50
b. Imperf., pair	*875.00*	
c. As "a," imperf., pair	*675.00*	
d. Tagging omitted (not Bureau precanceled)	75.00	—
e. As "a," tagged (error), dull gum	2.00	1.75
Pair	4.00	3.75
P# strip of 5, #33333	*150.00*	
P# single, #33333	—	*35.00*
Low gloss gum	*2.00*	
P# strip of 5, #33333	*150.00*	
P# single, #33333	—	*35.00*
2150 A1533 21.1c **multicolored,** *Oct. 22*	.40	.20
Pair	.80	.20
P# strip of 5, #111111	3.00	
P# strip of 5, #111121	4.25	
P# single, #111111	—	2.50
P# single, #111121	—	3.75
a. Untagged (Bureau Precancel)	.40	.40
Pair	.80	.80
P# strip of 5, #111111	3.50	
P# strip of 5, #111121	4.75	
P# single, #111111	—	2.50
P# single, #111121	—	3.75
b. As "a," tagged (error)	.50	.50
Pair	1.00	1.00
P# strip of 5, #111111	2.50	
P# strip of 5, #111121	3.00	
P# single, #111111	—	*95.00*
P# single, #111121	—	5.00

Precancellations on Nos. 2149a ("PRESORTED FIRST-CLASS"), 2150a and 2150b ("ZIP+4") do not have lines.

KOREAN WAR VETERANS

American Troops in Korea
A1535

Designed by Richard Sheaff from a photograph by David D. Duncan.

ENGRAVED
Plates of 200 in four panes of 50.

1985, July 26 **Tagged** ***Perf. 11***

2152 A1535 22c **gray green & rose red**	.40	.20
P# block of 4	2.50	—
Zip block of 4	1.75	—

SOCIAL SECURITY ACT, 50th ANNIV.

Men, Women, Children, Corinthian Columns
A1536

Designed by Robert Brangwynne.

Printed by American Bank Note Company.

PHOTOGRAVURE
Plates of 200 in four panes of 50.

1985, Aug. 14 **Tagged** ***Perf. 11***

2153 A1536 22c **deep & light blue**	.40	.20
P# block of 4, 2#+A	1.90	—
Zip block of 4	1.70	—

WORLD WAR I VETERANS

The Battle of Marne, France
A1537

Designed by Richard Sheaff from Harvey Dunn's charcoal drawing.

ENGRAVED
Plates of 200 in four panes of 50.

1985, Aug. 26 **Tagged** ***Perf. 11***

2154 A1537 22c **gray green & rose red**	.40	.20
P# block of 4	2.25	—
Zip block of 4	1.85	—
a. Red missing (PS)	*400.00*	
b. Tagging omitted		—

HORSES

Quarter Horse
A1538

Morgan
A1539

Saddlebred
A1540

Appaloosa A1541

Designed by Roy Andersen.

PHOTOGRAVURE

Plates of 160 in four panes of 40.

1985, Sept. 25	Tagged	*Perf. 11*	
2155 A1538 22c **multicolored**		1.25	.20
2156 A1539 22c **multicolored**		1.25	.20
2157 A1540 22c **multicolored**		1.25	.20
2158 A1541 22c **multicolored**		1.25	.20
a. Block of 4, #2155-2158		6.00	4.00
P# block of 4, 5#		7.50	—
Zip block of 4		6.25	—

PUBLIC EDUCATION IN AMERICA

Quill Pen, Apple, Spectacles, Penmanship Quiz — A1542

Designed by Uldis Purins.

Printed by American Bank Note Company

PHOTOGRAVURE

Plates of 200 in four panes of 50.

1985, Oct. 1	Tagged	*Perf. 11*	
2159 A1542 22c **multicolored**		.45	.20
P# block of 4, 5#+A		2.75	—
Zip block of 4		1.85	—
a. Tagging omitted			—

INTERNATIONAL YOUTH YEAR

YMCA Youth Camping, Cent. — A1543

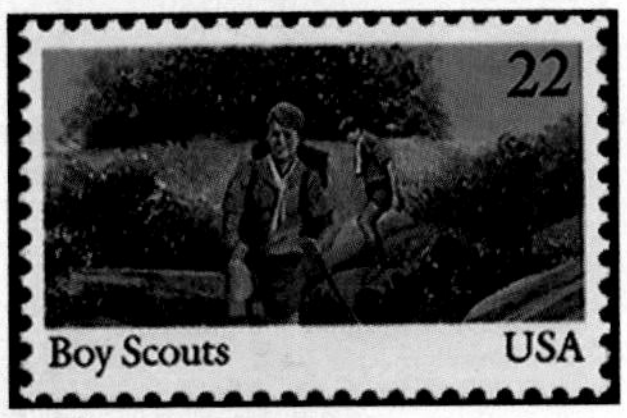

Boy Scouts, 75th Anniv. A1544

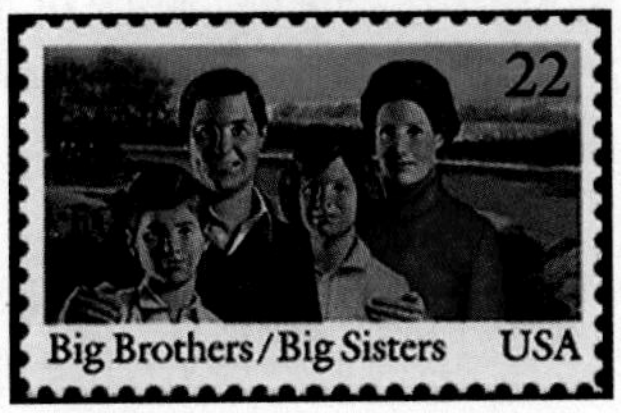

Big Brothers / Big Sisters Federation, 40th Anniv. A1545

Camp Fire Inc., 75th Anniv. A1546

Designed by Dennis Luzak.

Printed by American Bank Note Company.

PHOTOGRAVURE

Plates of 200 in four panes of 50.

1985, Oct. 7	Tagged	*Perf. 11*	
2160 A1543 22c **multicolored**		.70	.20
2161 A1544 22c **multicolored**		.70	.20
2162 A1545 22c **multicolored**		.70	.20
2163 A1546 22c **multicolored**		.70	.20
a. Block of 4, #2160-2163		3.00	2.25
P# block of 4, 5#+A		4.00	—
Zip block of 4		3.25	—

HELP END HUNGER

Youths and Elderly Suffering from Malnutrition A1547

Designed by Jerry Pinkney.

Printed by the American Bank Note Company.

PHOTOGRAVURE

Plates of 200 in four panes of 50.

1985, Oct. 15	Tagged	*Perf. 11*	
2164 A1547 22c **multicolored**		.45	.20
P# block of 4, 5#+A		2.25	—
Zip block of 4		1.90	—
a. Tagging omitted			—

CHRISTMAS

Genoa Madonna, Enameled Terra-Cotta by Luca Della Robbia (1400-1482) — A1548

Poinsettia Plants A1549

Designed by Bradbury Thompson (No. 2165) and James Dean (No. 2166).

PHOTOGRAVURE

Plates of 200 in panes of 50.

1985, Oct. 30	Tagged	*Perf. 11*	
2165 A1548 22c **multicolored**		.40	.20
P# block of 4, 4#		1.75	—
Zip block of 4		1.65	—
a. Imperf., pair		*70.00*	
b. Tagging omitted			—
2166 A1549 22c **multicolored**		.40	.20
P# block of 4, 5#		1.70	—
Zip block of 4		1.65	—
Vert. pair with full horiz. gutter between		—	
a. Imperf., pair		*110.00*	

ARKANSAS STATEHOOD, 150th ANNIV.

Old State House, Little Rock — A1550

Designed by Roger Carlisle.

Printed by the American Bank Note Company

PHOTOGRAVURE

Plates of 200 in four panes of 50.

1986, Jan. 3	Tagged	*Perf. 11*	
2167 A1550 22c **multicolored**		.75	.20
P# block of 4, 6#+A		3.75	—
Zip block of 4		3.10	—
a. Vert. pair, imperf. horiz.		—	
b. Tagging omitted			—

Marginal Inscriptions

Beginning with the Luis Munoz Marin issue a number of stamps include a descriptive inscription in the selvage.

GREAT AMERICANS ISSUE

A1551

A1552

Designed by Ron Adair.

Printed by the Bureau of Engraving & Printing.

ENGRAVED

Panes of 100 (#2168-2193, 2195), Panes of 20 (#2194, 2196)

Perf. 11, 11½x11 (#2185), 11.2x11.1 (20c)

1986-94	Tagged		
2168 A1551 1c **brownish vermilion,** large block tagging, *June 30*		.20	.20
P# block of 4		.25	—
Zip block of 4		.20	—
a. Tagging omitted		*5.00*	
2169 A1552 2c **bright blue,** large block tagging, *Feb. 28, 1987*		.20	.20
P# block of 4		.30	—
Zip block of 4		.20	—
a. Untagged		.20	.20
P# block of 4		.35	—
Zip block of 4		.20	—
b. Tagging omitted		—	—

The tagging omitted error No. 2169b appeared before No. 2169a was issued. Plate blocks from plate 1 are the error if untagged. No. 2169a is from plate 2. Other blocks and singles can be distinguished if se-tenant with tagged stamps. No. 2169a and 2169b also can be distinguished using a long wave ultraviolet light. The paper of No. 2169b will appear brownish, while the paper of No. 2169a appears almost white.

A1553

A1554

Designed by Christopher Calle.

Printed by the Bureau of Engraving & Printing.

2170 A1553 3c **bright blue,** large block tagging, dull gum, *Sept. 15*		.20	.20
P# block of 4		.50	—
Zip block of 4		.25	—
a. Untagged, dull gum, *1994*		.20	.20
P# block of 4		.50	—
Zip block of 4		.25	—
Shiny gum, *1994*		.20	

		P# block of 4	.50	—
		Zip block of 4	.25	—
b.		Tagging omitted	—	—

The tagging omitted error No. 2170b appeared before No. 2170a was issued. Plate blocks from plates 2 and 3 are the error if untagged. No. 2170a is from plate 4. Other blocks and singles are indistiguishable, unless se-tenant with tagged stamps.

2171	A1554	4c **blue violet,** large block tagging, *July 14*	.20	.20
		P# block of 4	.60	—
		Zip block of 4	.40	—
a.		4c **grayish violet,** untagged	.20	.20
		P# block of 4	.40	—
		Zip block of 4	.35	—
b.		4c **deep grayish blue,** untagged, *1993*	.20	.20
		P# block of 4	.50	—
		Zip block of 4	.40	—
c.		As No. 2171, tagging omitted		—

No. 2171c was found on a USPS souvenir page with first day cancel. No. 2171a and 2171b were not available on the first day of issue.

A1555

A1556

Designers: No. 2172, Christopher Calle. No. 2173, Juan Maldonado.

Printed by the Bureau of Engraving & Printing.

2172	A1555	5c **dark olive green,** large block tagging, *Feb. 27*	.20	.20
		P# block of 4	1.00	—
		Zip block of 4	.45	—
a.		Tagging omitted	*150.00*	—
2173	A1556	5c **carmine,** overall tagging, *Feb. 18, 1990*	.20	.20
		P# block of 4	.75	—
		P# zip block of 4	.90	—
		Zip block of 4	.45	—
a.		Untagged, *1991*	.20	.20
		P# block of 4	.60	—
		P# zip block of 4	.75	—
		Zip block of 4	.45	—
b.		Tagging omitted	—	—

The tagging omitted error No. 2173b appeared before No. 2173a was issued. Plate blocks from plate 1 are the error if untagged. No. 2173a is from plate 2. Other blocks and singles are indistiguishable, unless se-tenant with tagged stamps.

A1557

A1558

Designers: 10c, Robert Anderson. 14c, Ward Brackett.

Printed by the Bureau of Engraving & Printing.

2175	A1557	10c **lake,** large block tagging, dull gum, *Aug. 15, 1987*	.25	.20
		P# block of 4	1.10	—
		Zip block of 4	1.00	—
a.		Overall tagging, dull gum, *1990*	.60	.25
		P# block of 4	10.00	—
		Zip block of 4	2.00	—
b.		Tagging omitted	*12.50*	
c.		Prephosphored coated paper (solid tagging), dull gum, *1991*	.90	.20
		P# block of 4	4.00	—
		Zip block of 4	3.60	—
d.		Prephosphored uncoated paper (mottled tagging), shiny gum, *1993*	.90	.20
		P# block of 4	4.00	—
		Zip block of 4	3.60	—
e.		10c **carmine,** prephosphored uncoated paper (mottled tagging), shiny gum, *1994*	.40	.20
		P# block of 4	2.00	—
		Zip block of 4	1.75	—
f.		As "c," all color omitted		—

No. 2157f must be collected se-tenant with a partially printed stamp or longer vertical strip.

2176	A1558	14c **crimson,** large block tagging, *Feb. 12, 1987*	.30	.20
		P# block of 4	1.50	—
		Zip block of 4	1.20	—
a.		Tagging omitted		—

A1559

A1560

Designers: 15c, Jack Rosenthal. 17c, Christopher Calle.

Printed by the Bureau of Engraving & Printing.

2177	A1559	15c **claret,** large block tagging, *June 6, 1988*	.35	.20
		P# block of 4	10.00	—
		Zip block of 4	1.50	—
a.		Overall tagging, *1990*	.30	—
		P# block of 4	3.25	—
		Zip block of 4	1.20	—
b.		Prephosphored coated paper (solid tagging)	.40	—
		P# block of 4	3.25	—
		Zip block of 4	1.60	—
c.		Tagging omitted	*15.00*	—
d.		All color omitted		—

No. 2177d resulted from partially printed panes. It must be collected se-tenant with a partially printed stamp or in a longer horizontal strip showing error stamps plus partially/completely printed stamps.

2178	A1560	17c **dull blue green,** large block tagging, *June 18*	.35	.20
		P# block of 4	2.00	—
		Zip block of 4	1.40	—
		Pair with full horizontal gutter between		—
a.		Tagging omitted	*10.00*	

A1561

A1562

Designers: 20c, Robert Anderson. 21c, Susan Sanford.

Printed by: 20c, Banknote Corporation of America. 21c, Bureau of Engraving & Printing.

2179	A1561	20c **red brown,** prephosphored coated paper (grainy solid tagging), *Oct. 24, 1994*	.40	.20
		P# block of 4, 1#+B	2.00	—
a.		20c **orange brown,** prephosphored coated paper (grainy solid tagging)	.45	.20
		P# block of 4, 1#+B	2.25	—
b.		20c **bright red brown,** prephosphored coated paper (grainy solid tagging)	1.00	.25
		P# block of 4, 1#+B	6.00	—
2180	A1562	21c **blue violet,** large block tagging, *Oct. 21, 1988*	.45	.20
		P# block of 4	2.50	—
		Zip block of 4	1.65	—
a.		Tagging omitted		—

No. 2180 is known with worn tagging mats on which horizontal untagged areas have taggant giving the appearance of vertical band tagging.

A1563

A1564

A1565

Designers: 23c, Dennis Lyall. 25c, Richard Sparks. 28c, Robert Anderson.

Printed by the Bureau of Engraving & Printing.

2181	A1563	23c **purple,** large block tagging, dull gum, *Nov. 4, 1988*	.45	.20
		P# block of 4	2.50	—
		Zip block of 4	1.90	—
a.		Overall tagging, dull gum	.75	—
		P# block of 4	5.75	—
		Zip block of 4	3.25	—
b.		Prephosphored coated paper (solid tagging), dull gum	.65	—
		P# block of 4	5.00	—
		Zip block of 4	2.75	—
c.		Prephosphored uncoated paper (mottled tagging), shiny gum	.75	.20
		P# block of 4	5.75	—
		Zip block of 4	3.25	—
d.		Tagging omitted	*7.50*	
2182	A1564	25c **blue,** large block tagging, *Jan. 11*	.50	.20
		P# block of 4	2.75	—
		Zip block of 4	2.00	—
a.		Booklet pane of 10, *May 3, 1988*	5.00	3.75
b.		As #2182, tagging omitted	—	—
c.		As "a," tagging omitted	—	
d.		Horiz. pair, imperf between	—	
e.		As "a," all color omitted on right stamps	—	
f.		As No. 2182 (sheet stamp), vert. pair, bottom stamp all color omitted	—	

No. 2182f may be collected se-tenant with a partially printed stamp or longer vertical strip.
See Nos. 2197, 2197a.

2183	A1565	28c **myrtle green,** large block tagging, *Sept. 14, 1989*	.65	.35
		P# block of 4	3.50	—
		Zip block of 4	2.60	—

A1566

A1567

Designed by Christopher Calle.

Printed by: No. 2184, Canadian Bank Note Co. for Stamp Venturers. No. 2185, Stamp Venturers.

2184	A1566	29c **blue,** prephosphored uncoated paper (mottled tagging), *Mar. 9, 1992*	.70	.20
		P# block of 4, #+S	5.00	—
		Zip block of 4	3.00	—
2185	A1567	29c **indigo,** prephosphored coated paper (solid tagging), *Apr. 13, 1993*	.65	.20
		P# block of 4, 1#+S	3.50	—
		Zip block of 4	2.60	—

A1568

A1569

A1570

Designers: 35c, 40c, Christopher Calle. 45c, Bradbury Thompson.

Printed by: 35c, Canadian Bank Note Co. for Stamp Venturers. 40c, 45c, Bureau of Engraving & Printing.

2186	A1568	35c **black,** prephosphored uncoated paper (mottled tagging), *Apr. 3, 1991*	.75	.20
		P# block of 4, #+S	4.25	—
		Zip block of 4	3.00	—
2187	A1569	40c **dark blue,** overall tagging, dull gum, *Sept. 6, 1990*	.85	.20
		P# block of 4	4.50	—
		Zip block of 4	3.40	—
a.		Prephosphored coated paper (solid tagging), dull gum	1.00	.35

P# block of 4 5.50 —
Zip block of 4 4.00 —
b. Prephosphored coated paper (grainy solid tagging), low gloss gum, *1998* .85 .35
P# block of 4 4.50 —
Zip block of 4 3.40 —
c. Prephosphored uncoated paper (mottled tagging), shiny gum, *1994* 1.00 .20
P# block of 4 10.00 —
Zip block of 4 4.00 —
d. Tagging omitted —

2188 A1570 45c **bright blue,** large block tagging, *June 17, 1988* 1.00 .20
P# block of 4 5.00 —
Zip block of 4 4.00 —
a. 45c **blue,** overall tagging, *1990* 2.25 .20
P# block of 4 22.50 —
Zip block of 4 8.00 —
b. Tagging omitted *17.50*

The blue on No. 2188a is noticeably lighter than on No. 2188. Color variety specialists, as well as tagging specialists, will want to consider it as a second variety of this stamp.

A1571

A1572

Designers: 52c, John Berkey. 56c, Robert Anderson.

Printed by the Bureau of Engraving & Printing.

2189 A1571 52c **purple,** prephosphored coated paper (solid tagging), dull gum, *June 3, 1991* 1.10 .20
P# block of 4 7.50 —
Zip block of 4 4.50 —
a. Prephosphored uncoated paper (mottled tagging), shiny gum, *1993* 1.25 —
P# block of 4 8.00 —
Zip block of 4 5.00 —

Selvage inscriptions from the original printing of No. 2189 from plate 1 show the incorrect dates for Humphrey's vice-presidential term ("1964 to 1968"). Corrected plate 1 and plate 2 printings (No. 2189a) show the dates correctly as 1965 to 1969. Values for the two varieties of inscription blocks of 6 are approximately the same: $8.50.

2190 A1572 56c **scarlet,** large block tagging, *Sept. 3* 1.20 .20
P# block of 4 7.00 —
Zip block of 4 4.80 —
a. Tagging omitted —

No. 2190 known with a "tagging spill" making stamp appear overall tagged.

A1573

A1574

Designed by Christopher Calle.

Printed by the Bureau of Engraving & Printing.

2191 A1573 65c **dark blue,** large block tagging, *Nov. 5, 1988* 1.30 .20
P# block of 4 6.50 —
Zip block of 4 5.20 —
a. Tagging omitted *22.50*

2192 A1574 75c **deep magenta,** prephosphored coated paper (solid tagging), dull gum, *Feb. 16, 1992* 1.60 .20
P# block of 4 7.50 —
Zip block of 4 6.40 —
a. Prephosphored uncoated paper (mottled tagging), shiny gum 1.75 —
P# block of 4 9.00 —
Zip block of 4 7.00 —

A1575

A1576

"Lipstick on Shirt Front" double gouge plate flaw

Designers: No. 2193, Tom Broad. No. 2194, Bradbury Thompson.

Printed by the Bureau of Engraving & Printing.

2193 A1575 $1 **dark Prussian green,** large block tagging, *Sept. 23* 3.00 .50
P# block of 4 15.00 —
Zip block of 4 12.00 —
a. All color omitted —

No. 2193a must be collected se-tenant vertically with partially printed stamps.

2194 A1576 $1 **intense deep blue,** large block tagging, dull gum, *June 7, 1989* 2.25 .50
P# block of 4 12.00 —
Pane of 20 48.00
Double gouge plate flaw ("Lipstick on Shirt Front"), (pos. 6 on one plate #1 pane) —
b. $1 **deep blue,** overall tagging, dull gum, *1990* 2.50 .50
P# block of 4 13.00 —
Pane of 20 52.50
c. Tagging omitted *10.00*
d. $1 **dark blue,** prephosphored coated paper (solid tagging), dull gum, *1992* 2.50 .50
P# block of 4 13.00 —
Pane of 20 52.50
e. $1 **blue,** prephosphored uncoated paper (mottled tagging), shiny gum, *1993* 2.75 .60
P# block of 4 14.00 —
Pane of 20 58.00
f. $1 **blue,** prephosphored coated paper (grainy solid tagging), low gloss gum, *1998* 2.75 .50
P# block of 4 14.00 —
Pane of 20 58.00

No. 2194 issued in pane of 20 (see No. 2196.)
The intense deep blue of No. 2194 is much deeper than the deep blue and dark blue of the other $1 varieties.
The "Lipstick on Shirt Front" flaw was discovered during production and the position was repaired. Very few have been found.

A1577

A1578

Designers: $2, Tom Broad. $5, Arthur Lidov.

Printed by the Bureau of Engraving & Printing.

2195 A1577 $2 **bright violet,** large block tagging, *Mar. 19* 4.50 .50
P# block of 4 20.00 —
Zip block of 4 17.00 —
a. Tagging omitted *250.00*

No. 2195 is known with worn tagging mats on which horizontal untagged areas have taggant giving the appearance of vertical band tagging.

2196 A1578 $5 **copper red,** large block tagging, *Aug. 25, 1987* 9.00 1.00
P# block of 4 42.50 —
Pane of 20 185.00
a. Tagging omitted *225.00* —
b. Prephosphored coated paper (solid tagging), *1992* 11.00 —
P# block of 4 45.00 —
Pane of 20 220.00
Nos. 2168-2196 (28) 32.80 7.45

Booklet Stamp

Perf. 10 on 2 or 3 sides

2197 A1564 25c **blue,** large block tagging, *May 3, 1988* .55 .20
a. Booklet pane of 6 3.30 2.50
b. Tagging omitted 8.00
c. As "b," booklet pane of 6 50.00

UNITED STATES - SWEDEN STAMP COLLECTING

Handstamped Cover, Philatelic Memorabilia A1581

Boy Examining Stamp Collection A1582

No. 836 Under Magnifying Glass, Sweden Nos. 268, 271 — A1583

1986 Presidents Miniature Sheet on First Day Cover — A1584

Designed by Richard Sheaff and Eva Jern (No. 2200).

BOOKLET STAMPS
LITHOGRAPHED & ENGRAVED

Perf. 10 Vert. on 1 or 2 Sides

1986, Jan. 23 **Tagged**

2198 A1581 22c **multicolored** .45 .20
2199 A1582 22c **multicolored** .45 .20
2200 A1583 22c **multicolored** .45 .20
2201 A1584 22c **multicolored** .45 .20
a. Bklt. pane of 4, #2198-2201 2.00 1.75
b. As "a," black omitted on Nos. 2198, 2201 40.00 —
c. As "a," blue (litho.) omitted on Nos. 2198-2200 *2,250.*
d. As "a," buff (litho.) omitted —

See Sweden Nos. 1585-1588.

LOVE ISSUE

A1585

Designed by Saul Mandel.

Plates of 200 in four panes of 50.
PHOTOGRAVURE

1986, Jan. 30 **Tagged** ***Perf. 11***
2202 A1585 22c **multicolored** .55 .20
P# block of 4, 5# 2.75 —
Zip block of 4 2.25 —
a. Tagging omitted —

Sojourner Truth (c. 1797-1883), Human Rights Activist — A1586

Texas State Flag and Silver Spur — A1587

BLACK HERITAGE SERIES

Designed by Jerry Pinkney.

Printed by American Bank Note Co.

Plates of 200 in four panes of 50
PHOTOGRAVURE

1986, Feb. 4 **Tagged** ***Perf. 11***
2203 A1586 22c **multicolored** .55 .20
P# block of 4, 6#+A 2.75 —
Zip block of 4 2.25 —

REPUBLIC OF TEXAS, 150th ANNIV.

Designed by Don Adair.

Printed by the American Bank Note Co.

Plates of 200 in four panes of 50.
PHOTOGRAVURE

1986, Mar. 2 **Tagged** ***Perf. 11***
2204 A1587 22c **dark blue, dark red & grayish black** .55 .20
P# block of 4, 3#+A 2.75 —
Zip block of 4 2.25 —
a. Horiz. pair, imperf. vert. *900.00*
b. Dark red omitted *2,350.*
c. Dark blue omitted *8,000.*

FISH

Muskellunge — A1588

Atlantic Cod A1589

Largemouth Bass — A1590

Bluefin Tuna A1591

Catfish A1592

Designed by Chuck Ripper.

BOOKLET STAMPS
PHOTOGRAVURE

1986, Mar. 21 **Tagged** ***Perf. 10 Horiz.***
2205 A1588 22c **multicolored** 1.00 .20
2206 A1589 22c **multicolored** 1.00 .20
2207 A1590 22c **multicolored** 1.00 .20
2208 A1591 22c **multicolored** 1.00 .20
2209 A1592 22c **multicolored** 1.00 .20
a. Bklt. pane of 5, #2205-2209 5.50 2.75

The magenta used to print this issue is extremely fugitive. Dangerous fakes purported to be magenta omitted exist. No genuine examples are known. Panes apparently lacking red must be certified, and examples presently with certificates should be recertified.

PUBLIC HOSPITALS

A1593

Designed by Uldis Purins.

Printed by the American Bank Note Co.

PHOTOGRAVURE
Plates of 200 in four panes of 50.

1986, Apr. 11 **Tagged** ***Perf. 11***
2210 A1593 22c **multicolored** .40 .20
P# block of 4, 5#+A 1.75 —
Zip block of 4 1.65 —
a. Vert. pair. imperf. horiz. *275.00*
b. Horiz. pair, imperf. vert. *1,150.*

PERFORMING ARTS

Edward Kennedy "Duke" Ellington (1899-1974), Jazz Composer — A1594

Designed by Jim Sharpe.
Printed by the American Bank Note Co.

PHOTOGRAVURE
Plates of 200 in four panes of 50.

1986, Apr. 29 **Tagged** ***Perf. 11***
2211 A1594 22c **multicolored** .40 .20
P# block of 4, 6#+A 1.90 —
Zip block of 4 1.75 —
a. Vert. pair. imperf. horiz. *800.00*

AMERIPEX '86 ISSUE

Miniature Sheets

35 Presidents — A1599a

A1599b

A1599c

A1599d

Illustrations reduced.

Designs: No. 2216: a, George Washington. b, John Adams. c, Thomas Jefferson. d, James Madison. e, James Monroe. f, John Quincy Adams. g, Andrew Jackson. h, Martin Van Buren. i, William H. Harrison.

No. 2217: a, John Tyler. b, James Knox Polk. c, Zachary Taylor. d, Millard Fillmore. e, Franklin Pierce. f, James Buchanan. g, Abraham Lincoln. h, Andrew Johnson. i, Ulysses S. Grant.

No. 2218: a, Rutherford B. Hayes. b, James A. Garfield. c, Chester A. Arthur. d, Grover Cleveland. e, Benjamin Harrison. f, William McKinley. g, Theodore Roosevelt. h, William H. Taft. i, Woodrow Wilson.

No. 2219: a, Warren G. Harding. b, Calvin Coolidge. c, Herbert Hoover. d, Franklin Delano Roosevelt. e, White House. f, Harry S. Truman. g, Dwight D. Eisenhower. h, John F. Kennedy. i, Lyndon B. Johnson.

Designed by Jerry Dadds.

LITHOGRAPHED & ENGRAVED

1986, May 22 **Tagged** ***Perf. 11***

2216	A1599a Sheet of 9	7.50	4.00
a.-i.	22c, any single	.75	.40
j.	Blue (engr.) omitted	*2,500.*	
k.	Black inscription omitted	*2,000.*	
l.	Imperf.	*10,500.*	
m.	As "k," double impression of red	—	
n.	Blue omitted on stamps 1-3, 5-6, 8, 9	—	
2217	A1599b Sheet of 9	7.50	4.00
a-i.	22c, any single	.75	.40
j.	Black inscription omitted	*2,500.*	
k.	Tagging omitted	—	
2218	A1599c Sheet of 9	7.50	4.00
a.-i.	22c, any single	.75	.40
j.	Brown (engr.) omitted	—	
k.	Black inscription omitted	*2,500.*	
l.	Tagging omitted	—	
2219	A1599d Sheet of 9	7.50	4.00
a.-i.	22c, any single	.75	.40
j.	Blackish blue (engr.) inscription omitted on a-b, d-e, g-h	*2,500.*	
k.	Tagging omitted on c, f, i	*4,000.*	
l.	Blackish blue (engr.) omitted on all stamps	—	
	Nos. 2216-2219 (4)	30.00	16.00

Issued in conjunction with AMERIPEX '86 Intl. Philatelic Exhibition, Chicago, IL May 22-June 1. Sheet size: 120x207mm (sheet size varied).

ARCTIC EXPLORERS

Elisha Kent Kane — A1600

Adolphus W. Greely A1601

Vilhjalmur Stefansson A1602

Robert E. Peary, Matthew Henson A1603

Designed by Dennis Lyall.
Printed by the American Bank Note Company

PHOTOGRAVURE

Plates of 200 in four panes of 50.

1986, May 28 **Tagged** ***Perf. 11***

2220	A1600 22c **multicolored**	.65	.20
2221	A1601 22c **multicolored**	.65	.20
2222	A1602 22c **multicolored**	.65	.20
2223	A1603 22c **multicolored**	.65	.20
a.	Block of 4, #2220-2223	2.75	2.25
	P# block of 4, 5#+A	4.50	—
	Zip block of 4	3.00	—
b.	As "a," black omitted	*5,000.*	
c.	As "a," Nos. 2220, 2221 black omitted	—	
d.	As "a," Nos. 2222, 2223 black omitted	—	

STATUE OF LIBERTY, 100th ANNIV.

A1604

Designed by Howard Paine.

ENGRAVED

Plates of 200 in four panes of 50.

1986, July 4 **Tagged** ***Perf. 11***

2224	A1604 22c **scarlet & dark blue**	.40	.20
	P# block of 4	2.25	—
	Zip block of 4	1.65	—
a.	Scarlet omitted	—	

On No. 2224a, virtually all of the dark blue also is omitted, so the error stamp should be collected as part of a transition strip. See France No. 2014.

Coil Plate No. Strips of 3

Beginning with No. 2123, coil plate no. strips of 3 usually sell at the level of strips of 5 minus the face value of two stamps.

TRANSPORTATION ISSUE

A1604a

A1604b

Designers: 1c, 2c, David Stone.

COIL STAMPS
ENGRAVED

1986-87 Tagged *Perf. 10 Vert.*

2225 A1604a 1c **violet,** large block tagging, dull gum, *Nov. 26*	.20	.20
Pair	.20	.20
P# strip of 5, #1, 2	.50	
P# single, #1, 2	—	.40
a. Prephosphored uncoated paper (mottled tagging) (error), shiny gum	.20	.20
Pair	.20	.20
P# strip of 5, #3	32.50	
P# single, #3	—	25.00
b. Untagged, dull gum	.20	.20
Pair	.20	.20
P# strip of 5, #2-3	.55	
P# single, #2-3	—	.45
Shiny gum	.20	
P# strip of 5, #3	.60	
Low gloss gum	.20	
P# strip of 5, #3	2.50	
c. Imperf., pair	*2,000.*	
2226 A1604b 2c **black,** dull gum, *Mar. 6, 1987*	.20	.20
Pair	.20	.20
P# strip of 5, #1	.50	
P# single, #1	—	.35
a. Untagged, dull gum	.20	.20
Pair	.20	.20
P# strip of 5, #2	1.00	
P# single, #2	—	.50
Shiny gum	.20	
P# strip of 5, #2	2.00	

REDUCED SIZE

2228 A1285 4c **reddish brown,** large block tagging, *Aug.*	.20	.20
Pair	.20	.20
P# strip of 5, #1	1.50	
P# single, #1	—	.95
a. Overall tagging, *1990*	.70	.20
Pair	1.40	.20
P# strip of 5, #1	11.00	
P# single, #1	—	9.00
b. Imperf., pair	250.00	

Earliest known usage of No. 2228: Aug. 15, 1986.

On No. 2228 "Stagecoach 1890s" is 17¾mm long; on No. 1898A, 19½mm long.

UNTAGGED

2231 A1511 8.3c **green** (Bureau precancel, Blk. Rt./CAR-RT/SORT), *Aug. 29*	.50	.20
Pair	1.00	.40
P# strip of 5, #1	5.00	
P# strip of 5, #2	5.75	
P# single, #1	—	3.00
P# single, #2	—	5.00

On No. 2231 "Ambulance 1860s" is 18mm long; on No. 2128, 18⅓mm long.

Joint lines do not appear on Nos. 2225-2231.

AMERICAN FOLK ART SERIES
Navajo Art

A1605

A1606

A1607

A1608

Designed by Derry Noyes.

LITHOGRAPHED & ENGRAVED
Plates of 200 in four panes of 50.

1986, Sept. 4 Tagged *Perf. 11*

2235 A1605 22c **multicolored**	.80	.20
2236 A1606 22c **multicolored**	.80	.20
2237 A1607 22c **multicolored**	.80	.20
2238 A1608 22c **multicolored**	.80	.20
a. Block of 4, #2235-2238	3.25	2.25
P# block of 4, 5#	4.25	—
Zip block of 4	3.50	—
b. As "a," black (engr.) omitted	*325.00*	

LITERARY ARTS SERIES

T.S. Eliot (1888-1965), Poet — A1609

Designed by Bradbury Thompson.

ENGRAVED
Plates of 200 in four panes of 50.

1986, Sept. 26 Tagged *Perf. 11*

2239 A1609 22c **copper red**	.55	.20
P# block of 4	2.75	—
Zip block of 4	2.25	—
a. Tagging omitted		—

AMERICAN FOLK ART SERIES
Woodcarved Figurines

A1610

A1611

A1612

A1613

Designed by Bradbury Thompson.
Printed by the American Bank Note Company

PHOTOGRAVURE
Plates of 200 in four panes of 50.

1986, Oct. 1 Tagged *Perf. 11*

2240 A1610 22c **multicolored**	.50	.20
2241 A1611 22c **multicolored**	.50	.20
2242 A1612 22c **multicolored**	.50	.20
2243 A1613 22c **multicolored**	.50	.20
a. Block of 4, #2240-2243	2.00	1.50
P# block of 4, 5#+A	3.75	—
Zip block of 4	2.25	—
b. As "a," imperf. vert.	*1,250.*	

CHRISTMAS

Madonna, National Gallery, by Perugino (c. 1450-1513)
A1614

Village Scene
A1615

Designed by Bradbury Thompson (#2244) & Dolli Tingle (#2245).

PHOTOGRAVURE
Plates of 200 in four panes of 50.

1986, Oct. 24 Tagged *Perf. 11*

2244 A1614 22c **multicolored**	.40	.20
P# block of 4, 5#	2.00	—
Zip block of 4	1.65	—
a. Imperf., pair	*600.00*	
2245 A1615 22c **multicolored**	.40	.20
P# block of 4, 6#	1.90	—
Zip block of 4	1.65	—

MICHIGAN STATEHOOD, 150th ANNIV.

White Pine — A1616

Designed by Robert Wilbert.

PHOTOGRAVURE
Plates of 200 in four panes of 50.

1987, Jan. 26 Tagged *Perf. 11*

2246 A1616 22c **multicolored**	.55	.20
P# block of 4, 5#	2.75	—
Zip block of 4	2.25	—
Pair with full vert. gutter between	—	

PAN AMERICAN GAMES
Indianapolis, Aug. 7-25

Runner in Full Stride
A1617

Designed by Lon Busch.

PHOTOGRAVURE
Plates of 200 in four panes of 50.

1987, Jan. 29 Tagged *Perf. 11*

2247 A1617 22c **multicolored**	.40	.20
P# block of 4, 5#	1.90	—
Zip block of 4	1.65	—
a. Silver omitted	*1,500.*	

No. 2247a is valued in the grade of fine.

LOVE ISSUE

A1618

Designed by John Alcorn.

PHOTOGRAVURE
Panes of 100

1987, Jan. 30 — Tagged — *Perf. 11½x11*

2248 A1618 22c **multicolored** .40 .20
P# block of 4, 5# 1.90 —
Zip block of 4 1.65 —
Pair with full horiz. gutter between —

BLACK HERITAGE SERIES

Jean Baptiste Pointe du Sable (c. 1750-1818), Pioneer Trader, Founder of Chicago — A1619

Designed by Thomas Blackshear.

PHOTOGRAVURE
Plates of 200 in four panes of 50.

1987, Feb. 20 — Tagged — *Perf. 11*

2249 A1619 22c **multicolored** .50 .20
P# block of 4, 5# 2.60 —
Zip block of 4 2.10 —
a. Tagging omitted *10.00*

Enrico Caruso (1873-1921), Opera Tenor — A1620

Fourteen Achievement Badges — A1621

PERFORMING ARTS SERIES

Designed by Jim Sharpe.
Printed by American Bank Note Co.

PHOTOGRAVURE & ENGRAVED
Plates of 200 in four panes of 50.

1987, Feb. 27 — Tagged — *Perf. 11*

2250 A1620 22c **multicolored** .40 .20
P# block of 4, 4#+A 1.90 —
Zip block of 4 1.65 —
a. Black (engr.) omitted *5,000.*

GIRL SCOUTS, 75TH ANNIVERSARY

Designed by Richard Sheaff.

LITHOGRAPHED & ENGRAVED
Plates of 200 in four panes of 50.

1987, Mar. 12 — Tagged — *Perf. 11*

2251 A1621 22c **multicolored** .40 .20
P# block of 4, 6# 1.90 —
Zip block of 4 1.65 —
a. All litho. colors omitted *2,450.*
b. Red & black (engr.) omitted *1,950.*

All known examples of No. 2251a have been expertized and certificate must accompany purchase. The unique pane of No. 2251b has been expertized and a certificate exists for the pane of 50.

Coil Plate No. Strips of 3
Beginning with No. 2123, coil plate no. strips of 3 usually sell at the level of strips of 5 minus the face value of two stamps.

TRANSPORTATION ISSUE

A1622

A1623

A1624

A1625

A1626

A1627

A1628

A1629

A1630

A1631

A1632

A1633

A1634

A1635

A1636

Designers: 3c, 7.6c, 13.2c, 15c, Richard Schlecht. 5c, 5.3c, 16.7c, Lou Nolan. 8.4c, 20.5c, 24.1c, Christopher Calle. 10c, William H. Bond. 13c, Joe Brockert. 17.5c, Tom Broad. 20c, Dan Romano. 21c, David Stone.

COIL STAMPS
ENGRAVED

1987-88 — *Perf. 10 Vert.*
Tagged, Untagged (5.3c, 7.6c, 8.4c, 13c, 13.2c, 16.7c, 20.5c, 21c, 24.1c)

2252 A1622 3c **claret,** dull gum, *Feb. 29, 1988* .20 .20
Pair .20 .20
P# strip of 5, #1 .70
P# single, #1 — .60
a. Untagged, dull gum .20 .20
P# strip of 5, #2-3 1.50
P# single, #2 — .95
P# single, #3 — .80
Shiny gum, *1995* .20
P# strip of 5, #3 1.25
P# strip of 5, #5 6.00
P# strip of 5, #6 1.40
P# single, #5 — 7.00
P# single, #6 — 1.25
Low gloss gum .40
P# strip of 5, #5 8.00
P# single, #5 6.75
b. As "a," imperf pair, shiny gum —

The plate #5 on No. 2252a with low gloss gum is smaller than the #5 on No. 2252a with shiny gum. The smaller plate #5 represents a different printing sleeve (plate).

2253 A1623 5c **black,** *Sept. 25* .20 .20
Pair .20 .20
P# strip of 5, #1 .80
P# single, #1 — .75

2254 A1624 5.3c **black** (Bureau precancel "Nonprofit Carrier Route Sort" in red), *Sept. 16, 1988* .20 .20
Pair .20 .20
P# strip of 5, #1 1.40
P# single, #1 — .70

2255 A1625 7.6c **brown** (Bureau precancel "Nonprofit" in red), *Aug. 30, 1988* .20 .20
Pair .30 .30
P# strip of 5, #1-2 1.75
P# strip of 5, #3 3.50
P# single, #1-2 — 1.50
P# single, #3 — 4.00

2256 A1626 8.4c **deep claret** (Bureau precancel "Nonprofit" in red), *Aug. 12, 1988* .20 .20
Pair .30 .30
P# strip of 5, #1-2 1.90
P# strip of 5, #3 7.50
P# single, #1-2 — 1.00
P# single, #3 — 5.50
a. Imperf., pair *575.00*

2257 A1627 10c **blue,** large block tagging, dull gum, *Apr. 11* .40 .20
Pair .80 .20
P# strip of 5, #1 2.00
P# single, #1 — 1.00
a. Overall tagging, dull gum, *1993* 1.50 .20
Pair 3.00 .20
P# strip of 5, #1 12.00
P# single, #1 — 4.75
Shiny gum, *1994* .20 .20
Pair .20 .20
P# strip of 5, #4 3.50
P# single, #4 — 2.00
b. Prephosphored uncoated paper (mottled tagging), shiny gum .20 .20
Pair .40 .20
P# strip of 5, #1, 2 2.75
P# strip of 5, #3, 4 3.25
P# single, #1, 2 — 2.50
P# single, #3, 4 — 2.75
c. Prephosphored coated paper (solid tagging), low gloss gum .25 .20
Pair .50 .20
P# strip of 5, #5 4.75
P# single, #5 — 4.00
d. Tagging omitted *30.00*
e. Imperf, pair, large block tagging *1,750.*

2258 A1628 13c **black** (Bureau precancel "Presorted First-Class" in red), *Oct. 29, 1988* .65 .25
Pair 1.30 .50
P# strip of 5, #1 5.00
P# single, #1 — 2.00

2259 A1629 13.2c **slate green** (Bureau precancel "Bulk Rate" in red), *July 19, 1988* .25 .25
Pair .50 .50
P# strip of 5, #1-2 2.75
P# single, #1-2 — 1.50
a. Imperf., pair 95.00

2260 A1630 15c **violet,** large block tagging, *July 12, 1988* .25 .20
Pair .50 .20
P# strip of 5, #1 1.75
P# strip of 5, #2 2.25
P# single, #1-2 — 1.50
a. Overall tagging, *1990* .25 .20
Pair .50 .20
P# strip of 5, #2 3.25
P# single, #2 — 2.75
b. Tagging omitted *3.75*
c. Imperf., pair *650.00*

2261 A1631 16.7c **rose** (Bureau precancel "Bulk Rate " in black), *July 7, 1988* .30 .30
Pair .60 .60
P# strip of 5, #1 2.25
P# strip of 5, #2 2.50

			P# single, #1	—	1.60
			P# single, #2	—	2.50
a.			Imperf., pair	*165.00*	

All known examples of No. 2261a are miscut top to bottom.

2262	A1632	17.5c	**dark violet,** *Sept. 25*	.65	.20
			Pair	1.30	.20
			P# strip of 5, #1	4.00	
			P# single, #1	—	2.50
a.			Untagged (Bureau Precancel "ZIP + 4 Presort" in red)	.65	.30
			P# strip of 5, #1	4.00	
			P# single, #1	—	2.50
b.			Imperf., pair	*2,250.*	
2263	A1633	20c	**blue violet,** large block tagging, *Oct. 28, 1988*	.35	.20
			Pair	.70	.20
			P# strip of 5, #1-2	3.00	
			P# single, #1-2	—	1.75
a.			Imperf., pair	50.00	
b.			Overall tagging, *1990*	1.00	.20
			Pair	2.00	.20
			P# strip of 5, #2	8.00	
			P# single, #2	—	5.00
2264	A1634	20.5c	**rose** (Bureau precancel "ZIP + 4 Presort" in black), *Sept. 28, 1988*	.75	.40
			Pair	1.50	.80
			P# strip of 5, #1	5.75	
			P# single, #1	—	3.00
2265	A1635	21c	**olive green** (Bureau precancel "Presorted First-Class" in red), *Aug. 16, 1988*	.40	.40
			Pair	.80	.80
			P# strip of 5, #1-2	3.00	
			P# single, #1-2	—	2.50
a.			Imperf., pair	42.50	
2266	A1636	24.1c	**deep ultra** (Bureau precancel ZIP + 4 in red), *Oct. 26, 1988*	.80	.45
			Pair	1.60	.90
			P# strip of 5, #1	3.75	
			P# single, #1	—	2.25
			Nos. 2252-2266 (15)	5.80	3.85

5.3c, 7.6c, 8.4c, 13.2c, 16.7c, 20.5c, 21c and 24.1c only available precanceled.

SPECIAL OCCASIONS

A1637

A1638

A1639

A1640

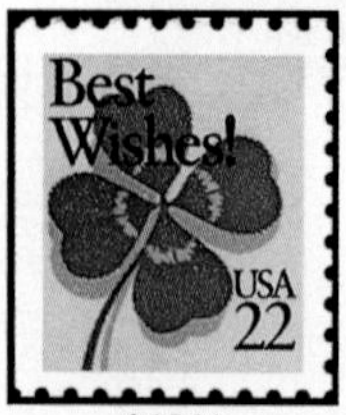

A1641

A1642

A1643

A1644

Designed by Oren Sherman.

BOOKLET STAMPS
PHOTOGRAVURE

1987, Apr. 20 Tagged *Perf. 10 on 1, 2 or 3 Sides*

2267	A1637	22c	**multicolored**	.65	.20
2268	A1638	22c	**multicolored**	.80	.20
2269	A1639	22c	**multicolored**	.80	.20
2270	A1640	22c	**multicolored**	.80	.20
2271	A1641	22c	**multicolored**	.80	.20
2272	A1642	22c	**multicolored**	.65	.20
2273	A1643	22c	**multicolored**	1.40	.20
2274	A1644	22c	**multicolored**	.80	.20
a.			Bklt. pane of 10 (#2268-2271, 2273-2274, 2 each #2267, 2272)	10.00	5.00

UNITED WAY, 100th ANNIV.

Six Profiles
A1645

Designed by Jerry Pinkney.

LITHOGRAPHED & ENGRAVED
Plates of 200 in four panes of 50.

1987, Apr. 28 Tagged *Perf. 11*

2275	A1645	22c	**multicolored**	.40	.20
			P# block of 4, 6#	1.90	—
			Zip block of 4	1.65	—

A1646

A1647

A1648

A1649

Pheasant — A1649a

Grosbeak — A1649b

Owl — A1649c

Honeybee — A1649d

Designs: Nos. 2276, 2278, 2280, Peter Cocci. Nos. 2277, 2279, 2282, Robert McCall. Nos. 2281, 2283-2285, Chuck Ripper.

PHOTOGRAVURE (Nos. 2276-2279)
Panes of 100

1987-88 Tagged *Perf. 11*

2276	A1646	22c	**multicolored,** *May 9*	.40	.20
			P# block of 4, 4#	1.90	—
			Zip block of 4	1.65	—
a.			Booklet pane of 20, *Nov. 30*	8.50	—
b.			As "a," vert. pair, imperf. btwn.	*1,500.*	
2277	A1647	(25c)	**multi,** *Mar. 22, 1988*	.45	.20
			P# block of 4, 4#	2.00	—
			Zip block of 4	1.85	—
2278	A1648	25c	**multi,** *May 6, 1988*	.45	.20
			P# block of 4, 4#	1.90	—
			Zip block of 4	1.85	—
			Pair with full vert. gutter between	*125.00*	

COIL STAMPS

Perf. 10 Vert.

2279	A1647	(25c)	**multi,** *Mar. 22, 1988*	.45	.20
			Pair	.90	.20
			P# strip of 5, #1111	2.75	
			P# strip of 5, #1211	4.00	
			P# strip of 5, #1222	2.75	
			P# strip of 5, #2222	3.25	
			P# single, #1111	—	.50
			P# single, #1211	—	1.10
			P# single, #1222	—	.80
			P# single, #2222	—	3.25
a.			Imperf., pair	*65.00*	—

ENGRAVED

2280	A1649	25c	**multi,** large block tagging, *May 20, 1988*	.45	.20
			Pair	.90	.20
			P# strip of 5, #1	5.75	
			P# strip of 5, #2-5	3.25	
			P# strip of 5, #7	6.00	
			P# strip of 5, #8	3.00	
			P# strip of 5, #9	8.50	
			P# single, #1	—	2.50
			P# single, #2-5	—	.75
			P# single, #7	—	2.00
			P# single, #8	—	.75
			P# single, #9	—	2.00
a.			Prephosphored uncoated paper (mottled tagging) *Feb. 14, 1989*	.45	.20
			P# strip of 5, #1	30.00	
			P# strip of 5, #2, 3	3.25	
			P# strip of 5, #5	6.00	
			P# strip of 5, #6	10.00	
			P# strip of 5, #7-11, 13-14	3.25	
			P# strip of 5, #15	6.00	
			P# single, #1	—	25.00
			P# single, #2	—	.60
			P# single, #3	—	.60
			P# single, #5	—	1.25
			P# single, #6	—	5.25
			P# single, #7-11, 13-14	—	.60
			P# single, #15	—	2.00
b.			Imperf., pair, large block tagging	25.00	
c.			Imperf., pair, prephosphored paper (mottled tagging)	10.00	
d.			Tagging omitted	*5.00*	
e.			Black trees	*100.00*	—
			P# strip of 5, #4, 5, 9	*700.00*	
f.			Pair, imperf. between	*500.00*	

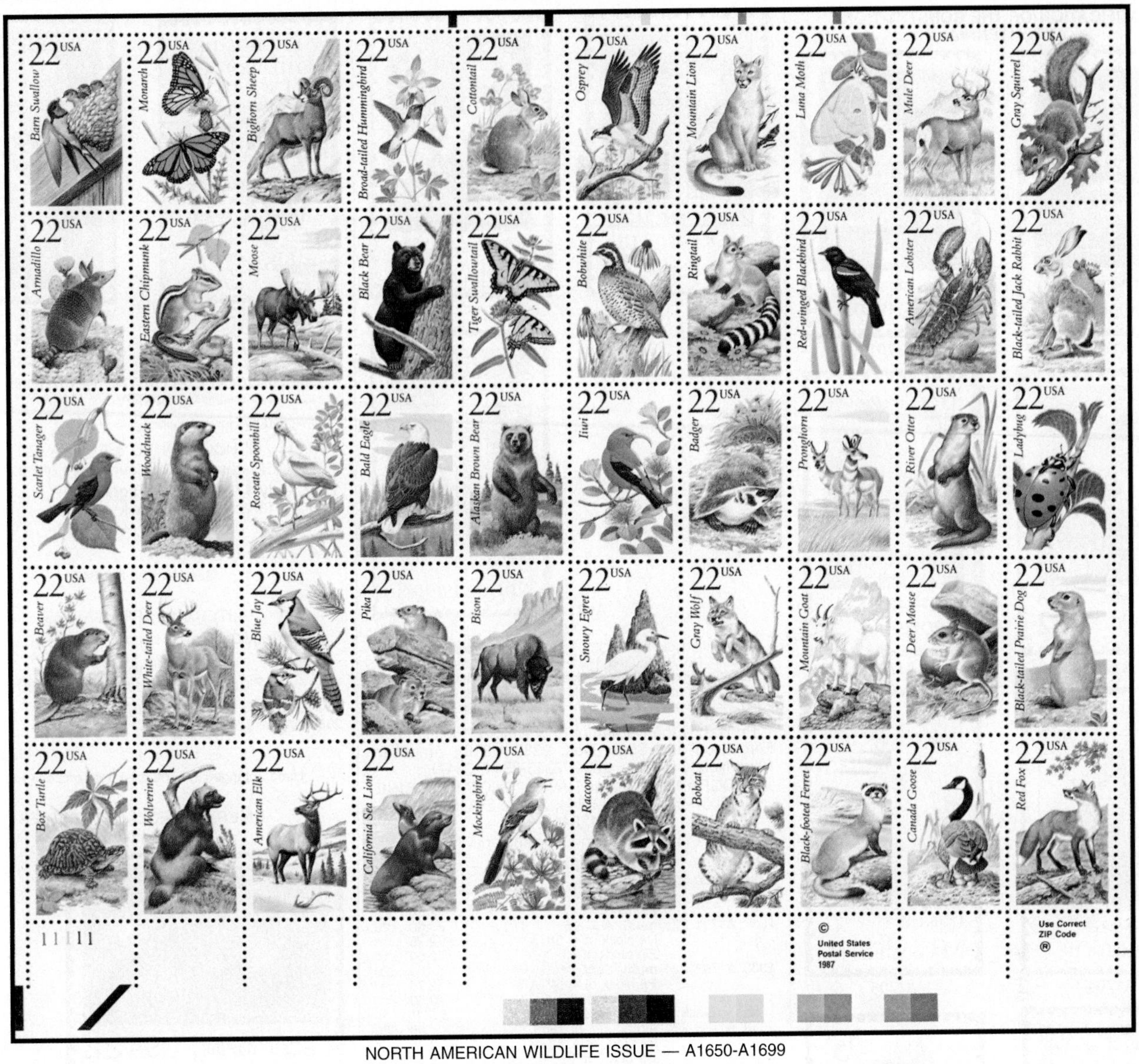

NORTH AMERICAN WILDLIFE ISSUE — A1650-A1699

LITHOGRAPHED AND ENGRAVED

2281 A1649d 25c **multi,** small block tagging *Sept. 2, 1988* .45 .20
Pair .90 .20
P# strip of 5, #1 3.50
P# single, #1 — .50
a. As No. 2281, imperf., pair 45.00
P#1-2
b. Black (engr.) omitted *50.00* —
c. Black (litho.) omitted *450.00*
d. Pair, imperf. between *700.00*
e. Yellow (litho.) omitted *1,000.*
f. Large block tagging .45 .20
Pair .90
P# strip of 5, #2 3.50
P# single, #2 — .50
g. As "f," imperf, pair 45.00
h. As "f," tagging omitted 85.00 —

No. 2281h can be distinguished as having come from the large block tagging stamp by its deeper colors and jet black "25," which is a characteristic of the plate 2 large block tagged printing.

No. 2281 from plate #1 is known with two types of "1" on the plate-numbered stamps. The original tall "1" was later shortened manually by removing the top of the "1," including the serif, so it would not penetrate the design. Value of plate # strip of 5 with tall "1," $24.

Beware of stamps with traces of the litho. black that are offered as No. 2281c.

Vertical pairs or blocks of No. 2281 and imperfs. with the engr. black missing are from printer's waste.

BOOKLET STAMPS

Printed by American Bank Note Co. (#2283)

PHOTOGRAVURE
Perf. 10, 11 (#2283)

2282 A1647 (25c) **multi,** *Mar. 22, 1988* .50 .20
a. Booklet pane of 10 6.50 3.50

2283 A1649a 25c **multi,** *Apr. 29, 1988* .50 .20
a. Booklet pane of 10 6.00 3.50
b. 25c multicolored, red removed from sky 6.50 .20
c. As "b," bklt. pane of 10 *70.00* —
d. Vert. pair, imperf. btwn. —

Imperf. panes exist from printers waste, and a large number exist. No. 2283d resulted from a foldover. Non-foldover pairs and multiples are printer's waste.

2284 A1649b 25c **multi,** *May 28, 1988* .50 .20
2285 A1649c 25c **multi,** *May 28, 1988* .50 .20
b. Bklt. pane of 10, 5 each #2284-2285 5.00 3.50
d. Pair, Nos. 2284-2285 1.10 .25
e. As "d," tagging omitted 12.50
2285A A1648 25c **multi,** *July 5, 1988* .50 .20
c. Booklet pane of 6 3.00 2.00

NORTH AMERICAN WILDLIFE

Illustration reduced.

Designed by Chuck Ripper.

PHOTOGRAVURE
Plates of 200 in four panes of 50.

1987, June 13 **Tagged** ***Perf. 11***

2286 A1650 22c Barn swallow 1.00 .50
2287 A1651 22c Monarch butterfly 1.00 .50
2288 A1652 22c Bighorn sheep 1.00 .50
2289 A1653 22c Broad-tailed hummingbird 1.00 .50
2290 A1654 22c Cottontail 1.00 .50
2291 A1655 22c Osprey 1.00 .50
2292 A1656 22c Mountain lion 1.00 .50
2293 A1657 22c Luna moth 1.00 .50
2294 A1658 22c Mule deer 1.00 .50
2295 A1659 22c Gray squirrel 1.00 .50
2296 A1660 22c Armadillo 1.00 .50
2297 A1661 22c Eastern chipmunk 1.00 .50
2298 A1662 22c Moose 1.00 .50
2299 A1663 22c Black bear 1.00 .50
2300 A1664 22c Tiger swallowtail 1.00 .50
2301 A1665 22c Bobwhite 1.00 .50
2302 A1666 22c Ringtail 1.00 .50
2303 A1667 22c Red-winged blackbird 1.00 .50
2304 A1668 22c American lobster 1.00 .50
2305 A1669 22c Black-tailed jack rabbit 1.00 .50
2306 A1670 22c Scarlet tanager 1.00 .50
2307 A1671 22c Woodchuck 1.00 .50
2308 A1672 22c Roseate spoonbill 1.00 .50
2309 A1673 22c Bald eagle 1.00 .50
2310 A1674 22c Alaskan brown bear 1.00 .50
2311 A1675 22c Iiwi 1.00 .50
2312 A1676 22c Badger 1.00 .50
2313 A1677 22c Pronghorn 1.00 .50
2314 A1678 22c River otter 1.00 .50
2315 A1679 22c Ladybug 1.00 .50
2316 A1680 22c Beaver 1.00 .50
2317 A1681 22c White-tailed deer 1.00 .50
2318 A1682 22c Blue jay 1.00 .50
2319 A1683 22c Pika 1.00 .50
2320 A1684 22c American buffalo 1.00 .50
2321 A1685 22c Snowy egret 1.00 .50
2322 A1686 22c Gray wolf 1.00 .50
2323 A1687 22c Mountain goat 1.00 .50
2324 A1688 22c Deer mouse 1.00 .50
2325 A1689 22c Black-tailed prairie dog 1.00 .50
2326 A1690 22c Box turtle 1.00 .50
2327 A1691 22c Wolverine 1.00 .50
2328 A1692 22c American elk 1.00 .50
2329 A1693 22c California sea lion 1.00 .50
2330 A1694 22c Mockingbird 1.00 .50
2331 A1695 22c Raccoon 1.00 .50
2332 A1696 22c Bobcat 1.00 .50
2333 A1697 22c Black-footed ferret 1.00 .50
2334 A1698 22c Canada goose 1.00 .50
2335 A1699 22c Red fox 1.00 .50
a. A1650-A1699 Pane of 50, #2286-2335 50.00 35.00
2286b-2335b Any single, red omitted *2,500.*

RATIFICATION OF THE CONSTITUTION BICENTENNIAL

A1700

A1701

A1702

A1703

A1704

A1705

A1706

A1707

A1708

A1709

A1710

A1711

A1712

Designers: Nos. 2336-2337, 2341 Richard Sheaff. No. 2338, Jim Lamb. No. 2339, Greg Harlin. No. 2340, Christopher Calle. No. 2342, Stephen Hustvedt. Nos. 2343, 2347, Bob Timberlake. No. 2344, Thomas Szumowski. No. 2345, Pierre Mion. No. 2346, Bradbury Thompson. No. 2348, Robert Brangwynne.

Printed by the Bureau of Engraving & Printing, J.W. Fergusson and Sons (Nos. 2337, 2338), American Bank Note Co. (Nos. 2339, 2343-2344, 2347).

LITHOGRAPHED & ENGRAVED, PHOTOGRAVURE (#2337-2339, 2343-2344, 2347), ENGRAVED (#2341).

Plates of 200 in four panes of 50.

1987-90		**Tagged**	**Perf. 11**	
2336	A1700 22c	**multi**, *July 4*	.60	.20
		P# block of 4, 5#	2.75	—
		Zip block of 4	2.50	—
2337	A1701 22c	**multi**, *Aug. 26*	.60	.20
		P# block of 4, 5#+A	2.75	—
		Zip block of 4	2.50	—
2338	A1702 22c	**multi**, *Sept. 11*	.60	.20
		P# block of 4, 5#+A	2.75	—
		Zip block of 4	2.50	—
a.		Black (engr.) omitted	*5,500.*	
2339	A1703 22c	**multi**, *Jan. 6, 1988*	.60	.20
		P# block of 4, 5#+A	2.75	—
		Zip block of 4	2.50	—
2340	A1704 22c	**multi**, *Jan. 9, 1988*	.60	.20
		P# block of 4, 5#	2.75	—
		Zip block of 4	2.50	—
2341	A1705 22c	**dark blue & dark red**, *Feb. 6, 1988*	.60	.20
		P# block of 4, 1#	2.75	—
		Zip block of 4	2.50	—
2342	A1706 22c	**multi**, *Feb. 15, 1988*	.60	.20
		P# block of 4, 6#	2.75	—
		Zip block of 4	2.50	—
2343	A1707 25c	**multi**, *May 23, 1988*	.60	.20
		P# block of 4, 5#+A	2.75	—
		Zip block of 4	2.50	—
a.		Strip of 3, vert. imperf btwn.	*12,500.*	
b.		Red missing (PS)	—	
2344	A1708 25c	**multi**, *June 21, 1988*	.60	.20
		P# block of 4, 4#+A	2.75	—
		Zip block of 4	2.50	—
2345	A1709 25c	**multi**, *June 25, 1988*	.60	.20
		P# block of 4, 5#	2.75	—
		Zip block of 4	2.50	—
2346	A1710 25c	**multi**, *July 26, 1988*	.60	.20
		P# block of 4, 5#	2.75	—
		Zip block of 4	2.50	—
2347	A1711 25c	**multi**, *Aug. 22, 1989*	.60	.20
		P# block of 4, 5#+A	2.75	—
		Zip block of 4	2.50	—
2348	A1712 25c	**multi**, *May 29, 1990*	.60	.20
		P# block of 4, 7#	3.00	—
		Zip block of 4	2.50	—
		Nos. 2336-2348 (13)	7.80	2.60

No. 2343b resulted either from a shifting of all colors or from a shift of both the perforations and the cutting of the pane.

Arabesque, Dar Batha Palace Door, Fez — A1713

William Faulkner (1897-1962), Novelist — A1714

US-MOROCCO DIPLOMATIC RELATIONS, 200th ANNIV.

Designed by Howard Paine.

LITHOGRAPHED & ENGRAVED

Plates of 200 in four panes of 50.

1987, July 17		**Tagged**	**Perf. 11**	
2349	A1713 22c	**scarlet & black**	.55	.20
		P# block of 4, 2#	1.75	—
		Zip block of 4	1.65	—
a.		Black (engr.) omitted	*250.00*	

See Morocco No. 642.

LITERARY ARTS SERIES

Designed by Bradbury Thompson.

ENGRAVED

Plates of 200 in four panes of 50

1987, Aug. 3		**Tagged**	**Perf. 11**	
2350	A1714 22c	**bright green**	.55	.20
		P# block of 4	2.75	—
		Zip block of 4	2.25	—

Used untagged imperfs exist from printer's waste.

AMERICAN FOLK ART SERIES

Lacemaking

A1715

A1716

A1717

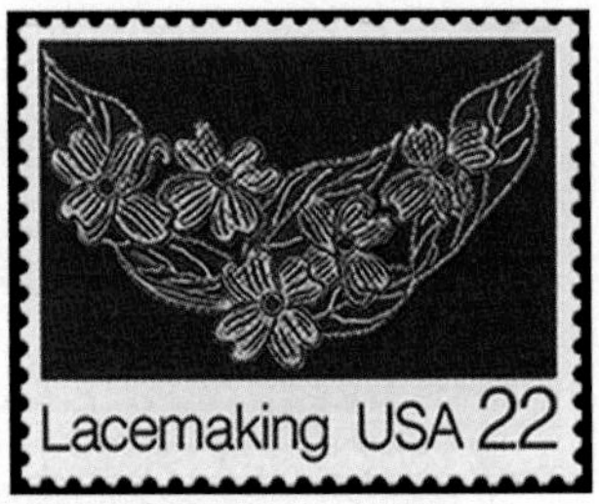

A1718

Designed by Libby Thiel.

LITHOGRAPHED & ENGRAVED
Plates of 160 in four panes of 40.

1987, Aug. 14	**Tagged**	***Perf. 11***	
2351 A1715 22c **ultra & white**		.45	.20
2352 A1716 22c **ultra & white**		.45	.20
2353 A1717 22c **ultra & white**		.45	.20
2354 A1718 22c **ultra & white**		.45	.20
a. Block of 4, #2351-2354		1.90	1.90
P# block of 4, 4#		3.25	—
Zip block of 4		2.00	—
b. As "a," white omitted		*550.00*	

DRAFTING OF THE CONSTITUTION BICENTENNIAL
Excerpts from the Preamble

A1719

A1720

A1721

A1722

A1723

Designed by Bradbury Thompson.

BOOKLET STAMPS
PHOTOGRAVURE

1987, Aug. 28	**Tagged**	***Perf. 10 Horiz.***	
2355 A1719 22c **multicolored**		.90	.20
a. Grayish green (background) omitted		—	
2356 A1720 22c **multicolored**		.90	.20
a. Grayish green (background) omitted		—	
2357 A1721 22c **multicolored**		.90	.20
a. Grayish green (background) omitted		—	
2358 A1722 22c **multicolored**		.90	.20
a. Grayish green (background) omitted		—	
2359 A1723 22c **multicolored**		.90	.20
a. Bklt. pane of 5, #2355-2359		4.50	2.25
b. Grayish green (background) omitted		—	
c. As No. 2359a, grayish green (background) omitted		—	

A1724

A1725

SIGNING OF THE CONSTITUTION

Designed by Howard Koslow.

LITHOGRAPHED & ENGRAVED
Plates of 200 in four panes of 50.

1987, Sept. 17	**Tagged**	***Perf. 11***	
2360 A1724 22c **multicolored**		.55	.20
P# block of 4, 6#		2.75	—
Zip block of 4		2.25	—

CERTIFIED PUBLIC ACCOUNTING

Designed by Lou Nolan.

LITHOGRAPHED & ENGRAVED
Plates of 200 in four panes of 50.

1987, Sept. 21	**Tagged**	***Perf. 11***	
2361 A1725 22c **multicolored**		1.00	.20
P# block of 4, 5#		5.50	—
Zip block of 4		4.00	—
a. Black (engr.) omitted		*675.00*	

LOCOMOTIVES

Stourbridge Lion, 1829
A1726

Best Friend of Charleston, 183
A1727

John Bull, 1831
A1728

Brother Jonathan, 1832
A1729

Gowan & Marx, 1839
A1730

Designed by Richard Leech.

BOOKLET STAMPS
LITHOGRAPHED & ENGRAVED

1987, Oct. 1	**Tagged**	***Perf. 10 Horiz.***	
2362 A1726 22c **multicolored**		.55	.20
2363 A1727 22c **multicolored**		.55	.20
2364 A1728 22c **multicolored**		.55	.20
2365 A1729 22c **multicolored**		.55	.20
a. Red omitted		*1,100.*	*225.00*
2366 A1730 22c **multicolored**		.55	.20
a. Bklt. pane of 5, #2362-2366		2.75	2.50
b. As No. 2366, black (engr.) omitted (single)		—	
c. As No. 2366, blue omitted (single)		—	

CHRISTMAS

Moroni Madonna — A1731

Christmas Ornaments — A1732

Designed by Bradbury Thompson (No. 2367) and Jim Dean (No. 2368).

PHOTOGRAVURE
Plates of 800 in eight panes of 100.

1987, Oct. 23	**Tagged**	***Perf. 11***	
2367 A1731 22c **multicolored**		.45	.20
P# block of 4, 6#		2.25	—
Zip block of 4		1.90	—
2368 A1732 22c **multicolored**		.45	.20
P# block of 4, 6#		2.10	—
Zip block of 4		1.90	—
Pair with full vert. gutter between		—	

1988 WINTER OLYMPICS, CALGARY

Skiing — A1733

Designed by Bart Forbes.

Printed by the American Bank Note Company

PHOTOGRAVURE
Plates of 200 in four panes of 50.

1988, Jan. 10	**Tagged**	***Perf. 11***	
2369 A1733 22c **multicolored**		.50	.20
P# block of 4, 4#+A		2.25	—
Zip block of 4		2.10	—

AUSTRALIA BICENTENNIAL

Caricature of an Australian Koala and an American Bald Eagle — A1734

Designed by Roland Harvey.

PHOTOGRAVURE
Plates of 160 in four panes of 40.

1988, Jan. 26	**Tagged**	***Perf. 11***	
2370 A1734 22c **multicolored**		.45	.20
P# block of 4, 5#		2.10	—
Zip block of 4		1.90	—

See Australia No. 1052.

BLACK HERITAGE SERIES

James Weldon Johnson (1871-1938), Author and Lyricist — A1735

Designed by Thomas Blackshear.

Printed by the American Bank Note Co.

PHOTOGRAVURE
Plates of 200 in four panes of 50.

1988, Feb. 2				Tagged	
2371	A1735	22c	**multicolored**	.50	.20
			P# block of 4, 5#+A	2.60	—
			Zip block of 4	2.10	—
a.			Tagging omitted		—

CATS

Siamese and Exotic Shorthair A1736

Abyssinian and Himalayan A1737

Maine Coon and Burmese A1738

American Shorthair and Persian A1739

Designed by John Dawson.

Printed by the American Bank Note Co.

PHOTOGRAVURE
Plates of 160 in four panes of 40.

1988, Feb. 5				Tagged	
2372	A1736	22c	**multicolored**	.70	.20
2373	A1737	22c	**multicolored**	.70	.20
2374	A1738	22c	**multicolored**	.70	.20
2375	A1739	22c	**multicolored**	.70	.20
a.			Block of 4, #2372-2375	2.80	1.90
			P# block of 4, 5#+A	4.00	—
			Zip block of 4	3.00	—

AMERICAN SPORTS

Knute Rockne (1883-1931), Notre Dame football coach.

Francis Ouimet (1893-1967), 1st amateur golfer to win the US Open championship.

A1740

A1741

Designed by Peter Cocci and Thomas Hipschen.

LITHOGRAPHED & ENGRAVED
Plates of 200 in four panes of 50.

1988, Mar. 9				Tagged	
2376	A1740	22c	**multicolored**	.50	.20
			P# block of 4, 7#	2.60	—
			Zip block of 4	2.10	—

Designed by M. Gregory Rudd.
Printed by the American Bank Note Co.

PHOTOGRAVURE
Plates of 200 in four panes of 50.

1988, June 13				Tagged	
2377	A1741	25c	**multicolored**	.60	.20
			P# block of 4, 5#+A	3.00	—
			Zip block of 4	2.50	—

LOVE ISSUE

Roses

A1742

A1743

Designed by Richard Sheaff.

PHOTOGRAVURE
Plates of 400 in four panes of 100 (25c).
Plates of 200 in four panes of 50 (45c).

1988				Tagged	
2378	A1742	25c	**multicolored,** *July 4*	.50	.20
			P# block of 4, 5#	2.25	—
			Zip block of 4	2.10	—
			Pair with full horiz. gutter between	—	
a.			Imperf., pair	*1,750.*	
2379	A1743	45c	**multicolored,** *Aug, 8*	.85	.20
			P# block of 4, 4#	3.75	—
			Zip block of 4	3.50	—

1988 SUMMER OLYMPICS, SEOUL

Gymnastic Rings A1744

Designed by Bart Forbes.

PHOTOGRAVURE
Plates of 200 in four panes of 50

1988, Aug. 19				Tagged	
2380	A1744	25c	**multicolored**	.50	.20
			P# block of 4, 5#	2.25	—
			Zip block of 4	2.10	—

CLASSIC AUTOMOBILES

1928 Locomobile A1745

1929 Pierce-Arrow — A1746

1931 Cord A1747

1932 Packard A1748

1935 Duesenberg — A1749

Designed by Ken Dallison.

LITHOGRAPHED & ENGRAVED
BOOKLET STAMPS

1988, Aug. 25		Tagged		*Perf. 10 Horiz.*	
2381	A1745	25c	**multicolored**	.80	.20
2382	A1746	25c	**multicolored**	.80	.20
2383	A1747	25c	**multicolored**	.80	.20
2384	A1748	25c	**multicolored**	.80	.20
2385	A1749	25c	**multicolored**	.80	.20
a.			Bklt. pane of 5, #2381-2385	6.00	3.50

ANTARCTIC EXPLORERS

Nathaniel Palmer (1799-1877) A1750

Lt. Charles Wilkes (1798-1877) A1751

Richard E. Byrd (1888-1957) A1752

Lincoln Ellsworth (1880-1951) A1753

Designed by Dennis Lyall.

Printed by the American Bank Note Co.

PHOTOGRAVURE

Plates of 160 in four panes of 40.

1988, Sept. 14 **Tagged** ***Perf. 11***

2386	A1750	25c	**multicolored**	.65	.20
2387	A1751	25c	**multicolored**	.65	.20
2388	A1752	25c	**multicolored**	.65	.20
2389	A1753	25c	**multicolored**	.65	.20
a.			Block of 4, #2386-2389	2.75	2.00
			P# block of 4, 6#+A	4.50	—
			Zip block of 4	3.00	—
b.			As "a," black omitted	*1,250.*	
c.			As "a," imperf. horiz.	*1,950.*	

AMERICAN FOLK ART SERIES

Carousel Animals

Deer — A1754

Horse — A1755

Camel — A1756

Goat — A1757

Designed by Paul Calle.

LITHOGRAPHED & ENGRAVED

Plates of 200 in four panes of 50.

1988, Oct. 1 **Tagged** ***Perf. 11***

2390	A1754	25c	**multicolored**	.65	.20
2391	A1755	25c	**multicolored**	.65	.20
2392	A1756	25c	**multicolored**	.65	.20
2393	A1757	25c	**multicolored**	.65	.20
a.			Block of 4, #2390-2393	3.00	2.00
			P# block of 4, 7#	4.00	—
			Zip block of 4	3.25	—
b.			As "a," red omitted	—	

EXPRESS MAIL RATE

Eagle and Moon — A1758

Designed by Ned Seidler.

LITHOGRAPHED & ENGRAVED

Panes of 20

1988, Oct. 4 **Tagged** ***Perf. 11***

2394	A1758	$8.75	**multicolored**	13.50	8.00
			P# block of 4, 7#	54.00	—

SPECIAL OCCASIONS

Happy Birthday A1759

Best Wishes A1760

Thinking of You A1761

Love You A1762

Designed by Harry Zelenko

Printed by the American Bank Note Co.

BOOKLET STAMPS

PHOTOGRAVURE

1988, Oct. 22 **Tagged** ***Perf. 11***

2395	A1759	25c	**multicolored**	.50	.20
2396	A1760	25c	**multicolored**	.50	.20
a.			Bklt. pane of 6, 3 #2395 + 3 #2396 with gutter between	3.50	3.25
2397	A1761	25c	**multicolored**	.50	.20
2398	A1762	25c	**multicolored**	.50	.20
a.			Bklt. pane of 6, 3 #2397 + 3 #2398 with gutter between	3.50	3.25
b.			As "a," imperf. horiz.	—	
c.			As "a," imperf.	—	

CHRISTMAS

Madonna and Child, by Botticelli — A1763

One-horse Open Sleigh and Village Scene — A1764

"Missing Curlicue on Sleigh Runner" Cylinder Flaw

Designed by Bradbury Thompson (No. 2399) and Joan Landis (No. 2400).

LITHOGRAPHED & ENGRAVED (No. 2399), PHOTOGRAVURE (No. 2400)

Plates of 300 in 6 Panes of 50

1988, Oct. 20 **Tagged** ***Perf. 11½***

2399	A1763	25c	**multicolored**	.50	.20
			P# block of 4, 5+1#	2.25	—
			Zip, copyright block of 4	2.10	—
			Pair with full vert. gutter btwn.	—	
a.			Gold omitted	25.00	
2400	A1764	25c	**multicolored**	.50	.20
			P# block of 4, 5#	2.25	—
			Zip, copyright block of 4	2.10	—
			Pair with full vert. gutter btwn.	—	
			Cylinder flaw (missing curlicue on sleigh runner, 11111 UR19)	9.00	

MONTANA STATEHOOD, 100th ANNIV.

C.M. Russell and Friends, by Charles M. Russell (1865-1926) A1765

Designed by Bradbury Thompson.

LITHOGRAPHED & ENGRAVED

Plates of 200 in four panes of 50.

1989, Jan. 15 **Tagged** ***Perf. 11***

2401	A1765	25c	**multicolored**	.55	.20
			P# block of 4, 5#	2.75	—
			Zip block of 4	2.25	—

Imperfs without gum exist from printer's waste.

BLACK HERITAGE SERIES

Asa Philip Randolph (1889-1979), Labor and Civil Rights Leader — A1766

Designed by Thomas Blackshear.

PHOTOGRAVURE

Plates of 200 in four panes of 50.

1989, Feb. 3 **Tagged** ***Perf. 11***

2402	A1766	25c	**multicolored**	.50	.20
			P# block of 4, 5#	2.25	—
			Zip block of 4	2.10	—

NORTH DAKOTA STATEHOOD, 100th ANNIV.

Grain Elevator on the Prairie A1767

Designed by Wendell Minor.

Printed by the American Bank Note Co.

PHOTOGRAVURE
Plates of 200 in four panes of 50.

1989, Feb. 21 **Tagged** ***Perf. 11***

2403	A1767	25c	**multicolored**	.50	.20
			P# block of 4, 4#+A	2.25	—
			Zip block of 4	2.10	—

WASHINGTON STATEHOOD, 100th ANNIV.

Mt. Rainier — A1768

Designed by Howard Rogers.

Printed by the American Bank Note Co.

PHOTOGRAVURE
Plates of 200 in four panes of 50.

1989, Feb. 22 **Tagged** ***Perf. 11***

2404	A1768	25c	**multicolored**	.50	.20
			P# block of 4, 4#+A	2.25	—
			Zip block of 4	2.10	—

STEAMBOATS

Experiment, 1788-90 — A1769

Phoenix, 1809 A1770

New Orleans, 1812 A1771

Washington, 1816 — A1772

Walk in the Water, 1818 A1773

Designed by Richard Schlecht.

LITHOGRAPHED & ENGRAVED
BOOKLET STAMPS
Perf. 10 Horiz. on 1 or 2 Sides

1989, Mar. 3 **Tagged**

2405	A1769	25c	**multicolored**	.50	.20
2406	A1770	25c	**multicolored**	.50	.20
2407	A1771	25c	**multicolored**	.50	.20
2408	A1772	25c	**multicolored**	.50	.20
2409	A1773	25c	**multicolored**	.50	.20
a.			Booklet pane of 5, #2405-2409	2.50	1.75
b.			As "a," tagging omitted		—

No. 122 — A1774

Arturo Toscanini (1867-1957), Conductor — A1775

WORLD STAMP EXPO '89

Nov. 17-Dec. 3. Washington, D.C.

Designed by Richard Sheaff.

LITHOGRAPHED & ENGRAVED
Plates of 200 in four panes of 50.

1989, Mar. 16 **Tagged** ***Perf. 11***

2410	A1774	25c	**grayish brn, blk & car rose**	.50	.20
			P# block of 4, 4#	2.25	—
			Zip block of 4	2.10	—

PERFORMING ARTS

Designed by Jim Sharpe

Printed by the American Bank Note Co.

PHOTOGRAVURE
Plates of 200 in four panes of 50.

1989, Mar. 25 **Tagged** ***Perf. 11***

2411	A1775	25c	**multicolored**	.50	.20
			P# block of 4, 5#+A	2.25	—
			Zip block of 4	2.10	—

CONSTITUTION BICENTENNIAL SERIES

House of Representatives A1776

Senate A1777

Executive Branch — A1778

Supreme Court — A1779

Designed by Howard Koslow

LITHOGRAPHED & ENGRAVED
Plates of 200 in four panes of 50.

1989-90 **Tagged** ***Perf. 11***

2412	A1776	25c	**multi,** *Apr. 4, 1989*	.50	.20
			P# block of 4, 4#	2.25	—
			Zip block of 4	2.10	—
2413	A1777	25c	**multi,** *Apr. 6, 1989*	.50	.20
			P# block of 4, 4#	2.75	—
			Zip block of 4	2.10	—
2414	A1778	25c	**multi,** *Apr. 16, 1989*	.50	.20
			P# block of 4, 4#	2.25	—
			Zip block of 4	2.10	—
2415	A1779	25c	**multi,** *Feb. 2, 1990*	.50	.20
			P# block of 4, 4#	2.25	—
			Zip block of 4	2.10	—

SOUTH DAKOTA STATEHOOD, 100th ANNIV.

Pasque Flowers, Pioneer Woman and Sod House on Grasslands A1780

Designed by Marian Henjum.

Printed by the American Bank Note Co.

PHOTOGRAVURE
Plates of 200 in four panes of 50.

1989, May 3 **Tagged** ***Perf. 11***

2416	A1780	25c	**multicolored**	.60	.20
			P# block of 4, 4#+A	2.75	—
			Zip block of 4	2.50	—

AMERICAN SPORTS

Henry Louis "Lou" Gehrig (1903-1941), New York Yankee Baseball Player — A1781

Designed by Bart Forbes.

Printed by the American Bank Note Co.

PHOTOGRAVURE
Plates of 200 in four panes of 50.

1989, June 10 **Tagged** ***Perf. 11***

2417	A1781	25c	**multicolored**	.60	.20
			P# block of 4, 6#+A	3.00	—
			Zip block of 4	2.50	—

LITERARY ARTS SERIES

Ernest Miller Hemingway (1899-1961), Nobel Prize winner for Literature in 1954 — A1782

Designed by M. Gregory Rudd.

Printed by the American Bank Note Co.

PHOTOGRAVURE
Plates of 200 in four panes of 50.

1989, July 17 **Tagged** ***Perf. 11***

2418 A1782 25c **multicolored**		.50	.20
	P# block of 4, 5#+A	2.25	—
	Zip block of 4	2.10	—
a.	Vert. pair, imperf horiz.	*1,750.*	

Imperforates on gummed stamp paper, including gutter pairs and blocks, are proofs from the ABNCo. archives.

MOON LANDING, 20TH ANNIVERSARY

Raising of the Flag on the Lunar Surface, July 20, 1969 — A1783

Designed by Christopher Calle.

LITHOGRAPHED & ENGRAVED
Panes of 20

1989, July 20 **Tagged** ***Perf. 11x11½***

2419 A1783 $2.40 **multicolored**		4.75	2.00
	P# block of 4, 6#	20.00	—
	Pane of 20	100.00	—
a.	Black (engr.) omitted	*2,000.*	
b.	Imperf., pair	*650.00*	
c.	Black (litho.) omitted	*2,250.*	

No. 2419 exists with a gray background instead of the normal dark blue. Some of these may have been caused by a chemical wiping of the blue plate. However, the same or extremely similar stamps can be produced by exposing normal stamps to sunlight or fluorescent light for varying time periods.

LETTER CARRIERS

A1784

Designed by Jack Davis.

Printed by the American Bank Note Co.

PHOTOGRAVURE
Plates of 160 in four panes of 40.

1989, Aug. 30 **Tagged** ***Perf. 11***

2420 A1784 25c **multicolored**		.50	.20
	P# block of 4, 5#+A	2.25	—
	Zip block of 4	2.10	—

CONSTITUTION BICENTENNIAL

Bill of Rights — A1785

Designed by Lou Nolan.

LITHOGRAPHED & ENGRAVED
Plates of 200 in four panes of 50.

1989, Sept. 25 **Tagged** ***Perf. 11***

2421 A1785 25c **multicolored**		.50	.20
	P# block of 4	3.25	—
	Zip block of 4	2.10	—
a.	Black (engr.) omitted	*250.00*	

PREHISTORIC ANIMALS

Tyrannosaurus Rex — A1786

Pteranodon A1787

Stegosaurus A1788

Brontosaurus A1789

Designed by John Gurche.

LITHOGRAPHED & ENGRAVED
Plates of 160 in four panes of 40.

1989, Oct. 1 **Tagged** ***Perf. 11***

2422 A1786 25c **multicolored**		.70	.20
a.	Black (engr.) omitted		—
2423 A1787 25c **multicolored**		.70	.20
2424 A1788 25c **multicolored**		.70	.20
2425 A1789 25c **multicolored**		.70	.20
a.	Block of 4, #2422-2425	2.80	2.00
	P# block of 4, 6#	4.00	—
	Zip block of 4	3.00	—
b.	As "a," black (engr.) omitted	*425.00*	

The correct scientific name for Brontosaurus is Apatosaurus.

No. 2425b is valued in the grade of fine. Very fine blocks exist and sell for approximately $600.

PRE-COLUMBIAN AMERICA ISSUE

Southwest Carved Figure, A.D. 1150-1350 — A1790

Designed by Lon Busch.

Printed by the American Bank Note Company.

PHOTOGRAVURE
Plate of 200 in four panes of 50.

1989, Oct. 12 **Tagged** ***Perf. 11***

2426 A1790 25c **multicolored**		.60	.20
	P# block of 4, 6#+A	3.00	—
	Zip block of 4	2.50	—
a.	Tagging omitted		—

See No. C121.

CHRISTMAS

Madonna and Child, by Caracci — A1791

Sleigh Full of Presents — A1792

Designed by Bradbury Thompson (#2427 & 2429) and Steven Dohanos (#2428).

Printed by the Bureau of Engraving and Printing (#2427 & 2429) and American Bank Note Company (#2428).

LITHOGRAPHED & ENGRAVED,
PHOTOGRAVURE (#2428-2429)
Sheets of 300 in six panes of 50.

1989, Oct. 19 **Tagged** ***Perf. 11½***

2427 A1791 25c **multicolored**		.50	.20
	P# block of 4, 5#	2.25	—
	Zip, copyright block of 4	2.10	—
	Pair with full horiz. gutter between	—	
a.	Booklet pane of 10	5.00	3.50
b.	Red (litho.) omitted	*650.00*	
c.	As "a," imperf.	—	

Perf. 11

2428 A1792 25c **multicolored**		.50	.20
	P# block of 4, 5#+A	2.25	—
	Zip, copyright block of 4	2.10	—
a.	Vert. pair, imperf. horiz.	*750.00*	

BOOKLET STAMP

Perf. 11½ on 2 or 3 sides

2429 A1792 25c **multicolored**		.50	.20
a.	Booklet pane of 10	5.00	3.50
b.	Vert. pair, imperf between	—	
c.	As "a," imperf between	—	
d.	As "a," red omitted	*3,250.*	
e.	Imperf., pair	—	

Marked differences exist between Nos. 2428 and 2429: No. 2429 was printed in four colors, No. 2428 in five colors. The runners on the sleigh in No. 2429 are twice as thick as those on No. 2428. On No. 2429 the package at the upper left in the sleigh has a red bow, whereas the same package in No. 2428 has a red and black bow; and the ribbon on the upper right package in No. 2429 is green, whereas the same ribbon in No. 2428 is black.

Eagle and Shield — A1793

Designed by Jay Haiden.

Printed by the American Bank Note Company.

PHOTOGRAVURE
BOOKLET STAMP

1989, Nov. 10 Tagged Self-Adhesive *Die Cut*

2431	A1793 25c **multicolored**	.50	.20
a.	Booklet pane of 18	11.00	
b.	Vert. pair, die cutting omitted between	*450.00*	
c.	Die cutting omitted, pair	*250.00*	

Panes sold for $5.

Also available in strips of 18 with stamps spaced for use in affixing machines to service first day covers. Sold for $5.

No. 2431c will include part of the margins around the stamps.

Sold only in 15 test cities (Atlanta, Chicago, Cleveland, Columbus, OH, Dallas, Denver, Houston, Indianapolis, Kansas City, MO, Los Angeles, Miami, Milwaukee, Minneapolis, Phoenix, St. Louis) and through the philatelic agency.

WORLD STAMP EXPO '89
Washington, DC, Nov. 17-Dec. 3

WORLD STAMP EXPO'89
The classic 1869 U.S. Abraham Lincoln stamp is reborn in these four larger versions commemorating World Stamp Expo'89, held in Washington, D.C. during the 20th Universal Postal Congress of the UPU. These stamps show the issued colors and three of the trial proof color combinations.

A1794

Illustration reduced.

Designed by Richard Sheaff.

LITHOGRAPHED & ENGRAVED

1989, Nov. 17 Tagged *Imperf.*

2433	A1794 Sheet of 4	10.00	10.00
a.	90c like No. 122	2.50	2.50
b.	90c like 132TC (blue frame, brown center)	2.50	2.50
c.	90c like 132TC (green frame, blue center)	2.50	2.50
d.	90c like 132TC (scarlet frame, blue center)	2.50	2.50
e.	As No. 2433, tagging omitted	—	

20th UPU CONGRESS
Traditional Mail Delivery

Stagecoach, c. 1850 — A1795

Paddlewheel Steamer — A1796

Biplane — A1797

Depot-hack Type Automobile — A1798

Designed by Mark Hess.

LITHOGRAPHED & ENGRAVED
Plates of 160 in four panes of 40.

1989, Nov. 19 Tagged *Perf. 11*

2434	A1795 25c **multicolored**	.50	.20
2435	A1796 25c **multicolored**	.50	.20
2436	A1797 25c **multicolored**	.50	.20
2437	A1798 25c **multicolored**	.50	.20
a.	Block of 4, #2434-2437	2.00	1.75
	P# block of 4, 5#	3.75	—
	Zip block of 4	2.25	—
b.	As "a," dark blue (engr.) omitted	*475.00*	
c.	As No. 2437a, tagging omitted	—	

No. 2437b is valued in the grade of fine. Very fine blocks exist and sell for approximately $700.

Souvenir Sheet
LITHOGRAPHED & ENGRAVED

1989, Nov. 28 Tagged *Imperf.*

2438	Sheet of 4	5.00	3.75
a.	A1795 25c multicolored	1.10	.80
b.	A1796 25c multicolored	1.10	.80
c.	A1797 25c multicolored	1.10	.80
d.	A1798 25c multicolored	1.10	.80
e.	Dark blue & gray (engr.) omitted	*5,000.*	

20th Universal Postal Union Congress.

VALUES FOR HINGED STAMPS AFTER NO. 771
This catalogue does not value unused stamps after No. 771 in hinged condition. Hinged unused stamps from No. 772 to the present are worth considerably less than the values given for unused stamps, which are for never-hinged examples.

IDAHO STATEHOOD, 100th ANNIV.

Mountain Bluebird, Sawtooth Mountains — A1799

Designed by John Dawson.

Printed by the American Bank Note Company.

PHOTOGRAVURE
Plates of 200 in four panes of 50.

1990, Jan. 6 Tagged *Perf. 11*

2439	A1799 25c **multicolored**	.55	.20
	P# block of 4, 5#+A	3.00	—
	Zip block of 4	2.25	—

LOVE

A1800

Designed by Jayne Hertko.

Printed by the U.S. Banknote Company (#2440) and the Bureau of Engraving and Printing (#2441).

PHOTOGRAVURE
Plates of 200 in four panes of 50.

1990, Jan. 18 Tagged *Perf. 12½x13*

2440	A1800 25c **black, bright blue, dark pink & emerald green**	.50	.20
	P# block of 4, 4#	2.25	—
	Zip, copyright block of 4	2.10	—
a.	Imperf., pair	*675.00*	

BOOKLET STAMP
Perf. 11½ on 2 or 3 sides

2441	A1800 25c **black, ultramarine, bright pink & dark green**	.50	.20
a.	Booklet pane of 10	5.00	3.50
b.	Bright pink omitted	*150.00*	
c.	As "a," bright pink omitted	*1,650.*	

No. 2441b may be obtained from booklet panes containing both normal and color-omitted stamps.

BLACK HERITAGE SERIES

Ida B. Wells (1862-1931), Journalist — A1801

Designed by Thomas Blackshear.

Printed by American Bank Note Company.

PHOTOGRAVURE
Plates of 200 in four panes of 50.

1990, Feb. 1 Tagged *Perf. 11*

2442	A1801 25c **multicolored**	.75	.20
	P# block of 4, 5#+A	3.75	—
	Zip block of 4	3.25	—

Beach Umbrella — A1802

Designed by Pierre Mion.

BOOKLET STAMP
PHOTOGRAVURE

1990, Feb. 3 Tagged *Perf. 11*

2443	A1802 15c **multicolored**	.30	.20
a.	Booklet pane of 10	3.00	2.00
b.	Blue omitted	*125.00*	
c.	As "a," blue omitted	*1,250.*	

WYOMING STATEHOOD, 100th ANNIV.

High Mountain Meadows, by Conrad Schwiering A1803

Designed by Jack Rosenthal.

LITHOGRAPHED & ENGRAVED
Plates of 200 in four panes of 50.

1990, Feb. 23 Tagged *Perf. 11*

2444	A1803 25c **multicolored**	.50	.20
	P# block of 4, 5#	3.25	—
	Zip block of 4	2.10	—
a.	Black (engr.) omitted	*1,350.*	—

CLASSIC FILMS

Judy Garland and Toto (The Wizard of Oz) — A1804

Clark Gable & Vivien Leigh (Gone With the Wind) — A1805

Gary Cooper (Beau Geste) — A1806

John Wayne (Stagecoach) A1807

Designed by Thomas Blackshear.

Printed by the American Bank Note Company.

PHOTOGRAVURE

Plates of 160 in four panes of 40.

1990, Mar. 23 **Tagged** ***Perf. 11***

2445	A1804 25c **multicolored**	1.50	.20
2446	A1805 25c **multicolored**	1.50	.20
2447	A1806 25c **multicolored**	1.50	.20
2448	A1807 25c **multicolored**	1.50	.20
a.	Block of 4, #2445-2448	6.00	3.50
	P# block of 4, 5#+A	6.50	—
	Zip block of 4	6.25	—

LITERARY ARTS SERIES

Marianne Moore (1887-1972), Poet — A1808

Designed by M. Gregory Rudd.

Printed by the American Bank Note Company.

PHOTOGRAVURE

Plates of 200 in four panes of 50.

1990, Apr. 18 **Tagged** ***Perf. 11***

2449	A1808 25c **multicolored**	.60	.20
	P# block of 4, 3#+A	2.75	—
	Zip block of 4	2.50	—
a.	All colors missing (EP)	—	

No. 2449a must be collected se-tenant with a partially printed stamp or in longer horizontal strips with a partially printed stamp and normal stamps.

Coil Plate No. Strips of 3
Beginning with No. 2123, coil plate no. strips of 3 usually sell at the level of strips of 5 minus the face value of two stamps.

TRANSPORTATION ISSUE

A1810

A1811

A1811a

A1812

A1816

A1822

A1823

A1825

A1827

Designers: 4c, 32c, Richard Schlecht. Nos. 2452, 2452B, 2452D, Susan Sanford. No. 2453, Paul Calle. 10c, David K. Stone. 20c, 23c, Robert Brangwynne. $1, Chuck Hodgson.

Printed by: Guilford Gravure for American Bank Note Co. (No. 2452B), J.W. Fergusson & Sons for Stamp Venturers (No. 2454), Stamp Venturers (No, 2452D), others by BEP.

COIL STAMPS

ENGRAVED, PHOTOGRAVURE (#2452B, 2452D, 2454, 2458)

Tagged, Untagged (Nos. 2452B, 2452D, 2453, 2454, 2457-2458)

1990-95 ***Perf. 9.8 Vert.***

2451	A1810	4c **claret,** *Jan. 25, 1991*	.20	.20
		Pair	.20	.20
		P# strip of 5, #1	.80	
		P# single, #1	—	.75
a.		Imperf., pair	*550.00*	
b.		Untagged	.20	.20
		Pair	.20	.20
		P# strip of 5, #1	.90	
		P# single, #1	—	.75
2452	A1811	5c **carmine,** dull gum, *Aug. 31*	.20	.20
		Pair	.20	.20
		P# strip of 5, #1	.85	
		P# single, #1	—	.85
a.		Untagged, dull gum	.20	.20
		Pair	.20	.20
		P# strip of 5, #1	3.00	
		P# single, #1	—	2.25
		Low gloss gum	.20	.20
		Pair	.20	.20
		P# strip of 5, #2	2.25	
		P# single, #2	—	1.60
c.		Imperf., pair	*600.00*	
2452B	A1811	5c **carmine,** *Dec. 8, 1992*	.20	.20
		Pair	.25	.20
		P# strip of 5, #A1-A2	1.25	
		P# single, #A1-A2	—	1.10
f.		Printed with luminescent ink	.20	.20
		Pair	.20	.20
		P# strip of 5, #A3	2.75	
		P# single, #A3	—	2.25
2452D	A1811a	5c **carmine,** low gloss gum, *Mar. 20, 1995*	.20	.20
		Pair	.20	.20
		P# strip of 5, #S1-S2	1.25	
		P# single, #S1-S2	—	1.25
e.		Imperf., pair	*135.00*	
g.		Printed with luminescent ink, shiny gum	.20	.20
		Pair	.20	.20
		P# strip of 5, #S2	2.25	
		P# single, #S2	—	1.75
		Low gloss gum	.20	
		P# strip of 5, #S3	2.25	
		P# single, #S3	—	2.50
h.		As "g," low gloss gum, imperf. pair	—	
2453	A1812	5c **brown** (Bureau precancel, Additional Nonprofit Postage Paid, in gray), *May 25, 1991*	.20	.20
		Pair	.50	.20
		P# strip of 5, #1-3	1.50	
		P# single, #1-3	—	.85
a.		Imperf., pair	*225.00*	
b.		Gray omitted	—	
2454	A1812	5c **red** (Bureau precancel, Additional Nonprofit Postage Paid, in gray), shiny gum, *Oct. 22, 1991*	.45	.20
		Pair	.90	.20
		P# strip of 5, #S11	1.25	
		P# single, #S11	—	1.00
		Low gloss gum	.65	
		Pair	1.30	
		P# strip of 5, #S11	6.00	
2457	A1816	10c **green** (Bureau precancel, Additional Presort Postage Paid, in gray), *May 25, 1991*	.35	.20
		Pair	.70	.40
		P# strip of 5, #1	2.50	
		P# single, #1	—	1.25
a.		Imperf., pair	*130.00*	
b.		All color omitted	—	

No. 2457b must be collected as part of a transitional strip with normal stamps having freak perfs.

2458	A1816	10c **green** (Bureau precancel, Additional Presort Postage Paid, in black), *May 25, 1994*	.45	.20
		Pair	.90	.40
		P# strip of 5, #11, 22	3.50	
		P# single, #11, 22	—	1.75
2463	A1822	20c **green,** *June 9, 1995*	.40	.20
		Pair	.80	.20
		P# strip of 5, #1-2	3.00	
		P# single, #1-2	—	2.00
a.		Imperf., pair	*90.00*	
2464	A1823	23c **dark blue,** prephosphored coated paper (solid tagging), dull gum, *Apr. 12, 1991*	.45	.20
		Pair	.90	.20
		P# strip of 5, #2-3	3.25	
		P# single, #2-3	—	2.00
a.		Prephosphored uncoated paper (mottled tagging), dull gum, *1993*	1.20	.20
		Pair	2.40	.20
		P# strip of 5, #3	9.00	
		Shiny gum, *1993*	.45	

		Pair	.90	
		P# strip of 5, #3	3.75	
		P# strip of 5, #4	10.00	
		P# strip of 5, #5	4.50	
		P# single, #3-4	—	4.00
		P# single, #5	—	5.50
b.		Imperf., pair	*110.00*	
2466	A1825	32c **blue,** prephosphored uncoated paper (mottled tagging), shiny gum, *June 2, 1995*	.80	.20
		Pair	1.60	.30
		P# strip of 5, #2	4.50	
		P# strip of 5, #3	4.75	
		P# strip of 5, #4	5.00	
		P# strip of 5, #5	9.00	
		P# single, #2, 3	—	2.25
		P# single, #4	—	2.75
		P# single, #5	—	3.50
		Low gloss gum	1.10	
		Pair	2.20	
		P# strip of 5, #3	10.00	
		P# strip of 5, #4	13.00	
		P# strip of 5, #5	10.00	
		P# single, #3	—	
		P# single, #4	—	
		P# single, #5	—	
a.		Imperf., pair, shiny gum	*500.00*	
		Low gloss gum	*500.00*	
b.		32c **bright blue,** prephosphored uncoated paper (mottled tagging), low gloss gum	6.00	4.50
		Pair	12.00	11.00
		P# strip of 5, #5	95.00	
		P# single, #5	—	*110.00*

Some specialists refer to No. 2466b as "Bronx blue," and it is considered to be an error of color.

2468	A1827	$1 **blue & scarlet,** overall tagging, dull gum, *Apr. 20*	2.25	.50
		Pair	4.50	1.00
		P# strip of 5, #1	13.00	
		P# single, #1	—	5.00
a.		Imperf., pair	*2,500.*	—
b.		Prephosphored uncoated paper (mottled tagging), shiny gum, *1993*	2.40	.50
		Pair	4.80	1.00
		P# strip of 5, #3	13.00	
		P# single, #3	—	5.00
c.		Prephosphored coated paper (grainy solid tagging), low gloss gum, *1998*	3.50	.50
		Pair	7.00	1.00
		P# strip of 5, #3	18.00	
		P# single, #3	—	10.00
		Nos. 2451-2468 (12)	6.15	2.70

Some mint pairs of No. 2468 appear to be imperf. but have faint blind perforations on the gum. Beware of examples with the gum removed.

LIGHTHOUSES

Admiralty Head, WA — A1829

Cape Hatteras, NC — A1830

West Quoddy Head, ME — A1831

American Shoals, FL — A1832

Sandy Hook, NJ — A1833

Designed by Howard Koslow.

BOOKLET STAMPS
LITHOGRAPHED & ENGRAVED

Perf. 10 Vert. on 1 or 2 sides

1990, Apr. 26 **Tagged**

2470	A1829	25c **multicolored**	1.90	.20
2471	A1830	25c **multicolored**	1.90	.20
2472	A1831	25c **multicolored**	1.90	.20
2473	A1832	25c **multicolored**	1.90	.20
2474	A1833	25c **multicolored**	1.90	.20
a.		Bklt. pane of 5, #2470-2474	9.50	2.00
b.		As "a," white ("USA 25") omitted	80.00	—

Perforations on Lighthouse booklet panes separate very easily. Careful handling is required.

FLAG

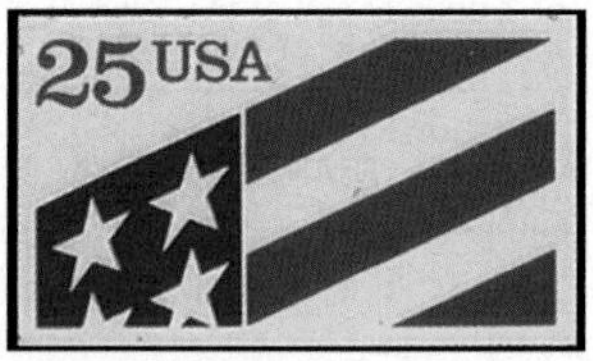

A1834

Designed by Harry Zelenko.

Printed by Avery International Corp.

PHOTOGRAVURE

1990, May 18 Untagged Self-adhesive *Die Cut*
Printed on Plastic

2475	A1834	25c **dark red & dark blue**	.55	.25
a.		Pane of 12	6.60	

Sold only in panes of 12; peelable plastic backing inscribed in light ultramarine. Available for a test period of six months at 22 First National Bank automatic teller machines in Seattle.

FLORA and FAUNA

American Kestrel — A1840

A1841

Eastern Bluebird — A1842

Fawn — A1843

Cardinal — A1844

Pumpkinseed Sunfish — A1845

Bobcat A1846

Designers: 1c, 3c, 45c, Michael Matherly. 19c, Peter Cocci. 30c, Robert Giusti. $2, Chuck Ripper.

Printed by: No. 2476 and No. 2478, American Bank Note Co. No. 2477, No. 2479, and No. 2482, Bureau of Engraving & Printing. No. 2480 and No. 2482, Stamp Venturers. No. 2481, Stamp Venturers (engraved) and The Press, Inc. (lithographed).

LITHOGRAPHED
Panes of 100

1990-95 Untagged *Perf. 11, 11.2 (#2477)*

2476	A1840	1c **multicolored,** *June 22, 1991*	.20	.20
		P# block of 4, 4#+A	.20	—
		Zip block of 4	.20	—

Imperforates on gummed stamp paper, plus imperforate and perforated gutter pairs and blocks (including imperforate and perforated gutter pairs and blocks of No. 2476 se-tenant with No. 2478), are proofs from the ABNCo. archives.

2477	A1841	1c **multicolored,** shiny gum, *May 10, 1995*	.20	.20
		P# block of 4, 4#	.20	—
		Low gloss gum	.20	
		P# block of 4, 4#	.20	
a.		Tagged (error), shiny gum	—	
2478	A1842	3c **multicolored,** *June 22, 1991*	.20	.20
		P# block of 4, 4#+A	.30	—
		Zip block of 4	.25	—
a.		Vert. pair, imperf horiz.	—	
b.		Double impression of all colors except yellow	—	

Note for No. 2476 also applies to No. 2478.

See Nos. 3032/3053. Compare design A1842 with design A2336.

PHOTOGRAVURE
Plates of 400 in four panes of 100.

Tagged ***Perf. 11***

2479	A1843	19c **multicolored,** *Mar. 11, 1991*	.35	.20
		P# block of 4, 5#	1.75	—
		Zip block of 4	1.50	—
a.		Tagging omitted	*10.00*	
b.		Red omitted	*725.00*	
c.		Imperf, pair	—	

On No. 2479b other colors are shifted.

2480	A1844	30c **multicolored,** *June 22, 1991*	.60	.20
		P# block of 4, 4#+S	2.75	—
		Zip block of 4	2.50	—

LITHOGRAPHED & ENGRAVED
Panes of 100
Perf. 11

2481	A1845	45c **multicolored,** *Dec. 2, 1992*	.90	.20
		P# block of 4, 5#+S	4.25	—
		Zip block of 4	3.75	—
a.		Black (engr.) omitted	*425.00*	—

Panes of 20

2482	A1846	$2 **multicolored,** *June 1, 1990*	3.50	1.25
		P# block of 4, 5#	14.00	—
		Pane of 20	70.00	
a.		Black (engr.) omitted	*225.00*	
b.		Tagging omitted	12.50	

Blue Jay — A1847

Wood Duck — A1848

African Violets — A1849

Peach — A1850

Pear — A1851

Red Squirrel — A1852

Rose — A1853

Pine Cone — A1854

Designed by Robert Giusti (#2483-2485), Ned Seidler (#2486-2488, 2493-2495A), Michael R. Matherly (#2489), Gyo Fujikawa (#2490), Paul Breeden (#2491), Gyo Fujikawa (#2492).

Printed by Stamp Venturers (#2483, 2492), Bureau of Engraving and Printing (#2484, 2487-2488), J.W. Fergusson & Sons for KCS Industries, Inc. (#2485), KCS Industries (#2486), Dittler Brothers, Inc. (#2489), Stamp Venturers (#2490), Banknote Corporation of America (#2491), Avery-Dennison (#2493-2495, 2495A).

PHOTOGRAVURE
BOOKLET STAMPS

1991-95 *Perf. 10.9x9.8*

Tagged

2483 A1847 20c **multicolored,** *June 15, 1995* .50 .20
a. Booklet pane of 10 5.25 2.25
b. As "a," imperf —

Perf. 10 on 2 or 3 sides

2484 A1848 29c **black & multi,** overall tagging, *Apr. 12, 1991* .60 .20
a. Booklet pane of 10 6.00 3.75
b. Vert. pair, imperf. horiz. *190.00*
c. As "b," bklt. pane of 10 *950.00*
d. Prephosphored coated paper (solid tagging) .60 .20
e. As "d," booklet pane of 10 6.00 3.75
f. Vert. pair, imperf between and with natural straight edge at top or bottom —
g. As "f," bklt. pane of 10 —

Perf. 11 on 2 or 3 Sides

2485 A1848 29c **red & multi,** *Apr. 12, 1991* .60 .20
a. Booklet pane of 10 6.00 4.00
b. Vert. pair, imperf. between *3,000.*
c. Imperf, pair *2,500.*

Perf. 10x11 on 2 or 3 Sides

2486 A1849 29c **multicolored,** *Oct. 8, 1993* .60 .20
a. Booklet pane of 10 6.00 4.00

Perf. 11x10 on 2 or 3 Sides

2487 A1850 32c **multicolored,** *July 8, 1995* .65 .20
2488 A1851 32c **multicolored,** *July 8, 1995* .65 .20
a. Booklet pane, 5 each #2487-2488 6.50 4.25
b. Pair, #2487-2488 1.30 .30

1993-95 **Tagged**

Die Cut

2489 A1852 29c **multicolored,** *June 25* .65 .20
a. Booklet pane of 18 12.00
b. As "a," die cutting omitted —
2490 A1853 29c **red, green & black,** *Aug. 19* .65 .20
a. Booklet pane of 18 12.00

Nos. 2489-2490 also available in strips with stamps spaced for use in affixing machines to service first day covers. No plate numbers. Stamps removed from strips are indistinquishable from booklet stamps.

2491 A1854 29c **multicolored,** *Nov. 5* .60 .20
a. Booklet pane of 18 11.00
b. Horiz. pair, die cutting omitted between *200.00*
c. Coil with plate # B1 — 6.00
P# strip of 5, #B1 8.50

Stamps without plate # from coil strips are indistinquishable from booklet stamps once they are removed from the backing paper.

Serpentine Die Cut 11.3x11.7 on 2, 3 or 4 Sides

2492 A1853 32c **pink, green & black,** prephosphored coated paper (solid tagging) *June 2, 1995* .65 .20
a. Booklet pane of 20+label 13.00
b. Booklet pane of 15+label 9.75
c. Horiz. pair, die cutting omitted between (grainy solid tagging) —
d. As "a," 2 stamps and parts of 7 others printed on backing liner (grainy solid tagging) —
e. Booklet pane of 14 (solid tagging) 21.00
f. Booklet pane of 16 (solid tagging) 21.00
g. Coil with plate # S111 (solid tagging) — 5.50
P# strip of 5, #S111 8.00
h. Vert. pair, die cutting omitted between (from No. 2492b) (grainy solid tagging) —
i. On prephosphored paper (grainy solid tagging) .65 .20
j. As "i," booklet pane of 20 + label 13.00
k. As "i," booklet pane of 15 + label 9.75

Stamps on plate # strips are separated on backing larger than the stamps. Stamps without plate # from coil strips are indistinquishable from interior position booklet stamps once they are removed from the backing paper.

For booklet panes containing No. 2492f with one stamp removed, see Nos. BK178B, BK178D-BK178E in Booklets section.

Serpentine Die Cut 8.8 on 2, 3 or 4 Sides

2493 A1850 32c **multicolored,** *July 8, 1995* .65 .20
2494 A1851 32c **multicolored,** *July 8, 1995* .65 .20
a. Booklet pane, 10 each #2493-2494+label 13.00
b. Pair, #2493-2494 1.30
c. As "b," die cutting omitted —

COIL STAMPS

Serpentine Die Cut 8.8 Vert.

2495 A1850 32c **multicolored,** *July 8, 1995* 2.00 .20
2495A A1851 32c **multicolored,** *July 8, 1995* 2.00 .20
b. Pair, #2495-2495A 4.00
P# strip of 5, 3 #2495A, 2 #2495, P#V11111 13.00
P# single, #V11111 — 6.00

See Nos. 3048, 3053-3054.

Scott values for used self-adhesive stamps are for examples either on piece or off piece.

OLYMPIANS

Jesse Owens, 1936 — A1855

Ray Ewry, 1900-08 A1856

Hazel Wightman, 1924 — A1857

Eddie Eagan, 1920, 1932 — A1858

Helene Madison, 1932 — A1859

Designed by Bart Forbes.

Printed by the American Bank Note Company.

PHOTOGRAVURE
Panes of 35.

1990, July 6 **Tagged** *Perf. 11*

2496 A1855 25c **multicolored** .60 .20
2497 A1856 25c **multicolored** .60 .20
2498 A1857 25c **multicolored** .60 .20
2499 A1858 25c **multicolored** .60 .20
2500 A1859 25c **multicolored** .60 .20
a. Strip of 5, #2496-2500 3.25 2.50
P# block of 10, 4#+A 8.00 —
Zip, inscription block of 10 6.50 —
b. As "a," blue omitted —

Imperforates on gummed stamp paper, including gutter pairs, strips and blocks, are proofs from the ABNCo. archives.

INDIAN HEADDRESSES

Assiniboin A1860

Cheyenne A1861

Comanche A1862

Flathead A1863

Shoshone A1864

Designed by Lunda Hoyle Gill.

LITHOGRAPHED & ENGRAVED
BOOKLET STAMPS

1990, Aug. 17 **Tagged** ***Perf. 11 on 2 or 3 Sides***

2501 A1860 25c **multicolored** 1.50 .20
2502 A1861 25c **multicolored** 1.50 .20
2503 A1862 25c **multicolored** 1.50 .20
2504 A1863 25c **multicolored** 1.50 .20

2505 A1864 25c **multicolored** 1.50 .20
a. Bklt. pane of 10, 2 each #2501-2505 15.00 7.50
b. As "a," black (engr.) omitted *3,500.*
c. Strip of 5, #2501-2505 7.50 2.50
d. As "a," horiz. imperf. between —

The one example of No. 2505d that has been reported is actually split at the booklet fold and is a block of 4 and a block of 6.

MICRONESIA & MARSHALL ISLANDS

Canoe and Flag of the Federated States of Micronesia A1865

Stick Chart, Canoe and Flag of the Republic of the Marshall Islands A1866

LITHOGRAPHED & ENGRAVED
Sheets of 200 in four panes of 50.

1990, Sept. 28 **Tagged** ***Perf. 11***
2506 A1865 25c **multicolored** .50 .20
2507 A1866 25c **multicolored** .50 .20
a. Pair, #2506-2507 1.00 .75
P# block of 4, 6# 2.50 —
Zip block of 4 2.10 —
b. As "a," black (engr.) omitted *2,750.*

See Micronesia Nos. 124-126, Marshall Islands No. 381.

SEA CREATURES

Killer Whales A1867

Northern Sea Lions — A1868

Sea Otter — A1869

Common Dolphin A1870

Designed by Peter Cocci (Nos. 2508, 2511), Vladimir Beilin, USSR (Nos. 2509-2510).

LITHOGRAPHED & ENGRAVED
Sheets of 160 in four panes of 40.

1990, Oct. 3 **Tagged** ***Perf. 11***
2508 A1867 25c **multicolored** .55 .20
2509 A1868 25c **multicolored** .55 .20
2510 A1869 25c **multicolored** .55 .20
2511 A1870 25c **multicolored** .55 .20
a. Block of 4, #2508-2511 2.25 1.90
P# block of 4, 5# 2.50 —
Zip block of 4 2.30 —
b. As "a," black (engr.) omitted *400.00*
c. As "a," tagging omitted —

See Russia Nos. 5933-5936.

PRE-COLUMBIAN AMERICA ISSUE

Grand Canyon A1871

Designed by Mark Hess.

Printed by the American Bank Note Company.

PHOTOGRAVURE
Plates of 200 in four panes of 50.
(3 panes of #2512, 1 pane of #C127)

1990, Oct. 12 **Tagged** ***Perf. 11***
2512 A1871 25c **multicolored** .55 .20
P# block of 4, 4#+A, UR, LL, LR 2.75 —
Zip block of 4 2.25 —

See No. C127.

DWIGHT D. EISENHOWER, BIRTH CENTENARY

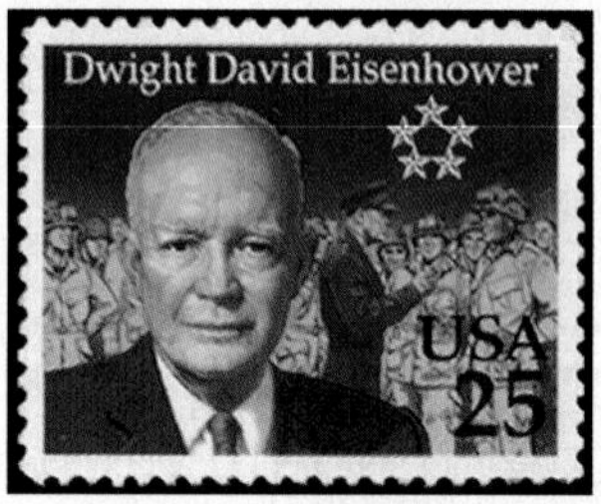

A1872

Designed by Ken Hodges.

Printed by the American Bank Note Company.

PHOTOGRAVURE
Plates of 160 in four panes of 40.

1990, Oct. 13 **Tagged** ***Perf. 11***
2513 A1872 25c **multicolored** .90 .20
P# block of 4, 5#+A 4.00 —
P# block of 8, 5#+A and inscriptions 8.00 —
Zip block of 4 3.75 —

Imperforates on gummed stamp paper are proofs from the ABNCo. archives.

CHRISTMAS

Madonna & Child, by Antonello — A1873

Christmas Tree — A1874

Designed by Bradbury Thompson (#2514) and Libby Thiel (#2515-2516).

Printed by the Bureau of Engraving and Printing or the American Bank Note Company (#2515).

LITHOGRAPHED & ENGRAVED
Sheets of 300 in six panes of 50 (#2414-2415).

1990, Oct. 18 **Tagged** ***Perf. 11½***
2514 A1873 25c **multicolored**, large block tagging .50 .20
P# block of 4, 5# 2.25 —
Zip, copyright block of 4 2.10 —
a. Large block tagging over prephosphored coated paper (solid tagging) .50 .20
b. As "a," bklt. pane of 10 5.00 3.25

PHOTOGRAVURE
Perf. 11

2515 A1874 25c **multicolored** .50 .20
P# block of 4, 4#+A 2.25 —
Zip block of 4 2.10 —
a. Vert. pair, imperf. horiz. *1,000.*
b. All colors missing (EP) —

No. 2515b must be collected se-tenant with normal and/or partially printed stamp(s).

BOOKLET STAMP

Perf. 11½x11 on 2 or 3 sides

2516 A1874 25c **multicolored** .50 .20
a. Booklet pane of 10 5.00 3.25

Marked differences exist between Nos. 2515 and 2516. The background red on No. 2515 is even while that on No. 2516 is splotchy. The bands across the tree and "Greetings" are blue green on No. 2515 and yellow green on No. 2516.

A1875

A1876

Designed by Wallace Marosek (Nos. 2517-2520), Richard Sheaff (No. 2521).

Printed by U.S. Bank Note Company (No. 2517), Bureau of Engraving and Printing (No. 2518-2519), KCS Industries (No. 2520), American Bank Note Company (No. 2521).

PHOTOGRAVURE
Sheets of 100

1991, Jan. 22 **Tagged** ***Perf. 13***
2517 A1875 (29c) **yel, blk, red & yel grn** .60 .20
P# block of 4, 4# 2.75 —
Zip block of 4 2.50 —
b. Horiz. pair, imperf. vert. *1,150.*

Do not confuse imperforate proofs of No. 2517 with No. 2518a. See note after No. 2518.

Imperforates on gummed stamp paper, including gutter pairs and blocks, are proofs from the ABNCo. archives.

COIL STAMP

Perf. 10 Vert.

2518 A1875 (29c) **yel, blk, dull red & dk yel grn** .60 .20
Pair 1.20 .20
P# strip of 5, #1111 3.00
P# strip of 5, #1211 10.00
P# strip of 5, #1222 3.50
P# strip of 5, #2211 3.75
P# strip of 5, #2222 3.50
P# single, #1111 — .60
P# single, #1211 — 12.00
P# single, #1222 — .60
P# single, #2211 — 3.00
P# single, #2222 — .60
a. Imperf., pair 27.50

"For U.S. addresses only" is 17½mm long on No. 2517, 16½mm long on No. 2518. Design of No. 2517 measures 21½x17½mm, No. 2518, 21x18mm.

BOOKLET STAMPS

Perf. 11 on 2 or 3 Sides

2519 A1875 (29c) **yel, blk, dull red & dk grn** .60 .20
a. Booklet pane of 10 6.50 4.50
2520 A1875 (29c) **pale yel, blk, red & brt grn** 1.75 .20
a. Booklet pane of 10 18.00 4.50
b. As "a," imperf. horiz. —
c. Horiz. pair, imperf btwn., in error booklet pane of 12 stamps *500.00*

No. 2519 has bullseye perforations that measure approximately 11.2. No. 2520 has less pronounced black lines in the leaf, which is a much brighter green than on No. 2519.

No. 2520c is from a paper foldover before perforating.

LITHOGRAPHED
Panes of 100

1991, Jan. 22 **Untagged** ***Perf. 11***
2521 A1876 (4c) **bister & carmine** .20 .20
P# block of 4, 2# .40 —
Zip block of 4 .30 —
a. Vert. pair, imperf. horiz. 95.00
b. Imperf., pair 60.00

FLAG

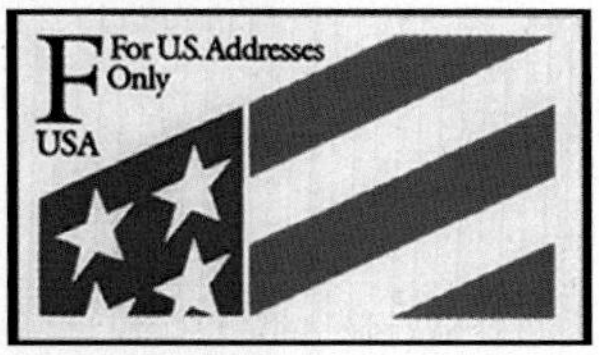

A1877

Designed by Harry Zelenko. Printed by Avery International Corp.

PHOTOGRAVURE

1991, Jan. 22 Untagged Self-Adhesive *Die Cut*
Printed on Plastic

2522 A1877 (29c) **blk, blue & dk red** .60 .25
a. Pane of 12 7.25

Sold only in panes of 12; peelable plastic backing inscribed in light ultramarine. Available during a test period at First National Bank automatic teller machines in Seattle.

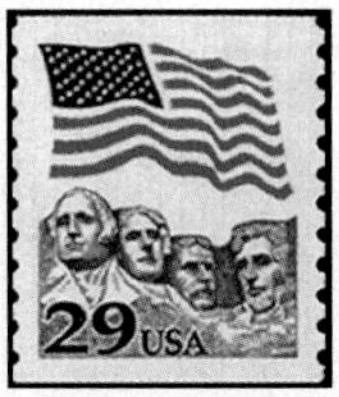

Flag Over Mt. Rushmore — A1878

Designed by Clarence Holbert.

COIL STAMP
ENGRAVED

1991, Mar. 29 Tagged *Perf. 10 Vert.*

2523 A1878 29c **blue, red & claret,** prephosphored uncoated paper (mottled tagging) .65 .20
Pair 1.30 .20
P# strip of 5, #1-7 4.00
P# strip of 5, #8 5.75
P# strip of 5, #9 7.50
P# single, #1 — .40
P# single, #2-4 — .50
P# single, #5 — 2.25
P# single, #6, 7 — .50
P# single, #8 — 2.00
P# single, #9 — 2.00
b. Imperf., pair 20.00
c. 29c **blue, red & brown,** prephosphored uncoated paper (mottled tagging) 3.00 —
Pair 6.00
P# strip of 5, #1 *4,000.*
P# strip of 5, #7 *160.00*
P# single, #1 — *1,450.*
P# single, 7 — *140.00*
d. Prephosphored coated paper (solid tagging) 5.00 —
Pair 10.00 —
P# strip of 5, #2 *1,400.*
P# strip of 5, #6 *260.00*
P# single, #2 — *250.00*
P# single, #6 — *150.00*

Specialists often call No. 2523c the "Toledo brown" variety, and No. 2523d "Lenz paper." It was from No. 2523d that it was discovered that "solid tagging" on prephosphored paper resulted from the application of taggant to coated paper.

COIL STAMP
PHOTOGRAVURE

Printed by American Bank Note Co.

1991, July 4 *Perf. 10 Vert.*

2523A A1878 29c **blue, red & brown** .75 .20
Pair 1.50 .20
P# strip of 5, #A11111, A22211 4.00
P# single, #A11111, A22211 — 2.25

On No. 2523A, USA and 29 are not outlined in white and are farther from the bottom of the design.

A1879

Designed by Wallace Marosek.

Printed by U.S. Bank Note Co. (#2524), J.W. Fergusson & Sons for Stamp Venturers (#2525, 2526), J.W. Fergusson & Sons, Inc. for KCS Industries, Inc. (#2527).

PHOTOGRAVURE
Panes of 100

1991-92 Tagged *Perf. 11*

2524 A1879 29c **dull yel, blk, red & yel grn,** *Apr. 5, 1991* .60 .20
P# block of 4, 4#+U 2.75 —
Zip block of 4 2.50 —

See note after No. 2527.

Perf. 13x12¾

2524A A1879 29c **dull yel, blk, red & yel grn,** *Apr. 5, 1991* 1.00 .20
P# block of 4, 4#+U 50.00 —
Zip block of 4 7.50 —

COIL STAMPS
Rouletted 10 Vert.

2525 A1879 29c **pale yel, blk, red & yel grn,** *Aug. 16, 1991* .60 .20
Pair 1.20 .30
P# strip of 5, #S1111, S2222 4.00
P# single, #S1111, S2222 — .75

No. 2525 was issued in attached coils so that "blocks" and "vertical pairs" exist.

Perf. 10 Vert.

2526 A1879 29c **pale yel, blk, red & yel grn,** *Mar. 3, 1992* .80 .20
Pair 1.60 .30
P# strip of 5, #S2222 4.25
P# single, #S2222 — 2.25

BOOKLET STAMP
Perf. 11 on 2 or 3 Sides

2527 A1879 29c **pale yel, blk, red & bright grn,** *Apr. 5* .60 .20
a. Booklet pane of 10 6.00 3.50
b. Horiz. pair, imperf. between —
c. Horiz. pair, imperf. vert. *175.00*
d. As "a," imperf. horiz. *900.00*

Flower on Nos. 2524-2524A has grainy appearance, inscriptions look rougher.
No. 2527b resulted from a foldover.

Flag, Olympic Rings — A1880

Designed by John Boyd.

Printed by KCS Industries, Inc.

BOOKLET STAMP
PHOTOGRAVURE

1991, Apr. 21 Tagged *Perf. 11 on 2 or 3 Sides*

2528 A1880 29c **multicolored** .60 .20
a. Booklet pane of 10 6.00 3.50
c. Vert. pair, imperf between, perfed at top and bottom *250.00*
d. Vert. strip of 3, top or bottom pair imperf between —
e. Vert. pair, imperf horiz. *700.00*

No. 2528c comes from misperfed booklet panes. No. 2528d resulted from paper foldovers after normal perforating and before cutting into panes. Two No. 2528d are known. No. 2528e is valued in the grade of fine.

Fishing Boat — A1881

Balloon — A1882

Designed by Pierre Mion.

Printed by: Multi-Color Corp. for American Bank Note Co (type I); Guilford Gravure (type II); J. W. Fergusson & Sons for Stamp Venturers (No. 2529C).

COIL STAMPS
PHOTOGRAVURE

1991, Aug. 8 Tagged *Perf. 9.8 Vert.*

2529 A1881 19c **multicolored** .40 .20
Pair .80 .30
P# strip of 5, #A1111, A1212, A2424 3.00
P# strip of 5, #A1112 5.25
P# single, #A1111, A1212, A2424 — 2.25
P# single, #A1112 — 5.00
a. Type II, *1993* .40 .20
Pair .80 .30
P# strip of 5, #A5555, A5556, A6667, A7667, A7679, A7766, A7779 3.50
P# single, same # — 2.25
b. As "a," untagged, *1993* 1.00 .40
Pair 2.00 .80
P# strip of 5, #A5555 8.50
P# single, #A5555 — 6.00

Design on Type II stamps is created by a finer dot pattern. Vertical sides of "1" are smooth on Type II and jagged on Type I stamps.

Imperforates are from printer's waste. Also, No. 2529a, Plate #A7767 is known only from printer's waste.

1994, June 25 Tagged *Perf. 9.8 Vert.*

2529C A1881 19c **multicolored** .50 .20
Pair 1.00 .30
P# strip of 5, #S111 4.00
P# single, #S111 — 2.75

No. 2529C has one loop of rope tying boat to piling.

BOOKLET STAMP

1991, May 17 Tagged *Perf. 10 on 2 or 3 Sides*

2530 A1882 19c **multicolored** .40 .20
a. Booklet pane of 10 4.00 2.75

Flags on Parade — A1883

Designed by Frank J. Waslick and Peter Cocci.

PHOTOGRAVURE
Panes of 100

1991, May 30 Tagged *Perf. 11*

2531 A1883 29c **multicolored**, overall tagging .60 .20
P# block of 4, 4# 2.75 —
Zip block of 4 2.50 —
b. Prephosphored coated paper (solid tagging) .75 .25
P# block of 4, 4# 6.50 —
Zip block of 4 3.25 —

Liberty Torch — A1884

Designed by Harry Zelenko.

Printed by Avery Dennison Co.

PHOTOGRAVURE

1991, June 25 Tagged *Die Cut*
Self-Adhesive

2531A A1884 29c **black, gold & green,** prephosphored coated paper (solid tagging) .60 .25
b. Booklet pane of 18 11.00
c. Die cutting omitted, pair *1,850.*
d. Overall tagging, *1992* .60 .25
e. As "d," booklet pane of 18 11.00

Sold only in panes of 18; peelable paper backing inscribed in light blue. Available for consumer testing at First National Bank automatic teller machines in Seattle, WA.

SWITZERLAND

Switzerland, 700th Anniv. A1887

Designed by Hans Hartman, Switzerland.

Printed by the American Bank Note Company.

PHOTOGRAVURE

Plates of 160 in four panes of 40

1991, Feb. 22 **Tagged** ***Perf. 11***

2532 A1887 50c **multicolored** 1.00 .25
P# block of 4, 5#+A 5.00 —
Zip block of 4 4.25 —
a. Vert. pair, imperf. horiz. *2,250.*

See Switzerland No. 888.

Imperfs exist from printer's waste.

A1888

A1889

VERMONT STATEHOOD, 200th ANNIV.

Designed by Sabra Field.

Printed by the American Bank Note Company.

PHOTOGRAVURE

Plates of 200 in four panes of 50

1991, Mar. 1 **Tagged** ***Perf. 11***

2533 A1888 29c **multicolored** .90 .20
P# block of 4, 4#+A 4.50 —
Zip block of 4 3.75 —

SAVINGS BONDS, 50TH ANNIVERSARY

Designed by Primo Angeli.

1991, Apr. 30 **Tagged** ***Perf. 11***

2534 A1889 29c **multicolored** .60 .20
P# block of 4, 6# 2.75 —
Zip block of 4 2.50 —
a. Tagging omitted —

LOVE

A1890

A1891

Designed by Harry Zelenko (#2535-2536) and Nancy L. Krause (#2537).

Printed by U.S. Banknote Co. (#2535), the Bureau of Engraving and Printing (#2536) and American Bank Note Co. (#2537).

PHOTOGRAVURE

Panes of 50

1991, May 9 **Tagged** ***Perf. 12½x13***

2535 A1890 29c **multicolored** .60 .20
P# block of 4, 5#+U 2.75 —
Zip, copyright block of 4 2.50 —
b. Imperf., pair *1,850.*

Perf. 11

2535A A1890 29c **multicolored** .85 .20
P# block of 4, 5#+U 4.00 —
Zip, copyright block of 4 3.50 —

BOOKLET STAMP

Perf. 11.1x11.3 on 2 or 3 Sides

2536 A1890 29c **multicolored** .60 .20
a. Booklet pane of 10 6.00 3.50

"29" is closer to edge of design on No. 2536 than on No. 2535.

Sheets of 200 in panes of 50

Perf. 11

2537 A1891 52c **multicolored** .90 .20
P# block of 4, 3#+A 4.50 —
Zip block of 4 4.00 —

LITERARY ARTS SERIES

William Saroyan
A1892

Designed by Ren Wicks.

Printed by J.W. Fergusson for American Bank Note Co.

PHOTOGRAVURE

Sheets of 200 in four panes of 50

1991, May 22 **Tagged** ***Perf. 11***

2538 A1892 29c **multicolored** .60 .20
P# block of 4, 5#+A 2.75 —
Zip block of 4 2.50 —

See Russia No. 6002.

Eagle, Olympic Rings — A1893

A1894

A1895

A1896

Futuristic Space Shuttle
A1897

Space Shuttle Challenger
A1898

Space Shuttle Endeavour — A1898a

Designed by: Terrence McCaffrey (Nos. 2539-2541), Timothy Knapp (No. 2542), Ken Hodges (No. 2543), Phil Jordan (Nos. 2544-2544A).

Printed by: J.W. Fergusson & Sons for Stamp Venturers (No. 2539); American Bank Note Co (Nos. 2540-2541); Jeffries Banknote Co. for the American Bank Note Co (No. 2542).

Nos. 2540, 2543-2544 for priority mail rate. Nos. 2541, 2544A for domestic express mail rate. No. 2542 for international express mail rate.

Nos. 2544-2544A printed by Ashton-Potter (USA) Ltd.

Sheet of 180 in nine panes of 20 (No. 2539)

Sheet of 120 in six panes of 20 (Nos. 2540-2542, 2544-2544A)

Pane of 40 (No. 2543)

PHOTOGRAVURE

Copyright information appears in the center of the top and bottom selvage.

1991, Sept. 29 **Tagged** ***Perf. 11***

2539 A1893 $1 **gold & multi** 1.90 .50
P# block of 4, 6#+S 8.00 —
Pane of 20 40.00
a. Black omitted —

LITHOGRAPHED & ENGRAVED

1991, July 7 **Tagged** ***Perf. 11***

2540 A1894 $2.90 **multicolored** 6.00 1.50
P# block of 4, 5#+A 24.00 —
Pane of 20 120.00
a. Vert. pair, imperf horiz. —
b. Black (engr.) omitted —

Imperforates on gummed stamp paper, including gutter pairs and blocks, are proofs from the ABNCo. archives. From the same source also come imperforate progressive proofs.

1991, June 16 **Untagged** ***Perf. 11***

2541 A1895 $9.95 **multicolored** 20.00 6.00
P# block of 4, 5#+A 80.00 —
Pane of 20 400.00
a. Imperf., pair —

No. 2541 exists imperf plus black (engr.) omitted from printer's waste.

1991, Aug. 31 **Untagged** ***Perf. 11***

2542 A1896 $14 **multicolored** 25.00 15.00
P# block of 4, 5#+A 100.00 —
Pane of 20 500.00
a. Red (engr. inscriptions) omitted —

No. 2542 exists imperf plus red omitted from printer's waste.

1993, June 3 **Tagged** ***Perf. 11x10½***

2543 A1897 $2.90 **multicolored** 6.00 1.75
P# block of 4, 6# 27.50 —
Zip block of 4 25.00 —
a. Tagging omitted —

1995, June 22 — Tagged — *Perf. 11.2*

2544	A1898 $3 **multicolored,** dated "1995"	5.75	1.75
b.	Dated "1996"	5.75	1.75
	P# block of 4, 5#+P	23.50	—
	Pane of 20	120.00	—
c.	As "b," horiz. pair, imperf between	—	
d.	As "b," imperf pair	*1,250.*	

1995, Aug. 4 — Tagged — *Perf. 11*

2544A	A1898a $10.75 **multicolored**	20.00	9.00
	P# block of 4, 5#+P	82.50	—
	Pane of 20	425.00	—

FISHING FLIES

Royal Wulff — A1899

Jock Scott — A1900

Apte Tarpon Fly — A1901

Lefty's Deceiver A1902

Muddler Minnow A1903

Designed by Chuck Ripper.

Printed by American Bank Note Co.

PHOTOGRAVURE
BOOKLET STAMPS

1991, May 31 — Tagged — *Perf. 11 Horiz.*

2545	A1899 29c **multicolored**	2.50	.20
a.	Black omitted	—	
b.	Horiz. pair, imperf between	—	
2546	A1900 29c **multicolored**	2.50	.20
a.	Black omitted	—	
2547	A1901 29c **multicolored**	2.50	.20
a.	Black omitted	—	
2548	A1902 29c **multicolored**	2.50	.20
2549	A1903 29c **multicolored**	2.50	.20
a.	Bklt. pane of 5, #2545-2549	12.50	*3.50*

Horiz. pairs, imperf vert,. exist from printer's waste.

No. 2545b is unique and resulted from a foldover after perfing but before cutting. Both stamps are creased.

Cole Porter (1891-1964), Composer — A1904

S. W. Asia Service Medal — A1905

PERFORMING ARTS

Designed by Jim Sharpe.

Printed by American Bank Note Co.

PHOTOGRAVURE
Panes of 50

1991, June 8 — Tagged — *Perf. 11*

2550	A1904 29c **multicolored**	.60	.20
	P# block of 4, 5#+A	2.75	—
	Zip block of 4	2.50	—
a.	Vert. pair, imperf. horiz.	*525.00*	

OPERATIONS DESERT SHIELD & DESERT STORM

Designed by Jack Williams.

Printed by J.W. Fergusson Co. for Stamp Venturers (No. 2551), Multi-Color Corp. for the American Bank Note Co. (No. 2552).

PHOTOGRAVURE
Panes of 50

1991, July 2 — Tagged — *Perf. 11*

2551	A1905 29c **multicolored**	.60	.20
	P# block of 4, 7#+S	2.75	—
	Zip block of 4	2.50	—
a.	Vert. pair, imperf. horiz.	*1,350.*	

No. 2551 is 21mm wide.

BOOKLET STAMP
Perf. 11 Vert. on 1 or 2 Sides

2552	A1905 29c **multicolored**	.60	.20
a.	Booklet pane of 5	3.00	2.25

No. 2552 is 20½mm wide. Inscriptions are shorter than on No. 2551.

No. 2552 Vert. pairs, imperf horiz., are from printer's waste.

1992 SUMMER OLYMPICS, BARCELONA

Pole Vault — A1907

Discus A1908

Women's Sprints A1909

Javelin A1910

Women's Hurdles A1911

Designed by Joni Carter.

Printed by the American Bank Note Co.

PHOTOGRAVURE
Panes of 40

1991, July 12 — Tagged — *Perf. 11*

2553	A1907 29c **multicolored**	.60	.20
2554	A1908 29c **multicolored**	.60	.20
2555	A1909 29c **multicolored**	.60	.20
2556	A1910 29c **multicolored**	.60	.20
2557	A1911 29c **multicolored**	.60	.20
a.	Strip of 5, #2553-2557	3.00	2.25
	P# block of 10, 5#+A	8.00	—
	Zip block of 10	6.00	—

NUMISMATICS

1858 Flying Eagle Cent, 1907 Standing Liberty Double Eagle, Series 1875 $1 Note, Series 1902 $10 National Currency Note — A1912

Designed by V. Jack Ruther.

LITHOGRAPHED & ENGRAVED
Sheets of 200 in four panes of 50

1991, Aug. 13 — Tagged — *Perf. 11*

2558	A1912 29c **multicolored**	.60	.20
	P# block of 4, 7#	2.75	—
	Zip block of 4	2.50	—

WORLD WAR II

A1913

Illustration reduced.

Designed by William H. Bond.

Designs and events of 1941: a, Military vehicles (Burma Road, 717-mile lifeline to China). b, Recruits (America's first peacetime draft). c, Shipments for allies (U.S. supports allies with Lend-Lease Act). d, Franklin D. Roosevelt, Winston Churchill (Atlantic Charter sets war aims of allies). e, Tank (America becomes the "arsenal of democracy.") f, Sinking of Destoyer Reuben James, Oct. 31. g, Gas mask, helmet (Civil defense mobilizes Americans at home). h, Liberty Ship, sea gull (First Liberty ship delivered December 30). i, Sinking ships (Japanese bomb Pearl Harbor, December 7). j, Congress in session (U.S.

declares war on Japan, December 8). Central label is the size of 15 stamps and shows world map, extent of axis control.

LITHOGRAPHED & ENGRAVED

Plates of eight subjects in four panes of 2 each

1991, Sept. 3		Tagged		*Perf. 11*
2559	A1913	Block of 10	7.50	5.00
		Pane of 20	15.00	—
a.-j.		29c any single	.75	.45
k.		Black (engr.) omitted	*12,500.*	

No. 2559 has selvage at left and right and either top or bottom.

BASKETBALL, 100TH ANNIVERSARY

Basketball, Hoop, Players' Arms — A1914

Designed by Lon Busch.

PHOTOGRAVURE

Sheets of 200 in four panes of 50

1991, Aug. 28			Tagged		*Perf. 11*
2560	A1914	29c	**multicolored**	.60	.20
			P# block of 4, 4#	2.75	—
			Zip block of 4	2.50	—

DISTRICT OF COLUMBIA BICENTENNIAL

Capitol Building from Pennsylvania Avenue, Circa 1903 — A1915

Designed by Pierre Mion.

LITHOGRAPHED & ENGRAVED

Plates of 200 in four panes of 50

1991, Sept. 7			Tagged		*Perf. 11*
2561	A1915	29c	**multicolored**	.60	.20
			P# block of 4, 5#	2.75	—
			Zip block of 4	2.50	—
a.			Black (engr.) omitted	*100.00*	

COMEDIANS

Stan Laurel (1890-1965) and Oliver Hardy (1892-1957) A1916

Edgar Bergen (1903-1978) and Charlie McCarthy A1917

Jack Benny (1894-1974) A1918

Fanny Brice (1891-1951) A1919

Bud Abbott (1895-1974) and Lou Costello (1908-1959) A1920

Designed by Al Hirschfeld.

LITHOGRAPHED & ENGRAVED

BOOKLET STAMPS

1991, Aug. 29			Tagged	*Perf. 11 on 2 or 3 Sides*	
2562	A1916	29c	**multicolored**	1.00	.20
2563	A1917	29c	**multicolored**	1.00	.20
2564	A1918	29c	**multicolored**	1.00	.20
2565	A1919	29c	**multicolored**	1.00	.20
2566	A1920	29c	**multicolored**	1.00	.20
a.			Bklt. pane of 10, 2 each #2562-2566	10.00	5.00
b.			As "a," scar & brt violet (engr.) omitted	*650.00*	
c.			Strip of 5, #2562-2566	5.00	2.50

BLACK HERITAGE SERIES

Jan E. Matzeliger (1852-1889), Inventor — A1921

Designed by Higgins Bond.
Printed by J.W. Fergusson & Sons for the American Bank Note Co.

PHOTOGRAVURE

Plates of 200 in four panes of 50

1991, Sept. 15			Tagged		*Perf. 11*
2567	A1921	29c	**multicolored**	.60	.20
			P# block of 4, 6#+A	2.75	—
			Zip block of 4	2.40	—
a.			Horiz. pair, imperf. vert.	*1,250.*	
b.			Vert. pair, imperf. horiz.	*1,250.*	
c.			Imperf., pair	*425.00*	

SPACE EXPLORATION

Mercury, Mariner 10 A1922

Venus, Mariner 2 A1923

Earth, Landsat A1924

Moon, Lunar Orbiter A1925

Mars, Viking Orbiter A1926

Jupiter, Pioneer 11 A1927

Saturn, Voyager 2 A1928

Uranus, Voyager 2 A1929

Neptune, Voyager 2 A1930

Pluto — A1931

Designed by Ron Miller.

PHOTOGRAVURE

BOOKLET STAMPS

1991, Oct. 1			Tagged	*Perf. 11 on 2 or 3 Sides*	
2568	A1922	29c	**multicolored**	1.00	.20
2569	A1923	29c	**multicolored**	1.00	.20
2570	A1924	29c	**multicolored**	1.00	.20
2571	A1925	29c	**multicolored**	1.00	.20
2572	A1926	29c	**multicolored**	1.00	.20

No.	Design	Denom.	Description	Unused	Used
2573	A1927	29c	**multicolored**	1.00	.20
2574	A1928	29c	**multicolored**	1.00	.20
2575	A1929	29c	**multicolored**	1.00	.20
2576	A1930	29c	**multicolored**	1.00	.20
2577	A1931	29c	**multicolored**	1.00	.20
a.			Bklt. pane of 10, #2568-2577	10.00	4.50

CHRISTMAS

Madonna and Child by Antoniazzo Romano — A1933

Santa Claus in Chimney — A1934

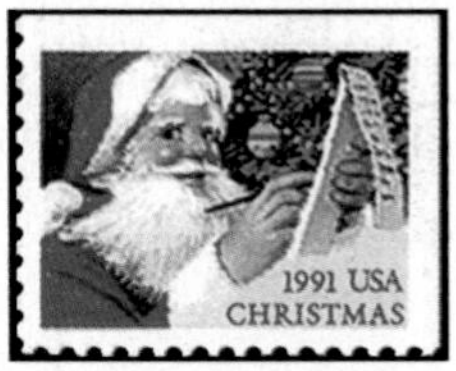

Santa Checking List — A1935

Santa with Present — A1936

Santa at Fireplace — A1937

Santa and Sleigh — A1938

Designed by Bradbury Thompson (#2578) and John Berkey (#2579-2585).

Printed by the Bureau of Engraving and Printing (#2578); J.W. Fergusson & Sons (#2579) and Multi-Color Corp. (#2580-2585) for the American Bank Note Co.

LITHOGRAPHED & ENGRAVED

Sheets of 300 in six panes of 50

1991, Oct. 17 — Tagged — *Perf. 11*

No.	Design	Denom.	Description	Unused	Used
2578	A1933	(29c)	**multicolored**	.60	.20
			P# block of 4, 5#	2.75	—
			Zip, copyright block of 4	2.50	—
a.			Booklet pane of 10	6.00	3.25
b.			Red & black (engr.) omitted	*3,250.*	

PHOTOGRAVURE

No.	Design	Denom.	Description	Unused	Used
2579	A1934	(29c)	**multicolored**	.60	.20
			P# block of 4, 3#+A	2.50	—
			Zip block of 4	2.25	—
a.			Horiz. pair, imperf. vert.	*250.00*	
b.			Vert. pair, imperf. horiz.	*375.00*	

Booklet Stamps

Size: 25x18½mm

Perf. 11 on 2 or 3 Sides

No.	Design	Denom.	Description	Unused	Used
2580	A1934	(29c)	Type I	2.00	.20
2581	A1934	(29c)	Type II	2.40	.20
a.			Pair, #2580-2581	4.80	.50
b.			Bklt. pane, 2 each, #2580, 2581	10.00	1.25
2582	A1935	(29c)	**multicolored**	.60	.20
a.			Bklt. pane of 4	2.40	1.25
2583	A1936	(29c)	**multicolored**	.60	.20
a.			Bklt. pane of 4	2.40	1.25
2584	A1937	(29c)	**multicolored**	.60	.20
a.			Bklt. pane of 4	2.40	1.25
2585	A1938	(29c)	**multicolored**	.60	.20
a.			Bklt. pane of 4	2.40	1.25
			Nos. 2578-2585 (8)	8.00	1.60

The far left brick from the top row of the chimney is missing from Type II, No. 2581.

Imperfs of Nos. 2581, 2583-2585 are printer's waste.

James K. Polk (1795-1849) A1939

"The Surrender of General Burgoyne at Saratoga," by John Trumbull A1942

Washington and Jackson — A1944

Designed by John Thompson (No. 2587), based on painting by John Trumbull (No. 2590), Richard D. Sheaff (No. 2592).

Printed by Banknote Corporation of America (No. 2587), Stamp Venturers (Nos. 2590, 2592).

ENGRAVED

Sheets of 400 in four panes of 100 (No. 2587)

Sheets of 120 in six panes of 20 (Nos. 2590, 2592)

1994-95 — Tagged — *Perf. 11.2*

No.	Design	Denom.	Description	Unused	Used
2587	A1939	32c	**red brown,** *Nov. 2, 1995*	.65	.20
			P# block of 4, 1#+B	3.25	—

Perf. 11.5

No.	Design	Denom.	Description	Unused	Used
2590	A1942	$1	**blue,** *May 5, 1994*	1.90	.50
			P# block of 4, 1#+S	7.60	—
			Pane of 20	38.00	—
2592	A1944	$5	**slate green,** *Aug. 19, 1994*	8.00	2.50
			P# block of 4, 1#+S	40.00	—
			Pane of 20	160.00	—

Some plate blocks contain either inscription or plate position diagram.

A1946

Eagle and Shield — A1947

A1950

Statue of Liberty — A1951

Designed by Lou Nolan (#2593-2594), Jay Haiden (#2595-2597), Richard Sheaff (#2598), Tom Engeman (#2599).

Printed by Bureau of Engraving & Printing (#2593), Stamp Venturers for KCS Industries (#2594), Banknote Corporation of America (#2595), Dittler Brothers, Inc. (#2596, 2599), Stamp Venturers (#2597), National Label Co. for 3M (#2598).

BOOKLET STAMPS

PHOTOGRAVURE

1992, Sept. 8 — Tagged — *Perf. 9.8 on 2 or 3 sides*

No.	Design	Denom.	Description	Unused	Used
2593	A1946	29c	**black & multi**	.60	.20
a.			Booklet pane of 10	6.00	4.25
d.			Imperf, pair	—	

Perf. 11x10 on 2 or 3 sides

No.	Design	Denom.	Description	Unused	Used
2593B	A1946	29c	**black & multi,** shiny gum	1.70	.50
			Low gloss gum	3.00	
c.			Bklt. pane of 10, shiny gum	17.00	7.50
			Low gloss gum	35.00	

1993, Apr. 8(?) — *Perf. 11x10 on 2 or 3 Sides*

No.	Design	Denom.	Description	Unused	Used
2594	A1946	29c	**red & multi**	.65	.20
a.			Booklet pane of 10	6.50	4.25

Denomination is red on #2594 and black on #2593 and 2593B.

LITHOGRAPHED & ENGRAVED

1992, Sept. 25 — Tagged — *Die Cut*

Self-Adhesive

No.	Design	Denom.	Description	Unused	Used
2595	A1947	29c	**brown & multicolored**	.60	.25
a.			Bklt. pane of 17 + label	13.00	
b.			Die cutting omitted, pair	*135.00*	
c.			Brown omitted	*350.00*	
d.			As "a," die cutting omitted	*1,150.*	
2596	A1947	29c	**green & multicolored**	.60	.25
a.			Bklt. pane of 17 + label	12.00	

PHOTOGRAVURE

No.	Design	Denom.	Description	Unused	Used
2597	A1947	29c	**red & multicolored**	.60	.25
a.			Bklt. pane of 17 + label	10.50	

Plate No. and inscription reads down on No. 2595a and up on Nos. 2596a-2597a. Design is sharper and more finely detailed on Nos. 2595, 2597.

Nos. 2595a-2597a sold for $5 each.

Nos. 2595-2597 also available in strips with stamps spaced for use in affixing machines to service first day covers.

PHOTOGRAVURE

1994 — Tagged — *Die Cut*

Self-Adhesive

No.	Design	Denom.	Description	Unused	Used
2598	A1950	29c	**red, cream & blue,** *Feb. 4*	.60	.20
a.			Booklet pane of 18	11.00	
b.			Coil with P#111	—	5.00
			P# strip of 5, #111	9.00	
2599	A1951	29c	**multicolored,** *June 24*	.60	.20
a.			Booklet pane of 18	11.00	
b.			Coil with P#D1111	—	5.00
			P# strip of 5, #D1111	9.00	

Except for Nos. 2598b and 2599b with plate numbers, coil stamps of these issues are indistinguishable from booklet stamps once they are removed from the backing paper.

See Nos. 3122-3122E.

Scott values for used self-adhesvive stamps are for examples either on piece or off piece.

Eagle and Shield — A1956

Eagle and Shield — A1957

A1959

A1960

Flag Over White House — A1961

Designed by Chris Calle (#2602-2604), Terrence McCaffrey (#2605), Lon Busch (#2606-2608), V. Jack Ruther (29c).

Printed by Guildford Gravure, Inc. for the American Bank Note Co. (#2602, 2606), Bureau of Engraving and Printing (#2603, 2607), Stamp Venturers (#2604, 2608), American Bank Note Co. (#2605)

PHOTOGRAVURE
COIL STAMPS

1991-93 Untagged ***Perf. 10 Vert.***

2602 A1956 (10c) **multi** (Bureau precancel, Bulk Rate, in blue), *Dec. 13* .30 .20
Pair .40 .40
P# strip of 5, #A11111, A11112, A21112, A21113, A22112, A22113, A33333, A43325, A43326, A43334, A43335, A53335, A54444, A54445, A77777, A88888 2.00
P# strip of 5, #A12213 12.00
P# strip of 5, #A34424, A34426, A43324, A88889 3.00
P# strip of 5, #A32333 *250.00*
P# strip of 5, #A33334 *75.00*
P# strip of 5, #A33335, A43426, A89999, A99998, A99999, A1010101010, A1011101011, A1011101012, A1110101010, A1110111010, A1111101010, A1111111010, A1411101010, A1411101011, A1412111110, A1412111111 2.50
P# strip of 5, #A1011101010 3.75
P# strip of 5, #A1211101010 4.00
P# strip of 5, #A1110101011 11.50
P# single, #A11111, A11112, A21112, A21113, A22112, A22113, A43324, A43325, A43326, A43334, A43335, A43426, A54444, A54445, A77777, A88888, A89999, A99998, A99999 — 2.00
P# single, #A12213 — 15.00
P# single, #A32333 — 250.00
P# single, #A33333, A33335, A34424, A34426 — 2.50
P# single, #A33334 — 75.00
P# single, #A53335, A88889, A1010101010, A1011101011, A1011101012, A1110101010, A1110111010, A1111101010, A1111111010, A1411101010, A1411101011, A1412111110, A1412111111 — 2.50
P# single, #A1011101010 — 3.00
P# single, #A1211101010 — 4.00
P# single, #A1110101011 — 9.00
a. Imperf., pair —

2603 A1957 (10c) **org yel & multi,** shiny gum (Bureau precancel, Bulk Rate, in red), *May 29, 1993* .30 .20
Pair .40 .40
P# strip of 5, #11111, 22221, 22222 2.25
P# single, same — 1.75
Low gloss gum .20
Pair .40
P# strip of 5, #22222, 33333, 44444 3.00
P# strip of 5, #11111 50.00
P# single, #33333, 44444 — 2.00
a. Imperf., pair 20.00
b. Tagged (error), shiny gum 2.00 1.50
Pair 4.00 3.50
P# strip of 5, #11111, 22221 10.00
P# strip of 5, #22222 *400.00*
P# single, #11111, 22221 — 10.00
P# single, #22222 — *300.00*

All examples of Nos. 2603, 2603a and 2603b were printed with luminescent ink.
See No. 2907.

2604 A1957 (10c) **gold & multi,** shiny gum (Bureau precancel, Bulk Rate, in red), *May 29, 1993* .30 .20
Pair .40 .40
P# strip of 5, #S22222 3.25
P# single, same — 2.00
Low gloss gum .20
Pair .40
P# strip of 5, #S11111 3.00
P# strip of 5, #S22222 2.75
P# single, #S11111 — 1.75

2605 A1959 23c **multi** (Bureau precancel in blue), *Sept. 27* .45 .40
Pair .90 .80
P# strip of 5, #A111, A212, A222 3.25
P# strip of 5, #A112, A122, A333 3.75
P# single, #A111, A112, A122, A212, A222, A333 — 2.25
a. Imperf, pair —

Vertical pairs uncut between on gummed stamp paper are proofs from the ABNCo. archives.

2606 A1960 23c **multi** (Bureau precanceled), *July 21, 1992* .45 .40
Pair .90 .80
P# strip of 5, #A1111, A2222, A2232, A2233, A3333, A4364, A4443, A4444, A4453 3.75
P# single, same # — 2.50

"First-Class" is 9½mm long and "23" is 6mm long on No. 2606.

2607 A1960 23c **multi,** shiny gum (Bureau precanceled), *Oct. 9, 1992* .45 .40
Pair .90 .80
P# strip of 5, #1111 4.00
P# single, #1111 — 2.00
Low gloss gum .45
Pair .90
P# strip of 5, #1111 4.00
a. Tagged (error), shiny gum 5.00 4.50
Pair 10.00 9.00
P# strip of 5, #1111 100.00
P# single, #1111 — 85.00
c. Imperf., pair 70.00

"First-Class" is 9mm long and "23" is 6½mm long on No. 2607.

2608 A1960 23c **vio bl, red & blk** (Bureau precanceled), *May 14, 1993* .75 .40
Pair 1.50 .80
P# strip of 5, #S111 4.00
P# single, #S111 — 2.25

"First-Class" is 8½mm long and "23" is 6½mm long on No. 2608.

ENGRAVED
Tagged

2609 A1961 29c **blue & red,** *Apr. 23, 1992* .60 .20
Pair 1.20 .20
P# strip of 5, #1-8 4.00
P# strip of 5, #9-16, 18 5.00
P# single, #1-4 — .50
P# single, #5 — 2.25
P# single, #6-8 — .50
P# single, #9 — 2.50
P# single, #10-16 — .80
P# single, #18 — 4.00
a. Imperf., pair 15.00
b. Pair, imperf. between 90.00

Beware of pairs with blind perfs sometimes offered as No. 2609b.

WINTER OLYMPICS

Hockey
A1963

Figure Skating
A1964

Speed Skating
A1965

Skiing
A1966

Bobsledding
A1967

Designed by Lon Busch. Printed by J.W. Fergusson & Sons for Stamp Venturers.

PHOTOGRAVURE
Panes of 35

1992, Jan. 11 Tagged ***Perf. 11***

2611 A1963 29c **multicolored** .60 .20
2612 A1964 29c **multicolored** .60 .20
2613 A1965 29c **multicolored** .60 .20
2614 A1966 29c **multicolored** .60 .20
2615 A1967 29c **multicolored** .60 .20
a. Strip of 5, #2611-2615 3.00 2.50
P# block of 10, 4#+S 7.00 —
Zip, copyright block of 15 9.00 —

Inscriptions on six marginal tabs.

Features detail from No. 129 — A1968

W.E.B. Du Bois (1868-1963) — A1969

WORLD COLUMBIAN STAMP EXPO

Designed by Richard Sheaff.

LITHOGRAPHED & ENGRAVED
Plates of 200 in four panes of 50

1992, Jan. 24 Tagged ***Perf. 11***

2616 A1968 29c **multicolored** .60 .20
P# block of 4, 4# 2.75 —
Zip block of 4 2.50 —
a. Tagging omitted 7.50

BLACK HERITAGE SERIES

W.E.B. Du Bois (1868-1963), Writer and Civil Rights Leader

Designed by Higgins Bond.

LITHOGRAPHED & ENGRAVED
Plates of 200 in four panes of 50

1992, Jan. 31 Tagged ***Perf. 11***

2617 A1969 29c **multicolored** .60 .20
P# block of 4, 7# 2.75 —
Zip block of 4 2.50 —

A1970

A1971

LOVE

Designed by Uldis Purins. Printed by the U.S. Bank Note Co.

PHOTOGRAVURE
Panes of 50

1992, Feb. 6		Tagged	Perf. 11	
2618	A1970 29c	**multicolored**	.60	.20
		P# block of 4, U+5#	2.75	—
		Zip, copyright block of 4	2.50	—
a.		Horiz. pair, imperf. vert.	*625.00*	
b.		As "a," green omitted on right stamp	*3,000.*	

OLYMPIC BASEBALL

Designed by Anthony DeLuz.

PHOTOGRAVURE
Plates of 200 in four panes of 50

1992, Apr. 3		Tagged	Perf. 11	
2619	A1971 29c	**multicolored**	.60	.20
		P# block of 4, 5#	2.75	—
		Zip block of 4	2.50	—

VOYAGES OF COLUMBUS

Seeking Queen Isabella's Support
A1972

Crossing the Atlantic
A1973

Approaching Land
A1974

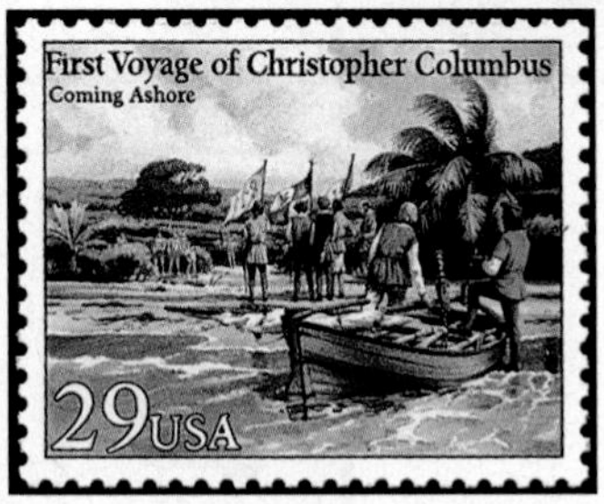

Coming Ashore
A1975

Designed by Richard Schlecht.

LITHOGRAPHED & ENGRAVED
Plates of 160 in four panes of 40

1992, Apr. 24		Tagged	Perf. 11	
2620	A1972 29c	**multicolored**	.60	.20
2621	A1973 29c	**multicolored**	.60	.20
2622	A1974 29c	**multicolored**	.60	.20
2623	A1975 29c	**multicolored**	.60	.20
a.		Block of 4, #2620-2623	2.40	2.00
		P# block of 4, 5#	2.75	—
		Zip block of 4	2.50	—

See Italy Nos. 1877-1880.

Souvenir Sheets

A1976

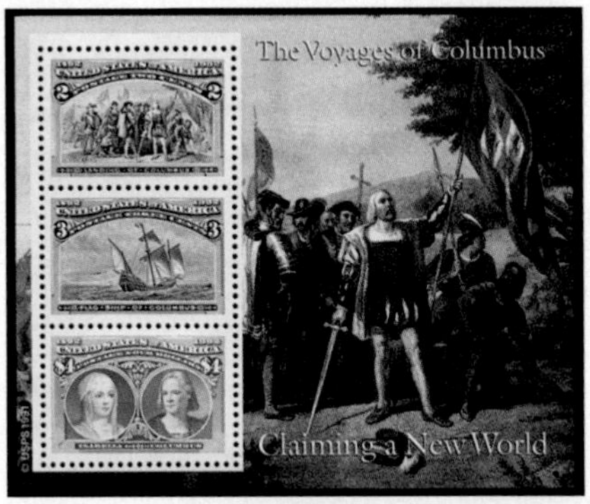

A1977

A1978

A1979

A1980

A1981

Illustrations reduced.

Designed by Richard Sheaff.

Printed by the American Bank Note Co. Margins on Nos. 2624-2628 are lithographed. Nos. 2624a-2628c, 2629 are similar in design to Nos. 230-245 but are dated 1492-1992.

LITHOGRAPHED & ENGRAVED

1992, May 22			Perf. 10½	
		Tagged (15c-$5), Untagged		
2624	A1976	Sheet of 3	2.00	1.25
a.	A71 1c	**deep blue**	.20	.20
b.	A74 4c	**ultramarine**	.20	.20
c.	A82 $1	**salmon**	1.75	1.00
d.		As No. 2624, tagging omitted on "c"	—	
2625	A1977	Sheet of 3	7.25	5.00
a.	A72 2c	**brown violet**	.20	.20
b.	A73 3c	**green**	.20	.20
c.	A85 $4	**crimson lake**	7.00	4.00
2626	A1978	Sheet of 3	1.60	1.25
a.	A75 5c	**chocolate**	.20	.20
b.	A80 30c	**orange brown**	.60	.30
c.	A81 50c	**slate blue**	.90	.50
d.		As No. 2626, tagging omitted on "c"	—	—
2627	A1979	Sheet of 3	5.75	3.50
a.	A76 6c	**purple**	.20	.20
b.	A77 8c	**magenta**	.20	.20
c.	A84 $3	**yellow green**	5.50	3.00
2628	A1980	Sheet of 3	4.00	3.00
a.	A78 10c	**black brown**	.20	.20
b.	A79 15c	**dark green**	.30	.20
c.	A83 $2	**brown red**	3.50	2.00
d.		As No. 2628, tagging omitted on "b"	—	
2629	A1981 $5	Sheet of 1	8.75	6.00
a.	A86 $5	**black**, single stamp	8.50	5.00
		Nos. 2624-2629 (6)	29.35	20.00

See Italy Nos. 1883-1888, Portugal Nos. 1918-1923 and Spain Nos. 2677-2682.

Imperforate souvenir sheets on gummed stamp paper, singly or in pairs and blocks, are proofs from the ABNCo. archives. Additionally, one imperforate essay, with the background of No. 2622 combined with the stamps of No. 2620, is recorded.

NEW YORK STOCK EXCHANGE BICENTENNIAL

A1982

Designed by Richard Sheaff.

Printed by the Jeffries Bank Note Co. for the American Bank Note Co.

LITHOGRAPHED & ENGRAVED

1992, May 17	Tagged	Perf. 11	
2630 A1982 29c **green, red & black**		.60	.20
	P# block of 4, 3#+A	2.75	—
	Zip, Olympic block of 4	2.50	—
a. Black missing (EP)		—	
b. Black missing (CM)		*8,000.*	
c. Center (black engr.) inverted		*26,000.*	

No. 2630a must be collected se-tenant with a normal stamp or with a stamp with half of black engraving missing, or se-tenant with a normal stamp and an additional 2630a.

No. 2630b may be collected alone or se-tenant with No. 2630c.

Two panes, each containing 28 No. 2630c and 12 No. 2630b, have been documented.

The unique pane containing 4 No. 2630a, one stamp with half of black center missing and 35 normal stamps sold at a 2002 auction for $18,400.

SPACE ACCOMPLISHMENTS

Cosmonaut, US Space Shuttle — A1983

Astronaut, Russian Space Station, Russian Space Shuttle — A1984

Sputnik, Vostok, Apollo Command & Lunar Modules — A1985

Soyuz, Mercury & Gemini Spacecraft — A1986

Designed by Vladimir Beilin (Russia) and Robert T. McCall.

PHOTOGRAVURE
Plates of 200 in four panes of 50

1992, May 29	Tagged	Perf. 11	
2631 A1983 29c **multicolored**		.60	.20
2632 A1984 29c **multicolored**		.60	.20
2633 A1985 29c **multicolored**		.60	.20
2634 A1986 29c **multicolored**		.60	.20
a. Block of 4, #2631-2634		2.40	1.90
	P# block of 4, 4#	3.25	—
	Zip block of 4	2.50	—
b. As "a," yellow omitted		—	

See Russia Nos. 6080-6083.

ALASKA HIGHWAY, 50th ANNIVERSARY

A1987

Designed by Byron Birdsall.

LITHOGRAPHED & ENGRAVED
Plates of 200 in four panes of 50

1992, May 30	Tagged	Perf. 11	
2635 A1987 29c **multicolored**		.60	.20
	P# block of 4, 6#	2.75	—
	Zip block of 4	2.50	—
a. Black (engr.) omitted		*750.00*	—

Almost half the recorded No. 2635a errors are poorly centered. These sell for approximately $475.

KENTUCKY STATEHOOD BICENTENNIAL

A1988

Designed by Joseph Petro.

Printed by J.W. Fergusson & Sons for Stamp Venturers.

PHOTOGRAVURE
Plates of 200 in four panes of 50

1992, June 1	Tagged	Perf. 11	
2636 A1988 29c **multicolored**		.60	.20
	P# block of 4, 5#+S	2.75	—
	Zip block of 4	2.50	—
a. Dark blue missing (EP)		—	
b. Dark blue and red missing (EP)		—	
c. All colors missing (EP)		—	

Nos. 2636a-2636c must be collected se-tenant with normal stamps.

SUMMER OLYMPICS

Soccer
A1989

Gymnastics
A1990

Volleyball
A1991

Boxing
A1992

Swimming
A1993

Designed by Richard Waldrep.

Printed by J.W. Fergusson & Sons for Stamp Venturers.

PHOTOGRAVURE
Panes of 35

1992, June 11	Tagged	Perf. 11	
2637 A1989 29c **multicolored**		.60	.20
2638 A1990 29c **multicolored**		.60	.20
2639 A1991 29c **multicolored**		.60	.20
2640 A1992 29c **multicolored**		.60	.20
2641 A1993 29c **multicolored**		.60	.20
a. Strip of 5, #2637-2641		3.00	2.50
	P# block of 10, 5#+S	6.50	—
	Zip, copyright block of 15	9.00	—

Inscriptions on six marginal tabs.

HUMMINGBIRDS

Ruby-throated
A1994

Broad-billed
A1995

Costa's — A1996

Rufous — A1997

Calliope — A1998

Designed by Chuck Ripper.

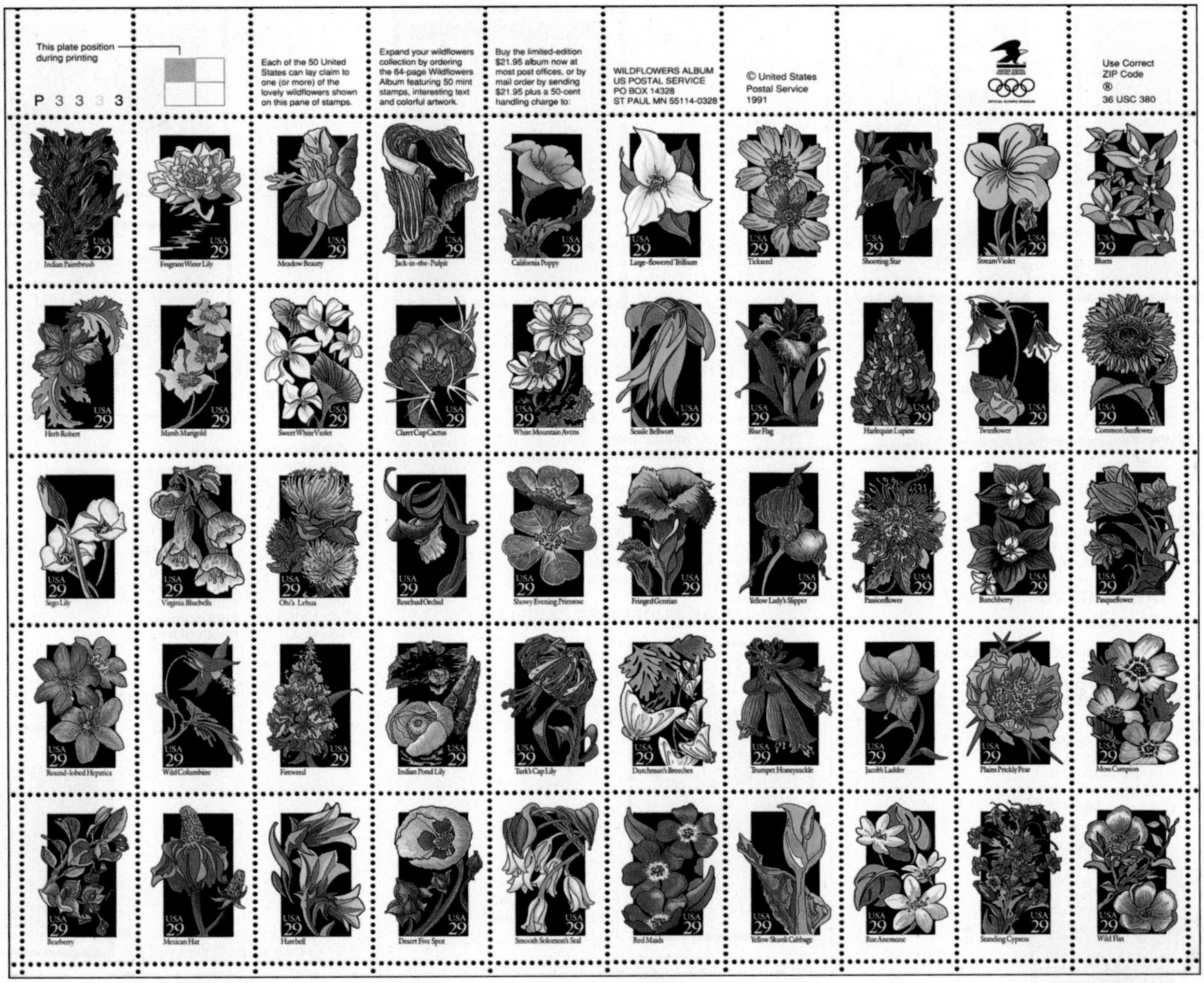

This plate position during printing
P 3 3 3 3
Each of the 50 United States can lay claim to one (or more) of the lovely wildflowers shown on this pane of stamps.
Expand your wildflowers collection by ordering the 64-page Wildflowers Album featuring 50 mint stamps, interesting text and colorful artwork.
Buy the limited-edition $21.95 album now at most post offices, or by mail order by sending $21.95 plus a 50-cent handling charge to:
WILDFLOWERS ALBUM
US POSTAL SERVICE
PO BOX 14328
ST PAUL MN 55114-0328
© United States Postal Service 1991
Use Correct ZIP Code
®
36 USC 380

WILDFLOWERS
A1999-A2048

Printed by Multi-Color Corp. for the American Bank Note Co.

PHOTOGRAVURE
BOOKLET STAMPS

Perf. 11 Vert. on 1 or 2 sides

1992, June 15			Tagged	
2642	A1994	29c **multicolored**	.60	.20
2643	A1995	29c **multicolored**	.60	.20
2644	A1996	29c **multicolored**	.60	.20
2645	A1997	29c **multicolored**	.60	.20
2646	A1998	29c **multicolored**	.60	.20
a.		Bklt. pane of 5, #2642-2646	3.00	2.50

Imperforate singles, booklet panes and pane multiples or varieties on gummed stamp paper are proofs from the ABNCo. archives. From the same source also come imperforate progressive proofs.

WILDFLOWERS

Illustration reduced.

Designed by Karen Mallary.

Printed by Ashton-Potter America, Inc.

LITHOGRAPHED
Plates of 300 in six panes of 50 and
Plates of 200 in four panes of 50

1992, July 24		Tagged	*Perf. 11*	
2647	A1999	29c Indian paintbrush	.80	.60
2648	A2000	29c Fragrant water lily	.80	.60
2649	A2001	29c Meadow beauty	.80	.60
2650	A2002	29c Jack-in-the-pulpit	.80	.60
2651	A2003	29c California poppy	.80	.60
2652	A2004	29c Large-flowered trillium	.80	.60
2653	A2005	29c Tickseed	.80	.60
2654	A2006	29c Shooting star	.80	.60
2655	A2007	29c Stream violet	.80	.60
2656	A2008	29c Bluets	.80	.60
2657	A2009	29c Herb Robert	.80	.60
2658	A2010	29c Marsh marigold	.80	.60
2659	A2011	29c Sweet white violet	.80	.60
2660	A2012	29c Claret cup cactus	.80	.60
2661	A2013	29c White mountain avens	.80	.60
2662	A2014	29c Sessile bellwort	.80	.60
2663	A2015	29c Blue flag	.80	.60
2664	A2016	29c Harlequin lupine	.80	.60
2665	A2017	29c Twinflower	.80	.60
2666	A2018	29c Common sunflower	.80	.60
2667	A2019	29c Sego lily	.80	.60
2668	A2020	29c Virginia bluebells	.80	.60
2669	A2021	29c Ohi'a lehua	.80	.60
2670	A2022	29c Rosebud orchid	.80	.60
2671	A2023	29c Showy evening primrose	.80	.60
2672	A2024	29c Fringed gentian	.80	.60
2673	A2025	29c Yellow lady's slipper	.80	.60
2674	A2026	29c Passionflower	.80	.60
2675	A2027	29c Bunchberry	.80	.60
2676	A2028	29c Pasqueflower	.80	.60
2677	A2029	29c Round-lobed hepatica	.80	.60
2678	A2030	29c Wild columbine	.80	.60
2679	A2031	29c Fireweed	.80	.60
2680	A2032	29c Indian pond lily	.80	.60
2681	A2033	29c Turk's cap lily	.80	.60
2682	A2034	29c Dutchman's breeches	.80	.60
2683	A2035	29c Trumpet honeysuckle	.80	.60
2684	A2036	29c Jacob's ladder	.80	.60
2685	A2037	29c Plains prickly pear	.80	.60
2686	A2038	29c Moss campion	.80	.60
2687	A2039	29c Bearberry	.80	.60
2688	A2040	29c Mexican hat	.80	.60
2689	A2041	29c Harebell	.80	.60
2690	A2042	29c Desert five spot	.80	.60
2691	A2043	29c Smooth Solomon's seal	.80	.60
2692	A2044	29c Red maids	.80	.60
2693	A2045	29c Yellow skunk cabbage	.80	.60
2694	A2046	29c Rue anemone	.80	.60
2695	A2047	29c Standing cypress	.80	.60
2696	A2048	29c Wild flax	.80	.60
a.		A1999-A2048 Pane of 50, #2647-2696	40.00	—

Sheet margin selvage contains a diagram of the plate layout with each pane's position shaded in gray.

WORLD WAR II

A2049

Illustration reduced.

Designed by William H. Bond.

Designs and events of 1942: a, B-25's take off to raid Tokyo, Apr. 18. b, Ration coupons (Food and other commodities rationed). c, Divebomber and deck crewman (US wins Battle of the Coral Sea, May). d, Prisoners of war (Corregidor falls to Japanese, May 6). e, Dutch Harbor buildings on fire (Japan invades Aleutian Islands, June). f, Headphones, coded message (Allies decipher secret enemy codes). g, Yorktown lost, U.S. wins at Midway. h, Woman with drill (Millions of women join war effort). i, Marines land on Guadalcanal, Aug. 7. j, Tank in desert (Allies land in North Africa, Nov.).

Central label is the size of 15 stamps and shows world map, extent of axis control.

LITHOGRAPHED & ENGRAVED
Plates of 80 in four panes of 20 each

1992, Aug. 17		Tagged	*Perf. 11*	
2697	A2049	Block of 10	7.50	5.00
		Pane of 20	15.00	—
a.-j.		29c any single	.75	.30
k.		Red (litho.) omitted	*5,000.*	

No. 2697 has selvage at left and right and either top or bottom.

Dorothy Parker — A2050

Von Karman (1881-1963), Rocket Scientist — A2051

LITERARY ARTS SERIES

Designed by Greg Rudd.

Printed by J.W. Fergusson & Sons for Stamp Venturers.

PHOTOGRAVURE
Plates of 200 in four panes of 50

1992, Aug. 22	**Tagged**	***Perf. 11***	
2698 A2050 29c **multicolored**		.60	.20
	P# block of 4, 5# + S	2.75	—
	Zip block of 4	2.50	—

THEODORE VON KARMAN

Designed by Chris Calle.

Printed by J.W. Fergusson & Sons for Stamp Venturers.

PHOTOGRAVURE
Plates of 200 in four panes of 50

1992, Aug. 31	**Tagged**	***Perf. 11***	
2699 A2051 29c **multicolored**		.60	.20
	P# block of 4, 4# + S	2.75	—
	Zip block of 4	2.50	—

MINERALS

Azurite — A2052

Copper — A2053

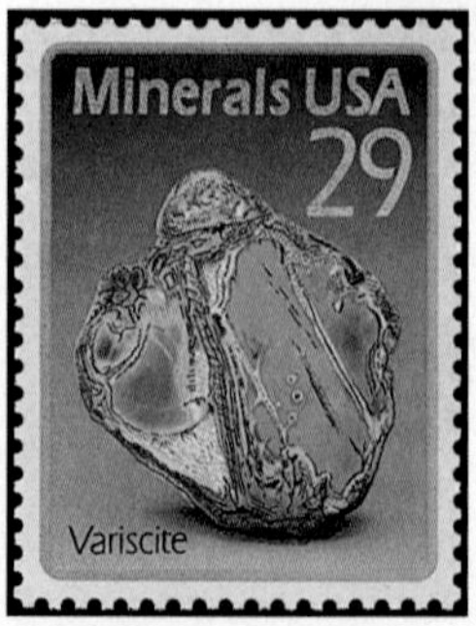

Variscite — A2054

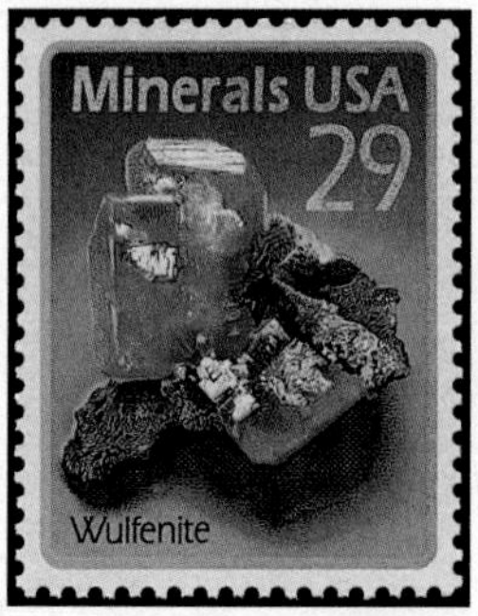

Wulfenite — A2055

Designed by Len Buckley.

LITHOGRAPHED & ENGRAVED
Sheets of 160 in four panes of 40.

1992, Sept. 17	**Tagged**	***Perf. 11***	
2700 A2052 29c **multicolored**		.60	.20
2701 A2053 29c **multicolored**		.60	.20
2702 A2054 29c **multicolored**		.60	.20
2703 A2055 29c **multicolored**		.60	.20
a.	Block or strip of 4, #2700-2703	2.40	2.00
	P# block of 4, 6#	3.50	—
	Zip block of 4	2.50	—
b.	As "a," silver (litho.) omitted	*8,250.*	
c.	As "a," red (litho.) omitted	—	
d.	As "a," silver omitted on two stamps	—	

JUAN RODRIGUEZ CABRILLO

Cabrillo (d. 1543), Ship, Map of San Diego Bay Area — A2056

Designed by Ren Wicks.

Printed by The Press and J.W. Fergusson & Sons for Stamp Venturers.

LITHOGRAPHED & ENGRAVED
Plates of 200 in four panes of 50

1992, Sept. 28	**Tagged**	***Perf. 11***	
2704 A2056 29c **multicolored**		.60	.20
	P# block of 4, 7# + 2 "S"s	3.50	—
	Zip, Olympic block of 4	2.50	—
a.	Black (engr.) omitted	*3,250.*	

WILD ANIMALS

Giraffe A2057

Giant Panda A2058

Flamingo A2059

King Penguins A2060

White Bengal Tiger — A2061

Designed by Robert Giusti.

Printed by J.W. Fergusson & Sons for Stamp Venturers.

PHOTOGRAVURE
BOOKLET STAMPS

1992, Oct. 1	**Tagged**	***Perf. 11 Horiz.***	
2705 A2057 29c **multicolored**		.65	.20
2706 A2058 29c **multicolored**		.65	.20
2707 A2059 29c **multicolored**		.65	.20
2708 A2060 29c **multicolored**		.65	.20
2709 A2061 29c **multicolored**		.65	.20
a.	Booklet pane of 5, #2705-2709	3.25	2.25
b.	As "a," imperf.	*2,250.*	

CHRISTMAS

Madonna and Child, by Giovanni Bellini — A2062

A2063

A2064

A2065

A2066

Designed by Bradbury Thompson (#2710) and Lou Nolan (#2711-2719).

Printed by the Bureau of Engraving and Printing, Ashton-Potter America, Inc. (#2711-2714), the Multi-Color Corporation for American Bank Note Company (#2715-2718), and Avery Dennison (#2719).

LITHOGRAPHED & ENGRAVED

Sheets of 300 in six panes of 50 (#2710, 2714a)

1992 **Tagged** ***Perf. 11½x11***

2710	A2062	29c	**multicolored,** *Oct. 22*	.60	.20
			P# block of 4, 5#	2.75	—
			Zip, copyright block of 4	2.50	—
a.			Booklet pane of 10	6.00	3.50

LITHOGRAPHED

2711	A2063	29c	**multicolored,** *Oct. 22*	.75	.20
2712	A2064	29c	**multicolored,** *Oct. 22*	.75	.20
2713	A2065	29c	**multicolored,** *Oct. 22*	.75	.20
2714	A2066	29c	**multicolored,** *Oct. 22*	.75	.20
a.			Block of 4, #2711-2714	3.00	1.10
			P# block of 4, 5# + P	3.75	—
			Zip, copyright block of 6	4.50	—

Booklet Stamps

PHOTOGRAVURE

Perf. 11 on 2 or 3 Sides

2715	A2063	29c	**multicolored,** *Oct. 22*	.85	.20
2716	A2064	29c	**multicolored,** *Oct. 22*	.85	.20
2717	A2065	29c	**multicolored,** *Oct. 22*	.85	.20
2718	A2066	29c	**multicolored,** *Oct. 22*	.85	.20
a.			Booklet pane of 4, #2715-2718	3.50	1.25

Imperforates and part-perforates on gummed stamp paper are proofs from the ABNCo. archives. From the same source come imperforates with Toys only and imperforates without denominations.

Self-Adhesive

Die Cut

2719	A2065	29c	**multicolored,** *Oct. 28*	.60	.20
a.			Booklet pane of 18	11.00	

"Greetings" is 27mm long on Nos. 2711-2714, 25mm long on Nos. 2715-2718 and 21½mm long on No. 2719. Nos. 2715-2719 differ in color from Nos. 2711-2714.

CHINESE NEW YEAR

Year of the Rooster A2067

Designed by Clarence Lee.

Printed by the American Bank Note Co.

LITHOGRAPHED & ENGRAVED

Panes of 20

1992, Dec. 30 **Tagged** ***Perf. 11***

2720	A2067	29c	**multicolored,** prephosphored paper (mottled tagging) plus block tagging under the engraved portion of the design	.60	.20
			P# block of 4, 5#+A	2.50	—
			Pane of 20	11.50	—
a.			Prephosphored paper (mottled tagging) plus block tagging on top of printed design	3.00	—
			P# block of 4, 5#+A	—	
b.			Prephosphored paper (mottled tagging)	*100.00*	—

See No. 3895i.

AMERICAN MUSIC SERIES

Elvis Presley A2068

Oklahoma! A2069

Hank Williams A2070

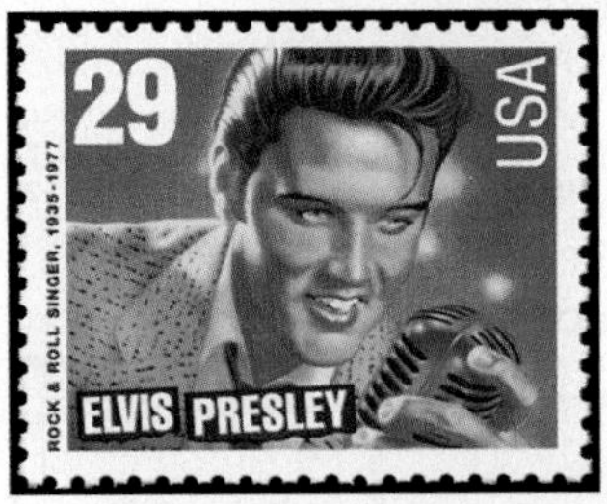

Elvis Presley A2071

Bill Haley A2072

Clyde McPhatter A2073

Ritchie Valens A2074

Otis Redding A2075

Buddy Holly — A2076

Dinah Washington A2077

Designed by Mark Stutzman (#2721, 2724-2725, 2727, 2729, 2731-2732, 2734, 2736), Wilson McLean (#2722), Richard Waldrep (#2723), John Berkey (#2726, 2728, 2730, 2733, 2735, 2737).

Printed by the Bureau of Engraving and Printing (#2721), Stamp Venturers (#2722-2730), Multi-color Corp. for American Bank Note Co. (#2731-2737).

PHOTOGRAVURE

Panes of 40, Panes of 35 (#2724-2730)

1993 **Tagged** ***Perf. 11***

2721	A2068	29c	**multicolored,** *Jan. 8*	.60	.20
			P# block of 4, 5#	2.75	—
			Zip, copyright block of 4	2.50	—
a.			Imperf, pair	—	

Perf. 10

2722	A2069	29c	**multicolored,** *Mar. 30*	.60	.20
			P# block of 4, 4#+S	4.00	—
			Zip block of 4	2.50	—
2723	A2070	29c	**multicolored,** *June 9*	.75	.20
			P# block of 4, 6#+S	4.25	—
			Zip block of 4	3.25	—

Perf. 11.2x11.5

2723A	A2070	29c	**multicolored,** *June 9*	20.00	10.00
			P# block of 4, 6#+S	140.00	—
			Zip block of 4	90.00	—

1993, June 16 ***Perf. 10***

2724	A2071	29c	**multicolored**	.70	.20
2725	A2072	29c	**multicolored**	.70	.20
2726	A2073	29c	**multicolored**	.70	.20
2727	A2074	29c	**multicolored**	.70	.20
2728	A2075	29c	**multicolored**	.70	.20
2729	A2076	29c	**multicolored**	.70	.20
2730	A2077	29c	**multicolored**	.70	.20
a.			Vert. strip of 7, #2724-2730	5.50	
			Horiz. P# block of 10, 2 sets of 6P#+S, + top label	10.00	—
			Vert. P# block of 8, 6#+S	7.75	—
			Pane of 35	29.00	—

No. 2730a with Nos. 2724-2730 in numerical sequence cannot be obtained from the pane of 35.

Booklet Stamps

Perf. 11 Horiz.

2731	A2071	29c	**multicolored**	.60	.20
2732	A2072	29c	**multicolored**	.60	.20
2733	A2073	29c	**multicolored**	.60	.20
2734	A2074	29c	**multicolored**	.60	.20
2735	A2075	29c	**multicolored**	.60	.20
2736	A2076	29c	**multicolored**	.60	.20
2737	A2077	29c	**multicolored**	.60	.20
a.			Booklet pane, 2 #2731, 1 each #2732-2737	5.00	2.25
b.			Booklet pane, #2731, 2735-2737 + tab	2.40	1.50

Nos. 2731-2737 have smaller design sizes, brighter colors and shorter inscriptions than Nos. 2724-2730, as well as framelines around the designs and other subtle design differences.

No. 2737b without tab is indistinguishable from broken No. 2737a.

Imperforates of both No. 2737a and 2737b on gummed stamp paper are proofs from the ABNCo. archives. Perforated booklet pane multiples and varieties also exist from the same source.

See Nos. 2769, 2771, 2775 and designs A2112-A2117.

SPACE FANTASY

A2086

A2087

A2088

A2089

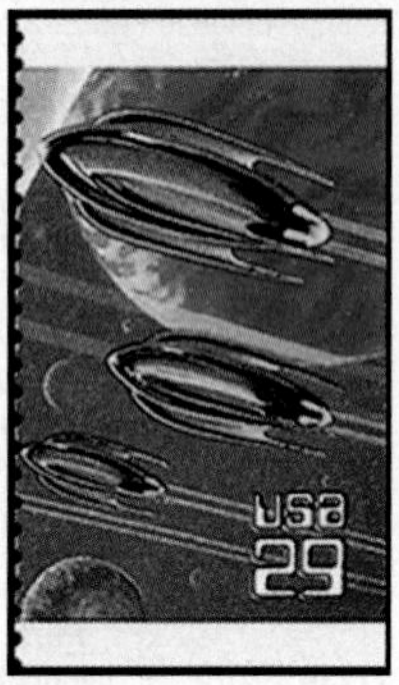

A2090

Designed by Stephen Hickman.

PHOTOGRAVURE
BOOKLET STAMPS

1993, Jan. 25	**Tagged**	***Perf. 11 Vert.***	
2741 A2086 29c **multicolored**		.60	.20
2742 A2087 29c **multicolored**		.60	.20
2743 A2088 29c **multicolored**		.60	.20
2744 A2089 29c **multicolored**		.60	.20
2745 A2090 29c **multicolored**		.60	.20
a. Booklet pane of 5, #2741-2745		3.00	2.25

BLACK HERITAGE SERIES

Percy Lavon Julian (1899-1975), Chemist — A2091

Designed by Higgins Bond.

LITHOGRAPHED & ENGRAVED
Panes of 50

1993, Jan. 29	**Tagged**	***Perf. 11***	
2746 A2091 29c **multicolored**		.60	.20
P# block of 4, 7#		2.75	—
Zip block of 4		2.50	—

OREGON TRAIL

A2092

Designed by Jack Rosenthal.

LITHOGRAPHED & ENGRAVED
Panes of 50

1993, Feb. 12	**Tagged**	***Perf. 11***	
2747 A2092 29c **multicolored**		.60	.20
P# block of 4, 6#		2.75	—
Zip block of 4		2.50	—
a. Tagging omitted		22.50	
b. Blue omitted		—	

WORLD UNIVERSITY GAMES

A2093

Designed by David Buck.

PHOTOGRAVURE
Panes of 50

1993, Feb. 25	**Tagged**	***Perf. 11***	
2748 A2093 29c **multicolored**		.60	.20
P# block of 4, 5#		2.75	—
Zip block of 4		2.50	—

GRACE KELLY (1929-1982)

Actress, Princess of Monaco — A2094

Designed by Czeslaw Slania.

Printed by Stamp Venturers.

ENGRAVED
Panes of 50

1993, Mar. 24	**Tagged**	***Perf. 11***	
2749 A2094 29c **blue**		.60	.20
P# block of 4, 1# +S		2.75	—
Zip block of 4		2.50	—

See Monaco No. 1851.

CIRCUS

Clown — A2095

Ringmaster — A2096

Trapeze Artist — A2097

Elephant — A2098

Designed by Steve McCracken.

Printed by Ashton Potter America.

LITHOGRAPHED
Panes of 40

1993, Apr. 6	**Tagged**	***Perf. 11***	
2750 A2095 29c **multicolored**		.60	.20
2751 A2096 29c **multicolored**		.60	.20
2752 A2097 29c **multicolored**		.60	.20
2753 A2098 29c **multicolored**		.60	.20
a. Block of 4, #2750-2753		2.40	1.75
P# block of 6, 5#+P		5.75	—
Zip block of 6		3.75	—

Plate and zip blocks of 6 and copyright blocks of 9 contain one #2753a with continuous design (complete spotlight).

CHEROKEE STRIP LAND RUN, CENTENNIAL

A2099

Designed by Harold T. Holden.

Printed by American Bank Note. Co.

LITHOGRAPHED & ENGRAVED
Panes of 20

1993, Apr. 17	**Tagged**	***Perf. 11***	
2754 A2099 29c **multicolored**		.60	.20
P# block of 4, 5#+A		2.50	—
Pane of 20		12.50	—

Imperforates on gummed stamp paper, including gutter pairs and blocks, are proofs from the ABNCo. archives. From the same source also come perforated gutter pairs and blocks, plus imperforates missing the red text and black denomination and "USA." An approved die proof also is recorded.

DEAN ACHESON (1893-1971)

Secretary of State — A2100

Designed by Christopher Calle.

Printed by Stamp Venturers.

ENGRAVED
Sheets of 300 in six panes of 50

1993, Apr. 21				*Perf. 11*	
2755	A2100	29c	**greenish gray**	.60	.20
			P# block of 4, 1#+S	2.75	—
			Zip block of 4	2.50	—

SPORTING HORSES

Steeplechase A2101

Thoroughbred Racing A2102

Harness Racing A2103

Polo — A2104

Designed by Michael Dudash.

Printed by Stamp Venturers.

LITHOGRAPHED & ENGRAVED
Panes of 40

1993, May 1			**Tagged**	*Perf. 11x11½*	
2756	A2101	29c	**multicolored**	.60	.20
2757	A2102	29c	**multicolored**	.60	.20
2758	A2103	29c	**multicolored**	.60	.20
2759	A2104	29c	**multicolored**	.60	.20
a.			Block of 4, #2756-2759	2.40	2.00
			P# block of 4, 5#+S	2.75	—
			Zip block of 4	2.50	—
b.			As "a," black (engr.) omitted	*750.00*	

GARDEN FLOWERS

Hyacinth — A2105

Daffodil — A2106

Tulip — A2107

Iris — A2108

Lilac — A2109

Designed by Ned Seidler.

LITHOGRAPHED & ENGRAVED
BOOKLET STAMPS

1993, May 15			**Tagged**	*Perf. 11 Vert.*	
2760	A2105	29c	**multicolored**	.60	.20
2761	A2106	29c	**multicolored**	.60	.20
2762	A2107	29c	**multicolored**	.60	.20
2763	A2108	29c	**multicolored**	.60	.20
2764	A2109	29c	**multicolored**	.60	.20
a.			Booklet pane of 5, #2760-2764	3.00	2.25
b.			As "a," black (engr.) omitted	*175.00*	
c.			As "a," imperf.	*1,000.*	

WORLD WAR II

A2110

Illustration reduced.

Designed by William H. Bond.

Designs and events of 1943: a, Destroyers (Allied forces battle German U-boats). b, Military medics treat the wounded. c, Amphibious landing craft on beach (Sicily attacked by Allied forces, July). d, B-24s hit Ploesti refineries, August. e, V-mail delivers letters from home. f, PT boat (Italy invaded by Allies, Sept.).

g, Nos. WS7, WS8, savings bonds, (Bonds and stamps help war effort). h, "Willie and Joe" keep spirits high. i, Banner in window (Gold Stars mark World War II losses). j, Marines assault Tarawa, Nov.

Central label is the size of 15 stamps and shows world map with extent of Axis control and Allied operations.

LITHOGRAPHED & ENGRAVED
Plates of 80 in four panes of 20 each

1993, May 31		**Tagged**	*Perf. 11*	
2765	A2110	Block of 10	7.50	5.00
		Pane of 20	15.00	—
a.-j.		29c any single	.75	.40
k.		As No. 2765, tagging omitted on a.-e.	—	
l.		As No. 2765, tagging omitted on f.-j.	—	

No. 2765 has selvage at left and right and either top or bottom.

JOE LOUIS (1914-1981)

A2111

Designed by Thomas Blackshear.

LITHOGRAPHED & ENGRAVED
Plates of 200 in four panes of 50

1993, June 22			**Tagged**	*Perf. 11*	
2766	A2111	29c	**multicolored**	.60	.20
			P# block of 4, 5#	2.75	—
			Zip block of 4	2.50	—

AMERICAN MUSIC SERIES

Oklahoma! Type and

Show Boat — A2112

Porgy & Bess — A2113

My Fair Lady — A2114

Designed by Wilson McLean.

Printed by Multi-Color Corp.

BOOKLET STAMPS
PHOTOGRAVURE
Perf. 11 Horiz. on 1 or 2 Sides

1993, July 14				**Tagged**	
2767	A2112	29c	**multicolored**	.60	.20
2768	A2113	29c	**multicolored**	.60	.20
2769	A2069	29c	**multicolored**	.60	.20
2770	A2114	29c	**multicolored**	.60	.20
a.			Booklet pane of 4, #2767-2770	2.75	2.25

No. 2769 has smaller design size, brighter colors and shorter inscription than No. 2722, as well as a frameline around the design and other subtle design differences.

Imperforate booklet panes, singly or in multiples, on gummed stamp paper are proofs from the ABNCo. archives. From the same source come imperforate progressive proofs, plus imperforate proofs/essays showing slightly altered designs.

AMERICAN MUSIC SERIES

Hank Williams Type and

Patsy Cline — A2115

The Carter Family A2116

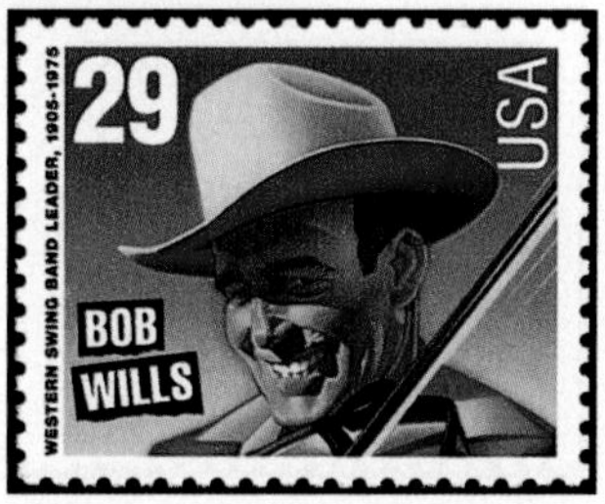

Bob Wills — A2117

Designed by Richard Waldrep.

Printed by Stamp Venturers (#2771-2774) and American Bank Note Co. (#2775-2778).

PHOTOGRAVURE

Panes of 20

1993, Sept. 25	Tagged		Perf. 10	
2771	A2070 29c multicolored		.75	.20
2772	A2115 29c multicolored		.75	.20
2773	A2116 29c multicolored		.75	.20
2774	A2117 29c multicolored		.75	.20
a.	Block or horiz. strip of 4, #2771-2774		3.00	1.75
	Horiz. P# block of 8, 2 sets of 6#+S + top label		6.50	—
	P# block of 4, 6#+S		3.25	—
	Pane of 20		16.00	—

Booklet Stamps

Perf. 11 Horiz. on one or two sides

With Black Frameline

2775	A2070 29c multicolored		.60	.20
2776	A2116 29c multicolored		.60	.20
2777	A2115 29c multicolored		.60	.20
2778	A2117 29c multicolored		.60	.20
a.	Booklet pane of 4, #2775-2778		2.50	2.00

Inscription at left measures 27½mm on No. 2723, 27mm on No. 2771 and 22mm on No. 2775. No. 2723 shows only two tuning keys on guitar, while No. 2771 shows those two and parts of two others.

Imperforate booklet panes on gummed stamp paper, singly or in multiples, are proofs from the ABNCo. archives. From the same source come panes perfed horiz. but uncut vertically, plus imperforate progressive proofs and other die proof varieties.

NATIONAL POSTAL MUSEUM

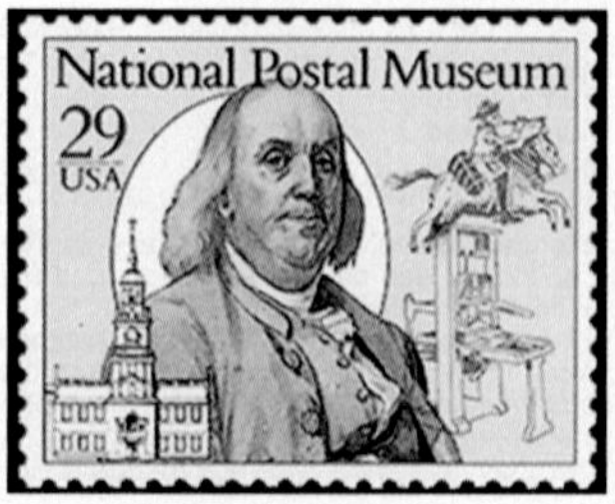

Independence Hall, Benjamin Franklin, Printing Press, Colonial Post Rider — A2118

Pony Express Rider, Civil War Soldier, Concord Stagecoach A2119

JN-4H Biplane, Charles Lindbergh, Railway Mail Car, 1931 Model A Ford Mail Truck — A2120

California Gold Rush Miner's Letter, Nos. 39, 295, C3a, C13, Barcode and Circular Date Stamp A2121

Designed by Richard Schlecht.

Printed by American Bank Note Co.

LITHOGRAPHED AND ENGRAVED

1993, July 30	Tagged		Perf. 11	
2779	A2118 29c multicolored		.60	.20
2780	A2119 29c multicolored		.60	.20
2781	A2120 29c multicolored		.60	.20
2782	A2121 29c multicolored		.60	.20
a.	Block or strip of 4, #2779-2782		2.40	2.00
	P# block of 4, 7#+A		2.50	—
	Pane of 20		12.50	—
b.	As "a," engr. maroon (USA/29) and black ("My dear...") omitted			—
c.	As "a," imperf		*3,250.*	

AMERICAN SIGN LANGUAGE

A2122

A2123

Designed by Chris Calle.

Printed by Stamp Venturers.

PHOTOGRAVURE

1993, Sept. 20	Tagged		Perf. 11½	
2783	A2122 29c multicolored		.60	.20
2784	A2123 29c multicolored		.60	.20
a.	Pair, #2783-2784		1.20	.75
	P# block of 4, 4#+S		2.50	—
	Pane of 20		12.50	—

CLASSIC BOOKS

A2124

A2125

A2126

A2127

Designed by Jim Lamb.

Printed by American Bank Note Co.

Designs: No. 2785, Rebecca of Sunnybrook Farm, by Kate Douglas Wiggin. No. 2786, Little House on the Prairie, by Laura Ingalls Wilder. No. 2787, The Adventures of Huckleberry Finn, by Mark Twain. No. 2788, Little Women, by Louisa May Alcott.

LITHOGRAPHED & ENGRAVED

Panes of 40

1993, Oct. 23	Tagged		Perf. 11	
2785	A2124 29c multicolored		.60	.20
2786	A2125 29c multicolored		.60	.20
2787	A2126 29c multicolored		.60	.20
2788	A2127 29c multicolored		.60	.20
a.	Block or horiz. strip of 4, #2785-2788		2.40	2.00
	P# block of 4, 5#+A		5.00	—
	Zip block of 4		2.50	—

Imperforates on gummed stamp paper, including gutter pairs and blocks, are proofs from the ABNCo. archives.

CHRISTMAS

Madonna and Child in a Landscape, by Giovanni Battista Cima — A2128

Jack-in-the-Box A2129

Red-Nosed Reindeer A2130

Snowman — A2131

Toy Soldier Blowing Horn — A2132

Designed by Bradbury Thompson (#2789-2790), Peter Good (#2791-2803).

Printed by Bureau of Engraving and Printing (#2789, 2791-2798), KCS Industries (#2790), Avery Dennison (#2799-2803).

LITHOGRAPHED & ENGRAVED

Panes of 50 (#2789, 2791-2794)

1993, Oct. 21 **Tagged** ***Perf. 11***

2789 A2128 29c **multicolored**	.60	.20
P# block of 4, 4#	2.75	—
Zip, copyright block of 4	2.50	—

Booklet Stamp

Size: 18x25mm

Perf. 11½x11 on 2 or 3 Sides

2790 A2128 29c **multicolored**	.60	.20
a. Booklet pane of 4	2.40	1.75
b. Imperf., pair	—	
c. As "a," imperf	—	

Nos. 2789-2790 have numerous design differences.

1993

PHOTOGRAVURE

Perf. 11½

2791 A2129 29c **multicolored,** *Oct. 21*	.60	.20
2792 A2130 29c **multicolored,** *Oct. 21*	.60	.20
2793 A2131 29c **multicolored,** *Oct. 21*	.60	.20
2794 A2132 29c **multicolored,** *Oct. 21*	.60	.20
a. Block or strip of 4, #2791-2794	2.40	2.00
P# block of 4, 6#	4.00	—
Zip, copyright block of 4	2.50	—

Snowman on Nos. 2793, 2799 has three buttons and seven snowflakes beneath nose (placement differs on both stamps). No. 2796 has two buttons and five snowflakes beneath nose. No. 2803 has two orange buttons and four snowflakes beneath nose.

Booklet Stamps

Size: 18x21mm

Perf. 11x10 on 2 or 3 Sides

2795 A2132 29c **multicolored,** *Oct. 21*	.85	.20
2796 A2131 29c **multicolored,** *Oct. 21*	.85	.20
2797 A2130 29c **multicolored,** *Oct. 21*	.85	.20
2798 A2129 29c **multicolored,** *Oct. 21*	.85	.20
a. Booklet pane, 3 each #2795-2796, 2 each #2797-2798	8.50	4.00
b. Booklet pane, 3 each #2797-2798, 2 each #2795-2796	8.50	4.00
c. Block of 4, #2795-2798	3.40	1.75

Self-Adhesive

Size: 19½x26½mm

Die Cut

2799 A2131 29c **multicolored,** *Oct. 28*	.65	.20
a. Coil with plate # V1111111	—	6.00
P# strip of 5, 1 each #2799-2801, 2 #2802, P#V1111111	10.00	
P# strip of 8, 2 each #2799-2802, P#V1111111	12.00	
2800 A2132 29c **multicolored,** *Oct. 28*	.65	.20
2801 A2129 29c **multicolored,** *Oct. 28*	.65	.20
2802 A2130 29c **multicolored,** *Oct. 28*	.65	.20
a. Booklet pane, 3 each #2799-2802	8.00	
b. Block of 4, #2799-2802	2.60	

Except for No. 2799a with plate number, coil stamps are indistinguishable from booklet stamps once they are removed from the backing paper.

Size: 17x20mm

2803 A2131 29c **multicolored,** *Oct. 28*	.60	.20
a. Booklet pane of 18	11.00	

Snowman on Nos. 2793, 2799 has three buttons and seven snowflakes beneath nose (placement differs on both stamps). No. 2796 has two buttons and five snowflakes beneath nose. No. 2803 has two orange buttons and four snowflakes beneath nose.

MARIANA ISLANDS

A2133

Designed by Herb Kane.

LITHOGRAPHED AND ENGRAVED

1993, Nov. 4 **Tagged** ***Perf. 11***

2804 A2133 29c **multicolored**	.60	.20
P# block of 4, 6#	2.50	—
Pane of 20	12.50	—

COLUMBUS' LANDING IN PUERTO RICO, 500th ANNIVERSARY

A2134

Designed by Richard Schlecht.

Printed by Stamp Venturers.

PHOTOGRAVURE

Panes of 50

1993, Nov. 19 **Tagged** ***Perf. 11.2***

2805 A2134 29c **multicolored**	.60	.20
P# block of 4, 5#+S	2.75	—
Zip block of 4	2.50	—

AIDS AWARENESS

A2135

Designed by Tom Mann.
Printed by Stamp Venturers.

PHOTOGRAVURE

Panes of 50

1993, Dec. 1 **Tagged** ***Perf. 11.2***

2806 A2135 29c **black & red**	.60	.20
P# block of 4, 3#+S	2.75	—
Zip, copyright block of 6	2.50	—
a. Perf. 11 vert. on 1 or 2 sides, from bklt. pane	.70	.20
b. As "a," booklet pane of 5	3.50	2.00

WINTER OLYMPICS

Slalom — A2136

Luge — A2137

Ice Dancing — A2138

Cross-Country Skiing — A2139

Ice Hockey — A2140

Designed by Lon Busch.
Printed by Ashton-Potter.

LITHOGRAPHED

Sheets of 120 in six panes of 20

1994, Jan. 6 **Tagged** ***Perf. 11.2***

2807 A2136 29c **multicolored**	.60	.20
2808 A2137 29c **multicolored**	.60	.20
2809 A2138 29c **multicolored**	.60	.20
2810 A2139 29c **multicolored**	.60	.20
2811 A2140 29c **multicolored**	.60	.20
a. Strip of 5, #2807-2811	3.00	2.50
Horiz. P# block of 10, 2 sets of 4#+P and inscriptions	6.50	—
Horiz. P# block of 10, 2 sets of 4#+P	6.00	—
Pane of 20	12.50	—

EDWARD R. MURROW, JOURNALIST (1908-65)

A2141

Designed by Chris Calle.

ENGRAVED

Panes of 50

1994, Jan. 21 **Tagged** ***Perf. 11.2***

2812 A2141 29c **brown**	.60	.20
P# block of 4, 1#	3.25	—

LOVE

A2142

A2143

A2144

Designed by Peter Goode (#2813), Lon Busch (#2814-2815).

Printed by Banknote Corp. of America (#2813), American Banknote Co. (#2814) and Bureau of Engraving and Printing (#2814C, 2815).

Booklet Stamps
LITHOGRAPHED & ENGRAVED

1994 **Tagged** ***Die Cut***
Self-adhesive

2813	A2142 29c **multicolored,** *Jan. 27*	.60	.20
a.	Booklet pane of 18	11.00	
b.	Coil with plate # B1	—	3.75
	P# strip of 5, #B1	6.75	

Except for No. 2813b with plate number, coil stamps are indistinguishable from booklet stamps once they are removed from the backing paper.

PHOTOGRAVURE
Perf. 10.9x11.1 on 2 or 3 sides

2814	A2143 29c **multicolored,** *Feb. 14*	.60	.20
a.	Booklet pane of 10	6.00	3.50
b.	Imperf, pair		—

Horiz. pairs, imperf between, are printer's waste.

LITHOGRAPHED & ENGRAVED
Sheets of 300 in six panes of 50
Tagged
Perf. 11.1

2814C	A2143 29c **multicolored,** *June 11*	.70	.20
	P# block of 4, 5#	3.00	—

Size of No. 2814C is 20x28mm. No. 2814 is 18x24½mm.

PHOTOGRAVURE & ENGRAVED
Sheet of 300 in six panes of 50
Perf. 11.2

2815	A2144 52c **multicolored,** *Feb. 14*	1.00	.20
	P# block of 4, 5#	5.00	—
	P# block of 10, 2 sets of 5#, plate diagram, copyright and pane price inscriptions	11.00	—

BLACK HERITAGE SERIES

Dr. Allison Davis (1902-83), Social Anthropologist, Educator — A2145

Designed by Chris Calle.

Printed by Stamp Venturers.

ENGRAVED

1994, Feb. 1 **Tagged** ***Perf. 11.2***

2816	A2145 29c **red brown & brown**	.60	.20
	P# block of 4, 1#+S	2.50	—
	Pane of 20	12.50	—

CHINESE NEW YEAR

Year of the Dog — A2146

Designed by Clarence Lee.

Printed by J.W. Fergusson & Sons for Stamp Venturers.

PHOTOGRAVURE
Sheets of 180 in nine panes of 20

1994, Feb. 5 **Tagged** ***Perf. 11.2***

2817	A2146 29c **multicolored**	.80	.20
	P# block of 4, 4#+S	3.50	—
	Pane of 20	17.50	—

See No. 3895j.

BUFFALO SOLDIERS

A2147

Designed by Mort Kuntsler.

Printed by Stamp Venturers.

LITHOGRAPHED & ENGRAVED
Plates of 180 in nine panes of 20

1994, Apr. 22 **Tagged** ***Perf. 11.5x11.2***

2818	A2147 29c **multicolored**	.60	.20
	P# block of 4, 5#+S	2.50	—
	Pane of 20	12.50	—
a.	Double impression (second impression light) of red brown (engr. inscriptions)	—	

SILENT SCREEN STARS

Rudolph Valentino (1895-1926) — A2148

Clara Bow (1905-65) — A2149

Charlie Chaplin (1889-1977) — A2150

Lon Chaney (1883-1930) — A2151

John Gilbert (1895-1936) — A2152

Zasu Pitts (1898-1963) — A2153

Harold Lloyd (1894-1971) — A2154

Keystone Cops — A2155

Theda Bara (1885-1955) — A2156

Buster Keaton (1895-1966) — A2157

Designed by Al Hirschfeld.

LITHOGRAPHED & ENGRAVED
Plates of 160 in four panes of 40

1994, Apr. 27 **Tagged** ***Perf. 11.2***

2819	A2148 29c **red, black & bright violet**	1.10	.30
2820	A2149 29c **red, black & bright violet**	1.10	.30
2821	A2150 29c **red, black & bright violet**	1.10	.30
2822	A2151 29c **red, black & bright violet**	1.10	.30
2823	A2152 29c **red, black & bright violet**	1.10	.30
2824	A2153 29c **red, black & bright violet**	1.10	.30
2825	A2154 29c **red, black & bright violet**	1.10	.30
2826	A2155 29c **red, black & bright violet**	1.10	.30
2827	A2156 29c **red, black & bright violet**	1.10	.30
2828	A2157 29c **red, black & bright violet**	1.10	.30
a.	Block of 10, #2819-2828	11.00	4.00
	P# block of 10, 4#, plate diagram and copyright inscription	12.00	—
	Half pane of 20	23.00	—
b.	As "a," black (litho.) omitted		—
c.	As "a," blk, red & brt vio (litho.) omitted		—

GARDEN FLOWERS

Lily — A2158

Zinnia — A2159

Gladiola — A2160

Marigold — A2161

Rose — A2162

Designed by Ned Seidler.

LITHOGRAPHED & ENGRAVED

1994, Apr. 28 Tagged *Perf. 10.9 Vert.*

Booklet Stamps

2829	A2158 29c	**multicolored**	.60	.20
2830	A2159 29c	**multicolored**	.60	.20
2831	A2160 29c	**multicolored**	.60	.20
2832	A2161 29c	**multicolored**	.60	.20
2833	A2162 29c	**multicolored**	.60	.20
a.		Booklet pane of 5, #2829-2833	3.00	2.25
b.		As "a," imperf	*1,500.*	
c.		As "a," black (engr.) omitted	*225.00*	
d.		As "a," tagging omitted	—	

1994 WORLD CUP SOCCER CHAMPIONSHIPS

A2163

A2164

A2165

Illustration reduced.

Designed by Michael Dudash.

Printed by J.W. Fergusson & Sons for Stamp Venturers. Design: 40c, Soccer player, diff.

PHOTOGRAVURE

Plates of 180 in nine panes of 20

1994, May 26 Tagged *Perf. 11.1*

2834	A2163 29c	**multicolored**	.60	.20
		P# block of 4, 4#+S	2.50	—
		Pane of 20	12.50	—
2835	A2163 40c	**multicolored**	.80	.20
		P# block of 4, 4#+S	3.20	—
		Pane of 20	16.00	—
2836	A2164 50c	**multicolored**	1.00	.20
		P# block of 4, 4#+S	4.00	—
		Pane of 20	20.00	—

Souvenir Sheet

2837	A2165	Sheet of 3, #a.-c.	4.00	3.00

Nos. 2834-2836 are printed on phosphor-coated paper while Nos. 2837a (29c), 2837b (40c), 2837c (50c) are block tagged. No. 2837c has a portion of the yellow map in the LR corner.

WORLD WAR II

A2166

Illustration reduced.

Designed by William H. Bond.

Designs and events of 1944: a, Allied forces retake New Guinea. b, P-51s escort B-17s on bombing raids. c, Troops running from landing craft (Allies in Normandy, D-Day, June 6). d, Airborne units spearhead attacks. e, Officer at periscope (Submarines shorten war in Pacific). f, Parade (Allies free Rome, June 4; Paris, Aug. 25).

g, Soldier firing flamethrower (US troops clear Saipan bunkers). h, Red Ball Express speeds vital supplies. i, Battleship firing main battery (Battle for Leyte Gulf, Oct. 23-26). j, Soldiers in snow (Bastogne and Battle of the Bulge, Dec.).

Central label is size of 15 stamps and shows world map with extent of Axis control and Allied operations.

LITHOGRAPHED & ENGRAVED

Plates of eight subjects in four panes of 2 each

1994, June 6 Tagged *Perf. 10.9*

2838	A2166	Block of 10	18.00	10.00
		Pane of 20	36.00	—
a.-j.		29c any single	1.80	.50

No. 2838 has selvage at left and right and either top or bottom.

NORMAN ROCKWELL

A2167

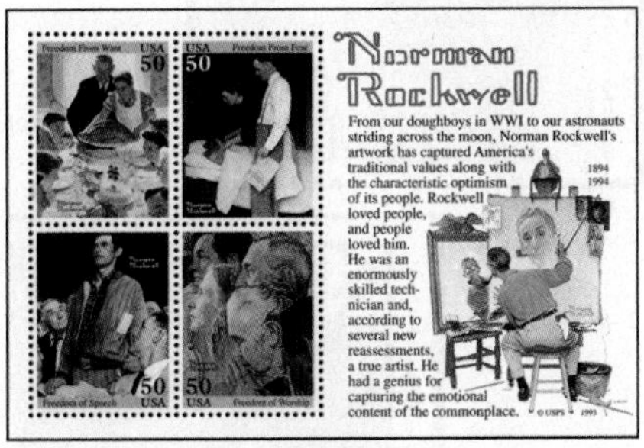

A2168

Illustration reduced.

Designed by Richard Sheaff based on Rockwell's works.

LITHOGRAPHED & ENGRAVED

Sheets of 200 in four panes of 50

1994, July 1 Tagged *Perf. 10.9x11.1*

2839	A2167 29c	**multicolored**	.60	.20
		P# block of 4, 5#	2.75	—

Souvenir Sheet

LITHOGRAPHED

2840	A2168	Sheet of 4	4.50	2.75
a.		50c Freedom From Want	1.10	.65
b.		50c Freedom From Fear	1.10	.65
c.		50c Freedom of Speech	1.10	.65
d.		50c Freedom of Worship	1.10	.65

Panes of No. 2839 contain two plate blocks, one containing a plate position diagram.

Moon Landing, 25th Anniv.

A2169

A2170

Designed by Paul and Chris Calle.

Printed by Stamp Venturers (#2841) and Banknote Corp. of America (#2842).

Miniature Sheet

LITHOGRAPHED

1994, July 20 Tagged *Perf. 11.2x11.1*

2841	A2169	29c Sheet of 12	11.00	—
a.		Single stamp	.90	.60

LITHOGRAPHED & ENGRAVED

Sheets of 120 in six panes of 20

Perf. 10.7x11.1

2842	A2170 $9.95	**multicolored**	20.00	16.00
		P# block of 4, 5#+B	82.50	—

LOCOMOTIVES

Hudson's General A2171

McQueen's Jupiter A2172

Eddy's No. 242 — A2173

Ely's No. 10 — A2174

Buchanan's No. 999 — A2175

Designed by Richard Leech.

Printed by J.W. Ferguson & Sons for Stamp Venturers.

PHOTOGRAVURE

1994, July 28 **Tagged** ***Perf. 11 Horiz.***

Booklet Stamps

2843	A2171	29c	**multicolored**	.70	.20
2844	A2172	29c	**multicolored**	.70	.20
2845	A2173	29c	**multicolored**	.70	.20
2846	A2174	29c	**multicolored**	.70	.20
2847	A2175	29c	**multicolored**	.70	.20
a.	Booklet pane of 5, #2843-2847			3.50	2.00
b.	As "a," imperf.			—	

GEORGE MEANY, LABOR LEADER (1894-1980)

A2176

Designed by Chris Calle.

ENGRAVED

Sheets of 200 in four panes of 50

1994, Aug. 16 **Tagged** ***Perf. 11.1x11***

2848	A2176	29c	**blue**	.60	.20
	P# block of 4, 1#			2.50	—

Panes of No. 2848 contain two plate blocks, one containing a plate position diagram.

AMERICAN MUSIC SERIES
Popular Singers

Al Jolson (1886-1950) A2177

Bing Crosby (1904-77) A2178

Ethel Waters (1896-1977) A2179

Nat "King" Cole (1919-65) A2180

Ethel Merman (1908-84) A2181

Jazz Singers

Bessie Smith (1894-1937) A2182

Muddy Waters (1915-83) A2183

Billie Holiday (1915-59) A2184

Robert Johnson (1911-38) A2185

Jimmy Rushing (1902-72) A2186

"Ma" Rainey (1886-1939) A2187

Mildred Bailey (1907-51) A2188

Howlin' Wolf (1910-76) A2189

Designed by Chris Payne (#2849-2853), Howard Koslow (#2854, 2856, 2858, 2860), Julian Allen (#2855, 2857, 2859, 2861).

Printed by J.W. Fergusson & Sons for Stamp Venturers (#2849-2853), Manhardt-Alexander for Ashton-Potter (USA) Ltd. (#2854-2861).

PHOTOGRAVURE

Plates of 180 in nine panes of 20, Plates of 210 in six panes of 35 (#2854-2861)

1994, Sept. 1 **Tagged** ***Perf. 10.1x10.2***

2849	A2177	29c	**multicolored**	.75	.20
2850	A2178	29c	**multicolored**	.75	.20
2851	A2179	29c	**multicolored**	.75	.20
2852	A2180	29c	**multicolored**	.75	.20
2853	A2181	29c	**multicolored**	.75	.20
a.	Vert. strip of 5, #2849-2853			3.75	2.00
	Vert. P# block of 6, 6#+S			8.00	—
	Horiz. P# block of 12, 2 sets of 6#+S, + top label			15.00	—
	Pane of 20			21.00	—
b.	Pane of 20, imperf			*4,600.*	

Some plate blocks of 6 will contain plate position diagram and copyright inscription, others will contain pane price inscription.

1994, Sept. 17 ***Perf. 11x10.8***

LITHOGRAPHED

2854	A2182	29c	**multicolored**	.75	.20
2855	A2183	29c	**multicolored**	.75	.20
2856	A2184	29c	**multicolored**	.75	.20
2857	A2185	29c	**multicolored**	.75	.20
2858	A2186	29c	**multicolored**	.75	.20
2859	A2187	29c	**multicolored**	.75	.20

2860	A2188 29c **multicolored**		.75	.20
2861	A2189 29c **multicolored**		.75	.20
a.	Block of 8, #2854-2861 +2 additional stamps		7.50	4.50
		Vert. P# block of 10, 5#+P	9.00	—
		P# block of 10, 2 sets of 5#+P, + top label	9.00	—
		Pane of 35	27.50	—

Vertical plate blocks contain either pane price inscription or copyright inscription.

Nos. 2854-2861 were available on the first day in 9 other cities.

LITERARY ARTS SERIES

James Thurber (1894-1961) — A2190

Designed by Richard Sheaff based on drawing by James Thurber.

LITHOGRAPHED & ENGRAVED
Plates of 200 in four panes of 50

1994, Sept. 10 **Tagged** ***Perf. 11***

2862	A2190 29c **multicolored**		.60	.20
		P# block of 4, 2#	2.75	—

Panes of No. 2862 contain two plate blocks, one containing a plate position diagram.

WONDERS OF THE SEA

Diver, Motorboat A2191

Diver, Ship — A2192

Diver, Ship's Wheel A2193

Diver, Coral — A2194

Designed by Charles Lynn Bragg.

Printed by Barton Press for Banknote Corporation of America.

LITHOGRAPHED
Plates of 216 in nine panes of 24

1994, Oct. 3 **Tagged** ***Perf. 11x10.9***

2863	A2191 29c **multicolored**		.60	.20
2864	A2192 29c **multicolored**		.60	.20
2865	A2193 29c **multicolored**		.60	.20
2866	A2194 29c **multicolored**		.60	.20
a.	Block of 4, #2863-2866		2.40	1.50
		P# block of 4, 4#+B	2.50	—
		Pane of 24	16.00	—
b.	As "a," imperf		*1,250.*	

CRANES

Black-Necked A2195

Whooping — A2196

Designed by Clarence Lee based on illustrations by Zhan Gengxi.

Printed by Barton Press for Banknote Corporation of America.

LITHOGRAPHED & ENGRAVED
Sheets of 120 in six panes of 20

1994, Oct. 9 **Tagged** ***Perf. 10.8x11***

2867	A2195 29c **multicolored**		.70	.20
2868	A2196 29c **multicolored**		.70	.20
a.	Pair, #2867-2868		1.40	.75
		P# block of 4, 5#+B	3.00	—
		Pane of 20	14.50	
b.	As "a," black & magenta (engr.) omitted		*1,650.*	
c.	As "a," double impression of engr. black (Birds' names and "USA") & magenta ("29")		*4,750.*	
d.	As "a," double impression of engr. black ("USA") & magenta ("29")			—

LEGENDS OF THE WEST

A2197

Illustration reduced.

g. Bill Pickett (1870-1932) (Revised)

Vertical Pair with Horizontal Gutter

Horizontal Pair with Vertical Gutter

Illustration reduced.

Designed by Mark Hess.

Printed by J.W. Fergusson & Sons for Stamp Venturers.

Designs: a, Home on the Range. b, Buffalo Bill Cody (1846-1917). c, Jim Bridger (1804-81). d, Annie Oakley (1860-1926). e, Native American Culture. f, Chief Joseph (c. 1840-1904). h, Bat Masterson (1853-1921). i, John C. Fremont (1813-90). j, Wyatt Earp (1848-1929). k, Nellie Cashman (c. 1849-1925). l, Charles Goodnight (1826-1929). m, Geronimo (1823-1909). n, Kit Carson (1809-68). o, Wild Bill Hickok (1837-76). p, Western Wildlife. q, Jim Beckwourth (c. 1798-1866). r, Bill Tilghman (1854-1924). s, Sacagawea (c. 1787-1812). t, Overland Mail.

PHOTOGRAVURE
Sheets of 120 in six panes of 20

1994, Oct. 18 **Tagged** ***Perf. 10.1x10***

2869	A2197	Pane of 20	15.00	10.00
a.-t.	29c any single		.75	.50
		Sheet of 120 (6 panes)	90.00	
		Cross gutter block of 20	25.00	—
		Vert. pairs with horiz. gutter (each)	2.50	—
		Horiz. pairs with vert. gutter (each)	2.50	—
u.	As No. 2869, a.-e. imperf. f.-j. part perf.			—

Cross gutter block of 20 consists of six stamps from each of two panes and four stamps from each of two other panes with the cross gutter between.

LEGENDS OF THE WEST (Recalled)

g. Bill Pickett (Recalled)

Nos. 2870b-2870d, 2870f-2870o, 2870q-2870s have a frameline around the vignette that is half the width of the frameline on similar stamps in No. 2869. Other design differences may exist.

PHOTOGRAVURE
Sheets of 120 in six panes of 20

1994 **Tagged** ***Perf. 10.1x10***
2870 A2197 29c Pane of 20 *260.00* —

150,000 panes of No. 2870 were made available through a drawing. Panes were delivered in an envelope. Value is for pane without envelope.

CHRISTMAS

Madonna and Child, by Elisabetta Sirani — A2200

Stocking — A2201

Santa Claus — A2202

Cardinal in Snow — A2203

Designed by Bradbury Thompson (#2871), Lou Nolan (#2872), Harry Zelenko (#2873), Peter Good (#2874).

Printed by Bureau of Engraving and Printing (#2871), Ashton-Potter USA, Ltd. (#2872), Avery Dennison (#2873-2874).

LITHOGRAPHED & ENGRAVED
Sheets of 300 in six panes of 50

1994, Oct. 20 **Tagged** ***Perf. 11¼***
2871 A2200 29c **multicolored,** shiny gum .70 .20
P# block of 4, 5# 3.00 —
Low gloss gum .70
P# block of 4, 5# 3.00

BOOKLET STAMP
Perf. 9¾x11

2871A A2200 29c **multicolored** .60 .20
b. Booklet pane of 10 6.25 3.50
c. Imperf, pair *500.00*

LITHOGRAPHED
Sheets of 400 in eight panes of 50
Perf. 11¼

2872 A2201 29c **multicolored** .60 .20
P# block of 4, 5#+P 2.50 —
a. Booklet pane of 20 12.50 4.00
b. Imperf., pair —
c. Vert. pair, imperf. horiz. —
d. Quadruple impression of black, triple impression of blue, double impression of red and yellow, green normal —
e. Vert. pair, imperf between —

Panes of Nos. 2871-2872 contain four plate blocks, one containing pane position diagram.

PHOTOGRAVURE
BOOKLET STAMPS
Self-Adhesive
Die Cut

2873 A2202 29c **multicolored** .70 .20
a. Booklet pane of 12 8.50
b. Coil with plate # V1111 — 6.00
P# strip of 5, P#V1111 9.00

Except for No. 2873b with plate number, coil stamps are indistinguishable from booklet stamps once they are removed from the backing paper.

2874 A2203 29c **multicolored** .60 .20
a. Booklet pane of 18 11.00

BUREAU OF ENGRAVING & PRINTING
Souvenir Sheet

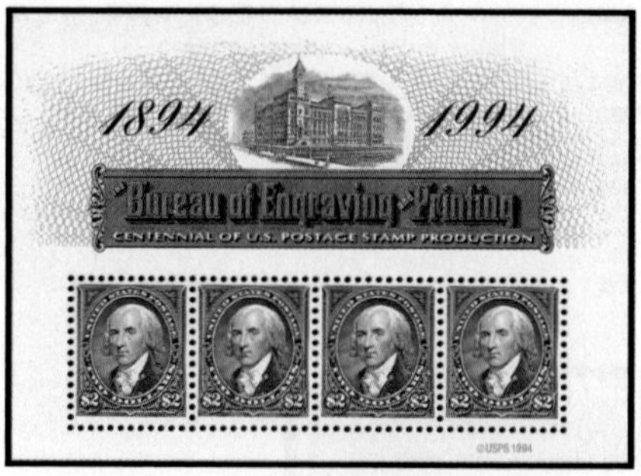

A2204

Illustration reduced.

Major Double Transfer

Minor Double Transfer

Designed by Peter Cocci, using original die for Type A98.

LITHOGRAPHED & ENGRAVED

1994, Nov. 3 **Tagged** ***Perf. 11***
2875 A2204 $2 Sheet of 4 16.00 13.50
a. Single stamp 4.00 2.00
Sheet of 4 with major double transfer on right stamp *90.00* —
Major double transfer, single stamp — —
Sheet of 4 with minor double transfer on right stamp *35.00* —
Minor double transfer, single stamp — —

CHINESE NEW YEAR

Year of the Boar — A2205

Designed by Clarence Lee.

Printed by Stamp Venturers.

PHOTOGRAVURE
Panes of 20

1994, Dec. 30 **Tagged** ***Perf. 11.2x11.1***
2876 A2205 29c **multicolored** .70 .20
P# block of 4, 5#+S 3.00 —
Pane of 20 15.00 —

See No. 3895k.

The first class rate was increased to 32c on Jan. 1, 1995.

A2206

A2207

A2208

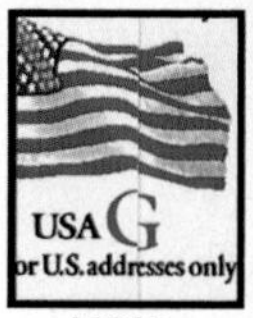

A2208a

A2209

Designed by Richard D. Sheaff (#2877-2878), Lou Nolan (#2879-2892).

Printed by American Bank Note Co. (#2877, 2884, 2890), Bureau of Engraving and Printing (#2879, 2881, 2883, 2889), Stamp Venturers (#2878, 2880, 2882, 2888, 2891-2892), KCS Industries (#2885), Avery-Dennison (#2886-2887).

Coil Plate No. Strips of 3
Beginning with No. 2123, coil plate no. strips of 3 usually sell at the level of strips of 5 minus the face value of two stamps.

LITHOGRAPHED
Sheets of 100

1994, Dec. 13 **Untagged** ***Perf. 11x10.8***
2877 A2206 (3c) **tan, bright blue & red** .20 .20
P# block of 4, 3#+A .30 —
Zip block of 4 .25 —
a. Imperf., pair *135.00*
b. Double impression of red *190.00*

No. 2877 imperf and with blue omitted is known from printer's waste.

Perf. 10.8x10.9

2878 A2206 (3c) **tan, dark blue & red** .20 .20
P# block of 4, 3#+S .40 —
Zip block of 4 .25 —

Inscriptions on #2877 are in a thin typeface. Those on #2878 are in heavy, bold type.

PHOTOGRAVURE
Tagged
Perf. 11.2x11.1

2879 A2207 (20c) **black "G," yellow & multi** .40 .20
P# block of 4, 5# 8.50 —
Zip block of 4 1.75 —
a. Imperf., pair —

Perf. 11x10.9

2880 A2207 (20c) **red "G," yellow & multi** .75 .20
P# block of 4, 5#+S 17.50 —
Zip block of 4 3.25 —

Perf. 11.2x11.1

2881 A2208 (32c) **black "G" & multi** 1.00 .20
P# block of 4, 4# *70.00* —
Zip block of 4 *5.50* —
a. Booklet pane of 10 6.00 3.75

Perf. 11x10.9

2882 A2208a (32c) **red "G" & multi** .60 .20
P# block of 4, 4#+S 4.00 —
Zip block of 4 2.75 —

Distance on #2882 from bottom of red G to top of flag immediately above is 13¾mm. Illustration A2208a shows #2885 superimposed over #2882.

BOOKLET STAMPS
Perf. 10x9.9 on 2 or 3 Sides

2883 A2208 (32c) **black "G" & multi** .65 .20
a. Booklet pane of 10 6.50 3.75

Perf. 10.9 on 2 or 3 Sides

2884 A2208 (32c) **blue "G" & multi** .65 .20
a. Booklet pane of 10 6.50 3.75

b. As "a," imperf *1,700.*

Perf. 11x10.9 on 2 or 3 Sides

2885 A2208a (32c) **red "G" & multi** .90 .20
a. Booklet pane of 10 9.00 4.50
b. Horiz. pair, imperf vert. —
c. Horiz. pair, imperf between —

Distance on #2885 from bottom of red G to top of flag immediately above is 13½mm. See note below #2882.

No. 2885c resulted from a paper foldover after perforating and before cutting into panes.

A2208b

A2208c

Self-Adhesive *Die Cut*

2886 A2208b (32c) **gray, blue, light blue, red & black** .75 .20
a. Booklet pane of 18 14.00
b. Coil with plate # V11111 — 10.00
P# strip of 5, same # 11.50

No. 2886 is printed on surface-tagged paper which is opaque, thicker and brighter than that of No. 2887 and has only a small number of blue shading dots in the white stripes immediately below the flag's blue field.

Except for No. 2886b with plate number, coil stamps are indistinguishable from booklet stamps once they are removed from the backing paper.

2887 A2208c (32c) **black, blue & red** .75 .20
a. Booklet pane of 18 14.00

No. 2887 has noticeable blue shading in the white stripes immediately below the blue field and has overall tagging. The paper is translucent, thinner and duller than No. 2886.

COIL STAMPS

Perf. 9.8 Vert.

2888 A2209 (25c) **black "G," blue & multi** .90 .50
Pair 1.80 1.00
P# strip of 5, #S11111 4.00
P# single, #S11111 2.50
2889 A2208 (32c) **black "G" & multi** 1.50 .20
Pair 3.00 .30
P# strip of 5, #1111, 2222 10.00
P# single, #1111, 2222 — 4.50
a. Imperf., pair *275.00*
2890 A2208 (32c) **blue "G" & multi** .65 .20
Pair 1.25 .30
P# strip of 5, #A1111, A1112, A1113, A1211, A1212, A1311, A1313, A1324, A2211, A2212, A2213, A2214, A3113, A3314, A3323, A3324, A3433, A3435, A3436, A4427, A5327, A5417, A5427 4.75
P# strip of 5, #A1222, A1314, A4426, A5437 6.25
P# strip of 5, #A1417, A2223 8.75
P# strip of 5, #A1433 9.25
P# strip of 5, #A2313 9.00
P# strip of 5, #A3114, A3315, A3423 8.50
P# strip of 5, #A3426 6.75
P# strip of 5, #A4435 *240.00*
P# single, #A1111, A1313, A2214, A3113, A3314, A3324, A4427, A5427 — 1.00
P# single, #A1212, A3323 — 3.00
P# single, #A2212, A3435 — 3.50
P# single, #A1112, A1311, A1324, A2213, A5327 — 2.50
P# single, #A1113, A5437 — 3.75
P# single, #A3315, A3423, A3426 4.75
P# single, #A1222, A2211, A3114 — 4.25
P# single, #A1211, A1314, A4426 4.00
P# single, #A1417, A1433 — 6.75
P# single, #A2223, A2313 — 6.00
P# single, #A3433, A3436 — 2.00
P# single, #A4435 — *240.00*
P# single, #A5417 3.00
2891 A2208 (32c) **red "G" & multi** .85 .20
Pair 1.70 .30
P# strip of 5, #S1111 4.75
P# single, #S1111 — 1.00

Rouletted 9.8 Vert.

2892 A2208 (32c) **red "G" & multi** .75 .20
Pair 1.50 .30
P# strip of 5, #S1111, S2222 5.25
P# single, #S1111, S2222 — 1.00

See note under No. 2525.

A2210

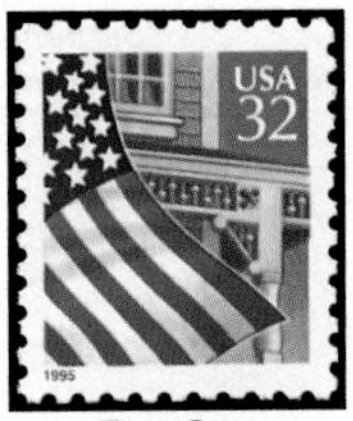

Flag Over Porch — A2212

Designed by Lou Nolan (#2893), Dave LaFleur (#2897).

Printed by American Bank Note Co. (#2893), Stamp Venturers (#2897).

PHOTOGRAVURE
COIL STAMP

1995 **Untagged** ***Perf. 9.8 Vert.***

2893 A2210 (5c) **green & multi** .50 .20
Pair 1.00 .20
P# strip of 5, #A11111, A21111 3.50
P# single, #A11111, A21111 — 1.60

No. 2893 was only available through the Philatelic Fullfillment Center (and, for a short time, at the L'Enfant Plaza Philatelic Center in Washington, DC) after its announcement 1/12/95. Covers submitted for first day cancels received a 12/13/94 cancel, even though the stamps were not available on that date.

Sheets of 400 in four panes of 100

1995, May 19 **Tagged** ***Perf. 10.4***

2897 A2212 32c **multicolored,** .65 .20
P# block of 4, 5#+S 4.25 —
a. Imperf., vert. pair *65.00*

See Nos. 2913-2916, 2920-2921, 3133. For booklet see No. BK243.

Butte — A2217

Mountain — A2218

Auto — A2220

Auto Tail Fin — A2223

Juke Box — A2225

Flag Over Field — A2230

Designed by Tom Engeman (#2902-2904B), Robert Brangwynne (#2905-2906), Chris Calle (#2907), Bill Nelson (#2908-2912B), Dave LaFleur (#2913-2916, 2921), Sabra Field (#2919).

Printed by J.W. Fergusson & Sons for Stamp Venturers (#2902, 2905, 2909, 2912, 2914), Bureau of Engraving and Printing (#2903, 2904B, 2908, 2911, 2912B, 2913, 2915A, 2915C-2915D, 2916, 2921), Stamp Venturers (#2902B, 2904, 2906-2907, 2910, 2912A, 2915B), Avery Dennison (#2904A, 2915, 2919, 2920).

Coil Plate No. Strips of 3
Beginning with No. 2123, coil plate No. strips of 3 usually sell at the level of strips of 5 minus the face value of two stamps.

COIL STAMPS
PHOTOGRAVURE

1995-97 **Untagged** ***Perf. 9.8 Vert.***

Self-Adhesive (#2902B, 2904A-2904B, 2906-2907, 2910, 2912A, 2912B, 2915-2915D, 2919-2921)

2902 A2217 (5c) **yellow, red & blue,** *Mar. 10* .20 .20
Pair .20 .20
P# strip of 5, #S111, S222, S333 1.25
P# single, #S111, S222, S333 — .70
a. Imperf., pair 600.00

Serpentine Die Cut 11.5 Vert.

2902B A2217 (5c) **yellow, red & blue,** *June 15, 1996* .35 .20
Pair .70
P# strip of 5, #S111 2.10
P# single, #S111 — .80

Perf. 9.8 Vert.

2903 A2218 (5c) **purple & multi,** *Mar. 16, 1996* .25 .20
Pair .50 .20
P# strip of 5, #11111 1.25
P# single, #11111 — .90
a. Tagged (error) 4.00 3.50
P# strip of 5, #11111 65.00
P# single, #11111 — 70.00

Letters of inscription "USA NONPROFIT ORG." outlined in purple on #2903.

2904 A2218 (5c) **blue & multi,** *Mar. 16, 1996* .20 .20
Pair .40 .20
P# strip of 5, #S111 1.25
P# single, #S111 — .80
c. Imperf., pair 425.00

Letters of inscription have no outline on #2904.

Serpentine Die Cut 11.2 Vert.

2904A A2218 (5c) **purple & multi,** *June 15, 1996* .40 .20
Pair .80
P# strip of 5, #V222222, V333323, V333342 4.00
P# strip of 5, #V333333 2.75
P# strip of 5, #V333343 3.00
P# single, #V222222, V333323, V333333, V333342 — 2.25
P# single, #V333343 3.75

Serpentine Die Cut 9.8 Vert.

2904B A2218 (5c) **purple & multi,** *Jan. 24, 1997* .20 .20
pair .40
P# strip of 5, #1111 1.40
P# single, #1111 — 1.00

Letters of inscription outlined in purple on #2904B, not outlined on No. 2904A.

Perf. 9.8 Vert.

2905 A2220 (10c) **black, red brown & brown,** small "1995" date, *Mar. 10* .20 .20
Pair .40 .40
P# strip of 5, #S111, S222 2.00
P# single, #S111, S222 — 1.25
a. Large "1995" date, *1996* .20 .20
Pair .40 .40
P# strip of 5, #S333 2.25
P# single, #S333 — 1.50
b. As "a," brown omitted, P#S33 single —

Date on 2905 is approximately 1.9mm long, on No. 2905a 2.1mm long.

Serpentine Die Cut 11.5 Vert.

2906 A2220 (10c) **black, brown & red brown,** *June 15, 1996* .40 .20
Pair .80
P# strip of 5, #S111 2.25
P# single, #S111 — 1.50
2907 A1957 (10c) **gold & multi,** *May 21, 1996* .75 .20
Pair 1.50
P# strip of 5, #S11111 4.00
P# single, #S11111 — 2.25

Perf. 9.8 Vert.

2908 A2223 (15c) **dark orange yellow & multi,** tagged, *Mar. 17* .30 .30
Pair .60 .60
P# strip of 5, #11111 2.50
P# single, #11111 — 2.00

No. 2908 has dark, bold colors, heavy shading lines and heavily shaded chrome.

2909 A2223 (15c) **buff & multi,** *Mar. 17* .30 .30

Pair .60 .60
P# strip of 5, #S11111 2.50
P# single, #S11111 — 1.75

No. 2909 has shinier chrome, more subdued colors and finer details than No. 2908.

Serpentine Die Cut 11.5 Vert.

2910 A2223 (15c) **buff & multi,** *June 15, 1996* .30 .30
Pair .60
P# strip of 5, #S11111 2.50
P# single, #S11111 — 1.75

Perf. 9.8 Vert.

2911 A2225 (25c) **dark red, dark yellow green & multi,** *Mar. 17* .50 .50
Pair 1.00 1.00
P# strip of 5, #111111, 212222, 222222, 332222 4.00
P# single, #111111, 212222, 222222 — 2.25
P# single, #332222 — 2.75
a. Imperf, pair —

No. 2911 has dark, saturated colors and dark blue lines in the music selection board.

2912 A2225 (25c) **bright orange red, bright yellow green & multi,** *Mar. 17* .50 .50
Pair 1.00 1.00
P# strip of 5, #S11111, S22222 3.50
P# single, same # — 2.00

No. 2912 has bright colors, less shading and light blue lines in the music selection board.

Serpentine Die Cut 11.5 Vert.

2912A A2225 (25c) **bright orange red, bright yellow green & multi,** *June 15, 1996* .50 .50
Pair 1.00
P# strip of 5, #S11111, S22222 3.75
P# single, same # — 1.60

Serpentine Die Cut 9.8 Vert.

2912B A2225 (25c) **dark red, dark yellow green & multi,** *Jan. 24, 1997* .75 .50
pair 1.50
P# strip of 5, #111111 4.00
P# strip of 5, #222222 5.00
P# single, #111111 — 1.50
P# single, #222222 — 3.50

See No. 3132.

Tagged

Perf. 9.8 Vert.

2913 A2212 32c **blue, tan, brown, red & light blue,** shiny gum, *May 19* .65 .20
Pair 1.30 .30
P# strip of 5, #11111, 22221 5.00
P# strip of 5, #22222 5.25
P# single, #11111, 22222 — 2.75
P# single, #22221 — 3.50
Low gloss gum .65
Pair 1.30
P# strip of 5, #11111, 22222, 33333, 34333, 44444, 45444, 66646, 77767, 78767, 91161, 99969 4.50
P# strip of 5, #22322 8.00
P# strip of 5, #66666 11.00
P# single, #22322 — 5.75
P# single, #33333, 34333, 44444, 45444, 66646, 77767 — 1.50
P# single, #66666 — 8.00
P# single, #78767, 91161, 99969 — 2.25
a. Imperf., pair 32.50

No. 2913 has pronounced light blue shading in the flag and red "1995" at left bottom. See No. 3133.

2914 A2212 32c **blue, yellow brown, red & gray,** *May 19* .80 .20
Pair 1.60 .30
P# strip of 5, #S11111 4.50
P# single, #S11111 — 2.00

No. 2914 has pale gray shading in the flag and blue "1995" at left bottom.

Serpentine Die Cut 8.7 Vert.

2915 A2212 32c **multicolored,** *Apr. 18* 1.25 .30
Pair 2.50
P# strip of 5, #V11111 10.50
P# single, #V11111 — 8.75

Serpentine Die Cut 9.8 Vert.

2915A A2212 32c **dk blue, tan, brown, red & light blue,** *May 21, 1996* .65 .20
Pair 1.30
P# strip of 5, #11111, 22222, 23222, 33333, 44444, 45444, 55555, 66666, 78777, 88888, 99999, 11111A, 13231A, 13311A, 22222A, 33333A, 44444A, 55555A, 66666A, 77777A, 78777A, 88888A 4.25
P# strip of 5, #87888 52.50
P# strip of 5, #87898 12.00
P# strip of 5, #88898 *210.00*
P# strip of 5, #89878, 97898 9.00
P# strip of 5, #89888 16.00
P# strip of 5, #89898 8.00
P# strip of 5, #89899 *450.00*
P# strip of 5, #99899 15.00
P# strip of 5, #13211A 80.00
P# single, #11111, 22222, 23222, 33333, 44444, 45444, 55555, 66666, 78777, 88888, 99999, 11111A, 13231A,13311A, 22222A, 33333A, 44444A, 55555A, 66666A, 77777A, 78777A, 88888A — 1.00
P# single, #87888 — *30.00*
P# single, #87898, 89878, 97898 — 4.00
P# single, #88898 — *175.00*
P# single, #89888 — 10.00
P# single, #89898 — 2.75
P# single, #89899 — 225.00
P# single, #99899 — 32.50
P# single, #13211A — *75.00*
h. Die cutting omitted, pair 32.50
i. Tan omitted *2,000.*
j. Double die cutting 30.00

No. 2915A has red "1996" at left bottom.

Die cutting on No. 2915A shows either 10 serpentine "peaks" on each side, 11 "peaks" on the left side and 10 "peaks" on the right side, or 10 "peaks" on the left side and 11 "peaks" on the right side. The last configuration is considered by specialists to be an error, and it is rare.

Sky on No. 3133 shows color gradation at LR not on No. 2915A.

On No. 2915Ai all other colors except brown are severely shifted.

On No. 2915Aj, the second die cutting is a different gauge than the normal 9.8.

Plate number 99999 strips of No. 2915A are known with the brown date number shifted one stamp to the right of the stamp with the other plate numbers. Such strips are scarce. Value of mint never hinged P# strip of 5 or 6, $1,500. Used examples are rare.

Serpentine Die Cut 11.5 Vert.

2915B A2212 32c **dk blue, tan, brown, red & light blue,** *June 15, 1996* 1.00 *.90*
Pair 2.00
P# strip of 5, #S11111 6.00
P# single, #S11111 — 2.75

Serpentine Die Cut 10.9 Vert.

2915C A2212 32c **dk blue, tan, brown, red & light blue,** *May 21, 1996* 2.00 .40
Pair 4.00
P# strip of 5, #55555, 66666 27.50
P# single, #55555, 66666 — 4.75
P# single, #88888 *3,000.*

Plate number 55555 strips of No. 2915C are known with the tan plate number shifted one stamp to the left of the stamp with the other plate numbers. Extremely scarce. Last reported auction sale price (2006) was approximately $5,250.

Serpentine Die Cut 9.8 Vert.

2915D A2212 32c **dark blue, tan, brown, red & light blue,** *Jan. 24, 1997* 2.00 *.90*
pair 4.00
P# strip of 5, #11111 9.00
P# single, #11111 — 3.00

No. 2915D shows 9 "peaks" at left and 10 at right or 10 "peaks" at left and 10 at right.

Stamps on multiples of No. 2915A touch, and are on a peelable backing the same size as the stamps, while those of No. 2915D are separated on the peelable backing, which is larger than the stamps.

No. 2915D has red "1997" at left bottom; No. 2915A has red "1996" at left bottom.

Sky on No. 3133 shows color gradation at LR not on No. 2915D, and it has blue "1996" at left bottom.

BOOKLET STAMPS

Perf. 10.8x9.8 on 2 or 3 Adjacent Sides

2916 A2212 32c **blue, tan, brown, red & light blue,** *May 19* .65 .20
a. Booklet pane of 10 6.50 3.25
b. As "a," imperf. —

Die Cut

2919 A2230 32c **multicolored,** *Mar. 17* .65 .20
a. Booklet pane of 18 12.00
b. Vert. pair, die cutting omitted btwn. —

Serpentine Die Cut 8.7 on 2, 3 or 4 Adjacent Sides

2920 A2212 32c **multicolored,** dated blue "1995," *Apr. 18* .65 .20
a. Booklet pane of 20+label 13.00
b. Small date 5.50 .35
c. As "b," booklet pane of 20+label *110.00*
f. As No. 2920, pane of 15+label *10.00*
g. As "a," partial pane of 10, 3 stamps and parts of 7 stamps printed on backing liner —
h. As No. 2920, booklet pane of 15 *35.00*
i. As No. 2920, die cutting omitted, pair —
j. Dark blue omitted (from No. 2920a) —
k. Vert. pair, die cutting missing between (PS) (from No. 2920a) —

Date on No. 2920 is nearly twice as large as date on No. 2920b. No. 2920f comes in various configurations.

No. 2920h is a pane of 16 with one stamp removed. The missing stamp is the lower right stamp in the pane or (more rarely) the upper left stamp. No. 2920h cannot be made from No. 2920f, a pane of 15 + label. The label is located in the sixth or seventh row of the pane and is die cut. If the label is removed, an impression of the die cutting appears on the backing paper.

Serpentine Die Cut 11.3 on 3 sides

2920D A2212 32c **multicolored,** dated blue "1996," *Jan. 20, 1996* .80 .25
e. Booklet pane of 10 8.00

Serpentine Die Cut 9.8 on 2 or 3 Adjacent Sides

2921 A2212 32c **dk bl, tan, brn, red & lt bl,** dated red 1996, *May 21, 1996* .90 .20
a. Booklet pane of 10, dated red "1996" 9.00
b. As No. 2921, dated red "1997," *Jan. 24, 1997* 1.20 .20
c. As "a," dated red "1997" 12.00
d. Booklet pane of 5 + label, dated red "1997," *Jan. 24, 1997* 7.00
e. As "a," die cutting omitted *225.00*

Scott values for used self-adhesive stamps are for examples either on piece or off piece.

GREAT AMERICANS ISSUE

A2248

A2249

A2250

A2251

A2253

A2255

A2256

A2257

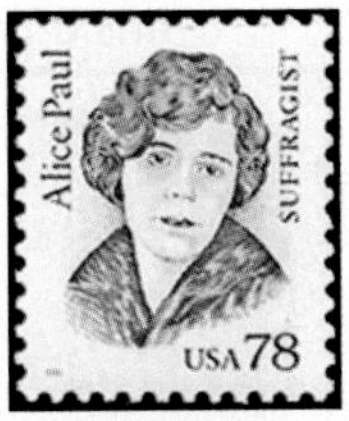

A2258

Designed by Dennis Lyall (#2933-2934), Richard Sheaff (#2935), Howard Paine (#2936, 2941-2942), Roy Andersen (#2938), Chris Calle (#2940, 2943).
Printed by Banknote Corporation of America (#2933-2935, 2940-2943), Ashton-Potter (USA) Ltd. (#2936), Bureau of Engraving & Printing (#2938).

ENGRAVED
Sheets of 400 in four panes of 100
Sheets of 160 in eight panes of 20 (#2935)
Sheets of 120 in six panes of 20 (#2936, 2941-2942)

1995-99 **Tagged**

Self-Adhesive (#2941-2942)

Perf. 11.2, Serpentine Die Cut 11.7x11.5 (#2941-2942)

2933 A2248 32c **brown,** prephosphored coated paper (solid tagging), *Sept. 13, 1995* .65 .20
P# block of 4, 1#+B 3.00 —
2934 A2249 32c **green,** prephosphored coated paper (solid tagging), *Apr. 26, 1996* .65 .25
P# block of 4, 1#+B 3.00 —
a. Prephosphored coated paper (grainy solid tagging) —
2935 A2250 32c **lake,** prephosphored coated paper (grainy solid tagging), *Apr. 3, 1998* .65 .35
P# block of 4, 1#+B 3.00 —
Pane of 20 14.75
2936 A2251 32c **blue,** prephosphored coated paper (solid tagging), *July 16, 1998* .65 .35
P# block of 4, 1#+P 3.00 —
Pane of 20 14.75 —
a. 32c **light blue** .65 .35
P# block of 4, 1#+P 3.00 —
Pane of 20 14.75 —
2938 A2253 46c **carmine,** prephosphored uncoated paper (mottled tagging), *Oct. 20, 1995* .90 .30
P# block of 4, 1# 4.50 —
2940 A2255 55c **green,** prephosphored coated paper (grainy solid tagging), *July 11, 1995* 1.10 .20
P# block of 4, 1#+B 5.50 —
a. Imperf, pair —
2941 A2256 55c **black,** prephosphored coated paper (solid tagging), *July 17, 1999* 1.10 .20
P# block of 4, 1#+B 4.40
Pane of 20 22.00
2942 A2257 77c **blue,** prephosphored coated paper (solid tagging), *Nov. 9, 1998* 1.50 .40
P# block of 4, 1#+B 6.00
Pane of 20 30.00
2943 A2258 78c **bright violet,** prephosphored coated paper (solid tagging), *Aug. 18, 1995* 1.60 .20
P# block of 4, 1#+B 7.50 —
a. 78c **dull violet,** prephosphored coated paper (grainy solid tagging) 1.60 .25
P# block of 4, 1#+B 7.50 —
b. 78c **pale violet,** prephosphored coated paper (grainy solid tagging) 1.75 .30
P# block of 4, 1#+B 12.00 —

The pale violet ink on No. 2943b luminesces bright pink under long-wave ultraviolet light.

LOVE

Cherub from Sistine Madonna, by Raphael
A2263 A2264

Designed by Terry McCaffrey.

Printed by the Bureau of Engraving and Printing (#2948) and Banknote Corp. of America (#2949).

LITHOGRAPHED & ENGRAVED
Sheets of 300 in six panes of 50

1995, Feb. 1 **Tagged** ***Perf. 11.2***

2948 A2263 (32c) **multicolored** .65 .20
P# block of 4, 5# 3.00 —

Self-Adhesive

Die Cut

2949 A2264 (32c) **multicolored** .65 .20
a. Booklet pane of 20 + label 13.00
b. Red (engr.) omitted *375.00*
c. As "a," red (engr.) omitted *7,500.*
d. Red (engr.) missing (CM) —

No. 2949d must be collected se-tenant with a normal stamp. See Nos. 2957-2960, 3030.

Florida Statehood, 150th Anniv.
A2265

Designed by Laura Smith.
Printed by Ashton-Potter (USA) Ltd.

LITHOGRAPHED
Sheets of 160 in eight panes of 20

1995, Mar. 3 **Tagged** ***Perf. 11.1***

2950 A2265 32c **multicolored** .65 .20
P# block of 4, 5#+P 2.60 —
Pane of 20 13.00 —

EARTH DAY

Earth Clean-Up
A2266

Solar Energy
A2267

Tree Planting
A2268

Beach Clean-Up
A2269

Designed by Christy Millard (#2951), Jennifer Michalove (#2952), Brian Hailes (#2953) and Melody Kiper (#2954).
Printed by Ashton-Potter (USA) Ltd.

LITHOGRAPHED
Sheets of 96 in six panes of 16

1995, Apr. 20 **Tagged** ***Perf. 11.1x11***

2951 A2266 32c **multicolored** .65 .20
2952 A2267 32c **multicolored** .65 .20
2953 A2268 32c **multicolored** .65 .20
2954 A2269 32c **multicolored** .65 .20
a. Block of 4, #2951-2954 2.60 1.75

P# block of 4, 5#+P 2.60 —
Horiz. P# block of 8, 2 sets of 5#+P, + top or bottom label 5.25 —
Pane of 16 10.50 —

A2270 A2271

RICHARD M. NIXON

37th President (1913-94)

Designed by Daniel Schwartz.
Printed by Barton Press and Bank Note Corp. of America.

LITHOGRAPHED & ENGRAVED
Sheets of 200 in four panes of 50

1995, Apr. 26 **Tagged** ***Perf. 11.2***

2955 A2270 32c **multicolored** .65 .20
P# block of 4, 5#+B 3.00 —
a. Red (engr.) missing (CM) *1,100.*

No. 2955 is known with red (engr. "Richard Nixon") inverted, and with red engr. omitted but only half the Nixon portrait present, both from printer's waste. No. 2955a shows a complete Nixon portrait.

BLACK HERITAGE SERIES

Bessie Coleman (d. 1926), Aviator

Designed by Chris Calle.

ENGRAVED
Sheets of 200 in four panes of 50

1995, Apr. 27 **Tagged** ***Perf. 11.2***

2956 A2271 32c **red & black** .85 .20
P# block of 4, 1# 3.75 —

LOVE

A2272 A2273

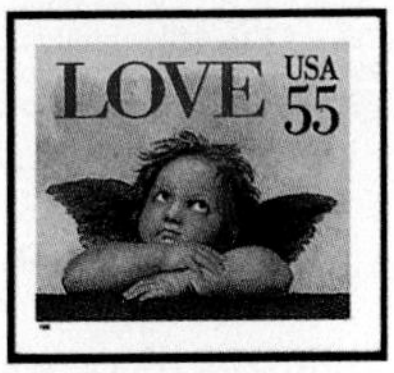

Cherubs from Sistine Madonna, by Raphael — A2274

Designed by Terry McCaffrey.
Printed by Bureau of Engraving and Printing (#2957-2959), Bank Note Corp. of America (#2960).

LITHOGRAPHED & ENGRAVED
Sheets of 300 in six panes of 50

1995, May 12 **Tagged** ***Perf. 11.2***

2957 A2272 32c **multicolored** .65 .20
P# block of 4, 5# 3.00 —
Copyright block of 6 4.25 —

Compare with No. 3030. For booklet see No. BK244.

2958 A2273 55c **multicolored** 1.10 .20
P# block of 4, 5# 5.50 —

BOOKLET STAMPS

Perf. 9.8x10.8

2959 A2272 32c **multicolored** .65 .20
a. Booklet pane of 10 6.50 3.25
b. Imperf, pair —

Self-Adhesive

Die Cut

2960 A2274 55c **multicolored** 1.10 .20
a. Booklet pane of 20 + label 22.50

RECREATIONAL SPORTS

Volleyball
A2275

Softball
A2276

Bowling
A2277

Tennis
A2278

Golf — A2279

Designed by Don Weller.
Printed by Bank Note Corp. of America.

LITHOGRAPHED
Sheets of 120 in six panes of 20

1995, May 20	**Tagged**	***Perf. 11.2***	
2961 A2275 32c **multicolored**		.65	.20
2962 A2276 32c **multicolored**		.65	.20
2963 A2277 32c **multicolored**		.65	.20
2964 A2278 32c **multicolored**		.65	.20
2965 A2279 32c **multicolored**		.65	.20
a. Vert. strip of 5, #2961-2965		3.25	2.00
P# block of 10, 2 sets of 4#+B		6.50	—
Pane of 20		13.00	—
b. As "a," imperf		*2,250.*	
c. As "a," yellow omitted		*2,000.*	
d. As "a," yellow, blue & magenta omitted		*2,000.*	

PRISONERS OF WAR & MISSING IN ACTION

A2280

Designed by Carl Herrman.
Printed by Ashton-Potter (USA) Ltd.

LITHOGRAPHED
Sheets of 160 in eight panes of 20

1995, May 29	**Tagged**	***Perf. 11.2***	
2966 A2280 32c **multicolored**		.65	.20
P# block of 4, 5#+P		2.50	—
Pane of 20		12.50	—

The five plate numbers do not include a sixth plate number for the plate that applied a transparent laquer "color."

LEGENDS OF HOLLYWOOD

Marilyn Monroe (1926-62) — A2281

Cross Gutter Block of 8

Illustration reduced.

Designed by Michael Deas.
Printed by Stamp Venturers.

PHOTOGRAVURE
Sheets of 120 in six panes of 20

1995, June 1	**Tagged**	***Perf. 11.1***	
2967 A2281 32c **multicolored**		.85	.20
P# block of 4, 6#+S		5.50	—
Pane of 20		25.00	
Sheet of 120 (six panes)		150.00	
Cross gutter block of 8		55.00	—
Block of 8 with vertical gutter		45.00	—
Horiz. pair with vert. gutter		7.50	—
Vert. pair with horiz. gutter		4.00	—
a. Imperf., pair		*475.00*	
Pane of 20, imperf.		*5,250.*	

Perforations in corner of each stamp are star-shaped.

TEXAS STATEHOOD

A2282

Designed by Laura Smith.
Printed by Sterling Sommer for Ashton-Potter (USA) Ltd.

LITHOGRAPHED
Sheets of 120 in six panes of 20

1995, June 16	**Tagged**	***Perf. 11.2***	
2968 A2282 32c **multicolored**		.75	.20
P# block of 4, 6#+P		3.00	—
Pane of 20		15.00	—

GREAT LAKES LIGHTHOUSES

Split Rock, Lake Superior — A2283

St. Joseph, Lake Michigan — A2284

Spectacle Reef, Lake Huron — A2285

Marblehead, Lake Erie — A2286

Thirty Mile Point, Lake Ontario — A2287

Designed by Howard Koslow.
Printed by Stamp Venturers.

PHOTOGRAVURE
BOOKLET STAMPS

1995, June 17	**Tagged**	***Perf. 11.2 Vert.***	
2969 A2283 32c **multicolored**		1.25	.30
2970 A2284 32c **multicolored**		1.25	.30
2971 A2285 32c **multicolored**		1.25	.30
2972 A2286 32c **multicolored**		1.25	.30
2973 A2287 32c **multicolored**		1.25	.30
a. Booklet pane of 5, #2969-2973		6.25	3.00

U.N., 50th ANNIV.

A2288

Designed by Howard Paine.
Printed by Banknote Corp. of America.

ENGRAVED
Sheets of 180 in nine panes of 20

1995, June 26	**Tagged**	***Perf. 11.2***	
2974 A2288 32c **blue**		.65	.20
P# block of 4, 1#+B		2.60	—
Pane of 20		13.00	—

CIVIL WAR

A2289

Illustration reduced.

Designed by Mark Hess.

Printed by Stamp Venturers.

Designs: a, Monitor and Virginia. b, Robert E. Lee. c, Clara Barton. d, Ulysses S. Grant. e, Battle of Shiloh. f, Jefferson Davis. g, David Farragut. h, Frederick Douglass. i, Raphael Semmes. j, Abraham Lincoln. k, Harriet Tubman. l, Stand Watie. m, Joseph E. Johnston. n, Winfield Hancock. o, Mary Chesnut. p, Battle of Chancellorsville. q, William T. Sherman. r, Phoebe Pember. s, "Stonewall" Jackson. t, Battle of Gettysburg.

PHOTOGRAVURE

Sheets of 120 in six panes of 20

1995, June 29 Tagged *Perf. 10.1*

2975	A2289 Pane of 20	35.00	17.50
a.-t.	32c any single	1.50	.60
	Sheet of 120 (6 panes)	200.00	
	Cross gutter block of 20	42.50	—
	Vert. pairs with horiz. gutter (each)	5.00	—
	Horiz. pairs with vert. gutter (each)	5.00	—
u.	As No. 2975, a.-e. imperf, f.-j. part perf, others perf	—	
v.	As No. 2975, k.-t. imperf, f.-j. part perf, others perf	—	
w.	As No. 2975, imperf	*1,500.*	
x.	Block of 9 (f.-h., k.-m., p.-r.) k.-l. & p.-q. imperf. vert.	—	
y.	As No. 2975, a.-b. perf, c., f.-h. part perf, others imperf	—	
z.	As No. 2975, o. and t. imperf, j., n. & s. part perf, others perf	—	

Cross gutter block of 20 consists of six stamps from each of two panes and four stamps from each of two other panes with the cross gutter between.

AMERICAN FOLK ART SERIES
Carousel Horses

A2290

A2291

A2292

A2293

Designed by Paul Calle.
Printed at Sterling Sommer for Ashton-Potter (USA) Ltd.

LITHOGRAPHED

Sheets of 160 in eight panes of 20

1995, July 21 Tagged *Perf. 11*

2976	A2290 32c **multicolored**	.65	.20
2977	A2291 32c **multicolored**	.65	.20
2978	A2292 32c **multicolored**	.65	.20
2979	A2293 32c **multicolored**	.65	.20
a.	Block of 4, #2976-2979	2.60	2.00
	P# block of 4, 5#+P	2.60	—
	Pane of 20	13.00	—

WOMAN SUFFRAGE

A2294

Designed by April Greiman.
Printed by Ashton-Potter (USA) Ltd.

LITHOGRAPHED & ENGRAVED

Sheets of 160 in four panes of 40

1995, Aug. 26 Tagged *Perf. 11.1x11*

2980	A2294 32c **multicolored**	.65	.20
	P# block of 4, 5#+P	3.00	—
a.	Black (engr.) omitted	*375.00*	
b.	Imperf., pair	*1,250.*	
c.	Vert. pair, imperf between and at bottom	—	

No. 2980a is valued in the grade of fine. Very fine examples exist and sell for much more.

WORLD WAR II

A2295

Illustration reduced.

Designed by Bill Bond.

Designs and events of 1945: a, Marines raise flag on Iwo Jima. b, Fierce fighting frees Manila by March 3, 1945. c, Soldiers advancing (Okinawa, the last big battle). d, Destroyed bridge (US and Soviets link up at Elbe River). e, Allies liberate Holocaust survivors. f, Germany surrenders at Reims. g, Refugees (By 1945, World War II has uprooted millions). h, Truman announces Japan's surrender. i, Sailor kissing nurse (News of victory hits home). j, Hometowns honor their returning veterans.

Central label is size of 15 stamps and shows world map with extent of Axis control and Allied operations.

LITHOGRAPHED & ENGRAVED

Plates of eight subjects in four panes of 2 each

1995, Sept. 2 Tagged *Perf. 11.1*

2981	A2295 Block of 10	15.00	7.50
	Pane of 20	30.00	—
a.-j.	32c any single	1.50	.50

No. 2981 has selvage at left and right and either top or bottom.

AMERICAN MUSIC SERIES

Louis Armstrong (1901-71) A2296

Coleman Hawkins (1904-69) A2297

James P. Johnson (1894-1955) A2298

Jelly Roll Morton (1890-1941) A2299

Charlie Parker (1920-55) A2300

Eubie Blake (1883-1983) A2301

Charles Mingus (1922-79) A2302

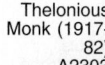

Thelonious Monk (1917-82)
A2303

John Coltrane (1926-67)
A2304

Erroll Garner (1921-77)
A2305

Designed by Dean Mitchell (#2982-2984, 2987, 2989, 2991-2992) and Thomas Blackshear (others).

Printed by Ashton-Potter (USA) Ltd. (#2982), Sterling Sommer for Ashton-Potter (USA) Ltd. (#2983-2992).

LITHOGRAPHED
Plates of 120 in six panes of 20

1995 **Tagged** ***Perf. 11.1x11***

2982	A2296	32c	**white denomination,** *Sept. 1*	.80	.25
			P# block of 4, 4#+P	3.20	—
			Pane of 20	16.00	—
a.			Imperf, pair	—	
2983	A2297	32c	**multicolored,** *Sept. 16*	1.50	.30
2984	A2296	32c	**black denomination,** *Sept. 16*	1.50	.30
2985	A2298	32c	**multicolored,** *Sept. 16*	1.50	.30
2986	A2299	32c	**multicolored,** *Sept. 16*	1.50	.30
2987	A2300	32c	**multicolored,** *Sept. 16*	1.50	.30
2988	A2301	32c	**multicolored,** *Sept. 16*	1.50	.30
2989	A2302	32c	**multicolored,** *Sept. 16*	1.50	.30
2990	A2303	32c	**multicolored,** *Sept. 16*	1.50	.30
2991	A2304	32c	**multicolored,** *Sept. 16*	1.50	.30
2992	A2305	32c	**multicolored,** *Sept. 16*	1.50	.30
a.			Vert. block of 10, #2983-2992	15.00	7.50
			P# block of 10	15.00	—
			Pane of 20	30.00	—
b.			Pane of 20, dark blue (inscriptions) omitted	—	
c.			Imperf pair of Nos. 2991-2992	—	

GARDEN FLOWERS

Aster
A2306

Chrysanthemum
A2307

Dahlia — A2308

Hydrangea — A2309

Rudbeckia — A2310

Designed by Ned Seidler.

LITHOGRAPHED & ENGRAVED
BOOKLET STAMPS

1995, Sept. 19 **Tagged** ***Perf. 10.9 Vert.***

2993	A2306	32c	**multicolored**	.65	.20
2994	A2307	32c	**multicolored**	.65	.20
2995	A2308	32c	**multicolored**	.65	.20
2996	A2309	32c	**multicolored**	.65	.20
2997	A2310	32c	**multicolored**	.65	.20
a.			Booklet pane of 5, #2993-2997	3.25	2.25
b.			As "a," imperf	—	

EDDIE RICKENBACKER (1890-1973), AVIATOR

A2311

Designed by Davis Meltzer.

PHOTOGRAVURE
Panes of 50

1995, Sept. 25 **Tagged** ***Perf. 11¼***

2998	A2311	60c	**multicolored,** small "1995" year date	1.40	.50
			P# block of 4, 5#	9.00	—
a.			Large "1995" date, *Oct., 1999*	2.00	.50
			P# block of 4, 5#	12.00	—

Date on No. 2998 is 1mm long, on No. 2998a 1½mm long.

REPUBLIC OF PALAU

A2312

Designed by Herb Kane.
Printed by Sterling Sommer for Ashton-Potter (USA) Ltd.

LITHOGRAPHED
Sheets of 200 in four panes of 50

1995, Sept. 29 **Tagged** ***Perf. 11.1***

2999	A2312	32c	**multicolored**	.65	.20
			P# block of 4, 5#+P	3.00	—

See Palau Nos. 377-378.

COMIC STRIPS

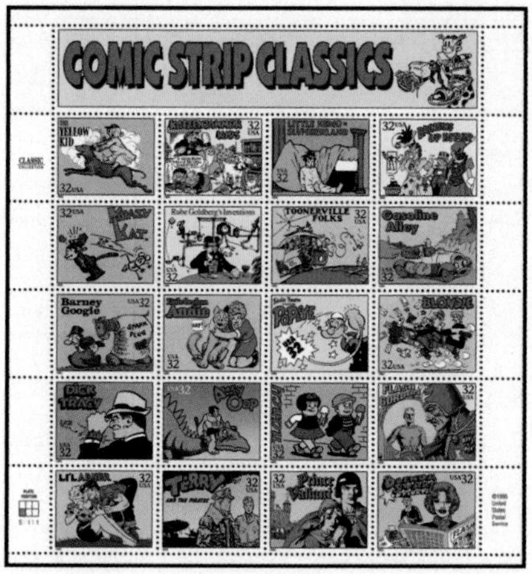

A2313

Illustration reduced.

Designed by Carl Herrman.

Printed by Stamp Venturers.

Designs: a, The Yellow Kid. b, Katzenjammer Kids. c, Little Nemo in Slumberland. d, Bringing Up Father. e, Krazy Kat. f, Rube Goldberg's Inventions. g, Toonerville Folks. h, Gasoline Alley. i, Barney Google. j, Little Orphan Annie. k, Popeye. l, Blondie. m, Dick Tracy. n, Alley Oop. o, Nancy. p, Flash Gordon. q, Li'l Abner. r, Terry and the Pirates. s, Prince Valiant. t, Brenda Starr, Reporter.

PHOTOGRAVURE
Sheets of 120 in six panes of 20

1995, Oct. 1 **Tagged** ***Perf. 10.1***

3000	A2313		Pane of 20	13.00	10.00
a.-t.		32c	any single	.65	.50
			Sheet of 120 (6 panes)	105.00	
			Cross gutter block of 20	35.00	—
			Vert. pairs with horiz. gutter (each)	3.75	—
			Horiz. pairs with vert. gutter (each)	3.75	—
u.			As No. 3000, a.-h. imperf., i.-l. part perf	—	
v.			As No. 3000, m.-t. imperf., i.-l. part perf	—	
w.			As No. 3000, a.-l. imperf.,m.-t. imperf vert.	—	
x.			As No. 3000, imperf	—	

Inscriptions on back of each stamp describe the comic strip.
Cross gutter block of 20 consists of six stamps from each of two panes and four stamps from each of two other panes with the cross gutter between.

U.S. NAVAL ACADEMY, 150th ANNIVERSARY

A2314

Designed by Dean Ellis. Printed by Sterling-Sommer for Aston-Potter (USA) Ltd.

LITHOGRAPHED
Sheets of 160 in eight panes of 20

1995, Oct. 10 **Tagged** ***Perf. 10.9***

3001	A2314	32c	**multicolored**	.65	.20
			P# block of 4, 5#+P	2.60	—
			Pane of 20	13.00	—

LITERARY ARTS SERIES

Tennessee Williams (1911-83)
A2315

Designed by Michael Deas. Printed by Sterling-Sommer for Ashton-Potter (USA) Ltd.

LITHOGRAPHED
Sheets of 160 in eight panes of 20

1995, Oct. 13	**Tagged**		***Perf. 11.1***	
3002	A2315 32c **multicolored**		.65	.20
	P# block of 4, 5#+P		2.80	—
	Pane of 20		14.00	—

CHRISTMAS

Madonna and Child, by Giotto di Bondone — A2316

Santa Claus Entering Chimney — A2317

Child Holding Jumping Jack — A2318

Child Holding Tree — A2319

Santa Claus Working on Sled — A2320

Midnight Angel — A2321

Children Sledding — A2322

Designed by Richard Sheaff (#3003), John Grossman & Laura Alders (#3004-3018).

Printed by Bureau of Engraving and Printing (#3003), Sterling-Sommer for Ashton-Potter (USA) Ltd. (#3004-3007), Avery Dennison (#3008-3011, 3013-3017), Banknote Corporation of America (#3012, 3018).

LITHOGRAPHED & ENGRAVED
Sheets of 300 in six panes of 50

1995	**Tagged**	***Perf. 11.2***	
3003	A2316 32c **multicolored,** *Oct. 19*	.65	.20
	P# block of 4, 5#	3.00	—
c.	Black (engr., denomination) omitted	*200.00*	

BOOKLET STAMP
Perf. 9.8x10.9

3003A	A2316 32c **multicolored,** *Oct. 19*	.65	.20
b.	Booklet pane of 10	6.50	4.00

LITHOGRAPHED
Sheets of 200 in four panes of 50
Perf. 11.25

3004	A2317 32c **multicolored,** *Sept. 30*	.70	.20
3005	A2318 32c **multicolored,** *Sept. 30*	.70	.20
3006	A2319 32c **multicolored,** *Sept. 30*	.70	.20
3007	A2320 32c **multicolored,** *Sept. 30*	.70	.20
a.	Block or strip of 4, #3004-3007	2.80	1.25
	P# block of 4, 4#+P	3.25	—
b.	Booklet pane of 10, 3 each #3004-3005, 2 each #3006-3007	7.00	4.00
c.	Booklet pane of 10, 2 each #3004-3005, 3 each #3006-3007	7.00	4.00
d.	As "a," imperf	*550.00*	

PHOTOGRAVURE
Self-Adhesive Stamps
Serpentine Die Cut 11.25 on 2, 3 or 4 sides

3008	A2320 32c **multicolored,** *Sept. 30*	.95	.20
3009	A2318 32c **multicolored,** *Sept. 30*	.95	.20
3010	A2317 32c **multicolored,** *Sept. 30*	.95	.20
3011	A2319 32c **multicolored,** *Sept. 30*	.95	.20
a.	Booklet pane of 20, 5 each #3008-3011 + label	19.00	

LITHOGRAPHED
Serpentine Die Cut 11.3x11.6 on 2, 3 or 4 sides

3012	A2321 32c **multicolored,** *Oct. 19*	.65	.20
a.	Booklet pane of 20 + label	13.00	
b.	Vert. pair, die cutting omitted between	—	
c.	Booklet pane of 15 + label, *1996*	13.00	
d.	Booklet pane of 15	*30.00*	

No. 3012a comes either with no die cutting in the label (1995 printing) or with the die cutting (and deeper colors) from the 1996 printing.

No. 3012d is a pane of 16 with one stamp removed. The missing stamp can be from either row 1, 2, 3, 7 or 8 of the pane. No. 3012d cannot be made from No. 3012c, a pane of 15 + label. The label is die cut. If the label is removed, an impression of the die cutting appears on the backing paper.

PHOTOGRAVURE
Die Cut

3013	A2322 32c **multicolored,** *Oct. 19*	.65	.20
a.	Booklet pane of 18	12.00	
b.	As "a," tagging omitted	—	

Self-Adhesive Coil Stamps
Serpentine Die Cut 11.2 Vert.

3014	A2320 32c **multicolored,** *Sept. 30*	2.50	.30
3015	A2318 32c **multicolored,** *Sept. 30*	2.50	.30
3016	A2317 32c **multicolored,** *Sept. 30*	2.50	.30
3017	A2319 32c **multicolored,** *Sept. 30*	2.50	.30
a.	Strip of 4, #3014-3017	10.00	
	P# strip of 5, 1 each #3014-3017 + 1 stamp, P#V1111	15.00	
	P# strip of 8, 2 each #3014-3017, P#V1111	30.00	
	P# single (#3017), #V1111	—	10.00

LITHOGRAPHED
Serpentine Die Cut 11.6 Vert.

3018	A2321 32c **multicolored,** *Oct. 19*	1.10	.30
	P# strip of 5, #B1111	9.00	
	P# single, #B1111	—	6.00

Nos. 3014-3018 were only available through the Philatelic Fullfillment Center in Kansas City.

Nos. 3005-3006 have "USA" printed in green. It is red on the self-adhesive stamps.

ANTIQUE AUTOMOBILES

1893 Duryea A2323

1894 Haynes A2324

1898 Columbia A2325

1899 Winton A2326

1901 White A2327

Designed by Ken Dallison.
Printed by Stamp Venturers.

PHOTOGRAVURE
Sheets of 200 in eight panes of 25

1995, Nov. 3	**Tagged**	***Perf. 10.1x11.1***	
3019	A2323 32c **multicolored**	.90	.20
3020	A2324 32c **multicolored**	.90	.20
3021	A2325 32c **multicolored**	.90	.20
3022	A2326 32c **multicolored**	.90	.20
3023	A2327 32c **multicolored**	.90	.20
a.	Vert. or horiz. strip of 5, #3019-3023	4.50	2.00
	Vert. or Horiz. P# block of 10, 2 sets of 4#+S	10.00	—
	Pane of 25	24.00	—

Vert. and horiz. strips are all in different order.

UTAH STATEHOOD CENTENARY

Delicate Arch, Arches Natl. Park — A2328

Designed by McRay Magleby.
Printed by Sterling Sommer for Ashton-Potter (USA) Ltd.

LITHOGRAPHED
Sheets of 200 in four panes of 50

1996, Jan. 4	**Tagged**	***Perf. 11.1***	
3024	A2328 32c **multicolored**	.75	.20
	P# block of 4, 5#+P	4.00	—

For booklet see No. BK245.

GARDEN FLOWERS

Crocus — A2329

Winter Aconite — A2330

Pansy — A2331

Snowdrop — A2332

Anemone — A2333

Designed by Ned Seidler.

LITHOGRAPHED & ENGRAVED
BOOKLET STAMPS

1996, Jan. 19 Tagged *Perf. 10.9 Vert.*

3025	A2329	32c	**multicolored**	.75	.20
3026	A2330	32c	**multicolored**	.75	.20
3027	A2331	32c	**multicolored**	.75	.20
3028	A2332	32c	**multicolored**	.75	.20
3029	A2333	32c	**multicolored**	.75	.20
a.			Booklet pane of 5, #3025-3029	3.75	2.50
b.			As "a," imperf.	—	

LOVE

Cherub from Sistine Madonna, by Raphael — A2334

Designed by Terry McCaffrey.
Printed by Banknote Corporation of America.

LITHOGRAPHED & ENGRAVED
BOOKLET STAMP

Serpentine Die Cut 11.3x11.7

1996, Jan. 20 Tagged

Self-Adhesive

3030	A2334	32c	**multicolored**	.65	.20
a.			Booklet pane of 20 + label	13.00	
b.			Booklet pane of 15 + label	10.00	
c.			Red (engr.) omitted	*200.00*	
d.			Red (engr.) missing (CM)	—	
e.			Double impression of red (engr.)	—	
f.			Die cutting omitted, pair	*275.00*	

No. 3030d must be collected se-tenant with a stamp bearing the red engraving.

FLORA AND FAUNA SERIES

Kestrel, Blue Jay and Rose Types of 1993-95 and

Red-headed Woodpecker A2335

Eastern Bluebird A2336

Red Fox — A2339

Ring-necked Pheasant — A2350

Coral Pink Rose — A2351

Designed by Michael Matherly (#3031-3033, 3044-3045); Terry McCaffrey (#3050-3051, 3055); Derry Noyes (#3036, 3052, 3052E).

Printed by Banknote Corporation of America (#3031A, 3036); Bureau of Engraving & Printing (#3031-3033, 3044-3045); Stamp Venturers (#3048-3049, 3053); Avery Dennison (#3050-3051A). American Packaging Corp. for Sennett Security Products (#3052); Sennett Security Products (#3052E).

LITHOGRAPHED

Sheets of 300 in six panes of 50 (#3031).
Sheets of 400 in eight panes of 50 (#3031A).
Sheets of 400 in four panes of 100 (#3032-3033).
Sheets of 120 in six panes of 20 (#3036).
Sheets of 200 in ten panes of 20 (#3036a)

1996-2002 Untagged *Serpentine Die Cut 10½*
Self-Adhesive (#3031, 3031A)

3031	A1841	1c	**multicolored,** *Nov. 19, 1999*	.20	.20
			P# block of 4, 4# or 4# + A	.25	

Serpentine Die Cut 11¼

3031A	A1841	1c	**multicolored,** *Oct. 2000*	.20	.20
			P# block of 4, 6# + B	.20	
b.			Die cutting omitted, pair	—	

No. 3031A has blue inscription and year.

Perf. 11

3032	A2335	2c	**multicolored,** *Feb. 2*	.20	.20
			P# block of 4, 5#	.25	—
3033	A2336	3c	**multicolored,** *Apr. 3*	.20	.20
			P# block of 4, 5#	.25	—

Some plate blocks contain plate position diagram.

Tagged

Serpentine Die Cut 11½x11¼

Self-Adhesive

3036	A2339	$1	**multicolored,** *Aug. 14, 1998*	2.00	.50
			P# block of 4, 4#+B	8.00	
			Pane of 20	40.00	
a.			Serpentine die cut 11¾x11, *2002*	2.75	.50
			P# block of 4, 4#+B	11.00	
			Pane of 20	55.00	

The tagging of No. 3036 has a bright yellow-green appearance under shortwave ultraviolet light while that of No. 3036a appears light blue green.

COIL STAMPS

Untagged

Perf. 9¾ Vert.

3044	A1841	1c	**multicolored,** small date, *Jan. 20*	.20	.20
			Pair	.20	.20
			P# strip of 5, #1111 in black, yellow, blue, magenta order	.50	
			P# single, same	—	.60
			P# strip of 5, #1111 in black, blue, yellow, magenta order	3.00	
			P# single, same	—	3.00
a.			Large date	.20	.20
			Pair	.20	.20
			P# strip of 5, #1111, 2222, 3333, 4444 in yellow, magenta, blue, black order	.70	
			P# single, same	—	.80

Date on No. 3044 is 1mm long, on No. 3044a 1.5mm long.

Untagged

3045	A2335	2c	**multicolored,** *June 22, 1999*	.20	.20
			Pair	.20	.20
			P# strip of 5, #11111	.60	—
			P# strip of 5, #22222	1.25	
			P# single, #11111	—	.65
			P# single, #22222	—	1.50

BOOKLET STAMPS

PHOTOGRAVURE

Serpentine Die Cut 10.4x10.8 on 3 Sides

1996-2000 Tagged

Self-Adhesive

3048	A1847	20c	**multicolored,** *Aug. 2, 1996*	.40	.20
a.			Booklet pane of 10	4.00	
b.			Booklet pane of 4	22.50	
c.			Booklet pane of 6	37.50	

Nos. 3048b-3048c are from the vending machine booklet No. BK237 that has a glue strip at the top edge of the top pane, the peelable strip removed and the rouletting line 2mm lower than on No. 3048a on some booklets, when the panes are compared with bottoms aligned. Vending booklets with plate #S2222 always have gauge 8½ rouletting on booklet covers. Convertible booklets (No. 3048a) with plate #S2222 always have gauge 12½ rouletting on booklet covers. Vending booklets with plate #S1111 can have either 8½ or 12½ gauge rouletting on booklet cover, and it may be impossible to tell a vending booklet with 12½ gauge rouletting and plate #S1111 from a convertible booklet with peelable strip removed.

Serpentine Die Cut 11.3x11.7 on 2, 3 or 4 Sides

3049	A1853	32c	**yellow, orange, green & black,** *Oct. 24, 1996*	.65	.20
a.			Booklet pane of 20 + label	13.00	
b.			Booklet pane of 4, *Dec. 1996*	2.60	
c.			Booklet pane of 5 + label, *Dec. 1996*	3.50	
			P# single, #S1111	.85	*1.00*
d.			Booklet pane of 6, *Dec. 1996*	4.00	
			Booklet pane of 6 containing P# single	6.00	
			P# single, #S1111	2.50	*1.00*

The plate # single in No. 3049c is on the lower left stamp. In No. 3049d it is the lower right stamp on the bottom pane of the booklet.

Serpentine Die Cut 11.2 on 3 Sides

3050	A2350	20c	**multicolored,** *July 31, 1998*	.50	.20
a.			Booklet pane of 10, all stamps upright	5.00	
b.			Serpentine die cut 11	1.25	.20
c.			As "b," booklet pane of 10, all stamps upright	12.50	

Serpentine Die Cut 10½x11 on 3 Sides

3051	A2350	20c	**multicolored,** *July 1999*	.75	.20

No. 3051 represents the eight upright stamps on the booklet panes Nos. 3051Ab and 3051Ac. The two stamps turned sideways on those panes are No. 3051A.

Specialists should note that 3051 can be either die cut 10.4 at top and 10.6 at bottom or 10.6 at top and 10.4 at bottom. These two varieties exist in equal numbers.

Serpentine Die Cut 10.6x10.4 on 3 Sides

3051A	A2350	20c	**multicolored,**	6.00	.50
b.			Booklet pane of 5, 4 #3051, 1 #3051A turned sideways at top	9.00	
c.			Booklet pane of 5, 4 #3051, 1 #3051A turned sideways at bottom	9.00	

Serpentine Die Cut 11½x11¼ on 2, 3 or 4 Sides

3052	A2351	33c	**multicolored,** *Aug. 13, 1999*	.90	.20
a.			Booklet pane of 4	3.60	
b.			Booklet pane of 5 + label	4.50	
c.			Booklet pane of 6	5.50	
d.			Booklet pane of 20 + label	17.50	
j.			Die cutting omitted, pair	—	

Serpentine Die Cut 10¾x10½ on 2 or 3 sides

3052E	A2351	33c	**multicolored,** *Apr. 7, 2000*	.80	.20
f.			Booklet pane of 20	16.00	
g.			Black ("33 USA," etc.) omitted	375.00	
h.			As "f," all 12 stamps on one side with black omitted	—	
i.			Horiz. pair, die cutting omitted between	—	

No. 3052Ef is a double-sided booklet pane with 12 stamps on one side and 8 stamps plus label on the other side.

COIL STAMPS

Serpentine Die Cut 11½ Vert.

3053	A1847	20c	**multicolored,** *Aug. 2, 1996*	.50	.20
			Pair	1.00	
			P# strip of 5, #S1111	4.00	
			P# single, #S1111	—	1.00

Yellow Rose, Ring-necked Pheasant Types of 1996-98

Printed by Bureau of Engraving and Printing (#3054-3055).

COIL STAMPS
LITHOGRAPHED

1997-98 Tagged *Serpentine Die Cut 9¾ Vert.*

Self-Adhesive

3054	A1853	32c	**yellow, magenta, black & green,** *Aug. 1, 1997*	.65	.20
			Pair	1.30	
			P# strip of 5, #1111, 1112, 1122, 2222, 2223, 2333, 3344, 4455, 5455, 5555, 5556, 5566, 5666, 6666, 7777	4.50	
			P# strip of 5, #2233, 3444	6.00	
			P# strip of 5, #6677, 6777, 8888	7.50	
			P# single, #1111, 1112, 1122, 4455, 5555, 5556, 5566, 5666, 6666, 7777	—	1.75
			P# single, #2222, 2333	—	2.50
			P# single, #2223, 8888	—	2.75
			P# single, #2233, 3444	—	3.75
			P# single, #3344, 5455, 6677	—	3.50
			P# single, #6777	—	5.50
a.			Die cutting omitted, pair	*85.00*	
b.			Black, yellow & green omitted	—	
c.			Black, yellow & green omitted, die cutting omitted, pair	—	
d.			Black omitted	—	
e.			Black omitted, die cutting omitted, pair	—	
f.			All colors omitted, die cutting omitted	—	
g.			Pair, die cutting omitted, containing one stamp each of "c" and "e"	—	

Nos. 3054b and 3054d also are miscut and with shifted die cuttings.

No. 3054f must be collected se-tenant with a partially printed stamp(s).

3055	A2350	20c	**multicolored,** *July, 31, 1998*	.40	.20
			Pair	.80	
			P# strip of 5, P#1111, 2222	3.00	
			P# single, same	—	1.50
a.			Die cutting omitted, pair	*175.00*	

BLACK HERITAGE SERIES

Ernest E. Just (1883-1941), Marine Biologist — A2358

Designed by Richard Sheaff.
Printed by Banknote Corporation of America.

LITHOGRAPHED
Sheets of 160 in eight panes of 20

1996, Feb. 1	Tagged	*Perf. 11.1*	
3058 A2358 32c **gray & black**		.65	.20
	P# block of 4, 4#+B	2.60	—
	Pane of 20	13.00	—

SMITHSONIAN INSTITUTION, 150TH ANNIVERSARY

A2359

Designed by Tom Engeman.
Printed by Ashton-Potter (USA) Ltd.

LITHOGRAPHED
Sheets of 160 in eight panes of 20

1996, Feb. 7	Tagged	*Perf. 11.1*	
3059 A2359 32c **multicolored**		.65	.20
	P# block of 4, 4#+P	2.60	—
	Pane of 20	13.00	—

CHINESE NEW YEAR

Year of the Rat — A2360

Designed by Clarence Lee.
Printed by Stamp Venturers.

PHOTOGRAVURE
Sheets of 180 in nine panes of 20

1996, Feb. 8	Tagged	*Perf. 11.1*	
3060 A2360 32c **multicolored**		.90	.20
	P# block of 4, 4#+S	4.25	—
	Pane of 20	19.00	—
a. Imperf., pair		*775.00*	

See No. 3895a.

PIONEERS OF COMMUNICATION

Eadweard Muybridge (1830-1904), Photographer A2361

Ottmar Mergenthaler (1854-99), Inventor of Linotype A2362

Frederic E. Ives (1856-1937), Developer of Halftone Process A2363

William Dickson (1860-1935), Co-developer of Kinetoscope A2364

Designed by Fred Otnes.
Printed by Ashton-Potter USA.

LITHOGRAPHED
Sheets of 120 in six panes of 20

1996, Feb. 22	Tagged	*Perf. 11.1x11*	
3061 A2361 32c **multicolored**		.65	.20
3062 A2362 32c **multicolored**		.65	.20
3063 A2363 32c **multicolored**		.65	.20
3064 A2364 32c **multicolored**		.65	.20
a. Block or strip of 4, #3061-3064		2.60	2.00
	P# block of 4, 5#+P	2.60	—
	Pane of 20	13.00	—

FULBRIGHT SCHOLARSHIPS, 50th ANNIVERSARY

A2365

Designed by Richard D. Sheaff.

LITHOGRAPHED & ENGRAVED
Sheets of 200 in four panes of 50

1996, Feb. 28	Tagged	*Perf. 11.1*	
3065 A2365 32c **multicolored**		.75	.20
	P# block of 4, 5#	4.25	—

For booklet see No. BK246.

JACQUELINE COCHRAN (1910-80), PILOT

A2366

Designed by Davis Meltzer.

LITHOGRAPHED & ENGRAVED
Sheets of 300 in six panes of 50

1996, Mar. 9	Tagged	*Perf. 11.1*	
3066 A2366 50c **multicolored**		1.00	.40
	P# block of 4, 5#	5.00	—
a. Black (engr.) omitted		55.00	

MARATHON

A2367

Designed by Michael Bartalos.

Printed by Banknote Corporation of America.

LITHOGRAPHED
Sheets of 160 in eight panes of 20

1996, Apr. 11	Tagged	*Perf. 11.1*	
3067 A2367 32c **multicolored**		.65	.20
	P# block of 4, 4#+B	2.60	—
	Pane of 20	13.00	—

1996 SUMMER OLYMPIC GAMES

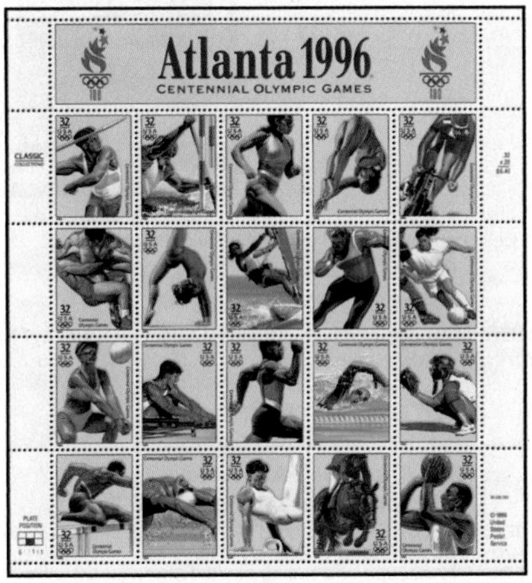

A2368

Illustration reduced.

Designed by Richard Waldrep. Printed by Stamp Venturers.

Designs: a, Decathlon (javelin). b, Men's canoeing. c, Women's running. d, Women's diving. e, Men's cycling. f, Freestyle wrestling. g, Women's gymnastics. h, Women's sailboarding. i, Men's shot put. j, Women's soccer. k, Beach volleyball. l, Men's rowing. m, Men's sprints. n, Women's swimming. o, Women's softball. p, Men's hurdles. q, Men's swimming. r, Men's gymnastics (pommel horse). s, Equestrian. t, Men's basketball.

PHOTOGRAVURE
Sheets of 120 in six panes of 20

1996, May 2	Tagged	*Perf. 10.1*	
3068 A2368 Pane of 20		13.00	10.00
a.-t. 32c any single		.65	.50
	Sheet of 120 (6 panes)	120.00	
	Cross gutter block of 20	45.00	—
	Vert. pairs with horiz. gutter (each)	4.00	—
	Horiz. pairs with vert. gutter (each)	4.00	—
u. As No. 3068, imperf		*1,100.*	
v. As No. 3068, back inscriptions omitted on a., f., k. & p., incorrect back inscriptions on others			—
w. As No. 3068, e. imperf, d., i.-j. part perf, all others perf			—

Inscription on back of each stamp describes the sport shown.
Cross gutter block of 20 consists of six stamps from each of two panes and four stamps from each of two other panes with the cross gutter between.

GEORGIA O'KEEFFE (1887-1986)

A2369

Designed by Margaret Bauer. Printed by Stamp Venturers.

PHOTOGRAVURE

Sheets of 90 in six panes of 15

1996, May 23	Tagged	*Perf. 11.6x11.4*	
3069 A2369 32c **multicolored**		.85	.20
	P# block of 4, 5#+S	5.00	—
	Pane of 15	14.50	9.00
a. Imperf., pair		*135.00*	
	Pane of 15, imperf.	*1,050.*	—

For booklet see No. BK247.

TENNESSEE STATEHOOD BICENTENNIAL

A2370

Designed by Phil Jordan. Printed by Stamp Venturers.

PHOTOGRAVURE

Sheets of 200 in four panes of 50.

1996, May 31	Tagged	*Perf. 11.1*	
3070 A2370 32c **multicolored**		.65	.20
	P# block of 4, 5#+S	3.00	—

For booklet see No. BK248.

Booklet Stamp

Self-Adhesive

Serpentine Die Cut 9.9x10.8

3071 A2370 32c **multicolored**		.75	.30
a.	Booklet pane of 20, #S11111	15.00	
b.	Horiz. pair, die cutting omitted btwn.	—	
c.	Die cutting omitted, pair	—	
d.	Horiz. pair, die cutting omitted vert.	—	—

AMERICAN INDIAN DANCES

Fancy — A2371

Butterfly — A2372

Traditional — A2373

Raven — A2374

Hoop — A2375

Designed by Keith Birdsong. Printed by Ashton-Potter (USA) Ltd.

LITHOGRAPHED

Sheets of 120 in six panes of 20.

1996, June 7	Tagged	*Perf. 11.1*	
3072 A2371 32c **multicolored**		1.00	.20
3073 A2372 32c **multicolored**		1.00	.20
3074 A2373 32c **multicolored**		1.00	.20
3075 A2374 32c **multicolored**		1.00	.20
3076 A2375 32c **multicolored**		1.00	.20
a.	Strip of 5, #3072-3076	5.00	2.50
	P# block of 10, 4#+P	12.00	—
	Pane of 20	24.00	—

For booklet see No. BK249.

PREHISTORIC ANIMALS

Eohippus A2376

Woolly Mammoth A2377

Mastodon A2378

Saber-tooth Cat — A2379

Designed by Davis Meltzer. Printed by Ashton-Potter (USA) Ltd.

LITHOGRAPHED

Sheets of 120 in six panes of 20

1996, June 8	Tagged	*Perf. 11.1x11*	
3077 A2376 32c **multicolored**		.65	.20
3078 A2377 32c **multicolored**		.65	.20
3079 A2378 32c **multicolored**		.65	.20
3080 A2379 32c **multicolored**		.65	.20
a.	Block or strip of 4, #3077-3080	2.60	2.00
	P# block of 4, 4#+P	2.60	—
	Pane of 20	13.00	—

A2380

A2381

BREAST CANCER AWARENESS

Designed by Tom Mann. Printed by Ashton-Potter (USA) Ltd.

LITHOGRAPHED

Sheets of 120 in six panes of 20

1996, June 15	Tagged	*Perf. 11.1*	
3081 A2380 32c **multicolored**		.65	.20
	P# block of 4, 5#+P	2.60	—
	Pane of 20	13.00	—

LEGENDS OF HOLLYWOOD

James Dean (1931-55)

Designed by Michael Deas.

Printed by Stamp Venturers.

PHOTOGRAVURE

Sheets of 120 in six panes of 20.

1996, June 24	Tagged	*Perf. 11.1*	
3082 A2381 32c **multicolored**		.65	.20
	P# block of 4, 7#+S	4.00	—
	Pane of 20	18.50	10.00
	Sheet of 120 (six panes)	110.00	
	Cross gutter block of 8	30.00	—
	Block of 8 with vertical gutter	20.00	—
	Horiz. pair with vert. gutter	4.75	—
	Vert. pair with horiz. gutter	3.00	—
a.	Imperf., pair	*175.00*	
	Pane of 20, imperf.	*1,900.*	—
b.	As "a," red (USA 32c) missing (CM) and tan (JAMES DEAN) omitted	—	
c.	As "a," tan (JAMES DEAN) omitted	—	
d.	As "a," top stamp red missing (CM) and tan (JAMES DEAN) omitted, bottom stamp tan omitted	—	

Perforations in corner of each stamp are star-shaped. No. 3082 was also available on the first day of issue in at least 127 Warner Bros. Studio stores.

Cross-gutter block consists of 3 stamps vertically from 2 upper panes and 1 stamp each from 2 lower panes.

For booklet see No. BK250.

Nos. 3082b-3082d come from the same error pane. The top row is No. 3082b; rows 2-4 are No. 3082c. No. 3082d is a vertical pair with one stamp from No. 3082b at top and one stamp from No. 3082c at bottom.

FOLK HEROES

A2382

A2383

A2384

A2385

Designed by David LaFleur.

Printed by Ashton-Potter (USA) Ltd.

LITHOGRAPHED
Sheets of 120 in six panes of 20

1996, July 11 **Tagged** ***Perf. 11.1x11***

3083	A2382 32c **multicolored**	.65	.20
3084	A2383 32c **multicolored**	.65	.20
3085	A2384 32c **multicolored**	.65	.20
3086	A2385 32c **multicolored**	.65	.20
a.	Block or strip of 4, #3083-3086	2.60	2.00
	P# block of 4, 4#+P	2.60	—
	Pane of 20	13.00	—

For booklet see No. BK251.

Myron's Discobolus — A2386

Young Corn, by Grant Wood — A2387

CENTENNIAL OLYMPIC GAMES

Designed by Carl Herrman.

Printed by Ashton-Potter (USA) Ltd.

ENGRAVED
Sheets of 80 in four panes of 20

1996, July 19 **Tagged** ***Perf. 11.1***

3087	A2386 32c **brown**	.80	.20
	P# block of 4, 1#+P	4.50	—
	Pane of 20	21.50	10.00

Sheet margin of the pane of 20 is lithographed.
For booklet see No. BK252.

IOWA STATEHOOD, 150TH ANNIVERSARY

Designed by Carl Herrman.

Printed by Ashton-Potter (USA) Ltd. (#3088), Banknote Corporation of America (#3089)

LITHOGRAPHED
Sheets of 200 in four panes of 50

1996, Aug. 1 **Tagged** ***Perf. 11.1***

3088	A2387 32c **multicolored**	.80	.20
	P# block of 4, 4#+P	3.75	—

For booklet see No. BK253.

BOOKLET STAMP

Self-Adhesive
Serpentine Die Cut 11.6x11.4

3089	A2387 32c **multicolored**	.70	.30
a.	Booklet pane of 20	14.00	

RURAL FREE DELIVERY, CENT.

A2388

Designed by Richard Sheaff.

LITHOGRAPHED & ENGRAVED
Sheets of 120 in six panes of 20

1996, Aug. 7 **Tagged** ***Perf. 11.2x11***

3090	A2388 32c **multicolored**	.80	.20
	P# block of 4, 5#	3.25	—
	Pane of 20	16.50	—

For booklet see No. BK254.

RIVERBOATS

Robt. E. Lee — A2389

Sylvan Dell — A2390

Far West A2391

Rebecca Everingham A2392

Bailey Gatzert A2393

Designed by Dean Ellis.

Printed by Avery Dennison.

PHOTOGRAVURE
Sheets of 200 in 10 panes of 20
Serpentine Die Cut 11x11.1

1996, Aug. 22 **Tagged**

Self-Adhesive

3091	A2389 32c **multicolored**	.65	.20
3092	A2390 32c **multicolored**	.65	.20
3093	A2391 32c **multicolored**	.65	.20
3094	A2392 32c **multicolored**	.65	.20
3095	A2393 32c **multicolored**	.65	.20
a.	Vert. strip of 5, #3091-3095	3.25	
	P# block of 10, 5#+V	6.50	
	Pane of 20	13.00	
b.	Strip of 5, #3091-3095, with special die cutting, die cut 11¼	*80.00*	*50.00*
	P# block of 10, 5#+V	*160.00*	
	Pane of 20	*320.00*	

The serpentine die cutting runs through the peelable backing to which Nos. 3091-3095 are affixed. No. 3095a exists with stamps in different sequences.

On the long side of each stamp in No. 3095b, the die cutting is missing 3 "perforations" between the stamps, one near each end and one in the middle. This allows a complete strip to be removed from the backing paper for use on a first day cover. No. 3095b was also used to make Souvenir Page No. 1215.

For booklet see No. BK255.

AMERICAN MUSIC SERIES
Big Band Leaders

Count Basie A2394

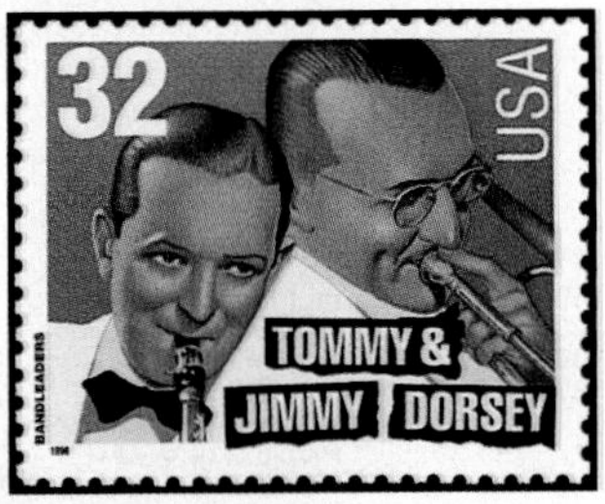

Tommy & Jimmy Dorsey A2395

Glenn Miller A2396

Benny Goodman A2397

Songwriters

Harold Arlen — A2398

Johnny Mercer A2399

Dorothy Fields A2400

Hoagy Carmichael A2401

Designed by Bill Nelson (#3096-3099), Gregg Rudd (#3100-3103).

Printed by Ashton-Potter (USA) Ltd.

LITHOGRAPHED
Sheets of 120 in six panes of 20

1996, Sept. 11 **Tagged** ***Perf. 11.1x11***

3096	A2394 32c **multicolored**		.75	.20
3097	A2395 32c **multicolored**		.75	.20
3098	A2396 32c **multicolored**		.75	.20
3099	A2397 32c **multicolored**		.75	.20
a.	Block or strip of 4, #3096-3099		3.00	2.00
	P# block of 4, 6#+P		4.00	—
	P# block of 8, 2 sets of P# + top label		6.75	—
	Pane of 20		19.00	—
3100	A2398 32c **multicolored**		.75	.20
3101	A2399 32c **multicolored**		.75	.20
3102	A2400 32c **multicolored**		.75	.20
3103	A2401 32c **multicolored**		.75	.20
a.	Block or strip of 4, #3100-3103		3.00	2.00
	P# block of 4, 6#+P		3.50	—
	P# block of 8, 2 sets of P# + top label		5.75	—
	Pane of 20		16.00	—

LITERARY ARTS SERIES

F. Scott Fitzgerald (1896-1940) A2402

Designed by Michael Deas.

PHOTOGRAVURE
Sheets of 200 in four panes of 50

1996, Sept. 27 **Tagged** ***Perf. 11.1***

3104	A2402 23c **multicolored**	.55	.20
	P# block of 4, 4#	4.00	—

ENDANGERED SPECIES

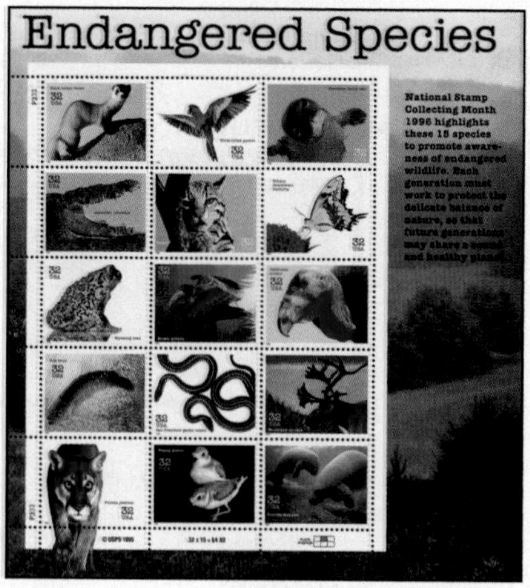

A2403

Illustration reduced.

Designed by James Balog. Printed by Ashton-Potter (USA) Ltd.

Designs: a, Black-footed ferret. b, Thick-billed parrot. c, Hawaiian monk seal. d, American crocodile. e, Ocelot. f, Schaus swallowtail butterfly. g, Wyoming toad. h, Brown pelican. i, California condor. j, Gila trout. k, San Francisco garter snake. l, Woodland caribou. m, Florida panther. n, Piping plover. o, Florida manatee.

LITHOGRAPHED
Sheets of 90 in six panes of 15

1996, Oct. 2 **Tagged** ***Perf. 11.1x11***

3105	A2403 Pane of 15	10.50	8.00
a.-o.	32c any single	.70	.50

See Mexico No. 1995. For booklet see No. BK256.

COMPUTER TECHNOLOGY

A2404

Designed by Nancy Skolos & Tom Wedell.

Printed by Ashton-Potter (USA) Ltd.

LITHOGRAPHED & ENGRAVED
Sheets of 160 in four panes of 40

1996, Oct. 8 **Tagged** ***Perf. 10.9x11.1***

3106	A2404 32c **multicolored**	.65	.20
	P# block of 4, 6#+P	3.00	—

CHRISTMAS

Madonna and Child from Adoration of the Shepherds, by Paolo de Matteis — A2405

Family at Fireplace — A2406

Decorating Tree — A2407

Dreaming of Santa Claus — A2408

Holiday Shopping — A2409

Skaters — A2410

Designed by Richard D. Sheaff (#3107, 3112), Julia Talcott (#3108-3111, 3113-3117).

Printed by Bureau of Engraving and Printing (#3107, 3112), Ashton-Potter (USA) Ltd. (#3108-3111), Banknote Corporation of America (#3113-3116), Avery-Dennison (#3117).

LITHOGRAPHED & ENGRAVED
Sheets of 300 in six panes of 50

1996 **Tagged** ***Perf. 11.1x11.2***

3107	A2405 32c **multicolored**, *Nov. 1*	.65	.20
	P# block of 4, 5#	3.00	—

For booklet see No. BK257.

LITHOGRAPHED
Perf. 11.3

3108	A2406 32c **multicolored**, *Oct. 8*	.65	.20
3109	A2407 32c **multicolored**, *Oct. 8*	.65	.20
3110	A2408 32c **multicolored**, *Oct. 8*	.65	.20
3111	A2409 32c **multicolored**, *Oct. 8*	.65	.20
a.	Block or strip of 4, #3108-3111	2.60	1.75
	P# block of 4, 4#+P	3.00	—
b.	Strip of 4, #3110-3111, 3108-3109, with #3109 imperf., #3108 imperf. at right		—
c.	Strip of 4, #3108-3111, with #3111 imperf, #3110 imperf at right		—

BOOKLET STAMPS
Self-Adhesive

LITHOGRAPHED & ENGRAVED
Serpentine Die Cut 10 on 2, 3 or 4 Sides

3112	A2405 32c **multicolored**, *Nov. 1*	.75	.20
a.	Booklet pane of 20 + label	15.00	
b.	Die cutting omitted, pair	75.00	
c.	As "a," die cutting omitted	—	

LITHOGRAPHED
Serpentine Die Cut 11.8x11.5 on 2, 3 or 4 Sides

3113	A2406 32c **multicolored**, *Oct. 8*	.75	.20
3114	A2407 32c **multicolored**, *Oct. 8*	.75	.20
3115	A2408 32c **multicolored**, *Oct. 8*	.75	.20
3116	A2409 32c **multicolored**, *Oct. 8*	.75	.20
a.	Booklet pane of 20, 5 ea #3113-3116	15.00	
b.	Strip of 4, #3113-3116, die cutting omitted	*550.00*	
c.	Block of 6, die cutting omitted	*775.00*	
d.	As "a," die cutting omitted	*2,100.*	

PHOTOGRAVURE
Die Cut

3117	A2410 32c **multicolored**, *Oct. 8*	.65	.20
a.	Booklet pane of 18	12.00	

HANUKKAH

A2411

Designed by Hannah Smotrich.

Printed by Avery Dennison.

PHOTOGRAVURE

Sheets of 200 in 10 panes of 20

1996, Oct. 22 Tagged *Serpentine Die Cut 11.1*

Self-Adhesive

3118 A2411 32c **multicolored**		.65	.20
	P# block of 4, 5#+V	2.60	
	Pane of 20	13.00	

Backing on No. 3118 is die cut with a continuous horizontal wavy line. The 1997 reprint is die cut with two short horizontal lines on each side of a semi-circle on the backing of each stamp.

See Nos. 3352, 3547, 3672, Israel No. 1289. For booklet see No. BK258.

CYCLING

Souvenir Sheet

A2412

Illustration reduced.

Designed by McRay Magleby.

Printed by Stamp Venturers.

PHOTOGRAVURE

1996, Nov. 1 Tagged *Perf. 11x11.1*

3119 A2412 Sheet of 2		2.50	2.00
a.	50c orange & multi	1.25	1.00
b.	50c blue green & multi	1.25	1.00

No. 3119 exists overprinted in gold for the Tour of China '96. This overprint is a private production.

CHINESE NEW YEAR

Year of the Ox — A2413

Designed by Clarence Lee.

Printed by Stamp Venturers.

PHOTOGRAVURE

Sheets of 180 in 9 panes of 20

1997, Jan. 5 Tagged *Perf. 11.2*

3120 A2413 32c **multicolored**		.80	.20
	P# block of 4, 4#+S	3.20	—
	Pane of 20	16.00	—

See No. 3895b.

BLACK HERITAGE SERIES

Brig. Gen. Benjamin O. Davis, Sr. (1880-1970) — A2414

Designed by Richard Sheaff.

Printed by Banknote Corp. of America.

LITHOGRAPHED

Sheets of 120 in six panes of 20

1997, Jan. 28 Tagged *Serpentine Die Cut 11.4*

Self-Adhesive

3121 A2414 32c **multicolored**		.65	.20
	P# block of 4, 4#+B	2.60	
	Pane of 20	13.00	

Statue of Liberty Type of 1994

Printed by Avery-Dennison.

PHOTOGRAVURE

Serpentine Die Cut 11 on 2, 3 or 4 Sides

1997, Feb. 1 Tagged

Self-Adhesive

3122 A1951 32c **red, light blue, dark blue & yellow**		.65	.20
a.	Booklet pane of 20 + label	13.00	
b.	Booklet pane of 4	2.60	
c.	Booklet pane of 5 + label	3.50	
	P# single, #V1111	.85	1.00
d.	Booklet pane of 6	4.00	
	Booklet pane of 6 containing P# single	6.00	
	P# single, #V1111	2.50	1.00
h.	As "a," die cutting omitted	—	

The plate # single in No. 3122c is the lower left stamp and should be collected unused with the reorder label to its right to differentiate it from the plate # single in No. 3122d which is the lower left stamp in the bottom pane of the booklet and should be collected with a normal stamp adjoining it at right. In used condition, these plate # singles are indistinguishable.

Serpentine Die Cut 11.5x11.8 on 2, 3 or 4 Sides

1997 Tagged

Self-Adhesive

3122E A1951 32c **red, light blue, dark blue & yellow**		1.25	.20
f.	Booklet pane of 20 + label	40.00	
g.	Booklet pane of 6	8.00	
	Booklet pane of 6 containing P# single	13.50	
	P# single, #V1111	5.50	2.00

The plate # single in No. 3122Eg is the lower left stamp in the bottom pane of the booklet.

LOVE

Swans

A2415 A2416

Designed by Marvin Mattelson.

Printed by Banknote Corp. of America.

LITHOGRAPHED

Serpentine Die Cut 11.8x11.6 on 2, 3 or 4 Sides

1997, Feb. 4 Tagged

Self-Adhesive

3123 A2415 32c **multicolored**		.65	.20
a.	Booklet pane of 20 + label	13.00	
b.	Die cutting omitted, pair	*135.00*	
c.	As "a," die cutting omitted	*1,350.*	
d.	As "a," black omitted	*575.00*	

Serpentine Die Cut 11.6x11.8 on 2, 3 or 4 Sides

3124 A2416 55c **multicolored**		1.10	.20
a.	Booklet pane of 20 + label	22.00	

HELPING CHILDREN LEARN

A2417

Designed by Chris Van Allsburg.

Printed by Avery-Dennison.

PHOTOGRAVURE

Sheets of 160 in eight panes of 20

Serpentine Die Cut 11.6x11.7

1997, Feb. 18 Tagged

Self-Adhesive

3125 A2417 32c **multicolored**		.65	.20
	P# block of 4, 4#+V	2.60	
	Pane of 20	13.00	

The die cut perforations of #3125 are fragile and separate easily.

MERIAN BOTANICAL PRINTS

Citron, Moth, Larvae, Pupa, Beetle A2418

Flowering Pineapple, Cockroaches A2419

No. 3128 (r), No. 3129 (l), No. 3128a below

Designed by Phil Jordan based on works by Maria Sibylla Merian (1647-1717).

Printed by Stamp Venturers.

PHOTOGRAVURE

Serpentine Die Cut 10.9x10.2 on 2, 3 or 4 Sides

1997, Mar. 3 Tagged

Self-Adhesive

3126 A2418 32c **multicolored**		.65	.20
3127 A2419 32c **multicolored**		.65	.20
a.	Booklet pane, 10 ea #3126-3127 + label	13.00	
b.	Pair, #3126-3127	1.30	
c.	Vert. pair, die cutting omitted between	*475.00*	

Size: 18.5x24mm

Serpentine Die Cut 11.2x10.8 on 2 or 3 Sides

3128 A2418 32c **multicolored**		1.00	.20
a.	See footnote	3.00	.25
b.	Booklet pane, 2 ea #3128-3129, 1 #3128a	7.00	

3129 A2419 32c **multicolored** 1.00 .20
a. See footnote 4.50 .35
b. Booklet pane, 2 ea #3128-3129, 1 #3129a 9.00
c. Pair, #3128-3129 2.00

Nos. 3128a-3129a are placed sideways on the pane and are serpentine die cut 11.2 on top and bottom, 10.8 on left side. The right side is 11.2 broken by a lsloping die cut where the stamp meets the vertical die cutting of the two stamps above it. See illustration above.

PACIFIC 97

Sailing Ship — A2420

Stagecoach — A2421

Designed by Richard Sheaff.

Printed by Banknote Corporation of America.

ENGRAVED
Sheets of 96 in six panes of 16

1997, Mar. 13 **Tagged** ***Perf. 11.2***

3130 A2420 32c **blue** .65 .30
3131 A2421 32c **red** .65 .30
a. Pair, #3130-3131 1.30 .75
P# block of 4, 1#+B 2.60 —
Pane of 16 10.50 7.50
Sheet of 96 (6 panes) 80.00
Cross gutter block of 16 (8 #3131a) 30.00 —
Vert. pairs with horiz. gutter (each) 10.00 —
Horiz. pairs with vert. gutter (each) 5.00 —

Juke Box and Flag Over Porch Types of 1995

Designed by Bill Nelson (#3132), Dave LaFleur (#3133).

Printed by Stamp Venturers.

PHOTOGRAVURE
COIL STAMPS

1997, Mar. 14 **Untagged** ***Imperf.***
Self-Adhesive

3132 A2225 (25c) **bright orange red, bright yellow green & multi** 1.50 .50
Pair 3.00
P# strip of 5, #M11111 8.00
P#, single, #M11111 6.50

Tagged
Serpentine Die Cut 9.9 Vert.

3133 A2212 32c **dark blue, tan, brown, red & light blue** 1.50 .20
Pair 3.00
P# strip of 5, #M11111 7.25
P#, single, #M11111 4.00

Nos. 3132-3133 were issued without backing paper. No. 3132 has simulated perforations ending in black bars at the top and bottom edges of the stamp. Sky on No. 3133 shows color gradation at LR not on Nos. 2915A or 2915D, and it has blue "1996" at left bottom.

LITERARY ARTS SERIES

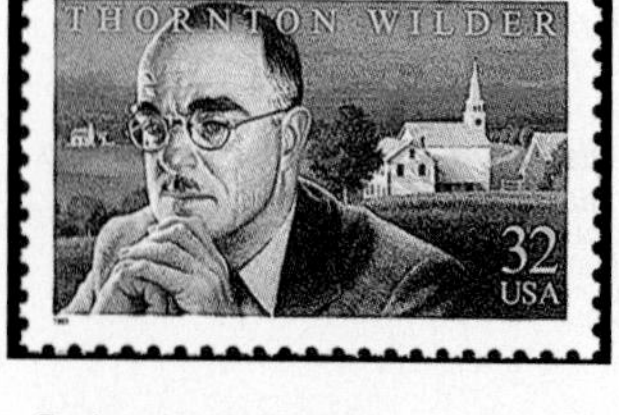

Thornton Wilder (1897-1975)
A2422

Designed by Phil Jordan.

Printed by Ashton-Potter (USA) Ltd.

LITHOGRAPHED
Sheets of 180 in nine panes of 20

1997, Apr. 17 **Tagged** ***Perf. 11.1***

3134 A2422 32c **multicolored** .65 .20
P# block of 4, 4#+P 2.60 —
Pane of 20 13.00 —

RAOUL WALLENBERG (1912-47)

Wallenberg and Jewish Refugees
A2423

Designed by Howard Paine.

Printed by Sterling Sommer for Ashton-Potter (USA) Ltd.

LITHOGRAPHED
Sheets of 180 in nine panes of 20

1997, Apr. 24 **Tagged** ***Perf. 11.1***

3135 A2423 32c **multicolored** .65 .20
P# block of 4, 4#+P 2.60 —
Pane of 20 13.00 —

DINOSAURS

A2424

Illustration reduced.

Designed by James Gurney.
Printed by Sterling Sommer for Ashton-Potter (USA) Ltd.

Designs: a, Ceratosaurus. b, Camptosaurus. c, Camarasaurus. d, Brachiosaurus. e, Goniopholis. f, Stegosaurus. g, Allosaurus. h, Opisthias. i, Edmontonia. j, Einiosaurus. k, Daspletosaurus. l, Palaeosaniwa. m, Corythosaurus. n, Ornithomimus. o, Parasaurolophus.

LITHOGRAPHED

1997, May 1 **Tagged** ***Perf. 11x11.1***

3136 A2424 Sheet of 15 10.00 8.00
a.-o. 32c any single .65 .50
p. As No. 3136, bottom 7 stamps imperf. *3,750.*
q. As No. 3136, top 8 stamps imperf *3,750.*
r. As No. 3136, all colors and tagging missing (EP) —

No. 3136r resulted from double sheeting in the sheet-fed press. It is properly gummed and perforated.

BUGS BUNNY

A2425

Cross Gutter Block of 12

Illustration reduced.

Designed by Warner Bros.

Printed by Avery Dennison.

PHOTOGRAVURE

1997, May 22 **Tagged** ***Serpentine Die Cut 11***
Self-Adhesive

3137 Pane of 10 6.75
a. A2425 32c single .65 .20
b. Pane of 9 #3137a 6.00
c. Pane of 1 #3137a .65
Sheet of 60 (six panes) top *375.00*
Sheet of 60 (six panes) bottom, with plate # *625.00*
Pane of 10 from uncut press sheet *70.00*
Pane of 10 with plate # *350.00*
Cross gutter block of 9 or 10 *200.00*
Cross gutter block of 12 *250.00*
Vert. pair with horiz. gutter *25.00*
Horiz. pair with vert. gutter *50.00*

Die cutting on #3137 does not extend through the backing paper.

Pane of 10 with P# comes from bottom uncut sheet of 60.

Nos. 3137b-3137c and 3138b-3138c are separated by a vertical line of microperforations that are absent on the uncut sheet of 60.

The horiz. pair with vert. gutter consists of a stamp at the left, from No. 3137b, part of the illustration of Bugs Bunny, the small gutter between the panes, and a stamp at the right from the left row of 3137b. Some pairs may include the single stamp from No. 3137c in addition to the two stamps at the right and left.

3138 Pane of 10 150.00
a. A2425 32c single 3.50
b. Pane of 9 #3138a 32.50
c. Pane of 1, no die cutting 110.00

Die cutting on #3138b extends through the backing paper.

An untagged promotional piece similar to No. 3137c exists on the same backing paper as the pane, with the same design image, but without Bugs' signature and the single stamp. Replacing the stamp is an enlarged "32 / USA" in the same style as used on the stamp. This promotional piece was not valid for postage.

PACIFIC 97

Franklin — A2426

Washington — A2427

Designed by Richard Sheaff. Selvage on Nos. 3139-3140 is lithographed.

LITHOGRAPHED & ENGRAVED

1997	Tagged	*Perf. 10.5x10.4*	
3139	Pane of 12, *May 29*	12.00	9.00
a.	A2426 50c single	1.00	.50
3140	Pane of 12, *May 30*	14.50	11.00
a.	A2427 60c single	1.20	.60

Nos. 3139-3140 were sold through June 8.

MARSHALL PLAN, 50TH ANNIV.

Gen. George C. Marshall, Map of Europe
A2428

Designed by Richard Sheaff.

Printed by Stevens Security Press for Ashton-Potter (USA) Ltd.

LITHOGRAPHED & ENGRAVED
Sheets of 120 in six panes of 20

1997, June 4	Tagged	*Perf. 11.1*	
3141 A2428 32c	**multicolored**	.65	.20
	P# block of 4, 5#+P	2.60	—
	Pane of 20	13.00	—

CLASSIC AMERICAN AIRCRAFT

A2429

Illustration reduced.

Designed by Phil Jordan.

Printed by Stamp Venturers.

Designs: a, Mustang. b, Model B. c, Cub. d, Vega. e, Alpha. f, B-10. g, Corsair. h, Stratojet. i, GeeBee. j, Staggerwing. k, Flying Fortress. l, Stearman. m, Constellation. n, Lightning. o, Peashooter. p, Tri-Motor. q, DC-3. r, 314 Clipper. s, Jenny. t, Wildcat.

PHOTOGRAVURE
Sheets of 120 in six panes of 20

1997, July 19	Tagged	*Perf. 10.1*	
3142 A2429	Pane of 20	13.00	10.00
a.-t.	32c any single	.65	.50
	Sheet of 120 (6 panes)	85.00	
	Cross gutter block of 20	22.50	
	Vert. pairs with horiz. gutter (each)	2.40	—
	Horiz. pairs with vert. gutter (each)	2.40	—

Inscriptions on back of each stamp describe the airplane.
Cross gutter block of 20 consists of six stamps from each of two panes and four stamps from each of two other panes with the cross gutter between.

FOOTBALL COACHES

Bear Bryant
A2430

Pop Warner
A2431

Vince Lombardi
A2432

George Halas
A2433

Designed by Carl Herrman.

Printed by Sterling Sommer for Ashton-Potter (USA) Ltd.

LITHOGRAPHED
Sheets of 120 in six panes of 20

1997	Tagged	*Perf. 11.2*	
3143 A2430 32c	**multicolored,** *July 25*	.65	.25
3144 A2431 32c	**multicolored,** *July 25*	.65	.25
3145 A2432 32c	**multicolored,** *July 25*	.65	.25
3146 A2433 32c	**multicolored,** *July 25*	.65	.25
a.	Block or strip of 4, #3143-3146	2.60	—
	P# block of 4, 5#+P	2.60	1.75
	P# block of 8, 2 sets of P# + top label	5.25	—
	Pane of 20	13.00	

With Red Bar Above Coach's Name

Perf. 11

3147 A2432 32c	**multicolored,** *Aug. 5*	.65	.45
	P# block of 4, 4#+P	3.00	—
	Pane of 20	14.50	—
3148 A2430 32c	**multicolored,** *Aug. 7*	.65	.45
	P# block of 4, 4#+P	3.00	—
	Pane of 20	14.50	—
3149 A2431 32c	**multicolored,** *Aug. 8*	.65	.45
	P# block of 4, 4#+P	3.00	—
	Pane of 20	14.50	—
3150 A2433 32c	**multicolored,** *Aug. 16*	.65	.45
	P# block of 4, 4#+P	3.00	—
	Pane of 20	14.50	—

AMERICAN DOLLS

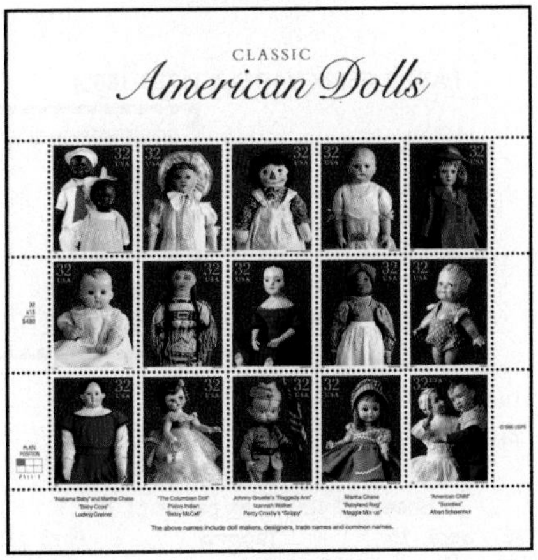

A2434

Illustration reduced.

Designed by Derry Noyes.

Printed by Sterling Sommer for Ashton-Potter (USA) Ltd.

Designs: a, "Alabama Baby," and doll by Martha Chase. b, "Columbian Doll." c, Johnny Gruelle's "Raggedy Ann." d, Doll by Martha Chase. e, "American Child." f, "Baby Coos." g, Plains Indian. h, Doll by Izannah Walker. i, "Babyland Rag." j, "Scootles." k, Doll by Ludwig Greiner. l, "Betsy McCall." m, Percy Crosby's "Skippy." n, "Maggie Mix-up." o, Dolls by Albert Schoenhut.

LITHOGRAPHED
Sheets of 90 in six panes of 15

1997, July 28	Tagged	*Perf. 10.9x11.1*	
3151 A2434	Pane of 15	13.50	—
a.-o.	32c any single	.90	.60

For booklet see No. BK266.

A2435

A2436

LEGENDS OF HOLLYWOOD

Humphrey Bogart (1899-1957).

Designed by Carl Herrman.

Printed by Stamp Venturers.

PHOTOGRAVURE
Sheets of 120 in six panes of 20

1997, July 31	Tagged	*Perf. 11.1*	
3152 A2435 32c	**multicolored**	.85	.20
	P# block of 4, 5#+S	3.50	—
	Pane of 20	18.50	—
	Sheet of 120 (6 panes)	95.00	—
	Cross gutter block of 8	17.50	—
	Block of 8 with vertical gutter	13.50	—
	Horiz. pair with vert. gutter	3.50	—
	Vert. pair with horiz. gutter	2.50	—

Perforations in corner of each stamp are star-shaped. Cross-gutter block consists of 6 stamps from upper panes and 2 stamps from panes below.
For booklet see No. BK267.

"THE STARS AND STRIPES FOREVER!"

Designed by Richard Sheaff.

Sheets of 300 in six panes of 50
PHOTOGRAVURE

1997, Aug. 21	Tagged	*Perf. 11.1*	
3153 A2436 32c	**multicolored**	.65	.20
	P# block of 4, 4#	3.00	—

For booklet see No. BK268.

AMERICAN MUSIC SERIES
Opera Singers

Lily Pons — A2437

Richard Tucker
A2438

Lawrence Tibbett A2439

Rosa Ponselle A2440

Classical Composers & Conductors

Leopold Stokowski A2441

Arthur Fiedler A2442

George Szell — A2443

Eugene Ormandy A2444

Samuel Barber A2445

Ferde Grofé A2446

Charles Ives — A2447

Louis Moreau Gottschalk A2448

Designed by Howard Paine.

Printed by Ashton-Potter (USA) Ltd.

LITHOGRAPHED
Sheets of 120 in six panes of 20

1997		**Tagged**		***Perf. 11***	
3154	A2437	32c	**multicolored**, *Sept. 10*	.75	.20
3155	A2438	32c	**multicolored**, *Sept. 10*	.75	.20
3156	A2439	32c	**multicolored**, *Sept. 10*	.75	.20
3157	A2440	32c	**multicolored**, *Sept. 10*	.75	.20
a.			Block or strip of 4, #3154-3157	3.00	2.00
			P# block of 4, 5#+P	3.00	—
			P# block of 8, 2 sets of P# + top label	6.00	—
			Pane of 20	15.00	—
3158	A2441	32c	**multicolored**, *Sept. 12*	1.00	.20
3159	A2442	32c	**multicolored**, *Sept. 12*	1.00	.20
3160	A2443	32c	**multicolored**, *Sept. 12*	1.00	.20
3161	A2444	32c	**multicolored**, *Sept. 12*	1.00	.20
3162	A2445	32c	**multicolored**, *Sept. 12*	1.00	.20
3163	A2446	32c	**multicolored**, *Sept. 12*	1.00	.20
3164	A2447	32c	**multicolored**, *Sept. 12*	1.00	.20
3165	A2448	32c	**multicolored**, *Sept. 12*	1.00	.20
a.			Block of 8, #3158-3165	8.00	4.00
			P# block of 8, 2 sets of 5P#+P + top label	10.00	—
			Pane of 20	22.00	

PADRE FÉLIX VARELA (1788-1853)

A2449

Designed by Carl Herrman.

Printed by Sterling Sommer for Ashton-Potter (USA) Ltd.

LITHOGRAPHED
Sheets of 120 in six panes of 20

1997, Sept. 15			**Tagged**	***Perf. 11.2***	
3166	A2449	32c	**purple**	.65	.20
			P# block of 4, 1#+P	2.60	—
			Pane of 20	13.00	—

DEPARTMENT OF THE AIR FORCE, 50TH ANNIV.

Thunderbirds Aerial Demonstration Squadron A2450

Designed by Phil Jordan.

Printed by Sterling Sommer for Ashton-Potter (USA) Ltd.

LITHOGRAPHED
Sheets of 180 in nine panes of 20

1997, Sept. 18			**Tagged**	***Perf. 11.2x11.1***	
3167	A2450	32c	**multicolored**	.65	.20
			P# block of 4, 4#+P	2.60	—
			Pane of 20	13.00	—

A hidden 3-D design can be seen on the stamp when it is viewed with a special viewer sold by the post office.

CLASSIC MOVIE MONSTERS

Lon Chaney as The Phantom of the Opera — A2451

Bela Lugosi as Dracula — A2452

Boris Karloff as Frankenstein's Monster — A2453

Boris Karloff as The Mummy — A2454

Lon Chaney, Jr. as The Wolf Man — A2455

Cross Gutter Block of 8

Illustration reduced.

Designed by Derry Noyes.

Printed by Stamp Venturers.

PHOTOGRAVURE

Sheets of 180 in nine panes of 20

1997, Sept. 30 **Tagged** ***Perf. 10.2***

3168	A2451 32c	**multicolored**	.75	.20
3169	A2452 32c	**multicolored**	.75	.20
3170	A2453 32c	**multicolored**	.75	.20
3171	A2454 32c	**multicolored**	.75	.20
3172	A2455 32c	**multicolored**	.75	.20
a.		Strip of 5, #3168-3172	3.75	2.25
		P# block of 10, 5#+S	7.50	—
		Pane of 20	15.00	—
		Sheet of 180 (9 panes)	130.00	
		Cross-gutter block of 8	17.50	
		Block of 10 with horiz. gutter	12.50	
		Vert. pairs with horiz. gutter (each)	2.50	—
		Horiz. pairs with vert. gutter (each)	2.50	—

Plate blocks may contain top label. See note after No. 3167.
For booklet see No. BK269.

FIRST SUPERSONIC FLIGHT, 50TH ANNIV.

A2456

Designed by Phil Jordan.

Printed by Banknote Corporation of America.

LITHOGRAPHED

Sheets of 180 in nine panes of 20

1997, Oct. 14 **Tagged** ***Serpentine Die Cut 11.4***

Self-Adhesive

3173	A2456 32c	**multicolored**	.65	.20
		P# block of 4, 4#+B	2.60	
		Pane of 20	13.00	

WOMEN IN MILITARY SERVICE

A2457

Designed by Derry Noyes.

Printed by Banknote Corporation of America.

LITHOGRAPHED

Sheets of 120 in six panes of 20

1997, Oct. 18 **Tagged** ***Perf. 11.1***

3174	A2457 32c	**multicolored**	.65	.20
		P# block of 4, 6#+B	2.60	—
		Pane of 20	13.00	

KWANZAA

A2458

Designed by Synthia Saint James. Printed by Avery Dennison.

PHOTOGRAVURE

Sheets of 250 in five panes of 50

1997, Oct. 22 **Tagged** ***Serpentine Die Cut 11***

Self-Adhesive

3175	A2458 32c	**multicolored**	.65	.20
		P# block of 4, 4#+V	3.00	
		Sheet of 250 (5 panes)	*550.00*	
		P# block of 4, 4#+V and 4 sets of #+VO	*225.00*	
		Horiz. pair with vert. gutter	*11.00*	

See Nos. 3368, 3548, 3673.

CHRISTMAS

Madonna and Child, by Sano di Pietro — A2459

Holly — A2460

Designed by Richard D. Sheaff (#3176), Howard Paine (#3177).

Printed by Bureau of Engraving and Printing (#3176), Banknote Corporation of America (#3177).

LITHOGRAPHED

Serpentine Die Cut 9.9 on 2, 3 or 4 Sides

1997 **Tagged**

Booklet Stamps

Self-Adhesive

3176	A2459 32c	**multicolored,** *Oct. 27*	.65	.20
a.		Booklet pane of 20 + label	13.00	

Serpentine Die Cut 11.2x11.6 on 2, 3 or 4 Sides

3177	A2460 32c	**multicolored,** *Oct. 30*	.65	.20
a.		Booklet pane of 20 + label	13.00	
b.		Booklet pane of 4	2.60	
c.		Booklet pane of 5 + label	3.25	
d.		Booklet pane of 6	3.90	

MARS PATHFINDER

Souvenir Sheet

Mars Rover Sojourner — A2461

Illustration reduced.

Designed by Terry McCaffrey. Printed by Stamp Venturers.

PHOTOGRAVURE

1997, Dec. 10 **Tagged** ***Perf. 11x11.1***

3178	A2461 $3	**multicolored**	6.00	4.00
a.		$3, single stamp	5.50	3.00
b.		Single souvenir sheet from sheet of 18	7.00	—
		Sheet of 18	125.00	
		Vert. pair with horiz. gutter	15.00	—

The perforations at the bottom of the stamp contain the letters "USA." Vertical rouletting extends from the vertical perforations of the stamp to the bottom of the souvenir sheet.

Sheet of 18 has vertical perforations separating the three columns of souvenir sheets. These were cut away when No. 3178 was produced. Thus, the souvenir sheet from the sheet of 18 is wider and has vertical perforations on one or two sides.

See note after No. 3167.

CHINESE NEW YEAR

Year of the Tiger A2462

Designed by Clarence Lee. Printed by Stamp Venturers.

PHOTOGRAVURE

Sheets of 180 in nine panes of 20

1998, Jan. 5 **Tagged** ***Perf. 11.2***

3179	A2462 32c	**multicolored**	.80	.20
		P# block of 4, 4#+S	3.75	—
		Pane of 20	18.00	

See No. 3895c.

A2463

A2464

ALPINE SKIING

Designed by Michael Schwab.

Printed by Banknote Corporation of America.

LITHOGRAPHED

Sheets of 180 in nine panes of 20

1998, Jan. 22 **Tagged** ***Perf. 11.2***

3180	A2463 32c	**multicolored**	.65	.20
		P# block of 4, 6#+B	2.60	—
		Pane of 20	13.00	

BLACK HERITAGE SERIES

Madam C.J. Walker (1867-1919), Entrepreneur

Designed by Richard Sheaff. Printed by Banknote Corp. of America.

LITHOGRAPHED

Sheets of 180 in nine panes of 20

Serpentine Die Cut 11.6x11.3

1998, Jan. 28 **Tagged**

Self-Adhesive

3181	A2464 32c	**sepia & black**	.65	.20
		P# block of 4, 3#+B	2.75	
		Pane of 20	13.00	

CELEBRATE THE CENTURY

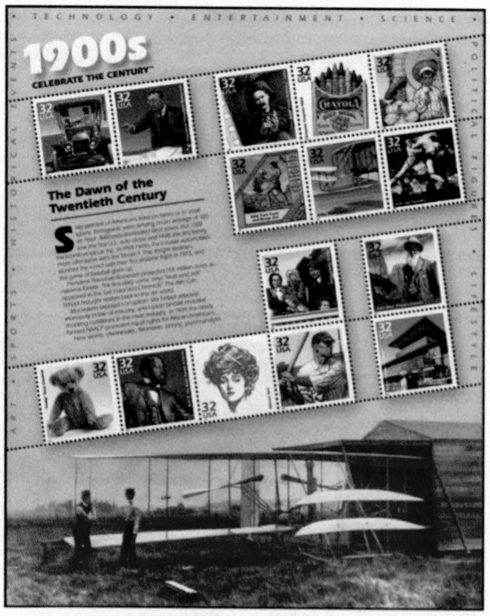

1900s — A2465

No. 3182: a, Model T Ford. b, Theodore Roosevelt. c, Motion picture "The Great Train Robbery," 1903. d, Crayola Crayons introduced, 1903. e, St. Louis World's Fair, 1904. f, Design used on Hunt's Remedy stamp (#RS56), Pure Food & Drug Act, 1906. g, Wright Brothers first flight, Kitty Hawk, 1903. h, Boxing match shown in painting "Stag at Sharkey's," by George Bellows of the Ash Can School. i, Immigrants arrive. j, John Muir, preservationist. k, "Teddy" Bear created. l, W.E.B. Du Bois, social activist. m, Gibson Girl. n, First baseball World Series, 1903. o, Robie House, Chicago, designed by Frank Lloyd Wright.

1910s — A2466

No. 3183: a, Charlie Chaplin as the Little Tramp. b, Federal Reserve System created, 1913. c, George Washington Carver. d, Avant-garde art introduced at Armory Show, 1913. e, First transcontinental telephone line, 1914. f, Panama Canal opens, 1914. g, Jim Thorpe wins decathlon at Stockholm Olympics, 1912. h, Grand Canyon National Park, 1919. i, U.S. enters World War I. j, Boy Scouts started in 1910, Girl Scouts formed in 1912. k, Woodrow Wilson. l, First crossword puzzle published, 1913. m, Jack Dempsey wins heavyweight title, 1919. n, Construction toys. o, Child labor reform.

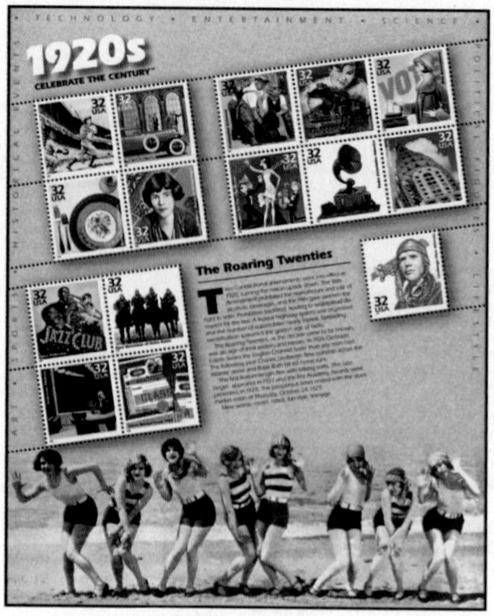

1920s — A2467

No. 3184: a, Babe Ruth. b, The Gatsby style. c, Prohibition enforced. d, Electric toy trains. e, 19th Amendment (woman voting). f, Emily Post's Etiquette. g, Margaret Mead, anthropologist. h, Flappers do the Charleston. i, Radio entertains America. j, Art Deco style (Chrysler Building). k, Jazz flourishes. l, Four Horsemen of Notre Dame. m, Lindbergh flies the Atlantic. n, American realism (The Automat, by Edward Hopper). o, Stock Market crash, 1929.

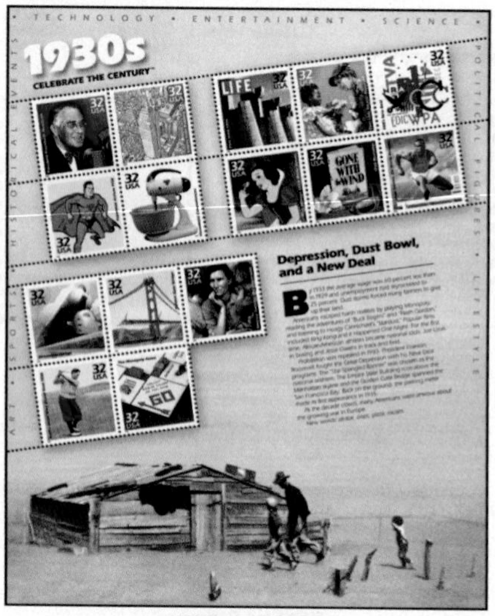

1930s — A2468

No. 3185: a, Franklin D. Roosevelt. b, The Empire State Building. c, 1st Issue of Life Magazine, 1936. d, Eleanor Roosevelt. e, FDR's New Deal. f, Superman arrives, 1938. g, Household conveniences. h, "Snow White and the Seven Dwarfs," 1937. i, "Gone with the Wind," 1936. j, Jesse Owens. k, Streamline design. l, Golden Gate Bridge. m, America survives the Depression. n, Bobby Jones wins golf Grand Slam, 1938. o, The Monopoly Game.

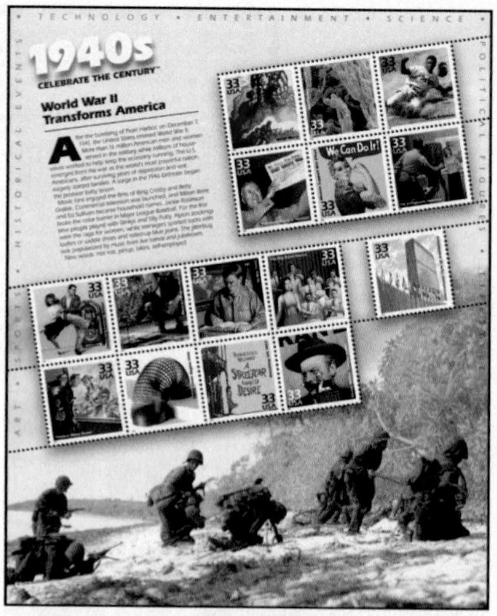

1940s — A2469

No. 3186: a, World War II. b, Antibiotics save lives. c, Jackie Robinson. d, Harry S Truman. e, Women support war effort. f, TV entertains America. g, Jitterbug sweeps nation. h, Jackson Pollock, Abstract Expressionism. i, GI Bill, 1944. j, Big Band Sound. k, Intl. style of architecture (UN Headquarters). l, Postwar baby boom. m, Slinky, 1945. n, "A Streecar Named Desire," 1947. o, Orson Welles' "Citizen Kane."

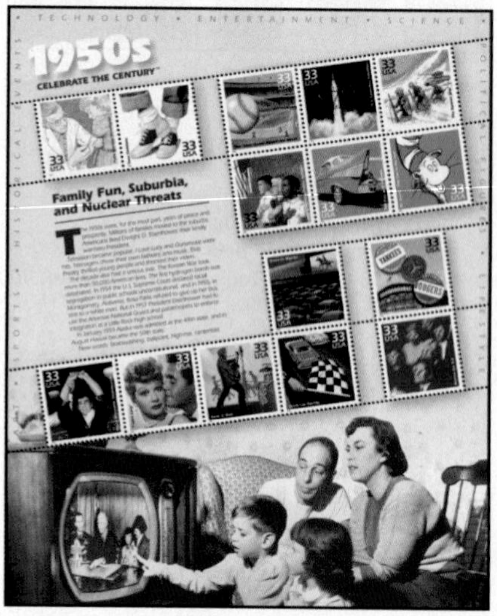

1950s — A2470

No. 3187: a, Polio vaccine developed. b, Teen fashions. c, The "Shot Heard 'Round the World." d, US launches satellites. e, Korean War. f, Desegregating public schools. g, Tail fins, chrome. h, Dr. Seuss' "The Cat in the Hat." i, Drive-in movies. j, World Series rivals. k, Rocky Marciano, undefeated boxer. l, "I Love Lucy." m, Rock 'n Roll. n, Stock car racing. o, Movies go 3-D.

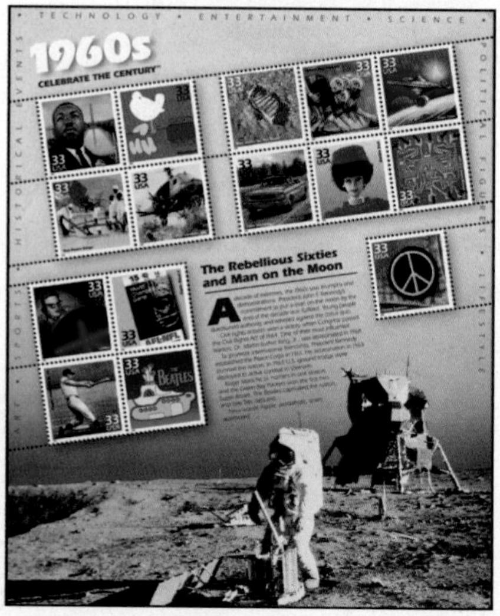

1960s — A2471

No. 3188: a, Martin Luther King, Jr., "I Have a Dream." b, Woodstock. c, Man walks on the moon. d, Green Bay Packers. e, Star Trek. f, The Peace Corps. g, Viet Nam War. h, Ford Mustang. i, Barbie Doll. j, Integrated circuit. k, Lasers. l, Super Bowl I. m, Peace symbol. n, Roger Maris, 61 in '61. o, The Beatles "Yellow Submarine."

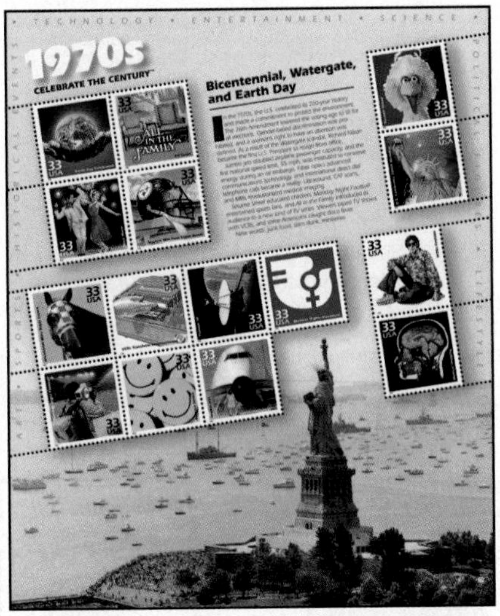

1970s — A2472

No. 3189: a, Earth Day celebrated. b, "All in the Family" television series. c, "Sesame Street" television series character, Big Bird. d, Disco music. e, Pittsburgh Steelers win four Super Bowls. f, US Celebrates 200th birthday. g, Secretariat wins Triple Crown. h, VCRs transform entertainment. i, Pioneer 10. j, Women's rights movement. k, 1970s fashions. l, "Monday Night Football." m, Smiley face buttons. n, Jumbo jets. o, Medical imaging.

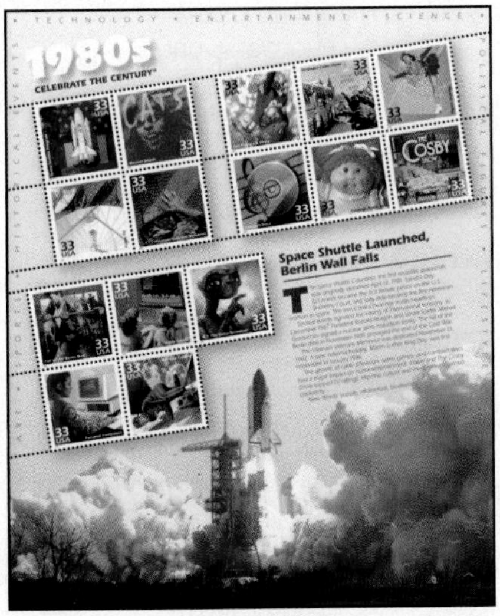

1980s — A2473

No. 3190: a, Space shuttle program. b, "Cats" Broadway show. c, San Francisco 49ers. d, Hostages in Iran come home. e, Figure skating. f, Cable TV. g, Vietnam Veterans Memorial. h, Compact discs. i, Cabbage Patch Kids. j, "The Cosby Show" television series. k, Fall of the Berlin Wall. l, Video games. m, "E. T. The Extra-Terrestrial" movie. n, Personal computers. o, Hip-hop culture.

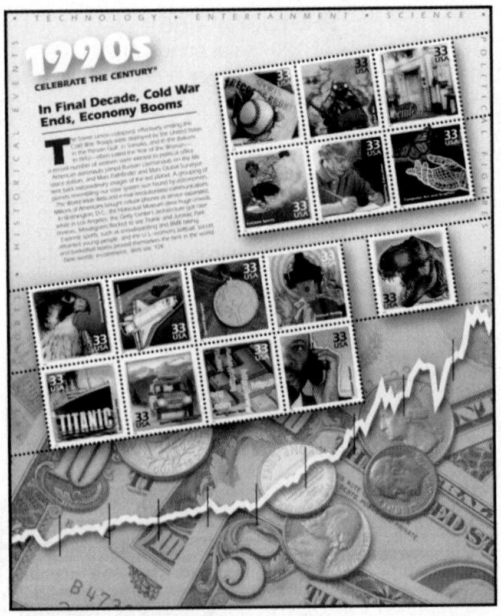

1990s — A2474

No. 3191: a, New baseball records. b, Gulf War. c, "Seinfeld" television series. d, Extreme sports. e, Improving education. f, Computer art and graphics. g, Recovering species. h, Return to space. i, Special Olympics. j, Virtual reality. k, Movie "Jurassic Park." l, Movie "Titanic." m, Sport utility vehicles. n, World Wide Web. o, Cellular phones.

Designed by Richard Waldrep (#3182), Dennis Lyall (#3183), Carl Herrman (#3184, 3188, 3190), Howard Paine (#3185-3187, 3189, 3191).

All illustrations reduced.

Printed by Ashton-Potter (USA) Ltd.

LITHOGRAPHED, ENGRAVED (#3182m, 3183f, 3184m, 3185b, 3186k, 3187a, 3188c, 3189h)

1998-2000 **Tagged** ***Perf. 11½***

3182	A2465	Pane of 15, *Feb. 3, 1998*	12.50	8.50
a.-o.		32c any single	.80	.65
		Sheet of 4 panes	50.00	
p.		Engr. red (No. 3182m, Gibson girl) omitted, in pane of 15	—	
3183	A2466	Pane of 15, *Feb. 3, 1998*	12.50	8.50
a.-o.		32c any single	.80	.65
		Sheet of 4 panes	50.00	
p.		Nos. 3183g, 3183 l-3183o imperf, in pane of 15	*1,250.*	
3184	A2467	Pane of 15, *May 28, 1998*	12.50	8.50
a.-o.		32c any single	.80	.65
		Sheet of 4 panes	50.00	
3185	A2468	Pane of 15, *Sept. 10, 1998*	12.50	8.50
a.-o.		32c any single	.80	.65
		Sheet of 4 panes	50.00	
3186	A2469	Pane of 15, *Feb. 18, 1999*	13.00	8.50
a.-o.		33c any single	.85	.65
		Sheet of 4 panes	52.00	
p.		Tagging omitted on b-j and m-o	—	
3187	A2470	Pane of 15, *May 26, 1999*	13.00	8.50
a.-o.		33c any single	.85	.65
		Sheet of 4 panes	52.00	
p.		Tagging omitted	—	
3188	A2471	Pane of 15, *Sept. 17, 1999*	13.00	8.50
a.-o.		33c any single	.85	.65
		Sheet of 4 panes	52.00	
3189	A2472	Pane of 15, *Nov. 18, 1999*	13.00	8.50
a.-o.		33c any single	.85	.65
		Sheet of 4 panes	52.00	
3190	A2473	Pane of 15, *Jan. 12, 2000*	13.00	8.50
a.-o.		33c any single	.85	.65
		Sheet of 4 panes	52.00	
3191	A2474	Pane of 15, *May 2, 2000*	13.00	8.50
a.-o.		33c any single	.85	.65
		Sheet of 4 panes	52.00	
		Nos. 3182-3191 (10)	128.00	85.00

"REMEMBER THE MAINE"

A2475

Designed by Richard Sheaff.

LITHOGRAPHED & ENGRAVED
Sheets of 120 in six panes of 20

1998, Feb. 15 **Tagged** ***Perf. 11.2x11***

3192	A2475	32c	**red & black**	.65	.20
			P# block of 4, 2#	2.60	—
			Pane of 20	13.00	

FLOWERING TREES

Southern Magnolia — A2476

Blue Paloverde — A2477

Yellow Poplar — A2478

Prairie Crab Apple — A2479

Pacific Dogwood — A2480

Designed by Howard Paine.

Printed by Banknote Corporation of America.

LITHOGRAPHED
Sheets of 120 in six panes of 20

1998, Mar. 19 **Tagged** ***Die Cut Perf 11.3***
Self-Adhesive

3193	A2476	32c	**multicolored**	.65	.20
3194	A2477	32c	**multicolored**	.65	.20
3195	A2478	32c	**multicolored**	.65	.20
3196	A2479	32c	**multicolored**	.65	.20

3197 A2480 32c **multicolored**		.65	.20
a.	Strip of 5, #3193-3197	3.25	
	P# block of 10, 2 sets of B+6#	6.50	
	Pane of 20	13.00	
b.	As "a," die cutting omitted	—	

ALEXANDER CALDER (1898-1976), SCULPTOR

Black Cascade, 13 Verticals, 1959 — A2481

Untitled, 1965 — A2482

Rearing Stallion, 1928 — A2483

Portrait of a Young Man, c. 1945 — A2484

Un Effet du Japonais, 1945 — A2485

Designed by Derry Noyes. Printed by Stamp Venturers.

PHOTOGRAVURE
Sheets of 120 in six panes of 20

1998, Mar. 25 **Tagged** ***Perf. 10.2***

3198 A2481 32c **multicolored**		.65	.20
3199 A2482 32c **multicolored**		.65	.20
3200 A2483 32c **multicolored**		.65	.20
3201 A2484 32c **multicolored**		.65	.20
3202 A2485 32c **multicolored**		.65	.20
a.	Strip of 5, #3198-3202	3.25	2.25
	P# block of 10, 2 sets of S+6#	6.50	—
	Pane of 20	13.00	—
	Sheet of 120 (6 panes)	*110.00*	
	Cross gutter block of 20	*37.50*	—
	Block of 10 with horiz. gutter	*22.50*	—
	Vert. pairs with horiz. gutter (each)	*4.00*	—
	Horiz. pairs with vert. gutter (each)	*5.50*	—

Cross gutter block of 20 consists of six stamps from each of two panes and four stamps from each of two other panes with the cross gutter between. The sheet of 120 was quickly sold out.

A2486

CINCO DE MAYO

Designed by Carl Herrman.

Printed by Stamp Venturers.

PHOTOGRAVURE
Sheets of 180 in nine panes of 20
Serpentine Die Cut 11.7x10.9

1998, Apr. 16 **Tagged**

Self-Adhesive

3203 A2486 32c **multicolored**		.65	.20
	P# block of 4, 5#+S	2.60	
	Pane of 20	13.00	
	Sheet of 180 (9 panes)	*115.00*	
	Cross gutter block of 4	*13.00*	
	Vert. pair with horiz. gutter	*2.25*	
	Horiz. pair with vert. gutter	*2.25*	

See Mexico #2066. For 33c version, see #3309.

A2487

A2488

SYLVESTER & TWEETY

Designed by Brenda Guttman.

Printed by Avery Dennison.

PHOTOGRAVURE

1998, Apr. 27 **Tagged** ***Serpentine Die Cut 11.1***

Self-Adhesive

3204	Pane of 10	6.75	
a.	A2487 32c single	.65	.20
b.	Pane of 9 #3204a	6.00	
c.	Pane of 1 #3204a	.65	
	Sheet of 60 (six panes) top	*70.00*	
	Sheet of 60 (six panes) bottom, with plate #	*110.00*	
	Pane of 10 from sheet of 60	*12.50*	
	Pane of 10 with plate #	*50.00*	
	Cross gutter block of 9 or 10	*45.00*	
	Cross gutter block of 12	*50.00*	
	Vert. pair with horiz. gutter	*7.00*	
	Horiz. pair with vert. gutter	*14.00*	

Die cutting on #3204b does not extend through the backing paper. Pane with plate number comes from bottom uncut sheet of 60.

The horiz. pair with vert. gutter consists of a stamp at the left from either No. 3204b, part of the illustration of Sylvester & Tweety, the small gutter between the panes, and a stamp at the right from the left row of No. 3204b. Some pairs may include the single stamp from No. 3204c in addition to the two stamps at the right and left.

3205	Pane of 10	12.50	
a.	A2487 32c single	1.00	
b.	Pane of 9 #3205a	*9.00*	
c.	Pane of 1, no die cutting	*2.00*	

Die cutting on #3205a extends through the backing paper.

Nos. 3204b-3204c and 3205b-3205c are separated by a vertical line of microperforations, which is absent on the uncut sheets of 60.

WISCONSIN STATEHOOD

Designed by Phil Jordan.

Printed by Sennett Security Products.

PHOTOGRAVURE
Sheets of 120 in six panes of 20
Serpentine Die Cut 10.8x10.9

1998, May 29 **Tagged**

Self-Adhesive

3206 A2488 32c **multicolored**		.65	.30
	P# block of 4, 4#+S	3.00	
	Pane of 20	13.00	

See note after No. 3167.

Wetlands — A2489

Diner — A2490

Designer by Phil Jordan (#3207-3207A), Carl Herrman (#3208, 308A).

Printed by Sennett Security Printers (#3207, 3208), Bureau of Engraving and Printing (#3207A, 3208A).

PHOTOGRAVURE
COIL STAMPS

1998 **Untagged** ***Perf. 10 Vert.***

3207 A2489 (5c) **multicolored,** *June 5*		.20	.20
	Pair	.20	.20
	P# strip of 5, #S1111	1.40	
	P#, single, #S1111	—	.75

Serpentine Die Cut 9.8 Vert.

Self-adhesive

3207A A2489 (5c) **multicolored,** small date, *Dec.14*		.20	.20
	Pair	.20	
	P# strip of 5, #1111, 2222, 3333	1.40	
	P# single, same #	—	.75
b.	Large date	.30	.20
	Pair	.60	
	P# strip of 5, #4444, 5555, 6666	1.40	
	P# single, same #	—	.75

Date on No. 3207A is approximately 1.4mm long, on No. 3207Ab approx. 1.6mm long.

Perf. 10 Vert.

3208 A2490 (25c) **multicolored,** *June 5*		.50	.50
	Pair	1.00	1.00
	P# strip of 5, #S11111	3.50	
	P#, single, #S11111	—	2.00

Serpentine Die Cut 9.8 Vert.

Self-Adhesive

3208A A2490 (25c) **multicolored,** *Sept. 30*		.50	.50
	Pair	1.00	
	P# strip of 5, #11111, 22211, 22222, 33333, 44444, 55555	3.50	
	P# single, same #	—	1.75

1898 TRANS-MISSISSIPPI STAMPS, CENT.

A2491

Illustration reduced.

Designed by Raymond Ostrander Smith (1898), Richard Sheaff (1998).
Printed by Banknote Corporation of America.

LITHOGRAPHED & ENGRAVED
Sheets of 54 in six panes of 9

1998, June 18 **Tagged** ***Perf. 12x12.4***

3209	A2491	Pane of 9	9.00	7.00
a.	A100	1c green & black	.20	.20
b.	A108	2c red brown & black	.20	.20
c.	A102	4c orange & black	.20	.20
d.	A103	5c blue & black	.20	.20
e.	A104	8c dark lilac & black	.20	.20
f.	A105	10c purple & black	.20	.20
g.	A106	50c green & black	1.25	.60
h.	A107	$1 red & black	2.25	1.25
i.	A101	$2 red brown & black	4.25	2.50
		Block of 9 with horiz. gutter	35.00	
		Vert. pairs with horiz. gutter (each)	10.00	

Vignettes on Nos. 3209b and 3209i are reversed in comparison to the original issue.
Vert. pairs consist of #3209g-3209a, 3209h-3209b, 3209i-3209c.

3210 A107	$1	Pane of 9 #3209h	18.00	—
		Sheet of 6 panes, 3 each #3209-3210	*125.00*	
		Cross gutter block of 12	55.00	—
		Block of 18 (2 panes) with vert. gutter between & selvage on 4 sides	*47.50*	—
		Block of 12 with vert. gutter	*32.50*	—
		Vert. pair #3209h with horiz. gutter	10.00	
		Horiz. pairs with vert. gutter (each)	10.00	

Block of 12 contains #3209 and one column of 3 #3209h from #3210 separated by vert. gutter.

BERLIN AIRLIFT, 50th ANNIV.

A2492

Designed by Bill Bond.
Printed by Banknote Corporation of America.

PHOTOGRAVURE
Sheets of 120 in six panes of 20

1998, June 26 **Tagged** ***Perf. 11.2***

3211	A2492	32c	**multicolored**	.65	.20
			P# block of 4, 4#+B	2.60	—
			Pane of 20	13.00	—

AMERICAN MUSIC SERIES
Folk Singers

Huddie "Leadbelly" Ledbetter (1888-1949) A2493

Woody Guthrie (1912-67) A2494

Sonny Terry (1911-86) A2495

Josh White (1908-69) A2496

Designed by Howard Paine.
Printed by American Packaging Corp. for Sennett Security Products.

PHOTOGRAVURE
Sheets of 180 in nine panes of 20

1998, June 26 **Tagged** ***Perf. 10.1x10.2***

3212	A2493	32c	**multicolored**	.75	.20
3213	A2494	32c	**multicolored**	.75	.20
3214	A2495	32c	**multicolored**	.75	.20
3215	A2496	32c	**multicolored**	.75	.20
a.			Block or strip of 4, #3212-3215	3.00	2.00
			P# block of 4, 5#+S	3.00	—
			P# block of 8, 2 sets of P# + top label	6.00	—
			Pane of 20	15.00	—

AMERICAN MUSIC SERIES
Gospel Singers

Mahalia Jackson (1911-72) A2497

Roberta Martin (1917-69) A2498

Clara Ward (1924-73) A2499

Sister Rosetta Tharpe (1921-73) A2500

Designed by Howard Paine.
Printed by American Packaging Corp. for Sennett Security Products.

PHOTOGRAVURE
Sheets of 120 in six panes of 20

1998, July 15 **Tagged** ***Perf. 10.1x10.3***

3216	A2497	32c	**multicolored**	.65	.20
3217	A2498	32c	**multicolored**	.65	.20
3218	A2499	32c	**multicolored**	.65	.20
3219	A2500	32c	**multicolored**	.65	.20
a.			Block or strip of 4, #3216-3219	2.60	2.00
			P# block of 4, 6#+S	3.50	—
			P# block of 8, 2 sets of P# + top label	7.00	—
			Pane of 20	17.00	—

SPANISH SETTLEMENT OF THE SOUTHWEST

La Mision de San Miguel de San Gabriel, Espanola, NM — A2501

Designed by Richard Sheaff.
Printed by Banknote Corporation of America.

LITHOGRAPHED
Sheets of 180 in nine panes of 20

1998, July 11 **Tagged** ***Perf. 11.2***

3220	A2501	32c	**multicolored**	.65	.20
			P# block of 4, 4#+B	2.60	—
			Pane of 20	13.00	—

LITERARY ARTS SERIES

Stephen Vincent Benét (1898-43) A2502

Designed by Carl Herrman.
Printed by Ashton-Potter (USA) Ltd.

LITHOGRAPHED
Sheets of 180 in nine panes of 20

1998, July 22 **Tagged** ***Perf. 11.2***

3221	A2502	32c	**multicolored**	.65	.20
			P# block of 4, 4#+P	2.60	—
			Pane of 20	13.00	—

TROPICAL BIRDS

Antillean Euphonia A2503

Green-throated Carib — A2504

Crested Honeycreeper
A2505

Cardinal Honeyeater
A2506

Designed by Phil Jordan.

Printed by Banknote Corporation of America.

LITHOGRAPHED

Sheets of 180 in nine panes of 20

1998, July 29 Tagged *Perf. 11.2*

3222	A2503	32c	**multicolored**	.65	.20
3223	A2504	32c	**multicolored**	.65	.20
3224	A2505	32c	**multicolored**	.65	.20
3225	A2506	32c	**multicolored**	.65	.20
a.			Block or strip of 4, #3222-3225	2.60	2.00
			P# block of 4, 4#+B	2.60	—
			Pane of 20	13.00	—

For booklet see No. BK272.

LEGENDS OF HOLLYWOOD

Alfred Hitchcock (1899-1980) — A2507

Designed by Richard Sheaff.

Printed at American Packaging Corp. for Sennett Security Products.

PHOTOGRAVURE

Sheets of 120 in six panes of 20

1998, Aug. 3 Tagged *Perf. 11.1*

3226	A2507	32c	**multicolored**	.75	.20
			P# block of 4, 4#+S	4.50	—
			Pane of 20	20.00	12.50
			Sheet of 120 (6 panes)	85.00	
			Cross gutter block of 8	19.00	—
			Block of 8 with vert. gutter	13.50	—
			Horiz. pair with vert. gutter	3.50	—
			Vert. pair with horiz. gutter	2.25	—

Perforations in corner of each stamp are star-shaped. Cross-gutter block consists of 6 stamps from upper panes and 2 stamps from panes below. Hitchcock's profile in the UL corner of each stamp is laser cut.

ORGAN & TISSUE DONATION

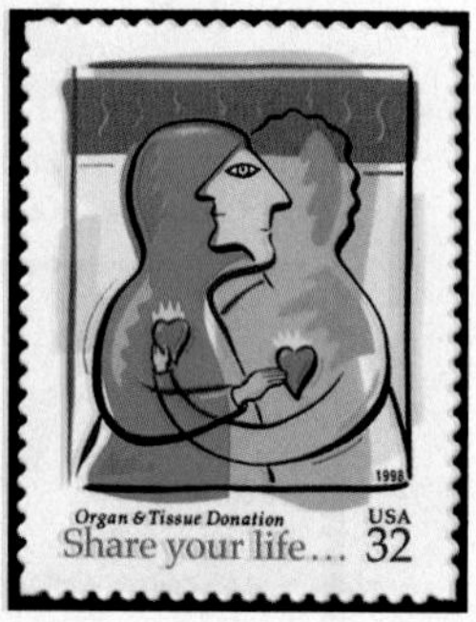

A2508

Designed by Richard Sheaff. Printed by Avery Dennison.

PHOTOGRAVURE

Sheets of 160 in eight panes of 20

1998, Aug. 5 Tagged *Serpentine Die Cut 11.7*

Self-Adhesive

3227	A2508	32c	**multicolored**	.65	.20
			P# block of 4 5#+V	2.60	
			Pane of 20	13.00	

MODERN BICYCLE

A2509

Designed by Richard Sheaff. Printed by Bureau of Engraving and Printing (#3228), Sennett Security Printers (#3229).

PHOTOGRAVURE

COIL STAMP

Serpentine Die Cut 9.8 Vert.

1998, Aug. 14 Untagged

Self-Adhesive (#3228)

3228	A2509	(10c)	**multicolored,** small "1998" year date	.20	.20
			Pair	.40	
			P# strip of 5, P#111, 221, 222, 333, 344, 444, 555	2.25	
			P# single, same #		1.75
a.			Large date	.25	.20
			Pair	.50	
			P# strip of 5, #666, 777, 888, 999	2.25	
			P# single, #666, 777, 888, 999	—	2.25

Date on No. 3228a is approximately 1½mm; on No. 3228 approximately 1mm.

Untagged

Perf. 9.9 Vert.

3229	A2509	(10c)	**multicolored**	.20	.20
			Pair	.40	.25
			P# strip of 5, P#S111	2.50	
			P# single, same #	—	1.75

BRIGHT EYES

Dog — A2510

Fish — A2511

Cat — A2512

Parakeet
A2513

Hamster
A2514

Designed by Carl Herrman. Printed at Guilford Gravure for Banknote Corp. of America.

PHOTOGRAVURE

Sheets of 180 in nine panes of 20

1998, Aug. 20 Tagged *Serpentine Die Cut 9.9*

Self-Adhesive

3230	A2510	32c	**multicolored**	.75	.20
3231	A2511	32c	**multicolored**	.75	.20
3232	A2512	32c	**multicolored**	.75	.20
3233	A2513	32c	**multicolored**	.75	.20
3234	A2514	32c	**multicolored**	.75	.20
a.			Strip of 5, #3230-3234	3.75	
			P# block of 8, 2 sets of 6#+B	7.50	
			Pane of 20	15.00	

Hidden 3-D designs can be seen on each stamp when viewed with a special viewer sold by the post office.

Plate blocks may contain top label.

KLONDIKE GOLD RUSH, CENTENNIAL

A2515

Designed by Howard Paine. Printed at Sterling Sommer for Ashton Potter (USA) Ltd.

LITHOGRAPHED

Sheets of 180 in nine panes of 20

1998, Aug. 21 Tagged *Perf. 11.1*

3235	A2515	32c	**multicolored**	.65	.20
			P# block of 4, 5#+P	2.60	—
			Pane of 20	13.00	—

AMERICAN ART

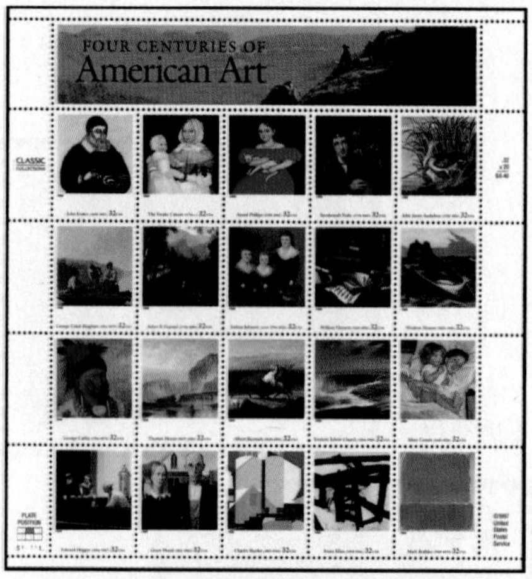

A2516

Illustration reduced.

Designed by Howard Paine. Printed by Sennett Security Products.

Paintings: a, "Portrait of Richard Mather," by John Foster. b, "Mrs. Elizabeth Freake and Baby Mary," by The Freake Limner. c, "Girl in Red Dress with Cat and Dog," by Ammi Phillips. d, "Rubens Peale with a Geranium," by Rembrandt Peale. e, "Long-billed Curlew, Numenius Longrostris," by John James Audubon. f, "Boatmen on the Missouri," by George Caleb Bingham. g, "Kindred Sprits," by Asher B. Durand. h, "The Westwood Children," by Joshua Johnson. i, "Music and Literature," by William Harnett. j, "The Fog Warning," by Winslow Homer. k, "The White Cloud, Head Chief of the Iowas," by George Catlin. l, "Cliffs of Green River," by Thomas Moran. m, "The Last of the Buffalo," by Alfred Bierstadt. n, "Niagara," by Frederic Edwin Church. o, "Breakfast in Bed," by Mary Cassatt. p, "Nighthawks," by Edward Hopper. q, "American Gothic," by Grant Wood. r, "Two Against the White," by Charles Sheeler. s, "Mahoning," by Franz Kline. t, "No. 12," by Mark Rothko.

PHOTOGRAVURE

Sheets of 120 stamps in six panes of 20

1998, Aug. 27 Tagged *Perf. 10.2*

3236	A2516 Pane of 20	17.50	10.00
a.-t.	32c any single	.85	.60
	Sheet of 120 (six panes)	100.00	
	Cross gutter block of 20	30.00	—
	Vert. pairs with horiz. gutter (each)	3.25	—
	Horiz. pairs with vert. gutter (each)	3.25	—

Inscriptions on the back of each stamp describe the painting and the artist.

Cross gutter block of 20 consists of six stamps from each of two panes and four stamps from each of two other panes with the cross gutter between.

AMERICAN BALLET

A2517

Designed by Derry Noyes. Printed by Sterling Sommer for Ashton-Potter (USA) Ltd.

LITHOGRAPHED

Sheets of 120 in six panes of 20

1998, Sept. 16 Tagged *Perf. 10.9x11.1*

3237 A2517 32c **multicolored**	.65	.20
P# block of 4, 4#+P	3.00	—
Pane of 20	14.50	—
Sheet of 120 (six panes)	85.00	
Cross gutter block of 4	14.00	—
Vert. pair with horiz. gutter	2.25	—
Horiz. pair with vert. gutter	2.25	—

For booklet see No. BK273.

SPACE DISCOVERY

A2518

A2519

A2520

A2521

A2522

Designed by Phil Jordan. Printed at American Packaging Corp. for Sennett Security Products.

PHOTOGRAVURE

Sheets of 180 in nine panes of 20

1998, Oct. 1 Tagged *Perf. 11.1*

3238	A2518 32c **multicolored**	.65	.20
3239	A2519 32c **multicolored**	.65	.20
3240	A2520 32c **multicolored**	.65	.20
3241	A2521 32c **multicolored**	.65	.20
3242	A2522 32c **multicolored**	.65	.20
a.	Strip of 5, #3238-3242	3.25	2.25
	P# block of 10, 2 sets of 5#+S	6.50	—
	Pane of 20	13.00	
	Sheet of 180 (9 panes)	110.00	
	Cross gutter block of 10	17.50	—
	Vert. block of 10 with horiz. gutter	10.00	—
	Horiz. pair (#3238, 3242) with vert. gutter	2.00	—
	Vert. pairs with horiz. gutter (each)	2.00	
	Pane of 20 from sheet of 180	12.00	—

Hidden 3-D designs can be seen on each stamp when viewed with a special viewer sold by the post office.

Plate blocks may contain top label.

Cross gutter block of 10 consists of two stamps from each of two panes and three stamps from each of two other panes with the cross gutter between. Pane of 20 from sheet of 180 has vertical perforations on one or both sides and is wider than pane sold in local post offices.

For booklet see No. BK274.

GIVING AND SHARING

A2523

Designed by Bob Dinetz.

Printed by Avery Dennison.

PHOTOGRAVURE

Sheets of 200 in ten panes of 20

1998, Oct. 7 Tagged *Serpentine Die Cut 11.1*

Self-Adhesive

3243 A2523 32c **multicolored**	.65	.20
P# block of 4, 4#+V	2.60	—
Pane of 20	13.00	—

CHRISTMAS

Madonna and Child, Florence, 15th Cent. — A2524

Evergreen Wreath — A2525

Victorian Wreath — A2526

Chili Pepper Wreath — A2527

Tropical Wreath — A2528

Designed by Richard D. Sheaff (#3244), Lilian Dinihanian (A2525), George de Bruin (A2526), Chris Crinklaw (A2527), Micheale Thunin (A2528).

Printed by Bureau of Engraving and Printing (#3244), Banknote Corporation of America (#3245-3252).

LITHOGRAPHED

Sheets of 160 in 8 panes of 20 (#3249-3252)

Serpentine Die Cut 10.1x9.9 on 2, 3 or 4 Sides

1998, Oct. 15 Tagged

Self-Adhesive

Booklet Stamps

3244	A2524 32c **multicolored**	.65	.20
a.	Booklet pane of 20 + label	13.00	
b.	Die cutting omitted, pair	—	

Serpentine Die Cut 11.3x11.7 on 2 or 3 Sides

3245	A2525 32c **multicolored**	6.00	.20
3246	A2526 32c **multicolored**	6.00	.20
3247	A2527 32c **multicolored**	6.00	.20
3248	A2528 32c **multicolored**	6.00	.20
a.	Booklet pane of 4, #3245-3248	25.00	
b.	Booklet pane of 5, #3245-3246, 3248, 2 #3247 + label	32.50	
c.	Booklet pane of 6, #3247-3248, 2 each #3245-3246	40.00	
d.	As "a," die cutting omitted	—	
e.	As "b," die cutting omitted	—	
f.	As "c," die cutting omitted	—	

Size: 23x30mm

Serpentine Die Cut 11.4x11.5 on 2, 3, or 4 Sides

3249	A2525 32c **multicolored**	1.75	.20
a.	Serp. die cut 11.7x11.6 on 2, 3, or 4 sides	1.75	.20
3250	A2526 32c **multicolored**	1.75	.20
a.	Serp. die cut 11.7x11.6 on 3 or 4 sides	1.75	.20
3251	A2527 32c **multicolored**	1.75	.20
a.	Serp. die cut 11.7x11.6 on 3 or 4 sides	1.75	.20
3252	A2528 32c **multicolored + label**	1.75	.20
a.	Serp. die cut 11.7x11.6 on 2, 3, or 4 sides	1.75	.20
b.	Block or strip of 4, #3249-3252	7.00	
	P#block of 4, 6#+B	7.50	
	Pane of 20	37.50	
c.	Booklet pane of 20, 5 each #3249-3252 + label	35.00	
d.	Block or strip of 4, #3249a-3252a	7.00	
e.	Booklet pane of 20, 5 each #3249a-3252a + label	35.00	
f.	Block or strip of 4, #3249-3252, red ("Greetings 32 USA" and "1998") omitted on #3249, 3252	*700.00*	
g.	Block or strip of 4, #3249-3252, red ("Greetings 32 USA" and "1998") omitted on #3249, 3252; green (same) omitted on #3250, 3251	—	
h.	As "b," die cutting omitted	—	
i.	As "c," die cutting omitted	—	

Dedicated printing plates were used to print the red and green denominations, salutations and dates. Red and green appearing in the wreaths come from other plates and, therefore, are not part of the color omissions.

Specialists will want to note that the "1998" date on the flat pane of 20 is about .1mm wider than the date on the corresponding booklet pane (No. 3252c). The measurements are approximately 1.3mm versus 1.2mm, respectively. Therefore, unused and used singles can be distinguished.

Weather Vane — A2529

Uncle Sam — A2530

Uncle Sam's Hat — A2531

Space Shuttle Landing
A2532

Piggyback Space Shuttle
A2533

Designed by Terry McCaffrey (#3257-3258, 3260, 3264-3269), Richard Sheaff (#3259, 3263), Phil Jordan (#3261-3262).

Printed by Ashton Potter (USA) Ltd. (#3257), American Packaging Corp. for Sennett Security Products (#3259), Stamp Venturers (#3260), Banknote Corporation of America (#3258, 3261-3262), Bureau of Engraving and Printing (#3263-3267), Avery Dennison (#3268-3269).

LITHOGRAPHED

Sheets of 400 in eight panes of 50 (#3257, 3260), Sheets of 300 in six panes of 50 (#3258), Sheets of 160 in eight panes of 20 (#3259), Sheets of 120 in six panes of 20 (#3261-3262)

1998 Untagged *Perf. 11.2*

3257 A2529 (1c) **multicolored** *Nov. 9* .20 .20
P# block of 4, 5# + P .25 —
a. Black omitted 135.00
3258 A2529 (1c) **multicolored**, *Nov. 9* .20 .20
P# block of 4, 5# + B .25 —

No. 3257 is 18mm high, has thin letters, white USA, and black 1998. No. 3258 is 17mm high, has thick letters, pale blue USA and blue 1998.

PHOTOGRAVURE

Tagged

Serpentine Die Cut 10.8

Self-Adhesive (#3259, 3261-3263, 3265-3269)

3259 A2530 22c **multicolored**, *Nov. 9* .45 .20
a. Die cut 10.8x10.5 2.50 .25
b. Vert. pair, No. 3259 + 3259a 3.50
P# block of 4, 4# + S, all No. 3259 2.50
P# block of 4, top stamps No. 3259, bottom stamps No. 3259a —
P# block of 4, top stamps No. 3259a, bottom stamps No. 3259 7.50
Pane of 20, all No. 3259 9.00
Pane of 20, row 1 No. 3259a, rows 2-4 No. 3259 —
Pane of 20, row 2 No. 3259a, rows 1, 3-4 No. 3259 35.00
Pane of 20, row 3 No. 3259a, rows 1-2, 4 No. 3259 15.00
Pane of 20, row 4 No. 3259a, rows 1-3 No. 3259 30.00

See No. 3353.

Perf. 11.2

3260 A2531 (33c) **multicolored**, shiny gum, *Nov. 9* .65 .20
P# block of 4 4#+S 2.75 —
Low-gloss gum .65 .20
P# block of 4 4#+S 2.75 —

LITHOGRAPHED

Serpentine Die Cut 11.5

3261 A2532 $3.20 **multicolored**, *Nov. 9* 6.00 1.50
P# block of 4, 4#+B 24.00
Pane of 20 120.00
3262 A2533 $11.75 **multicolored**, *Nov. 19* 22.50 10.00
P# block of 4, 4#+B 90.00
Pane of 20 450.00

COIL STAMPS

PHOTOGRAVURE

Serpentine Die Cut 9.9 Vert.

3263 A2530 22c **multicolored**, *Nov. 9* .45 .20
Pair .90
P# strip of 5, #1111 4.00
P# single, same # 1.75
a. Die cutting omitted, pair —

See No. 3353.

Perf. 9.8 Vert.

3264 A2531 (33c) **multicolored**, *Nov. 9* .65 .20
Pair 1.30 .30
P# strip of 5, #1111, 3333, 3343, 3344, 3444 6.50
P# single, same # 3.75
a. Imperf, pair 35.00

On No. 3264, the black plate #1 of plate #1111 used in printing rolls of 100 places the plate digit "1" farther from the black printing in the vignette than does the black plate #1 of plate #1111 used in printing rolls of 3,000. These are referred to as "Low black 1" and "Hi black 1" and are used by plate number specialists to distinguish the different printings from plate #1111.

Serpentine Die Cut 9.9 Vert.

3265 A2531 (33c) **multicolored**, *Nov. 9* .80 .20
Pair 1.60
P# strip of 5, #1111, 1131, 2222, 3333 7.50
P# single, same # 4.50
a. Die cutting omitted, pair 75.00 —
b. Red omitted *625.00*
c. Black omitted —
d. Black omitted, die cutting omitted, pair —
e. Red omitted, die cutting omitted, pair —

Unused examples of No. 3265 are on backing paper the same size as the stamps. Corners of the stamp are 90 degree angles.

On No. 3265b, the blue and gray colors are shifted down and to the right.

Serpentine Die Cut 9.9 Vert.

3266 A2531 (33c) **multicolored**, *Nov. 9* 1.75 .20
Pair 3.50
P# strip of 5, #1111 12.50
P# single, same # 3.50

Unused examples of No. 3266 are on backing paper larger than the stamps, and the stamps are spaced approximately 2mm. apart. Corners of stamps are rounded.

BOOKLET STAMPS

Serpentine Die Cut 9.9 on 2 or 3 Sides

3267 A2531 (33c) **multicolored**, *Nov. 9* .75 .20
a. Booklet pane of 10 7.50

Serpentine Die Cut 11¼ on 3 Sides (#3268, 3268a)

or 11 on 2, 3 or 4 sides (#3268b, 3268c)

3268 A2531 (33c) **multicolored**, *Nov. 9* .75 .20
a. Booklet pane of 10 7.50
b. Serpentine die cut 11 .75 .20
c. As "b," booklet pane of 20 + label 15.00

Die Cut 8 on 2, 3 or 4 Sides

3269 A2531 (33c) **multicolored**, *Nov. 9* .65 .20
a. Booklet pane of 18 12.00

Unused and used examples of an "H" nondenominated stamp inscribed "Postcard Rate" exist in the marketplace. There is no evidence that these stamps were ever officially issued.

A2534

Designed by Chris Calle.

PHOTOGRAVURE

COIL STAMPS

1998, Dec. 14 Untagged *Perf. 9.8 Vert.*

3270 A2534 (10c) **multicolored**, small date .20 .20
Pair .40 .40
P# strip of 5, #11111 2.25
P# single, #11111 2.00
a. Large date .45 .20
Pair .90 .40
P# strip of 5, #22222 6.00 —
P# single, same # — 5.00

Self-Adhesive

Serpentine Die Cut 9.9 Vert.

3271 A2534 (10c) **multicolored**, small date .20 .20
Pair .40
P# strip of 5, #11111, 22222 2.25
P# single, #11111, 22222 1.75
a. Large date 1.00 .20
Pair 2.00
P# strip of 5, #33333 5.00
P# single, #33333 — 6.00
b. Tagged (error) 1.25 .75
Pair 2.50
P# strip of 5, #11111 10.00
P# single, #11111 — 9.50

No. 3271 is known with eagle in red brown rather than the normal golden brown, apparently from contaminated ink. Values slightly higher than normal No. 3271.

Dates on Nos. 3270a and 3271a are approximately 1¾mm; on Nos. 3270-3271 approximately 1¼mm.

Compare to Nos. 2602-2604, 2907.

Scott values for used self-adhesive stamps are for examples either on piece or off piece.

CHINESE NEW YEAR

Year of the Rabbit
A2535

Designed by Clarence Lee.

Printed at American Packaging Corp. for Sennett Security Printers.

PHOTOGRAVURE

Sheets of 180 in nine panes of 20

1999, Jan. 5 Tagged *Perf. 11.2*

3272 A2535 33c **multicolored** .80 .20
P# block of 4, 4#+S 3.25 —
Pane of 20 17.00 —

See No. 3895d.

BLACK HERITAGE SERIES

Malcolm X (1925-65), Civil Rights Activist — A2536

Designed by Richard Sheaff. Printed by Banknote Corp. of America.

LITHOGRAPHED

Sheets of 180 in nine panes of 20

1999, Jan. 20 Tagged *Serpentine Die Cut 11.4*

Self-Adhesive

3273 A2536 33c **multicolored** .85 .20
P# block of 4, 3#+B 3.40
Pane of 20 17.00

LOVE

A2537

A2538

Designed by John Grossman, Holly Sudduth.

Printed by Avery Dennison.

PHOTOGRAVURE

1999, Jan. 28 Tagged *Die Cut*

Booklet Stamp

Self-Adhesive

3274 A2537 33c **multicolored** .65 .20
a. Booklet pane of 20 13.00
b. Die cutting omitted, pair *175.00*
c. As "a," die cutting omitted *1,800.*

Sheets of 160 in eight panes of 20

3275 A2538 55c **multicolored** 1.10 .20
P# block of 4, 7#+B 4.40
Pane of 20 22.00

HOSPICE CARE

A2539

Designed by Phil Jordan.

Printed by Banknote Corp. of America.

LITHOGRAPHED

Sheets of 120 in six panes of 20

1999, Feb. 9 Tagged *Serpentine Die Cut 11.4*

3276	A2539 33c **multicolored**		.65	.20
		P# block of 4, 4#+B	2.80	
		Pane of 20	13.50	

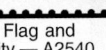

Flag and City — A2540

Flag and Chalkboard — A2541

Designed by Richard Sheaff. Printed by Bureau of Engraving and Printing (#3277, 3279-3282), Avery Dennison (#3278, 3278F, 3283).

PHOTOGRAVURE

Sheets of 400 in four panes of 100 (#3277),

Sheets of 200 in ten panes of 20 (#3278)

1999, Feb. 25 Tagged *Perf. 11.2*

Self-Adhesive (#3278, 3278F, 3279, 3281-3282)

3277	A2540 33c **multicolored**		.70	.20
		P# block of 4, 4#	47.50	—

No. 3277 has red date.

Serpentine Die Cut 11 on 2, 3 or 4 Sides

3278	A2540 33c **multicolored**		.65	.20
		P# block of 4, 4#+V	4.25	
		Pane of 20	20.00	
a.	Booklet pane of 4		2.60	
b.	Booklet pane of 5 + label		3.25	
		P# single, #V1111, V1112, V1121, V1122, V1212, V2212	.80	1.00
c.	Booklet pane of 6		3.90	
d.	Booklet pane of 10		12.50	
e.	Booklet pane of 20 + label		17.00	
h.	As "e," die cutting omitted		—	
i.	Serpentine die cut 11¼		1.40	.20
j.	As "i," booklet pane of 10		14.00	

No. 3278 has black date.

The plate # single in No. 3278b is the lower left single.

BOOKLET STAMPS

Serpentine Die Cut 11½x11¾ on 2, 3 or 4 Sides

3278F	A2540 33c **multicolored**	1.10	.20
g.	Booklet pane of 20 + label	22.50	

No. 3278F has black date.

Serpentine Die Cut 9.8 on 2 or 3 Sides

3279	A2540 33c **multicolored**	.85	.20
a.	Booklet pane of 10	8.50	

No. 3279 has red date.

COIL STAMPS

Perf. 9.9 Vert.

3280	A2540 33c **multicolored,** small "1999" year date		.65	.20
		Pair	1.30	.30
		P# strip of 5, #1111, 2222	4.00	—
		P# single, same #		1.50
a.	Large date		1.25	.20
		Pair	2.50	.30
		P# strip of 5, #3333	9.00	—
		P# single, same #	—	5.00
b.	As No. 3280, imperf pair		—	

Serpentine Die Cut 9.8 Vert.

Two types of No. 3281: Type I, Long vertical feature at left and right of tallest building consists of 3 separate lines; Type II, Same features consist of solid color.

3281	A2540 33c **multicolored,** type I, large "1999" year date		.65	.20
		Pair	1.30	
		P# strip of 5, #6666, 7777, 8888, 9999, 1111A, 2222A, 3333A, 4444A, 5555A, 6666A, 7777A, 8888A, 1111B, 2222B	4.75	
		P# single, same #		1.00
		P# single, #7777A, 8888A, 1111B, 2222B	—	1.50
a.	Die cutting omitted, pair		30.00	
b.	Light blue and yellow omitted		*575.00*	
c.	Small date, type II		.65	.20
		Pair	1.30	
		P# strip of 5, #1111, 2222, 3333, 3433, 4443, 4444, 5555	5.50	
		P# single, same #	—	1.25
d.	Small date, type I		5.00	.30
		Pair	10.00	
		P# strip of 5, #9999A	30.00	
		P# single, same #		3.50
e.	As "c," die cutting omitted, pair		—	

Corners are square on #3281. Unused examples are on backing paper the same size as the stamps, and the stamps are adjoining.

Date on Nos. 3280a and 3281 is approximately 1¾mm; on Nos. 3280, 3281c and 3281d approximately 1¼mm.

3282	A2540 33c **multicolored**		.65	.20
		Pair	1.30	
		P# strip of 5, #1111, 2222	4.00	
		P# single, same #		3.25

Corners are rounded on #3282. Unused examples are on backing paper larger than the stamps, and the stamps are spaced approximately 2mm. apart.

PHOTOGRAVURE

Serpentine Die Cut 7.9 on 2, 3 or 4 Sides

1999, Mar. 13 Tagged

Self-Adhesive

BOOKLET STAMP

3283	A2541 33c **multicolored**	.65	.20
a.	Booklet pane of 18	12.00	

IRISH IMMIGRATION

A2542

Designed by Howard Paine. Printed by Ashton-Potter (USA) Ltd.

LITHOGRAPHED

Sheets of 180 in nine panes of 20

1999, Feb. 26 Tagged *Perf. 11.2*

3286	A2542 33c **multicolored**		.65	.20
		P# block of 4, 4#+P	2.60	—
		Pane of 20	13.00	—

See Ireland No. 1168.

PERFORMING ARTS SERIES

Alfred Lunt (1892-1977), Lynn Fontanne (1887-1983), Actors

A2543

Designed by Carl Herrman. Printed by Sterling Sommer for Ashton-Potter (USA) Ltd.

LITHOGRAPHED

Sheets of 180 in nine panes of 20

1999, Mar. 2 Tagged *Perf. 11.2*

3287	A2543 33c **multicolored**		.65	.20
		P# block of 4, 4#+P	2.60	—
		Pane of 20	13.00	—

ARCTIC ANIMALS

Arctic Hare — A2544

Arctic Fox — A2545

Snowy Owl — A2546

Polar Bear — A2547

Gray Wolf — A2548

Designed by Derry Noyes. Printed by Banknote Corp. of America.

LITHOGRAPHED

Sheets of 90 in six panes of 15

1999, Mar. 12 Tagged *Perf. 11*

3288	A2544 33c **multicolored**	.85	.20
3289	A2545 33c **multicolored**	.85	.20
3290	A2546 33c **multicolored**	.85	.20
3291	A2547 33c **multicolored**	.85	.20

3292 A2548 33c **multicolored** .85 .20
a. Strip of 5, #3288-3292 4.25 —
Pane of 15, 6#+B 13.00 —

While the normal definition of a plate block dictates a block of 10, this would require collectors to discard the decorative label and top row of stamps from the pane of 15. To avoid destroying the more collectible entire, We list the entire pane as the plate block.

SONORAN DESERT

A2549

Illustration reduced.

Designed by Ethel Kessler. Printed by Banknote Corporation of America.

Designs: a, Cactus wren, brittlebush, teddy bear cholla. b, Desert tortoise. c, White-winged dove, prickly pear. d, Gambel quail. e, Saguaro cactus. f, Desert mule deer. g, Desert cotton-tail, hedgehog cactus. h, Gila monster. i, Western diamondback rattlesnake, cactus mouse. j, Gila woodpecker.

LITHOGRAPHED
Sheets of 60 in six panes of 10
Serpentine Die Cut Perf 11.2
1999, Apr. 6 **Tagged**
Self-Adhesive

3293 A2549 Pane of 10 6.50
a.-j. 33c any single .65 .50
Sheet of 6 panes 40.00

BERRIES

Blueberries
A2550

Raspberries
A2551

Strawberries
A2552

Blackberries
A2553

Designed by Howard Paine. Printed by Guilford Gravure for Banknote Corporation of America.

PHOTOGRAVURE
Serpentine Die Cut 11¼x11½ on 2, 3 or 4 Sides (Nos. 3294-3297), or 2 or 3 sides (Nos. 3294a-3297a)
1999, Apr. 10 **Tagged**
Self-Adhesive

3294 A2550 33c **multicolored** .75 .20
a. Dated "2000," *Mar. 15, 2000* 1.00 .20
3295 A2551 33c **multicolored** .75 .20
a. Dated "2000," *Mar. 15, 2000* 1.00 .20
3296 A2552 33c **multicolored** .75 .20
a. Dated "2000," *Mar. 15, 2000* 1.00 .20
3297 A2553 33c **multicolored** .75 .20
a. Dated "2000," *Mar. 15, 2000* 1.00 .20
b. Booklet pane of 20, 5 each #3294-3297 + label 15.00
c. Block of 4, #3294-3297 3.00
d. Booklet pane of 20, 5 #3297e + label 20.00
e. Block of 4, #3294a-3297a 4.00

No. 3297d is a double-sided booklet pane, with 12 stamps on one side and eight stamps plus label on the other side.

Serpentine Die Cut 9½x10 on 2 or 3 Sides

3298 A2550 33c **multicolored** .90 .20
3299 A2552 33c **multicolored** .90 .20
3300 A2551 33c **multicolored** .90 .20
3301 A2553 33c **multicolored** .90 .20
a. Booklet pane of 4, #3298-3301 3.60
b. Booklet pane of 5, #3298, 3299, 3301, 2 #3300 + label 4.50
c. Booklet pane of 6, #3300, 3301, 2 #3298, 3299 5.50
d. Block of 4, #3298-3301 3.40

COIL STAMPS
Serpentine Die Cut 8.5 Vert.

3302 A2550 33c **multicolored** 1.00 .20
3303 A2551 33c **multicolored** 1.00 .20
3304 A2553 33c **multicolored** 1.00 .20
3305 A2552 33c **multicolored** 1.00 .20
a. Strip of 4, #3302-3305 4.00
P# strip of 5, 2 #3302, 1 ea #3303-3305, P#B1111, B1112, B2211, B2221, B2222 5.25
P# strip of 9, 2 ea #3302-3303, 3305, 3 #3304, same P# 8.00
P# single (#3304), same P# — 1.25

A2554

A2555

DAFFY DUCK

Designed by Ed Wieczyk.
Printed by Avery Dennison.

PHOTOGRAVURE
1999, Apr. 16 **Tagged** ***Serpentine Die Cut 11.1***
Self-Adhesive

3306 Pane of 10 6.75
a. A2554 33c single .65 .20
b. Pane of 9 #3306a 6.00
c. Pane of 1 #3306a .65
Sheet of 60 (six panes) top 40.00
Sheet of 60 (six panes) bottom, with plate # in selvage 47.50
Pane of 10 from sheet of 60 8.00
Pane of 10 with plate # in selvage 15.00
Cross gutter block of 9 or 10 15.00
Cross gutter block of 12 18.00
Vert. pair with horiz. gutter 2.00
Horiz. pair with vert. gutter 4.00

Nos. 3306b-3306c and 3307b-3307c are separated by a vertical line of microperforations, which is absent on the uncut sheet of 60.

Die cutting on #3306b does not extend through the backing paper.

3307 Pane of 10 14.00
a. A2554 33c single 1.25
b. Pane of 9 #3307a 12.00
c. Pane of 1, no die cutting 1.75
d. As "a," vert. pair, die cutting omitted between —

Die cutting on #3307a extends through the backing paper.

Nos. 3306b-3306c and 3307b-3307c are separated by a vertical line of microperforations.

LITERARY ARTS SERIES

Ayn Rand (1905-82).

Designed by Phil Jordan.

Printed by Sterling Sommer for Ashton-Potter (USA) Ltd.

LITHOGRAPHED
Sheets of 180 in nine panes of 20
1999, Apr. 22 **Tagged** ***Perf. 11.2***

3308 A2555 33c **multicolored** .65 .20
P# block of 4, 4#+P 2.60 —
Pane of 20 13.00 —

Cinco De Mayo Type of 1998

Designed by Carl Herrman.

Printed by Banknote Corporation of America.

LITHOGRAPHED
Sheets of 160 in eight panes of 20
Serpentine Die Cut 11.6x11.3
1999, Apr. 27 **Tagged**
Self-Adhesive

3309 A2486 33c **multicolored** .65 .20
P# block of 4, 6#+B 2.60
Pane of 20 13.00

TROPICAL FLOWERS

Bird of Paradise
A2556

Royal Poinciana
A2557

Gloriosa Lily — A2558

Chinese Hibiscus
A2559

Designed by Carl Herrman.

Printed by Sennett Security Products.

PHOTOGRAVURE
BOOKLET STAMPS
Serpentine Die Cut 10.9 on 2 or 1 Sides
1999, May 1 **Tagged**
Self-Adhesive

3310 A2556 33c **multicolored** .65 .20
3311 A2557 33c **multicolored** .65 .20
3312 A2558 33c **multicolored** .65 .20
3313 A2559 33c **multicolored** .65 .20
a. Block of 4, #3310-3313 2.60
b. Booklet pane, 5 each #3313a 13.00

No. 3313b is a double-sided booklet pane with 12 stamps on one side and 8 stamps plus label on the other side.

A2560

A2561

JOHN (1699-1777) & WILLIAM (1739-1823) BARTRAM, BOTANISTS

Designed by Phil Jordan. Printed by Banknote Corporation of America.

LITHOGRAPHED
Sheets of 180 in nine panes of 20

1999, May 18 Tagged *Serpentine Die Cut 11½*
Self-Adhesive

3314 A2560 33c	Franklinia alatamaha, by William Bartram	.65	.20
	P# block of 4, 4#+B	2.60	
	Pane of 20	13.00	

PROSTATE CANCER AWARENESS

Designed by Michael Cronan. Printed by Avery Dennison.

PHOTOGRAVURE
Sheets of 200 in ten panes of 20

1999, May 28 Tagged *Serpentine Die Cut 11*
Self-Adhesive

3315 A2561 33c	**multicolored**	.65	.20
	P# block of 4, 5#+V	2.60	
	Pane of 20	13.00	

CALIFORNIA GOLD RUSH, 150TH ANNIV.

A2562

Designed by Howard Paine. Printed by Ashton-Potter (USA) Ltd.

LITHOGRAPHED
Sheets of 180 in nine panes of 20

1999, June 18 Tagged *Perf. 11¼*

3316 A2562 33c	**multicolored**	.65	.20
	P# block of 4, 5#+P	2.60	—
	Pane of 20	13.00	—

AQUARIUM FISH
Reef Fish

A2563

A2564

A2565

A2566

Designed by Richard Sheaff. Printed by Banknote Corporation of America.

Designs: No. 3317, Yellow fish, red fish, cleaner shrimp. No. 3318, Fish, thermometer. No. 3319, Red fish, blue & yellow fish. No. 3320, Fish, heater/aerator.

LITHOGRAPHED
Sheets of 120 in six panes of 20

1999, June 24 Tagged *Serpentine Die Cut 11½*
Self-Adhesive

3317 A2563 33c	**multicolored**, block tagging	.65	.20
a.	Overall tagging	12.50	*10.00*
3318 A2564 33c	**multicolored**, block tagging	.65	.20
a.	Overall tagging	12.50	*10.00*
3319 A2565 33c	**multicolored**, block tagging	.65	.20
a.	Overall tagging	12.50	*10.00*
3320 A2566 33c	**multicolored**, block tagging	.65	.20
a.	Overall tagging	12.50	*10.00*
b.	Strip of 4, #3317-3320	2.60	
	P# block of 8, 2 sets of 4#+B	5.20	
	Pane of 20	13.00	
	Sheet of 6 panes	80.00	
	Cross gutter block of 8	20.00	
	Block of 8 with horiz. gutter	9.00	
	Horiz. pair with vert. gutter	2.00	
	Vert. pairs with horiz. gutter (each)	2.25	
c.	Strip of 4, #3317a-3320a	55.00	
	P# block of 8, 2 sets of 4#+B	125.00	
	Pane of 20	300.00	

Plate blocks will have either top label or list of fish shown on bottom selvage. Cross gutter block of 8 consists of 4 horiz. pairs separated by vert. gutter with horiz. gutter between.

Press sheets were printed with large block tagging.

EXTREME SPORTS

Skateboarding — A2567

BMX Biking — A2568

Snowboarding — A2569

Inline Skating — A2570

Designed by Carl Herrman. Printed by Avery Dennison.

PHOTOGRAVURE
Sheets of 160 in eight panes of 20

1999, June 25 Tagged *Serpentine Die Cut 11*
Self-Adhesive

3321 A2567 33c	**multicolored**	.75	.20
3322 A2568 33c	**multicolored**	.75	.20
3323 A2569 33c	**multicolored**	.75	.20
3324 A2570 33c	**multicolored**	.75	.20
a.	Block or strip of 4, #3321-3324	3.00	
	P# block of 4, 4#+V	3.00	
	Pane of 20	15.00	
	Sheet of 80 (four panes) top	62.50	
	Sheet of 80 (four panes) bottom, with plate # in sheet margin	67.50	
	Pane of 20 with extra selvage from sheet of 80	15.00	
	Pane of 20 with plate # in sheet margin	22.50	
	Cross gutter block of 8	7.50	
	Vert. pairs with horiz. gutter (each)	2.00	
	Horiz. pairs with vert. gutter (each)	2.00	
	Block of 4 with horiz. gutter	5.00	
	Block of 8 with vert. gutter	10.00	

Cross gutter block of 8 consists of 4 horiz. pairs separated by vert. gutter with horiz. gutter between

AMERICAN GLASS

Free-Blown Glass — A2571

Mold-Blown Glass — A2572

Pressed Glass — A2573

Art Glass — A2574

Designed by Richard Sheaff. Printed by Sterling Sommer for Ashton-Potter (USA) Ltd.

LITHOGRAPHED
Sheets of 90 in six panes of 15

1999, June 29 Tagged *Perf. 11*

3325 A2571 33c	**multicolored**	1.25	.20
3326 A2572 33c	**multicolored**	1.25	.20
3327 A2573 33c	**multicolored**	1.25	.20
3328 A2574 33c	**multicolored**	1.25	.20
a.	Strip or block of 4, #3325-3328	5.00	3.00
	Pane of 15, 4 each #3325, 3327-3328, 3 #3326	19.00	12.50

A2575

A2576

LEGENDS OF HOLLYWOOD
James Cagney (1899-1986)

Designed by Howard Paine.

Printed by Sennett Security Products.

PHOTOGRAVURE
Sheets of 120 in six panes of 20

1999, July 22 Tagged *Perf. 11*

3329 A2575 33c	**multicolored**	.80	.20
	P# block of 4, 5#+S	4.25	—
	Pane of 20	20.00	—
	Sheet of 120 (6 panes)	85.00	—
	Cross gutter block of 8	17.50	—
	Block of 8 with vertical gutter	11.00	—
	Horiz. pair with vert. gutter	3.00	—
	Vert. pair with horiz. gutter	2.00	—

Perforations in corner of each stamp are star-shaped. Cross-gutter block consists of 2 stamps from upper panes and 6 stamps from panes below.

GEN. WILLIAM "BILLY" L. MITCHELL (1879-1936), AVIATION PIONEER

Designed by Phil Jordan.
Printed by Guilford Gravure for Banknote Corporation of America.

PHOTOGRAVURE
Sheets of 180 in nine panes of 20

1999, July 30 Tagged *Serpentine Die Cut 9¾x10*
Self-Adhesive

3330	A2576	55c	**multicolored**	1.10	.30
			P# block of 4, 5#+B	4.40	
			Pane of 20	22.00	

HONORING THOSE WHO SERVED

A2577

Designed by Richard Sheaff and Uldis Purins.
Printed by Avery Dennison.

PHOTOGRAVURE
Sheets of 200 in 10 panes of 20

1999, Aug. 16 Tagged *Serpentine Die Cut 11*
Self-Adhesive

3331	A2577	33c	**black, blue & red**	.65	.20
			P# block of 4, 3#+V	2.60	
			Pane of 20	13.00	

UNIVERSAL POSTAL UNION

A2578

Designed by Gerald Gallo.
Printed by Sterling Sommer for Ashton-Potter (USA) Ltd.

LITHOGRAPHED
Sheets of 180 in nine panes of 20

1999, Aug. 25 Tagged *Perf. 11*

3332	A2578	45c	**multicolored**	.90	.45
			P# block of 4, 3#+P	3.60	—
			Pane of 20	18.00	—

FAMOUS TRAINS

Daylight
A2579

Congressional
A2580

20th Century
Limited
A2581

Hiawatha
A2582

Super Chief
A2583

Designed by Howard Paine.
Printed by Ashton-Potter (USA) Ltd.

LITHOGRAPHED
Sheets of 120 in six panes of 20

1999, Aug. 26 Tagged *Perf. 11*

3333	A2579	33c	**multicolored**	.75	.20
3334	A2580	33c	**multicolored**	.75	.20
3335	A2581	33c	**multicolored**	.75	.20
3336	A2582	33c	**multicolored**	.75	.20
3337	A2583	33c	**multicolored**	.75	.20
a.			Strip of 5, #3333-3337	3.75	—
			Pane of 20, 4 #3337a	15.00	—
			P# block of 8, 2 sets of 4#+P	6.00	—
			Sheet of 120 (6 panes)	90.00	—
			Block of 10 with vert. gutter	15.00	—
			Cross gutter block of 8	17.50	—
			Horiz. pairs with vert. gutter (each)	2.25	—
			Vert. pairs with horiz. gutter (each)	2.25	—

Stamps in No. 3337a are arranged in four different orders. Plate block may contain top label.

FREDERICK LAW OLMSTED (1822-1903), LANDSCAPE ARCHITECT

A2584

Designed by Ethel Kessler.
Printed by Ashton-Potter (USA) Ltd.

LITHOGRAPHED
Sheets of 120 in six panes of 20

1999, Sept. 12 Tagged *Perf. 11*

3338	A2584	33c	**multicolored**	.65	.20
			P# block of 4, 4#+P	2.60	—
			Pane of 20	13.00	—

AMERICAN MUSIC SERIES
Hollywood Composers

Max Steiner
(1888-1971)
A2585

Dimitri
Tiomkin
(1894-1975)
A2586

Bernard
Herrmann
(1911-75)
A2587

Franz
Waxman
(1906-67)
A2588

Alfred
Newman
(1907-70)
A2589

Erich
Wolfgang
Korngold
(1897-1957)
A2590

Designed by Howard Paine.
Printed by Sterling Sommer for Ashton-Potter (USA) Ltd.

LITHOGRAPHED
Sheets of 120 in six panes of 20

1999, Sept. 16 Tagged *Perf. 11*

3339	A2585	33c	**multicolored**	1.25	.20
3340	A2586	33c	**multicolored**	1.25	.20
3341	A2587	33c	**multicolored**	1.25	.20
3342	A2588	33c	**multicolored**	1.25	.20
3343	A2589	33c	**multicolored**	1.25	.20
3344	A2590	33c	**multicolored**	1.25	.20
a.			Block of 6, #3339-3344	7.50	4.50
			P# block of 6, 5#+P	7.50	—
			P# block of 8, 2 sets of 5#+P + top label	10.00	—
			Pane of 20	25.00	—

AMERICAN MUSIC SERIES
Broadway Songwriters

Ira (1896-1983) & George (1898-1937) Gershwin A2591

Alan Jay Lerner (1918-86) & Frederick Loewe (1901-88) A2592

Lorenz Hart (1895-1943) A2593

Richard Rodgers (1902-79) & Oscar Hammerstein II (1895-1960) A2594

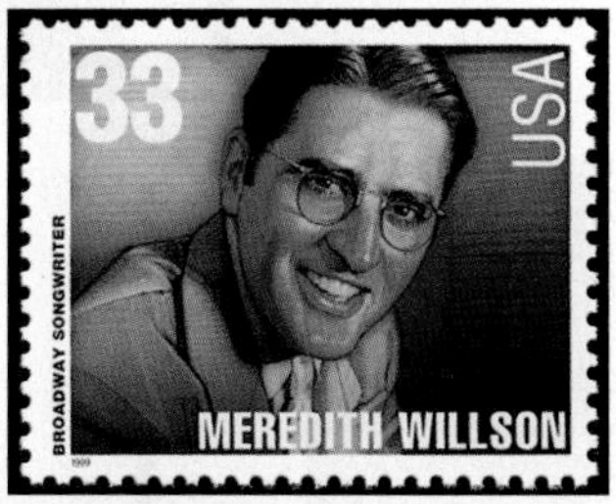

Meredith Willson (1902-84) A2595

Frank Loesser (1910-69) A2596

Designed by Howard Paine.
Printed by Sterling Sommer for Ashton-Potter (USA) Ltd.

LITHOGRAPHED
Sheets of 120 in six panes of 20

1999, Sept. 21 Tagged *Perf. 11*

3345	A2591	33c	**multicolored**	1.25	.20
3346	A2592	33c	**multicolored**	1.25	.20
3347	A2593	33c	**multicolored**	1.25	.20
3348	A2594	33c	**multicolored**	1.25	.20
3349	A2595	33c	**multicolored**	1.25	.20
3350	A2596	33c	**multicolored**	1.25	.20
a.			Block of 6, #3345-3350	7.50	4.50
			P# block of 6, 5#+P	7.50	—
			P# block of 8, 2 sets of 5#+P + top label	10.00	—
			Pane of 20	25.00	—

INSECTS & SPIDERS

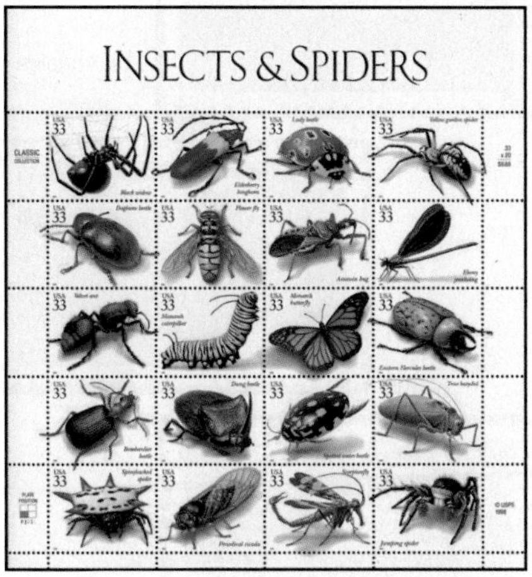

A2597

Illustration reduced.

Designed by Carl Herrman.
Printed by Ashton-Potter (USA) Ltd.

Designs: a, Black widow. b, Elderberry longhorn. c, Lady beetle. d, Yellow garden spider. e, Dogbane beetle. f, Flower fly. g, Assassin bug. h, Ebony jewelwing. i, Velvet ant. j, Monarch caterpillar. k, Monarch butterfly. l, Eastern Hercules beetle. m, Bombardier beetle. n, Dung beetle. o, Spotted water beetle. p, True katydid. q, Spinybacked spider. r, Periodical cicada. s, Scorpionfly. t, Jumping spider.

LITHOGRAPHED
Sheets of 80 in four panes of 20

1999, Oct. 1 Tagged *Perf. 11*

3351	A2597	Pane of 20	13.00	10.00
a.-t.		33c any single	.65	.50
		Sheet of 4 panes	52.50	
		Cross gutter block of 20	20.00	
		Vert. pair with horiz. gutter (each)	1.60	
		Horiz. pair with vert. gutter (each)	1.60	

Cross gutter block of 20 consists of six stamps from each of two panes and four stamps from each of the two other panes with the cross gutter between.

Hanukkah Type of 1996

Designed by Hannah Smotrich.
Printed by Avery Dennison.

PHOTOGRAVURE
Sheets of 200 in 10 panes of 20

1999, Oct. 8 Tagged *Serpentine Die Cut 11*
Self-Adhesive

3352	A2411	33c	**multicolored**	.65	.20
			P# block of 4, 5#+V	2.60	
			Pane of 20	13.00	

Uncle Sam Type of 1998

Designed by Richard Sheaff.
Printed by Bureau of Engraving and Printing.

COIL STAMP
PHOTOGRAVURE

1999, Oct. 8 Tagged *Perf. 9¾ Vert.*

3353	A2530	22c	**multicolored**	.45	.20
			Pair	.90	.30
			P# strip of 5, #1111	3.25	—
			P# single, same #	—	2.25

NATO, 50TH ANNIV.

A2598

Designed by Michael Cronan.
Printed by Ashton-Potter (USA) Ltd.

LITHOGRAPHED
Sheets of 180 in nine panes of 20

1999, Oct. 13 Tagged *Perf. 11¼*

3354	A2598	33c	**multicolored**	.65	.20
			P# block of 4, 4#+P	2.60	—
			Pane of 20	13.00	—

CHRISTMAS

Madonna and Child, by Bartolomeo Vivarini — A2599

Deer — A2600

Designed by Richard Sheaff (#3355), Tom Nikosey (#3356-3367).
Printed by Banknote Corp. of America.

LITHOGRAPHED
Serpentine Die Cut 11¼ on 2 or 3 sides

1999, Oct. 20 Tagged

Booklet Stamp
Self-Adhesive

3355	A2599	33c	**multicolored**	1.00	.20
a.			Booklet pane of 20	20.00	

Sheets of 120 in six panes of 20
Serpentine Die Cut 11¼

3356	A2600	33c	**gold & red**	1.20	.20
3357	A2600	33c	**gold & blue**	1.20	.20
3358	A2600	33c	**gold & purple**	1.20	.20
3359	A2600	33c	**gold & green**	1.20	.20
a.			Block or strip of 4, #3356-3359	4.80	
			P# block of 4, 6#+B	4.80	
			Pane of 20	24.00	

Booklet Stamps
Serpentine Die Cut 11¼ on 2, 3 or 4 sides

3360	A2600	33c	**gold & red**	1.50	.20
3361	A2600	33c	**gold & blue**	1.50	.20
3362	A2600	33c	**gold & purple**	1.50	.20
3363	A2600	33c	**gold & green**	1.50	.20
a.			Booklet pane of 20, 5 each #3360-3363	30.00	
b.			Block of 4, #3360-3363	6.00	
c.			As "b," die cutting omitted	—	
d.			As "a," die cutting omitted	—	

Size: 21x19mm
Serpentine Die Cut 11½x11¼ on 2 or 3 sides

3364	A2600	33c	**gold & red**	2.00	.20
3365	A2600	33c	**gold & blue**	2.00	.20
3366	A2600	33c	**gold & purple**	2.00	.20
3367	A2600	33c	**gold & green**	2.00	.20
a.			Booklet pane of 4, #3364-3367	8.00	
b.			Booklet pane of 5, #3364, 3366, 3367, 2 #3365 + label	10.00	
c.			Booklet pane of 6, #3365, 3367, 2 each #3364 & 3366	12.00	
d.			Block of 4, #3364-3367	8.00	

The frame on Nos. 3356-3359 is narrow and the space between it and the hoof is a hairline. The frame on Nos. 3360-3363 is much thicker, and the space between it and the hoof is wider.

Kwanzaa Type of 1997

Designed by Synthia Saint James
Printed by Avery Dennison.

PHOTOGRAVURE
Sheets of 240 in twelve pane of 20

1999, Oct. 29 Tagged *Serpentine Die Cut 11*
Self-Adhesive

3368	A2458	33c	**multicolored**	.65	.20
			P# block of 4, 4#+V	2.60	
			Pane of 20	13.00	

YEAR 2000

Baby New Year — A2601

Designed by Carl Herrman.
Printed by Banknote Corporation of America.

LITHOGRAPHED
Sheets of 120 in six panes of 20

1999, Dec. 27 Tagged *Serpentine Die Cut 11¼*
Self-Adhesive

3369 A2601 33c **multicolored** .65 .20
P# block of 4, 5#+B 3.00
Pane of 20 14.50

CHINESE NEW YEAR

Year of the Dragon A2602

Designed by Clarence Lee.
Printed by Sterling Sommer.

LITHOGRAPHED
Sheets of 180 in nine panes of 20

2000, Jan. 6 Tagged *Perf. 11¼*

3370 A2602 33c **multicolored** .80 .20
P# block of 4, 4#+P 3.25 —
Pane of 20 15.50 —

See No. 3895e.

BLACK HERITAGE SERIES

Patricia Roberts Harris (1924-85), First Black Woman Cabinet Secretary — A2603

Designed by Richard Sheaff.
Printed by Ashton-Potter (USA) Ltd.

LITHOGRAPHED
Sheets of 180 in nine panes of 20
Serpentine Die Cut 11½x11¼

2000, Jan. 27 Tagged
Self-Adhesive

3371 A2603 33c **indigo** .65 .20
P# block of 4, 4#+P 2.75
Pane of 20 13.50

SUBMARINES

S Class A2604

Los Angeles Class A2605

Ohio Class A2606

USS Holland A2607

Gato Class — A2608

Illustration of No. 3377 reduced.

Designed by Carl Herrman.
Printed by Banknote Corporation of America.

LITHOGRAPHED
Sheets of 180 in nine panes of 20

2000, Mar. 27 Tagged *Perf. 11*

3372 A2605 33c **multicolored,** with microprinted "USPS" at base of sail .75 .20
P# block of 4, 4#+B 3.00 —
Pane of 20 15.00 —

BOOKLET STAMPS

3373 A2604 22c **multicolored** 1.25 .75
3374 A2605 33c **multicolored,** no microprinting 1.75 1.00
3375 A2606 55c **multicolored** 2.75 1.25
3376 A2607 60c **multicolored** 3.00 1.50
3377 A2608 $3.20 **multicolored** 16.00 5.00
a. Booklet pane of 5, #3373-3377 25.00 —

No. 3377a was issued with two types of text in the selvage.

PACIFIC COAST RAIN FOREST

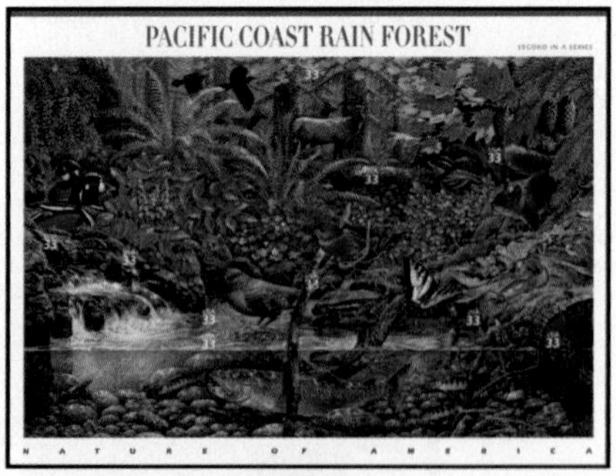

A2609

Illustration reduced.

Designed by Ethel Kessler.
Printed by Banknote Corporation of America.

Designs: a, Harlequin duck. b, Dwarf oregongrape, snail-eating ground beetle. c, American dipper, horiz. d, Cutthroat trout, horiz. e, Roosevelt elk. f, Winter wren. g, Pacific giant salamander, Rough-skinned newt. h, Western tiger swallowtail, horiz. i, Douglas squirrel, foliose lichen. j, Foliose lichen, banana slug.

LITHOGRAPHED
Sheets of 60 in six panes of 10
Serpentine Die Cut 11¼x11½, 11½ (horiz. stamps)

2000, Mar. 29 Tagged
Self-Adhesive

3378 A2609 Pane of 10 8.00
a.-j. 33c any single .80 .50
Sheet of 6 panes 50.00

LOUISE NEVELSON (1899-1988), SCULPTOR

Silent Music I — A2610

Royal Tide I — A2611

Black Chord — A2612

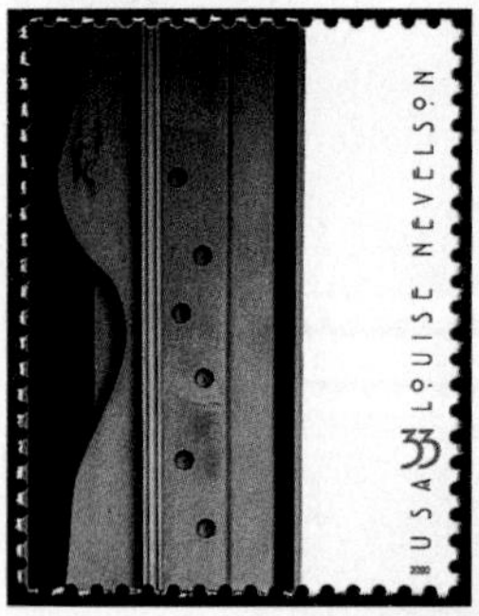

Nightsphere-Light A2613

Dawn's Wedding Chapel I — A2614

Designed by Ethel Kessler.

Printed by Ashton-Potter (USA) Ltd.

LITHOGRAPHED

Sheets of 80 in four panes of 20.

2000, Apr. 6	Tagged	*Perf. 11x11¼*		
3379 A2610 33c	**multicolored**		.65	.20
3380 A2611 33c	**multicolored**		.65	.20
3381 A2612 33c	**multicolored**		.65	.20
3382 A2613 33c	**multicolored**		.65	.20
3383 A2614 33c	**multicolored**		.65	.20
a.	Strip of 5, #3379-3383		3.25	—
	P# block of 10, 4#+P		6.50	—
	Pane of 20		13.00	—

HUBBLE SPACE TELESCOPE IMAGES

Eagle Nebula — A2615

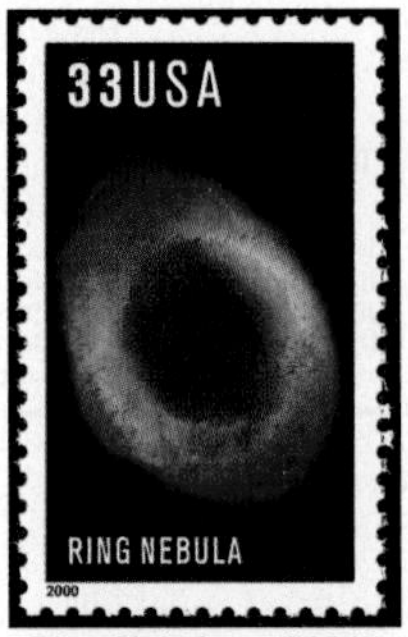

Ring Nebula — A2616

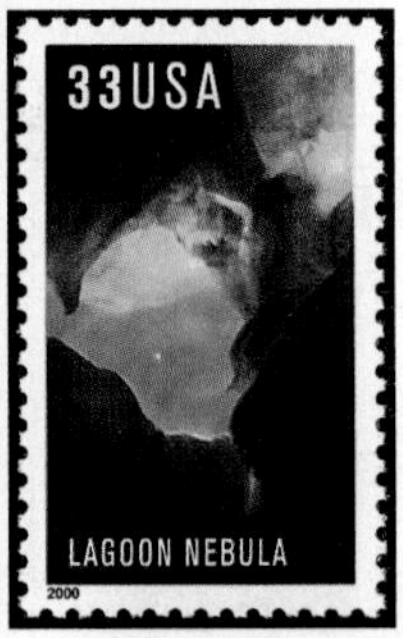

Lagoon Nebula — A2617

Egg Nebula — A2618

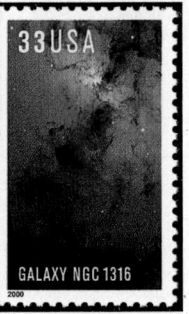

Galaxy NGC 1316 — A2619

Designed by Phil Jordan. Printed at American Packaging Corp. for Sennett Security Products.

PHOTOGRAVURE

Sheets of 120 in six panes of 20.

2000, Apr. 10	Tagged	*Perf. 11*		
3384 A2615 33c	**multicolored**		.65	.20
3385 A2616 33c	**multicolored**		.65	.20
3386 A2617 33c	**multicolored**		.65	.20
3387 A2618 33c	**multicolored**		.65	.20
3388 A2619 33c	**multicolored**		.65	.20
a.	Strip of 5, #3384-3388		3.25	—
	P# block of 10, 6#+S		6.50	—
	Pane of 20		13.00	—
b.	As "a," imperf		*1,250.*	
	As "b," pane of 20		*5,000.*	

AMERICAN SAMOA

Samoan Double Canoe A2620

Designed by Howard Paine.
Printed by Ashton-Potter (USA) Ltd.

LITHOGRAPHED

Sheets of 120 in six panes of 20

2000, Apr. 17	Tagged	*Perf. 11*		
3389 A2620 33c	**multicolored**		.65	.20
	P# block of 4, 4#+P		2.60	—
	Pane of 20		13.00	—

LIBRARY OF CONGRESS

Interior Dome and Arched Windows in Main Reading Room, Thomas Jefferson Building — A2621

Designed by Ethel Kessler.
Printed by Ashton-Potter (USA) Ltd.

LITHOGRAPHED

Sheets of 120 in six panes of 20

2000, Apr. 24	Tagged	*Perf. 11*		
3390 A2621 33c	**multicolored**		.65	.20
	P# block of 4, 5#+P		2.60	—
	Pane of 20		13.00	—

ROAD RUNNER & WILE E. COYOTE

A2622

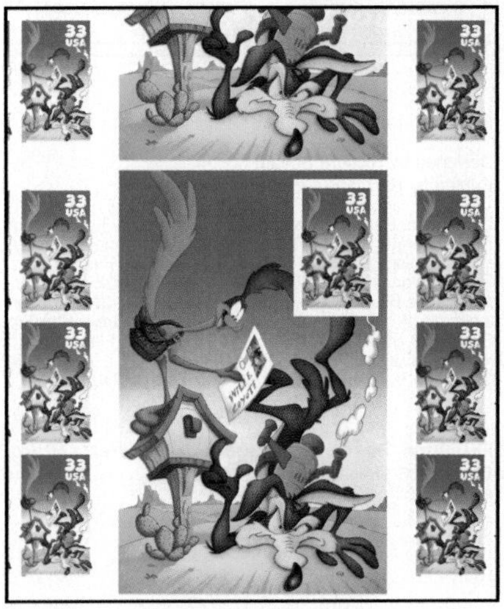

Cross Gutter Block of 9

Illustration reduced.

Designed by Ed Wleczyk, Warner Bros.
Printed by Banknote Corp. of America, Inc.

LITHOGRAPHED

2000, Apr. 26 Tagged *Serpentine Die Cut 11*

Self-Adhesive

3391	Pane of 10	9.00	
a.	A2622 33c single	.85	.20
b.	Pane of 9 #3391a	7.75	
c.	Pane of 1 #3391a	1.25	
	Sheet of 60 (six panes) top, with plate # in selvage on reverse	55.00	
	Sheet of 60 (six panes) bottom, with plate # in selvage	57.50	
	Pane of 10 from sheet of 60	9.50	
	Two panes of 10 with plate numbers on front	22.50	
	Cross gutter block of 9 or 10	16.00	
	Vert. pair with horiz. gutter	2.00	
	Horiz. pair with vert. gutter	4.00	
d.	All die cutting omitted, pane of 10	*2,400.*	

Die cutting on #3391b does not extend through the backing paper.

3392	Pane of 10	*40.00*
a.	A2622 33c single	*2.75*
b.	Pane of 9 #3392a	*30.00*
c.	Pane of 1, imperf.	*5.00*

Die cutting on #3392a extends through the backing paper. Used examples of No. 3392a are identical to those of No. 3391a.

Nos. 3391b-3391c and 3392b-3392c are separated by a vertical line of microperforations.

DISTINGUISHED SOLDIERS

Maj. Gen. John L. Hines (1868-1968) A2623

Gen. Omar N. Bradley (1893-1981) A2624

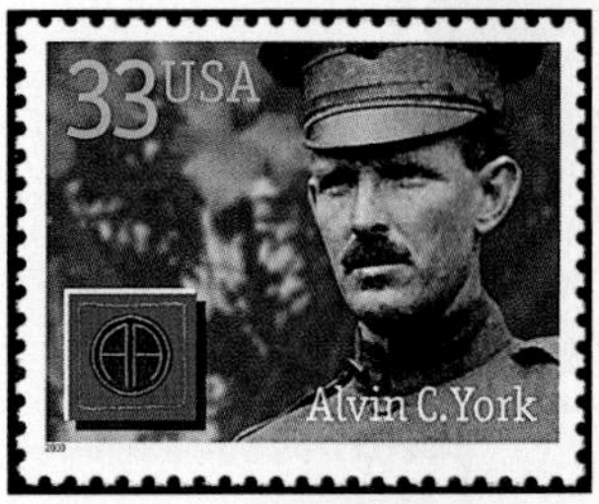

Sgt. Alvin C. York (1887-1964) A2625

Second Lt. Audie L. Murphy (1924-71) A2626

Designed by Phil Jordan.
Printed by Sterling Sommer for Ashton-Potter (USA) Ltd.

LITHOGRAPHED

Sheets of 120 in six panes of 20

2000, May 3	Tagged	*Perf. 11*		
3393 A2623 33c	**multicolored**		.65	.20
3394 A2624 33c	**multicolored**		.65	.20
3395 A2625 33c	**multicolored**		.65	.20
3396 A2626 33c	**multicolored**		.65	.20
a.	Block or strip of 4, #3393-3396		2.60	—
	P# block of 4, 4#+P		2.60	—
	Pane of 20		13.00	—

SUMMER SPORTS

Runners A2627

Designed by Richard Sheaff.
Printed by Ashton-Potter (USA) Ltd.

LITHOGRAPHED

Sheets of 120 in six panes of 20

2000, May 5 **Tagged** ***Perf. 11***

3397	A2627	33c	**multicolored**	.65	.20
			P# block of 4, 4#+P	2.60	—
			Pane of 20	13.00	—

ADOPTION

Stick Figures — A2628

Designed by Greg Berger.
Printed by Banknote Corporation of America.

LITHOGRAPHED

Sheets of 120 in six panes of 20

2000, May 10 **Tagged** ***Serpentine Die Cut 11½***

Self-Adhesive

3398	A2628	33c	**multicolored**	.75	.20
			P# block of 4, 5#+B	3.00	
			Pane of 20	15.00	
a.			Die cutting omitted, pair	—	

YOUTH TEAM SPORTS

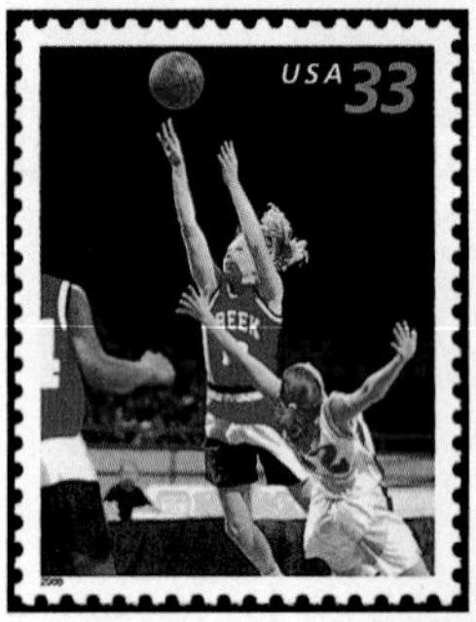

Basketball — A2629

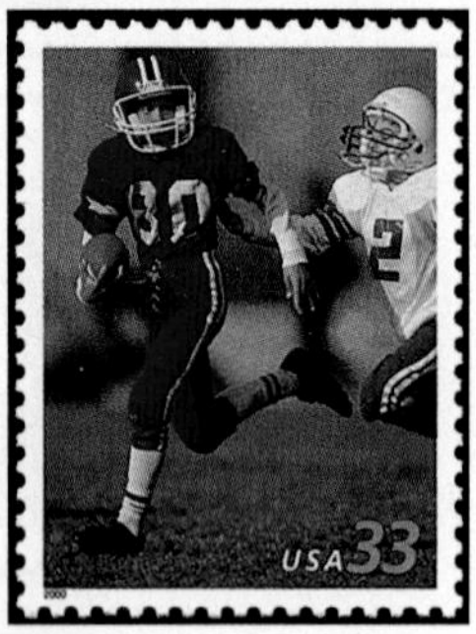

Football — A2630

Soccer — A2631

Baseball — A2632

Designed by Derry Noyes.
Printed by Sterling Sommer for Ashton-Potter (USA) Ltd.

LITHOGRAPHED

Sheets of 120 in six panes of 20

2000, May 27 **Tagged** ***Perf. 11***

3399	A2629	33c	**multicolored**	.65	.20
3400	A2630	33c	**multicolored**	.65	.20
3401	A2631	33c	**multicolored**	.65	.20
3402	A2632	33c	**multicolored**	.65	.20
a.			Block or strip of 4, #3399-3402	2.60	—
			P# block of 4, 4#+P	2.60	—
			Pane of 20	13.00	—

THE STARS AND STRIPES

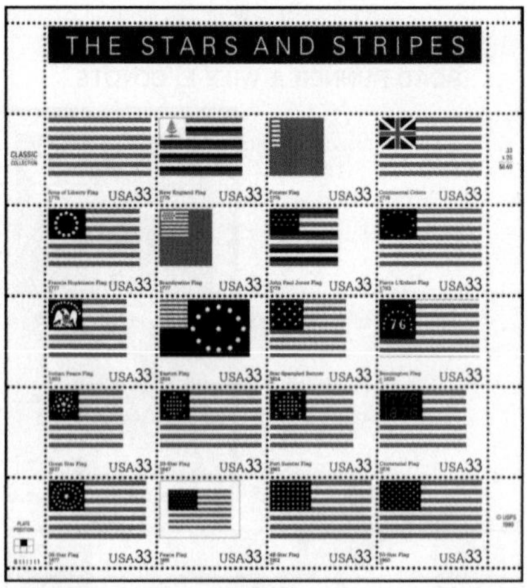

A2633

Illustration reduced.

Designed by Richard Sheaff.
Printed by Banknote Corp. of America.

Designs: a, Sons of Liberty Flag, 1775. b, New England Flag, 1775. c, Forster Flag, 1775. d, Continental Colors, 1776. e, Francis Hopkinson Flag, 1777. f, Brandywine Flag, 1777. g, John Paul Jones Flag, 1779. h, Pierre L'Enfant Flag, 1783. i, Indian Peace Flag, 1803. j, Easton Flag, 1814. k, Star-Spangled Banner, 1814. l, Bennington Flag, c. 1820. m, Great Star Flag, 1837. n, 29-Star Flag, 1847. o, Fort Sumter Flag, 1861. p, Centennial Flag, 1876. q, 38-Star Flag, 1877. r, Peace Flag, 1891. s, 48-Star Flag, 1912. t, 50-Star Flag, 1960.

LITHOGRAPHED

2000, June 14 **Tagged** ***Perf. 10½x11***

3403	A2633	Pane of 20	15.00	11.00
a.-t.		33c any single	.75	.50
		Sheet of 120 (6 panes)	85.00	
		Cross gutter block of 20	25.00	—
		Vert. pairs with horiz. gutter (each)	2.50	—
		Horiz. pairs with vert. gutter (each)	2.50	—

Inscriptions on the back of each stamp describe the flag.

Cross gutter block of 20 consists of six stamps from each of two panes and four stamps from each of two other panes with the cross gutter between.

BERRIES

Blueberries — A2634

Strawberries — A2635

Blackberries — A2636

Raspberries — A2637

Designed by Howard Paine. Printed by Guilford Gravure.

See designs A2550-A2553.

PHOTOGRAVURE

COIL STAMPS

Serpentine Die Cut 8½ Horiz.

2000, June 16 **Tagged**

Self-Adhesive

3404	A2634	33c	**multicolored**	2.50	.20
3405	A2635	33c	**multicolored**	2.50	.20
3406	A2636	33c	**multicolored**	2.50	.20
3407	A2637	33c	**multicolored**	2.50	.20
a.			Strip of 4, #3404-3407	10.00	
			P# strip of 5, 2 #3404, 1 each #3405-3407, #G1111	12.50	
			P# strip of 9, 2 each #3404-3405, 3407, 3 #3406, #G1111	17.00	
			P# single (#3406), #G1111	—	1.25

Nos. 3404-3407 are linerless coils issued without backing paper. The adhesive is strong and can remove the ink from stamps in the roll.

LEGENDS OF BASEBALL

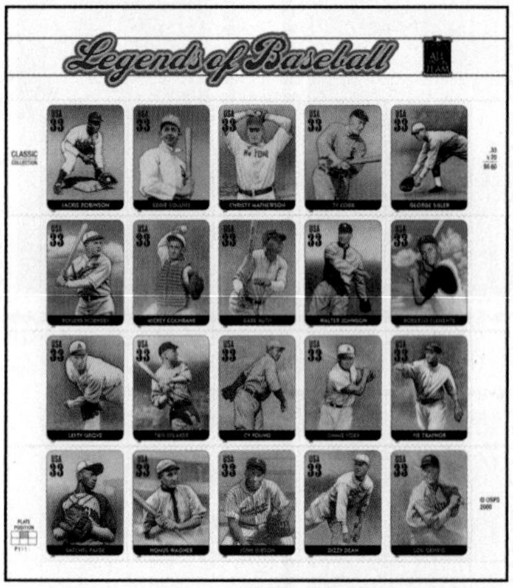

A2638

Illustration reduced.

Designed by Phil Jordan. Printed by Ashton-Potter (USA) Ltd.

Designs: a, Jackie Robinson. b, Eddie Collins. c, Christy Mathewson. d, Ty Cobb. e, George Sisler. f, Rogers Hornsby. g, Mickey Cochrane. h, Babe Ruth. i, Walter Johnson. j, Roberto Clemente. k, Lefty Grove. l, Tris Speaker. m, Cy Young. n, Jimmie Foxx. o, Pie Traynor. p, Satchel Paige. q, Honus Wagner. r, Josh Gibson. s, Dizzy Dean. t, Lou Gehrig.

LITHOGRAPHED

Sheets of 120 in six panes of 20

2000, July 6 **Tagged** ***Serpentine Die Cut 11¼***

Self-Adhesive

3408	A2638	Pane of 20	13.00	
a.-t.		33c any single	.65	.50
		Sheet of 120 (6 panes)	80.00	
		Cross gutter block of 20	22.50	—
		Vert. pairs with horiz. gutter (each)	2.25	—
		Horiz. pairs with vert. gutter (each)	2.25	—

Cross gutter block of 20 consists of six stamps from each of two panes and four stamps from each of two other panes with the cross gutter between.

SPACE
Souvenir Sheets

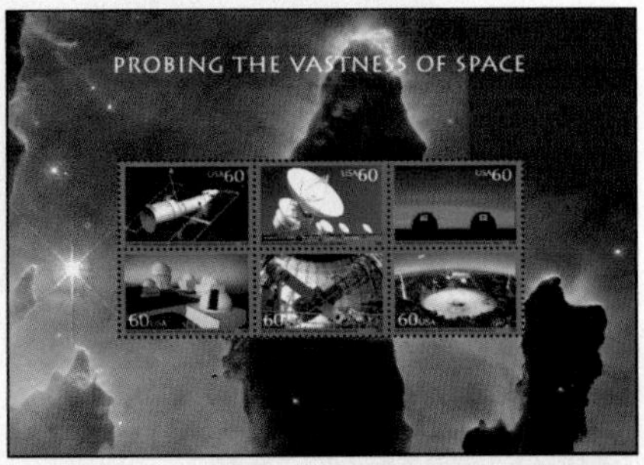

Probing the Vastness of Space — A2639

Exploring the Solar System — A2640

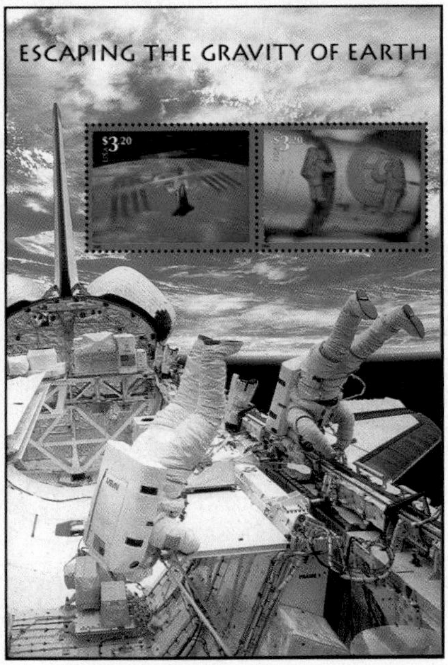

Escaping the Gravity of Earth — A2641

Space Achievement and Exploration — A2642

Landing on the Moon — A2643

Illustrations reduced.

Designed by Richard Sheaff. Printed by American Packaging Corporation for Sennett Security Products.

Designs: No. 3409: a, Hubble Space Telescope. b, Radio interferometer very large array, New Mexico. c, Optical and infrared telescopes, Keck Observatory, Hawaii. d, Optical telescopes, Cerro Tololo Observatory, Chile. e, Optical telescope, Mount Wilson Observatory, California. f, Radio telescope, Arecibo Observatory, Puerto Rico.

No. 3410: a, Sun and corona. b, Cross-section of sun. c, Sun and earth. d, Sun and solar flare. e, Sun and clouds.

No. 3411: a, Space Shuttle and Space Station. b, Astronauts working in space.

PHOTOGRAVURE

2000 **Tagged** ***Perf. 10½x11***

3409	A2639	Sheet of 6, *July 10*	12.50	7.00
a.-f.		60c any single	2.00	1.00

Perf. 10¾

3410	A2640	Sheet of 5 + label, *July 11*	16.00	10.00
a.-e.		$1 any single	3.00	1.75
f.		As No. 3410, imperf	*3,250.*	
g		As No. 3410, with hologram from No. 3411b applied	—	

Untagged

Photogravure with Hologram Affixed

Perf. 10½, 10¾ (#3412)

3411	A2641	Sheet of 2, *July 9*	21.00	10.00
a.-b.		$3.20 any single	10.00	4.00
c.		Hologram omitted on right stamp	—	
3412	A2642	**multicolored,** *July 7*	37.50	17.50
a.		$11.75 single	35.00	15.00
b.		Hologram omitted	—	
c.		Hologram omitted on No. 3412 in uncut sheet of 5 panes	—	
3413	A2643	**multicolored,** *July 8*	37.50	17.50
		Uncut sheet of 5 panes, #3409-3413	115.00	
a.		$11.75 single	35.00	15.00
b.		Double hologram	—	
c.		Double hologram on No. 3413 in uncut sheet of 5 panes	—	
d.		Hologram omitted on No. 3413 in uncut sheet of 5 panes	—	
		Nos. 3409-3413 (5)	124.50	62.00

Warning: Soaking in water may affect holographic images.

STAMPIN' THE FUTURE CHILDREN'S STAMP DESIGN CONTEST WINNERS

By Zachary Canter A2644

By Sarah Lipsey A2645

By Morgan Hill — A2646

By Ashley Young A2647

Designed by Richard Sheaff. Printed by Ashton-Potter (USA) Ltd.

LITHOGRAPHED

Sheets of 120 in six panes of 20

2000, July 13 **Tagged** ***Serpentine Die Cut 11¼***

Self-Adhesive

3414	A2644 33c **multicolored**		.65	.20
3415	A2645 33c **multicolored**		.65	.20
3416	A2646 33c **multicolored**		.65	.20
3417	A2647 33c **multicolored**		.65	.20
a.	Horiz. strip of 4, #3414-3417		2.60	
		P# block of 8, 2 sets of 5#+P	5.25	
		Pane of 20	13.00	

Plate block may contain top label.

DISTINGUISHED AMERICANS

Gen. Joseph W. Stilwell (1883-1946) A2650

Wilma Rudolph (1940-94), Athlete A2652

Sen. Claude Pepper (1900-89) A2656

Sen. Margaret Chase Smith (1897-1995) A2657

James A. Michener (1907-97), Author — A2657a

Dr. Jonas Salk (1914-95), Polio Vaccine Pioneer — A2658

Harriet Beecher Stowe (1811-96), Author A2660

Sen. Hattie Caraway (1878-1950) A2661

Edward Trudeau (1848-1915), Phthisiologist — A2661a — 3432A

Edna Ferber (1887-1968), Writer — A2662

Edna Ferber (With Curving Shoulder) — A2663

Dr. Albert Sabin (1906-93), Polio Vaccine Pioneer — A2664

Designed by: 10c, 23c, 33c, 58c, 59c, 63c, 75c, 76c, 83c, 87c Richard Sheaff; 76c, Howard E. Paine.

Printed by Banknote Corporation of America (#3420-3433). Ashton-Potter (USA) Ltd. (#3422, 3427, 3428, 3432A, 3434). Banknote Corporation of America for Sennett Security Products, (#3427A, 3430).

LITHOGRAPHED & ENGRAVED, LITHOGRAPHED (#3436)

Sheets of 120 in six panes of 20

Sheets of 300 in fifteen panes of 20 (#3427A)

Perf. 11 (#3420, 3426), Serpentine Die Cut 11¼x10¾ (#3422, 3430), 11¼x11 (#3428, 3435), 11 (#3427, 3431), 11½x11 (#3432), 11x11¾ (#3433), 11¼ (#3434),

2000-07 **Tagged**

Self-Adhesive (#3422, 3431-3434, 3436)

3420	A2650	10c	**red & black,** *Aug. 24*	.20	.20
			P# block of 4, 3#+B	.80	—
			Pane of 20	4.00	—
a.			Imperf, pair	*500.00*	
3422	A2652	23c	**red & black,** *July 14, 2004*	.45	.20
			P# block of 4, 2#+P	1.80	
			Pane of 20	9.00	
3426	A2656	33c	**red & black,** *Sept. 7*	.65	.20
			P# block of 4, 3#+B	2.60	—
			Pane of 20	13.00	—
3427	A2657	58c	**red & black,** *June 13, 2007*	1.25	.20
			P# block of 4, 3#+P	5.00	
			Pane of 20	25.00	
3427A	A2657a	59c	**multicolored,** *May 12, 2008*	1.25	.20
			P# block of 4, 5#+S	5.00	
			Pane of 20	25.00	
3428	A2658	63c	**red & black** *Mar. 8, 2006*	1.25	.20
			P# block of 4, 3#+P	5.00	
			Pane of 20	25.00	
a.			Black (litho.) omitted	—	
3430	A2660	75c	**red & black,** *June 13, 2007*	1.50	.20
			P# block of 4, 3#+S	6.00	
			Pane of 20	30.00	
3431	A2661	76c	**red & black,** *Feb. 21, 2001*	1.50	.20
			P# block of 4, 3#+B	6.00	
			Pane of 20	30.00	
3432	A2661	76c	**red & black,**	*3.50*	*2.00*
			P# block of 4, 3#+B	*14.00*	
			Pane of 20	*70.00*	
3432A	A2661a	76c	**multicolored,** *May 12, 2008*	1.50	.20
			P# block of 4, 4#+P	6.00	
			Pane of 20	30.00	
3433	A2662	83c	**red & black,** *July 29, 2002*	1.60	.30
			P# block of 4, 3#+B1	6.50	
			Pane of 20	32.50	

The previously listed "Big Mouth" flaw on No. 3433 has been discovered to be not a constant plate flaw but rather the result of extraneous matter on the plate affecting a reported 15 panes before the matter fell off, or was removed from, the plate.

3434	A2663	83c	**red & black,** *Aug. 2003*	1.60	.30
			P# block of 4, 3#+P	6.50	
			Pane of 20	32.50	
3435	A2664	87c	**red & black,** *Mar. 8, 2006*	1.75	.30
			P# block of 4, 2#+S	7.00	
			Pane of 20	35.00	

BOOKLET STAMP

Serpentine Die Cut 11¼x10¾ on 3 Sides

Self-Adhesive

3436	A2652	23c	**red & black,** *July 14, 2004*	.45	.20
a.			Booklet pane of 4	1.80	
b.			Booklet pane of 6	2.70	
c.			Booklet pane of 10	4.50	
d.			As "c," die cutting omitted	—	

This is an ongoing set. Numbers may change.

CALIFORNIA STATEHOOD, 150TH ANNIV.

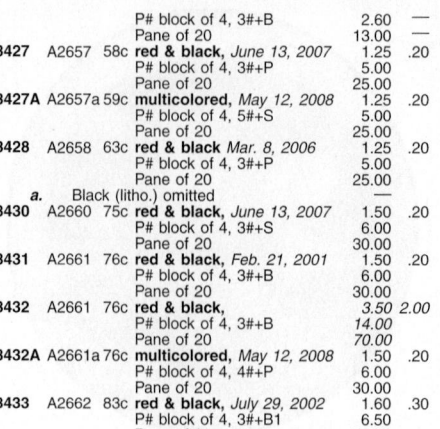

Big Sur and Iceplant — A2668

Designed by Carl Herrman.
Printed by Avery Dennison.

PHOTOGRAVURE

Sheets of 200 in ten panes of 20

2000, Sept. 8 **Tagged** ***Serpentine Die Cut 11***

Self-Adhesive

3438	A2668	33c	**multicolored**	.75	.20
			P# block of 4, 5#+V	3.00	
			Pane of 20	15.00	

DEEP SEA CREATURES

Fanfin Anglerfish A2669

Sea Cucumber A2670

Fangtooth A2671

Amphipod A2672

Medusa A2673

Designed by Ethel Kessler.
Printed by American Packaging Corp. for Sennett Security Products.

PHOTOGRAVURE

Sheets of 135 in nine panes of 15

2000, Oct. 2 **Tagged** ***Perf. 10x10¼***

3439	A2669	33c	**multicolored**	.65	.20
3440	A2670	33c	**multicolored**	.65	.20
3441	A2671	33c	**multicolored**	.65	.20
3442	A2672	33c	**multicolored**	.65	.20
3443	A2673	33c	**multicolored**	.65	.20
a.			Vert. strip of 5, #3439-3443	3.25	2.00
			Pane of 15, 4#+S	9.75	—
			Sheet of 135 (nine panes)	90.00	—
			Cross gutter block of 10	15.00	—
			Horiz. block of 10 with vert. gutter	10.00	—
			Horiz. pairs with vert. gutter (each)	2.00	—
			Vert. pair with horiz. gutter	1.75	—

See note under No. 3292 regarding lack of plate block listing.

Cross gutter block of 10 consists of three stamps from each of two panes and two stamps from each of the other two panes with the cross gutter between.

LITERARY ARTS SERIES

Thomas Wolfe (1900-38), Novelist A2674

Designed by Phil Jordan.
Printed by Ashton-Potter (USA) Ltd.

LITHOGRAPHED

Sheets of 120 in six panes of 20

2000, Oct. 3 **Tagged** ***Perf. 11***

3444	A2674	33c	**multicolored**	.65	.20
			P# block of 4, 5#+P	2.60	—
			Pane of 20	13.00	—

WHITE HOUSE, 200TH ANNIV.

A2675

Designed by Derry Noyes.

Printed by Ashton-Potter (USA) Ltd.

LITHOGRAPHED

Sheets of 180 in nine panes of 20

2000, Oct. 18 Tagged *Serpentine Die Cut 11¼*

Self-Adhesive

3445 A2675 33c **multicolored** 1.00 .20
P# block of 4, 4#+P 4.00
Pane of 20 20.00

LEGENDS OF HOLLYWOOD

Edward G. Robinson (1893-1973), Actor — A2676

Designed by Howard Paine.
Printed by American Packaging Corporation for Sennett Security Products.

PHOTOGRAVURE

Sheets of 120 in six panes of 20

2000, Oct. 24 Tagged *Perf. 11*

3446 A2676 33c **multicolored** 1.50 .20
P# block of 4, 7#+S 7.00 —
Pane of 20 34.00 12.50
Sheet of 120 (6 panes) 160.00
Cross gutter block of 8 25.00
Block of 8 with vertical gutter 15.00
Horiz. pair with vert. gutter 4.00
Vert. pair with horiz. gutter 3.00

Perforations in corner of each stamp are star-shaped. Cross gutter block consists of 6 stamps from upper panes and 2 stamps from panes below.

New York Public Library Lion — A2677

Designed by Carl Herrman.
Printed by American Packaging Corporation for Sennett Security Products.

PHOTOGRAVURE

COIL STAMP

Serpentine Die Cut 11½ Vert.

2000, Nov. 9 Untagged

Self-Adhesive

3447 A2677 (10c) **multicolored,** "2000" year date .20 .20
Pair .40
P# strip of 5, #S11111, S22222, S33333, S44444, S66666 2.25
P# single, #S11111, S22222, S33333, S44444, S66666, S77777 — 1.75
a. "2003" year date .20 .20
Pair .40
P# strip of 5, #S55555 3.00
P# single, #S55555 — 2.00
b. As No. 3447, prephosphored coated paper (solid tagging) (error) —

No. 3447 also is known with extremely faint phosphor splotches. No. 3447b has full-strength tagging. Values with faint tagging: unused and used singles, $2; P# strip of 5 unused, $23; P# single used, $17.50.

See No. 3769.

Flag Over Farm — A2678

Designed by Richard Sheaff.

Printed by Sterling Sommer for Ashton-Potter (USA) Ltd. (#3448), Ashton-Potter (USA) Ltd. (#3449), Avery Dennison (#3450).

LITHOGRAPHED (#3448-3449), PHOTOGRAVURE (#3450)

Sheets of 120 in six panes of 20

2000, Dec. 15 Tagged *Perf. 11¼*

3448 A2678 (34c) **multicolored** .75 .20
P# block of 4, 4# + P 3.25 —
Pane of 20 16.00 —

Self-Adhesive

Serpentine Die Cut 11¼

3449 A2678 (34c) **multicolored** 1.00 .20
P# block of 4, 4# + P 5.00
Pane of 20 24.00

Booklet Stamp

Self-Adhesive

Serpentine Die Cut 8 on 2, 3 or 4 sides

3450 A2678 (34c) **multicolored** .85 .20
a. Booklet pane of 18 16.00
b. Die cutting omitted, pair —

A2679

Statue of Liberty — A2680

Designed by Derry Noyes.
Printed by Avery Dennison (#3451), Bureau of Engraving and Printing (#3452-3453).

PHOTOGRAVURE

Serpentine Die Cut 11 on 2, 3 or 4 sides

2000, Dec. 15 Tagged

Self-Adhesive (#3451, 3453)

Booklet Stamp

3451 A2679 (34c) **multicolored** .70 .20
a. Booklet pane of 20 14.00
b. Booklet pane of 4 2.80
Booklet pane of 4 containing P# single 3.50
P# single, #V1111 1.00 .70
c. Booklet pane of 6 5.25
d. As "a," die cutting omitted —

Coil Stamps

Perf. 9¾ Vert.

3452 A2680 (34c) **multicolored** .70 .20
Pair 1.30 .30
P# strip of 5, #1111 5.00 —
P# single, same # — 2.25

Serpentine Die Cut 10 Vert.

3453 A2680 (34c) **multicolored,** small date .70 .20
Pair 1.40
P# strip of 5, #1111 6.50
P# single, same # — 1.50
a. Die cutting omitted, pair —
b. Large date .75 .20
Pair 1.50
P# strip of 5, #1111 8.00
P# single, same # — 1.50

The date on No. 3453 is 1.4mm long, on No. 3453b 1.55mm long and darker in color.

A2681

A2682

A2683

Flowers — A2684

Designed by Derry Noyes.
Printed by American Packaging Corporation for Sennett Security Products (#3454-3461), Guilford Gravure for Banknote Corporation of America, Inc. (#3462-3465).

PHOTOGRAVURE

Serpentine Die Cut 10½x10¾ on 2 or 3 sides

2000, Dec. 15 Tagged

Booklet Stamps

Self-Adhesive

3454 A2681 (34c) **purple & multi** 1.00 .20
3455 A2682 (34c) **tan & multi** 1.00 .20
3456 A2683 (34c) **green & multi** 1.00 .20
3457 A2684 (34c) **red & multi** 1.00 .20
a. Block of 4, #3454-3457 4.00
b. Booklet pane of 4, #3454-3457 4.00
c. Booklet pane of 6, #3456, 3457, 2 each #3454-3455 6.00
d. Booklet pane of 6, #3454, 3455, 2 each #3456-3457 6.00
e. Booklet pane of 20, 5 each #3454-3457 + label 20.00

No. 3457e is a double-sided booklet pane, with 12 stamps on one side and eight stamps plus label on the other side.

Serpentine Die Cut 11½x11¾ on 2 or 3 sides

3458 A2681 (34c) **purple & multi** 3.00 .25
3459 A2682 (34c) **tan & multi** 3.00 .25
3460 A2683 (34c) **green & multi** 3.00 .25
3461 A2684 (34c) **red & multi** 3.00 .25
a. Block of 4, #3458-3461 12.00
b. Booklet pane of 20, 2 each #3461a, 3 each #3457a 36.50
c. Booklet pane of 20, 2 each #3457a, 3 each #3461a 45.00

Nos. 3461b and 3461c are double-sided booklet panes, with 12 stamps on one side and eight stamps plus label on the other side.

Coil Stamps

Serpentine Die Cut 8½ Vert.

3462 A2683 (34c) **green & multi** 3.50 .20
3463 A2684 (34c) **red & multi** 3.50 .20
3464 A2682 (34c) **tan & multi** 3.50 .20
3465 A2681 (34c) **purple & multi** 3.50 .20
a. Strip of 4, #3462-3465 14.00
P# strip of 5, 2 #3462, 1 each #3463-3465, P#B1111 15.00
P# strip of 9, 2 each #3462-3463, 3465, 3 #3464, same P# 22.50
P# single (#3464) — 1.25

Lettering on No. 3462 has black outline not found on No. 3456. Zeroes of "2000" are rounder on Nos. 3454-3457 than on Nos. 3462-3465.

Statue of Liberty A2685

George Washington A2686

American Buffalo — A2687

Flag Over Farm — A2688

Statue of Liberty — A2689

A2690

A2691

A2692

Flowers — A2693

Apple — A2694

Orange — A2695

Eagle — A2696

Capitol Dome — A2697

Washington Monument — A2698

Designed by Sterling Sommer for Ashton-Potter (USA) Ltd. (#3467), Carl Herrman (#3467, 3468, 3471, 3471A, 3475, 3484, 3484A), Richard Sheaff (#3468A, 3469, 3470, 3475A, 3482-3483, 3495), Derry Noyes (#3466, 3472-3473, 3476, 3477-3481, 3485, 3487-3490), Ned Seidler (#3491-3494).

Printed by Avery Dennison (#3468, 3475, 3485, 3495) Ashton-Potter (USA) Ltd. (#3469-3470, 3482-3484A), American Packaging Corporation for Sennett Security Printers (#3471, 3471A, 3487-3490), Bureau of Engraving and Printing (#3466, 3476-3477), Guilford Gravure, Inc. for Banknote Corporation of America (#3475A, 3478-3481), Banknote Corporation of America (#3468A, 3472-3473, 3491-3494).

PHOTOGRAVURE

Serpentine Die Cut 9¾ Vert.

2001, Jan. 7 **Tagged**

Coil Stamp

Self-Adhesive

3466 A2685 34c **multicolored** .70 .20
Pair 1.40
P# strip of 5, #1111, 2222 5.00
P# single, same # — 2.50

Sheets of 400 in four panes of 100 (#3467), Sheets of 200 in ten panes of 20 (#3468), Sheets of 200 in two panes of 100 (#3469), Sheets of 120 in six panes of 20 (#3468A, 3470-3473), Sheets of 160 in eight panes of 20 (#3471A)

Self-Adhesive (#3468-3468A, 3470-3473)

2001 **Photo.** **Tagged** ***Perf. 11¼x11***

3467 A2687 21c **multicolored,** *Sept. 20* .50 .20
P# block of 4, 6#+P 21.00 —

Serpentine Die Cut 11

3468 A2687 21c **multicolored,** *Feb. 22* .40 .20
P# block of 4, 4#+V 1.60
Pane of 20 8.00

Litho.

Serpentine Die Cut 11¼x11¾

3468A A2686 23c **green,** *Sept. 20* .45 .20
P# block of 4, 3#+B 1.80
Pane of 20 9.00

Photo.

Perf. 11¼

3469 A2688 34c **multicolored,** *Feb. 7* .75 .20
P# block of 4, 4#+P 25.00 —

Serpentine Die Cut 11¼

3470 A2688 34c **multicolored,** *Mar. 6* .75 .20
P# block of 4, 4#+P 3.00
Pane of 20 15.00

Photo.

Serpentine Die Cut 10¾

3471 A2696 55c **multicolored,** *Feb. 22* 1.10 .20
P# block of 4, 5#+S 4.40
Pane of 20 22.00

Serpentine Die Cut 10¾

3471A A2696 57c **multicolored,** *Sept. 20* 1.10 .20
P# block of 4, 5#+S 4.40
Pane of 20 22.00

LITHOGRAPHED

Serpentine Die Cut 11¼x11½

3472 A2697 $3.50 **multicolored,** *Jan. 29* 7.00 2.00
P# block of 4, 4#+B 28.00
Pane of 20 140.00
a. Die cutting omitted, pair —

3473 A2698 $12.25 **multicolored,** *Jan. 29* 22.50 10.00
P# block of 4, 4#+B 90.00
Pane of 20 450.00

COIL STAMPS

Self-Adhesive (#3475-3475A, 3477-3481)

Photo.

Serpentine Die Cut 8½ Vert.

3475 A2687 21c **multicolored,** *Feb. 22* .50 .20
Pair 1.00 .30
P# strip of 5, #V1111, V2222 3.00 —
P# single, same # — 1.00

3475A A2686 23c **green,** *Sept. 20* .50 .20
Pair 1.00
P# strip of 5, #B11 3.00
P# single, same # — 1.00

Compare No. 3475A ("2001" date at lower left) with No. 3617 ("2002" date at lower left).

Perf. 9¾ Vert.

3476 A2685 34c **multicolored,** prephosphored coated paper (grainy solid tagging), *Feb. 7* .70 .20
Pair 1.40 .30
P# strip of 5, #1111 5.00 —
P# single, same # — 2.75
a. Prephosphored coated paper (solid tagging) .65 .20
Pair 1.30 .30
P# strip of 5, #1111 6.00 —
P# single, same # — 4.00

Serpentine Die Cut 9¾ Vert.

3477 A2685 34c **multicolored,** *Feb. 7* .80 .20
Pair 1.60 .30
P# strip of 5, #1111, 2222, 3333, 4444, 5555, 6666 5.00 —
P# single, same # — 1.00
P# strip of 5, #7777 11.00
P# single, #7777 — 8.50
a. Die cutting omitted, pair *225.00*

No. 3477 has right angle corners and backing paper as high as the stamp. No. 3466 has rounded corners and is on backing paper larger than the stamp.

Serpentine Die Cut 8½ Vert.

3478 A2690 34c **green & multi,** *Feb. 7* .70 .20
3479 A2691 34c **red & multi,** *Feb. 7* .70 .20
3480 A2692 34c **tan & multi,** *Feb. 7* .70 .20
3481 A2693 34c **purple & multi,** *Feb. 7* .70 .20
a. Strip of 4, #3478-3481 2.80
P# strip of 5, 2 #3478, 1 each #3479-3481, P#B1111, B2111, B2122, B2211, B2222 5.50
P# strip of 9, 3 #3480, 2 each #3478-3479, 3481, P# B1111, B2111, B2122, B2211, B2222 8.00 —
P# single, (#3480), same # — 2.00

BOOKLET STAMPS

Litho.

Self-Adhesive, Tagged

Serpentine Die Cut 11¼x11 on 3 Sides

3482 A2686 20c **dark carmine,** *Feb. 22* .45 .20
a. Booklet pane of 10 4.50
b. Booklet pane of 4 1.80
c. Booklet pane of 6 2.70

Serpentine Die Cut 10½x11 on 3 Sides

3483 A2686 20c **dark carmine,** *Feb. 22* 5.00 1.25
a. Booklet pane of 4, 2 #3482 at L, 2 #3483 at R 12.00
b. Booklet pane of 6, 3 #3482 at L, 3 #3483 at R 20.00
c. Booklet pane of 10, 5 #3482 at L, 5 #3483 at R 25.00
d. Booklet pane of 4, 2 #3483 at L, 2 #3482 at R 12.00
e. Booklet pane of 6, 3 #3483 at L, 3 #3482 at R 20.00
f. Booklet pane of 10, 5 #3483 at L, 5 #3482 at R 25.00
g. Pair, #3482 at L, #3483 at R 5.50
h. Pair, #3483 at L, #3482 at R 5.50

Serpentine Die Cut 11¼ on 3 Sides

3484 A2687 21c **multicolored,** *Sept. 20* .50 .20
b. Booklet pane of 4 2.00
c. Booklet pane of 6 3.00
d. Booklet pane of 10 5.00

Serpentine Die Cut 10½x11¼

3484A A2687 21c **multicolored,** *Sept. 20* 5.00 1.50
e. Booklet pane of 4, 2 #3484 at L, 2 #3484A at R 12.00
f. Booklet pane of 6, 3 #3484 at L, 3 #3484A at R 20.00
g. Booklet pane of 10, 5 #3484 at L, 5 #3484A at R 25.00
h. Booklet pane of 4, 2 #3484A at L, 2 #3484 at R 12.00
i. Booklet pane of 6, 3 #3484A at L, 3 #3484 at R 20.00
j. Booklet pane of 10, 5 #3484A at L, 5 #3484 at R 25.00
k. Pair, #3484 at L, #3484A at R 5.50
l. Pair, #3484A at L, #3484 at R 5.50

Photo.

Serpentine Die Cut 11 on 2, 3 or 4 Sides

3485 A2689 34c **multicolored,** *Feb. 7* .70 .20
a. Booklet pane of 10 7.00
b. Booklet pane of 20 14.00
c. Booklet pane of 4 3.00
Booklet pane of 4 containing P# single 4.00
P# single, #V1111, V1122, V2212, V2222 1.50 1.50
P# single, #V1112, V1121 — —
d. Booklet pane of 6 4.50
e. Die cutting omitted, pair (from No. 3485b) —
f. As "e," booklet pane of 20 —

Serpentine Die Cut 10½x10¾ on 2 or 3 Sides

3487 A2693 34c **purple & multi,** *Feb. 7* .75 .20
3488 A2692 34c **tan & multi,** *Feb. 7* .75 .20
3489 A2690 34c **green & multi,** *Feb. 7* .75 .20
3490 A2691 34c **red & multi,** *Feb. 7* .75 .20
a. Block of 4, #3487-3490 3.00
b. Booklet pane of 4, #3487-3490 3.00
c. Booklet pane of 6, #3489-3490, 2 each #3487-3488 4.50
d. Booklet pane of 6, #3487-3488, 2 each #3489-3490 4.50
e. Booklet pane of 20, 5 each #3490a + label 15.00

No. 3490e is a double-sided booklet pane, with 12 stamps on one side and eight stamps plus label on the other side.

Litho.

Serpentine Die Cut 11¼ on 2, 3 or 4 Sides

3491 A2694 34c **multicolored,** *Mar. 6* .70 .20
3492 A2695 34c **multicolored,** *Mar. 6* .70 .20
a. Pair, #3491-3492 1.40
b. Booklet pane, 10 each #3491-3492 14.00
c. As "a," black ("34 USA") omitted —
d. As "a," die cutting omitted —
e. As "b," die cutting omitted —

Serpentine Die Cut 11½x10¾ on 2 or 3 Sides

3493 A2694 34c **multicolored,** *May* 1.00 .20
3494 A2695 34c **multicolored,** *May* 1.00 .20
a. Pair, #3493-3494 2.00
b. Booklet pane, 2 each #3493-3494 4.00
Booklet pane, 2 each #3493-3494, containing P# single 6.00
P# single, #B1111 2.00 2.00
c. Booklet pane, 3 each #3493-3494, #3493 at UL 6.00
d. Booklet pane, 3 each #3493-3494, #3494 at UL 6.00

Serpentine Die Cut 8 on 2, 3 or 4 sides

3495 A2688 34c **multicolored,** *Dec. 17* .90 .20
a. Booklet pane of 18 16.50

LOVE

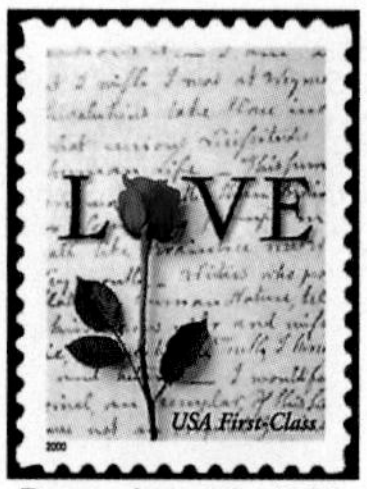

Rose, Apr. 20, 1763 Love Letter by John Adams — A2699

Rose, Apr. 20, 1763 Love Letter by John Adams — A2700

Rose, Aug. 11, 1763 Love Letter by Abigail Smith (Abigail Adams in 1764) — A2701

Designed by Lisa Catalone. Printed by Banknote Corporation of America, Inc.

LITHOGRAPHED

Sheets of 180 in nine panes of 20 (#3499)

Serpentine Die Cut 11¼ on 2, 3 or 4 Sides

2001 Tagged

Self-Adhesive

Booklet Stamps (Nos. 3496-3498)

3496 A2699 (34c) **multicolored,** *Jan. 19*		.90	.20
a.	Booklet pane of 20	18.00	
b.	Vert. pair, die cutting omitted between	—	

Serpentine Die Cut 11¼ on 2, 3 or 4 Sides

3497 A2700 34c **multicolored,** *Feb. 14*		.90	.20
a.	Booklet pane of 20	18.00	
b.	Vertical pair, die cutting omitted between	—	

Size: 18x21mm

Serpentine Die Cut 11½x10¾ on 2 or 3 Sides

3498 A2700 34c **multicolored,** *Feb. 14*		1.00	.20
a.	Booklet pane of 4	4.00	
	Booklet pane of 4 containing P# single	6.00	
	P# single, #B1111	2.00	2.00
b.	Booklet pane of 6	6.00	

Plate number single on No. 3498 is on the lower left stamp of the bottom pane of 4 of the booklet.

Serpentine Die Cut 11¼

3499 A2701 55c **multicolored,** *Feb. 14*		1.10	.20
	P# block of 4, 4#+B	4.50	
	Pane of 20	22.50	

See No. 3551.

CHINESE NEW YEAR

Year of the Snake — A2702

Designed by Clarence Lee. Printed by Sterling Sommer for Ashton-Potter (USA) Ltd.

LITHOGRAPHED

Sheets of 180 in nine panes of 20

2001, Jan. 20 Tagged *Perf. 11¼*

3500 A2702 34c **multicolored**		.70	.20
	P# block of 4, 5#+P	2.80	—
	Pane of 20	14.00	—

See No. 3895f.

BLACK HERITAGE SERIES

Roy Wilkins (1901-81), Civil Rights Leader — A2703

Designed by Richard Sheaff. Printed by Ashton-Potter (USA) Ltd.

LITHOGRAPHED

Sheets of 180 in nine panes of 20

Serpentine Die Cut 11½x11¼

2001, Jan. 24 Tagged

Self-Adhesive

3501 A2703 34c **blue**		.70	.20
	P# block of 4, 2#+P	2.80	
	Pane of 20	14.00	

AMERICAN ILLUSTRATORS

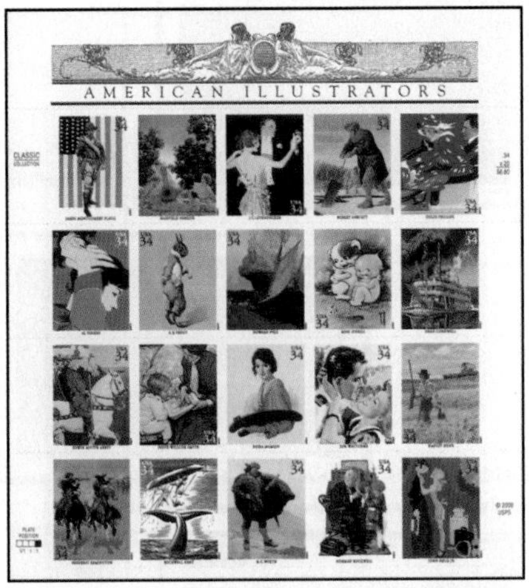

A2704

Illustration reduced.

Designed by Carl Herrman.
Printed by Avery Dennison.

Designs: a, Marine Corps poster "First in the Fight, Always Faithful," by James Montgomery Flagg. b, "Interlude (The Lute Players)," by Maxfield Parrish. c, Advertisement for Arrow Collars and Shirts, by J. C. Leyendecker. d, Advertisement for Carrier Corp. Refrigeration, by Robert Fawcett. e, Advertisement for Luxite Hosiery, by Coles Phillips. f, Illustration for correspondence school lesson, by Al Parker. g, "Br'er Rabbit," by A. B. Frost. h, "An Attack on a Galleon," by Howard Pyle. i, Kewpie and Kewpie Doodle Dog, by Rose O'Neill. j, Illustration for cover of True Magazine, by Dean Cornwell. k, "Galahad's Departure," by Edwin Austin Abbey. l, "The First Lesson," by Jessie Willcox Smith. m, Illustration for cover of McCall's Magazine, by Neysa McMein. n, "Back Home For Keeps," by Jon Whitcomb. o, "Something for Supper," by Harvey Dunn. p, "A Dash for the Timber," by Frederic Remington. q, Illustration for "Moby Dick," by Rockwell Kent. r, "Captain Bill Bones," by N. C. Wyeth. s, Illustration for cover of The Saturday Evening Post, by Norman Rockwell. t, "The Girl He Left Behind," by John Held, Jr.

PHOTOGRAVURE

Sheets of 80 in four panes of 20

2001, Feb. 1 Tagged *Serpentine Die Cut 11¼*

Self-Adhesive

3502 A2704	Pane of 20	17.50	
a.-t. 34c	any single	.85	.60
	Sheet of 80 (4 panes)	52.50	
	Block of 20 different stamps with vert. gutter between any 2 columns	27.50	
	Pairs with vert. gutter between (each)	2.00	

DIABETES AWARENESS

A2705

Designed by Richard Sheaff. Printed by Ashton-Potter (USA) Ltd.

LITHOGRAPHED

Sheets of 180 in nine panes of 20

Serpentine Die Cut 11¼x11½

2001, Mar. 16 Tagged

Self-Adhesive

3503 A2705 34c **multicolored**		.65	.20
	P# block of 4, 4#+P	2.60	
	Pane of 20	13.00	

NOBEL PRIZE CENTENARY

Alfred Nobel and Obverse of Medals A2706

Designed by Olof Baldursdottir of Sweden. Printed by De La Rue Security Printing.

LITHOGRAPHED & ENGRAVED

Sheets of 120 in six panes of 20

2001, Mar. 22 Tagged *Perf. 11*

3504 A2706 34c **multicolored**		.70	.20
	P# block of 4, 3#+S	2.80	—
	Pane of 20	14.00	—
a.	Imperf, pair	—	

See Sweden No. 2415.

PAN-AMERICAN EXPOSITION INVERT STAMPS, CENT.

A2707

Illustration reduced.

Reproductions (dated 2001) of: a, #294a. b, #295a. c, #296a. d, Commemorative "cinderella" stamp depicting a buffalo.

Designed by Richard Sheaff. Printed by Banknote Corporation of America.

LITHOGRAPHED (#3505d), ENGRAVED (others)

Sheets of 28 in four panes of 7

2001, Mar. 29 *Perf. 12 (#3505d), 12½x12 (others)*

Tagged (#3505d), Untagged (others)

3505 A2707	Pane of 7, #3505a-3505c, 4 #3505d	9.00	7.00
a.	A109 1c **green & black**	.60	.20
b.	A110 2c **carmine & black**	.60	.20
c.	A111 4c **deep red brown & black**	.60	.20
d.	80c **red & blue**	1.75	.35
	Sheet of 4 panes	45.00	
	Pane with vertical gutter, 80c stamps at left; "a," "b" & "c" at right (from sheet of 4 panes)	20.00	

GREAT PLAINS PRAIRIE

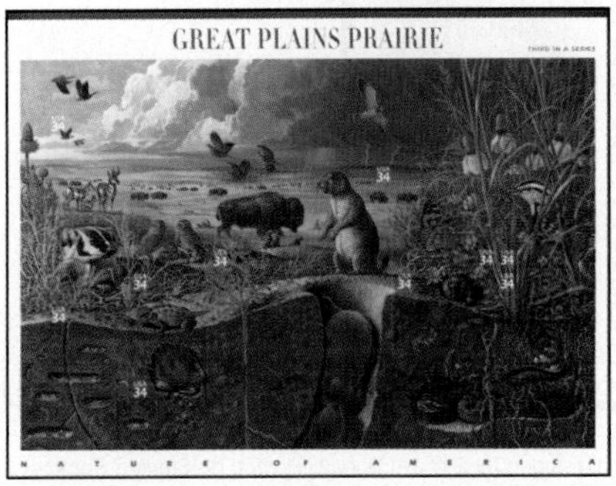

A2708

Illustration reduced.

Designed by Ethel Kessler. Printed by Ashton-Potter (USA) Ltd.

Wildlife and flowers: a, Pronghorns, Canada geese. b, Burrowing owls, American buffalos. c, American buffalo, Black-tailed prairie dogs, wild alfalfa, horiz. d, Black-tailed prairie dog, American buffalos,. e, Painted lady butterfly, American buffalo, prairie coneflowers, prairie wild roses, horiz. f, Western meadowlark, camel cricket, prairie coneflowers, prairie wild roses. g, Badger, harvester ants. h, Eastern short-horned lizard, plains pocket gopher. i, Plains spadefoot, dung beetle, prairie wild roses, horiz. j, Two-striped grasshopper, Ord's kangaroo rat.

LITHOGRAPHED
Sheets of 60 in six panes of 10

2001, Apr. 19 Tagged *Serpentine Die Cut 10*
Self-Adhesive

3506	A2708	Pane of 10	11.00	
a.-j.		34c Any single	1.00	.50
		Sheet of 6 panes	65.00	

PEANUTS COMIC STRIP

Snoopy
A2709

Designed by Paige Braddock. Printed by Ashton-Potter (USA) Ltd.

LITHOGRAPHED
Sheets of 180 in nine panes of 20
Serpentine Die Cut 11¼x11½

2001, May 17 Tagged
Self-Adhesive

3507	A2709 34c	**multicolored**	.75	.20
		P# block of 4, 5#+P	3.00	
		Pane of 20	15.00	

HONORING VETERANS

A2710

Designed by Carl Herrman. Printed by Ashton-Potter (USA) Ltd.

LITHOGRAPHED
Sheets of 180 in nine panes of 20
Serpentine Die Cut 11¼x11½

2001, May 23 Tagged
Self-Adhesive

3508	A2710 34c	**multicolored**	.70	.20
		P# block of 4, 4#+P	2.80	
		Pane of 20	14.00	11.00

FRIDA KAHLO (1907-54), PAINTER

Self-portrait — A2711

Designed by Richard Sheaff. Printed by Sterling Sommer for Ashton-Potter (USA) Ltd..

LITHOGRAPHED
Sheets of 80 in four panes of 20

2001, June 21 Tagged *Perf. 11¼*

3509	A2711 34c	**multicolored**	.70	.20
		P# block of 4, 4#+P	2.80	—
		Pane of 20	14.00	—

LEGENDARY PLAYING FIELDS

Ebbets Field — A2712

Tiger Stadium A2713

Crosley Field — A2714

Yankee Stadium A2715

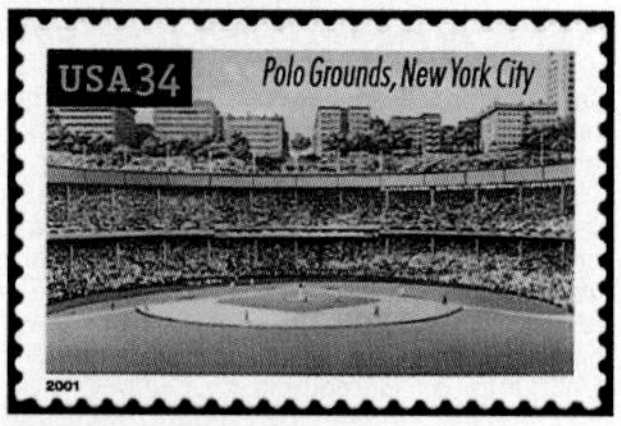

Polo Grounds A2716

Forbes Field — A2717

Fenway Park — A2718

Comiskey Park — A2719

Shibe Park — A2720

Wrigley Field — A2721

Designed by Phil Jordan. Printed by Avery Dennison.

PHOTOGRAVURE
Sheets of 160 in eight panes of 20
Serpentine Die Cut 11¼x11½

2001, June 27 Tagged Self-Adhesive

3510	A2712 34c	**multicolored**	.90	.60
3511	A2713 34c	**multicolored**	.90	.60
3512	A2714 34c	**multicolored**	.90	.60
3513	A2715 34c	**multicolored**	.90	.60
3514	A2716 34c	**multicolored**	.90	.60
3515	A2717 34c	**multicolored**	.90	.60
3516	A2718 34c	**multicolored**	.90	.60
3517	A2719 34c	**multicolored**	.90	.60
3518	A2720 34c	**multicolored**	.90	.60
3519	A2721 34c	**multicolored**	.90	.60
a.		Block of 10, #3510-3519	9.00	
		P# block of 10, 4#+V	9.00	
		Pane of 20	18.00	
		Sheet of 160 (8 panes)	125.00	
		Cross-gutter block of 12	20.00	
		Horiz. block of 10 with vert. gutter	10.00	
		Block of 4 with horiz. gutter	4.50	
		Vert. pairs with horiz. gutter (each)	2.00	
		Horiz. pairs with vert. gutter (each)	2.00	

Cross gutter block contains one each Nos. 3510-3517, two each of Nos. 3518-3519, and vertical and horizontal gutters.

ATLAS STATUE, NEW YORK CITY

A2722

Designed by Kevin Newman. Printed by Banknote Corporation of America.

PHOTOGRAVURE
COIL STAMP
Serpentine Die Cut 8½ Vert.

2001, June 29 Untagged
Self-Adhesive

3520	A2722 (10c)	**multicolored**	.20	.20
		Pair	.40	
		P# strip of 5, #B1111	2.25	
		P# single, same #	—	1.25

See No. 3770.

LEONARD BERNSTEIN (1918-90), CONDUCTOR

A2723

Designed by Howard Paine. Printed by Sterling Sommer for Ashton-Potter (USA) Ltd.

LITHOGRAPHED
Sheets of 180 in nine panes of 20

2001, July 10 Tagged *Perf. 11¼*

3521	A2723 34c	**multicolored**	.70	.20
		P# block of 4, 4#+P	2.80	—
		Pane of 20	14.00	—

WOODY WAGON

A2724

Designed by Kevin Newman. Printed by American Packaging Corporation for Sennett Security Products.

PHOTOGRAVURE
COIL STAMP

Serpentine Die Cut 11½ Vert.

2001, Aug. 3 **Untagged**

Self-Adhesive

3522	A2724 (15c) **multicolored**	.30	.20
	Pair	.60	
	P# strip of 5, #S11111	3.00	
	P# single, same #	—	2.00

LEGENDS OF HOLLYWOOD

Lucille Ball (1911-89) — A2725

Designed by Derry Noyes. Printed by Banknote Corporation of America.

LITHOGRAPHED
Sheets of 180 in nine panes of 20

2001, Aug. 6 **Tagged** ***Serpentine Die Cut 11***

Self-Adhesive

3523	A2725 34c **multicolored**	1.00	.20
	P# block of 4, 4#+B	4.50	
	Pane of 20	22.00	13.00
	Sheet of 180 (9 panes)	145.00	
	Cross-gutter block of 8	20.00	
	Block of 8 with vert. gutter	11.50	
	Horiz. pair with vert. gutter	3.25	
	Vert. pairs with horiz. gutter	2.25	
a.	Die cutting omitted, pair	—	
	As "a," pane of 20	—	

Cross gutter block consists of 6 stamps from upper panes and 2 stamps from lower panes.

AMERICAN TREASURES SERIES
Amish Quilts

Diamond in the Square, c. 1920 — A2726

Lone Star, c. 1920 — A2727

Sunshine and Shadow, c. 1910 — A2728

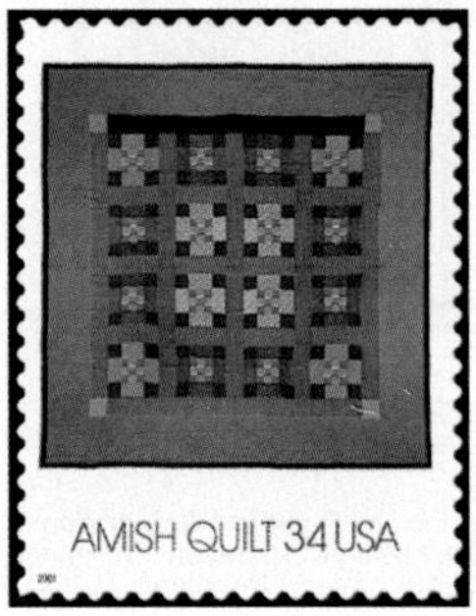

Double Ninepatch Variation — A2729

Designed by Derry Noyes. Printed by Ashton-Potter (USA) Ltd.

LITHOGRAPHED
Sheets of 120 in six panes of 20

Serpentine Die Cut 11¼x11½

2001, Aug. 9 **Tagged**

Self-Adhesive

3524	A2726 34c **multicolored**	.70	.20
3525	A2727 34c **multicolored**	.70	.20
3526	A2728 34c **multicolored**	.70	.20
3527	A2729 34c **multicolored**	.70	.20
a.	Block or strip of 4, #3524-3527	2.80	
	P# block of 4, 5#+P	2.80	
	Pane of 20	14.00	

CARNIVOROUS PLANTS

Venus Flytrap — A2730

Yellow Trumpet — A2731

Cobra Lily — A2732

English Sundew — A2733

Designed by Steve Buchanan.
Printed by Avery Dennison.

PHOTOGRAVURE
Sheets of 160 in eight panes of 20

2001, Aug. 23 **Tagged** ***Serpentine Die Cut 11½***

Self-Adhesive

3528	A2730 34c **multicolored**	.70	.20
3529	A2731 34c **multicolored**	.70	.20
3530	A2732 34c **multicolored**	.70	.20
3531	A2733 34c **multicolored**	.70	.20
a.	Block or strip of 4, #3528-3531	2.80	
	P# block of 4, 4#+V	2.80	
	Pane of 20	14.00	

EID

"Eid Mubarak" — A2734

Designed by Mohamed Zakariya.
Printed by Avery Dennison.

PHOTOGRAVURE
Sheets of 240 in twelve panes of 20

2001, Sept. 1 **Tagged** ***Serpentine Die Cut 11¼***

Self-Adhesive

3532	A2734 34c **multicolored**	.70	.20
	P# block of 4, 3#+V	2.80	
	Pane of 20	14.00	

See No. 3674.

ENRICO FERMI (1901-54), PHYSICIST

A2735

Designed by Richard Sheaff. Printed by Sterling Sommer for Ashton-Potter (USA) Ltd.

LITHOGRAPHED
Sheets of 180 in nine panes of 20

2001, Sept. 29 **Tagged** ***Perf. 11***

3533	A2735 34c **multicolored**	.70	.20
	P# block of 4, 4#+P	2.80	—
	Pane of 20	14.00	—

THAT'S ALL FOLKS!

Porky Pig at Mailbox — A2736

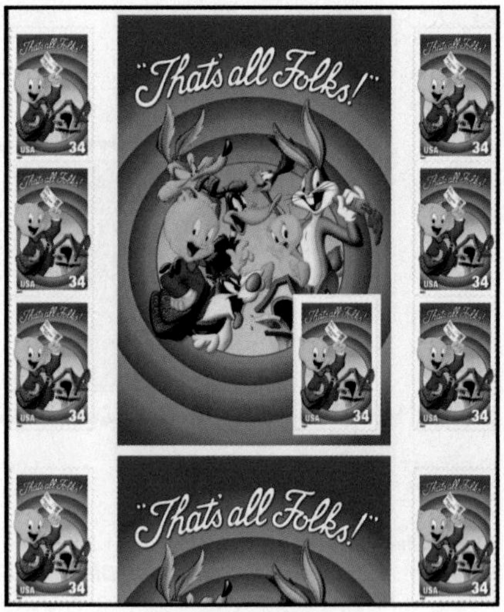

Cross Gutter Block of 9

Illustration reduced.

Designed by Ed Wleczyk, Warner Bros.

Printed by Avery Dennison.

PHOTOGRAVURE

2001, Oct. 1 Tagged *Serpentine Die Cut 11*

Self-Adhesive

3534	Pane of 10	7.00	
a.	A2736 34c single	.70	.20
b.	Pane of 9 #3534a	6.25	
c.	Pane of 1 #3534a	.70	
	Sheet of 60 (six panes) no plate numbers	47.50	
	Sheet of 60 (six panes) with plate # in selvage on front and reverse	50.00	
	Pane of 10 from sheet of 60	8.00	
	Pane of 10 with plate numbers on front	12.50	
	Cross gutter block of 9 or 10	16.00	
	Cross gutter block of 12	18.00	
	Vert. pair with horiz. gutter	2.00	
	Horiz. pair with vert. gutter	4.00	

Die cutting on No. 3534b does not extend through the backing paper.

3535	Pane of 10	60.00	
a.	A2736 34c single	3.00	
b.	Pane of 9 #3535a	27.50	
c.	Pane of 1, no die cutting	30.00	

Die cutting on No. 3535a extends through backing paper.

Nos. 3534b-3534c and 3535b-3535c are separated by a vertical line of microperforations.

CHRISTMAS

Virgin and Child, by Lorenzo Costa — A2737

A2738 A2739

A2740 A2741

19th Century Chromolithographs of Santa Claus

Designed by Richard Sheaff.

Printed by Guilford Gravure, Inc., for Banknote Corporation of America (#3536), American Packaging Corporation for Sennett Security Products (#3537-3540), Avery Dennison (#3541-3544).

PHOTOGRAVURE

Sheets of 160 in eight panes of 20 (#3537-3540)

Serpentine Die Cut 11½ on 2, 3 or 4 Sides

2001, Oct. 10 Tagged

Self-Adhesive

Booklet Stamps (#3536, 3537a-3540a, 3537b, 3538b, 3539b, 3540e, 3541-3544)

3536	A2737 34c **multicolored**	.75	.20
a.	Booklet pane of 20	15.00	

Serpentine Die Cut 10¾x11

Black Inscriptions

3537	A2738 34c **multicolored,** large date	.70	.20
a.	Small date (from booklet pane)	.75	.20
b.	Large date (from booklet pane)	2.00	.20
3538	A2739 34c **multicolored,** large date	.70	.20
a.	Small date (from booklet pane)	.75	.20
b.	Large date (from booklet pane)	2.00	.20
3539	A2740 34c **multicolored,** large date	.70	.20
a.	Small date (from booklet pane)	.75	.20
b.	Large date (from booklet pane)	2.00	.20
3540	A2741 34c **multicolored,** large date	.70	.20
a.	Small date (from booklet pane)	.75	.20
b.	Block of 4, #3537-3540	2.80	
	P# block of 4, 4#+S	2.80	
	Pane of 20	14.00	
c.	Block of 4, small date, #3537a-3540a	3.00	
d.	Booklet pane of 20, 5 #3540c + label	15.00	
e.	Large date (from booklet pane)	2.00	.20
f.	Block of 4, large date, #3537b-3539b, 3540e	8.00	
g.	Booklet pane of 20, 5 #3540f + label	40.00	

Nos. 3540d and 3540g are double-sided booklet panes, with 12 stamps on one side and eight stamps plus label on the other side.

Numerals "3" and "4" are distinctly separate on Nos. 3537-3540, and touching or separated by a slight hairline on the booklet pane stamps.

Designs of Nos. 3537a-3540a are slightly taller than Nos. 3537-3540.

Serpentine Die Cut 11 on 2 or 3 Sides

Size: 21x18½mm

Green and Red Inscriptions

3541	A2738 34c **multicolored**	.70	.20
3542	A2739 34c **multicolored**	.70	.20
3543	A2740 34c **multicolored**	.70	.20
3544	A2741 34c **multicolored**	.70	.20
a.	Block of 4, #3541-3544	2.80	
b.	Booklet pane of 4, #3541-3544	2.80	
c.	Booklet pane of 6, #3543-3544, 2 #3541-3542	4.25	
d.	Booklet pane of 6, #3541-3542, 2 #3543-3544	4.25	
	Nos. 3536-3544 (9)	6.35	1.80

JAMES MADISON (1751-1836)

Madison and His Home, Montpelier A2742

Designed by John Thompson.

Printed by Banknote Corporation of America.

LITHOGRAPHED & ENGRAVED

Sheets of 120 in six panes of 20

2001, Oct. 18 Tagged *Perf. 11x11¼*

3545	A2742 34c **green & black**	.70	.20
	P# block of 4, 2#+B	2.80	—
	Pane of 20	14.00	—
	Sheet of 120 (6 panes)	80.00	
	Cross gutter block of 4	8.25	—
	Horiz. pair with vert. gutter	3.00	—
	Vert. pair with horiz. gutter	2.00	—

THANKSGIVING

Cornucopia — A2743

Designed by Richard Sheaff.

Printed by Ashton-Potter (USA) Ltd.

LITHOGRAPHED

Sheets of 180 in nine panes of 20

2001, Oct. 19 Tagged *Serpentine Die Cut 11¼*

Self-Adhesive

3546	A2743 34c **multicolored**	.70	.20
	P# block of 4, 4#+P	2.80	
	Pane of 20	14.00	

Hanukkah Type of 1996

Designed by Hannah Smotrich.

Printed by Avery Dennison.

PHOTOGRAVURE

Sheets of 200 in ten panes of 20

2001, Oct. 21 Tagged *Serpentine Die Cut 11*

Self-Adhesive

3547	A2411 34c **multicolored**	.70	.20
	P# block of 4, 5#+V	2.80	
	Pane of 20	14.00	

Kwanzaa Type of 1997

Designed by Synthia Saint James.

Printed by Avery Dennison.

PHOTOGRAVURE

Sheets of 240 in twelve panes of 20

2001, Oct. 21 Tagged *Serpentine Die Cut 11*

Self-Adhesive

3548	A2458 34c **multicolored**	.70	.20
	P# block of 4, 4#+V	2.80	
	Pane of 20	14.00	

UNITED WE STAND

A2744

Designed by Terry McCaffrey.

Printed by Banknote Corporation of America (#3549), Bureau of Engraving and Printing (#3550).

LITHOGRAPHED

BOOKLET STAMPS

Serpentine Die Cut 11¼ on 2, 3, or 4 Sides

2001, Oct. 24 Tagged

Self-Adhesive

3549	A2744 34c **multicolored**	.75	.20
a.	Booklet pane of 20	15.00	

PHOTOGRAVURE

Serpentine Die Cut 10½x10¾ on 2 or 3 Sides

2002, Jan. Tagged

Self-Adhesive

3549B	A2744 34c **multicolored,** *Jan. 2002*	.90	.20
c.	Booklet pane of 4	3.60	
d.	Booklet pane of 6	5.40	
e.	Booklet pane of 20	18.00	

No. 3549Be is a double-sided booklet pane, with 12 stamps on one side and eight stamps plus label on the other side.

"First day covers" of No. 3549B are dated Oct. 24, 2001.

COIL STAMP

Serpentine Die Cut 9¾ Vert.

2001, Oct. 24 **Tagged**

Self-Adhesive

3550	A2744	34c	**multicolored, perpendicular corners**	.95	.20
			Pair	1.90	
			P# strip of 5, #1111, 2222	6.00	
			P# strip of 5, #3333	8.00	
			P# single, same #	—	1.00
			P# single, #3333	—	3.00
3550A	A2744	34c	**multicolored**	1.10	.20
			Pair	2.20	
			P# strip of 5, #1111	6.50	
			P# single, same #	—	3.00

No. 3550 has right angle corners and backing paper as high as the stamp. No. 3550A has rounded corners, the backing paper larger than the stamp, and the stamps are spaced approximately 2mm apart.

Love Letters Type of 2001

Designed by Lisa Catalone.
Printed by Banknote Corporation of America.

LITHOGRAPHED

Sheets of 160 in eight panes of 20

2001, Nov. 19 **Tagged** ***Serpentine Die Cut 11¼***

Self-Adhesive

3551	A2701	57c	**multicolored**	1.10	.20
			P# block of 4, 4# + B	5.00	
			Pane of 20	24.00	

WINTER OLYMPICS

Ski Jumping
A2745

Snowboarding
A2746

Ice Hockey
A2747

Figure Skating
A2748

Designed by Jager Di Paola Kemp. Printed by American Packaging Corporation for Sennett Security Products.

PHOTOGRAVURE

Sheets of 180 in nine panes of 20

Serpentine Die Cut 11½x10¾

2002, Jan. 8 **Tagged**

Self-Adhesive

3552	A2745	34c	**multicolored**	.70	.20
3553	A2746	34c	**multicolored**	.70	.20
3554	A2747	34c	**multicolored**	.70	.20
3555	A2748	34c	**multicolored**	.70	.20
a.			Block or strip of 4, #3552-3555	2.80	
			P# block of 4, 6#+S (UL and UR only)	3.00	
			Pane of 20	15.00	
			Sheet of 180 (9 panes)	125.00	
			Cross gutter block of 8	15.00	
			Block of 4 with vert. gutter	4.00	
			Block of 8 with horiz. gutter	8.00	
			Vert. pair with horiz. gutter, each	1.75	
			Horiz. pair with vert. gutter, each	1.75	
b.			Die cutting inverted, pane of 20	—	
c.			Die cutting omitted, block of 4	*825.00*	
			As "c," pane of 20	—	

Cross gutter blocks of 8 may be either 2x4 or 4x2 in configuration. The former will not show equal numbers of each stamp; the latter will.

Blocks of 4 with vertical gutter must show one of each of the stamps.

MENTORING A CHILD

Child and Adult — A2749

Designed by Lance Hidy. Printed by American Packaging Corporation for Sennett Security Products.

PHOTOGRAVURE

Sheets of 120 in six panes of 20

Serpentine Die Cut 11x10¾

2002, Jan. 10 **Tagged**

Self-Adhesive

3556	A2749	34c	**multicolored**	.70	.20
			P# block of 4, 5#+S	2.80	
			Pane of 20	14.00	

BLACK HERITAGE SERIES

Langston Hughes (1902-67), Writer — A2750

Designed by Richard Sheaff. Printed by Banknote Corporation of America.

LITHOGRAPHED

Sheets of 120 in six panes of 20

Serpentine Die Cut 10¼x10½

2002, Feb. 1 **Tagged**

Self-Adhesive

3557	A2750	34c	**multicolored**	.70	.20
			P# block of 4, 5#+B	3.00	
			Pane of 20	15.00	
a.			Die cutting omitted, pair	—	
			As "a," pane of 20	—	

Beware of pairs/panes with extremely faint die cutting offered as imperf errors.

HAPPY BIRTHDAY

A2751

Designed by Harry Zelenko. Printed by Avery Dennison.

PHOTOGRAVURE

Sheets of 200 in ten panes of 20

2002, Feb. 8 **Tagged** ***Serpentine Die Cut 11***

Self-Adhesive

3558	A2751	34c	**multicolored**	.70	.20
			P# block of 4, 4#+V	2.80	
			Pane of 20	14.00	

See No. 3695.

CHINESE NEW YEAR

Year of the Horse
A2752

Designed by Clarence Lee. Printed by Banknote Corporation of America.

LITHOGRAPHED

Sheets of 120 in six panes of 20

Serpentine Die Cut 10½x10¼

2002, Feb. 11 **Tagged**

Self-Adhesive

3559	A2752	34c	**multicolored**	.75	.20
			P# block of 4, 5#+B	3.00	
			Pane of 20	15.00	

See No. 3895g.

U.S. MILITARY ACADEMY, BICENT.

Military Academy Coat of Arms — A2753

Designed by Derry Noyes. Printed by American Packaging Corp. for Sennett Security Products.

PHOTOGRAVURE

Sheets of 180 in nine panes of 20

Serpentine Die Cut 10½x11

2002, Mar. 16 **Tagged**

Self-Adhesive

3560	A2753	34c	**multicolored**	.70	.20
			P# block of 4, 6#+S	2.80	
			Pane of 20	14.00	

GREETINGS FROM AMERICA

A2754-A2803

Illustration reduced.

Designed by Richard Sheaff. Printed by American Packaging Corp. for Sennett Security Products.

PHOTOGRAVURE

Sheets of 100 in two panes of 50

2002, Apr. 4 **Tagged** ***Serpentine Die Cut 10¾***

Self-Adhesive

3561	A2754	34c	Alabama	.70	.45
3562	A2755	34c	Alaska	.70	.45
3563	A2756	34c	Arizona	.70	.45

3564 A2757 34c Arkansas .70 .45
3565 A2758 34c California .70 .45
3566 A2759 34c Colorado .70 .45
3567 A2760 34c Connecticut .70 .45
3568 A2761 34c Delaware .70 .45
3569 A2762 34c Florida .70 .45
3570 A2763 34c Georgia .70 .45
3571 A2764 34c Hawaii .70 .45
3572 A2765 34c Idaho .70 .45
3573 A2766 34c Illinois .70 .45
3574 A2767 34c Indiana .70 .45
3575 A2768 34c Iowa .70 .45
3576 A2769 34c Kansas .70 .45
3577 A2770 34c Kentucky .70 .45
3578 A2771 34c Louisiana .70 .45
3579 A2772 34c Maine .70 .45
3580 A2773 34c Maryland .70 .45
3581 A2774 34c Massachusetts .70 .45
3582 A2775 34c Michigan .70 .45
3583 A2776 34c Minnesota .70 .45
3584 A2777 34c Mississippi .70 .45
3585 A2778 34c Missouri .70 .45
3586 A2779 34c Montana .70 .45
3587 A2780 34c Nebraska .70 .45
3588 A2781 34c Nevada .70 .45
3589 A2782 34c New Hampshire .70 .45
3590 A2783 34c New Jersey .70 .45
3591 A2784 34c New Mexico .70 .45
3592 A2785 34c New York .70 .45
3593 A2786 34c North Carolina .70 .45
3594 A2787 34c North Dakota .70 .45
3595 A2788 34c Ohio .70 .45
3596 A2789 34c Oklahoma .70 .45
3597 A2790 34c Oregon .70 .45
3598 A2791 34c Pennsylvania .70 .45
3599 A2792 34c Rhode Island .70 .45
3600 A2793 34c South Carolina .70 .45
3601 A2794 34c South Dakota .70 .45
3602 A2795 34c Tennessee .70 .45
3603 A2796 34c Texas .70 .45
3604 A2797 34c Utah .70 .45
3605 A2798 34c Vermont .70 .45
3606 A2799 34c Virginia .70 .45
3607 A2800 34c Washington .70 .45
3608 A2801 34c West Virginia .70 .45
3609 A2802 34c Wisconsin .70 .45
3610 A2803 34c Wyoming .70 .45
a. Pane of 50, #3561-3610 35.00
Sheet of 100 (two panes) 70.00
Block of 50 different stamps with vert. gutter between any 2 columns 35.00
Pair with vert. gutter between (each) 2.00

LONGLEAF PINE FOREST

A2804

Illustration reduced.

Designed by Ethel Kessler. Printed by American Packaging Corp. for Sennett Security Products.

Wildlife and flowers: a, Bachman's sparrow. b, Northern bobwhite, yellow pitcher plants. c, Fox squirrel, red-bellied woodpecker. d, Brown-headed nuthatch. e, Broadhead skink, yellow pitcher plants, pipeworts. f, Eastern towhee, yellow pitcher plants, Savannah meadow beauties, toothache grass. g, Gray fox, gopher tortoise, horiz. h, Blind click beetle, sweetbay, pine woods treefrog. i, Rosebud orchid, pipeworts, southern toad, yellow pitcher plants. j, Grass-pink orchid, yellow-sided skimmer, pipeworts, yellow pitcher plants, horiz.

PHOTOGRAVURE
Sheets of 90 in nine panes of 10
Serpentine Die Cut 10½x10¾, 10¾x10½
2002, Apr. 26 **Tagged**
Self-Adhesive

3611 A2804 Pane of 10 16.00
a.-j. 34c Any single 1.60 .50
Sheet of 9 panes 145.00
k. As No. 3611, die cutting omitted —

AMERICAN DESIGN SERIES

Toleware Coffeepot — A2805

Designed by Derry Noyes.
Printed by American Packaging Corp. for Sennett Security Products.

PHOTOGRAVURE
COIL STAMP
2002, May 31 **Untagged** ***Perf. 9 ¾ Vert.***

3612 A2805 5c **multicolored** .20 .20
Pair .20 .20
P# strip of 5, #S1111111 1.25 —
P# single, #S1111111 — .75
a. Imperf, pair —

No. 3612a is valued with disturbed gum.

Star — A2806

Designed by Phil Jordan. Printed by Banknote Corporation of America.

LITHOGRAPHED, PHOTOGRAVURE (No. 3614, 3615)
Sheets of 400 in eight panes of 50
2002, June 7 **Untagged** ***Serpentine Die Cut 11***
Self-Adhesive (#3613-3614)
Year at Lower Left

3613 A2806 3c **red, blue & black** .20 .20
P# block of 4, 3#+B .25
a. Die cutting omitted, pair —

Serpentine Die Cut 10
Year at Lower Right

3614 A2806 3c **red, blue & black** .20 .20
P# block of 4, 3#+B .25

Coil Stamp
Perf. 10 Vert.
Year at Lower Left

3615 A2806 3c **red, blue & black** .20 .20
Pair .20 .20
P# strip of 5, #S111 .85 —
P# single, same # — .75
a. Prephosphored paper (solid tagging) (error) .40 .20
Pair .80 .20
P# strip of 5, #S111 4.00 —
P# single, same # — 4.00

Washington Type of 2001

Designed by Richard Sheaff. Printed by Ashton-Potter (USA) Ltd. (#3616, 3618, 3619), Avery Dennison (#3617).

LITHOGRAPHED, PHOTOGRAVURE (#3617)
Sheets of 400 in four panes of 100 (#3616)
2002, June 7 **Tagged** ***Perf. 11¼***

3616 A2686 23c **green** .50 .20
P# block of 4, 1#+P 17.50 —

Self-Adhesive
Coil Stamp
Serpentine Die Cut 8½ Vert.

3617 A2686 23c **gray green** .45 .20
Pair .90
P# strip of 5, #V11, V13, V21, V22, V24, V35, V36, V45, V46 3.00
P# single, same # — 1.00
a. Die cutting omitted, pair —

Compare No. 3617 ("2002" date at lower left) with No. 3475A ("2001" date at lower left).

Booklet Stamps
Serpentine Die Cut 11¼x11 on 3 Sides

3618 A2686 23c **green** .45 .20
a. Booklet pane of 4 1.80
b. Booklet pane of 6 2.70
c. Booklet pane of 10 4.50

Serpentine Die Cut 10½x11 on 3 Sides

3619 A2686 23c **green** 3.00 1.75
a. Booklet pane of 4, 2 #3619 at L, 2 #3618 at R 7.00
b. Booklet pane of 6, 3 #3619 at L, 3 #3618 at R 12.50
c. Booklet pane of 4, 2 #3618 at L, 2 #3619 at R 7.00
d. Booklet pane of 6, 3 #3618 at L, 3 #3619 at R 12.50
e. Booklet pane of 10, 5 #3619 at L, 5#3618 at R 15.00
f. Booklet pane of 10, 5 #3618 at L, 5 #3619 at R 15.00
g. Pair, #3619 at L, #3618 at R 3.50
h. Pair, #3618 at L, #3619 at R 3.50

Flag — A2807

Designed by Terrence W. McCaffrey. Printed by Sterling Sommer for Ashton-Potter (USA) Ltd. (#3620), Ashton-Potter (USA) Ltd. (#3621), Bureau of Engraving and Printing (#3622), Banknote Corporation of America (#3623), American Packaging Corporation for Sennett Security Products (#3624), Avery Dennison (#3625).

LITHOGRAPHED, PHOTOGRAVURE (#3622, 3624, 3625)
Sheets of 400 in four panes of 100 (#3620), Sheets of 120 in six panes of 20 (#3621)
2002, June 7 **Tagged** ***Perf. 11¼x11***

3620 A2807 (37c) **multicolored** .85 .20
P# block of 4, 4#+P 25.00 —

Self-Adhesive
Serpentine Die Cut 11¼x11

3621 A2807 (37c) **multicolored** 1.00 .20
P# block of 4, 4#+P 7.50
Pane of 20 35.00

Coil Stamp
Serpentine Die Cut 10 Vert.

3622 A2807 (37c) **multicolored** .75 .20
Pair 1.50
P# strip of 5, #1111, 2222 6.50
P# single, same # — 1.00
a. Die cutting omitted, pair —

Booklet Stamps
Serpentine Die Cut 11¼ on 2, 3 or 4 Sides

3623 A2807 (37c) **multicolored** .75 .20
a. Booklet pane of 20 15.00

Serpentine Die Cut 10½x10¾ on 2 or 3 Sides

3624 A2807 (37c) **multicolored** .75 .20
a. Booklet pane of 4 3.00
b. Booklet pane of 6 4.50
c. Booklet pane of 20 15.00

Serpentine Die Cut 8 on 2, 3 or 4 sides

3625 A2807 (37c) **multicolored** .75 .20
a. Booklet pane of 18 13.50

Toy Mail Wagon — A2808

Toy Locomotive — A2809

Toy Taxicab — A2810

Toy Fire Pumper — A2811

Designed by Derry Noyes. Printed by Avery Dennison

PHOTOGRAVURE
Serpentine Die Cut 11 on 2, 3 or 4 Sides
2002, June 7 **Tagged**
Booklet Stamps
Self-Adhesive

3626 A2808 (37c) **multicolored** .75 .20
3627 A2809 (37c) **multicolored** .75 .20
3628 A2810 (37c) **multicolored** .75 .20
3629 A2811 (37c) **multicolored** .75 .20
a. Block of 4, #3626-3629 3.00
b. Booklet pane of 4, #3626-3629 3.00
c. Booklet pane of 6, #3627, 3629, 2 each #3626, 3628 4.50

d. Booklet pane of 6, #3626, 3628, 2 each #3627, 3629 — 4.50
e. Booklet pane of 20, 5 each #3626-3629 — 15.00

Flag — A2812

Designed by Terrence W. McCaffrey. Printed by Ashton-Potter (USA) Ltd. (#3629F, 3630, 3633B), American Packaging Corporation for Sennett Security Products (#3631, 3632A, 3632C, 3636), Bureau of Engraving and Printing (#3632), Banknote Corporation of America (#3633, 3635), Guilford Gravure for Banknote Corporation of America (#3633A), Avery Dennison (#3634, 3634b, 3636D, 3637).

LITHOGRAPHED, PHOTOGRAVURE (#3631-3633, 3634, 3636, 3636D)

Sheets of 400 in four panes of 100

2002-05 — Tagged — *Perf. 11¼*

3629F A2812 37c **multicolored,** *Nov. 24, 2003* — .90 .20
P# block of 4, 4#+P — 25.00 —

No. 3629F has microprinted "USA" in top red stripe of flag.

Sheets of 120 in six panes of 20

Serpentine Die Cut 11¼x11

Self-Adhesive

3630 A2812 37c **multicolored** *June 7* — .90 .20
P# block of 4, 4#+P — 5.00
Pane of 20 — 23.50

No. 3630 has microprinted "USA" in top red stripe of flag.

COIL STAMPS

Water-Activated Gum

Perf. 10 Vert.

3631 A2812 37c **multicolored,** *June 7* — .95 .20
Pair — 1.90 —
P# strip of 5, #S1111 — 6.00 —
P# single, same # — — 2.00

No. 3631 is known printed with non-reactive red ink and also with luminescent yellow ink that glows orange under long wave ultraviolet light.

Self-Adhesive

Serpentine Die Cut 9¾ Vert.

3632 A2812 37c **multicolored,** *June 7* — .75 .20
Pair — 1.50
P# strip of 5, #1111, 2222, 3333, 4444, 5555, 6666, 7777, 8888, 9999, 1111A, 2222A, 3333A, 4444A, 5555A, 6666A — 4.75
P# single, same # — — 1.00
b. Die cutting omitted, pair — *95.00*

On plate #s 1111 through 9999 and 5555A-6666A, the color laydown order of plate numbers is yellow, magenta, cyan, black. Plate #s 1111A through 4444A have a laydown order of cyan, magenta, yellow, black.

Serpentine Die Cut 10¼ Vert.

3632A A2812 37c **multicolored,** prephosphored paper (solid tagging), *Aug. 7, 2003* — .75 .20
Pair — 1.50
P# strip of 5, #S1111, S2222, S3333 — 5.25
P# strip of 5, #S4444 — *150.00*
P# single, #S1111, S2222, S3333 — — 1.25
P# single, P#S4444 — — 50.00
e. Prephosphored paper (mottled tagging) — .75 .20
Pair — 1.50
P# strip of 5, #S3333, S4444 — 6.00
P# single, P#S3333, S4444 — — 3.00
f. Die cutting omitted, pair — —

No. 3632A lacks points of stars at margin at left top, and was printed in "logs" of adjacent coil rolls that are connected at the top or bottom, wherein each roll could be separated from an adjacent roll as needed.

No. 3632 has "2002" date at left bottom. No. 3632A has "2003" date at left bottom.

On No. 3632A, P# S3333 was printed with yellow ink that glows orange under long wave ultraviolet light as well as with non-reactive red ink. P# S4444 was printed with and without luminescent red ink. Values the same.

Serpentine Die Cut 11¾ Vert.

3632C A2812 37c **multicolored,** prephosphored paper (solid tagging), *2004* — .75 .20
Pair — 1.50
P# strip of 5, #S1111 — 5.50
P# single, same # — — 2.50
d. Prephosphored paper (mottled tagging) — .75 .20
Pair — 1.50
P# strip of 5, #S1111 — 5.50
P# single, same # — — 2.50

Serpentine Die Cut 8½ Vert.

3633 A2812 37c **multicolored,** *June 7* — .75 .20
Pair — 1.50
P# strip of 5, #B1111 — 5.00
P# single, same # — — 1.50

Backing paper of No. 3633 is larger than the stamp.

3633A A2812 37c **multicolored** *April, 2003* — 2.00 .20
Pair — 4.00
P# strip of 5 #B1111 — 11.00
P# single, same # — — 1.50

No. 3633A has right angle corners and backing paper as high as the stamp, and is dated "2003." No. 3633 is dated "2002," has rounded corners, the backing paper larger than the stamp, and the stamps are spaced approximately 2mm apart.

Serpentine Die Cut 9½ Vert.

3633B A2812 37c **multicolored** *June 7, 2005* — 3.00 .20
Pair — 6.00
P# strip of 5, #P1111 — 22.50
P# single, #P1111 — — 3.00

No. 3633B has microprinted "USA" in top red stripe of flag, and has "2005" date at bottom left.

Booklet Stamps

Serpentine Die Cut 11.1 on 3 Sides (#3634) or 2 or 3 sides (#3634b-3634d)

3634 A2812 37c **multicolored,** large "2002" year date, *June 7* — .75 .20
a. Booklet pane of 10 — 7.50
b. Small "2003," *Oct. 23, 2003* — .75 .20
c. Booklet pane, 4 #3634b — 3.00
d. Booklet pane, 6 #3634b — 4.50
e. As #3634, die cut 11.3 — .75 .20
f. As "e," booklet pane of 10 — 7.50

Serpentine Die Cut 11.3 on 2, 3 or 4 Sides

3635 A2812 37c **multicolored,** *June 7* — .75 .20
a. Booklet pane of 20 — 15.00

No. 3635 has "USPS" microprinted in the top red flag stripe and has a small "2002" year date.

Serpentine Die Cut 10½x10¾ on 2 or 3 Sides

3636 A2812 37c **multicolored,** *June 7* — .75 .20
a. Booklet pane of 4 — 3.00
b. Booklet pane of 6 — 4.50
c. Booklet pane of 20 — 15.00
d. As "c," 11 stamps and part of 12th stamp on reverse printed on backing liner, the 8 stamps on front side imperf — —

No. 3636c is a double-sided booklet pane, with 12 stamps on one side and eight stamps plus label on the other side.

Nos. 3636a and 3636b were issued on three types of prephosphored paper, with solid, grainy solid and mottled tagging characteristics. No. 3636c was issued on two types of prephosphored paper, with solid and mottled tagging.

Serpentine Die Cut 11¼x11 on 2 or 3 Sides

3636D A2812 37c **multicolored,** *July, 2004* — .90 .20
e. Booklet pane of 20 — 18.00

No. 3636D lacks points of stars at margin at UL. No. 3636De is a double-sided booklet pane with 12 stamps on one side and eight stamps plus label on the other side.

Serpentine Die Cut 8 on 2, 3 or 4 Sides

Tagged

3637 A2812 37c **multicolored,** *Feb. 4, 2003* — .75 .20
a. Booklet pane of 18 — 13.50

Toy Locomotive — A2813

Toy Mail Wagon — A2814

Toy Fire Pumper — A2815

Toy Taxicab — A2816

Designed by Derry Noyes. Printed by Banknote Corporation of America, Avery Dennison (#3642-3645)

PHOTOGRAVURE

Serpentine Die Cut 8½ Horiz.

2002, July 26 — Tagged

Self-Adhesive

Coil Stamps

3638 A2813 37c **multicolored** — .85 .20
3639 A2814 37c **multicolored** — .85 .20
3640 A2815 37c **multicolored** — .85 .20
3641 A2816 37c **multicolored** — .85 .20
a. Strip of 4, #3638-3641 — 3.40
P# strip of 5, 2 #3638, 1 each #3639-3641, #B11111, B12222 — 5.00
P# strip of 9, 2 each #3638-3639, 3641, 3 #3640, #B11111, B12222 — 8.00
P# single (#3640), #B11111, B12222 — — 1.25

Serpentine Die Cut 11 on 2, 3 or 4 Sides

Booklet Stamps

3642 A2814 37c **multicolored,** "2002" year date — .75 .20
a. Serpentine die cut 11x11¼ on 2 or 3 sides, dated "2003," *Sept. 3, 2003* — .75 .20
3643 A2813 37c **multicolored,** "2002" year date — .75 .20
a. Serpentine die cut 11x11¼ on 2 or 3 sides, dated "2003," *Sept. 3, 2003* — .75 .20
3644 A2816 37c **multicolored,** "2002" year date — .75 .20
a. Serpentine die cut 11x11¼ on 2 or 3 sides, dated "2003," *Sept. 3, 2003* — .75 .20
3645 A2815 37c **multicolored,** "2002" year date — .75 .20
a. Block of 4, #3642-3645 — 3.00
b. Booklet pane of 4, #3642-3645 — 3.00
c. Booklet pane of 6, #3643, 3645, 2 each #3642, 3644 — 4.50
d. Booklet pane of 6, #3642, 3644, 2 each #3643, 3645 — 4.50
e. Booklet pane of 20, 5 each #3642-3645 — 15.00
f. Serpentine die cut 11x11¼ on 2 or 3 sides, dated "2003," *Sept. 3, 2003* — .75 .20
g. Block of 4, #3642a, 3643a, 3644a, 3645f — 3.00
h. Booklet pane of 20, 5 #3645g — 15.00

No. 3645h is a double-sided booklet with 12 stamps on one side and 8 stamps plus label (booklet cover) on the other side. Nos. 3642a, 3643a, 3644a and 3645f have slightly narrower designs than Nos. 3642-3645.

Coverlet Eagle — A2817

Designed by Richard Sheaff. Printed by Ashton-Potter (USA) Ltd.

LITHOGRAPHED

Sheets of 120 in six panes of 20

Serpentine Die Cut 11x11¼

2002, July 12 — Tagged

Self-Adhesive

3646 A2817 60c **multicolored** — 1.25 .25
P# block of 4, 4#+P — 5.00
Pane of 20 — 25.00

Jefferson Memorial A2818

Capitol Dome — A2819

Designed by Derry Noyes. Printed by Banknote Corporation of America (#3647-3648), American Packaging Corporation for Sennett Security Printers (#3647A).

LITHOGRAPHED

Sheets of 180 in nine panes of 20

Serpentine Die Cut 11¼ (#3647, 3648), 11x10¾ (#3647A)

2002-03 — Tagged

Self-Adhesive

3647 A2818 $3.85 **multicolored,** *July 30* — 7.50 2.00
P# block of 4, 4#+B — 30.00
Pane of 20 — 150.00

3647A A2818 $3.85 **multicolored,** *Nov. 2003* 8.50 2.00
P# block of 4, 5#+S 35.00
Pane of 20 175.00
3648 A2819 $13.65 **multicolored,** *July 30* 27.50 10.00
P# block of 4, 4#+B 110.00
Pane of 20 550.00

No. 3647A is dated 2003.

MASTERS OF AMERICAN PHOTOGRAPHY

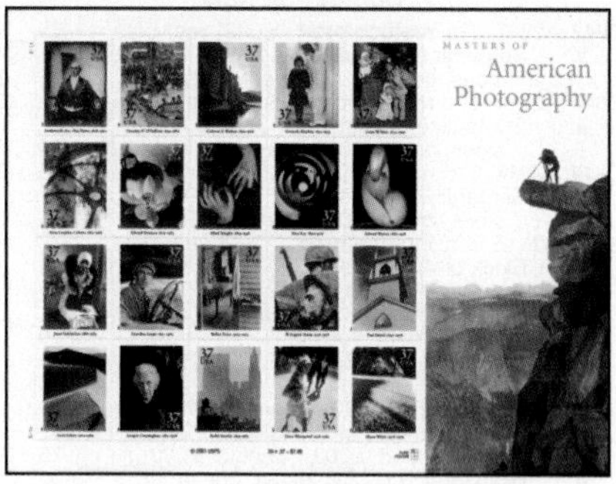

A2820

Illustration reduced.

Designed by Derry Noyes. Printed by American Packaging Corporation for Sennett Security Products.

Designs: a, Portrait of Daniel Webster, by Albert Sands Southworth and Josiah Johnson Hawes. b, Gen. Ulysses S. Grant and Officers, by Timothy H. O'Sullivan. c, "Cape Horn, Columbia River," by Carleton E. Watkins. d, "Blessed Art Thou Among Women," by Gertrude Käsebier. e, "Looking for Lost Luggage, Ellis Island," by Lewis W. Hine. f, "The Octopus," by Alvin Langdon Coburn. g, "Lotus, Mount Kisco, New York," by Edward Steichen. h, "Hands and Thimble," by Alfred Stieglitz. i, "Rayograph," by Man Ray. j, "Two Shells," by Edward Weston. k, "My Corsage," by James VanDerZee. l, "Ditched, Stalled, and Stranded, San Joaquin Valley, California," by Dorothea Lange. m, "Washroom and Dining Area of Floyd Burroughs' Home, Hale County, Alabama," by Walker Evans. n, "Frontline Soldier with Canteen, Saipan," by W. Eugene Smith. o, "Steeple," by Paul Strand. p, "Sand Dunes, Sunrise," by Ansel Adams. q, "Age and Its Symbols," by Imogen Cunningham. r, New York cityscape, by André Kertész. s, Photograph of pedestrians, by Garry Winogrand. t, "Bristol, Vermont," by Minor White.

PHOTOGRAVURE
Sheets of 120 in six panes of 20
Serpentine Die Cut 10½x10¾

2002, June 13 **Tagged**
Self-Adhesive

3649 A2820 Pane of 20 15.00
a.-t. 37c Any single .75 .50
Sheet of 120 (6 panes) 90.00
Cross-gutter block of 20 30.00
Horiz. block of 8 with vert. gutter 11.00
Vert. block of 10 with horiz. gutter 14.00
Vert. pairs with horiz. gutter (each) 2.50
Horiz. pairs with vert. gutter (each) 2.50

Cross gutter block of 20 consists of six stamps from each of two panes and four stamps from each of two other panes with the cross gutter between.

AMERICAN TREASURES SERIES

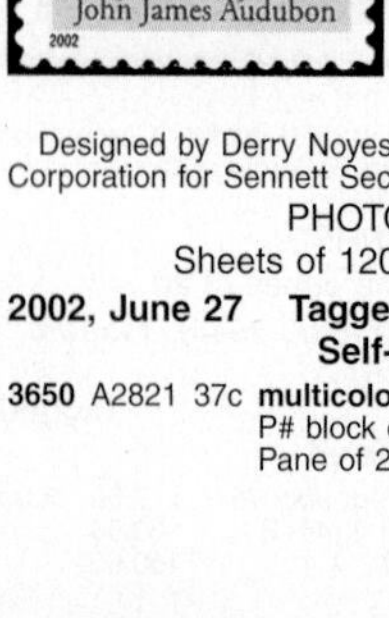

Scarlet and Louisiana Tanagers, by John James Audubon — A2821

Designed by Derry Noyes. Printed by American Pacakaging Corporation for Sennett Security Products.

PHOTOGRAVURE
Sheets of 120 in six panes of 20

2002, June 27 **Tagged** ***Serpentine Die Cut 10¾***
Self-Adhesive

3650 A2821 37c **multicolored** 1.00 .20
P# block of 4, 7#+S 6.00
Pane of 20 27.50

HARRY HOUDINI (1874-1926), MAGICIAN

A2822

Designed by Richard Sheaff. Printed by Ashton-Potter (USA) Ltd.

LITHOGRAPHED
Sheets of 180 in nine panes of 20

2002, July 3 **Tagged** ***Serpentine Die Cut 11¼***
Self-Adhesive

3651 A2822 37c **multicolored** .75 .20
P# block of 4, 4#+P 3.00 —
Pane of 20 15.00 —

ANDY WARHOL (1928-87), ARTIST

Self-Portrait — A2823

Designed by Richard Sheaff.
Printed by American Packaging Corporation for Sennett Security Products.

PHOTOGRAVURE
Sheets of 80 in four panes of 20
Serpentine Die Cut 10½x10¾

2002, Aug. 9 **Tagged**
Self-Adhesive

3652 A2823 37c **multicolored** .75 .20
P# block of 4, 6#+S 3.00
Pane of 20 15.00

TEDDY BEARS, CENTENNIAL

Bruin Bear, c. 1907 — A2824

"Stick" Bear, 1920s — A2825

Gund Bear, c. 1948 — A2826

Ideal Bear, c. 1905 — A2827

Designed by Margaret Bauer.
Printed by American Packaging Corporation for Sennett Security Products.

PHOTOGRAVURE
Sheets of 120 in six panes of 20

2002, Aug. 15 **Tagged** ***Serpentine Die Cut 10½***
Self-Adhesive

3653 A2824 37c **multicolored** 1.00 .20
3654 A2825 37c **multicolored** 1.00 .20
3655 A2826 37c **multicolored** 1.00 .20
3656 A2827 37c **multicolored** 1.00 .20
a. Block or vert. strip of 4, #3653-3656 4.00
P# block of 4, 7#+S 5.00
P# block of 10, 2 sets of P# + top label 15.00
Pane of 20 27.50
Sheet of 120 (six panes) 125.00
Cross gutter block of 8 22.50
Block of 8 with vert. gutter 11.00
Block of 4 with horiz. gutter 6.00
Vert. pair with horiz. gutter (each) 2.50
Horiz. pair with vert. gutter (each) 2.50

Cross gutter block can be either a vertical or horizontal block showing all designs.

LOVE

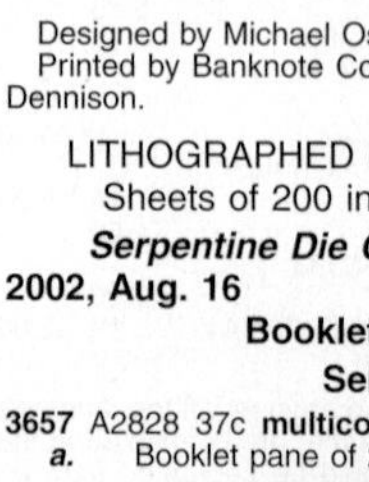

A2828

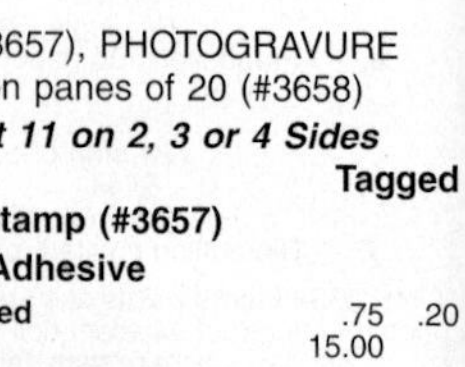

A2829

Designed by Michael Osborne.
Printed by Banknote Corporation of America (#3657), Avery Dennison.

LITHOGRAPHED (#3657), PHOTOGRAVURE
Sheets of 200 in ten panes of 20 (#3658)
Serpentine Die Cut 11 on 2, 3 or 4 Sides

2002, Aug. 16 **Tagged**
Booklet Stamp (#3657)
Self-Adhesive

3657 A2828 37c **multicolored** .75 .20
a. Booklet pane of 20 15.00

Serpentine Die Cut 11

3658 A2829 60c **multicolored** 1.25 .25
P# block of 4, 5#+V 5.00
Pane of 20 25.00

LITERARY ARTS

Ogden Nash (1902-71), Poet — A2830

Designed by Carl T. Herrman.
Printed by Avery Dennison.

PHOTOGRAVURE
Sheets of 200 in ten panes of 20

2002, Aug. 19 Tagged *Serpentine Die Cut 11*
Self-Adhesive

3659	A2830 37c **multicolored**		.75	.20
	P# block of 4, 8#+V		3.00	
	Pane of 20		15.00	

DUKE KAHANAMOKU (1890-1968), "FATHER OF SURFING" AND OLYMPIC SWIMMER

Kahanamoku and Surfers at Waikiki Beach — A2831

Designed by Carl T. Herrman.
Printed by Avery Dennison.

PHOTOGRAVURE
Sheets of 200 in ten panes of 20
Serpentine Die Cut 11½x11¾

2002, Aug. 24 Tagged
Self-Adhesive

3660	A2831 37c **multicolored**		.75	.20
	P# block of 4, 4#+V		3.00	
	Pane of 20		15.00	

AMERICAN BATS

Red Bat — A2832

Leaf-nosed Bat — A2833

Pallid Bat — A2834

Spotted Bat — A2835

Designed by Phil Jordan.
Printed by American Packaging Corporation for Sennett Security Products.

PHOTOGRAVURE
Sheets of 120 in six panes of 20

2002, Sept. 13 Tagged *Serpentine Die Cut 10¾*
Self-Adhesive

3661	A2832 37c **multicolored**		.75	.20
3662	A2833 37c **multicolored**		.75	.20
3663	A2834 37c **multicolored**		.75	.20
3664	A2835 37c **multicolored**		.75	.20
a.	Block or horiz. strip of 4, #3661-3664		3.00	
	P# block of 4, 7#+S		3.25	
	P# block of 8, 2 sets of P# + top label		6.50	
	Pane of 20		16.00	

WOMEN IN JOURNALISM

Nellie Bly (1864-1922) A2836

Ida M. Tarbell (1857-1944) A2837

Ethel L. Payne (1911-91) A2838

Marguerite Higgins (1920-66) A2839

Designed by Fred Otnes.
Printed by American Packaging Corporation for Sennett Security Products.

PHOTOGRAVURE
Sheets of 120 in six panes of 20
Serpentine Die Cut 11x10½

2002, Sept. 14 Tagged
Self-Adhesive

3665	A2836 37c **multicolored**		.75	.20
3666	A2837 37c **multicolored**		.75	.20
3667	A2838 37c **multicolored**		.75	.20
3668	A2839 37c **multicolored**		.75	.20
a.	Block or horiz. strip of 4, #3665-3668		3.00	
	P# block of 4, 5#+S		3.25	
	P# block of 8, 2 sets of P# + top label		6.50	
	Pane of 20		16.00	

IRVING BERLIN (1888-1989), COMPOSER

Berlin and Score of "God Bless America" — A2840

Designed by Greg Berger.
Printed by Avery Dennison.

PHOTOGRAVURE
Sheets of 200 in ten panes of 20

2002, Sept. 15 Tagged *Serpentine Die Cut 11*
Self-Adhesive

3669	A2840 37c **multicolored**		.75	.20
	P# block of 4, 4#+V		3.00	
	Pane of 20		15.00	

NEUTER AND SPAY

Kitten — A2841

Puppy A2842

Designed by Derry Noyes. Printed by American Packaging Corporation for Sennett Security Products.

PHOTOGRAVURE
Sheets of 120 in six panes of 20
Serpentine Die Cut 10¾x10½

2002, Sept. 20 Tagged
Self-Adhesive

3670	A2841 37c **multicolored**		1.00	.20
3671	A2842 37c **multicolored**		1.00	.20
a.	Horiz. or vert. pair, #3670-3671		2.00	
	P# block of 4, 5#+S		4.00	
	P# block of 8, 2 sets of P# + top label		8.00	
	Pane of 20		20.00	

Hanukkah Type of 1996

Designed by Hannah Smotrich.
Printed by Avery Dennison.

PHOTOGRAVURE
Sheets of 200 in ten panes of 20

2002, Oct. 10 Tagged *Serpentine Die Cut 11*
Self-Adhesive

3672	A2411 37c **multicolored**		.75	.20
	P# block of 4, 5#+V		3.00	
	Pane of 20		15.00	

Kwanzaa Type of 1997

Designed by Synthia Saint James.
Printed by Avery Dennison.

PHOTOGRAVURE
Sheets of 200 in ten panes of 20

2002, Oct. 10 Tagged *Serpentine Die Cut 11*
Self-Adhesive

3673	A2458 37c **multicolored**		.75	.20
	P# block of 4, 4#+V		3.00	
	Pane of 20		15.00	

Eid Type of 2001

Designed by Mohamed Zakariya.
Printed by Avery Dennison.

PHOTOGRAVURE
Sheets of 240 in twelve panes of 20

2002, Oct. 10 Tagged *Serpentine Die Cut 11*
Self-Adhesive

3674	A2734 37c **multicolored**		.75	.20
	P# block of 4, 3#+V		3.00	
	Pane of 20		15.00	

CHRISTMAS

Madonna and Child, by Jan Gossaert — A2843

Designed by Richard Sheaff.
Printed by Banknote Corporation of America.

LITHOGRAPHED

Serpentine Die Cut 11x11¼ on 2, 3 or 4 Sides

2002, Oct. 10 **Tagged**

Self-Adhesive

Booklet Stamp

Design size: 19x27mm

3675	A2843	37c	**multicolored**	.75	.20
a.			Booklet pane of 20	15.00	

Compare to No. 3820, which measures 19½x28mm

CHRISTMAS

Snowman with Red and Green Plaid Scarf — A2844

Snowman with Blue Plaid Scarf — A2845

Snowman with Pipe — A2846

Snowman with Top Hat — A2847

Snowman with Blue Plaid Scarf — A2848

Snowman with Pipe — A2849

Snowman with Top Hat — A2850

Snowman with Red and Green Plaid Scarf — A2851

Designed by Derry Noyes.

Printed by Avery Dennison (#3676-3679, 3688-3691), Guilford Gravure (#3680-3683), and American Packaging Corp. for Sennett Security Products (#3684-3687).

PHOTOGRAVURE

Sheets of 200 in ten panes of 20

2002, Oct. 28 **Tagged** ***Serpentine Die Cut 11***

Self-Adhesive

3676	A2844	37c	**multicolored**	.85	.20
3677	A2845	37c	**multicolored**	.85	.20
3678	A2846	37c	**multicolored**	.85	.20
3679	A2847	37c	**multicolored**	.85	.20
a.			Block or vert. strip of 4, #3676-3679	3.40	
			P# block of 4, 4#+V	3.40	
			Pane of 20	17.00	

COIL STAMPS

Serpentine Die Cut 8½ Vert.

3680	A2848	37c	**multicolored**	1.75	.20
3681	A2849	37c	**multicolored**	1.75	.20
3682	A2850	37c	**multicolored**	1.75	.20
3683	A2851	37c	**multicolored**	1.75	.20
a.			Strip of 4, #3680-3683	7.00	
			P# strip of 5, 2 #3680, 1 each #3681-3683, #G1111, G1112	9.00	
			P# strip of 9, 2 each #3680, 3681, 3683, 3 #3682, same #	15.00	
			P# single (#3682), same #	—	2.00

BOOKLET STAMPS

Serpentine Die Cut 10¾x11 on 2 or 3 Sides

3684	A2844	37c	**multicolored**	1.00	.20
3685	A2845	37c	**multicolored**	1.00	.20
3686	A2846	37c	**multicolored**	1.00	.20
3687	A2847	37c	**multicolored**	1.00	.20
a.			Block of 4, #3684-3687	4.00	
b.			Booklet pane of 20, 5 #3687a + label	20.00	

No. 3687b is a double-sided booklet pane with 12 stamps on one side and eight stamps plus label on the other side.

Serpentine Die Cut 11 on 2 or 3 Sides

3688	A2851	37c	**multicolored**	1.00	.20
3689	A2848	37c	**multicolored**	1.00	.20
3690	A2849	37c	**multicolored**	1.00	.20
3691	A2850	37c	**multicolored**	1.00	.20
a.			Block of 4, #3688-3691	4.00	
b.			Booklet pane of 4, #3688-3691	4.00	
c.			Booklet pane of 6, #3690-3691, 2 each #3688-3689	6.00	
d.			Booklet pane of 6, #3688-3689, 2 each #3690-3691	6.00	
			Nos. 3676-3691 (16)	11.20	3.20

Colors of Nos. 3684-3687 are deeper and designs are slightly smaller than those found on Nos. 3676-3679.

LEGENDS OF HOLLYWOOD

Cary Grant (1904-86), Actor — A2852

Designed by Carl Herrman.

Printed by American Packaging Corporation for Sennett Security Products.

PHOTOGRAVURE

Sheets of 120 in six panes of 20

2002, Oct. 15 **Tagged** ***Serpentine Die Cut 10¾***

Self-Adhesive

3692	A2852	37c	**multicolored**	.90	.20
			P# block of 4, 6#+S	3.60	
			Pane of 20	18.00	
			Sheet of 120 (6 panes)	90.00	
			Cross gutter block of 8	17.50	
			Block of 8 with vertical gutter	12.50	
			Horiz. pair with vert. gutter	3.00	
			Vert. pair with horiz. gutter	2.00	

Cross gutter block consists of 6 stamps from upper panes and 2 stamps from panes below.

Sea Coast — A2853

Designed by Tom Engelman.

Printed by Banknote Corporation Of America.

PHOTOGRAVURE

COIL STAMP

Serpentine Die Cut 8½ Vert.

2002, Oct. 21 **Tagged**

Self-Adhesive

3693	A2853	(5c)	**multicolored**	.20	.20
			Pair	.20	
			P# strip of 5, #B111	1.25	
			P# single, #B111	—	1.00

See Nos. 3775, 3785, 3864, 3874, 3875.

HAWAIIAN MISSIONARY STAMPS

A2854

Illustration reduced.

Designed by Richard Sheaff.

Printed by Banknote Corporation of America.
Designs: a, 2c stamp of 1851 (Hawaii Scott 1). b, 5c stamp of 1851 (Hawaii Scott 2) c, 13c stamp of 1851 (Hawaii Scott 3). d, 13c stamp of 1852 (Hawaii Scott 4).

LITHOGRAPHED

Sheets of 24 in six panes of 4

2002, Oct. 24 **Tagged** ***Perf. 11***

3694	A2854		Pane of 4	3.50	2.50
a.-d.		37c	Any single	.85	.50
			Sheet of 6 panes	25.00	

Happy Birthday Type of 2002

Designed by Harry Zelenko.

Printed by Avery Dennison.

PHOTOGRAVURE

Sheets of 200 in ten panes of 20

2002, Oct. 25 **Tagged** ***Serpentine Die Cut 11***

Self-Adhesive

3695	A2751	37c	**multicolored**	.75	.20
			P# block of 4, 4#+V	3.00	
			Pane of 20	15.00	

Greetings From America Type of 2002

Designed by Richard Sheaff. Printed by American Packaging Corp. for Sennett Security Products.

PHOTOGRAVURE

Sheets of 100 in two panes of 50

2002, Oct. 25 **Tagged** ***Serpentine Die Cut 10¾***

Self-Adhesive

3696	A2754	37c	Alabama	.75	.60
3697	A2755	37c	Alaska	.75	.60
3698	A2756	37c	Arizona	.75	.60
3699	A2757	37c	Arkansas	.75	.60
3700	A2758	37c	California	.75	.60
3701	A2759	37c	Colorado	.75	.60
3702	A2760	37c	Connecticut	.75	.60
3703	A2761	37c	Delaware	.75	.60
3704	A2762	37c	Florida	.75	.60
3705	A2763	37c	Georgia	.75	.60
3706	A2764	37c	Hawaii	.75	.60
3707	A2765	37c	Idaho	.75	.60
3708	A2766	37c	Illinois	.75	.60
3709	A2767	37c	Indiana	.75	.60
3710	A2768	37c	Iowa	.75	.60
3711	A2769	37c	Kansas	.75	.60
3712	A2770	37c	Kentucky	.75	.60
3713	A2771	37c	Louisiana	.75	.60
3714	A2772	37c	Maine	.75	.60
3715	A2773	37c	Maryland	.75	.60
3716	A2774	37c	Massachusetts	.75	.60
3717	A2775	37c	Michigan	.75	.60
3718	A2776	37c	Minnesota	.75	.60
3719	A2777	37c	Mississippi	.75	.60
3720	A2778	37c	Missouri	.75	.60
3721	A2779	37c	Montana	.75	.60
3722	A2780	37c	Nebraska	.75	.60
3723	A2781	37c	Nevada	.75	.60
3724	A2782	37c	New Hampshire	.75	.60

3725 A2783 37c New Jersey .75 .60
3726 A2784 37c New Mexico .75 .60
3727 A2785 37c New York .75 .60
3728 A2786 37c North Carolina .75 .60
3729 A2787 37c North Dakota .75 .60
3730 A2788 37c Ohio .75 .60
3731 A2789 37c Oklahoma .75 .60
3732 A2790 37c Oregon .75 .60
3733 A2791 37c Pennsylvania .75 .60
3734 A2792 37c Rhode Island .75 .60
3735 A2793 37c South Carolina .75 .60
3736 A2794 37c South Dakota .75 .60
3737 A2795 37c Tennessee .75 .60
3738 A2796 37c Texas .75 .60
3739 A2797 37c Utah .75 .60
3740 A2798 37c Vermont .75 .60
3741 A2799 37c Virginia .75 .60
3742 A2800 37c Washington .75 .60
3743 A2801 37c West Virginia .75 .60
3744 A2802 37c Wisconsin .75 .60
3745 A2803 37c Wyoming .75 .60
a. Pane of 50, #3696-3745 37.50

BLACK HERITAGE SERIES

Thurgood Marshall (1908-93), Supreme Court Justice — A2855

Designed by Richard Sheaff. Printed by Ashton-Potter (USA) Ltd.

LITHOGRAPHED
Sheets of 180 in nine panes of 20

2003, Jan. 7 Tagged *Serpentine Die Cut 11½*
Self-Adhesive

3746 A2855 37c **black & gray** .75 .20
P# block of 4, 3#+P 3.00
Pane of 20 15.00

CHINESE NEW YEAR

Year of the Ram — A2856

Designed by Clarence Lee. Printed by Banknote Corporation of America.

LITHOGRAPHED
Sheets of 120 in six panes of 20

2003, Jan. 15 Tagged *Serpentine Die Cut 11½*
Self-Adhesive

3747 A2856 37c **multicolored** .75 .20
P# block of 4, 4#+B 3.00
Pane of 20 15.00
a. Tagging omitted —

See No. 3895h.

LITERARY ARTS

Zora Neale Hurston (1891-1960), Writer A2857

Designed by Howard E. Paine. Printed by American Packaging Corporation for Sennett Security Products.

PHOTOGRAVURE
Sheets of 120 in six panes of 20

2003, Jan. 24 Tagged *Serpentine Die Cut 10¾*
Self-Adhesive

3748 A2857 37c **multicolored** .80 .20
P# block of 4, 5#+S 3.25
Pane of 20 16.00

AMERICAN DESIGN SERIES

Navajo Necklace — A2858

Chippendale Chair — A2859

American Clock — A2860

Tiffany Lamp — A2866

Silver Coffeepot — A2868

Designed by Derry Noyes. Printed by Ashton-Potter (USA) Ltd. (#3749, 3752, 3755, 3757), American Packaging Corp. for Sennett Security Products (#3751, 3754, 3756, 3758, 3759, 3761), Banknote Corporation of America for Sennett Security Products (#3749A, 3753, 3758A).

LITHOGRAPHED, PHOTOGRAVURE (#3751, 3756)
Sheets of 300 in fifteen panes of 20 (#3749A), Sheets of 280 in fourteen panes of 20, Sheets of 240 in twelve panes of 20 (#3757), Sheets of 200 in ten panes of 20 (#3749, 3753, 3754), Sheets of 120 in six panes of 20 (#3755), Sheets of 160 in eight panes of 20 (#3756).
Self-Adhesive

2003-07 Untagged

Serpentine Die Cut 11¼x11

3749 A2866 1c **multicolored,** *Mar. 16, 2007* .20 .20
P# block of 4, 6#+P .20
Pane of 20 .40
3749A A2866 1c **multicolored,** *Mar. 7, 2008* .20 .20
P# block of 4, 5#+S .20
Pane of 20 .40

No. 3749A has "USPS" microprinted on a white field high on the lamp stand, just below the shade and is dated "2008." No. 3749 has "USPS" microprinted lower on the lamp stand and not on a white field and is dated "2007."

Serpentine Die Cut 11

3750 A2858 2c **multicolored,** *Aug. 20, 2004* .20 .20
P# block of 4, 5#+V .20
Pane of 20 .80

A reprinting of No. 3750 shows the borders in a much brighter deep turquoise blue shade.

Serpentine Die Cut 11¼x11½

3751 A2858 2c **multicolored,** *Dec. 8, 2005* .20 .20
P# block of 4, 6#+S .20
Pane of 20 .80

Serpentine Die Cut 11¼x11
With "USPS" Microprinting

3752 A2858 2c **multicolored,** *Dec. 8, 2005* .20 .20
P# block of 4, 5#+P .20
Pane of 20 .80

Serpentine Die Cut 11¼x10¾

3753 A2858 2c **multicolored,** *May 12, 2007* .20 .20
P# block of 4, 6#+S .20
Pane of 20 .80

Serpentine Die Cut 11¼x11

3754 A2868 3c **multicolored,** *Mar. 16, 2007* .20 .20
P# block of 4, 4#+S .25
Pane of 20 1.25

Microprinted "USPS" on No. 3752 is found on top silver appendage next to and below the middle turquoise stone on the right side of the necklace. Microprinting on No. 3753 is found on the top silver appendage next to and below the middle turquoise stone on the left side of the necklace. Nos. 3751 and 3752 are dated "2006." No. 3753 is dated "2007."

Serpentine Die Cut 10¾x10¼

3755 A2859 4c **multicolored,** *Mar. 5, 2004* .20 .20
P# block of 4, 4#+P .35
Pane of 20 1.60

Serpentine Die Cut 11¼x11¾

3756 A2805 5c **multicolored,** *June 25, 2004* .20 .20
P# block of 4, 7#+S .40
Pane of 20 2.00

Serpentine Die Cut 11¼x11
Tagged

3757 A2860 10c **multicolored,** *Jan. 24* .20 .20
P# block of 4, 4#+P .80
Pane of 20 4.00
a. Die cutting omitted, pair —

PHOTOGRAVURE
COIL STAMPS
Untagged

Perf. 9¾ Vert.

3758 A2866 1c **multicolored,** *Mar. 1* .20 .20
Pair .20 .20
P# strip of 5, #S11111 .50 —
P# single, #S11111 — .40
3758A A2866 1c **multicolored,** *June 7, 2008* .20 .20
Pair .20 .20
P# strip of 5, #S11111 .60 —
P# single, #S11111 — .40

No. 3758A has microprinted "USPS" on lamp stand just below the lampshade and is dated "2008." No. 3758 lacks microprinting and is dated "2003."

3759 A2868 3c **multicolored,** *Sept. 16, 2005* .20 .20
Pair .20 .20
P# strip of 5, #S1111 .75 —
P# single, #S1111 — .65

Serpentine Die Cut 11 Vert.

3761 A2859 4c **multicolored,** *July 4, 2007* .20 .20
Pair .20 .20
P# strip of 5, #S1111 1.25 —
P# single, #S1111 — .75

Perf. 9¾ Vert.

3762 A2860 10c **multicolored,** *Aug. 4, 2006* .20 .20
Pair .40 .20
P# strip of 5, #S1111 2.00 —
P# single, #S1111 — 1.50

This is an ongoing set. Numbers may change.
See No. 3612

AMERICAN CULTURE SERIES

Wisdom, Rockefeller Center, New York City — A2875

Designed by Carl Herrman. Printed by Ashton-Potter (USA) Ltd.

LITHOGRAPHED
Sheets of 120 in six panes of 20
Serpentine Die Cut 11¼x11

2003, Feb. 28 Tagged
Self-Adhesive

3766 A2875 $1 **multicolored** 2.00 .40
P# block of 4, 5# + P 8.00
Pane of 20 40.00

New York Public Library Lion Type of 2000

Designed by Carl Herrman. Printed by American Packaging Corporation for Sennett Security Products.

PHOTOGRAVURE
COIL STAMP

2003, Feb. 4 Untagged *Perf. 10 Vert.*

3769 A2677 (10c) **multicolored** .20 .20
Pair .40 .20
P# strip of 5, #S11111 3.00 —
P# single, #S11111 — 1.75

Atlas Statue Type of 2001

Designed by Kevin Newman. Printed by Avery Dennison.

PHOTOGRAVURE

2003, Oct. Untagged *Serpentine Die Cut 11 Vert.*
Coil Stamp
Self-Adhesive

3770 A2722 (10c) **multicolored** .20 .20
Pair .40
P# strip of 5, #V11111, V11222, V12222, V21111, V21211, V22111, V22112, V22211, V23113, V32332, V33333, V33332 3.00
P# strip of 5, #V12111 *190.00*
P# strip of 5, #V22222 5.00
P# single, #V11111, V11222, V12222, V21111, V21211, V22111, V22112, V22211, V23113, V32332, V33333, V33332 — 1.75
P# single, # V12111 *125.00*

	P# single, # V13222	150.00	
	P# single, # V22222	3.00	
	P# single, # V21113	—	
a.	Tagged, error	—	
	P# single, # V21211	—	

No. 3770 is dated 2003.

SPECIAL OLYMPICS

Athlete with Medal — A2879

Designed by Lance Hidy. Printed by Avery Dennison.

PHOTOGRAVURE

Sheets of 200 in ten panes of 20

2003, Feb. 13 **Tagged** ***Serpentine Die Cut 11***

Self-Adhesive

3771 A2879 80c **multicolored**		1.60	.35
	P# block of 4, 6# + V	6.40	
	Pane of 20	32.00	

AMERICAN FILMMAKING: BEHIND THE SCENES

A2880

Block of 10 With Vertical Gutter Between

Illustrations reduced.

Designed by Imaginary Forces. Printed by American Packaging Corporation for Sennett Security Products.

Designs: a, Screenwriting (segment of script from *Gone With the Wind*). b, Directing (John Cassavetes). c, Costume design (Edith Head). d, Music (Max Steiner working on score). e, Makeup (Jack Pierce working on Boris Karloff's makeup for *Frankenstein*). f, Art direction (Perry Ferguson working on sketch for *Citizen Kane*). g, Cinematography (Paul Hill, assistant cameraman for *Nagana*). h, Film editing (J. Watson Webb editing *The Razor's Edge*). i, Special effects (Mark Siegel working on model for *E.T. The Extra-Terrestrial*). j, Sound (Gary Summers works on control panel).

PHOTOGRAVURE

Sheets of 60 in six panes of 10

Serpentine Die Cut 11 Horiz.

2003, Feb. 25 **Tagged**

Self-Adhesive

3772 A2880	Pane of 10	10.00	
a.-j.	37c Any single	1.00	.50
	Sheet of 6 panes	60.00	
	Block of 10 with vertical gutter between	12.50	

OHIO STATEHOOD BICENTENNIAL

Aerial View of Farm Near Marietta — A2881

Designed by Phil Jordan. Printed by Banknote Corporation of America.

LITHOGRAPHED

Sheets of 120 in six panes of 20

Serpentine Die Cut 11¾x11½

2003, Mar. 1 **Tagged**

Self-Adhesive

3773 A2881 37c **multicolored**		.75	.20
	P# block of 4, 4# + B	3.00	
	Pane of 20	15.00	

PELICAN ISLAND NATIONAL WILDLIFE REFUGE, CENT.

Brown Pelican — A2882

Designed by Carl T. Herrman. Printed by Banknote Corporation of America.

LITHOGRAPHED

Sheets of 120 in six panes of 20

Serpentine Die Cut 12x11½

2003, Mar. 14 **Tagged**

Self-Adhesive

3774 A2882 37c **multicolored**		.75	.20
	P# block of 4, 4#+B	3.00	
	Pane of 20	15.00	

Sea Coast Type of 2002

Designed by Tom Engeman. Printed by Banknote Corporation of America.

PHOTOGRAVURE

COIL STAMP

2003, Mar. 19 **Untagged** ***Perf. 9¾ Vert.***

3775 A2853 (5c) **multicolored**		.20	.20
	Pair	.20	—
	P# strip of 5, #B111	1.25	
	P# single, #B111		1.00

See No. 3864. No. 3775 has "2003" year date in blue, dots that run together in surf area, and a distinct small orange cloud. No. 3864 has "2004" year date in black, rows of distinctly separated dots in surf area, and the small orange cloud is indistinct.

OLD GLORY

Uncle Sam on Bicycle with Liberty Flag, 20th Cent. — A2883

1888 Presidential Campaign Badge — A2884

1893 Silk Bookmark — A2885

Modern Hand Fan — A2886

Carving of Woman with Flag and Sword, 19th Cent. — A2887

Designed by Richard Sheaff. Printed by Ashton-Potter (USA) Ltd.

LITHOGRAPHED

BOOKLET STAMPS

2003, Apr. 3 **Tagged** ***Serpentine Die Cut 10x9¾***

Self-Adhesive

3776 A2883 37c **multicolored**		.75	.50
3777 A2884 37c **multicolored**		.75	.50
3778 A2885 37c **multicolored**		.75	.50
3779 A2886 37c **multicolored**		.75	.50
3780 A2887 37c **multicolored**		.75	.50
a.	Horiz. strip of 5, #3776-3780	3.75	
b.	Booklet pane, 2 #3780a	7.50	

No. 3780b was issued with two types of backing.

CESAR E. CHAVEZ (1927-93), LABOR ORGANIZER

A2888

Designed by Carl Herrman. Printed by Banknote Corporation of America.

LITHOGRAPHED
Sheets of 120 in six panes of 20
Serpentine Die Cut 11¾x11½

2003, Apr. 23 **Tagged**

Self-Adhesive

3781 A2888 37c **multicolored**	.75	.20
P# block of 4, 4# + B	3.00	
Pane of 20	15.00	

LOUISIANA PURCHASE, BICENT.

English Translation of Treaty, Map of U.S., Treaty Signers — A2889

Designed by Richard Sheaff. Printed by American Packaging Corporation for Sennett Security Products

PHOTOGRAVURE
Sheets of 120 in six panes of 20

2003, Apr. 30 Tagged ***Serpentine Die Cut 10¾***

Self-Adhesive

3782 A2889 37c **multicolored**	.95	.40
P# block of 4, 6# + S	4.00	
Pane of 20	20.00	

FIRST FLIGHT OF WRIGHT BROTHERS, CENT.

Orville Wright Piloting 1903 Wright Flyer — A2890

Designed by McRay Magleby. Printed by Avery Dennison.

PHOTOGRAVURE

2003, May 22 Tagged ***Serpentine Die Cut 11***

Self-Adhesive

3783 A2890 37c **multicolored**	.75	.40
a. Pane of 9	6.75	
b. Pane of 1	.75	

PURPLE HEART

A2891

Designed by Carl Herrman. Printed by Banknote Corporation of America (#3784), Ashton-Potter (USA) Ltd. (#3784A).

LITHOGRAPHED
Sheets of 200 in ten panes of 20 (#3784), Sheets of 120 in six panes of 20 (#3784A)

2003 Tagged ***Serpentine Die Cut 11¼x10¾***

Self-Adhesive

3784 A2891 37c **multicolored**, *May 30*	.75	.20
P# block of 4, 4#+B	3.00	
Pane of 20	15.00	
b. Printed on back of backing paper	—	
d. Die cutting omitted, pair	—	

Serpentine Die Cut 10¾x10¼

3784A A2891 37c **multicolored**, *Aug. 1*	.75	.20
P# block of 4, 4#+P	3.00	
Pane of 20	15.00	
c. Die cutting omitted, pane of 20	*1,600.*	

Sea Coast Type of 2002

Designed by Tom Engeman. Printed by J.W. Ferguson & Sons for Ashton-Potter (USA) Ltd.

PHOTOGRAVURE
COIL STAMP

2003, June Untagged ***Serpentine Die Cut 9½x10***

Self-Adhesive

3785 A2853 (5c) **multicolored**	.20	.20
Pair	.20	
P# strip of 5, #P1111	1.50	
P# single, same #	—	1.00
a. Serp. die cut 9¼x10	.20	.20
Pair	.20	
P# strip of 5, #P2222	1.50	
P# single, same #	—	1.00
b. As "a," tagged (error)	3.25	2.00
P# strip of 5, #P2222	40.00	
P# single, same #	—	7.00

No. 3785 has more of a scarlet shade in sky than does No. 3785a. Both have black "2003" year date.

LEGENDS OF HOLLYWOOD

Audrey Hepburn (1929-93), Actress — A2892

Designed by Michael J. Deas. Printed by American Packaging Corporation for Sennett Security Products.

PHOTOGRAVURE
Sheets of 120 in six panes of 20

2003, June 11 Tagged ***Serpentine Die Cut 10¾***

Self-Adhesive

3786 A2892 37c **multicolored**	.90	.20
P# block of 4, 6#+S	3.75	
Pane of 20	19.00	
Sheet of 120 (6 panes)	85.00	
Cross gutter block of 8	17.50	
Block of 8 with vertical gutter	10.00	
Horiz. pair with vert. gutter	3.00	
Vert. pair with horiz. gutter	2.00	

Cross gutter block consists of 6 stamps from upper panes and 2 stamps from panes below.

SOUTHEASTERN LIGHTHOUSES

Old Cape Henry, Virginia — A2893

Cape Lookout, North Carolina — A2894

Morris Island, South Carolina — A2895

Tybee Island, Georgia — A2896

Hillsboro Inlet, Florida — A2897

Designed by Howard E. Paine. Printed by American Packaging Corporation for Sennett Security Products.

PHOTOGRAVURE
Sheets of 120 in six panes of 20

2003, June 13 Tagged ***Serpentine Die Cut 10¾***

Self-Adhesive

3787 A2893 37c **multicolored**	1.10	.20
3788 A2894 37c **multicolored**	1.10	.20
a. Bottom of "USA" even with top of upper half-diamond of lighthouse (pos. 2)	4.00	2.50
3789 A2895 37c **multicolored**	1.10	.20
3790 A2896 37c **multicolored**	1.10	.20
3791 A2897 37c **multicolored**	1.10	.20
a. Strip of 5, #3587-3791	5.50	
b. Strip of 5, #3787, 3788a, 3789-3791	9.00	
P# block of 10, 2 sets of 6#+S	14.00	
Pane of 20	28.00	

Eagle in Gold on Colored Background A2898

Colored Eagle on Gold Background A2899

Designed by Tom Engeman. Printed by American Packaging Corporation for Sennett Security Products.

PHOTOGRAVURE
COIL STAMPS
Dated "2003"

Serpentine Die Cut 11¾ Vert.

2003, June 26 **Untagged**

Self-Adhesive

3792 A2898 (25c) **gray & gold**	.50	.20
3793 A2899 (25c) **gold & red**	.50	.20
3794 A2898 (25c) **dull blue & gold**	.50	.20
3795 A2899 (25c) **gold & Prussian blue**	.50	.20
3796 A2898 (25c) **green & gold**	.50	.20
3797 A2899 (25c) **gold & gray**	.50	.20
3798 A2898 (25c) **Prussian blue & gold**	.50	.20
3799 A2899 (25c) **gold & dull blue**	.50	.20
3800 A2898 (25c) **red & gold**	.50	.20
3801 A2899 (25c) **gold & green**	.50	.20
a. Strip of 10, #3792-3801	5.00	
P# strip of 11, 2 # 3801, 1 each #3792-3800, #S1111111, S2222222, S3333333	8.00	
P# strip of 21, 3 # 3796, 2 each #3792-3795, 3797-3801, same #	16.00	
P# single (#3796), same #	—	2.75

Dated "2005"

2005, Aug. 5 ***Serpentine Die Cut 11½ Vert.***

3792a A2898 (25c) **gray & gold**	.50	.20
3793a A2899 (25c) **gold & red**	.50	.20
3794a A2898 (25c) **dull blue & gold**	.50	.20
3795a A2899 (25c) **gold & Prussian blue**	.50	.20
3796a A2898 (25c) **green & gold**	.50	.20
3797a A2899 (25c) **gold & gray**	.50	.20
3798a A2898 (25c) **Prussian blue & gold**	.50	.20
3799a A2899 (25c) **gold & dull blue**	.50	.20
3800a A2898 (25c) **red & gold**	.50	.20
3801b A2899 (25c) **gold & green**	.50	.20
c. Strip of 10, #3792a-3801b	5.00	
P# strip of 11, 2 #3801b, 1 each #3792a-3800a, P#S1111111	8.50	
P# strip of 21, 3 #3796a, 2 each #3792a-3795a, 3797a-3800a, 3801b, P#S1111111	17.00	
P# single (#3796a), #S1111111		3.25

ARCTIC TUNDRA

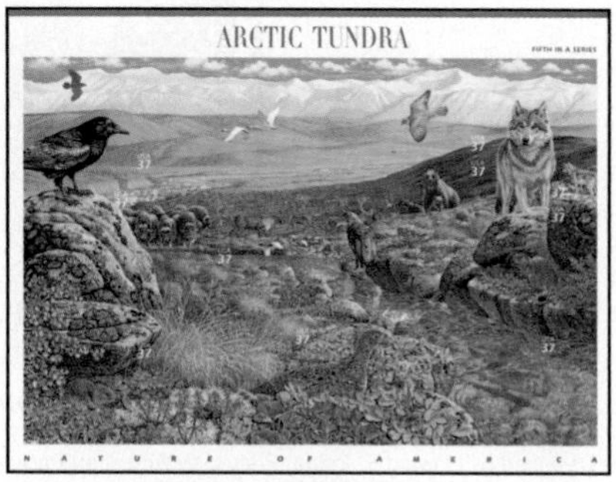

A2900

Illustration reduced.

Designed by Ethel Kessler. Printed by Banknote Corporation of America.

Wildlife and vegetation: a, Gyrfalcon. b, Gray wolf, vert. c, Common raven, vert. d, Musk oxen and caribou, vert. e, Grizzly bears, caribou. f, Caribou, willow ptarmigans. g, Arctic ground squirrel, vert. h, Willow ptarmigan, bearberry. i, Arctic grayling. j, Singing vole, thin-legged wolf spider, lingonberry, Labrador tea.

LITHOGRAPHED

Sheets of 80 in eight panes of 10

Serpentine Die Cut 10¾x10½, 10½x10¾

2003, July 2 **Tagged**

Self-Adhesive

3802	A2900	Pane of 10	7.50	
a.-j.	37c	Any single	.75	.50
		Sheet of 8 panes	65.00	
		Pair of tete-beche panes	15.00	

KOREAN WAR VETERANS MEMORIAL

Memorial in Snow — A2901

Designed by Richard Sheaff. Printed by Banknote Corporation of America.

LITHOGRAPHED

Sheets of 120 in six panes of 20

Serpentine Die Cut 11½x11¾

2003, July 27 **Tagged**

Self-Adhesive

3803	A2901	37c	**multicolored**	.75	.20
			P# block of 4, 4#+B	3.00	
			Pane of 20	15.00	

MARY CASSATT PAINTINGS

Young Mother, 1888 — A2902

Children Playing on the Beach, 1884 — A2903

On a Balcony, 1878-79 — A2904

Child in a Straw Hat, c. 1886 — A2905

Designed by Derry Noyes. Printed by American Packaging Corporation for Sennett Security Products.

PHOTOGRAVURE

Serpentine Die Cut 10¾ on 2 or 3 Sides

2003, Aug. 7 **Tagged**

Self-Adhesive

Booklet Stamps

3804	A2902	37c	**multicolored**	.75	.20
3805	A2903	37c	**multicolored**	.75	.20
3806	A2904	37c	**multicolored**	.75	.20
3807	A2905	37c	**multicolored**	.75	.20
a.			Block of 4, #3804-3807	3.00	
b.			Booklet pane of 20, 5 #3807a	15.00	

No. 3807b is a double-sided booklet with 12 stamps on one side and 8 stamps plus label (booklet cover) on the other side.

EARLY FOOTBALL HEROES

Bronko Nagurski (1908-90) — A2906

Ernie Nevers (1903-76) — A2907

Walter Camp (1859-1925) — A2908

Red Grange (1903-91) — A2909

Designed by Richard Sheaff. Printed by Avery Dennison.

PHOTOGRAVURE

Sheets of 200 in ten panes of 20

Serpentine Die Cut 11½x11¾

2003, Aug. 8 **Tagged**

Self-Adhesive

3808	A2906	37c	**multicolored**	.75	.20
3809	A2907	37c	**multicolored**	.75	.20
3810	A2908	37c	**multicolored**	.75	.20
3811	A2909	37c	**multicolored**	.75	.20
a.			Block of 4, #3808-3811	3.00	
			P# block of 4, 7#+V	3.00	
			Pane of 20	15.00	

ROY ACUFF

Acuff (1903-92), Country Music Artist, and Fiddle — A2910

Designed by Richard Sheaff.
Printed by Avery Dennison.

PHOTOGRAVURE

Sheets of 200 in ten panes of 20

2003, Sept. 13 **Tagged** ***Serpentine Die Cut 11***

Self-Adhesive

3812	A2910	37c	**multicolored**	.75	.20
			P# block of 4, 4#+V	3.00	
			Pane of 20	15.00	

DISTRICT OF COLUMBIA

Map, National Mall, Row Houses and Cherry Blossoms — A2911

Designed by Greg Berger.
Printed by American Packaging Corporation for Sennett Security Products.

PHOTOGRAVURE

Sheets of 128 in eight panes of 16

2003, Sept. 23 **Tagged** ***Serpentine Die Cut 11***

Self-Adhesive

3813	A2911	37c	**multicolored**	.75	.20
			P# block of 4, 8#+S	3.75	
			Pane of 16	18.00	

REPTILES AND AMPHIBIANS

Scarlet Kingsnake A2912

Blue-Spotted Salamander A2913

Reticulate Collared Lizard A2914

Ornate Chorus Frog — A2915

Ornate Box Turtle A2916

Designed by Steve Buchanan. Printed by Avery Dennison.

PHOTOGRAVURE

Sheets of 200 in ten panes of 20

2003, Oct. 7 Tagged *Serpentine Die Cut 11*

Self-Adhesive

3814 A2912 37c **multicolored**	.75	.20
3815 A2913 37c **multicolored**	.75	.20
3816 A2914 37c **multicolored**	.75	.20
3817 A2915 37c **multicolored**	.75	.20
3818 A2916 37c **multicolored**	.75	.20
a. Vert. strip of 5, #3814-3818	3.75	
P# block of 10, 4#+V	7.50	
Pane of 20	15.00	

Washington Type of 2002

Designed by Richard Sheaff.

Printed by Avery Dennison.

PHOTOGRAVURE

Sheets of 200 in ten panes of 20

2003, Oct. Tagged *Serpentine Die Cut 11*

Self-Adhesive

3819 A2686 23c **gray green**	.70	.20
P# block of 4, 2#+V	7.50	
Pane of 20	32.50	

Christmas Type of 2002

Designed by Richard Sheaff.

Printed by Ashton-Potter (USA) Ltd.

LITHOGRAPHED

Serpentine Die Cut 11¼ on 2 or 3 Sides

2003, Oct. 23 Tagged

Self-Adhesive

Booklet Stamp

Size: 19½x28mm

3820 A2843 37c **multicolored**	.75	.20
a. Booklet pane of 20	15.00	
b. Die cutting omitted, pair	—	

No. 3820a is a double-sided booklet with 12 stamps on one side and 8 stamps plus label (booklet cover) on the other side. Compare to No. 3675, which measures 19x27mm.

CHRISTMAS

Reindeer with Pan Pipes — A2917

Santa Claus with Drum — A2918

Santa Claus with Trumpet — A2919

Reindeer with Horn — A2920

Reindeer with Pan Pipes — A2921

Santa Claus with Drum — A2922

Santa Claus with Trumpet — A2923

Reindeer with Horn — A2924

Designed by Ethel Kessler.

Printed by American Packaging Corp. for Sennett Security Products.

PHOTOGRAVURE

Sheets of 160 in eight panes of 20

Serpentine Die Cut 11¾x11

2003, Oct. 23 Tagged

Self-Adhesive

3821 A2917 37c **multicolored**	.80	.20
3822 A2918 37c **multicolored**	.80	.20
3823 A2919 37c **multicolored**	.80	.20
3824 A2920 37c **multicolored**	.80	.20
a. Block of 4, #3821-3824	3.20	
P# block of 4, 4#+S	3.20	
Pane of 20	16.00	
b. Booklet pane of 20, 5 each #3821-3824	16.00	

BOOKLET STAMPS

Serpentine Die Cut 10½x10¾ on 2 or 3 Sides

3825 A2921 37c **multicolored**	.85	.20
3826 A2922 37c **multicolored**	.85	.20
3827 A2923 37c **multicolored**	.85	.20
3828 A2924 37c **multicolored**	.85	.20
a. Block of 4, #3825-3828	3.40	
b. Booklet pane of 4, #3825-3828	3.40	
c. Booklet pane of 6, #3827-3828, 2 each #3825-3826	5.25	
d. Booklet pane of 6, #3825-3826, 2 each #3827-3828	5.25	

No. 3824b is a double-sided booklet with 12 stamps on one side and 8 stamps plus label (booklet cover) on the other side.

Snowy Egret — A2925

Designed by Carl T. Herrman.

Printed by Avery Dennison (#3829), Ashton-Potter (USA) Ltd. (#3829A, 3830, 3830D).

COIL STAMPS

2003-05 Tagged *Serpentine Die Cut 8½ Vert.*

Self-Adhesive

PHOTOGRAVURE

3829 A2925 37c **multicolored,** *Oct. 24, 2003*	.75	.20
Pair	1.50	
P# strip of 5, #V1111, V2111, V3212, V3222	4.50	
P# strip of 5, #V3211	—	
P# strip of 5, #V3221	225.00	
P# single, #V1111, V2111, V3212, V3222	—	1.25
P# single, #V2121	—	—
P# single, #V3211	—	—
P# single, #V3221	—	—

LITHOGRAPHED

Serpentine Die Cut 9½ Vert.

3829A A2925 37c **multicolored,** Mar., 2004	.75	.20
Pair	1.50	
P# strip of 5, #P11111, P22222, P33333, P44444, P55555	6.00	
P# single, same #	—	2.25

Serpentine Die Cut 11½x11 on 2, 3 or 4 Sides

Booklet Stamps

PHOTOGRAVURE

3830 A2925 37c **multicolored,** *Jan. 30, 2004*	.75	.20
a. Booklet pane of 20	15.00	
b. Die cutting omitted, pair	—	
c. As "a," die cutting omitted	—	

With "USPS" Microprinted on Bird's Breast

3830D A2925 37c **multicolored,** *2004*	*5.00*	.25
e. Booklet pane of 20	*100.00*	
f. Die cutting omitted, pair	—	

PACIFIC CORAL REEF

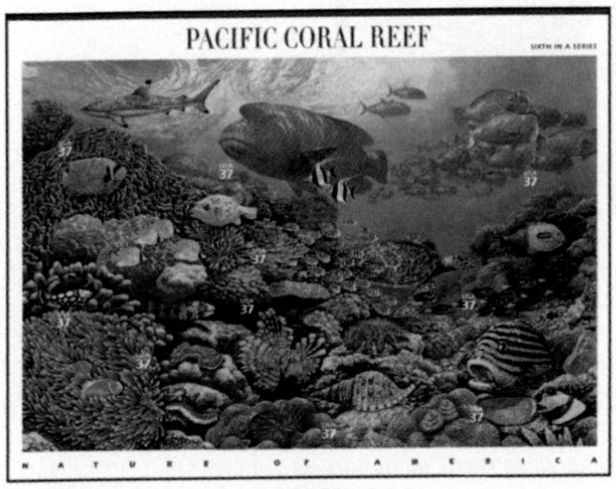

A2926

Illustration reduced.

Designed by Ethel Kessler. Printed by Avery Dennison.

Marine life: a, Emperor angelfish, blue coral, mound coral, vert. b, Humphead wrasse, Moorish idol. c, Bumphead parrotfish, vert. d, Black-spotted puffer, threadfin butterflyfish, staghorn coral. e, Hawksbill turtle, palette surgeonfish. f, Pink anemonefish, magnificent sea anemone, vert. g, Snowflake moray eel, Spanish dancer. h, Lionfish, vert. i, Triton's trumpet. j, Oriental sweetlips, bluestreak cleaner wrasse, mushroom coral, vert.

PHOTOGRAVURE

Sheets of 80 in eight panes of 10

2004, Jan. 2 Tagged *Serpentine Die Cut 10¾*

Self-Adhesive

3831 A2926 Pane of 10	7.50	
a.-j. 37c Any single	.75	.20
Sheet of 8 panes	57.50	

CHINESE NEW YEAR

Year of the Monkey A2927

Designed by Clarence Lee. Printed by American Packaging Corporation for Sennett Security Products.

PHOTOGRAVURE
Sheets of 120 in six panes of 20

2004, Jan. 13 Tagged *Serpentine Die Cut 10¾*
Self-Adhesive

3832 A2927 37c **multicolored** .75 .20
P# block of 4, 4# + S 3.00
Pane of 20 15.00

See No. 3895i.

LOVE

Candy Hearts — A2928

Designed by Michael Osborne. Printed by Avery Dennison.

PHOTOGRAVURE
BOOKLET STAMP
Serpentine Die Cut 10¾ on 2, 3 or 4 Sides

2004, Jan. 14 Tagged
Self-Adhesive

3833 A2928 37c **multicolored** .75 .20
a. Booklet pane of 20 15.00

BLACK HERITAGE SERIES

Paul Robeson (1898-1976), Actor, Singer, Athlete and Activist — A2929

Designed by Richard Sheaff. Printed by American Packaging Corporation for Sennett Security Products.

PHOTOGRAVURE
Sheets of 120 in six panes of 20

2004, Jan. 20 Tagged *Serpentine Die Cut 10¾*
Self-Adhesive

3834 A2929 37c **multicolored** .75 .20
P# block of 4, 4# + S 3.00
Pane of 20 15.00

THEODOR SEUSS GEISEL (DR. SEUSS)

Dr. Seuss (1904-91), Children's Book Writer, and Book Characters A2930

Designed by Carl T. Herrman. Printed by American Packaging Corporation for Sennett Security Products.

PHOTOGRAVURE
Sheets of 180 in nine panes of 20
Serpentine Die Cut 10¾x10½

2004, Mar. 2 Tagged
Self-Adhesive

3835 A2930 37c **multicolored** .85 .20
P# block of 4, 6#+S 3.50
Pane of 20 17.50
a. Die cutting omitted, pair —

FLOWERS

White Lilacs and Pink Roses — A2931

Five Varieties of Pink Roses — A2932

Designed by Richard Sheaff. Printed by Ashton-Potter (USA) Ltd. (#3836), American Packaging Corporation for Sennett Security Products.

LITHOGRAPHED (#3836), PHOTOGRAVURE
BOOKLET STAMP (#3836)
Sheets of 160 in eight panes of 20 (#3837)
Serpentine Die Cut 10¾ on 2, 3 or 4 Sides

2004, Mar. 4 Tagged
Self-Adhesive

3836 A2931 37c **multicolored** .75 .20
a. Booklet pane of 20 15.00

Serpentine Die Cut 11½x11

3837 A2932 60c **multicolored** 1.25 .25
P# block of 4, 5#+S 5.00
Pane of 20 25.00

UNITED STATES AIR FORCE ACADEMY, 50TH ANNIV.

Cadet Chapel A2933

Designed by Phil Jordan. Printed by American Packaging Corporation for Sennett Security Products.

PHOTOGRAVURE
Sheets of 120 in six panes of 20

2004, Apr. 1 Tagged *Serpentine Die Cut 10¾*
Self-Adhesive

3838 A2933 37c **multicolored** .75 .20
P# block of 4, 6# + S 3.00
Pane of 20 15.00

HENRY MANCINI

Henry Mancini (1924-94), Composer, and Pink Panther A2934

Designed by Carl Herrman. Printed by American Packaging Corporation for Sennett Security Products.

PHOTOGRAVURE
Sheets of 120 in six panes of 20

2004, Apr. 13 Tagged *Serpentine Die Cut 10¾*
Self-Adhesive

3839 A2934 37c **multicolored** .75 .20
P# block of 4, 6#+S 3.00
Pane of 20 15.00

AMERICAN CHOREOGRAPHERS

Martha Graham (1893-1991) A2935

Alvin Ailey (1931-89), and Dancers A2936

Agnes de Mille (1909-93), and Dancers A2937

George Balanchine (1904-83), and Dancers A2938

Designed by Ethel Kessler. Printed by Ashton-Potter (USA) Ltd.

LITHOGRAPHED
Sheets of 120 in six panes of 20

2004, May 4 Tagged *Serpentine Die Cut 10¾*
Self-Adhesive

3840 A2935 37c **multicolored** .75 .20
3841 A2936 37c **multicolored** .75 .20
3842 A2937 37c **multicolored** .75 .20
3843 A2938 37c **multicolored** .75 .20
a. Horiz. strip of 4, #3840-3843 3.00
P# block of 8, 2 sets of P#, 6#+P 6.00
Pane of 20 15.00
b. Strip of 4, die cutting omitted —
As "b," pane of 20 —

Eagle Types of 2003

Designed by Tom Engeman. Printed by American Packaging Corporation for Sennett Security Products.

PHOTOGRAVURE
COIL STAMPS

2004, May 12 Untagged *Perf. 9¾ Vert.*

3844 A2898 (25c) **gray & gold** .65 .20
3845 A2899 (25c) **gold & green** .65 .20
3846 A2898 (25c) **red & gold** .65 .20
3847 A2899 (25c) **gold & dull blue** .65 .20
3848 A2898 (25c) **Prussian blue & gold** .65 .20
3849 A2899 (25c) **gold & gray** .65 .20
3850 A2898 (25c) **green & gold** .65 .20
3851 A2899 (25c) **gold & Prussian blue** .65 .20
3852 A2898 (25c) **dull blue & gold** .65 .20
3853 A2899 (25c) **gold & red** .65 .20
a. Strip of 10, #3844-3853 6.50 —
P# strip of 11, 2 # 3844, 1 each # 3845-3853, #S1111111 9.50 —
P# single (#3849), same # — 2.75

LEWIS & CLARK EXPEDITION, BICENT.

Meriwether Lewis (1774-1809) and William Clark (1770-1838) On Hill — A2939

Lewis — A2940

Clark — A2941

Designed by Michael J. Deas. Printed by Banknote Corporation of America for Sennett Security Products (#3854), Ashton-Potter (USA) Ltd.

LITHOGRAPHED & ENGRAVED

Sheets of 180 in nine panes of 20

2004, May 14 Tagged *Serpentine Die Cut 10¾*

Self-Adhesive

3854	A2939	37c	**green & multicolored**	.90	.20
			P# block of 4, 6#+S	3.75	
			Pane of 20	19.00	
			Sheet of 180 (9 panes)	175.00	
			Cross gutter block of 4	14.00	
			Horiz. pair with vert. gutter	2.25	
			Vert. pair with horiz. gutter	2.25	

Booklet Stamps

Serpentine Die Cut 10½x10¾

3855	A2940	37c	**blue & multicolored**	.90	.45
3856	A2941	37c	**red & multicolored**	.90	.45
a.			Horiz. or vert. pair, #3855-3856	1.80	
b.			Booklet pane, 5 each #3855-3856	9.00	

Nos. 3855-3856 were issued in booklets containing two No. 3856b, each with a different backing. The booklets sold for $8.95.

ISAMU NOGUCHI (1904-88), SCULPTOR

Akari 25N — A2942

Margaret La Farge Osborn — A2943

Black Sun — A2944

Mother and Child — A2945

Figure (Detail) — A2946

Designed by Derry Noyes. Printed by Ashton-Potter (USA) Ltd.

LITHOGRAPHED

Sheets of 120 in six panes of 20

Serpentine Die Cut 10½x10¾

2004, May 18 Tagged

Self-Adhesive

3857	A2942	37c	**black**	.75	.20
3858	A2943	37c	**black**	.75	.20
3859	A2944	37c	**black**	.75	.20
3860	A2945	37c	**black**	.75	.20
3861	A2946	37c	**black**	.75	.20
a.			Horiz. strip of 5, #3857-3861	3.75	
			P# block of 6 (3 across x 2 down), 2#+P	4.50	
			P# block of 8, 2 sets of 2#+P + left label	6.00	
			Pane of 20	15.00	
			Sheet of 120 (6 panes)	85.00	
			Cross gutter block of 8	17.50	
			Block of 8 with vert. gutter	10.00	
			Block of 10 with horiz. gutter	11.00	
			Horiz. pair with vert. gutter	2.25	
			Vert. pair with horiz. gutter	2.25	

The cross gutter block consists of 1 stamp from each of the two upper panes and three stamps vertically from each of the two lower panes.

NATIONAL WORLD WAR II MEMORIAL

A2947

Designed by Howard E. Paine. Printed by Ashton-Potter (USA) Ltd.

LITHOGRAPHED

Sheets of 180 in nine panes of 20

2004, May 29 Tagged *Serpentine Die Cut 10¾*

Self-Adhesive

3862	A2947	37c	**multicolored**	.75	.20
			P# block of 4, 4#+P	3.00	
			Pane of 20	15.00	

Scott values for used self-adhesive stamps are for examples either on piece or off piece.

SUMMER OLYMPIC GAMES, ATHENS, GREECE

Stylized Runner A2948

Designed by Richard Sheaff. Printed by Ashton-Potter (USA) Ltd.

LITHOGRAPHED

Sheets of 120 in six panes of 20

2004, June 9 Tagged *Serpentine Die Cut 10¾*

Self-Adhesive

3863	A2948	37c	**multicolored**	.75	.20
			P# block of 4, 4#+P	3.00	
			Pane of 20	15.00	

Sea Coast Type of 2002

Designed by Tom Engeman. Printed by American Packaging Corp. for Sennett Security Products.

PHOTOGRAVURE

COIL STAMP

2004, June 11 Untagged *Perf. 9¾ Vert.*

3864	A2853	(5c)	**multicolored**	.20	.20
			Pair	.20	—
			P# strip of 5, #S1111	1.50	—
			P# single, same #	—	1.00

No. 3864 has "2004" year date in black, rows of distinctly separated dots in surf area, and the small orange cloud is indistinct. No. 3775 has "2003" year date in blue, dots that run together in surf area, and a distinct small orange cloud.

No. 3864 known with red ink that glows orange under long wave ultraviolet light. Values the same.

THE ART OF DISNEY: FRIENDSHIP

Goofy, Mickey Mouse, Donald Duck — A2949

Bambi, Thumper — A2950

Mufasa, Simba — A2951

Jiminy Cricket, Pinocchio — A2952

Designed by David Pacheco. Printed by American Packaging Corporation for Bamknote Corporation of America/Sennett Security Products.

LITHOGRAPHED
Sheets of 180 in nine panes of 20
Serpentine Die Cut 10½x10¾

2004, June 23 **Tagged**

Self-Adhesive

3865	A2949	37c	**multicolored**	1.00	.20
3866	A2950	37c	**multicolored**	1.00	.20
3867	A2951	37c	**multicolored**	1.00	.20
3868	A2952	37c	**multicolored**	1.00	.20
a.			Block or vert. strip of 4, #3865-3868	4.00	
			P# block of 4, 4#+S	4.00	
			Pane of 20	20.00	

U.S.S. CONSTELLATION

A2953

Designed by Howard E. Paine. Printed by Ashton-Potter (USA) Ltd.

ENGRAVED
Sheets of 180 in nine panes of 20

2004, June 30 **Tagged** ***Serpentine Die Cut 10½***

Self-Adhesive

3869	A2953	37c	**brown**	.75	.20
			P# block of 4, 1#+P	3.00	
			Pane of 20	15.00	

R. BUCKMINSTER FULLER (1895-1983), ENGINEER

Time Magazine Cover Depicting Fuller, by Boris Artzybasheff — A2954

Designed by Carl T. Herrman. Printed by Ashton-Potter (USA) Ltd.

LITHOGRAPHED
Sheets of 120 in six panes of 20
Serpentine Die Cut 10½x10¾

2004, July 12 **Tagged**

Self-Adhesive

3870	A2954	37c	**multicolored**	.75	.20
			P# block of 4, 5#+P	3.00	
			Pane of 20	15.00	

LITERARY ARTS

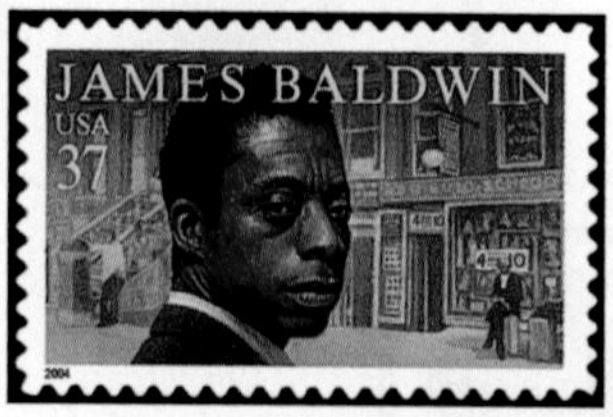

James Baldwin (1924-87), Writer A2955

Designed by Phil Jordan. Printed by Ashton-Potter (USA) Ltd.

LITHOGRAPHED
Sheets of 180 in nine panes of 20

2004, July 23 **Tagged** ***Serpentine Die Cut 10¾***

Self-Adhesive

3871	A2955	37c	**multicolored**	.75	.20
			P# block of 4, 5#+P	3.00	
			Pane of 20	15.00	

AMERICAN TREASURES SERIES

Giant Magnolias on a Blue Velvet Cloth, by Martin Johnson Heade A2956

Designed by Derry Noyes. Printed by American Packaging Corporation for Sennett Security Products.

PHOTOGRAVURE
BOOKLET STAMP
Serpentine Die Cut 10¾ on 2 or 3 Sides

2004, Aug. 12 **Tagged**

Self-Adhesive

3872	A2956	37c	**multicolored**	.70	.20
a.			Booklet pane of 20	15.00	
b.			Die cutting omitted, pair	—	

No. 3872a is a double-sided booklet pane with 12 stamps on one side and eight stamps plus label on the other side.

ART OF THE AMERICAN INDIAN

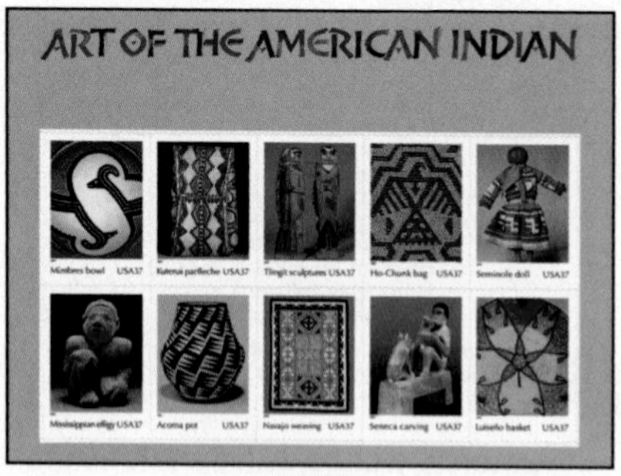

A2957

Illustration reduced.

Designed by Richard Sheaff. Printed by Avery Dennison.

Designs: a, Mimbres bowl. b, Kutenai parfleche. c, Tlingit sculptures. d, Ho-Chunk bag. e, Seminole doll. f, Mississippian effigy. g, Acoma pot. h, Navajo weaving. i, Seneca carving. j, Luiseño basket.

PHOTOGRAVURE
Serpentine Die Cut 10¾x11

2004, Aug. 21 **Tagged**

Self-Adhesive

3873	A2957	Pane of 10	12.00	
a.-j.		37c Any single	1.20	.20

Sea Coast Type of 2002

Designed by Tom Engeman.

Printed by Ashton-Potter (USA), Ltd. (#3874); American Packaging Corporation for Sennett Security Products (#3875).

PHOTOGRAVURE
COIL STAMPS

2004-05 **Untagged** ***Serpentine Die Cut 10 Vert.***

Self-Adhesive

3874	A2853	(5c)	**multicolored,** large "2003" year date	.20	.20
			Pair	.20	
			P# strip of 5, #P2222	1.60	
			P# single, #P2222	—	1.00
a.			Small "2003" year date ('05)	.20	.20
			Pair	.20	
			P# strip of 5, #P3333, P4444, P5555, P6666, P7777, P8888, P9999	1.60	
			P# single, same numbers	—	1.00

On Nos. 3874 and 3874a, the stamps are spaced on backing paper that is taller than the stamps.

On No. 3874 the color laydown order of plate numbers is cyan, magenta, yellow, black. On No. 3874a, the order is BCMY.

Serpentine Die Cut 11½ Vert.

3875	A2853	(5c)	**multicolored,** "2004" year date	.20	.20
			Pair	.20	
			P# strip of 5, #S1111	1.50	
			P# single, #S1111	—	1.00

On No. 3875, the stamps are spaced on backing paper that is taller than the stamps.

No. 3875 exists with very faint traces of tagging.

LEGENDS OF HOLLYWOOD

John Wayne (1907-79), Actor — A2958

Designed by Derry Noyes.

Printed by American Packaging Corporation for Sennett Security Products.

PHOTOGRAVURE
Sheets of 120 in six panes of 20

2004, Sept. 9 **Tagged** ***Serpentine Die Cut 10¾***

Self-Adhesive

3876	A2958	37c	**multicolored**	.75	.20
			P# block of 4, 6#+S	3.00	
			Pane of 20	15.00	
			Sheet of 120 (6 panes)	85.00	
			Cross gutter block of 8	17.50	
			Block of 8 with vertical gutter	10.00	
			Horiz. pair with vert. gutter	3.00	
			Vert. pair with horiz. gutter	2.00	

SICKLE CELL DISEASE AWARENESS

Mother and Child — A2959

Designed by Howard Paine.

Printed by Avery Dennison.

PHOTOGRAVURE
Sheets of 200 in ten panes of 20

2004, Sept. 29 **Tagged** ***Serpentine Die Cut 11***

Self-Adhesive

3877	A2959	37c	**multicolored**	.75	.20
			P# block of 4, 6#+V	3.00	
			Pane of 20	15.00	

CLOUDSCAPES

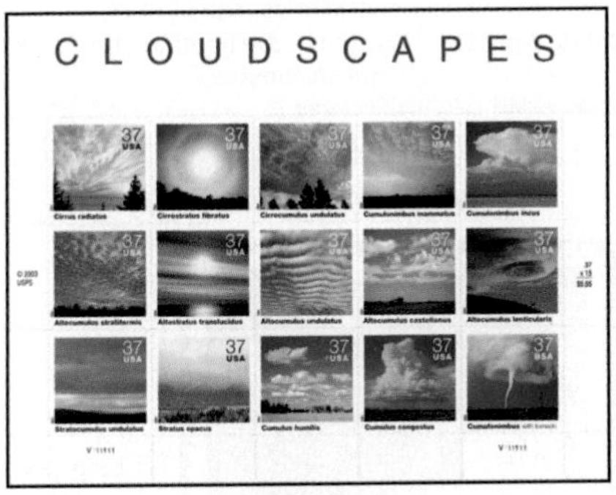

A2960

Illustration reduced.

Designed by Howard E. Paine.

Printed by Avery Dennison.

Clouds: a, Cirrus radiatus. b, Cirrostratus fibratus. c, Cirrocumulus undulatus. d, Cumulonimbus mammatus. e, Cumulonimbus incus. f, Altocumulus stratiformis. g, Altostratus translucidus. h, Altocumulus undulatus. i, Altocumulus castellanus. j, Altocumulus lenticularis. k, Stratocumulus undulatus. l, Stratus opacus. m, Cumulus humilis. n, Cumulus congestus. o, Cumulonimbus with tornado.

PHOTOGRAVURE

2004, Oct. 4 Tagged ***Serpentine Die Cut 11***

Self-Adhesive

3878	A2960	Pane of 15	12.50	
a.-o.		37c Any single	.80	.20

CHRISTMAS

Madonna and Child, by Lorenzo Monaco — A2961

Designed by Richard Sheaff.
Printed by Ashton-Potter (USA), Ltd.

LITHOGRAPHED
BOOKLET STAMP

Serpentine Die Cut 10¾x11 on 2 or 3 Sides

2004, Oct. 14 Tagged

Self-Adhesive

3879	A2961 37c	**multicolored**	.75	.20
a.		Booklet pane of 20	15.00	
b.		As "a," die cutting omitted	—	

No. 3879a is a double-sided booklet pane with 12 stamps on one side and eight stamps plus label that serves as a booklet cover on the other side.

HANUKKAH

Dreidel — A2962

Designed by Ethel Kessler.
Printed by Banknote Corporation of America for Sennett Security Products.

LITHOGRAPHED

Sheets of 300 in fifteen panes of 20

2004, Oct. 15 Tagged ***Serpentine Die Cut 10¾***

Self-Adhesive

3880	A2962 37c	**multicolored**	.75	.20
		P# block of 4, 4#+S	3.00	
		Pane of 20	15.00	
a.		Die cuts applied to wrong sides of stamp (hyphen-hole die cuts and wavy line on face, die cut 10¾ on reverse)	—	—

KWANZAA

People in Robes — A2963

Designed by Derry Noyes.
Printed by Ashton-Potter (USA), Ltd.

LITHOGRAPHED

Sheets of 160 in eight panes of 20

2004, Oct. 16 Tagged ***Serpentine Die Cut 10¾***

Self-Adhesive

3881	A2963 37c	**multicolored**	.75	.20
		P# block of 4, 6#+P	3.00	
		Pane of 20	15.00	

LITERARY ARTS

Moss Hart (1904-61), Playwright A2964

Designed by Ethel Kessler.
Printed by Avery Dennison.

PHOTOGRAVURE

Sheets of 200 in ten panes of 20

2004, Oct. 25 Tagged ***Serpentine Die Cut 11***

Self-Adhesive

3882	A2964 37c	**multicolored**	.75	.20
		P# block of 4, 5#+V	3.00	
		Pane of 20	15.00	

CHRISTMAS

Purple Santa Ornament — A2965

Green Santa Ornament — A2966

Blue Santa Ornament — A2967

Red Santa Ornament — A2968

Purple Santa Ornament — A2969

Green Santa Ornament — A2970

Blue Santa Ornament — A2971

Red Santa Ornament — A2972

Designed by Derry Noyes. Printed by American Packaging Corporation for Sennett Security Printers. (#3883-3890), Avery Dennison (#3891-3894).

PHOTOGRAVURE

Sheets of 160 in eight panes of 20

Serpentine Die Cut 11½x11

2004, Nov. 16 Tagged

Self-Adhesive

3883	A2965 37c	**purple & multicolored**	.80	.20
3884	A2966 37c	**green & multicolored**	.80	.20
3885	A2967 37c	**blue & multicolored**	.80	.20
3886	A2968 37c	**red & multicolored**	.80	.20
a.		Block or strip of 4, #3883-3886	3.20	
		P# block of 4, 4#+S	3.20	
		Pane of 20	16.00	
b.		Booklet pane of 20, 5 #3886a blocks	16.00	

Booklet Stamps

Serpentine Die Cut 10¼x10¾ on 2 or 3 Sides

3887	A2969 37c	**purple & multicolored**	.75	.20
3888	A2970 37c	**green & multicolored**	.75	.20
3889	A2971 37c	**blue & multicolored**	.75	.20
3890	A2972 37c	**red & multicolored**	.75	.20
a.		Block of 4, #3887-3890	3.00	
b.		Booklet pane of 4, #3887-3890	3.00	
c.		Booklet pane of 6, #3889-3890, 2 each #3887-3888	4.50	
d.		Booklet pane of 6, #3887-3888, 2 each #3889-3890	4.50	

Serpentine Die Cut 8 on 2, 3 or 4 Sides

3891	A2970 37c	**green & multicolored**	.90	.20
3892	A2969 37c	**purple & multicolored**	.90	.20
3893	A2972 37c	**red & multicolored**	.90	.20
3894	A2971 37c	**blue & multicolored**	.90	.20
a.		Block of 4, #3891-3894	3.60	
b.		Booklet pane of 18, 6 each #3891, 3893, 3 each # 3892, 3894	18.00	
		Nos. 3883-3894 (12)	9.80	2.40

No. 3886b is a double-sided booklet with 12 stamps on one side and 8 stamps plus label that serves as a booklet cover on the other side.

The design of No. 3894b shows ornaments in a wooden box. The pattern of the wooden box dividers creates three types of each design. Rows 1 and 4 are Type 1, with a top horizontal strip of frame extending from edge to edge while the bottom strip of frame stops at the design's width. Rows 2 and 5 are Type 2, with both top and bottom strips of frame stopping at the design's width. Rows 3 and 6 are Type 3, with the top strip of frame stopping at design's width while the bottom strip of frame extends from edge to edge. Each variety is equally common.

Chinese New Year Types of 1992-2004

Designed by Clarence Lee. Printed by American Packaging Corporation for Sennett Security Products.

PHOTOGRAVURE

2005, Jan. 6 Tagged ***Serpentine Die Cut 10¾***

Self-Adhesive

3895		Double sided pane of 24, 2 each #a-l	18.00	
a.	A2360 37c	Rat	.75	.20
b.	A2413 37c	Ox	.75	.20
c.	A2462 37c	Tiger	.75	.20
d.	A2535 37c	Rabbit	.75	.20
e.	A2602 37c	Dragon	.75	.20
f.	A2702 37c	Snake	.75	.20
g.	A2752 37c	Horse	.75	.20
h.	A2856 37c	Ram	.75	.20
i.	A2927 37c	Monkey	.75	.20
j.	A2067 37c	Rooster	.75	.20
k.	A2146 37c	Dog	.75	.20
l.	A2205 37c	Boar	.75	.20
m.		As No. 3895, die cutting omitted on "a," "b," and "c" on reverse side	*1,250.*	

No. 3895h has "2005" year date and is photogravure while No. 3747 has "2003" year date and is lithographed.

Stamps are on the right side of the front and on the left side of the reverse.

BLACK HERITAGE SERIES

Marian Anderson (1897-1993), Singer — A2973

Designed by Richard Sheaff. Printed by American Packaging Corporation for Sennett Security Products.

PHOTOGRAVURE
Sheets of 120 in six panes of 20

2005, Jan. 27 Tagged *Serpentine Die Cut 10¾*
Self-Adhesive

3896 A2973 37c **multicolored**		.75	.20
	P# block of 4, 4# + S	3.00	
	Pane of 20	15.00	

RONALD REAGAN

Ronald Reagan (1911-2004), 40th President — A2974

Designed by Howard E. Paine. Printed by American Packaging Corporation for Sennett Security Products.

PHOTOGRAVURE
Sheets of 120 in six panes of 20

2005, Feb. 9 Tagged *Serpentine Die Cut 10¾*
Self-Adhesive

3897 A2974 37c **multicolored**		.75	.20
	P# block of 4, 4#+S	3.00	
	Pane of 20	15.00	
	Sheet of 120 (6 panes)	90.00	
	Cross gutter block of 4	8.25	
	Horiz. pair with vert. gutter	3.00	
	Vert. pair with horiz. gutter	2.00	

The bottom center stamp (pos. 18) shows a small portion of the pane position diagram in the bottom margin, due to the too-high placement of the diagram in the selvage. There are three varieties of the portion appearing on the stamp, depending on the pane position on the press sheet.

LOVE

Hand and Flower Bouquet — A2975

Designed by Derry Noyes. Printed by Avery Dennison.

PHOTOGRAVURE
BOOKLET STAMP

Serpentine Die Cut 10¾x11 on 2, 3 or 4 Sides
2005, Feb. 18 Tagged
Self-Adhesive

3898 A2975 37c **multicolored**		.75	.20
a.	Booklet pane of 20	15.00	

NORTHEAST DECIDUOUS FOREST

A2976

Illustration reduced.

Designed by Ethel Kessler. Printed by Avery Dennison.

Wildlife: a, Eastern buckmoth, vert. b, Red-shouldered hawk. c, Eastern red bat. d, White-tailed deer. e, Black bear. f, Long-tailed weasel, vert. g, Wild turkey, vert. h, Ovenbird, vert. i, Red eft. j, Eastern chipmunk.

PHOTOGRAVURE
Sheets of 80 in eight panes of 10

2005, Mar. 3 Tagged *Serpentine Die Cut 10¾*
Self-Adhesive

3899 A2976	Pane of 10	7.50	
a.-j.	37c Any single	.75	.20
	Sheet of 8 panes	60.00	

SPRING FLOWERS

Hyacinth — A2977

Daffodil — A2978

Tulip — A2979

Iris — A2980

Designed by Derry Noyes. Printed by Ashton-Potter (USA) Ltd.

LITHOGRAPHED
BOOKLET STAMPS

Serpentine Die Cut 10¾ on 2 or 3 Sides
2005, Mar. 15 Tagged
Self-Adhesive

3900 A2977 37c **multicolored**		.75	.20
3901 A2978 37c **multicolored**		.75	.20
3902 A2979 37c **multicolored**		.75	.20
3903 A2980 37c **multicolored**		.75	.20
a.	Block of 4, #3900-3903	3.00	
b.	Booklet pane, 5 each #3900-3903	15.00	
c.	As "b," die cutting omitted on side with 8 stamps	—	

No. 3903b is a double-sided booklet with 12 stamps on one side and 8 stamps plus label (booklet cover) on the other side.

LITERARY ARTS

Robert Penn Warren (1905-89), Writer A2981

Designed by Carl Herrman. Printed by American Packaging Corporation for Sennett Security Products.

PHOTOGRAVURE
Sheets of 120 in six panes of 20

2005, Apr. 22 Tagged *Serpentine Die Cut 10¾*
Self-Adhesive

3904 A2981 37c **multicolored**		.75	.20
	P# block of 4, 5#+S	3.00	
	Pane of 20	15.00	

EDGAR Y. "YIP" HARBURG

Harburg (1896-1981), Lyricist A2982

Designed by Ethel Kessler. Printed by Banknote Corporation of America for Sennett Security Products.

LITHOGRAPHED
Sheets of 120 in six panes of 20

2005, Apr. 28 Tagged *Serpentine Die Cut 10¾*
Self-Adhesive

3905 A2982 37c **multicolored**		.75	.20
	P# block of 4, 4#+S	3.00	
	Pane of 20	15.00	

AMERICAN SCIENTISTS

Barbara McClintock (1902-92), Geneticist A2983

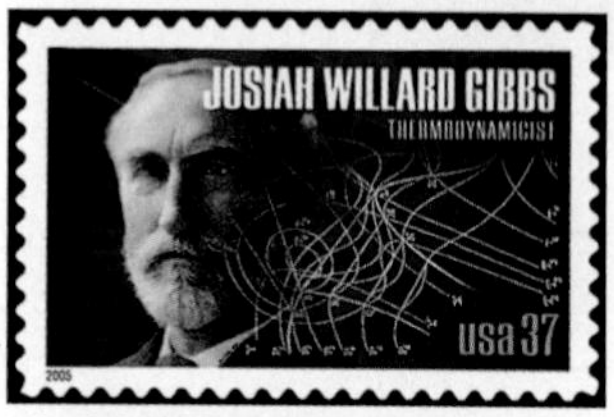

Josiah Willard Gibbs (1839-1903), Thermodynamicist — A2984

John von Neumann (1903-57), Mathematician A2985

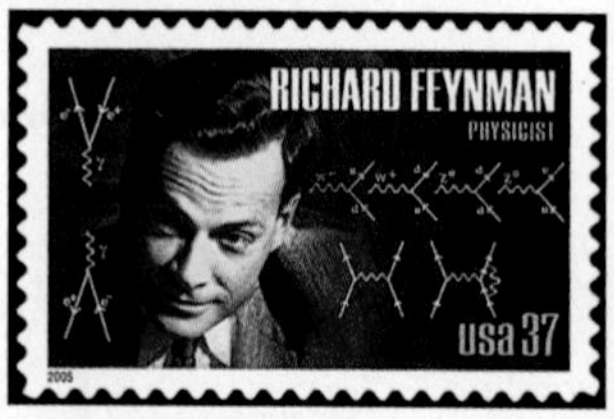

Richard Feynman (1918-88), Physicist A2986

Designed by Carl Herrman. Printed by Banknote Corporation of America for Sennett Security Products.

LITHOGRAPHED
Sheets of 180 in nine panes of 20

2005, May 4 Tagged *Serpentine Die Cut 10¾*
Self-Adhesive

3906 A2983 37c **multicolored**		.75	.20
3907 A2984 37c **multicolored**		.75	.20
3908 A2985 37c **multicolored**		.75	.20
a.	Vert. pair, die cutting omitted, #3906 & 3908	—	
3909 A2986 37c **multicolored**		.75	.20
a.	Block or horiz. strip of 4, #3906-3909	3.00	
	P# block of 8, 2 sets of P# + top label, 5#+S	6.00	
	P# block of 4, 5#+S	3.00	
	Pane of 20	15.00	
b.	All colors omitted, tagging omitted, pane of 20	—	

c.	As "a," printing on back of stamps omitted	—	
d.	Vert. pair, die cutting omitted, #3907 & 3909	—	

On No. 3909b, the printing on the back of the pane and all die cutting is normal.

MODERN AMERICAN ARCHITECTURE

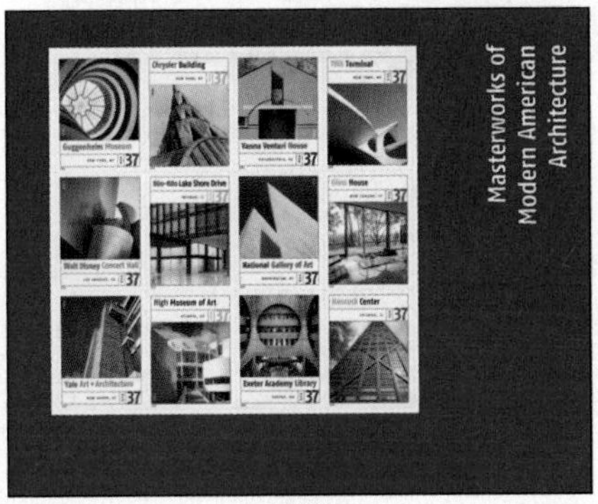

A2987

Illustration reduced.

Designed by Margaret Bauer. Printed by Ashton-Potter (USA) Ltd.

Buildings: a, Guggenheim Museum, New York. b, Chrysler Building, New York. c, Vanna Venturi House, Philadelphia. d, TWA Terminal, New York. e, Walt Disney Concert Hall, Los Angeles. f, 860-880 Lake Shore Drive, Chicago. g, National Gallery of Art, Washington, DC. h, Glass House, New Canaan, CT. i, Yale Art and Architecture Building, New Haven, CT. j, High Museum of Art, Atlanta. k, Exeter Academy Library, Exeter, NH. l, Hancock Center, Chicago.

LITHOGRAPHED

Serpentine Die Cut 10¾x11

2005, May 19 **Tagged**

Self-Adhesive

3910	A2987	Pane of 12	9.00	
a.-l.		37c Any single	.75	.20
m.		As No. 3910, orange yellow omitted	—	—

No. 3910m exists on a first day cover.

LEGENDS OF HOLLYWOOD

Henry Fonda (1905-82), Actor — A2988

Designed by Derry Noyes. Printed by Ashton-Potter (USA) Ltd.

LITHOGRAPHED

Sheets of 180 in nine panes of 20

Serpentine Die Cut 11x10¾

2005, May 20 **Tagged**

Self-Adhesive

3911	A2988 37c	**multicolored**	.75	.20
		P# block of 4, 5#+P	3.00	
		Pane of 20	15.00	
		Sheet of 180 (9 panes)	135.00	
		Cross gutter block of 8	17.50	
		Block of 8 with vert. gutter	10.00	
		Horiz. pair with vert. gutter	3.00	
		Vert. pair with horiz. gutter	2.00	

The cross gutter block consists of 4 stamps from the two upper panes and 4 stamps from the two lower panes.

THE ART OF DISNEY: CELEBRATION

Pluto, Mickey Mouse — A2989

Mad Hatter, Alice — A2990

Flounder, Ariel — A2991

Snow White, Dopey — A2992

Designed by David Pacheco. Printed by Banknote Corporation of America for Sennett Security Products.

LITHOGRAPHED

Sheets of 180 in nine panes of 20

Serpentine Die Cut 10½x10¾

2005, June 30 **Tagged**

Self-Adhesive

3912	A2989 37c	**multicolored**	.75	.20
3913	A2990 37c	**multicolored**	.75	.20
3914	A2991 37c	**multicolored**	.75	.20
3915	A2992 37c	**multicolored**	.75	.20
a.		Block or vert. strip of 4, #3912-3915	3.00	
		P# block of 4, 6#+S	3.00	
		P# block of 10, 2 sets of P# + top label	7.50	
		Pane of 20	15.00	
b.		Die cutting omitted, pane of 20	—	
c.		Printed on backing paper, pane of 20	—	

ADVANCES IN AVIATION

Boeing 247 — A2993

Consolidated PBY Catalina A2994

Grumman F6F Hellcat A2995

Republic P-47 Thunderbolt A2996

Engineering and Research Corporation Ercoupe 415 — A2997

Lockheed P-80 Shooting Star — A2998

Consolidated B-24 Liberator A2999

Boeing B-29 Superfortress A3000

Beechcraft 35 Bonanza A3001

Northrop YB-49 Flying Wing — A3002

Designed by Phil Jordan. Printed by Ashton-Potter (USA) Ltd.

LITHOGRAPHED
Sheets of 180 in nine panes of 20
Serpentine Die Cut 10¾x10½

2005, July 29 **Tagged**

Self-Adhesive

3916	A2993	37c	**multicolored**	.75	.20
3917	A2994	37c	**multicolored**	.75	.20
3918	A2995	37c	**multicolored**	.75	.20
3919	A2996	37c	**multicolored**	.75	.20
3920	A2997	37c	**multicolored**	.75	.20
3921	A2998	37c	**multicolored**	.75	.20
3922	A2999	37c	**multicolored**	.75	.20
3923	A3000	37c	**multicolored**	.75	.20
3924	A3001	37c	**multicolored**	.75	.20
3925	A3002	37c	**multicolored**	.75	.20
a.			Block of 10, #3916-3925	7.50	
			P# block of 10, 7#+P	7.50	
			Pane of 20	15.00	

RIO GRANDE BLANKETS

A3003

A3004

A3005

A3006

Designed by Derry Noyes. Printed by Ashton-Potter (USA) Ltd.

LITHOGRAPHED
BOOKLET STAMPS
Serpentine Die Cut 10¾ on 2 or 3 Sides

2005, July 30 **Tagged**

Self-Adhesive

3926	A3003	37c	**multicolored**	.75	.20
3927	A3004	37c	**multicolored**	.75	.20
3928	A3005	37c	**multicolored**	.75	.20
3929	A3006	37c	**multicolored**	.75	.20
a.			Block of 4, #3926-3929	3.00	
b.			Booklet pane, 5 each #3926-3929	15.00	

No. 3929b is a double-sided booklet with 12 stamps on one side and 8 stamps plus label (booklet cover) on the other side.

PRESIDENTIAL LIBRARIES ACT, 50th ANNIV.

Presidential Seal — A3007

Designed by Howard E. Paine. Printed by Banknote Corporation of America for Sennett Security Products.

LITHOGRAPHED
Sheets of 180 in nine panes of 20

2005, Aug. 4 **Tagged** ***Serpentine Die Cut 10¾***

Self-Adhesive

3930	A3007	37c	**multicolored**	.75	.20
			P# block of 4, 3#+S	3.00	
			Pane of 20	15.00	
			Sheet of 180 (9 panes)	135.00	
			Cross gutter block of 4	8.25	
			Horiz. pair with vert. gutter	3.00	
			Vert. pair with horiz. gutter	2.00	

SPORTY CARS OF THE 1950S

1953 Studebaker Starliner A3008

1954 Kaiser Darren A3009

1953 Chevrolet Corvette A3010

1952 Nash Healey A3011

1955 Ford Thunderbird A3012

Designed by Art M. Fitzpatrick. Printed by Ashton-Potter (USA) Ltd.

LITHOGRAPHED
BOOKLET STAMPS
Serpentine Die Cut 10¾ on 2 or 3 Sides

2005, Aug. 20 **Tagged**

Self-Adhesive

3931	A3008	37c	**multicolored**	.80	.20
3932	A3009	37c	**multicolored**	.80	.20
3933	A3010	37c	**multicolored**	.80	.20
3934	A3011	37c	**multicolored**	.80	.20
3935	A3012	37c	**multicolored**	.80	.20
a.			Vert. strip of 5, #3931-3935	4.00	
b.			Booklet pane, 4 each #3931-3935	16.00	

Stamps in No. 3935a are not adjacent, as rows of selvage are between stamps one and two, and between stamps three and four.

No. 3935b is a double-sided booklet pane with 12 stamps on one side (2 each #3931, 3933, 3935, and 3 each #3932, 3934) and eight stamps (1 each #3932, 3934, and 2 each #3931, 3933, 3935) plus label on the other side.

ARTHUR ASHE

Arthur Ashe (1943-93), Tennis Player — A3013

Designed by Carl T. Herrman. Printed by Ashton-Potter (USA) Ltd.

LITHOGRAPHED
Sheets of 240 in twelve panes of 20

2005, Aug. 27 **Tagged** ***Serpentine Die Cut 10¾***

Self-Adhesive

3936	A3013	37c	**multicolored**	.75	.20
			P# block of 4, 5#+P	3.00	
			Pane of 20	15.00	

TO FORM A MORE PERFECT UNION

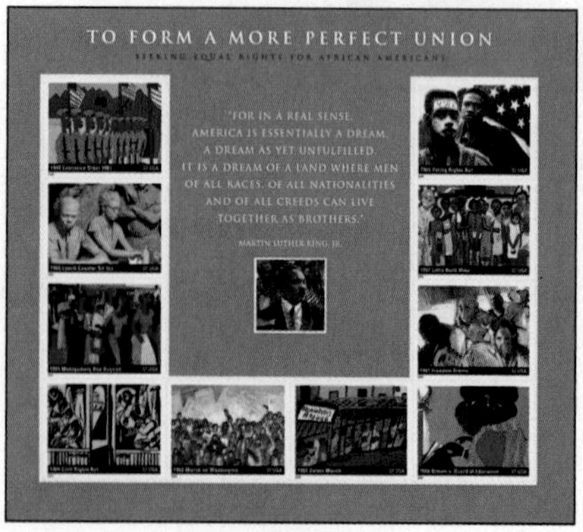

A3014

Illustration reduced.

Designed by Ethel Kessler. Printed by Ashton-Potter (USA) Ltd.

Inscriptions and artwork: a, 1948 Executive Order 9981 (Training for War, by William H. Johnson). b, 1965 Voting Rights Act (Youths on the Selma March, 1965, photograph by Bruce Davidson). c, 1960 Lunch Counter Sit-ins (National Civil Rights Museum exhibits, by StudioEIS). d, 1957 Little Rock Nine (America Cares, by George Hunt). e, 1955 Montgomery Bus Boycott (Walking, by Charles Alston). f, 1961 Freedom Riders (Freedom Riders, by May Stevens). g, 1964 Civil Rights Act (Dixie Café, by Jacob Lawrence). h,

1963 March on Washington (March on Washington, by Alma Thomas). i, 1965 Selma March (Selma March, by Bernice Sims). j, 1954 Brown v. Board of Education (The Lamp, by Romare Bearden).

LITHOGRAPHED

Serpentine Die Cut 10¾x10½

2005, Aug. 30 **Tagged**

Self-Adhesive

3937	A3014	Pane of 10	7.50	
a.-j.		37c Any single	.75	.20

CHILD HEALTH

Child and Doctor — A3015

Designed by Craig Frazier.

Printed by Avery Dennison.

PHOTOGRAVURE

Sheets of 200 in ten panes of 20

Serpentine Die Cut 10½x11

2005, Sept. 7 **Tagged**

Self-Adhesive

3938	A3015	37c	**multicolored**	.75	.20
			P# block of 4, 4#+V	3.00	
			Pane of 20	15.00	

LET'S DANCE

Merengue — A3016

Salsa — A3017

Cha Cha Cha — A3018

Mambo — A3019

Designed by Ethel Kessler.

Printed by American Packaging Corporation for Sennett Security Products.

PHOTOGRAVURE

Sheets of 120 in six panes of 20

2005, Sept. 17 **Tagged** ***Serpentine Die Cut 10¾***

Self-Adhesive

3939	A3016	37c	**multicolored**	.75	.20
3940	A3017	37c	**multicolored**	.75	.20
3941	A3018	37c	**multicolored**	.75	.20
3942	A3019	37c	**multicolored**	.75	.20
a.			Vert. strip of 4, #3939-3942	3.00	
			P# block of 8, 8#+S	6.00	
			Pane of 20	15.00	

Stamps in the vertical strip are not adjacent as rows of selvage are between the stamps. The backing paper of stamps from the 2nd and 4th columns have Spanish inscriptions, while the other columns have English inscriptions.

GRETA GARBO

Garbo (1905-90), Actress — A3020

Designed by Carl T. Herrman.

Printed by Banknote Corporation of America for Sennett Security Products.

ENGRAVED

Sheets of 120 in six panes of 20

2005, Sept. 23 **Tagged** ***Serpentine Die Cut 10¾***

Self-Adhesive

3943	A3020	37c	**black**	.75	.20
			P# block of 4, 1#+S	3.00	
			Pane of 20	15.00	

See Sweden No. 2517.

JIM HENSON AND THE MUPPETS

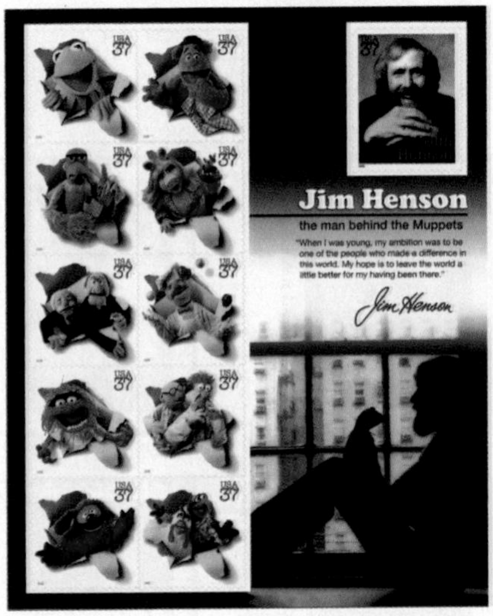

A3021

Illustration reduced.

Designed by Edward Eyth.

Printed by Avery Dennison.

No. 3944: a, Kermit the Frog. b, Fozzie Bear. c, Sam the Eagle and flag. d, Miss Piggy. e, Statler and Waldorf. f, The Swedish Chef and fruit. g, Animal. h, Dr. Bunsen Honeydew and Beaker. i, Rowlf the Dog. j, The Great Gonzo and Camilla the Chicken. k, Jim Henson.

Nos. 3944a-3944j are 30x30mm; No. 3944k, 28x37mm.

PHOTOGRAVURE

Serpentine Die Cut 10½, 10½x10¾ (#3944k)

2005, Sept. 28 **Tagged**

Self-Adhesive

3944	A3021	Pane of 11	8.25	
a.-k.		37c Any single	.75	.20

CONSTELLATIONS

Leo — A3022

Orion — A3023

Lyra — A3024

Pegasus — A3025

Designed by McRay Magleby.

Printed by Ashton-Potter (USA) Ltd.

LITHOGRAPHED

Sheets of 240 in twelve panes of 20

2005, Oct. 3 **Tagged** ***Serpentine Die Cut 10¾***

Self-Adhesive

3945	A3022	37c	**multicolored**	.75	.20
3946	A3023	37c	**multicolored**	.75	.20
3947	A3024	37c	**multicolored**	.75	.20

3948 A3025 37c **multicolored** .75 .20
a. Block or vert. strip of 4, #3945-3948 3.00
P# block of 4, 6#+P 3.00
P# block of 10, 2 sets of P# + top label 7.50
Pane of 20 15.00
b. As "a," die cutting omitted —

CHRISTMAS COOKIES

Santa Claus — A3026

Snowmen — A3027

Angel — A3028

Elves — A3029

Santa Claus — A3030

Snowmen — A3031

Angel — A3032

Elves — A3033

Designed by Derry Noyes.
Printed by Banknote Corporation of America for Sennett Security Products (#3949-3952), American Packaging Corporation for Sennett Security Products (#3953-3960).

LITHOGRAPHED, PHOTOGRAVURE (#3953-3960)

Serpentine Die Cut 10¾x11

2005, Oct. 20 **Tagged**

Self-Adhesive

Design Size: 19x26mm

3949 A3026 37c **multicolored** .75 .20
3950 A3027 37c **multicolored** .75 .20
3951 A3028 37c **multicolored** .75 .20
3952 A3029 37c **multicolored** .75 .20
a. Block or vert. strip of 4, #3949-3952 3.00
P# block of 4, 4#+S 3.00
Pane of 20 15.00

Booklet Stamps

Serpentine Die Cut 10¾x11 on 2 or 3 Sides

Design Size: 19½x27mm

3953 A3026 37c **multicolored** .75 .20
3954 A3027 37c **multicolored** .75 .20
3955 A3028 37c **multicolored** .75 .20
3956 A3029 37c **multicolored** .75 .20
a. Block of 4, #3953-3956 3.00
b. Booklet pane of 20, 5 #3956a 15.00

Serpentine Die Cut 10½x10¾

3957 A3030 37c **multicolored** 1.50 .20
3958 A3031 37c **multicolored** 1.50 .20
3959 A3032 37c **multicolored** 1.50 .20
3960 A3033 37c **multicolored** 1.50 .20
a. Block of 4, #3957-3960 6.00
b. Booklet pane of 4, #3957-3960 6.00
c. Booklet pane of 6, #3959-3960, 2 each #3957-3958 9.00
d. Booklet pane of 6, #3957-3958, 2 each #3959-3960 9.00

No. 3956b is a double-sided booklet pane with 12 stamps on one side and eight stamps plus label that serves as a booklet cover on the other side. Nos. 3949-3952 have a small "2005" year date, while Nos. 3953-3956 have a large year date. Other design differences caused by different cropping of the images can be found, with Nos. 3953-3956 showing slightly more design features on one or more sides.

DISTINGUISHED MARINES

Lt. Gen. John A. Lejeune (1867-1942), 2nd Infantry Division Insignia A3034

Lt. Gen. Lewis B. Puller (1898-1971), 1st Marine Division Insignia A3035

Sgt. John Basilone (1916-45), 5th Marine Division Insignia A3036

Sgt. Major Daniel J. Daly (1873-1937), 73rd Machine Gun Company, 6th Marine Regiment Insignia A3037

Designed by Phil Jordan. Printed by Ashton-Potter (USA) Ltd.

LITHOGRAPHED

Sheets of 180 in nine panes of 20

Serpentine Die Cut 11x10½

2005, Nov. 10 **Tagged**

Self-Adhesive

3961 A3034 37c **multicolored** 1.00 .20
3962 A3035 37c **multicolored** 1.00 .20
3963 A3036 37c **multicolored** 1.00 .20
3964 A3037 37c **multicolored** 1.00 .20
a. Block or horiz. strip of 4, #3961-3964 4.00
P# block of 4, 6#+P 4.00
P# block of 8, 2 sets of P# + top panel 8.00
Pane of 20 20.00

Flag and Statue of Liberty — A3038

Designed by Carl and Ann Purcell. Printed by Sterling Sommer, Inc. for Ashton-Potter (USA) Ltd. (#3965), Ashton-Potter (USA) Ltd. (#3966, 3970), American Packaging Corporation for Sennett Security Printers (#3967, 3969, 3973), Avery Dennison (#3968, 3972, 3975), Banknote Corporation of America for Sennett Security Products (#3974).

LITHOGRAPHED (#3965, 3966, 3970, 3974), PHOTOGRAVURE

Sheets of 400 in four panes of 100 (#3965), Sheets of 120 in six panes of 20 (#3966)

2005, Dec. 8 **Tagged** ***Perf. 11¼***

3965 A3038 (39c) **multicolored** .80 .20
P# block of 4, 4#+P 5.00 —

Self-Adhesive (#3966, 3968-3975)

Serpentine Die Cut 11¼x10¾

3966 A3038 (39c) **multicolored** .80 .20
P# block of 4, 4#+P 3.20
Pane of 20 16.00
a. Booklet pane of 20 16.00
b. As "a," die cutting omitted —

COIL STAMPS

Perf. 9¾ Vert.

3967 A3038 (39c) **multicolored** .80 .20
Pair 1.60 —
P# strip of 5, #S1111 5.25 —
P# single, #S1111 2.00

Serpentine Die Cut 8½ Vert.

3968 A3038 (39c) **multicolored** .80 .20
Pair 1.60
P# strip of 5, #V1111 5.25
P# single, #V1111 1.50

Serpentine Die Cut 10¼ Vert.

3969 A3038 (39c) **multicolored** .80 .20
Pair 1.60
P# strip of 5, #S1111 5.25
P# single, #S1111 1.50

Serpentine Die Cut 9½ Vert.

3970 A3038 (39c) **multicolored** .80 .20
Pair 1.60
P# strip of 5, #P1111 7.00
P# strip of 5, #P2222 5.75
P# single, #P1111, P2222 2.00

BOOKLET STAMPS

Serpentine Die Cut 11¼x10¾ on 2 or 3 Sides

3972 A3038 (39c) **multicolored** .80 .20
a. Booklet pane of 20 16.00

Serpentine Die Cut 10½x10¾ on 2 or 3 Sides

3973 A3038 (39c) **multicolored** .80 .20
a. Booklet pane of 20 16.00

On both Nos. 3972 and 3973, the sky immediately above the date is bright blue and extends from the left side to beyond the "6" in the date, the left arm of the star at the upper left barely touches the frame line and is without the "USPS" microprinting. They are distinguishable by the die cutting. Nos. 3872a and 3973a are double-sided booklet panes with 12 stamps on one side and eight stamps plus label that serves as a booklet cover on the other side.

No. 3973 was not available until January 2006.

Serpentine Die Cut 11¼x10¾ on 2 or 3 Sides

3974 A3038 (39c) **multicolored** .80 .20
a. Booklet pane of 4 3.20
b. Booklet pane of 6 4.80

Serpentine Die Cut 8 on 2, 3 or 4 Sides

3975 A3038 (39c) **multicolored** .80 .20
a. Booklet pane of 18 14.50
Nos. 3965-3975 (10) 8.00 2.00

Nos. 3965-3975 are dated "2006."

On No. 3966, the sky immediately above the date is bright blue and extends from the left side to beyond the "6" in the date, the left arm of the star at upper left is clear of the top frame, and "USPS" is microprinted on the top red flag stripe.

On No. 3974, the sky immediately above the date is dark blue and extends from the left side to the second "0" in the date, the left arm of the star at upper left touches the top frame, and lacks the microprinting found on No. 3966.

Nos. 3965 and 3970 also have "USPS" microprinted on the top red flag stripe.

Nos. 3966a and 3972a are double-sided booklet panes with 12 stamps on one side and eight stamps plus label that serves as a booklet cover on the other side. On No. 3966a, the stamps on one side are upside-down with relation to the stamps on the other side. On No. 3972a the stamps are all aligned the same on both sides.

LOVE

Birds — A3039

Designed by Craig Frazier. Printed by Avery Dennison.

PHOTOGRAVURE

Serpentine Die Cut 11 on 2, 3, or 4 Sides

2006, Jan. 3 **Tagged**

BOOKLET STAMP

Self-Adhesive

3976 A3039 (39c) **multicolored** .90 .20
a. Booklet pane of 20 18.00

Flag and Statue of Liberty — A3040

Designed by Carl and Ann Purcell. Printed by American Packaging Corporation for Sennett Security Products (#3979, 3982), Ashton-Potter (USA) Ltd. (#3978, 3981). Avery Dennison (#3980).

LITHOGRAPHED (#3978, 3981), PHOTOGRAVURE (#3979-3980, 3983, 3985)

Sheets of 120 in six panes of 20

2006 Tagged ***Serpentine Die Cut 11¼x10¾***

Self-Adhesive

3978 A3040	39c **multicolored,** *Apr. 8*		.80	.20
	P# block of 4, 4#+P		3.20	
	Pane of 20		16.00	
a.	Booklet pane of 10		8.00	
b.	Booklet pane of 20		16.00	
c.	As "b," die cutting omitted on side with 8 stamps		—	

No. 3978 has "USPS" microprinted on top red flag stripe.

No. 3978b is a double-sided booklet with 12 stamps on one side and 8 stamps plus label (booklet cover) on the other side.

Perf. 10 Vert.

COIL STAMPS

3979 A3040	39c **multicolored,** *Mar. 8*	.80	.20
	Pair	1.60	—
	P# strip of 5, #S1111	5.25	—
	P# single, #S1111	—	2.50

Serpentine Die Cut 11 Vert.

3980 A3040	39c **multicolored,** *Jan. 9*	.80	.20
	Pair	1.60	
	P# strip of 5, #V1111	5.25	
	P# single, #V1111		2.50

No. 3980 has rounded corners and lacks microprinting. Unused examples are on backing paper taller than the stamp, and the stamps are spaced approximately 3mm apart.

Serpentine Die Cut 9½ Vert.

3981 A3040	39c **multicolored,** *Apr. 8*	.80	.20
	Pair	1.60	
	P# strip of 5, #P1111	6.25	
	P# single, #P1111		2.00
a.	Die cutting omitted, pair	—	

No. 3981 has "USPS" microprinted on top red flag stripe.

Serpentine Die Cut 10¼ Vert.

3982 A3040	39c **multicolored,** *Apr. 8*	.80	.20
	Pair	1.60	
	P# strip of 5, #S1111	5.25	
	P# single, #S1111		2.00
a.	Vert. pair, unslit between	—	

No. 3982 was not made available until June, despite the official first day of issue.

Serpentine Die Cut 8½ Vert.

3983 A3040	39c **multicolored,** *Apr. 8*	.80	.20
	Pair	1.60	
	P# strip of 5, #V1111	5.25	
	P# single, #V1111	—	2.00

BOOKLET STAMP

Serpentine Die Cut 11¼x10¾ on 2 or 3 Sides

3985 A3040	39c **multicolored,** *Apr. 8*	.80	.20
a.	Booklet pane of 20	16.00	
b.	Serpentine die cut 11.1 on 2 or 3 sides	.80	.20
c.	Booklet pane of 4 #3985b	3.20	
d.	Booklet pane of 6 #3985b	4.80	

Nos. 3983 and 3985 lack the microprinting found on Nos. 3978 and 3981. No. 3983 was not made available until July and No. 3985 was not made available until August, despite the official first day of issue. No. 3985a is a double-sided booklet with 12 stamps on one side and 8 stamps plus label (booklet cover) on the other side.

CHILDREN'S BOOK ANIMALS

The Very Hungry Caterpillar, from *The Very Hungry Caterpillar,* by Eric Carle — A3041

Wilbur, from *Charlotte's Web,* by E. B. White — A3042

Fox in Socks, from *Fox in Socks,* by Dr. Seuss — A3043

Maisy, from *Maisy's ABC,* by Lucy Cousins — A3044

Wild Thing, from *Where the Wild Things Are,* by Maurice Sendak — A3045

Curious George, from *Curious George,* by Margaret and H. A. Rey — A3046

Olivia, from *Olivia,* by Ian Falconer — A3047

Frederick, from *Frederick,* by Leo Lionni — A3048

Designed by Derry Noyes. Printed by American Packaging Corporation for Sennett Security Products.

PHOTOGRAVURE

Sheets of 96 in six panes of 16

2006, Jan. 10 Tagged ***Serpentine Die Cut 10¾***

Self-Adhesive

3987 A3041	39c **multicolored**	.80	.20
3988 A3042	39c **multicolored**	.80	.20
3989 A3043	39c **multicolored**	.80	.20
3990 A3044	39c **multicolored**	.80	.20
3991 A3045	39c **multicolored**	.80	.20
3992 A3046	39c **multicolored**	.80	.20
3993 A3047	39c **multicolored**	.80	.20
3994 A3048	39c **multicolored**	.80	.20
a.	Block of 8, #3987-3994	6.50	
	P# block of 8, 9# + S	6.50	
	Pane of 16	13.00	
	Sheet of 96 (6 panes)	80.00	
	Cross gutter block of 8	15.00	
	Block of 8 with horiz. gutter	9.00	
	Block of 8 different stamps with vert. gutter	8.00	
	Horiz. pair with vert. gutter	2.00	
	Vert. pair with horiz. gutter	2.00	

See Great Britain Nos. 2340-2341.

2006 WINTER OLYMPICS, TURIN, ITALY

Skier — A3049

Designed by Derry Noyes. Printed by Banknote Corporation of America for Sennett Security Products.

LITHOGRAPHED

Sheets of 240 in twelve panes of 20

2006, Jan. 11 Tagged ***Serpentine Die Cut 10¾***

Self-Adhesive

3995 A3049	39c **multicolored**	.80	.20
	P# block of 4, 4# + S	3.20	
	Pane of 20	16.00	

BLACK HERITAGE SERIES

Hattie McDaniel (1895-1952), Actress — A3050

Designed by Ethel Kessler. Printed by Banknote Corporation of America for Sennett Security Products.

LITHOGRAPHED

Sheets of 240 in twelve panes of 20

2006, Jan. 25 Tagged ***Serpentine Die Cut 10¾***

Self-Adhesive

3996 A3050	39c **multicolored**	.80	.20
	P# block of 4, 4# + S	3.20	
	Pane of 20	16.00	

Chinese New Year Types of 1992-2004

Designed by Clarence Lee. Printed by Banknote Corporation of America for Sennett Security Products.

LITHOGRAPHED

2006, Jan. 29 Tagged ***Serpentine Die Cut 10¾***

Self-Adhesive

No.	Description	Unused	Used
3997	Pane of 12	9.75	
a.	A2360 39c Rat	.80	.20
b.	A2413 39c Ox	.80	.20
c.	A2462 39c Tiger	.80	.20
d.	A2535 39c Rabbit	.80	.20
e.	A2602 39c Dragon	.80	.20
f.	A2702 39c Snake	.80	.20
g.	A2752 39c Horse	.80	.20
h.	A2856 39c Ram	.80	.20
i.	A2927 39c Monkey	.80	.20
j.	A2067 39c Rooster	.80	.20
k.	A2146 39c Dog	.80	.20
l.	A2205 39c Boar	.80	.20

WEDDING DOVES

Dove Facing Left — A3051

Dove Facing Right — A3052

Designed by Michael Osborne. Printed by Ashton-Potter (USA) Ltd.

LITHOGRAPHED

BOOKLET STAMPS

Serpentine Die Cut 10¾x11 on 2, 3 or 4 Sides

2006, Mar. 1 Tagged

Self-Adhesive

No.	Description	Unused	Used
3998	A3051 39c **pale lilac & bluish lilac**	.80	.20
a.	Booklet pane of 20	16.00	
b.	As "a," die cutting omitted	—	

Serpentine Die Cut 10¾x11

No.	Description	Unused	Used
3999	A3052 63c **pale green & dull green**	1.25	.50
a.	Booklet pane, 20 each #3998-3999	37.50	
b.	Horiz. pair, #3998-3999 with vertical gutter between	2.10	1.50

Common Buckeye Butterfly — A3053

Designed by Carl T. Herrman. Printed by Sterling Sommer, Inc. for Ashton-Potter (USA) Ltd. (#4000), Avery Dennison (#4001-4002).

LITHOGRAPHED (#4000), PHOTOGRAVURE (#4001-4002)

Sheets of 400 in four panes of 100 (#4000), Sheets of 280 in fourteen panes of 20 (#4001)

2006, Mar. 8 Tagged ***Perf. 11¼***

No.	Description	Unused	Used
4000	A3053 24c **multicolored**	.50	.20
	P# block of 4, 4#+P	8.00	—

Self-Adhesive

Serpentine Die Cut 11

No.	Description	Unused	Used
4001	A3053 24c **multicolored**	.50	.20
	P# block of 4, 4#+V	2.00	
	Pane of 20	10.00	
a.	Serpentine die cut 10¾x11¼ on 3 sides (from booklet panes)	.50	.20
b.	Booklet pane of 10 #4001a	5.00	
c.	Booklet pane of 4 #4001a	2.00	
d.	Booklet pane of 6 #4001a	3.00	

Some panes of No. 4001 contain bottom-row stamps that are 1mm taller than the other stamps on the pane. This most likely was caused by a shift of the die cutting blade cylinder on a low percentage of sheets in the press run.

COIL STAMP

Serpentine Die Cut 8½ Horiz.

No.	Description	Unused	Used
4002	A3053 24c **multicolored**	.50	.20
	Pair	1.00	
	P# strip of 5, #V1111	3.75	
	P# single, #V1111	—	2.00

No. 4001b is a convertible booklet that was sold flat. It has a self-adhesive panel that covers the rouletting on the inside of the booklet cover. Nos. 4001c and 4001d are component panes of a vending machine booklet, which was sold pre-folded and sealed, and which does not have the self-adhesive panel covering the rouletting on the inside of the booklet cover.

CROPS OF THE AMERICAS

Chili Peppers — A3054

Beans — A3055

Sunflower and Seeds — A3056

Squashes — A3057

Corn — A3058

Designed by Phil Jordan. Printed by American Packaging Corporation for Sennett Security Products (#4003-4012), Banknote Corporation of America for Sennett Security Products (#4013-4017).

PHOTOGRAVURE (#4003-4012), LITHOGRAPHED (#4013-4017)

Serpentine Die Cut 10¼ Horiz.

2006, Mar. 16 Tagged

Self-Adhesive

Coil Stamps

No.	Description	Unused	Used
4003	A3054 39c **multicolored**	.85	.20
4004	A3055 39c **multicolored**	.85	.20
4005	A3056 39c **multicolored**	.85	.20
4006	A3057 39c **multicolored**	.85	.20
4007	A3058 39c **multicolored**	.85	.20
a.	Strip of 5, #4003-4007	4.25	
	P# strip of 5, #4003-4007, #S1111	7.00	—
	P# strip of 11, 3 #4005, 2 each #4003-4004, 4006-4007	12.50	
	P# single (#4005), #S1111	—	2.00

Booklet Stamps

Serpentine Die Cut 10¾x10½ on 2 or 3 Sides

No.	Description	Unused	Used
4008	A3058 39c **multicolored**	.80	.20
4009	A3057 39c **multicolored**	.80	.20
4010	A3056 39c **multicolored**	.80	.20
4011	A3055 39c **multicolored**	.80	.20
4012	A3054 39c **multicolored**	.80	.20
a.	Horiz. strip of 5, #4008-4012	4.00	
b.	Booklet pane, 4 each #4008-4012	16.00	

Stamps in Nos. 4012a and 4017a are not adjacent, as one or two rows of selvage is between stamps (or a blank space where selvage was removed by the manufacturer).

No. 4012b is a double-sided booklet with 12 stamps on one side and 8 stamps plus label (booklet cover) on the other side.

"USA" is at right of "39" on No. 4004, at left of "39" on Nos. 4011, 4017. Top of "USA" is aligned with top of "39" on No. 4013, with bottom of "39" on Nos. 4003, 4012.

Serpentine Die Cut 10¾x11¼on 2 or 3 Sides

No.	Description	Unused	Used
4013	A3054 39c **multicolored**	.80	.20
4014	A3058 39c **multicolored**	.80	.20
4015	A3057 39c **multicolored**	.80	.20
4016	A3056 39c **multicolored**	.80	.20
a.	Booklet pane of 4, #4013-4016	3.20	
4017	A3055 39c **multicolored**	.80	.20
a.	Horiz. strip of 5, #4013-4017	4.00	
b.	Booklet pane of 4, #4013-4015, 4017	3.20	
c.	Booklet pane of 6, #4013-4016, 2 #4017	4.80	
d.	Booklet pane of 6, #4013-4015, 4017, 2 #4016	4.80	

The peelable selvage strips were removed by the manufacturer from 1 million of the 11 million vending booklets produced (containing Nos. 4017b, 4017c and 4017d).

X-PLANES

A3059

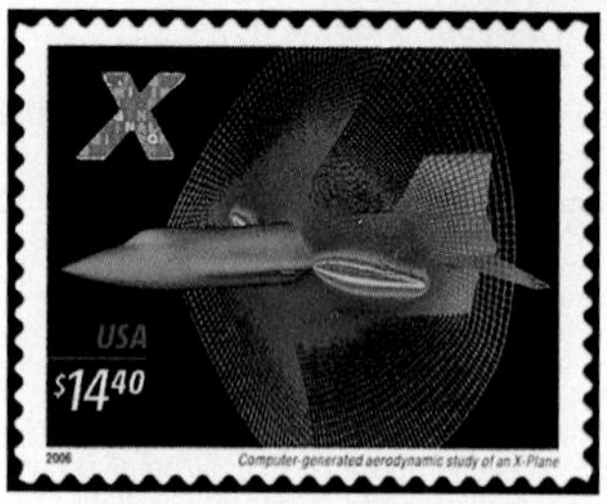

A3060

Designed by Phil Jordan. Printed by Banknote Corporation of America for Sennett Security Products.

LITHOGRAPHED WITH HOLOGRAM AFFIXED

Sheets of 120 in six panes of 20

Serpentine Die Cut 10¾x10½

2006, Mar. 17 Tagged

Self-Adhesive

No.	Description	Unused	Used
4018	A3059 $4.05 **multicolored**	8.00	5.00
	P# block of 4, 4#+S	40.00	
	Pane of 20	160.00	
a.	Silver foil ("X") omitted	—	
4019	A3060 $14.40 **multicolored**	27.50	15.00
	P# block of 4, 4#+S	110.00	
	Pane of 20	550.00	

SUGAR RAY ROBINSON (1921-89), BOXER

A3061

Designed by Carl T. Herrman. Printed by Avery Dennison.

PHOTOGRAVURE

Sheets of 200 in ten panes of 20

2006, Apr. 7 Tagged ***Serpentine Die Cut 11***

Self-Adhesive

No.	Description	Unused	Used
4020	A3061 39c **red & blue**	.80	.20
	P# block of 4, 2#+V	3.20	
	Pane of 20	16.00	

BENJAMIN FRANKLIN (1706-90)

Statesman A3062

Scientist A3063

Printer
A3064

Postmaster
A3065

Designed by Richard Sheaff. Printed by Avery Dennison.

PHOTOGRAVURE

Sheets of 200 in ten panes of 20

2006, Apr. 7 Tagged *Serpentine Die Cut 11*

Self-Adhesive

4021	A3062	39c	**multicolored**	1.10	.20
4022	A3063	39c	**multicolored**	1.10	.20
4023	A3064	39c	**multicolored**	1.10	.20
4024	A3065	39c	**multicolored**	1.10	.20
a.			Block or horiz. strip of 4	4.40	
			P# block of 4, 4#+V	4.50	
			Pane of 20	20.00	

THE ART OF DISNEY: ROMANCE

Mickey and Minnie Mouse — A3066

Cinderella and Prince Charming — A3067

Beauty and the Beast — A3068

Lady and Tramp — A3069

Designed by David Pacheco. Printed by Ashton-Potter (USA) Ltd.

LITHOGRAPHED

Sheets of 180 in nine panes of 20

Serpentine Die Cut 10½x10¾

2006, Apr. 21 Tagged

Self-Adhesive

4025	A3066	39c	**multicolored**	.80	.20
4026	A3067	39c	**multicolored**	.80	.20
4027	A3068	39c	**multicolored**	.80	.20
4028	A3069	39c	**multicolored**	.80	.20
a.			Block or vert. strip of 4, #4025-4028	3.20	
			P# block of 4, 6#+P	3.20	
			Pane of 20	16.00	

LOVE

Birds — A3070

Designed by Craig Frazier. Printed by Avery Dennison.

PHOTOGRAVURE

Serpentine Die Cut 11 on 2, 3 or 4 Sides

2006, May 1 Tagged

Self-Adhesive

Booklet Stamp

4029	A3070	39c	**multicolored**	.80	.20
a.			Booklet pane of 20	16.00	

LITERARY ARTS

Katherine Anne Porter (1890-1980), Author
A3071

Designed by Derry Noyes. Printed by Banknote Corporation of America for Sennett Security Products.

LITHOGRAPHED

Sheets of 240 in twelve panes of 20

2006, May 15 Tagged *Serpentine Die Cut 10¾*

Self-Adhesive

4030	A3071	39c	**multicolored**	.80	.20
			P# block of 4, 4#+S	3.20	
			Pane of 20	16.00	

AMBER ALERT

Mother and Child — A3072

Designed by Derry Noyes. Printed by Avery Dennison.

PHOTOGRAVURE

Sheets of 160 in eight panes of 20

2006, May 25 Tagged *Serpentine Die Cut 10¾*

Self-Adhesive

4031	A3072	39c	**multicolored**	.80	.20
			P# block of 4, 6#+V	3.20	
			Pane of 20	16.00	

Purple Heart Type of 2003

Designed by Carl T. Herrman. Printed by Ashton-Potter (USA) Ltd.

LITHOGRAPHED

Sheets of 120 in six panes of 20

Serpentine Die Cut 11¼x11

2006, May 26 Tagged

Self-Adhesive

4032	A2891	39c	**multicolored**	.80	.20
			P# block of 4, 4#+P	3.20	
			Pane of 20	16.00	

WONDERS OF AMERICA

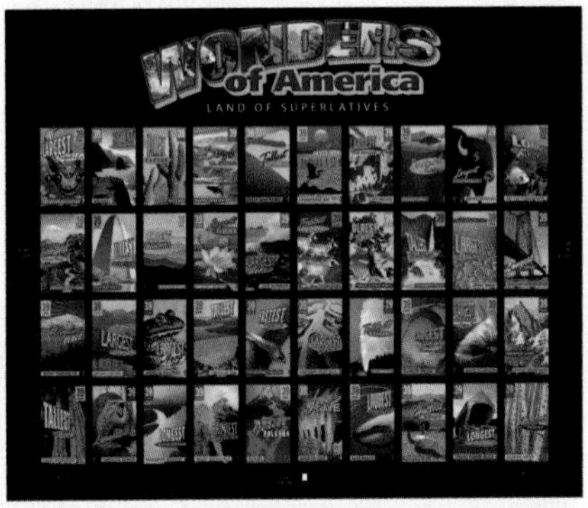

A3073-A3112

Illustration reduced.

Designed by Richard Sheaff. Printed by Avery Dennison.

Designs: No. 4033, American alligator, largest reptile. No. 4034, Moloka'i, highest sea cliffs. No. 4035, Saguaro, tallest cactus. No. 4036, Bering Glacier, largest glacier. No. 4037, Great Sand Dunes, tallest dunes. No. 4038, Chesapeake Bay, largest estuary. No. 4039, Cliff Palace, largest cliff dwelling. No. 4040, Crater Lake, deepest lake. No. 4041, American bison, largest land mammal. No. 4042, Off the Florida Keys, longest reef. No. 4043, Pacific Crest Trail, longest hiking trail. No. 4044, Gateway Arch, tallest man-made monument. No. 4045, Appalachians, oldest mountains. No. 4046, American lotus, largest flower. No. 4047, Lake Superior, largest lake. No. 4048, Pronghorn, fastest land animal. No. 4049, Bristlecone pines, oldest trees. No. 4050, Yosemite Falls, tallest waterfall. No. 4051, Great Basin, largest desert. No. 4052, Verrazano-Narrows Bridge, longest span. No. 4053, Mount Washington, windiest place. No. 4054, Grand Canyon, largest canyon. No. 4055, American bullfrog, largest frog. No. 4056, Oroville Dam, tallest dam. No. 4057, Peregrine falcon, fastest bird. No. 4058, Mississippi River Delta, largest delta. No. 4059, Steamboat, tallest geyser. No. 4060, Rainbow Bridge, largest natural bridge. No. 4061, White sturgeon, largest freshwater fish. No. 4062, Rocky Mountains, longest mountain chain. No. 4063, Coast redwoods, tallest trees. No. 4064, American beaver, largest rodent. No. 4065, Mississippi-Missouri, longest river system. No. 4066, Mount Wai'ale'ale, rainiest spot. No. 4067, Kilauea, most active volcano. No. 4068, Mammoth Cave, longest cave. No. 4069, Blue whale, loudest animal. No. 4070, Death Valley, hottest spot. No. 4071, Cornish-Windsor Bridge, longest covered bridge. No. 4072, Quaking aspen, largest plant.

PHOTOGRAVURE

Sheets of 80 in two panes of 40

2006, May 27 Tagged *Serpentine Die Cut 10¾*

Self-Adhesive

4033	A3073	39c	**multicolored**	.80	.45
4034	A3074	39c	**multicolored**	.80	.45
4035	A3075	39c	**multicolored**	.80	.45
4036	A3076	39c	**multicolored**	.80	.45
4037	A3077	39c	**multicolored**	.80	.45
4038	A3078	39c	**multicolored**	.80	.45
4039	A3079	39c	**multicolored**	.80	.45
4040	A3080	39c	**multicolored**	.80	.45
4041	A3081	39c	**multicolored**	.80	.45
4042	A3082	39c	**multicolored**	.80	.45
4043	A3083	39c	**multicolored**	.80	.45
4044	A3084	39c	**multicolored**	.80	.45
4045	A3085	39c	**multicolored**	.80	.45
4046	A3086	39c	**multicolored**	.80	.45
4047	A3087	39c	**multicolored**	.80	.45
4048	A3088	39c	**multicolored**	.80	.45
4049	A3089	39c	**multicolored**	.80	.45
4050	A3090	39c	**multicolored**	.80	.45
4051	A3091	39c	**multicolored**	.80	.45
4052	A3092	39c	**multicolored**	.80	.45
4053	A3093	39c	**multicolored**	.80	.45
4054	A3094	39c	**multicolored**	.80	.45
4055	A3095	39c	**multicolored**	.80	.45
4056	A3096	39c	**multicolored**	.80	.45
4057	A3097	39c	**multicolored**	.80	.45
4058	A3098	39c	**multicolored**	.80	.45
4059	A3099	39c	**multicolored**	.80	.45

4060	A3100	39c **multicolored**	.80	.45
4061	A3101	39c **multicolored**	.80	.45
4062	A3102	39c **multicolored**	.80	.45
4063	A3103	39c **multicolored**	.80	.45
4064	A3104	39c **multicolored**	.80	.45
4065	A3105	39c **multicolored**	.80	.45
4066	A3106	39c **multicolored**	.80	.45
4067	A3107	39c **multicolored**	.80	.45
4068	A3108	39c **multicolored**	.80	.45
4069	A3109	39c **multicolored**	.80	.45
4070	A3110	39c **multicolored**	.80	.45
4071	A3111	39c **multicolored**	.80	.45
4072	A3112	39c **multicolored**	.80	.45
a.		Pane of 40, #4033-4072	32.00	
		Sheet of 80 (two panes)	65.00	
		Block of 40 different stamps with horiz. gutter between any two rows	32.00	
		Pair with horiz. gutter between (each)	2.00	

EXPLORATION OF EAST COAST BY SAMUEL DE CHAMPLAIN, 400TH ANNIV.

Ship and Map — A3113

A3114

Illustration reduced.

Designed by Rejean Myette and Francois Martin, Canada (#4073), Terrence W. McCaffrey and Francois Martin (#4074). Printed by Ashton-Potter (USA) Ltd. Illustration A3114 is reduced.

LITHOGRAPHED & ENGRAVED

Sheets of 120 in six panes of 20 (#4073), Sheets of 24 in six panes of 4 (#4074)

2006, May 28 Tagged *Serpentine Die Cut 10¾*

Self-Adhesive (#4073)

4073	A3113	39c **multicolored**	.85	.20
		P# block of 4, 6#+P	3.50	
		Pane of 20	17.50	

Souvenir Sheet

Perf. 11

4074	A3114	Sheet, 2 each #4074a, Canada #2156a	4.25	2.00
a.	A3113	39c **multicolored**	.85	.20
		Sheet of 24 (6 panes)	25.00	—
		Cross gutter block of 4 Canadian and 4 American stamps	9.00	—
		Block of 2 Canadian and 2 American stamps with horiz. gutter between	4.75	—
		Horiz. pair of Canadian and American stamps with vert. gutter between	2.25	—

Washington 2006 World Philatelic Exhibition (#4074). Canada No. 2156, which was sold only by Canada Post, has a bar code in the lower left margin of the sheet. No. 4074, which was sold only by the United States Postal Service for $1.75, lacks this bar code.

WASHINGTON 2006 WORLD PHILATELIC EXHIBITION

Souvenir Sheet

A3115

Illustration reduced.

Designed by Richard Sheaff. Printed by Banknote Corporation of America for Sennett Security Products.

LITHOGRAPHED (MARGIN) & ENGRAVED

Sheets of 18 in six panes of 3

2006, May 29 Tagged *Perf. 10¾x10½*

4075	A3115	Pane of 3	16.00	6.00
a.	A174	$1 **violet brown**	2.00	.50
b.	A175	$2 **deep blue**	4.00	1.00
c.	A176	$5 **carmine & blue**	10.00	2.50
		Sheet of 6 panes	96.00	—
		Cross gutter block of 4 panes	64.00	—
		Vert. pair of panes with horiz. gutter between	32.00	—
		Horiz. pair of panes with vert. gutter between	32.00	—

DISTINGUISHED AMERICAN DIPLOMATS

Souvenir Sheet

A3116

Illustration reduced.

Designed by Howard E. Paine. Printed by Avery Dennison.

No. 4076: a, Robert D. Murphy (1894-1978). b, Frances E. Willis (1899-1983). c, Hiram Bingham IV (1903-88). d, Philip C. Habib (1920-92). e, Charles E. Bohlen (1904-74). f, Clifton R. Wharton, Sr. (1899-1990).

PHOTOGRAVURE

Sheets of 90 in fifteen panes of 6

2006, May 29 Tagged *Serpentine Die Cut 10¾*

Self-Adhesive

4076	A3116	Pane of 6	4.80	
a.-f.		39c any single	.80	.20
		Sheet of 15 panes	72.00	
		Cross gutter block of 6	7.00	
		Block of 6 with vert. gutter between	7.00	
		Block of 6 with horiz. gutter between	7.00	
		Horiz. pair with vert. gutter (each)	2.00	
		Vert. pair with horiz. gutter (each)	2.00	

The cross gutter block consists of 1 stamp from each of two panes and 2 stamps from each of two adjacent panes. Plate number, 1#+V, is on margin of backing paper.

LEGENDS OF HOLLYWOOD

Judy Garland (1922-69), Actress — A3117

Designed by Ethel Kessler. Printed by Banknote Corporation of America for Sennett Security Products.

LITHOGRAPHED

Sheets of 120 in six panes of 20

2006, June 10 Tagged *Serpentine Die Cut 10¾*

Self-Adhesive

4077	A3117	39c **multicolored**	.80	.20
		P# block of 4, 4#+S	3.20	
		Pane of 20	16.00	
		Sheet of 120 (6 panes)	97.50	
		Cross gutter block of 8	17.50	
		Block of 8 with vertical gutter	10.00	
		Horiz. pair with vert. gutter	3.00	
		Vert. pair with horiz. gutter	2.00	
a.		Pair, die cutting omitted	—	

Cross gutter block consists of 6 stamps from upper panes and 2 stamps from panes below.

Ronald Reagan Type of 2005

Designed by Howard E. Paine. Printed by American Packaging Corporation for Sennett Security Products.

PHOTOGRAVURE

Sheets of 120 in six panes of 20

2006, June 14 Tagged *Serpentine Die Cut 10¾*

Self-Adhesive

4078	A2974	39c **multicolored**	.80	.20
		P# block of 4, 4#+S	3.20	
		Pane of 20	16.00	

Happy Birthday Type of 2002

Designed by Harry Zelenko. Printed by Avery Dennison.

PHOTOGRAVURE

Sheets of 200 in ten panes of 20

2006, June 23 Tagged *Serpentine Die Cut 11*

Self-Adhesive

4079	A2751	39c **multicolored**	.80	.20
		P# block of 4, 4#+V	3.20	
		Pane of 20	16.00	

BASEBALL SLUGGERS

Roy Campanella (1921-93) — A3118

Hank Greenberg (1911-86) — A3119

Mel Ott (1909-58) — A3120

Mickey Mantle (1931-95) — A3121

Designed by Phil Jordan. Printed by Avery Dennison.

PHOTOGRAVURE

Sheets of 120 in six panes of 20

2006, July 15 Tagged *Serpentine Die Cut 10¾*

Self-Adhesive

4080	A3118 39c **multicolored**		.80	.20
4081	A3119 39c **multicolored**		.80	.20
4082	A3120 39c **multicolored**		.80	.20
4083	A3121 39c **multicolored**		.80	.20
a.	Block or vert. strip of 4, #4080-4083		3.20	
		P# block of 4, 6#+V	3.20	
		P# block of 10, 2 sets of P# + top label	8.00	
		Pane of 20	16.00	
		Sheet of 120 (6 panes)	97.50	
		Cross gutter block of 8	17.50	
		Block of 4 with horiz. gutter	6.00	
		Horiz. pair with vert. gutter	3.00	
		Vert. pair with horiz. gutter	3.00	

Cross gutter block of 8 consists of four stamps from top two panes and four stamps from bottom two panes with the cross gutter between.

DC COMICS SUPERHEROES

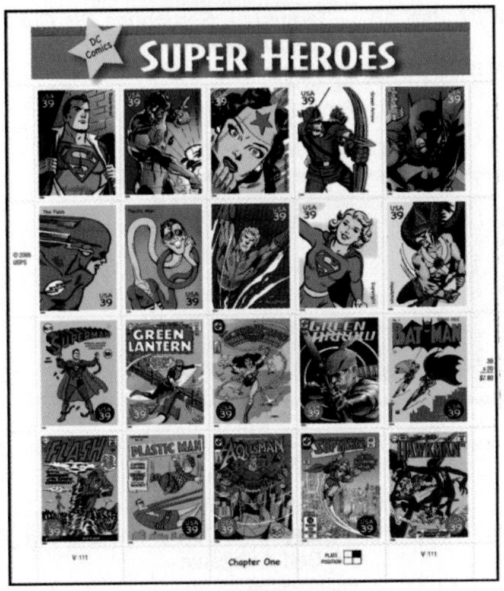

A3122

Illustration reduced.

Designed by Carl T. Herrman. Printed by Avery Dennison.

No. 4084: a, Superman. b, Green Lantern. c, Wonder Woman. d, Green Arrow. e, Batman. f, The Flash. g, Plastic Man. h, Aquaman. i, Supergirl. j, Hawkman. k, Cover of *Superman #11.* l, Cover of *Green Lantern #4.* m, Cover of *Wonder Woman #22 (Second Series).* n, Cover of *Green Arrow #15.* o, Cover of *Batman #1.* p, Cover of *The Flash #111.* q, Cover of *Plastic Man #4.* r, Cover of *Aquaman #5 (of 5).* s, Cover of *The Daring New Adventures of Supergirl #1.* t, Cover of *The Brave and the Bold Presents Hawkman #36.*

PHOTOGRAVURE

Sheets of 80 in four panes of 20

Serpentine Die Cut 10½x10¾

2006, July 20 Tagged

Self-Adhesive

4084	A3122	Pane of 20	16.00	
a.-t.	39c Any single		.80	.20
		Sheet of 80 (4 panes)	65.00	
		Cross gutter block of 20	24.00	
		Horiz. pair with vert. gutter (each)	3.00	
		Vert. pair with horiz. gutter (each)	3.00	

Cross gutter block consists of 12 stamps from the panes on one side of the sheet and 8 stamps from the panes on the other side of the sheet.

MOTORCYCLES

1940 Indian Four — A3123

1918 Cleveland A3124

Generic "Chopper," c. 1970 — A3125

1965 Harley-Davidson Electra-Glide — A3126

Designed by Richard Sheaff. Printed by Avery Dennison.

PHOTOGRAVURE

Sheets of 160 in eight panes of 20

Serpentine Die Cut 10¾x10½

2006, Aug. 7 Tagged

Self-Adhesive

4085	A3123 39c **multicolored**		.90	.20
4086	A3124 39c **multicolored**		.90	.20
4087	A3125 39c **multicolored**		.90	.20
4088	A3126 39c **multicolored**		.90	.20
a.	Block or horiz. strip of 4, #4085-4088		3.60	
		P# block of 4, 5#+V	3.60	
		P# block of 8, 2 sets of P# + top label	7.20	
		Pane of 20	18.00	

AMERICAN TREASURES SERIES
Quilts of Gee's Bend, Alabama

Housetop Variation, by Mary Lee Bendolph — A3127

Pig in a Pen Medallion, by Minnie Sue Coleman — A3128

Nine Patch, by Ruth P. Mosely — A3129

Housetop Four Block Half Log Cabin Variation, by Lottie Mooney — A3130

Roman Stripes Variation, by Loretta Pettway — A3131

Chinese Coins Variation, by Arlonzia Pettway — A3132

Blocks and Strips, by Annie Mae Young — A3133

Medallion, by Loretta Pettway — A3134

Bars and String-pieced Columns, by Jessie T. Pettway — A3135

Medallion With Checkerboard Center, by Patty Ann Williams — A3136

Designed by Derry Noyes. Printed by American Packaging Corporation for Sennett Security Products.

PHOTOGRAVURE

BOOKLET STAMPS

Serpentine Die Cut 10¾ on 2 or 3 Sides

2006, Aug. 24 Tagged

Self-Adhesive

4089	A3127 39c **multicolored**	.80	.20
4090	A3128 39c **multicolored**	.80	.20
4091	A3129 39c **multicolored**	.80	.20
4092	A3130 39c **multicolored**	.80	.20
4093	A3131 39c **multicolored**	.80	.20
4094	A3132 39c **multicolored**	.80	.20
4095	A3133 39c **multicolored**	.80	.20
4096	A3134 39c **multicolored**	.80	.20
4097	A3135 39c **multicolored**	.80	.20

4098 A3136 39c **multicolored** .80 .20
a. Block of 10, #4089-4098 8.00
b. Booklet pane of 20, 2 each #4089-4098 16.00

No. 4098b is a double-sided booklet pane with 12 stamps on one side (1 each #4090-4093, 4095-4098, and 2 each #4089, 4094) and eight stamps (1 each #4090-4093, 4095-4098) plus label (booklet cover) on the other side.

SOUTHERN FLORIDA WETLAND

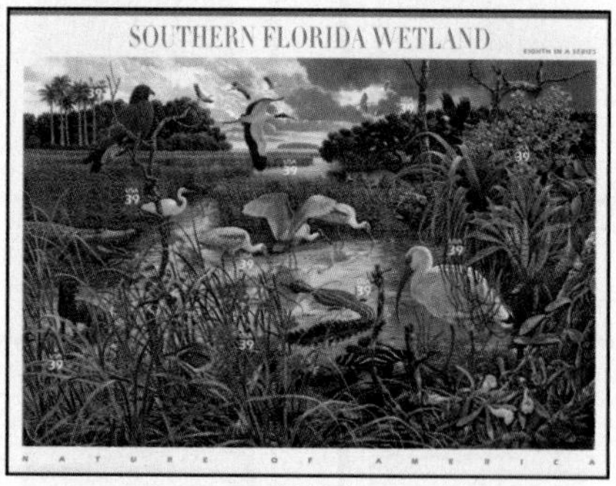

A3137

Illustration reduced.

Designed by Ethel Kessler.

Printed by Avery Dennison.

Wildlife: a, Snail kite. b, Wood storks. c, Florida panther. d, Bald eagle, horiz. e, American crocodile, horiz. f, Roseate spoonbills, horiz. g, Everglades mink. h, Cape Sable seaside sparrow, horiz. i, American alligator, horiz. j, White ibis.

PHOTOGRAVURE
Sheets of 80 in eight panes of 10

2006, Oct. 4 Tagged ***Serpentine Die Cut 10¾***
Self-Adhesive

4099 A3137 Pane of 10 8.00
a.-j. 39c any single .80 .20
Sheet of 8 panes 65.00

CHRISTMAS

Madonna and Child with Bird, by Ignacio Chacón — A3138

Snowflake — A3139

Snowflake — A3140

Snowflake — A3141

Snowflake — A3142

Designed by Michael Osborne (#4100), Richard Sheaff. Printed by Ashton-Potter (USA) Ltd. (#4100), Banknote Corporation of America for Sennett Security Products (#4101-4112), Avery Dennison (#4113-4116).

LITHOGRAPHED, PHOTOGRAVURE (#4113-4116)
Sheets of 240 in twelve panes of 20 (#4101-4104)

Serpentine Die Cut 10¾x11 on 2 or 3 Sides
2006 Tagged
Self-Adhesive
Booklet Stamps (#4100, 4105-4116)

4100 A3138 39c **multicolored,** *Oct. 17* .80 .20
a. Booklet pane of 20 16.00

Base of Denomination Higher Than Year Date
Serpentine Die Cut 11¼x11

4101 A3139 39c **multicolored,** *Oct. 5* .90 .20
4102 A3140 39c **multicolored,** *Oct. 5* .90 .20
4103 A3141 39c **multicolored,** *Oct. 5* .90 .20
4104 A3142 39c **multicolored,** *Oct. 5* .90 .20
a. Block or vert. strip of 4, #4101-4104 3.60
P# block of 4, 4#+S 3.60
Pane of 20 18.00

Base of Denominations Even With Year Date
Serpentine Die Cut 11¼x11½ on 2 or 3 Sides

4105 A3139 39c **multicolored,** *Oct. 5* .80 .20
a. Red missing (PS) —
4106 A3140 39c **multicolored,** *Oct. 5* .80 .20
a. Red missing (PS) —
4107 A3141 39c **multicolored,** *Oct. 5* .80 .20
4108 A3142 39c **multicolored,** *Oct. 5* .80 .20
a. Block of 4, #4105-4108 3.20
b. Booklet pane of 20, 5 #4108a 16.00

Serpentine Die Cut 11¼x11 on 2 or 3 Sides

4109 A3139 39c **multicolored,** *Oct. 5* .80 .20
4110 A3140 39c **multicolored,** *Oct. 5* .80 .20
4111 A3141 39c **multicolored,** *Oct. 5* .80 .20
4112 A3142 39c **multicolored,** *Oct. 5* .80 .20
a. Block of 4, #4109-4112 3.20
b. Booklet pane of 4, #4109-4112 3.20
c. Booklet pane of 6, #4111-4112, 2 each #4109-4110 4.80
d. Booklet pane of 6, #4109-4110, 2 each #4111-4112 4.80

Serpentine Die Cut 8 on 2, 3 or 4 Sides

4113 A3139 39c **multicolored,** *Oct. 5* 1.00 .20
a. Red and green missing (PS) —
4114 A3141 39c **multicolored,** *Oct. 5* 1.00 .20
4115 A3140 39c **multicolored,** *Oct. 5* 1.00 .20
4116 A3142 39c **multicolored,** *Oct. 5* 1.00 .20
a. Block of 4, #4113-4116 4.00
b. Booklet pane of 18, 4 each #4114, 4116, 5 each #4113, 4115 20.00
Nos. 4100-4116 (17) 14.80 3.40

No. 4108b is a double-sided booklet pane with 12 stamps on one side and eight stamps plus label that serves as a booklet cover on the other side. Snowflakes on Nos. 4101-4104 are slightly smaller than those on Nos. 4105-4116.

Eid Type of 2001

Designed by Mohamed Zakariya. Printed by Avery Dennison.

PHOTOGRAVURE
Sheets of 240 in twelve panes of 20

2006, Oct. 6 Tagged ***Serpentine Die Cut 11***
Self-Adhesive

4117 A2734 39c **multicolored** .80 .20
P# block of 4, 3#+V 3.20
Pane of 20 16.00

Hanukkah Type of 2004

Designed by Ethel Kessler. Printed by Banknote Corporation of America for Sennett Security Products.

LITHOGRAPHED
Sheets of 240 in twelve panes of 20

2006, Oct. 6 Tagged ***Serpentine Die Cut 10¾x11***
Self-Adhesive

4118 A2962 39c **multicolored** .80 .20
P# block of 4, 4#+S 3.20
Pane of 20 16.00

Kwanzaa Type of 2004

Designed by Derry Noyes. Printed by Ashton-Potter (USA) Ltd.

LITHOGRAPHED
Sheets of 160 in eight panes of 20

2006, Oct. 6 Tagged ***Serpentine Die Cut 11x10¾***
Self-Adhesive

4119 A2963 39c **multicolored** .80 .20
P# block of 4, 6#+P 3.20
Pane of 20 16.00

BLACK HERITAGE SERIES

Ella Fitzgerald (1917-96), Singer — A3143

Designed by Ethel Kessler. Printed by Ashton-Potter (USA) Ltd.

LITHOGRAPHED
Sheets of 120 in six panes of 20

2007, Jan. 10 Tagged ***Serpentine Die Cut 11***
Self-Adhesive

4120 A3143 39c **multicolored** .80 .20
P# block of 4, 6# + P 3.20
Pane of 20 16.00

OKLAHOMA STATEHOOD, 100TH ANNIV.

Cimarron River — A3144

Designed by Phil Jordan. Printed by Ashton-Potter (USA) Ltd.

LITHOGRAPHED
Sheets of 120 in six panes of 20

2007, Jan. 11 Tagged ***Serpentine Die Cut 11***
Self-Adhesive

4121 A3144 39c **multicolored** .80 .20
P# block of 4, 5# + P 3.20
Pane of 20 16.00

LOVE

Hershey's Kiss — A3145

Designed by Derry Noyes. Printed by Avery Dennison.

PHOTOGRAVURE

Serpentine Die Cut 10¾x11 on 2, 3 or 4 Sides
2007, Jan. 13 Tagged
BOOKLET STAMP
Self-Adhesive

4122 A3145 39c **multicolored** .80 .20
a. Booklet pane of 20 16.00

INTERNATIONAL POLAR YEAR

Souvenir Sheet

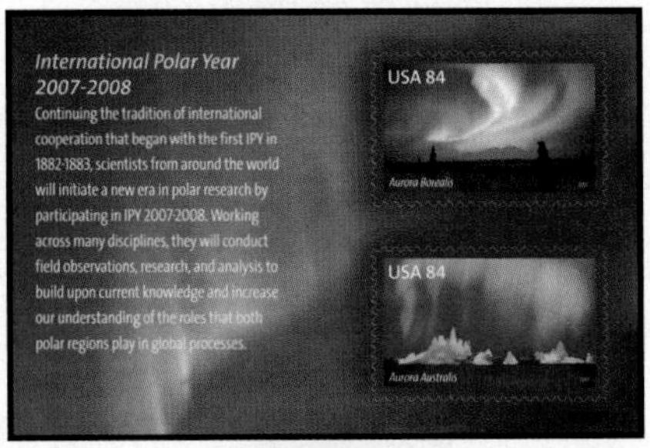

A3146

Illustration reduced.

Designed by Phil Jordan. Printed by Ashton-Potter (USA) Ltd.

No. 4123: a, Aurora borealis. b, Aurora australis.

LITHOGRAPHED

Sheets of 30 in fifteen panes of 2

2007, Feb. 21 Tagged *Serpentine Die Cut 10¾*

Self-Adhesive

4123 A3146 Pane of 2 3.50
a.-b. 84c Either single 1.75 .50
Sheet of 15 panes 52.50
Cross gutter block of 4 stamps 9.00
Vert. pair of panes with horiz. gutter between 7.00
Horiz. pair of panes with vert. gutter between 7.00
Vert. pair of stamps with horiz. gutter between 3.50

LITERARY ARTS

Henry Wadsworth Longfellow (1807-82), Poet — A3147

Designed by Howard E. Paine. Printed by Ashton-Potter (USA) Ltd.

LITHOGRAPHED

Sheets of 120 in six panes of 20

2007, Mar. 15 Tagged *Serpentine Die Cut 10¾*

Self-Adhesive

4124 A3147 39c **multicolored** .80 .20
P# block of 4, 5#+P 3.20
Pane of 20 16.00

"FOREVER" STAMP

Liberty Bell — A3148

Large Microprinting (#4125, 4128)

Small Microprinting (#4126)

Medium Microprinting (#4127)

Designed by Carl T. Herrman. Printed by Avery Dennison (#4125, 4128), Ashton-Potter (USA) Ltd. (#4126), Banknote Corporation of America for Sennett Security Products (#4127)

PHOTOGRAVURE, LITHOGRAPHED (#4126, 4127)

Serpentine Die Cut 11¼x10¾ on 2 or 3 Sides

2007, Apr. 12 Tagged

Booklet Stamps

Self-Adhesive

Large Microprinting, Bell 16mm Wide

4125 A3148 (41c) **multicolored** .85 .20
a. Booklet pane of 20 17.00

Small Microprinting, Bell 16mm Wide

4126 A3148 (41c) **multicolored** .85 .20
a. Booklet pane of 20 17.00

Medium Microprinting, Bell 15mm Wide

4127 A3148 (41c) **multicolored** "2007" year date, prephosphored coated paper (solid tagging) .85 .20
a. Booklet pane of 20 17.00
b. Booklet pane of 4 3.40
c. Booklet pane of 6 5.10
d. Prephosphored paper (mottled tagging) .85 .20
e. Ad "d," booklet pane of 20 17.00
f. (42c) Dated "2008," prephosphored coated paper (solid tagging) .85 .20
g. As "f," booklet pane of 20 17.00
h. (42c) Dated "2008," prephosphored paper (mottled tagging) .85 .20
i. Booklet pane of 20, 8 #4127f, 12 #4127h —

Large Microprinting, Bell 16mm Wide

Serpentine Die Cut 8 on 2, 3 or 4 Sides

4128 A3148 (41c) **multicolored** .85 .20
a. Booklet pane of 18 15.50
Nos. 4125-4128 (4) 3.40 .80

Nos. 4125-4128 were sold for 41c on the day of issue and will be valid for the one ounce first class postage rate after any new rates go into effect. As of May 12, 2008, any "Forever" stamp (Nos. 4125-4128 and 4127d) in stock was sold for 42c.

Nos. 4125a, 4126a, 4127a and 4127e are double-sided booklet panes, with 12 stamps on one side and eight stamps plus a label that serves as a booklet cover on the other side.

Nos. 4127b and 4127c exist with rouletting on backing paper of either gauge 9 1/2 or 13.

Flag — A3149

Designed by Richard Sheaff. Printed by Ashton-Potter (USA) Ltd. (#4129, 4130, 4132), Banknote Corporation of America for Sennett Security Products (#4131, 4133), Avery Dennison (#4134, 4135).

LITHOGRAPHED, PHOTOGRAVURE (#4134, 4135)

Sheets of 400 in four panes of 100 (#4129), Sheets of 120 in six panes of 20 (#4130)

2007, Apr. 12 Tagged *Perf. 11¼*

4129 A3149 (41c) **multicolored** .85 .40
P# block of 4, 4#+P 4.50 —

Self-Adhesive (#4130, 4132-4135)

Serpentine Die Cut 11¼x10¾

4130 A3149 (41c) **multicolored** .85 .20
P# block of 4, 4#+P 3.50
Pane of 20 17.00

COIL STAMPS

Perf. 9¾ Vert.

4131 A3149 (41c) **multicolored** .85 .40
Pair 1.70 .80
P# strip of 5, #S1111 6.00 —
P# single, #S1111 — 2.00

With Perpendicular Corners

Serpentine Die Cut 9½ Vert.

4132 A3149 (41c) **multicolored** .85 .20
Pair 1.70
P# strip of 5, #P1111 6.00
P# single, #P1111 — 2.00

Serpentine Die Cut 11 Vert.

4133 A3149 (41c) **multicolored** .85 .20
Pair 1.70
P# strip of 5, #S1111 6.00
P# single, #S1111 — 2.00
a. Die cutting omitted, pair —

Serpentine Die Cut 8½ Vert.

4134 A3149 (41c) **multicolored** .85 .20
Pair 1.70
P# strip of 5, #V1111 6.00
P# single, #V1111 — 2.00

With Rounded Corners

Serpentine Die Cut 11 Vert.

4135 A3149 (41c) **multicolored** .85 .20
Pair 1.70
P# strip of 5, #V1111 6.00
P# single, #V1111 — 2.00
Nos. 4129-4135 (7) 5.95 1.80

Nos. 4132-4134 are on backing paper as high as the stamp. No. 4135 is on backing paper that is larger than the stamp.

SETTLEMENT OF JAMESTOWN, 400TH ANNIV.

Ships Susan Constant, Godspeed and Discovery — A3150

Illustration reduced.

Designed by Richard Sheaff. Printed by Banknote Corporation of America for Sennett Security Products.

LITHOGRAPHED

Double-sided panes of 20 (19 on one side, 1 on other side)

Serpentine Die Cut 10½x10½x10¾

2007, May 11 Tagged

Self-Adhesive

4136 A3150 41c **multicolored** 1.00 .20
Pane of 20 20.00

WILDLIFE

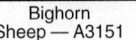

Bighorn Sheep — A3151

Florida Panther — A3152

Designed by Carl T. Herrman. Printed by Ashton-Potter (USA) Ltd. (#4137, 4139), Avery Dennison (#4138, 4142), Banknote Corporation of America for Sennett Security Products (#4140, 4141).

LITHOGRAPHED, PHOTOGRAVURE (#4138, 4142)

Sheets of 400 in four panes of 100 (#4137), Sheets of 280 in fourteen panes of 20 (#4138), Sheets of 120 in six panes of 20 (#4139)

2007 Tagged *Perf. 11¼x11*

4137 A3152 26c **multicolored,** *May 12* .55 .20
P# block of 4, 4#+P 3.25 —

Self-Adhesive

Serpentine Die Cut 11

4138 A3151 17c **multicolored,** *May 14* .35 .20
P# block of 4, 4#+V 1.40
Pane of 20 7.00

Serpentine Die Cut 11¼x11

4139 A3152 26c **multicolored,** *May 12* .55 .20
P# block of 4, 4#+P 2.25
Pane of 20 11.00

Coil Stamps

Serpentine Die Cut 11 Vert.

4140 A3151 17c **multicolored,** *May 21* .35 .20
Pair .70
P# strip of 5, #S11111111 3.25
P# single, #S11111111 — 1.75

4141 A3152 26c **multicolored,** *May 12* .55 .20
Pair 1.10
P# strip of 5, #S1111 4.00
P# single, #S1111 — 2.00
a. Die cutting omitted, pair —

Booklet Stamp

Serpentine Die Cut 11¼x11 on 3 Sides

4142 A3152 26c **multicolored,** *May 12* .55 .20
a. Booklet pane of 10 5.50

Nos. 4137 and 4139 have microprinted "USPS" to the left and above the lower left whisker. No. 4140 has microprinted "USPS" on right horn. No. 4141 has microprinted "USPS" along the right edge of the stamp just above the panther. Nos. 4138 and 4142 lack microprinting.

PREMIERE OF MOVIE "STAR WARS," 30TH ANNIV.

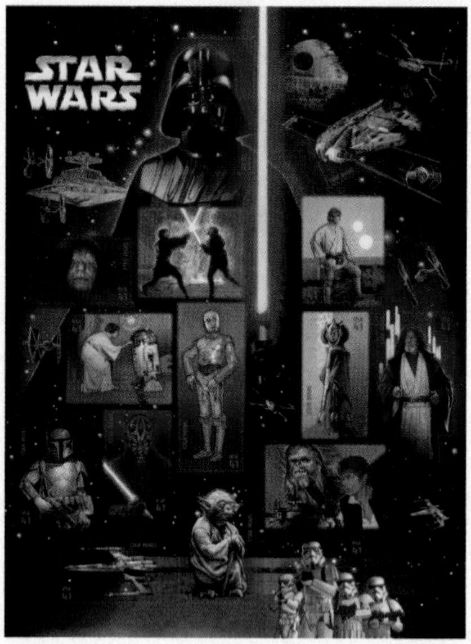

A3153

Designed by Terrence McCaffrey and William J. Gicker, Jr.. Printed by Banknote Corporation of America for Sennett Security Products.

No. 4143: a, Darth Vader (40x53mm). b, Millennium Falcon (47x25mm). c, Emperor Palpatine (41x26mm). d, Anakin Skywalker and Obi-Wan Kenobi (41x33mm). e, Luke Skywalker (31x41mm). f, Princess Leia and R2-D2 (41x33mm). g, C-3PO (21x65mm). h, Queen Padmé Amidala (26x48mm). i, Obi-Wan Kenobi (31x48mm). j, Boba Fett (32x40mm). k, Darth Maul (26x41mm). l, Chewbacca and Han Solo (48x31mm). m, X-wing Starfighter (41x26mm). n, Yoda (31x48mm). o, Stormtroopers (41x31mm).

LITHOGRAPHED

Sheets of 45 in three panes of 15

2007, May 27 Tagged *Serpentine Die Cut 11*

Self-Adhesive

4143	A3153	Pane of 15	13.00	
a.-o.		41c Any single	.85	.20
		Sheet of 45 (3 panes)	40.00	
		Block of 15 with vertical gutter (6 stamps at left and 9 stamps at right)	16.50	

PRESIDENTIAL AIRCRAFT

Air Force One — A3154

Marine One — A3155

Designed by Phil Jordan. Printed by Ashton-Potter (USA) Ltd. (#4144), Banknote Corporation of America for Sennett Security Products (#4145).

LITHOGRAPHED & ENGRAVED (#4144), LITHOGRAPHED (#4145)

Sheets of 120 in six panes of 20

2007, June 13 Tagged *Serpentine Die Cut 10¾*

Self-Adhesive

4144	A3154	$4.60	**multicolored**	9.25	5.00
			P# block of 4, 6#+P	37.50	
			Pane of 20	190.00	
a.		Black (engr.) omitted		—	
4145	A3155	$16.25	**multicolored**	27.50	16.00
			P# block of 4, 5#+S	110.00	
			Pane of 20	550.00	

PACIFIC LIGHTHOUSES

Diamond Head Lighthouse, Hawaii — A3156

Five Finger Lighthouse, Alaska — A3157

Grays Harbor Lighthouse, Washington — A3158

Umpqua River Lighthouse, Oregon — A3159

St. George Reef Lighthouse, California — A3160

Designed by Howard E. Paine. Printed by Avery Dennison.

PHOTOGRAVURE

Sheets of 160 in eight panes of 20

2007, June 21 Tagged *Serpentine Die Cut 11*

Self-Adhesive

4146	A3156	41c	**multicolored**	.85	.20
4147	A3157	41c	**multicolored**	.85	.20
4148	A3158	41c	**multicolored**	.85	.20
4149	A3159	41c	**multicolored**	.85	.20
4150	A3160	41c	**multicolored**	.85	.20
a.		Horiz. strip of 5, #4146-4150		4.25	
			P# block of 10, 5#+V	8.50	
			Pane of 20	17.00	

WEDDING HEARTS

Heart With Lilac Background — A3161

Heart With Pink Background — A3162

Designed by Carl T. Herrman. Printed by Ashton-Potter (USA) Ltd. (#4151), Avery Dennison (#4152).

LITHOGRAPHED (#4151), PHOTOGRAVURE (#4152)

BOOKLET STAMP (#4151)

Sheets of 240 in twelve panes of 20 (#4152)

Serpentine Die Cut 10¾ on 2, 3 or 4 Sides

2007, June 27 Tagged

Self-Adhesive

4151	A3161	41c	**multicolored**	.85	.20
a.		Booklet pane of 20		17.00	

Serpentine Die Cut 10¾x11

4152	A3162	58c	**multicolored**	1.25	.25
			P# block of 4, 4#+V	5.00	
			Pane of 20	25.00	

POLLINATION

Purple Nightshade, Morrison's Bumblebee A3163

Hummingbird Trumpet, Calliope Hummingbird A3164

Saguaro, Lesser Long-nosed Bat — A3165

Prairie Ironweed, Southern Dogface Butterfly A3166

Designed by Steve Buchanan. Printed by Ashton-Potter (USA) Ltd.

No. 4153: Type I, Tip of bird wing is directly under center of "U" in "USA," straight edge at left. Type II, Tip of bird wing is directly under the right line of the "U" in "USA," straight edge at right.

No. 4154: Type I, Tip of bird wing is even with the top of denomination, straight edge at right. Type II, Tip of bird wing is well above denomination, straight edge at left.

No. 4155: Type I, Top of "USA" is even with the lower portion of the nearest unopened green saguaro flower bud, straight edge at left. Type II, Top of "USA" is even with the point where the flower and unopened green saguaro bud meet, straight edge at right.

No. 4156: Type I, Bottom of denomination is even with top point of the white triangle found between the bottom of the purple flower and the green leaf below it, straight edge at right. Type II, Bottom of denomination is even with the lower point of the white triangle found between the bottom of the purple flower and the green leaf below it, straight edge at left.

LITHOGRAPHED

Serpentine Die Cut 11 on 2, 3 or 4 Sides

2007, June 29 Tagged

Self-Adhesive

Booklet Stamps

4153	A3163	41c	**multicolored,** Type I	.85	.20
a.		Type II		.85	.20
4154	A3164	41c	**multicolored,** Type I	.85	.20
a.		Type II		.85	.20
4155	A3165	41c	**multicolored,** Type I	.85	.20
a.		Type II		.85	.20
4156	A3166	41c	**multicolored,** Type I	.85	.20
a.		Type II		.85	.20
b.		Block of 4, #4153-4156		3.40	
c.		Block of 4, #4153a-4156a		3.40	
d.		Booklet pane of 20, 3 each #4153-4156, 2 each #4153a-4156a		17.00	

No. 4156d is a double-sided booklet with 12 stamps (2 each #4153-4156, 1 each #4153a-4156a) on one side and 8 stamps plus label (booklet cover) on the other side.

Patriotic Banner — A3167

Designed by Michael Osborne. Printed by Avery-Dennison (#4157), Banknote Corporation of America for Sennett Security Products (#4158).

PHOTOGRAVURE (#4157), LITHOGRAPHED (#4158)

Serpentine Die Cut 11 Vert.

2007, July 4 **Untagged**

Coil Stamps

Self-Adhesive

4157 A3167 (10c) **multicolored**		.20	.20
	Pair	.40	
	P# strip of 5, #V111	2.50	
	P# single, #V111	—	1.75

Serpentine Die Cut 11¾ Vert.

4158 A3167 (10c) **multicolored**		.20	.20
	Pair	.40	
	P# strip of 5, #S111	2.50	
	P# single, #S111	—	1.75

MARVEL COMICS SUPERHEROES

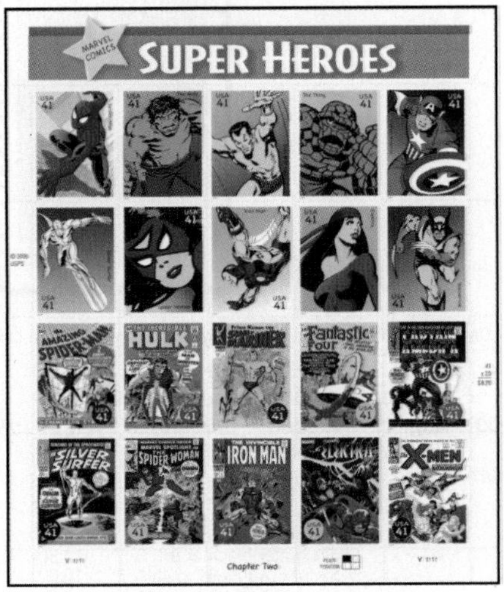

A3168

Illustration reduced.

Designed by Carl T. Herrman. Printed by Avery Dennison.

No. 4159: a, Spider-man. b, The Hulk. c, Sub-Mariner. d, The Thing. e, Captain America. f, Silver Surfer. g, Spider-Woman. h, Iron Man. i, Elektra. j, Wolverine. k, Cover of *The Amazing Spider-Man #1*. l, Cover of *The Incredible Hulk #1*. m, Cover of *Sub-Mariner #1*. n, Cover of *The Fantastic Four #3*. o, Cover of *Captain America #100*. p, Cover of *The Silver Surfer #1*. q, Cover of *Marvel Spotlight on The Spider-Woman #32*. r, Cover of *Iron Man #1*. s, Cover of *Daredevil #176 Featuring Elektra*. t, Cover of *The X-Men #1*.

PHOTOGRAVURE

Sheets of 80 in four panes of 20

Serpentine Die Cut 10½x10¾

2007, July 26 **Tagged**

Self-Adhesive

4159 A3168	Pane of 20	17.00	
a.-t.	41c Any single	.85	.20
	Sheet of 80 (4 panes)	68.00	
	Cross gutter block of 20	25.00	
	Horiz. pair with vert. gutter (each)	3.00	
	Vert. pair with horiz. gutter (each)	3.00	

Cross gutter block consists of 12 stamps from the panes on one side of the sheet and 8 stamps from the panes on the other side of the sheet.

VINTAGE MAHOGANY SPEEDBOATS

1915 Hutchinson — A3169

1954 Chris-Craft — A3170

1939 Hacker-Craft A3171

1931 Gar Wood — A3172

Designed by Carl T. Herrman. Printed by Ashton-Potter (USA) Ltd.

LITHOGRAPHED

Sheets of 72 in six panes of 12

2007, Aug. 4 **Tagged** ***Serpentine Die Cut 10½***

Self-Adhesive

4160 A3169 41c **multicolored**		.85	.20
4161 A3170 41c **multicolored**		.85	.20
4162 A3171 41c **multicolored**		.85	.20
4163 A3172 41c **multicolored**		.85	.20
a.	Horiz. strip of 4, #4160-4163	3.40	
	P# block of 8, 4#+P	6.80	
	Pane of 12	10.20	

Purple Heart Type of 2003

Designed by Carl T. Herrman. Printed by Ashton-Potter (USA) Ltd.

LITHOGRAPHED

Sheets of 120 in six panes of 20

Serpentine Die Cut 11¼x10¾

2007, Aug. 7 **Tagged**

Self-Adhesive

4164 A2891 41c **multicolored**		.85	.20
	P# block of 4, 4#+P	3.40	
	Pane of 20	17.00	

AMERICAN TREASURES SERIES

Magnolia and Irises, Stained Glass by Louis Comfort Tiffany — A3173

Designed by Derry Noyes. Printed by Ashton-Potter (USA) Ltd.

LITHOGRAPHED

BOOKLET STAMP

Serpentine Die Cut 10¾ on 2 or 3 Sides

2007, Aug. 9 **Tagged**

Self-Adhesive

4165 A3173 41c **multicolored**		.85	.20
a.	Booklet pane of 20	17.00	

No. 4165a is a double-sided booklet pane with 12 stamps on one side and eight stamps plus label (booklet cover) on the other side.

FLOWERS

Iris — A3174

Dahlia — A3175

Magnolia — A3176

Red Gerbera Daisy — A3177

Coneflower — A3178

Tulip — A3179

Water Lily — A3180

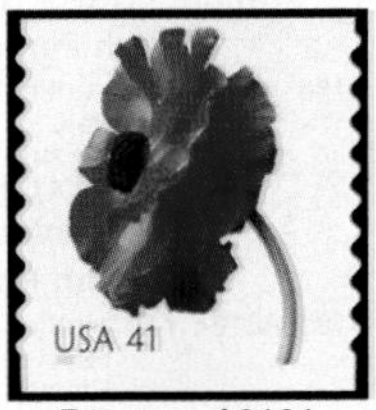

Poppy — A3181

Chrysanthemum A3182

Orange Gerbera Daisy A3183

Designed by Carl T. Herrman. Printed by Ashton-Potter (USA) Ltd. (#4166-4175), Avery Dennison (#4176-4185)

LITHOGRAPHED, PHOTOGRAVURE (#4176-4185)

Serpentine Die Cut 9½ Vert.

2007, Aug. 10 **Tagged**

COIL STAMPS

Self-Adhesive

4166	A3174	41c	**multicolored**	.85	.20
4167	A3175	41c	**multicolored**	.85	.20
4168	A3176	41c	**multicolored**	.85	.20
4169	A3177	41c	**multicolored**	.85	.20
4170	A3178	41c	**multicolored**	.85	.20
4171	A3179	41c	**multicolored**	.85	.20
4172	A3180	41c	**multicolored**	.85	.20
4173	A3181	41c	**multicolored**	.85	.20
4174	A3182	41c	**multicolored**	.85	.20
4175	A3183	41c	**multicolored**	.85	.20
a.			Strip of 10, #4166-4175	8.50	
			P# strip of 11, 2 # 4175, 1 each #4166-4174, #P1111	13.00	—
			P# single (#4170), #P1111	—	2.00

BOOKLET STAMPS

Serpentine Die Cut 11¼x11½ on 2 or 3 Sides

4176	A3182	41c	**multicolored**	.85	.20
4177	A3183	41c	**multicolored**	.85	.20
4178	A3174	41c	**multicolored**	.85	.20
4179	A3175	41c	**multicolored**	.85	.20
4180	A3176	41c	**multicolored**	.85	.20
4181	A3177	41c	**multicolored**	.85	.20
4182	A3180	41c	**multicolored**	.85	.20
4183	A3181	41c	**multicolored**	.85	.20
4184	A3178	41c	**multicolored**	.85	.20
4185	A3179	41c	**multicolored**	.85	.20
a.			Booklet pane of 20, 2 each #4176-4185	17.00	
b.			As "a," Die cutting missing on Nos. 4178 & 4183 on pront side (PS)		—

No. 4185a is a double-sided booklet pane with 12 stamps on one side (2 each #4176-4177, 1 each #4178-4185) and eight stamps (#4178-4185) plus label (booklet cover) on the other side.

Flag — A3184

Designed by Richard Sheaff. Printed by Avery Dennison (#4188, 4189), Ashton-Potter (USA) Ltd. (#4186, 4190), Banknote Corporation of America for Sennett Security Products (#4187, 4191).

LITHOGRAPHED, PHOTOGRAVURE (#4188, 4189)

Serpentine Die Cut 8½ Vert.

2007, Aug. 15 **Tagged**

COIL STAMPS

Self-Adhesive

With "USPS" Microprinted on Right Side of Flagpole

4186	A3184	41c	**multicolored**	.85	.20
			Pair	1.60	
			P# strip of 5, #P11111	6.00	
			P# single, #P11111	—	2.00

With "USPS" Microprinted on Left Side of Flagpole

Serpentine Die Cut 11 Vert.

4187	A3184	41c	**multicolored**	.85	.20
			Pair	1.60	
			P# strip of 5, #S11111	6.00	
			P# single, #S11111	—	2.00

Without "USPS" Microprinting on Flagpole

With Perpendicular Corners

4188	A3184	41c	**multicolored**	.85	.20
			Pair	1.60	
			P# strip of 5, #V11111	6.00	
			P# single, #V11111	—	2.00

Serpentine Die Cut 11 Vert.

With Rounded Corners

4189	A3184	41c	**multicolored**	.85	.20
			Pair	1.60	
			P# strip of 5, #V11111	6.00	
			P# single, #V11111	—	2.00

BOOKLET STAMPS

Serpentine Die Cut 11¼x10¾ on 3 Sides

With "USPS" Microprinted on Right Side of Flagpole

4190	A3184	41c	**multicolored**	.85	.20
a.			Booklet pane of 10	8.50	

With "USPS" Microprinted on Left Side of Flagpole

Serpentine Die Cut 11¼x10¾ on 2 or 3 Sides

4191	A3184	41c	**multicolored**	.85	.20
a.			Booklet pane of 20	17.00	

No. 4188 is on backing paper as high as the stamp. No. 4189 is on backing paper that is larger than the stamp. The microprinting on Nos. 4190 and 4191 is under the ball of the flagpole. The flagpole is light gray on No. 4190 and dark gray on No. 4191. No. 4191a is a double-sided booklet with 12 stamps on one side and 8 stamps plus label (booklet cover) on the other side.

Nos. 4188-4189 lack "USPS" microprinting on the flagpole. No. 4186 was not sold to the public until October 2007 and No. 4187 was not sold to the public until November 2007.

THE ART OF DISNEY: MAGIC

Mickey Mouse — A3185

Peter Pan and Tinker Bell — A3186

Dumbo and Timothy Mouse — A3187

Aladdin and Genie — A3188

Designed by David Pacheco. Printed by Avery Dennison.

PHOTOGRAVURE

Sheets of 160 in eight panes of 20

Serpentine Die Cut 10½x10¾

2007, Aug. 16 **Tagged**

Self-Adhesive

4192	A3185	41c	**multicolored**	.85	.20
4193	A3186	41c	**multicolored**	.85	.20
4194	A3187	41c	**multicolored**	.85	.20
4195	A3188	41c	**multicolored**	.85	.20
a.			Block of 4, #4192-4195	3.40	
			P# block of 4, 6#+V	3.40	
			P# block of 10, 2 sets of P# + top label	8.50	
			Pane of 20	17.00	

CELEBRATE

A3189

Designed by Ethel Kessler. Printed by Banknote Corporation of America for Sennett Security Products.

LITHOGRAPHED

Sheets of 160 in eight panes of 20

2007, Aug. 17 **Tagged** ***Serpentine Die Cut 10¾***

Self-Adhesive

4196	A3189	41c	**multicolored**	.85	.20
			P# block of 4, 4#+S	3.40	
			Pane of 20	17.00	

LEGENDS OF HOLLYWOOD

James Stewart (1908-97), Actor — A3190

Designed by Phil Jordan. Printed by Ashton-Potter (USA) Ltd.

LITHOGRAPHED

Sheets of 180 in nine panes of 20

2007, Aug. 17 **Tagged** ***Serpentine Die Cut 10¾***

Self-Adhesive

4197	A3190	41c	**multicolored**	.85	.20
			P# block of 4, 4#+P	3.40	
			Pane of 20	17.00	
			Sheet of 180 (9 panes)	155.00	
			Cross gutter block of 8	17.50	
			Block of 8 with vert. gutter	10.00	
			Horiz. pair with vert. gutter	3.00	
			Vert. pair with horiz. gutter	2.00	

The cross gutter block consists of 2 stamps from the two upper panes and 6 stamps from the two lower panes.

ALPINE TUNDRA

A3191

Illustration reduced.

Designed by Ethel Kessler. Printed by Banknote Corporation of America for Sennett Security Products.

Wildlife: a, Elk. b, Golden eagle, horiz. c, Yellow-bellied marmot. d, American pika. e, Bighorn sheep. f, Magdalena alpine butterfly. g, White-tailed ptarmigan. h, Rocky Mountain parnassian butterfly. i, Melissa arctic butterfly, horiz. j, Brown-capped rosy-finch, horiz.

PHOTOGRAVURE

Sheets of 80 in eight panes of 10

2007, Aug. 28 **Tagged** ***Serpentine Die Cut 10¾***

Self-Adhesive

4198	A3191	Pane of 10	8.50	
a.-j.		41c any single	.85	.20
		Sheet of 8 panes	67.50	

GERALD R. FORD

Gerald R. Ford (1913-2006), 38th President — A3192

Designed by Ethel Kessler. Printed by Ashton-Potter (USA) Ltd.

LITHOGRAPHED
Sheets of 120 in six panes of 20

2007, Aug. 31 **Tagged** ***Serpentine Die Cut 11***
Self-Adhesive

4199	A3192 41c **multicolored**	.85	.20
	P# block of 4, 5#+P	3.40	
	Pane of 20	17.00	
	Sheet of 120 (6 panes)	105.00	
	Cross gutter block of 4	8.50	
	Horiz. pair with vert. gutter	3.00	
	Vert. pair with horiz. gutter	2.00	

JURY DUTY

Twelve Jurors — A3193

Designed by Carl T. Herrman. Printed by Ashton-Potter (USA) Ltd.

LITHOGRAPHED
Sheets of 120 in six panes of 20

2007, Sept. 12 **Tagged** ***Serpentine Die Cut 10½***
Self-Adhesive

4200	A3193 41c **multicolored**	.85	.20
	P# block of 4, 5#+P	3.40	
	Pane of 20	17.00	

MENDEZ V. WESTMINSTER, 60th ANNIV.

A3194

Designed by Ethel Kessler. Printed by Ashton-Potter (USA) Ltd.

LITHOGRAPHED
Sheets of 120 in six panes of 20

2007, Sept. 14 **Tagged** ***Serpentine Die Cut 11***
Self-Adhesive

4201	A3194 41c **multicolored**	.85	.20
	P# block of 4, 4#+P	3.40	
	Pane of 20	17.00	

Eid Type of 2001

Designed by Mohamed Zakariya. Printed by Avery Dennison.

PHOTOGRAVURE
Sheets of 240 in twelve panes of 20

2007, Sept. 28 **Tagged** ***Serpentine Die Cut 11***
Self-Adhesive

4202	A2734 41c **multicolored**	.85	.20
	P# block of 4, 3#+V	3.40	
	Pane of 20	17.00	

AURORAS

Aurora Borealis A3195

Aurora Australis A3196

Designed by Phil Jordan. Printed by Ashton-Potter (USA) Ltd.

LITHOGRAPHED
Sheets of 120 in six panes of 20

2007, Oct. 1 **Tagged** ***Serpentine Die Cut 10¾***
Self-Adhesive

4203	A3195 41c **multicolored**	.90	.20
4204	A3196 41c **multicolored**	.90	.20
a.	Horiz. or vert. pair, #4203-4204	1.80	
	P# block of 4, 5#+P	4.00	
	Pane of 20	20.00	

YODA

A3197

Designed by Greg Breeding. Printed by Banknote Corporation of America for Sennett Security Products.

LITHOGRAPHED
Sheets of 120 in six panes of 20
Serpentine Die Cut 10½x10¾

2007, Oct. 25 **Tagged**
Self-Adhesive

4205	A3197 41c **multicolored**	.85	.20
	P# block of 4, 5#+S	3.40	
	Pane of 20	17.00	
	Sheet of 60 (left or right)	51.00	
	Vert. pair with horiz. gutter	2.00	

CHRISTMAS

Madonna of the Carnation, by Bernardino Luini — A3198

Knit Reindeer — A3199

Knit Christmas Tree — A3200

Knit Snowman — A3201

Knit Bear — A3202

Knit Reindeer — A3203

Knit Christmas Tree — A3204

Knit Snowman — A3205

Knit Bear — A3206

Designed by Richard Sheaff (#4206), Carl T. Herrman. Printed by Ashton-Potter (USA) Ltd. (#4206), Banknote Corporation of America for Sennett Security Products (#4207-4214), Avery Dennison (#4215-4218).

LITHOGRAPHED, PHOTOGRAVURE (#4215-4218)
Sheets of 160 in eight panes of 20 (#4207-4210)
Serpentine Die Cut 10¾x11 on 2 or 3 Sides

2007, Oct. 25 **Tagged**
Self-Adhesive
Booklet Stamps (#4206, 4211-4218)

4206	A3198 41c **multicolored**	.85	.20
a.	Booklet pane of 20	17.00	
	Serpentine Die Cut 10¾		
4207	A3199 41c **multicolored**	.85	.20
a.	Overall tagging	.85	.20
4208	A3200 41c **multicolored**	.85	.20
a.	Overall tagging	.85	.20
4209	A3201 41c **multicolored**	.85	.20
a.	Overall tagging	.85	.20
4210	A3202 41c **multicolored**	.85	.20
a.	Overall tagging	.85	.20
b.	Block or vert. strip of 4, #4207-4210	3.40	
	P# block of 4, 4#+S	3.40	
	Pane of 20	17.00	
c.	Block of 4, #4207a-4210a	3.40	
d.	Booklet pane of 20, 5 each #4207-4210	17.00	
	Serpentine Die Cut 11¼x11 on 2 or 3 Sides		
4211	A3203 41c **multicolored**	.85	.20
4212	A3204 41c **multicolored**	.85	.20
4213	A3205 41c **multicolored**	.85	.20
4214	A3206 41c **multicolored**	.85	.20
a.	Block of 4, #4211-4214	3.40	
b.	Booklet pane of 4, #4211-4214	3.40	
c.	Booklet pane of 6, #4213-4214, 2 each #4211-4212	5.10	
d.	Booklet pane of 6, #4211-4212, 2 each #4213-4214	5.10	
	Serpentine Die Cut 8 on 2, 3 or 4 Sides		
4215	A3203 41c **multicolored**	.85	.20
4216	A3204 41c **multicolored**	.85	.20
4217	A3205 41c **multicolored**	.85	.20

4218 A3206 41c **multicolored** .85 .20
a. Block of 4, #4215-4218 3.40
b. Booklet pane of 18, 4 each #4215, 4218, 5 each #4216, 4217 15.50
Nos. 4206-4218 (13) 11.05 2.60

No. 4206a is a double-sided booklet pane with 12 stamps on one side and eight stamps plus label that serves as a booklet cover on the other side.

Nos. 4207-4210 were printed on prephosphored paper (solid tagging).

No. 4210d is a double-sided booklet pane with 12 stamps on one side (3 each of Nos. 4207a-4210a) and eight stamps (2 each of Nos. 4207a-4210a) plus label that serves as a booklet cover on the other side.

Hanukkah Type of 2004

Designed by Ethel Kessler. Printed by Banknote Corporation of America for Sennett Security Products.

LITHOGRAPHED
Sheets of 160 in eight panes of 20
Serpentine Die Cut 10¾x11

2007, Oct. 26 **Tagged**
Self-Adhesive

4219 A2962 41c **multicolored** .85 .20
P# block of 4, 4#+S 3.40
Pane of 20 17.00

Kwanzaa Type of 2004

Designed by Derry Noyes. Printed by Ashton-Potter (USA) Ltd.

LITHOGRAPHED
Sheets of 160 in eight panes of 20
Serpentine Die Cut 11x10¾

2007, Oct. 26 **Tagged**
Self-Adhesive

4220 A2963 41c **multicolored** .85 .20
P# block of 4, 6#+P 3.40
Pane of 20 17.00

CHINESE NEW YEAR

Year of the Rat — A3207

Designed by Ethel Kessler. Printed by Avery Dennison

PHOTOGRAVURE
Sheets of 108 in nine panes of 12

2008, Jan. 9 **Tagged** ***Serpentine Die Cut 10¾***
Self-Adhesive

4221 A3207 41c **multicolored** .85 .20
Pane of 12 10.50
Sheet of 108 (9 panes) 95.00
Cross gutter block of 4 8.00
Horiz. pair with vert. gutter 2.00
Vert. pair with horiz. gutter 2.00

BLACK HERITAGE SERIES

Charles W. Chesnutt (1858-1932), Writer — A3208

Designed by Howard E. Paine. Printed by Avery Dennison.

PHOTOGRAVURE
Sheets of 200 in ten panes of 20

2008, Jan. 31 **Tagged** ***Serpentine Die Cut 11***
Self-Adhesive

4222 A3208 41c **multicolored** .85 .20
P# block of 4, 4# + V 3.40
Pane of 20 17.00

FIRST DAY COVERS

2008
4221 41c **Chinese New Year,** *Jan. 9,* San Francisco, CA 2.10
4222 41c **Charles W. Chesnutt,** *Jan. 31,* Cleveland, OH 2.10

LITERARY ARTS SERIES

Marjorie Kinnan Rawlings (1896-1953), Writer A3209

Designed by Carl T. Herrman. Printed by Avery Dennison.

PHOTOGRAVURE
Sheets of 200 in ten panes of 20

2008, Feb. 21 **Tagged** ***Serpentine Die Cut 11***
Self-Adhesive

4223 A3209 41c **multicolored** .85 .20
P# block of 4, 4# + V 3.40
Pane of 20 17.00

AMERICAN SCIENTISTS

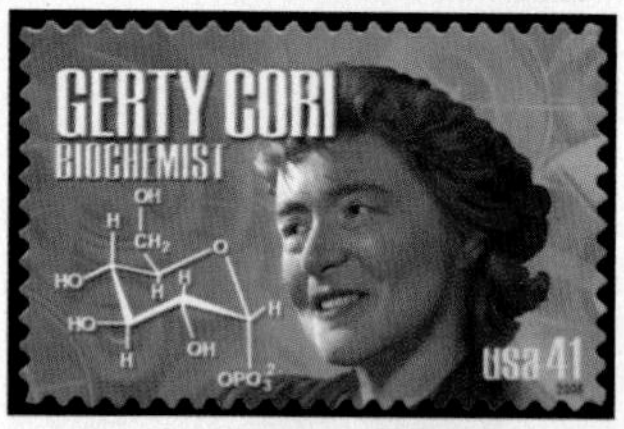

Gerty Cori (1896-1957), Biochemist A3210

Linus Pauling (1901-94), Structural Chemist A3211

Edwin Hubble (1889-1953), Astronomer A3212

John Bardeen (1908-91), Theoretical Physicist A3213

Designed by Victor Stabin. Printed by Avery Dennison.

PHOTOGRAVURE
Sheets of 160 in eight panes of 20

2008, Mar. 6 **Tagged** ***Serpentine Die Cut 11***
Self-Adhesive

4224 A3210 41c **multicolored** .85 .20
4225 A3211 41c **multicolored** .85 .20
4226 A3212 41c **multicolored** .85 .20
4227 A3213 41c **multicolored** .85 .20
a. Horiz. strip of 4, #4224-4227 3.40
P# block of 8, 2 sets of 4# + V 6.80
Pane of 20 17.00

Plate block may contain top label.

Flag at Dusk — A3214

Flag at Night — A3215

Flag at Dawn — A3216

Flag at Midday — A3217

Designed by Phil Jordan. Printed by American Packaging Corporation for Sennett Security Products (#4228-4231), Ashton-Potter (USA) Ltd. (#4232-4235), Banknote Corporation of America for Sennett Security Products (#4236-4239), Avery Dennison (#4240-4247).

PHOTOGRAVURE (#4228-4231, 4240-4247),
LITHOGRAPHED (#4232-4239)

2008, Apr. 18 **Tagged** ***Perf. 10 Vert.***
COIL STAMPS

4228 A3214 42c **multicolored** .85 .40
4229 A3215 42c **multicolored** .85 .40
4230 A3216 42c **multicolored** .85 .40
4231 A3217 42c **multicolored** .85 .40
a. Horiz. strip of 4, #4228-4231 3.40 1.60
P# strip of 5, 2 #4228, 1 each #4229-4231, #S1111111 6.00 —
P# strip of 9, 3 #4230, 2 each #4228-4229, 4230, P#S1111111 8.75 —
P# single, #S1111111 (#4230) — 2.00

Self-Adhesive
With Perpendicular Corners
Serpentine Die Cut 9½ Vert.

4232 A3214 42c **multicolored** .85 .20
4233 A3215 42c **multicolored** .85 .20
4234 A3216 42c **multicolored** .85 .20
4235 A3217 42c **multicolored** .85 .20
a. Horiz. strip of 4, #4232-4235 3.40
P# strip of 5, 2 #4232, 1 each #4233-4235, #P1111 6.00
P# strip of 9, 3 #4234, 2 each #4232-4233, 4235, P#P1111 8.75
P# single, #P1111 (#4234) — 2.00

Serpentine Die Cut 11 Vert.

4236 A3214 42c **multicolored** .85 .20
4237 A3215 42c **multicolored** .85 .20
4238 A3216 42c **multicolored** .85 .20
4239 A3217 42c **multicolored** .85 .20
a. Horiz. strip of 4, #4236-4239 3.40
P# strip of 5, 2 #4236, 1 each #4237-4239, #S1111 6.00
P# strip of 9, 3 #4238, 2 each #4236-4237, 4239, P#S1111 8.75
P# single, #S1111 (#4238) — 2.00

Serpentine Die Cut 8½ Vert.

4240 A3214 42c **multicolored** .85 .20
4241 A3215 42c **multicolored** .85 .20
4242 A3216 42c **multicolored** .85 .20
4243 A3217 42c **multicolored** .85 .20
a. Horiz. strip of 4, #4240-4243 3.40
P# strip of 5, 2 #4240, 1 each #4241-4243, #V1111 6.00
P# strip of 9, 3 #4242, 2 each #4240-4241, 4244, P#V1111 8.75
P# single, #V1111 (#4242) — 2.00

Serpentine Die Cut 11 Vert.
With Rounded Corners

4244 A3214 42c **multicolored** .85 .30
4245 A3215 42c **multicolored** .85 .30
4246 A3216 42c **multicolored** .85 .30
4247 A3217 42c **multicolored** .85 .30
a. Horiz. strip of 4, #4244-4247 3.40
P# strip of 5, 2 #4244, 1 each #4245-4247, #V1111 6.00
P# strip of 9, 3 #4246, 2 each #4244-4245, 4247, P#V1111 8.75
P# single, #V1111 (#4246) — 2.00
Nos. 4228-4247 (20) 17.00 5.20

Nos. 4232-4243 are on backing paper as high as the stamp. Nos. 4244-4247 are on backing paper that is larger than the stamp. Nos. 4232-4235 have "USPS" microprinted on the right side of a white flag stripe. On Nos. 4244-4247, the paper, vignette size and "2008" year date are slightly larger than those features on Nos. 4236-4239.

AMERICAN JOURNALISTS

Martha Gellhorn (1908-98) A3218

John Hersey (1914-93) A3219

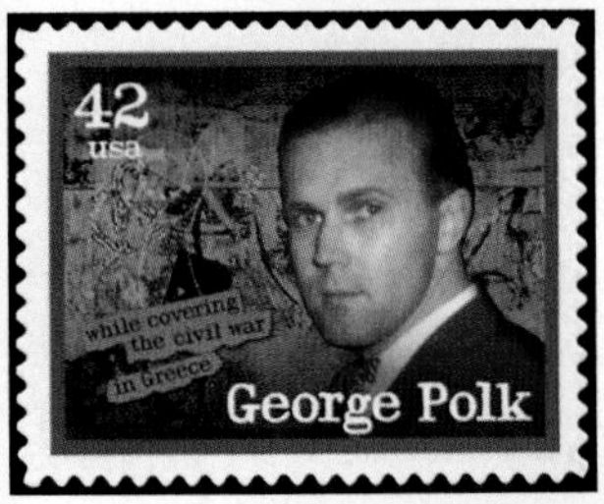

George Polk (1913-48) A3220

Ruben Salazar (1928-70) A3221

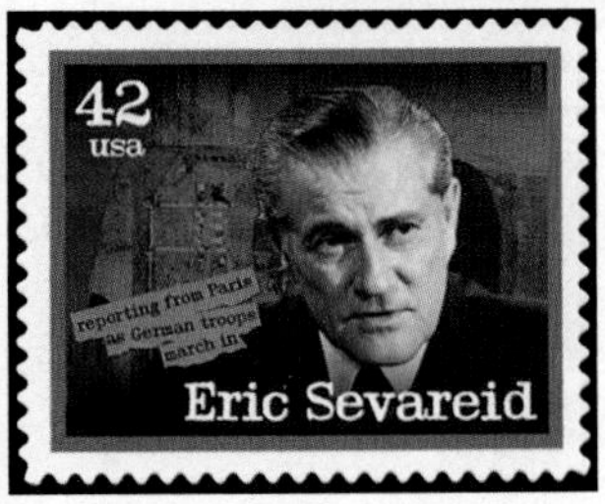

Eric Sevareid (1912-92) A3222

Designed by Howard E. Paine. Printed by Ashton-Potter (USA) Ltd.

LITHOGRAPHED

Serpentine Die Cut 10¾x10½

2008, Apr. 22 **Tagged**

Self-Adhesive

4248	A3218	42c	**multicolored**	.85	.20
4249	A3219	42c	**multicolored**	.85	.20
4250	A3220	42c	**multicolored**	.85	.20
4251	A3221	42c	**multicolored**	.85	.20
4252	A3222	42c	**multicolored**	.85	.20
a.			Vert. strip of 5, #4248-4252	4.25	
			P# block of 10, 2 sets of 4# + P	8.50	
			P# block of 8, 2 sets of 4# +P	7.00	
			Pane of 20	17.00	

TROPICAL FRUIT

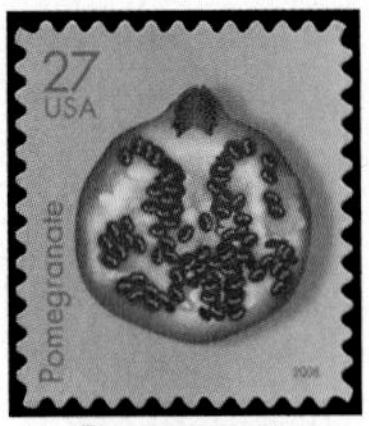

Pomegranate A3223

Star Fruit A3224

Kiwi — A3225

Papaya — A3226

Guava — A3227

Designed by Ethel Kessler. Printed by Ashton-Potter (USA) Ltd. (#4253-4257), Avery Dennison (#4258-4262)

LITHOGRAPHED (#4253-4257), PHOTOGRAVURE (#4258-4262)

Serpentine Die Cut 11¼x10¾

2008, Apr. 25 **Tagged**

Self-Adhesive

4253	A3223	27c	**multicolored**	.55	.20
4254	A3224	27c	**multicolored**	.55	.20
4255	A3225	27c	**multicolored**	.55	.20
4256	A3226	27c	**multicolored**	.55	.20
4257	A3227	27c	**multicolored**	.55	.20
a.			Horiz. strip of 5, #4253-4257	2.75	
			P# block of 10, 2 sets of 4# + P	5.50	
			Pane of 20	11.00	

COIL STAMPS

Serpentine Die Cut 8½ Vert.

4258	A3226	27c	**multicolored**	.55	.20
4259	A3227	27c	**multicolored**	.55	.20
4260	A3223	27c	**multicolored**	.55	.20
4261	A3224	27c	**multicolored**	.55	.20
4262	A3225	27c	**multicolored**	.55	.20
a.			Horiz. strip of 5, #4258-4262	2.75	
			P# strip of 5, #V1111111	4.00	
			P# strip of 11, 3 #4260, 2 each #4258-4259, 4261, 4262, #V1111111	7.75	
			P# single, #V1111111 (#4260)	—	2.00
			Nos. 4253-4262 (10)	5.50	2.00

Purple Heart Type of 2003

Designed by Carl T. Herrman. Printed by Ashton-Potter (USA) Ltd.

LITHOGRAPHED

Sheets of 400 in four panes of 100 (#4263), Sheets of 120 in six panes of 20 (#4264)

2008, Apr. 30 **Tagged** *Perf. 11¼*

4263	A2891	42c	**multicolored**	.85	.25
			P# block of 4, 4#+P	3.40	—

Self-Adhesive

Serpentine Die Cut 11¼x10¾

4264	A2891	42c	**multicolored**	.85	.20
			P# block of 4, 4#+V	3.40	
			Pane of 20	17.00	

FRANK SINATRA

Frank Sinatra (1915-98), Singer and Actor — A3228

Designed by Richard Sheaff. Printed by Ashton-Potter (USA) Ltd.

LITHOGRAPHED
Sheets of 120 in six panes of 20

2008, May 13 Tagged *Serpentine Die Cut 10¾*

Self-Adhesive

4265	A3228	42c	**multicolored**	.85	.20
			P# block of 4, 4#+P	3.40	
			Pane of 20	17.00	
			Sheet of 120 (6 panes)	105.00	
			Cross gutter block of 4	8.00	
			Horiz. pair with vert. gutter	2.00	
			Vert. pair with horiz. gutter	2.00	

MINNESOTA STATEHOOD, 150th ANNIV.

Bridge Over Mississippi River Near Winona — A3229

Designed by Ethel Kessler. Printed by Ashton-Potter (USA) Ltd.

LITHOGRAPHED
Sheets of 120 in six panes of 20

2008, May 17 Tagged *Serpentine Die Cut 10¾*

Self-Adhesive

4266	A3229	42c	**multicolored**	.85	.20
			P# block of 4, 4#+P	3.40	
			Pane of 20	17.00	

Dragonfly — A3230

Designed by Carl T. Herrman. Printed by Banknote Corporation of America for Sennett Security Products.

LITHOGRAPHED
Sheets of 400 in twenty panes of 20
Serpentine Die Cut 11¼x11

2008, May 19 Tagged

Self-Adhesive

4267	A3230	62c	**multicolored**	1.25	.20
			P# block of 4, 4#+S	5.00	
			Pane of 20	25.00	

AMERICAN LANDMARKS

Mount Rushmore A3231

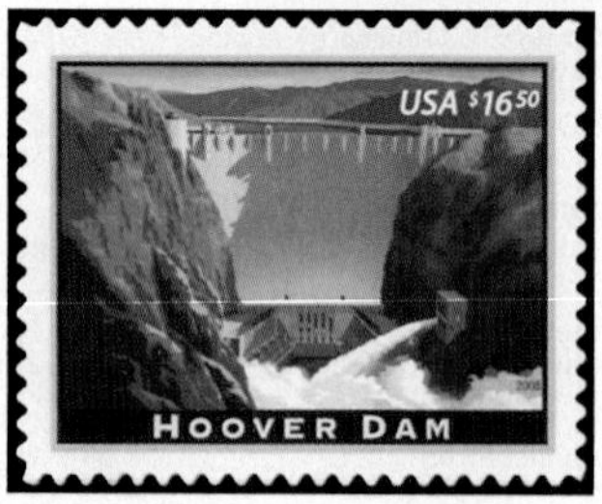

Hoover Dam — A3232

Designed by Carl T. Herrman. Printed by Ashton-Potter (USA) Ltd. (#4268), Banknote Corporation of America for Sennett Security Products (#4269).

LITHOGRAPHED
Sheets of 180 in nine panes of 20 (#4268), Sheets of 120 in six panes of 20 (#4269)

2008 Tagged *Serpentine Die Cut 10¾x10½*

Self-Adhesive

4268	A3231	$4.80	**multicolored,** *June 6*	9.75	5.00
			P# block of 4, 4#+P	40.00	
			Pane of 20	200.00	
4269	A3232	$16.50	**multicolored,** *June 20*	30.00	17.00
			P# block of 4, 5#+S	120.00	
			Pane of 20	600.00	

LOVE

Man Carrying Heart — A3233

Designed by Ethel Kessler. Printed by Avery Dennison.

PHOTOGRAVURE
Serpentine Die Cut 10¾ on 2, 3, or 4 Sides

2008, June 10 Tagged

Booklet Stamp

Self-Adhesive

4270	A3233	42c	**multicolored**	.85	.20
a.			Booklet pane of 20	17.00	

WEDDING HEARTS

Heart With Light Green Background — A3234

Heart With Buff Background — A3235

Designed by Carl T. Herrman. Printed by Ashton-Potter (USA) Ltd. (#4271), Avery Dennison (#4272).

LITHOGRAPHED (#4271), PHOTOGRAVURE (#4272)
BOOKLET STAMP (#4271)
Sheets of 240 in twelve panes of 20 (#4272)
Serpentine Die Cut 10¾ on 2, 3 or 4 Sides

2008, June 10 Tagged

Self-Adhesive

4271	A3234	42c	**multicolored**	.85	.20
a.			Booklet pane of 20	17.00	

Serpentine Die Cut 10¾

4272	A3235	59c	**multicolored**	1.25	.25
			P# block of 4, 3#+V	5.00	
			Pane of 20	25.00	

FLAGS OF OUR NATION

American Flag and Clouds A3236

Alabama Flag and Shrimp Boat A3237

Alaska Flag and Humpback Whale — A3238

American Samoa Flag and Island Peaks and Trees A3239

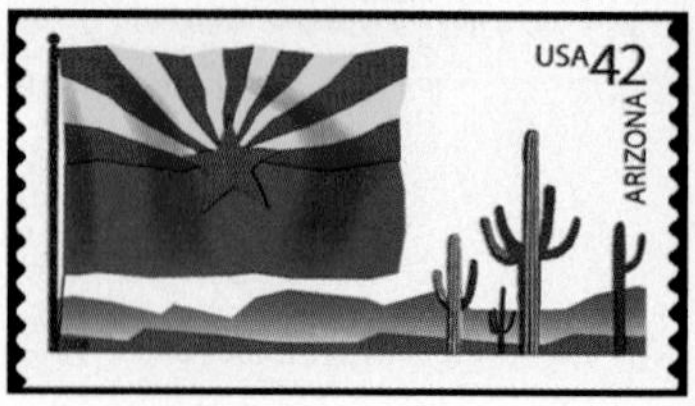

Arizona Flag and Saguaro Cacti A3240

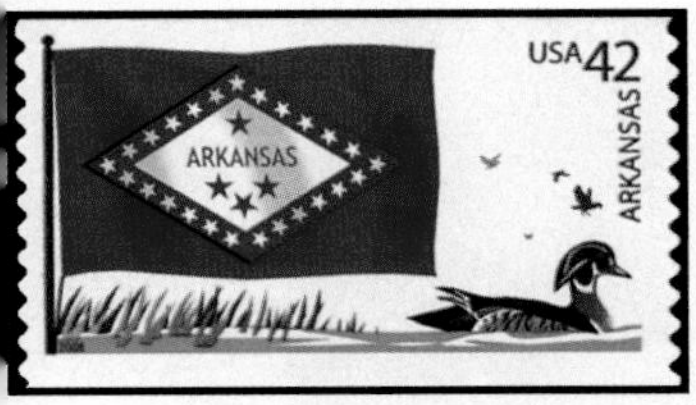

Arkansas Flag and Wood Duck
A3241

California Flag and Coast
A3242

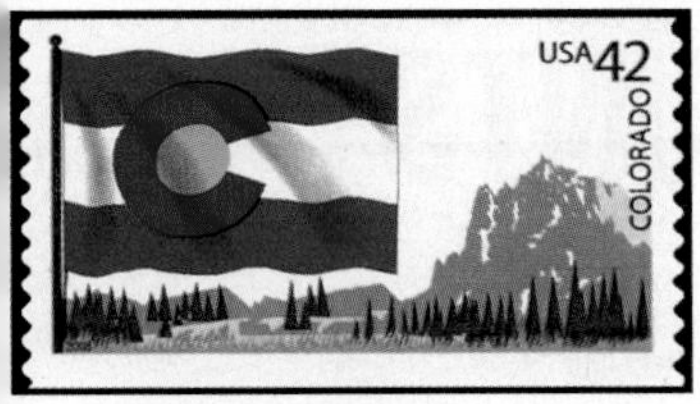

Colorado Flag and Mountain
A3243

Connecticut Flag, Sailboats and Buoy — A3244

Delaware Flag and Beach
A3245

Designed by Howard E. Paine. Printed by American Packaging Corp. for Sennett Security Products.

PHOTOGRAVURE

Serpentine Die Cut 11 Vert.

2008, June 14 **Tagged**

Self-Adhesive

Coil Stamps

4273	A3236	42c	**multicolored**	.85	.25
4274	A3237	42c	**multicolored**	.85	.25
4275	A3238	42c	**multicolored**	.85	.25
4276	A3239	42c	**multicolored**	.85	.25
4277	A3240	42c	**multicolored**	.85	.25
a.			Strip of 5, #4273-4277	4.25	
4278	A3241	42c	**multicolored**	.85	.25
4279	A3242	42c	**multicolored**	.85	.25
4280	A3243	42c	**multicolored**	.85	.25
4281	A3244	42c	**multicolored**	.85	.25
4282	A3245	42c	**multicolored**	.85	.25
a.			Strip of 5, #4278-4282	4.25	
b.			P # set of 10, #4277a + 4182a	8.50	
			P# strip of 11, #4273-4277, 4279-4282, 2 #4278, P#111111111	12.50	

No. 4273 always has a plate number. No. 4282b may be collected as one continuous strip, but the item will not fit in any standard album.

CHARLES (1907-78) AND RAY (1912- 88) EAMES, DESIGNERS

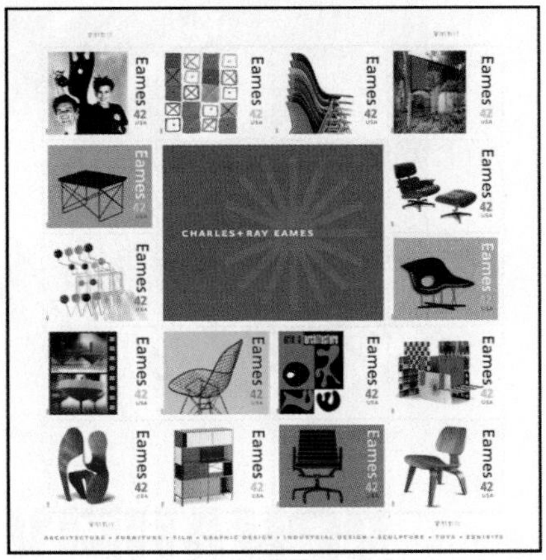

A3296

Illustration reduced.

Designed by Derry Noyes. Printed by Avery Dennison.

No. 4333: a, Christmas card depicting Charles and Ray Eames. b, "Crosspatch" fabric design. c, Stacking chairs. d, Case Study House #8, Pacific Palisades, CA. e, Wire-base table. f, Lounge chair and ottoman. g, Hang-it-all. h, La Chaise. i, Scene from film, "Tops." j, Wire mesh chair. k, Cover of May 1943 edition of *California Arts & Architecture* Magazine. l, House of Cards. m, Molded plywood sculpture. n, Eames Storage Unit. o, Aluminum group chair. p, Molded plywood chair.

PHOTOGRAVURE

Sheets of 160 in ten panes of 16

Serpentine Die Cut 10¾x10½

2008, June 17 **Tagged**

Self-Adhesive

4333	A3296		Pane of 16 + label	14.00	
a.-p.		42c	Any single	.85	.20

SUMMER OLYMPIC GAMES, BEIJING, CHINA

Gymnast
A3297

Designed by Clarence Lee. Printed by Banknote Corporation of America for Sennett Security Products.

LITHOGRAPHED

Sheets of 180 in nine panes of 20

2008, June 19 **Tagged** ***Serpentine Die Cut 10¾***

Self-Adhesive

4334	A3297	42c	**multicolored**	.85	.20
			P# block of 4, 6#+S	3.40	
			Pane of 20	17.00	

2008 END-OF-YEAR ISSUES

The USPS has announced that the following items will be released in late 2008. Dates, denominations and cities are tentative.

Celebrate, (42c) self-adhesive stamp, *July 10,* Washington, DC.

American Clock, American Design Series, (10c) lithographed coil stamp, *July 15,* Washington, DC.

Take Me Out to the Ball Game, 42c self-adhesive stamp, *July 16,* Washington, DC.

Vintage Black Cinema, 5 42c self-adhesive stamps depicting Black and Tan, The Sport of the Gods, Prinsesse Tam-Tam, Caldonia, Hallelujah, *July 16,* Newark NJ.

Disney Characters, 4 42c self-adhesive stamps depicting Mickey Mouse as Steamboat Willie, Sleeping Beauty, Jungle Book characters Mowgli and Baloo, Pongo and puppy from 101 Dalmatians, *Aug. 7,* Anaheim, CA.

Disney Characters, 4 27c postal cards depicting Mickey Mouse as Steamboat Willie, Sleeping Beauty, Jungle Book characters Mowgli and Baloo, Pongo and puppy from 101 Dalmatians, in a booklet of 20 containing five each *Aug. 7,* Anaheim, CA.

Valley of the Yosemite, by Albert Bierstadt, American Treasures Series, self-adhesive 42c booklet stamp in booklet pane of 20 stamps, *Aug. 14,* Hartford, CT.

Sunflower, self-adhesive 42c booklet stamp in booklet pane of 20 stamps, *Aug. 15,* Hartford, CT.

Sunflower, 42c letter sheet, *Aug. 15,* Hartford, CT.

Flags of Our Nation, strip of 10 42c self-adhesive coil stamps depicting flags and scenery of District of Columbia, Florida, Georgia, Guam, Hawaii, Idaho, Illinois, Indiana, Iowa and Kansas, *Sept. 2,* Washington, DC.

Sea Coast, (5c) coil stamp, *Sept. 5,* Washington, DC.

Latin Jazz, 42c self-adhesive stamp, *Sept. 8,* Washington, DC.

Bette Davis, Legends of Hollywood Series, 42c self-adhesive stamp, *Sept. 18,* Boston, MA.

Eid, 42c self-adhesive stamp, *Sept. 23,* Washington, DC.

Great Lakes Dunes, Nature of America Series, pane of 10 42c self-adhesive stamps, *Oct. 2,* Empire, MI.

America on the Move: Tail Fins and Chrome, 5 42c self-adhesive stamps depicting 1957 Studebaker Golden Hawk, 1957 Lincoln Premier, 1957 Chrysler 300C, 1957 Pontiac Safari and 1959 Cadillac Eldorado, *Oct. 3,* Carlisle, PA

America on the Move: Tail Fins and Chrome, 5 27c postal cards depicting 1957 Studebaker Golden Hawk, 1957 Lincoln Premier, 1957 Chrysler 300C, 1957 Pontiac Safari and 1959 Cadillac Eldorado, *Oct. 3,* Carlisle, PA.

Alzheimer's Disease Awareness, 42c self-adhesive stamp, *Oct. 17,* Morgantown, WV.

Christmas, Virgin and Child with the Young John the Baptist by Sandro Botticelli, 42c self-adhesive booklet stamp in booklet pane of 20, *Oct. 23,* New York, NY.

Holiday Nutcrackers, 4 42c self-adhesive booklet stamps depicting Drummer, Santa Claus, King and Soldier, in convertible booklet of 20, *Oct. 23,* New York, NY.

Holiday Nutcrackers, 4 42c self-adhesive vending machine booklet stamps depicting Drummer, Santa Claus, King and Soldier, in booklet pane of 20, *Oct. 23,* New York, NY.

Holiday Nutcrackers, 4 42c self-adhesive ATM booklet stamps depicting Drummer, Santa Claus, King and Soldier, in vending booklet of 18, *Oct. 23,* New York, NY.

Hanukkah, 42c self-adhesive stamp, *Oct. 24,* New York, NY.

Kwanzaa, 42c self-adhesive stamp, *Oct. 24,* New York, NY.

Listings as of 5PM, July 30, 2008.

SEMI-POSTAL STAMPS

The genesis of the U.S. semi-postal stamp program was a July 1997 bill passed by both houses of Congress that directed the USPS to issue a stamp to benefit breast-cancer research. On August 13, the President signed it into law. The surcharge was to be up to 25% of the current first-class rate.

BREAST CANCER RESEARCH

SP1

Designed by Ethel Kessler. Printed by Avery Dennison.

PHOTOGRAVURE
Sheets of 160 in eight panes of 20

1998, July 29 Tagged *Serpentine Die Cut 11*
Self-Adhesive

B1	SP1	(32c+8c)	**multicolored**	.80	.20
			P# block of 4, 6#+V	3.25	
			Pane of 20	16.00	

The 8c surtax was for cancer research. After the Jan. 10, 1999, first class postage rate changes, No. B1 became a 33c stamp with a 7c surtax; after Jan. 7, 2001, it became a 34c stamp with a 6c surtax. Effective Mar. 23, 2002, the stamp was sold for 45c, but the face value remained at 34c until June 30, 2002, at which time the face value rose to 37c. On Jan. 8, 2006, the face value rose to 39c, and on May 14, 2007, the face value rose to 41c and the stamp sold for 55c.

Sales of No. B1 were suspended Jan. 1, 2004, but resumed Feb. 2, 2004, after Congress extended the sales period through Dec. 31, 2005. Subsequently, the sales period was again extended.

HEROES OF 2001

Firemen Atop World Trade Center Rubble — SP2

Designed by Derry Noyes. Printed by Ashton-Potter (USA) Ltd..

LITHOGRAPHED
Sheets of 120 in six panes of 20

2002, June 7 Tagged *Serpentine Die Cut 11¼*
Self-Adhesive

B2	SP2	(34c+11c)	**multicolored**	.80	.35
			P# block of 4, 4#+P	3.25	
			Pane of 20	16.00	

The 11c surtax was for assistance to families of emergency relief personnel killed or permanently disabled in the line of duty in connection with the terrorist attacks of Sept. 11, 2001. No. B2 became a 37c stamp with an 8c surtax June 30, 2002.

STOP FAMILY VIOLENCE

SP3

Designed by Carl T. Herrman.

Printed by Avery Dennison.

PHOTOGRAVURE
Sheets of 200 in ten panes of 20

2003, Oct. 8 Tagged *Serpentine Die Cut 11*
Self-Adhesive

B3	SP3	(37c+8c)	**multicolored**	.85	.45
			P# block of 4, 4#+V	3.50	
			Pane of 20	17.50	

AIR POST STAMPS

Air mail in the U. S. postal system developed in three stages: pioneer period (with many unofficial or semi-official flights before 1918), government flights and contract air mail (C.A.M.). Contract air mail began on February 15, 1926.

All C.A.M. contracts were canceled on February 19, 1934, and air mail was carried by Army planes for six months. After that the contract plan was resumed. Separate domestic airmail service was abolished Oct. 11, 1975.

See Domestic Air Mail Rates chart in introduction.

Curtiss Jenny — AP1

No. C3 first used on airplane mail service between Washington, Philadelphia and New York, on May 15, 1918, but was valid for ordinary postage. The rate of postage was 24 cents per ounce, which included immediate individual delivery.

Rate of postage was reduced to 16 cents for the first ounce and 6 cents for each additional ounce, which included 10 cents for immediate individual delivery, on July 15, 1918, by Postmaster General's order of June 26, 1918. No. C2 was first used for air mail in the tri-city service on July 15.

Rate of postage was reduced on December 15, 1918, by Postmaster General's order of November 30, 1918, to 6 cents per ounce. No. C1 was first used for air mail (same three-way service) on Dec. 16.

FLAT PLATE PRINTINGS
Plates of 100 subjects.

1918 Unwmk. Engr. *Perf. 11*

C1	AP1	6c	**orange,** *Dec. 10*	65.	30.
			pale orange	65.	30.
			Never hinged	135.	
			On cover		50.
			First flight cover, *Dec. 16*		2,000.
			Margin block of 4, arrow top or left	290.	140.
			Center line block	300.	150.
			P# block of 6, arrow	775.	—
			Never hinged	1,125.	
			Double transfer (#9155-14)	90.	45.
C2	AP1	16c	**green,** *July 11*	70.	35.
			dark green	70.	35.
			Never hinged	150.	
			On cover		55.
			First flight cover, *July 15*		800.
			Margin block of 4, arrow top or left	310.	175.
			Center line block	340.	190.
			P# block of 6, arrow	1,000.	—
			Never hinged	1,500.	
C3	AP1	24c	**carmine rose & blue,** *May 13*	70.	35.
			dark carmine rose & blue	75.	35.
			Never hinged	150.	
			On cover		75.
			First flight cover, *May 15*		750.
			Margin block of 4, arrow top or left	310.	150.
			Margin block of 4, arrow bottom	360.	160.
			Margin block of 4, arrow right	400.	200.
			Center line block	350.	175.
			P# block of 4, red P# only	400.	—
			P# block of 12, two P#, arrow & two "TOP"	1,300.	—
			Never hinged	2,100.	
			P# block of 12, two P#, arrow & blue "TOP" only	*12,500.*	
a.			Center inverted	*500,000.*	
			Never hinged	*1,100,000.*	
			Block of 4	*2,000,000.*	
			Block of 4 with horiz. guide line	*2,150,000.*	
			Corner margin block of 4 with siderographer's initials	*2,400,000.*	
			Center line block	*2,150,000.*	
			P# block of 4, blue P#	*3,500,000.*	
			Nos. C1-C3 (3)	205.00	100.00
			Nos. C1-C3, never hinged	435.00	

Plate Blocks

Scott values for plate blocks printed from flat plates are for very fine side and bottom positions. Top position plate blocks with full wide selvage sell for more.

Airplane Radiator and Wooden Propeller — AP2

Air Service Emblem — AP3

DeHavilland Biplane — AP4

Nos. C4-C6 were issued primarily for use in the new night-flying air mail service between New York and San Francisco, but valid for all purposes. Three zones were established; New York-Chicago, Chicago-Cheyenne, Cheyenne-San Francisco, and the rate of postage was 8 cents an ounce for each zone. Service was inaugurated on July 1, 1924.

These stamps were placed on sale at the Philatelic Agency at Washington on the dates indicated in the listings but were not issued to postmasters at that time.

Plates of 400 subjects in four panes of 100 each.

1923			**Unwmk.**	***Perf. 11***	
C4	AP2	8c	**dark green,** *Aug. 15*	21.00	14.00
			deep green	21.00	14.00
			Never hinged	42.50	
			On cover		22.50
			P# block of 6	250.00	—
			Never hinged	350.00	
			Double transfer	40.00	22.50
C5	AP3	16c	**dark blue,** *Aug. 17*	70.00	30.00
			Never hinged	150.00	
			On cover		47.50
			P# block of 6	1,550.	—
			Never hinged	2,350.	
			Double transfer	120.00	50.00
C6	AP4	24c	**carmine,** *Aug. 21*	75.00	30.00
			Never hinged	160.00	
			On cover		42.50
			P# block of 6	2,050.	—
			Never hinged	3,100.	
			Double transfer (Pl. 14841)	160.00	42.50
			Nos. C4-C6 (3)	166.00	74.00
			Nos. C4-C6, never hinged	365.00	

Map of United States and Two Mail Planes — AP5

Double Transfer

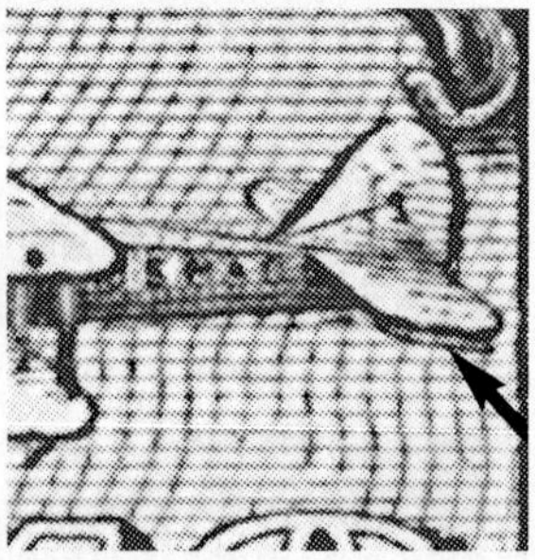

The Act of Congress of February 2, 1925, created a rate of 10 cents per ounce for distances to 1000 miles, 15 cents per ounce for 1500 miles and 20 cents for more than 1500 miles on contract air mail routes.

Plates of 200 subjects in four panes of 50 each.

1926-27			**Unwmk.**	***Perf. 11***	
C7	AP5	10c	**dark blue,** *Feb. 13, 1926*	2.50	.35
			light blue	2.50	.35
			Never hinged	4.50	
			P# block of 6	35.00	—
			Never hinged	47.50	
			Double transfer (18246 UL 11)	5.75	1.10
C8	AP5	15c	**olive brown,** *Sept. 18, 1926*	2.75	2.50
			light brown	2.75	2.50
			Never hinged	5.25	
			P# block of 6	35.00	—
			Never hinged	50.00	
C9	AP5	20c	**yellow green,** *Jan. 25, 1927*	7.00	2.00
			green	7.00	2.00
			Never hinged	13.50	
			P# block of 6	75.00	—
			Never hinged	105.00	
			Nos. C7-C9 (3)	12.25	4.85
			Nos. C7-C9, never hinged	23.25	

Lindbergh's Plane "Spirit of St. Louis" and Flight Route — AP6

A tribute to Col. Charles A. Lindbergh, who made the first non-stop (and solo) flight from New York to Paris, May 20-21, 1927.

Plates of 200 subjects in four panes of 50 each.

1927, June 18			**Unwmk.**	***Perf. 11***	
C10	AP6	10c	**dark blue**	7.00	2.50
			Never hinged	13.00	
			P# block of 6	90.00	—
			Never hinged	130.00	
			Double transfer	11.50	3.25
a.			Booklet pane of 3, *May 26, 1928*	80.00	*65.00*
			Never hinged	130.00	

Beacon on Rocky Mountains AP7

Issued to meet the new rate, effective August 1, of 5 cents per ounce.

Plates of 100 subjects in two panes of 50

1928, July 25			**Unwmk.**	***Perf. 11***	
C11	AP7	5c	**carmine and blue**	5.00	.75
			Never hinged	9.50	
			On cover, first day of 5c airmail rate, Aug. 1		3.00
			Margin block of 4, arrow, (line) right or left	24.00	4.50
			P# block of 6, two P# & red "TOP"	40.00	—
			Never hinged	55.00	
			P# block of 6, two P# & blue "TOP"	40.00	—
			Never hinged	55.00	
			P# block of 6, two P# & double "TOP"	110.00	—
			Never hinged	160.00	
			P# block of 8, two P# only (no "TOP")	200.00	—
			Never hinged	300.00	
			Recut frame line at left	7.50	1.50
			Double transfer	—	—
a.			Vert. pair, imperf. between	*7,000.*	

Winged Globe — AP8

Plates of 200 subjects in four panes of 50 each.

1930, Feb. 10			**Unwmk.**	***Perf. 11***	
			Stamp design: 46½x19mm		
C12	AP8	5c	**violet**	9.50	.50
			Never hinged	18.00	
			P# block of 6	140.00	—
			Never hinged	210.00	
			Double transfer (Pl. 20189)	19.00	1.25
a.			Horiz. pair, imperf. between	*4,500.*	

See Nos. C16-C17, C19.

GRAF ZEPPELIN ISSUE

Zeppelin Over Atlantic Ocean — AP9

Zeppelin Between Continents — AP10

Zeppelin Passing Globe — AP11

Issued for use on mail carried on the first Europe-Pan-America round trip flight of the Graf Zeppelin in May, 1930. They were withdrawn from sale June 30, 1930.

Plates of 200 subjects in four panes of 50 each.

1930, Apr. 19			**Unwmk.**	***Perf. 11***	
C13	AP9	65c	**green**	240.	160.
			Never hinged	425.	
			On cover or card		175.
			Block of 4	1,050.	700.
			P# block of 6	2,300.	—
			Never hinged	3,250.	
C14	AP10	$1.30	**brown**	500.	375.
			Never hinged	900.	
			On cover		400.
			Block of 4	2,250.	1,500.
			P# block of 6	5,750.	—
			Never hinged	8,000.	
C15	AP11	$2.60	**blue**	700.	575.
			Never hinged	1,275.	
			On cover		600.
			Block of 4	3,400.	2,500.
			P# block of 6	8,500.	—
			Never hinged	12,000.	
			Nos. C13-C15 (3)	1,440.	1,110.
			Nos. C13-C15, never hinged	2,600.	

ROTARY PRESS PRINTING

Plates of 200 subjects in four panes of 50 each.

1931-32			**Unwmk.**	***Perf. 10½x11***	
			Stamp design: 47½x19mm		
C16	AP8	5c	**violet,** *Aug. 19, 1931*	5.00	.60
			Never hinged	8.75	
			Block of 4	22.00	2.00
			P# block of 4	75.00	—
			Never hinged	100.00	

Issued to conform with new air mail rate of 8 cents per ounce which became effective July 6, 1932.

C17	AP8	8c	**olive bister,** *Sept. 26, 1932*	2.25	.40
			Never hinged	4.00	
			Block of 4	10.00	2.00
			P# block of 4	27.50	—
			Never hinged	37.50	

CENTURY OF PROGRESS ISSUE

"Graf Zeppelin," Federal Building at Chicago Exposition and Hangar at Friedrichshafen — AP12

Issued in connection with the flight of the airship "Graf Zeppelin" in October, 1933, to Miami, Akron and Chicago and from the last city to Europe.

FLAT PLATE PRINTING

Plates of 200 subjects in four panes of 50 each.

1933, Oct. 2			**Unwmk.**	***Perf. 11***	
C18	AP12	50c	**green**	55.00	55.00
			Never hinged	100.00	
			On cover		80.00

Block of 4	230.00	290.00
P# block of 6	500.00	—
Never hinged	750.00	

Catalogue values for unused stamps in this section, from this point to the end, are for Never Hinged items.

Type of 1930 Issue
ROTARY PRESS PRINTING

Issued to conform with new air mail rate of 6 cents per ounce which became effective July 1, 1934.

Plates of 200 subjects in four panes of 50 each.

1934, June 30 Unwmk. *Perf. 10½x11*

C19 AP8 6c **dull orange**	3.50	.25
On cover, first day of 6c airmail rate, July 1		10.00
Block of 4	14.00	1.10
P# block of 4	20.00	—
Horiz. pair with full vert. gutter btwn.	*425.00*	
Vert. pair with full horiz. gutter btwn.	*600.00*	

TRANSPACIFIC ISSUES

"China Clipper" over Pacific AP13

Issued to pay postage on mail transported by the Transpacific air mail service, inaugurated Nov. 22, 1935.

FLAT PLATE PRINTING
Plates of 200 subjects in four panes of 50 each.

1935, Nov. 22 Unwmk. *Perf. 11*

C20 AP13 25c **blue**	1.40	1.00
P# block of 6	22.50	—

"China Clipper" over Pacific — AP14

Issued primarily for use on the Transpacific service to China, but valid for all air mail purposes.

FLAT PLATE PRINTING
Plates of 200 subjects in four panes of 50 each.

1937, Feb. 15 Unwmk. *Perf. 11*

C21 AP14 20c **green**	11.00	1.75
dark green	11.00	1.75
Block of 4	45.00	8.50
P# block of 6	90.00	—
C22 AP14 50c **carmine**	11.00	5.00
Block of 4	45.00	21.00
P# block of 6	90.00	—

Wide full selvage top margin plate blocks of No. C22 are extremely scarce and sell for 10 or more times the value listed.

Eagle Holding Shield, Olive Branch and Arrows — AP15

FLAT PLATE PRINTING

Frame plates of 100 subjects in two panes of 50 each separated by a 1½-inch wide vertical gutter with central guide line, and vignette plates of 50 subjects. Some plates were made of iron, then chromed; several of these carry an additional imprint, "E.I." (Electrolytic Iron).

1938, May 14 Unwmk. *Perf. 11*

C23 AP15 6c **dark blue & carmine**	.50	.20
Margin block of 4, bottom or side arrow	2.25	.55
P# block of 4, 2 P#	8.00	—
Center line block	2.75	.95
Top P# block of 10, with two P#, arrow, two "TOP" and two registration markers	15.00	
a. Vert. pair, imperf. horiz.	*325.00*	—
On cover	1,750.	
P# block of 4, 2 P#	*1,250.*	
b. Horiz. pair, imperf. vert.	*12,500.*	
P# block of 4, 2 P#	*37,500.*	
c. 6c **ultramarine & carmine**	150.00	*1,500.*
Center line block	*1,200.*	
P# block of 4, 2 P#	*1,500.*	

Top plate number blocks of No. C23 are found both with and without top arrow.

The plate block of No. C23b is unique and never hinged; value is based on 1994 auction sale.

TRANSATLANTIC ISSUE

Winged Globe — AP16

Inauguration of Transatlantic air mail service.

FLAT PLATE PRINTING
Plates of 200 subjects in four panes of 50 each.

1939, May 16 Unwmk. *Perf. 11*

C24 AP16 30c **dull blue**	12.00	1.50
P# block of 6	130.00	—

Twin-Motored Transport Plane — AP17

ROTARY PRESS PRINTING
E. E. Plates of 200 subjects in four panes of 50 each.

1941-44 Unwmk. *Perf. 11x10½*

C25 AP17 6c **carmine**, *June 25, 1941*	.20	.20
P# block of 4	.60	—
Pair with full vert. gutter btwn.	*225.00*	
Pair with full horiz. gutter btwn.	—	
a. Booklet pane of 3, *Mar. 18, 1943*	5.00	1.50
b. Horiz. pair, imperf. between	*2,250.*	

Singles from No. C25a are imperf. at sides or at sides and bottom.

Value of No. C25b is for pair without blue crayon P. O. rejection mark on front. Very fine pairs with crayon mark sell for about $1,750.

C26 AP17 8c **olive green**, *Mar. 21, 1944*	.20	.20
P# block of 4	1.10	—
Pair with full horiz. gutter btwn.	*325.00*	
a. All color omitted	—	

No. C26a has an albino impression and exists as a pair of stamps within a double-paper spliced strip of six stamps.

C27 AP17 10c **violet**, *Aug. 15, 1941*	1.25	.20
P# block of 4	5.50	—
C28 AP17 15c **brown carmine**, *Aug. 19, 1941*	2.25	.35
P# block of 4	9.50	—
C29 AP17 20c **bright green**, *Aug. 27, 1941*	2.25	.30
P# block of 4	9.50	—
C30 AP17 30c **blue**, *Sept. 25, 1941*	2.25	.35
P# block of 4	9.50	—
C31 AP17 50c **orange**, *Oct. 29, 1941*	11.00	3.25
P# block of 4	50.00	—
Nos. C25-C31 (7)	19.40	4.85

DC-4 Skymaster AP18

ROTARY PRESS PRINTING
E. E. Plates of 200 subjects in four panes of 50 each.

1946, Sept. 25 Unwmk. *Perf. 11x10½*

C32 AP18 5c **carmine**	.20	.20
P# block of 4	.45	—

DC-4 Skymaster — AP19

ROTARY PRESS PRINTING
E. E. Plates of 400 subjects in four panes of 100 each.

1947, Mar. 26 Unwmk. *Perf. 10½x11*

C33 AP19 5c **carmine**	.20	.20
P# block of 4	.60	—

Pan American Union Building, Washington, D.C., and Martin 2-0-2 — AP20

Statue of Liberty, New York Skyline and Lockheed Constellation AP21

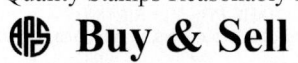

San Francisco-Oakland Bay Bridge and Boeing B377 Stratocruiser — AP22

Designed by Victor S. McCloskey, Jr., Leon Helguera and William K. Schrage.

ROTARY PRESS PRINTING
E. E. Plates of 200 subjects in four panes of 50 each.

1947 Unwmk. *Perf. 11x10½*

C34 AP20 10c **black**, *Aug. 30*	.25	.20
P# block of 4	1.10	—
a. Dry printing	.40	.20
P# block of 4 (#25613, 25614)	1.75	—
C35 AP21 15c **bright blue green**, *Aug. 20*	.35	.20
blue green	.35	.20
P# block of 4	1.50	—

Pair with full horiz. gutter btwn. *650.00*
a. Horiz. pair, imperf. between *2,750.*
b. Dry printing .55 .20
P# block of 4 (#25492 and up) 2.50 —
C36 AP22 25c **blue,** *July 30* .90 .20
P# block of 4 4.00 —
a. Dry printing 1.20 .20
P# block of 4 (#25615 and up) 5.25 —
Nos. C34-C36 (3) 1.50 .60

See note on wet and dry printings following No. 1029.
No. C35a is valued in the grade of fine.

ROTARY PRESS COIL STAMP
Type of 1947

1948, Jan. 15 Unwmk. *Perf. 10 Horizontally*
C37 AP19 5c **carmine** 1.00 .80
Pair 2.10 1.75
Joint line pair 10.00 3.00

NEW YORK CITY ISSUE

Map of Five Boroughs, Circular Band and Planes — AP23

50th anniv. of the consolidation of the five boroughs of New York City.

ROTARY PRESS PRINTING
E. E. Plates of 400 subjects in four panes of 100 each.

1948, July 31 Unwmk. *Perf. 11x10½*
C38 AP23 5c **bright carmine** .20 .20
P# block of 4 3.50 —

Type of 1947
ROTARY PRESS PRINTING
E. E. Plates of 400 subjects in four panes of 100 each.

1949 Unwmk. *Perf. 10½x11*
C39 AP19 6c **carmine,** *Jan. 18* .20 .20
P# block of 4 .50 —
Pair with full horiz. gutter btwn. *600.00*
a. Booklet pane of 6, *Nov. 18* 10.00 5.00
b. Dry printing .50 .20
P# block of 4 (#25340 and up) 2.25 —
c. As "a," dry printing 25.00 —

See note on wet and dry printings following No. 1029.

ALEXANDRIA BICENTENNIAL ISSUE

Home of John Carlyle, Alexandria Seal and Gadsby's Tavern AP24

200th anniv. of the founding of Alexandria, Va.

ROTARY PRESS PRINTING
E. E. Plates of 200 subjects in four panes of 50 each.

1949, May 11 Unwmk. *Perf. 11x10½*
C40 AP24 6c **carmine** .20 .20
P# block of 4 .50 —

ROTARY PRESS COIL STAMP
Type of 1947

1949, Aug. 25 Unwmk. *Perf. 10 Horizontally*
C41 AP19 6c **carmine** 3.00 .20
Pair 6.25 .20
Joint line pair 14.00 1.35

UNIVERSAL POSTAL UNION ISSUE

Post Office Department Building AP25

Globe and Doves Carrying Messages AP26

Boeing Stratocruiser and Globe — AP27

Universal Postal Union, 75th Anniv.

ROTARY PRESS PRINTING
E. E. Plates of 200 subjects in four panes of 50 each.

1949 Unwmk. *Perf. 11x10½*
C42 AP25 10c **violet,** *Nov. 18* .20 .20
P# block of 4 1.40 —
C43 AP26 15c **ultramarine,** *Oct. 7* .30 .25
P# block of 4 1.25 —
C44 AP27 25c **rose carmine,** *Nov. 30* .60 .40
P# block of 4 4.00 —
Nos. C42-C44 (3) 1.10 .85

WRIGHT BROTHERS ISSUE

Wilbur and Orville Wright and their Plane, 1903 — AP28

46th anniv. of the 1st successful flight in a motor-powered airplane, Dec. 17, 1903, at Kill Devil Hill near Kitty Hawk, NC, by Wilbur (1867-1912) and Orville Wright (1871-1948) of Dayton, OH. The plane flew 852 feet in 59 seconds.

ROTARY PRESS PRINTING
E. E. Plates of 200 subjects in four panes of 50 each.

1949, Dec. 17 Unwmk. *Perf. 11x10½*
C45 AP28 6c **magenta** .20 .20
P# block of 4 .70 —

Diamond Head, Honolulu, Hawaii AP29

ROTARY PRESS PRINTING
E. E. Plates of 200 subjects in four panes of 50 each.

1952, Mar. 26 Unwmk. *Perf. 11x10½*
C46 AP29 80c **bright red violet** 5.00 1.25
P# block of 4 22.50 —

POWERED FLIGHT, 50th ANNIV.

First Plane and Modern Plane — AP30

ROTARY PRESS PRINTING
E. E. Plates of 200 subjects in four panes of 50 each.

1953, May 29 Unwmk. *Perf. 11x10½*
C47 AP30 6c **carmine** .20 .20
P# block of 4 .55 —

Eagle in Flight — AP31

Issued primarily for use on domestic post cards.

ROTARY PRESS PRINTING
E. E. Plates of 400 subjects in four panes of 100 each.

1954, Sept. 3 Unwmk. *Perf. 11x10½*
C48 AP31 4c **bright blue** .20 .20
P# block of 4 1.10 —

AIR FORCE, 50th ANNIV.

B-52 Stratofortress and F-104 Starfighters AP32

Designed by Alexander Nagy, Jr.

ROTARY PRESS PRINTING
E. E. Plates of 200 subjects in four panes of 50 each.

1957, Aug. 1 Unwmk. *Perf. 11x10½*
C49 AP32 6c **blue** .20 .20
P# block of 4 .70 —

Type of 1954

Issued primarily for use on domestic post cards.

1958, July 31 Unwmk. *Perf. 11x10½*
C50 AP31 5c **red** .20 .20
P# block of 4 1.00 —

Silhouette of Jet Airliner — AP33

Designed by William H. Buckley and Sam Marsh.

ROTARY PRESS PRINTING
E. E. Plates of 400 subjects in four panes of 100 each.

1958, July 31 Unwmk. *Perf. 10½x11*
C51 AP33 7c **blue** .20 .20
P# block of 4 .60 —
a. Booklet pane of 6 9.00 7.00
b. Vert. pair, imperf. between (from booklet pane) —

No. C51b resulted from a paper foldover after perforating and before cutting into panes. Two pairs are known.

ROTARY PRESS COIL STAMP
Perf. 10 Horizontally

C52 AP33 7c **blue** 2.00 .20
Pair 4.25 .40
Joint line pair 14.00 1.25
Small holes 10.00 —
Pair 20.00
Joint line pair 200.00

ALASKA STATEHOOD ISSUE

Big Dipper, North Star and Map of Alaska — AP34

Designed by Richard C. Lockwood.

ROTARY PRESS PRINTING

E. E. Plates of 200 subjects in four panes of 50 each.

1959, Jan. 3	Unwmk.	*Perf. 11x10½*		
C53 AP34 7c	**dark blue**		.20	.20
	P# block of 4		.75	—

BALLOON JUPITER ISSUE

Balloon and Crowd — AP35

Designed by Austin Briggs.

Centenary of the carrying of mail by the balloon Jupiter from Lafayette to Crawfordsville, Ind.

GIORI PRESS PRINTING

Plates of 200 subjects in four panes of 50 each.

1959, Aug. 17	Unwmk.	*Perf. 11*		
C54 AP35 7c	**dark blue & red**		.30	.20
	P# block of 4		1.40	—

HAWAII STATEHOOD ISSUE

Alii Warrior, Map of Hawaii and Star of Statehood AP36

Designed by Joseph Feher.

ROTARY PRESS PRINTING

E. E. Plates of 200 subjects in four panes of 50 each.

1959, Aug. 21	Unwmk.	*Perf. 11x10½*		
C55 AP36 7c	**rose red**		.20	.20
	P# block of 4		.75	—

PAN AMERICAN GAMES ISSUE

Runner Holding Torch — AP37

Designed by Suren Ermoyan.

3rd Pan American Games, Chicago, Aug. 27-Sept. 7, 1959.

GIORI PRESS PRINTING

Plates of 200 subjects in four panes of 50 each.

1959, Aug. 27	Unwmk.	*Perf. 11*		
C56 AP37 10c	**violet blue & bright red**		.25	.25
	P# block of 4		1.25	—

Liberty Bell — AP38

Statue of Liberty AP39

Abraham Lincoln AP40

GIORI PRESS PRINTING

Plates of 200 subjects in four panes of 50 each.

1959-66	Unwmk.	*Perf. 11*		
C57 AP38 10c	**black & green,** *June 10, 1960*		1.00	.70
	P# block of 4		6.00	—
C58 AP39 15c	**black & orange,** *Nov. 20, 1959*		.35	.20
	P# block of 4		1.50	—
C59 AP40 25c	**black & maroon,** *Apr. 22, 1960*		.50	.20
	P# block of 4		2.00	—
a.	Tagged, *Dec. 29, 1966*		.60	.30
	P# block of 4		2.50	—
	Nos. C57-C59 (3)		1.85	1.10

See Luminescence data in Information for Collectors section.

Type of 1958

ROTARY PRESS PRINTING

E. E. Plates of 400 subjects in four panes of 100 each.

1960, Aug. 12	Unwmk.	*Perf. 10½x11*		
C60 AP33 7c	**carmine**		.20	.20
	P# block of 4		.60	—
	Pair with full horiz. gutter btwn.		125.00	
a.	Booklet pane of 6, *Aug. 19*		10.00	8.00
b.	Vert. pair, imperf between (from booklet pane)		*5,500.*	

No. C60b resulted from a paper foldover after perforating and before cutting into panes. Two pairs are known.

Type of 1958

ROTARY PRESS COIL STAMP

1960, Oct. 22	Unwmk.	*Perf. 10 Horizontally*		
C61 AP33 7c	**carmine**		4.00	.25
	Pair		8.25	.55
	Joint line pair		35.00	3.75

Type of 1959-60 and

Statue of Liberty AP41

GIORI PRESS PRINTING

Plates of 200 subjects in four panes of 50 each.

1961-67	Unwmk.	*Perf. 11*		
C62 AP38 13c	**black & red,** *June 28, 1961*		.40	.20
	P# block of 4		1.65	—
a.	Tagged, *Feb. 15, 1967*		.75	.50
	P# block of 4		6.00	—
C63 AP41 15c	**black & orange,** *Jan. 13, 1961*		.30	.20
	P# block of 4		1.25	—
a.	Tagged, *Jan. 11, 1967*		.35	.20
	P# block of 4		1.50	—
b.	As "a," horiz. pair, imperf. vert.		*15,000.*	
c.	As "a," horiz. pair, imperf between and at left		*2,750.*	
d.	All color omitted		—	

On No. C63d, there is a clear albino plate impression.

Jet Airliner over Capitol — AP42

Designed by Henry K. Bencsath.

ROTARY PRESS PRINTING

E.E. Plates of 400 subjects in four panes of 100 each.

1962, Dec. 5	Unwmk.	*Perf. 10½x11*		
C64 AP42 8c	**carmine**		.20	.20
	P# block of 4		.65	—
a.	Tagged, *Aug. 1, 1963*		.20	.20
	P# block of 4		.65	—
	As "a," pair with full horiz. gutter between		—	
b.	Booklet pane of 5 + label		7.00	3.00
c.	As "b," tagged, *1964*		2.00	.75

Nos. C64a and C64c were made by overprinting Nos. C64 and C64b with phosphorescent ink. No. C64a was first issued at Dayton, O., for experiments in high speed mail sorting. The tagging is visible in ultraviolet light.

COIL STAMP; ROTARY PRESS

Perf. 10 Horizontally

C65 AP42 8c	**carmine**		.40	.20
	Pair		.80	.20
	Joint line pair		3.75	.35
a.	Tagged, *Sept. 1964*		.35	.20
	Pair		.70	.20
	Joint line pair		1.75	.30

Earliest documented use of C65a: Jan. 14, 1965.

MONTGOMERY BLAIR ISSUE

Montgomery Blair — AP43

Designed by Robert J. Jones

Montgomery Blair (1813-83), Postmaster General (1861-64), who called the 1st Intl. Postal Conf., Paris, 1863, forerunner of the UPU.

GIORI PRESS PRINTING

Plates of 200 subjects in four panes of 50 each.

1963, May 3	Unwmk.	*Perf. 11*		
C66 AP43 15c	**dull red, dark brown & blue**		.60	.55
	P# block of 4		2.50	—

Bald Eagle — AP44

Designed by V. S. McCloskey, Jr.

Issued primarily for use on domestic post cards.

ROTARY PRESS PRINTING

E.E. Plates of 400 subjects in four panes of 100 each.

1963, July 12	Unwmk.	*Perf. 11x10½*		
C67 AP44 6c	**red**		.20	.20
	P# block of 4		1.40	—
a.	Tagged, *Feb. 15, 1967*		4.00	3.00
	P# block of 4		62.50	—

AMELIA EARHART ISSUE

Amelia Earhart and Lockheed Electra — AP45

Designed by Robert J. Jones.

Amelia Earhart (1898-1937), 1st woman to fly across the Atlantic.

GIORI PRESS PRINTING

Plates of 200 subjects in four panes of 50 each.

1963, July 24 **Unwmk.** ***Perf. 11***

C68 AP45 8c **carmine & maroon**	.20	.20
P# block of 4	1.00	—

ROBERT H. GODDARD ISSUE

Robert H. Goddard, Atlas Rocket and Launching Tower, Cape Kennedy AP46

Designed by Robert J. Jones.

Dr. Robert H. Goddard (1882-1945), physicist and pioneer rocket researcher.

GIORI PRESS PRINTING

Plates of 200 subjects in four panes of 50 each.

1964, Oct. 5 **Tagged** ***Perf. 11***

C69 AP46 8c **blue, red & bister**	.40	.20
P# block of 4	1.75	—
Margin block of 4, Mr. Zip and "Use Zip Code"	1.65	—
a. Tagging omitted		—

Luminescence

Air Post stamps issued after mid-1964 are tagged.

ALASKA PURCHASE ISSUE

Tlingit Totem, Southern Alaska — AP47

Designed by Willard R. Cox

Centenary of the Alaska Purchase. The totem pole shown is in the Alaska State Museum, Juneau.

GIORI PRESS PRINTING

Plates of 200 subjects in four panes of 50 each.

1967, Mar. 30 **Unwmk.** ***Perf. 11***

C70 AP47 8c **brown**	.25	.20
P# block of 4	1.10	—
Margin block of 4, Mr. Zip and "Use Zip Code"	1.05	—

"Columbia Jays" by John James Audubon — AP48

Fifty-Star Runway — AP49

GIORI PRESS PRINTING

Designed by Robert J. Jones.

Plates of 200 subjects in four panes of 50 each.

1967, Apr. 26 ***Perf. 11***

C71 AP48 20c **multicolored**	.80	.20
P# block of 4	3.50	—
Margin block of 4, Mr. Zip and "Use Zip Code"	3.25	—
a. Tagging omitted	*10.00*	

See note over No. 1241.

ROTARY PRESS PRINTING

Designed by Jaan Born.

E. E. Plates of 400 subjects in four panes of 100 each.

1968, Jan. 5 **Unwmk.** ***Perf. 11x10½***

C72 AP49 10c **carmine**	.20	.20
P# block of 4	.90	—
Margin block of 4, "Use Zip Codes"	.85	—
Vert. pair with full horiz. gutter between	—	
b. Booklet pane of 8	2.00	.75
c. Booklet pane of 5 + label, *Jan. 6*	3.75	.75
d. Vert. pair, imperf. between (from bklt. pane)	*4,000.*	
e. Tagging omitted	*12.00*	—
f. As "b," tagging omitted		—

Red is the normal color of the tagging. Copies of No. C72b exist that have a mixture of the two tagging compounds.

No. C72d resulted from a paper foldover after perforating and before cutting into panes. Two pairs are recorded from different panes.

ROTARY PRESS COIL STAMP

Perf. 10 Vertically

C73 AP49 10c **carmine**	.30	.20
Pair	.65	.20
Joint line pair	1.75	.20
a. Imperf., pair	*600.00*	
Joint line pair	*900.00*	

$1 Air Lift

This stamp, listed as No. 1341, was issued Apr. 4, 1968, to pay for airlift of parcels to and from U.S. ports to servicemen overseas and in Alaska, Hawaii and Puerto Rico.

It was "also valid for paying regular rates for other types of mail," the Post Office Department announced to the public in a philatelic release dated Mar. 10, 1968. The stamp is inscribed "U.S. Postage" and is untagged.

On Apr. 26, 1969, the P.O.D. stated in its Postal Manual (for postal employees) that this stamp "may be used toward paying the postage or fees for special services on *airmail* articles." On Jan. 1, 1970, the Department told postal employees through its Postal Bulletin that this $1 stamp "can only be used to pay the airlift fee or toward payment of postage or fees on *airmail* articles."

Some collectors prefer to consider No. 1341 an airmail stamp.

50th ANNIVERSARY OF AIR MAIL ISSUE

Curtiss Jenny — AP50

Designed by Hordur Karlsson.

50th anniv. of regularly scheduled air mail service.

LITHOGRAPHED, ENGRAVED (GIORI)

Plates of 200 subjects in four panes of 50 each.

1968, May 15 ***Perf. 11***

C74 AP50 10c **blue, black & red**	.25	.20
P# block of 4	1.40	—
Margin block of 4, Mr. Zip and "Use Zip Code"	1.05	—
b. Tagging omitted	*8.00*	

"USA" and Jet — AP51

Designed by John Larrecq.

LITHOGRAPHED, ENGRAVED (GIORI)

Plates of 200 subjects in four panes of 50 each.

1968, Nov. 22 ***Perf. 11***

C75 AP51 20c **red, blue & black**	.35	.20
P# block of 4	1.75	—
Margin block of 4, Mr. Zip and "Use Zip Code"	1.50	—
a. Tagging omitted	*10.00*	

MOON LANDING ISSUE

First Man on the Moon AP52

Designed by Paul Calle.

Man's first landing on the moon July 20, 1969, by U.S. astronauts Neil A. Armstrong and Col. Edwin E. Aldrin, Jr., with Lieut. Col. Michael Collins piloting Apollo 11.

LITHOGRAPHED, ENGRAVED (GIORI)

Plates of 128 subjects in four panes of 32 each.

1969, Sept. 9 ***Perf. 11***

C76 AP52 10c **yellow, black, lt. blue, ultra., rose red & carmine**	.25	.20
P# block of 4	1.10	—
Margin block of 4, Mr. Zip and "Use Zip Code"	1.05	—
a. Rose red (litho.) omitted	*525.00*	—
b. Tagging omitted		—

On No. C76a, the lithographed rose red is missing from the entire vignette-the dots on top of the yellow areas as well as the flag shoulder patch.

Silhouette of Delta Wing Plane — AP53

Silhouette of Jet Airliner — AP54

Winged Airmail Envelope — AP55

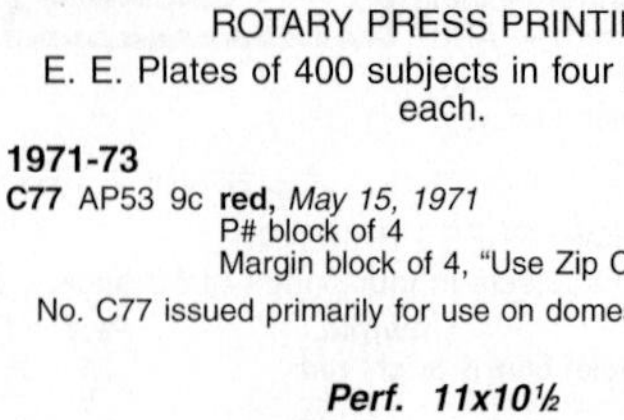

Statue of Liberty AP56

Designed by George Vander Sluis (9c, 11c), Nelson Gruppo (13c) and Robert J. Jones (17c).

ROTARY PRESS PRINTING

E. E. Plates of 400 subjects in four panes of 100 each.

1971-73 ***Perf. 10½x11***

C77 AP53 9c **red,** *May 15, 1971*	.20	.20
P# block of 4	.90	—
Margin block of 4, "Use Zip Codes"	.85	—

No. C77 issued primarily for use on domestic post cards.

Perf. 11x10½

C78 AP54 11c **carmine,** *May 7, 1971*	.20	.20
P# block of 4	.90	—
Margin block of 4, "Use Zip Codes"	.85	—
Pair with full vert. gutter btwn.	—	
a. Booklet pane of 4 + 2 labels	1.25	.75
b. Untagged (Bureau precanceled)	.85	.85
P# block of 4	27.50	—
Margin block of 4, "Use Zip Codes"	13.75	—
c. Tagging omitted (not Bureau precanceled)	7.50	
C79 AP55 13c **carmine,** *Nov. 16, 1973*	.25	.20
P# block of 4	1.10	—
Margin block of 4, "Use Zip Codes"	1.05	—
a. Booklet pane of 5 + label, *Dec. 27, 1973*	1.50	.75
b. Untagged (Bureau precanceled)	.85	.85

P# block of 4 11.50 —
Margin block of 4, "Use Zip Codes" 9.50 —
c. Green instead of red tagging (single from booklet pane) —
d. Tagging omitted (not precanceled) 7.50 —

No. C78b Bureau precanceled "WASHINGTON D.C." (or "DC" - more valuable thus), No. C79b "WASHINGTON DC" only; both for use of Congressmen, but available to any permit holder.

Red is the normal color of the tagging. Copies also exist that have a mixture of the two tagging compounds.

GIORI PRESS PRINTING

Panes of 200 subjects in four panes of 50 each.

Perf. 11

C80 AP56 17c **bluish black, red, & dark green,** *July 13, 1971* .35 .20
P# block of 4 1.60 —
Margin block of 4, Mr. Zip and "Use Zip Code" 1.50 —
a. Tagging omitted 10.00 —

"USA" & Jet Type of 1968

LITHOGRAPHED, ENGRAVED (GIORI)

Plates of 200 subjects in four panes of 50 each.

Perf. 11

C81 AP51 21c **red, blue & black,** *May 21, 1971* .40 .20
P# block of 4 2.00 —
Margin block of 4, Mr. Zip and "Use Zip Code" 1.75 —
a. Tagging omitted *10.00*
b. Black (engr.) missing (FO) *2,750.*

The two recorded examples of No. C81b are in a single full pane. Catalogue value is for both errors.

COIL STAMPS

ROTARY PRESS PRINTING

1971-73 ***Perf. 10 Vertically***

C82 AP54 11c **carmine,** *May 7, 1971* .25 .20
Pair .50 .25
Joint line pair .85 .35
a. Imperf., pair *250.00*
Joint line pair *425.00*
b. Tagging omitted 11.00
C83 AP55 13c **carmine,** *Dec. 27, 1973* .30 .20
Pair .60 .25
Joint line pair 1.10 —
a. Imperf., pair 75.00
Joint line pair 150.00
b. Tagging omitted —

NATIONAL PARKS CENTENNIAL ISSUE

City of Refuge, Hawaii

Kii Statue and Temple — AP57

Designed by Paul Rabut.

Centenary of national parks. This 11c honors the City of Refuge National Historical Park, established in 1961 at Honaunau, island of Hawaii.

LITHOGRAPHED, ENGRAVED (GIORI)

Plates of 200 subjects in four panes of 50 each.

1972, May 3 ***Perf. 11***

C84 AP57 11c **orange & multicolored** .20 .20
P# block of 4 .90 —
Margin block of 4, Mr. Zip and "Use Zip Code" .85 —
a. Blue & green (litho.) omitted *750.00*
b. Tagging omitted — —

OLYMPIC GAMES ISSUE

Skiing and Olympic Rings — AP58

Designed by Lance Wyman.

11th Winter Olympic Games, Sapporo, Japan, Feb. 3-13, and 20th Summer Olympic Games, Munich, Germany, Aug. 26-Sept. 11.

PHOTOGRAVURE (Andreotti)

Plates of 200 subjects in four panes of 50 each.

1972, Aug. 17 ***Perf. 11x10½***

C85 AP58 11c **black, blue, red, emerald & yellow** .20 .20
P# block of 10, 5 P# 2.40 —
Margin block of 4, "Use Zip Code" .85 —

ELECTRONICS PROGRESS ISSUE

De Forest Audions AP59

Designed by Walter and Naiad Einsel.

LITHOGRAPHED, ENGRAVED (GIORI)

Plates of 200 subjects in four panes of 50 each.

1973, July 10 ***Perf. 11***

C86 AP59 11c **vermilion, lilac, pale lilac, olive, brown, deep carmine & black** .30 .20
P# block of 4 1.25 —
Margin block of 4, Mr. Zip and "Use Zip Code" 1.20 —
a. Vermilion & olive (litho.) omitted *900.00*
b. Tagging omitted *25.00*
c. Olive omitted —

Statue of Liberty AP60

Mt. Rushmore National Memorial AP61

Designed by Robert (Gene) Shehorn.

GIORI PRESS PRINTING

Panes of 200 subjects in four panes of 50 each.

1974 ***Perf. 11***

C87 AP60 18c **carmine, black & ultramarine,** *Jan. 11* .35 .30
P# block of 4, 2# 1.50 —
Margin block of 4, Mr. Zip and "Use Zip Code" 1.45 —
a. Tagging omitted *20.00*
C88 AP61 26c **ultramarine, black & carmine,** *Jan. 2* .60 .20
P# block of 4 2.30 —
Margin block of 4, Mr. Zip and "Use Zip Code" 2.20 —
Pair with full vert. gutter btwn. —
a. Tagging omitted *17.50*
b. Yellow-green instead of orange-red tagging — —

Plane and Globes AP62

Plane, Globes and Flags — AP63

Designed by David G. Foote.

GIORI PRESS PRINTING

Panes of 200 subjects in four panes of 50 each.

1976, Jan. 2 ***Perf. 11***

C89 AP62 25c **red, blue & black** .50 .20
P# block of 4 2.25 —
Margin block of 4, Mr. Zip and "Use Zip Code" 2.10 —
a. Tagging omitted *45.00* —
C90 AP63 31c **red, blue & black** .60 .20
P# block of 4 2.60 —
Margin block of 4, Mr. Zip and "Use Zip Code" 2.50 —
a. Tagging omitted *10.00*

WRIGHT BROTHERS ISSUE

Orville and Wilbur Wright, and Flyer A — AP64

Wright Brothers, Flyer A and Shed — AP65

Designed by Ken Dallison.

75th anniv. of 1st powered flight, Kill Devil Hill, NC, Dec. 17, 1903.

LITHOGRAPHED, ENGRAVED (GIORI)

Plates of 400 subjects in four panes of 100 each.

1978, Sept. 23 ***Perf. 11***

C91 AP64 31c **ultramarine & multicolored** .65 .30
C92 AP65 31c **ultramarine & multicolored** .65 .30
a. Vert. pair, #C91-C92 1.30 1.20
P# block of 4 3.00 —
Margin block of 4, "Use Correct Zip Code" 2.75 —
b. As "a," ultra. & black (engr.) omitted *700.00*
c. As "a," black (engr.) omitted *2,500.*
d. As "a," black, yellow, magenta, blue & brown (litho.) omitted *2,250.*

OCTAVE CHANUTE ISSUE

Chanute and Biplane Hang-glider — AP66

Biplane Hang-glider and Chanute — AP67

Designed by Ken Dallison.

Octave Chanute (1832-1910), civil engineer and aviation pioneer.

LITHOGRAPHED, ENGRAVED (GIORI)

Plates of 400 subjects in four panes of 100 each.

1979, Mar. 29 **Tagged** ***Perf. 11***

C93 AP66 21c **blue & multicolored** .70 .35
C94 AP67 21c **blue & multicolored** .70 .35
a. Vert. pair, #C93-C94 1.40 1.20
P# block of 4 3.00 —
Margin block of 4, Mr. Zip 2.85 —
b. As "a," ultra & black (engr.) omitted *3,750.*

WILEY POST ISSUE

Wiley Post and "Winnie Mae" — AP68

NR-105-W, Post in Pressurized Suit, Portrait — AP69

Designed by Ken Dallison.

Wiley Post (1899-1935), first man to fly around the world alone and high-altitude flying pioneer.

LITHOGRAPHED, ENGRAVED (GIORI)

Plates of 400 subjects in four panes of 100 each.

1979, Nov. 20	Tagged	Perf. 11	
C95 AP68 25c **blue & multicolored**		1.10	.45
C96 AP69 25c **blue & multicolored**		1.10	.45
a. Vert. pair, #C95-C96		2.25	1.50
P# block of 4		4.75	—
Margin block of 4, Mr. Zip		4.50	—

OLYMPIC GAMES ISSUE

High Jump — AP70

Designed by Robert M. Cunningham.

22nd Olympic Games, Moscow, July 19-Aug. 3, 1980.

PHOTOGRAVURE

Plates of 200 subjects in four panes of 50 each.

1979, Nov. 1	Tagged	Perf. 11	
C97 AP70 31c **multicolored**		.70	.30
P# block of 12, 6#		9.50	—
Zip block of 4		3.00	—

PHILIP MAZZEI (1730-1816)

Italian-born Political Writer — AP71

Designed by Sante Graziani

PHOTOGRAVURE

Plates of 200 subjects in four panes of 50 each.

1980, Oct. 13	Tagged	Perf. 11	
C98 AP71 40c **multicolored**		.80	.20
P# block of 12, 6#		10.00	—
Zip block of 4		3.50	—
b. Imperf., pair		*3,500.*	
d. Tagging omitted		*11.00*	

1982	Tagged	Perf. 10½x11¼	
C98A AP71 40c **multicolored**		8.00	1.50
P# block of 12, 6#		125.00	—
c. Horiz. pair, imperf. vert.		*4,250.*	

BLANCHE STUART SCOTT (1886-1970)

First Woman Pilot — AP72

Designed by Paul Calle.

PHOTOGRAVURE

Plates of 200 subjects in four panes of 50.

1980, Dec. 30	Tagged	Perf. 11	
C99 AP72 28c **multicolored**		.60	.20
P# block of 12, 6#		8.50	—
Zip block of 4		2.50	—
a. Imperf., pair		*2,500.*	

GLENN CURTISS (1878-1930)

Aviation Pioneer and Aircraft Designer AP73

Designed by Ken Dallison.

PHOTOGRAVURE

Plates of 200 subjects in four panes of 50.

1980, Dec. 30	Tagged	Perf. 11	
C100 AP73 35c **multicolored**		.65	.20
P# block of 12, 6#		9.00	—
Zip block of 4		2.75	—
a. Light blue (background) omitted		*2,000.*	

SUMMER OLYMPICS 1984

Women's Gymnastics — AP74

Hurdles — AP75

Women's Basketball — AP76

Soccer — AP77

Shot Put — AP78

Men's Gymnastics AP79

Women's Swimming AP80

Weight Lifting — AP81

Women's Fencing AP82

Cycling AP83

Women's Volleyball AP84

Pole Vaulting AP85

Designed by Robert Peak.

23rd Olympic Games, Los Angeles, July 28-Aug. 12, 1984.

PHOTOGRAVURE

Plates of 200 subjects in four panes of 50.

1983, June 17	Tagged	Perf. 11	
C101 AP74 28c **multicolored**		1.00	.30
C102 AP75 28c **multicolored**		1.00	.30
C103 AP76 28c **multicolored**		1.00	.30
C104 AP77 28c **multicolored**		1.00	.30
a. Block of 4, #C101-C104		4.25	2.50
P# block of 4, 4#		5.50	—
Zip block of 4		4.25	—
b. As "a," imperf. vert.		*7,500.*	

1983, Apr. 8	Tagged	Perf. 11.2 Bullseye	
C105 AP78 40c **multicolored**		.90	.40
a. Perf. 11 line		1.00	.45
C106 AP79 40c **multicolored**		.90	.40
a. Perf. 11 line		1.00	.45
C107 AP80 40c **multicolored**		.90	.40
a. Perf. 11 line		1.00	.45
C108 AP81 40c **multicolored**		.90	.40
a. Perf. 11 line		1.00	.45
b. Block of 4, #C105-C108		4.25	3.00
P# block of 4, 4#		5.00	—
Zip block of 4		4.50	—
c. Block of 4, #C105a-C108a		5.00	4.00
P# block of 4, 4#		7.50	—
d. Block of 4, imperf.		*1,000.*	

1983, Nov. 4	Tagged	*Perf. 11*	
C109 AP82 35c **multicolored**		.90	.55
C110 AP83 35c **multicolored**		.90	.55
C111 AP84 35c **multicolored**		.90	.55
C112 AP85 35c **multicolored**		.90	.55
a. Block of 4, #C109-C112		4.00	3.25
P# block of 4, 4#		6.50	—
Zip block of 4		4.25	—

AVIATION PIONEERS

Alfred V. Verville (1890-1970), Inventor, Verville-Sperry R-3 Army Racer — AP86

Lawrence Sperry (1892-1931), Aircraft Designer, and Father Elmer (1860-1930), Designer and Pilot, 1st Seaplane AP87

Designed by Ken Dallison (No. C113) and Howard Koslow (No. C114)

PHOTOGRAVURE
Plates of 200 in four panes of 50
(2 panes each, No. C113 and No. C114)
Plates of 200 in four panes of 50 (No. C114)

1985, Feb. 13	Tagged	*Perf. 11*	
C113 AP86 33c **multicolored**		.65	.20
P# block of 4, 5#, UL, LR		3.25	—
Zip block of 4		2.90	—
a. Imperf., pair		*850.00*	
C114 AP87 39c **multicolored**		.80	.25
P# block of 4, 5#, UR, LL		3.75	—
P# block of 4, 4#		3.75	—
Zip block of 4		3.50	—
a. Imperf., pair		*1,750.*	

Philatelic Foundation certificates issued prior to August 1994 for No. C114 with magenta missing have been rescinded. At this time no true magenta missing copies are known.

TRANSPACIFIC AIRMAIL
50th Anniversary

Martin M-130 China Clipper AP88

Designed by Chuck Hodgson.

PHOTOGRAVURE
Plates of 200 in four panes of 50

1985, Feb. 15	Tagged	*Perf. 11*	
C115 AP88 44c **multicolored**		.85	.25
P# block of 4, 4#		4.00	—
Zip block of 4		3.50	—
a. Imperf., pair		*750.00*	

FR. JUNIPERO SERRA (1713-1784)
California Missionary

Outline Map of Southern California, Portrait, San Gabriel Mission AP89

Designed by Richard Schlecht from a Spanish stamp.

PHOTOGRAVURE
Plates of 200 in four panes of 50

1985, Aug. 22	Tagged	*Perf. 11*	
C116 AP89 44c **multicolored**		1.00	.35
P# block of 4		7.50	—
Zip block of 4		4.25	—
a. Imperf., pair		*1,500.*	

SETTLING OF NEW SWEDEN, 350th ANNIV.

Settler, Two Indians, Map of New Sweden, Swedish Ships "Kalmar Nyckel" and "Fogel Grip" — AP90

Designed by Goran Osterland based on an 18th century illustration from a Swedish book about the Colonies.

LITHOGRAPHED AND ENGRAVED
Plates of 200 in four panes of 50

1988, Mar. 29	Tagged	*Perf. 11*	
C117 AP90 44c **multicolored**		1.00	.25
P# block of 4, 5#		6.50	—
Zip block of 4		5.00	—

See Sweden No. 1672 and Finland No. 768.

SAMUEL P. LANGLEY (1834-1906)

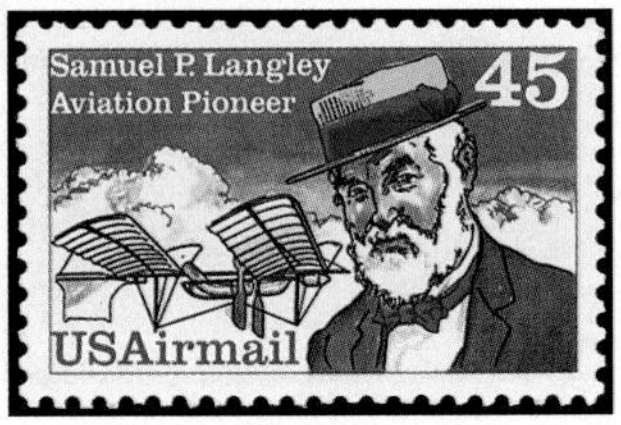

Langley and Unmanned Aerodrome No. 5 — AP91

Designed by Ken Dallison.

LITHOGRAPHED AND ENGRAVED
Plates of 200 in four panes of 50

1988, May 14	Tagged	*Perf. 11*	
C118 AP91 45c **multicolored,** large block tagging		.90	.20
P# block of 4, 7#		4.00	—
Zip block of 4		4.00	—
a. Overall tagging		3.00	.50
P# block of 4, 7#		30.00	—
Zip block of 4		14.00	—

IGOR SIKORSKY (1889-1972)

Sikorsky and 1939 VS300 Helicopter AP92

Designed by Ren Wicks.

PHOTOGRAVURE AND ENGRAVED
Plates of 200 in four panes of 50

1988, June 23	Tagged	*Perf. 11*	
C119 AP92 36c **multicolored**		.70	.25
P# block of 4, 6#		3.25	—
Zip block of 4		3.10	—
a. Red, dk blue & black (engraved) omitted		—	

Beware of copies with traces of engraved red offered as "red omitted" varieties.

FRENCH REVOLUTION BICENTENNIAL

Liberty, Equality and Fraternity — AP93

Designed by Richard Sheaff.

LITHOGRAPHED AND ENGRAVED
Plates of 120 in four panes of 30.

1989, July 14	Tagged	*Perf. 11½x11*	
C120 AP93 45c **multicolored**		.95	.20
P# block of 4, 4#		4.75	—
Zip block of 4		4.00	—

See France Nos. 2143-2145a.

PRE-COLUMBIAN AMERICA ISSUE

Southeast Carved Figure, 700-1430 A.D. — AP94

Designed by Lon Busch.
Printed by American Bank Note Co.

PHOTOGRAVURE
Plates of 200 in four panes of 50

1989, Oct. 12		*Perf. 11*	
C121 AP94 45c **multicolored**		.90	.20
P# block of 4, 4#		5.25	—
Zip block of 4		3.75	—

20th UPU CONGRESS
Futuristic Mail Delivery

Spacecraft — AP95

Air-suspended Hover Car — AP96

Moon Rover — AP97

Space Shuttle — AP98

Designed by Ken Hodges.

LITHOGRAPHED & ENGRAVED

Plates of 160 in four panes of 40.

1989, Nov. 27 **Tagged** ***Perf. 11***

C122 AP95 45c **multicolored**		1.00	.50
C123 AP96 45c **multicolored**		1.00	.50
C124 AP97 45c **multicolored**		1.00	.50
C125 AP98 45c **multicolored**		1.00	.50
a.	Block of 4, #C122-C125	4.00	3.00
	P# block of 4, 5#	5.50	—
	Zip block of 4	4.50	—
b.	As "a," light blue (engr.) omitted	*750.00*	

Souvenir Sheet

LITHOGRAPHED & ENGRAVED

1989, Nov. 24 **Tagged** ***Imperf.***

C126	Sheet of 4	5.00	4.00
a.	AP95 45c multicolored	1.25	.50
b.	AP96 45c multicolored	1.25	.50
c.	AP97 45c multicolored	1.25	.50
d.	AP98 45c multicolored	1.25	.50
e.	As No. C126, tagging omitted	—	

PRE-COLUMBIAN AMERICA ISSUE

Tropical Coast — AP99

Designed by Mark Hess.
Printed by the American Bank Note Company.

PHOTOGRAVURE

Plates of 200 in four panes of 50

(3 panes of #2512, 1 pane of #C127)

1990, Oct. 12 **Tagged** ***Perf. 11***

C127 AP99 45c **multicolored**		.90	.20
	P# block of 4, 4#, UL only	7.00	—
	Zip block of 4	3.75	—

HARRIET QUIMBY, 1ST AMERICAN WOMAN PILOT

Quimby (1884-1912), Bleriot Airplane AP100

Designed by Howard Koslow. Printed by Stamp Venturers.

PHOTOGRAVURE

Panes of 200 in four panes of 50

1991, Apr. 27 **Tagged** ***Perf. 11***

C128 AP100 50c **multicolored**, overall tagging		1.00	.25
	P# block of 4, #S1111	5.25	—
	Zip block of 4	4.25	—
a.	Vert. pair, imperf. horiz.	1,750.	
b.	Perf. 11.2, prephosphored uncoated paper (mottled tagging), *1993*	1.10	.25
	P# block of 4, #S2222	5.75	—
	Zip block of 6	4.50	—

WILLIAM T. PIPER, AIRCRAFT MANUFACTURER

Piper and Piper Cub — AP101

Designed by Ren Wicks.
Printed by J. W. Fergusson and Sons for American Bank Note Co.

PHOTOGRAVURE

Panes of 200 in four panes of 50

1991, May 17 **Tagged** ***Perf. 11***

C129 AP101 40c **multicolored**		.80	.20
	P# block of 4, 4#+A	3.75	—
	Zip block of 4	3.50	—

Blue sky is plainly visible all the way across stamp above Piper's head.

See No. C132.

ANTARCTIC TREATY, 30TH ANNIVERSARY

AP102

Designed by Howard Koslow. Printed by Stamp Venturers.

PHOTOGRAVURE

Panes of 50

1991, June 21 **Tagged** ***Perf. 11***

C130 AP102 50c **multicolored**		1.00	.35
	P# block of 4, 4#+S	5.00	—
	Zip block of 4	4.25	—

PRE-COLUMBIAN AMERICA ISSUE

Bering Land Bridge AP103

Designed by Richard Schlect.

PHOTOGRAVURE

Plates of 200 in 4 panes of 50

1991, Oct. 12 **Tagged** ***Perf. 11***

C131 AP103 50c **multicolored**		1.00	.35
	P# block of 4, 6#	5.25	—
	Zip block of 4	4.75	—

Piper Type of 1991

Printed by Stamp Venturers.

PHOTOGRAVURE

Panes of 200 in four panes of 50

1993 **Tagged** ***Perf. 11.2***

C132 AP101 40c **multicolored**		2.75	.65
	P# block of 4, 4#+S	52.50	—
	Zip block of 4	12.00	—

Piper's hair touches top edge of design. No inscriptions. Bullseye perf.

"All LC (Letters and Cards) mail receives First-Class Mail service in the United States, is dispatched by the fastest transportation available, and travels by airmail or priority service in the destination country. All LC mail should be marked 'AIRMAIL' or 'PAR AVION.'" (U.S. Postal Service, Pub. 51).

No. C133 listed below was issued to meet the LC rate to Canada and Mexico and is inscribed with the silhouette of a jet plane next to the denomination indicating the need for airmail service. This is unlike No. 2998, which met the LC rate to other countries, but contained no indication that it was intended for that use.

Future issues that meet a specific international airmail rate and contain the airplane silhouette will be treated by Scott as Air Post stamps. Stamps similar to No. 2998 will be listed in the Postage section.

SCENIC AMERICAN LANDSCAPES

Niagara Falls AP104

Designed by Ethel Kessler. Printed by Avery Dennison.

PHOTOGRAVURE

Sheets of 200 in ten panes of 20

1999, May 12 **Tagged** ***Serpentine Die Cut 11***

Self-Adhesive

C133 AP104 48c **multicolored**		.95	.20
	P# block of 4, 5#+V	4.00	
	Pane of 20	20.00	

Rio Grande AP105

Designed by Ethel Kessler. Printed by Avery Dennison.

PHOTOGRAVURE

Sheets of 200 in ten panes of 20

1999, July 30 **Tagged** ***Serpentine Die Cut 11***

Self-Adhesive

C134 AP105 40c **multicolored**		.80	.60
	P# block of 4, 5#+V	3.20	
	Pane of 20	16.00	

Grand Canyon AP106

Designed by Ethel Kessler.
Printed by Banknote Corp. of America.

LITHOGRAPHED

Sheets of 180 in nine panes of 20

Serpentine Die Cut 11¼x11½

2000, Jan. 20 **Tagged**

Self-Adhesive

C135 AP106 60c **multicolored**		1.25	.25
	P# block of 4, 4#+B	5.00	
	Pane of 20	25.00	
a.	Die cutting omitted, pair	*2,250.*	
b.	Vert. pair, die cutting omitted horiz.	—	
c.	Horiz. pair, die cutting omitted between	—	
d.	Horiz. pair, vert. die cutting omitted	—	

Nine-Mile Prairie, Nebraska AP107

Designed by Ethel Kessler. Printed by Ashton-Potter (USA) Ltd.

LITHOGRAPHED

Sheets of 180 in nine panes of 20

Serpentine Die Cut 11¼x11½

2001, Mar. 6 **Tagged**

Self-Adhesive

C136 AP107 70c **multicolored**		1.40	.30
	P# block of 4, 5#+P	5.60	
	Pane of 20	28.00	

Mt. McKinley AP108

Designed by Ethel Kessler. Printed by Avery Dennison.

PHOTOGRAVURE

Sheets of 200 in ten panes of 20.

2001, Apr. 17 **Tagged** ***Serpentine Die Cut 11***

Self-Adhesive

C137 AP108 80c **multicolored**		1.60	.35
	P# block of 4, 5 #+V	6.40	
	Pane of 20	32.00	

Acadia National Park — AP109

Designed by Ethel Kessler. Printed by Banknote Corporation of America.

LITHOGRAPHED

Sheets of 180 in nine panes of 20 (#C138), Sheets of 120 in six panes of 20 (#C138a)

Serpentine Die Cut 11.25x11.5 (No. C138), 11.5x11.9 (No. C138a)

2001-05 **Tagged**

Self-Adhesive

C138 AP109 60c **multicolored**, prephosphored coated paper (solid tagging), *May 30, 2001* 1.25 .25
P# block of 4, 4# + B 5.00
Pane of 20 25.00
a. Overall tagging, *March 2003* 1.25 .25
P# block of 4, 4# + B 5.00
Pane of 20 25.00
b. As "a," with "2005" year date, *Jan. 2005* 1.25 .25
P# block of 4, 4#+S 5.00
Pane of 20 25.00
c. As "b," printed on back of backing paper —

Bryce Canyon National Park — AP110

Great Smoky Mountains National Park — AP111

Designed by Ethel Kessler. Printed by Banknote Corporation of America for Sennett Security Products (#C139), Ashton-Potter (USA) Ltd. (#C140), Avery Dennison (#C141).

LITHOGRAPHED, PHOTOGRAVURE (#C141)

Sheets of 180 in nine panes of 20 and sheets of 160 in eight panes of 20 (#C139), Sheets of 120 in six panes of 20 (#C140), Sheets of 200 in ten panes of 20 (#C141)

2006, Feb. 24 **Tagged** ***Serpentine Die Cut 10¾***

Self-Adhesive

C139 AP110 63c **multicolored** 1.25 .25
P# block of 4, 5#+S 5.00
Pane of 20 25.00
a. Die cutting omitted, pair —
C140 AP111 75c **multicolored** 1.50 .35
P# block of 4, 5#+P 6.00
Pane of 20 30.00
a. Die cutting omitted, pair —

Two printings of No. C139 with different plate # order. Sheet of 180 has gray plate # first (and has glossier finish). Sheet of 160 has gray plate # last.

Yosemite National Park — AP112

Serpentine Die Cut 11

C141 AP112 84c **multicolored** 1.75 .35
P# block of 4, 5#+V 7.00
Pane of 20 35.00
Nos. C139-C141 (3) 4.50 .95

Okefenokee Swamp, Georgia and Florida AP113

Hagatña Bay, Guam AP114

Designed by Ethel Kessler. Printed by Ashton-Potter (USA) Ltd. (#C142), Avery Dennison (#C143).

LITHOGRAPHED (#C142), PHOTOGRAVURE (#C143)

Sheets of 120 in six panes of 20 (#C142), Sheets of 200 in ten panes of 20 (#C143)

2007, June 1 **Tagged** ***Serpentine Die Cut 10¾***

Self-Adhesive

C142 AP113 69c **multicolored** 1.40 .30
P# block of 4, 5#+P 5.60
Pane of 20 28.00

Serpentine Die Cut 11

C143 AP114 90c **multicolored** 1.80 .40
P# block of 4, 5#+V 7.20
Pane of 20 36.00

13-Mile Woods, New Hampshire AP115

Trunk Bay, St. John, Virgin Islands AP116

Designed by Ethel Kessler. Printed by Banknote Corporation of America for Sennett Security Products (#C144), Avery Dennison (#C145).

LITHOGRAPHED (#C144), PHOTOGRAVURE (#C145)

Sheets of 180 in nine panes of 20 (#C144), Sheets of 200 in ten panes of 20 (#C145)

2008, May 16 **Tagged** ***Serpentine Die Cut 10¾***

Self-Adhesive

C144 AP115 72c **multicolored** 1.50 .30
P# block of 4, 5#+S 6.00
Pane of 20 30.00

Serpentine Die Cut 11

C145 AP116 94c **multicolored** 1.90 .45
P# block of 4, 5#+V 7.60
Pane of 20 38.00

AIR POST SPECIAL DELIVERY STAMPS

Great Seal of United States APSD1

No. CE1 was issued for the prepayment of the air postage and the special delivery fee in one stamp. First day sale was at the American Air Mail Society Convention.

FLAT PLATE PRINTING

Plates of 200 subjects in four panes of 50 each.

1934, Aug. 30 **Unwmk.** ***Perf. 11***

CE1 APSD1 16c **dark blue** .60 .70
blue .60 .70
Never hinged .80
P# block of 6 15.00 —
Never hinged 22.50
First day cover, Chicago *(40,171)* 25.00
First day cover, Washington, D.C., *Aug. 31* 15.00

For imperforate variety see No. 771.

Type of 1934

Frame plates of 100 subjects in two panes of 50 each separated by a 1½ inch wide vertical gutter with central guide line, and vignette plates of 50 subjects.

The "seal" design for No. CE2 was from a new engraving, slightly smaller than that used for No. CE1.

Top plate number blocks of No. CE2 are found both with and without top arrow.

Issued in panes of 50 each.

1936, Feb. 10

CE2 APSD1 16c **red & blue** .45 .25
Never hinged .60
Margin block of 4, bottom or side arrow 2.00 1.50
Center line block 2.50 2.25
P# block of 4, 2# 8.50 —
Never hinged 12.00
P# block of 4, 2#, blue dotted registration marker 85.00
Never hinged 110.00
Same, arrow, thick red registration marker 80.00
Never hinged 100.00
P# block of 10, 2#, two "TOP" and two registration markers 20.00 6.00
Never hinged 25.00
First day cover Washington, D.C. *(72,981)* 17.50
a. Horiz. pair, imperf. vert. *3,750.*
P# block of 6, 2#, two "TOP" and registration markers *40,000.*

The No. CE2a plate block is unique. Value represents sale in 1997.

Quantities issued: #CE1, 9,215,750; #CE2, 72,517,850.

AIR POST SEMI-OFFICIAL STAMPS

Buffalo Balloon

This stamp was privately issued by John F. B. Lillard, a Nashville reporter. It was used on covers carried on a balloon ascension of June 18, 1877, which began at Nashville and landed at Gallatin, Tenn., and possibly on other flights. The balloon was owned and piloted by Samuel Archer King. The stamp was reported to have been engraved by (Mrs.?) J. H. Snively and printed in tete beche pairs from a single die. Lillard wrote that 300 were printed and 23 used.

Buffalo Balloon — APSO1

1877, June 18	**Typo.**		***Imperf.***
CL1 APSO1 5c **deep blue**		*7,500.*	
Never hinged		*10,000.*	
On cover with 3c #158			*150,000.*
On cover with 1c #156 & 2c #178			*130,000.*
a. Tête bêche pair, vertical		*22,500.*	
Never hinged		—	

A black proof exists of No. CL1, value *$7,500.*

Rodgers Aerial Post

This stamp was privately issued by Calbraith Perry Rodgers' wife who acted as unofficial postmaster during her husband's cross-country airplane flight in 1911. Rodgers was competing for the $50,000 prize offered by William Randolph Hearst to whomever completed the trip within a 30-day period. Rodgers' flight was sponsored by the Armour meat-packing company, makers of the soft drink, Vin Fiz.

The stamp probably was first available in Texas about October 19. Recorded dated examples exist from Oct. 19 to Nov. 8.

Each of the thirteen known examples is trimmed close to the design on one or more sides.

APSO2

1911, Oct.		***Imperf.***
CL2 APSO2 25c **black**	*55,000.*	
On postcard with 1c #374		*75,000.*
Tied on cover with 1c #374		*115,000.*

No. CL2 is the first stamp in the world to picture an airplane.

Four examples are recorded off cover and without cancel (unused column). Only one of these has original gum. The unused value is for a stamp without gum. The example tied on cover is unique. Seven examples are recorded used on postcards.

R.F. OVERPRINTS

Authorized as a control mark by the United States Fleet Post Office during 1944-45 for the accommodation of and exclusive use by French naval personnel on airmail correspondence to the United States and Canada. All "R.F." (Republique Francaise) mail had to be posted on board French ships or at one of their western Mediterranean or northwest African naval bases and had to bear the return address, rank and/or serial number of a French officer or seaman. It also had to be reviewed by a censor.

All "R.F." overprints were handstamped by the French naval authorities after the stamps were affixed for mailing. The stamps had to be canceled by a special French naval cancellation. The status of unused stamps seems questionable; they are alleged to have been handstamped at a later date.

Several types of "R.F." overprints other than those illustrated are known, but their validity is doubtful.

United States No. C25 Handstamped in Black

a

b

c

d

e

f

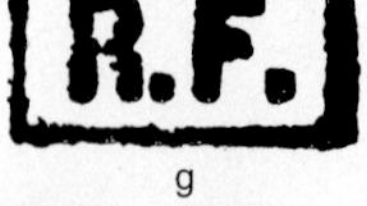

g

h

i

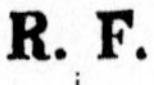

j

k

l

1944-45	**Unwmk.**	***Perf. 11x10½***
CM1	AP17 (a) 6c **carmine,** on cover	300.00
CM2	AP17 (b) 6c **carmine,** on cover	475.00
CM3	AP17 (c) 6c **carmine,** on cover	300.00
CM4	AP17 (d) 6c **carmine,** on cover	350.00
CM5	AP17 (e) 6c **carmine,** on cover	425.00
CM6	AP17 (f) 6c **carmine,** on cover	350.00
CM7	AP17 (g) 6c **carmine,** on cover	600.00
CM8	AP17 (h) 6c **carmine,** on cover	600.00
CM9	AP17 (i) 6c **carmine,** on cover	750.00
CM10	AP17 (j) 6c **carmine,** on cover	—
CM11	AP17 (k) 6c **carmine,** on cover	—
CM12	AP17 (l) 6c **carmine,** on cover	—

Counterfeits of several types exist.

No. 907 is known with type "c" overprint; Nos. 804 and 928 with type "f"; No. C19 with type "e"; No. C25a (single) with type "c","d," "f," and "l"; No. C26 with type "a," "d" or "f."; and No. C28 with type "c." Type "i" exists in several very minor variations.

STAMPED ENVELOPES

Nos. UC3, UC4 or UC6 Handstamped in Black

1944-45		
UCM1	UC2 (a) 6c **orange,** entire	300.00
UCM2	UC2 (b) 6c **orange,** entire	550.00
UCM3	UC2 (d) 6c **orange,** entire	450.00
UCM3A	UC2 (e) 6c **orange,** entire	1,000.
UCM4	UC2 (f) 6c **orange,** entire	550.00
UCM5	UC2 (h) 6c **orange,** entire	—
UCM6	UC2 (i) 6c **orange,** entire	—
UCM7	UC2 (j) 6c **orange,** entire	—
UCM8	UC2 (k) 6c **orange,** entire	—

Values for Nos. UCM1-UCM8 reflect the scarcity of the actual overprint types. Use of No. UC6 envelopes was by far the most common. Overprints on Nos. UC3 or UC4 merit a premium.

Specialist collectors question the existence of No. UCM6. The editors will be deleting this number if authenticated evidence of its existence is not provided.

SPECIAL DELIVERY STAMPS

Special Delivery service was instituted by the Act of Congress of March 3, 1885, and put into operation on October 1, 1885. The Act limited the service to free delivery offices and such others as served places with a population of 4,000 or more, and its privileges were thus operative in but 555 post offices. The Act of August 4, 1886, made the stamps and service available at all post offices and upon any article of mailable matter, beginning Oct. 1, 1886. To consume the supply of stamps of the first issue, Scott No. E2 was withheld until September 6, 1888.

A Special Delivery stamp, when affixed to any stamped letter or article of mailable matter, secured later delivery during daytime and evening at most post offices, so that the item did not have to wait until the next day for delivery.

Messenger Running — SD1

ENGRAVED

Printed by the American Bank Note Co.

Plates of 100 subjects in two panes of 50 each

1885 **Unwmk.** ***Perf. 12***

E1 SD1 10c	**blue**	550.00	70.00
	deep blue	550.00	70.00
	Never hinged	1,250.	
	On cover		130.00
	First day of service cover (Oct. 1)		*20,000.*
	Block of four	2,500.	
	P# block of 8, Impt. 495 or 496	*17,500.*	
	Margin strip of 4, same	5,000.	
	Double transfer at top	850.00	200.00

Earliest documented use: Sept. 29, 1885, on a cover delivered Oct. 1. There is also a Sept. 30 cover recorded, received for delivery at 7:00 a.m. Oct. 1.

Messenger Running SD2

1888, Sept. 6

E2 SD2 10c	**blue**	500.00	35.00
	deep blue	500.00	35.00
	Never hinged	1,150.	
	On cover		95.00
	Block of four	2,250.	
	P# block of 8, Impt. 73 or 552	*16,000.*	
	Never hinged	*22,500.*	
	Margin strip of 4, same	4,750.	

Earliest documented use: Dec. 18, 1888.

See note above No. E3.

COLUMBIAN EXPOSITION ISSUE

Though not issued expressly for the Exposition, No. E3 is considered to be part of that issue. It was released in orange because No. E2 was easily confused with the 1c Columbian, No. 230.

From Jan. 24, 1893, until Jan. 5, 1894, the special delivery stamp was printed in orange; the issue in that color continued until May 19, 1894, when the stock on hand was exhausted. The stamp in blue was not issued from Jan. 24, 1893 to May 19, 1894. However, on Jan. 5, 1894, printing of the stamp in blue was resumed. Presumably it was reissued from May 19, 1894 until the appearance of No. E4 on Oct. 10, 1894. The emissions of the blue stamp of this design before Jan. 24, 1893 and after Jan. 5, 1894 are indistinguishable.

1893, Jan. 24

E3 SD2 10c	**orange**	260.00	40.00
	deep orange	260.00	40.00
	Never hinged	600.00	
	On cover		130.00
	On cover, Columbian Expo. station machine canc.		1,000.
	On cover, Columbian Expo. station duplex handstamp cancel		1,250.
	Block of four	1,150.	
	P# block of 8, Impt. 73 or 552	*11,000.*	
	Never hinged	*15,000.*	
	Margin strip of 4, same	3,750.	

Earliest documented use: Feb. 11, 1893.

Messenger Running — SD3

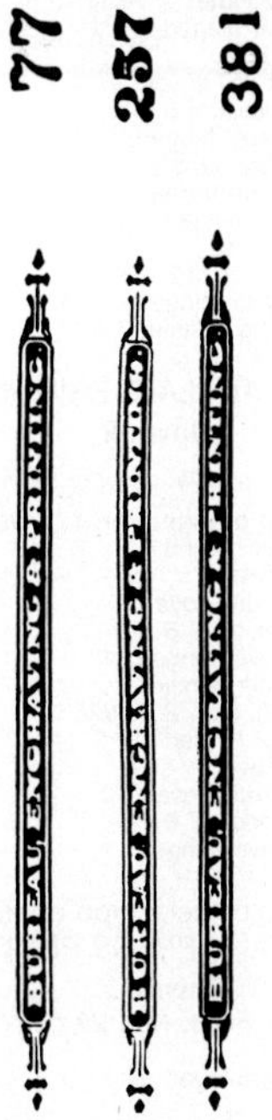

Type III Type VI Type VII

Printed by the Bureau of Engraving and Printing.

1894, Oct. 10

Line under "TEN CENTS"

E4 SD3 10c	**blue**	850.00	55.00
	dark blue	850.00	55.00
	bright blue	1,000.	75.00
	Never hinged	2,100.	
	On cover		210.00
	Block of four	3,750.	
	Margin block of 4, arrow	3,900.	
	P#77 block of 6, T III Impt.	*17,500.*	
	Never hinged	*25,000.*	
	Margin strip of 3, same	5,000.	
	Never hinged	7,500.	
	Double transfer	—	—

Earliest documented use: Oct. 25, 1894.

Imperfs of No. E4 on stamp paper, currently listed as No. E4aP, may not be proofs, but it is also unlikely that they were regularly issued. They most likely are from printer's waste.

1895, Aug. 16 **Wmk. 191**

E5 SD3 10c	**blue**	210.00	10.00
	dark blue	210.00	10.00
	deep blue	210.00	10.00
	Never hinged	475.00	
	On cover		20.00
	Block of four	900.00	
	Margin block of 4, arrow	925.00	
	P# block of 6, T III, VI or VII Impt.	*4,750.*	
	Never hinged	*6,750.*	
	Margin strip of 3, same	900.00	
	Never hinged	1,600.	
	Double transfer	—	32.50
	Line of color through "POSTAL DELIVERY," from bottom row of Plates 1257-1260	300.00	35.00
	Never hinged	625.00	
a.	Dots in curved frame above messenger (Pl. 882)	300.00	20.00
	Never hinged	650.00	
b.	Printed on both sides		—

Earliest documented use: Oct. 3, 1895.

The existence of No. E5b has been questioned by specialists. The editors would like to see authenticated evidence of its existence.

See Die and Plate Proofs for imperf. on stamp paper.

Messenger on Bicycle — SD4

1902, Dec. 9

E6 SD4 10c	**ultramarine**	230.00	10.00
	pale ultramarine	230.00	10.00
	dark ultramarine	240.00	10.00
	Never hinged	525.00	
	On cover		20.00
	Block of four	1,000.	
	Margin block of 4, arrow	1,050.	
	P# block of 6, T VII Impt.	*3,250.*	
	Never hinged	*4,750.*	
	Margin strip of 3, same	825.00	
	Never hinged	1,450.	
	P# block of 6, "09"	*3,000.*	
	Never hinged	*4,500.*	
	Margin strip of 3, same	850.	
	Never hinged	1,500.	
	Double transfer	—	—
	Damaged transfer under "N" of "CENTS"	250.00	15.00
a.	10c **blue**	250.00	10.00
	Never hinged	575.00	
	On cover		25.00
	Block of four	1,100.	
	Margin block of 4, arrow	1,150.	
	P# block of 6, T VII Impt.	*3,500.*	
	Never hinged	*5,000.*	
	Margin strip of 3, same	925.00	
	Never hinged	1,650.	
	Double transfer	—	—

Earliest documented use: Jan. 22, 1903.

No. E6 was re-issued in 1909 from new plates 5240, 5243-5245. After a few months use the Bureau added "09" to these plate numbers. The stamp can be identified only by plate number. The plate numbers without the "09" are scarcer and worth more.

Helmet of Mercury — SD5

Designed by Whitney Warren.

Plates of 280 subjects in four panes of 70 each

1908, Dec. 12

E7 SD5 10c	**green**	70.00	45.00
	dark green	70.00	45.00
	yellowish green	70.00	45.00
	Never hinged	150.00	
	On cover		200.00
	Block of four	300.00	
	P# block of 6, T V Impt.	*1,000.*	—
	Never hinged	*1,400.*	
	Margin strip of 3, same	300.00	
	Never hinged	500.00	
	Double transfer	160.00	100.00

Earliest documented use: Dec. 14, 1908.

Plates of 200 subjects in four panes of 50 each

1911, Jan. **Wmk. 190** ***Perf. 12***

E8	SD4 10c **ultramarine**	110.00	10.00
	pale ultramarine	110.00	10.00
	dark ultramarine	110.00	10.00
	Never hinged	240.00	
	On cover		20.00
	Block of four	460.00	
	P# block of 6, T VII Impt.	*1,850.*	
	Never hinged	*2,750.*	
	P# block of 6	*1,700.*	
	Never hinged	*2,500.*	
	Top frame line missing (Pl. 5514)	150.00	22.50
	Never hinged	325.00	
b.	10c **violet blue**	125.00	12.00
	Never hinged	275.00	
	On cover		25.00
	Block of four	550.00	
	P# block of 6, T VII Impt.	*1,950.*	
	Never hinged	*2,900.*	
	P# block of 6	*1,800.*	
	Never hinged	*2,650.*	

Earliest documented use: Jan. 14, 1911.

1914, Sept. ***Perf. 10***

E9	SD4 10c **ultramarine**	190.00	12.00
	pale ultramarine	190.00	12.00
	Never hinged	425.00	
	On cover		45.00
	Block of four	800.00	
	P# block of 6, T VII Impt.	*4,000.*	—
	Never hinged	*6,000.*	
	P# block of 6	*3,000.*	—
	Never hinged	*4,500.*	
	Margin block of 8, T VII Impt. & P# (side)	—	
a.	10c **blue**	240.00	15.00
	Never hinged	525.00	
	On cover		45.00
	Block of four	1,050.	
	P# block of 6, T VII Impt.	*5,000.*	—
	Never hinged	*7,500.*	
	P# block of 6	*4,000.*	—
	Never hinged	*6,000.*	
	Margin block of 8, T VII Impt. & P# (side)	—	

Earliest documented use: Oct. 26, 1914.

1916, Oct. 19 **Unwmk.** ***Perf. 10***

E10	SD4 10c **pale ultramarine**	320.00	45.00
	ultramarine	340.00	50.00
	Never hinged	700.00	
	On cover		100.00
	Block of four	1,400.	
	P# block of 6, T VII Impt. 5520	*5,500.*	—
	Never hinged	*7,750.*	
	P# block of 6	*5,000.*	—
	Never hinged	*7,250.*	
a.	10c **blue**	350.00	50.00
	Never hinged	750.00	
	On cover		110.00
	Block of four	1,550.	
	P# block of 6, T VII Impt. 5520	*5,750.*	—
	P# block of 6	*5,000.*	—

Earliest documented use: Nov. 4, 1916.

1917, May 2 **Unwmk.** ***Perf. 11***

E11	SD4 10c **ultramarine**	20.00	.75
	pale ultramarine	20.00	.75
	dark ultramarine	25.00	2.00
	Never hinged	45.00	
	On cover		4.00
	Block of four	85.00	
	P# block of 6, T VII Impt.	725.00	—
	Never hinged	1,100.	
	P# block of 6	225.00	—
	Never hinged	340.00	
	Margin block of 8, T VII Impt. & P# (side)	—	
b.	10c **gray violet**	30.00	3.00
	Never hinged	65.00	
	On cover		4.00
	Block of four	130.00	
	P# block of 6, T VII Impt.	850.00	—
	Never hinged	1,300.	
	P# block of 6	300.00	—
	Never hinged	450.00	
	Margin block of 8, T VII Impt. & P# (side)	—	
c.	10c **blue**	65.00	4.00
	Never hinged	140.00	
	On cover		15.00
	Block of four	275.00	
	P# block of 6, T VII Impt.	2,000.	
	P# block of 6	625.00	
	Margin block of 8, T VII Impt. & P# (side)	—	
d.	Perf. 10 at left	—	

Earliest documented use: June 12, 1917.

The aniline ink used on some printings of No. E11 permeated the paper causing a pink tinge to appear on the back. Such stamps are called "pink backs." They are scarce and valued higher than the normal stamp.

Motorcycle Delivery SD6

Post Office Truck — SD7

1922, July 12 **Unwmk.** ***Perf. 11***

E12	SD6 10c **gray violet**	42.50	1.25
	Never hinged	90.00	
	On cover		2.00
	First day cover		500.00
	P# block of 6	475.00	—
	Never hinged	750.00	
	Double transfer	—	—
a.	10c **deep ultramarine**	50.00	2.00
	Never hinged	115.00	
	On cover		3.50
	P# block of 6	525.00	—
	Never hinged	800.00	
	Double transfer	—	—

FLAT PLATE PRINTING

1925 **Unwmk.** ***Perf. 11***

Issued to facilitate special delivery service for parcel post.

E13	SD6 15c **deep orange,** *Apr. 11, 1925*	27.50	1.75
	Never hinged	55.00	
	On cover		17.50
	First day cover		350.00
	P# block of 6	350.00	—
	Never hinged	500.00	
	Double transfer	37.50	3.00
E14	SD7 20c **black,** *Apr. 25, 1925*	2.00	1.00
	Never hinged	4.25	
	On cover		5.00
	First day cover		125.00
	P# block of 6	40.00	
	Never hinged	60.00	

Motorcycle Type of 1922
ROTARY PRESS PRINTING

1927-31 **Unwmk.** ***Perf. 11x10½***

E15	SD6 10c **gray violet,** *Nov. 29, 1927*	.65	.25
	violet	.65	.25
	Never hinged	1.20	
a.	10c **red lilac**	.65	.25
	Never hinged	1.20	
b.	10c **gray lilac**	.65	.25
	Never hinged	1.20	
	On cover		.30
	First day cover		110.00
	First day cover, electric eye plate, *Sept. 8, 1941*		30.00
	P# block of 4	3.75	—
	Never hinged	6.25	
	Gouged plate	—	
	Cracked plate 19280 LR	35.00	
c.	Horizontal pair, imperf. between	325.00	
	Never hinged	*550.00*	
E16	SD6 15c **orange,** *Aug. 1931*	.70	.25
	Never hinged	1.05	
	On cover		1.50
	First day cover, Washington, D.C., *Aug. 13, 1931*		125.00
	P# block of 4	2.75	—
	Never hinged	4.50	

The Washington, D.C. Aug. 13, 1931 first day cover reflects the first day of sale at the philatelic agency. The actual earliest documented use of No. E16 is Aug. 6, 1931, at Easton, PA; value, $2,500.

Catalogue values for unused stamps in this section, from this point to the end, are for Never Hinged items.

Motorcycle Type of 1922
ROTARY PRESS PRINTING
E. E. Plates of 200 subjects in four panes of 50 each.

1944-51 **Unwmk.** ***Perf. 11x10½***

E17	SD6 13c **blue,** *Oct. 30, 1944*	.60	.20
	First day cover		15.00
	P# block of 4	2.75	—
E18	SD6 17c **orange yellow,** *Oct. 30, 1944*	3.50	2.50
	First day cover		12.00
	First day cover, Nos. E17 & E18		30.00
	P# block of 4	24.00	—
E19	SD7 20c **black,** *Nov. 30, 1951*	1.25	.20
	First day cover		5.00
	P# block of 4	5.50	—

Special Delivery Letter, Hand to Hand — SD8

ROTARY PRESS PRINTING
E.E. Plates of 200 subjects in four panes of 50 each

1954, Oct. 13 **Unwmk.** ***Perf. 11x10½***

E20	SD8 20c **deep blue**	.40	.20
	light blue	—	—
	First day cover, Boston *(194,043)*		3.00
	P# block of 4	2.00	—

1957, Sept. 3

E21	SD8 30c **lake**	.50	.20
	First day cover, Indianapolis, Ind. *(111,451)*		2.25
	P# block of 4	2.25	—

Arrows SD9

Designed by Norman Ives.

GIORI PRESS PRINTING
Plates of 200 subjects in four panes of 50 each

1969, Nov. 21 **Unwmk.** ***Perf. 11***

E22	SD9 45c **carmine & violet blue**	1.25	.25
	First day cover, New York, N.Y.		4.00
	P# block of 4	5.50	—
	Margin block of 4, Mr. Zip and "Use Zip Code"	5.10	—

1971, May 10 ***Perf. 11***

E23	SD9 60c **violet blue & carmine**	1.25	.20
	First day cover, Phoenix, Ariz. *(129,562)*		3.50
	P# block of 4	5.50	—
	Margin block of 4, Mr. Zip and "Use Zip Code"	5.25	—

REGISTRATION STAMP

The Registry System for U.S. mail went into effect July 1, 1855, the fee being 5 cents. On June 30, 1863, the fee was increased to 20 cents.
On January 1, 1869, the fee was reduced to 15 cents and on January 1, 1874, to 8 cents. On July 1, 1875, the fee was increased to 10 cents. On January 1, 1893 the fee was again reduced to 8 cents and again it was increased to 10 cents on November 1, 1909.
Early registered covers with various stamps, rates and postal markings are of particular interest to collectors.
Registry stamps (10c ultramarine) were issued on December 1, 1911, to prepay registry fees (not postage), but ordinary stamps were valid for registry fees then as now. These special stamps were abolished May 28, 1913, by order of the Postmaster General, who permitted their use until supplies on hand were exhausted.

Eagle — RS1

ENGRAVED

1911, Dec. 1 **Wmk. 190** ***Perf. 12***

F1	RS1 10c **ultramarine**		70.00	10.00
		pale ultramarine	70.00	10.00
		Never hinged	150.00	
		On cover		50.00
		Block of 4	325.00	*80.00*
		P# block of 6, Impt. & "A"	*1,600.*	—
		Never hinged	*2,500.*	
		First day cover		*17,500.*

CERTIFIED MAIL STAMP

Certified Mail service was started on June 6, 1955, for use on first class mail for which no indemnity value is claimed, but for which proof of mailing and proof of delivery are available at less cost than registered mail. The mailer receives one receipt and the addressee signs another when the postman delivers the letter. The second receipt is kept on file at the post office for six months. The Certified Mail charge, originally 15 cents, is in addition to regular postage, whether surface mail, air mail, or special delivery.

Catalogue value for the unused stamp in this section is for a Never Hinged item.

Letter Carrier — CM1

ROTARY PRESS PRINTING

E. E. Plates of 200 subjects in four panes of 50

1955, June 6 **Unwmk.** ***Perf. 10½x11***

FA1	CM1 15c **red**		.45	.30
		P# block of 4	4.25	—
		First day cover		7.50

POSTAGE DUE STAMPS

Postage due stamps were authorized by an act of Congress, approved March 3, 1879, and effective July 1, 1879. By law, postage due stamps were to be affixed by clerks to any piece of mailable matter to denote the amount collected from the addressee because of insufficient prepayment of postage.

Although the Post Office Department required postage to be prepaid beginning in 1855, there were many instances when full postage was not required, and postage due payment had to be collected in cash from the addressees. These instances included insufficiently prepaid letters, advertised letters, and unpaid ship letters and steamboat letters.

The reason for the appearance of postage due stamps may be summed up in one word: accountability. The 1880 *Report of the Postmaster General* noted that the former system of collecting postage due had one great weakness: "In securing the full returns of (the postage due collected in cash) the department was entirely dependent on the fidelity of the postmasters." Postage due stamps, affixed to underpaid mail as receipts for the underpayment collected, solved that problem by requiring postmasters to account for cash receipts that would balance any postage due stamps no longer in stock, in the same way that they had to account for regular postage stamp sales.

The last postage due stamps were printed in early November, 1985. With the advent of postage meters, the scrapping of the last Cottrell press in November 1985 (the last press capable of printing the current postage due stamps as designed), and finally new regulations requiring full prepayment of postage in all cases, postage due stamps became anachronistic, and their use ceased.

Printed by the American Bank Note Co.
Plates of 200 subjects in two panes of 100 each.

D1

D2

1879 Unwmk. Engr. *Perf. 12*

J1 D1 1c	**brown**	95.00	14.00
	pale brown	95.00	14.00
	deep brown	95.00	14.00
	Never hinged	275.00	
	Block of 4	425.00	75.00
	P# block of 10, Impt.	*1,650.*	

Earliest documented use: July 5, 1879.

J2 D1 2c	**brown**	425.00	18.00
	pale brown	425.00	18.00
	Never hinged	1,100.	
	Block of 4	1,800.	—

Earliest documented use: July 27, 1879.

J3 D1 3c	**brown**	105.00	6.00
	pale brown	105.00	6.00
	deep brown	105.00	6.00
	yellowish brown	115.00	7.00
	Never hinged	300.00	
	Block of 4	460.00	32.50
	P# block of 10, Impt.	*1,800.*	

Earliest documented use: June 18, 1879.

J4 D1 5c	**brown**	825.00	70.00
	Never hinged	2,100.	
	pale brown	825.00	70.00
	deep brown	825.00	70.00
	Block of 4	3,500.	—

Earliest documented use: July 7, 1879.

J5 D1 10c	**brown,** *Sept. 19*	1,000.	70.00
	pale brown	1,000.	70.00
	deep brown	1,000.	70.00
	Never hinged	*2,750.*	
	Block of 4	4,500.	—
a.	Imperf., pair	*3,000.*	

Earliest documented use: Oct. 7, 1879.

J6 D1 30c	**brown,** *Sept. 19*	400.00	65.00
	pale brown	400.00	65.00
	Never hinged	900.00	
	Block of 4	1,700.	—
	P# block of 10, Impt.	*5,000.*	
J7 D1 50c	**brown,** *Sept. 19*	650.00	90.00
	pale brown	650.00	90.00
	Never hinged	1,750.	
	Block of 4	2,900.	—
	P# block of 10, Impt.	*12,500.*	

SPECIAL PRINTING

1879 Unwmk. *Perf. 12*

Soft porous paper

Printed by the American Bank Note Co.

J8 D1	1c deep brown *(9,420)*	*22,500.*
J9 D1	2c deep brown *(1,361)*	*20,000.*
J10 D1	3c deep brown *(436)*	*25,000.*
J11 D1	5c deep brown *(249)*	*15,000.*
J12 D1	10c deep brown *(174)*	*9,000.*
J13 D1	30c deep brown *(179)*	*10,000.*
J14 D1	50c deep brown *(179)*	*9,000.*

Identifying characteristics for the final 8,920 copies of No. J8 delivered to the Post Office are unknown, and it is likely that these were regular issue stamps (No. J1) that were then sold as special printings.

1884 Unwmk. *Perf. 12*

J15 D1 1c	**red brown**	75.00	7.00
	pale red brown	75.00	7.00
	deep red brown	75.00	7.00
	Never hinged	200.00	
	Block of 4	350.00	45.00
	P# block of 10, Impt.	*1,450.*	
J16 D1 2c	**red brown**	90.00	6.00
	pale red brown	90.00	6.00
	deep red brown	90.00	6.00
	Never hinged	250.00	
	Block of 4	400.00	37.50
	P# block of 10, Impt.	*1,650.*	
J17 D1 3c	**red brown**	1,150.	300.00
	deep red brown	1,150.	300.00
	Never hinged	2,750.	
	Block of 4	5,000.	—
J18 D1 5c	**red brown**	625.00	45.00
	pale red brown	625.00	45.00
	deep red brown	625.00	45.00
	Never hinged	1,500.	
	Block of 4	2,850.	—
J19 D1 10c	**red brown**	625.00	35.00
	deep red brown	625.00	35.00
	Never hinged	1,500.	
	Block of 4	2,850.	—
	P# block of 10, Impt.	*14,000.*	
J20 D1 30c	**red brown**	225.00	60.00
	deep red brown	225.00	60.00
	Never hinged	550.00	
	Block of 4	1,050.	350.00
	P# block of 10, Impt.	*3,500.*	
J21 D1 50c	**red brown**	1,900.	225.00
	Never hinged	4,250.	
	Block of 4	8,250.	—

1891 Unwmk. *Perf. 12*

J22 D1 1c	**bright claret**	35.00	2.00
	light claret	35.00	2.00
	dark claret	35.00	2.00
	Never hinged	95.00	
	Block of 4	160.00	11.00
	P# block of 10, Impt.	*625.00*	
J23 D1 2c	**bright claret**	37.50	2.00
	light claret	37.50	2.00
	dark claret	37.50	2.00
	Never hinged	100.00	
	Block of 4	170.00	11.00
	P# block of 10, Impt.	*700.00*	
J24 D1 3c	**bright claret**	75.00	16.00
	dark claret	75.00	16.00
	Never hinged	200.00	
	Block of 4	350.00	80.00
	P# block of 10, Impt.	*1,100.*	
J25 D1 5c	**bright claret**	110.00	16.00
	light claret	110.00	16.00
	dark claret	110.00	16.00
	Never hinged	325.00	
	Block of 4	500.00	80.00
	P# block of 10, Impt.	*1,500.*	
J26 D1 10c	**bright claret**	180.00	30.00
	light claret	180.00	30.00
	Never hinged	550.00	
	Block of 4	800.00	190.00
	P# block of 10, Impt.	*2,500.*	
J27 D1 30c	**bright claret**	650.00	225.00
	Never hinged	1,900.	
	Block of 4	2,750.	—
	P# block of 10, Impt.	*8,750.*	
J28 D1 50c	**bright claret**	700.00	210.00
	dark claret	700.00	210.00
	Never hinged	2,000.	
	Block of 4	3,000.	—
	P# block of 10, Impt.	*10,500.*	
	Nos. J22-J28 (7)	1,787.	501.00

See Die and Plate Proofs for imperfs. on stamp paper.

Printed by the Bureau of Engraving and Printing.

1894 Unwmk. *Perf. 12*

J29 D2 1c	**vermilion**	2,750.	725.
	pale vermilion	2,750.	725.
	Never hinged	*6,750.*	
	Block of 4	*12,000.*	*3,250.*
	P# block of 6, Impt.	—	
J30 D2 2c	**vermilion**	850.	350.
	deep vermilion	850.	350.
	Never hinged	2,100.	
	Block of 4	3,750.	
	P# block of 6, Impt.	*7,000.*	

1894-95

J31 D2 1c	**deep claret,** *Aug. 14, 1894*	80.00	12.00
	claret	80.00	12.00
	lake	80.00	12.00
	Never hinged	300.00	
	Block of 4	360.00	65.00
	P# block of 6, Impt.	675.00	
	Never hinged	1,900.	
b.	Vertical pair, imperf. horiz.	—	

See Die and Plate Proofs for imperf. on stamp paper.

J32 D2 2c	**deep claret,** *July 20, 1894*	70.00	10.00
	claret	70.00	10.00
	lake	70.00	10.00
	Never hinged	275.00	
	Block of 4	300.00	65.00
	P# block of 6, Impt.	625.00	
	Never hinged	1,750.	
J33 D2 3c	**deep claret,** *Apr. 27, 1895*	220.00	50.00
	lake	220.00	50.00
	Never hinged	675.00	
	Block of 4	950.00	—
	P# block of 6, Impt.	2,750.	
	Never hinged	*5,000.*	
J34 D2 5c	**deep claret,** *Apr. 27, 1895*	350.00	55.00
	claret	350.00	55.00
	Never hinged	1,000.	
	Block of 4	1,500.	—
	P# block of 6, Impt.	3,000.	
	Never hinged	*6,500.*	
J35 D2 10c	**deep claret,** *Sept. 24, 1894*	400.00	40.00
	Never hinged	1,100.	
	Block of 4	1,750.	—
	P# block of 6, Impt.	3,250.	
J36 D2 30c	**deep claret,** *Apr. 27, 1895*	600.00	225.00
	claret	600.00	225.00
	Never hinged	1,400.	
	Block of 4	2,750.	—
	P# block of 6, Impt.	4,750.	
	Never hinged	9,000.	
a.	30c **carmine**	750.00	275.00
	Never hinged	1,750.	
	Block of 4	3,500.	—
	P# block of 6, Impt.	5,750.	
	Never hinged	*11,000.*	
b.	30c **pale rose**	500.00	200.00
	Never hinged	1,250.	
	Block of 4	2,250.	—
	P# block of 6, Impt.	4,250.	
	Never hinged	*8,000.*	
J37 D2 50c	**deep claret,** *Apr. 27, 1895*	2,000.	800.00
	Never hinged	4,750.	
	Block of 4	8,750.	—
	P# block of 6, Impt.	*15,000.*	
a.	50c **pale rose**	1,800.	725.00
	Never hinged	4,250.	
	Block of 4	7,750.	—
	P# block of 6, Impt.	*13,000.*	

Shades are numerous in the 1894 and later issues.

Wmk. 191 Horizontally or Vertically

1895-97 *Perf. 12*

J38 D2 1c	**deep claret,** *Aug. 29, 1895*	15.00	1.00
	claret	15.00	1.00
	carmine	15.00	1.00
	lake	15.00	1.00
	Never hinged	45.00	
	Block of 4	65.00	8.50
	P# block of 6, Impt.	275.00	
	Never hinged	450.00	
J39 D2 2c	**deep claret,** *Sept. 14, 1895*	15.00	1.00
	claret	15.00	1.00
	carmine	15.00	1.00
	lake	15.00	1.00
	Never hinged	45.00	
	Block of 4	65.00	8.50
	P# block of 6, Impt.	275.00	
	Never hinged	450.00	
	Double transfer	—	—

In October, 1895, the Postmaster at Jefferson, Iowa, surcharged a few 2 cent stamps with the words "Due I cent" in black on each side, subsequently dividing the stamps vertically and using each half as a 1 cent stamp. Twenty of these were used.

J40 D2 3c	**deep claret,** *Oct. 30, 1895*	110.00	4.00
	claret	110.00	4.00
	rose red	110.00	4.00
	carmine	110.00	4.00

	Never hinged	275.00	
	Block of 4	475.00	22.50
	P# block of 6, Impt.	1,000.	
	Never hinged	1,800.	
J41 D2	5c **deep claret,** *Oct. 15, 1895*	120.00	4.00
	claret	120.00	4.00
	carmine rose	120.00	4.00
	Never hinged	300.00	
	Block of 4	525.00	22.50
	P# block of 6, Impt.	1,050.	
	Never hinged	2,000.	
J42 D2	10c **deep claret,** *Sept. 14, 1895*	120.00	6.00
	claret	120.00	6.00
	carmine	120.00	6.00
	lake	120.00	6.00
	Never hinged	300.00	
	Block of 4	525.00	37.50
	P# block of 6, Impt.	1,050.	
	Never hinged	2,000.	
J43 D2	30c **deep claret,** *Aug. 21, 1897*	700.00	70.00
	claret	700.00	70.00
	Never hinged	1,800.	
	Block of 4	3,000.	425.00
	P# block of 6, Impt.	*6,500.*	
J44 D2	50c **deep claret,** *Mar. 17, 1896*	450.00	50.00
	claret	450.00	50.00
	Never hinged	1,200.	
	Block of 4	2,000.	250.00
	P# block of 6, Impt.	*4,750.*	—
	Nos. J38-J44 (7)	1,530.	136.00

Plates of 400 subjects in four panes of 100.

1910-12 Wmk. 190 *Perf. 12*

J45 D2	1c **deep claret,** *Dec., 1910*	45.00	5.00
	Never hinged	130.00	
a.	1c **rose carmine**	40.00	5.00
	Never hinged	120.00	
	Block of 4 (2 or 3mm spacing)	200.00	20.00
	P# block of 6, Impt. & star	525.00	
	Never hinged	875.00	
J46 D2	2c **deep claret,** *Nov. 25, 1910*	45.00	2.00
	lake	45.00	2.00
	Never hinged	130.00	
a.	2c **rose carmine**	40.00	2.00
	Never hinged	120.00	
	Block of 4 (2 or 3mm spacing)	200.00	7.50
	P# block of 6, Impt. & star	500.00	—
	Never hinged	850.00	
	P# block of 6	550.00	
	Never hinged	900.00	
	Double transfer	—	—
J47 D2	3c **deep claret,** *Aug. 31, 1910*	675.00	50.00
	lake	675.00	50.00
	Never hinged	1,750.	
	Block of 4 (2 or 3mm spacing)	2,900.	275.00
	P# block of 6, Impt. & star	6,000.	
	Never hinged	*11,500.*	
J48 D2	5c **deep claret,** *Aug. 31, 1910*	130.00	12.00
	Never hinged	300.00	
a.	5c **rose carmine**	130.00	12.00
	Never hinged	300.00	
	Block of 4 (2 or 3mm spacing)	550.00	60.00
	P# block of 6, Impt. & star	1,150.	
	Never hinged	*2,000.*	
J49 D2	10c **deep claret,** *Aug. 31, 1910*	140.00	20.00
	Never hinged	360.00	
	Block of 4 (2 or 3mm spacing)	600.00	120.00
	P# block of 6, Impt. & star	1,500.	
a.	10c **rose carmine**	140.00	20.00
	Never hinged	360.00	
J50 D2	50c **deep claret,** *Sept. 23, 1912*	1,150.	175.00
	Never hinged	3,000.	
	Block of 4 (2 or 3mm spacing)	5,000.	
	P# block of 6, Impt. & star	*10,000.*	
a.	50c **rose carmine**	1,200.	190.00
	Never hinged	*3,250.*	

1914 *Perf. 10*

J52 D2	1c **carmine lake**	90.00	15.00
	deep carmine lake	90.00	15.00
	Never hinged	260.00	
	Block of 4 (2 or 3mm spacing)	400.00	80.00
	P# block of 6, Impt. & star	750.00	—
	Never hinged	1,750.	
a.	1c **dull rose**	95.00	15.00
	Never hinged	270.00	
	Block of 4 (2 or 3mm spacing)	425.00	85.00
	P# block of 6, Impt. & star	775.00	—
	Never hinged	1,800.	
J53 D2	2c **carmine lake**	70.00	1.00
	Never hinged	200.00	
	Block of 4	300.00	8.00
	P# block of 6	650.00	—
	Never hinged	1,250.	
a.	2c **dull rose**	75.00	2.00
	Never hinged	210.00	
	Block of 4		15.00
b.	2c **vermilion**	75.00	2.00
	Never hinged	210.00	
	Block of 4	325.00	14.00
	P# block of 6	675.00	—
	Never hinged	1,400.	
J54 D2	3c **carmine lake**	1,150.	75.00
	Never hinged	3,300.	
	Block of 4 (2 or 3mm spacing)	5,250.	—
	P# block of 6, Impt. & star	*9,500.*	—
a.	3c **dull rose**	1,100.	75.00
	Never hinged	3,250.	
	Block of 4 (2 or 3mm spacing)	5,000.	—
	P# block of 6, Impt. & star	*9,000.*	—
J55 D2	5c **carmine lake**	55.00	6.00
	Never hinged	160.00	
	Block of 4 (2 or 3mm spacing)	240.00	30.00
	P# block of 6, Impt. & star	475.00	—
	Never hinged	1,150.	
a.	5c **dull rose**	50.00	4.00
	carmine rose	50.00	4.00
	Never hinged	150.00	
	deep claret	—	—
	Block of 4 (2 or 3mm spacing)	225.00	20.00
	P# block of 6, Impt. & star	450.00	—
	Never hinged	1,100.	
J56 D2	10c **carmine lake**	85.00	4.00
	Never hinged	240.00	
	Block of 4 (2 or 3mm spacing)	375.00	22.50
	P# block of 6, Impt. & star	825.00	—
a.	10c **dull rose**	90.00	5.00
	carmine rose	90.00	5.00
	Never hinged	250.00	
	Block of 4 (2 or 3mm spacing)	400.00	25.00
	P# block of 6, Impt. & star	950.00	—
	Never hinged	1,700.	
J57 D2	30c **carmine lake**	250.00	55.00
	Never hinged	600.00	
	Block of 4 (2 or 3mm spacing)	1,100.	325.00
	P# block of 6, Impt. & star	2,900.	—
J58 D2	50c **carmine lake**	*17,500.*	1,500.
	Never hinged	*32,500.*	
	Precanceled		750.00
	Block of 4 (2 or 3mm spacing)	*75,000.*	*6,500.*
	P# block of 6, Impt. & star	*125,000.*	

No. J58 unused is valued in the grade of fine.

No. J58, precanceled, was used at Buffalo (normal, inverted) and Chicago (normal, inverted, double, double inverted).

1916 Unwmk. *Perf. 10*

J59 D2	1c **rose**	4,500.	700.00
	Never hinged	10,000.	
	Block of 4 (2 or 3mm spacing)	21,000.	*3,400.*
	P# block of 6, Impt. & star	*31,500.*	
	Experimental bureau precancel, New Orleans		*350.00*
J60 D2	2c **rose**	300.00	75.00
	Never hinged	850.00	
	Block of 4	1,350.	350.00
	P# block of 6	2,500.	—
	Experimental bureau precancel, New Orleans		35.00

1917 Unwmk. *Perf. 11*

J61 D2	1c **carmine rose**	3.00	.25
	dull rose	3.00	.25
	Never hinged	10.00	
a.	1c **rose red**	3.00	.25
	Never hinged	10.00	
b.	1c **deep claret**	3.00	.25
	claret brown	3.00	.25
	Never hinged	10.00	
	Block of 4 (2 or 3mm spacing)	13.00	2.00
	P# block of 6, Impt. & star	150.00	—
	Never hinged	350.00	
	P# block of 6	45.00	—
	Never hinged	100.00	
J62 D2	2c **carmine rose**	3.00	.25
	Never hinged	10.00	
a.	2c **rose red**	3.00	.25
	Never hinged	10.00	
b.	2c **deep claret**	3.00	.25
	claret brown	3.00	1.10
	Never hinged	10.00	
	Block of 4	13.00	2.00
	Never hinged	42.50	
	P# block of 6	55.00	—
	Never hinged	125.00	
	Double transfer	—	—
J63 D2	3c **carmine rose**	15.00	.80
	Never hinged	40.00	
a.	3c **rose red**	15.00	.80
	Never hinged	40.00	
b.	3c **deep claret**	15.00	.80
	claret brown	15.00	.80
	Never hinged	40.00	
	Block of 4 (2 or 3mm spacing)	65.00	5.00
	P# block of 6, Impt. & star	150.00	—
	Never hinged	300.00	
	P# block of 6	125.00	—
	Never hinged	275.00	
J64 D2	5c **carmine**	12.50	.80
	carmine rose	12.50	.80
	Never hinged	37.50	
a.	5c **rose red**	12.50	.80
	Never hinged	37.50	
b.	5c **deep claret**	12.50	.80
	claret brown	12.50	.80
	Never hinged	37.50	
	Block of 4 (2 or 3mm spacing)	52.50	6.00
	P# block of 6, Impt. & star	125.00	—
	Never hinged	275.00	
	P# block of 6	105.00	—
	Never hinged	250.00	
J65 D2	10c **carmine rose**	25.00	1.00
	Never hinged	70.00	
a.	10c **rose red**	25.00	1.00
	Never hinged	70.00	
b.	10c **deep claret**	25.00	1.00
	claret brown	25.00	1.00
	Never hinged	70.00	
	Block of 4 (2 or 3mm spacing)	110.00	7.50
	P# block of 6, Impt. & star	220.00	—
	Never hinged	475.00	
	P# block of 6	240.00	—
	Never hinged	525.00	
	Double transfer	—	—
J66 D2	30c **carmine rose**	90.00	2.00
	Never hinged	260.00	
a.	30c **deep claret**	90.00	2.00
	claret brown	90.00	2.00
	Never hinged	260.00	
	Block of 4 (2 or 3mm spacing)	390.00	14.00
	P# block of 6, Impt. & star	750.00	—
	P# block of 6	800.00	—
b.	As "a," perf 10 at top, precanceled		*21,000.*

No. J66b is valued with small faults and fine centering, as the two recorded examples are in this condition and grade. One is precanceled St. Louis, Mo., and the other is precanceled Minneapolis, Minn.

J67 D2	50c **carmine rose**	150.00	1.00
	Never hinged	370.00	
a.	50c **rose red**	150.00	1.00
	Never hinged	370.00	
b.	50c **deep claret**	150.00	1.00
	claret brown	150.00	1.00
	Never hinged	370.00	
	Block of 4 (2 or 3mm spacing)	625.00	7.50
	P# block of 6, Impt. & star	1,150.	—
	Never hinged	2,500.	
	P# block of 6	1,250.	—

1925, Apr. 13

J68 D2	½c **dull red**	1.00	.25
	Never hinged	1.75	
	Block of 4	4.00	1.50
	P# block of 6	12.50	—
	Never hinged	17.50	

D3

D4

1930 **Unwmk.** ***Perf. 11***

Design measures 19x22mm

No.	Type	Description	Unused	Used
J69	D3	½c **carmine**	4.50	1.90
		Never hinged	10.00	
		P# block of 6	50.00	—
		Never hinged	80.00	
J70	D3	1c **carmine**	3.00	.35
		Never hinged	7.00	
		P# block of 6	55.00	—
		Never hinged	100.00	
J71	D3	2c **carmine**	4.00	.35
		Never hinged	9.00	
		P# block of 6	50.00	—
		Never hinged	95.00	
J72	D3	3c **carmine**	21.00	2.75
		Never hinged	50.00	
		P# block of 6	300.00	—
		Never hinged	500.00	
J73	D3	5c **carmine**	19.00	5.00
		Never hinged	45.00	
		P# block of 6	300.00	—
		Never hinged	500.00	
J74	D3	10c **carmine**	45.00	2.00
		Never hinged	100.00	
		P# block of 6	475.00	—
		Never hinged	875.00	
J75	D3	30c **carmine**	150.00	4.00
		Never hinged	325.00	
		P# block of 6	1,150.	—
		Never hinged	*2,250.*	
J76	D3	50c **carmine**	200.00	2.00
		Never hinged	450.00	
		P# block of 6	1,750.	—
		Never hinged	*3,250.*	

Design measures 22x19mm

No.	Type	Description	Unused	Used
J77	D4	$1 **carmine**	35.00	.35
		Never hinged	70.00	
		P# block of 6	250.00	—
		Never hinged	475.00	
a.		$1 **scarlet**	30.00	.35
		Never hinged	60.00	
		P# block of 6	275.00	—
		Never hinged	500.00	
J78	D4	$5 **carmine**	40.00	.35
		Never hinged	90.00	
		P# block of 6	300.00	—
		Never hinged	600.00	—
a.		$5 **scarlet**	35.00	.35
		Never hinged	75.00	
		P# block of 6	260.00	—
		Never hinged	525.00	
b.		As "a," wet printing	40.00	.35
		Never hinged	90.00	
		P# block of 6	300.00	—
		Never hinged	600.00	

See note on Wet and Dry Printings following No. 1029.

Type of 1930-31 Issue
Rotary Press Printing
Ordinary and Electric Eye Plates
Design measures 19x22½mm

1931 **Unwmk.** ***Perf. 11x10½***

No.	Type	Description	Unused	Used
J79	D3	½c **dull carmine**	.90	.20
		Never hinged	1.30	
a.		½c **scarlet**	.90	.20
		Never hinged	1.30	
		P# block of 4	20.00	—
		Never hinged	30.00	
J80	D3	1c **dull carmine**	.20	.20
		Never hinged	.30	
a.		1c **scarlet**	.20	.20
		Never hinged	.30	
		P# block of 4 (#25635, 25636)	1.50	—
		Never hinged	2.25	
b.		As "a," wet printing	.20	.20
		Never hinged	.20	
		P# block of 4	1.75	—
		Never hinged	2.60	
		Pair with full vertical gutter between	—	
J81	D3	2c **dull carmine**	.20	.20
		Never hinged	.30	
a.		2c **scarlet**	.20	.20
		Never hinged	.30	
		P# block of 4 (#25637, 25638)	1.50	—
		Never hinged	2.25	
b.		As "a," wet printing	.20	.20
		Never hinged	.30	
		P# block of 4	2.00	—
		Never hinged	3.00	
J82	D3	3c **dull carmine**	.25	.20
		Never hinged	.40	
a.		3c **scarlet**	.25	.20
		Never hinged	.40	
		P# block of 4 (#25641, 25642)	2.25	—
		Never hinged	3.40	
b.		As "a," wet printing	.30	.20
		Never hinged	.45	
		P# block of 4	2.50	—
		Never hinged	3.75	
J83	D3	5c **dull carmine**	.40	.20
		Never hinged	.60	
a.		5c **scarlet**	.40	.20
		Never hinged	.60	
		P# block of 4 (#25643, 25644)	3.00	—
		Never hinged	4.50	
b.		As "a," wet printing	.50	.20
		Never hinged	.75	
		P# block of 4	3.50	—
		Never hinged	5.25	
J84	D3	10c **dull carmine**	1.10	.20
		Never hinged	1.80	
a.		10c **scarlet**	1.10	.20
		Never hinged	1.80	
		P# block of 4 (#25645, 25646)	6.50	—
		Never hinged	9.75	
b.		As "a," wet printing	1.25	.20
		Never hinged	1.90	
		P# block of 4	7.00	—
		Never hinged	10.50	
J85	D3	30c **dull carmine**	7.50	.25
		Never hinged	11.50	
a.		30c **scarlet**	7.50	.25
		Never hinged	11.50	
		P# block of 4	35.00	—
		Never hinged	60.00	
J86	D3	50c **dull carmine**	9.00	.25
		Never hinged	15.00	
a.		50c **scarlet**	9.00	.25
		Never hinged	15.00	
		P# block of 4	52.50	—
		Never hinged	85.00	

Design measures 22½x19mm

1956 ***Perf. 10½x11***

No.	Type	Description	Unused	Used
J87	D4	$1 **scarlet**	30.00	.25
		Never hinged	47.50	
		P# block of 4	190.00	—
		Never hinged	290.00	
		Nos. J79-J87 (9)	49.55	1.95

Catalogue values for unused stamps in this section, from this point to the end, are for Never Hinged items.

D5

Rotary Press Printing

Denominations added in black by rubber plates in an operation similar to precanceling.

1959, June 19 **Unwmk.** ***Perf. 11x10½***

Denomination in Black

No.	Type	Description	Unused	Used
J88	D5	½c **carmine rose**	1.50	1.10
		P# block of 4	130.00	—
J89	D5	1c **carmine rose**, shiny gum	.20	.20
		P# block of 4	.35	—
		Dull gum	.25	
		P# block of 4	4.50	
a.		Denomination omitted	225.00	
		P# block of 4	—	—
b.		Pair, one without "1 CENT"	*475.00*	
J90	D5	2c **carmine rose**, shiny gum	.20	.20
		P# block of 4	.45	—
		Wide spacing, pair	*120.00*	
		Dull gum	.40	
		P# block of 4	12.50	
J91	D5	3c **carmine rose**, shiny gum	.20	.20
		P# block of 4	.50	—
		Dull gum	.50	
		P# block of 4	15.00	
a.		Pair, one without "3 CENTS"	*675.00*	
J92	D5	4c **carmine rose**	.20	.20
		P# block of 4	.60	—
		Wide spacing, pair	*120.00*	
J93	D5	5c **carmine rose**, shiny gum	.20	.20
		P# block of 4	.65	—
		Dull gum	.45	
		P# block of 4	8.00	
a.		Pair, one without "5 CENTS"	*1,500.*	
J94	D5	6c **carmine rose**, shiny gum	.20	.20
		P# block of 4	.70	—
		Pair with full vertical gutter between	—	
		Dull gum	*90.00*	
		P# block of 4	*1,250.*	
a.		Pair, one without "6 CENTS"	*850.00*	
J95	D5	7c **carmine rose**, shiny gum	.20	.20
		P# block of 4	.80	—
		Wide spacing, pair	*120.00*	
		Dull gum	*700.00*	
		P# block of 4	*7,500.*	
J96	D5	8c **carmine rose**	.20	.20
		P# block of 4	.90	—
		Wide spacing, pair	*120.00*	
a.		Pair, one without "8 CENTS"	*850.00*	
J97	D5	10c **carmine rose**, shiny gum	.20	.20
		P# block of 4	1.00	—
		Dull gum	.35	
		P# block of 4	5.00	
J98	D5	30c **carmine rose**, shiny gum	.75	.20
		P# block of 4	3.50	—
		Dull gum	1.00	
		P# block of 4	16.00	
J99	D5	50c **carmine rose**, shiny gum	1.10	.20
		P# block of 4	5.00	—
		Dull gum	1.75	
		P# block of 4	20.00	

Straight Numeral Outlined in Black

No.	Type	Description	Unused	Used
J100	D5	$1 **carmine rose, shiny gum**	2.00	.20
		P# block of 4	8.50	—
		Dull gum	2.50	
		P# block of 4	22.50	
J101	D5	$5 **carmine rose**, shiny gum	9.00	.20
		P# block of 4	40.00	—
		Dull gum	11.00	
		P# block of 4	65.00	
		Nos. J88-J101 (14)	16.15	3.70

All single stamps with denomination omitted are catalogued as No. J89a.

Rotary Press Printing

1978-85 ***Perf. 11x10½***

Denomination in Black

No.	Type	Description	Unused	Used
J102	D5	11c **carmine rose**, *Jan. 2, 1978*	.25	.20
		P# block of 4	2.00	—
J103	D5	13c **carmine rose**, *Jan. 2, 1978*	.25	.20
		P# block of 4	2.00	—
J104	D5	17c **carmine rose**, *June 10, 1985*	.40	.35
		P# block of 4	22.50	—

U.S. POSTAL AGENCY IN CHINA

Postage stamps of the 1917-19 U.S. series (then current) were issued to the U.S. Postal Agency, Shanghai, China, surcharged at double the original value of the stamps.

These stamps were intended for sale at Shanghai at their surcharged value in local currency, valid for prepayment on mail despatched from the U.S. Postal Agency at Shanghai to addresses in the U.S.

Stamps were first issued May 24, 1919, and were placed on sale at Shanghai on July 1, 1919. These stamps were not issued to postmasters in the U.S. The Shanghai post office, according to the U.S.P.O. Bulletin, was closed in December 1922. The stamps were on sale at the Philatelic Agency in Washington, D.C. for a short time after that.

Italicized numbers in parentheses indicate quantities shipped to the postal agency in Shanghai and to the Washington Philatelic Agency. In the case of Nos. K17-K18, the numbers are the quantity locally overprinted. All Nos. K16a, K17 and K18 are believed to have been sold. The final disposition of remainders of the others is not known. Neither the records of the Shanghai Postal Agency nor the records of the Washington Philatelic Agency have been located at this time. Authority for quantities shipped is the research of Joseph M. Napp, who in turn benefitted by the research of Meyer Tuchinsky.

The cancellations of the China office included "U.S. Postal Agency Shanghai China", "U.S. Pos. Service Shanghai China" duplexes, and the Shanghai parcel post roller cancel. Used stamps are valued bearing legible cancels showing Chinese origin.

United States Stamps #498-499, 502-504, 506-510, 512, 514-518 Surcharged in Black or Red (Nos. K7, K16)

1919 **Unwmk.** ***Perf. 11***

K1	A140	2c on 1c **green** *(355,000)*	25.00	*55.00*
		Never hinged	70.00	
		Block of 4	110.00	*325.00*
		P# block of 6	300.00	—
		Never hinged	600.00	
		Double transfer	42.50	
		Never hinged	110.00	
		Earliest documented use: July 2, 1919.		
K2	A140	4c on 2c **rose,** type I *(355,000)*	25.00	*55.00*
		Never hinged	70.00	
		Block of 4	110.00	*325.00*
		P# block of 6	300.00	—
		Never hinged	600.00	
		Earliest documented use: July 2, 1919.		
K3	A140	6c on 3c **violet,** type II, *(113,000)*	60.00	*120.00*
		Never hinged	150.00	
		Block of 4	260.00	*600.00*
		P# block of 6	675.00	—
		Never hinged	1,150.	
K4	A140	8c on 4c **brown** *(113,000)*	60.00	*120.00*
		Never hinged	150.00	
		Block of 4	260.00	*600.00*
		P# block of 6	675.00	—
		Never hinged	1,150.	
K5	A140	10c on 5c **blue** *(113,000)*	65.00	*120.00*
		Never hinged	170.00	
		Block of 4	280.00	*600.00*
		P# block of 6	600.00	
		Never hinged	1,100.	
K6	A140	12c on 6c **red orange** *(113,000)*	85.00	*175.00*
		Never hinged	220.00	
		Block of 4	375.00	*925.00*
		P# block of 6	800.00	
		Never hinged	*1,500.*	
K7	A140	14c on 7c **black** *(113,000)*	87.50	*190.00*
		Never hinged	225.00	
		Block of 4	400.00	*1,050.*
		P# block of 6	1,050.	
		Never hinged	*1,650.*	
K8	A148	16c on 8c **olive bister** *(13,000)*	70.00	*135.00*
		Never hinged	180.00	
		Block of 4	300.00	*750.00*
		P# block of 6	625.00	
		Never hinged	1,150.	
a.		16c on 8c **olive green** *(100,000)*	60.00	*110.00*
		Never hinged	160.00	
		Block of 4	260.00	*650.00*
		P# block of 6	575.00	
		Never hinged	1,000.	
K9	A148	18c on 9c **salmon red** *(113,000)*	65.00	*155.00*
		Never hinged	170.00	
		Block of 4	280.00	*775.00*
		P# block of 6	700.00	
		Never hinged	*1,200.*	
K10	A148	20c on 10c **orange yellow** *(113,000)*	60.00	*120.00*
		Never hinged	160.00	
		Block of 4	260.00	*600.00*
		P# block of 6	725.00	
		Never hinged	1,300.	
K11	A148	24c on 12c **brown carmine** *(50,000)*	80.00	*140.00*
		Never hinged	200.00	
		Block of 4	350.00	*650.00*
		P# block of 6	1,000.	
a.		24c on 12c **claret brown** *(8,000)*	110.00	*185.00*
		Never hinged	275.00	
		Block of 4	475.00	*900.00*
		P# block of 6	1,200.	
		Never hinged	*2,100.*	
K12	A148	30c on 15c **gray** *(58,000)*	87.50	*210.00*
		Never hinged	210.00	
		Block of 4	375.00	—
		P# block of 6	1,150.	
		Never hinged	*2,000.*	
K13	A148	40c on 20c **deep ultramarine** *(58,000)*	130.00	*300.00*
		Never hinged	300.00	
		Block of 4	550.00	*1,700.*
		P# block of 6	1,300.	
		Never hinged	*2,250.*	
K14	A148	60c on 30c **orange red** *(58,000)*	120.00	*250.00*
		Never hinged	280.00	
		Block of 4	525.00	*1,400.*
		P# block of 6	1,050.	
		Never hinged	*1,800.*	
K15	A148	$1 on 50c **light violet** *(14,000)*	575.00	*875.00*
		Never hinged	1,300.	
		Block of 4	2,500.	*5,250.*
		P# block of 6	*17,500.*	
K16	A148	$2 on $1 **violet brown** *(13,800)*	450.00	*700.00*
		Never hinged	1,000.	
		Block of 4	2,000.	*4,750.*
		Margin block of 4, arrow, right or left	2,100.	
		P# block of 6	*7,000.*	
		Never hinged	*11,000.*	
a.		Double surcharge *(200)*	*8,500.*	*8,000.*
		Never hinged	*14,000.*	
		Block of 4	—	
		Nos. K1-K16 (16)	2,045.	*3,720.*

Fake surcharges exist, but most are rather crudely made.

United States Stamps Nos. 498 and 528B Locally Surcharged

1922, July 3

K17	A140	2c on 1c **green** *(10,000)*	110.00	*175.00*
		Never hinged	250.00	
		Block of 4	475.00	*825.00*
		P# block of 6	850.00	
		Never hinged	1,750.	
K18	A140	4c on 2c **carmine,** type VII *(10,000)*	100.00	*155.00*
		Never hinged	230.00	
		Block of 4	425.00	*725.00*
		P# block of 6	800.00	
		Never hinged	1,400.	
a.		"SHANGHAI" omitted	*7,500.*	
b.		"CHINA" only	*15,000.*	

OFFICIAL STAMPS

The original official stamps were authorized by Act of Congress, approved March 3, 1873, abolishing the franking privilege. Stamps for each executive government department were issued July 1, 1873.

Penalty franks were first authorized in 1877, and their expanded use after 1879 reduced the need for official stamps, the use of which was finally abolished on July 5, 1884.

DESIGNS. Stamps for departments other than the Post Office picture the same busts used in the regular postage issue: 1c Franklin, 2c Jackson, 3c Washington, 6c Lincoln, 7c Stanton, 10c Jefferson, 12c Clay, 15c Webster, 24c Scott, 30c Hamilton, and 90c Perry. William H. Seward appears on the $2, $5, $10 and $20.

Designs of the various denominations are not identical, but resemble those illustrated.

PLATES. Plates of 200 subjects in two panes of 100 were used for Post Office Department 1c, 3c, 6c; Treasury Department 1c, 2c, 3c, and War Department 2c, 3c. Plates of 10 subjects were used for State Department $2, $5, $10 and $20. Plates of 100 subjects were used for all other Official stamps up to No. O120.

CANCELLATIONS. Odd or Town cancellations on Departmental stamps are relatively much scarcer than those appearing on the general issues of the same period. Town cancellations, especially on the 1873 issue, are scarce. The "Kicking Mule" cancellation is found used on stamps of the War Department and has also been seen on some stamps of the other Departments. Black is usual.

Grade, condition and presence of original gum are very important in valuing Nos. O1-O120.

As is done elsewhere in this catalogue, all Officials are valued in the grade of very fine. If unused, they will have original gum. Values for never-hinged stamps and unused stamps without gum are also given.

Printed by the Continental Bank Note Co.
Thin Hard Paper

O1

Franklin — O2

AGRICULTURE

1873 **Engr.** **Unwmk.** ***Perf. 12***

O1	O1	1c **yellow**	280.00	*180.00*
		Never hinged	600.00	
		No gum	160.00	
		On wrapper		*2,500.*
		Block of 4	1,250.	
		Ribbed paper	340.00	200.00
		Cancellations		
		Magenta		+7.50
		Violet		+7.50
		Blue		+5.00
		Red		+50.00
		Town		+7.50
		Fort		+150.00
O2	O1	2c **yellow**	240.00	85.00
		Never hinged	500.00	
		No gum	100.00	
		On cover		*4,000.*
		Block of 4	1,050.	
		P# block of 12	—	
		Ribbed paper	240.00	95.00
		Cancellations		
		Blue		+3.00
		Violet		+3.00
		Red		+15.00
		Magenta		+5.00
		Town		+5.00
O3	O1	3c **yellow**	220.00	16.00
		Never hinged	460.00	
		No gum	80.00	
		On cover		*900.00*
		Block of 4	1,000.	—
		P# block of 12, Impt., never hinged	*3,900.*	
		Ribbed paper	240.00	16.00
		Double transfer	—	—
		Short transfer at upper left (pos. 10, 18, 28)	—	—

The never hinged, bottom left plate block of No. O3 is the only plate block of this number recorded.

		Cancellations		
		Blue		+.50
		Purple		+1.00
		Magenta		+1.00
		Violet		+1.00
		Red		+17.50
		Indigo		+10.00
		Green		+200.00
		Brown		+20.00
		Town		+4.00
		"Paid"		+27.50
		Numeral		+35.00
		Railroad		+75.00
		Express Company		+900.00
O4	O1	6c **yellow**	260.00	60.00
		Never hinged	550.00	
		No gum	95.00	
		On cover		*8,500.*
		Block of 4	1,250.	

			Cancellations		
			Blue		+3.00
			Magenta		+4.00
			Violet		+5.00
			Red		+50.00
			Town		+7.00
			"Paid"		+27.50
			Numeral		+35.00
			Express Company		—
			Revenue		—
O5	O1	10c	**yellow**	525.00	200.00
			Never hinged	1,150.	
			No gum	220.00	
			On cover (parcel label)		*6,000.*
			Block of 4	2,500.	
			Cancellations		
			Violet		+5.00
			Blue		+5.00
			Red		+50.00
			Town		+25.00
O6	O1	12c	**yellow**	450.00	260.00
			Never hinged	950.00	
			No gum	250.00	
			On cover		*12,000.*
			Block of 4	1,950.	
			Cancellations		
			Violet		+10.00
			Blue		+10.00
			Red		+50.00
			Town		+30.00
O7	O1	15c	**yellow**	425.00	230.00
			Never hinged	950.00	
			No gum	225.00	
			Block of 4	1,850.	
			Recut top left frame line (pos. 100)	—	—
			Cancellations		
			Purple		+10.00
			Blue		+10.00
O8	O1	24c	**yellow**	425.00	220.00
			Never hinged	950.00	
			No gum	225.00	
			On parcel label		—
			Block of 4	1,850.	
			Cancellation		
			Violet		+10.00
O9	O1	30c	**yellow**	550.00	270.00
			Never hinged	1,200.	
			No gum	275.00	
			Block of 4	2,500.	
			Cancellations		
			Blue		+10.00
			Red		+65.00

EXECUTIVE

1873

O10	O2	1c	**carmine**	850.00	475.00
			deep carmine	850.00	475.00
			Never hinged	2,250.	
			No gum	450.00	
			On cover with No. O11		*3,250.*
			On cover, single franking		*3,000.*
			Block of 6	*4,250.*	

The only known block is with original gum and is off-center with perfs just cutting into design. It is valued thus.

			Cancellations		
			Violet		+10.00
			Blue favor		+10.00
			Red		+50.00
			Town		+30.00
O11	O2	2c	**carmine**	550.00	240.00
			deep carmine	550.00	240.00
			Never hinged	1,250.	
			No gum	240.00	
			On cover, single franking		*3,750.*
			Block of 4	*3,250.*	
			Foreign entry of 6c Agriculture (pos. 40)	*2,500.*	*1,000.*
			Cancellations		
			Violet		+10.00
			Blue favor		+10.00
			Red		+50.00
O12	O2	3c	**carmine**	700.00	210.00
			Never hinged	1,600.	
			No gum	270.00	
			On cover		*1,000.*
			On cover from Long Branch, N.J.		*4,500.*
			Block of 4	*3,250.*	
	a.	3c	**violet rose**	850.00	210.00
			Never hinged	1,950.	
			No gum	325.00	
			Cancellations		
			Blue favor		+10.00
			Violet		+10.00
			Indigo		+20.00
			Red		+50.00
			Town		+35.00
O13	O2	6c	**carmine**	900.00	550.00
			pale carmine	900.00	550.00
			deep carmine	900.00	550.00
			Never hinged	—	
			No gum	325.00	
			On cover		*5,000.*
			Double transfer (pos. 6)	*2,600.*	*1,000.*
			Cancellations		
			Violet		+15.00
			Blue favor		+15.00
			Town		+50.00
			New York Foreign Mail		—
O14	O2	10c	**carmine**	1,200.	650.00
			pale carmine	1,200.	650.00
			deep carmine	1,200.	650.00
			Never hinged	—	
			No gum	600.00	
			On cover		—
			Block of 4	*5,500.*	
			Cancellations		
			Violet		+15.00
			Blue favor		+15.00

O3

O4

INTERIOR

1873

O15	O3	1c	**vermilion**	75.00	10.00
			dull vermilion	75.00	10.00
			bright vermilion	75.00	10.00
			Never hinged	170.00	
			No gum	30.00	
			On cover		160.00
			Block of 4	325.00	*325.00*
			P# block of 10, Impt.	*1,000.*	
			Never hinged	*1,850.*	
			Ribbed paper	85.00	20.00
			Short transfer at bottom right (pos. 91)	—	—
			Cancellations		
			Violet		+1.00
			Blue		+1.00
			Red		+12.50
			Ultramarine		+8.00
			Town		+3.00
O16	O3	2c	**vermilion**	70.00	12.00
			dull vermilion	70.00	12.00
			bright vermilion	70.00	12.00
			Never hinged	160.00	
			No gum	30.00	
			On cover		65.00
			Block of 4	300.00	*300.00*
			P# block of 10, Impt.	*950.00*	
			P# block of 12, Impt.	*1,050.*	
			Cancellations		
			Purple		+.75
			Violet		+75
			Blue		+.75
			Red		+6.00
			Town		+7.50
			Numeral		+20.00
			"Paid"		+20.00
O17	O3	3c	**vermilion**	80.00	6.00
			dull vermilion	80.00	6.00
			bright vermilion	80.00	6.00
			Never hinged	175.00	
			No gum	35.00	
			On cover		40.00
			First day cover, Nos. O17, O18, *July 1, 1873*		*9,000.*
			Block of 4	350.00	*350.00*
			P# block of 10, Impt.	*975.00*	
			Ribbed paper	100.00	10.00
			Cancellations		
			Violet		+1.00
			Blue		+1.00
			Indigo		+3.00
			Magenta		+5.00
			Red		+15.00
			Green		+65.00
			Town		+7.50
			Numeral		+20.00
			Express Company		+75.00
			"Paid"		+20.00
			Fort		—
O18	O3	6c	**vermilion**	70.00	10.00
			dull vermilion	70.00	10.00
			bright vermilion	70.00	10.00
			scarlet vermilion	70.00	10.00
			Never hinged	160.00	
			No gum	27.50	
			On cover		95.00
			Block of 4	350.00	—
			P# block of 10, Impt.	*950.00*	
			Cancellations		
			Violet		+1.00
			Blue		+1.00
			Red		+15.00
			Town		+7.50
			Express Company		—
			Railroad		—
			Fort		—

See No. O17 for first day cover listing.

O19	O3	10c	**vermilion**	70.00	20.00
			dull vermilion	70.00	20.00
			bright vermilion	70.00	20.00
			Never hinged	160.00	
			No gum	27.50	
			On cover		*600.00*
			Block of 4	350.00	—
			P# block of 12, Impt.	*1,000.*	
			Cancellations		
			Violet		+1.00
			Blue		+1.00
			Indigo		+10.00
			Red		+25.00
			Town		+10.00
			Fort		—
			New York Foreign Mail		+300.00
O20	O3	12c	**vermilion**	90.00	12.00
			bright vermilion	90.00	12.00
			Never hinged	200.00	
			No gum	35.00	
			On cover		*575.00*
			Block of 4	400.00	500.00
			P# block of 10, Impt.	*1,150.*	
			Short transfer at right (pos. 6)	—	—
			Cancellations		
			Violet		+1.00
			Magenta		+1.00
			Blue		+1.00
			Red		+15.00
			Brown		+20.00
			Town		+7.50
			Fort		—
O21	O3	15c	**vermilion**	200.00	25.00
			bright vermilion	200.00	25.00
			Never hinged	450.00	
			No gum	80.00	
			On cover		*650.00*
			Block of 4	900.00	—
			P# block of 12, Impt.	—	
			Double transfer of left side	275.00	37.50
			Cancellations		
			Blue		+1.50
			Violet		+1.50
			Town		+5.00
O22	O3	24c	**vermilion**	180.00	20.00
			dull vermilion	180.00	20.00
			bright vermilion	180.00	20.00
			Never hinged	400.00	
			No gum	60.00	
			On cover		*2,500.*
			Block of 4	775.00	*2,000.*
			P# block of 12, Impt.	*2,500.*	
	a.		Double impression		—
			Cancellations		
			Violet		+1.50
			Blue		+1.50
			Red		+15.00
			Town		+5.00
O23	O3	30c	**vermilion**	290.00	20.00
			bright vermilion	290.00	20.00
			Never hinged	625.00	
			No gum	110.00	
			On parcel label		*6,000.*
			Block of 4	1,250.	—
			P# block of 12, Impt.	*4,250.*	
			Cancellations		
			Violet		+2.00
			Blue		+2.00
			Red		+50.00
			Town		+7.50
O24	O3	90c	**vermilion**	325.00	50.00
			bright vermilion	325.00	50.00
			Never hinged	700.00	
			No gum	120.00	
			On cover		*4,500.*
			Block of 4	1,650.	—
			P# block of 12, Impt.	*5,000.*	
			Double transfer	390.00	
			Major double transfer (Pos. 17)	*600.00*	*250.00*
			Short transfer at right (Pos. 56)		—
			Silk paper	—	
			Cancellations		
			Violet		+4.00
			Blue		+4.00
			Magenta		+10.00

Red +50.00
Brown +60.00
Town +17.50

JUSTICE

1873
O25 O4 1c **purple** 250.00 100.00
dark purple 250.00 100.00
Never hinged 550.00
No gum 100.00
On cover *1,750.*
On cover with No. O26 *4,000.*
Block of 4 1,100.
Double transfer — —

Cancellations
Violet +3.00
Blue +3.00
Indigo +5.00
Magenta +5.00
Red +20.00
Town +7.50

O26 O4 2c **purple** 310.00 110.00
light purple 310.00 110.00
Never hinged 700.00
No gum 120.00
On cover *1,500.*
Block of 4 1,400.
Short transfer at right side (pos. 3) —

Cancellations
Violet +4.00
Blue +4.00
Ultramarine +10.00
Indigo +5.00
Magenta +5.00
Red +20.00
Town +20.00

O27 O4 3c **purple** 320.00 35.00
dark purple 320.00 35.00
bluish purple 320.00 35.00
Never hinged 725.00
No gum 110.00
On cover *575.00*
Block of 4 1,450.
Double transfer —

Cancellations
Violet +2.00
Magenta +2.00
Blue +2.00
Ultramarine +10.00
Indigo +5.00
Red +12.00
Green +100.00
Town +15.00

O28 O4 6c **purple** 310.00 45.00
light purple 310.00 45.00
bluish purple 310.00 45.00
Never hinged 700.00
No gum 110.00
On cover *1,200.*
Block of 4 1,400.

Cancellations
Violet +2.00
Blue +2.00
Indigo +5.00
Magenta +5.00
Red +15.00
Town +17.50

O29 O4 10c **purple** 310.00 100.00
bluish purple 310.00 100.00
Never hinged 700.00
No gum 120.00
On cover *3,750.*
Block of 4 1,400.
P# block of 10, Impt. *6,000.*
Double transfer — —

Cancellations
Violet +4.00
Blue +4.00
Magenta +5.00
Town +17.50

O30 O4 12c **purple** 260.00 75.00
dark purple 260.00 75.00
Never hinged 575.00
No gum 95.00
On cover *1,750.*
Block of 4 1,200.

Cancellations
Purple +2.00
Violet +2.00
Blue +2.00
Magenta +5.00
Red +35.00
Town +17.50

O31 O4 15c **purple** 475.00 200.00
Never hinged 1,050.
No gum 210.00
On cover *1,250.*
Block of 4 *2,400.*
Double transfer — —

Cancellations
Violet +5.00
Blue +5.00
Indigo +5.00
Magenta +10.00
Red +35.00
Town +10.00

The block of 4 of No. O31 is unique. It is in the grade of fine and is valued thus.

O32 O4 24c **purple** 1,250. 425.00
Never hinged —
No gum 550.00
On cover *8,000.*
Short transfer (pos. 98) — —

Cancellations
Violet +10.00
Blue +10.00
Magenta +10.00
Red +35.00
Town +40.00

O33 O4 30c **purple** 1,300. 350.00
Never hinged —
No gum 550.00
On cover with Nos. O27 & O28 22,000.
Double transfer at top 1,400. 375.00

Cancellations
Purple +10.00
Violet +10.00
Blue +10.00
Magenta +10.00
Red +50.00
Town +40.00

The block of 4 of No. O33 is unique. It is in the grade of fine and is valued thus.

O34 O4 90c **purple** 1,900. 900.00
dark purple 1,900. 900.00
Never hinged —
No gum 800.00
On cover with No. O33 *26,000.*
Pair —
Double plate scratch — —
Triple transfer at top — —

Cancellations
Purple +25.00
Violet +25.00
Blue +25.00
Magenta +25.00

No. O34 on cover is unique. The cover bears three No. O34 and four No. O33.

O5

O6

NAVY

1873
O35 O5 1c **ultramarine** 160.00 50.00
dark ultramarine 160.00 50.00
Never hinged 350.00
No gum 65.00
On cover *750.00*
On cover with No. O36 *2,000.*
Block of 4 750.00
P# block of 12, Impt. *2,250.*
a. 1c **dull blue** 160.00 50.00
Never hinged 350.00
No gum 65.00

Cancellations
Violet +2.00
Blue +2.00
Indigo +5.00
Red +20.00
Town +7.50
Steamship +100.00
New York Foreign Mail —

O36 O5 2c **ultramarine** 160.00 25.00
dark ultramarine 160.00 25.00
Never hinged 350.00
No gum 65.00
On cover *500.00*
Block of 4 750.00
P# block of 12, Impt. *2,250.* —
Double transfer — —
a. 2c **dull blue** 160.00 25.00
gray blue 160.00 25.00
Never hinged 350.00
No gum 65.00
Block of 4 750.00

The 2c deep green and the 2c black, both perforated and imperforate, are trial color proofs.

Cancellations
Violet +1.50
Blue +1.50
Indigo +5.00
Red +15.00
Green +75.00
Town +10.00
Steamship +100.00

O37 O5 3c **ultramarine** 170.00 15.00
pale ultramarine 170.00 15.00
dark ultramarine 170.00 15.00
Never hinged 375.00
No gum 60.00
On cover *250.00*
Block of 4 775.00 *1,000.*
P# block of 12, Impt. *2,500.*
Double transfer — —
a. 3c **dull blue** 170.00 15.00
Never hinged 375.00
No gum 60.00

Cancellations
Violet +1.50
Blue +1.50
Indigo +5.00
Ultramarine +10.00
Magenta +5.00
Red +15.00
Town +5.00
Blue town +15.00
Steamship +75.00

O38 O5 6c **ultramarine** 150.00 25.00
bright ultramarine 150.00 25.00
Never hinged 325.00
No gum 55.00
On cover *750.00*
Block of 4 700.00 —
P# block of 12, Impt. *2,400.*
Vertical line through "N" of "Navy" 175.00 35.00
Double transfer — —
a. 6c **dull blue** 150.00 25.00
Never hinged 325.00
No gum 55.00

Cancellations
Violet +1.50
Purple +1.50
Blue +1.50
Magenta +10.00
Red +17.50
Green +100.00
Town +5.00
Steamship +100.00
New York Foreign Mail —

O39 O5 7c **ultramarine** 650.00 230.00
dark ultramarine 650.00 230.00
Never hinged —
No gum 250.00
On cover *3,000.*
Block of 4 *2,800.*
Double transfer — —
a. 7c **dull blue** 650.00 230.00
Never hinged —
No gum 250.00

Cancellations
Blue +10.00
Violet +10.00
Magenta +10.00
Red +45.00
Town +25.00

O40 O5 10c **ultramarine** 210.00 45.00
dark ultramarine 210.00 45.00
Never hinged 475.00
No gum 75.00
On cover *4,000.*
Block of 4 1,150.
P# block of 12, Impt. *2,900.* —
Plate scratch (pos. 3) *325.00* —
Ribbed paper 225.00 60.00
a. 10c **dull blue** 210.00 45.00
Never hinged 475.00
No gum 75.00

Cancellations
Violet +2.00
Blue +2.00
Brown +20.00
Red +25.00
Town +10.00
Steamship +100.00
New York Foreign Mail —

O41 O5 12c **ultramarine** 220.00 45.00
pale ultramarine 220.00 45.00
dark ultramarine 220.00 45.00
Never hinged 500.00
No gum 80.00
On cover *3,000.*
Block of 4 1,100.
P# strip of 6, Impt. —
Short transfer at lower right (pos. 10) — —
Double transfer of left side (pos. 50) 400.00 250.00

Cancellations
Violet +2.50
Magenta +2.50
Blue +2.50
Red +25.00
Town +10.00
Supplementary Mail +80.00
Steamship +200.00
New York Foreign Mail +325.00

O42 O5 15c **ultramarine** 375.00 75.00
dark ultramarine 375.00 75.00
Never hinged —
No gum 135.00
On cover *21,000.*
Block of 4 1,700.
P# strip of 6, Impt. —
Short transfer at upper left (pos. 26) —

Cancellations
Violet +2.50
Blue +2.50
Red +35.00
Yellow —
Town +20.00

O43 O5 24c **ultramarine** 400.00 85.00
dark ultramarine 400.00 85.00
Never hinged —
No gum 160.00
On cover *30,000.*
Block of 4 2,000.
Recut at upper right (pos. 33, 92) — —
a. 24c **dull blue** 375.00 80.00
Never hinged —
No gum 150.00

Cancellations
Violet +5.00
Magenta +5.00
Red +50.00

	Blue		+5.00
	Green		+150.00
	Town		+40.00
	Steamship		+125.00
	New York Foreign Mail		—
O44 O5 30c	**ultramarine**	325.00	50.00
	dark ultramarine	325.00	50.00
	Never hinged	—	
	No gum	125.00	
	On cover		*42,500.*
	Block of 4	1,600.	*3,000.*
	Double transfer	350.00	55.00
	Cancellations		
	Blue		+4.00
	Red		+30.00
	Violet		+4.00
	Town		+20.00
	Supplementary Mail		+125.00
	New York Foreign Mail		+400.00
O45 O5 90c	**ultramarine**	1,050.	375.00
	Never hinged	—	
	No gum	450.00	
	Block of 4	*6,250.*	
	Short transfer at upper left (pos. 1, 5)	—	—
a.	Double impression		*20,000.*
	Cancellations		
	Purple		+15.00
	Violet		+15.00
	Red		+75.00
	Town		+40.00

POST OFFICE

Stamps of the Post Office Department are often on paper with a gray surface. This is due to insufficient wiping of the excess ink off plates during printing.

1873

O47 O6 1c	**black**	25.00	12.00
	gray black	25.00	12.00
	Never hinged	60.00	
	No gum	12.00	
	On cover		60.00
	Block of 4	110.00	—
	P# block of 12, Impt.	400.00	
	Never hinged	550.00	
	Cancellations		
	Purple		+1.00
	Violet		+1.00
	Magenta		+1.00
	Blue		+1.00
	Red		+12.50
	Town		+3.50
O48 O6 2c	**black**	30.00	10.00
	gray black	30.00	10.00
	Never hinged	75.00	
	No gum	13.00	
	On cover		160.00
	Block of 4	140.00	—
	P# block of 12, Impt.	475.00	
a.	Double impression	600.00	400.00
	Cancellations		
	Purple		+1.00
	Violet		+1.00
	Blue		+1.00
	Indigo		+5.00
	Magenta		+1.00
	Red		+12.50
	Town		+3.50
	Blue town		+7.50
	New York Foreign Mail		—
O49 O6 3c	**black**	10.00	2.00
	gray black	10.00	2.00
	Never hinged	25.00	
	No gum	3.00	
	On cover		20.00
	Block of 4	45.00	—
	P# block of 12, Impt.	*200.00*	
	Never hinged	*350.00*	
	Cracked plate	—	—
	Double transfer at bottom	—	—
	Double paper	—	—
	Vertical ribbed paper	—	—
a.	Printed on both sides		*7,500.*
	Cancellations		
	Purple		+.75
	Violet		+.75
	Blue		+.75
	Indigo		+5.00
	Ultramarine		+1.50
	Magenta		+.75
	Red		+10.00
	Brown		+20.00
	Green		+60.00
	Numeral		+20.00
	Town		+1.50
	Railroad		+25.00
	"Paid"		+12.00
O50 O6 6c	**black**	30.00	8.00
	gray black	30.00	8.00
	Never hinged	75.00	
	No gum	12.00	
	On cover		75.00
	Block of 4	150.00	—
	P# block of 14, Impt.	550.00	
	Vertical ribbed paper	—	12.50
	Double transfer of top frame (pos. 96L, 99L)	—	—
a.	Diagonal half used as 3c on cover		*4,750.*
b.	Double impression		*3,000.*
	Cancellations		
	Purple		+.75
	Violet		+.75
	Magenta		+.75
	Blue		+.75
	Indigo		+5.00
	Red		+12.00
	Brown		+20.00
	Numeral		+20.00
	Town		+2.50
	"Paid"		+15.00
O51 O6 10c	**black**	140.00	55.00
	gray black	140.00	55.00
	Never hinged	325.00	
	No gum	60.00	
	On cover		*400.00*
	Block of 4	700.00	—
	P# block of 12, Impt.	*1,950.*	
	Cancellations		
	Violet		+3.50
	Red		+15.00
	Magenta		+3.50
	Blue		+3.50
	Town		+10.00
O52 O6 12c	**black**	120.00	12.00
	gray black	120.00	12.00
	Never hinged	275.00	
	No gum	40.00	
	On cover		*1,000.*
	Block of 4	575.00	*1,250.*
	P# block of 12, Impt.	*1,850.*	
	Plate scratch above small "12"	—	—
	Cancellations		
	Purple		+1.00
	Magenta		+1.00
	Blue		+1.00
	Indigo		+5.00
	Red		+12.50
	Town		+4.00
O53 O6 15c	**black**	140.00	20.00
	gray black	140.00	20.00
	Never hinged	325.00	
	No gum	50.00	
	On cover		*5,000.*
	Block of 4	675.00	—
	P# block of 14, Impt.	*2,250.*	
	Double transfer	—	—
	Cancellations		
	Violet		+1.50
	Magenta		+1.50
	Red		+20.00
	Blue		+1.50
	Town		+7.50
	New York Foreign Mail		—
O54 O6 24c	**black**	200.00	25.00
	gray black	200.00	25.00
	Never hinged	450.00	
	No gum	70.00	
	Block of 4	900.00	—
	P# block of 12, Impt.	—	
	Double paper	—	—
	Cancellations		
	Violet		+1.50
	Blue		+1.50
	Red		+20.00
	Town		+7.50
	New York Foreign Mail		—
O55 O6 30c	**black**	200.00	25.00
	gray black	200.00	25.00
	Never hinged	450.00	
	No gum	70.00	
	On cover		—
	Block of 4	900.00	750.00
	P# block of 12, Impt.	*2,900.*	
	Cancellations		
	Purple		+1.50
	Blue		+1.50
	Red		+20.00
	Magenta		+1.50
	Town		+12.50
O56 O6 90c	**black**	220.00	25.00
	gray black	220.00	25.00
	Never hinged	500.00	
	No gum	80.00	
	Block of 4	950.00	*1,250.*
	P# block of 12, Impt.	*3,000.*	
	Double transfer	—	—
	Double paper	—	—
	Silk paper	—	
	Cancellations		
	Purple		+1.50
	Magenta		+1.50
	Blue		+1.50
	Town		+6.50

STATE

Franklin — O7

William H. Seward — O8

1873

O57 O7 1c	**dark green**	260.00	75.00
	dark yellow green	260.00	75.00
	light green	260.00	75.00
	Never hinged	575.00	
	No gum	110.00	
	On cover		—
	Block of 4	1,250.	—
	Plate scratch at left (pos. 51)	—	—
	Cancellations		
	Violet		+2.00
	Blue favor		+2.00
	Red		+17.50
	Town		+7.50
O58 O7 2c	**dark green**	310.00	100.00
	dark yellow green	310.00	100.00
	yellow green	—	—
	Never hinged	700.00	
	No gum	120.00	
	On cover		*1,000.*
	Double transfer at bottom (pos. 98)	600.00	—
	Cancellations		
	Violet		+5.00
	Blue favor		+5.00
	Indigo		+5.00
	Red		+50.00
	Town		+25.00
O59 O7 3c	**bright green**	220.00	25.00
	yellow green	220.00	25.00
	dark green	220.00	25.00
	Never hinged	500.00	
	No gum	85.00	
	On cover		*600.00*
	First day cover, *July 1, 1873*		—
	Block of 4	1,100.	—
	Double paper	—	—
	Short transfer at right (pos. 85)		—
	Cancellations		
	Violet		+1.50
	Blue favor		+1.50
	Indigo		+1.50
	Red		+10.00
	Town		+6.50
O60 O7 6c	**bright green**	220.00	30.00
	dark green	220.00	30.00
	yellow green	220.00	30.00
	Never hinged	500.00	
	No gum	85.00	
	On cover		*800.00*
	Block of 4	1,100.	
	P# block of 12, Impt.	—	
	Double transfer	—	—
	Foreign entry of 6c Executive (pos. 41, 91)	—	*500.00*
	Double transfer plus foreign entry of 6c Executive (pos. 61)	—	
	Plate scratch in margin (pos. 26, right; 27, left)	*325.00*	*275.00*
	Cancellations		
	Violet		+2.00
	Blue favor		+10.00
	Indigo		+2.00
	Red		+20.00
	Town		+17.50
O61 O7 7c	**dark green**	290.00	65.00
	dark yellow green	290.00	65.00
	Never hinged	650.00	
	No gum	95.00	
	On cover		*1,000.*
	Block of 4	1,500.	
	Ribbed paper	310.00	70.00
	Cancellations		
	Violet		+2.00
	Blue favor		+2.00
	Indigo		+2.00
	Red		+25.00
	Town		+10.00
O62 O7 10c	**dark green**	230.00	55.00
	bright green	230.00	55.00
	yellow green	230.00	—
	Never hinged	525.00	
	No gum	100.00	
	On cover		*2,000.*
	Block of 4	1,150.	
	P# block of 12, Impt.	—	
	Short transfer (pos. 34)	275.00	67.50
	Cancellations		
	Violet		+2.50
	Blue favor		+2.50
	Indigo		+2.50
	Red		+35.00
	Town		+25.00
	New York Foreign Mail		+325.00
O63 O7 12c	**dark green**	310.00	125.00
	dark yellow green	—	—
	Never hinged	700.00	
	No gum	140.00	
	On cover		*1,500.*
	Block of 4	1,650.	
	Cancellations		
	Violet		+5.00
	Blue favor		+5.00
	Red		+30.00
	Town		+15.00
O64 O7 15c	**dark green**	320.00	90.00
	dark yellow green	320.00	90.00
	Never hinged	725.00	
	No gum	130.00	
	On cover		*5,750.*
	Block of 4	1,750.	
	Short transfer at upper right		450.00
	Plate scratch at lower left (pos. 91)	*450.00*	

Plate scratch in margin (pos. 95, right; 96, left)	—	
Damaged plate at left (pos. 63)	—	
Cancellations		
Violet		+2.50
Blue favor		+2.50
Red		+30.00
Town		+30.00
O65 O7 24c **dark green**	525.00	230.00
dark yellow green	525.00	230.00
Never hinged	—	
No gum	275.00	
On cover		*17,500.*
Block of 4	*3,100.*	
Short transfer at bottom left (pos. 10)	*600.00*	
Plate gashes in forehead (pos. 76)	*750.00*	725.00
Plate scratch (pos. 66)	*800.00*	—
Cancellations		
Violet		+15.00
Blue favor		+15.00
Indigo		+15.00
Red		+85.00
Town		+55.00
O66 O7 30c **dark green**	500.00	180.00
dark yellow green	500.00	180.00
Never hinged	—	
No gum	240.00	
On cover		*12,500.*
Block of 4	*4,500.*	
Cancellations		
Violet		+5.00
Blue favor		+5.00
Indigo		+5.00
Red		+50.00
Town		+50.00
O67 O7 90c **dark green**	1,050.	325.00
dark yellow green	—	
Never hinged	—	
No gum	525.00	
On parcel wrapper front with Nos. O60 & O66		*62,500.*
Cancellations		
Violet		+15.00
Blue favor		+15.00
Red		+85.00
Red New York Foreign Mail		—
Town		+90.00
O68 O8 $2 **green & black**	1,500.	1,500.
yellow green & black	1,500.	1,500.
Never hinged	3,350.	
No gum	750.00	
On parcel label		*175,000.*
Block of 4	*18,000.*	
Ribbed paper		—
Cancellations		
Violet		+25.00
Blue favor		+25.00
Red		+175.00
Town		+125.00
Red New York Foreign Mail		+3,000.
Pen		*300.00*
O69 O8 $5 **green & black**	7,500.	*12,000.*
yellow green & black	7,500.	*12,000.*
Never hinged	—	
No gum	3,250.	
Irregular block of 6	*60,000.*	
Cancellations		
Blue favor		+250.00
Red favor		+250.00
Pen		*1,600.*
O70 O8 $10 **green & black**	5,000.	*7,000.*
yellow green & black	5,000.	*7,000.*
Never hinged	11,500.	
No gum	2,750.	
Block of 4	*26,500.*	
P# sheet of 10, Impt.	*62,500.*	
Ribbed paper	—	
Cancellations		
Blue favor		+200.00
Pen		*1,250.*
O71 O8 $20 **green & black**	5,250.	5,000.
yellow green & black	5,250.	5,000.
Never hinged	12,500.	
No gum	2,500.	
Block of 4	*27,500.*	
Block of 4, presentation pen cancel		*10,000.*
P# sheet of 10, Impt.	*67,500.*	

No. O71 used is valued with a blue or red favor cancel.

Cancellations	
Blue favor	5,000.
Red favor	5,000.
Pen presentation	1,750.

The design of Nos. O68 to O71 measures 25½x39½mm.

O9

O10

TREASURY

1873

O72 O9 1c **brown**	120.00	10.00
dark brown	120.00	10.00
yellow brown	120.00	10.00
Never hinged	250.00	
No gum	45.00	
On cover		100.00
Block of 4	525.00	*325.00*
P# block of 14, Impt.	*2,100.*	
Never hinged	*4,000.*	
Double transfer	135.00	12.50
Cancellations		
Purple		+1.00
Violet		+1.00
Magenta		+1.00
Blue		+1.00
Red		+10.00
Brown		+20.00
Green		+200.00
Town		+2.00
Blue town		+4.00
New York Foreign Mail		—
O73 O9 2c **brown**	125.00	8.00
dark brown	125.00	8.00
yellow brown	125.00	8.00
Never hinged	275.00	
No gum	45.00	
On cover		75.00
Block of 4	550.00	*325.00*
P# block of 14, Impt.	*2,000.*	
Double transfer	—	12.50
Plate scratch (pos. 3R)		—
Cancellations		
Purple		+1.00
Violet		+1.00
Magenta		+1.00
Blue		+1.00
Indigo		+3.00
Red		+10.00
Town		+2.00
Blue town		+4.00
New York Foreign Mail		+275.00
O74 O9 3c **brown**	110.00	2.00
dark brown	110.00	2.00
yellow brown	110.00	2.00
Never hinged	230.00	
No gum	40.00	
On cover		100.00
First day cover, *July 1, 1873*		*11,000.*
Block of 4	475.00	*250.00*
P# block of 14, Impt.	*1,850.*	
Double paper	—	
Shaded circle outside of right frame line	—	—
Short transfer at bottom (pos. 36 R 29)	—	—
a. Double impression		*5,000.*
Cancellations		
Purple		+.50
Violet		+.50
Blue		+.50
Indigo		+3.00
Ultramarine		+2.00
Magenta		+.50
Red		+3.50
Brown		+20.00
Green		+200.00
Town		+1.00
Railroad		+20.00
"Paid"		+10.00
O75 O9 6c **brown**	120.00	4.00
dark brown	120.00	4.00
yellow brown	120.00	4.00
Never hinged	250.00	
No gum	45.00	
On cover		75.00
Block of 4	525.00	*500.00*
P# block of 12, Impt.	*1,900.*	
Never hinged	*3,500.*	
Dirty plate	120.00	6.00
Double transfer		—
Cancellations		
Purple		+.50
Violet		+.50
Magenta		+.50
Blue		+.50
Indigo		+3.00
Ultramarine		+1.50
Red		+5.00
Green		+200.00
"Paid"		+20.00
Town		+1.50
New York Foreign Mail		—
O76 O9 7c **brown**	250.00	35.00
dark brown	250.00	35.00
yellow brown	250.00	35.00
Never hinged	550.00	
No gum	95.00	
On cover		750.00
On cover with 6c War #O86		*12,000.*
Block of 4	1,100.	*1,000.*
P# block of 12, Impt.	—	
Cancellations		
Purple		+2.00
Violet		+2.00
Blue		+2.00
Indigo		+3.00
Red		+30.00
Green		+200.00
Town		+7.50
Blue town		+12.50
New York Foreign Mail		—
O77 O9 10c **brown**	240.00	12.00
dark brown	240.00	12.00
yellow brown	240.00	12.00
Never hinged	525.00	
No gum	90.00	
On cover		*450.00*
Block of 4	1,075.	*325.00*
P# block of 12, Impt.	—	
Double paper	—	—
Double transfer		—
Cancellations		
Purple		+1.00
Violet		+1.00
Blue		+1.00
Indigo		+3.00
Ultramarine		+4.00
Magenta		+1.00
Red		+12.00
Brown		+20.00
Green		+200.00
Town		+4.00
Blue town		+8.50
O78 O9 12c **brown**	300.00	10.00
dark brown	300.00	10.00
yellow brown	300.00	10.00
Never hinged	650.00	
No gum	100.00	
On cover		600.00
Block of 4	1,400.	*325.00*
Cancellations		
Purple		+.50
Blue		+.50
Ultramarine		+10.00
Red		+10.00
Green		+200.00
Town		+2.50
Railroad		+20.00
O79 O9 15c **brown**	300.00	12.00
yellow brown	300.00	12.00
Never hinged	650.00	
No gum	100.00	
On cover		*850.00*
Block of 4	1,400.	*325.00*
P# block of 12, Impt.	*4,250.*	
Never hinged	*6,000.*	
Cancellations		
Blue		+1.00
Purple		+1.00
Red		+10.00
Green		+200.00
Town		+2.50
Blue town		+7.50
Numeral		+15.00
Steamship		+100.00
O80 O9 24c **brown**	675.00	100.00
dark brown	675.00	90.00
yellow brown	675.00	90.00
Never hinged	—	
No gum	270.00	
Block of 4	3,250.	
Block of 14		—
Double transfer at top	725.00	—
Short transfer at top (pos. 61)		—
Cancellations		
Violet		+10.00
Blue		+5.00
Ultramarine		+10.00
Magenta		+5.00
Red		+30.00
Brown		+20.00
Town		+15.00
Blue town		+25.00
New York Foreign Mail		—
O81 O9 30c **brown**	400.00	12.00
dark brown	400.00	12.00
yellow brown	400.00	12.00
Never hinged	—	
No gum	140.00	
On cover		*5,000.*
Block of 4	1,750.	*500.00*
Short transfer at left top (pos. 95)	450.00	25.00
Short transfer at right top (pos. 45)	450.00	25.00
Block of 4, one pos. 45	—	
Short transfer across entire top (pos. 41)	450.00	25.00
Cancellations		
Purple		+1.00
Blue		+1.00
Magenta		+1.00
Red		+12.00
Green		+200.00
Town		+3.50
Blue town		+7.50
O82 O9 90c **brown**	400.00	15.00
dark brown	400.00	15.00
yellow brown	400.00	15.00
Never hinged	—	
No gum	140.00	
Block of 4	1,750.	*375.00*
Double paper	—	—

Cancellations		
Purple		+1.00
Magenta		+1.00
Blue		+1.00
Red		+30.00
Brown		+7.50
Green		+200.00
Town		+3.50
Blue town		+7.50

WAR

1873

O83 O10 1c **rose**	240.00	15.00
rose red	240.00	15.00
Never hinged	525.00	
No gum	90.00	
On cover		140.00
Block of 4	1,050.	
Block of 10		—
P# block of 12, Impt.	*3,250.*	
Cancellations		
Purple		+1.00
Blue		+1.00
Magenta		+5.00
Red		+15.00
Town		+3.50
Fort		+100.00
Numeral		+12.50
"Paid"		—
O84 O10 2c **rose**	240.00	15.00
rose red	240.00	15.00
Never hinged	525.00	
No gum	90.00	
On cover		70.00
Block of 4	1,025.	—
P# block of 14, Impt.	*3,750.*	
Ribbed paper	250.00	17.50
Cancellations		
Purple		+1.50
Magenta		+1.50
Blue		+1.50
Red		+15.00
Town		+4.00
Fort		+100.00
O85 O10 3c **rose**	240.00	5.00
rose red	240.00	5.00
Never hinged	525.00	
No gum	90.00	
On cover		40.00
Block of 4	1,025.	*550.00*
P# block of 14, Impt.	*3,750.*	
Cancellations		
Purple		+1.00
Blue		+1.00
Ultramarine		+10.00
Magenta		+1.00
Red		+20.00
Green		+35.00
Town		+1.50
Fort		+100.00
"Paid"		+12.00
O86 O10 6c **rose**	625.00	10.00
pale rose	625.00	10.00
Never hinged	1,350.	
No gum	250.00	
On cover		60.00
Block of 4	*3,000.*	—
P# block of 12, Impt.	—	
Cancellations		
Purple		+1.50
Blue		+1.50
Indigo		+3.00
Magenta		+3.00
Red		+15.00
Town		+3.50
Blue town		+6.50
Fort		+100.00
O87 O10 7c **rose**	160.00	90.00
pale rose	160.00	90.00
rose red	160.00	90.00
Never hinged	360.00	
No gum	80.00	
On cover		—
Block of 4	675.00	
P# block of 10, Impt.	*2,250.*	
Cancellations		
Purple		+2.50
Blue		+3.50
Magenta		+10.00
Red		+25.00
Town		+7.50
O88 O10 10c **rose**	140.00	25.00
rose red	140.00	25.00
Never hinged	300.00	
No gum	45.00	
On cover		*2,000.*
Block of 4	600.00	*900.00*
P# block of 12, Impt.	*2,000.*	

All examples of No. O88 show a crack at lower left. It was on the original die.

Cancellations		
Purple		+1.00
Blue		+1.00
Town		+3.50
Fort		+100.00
O89 O10 12c **rose**	275.00	12.00
Never hinged	600.00	
No gum	110.00	
On cover		450.00
Block of 4	1,250.	*550.00*
P# block of 12, Impt.	*3,850.*	
Never hinged	*7,750.*	
Ribbed paper	300.00	20.00
Cancellations		
Purple		+1.00
Magenta		+1.00
Blue		+1.00
Indigo		+5.00
Red		+10.00
Town		+3.00
Fort		+100.00
O90 O10 15c **rose**	85.00	15.00
pale rose	85.00	15.00
rose red	85.00	15.00
Never hinged	190.00	
No gum	30.00	
On cover		3,250.
Block of 4	375.00	—
P# block of 10, Impt.	*1,100.*	
Ribbed paper	92.50	20.00
Short transfer at upper right (pos. 74)		—
Cancellations		
Purple		+1.00
Blue		+1.00
Ultramarine		+10.00
Magenta		+3.00
Red		+10.00
Town		+2.50
Fort		+200.00
Express Company		—
O91 O10 24c **rose**	85.00	12.00
pale rose	85.00	12.00
rose red	85.00	12.00
Never hinged	190.00	
No gum	30.00	
On cover		—
Block of 4	375.00	*2,250.*
P# block of 10, Impt.	*1,300.*	
Cancellations		
Purple		+1.00
Blue		+1.00
Magenta		+5.00
Town		+2.50
Fort		+100.00
O92 O10 30c **rose**	130.00	12.00
rose red	130.00	12.00
Never hinged	275.00	
No gum	45.00	
On cover		—
Block of 4	575.00	*350.00*
P# block of 12, Impt.	*1,850.*	
Ribbed paper	140.00	15.00
Cancellations		
Purple		+1.00
Magenta		+1.00
Blue		+1.00
Red		+20.00
Town		+2.50
Fort		+100.00
O93 O10 90c **rose**	225.00	50.00
rose red	225.00	50.00
Never hinged	500.00	
No gum	80.00	
On cover		—
Block of 4	975.00	*975.00*
P# block of 12, Impt.	*3,750.*	
Cancellations		
Purple		+2.00
Magenta		+2.00
Blue		+2.00
Red		+20.00
Numeral		+40.00
Town		+7.50
Fort		+125.00

Printed by the American Bank Note Co.

The Continental Bank Note Co. was consolidated with the American Bank Note Co. on February 4, 1879. The American Bank Note Company used many plates of the Continental Bank Note Company to print the ordinary postage, Departmental and Newspaper stamps. Therefore, stamps bearing the Continental Company's imprint were not always its product.

1879 — Soft Porous Paper

AGRICULTURE

O94 O1 1c **yellow** (issued without gum)	6,000.	
Block of 4	*30,000.*	
O95 O1 3c **yellow**	550.00	110.00
Never hinged	1,250.	
No gum	240.00	
Block of 4	2,750.	*1,350.*
P# block of 12, Impt.	*7,250.*	
Cancellations		
Purple		+5.00
Blue		+5.00
Town		+30.00

INTERIOR

O96 O3 1c **vermilion**	300.00	*275.00*
pale vermilion	300.00	*275.00*
Never hinged	550.00	
No gum	160.00	
Block of 4	1,450.	—
P# block of 12, Impt.	*4,500.*	
Short transfer at lower right (pos. 91)	600.00	
Cancellations		
Purple		+5.00
Blue		+5.00
Town		+15.00
O97 O3 2c **vermilion**	10.00	3.00
pale vermilion	10.00	3.00
scarlet vermilion	10.00	3.00
Never hinged	17.50	
No gum	3.00	
On cover		150.00
Block of 4	47.50	*250.00*
P# block of 12, Impt.	*225.00*	
Cancellations		
Purple		+.50
Violet		+.50
Blue		+.50
Red		+5.00
Town		+1.50
Blue town		+3.00
Railroad		+40.00
Fort		+100.00
O98 O3 3c **vermilion**	10.00	3.00
pale vermilion	10.00	3.00
Never hinged	22.50	
No gum	3.00	
On cover		30.00
Block of 4	47.50	—
P# block of 10, Impt.	*225.00*	
Cancellations		
Purple		+.50
Violet		+.50
Blue		+.50
Red		+5.00
Town		+1.50
Blue town		+3.00
Railroad		+40.00
Numeral		+5.00
O99 O3 6c **vermilion**	10.00	12.50
pale vermilion	10.00	12.50
scarlet vermilion	10.00	12.50
Never hinged	17.50	
No gum	3.00	
On cover		200.00
Block of 4	47.50	—
P# block of 10, Impt.	*225.00*	
Cancellations		
Purple		+.50
Blue		+.50
Red		+5.00
Town		+1.50
Fort		+100.00
O100 O3 10c **vermilion**	110.00	75.00
pale vermilion	110.00	75.00
Never hinged	250.00	
No gum	60.00	
On cover		*1,200.*
Block of 4	500.00	
P# block of 12, Impt.	*1,650.*	
Cancellations		
Purple		+5.00
Blue		+5.00
Town		+10.00
O101 O3 12c **vermilion**	230.00	115.00
pale vermilion	230.00	115.00
Never hinged	525.00	
No gum	130.00	
On cover		—
Block of 4	1,075.	*575.00*
Block of 6		*1,500.*
P# block of 12, Impt.	*2,900.*	
Short transfer at lower right (pos. 6)	—	—
Cancellation		
Violet		+5.00
O102 O3 15c **vermilion**	400.00	260.00
Never hinged	900.00	
No gum	200.00	
Block of 4	1,750.	
P# block of 12, Impt.	—	
On cover		*6,500.*
Double transfer	450.00	—
Cancellations		
Purple		+5.00
Blue		+5.00
O103 O3 24c **vermilion**	4,500.	—
Never hinged	10,000.	
No gum	2,100.	
Block of 4	*25,000.*	
P# strip of 6, Impt.	—	
Cancellation		
Blue		—

JUSTICE

O106 O4 3c **bluish purple**	175.00	100.00
deep bluish purple	175.00	100.00
Never hinged	400.00	
No gum	80.00	
On cover		1,250.
Block of 4	750.00	
Cancellations		
Violet		+5.00
Blue		+5.00
Indigo		+5.00
Ultramarine		+10.00
O107 O4 6c **bluish purple**	475.00	275.00
Never hinged	1,050.	
No gum	210.00	
On cover		—
Block of 4	2,250.	
Cancellations		
Blue		+10.00
Indigo		+5.00
Town		+20.00

POST OFFICE

O108 O6 3c **black**	30.00	10.00
gray black	30.00	10.00
Never hinged	70.00	
No gum	10.00	
On cover		—
Block of 4	130.00	—
P# block of 14, Impt.	*475.00*	
Cancellations		
Purple		+1.00
Violet		+1.00
Blue		+1.00
Indigo		+10.00

Magenta +1.00
Red +20.00
Green +40.00
Town +2.00
"Paid" +12.00

TREASURY

O109 O9 3c **brown** 80.00 10.00
yellow brown 80.00 10.00
Never hinged 175.00
No gum 35.00
On cover 110.00
Block of 4 400.00 *900.00*
P# block of 14, Impt. *1,450.*

Cancellations
Purple +1.50
Blue +1.50
Indigo +3.00
Town +2.00
Numeral +7.50

O110 O9 6c **brown** 200.00 50.00
yellow brown 200.00 50.00
dark brown 200.00 50.00
Never hinged 450.00
No gum 65.00
On cover 300.00
Block of 4 950.00 —
P# block of 12, Impt. *2,900.*

Cancellations
Purple +6.00
Magenta +6.00
Blue +6.00

O111 O9 10c **brown** 260.00 80.00
yellow brown 260.00 80.00
dark brown 260.00 80.00
Never hinged 575.00
No gum 90.00
On cover *750.00*
Block of 4 1,250. —
P# block of 12, Impt. *4,500.*

Cancellations
Purple +2.50
Blue +2.50
Magenta +5.00
Town +7.50

O112 O9 30c **brown** 2,400. 425.00
Never hinged —
No gum 875.00
Block of 4 *12,000.*

Cancellations
Blue +25.00
Indigo +25.00
Town +50.00

O113 O9 90c **brown** 4,500. 525.00
dark brown 4,500. 525.00
Never hinged —
No gum 1,650.
Block of 4 *20,000.*

Cancellations
Purple +25.00
Blue +25.00
Town +75.00

WAR

O114 O10 1c **rose red** 6.00 4.00
rose 6.00 4.00
dull rose red 6.00 4.00
brown rose 6.00 4.00
Never hinged 11.00
No gum 2.50
On cover 55.00
Block of 4 27.50 —
P# block of 12, Impt. *150.00*
Never hinged *220.00*

Cancellations
Purple +.50
Blue +.50
Town +1.00
Fort +100.00

O115 O10 2c **rose red** 12.00 4.00
dark rose red 12.00 4.00
dull vermilion 12.00 4.00
Never hinged 22.50
No gum 4.00
On cover 40.00
Block of 4 52.50 —
P# block of 12, Impt. *200.00*
Never hinged *325.00*

Cancellations
Purple +.50
Blue +.50
Magenta +.50
Green +35.00
Town +2.00
Fort +100.00

O116 O10 3c **rose red** 12.00 2.00
dull rose red 12.00 2.00
Never hinged 22.50
No gum 4.00
On cover 35.00
Block of 4 52.50 —
P# block of 12, Impt. *200.00*
Never hinged *325.00*
Double transfer 17.50 6.00
Plate flaw at upper left (32 R 20) — —
a. Imperf., pair *5,000.*
b. Double impression *6,500.*

Cancellations
Purple +.50
Violet +.50
Blue +.50
Ultramarine +5.00
Magenta +1.00
Red +5.00
Town +1.00
Fort +100.00

O117 O10 6c **rose red** 11.00 3.00
dull rose red 11.00 3.00
dull vermilion — —
Never hinged 20.00
No gum 4.00
On cover 50.00
Block of 4 47.50 —
P# block of 12, Impt. *190.00*

Cancellations
Purple +.50
Blue +.50
Magenta +1.00
Brown +20.00
Town +1.00
Fort +100.00
Numeral +7.50

O118 O10 10c **rose red** 65.00 50.00
dull rose red 65.00 50.00
Never hinged 120.00
No gum 26.00
On cover *1,800.*
Block of 4 300.00
P# block of 10, Impt. *950.00*

Cancellations
Violet +3.00
Town +5.00
Fort +100.00

O119 O10 12c **rose red** 60.00 14.00
dull rose red 60.00 14.00
brown rose 60.00 14.00
Never hinged 110.00
No gum 20.00
On cover —
Block of 4 260.00 —
P# block of 10, Impt. *775.00*

Cancellations
Purple +1.00
Violet +1.00
Red +10.00
Town +2.50
Fort +150.00

O120 O10 30c **rose red** 225.00 100.00
dull rose red 225.00 100.00
Never hinged 450.00
No gum 90.00
Block of 4 975.00 —
P# block of 10, Impt. *3,500.*

Cancellations
Violet +5.00
Town +10.00
Fort +125.00

SPECIAL PRINTINGS

Special printings of Official stamps were made in 1875 at the time the other Reprints, Re-issues and Special Printings were printed. They are ungummed. Though overprinted "SPECIMEN," these stamps are Special Printings, and they are not considered to be in the same category as the stamps listed in the Specimen section of this catalogue.

Although perforated, these stamps were sometimes (but not always) cut apart with scissors. As a result the perforations may be mutilated and the design damaged.

Number sold indicated in parentheses.

All values exist imperforate.

Blocks of 4 are now listed. All are scarce, a few are rare. They will be valued when sufficient information has been received. Imprint and plate number strips or blocks are very scarce.

The "SEPCIMEN" error appears once on some panes of 100. The error was discovered and corrected part way through the printing. Blocks of 4 or larger with the "SEPCIMEN" error are rare and worth much more than the value of the individual stamps.

Printing flaws which resemble broken type (but are not) are commonly found on the SPECIMEN overprint on these and other overprinted stamps. The variety listed as a "small dotted i" is actually an "i"; it is not one of the printing flaws noted in the preceding sentence. All "small dotted 'i'" varieties are on ribbed paper from the second special printings. They occur in positions 7 and 26.

Printed by the Continental Bank Note Co.

Overprinted in Block Letters

1875 Thin, hard white paper *Perf. 12*

Type D

AGRICULTURE

Carmine Overprint

O1S D 1c **yellow** (10,234) 30.00
Block of 4 *350.00*
a. "Sepcimen" error 2,500.
b. Horiz. ribbed paper (10,000) 37.50
Block of 4 *425.00*
c. As "b," small dotted "i" in "Specimen" 500.00
O2S D 2c **yellow** (4,192) 55.00
Block of 4 *625.00*
a. "Sepcimen" error 3,000.
O3S D 3c **yellow** (389) 300.00
a. "Sepcimen" error *11,000.*
O4S D 6c **yellow** (373) 325.00
a. "Sepcimen" error *17,500.*
O5S D 10c **yellow** (390) 325.00
a. "Sepcimen" error *17,500.*
O6S D 12c **yellow** (379) 325.00
a. "Sepcimen" error *11,000.*
O7S D 15c **yellow** (370) 325.00
a. "Sepcimen" error *11,000.*
O8S D 24c **yellow** (352) 325.00
a. "Sepcimen" error *11,000.*
O9S D 30c **yellow** (354) 325.00
a. "Sepcimen" error *13,500.*

EXECUTIVE

Blue Overprint

O10S D 1c **carmine** (10,000) 30.00
Block of 4 *350.00*
P# block of 14, Impt. *18,000.*
a. Horiz. ribbed paper (10,000) 35.00
Block of 4 *375.00*
b. As "a," small dotted "i" in "Specimen" 500.00
O11S D 2c **carmine** (7,430) 55.00
Block of 4 650.00
Foreign entry of 6c Agriculture (pos. 40) *2,250.*
O12S D 3c **carmine** (3,735) 67.50
Block of 4 —
O13S D 6c **carmine** (3,485) 67.50
Block of 4 —
O14S D 10c **carmine** (3,461) 67.50
Block of 4 —

INTERIOR

Blue Overprint

O15S D 1c **vermilion** (7,194) 55.00
Block of 4 *650.00*
P# block of 12, impt. *5,750.*
O16S D 2c **vermilion** (1,263) 120.00
Block of 4 1,500.
P# Block of 12, Impt. *10,000.*
a. "Sepcimen" error *11,000.*
O17S D 3c **vermilion** (88) 1,400.
O18S D 6c **vermilion** (83) 1,400.
O19S D 10c **vermilion** (82) 1,400.
O20S D 12c **vermilion** (75) 1,400.
O21S D 15c **vermilion** (78) 1,400.
Double transfer at left 2,250.
O22S D 24c **vermilion** (77) 1,400.
O23S D 30c **vermilion** (75) 1,400.
O24S D 90c **vermilion** (77) 1,400.

JUSTICE

Blue Overprint

O25S D 1c **purple** (10,000) 30.00
Block of 4 *350.00*
P# block of 12, Impt. *3,250.*
a. "Sepcimen" error 1,900.
b. Horiz. ribbed paper (9,729) 35.00
Block of 4 *550.00*
P# block of 12, Impt. *4,000.*
c. As "b," small dotted "i" in "Specimen" 500.00
O26S D 2c **purple** (3,395) 55.00
Block of 4 650.00
P# block of 12, Impt. *5,500.*
a. "Sepcimen" error 2,500.
O27S D 3c **purple** (178) 900.00
Plate scratches —
a. "Sepcimen" error *8,750.*
O28S D 6c **purple** (163) 900.00
O29S D 10c **purple** (163) 900.00
O30S D 12c **purple** (154) 900.00
a. "Sepcimen" error *15,000.*
O31S D 15c **purple** (157) 900.00
a. "Sepcimen" error *13,500.*
O32S D 24c **purple** (150) 900.00
a. "Sepcimen" error *15,000.*
O33S D 30c **purple** (150) 900.00
a. "Sepcimen" error *13,500.*
O34S D 90c **purple** (152) 900.00

NAVY

Carmine Overprint

O35S D 1c **ultramarine** (10,000) 32.50
Block of 4 *375.00*
a. "Sepcimen" error 2,500.
b. Double "Specimen" overprint *1,900.*
O36S D 2c **ultramarine** (1,748) 60.00
Block of 4 *750.00*
a. "Sepcimen" error 3,250.
O37S D 3c **ultramarine** (126) 1,000.
O38S D 6c **ultramarine** (116) 1,100.
Vertical line through "N" of "Navy" *1,650.*
O39S D 7c **ultramarine** (501) 450.00
Block of 4 *5,000.*
a. "Sepcimen" error 8,250.
O40S D 10c **ultramarine** (112) 1,100.
a. "Sepcimen" error *17,500.*
O41S D 12c **ultramarine** (107) 1,000.
Double transfer at left side, pos. 50 —
a. "Sepcimen" error *17,500.*
O42S D 15c **ultramarine** (107) 1,000.
a. "Sepcimen" error *13,500.*
O43S D 24c **ultramarine** (106) 1,000.
a. "Sepcimen" error *13,500.*

O44S D 30c **ultramarine** (104) 1,000.
Double transfer —
a. "Sepcimen" error *17,500.*
O45S D 90c **ultramarine** (102) 1,000.

POST OFFICE

Carmine Overprint

O47S D 1c **black** (6,015) 42.50
Block of 4 *475.00*
a. "Sepcimen" error 1,900.
Block of 4, one stamp "SEPCIMEN" error *6,000.*
b. Inverted overprint *2,750.*
O48S D 2c **black** (590) 250.00
Block of 4 *3,250.*
a. "Sepcimen" error 3,250.
O49S D 3c **black** (91) 1,200.
a. "Sepcimen" error —
O50S D 6c **black** (87) 1,100.
O51S D 10c **black** (177) 900.00
a. "Sepcimen" error *11,000.*
O52S D 12c **black** (93) 1,000.
O53S D 15c **black** (82) 1,100.
a. "Sepcimen" error *13,500.*
O54S D 24c **black** (84) 1,100.
a. "Sepcimen" error *11,000.*
O55S D 30c **black** (81) 1,200.
O56S D 90c **black** (82) 1,100.
a. "Sepcimen" error —

STATE

Carmine Overprint

O57S D 1c **bluish green** (10,000) 30.00
Block of 4 *350.00*
a. "Sepcimen" error 1,900.
b. Horiz. ribbed paper (10,000) 35.00
Block of 4 *425.00*
c. As "b," small dotted "i" in "Specimen" 550.00
d. Double "Specimen" overprint *3,850.*
Block of 4 —
O58S D 2c **bluish green** (5,145) 90.00
Block of 4 *850.00*
a. "Sepcimen" error *2,500.*
O59S D 3c **bluish green** (793) 120.00
Block of 4 —
a. "Sepcimen" error 6,000.
O60S D 6c **bluish green** (467) 275.00
Double transfer *600.00*
a. "Sepcimen" error 8,250.
O61S D 7c **bluish green** (791) 120.00
Block of 4 *1,500.*
a. "Sepcimen" error 8,250.
O62S D 10c **bluish green** (346) 500.00
Short transfer, pos. 34 *2,200.*
a. "Sepcimen" error *17,500.*
O63S D 12c **bluish green** (280) 550.00
a. "Sepcimen" error *11,000.*
O64S D 15c **bluish green** (257) 550.00
O65S D 24c **bluish green** (253) 550.00
a. "Sepcimen" error *11,000.*
O66S D 30c **bluish green** (249) 550.00
a. "Sepcimen" error *15,000.*
O67S D 90c **bluish green** (245) 550.00
a. "Sepcimen" error *11,000.*
O68S D $2 **green & black** (32) *20,000.*
O69S D $5 **green & black** (12) *25,000.*
O70S D $10 **green & black** (8) *50,000.*
O71S D $20 **green & black** (7) *85,000.*

TREASURY

Blue Overprint

O72S D 1c **dark brown** (2,185) 75.00
Block of 4 *975.00*
Double transfer —
O73S D 2c **dark brown** (309) 350.00
Block of 4 *4,250.*
O74S D 3c **dark brown** (84) 1,400.
O75S D 6c **dark brown** (85) 1,400.
O76S D 7c **dark brown** (198) 850.00
Block of 4 9,000.
P# block of 12, impt. 30,000.

The only recorded plate block of No. O76S is contained in a half sheet of 50 stamps.

O77S D 10c **dark brown** (82) 1,350.
O78S D 12c **dark brown** (75) 1,350.
O79S D 15c **dark brown** (75) 1,350.
O80S D 24c **dark brown** (99) 1,350.
O81S D 30c **dark brown** (74) 1,350.
Short transfer at left top (pos. 95) (1) —
Short transfer at right top (pos. 45) (1) —
O82S D 90c **dark brown** (72) 1,350.

WAR

Blue Overprint

O83S D 1c **deep rose** (9,610) 30.00
Block of 4 *375.00*
a. "Sepcimen" error 1,600.
O84S D 2c **deep rose** (1,618) 120.00
Block of 4 *1,400.*
P# block of 12 *9,000.*
a. "Sepcimen" error 2,000.
O85S D 3c **deep rose** (118) 1,000.
a. "Sepcimen" error *11,000.*
O86S D 6c **deep rose** (111) 1,000.
a. "Sepcimen" error *15,000.*
O87S D 7c **deep rose** (539) 325.00
Block of 4 *2,750.*
a. "Sepcimen" error 10,000.
O88S D 10c **deep rose** (119) 1,000.
a. "Sepcimen" error *13,500.*
O89S D 12c **deep rose** (105) 1,000.
a. "Sepcimen" error *13,500.*
O90S D 15c **deep rose** (105) 1,000.
a. "Sepcimen" error *13,500.*
O91S D 24c **deep rose** (106) 1,000.
a. "Sepcimen" error *13,500.*
O92S D 30c **deep rose** (104) 1,000.
a. "Sepcimen" error *13,500.*
O93S D 90c **deep rose** (106) 1,000.
a. "Sepcimen" error *13,500.*

Printed by the American Bank Note Co.
SOFT POROUS PAPER
EXECUTIVE

1881

Blue Overprint

O10xS D 1c **violet rose** (4,652) 95.00
Block of 4 *1,100.*

NAVY

Carmine Overprint

O35xS D 1c **gray blue** (4,182) 100.00
deep blue 100.00
Block of 4 *1,150.*
P# strip of 6, Impt. *4,000.*
a. Double overprint 1,200.

STATE

O57xS D 1c **yellow green** (1,672) 180.00
Block of 4 *2,500.*

POSTAL SAVINGS MAIL

The Act of Congress, approved June 25, 1910, establishing postal savings depositories, provided:

"Sec. 2. That the Postmaster General is hereby directed to prepare and issue special stamps of the necessary denominations for use, in lieu of penalty or franked envelopes, in the transmittal of free mail resulting from the administration of this act."

The use of postal savings official stamps was discontinued by the Act of Congress, approved September 23, 1914. Postmasters were notified of the discontinuance in mid-October 1914. The unused stamps in the hands of postmasters were returned and destroyed.

O11

Printed by the Bureau of Engraving & Printing

1910-11 **Engr.** **Wmk. 191**

O121 O11 2c **black,** *Dec. 22, 1910* 17.50 2.00
Never hinged 40.00
On cover 12.50
Block of 4 (2mm spacing) 80.00 11.00
Block of 4 (3mm spacing) 77.50 10.00
P# block of 6, Impt. & Star 350.00
Double transfer 22.50 4.00
O122 O11 50c **dark green,** *Feb. 1, 1911* 160.00 60.00
Never hinged 375.00
On cover 225.00
Block of 4 (2mm spacing) 675.00 300.00
Block of 4 (3mm spacing) 650.00 300.00
Margin block of 4, arrow 675.00
P# block of 6, Impt. & Star 2,400.
Never hinged *3,500.*
O123 O11 $1 **ultramarine,** *Feb. 1, 1911* 200.00 15.00
Never hinged 450.00
On cover 110.00
Block of 4 (2mm spacing) 850.00 75.00
Block of 4 (3mm spacing) 825.00 75.00
Margin block of 4, arrow 850.00
P# block of 6, Impt. & Star 2,400. —

Wmk. 190

O124 O11 1c **dark violet,** *Mar. 27, 1911* 10.00 2.00
Never hinged 22.50
On cover 15.00
Block of 4 (2mm spacing) 45.00 9.00
Block of 4 (3mm spacing) 42.50 8.50
P# block of 6, Impt. & Star 190.00
O125 O11 2c **black** 55.00 7.00
Never hinged 135.00
On cover 25.00
Block of 4 (2mm spacing) 240.00 32.50
Block of 4 (3mm spacing) 225.00 32.50
P# block of 6, Impt. & Star 700.00
Double transfer 60.00 8.00
O126 O11 10c **carmine,** *Feb. 1, 1911* 20.00 2.00
Never hinged 50.00
On cover 20.00
Block of 4 (2mm spacing) 87.50 30.00
Block of 4 (3mm spacing) 82.50 10.00
P# block of 6, Impt. & Star 370.00
Double transfer 25.00 3.50

Catalogue values for unused stamps in this section, from this point to the end, are for Never Hinged items.

From No. O127 onward, all official stamps are tagged unless noted.

OFFICIAL MAIL

O12

Designed by Bradbury Thompson

Engraved

1983, Jan. 12-1985 **Unwmk.** **Tagged** ***Perf. 11***

O127 O12 1c **red, blue & black** .20 .20
FDC, Washington, DC 1.00
P# block of 4, UL or UR .25
O128 O12 4c **red, blue & black** .20 .25
FDC, Washington, DC 1.00
P# block of 4, LR only .40
O129 O12 13c **red, blue & black** .45 *15.00*
FDC, Washington, DC 1.00
P# block of 4, UR only 2.00
O129A O12 14c **red, blue & black,** *May 15, 1985* .45 .50
FDC, Washington, DC 1.00
Zip-copyright block of 6 2.90
O130 O12 17c **red, blue & black** .60 .40
FDC, Washington, DC 1.00
P# block of 4, LL only 3.00
O132 O12 $1 **red, blue & black** 2.25 1.00
FDC, Washington, DC 2.25
P# block of 4, UL only 10.00
O133 O12 $5 **red, blue & black** 9.00 5.00
FDC, Washington, DC 12.50
P# block of 4, LL only 42.50
Nos. O127-O133 (7) 13.15 22.35

No. O129A does not have a "c" after the "14."

COIL STAMPS

Perf. 10 Vert.

O135 O12 20c **red, blue & black** 1.75 2.00
FDC, Washington, DC 1.00
Pair 3.50 4.00
P# strip of 3, P# 1 12.00
P# strip of 5, P# 1 55.00
P# single, #1 — 20.00
a. Imperf., pair *2,000.*
O136 O12 22c **red, blue & blk, low gloss gum,** *May 15, 1985* 1.00 *2.00*
FDC, Washington, DC 1.00
Pair 2.00 *4.00*
Dull finish gum *75.00*
a. Tagging omitted —

Used Values
of Nos. O135-O138, O140, etc., do not apply to stamps removed from first day covers.

Inscribed: Postal Card Rate D

1985, Feb. 4 ***Perf. 11***

O138 O12 (14c) **red, blue & black** 5.25 *10.00*
FDC, Washington, DC 1.00
P# block of 4, LR only 42.50 —

Frame line completely around the design — O13

Inscribed: No. O139, Domestic Letter Rate D; No. O140, Domestic Mail E.

COIL STAMPS

1985-88 **Litho., Engr. (#O139)** ***Perf. 10 Vert.***

O138A O13 15c **red, blue & blk,** *June 11, 1988* .45 .50
FDC, Corpus Christi, TX 1.25
Pair .90 1.00
O138B O13 20c **red, blue & blk,** *May 19, 1988* .45 .30
FDC, Washington 1.25
Pair .90 .60
O139 O12 (22c) **red, blue & blk,** *Feb. 4* 5.25 *10.00*

FDC, Washington, DC 1.00
Pair 10.50 —
P# strip of 3, P# 1 27.50
P# strip of 5, P# 1 55.00
P# single, #1 — 32.50

O140 O13 (25c) **red, blue & black,** *Mar. 22, 1988* .75 *2.00*
FDC, Washington 1.25
Pair 1.50 —

O141 O13 25c **red, blue & blk,** *June 11, 1988* .65 .50
FDC, Corpus Christi, TX 1.25
Pair 1.30 1.00
a. Imperf., pair *1,500.* —
Nos. O138A-O141 (5) 7.55 *13.30*

First day cancellation was applied to 137,721 covers bearing Nos. O138A and O141.

Plates of 400 in four panes of 100.

1989, July 5 **Litho.** ***Perf. 11***

O143 O13 1c **red, blue & black** .20 .20
FDC, Washington, DC 1.25

Type of 1985 and

O14

COIL STAMPS

1991 **Litho.** ***Perf. 10 Vert.***

O144 O14 (29c) **red, blue & blk,** *Jan. 22* .80 .50
FDC, Washington, DC 1.25
Pair 1.60 —

O145 O13 29c **red, blue & blk,** *May 24* .65 .30
FDC, Seattle, WA 1.25
Pair 1.30 .60

Plates of 400 in four panes of 100.

1991-93 **Litho.** ***Perf. 11***

O146 O13 4c **red, blue & blk,** *Apr. 6* .20 *.30*
FDC, Oklahoma City, OK 1.25

O146A O13 10c **red, blue & black,** *Oct. 19, 1993* .25 *.30*
FDC, Washington, DC 1.25

O147 O13 19c **red, blue & blk,** *May 24* .40 *.50*
FDC, Seattle, WA 1.25

O148 O13 23c **red, blue & blk,** *May 24* .45 .30
FDC, Seattle, WA 1.25
Horiz. pair with full vert. gutter between —
Vert. pair with full horiz. gutter between —

Imperfs of No. O148 are printer's waste.

Perf. 11¼

O151 O13 $1 **red, blue & black,** *Sept. 1993* 4.75 .75
Nos. O146-O151 (5) 6.05 2.15

COIL STAMPS

Inscribed: No. O152, For U.S. addresses only G.

Perf. 9.8 Vert.

O152 O14 (32c) **red, blue & black,** *Dec. 13, 1994* .65 .50
FDC, Washington, DC 1.25
Pair 1.30 —

O153 O13 32c **red, blue & black,** *May 9, 1995* 1.25 .50
FDC, Washington, DC 1.25
Pair 2.50 —

Nos. O146A, O151, O153 have a line of microscopic text below the eagle.

1995, May 9 **Litho.** ***Perf. 11.2***

O154 O13 1c **red, blue & black,** untagged .20 *.50*
FDC, Washington, DC 1.25
Pair .20 —

O155 O13 20c **red, blue & black** .45 *.50*
FDC, Washington, DC 1.25
Pair .90 —

O156 O13 23c **red, blue & black** .55 .50
FDC, Washington, DC 1.25
Pair 1.10 —

COIL STAMP

1999, Oct. 8 **Litho.** ***Perf. 9¾ Vert.***

O157 O13 33c **red, blue & black** .65 —
FDC, Washington, DC 1.25
Pair 1.30 —

Type of 1985
COIL STAMP

2001, Feb. 27 **Litho.** **Tagged** ***Perf. 9¾ Vert.***

O158 O13 34c **red, blue & black** .65 .50
FDC, Washington, DC 1.25
Pair 1.30 —

Nos. O154-O158 have a line of microscopic text below the eagle.

Type of 1985
COIL STAMP

2002, Aug. 2 **Photo.** **Tagged** ***Perf. 10 Vert.***

O159 O13 37c **red, blue & black** .70 .50
First day cover, Washington, DC 1.25
First day cover, any other city 1.25
Pair 1.40 —
P# strip of 5, P#S111 5.25 —
P# single, same # — .70

Type of 1985
COIL STAMP

2006, Mar. 8 **Photo.** **Tagged** ***Perf. 10 Vert.***

O160 O13 39c **red, blue & black** .80 .40
First day cover, Washington, DC 1.25
First day cover, any other city 1.25
Pair 1.60 —
P# strip of 5, #S111 5.75 —
P# single, #S111 — 2.00

Type of 1988

Designed by Bradbury Thompson.

Printed by Sterling Sommer for Ashton-Potter (USA) Ltd.

LITHOGRAPHED

Sheets of 240 in twelve panes of 20

2006, Sept. 29 **Tagged** ***Perf. 11¼***

O161 O13 $1 **red, blue & black** 2.00 .75
First day cover, Washington, DC 3.25
First day cover, any other city 3.25
Pane of 20 40.00

No. O161 has a solid blue background. No. O151 has a background of crosshatched lines.

Type of 1985
COIL STAMP

2007, June 25 **Litho.** **Tagged** ***Perf. 9¾***

O162 O13 41c **red, blue & black** .85 .40
First day cover, Kansas City, MO 2.10
Pair 1.75 —
P# strip of 5, #S111 6.00 —
P# single, #S111 — 2.00

Nos. O159-O162 have solid blue backgrounds. Nos. O138A-O158 have a background of crosshatched lines.

NEWSPAPER AND PERIODICAL STAMPS

First issued in September 1865 for prepayment of postage on bulk shipments of newspapers and periodicals. From 1875 on, the stamps were affixed to pages of receipt books, sometimes canceled, and retained by the post office.

Virtually all used stamps of Nos. PR1-PR4 are canceled by blue brush strokes and have faults such as tears, stains, creases, etc. All are rare. Most used stamps of Nos. PR9-PR32, PR57-PR79 and PR81-PR89 are pen canceled (or uncanceled), with some of Nos. PR9-PR32 also known canceled by a thick blue brush stroke or a handstamp cancellation. Used values for Nos. PR90-PR125 are for stamps with handstamp cancellations.

Discontinued on July 1, 1898.

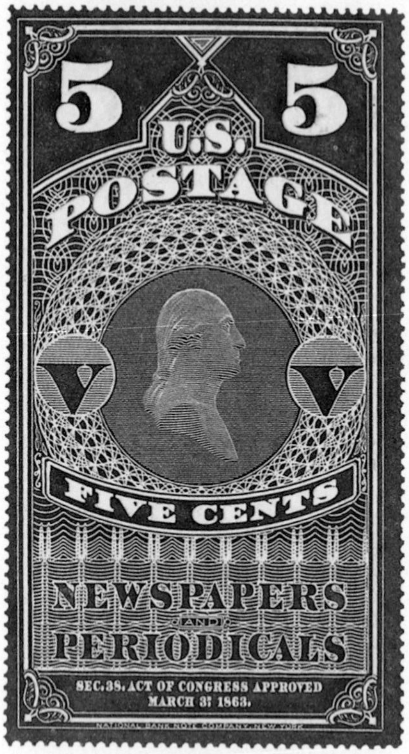

Washington — N1

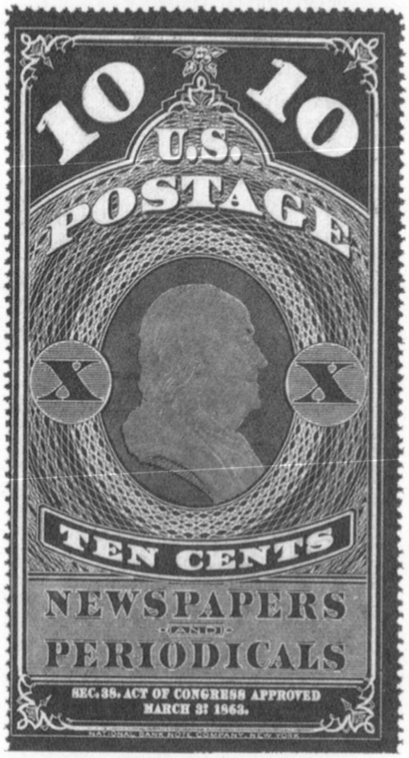

Franklin — N2

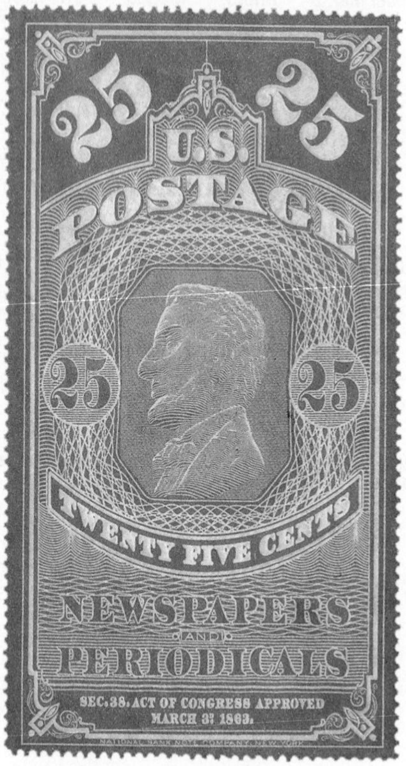

Lincoln — N3

Values for Nos. PR1-PR8 are for examples with perforations on all four sides. Examples with natural straight edges sell for somewhat less. Some panes were fully perforated, while others have natural straight edges either at top or bottom affecting five stamps in the pane of ten.

Printed by the National Bank Note Co.
Plates of 20 subjects in two panes of 10 each.

Typographed and Embossed

1865 Unwmk. *Perf. 12*

Thin hard paper, without gum

Size of design: 51x95mm

Colored Border

PR1	N1	5c	**dark blue**	750.00	*2,000.*
			blue	750.00	*2,000.*
			Block of 4	3,750.	—
a.		5c	**light blue**	1,000.	—
PR2	N2	10c	**blue green**	300.00	*1,800.*
a.		10c	**green**	300.00	*1,800.*
			Block of 4	1,400.	—
b.			Pelure paper	350.00	*1,800.*
PR3	N3	25c	**orange red**	375.00	*2,400.*
			Block of 4	1,600.	—
a.		25c	**carmine red**	350.00	*2,400.*
			Block of 4	1,600.	—
b.			Pelure paper	375.00	

Nos. PR1-PR3 used are valued with faults.

White Border

Yellowish paper

PR4	N1	5c	**light blue**	250.00	*2,400.*
			blue	225.00	—
			Block of 4	1,250.	
a.		5c	**dark blue**	250.00	—
b.			Pelure paper	300.00	—

REPRINTS of 1865 ISSUE

Printed by the Continental Bank Note Co. using the original National Bank Note Co. plates

1875 ***Perf. 12***

Hard white paper, without gum

5c White Border, 10c and 25c Colored Border

PR5	N1	5c	**dull blue** *(10,000)*	200.00	
			dark blue	200.00	
			Block of 4	900.00	
a.			Printed on both sides	*5,750.*	
PR6	N2	10c	**dark bluish green** *(7765)*	225.00	
			deep green	225.00	
			Block of 4	975.00	
a.			Printed on both sides	*4,250.*	
PR7	N3	25c	**dark carmine** *(6684)*	250.00	
			dark carmine red	250.00	
			Block of 4	1,125.	

750 examples of each value, which were remainders from the regular issue, were sold as reprints because of delays in obtaining Nos. PR5-PR7. These remainders cannot be distinguished from Nos. PR2-PR4, and are not included in the reprint quantities.

The Continental Bank Note Co. made another special printing from new plates, which did not have the colored border. These exist imperforate and perforated, but they were not regularly issued.

On No. PR5, there is no thin line of color in the second white area on each side of the stamp. On No. PR8, there is often a thin line of color in this area, but not all examples of No. PR8 show this line (see illustration below). Expertization is based on color and paper.

#PR5

#PR8

Printed by the American Bank Note Co.
Soft porous paper, without gum
White Border

1881

PR8	N1	5c	**dark blue** (5645)	800.00	
			Block of 4	4,000.	

Statue of Freedom on Capitol Dome, by Thomas Crawford — N4

"Justice" — N5

Ceres — N6

"Victory" — N7

Clio — N8

Minerva — N9

Vesta — N10

"Peace" — N11

"Commerce" — N12

Hebe — N13

Indian Maiden — N14

Values for used examples of Nos. PR9-PR113 are for fine-very fine examples for denominations to $3, and fine for denominations of $3 or higher. Some used Scott numbers may not exist without faults.

Printed by the Continental Bank Note Co.
Plates of 100 subjects in two panes of 50 each
Size of design: 24x35mm

1875, Jan. 1 **Engr.** ***Perf. 12***

Thin hard paper

No.	Design	Denom.	Color / Variety	Unused	Used
PR9	N4	2c	**black**	280.00	30.00
			gray black	280.00	30.00
			greenish black	280.00	30.00
			No gum	125.00	
			Handstamp or blue brush cancel		65.00
			Block of 4	1,250.	190.00
PR10	N4	3c	**black**	280.00	32.50
			gray black	280.00	32.50
			No gum	125.00	
			Handstamp or blue brush cancel		65.00
			Block of 4	1,250.	160.00
PR11	N4	4c	**black**	280.00	30.00
			gray black	280.00	30.00
			greenish black	280.00	30.00
			No gum	125.00	
			Handstamp or blue brush cancel		65.00
			Block of 4	1,250.	
PR12	N4	6c	**black**	280.00	32.50
			gray black	280.00	32.50
			greenish black	280.00	32.50
			No gum	125.00	
			Handstamp or blue brush cancel		65.00
			Block of 4	1,250.	
PR13	N4	8c	**black**	325.00	47.50
			gray black	325.00	47.50
			greenish black	325.00	47.50
			No gum	140.00	
			Handstamp or blue brush cancel		100.00
PR14	N4	9c	**black**	475.00	95.00
			gray black	475.00	95.00
			No gum	200.00	
			Handstamp or blue brush cancel		210.00
			Double transfer at top	525.00	110.00
PR15	N4	10c	**black**	350.00	37.50
			gray black	350.00	37.50
			greenish black	350.00	37.50
			No gum	140.00	
			Handstamp or blue brush cancel		75.00
			Block of 4	1,600.	
PR16	N5	12c	**rose**	800.00	100.00
			pale rose	800.00	100.00
			No gum	350.00	
			Handstamp or blue brush cancel		175.00
PR17	N5	24c	**rose**	875.00	125.00
			pale rose	875.00	125.00
			No gum	400.00	
			Handstamp or blue brush cancel		210.00
			Paper with silk fibers	*2,000.*	
PR18	N5	36c	**rose**	875.00	150.00
			pale rose	875.00	150.00
			No gum	400.00	
			Handstamp or blue brush cancel		275.00
PR19	N5	48c	**rose**	1,250.	200.00
			pale rose	1,250.	200.00
			No gum	500.00	
			Handstamp or blue brush cancel		375.00
PR20	N5	60c	**rose**	1,250.	115.00
			pale rose	1,250.	115.00
			No gum	500.00	
			Handstamp or blue brush cancel		225.00
PR21	N5	72c	**rose**	1,250.	250.00
			pale rose	1,250.	250.00
			No gum	500.00	
			Handstamp or blue brush cancel		475.00
PR22	N5	84c	**rose**	1,850.	375.00
			pale rose	1,850.	375.00
			No gum	700.00	
			Handstamp or blue brush cancel		625.00
PR23	N5	96c	**rose**	1,350.	250.00
			pale rose	1,350.	250.00
			No gum	550.00	
			Handstamp or blue brush cancel		575.00
PR24	N6	$1.92	**dark brown**	1,650.	250.00
			No gum	725.00	
			Handstamp or blue brush cancel		400.00
PR25	N7	$3	**vermilion**	1,800.	450.00
			No gum	725.00	
			Handstamp or blue brush cancel		700.00
PR26	N8	$6	**ultramarine**	3,600.	550.00
			dull ultramarine	3,600.	550.00
			No gum	1,500.	
			Handstamp or blue brush cancel		800.00
PR27	N9	$9	**yellow orange**	4,000.	600.00
			No gum	1,700.	
			Handstamp or blue brush cancel		1,000.
PR28	N10	$12	**blue green**	4,500.	750.00
			No gum	1,750.	
			Handstamp or blue brush cancel		1,250.
PR29	N11	$24	**dark gray violet**	4,750.	800.00
			No gum	1,850.	
			Handstamp or blue brush cancel		1,350.
PR30	N12	$36	**brown rose**	5,000.	950.00
			No gum	2,000.	
			Handstamp or blue brush cancel		1,600.
PR31	N13	$48	**red brown**	6,250.	1,150.
			No gum	2,300.	
			Handstamp or blue brush cancel		1,900.
PR32	N14	$60	**violet**	6,500.	1,250.
			No gum	2,400.	
			Handstamp or blue brush cancel		2,500.

SPECIAL PRINTING of 1875 ISSUE

Printed by the Continental Bank Note Co.
Hard white paper, without gum

1875 ***Perf. 12***

No.	Design	Denom.	Color / Variety	Unused	Used
PR33	N4	2c	**gray black** *(5,000)*	600.00	
			Block of 4	3,000.	
a.			Horizontally ribbed paper (10,000)	450.00	
PR34	N4	3c	**gray black** *(5,000)*	600.00	
			Block of 4	3,000.	
a.			Horizontally ribbed paper (1,952)	450.00	
PR35	N4	4c	**gray black** *(4451)*	650.00	
			Block of 4	3,250.	
a.			Horizontally ribbed paper	900.00	
PR36	N4	6c	**gray black** *(2348)*	850.00	
PR37	N4	8c	**gray black** *(1930)*	950.00	
PR38	N4	9c	**gray black** *(1795)*	1,050.	
PR39	N4	10c	**gray black** *(1499)*	1,300.	
PR40	N5	12c	**pale rose** *(1313)*	1,500.	
PR41	N5	24c	**pale rose** *(411)*	2,100.	
PR42	N5	36c	**pale rose** *(330)*	2,800.	
PR43	N5	48c	**pale rose** *(268)*	4,000.	
PR44	N5	60c	**pale rose** *(222)*	4,000.	
PR45	N5	72c	**pale rose** *(174)*	4,500.	
PR46	N5	84c	**pale rose** *(164)*	5,000.	
PR47	N5	96c	**pale rose** *(141)*	*8,500.*	
PR48	N6	$1.92	**dark brown** *(41)*	*22,500.*	
PR49	N7	$3	**vermilion** *(20)*	*45,000.*	
PR50	N8	$6	**ultramarine** *(14)*	*80,000.*	
PR51	N9	$9	**yellow orange** *(4)*	*160,000.*	
PR52	N10	$12	**blue green** *(5)*	*125,000.*	
PR53	N11	$24	**dark gray violet** *(2)*	—	
PR54	N12	$36	**brown rose** *(2)*	*250,000.*	
PR55	N13	$48	**red brown** *(1)*	—	
PR56	N14	$60	**violet** *(1)*	—	

Although four examples of No. PR51 were sold, only one is currently documented.

No. PR54 is valued in the grade of fine. Although two stamps were sold, only one is currently documented.

All values of this issue, Nos. PR33 to PR56, exist imperforate but were not regularly issued thus. Value, set $60,000.

Numbers in parentheses are quantities sold.

Printed by the American Bank Note Co.
Soft porous paper

1879 **Unwmk.** ***Perf. 12***

No.	Design	Denom.	Color / Variety	Unused	Used
PR57	N4	2c	**black**	50.00	8.50
			gray black	50.00	8.50
			greenish black	50.00	8.50
			No gum	20.00	
			Handstamp cancel		25.00
			Block of 4	225.00	
			Double transfer at top	55.00	14.00
			Cracked plate	—	—
PR58	N4	3c	**black**	60.00	10.50
			gray black	60.00	10.50
			intense black	60.00	10.50
			No gum	25.00	
			Handstamp cancel		35.00
			Block of 4	250.00	
			Double transfer at top	65.00	15.00
PR59	N4	4c	**black**	60.00	10.50
			gray black	60.00	10.50
			intense black	60.00	10.50
			greenish black	60.00	10.50
			No gum	25.00	
			Handstamp cancel		35.00
			Block of 4	250.00	
			Double transfer at top	65.00	15.00
PR60	N4	6c	**black**	105.00	21.00
			gray black	105.00	21.00
			intense black	105.00	21.00
			greenish black	105.00	21.00
			No gum	45.00	
			Handstamp cancel		75.00
			Block of 4	500.00	
			Double transfer at top	115.00	26.00
PR61	N4	8c	**black**	115.00	21.00
			gray black	115.00	21.00
			greenish black	115.00	21.00
			No gum	47.50	
			Handstamp cancel		75.00
			Block of 4	525.00	
			Double transfer at top	125.00	26.00
PR62	N4	10c	**black**	115.00	21.00
			gray black	115.00	21.00
			greenish black	115.00	21.00
			No gum	47.50	
			Handstamp cancel		75.00
			Block of 4	525.00	
			Double transfer at top	125.00	
PR63	N5	12c	**red**	475.00	85.00
			No gum	200.00	
			Handstamp cancel		225.00
			Block of 4	2,150.	
PR64	N5	24c	**red**	475.00	85.00
			No gum	200.00	
			Handstamp cancel		225.00
			Block of 4	2,150.	
PR65	N5	36c	**red**	1,000.	240.00
			No gum	475.00	
			Handstamp cancel		500.00
			Block of 4	4,500.	
PR66	N5	48c	**red**	1,000.	180.00
			No gum	450.00	
			Handstamp cancel		450.00
PR67	N5	60c	**red**	1,000.	160.00
			No gum	450.00	
			Handstamp cancel		400.00
			Block of 4	4,500.	
a.			Imperf., pair	*4,000.*	
PR68	N5	72c	**red**	1,250.	300.00
			No gum	575.00	
			Handstamp cancel		700.00
PR69	N5	84c	**red**	1,250.	225.00
			No gum	575.00	
			Handstamp cancel		575.00
			Block of 4	—	
PR70	N5	96c	**red**	1,200.	160.00
			No gum	525.00	
			Handstamp cancel		400.00
			Block of 4	5,500.	
PR71	N6	$1.92	**pale brown**	550.00	135.00
			brown	550.00	135.00
			No gum	225.00	
			Handstamp cancel		300.00
			Block of 4	2,500.	
			Cracked plate	600.00	
PR72	N7	$3	**red vermilion**	625.00	150.00
			No gum	250.00	
			Handstamp cancel		350.00
			Block of 4	2,850.	
PR73	N8	$6	**blue**	1,050.	230.00
			ultramarine	1,100.	230.00
			No gum	400.00	
			Handstamp cancel		500.00
PR74	N9	$9	**orange**	800.00	160.00
			No gum	325.00	

			Handstamp cancel		375.00
PR75	N10	$12	**yellow green**	850.00	210.00
			No gum	325.00	
			Handstamp cancel		500.00
PR76	N11	$24	**dark violet**	800.00	260.00
			No gum	300.00	
			Handstamp cancel		600.00
PR77	N12	$36	**Indian red**	850.00	280.00
			No gum	350.00	
			Handstamp cancel		650.00
PR78	N13	$48	**yellow brown**	900.00	390.00
			No gum	350.00	
			Handstamp cancel		775.00
PR79	N14	$60	**purple**	850.00	360.00
			bright purple	850.00	360.00
			No gum	350.00	
			Handstamp cancel		750.00

See Die and Plate Proofs for other imperfs. on stamp paper.

SPECIAL PRINTING of 1879 ISSUE

Printed by the American Bank Note Co.

Without gum

1883

PR80	N4	2c	**intense black** (4,514)	1,350.	
			Block of 4	6,250.	

REGULAR ISSUE

Printed by the American Bank Note Co.

With gum

1885, July 1 **Unwmk.** ***Perf. 12***

PR81	N4	1c	**black**	85.00	8.50
			gray black	70.00	8.50
			intense black	70.00	8.50
			No gum	35.00	
			Handstamp cancel		30.00
			Block of 4	375.00	
			Double transfer at top	90.00	11.00
PR82	N5	12c	**carmine**	180.00	20.00
			deep carmine	180.00	20.00
			rose carmine	180.00	20.00
			No gum	75.00	
			Handstamp cancel		75.00
			Block of 4	875.00	
			Plate crack (pos. 41)	*240.00*	
PR83	N5	24c	**carmine**	180.00	22.50
			deep carmine	180.00	22.50
			rose carmine	180.00	22.50
			No gum	75.00	
			Handstamp cancel		100.00
			Block of 4	875.00	
PR84	N5	36c	**carmine**	280.00	37.50
			deep carmine	280.00	37.50
			rose carmine	280.00	37.50
			No gum	115.00	
			Handstamp cancel		125.00
			Block of 4	1,300.	
PR85	N5	48c	**carmine**	400.00	55.00
			deep carmine	400.00	55.00
			No gum	175.00	
			Handstamp cancel		200.00
			Block of 4	1,750.	
PR86	N5	60c	**carmine**	525.00	80.00
			deep carmine	525.00	80.00
			No gum	230.00	
			Handstamp cancel		280.00
			Block of 4	2,400.	
PR87	N5	72c	**carmine**	525.00	85.00
			deep carmine	525.00	85.00
			rose carmine	525.00	85.00
			No gum	230.00	
			Handstamp cancel		310.00
			Block of 4	2,400.	
PR88	N5	84c	**carmine**	800.00	200.00
			rose carmine	800.00	200.00
			No gum	300.00	
			Handstamp cancel		475.00
			Block of 4	3,650.	
PR89	N5	96c	**carmine**	700.00	160.00
			rose carmine	700.00	160.00
			No gum	275.00	
			Handstamp cancel		425.00
			Block of 4	3,150.	

See Die and Plate Proofs for imperfs. on stamp paper.

Printed by the Bureau of Engraving and Printing

1894 **Unwmk.** ***Perf. 12***

Soft wove paper, with pale, whitish gum

PR90	N4	1c	**intense black**	425.00	*750.00*
			Never hinged	1,000.	
			No gum	175.00	
			Block of 4	1,850.	
			Double transfer at top	450.00	
PR91	N4	2c	**intense black**	475.00	
			Never hinged	1,100.	
			No gum	200.00	
			Block of 4	2,150.	
			Double transfer at top	500.00	
PR92	N4	4c	**intense black**	500.00	—
			Never hinged	1,350.	
			No gum	225.00	
			Block of 4	2,400.	
PR93	N4	6c	**intense black**	3,750.	
			No gum	1,750.	
			Block of 4	—	
PR94	N4	10c	**intense black**	1,150.	
			No gum	500.00	
			Block of 4	5,000.	
PR95	N5	12c	**pink**	2,600.	*1,500.*
			No gum	1,100.	
			Block of 4	12,000.	
PR96	N5	24c	**pink**	3,750.	*1,750.*
			No gum	1,850.	
			Block of 4	17,500.	
PR97	N5	36c	**pink**	*50,000.*	
			Block of 4	—	
PR98	N5	60c	**pink**	*55,000.*	*7,500.*
			Block of 4	—	
PR99	N5	96c	**pink**	*52,500.*	
PR100	N7	$3	**scarlet**	*60,000.*	
			Block of 4	—	
PR101	N8	$6	**pale blue**	*60,000.*	—
			No gum	*30,000.*	

Nos. PR90, PR95-PR98 used are valued with fine centering and small faults.

No. PR97 unused is valued in the grade of very good to fine. No. PR98 unused is valued in the grade of fine. Nos. PR99-PR100 unused are valued in the grade of fine-very fine.

Statue of Freedom — N15

N16

N17

N18

N19

N20

N21

N22

1895, Feb. 1 **Unwmk.** ***Perf. 12***

Size of designs: 1c-50c, 21x34mm

$2-$100, 24x35mm

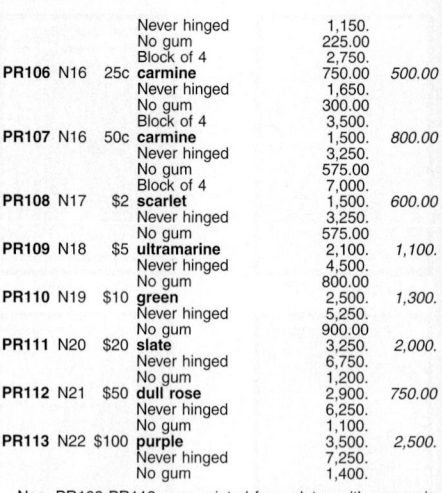

PR102	N15	1c	**black**	230.00	*100.00*
			Never hinged	500.00	
			No gum	90.00	
			Block of 4	1,050.	*500.00*
PR103	N15	2c	**black**	230.00	*100.00*
			gray black	230.00	*100.00*
			Never hinged	500.00	
			No gum	90.00	
			Block of 4	1,050.	—
			Double transfer at top	250.00	—
PR104	N15	5c	**black**	300.00	*150.00*
			gray black	300.00	*150.00*
			Never hinged	650.00	
			No gum	125.00	
			Block of 4	1,350.	
PR105	N15	10c	**black**	550.00	*350.00*
			Never hinged	1,150.	
			No gum	225.00	
			Block of 4	2,750.	
PR106	N16	25c	**carmine**	750.00	*500.00*
			Never hinged	1,650.	
			No gum	300.00	
			Block of 4	3,500.	
PR107	N16	50c	**carmine**	1,500.	*800.00*
			Never hinged	3,250.	
			No gum	575.00	
			Block of 4	7,000.	
PR108	N17	$2	**scarlet**	1,500.	*600.00*
			Never hinged	3,250.	
			No gum	575.00	
PR109	N18	$5	**ultramarine**	2,100.	*1,100.*
			Never hinged	4,500.	
			No gum	800.00	
PR110	N19	$10	**green**	2,500.	*1,300.*
			Never hinged	5,250.	
			No gum	900.00	
PR111	N20	$20	**slate**	3,250.	*2,000.*
			Never hinged	6,750.	
			No gum	1,200.	
PR112	N21	$50	**dull rose**	2,900.	*750.00*
			Never hinged	6,250.	
			No gum	1,100.	
PR113	N22	$100	**purple**	3,500.	*2,500.*
			Never hinged	7,250.	
			No gum	1,400.	

Nos. PR102-PR113 were printed from plates with arrows in the top, bottom and side margins, but no guidelines between the stamps.

1895-97 **Wmk. 191** ***Perf. 12***

PR114	N15	1c	**black,** *Jan. 11, 1896*	8.00	*25.00*
			gray black	8.00	*25.00*
			Never hinged	20.00	
			No gum	2.75	
			Block of 4	35.00	—
PR115	N15	2c	**black,** *Nov. 21, 1895*	8.00	*25.00*
			gray black	15.00	*25.00*
			Never hinged	20.00	
			No gum	2.75	
			Block of 4	35.00	—
PR116	N15	5c	**black,** *Feb. 12, 1896*	13.00	*40.00*
			gray black	13.00	*40.00*
			Never hinged	27.50	
			No gum	4.25	
			Block of 4	57.50	—
PR117	N15	10c	**black,** *Sept. 13, 1895*	13.00	*25.00*
			gray black	13.00	*25.00*
			Never hinged	27.50	
			No gum	4.25	
			Block of 4	57.50	—
PR118	N16	25c	**carmine,** *Oct. 11, 1895*	20.00	*65.00*
			lilac rose	20.00	*65.00*
			Never hinged	45.00	
			No gum	7.00	
			Block of 4	87.50	—
PR119	N16	50c	**carmine,** *Sept. 19, 1895*	25.00	*75.00*
			rose carmine	25.00	*75.00*
			lilac rose	25.00	*75.00*
			Never hinged	55.00	
			No gum	8.50	
			Block of 4	110.00	—
PR120	N17	$2	**scarlet,** *Jan. 23, 1897*	30.00	*110.00*
			scarlet vermilion	30.00	*110.00*
			Never hinged	75.00	
			No gum	10.00	
			Block of 4	130.00	—
PR121	N18	$5	**dark blue,** *Jan. 16, 1896*	40.00	*160.00*
			Never hinged	100.00	
			No gum	13.50	
			Block of 4	200.00	
a.			$5 light blue	200.00	*500.00*
			Never hinged	500.00	
			No gum	67.50	
			Block of 4	*875.00*	*2,500.*
PR122	N19	$10	**green,** *Mar. 5, 1896*	42.50	*160.00*
			Never hinged	105.00	
			No gum	14.00	
			Block of 4	200.00	—
PR123	N20	$20	**slate,** *Jan. 27, 1896*	45.00	*180.00*
			Never hinged	110.00	
			No gum	15.00	
			Block of 4	210.00	—
PR124	N21	$50	**dull rose,** *July 31, 1897*	75.00	*225.00*
			Never hinged	170.00	
			No gum	27.50	
			Block of 4	350.00	
PR125	N22	$100	**purple,** *Jan. 23, 1896*	65.00	*240.00*
			Never hinged	150.00	
			No gum	22.50	
			Block of 4	300.00	
			Nos. PR114-PR125 (12)	384.50	1,330.
			Nos. PR114-PR125, never hinged	905.00	

Nos. PR114-PR125 were printed from the original plates with guide lines added in November 1895. Top and bottom plate strips and blocks of Nos. PR114-PR119 exist both with and without vertical guidelines.

In 1899 the Government sold 26,989 sets of these stamps, but, as the stock of high values was not sufficient to make up the required number, an additional printing was made of the $5, $10, $20, $50 and $100. These are virtually indistinguishable from earlier printings.

POSTAL NOTE STAMPS

Postal note stamps were issued to supplement the regular money order service. They were a means of sending amounts under $1. One or two Postal note stamps, totaling 1c to 99c, were affixed to United States Postal Notes and canceled by the clerk. The stamps were on the second of three parts, the one retained by the post office redeeming the Postal Note. They were discontinued March 31, 1951.

Catalogue Values for Unused Postal Note stamps are for Never Hinged items.

MO1

ROTARY PRESS PRINTING

1945, Feb. 1 **Unwmk.** *Perf. 11x10½*

PN1	MO1	1c **black** (155950-155951)	.35	.25
PN2	MO1	2c **black** (156003-156004)	.35	.25
PN3	MO1	3c **black** (156062-156063)	.35	.25
PN4	MO1	4c **black** (156942-156943)	.35	.25
PN5	MO1	5c **black** (156261-156262)	.40	.25
PN6	MO1	6c **black** (156064-156065)	.45	.25
PN7	MO1	7c **black** (156075-156076)	.60	.25
PN8	MO1	8c **black** (156077-156078)	.85	.25
PN9	MO1	9c **black** (156251-156252)	1.00	.25
PN10	MO1	10c **black** (156274-156275)	1.20	.25
PN11	MO1	20c **black** (156276-156277)	1.80	.25
PN12	MO1	30c **black** (156303-156304)	2.50	.25
PN13	MO1	40c **black** (156283-156284)	3.50	.25
PN14	MO1	50c **black** (156322-156323)	3.75	.25
PN15	MO1	60c **black** (156324-156325)	4.50	.25
PN16	MO1	70c **black** (156344-156345)	7.00	.25
PN17	MO1	80c **black** (156326-156327)	8.25	.25
PN18	MO1	90c **black** (156352-156353)	10.00	.25
		Nos. PN1-PN18 (18)	47.20	4.50

Blocks of four and plate number blocks of four are valued at 4 and 15 times the unused single value.

Postal note stamps exist on postal note cards with first day cancellation.

Numbers in parentheses are plate Nos.

PARCEL POST STAMPS

The Act of Congress approved Aug. 24, 1912, created postage rates on 4th class mail weighing 4 ounces or less at 1 cent per ounce or fraction. On mail over 4 ounces, the rate was by the pound. These rates were to be prepaid by distinctive postage stamps. Under this provision, the Post Office Department prepared 12 parcel post and 5 parcel post postage due stamps, usable only on parcel post packages starting Jan. 1, 1913. Other stamps were not usable on parcel post starting on that date.

Beginning on Nov. 27, 1912, the stamps were shipped to post offices offering parcel post service. Approximate shipping dates were: 1c, 2c, 5c, 25c, 1c due, 5c due, Nov. 27; 10c, 2c due, Dec. 9; 4c, 10c due, Dec. 12; 15c, 20c, 25c due, Dec. 16; 75c, Dec. 18. There was no prohibition on sale of the stamps prior to Jan. 1, 1913. Undoubtedly many were used on 4th class mail in Dec. 1912. Fourth class mail was expanded by adding former 2nd and 3rd class categories and was renamed "parcel post" effective Jan. 1, 1913. Normally 4th class (parcel post) mail did not receive a dated cancel unless a special service was involved. Small pieces, such as samples, are known with 1st class cancels.

With the approval of the Interstate Commerce Commission, the Postmaster General directed, in Order No. 7241 dated June 26, 1913, and effective July 1, 1913, that regular postage stamps should be valid on parcels. Parcel post stamps then became usable as regular stamps.

Parcel post and parcel post postage due stamps remained on sale, but no further printings were made. Remainders, consisting of 3,510,345 of the 75c, were destroyed in Sept. 1921.

The 20c was the first government-issued postage stamp of any country to show an airplane.

Post Office Clerk — PP1

City Carrier — PP2

Railway Postal Clerk — PP3

Rural Carrier — PP4

Mail Train and Mail Bag on Rack — PP5

Steamship "Kronprinz Wilhelm" and Mail Tender, New York — PP6

Automobile Service — PP7

Airplane Carrying Mail — PP8

Manufacturing (Steel Plant, South Chicago) — PP9

Dairying — PP10

Harvesting PP11

Fruit Growing (Florida Orange Grove) — PP12

6161 TEN

Plate number and imprint consisting of value in words.

Marginal imprints, consisting of value in words, were added to the plates on January 27, 1913.

Designed by Clair Aubrey Huston.

Plates of 180 subjects in four panes of 45 each.

1913 Wmk. 190 Engr. *Perf. 12*

Q1	PP1	1c	**carmine rose** *(209,691,094)*	5.75	1.75
			carmine	5.75	1.75
			Never hinged	14.00	
			First day cover, *July 1, 1913*		*1,500.*
			On cover, 1913-25		6.00
			Block of 4	25.00	9.00
			P# block of 4, Impt.	45.00	
			P# block of 6, Impt.	105.00	
			P# block of 6	110.00	
			Never hinged	180.00	
			Double transfer	9.50	4.00
Q2	PP2	2c	**carmine rose** *(206,417,253)*	6.75	1.40
			carmine	6.75	1.40
			Never hinged	19.00	
			First day cover, *July 1, 1913*		*1,750.*
			On cover, 1913-25		5.75
			Block of 4	30.00	6.50
			P# block of 4, Impt.	47.50	
			P# block of 6, Impt.	125.00	
			P# block of 6	145.00	
			Never hinged	240.00	
			Double transfer	—	—
a.			2c **lake**	*1,750.*	
b.			2c **carmine lake**	*350.00*	

No. Q2a is valued in the grade of fine to very fine.

Q3	PP3	3c	**carmine,** *Apr. 5, 1913 (29,027,433)*	13.50	6.50
			deep carmine	13.50	6.50
			Never hinged	37.50	
			First day cover, *July 1, 1913*		*3,500.*
			On cover, 1913-25		19.00
			Block of 4	57.50	37.50
			P# block of 4, Impt.	100.00	
			P# block of 6, Impt.	260.00	
			P# block of 6	235.00	
			P# block of 8, Impt. (side)	310.00	
			Never hinged	550.00	
			Retouched at lower right corner (No. 6257 LL 7)	26.00	14.50
			Double transfer (No. 6257 LL 6)	26.00	14.50
Q4	PP4	4c	**carmine rose** *(76,743,813)*	37.50	3.50
			carmine	37.50	3.50
			Never hinged	110.00	
			First day cover, *July 1, 1913*		*3,500.*
			On cover, 1913-25		65.00
			Block of 4	160.00	17.50
			P# block of 4, Impt.	360.00	
			P# block of 6, Impt.	1,050.	
			P# block of 6	1,000.	
			Never hinged	1,700.	
			Double transfer	—	—
Q5	PP5	5c	**carmine rose** *(108,153,993)*	32.50	2.50
			carmine	32.50	2.50
			Never hinged	90.00	
			First day cover, *July 1, 1913*		*3,500.*
			On cover, 1913-25		42.50
			Block of 4	135.00	15.00
			P# block of 4, Impt.	350.00	
			P# block of 6, Impt.	1,000.	
			P# block of 6	975.00	
			Never hinged	1,600.	
			Double transfer	45.00	6.25
Q6	PP6	10c	**carmine rose** *(56,896,653)*	52.50	3.50
			carmine	52.50	3.50
			Never hinged	120.00	
			First day cover, *July 1, 1913*		*12,500.*
			On cover, 1913-25		55.00
			Block of 4	240.00	30.00
			P# block of 4, Impt.	440.00	
			P# block of 6, Impt.	1,150.	
			P# block of 6	1,000.	
			Never hinged	1,650.	
			Double transfer	—	—
Q7	PP7	15c	**carmine rose** *(21,147,033)*	67.50	15.00
			carmine	67.50	15.00
			Never hinged	180.00	
			First day cover, *July 1, 1913*		—
			On cover, 1913-25		350.00
			Block of 4	310.00	100.00
			P# block of 4, Impt.	700.00	
			P# block of 6, Impt.	2,600.	
			P# block of 8, Impt.	3,100.	
			P# block of 6	2,300.	
			Never hinged	*3,700.*	
Q8	PP8	20c	**carmine rose** *(17,142,393)*	150.00	30.00
			carmine	150.00	30.00
			Never hinged	325.00	
			On cover, 1913-25		750.00
			Block of 4	650.00	150.00
			P# block of 4, Impt.	1,500.	
			P# block of 6, Impt.	6,500.	
			P# block of 8, Impt. (side)	7,000.	
			P# block of 6	6,500.	
			Never hinged	*10,000.*	
Q9	PP9	25c	**carmine rose** *(21,940,653)*	67.50	8.50
			carmine	67.50	8.50
			Never hinged	180.00	
			On cover, 1913-25		300.00
			Block of 4	310.00	60.00
			P# block of 6, Impt.	2,700.	
			P# block of 8, Impt. (side)	3,500.	
			P# block of 6	2,400.	
			Never hinged	*3,850.*	
Q10	PP10	50c	**carmine rose,** *Mar. 15, 1913 (2,117,793)*	300.00	50.00
			carmine	300.00	50.00
			Never hinged	700.00	
			On cover, 1913-25		—
			Block of 4	1,350.	325.00
			P# block of 4, Impt.	2,000.	
			Never hinged	3,000.	
			P# block of 6, Impt.	*22,500.*	
			Never hinged	*30,000.*	
Q11	PP11	75c	**carmine rose** *(2,772,615)*	110.00	40.00
			carmine	110.00	40.00
			Never hinged	240.00	
			On cover, 1913-25		—
			Block of 4	500.00	225.00
			P# block of 6, Impt.	4,000.	
			P# block of 8, Impt. (side)	3,600.	
			P# block of 6	3,000.	
			Never hinged	*4,500.*	
Q12	PP12	$1	**carmine rose,** *Jan. 3, 1913 (1,053,273)*	375.00	45.00
			carmine	375.00	45.00
			Never hinged	850.00	
			On cover, 1913-25		1,250.
			Block of 4	1,650.	225.00
			P# block of 6, Impt.	*20,000.*	
			Never hinged	*29,000.*	
			P# block of 8, Impt. (side)	*21,000.*	
			P# block of 6	*18,000.*	
			Never hinged	*27,500.*	
			Nos. Q1-Q12 (12)	1,218.	207.65
			Nos. Q1-Q12, never hinged	2,865.	

The 1c, 2c, 4c and 5c are known in parcel post usage postmarked Jan. 1, 1913.

PARCEL POST POSTAGE DUE STAMPS

See notes preceding Scott No. Q1. Parcel Post Postage Due stamps were allowed to be used as regular postage due stamps from July 1, 1913.

PPD1

Designed by Clair Aubrey Huston

Plates of 180 subjects in four panes of 45

1913 Wmk. 190 Engr. *Perf. 12*

JQ1	PPD1	1c	**dark green** (7,322,400)	10.50	4.50
			yellowish green	10.50	4.50
			Never hinged	27.50	
			On cover, 1913-25		150.00
			Block of 4	47.50	35.00
			P# block of 6	550.00	
			Never hinged	900.00	

Earliest documented use: Feb. 26, 1913.

JQ2	PPD1	2c	**dark green** (3,132,000)	85.00	17.50
			yellowish green	85.00	17.50
			Never hinged	210.00	
			On cover, 1913-25		200.00
			Block of 4	375.00	125.00
			P# block of 6	*3,750.*	
			Never hinged	*6,000.*	

Earliest documented use: July 7, 1913.

JQ3	PPD1	5c	**dark green** (5,840,100)	14.00	5.50
			yellowish green	14.00	5.50
			Never hinged	35.00	
			On cover, 1913-25		185.00
			Block of 4	60.00	37.50
			P# block of 6	600.00	
			Never hinged	975.00	

Earliest documented use: Jan. 15, 1913 (dated cancel on off-cover stamp).

JQ4	PPD1	10c	**dark green** (2,124,540)	175.00	45.00
			yellowish green	175.00	45.00
			Never hinged	425.00	
			On cover, 1913-25		650.00
			Block of 4	775.00	375.00
			P# block of 6	*9,750.*	
			Never hinged	*14,000.*	

Earliest documented use: July 19, 1913.

JQ5	PPD1	25c	**dark green** (2,117,700)	100.00	5.00
			yellowish green	100.00	5.00
			Never hinged	260.00	
			On cover, 1913-25		—
			Block of 4	450.00	35.00
			P# block of 6	*5,000.*	
			Never hinged	*8,000.*	

Earliest documented use: Aug. 30, 1913.

Nos. JQ1-JQ5 (5)	384.50	77.50
Nos. JQ1-JQ5, never hinged	956.00	

SPECIAL HANDLING STAMPS

The Postal Service Act, approved February 28, 1925, provided for a special handling stamp of the 25-cent denomination for use on fourth-class mail matter, which would secure for such mail matter the expeditious handling accorded to mail matter of the first class.

PP13

FLAT PLATE PRINTING
Plates of 200 subjects in four panes of 50

1925-55 **Unwmk.** ***Perf. 11***

QE1 PP13 10c **yellow green,** wet printing, *June 25, 1928*		2.50	1.00
	Never hinged	4.25	
	Block of 4	10.50	—
	P# block of 6	25.00	
	Never hinged	40.00	
	First day cover		45.00
a.	Dry printing, *1955*	3.75	—
	Never hinged	6.50	
	Block of 4	16.00	
	P# block of 6	40.00	
	Never hinged	65.00	
QE2 PP13 15c **yellow green,** wet printing, *June 25, 1928*		3.00	.90
	Never hinged	5.00	
	Block of 4	12.50	—
	P# block of 6	30.00	
	Never hinged	47.50	
	First day cover		45.00
a.	Dry printing, *1955*	5.00	—
	Never hinged	8.00	
	Block of 4	21.00	
	P# block of 6	50.00	
	Never hinged	75.00	
QE3 PP13 20c **yellow green,** wet printing, *June 25, 1928*		4.50	1.50
	Never hinged	7.75	
	Block of 4	19.00	—
	P# block of 6	37.50	
	Never hinged	60.00	
	First day cover		45.00
	First day cover, Nos. QE1-QE3		350.00
a.	Dry printing, *1955*	7.50	—
	Never hinged	12.50	
	Block of 4	32.50	
	P# block of 6	57.50	
	Never hinged	85.00	

"AT" joined at top

"TA" joined at top

QE4 PP13 25c **deep green,** *April 11, 1925*		25.00	3.75
	Never hinged	45.00	
	Block of 4	125.00	24.00
	P# block of 6	350.00	
	Never hinged	525.00	
	"A" and second "T" of "States" joined at top (Pl. 17103)	70.00	30.00
	Never hinged	120.00	
	"A" and second "T" of "States" and "T" and "A" of "Postage" joined at top (Pl. 17103)	110.00	100.00
	Never hinged	190.00	
	First day cover		225.00
a.	25c **yellow green,** *1928*	20.00	15.00
	Never hinged	37.50	
	Block of 4	100.00	75.00
	P# block of 6	250.00	
	Never hinged	360.00	
	Nos. QE1-QE4 (4)	35.00	7.15
	Nos. QE1-QE4, never hinged	62.00	

See note on Wet and Dry Printings following No. 1029.

POSTAL INSURANCE STAMPS

Postal insurance stamps were issued to pay insurance on parcels for loss or damage. The stamps come in a booklet of one which also carries instructions for use and a receipt form for use if there is a claim. The booklets were sold by vending machine. Values in unused column are for complete booklets. Values in used column are for used stamps.

PPI1

1965, Aug. **Typo.** ***Rouletted 9 at Top***

QI1 PPI1 (10c) **dark red** 135.00 —

No. QI1 paid insurance up to $10. It was sold at the Canoga Park, Calif., automatic post office which opened Aug. 19, 1965. The "V" stands for "Vended."

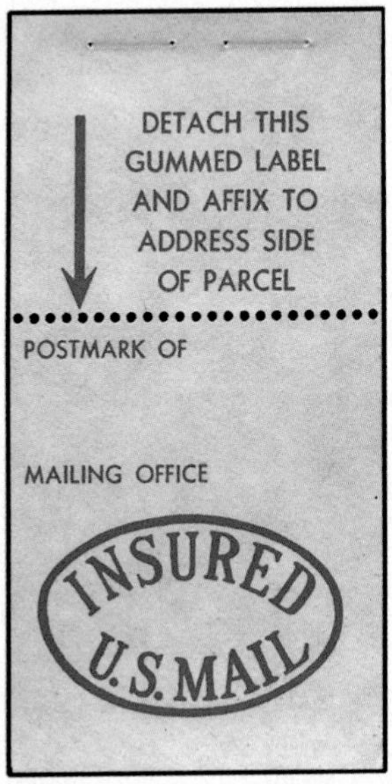

PPI2

1966, Mar. 26 **Litho.** ***Perf. 11 at Top***

QI2 PPI2 (20c) **red** 4.00 —

No. QI2 paid insurance up to $15. The rate increased from 20c to 25c on Apr. 18, 1976, and to 40c on July 18, 1976.

The QI2 booklet comes with two types of front covers, the first beginning "Vended..." and the second "Domestic Vended...." There also are two types of back covers, the first with some white on black lettering, the second with all black on white lettering.

No 25c postal insurance stamps were printed. Existing examples of No. QI2 had 5c postage stamps added and the value on the cover was changed to 25c, usually by hand, but sometimes by handstamp or label. Twenty-cent stamps were added to make the 40c rate since new postal insurance stamps were not issued until 1977. Some 25c provisional booklets were further revalued to 40c by the addition of a 15c stamp. Each provisional booklet comes with both cover types.

Type PPI2 with "FEE PAID THROUGH VENDING MACHINE" Added Below

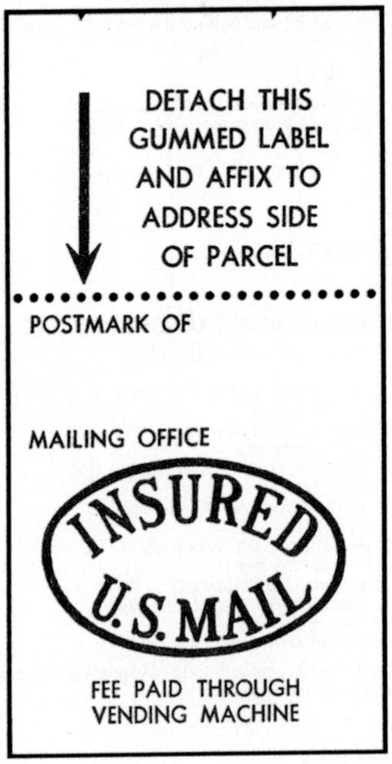

1977-81 **Litho.** ***Perf. 11 at Top***

QI3 PPI2 (40c) **black** 10.00 —

Available for use by Nov. 28, 1977 or earlier.

QI3 is often found misperfed with vertical perforations running through "Postmark of" and "Mailing Office." This variety is common and does not merit a premium.

QI4	PPI2 (50c) **green**	9.00 —

The rate increased to 50c on May 29, 1978. Examples of QI2 and QI3 exist revalued to 50c by the addition of stamps.

QI5	PPI2 (45c) **red,** *1981*	10.00 —

No. QI3 booklets exist revalued to 45c by the addition of a 5c stamp, and the QI4 booklet is known revalued to 45c on its cover.

FIRST DAY COVERS

All envelopes or cards are postmarked Washington, D.C., unless otherwise stated. Minors and sublistings without dates have the same date and city (if none is otherwise mentioned) as the previous listing. Minors and sublistings with dates differing from the previous listing are postmarked in Washington, D.C. unless otherwise stated.

Values are for first day covers in very fine condition, without tears, stains or smeared postmarks, and with sound stamps that have fresh color and are not badly off center.

Printed cachets on covers before Scott Nos. 772 and C20 sell at a substantial premium. Values for covers of Nos. 772-986 and C20-C45 are for those with the most common cachets and addressed. Unaddressed covers sell at a substantial premium and covers without cachet sell at a substantial discount. Values for covers from Scott 987 and C46 onward are for those with the most common cachets and unaddressed.

Values for 1st class rate stamps are for covers bearing single stamps. Blocks of 4 on first day covers usually sell for about 1½ times as much as singles; Plate number blocks of 4 at about 3 times; Plate number blocks of 6 at about 4 times; coil line pairs at about 3 times. Stamps with denominations less than the first class rate will have the proper multiple to make the rate if practical or additional postage. (See Nos. 899, 907-908, 930-931, etc.)

Dates given are those on which the stamps were first *officially* placed on sale. Many instances are known of stamps being sold in advance, contrary to regulations.

Numbers in parentheses are quantities stated to have received the first day cancel.

Listings from Scott Nos. 551 and C4 are for covers canceled at cities officially designated by the Post Office Department or Postal Service. Some tagged varieties and cities of special interest are exceptions.

Air post first day covers are listed following the Postage first day covers. Envelope, postal card and other first day covers are with the regular listings. Quantities given for se-tenant issues include the multiple and any single or combination of singles (see No. 2375a).

1851-57

5A	1c **blue, type Ib,** *July 1, 1851,* Boston, Mass.	*120,000.*
7	1c **blue, type II,** *July 1, 1851,* any city	*25,000.*
	Same on printed circular	*4,000.*
10	3c **orange brown,** *July 1, 1851,* any city	*12,500.*

The No. 5A cover is unique. Value is based on 1996 auction sale. The No. 7 cover also is unique.

1861

64	3c **pink,** *Aug. 17, 1861,* Baltimore, Md.	*22,000.*
64b	3c **rose pink,** *Aug. 17, 1861,* Baltimore, Md.	*23,000.*

The Nos. 64 and 64b covers are each unique.

1883

210	2c **red brown,** *Oct. 1,* any city	*2,000.*
210, 211	2c, 4c **blue green,** *Oct. 1,* New York, N.Y.	*50,000.*

The Nos. 210, 211 cover is unique.

1890

219D	2c **lake,** *Feb. 22,* any city	*35,000.*

1893

COLUMBIAN EXPOSITION ISSUE

230	1c **deep blue,** *Jan. 1,* any city	*20,000.*
	Jan. 2, any city	*5,000.*
231	2c **brown violet,** *Jan. 1,* any city	*20,000.*
	Jan. 2, any city	*5,000.*
232	3c **green,** *Jan. 1,* any city	*20,000.*
	Jan. 2, any city	*7,000.*
	230, 232 on one cover, *Jan. 2,* Boston, Mass.	*8,250.*
233	4c **ultramarine,** *Jan. 1,* any city	*20,000.*
	Jan. 2, any city	*14,000.*
234	5c **chocolate,** *Jan. 1,* any city	*27,500.*
	Jan. 2, any city	*17,500.*
235	6c **purple,** *Jan. 2,* any city	*22,500.*
237	10c **black brown,** *Jan. 1,* any city	*32,500.*
	Jan. 2, any city	*27,500.*
242	$2 **brown red,** *Jan. 2,* any city	*65,000.*

As Jan. 1, 1893, was a Sunday, specialists recognize both Jan. 1 and 2 as "first day."

1898

TRANS-MISSISSIPPI EXPOSITION ISSUE

285	1c **green,** *June 17,* any city	*12,000.*
286	2c **copper red,** *June 17,* any city	*14,000.*
	Pittsburgh, Pa,	*13,000.*
287	4c **orange,** *June 17*	*27,500.*
288	5c **dull blue,** *June 17,* any city	*16,000.*
	285, 287-288 on one cover	*75,000.*
	285-288 on one cover	*75,000.*
289	8c **violet brown,** *June 17,* any city	*22,500.*
290	10c **gray violet,** *June 17*	*27,500.*
	285-290, all 6 on one cover, *June 17*	*100,000.*
291	50c **sage green,** *June 17,* any city	*50,000.*
292	$1 **black,** *June 17,* any city	*55,000.*

1901

PAN AMERICAN EXPOSITION ISSUE

294	1c **green & black,** *May 1,* any city	*4,000.*
295	2c **carmine & black,** *May 1,* any city	*2,500.*
297	5c **ultra. & blk.,** *May 1,* any city	*35,000.*
	294, 295, 297 on one cover, *May 1,* Boston, Mass.	*17,500.*
	294, 296, 297 on one cover, *May 1,* Boston, Mass.	*16,000.*
	295, 298 on one cover, *May 1,* Washington, D.C.	*33,500.*
	296, 298 on one cover, *May 1,* Boston, Mass.	*27,500.*
	297, 298 on one cover, *May 1,* Philadelphia, Pa.	*27,500.*
	294-299, complete set of 6 on one cover *May 1,* any city	*30,000.*

1904

LOUISIANA PURCHASE EXPOSITION ISSUE

323	1c **green,** *Apr. 30,* any city	*7,500.*
324	2c **carmine,** *Apr. 30,* any city	*5,000.*
325	3c **violet,** *Apr. 30,* any city	*20,000.*
326	5c **dark blue,** *Apr. 30,* any city	*22,500.*
327	10c **red brown,** *Apr. 30,* any city	*24,000.*
	323-327, all 5 on one cover, *Apr. 30,* New York	*65,000.*

The Nos. 323-327 combination cover is unique.

1907

328	1c **Jamestown,** *Apr. 26,* any city	*10,000.*
329	2c **Jamestown,** *Apr. 26,* any city	*15,000.*

1908

331a	1c **green,** booklet single, *Dec. 2,* Washington, D.C.	*17,500.*

1909

367	2c **Lincoln,** *Feb. 12,* any city	*500.*
	On pictorial postcard, *Feb. 12,* Boston	*425.*

Imperf

368	2c **Lincoln,** *Feb. 12,* any city	*13,000.*

1909

ALASKA-YUKON ISSUE

370	2c **carmine,** *June 1,* any city	*3,000.*
	On Expo-related picture postcard, *June 1*	*5,000.*

1909

HUDSON-FULTON ISSUE

372	2c **carmine,** *Sept. 25,* any city	*900.*
	On Expo-related picture postcard, *Sept. 25*	*1,400.*

Imperf

373	2c **carmine,** *Sept. 25,* any city	*8,000.*

1913

PANAMA-PACIFIC ISSUE

397	1c **green,** *Jan. 1,* any city	*5,000.*
399	5c **blue,** *Jan. 1*	*31,000.*
400	10c **orange yellow,** *Jan. 1*	*10,000.*
	397, 399 & 400, all 3 on one cover, San Francisco, Cal.	—

The editors would like to see expertization of the above 3-stamp cover.

1916-22

COIL STAMP

497	10c **orange yellow,** *Jan. 31, 1922,* any city	*6,000.*

1918-20

OFFSET PRINTING

526	2c **carmine,** type IV, *Mar. 15, 1920*	*850.*

1919

537	3c **Victory,** *Mar. 3,* any city	*800.*

1919 ***Perf. 11x10***

541	3c **violet,** type II, *June 14, 1919,* any city	*9,000.*

1920 ***Perf. 10x11***

REGULAR ISSUE

542	1c **green,** *May 26*	*1,750.*

1920

548	1c **Pilgrim,** *Dec. 21,* any city, pair	*1,000.*
	Plymouth, Mass.	*5,000.*
549	2c **Pilgrim,** *Dec. 21,* any city	*700.*
	Plymouth, Mass.	*5,000.*
550	5c **Pilgrim,** *Dec. 21,* any city	*2,500.*
	548-550, complete set of 3 on one cover, *Dec. 21,* any city	*1,750.*
	Washington, D.C.	*3,000.*

1922-26 ***Perf. 11***

551	½c **Hale,** *Apr. 4, 1925,* block of 4	19.00
	New Haven, Conn.	*25.00*
	551 & 576 on one cover, *Apr. 4, 1925,* New Haven, Conn.	*165.00*
552	1c **Franklin,** *Jan. 17, 1923,* pair	27.50
	Philadelphia, Pa.	*47.50*
553	1½c **Harding,** *Mar. 19, 1925,* pair	52.50
	553, 582, 598 on one cover, *Mar. 19, 1925*	*190.00*
554	2c **Washington,** *Jan. 15, 1923*	42.50
555	3c **Lincoln,** *Feb. 12, 1923*	40.00
	Hodgenville, Ky.	*325.00*
556	4c **Martha Washington,** *Jan. 15, 1923*	65.00
557	5c **Roosevelt,** *Oct. 27, 1922*	*135.00*
	New York, N.Y.	*190.00*
	Oyster Bay, N.Y.	*1,750.*
558	6c **Garfield,** *Nov. 20, 1922*	235.00
559	7c **McKinley,** *May 1, 1923*	185.00
	Niles, O.	*275.00*
560	8c **Grant,** *May 1, 1923*	190.00

561	9c	**Jefferson**, *Jan. 15, 1923*	190.00
562	10c	**Monroe**, *Jan. 15, 1923*	190.00
		554, 556, 561 & 562, all 4 stamps issued *Jan. 15* on one cover	*3,500.*
563	11c	**Hayes**, *Oct. 4, 1922*	650.00
		Fremont, O.	*3,750.*
564	12c	**Cleveland**, *Mar. 20, 1923*	185.00
		Boston, Mass. (Philatelic Exhibition)	*185.00*
		Caldwell, N.J.	*210.00*
565	14c	**American Indian**, *May 1, 1923*	400.00
		Muskogee, Okla.	*1,250.*
566	15c	**Statue of Liberty**, *Nov. 11, 1922*	575.00
567	20c	**Golden Gate**, *May 1, 1923*	*600.00*
		San Francisco, Cal.	*2,000.*
		559, 560, 565 & 567, all 4 stamps issued *May 1* on one cover	*10,000.*
568	25c	**Niagara Falls**, *Nov. 11, 1922*	*650.00*
569	30c	**American Buffalo**, *Mar. 20, 1923*	*800.00*
570	50c	**Arlington**, *Nov. 11, 1922*	*1,250.*
571	$1	**Lincoln Memorial**, *Feb. 12, 1923*	*7,000.*
		Springfield, Ill.	*6,500.*
572	$2	**U.S. Capitol**, *Mar. 20, 1923*	*17,500.*
573	$5	**America**, *Mar. 20, 1923*	*32,500.*

Imperf

576	1½c	**Harding**, *Apr. 4, 1925*	42.50

Perf. 10

581	1c	**Franklin**, *Oct. 17, 1923*, not precanceled	*6,000.*
582	1½c	**Harding**, *Mar. 19, 1925*	40.00
583a	2c	**Washington booklet pane of 6**, *Aug. 27, 1926*	*1,500.*
584	3c	**Lincoln**, *Aug. 1, 1925*	55.00
585	4c	**Martha Washington**, *Apr. 4, 1925*	50.00
586	5c	**Roosevelt**, *Apr. 4, 1925*	60.00
587	6c	**Garfield**, *Apr. 4, 1925*	60.00
		585-587, all 3 stamps issued *April 4* on one cover	*1,000.*
588	7c	**McKinley**, *May 29, 1926*	60.00
589	8c	**Grant**, *May 29, 1926*	70.00
590	9c	**Jefferson**, *May 29, 1926*	77.50
591	10c	**Monroe**, *June 8, 1925*	95.00

Perf. 10 Vertically

597	1c	**Franklin**, *July 18, 1923*	*600.00*
598	1½c	**Harding**, *Mar. 19, 1925*	65.00
599	2c	**Washington**, *Jan. 15, 1923*	*1,750.*
600	3c	**Lincoln**, *May 10, 1924*	90.00
602	5c	**Roosevelt**, *Mar. 5, 1924*	95.00
603	10c	**Monroe**, *Dec. 1, 1924*	110.00

No. 599 is known used on Jan. 10, 11 and 13, 1923 (one each day). Jan. 15 was the first day of sale in Washington, D. C.

Perf. 10 Horizontally

604	1c	**Franklin**, *July 19, 1924*	90.00
605	1½c	**Harding**, *May 9, 1925*	70.00
606	2c	**Washington**, *Dec. 31, 1923*	125.00

1923

610	2c	**Harding**, perf. 11, *Sept. 1*	37.50
		Marion, O.	22.50
611	2c	**Harding**, imperf., *Nov. 15*	90.00
612	2c	**Harding**, perf. 10, *Sept. 12*	100.00

1924

614	1c	**Huguenot-Walloon**, *May 1*, pair	35.00
		Albany, N.Y	35.00
		Allentown, Pa.	35.00
		Charleston, S.C.	35.00
		Jacksonville, Fla.	35.00
		Lancaster, Pa.	35.00
		Mayport, Fla.	35.00
		New Rochelle, N.Y.	35.00
		New York, N.Y.	35.00
		Philadelphia, Pa.	35.00
		Reading, Pa.	35.00
615	2c	**Huguenot-Walloon**, *May 1*	50.00
		Albany, N.Y.	50.00
		Allentown, Pa.	50.00
		Charleston, S.C.	50.00
		Jacksonville, Fla.	50.00
		Lancaster, Pa.	50.00
		Mayport, Fla.	50.00
		New Rochelle, N.Y.	50.00
		New York, N.Y.	50.00
		Philadelphia, Pa.	50.00
		Reading, Pa.	50.00
616	5c	**Huguenot-Walloon**, *May 1*	75.00
		Albany, N.Y.	75.00
		Allentown, Pa.	75.00
		Charleston, S.C.	75.00
		Jacksonville, Fla.	75.00
		Lancaster, Pa.	75.00
		Mayport, Fla.	75.00
		New Rochelle, N.Y.	75.00
		New York, N.Y.	75.00
		Philadelphia, Pa.	75.00
		Reading, Pa.	75.00
		614-616 on one cover, any city	160.00

1925

617	1c	**Lexington-Concord**, *Apr. 4*, pair	30.00
		Boston, Mass.	30.00
		Cambridge, Mass.	30.00
		Concord, Mass.	32.50
		Concord Junction, Mass.	30.00
		Lexington, Mass.	30.00
618	2c	**Lexington-Concord**, *Apr. 4*	35.00
		Boston, Mass.	35.00
		Cambridge, Mass.	35.00
		Concord, Mass	35.00
		Concord Junction, Mass.	35.00
		Lexington, Mass.	42.50
619	5c	**Lexington-Concord**, *Apr. 4*	75.00
		Boston, Mass.	75.00
		Cambridge, Mass.	75.00
		Concord, Mass.	75.00
		Concord Junction, Mass.	75.00
		Lexington, Mass.	75.00
		617-619 on one cover, Concord Junction or Lexington	175.00
		Set of 3 on one cover, any other city	150.00

1925

620	2c	**Norse-American**, *May 18*	20.00
		Algona, Iowa	20.00
		Benson, Minn.	20.00
		Decorah, Iowa	20.00
		Minneapolis, Minn.	20.00
		Northfield, Minn.	20.00
		St. Paul, Minn.	20.00
621	5c	**Norse-American**, *May 18*	32.50
		Algona, Iowa	32.50
		Benson, Minn.	32.50
		Decorah, Iowa	32.50
		Minneapolis, Minn.	32.50
		Northfield, Minn.	32.50
		St. Paul, Minn.	32.50
		620-621 on one cover, any city	50.00

1925-26

622	13c	**Harrison**, *Jan. 11, 1926*	25.00
		Indianapolis, Ind.	37.50
		North Bend, Ohio *(500)*	175.00
623	17c	**Wilson**, *Dec. 28, 1925*	15.00
		New York, N.Y.	15.00
		Princeton, N.J.	15.00
		Staunton, Va.	30.00

1926

627	2c	**Sesquicentennial**, *May 10*	15.00
		Boston, Mass.	15.00
		Philadelphia, Pa.	15.00
628	5c	**Ericsson**, *May 29*	40.00
		Chicago, Ill.	40.00
		Minneapolis, Minn.	40.00
		New York, N.Y.	40.00
629	2c	**White Plains**, New York, N.Y., *Oct. 18*	6.25
		New York, N.Y., Inter-Philatelic Exhibition Agency cancellation	6.25
		White Plains, N.Y.	6.25
		Washington, D.C., *Oct. 28*	3.50
630		Sheet of 25, *Oct. 18*	1,500.
		Sheet of 25, *Oct. 28*	1,000.

1926-34 ***Imperf.***

631	1½c	**Harding**, *Aug. 27, 1926*, pair	35.00

Perf. 11x10½

632	1c	**Franklin**, *June 10, 1927*, pair	45.00
632a		Booklet pane of 6, *Nov. 2, 1927*	*3,250.*
633	1½c	**Harding**, *May 17, 1927*, pair	45.00
634	2c	**Washington**, *Dec. 10, 1926*	47.50
635	3c	**Lincoln**, *Feb. 3, 1927*	47.50
635a	3c	**bright violet**, *Feb. 7, 1934*	25.00
636	4c	**Martha Washington**, *May 17, 1927*	50.00
637	5c	**Roosevelt**, *Mar. 24, 1927*	50.00
638	6c	**Garfield**, *July 27, 1927*	57.50
639	7c	**McKinley**, *Mar. 24, 1927*	57.50
		637, 639, both stamps issued *Mar. 24*	500.00
640	8c	**Grant**, *June 10, 1927*	67.50
		632, 640, both stamps issued *June 10*	350.00
641	9c	**Jefferson**, *May 17, 1927*	72.50
		633, 636, 641 all three stamps issued *May 17*	550.00
642	10c	**Monroe**, *Feb. 3, 1927*	90.00

1927

643	2c	**Vermont**, *Aug. 3*	6.00
		Bennington, Vt.	6.00
644	2c	**Burgoyne**, *Aug. 3*	12.50
		Albany, N.Y.	12.50
		Rome, N.Y.	12.50
		Syracuse, N.Y.	12.50
		Utica, N.Y.	12.50

1928

645	2c	**Valley Forge**, *May 26*	4.00
		Cleveland, O.	67.50
		Lancaster, Pa.	4.00
		Norristown, Pa.	4.00
		Philadelphia, Pa.	4.00
		Valley Forge, Pa.	4.00
		West Chester, Pa.	4.00
		Cleveland, Midwestern Philatelic Sta. cancellation	4.00
646	2c	**Molly Pitcher**, *Oct. 20*	15.00
		Freehold, N.J.	15.00
		Red Bank, N.J.	15.00

1928

647	2c	**Hawaii**, *Aug. 13*	15.00
		Honolulu, Hawaii	17.50
648	5c	**Hawaii**, *Aug. 13*	22.50
		Honolulu, Hawaii	25.00
		647-648 on one cover	40.00
649	2c	**Aero Conf.**, *Dec. 12*	7.00
650	5c	**Aero Conf.**, *Dec. 12*	10.00
		649-650 on one cover	15.00

1929

651	2c	**Clark**, Vincennes, Indiana, *Feb. 25*	6.00
		Washington, *Feb. 26*, first day of sale by Philatelic Agency	3.00

Perf. 11x10½

653	½c	**olive brown**, *May 25*, block of four	27.50
654	2c	**Electric Light**, perf. 11, Menlo Park, N.J., *June 5*	10.00
		Washington, D.C., *June 6*, first day of sale by Philatelic Agency	4.00
655	2c	**Electric Light**, perf. 11x10½, *June 11*	80.00
656	2c	**Electric Light**, perf. 10 vert., *June 11*	90.00
657	2c	**Sullivan**, Auburn, N.Y., *June 17*	4.00
		Binghamton, N.Y.	4.00
		Canajoharie, N.Y.	4.00
		Canandaigua, N.Y.	4.00
		Elmira, N.Y.	4.00
		Geneseo, N.Y.	4.00
		Geneva, N.Y.	4.00
		Horseheads, N.Y.	4.00
		Owego, N.Y.	4.00
		Penn Yan, N.Y	4.00
		Perry, N.Y.	4.00
		Seneca Falls, N.Y.	4.00
		Waterloo, N.Y.	4.00
		Watkins Glen, N.Y.	4.00
		Waverly, N.Y.	4.00
		Washington, D.C., *June 18*	2.00

1929

658	1c	**Kansas**, *May 1*, pair	50.00
		Newton, Kan., *Apr. 15*	325.00
659	1½c	**Kansas**, *May 1*, pair	57.50
		Colby, Kan., *Apr. 16*	—
660	2c	**Kansas**, *May 1*	57.50
		Colby, Kan., *Apr. 16*	—
661	3c	**Kansas**, *May 1*	65.00
		Colby, Kan., *Apr. 16*	—
662	4c	**Kansas**, *May 1*	100.00
		Colby, Kan., *Apr. 16*	—
663	5c	**Kansas**, *May 1*	100.00
		Colby, Kan., *Apr. 16*	—
664	6c	**Kansas**, *May 1*	125.00
		Newton, Kan., *Apr. 15*	600.00
665	7c	**Kansas**, *May 1*	125.00
		Colby, Kan., *Apr. 16*	—
666	8c	**Kansas**, *May 1*	125.00
		Newton, Kan., *Apr. 15*	575.00
667	9c	**Kansas**, *May 1*	150.00
		Colby, Kan., *Apr. 16*	—
668	10c	**Kansas**, *May 1*	200.00
		Colby, Kan., *Apr. 16*	—
		658-668 on 1 cover, Washington, D.C., *May 1*	1,500.
669	1c	**Nebraska**, *May 1*, pair	50.00
		Beatrice, Neb., *Apr. 15*	125.00
670	1½c	**Nebraska**, *May 1*, pair	52.50
		Hartington, Neb., *Apr. 15*	275.00
671	2c	**Nebraska**, *May 1*	57.50
		Auburn, Neb., *Apr. 15*	1,200.
		Beatrice, Neb., *Apr. 15*	—
		Hartington, Neb., *Apr. 15*	225.00
672	3c	**Nebraska**, *May 1*	70.00
		Beatrice, Neb., *Apr. 15*	275.00
		Hartington, Neb., *Apr. 15*	275.00
673	4c	**Nebraska**, *May 1*	100.00
		Beatrice, Neb., *Apr. 15*	240.00
		Hartington, Neb., *Apr. 15*	275.00
674	5c	**Nebraska**, *May 1*	100.00
		Beatrice, Neb., *Apr. 15*	275.00
		Hartington, Neb., *Apr. 15*	275.00
675	6c	**Nebraska**, *May 1*	125.00
		Ravenna, Neb., *Apr. 17*	—
		Wahoo, Neb., *Apr. 17*	—
676	7c	**Nebraska**, *May 1*	150.00
		Auburn, Neb., *Apr. 17*	275.00
677	8c	**Nebraska**, *May 1*	125.00
		Humbolt, Neb., *Apr. 17*	250.00
		Pawnee City, Neb., *Apr. 17*	275.00
678	9c	**Nebraska**, *May 1*	150.00
		Cambridge, Neb., *Apr. 17*	250.00
679	10c	**Nebraska**, *May 1*	200.00
		Tecumseh, Neb., *Apr. 18*	—
		669-679 on 1 cover, Washington, D.C., *May 1*	1,500.
		658-679 on 1 cover, Washington, D.C., *May 1*	*4,250.*
680	2c	**Fallen Timbers**, Erie, Pa., *Sept. 14*	3.50
		Maumee, O.	3.50
		Perrysburg, O.	3.50
		Toledo, O.	3.50
		Waterville, O.	3.50
		Washington, D.C., *Sept. 16*	2.00
681	2c	**Ohio River**, Cairo, Ill., *Oct. 19*	3.50
		Cincinnati, O.	3.50
		Evansville, Ind.	3.50
		Homestead, Pa.	3.50
		Louisville, Ky.	3.50
		Pittsburgh, Pa.	3.50
		Wheeling, W. Va.	3.50
		Washington, D.C., *Oct. 21*	2.00

1930

682	2c	**Massachusetts Bay Colony**, Boston, Mass. *Apr. 8 (60,000)*	3.50
		Salem, Mass.	3.50
		Washington, D.C., *Apr. 11*	2.00
683	2c	**Carolina-Charleston**, Charleston, S.C. *Apr. 10*	3.50
		Washington, D.C., *Apr. 11*	2.00

Perf. 11x10½

684	1½c	**Harding**, Marion, O., *Dec. 1*, pair	4.50
		Washington, D.C., *Dec. 2*	2.50
685	4c	**Taft**, Cincinnati, O., *June 4*	6.00
		Washington, D.C., *June 5*	3.00

Perf. 10 Vertically

686	1½c	**Harding**, Marion, Ohio, *Dec. 1*	5.00
		Washington, D.C., *Dec. 2*	3.00
687	4c	**Taft**, *Sept. 18*	20.00

Perf. 11

688 2c **Braddock,** Braddock, Pa., *July 9* 4.00
Washington, D.C., *July 10* 2.00
689 2c **Von Steuben,** New York, N.Y., *Sept. 17* 4.00
Washington, D.C., *Sept. 18* 2.00

1931

690 2c **Pulaski,** Brooklyn, N.Y., *Jan. 16* 4.00
Buffalo, N.Y. 4.00
Chicago, Ill. 4.00
Cleveland, O. 4.00
Detroit, Mich. 4.00
Gary, Ind. 4.00
Milwaukee, Wis. 4.00
New York, N.Y. 4.00
Pittsburgh, Pa. 4.00
Savannah, Ga. 4.00
South Bend, Ind. 4.00
Toledo, O. 4.00
Washington, D.C., *Jan. 17* 2.00

1931 ***Perf. 11x10½, 10½x11***

692 11c **Hayes,** *Sept. 4* 100.
693 12c **Cleveland,** *Aug. 25* 100.
694 13c **Harrison,** *Sept. 4* 100.
695 14c **American Indian,** *Sept. 8* 100.
696 15c **Liberty,** *Aug. 27* 120.
697 17c **Wilson,** *July 25,* Brooklyn, N.Y. *2,750.*
Washington, D.C., *July 27* 400.
698 20c **Golden Gate,** *Sept. 8* 300.
699 25c **Niagara Falls,** *July 25,* Brooklyn, N.Y. *2,000.*
Washington, D.C., *July 27* 350.
697, 699 on one cover, Brooklyn, *July 25* *5,750.*
697, 699 on one cover, Washington, *July 27* *2,500.*
700 30c **American Buffalo,** *Sept. 8* 300.
701 50c **Arlington,** *Sept. 4* 400.
Woolrich, Pa., *Sept. 4* 625.

1931

702 2c **Red Cross,** *May 21* 3.00
Dansville, N.Y. 3.00
703 2c **Yorktown,** *Oct. 19,* Wethersfield, Conn. 3.50
Yorktown, Va. 3.50
Washington, D.C., *Oct. 20* 2.00

1932

WASHINGTON BICENTENNIAL ISSUE

704 ½c *Jan. 1,* block of 4 5.00
705 1c *Jan. 1,* pair 4.00
706 1½c *Jan. 1,* pair 4.00
707 2c *Jan. 1* 4.00
708 3c *Jan. 1* 4.00
709 4c *Jan. 1* 4.00
710 5c *Jan. 1* 4.00
711 6c *Jan. 1* 4.00
712 7c *Jan. 1* 4.00
713 8c *Jan. 1* 4.50
714 9c *Jan. 1* 4.50
715 10c *Jan. 1* 4.50
704-715, set of 12 on one cover, *Jan. 1* 70.00

1932

716 2c **Olympic Winter Games,** *Jan. 25,* Lake Placid, N.Y. 6.00
Washington, D.C., *Jan. 26* 1.50
717 2c **Arbor Day,** *Apr. 22,* Nebraska City, Neb. 4.00
Washington, D.C., *Apr. 23* 1.50
Adams, N.Y., *Apr. 23* 6.50
718 3c **Olympic Summer Games,** *June 15,* Los Angeles, Cal. 6.00
Washington, D.C., *June 16* 2.75
719 5c **Olympic Summer Games,** *June 15,* Los Angeles, Cal. 8.00
Washington, D.C., *June 16* 2.75
718, 719 on one cover, Los Angeles, Cal. 10.00
718, 719 on one cover, Washington, D.C. 4.50
720 3c **Washington,** *June 16* 7.50
720b Booklet pane of 6, *July 25* 100.00
721 3c **Washington Coil,** Sideways, *June 24* 15.00
722 3c **Washington Coil,** Endways, *Oct. 12* 15.00
723 6c **Garfield Coil,** Sideways, *Aug. 18,* Los Angeles, Cal. 15.00
Washington, D.C., *Aug. 19* 4.00
724 3c **William Penn,** *Oct. 24,* New Castle, Del. 3.25
Chester, Pa. 3.25
Philadelphia, Pa. 3.25
Washington, D.C., *Oct. 25* 1.25
725 3c **Daniel Webster,** *Oct. 24,* Franklin, N.H. 3.25
Exeter, N.H. 3.25
Hanover, N.H. 3.25
Washington, D.C., *Oct. 25* 1.25

1933

726 3c **Gen. Oglethorpe,** *Feb. 12,* Savannah, Ga., *(200,000)* 3.25
Washington, D.C., *Feb. 13* 1.50
727 3c **Peace Proclamation,** *Apr. 19,* Newburgh, N.Y. *(349,571)* 3.50
Washington, D.C., *Apr. 20* 1.25
728 1c **Century of Progress,** *May 25,* Chicago, Ill., strip of 3 3.00
Washington, D.C., *May 26* 1.00
729 3c **Century of Progress,** *May 25,* Chicago, Ill. 3.00
Washington, D.C., *May 26* 1.00
728, 729 on one cover 5.00

Covers mailed May 25, bearing Nos. 728 and 729 total 232,251.

730 1c **American Philatelic Society,** sheet of 25, *Aug. 25,* Chicago, Ill. 100.00
730a 1c **A.P.S.,** imperf., *Aug. 25,* Chicago, Ill., strip of 3 3.25
Washington, D.C., *Aug. 28* 1.25
731 3c **American Philatelic Society,** sheet of 25, *Aug. 25,* Chicago, Ill. 100.00
731a 3c **A.P.S.,** single, imperf., *Aug. 25,* Chicago, Ill. 3.25
Washington, D.C., *Aug. 28* 1.25
730a, 731a on one cover 5.50

Covers mailed Aug. 25 bearing Nos. 730, 730a, 731, 731a total 65,218.

732 3c **National Recovery Administration,** *Aug. 15,(65,000)* 3.25
Nira, Iowa, *Aug. 17* 2.50
733 3c **Byrd Antarctic,** *Oct. 9* 10.00
734 5c **Kosciuszko,** *Oct. 13,* Boston, Mass. *(23,025)* 4.50
Buffalo, N.Y. *(14,981)* 5.50
Chicago, Ill, *(26,306)* 4.50
Detroit, Mich. *(17,792)* 5.25
Pittsburgh, Pa. *(6,282)* 15.00
Kosciuszko, Miss. *(27,093)* 5.25
St. Louis, Mo. *(17,872)* 5.25
Washington, D.C., *Oct. 14* 1.60

1934

735 3c **National Exhibition,** sheet of 6, Byrd imperf., *Feb. 10,* New York, N.Y. 40.00
Washington, D.C., *Feb. 19* 27.50
735a 3c **National Exhibition,** single, imperf., New York, N.Y., *Feb. 10 (450,715)* 5.00
Washington, D.C., *Feb. 19* 2.75
736 3c **Maryland Tercentenary,** *Mar. 23* St. Mary's City, Md. *(148,785)* 1.60
Washington, D.C., *Mar. 24* 1.00
737 3c **Mothers of America,** perf. 11x10½, *May 2, any city* 1.60
738 3c **Mothers of America,** perf. 11, *May 2, any city* 1.60
737, 738 on one cover 4.00

Covers mailed at Washington, May 2 bearing Nos. 737 and 738 total 183,359.

739 3c **Wisconsin,** *July 7,* Green Bay, Wisc. *(130,000)* 1.10
Washington, D.C., *July 9* 1.00
740 1c **Parks, Yosemite,** *July 16* 2.25
Yosemite, Cal., *(60,000),* strip of 3 2.75
741 2c **Parks, Grand Canyon,** *July 24* 2.25
Grand Canyon, Ariz., *(75,000),* pair 2.75
742 3c **Parks, Mt. Rainier,** *Aug. 3* 2.50
Longmire, Wash., *(64,500)* 3.00
743 4c **Parks, Mesa Verde,** *Sept. 25* 2.25
Mesa Verde, Colo., *(51,882)* 2.75
744 5c **Parks, Yellowstone,** *July 30* 2.25
Yellowstone, Wyo., *(87,000)* 2.50
745 6c **Parks, Crater Lake,** *Sept. 5* 3.00
Crater Lake, Ore., *(45,282)* 3.25
746 7c **Parks, Arcadia,** *Oct. 2* 3.00
Bar Harbor, Maine *(51,312)* 3.25
747 8c **Parks, Zion,** *Sept. 18* 3.25
Zion, Utah, *(43,650)* 3.75
748 9c **Parks, Glacier Park,** *Aug. 27* 3.50
Glacier Park, Mont., *(52,626)* 3.75
749 10c **Parks, Smoky Mountains,** *Oct. 8* 6.00
Sevierville, Tenn., *(39,000)* 7.50

Imperf

750 3c **American Philatelic Society,** sheet of 6, *Aug. 28,* Atlantic City, N.J. 40.00
750a 3c **A.P.S.,** single, *Aug. 28,* Atlantic City, N.J. *(40,000)* 3.25
Washington, D.C., *Sept. 4* 2.00
751 1c **Trans-Mississippi Philatelic Expo.,** sheet of 6, *Oct. 10,* Omaha, Neb. 35.00
751a 1c **Trans-Miss. Phil. Expo.,** Omaha. Neb., *Oct. 10 (125,000),* strip of 3 3.25
Washington, D.C., Oct. 15 2.00

1935

SPECIAL PRINTING

Nos. 752-771 issued Mar. 15

752 3c **Peace Commemoration** 5.00
753 3c **Byrd** 6.00
754 3c **Mothers of America** 6.00
755 3c **Wisconsin Tercentenary** 6.00
756 1c **Parks, Yosemite,** strip of 3 6.00
757 2c **Parks, Grand Canyon,** pair 6.00
758 3c **Parks, Mount Rainier** 6.00
759 4c **Parks, Mesa Verde** 6.50
760 5c **Parks, Yellowstone** 6.50
761 6c **Parks, Crater Lake** 6.50
762 7c **Parks, Acadia** 6.50
763 8c **Parks, Zion** 7.50
764 9c **Parks, Glacier Park** 7.50
765 10c **Parks, Smoky Mountains** 7.50
766a 1c **Century of Progress,** strip of 3 5.50
Pane of 25 *250.00*
767a 3c **Century of Progress** 5.50
Pane of 25 *250.00*
768a 3c **Byrd** 6.50
Pane of 6 *250.00*
769a 1c **Parks, Yosemite,** strip of 3 4.00
Pane of 6 *250.00*
770a 3c **Parks, Mount Rainier** 5.00
Pane of 6 *250.00*
771 16c **Airmail Special Delivery** 12.50

Catalogue values from this point to No. 986 are for addressed covers with the most common cachets.

772 3c **Connecticut Tercentenary,** *Apr. 26,* Hartford, Conn. *(217,800)* 14.00
Washington, D.C., *Apr. 27* 2.25
773 3c **California Exposition,** *May 29,* San Diego, Cal. *(214,042)* 14.00
Washington, D.C., *May 31* 1.50
774 3c **Boulder Dam,** *Sept. 30,* Boulder City, Nev. *(166,180)* 15.00
Washington, D.C., *Oct. 1* 2.00
775 3c **Michigan Centenary,** *Nov. 1,* Lansing, Mich. *(176,962)* 15.00
Washington, D.C., *Nov. 2* 1.50

1936

776 3c **Texas Centennial,** *Mar. 2,* Gonzales, Texas *(319,150)* 20.00
Washington, D.C., *Mar. 3* 2.00
777 3c **Rhode Island Tercentenary,** *May 4,* Providence, R.I. *(245,400)* 12.50
Washington, D.C., *May 5* 2.25
778 **TIPEX** souvenir sheet, *May 9 (297,194)* *New York, N.Y.* (TIPEX cancellation) 14.00
Washington, D.C., *May 11* 3.50
782 3c **Arkansas Centennial,** *June 15,* Little Rock, Ark. *(376,693)* 13.00
Washington, D.C, *June 16* 1.25
783 3c **Oregon Territory Centennial,** *July 14,* Astoria, Ore. *(91,110)* 10.00
Daniel, Wyo., *(67,013)* 10.00
Lewiston, Ida., *(86,100)* 10.00
Missoula, Mont., *(59,883)* 11.00
Walla Walla, Wash., *(106,150)* 9.00
Washington, D.C., *July 15* 1.25
784 3c **Susan B. Anthony,** *Aug. 26 (178,500)* 15.00

1936-37

785 1c **Army,** *Dec. 15, 1936,* strip of 3 8.00
786 2c **Army,** *Jan. 15, 1937,* pair 8.00
787 3c **Army,** *Feb. 18, 1937* 8.00
788 4c **Army,** *Mar. 23, 1937* 8.00
789 5c **Army,** *May 26, 1937,* West Point, N.Y., *(160,000)* 8.00
Washington, D.C., *May 27* 4.00
790 1c **Navy,** *Dec. 15, 1936,* strip of 3 8.00
791 2c **Navy,** *Jan. 15, 1937,* pair 8.00
792 3c **Navy,** *Feb. 18, 1937* 8.00
793 4c **Navy,** *Mar. 23, 1937* 8.00
794 5c **Navy,** *May 26, 1937,* Annapolis, Md., *(202,806)* 8.00
Washington, D.C., *May 27* 4.00

Covers for #785 & 790 total 390, 749; #786 & 791 total 292,570; #787 & 792 total 320,888; #788 & 793 total 331,000.

1937

795 3c **Ordinance of 1787,** *July 13* Marietta, Ohio *(130,531)* 9.00
New York, N.Y. *(125,134)* 9.00
Washington, D.C., *July 14* 1.25
796 5c **Virginia Dare,** *Aug. 18,* Manteo, N.C. *(226,730)* 11.00
797 10c **Souvenir Sheet,** *Aug. 26,* Asheville, N.C. *(164,215)* 11.00
798 3c **Constitution,** *Sept. 17,* Philadelphia, Pa. *(281,478)* 9.00
799 3c **Hawaii,** *Oct. 18,* Honolulu, Hawaii *(320,334)* 11.00
800 3c **Alaska,** *Nov. 12,* Juneau, Alaska *(230,370)* 10.00
801 3c **Puerto Rico,** *Nov. 25,* San Juan, P.R. *(244,054)* 10.00
802 3c **Virgin Islands,** *Dec. 15,* Charlotte Amalie, V.I. *(225,469)* 10.00

1938

PRESIDENTIAL ISSUE

803 ½c **Franklin,** *May 19,* Philadelphia, Pa. *(224,901),* block of 6 3.50
804 1c **G. Washington,** *Apr. 25 (124,037),* strip of 3 3.50
804b Booklet pane of 6, *Jan. 27, 1939* 12.50
805 1½c **M. Washington,** *May 5 (128,339),* pair 3.50
806 2c **J. Adams,** *June 3 (127,806),* pair 3.50
806b Booklet pane of 6, *Jan. 27, 1939* 15.00
807 3c **Jefferson,** *June 16 (118,097)* 3.50
807a Booklet pane of 6, *Jan. 27, 1939* 17.50
808 4c **Madison,** *July 1 (118,765)* 3.50
809 4½c **White House,** *July 11 (115,820)* 3.50
810 5c **Monroe,** *July 21 (98,282)* 3.50
811 6c **J.Q. Adams,** *July 28 (97,428)* 3.50
812 7c **Jackson,** *Aug. 4 (98,414)* 3.50
813 8c **Van Buren,** *Aug. 11 (94,857)* 3.50
814 9c **W.H. Harrison,** *Aug. 18 (91,229)* 3.50
815 10c **Tyler,** *Sept. 2 (83,707)* 3.50
816 11c **Polk,** *Sept. 8 (63,966)* 5.00
817 12c **Taylor,** *Sept. 14 (62,935)* 5.00
818 13c **Fillmore,** *Sept. 22 (58,965)* 5.00
819 14c **Pierce,** *Oct. 6 (49,819)* 5.00
820 15c **Buchanan,** *Oct. 13 (52,209)* 5.00
821 16c **Lincoln,** *Oct. 20 (59,566)* 7.00
822 17c **A. Johnson,** *Oct. 27 (55,024)* 6.00
823 18c **Grant,** *Nov. 3 (53,124)* 6.00
824 19c **Hayes,** *Nov. 10 (54,124)* 6.00
825 20c **Garfield,** *Nov. 10 (51,971)* 7.00
826 21c **Arthur,** *Nov. 22 (44,367)* 7.00
827 22c **Cleveland,** *Nov. 22 (44,358)* 8.00
828 24c **B. Harrison,** *Dec. 2 (46,592)* 8.00
829 25c **McKinley,** *Dec. 2 (45,691)* 8.00

830 30c **T. Roosevelt**, *Dec. 8 (43,528)* 9.00
831 50c **Taft**, *Dec. 8 (41,984)* 12.50
832 $1 **Wilson, purple & black**, *Aug. 29 (24,618)* 50.00
832c **red violet & black**, *Aug. 31, 1954 (20,202)* 25.00
833 $2 **Harding**, *Sept. 29 (19,895)* 100.00
834 $5 **Coolidge**, *Nov. 17 (15,615)* 175.00

1938

835 3c **Constitution**, *June 21*, Philadelphia, Pa. *(232,873)* 15.00
836 3c **Swedes and Finns**, *June 27*, Wilmington, Del. *(225,617)* 15.00
837 3c **Northwest Sesqui.**, *July 15*, Marietta, Ohio *(180,170)* 15.00
838 3c **Iowa**, *Aug. 24*, Des Moines, Iowa *(209,860)* 15.00

1939

COIL STAMPS

Perf. 10 Vertically

839 1c **G. Washington**, *Jan. 20*, strip of 3 5.00
840 1½c **M. Washington**, *Jan. 20*, pair 5.00
841 2c **J. Adams**, *Jan. 20*, pair 5.00
842 3c **Jefferson**, *Jan. 20* 5.00
843 4c **Madison**, *Jan. 20* 5.00
844 4½c **White House**, *Jan. 20* 5.00
845 5c **Monroe**, *Jan. 20* 5.00
846 6c **J.Q. Adams**, *Jan. 20* 6.50
847 10c **Tyler**, *Jan. 20* 9.00
839-847 on one cover, *Jan. 20* 45.00

Perf. 10 Horizontally

848 1c Strip of 3, *Jan. 27* 5.00
849 1½c Pair, *Jan. 27* 5.00
850 2c Pair, *Jan. 27* 5.00
851 3c *Jan. 27* 5.50
848-851 on one cover, *Jan. 27* 25.00

1939

852 3c **Golden Gate Expo**, *Feb. 18*, San Francisco, Cal. *(352,165)* 16.00
853 3c **N.Y. World's Fair**, *Apr. 1*, New York, N.Y. *(585,565)* 20.00
854 3c **Washington Inauguration**, *Apr. 30*, New York, N.Y. *(395,644)* 17.50
855 3c **Baseball Centennial**, *June 12*, Cooperstown, N.Y. *(398,199)* 40.00
856 3c **Panama Canal**, *Aug. 15*, U.S.S. Charleston, Canal Zone *(230,974)* 18.00
857 3c **Printing Tercentenary**, *Sept. 25*, New York, N.Y. *(295,270)* 15.00
858 3c **50th Statehood Anniversary**, Bismarck, N.D. *Nov. 2 (142,106)* 12.50
Pierre, S.D., *Nov. 2 (150,429)* 12.50
Helena, Mont., *Nov. 8 (130,273)* 12.50
Olympia, Wash., *Nov. 11 (150,429)* 12.50

1940

FAMOUS AMERICANS

859 1c **Washington Irving**, *Jan. 29*, Tarrytown, N.Y. *(170,969)*, strip of 3 4.50
860 2c **James Fenimore Cooper**, *Jan. 29*, Cooperstown, N.Y. *(154,836)*, pair 3.00
861 3c **Ralph Waldo Emerson**, *Feb. 5*, Boston, Mass. *(185,148)* 3.00
862 5c **Louisa May Alcott**, *Feb. 5*, Concord, Mass. *(134,325)* 4.00
863 10c **Samuel L. Clemens**, *Feb. 13*, Hannibal, Mo. *(150,492)* 8.00
864 1c **Henry W. Longfellow**, *Feb. 16*, Portland, Me. *(160,508)*, strip of 3 3.00
865 2c **John Greenleaf Whittier**, *Feb. 16*, Haverhill, Mass. *(148,423)*, pair 3.00
866 3c **James Russell Lowell**, *Feb. 20*, Cambridge, Mass. *(148,735)* 3.00
867 5c **Walt Whitman**, *Feb. 20*, Camden, N.J. *(134,185)* 4.00
868 10c **James Whitcomb Riley**, *Feb. 24*, Greenfield, Ind. *(131,760)* 6.00
869 1c **Horace Mann**, *Mar. 14*, Boston, Mass. *(186,854)*, strip of 3 3.00
870 2c **Mark Hopkins**, *Mar. 14*, Williamstown, Mass. *(140,286)*, pair 3.00
871 3c **Charles W. Eliot**, *Mar. 28*, Cambridge, Mass. *(155,708)* 3.00
872 5c **Frances E. Willard**, *Mar. 28*, Evanston, Ill. *(140,483)* 4.00
873 10c **Booker T. Washington**, *Apr. 7*, Tuskegee Institute, Ala. *(163,507)* 10.00
874 1c **John James Audubon**, *Apr. 8*, St. Francisville, La. *(144,123)*, strip of 3 3.00
875 2c **Dr. Crawford W. Long**, *Apr. 8*, Jefferson, Ga. *(158,128)*, pair 3.00
876 3c **Luther Burbank**, *Apr. 17*, Santa Rosa, Cal. *(147,033)* 3.00
877 5c **Dr. Walter Reed**, *Apr. 17 (154,464)* 4.00
878 10c **Jane Addams**, *Apr. 26*, Chicago, Ill. *(132,375)* 6.00
879 1c **Stephen Collins Foster**, *May 3*, Bardstown, Ky. *(183,461)*, strip of 3 3.00
880 2c **John Philip Sousa**, *May 3 (131,422)*, pair 4.00
881 3c **Victor Herbert**, *May 13*, New York, N.Y. *(168,200)* 3.00
882 5c **Edward A. MacDowell**, *May 13*, Peterborough, N.H. *(135,155)* 4.00
883 10c **Ethelbert Nevin**, *June 10*, Pittsburgh, Pa. *(121,951)* 6.00
884 1c **Gilbert Stuart**, *Sept. 5*, Narragansett, R.I. *(131,965)*, strip of 3 3.00
885 2c **James A. McNeill Whistler**, *Sept. 5*, Lowell, Mass. *(130,962)*, pair 3.00
886 3c **Augustus Saint-Gaudens**, *Sept. 16*, New York, N.Y. *(138,200)* 3.00
887 5c **Daniel Chester French**, *Sept. 16*, Stockbridge, Mass. *(124,608)* 4.00
888 10c **Frederic Remington**, *Sept. 30*, Canton, N.Y. *(116,219)* 7.00
889 1c **Eli Whitney**, *Oct. 7*, Savannah, Ga. *(140,868)*, strip of 3 3.00
890 2c **Samuel F.B. Morse**, *Oct. 7*, New York, N.Y. *(135,388)*, pair 3.00
891 3c **Cyrus Hall McCormick**, *Oct. 14*, Lexington, Va. *(137,415)* 3.00
892 5c **Elias Howe**, *Oct. 14*, Spencer, Mass. *(126,334)* 4.00
893 10c **Alexander Graham Bell**, *Oct. 28*, Boston, Mass. *(125,372)* 10.00

1940

894 3c **Pony Express**, *Apr. 3*, St. Joseph, Mo. *(194,589)* 12.00
Sacramento, Cal. *(160,849)* 12.00
895 3c **Pan American Union**, *Apr. 14 (182,401)* 9.50
896 3c **Idaho Statehood**, *July 3*, Boise, Idaho *(156,429)* 9.50
897 3c **Wyoming Statehood**, *July 10* Cheyenne, Wyo. *(156,709)* 9.50
898 3c **Coronado Expedition**, *Sept. 7*, Albuquerque, N.M. *(161,012)* 9.50
899 1c **Defense**, *Oct. 16*, strip of 3 7.00
900 2c **Defense**, *Oct. 16*, pair 7.00
901 3c **Defense**, *Oct. 16* 7.00
899-901 on one cover 12.00

First day cancel was applied to 450,083 covers bearing one or more of Nos. 899-901.

902 3c **Thirteenth Amendment**, *Oct. 20*, World's Fair, N.Y. *(156,146)* 10.00

1941

903 3c **Vermont Statehood**, *Mar. 4*, Montpelier, Vt. *(182,423)* 10.00

MacArthur, W. Va.
Apr 15, 1942
First Day Cover

Covers exist with this cancellation. "First Day" refers to the first day of the new name of the town, previously known as Hollywood, W. Va.

1942

904 3c **Kentucky Statehood**, *June 1*, Frankfort, Ky. *(155,730)* 10.00
905 3c **"Win the War"**, *July 4 (191,168)* 10.00
906 5c **Chinese Resistance**, *July 7*, Denver, Colo. *(168,746)* 12.00

1943-44

907 2c **Allied Nations**, *Jan. 14, 1943 (178,865)*, pair 6.00
908 1c **Four Freedoms**, *Feb. 12, 1943 (193,800)*, strip of 3 6.00
909 5c **Poland**, *June 22, 1943*, Chicago, Ill. *(88,170)* 5.00
Washington, D.C. *(136,002)* 4.00
910 5c **Czechoslovakia**, *July 12, 1943 (145,112)* 4.00
911 5c **Norway**, *July 27, 1943 (155,054)* 4.00
912 5c **Luxemborg**, *Aug. 10, 1943 (166,367)* 4.00
913 5c **Netherlands**, *Aug. 24, 1943 (148,763)* 4.00
914 5c **Belgium**, *Sept. 14, 1943 (154,220)* 4.00
915 5c **France**, *Sept. 28, 1943 (163,478)* 4.00
916 5c **Greece**, *Oct. 12, 1943 (166,553)* 4.00
917 5c **Yugoslavia**, *Oct. 26, 1943 (161,835)* 4.00
918 5c **Albania**, *Nov. 9, 1943 (162,275)* 4.00
919 5c **Austria**, *Nov. 23, 1943 (172,285)* 4.00
920 5c **Denmark**, *Dec. 7, 1943 (173,784)* 4.00
921 5c **Korea**, *Nov. 2, 1944 (192,860)* 5.00

1944

922 3c **Railroad**, *May 10*, Ogden, Utah *(151,324)* 10.00
Omaha, Neb. *(171,000)* 10.00
San Francisco, Cal. *(125,000)* 10.00
923 3c **Steamship**, *May 22*, Kings Point, N.Y. *(152,324)* 9.00
Savannah, Ga. *(181,472)* 9.00
924 3c **Telegraph**, *May 24 (141,907)* 9.00
Baltimore, Md. *(136,480)* 9.00
925 3c **Philippines**, *Sept. 27 (214,865)* 9.00
926 3c **Motion Picture**, *Oct. 31*, Hollywood, Cal. *(190,660)* 10.00
New York, N.Y. *(176,473)* 9.00

1945

927 3c **Florida**, *Mar. 3*, Tallahassee, Fla. *(228,435)* 9.00
928 5c **United Nations Conference**, *Apr. 25*, San Francisco, Cal. *(417,450)* 9.00
929 3c **Iwo Jima**, *July 11 (391,650)* 15.00

1945-46

930 1c **Roosevelt**, *July 26, 1945*, Hyde Park, N.Y. *(390,219)*, strip of 3 4.50
931 2c **Roosevelt**, *Aug. 24, 1945*, Warm Springs, Ga. *(426,142)*, pair 4.50
932 3c **Roosevelt**, *June 27, 1945 (391,650)* 4.50
933 5c **Roosevelt**, *Jan. 30, 1946 (466,766)* 4.50

1945

934 3c **Army**, *Sept. 28 (392,300)* 11.00
935 3c **Navy**, *Oct. 27*, Annapolis, Md. *(460,352)* 11.00
936 3c **Coast Guard**, *Nov. 10* New York, N.Y. *(405,280)* 11.00
937 3c **Alfred E. Smith**, *Nov. 26* New York, N.Y. *(424,950)* 3.00
938 3c **Texas**, *Dec. 29*, Austin, Tex. *(397,860)* 9.00

1946

939 3c **Merchant Marine**, *Feb. 26 (432,141)* 9.00
940 3c **Veterans of WWII**, *May 9 (492,786)* 11.00
941 3c **Tennessee**, *June 1, 1946*, Nashville, Tenn. *(463,512)* 4.00
942 3c **Iowa**, *Aug. 3*, Iowa City, Iowa *(517,505)* 4.00
943 3c **Smithsonian**, *Aug. 10 (402,448)* 4.00
944 3c **Kearny Expedition**, *Oct. 16*, Santa Fe, N.M. *(384,300)* 4.00

1947

945 3c **Thomas A. Edison**, *Feb. 11*, Milan, Ohio *(632,473)* 5.00
946 3c **Joseph Pulitzer**, *Apr. 10*, New York, N.Y. *(580,870)* 4.00
947 3c **Stamp Centenary**, *May 17*, New York, N.Y. *(712,873)* 4.00
948 5c and 10c **Centenary Exhibition Sheet**, *May 19*, New York, N.Y. *(502,175)* 4.50
949 3c **Doctors**, *June 9*, Atlantic City, N.J. *(508,016)* 9.00
950 3c **Utah**, *July 24*, Salt Lake City, Utah *(456,416)* 3.00
951 3c **"Constitution,"** *Oct. 21*, Boston, Mass. *(683,416)* 8.00
952 3c **Everglades Park**, *Dec. 5*, Florida City, Fla. *(466,647)* 3.00

1948

953 3c **Carver**, *Jan. 5*, Tuskegee Institute, Ala. *(402,179)* 3.00
954 3c **California Gold**, *Jan. 24*, Coloma, Calif. *(526,154)* 3.50
955 3c **Mississippi Territory**, *Apr. 7*, Natchez, Miss. *(434,804)* 2.00
956 3c **Four Chaplains**, *May 28 (459,070)* 8.00
957 3c **Wisconsin Centennial**, *May 29*, Madison, Wis. *(470,280)* 3.00
958 5c **Swedish Pioneers**, *June 4* Chicago, Ill. *(364,318)* 4.00
959 3c **Women's Progress**, *July 19*, Seneca Falls, N.Y. *(401,923)* 3.00
960 3c **William Allen White**, *July 31*, Emporia, Kans. *(385,648)* 2.50
961 3c **U.S.-Canada Friendship**, *Aug. 2*, Niagara Falls, N.Y. *(406,467)* 3.00
962 3c **Francis Scott Key**, *Aug. 9*, Frederick, Md. *(505,930)* 2.50
963 3c **Salute to Youth**, *Aug. 11 (347,070)* 2.50
964 3c **Oregon Territory Establishment**, *Aug. 14*, Oregon City, Ore. *(365,898)* 3.00
965 3c **Harlan Fiske Stone**, *Aug. 25*, Chesterfield, N.H. *(362,170)* 2.50
966 3c **Palomar Observatory**, *Aug. 30*, Palomar Mountain, Calif. *(401,365)* 5.00
967 3c **Clara Barton**, *Sept. 7*, Oxford, Mass. *(362,000)* 3.00
968 3c **Poultry Industry**, *Sept. 9*, New Haven, Conn. *(475,000)* 3.00
969 3c **Gold Star Mothers**, *Sept. 21 (386,064)* 2.00
970 3c **Fort Kearny**, *Sept. 22*, Minden, Neb. *(429,633)* 2.00
971 3c **Volunteer Firemen**, *Oct. 4*, Dover, Del. *(399,630)* 10.00
972 3c **Indian Centennial**, *Oct. 15*, Muskogee, Okla. *(459,528)* 3.50
973 3c **Rough Riders**, *Oct. 27*, Prescott, Ariz. *(399,198)* 2.50
974 3c **Juliette Low**, *Oct. 29*, Savannah, Ga. *(476,573)* 8.00
975 3c **Will Rogers**, *Nov. 4*, Claremore, Okla. *(450,350)* 2.00
976 3c **Fort Bliss**, *Nov. 5*, El Paso, Tex. *(421,000)* 5.00
977 3c **Moina Michael**, *Nov. 9*, Athens, Ga. *(374,090)* 2.50
978 3c **Gettysburg Address**, *Nov. 19*, Gettysburg, Pa. *(511,990)* 2.75
979 3c **American Turners Society**, *Nov. 20*, Cincinnati, Ohio *(434,090)* 2.00
980 3c **Joel Chandler Harris**, *Dec. 9*, Eatonton, Ga. *(426,199)* 2.25

1949

981 3c **Minnesota Territory**, *Mar. 3*, St. Paul, Minn. *(458,750)* 2.25
982 3c **Washington and Lee University**, *Apr. 12*, Lexington, Va. *(447,910)* 2.25
983 3c **Puerto Rico Election**, *Apr. 27*, San Juan, P.R. *(390,416)* 2.25
984 3c **Annapolis, Md.**, *May 23*, Annapolis, Md. *(441,802)* 3.00
985 3c **G.A.R.**, *Aug. 29*, Indianapolis, Ind. *(471,696)* 3.25
986 3c **Edgar Allan Poe**, *Oct. 7*, Richmond, Va. *(371,020)* 4.00

Catalogue values from this point to the end of the section are for unaddressed covers with the most common cachets.

1950

987 3c **American Bankers Assoc.**, *Jan. 3*, Saratoga Springs, N.Y. *(388,622)* 2.75

988 3c **Samuel Gompers,** *Jan. 27 (332,023)* 1.75

National Capital Sesquicentennial

989 3c **Freedom,** *Apr. 20 (371,743)* 1.50
990 3c **Executive,** *June 12 (376,789)* 1.50
991 3c **Judicial,** *Aug. 2 (324,007)* 1.50
992 3c **Legislative,** *Nov. 22 (352,215)* 1.50
993 3c **Railroad Engineers,** *Apr. 29,* Jackson, Tenn. *(420,830)* 4.00
994 3c **Kansas City Centenary,** *June 3,* Kansas City, Mo. *(405,390)* 1.50
995 3c **Boy Scouts,** *June 30,* Valley Forge, Pa. *(622,972)* 12.00
996 3c **Indiana Territory Sesquicentennial,** *July 4,* Vincennes, Ind. *(359,643)* 1.75
997 3c **California Statehood,** *Sept. 9,* Sacramento, Cal. *(391,919)* 2.50

1951

998 3c **United Confederate Veterans,** *May 30,* Norfolk, Va. *(374,235)* 3.00
999 3c **Nevada Centennial,** *July 14,* Genoa, Nev. *(336,890)* 1.50
1000 3c **Landing of Cadillac,** *July 24,* Detroit, Mich. *(323,094)* 1.50
1001 3c **Colorado Statehood,** *Aug. 1,* Minturn, Colo. *(311,568)* 1.50
1002 3c **American Chemical Society,** *Sept. 4,* New York, N.Y. *(436,419)* 1.75
1003 3c **Battle of Brooklyn,** *Dec. 10,* Brooklyn, N.Y. *(420,000)* 1.50

1952

1004 3c **Betsy Ross,** *Jan. 2,* Philadelphia, Pa. *(314,312)* 1.50
1005 3c **4-H Club,** *Jan. 15,* Springfield, Ohio *(383,290)* 3.25
1006 3c **B. & O. Railroad,** *Feb. 28,* Baltimore, Md. *(441,600)* 4.50
1007 3c **American Automobile Association,** *Mar. 4,* Chicago, Ill. *(520,123)* 1.75
1008 3c **NATO,** *Apr. 4 (313,518)* 1.50
1009 3c **Grand Coulee Dam,** *May 15,* Grand Coulee, Wash. *(341,680)* 1.50
1010 3c **Lafayette,** *June 13,* Georgetown, S.C. *(349,102)* 1.50
1011 3c **Mt. Rushmore Memorial,** *Aug. 11,* Keystone, S.D. *(337,027)* 1.50
1012 3c **Civil Engineers,** *Sept. 6,* Chicago, Ill. *(318,483)* 1.50
1013 3c **Service Women,** *Sept. 11 (308,062)* 1.75
1014 3c **Gutenberg Bible,** *Sept. 30 (387,078)* 1.50
1015 3c **Newspaper Boys,** *Oct. 4,* Philadelphia, Pa. *(626,000)* 1.50
1016 3c **Red Cross,** *Nov. 21,* New York, N.Y. *(439,252)* 2.00

1953

1017 3c **National Guard,** *Feb. 23 (387,618)* 2.00
1018 3c **Ohio Sesquicentennial,** *Mar. 2,* Chillicothe, Ohio *(407,983)* 1.50
1019 3c **Washington Territory,** *Mar. 2,* Olympia, Wash. *(344,047)* 1.50
1020 3c **Louisiana Purchase,** *Apr. 30,* St. Louis, Mo. *(425,600)* 1.50
1021 5c **Opening of Japan,** *July 14 (320,541)* 1.75
1022 3c **American Bar Association,** *Aug. 24,* Boston, Mass. *(410,036)* 6.50
1023 3c **Sagamore Hill,** *Sept. 14,* Oyster Bay, N.Y. *(379,750)* 1.50
1024 3c **Future Farmers,** *Oct. 13,* Kansas City, Mo. *(424,193)* 1.50
1025 3c **Trucking Industry,** *Oct. 27,* Los Angeles, Calif. *(875,021)* 1.50
1026 3c **Gen. G.S. Patton, Jr.,** *Nov. 11,* Fort Knox, Ky. *(342,600)* 4.50
1027 3c **New York City,** *Nov. 20,* New York, N.Y. *(387,914)* 1.50
1028 3c **Gadsden Purchase,** *Dec. 30,* Tucson, Ariz. *(363,250)* 1.50

1954

1029 3c **Columbia University,** *Jan. 4,* New York, N.Y. *(550,745)* 1.50

1954-67

LIBERTY ISSUE

1030a ½c **Franklin,** *Oct. 20, 1955 (223,122),* block of 6 1.00
1031b 1c **Washington,** *Aug. 26, 1954,* Chicago, Ill. *(272,581),* strip of 3 1.00
1031A 1¼c **Palace of Governors,** *June 17, 1960,* Santa Fe, N.M., strip of 3 1.00
1031A and 1054A on one cover 1.50

First day cancel was applied to 501,848 covers bearing one or more of Nos. 1031A, 1054A.

1032 1½c **Mt. Vernon,** *Feb. 22, 1956,* Mount Vernon, Va. *(270,109),* pair 1.00
1033 2c **Jefferson,** *Sept. 15, 1954,* San Francisco, Cal. *(307,300),* pair 1.00
1034 2½c **Bunker Hill,** *June 17, 1959,* Boston, Mass. *(315,060),* pair 1.00
1035e 3c **Statue of Liberty,** *June 24, 1954,* Albany, N.Y. *(340,001)* 1.00
1035a Booklet pane of 6, *June 30, 1954* 3.50
1035b 3c Tagged, *July 6, 1966* 40.00
1036c 4c **Lincoln,** *Nov. 19, 1954,* New York, N.Y. *(374,064)* 1.50
1036a Booklet pane of 6, *July 31, 1958,* Wheeling, W. Va. *(135,825)* 4.00
1036b 4c Tagged, *Nov. 2, 1963* 50.00

No. 1036b was supposed to have been issued at Dayton Nov. 2, but a mix-up delayed its issuance there until Nov. 4. About 510 Covers received the Nov. 2 cancellation.

1037 4½c **Hermitage,** *Mar. 16, 1959,* Hermitage, Tenn. *(320,000)* 1.00
1038 5c **Monroe,** *Dec. 2, 1954,* Fredericksburg, Va. *(255,650)* 1.00
1039a 6c **T. Roosevelt,** *Nov. 18, 1955,* New York, N.Y. *(257,551)* 1.00
1040 7c **Wilson,** *Jan. 10, 1956,* Staunton, Va. *(200,111)* 1.00
1041 8c **Statue of Liberty** (flat plate), *Apr. 9, 1954* 1.00
1041B 8c **Statue of Liberty** (rotary press), *Apr. 9, 1954* 1.00

First day cancellation was applied to 340,077 covers bearing one or more of Nos. 1041-1041B.

1042 8c **Statue of Liberty** (Giori press), *Mar. 22, 1958,* Cleveland, O. *(223,899)* 1.00
1042A 8c **Pershing,** *Nov. 17, 1961,* New York, N.Y. *(321,031)* 1.25
1043 9c **Alamo,** *June 14, 1956,* San Antonio, Texas *(207,086)* 1.50
1044 10c **Independence Hall,** *July 4, 1956,* Philadelphia, Pa., *(220,930)* 1.00
1044d 10c Tagged, *July 6, 1966* 40.00
1044A 11c **Statue of Liberty,** *June 15, 1961 (238,905)* 1.25
1044Ac 11c Tagged, *Jan. 11, 1967* 40.00
1045 12c **B. Harrison,** *June 6, 1959,* Oxford, O. *(225,869)* 1.25
1045a 12c Tagged, *May 6, 1968* 40.00
1046 15c **Jay,** *Dec. 12, 1958 (205,680)* 1.25
1046a 15c Tagged, *July 6, 1966* 40.00
1047 20c **Monticello,** *Apr. 13, 1956,* Charlottesville, Va. *(147,860)* 1.25
1048 25c **Revere,** *Apr. 18, 1958,* Boston, Mass. *(196,530)* 1.25
1049a 30c **Lee,** *Sept. 21, 1955,* Norfolk, Va. *(120,166)* 2.00
1050a 40c **Marshall,** *Sept. 24, 1955,* Richmond, Va. *(113,972)* 2.00
1051a 50c **Anthony,** *Aug. 25, 1955,* Louisville, Ky. *(110,220)* 6.00
1052a $1 **Henry,** *Oct. 7, 1955,* Joplin, Mo. *(80,191)* 15.00
1053 $5 **Hamilton,** *Mar. 19, 1956,* Paterson, N.J. *(34,272)* 50.00

1954-73

COIL STAMPS

1054c 1c **Washington,** *Oct. 8, 1954,* Baltimore, Md. *(196,318),* strip of 3 1.00
1054A 1¼c **Palace of Governors,** *June 17, 1960,* Santa Fe, N.M., strip of 3 1.00
1055d 2c **Jefferson,** *Oct. 22, 1954,* St. Louis, Mo. *(162,050),* pair 1.00
1055a 2c Tagged, *May 6, 1968,* pair 32.50
1056 2½c **Bunker Hill,** *Sept. 9, 1959,* Los Angeles, Calif. *(198,680),* pair 2.00
1057c 3c **Statue of Liberty,** *July 20, 1954 (137,139)* 1.00
1058 4c **Lincoln,** *July 31, 1958,* Mandan, N.D. *(184,079)* 1.50
1059 4½c **Hermitage,** *May 1, 1959,* Denver, Colo. *(202,454)* 1.75
1059A 25c **Revere,** *Feb. 25, 1965,* Wheaton, Md. *(184,954)* 1.25
1059Ab 25c Tagged, *Apr. 3, 1973,* New York, N.Y. 40.00

1954

1060 3c **Nebraska Territory,** *May 7,* Nebraska City, Neb. *(401,015)* 1.00
1061 3c **Kansas Territory,** *May 31,* Fort Leavenworth, Kans. *(349,145)* 1.00
1062 3c **George Eastman,** *July 12,* Rochester, N.Y. *(630,448)* 1.00
1063 3c **Lewis & Clark Expedition,** *July 28,* Sioux City, Iowa *(371,557)* 1.50

1955

1064 3c **Pennsylvania Academy of the Fine Arts,** *Jan. 15,* Philadelphia, Pa. *(307,040)* 1.00
1065 3c **Land Grant Colleges,** *Feb. 12,* East Lansing, Mich. *(419,241)* 1.25
1066 8c **Rotary International,** *Feb. 23,* Chicago, Ill. *(350,625)* 3.00
1067 3c **Armed Forces Reserve,** *May 21 (300,436)* 1.25
1068 3c **New Hampshire,** *June 21,* Franconia, N.H. *(330,630)* 2.00
1069 3c **Soo Locks,** *June 28,* Sault Sainte Marie, Mich. *(316,616)* 1.00
1070 3c **Atoms for Peace,** *July 28 (351,940)* 1.00
1071 3c **Fort Ticonderoga,** *Sept. 18,* Fort Ticonderoga, N.Y. *(342,946)* 1.00
1072 3c **Andrew W. Mellon,** *Dec. 20 (278,897)* 1.00

1956

1073 3c **Benjamin Franklin,** *Jan. 17,* Philadelphia, Pa. *(351,260)* 1.25
1074 3c **Booker T. Washington,** *Apr. 5,* Booker T. Washington Birthplace, Va. *(272,659)* 2.00
1075 11c **FIPEX Souvenir Sheet,** *Apr. 28,* New York, N.Y. *(429,327)* 5.00
1076 3c **FIPEX,** *Apr. 30,* New York, N.Y. *(526,090)* 1.00
1077 3c **Wildlife (Turkey),** *May 5,* Fond du Lac, Wis. *(292,121)* 1.75
1078 3c **Wildlife (Antelope),** *June 22,* Gunnison, Colo. *(294,731)* 1.75
1079 3c **Wildlife (Salmon),** *Nov. 9,* Seattle, Wash. *(346,800)* 1.75
1080 3c **Pure Food and Drug Laws,** *June 27,* Washington, D.C. *(411,761)* 1.00
1081 3c **Wheatland,** *Aug. 5,* Lancaster, Pa. *(340,142)* 1.00
1082 3c **Labor Day,** *Sept. 3,* Camden, N.J. *(338,450)* 1.00
1083 3c **Nassau Hall,** *Sept. 22,* Princeton, N.J. *(350,756)* 1.00
1084 3c **Devils Tower,** *Sept. 24,* Devils Tower, Wyo. *(285,090)* 1.25
1085 3c **Children,** *Dec. 15 (305,125)* 1.00

1957

1086 3c **Alexander Hamilton,** *Jan. 11,* New York, N.Y. *(305,117)* 1.00
1087 3c **Polio,** *Jan. 15 (307,630)* 1.50
1088 3c **Coast & Geodetic Survey,** *Feb. 11,* Seattle, Wash. *(309,931)* 1.00
1089 3c **Architects,** *Feb. 23,* New York, N.Y. *(368,840)* 1.25
1090 3c **Steel Industry,** *May 22,* New York, N.Y. *(473,284)* 1.00
1091 3c **Naval Review,** *June 10,* U.S.S. Saratoga, Norfolk, Va. *(365,933)* 1.25
1092 3c **Oklahoma Statehood,** *June 14,* Oklahoma City, Okla. *(327,172)* 1.00
1093 3c **School Teachers,** *July 1,* Philadelphia, Pa. *(357,986)* 2.00
(Spelling error) Philadelpia 8.00
1094 4c **Flag,** *July 4 (523,879)* 1.00
1095 3c **Shipbuilding,** *Aug. 15,* Bath, Maine *(347,432)* 1.25
1096 8c **Ramon Magsaysay,** *Aug. 31 (334,558)* 1.50
1097 3c **Lafayette Bicentenary,** *Sept. 6,* Easton, Pa. *(260,421)* 1.00
Fayetteville, N.C. *(230,000)* 1.00
Louisville, Ky. *(207,856)* 1.00
1098 3c **Wildlife** (Whooping Cranes), *Nov. 22,* New York, N.Y. *(342,970)* 1.25
New Orleans, La. *(154,327)* 1.25
Corpus Christi, Tex. *(280,990)* 1.25
1099 3c **Religious Freedom,** *Dec. 27,* Flushing, N.Y. *(357,770)* 1.00

1958

1100 3c **Gardening-Horticulture,** *Mar. 15,* Ithaca, N.Y. *(451,292)* 1.00
1104 3c **Brussels Exhibition,** *Apr. 17,* Detroit, Mich. *(428,073)* 1.00
1105 3c **James Monroe,** *Apr. 28,* Montross, Va. *(326,988)* 1.00
1106 3c **Minnesota Statehood,** *May 11,* Saint Paul, Minn. *(475,552)* 1.00
1107 3c **International Geophysical Year,** *May 31,* Chicago, Ill. *(397,000)* 1.00
1108 3c **Gunston Hall,** *June 12,* Lorton, Va. *(349,801)* 1.00
1109 3c **Mackinac Bridge,** *June 25,* Mackinac Bridge, Mich. *(445,605)* 1.00
1110 4c **Simon Bolivar,** *July 24* 1.50
1111 8c **Simon Bolivar,** *July 24* 2.25
1110-1111 on one cover 2.00

First day cancellation was applied to 708, 777 covers bearing one or more of Nos. 1110-1111.

1112 4c **Atlantic Cable,** *Aug. 15,* New York, N.Y. *(365,072)* 1.00

1958-59

1113 1c **Lincoln Sesquicentennial,** *Feb. 12, 1959,* Hodgenville, Ky. *(379,862)* block of four 2.00
1114 3c **Lincoln Sesquicentennial,** *Feb. 27, 1959,* New York, N.Y. *(437,737)* 2.00
1115 4c **Lincoln-Douglas Debates,** *Aug. 27, 1958,* Freeport, Ill. *(373,063)* 2.00
1116 4c **Lincoln Sesquicentennial,** *May, 30, 1959 (894,887)* 2.00

1958

1117 4c **Lajos Kossuth,** *Sept. 19* 1.25
1118 8c **Lajos Kossuth,** *Sept. 19* 1.50
1117-1118 on one cover 2.25

First day cancellation was applied to 722,188 covers bearing one or more of Nos. 1117-1118.

1119 4c **Freedom of Press,** *Sept. 22,* Columbia, Mo. *(411,752)* 1.00
1120 4c **Overland Mail,** *Oct. 10,* San Francisco, Cal. *(352,760)* 1.00
1121 4c **Noah Webster,** *Oct. 16,* West Hartford, Conn. *(364,608)* 1.00
1122 4c **Forest Conservation,** *Oct. 27,* Tucson, Ariz. *(405,959)* 1.00
1123 4c **Fort Duquesne,** *Nov. 25,* Pittsburgh, Pa. *(421,764)* 1.00

1959

1124 4c **Oregon Statehood,** *Feb. 14,* Astoria, Ore. *(452,764)* 1.00
1125 4c **San Martin,** *Feb. 25* 1.50
1126 8c **San Martin,** *Feb. 25* 2.25
1125-1126 on one cover 2.00

First day cancellation was applied to 910,208 covers bearing one or more of No. 1125-1126.

1127 4c **NATO,** *Apr. 1 (361,040)* 1.25
1128 4c **Arctic Exploration,** *Apr. 6,* Cresson, Pa. *(397,770)* 1.00
1129 8c **World Trade,** *Apr. 20 (503,618)* 1.00
1130 4c **Silver Centennial,** *June 8,* Virginia City, Nev. *(337,233)* 1.00
1131 4c **St. Lawrence Seaway,** *June 26,* Massena, N.Y. *(543,211)* 1.25
1132 4c **Flag** (49 stars), *July 4,* Auburn, N.Y. *(523,773)* 1.00

1133 4c **Soil Conservation,** *Aug. 26,* Rapid City, S.D. *(400,613)* 1.00
1134 4c **Petroleum Industry,** *Aug. 27,* Titusville, Pa. *(801,859)* 1.50
1135 4c **Dental Health,** *Sept. 14,* New York, N.Y. *(649,813)* 3.50
1136 4c **Reuter,** *Sept. 29* 1.25
1137 8c **Reuter,** *Sept. 29* 1.50
1136-1137 on one cover 2.25

First day cancellation was applied to 1,207,933 covers bearing one or more of Nos. 1136-1137.

1138 4c **Dr. Ephraim McDowell,** *Dec. 3,* Danville, Ky. *(344,603)* 1.25

1960-61

1139 4c **Washington "Credo,"** *Jan. 20, 1960,* Mount Vernon, Va. *(438,335)* 1.25
1140 4c **Franklin "Credo,"** *Mar. 31, 1960,* Philadelphia, Pa. *(497,913)* 1.25
1141 4c **Jefferson "Credo,"** *May 18, 1960,* Charlottesville, Va. *(454,903)* 1.25
1142 4c **Francis Scott Key "Credo,"** *Sept. 14, 1960,* Baltimore, Md. *(501,129)* 1.25
1143 4c **Lincoln "Credo,"** *Nov. 19, 1960,* New York, N.Y. *(467,780)* 1.50
1144 4c **Patrick Henry "Credo,"** *Jan. 11, 1961,* Richmond, Va. *(415,252)* 1.25

1960

1145 4c **Boy Scouts,** *Feb. 8 (1,419,955)* 4.00
1146 4c **Olympic Winter Games,** *Feb. 18,* Olympic Valley, Calif, *(516,456)* 1.00
1147 4c **Masaryk,** *Mar. 7* 1.25
1148 8c **Masaryk,** *Mar. 7* 1.50
1147-1148 on one cover 2.25

First day cancellation was applied to 1,710,726 covers bearing one or more of Nos. 1147-1148.

1149 4c **World Refugee Year,** *Apr. 7 (413,298)* 1.00
1150 4c **Water Conservation,** *Apr. 18 (648,988)* 1.00
1151 4c **SEATO,** *May 31 (514,926)* 1.00
1152 4c **American Woman,** *June 2 (830,385)* 1.25
1153 4c **50-Star Flag,** *July 4,* Honolulu, Hawaii *(820,900)* 1.00
1154 4c **Pony Express Centennial,** *July 19,* Sacramento, Calif, *(520,223)* 1.75
1155 4c **Employ the Handicapped,** *Aug. 28,* New York, N.Y. *(439,638)* 1.50
1156 4c **World Forestry Congress,** *Aug. 29,* Seattle, Wash. *(350,848)* 1.00
1157 4c **Mexican Independence,** *Sept. 16,* Los Angeles, Calif, *(360,297)* 1.00
1158 4c **U.S.-Japan Treaty,** *Sept. 28 (545,150)* 1.00
1159 4c **Paderewski,** *Oct. 8* 1.25
1160 8c **Paderewski,** *Oct. 8* 1.50
1159-1160 on one cover 2.25

First day cancellation was applied to 1,057,438 covers bearing one or more of Nos. 1159-1160.

1161 4c **Robert A. Taft,** *Oct. 10,* Cincinnati, Ohio *(312,116)* 1.00
1162 4c **Wheels of Freedom,** *Oct. 15,* Detroit, Mich. *(380,551)* 1.00
1163 4c **Boys' Clubs,** *Oct. 18,* New York, N.Y. *(435,009)* 1.00
1164 4c **Automated P.O.,** *Oct. 20,* Providence, R.I. *(458,237)* 1.00
1165 4c **Mannerheim,** *Oct. 26* 1.25
1166 8c **Mannerheim,** *Oct. 26* 1.50
1165-1166 on one cover 2.25

First day cancellation was applied to 1,168,770 covers bearing one or more of Nos. 1165-1166.

1167 4c **Camp Fire Girls,** *Nov. 1,* New York, N.Y. *(324,944)* 3.00
1168 4c **Garibaldi,** *Nov. 2* 1.25
1169 8c **Garibaldi,** *Nov. 2* 1.50
1168-1169 on one cover 2.25

First day cancellation was applied to 1,001,490 covers bearing one or more of Nos. 1168-1169.

1170 4c **Senator George,** *Nov. 5,* Vienna, Ga. *(278,890)* 1.00
1171 4c **Andrew Carnegie,** *Nov. 25,* New York, N.Y. *(318,180)* 1.00
1172 4c **John Foster Dulles,** *Dec. 6 (400,055)* 1.00
1173 4c **Echo I,** *Dec. 15 (583,747)* 2.50

1961-65

1174 4c **Gandhi,** *Jan. 26, 1961* 1.25
1175 8c **Gandhi,** *Jan. 26, 1961* 1.75
1174-1175 on one cover 2.50

First day cancellation was applied to 1,013,515 covers bearing one or more of Nos. 1174-1175.

1176 4c **Range Conservation,** *Feb. 2, 1961,* Salt Lake City, Utah *(357,101)* 1.00
1177 4c **Horace Greeley,** *Feb. 3, 1961,* Chappaqua, N.Y. *(359,205)* 1.00
1178 4c **Fort Sumter,** *Apr. 12, 1961,* Charleston, S.C. *(602,599)* 4.00
1179 4c **Battle of Shiloh,** *Apr. 7, 1962,* Shiloh, Tenn. *(526,062)* 4.00
1180 5c **Battle of Gettysburg,** *July 1, 1963,* Gettysburg, Pa. *(600,205)* 4.00
1181 5c **Battle of Wilderness,** *May 5, 1964,* Fredericksburg, Va. *(450,904)* 4.00
1182 5c **Appomattox,** *Apr. 9, 1965,* Appomattox, Va. *(653,121)* 4.00

1961

1183 4c **Kansas Statehood,** *May 10,* Council Grove, Kansas *(480,561)* 1.00
1184 4c **Senator Norris,** *July 11 (482,875)* 1.00
1185 4c **Naval Aviation,** *Aug. 20,* San Diego, Calif. *(416,391)* 1.50
1186 4c **Workmen's Compensation,** *Sept. 4,* Milwaukee, Wis, *(410,236)* 1.00
1187 4c **Frederic Remington,** *Oct. 4 (723,443)* 1.25
1188 4c **China Republic,** *Oct. 10 (463,900)* 5.50
1189 4c **Naismith-Basketball,** *Nov. 6,* Springfield, Mass. *(479,917)* 7.50
1190 4c **Nursing,** *Dec. 28 (964,005)* 10.00

1962

1191 4c **New Mexico Statehood,** *Jan. 6,* Sante Fe, N.M. *(365,330)* 2.00
1192 4c **Arizona Statehood,** *Feb. 14,* Phoenix, Ariz. *(508,216)* 1.75
1193 4c **Project Mercury,** *Feb. 20,* Cape Canaveral, Fla. *(3,000,000)* 3.00
Any other city 5.00
1194 4c **Malaria Eradication,** *Mar. 30 (554,175)* 1.00
1195 4c **Charles Evans Hughes,** *Apr. 11 (544,424)* 1.00
1196 4c **Seattle World's Fair,** *Apr. 25,* Seattle, Wash. *(771,856)* 1.25
1197 4c **Louisiana Statehood,** *Apr. 30,* New Orleans, La. *(436,681)* 1.00
1198 4c **Homestead Act,** *May 20,* Beatrice, Nebr. *(487,450)* 1.00
1199 4c **Girl Scouts,** *July 24,* Burlington, Vt. *(634,347)* 5.00
1200 4c **Brien McMahon,** *July 28,* Norwalk, Conn. *(384,419)* 1.00
1201 4c **Apprenticeship,** *Aug. 31 (1,003,548)* 1.00
1202 4c **Sam Rayburn,** *Sept. 16,* Bonham, Texas *(401,042)* 1.50
1203 4c **Dag Hammarskjold,** *Oct. 23,* New York, N.Y. *(500,683)* 1.00
1203a 4c **Dag Hammarskjold,** original yellow inverted, *Oct. 23,* New York, N.Y. *2,000.*
1204 4c **Hammarskjold,** yellow inverted, *Nov. 16,* (about *75,000)* 5.00
1205 4c **Christmas,** *Nov. 1,* Pittsburgh, Pa. *(491,312)* 1.10
1206 4c **Higher Education,** *Nov. 14 (627,347)* 1.25
1207 4c **Winslow Homer,** *Dec. 15,* Gloucester, Mass. *(498,866)* 1.25

1963-66

1208 5c **Flag,** *Jan. 9, 1963 (696,185)* 1.00
1208a 5c Tagged, *Aug. 25, 1966* 30.00

1962-66

REGULAR ISSUE

1209 1c **Jackson,** *Mar. 22, 1963,* New York, N.Y. *(392,363),* block of 5 or 6 1.00
1209a 1c Tagged, *July 6, 1966,* block of 5 or 6 30.00
1213 5c **Washington,** *Nov. 23, 1962,* New York, N.Y. *(360,531)* 1.00
1213a Booklet pane of 5 + label, *Nov. 23, 1962,* New York, N.Y. *(111,452)* 4.00
1213b 5c Tagged, *Oct. 28, 1963,* Dayton, Ohio (about *15,000)* 30.00
1213c Booklet pane of 5 + label, tagged, *Oct. 28, 1963,* Dayton, Ohio 100.00
Washington, D.C. *(750)* 110.00
1225 1c **Jackson,** Coil, *May 31, 1963,* Chicago, Ill. *(238,952),* pair and strip of 3 1.00
1225a 1c Coil, tagged, *July 6, 1966,* pair and strip of 3 30.00
1229 5c **Washington,** Coil, *Nov. 23, 1962,* New York, N.Y. *(184,627)* 1.00
1229a 5c Coil, tagged, *Oct. 28, 1963,* Dayton, Ohio (about *2,000)* 30.00

1963

1230 5c **Carolina Charter,** *Apr. 6,* Edenton, N.C. *(426,200)* 1.00
1231 5c **Food for Peace,** *June 4 (624,342)* 1.00
1232 5c **West Virginia Statehood,** *June 20,* Wheeling, W. Va. *(413,389)* 1.00
1233 5c **Emancipation Proclamation,** *Aug. 16,* Chicago, Ill, *(494,886)* 1.75
1234 5c **Alliance for Progress,** *Aug. 17 (528,095)* 1.00
1235 5c **Cordell Hull,** *Oct. 5* Carthage, Tenn. *(391,631)* 1.00
1236 5c **Eleanor Roosevelt,** *Oct. 11 (860,155)* 1.25
1237 5c **Science,** *Oct. 14 (504,503)* 1.25
1238 5c **City Mail Delivery,** *Oct. 26 (544,806)* 1.25
1239 5c **Red Cross,** *Oct. 29 (557,678)* 2.00
1240 5c **Christmas,** *Nov. 1,* Santa Claus, Ind. *(458,619)* 1.25
1240a 5c **Christmas,** tagged, *Nov. 2,* (about *500)* 60.00

Note below No. 1036b also applies to No. 1240a.

1241 5c **Audubon,** *Dec. 7,* Henderson, Ky. *(518,855)* 1.25

1964

1242 5c **Sam Houston,** *Jan. 10,* Houston, Tex. *(487,986)* 1.75
1243 5c **Charles Russell,** *Mar. 19,* Great Falls, Mont. *(658,745)* 1.25
1244 5c **N.Y. World's Fair,** *Apr. 22,* World's Fair, N.Y. *(1,656,346)* 2.00
1245 5c **John Muir,** *Apr. 29,* Martinez, Calif. *(446,925)* 1.50
1246 5c **John F. Kennedy,** *May 29,* Boston, Mass. *(2,003,096)* 2.50
Any other city 4.50
1247 5c **New Jersey Tercentenary,** *June 15,* Elizabeth, N.J. *(526,879)* 1.00
1248 5c **Nevada Statehood,** *July 22,* Carson City, Nev. *(584,973)* 1.00
1249 5c **Register & Vote,** *Aug. 1 (533,439)* 1.25
1250 5c **Shakespeare,** *Aug. 14,* Stratford, Conn. *(524,053)* 2.00
1251 5c **Drs. Mayo,** *Sept. 11,* Rochester, Minn. *(674,846)* 3.00
1252 5c **American Music,** *Oct. 15,* New York, N.Y. *(466,107)* 1.50
1253 5c **Homemakers,** *Oct. 26,* Honolulu, Hawaii *(435,392)* 1.00
1257b 5c **Christmas,** *Nov. 9,* Bethlehem, Pa. 3.00
1254-1257, any single 1.00
1257c 5c Tagged, *Nov. 10,* Dayton, O. 57.50
1254a-1257a, any single 30.00

First day cancellation was applied to 794,900 covers bearing Nos. 1254-1257 in singles or multiples and at Dayton to about 2,700 covers bearing Nos. 1254a-1257a in singles or multiples.

1258 5c **Verrazano-Narrows Bridge,** *Nov. 21,* Staten Island, N.Y. *(619,780)* 1.00
1259 5c **Fine Arts,** *Dec. 2 (558,046)* 1.00
1260 5c **Amateur Radio,** *Dec. 15,* Anchorage, Alaska *(452,255)* 5.00

1965

1261 5c **Battle of New Orleans,** *Jan. 8,* New Orleans, La. *(466,029)* 1.00
1262 5c **Physical Fitness-Sokol,** *Feb. 15 (864,848)* 1.25
1263 5c **Cancer Crusade,** *Apr. 1 (744,485)* 2.50
1264 5c **Churchill,** *May 13,* Fulton, Mo. *(773,580)* 2.00
1265 5c **Magna Carta,** *June 15,* Jamestown, Va. *(479,065)* 1.00
1266 5c **Intl. Cooperation Year,** *June 26,* San Francisco, Cal. *(402,925)* 1.00
1267 5c **Salvation Army,** *July 2,* New York, N.Y. *(634,228)* 3.00
1268 5c **Dante,** *July 17,* San Francisco, Cal. *(424,893)* 1.00
1269 5c **Herbert Hoover,** *Aug. 10,* West Branch, Iowa *(698,182)* 1.00
1270 5c **Robert Fulton,** *Aug. 19,* Clermont, N.Y. *(550,330)* 1.00
1271 5c **Florida Settlement,** *Aug. 28,* St. Augustine, Fla. *(465,000)* 1.00
1272 5c **Traffic Safety,** *Sept. 3,* Baltimore, Md. *(527,075)* 1.00
1273 5c **Copley,** *Sept. 17 (613,484)* 1.00
1274 11c **Intl. Telecommunication Union,** *Oct. 6 (332,818)* 1.10
1275 5c **Adlai Stevenson,** *Oct. 23,* Bloomington, Ill. *(755,656)* 1.00
1276 5c **Christmas,** *Nov. 2,* Silver Bell, Ariz. *(705,039)* 1.00
1276a 5c Tagged, *Nov. 15,* (about *300)* 50.00

1965-78

PROMINENT AMERICANS ISSUE

1278 1c **Jefferson,** *Jan. 12, 1968,* Jeffersonville, Ind., block of 5 or 6 1.00
1278a Booklet pane of 8, *Jan. 12, 1968,* Jeffersonville, Ind. 2.50
1278b Booklet pane of 4 + 2 labels, *May 10, 1971* 11.50

First day cancellation was applied to 655,680 covers bearing one or more of Nos. 1278, 1278a and 1299.

1279 1¼c **Gallatin,** *Jan. 30, 1967,* Gallatin, Mo. *(439,010)* 1.00
1280 2c **Wright,** *June 8, 1966,* Spring Green, Wis. *(460,427)* 1.00
1280a Booklet pane of 5 + label, *Jan. 8, 1968,* Buffalo, N.Y. *(147,244)* 3.50
1280c Booklet pane of 6, *May 7, 1971,* Spokane, Wash. 15.00
1281 3c **Parkman,** *Sept. 16, 1967,* Boston, Mass. *(518,355)* 1.00
1282 4c **Lincoln,** *Nov. 19, 1965,* New York, N.Y. *(445,629)* 1.50
1282a 4c Tagged, *Dec. 1, 1965,* Dayton, O. (about *2,000)* 30.00
Washington, D.C. *(1,200)* 32.50
1283 5c **Washington,** *Feb. 22, 1966 (525,372)* 1.00
1283a 5c Tagged, *Feb. 23, 1966,* (about *900)* 30.00
Dayton, Ohio (about *200)* 75.00
1283B 5c **Washington,** Redrawn, *Nov. 17, 1967,* New York, N.Y. *(328,983)* 1.00
1284 6c **Roosevelt,** *Jan. 29, 1966,* Hyde Park, N.Y. *(448,631)* 1.00
1284a 6c Tagged, *Dec. 29, 1966* 40.00
1284b Booklet pane of 8, *Dec. 28, 1967* 2.75
1284c Booklet pane of 5 + label, *Jan. 9, 1968* 100.00
1285 8c **Einstein,** *Mar. 14, 1966,* Princeton, N.J. *(366,803)* 3.00
1285a 8c Tagged, *July 6, 1966* 40.00
1286 10c **Jackson,** *Mar. 15, 1967,* Hermitage, Tenn. *(255,945)* 1.00
1286A 12c **Ford,** *July 30, 1968,* Greenfield Village, Mich. *(342,850)* 1.50
1287 13c **Kennedy,** *May 29, 1967,* Brookline, Mass. *(391,195)* 1.75
1288 15c **Holmes,** type I, *Mar. 8, 1968 (322,970)* 1.00
1288B 15c **Holmes,** from bklt., *June 14, 1978,* Boston, Mass. 1.00
1288Bc Booklet pane of 8 3.00

First day cancellation was applied to 387,119 covers bearing one or more of Nos. 1288B and 1305E.

1289 20c **Marshall,** *Oct. 24, 1967,* Lexington, Va. *(221,206)* 1.10
1289a 20c Tagged, *Apr. 3, 1973,* New York, N.Y. 40.00
1290 25c **Douglass,** *Feb. 14, 1967 (213,730)* 2.50
1290a 25c Tagged, *Apr. 3, 1973,* New York, N.Y. 45.00
1291 30c **Dewey,** *Oct. 21, 1968,* Burlington, Vt. *(162,790)* 1.75
1291a 30c Tagged, *Apr. 3, 1973,* New York, N.Y. 45.00
1292 40c **Paine,** *Jan. 29, 1968,* Philadelphia, Pa. *(157,947)* 1.75
1292a 40c Tagged, *Apr. 3, 1973,* New York, N.Y. 45.00
1293 50c **Stone,** *Aug. 13, 1968,* Dorchester, Mass. *(140,410)* 2.50
1293a 50c Tagged, *Apr. 3, 1973,* New York, N.Y. 45.00
1294 $1 **O'Neill,** *Oct. 16, 1967,* New London, Conn. *(103,102)* 6.00
1294a $1 Tagged, *Apr. 3, 1973,* New York, N.Y. 60.00
1295 $5 **Moore,** *Dec. 3, 1966,* Smyrna, Del. *(41,130)* 40.00
1295a $5 Tagged, *Apr. 3, 1973,* New York, N.Y. 120.00

First day cancellation was applied to 17,533 covers bearing one or more of Nos. 1059b, 1289a, 1290a, 1291a, 1292a, 1293a, 1294a and 1295a.

COIL STAMPS

1297 3c **Parkman,** *Nov. 4, 1975,* Pendleton, Ore. *(166,798)* 1.00
1298 6c **Roosevelt,** Perf. 10 Horiz., *Dec. 28, 1967* 1.00

First day cancellation was applied to 312,330 covers bearing one or more of Nos. 1298 and 1284b.

1299 1c **Jefferson,** *Jan. 12, 1968,* Jeffersonville, Ind., pair and strip of 3 1.00
1303 4c **Lincoln,** *May 28, 1966,* Springfield, Ill. *(322,563)* 1.50
1304 5c **Washington,** *Sept. 8, 1966,* Cincinnati, O. *(245,400)* 1.00
1305 6c **Roosevelt,** Perf. 10 vert., *Feb. 28, 1968 (317,199)* 1.00
1305E 15c **Holmes,** type I, *June 14, 1978,* Boston, Mass. 1.00
1305C $1 **O'Neill,** *Jan. 12, 1973,* Hempstead, N.Y. *(121,217)* 4.00

1966

1306 5c **Migratory Bird Treaty,** *Mar. 16,* Pittsburgh, Pa. *(555,485)* 1.75
1307 5c **Humane Treatment of Animals,** *Apr. 9,* New York, N.Y. *(524,420)* 1.25
1308 5c **Indiana Statehood,** *Apr. 16,* Corydon, Ind. *(575,557)* 1.00
1309 5c **Circus,** *May 2,* Delavan, Wis. *(754,076)* 2.00
1310 5c **SIPEX,** *May 21 (637,802)* 1.00
1311 5c **SIPEX, souvenir sheet,** *May 23 (700,882)* 1.10
1312 5c **Bill of Rights,** *July 1,* Miami Beach, Fla. *(562,920)* 1.75
1313 5c **Polish Millennium,** *July 30 (715,603)* 1.50
1314 5c **Natl. Park Service,** *Aug. 25,* Yellowstone National Park, Wyo. *(528,170)* 1.00
1314a 5c Tagged, *Aug. 26* 35.00
1315 5c **Marine Corps Reserve,** *Aug. 29 (585,923)* 1.50
1315a 5c Tagged, *Aug. 29* 35.00
1316 5c **Gen. Fed. of Women's Clubs,** *Sept. 12,* New York, N.Y. *(383,334)* 1.25
1316a 5c Tagged, *Sept. 13* 35.00
1317 5c **Johnny Appleseed,** *Sept. 24,* Leominster, Mass. *(794,610)* 1.50
1317a 5c Tagged, *Sept. 26* 35.00
1318 5c **Beautification of America,** *Oct. 5 (564,440)* 1.00
1318a 5c Tagged, *Oct. 5* 35.00
1319 5c **Great River Road,** *Oct. 21,* Baton Rouge, La. *(330,933)* 1.00
1319a 5c Tagged, *Oct. 22* 35.00
1320 5c **Savings Bond-Servicemen,** *Oct. 26,* Sioux City, Iowa *(444,421)* 1.00
1320a 5c Tagged, *Oct. 27* 35.00
1321 5c **Christmas,** *Nov. 1,* Christmas, Mich. *(537,650)* 1.00
1321a 5c Tagged, *Nov. 2* 35.00
1322 5c **Mary Cassatt,** *Nov. 17 (593,389)* 1.00
1322a 5c Tagged, *Nov. 17* 35.00

1967

1323 5c **National Grange,** *Apr. 17 (603,460)* 1.00
1324 5c **Canada Centenary,** *May 25,* Montreal, Canada *(711,795)* 1.00
1325 5c **Erie Canal,** *July 4,* Rome, N.Y. *(784,611)* 1.00
1326 5c **Search for Peace-Lions,** *July 5,* Chicago, Ill. *(393,197)* 1.00
1327 5c **Thoreau,** *July 12,* Concord, Mass. *(696,789)* 1.00
1328 5c **Nebraska Statehood,** *July 29,* Lincoln, Nebr. *(1,146,957)* 1.00
1329 5c **Voice of America,** *Aug. 1 (455,190)* 2.00
1330 5c **Davy Crockett,** *Aug. 17,* San Antonio, Tex. *(462,291)* 1.25
1331a 5c **Space Accomplishments,** *Sept. 29,* Kennedy Space Center, Fla. *(667,267)* 8.00
1331-1332, any single 3.00
1333 5c **Urban Planning,** *Oct. 2 (389,009)* 1.00
1334 5c **Finland Independence,** *Oct. 6,* Finland, Minn. *(408,532)* 1.00
1335 5c **Thomas Eakins,** *Nov. 2 (648,054)* 1.40
1336 5c **Christmas,** *Nov. 6,* Bethlehem, Ga. *(462,118)* 1.25
1337 5c **Mississippi Statehood,** *Dec. 11,* Natchez, Miss. *(379,612)* 1.00

1968-71

1338 6c **Flag** (Giori), *Jan. 24, 1968 (412,120)* 1.00
1338A 6c **Flag coil,** *May 30, 1969,* Chicago, Ill. *(248,434)* 1.00
1338D 6c **Flag** (Huck) *Aug. 7, 1970 (365,280)* 1.00
1338F 8c **Flag,** *May 10, 1971* 1.00
1338G 8c **Flag coil,** *May 10, 1971* 1.00

First day cancellation (May 10) was applied to 235,543 covers bearing one or more of Nos. 1338F-1338G.

1968

1339 6c **Illinois Statehood,** *Feb. 12,* Shawneetown, Ill. *(761,640)* 1.00
1340 6c **HemisFair'68,** *Mar. 30,* San Antonio, Tex. *(469,909)* 1.00
1341 $1 **Airlift,** *Apr. 4,* Seattle, Wash. *(105,088)* 7.00
1342 6c **Youth-Elks,** *May 1,* Chicago, Ill. *(354,711)* 1.00
1343 6c **Law and Order,** *May 17 (407,081)* 2.50
1344 6c **Register and Vote,** *June 27 (355,685)* 1.00
1354a 6c **Historic Flag series of 10,** *July 4,* Pittsburgh, Pa. *(2,924,962)* 15.00
1345-1354, any single 3.00
1355 6c **Disney,** *Sept. 11,* Marceline, Mo. *(499,505)* 25.00
1356 6c **Marquette,** *Sept. 20,* Sault Ste. Marie, Mich. *(379,710)* 1.00
1357 6c **Daniel Boone,** *Sept. 26,* Frankfort, Ky. *(333,440)* 1.25
1358 6c **Arkansas River,** *Oct. 1,* Little Rock, Ark. *(358,025)* 1.00
1359 6c **Leif Erikson,** *Oct. 9,* Seattle, Wash. *(376,565)* 1.00
1360 6c **Cherokee Strip,** *Oct. 15,* Ponca, Okla. *(339,330)* 1.00
1361 6c **John Trumbull,** *Oct. 18,* New Haven, Conn. *(378,285)* 2.00
1362 6c **Waterfowl Conservation,** *Oct. 24,* Cleveland, Ohio, *(349,719)* 1.25
1363 6c **Christmas,** tagged, *Nov. 1 (739,055)* 1.25
1363a 6c Untagged, *Nov. 2* 10.00
1364 6c **American Indian,** *Nov. 4 (415,964)* 1.25

1969

1368a 6c **Beautification of America,** *Jan. 16 (1,094,184)* 4.00
1365-1368, any single 1.00
1369 6c **American Legion,** *Mar. 15 (632,035)* 1.00
1370 6c **Grandma Moses,** *May 1 (367,880)* 1.50
1371 6c **Apollo 8,** *May 5,* Houston, Texas *(908,634)* 2.25
1372 6c **W.C. Handy,** *May 17,* Memphis, Tenn. *(398,216)* 2.25
1373 6c **California Bicentenary,** *July 16,* San Diego, Calif, *(530,210)* 1.00
1374 6c **J.W. Powell,** *Aug. 1,* Page, Ariz. *(434,433)* 1.00
1375 6c **Alabama Statehood,** *Aug. 2,* Huntsville, Ala. *(485,801)* 1.00
1379a 6c **Botanical Congress,** *Aug. 23,* Seattle, Wash. *(737,935)* 5.00
1376-1379, any single 1.50
1380 6c **Dartmouth Case,** *Sept. 22,* Hanover, N.H. *(416,327)* 1.00
1381 6c **Professional Baseball,** *Sept. 24,* Cincinnati, Ohio *(414,942)* 12.00
1382 6c **Intercollegiate Football,** *Sept. 26,* New Brunswick, N.J. *(414,860)* 6.50
1383 6c **Dwight D. Eisenhower,** *Oct. 14,*Abilene, Kans. *(1,009,560)* 1.00
1384 6c **Christmas,** *Nov. 3,* Christmas, Fla. *(555,500)* 1.25
1385 6c **Hope for Crippled,** *Nov. 20,* Columbus, Ohio *(342,676)* 1.25
1386 6c **William M. Harnett,** *Dec. 3,* Boston, Mass. *(408,860)* 1.00

1970-74

1390a 6c **National History,** *May 6, 1970,* New York, N.Y. *(834,260)* 4.00
1387-1390, any single 1.50
1391 6c **Maine Statehood,** *July 9, 1970,* Portland, Maine, *(472,165)* 2.75
1392 6c **Wildlife Conservation,** *July 20, 1970,* Custer, S.D. *(309,418)* 1.00
1393 6c **Eisenhower,** *Aug. 6, 1970* 1.00
1393a Booklet pane of 8 3.00
1393b Booklet pane of 5 + label 1.50

First day cancellations were applied to 823,540 covers bearing one or more of Nos. 1393 and 1401.

1393D 7c **Franklin,** *Oct. 20, 1972,* Philadelphia, Pa. *(309,276)* 1.00
1394 8c **Eisenhower** (multi), *May 10, 1971* 1.00
1395 8c **Eisenhower** (claret), *May 10, 1971* 1.00
1395a Booklet pane of 8 2.50
1395b Booklet pane of 6 2.50
1395c Booklet pane of 4 + 2 labels, *Jan. 28, 1972,* Casa Grande, Ariz. 2.25
1395d Booklet pane of 7 + label, *Jan. 28, 1972,* Casa Grande, Ariz. 2.25

First day cancellations were applied to 813,947 covers bearing one or more of Nos. 1394, 1395 and 1402. First day cancellations were applied to 181,601 covers bearing one or more of Nos. 1395c or 1395d.

1396 8c **Postal Service Emblem,** *July 1, 1971, any city (est. 16,300,000)* 1.00

First day cancels from over 16,000 different cities are known. Some are rare.

1397 14c **Fiorello H. LaGuardia,** *Apr. 24, 1972,* New York, N.Y. *(180,114)* 1.00
1398 16c **Ernie Pyle,** *May 7, 1971 (444,410)* 1.50
1399 18c **Elizabeth Blackwell,** *Jan. 23, 1974,* Geneva, N.Y. *(217,938)* 1.25
1400 21c **Amadeo Giannini,** *June 27, 1973,* San Mateo, Calif. *(282,520)* 1.50
1401 6c **Eisenhower coil,** *Aug. 6, 1970* 1.00
1402 8c **Eisenhower coil,** *May 10, 1971* 1.00

1970

1405 6c **Edgar Lee Masters,** *Aug. 22,* Petersburg Ill. *(372,804)* 1.00
1406 6c **Woman Suffrage,** *Aug. 26,* Adams, Mass. *(508,142)* 1.00
1407 6c **South Carolina Anniv.** *Sept. 12,* Charleston, S.C. *(533,000)* 1.00
1408 6c **Stone Mt. Memorial,** *Sept. 19,* Stone Mountain, Ga. *(558,546)* 1.00
1409 6c **Fort Snelling,** *Oct. 17,* Fort Snelling, Minn. *(497,611)* 1.00
1413a 6c **Anti-Pollution,** *Oct. 28,* San Clemente, Calif. *(1,033,147)* 4.00
1410-1413, any single 1.25
1414 6c **Christmas (Nativity),** *Nov. 5* 1.25
1414a 6c Precanceled, *Nov. 5* 7.50
1418b 6c **Christmas,** *Nov. 5* 5.50
1415-1418, any single 1.50
1414-1418 on one cover 8.50
1418c 6c Precanceled, *Nov. 5* 15.00
1415a-1418a, any single 5.00
1414a-1418a on one cover 30.00

First day cancellation was applied to 2,014,450 covers bearing one or more of Nos. 1414-1418 or 1414a-1418a.

1419 6c **United Nations,** *Nov. 20,* New York, N.Y. *(474,070)* 1.50
1420 6c **Pilgrims' Landing,** *Nov. 21,* Plymouth, Mass. *(629,850)* 1.00
1421 6c **Disabled Veterans,** *Nov. 24,* Cincinnati, Ohio, or Montgomery, Ala. 2.00
1422 6c **U.S. Servicemen,** *Nov. 24,* Cincinnati, Ohio, or Montgomery, Ala. 2.00
1421a 3.00

First day cancellation was applied to 476,610 covers at Cincinnati and 336,417 at Montgomery, each cover bearing one or more of Nos. 1421-1422.

1971

1423 6c **Wool Industry,** *Jan. 19,* Las Vegas, Nev. *(379,911)* 1.00
1424 6c **MacArthur,** *Jan. 26,* Norfolk, Va. *(720,035)* 1.75
1425 6c **Blood Donor,** *Mar. 12,* New York, N.Y. *(644,497)* 1.00
1426 8c **Missouri Sesquicentennial,** *May 8,* Independence, Mo. *(551,000)* 1.00
1430a 8c **Wildlife Conservation,** *June 12,* Avery Island, La. *(679,483)* 3.00
1427-1430, any single 1.25
1431 8c **Antarctic Treaty,** *June 23 (419,200)* 1.00
1432 8c **American Revolution Bicentennial,** *July 4 (434,930)* 1.00
1433 8c **John Sloan,** *Aug. 2,* Lock Haven, Pa. *(482,265)* 1.00
1434a 8c **Space Achievement Decade,** *Aug. 2,* Kennedy Space Center, Fla. *(1,403,644)* 2.00
Houston, Texas *(811,560)* 2.00
Huntsville, Ala. *(524,000)* 2.00
1436 8c **Emily Dickinson,** *Aug. 28,* Amherst, Mass. *(498,180)* 1.00
1437 8c **San Juan,** *Sept. 12,* San Juan, P.R. *(501,668)* 1.00
1438 8c **Drug Abuse,** *Oct. 4,* Dallas, Texas *(425,330)* 1.00
1439 8c **CARE,** *Oct. 27,* New York, N.Y. *(402,121)* 1.00
1443a 8c **Historic Preservation,** *Oct. 29,* San Diego, Calif. *(783,242)* 3.00
1440-1443, any single 1.25
1444 8c **Christmas (religious),** *Nov. 10* 1.25
1445 8c **Christmas (secular),** *Nov. 10* 1.25
1444-1445 on one cover 1.50

First day cancellation was applied to 348,038 covers with No. 1444 and 580,062 with No. 1445.

1972

1446 8c **Sidney Lanier,** *Feb. 3,* Macon Ga. *(394,800)* 1.00
1447 8c **Peace Corps,** *Feb. 11 (453,660)* 1.00
1451a 2c **National Parks Centennial,** *Apr. 5,* Hatteras, N.C., block of 4 *(505,697)* 3.00
1452 6c **National Parks,** *June 26,* Vienna, Va. *(403,396)* 1.00
1453 8c **National Parks,** *Mar. 1,* Yellowstone National Park, Wyo. 1.00
Washington, D.C. *(847,500)* 1.00
1454 15c **National Parks,** *July 28,* Mt. McKinley National Park, Alaska *(491,456)* 1.00

1455 8c **Family Planning,** *Mar. 18,* New York, N.Y. *(691,385)* 1.00
1459a 8c **Colonial Craftsmen** (Rev. Bicentennial), *July 4,* Williamsburg, Va. *(1,914,976)* 2.50
1456-1459, any single 1.00
1460 6c **Olympics,** *Aug. 17* 1.00
1461 8c **Winter Olympics,** *Aug. 17* 1.00
1462 15c **Olympics,** *Aug. 17* 1.00
1460-1462 and C85 on one cover 2.00

First day cancellation was applied to 971,536 covers bearing one or more of Nos. 1460-1462 and C85.

1463 8c **P.T.A.,** *Sept. 15,* San Francisco, Cal. *(523,454)* 1.00
1467a 8c **Wildlife,** *Sept. 20,* Warm Springs, Ore. *(733,778)* 3.00
1464-1467, any single 1.50
1468 8c **Mail Order,** *Sept. 27,* Chicago, Ill. *(759,666)* 1.00
1469 8c **Osteopathy,** *Oct. 9,* Miami, Fla. *(607,160)* 1.50
1470 8c **Tom Sawyer,** *Oct. 13,* Hannibal, Mo. *(459,013)* 1.50
1471 8c **Christmas (religious),** *Nov. 9* 1.00
1472 8c **Christmas (secular),** *Nov. 9* 1.00
1471-1472 on one cover 2.00

First day cancellation was applied to 713,821 covers bearing one or more of Nos. 1471-1472.

1473 8c **Pharmacy,** *Nov. 10,* Cincinnati, Ohio *(804,320)* 8.00
1474 8c **Stamp Collecting,** *Nov. 17,* New York, N.Y. *(434,680)* 1.25

1973

1475 8c **Love,** *Jan. 26,* Philadelphia, Pa. *(422,492)* 2.00
1476 8c **Pamphleteer** (Rev. Bicentennial), *Feb. 16,* Portland, Ore. *(431,784)* 1.00
1477 8c **Broadside** (Rev. Bicentennial), *Apr. 13,* Atlantic City, N.J. *(423,437)* 1.00
1478 8c **Post Rider** (Rev. Bicentennial), *June 22,* Rochester, N.Y. *(586,850)* 1.00
1479 8c **Drummer** (Rev. Bicentennial), *Sept. 28,* New Orleans, La. *(522,427)* 1.00
1483a 8c **Boston Tea Party** (Rev. Bicentennial), *July 4,* Boston, Mass. *(897,870)* 3.00
1480-1483, any single 1.00
1484 8c **George Gershwin,** *Feb. 28,* Beverly Hills, Calif. *(448,814)* 1.00
1485 8c **Robinson Jeffers,** *Aug. 13,* Carmel, Calif. *(394,261)* 1.00
1486 8c **Henry O. Tanner,** *Sept. 10,* Pittsburgh, Pa. *(424,065)* 2.50
1487 8c **Willa Cather,** *Sept. 20,* Red Cloud, Nebr. *(435,784)* 1.00
1488 8c **Nicolaus Copernicus,** *Apr. 23* *(734,190)* 1.50
1498a 8c **Postal People,** *Apr. 30, any city* 5.00
1489-1498, any single 1.00

First day cancellation was applied at Boston to 1,205,212 covers bearing one or more of Nos. 1489-1498. Cancellations at other cities unrecorded.

1499 8c **Harry S Truman,** *May 8,* Independence, Mo. *(938,636)* 1.50
1500 6c **Electronics,** *July 10,* New York, N.Y. 1.00
1501 8c **Electronics,** *July 10,* New York, N.Y. 1.00
1502 15c **Electronics,** *July 10,* New York, N.Y. 1.00
1500-1502 and C86 on one cover 4.00

First day cancellation was applied to 1,197,700 covers bearing one or more of Nos. 1500-1502 and C86.

1503 8c **Lyndon B. Johnson,** *Aug. 27,* Austin, Texas *(701,490)* 1.00

1973-74

1504 8c **Angus Cattle,** *Oct. 5, 1973,* St. Joseph, Mo. *(521,427)* 1.00
1505 10c **Chautauqua,** *Aug. 6, 1974,* Chautauqua, N.Y. *(411,105)* 1.00
1506 10c **Wheat,** *Aug. 16, 1974,* Hillsboro, Kans. *(468,280)* 1.00
1507 8c **Christmas (religious),** *Nov. 7, 1973* 1.00
1508 8c **Christmas (secular),** *Nov. 7, 1973* 1.00
1507-1508 on one cover 1.10

First day cancellation was applied to 807,468 covers bearing one or both of Nos. 1507-1508.

1509 10c **Crossed Flags,** *Dec. 8, 1973,* San Francisco, Calif. 1.00

First day cancellation was applied to 341,528 covers bearing one or more of Nos. 1509 and 1519.

1510 10c **Jefferson Memorial,** *Dec. 14, 1973* 1.00
1510b Booklet pane of 5 + label 2.25
1510c Booklet pane of 8 2.50
1510d Booklet pane of 6, *Aug. 5, 1974,* Oakland, Calif. 3.00

First day cancellation was applied to 686,300 covers bearing one or more of Nos. 1510, 1510b, 1510c, 1520.

1511 10c **Zip Code,** *Jan. 4, 1974 (335,220)* 1.00
1518 6.3c **Bell Coil,** *Oct. 1, 1974 (221,141)* 1.00
1519 10c **Crossed Flags coil,** *Dec. 8, 1973,* San Francisco, Calif. 1.00
1520 10c **Jefferson Memorial coil,** *Dec. 14, 1973* 1.00

1974

1525 10c **Veterans of Foreign Wars,** *Mar. 11* *(543,598)* 1.50
1526 10c **Robert Frost,** *Mar. 26,* Derry, N.H. *(500,425)* 1.00
1527 10c **EXPO '74,** *Apr. 18,* Spokane, Wash. *(565,548)* 1.00
1528 10c **Horse Racing,** *May 4,* Louisville, Ky. *(623,983)* 3.00
1529 10c **Skylab,** *May 14,* Houston, Tex. *(972,326)* 1.50
1537a 10c **UPU Centenary,** *June 6 (1,374,765)* 4.00
1530-1537, any single 1.00
1541a 10c **Mineral Heritage,** *June 13,* Lincoln, Neb. *(865,368)* 2.75
1538-1541, any single 1.00
1542 10c **Kentucky Settlement,** *June 15,* Harrodsburg, Ky. *(478,239)* 1.00
1546a 10c **Continental Congress** (Rev. Bicentennial), *July 4,* Philadelphia, Pa. *(2,124,957)* 2.75
1543-1546, any single 1.00
1547 10c **Energy Conservation,** *Sept. 23,* Detroit, Mich. *(587,210)* 1.00
1548 10c **Sleepy Hollow,** *Oct. 10,* North Tarrytown, N.Y. *(514,836)* 3.00
1549 10c **Retarded Children,** *Oct. 12,* Arlington Tex. *(412,882)* 1.00
1550 10c **Christmas (Religious),** *Oct. 23,* New York, N.Y. *(634,990)* 1.00
1551 10c **Christmas (Currier & Ives),** *Oct. 23,* New York, N.Y. *(634,990)* 1.00
1550-1551 on one cover 1.10
1552 10c **Christmas (Dove),** *Nov. 15,* New York, N.Y. *(477,410)* 1.50

1975

1553 10c **Benjamin West,** *Feb. 10,* Swarthmore, Pa. *(465,017)* 1.00
1554 10c **Paul L. Dunbar,** *May 1,* Dayton, Ohio *(397,347)* 1.50
1555 10c **D.W. Griffith,** *May 27,* Beverly Hills, Calif. *(424,167)* 1.00
1556 10c **Pioneer-Jupiter,** *Feb. 28,* Mountain View, Calif. *(594,896)* 1.25
1557 10c **Mariner 10,** *Apr. 4,* Pasadena, Calif. *(563,636)* 1.25
1558 10c **Collective Bargaining,** *Mar. 13* *(412,329)* 1.00
1559 8c **Sybil Ludington** (Rev. Bicentennial), *Mar. 25,* Carmel, N.Y. *(394,550)* 1.00
1560 10c **Salem Poor** (Rev. Bicentennial, *Mar. 25,* Cambridge, Mass. *(415,565)* 1.50
1561 10c **Haym Salomon** (Rev. Bicentennial), *Mar. 25,* Chicago, Ill. *(442,630)* 1.00
1562 18c **Peter Francisco** (Rev. Bicentennial), *Mar. 25,* Greensboro, N.C. *(415,000)* 1.00
1563 10c **Lexington-Concord** (Rev. Bicentennial), *Apr. 19,* Lexington, Mass., or Concord, Mass, *(975,020)* 1.00
1564 10c **Bunker Hill** (Rev. Bicentennial), *June 17,* Charlestown, Mass. *(557,130)* 1.00
1568a 10c **Military Services** (Rev. Bicentennial), *July 4 (1,134,831)* 2.50
1565-1568, any single 1.00
1569a 10c **Apollo-Soyuz,** *July 15,* Kennedy Space Center, Fla. *(1,427,046)* 5.00
1569-1570, any single 3.00
1571 10c **International Women's Year,** *Aug. 26,* Seneca Falls, N.Y. *(476,769)* 1.00
1575a 10c **Postal Service Bicentenary,** *Sept. 3,* Philadelphia, Pa. *(969,999)* 2.50
1572-1575, any single 1.00
1576 10c **World Peace through Law,** *Sept. 29 (386,736)* 1.25
1577a 10c **Banking-Commerce,** *Oct. 6,* New York, N.Y. *(555,580)* 1.75
1577-1578, any single 1.00
1579 (10c) **Christmas (religious),** *Oct. 14* 1.00
1580 (10c) **Christmas (secular),** *Oct. 14* 1.00
1579-1580 on one cover 2.00

First day cancellation was applied to 730,079 covers bearing one or more of Nos. 1579-1580.

1975-79

AMERICANA ISSUE

1581 1c **Inkwell,** *Dec. 8, 1977,* St. Louis, Mo., multiple for 1st class rate 1.00
1582 2c **Speaker's Stand,** *Dec. 8, 1977,* St. Louis, Mo., multiple for 1st class rate 1.00
1584 3c **Ballot Box,** *Dec. 8, 1977,* St. Louis, Mo., multiple for 1st class rate 1.00
1585 4c **Books and Eyeglasses,** *Dec. 8, 1977,* St. Louis, Mo., multiple for 1st class rate 1.00

First day cancellation was applied to 530,033 covers bearing one or more of Nos. 1581-1582, 1584-1585.

1590 9c **Capitol Dome,** from bklt.,*Mar. 11, 1977,* New York, N.Y., plus postage for 1st class rate 1.00
1591 9c **Capitol Dome,** *Nov. 24, 1975 (190,117),* multiple for 1st class rate 1.00
1592 10c **Justice,** *Nov. 17, 1977,* New York, N.Y. *(359,050),* multiple for 1st class rate 1.00
1593 11c **Printing Press,** *Nov. 13, 1975,* Philadelphia, Pa. *(217,755),* multiple for 1st class rate 1.00
1594 12c **Torch,** *Apr. 8, 1981,* Dallas, TX, multiple for 1st class rate 1.00

First day cancellation was applied to 280,930 covers bearing one or more of Nos. 1594 and 1816.

1595 13c **Liberty Bell,** *Oct. 31, 1975,* Cleveland, Ohio *(256,734)* 1.00
1595a Booklet pane of 6 2.00
1595b Booklet pane of 7 + label 2.75
1595c Booklet pane of 8 2.50
1595d Booklet pane of 5 + label, *Apr. 2, 1976,* Liberty, Mo. 2.25
1596 13c **Eagle and Shield,** *Dec. 1, 1975,* Juneau, Alaska *(418,272)* 1.00
1597 15c **Flag,** *June 30, 1978,* Baltimore, Md. 1.00
1598 15c **Flag,** from bklt., *June 30, 1978,* Baltimore, Md. 1.00
1598a Booklet pane of 8 2.50

First day cancellation was applied to 315,359 covers bearing one or more of Nos. 1597, 1598, and 1618C.

1599 16c **Statue of Liberty,** *Mar. 31, 1978,* New York, N.Y. 1.00
1603 24c **Old North Church,** *Nov. 14, 1975,* Boston, Mass. *(208,973)* 1.00
1604 28c **Fort Nisqually,** *Aug. 11, 1978,* Tacoma, Wash. *(159,639)* 1.00
1605 29c **Sandy Hook Lighthouse,** *Apr. 14, 1978,* Atlantic City, N.J. *(193,476)* 1.50
1606 30c **Schoolhouse,** *Aug. 27, 1979,* Devils Lake, N.D. *(186,882)* 1.25
1608 50c **Betty Lamp,** *Sept. 11, 1979,* San Juan, P.R. *(159,540)* 1.50
1610 $1 **Rush Lamp,** *July 2, 1979,* San Francisco, Calif. *(255,575)* 3.00
1611 $2 **Kerosene Lamp,** *Nov. 16, 1978,* New York, N.Y. *(173,596)* 5.00
1612 $5 **Railroad Lantern,** *Aug. 23, 1979,* Boston, Mass. *(129,192)* 12.50

COIL STAMPS

1613 3.1c **Guitar,** *Oct. 25, 1979,* Shreveport, La. *(230,403)* 1.00
1614 7.7c **Saxhorns,** *Nov. 20, 1976,* New York, N.Y. *(285,290)* 1.00
1615 7.9c **Drum,** *Apr. 23, 1976,* Miami, Fla. *(193,270)* 1.00
1615C 8.4c **Piano,** *July 13, 1978,* Interlochen, Mich. *(200,392)* 1.00
1616 9c **Capitol Dome,** *Mar. 5, 1976,* Milwaukee, Wis. *(128,171)* 1.00
1617 10c **Justice,** *Nov. 4, 1977,* Tampa, Fla. *(184,954)* 1.00
1618 13c **Liberty Bell,** *Nov. 25, 1975,* Allentown, Pa. *(320,387)* 1.00
1618C 15c **Flag,** *June 30, 1978,* Baltimore, Md. 1.00
1619 16c **Statue of Liberty,** *Mar. 31, 1978,* New York, N.Y. 1.00

First day cancellation was applied to 376,338 covers bearing one or more of Nos. 1599 and 1619.

1975

1622 13c **13-Star Flag,** *Nov. 15,* Philadelphia, Pa. 1.00
1623 13c **Flag over Capitol,** *Mar. 11,* New York, N.Y. 1.50
1623a Booklet pane of 8, perf 11 (1 #1590 +7 #1623) 25.00
1623Bc Booklet pane of 8, perf. 10x9¾ (1 #1590A + 7 #1623B) 15.00

First day cancellation was applied to 242,208 covers bearing Nos. 1623, 1623a, 1623B or 1623Bc.

1625 13c **13-Star Flag coil,** *Nov. 15,* Philadelphia, PA 1.00

First day cancellation was applied to 362,959 covers bearing one or more of Nos. 1622 and 1625.

1976

1631a 13c **Spirit of '76,** *Jan. 1,* Pasadena, CA *(1,013,067)* 2.00
1629-1631, any single 1.25
1632 13c **Interphil '76,** *Jan. 17,* Philadelphia, Pa. *(519,902)* 1.00
1682a 13c **State Flags,** *Feb. 23* 27.50
1633-1682, any single 1.50
1683 13c **Telephone,** *Mar. 10,* Boston, Mass. *(662,515)* 1.00
1684 13c **Commercial Aviation,** *Mar. 19,* Chicago Ill. *(631,555)* 1.50
1685 13c **Chemistry,** *Apr. 6,* New York, N.Y. *(557,600)* 1.50

Bicentennial Souvenir Sheets of 5

1686 13c **Surrender of Cornwallis,** *May 29,* Philadelphia, Pa. 7.50
1687 18c **Declaration of Independence,** *May 29,* Philadelphia, Pa. 7.50
1688 24c **Declaration of Independence,** *May 29,* Philadelphia, Pa. 7.50
1689 31c **Washington at Valley Forge,** *May 29,* Philadelphia, Pa. 7.50

First day cancellation was applied to 879,890 covers bearing singles, multiples or complete sheets of Nos. 1686-1689.

1690 13c **Franklin,** *June 1,* Philadelphia, Pa. *(588,740)* 1.00
1694a 13c **Declaration of Independence,** *July 4,* Philadelphia, Pa. *(2,093,880)* 2.00
1691-1694, any single 1.00
1698a 13c **Olympic Games,** *July 16,* Lake Placid, N.Y. *(1,140,189)* 2.00
1695-1698, any single 1.00
1699 13c **Clara Maass,** *Aug. 18,* Belleville, N.J. *(646,506)* 2.50
1700 13c **Adolph S. Ochs,** *Sept. 18,* New York, N.Y. *(582,580)* 1.00
1701 13c **Christmas (religious),** *Oct. 27,* Boston, Mass. (540,050) 1.00
1702 13c **Christmas (secular),** *Oct. 27,* Boston, Mass. (181,410) 1.00
1703 13c **Christmas (secular),** block tagged, *Oct. 27,* Boston, Mass. (330,450) 1.00
1701 and 1702 or 1703 on one cover 1.25

1977

1704 13c **Washington at Princeton**, *Jan. 3*, Princeton, N.J. *(695,335)* 1.00
1705 13c **Sound Recording**, *Mar. 23 (632,216)* 1.25
1709a 13c **Pueblo Art**, *Apr. 13*, Santa Fe, N.M. *(1,194,554)* 2.00
1706-1709, any single 1.00
1710 13c **Lindbergh Flight**, *May 20*, Roosevelt Sta., N.Y. *(3,985,989)* 3.50
1711 13c **Colorado Statehood**, *May 21*, Denver, Colo. *(510,880)* 1.00
1715a 13c **Butterflies**, *June 6*, Indianapolis, Ind. *(1,218,278)* 2.00
1712-1715, any single 2.00
1716 13c **Lafayette's Landing**, *June 13*, Charleston, S.C. *(514,506)* 1.00
1720a 13c **Skilled Hands**, *July 4*, Cincinnati, Ohio *(1,263,568)* 2.00
1717-1720, any single 1.00
1721 13c **Peace Bridge**, *Aug. 4*, Buffalo, N.Y. *(512,995)* 1.00
1722 13c **Battle of Oriskany**, *Aug. 6*, Utica, N.Y. *(605,906)* 1.00
1723a 13c **Energy Conservation**, *Oct. 20 (410,299)* 1.50
1723-1724, any single 1.25
1725 13c **Alta California**, *Sept. 9*, San Jose, Calif. *(709,457)* 1.00
1726 13c **Articles of Confederation**, *Sept. 30*, York, Pa. *(605,455)* 1.00
1727 13c **Talking Pictures**, *Oct. 6*, Hollywood, Calif. *(570,195)* 1.50
1728 13c **Surrender at Saratoga** *Oct. 7*, Schuylerville, N.Y. *(557,529)* 1.00
1729 13c **Christmas (Valley Forge)**, *Oct. 21*, Valley Forge, Pa. *(583,139)* 1.00
1730 13c **Christmas (mailbox)**, *Oct. 21*, Omaha, Nebr. *(675,786)* 1.00

1978

1731 13c **Carl Sandburg**, *Jan. 6*, Galesburg, Ill. *(493,826)* 1.00
1732a 13c **Captain Cook**, *Jan. 20*, Honolulu, Hawaii, or Anchorage, Alaska 1.75
1732-1733, any single 1.25

First day cancellation was applied to 823,855 covers at Honolulu, and 672,804 at Anchorage, each cover bearing one or both of Nos. 1732-1733.

1734 13c **Indian Head Penny**, *Jan. 11*, Kansas City, Mo. *(512,426)* 1.00

1978-80

REGULAR ISSUE

1735 (15c) **"A" Eagle**, *May 22*, Memphis, Tenn. 1.00
1736 (15c) **"A" Eagle**, bklt. single *May 22*, Memphis, Tenn. 1.00
1736a Booklet pane of 8 2.50
1737 15c **Roses**, *July 11*, Shreveport, La. *(445,003)* 1.00
1737a Booklet pane of 8 2.50
1742a 15c **Windmills Booklet pane of 10**, *Feb. 7, 1980*, Lubbock, TX 3.50
1738-1742, any single 1.00
1743 15c **"A" Eagle coil**, *May 22*, Memphis, Tenn. 1.00

First day cancellation was applied to 689,049 covers bearing one or more of Nos. 1735, 1736 and 1743. First day cancellation was applied to 708,411 covers bearing one or more of Nos. 1738-1742a.

1978

1744 13c **Harriet Tubman**, *Feb. 1 (493,495)* 1.75
1748a 13c **American Quilts**, *Mar. 8*, Charleston, W.Va. 2.00
1745-1748, any single 1.00

First day cancellation was applied to 1,081,827 covers bearing one or more of Nos. 1745-1748.

1752a 13c **American Dance**, *Apr. 26*, New York, N.Y. *(1,626,493)* 2.00
1749-1752, any single 1.00
1753 13c **French Alliance**, *May 4*, York, Pa. *(705,240)* 1.00
1754 13c **Papanicolaou**, *May 18 (535,584)* 1.00
1755 13c **Jimmie Rodgers**, *May 24*, Meridian, Miss. *(599,287)* 1.00
1756 15c **George M. Cohan**, *July 3*, Providence, R.I. *(740,750)* 1.25
1757 **CAPEX** souv. sheet, *June 10*, Toronto, Canada *(1,994,067)* 2.75
1758 15c **Photography**, *June 26*, Las Vegas, Nev. *(684,987)* 1.00
1759 15c **Viking Missions**, *July 20*, Hampton, Va. *(805,051)* 1.00
1763a 15c **American Owls**, *Aug. 26*, Fairbanks, Alas. *(1,690,474)* 2.00
1760-1763, any single 1.25
1767a 15c **American Trees**, *Oct. 9*, Hot Springs National Park, Ark. *(1,139,100)* 2.00
1764-1767, any single 1.25
1768 15c **Christmas (Madonna)**, *Oct. 18 (553,064)* 1.00
1769 15c **Christmas (Hobby Horse)**, *Oct. 18*, Holly, Mich. *(603,008)* 1.00

1979-80

1770 15c **Robert Kennedy**, *Jan. 12 (624,582)* 1.50
1771 15c **Martin L. King**, *Jan. 13*, Atlanta, Ga. *(726,149)* 2.00
1772 15c **Year of Child**, *Feb. 15*, Philadelphia, Pa. *(716,782)* 1.00
1773 15c **John Steinbeck**, *Feb. 27*, Salinas, Calif. *(709,073)* 1.00
1774 15c **Albert Einstein**, *Mar. 4*, Princeton, N.J. *(641,423)* 3.50
1778a 15c **Toleware**, *Apr. 19*, Lancaster, Pa. *(1,581,962)* 2.00
1775-1778, any single 1.00
1782a 15c **American Architecture**, *June 4*, Kansas City, Mo. *(1,219,258)* 2.00
1779-1782, any single 1.00
1786a 15c **Endangered Flora**, *June 7*, Milwaukee, Wis. *(1,436,268)* 2.00
1783-1786, any single 1.00
1787 15c **Guide Dogs**, *June 15*, Morristown, N.J. *(588,826)* 1.25
1788 15c **Special Olympics**, *Aug. 9*, Brockport, N.Y. *(651,344)* 1.25
1789 15c **John Paul Jones**, *Sept. 23*, Annapolis, Md. 1.50
1789A 15c **John Paul Jones**, *Sept. 23*, Annapolis, Md. 1.50

Total for 1789 and 1789A is 587,018.

1790 10c **Olympic Javelin**, *Sept. 5*, Olympia, Wash. *(305,122)* 1.00
1794a 15c **Olympics 1980**, *Sept. 28*, Los Angeles, Calif. *(1,561,366)* 2.00
1791-1794, any single 1.25
1798b 15c **Winter Olympics**, *Feb. 1, 1980*, Lake Placid, N.Y. *(1,166,302)* 2.00
1795-1798, any single 1.25

1979

1799 15c **Christmas (Madonna)**, *Oct. 18 (686,990)* 1.25
1800 15c **Christmas (Santa Claus)**, *Oct. 18*, North Pole, Alaska *(511,829)* 1.25
1799-1800, both stamps issued *Oct. 18* 2.00
1801 15c **Will Rogers**, *Nov. 4*, Claremore, Okla. *(1,643,151)* 1.50
1802 15c **Viet Nam Veterans**, *Nov. 11*, Arlington, VA *(445,934)* 3.25

1980

1803 15c **W.C. Fields**, *Jan. 29*, Beverly Hills, CA *(633,303)* 2.00
1804 15c **Benjamin Banneker**, *Feb. 15*, Annapolis, MD *(647,126)* 2.00
1810a 15c **Letter Writing**, *Feb. 25 (1,083,360)* 2.50
1805-1810, any single 1.00

1980-81

DEFINITIVES

1811 1c **Quill Pen**, coil, *Mar. 6, 1980*, New York, NY *(262,921)* 1.00
1813 3.5c **Violins**, coil, *June 23, 1980*, Williamsburg, PA 1.00

FD cancel was applied to 716,988 covers bearing Nos. 1813 or U590.

1816 12c **Torch**, coil, *Apr. 8, 1981*, Dallas, TX 1.00
1818 (18c) **"B" Eagle**, *Mar. 15, 1981*, San Francisco, CA 1.25

FD cancel was applied to 511,688 covers bearing one or more of Nos. 1818-1820, U592 or UX88.

1819 (18c) **"B" Eagle**, bklt. single, *Mar. 15, 1981*, San Francisco, CA 1.00
1819a Booklet pane of 8 3.00
1820 (18c) **"B" Eagle**, coil, *Mar. 15, 1981*, San Francisco, CA 1.00

1980

1821 15c **Frances Perkins**, *Apr. 10 (678,966)* 1.00
1822 15c **Dolley Madison**, *May 20 (331,048)* 1.00
1823 15c **Emily Bissell**, *May 31*, Wilmington, DE *(649,509)* 1.00
1824 15c **Helen Keller, Anne Sullivan**, *June 27*, Tuscumbia, AL *(713,061)* 1.25
1825 15c **Veterans Administration**, *July 21 (634,101)* 1.50
1826 15c **Bernardo de Galvez**, *July 23*, New Orleans, LA *(658,061)* 1.00
1830a 15c **Coral Reefs**, *Aug. 26*, Charlotte Amalie, VI *(1,195,126)* 2.00
1827-1830, any single 1.00
1831 15c **Organized Labor**, *Sept. 1 (759,973)* 1.00
1832 15c **Edith Wharton**, *Sept. 5*, New Haven, CT *(633,917)* 1.00
1833 15c **Education**, *Sept. 12*,Franklin, MA *(672,592)* 1.50
1837a 15c **Indian Masks**, *Sept. 25*, Spokane, WA *(2,195,136)* 2.00
1834-1837, any single 1.00
1841a 15c **Architecture**, *Oct. 9*, New York, NY *(2,164,721)* 1.75
1838-1841, any single 1.00
1842 15c **Christmas (Madonna)**, *Oct. 31 (718,614)* 1.25
1843 15c **Christmas (Toys)**, *Oct. 31*, Christmas, MI *(755,108)* 1.25

1980-85

GREAT AMERICANS ISSUE

1844 1c **Dorothea Dix**, *Sept. 23, 1983*, Hampden, ME *(164,140)* 1.00
1845 2c **Igor Stravinsky**, *Nov. 18, 1982*, New York, NY *(501,719)* 1.00
1846 3c **Henry Clay**, *July 13, 1983 (204,320)* 1.00
1847 4c **Carl Schurz**, *June 3, 1983*, Watertown, WI *(165,010)* 1.00
1848 5c **Pearl Buck**, *June 25, 1983*, Hillsboro, WV *(231,852)* 1.00
1849 6c **Walter Lippman**, *Sept. 19, 1985*, Minneapolis, MN *(371,990)* 1.00
1850 7c **Abraham Baldwin**, *Jan. 25, 1985*, Athens, GA *(402,285)* 1.25
1851 8c **Henry Knox**, *July 25, 1985*, Thomaston, ME *(315,937)* 1.00
1852 9c **Sylvanus Thayer**, *June 7, 1985*, Braintree, MA *(345,649)* 1.25
1853 10c **Richard Russell**, *May 31, 1984*, Winder, GA *(183,581)* 1.00
1854 11c **Alden Partridge**, *Feb. 12, 1985*, Northfield, VT *(442,311)* 1.25
1855 13c **Crazy Horse**, *Jan. 15, 1982*, Crazy Horse, SD 1.50
1856 14c **Sinclair Lewis**, *Mar. 21, 1985*, Sauk Centre, MN *(308,612)* 1.00
1857 17c **Rachel Carson**, *May 28, 1981*, Springdale, PA *(273,686)* 1.00
1858 18c **George Mason**, *May 7, 1981*, Gunston Hall, VA *(461,937)* 1.00
1859 19c **Sequoyah**, *Dec. 27, 1980*, Tahlequah, OK *(241,325)* 1.25
1860 20c **Ralph Bunche**, *Jan. 12, 1982*, New York, NY 1.75
1861 20c **Thomas H. Gallaudet**, *June 10, 1983*, West Hartford, CT *(261,336)* 1.25
1862 20c **Harry S Truman**, *Jan. 26, 1984 (267,631)* 1.25
1863 22c **John J. Audubon**, *Apr. 23, 1985*, New York, NY *(516,249)* 1.25
1864 30c **Frank Laubach**, *Sept. 2, 1984*, Benton, PA *(118,974)* 1.25
1865 35c **Charles Drew**, *June 3, 1981 (383,882)* 1.75
1866 37c **Robert Millikan**, *Jan. 26, 1982*, Pasadena, CA 1.25
1867 39c **Grenville Clark**, *Mar. 20, 1985*, Hanover, NH *(297,797)* 1.25
1868 40c **Lillian Gilbreth**, *Feb. 24, 1984*, Montclair, NJ *(110,588)* 1.50
1869 50c **Chester W. Nimitz**, *Feb. 22, 1985*, Fredericksburg, TX *(376,166)* 2.00

1981

1874 15c **Everett Dirksen**, *Jan. 4*, Pekin, IL *(665,755)* 1.00
1875 15c **Whitney M. Young**, *Jan. 30*, New York, NY *(963,870)* 1.75
1879a 18c **Flowers**, *Apr. 23*, Fort Valley, GA *(1,966,599)* 2.50
1876-1879, any single 1.00

DEFINITIVES

1889a 18c **Animals Booklet pane of 10**, *May 14*, Boise, ID 5.00
1880-1889, any single 1.00
1890 18c **Flag-Anthem (grain)**, *Apr. 24*, Portland, ME 1.00
1891 18c **Flag-Anthem (sea)**, *Apr. 24*, Portland, ME 1.50
1892 6c **Star Circle**, *Apr. 24*, Portland, ME 1.00
1893 18c **Flag-Anthem (mountain)**, *Apr. 24*, Portland, ME 1.00
1893a Booklet pane of 8 (2 #1892, 6 #1893) 2.50

FDC cancel was applied to 691,526 covers bearing one or more of Nos. 1890-1893 & 1893a.

1894 20c **Flag-Court**, *Dec. 17* 1.00
1895 20c **Flag-Court**, coil, *Dec. 17* 1.00
1896 20c **Flag-Court**, perf. 11x10½, *Dec. 17 (185,543)* 1.00
1896a Booklet pane of 6 6.00
1896b Booklet pane of 10, *June 1, 1982* *10.00*

First day cancellations were applied to 598,169 covers bearing one or more of Nos. 1894-1896.

1981-84

TRANSPORTATION ISSUE

1897 1c **Omnibus**, *Aug. 19, 1983*, Arlington, VA *(109,463)* 1.00
1897A 2c **Locomotive**, *May 20, 1982*, Chicago, IL *(290,020)* 1.50
1898 3c **Handcar**, *Mar. 25, 1983*, Rochester, NY *(77,900)* 1.00
1898A 4c **Stagecoach**, *Aug. 19, 1982*, Milwaukee, WI *(152,940)* 1.00
1899 5c **Motorcycle**, *Oct. 10, 1983*, San Francisco, CA *(188,240)* 2.00
1900 5.2c **Sleigh**, *Mar. 21, 1983*, Memphis, TN *(141,979)* 1.00
1901 5.9c **Bicycle**, *Feb. 17, 1982*, Wheeling, WV *(814,419)* 1.50
1902 7.4c **Baby Buggy**, *Apr. 7, 1984*, San Diego, CA 1.00
1903 9.3c **Mail Wagon**, *Dec. 15, 1981*, Shreveport, LA *(199,645)* 1.00
1904 10.9c **Hansom**, *Mar. 26, 1982*, Chattanooga, TN 1.00
1905 11c **Railroad Caboose**, *Feb. 3, 1984*, Chicago, IL *(172,753)* 1.50
1906 17c **Electric Auto**, *June 25, 1982*, Greenfield Village, MI *(239,458)* 1.00
1907 18c **Surrey**, *May 18, 1981*, Notch, MO *(207,801)* 1.00
1908 20c **Fire Pumper**, *Dec. 10, 1981*, Alexandria, VA *(304,668)* 2.00
1909 $9.35 **Eagle**, *Aug. 12, 1983*, Kennedy Space Center, FL *(77,858)* 50.00
1909a Booklet pane of 3 *125.00*

1981

1910 18c **Red Cross**, *May 1 (874,972)* 1.75
1911 18c **Savings & Loan**, *May 8*, Chicago, IL *(740,910)* 1.00

1919a 18c **Space Achievement,** *May 21,* Kennedy Space Center, FL *(7,027,549)* 3.00
1912-1919, any single 1.00
1920 18c **Professional Management,** *June 18,* Philadelphia, PA *(713,096)* 1.00
1924a 18c **Wildlife Habitats,** *June 26,* Reno, NV *(2,327,609)* 2.50
1921-1924, any single 1.00
1925 18c **Year of Disabled,** *June 29,* Milford, MI *(714,244)* 1.00
1926 18c **Edna St. V. Millay,** *July 10,* Austerlitz, NY *(725,978)* 1.00
1927 18c **Alcoholism,** *Aug. 19 (874,972)* 3.00
1931a 18c **Architecture,** *Aug. 28,* New York, NY *(1,998,208)* 2.50
1928-1931, any single 1.00
1932 18c **Babe Zaharias,** *Sept. 22,* Pinehurst, NC 6.50
1933 18c **Bobby Jones,** *Sept. 22,* Pinehurst, NC 10.00
1932-1933, both stamps issued *Sept. 22,* Pinehurst, NC 12.50

First day cancel was applied to 1,231,543 covers bearing one or more of Nos. 1932-1933.

1934 18c **Frederic Remington,** *Oct. 9,* Oklahoma City, OK *(1,367,099)* 1.25
1935 18c **James Hoban,** *Oct. 13* 1.00
1936 20c **James Hoban,** *Oct. 13* 1.00
1935-1936, both stamps issued *Oct. 13* 2.50

FD cancel was applied to 635,012 covers bearing Nos. 1935-1936.

1938a 18c **Yorktown-Va. Capes Battle,** *Oct. 16,* Yorktown, VA *(1,098,278)* 1.50
1937-1938, any single 1.00
1939 (20c) **Christmas (Madonna),** *Oct. 28,* Chicago, IL *(481,395)* 1.00
1940 (20c) **Christmas (Teddy Bear),** *Oct. 28,* Christmas Valley, OR *(517,898)* 1.00
1941 20c **John Hanson,** *Nov. 5,* Frederick, MD *(605,616)* 1.00
1945a 20c **Desert Plants,** *Dec. 11,* Tucson, AZ *(1,770,187)* 2.50
1942-1945, any single 1.00

REGULAR ISSUE

1946 (20c) **"C" Eagle,** *Oct. 11,* Memphis, TN 1.00
1947 (20c) **"C" Eagle,** coil, *Oct. 11,* Memphis, TN 1.00
1948 (20c) **"C" Eagle,** bklt. single, *Oct. 11,* Memphis, TN 1.00
1948a Booklet pane of 10 *3.50*

First day cancellations were applied to 304,404 covers bearing one or more of Nos. 1946-1948.

1982

1949 20c **Bighorn,** *Jan. 8,* Bighorn, MT 1.25
1949a Booklet pane of 10 *6.00*
1950 20c **F.D. Roosevelt,** *Jan. 30,* Hyde Park, NY 1.00
1951 20c **Love,** *Feb. 1,* Boston, MA *(325,727)* 1.00
1952 20c **Washington,** *Feb. 22,* Mt. Vernon, VA 1.25
2002b 20c **Birds-Flowers,** perf 10½x11¼ *Apr. 14,* Washington, DC, or State Capital 30.00
1953-2002, any single 1.25
2002Ac 20c **Birds-Flowers,** perf 11¼x11 *Apr. 14,* Washington, DC —
2003 20c **U.S.-Netherlands,** *Apr. 20* 1.00
2004 20c **Library of Congress,** *Apr. 21* 1.00
2005 20c **Consumer Education,** *Apr. 27* 1.00
2009a 20c **Knoxville Fair,** *Apr. 29,* Knoxville, TN 2.50
2006-2009, any single 1.00
2010 20c **Horatio Alger,** *Apr. 30,* Willow Grove, PA 1.00
2011 20c **Aging,** *May 21,* Sun City, AZ *(510,677)* 1.00
2012 20c **Barrymores,** *June 8,* New York, NY 1.00
2013 20c **Dr. Mary Walker,** *June 10,* Oswego, NY 1.00
2014 20c **Peace Garden,** *June 30,* Dunseith, ND 1.00
2015 20c **America's Libraries,** *July 13,* Philadelphia, PA 1.00
2016 20c **Jackie Robinson,** *Aug. 2,* Cooperstown, NY 6.00
2017 20c **Touro Synagogue,** *Aug. 22,* Newport, RI *(517,264)* 1.50
2018 20c **Wolf Trap Farm Park,** *Sept. 1,* Vienna, VA *(704,361)* 1.00
2022a 20c **Architecture,** *Sept. 30 (1,552,567)* 2.50
2019-2022, any single 1.00
2023 20c **St. Francis,** *Oct. 7,* San Francisco, CA *(530,275)* 1.25
2024 20c **Ponce de Leon,** *Oct. 12,* San Juan, PR *(530,275)* 1.00
2025 13c **Puppy, Kitten,** *Nov. 3,* Danvers, MA *(239,219)* 1.25
2026 20c **Christmas (Madonna),** *Oct. 28 (462,982)* 1.00
2030a 20c **Christmas (Children),** *Oct. 28,* Snow, OK *(676,950)* 2.50
2027-2030, any single 1.00

1983

2031 20c **Science & Industry,** *Jan. 19,* Chicago, IL *(526,693)* 1.00
2035a 20c **Balloons,** *Mar. 31,* Albuquerque, NM or Washington, DC *(989,305)* 2.50
2032-2035, any single 1.00
2036 20c **U.S.-Sweden,** *Mar. 24,* Philadelphia, PA *(526,373)* 1.00
2037 20c **Civilian Conservation Corps.,** *Apr. 5,* Luray, VA *(483,824)* 1.00
2038 20c **Joseph Priestley,** *Apr. 13,* Northumberland, PA *(673,266)* 1.00
2039 20c **Voluntarism,** *Apr. 20 (574,708)* 1.00
2040 20c **U.S.-Germany,** *Apr. 29,* Germantown, PA *(611,109)* 1.00
2041 20c **Brooklyn Bridge,** *May 17,* Brooklyn, NY *(815,085)* 1.75
2042 20c **TVA,** *May 18,* Knoxville, TN *(837,588)* 1.00
2043 20c **Physical Fitness,** *May 14,* Houston, TX *(501,336)* 1.25
2044 20c **Scott Joplin,** *June 9,* Sedalia, MO *(472,667)* 1.75
2045 20c **Medal of Honor,** *June 7 (1,623,995)* 5.50
2046 20c **Babe Ruth,** *July 6,* Chicago, IL *(1,277,907)* 5.00
2047 20c **Nathaniel Hawthorne,** *July 8,* Salem, MA *(442,793)* 1.00
2051a 13c **Summer Olympics,** *July 28,* South Bend, IN *(909,332)* 2.50
2048-2051, any single 1.25
2052 20c **Treaty of Paris,** *Sept. 2 (651,208)* 1.00
2053 20c **Civil Service,** *Sept. 9 (422,206)* 1.00
2054 20c **Metropolitan Opera,** *Sept. 14,* New York, NY *(807,609)* 1.50
2058a 20c **American Inventors,** *Sept. 21 (1,006,516)* 2.50
2055-2058, any single 1.00
2062a 20c **Streetcars,** *Oct. 8,* Kennebunkport, ME *(1,116,909)* 2.50
2059-2062, any single 1.00
2063 20c **Christmas (Madonna),** *Oct. 28 (361,874)* 1.00
2064 20c **Christmas (Santa),** *Oct. 28,* Santa Claus, IN *(388,749)* 1.00
2065 20c **Martin Luther,** *Nov. 11 (463,777)* 1.50

1984

2066 20c **Alaska Statehood,** *Jan. 3,* Fairbanks, AK *(816,591)* 1.00
2070a 20c **Winter Olympics,** *Jan. 6,* Lake Placid, NY *(1,245,807)* 2.50
2067-2070, any single 1.00
2071 20c **Federal Deposit Ins. Corp.,** *Jan. 12 (536,329)* 1.00
2072 20c **Love,** *Jan. 31 (327,727)* 1.00
2073 20c **Carter Woodson,** *Feb. 1 (387,583)* 1.75
2074 20c **Soil & Water Conservation,** *Feb. 6,* Denver, CO *(426,101)* 1.00
2075 20c **Credit Union Act,** *Feb. 10,* Salem, MA *(523,583)* 1.00
2079a 20c **Orchids,** *Mar. 5,* Miami, FL *(1,063,237)* 2.50
2076-2079, any single 1.00
2080 20c **Hawaii Statehood,** *Mar. 12,* Honolulu, HI *(546,930)* 1.00
2081 20c **National Archives,** *Apr. 16 (414,415)* 1.00
2085a 20c **Olympics 1984,** *May 4,* Los Angeles, CA *(1,172,313)* 2.50
2082-2085, any single 1.25
2086 20c **Louisiana Exposition,** *May 11,* New Orleans, LA *(467,408)* 1.00
2087 20c **Health Research,** *May 17,* New York, NY *(845,007)* 1.00
2088 20c **Douglas Fairbanks,** *May 23,* Denver CO *(547,134)* 1.00
2089 20c **Jim Thorpe,** *May 24,* Shawnee, OK *(568,544)* 3.00
2090 20c **John McCormack,** *June 6,* Boston, MA *(464,117)* 1.00
2091 20c **St. Lawrence Seaway,** *June 26,* Massena, NY *(550,173)* 1.00
2092 20c **Waterfowl Preservation Act,** *July 2,* Des Moines, IA *(549,388)* 1.00
2093 20c **Roanoke Voyages,** *July 13,* Manteo, NC *(443,725)* 1.00
2094 20c **Herman Melville,** *Aug. 1,* New Bedford, MA *(378,293)* 1.75
2095 20c **Horace A. Moses,** *Aug. 6,* Bloomington, IN *(459,386)* 1.00
2096 20c **Smokey Bear,** *Aug. 13,* Capitan, NM *(506,833)* 3.50
2097 20c **Roberto Clemente,** *Aug. 17,* Carolina, PR *(547,387)* 9.00
2101a 20c **Dogs,** *Sept. 7,* New York, NY *(1,157,373)* 3.00
2098-2101, any single 1.50
2102 20c **Crime Prevention,** *Sept. 26 (427,564)* 1.25
2103 20c **Hispanic Americans,** *Oct. 31 (416,796)* 1.75
2104 20c **Family Unity,** *Oct. 1,* Shaker Heights, OH *(400,659)* 1.00
2105 20c **Eleanor Roosevelt,** *Oct. 11,* Hyde Park, NY *(479,919)* 1.00
2106 20c **Nation of Readers,** *Oct. 16 (437,559)* 1.00
2107 20c **Christmas (Madonna),** *Oct. 30 (386,385)* 1.00
2108 20c **Christmas (Santa),** *Oct. 30,* Jamaica, NY *(430,843)* 1.00
2109 20c **Vietnam Veterans' Memorial,** *Nov. 10 (434,489)* 5.00

1985

2110 22c **Jerome Kern,** *Jan. 23,* New York, NY (503,855) 1.00

REGULAR ISSUE

2111 (22c) **"D" Eagle,** *Feb. 1,* Los Angeles, CA 1.00
2112 (22c) **"D" Eagle, coil,** *Feb. 1,* Los Angeles, CA 1.00
2113 (22c) **"D" Eagle, bklt. single,** *Feb. 1,* Los Angeles, CA 1.00
2113a Booklet pane of 10 *7.50*

First Day cancel was applied to 513,027 covers bearing one or more of Nos. 2111-2113.

2114 22c **Flag over Capitol Dome,** *Mar. 29* 1.00
2115 22c **Flag over Capitol Dome,** coil, *Mar. 29* 1.00
2115b Inscribed "T" at bottom, *May 23, 1987,* Secaucus, NJ *1.00*

First Day Cancel was applied to 268,161 covers bearing one or more of Nos. 2114-2115.

2116 22c **Flag Over Capitol Dome,** bklt. single, *Mar. 29,* Waubeka, WI *(234,318)* 1.00
2116a Booklet pane of 5 3.50
2121a 22c **Seashells Booklet pane of 10,** *Apr. 4,* Boston, MA *(426,290)* *7.50*
2117-2121, any single 1.00
2122 $10.75 **Eagle and Half Moon,** type I, *Apr. 29,* San Francisco, CA *(93,154)* 50.00
2122a Booklet pane of 3 *125.00*
2122b Type II, *June 19, 1989* *350.00*
2122c Booklet pane of 3, type II *700.00*

1985-87

TRANSPORTATION ISSUE

2123 3.4c **School Bus,** *June 8, 1985,* Arlington, VA *(131,480)* 1.00
2124 4.9c **Buckboard,** *June 21, 1985,* Reno, NV 1.00
2125 5.5c **Star Route Truck,** *Nov. 1, 1986,* Fort Worth, TX *(136,021)* 1.00
2126 6c **Tricycle,** *May 6, 1985,* Childs, MD *(151,494)* 1.25
2127 7.1c **Tractor,** *Feb. 6, 1987,* Sarasota, FL *(167,555)* 1.00
2127a 7.1c **Tractor,** Zip+4 precancel, untagged, *May 26, 1989,* Rosemont, IL *(202,804)* 5.00
2128 8.3c **Ambulance,** *June 21, 1986,* Reno, NV 1.00

First day cancel was applied to 338,765 covers bearing one or more of Nos. 2124 and 2128.

2129 8.5c **Tow Truck,** *Jan. 24, 1987,* Tucson, AZ *(224,285)* 1.25
2130 10.1c **Oil Wagon,** *Apr. 18, 1985,* Oil Center, NM 1.25
2130a 10.1c "Bulk Rate Carrier Route Sort" precancel, *June 27, 1988 (136,428)* 1.25
2131 11c **Stutz Bearcat,** *June 11, 1985,* Baton Rouge, LA *(135,037)* 1.25
2132 12c **Stanley Steamer,** *Apr. 2, 1985,* Kingfield, ME *(173,998)* 1.25
2133 12.5c **Pushcart,** *Apr. 18, 1985,* Oil Center, NM 1.25

First day cancel was applied to 319,953 covers bearing one or more of Nos. 2130 and 2133.

2134 14c **Ice Boat,** *Mar. 23, 1985,* Rochester, NY *(324,710)* 1.25
2135 17c **Dog Sled,** *Aug. 20, 1986,* Anchorage, AK 1.50
2136 25c **Bread Wagon,** *Nov. 22, 1986,* Virginia Beach, VA *(151,950)* 1.25

1985

2137 22c **Mary McLeod Bethune,** *Mar. 5 (413,244)* 1.50
2141a 22c **Duck Decoys,** *Mar. 22,* Shelburne, VT *(932,249)* 2.50
2138-2141, any single 1.00
2142 22c **Winter Special Olympics,** *Mar. 25,* Park City, UT *(253,074)* 1.00
2143 22c **Love,** *Apr. 17,* Hollywood, CA *(283,072)* 1.00
2144 22c **Rural Electrification Administration,** *May 11,* Madison, SD *(472,895)* 1.00
2145 22c **AMERIPEX '86,** *May 25,* Rosemont, IL *(457,038)* 1.00
2146 22c **Abigail Adams,** *June 14,* Quincy, MA *(491,026)* 1.00
2147 22c **Frederic Auguste Bartholdi,** *July 18,* New York, NY *(594,896)* 1.00
2149 18c **George Washington, Washington Monument,** *Nov. 6 (376,238)* 1.00
2150 21.1c **Envelopes,** *Oct. 22 (119,941)* 1.00
2152 22c **Korean War Veterans,** *July 26 (391,754)* 3.00
2153 22c **Social Security Act,** *Aug. 14,* Baltimore, MD *(265,143)* 1.00
2154 22c **World War I Veterans,** *Aug. 26,* Milwaukee, WI 1.50
2158a 22c **Horses,** *Sept. 25,* Lexington, KY *(1,135,368)* 2.50
2155-2158, any single 1.50
2159 22c **Public Education in America,** *Oct. 1,* Boston, MA *(356,030)* 1.00
2163a 22c **International Youth Year,** *Oct. 7,* Chicago, IL *(1,202,541)* 2.50
2160, 2162-2163, any single 1.00
2161 2.00
2164 22c **Help End Hunger,** *Oct. 15 (299,485)* 1.00
2165 22c **Christmas (Madonna & Child),** *Oct. 30,* Detroit, MI 1.00
2166 22c **Christmas (Poinsettia),** *Oct. 30,* Nazareth, MI *(524,929)* 1.00

1986

2167 22c **Arkansas Statehood,** *Jan. 3,* Little Rock, AR *(364,729)* 1.00

1986-94

GREAT AMERICANS ISSUE

2168 1c **Margaret Mitchell,** *June 30, 1986,* Atlanta, GA *(316,764)* 2.00
2169 2c **Mary Lyon,** *Feb. 28, 1987,* South Hadley, MA *(349,831)* 1.00
2170 3c **Dr. Paul Dudley White,** *Sept. 15, 1986* 1.00
2171 4c **Father Flanagan,** *July 14, 1986,* Boys Town, NE *(367,883)* 1.25
2172 5c **Hugo Black,** *Feb. 27, 1986 (303,012)* 1.00
2173 5c **Luis Munoz Marin,** *Feb. 18, 1990,* San Juan, PR *(269,618)* 1.00
2175 10c **Red Cloud,** *Aug. 15, 1987,* Red Cloud, NE *(300,472)* 1.50
2176 14c **Julia Ward Howe,** *Feb. 12, 1987,* Boston, MA *(454,829)* 1.00
2177 15c **Buffalo Bill Cody,** *June 6, 1988* Cody, WY *(356,395)* 2.00
2178 17c **Belva Ann Lockwood,** *June 18, 1986,* Middleport, NY *(249,215)* 1.00
2179 20c **Virginia Apgar,** *Oct. 24, 1994,* Dallas, TX *(28,461)* 1.00
2180 21c **Chester Carlson,** *Oct. 21, 1988,* Rochester, NY *(288,073)* 1.00
2181 23c **Mary Cassatt,** *Nov. 4, 1988,* Philadelphia, PA *(322,537)* 1.00
2182 25c **Jack London,** *Jan. 11, 1986,* Glen Ellen, CA *(358,686)* 1.25
2182a Booklet pane of 10, *May 3, 1988,* San Francisco, CA 6.00
2183 28c **Sitting Bull,** *Sept. 14, 1989,* Rapid City, SD *(126,777)* 1.50
2184 29c **Earl Warren,** *Mar. 9, 1992 (175,517)* 1.25
2185 29c **Thomas Jefferson,** *Apr. 13, 1993,* Charlottesville, VA *(202,962)* 1.25
2186 35c **Dennis Chavez,** *Apr. 3, 1991,* Albuquerque, NM *(285,570)* 1.25
2187 40c **Claire Chennault,** *Sept. 6, 1990,* Monroe, LA *(186,761)* 2.00
2188 45c **Harvey Cushing,** *June 17, 1988,* Cleveland, OH *(135,140)* 1.25
2189 52c **Hubert Humphrey,** *June 3, 1991,* Minneapolis, MN *(93,391)* 1.40
2190 56c **John Harvard,** *Sept. 3, 1986,* Cambridge, MA 2.50
2191 65c **Hap Arnold,** *Nov. 5, 1988,* Gladwyne, PA *(129,829)* 2.50
2192 75c **Wendell Willkie,** *Feb. 18, 1992,* Bloomington, IN *(47,086)* 2.50
2193 $1 **Dr. Bernard Revel,** *Sept. 23, 1986,* New York, NY 5.00
2194 $1 **Johns Hopkins,** *June 7, 1989,* Baltimore, MD *(159,049)* 3.00
2195 $2 **William Jennings Bryan,** *Mar. 19, 1986,* Salem, IL *(123,430)* 6.00
2196 $5 **Bret Harte,** *Aug. 25, 1987,* Twain Harte, CA *(111,431)* 15.00
2197 25c **Jack London,** bklt. single, *May 3, 1988,* San Francisco, CA 1.00
2197a Booklet pane of 6 4.00

First day cancel was applied to 94,655 covers bearing one or more of Nos. 2183a, 2197, and 2197a.

1986

2201a 22c **Stamp Collecting Booklet pane of 4,** *Jan. 23,* State College, PA 4.00
2198-2201, any single 1.00

First day cancellation was applied to 675,924 covers bearing one or more of Nos. 2198-2201a.

2202 22c **Love,** *Jan. 30,* New York, NY 1.00
2203 22c **Sojourner Truth,** *Feb. 4,* New Paltz, NY *(342,985)* 1.75
2204 22c **Republic of Texas,** *Mar. 2,* San Antonio, TX *(380,450)* 1.75
2209a 22c **Fish Booklet pane of 5,** *Mar. 21,* Seattle, WA 5.00
2205-2209, any single 1.25

First day cancellation was applied to 988,184 covers bearing one or more of Nos. 2205-2209a.

2210 22c **Public Hospitals,** *Apr. 11,* New York, NY *(403,665)* 1.00
2211 22c **Duke Ellington,** *Apr. 29,* New York, NY *(397,894)* 2.25
2216 22c **Presidents Souvenir Sheet of 9 (Washington-Harrison),** *May 22,* Chicago, IL 4.00
2217 22c **Presidents Souvenir Sheet of 9 (Tyler-Grant),** *May 22,* Chicago, IL 4.00
2218 22c **Presidents Souvenir Sheet of 9 (Hayes-Wilson),** *May 22,* Chicago, IL 4.00
2219 22c **Presidents Souvenir Sheet of 9 (Harding-Johnson),** *May 22,* Chicago, IL 4.00
2216a-2219g, 2219i, any single 1.50
2219h 2.50

First day cancellation was applied to 9,009,599 covers bearing one or more of Nos. 2216-2219, 2216a-2219i.

2223a 22c **Polar Explorers,** *May 28,* North Pole, AK *(760,999)* 3.75
2220-2223, any single 1.25
2224 22c **Statue of Liberty,** *July 4,* New York, NY *(1,540,308)* 1.25

1986-87

TRANSPORTATION ISSUE

2225 1c **Omnibus,** *Nov. 26, 1986 (57,845)* 1.00
2226 2c **Locomotive,** *Mar. 6, 1987,* Milwaukee, WI *(169,484)* 1.50

1986

2238a 22c **Navajo Art,** *Sept. 4,* Window Rock, AZ *(1,102,520)* 2.00
2235-2238, any single 1.00
2239 22c **T.S. Eliot,** *Sept. 26,* St. Louis, MO *(304,764)* 1.00
2243a 22c **Woodcarved Figurines,** *Oct. 1 (629,399)* 2.00
2240-2243, any single 1.00
2244 22c **Christmas (Madonna),** *Oct. 24 (467,999)* 1.00
2245 22c **Christmas (Winter Village),** *Oct. 24,* Snow Hill, MD *(504,851)* 1.00

1987

2246 22c **Michigan Statehood Sesquicent.,** *Jan. 26,* Lansing, MI *(379,117)* 1.00
2247 22c **Pan American Games,** *Jan. 29,* Indianapolis, IN *(344,731)* 1.00
2248 22c **Love,** *Jan. 30,* San Francisco, CA *(333,329)* 1.00
2249 22c **Pointe du Sable,** *Feb. 20,* Chicago, IL *(313,054)* 1.50
2250 22c **Enrico Caruso,** *Feb. 27,* New York, NY *(389,834)* 1.00
2251 22c **Girl Scouts of America,** *Mar. 12 (556,391)* 2.50

1987-88

TRANSPORTATION ISSUE

2252 3c **Conestoga Wagon,** *Feb. 29, 1988,* Conestoga, PA *(155,203)* 1.00
2253 5c **Milk Wagon,** *Sept. 25, 1987,* Indianapolis, IN 1.00

First day cancel was applied to 162,571 covers bearing one or more of Nos. 2253 and 2262.

2254 5.3c **Elevator,** *Sept. 16, 1988,* New York, NY *(142,705)* 1.00
2255 7.6c **Carretta,** *Aug. 30, 1988,* San Jose, CA *(140,024)* 1.00
2256 8.4c **Wheelchair,** *Aug. 12, 1988,* Tucson, AZ *(136,337)* 1.00
2257 10c **Canal Boat,** *Apr. 11, 1987,* Buffalo, NY *(171,952)* 1.00
2258 13c **Police Patrol Wagon,** *Oct. 29, 1988,* Anaheim, CA *(132,928)* 1.50
2259 13.2c **Railway Coal Car,** *July 19, 1988,* Pittsburgh, PA *(123,965)* 1.00
2260 15c **Tugboat,** *July 12, 1988,* Long Beach, CA *(134,926)* 1.00
2261 16.7c **Popcorn Wagon,** *July 7, 1988,* Chicago, IL *(117,908)* 1.00
2262 17.5c **Racing Car,** *Sept. 25, 1987,* Indianapolis, IN 1.25
2263 20c **Cable Car,** *Oct. 28, 1988,* San Francisco, CA *(150,068)* 1.00
2264 20.5c **Fire Engine,** *Sept. 28, 1988,* San Angelo, TX *(123,043)* 1.50
2265 21c **Railway Mail Car,** *Aug. 16, 1988,* Santa Fe, NM *(124,430)* 1.00
2266 24.1c **Tandem Bicycle,** *Oct. 26, 1988,* Redmond, WA *(138,593)* 1.50

1987

2274a 22c **Special Occasions Booklet pane of 10,** *Apr. 20,* Atlanta, GA 5.00
2267-2274, any single 1.00

First day cancellation was applied to 1,588,129 covers bearing one or more of Nos. 2267-2274a.

2275 22c **United Way,** *Apr. 28 (556,391)* 1.00

1987-89

2276 22c **Flag and Fireworks,** *May 9, 1987* Denver, CO *(398,855)* 1.00
2276a Booklet pane of 20, *Nov. 30, 1987* 8.00
2277 (25c) **"E" Earth,** *Mar. 22, 1988* 1.25
2278 25c **Flag and Clouds,** *May 6, 1988,* Boxborough, MA *(131,265)* 1.25
2279 (25c) **"E" Earth,** coil, *Mar. 22, 1988* 1.25
2280 25c **Flag over Yosemite,** large block tagging, *May 20, 1988,* Yosemite, CA *(144,339)* 1.25
2280a 25c Prephosphored paper, *Feb. 14, 1989,* Yosemite, CA *(118,874)* 1.25
2281 25c **Honey Bee,** *Sept. 2, 1988,* Omaha, NE *(122,853)* 1.25
2282 (25c) **"E" Earth,** bklt. single, *Mar. 22, 1988* 1.25
2282a Booklet pane of 10 6.00

First day cancel was applied to 363,639 covers bearing one or more of Nos. 2277, 2279 and 2282.

2283 25c **Pheasant,** *Apr. 29, 1988,* Rapid City, SD *(167,053)* 1.25
2283a Booklet pane of 10 6.00
2285b 25c **Grosbeak & Owl, booklet pane of 10** *May 28, 1988,* Arlington, VA 6.00
2284-2285, any single 1.25

First day cancel was applied to 272,359 covers bearing one or more of Nos. 2284 and 2285.

2285A 25c **Flag and Clouds,** bklt. single, *July 5, 1988 (117,303)* 1.00
2285Ac Booklet pane of 6 4.00

2335a 22c **American Wildlife,** *June 13, 1987,* Toronto, Canada 50.00
2286-2335, any single 1.50

1987-90 RATIFICATION OF THE CONSTITUTION

2336 22c **Delaware,** *July 4, 1987,* Dover, DE *(505,770)* 1.50
2337 22c **Pennsylvania,** *Aug. 26, 1987,* Harrisburg, PA *(367,184)* 1.50
2338 22c **New Jersey,** *Sept. 11, 1987,* Trenton, NJ *(432,899)* 1.50
2339 22c **Georgia,** *Jan. 6, 1988,* Atlanta, GA *(467,804)* 1.50
2340 22c **Connecticut,** *Jan. 9, 1988,* Hartford, CT *(379,706)* 1.50
2341 22c **Massachusetts,** *Feb. 6, 1988,* Boston, MA *(412,616)* 1.50
2342 22c **Maryland,** *Feb. 15, 1988,* Annapolis, MD *(376,403)* 1.50
2343 25c **South Carolina,** *May 23, 1988,* Columbia, SC *(322,938)* 1.50
2344 25c **New Hampshire,** *June 21, 1988,* Concord, NH *(374,402)* 1.50
2345 25c **Virginia,** *June 25, 1988,* Williamsburg, VA *(474,079)* 1.50
2346 25c **New York,** *July 26, 1988,* Albany, NY *(385,793)* 1.50
2347 25c **North Carolina,** *Aug. 22, 1989,* Fayetteville, NC *(392,953)* 1.50
2348 25c **Rhode Island,** *May 29, 1990,* Pawtucket, RI *(305,566)* 1.50

1987

2349 22c **U.S.-Morocco Diplomatic Relations Bicent.,** *July 17 (372,814)* 1.00
2350 22c **William Faulkner,** *Aug. 3,* Oxford, MS *(480,024)* 1.00
2354a 22c **Lacemaking,** *Aug. 14,* Ypsilanti, MI 2.50
2351-2354, any single 1.00
2359a 22c **Drafting of Constitution Bicent. Booklet pane of 5,** *Aug. 28* 4.00
2355-2359, any single 1.25

First day cancellation was applied to 1,008,799 covers bearing one or more of Nos. 2355-2359a.

2360 22c **Signing of Constitution Bicent.,** *Sept. 17,* Philadelphia, PA *(719,975)* 1.25
2361 22c **Certified Public Accounting,** *Sept. 21,* New York, NY *(362,099)* 7.50
2366a 22c **Locomotives booklet pane of 5,** *Oct. 1,* Baltimore, MD 3.00
2362-2366, any single 1.25

First day cancellation was applied to 976,694 covers bearing one or more of Nos. 2362-2366a.

2367 22c **Christmas (Madonna),** *Oct. 23 (320,406)* 1.25
2368 22c **Christmas (Ornaments),** *Oct. 23,* Holiday-Anaheim, CA *(375,858)* 1.25

1988

2369 22c **Winter Olympics, Calgary,** *Jan. 10,* Anchorage, AK *(395,198)* 1.00
2370 22c **Australia Bicentennial,** *Jan. 26 (523,465)* 1.75
2371 22c **James Weldon Johnson,** *Feb. 2,* Nashville, TN *(465,282)* 1.75
2375a 22c **Cats,** *Feb. 5,* New York, NY *(872,734)* 4.50
2372-2375, any single 2.00
2376 22c **Knute Rockne,** *Mar. 9,* Notre Dame, IN *(404,311)* 4.00
2377 25c **Francis Ouimet,** *June 13,* Brookline, MA *(383,168)* 4.50
2378 25c **Love,** *July 4,* Pasadena, CA *(399,038)* 1.00
2379 45c **Love,** *Aug. 8,* Shreveport, LA *(121,808)* 1.25
2380 25c **Summer Olympics, Seoul,** *Aug. 19,* Colorado Springs, CO *(402,616)* 1.25
2385a 25c **Automobiles booklet pane of 5,** *Aug. 25,* Detroit, MI 4.00
2381-2385, any single 1.25

First day cancel was applied to 875,801 covers bearing one or more of Nos. 2381-2385a.

2389a 25c **Antarctic Explorers,** *Sept. 14 (720,537)* 3.00
2386-2389, any single 1.25
2393a 25c **Carousel Animals,** *Oct. 1,* Sandusky, OH *(856,380)* 3.50
2390-2393, any single 1.50
2394 $8.75 **Express Mail,** *Oct. 4,* Terre Haute, IN *(66,558)* 27.50
2396a 25c **Special Occasions (Happy Birthday, Best Wishes),** *Oct. 22,* King of Prussia, PA 4.00
2395-2396, any single 1.25
2398a 25c **Special Occasions (Thinking of You, Love You),** *Oct. 22,* King of Prussia, PA 4.00
2397-2398, any single 1.25

First day cancel was applied to 126,767 covers bearing one or more of Nos. 2395-2398, 2396a, 2398a.

2399 25c **Christmas (Madonna),** *Oct. 20 (247,291)* 1.25
2400 25c **Christmas (Contemporary),** *Oct. 20,* Berlin, NH *(412,213)* 1.25

1989

2401 25c **Montana,** *Jan. 15,* Helena, MT *(353,319)* 1.25
2402 25c **A. Philip Randolph,** *Feb. 3,* New York, NY *(363,174)* 1.75

2403 25c **North Dakota,** *Feb. 21,* Bismarck, ND *(306,003)* 1.00
2404 25c **Washington Statehood,** *Feb. 22,* Olympia, WA *(445,174)* 1.00
2409a 25c **Steamboats Booklet pane of 5,** *Mar. 3,* New Orleans, LA 3.00
2405-2409, any single 1.25

First day cancel was applied to 981,674 covers bearing one or more of Nos. 2405-2409a.

2410 25c **World Stamp Expo,** *Mar. 16,* New York, NY *(296,310)* 1.00
2411 25c **Arturo Toscanini,** *Mar. 25,* New York, NY *(309,441)* 1.00

1989-90

BRANCHES OF GOVERNMENT

2412 25c **House of Representatives,** *Apr. 4, 1989 (327,755)* 1.25
2413 25c **Senate,** *Apr. 6, 1989 (341,288)* 1.25
2414 25c **Executive Branch,** *Apr. 16, 1989* Mount Vernon, VA *(387,644)* 1.25
2415 25c **Supreme Court,** *Feb. 2, 1990 (233,056)* 1.25

1989

2416 25c **South Dakota,** *May 3,* Pierre, SD *(348,370)* 1.00
2417 25c **Lou Gehrig,** *June 10,* Cooperstown, NY *(694,227)* 4.00
2418 25c **Ernest Hemingway,** *July 17,* Key West, FL *(345,436)* 1.25
2419 $2.40 **Moon Landing,** *July 20 (208,982)* 7.50
2420 25c **Letter Carriers,** *Aug. 30,* Milwaukee, WI *(372,241)* 1.25
2421 25c **Bill of Rights,** *Sept. 25,* Philadelphia, PA *(900,384)* 1.00
2425a 25c **Dinosaurs,** *Oct. 1,* Orlando, FL *(871,634)* 3.00
2422-2425, any single 1.50
2426 25c **Southwest Carved Figure,** *Oct. 12,* San Juan, PR *(215,285)* 1.00
2427 25c **Christmas (Madonna),** *Oct. 19 (395,321)* 1.00
2427a Booklet pane of 10 6.00
2428 25c **Christmas (Sleigh with Presents),** *Oct. 19,* Westport, CT 1.00
2429 25c **Christmas (Sleigh with Presents) from bklt.,** *Oct. 19,* Westport, CT 1.00
2429a Booklet pane of 10 6.00

First day cancel was applied to 345,931 covers bearing one or more of Nos. 2428-2429a.

2431 25c **Eagle and Shield,** *Nov. 10,* Virginia Beach, VA 1.25
2433 90c **World Stamp Expo '89 Souvenir Sheet,** *Nov. 17 (281,725)* 7.00
2437a 25c **Classic Mail Transportation,** *Nov. 19 (916,389)* 2.50
2434-2437, any single 1.25
2438 25c **Classic Mail Transportation Souvenir Sheet,** *Nov. 28 (241,634)* 3.00

1990

2439 25c **Idaho Statehood,** *Jan. 6,* Boise, ID *(252,493)* 1.25
2440 25c **Love,** *Jan. 18,* Romance, AR 1.25
2441 25c **Love, from bklt.,** *Jan. 18,* Romance, AR 1.00
2441a Booklet pane of 10 6.00

First day cancel was applied to 257,788 covers bearing one or more of Nos. 2440-2441a.

2442 25c **Ida B. Wells,** *Feb. 1,* Chicago, IL *(229,226)* 2.00
2443 15c **Beach Umbrella,** *Feb. 3,* Sarasota, FL 1.25
2443a Booklet pane of 10 4.25

First day cancel was applied to 72,286 covers bearing one or more of Nos. 2443-2443a.

2444 25c **Wyoming Statehood,** *Feb. 23,* Cheyenne, WY *(317,654)* 1.00
2448a 25c **Classic Films,** *Mar. 23,* Hollywood, CA *(863,079)* 5.00
2445-2448, any single 2.50
2449 25c **Marianne Moore,** *Apr. 18,* Brooklyn, NY *(390,535)* 1.25

1990-95

TRANSPORTATION COILS

2451 4c **Steam Carriage,** *Jan. 25, 1991,* Tucson, AZ *(100,393)* 1.25
2452 5c **Circus Wagon,** engraved, *Aug. 31, 1990,* Syracuse, NY *(71,806)* 1.50
2452B 5c **Circus Wagon,** photogravure, *Dec. 8, 1992,* Cincinnati, OH 1.50
2452D 5c **Circus Wagon,** with cent sign, photogravure, *Mar. 20, 1995,* Kansas City MO *(20,835)* 2.00
2453 5c **Canoe,** engraved, *May 25, 1991,* Secaucus, NJ *(108,634)* 1.25
2454 5c **Canoe,** photogravure, *Oct. 22, 1991,* Secaucus, NJ 1.25
2457 10c **Tractor Trailer,** engr., *May 25, 1991,* Secaucus, NJ *(84,717)* 1.25
2458 10c **Tractor Trailer,** photo., *May 25, 1994,* Secaucus, NJ *(15,431)* 1.25
2463 20c **Cog Railway,** *June 9, 1995,* Dallas, TX *(28,883)* 1.25
2464 23c **Lunch Wagon,** *Apr. 12, 1991,* Columbus, OH *(115,830)* 1.25
2466 32c **Ferry Boat,** *June 2, 1995,* McLean VA 1.25

First day cancellation was applied to 59,100 covers bearing one or more of Nos. 2466, 2492.

2468 $1 **Seaplane,** *Apr. 20, 1990* Phoenix, AZ *(244,775)* 2.50

1990

2474a 25c **Lighthouses booklet pane of 5,** *Apr. 26* 4.00
2470-2474, any single 1.50

First day cancel was applied to 805,133 covers bearing one or more of Nos. 2470-2474a.

2475 25c **Flag,** *May 18,* Seattle, WA *(97,567)* 1.00

1990-95

FLORA AND FAUNA ISSUE

2476 1c **Kestrel,** *June 22,* Aurora, CO *(77,781)* 1.00
2477 1c **Kestrel, with cent sign,** *May 10, 1995* Aurora, CO *(21,767)* 1.00
2478 3c **Eastern Bluebird,** *June 22,* Aurora, CO *(76,149)* 1.00
2479 19c **Fawn,** *Mar. 11 (100,212)* 1.00
2480 30c **Cardinal,** *June 22,* Aurora, CO *(101,290)* 1.25
2481 45c **Pumpkinseed Sunfish,** *Dec. 2, 1992 (38,696)* 1.75
2482 $2 **Bobcat,** *June 1,* Arlington, VA *(49,660)* 5.00
2483 20c **Blue Jay,** booklet single, *June 15, 1995,* Kansas City MO 1.25

First day cancellation was applied to 16,847 covers bearing one or more of Nos. 2483, 2483a.

2484 29c **Wood Duck,** black denomination bklt. single, *Apr. 12,* Columbus, OH 1.00
2484a Booklet pane of 10 4.00
2485 29c **Wood Duck,** red denomination bklt. single, *Apr. 12,* Columbus, OH 1.00
2485a Booklet pane of 10 4.00

First day cancel was applied to 205,305 covers bearing one or more of Nos. 2484-2485, 2484a-2485a.

2486 29c **African Violet,** *Oct. 8, 1993,* Beaumont, TX 1.00
2486a Booklet pane of 10 4.00

First day cancellation was applied to 40,167 covers bearing one or more of Nos. 2486-2486a.

2487 32c **Peach,** booklet single, *July 8, 1995,* Reno NV 1.50
2488 32c **Pear,** booklet single, *July 8, 1995,* Reno NV 1.50

First day cancellation was applied to 71,086 covers bearing one or more of Nos. 2487-2488, 2488a, 2493-2495A.

2488a Booklet pane, 5 each #2488-2489 7.50
2489 29c **Red Squirrel,** self-adhesive, *June 25, 1993* Milwaukee, WI *(48,564)* 1.25
2490 29c **Red Rose,** self-adhesive, *Aug. 19, 1993* Houston, TX *(37,916)* 1.25
2491 29c **Pine Cone,** self-adhesive, *Nov. 5, 1993* Kansas City, MO *(110,924)* 1.25
2492 32c **Pink Rose,** self-adhesive, *June 2, 1995,* McLean VA 1.25

First day cancellation was applied to 59,100 covers bearing one or more of Nos. 2466, 2492.

2493 32c **Peach,** self-adhesive, *July 8, 1995,* Reno NV 1.25
2494 32c **Pear,** self-adhesive, *July 8, 1995,* Reno NV 1.25
2495 32c **Peach,** self-adhesive, serpentine die cut vert., *July 8, 1995,* Reno NV 1.25
2495A 32c **Pear,** self-adhesive, serpentine die cut vert., *July 8, 1995,* Reno NV 1.25

First day cancellation was applied to 71,086 covers bearing one or more of Nos. 2487-2488, 2488a, 2493-2495A.

1990

2500a 25c **Olympians,** *July 6,* Minneapolis, MN *(1,143,404)* 4.00
2496-2500, any single 1.25
2505a 25c **Indian Headdresses, booklet pane of 10** *Aug. 17,* Cody, WY 6.00
2501-2505, any single 1.25

First day cancel was applied to 979,580 covers bearing one or more of Nos. 2501-2505a.

2507a 25c **Micronesia, Marshall Islands,** *Sept. 28 (343,816)* 2.00
2506-2507, any single 1.25
2511a 25c **Sea Creatures,** *Oct. 3,* Baltimore, MD *(706,047)* 3.00
2508-2511, any single 1.25
2512 25c **Grand Canyon,** *Oct. 12,* Grand Canyon, AZ *(164,190)* 1.75
2513 25c **Dwight D. Eisenhower,** *Oct. 13,* Abilene, KS *(487,988)* 1.50
2514 25c **Christmas (traditional),** *Oct. 18* 1.25
2514a Booklet pane of 10 6.00

First day cancel was applied to 378,383 covers bearing one or more of Nos. 2514-2514a.

2515 25c **Christmas (secular),** *Oct. 18,* Evergreen, CO 1.25
2516 25c **Christmas (secular),** *Oct. 18,* Evergreen, CO 1.00
2516a Booklet pane of 10 6.00

First day cancel was applied to 230,586 covers bearing one or more of Nos. 2515-2516a.

1991-94

2517 (29c) **"F" Flower,** *Jan. 22, 1991 (106,698)* 1.25
2518 (29c) **"F" Flower,** coil, *Jan. 22, 1991 (39,311)* 1.25
2519 (29c) **"F" Flower,** bklt. single (bullseye perf. 11.2), *Jan. 22, 1991* 1.00
2519a Booklet pane of 10 7.25
2520 (29c) **"F" Flower,** bklt. single (perf. 11), *Jan. 22, 1991* 1.25
2520a Booklet pane of 10 8.00

First day cancel was applied to 32,971 covers bearing one or more of Nos. 2519-2520, 2519a-2520a.

2521 (4c) **Makeup Stamp,** *Jan. 22, 1991 (51,987)* 1.25
2522 (29c) **"F" Flag,** *Jan. 22, 1991 (48,821)* 1.25
2523 29c **Flag over Mt. Rushmore,** engraved, *Mar. 29, 1991* Mt. Rushmore, SD *(233,793)* 1.25
2523A 29c **Flag over Mt. Rushmore,** photogravure, *July 4, 1991* Mt. Rushmore, SD *(80,662)* 1.25
2524 29c **Flower,** *Apr. 5, 1991,* Rochester, NY *(132,233)* 1.00
2525 29c **Flower,** roulette 10 coil, *Aug. 16, 1991,* Rochester, NY *(144,750)* 1.00
2526 29c **Flower,** perf. 10 coil, *Mar. 3, 1992,* Rochester, NY *(35,877)* 1.00
2527 29c **Flower,** bklt. single, *Apr. 5, 1991,* Rochester, NY 1.00
2527a Booklet pane of 10 4.00

First day cancel was applied to 16,975 covers bearing one or more of Nos. 2527-2527a.

2528 29c **Flag and Olympic Rings,** bklt. single, *Apr. 21, 1991,* Atlanta, GA 1.25
2528a Booklet pane of 10 5.00

First day cancel was applied to 319,488 covers bearing one or more of Nos. 2528-2528a.

2529 19c **Fishing Boat,** two loops, *Aug. 8, 1991 (82,698)* 1.50
2529C 19c **Fishing Boat,** one loop, *June 25, 1994,* Arlington, VA *(14,538)* 1.50
2530 19c **Balloon,** *May 17, 1991,* Denver, CO 1.25
2530a Booklet pane of 10 5.00

First day cancel was applied to 96,351 covers bearing one or more of Nos. 2530-2530a.

2531 29c **Flags on Parade,** *May 30, 1991,* Waterloo, NY *(104,046)* 1.00
2531A 29c **Liberty Torch,** *June 25, 1991,* New York, NY *(68,456)* 1.25

1991-95

2532 50c **Switzerland,** *Feb. 22,* Washington, DC *(316,047)* 1.40
2533 29c **Vermont,** *Mar. 1,* Bennington, VT *(308,105)* 1.50
2534 29c **Savings Bonds,** *Apr. 30,* Washington, DC *(341,955)* 1.25
2535 29c **Love,** *May 9,* Honolulu, HI *(336,132)* 1.25
2536 29c **Love,** bklt. single, *May 9,* Honolulu, HI 1.25
2536a Booklet pane of 10 5.00

First day cancel was applied to 43,336 covers bearing one or more of Nos. 2536-2536a.

2537 52c **Love,** *May 9,* Honolulu, HI *(90,438)* 1.25
2538 29c **William Saroyan,** *May 22,* Fresno, CA *(334,373)* 1.50
2539 $1 **Eagle & Olympic Rings,** *Sept. 29,* Orlando, FL *(69,241)* 2.25
2540 $2.90 **Eagle & Olympic Rings,** *July 7,* San Diego, CA *(79,555)* 5.50
2541 $9.95 **Eagle & Olympic Rings,** *June 16,* Sacramento, CA *(68,657)* 15.00
2542 $14 **Eagle,** *Aug. 31,* Hunt Valley, MD *(54,727)* 27.50
2543 $2.90 **Futuristic Space Shuttle,** *June 3, 1993,* Kennedy Space Center, FL *(36,359)* 6.00
2544 $3 **Space Shuttle Challenger,** *June 22, 1995* Anaheim CA *(16,502)* 6.00
2544A $10.75 **Space Shuttle Endeavour,** *Aug. 4, 1995* Irvine CA *(10,534)* 15.00

1991

2549a 29c **Fishing Flies booklet pane of 5,** *May 31,* Cuddebackville, NY *(1,045,726)* 3.00
2545-2549, any single 1.25
2550 29c **Cole Porter,** *June 8,* Peru, IN *(304,363)* 1.25
2551 29c **Desert Storm/ Desert Shield,** *July 2* 2.50
2552 29c **Desert Storm/ Desert Shield,** bklt. single, *July 2* 2.50
2552a Booklet pane of 5 5.00

First day cancel was applied to 860,455 covers bearing one or more of Nos. 2551-2552, 2552a.

2557a 29c **Summer Olympics,** *July 12,* Los Angeles, CA *(886,984)* 3.00
2553-2557, any single 1.25
2558 29c **Numismatics,** *Aug. 13,* Chicago, IL *(288,519)* 1.25

2559 29c **World War II block of 10,** *Sept. 3,* Phoenix, AZ *(1,832,967)* 7.00
2559a-2559j, any single 2.00
2560 29c **Basketball,** *Aug. 28,* Springfield, MA *(295,471)* 2.25
2561 29c **District of Columbia,** *Sept. 7 (299,989)* 1.25
2566a 29c **Comedians booklet pane of 10,** *Aug. 29,* Hollywood, CA 3.00
2562-2566, any single 1.25

First day cancel was applied to 954,293 covers bearing one or more of Nos. 2562-2566a.

2567 29c **Jan Matzeliger,** *Sept. 15,* Lynn, MA *(289,034)* 1.75
2577a 29c **Space Exploration booklet pane of 10,** *Oct. 1,* Pasadena, CA 5.00
2568-2577, any single 1.25

First day cancel was applied to 1,465,111 covers bearing one or more of Nos. 2568-2577a.

2578 (29c) **Christmas (religious),** *Oct. 17,* Houston, TX 1.25
2579 (29c) **Christmas (secular),** *Oct. 17,* Santa, ID *(169,750)* 1.25
2581b (29c) **Christmas booklet pane of 4,** *Oct. 17,* Santa, ID 2.50
2580-2581, any single 1.25
2582 (29c) **Christmas,** bklt. single, *Oct. 17,* Santa, ID 1.25
2582a Booklet pane of 4 2.50
2583 (29c) **Christmas,** bklt. single, *Oct. 17,* Santa, ID 1.25
2583a Booklet pane of 4 2.50
2584 (29c) **Christmas,** bklt. single, *Oct. 17,* Santa, ID 1.25
2584a Booklet pane of 4 2.50
2585 (29c) **Christmas,** bklt. single, *Oct. 17,* Santa, ID 1.25
2585a Booklet pane of 4 2.50

First day cancel was applied to 168,794 covers bearing one or more of Nos. 2580-2585, 2581b, 2582a, 2583a, 2584a and 2585a.

1991-95

2587 32c **James K. Polk,** *Nov. 2, 1995,* Columbia TN *(189,429)* 1.25
2590 $1 **Surrender of Gen. John Burgoyne,** *May 5, 1994,* New York, NY *(379,629)* 2.50
2592 $5 **Washington & Jackson,** *Aug. 19, 1994,* Pittsburgh, PA *(16,303)* 12.50
2593 29c **Pledge of Allegiance,** black denomination, *Sept. 8, 1992,* Rome, NY 1.25
2593a Booklet pane of 10 5.00

First day cancel was applied to 61,464 covers bearing one or more of Nos. 2593-2593a.

2595 29c **Eagle & Shield,** brown denomination, *Sept. 25, 1992,* Dayton, OH 1.50
2596 29c **Eagle & Shield,** green denomination, *Sept. 25, 1992,* Dayton, OH 1.50
2597 29c **Eagle & Shield,** red denomination, *Sept. 25, 1992,* Dayton, OH 1.50

First day cancel was applied to 65,822 covers bearing one or more of Nos. 2595-2597.

2598 29c **Eagle,** *Feb. 4, 1994,* Sarasota, FL *(67,300)* 1.25
2599 29c **Statue of Liberty,** *June 24, 1994,* Haines City, FL *(39,810)* 1.25
2602 (10c) **Eagle & Shield,** Bulk Rate USA, *Dec. 13, 1991,* Kansas City, MO *(21,176)* 1.25
2603 (10c) **Eagle & Shield,** USA Bulk Rate, *May 29, 1993,* Secaucus, NJ 1.25
2604 (10c) **Eagle & Shield,** gold eagle, *May 29, 1993,* Secaucus, NJ 1.25

First day cancellation was applied to 36,444 covers bearing one or more of Nos. 2603-2604.

2605 23c **Flag,** *Sept. 27, 1991* 1.25
2606 23c **Reflected Flag,** *July 21, 1992,* Kansas City, MO *(35,673)* 1.25
2607 23c **Reflected Flag,** 7mm "23," *Oct. 9, 1992,* Kansas City, MO 1.25
2608 23c **Reflected Flag,** 8 ½mm "First Class" *May 14, 1993,* Denver, CO *(15,548)* 1.25
2609 29c **Flag over White House,** *Apr. 23, 1992 (56,505)* 1.25

1992

2615a 29c **Winter Olympics,** *Jan. 11,* Orlando, FL *(1,062,048)* 3.50
2611-2615, any single 1.25
2616 29c **World Columbian Stamp Expo,** *Jan. 24,* Rosemont, IL *(309,729)* 1.25
2617 29c **W.E.B. Du Bois,** *Jan. 31,* Atlanta, GA *(196,219)* 1.75
2618 29c **Love,** *Feb. 6,* Loveland, CO *(218,043)* 1.25
2619 29c **Olympic Baseball,** *Apr. 3,* Atlanta, GA *(105,996)* 2.00
2623a 29c **Voyages of Columbus,** *Apr. 24,* Christiansted, VI 2.75
2620-2623, any single 1.25

First day cancellation was applied to 509,270 covers bearing one or more of Nos. 2620-2623a.

2624 **First Sighting of Land Souvenir Sheet of 3,** *May 22,* Chicago, IL 3.50
2624a 1c 1.50
2624b 4c 1.50
2624c $1 2.50
2625 **Claiming a New World Souvenir Sheet of 3,** *May 22,* Chicago, IL 9.00
2625a 2c 1.50
2625b 3c 1.50
2625c $4 8.00
2626 **Seeking Royal Support Souvenir Sheet of 3,** *May 22,* Chicago, IL 3.00
2626a 5c 1.50
2626b 30c 1.50
2626c 50c 2.00
2627 **Royal Favor Restored Souvenir Sheet of 3,** *May 22,* Chicago, IL 7.50
2627a 6c 1.50
2627b 8c 1.50
2627c $3 7.50
2628 **Reporting Discoveries Souvenir Sheet of 3,** *May 22,* Chicago, IL 8.50
2628a 10c 1.50
2628b 15c 1.50
2628c $2 5.00
2629 $5 **Christopher Columbus Souvenir Sheet,** *May 22,* Chicago, IL 12.50

First day cancel was applied to 211,142 covers bearing one or more of Nos. 2624-2629.

2630 29c **New York Stock Exchange,** *May 17,* New York, NY *(261,897)* 2.50
2634a 29c **Space Accomplishments,** *May 29,* Chicago, IL 2.75
2631-2634, any single 1.50

First day cancel was applied to 277,853 covers bearing one or more of Nos. 2631-2634a.

2635 29c **Alaska Highway,** *May 30,* Fairbanks, AK *(186,791)* 1.25
2636 29c **Kentucky,** *June 1,* Danville, KY *(251,153)* 1.25
2641a 29c **Summer Olympics,** *June 11,* Baltimore, MD *(713,942)* 3.00
2637-2641, any single 1.25
2646a 29c **Hummingbirds booklet pane of 5,** *June 15* 3.00
2642-2646, any single 1.25

First day cancel was applied to 995,278 covers bearing one or more of Nos. 2642-2646a.

2696a 29c **Wildflowers,** *July 24,* Columbus, OH 30.00
2647-2696, any single 1.25

First day cancellation was applied to 3,693,972 covers bearing one or more of Nos. 2647-2696a.

2697 29c **World War II block of 10,** *Aug. 17,* Indianapolis, IN *(1,734,880)* 7.00
2697a-2697j, any single 2.00

First day cancellation was applied to 1,734,880 covers bearing one or more of Nos. 2697, 2697a-2697j.

2698 29c **Dorothy Parker,** *Aug. 22,* West End, NJ *(266,323)* 1.50
2699 29c **Theodore von Karman,** *Aug. 31 (256,986)* 1.50
2703a 29c **Minerals,** *Sept. 17* 2.75
2700-2703, any single 1.25

First day cancellation was applied to 681,416 covers bearing one or more of Nos. 2700-2703.

2704 29c **Juan Rodriguez Cabrillo,** *Sept. 28,* San Diego, CA *(290,720)* 1.25
2709a 29c **Wild Animals booklet pane of 5,** *Oct. 1,* New Orleans, LA 3.25
Any other city 4.00
2705-2709, any single 1.25

First day cancel was applied to 604,205 New Orleans covers bearing one or more of Nos. 2705-2709a.

2710 29c **Christmas (religious),** *Oct. 22* 1.25
2710a Booklet pane of 10 7.25

First day cancel was applied to 201,576 covers bearing one or more of Nos. 2710-2710a.

2714a 29c **Christmas (secular),** *Oct. 22,* Kansas City, MO 2.75
2711-2714, any single 1.25
2718a 29c **Christmas (secular) booklet pane of 4,** *Oct. 22,* Kansas City, MO 2.75
2715-2718, any single 1.25

First day cancel was applied to 461,937 covers bearing one or more of Nos. 2711-2714, 2715-2718 and 2718a.

2719 29c **Christmas (secular),** self-adhesive, *Oct. 28,* New York, NY *(48,873)* 1.25
2720 29c **Chinese New Year,** *Dec. 30,* San Francisco, CA *(138,238)* 2.25

1993

2721 29c **Elvis (Presley),** *Jan. 8,* Memphis, TN, AM cancellation, *(4,452,815)* 2.00
Any city, PM cancellation 3.00
2722 29c **Oklahoma!,** *Mar. 30,* Oklahoma City, OK *(283,837)* 1.25
2723 29c **Hank Williams,** perf 10, *June 9,* Nashville, TN 1.25
2723A 29c **Hank Williams,** perf 11.2x11.5, *June 9,* Nashville, TN —

First day cancel was applied to 311,106 covers bearing one or more of Nos. 2723-2723A.

2730a 29c **Rock & Roll/Rhythm & Blues Musicians,** *June 16,* Cleveland OH or Santa Monica CA 5.00
Any other city 5.00
2724-2730, any single 1.25
Any single, any other city 1.25

Value for No. 2730a is also for any se-tenant configuration of seven different stamps.

First day cancel was applied to 540,809 covers bearing one or more of Nos. 2724-2730a, 2731-2737b.

2737a 29c **Rock & Roll/Rhythm & Blues Musicians booklet pane of 8,** *June 16,* Cleveland, OH or Santa Monica CA 5.25
Any other city 5.25
2731-2737, any single 1.25
Any single, any other city 1.25
2737b 29c **Rock & Roll/Rhythm & Blues Musicians booklet pane of 4,** *June 16,* Cleveland, OH or Santa Monica CA 2.75
Any other city 2.75

For first day cancellation quantities, see No. 2730a.

2745a 29c **Space Fantasy booklet pane of 5,** *Jan. 25,* Huntsville, AL 3.25
2741-2745, any single 1.25

First day cancel was applied to 631,203 covers bearing one or more of Nos. 2741-2745a.

2746 29c **Percy Lavon Julian,** *Jan. 29,* Chicago, IL *(120,877)* 1.75
2747 29c **Oregon Trail,** *Feb. 12,* Salem, OR *(436,550)* 1.25

No. 2747 was also available on the first day of issue in 36 cities along the route of the Oregon Trail.

2748 29c **World University Games,** *Feb. 25,* Buffalo, NY *(157,563)* 1.50
2749 29c **Grace Kelly,** *Mar. 24,* Beverly Hills, CA *(263,913)* 3.00
2753a 29c **Circus,** *Apr. 6* 3.00
2750-2753, any single 1.50

First day cancel was applied to 676,927 covers bearing one or more of Nos. 2750-2753a.

2754 29c **Cherokee Strip Land Run,** *Apr. 17,* Enid, OK *(260,118)* 1.25
2755 29c **Dean Acheson,** *Apr. 21, (158,783)* 1.25
2759a 29c **Sporting Horses,** *May 1,* Louisville, KY 4.00
2756-2759, any single 2.00

First day cancel was applied to 448,059 covers bearing one or more of Nos. 2756-2759a.

2764a 29c **Garden Flowers booklet pane of 5,** *May 15,* Spokane, WA 3.00
2760-2764, any single 1.50

First day cancel was applied to 492,578 covers bearing one or more of Nos. 2760-2764a.

2765 29c **World War II block of 10,** *May 31,* 7.00
2765a-2765j, any single 2.00

First day cancel was applied to 543,511 covers bearing one or more of Nos. 2765, 2765a-2765j.

2766 29c **Joe Louis,** *June 22,* Detroit, MI *(229,272)* 3.00
2770a 29c **Broadway Musicals booklet pane of 4,** *July 14,* New York, NY 3.50
2767-2770, any single 1.25

First day cancel was applied to 308,231 covers bearing one or more of Nos. 2767-2770a.

2774a 29c **Country Music,** *Sept. 25,* Nashville, TN 3.00
2771-2774, any single 1.25
2778a 29c **Country Music booklet pane of 4,** *Sept. 25,* Nashville, TN 3.00
2775-2778, any single 1.25

First day cancel was applied to 362,904 covers bearing one or more of Nos. 2771-2774a, 2775-2778a.

2782a 29c **National Postal Museum,** *July 30* 2.75
2779-2782, any single 1.25

First day cancel was applied to 371,115 covers bearing one or more of Nos. 2779-2782a.

2784a 29c **Deafness/Sign Language,** *Sept. 20,* Burbank, CA 2.50
2783-2784, any single 1.50

First day cancel was applied to 112,350 covers bearing one or more of Nos. 2783-2784a.

2788a 29c **Classic Books,** *Oct. 23,* Louisville, KY 2.75
2785-2788, any single 1.25

First day cancel was applied to 269,457 covers bearing one or more of Nos. 2785-2788a.

2789 29c **Christmas (religious),** *Oct. 21,* Raleigh, NC 1.25
2790 29c **Christmas (religious),** booklet single, *Oct. 21,* Raleigh, NC 1.25
2790a Booklet pane of 4 2.50

First day cancellation was applied to 155,192 covers bearing one or more of Nos. 2789-2790a.

2794a 29c **Christmas (secular),** sheet stamps, *Oct. 21,* New York, NY 2.75
2791-2794, any single 1.25
2798a 29c **Christmas (secular) booklet pane of 10,** *Oct. 21,* New York, NY 6.50
2798b 29c **Christmas (secular) booklet pane of 10,** *Oct. 21,* New York, NY 6.50
2795-2798, any single 1.25
2799 29c **Christmas (snowman),** large self-adhesive, *Oct. 28,* New York, NY 1.25
2800 29c **Christmas (soldier),** self-adhesive, *Oct. 28,* New York, NY 1.25
2801 29c **Christmas (jack-in-the-box),** self-adhesive, *Oct. 28,* New York, NY 1.25
2802 29c **Christmas (reindeer),** self-adhesive, *Oct. 28,* New York, NY 1.25

2799-2802 on one cover 2.50

2803 29c **Christmas (snowman),** small self-adhesive, *Oct. 28,* New York, NY 1.25

First day cancel was applied to 384,262 covers bearing one or more of Nos. 2791-2794a, 2795-2798b, 2799-2803.

2804 29c **Mariana Islands,** *Nov. 4,* Saipan, MP *(157,410)* 1.25

2805 29c **Columbus' Landing in Puerto Rico,** *Nov. 19,* San Juan, PR *(222,845)* 1.25

2806 29c **AIDS Awareness,** *Dec. 1,* New York, NY 2.00

2806a Booklet single, perf. 11 vert. 2.00

2806b Booklet pane of 5 4.00

First day cancellation was applied to 209,200 covers bearing one or more of Nos. 2806-2806b.

1994

2811a 29c **Winter Olympics,** *Jan. 6,* Salt Lake City, UT 3.00

2807-2811, any single 1.25

First day cancellation was applied to 645,636 covers bearing one or more of Nos. 2807-2811a.

2812 29c **Edward R. Murrow,** *Jan. 21,* Pullman, WA *(154,638)* 1.25

2813 29c **Love,** self-adhesive, *Jan. 27,* Loveland, OH *(125,146)* 1.25

2814 29c **Love,** booklet single, *Feb. 14,* Niagara Falls, NY 1.25

2814a Booklet pane of 10 6.50

2814C 29c **Love,** *June 11,* Niagara Falls, NY *(42,109)* 1.25

2815 52c **Love,** *Feb. 14,* Niagara Falls, NY 1.50

2816 29c **Dr. Allison Davis,** *Feb. 1,* Williamstown, MA *(162,404)* 2.00

2817 29c **Chinese New Year,** *Feb. 5,* Pomona, CA *(148,492)* 2.00

2818 29c **Buffalo Soldiers,** *Apr. 22,* Dallas, TX *(107,223)* 2.75

No. 2818 was also available on the first day of issue in forts in Kansas, Texas and Arizona.

2828a 29c **Silent Screen Stars,** *Apr. 27,* San Francisco, CA 6.50

2819-2828, any single 1.50

First day cancellation was applied to 591,251 covers bearing one or more of Nos. 2819-2828a.

2833a 29c **Garden Flowers booklet pane of 5,** *Apr. 28,* Cincinnati, OH 3.25

2829-2833, any single 1.25

First day cancellation was applied to 153,069 covers bearing one or more of Nos. 2829-2833a.

2834 29c **World Cup Soccer,** *May 26,* New York, NY 2.00

2835 40c **World Cup Soccer,** *May 26,* New York, NY 2.00

2836 50c **World Cup Soccer,** *May 26,* New York, NY 2.00

First day cancellation was applied to 443,768 covers bearing one or more of Nos. 2834-2836.

2837 **World Cup Soccer souvenir sheet of 3,** *May 26,* New York, NY *(59,503)* 4.00

2838 29c **World War II block of 10,** *June 6,* USS Normandy 7.00

2838a-2838j, any single 2.00

No. 2838 was also available on the first day of issue in 13 other locations.

First day cancellation was applied to 744,267 covers bearing one or more of Nos. 2838, 2838a-2838j.

2839 29c **Norman Rockwell,** *July 1,* Stockbridge, MA *(232,076)* 1.25

2840 50c **Norman Rockwell Souvenir Sheet of 4,** *July 1,* Stockbridge, MA 3.50

2840a-2840d, any single 1.50

First day cancellation was applied to 19,734 covers bearing one or more of Nos. 2840-2840d.

2841 29c **Moon Landing Sheet of 12,** *July 20,* 6.50

2841a, single stamp 2.00

First day cancellation was applied to 303,707 covers bearing one or more of Nos. 2841-2841a.

2842 $9.95 **Moon Landing,** *July 20 (11,463)* 20.00

2847a 29c **Locomotives booklet pane of 5,** *July 28,* Chama, NM 4.00

2843-2847, any single 1.75

First day cancellation was applied to 169,016 covers bearing one or more of Nos. 2843-2847a.

2848 29c **George Meany,** *Aug. 16 (172,418)* 1.25

2853a 29c **American Music Series,** *Sept. 1,* New York, NY 4.50

2849-2853, any single 1.50

First day cancellation was applied to 156,049 covers bearing one or more of Nos. 2849-2853a.

2861a 29c **American Music Series,** *Sept. 17,* Greenville MS 6.00

2854-2861, any single 1.25

First day cancellation was applied to 483,737 covers bearing one or more of Nos. 2854-2861a.

2862 29c **James Thurber,** *Sept. 10,* Columbus OH *(39,064)* 1.25

2866a 29c **Wonders of the Sea,** *Oct. 3,* Honolulu HI 2.75

2863-2866, any single 1.25

First day cancellation was applied to 284,678 covers bearing one or more of Nos. 2863-2866a.

2868a 29c **Cranes,** *Oct. 9* 2.50

2867-2868, any single 1.25

First day cancellation was applied to 202,955 covers bearing one or more of Nos. 2867-2868a, 24,942 with the People's Republic of China stamps.

2869 29c **Legends of the West Pane of 20,** *Oct. 18,* Laramie WY *(429,680)* 15.00

Tucson, AZ *(220,417)* 15.00

Lawton, OK *(191,393)* 15.00

2869a-2869t, any single, any city 2.25

First day cancellation was applied to covers bearing one or more of Nos. 2869-2869t.

2871 29c **Christmas (religious),** perf 11¼, *Oct. 20 (155,192)* 1.25

2871A 29c **Christmas (religious),** perf 9¾x11, *Oct. 20 (155,192)* 1.25

2872 29c **Christmas (stocking),** *Oct. 20,* Harmony MN 1.25

2873 29c **Christmas (Santa Claus),** self-adhesive, *Oct. 20,* Harmony MN 1.25

2874 29c **Christmas (cardinal),** small self-adhesive, *Oct. 20,* Harmony MN 1.25

First day cancellation was applied to 132,005 covers bearing one or more of Nos. 2872, 2872a, 2873, 2874.

2875 $2 **Bureau of Printing and Engraving Souvenir sheet,** *Nov. 3,* New York, NY *(13,126)* 25.00

2875a $2 Single stamp 7.00

2876 29c **Chinese New Year (Boar),** *Dec. 30,* Sacramento CA 1.75

2877 (3c) **Dove, bright blue,** *Dec. 13* 1.25

2878 (3c) **Dove, dark blue,** *Dec. 13* 1.25

2879 (20c) **G, black,** *Dec. 13* 1.25

2880 (20c) **G, red,** *Dec. 13* 1.25

2881 (32c) **G, black,** *Dec. 13* 1.25

2881a Booklet pane of 10 6.75

2882 (32c) **G, red,** *Dec. 13* 1.25

2883 (32c) **G, black,** *Dec. 13* 1.25

2883a Booklet pane of 10 6.75

2884 (32c) **G, black,** *Dec. 13* 1.25

2884a Booklet pane of 10 6.75

2885 (32c) **G, red,** *Dec. 13* 1.25

2885a Booklet pane of 10 6.75

2886 (32c) **G, gray, blue, light blue, red & black,** self-adhesive, *Dec. 13* 1.25

2887 (32c) **G, black, blue & red,** self-adhesive, *Dec. 13* 1.25

2888 (25c) **G, black,** coil, *Dec. 13* 1.25

2889 (32c) **G, black,** coil, *Dec. 13* 1.25

2890 (32c) **G, blue,** coil, *Dec. 13* 1.25

2891 (32c) **G, red,** coil, *Dec. 13* 1.25

2892 (32c) **G, red,** rouletted coil, *Dec. 13* 1.25

Originally, No. 2893 (the 5c green Non-profit Presort G rate stamp) was only available through the Philatelic Fullfillment Center after their announcement 1/12/95. Requests for first day cancels received a 12/13/94 cancel, even though they were not available on that date. Value, $1.25.

First day cancellation was applied to 338,107 covers bearing one or more of Nos. 2877-2893(?), and U633-U634.

2897 32c **Flag Over Porch,** *May 19,* Denver CO 1.25

First day cancellation was applied to 66,609 covers bearing one or more of Nos. 2897, 2913-2914, 2916 and possibly, 2920.

1995-98

2902 (5c) **Butte,** coil, *Mar. 10,* State College PA 1.25

First day cancellation was applied to 80,003 covers bearing one or more of Nos. 2902, 2905, and U635-U636.

2902B (5c) **Butte,** self-adhesive coil, *June 15, 1996,* San Antonio TX 1.25

First day cancellation was applied to 87,400 covers bearing one or more of Nos. 2902B, 2904A, 2906, 2910, 2912A, 2915B.

2903 (5c) **Mountain,** purple & multi coil, *Mar. 16, 1996* San Jose CA 1.25

2904 (5c) **Mountain,** blue & multi coil, *Mar. 16,1996* San Jose CA 1.25

First day cancellation was applied to 28,064 covers bearing one or more of Nos. 2903-2904.

2904A (5c) **Mountain,** purple & multi self-adhesive coil, *June 15, 1996,* San Antonio TX 1.25

First day cancellation was applied to 87,400 covers bearing one or more of Nos. 2902B, 2904A, 2906, 2910, 2912A, 2915B.

2904B (5c) **Mountain,** purple & multi self-adhesive coil, inscription outlined, *Jan. 24, 1997,* Tucson, AZ 1.25

2905 (10c) **Auto,** coil, *Mar. 10,* State College PA 1.25

2906 (10c) **Auto,** self-adhesive coil, *June 15, 1996* San Antonio TX 1.25

First day cancellation was applied to 87,400 covers bearing one or more of Nos. 2902B, 2904A, 2906, 2910, 2912A, 2915B.

2907 (10c) **Eagle & Shield,** USA Bulk Rate self-adhesive coil, *May 21, 1996* 1.25

First day cancellation was applied to 54,102 covers bearing one or more of Nos. 2907, 2915A, 2915C, 2921.

2908 (15c) **Auto tail fin (dark orange yellow),** coil, *Mar. 17,* New York NY 1.25

2909 (15c) **Auto tail fin (buff),** coil, *Mar. 17,* New York, NY 1.25

First day cancellation was applied to 93,770 covers bearing one or more of Nos. 2908-2909, 2911-2912, 2919.

2910 (15c) **Auto tail fin (buff),** self-adhesive coil, *June 15, 1996,* San Antonio TX 1.25

First day cancellation was applied to 87,400 covers bearing one or more of Nos. 2902B, 2904A, 2906, 2910, 2915B.

2911 (25c) **Juke box,** coil, *Mar. 17,* New York NY 1.25

2912 (25c) **Juke box,** coil, *Mar. 17,* New York NY 1.25

First day cancellation was applied to 93,770 covers bearing one or more of Nos. 2908-2909, 2911-2912, 2919.

2912A (25c) **Juke box,** self-adhesive coil, bright orange red & multi, microperfs, *June 15, 1996,* New York NY 1.25

First day cancellation was applied to 87,400 covers bearing one or more of Nos. 2902B, 2904A, 2906, 2910, 2912A, 2915B.

2912B (25c) **Juke box,** self-adhesive coil, dark red & multi, *Jan. 24, 1997,* Tucson, AZ 1.25

2913 32c **Flag Over Porch,** coil, *May 19,* Denver CO 1.25

2914 32c **Flag Over Porch,** coil, *May 19,* Denver CO 1.25

2915 32c **Flag Over Porch,** self-adhesive, die cut 8.7 vert., *Apr. 18* 1.25

2915A 32c **Flag Over Porch,** self-adhesive, die cut 9.8 vert., 11 teeth, *May 21, 1996* 1.25

2915B 32c **Flag Over Porch,** self-adhesive die cut 11.5 vert., *June 15, 1996,* San Antonio TX 1.25

First day cancellation was applied to 87,400 covers bearing one or more of Nos. 2902B, 2904A, 2906, 2910, 2912A, 2915B.

2915C 32c **Flag Over Porch,** self-adhesive, die cut 10.9, *May 21, 1996* 2.00

2915D 32c **Flag Over Porch,** self-adhesive coil, self-adhesive die cut 9.8 vert., 9 teeth, *Jan. 24, 1997,* Tucson, AZ 1.25

First day cancellation was applied to 56,774 covers bearing one or more of Nos. 2904B, 2912B, 2915D and 2921b.

2916 32c **Flag Over Porch,** booklet single, *May 19,* Denver CO 1.25

2916a Booklet pane of 10 7.50

2919 32c **Flag Over Field,** self-adhesive, *Mar. 17,* New York NY 1.25

First day cancellation was applied to 93,770 covers bearing one or more of Nos. 2908-2909, 2911-2912, 2919.

2920 32c **Flag Over Porch,** self-adhesive, *Apr. 18* 1.25

First day cancellation was applied to 66,609 covers bearing one or more of Nos. 2897, 2913-2914, 2916 and possibly, 2920.

First day cancellation was applied to 57,639 covers bearing one or more of Nos. 2920d, 3030, 3044.

2921 32c **Flag Over Porch,** self-adhesive, booklet stamp, die cut 9.8 on 2 or 3 sides, *May 21, 1996* 1.25

First day cancellation was applied to 54,102 covers bearing one or more of Nos. 2907, 2915A, 2915C, 2921.

GREAT AMERICANS ISSUE

2933 32c **Milton Hershey,** *July 11,* Hershey PA *(121,228)* 1.25

2934 32c **Cal Farley,** *Apr. 26, 1996,* Amarillo TX *(109,440)* 1.25

2935 32c **Henry Luce,** *Apr. 3, 1998,* New York NY *(76,982)* 1.25

2936 32c **Wallace,** *July 16, 1998,* Pleasantville NY *(72,183)* 1.25

2938 46c **Ruth Benedict,** *Oct. 20,* Virginia Beach VA *(24,793)* 1.40

2940 55c **Alice Hamilton,** *July 11,* Boston MA *(24,225)* 1.40

2941 55c **Justin Morrill,** *July 17, 1999* Strafford VT *(19,699)* 1.40

2942 77c **Mary Breckinridge,** *Nov. 9, 1998* Troy, NY 1.75

First day cancellation was applied to 121,662 covers bearing one or more of Nos. 2942, 3257-3261, 3263-3269.

2943 78c **Alice Paul,** *Aug. 18,* Mount Laurel NJ *(25,071)* 1.75

1995

2948 (32c) **Love,** *Feb. 1,* Valentines VA 1.50

2949 (32c) **Love,** self-adhesive, *Feb. 1,* Valentines VA 1.50

First day cancellation was applied to 70,778 covers bearing one or more of Nos. 2948, 2949.

2950 32c **Florida Statehood,** *Mar. 3,* Tallahassee FL *(167,499)* 1.25

2954a 32c **Earth Day,** *Apr. 20* 2.75

2951-2954, any single 1.25

First day cancellation was applied to 328,893 covers bearing one or more of Nos. 2951-2954, 2954a.

2955 32c **Richard Nixon,** *Apr. 26,* Yorba Linda CA *(377,605)* 1.25

2956 32c **Bessie Coleman,** *Apr. 27,* Chicago IL *(299,834)* 1.75

2957 32c **Love,** *May 12,* Lakeville PA 1.25

2958 55c **Love,** *May 12,* Lakeville PA 1.25

2959 32c **Love,** booklet single, *May 12,* Lakeville PA 1.25
2959a Booklet pane of 10 7.50
2960 55c **Love,** self-adhesive, *May 12,* Lakeville PA 1.40

First day cancellation was applied to 273,350 covers bearing one or more of Nos. 2957-2959, 2959a, and U637.

2965a 32c **Recreational Sports,** *May 20,* Jupiter FL 3.25
2961-2965, any single 1.50

First day cancellation was applied to 909,807 covers bearing one or more of Nos. 2961-2965, 2965a.

2966 32c **Prisoners of War & Missing in Action,** *May 29 (231,857)* 2.25
2967 32c **Marilyn Monroe,** *June 1,* Universal City CA *(703,219)* 3.25
Any other city 2.00
2968 32c **Texas Statehood,** *June 16,* Austin TX *(177,550)* 1.75
2973a 32c **Great Lakes Lighthouses booklet pane of 5,** *June 17,* Cheboygan MI 5.00
2969-2973, any single 2.00

First day cancellation was applied to 626,055 covers bearing one or more of Nos. 2969-2973, 2973a.

2974 32c **UN, 50th Anniv.,** *June 26,* San Francisco CA *(160,383)* 1.50
2975 32c **Civil War pane of 20,** *June 29,* Gettysburg PA 16.00
Any other city 16.00
2975a-2975t, any single, Gettysburg PA 2.00
Any other city 1.75

First day cancellation was applied to 1,950,134 covers bearing one or more of Nos. 2975, 2975a-2975t, and UX200-UX219.

2979a 32c **Carousel Horses,** *July 21,* Lahaska PA 3.25
2976-2979, any single 1.25

First day cancellation was applied to 479,038 covers bearing one or more of Nos. 2976-2979, 2979a.

2980 32c **Woman Suffrage,** *Aug. 26 (196,581)* 1.25
2981 32c **World War II block of 10,** *Sept. 2,* Honolulu HI 7.00
2981a-2981j, any single 2.00

First day cancellation was applied to 1,562,094 covers bearing one or more of Nos. 2981, 2981a-2981j.

2982 32c **American Music Series,** *Sept. 1,* New Orleans LA *(258,996)* 1.75
2992a 32c **American Music Series,** *Sept. 16,* Monterey CA 6.50
2983-2992, any single 1.50

First day cancellation was applied to 629,956 covers bearing one or more of Nos. 2983-2992, 2992a.

2997a 32c **Garden Flowers booklet pane of 5,** *Sept. 19,* Encinitas CA 4.00
2993-2997, any single 1.25

First day cancellation was applied to 564,905 covers bearing one or more of Nos. 2993-2997, 2997a.

2998 60c **Eddie Rickenbacker,** *Sept. 25,* Columbus OH *(24,283)* 1.75
2999 32c **Republic of Palau,** *Sept. 29,* Agana GU *(157,377)* 1.25
3000 32c **Comic Strips Pane of 20,** *Oct. 1,* Boca Raton FL 13.00
3000a-3000t, any single 2.00

First day cancellation was applied to 1,362,990 covers bearing one or more of Nos. 3000, 3000a-3000t.

3001 32c **US Naval Academy,** *Oct. 10,* Annapolis, MD *(222,183)* 2.00
3002 32c **Tennessee Williams,** *Oct. 13,* Clarksdale MS *(209,812)* 1.25
3003 32c **Christmas, Madonna,** perf 11.2, *Oct. 19* 1.25
3003A 32c **Christmas, Madonna,** perf 9.8x10.9. *Oct. 19* 1.25
3003Ab Booklet pane of 10 7.25

First day cancellation was applied to 223,301 covers bearing one or more of Nos. 3003, 3003A-3003Ab.

3007a 32c **Christmas (secular) sheet,** *Sept. 30,* North Pole NY 3.25
3004-3007, any single 1.25
3007b 32c Booklet pane of 10, 3 #3004, etc. 7.25
3007c 32c Booklet pane of 10, 2 #3004, etc. 7.25

First day cancellation was applied to 487,816 covers bearing one or more of Nos. 3004-3007, 3007a.

3008-3011 32c **Christmas (secular) self-adhesive booklet stamps,** *Sept. 30,* North Pole NY 3.25
3008-3011, any single 1.25
3012 32c **Angel,** *Oct. 19,* Christmas FL 1.25
3013 32c **Children sledding,** *Oct. 19,* Christmas FL 1.25

First day cancellation was applied to 77,675 covers bearing one or more of Nos. 3012, 3013, 3018.

3014-3017 32c **Self-adhesive coils,** *Sept. 30,* North Pole NY 2.50
3014-3017, any single 1.25
3018 32c **Self-adhesive coil,** *Oct. 19,* Christmas FL 1.25

First day cancellation was applied to 77,675 covers bearing one or more of Nos. 3012, 3013, 3018.

3023a 32c **Antique Automobiles,** *Nov. 3,* New York NY 3.00
3019-3023, any single 1.25

First day cancellation was applied to 757,003 covers bearing one or more of Nos. 3019-3023, 3023a.

1996

3024 32c **Utah Statehood Cent.,** *Jan. 4,* Salt Lake City UT *(207,089)* 1.25
3029a 32c **Garden Flowers booklet pane,** *Jan. 19,* Kennett Square PA 3.50
3025-3029, any single 1.25

First day cancellation was applied to 876,176 covers bearing one or more of Nos. 3025-3029, 3029a.

3030 32c **Love self-adhesive,** *Jan. 20,* New York NY 1.25

First day cancellation was applied to 57,639 covers bearing one or more of Nos. 2920d, 3030, 3044.

1996-2000

FLORA AND FAUNA

3031 1c **Kestrel,** *Nov. 19, 1999,* New York, NY *(14,431)* 1.50
3032 2c **Red-headed woodpecker,** *Feb. 2,* Sarasota FL *(37,319)* 1.25
3033 3c **Eastern Bluebird,** *Apr. 3 (23,405)* 1.25
3036 $1 **Red Fox,** *Aug. 14, 1998* 3.50

First day cancellation was applied to 46,557 covers bearing one or more of Nos. 3228-3229, 3036.

3044 1c **American Kestrel, coil,** *Jan. 20,* New York NY 1.25

First day cancellation was applied to 57,639 covers bearing one or more of Nos. 2920d, 3030, 3044.

3045 2c **Red-Headed Woodpecker,** *June 22, 1999 (14,377)* 1.25
3048 20c **Blue Jay, booklet stamp, self-adhesive,** *Aug. 2,* St. Louis MO 1.25

First day cancellation was applied to 32,633 covers bearing one or more of Nos. 3048, 3053.

3049 32c **Yellow Rose, booklet stamp, self-adhesive,** *Oct. 24,* Pasadena, CA *(7,849)* 1.25
3050 20c **Ring-necked Pheasant, booklet stamp, self-adhesive,** *July 31, 1998* Somerset NJ 1.25

First day cancellation was applied to 32,220 covers bearing one or more of Nos. 3050, 3055.

3052 33c **Coral Pink Rose,** serpentine die cut 11½x11¼, *Aug. 13, 1999,* Indianapolis, IN 1.25
3052E 33c **Coral Pink Rose,** serpentine die cut 10¾x10½, *Apr. 7, 2000,* New York, NY *(18,199)* 1.25
3053 20c **Blue Jay, coil, self-adhesive,** *Aug. 2,* St. Louis MO 1.25
3054 32c **Yellow Rose, self-adhesive,** *Aug. 1, 1997,* Falls Church VA *(20,029)* 1.25
3055 20c **Ring-necked Pheasant,coil, self-adhesive,** *July 31, 1998* Somerset NJ 1.25

First day cancellation was applied to 32,220 covers bearing one or more of Nos. 3050, 3055.

1996

3058 32c **Ernest E. Just,** *Feb. 1 (191,360)* 1.75
3059 32c **Smithsonian, 150th anniv.,** *Feb. 7, (221,399)* 1.25
3060 32c **Chinese New Year,** *Feb. 8,* San Francisco CA *(237,451)* 1.75
3064a 32c **Pioneers of Communication,** *Feb. 22,* New York NY 2.50
3061-3064, any single 1.25

First day cancellation was applied to 567,205 covers bearing one or more of Nos. 3061-3064, 3064a.

3065 32c **Fulbright Scholarships,** *Feb. 28,* Fayetteville AR *(227,330)* 1.25
3066 50c **Jacqueline Cochran,** *Mar. 9,* Indio CA *(30,628)* 1.75
3067 32c **Marathon,** *Apr. 11,* Boston MA *(177,050)* 2.00
3068 32c **Olympics, pane of 20,** *May 2* 13.00
3068a-3068t, any single 1.25
Atlanta, GA —

Washington DC first day cancellation was applied to 1,807,316 covers bearing one or more of Nos. 3068, 3068a-3068t. Atlanta was also an official first day city, and covers postmarked there are scarce.

3069 32c **Georgia O'Keeffe,** *May 23,* Santa Fe NM *(200,522)* 1.50
3070 32c **Tennessee Statehood, Bicen.,** *May 31,* Knoxville, Memphis or Nashville TN 1.25
3071 32c **Tennessee, self-adhesive,** *May 31,* Knoxville, Memphis or Nashville TN 1.25

First day cancellation was applied to 217,281 covers bearing one or more of Nos. 3070-3071.

3076a 32c **American Indian Dances, strip of 5,** *June 7,* Oklahoma City OK 2.75
3072-3076, any single 1.25

First day cancellation was applied to 653,057 covers bearing one or more of Nos. 3072-3076, 3076a.

3080a 32c **Prehistoric Animals,** *June 8,* Toronto, Canada 2.75
3077-3080, any single 1.50

First day cancellation was applied to 485,929 covers bearing one or more of Nos. 3077-3080, 3080a.

3081 32c **Breast Cancer Awareness,** *June 15 (183,896)* 1.25
Any other city 1.25
3082 32c **James Dean,** *June 24,* Burbank CA *(263,593)* 2.00
3086a 32c **Folk Heroes,** *July 11,* Anaheim CA 2.75
3083-3086, any single 1.25

First day cancellation was applied to 739,706 covers bearing one or more of Nos. 3083-3086, 3086a.

3087 32c **Centennial Olympic Games,** *July 19,* Atlanta GA *(269,056)* 1.25
3088 32c **Iowa Statehood, 150th Anniv.,** *Aug. 1,* Dubuque IA 1.25
3089 32c **Iowa Statehood, self-adhesive** *Aug. 1,* Dubuque IA 1.25
3088, 3089, both stamps issued *Aug. 1,* Dubuque, IA 1.75

First day cancellation was applied to 215,181 covers bearing one or more of Nos. 3088-3089.

3090 32c **Rural Free Delivery,** *Aug. 7,* Charleston WV *(192,070)* 1.25
3091-3095 32c **Riverboats,** *Aug. 22,* Orlando FL 3.50
3091-3095, any single 1.25
3095b 32c **Riverboats, special die cutting,** *Aug. 22,* Orlando FL 3.50

First day cancellation was applied to 770,384 covers bearing one or more of Nos. 3091-3095, 3095b.

3099a 32c **Big Band Leaders,** *Sept. 11,* New York NY 3.25
3096-3099, any single 1.25

First day cancellation was applied to 1,235,166 covers bearing one or more of Nos. 3096-3103, 3099a, 3103a.

3103a 32c **Songwriters,** *Sept. 11,* New York NY 3.25
3100-3103, any single 1.25

First day cancellation was applied to 1,235,166 covers bearing one or more of Nos. 3096-3103, 3099a, 3103a.

3104 23c **F. Scott Fitzgerald,** *Sept. 27,* St. Paul MN *(150,783)* 1.25
3105 32c **Endangered Species,** *Oct. 2,* San Diego CA 7.50
3105a-3105o, any single 1.25

First day cancellation was applied to 941,442 covers bearing one or more of Nos. 3105, 3105a-3105o.

3106 32c **Computer Technology,** *Oct. 8,* Aberdeen Proving Ground MD *(153,688)* 1.75
3107 32c **Christmas Madonna,** *Nov. 1,* Richmond VA 1.25

First day cancellation was applied to 164,447 covers bearing one or more of Nos. 3107, 3112.

3111a 32c **Christmas (secular),** *Oct. 8,* North Pole AK 2.75
3108-3111, any single 1.25

First day cancellation was applied to 884,339 covers bearing one or more of Nos. 3108-3111, 3111a, 3113-3117.

3112 32c **As No. 3107, self-adhesive,** *Nov. 1,* Richmond VA 1.25
3113-3116 32c **Christmas (secular), self-adhesive,** *Oct. 8,* North Pole AK 3.25
3113-3116, any single 1.25
3117 32c **Skaters, self-adhesive,** *Oct. 8,* North Pole AK 1.25

First day cancellation was applied to 884,339 covers bearing one or more of Nos. 3108-3111, 3111a, 3113-3117.

3118 32c **Hanukkah,** *Oct. 22 (179,355)* 1.75
3119 50c **Cycling,** *Nov. 1,* New York NY 4.00
3119a-3119b, any single 2.00

First day cancellation was applied to 290,091 covers bearing one or more of Nos. 3119, 3119a-3119b.

1997

3120 32c **Chinese New Year,** *Jan. 5,* Honolulu *(233,638)* 1.75
3121 32c **Benjamin O. Davis, Sr.,** *Jan. 28 (166,527)* 1.75
3122 32c **Statue of Liberty, self-adhesive,** *Feb. 1,* San Diego CA *(40,003)* 1.25

3123 32c **Love, Swans, self-adhesive,** *Feb. 4,* Los Angeles CA 1.25
3124 55c **Love, Swans, self-adhesive,** *Feb. 4,* Los Angeles CA 1.50

First day cancellation was applied to 257,380 covers bearing one or more of Nos. 3123-3124.

3125 32c **Helping Children Learn, self-adhesive** *Feb. 18 (175,410)* 1.25
3126 32c **Merian Botanical Prints, Citron, etc., self-adhesive, die cut 10.9x10.2,** *Mar. 3* 1.25
3127 32c **Merian Botanical Prints, Pineapple, etc., self-adhesive, die cut 10.9x10.2,** *Mar. 3* 1.25
3128 32c **Merian Botanical Prints, Citron, etc., self-adhesive, die cut 11.2x10.8,** *Mar. 3* 1.25
3128a 32c **Merian Botanical Prints, Citron, etc., self-adhesive, die cut mixed perf,** *Mar. 3* 1.25
3129 32c **Merian Botanical Prints, Pineapple, etc., self-adhesive, die cut 11.2x10.8,** *Mar. 3* 1.25
3129a 32c **Merian Botanical Prints, Pineapple, etc., self-adhesive, die cut mixed perf,** *Mar. 3* 1.25

First day cancellation was applied to 336,897 covers bearing one or more of Nos. 3126-3129, 3128a-3129a.

3131a 32c **Pacific 97,** *Mar. 13,* New York NY 1.75
3130-3131, any single 1.25

First day cancellation was applied to 371,908 covers bearing one or more of Nos. 3130-3131, 3131a.

3132 (25c) **Juke Box, self-adhesive** *Mar. 14,* New York NY 1.25
3133 32c **Flag over Porch, Self-adhesive** *Mar. 14,* New York NY 1.25

First day cancellation was applied to 26,0820 covers bearing one or more of Nos. 3132-3133.

3134 32c **Thornton Wilder,** *Apr. 17,* Hamden CT *(157,299)* 1.25
3135 32c **Raoul Wallenberg,** *Apr. 24 (168,668)* 2.00
3136 32c **Dinosaurs, pane of 15** *May 1,* Grand Junction CO 7.50
3136a-3136o, any single 1.25

First day cancellation was applied to 1,782,1221 covers bearing one or more of Nos. 3136, 3136a-3136o.

3137a 32c **Bugs Bunny,** *May 22,* Burbank CA *(378,142)* 2.00
3139 50c **Pacific 97, Franklin, pane of 12** *May 29,* San Francisco CA 12.00
3139a, single 2.00
3140 60c **Pacific 97,, pane of 12,** *May 30,* San Francisco CA 12.00
3140a, single 2.00

First day cancellation was applied to 328,401 covers bearing one or more of Nos. 3139-3140, 3139a-3140b.

3141 32c **Marshall Plan,** *June 4,* Cambridge MA *(157,622)* 1.50
3142 32c **Classic American Aircraft,** *July 19,* Dayton OH 10.00
3142a-3142t, any single 1.25

First day cancellation was applied to 1,413,833 covers bearing one or more of Nos. 3142, 3142a-3142t.

3146a 32c **Football Coaches** *July 25,* Canton OH 3.00
3143-3146, any single 1.75

First day cancellation was applied to 586,946 covers bearing one or more of Nos. 3143-3146.

3147 32c **Bear Bryant,** *Aug. 5,* Green Bay WI *(119,428)* 1.75
3148 32c **Pop Warner,** *Aug. 7,* Tuscaloosa AL *(23,858)* 1.75
3149 32c **Vince Lombardi,** *Aug. 8,* Philadelphia PA *(37,839)* 1.75
3150 32c **George Halas,** *Aug. 16,* Chicago IL *(26,760)* 1.75
3151 32c **American Dolls,** *July 28,* Anaheim CA 8.00
3151a-3151o, any single 1.25

First day cancellation was applied to 831,359 covers bearing one or more of Nos. 3151, 3151a-3151o.

3152 32c **Humphrey Bogart,** *July 31,* Los Angeles CA *(220,254)* 1.75
3153 32c **"The Star and Stripes Forever,"** *Aug. 21,* Milwaukee WI *(36,666)* 1.25
3157a 32c **Opera Singers,** *Sept. 10,* New York NY 2.75
3154-3157, any single 1.25

First day cancellation was applied to 386,689 covers bearing one or more of Nos. 3154-3157.

3165a 32c **Classical Composers and Conductors,** *Sept. 12,* Cincinnati OH 5.25
3158-3165, any single 1.25

First day cancellation was applied to 424,344 covers bearing one or more of Nos. 3158-3165.

3166 32c **Padre Felix Varela,** *Sept. 15,* Miami FL *(120,079)* 1.25
3167 32c **Department of the Air Force,** *Sept. 18 (178,519)* 1.50
3172a 32c **Classic Movie Monsters,** *Sept. 30,* Universal City CA 3.75
3168-3172, any single 1.50

First day cancellation was applied to 476,993 covers bearing one or more of Nos. 3168-3172.

3173 32c **First Supersonic Flight,** *Oct. 14,* Edwards AFB CA *(173,778)* 1.50
3174 32c **Women in Military Service,** *Oct. 18 (106,121)* 1.75
3175 32c **Kwanzaa,** *Oct. 22,* Los Angeles CA *(92,489)* 1.75
3176 32c **Christmas Madonna,** *Oct. 27 (35,809)* 1.25
3177 32c **Holly,** *Oct. 30,* New York NY *(87,332)* 1.25
3178 $3 **Mars Pathfinder,** *Dec. 10* Pasadena CA *(11,699)* 9.00

1998

3179 32c **Chinese New Year,** *Jan. 5,* Seattle WA *(234,269)* 1.75
3180 32c **Alpine Skiing,** *Jan. 22,* Salt Lake City UT *(196,504)* 1.25
3181 32c **Madam C. J. Walker,** *Jan. 28,* Indianapolis IN *(146,348)* 1.75

1998-2000

CELEBRATE THE CENTURY

3182 32c **1900s,** *Feb. 3 (11,699)* 8.50
3182a-3182o, any single 1.50
3183 32c **1910s,** *Feb. 3* 8.50
3183a-3183o, any single 1.50

First day cancellation was applied to 3,896,387 covers bearing one or more of Nos. 3182-3182o, 3183-3183o.

3184 32c **1920s,** *May 28* 8.50
3184a-3184o, any single 1.75

First day cancellation was applied to 1,057,909 covers bearing one or more of Nos. 3184-3184o.

3185 32c **1930s,** *Sept. 10,* Cleveland OH 8.50
3185a-3185o, any single 1.75

First day cancellation was applied to 999,017 covers bearing one or more of Nos. 3185-3185o.

3186 33c **1940s,** *Feb. 18, 1999,* Dobbins AFB GA 8.50
3186a-3186o, any single 1.75

First day cancellation was applied to 1,459,138 covers bearing one or more of Nos. 3186-3186o.

3187 33c **1950s,** *May 26, 1999,* Springfield MA 8.50
3187a-3187o, any single 1.75

First day cancellation was applied to 1,454,906 covers bearing one or more of Nos. 3187-3187o.

3188 33c **1960s,** *Sept. 17, 1999,* Green Bay, WI 8.50
3188a-3188o, any single 1.75

First day cancellation was applied to 1,252,243 covers bearing one or more of Nos. 3188-3188o.

3189 33c **1970s,** *Nov. 18, 1999,* New York, NY 8.50
3189a-3189o, any single 1.75

First day cancellation was applied to 894,084 covers bearing one or more of Nos. 3189-3189o.

3190 33c **1980s,** *Jan. 12, 2000,* Kennedy Space Center, FL 8.50
3190a-3190o, any single 1.75
3191 33c **1990s,** *May 2, 2000,* Escondido, CA 8.50
3191a-3191o, any single 1.75

First day cancellation was applied to 1,172,962 covers bearing one or more of Nos. 3191-3190o.

1998

3192 32c **"Remember the Maine,"** *Feb. 15,* Key West FL *(161,657)* 1.75
3193-3197 32c **Flowering Trees,** *Mar. 19,* New York NY 3.75
3193-3197, any single 1.50

First day cancellation was applied to 666,199 covers bearing one or more of Nos. 3193-3197.

3202a 32c **Alexander Calder,** *Mar. 25* 3.75
3198-3202, any single 1.50

First day cancellation was applied to 588,887 covers bearing one or more of Nos. 3198-3202, 3202a.

3203 32c **Cinco de Mayo,** *Apr. 16,* San Antonio TX *(144,443)* 1.25
3204a 32c **Sylvester & Tweety,** *Apr. 27,* New York NY *(213,839)* 1.25
3206 32c **Wisconsin Statehood,** *May 29,* Madison WI *(130,810)* 1.25

1998-99

3207 (5c) **Wetlands,** *June 5,* McLean VA 1.25
3207A (5c) **Wetlands, Serpentine die cut,** *Dec. 14* 1.25
3208 (25c) **Diner,** *June 5,* McLean VA 1.25

First day cancellation was applied to 35,333 covers bearing one or more of Nos. 3207, 3208; 13,378 covers bearing one of more of Nos. 3207A, 3270-3271.

3208A (25c) **Diner, Serpentine die cut,** *June 5 (13,984)* 1.25

1998

1898 TRANS-MISSISSIPPI STAMPS, CENT.

3209 **Sheet of 9,** *June 18,* Anaheim CA 6.50
3209a 1c 1.50
3209b 2c 1.50
3209c 4c 1.50
3209d 5c 1.50
3209e 8c 1.50
3209f 10c 1.50
3209g 50c 2.00
3209h $1 2.50
3209i $2 4.50
3210 $1 **Sheet of 9,** *June 18,* Anaheim CA 15.00

First day cancellation was applied to 203,649 covers bearing one or more of Nos. 3209-3210, 3209a-3209i.

1998

3211 32c **Berlin Airlift,** *June 26,* Berlin, Germany *(137,894)* 1.50
3215a 32c **Folk Musicians,** *June 26* 3.25
3212-3215, any single 1.25

First day cancellation was applied to 341,015 covers bearing one or more of Nos. 3212-3215, 3215a.

3219a 32c **Gospel Music,** *July 15,* New Orleans LA 3.25
3216-3219, any single 1.25

First day cancellation was applied to 330,533 covers bearing one or more of Nos. 3216-3219, 3219a.

3220 32c **Spanish Settlement of the Southwest,** *July 11,* Española NM *(122,182)* 1.25
3221 32c **Stephen Vincent Benét,** *July 22,* Harpers Ferry WV *(107,412)* 1.25
3225a 32c **Tropical Birds,** *July 29,* Ponce PR 3.00
3222-3225, any single 1.25

First day cancellation was applied to 371,354 covers bearing one or more of Nos. 3222-3225, 3225a.

3226 32c **Alfred Hitchcock,** *Aug. 3,* Los Angeles CA *(140,628)* 1.50
3227 32c **Organ & Tissue Donation,** *Aug. 5,* Columbus OH *(110,601)* 1.25
3228 (10c) **Modern Bicycle, Serpentine die cut,** *Aug. 14* 1.25
3229 (10c) **Modern Bicycle,** *Aug. 14* 1.25

First day cancellation was applied to 46,557 covers bearing one or more of Nos. 3228-3229, 3036.

3230-3234 32c **Bright Eyes,** *Aug. 20,* Boston MA 3.25
3230-3234, any single 1.75

First day cancellation was applied to 394,280 covers bearing one or more of Nos. 3230-3234.

3235 32c **Klondike Gold Rush Cent.,** *Aug. 21,* Nome or Skagway AK *(123,559)* 1.50
3236 32c **American Art, pane of 20,** *Aug. 27,* Santa Clara CA 9.00
3236a-3236t, any single 1.25

First day cancellation was applied to 924,031 covers bearing one or more of Nos. 3236, 3236a-3236t.

3237 32c **American Ballet,** *Sept. 16,* New York NY *(133,034)* 1.25
3242a 32c **Space Discovery,** *Oct. 1,* Kennedy Space Center FL 3.75
3238-3242, any single 1.25

First day cancellation was applied to 399,807 covers bearing one or more of Nos. 3238-3242, 3242a.

3243 32c **Giving & Sharing,** *Oct. 7,* Atlanta GA *(124,051)* 1.25
3244 32c **Christmas, Madonna,** *Oct. 15 (105,835)* 1.25
3245-3248 32c **Christmas, Secular,** *Oct. 15,* Christmas MI 3.25
3245-3248, any single 1.25
3249-3252 32c **Christmas, Secular, size: 23x30mm,** *Oct. 15,* Christmas MI 3.00
3249-3252, any single 1.25

First day cancellation was applied to 328,199 covers bearing one or more of Nos. 3245-3252.

3257 (1c) **Weather Vane, white USA,** *Nov. 9,* Troy NY 1.25
3258 (1c) **Weather Vane, pale blue USA,** *Nov. 9,* Troy NY 1.25
3259 22c **Uncle Sam,** *Nov. 9,* Troy NY 1.25
3260 (33c) **Uncle Sam's Hat,** *Nov. 9,* Troy NY 1.25
3261 $3.20 **Space Shuttle Landing,** *Nov. 9,* 5.00

3262 $11.75 **Piggyback Space Shuttle,** *Nov. 9,* New York NY *(3,703)* 25.00
3263 22c **Uncle Sam, coil,** *Nov. 9,* Troy NY 1.25
3264 (33c) **Uncle Sam's Hat, coil,** *Nov. 9,* Troy NY 1.25
3265 (33c) **Uncle Sam's Hat, self-adhesive coil, die cut 9.9, round corners,** *Nov. 9,* Troy NY 1.25
3266 (33c) **Uncle Sam's Hat, self-adhesive coil, die cut 9.9, square corners,** *Nov. 9,* Troy NY 1.50
3267 (33c) **Uncle Sam's Hat, self-adhesive booklet single, die cut 9.9** *Nov. 9,* Troy NY 1.25
3268 (33c) **Uncle Sam's Hat, self-adhesive booklet single, die cut 11.2x11.1** *Nov. 9,* Troy NY 1.25
3269 (33c) **Uncle Sam's Hat, self-adhesive booklet single, die cut 8** *Nov. 9,* Troy NY 1.25

First day cancellation was applied to 121,662 covers bearing one or more of Nos. 2942, 3257-3261, 3263-3269.

3270 (10c) **Eagle & Shield, Presorted Std.,** *Dec. 14* 1.25
3271 (10c) **Eagle & Shield, Presorted Std., self-adhesive, Serpentine die cut,** *Dec. 14* 1.25

First day cancellation was applied to 13,378 covers bearing one of more of Nos. 3207A, 3270-3271.

1999

3272 33c **Chinese New Year,** *Jan. 5,* Los Angeles CA *(151,436)* 1.75
3273 33c **Malcolm X,** *Jan. 20,* New York NY *(107,226)* 2.00
3274 33c **Love,** *Jan. 28,* Loveland CO 1.25
3275 55c **Love,** *Jan. 28,* Loveland CO 1.50

First day cancellation was applied to 189,331 covers bearing one of more of Nos. 3274, 3275, UX300.

3276 33c **Hospice Care,** *Feb. 9,* Largo FL *(136,976)* 1.25
3277 33c **Flag & City,** *Feb. 25,* Orlando FL 1.25
3278 33c **Flag & City, self-adhesive, die cut 11.1** *Feb. 25,* Orlando FL 1.25
3279 33c **Flag & City, self-adhesive, die cut 9.8** *Feb. 25,* Orlando FL 1.25
3280 33c **Flag & City, coil, perf. 9.9 vert.** *Feb. 25,* Orlando FL 1.25
3281 33c **Flag & City, self-adhesive coil, die cut 9.8 vert, square corners,** *Feb. 25,* Orlando FL 1.25
3282 33c **Flag & City, self-adhesive coil, die cut 9.8 vert., round corners,** *Feb. 25,* Orlando FL 1.25

First day cancellation was applied to 88,569 covers bearing one of more of Nos. 3277-3282.

3283 33c **Flag & Blackboard, self-adhesive, die cut 7.9,** *Mar. 13 (26,067)* 1.25
3286 33c **Irish Immigration,** *Feb. 26,* Boston MA *(127,213)* 1.50
3287 33c **Lunt & Fontanne,** *Mar. 2,* New York NY *(120,423)* 1.25
3292a 33c **Arctic Animals,** *Mar. 12,* Barrow AK 3.25
3288-3292, any single 1.25

First day cancellation was applied to 476,863 covers bearing one of more of Nos. 3288-3292, 3292a.

3293 33c **Sonoran Desert, Pane of 10,** *Apr. 6,* Tucson AZ 6.75
3293a-3293j, any single 1.25

First day cancellation was applied to 410,985 covers bearing one of more of Nos. 3293-3293j.

3294-3297 33c **Christmas Berries, die cut 11.2x11.7** *Apr. 10,* Ponchatoula LA 3.25
3294-3297, any single 1.25
3297e, dated 2000, *Mar. 15, 2000,* Ponchatoula LA 3.25
3294a-3296a, 3297c, any single 1.25
3298-3301 33c **Christmas Berries, die cut 9.5x10** *Apr. 10,* Ponchatoula LA 3.25
3298-3301, any single 1.25
3302-3305 33c **Christmas Berries, die cut 8.5 vert.** *Apr. 10,* Ponchatoula LA 3.25
3302-3305, any single 1.25

First day cancellation was applied to 101,344 covers bearing one of more of Nos. 3294-3305.

3306a 33c **Daffy Duck,** *Apr. 16,* Los Angeles CA 1.50

First day cancellation was applied to 177,988 covers bearing one of more of Nos. 3306-3307c, UX304.

3308 33c **Ayn Rand,** *Apr. 22,* New York NY *(123,660)* 2.50
3309 33c **Cinco de Mayo,** *Apr. 27,* San Antonio TX *(20,904)* 1.25
3310-3313 33c **Tropical Flowers,** *May 1,* Honolulu HI 3.25
3310-3313, any single 1.25

First day cancellation was applied to 311,495 covers bearing one of more of Nos. 3310-3313, 3313a, 3313b.

3314 33c **Bartram,** *May 18,* Philadelphia PA *(110,381)* 1.25
3315 33c **Prostate Cancer Awareness,** *July 22,* Austin TX *(113,299)* 1.25
3316 33c **California Gold Rush,** *June 18,* Sacramento CA *(123,648)* 1.25
3317-3320 33c **Aquarium Fish,** *June 24,* Anaheim CA 3.25
3317-3320, any single 1.25

First day cancellation was applied to 301,719 covers bearing one of more of Nos. 3317-3320, 3320a-3320c.

3321-3324 33c **Extreme Sports,** *June 25,* San Francisco CA 3.00
3321-3324, any single 1.25

First day cancellation was applied to 278,068 covers bearing one of more of Nos. 3321-3324, 3324a.

3328a 33c **American Glass,** *June 29,* Corning NY 3.00
3325-3328, any single 1.25

First day cancellation was applied to 272,792 covers bearing one of more of Nos. 3325-3328, 3328a.

3329 33c **James Cagney,** *July 22,* Burbank CA *(135,867)* 1.75
3330 55c **"Billy" Mitchell,** *July 30,* Milwaukee WI 1.50

First day cancellation was applied to 42,144 covers bearing one of more of Nos. 3330, C134.

3331 33c **Honoring Those Who Served,** *Aug. 16,* Kansas City MO *(130,306)* 1.75
3332 45c **Universal Postal Union,** *Aug. 25,* Beijing, China (20,371) 1.25
3337a 33c **Famous Trains,** *Aug. 26,* Cleveland, OH 3.75
any other city 3.75
#3333-3337, any single, Cleveland, OH 1.50
#3333-3337, any single, any other city 1.50

First day cancellation was applied to 518,446 covers bearing one of more of Nos. 3333-3337, 3337a, UX307-UX311a.

3338 33c **Frederick Law Olmsted,** *Sept. 12,* Boston, MA (109,735) 1.25
3344a 33c **Hollywood Composers,** *Sept. 16,* Los Angeles, CA 3.75
#3339-3344, any single, Los Angeles, CA 1.25

First day cancellation was applied to 287,407 covers bearing one of more of Nos. 3339-3344, 3344a.

3350a 33c **Broadway Songwriters,** *Sept. 21,* New York, NY 3.75
#3345-3350, any single, New York, NY 1.25

First day cancellation was applied to 284,840 covers bearing one of more of Nos. 3345-3350, 3350a.

3351 33c **Insects & Spiders,** *Oct. 1,* Indianapolis, IN 10.00
#3351a-3351t, any single 1.25

First day cancellation was applied to 773,590 covers bearing one of more of Nos. 3351-3351t.

3352 33c **Hanukkah,** *Oct. 8,* Washington, DC 1.50
3353 22c **Uncle Sam perforated coil,** *Oct. 8,* Washington, DC 1.25

First day cancellation was applied to 44,534 covers bearing one of more of Nos. 3352-3353, O157.

3354 33c **NATO,** *Oct. 13,* Brussels, Belgium *(110,415)* 1.50
3355 33c **Christmas Madonna,** *Oct. 20,* Washington, DC *(110,460)* 1.25
3356-3359 33c **Christmas Deer, narrow frame (sheet),** *Oct. 20,* Rudolph, WI 3.00
3356-3359, any single 1.25
3360-3363 33c **Christmas Deer, thick frame (booklet),** *Oct. 20,* Rudolph, WI 3.00
3360-3363, any single 1.25
3364-3367 33c **Christmas Deer, smaller size (booklet),** *Oct. 20,* Rudolph, WI 3.00
3364-3367, any single 1.25

First day cancellation was applied to 239,350 covers bearing one of more of Nos. 3356-3367, 3359a, 3363a, 3367a-3367c.

3368 33c **Kwanzaa,** *Oct. 29,* Los Angeles, CA *(20,493)* 1.75
3369 33c **Year 2000,** *Dec. 27,* Washington, DC *(145,928)* 1.25

2000

3370 33c **Chinese New Year,** *Jan. 6,* San Francisco, CA *(155,586)* 1.75
3371 33c **Patricia Roberts Harris,** *Jan. 27,* Washington, DC *(82,211)* 1.75
3372 33c **Los Angeles Class Submarine,** with microprinting, *Mar. 27,* Groton, CT 1.50
3373 22c **S Class Submarine,** *Mar. 27,* Groton, CT 1.50
3374 33c **Los Angeles Class Submarine,** no microprinting, *Mar. 27,* Groton, CT 1.50
3375 55c **Ohio Class Submarine,** *Mar. 27,* Groton, CT 1.75
3376 60c **USS Holland,** *Mar. 27,* Groton, CT 1.75
3377 $3.20 **Gato Class Submarine,** *Mar. 27,* Groton, CT 6.00
3377a, Booklet pane of 5, #3373-3377, either selvage 8.00

First day cancellation was applied to 265,226 covers bearing one of more of Nos. 3372-3377, 3377a.

3378 33c **Pacific Coast Rain Forest Pane of 10,** *Mar. 29,* Seattle, WA 6.75
3378a-3378j, any single 1.25

First day cancellation was applied to 435,549 covers bearing one of more of Nos. 3378-3378j.

3383a 33c **Louise Nevelson,** *Apr. 6,* New York, NY 3.25
3379-3383, any single 1.25

First day cancellation was applied to 389,200 covers bearing one of more of Nos. 3379-3383, 3383a.

3388a 33c **Hubble Space Telescope,** *Apr. 10,* Greenbelt, MD 3.25
3384-3388, any single 1.25

First day cancellation was applied to 411,449 covers bearing one of more of Nos. 3384-3388, 3388a.

3389 33c **American Samoa,** *Apr. 17,* Pago Pago, AS *(107,346_* 1.25
3390 33c **Library of Congress,** *Apr. 24,* Washington, DC *(115,679)* 1.25
3391a 33c **Road Runner & Wile E. Coyote,** *Apr. 26,* Phoenix, AZ 1.25

First day cancellation was applied to 154,903 covers bearing one of more of Nos. 3391-3392, 3391a-3391c, 3392a-3392c.

3396a 33c **Distinguished Soldiers,** *May 3,* Washington, DC 3.25
Any other city 3.25
3393-3396, any single, Washington, DC 1.50
Any other city 1.25

First day cancellation was applied to 322,278 covers bearing one of more of Nos. 3393-3396, 3396a.

3397 33c **Summer Sports,** *May 5,* Spokane, WA *(110,768)* 1.25
3398 33c **Adoption,** *May 10,* Beverly Hills, CA 1.25

First day cancellation was applied to 137,903 covers bearing one of more of Nos. 3398, UX315.

3402a 33c **Youth Team Sports,** *May 27,* Lake Buena Vista, FL 3.25
3399-3402, any single 1.25

First day cancellation was applied to 309,349 covers bearing one of more of Nos. 3399-3402, 3402a.

3403 33c **The Stars and Stripes, pane of 20,** *June 14,* Baltimore, MD 10.00
3403a-3403t, any single 1.25

First day cancellation was applied to 1,121,071 covers bearing one of more of Nos. 3403-3403t.

3404-3407 33c **Berries,** die cut 8½ horiz., *June 16,* Buffalo, NY 3.25
3404-3707, any single 1.25

First day cancellation was applied to 35,671 covers bearing one of more of Nos. 3404-3407, 3407a.

3408 33c **Legends of Baseball, pane of 20,** *July 6,* Atlanta, GA 10.00
3408a-3708t, any single 1.75

First day cancellation was applied to 1,214,413 covers bearing one of more of Nos. 3408-3408t.

3409 60c **Probing the Vastness of Space,** *July 10,* Anaheim, CA 6.00
3409a-3409f, any single 1.50

First day cancellation was applied to 296,252 covers bearing one of more of Nos. 3409-3409f.

3410 $1 **Exploring the Solar System,** *July 11,* Anaheim, CA 9.00
3410a-3410e, any single 2.00

First day cancellation was applied to 49,500 covers bearing one of more of Nos. 3410-3410e.

3411 $3.20 **Escaping the Gravity of Earth,** *July 9,* Anaheim, CA 9.50
3411a-3411b, any single 3.75

First day cancellation was applied to 22,321 covers bearing one of more of Nos. 3411-3411b.

3412 $11.75 **Space Achievement and Exploration,** *July 7,* Anaheim, CA *(12,070)* 17.50
3413 $11.75 **Landing on the Moon,** *July 8,* Anaheim, CA *(11,639)* 17.50
3414-3417 33c **Stampin' The Future,** *July 13,* Anaheim, CA 3.25
3414-3417, any single 1.25

First day cancellation was applied to 294,434 covers bearing one of more of Nos. 3414-3417, 3417a.

Distinguished Americans Issue 2000-2008

3420 10c **Joseph W. Stilwell,** *Aug. 24,* Providence, RI *(21,669)* 1.50
3422 23c **Wilma Rudolph, litho. & engr.** *July 14, 2004,* Sacramento, CA 1.25
3426 33c **Claude Pepper,** *Sept. 7,* Washington, DC *(60,689)* 1.25
3427 58c **Margaret Chase Smith,** *June 13, 2007,* Washington, DC 2.40
3427A 59c **James A. Michener,** *May 12, 2008,* Washington, DC 2.40
3428 63c **Dr. Jonas Salk,** *Mar. 8,* Washington, DC 2.50
Any other city 2.50
3430 75c **Harriet Beecher Stowe,** *June 13, 2007* Washington, DC 2.75
3431 76c **Hattie Caraway,** *Feb. 21, 2001,* Little Rock, AR 1.75
3432A 76c **Edward Trudeau,** *May 12, 2008,* Washington, DC 2.75
3433 83c **Edna Ferber,** *July 29, 2002,* Appleton, WI 1.75
3435 87c **Dr. Albert Sabin,** *Mar. 8,* Washington, DC 3.00
Any other city 3.00
3436 23c **Wilma Rudolph, litho. booklet stamp** *July 14, 2004,* Sacramento, CA 1.25
3438 33c **California Statehood,** *Sept. 8,* Sacramento, CA *(119,729)* 1.25
3443a 33c **Deep Sea Creatures,** *Oct. 2,* Monterey, CA 3.75
#3439-3443, any single 1.25

First day cancellation was applied to 385,406 covers bearing one of more of Nos. 3439-3443, 3443a.

3444 33c **Thomas Wolfe,** *Oct. 3,* Asheville, NC *(112,293)* 1.25
3445 33c **White House,** *Oct. 18,* Washington, DC *(135,844)* 1.25
3446 33c **Edward G. Robinson,** *Oct. 24,* Los Angeles, CA *(120,125)* 1.75
3447 (10c) **New York Public Library Lion,** *Nov. 9,* New York, NY *(18,477)* 1.25
3448 (34c) **Flag Over Farm, perf,** *Dec. 15,* Washington, DC 1.25
3449 (34c) **Flag Over Farm, litho. self-adhesive,** *Dec. 15,* Washington, DC 1.25
3450 (34c) **Flag Over Farm, photo. self-adhesive,** *Dec. 15,* Washington, DC 1.25
3451 (34c) **Statue of Liberty, booklet stamp,** *Dec. 15,* Washington, DC 1.25
3452 (34c) **Statue of Liberty perforated coil,** *Dec. 15,* Washington, DC 1.25
3453 (34c) **Statue of Liberty self-adhesive coil,** *Dec. 15,* Washington, DC 1.25
3454-3457 (34c) **Flowers, booklet stamps die cut 10¼x10¾,** *Dec. 15,* Washington, DC 3.25
3454-3457, any single 1.25
3458-3461 (34c) **Flowers, booklet stamps die cut 11½x11¾,** *Dec. 15,* Washington, DC 3.25
3458-3461, any single 1.25
3462-3465 (34c) **Flowers, coil stamps,** *Dec. 15,* Washington, DC 3.25
3462-3465, any single 1.25

First day cancellation was applied to 178,635 covers bearing one of more of Nos. 3448-3465, 3450a, 3451a-3451d, 3457a-3457e, 3461a-3461c, 3465a.

2001

3466 34c **Statue of Liberty coil (rounded corners),** *Jan. 7,* Washington, DC 1.25
3467 21c **American Buffalo, perforated sheet stamp,** *Sept. 20,* Washington, DC 1.25
3468 21c **American Buffalo, perforated sheet stamp,** *Feb. 22,* Wall, SD 1.25
3468A 23c **George Washington, sheet stamp,** *Sept. 20,* Washington, DC 1.25
3469 34c **Flag Over Farm, perforated sheet stamp,** *Feb. 7,* New York, NY 1.25
3470 34c **Flag Over Farm, self-adhesive sheet stamp,** *Mar. 6,* Lincoln, NE 1.25
3471 55c **Eagle,** *Feb. 22,* Wall, SD 1.50
3471A 57c **Eagle,** *Sept. 20,* Washington, DC 1.50
3472 $3.50 **Capitol Dome,** *Jan. 29,* Washington, DC 6.25
3473 $12.25 **Washington Monument,** *Jan. 29,* Washington, DC 15.00
3475 21c **American Buffalo coil stamp,** *Feb. 22,* Wall, SD 1.25
3475A 23c **George Washington, coil stamp,** *Sept. 20,* Washington, DC 1.25
3476 34c **Statue of Liberty, perforated coil stamp,** *Feb. 7,* New York, NY 1.25
3477 34c **Statue of Liberty coil stamp (right angle corners),** *Feb. 7,* New York, NY 1.25
3478-3481 34c **Flower coil stamps,** *Feb. 7,* New York, NY 3.25
3478-3481, any single 1.25

Serpentine Die Cut 11¼

3482 20c **George Washington booklet stamp,** *Feb. 22,* Wall, SD 1.25

Serpentine Die Cut 10½x11¼

3483 21c **George Washington booklet stamp,** *Feb. 22,* Wall, SD 1.25
3484 21c **American Buffalo, booklet stamp, serp. die cut 11¼,** *Sept. 20,* Washington, DC 1.25
3484A 21c **American Buffalo, booklet stamp, serp. die cut 10½x11¼,** *Sept. 20,* Washington, DC *1.25*
3485 34c **Statue of Liberty booklet stamp,** *Feb. 7,* New York, NY 1.25
3487-3490 34c **Flower booklet stamps,** *Feb. 7,* New York, NY 3.25
3487-3490, any single 1.25
3491-3492 34c **Apple & Orange booklet stamps,** *Feb. 7,* Lincoln, NE 2.25
3491-3492, any single 1.25
3495 34c **Flag Over Farm, booklet stamp,** *Dec. 17,* Washington, DC 1.25
3496 (34c) **Love Letter,** *Jan. 19,* Tucson, AZ 1.25
3497 34c **Love Letters,** *Feb. 14,* Lovejoy, GA 1.25

Serpentine Die Cut 11½x10¾

3498 34c **Love Letters, die cut 11½x10¾,** *Feb. 14,* Lovejoy, GA 1.25
3499 55c **Love Letter,** *Feb. 14,* Lovejoy, GA 1.50
3500 34c **Chinese New Year,** *Jan. 20,* Oakland, CA 1.75
3501 34c **Roy Wilkins,** *Jan. 24,* Minneapolis, MN 1.25
3502 34c **American Illustratiors pane of 20,** *Feb. 1,* New York, NY 9.50
3502a-3502t, any single 1.25
3503 34c **Diabetes Awareness,** *Mar. 16,* Boston, MA 1.25
3504 34c **Nobel Prize Centenary,** *Mar. 22,* Washington, DC 1.50
3505 **Pan-American Inverts Pane,** *Mar. 29,* New York, NY 6.00
3505a 1c 1.25
3505b 2c 1.25
3505c 4c 1.25
3505d 80c 1.75
3506 34c **Great Plains Prairie Pane of 10,** *Apr. 19,* Lincoln, NE 7.00
3507 34c **Peanuts,** *May 17,* Santa Rosa, CA 1.50
3508 34c **Honoring Veterans,** *May 23,* Washington, DC 2.00
Any other city 1.25
3509 34c **Frida Kahlo,** *June 21,* Phoenix, AZ 1.25
3519a 34c **Legendary Playing Fields,** *June 27,* New York, NY, Boston, MA, Chicago, IL or Detroit, MI 6.50
3510-3519, any single, New York, NY, Boston, MA, Chicago, IL or Detroit, MI 1.50
3520 (10c) **Atlas Statue,** *June 29,* New York, NY 1.25
3521 34c **Leonard Bernstein,** *July 10,* New York, NY 1.25
3522 (15c) **Woody Wagon,** *Aug. 3,* Denver, CO 1.25
3523 34c **Lucille Ball,** *Aug. 6,* Los Angeles, CA 2.00
3527a 34c **Amish Quilts,** *Aug. 9,* Nappanee, IN 3.25
3524-3527, any single 1.25
3531a 34c **Carnivorous Plants,** *Aug. 23,* Des Plaines, IL 3.25
3528-3531, any single 1.25
3532 34c **Eid** *Sept. 1,* Des Plaines, IL 1.25
3533 34c **Enrico Fermi,** *Sept. 29,* Chicago, IL 1.25
3534a 34c **That's All Folks!,** *Oct. 1,* Beverly Hills, CA 1.25

First day cancellation was applied to 151,009 covers bearing one or more of Nos. 3534-3535, 3534a-3534c, 3535a-3535c.

3536 34c **Christmas, Madonna,** *Oct. 10,* Philadelphia, PA 1.25
3537-3540 34c **Christmas, Santas, black inscriptions, large date** *Oct. 10,* Santa Claus, IN 3.25
3537-3540, any single 1.25
3537a-3540a, small date (from booklet) 3.25
3537a-3540a, any single 1.25
3541-3544 34c **Christmas, Santas, green and red inscriptions,** *Oct. 10,* Santa Claus, IN 3.25
3541-3544, any single 1.25
3545 34c **James Madison,** *Oct. 18,* New York, NY 1.25
3546 34c **Thanksgiving,** *Oct. 19,* Dallas, TX 1.25
3547 34c **Hanukkah,** *Oct. 21,* New York, NY 1.25
3548 34c **Kwanzaa,** *Oct. 21,* New York, NY 1.25
3549 34c **United We Stand,** *Oct. 24,* Washington, DC 1.50

First day cancellation was applied to 451,053 covers bearing one or more of Nos. 3549, 3550, 3550A.

3549B 34c **United We Stand,** serpentine die cut 10½x10¾ booklet stamp *Oct. 24,* Washington, DC

2002

3552-3555 34c **Winter Sports,** *Jan. 8,* Park City, UT 3.25
3552-3555, any single 1.25
3556 34c **Mentoring a Child,** *Jan. 10,* Annapolis, MD 1.25
3557 34c **Langston Hughes,** *Feb. 1,* New York, NY 1.25
3558 34c **Happy Birthday,** *Feb. 8,* Riverside, CA 1.25
3559 34c **Chinese New Year,** *Feb. 11,* New York, NY 1.50
3560 34c **U.S. Military Academy Bicent.,** *Mar. 16,* West Point, NY 1.75
3610a 34c **Greetings from America Pane,** *Apr. 4,* New York, NY 32.50
3561-3610, Any single, New York, NY 1.25
3610a, Any other city 32.50
3561-3610, Any single, any other city 1.50
3561-3610, any state capital 2.00
3611 34c **Longleaf Pine Forest Pane of 10,** *Apr. 26,* Tallahassee, FL 7.00
3611a-3611j, any single 1.25
3612 5c **Toleware Coffeepot,** *May 31,* McLean, VA 1.25
3613 3c **Litho. Star sheet stamp,** *June 7,* Washington, DC 1.25
Any other city 1.25
3614 3c **Photo. Star sheet stamp,** *June 7,* Washington, DC 1.25
Any other city 1.25
3615 3c **Star coil stamp,** *June 7,* Washington, DC 1.25
3616 23c **George Washington,** water-activated gum sheet stamp, *June 7,* Washington, DC 1.00
3617 23c **George Washington,** gray green coil stamp, *June 7,* Washington, DC 1.00
3618 23c **George Washington,** booklet stamp, serp. die cut 11¼ on 3 sides, *June 7,* Washington, DC 1.00
3620 (37c) **Flag,** water-activated gum sheet stamp, *June 7,* Washington, DC 1.25
Any other city 1.25
3621 (37c) **Flag,** self-adhesive sheet stamp, serp. die cut 11¼x11, *June 7,* Washington, DC 1.25
Any other city 1.25
3622 (37c) **Flag,** coil stamp, *June 7,* Washington, DC 1.25
Any other city 1.25
3623 (37c) **Flag,** booklet stamp, serp. die cut 11¼ on 2, 3 or 4 sides, *June 7,* Washington, DC 1.25
Any other city 1.25
3624 (37c) **Flag,** booklet stamp, serp. die cut 10½x10¾ on 2 or 3 sides, *June 7,* Washington, DC 1.25
Any other city 1.25
3625 (37c) **Flag,** booklet stamp, serp. die cut 8 on 2, 3 or 4 sides, *June 7,* Washington, DC 1.25
Any other city 1.25
3626-3629 (37c) **Antique Toys,** booklet stamps, *June 7,* Washington, DC 3.25
Any other city 3.25
3626-3629, any single 1.25
3626-3629, any single, any other city 1.25
3629F 37c **Flag,** perf. 11¼, *Nov. 24,* Washington, DC 1.25
3630 37c **Flag,** self-adhesive sheet stamp, serp. die cut 11¼x11, *June 7,* Washington, DC 1.25
Any other city 1.25
3631 37c **Flag,** water-activated gum coil stamp, *June 7,* Washington, DC 1.25
3632 37c **Flag,** self-adhesive coil stamp, serp. die cut 10 vert., *June 7,* Washington, DC 1.25
3632A 37c **Flag coil, lacking star points at top** *Aug. 7, 2003* Columbus, OH —
3633 37c **Flag,** self-adhesive coil stamp, serp. die cut 8½ vert., *June 7,* Washington, DC 1.25
3634 37c **Flag,** self-adhesive booklet stamps, serp. die cut 11 on 3 sides, *June 7,* Washington, DC 1.25
3635 37c **Flag,** booklet stamp, serp. die cut 11¼ on 2, 3 or 4 sides, *June 7,* Washington, DC 1.25
3636 37c **Flag,** booklet stamp, serp. die cut 10½x10¾ on 2 or 3 sides, *June 7,* Washington, DC 1.25
3637 37c **Flag,** booklet stamp, serp. die cut 8 on 2, 3 or 4 sides, *Feb. 4, 2003* Washington, DC 1.25
3638-3641 37c **Antique Toys coil stamps,** *July 26,* Rochester, NY 3.25
3638-3641, any single 1.25
3642-3645 37c **Antique Toys booklet stamps,** *July 26,* Rochester, NY 3.25
3642-3645, any single 1.25
3642a-3645f 37c **Antique Toys,** booklet stamps, serp. die cut 11x11¼ on 2 or 3 sides, *Sept. 3,* Washington, DC 3.25
3642a-3645f, any single 1.25
3646 60c **Coverlet Eagle,** *July 12,* Oak Brook, IL 1.50
3647 $3.85 **Jefferson Memorial,** *July 30,* Washington, DC 7.00
Any other city 7.00
3648 $13.65 **Capitol Dome,** *July 30,* Washington, DC 25.00
Any other city 25.00
3649 37c **Masters of American Photography,** *June 13,* San Diego, CA 10.00

	3649a-3649t, any single	1.25
3650	37c **John James Audubon,** *June 27,* Santa Clara, CA	1.25
3651	37c **Harry Houdini,** *July 3,* New York, NY	1.50
3652	37c **Andy Warhol,** *Aug. 9,* Pittsburgh, PA	1.25
3653-3656	37c **Teddy Bears,** *Aug. 15,* Atlantic City, NJ	3.25
	3653-3656, any single	1.25
3657	37c **Love,** *Aug. 16,* Atlantic City, NJ	1.25
3658	60c **Love,** *Aug. 16,* Atlantic City, NJ	1.50
3659	37c **Ogden Nash,** *Aug. 19,* Baltimore, MD	1.25
3660	37c **Duke Kahanamoku,** *Aug. 24,* Honolulu, HI	1.25
3661-3664	37c **American Bats,** *Sept. 13,* Austin, TX	3.25
	3661-3664, any single	1.25
3665-3668	37c **Women in Journalism,** *Sept. 14,* Fort Worth, TX	3.25
	3665-3668, any single	1.25
3669	37c **Irving Berlin,** *Sept. 15,* New York, NY	1.25
3670-3671	37c **Neuter and Spay,** *Sept. 20,* Washington, DC	2.25
	Any other city	2.25
	3670-3671, either single, Washington, DC	1.25
	3670-3671, either single, any other city	1.25
3672	37c **Hanukkah,** *Oct. 10,* Washington, DC	1.25
3673	37c **Kwanzaa,** *Oct. 10,* Washington, DC	1.25
3674	37c **Eid,** *Oct. 10,* Washington, DC	1.25
3675	37c **Christmas Madonna,** design size 19x27mm,*Oct. 10,* Chicago, IL	1.25
3676-3679	37c **Christmas Snowmen,** serp. die cut 11 (sheet stamps), *Oct. 28,* Houghton, MI	3.25
	3676-3679, any single	1.25
3680-3683	37c **Christmas Snowmen,** serp. die cut 8½ vert. (coil stamps), *Oct. 28,* Houghton, MI	3.25
	3680-3683, any single	1.25
3684-3687	37c **Christmas Snowmen,** serp. die cut 10¾x11 on 2 or 3 sides (large booklet stamps), *Oct. 28,* Houghton, MI	3.25
	3684-3687, any single	1.25
3688-3691	37c **Christmas Snowmen,** serp. die cut 11 on 2 or 3 sides (small booklet stamps), *Oct. 28,* Houghton, MI	3.25
	3688-3691, any single	1.25
3692	37c **Cary Grant,** *Oct. 15,* Los Angeles, CA	1.50
3693	(5c) **Sea Coast,** *Oct. 21,* Washington, DC	1.25
3694	37c **Hawaiian Missionary Stamps sheet,** *Oct. 24,* New York, NY	4.00
	3694a-3694d, any single	1.25
3695	37c **Happy Birthday,** *Oct. 25,* New York, NY	1.25

2002

3745a	37c **Greetings From America,** *Oct. 25,* New York, NY	35.00
	3696-3745, any single	1.25
	3696-3745, any state capital	1.50

2003

3746	37c **Thurgood Marshall,** *Jan. 7,* Washington, DC	1.25
3747	37c **Chinese New Year,** *Jan. 15,* Chicago, IL	1.50
3748	37c **Zora Neale Hurston,** *Jan. 24,* Eatonville, FL	1.25

American Design Series 2003-08

3749	1c **Tiffany Lamp,** *Mar. 16, 2007,* New York, NY	2.00
3749A	1c **Tiffany Lamp,** *Mar. 7, 2008,* New York, NY	2.00
3750	2c **Navajo Necklace,** *Aug. 20, 2004,* Indianapolis, IN	1.25
3751	2c **Navajo Necklace,** photo., serpentine die cut 11¼x11½, *Dec. 8, 2005,* Washington, DC	2.00
	Any other city	2.00
3752	2c **Navajo Necklace,** litho., serpentine die cut 11¼x11, *Dec. 8, 2005,* Washington, DC	2.00
	Any other city	2.00
3753	2c **Navajo Necklace,** litho., serpentine die cut 11¼x10¾, microprinting at left, *May 12, 2007,* Washington, DC	2.00
3754	3c **Silver Coffeepot,** *Mar. 16, 2007,* New York, NY	2.00
3755	4c **Chippendale Chair,** *Mar. 5, 2004,* New York, NY	1.25
3756	5c **Toleware, serpentine die cut 11¼x11¾,** *June 25, 2004,* Santa Clara, CA	1.25
3757	10c **American Clock,** *Jan. 24, 2003,* Tucson, AZ	1.25
3758	1c **Tiffany Lamp Coil,** *Mar. 1, 2003,* Biloxi, MS	1.25
3758A	1c **Tiffany Lamp,** litho. coil stamp, *June 7, 2008,* McLean, VA	2.10
3759	3c **Silver Coffeepot Coil,** *Sept. 16, 2005,* Milwaukee, WI	2.00
3761	4c **Chippendale Chair coil,** *July 19, 2007,* Washington, DC	2.00
3762	10c **American Clock Coil,** *Aug. 4, 2006,* Independence, OH	2.00

American Culture Series

3766	$1 **Wisdom,** *Feb. 28,* Biloxi, MS	2.50
3769	(10c) **New York Public Library Lion,** perf. 10 vert., *Feb. 4,* Washington, DC	1.25
3771	80c **Special Olympics,** *Feb. 13,* Chicago, IL	1.75
3772	37c **American Filmmaking: Behind the Scenes Pane of 10,** *Feb. 25,* Beverly Hills, CA	7.25
	3772a-3772j, any single	1.25
3773	37c **Ohio Statehood Bicentennial,** *Mar. 1,* Chillicothe, OH	1.25
3774	37c **Pelican Island National Wildlife Refuge, Cent.,** *Mar. 14,* Sebastian, FL	1.25
3775	(5c) **Sea Coast,** perf. 9¾ vert. *Mar. 19,* Washington, DC	1.25
3776-3780	37c **Old Glory,** *Apr. 3,* New York, NY	4.00
	3776-3780, any single	1.25
3781	37c **Cesar E. Chavez,** *Apr. 23,* Los Angeles, CA	1.25
3782	37c **Louisiana Purchase, Bicent.,** *Apr. 30,* New Orleans, LA	1.25
3783	37c **First Flight,** *May 22,* Dayton, OH or Kill Devil Hills, NC	1.25
3784	37c **Purple Heart,** *May 30,* Mount Vernon, VA	1.50
3784A	37c **Purple Heart, serpentine die cut 10¾x10¼,** *Aug. 1,* Somerset, NJ	—
3786	37c **Audrey Hepburn,** *June 11,* Los Angeles, CA	1.75
3787-3791	37c **Southeastern Lighthouses,** *June 13,* Tybee Island, GA	4.00
	3787, 3788a, 3789-3791, Tybee Island, GA	4.00
	3787-3791, 3788a, any single	1.50
3792-3801	(25c) **Eagle coils,** *June 26,* Santa Clara, CA	6.00
	3792-3801, any single	1.25
3792a-3801b	(25c) **Eagle coil dated "2005",** *Aug. 5,* Grand Rapids, MI	6.00
	3792a-3801b, any single	1.25
3802	37c **Arctic Tundra,** *July 2,* Fairbanks, AK	7.50
	3802a-3802j, any single	1.25
3803	37c **Korean War Veterans Memorial,** *July 27,* Washington, DC	1.75
3804-3807	37c **Mary Cassatt booklet stamps,** *Aug. 7,* Columbus, OH	3.25
	3804-3807, any single	1.25
3808-3811	37c **Early Football Heroes,** *Aug. 8,* South Bend, IN	3.25
	3808-3811, any single	1.25
3812	37c **Roy Acuff,** *Sept. 13,* Nashville, TN	1.25
3813	37c **District of Columbia,** *Sept. 23,* Washington, DC	1.25
3814-3818	37c **Reptiles and Amphibians,** *Oct. 7,* San Diego, CA	4.00
	3814-3818, any single, San Diego, CA	1.25
3820	37c **Christmas Madonna,** design size 19½x28mm, *Oct. 23,* New York, NY	1.25
3821-3824	37c **Christmas Music Makers (sheet stamps),** serp. die cut 11x11¼, *Oct. 23,* New York, NY	3.25
	3821-3824, any single	1.25
3825-3828	37c **Christmas Music Makers (vending machine booklet stamps),** serp. die cut 11¾x11 on 3 sides, *Oct. 23,* New York, NY	3.25
	3825-3828, any single	1.25
3829	37c **Snowy Egret coil,** *Oct. 24,* New York, NY	1.25

2004

3830	37c **Snowy Egret booklet stamp,** *Jan. 30,* Norfolk, VA	1.25
3831	37c **Pacific Coral Reef,** *Jan. 2,* Honolulu, HI	7.50
	3831a-3831j, any single	1.25
3832	37c **Chinese New Year,** *Jan. 13,* San Francisco, CA	1.50
3833	37c **Love Candy Hearts,** *Jan. 14,* Revere, MA	1.25
3834	37c **Paul Robeson,** *Jan. 20,* Princeton, NJ	1.25
3835	37c **Theodor Seuss Geisel (Dr. Seuss),** *Mar. 2,* La Jolla, CA	1.25
3836	37c **Flowers,** *Mar. 4,* New York, NY	1.25
3837	60c **Flowers,** *Mar. 4,* New York, NY	1.50
3838	37c **U.S. Air Force Academy,** *Apr. 1,* Colorado Springs, CO	1.50
3839	37c **Henry Mancini,** *Apr. 13,* Los Angeles, CA	1.25
3840-3843	37c **American Choreographers,** *May 4,* Newark, NJ	3.25
	3840-3843, any single	1.25
3844-3853	(25c) **Eagle coils,** perf. 9¾ vert. *May 12,* Washington, DC	6.00
	3844-3853, any single	1.25
3854	37c **Lewis & Clark,** *May 14,* Astoria, OR	1.75
	Atchison, KS	1.75
	Great Falls, MT	1.75
	Hartford, IL	1.75
	Ilwaco, WA	1.75
	Orofino, ID	1.75
	Omaha, NE	1.75
	Pierre, SD	1.75
	Sioux City, IA	1.75
	St. Charles, MO	1.75
	Washburn, ND	1.75
3855-3856	37c **Lewis & Clark booklet stamps,** *May 14,* Astoria, OR	2.75
	Atchison, KS	2.75
	Great Falls, MT	2.75
	Hartford, IL	2.75
	Ilwaco, WA	2.75
	Orofino, ID	2.75
	Omaha, NE	2.75
	Pierre, SD	2.75
	Sioux City, IA	2.75
	St. Charles, MO	2.75
	Washburn, ND	2.75
	3855-3856, any single, any of the aforementioned 11 cities	1.40
3857-3861	37c **Isamu Noguchi,** *May 18,* Long Island City, NY	4.00
	3857-3861, any single	1.25
3862	37c **National World War II Memorial,** *May 29,* Washington, DC	1.50
	Any other city	1.75
3863	37c **Summer Olympics,** *June 9,* Philadelphia, PA	1.25
3864	(5c) **Sea Coast coil with black 2004 date,** *June 11,* Washington, DC	1.25
3865-3868	37c **Disney Characters,** *June 23,* Anaheim, CA	3.25
	3865-3868, any single	1.25
3869	37c **U.S.S. Constellation,** *June 30,* Baltimore, MD	1.25
3870	37c **R. Buckminster Fuller,** *July 12,* Stanford, CA	1.25
3871	37c **James Baldwin,** *July 23,* New York, NY	1.25
3872	37c **Martin Johnson Heade,** *Aug. 12,* Sacramento, CA	1.25
3873	37c **Art of the American Indian pane of 10,** *Aug. 21,* Santa Fe, NM	7.00
	3873a-3873j, any single, Santa Fe, NM	1.25
3876	37c **John Wayne,** *Sept. 9,* Los Angeles, CA	2.00
3877	37c **Sickle Cell Disease,** *Sept. 29,* Atlanta, GA	1.25
3878	37c **Cloudscapes,** *Oct. 4,* Milton, MA	9.00
	3878a-3878o any single	1.25
3879	37c **Christmas Madonna,** *Oct. 14,* New York, NY	1.25
3880	37c **Hanukkah,** *Oct. 15,* New York, NY	1.25
3881	37c **Kwanzaa,** *Oct. 16,* Chicago, IL	1.25
3882	37c **Moss Hart,** *Oct. 25,* New York, NY	1.25
3883-3886	37c **Christmas Santa Ornaments,** serpentine die cut 11½x11, *Nov. 16,* New York, NY	3.25
	3883-3886, any single	1.25
3887-3890	37c **Christmas Santa Ornaments,** serpentine die cut 10¼x10¾ on 2 or 3 sides, *Nov. 16,* New York, NY	3.25
	3887-3890, any single	1.25
3891-3894	37c **Christmas Santa Ornaments,** serpentine die cut 8 on 2, 3 or 4 sides, *Nov. 16,* New York, NY	3.25
	3891-3894, any single	1.25

2005

3895	37c **Chinese New Year double-sided pane,** *Jan. 6,* Honolulu, HI	20.00
	3895a-3895l, any single	1.25
3896	37c **Marian Anderson,** *Jan. 27,* Washington, DC	1.25
3897	37c **Ronald Reagan,** *Feb. 9,* Simi Valley, CA	1.75
	Any other city	1.50
3898	37c **Love,** *Feb. 18,* Atlanta, GA	1.25
3899	37c **Northeast Deciduous Forest,** *Mar. 3,* New York, NY	7.50
	3899a-3899j, any single	1.25
3900-3903	37c **Spring Flowers,** *Mar. 15,* Chicago, IL	3.25
	3900-3903, any single	1.25
3904	37c **Robert Penn Warren,** *Apr. 22,* Guthrie, KY	1.25
3905	37c **Yip Harburg,** *Apr. 28,* New York, NY	1.25
3906-3909	37c **American Scientists,** *May 4,* New Haven, CT	3.25
	3906-3909, any single	1.25
3910	37c **Modern American Architecture,** *May 19,* Las Vegas NV	9.00
	Any other city	9.00
	3910a-3910l, any single, Las Vegas, NV	1.25
	3910a-3910l, any single, any other city	1.25
3911	37c **Henry Fonda,** *May 20,* Los Angeles, CA	1.25
3912-3915	37c **Disney Characters,** *June 30,* Anaheim, CA	3.25
	3912-3915, any single	1.25
3916-3925	37c **Advances in Aviation,** *July 29,* Oshkosh, WI	7.50
	3916-3925, Vienna, VA	7.50
	3916-3925, any single, Oshkosh, WI	1.50
	3916-3925, any single, Vienna, VA	1.50
3926-3929	37c **Rio Grande Blankets,** *July 30,* Santa Fe, NM	3.25
	3926-3929, any single	1.25
3930	37c **Presidential Libraries Act, 50th Anniv.,** *Aug. 4,* Grand Rapids, MI	1.25
	Abilene, KS	1.50
	Ann Arbor, MI	1.25
	Atlanta, GA	1.25

		Austin, TX	1.25
		Boston, MA	1.50
		College Station, TX	1.25
		Hyde Park, NY	1.25
		Independence, MO	1.50
		Little Rock, AR	1.25
		Simi Valley, CA	1.50
		West Branch, IA	1.25
		Yorba Linda, CA	1.25
3931-3935	37c	**Sporty Cars of the 1950s,** *Aug. 20,* Detroit, MI	5.00
		3931-3935, any single	2.00
3936	37c	**Arthur Ashe,** *Aug. 27,* Flushing, NY	2.00
3937	37c	**To Form a More Perfect Union pane of 10,** *Aug. 30,* Washington, DC	8.75
		Greensboro, NC	8.75
		Jackson, MS	8.75
		Little Rock, AR	8.75
		Memphis, TN	8.75
		Montgomery, AL	8.75
		Selma, AL	8.75
		Topeka, KS	8.75
		Any other city	8.75
		3937a-3937j, any single, Washington, DC	2.00
		3937a-3937j, any single, Greensboro, NC	2.00
		3937a-3937j, any single, Jackson, MS	2.00
		3937a-3937j, any single, Little Rock, AR	2.00
		3937a-3937j, any single, Memphis, TN	2.00
		3937a-3937j, any single, Montgomery, AL	2.00
		3937a-3937j, any single, Selma, AL	2.00
		3937a-3937j, any single, Topeka, KS	2.00
		3937a-3937j, any single, any other city	2.00
3938	37c	**Child Health,** *Sept. 7,* Philadelphia, PA	2.00
		Any other city	2.00
3939-3942	37c	**Let's Dance,** *Sept. 17,* New York, NY	4.25
		Miami, FL	4.25
		3939-3942, any single, New York, NY	2.00
		3939-3942, any single, Miami, FL	2.00
3943	37c	**Greta Garbo,** *Sept. 23,* New York, NY	2.00
3944	37c	**Jim Henson and the Muppets,** *Sept. 28,* North Hollywood, CA	9.25
		3944a-3944k, any single	2.00
3945-3948	37c	**Constellations,** *Oct. 3,* Bloomfield Hills, MI	4.25
		3945-3948, any single	2.00
3949-3952	37c	**Christmas Cookies,** serpentine die cut 10¾x11, *Oct. 20,* New York, NY	4.25
		Minneapolis, MN	4.25
		3949-3952, any single, New York, NY	2.00
		3949-3952, any single, Minneapolis, MN	2.00
3953-3956	37c	**Christmas Cookies,** convertible booklet stamps, serpentine die cut 10¾x11 on 2 or 3 sides, *Oct. 20,* New York, NY	4.25
		Minneapolis, MN	4.25
		3949-3952, any single, New York, NY	2.00
		3949-3952, any single, Minneapolis, MN	2.00
3957-3960	37c	**Christmas Cookies,** vending machine booklet stamps, serpentine die cut 10½x10¾, *Oct. 20,* New York, NY	4.25
		Minneapolis, MN	4.25
		3949-3952, any single, New York, NY	2.00
		3949-3952, any single, Minneapolis, MN	2.00
3961-3964	37c	**Distinguished Marines,** *Nov. 10,* Washington, DC	4.25
		Oceanside, CA	4.25
		Any other city	4.25
		3961-3964, any single, Washington, DC	2.00
		3961-3964, any single, Oceanside, CA	2.00
		3961-3964, any single, any other city	2.00
3965	(39c)	**Flag and Statue of Liberty,** perf. 11¼, *Dec. 8,* Washington, DC	2.00
		Any other city	2.00
3966	(39c)	**Flag and Statue of Liberty,** self-adhesive, serpentine die cut 11¼x11, *Dec. 8,* Washington, DC	2.00
		Any other city	2.00
3967	(39c)	**Flag and Statue of Liberty,** coil stamp, perf. 9¾ vert., *Dec. 8,* Washington, DC	2.00
		Any other city	2.00
3968	(39c)	**Flag and Statue of Liberty,** self-adhesive coil stamp, photo., serpentine die cut 8½ vert., *Dec. 8,* Washington, DC	2.00
		Any other city	2.00
3969	(39c)	**Flag and Statue of Liberty,** self-adhesive coil stamp, photo., serpentine die cut 10¼ vert., *Dec. 8,* Washington, DC	2.00
		Any other city	2.00
3970	(39c)	**Flag and Statue of Liberty,** self-adhesive coil stamp, litho., serpentine die cut 9½ vert., *Dec. 8,* Washington, DC	2.00
3972	(39c)	**Flag and Statue of Liberty,** self-adhesive booklet stamp with bright blue spot over date, photo., serpentine die cut 11¼x10¾ on 2 or 3 sides, *Dec. 8,* Washington, DC	2.00
		Any other city	2.00
3973	(39c)	**Flag and Statue of Liberty,** self-adhesive booklet stamp, serpentine die cut 10¼x10¾, *Dec. 8,* Washington, DC	2.00
		Any other city	2.00

Although No. 3973 has an issue date of Dec. 8, it was not known to have been available until January 2006.

3974	(39c)	**Flag and Statue of Liberty,** self-adhesive booklet stamp with dark blue spot over date, litho., serpentine die cut 11¼x11 on 2 or 3 sides, *Dec. 8,* Washington, DC	2.00
		Any other city	2.00
3975	(39c)	**Flag and Statue of Liberty,** self-adhesive booklet stamp, photo., serpentine die cut 8 on 2, 3 or 4 sides, *Dec. 8,* Washington DC	2.00
		Any other city	2.00

2006

3976	(39c)	**Birds,** self-adhesive booklet stamp, *Jan. 3,* Washington, DC	2.00
		Any other city	2.00
3978	39c	**Flag and Statue of Liberty,** self-adhesive, *Apr. 8,* Washigton, DC	2.00
		Any other city	2.00
3979	39c	**Flag and Statue of Liberty,** coil stamp, perf. 10 vert. *Mar. 8,* Washington, DC	2.00
		Any other city	2.00
3980	39c	**Flag and Statue of Liberty,** self-adhesive coil stamp, serpentine die cut 11 vert. with rounded corners, *Jan. 9,* Washington, DC	2.00
		Any other city	2.00
3981	39c	**Flag and Statue of Liberty,** self-adhesive coil stamp, serpentine die cut 9½ vert., *Apr. 8,* Washington, DC	2.00
		Any other city	2.00
3985b	39c	**Flag and Statue of Liberty,** photo., serpentine die cut 11.1 on 2 or 3 sides, *Nov. 8,* Washington, DC	2.00
3987-3994	39c	**Children's Book Animals,** *Jan. 10,* Findlay, OH	7.50
		3987-3994, any single	2.00
3999	39c	**2006 Winter Olympics,** *Jan. 11,* Colorado Springs, CO	2.00
3996	39c	**Hattie McDaniel,** *Jan. 25,* Beverly Hills, CA	2.00
3997	39c	**Chinese New Year pane,** *Jan. 29,* Washington, DC	10.50
		3997a-3997l, any single	2.00
3998	39c	**Wedding Dove,** *Mar. 1,* New York, NY	2.00
3999	63c	**Wedding Dove,** *Mar. 1,* New York, NY	2.50
4000	24c	**Common Buckeye Butterfly,** perf. 11¼, *Mar. 8,* Washington, DC	2.00
		Any other city	2.00
4001	24c	**Common Buckeye Butterfly,** self-adhesive, serpentine die cut 11, *Mar. 8,* Washington, DC	2.00
		Any other city	2.00
4001a	24c	**Common Buckeye Butterfly,** self-adhesive booklet pane stamp, serpentine die cut 10¾x11¼, *Mar. 8,* Washington, DC	2.00
		Any other city	2.00
4002	24c	**Common Buckeye Butterfly,** self-adhesive coil stamp, serpentine die cut 8½ horiz., *Mar. 8,* Washington, DC	2.00
		Any other city	2.00
4003-4007	39c	**Crops of the Americas,** self-adhesive coil stamps, *Mar. 16,* New York, NY	5.25
		4003-4007, any single	2.00
4008-4012	39c	**Crops of the Americas,** self-adhesive booklet stamps, serpentine die cut 10¾x10½ on 2 or 3 sides, *Mar. 16,* New York, NY	5.25
		4008-4012, any single	2.00
4013-4017	39c	**Crops of the Americas,** self-adhesive booklet stamps, serpentine die cut 10¾x11¼ on 2 or 3 sides, *Mar. 16,* New York, NY	5.25
		4013-4017, any single	2.00
4018	$4.05	**X-Plane,** *Mar. 17,* New York, NY	8.00
		Any other city	8.00
4019	$14.40	**X-Plane,** *Mar. 17,* New York, NY	27.50
		Any other city	27.50
4020	39c	**Sugar Ray Robinson,** *Apr. 7,* New York, NY	2.00
4021-4024	39c	**Benjamin Franklin,** *Apr. 7,* Philadelphia, PA	4.50
		4021-4024, any single	2.00
4025-4028	39c	**Disney Characters,** *Apr. 21,* Orlando, FL	4.50
		4025-4028, any single	2.00
4029	39c	**Birds,** self-adhesive booklet stamp, *May 1,* Washington, DC	2.00
4030	39c	**Katherine Anne Porter,** *May 15,* Kyle, TX	2.00
4031	39c	**Amber Alert,** *May 25,* Arlington, TX	2.00
		Washington, DC	2.00
4032	39c	**Purple Heart,** *May 26,* Washington, DC	2.00
4072a	39c	**Wonders of America,** *May 27,* Washington, DC	32.50
		4033-4072, any single, Washington, DC	2.00
		4072a, any other city	32.50
		4033-4072, any single, any other city	2.00
4073	39c	**Samuel de Champlain,** self-adhesive stamp, *May 28,* Washington, DC	2.00
		Ticonderoga, NY	2.00
		Annapolis Royal, Nova Scotia, Canada	2.00
4074		**Samuel de Champlain,** souvenir sheet, *May 28,* Washington, DC	4.75
		Ticonderoga, NY	4.75
		Annapolis Royal, Nova Scotia, Canada	4.75
4075		**Washington 2006 World Philatelic Exhibition,** souvenir sheet, *May 29,* Washington, DC	16.00
4075a		$1	3.25
4075b		$2	5.25
4075c		$5	10.00
4076	39c	**Distinguished American Diplomats,** souvenir sheet, *May 30,* Washington, DC	6.00
		4076a-4076f, any single	2.00
4077	39c	**Judy Garland,** *June 10,* New York, NY	2.00
4078	39c	**Ronald Reagan,** *June 14,* Simi Valley, CA	2.00
4079	39c	**Happy Birthday,** *June 23,* Santa Clara, CA	2.00
4080-4083	39c	**Baseball Sluggers,** *July 15,* Bronx, NY	4.50
		4080-4083, any single	2.00
4084	39c	**DC Comics Superheroes,** *July 20,* San Diego, CA	16.00
		4084a-4084t, any single	2.00
4085-4088	39c	**Motorcycles,** *Aug. 7,* Sturgis, SD	4.50
		4085-4088, any single, Sturgis, SD	2.00
4089-4098	39c	**Quilts of Gee's Bend,** *Aug. 24,* Chicago, IL	8.00
		4089-4098, any single, Chicago, IL	2.00
4099	39c	**Southern Florida Wetland,** *Oct. 4,* Naples, FL	9.00
		4099a-4099j, any single	2.00
4100	39c	**Christmas Madonna,** *Oct. 17,* Denver, CO	2.00
4101-4104	39c	**Christmas Snowflakes,** denominations higher than year date, serpentine die cut 11¼x11, *Oct. 5,* New York, NY	4.50
		4101-4104, any single	2.00
4105-4108	39c	**Christmas Snowflakes,** denominations even with year date, serpentine die cut 11¼x11½ on 2 or 3 sides, *Oct. 5,* New York, NY	4.50
		4105-4108, any single	2.00
4109-4112	39c	**Christmas Snowflakes,** denominations even with year date, serpentine die cut 11¼x11 on 2 or 3 sides, *Oct. 5,* New York, NY	4.50
		4109-4112, any single	2.00
4113-4116	39c	**Christmas Snowflakes,** denominations even with year date, serpentine die cut 8 on 2, 3 or 4 sides, *Oct. 5,* New York, NY	4.50
		4113-4116, any single	2.00
4117	39c	**Eid,** *Oct. 6,* New York, NY	2.00
4118	39c	**Hanukkah,** *Oct. 6,* New York, NY	2.00
4119	39c	**Kwanzaa,** *Oct. 6,* New York, NY	2.00

2007

4120	39c	**Ella Fitzgerald,** *Jan. 10,* New York, NY	2.00
4121	39c	**Oklahoma Statehood,** *Jan. 11,* Oklahoma City, OK	2.00
4122	39c	**Love,** self-adhesive booklet stamp, *Jan. 13,* Hershey, PA	2.00
4123	84c	**International Polar Year,** *Feb. 21,* Fairbanks, AK	4.75
		4123a-4123b, either single	3.00
4124	39c	**Henry Wadsworth Longfellow,** *Mar. 15,* New York, NY	2.00
4125	(41c)	**Liberty Bell,** self-adhesive booklet stamp, large microprinting, 16mm bell, serpentine die cut 11¼x10¾, *Apr. 12,* Philadelphia, PA	2.10
4126	(41c)	**Liberty Bell,** self-adhesive booklet stamp, small microprinting, 16mm bell, serpentine die cut 11¼x10¾, *Apr. 12,* Philadelphia, PA	2.10
4127	(41c)	**Liberty Bell,** self-adhesive booklet stamp, medium microprinting, 15mm bell, serpentine die cut 11¼x10¾, *Apr. 12,* Philadelphia, PA	2.10
4127d	(42c)	**Forever,** dated "2008," *May 12, 2008* Washington, DC	2.10
4128	(41c)	**Liberty Bell,** self-adhesive booklet stamp, large microprinting, 16mm bell, serpentine die cut 8, *Apr. 12,* Philadelphia, PA	2.10

4129 (41c) **Flag,** perf. 11¼, *Apr. 12,* Washington, DC 2.10
4130 (41c) **Flag,** self-adhesive, serpentine die cut 11¼x10¾, *Apr. 12,* Washington, DC 2.10
4131 (41c) **Flag,** coil stamp, perf. 9¾ vert., *Apr. 12,* Washington, DC 2.10
4132 (41c) **Flag,** self-adhesive coil stamp, serpentine die cut 9½ vert., *Apr. 12,* Washington, DC 2.10
4133 (41c) **Flag,** self-adhesive coil stamp, serpentine die cut 11 vert., perpendicular corners, *Apr. 12,* Washington, DC 2.10
4134 (41c) **Flag,** self-adhesive coil stamp, serpentine die cut 8½ vert., *Apr. 12,* Washington, DC 2.10
4135 (41c) **Flag,** self-adhesive coil stamp, serpentine die cut 11 vert., rounded corners, *Apr. 12,* Washington, DC 2.10
4136 41c **Settlement of Jamestown,** *May 11,* Jamestown, VA 2.10
4137 26c **Florida Panther,** perf. 11¼x11 *May 12,* Washington, DC 2.10
4138 17c **Bighorn Sheep,** self-adhesive, serpentine die cut 11, *May 14,* Washington, DC 2.10
4139 26c **Florida Panther,** self-adhesive, serpentine die cut 11¼x11, *May 12,* Washington, DC 2.10
4140 17c **Bighorn Sheep,** self-adhesive coil, serpentine die cut 11 vert., *May 21,* Washington, DC 2.10
4141 26c **Florida Panther,** self-adhesive coil, serpentine die cut 11 vert., *May 12,* Washington, DC 2.10
4142 26c **Florida Panther,** self-adhesive booklet stamp, serpentine die cut 11¼x11 on 3 sides, *May 12,* Washington, DC 2.10
4143 39c **Star Wars,** *May 27,* Los Angeles, CA 12.50
4143a-4143o, any single 2.10
4144 $4.60 **Air Force One,** *June 13,* Washington, DC 9.25
4145 $16.25 **Marine One,** *June 13,* Washington, DC 32.50
4146-4150 41c **Pacific Lighthouses,** *June 21,* Westport, WA 5.50
4146-4150, any single 2.10
4151 41c **Wedding Heart,** *June 27,* Washington, DC 2.10
4152 58c **Wedding Heart,** *June 27,* Washington, DC 2.40
4153-4156 41c **Pollination,** type I, *June 29,* Washington, DC 4.50
4153-4156, type I, any single 2.10
4153a-4156a, type II 4.50
4153a-4156a, type II, any single 2.10
4157 (10c) **Patriotic Banner coil,** serpentine die cut 11 vert., *July 4,* Washington, DC 2.00
4158 (10c) **Patriotic Banner coil,** serpentine die cut 11½ vert., *July 4,* Washington, DC 2.00
4159 41c **Marvel Comics Superheroes,** *July 26,* San Diego, CA 17.00
4159a-4159t, any single 2.10
4160-4163 41c **Vintage Mahogany Speedboats,** *Aug. 4,* Clayton, NY 4.50
4160-4163, any single 2.10
4164 41c **Purple Heart,** *Aug. 7,* Washington, DC 2.10
4165 41c **Louis Comfort Tiffany,** *Aug. 9,* Portland, OR 2.10
4166-4175 41c **Flowers,** self-adhesive coil stamps, *Aug. 10,* Portland, OR 8.25
4166-4175, any single 2.10
4176-4185 41c **Flowers,** self-adhesive booklet stamps, *Aug. 10,* Portland, OR 8.25
4176-4185, any single 2.10
4186 41c **Flag,** self-adhesive coil stamp with microprinting on right side of flagpole, serpentine die cut 9½ vert., *Aug. 15,* Washington, DC 2.10
4187 41c **Flag,** self-adhesive coil stamp with microprinting on left side of flagpole, serpentine die cut 9½ vert., *Aug. 15,* Washington, DC 2.10
4188 41c **Flag,** self-adhesive coil stamp with perpendicular corners, serpentine die cut 8½ vert., *Aug. 15,* Washington, DC 2.10
4189 41c **Flag,** self-adhesive coil stamp with rounded corners, serpentine die cut 11 vert., *Aug. 15,* Washington, DC 2.10
4190 41c **Flag,** self-adhesive booklet stamp with microprinting on right side of flagpole, *Aug. 15,* Washington, DC 2.10
4191 41c **Flag,** self-adhesive booklet stamp with microprinting on left side of flagpole, *Aug. 15,* Washington, DC 2.10
4192-4195 41c **Disney Characters,** *Aug. 16,* Orlando, FL 4.50
4192-4195, any single 2.10
4196 41c **Celebrate,** *Aug. 17,* Stamford, CT 2.10
4197 41c **James Stewart,** *Aug. 17,* Universal City, CA 2.10
4198 41c **Alpine Tundra,** *Aug. 28,* Estes Park, CO 8.25
4198a-4198j, any single 2.10
4199 41c **Gerald R. Ford,** *Aug. 31,* Grand Rapids, MI 2.10
Rancho Mirage, CA 2.10
4200 41c **Jury Duty,** *Sept. 12,* New York, NY 2.10
4201 41c **Mendez v. Westminster,** *Sept. 14,* Santa Ana, CA 2.10
4202 41c **Eid,** *Sept. 28,* Washington, DC 2.10
4203-4204 41c **Auroras,** *Oct. 1,* Washington, DC 3.00
4203-4204, any single 2.10
4205 41c **Yoda,** *Oct. 25,* New York, NY 2.10
4206 41c **Christmas Madonna,** *Oct. 25,* New York, NY 2.10
4207-4210 41c **Christmas Knits,** serpentine die cut 10¾, *Oct. 25,* New York, NY 4.50
4207-4210, any single 2.10
4211-4214 41c **Christmas Knits,** serpentine die cut 11¼x11 on 2 or 3 sides, *Oct. 25,* New York, NY 4.50
4211-4214, any single 2.10
4215-4218 41c **Christmas Knits,** serpentine die cut 8 on 2, 3 or 4 sides, *Oct. 25,* New York, NY 4.50
4215-4218, any single 2.10
4219 41c **Hanukkah,** *Oct. 26,* New York, NY 2.10
4220 41c **Kwanzaa,** *Oct. 26,* New York, NY 2.10

2008

4221 41c **Chinese New Year,** *Jan. 9,* San Francisco, CA 2.10
4222 41c **Charles W. Chesnutt,** *Jan. 31,* Cleveland, OH 2.10
4223 41c **Marjorie Kinnan Rawlings,** *Feb. 21,* Hawthorne, FL 2.10
4224-4227 41c **American Scientists,** *Mar. 6,* New York, NY 4.50
4224-4227, any single 2.10
4228-4231 42c **Flags,** coil stamps, perf. 10 vert., *Apr. 18,* Washington, DC 4.75
4228-4231, any single 2.10
4232-4235 42c **Flags,** self-adhesive coil stamps, serpentine die cut 9½ vert., *Apr. 18,* Washington, DC 4.75
4232-4235, any single 2.10
4236-4239 42c **Flags,** self-adhesive coil stamps, serpentine die cut 11 vert. with perpendicular corners, *Apr. 18,* Washington, DC 4.75
4236-4239, any single 2.10
4240-4243 42c **Flags,** self-adhesive coil stamps, serpentine die cut 8½ vert., *Apr. 18,* Washington, DC 4.75
4240-4243, any single 2.10
4244-4247 42c **Flags,** self-adhesive coil stamps, serpentine die cut 11 vert. with rounded corners, *Apr. 18,* Washington, DC 4.75
4244-42471, any single 2.10
4248-4252 42c **American Journalists,** *Apr. 22,* Washington, DC 5.50
4248-4252, any single 2.10
4253-4257 27c **Tropical Fruit,** serpentine die cut 11¼x10¾, *Apr. 25,* Burlingame, CA 4.00
4253-4257, any single 1.75
4258-4262 27c **Tropical Fruit,** self-adhesive coil stamps, serpentine die cut 8½ vert., *Apr. 25,* Burlingame, CA 4.00
4258-4262, any single 1.75
4263 42c **Purple Heart,** perf. 11¼, *Apr. 30,* Washington, DC 2.10
4264 42c **Purple Heart,** self-adhesive, serpentine die cut 11¼x10¾, *Apr. 30,* Washington, DC 2.10
4265 42c **Frank Sinatra,** *May 13,* New York, NY 2.10
Las Vegas, NV 2.10
4266 42c **Minnesota Statehood, 150th Anniv.,** *May 17,* St. Paul, MN 2.10
4267 62c **Dragonfly,** *May 19,* Washington, DC 2.50
4268 $4.80 **Mount Rushmore,** *June 6,* McLean, VA 9.75
4269 $16.50 **Hoover Dam,** *June 20,* Washington, DC 33.00
4270 42c **Love,** *June 10,* Washington, DC 2.10
4271 42c **Wedding Heart,** *June 10,* Washington, DC 2.10
4272 59c **Wedding Heart,** *June 10,* Washington, DC 2.40
4273-4282 42c **Flags of Our Nation,** *June 14,* Washington, DC 8.50
4273-4282, any single 2.10
4333 42c **Charles and Ray Eames,** *June 17,* Santa Monica, CA 13.50
4333a-4333p, any single 2.10
4334 42c **Summer Olympics,** *June 19,* Philadelphia, PA 2.10

SEMI-POSTAL FIRST DAY COVERS

1998

B1 32c +8c **Breast Cancer,** *July 29,* Washington, DC (51,775) 2.00

2002

B2 (34c+11c) **Heroes of 2001,** *June 7,* New York, NY 3.00
Any other city 2.00

2003

B3 (37c+8c) **Stop Family Violence,** *Oct. 8,* Washington, DC 1.60
Any other city 1.60

AIR POST FIRST DAY COVERS

1918

C1 6c **orange,** *Dec. 10* — *25,000.*
C2 16c **green,** *July 11* — *32,500.*
C3 24c **carmine rose & blue,** *May 13* — *27,500.*

1923

C4 8c **dark green,** *Aug. 15* — 400.00
C5 16c **dark blue,** *Aug. 17* — 600.00
C6 24c **carmine,** *Aug. 21* — 750.00

1926-27

C7 10c **dark blue,** *Feb. 13, 1926* — 70.00
Chicago, Ill. — 85.00
Detroit, Mich. — 85.00
Cleveland, Ohio — 130.00
Dearborn, Mich. — 130.00
C8 15c **olive brown,** *Sept. 18, 1926* — 85.00
C9 20c **yellow green,** *Jan. 25, 1927* — 100.00
New York, N.Y. — 125.00
C10 10c **dark blue,** *June 18, 1927* — 25.00
St. Louis, Mo. — 25.00
Little Falls, Minn. — 35.00
Detroit, Mich. — 35.00
C10a Booklet pane of 3, *May 26, 1928* — 875.00
Cleveland Midwestern Philatelic Sta. cancel — 800.00
C10a & 645 on one cover, Washington, D.C. — 1,000.

1928-30

C11 5c **carmine & blue,** *July 25, 1928,* pair — 50.00
C12 5c **violet,** *Feb. 10, 1930* — 12.00
C13 65c **green,** *Apr. 19, 1930* — 1,200.
C14 $1.30 **brown,** *Apr. 19, 1930* — 1,100.
C15 $2.60 **blue,** *Apr. 19, 1930* — 1,200.
C13-C15 on one cover — 15,000.

Values are for first day covers flown on Zeppelin flights with appropriate markings. Non-flown covers sell for less.

1931-33

C16 5c **violet,** *Aug. 19, 1931* — 175.00
C17 8c **olive bister,** *Sept. 26, 1932* — 15.00
C18 50c **green,** *Oct. 2, 1933,* New York, N.Y. *(3,500)* — 200.00
Akron, Ohio, *Oct. 4* — 300.00
Washington, D.C., *Oct. 5* — 275.00
Miami, Fla., *Oct. 6* — 150.00
Chicago, Ill., *Oct. 7* — 250.00

1934-37

C19 6c **dull orange,** *June 30, 1934,* Baltimore, Md. — *190.00*
New York, N.Y. — *800.00*
Brooklyn, N.Y. — 1,200.
San Francisco, Calif. — 1,500.
Washington, D.C., *July 1* — 10.00

Catalogue values for Nos. C20-C45 are for addressed covers with the most common cachets.

C20 25c **blue,** *Nov. 22, 1935 (10,910)* — 40.00
San Francisco, Cal. *(15,000)* — 35.00
C21 20c **green,** *Feb. 15, 1937* — 45.00
C22 50c **carmine,** *Feb. 15, 1937* — 50.00
C21-C22 on one cover — 100.00

First day covers of Nos. C21 and C22 total 40,000.

1938-39

C23 6c **dark blue & carmine,** *May 14, 1938,* Dayton, Ohio *(116,443)* — 15.00
St. Petersburg, Fla. *(95,121)* — 15.00
Washington, D.C., *May 15* — 3.50
C24 30c **dull blue,** *May 16, 1939,* New York, N.Y. *(68,634)* — 47.50

1941-44

C25 6c **carmine,** *June 25, 1941 (99,986)* — 3.75
C25a Booklet pane of 3, *Mar. 18, 1943* — 25.00
C26 8c **olive green,** *Mar. 21, 1944 (147,484)* — 3.75
C27 10c **violet,** *Aug. 15, 1941,* Atlantic City, N.J. *(87,712)* — 8.00
C28 15c **brown carmine,** *Aug. 19, 1941,* Baltimore, Md. *(74,000)* — 10.00
C29 20c **bright green,** *Aug. 27, 1941,* Philadelphia, Pa. *(66,225)* — 12.50
C30 30c **blue,** *Sept. 25, 1941,* Kansas City, Mo. *(57,175)* — 20.00
C31 50c **orange,** *Oct. 29, 1941,* St. Louis, Mo. *(54,580)* — 40.00

1946-48

C32 5c **carmine,** *Sept. 25, 1946* — 2.00

First day covers of Nos. C32 & UC14 total 396,669.

C33 5c **carmine,** *Mar. 26, 1947 (342,634)* — 2.00
C34 10c **black,** *Aug. 30, 1947 (265,773)* — 2.00
C35 15c **bright blue green,** *Aug. 20, 1947,* New York, N.Y. *(230,338)* — 1.75
C36 25c **blue,** *July 30, 1947,* San Francisco, Cal. *(201,762)* — 2.25
C37 5c **carmine, coil,** *Jan. 15, 1948 (192,084)* — 1.75
C38 5c **New York City,** *July 31, 1948,* New York, N.Y. *(371,265)* — 1.75

1949

C39 6c **carmine,** *Jan. 18 (266,790)* — 1.50
C39a Booklet pane of 6, *Nov. 18, 1949,* New York, N.Y. — 10.00
C40 6c **Alexandria Bicentennial,** *May 11,* Alexandria, Va. *(386,717)* — 1.50
C41 6c **carmine coil,** *Aug. 25 (240,386)* — 1.25
C42 10c **U.P.U.,** *Nov. 18,* New Orleans, La. *(270,000)* — 1.75
C43 15c **U.P.U.,** *Oct. 7,* Chicago, Ill. *(246,833)* — 2.75
C44 25c **U.P.U.,** *Nov. 30,* Seattle, Wash. *(220,215)* — 3.75
C45 6c **Wright Brothers,** *Dec. 17,* Kitty Hawk, N.C. *(378,585)* — 2.75

Catalogue values from this point to the end of the section are for unaddressed covers with the most common cachets.

1952-59

C46 80c **Hawaii,** *Mar. 26, 1952,* Honolulu, Hawaii, *(89,864)* — 20.00
C47 6c **Powered Flight,** *May 29, 1953,* Dayton, Ohio *(359,050)* — 1.50
C48 4c **bright blue,** *Sept. 3, 1954,* Philadelphia, Pa. *(295,720)* — 1.00
C49 6c **Air Force,** *Aug. 1, 1957 (356,683)* — 2.75
C50 5c **red,** *July 31, 1958,* Colorado Springs, Colo. *(207,954)* — 1.00
C51 7c **blue,** *July 31, 1958,* Philadelphia, Pa. *(204,401)* — 1.00
C51a Booklet pane of 6, San Antonio, Tex. *(119,769)* — 9.00
C52 7c **blue coil,** *July 31, 1958,* Miami, Fla. *(181,603)* — 1.00
C53 7c **Alaska Statehood,** *Jan. 3, 1959,* Juneau, Alaska *(489,752)* — 1.50
C54 7c **Balloon Jupiter,** *Aug. 17, 1959,* Lafayette, Ind.*(383,556)* — 1.75
C55 7c **Hawaii Statehood,** *Aug. 21, 1959,* Honolulu, Hawaii *(533,464)* — 1.00
C56 10c **Pan American Games,** *Aug. 27, 1959,* Chicago, Ill. *(302,306)* — 1.00

1959-66

C57 10c **Liberty Bell,** *June 10, 1960,* Miami, Fla. *(246,509)* — 1.50
C58 15c **Statue of Liberty,** *Nov. 20, 1959,* New York, N.Y. *(259,412)* — 1.50
C59 25c **Abraham Lincoln,** *Apr. 22, 1960,* San Francisco, Cal. *(211,235)* — 1.50
C59a 25c Tagged, *Dec. 29, 1966 (about 3,000)* — 50.00
C60 7c **carmine,** *Aug. 12, 1960,* Arlington, Va. *(247,190)* — 1.00
C60a Booklet pane of 6, *Aug. 19, 1960,* St. Louis, Mo. *(143,363)* — 8.00
C61 7c **carmine coil,** *Oct. 22, 1960,* Atlantic City, N.J. *(197,995)* — 1.00

1961-67

C62 13c **Liberty Bell,** *June 28, 1961,* New York, N.Y. *(316,166)* — 1.00
C62a 13c Tagged, *Feb. 15, 1967* — 50.00
C63 15c **Redrawn Statue of Liberty,** *Jan. 13, 1961,* Buffalo, N.Y. *(192,976)* — 1.00
C63a 15c Tagged, *Jan. 11, 1967* — 50.00
C64 8c **carmine,** *Dec. 5, 1962 (288,355)* — 1.00
C64b Booklet pane of 5 + label *(146,835)* — 3.50
C64a 8c Tagged, *Aug. 1, 1963,* Dayton, Ohio *(262,720)* — 2.00
C65 8c **carmine coil,** *Dec. 5, 1962 (220,173)* — 1.00

1963-69

C66 15c **Montgomery Blair,** *May 3, 1963,* Silver Spring, Md. *(260,031)* — 1.50
C67 6c **Bald Eagle,** *July 12, 1963,* Boston, Mass. *(268,265)* — 1.00
C67a 6c Tagged, *Feb. 15, 1967* — 50.00
C68 8c **Amelia Earhart,** *July 24, 1963,* Atchison, Kan. *(437,996)* — 4.00
C69 8c **Robert H. Goddard,** *Oct. 5, 1964,* Roswell, N.M. *(421,020)* — 3.00
C70 8c **Alaska Purchase,** *Mar. 30, 1967,* Sitka, Alaska *(554,784)* — 1.50
C71 20c **Audubon,** *Apr. 26, 1967,* Audubon (Station of N.Y.C.), N.Y. *(227,930)* — 2.00
C72 10c **carmine,** *Jan. 5, 1968,* San Francisco, Cal. — 1.00
C72b Booklet pane of 8 — 3.75
C72c Booklet pane of 5 + label, slogan 4 *Jan. 6, 1968* — 125.00
With slogan 5 — 110.00
C73 10c **carmine coil,** *Jan. 5, 1968,* San Francisco, Cal. — 1.00
C74 10c **Air Mail Service,** *May 15, 1968 (521,084)* — 1.50
C75 20c **USA and Jet,** *Nov. 22, 1968,* New York, N.Y. *(276,244)* — 1.25
C76 10c **Moon Landing,** *Sept. 9, 1969 (8,743,070)* — 5.00

1971-73

C77 9c **red,** *May 15, 1971,* Kitty Hawk, N.C. — 1.00

First day cancellation was applied to 379,442 covers of Nos. C77 and UXC10.

C78 11c **carmine,** *May 7, 1971,* Spokane, Wash. — 1.00
C78a Booklet pane of 4 + 2 labels — 2.25
C79 13c **carmine,** *Nov. 16, 1973,* New York, N.Y. *(282,550)* — 1.00
C79a Booklet pane of 5 + label, *Dec. 27, 1973,* Chicago, Ill. — 2.25

First day cancellation was applied to 464,750 covers of Nos. C78, C78a and C82, and to 204,756 covers of Nos. C79a and C83.

C80 17c **Statue of Liberty,** *July 13, 1971,* Lakehurst, N.J. *(172,269)* — 1.50
C81 21c **USA and Jet,** *May 21, 1971 (293,140)* — 1.00
C82 11c **carmine coil,** *May 7, 1971,* Spokane, Wash. — 1.00
C83 13c **carmine coil,** *Dec. 27, 1973,* Chicago, Ill. — 1.00
C84 11c **National Parks Centennial,** *May 3, 1972,* Honaunau, Hawaii *(364,816)* — 1.00
C85 11c **Olympics,** *Aug. 17, 1972* — 1.00

First day cancellation was applied to 971,536 covers of Nos. 1460-1462 and C85.

C86 11c **Electronics,** *July 10, 1973,* New York, N.Y. — 1.00

First day cancellation was applied to 1,197,700 covers of Nos. 1500-1502 and C86.

1974-79

C87 18c **Statue of Liberty,** *Jan. 11, 1974,* Hempstead, N.Y. *(216,902)* — 1.25
C88 26c **Mt. Rushmore,** *Jan. 2, 1974,* Rapid City, S.D. *(210,470)* — 1.50
C89 25c **Plane and Globes,** *Jan. 2, 1976,* Honolulu, Hawaii — 1.00
C90 31c **Plane, Globes and Flag,** *Jan. 2, 1976,* Honolulu, Hawaii — 1.25
C92a 31c **Wright Brothers,** *Sept. 23, 1978,* Dayton, Ohio — 4.00
C91-C92, any single — 3.00
C94a 21c **Octave Chanute,** *Mar. 29, 1979,* Chanute, Kan. *(459,235)* — 4.00
C93-C94, any single — 3.00
C96a 25c **Wiley Post,** *Nov. 20, 1979,* Oklahoma City, Okla. — 4.00
C95-C96, any single — 3.00
C97 31c **Olympics,** *Nov. 1, 1979,* Colorado Springs, CO — 1.50

1980

C98 40c **Philip Mazzei,** *Oct. 13* — 1.50
C99 28c **Blanche Stuart Scott,** *Dec. 30,* Hammondsport, NY *(238,502)* — 1.50
C100 35c **Glenn Curtiss,** *Dec. 30,* Hammondsport, NY *(208,502)* — 1.50

1983

C104a 28c **Olympics,** *June 17,* San Antonio, TX *(901,028)* — 3.75
C101-C104, any single — 1.75
C108a 40c **Olympics,** *Apr. 8,* Los Angeles, CA *(1,001,657)* — 5.00
C105-C108, any single — 1.75
C112a 35c **Olympics,** *Nov. 4,* Colorado Springs, CO*(897,729)* — 4.50
C109-C112, any single — 1.75

1985

C113 33c **Alfred V. Verville,** *Feb. 13,* Garden City, NY — 1.50
C114 39c **Lawrence & Elmer Sperry,** *Feb. 13,* Garden City, NY — 1.50

First day cancel was applied to 429,290 covers bearing one more of Nos. C113-C114.

C115 44c **Transpacific Air Mail,** *Feb. 15,* San Francisco, CA *(269,229)* — 1.75

A total of 269,229 first day cancels were applied for Nos. C115 and UXC22.

C116 44c **Junipero Serra,** *Aug. 22,* San Diego, CA *(254,977)* — 2.00

1988

C117 44c **Settling of New Sweden,** *Mar. 29,* Wilmington, DE *(213,445)* — 1.50
C118 45c **Samuel P. Langley,** *May 14,* San Diego, CA — 1.50
C119 36c **Igor Sikorsky,** *June 23,* Stratford, CT *(162,986)* — 2.50

1989

C120 45c **French Revolution,** *July 14 (309,975)* — 1.50
C121 45c **Southeast Carved Figure,** *Oct. 12,* San Juan, PR *(93,569)* — 1.50

C125a 45c **Future Mail Transportation,** *Nov. 27 (765,479)* 6.50
C122-C125, any single 1.75
C126 45c **Future Mail Transportation Souvenir Sheet,** *Nov. 24 (257,826)* 6.50

1990

C127 45c **Tropical Coast,** *Oct. 12,* Grand Canyon, AZ *(137,068)* 1.50

1991

C128 50c **Harriet Quimby,** *Apr. 27,* Plymouth, MI 1.50
C129 40c **William T. Piper,** *May 17,* Denver, CO 1.50
C130 50c **Antarctic Treaty,** *June 21* 1.50
C131 50c **Bering Land Bridge,** *Oct. 12,* Anchorage, AK 1.50

1999

C133 48c **Niagara Falls,** *May 12,* Niagara Falls, NY *(20,878)* 1.75
C134 40c **Rio Grande,** *July 30,* Milwaukee, WI 2.00
any other city 2.00

First day cancel was applied to 42,144 covers bearing one more of Nos. 3330, C134.

C135 60c **Grand Canyon,** *Jan. 20,* Grand Canyon, AZ *(64,282)* 2.00

2001

C136 70c **Nine-mile Prairie,** *Mar. 6,* Lincoln, NE 2.00

C137 80c **Mt. McKinley,** *Apr. 17,* Fairbanks, AK 2.00

C138 60c **Acadia National Park,** *May 30,* Bar Harbor, ME 2.00

2006

C139 63c **Bryce Canyon National Park,** *Feb. 24,* St. Louis, MO 2.50
Any other city 2.50
C140 75c **Great Smoky Mountains National Park,** *Feb. 24,* St. Louis, MO 2.75
Any other city 2.75
C141 84c **Yosemite National Park,** *Feb. 24,* St. Louis, MO 3.00
Any other city 3.00

2007

C142 69c **Okefenokee Swamp,** *June 1,* McLean, VA 2.60
C143 90c **Hagatña Bay,** *June 1,* Barrigada, GU 3.00

BOOKLETS: PANES & COVERS

Most booklet panes issued before 1962 consist of a vertical block of 6 stamps perforated vertically through the center. The panes are perforated horizontally on all but the bottom edge and the top of the selvage tab. The selvage top, the two sides and the bottom are straight edged. Exceptions for panes issued before 1962 are the 1917 American Expeditionary Forces panes (30 stamps); Lindbergh and 6¢ 1943 air mails (3), and the Savings Stamps (10). Since 1962, panes have been issued with 3 to 20 stamps and various configurations. They have included one or more labels and two or more stamps se-tenant.

Flat plate booklet panes, with the exceptions noted above, were made from specially designed plates of 180 or 360 subjects. They are collected in plate positions. There are nine collectible positions on the 180-subject plate and 12 on the 360-subject plate.

Rotary booklet panes issued from 1926 to May 1978 (except for Nos. 1623a and 1623Bc) were made from specially designed plates of 180, 320, 360, and 400 subjects. They also are collected in plate positions. There are five collectible positions on the 360-subject plates which were printed before electric eye plates came into use, and 18 collectible positions on the Type II "new design" 360-subject rotary plates. There are 17 collectible positions in the rotary air mail 180-subject plate, and 21 collectible positions in the Type IV "modified design" 360-subject plate. There are 13 collectible positions on the 320-subject plates and 24 on the 400 subject plates. There are five collectible positions on Defense and War Savings 300-subject plates.

The generally accepted methods of designating pane positions as illustrated and explained hereafter are those suggested by George H. Beans in the May 1913 issue of "Everybody's Philatelist" and by B. H. Mosher in his monograph "Discovering U.S. Rotary Pane Varieties 1926-78." Some collectors seek all varieties possible, but the majority collect unused (A) panes and plate number (D) panes from flat plate issues, and plain panes and panes with electric eye bars and electric eye dashes, where available, from rotary plates.

Starting in 1977, BEP made two major changes in booklet production. Printing of panes was gradually moved from rotary plates to sleeves for modern high speed presses. Also, booklet production was transferred to Goebel booklet-forming machines. These changes virtually eliminated collectible pane positions for several years. However, beginning with No. BK156 (No. 2276a), BEP and other printers began placing printing process control marks in pane tabs. As a result, specialist booklet pane collectors actively resumed collecting pane positions. Collectible positions on these issues are not shown in this catalogue but can be found in the United States Stamp Society's Research Paper No. 2 "Folded Style Checklist," Michael O. Perry, editor. Also, because of the requirements of the Goebel machine, the subject size of printing plates or sleeves varied widely. For these reasons, plate layouts are not shown for each issue. The plate layout for No. 1288c and the sleeve layout for No. 1623a are shown as typical.

The following panes, issued after Mar. 11, 1977, were printed from pairs of rotary plates and assembled into booklets on the Goebel machine: Nos. 1288c, 1742a, 1819a, 1889a, and 1949a. One pane in 12 of those issues may have a join line along either long side of the pane, creating three collectible positions: no join line, join line top (or right) and join line bottom (or left). Except for Nos. 1736a and 2276a, all other booklet panes issued from Mar. 11, 1977 on were printed from intaglio sleeves, gravure cylinders, and/or offset plates.

At least one pane in every booklet produced on the BEP's Goebel machines contains two register marks in the tab: a cross register line (CRL) 1.5mm wide which runs across the width of the tab and a length register mark (LRM), typically 1.5x5mm, usually placed above the right hand (or top) stamp of the pane. Nos. 1623a and 1623Bc were regularly issued with the LRM over either stamp. Some examples of Nos. 1893a, 2121a and 3003Ab were issued with the LRM over the left stamp.

Starting with No. 1889a (except for No. 1948a), plate numbers (1 to 5 digits) were placed in the tab, normally over the left stamp. On booklets containing Nos. 1889a, 1949a and 2113a, the plate number is supposed to be on the top pane, the second pane not having a number. All subsequent multi-pane booklets have the plate number on each pane. Some multi-pane booklets contain panes with different plate numbers. The booklet value is determined by the top pane.

Most recent booklets have been printed by contractors other than the BEP so markings may differ or be absent.

Panes in all booklets assembled on the Goebel machine will be folded at least once. **Repeated handling of booklets with folded panes may cause the panes to fall apart.**

Booklet panes with tabs attached to the cover by adhesive instead of staples are valued on the basis of the tab intact. Minor damage on the back of the tab due to removal from the booklet does not affect the value. Some of these panes were furnished to first day cover processors unfolded and not pasted into covers. Around 1989, these panes were available to collectors through the Philatelic Agency.

All panes from 1967 to date are tagged, unless otherwise stated.

Dr. William R. Bush, Morton Dean Joyce, Robert E. Kitson, Richard F. Larkin, Dr. Robert Marks, Bruce H. Mosher, Michael O. Perry, the United States Stamp Society (formerly the Bureau Issues Association), and the Booklet Collectors Club helped the editors extensively in compiling the listings and preparing the illustrations of booklets, covers and plate layouts.

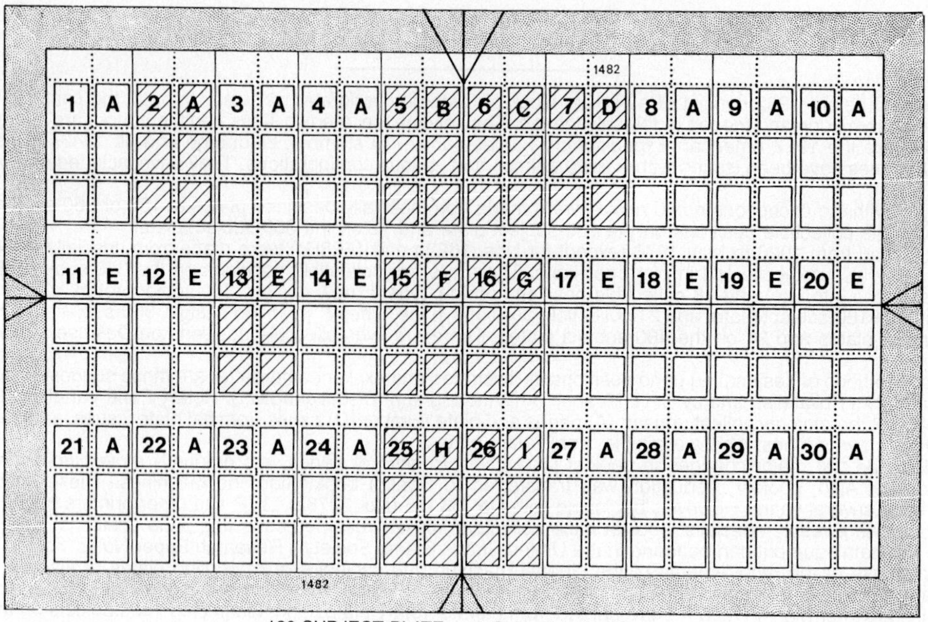

180-SUBJECT PLATE — 9 Collectible Positions

Beginning at upper left and reading from left to right, the panes are designated from 1 to 30. All positions not otherwise identifiable are designated by the letter A: Pane 1A, 2A, 3A, 4A, etc.

The identifiable positions are as follows:

A — The ordinary booklet pane without distinguishing features. Occurs in Position 1, 2, 3, 4, 8, 9, 10, 21, 22, 23, 24, 27, 28, 29, 30.
B — Split arrow and guide line at right. Occurs in Position 5 only.
C — Split arrow and guide line at left. Occurs in Position 6 only.
D — Plate number pane. Occurs in Position 7 only.
E — Guide line pane showing horizontal guide line between stamps 1-2 and 3-4 of the pane. Occurs in Positions 11, 12, 13, 14, 17, 18, 19, and 20.
F — Guide line through pane and at right. Occurs in Position 15 only.
G — Guide line through pane and at left. Occurs in Position 16 only.
H — Guide line at right. Occurs in Position 25 only.
I — Guide line at left. Occurs in Position 26 only.

Only positions B, F and H or C, G and I may be obtained from the same sheet, depending on whether the knife which separated the panes fell to right or left of the line.
Side arrows, bottom arrows, or bottom plate numbers are seldom found because the margin of the sheets is usually cut off, as are the sides and bottom of each pane.
In the illustrations, the dotted lines represent the rows of perforations, the unbroken lines represents the knife cut.

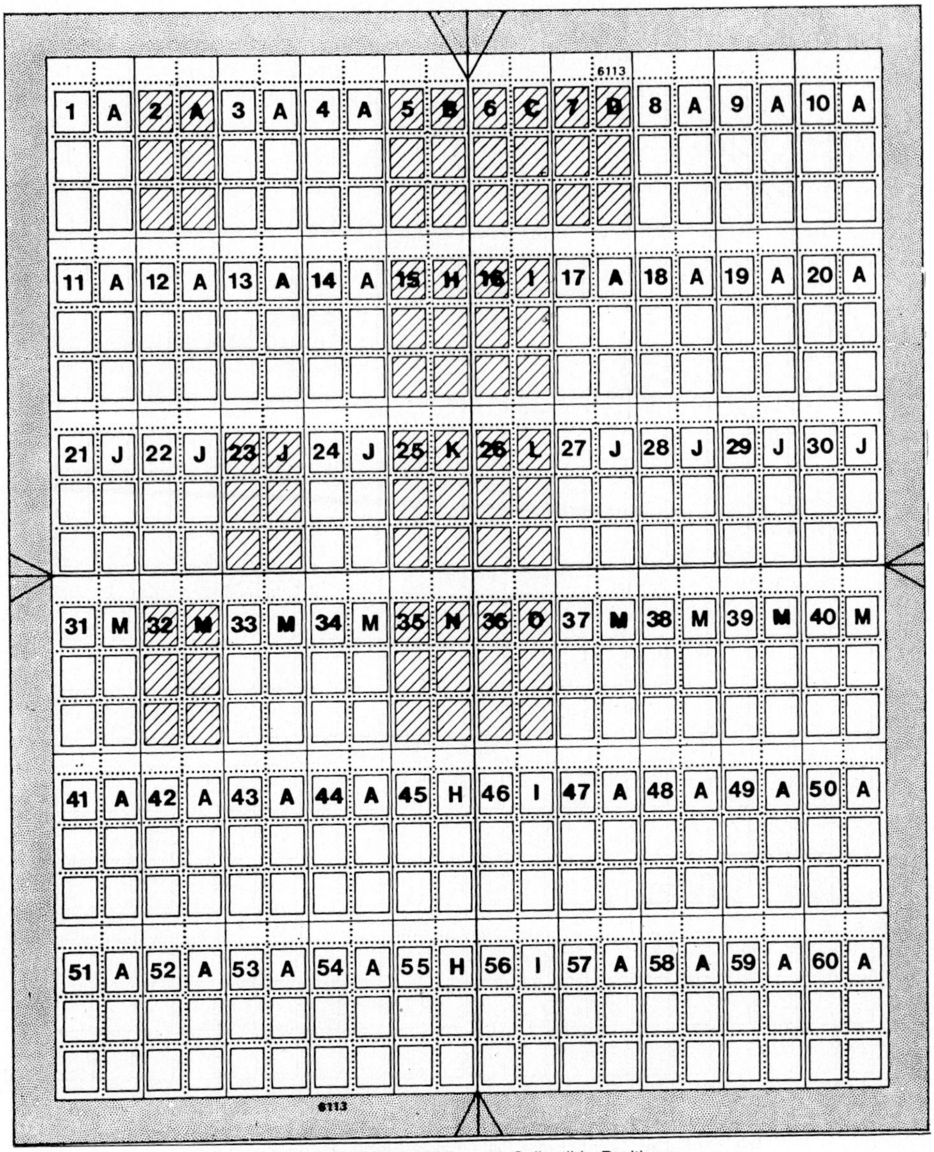

360-SUBJECT PLATE — 12 Collectible Positions

As with the 180-Subject Sheets, the position of the various panes is indicated by numbers beginning in the upper left corner with the No. 1 and reading from left to right to No. 60.

The identifiable positions are as follows:

A — The ordinary booklet pane without distinguishing features. Occurs in Positions 1, 2, 3, 4, 8, 9, 10, 11, 12, 13, 14, 17, 18, 19, 20, 41, 42, 43, 44, 47, 48, 49, 50, 51, 52, 53, 54, 57, 58, 59, and 60.

B — Split arrow and guide line at right. Occurs in Position 5 only.

C — Split arrow and guide line at left. Occurs in Position 6 only.

D — Plate number pane. Occurs in Position 7 only.

E, F, G — Do not occur in the 360-Subject Plate.

H — Guide line at right. Occurs in Positions 15, 45, and 55.

I — Guide line at left. Occurs in Positions 16, 46, and 56.

J — Guide line at bottom. Occurs in Positions 21, 22, 23, 24, 27, 28, 29 and 30.

K — Guide line at right and bottom. Occurs in Position 25 only.

L — Guide line at left and bottom. Occurs in Position 26 only.

M — Guide line at top. Occurs in Positions 31, 32, 33, 34, 37, 38, 39 and 40.

N — Guide line at top and right. Occurs in Position 35 only.

O — Guide line at top and left. Occurs in Position 36 only.

Only one each of Positions B or C, K, L, N or O; four positions of H or I, and eight or nine positions of J or M may be obtained from each 360 subject sheet, depending on whether the knife fell to the right or left, top or bottom of the guide lines.

Because the horizontal guide line appears so close to the bottom row of stamps on panes Nos. 21 to 30, Positions M, N, and O occur with great deal less frequency than Positions J, K and L.

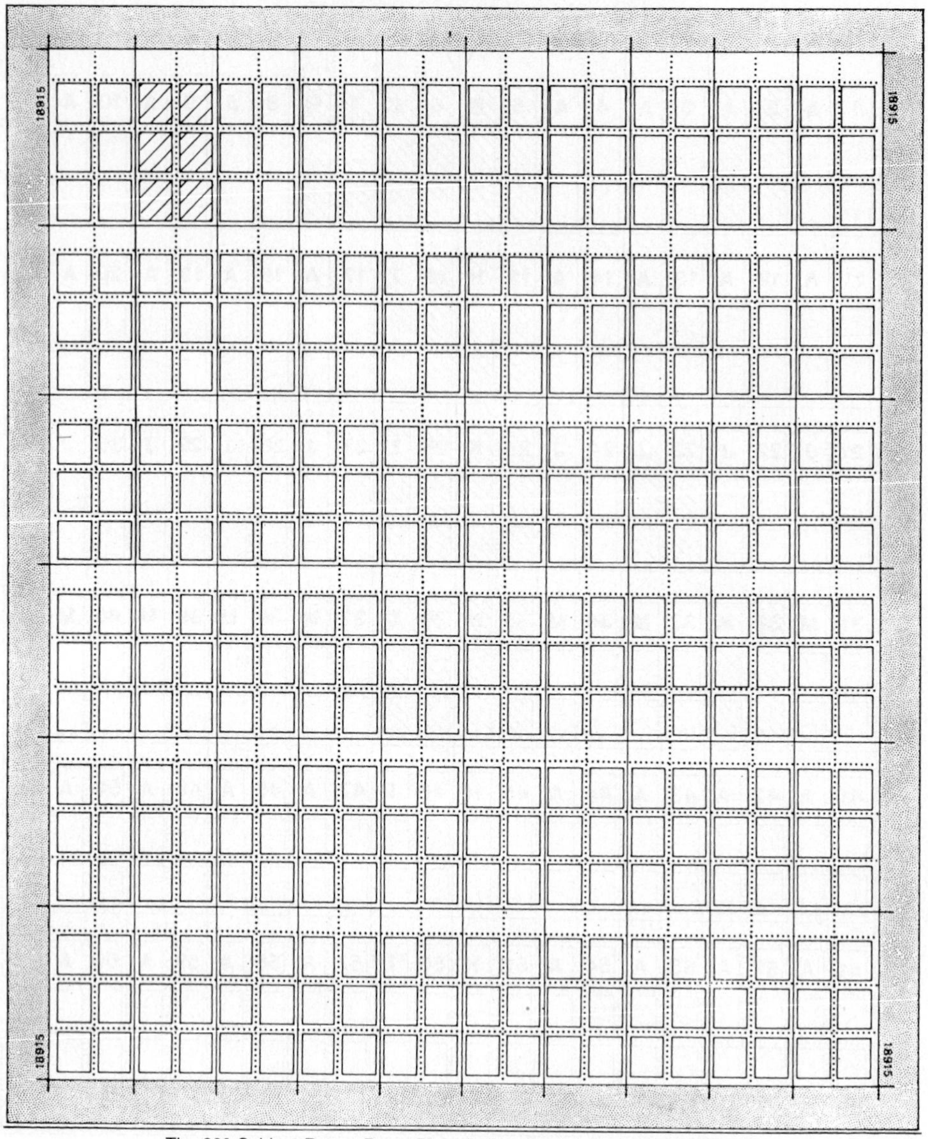

The 360-Subject Rotary Press Plate (before Electric Eye) Position A only

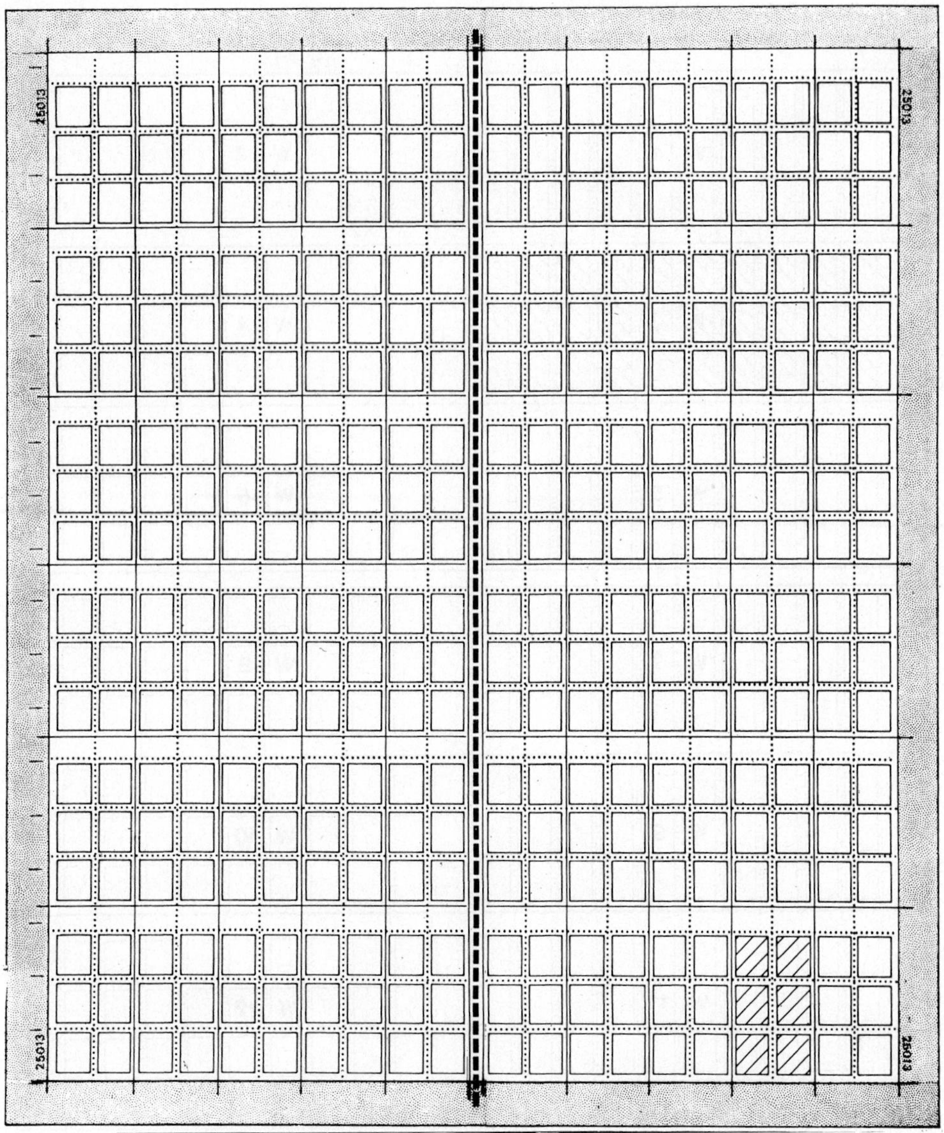

The 360-Subject Rotary Press Plate — Electric Eye

A modified design was put into use in 1956. The new plates have 20 frame bars instead of 17.

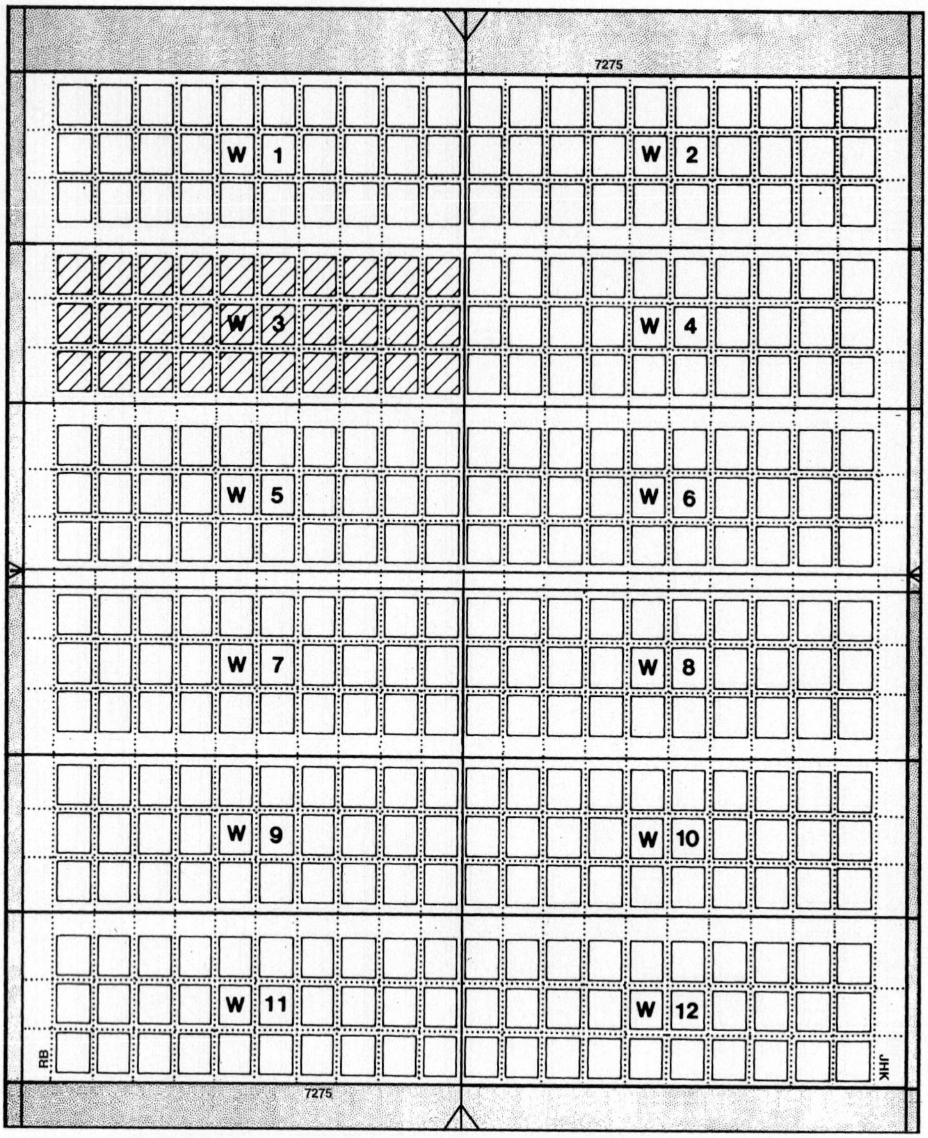

The A.E.F. Plate — 360-Subject Flat Plate — 8 Collectible Positions (See listings)

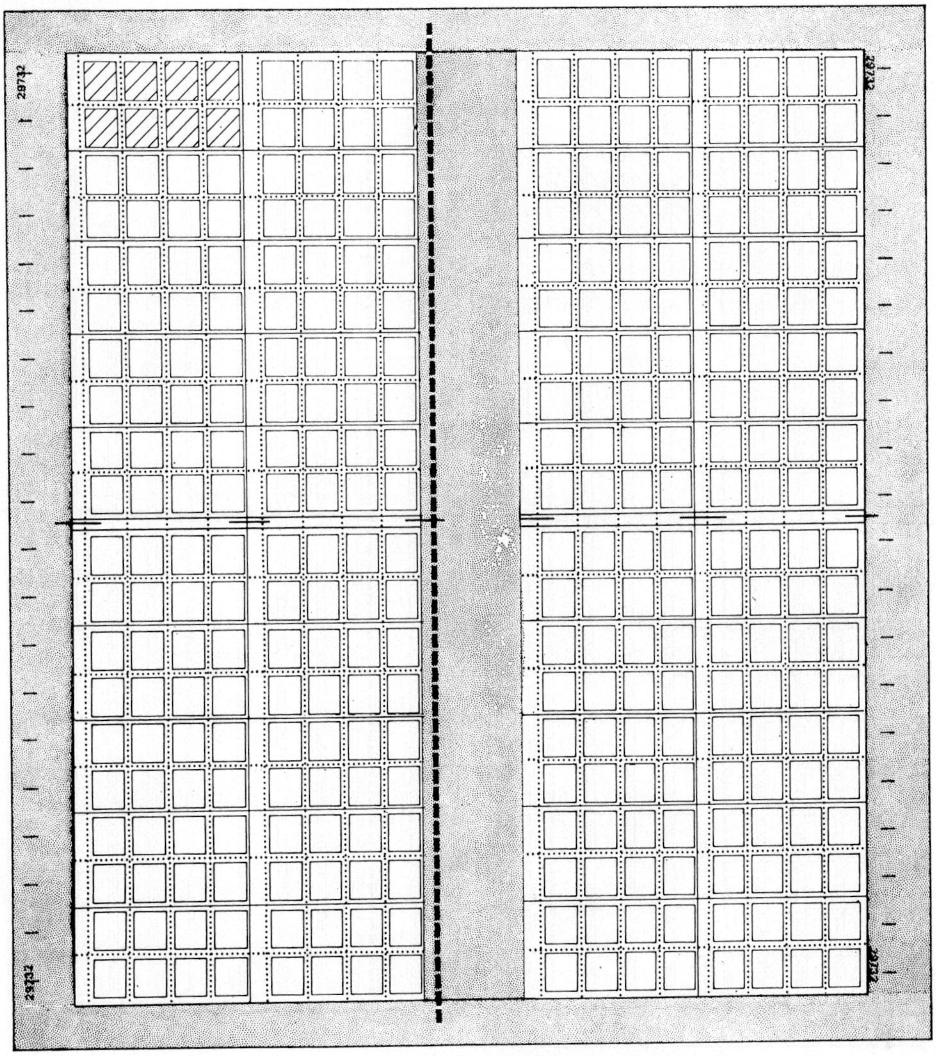

The 320-Subject Plate

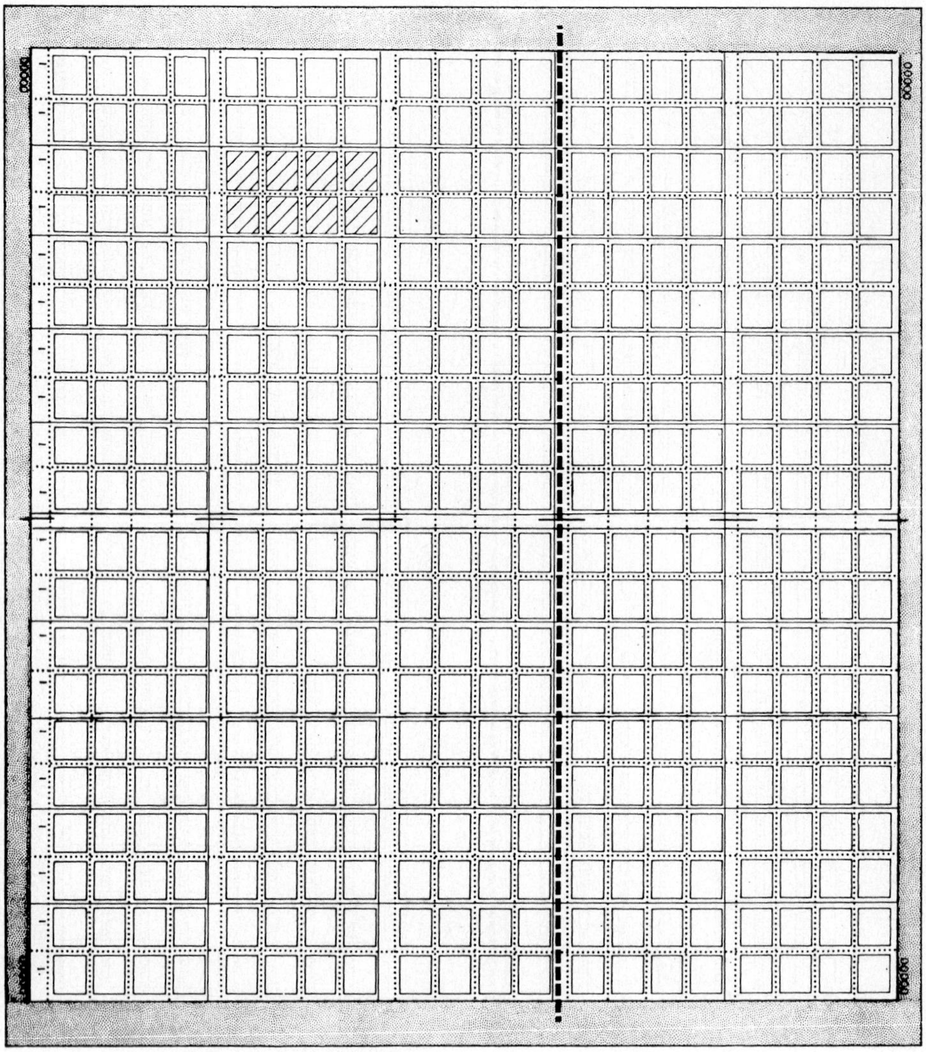

400-Subject Plate — The 300-Subject plate with double labels has the same layout.

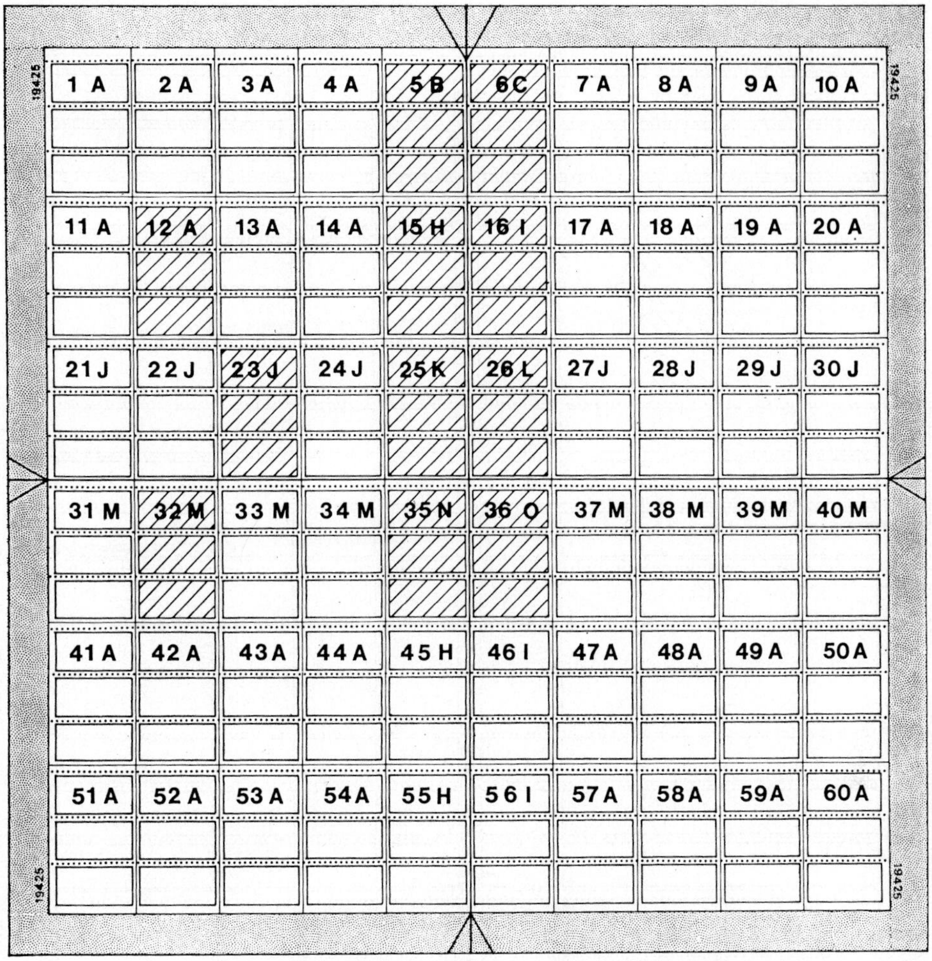

Lindbergh Booklet Plate-180 Subjects — 11 Collectible Positions

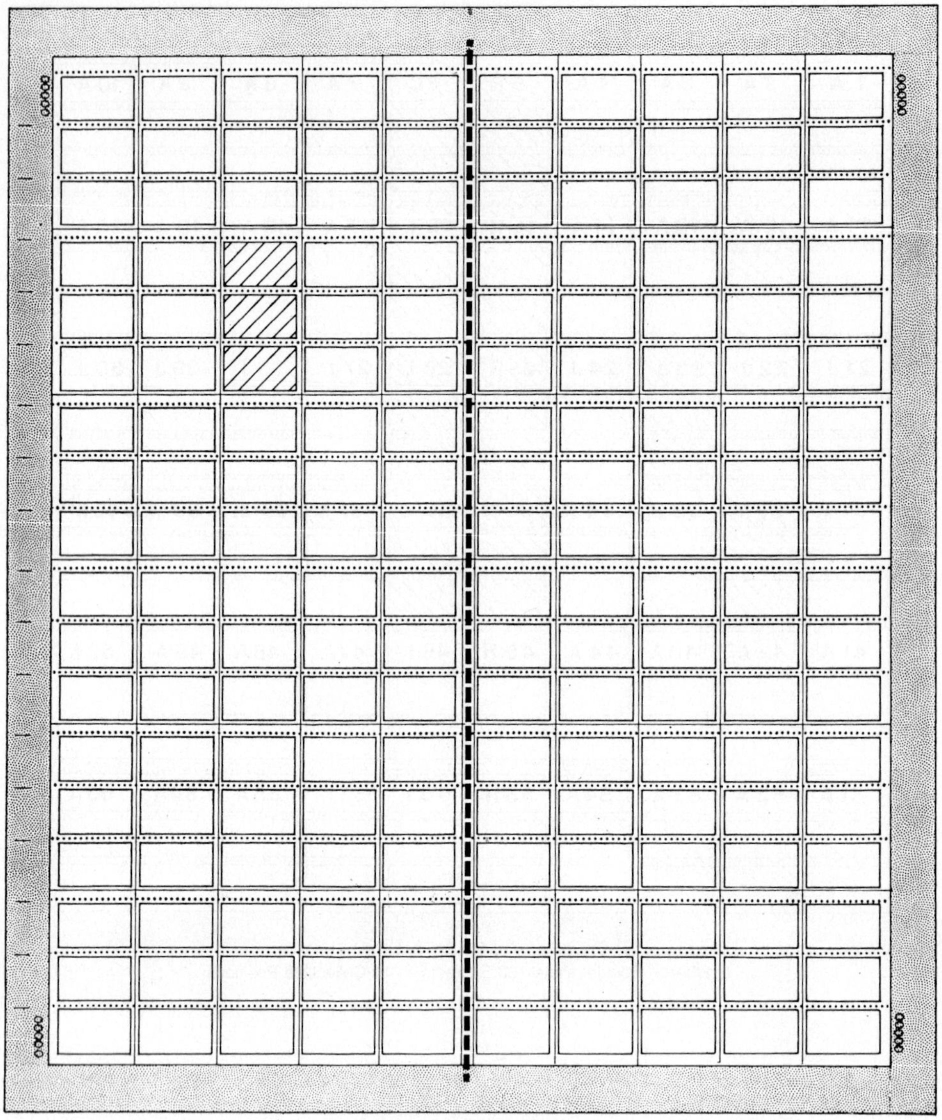

Airmail 180-Subject Rotary Press Plate — Electric Eye

Plate Sizes: No. 1288Bc to date.

Since 1978 numerous plate sizes from 78 to 1080 subjects have been used. Because plate size is not relevant to collecting these panes, we are not including this information in the catalogue.

BOOKLET PANES

Values for both unused and used booklet panes are for complete panes with selvage, and for panes of six unless otherwise stated. Panes in booklets are Never Hinged. Values for stapled booklets are for those with creasing along the lines of the staples. Values for booklets which were glued shut are for opened booklets without significant damage to the cover.

See other notes in the introduction to this section.

BOOKLET COVERS

Front covers of booklets of postage and airmail issues are illustrated and numbered.

Included are the Booklet Cover number (BC2A); and the catalogue numbers of the Booklet Panes (300b, 331a). The text of the inside and or back covers changes. Some modern issues have minor changes on the front covers also. When more than one combination of covers exists, the number of possible booklets is noted in parentheses after the booklet listing.

Washington — A88

Wmk. 191 Horizontally or Vertically

1900-03 ***Perf. 12***

279Bj	A88 2c **red,** horizontal wmk., *Apr. 18*	500.	*1,250.*
	light red	500.	
	orange red, *1902*	500.	
	Never hinged	1,000.	
	With plate number (D)	1,350.	*3,000.*
	Never hinged	2,150.	
279Bk	A88 2c **red,** vertical watermark	500.	*1,250.*
	Never hinged	1,000.	
	With plate number (D)	1,350.	
	Never hinged	2,150.	

360- (horiz. wmk.) and 180- (vert. wmk.) subject plates. All plate positions exist, except J, K, and L, due to the horizontal guide line being placed too far below stamps to appear on the upper panes.

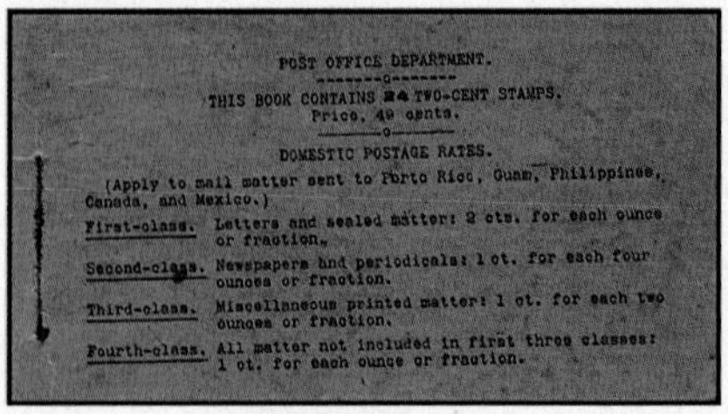

POST OFFICE DEPARTMENT.

THIS BOOK CONTAINS 24 TWO-CENT STAMPS.
Price, 49 cents.

DOMESTIC POSTAGE RATES.

(Apply to mail matter sent to Porto Rico, Guam, Philippines, Canada, and Mexico.)

First-class. Letters and sealed matter: 2 cts. for each ounce or fraction.

Second-class. Newspapers and periodicals: 1 ct. for each four ounces or fraction.

Third-class. Miscellaneous printed matter: 1 ct. for each two ounces or fraction.

Fourth-class. All matter not included in first three classes: 1 ct. for each ounce or fraction.

279Bj-279Bk — BC1

1900-03

Text only cover

25c booklet contains 2 panes of six 2c stamps.
49c booklet contains 4 panes of six 2c stamps.
97c booklet contains 8 panes of six 2c stamps.

Booklets sold for 1c more than the face value of the stamps.

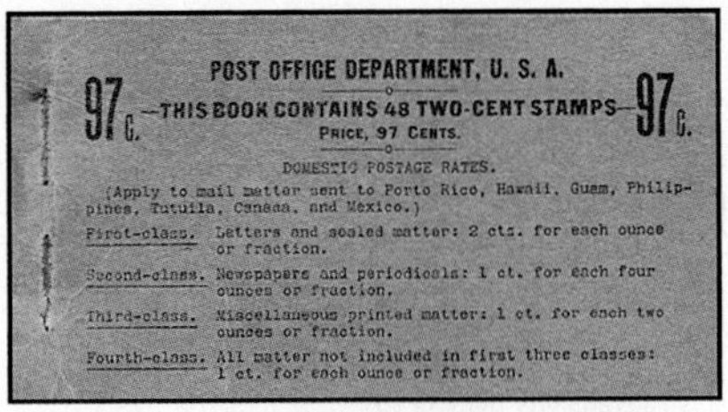

279Bj, 279Bk, 301c, 319, 332a — BC2B

1900-08

Text cover with price added in upper corners

25c booklets contain 4 panes of six 1c stamps or 2 panes of six 2c stamps.
49c booklet contains 4 panes of six 2c stamps.
97c booklet contains 8 panes of six 2c stamps.

Booklets

BK1	BC1	25c	**black,** *cream*	—
BK2	BC1	25c	**black,** *buff*	*6,000.*
BK3	BC1	49c	**green,** *cream*	—
BK4	BC1	49c	**black,** *buff*	—
BK5	BC1	97c	**red,** *cream*	—
BK6	BC1	97c	**black,** *gray*	—
BK7	BC2B	25c	**black,** *cream* (3)	*7,000.*
BK8	BC2B	49c	**black,** *buff* (3)	—
BK9	BC2B	97c	**black,** *gray* (3)	*15,000.*

Nos. BK1-BK6 and one type each of Nos. BK7-BK9 exist with specimen overprints handstamped on cover and individual stamps.

All covers of BK7-BK9 exist with "Philippines" overprint in 50mm or 48mm.

Franklin — A115

1903-07 **Wmk. 191 Vertically**

300b	A115	1c **blue green,** *Mar. 6, 1907*	600.	*12,500.*
		Never hinged	1,150.	
		With plate number (D)	1,300.	
		Never hinged	*2,250.*	
		With plate number 3472 over left stamp (D)	*4,000.*	

180-Subject Plates only. All plate positions exist.

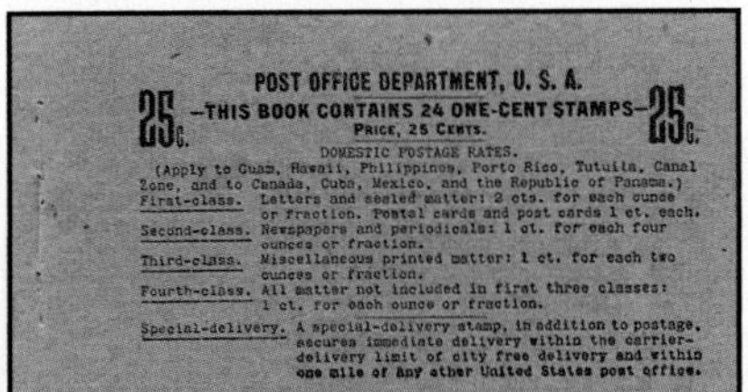

300b, 331a — BC2A

1900-08

Text cover with price added in upper corners

25c booklets contain 4 panes of six 1c stamps or 2 panes of six 2c stamps.
49c booklet contains 4 panes of six 2c stamps.

Booklet

BK10	BC2A	25c	**black,** *green* (6)	*6,500.*

Washington — A116

301c	A116	2c **carmine,** *Jan. 24, 1903*	500.	*2,250.*
		Never hinged	950.	
		With plate number (D)	1,500.	*3,000.*
		Never hinged	*2,500.*	

180-Subject Plates only. All plate positions exist.

Booklets

BK11	BC2B	25c	**black,** *cream*	*3,000.*
BK12	BC2B	49c	**black,** *buff*	*4,000.*
BK13	BC2B	97c	**black,** *gray*	—

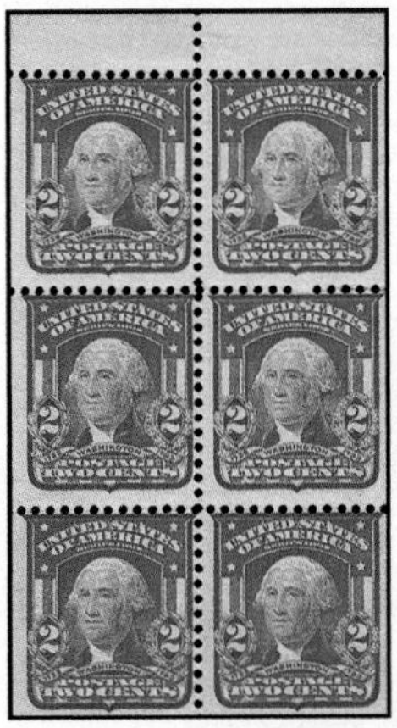

Washington — A129

1903 **Wmk. 191 Vertically**

319g	A129	2c **carmine,** type I, *Dec. 3, 1903*	125.00	*550.00*
		Never hinged	240.00	
		With plate number (D)	275.00	*850.00*
		Never hinged	500.00	
		Wmk. horizontal	*4,000.*	
		Never hinged	*6,500.*	
		With Plate number (D)	*9,500.*	
319n	A129	2c **carmine rose** (I)	250.00	*650.00*
		Never hinged	450.00	
		With plate number (D)	425.00	*950.00*
		Never hinged	725.00	
319p	A129	2c **scarlet** (I)	185.00	*575.00*
		Never hinged	350.00	
		With plate number (D)	350.00	*900.00*
		Never hinged	625.00	
319h	A129	2c **carmine,** type II, *1907*	900.00	
		Never hinged	1,500.	
		With plate number (D)	1,500.	
		Never hinged	2,500.	
319q	A129	2c **lake** (II)	300.00	*750.00*
		Never hinged	575.00	
		With plate number (D)	550.00	
		Never hinged	900.00	

180-Subject Plates only. All plate positions exist.

Booklets

BK14	BC2B	25c	**black,** *cream* (11)	1,100.
BK15	BC2A	49c	**black,** *buff* (11)	*1,350.*
BK16	BC2A	49c	**black,** *pink*	*2,500.*
BK17	BC2B	97c	**black,** *gray* (11)	*3,250.*

Booklet Covers

When more than one combination of covers exists, the number of possible booklets is noted in parentheses after the booklet listing.

Franklin — A138

1908 **Wmk. 191 Vertically**

331a	A138	1c **green,** *Dec. 1908*	160.00	*450.00*
		Never hinged	285.00	
		With plate number (D)	240.00	
		Never hinged	400.00	

180- and 360-Subject Plates. All plate positions exist.

No. 331 exists in horizontal pair, imperforate between, a variety resulting from booklet experiments. Not regularly issued. Value, unused $2,500.

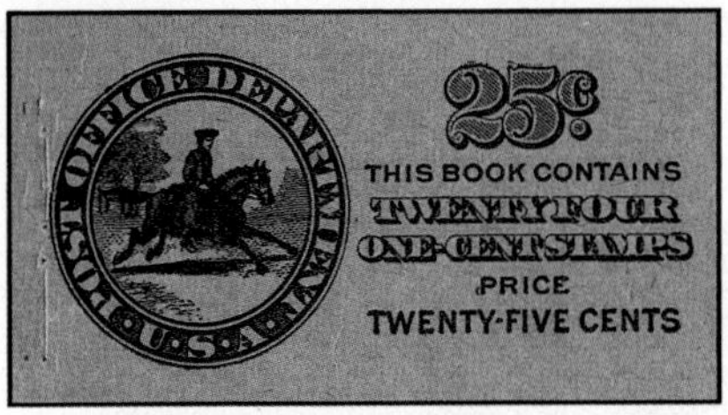

331a, 332a, 374a, 375a, 405b, 406a — BC3

1908-12 **Postrider**

25c booklet contains 4 panes of six 1c stamps.
25c booklet contains 2 panes of six 2c stamps.
49c booklet contains 4 panes of six 2c stamps.
97c booklet contains 8 panes of six 2c stamps.

Booklets

BK18 BC2A 25c **black,** *green* (3) *2,000.*
BK19 BC3 25c **black,** *green* *2,250.*

Washington — A139

332a A139 2c **carmine,** *Nov. 16, 1908* 135.00 *400.00*
Never hinged 230.00
With plate number (D) 175.00
Never hinged 300.00

180- and 360-Subject Plates. All plate positions exist.

Booklets

BK20 BC2B 25c **black,** *cream* (2) *1,250.*
BK21 BC2A 49c **black,** *buff* (2) *2,750.*
BK22 BC2A 49c **black,** *pink* *2,750.*
BK23 BC2B 97c **black,** *gray* (3) *3,000.*
BK24 BC3 25c **black,** *cream* *1,250.*
BK25 BC3 49c **black,** *pink* *2,500.*
BK26 BC3 97c **black,** *gray* *3,000.*

1910 **Wmk. 190 Vertically** ***Perf. 12***

374a A138 1c **green,** *Oct. 7, 1910* 225.00 *300.00*
Never hinged 375.00
With plate number (D) 300.00
Never hinged 475.00

360-Subject Plates only. All plate positions exist.

Booklet

BK27 BC3 25c **black,** *green* (2) *2,000.*

375a A139 2c **carmine,** *Nov. 30, 1910* 125.00 *200.00*
Never hinged 200.00
With plate number (D) 170.00
Never hinged 290.00

360-Subject Plates only. All plate positions exist.

Booklets

BK28 BC3 25c **black,** *cream* (2) *900.00*
BK29 BC3 49c **black,** *pink* (2) *2,500.*
BK30 BC3 97c **black,** *gray* (2) *3,000.*

Washington — A140

1912 **Wmk. 190 Vertically**

405b A140 1c **green,** *Feb. 8, 1912* 65.00 *75.00*
Never hinged 110.00
With plate number (D) 80.00
Never hinged 140.00

360-Subject Plates only. All plate positions exist.

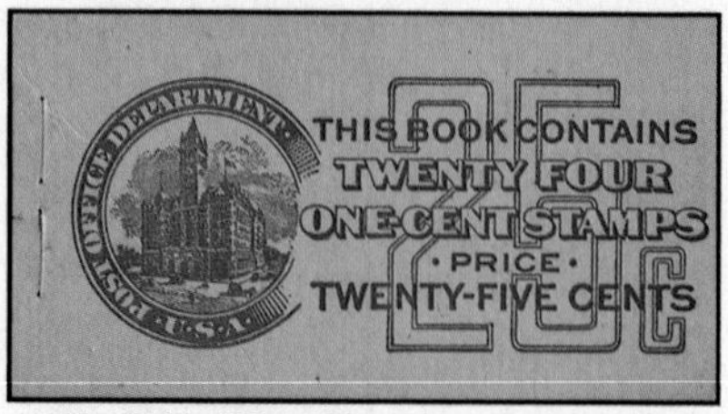

405b, 424d, 462a, 498e, 632a, 804b — BC4A

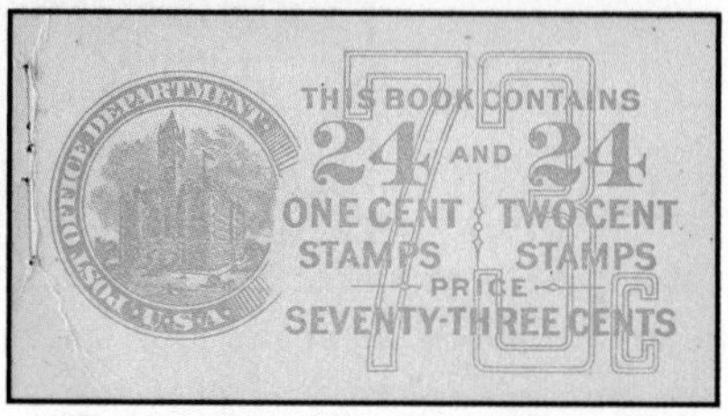

405b, 424d, 462a, 498e, 552a, 632a — BC4B

1912-39 **Washington P.O.**

Price of booklet in large numerals behind contents information

25c booklet contains 4 panes of six 1c stamps.
73c booklet contains 4 panes of six 1c stamps and 4 panes of six 2c stamps.
97c booklet contains 16 panes of six 1c stamps.

Ordinary Booklets

BK31 BC3 25c **black,** *green* (2) *1,000.*
BK32 BC4A 25c **green,** *green* (3) *1,250.*
BK33 BC4A 97c **green,** *lavender* *1,750.*

Combination Booklet

BK34 BC4B 73c **red,** 4 #405b + 4 #406a *3,000.*

Washington — A140

406a A140 2c **carmine,** *Feb. 8, 1912* 65.00 *90.00*
Never hinged 110.00
With plate number (D) 80.00
Never hinged 140.00

360-Subject Plates only. All plate positions exist.

406a, 425e, 463a, 499e, 554c, 583a, 632a, 634d, 804b, 806b — BC5A

1912-39 **Small Postrider**

Large background numerals

25c booklets contain 4 panes of six 1c stamps or 2 panes of six 2c stamps.
49c booklet contains 4 panes of six 2c stamps.
97c booklets contain 16 panes of six 1c stamps or 8 panes of six 2c stamps.

Ordinary Booklets

BK35 BC3 25c **black,** *cream* (2) *825.00*
BK36 BC3 49c **black,** *pink* (2) *1,500.*
BK37 BC3 97c **black,** *gray* (2) 2,000.
BK38 BC5A 25c **red,** *buff* (3) *1,000.*
BK39 BC5A 49c **red,** *pink* (3) 1,750.
BK40 BC5A 97c **red,** *blue,* (3) 2,250.

Combination Booklet

See No. BK34.

1914 **Wmk. 190 Vertically** ***Perf. 10***

424d A140 1c **green** 5.25 *7.50*
Never hinged 8.75
Double transfer, Plate 6363 — —
With plate number (D) 14.00
Never hinged 22.50
Cracked plate —
e. As "d," imperf. *2,000.*
With plate number (D) —

360-Subject Plates only. All plate positions exist.
All known examples of No. 424e are without gum.

Ordinary Booklets

BK41 BC4A 25c **green,** *green* (3) 300.00
BK42 BC4A 97c **green,** *lavender* (2) 135.00

Combination Booklet

BK43 BC4B 73c **red,** 4 #424d + 4 #425e (3) 300.00

425e A140 2c **carmine,** *Jan. 6, 1914* 17.50 *25.00*
Never hinged 30.00
With plate number (D) 42.50
Never hinged 70.00

360-Subject Plates only. All plate positions exist.

Ordinary Booklets

BK44 BC5A 25c **red,** *buff* (3) 500.00
BK45 BC5A 49c **red,** *pink* (3) 1,000.
BK46 BC5A 97c **red,** *blue* (3) 1,250.

Combination Booklet

See No. BK43.

1916 **Unwmk.** ***Perf. 10***

462a A140 1c **green,** *Oct. 15, 1916* 9.50 *12.50*
Never hinged 16.00
Cracked plate at right 225.00 —
Never hinged 325.00
Cracked plate at left 310.00
Never hinged 425.00
With plate number (D) 25.00
Never hinged 37.50

360-Subject Plates only. All plate positions exist.

Ordinary Booklets

BK47 BC4A 25c **green,** *green* 650.00
BK48 BC4A 97c **green,** *lavender* 500.00

Combination Booklets

BK49 BC4B 73c **red,** 4 #462a + 4 #463a (2) 900.00

463a A140 2c **carmine,** *Oct. 8, 1916* 110.00 *110.00*
Never hinged 180.00
With plate number (D) 150.00
Never hinged 240.00

360-Subject Plates only. All plate positions exist.

Ordinary Booklets

BK50 BC5A 25c **red,** *buff* *950.00*
BK51 BC5A 49c **red,** *pink* *1,500.*
BK52 BC5A 97c **red,** *blue* *2,500.*

Combination Booklets

See No. BK49.

1917-18 **Unwmk.** ***Perf. 11***

498e A140 1c **green,** *Apr. 6, 1917* 2.50 *2.00*
Never hinged 4.25
Double transfer — —
With plate number (D) 6.00 *2.00*
Never hinged 9.00

360-Subject Plates only. All plate positions exist.

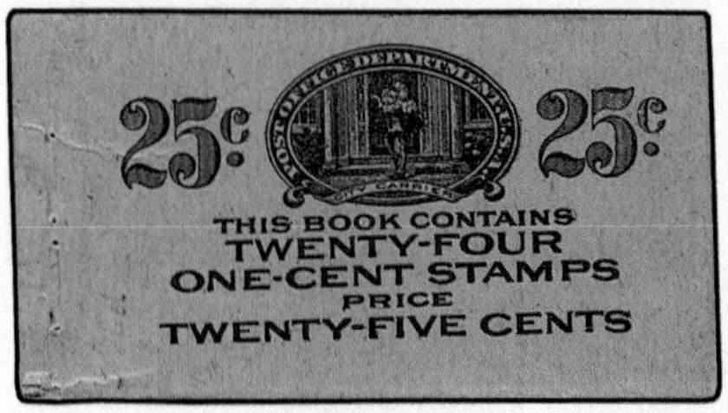

498e, 552a — BC6A

1917-23 **Oval designs**

25c booklet contains 4 panes of six 1c stamps.

Ordinary Booklets

BK53 BC4A 25c **green,** *green* (2) 300.00
BK54 BC4A 97c **green,** *lavender* (4) 85.00
BK55 BC6A 25c **green,** *green* (5) 120.00

Combination Booklets

BK56 BC4B 73c **red,** 4 #498e + 4 #499e (4) 80.00
BK57 BC4B 73c **red,** 4 #498e + 4 #554c (3) 100.00

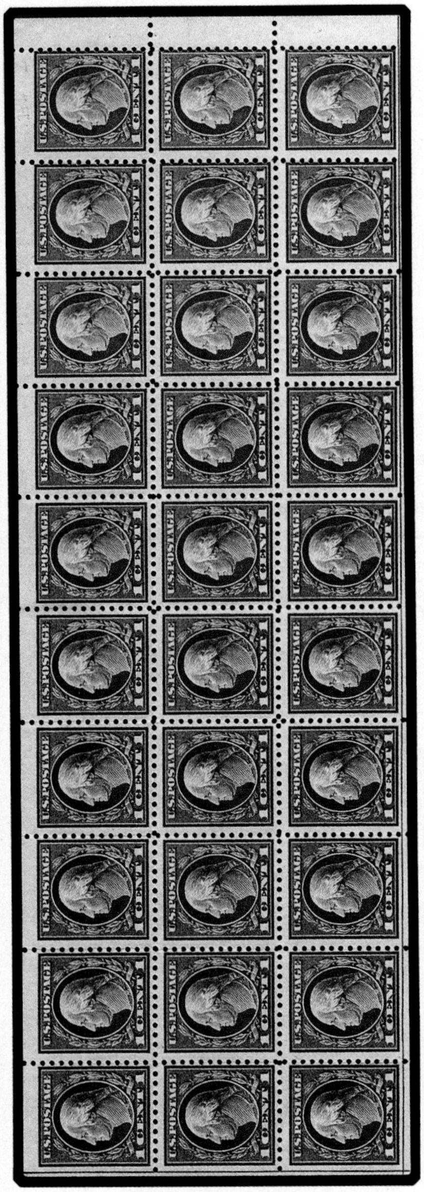

Washington — A140

A.E.F. Panes of 30

1917, Aug.

498f	A140	1c **green** (pane of 30)	*1,150.*	
		Never hinged	*1,800.*	

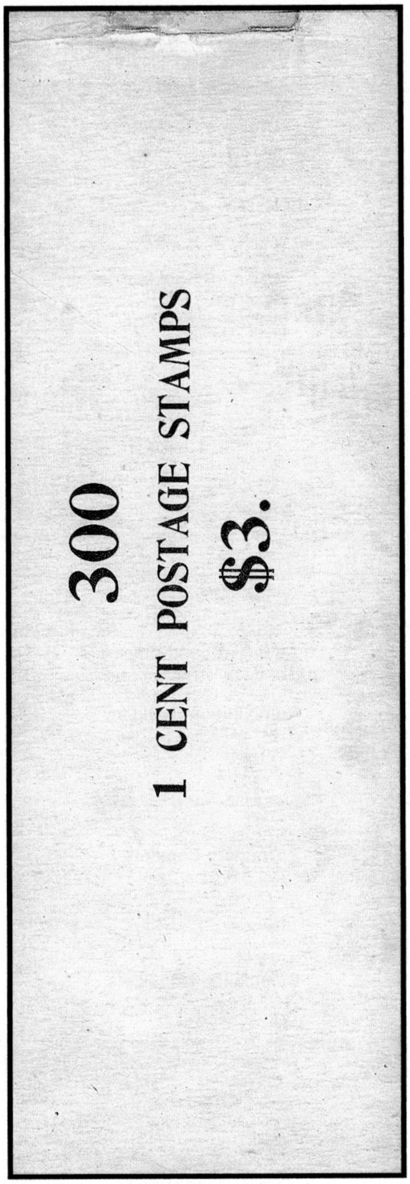

498f, 499f — BC7

Illustration reduced.

A.E.F.

1917

$3 booklet contains 10 panes of thirty 1c stamps.
$6 booklet contains 10 panes of thirty 2c stamps.

Booklets sold for face value.

Booklet

BK64	BC7	$3 **black,** *green*	*25,000.*

499e	A140	2c **rose,** type I, *Mar. 31, 1917*	4.00	*2.50*
		Never hinged	6.75	
		With plate number (D)	7.00	*2.25*
		Never hinged	10.00	

360-Subject Plates only. All plate positions exist.

499e, 554c, 583a, 634d — BC6C

1917-27 **Oval designs**

97c booklet contains 8 panes of six 2c stamps.

Ordinary Booklets

BK58	BC5A	25c **red,** *buff* (5)	250.00
BK59	BC5A	49c **red,** *pink* (4)	400.00
BK60	BC5A	97c **red,** *blue* (3)	750.00
BK61	BC6C	97c **red,** *blue* (2)	1,250.

Combination Booklets

See No. BK56.

499f	A140	2c **rose,** (pane of 30) type I	*28,000.*	—
		Never hinged	*38,000.*	

Booklet

BK65	BC7	$6 **black,** *pink*

No examples of No. BK65 are known. The number and description are provided only for specialist reference.

Nos. 498f and 499f were for use of the American Expeditionary Force in France.

They were printed from the ordinary 360-Subject Plates, the sheet being cut into 12 leaves of 30 stamps each in place of 60 leaves of 6 stamps each, and, of course, the lines of perforations changed accordingly.

The same system as used for designating plate positions on the ordinary booklet panes is used for designating the war booklet, only each war booklet pane is composed of 5 ordinary panes. Thus, No. W1 booklet pane would be composed of positions 1, 2, 3, 4, and 5 of an ordinary pane, etc.

The A. E. F. booklet panes were bound at side margins which accounts for side arrows sometimes being found on positions W5 and W6. As the top and bottom arrows were always removed when the sheets were cut, positions W1 and W2 cannot be distinguished from W7 and W8. Cutting may remove guidelines on these, but identification is possible by wide bottom margins. Positions W3 and W4 cannot be distinguished from W9 and W10.

There are thus just 8 collectible positions from the sheet as follows:

W1 or W7 Narrow top and wide bottom margins. Guide line at right.

W2 or W8 As W1, but guide line at left.

W3 or W9 Approximately equal top and bottom margins. Guide line at right.

W4 or W10 As W3, but guide line at left.

W5 Narrow bottom margin showing guideline very close to stamps. Wide top margin. Guide line at right. Pane with extra long tab may show part of split arrow at left.

W6 As W5, but guide line at left, split arrow at right. Guide line at left and at bottom. Arrow at lower right may or may not show.

W11 Narrow bottom and wide top margins. Guide line at right. Siderographer initials on left tab.

W12 Narrow bottom and wide top margins. Guide line at left. Finisher initials on right tab.

Washington — A140

501b	A140	3c **violet,** type I, *Oct. 17, 1917*	75.00	*60.00*
		Never hinged	125.00	
		With plate number (D)	105.00	
		Never hinged	160.00	

360-Subject Plates only. All plate positions exist.

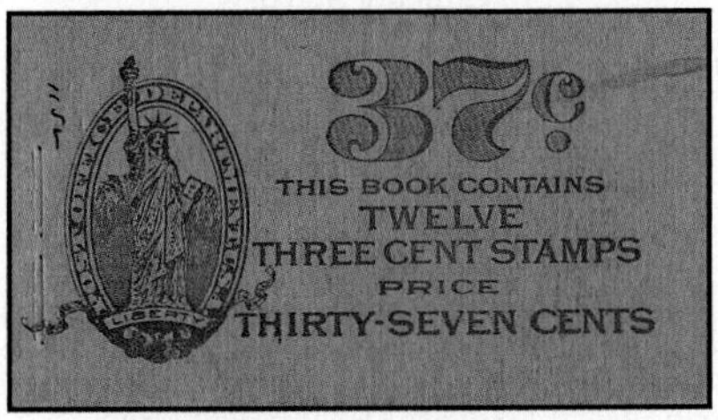

501b, 502b — BC6B

1917-18 **Oval designs**

37c booklet contains 2 panes of six 3c stamps.

Booklet

BK62 BC6B 37c **violet,** *sage* 500.00

502b A140 3c **violet,** type II, *Mar. 1918* 60.00 *55.00*
Never hinged 100.00
With plate number (D) 77.50
Never hinged 120.00

360-Subject Plates only. All plate positions exist.

Booklet

BK63 BC6B 37c **violet,** *sage* 235.00

Franklin — A155

1923 **Unwmk.** ***Perf. 11***

552a A155 1c **deep green,** *Aug. 1923* 7.50 *4.00*
Never hinged 12.50
With plate number (D) 13.00
Never hinged 21.00

360-Subject Plates only. All plate positions exist.

Ordinary Booklets

BK66 BC6A 25c **green,** *green* (2) 75.00
BK67 BC4A 97c **green,** *lavender* (3) *650.00*

Combination Booklet

BK68 BC4B 73c **white,** *red,* 4 #552a + 4 #554c (3) 85.00

Washington — A157

554c A157 2c **carmine** 7.00 *3.00*
Never hinged 12.00
With plate number (D) 12.00
Never hinged 20.00

360-Subject Plates only. All plate positions exist.

Ordinary Booklets

BK69 BC5A 25c **red,** *buff* (3) *400.00*
BK70 BC5A 49c **red,** *pink* (3) 950.00
BK71 BC6C 97c **red,** *blue* (3) 1,500.

Combination Booklets

See Nos. BK57 and BK68.

ROTARY PRESS PRINTINGS

Two experimental plates were used to print No. 583a. At least one guide line pane (H) is known from these plates. The rest of rotary press booklet panes were printed from specially prepared plates of 360-subjects in arrangement as before, but without the guide lines and the plate numbers are at the sides instead of at the top as on the flat plates.

The only varieties possible are the ordinary pane (A) and partial plate numbers appearing at the right or left of the upper or lower stamps of a booklet pane when the trimming of the sheets is off center. The note applies to Nos. 583a, 632a, 634d, 720b, 804b, 806b and 807a, before Electric Eyes.

1926 ***Perf. 10***

583a A157 2c **carmine,** *Aug. 1926* 95.00 *150.00*
Never hinged 175.00

Ordinary Booklets

BK72 BC5A 25c **red,** *buff* (3) *725.00*
BK73 BC5A 49c **red,** *pink* *1,000.*
BK74 BC6C 97c **red,** *blue* *1,250.*

1927 ***Perf. 11x10½***

632a A155 1c **green,** *Nov. 2, 1927* 5.00 *4.00*
Never hinged 8.00

Ordinary Booklets

BK75 BC5A 25c **green,** *green* (3) 65.00
BK76 BC4A 97c **green,** *lavender* 600.00
BK77 BC5A 97c **green,** *lavender* —

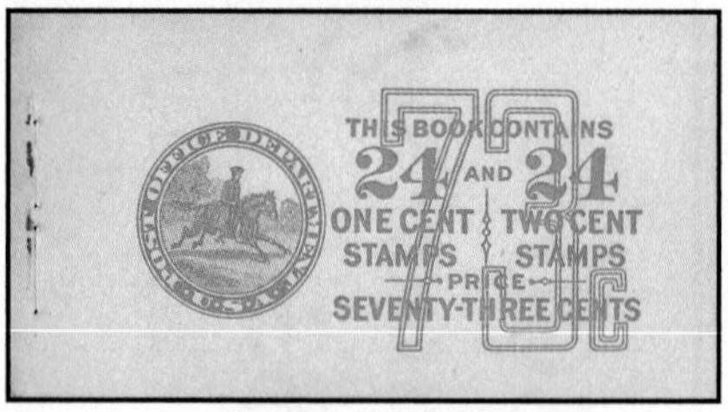

632a, 804b — BC5D

1927-39 **Small Postrider**

Large background numerals

73c booklet contains 4 panes of six 1c stamps and 4 panes of six 2c stamps.

Combination Booklets

BK78 BC4B 73c **red,** 4 #632a + 4 #634d —
BK79 BC5D 73c **red,** 4 #632a + 4 #634d (2) 90.00

634d A157 2c **carmine,** type I, *Feb. 25, 1927* 1.50 *1.50*
Never hinged 2.50

Ordinary Booklets

BK80 BC5A 25c **red,** *buff* (2) 10.00
a. With experimental cellophane interleaving *1,500.*
BK81 BC5A 49c **red,** *pink* (2) 15.00
BK82 BC5A 97c **red,** *blue* (3) 50.00
BK83 BC6C 97c **red,** *blue* 900.00

Combination Booklets

See Nos. BK78 and BK79.

56,000 booklets of BK80a were produced in 1928 using .00125 inch thick cellophane interleaving. Scarce, as few were saved.

Varieties

634e A157 2c **carmine lake,** type I *2,000.*
Never hinged *4,000.*

Booklet

BK82a BC5A 97c **red,** *blue,* containing 8 panes of No. 634e —

Washington — A226

1932

720b A226 3c **deep violet,** *July 25, 1932* 35.00 *12.50*
Never hinged 60.00

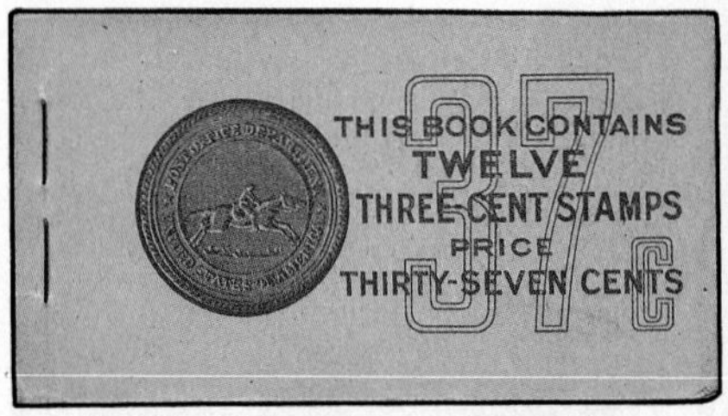

720b, 806b, 807a, 1035a — BC9A

1932-54 **Post Office Seal**

Large background numerals

25c booklet contains 2 panes of six 2c stamps.
37c booklet contains 2 panes of six 3c stamps.
49c booklet contains 4 panes of six 2c stamps.
73c booklets contain 4 panes of six 3c stamps or 4 panes of six 1c stamps and 4 panes of six 2c stamps.

Ordinary Booklets

BK84 BC9A 37c **violet,** *buff* (2) 135.00
a. With experimental cellophane interleaving *1,750.*
BK85 BC9A 73c **violet,** *pink* (2) 375.00

30,000 booklets of No. BK84a were made with .001 inch thick cellophane interleaving, similar to but thinner than the experimental interleaving used for No. BK80a. Poor handling qualities during booklet assembly plus higher cost prevented wider use. Placed on sale in Wash. D.C. post office in Sept., 1936. Extremely scarce, as few were saved.

Catalogue values for unused panes in this section, from this point to the end, are for Never Hinged items.

Washington — A276

In 1942 plates were changed to the Type II "new design" and the E. E. marks may appear at the right or left margins of panes of Nos. 804b, 806b and 807a. Panes printed from E. E. plates have 2½mm vertical gutter; those from pre-E. E. plates have 3mm vertical gutter.

1939-42 ***Perf. 11x10½***

804b A276 1c 3mm vert. gutter, *Jan. 27, 1939* 4.00 *.85*

Ordinary Booklets

BK86 BC5A 25c **green,** *green* 75.00
BK87 BC5A 97c **green,** *lavender* *450.00*
BK88 BC4A 97c **green,** *lavender* —

Combination Booklet

BK89 BC5D 73c **red,** 4 #804b + 4 #806b 135.00

804b A276 1c 2½mm vert. gutter, *Apr. 14, 1942* 2.00 *.50*

Ordinary Booklets

BK90 BC5A 25c **green,** *green* 8.25
BK91 BC5A 97c **green,** *lavender* 450.00

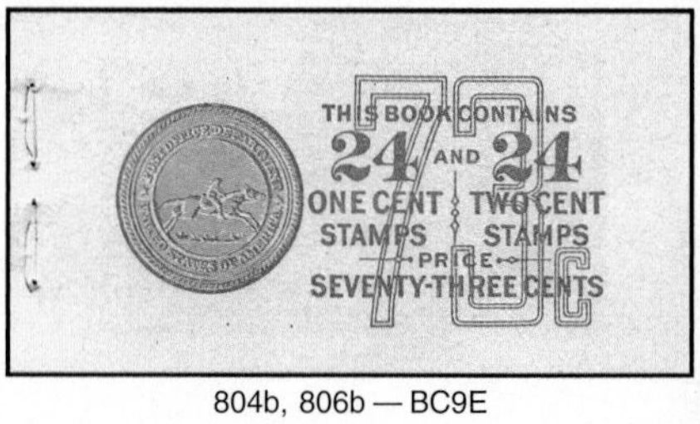

804b, 806b — BC9E

1939 **Post Office Seal**

Large background numerals

73c booklets contain 4 panes of six 3c stamps or 4 panes of six 1c stamps and 4 panes of six 2c stamps.

Combination Booklets

BK92	BC5D	73c **red,** 4 #804b + 4 #806b	30.00
BK93	BC9E	73c **red,** 4 #804b + 4 #806b	37.50

Adams — A278

806b	A278	2c 3mm vert. gutter, *Jan. 27, 1939*	22.50	*2.50*

Ordinary Booklets

BK94	BC5A	97c **red,** *blue*	*375.00*

Combination Booklet

See No. BK89.

806b	A278	2c 2½mm vert. gutter, *Apr. 25, 1942*	5.50	*1.00*

Ordinary Booklets

BK95	BC5A	97c **red,** *blue*	1,250.
BK96	BC5A	25c **red,** *buff*	19.00
BK97	BC9A	25c **red,** *buff*	90.00
BK98	BC5A	49c **red,** *pink*	45.00
BK99	BC9A	49c **red,** *pink*	75.00

Combination Booklets

See Nos. BK92 and BK93.

Jefferson — A279

807a	A279	3c 3mm vert. gutter, *Jan. 27, 1939*	30.00	*3.25*

Booklets

BK100	BC9A	37c **violet,** *buff*	85.00
BK101	BC9A	73c **violet,** *pink*	*750.00*

807a	A279	3c 2½mm vert. gutter, *Mar. 6, 1942*	8.50	*2.00*
		Horiz. pair with full vert. pane gutter btwn.	—	

Booklets

BK102	BC9A	37c **violet,** *buff* (3)	22.50
BK103	BC9A	73c **violet,** *pink* (3)	47.50

Variety

807d	A279	As "a," imperf between vert.	—

Statue of Liberty — A482

1954-58 ***Perf. 11x10½***

1035a	A482	3c pane of 6, *June 30, 1954*	4.00	*1.25*
1035f		Dry printing	5.00	*1.50*

Booklets

BK104	BC9A	37c **violet,** *buff,* with #1035a	22.50
a.		With #1035f	27.50
BK105	BC9A	73c **violet,** *pink,* with #1035a	27.50
a.		With #1035f	22.50

Variety

1035g		As "a," vert. imperf. betwn.	*5,000.*

Lincoln — A483

1036a	A483	4c pane of 6, *July 31, 1958*	2.75	*1.25*

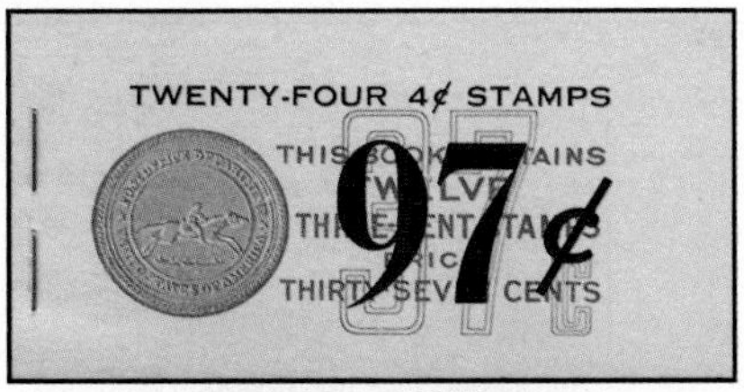

1036a — BC9F

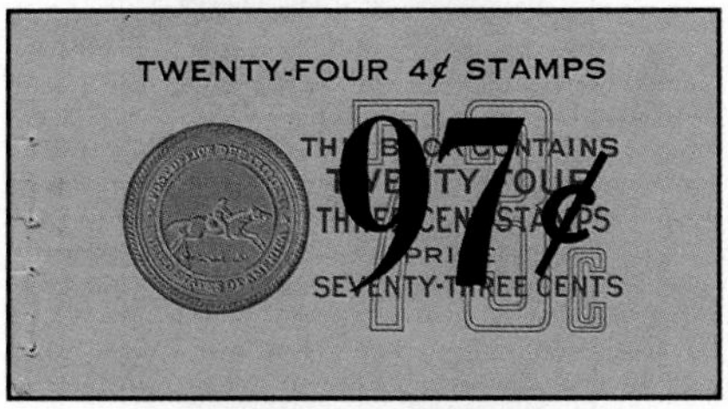

1036a — BC9G

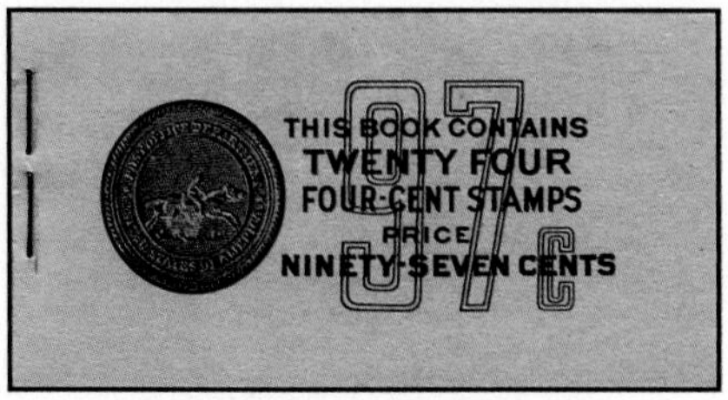

1036a — BC9H

1958

97c booklet contains 4 panes of six 4c stamps.

Booklets

BK106	BC9F	97c on 37c **violet,** *buff*	60.00
BK107	BC9G	97c on 73c **violet,** *pink*	30.00
BK108	BC9H	97c **blue,** *yellow*	150.00
BK109	BC9H	97c **blue,** *pink* (3)	18.00
a.		With experimental silicone interleaving	*150.00*

Variety

1036d	A483	As "a," imperf. horiz.	—

Washington (Slogan 1) — A650

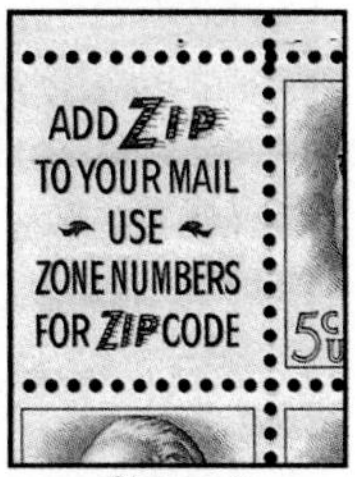

Slogan 2

Slogan 3

1962-64 ***Perf. 11x10½***

Plate of 300 stamps, 60 labels

1213a	A650	5c pane of 5+label, slogan 1, *Nov. 23, 1962*	7.00	*4.00*
		With slogan 2, *1963*	16.00	*7.00*
		With slogan 3, *1964*	3.00	*2.00*

1213a — BC12A

1962-63 **Small Postrider**

$1 booklet contains 4 panes of five 5c stamps.

1213a, 1213c — BC13A

1963-64 **Mr. Zip**

$1 booklet contains 4 panes of five 5c stamps.

Booklets

BK110	BC12A	$1 **blue,** slogan 1	30.00
BK111	BC12A	$1 **blue,** slogan 2	110.00
BK112	BC13A	$1 **blue,** slogan 2	90.00
BK113	BC13A	$1 **blue,** slogan 3 (3)	15.00

1213c	A650	As No. 1213a, tagged, slogan 2, *Oct. 28, 1963*	60.00	*10.00*
		With slogan 3, *1964*	2.00	*1.50*

Booklets

BK114	BC13A	$1 **blue,** slogan 2	240.00
BK115	BC13A	$1 **blue,** slogan 3 (4)	10.50

Jefferson — A710

1967-78 ***Perf. 11x10½***

1278a	A710	1c pane of 8, shiny gum, *Jan. 12, 1968*	1.00	*.75*
		Dull gum	2.00	

Combination Booklets

See Nos. BK116, BK117B, BK118 and BK119.

Variety

1278e	A710	As "a," dull gum, tagging omitted	*75.00*

Jefferson — A710

1278b	A710	1c pane of 4+2 labels, slogans 5 & 4, *May 10, 1971*	.80	.60

Combination Booklet

See No. BK122.

Wright — A712

Slogan 4

Slogan 5

1280a	A712	2c pane of 5+label, slogan 4, *Jan. 8, 1968*	1.25	.80
		With slogan 5	1.25	.80

Combination Booklets

See Nos. BK117 and BK120.

1280c	A712	2c pane of 6, shiny gum, *May 7, 1971*	1.00	.75
		Dull gum	1.10	

Combination Booklets

See Nos. BK127 and BKC22.

The 1c and 6c panes of 8, Nos. 1278a and 1284b, were printed from 320-subject plates and from 400-subject plates, both with electric eye markings. The 2c and 6c panes of 5 stamps plus label, Nos. 1280a and 1284c, were printed from 360-subject plates.

An experimental moisture-resistant gum was used on 1,000,000 panes of No. 1278a and 4,000,000 of No. 1393a released in March, 1971. This dull finish gum shows no breaker ridges. The booklets lack interleaving. This gum was also used for Nos. 1395c, 1395d, 1288c and all engraved panes from No. 1510b on unless noted.

Roosevelt — A716

Perf. 10½x11

1284b	A716	6c pane of 8, *Dec. 28, 1967*	1.50	1.00

1278a, 1284b, 1393a — BC14A

1967-70

$2 booklet contains 4 panes of eight 6c stamps and 1 pane of eight 1c stamps.

Combination Booklet

BK116	BC14A	$2 **brown,** 4 #1284b (6c)+1 #1278a(1c)(2)	7.75

Variety

1284e	A716	6c As "b," tagging omitted	*50.00*	—

Booklet

BK116a	BC14A	$2 with 4 #1284e + 1 #1278a (1c)	*250.00*

Roosevelt — A716

1284c	A716	6c pane of 5+label, slogan 4, *Jan. 9, 1968*	1.50	1.00
		With slogan 5	1.50	1.00

1278a, 1280a, 1284c, 1393b, 1395b — BC15

1968-71

$1 booklets contain 2 panes of six 8c stamps and 1 pane of four 1c stamps, or 3 panes of five 6c stamps and 1 pane of five 2c stamps.

Combination Booklet

BK117	BC15	$1 **brown,** 3 #1284c (6c) + 1 #1280a (2c) (2)	7.00

No. BK117 contains panes with slogan 4, slogan 5 or combinations of 4 and 5.

Oliver Wendell Holmes — A720

Perf. 10

1288Bc A720 15c pane of 8, *June 14, 1978* 2.80 1.75

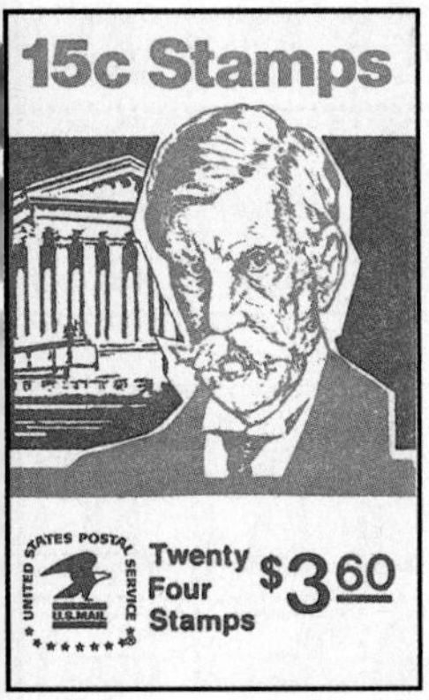

1288Bc — BC23

1978

$3.60 booklet contains 3 panes of eight 15c stamps.

Booklet

BK117A BC23 $3.60 **red & light blue,** no P# 8.75

Varieties

1288Be A720 As "c," vert. imperf. btwn. *1,750.*

1288Bi A720 As "c," tagging omitted *85.00* *50.00*

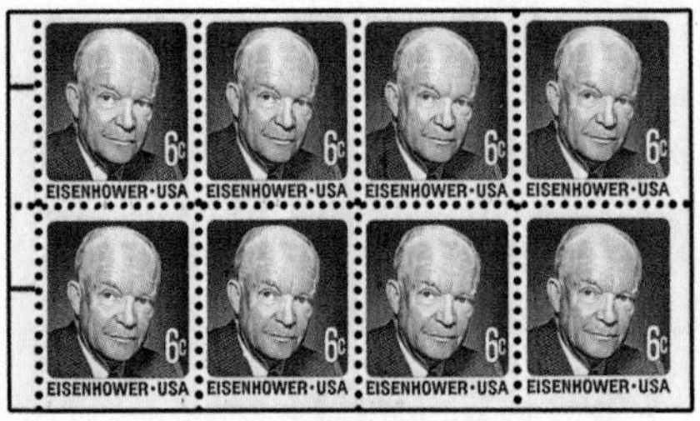

Eisenhower — A815

Plate of 400 subjects for No. 1393a.

1970 Tagged ***Perf. 11x10½***

1393a A815 6c pane of 8, shiny gum, *Aug. 6* 1.50 .75

Dull gum 1.90

1278a, 1393a, 1395a — BC16

1970-71 **Eisenhower**

$2 booklet contains 4 panes of eight 6c stamps and 1 pane of eight 1c stamps.

$1.92 booklet contains 3 panes of eight 8c stamps.

Combination Booklets

BK117B BC14A $2 **blue,** 4 #1393a (6c) + 1 #1278a (1c) 9.00

BK118 BC16 $2 **blue,** 4 #1393a (6c) + 1 #1278a (1c) (2) 7.25

BK119 BC16 $2 **blue,** dull gum, 4 #1393a (6c) + 1 #1278a (1c) (2) 8.75

Varieties

1393h A815 6c As "a," tagging omitted, shiny gum *250.00* —

Dull gum —

Eisenhower — A815

Plate of 300 stamps and 60 labels for No. 1393b.

1393b A815 6c pane of 5+label, slogan 4, *Aug. 6* 1.50 .75

With slogan 5 1.50 .75

Combination Booklet

BK120 BC15 $1 **blue,** 3 #1393b (6c) + 1 #1280a (2c) 6.00

No. BK120 contains panes with slogan 4, slogan 5 or combinations of 4 and 5.

Eisenhower — A815a

1971-72 **Shiny Gum** ***Perf. 11x10½***

1395a A815a 8c **deep claret,** pane of 8, *May 10, 1971* 1.80 1.25

Booklet

BK121 BC16 $1.92 **claret** (2) 6.50

Variety

1395f As "a," tagging omitted — —

Eisenhower — A815a

1395b A815a 8c pane of 6, *May 10, 1971* 1.25 1.10

Combination Booklet

BK122 BC15 $1 **claret,** 2 #1395b (8c) + 1 #1278b (1c) (2) 4.00

Variety

1395g As "b," tagging omitted *40.00* —

Slogans 6 and 7

Eisenhower — A815a

Dull Gum

1395c A815a 8c pane of 4 + 2 labels, slogans 6 and 7, *Jan. 28, 1972* 1.65 1.00

1395d A815a 8c pane of 7 + label, slogan 4, *Jan. 28, 1972* 1.90 1.10

With slogan 5 1.90 1.10

1395c, 1395d — BC17A

1972 **Postal Service Emblem**

$2 booklet contains 3 panes of seven 8c stamps and 1 pane of four 8c stamps.

Combination Booklet

BK123 BC17A $2 **claret,** *yellow,* 3 #1395d + 1 #1395c 7.75

Varieties

1395h As "c," tagging omitted *40.00* —

1395i As "d," tagging omitted —

Plate of 400 subjects for No. 1395a. Plate of 360 subjects for No. 1395b. Plate of 300 subjects (200 stamps and 100 double-size labels) for No. 1395c. Plate of 400 subjects (350 stamps and 50 labels) for No. 1395d.

A pane of No. 1395d is known with a foldover resulting in a vertical pair of stamp and label, imperf between.

No. BK123 exists with covers printed on both thin and thick card stock.

Booklet Covers
When more than one combination of covers exists, the number of possible booklets is noted in parentheses after the booklet listing.

Jefferson Memorial (Slogan 8) — A924

1973-74 *Perf. 11x10½*

1510b A924 10c pane of 5 + label, slogan 8, *Dec. 14, 1973* 1.65 .90

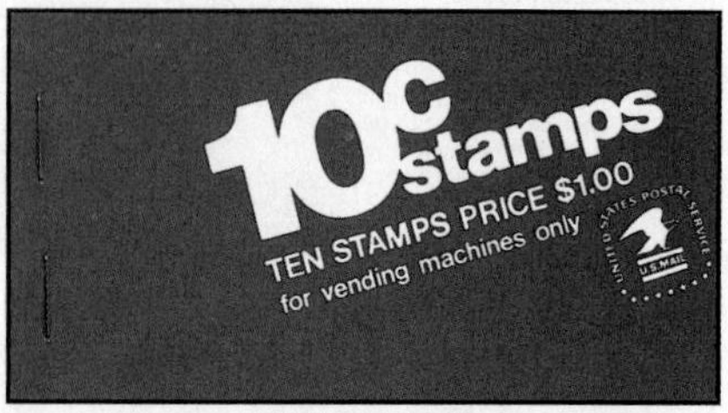

1510b — BC17B

1973 **Postal Service Emblem**

$1 booklet contains 2 panes of five 10c stamps.

Booklet

BK124 BC17B $1 **red & blue** 3.75

Jefferson Memorial — A924

1510c A924 10c pane of 8, *Dec. 14, 1973* 1.65 1.00

1510c — BC17C

1973 **Postal Service Emblem**

$4 booklet contains 5 panes of eight 10c stamps.

Booklet

BK125 BC17C $4 **red & blue** 8.50

Jefferson Memorial — A924

1510d A924 10c pane of 6, *Aug. 5, 1974* 5.25 1.75

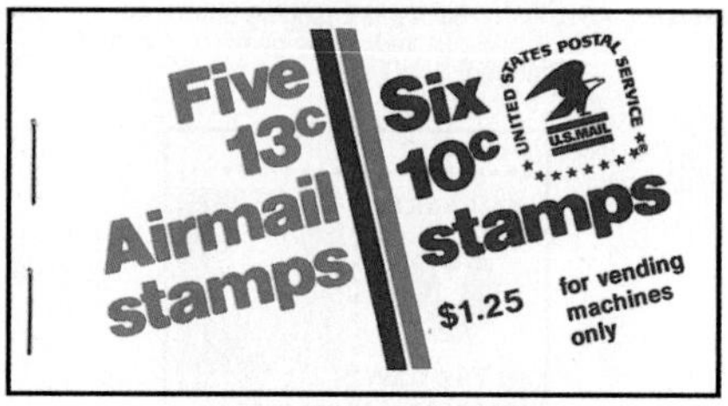

1510d, C79a — BC17D

1974 **Postal Service Emblem**

$1.25 booklet contains 1 pane of five 13c stamps and 1 pane of six 10c stamps.

Combination Booklet

BK126 BC17D $1.25 **red & blue,** 1 #1510d (10c) + 1 #C79a (13c) 7.25

No. BK125 exists with covers printed on both thin and thick card stock.

Variety

1510h As "c," tagging omitted —

1975-78 *Perf. 11x10½*

1595a A998 13c pane of 6, *Oct. 31, 1975* 2.25 1.00

1595a, 1595d, 1280c — BC19A

1975-76

90c booklet contains 1 pane of six 13c stamps and 1 pane of six 2c stamps.

$1.30 booklet contains 2 panes of five 13c stamps.

Combination Booklet

BK127 BC19A 90c **red & blue,** 1 #1595a (13c) + 1 #1280c (2c) (2) 3.25

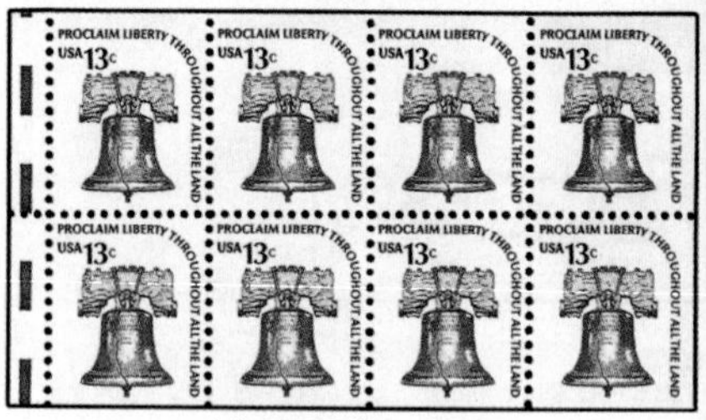

Liberty Bell — A998

1595b A998 13c pane of 7 + label, slogan 8, *Oct. 31, 1975* 2.25 1.00

1595c A998 13c pane of 8, *Oct. 31, 1975* 2.25 1.00

1595b, 1595c — BC19B

1975

$2.99 booklet contains 2 panes of eight 13c stamps and 1 pane of seven 13c stamps.

Combination Booklet

BK128 BC19B $2.99 **red & blue,** 2 #1595c (13c) + 1 #1595b (13c) (2) 7.75

No. BK128 exists with covers printed on both thin and thick card stock.

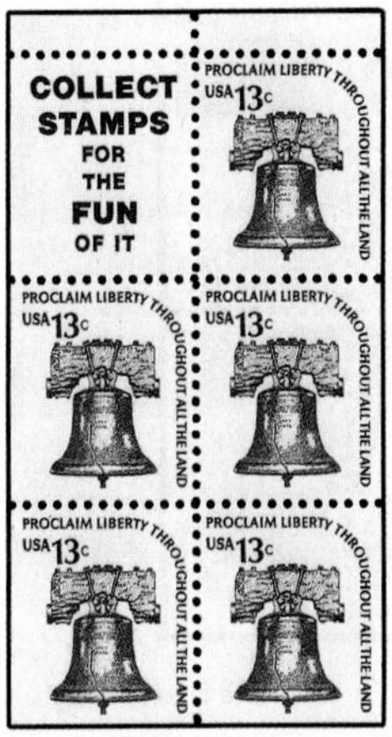

Liberty Bell (Slogan 9) — A998

1595d A998 13c pane of 5 + label, slogan 9, *Apr. 2, 1976* 1.75 1.00

Booklet

BK129 BC19A $1.30 **red & blue** 4.00

Fort McHenry Flag (15 Stars) — A1001

1977-78 *Perf. 11x10½*

1598a A1001 15c pane of 8, *June 30, 1978* 4.25 .80

1598a — BC21

1978

$1.20 booklet contains 1 pane of eight 15c stamps.

Booklet

BK130 BC21 $1.20 **red & light blue,** no P# 4.50

1623a — A994, A1018a

1623a A1018a Pane of 8 (1 #1590 + 7 #1623), *Mar. 11, 1977* 2.25 1.25

1623a — BC20

1977

$1 booklet contains 1 pane of one 9c stamp and seven 13c stamps.

Booklet

BK131 BC20 $1 **red & light blue,** no P# (3) 2.50

Variety

1623g As "a," tagging omitted —

Booklet

BK131a BC20 $1 with #1623g —

Perf. 10x9¾

1623Bc A1018a Pane of 8 (1 #1590A + 7 #1623B), *Mar. 11, 1977* 22.50 —

Booklet

BK132 BC20 $1 **red & light blue,** no P# (2) 23.00

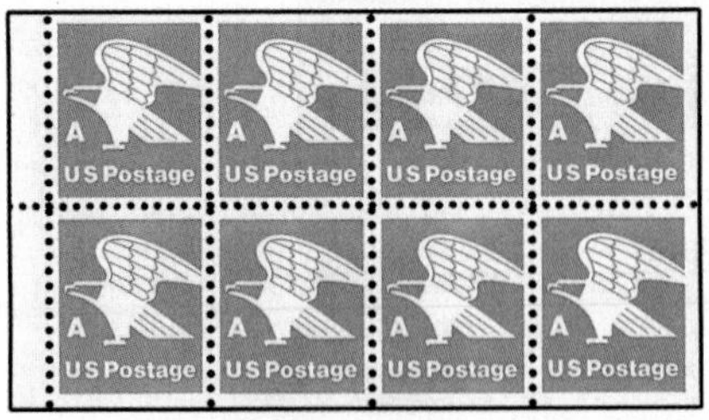

1736a — A1124

1978 **Tagged** *Perf. 11x10½*

1736a A1124 A pane of 8, *May 22* 2.50 1.50

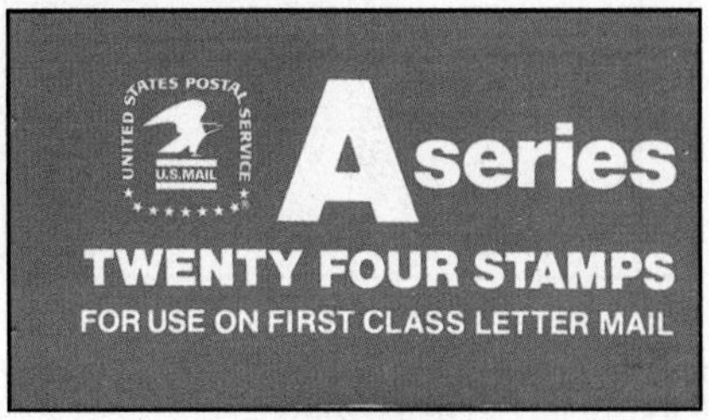

1736a — BC24

BC24 illustration reduced.

1978

$3.60 booklet contains 3 panes of eight A (15c) stamps.

Booklet

BK133 BC24 $3.60 **deep orange** 7.75

No. BK133 exists with covers printed on both thin and thick card stock.

Variety

1736b As "a," tagging omitted —

1737a — A1126

Perf. 10

1737a A1126 15c pane of 8, *July 11* 2.50 1.50

1737a — BC22

1978

$2.40 booklet contains 2 panes of eight 15c stamps.

Booklet

BK134 BC22 $2.40 **rose red & yel grn,** no P# (4) 5.25

Varieties

1737c	As "a," imperf.	*2,200.*	
1737d	As "a," tagging omitted	*50.00*	—

Windmills — A1127-A1131

1980 *Perf. 11*

1742a A1127 15c pane of 10, *Feb. 7* 3.50 3.00

1742a — BC25

1980

$3 booklet contains 2 panes of ten 15c stamps.

Booklet

BK135 BC25 $3 **light blue & dark blue,** *blue,* no P# 7.50

1819a — A1207

1981

1819a A1207 B pane of 8, *Mar. 15* 3.75 2.25

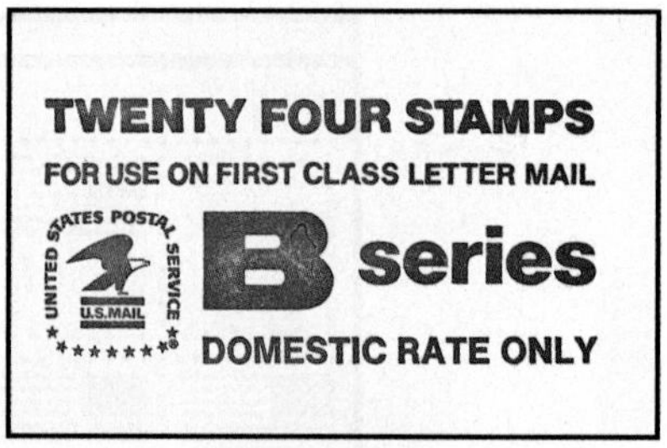

1819a — BC26

1981

$4.32 booklet contains 3 panes of eight B (18c) stamps.

Booklet

BK136 BC26 $4.32 **dull violet,** no P# 11.75

1889a — A1267-A1276

1889a A1267 18c pane of 10, *May 14* 8.50 6.00

1889a — BC28

1981

$3.60 booklet contains 2 panes of ten 18c stamps.

Booklet

BK137 BC28	$3.60	**gray & olive,** P#1-10	17.50
		P#11-13	40.00
		P#14-16	35.00

1893a — A1279-A1280

1893a	A1279	Pane of 8 (2 #1892, 6 #1893), *Apr. 24*	3.00	2.50

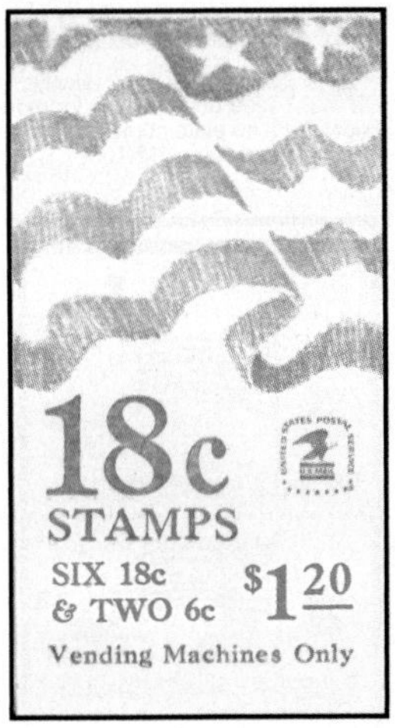

1893a — BC27

1981

$1.20 booklet contains 1 pane of two 6c and six 18c stamps.

Booklet

BK138	BC27	$1.20 **blue & red,** P#1	3.25	

Varieties

1893b	As "a," vert. imperf. btwn.	70.00	
1893d	As "a," tagging omitted	—	

Booklets

BK138a	BC27	$1.20	With No. 1893b, P#1	70.00
BK138b	BC27	$1.20	With No. 1893d, P#1	—

1896a — A1281

1981-83

1896a	A1281	20c pane of 6, small block tagging, *Dec. 17, 1981*	3.00	2.25
		Scored perforations	3.00	—

1896a — BC29

1982

$1.20 booklet contains 1 pane of six 20c stamps.

Booklet

BK139	BC29	$1.20 **blue & red,** P#1 (2)	3.25

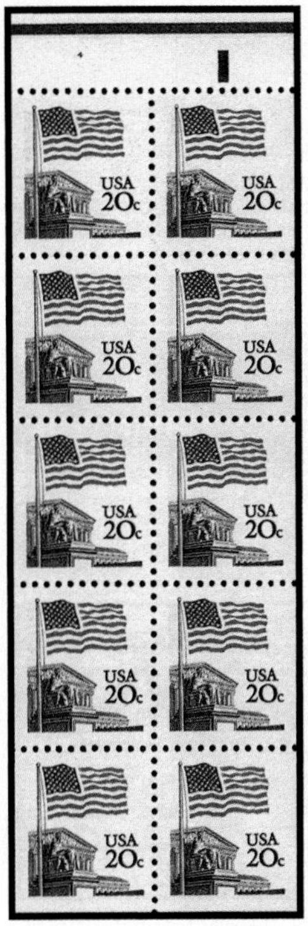

1896b — A1281

1896b	A1281	20c pane of 10, *June 1, 1982*	5.25	3.25

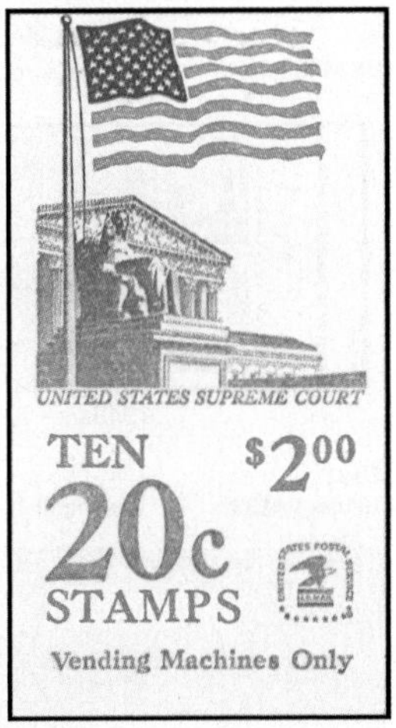

1896b — BC29A

1982

$2 booklet contains 1 pane of ten 20c stamps.

Booklet

BK140	BC29A	$2 **blue & red,** P#1 (4)	5.50
		P#4	47.50

1896e	A1281	20c pane of 10, large block tagging, *Nov. 17, 1983*	5.25	3.25
		Scored perforations	5.25	—

1896b — BC29B

1983

$4 booklet contains 2 panes of ten 20c stamps.

Booklet

BK140A	BC29B	$4 **blue & red,** *Nov. 17, 1983,* P#2	11.00
		P#3	17.50

P#4 *260.00*

Variety

1896f	As "a," tagging omitted		—	—

The small block tagging is 16x18mm (Nos. 1896a-1896b). The large block tagging is 18x21mm (No. 1896e).

Booklet Covers

When more than one combination of covers exists, the number of possible booklets is noted in parentheses after the booklet listing.

1909a — A1296

1983

1909a	A1296	$9.35 pane of 3, *Aug. 12*	60.00	—

1909a — BC31

1983

$28.05 booklet contains 1 pane of three $9.35 stamps.

Booklet

BK140B	BC31	28.05 **blue & red,** P#1111	62.50

1948a — A1333

1981

1948a	A1333	C pane of 10, *Oct. 11*	4.50	3.25

TWENTY STAMPS
FOR USE ON FIRST CLASS LETTER MAIL
C series
DOMESTIC RATE ONLY

1948a — BC26A

1981

$4 booklet contains 2 panes of ten C (20c) stamps.

Booklet

BK141	BC26A	$4 **brown,** *blue,* no P#	10.00

1949a — A1334

1982

1949a	A1334	20c pane of 10, type I, *Jan. 8*	5.50	2.50
1949d		As "a," type II	11.00	—

1949a — BC30

1982

$4 booklet contains 2 panes of ten 20c stamps.

Booklets

BK142	BC30	$4 **blue & yellow green,** P#1-6, 9-10	16.00
		P#11, 12, 15	40.00
		P#14	30.00
		P#16	75.00
		P#17-19	55.00
		P#20, 22-24	100.00
		P#21, 28, 29	*350.00*
		P#25-26	*150.00*
a.		Type II, P#34	22.00

Varieties

1949b	As "a," vert. imperf. btwn.	*95.00*	
1949f	As "a," tagging omitted	*50.00*	—

Booklets

BK142b	As BK142, with 2 #1949b		—
BK142c	As BK142, with 2 #1949f, P#4, 5, 6, 19	*100.00*	

Stamps in No. 1949a are 18¾mm wide and have overall tagging. Stamps in No. 1949d are 18½mm wide and have block tagging.

Plate number does not always appear on top pane in Nos. BK142, BK142a. These booklets sell for more, except P#14 and 15.

Booklet cover BC30 comes in blue & yellow green and in blue & olive green. Both are equally common.

2113a — A1497

1985 ***Perf. 11***

2113a	A1497	D pane of 10 *Feb. 1*	8.50	3.00

2113a BC26B

1985

$4.40 booklet contains 2 panes of ten D (22c) stamps.

Booklet

BK143	BC26B	$4.40 **green,** P#1, 3, 4	17.00
		P#2	*500.00*

Variety

2113b	As "a," imperf. between, horiz.	—

Plate number does not always appear on top pane in No. BK143. These booklets sell for more except P#4. No. BK143 is known with no plate number on top pane and plate number 2 on bottom pane; value, $2,100.

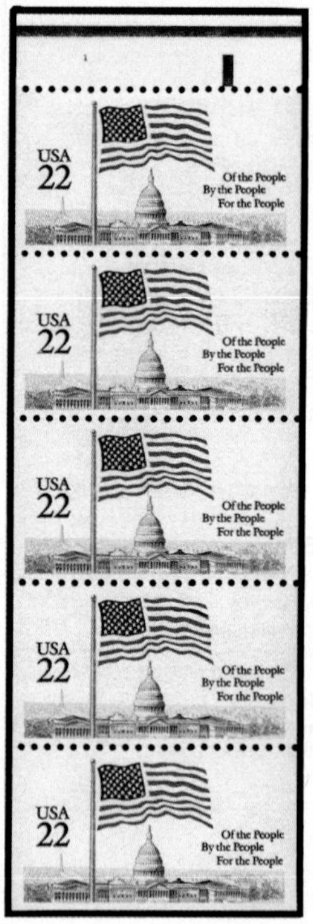

2116a — A1499

Perf. 10 Horiz.

2116a	A1499	22c pane of 5, *Mar. 29*	2.50	1.25
		Scored perforations	2.50	—

2116a — BC33C

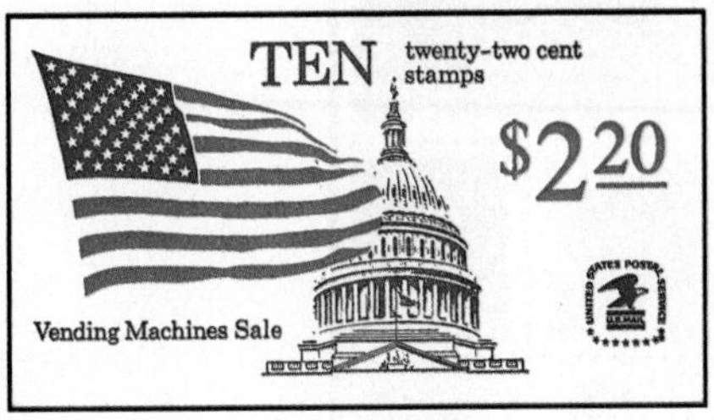

2116a — BC32

1985

$1.10 booklet contains one pane of five 22c stamps.
$2.20 booklet contains two panes of five 22c stamps.

Booklets

BK144	BC33C	$1.10	**blue & red,** P#1, 3 (2)	2.75
BK145	BC32	$2.20	**blue & red,** P#1, 3 (2)	5.25

2121a — A1500-A1504

Perf. 10

2121a	A1500	22c pane of 10, *Apr. 4*	4.00	3.00

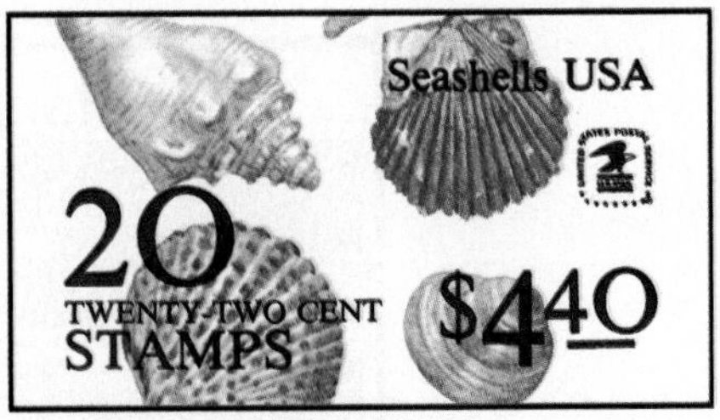

2121a — BC33A

Many different seashell configurations are possible on BC33A. Seven adjacent covers are necessary to show all 25 shells.

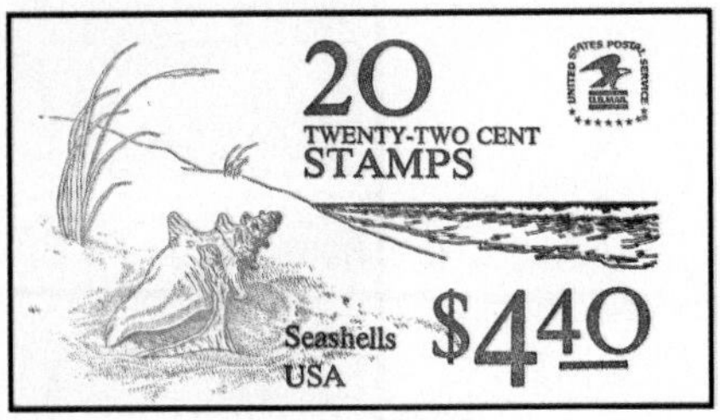

2121a — BC33B

1985

$4.40 booklet contains two panes of ten 22c stamps.

Booklets

BK146	BC33A	$4.40	**multicolored,** P#1, 3	8.50
			P#2	10.00
BK147	BC33B	$4.40	**brown & blue,** P#1, 3, 5, 6, 7, 10	8.50
			P#8	10.00

Varieties

2121b	As "a," violet omitted on both Nos. 2120	*550.00*
2121c	As "a," vert. imperf. btwn.	*500.00*
2121d	As "a," imperf.	—

2122a — A1505

1985-89 ***Perf. 10 Vert.***

2122a	A1505	10.75 type I, pane of 3, *Apr. 29, 1985*	60.00	—

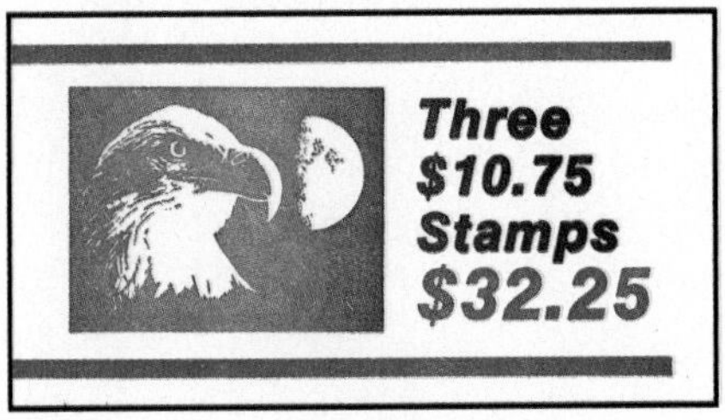

2122a — BC31A

1985

$32.25 booklet contains 1 pane of three $10.75 stamps.

Booklet

BK148	BC31A	32.25	**multicolored,** P#11111	62.50

2122c	A1505	10.75 type II, pane of 3, *June 19, 1989*	65.00	—

2122c — BC31B

1989

$32.25 booklet contains 1 pane of three $10.75 stamps.

Booklet

BK149	BC31B	32.25	**blue & red,** P#22222 (2)	67.50

2182a — A1564

1988 ***Perf. 11***

2182a	A1564	25c pane of 10, *May 3*	5.00	3.75

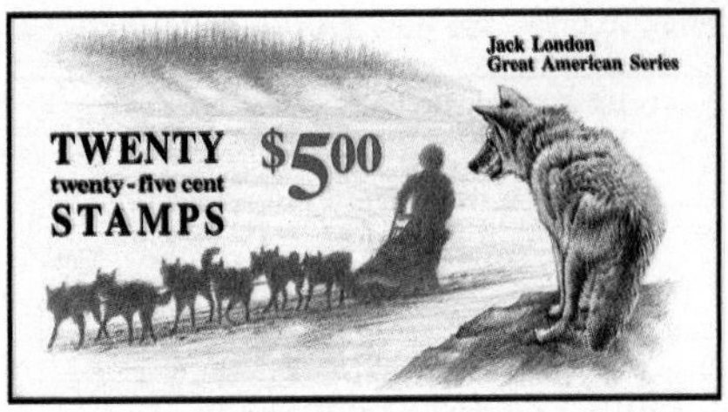

2182a, 2197a — BC43

1988

$1.50 booklet contains one pane of six 25c stamps.
$3 booklet contains two panes of six 25c stamps.
$5 booklet contains two panes of ten 25c stamps.

Booklet

BK150	BC43	$5	**multicolored,** P#1-2	10.50

Varieties

2182c	As "a," tagging omitted	—
2182e	As "a," all color omitted on right stamps	—

Booklet

BK150a	BC43	$5	As BK150, with #2182c	—

2197a — A1564

Perf. 10 on 2 or 3 Sides

2197a	A1564	25c	pane of 6, *May 3*	3.30	2.50

Booklets

BK151	BC43	$1.50	**blue & brown,** P#1	3.30
BK152	BC43	$3	**brown & blue,** P#1	6.60

BK151 and BK152 exist with covers printed on both thin and thick card stock.

Variety

2197c	A1564	25c	As "a," tagging omitted	50.00

Booklet

BK151a	BC43	$1.50	As BK151, with #2197c	57.50

2201a — A1581-A1584

1986

2201a	A1581	22c	pane of 4, *Jan. 23*	2.00	1.75

2201a — BC34

1986

$1.76 booklet contains 2 panes of four 22c stamps.

Booklet

BK153	BC34	$1.76	**purple & black,** P#1	4.00

Varieties

2201b	As "a," black omitted on Nos. 2198, 2201	40.00
2201c	As "a," blue (litho.) omitted on Nos. 2198-2200	*2,250.*
2201d	As "a," buff (litho.) omitted	—

Booklets

BK153a	BC34	$1.76	As No. BK153, with 2 #2201b	100.00
BK153b	BC34	$1.76	As No. BK153, with 2 #2201c	*5,000.*

2209a — A1588-A1592

2209a	A1588	22c	pane of 5, *Mar. 21*	5.50	2.75

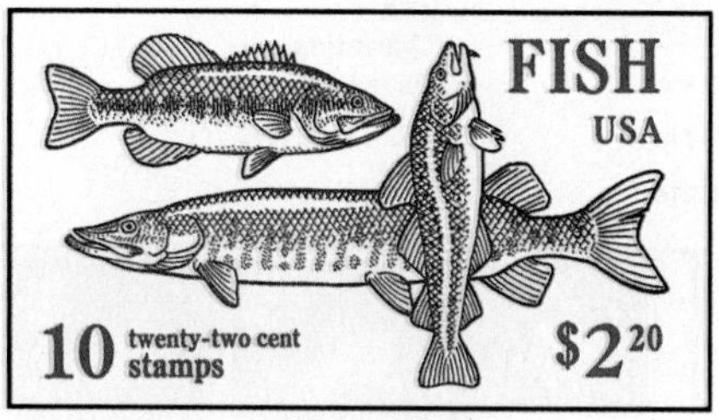

2209a — BC35

1986

$2.20 booklet contains 2 panes of five 22c stamps.

Booklet

BK154	BC35	$2.20	**blue green and red,** P#11111, 22222	12.00

2274a — A1637-A1644

1987

2274a	A1637	22c	pane of 10, *Apr. 20*	10.00	5.00

2274a — BC36

1987

$2.20 booklet contains 1 pane of ten 22c stamps.

Booklet

BK155	BC36	$2.20	**blue & red,** P#111111, 222222	12.50

2276a — A1646

Perf. 11

2276a A1646 22c pane of 20, *Nov. 30* 8.50 —

2276a — BC39

Illustration reduced.

1987

$4.40 booklet contains one pane of twenty 22c stamps.

Booklet

BK156	BC39	$4.40	**multicolored,** no P#	9.00
			P#1111, 2222	12.00
			P#2122	19.00

Variety

2276b	As "a," vert. pair, imperf. between	*1,500.*

No. 2276a was made from sheets of No. 2276 which had alternating rows of perforations removed and the right sheet margins trimmed off.

2282a — A1647

1988 ***Perf. 10***

2282a	A1647	E pane of 10, *Mar. 22*	6.50	3.50
		Scored perforations	6.50	—

2282a — BC40

1988

$5 booklet contains two panes of ten E stamps.

Booklet

BK157	BC40	$5	**blue,** P#1111, 2222	13.00
			P#2122	15.00

2283a — A1649a

Perf. 11

2283a	A1649a	25c pane of 10, *Apr. 29*	6.00	3.50

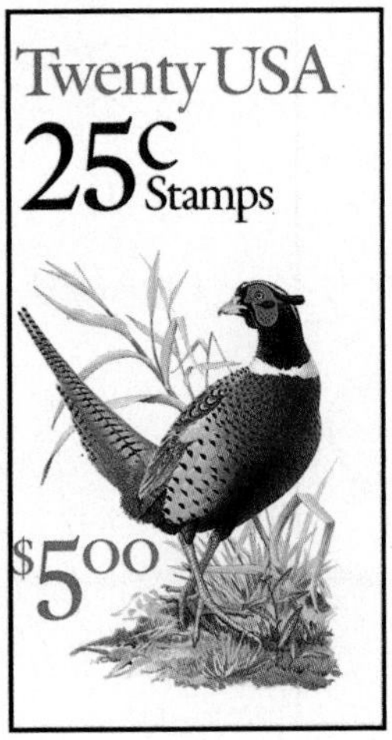

2283a, 2283c — BC41

1988

$5 booklet contains two panes of ten 25c stamps.

Booklet

BK158	BC41	$5	**multicolored,** P#A1111	12.00

Color Change

2283c	A1649a	25c red removed from sky, pane of 10	*70.00*	—

Booklet

BK159	BC41	$5	**multicolored,** P#A3111, A3222	*140.00*

2285b — A1649b-A1649c

Perf. 10

2285b	A1649b	25c pane of 10, *May 28*	5.00	3.50

2285b — BC45

1988

$5 booklet contains two panes of ten 25c stamps.

Booklet

BK160 BC45 $5 **red & black,** P#1111, 1112, 1211, 1433, 1434, 1734, 2121, 2321, 3333, 5955 (2) 12.00
P#1133, 2111, 2122, 2221, 2222, 3133, 3233, 3412, 3413, 3422, 3521, 4642, 4644, 4911, 4941 20.00
P#1414 95.00
P#1634, 3512 50.00
P#3822 40.00
P#5453 165.00

2285Ac — A1648

2285Ac A1648 25c pane of 6, *July 5* 3.00 2.00

2285Ac — BC46

1988

$3 booklet contains two panes of six 25c stamps.

Booklet

BK161 BC46 $3 **blue & red,** P#1111 6.00

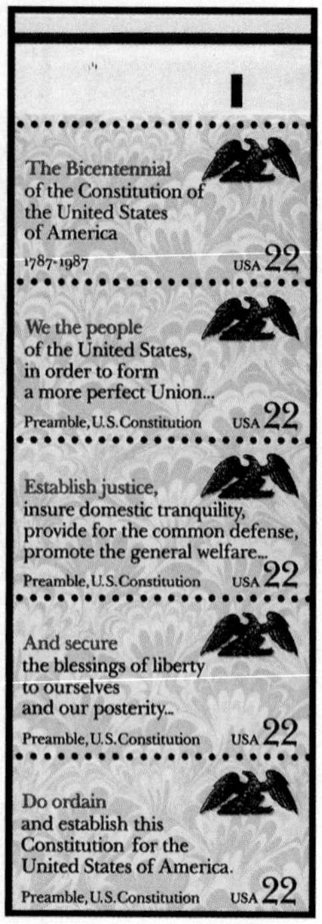

2359a — A1719-A1723

1987

2359a A1719 22c pane of 5, *Aug. 28* 4.50 2.25

2359a — BC37

1987

$4.40 booklet contains four panes of five 22c stamps.

Booklet

BK162 BC37 $4.40 **red & blue,** P#1111, 1112 18.00

Variety

2359c As No. 2359a, grayish green (background) omitted —

2366a — A1726-A1730

2366a A1726 22c pane of 5, *Oct. 1* 2.75 2.50

2366a — BC38

1987

$4.40 booklet contains four panes of five 22c stamps.

Booklet

BK163 BC38 $4.40 **black & yellow,** P#1, 2 11.00

2385a — A1745-A1749

1988

2385a A1745 25c pane of 5, *Aug. 25* 6.00 3.50

2385a — BC47

1988

$5 booklet contains four panes of five 25c stamps.

Booklet

BK164 BC47 $5 **black & red,** P#1 25.00

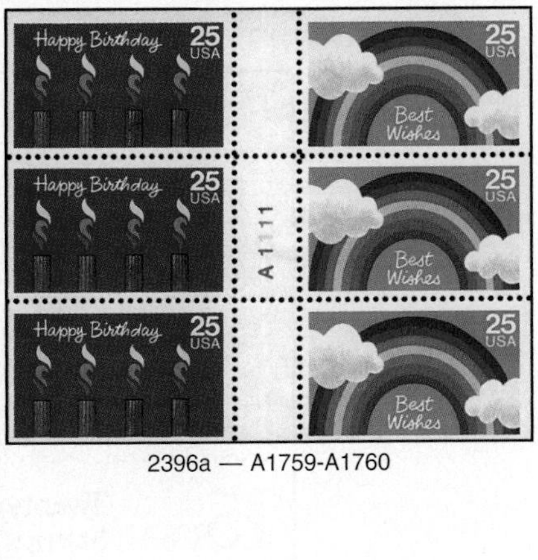

2396a — A1759-A1760

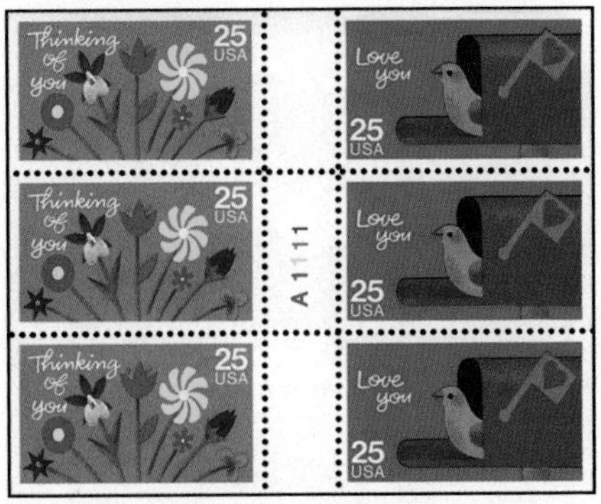

2398a — A1761-A1762

Perf. 11

2396a A1759 25c pane of 6, *Oct. 22* 3.50 3.25
2398a A1761 25c pane of 6, *Oct. 22* 3.50 3.25

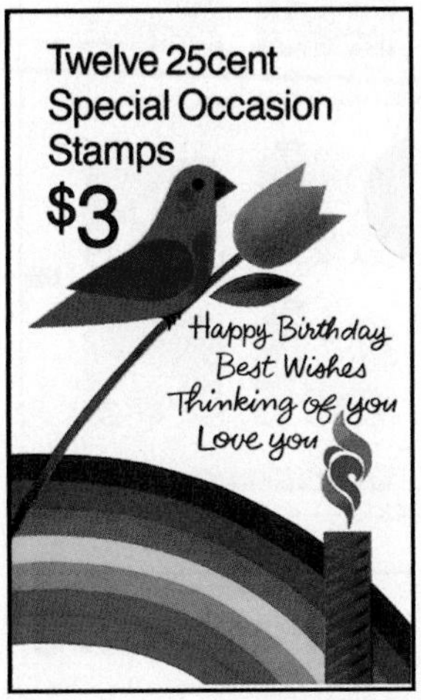

2396a, 2398a — BC48

1988

$3 booklet contains two panes of six 25c stamps.

Combination Booklet

BK165 BC48 $3 **multicolored,** 1 #2396a, 1 #2398a, P#A1111 (2) 7.00

Varieties

2398b As "a," imperf. horiz. —
2398c As "a," imperf —

One example of a never-folded pane of No. 2396a exists uncancelled, affixed to a USPS souvenir page.

2409a — A1769-A1773

1989 ***Perf. 10***

2409a A1769 25c pane of 5, *Mar. 3* 2.50 1.75
Never folded pane, P#1 8.00
P#2 20.00

2409a — BC49

1989

$5 booklet contains four panes of five 25c stamps.

Booklet

BK166 BC49 $5 **blue & black,** P#1, 2 10.00

Variety

2409b As "a," tagging omitted —

2427a — A1791

Perf. 11½

2427a A1791 25c pane of 10, *Oct. 19* 5.00 3.50
Never folded pane, P#1 10.00

2427a — BC50

1989

$5 booklet contains two panes of ten 25c stamps.

Booklet

BK167	BC50	$5 **multicolored,** P#1	10.00

Variety

2427c	As "a," imperf	—

2429a — A1792

2429a	A1792	25c pane of 10, *Oct. 19*	5.00	3.50
		Never folded pane, P#1111	17.50	

2429a — BC51

Illustration reduced.

1989

$5 booklet contains two panes of ten 25c stamps.

Booklet

BK168	BC51	$5 **multicolored,** P#1111, 2111	10.00

Varieties

2429c	As "a," imperf between	—
2429d	As "a," red omitted	*3,250.*

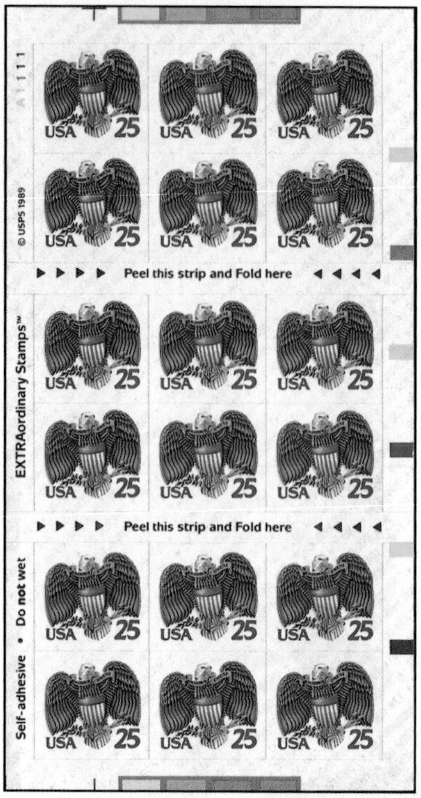

2431a — A1793

2431a — BC52

1989

$5 fold-it-yourself booklet contains eighteen self-adhesive 25c stamps.

Self-adhesive *Die cut*

2431a	A1793	25c pane of 18, *Nov. 10,* P#A1111	11.00

By its nature, No. 2431a constitutes a complete booklet. Blue & red peelable paper backing is booklet cover (BC52). Sold for $5.

2441a — A1800

1990 *Perf. 11½*

2441a	A1800	25c pane of 10, *Jan. 18*	5.00	3.50
		Never folded pane, P#1211	20.00	

2441a — BC53

Illustration reduced.

1990

$5 booklet contains two panes of ten 25c stamps.

Booklet

BK169	BC53	$5 **multicolored,** P#1211	10.50
		P#2111	20.00
		P#2211	30.00
		P#2222	17.50

Variety

2441c	As "a," bright pink omitted	*1,650.*

Panes exist containing both normal and bright pink omitted stamps. Value is less than that of No. 2441c.

2443a — A1802

Perf. 11

2443a	A1802	15c pane of 10, *Feb. 3*	3.00	2.00
		Never folded pane, P#111111	9.00	

2443a — BC54

1990

$3 booklet contains two panes of ten 15c stamps.

Booklet

BK170 BC54 $3 **multi,** P#111111 6.00
P#221111 10.00

Variety

2443c As "a," blue omitted *1,250.*

2474a — A1829-A1833

Perf. 10

2474a A1829 25c pane of 5, *Apr. 26* 8.00 2.00
Never folded pane,
P#1, 3, 5 8.50
P#2 10.50
P#4 —

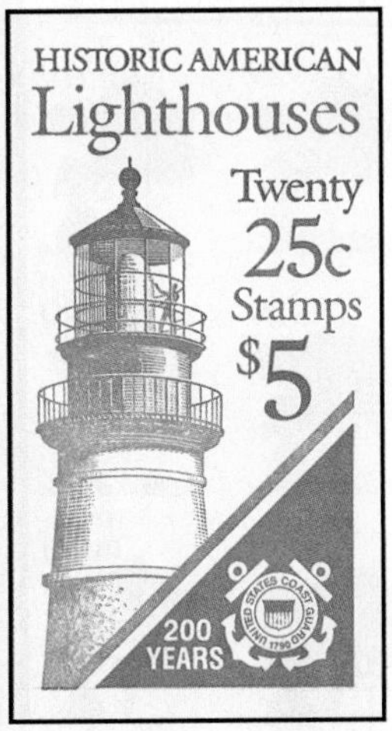

2474a — BC55

1990

$5 booklet contains four panes of five 25c stamps.

Booklet

BK171 BC55 $5 **blue & red,** P#1-5 (2) 32.00

Variety

2474b As "a," white omitted 80.00 —

Booklet

BK171a As No. BK171, with 4
No. 2474b 325.00

2483a — A1847

1991-95

2483a A1847 20c **multicolored,** pane of 10, *June 15, 1995* 5.25 2.25
Never folded pane 6.25

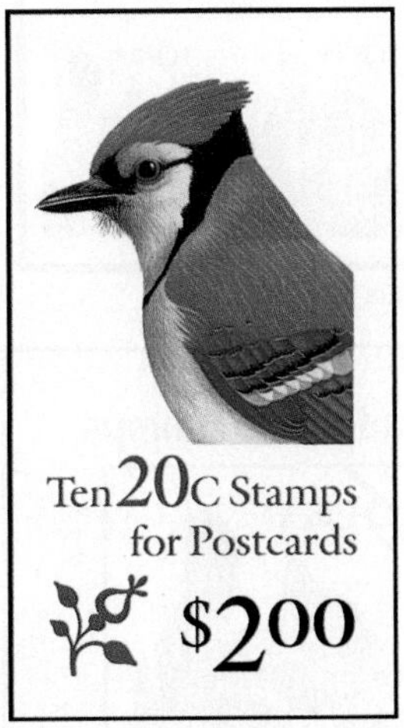

2483a — BC56

1995

$2 booklet contains one pane of 10 20c stamps.

Booklet

BK172 BC56 $2 **multicolored,**
P#S1111 5.25

Variety

2483b As "a," imperf —

2484a — A1848

Perf. 10

2484a A1848 29c **black & multi,** overall tagging, pane of 10, *Apr. 12, 1991* 6.00 3.75
Never folded pane,
P#1111 9.50

2484e A1848 29c **black & multi,** prephosphored paper (solid tagging), pane of 10, *1992* 6.00 3.75

2484a, 2485a — BC57

Illustration reduced.

1991-92

$2.90 booklet contains one pane of 10 29c stamps.
$5.80 booklet contains two panes of 10 29c stamps.

Booklets

BK173 BC57 $2.90 **black & green,** with No. 2484e, P#4444 6.25

BK174 BC57 $5.80 **black & red,** P#1111,
2222 12.00
P#1211 125.00
P#3222, 3333 20.00

BK174a As No. BK174, with 2 #2484e, P#2122,
2222, 3222, 3333 17.50
P#3221 100.00
P#3331 —
P#4444 15.00

Varieties

2484c As "a," imperf horiz. *950.00*

2484g As "a," imperf between and with natural straight edge at top or bottom —

2485a — A1848

Perf. 11

2485a A1848 29c **red & multi,** pane of 10, *Apr. 12, 1991* 6.00 4.00
Never folded pane,
P#K11111 12.50

Booklet

BK175 BC57 $5.80 **black & multi,**
P#K11111 13.00

2486a — A1849

2486a A1849 29c pane of 10, *Oct. 8, 1993* 6.00 4.00
Never folded pane,
P#K1111 6.75

2486a — BC58

1993

$2.90 booklet contains one pane of 10 29c stamps.
$5.80 booklet contains two panes of 10 29c stamps.

Booklets

BK176 BC58 $2.90 **multicolored,**
P#K1111 6.25

BK177 BC58 $5.80 **multicolored,**
P#K1111 12.50

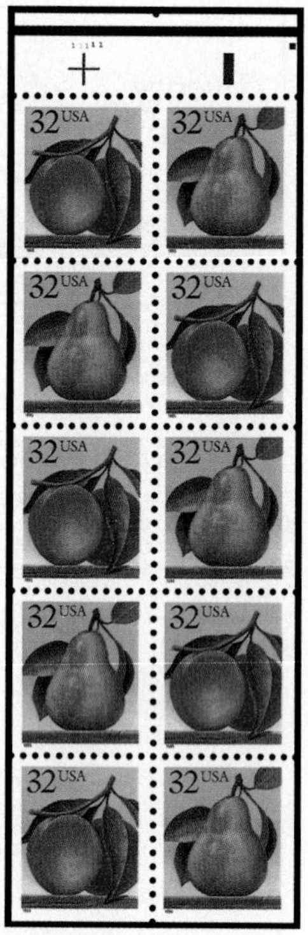

2488a — A1850-A1851

2488a A1850 32c **multicolored,** pane of 10, *July 8, 1995* 6.50 4.25
Never folded pane 7.25

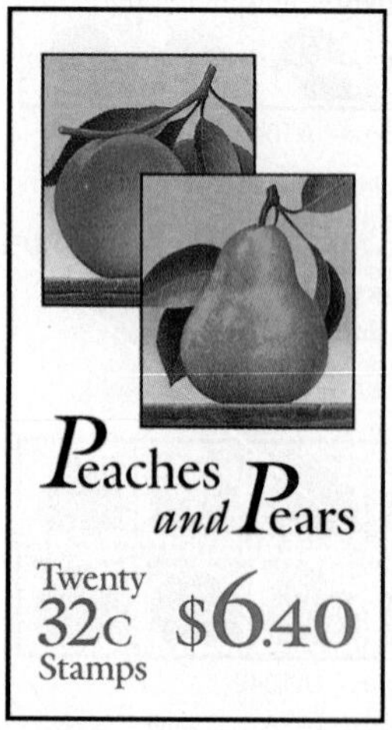

2488a — BC59

1995

$6.40 booklet contains two panes of 10 32c stamps.

Booklet

BK178 BC59 $6.40 **multicolored,** P#11111 13.00

2489a — A1852

2489a BC60

1993

$5.22 fold-it-yourself booklet contains 18 self-adhesive 29c stamps.

Self-Adhesive ***Die Cut***

2489a	A1852	29c pane of 18, *June 25, 1993*, P#D11111, D22211	12.00
		P#D22221, D22222, D23133	14.50

By its nature, No. 2489a constitutes a complete booklet (BC60). The peelable backing serves as a booklet cover.

Variety

2489b As "a," die cutting omitted —

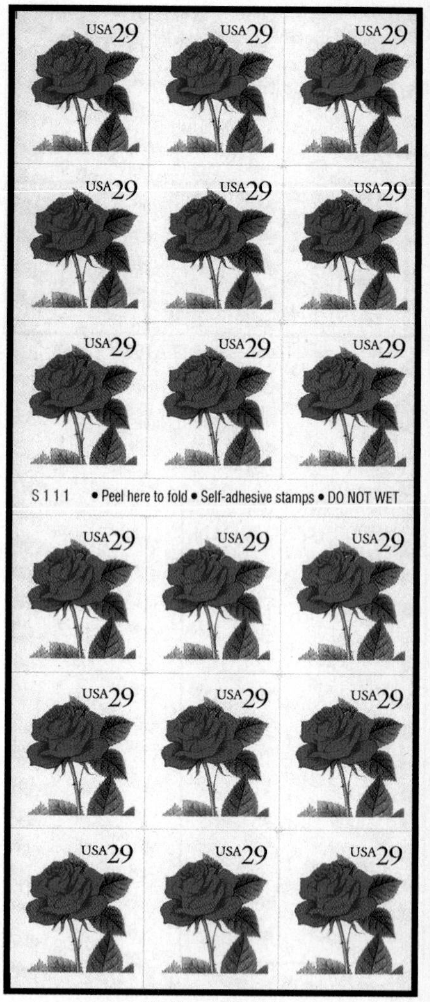

2490a — A1853

2490a BC61

1993

$5.22 fold-it-yourself booklet contains 18 self-adhesive 29c stamps.

Self-Adhesive ***Die Cut***

2490a A1853 29c pane of 18, *Aug. 19, 1993*, P#S111 12.00

By its nature, No. 2490a constitutes a complete booklet (BC61). The peelable backing, of which two types are known, serves as a booklet cover.

2491a — A1854

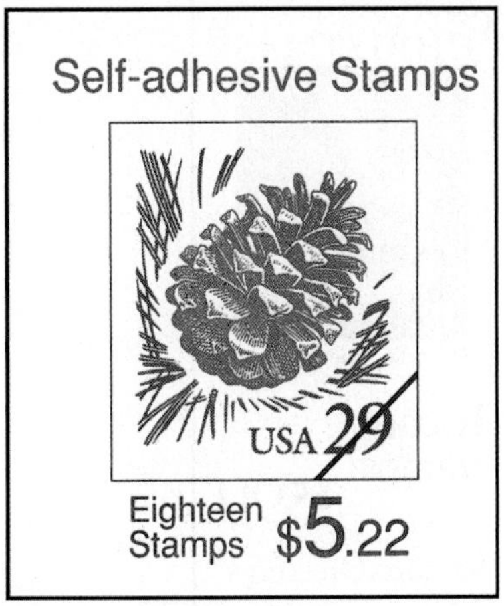

2491a — BC61A

1993

$5.22 fold-it-yourself booklet contains 18 self-adhesive stamps.

Self-Adhesive ***Die Cut***

2491a A1854 29c pane of 18, *Nov. 5, 1993,* P#B3-11, 13-14, 16		11.00
P#B1		17.50
P#B2, 12, 15		15.00

By its nature, No. 2491a constitutes a complete booklet (BC61A). The peelable backing serves as a booklet cover.

2492a — A1853

2492a — BC61B

1995

$6.40 fold-it-yourself booklet contains 20 self-adhesive 32c stamps.

Serpentine Die Cut 11.3x11.7 on 2, 3 or 4 Sides

Self-Adhesive

2492a A1853 32c pane of 20 + label, *June 2, 1995,* P#S111, S112, S333, prephosphored coated paper (solid tagging)	13.00
2492b A1853 32c pane of 15 + label, *1996* (solid tagging)	9.75
2492e A1853 32c pane of 14, *1996* (solid tagging)	21.00
2492f A1853 32c pane of 16, *1996* (solid tagging)	21.00
2492j A1853 32c pane of 20 + label, P#S444, S555, prephosphored coated paper (grainy solid tagging)	13.00
2492k A1853 32c pane of 15 + label (grainy solid tagging)	9.75

By its nature, No. 2492a is a complete booklet (BC61B). The peelable backing serves as a booklet cover.

Nos. 2492a, 2492b, 2492j and 2492k come either with no die cutting on the label or with die cutting.

No. 2492e contains blocks of 4, 6 and 4 stamps. No. 2492f contains blocks of 6, 6 and 4 stamps. The blocks are on rouletted backing paper. The peel-a-way strips that were between the blocks have been removed to fold the pane.

Booklets

See note before No. BK243.

BK178A BC126 $4.80 **blue,** No. 2492b (5) (solid tagging)	10.00
g. As No. BK178A, pane with grainy solid tagging	10.00
BK178B BC126 $4.80 **blue,** No. 2492f with bottom right stamp removed (solid tagging)	40.00
h. As No. BK178B, pane with grainy solid tagging	40.00
BK178C BC126 $9.60 **blue,** 2 #2492b, No P# (3) (grainy solid tagging only)	20.00
BK178D BC126 $9.60 **blue,** 2 panes of #2492f ea with a stamp removed from either the top or bottom row, No P# (3) (grainy solid tagging only)	45.00

Combination Booklets

See note before No. BK243.

BK178E BC126 $9.60 **blue,** 1 ea #2492e, 2492f, no P# (3) (solid tagging only)	47.50
BK178F BC126 $9.60 **blue,** #2492b, 2492f with bottom right stamp removed, no P# (grainy solid tagging only)	*225.00*

No. BK178A was issued wrapped in cellophane and not wrapped in cellophane. The two cellophane-wrapped versions are scarcer.

No. BK178E was sold wrapped in cellophane with the contents of the booklet listed on a label. Three versions exist. No. 2492f is affixed to the booklet cover, and No. 2492e is loose.

The panes of #2492f with one stamp removed that are contained in Nos. BK178B, BK178D and BK178F cannot be made from No. 2492b, a pane of 15 + label. The label is located in the sixth or seventh row of the pane and is sometimes die cut. The panes with one stamp removed all have the stamp removed from the top or bottom row of the pane.

Variety

2492d As "a," 2 stamps and parts of 7 others printed on backing liner (grainy solid tagging)	—

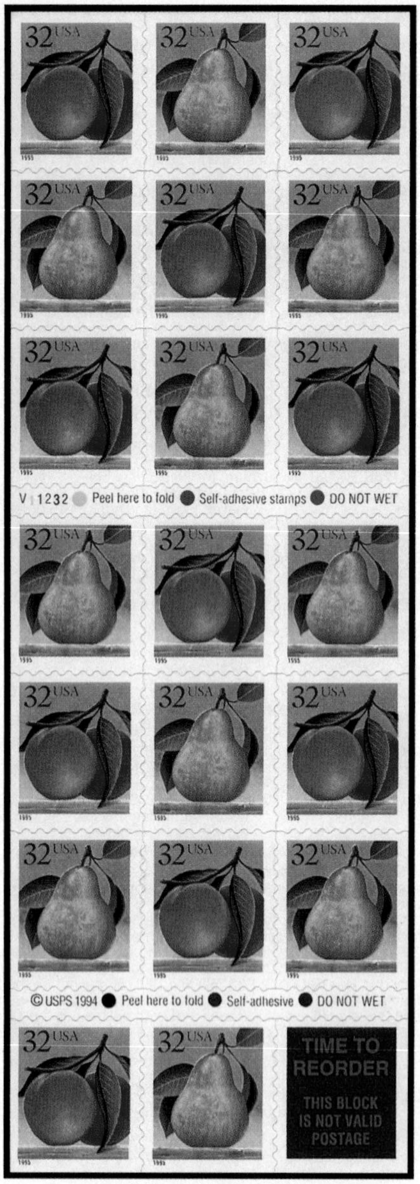

2494a — A1850-A1851

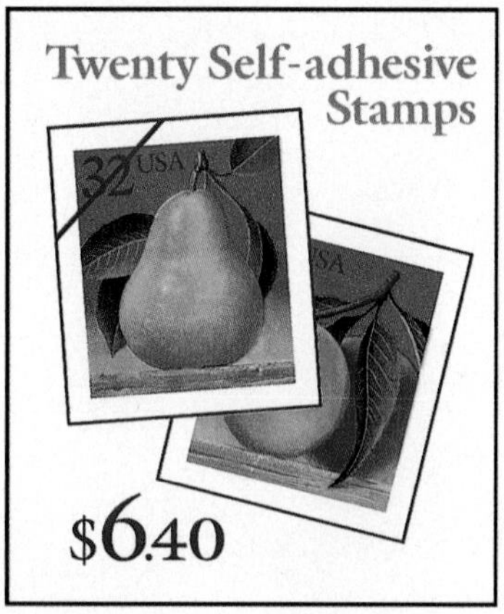

2494a
BC61C

1995

$6.40 fold-it-yourself booklet contains 20 self-adhesive 32c stamps.

Serpentine Die Cut 8.8

2494a	A1850	32c pane of 20+label, *July 8, 1995,* P# list 1	13.00
		P# list 2	18.00
		P#V11132, V33353	15.00
		P#V33323	25.00
		P#V11232	—

By its nature, No. 2494a is a complete booklet (BC61C). The peelable backing serves as a booklet cover. It comes either with no die cutting on the label or with die cutting.

List 1 — P#V11111, V11122, V12132, V12211, V12221, V22212, V22222, V33142, V33243, V33333, V33343, V33363, V44424, V44434, V44454, V45434, V45464, V54365, V54565, V55365, V55565.
List 2 — P#V11131, V12131, V12232, V22221, V33143, V33453.

2505a — A1860-A1864

1990 ***Perf. 11***

2505a A1860 25c pane of 10, *Aug. 17*	12.00	7.50
Never folded pane, P#1-2	17.50	

2505a — BC62

1990

$5 booklet contains two panes of 10 25c stamps.

Booklet

BK179 BC62 $5 **multicolored,** P#1, 2 25.00

Varieties

2505b	As "a," black (engr.) omitted	*3,500.*
2505d	As "a," horiz. imperf.	—

2514b — A1873

1990 ***Perf. 11½***

2514b A1873 25c pane of 10, *Oct. 18*	5.00	3.25
Never folded pane	12.50	

2514a — BC63

1990

$5 booklet contains two panes of 10 25c stamps.

Booklet

BK180 BC63 $5 **multicolored,** P#1 10.00

2516a — A1874

1990 *Perf. 11½x11*

2516a A1874 25c pane of 10, *Oct. 18* 5.00 3.25
Never folded pane, P#1111 —
Never folded pane, P#1211 15.00

2516a — BC64

1990

$5 booklet contains two panes of 10 25c stamps.

Booklet

BK181 BC64 $5 **multicolored,** P#1211 11.00
P#1111 —

2519a — A1875

1991 *Perf. 11.2 Bullseye*

2519a A1875 F pane of 10, *Jan. 22* 6.50 4.50

2519a, 2520a — BC65

1991

$2.90 booklet contains one pane of 10 F stamps.
$5.80 booklet contains two panes of 10 F stamps.

Booklets

BK182 BC65 ($2.90) **yellow & multi,** P#2222 6.50
BK183 BC65 ($5.80) **grn, red & blk,** P#1111, 2121, 2222 13.00
P#1222, 2111, 2212 25.00

2520a — A1875

Perf. 11

2520a A1875 F pane of 10, *Jan. 22* 18.00 4.50
Never folded pane, P#K1111 —

Booklet

BK184 BC65 ($2.90) like #BK182, **grn, red & blk,** P#K1111 18.00

Varieties

2520b As "a," imperf. horiz. —
2520c Horiz. pair, imperf between, in error booklet pane of 12 stamps *500.00*

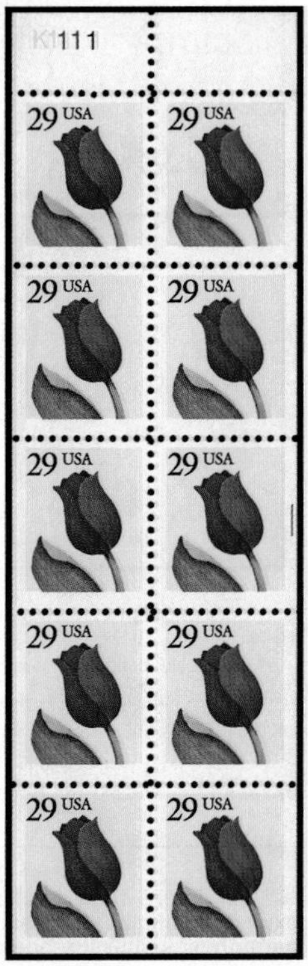

2527a — A1879

Perf. 11

2527a A1879 29c pane of 10, *Apr. 5* 6.00 3.50
Never folded pane, P#K1111 8.00

2527a — BC66

1991

$2.90 booklet contains one pane of 10 29c stamps.

Booklet

BK185 BC66 $5.80 **multicolored,** P#K1111, K2222, K3333 12.00

Variety

2527d As "a," imperf horiz. *900.00*

2528a — A1880

Perf. 11

2528a A1880 29c pane of 10, *Apr. 21* 6.00 3.50
Never folded pane 7.00

2528a — BC67

2528a — BC67A

1991

$2.90 booklet contains one pane of 10 29c stamps.

Booklets

BK186 BC67 $2.90 **black & multicolored,** P#K11111 5.75

BK186A BC67A $2.90 **red & multicolored,** P#K11111 (2) 6.75

Booklet Covers

When more than one combination of covers exists, the number of possible booklets is noted in parentheses after the booklet listing.

2530a — A1882

1991 ***Perf. 10***

2530a A1882 19c pane of 10, *May 17* 4.00 2.75
Never folded pane, P#1111 5.00

2530a — BC68

1991

$3.80 booklet contains two panes of 10 19c stamps.

Booklet

BK187 BC68 $3.80 **black & blue,** P#1111, 2222 8.00
P#1222 32.50

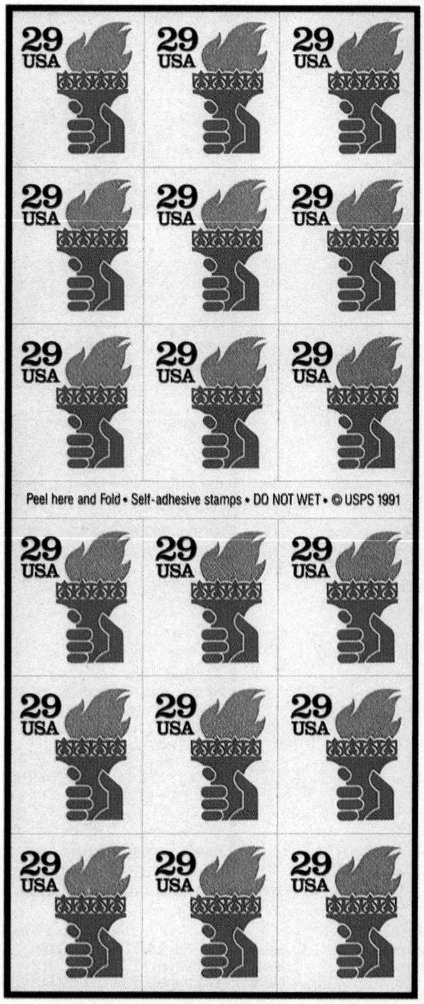
29 USA
Peel here and Fold • Self-adhesive stamps • DO NOT WET • © USPS 1991

2531Ab — A1884

2531Ab — BC68A

Self-adhesive Stamps
29 USA
Convenient: No Licking!
Strong Adhesive: Stays on Envelopes!
Easy to Use: No Tearing!
Eighteen Stamps

2531Ae — BC68B

1991-92

$5.22 fold-it-yourself booklet contains 18 self-adhesive 29c stamps.

Self-Adhesive

Die Cut

2531Ab A1884 29c pane of 18, prephosphored coated paper (solid tagging), *June 25*, no P# 11.00

By its nature, No. 2531Ab constitutes a complete booklet (BC68A). The peelable backing serves as a booklet cover.

Variety

2531Ae As "b," overall tagging (BC68B), *1992* 11.00

2536a — A1890

1991 ***Perf. 11***

2536a A1890 29c pane of 10, *May 9* 6.00 3.50
Never folded pane, P#1111, 1112 8.25

2536a — BC69

1991

$5.80 booklet contains two panes of 10 29c stamps.

Booklet

BK188 BC69 $5.80 **multicolored,**
P#1111, 1112 12.00
P#1113, 1123, 2223 16.00
P#1212 42.50

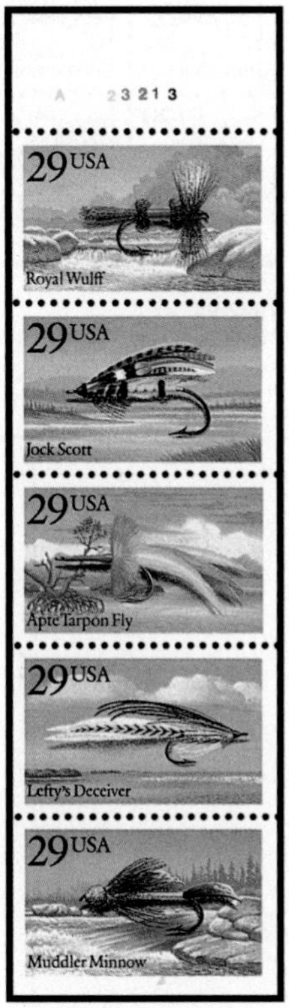

2549a — A1899-A1903

Perf. 11

2549a A1899 29c pane of 5, *May 31* 12.50 3.50
Never folded pane,
P#A23133, A23213 15.00
P#A11111, A22122, A22132, A33213 —
P#A23124 42.50
P#A32225, A33233 27.50

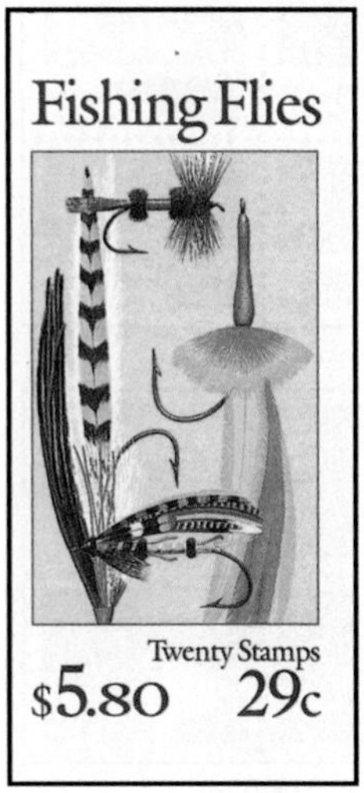

2549a — BC70

1991

$5.80 booklet contains four panes of 5 29c stamps.

Booklet

BK189 BC70 $5.80 **multicolored,**
P#A22122, A23123, A23124, A33235, A44446, A45546, A45547 50.00
P#A11111, A22133, A23133, A23213 57.50
P#A22132, A32224, A32225, A33233 52.50
P#A31224 —

No. BK189 exists assembled from panes with different plate numbers.

P#33213 has yet to be found as top pane in booklets.

2552a — A1905

Perf. 11

2552a A1905 29c pane of 5, *July 2* 3.00 2.25
Never folded pane, P#A11121111 4.75

2552a — BC71

1991

$5.80 booklet contains four panes of 5 29c stamps.

Booklet

BK190 BC71 $5.80 **multicolored,**
P#A11111111, A11121111 12.00

2566a — A1916-A1920

2566a A1916 29c pane of 10, *Aug. 29* 10.00 5.00
Never folded pane, P#1 11.50

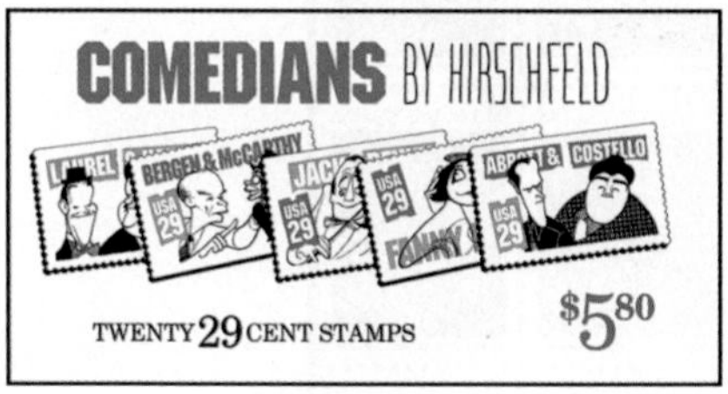

2566a — BC72

1991

$5.80 booklet contains two panes of ten 29c stamps.

Booklet

BK191 BC72 $5.80 **scar, blk & brt vio,**
P#1, 2 21.00

Variety

2566b As "a," scar & brt violet (engr.) omitted *650.00*

2577a — A1922-A1931

2577a A1922 29c pane of 10, *Oct. 1* 10.00 4.50
Never folded pane, P#111111 13.50

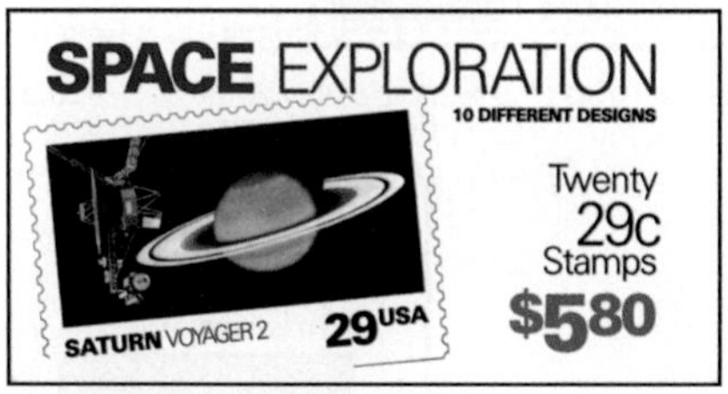

2577a — BC73

1991

$5.80 booklet contains two panes of 10 29c stamps.

Booklet

BK192 BC73 $5.80 **blue, black & red,**
P#111111 21.00
P#111112 25.00

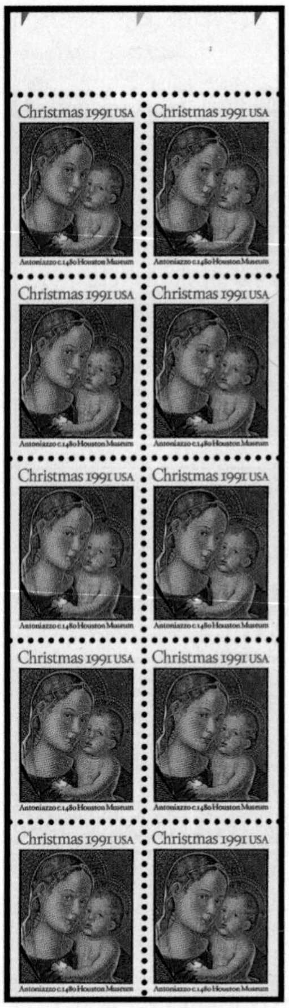

2578a — A1933

2578a A1933 (29c) pane of 10, *Oct. 17* 6.00 3.25
Never folded pane 8.00

2578a — BC74

1991

($5.80) booklet contains two panes of 10 (29c) stamps.

Booklet

BK193 BC74 ($5.80) **multicolored,** P#1 12.00

2581b — A1934

2582a — A1935

2583a — A1936

2584a — A1937

2585a — A1938

2581b A1934 (29c) pane, 2 each, #2580, 2581, *Oct. 17* 10.00 1.25
Never bound pane, P#A11111 11.00
2582a A1935 (29c) pane of 4, *Oct. 17* 2.40 1.25
Never bound pane, P#A11111 3.50
2583a A1936 (29c) pane of 4, *Oct. 17* 2.40 1.25
Never bound pane, P#A11111 3.50
2584a A1937 (29c) pane of 4, *Oct. 17* 2.40 1.25
Never bound pane, P#A11111 3.50
2585a A1938 (29c) pane of 4, *Oct. 17* 2.40 1.25
Never bound pane, P#A11111 3.50

2581b, 2582a-2585a — BC75

1991

($5.80) booklet contains five panes of 4 (29c) stamps.

Combination Booklet

BK194 BC75 ($5.80) **multicolored,** 1 each #2581b, 2582a-2585a, P#A11111, A12111 20.00

Nos. 2581b-2585a are unfolded panes.
Imperf examples of Nos. 2582a-2585a are printer's waste.

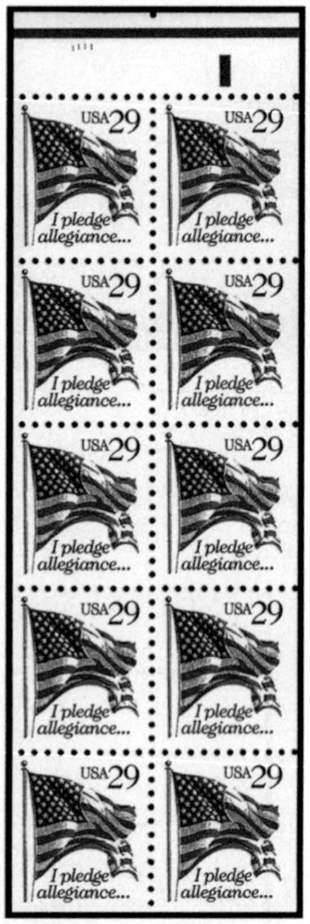

2593a — A1946

1992-94 ***Perf. 10***

2593a A1946 29c **black & multi,** pane of 10, *Sept. 8* 6.00 4.25
Never folded pane, P#1111 8.00

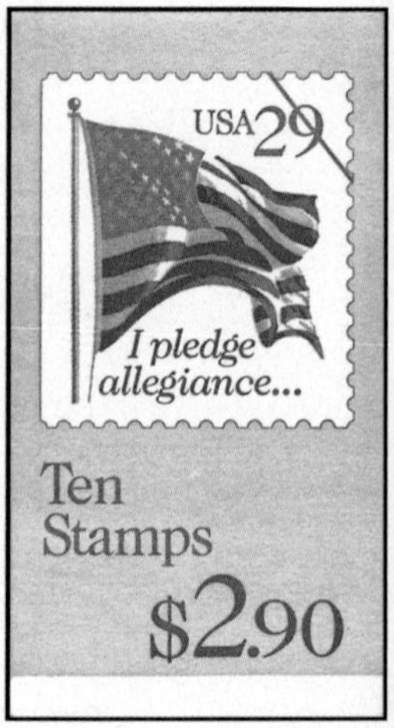

2593a, 2594a — BC76

1992

$2.90 booklet contains one pane of 10 29c stamps.

$5.80 booklet contains two panes of 10 29c stamps.

Booklets

BK195 BC76 $2.90 **blue & red,** P#1111, 2222 6.00

BK196 BC76 $5.80 **blue & red,** P#1111, 2222 12.00
P#1211, 2122 —

Perf. 11x10

2593Bc A1946 29c **black & multi,** pane of 10, shiny gum, *1993* 14.00 7.50
Low gloss gum 30.00

Booklet

BK197 BC76 $5.80 **blue & red,** P#1111, 1211, 2122, 2222, 2232, 3333 30.00
P#2232, low gloss gum 60.00
P#2333 —
P#3333, 4444, low gloss gum *125.00*

2594a A1946 29c **red & multi,** pane of 10, *1993* 6.50 4.25
Never folded pane 8.00

Booklet

BK198 BC76 $2.90 **black, red & blue,** P#K1111 6.00

BK199 BC76 $5.80 **multicolored,** *1994,* P#K1111 13.50

2595a — A1947

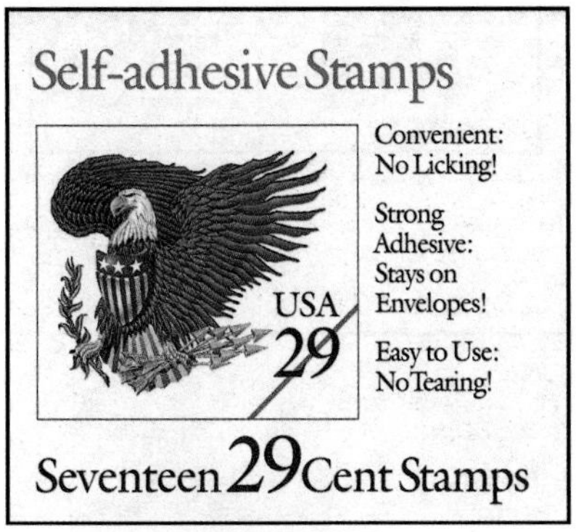

2595a — BC77

1992

$5 fold-it-yourself booklet contains 17 self-adhesive 29c stamps.

No. BC77 for Nos. 2595a, 2596a and 2597a differs in size and style of type as well as location of UPC labels.

Self-adhesive

Die Cut

2595a A1947 29c **brown & multi**, pane of 17 + label, *Sept. 25,* P#B1111-1, B1111-2, B2222-1, B2222-2, B3333-1, B3333-3, B3434-1, B3434-3, B4444-1 13.00
P#B4344-1, B4444-3 15.00
P#B4344-3 *200.00*

Variety

2595d As "a," no die cutting *1,150.*

2596a A1947 29c **green & multi**, pane of 17 + label, *Sept. 25, 1992,* P#D11111, D21221, D22322, D32322, D32332, D43352, D43452, D43453, D54563, D54573, D65784 12.00
P#D54571, D54673, D61384 15.00
P#D32342, D42342 35.00
P#D54561 25.00

2597a A1947 29c **red & multi,** pane of 17 + label, *Sept. 25,* P#S1111 10.50

By their nature, Nos. 2595a-2597a constitute complete booklets (BC77). A peelable paper backing serves as a booklet cover for each. No. 2595a has a black and multicolored backing with serifed type. No. 2596a has a blue and multicolored backing with serifed type, No. 2597a has a black and multicolored backing with unserifed type.

2598a — A1950

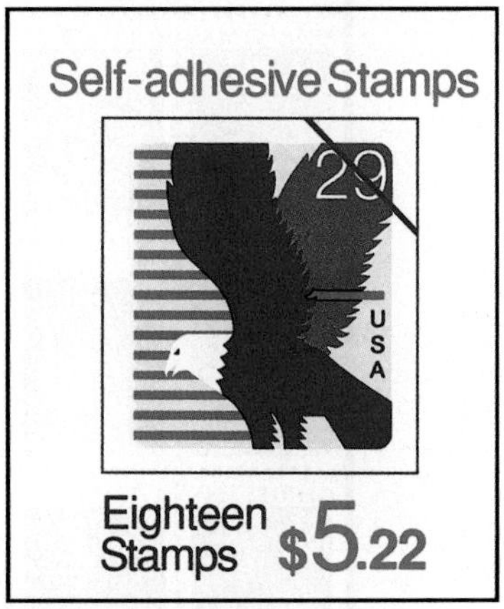

2598a BC78

1994

$5.22 fold-it-yourself booklet contains 18 self-adhesive 29c stamps.

Self-Adhesive ***Die Cut***

2598a A1950 29c pane of 18, *Feb. 4, 1994,* P#M111, M112 11.00

By its nature, No. 2598a constitutes a complete booklet (BC78). The peelable backing serves as a booklet cover.

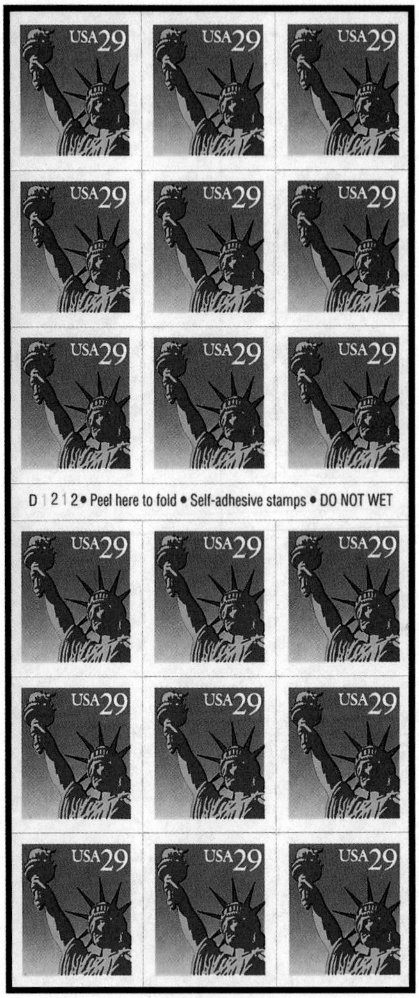

2599a — A1951

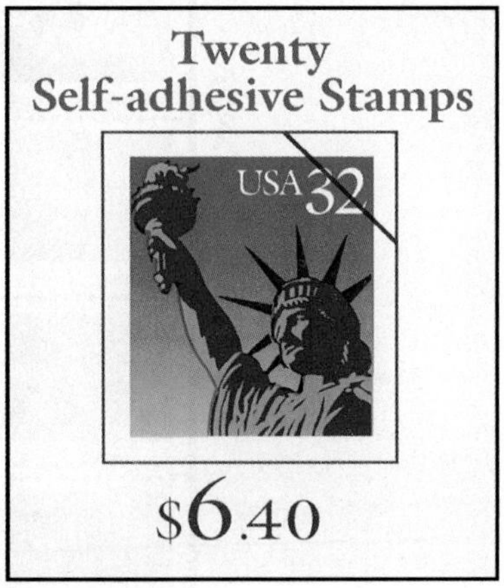

2599a BC79

1994

$5.22 fold-it-yourself booklet contains 18 self-adhesive 29c stamps.

Self-Adhesive ***Die Cut***

2599a A1951 29c pane of 18, *June 24, 1994,* P#D1111, D1212 11.00

By its nature, No. 2599a constitutes a complete booklet (BC79). The peelable backing serves as a booklet cover.

2646a — A1994-A1998

1992

2646a A1994 29c pane of 5, *June 15* 3.00 2.50
Never folded pane,
P#A2212112, A2212122,
A2222222 4.00
P#A1111111, A2212222 10.00

Imperforate panes are proofs.

2646a — BC80

1992

$5.80 booklet contains four panes of 5 29c stamps.

Booklet

BK201 BC80 $5.80 **multicolored,**
P#A1111111, A2212112,
A2212222, A2222222 12.00
P#A2212122 18.00

2709a — A2057-A2061

2709a A2057 29c pane of 5, *Oct. 1* 3.25 2.25
Never folded pane 4.25

2709a — BC83

1992

$5.80 booklet contains four panes of 5 29c stamps.

Booklet

BK202 BC83 $5.80 **multicolored,** P#K1111 12.00

Variety

2709b As "a," imperf. *2,250.*

2710a — A2062

2710a A2062 29c pane of 10, *Oct. 22* 6.00 3.50
Never folded pane 7.00

2710a — BC83A

1992

$5.80 booklet contains two panes of 10 29c stamps.

Booklet

BK202A BC83A $5.80 **multicolored,** P#1 12.00

2718a — A2063-A2066

2718a A2063 29c pane of 4, *Oct. 22* 3.50 1.25
Never bound pane,
P#A111111, A222222 4.50
P#A112211 —

2718a — BC84

1992

$5.80 booklet contains five panes of 4 29c stamps.

Booklet

BK203 BC84 $5.80 **multi,** P#A111111,
A112211, A222222 19.00

Imperfs and part-perfs of No. 2718a are proofs.

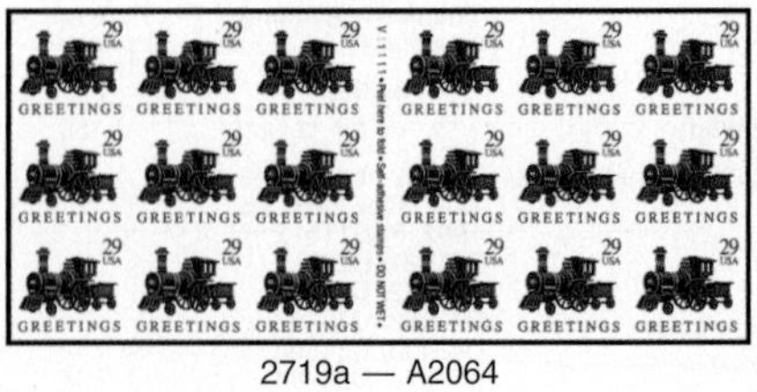

2719a — A2064

2719a
BC85

1992

$5.22 fold-it-yourself booklet contains 18 self-adhesive 29c stamps.

Self-Adhesive

Die Cut

2719a	A2064	29c	**multicolored,** pane of 18, *Oct. 29,* P#V11111	11.00

By its nature, No. 2719a constitutes a complete booklet (BC85). The peelable paper backing serves as a booklet cover.

2737a — A2071, A2075-A2077

Tab format on No. 2737a is similar to that shown for No. 2737b.

1993

2737a	A2071	29c	pane of 8, 2 #2731, 1 each #2732-2737, *June 16*	5.00	2.25
			Never folded pane, P#A22222	6.25	
			P#A13113	—	
2737b	A2071	29c	pane of 4, #2731, 2735-2737 + tab, *June 16*	2.40	1.50
			Never folded pane, P#A22222	3.50	
			P#A13113	—	

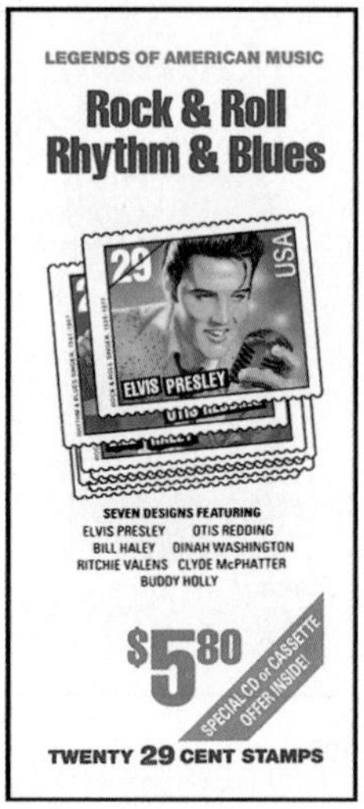

2737a, 2737b — BC86

1993

$5.80 booklet contains one pane of four 29c stamps and two panes of eight 29c stamps.

Combination Booklet

BK204	BC86	$5.80	**multicolored,** 2 #2737a + 1 #2737b, P#A11111, A22222	12.50
			P#A13113, A44444	15.00

No. 2737b without tab is indistinguishable from broken No. 2737a.

Never folded panes of No. 2737a with P#A11111 exist missing the bottom stamp (found in some USPS mint sets).

No. BK204 exists assembled from panes with different plate numbers.

Imperforate panes of Nos. 2737a and 2737b are proofs.

2745a — A2086-A2090

2745a	A2086	29c	pane of 5, *Jan. 25*	3.00	2.25
			Never folded pane, P#1111, 1211	4.00	
			P#2222	6.50	

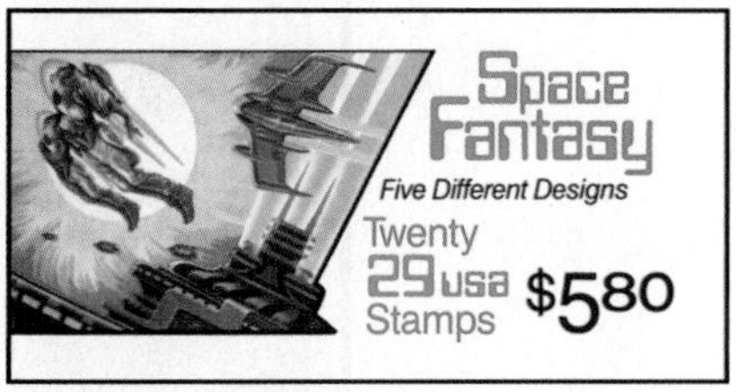

2745a — BC89

1993

$5.80 booklet contains four panes of 5 29c stamps.

Booklet

BK207	BC89	$5.80	**multi,** P#1111, 1211, 2222	12.00

2764a — A2105-A2109

2764a	A2105	29c	pane of 5, *May 15*	3.00	2.25
			Never folded pane, P#1	4.00	

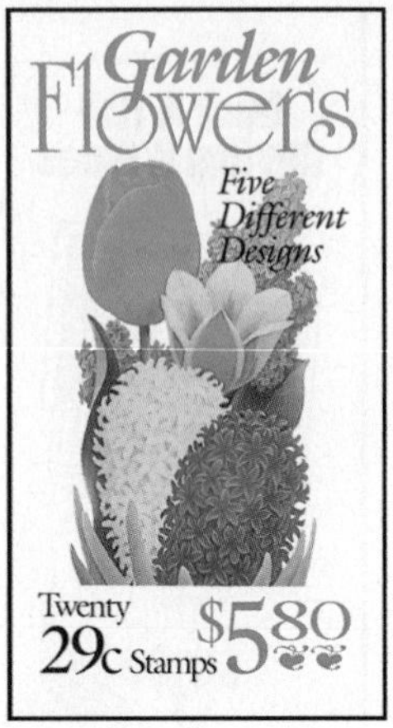

2764a — BC90

1993

$5.80 booklet contains four panes of 5 29c stamps.

Booklet

BK208 BC90 $5.80 **multicolored,** P#1, 2 12.00

Varieties

2764b As "a," black (engr.) omitted *175.00*
2764c As "a," imperf. *1,000.*

Booklet

BK208a As #BK208, with 4 #2764b *850.00*

2770a — A2069, A2112-A2114

2770a A2069 29c pane of 4, *July 14* 2.75 2.25
Never folded pane,
P#A11111, A11121,
A22222 3.75

Imperforate panes are proofs.

2770a — BC91

1993

$5.80 booklet contains five panes of 4 29c stamps.

Booklet

BK209 BC91 $5.80 **multicolored,** P#A11111, A11121, A22222, A23232, A23233 12.00

2778a — A2070, A2115-A2117

2778a A2070 29c pane of 4, *Sept. 25, 1993* 2.50 2.00
Never folded pane,
P#A222222 3.50

Imperforate panes are proofs.

2778a — BC92

1993

$5.80 booklet contains five panes of 4 29c stamps.

Booklet

BK210 BC92 $5.80 **multicolored,** P#A111111, A222222, A333333, A422222 11.00
P#A333323 —

2790a — A2128

2790a A2128 29c pane of 4, *Oct. 21, 1993* 2.40 1.7
Never bound pane,
P#K111111, K133333,
K144444 3.50
P#K255555 *85.00*

2790a — BC93

1993

$5.80 booklet contains five panes of 4 29c stamps.

Booklet

BK211 BC93 $5.80 **multicolored,** P#K111111, K133333, K144444, K255555, K266666 12.00
P#K222222 35.00

Variety

2790c As "a," imperf. —

2798a — A2129-A2132

2798a A2129 29c pane of 10, 3 each #2795-2796, 2 each #2797-2798, *Oct. 21, 1993* 8.50 4.00
Never folded pane, P#111111 10.00

2798b A2129 29c pane of 10, 3 each #2797-2798, 2 each #2795-2796, *Oct. 21, 1993* 8.50 4.00
Never folded pane, P#111111 10.00

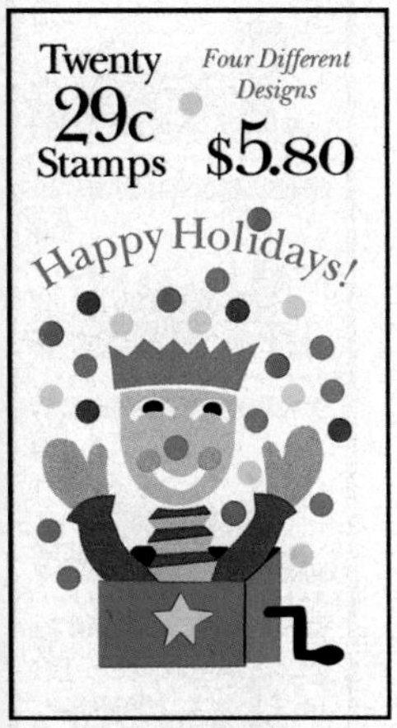

2798a — BC94

1993

$5.80 booklet contains two panes of 10 29c stamps.

Combination Booklet

BK212 BC94 $5.80 **multicolored,** 1 each #2798a, 2798b, P#111111, 222222 19.00

On No. 2798b the plate number appears close to the top row of perfs. Different selvage markings can be found there.

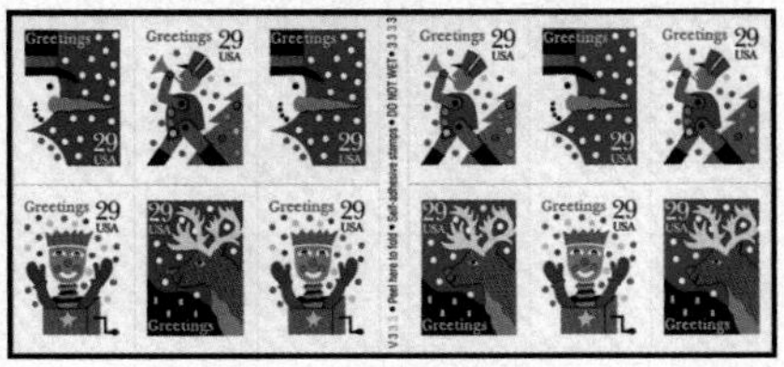

2802a — A2129-A2132

2802a — BC95

1993

$3.48 fold-it-yourself booklet contains 12 self-adhesive 29c stamps.

Self-Adhesive *Die Cut*

2802a A2129 29c pane of 12, 3 each #2799-2802, *Oct. 28, 1993,* P#V1111111, V2221222, V2222112, V2222122, V2222221, V2222222 8.00
P#V3333333 10.00

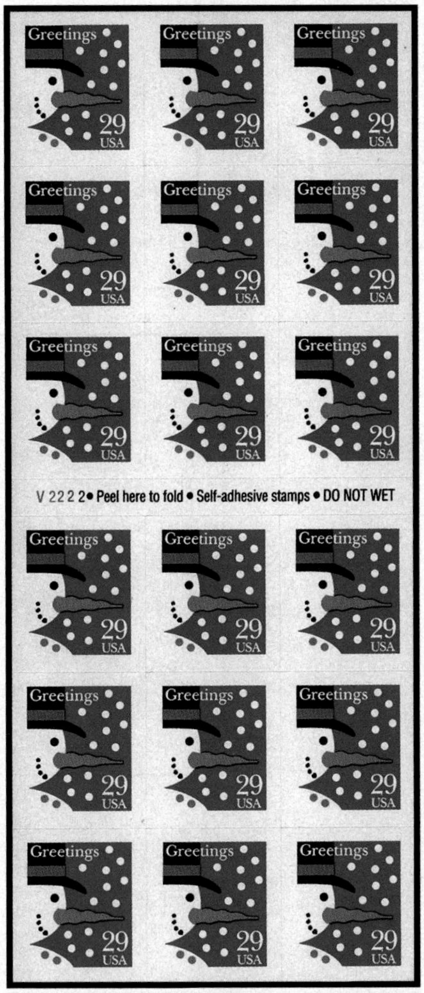

2803a — A2131

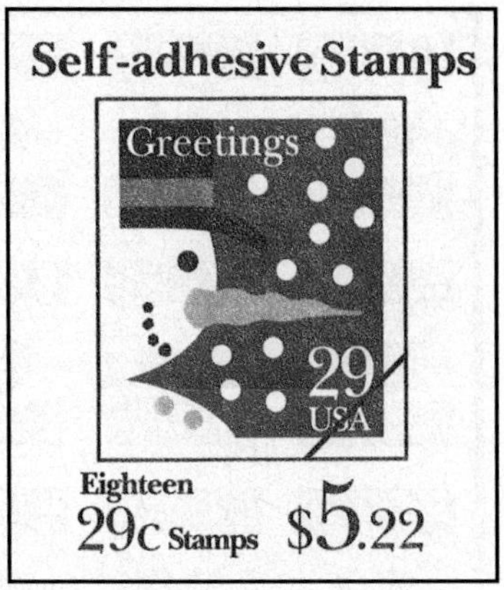

2803a BC96

1993

$5.22 fold-it-yourself booklet contains 18 self-adhesive 29c stamps.

2803a A2131 29c pane of 18, *Oct. 28, 1993,* P#V1111 11.00
P# V2222 14.00

By their nature, Nos. 2802a-2803a constitute complete booklets (BC95-BC96). The peelable backing serves as a booklet cover.

2806b — A2135

2806b A2135 29c pane of 5, *Dec. 1, 1993* 3.50 2.00
Never folded pane 4.50

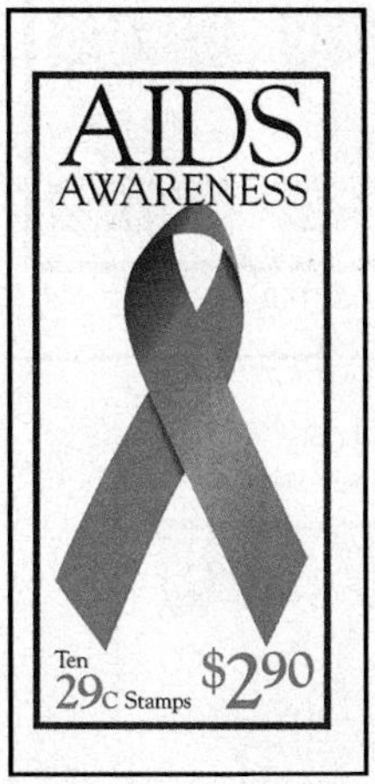

2806b — BC97

1993

$2.90 booklet contains two panes of 5 29c stamps.

Booklet

BK213 BC97 $2.90 **black & red,** P#K111 7.00

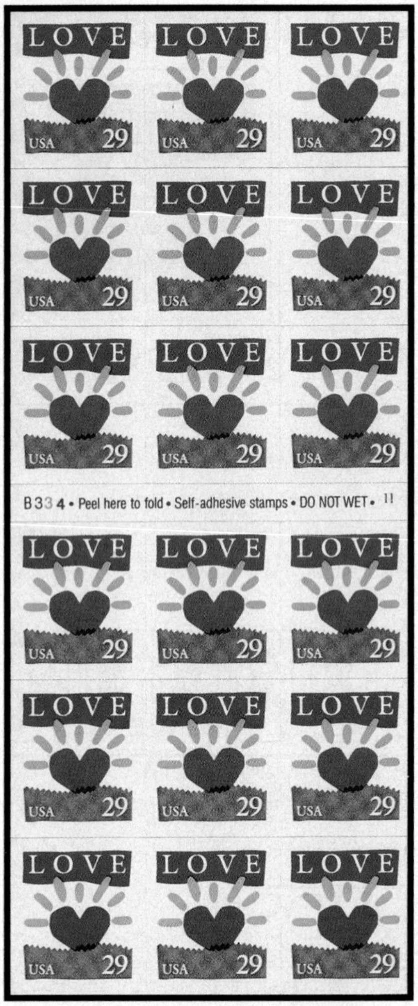

2813a — A2142

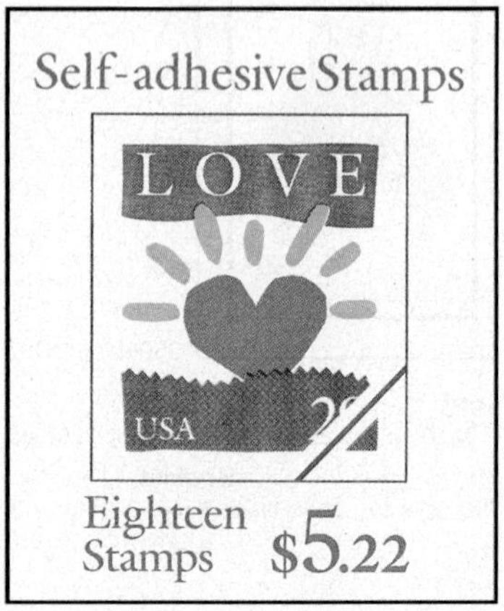

2813a
BC98

1994

$5.22 fold-it-yourself booklet contains 18 self-adhesive 29c stamps.

1994	**Self-Adhesive**	***Die Cut***
2813a A2142 29c	pane of 18, *Jan. 27*, P#, see list	11.00
	P#B111-5, B333-14	*75.00*
	P#B121-5, B444-7, B444-8, B444-9, B444-14	14.00
	P#B333-5, B333-7, B333-8	22.50
	P#B334-11	*750.00*
	P#B344-11	50.00
	P#B434-10	100.00

By its nature, No. 2813a constitutes a complete booklet (BC98). The peelable backing serves as a booklet cover.

List — #B111-1, B111-2, B111-3, B111-4, B221-5, B222-4, B222-5, B222-6, B333-9, B333-10, B333-11, B333-12, B333-17, B344-12, B344-13, B444-10, B444-13, B444-15, B444-16, B444-17, B444-18, B444-19, B555-20, B555-21

2814a — A2143

2814a	A2143	29c pane of 10, *Feb. 14, 1994*	6.00	3.50
		Never folded pane, P#A11111	7.50	

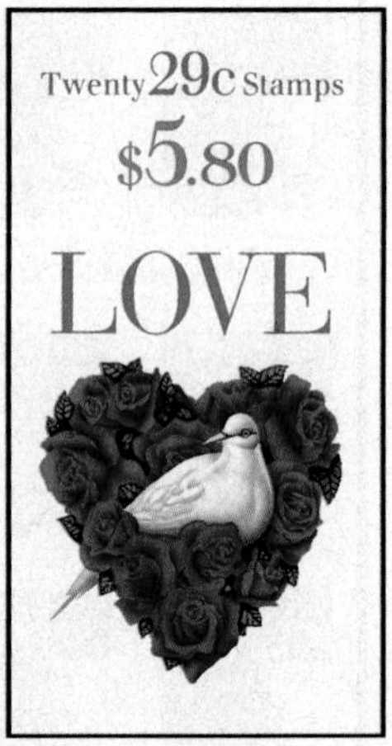

2814a — BC99

1994

$5.80 booklet contains two panes of 10 29c stamps.

Booklet

BK214 BC99 $5.80 **multicolored,** P#A11111, A11311, A12112, A21222, A22122, A22322	11.00
P#A12111, A12211, A12212, A21311	25.00
P#A22222	16.00

2833a — A2158-A2162

2833a	A2158	29c pane of 5, *Apr. 28, 1994*	3.00	2.25
		Never folded pane, P#2	3.50	

2833a — BC100

1994

$5.80 booklet contains four panes of 5 29c stamps.

Booklet

BK215 BC100 $5.80 **multicolored,** P#1, 2	12.00

Varieties

2833b	As "a," imperf	*1,500.*
2833c	As "a," black (engr.) omitted	*225.00*
2833d	As "a," tagging omitted	—

Booklet

BK215a	As #BK215, with 4 #2833c	*1,050.*

2847a — A2171-A2175

2847a	A2171	29c pane of 5, *July 28, 1994*	3.50	2.00
		Never folded pane	4.50	

2847a — BC101

1994

$5.80 booklet contains four panes of 5 29c stamps.

Booklet

BK216 BC101 $5.80 **multicolored,** P#S11111 14.00

Variety

2847b As "a," imperf —

2871Ab — A2200

2871Ab A2200 29c pane of 10, *Oct. 20, 1994* 6.25 3.50
Never folded pane, P#1, 2 7.00

2871Ab — BC102

1994

$5.80 booklet contains two panes of 10 29c stamps.

Booklet

BK217 BC102 $5.80 **multicolored,** P#1, 2 12.50

2872a — A2201

2872a A2201 29c pane of 20, *Oct. 20, 1994* 12.50 4.00
Never folded pane,
P#P11111, P22222,
P44444 14.00
P#P33333 —

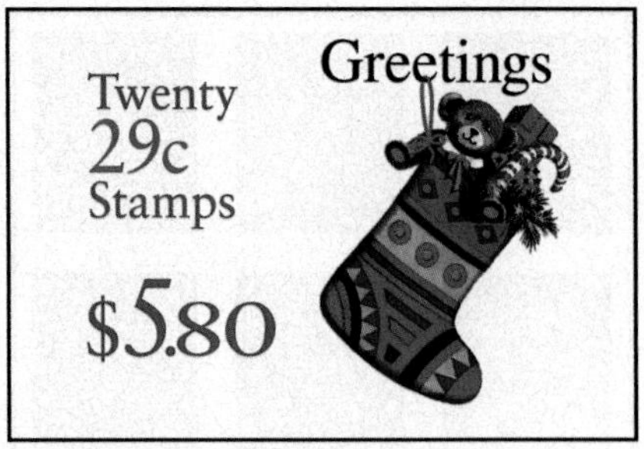

2872a — BC103

1994

$5.80 booklet contains one pane of 20 29c stamps.

Booklet

BK218 BC103 $5.80 **multicolored,** P#P11111, P22222, P33333, P44444 12.50

2873a — A2202

2873a — BC104

1994

$3.48 fold-it-yourself booklet contains 12 self-adhesive 29c stamps.

2873a A2202 29c pane of 12, *Oct. 20, 1994,* P#V1111 8.50

By its nature, No. 2873a constitutes a complete booklet (BC104). The peelable backing serves as a booklet cover.

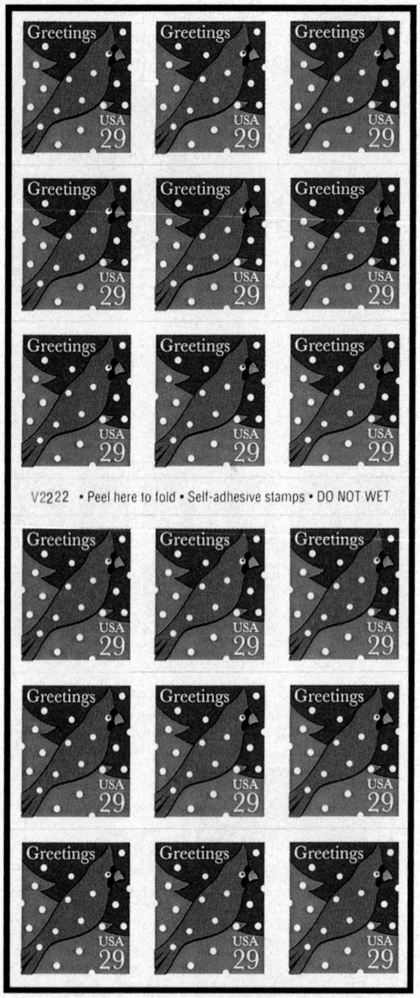

2874a — A2203

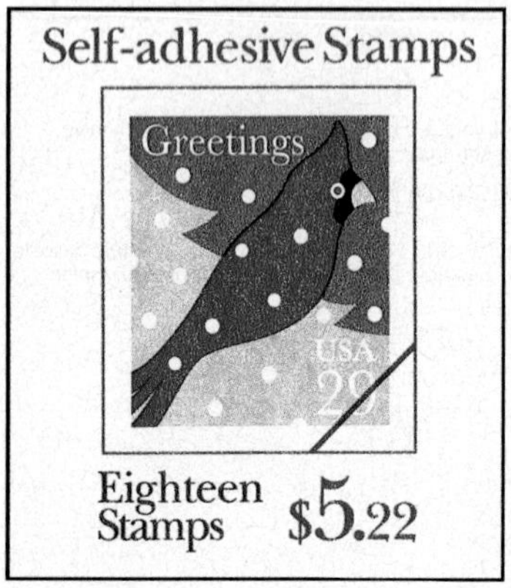

2874a
BC105

1994

$5.22 fold-it-yourself booklet contains 18 self-adhesive 29c stamps.

2874a A2203 29c pane of 18, *Oct. 20, 1994,* P#V1111, V2222 — 11.00

By its nature, No. 2874a constitutes a complete booklet (BC105). The peelable backing serves as a booklet cover.

2881a — A2208

1994 *Perf. 11.2x11.1*

2881a A2208 (32c) **black "G" & multi,** pane of 10, *Dec. 13, 1994* — 6.00 3.75

2881a, 2883a, 2884a, 2885a — BC106

1994

($3.20) booklet contains one pane of 10 G stamps.
($6.40) booklet contains two panes of 10 G stamps.

No. BC106 was printed by three different manufacturers in either two- or four-color formats, with G in different colors and with other minor design differences.

Booklet

BK219 BC106 ($3.20) **pale blue & red,** P#1111 — 6.00

Perf. 10x9.9

2883a A2208 (32c) **black "G" & multi,** pane of 10, *Dec. 13, 1994* — 6.50 3.75

Booklets

BK220 BC106 ($3.20) **pale blue & red,** P#1111, 2222 — 6.50

BK221 BC106 ($6.40) **blue & red,** P#1111, 2222 — 13.00

Perf. 10.9

2884a A2208 (32c) **blue "G" & multi,** pane of 10, *Dec. 13, 1994* — 6.50 3.75

Booklet

BK222 BC106 ($6.40) **blue "G" & multi,** P#A1111, A1211, A2222, A3333, A4444 — 13.00

No. BK222 exists with panes that have different plate numbers.

Variety

2884b As "a," imperf. — *1,750.*

Perf. 11x10.9

2885a A2208 (32c) **red "G" & multi,** pane of 10, *Dec. 13, 1994* — 9.00 4.50

Booklet

BK223 BC106 ($6.40) **red "G" & multi,** P#K1111 — 19.00

2886a — A2208b

2886a, 2887a
BC107

1994

($5.76) fold-it-yourself booklet contains 18 self-adhesive G stamps.

Self-Adhesive *Die Cut*

2886a A2208b (32c) **gray, blue, light blue, red & black,** pane of 18, *Dec. 13, 1994,* P#V11111, V22222 — 14.00

2887a A2208c (32c) **black, blue & red,** pane of 18, *Dec. 13, 1994,* no P# — 14.00

By their nature, Nos. 2886a and 2887a constitute complete booklets (BC107). The peelable backing serves as a booklet cover. The backing on No. 2886a contains a UPC symbol, while the backing on No. 2887a does not.

2916a — A2212

Perf. 10.8x9.8

2916a A2212 32c **blue, tan, brown, red & light blue,** pane of 10, *May 19, 1995* 6.50 3.25
Never folded pane, P#11111 7.25

2916a — BC108

1995

$3.20 booklet contains one pane of 10 32c stamps.
$6.40 booklet contains two panes of 10 32c stamps.

Booklets

BK225 BC108 $3.20 **blue & red,** P#11111, 22222, 33332 6.50
P#23222, 44444 —

BK226 BC108 $6.40 **multicolored,** P#11111, 22222, 23222, 33332, 44444 13.00

Variety

2916b As "a," imperf. —

2919a — A2230

2919a
BC113

1995

$5.76 fold-it-yourself booklet contains 18 self-adhesive 32c stamps.

Self-Adhesive *Die Cut*

2919a A2230 32c pane of 18, *Mar. 17, 1995,* P#V1111, V1311, V1433, V2222, V2322 12.00
P#V2111 45.00

By its nature No. 2919a is a complete booklet (BC113). The peelable backing serves as a booklet cover.

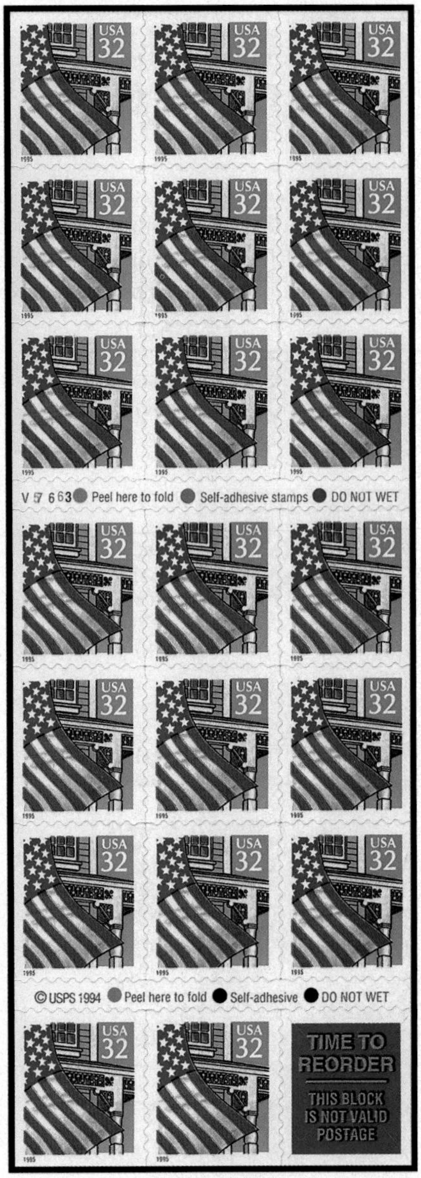

2920a — A2212

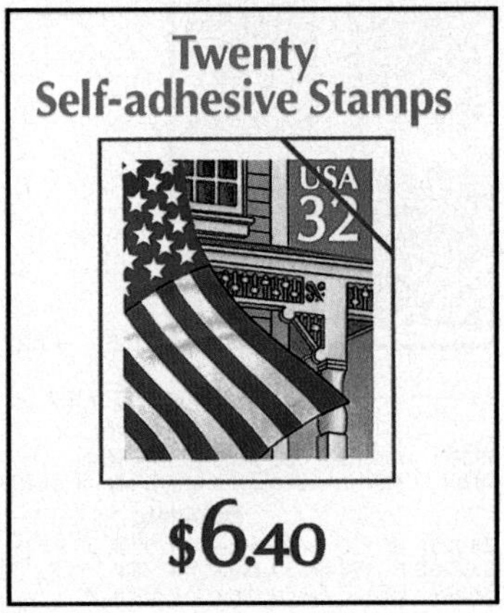

2920a
BC114

1995

$6.40 fold-it-yourself booklet contains 20 self-adhesive 32c stamps.

Serpentine Die Cut 8.7 on 2 or 3 Sides

Self-Adhesive

2920a A2212 32c pane of 20 + label, large date, *Apr. 18, 1995* (see List 1) 13.00
P#V23422 25.00
P#V23522 40.00
P#V57663 —

2920c A2212 32c pane of 20 + label, small date, *Apr. 18, 1995,* P#V11111 *110.00*

Variety

2920g As "a," partial pane of 10, 3 stamps and parts of 7 stamps printed on backing liner —

By their nature Nos. 2920a, 2920c are complete booklets (BC114). The rouletted peelable backing, of which two types are known, serves as a booklet cover.

Date on No. 2920a is nearly twice as large as date on No. 2920c.

No. 2920a comes either with no die cutting on the label or with die cutting.

List 1 — P#V12211, V12212, V12312, V12321, V12322, V12331, V13322, V13831, V13834, V13836, V22211, V23322, V23432, V34743, V34745, V36743, V42556, V45554, V56663, V56665, V56763, V65976, V78989.

2920f — A2212

Serpentine Die Cut 8.7
Self-Adhesive

2920f A2212 32c pane of 15 + label 10.00
2920h A2212 32c pane of 15, see note, *1996* *50.00*

Booklets

BK226A BC126 $4.80 **blue,** 1 #2920f, no P# (4) 10.00
BK226B BC126 $4.80 **blue,** 1 #2920h, no P# (3) 75.00
BK227 BC126 $9.60 **blue,** 2 #2920f (3) 18.00

No. 2920h is a pane of 16 with one stamp removed. The missing stamp is the lower right stamp in the pane or (more rarely) the upper left stamp. No. 2920h cannot be made from No. 2920f, a pane of 15 + label. The label is located in the sixth or seventh row of the pane and is die cut. If the label is removed, an impression of the die cutting appears on the backing paper.

2920De — A2212

Serpentine Die Cut 11.3
Self-Adhesive

2920De A2212 32c pane of 10, *Jan. 20, 1996* 8.00

By its nature No. 2920De is a complete booklet (BC114). The rouletted peelable backing serves as a booklet cover.

Below is a list of known plate numbers. Some numbers may be scarcer than the value indicated in the listing.

No. 2920De — P#V11111, V12111, V23222, V31121, V32111, V32121, V44322, V44333, V44444, V55555, V66666, V66886, V67886, V68886, V68896, V76989, V77666, V77668, V77766, V77776, V78698, V78886, V78896, V78898, V78986, V78989, V89999.

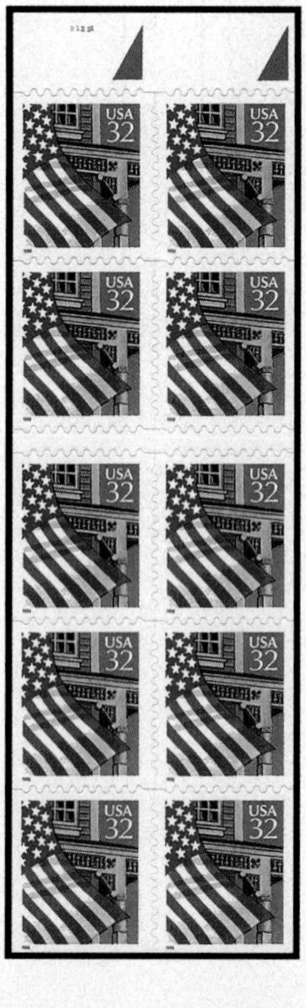

2921a — A2212

Serpentine Die Cut 9.8
Self-Adhesive

2921a A2212 32c pane of 10, dated red "1996," *May 21, 1996* 9.00
Never folded pane, P#21221, 22221, 22222 10.50
2921c A2212 32c pane of 10, dated red "1997," *Jan. 24, 1997* 12.00
Never folded pane, P#11111 14.00
2921d A2212 32c pane of 5 + label, dated red "1997," *Jan. 24, 1997* 7.00
Never folded pane, P#11111 8.50

Combination Booklet

BK227A BC108 $4.80 **multicolored,** 1 ea #2921c-2921d P#11111 19.00

No. BK227A is only source of No. 2921c with P# above right column of stamps and no length register marks or cross register lines in selvage tab.

Booklets

BK228 BC108 $6.40 **blue, red & black,** 2 #2921a (5) 18.00

Known numbers for BK228: P#11111, 12111, 21221, 22221, 22222, 44434, 44444, 55555, 55556, 66666, 77777, 88788, 88888, 99999. Some numbers may be scarcer than the value indicated in the listing.

No. BK228 is only source of No. 2921a, which has P# above left column of stamps.

BK228A BC108 $9.60 **multicolored,** 3 #2921c, P#11111 22.50

No. BK228A is only source of No. 2921c with P# above left column of stamps and length register marks and cross register lines in selvage tab.

Variety

2921e As "a," die cutting omitted *225.00*

Booklet

BK228b As #BK228, with 2 #2921e, P#11111, 13111 *450.00*

2949a — A2264

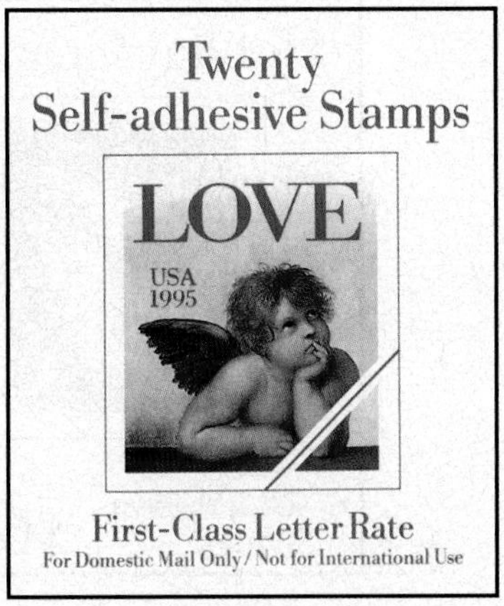

2949a
BC115

1995

($6.40) fold-it-yourself booklet contains 20 self-adhesive non-denominated 32c stamps.

Self-Adhesive ***Die Cut***

2949a A2264 (32c) pane of 20 + label, *Feb. 1, 1995,* P#B1111-1, B2222-1, B2222-2, B3333-2 13.00

By its nature, No. 2949a is a complete booklet (BC115). The peelable backing serves as a booklet cover.

Variety

2949c As "a," red (engr.) omitted *7,500.*

2959a — A2272

Perf. 9.8x10.8

2959a A2272 32c pane of 10, *May 12, 1995* 6.50 3.25
Never folded pane 6.75

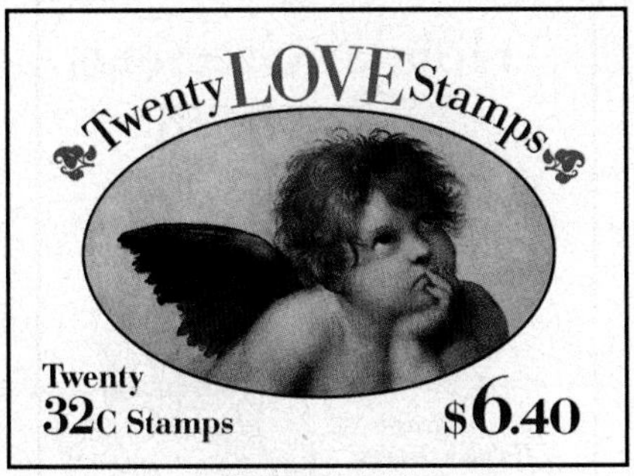

2959a — BC116

1995

$6.40 booklet contains two panes of 10 32c stamps.

Booklet

BK229 BC116 $6.40 **multicolored,** P#1 13.00

2960a — A2274

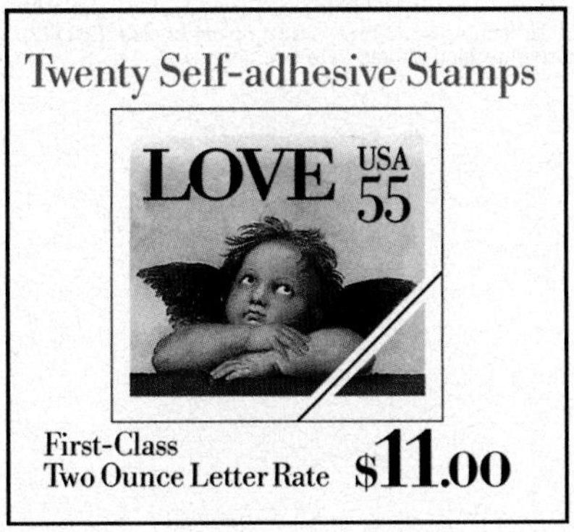

2960a — BC117

1995

$11 fold-it-yourself booklet contains 20 self-adhesive 55c stamps.

Self-Adhesive ***Die Cut***

2960a A2274 55c pane of 20 + label, *May 12, 1995,* P#B1111-1, B2222-1 22.50

By its nature, No. 2960a is a complete booklet (BC117). The peelable backing serves as a booklet cover. It comes either with no die cutting on the label or with die cutting.

2973a — A2283-A2287

2973a A2283 32c pane of 5, *June 17, 1995* 6.25 3.00
Never folded pane 6.75

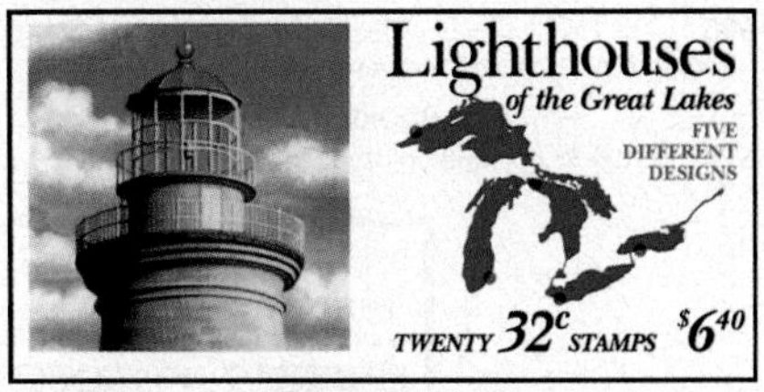

2973a — BC118

1995

$6.40 booklet contains four panes of 5 32c stamps.

Booklet

BK230 BC118 $6.40 **multicolored,** P#S11111 25.00

2997a — A2306-A2310

2997a A2306 32c pane of 5, *Sept. 19, 1995* 3.25 2.25
Never folded pane 4.25

2997a — BC119

1995

$6.40 booklet contains four panes of 5 32c stamps.

Booklet

BK231 BC119 $6.40 **multicolored,** P#2 13.00

Variety

2997b As "a," imperf. —

3003Ab — A2316

3003Ab A2316 32c pane of 10, *Oct. 19, 1995* 6.50 4.00
Never folded pane 7.50

3003b — BC120

1995

$6.40 booklet contains two panes of 10 32c stamps.

Booklet

BK232 BC120 $6.40 **multicolored,** P#1 13.00

3007b — A2317-A2320

3007b A2317 32c pane of 10, 3 each #3004-3005, 2 each #3006-3007, *Sept. 30, 1995* 7.00 4.00
Never folded pane, P#P1111 8.00

3007c A2317 32c pane of 10, 2 each #3004-3005, 3 each #3006-3007, *Sept. 30, 1995* 7.00 4.00
Never folded pane, P#P1111 8.00

3007b-3007c — BC121

1995

$6.40 booklet contains two panes of 10 32c stamps

Combination Booklet

BK233 BC121 $6.40 **multicolored,** 1 each #3007b, 3007c, P#P1111, P2222 14.00

3011a — A2317-A2320

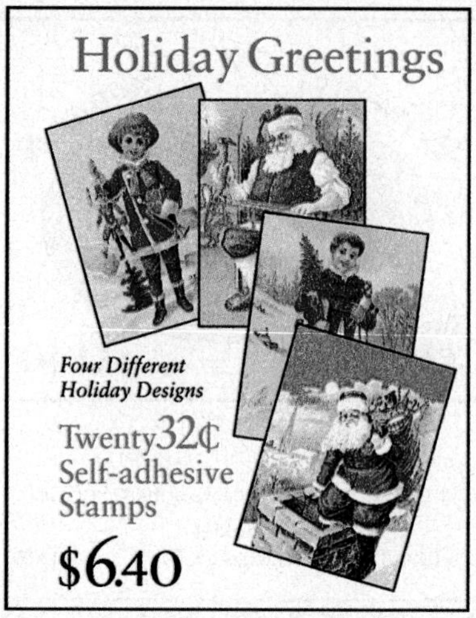

3011a — BC122

1995

$6.40 fold-it-yourself booklet contains 20 self-adhesive 32c stamps

Serpentine Die Cut

3011a A2317 32c pane of 20 +label, *Sept. 30, 1995,* P#V1111, V1211, V3233, V3333, V4444 19.00
P#V1212 26.00

By its nature, No. 3011a is a complete booklet (BC122). The peelable backing serves as a booklet cover.

3012a — A2321

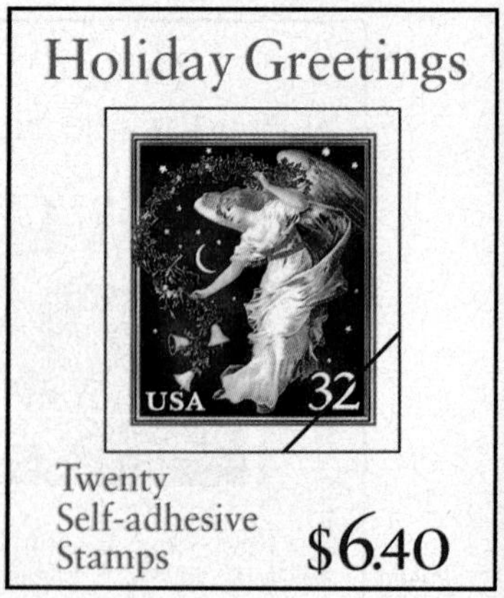

3012a BC123

1995

$6.40 fold-it-yourself booklet contains 20 self-adhesive 32c stamps

Serpentine Die Cut

3012a A2321 32c pane of 20 + label, *Oct. 19, 1995,* P#B1111, B2222, B3333 13.00

By its nature, No. 3012a is a complete booklet (BC123). The peelable backing serves as a booklet cover.

No. 3012a comes either with no die cutting on the label (1995 printing) or with die cutting from the 1996 printing.

3012c A2321 32c pane of 15 + label, *1996,* no P# 13.00

3012d A2321 32c pane of 15, see note, *1996* *30.00*

Booklets

BK233A BC126 $4.80 **blue,** #3012c (2) 13.00
BK233B BC126 $4.80 **blue,** #3012d —
BK233C BC126 $9.60 **blue** 2 #3012c (3) 26.00
BK233D BC126 $9.60 **blue,** 2 #3012d, no P# (3) 60.00
f. As No. BK233D, but one pane is of 16 stamps (thus 31 stamps in the booklet) (error) —

Combination Booklet

BK233E BC126 $9.60 **blue,** 1 ea #3012c, 3012d (2) 80.00

No. 3012d is a pane of 16 with one stamp removed. The missing stamp can be from either row 1, 2, 3, 7 or 8. No. 3012d cannot be made from No. 3012c, a pane of 15 + label. The label is die cut. If the label is removed, an impression of the die cutting appears on the backing paper.

3013a — A2322

3013a
BC124

1995
$5.76 fold-it-yourself booklet contains 18 self-adhesive 32c stamps

Die Cut

3013a A2322 32c Pane of 18, *Oct. 19, 1995,* P#V1111 12.00

Variety

3013b As "a," tagging omitted —

By its nature, No. 3013a is a complete booklet (BC124). The peelable backing serves as a booklet cover.

3029a — A2329-A2333

3029a A2329 32c pane of 5, *Jan. 19, 1996* 3.75 2.50
Never folded pane 4.25

3029a — BC125

1996
$6.40 booklet contains four panes of 5 32c stamps

Booklet

BK234 BC125 $6.40 **multicolored,** P#1 15.00

Variety

3029b As "a," imperf. —

3030a — A2334

Serpentine Die Cut 11.3x11.7

3030a A2334 32c pane of 20+label, *Jan. 20, 1996* 13.00

By its nature, No. 3030a is a complete booklet (BC115). The peelable backing serves as a booklet cover.
P#B1111-1, B1111-2, B2222-1, B2222-2.

3030b A2334 32c pane of 15 + label, *1996* 10.00

Booklet

BK235 BC126 $4.80 **blue,** #3030b (4) 10.00
BK236 BC126 $9.60 **blue,** 2 #3030b (3) 18.00

We Deliver For You.

3048a — A1847

Ten Self-adhesive Stamps for Postcards
USA 20
$2.00

3048a-3048c — BC128

1996

$2.00 fold-it-yourself booklet contains 10 self-adhesive 20c stamps
$2.00 booklet contains 10 self-adhesive 20c stamps

Serpentine Die Cut 10.4x10.8

3048a A1847 20c pane of 10, *Aug. 2, 1996,* P#S1111, S2222 4.00

By is nature, No. 3048a is a complete booklet (BC128). The peelable backing serves as a booklet cover.

We Deliver For You.

3048b, 3048c — A1847

3048b A1847 20c Booklet pane of 4 *22.50*
3048c A1847 20c Booklet pane of 6 *37.50*

Nos. 3048b-3048c are from the vending machine booklet No. BK237 that has a glue strip at the top edge of the top pane, the peelable strip removed and the rouletting line 2mm lower than on No. 3048a when the panes are compared with the bottoms aligned.

Combination Booklet

BK237 BC128 $2.00 **multicolored,** 1 ea #3048b, 3048c, P#S1111, S2222 *67.50*

3049a — A1853

Serpentine Die Cut 11.3x11.7

3049a A1853 32c pane of 20 + label, *Oct. 24, 1996,* P#S1111, S2222 13.00

By its nature, No. 3049a is a complete booklet (BC61B). The peelable backing, of which three types are known, serves as a booklet cover.

3049b, 3049c, 3049d — A1853

3049b A1853 32c pane of 4, *Dec. 1996,* no P# 2.60
3049c A1853 32c pane of 5 + label, *Dec. 1996,* P#S1111 3.50
3049d A1853 32c pane of 6, *Dec. 1996,* without P# 4.00

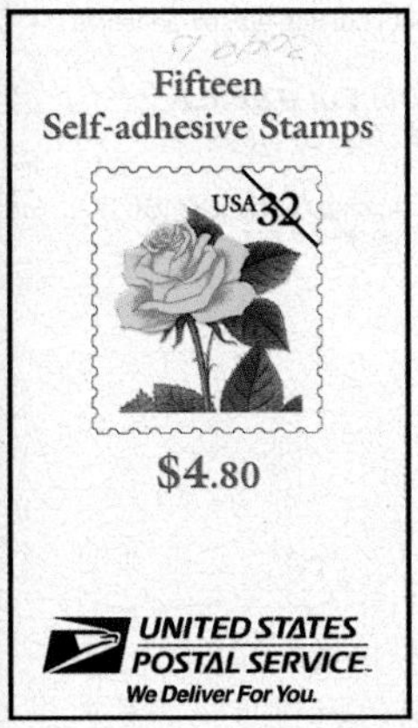

3049b, 3049c, 3049d — BC129

1996

$4.80 booklet contains 15 self-adhesive 32c stamps
$9.60 booklet contains 30 self-adhesive 32c stamps

Combination Booklet

BK241 BC129 $4.80 **multicolored,** 1 ea #3049b-3049d, P#S1111 10.25

Booklet

BK242 BC129 $9.60 **multicolored,** 5 #3049d, P#S1111 20.00

The backing on Nos. BK241-BK242 is rouletted between each pane.

P# single in No. 3049c from No. BK241 is on the lower left stamp. In No. 3049d from BK242, P# single is the lower right stamp on the bottom pane of the booklet.

Variety

3049d Pane of 6 containing P# single 6.00

3050a, 3050c — A2350

3050a, 3050c, 3051Ab-3051Ac
BC130

1998

$2.00 fold-it-yourself booklet contains 10 self-adhesive 20c stamps
$2.00 booklet contains 10 self-adhesive 20c stamps

1998 ***Serpentine Die Cut 11.2***

3050a A2350 20c pane of 10, *July 31, 1998,* P#V1111, V2222, V2232, V3233 5.00
P#V2342, V2343, V3232 —

Serpentine Die Cut 11

3050c A2350 20c pane of 10, *July 31, 1998,* P#V2333, V2342, V2343, V3232, V3243, V3333 12.50
P#V2232, V2332 —

By their nature Nos. 3050a and 3050c are complete booklets (BC130). The peelable backing serves as a booklet cover. All stamps in Nos. 3050a and 3050c are upright.

3051Ab, 3051Ac — A2350

Serpentine Die Cut 10½x11 on 3 Sides (#3051), 10.6x10.4 on 3 sides (#3051A)

1999

Self-Adhesive

3051Ab A2350 20c pane, 4 #3051, 1 #3051A turned sideways at top, *July 1999* 9.00
3051Ac A2350 20c pane, 4 #3051, 1 #3051A turned sideways at bottom, *July 1999* 9.00

Booklet

BK242A BC130 $2.00 **multicolored,** #3051Ab, 3051Ac, P#V1111, *July 1999* 19.00

3052a-3052c — A2351

Serpentine Die Cut 11½x11¼

3052a	A2351	33c pane of 4, no P#	3.60
3052b	A2351	33c pane of 5 + label, no P#	4.50
3052c	A2351	33c pane of 6	5.50

3052a-3052c — BC131A

1999

$4.95 booklet contains 15 self-adhesive 33c stamps + label

Combination Booklet

BK242B BC131A $4.95 **multicolored,** 1 each #3052a-3052c, P#S111, *Aug. 13, 1999* 13.75

No. BK242B has a self-adhesive strip on #3052b that adheres to the plastic-coated peelable backing of #3052a when the booklet is closed. When the booklet is opened, this strip is sticky and may adhere firmly to mounts, album pages, etc. Removal of this strip will damage the backing paper of #3052b.

Plate numbers for No. BK242B are on backing paper below bar code.

3052d — A2351

3052d — BC131

1999

$6.60 fold-it-yourself booklet contains 20 self-adhesive 33c stamps + label

3052d A2351 33c pane of 20 + label, P#S111, S222 17.50

No. 3052d is a complete booklet (BC131). The peelable backing serves as a booklet cover.

3052Ef — A2351

Serpentine Die Cut 10¾x10½ on 2 or 3 Sides

2000

3052Ef A2351 33c pane of 20, *Apr. 7, 2000,* P#S111, S222, S333 16.00

By its nature, No. 3052Ef is a complete booklet. Eight stamps and the booklet cover (similar to BC131) are printed on one side of the peelable backing and twelve stamps plus P# appear on the other side of the backing.

Variety

3052Eh As "f," all 12 stamps on one side with black ("33 USA," etc.) omitted —

3071a — A2370

3071a — BC127

1996

$6.40 fold-it-yourself booklet contains 20 self-adhesive 32c stamps

Serpentine Die Cut 9.9x10.8

3071a A2370 32c pane of 20, *May 31, 1996,* P#S11111 15.00

By its nature, No. 3071a is a complete booklet (BC127). The peelable backing serves as a booklet cover.

3089a — A2387

3089a — BC133

1996

$6.40 fold-it-yourself booklet contains 20 self-adhesive 32c stamps

Serpentine Die Cut 11.6x11.4

3089a A2387 32c pane of 20, *Aug. 1, 1996,* P#B1111 14.00

By its nature, No. 3089a is a complete booklet (BC133). The peelable backing serves as a booklet cover.

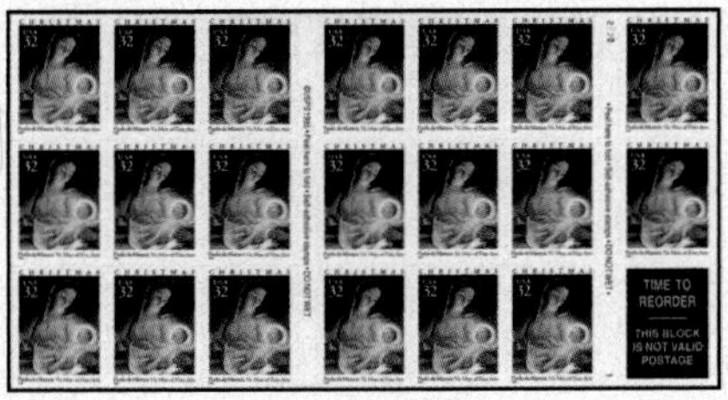

3112a — A2405

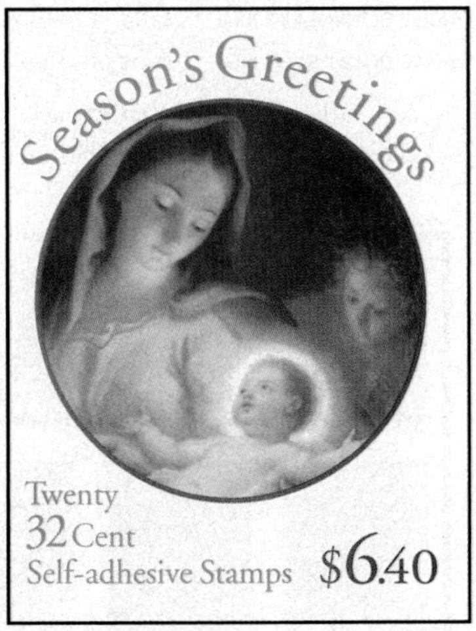

3112a
BC134

1996

$6.40 fold-it-yourself booklet contains 20 self-adhesive 32c stamps

Serpentine Die Cut 10 on 2, 3 or 4 Sides

3112a A2405 32c pane of 20 + label, *Nov. 1, 1996* 15.00

Variety

3112c As "a," die cutting omitted —

By its nature No. 3112a is a complete booklet (BC134). The peelable backing serves as a booklet cover.

Below is a list of known plate numbers. Some numbers may be scarcer than the value indicated in the listing.

P#1111-1, 1211-1, 2212-1, 2222-1, 2323-1, 3323-1, 3333-1, 3334-1, 4444-1, 5544-1, 5555-1, 5556-1, 5556-2, 5656-2, 6656-2, 6666-1, 6666-2, 6766-1, 7887-1, 7887-2, 7888-2, 7988-2.

3116a — A2406-2409

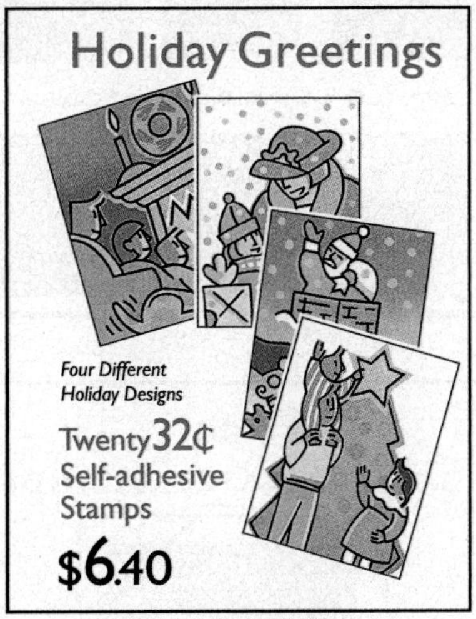

3116a — BC135

1996

$6.40 fold-it-yourself booklet contains 20 self-adhesive 32c stamps

Serpentine Die Cut 11.8x11.5 on 2, 3 or 4 Sides

3116a A2406 32c pane of 20 + label, *Oct. 8, 1996,* P#B1111, B2222, B3333 15.00

Variety

3116d As "a," die cutting omitted *2,100.*

By its nature No. 3116a is a complete booklet (BC135). The peelable backing serves as a booklet cover.

3117a — A2410

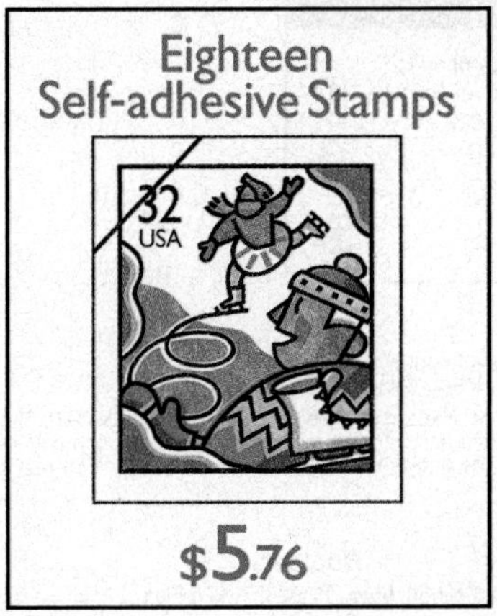

3117a
BC136

1996

$5.76 fold-it-yourself booklet contains 18 self-adhesive 32c stamps

Die Cut

3117a A2410 32c pane of 18, *Oct. 8, 1996,* P#V1111, V2111 12.00

By its nature No. 3117a is a complete booklet (BC136). The peelable backing serves as a booklet cover.

MAKESHIFT VENDING MACHINE BOOKLETS

The booklets listed below were released in 1996 to meet the need for $4.80 and $9.60 vending machine booklets. The booklets consist of blocks of sheet stamps folded and affixed to a standard cover (BC126) with a spot of glue.

The cover varies from issue to issue in the line of text on the front that indicates the number of stamps contained in the booklet and in the four lines of text on the back that describe the contents of the booklet and list the booklet's item number. Due to the folding required to make stamps fit within the covers, the stamp blocks may easily fall apart when booklets are opened. Stamps may also easily detach from booklet cover.

Front

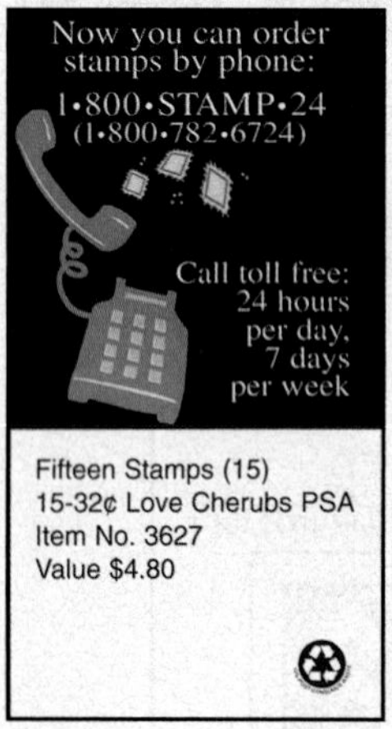

Back — BC126

1996

$4.80 booklet contains 15 32c stamps
$9.60 booklet contains 30 32c stamps

A number of different stamps have been sold in BC126. The text on the front and back changes to describe the contents of the booklet. The enclosed stamps are affixed to the cover with a spot of glue.

1996

Booklets

BK243	BC126	$4.80	**blue,** 15 #2897 (32c Flag Over Porch)	11.00
BK244	BC126	$4.80	**blue,** 15 #2957 (32c Cherub/Love)	11.00
BK245	BC126	$4.80	**blue,** 15 #3024 (32c Utah)	12.50
BK246	BC126	$4.80	**blue,** 15 #3065 (32c Fulbright Scholarships)	11.00
BK247	BC126	$4.80	**blue,** 15 #3069 (32c Georgia O'Keeffe)	11.00
BK248	BC126	$4.80	**blue,** 15 #3070 (32c Tennessee)	11.00
BK249	BC126	$4.80	**blue,** 3 #3076a (32c Indian Dances)	11.00
BK250	BC126	$4.80	**blue,** 15 #3082 (32c James Dean)	13.50
BK251	BC126	$4.80	**blue,** 15 (#3083-3086) (32c Folk Heroes)	11.00
BK252	BC126	$4.80	**blue,** 15 #3087 (32c Olympic Centennial)	15.00
BK253	BC126	$4.80	**blue,** 15 #3088 (32c Iowa)	11.00
BK254	BC126	$9.60	**blue,** 30 #3090 (32c Rural Free Delivery)	22.50
BK255	BC126	$4.80	**blue,** 3 #3095a (32c Riverboats)	12.50
BK256	BC126	$4.80	**blue,** #3105a-3105o (32c Endangered Species)	11.00
BK257	BC126	$4.80	**blue,** 15 #3107 (32c Madonna Christmas)	11.00
BK258	BC126	$4.80	**blue,** 15 #3118 (32c Hanukkah)	11.00

The contents of #BK251 may vary.

See Nos. BK178A-BK178F, BK226A-BK226B, BK227, BK233A-BK233E, BK235-BK236, BK266-BK269, BK272-BK274, BK277-BK278.

3122a — A1951

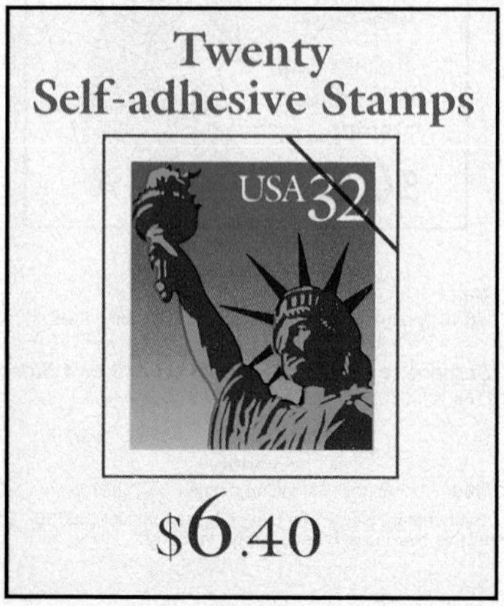

3122a — BC79A

1997

$6.40 fold-it-yourself booklet contains 20 self-adhesive 32c stamps

1997

Serpentine Die Cut 11

3122a	A1951	32c pane of 20 + label, *Feb. 1,* P#V1111, V1211, V1311, V2122, V2222, V2311, V2331, V3233, V3333, V3513, V4532	13.00

Variety

3122h	As "a," die cutting omitted	—

By its nature, No. 3122a is a complete booklet (BC79A). The peelable backing, of which two types are known, serves as a booklet cover.

3122b-3122d — A1951

3122b	A1951	32c pane of 4, *Feb. 1,* no P#	2.60
3122c	A1951	32c pane of 5 + label, *Feb. 1,* P#V1111	3.50

3122d A1951 32c pane of 6, *Feb. 1,* without P# 4.00

3122b-3122d — BC79B

1997

$4.80 fold-it-yourself booklet contains 15 self-adhesive 32c stamps
$9.60 fold-it-yourself booklet contains 30 self-adhesive 32c stamps

Combination Booklet

BK259 BC79B $4.80 **multicolored,** 1 ea #3122b-3122d, P#V1111 10.00

Booklet

BK260 BC79B $9.60 **multicolored,** 5 #3122d, P#V1111 19.00

The backing on Nos. BK259-BK260 is rouletted between each pane.

Variety

3122d pane of 6 containing P# single 6.00

The plate # single in No. 3122c is the lower left stamp and should be collected unused with the reorder label to its right to differentiate it from the plate # single in No. 3122d which is the lower left stamp in the bottom pane of the booklet and should be collected with a normal stamp adjoining it at right. In used condition, these plate # singles are indistinguishable.

Serpentine Die Cut 11.5x11.8 on 2, 3 or 4 Sides

3122Ef A1951 32c pane of 20 + label, P#V1111, V1211, V2122, V2222 40.00

By its nature, No. 3122Ef is a complete booklet (BC79A). The peelable backing serves as a booklet cover.

3122Eg A1951 32c pane of 6, *1997,* without plate # single 7.00

Booklet

BK260A BC79B $9.60 **multicolored,** 5 #3122Eg, P#V1111 42.50

Variety

3122Eg pane of 6 containing P# single 13.50

The plate # single in No. 3122Eg from No. BK260A is the lower left stamp in the bottom pane of the booklet.

3123a — A2415

3123a — BC137

1997

$6.40 fold-it-yourself booklet contains 20 self-adhesive 32c stamps

1997

Serpentine Die Cut 11.8x11.6 on 2, 3 or 4 Sides

3123a A2415 32c pane of 20 + label, *Feb. 4,* P#B1111, B2222, B3333, B4444, B5555, B6666, B7777 13.00

Varieties

3123c As "a," die cutting omitted *1,350.*
3123d As "a," black omitted *575.*

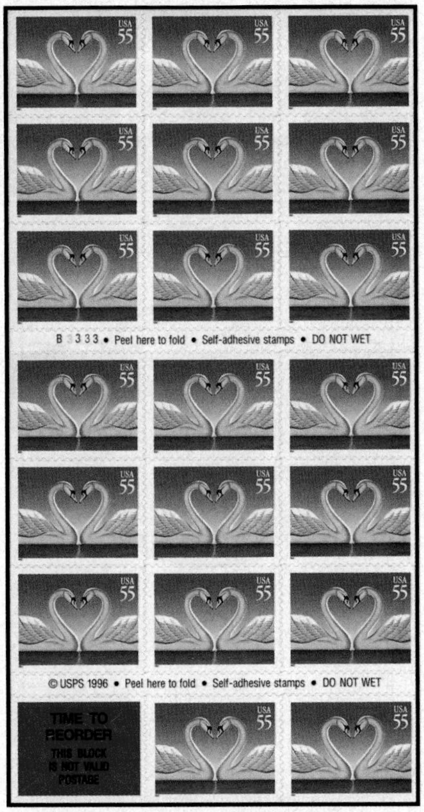

3124a — A2416

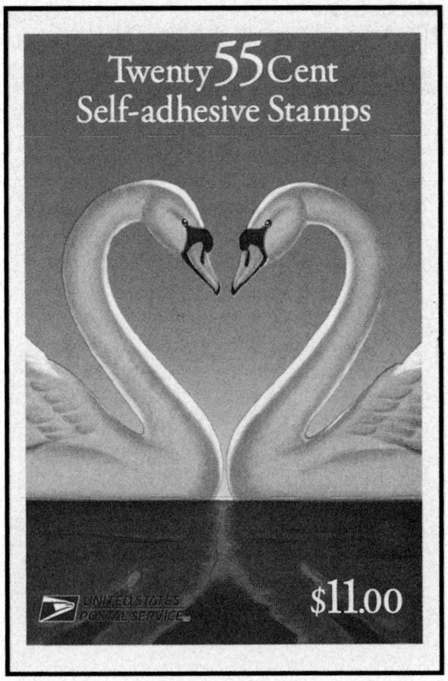

3124a — BC137A

1997

$11 fold-it-yourself booklet contains 20 self-adhesive 55c stamps

Serpentine Die Cut 11.6x11.8 on 2, 3 or 4 Sides

3124a A2416 55c pane of 20 + label, *Feb. 4,* P#B1111, B2222, B3333, B4444 22.00

By their nature, Nos. 3123a-3124a are complete booklets (BC137 and BC137A). The peelable backing serves as a booklet cover.

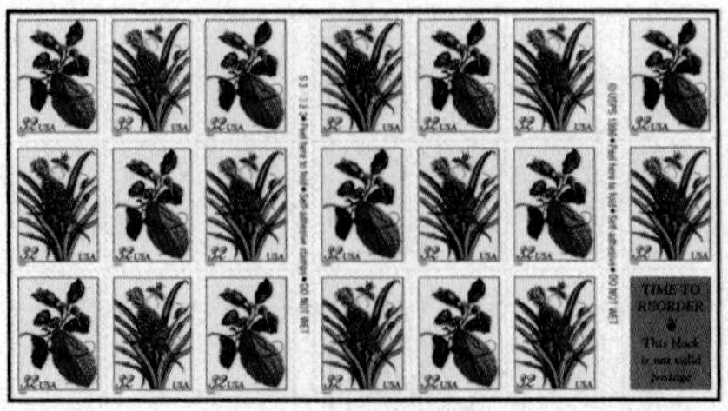

3127a — A2418-A2419

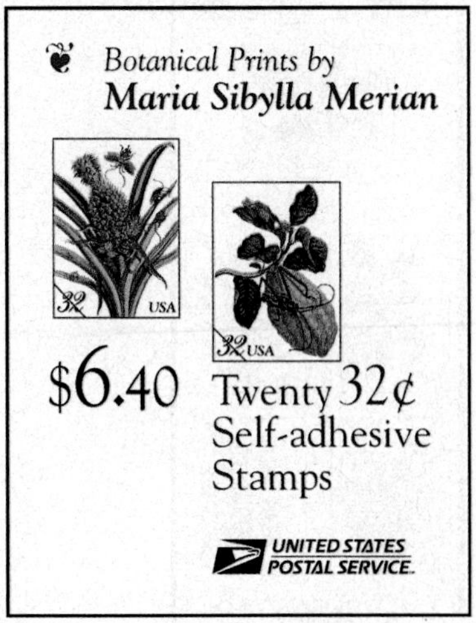

3127a BC138

1997

$6.40 fold-it-yourself booklet contains 20 32c stamps

Serpentine Die Cut 10.9x10.2 on 2, 3 or 4 Sides

1997

3127a A2418 32c pane of 20 + label, 10 ea #3126-3127, *Mar. 3,* P#S11111, S22222, S33333 13.00

By its nature, No. 3127a is a complete booklet (BC138). The peelable backing serves as a booklet cover.

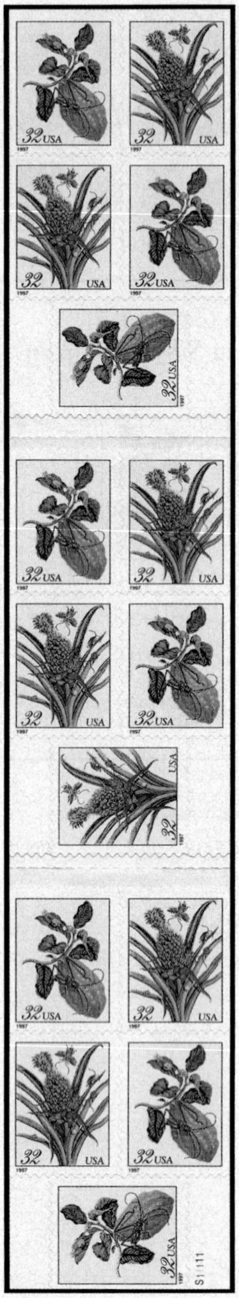

3128b, 3129b — A2418-A2419

3128b	A2418	32c pane of 5, 2 ea #3128-3129, 1 #3128a, *Mar. 3,* no P# or P#S11111	7.00
3129b	A2419	32c pane of 5, 2 ea #3128-3129, 1 #3129a, *Mar. 3,* no P#	9.00

3128b, 3129b — BCA138

1997

$4.80 booklet contains 15 32c stamps

Combination Booklet

BK261	BC138A $4.80	2 #3128b, 1 #3129b, P#S11111	25.00

In No. BK261, No. 3128b at top has no plate #, while the No. 3128b at bottom has a plate # in the selvage.

3176a — A2459

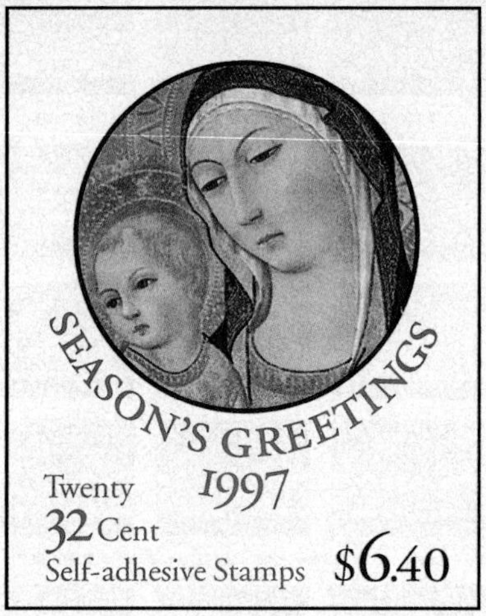

3176a — BC140

1997

$6.40 fold-it-yourself booklet contains 20 self-adhesive 32c stamps

Serpentine Die Cut 9.9 on 2, 3 or 4 Sides

1997, Oct. 27 **Tagged**

3176a	A2459	32c pane of 20 + label, P#1111, 2222, 3333	13.00

By its nature, No. 3176a is a complete booklet (BC140). The peelable backing serves as a booklet cover.

3177a — A2460

3177a BC141

1997

$6.40 fold-it-yourself booklet contains 20 self-adhesive 32c stamps

Serpentine Die Cut 11.2x11.6 on 2, 3 or 4 Sides

1997, Oct. 30 **Tagged**

Self-Adhesive

3177a	A2460	32c pane of 20 + label, P#B1111, B2222, B3333	13.00

By its nature No. 3177a is a complete booklet (BC141). The peelable backing serves as a booklet cover.

3177b-3177d — A2460

3177b A2460 32c Booklet pane of 4, no P# 2.60
3177c A2460 32c Booklet pane of 5 + label, no P# 3.25
3177d A2460 32c Booklet pane of 6, no P# or P#B1111 3.90

3177b-3177d — BC141A

1997

$4.80 booklet contains 15 self-adhesive 32c stamps

$9.60 booklet contains 30 self-adhesive 32c stamps

Combination Booklet

BK264 BC141A $4.80 **black & green,** 1 ea #3177b-3177d, P#B1111 9.75

Booklet

BK265 BC141A $9.60 **black & green,** 5 #3177d, P#B1111 20.00

Panes in Nos. BK264-BK265 are separated by rouletting between each pane.

MAKESHIFT VENDING MACHINE BOOKLETS

See note before No. BK243.

1997

BK266 BC126 $4.80 #3151a-3151o (32c Dolls) 9.00
BK267 BC126 $4.80 15 #3152 (32c Humphrey Bogart) 9.00
BK268 BC126 $4.80 15 #3153 (32c Stars & Stripes) 9.00
BK269 BC126 $4.80 3 ea #3168-3172 (32c Movie Monsters) 9.00

3244a — A2524

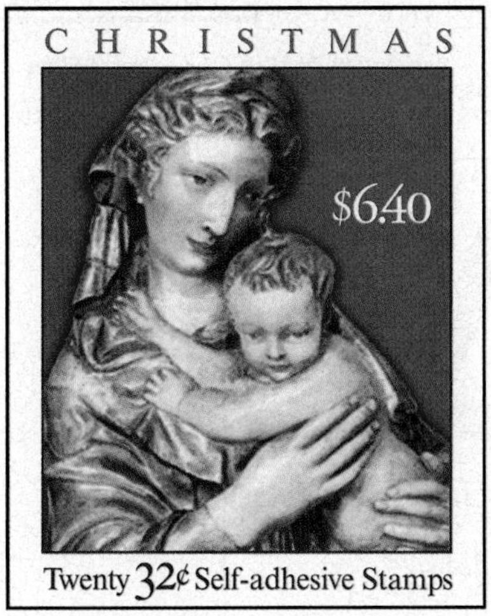

3244a — BC142

1998

$6.40 fold-it-yourself booklet contains 20 self-adhesive 32c stamps

Serpentine Die Cut 10.1x9.9 on 2, 3 or 4 Sides

1998, Oct. 15 **Tagged**

3244a A2524 32c pane of 20 + label, P#11111, 22222, 33333 13.00

No. 3244a is a complete booklet (BC142). The peelable backing serves as a booklet cover.

3248a-3248c — A2525-A2528

Serpentine Die Cut 11.3x11.6 on 2, or 3 Sides

1998, Oct. 15 **Tagged**

3248a A2525 32c pane of 4, #3245-3248, no P# 25.00
3248b A2525 32c pane of 5, #3245-3246, 3248, 2 #3247 + label, no P# 32.50
3248c A2525 32c pane of 6, #3247-3248, 2 each #3245-3246, P#B111111 40.00

3248a-3248c — BC143

1998

$4.80 booklet contains 15 self-adhesive 32c stamps

Combination Booklet

BK270 BC143 $4.80 **multi,** 1 each #3248a-3248c, P#B111111 100.00

Varieties

3248d	A2525	32c As "a," imperf	—
3248e	A2525	32c As "b," imperf	—
3248f	A2525	32c As "c," imperf	—

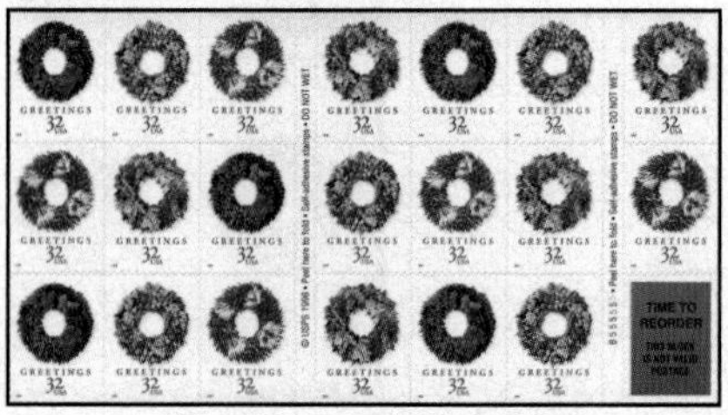

3252c, 3252e — A2525-A2528

3252c, 3252e — BC143A

1998

$6.40 fold-it-yourself booklet contains 20 self-adhesive 32c stamps

Serpentine Die Cut 11.4x11.5 on 2, 3 or 4 Sides

3252c A2525 32c pane of 20, 5 each #3249-3252 + label, P#B222222, B333333, B444444, B555555 35.00

Serpentine Die Cut 11.7x11.6 on 2, 3 or 4 Sides

3252e A2525 32c pane of 20, 5 each #3249a-3252a + label, P#B111111, B222222 35.00

Nos. 3252c and 3252e are complete booklets (BC143A). The peelable backing serves as a booklet cover.

3267a — A2531

Serpentine Die Cut 9.9 on 2 or 3 Sides

1998, Nov. 9

3267a A2531 (33c) pane of 10 7.50

3267a, 3268a — BC144

1998

($6.60) booklet contains 20 self-adhesive (33c) stamps

($3.30) fold-it-yourself booklet (#3268a) contains 10 self-adhesive (33c) stamps

Booklet

BK271 BC144 ($6.60) **multi,** 2 #3267a, P#1111, 2222, 3333 15.00

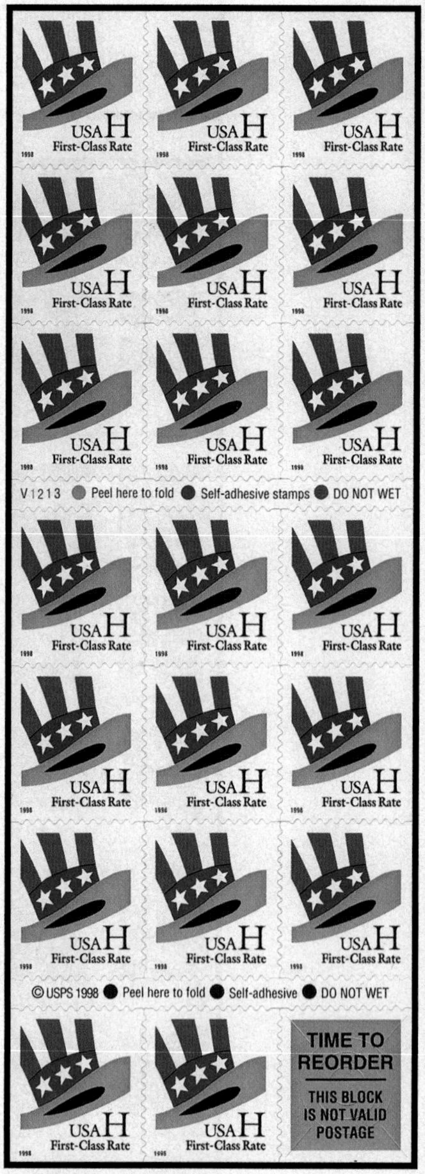

3268c — A2531

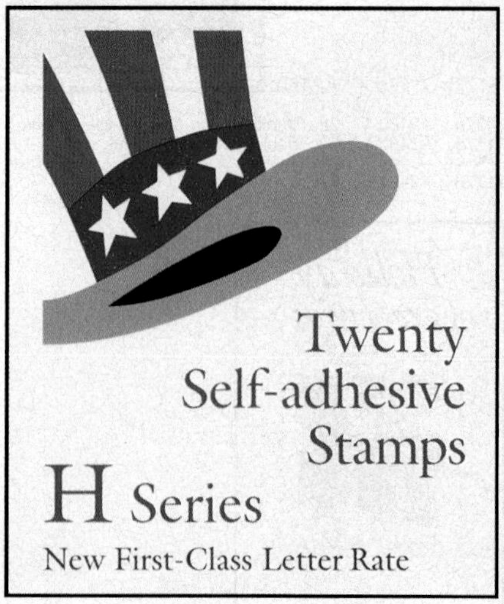

3268c — BC144A

1998

($6.60) fold-it-yourself booklet contains 20 self-adhesive (33c) stamps

Die cut 11¼ on 3 sides (No. 3268a), 11 on 2, 3 or 4 Sides (No. 3268c)

3268a	A2531	(33c) pane of 10, P#V1111, V1211, V2211, V2222	7.50
3268c	A2531	(33c) pane of 20 + label, P#V1111, V1112, V1113, V1213, V1222, V2113, V2122, V2213, V2223	15.00
		P# V1122, V2222	21.00

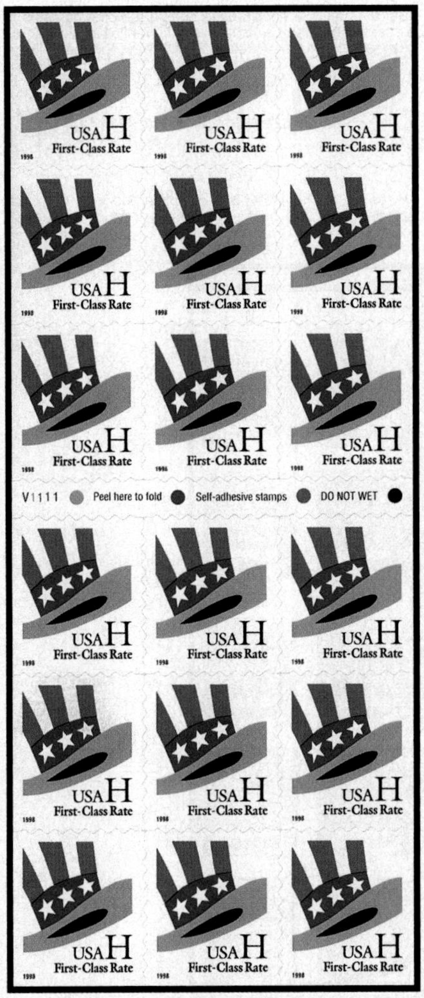

3269a — A2531

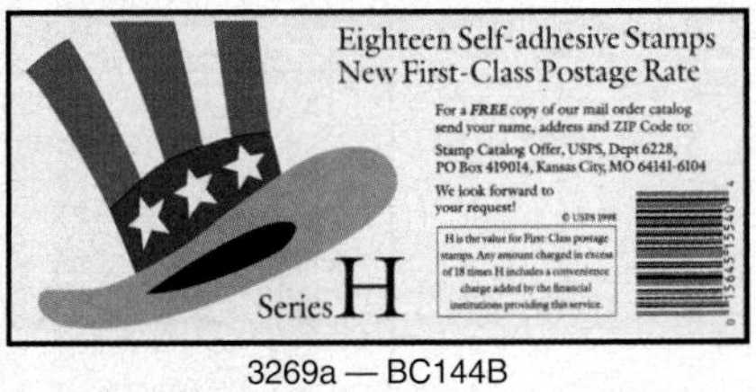

3269a — BC144B

1998

($5.94) fold-it-yourself booklet contains 18 self-adhesive (33c) stamps

Die Cut 8

3269a	A2531	(33c) pane of 18, P#V1111	12.00

Nos. 3268a, 3268c, 3269a are complete booklets (BC144, BC144A, BC144B). The peelable backing serves as a booket cover.

MAKESHIFT VENDING MACHINE BOOKLETS

See note before No. BK243.

1998

BK272	BC126	$4.80	15 (#3222-3225) (32c Tropical Birds)	9.00
BK273	BC126	$4.80	15 #3237 (32c Ballet)	9.00
BK274	BC126	$4.80	3 #3242a (32c Space Discovery)	9.00

Configuration of stamps in #BK272 may vary.

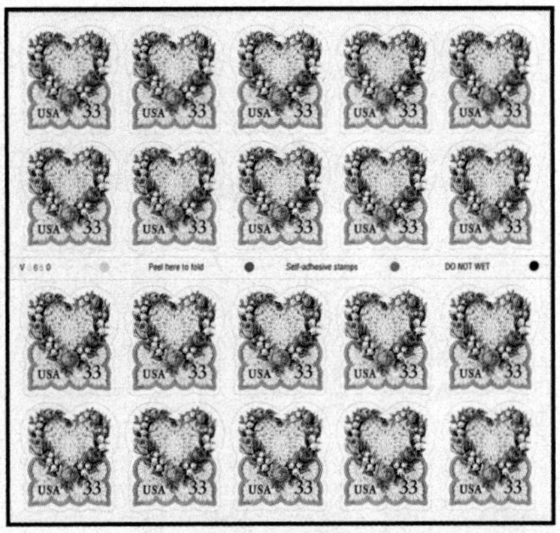

3274a — A2537

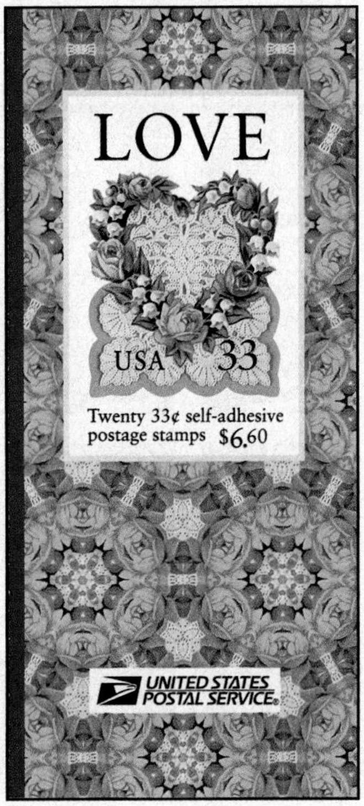

3274a
BC145

1999

$6.60 Fold-it-yourself booklet contains 20 self-adhesive 33c stamps

Tagged ***Die Cut***

3274a	A2537	33c pane of 20, *Jan. 28, 1999*	13.00

No. 3274a is a complete booklet (BC145). The peelable backing serves as a booklet cover.

Below is a list of known plate numbers. Some numbers may be scarcer than the value indicated in the listing.

P#V1111, V1112, V1117, V1118, V1211, V1212, V1213, V1233, V1313, V1314, V1333, V1334, V1335, V2123, V2221, V2222, V2223, V2424, V2425, V2426, V2324, V3123, V3124, V3125, V3133, V3134, V3323, V3327, V3333, V3334, V3336, V4549, V5650.

Variety

3274c	As "a," die cutting omitted	*1,800.*

3278a-3278c — A2540

Serpentine Die Cut 11 on 2, 3 or 4 Sides

1999 **Tagged**

Self-Adhesive

3278a	A2540	33c pane of 4, no P#	2.60
3278b	A2540	33c pane of 5 + label, P#V1111, V1112, V1121, V1122, V1212, V2212	3.25
3278c	A2540	33c pane of 6, no P#	3.90

3278a-3278c — BC146

1999

$4.95 booklet contains 15 self-adhesive 33c stamps

COMBINATION BOOKLET

BK275 BC146 $4.95 **multi,** 1 each #3278a-3278c, P#V1111, V1112, V1121, V1122, V1212, V2212 10.00

The plate # single in No. 3278b from No. BK275 is the lower left stamp.

3278d, 3278j — A2540

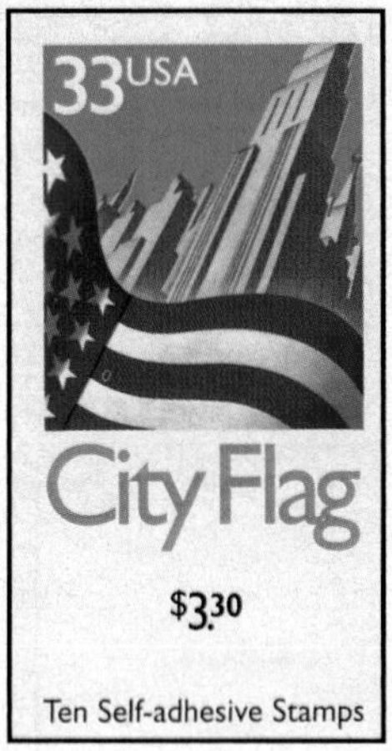

3278d — BC146A

1999

$3.30 Fold-it-yourself booklet contains 10 self-adhesive 33c stamps

3278d A2540 33c pane of 10, P#V1112, V1113, V2322, V2324, V3433, V3434, V3545 12.50
P#V1111 —

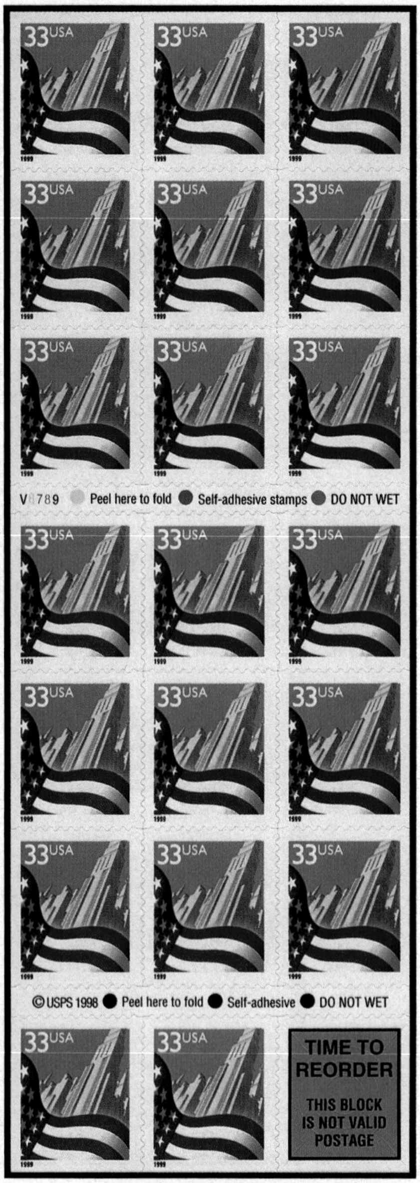

3278e, 3278Fg — A2540

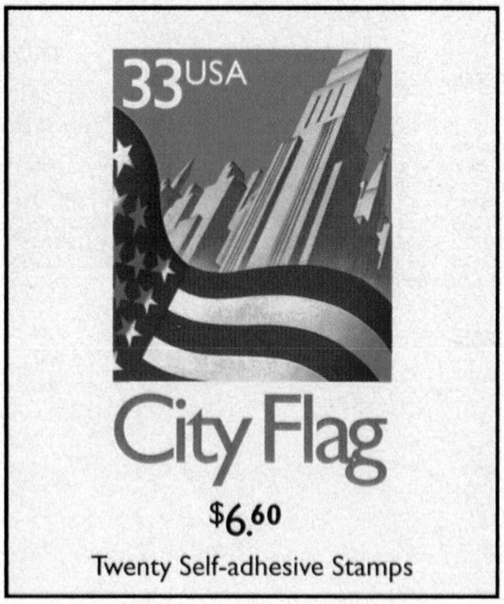

3278e, 3278Fg — BC146B

1999

$6.60 Fold-it-yourself booklet contains 20 self-adhesive 33c stamps

3278e A2540 33c pane of 20 + label, P#V1111, V1211, V2122, V2222, V2223, V3333, V4444 17.00
P#V8789 —

Nos. 3278d-3278e are complete booklets (BC146A, BC146B). The peelable backing serves as a booklet cover.

Serpentine Die Cut 11½x11¾ on 2, 3 or 4 Sides

3278Fg A2540 33c pane of 20 + label 22.50

No. 3278Fg is a complete booklet. The peelable backing serves as a booklet cover and is similar to BC146B.

Below is a list of known plate numbers. Some numbers may be scarcer than the value indicated in the listing.

P# V1111, V1131, V2222, V2223, V2227, V2243, V2323, V2423, V2443, V3333, V4444, V5428, V5445, V5446, V5576, V5578, V6423, V6456, V6546, V6556, V6575, V6576, V7567, V7663, V7667, V7676, V8789.

Serpentine Die Cut 11¼

3278j A2540 33c pane of 10, P#V1111, V2222 14.00
P#V1112, V1113, V2322 —

By its nature No. 3278j is a complete booklet. The peelable backing serves as a booklet cover and is similar to BC146A.

3279a — A2540

Serpentine Die Cut 9.8 on 2 or 3 Sides

3279a A2540 33c pane of 10 8.50

3279a — BC146C

1999

$6.60 Booklet contains 20 self-adhesive 33c stamps

BOOKLET

BK276 BC146C $6.60 **multi,** 2 #3279a, P#1111, 1121 17.00

Variety

3278h As "e," die cutting omitted —

3283a — A2541

3283a — BC147

1999

$5.94 fold-it-yourself booklet contains 18 self-adhesive 33c stamps

Serpentine Die Cut 7.9 on 2, 3 or 4 Sides

Tagged

3283a A2541 33c pane of 18, P#V1111 12.00

No. 3283a is a complete booklet (BC147). The peelable backing serves as a booklet cover.

3297b — A2550-A2553

3297b
BC148

1999

$6.60 fold-it-yourself booklet contains 20 self-adhesive 33c stamps + label

Serpentine Die Cut 11¼x11½ on 2, 3 or 4 Sides

1999-2000 **Tagged**

Self-Adhesive

3297b A2550 33c pane of 20, 5 ea #3294-3297 + label 15.00

No. 3297b is a complete booklet (BC148). The peelable backing serves as a booklet cover.

P#B1111, B1112, B2211, B2222, B3331, B3332, B3333, B4444, B5555.

3297d, BC148A — A2550-A2553

Serpentine Die Cut 11¼x11½ on 2 or 3 Sides

3297d A2550 33c pane of 20, 5 #3297e + label, *Mar. 15, 2000,* P#B1111 20.00

By its nature, No. 3297d is a double-sided complete booklet. Eight stamps and the booklet cover (BC148A) plus P# are printed on one side of the peelable backing and 12 stamps are printed on the other side of the backing.

3301a-3301c — A2550-A2553

Serpentine Die Cut 9½x10 on 2 or 3 sides

3301a	A2550	33c pane of 4, no P#	3.60
3301b	A2550	33c pane of 5 + label, no P#	4.50
3301c	A2550	33c pane of 6, P#B1111, B1112, B2212, B2222	5.50
		P#B2221	—

3301a-3301c — BC148B

1999

$4.95 booklet contains 15 self-adhesive 33c stamps + label

COMBINATION BOOKLET

BK276A BC148B $4.95 **multicolored,** 1 each #3301a-3301c, P# see 3301c 14.00

3313b, BC149 — A2556-A2559

Serpentine Die Cut 10.9 on 2 or 3 Sides

1999 **Tagged**

3313b	A2556	33c pane of 20, all P# (see below) except P#S22444	13.00
		P#S22444	—

By its nature, No. 3313b is a complete booklet. Eight stamps and the booklet cover (BC149) plus P# are printed on one side of the peelable backing and 12 stamps are printed on the other side of the backing.

P#S11111, S22222, S22244, S22344, S22444, S22452, S22462, S23222, S24222, S24224, S24242, S24244, S24422, S24442, S24444, S26462, S32323, S32333, S32444, S33333, S44444, S45552, S46654, S55452, S55552, S56462, S62544, S62562, S64452, S64544, S65544, S65552, S66462, S66544, S66552, S66562, S66652.

3355a, BC150 — A2599

1999, Oct. 20 ***Serpentine Die Cut 11¼***

Self-Adhesive

3355a	A2599	33c pane of 20, P#B1111, B2222, B3333	20.00

No. 3355a is a complete booklet. Eight stamps and the booklet cover (BC150) plus P# are printed on one side of the peelable backing and 12 stamps are printed on the other side of the backing.

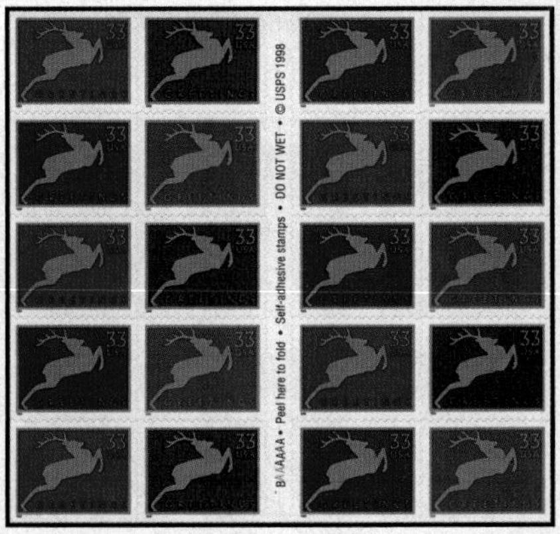

3363a — A2600

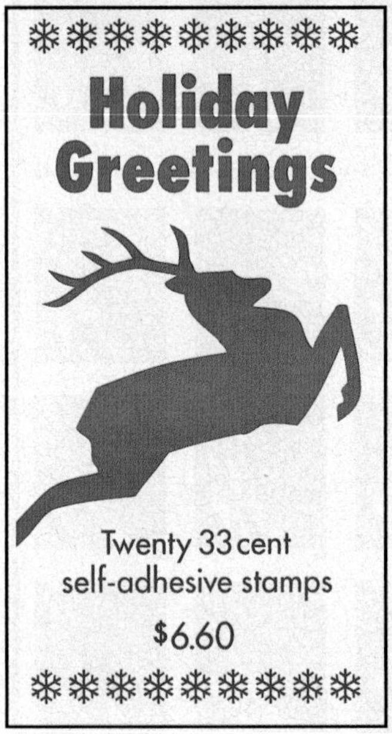

3363a
BC151

1999

$6.60 fold-it-yourself booklet contains 20 self-adhesive 33c stamps

1999, Oct. 20 ***Serpentine Die Cut 11¼***

Self-Adhesive

3363a	A2600	33c pane of 20, P#B111111, B222222, B333333, B444444, B555555, B666666, B777777, B888888, B999999, B000000, BAAAAAA, BBBBBBB	30.00

No. 3363a is a complete booklet (BC151). The peelable backing serves as a booklet cover.

Variety

3363d	As "a," die cutting omitted	—

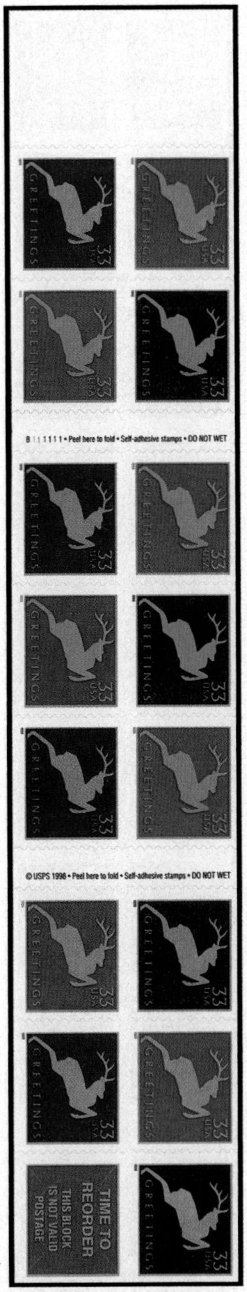

3367a-3367c — A2600

Serpentine Die Cut 11½x11¼ on 2 or 3 sides

Stamp Size: 21x19mm

3367a	A2600	33c pane of 4, no P#	8.00
3367b	A2600	33c pane of 5 + label, no P#	10.00
3367c	A2600	33c pane of 6, P#B111111, B222222	12.00

Fifteen 33 cent self-adhesive stamps

3367a-3367c — BC152

1999

$4.95 fold-it-yourself booklet contains 15 self-adhesive 33c stamps

COMBINATION BOOKLET

BK276B	BC152	$4.95	**green & gold,** 1 each #3367a-3367c, P# see 3367c	30.00

MAKESHIFT VENDING MACHINE BOOKLETS

See note before No. BK243.

1999

BK277	BC126	$4.95	4 each #3325, 3327-3328, 3 #3326 (33c American Glass)	11.00
BK278	BC126	$4.95	3 each #3333-3337 (33c Famous Trains)	11.00

3377a — A2604-A2608

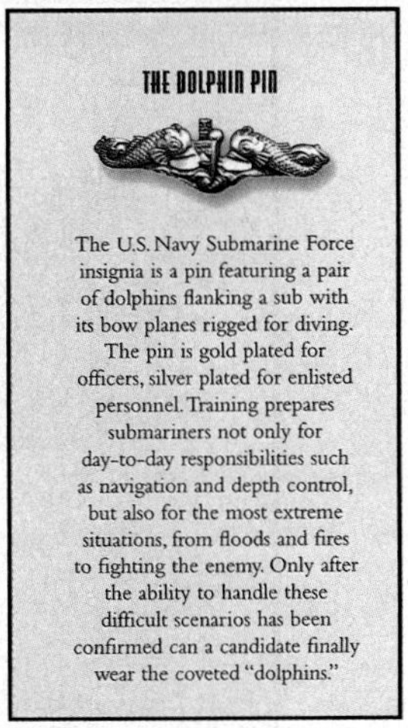
THE DOLPHIN PIN
The U.S. Navy Submarine Force insignia is a pin featuring a pair of dolphins flanking a sub with its bow planes rigged for diving. The pin is gold plated for officers, silver plated for enlisted personnel. Training prepares submariners not only for day-to-day responsibilities such as navigation and depth control, but also for the most extreme situations, from floods and fires to fighting the enemy. Only after the ability to handle these difficult scenarios has been confirmed can a candidate finally wear the coveted "dolphins."

Selvage 1

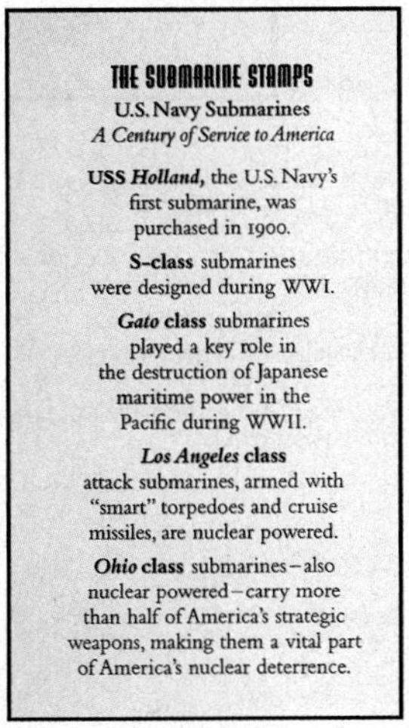

THE SUBMARINE STAMPS

A Century of Service to America
USS Holland, the U.S. Navy's first submarine, was purchased in 1900.
S-class submarines were designed during WWI.
Gato class submarines played a key role in the destruction of Japanese maritime power in the Pacific during WWII.
Los Angeles class attack submarines, armed with "smart" torpedoes and cruise missiles, are nuclear powered.
Ohio class submarines–also nuclear powered–carry more than half of America's strategic weapons, making them a vital part of America's nuclear deterrence.

Selvage 2

2000, Mar. 27 ***Perf. 11***

3377a	pane of 5 with selvage 1	25.00	—
	With selvage 2	25.00	—

A CENTURY OF SERVICE TO AMERICA

3377a — BC153

2000

$9.80 booklet contains 2 panes of one 22c, 33c, 55c, 60c and $3.20 stamps and 6 leaves of text.

Booklet

BK279	BC153	$9.80	**multicolored,** no P#	50.00

No. BK279 contains one pane with selvage 1 and one pane with selvage 2.

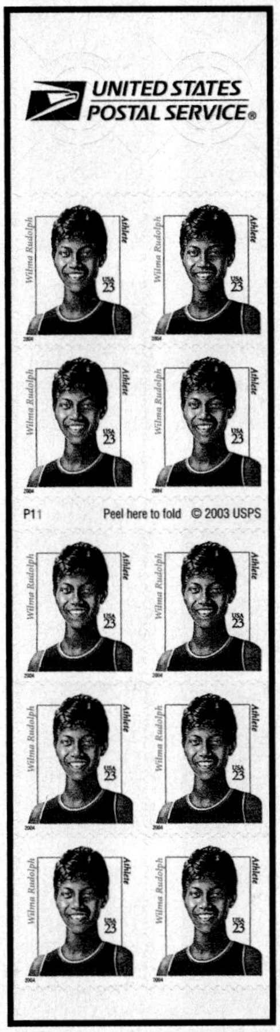

3436a, 3436b, 3436c — A2652

Serpentine Die Cut 11¼x10¾ on 3 Sides

2004, July 14 **Litho.**

Self-Adhesive

3436a	A2652	23c pane of 4, no P#	1.80
3436b	A2652	23c pane of 6, no P#	2.70
3436c	A2652	23c pane of 10, P#P11	4.50

3436a, 3436b, 3436c — BC153A

2004

$2.30 booklet contains 10 self-adhesive 23c stamps
$2.30 fold-it-yourself booklet contains 10 self-adhesive 23c stamps

COMBINATION BOOKLET

BK279A	BC153A	$2.30	**multi,** #3436a-3436b, no P#	4.50

By its nature, No. 3436c is a complete booklet (BC153A). The peelable backing serves as a booklet cover. No. BK279A lacks the self-adhesive panel that covers the rouletting. The backing on No. 3436b has a different product code (672900) than that found on the lower portion of No. 3436c (673000).

Variety

3436d A2652 23c As "c," die cutting omitted —

3450a — A2678

3450a BC154

2000

$6.12 fold-it-yourself booklet contains 18 self-adhesive (34c) stamps

2000 ***Serpentine Die Cut 8 on 2, 3 or 4 Sides***

Self-Adhesive

3450a A2678 (34c) pane of 18, P#V1111, *Dec. 15* 16.00

No. 3450a is a complete booklet (BC154). The peelable backing serves as a booklet cover.

3451a — A2679

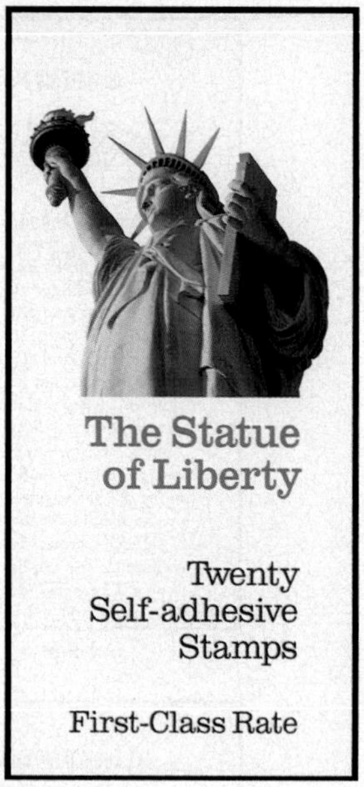

3451a — BC155

2000

$6.80 fold-it-yourself booklet contains 20 self-adhesive (34c) stamps

Serpentine Die Cut 11 on 2, 3 or 4 Sides

2000, Dec. 15

Self-Adhesive

3451a A2679 (34c) pane of 20, P#V1111, V2222 14.00

No. 3451a is a complete booklet (BC155). The peelable backing serves as a booklet cover.

3451b-3451c — A2679

3451b A2679 (34c) pane of 4, without plate # 2.80
3451c A2679 (34c) pane of 6, no P# 5.25

3451b, 3451c — BC156

2000

$6.80 booklet contains 20 self-adhesive (34c) stamps

COMBINATION BOOKLET

BK280 BC156 ($6.80) **multicolored,** 1 #3451b without P#, 1 #3451b with P#V1111 or V2222, 2 #3451c 17.50

P# on No. 3451b is on the lower right stamp of the right pane of 4 of the booklet.

Varieties

3451b pane of 4, containing P# single 3.10

3451d As "a," die cutting omitted —

3457b-3457d — A2681-A2684

Serpentine Die Cut 10½x10¾ on 2 or 3 Sides (#3454-3457), 11½x11¾ on 2 or 3 sides (#3458-3461)

2000

Self-Adhesive

3457b A2681 (34c) pane of 4, #3454-3457, *Dec. 15* 4.00

3457c A2681 (34c) pane of 6, #3456, 3457, 2 each #3454-3455, no P#, *Dec. 15* 6.00

3457d A2681 (34c) pane of 6, #3454, 3455, 2 each #3456-3457, no P#, *Dec. 15* 6.00

3457b-3457d — BC158

2000

$6.80 booklet contains 20 self-adhesive (34c) stamps

COMBINATION BOOKLET

BK281 BC158 ($6.80) **multicolored,** #3457c, 3457d, 2 #3457b, P#S1111 22.50

P# on No. BK281 is on the backing paper of the top pane of No. 3457b.

3457e, BC157 — A2681-A2684

3457e A2681 (34c) pane of 20, 5 each # 3454-3457, P#S1111, *Dec. 15* 20.00

No. 3457e is a complete booklet. Eight stamps and the booklet cover (BC157) are printed on one side of the peelable backing and 12 stamps plus P# are printed on the other side of the backing.

3461b A2681 pane of 20, 2 each #3461a, 3 each #3457a, #S1111, *Dec. 15* 36.50

3461c A2681 pane of 20, 2 each #3457a, 3 each #3461a, #S1111, *Dec. 15* 45.00

Nos. 3461b and 3461c are complete booklets. Two blocks of four with the same gauge die cutting and the booklet cover (BC157) are printed on one side of the peelable backing and three blocks of four with the other gauge die cutting plus P# are printed on the other side of the backing.

3482a, 3483c, 3483f — A2686

3482a, 3483c, 3483f — BC159

2001

$2 fold-it-yourself booklet contains 10 self-adhesive 20c stamps

$2 booklet contains 10 self-adhesive 20c stamps

Serpentine Die Cut 11¼x11 on 3 Sides

2001, Feb. 22

Self-Adhesive

3482a A2686 20c pane of 10, P#P1, P2, P3 4.00

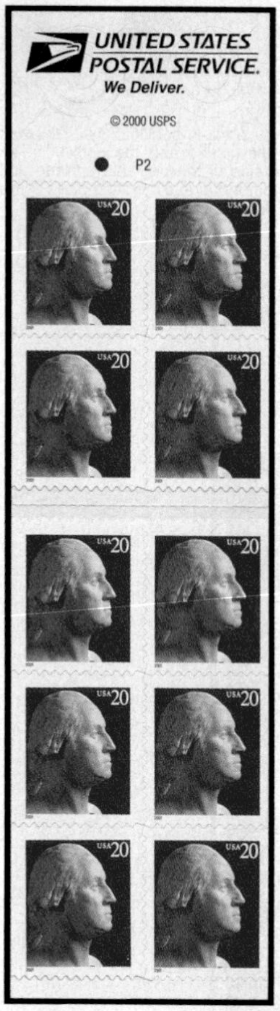

3482b, 3483c — A2686

3482b A2686 20c pane of 4, P#P1, P2, P3 1.80
3482c A2686 20c pane of 6, no P# 2.70

COMBINATION BOOKLET

BK281A BC159 $2 **multicolored,** #3482b-3482c, P#P1, P2, P3 4.50

No. BK281A has slightly smaller cover (BC159) than No. 3482a and lacks self-adhesive panel that covers the rouletting.

3483a A2686 20c pane of 4, 2 #3482 at L, 2 #3483 at R, P#P1, P2, P3 12.00
3483b A2686 20c pane of 6, 3 #3482 at L, 3 #3483 at R, no P# 20.00
3483c A2686 20c pane of 10, 5 #3482 at L, 5 #3483 at R, P#P1, P2, P3 25.00
3483d A2686 20c pane of 4, 2 #3483 at L, 2 #3282 at R, P#P1, P2, P3 12.00
3483e A2686 20c pane of 6, 3 #3483 at L, 3 #3282 at R, no P# 20.00
3483f A2686 20c pane of 10, 5 #3483 at L, 5 #3282 at R, P#P1, P2, P3 25.00

Nos. 3482a, 3483c and 3483f are complete booklets (BC159) and include a self-adhesive panel that covers the rouletting. The peelable backing, which is slightly longer than that on Nos. BK282 and BK282A, serves as a booklet cover.

COMBINATION BOOKLETS

BK282 BC159 $2 **multicolored,** #3483a-3483b, P#P1, P2, P3 32.50
BK282A BC159 $2 **multicolored,** #3483d-3483e, P#P1, P2, P3 32.50

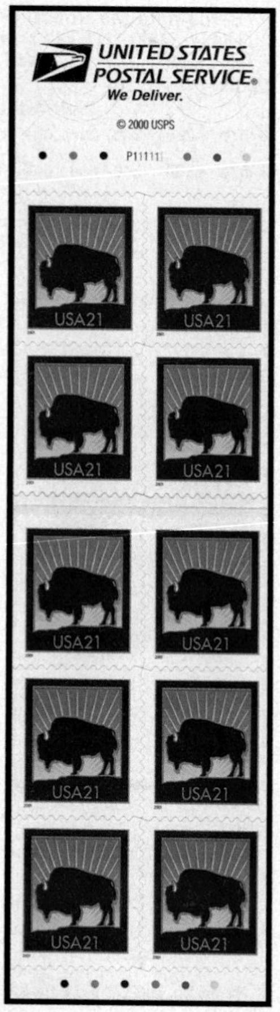

3484b, 3484c — A2687

3484d, 3484Ag, 3484Aj — BC159A

2001

$2.10 fold-it-yourself booklet contains 10 self-adhesive 21c stamps
$2.10 booklet contains 10 self-adhesive 21c stamps

Serpentine Die Cut 11¼ on 3 Sides

2001, Sept. 20

Self-Adhesive

3484b A2687 21c pane of 4, P#P111111, P333333, P444444 2.00
3484c A2687 21c pane of 6, no P# 3.00

COMBINATION BOOKLET

BK282B BC159A $2.10 **multi,** #3484b-3484c, P#P111111, P333333, P444444 5.00

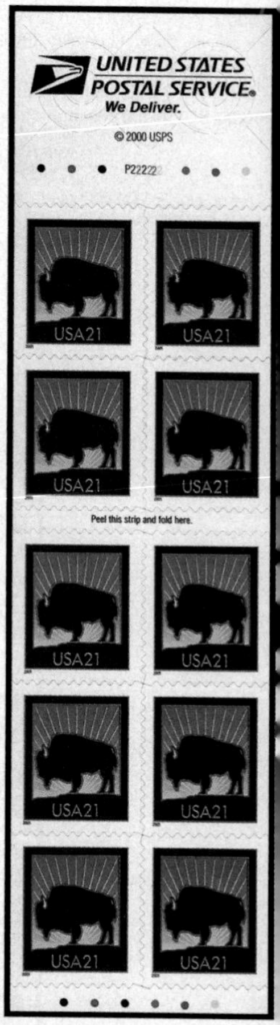

3484d, 3484Ag, 3484Aj — A2687

3484d A2687 21c pane of 10, P#P111111, P222222, P333333, P444444, P555555 5.00

Serpentine Die Cut 10½x11¼ on 3 Sides

3484Ae A2687 21c pane of 4, 2 #3484 at L, 2# 3484A at R, P#P111111, P333333, P444444 12.00
3484Af A2687 21c pane of 6, 3 #3484 at L, 3# 3484A at R, no P# 20.00
3484Ag A2687 21c pane of 10, 5 #3484 at L, 5# 3484A at R, P#P111111, P222222, P333333, P444444, P555555 25.00
3484Ah A2687 21c pane of 4, 2 #3484A at L, 2# 3484 at R, P#P111111, P333333, P444444 12.00
3484Ai A2687 21c pane of 6, 3 #3484A at L, 3# 3484 at R, no P# 20.00
3484Aj A2687 21c pane of 10, 5 #3484A at L, 5# 3484 at R, P#P111111, P222222, P333333, P444444, P555555 25.00

COMBINATION BOOKLETS

BK282C BC159A $2.10 **multi,** #3484Ae-3484Af, P#P111111, P333333, P444444 32.50
BK282D BC159A $2.10 **multi,** #3484Ah-3484Ai, P#P111111, P333333, P444444 32.50

Nos. 3484d, 3484Ag and 3484Aj are complete booklets (BC159A). The peelable backing serves as a booklet cover. Nos. BK282B-BK282D lack self-adhesive panel that covers the rouletting. Nos. BK282B-BK282D have a small 662900 UPC code on cover back, while Nos. 3484d, 3484Ag and 3484Aj have a large 662800 UPC code on cover back.

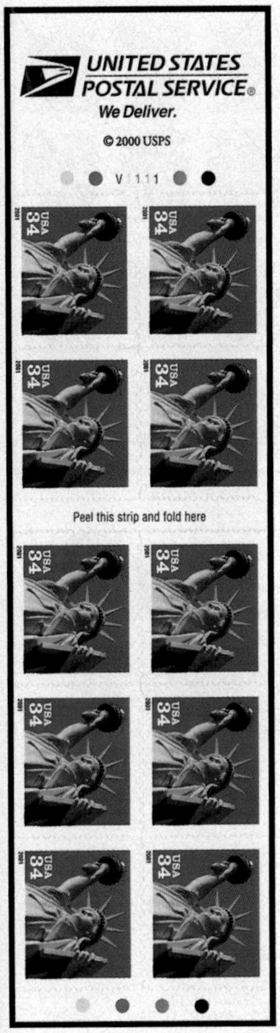

3485a — A2689

3485a — BC160

2001

$3.40 fold-it-yourself booklet contains 10 self-adhesive 34c stamps

2001, Feb. 7 ***Serpentine Die Cut 11 on 3 Sides***
Self-Adhesive

3485a A2689 34c pane of 10, P#V1111, V1221 7.00

3485b — A2689

3485b — BC160B

2001

$6.80 fold-it-yourself booklet contains 20 self-adhesive 34c stamps

3485b A2689 34c pane of 20, P#V1111, V1211, V1221, V2111, V2112, V2121, V2122, V2212, V2222 14.00

Nos. 3485a-3485b are complete booklets (BC160 and BC160B). The peelable backing serves as a booklet cover.

3485c, 3485d — A2689

3485c	A2689	34c pane of 4, without P#		3.00
3485d	A2689	34c pane of 6, no P#		4.50

3485c, 3485d — BC160A

OOKLET

olored, 1 #3485c with P#, 1 #3485c without P#, 2 3485d, P#V1111, V1122, V2212, V2222 15.00

P#V1112, V1121 —

P# on No. 3485c is on the lower right stamp of the right pane of 4 of No. BK283.

Varieties

3485c Pane of 4 containing P#V1111, V1122, V2212, V2222 4.00

Pane of 4 containing P#V1112, V1121 —

3485f As "b," die cutting omitted —

3490b, 3490c, 3490d — A2690-A2693

Serpentine Die Cut 10½x 10¾ on 2 or 3 Sides

2001, Feb. 7

Self-Adhesive

3490b 34c pane of 4 3.00

3490c 34c pane of 6, #3489-3490, 2 each #3487-3488 4.50

3490d 34c pane of 6, #3487-3488, 2 each #3489-3490 4.50

3490b, 3490c, 3490d — BC162

2001

$6.80 booklet contains 20 self-adhesive 34c stamps

COMBINATION BOOKLET

BK284 BC162 $6.80 **multicolored,** #3490c-3490d, 2 #3490b, P#S1111 15.00

P# on No. BK284 is on the backing paper of the bottom pane of No. 3490b.

3490e, BC161 — A2690-A2693

3490e 34c pane of 20, 5 #3490a, P#S1111, S2222 15.00

No. 3490e is a complete booklet with 12 stamps plus P# on one side and eight stamps plus booklet cover (BC161) on the other side. The peelable backing serves as a booklet cover.

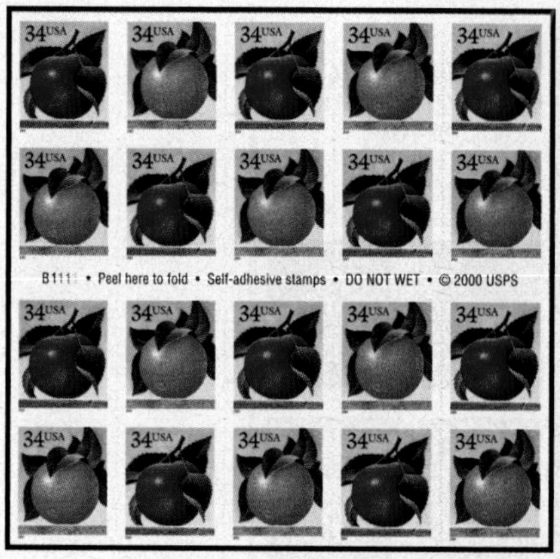

3492b — A2694-A2695

3492b — BC163

2001

$6.80 fold-it-yourself booklet contains 20 self-adhesive 34c stamps

Serpentine Die Cut 11¼ on 2, 3 or 4 sides

2001, Mar. 6

Self-Adhesive

3492b 34c pane of 20, 10 each #3491-3492, P# B1111, B2222, B3333, B4444, B5555, B6666, B7777 14.00

No. 3492b is a complete booklet (BC163). The peelable backing serves as a booklet cover.

Variety

3492e As "b," die cutting omitted —

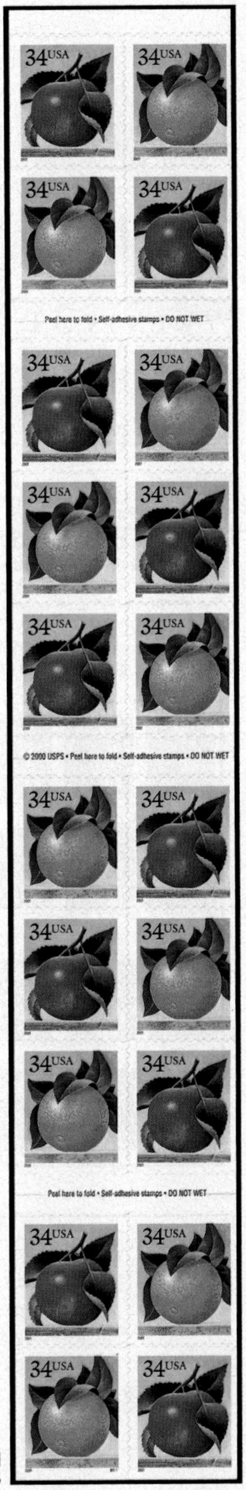

3494b, 3494c, 3494d — A2694-A2695

2001, May *Serpentine Die Cut 11½x10¾*

Self-Adhesive

3494b 34c pane of 4, 2 each #3493-3494, without P# 4.00
3494c 34c pane of 6, 3 each #3493-3494, #3493 at UL, no P# 6.00
3494d 34c pane of 6, 3 each #3493-3494, #3494 at UL, no P# 6.00

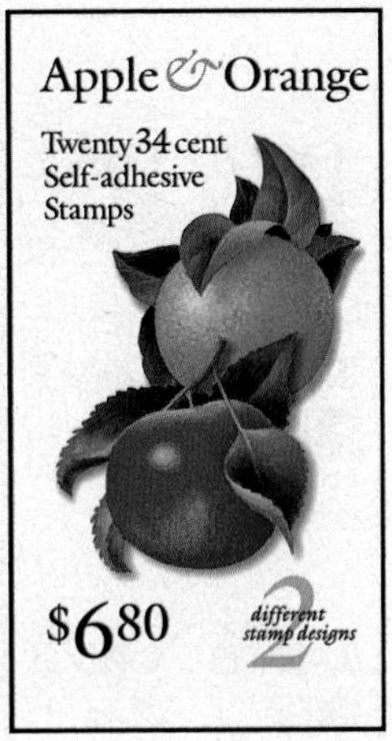

3494b, 3494c, 3494d — BC163A

2001

$6.80 booklet contains 20 self-adhesive 34c stamps

COMBINATION BOOKLET

BK284A BC163A $6.80 **multi,** #3494c, 3494d, 2 #3494b, P#B1111 22.00

P# on No. BK284A is on bottom left stamp in bottom pane of No. 3494b.

Variety

3494b Pane of 4 with P#B1111 6.00

3495a — A2688

3495a — BC163B

2001

$6.12 booklet contains 18 self-adhesive 34c stamps

Serpentine Die Cut 8 on 2, 3 or 4 Sides

2001, Dec. 17

Self-Adhesive

3495a 34c pane of 18, #V1111 16.50

Nos. 3495a is a complete booklet (BC163B). The peelable backing serves as a booklet cover.

3496a — A2699

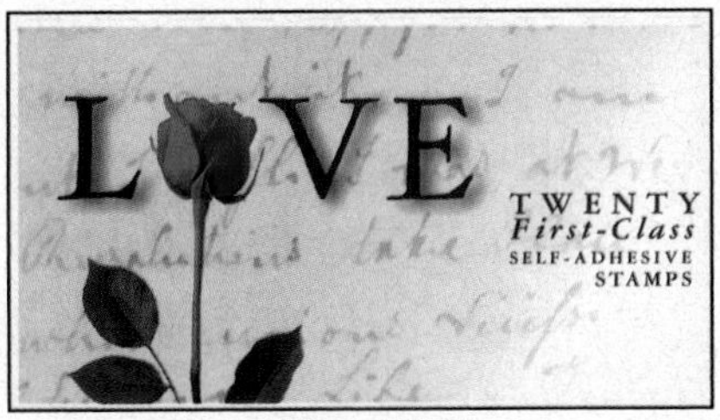

3496a — BC164

2001

$6.80 fold-it-yourself booklet contains 20 self-adhesive (34c) stamps

2001 *Serpentine Die Cut 11¼ on 2, 3, or 4 Sides*

Self-Adhesive

3496a A2699 (34c) pane of 20, P#B1111, B2222, *Jan. 19* 18.00

No. 3496a is a complete booklet (BC164). The peelable backing serves as a booklet cover.

3497a — A2700

3497a — BC165

2001

$6.80 fold-it-yourself booklet contains 20 self-adhesive 34c stamps

2001 ***Serpentine Die Cut 11¼ on 2, 3 or 4 Sides***

Self-Adhesive

3497a A2700 34c pane of 20, P#B1111, B2222, B3333, B4444, B5555, *Feb. 14* 18.00

No. 3497a is a complete booklet (BC165). The peelable backing serves as a booklet cover.

3498a, 3498b — A2700

Size: 18x21mm

Serpentine Die Cut 11½x10¾

3498a A2700 34c pane of 4, without P#, *Feb. 14* 4.00

3498b A2700 34c pane of 6, no P#, *Feb. 14* 6.00

3498a, 3498b — BC166

2001

$6.80 booklet contains 20 self-adhesive 34c stamps

COMBINATION BOOKLET

BK285 BC166 $6.80 **multicolored,** 2 each #3498a-3498b, P#B1111 22.50

P# on No. BK285 is on bottom left stamp in bottom pane of No. 3498a.

Variety

3498a pane of 4, containing P#B1111 6.00

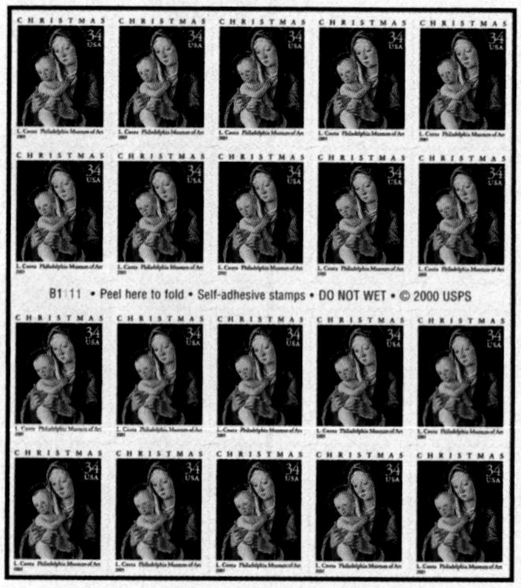

3536a — A2737

3536a — BC167

2001

$6.80 fold-it-yourself booklet contains 20 self-adhesive 34c stamps

Serpentine Die Cut 11½ on 2, 3 or 4 Sides

2001, Oct. 10

Self-Adhesive

3536a A2737 34c pane of 20, P#B1111 15.00

No. 3536a is a complete booklet (BC167). The peelable backing serves as a booklet cover.

3540d, 3540g, BC168 — A2738-A2741

Serpentine Die Cut 10¾x11 on 2 or 3 Sides

3540d A2738 34c pane of 20, small date, 5 #3540c + label, P#S1111 15.00

3540g A2738 34c pane of 20, large date, 5 #3540f + label, P#S3333, S4444 40.00

Nos. 3540d and 3540g are complete booklets with 12 stamps plus P# on one side and eight stamps plus booklet cover (BC168) on the other side. The peelable backing serves as a booklet cover.

3544b, 3544c, 3544d — A2738-A2741

Green Denomination

Stamp Size: 21x18½mm

Serpentine Die Cut 11 on 2 or 3 sides

3544b A2738 34c pane of 4, #3541-3544 2.80

3544c A2738 34c pane of 6, #3543-3544, 2 #3541-3542 4.25

3544d A2738 34c pane of 6, #3541-3542, 2 #3543-3544 4.25

3544b, 3544c, 3544d — BC169

2001

$6.80 booklet contains 20 self-adhesive 34c stamps

COMBINATION BOOKLET

BK286 BC169 $6.80 **multi,** #3544c-3544d, 2 #3544b, P#V1111 14.00

P# on No. BK286 is on the backing paper of the bottom pane of No. 3544b.

3549a — A2744

3549a — BC170

2001

$6.80 booklet contains 20 self-adhesive 34c stamps

Serpentine Die Cut 11¼ on 2, 3 or 4 Sides

2001, Oct. 24

Self-Adhesive

3549a A2744 34c Pane of 20, P#B1111, B2222, B3333, B4444 15.00

No. 3549a is a complete booklet (BC170). The peelable backing serves as a booklet cover.

3549Bc, 3549Bd — A2744

Serpentine Die Cut 10½x10¾ on 2 or 3 Sides

2002, Jan.

Self-Adhesive

3549Bc A2744 34c pane of 4		3.60
3549Bd A2744 34c pane of 6		5.40

3549Bc, 3549Bd — BC171

2002

$6.80 booklet contains 20 self-adhesive 34c stamps

COMBINATION BOOKLET

BK287 BC171 $6.80 **multi,** 2 each #3549Bc, 3549Bd, P#S1111		18.00

P# on No. BK287 is on the backing paper of the lower example of No. 3549Bd.

3549Be, BC172 — A2744

3549Be A2744 34c pane of 20, P#S1111		18.00

No. 3549Be is a complete booklet with 12 stamps plus P# on one side and eight stamps plus booklet cover (BC172) on the other side. The peelable backing serves as a booklet cover.

Washington Type of 2002

3618a, 3618b — A2686

Serpentine Die Cut 11¼x11 on 3 Sides

2002, June 7

Self-Adhesive

3618a A2686 23c pane of 4, P#P1, P2, P4		1.80
3618b A2686 23c pane of 6, no P#		2.70

3618c, 3619e, 3619f — BC173

2002

$2.30 booklet contains 10 self-adhesive 23c stamps

COMBINATION BOOKLET

BK288 BC173 $2.30 **multi,** #3618a-3618b, P#P1, P2, P4 4.50

No. BK288 has a 671800 UPC code on cover back, while No. 3618c has a 671000 UPC code on cover back.

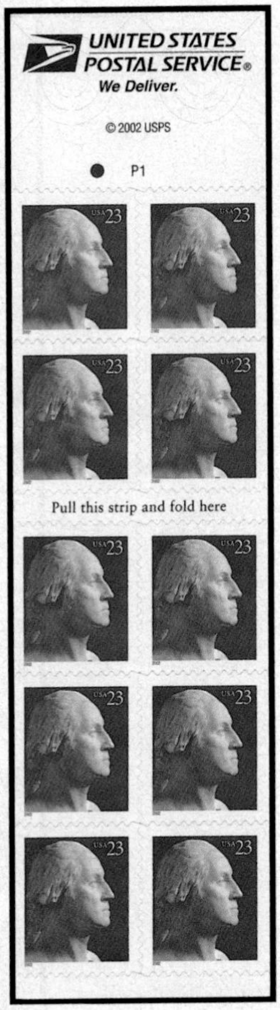

3618c — A2686

3618c A2686 23c pane of 10, P#P1, P2, P3 4.50

No. 3618c is a complete booklet and includes a self-adhesive panel that covers the rouletting. The peelable backing (BC173), which is slightly longer than on No. BK288, serves as a booklet cover.

Washington Type of 2002

Serpentine Die Cut 10½x11 on 3 Sides

2002, June 7

Self-Adhesive

3619a A2686 23c pane of 4, 2 #3619 at L, 2 #3618 at R, P#P1, P2, P4 7.00
3619b A2686 23c pane of 6, 3 #3619 at L, 3 #3618 at R, no P# 12.50
3619c A2686 23c pane of 4, 2 #3618 at L, 2 #3619 at R, P#P1, P2, P4 7.00
3619d A2686 23c pane of 6, 3 #3618 at L, 3 #3619 at R, no P# 12.50

COMBINATION BOOKLETS

BK289 BC173 $2.30 **multi,** #3619a-3619b, P#P1, P2, P4 20.00
BK289A BC173 $2.30 **multi,** #3619c-3619d, P#P1, P2, P4 20.00

Serpentine Die Cut 10½x11 on 3 Sides

Self-Adhesive

3619e A2686 23c pane of 10, 5 #3619 at L, 5 #3618 at R, P#P1, P2, P3 15.00
3619f A2686 23c pane of 10, 5 #3618 at L, 5 #3619 at R, P#P1, P2, P3 15.00

Nos. 3619e and 3619f are complete booklets and include a self-adhesive panel that covers the rouletting. The peelable backing (BC173), which is slightly longer than those on Nos. BK289 and BK289A, serves as a booklet cover.

3623a — A2807

3623a — BC174

2002

$7.40 fold-it-yourself booklet contains 20 self-adhesive (37c) stamps

Serpentine Die Cut 11¼ on 2, 3 or 4 Sides

2002, June 7 **Litho.**

Self-Adhesive

3623a A2807 (37c) pane of 20, P#B1111, B2222, B3333 15.00

No. 3623a is a complete booklet (BC174). The peelable backing serves as a booklet cover.

3624a, 3624b — A2807

Serpentine Die Cut 10½x10¾ on 2 or 3 Sides

2002, June 7 **Photo.**

Self-Adhesive

3624a A2807 (37c) pane of 4, no P# 3.00
3624b A2807 (37c) pane of 6 4.50

3624a, 3624b — BC175

2002

$7.40 booklet contains 20 self-adhesive (37c) stamps

COMBINATION BOOKLET

BK290 BC175 ($7.40) **multi,** 2 each #3624a, 3624b, P#S11111 15.00

Plate number on No. BK290 is on the backing paper of the lower example of No. 3624b.

3624c, BC176 — A2807

Serpentine Die Cut 10½x10¾ on 2 or 3 Sides

3624c A2807 (37c) pane of 20, P#S1111 15.00

No. 3624c is a complete booklet with 12 stamps plus P# on one side and eight stamps plus booklet cover (BC176) on the other side. The peelable backing serves as a booklet cover.

3625a — A2807

3625a BC177

2002

$6.66 fold-it-yourself booklet contains 18 self-adhesive (37c) stamps

Serpentine Die Cut 8 on 2, 3 or 4 Sides

2002, June 7 **Photo.**

Self-Adhesive

3625a A2807 (37c) pane of 18, P#V1111 13.50

No. 3625a is a complete booklet (BC177). The peelable backing serves as a booklet cover.

3629b, 3629c, 3629d — A2808-A2811

Serpentine Die Cut 11 on 2 or 3 Sides

2002, June 7 **Photo.**

Self-Adhesive

3629b A2808 (37c) pane of 4, #3626-3629, no P# 3.00

3629c A2808 (37c) pane of 6, #3627, 3629, 2 each #3626, 3628, no P# 4.50

3629d A2808 (37c) pane of 6, #3626, 3628, 2 each #3627, 3629, no P# 4.50

3629b, 3629c, 3629d — BC178

2002

$7.40 booklet contains 20 self-adhesive (37c) stamps

COMBINATION BOOKLET

BK291 BC178 ($7.40) **multi,** #3629c-3629d, 2 #3629b, no P# 15.00

3629e — A2808-A2811

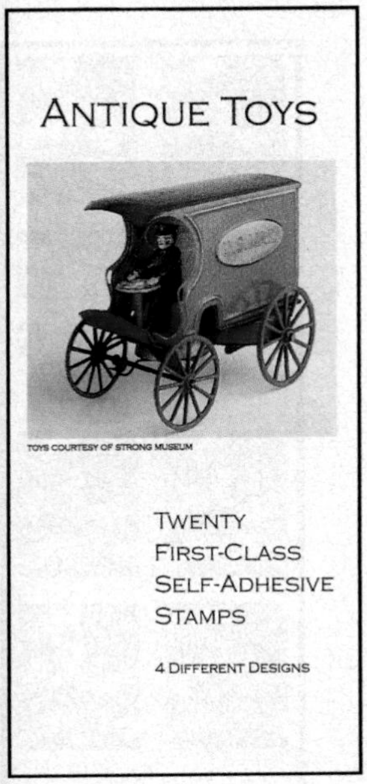

3629e — BC179

2002

$7.40 fold-it-yourself booklet contains 20 self-adhesive (37c) stamps

Serpentine Die Cut 11 on 2, 3 or 4 Sides

3629e A2808 (37c) pane of 20, 5 each #3626-3629, P#V1111, V1112, V2222 15.00

No. 3629e is a complete booklet (BC179). The peelable backing serves as a booklet cover.

3634a — A2812

3634a — BC180

2002

$3.70 fold-it-yourself booklet contains 10 self-adhesive 37c stamps

Serpentine Die Cut 11.1 on 3 Sides

2002, June 7 **Photo.**

Self-Adhesive

3634a A2812 37c pane of 10, P#V1111 7.50

No. 3634a is a complete booklet (BC180). The peelable backing serves as a booklet cover.

3634c, 3634d — A2812

Serpentine Die Cut 11 on 2 or 3 Sides

2003, Nov. **Photo.**

Self-Adhesive

3634c A2812 37c pane of 4 #3634b, no P# 3.00
3634d A2812 37c pane of 6 #3634b 4.50

3634c, 3634d — BC180A

2002

$7.40 booklet contains 20 self-adhesive 37c stamps.

COMBINATION BOOKLET

BK291A BC180A $7.40 **multi,** 2 each #3634c, 3634d, P#V1111 15.00

Plate number on No. BK291A is on the backing paper of the lower example of No. 3634d.

2002(?) ***Serpentine Die Cut 11.3 on 3 Sides***

Self-Adhesive

Photo.

3634f A2812 37c pane of 10, P#V1111 7.50

No. 3634f is a complete booklet (BC180). The peelable backing serves as a booklet cover.

3635a — A2812

3635a — BC181

2002

$7.40 fold-it-yourself booklet contains 20 self-adhesive 37c stamps

Serpentine Die Cut 11¼ on 2, 3 or 4 Sides

2002, June 7 **Litho.**

Self-Adhesive

3635a A2812 37c pane of 20, P#B1111, B2222, B3333, B4444, B5555, B6666, B7777 15.00

No. 3635a is a complete booklet (BC181). The peelable backing serves as a booklet cover.

3636a, 3636b — A2812

Serpentine Die Cut 10½x10¾ on 2 or 3 Sides

2002, June 7 **Photo.**

Self-Adhesive

3636a A2812 37c pane of 4, no P# 3.00
3636b A2812 37c pane of 6 4.50

3636a, 3636b — BC182

2002

$7.40 fold-it-yourself booklet contains 20 self-adhesive 37c stamps

COMBINATION BOOKLET

BK291B BC182 $7.40 **multi,** 2 each #3636a, 3636b, P#S11111 15.00

Plate number on No. BK291B is on the backing paper of the lower example of No. 3636b.

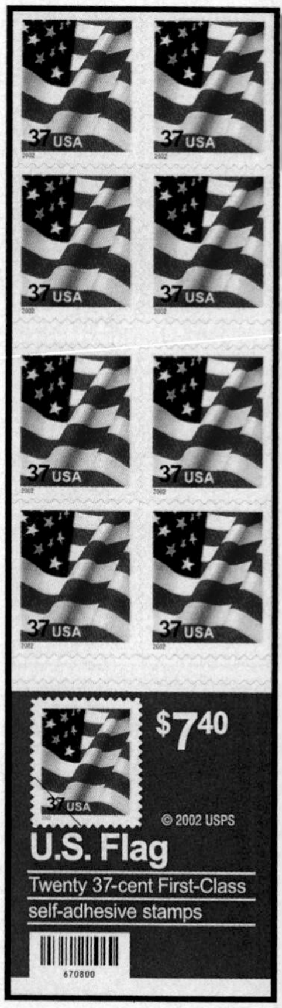

3636c, BC183 — A2812

Serpentine Die Cut 10½x10¾ on 2 or 3 Sides

2002, June 7 **Photo.**

Self-Adhesive

3636c A2812 37c pane of 20, P#S1111, S2222, S3333, S4444, S5555 15.00

No. 3636c is a complete booklet with 12 stamps plus P# on one side and eight stamps plus booklet cover (BC183) on the other side. The peelable backing serves as a booklet cover.

Variety

3636d As "c," 11 stamps and part of 12th stamp on reverse printed on backing liner, the 8 stamps on front side imperf —

Serpentine Die Cut 11¼x11 on 2 or 3 Sides

2004, July **Photo.**

Self-Adhesive

3636De A2812 37c pane of 20, P#V1111 18.00

No. 3636De is a complete booklet with 12 stamps plus P# on one side and eight stamps plus booklet cover (BC183) on the other side. The peelable backing serves as a booklet cover.

3637a — A2812

3637a—BC184

2003

$6.66 fold-it-yourself booklet contains 18 self-adhesive 37c stamps

Serpentine Die Cut 8 on 2, 3 or 4 Sides

2003, Feb. 4 **Photo.**

Self-Adhesive

3637a A2812 37c pane of 18, #V1111 13.50

No. 3637a is a complete booklet (BC184). The peelable backing serves as a booklet cover.

3645b, 3645c, 3645d — A2813-A2816

Serpentine Die Cut 11 on 2 or 3 Sides

2002, July 26 **Photo.**

Self-Adhesive

3645b A2813 37c pane of 4, #3642-3645, no P# 3.00
3645c A2813 37c pane of 6, #3643, 3645, 2 each #3642, 3644, no P# 4.50
3645d A2813 37c pane of 6, #3642, 3644, 2 each #3643, 3645 4.50

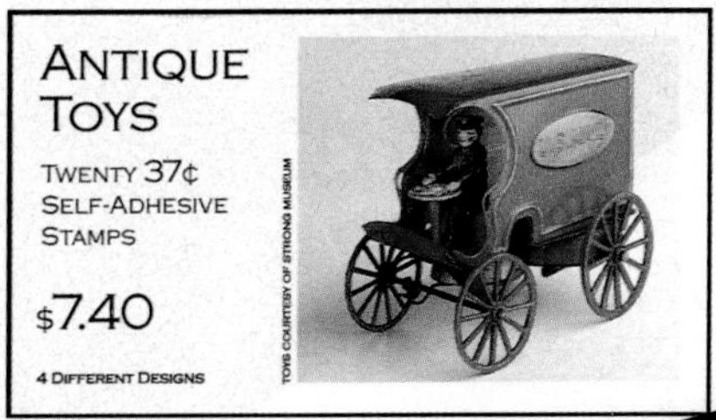

3645b, 3645c, 3645d — BC185

2002

$7.40 booklet contains 20 self-adhesive 37c stamps

COMBINATION BOOKLET

BK292 BC185 $7.40 **multi**,#3645c-3645d, 2 #3645b, P#V1111 15.00

Plate number on No. BK292 is on the backing paper of No. 3645d.

3645e — A2813-A2816

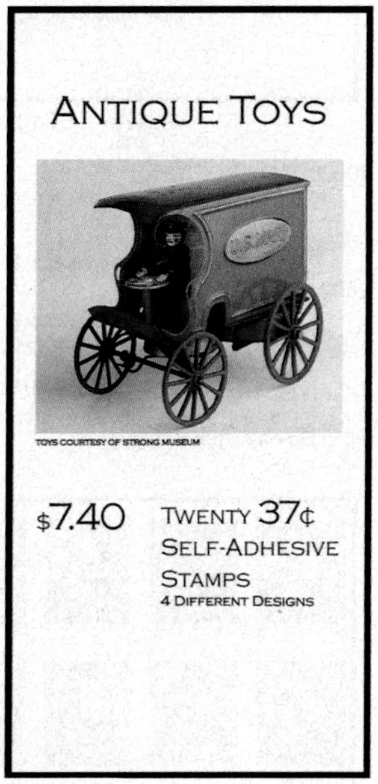

3645e — BC186

2002

$7.40 fold-it-yourself booklet contains 20 self-adhesive 37c stamps

Serpentine Die Cut 11 on 2, 3 or 4 Sides

3645e A2813 37c pane of 20, 5 each #3642-3645, P#V1111, V1112, V2221, V2222 15.00

No. 3645e is a complete booklet (BC186). The peelable backing serves as a booklet cover.

3645h, BC179A — A2813-A2816

Serpentine Die Cut 11x11¼ on 2 or 3 Si

2003, Sept. 3

Self-Adhe

3645h A2813 37c pa

No. 3645

and

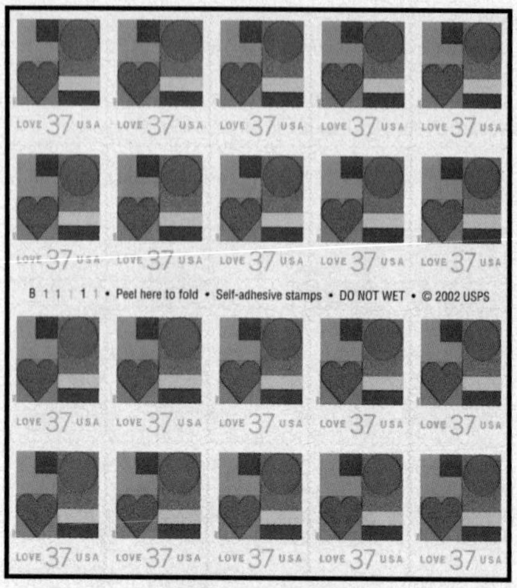

3657a — A2828

3657a — BC187

2002

$7.40 fold-it-yourself booklet contains 20 self-adhesive 37c stamps

Serpentine Die Cut 11 on 2, 3 or 4 Sides

2002, Aug. 16 **Litho.**

Self-Adhesive

3657a A2828 37c pane of 20, P#B11111, B22222, B33333, B44444, B55555, B66666, B77777 15.00

No. 3657a is a complete booklet (BC187). The peelable backing serves as a booklet cover.

Serpentine Die Cut 11x11¼ on 2, 3 or 4 Sides

2002, Oct. 10

Self-Adhesive

3675a A2843 37c pane of 20, P#B1111, B2222 15.00

No. 3675a is a complete booklet (BC188). The peelable backing serves as a booklet cover.

3687b, BC189 — A2844-A2847

Serpentine Die Cut 10¾ on 2 or 3 Sides

2002, Oct. 28

Self-Adhesive

3687b A2844 37c Pane of 20, P#S111, S1113, S2222, S4444 20.00

No. 3687b is a complete booklet with 12 stamps plus P# on one side and eight stamps plus booklet cover (BC189) on the other side. The peelable backing serves as a booklet cover.

3691b, 3691c, 3691d — A2848-A2851

Serpentine Die Cut 11 on 2 or 3 Sides

3691b A2848 37c	Pane of 4, #3688-3691	4.00
3691c A2848 37c	Pane of 6, #3690-3691, 2 each #3688-3689, no P#	6.00
3691d A2848 37c	Pane of 6, #3688-3689, 2 each #3690-3691	6.00

3691b, 3691c, 3691d — BC190

2002

$7.40 booklet contains 20 self-adhesive 37c stamps

COMBINATION BOOKLET

BK293 BC190 $7.40 **multi,** #3691c, 3691d, 2 #3691b, P#V1111 22.50

Plate number on No. BK293 is on the backing paper of the upper example of No. 3691b.

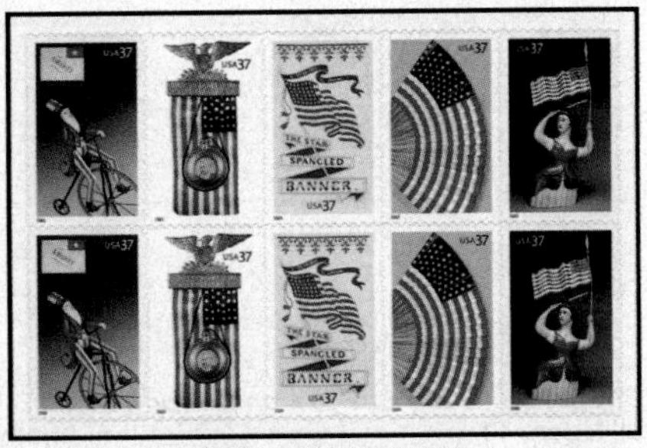

3780b — A2883-A2887

Backing 1

Backing 2

2003, Apr. 3 Litho. ***Serpentine Die Cut 10x9¾***

Self-Adhesive

3780b A2883 37c Pane of 2 #3780a with backing 1 7.50
With backing 2 7.50

3780b — BC191

2003

$7.40 booklet contains 20 self-adhesive stamps

Booklet

BK294 BC191 $7.40 **multi,** no P# 15.00

No. BK294 contains one No. 3780b with backing 1 and one No. 3780b with backing 2.

3807b, BC193 — A2902-A2905

Serpentine Die Cut 10¾ on 2 or 3 Sides

2003, Aug. 7 **Photo.**

Self-Adhesive

3807b A2902 37c pane of 20, 5 #3807a, P#S11111 15.00

No. 3807b is a complete double-sided booklet. Eight stamps and the booklet cover (BC193) are printed on one side of the peelable backing paper and 12 stamps plus P# are printed on the other side of the backing paper.

3820a, BC194 — A2843

Serpentine Die Cut 11x11¼ on 2 or 3 Sides

2003, Oct. 23

Self-Adhesive

Size: 28x19½mm

3820a A2843 37c pane of 20, P#P1111 15.00

No. 3820a is a complete double-sided booklet. Eight stamps, P# and the booklet cover (BC194) are printed on one side of the peelable backing paper, and 12 stamps plus P# are printed on the other side of the backing paper.

On one version of this pane (shown), an incorrect bar code was printed over with white ink, mostly covering the incorrect code, and the correct bar code was then added. This version is much scarcer; value $30.

3824b, BC195 — A2917-A2920

Serpentine Die Cut 11¾x11 on 2 or 3 Sides

2003, Oct. 23

Self-Adhesive

3824b A2917 37c Pane of 20, 5 each #3821-3824, P#S1111, S2222 16.00

No. 3824b is a complete double-sided booklet. Eight stamps plus P# and the booklet cover (BC195) are printed on one side of the peelable backing paper, and 12 stamps plus P# are printed on the other side of the backing paper.

3828b, 3828c, 3828d — A2921-A2924

Serpentine Die Cut 10½x10¾ on 2 or 3 Sides

3828b A2921 37c Pane of 4, #3825-3828, no P# 3.40
3828c A2921 37c Pane of 6, #3827-3828, 2 each #3825-3828, no P# 5.25
3828d A2921 37c Pane of 6, #3825-3826, 2 each #3827-3828, P#S111111 5.25

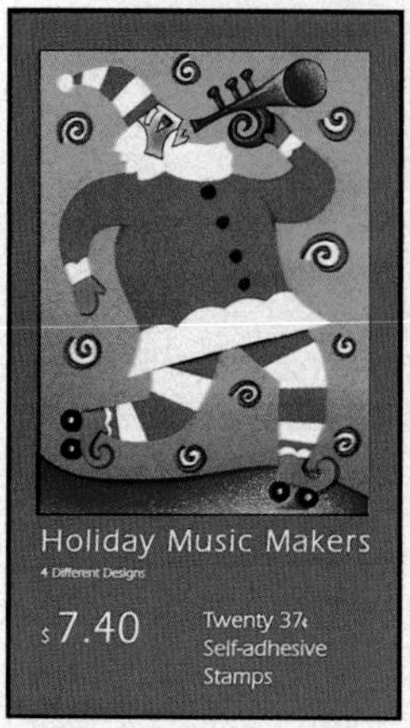

3828b, 3828c, 3828d — BC196

2003

$7.40 booklet contains 20 self-adhesive 37c stamps

COMBINATION BOOKLET

BK296 BC196 $7.40 **multi,** #3828c, 3828d, 2 each #3828b, P#S11111 17.50

Plate number on No. BK296 is printed on the backing paper of No. 3828d.

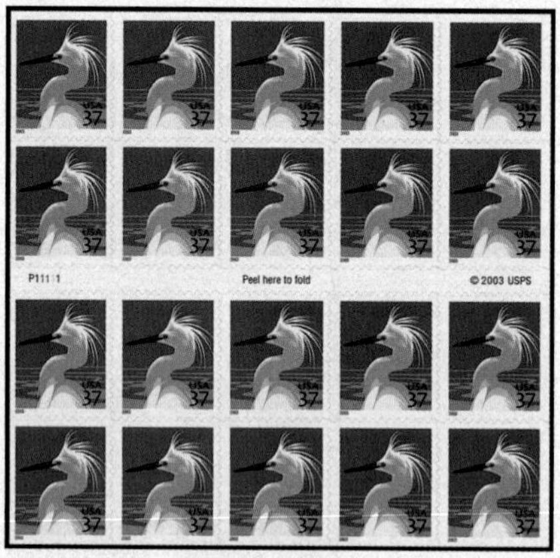

3830a — A2925

3830a — BC197

2004

$7.40 fold-it-yourself booklet contains 20 self-adhesive 37c stamps

Serpentine Die Cut 11½x11 on 2, 3 or 4 Sides

2004, Jan. 30 **Litho.**

Self-Adhesive

3830a A2925 37c pane of 20, P#P11111, P22222 15.00

No. 3830a is a complete booklet (BC197). The peelable backing serves as a booklet cover.

Variety

3830c As "a," die cutting omitted —

Serpentine Die Cut 11½x11 on 2, 3 or 4 Sides

2005? **Photo.**

Self-Adhesive

With "USPS" Microprinted on Bird's Breast

3830De A2925 37c pane of 20, P#P33333, P44444, P55555 *100.00*

No. 3830De is a complete booklet (BC197). The peelable backing serves as a booklet cover.

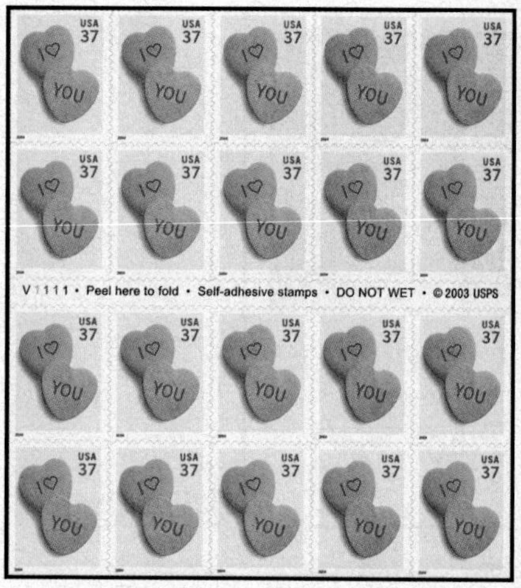

3833a — A2928

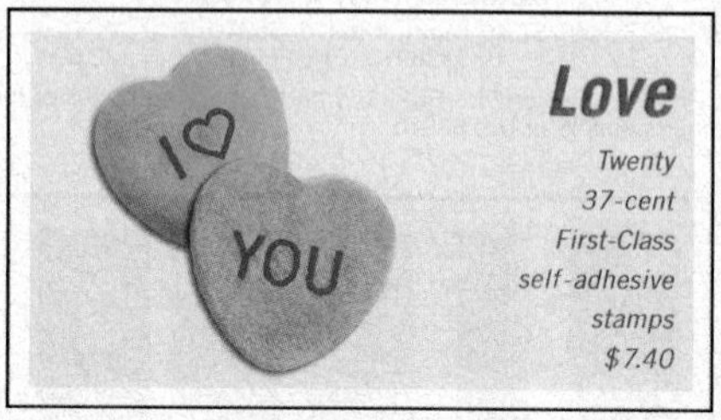

3833a — BC198

2004

$7.40 fold-it-yourself booklet contains 20 self-adhesive 37c stamps

Serpentine Die Cut 10¾ on 2, 3 or 4 Sides

2004, Jan. 14 **Photo.**

Self-Adhesive

3833a A2928 37c pane of 20, P#V1111 15.00

No. 3833a is a complete booklet (BC198). The peelable backing serves as a booklet cover.

3836a — A2931

3836a — BC199

2004

$7.40 booklet contains 20 self-adhesive stamps

Serpentine Die Cut 10¾ on 2, 3 or 4 Sides

2004, Mar. 4 **Litho.**

Self-Adhesive

3836a A2931 37c pane of 20, #P22222 15.00

No. 3836a is a complete booklet (BC199). The peelable backing serves as a booklet cover.

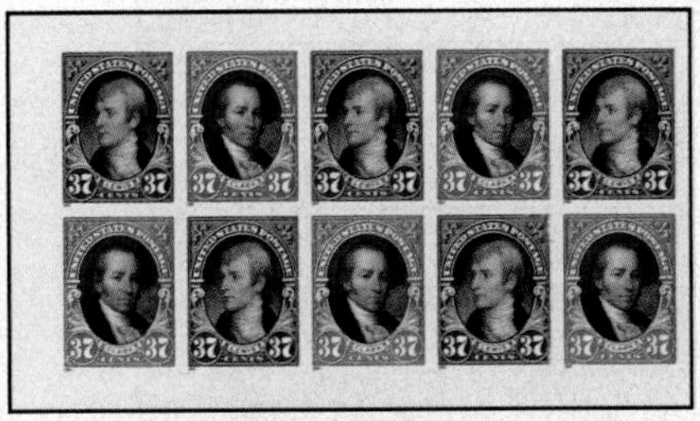

3856b — A2940-A2941

Backing 1

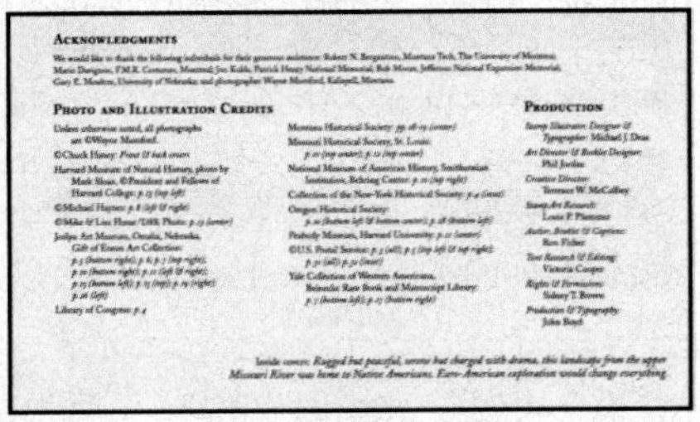

Backing 2

Serpentine Die Cut 10½x10¾

2004, May 14 **Litho. & Engr.**

Self-Adhesive

3856b A2940 37c Pane, 5 each #3855-3856 with backing 1 9.00
With backing 2 9.00

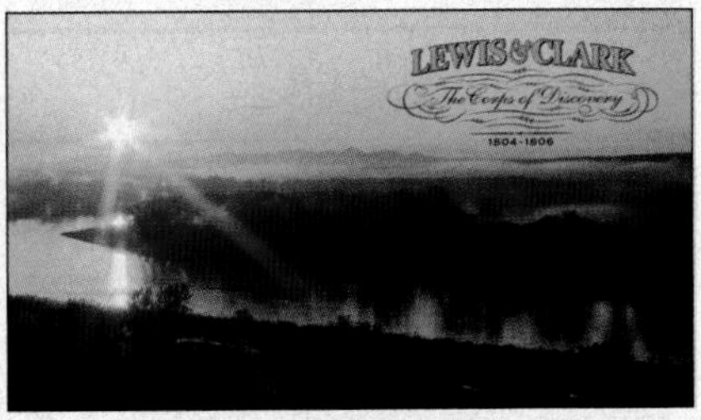

3856b — BC200

2004

$8.95 booklet contains 20 self-adhesive stamps

Booklet

BK297 BC200 $8.95 **multi,** no P# 18.00

No. BK297 contains one No. 3856b with backing 1 and one No. 3856b with backing 2.

3872a, BC201 — A2956

Serpentine Die Cut 10¾ on 2 or 3 Sides

2004, Aug. 12 **Photo.**

Self-Adhesive

3872a A2956 37c pane of 20, P#S1111 15.00

No. 3872a is a complete booklet with 12 stamps plus P# on one side and eight stamps plus booklet cover (BC201) on the other side. The peelable backing serves as a booklet cover.

3879a, BC202 — A2961

Serpentine Die Cut 10¾x11 on 2 or 3 Sides

2004, Oct. 14 **Litho.**

Self-Adhesive

3879a A2961 37c pane of 20, P#P1111 15.00

No. 3879a is a complete booklet with 12 stamps plus P# on one side and eight stamps plus P# and a label that serves as a booklet cover (BC202) on the other side.

Variety

3879b As "a," die cutting omitted —

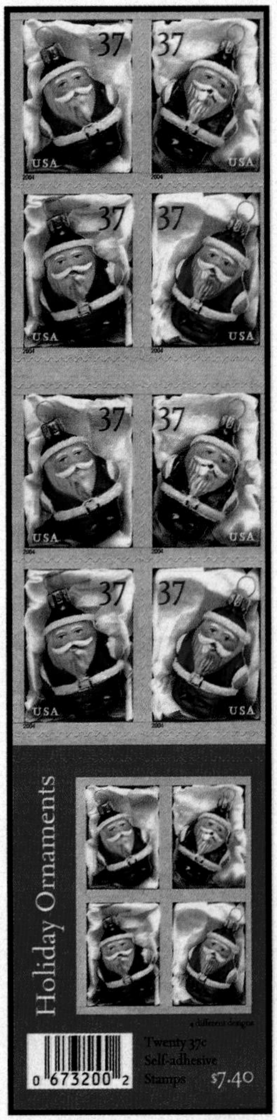

3886b, BC203 —A2965-A2968

Serpentine Die Cut 11½x11 on 2 or 3 Sides

2004, Nov. 16 **Photo.**

Self-Adhesive

3886b A2965 37c pane of 20, 5 #3886a, P#S1111 15.00

No. 3886b is a complete double-sided booklet. Eight stamps and the booklet cover (BC203) are on one side of the peelable backing paper and 12 stamps plus P# are on the other side of the backing paper.

3890b, 3890c, 3890d — A2969-A2972

Serpentine Die Cut 10¼x10¾ on 2 or 3 Sides

3890b A2969 37c pane of 4 #3887-3890, no P# 3.00
3890c A2969 37c pane of 6 #3889-3890, 2 each #3887-3888, no P# 4.50
3890d A2969 37c pane of 6 #3887-3888, 2 each #3889-3890, P#S11111 4.50

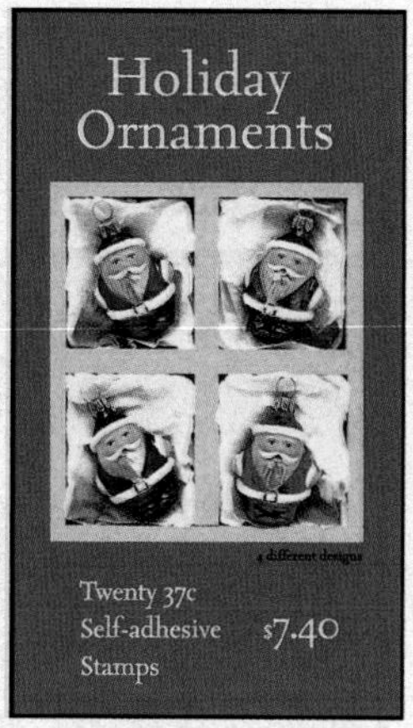

3890b, 3890c, 3890d — BC204

2004

$7.40 booklet contains 20 self-adhesive 37c stamps

COMBINATION BOOKLET

BK298 BC204 $7.40 **multi,** #3890c, 3890d, 2 #3890b, P#S11111 15.00

Plate number on No. BK298 is printed on the backing paper of No. 3890d.

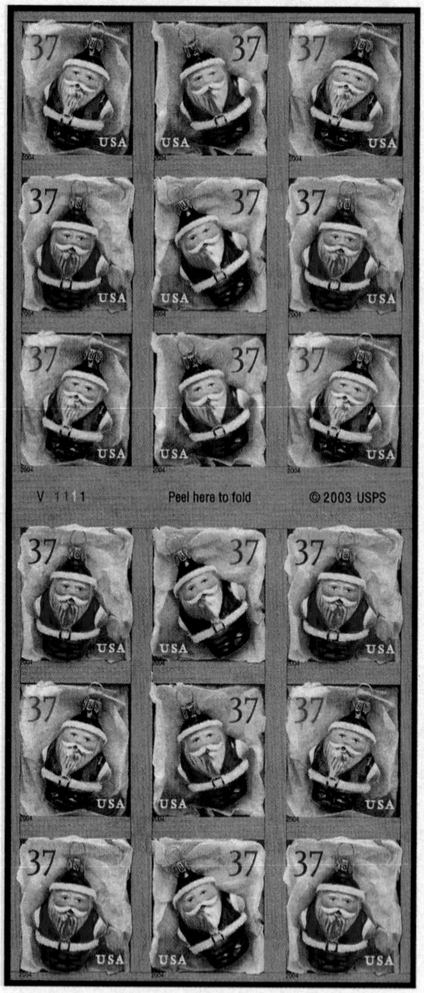

3894b — A2969-A2972

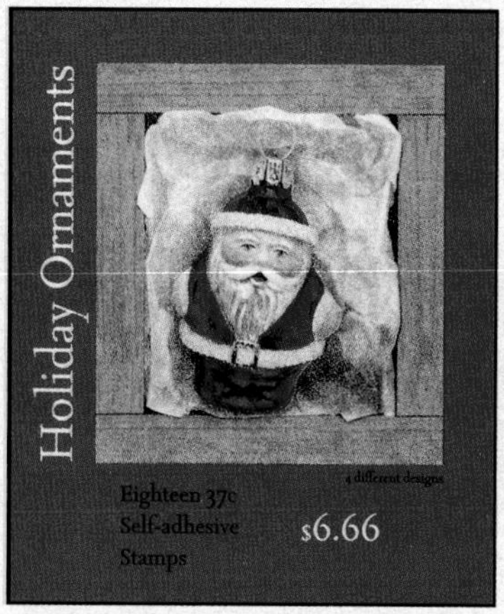

3894b BC205

2004

$6.66 fold-it-yourself booklet contains 18 self-adhesive 37c stamps

Serpentine Die Cut 8 on 2, 3 or 4 Sides

3894b A2969 37c pane of 18, 6 each #3891, 3893, 3 each #3892, 3894, P#V11111 18.00

No. 3894b is a complete booklet (BC205). The peelable backing serves as a booklet cover.

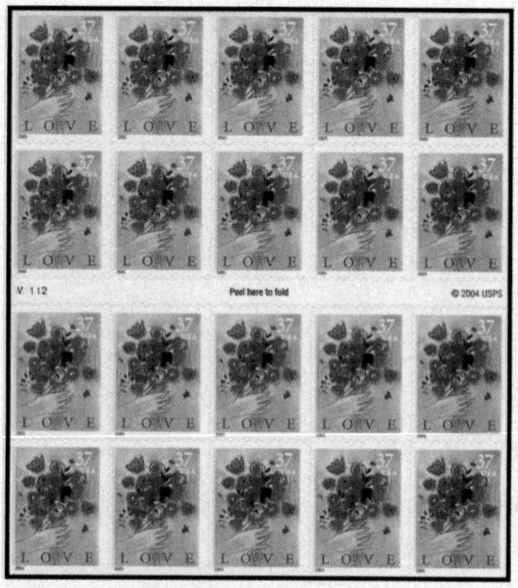

3898a — A2975

3898a — BC206

2005

$7.40 booklet contains 20 self-adhesive stamps

Serpentine Die Cut 10¾x11 on 2, 3 or 4 Sides

2005, Feb. 18 **Photo.**

Self-Adhesive

3898a A2975 37c pane of 20, #V1111, V1112 15.00

No. 3898a is a complete booklet (BC206). The peelable backing serves as a booklet cover.

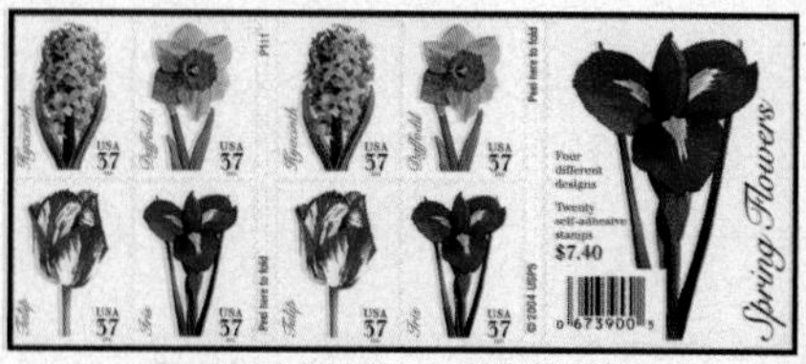

3903b, BC207 — A2977-A2980

Serpentine Die Cut 10¾ on 2 or 3 Sides

2005, Mar. 15 **Litho.**

Self-Adhesive

3903b A2977 37c pane of 20, P#P1111 15.00

Variety

3903c As "b," die cutting omitted on side with eight stamps —

No. 3903b is a complete booklet with 12 stamps plus P# on one side and eight stamps plus P# and a label that serves as a booklet cover (BC207) on the other side.

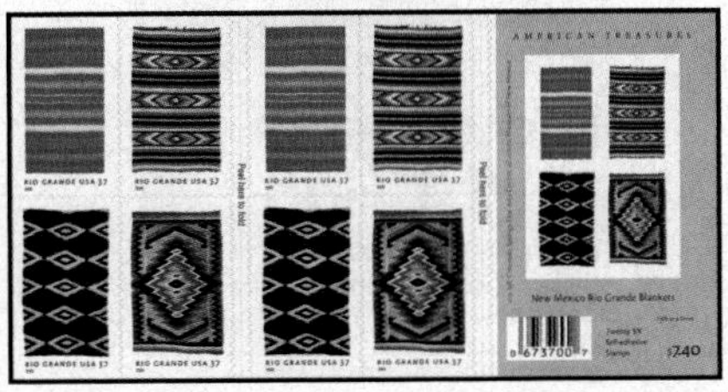

3929b, BC208 — A3003-A3006

Serpentine Die Cut 10¾ on 2 or 3 Sides

2005, July 30 **Litho.**

Self-Adhesive

3929b A3003 37c pane of 20, P#P1111 15.00

No. 3929b is a complete booklet with 12 stamps plus two P# on one side and eight stamps plus a label that serves as a booklet cover (BC208) on the other side.

3935b, BC209 — A3008-A3012

Serpentine Die Cut 10¾ on 2 or 3 Sides

2005, Aug. 20 **Litho.**

Self-Adhesive

3935b A3008 37c pane of 20, P#P1111 16.00

No. 3935b is a complete booklet with 12 stamps (2 each #3931, 3933, 3935, and 3 each #3932, 3934) plus P# on one side and eight stamps (1 each #3932, 3934, and 2 each #3931, 3933, 3935) plus a label that serves as the booklet cover (BC209) on the other side.

3956b, BC210 — A3026-A3029

Serpentine Die Cut 10¾x11 on 2 or 3 Sides

2005, Oct. 20 **Photo.**

Self-Adhesive

3956b A3026 37c pane of 5 #3956a, P#S1111 15.00

No. 3956b is a complete double-sided booklet. Eight stamps and the booklet cover (BC210) are on one side of the peelable backing paper and 12 stamps plus P# are on the other side of the backing.

3960b, 3960c, 3960d — A3030-A3033

Serpentine Die Cut 10½x10¾ on 2 or 3 Sides

3960b A3030 37c pane of 4 #3957-3960 6.00

3960c A3030 37c pane of 6 #3959-3960, 2 each #3957-3958, no P# 9.00

3960d A3030 37c pane of 6 #3957-3958, 2 each #3959-3960, no P# 9.00

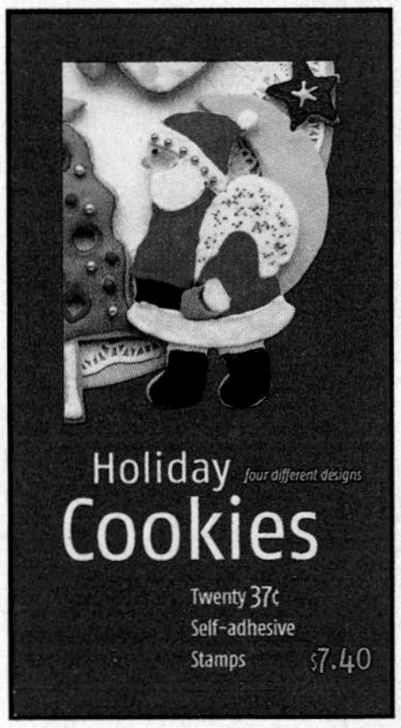

3960b, 3960c, 3960d — BC211

2005

$7.40 booklet contains 20 self-adhesive 37c stamps

COMBINATION BOOKLET

BK299 BC211 $7.40 **multi,** #3960c, 3960d, 2 #3960b, P#S1111 30.00

Plate number on No. BK299 is printed on the backing paper of the lower example of No. 3960b.

3966a, 3972a, 3973a, BC212 — A3038

Serpentine Die Cut 11¼x11 on 2 or 3 Sides

2005, Dec. 8 **Litho.**

Self-Adhesive

3966a A3038 (39c) pane of 20, P#P1111 16.00

Photo.

Serpentine Die Cut 11¼x10¾ on 2 or 3 Sides

3972a A3038 (39c) pane of 20, P#V1111 16.00

Serpentine Die Cut 10¼x10¾ on 2 or 3 Sides

3973a A3038 (39c) pane of 20, P#S1111 16.00

Nos. 3966a, 3972a and 3973a are complete double-sided booklets. Eight stamps and the booklet cover (BC212) are on one side of the peelable backing paper and 12 stamps plus P# are on the other side of the backing paper. On No. 3966a, the stamps on one side are upside-down with relation to the stamps on the other side. On Nos. 3972a and 3973a the stamps are all aligned the same on both sides.

3974a, 3974b — A3038

Serpentine Die Cut 11¼x11 on 2 or 3 Sides

Litho.

3974a A3038 (39c) pane of 4 3.20
3974b A3038 (39c) pane of 6, no P# 4.80

3974a, 3974b — BC213

2005

($7.80) booklet contains 20 self-adhesive (39c) stamps

COMBINATION BOOKLET

BK300 BC213 ($7.80) **multi,** 2 each #3974a, 3974b, P#S1111 16.00

Plate number on No. BK300 is printed on the backing paper of the upper example of No. 3974a.

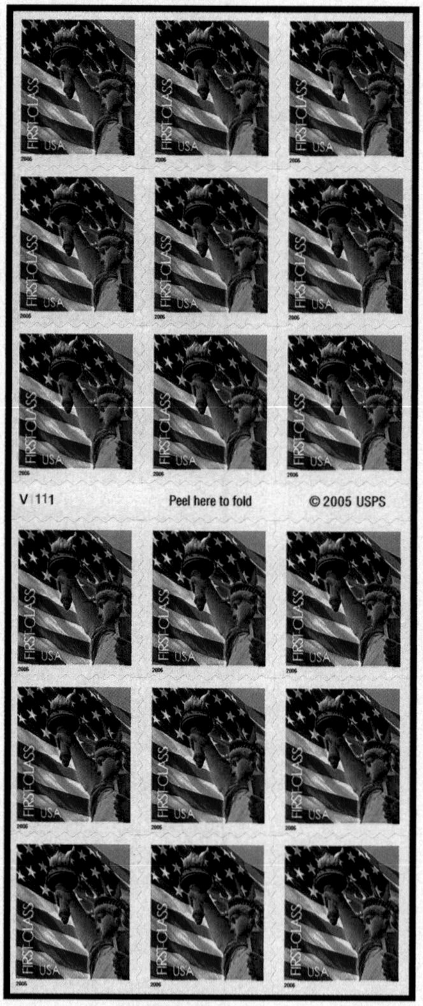

3975a — A3038

3975a
BC214

2005

($7.02) fold-it-yourself booklet contains 18 self-adhesive (39c) stamps

Serpentine Die Cut 8 on 2, 3 or 4 Sides

Photo.

3975a A3038 (39c) pane of 18, P#V1111 14.50

No. 3975a is a complete booklet (BC214). The peelable backing serves as a booklet cover.

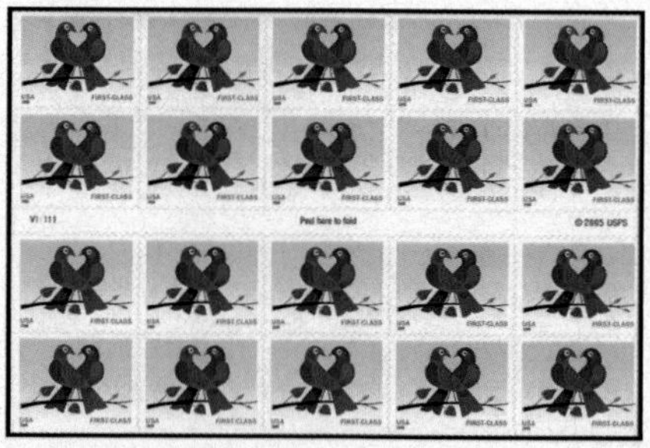

3976a — A3039

3976a — BC215

2006

($7.80) fold-it-yourself booklet contains 20 self-adhesive (39c) stamps

Serpentine Die Cut 11 on 2, 3 or 4 Sides

2006, Jan. 3 **Photo.**

Self-Adhesive

3976a A3039 (39c) pane of 20, P#V11111 18.00

No. 3976a is a complete booklet (BC215). The peelable backing serves as a booklet cover.

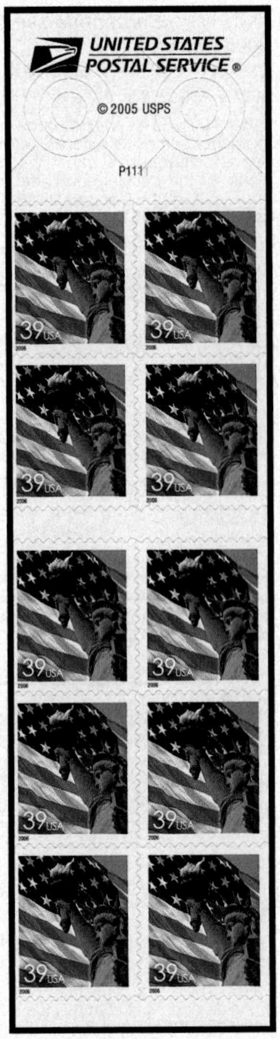

3978a — A3040

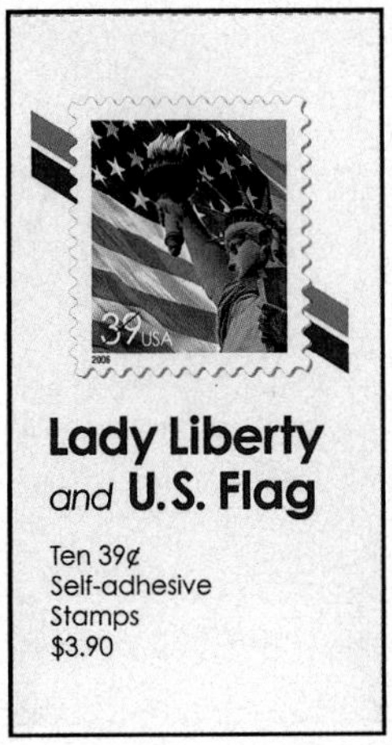

3978a — BC216

2006

$3.90 fold-it-yourself booklet contains 10 self-adhesive 39c stamps

Serpentine Die Cut 11¼x10¾ on 3 Sides

2006, Apr. 8 **Litho.**

Self-Adhesive

3978a A3040 39c pane of 10, P#P1111 8.00

No. 3978a is a complete booklet (BC216). The peelable backing serves as a booklet cover.

3978b, 3985a, BC217 — A3040

Serpentine Die Cut 11¼x10¾ on 2 or 3 Sides

2006, Apr. 8 **Litho.**

Self-Adhesive

3978b A3040 39c pane of 20, P#P1111 16.00

Variety

3978c As "b," die cutting omitted on the side with eight stamps —

No. 3978b is a complete booklet with 12 stamps plus P# on one side and eight stamps plus a label that serves as the booklet cover (BC217) on the other side.

Flag and Statue of Liberty (No. 3978b) Type of 2006

Serpentine Die Cut 11¼x10¾ on 2 or 3 Sides

2006, Apr. 8 **Photo.**

Self-Adhesive

Without Microprinting

3985a A3040 39c pane of 20, #V1111 16.00

No. 3985a is a complete booklet with 12 stamps plus P# on one side and eight stamps plus a label that serves as the booklet cover (BC217) on the other side. The fonts of the UPC code on the booklet cover for No. 3985a differ from those used on No. 3978b.

3985c, 3985d — A3040

Serpentine Die Cut 11.1 on 2 or 3 Sides

2006, Nov. 8 **Photo.**

Self-Adhesive

3985c A3040 39c pane of 4 3.20

3985d A3040 39c pane of 6, no P# 4.80

3985c,
3985d — BC216A

2006

$7.80 fold-it-yourself booklet contains 20 self-adhesive 39c stamps

COMBINATION BOOKLET

BK300A BC216A $7.80 **multi,** 2 each #3985c, 3985d P#V11111 16.00

Plate number on No. BK300A is printed on the backing paper of the lower example of No. 3985c.

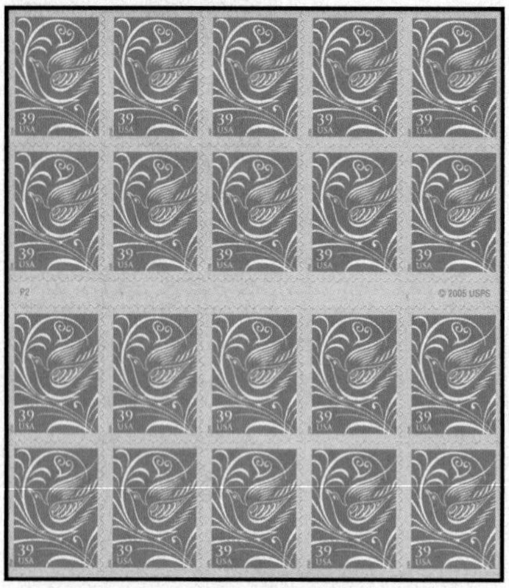

3998a — A3051

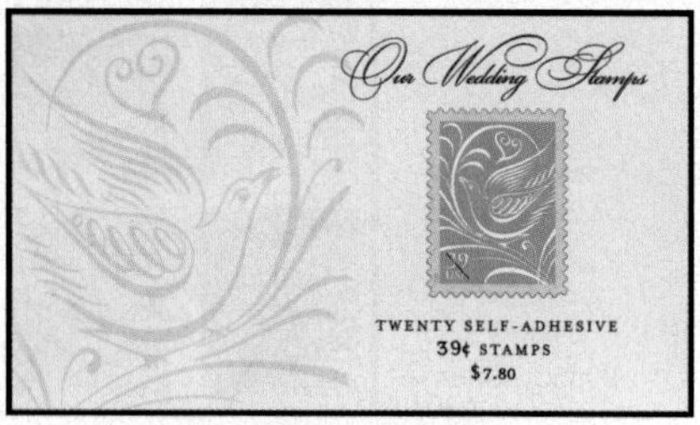

3998a — BC218

2006

$7.80 booklet contains 20 self-adhesive 39c stamps

Serpentine Die Cut 10¾x11 on 2, 3 or 4 Sides

2006, Mar. 1 **Litho.**

Self-Adhesive

3998a A3051 39c pane of 20, #P1 16.00

Variety

3998b As "a," die cutting omitted —

No. 3998a is a complete booklet (BC218). The peelable backing serves as a booklet cover.

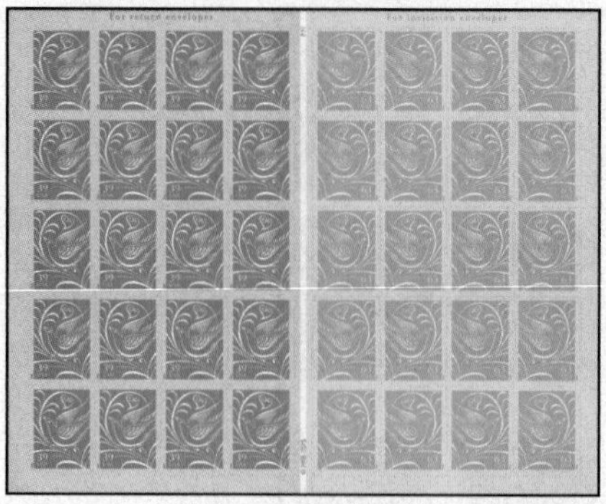

3999a — A3051-A3052

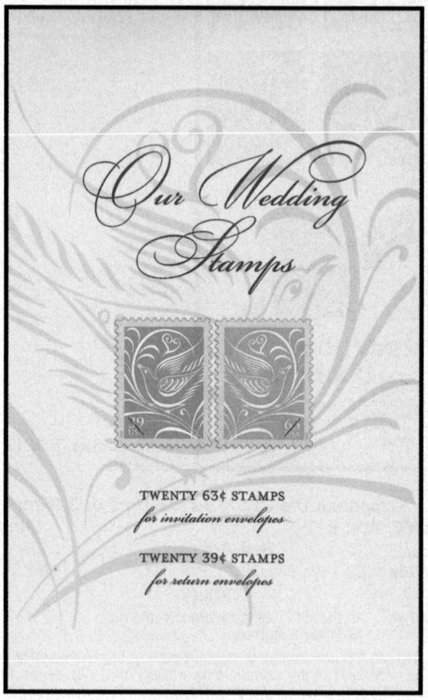

3999a — BC219

2006

$20.40 booklet contains 20 self-adhesive 39c stamps and 20 self-adhesive 63c stamps

Serpentine Die Cut 10¾x11

3999a Pane of 40 (20 each #3998-3999), #P11 37.50

No. 3999a is a complete booklet (BC219). The peelable backing serves as a booklet cover.

4001b — A3053

4001b — BC220

2006

$2.40 fold-it-yourself booklet contains 10 self-adhesive 24c stamps

Serpentine Die Cut 10¾x11¼

2006, Mar. 8 **Photo.**

Self-Adhesive

4001b A3053 24c pane of 10 #4001a, P#V1111 5.00

No. 4001b is a complete booklet (BC220). The peelable backing paper serves as a booklet cover. No. 4001b was sold flat. It has a self-adhesive panel that covers the rouletting on the inside of the booklet cover that is not found in BK301. Three large cuts of rouletting separate the two halves of the booklet cover on No. 4001b.

4001c, 4001d — A3053

4001c A3053 24c pane of 4 #4001a, P#V1111 2.00
4001d A3053 24c pane of 6 #4001a, no P# 3.00

COMBINATION BOOKLET

BK301 BC220 $2.40 **multi,** #4001c, 4001d, P#V1111 5.00

No. BK301 was sold glued shut. When the booklet is opened, the self-adhesive panel found on the right side of No. 4001d sticks to the left side of 4001c, as shown in the illustration above. Fine rouletting separates the two halves of the booklet cover on No. BK301.

4012b, BC221 — A3054-A3058

Serpentine Die Cut 10¾x10½ on 2 or 3 Sides

2006, Mar. 16 **Photo.**

Self-Adhesive

4012b A3054 39c pane of 20, P#S1111 16.00

No. 4012b is a complete booklet with 12 stamps plus P# on one side and eight stamps plus a label that serves as a booklet cover (BC221) on the other side.

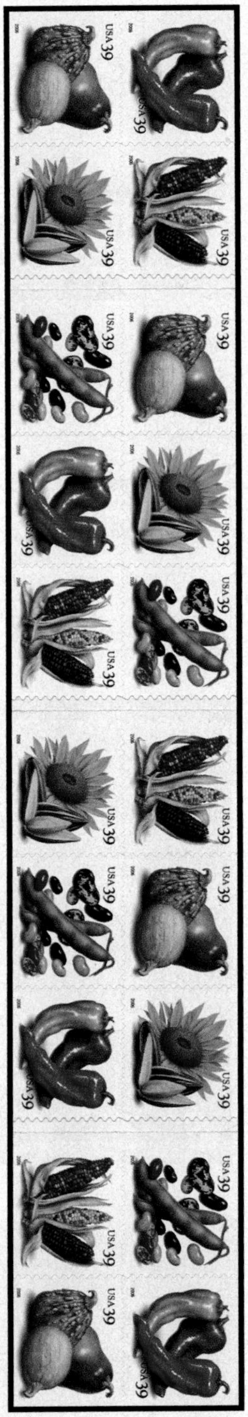

4016a, 4017b, 4017c, 4017d — A3054-A3058

Serpentine Die Cut 10¾x11¼ on 2 or 3 Sides

Litho.

4016a	A3054	39c	pane of 4, #4013-4016, no P#	3.20
4017b	A3054	39c	pane of 4, #4013-4015, 4017, no P#	3.20
4017c	A3054	39c	pane of 6, #4013-4016, 2 #4017, no P#	4.80
4017d	A3054	39c	pane of 6, #4013-4015, 4017, 2 #4016, no P#	4.80

4016a, 4017b, 4017c, 4017d — BC222

2006

$7.80 booklet contains 20 self-adhesive 39c stamps

COMBINATION BOOKLET

BK302 BC222 $7.80 **multi,** #4016a, 4017b, 4017c, 4017d, no P# 16.00

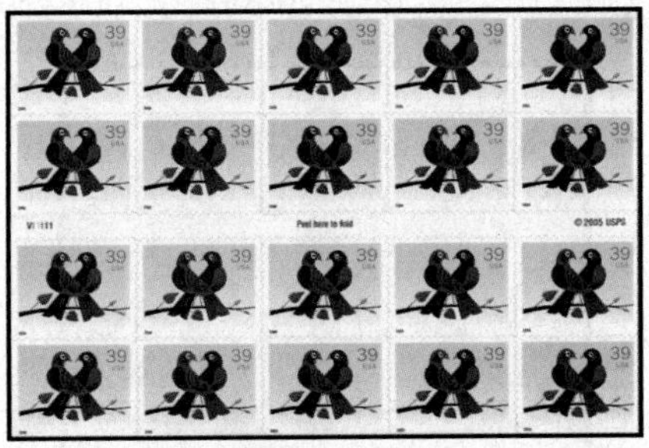

4029a — A3070

4029a — BC223

2006

$7.80 fold-it-yourself booklet contains 20 self-adhesive 39c stamps

Serpentine Die Cut 11 on 2, 3 or 4 Sides

2006, May 1 **Photo.**

Self-Adhesive

4029a A3070 39c pane of 20, P#V11111 16.00

No. 4029a is a complete booklet (BC223). The peelable backing serves as a booklet cover.

4098b, BC224 — A3127-A3136

Serpentine Die Cut 10¾ on 2 or 3 Sides

2006, Aug. 24 **Photo.**

Self-Adhesive

4098b A3127 39c pane of 20, P#S11111 16.00

No. 4098b is a complete booklet with 12 stamps (1 each #4090-4093, 4095-4098, and 2 each #4089, 4094) plus P# on one side and eight stamps (1 each #4090-4093, 4095-4098) plus a label that serves as the booklet cover (BC224) on the other side.

4100a, BC225 — A3138

Serpentine Die Cut 10¾x11 on 2 or 3 Sides

2006 **Litho.**

Self-Adhesive

4100a A3138 39c pane of 20, P#P1111, *Oct. 17* 16.00

No. 4100a is a complete double-sided booklet with 12 stamps plus P# on one side of the peelable backing and eight stamps plus P# and the label that serves as a booklet cover (BC225) on the other side of the backing.

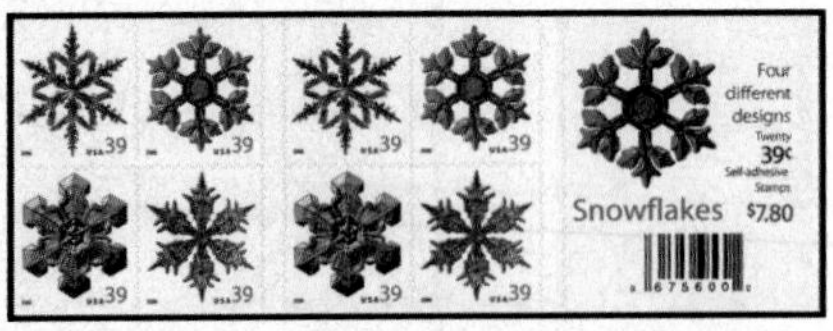

4108b, BC226 — A3139-A3142

Serpentine Die Cut 11¼x11½ on 2 or 3 Sides

4108b A3139 39c pane of 20, P#S1111, *Oct. 5* 16.00

No. 4108b is a complete double-sided booklet. Eight stamps and the label that serves as a booklet cover (BC226) are on one side of the peelable backing and 12 stamps plus P# are on the other side of the backing.

4112b, 4112c, 4112d — A3139-A3142

Serpentine Die Cut 11¼x11 on 2 or 3 Sides

4112b A3139 39c pane of 4, #4109-4112 *Oct. 5* 3.20
4112c A3139 39c pane of 6, #4111-4112, 2 each #4109-4110, no P#, *Oct. 5* 4.80
4112d A3139 39c pane of 6, #4109-4110, 2 each #4111-4112, *Oct. 5* 4.80

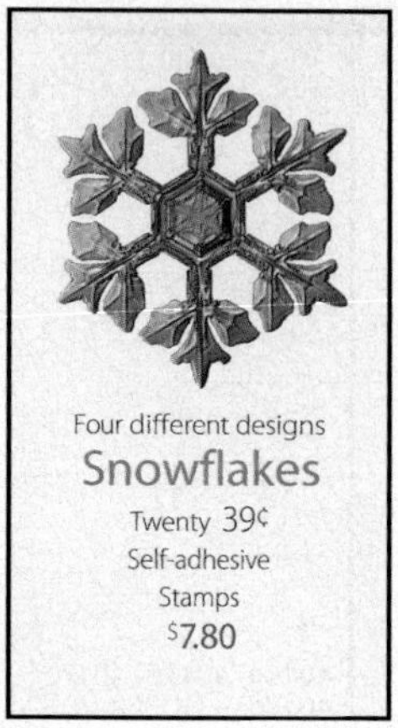

4112b, 4112c, 4112d — BC227

2006

$7.80 booklet contains 20 self-adhesive 39c stamps

COMBINATION BOOKLET

BK303 BC227 $7.80 **multi,** #4112c, 4112d, 2 #4112b, P#S1111 16.00

Plate number on No. BK303 is printed on the backing paper of No. 4112d.

4116b — A3139-A3142

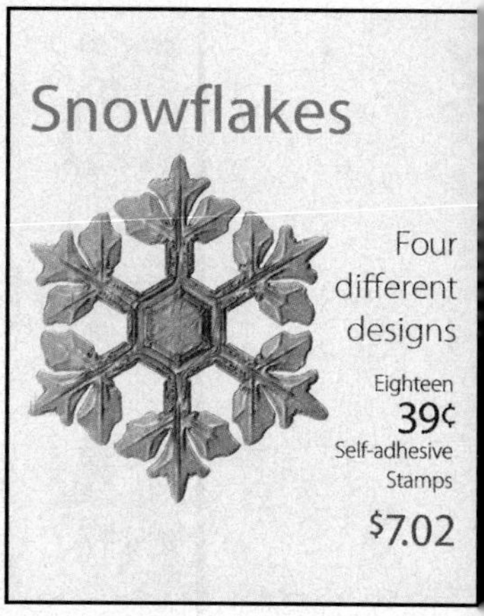

4116b
BC228

2006

$7.02 fold-it-yourself booklet contains 18 self-adhesive 39c stamps

Serpentine Die Cut 8 on 2, 3 or 4 Sides

Photo.

4116b A3139 39c pane of 18, 4 each #4114, 4116, 5 each #4113, 4115, P#V1111, *Oct. 5* 20.00

No. 4116b is a complete booklet (BC228). The peelable backing serves as a booklet cover.

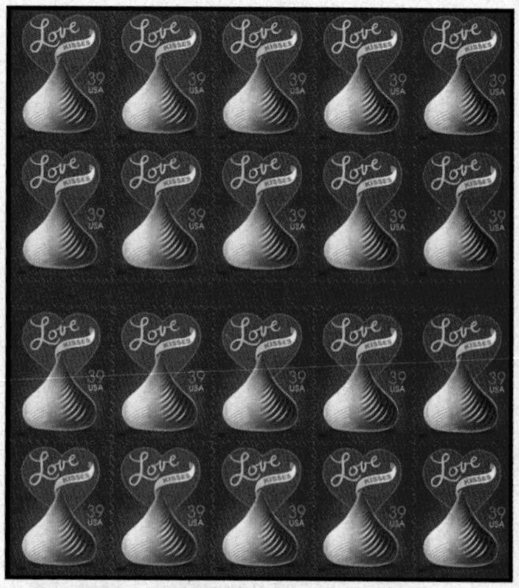

4122a — A3145

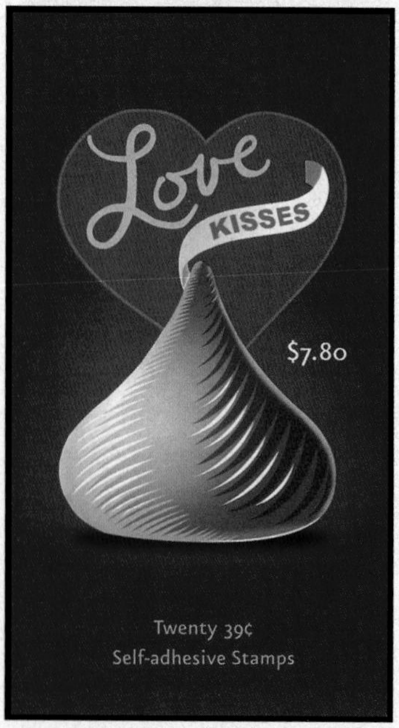

4122a
BC229

2007

$7.80 fold-it-yourself booklet contains 20 self-adhesive 39c stamps

Serpentine Die Cut 10¾x11 on 2, 3 or 4 Sides

2007, Jan. 13 **Photo.**

Self-Adhesive

4122a A3145 39c pane of 20 16.00

No. 4122a is a complete booklet (BC229). The peelable backing serves as a booklet cover. The plate number (V1111) is printed on the rear cover of the booklet.

4125a, 4126a, 4127a, BC230 — A3148

Serpentine Die Cut 11¼x10¾ on 2 or 3 Sides

2007, Apr. 12 **Photo.**

Self-Adhesive

Large Microprinting, Bell 16mm Wide

4125a A3148 (41c) pane of 20, P#V11111 17.00

Litho.

Small Microprinting, Bell 16mm Wide

4126a A3148 (41c) pane of 20, P#P11111 17.00

Medium Microprinting, Bell 15mm Wide

4127a A3148 (41c) pane of 20, P#S11111, "2007" year date, prephosphored coated paper (solid tagging) 17.00

4127e A3148 (41c) pane of 20, P#S11111, prephosphored paper (mottled tagging) 17.00

4127g A3148 (42c) pane of 20, P#S11111, "2008" year date, prephosphored coated paper (solid tagging) 17.00

4127i A3148 (42c) pane of 20, P#S11111, "2008" year date, prephosphored paper, solid tagging on side with 8 stamps, mottled tagging on side with 12 stamps —

Nos. 4125a, 4126a, 4127a, 4127e, 4127g and 4127i are complete double-sided booklets with 12 stamps plus P# on one side of the peelable backing and eight stamps and a label that serves as a booklet cover (BC230) on the other side of the backing.

No. BC230 was printed by three different manufacturers with differences in the fonts used in the UPC code.

4127b, 4127c — A3148

Medium Microprinting, Bell 15mm Wide

4127b A3148 (41c) pane of 4 3.40

4127c A3148 (41c) pane of 6, no P# 5.10

4127b, 4127c — BC231

2007

$8.20 booklet contains 20 self-adhesive (41c) stamps

COMBINATION BOOKLET

BK304 BC231 $8.20 **multi,** 2 each #4127b, 4127c, P#S11111 17.00

Plate number on No. BK304 is printed on the backing of the lower example of No. 4127b.

4128a — A3148

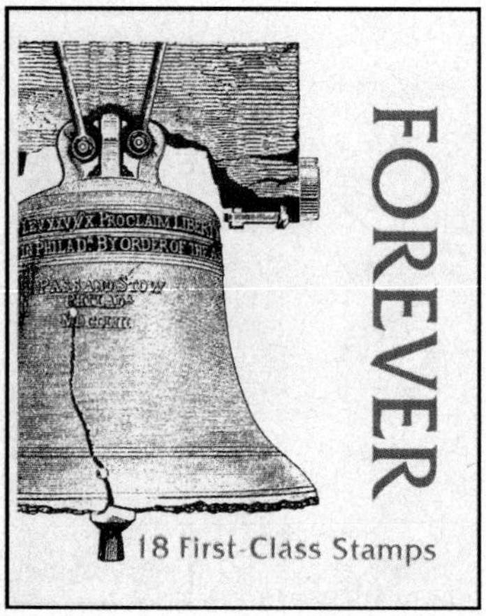

4128a
BC232

2007

$7.38 fold-it-yourself booklet contains 18 self-adhesive (41c) stamps

Large Microprinting, Bell 16mm Wide
Photo.

4128a A3148 (41c) pane of 18 15.50

No. 4128a is a complete booklet (BC232). The peelable backing serves as a booklet cover. Two versions exist. The original issue has P#V11 on the backing paper, while a second printing has P#V22222 on the peelable strip on the front.

4142a — A3152

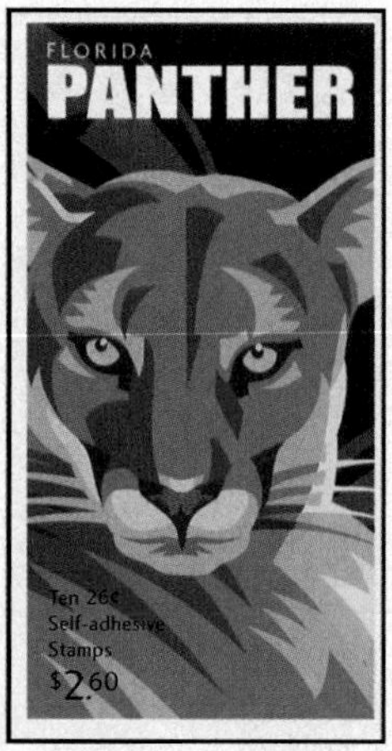

4142a — BC233

2007

$2.60 fold-it-yourself booklet contains 10 self-adhesive 26c stamps

Serpentine Die Cut 11¼x11 on 3 Sides

2007, May 12 **Photo.**

Self-Adhesive

4142a A3152 26c pane of 10, P#V11111 5.50

No. 4142a is a complete booklet (BC233). The peelable backing serves as a booklet cover.

4151a — A3161

4151a — BC234

2007

$8.20 fold-it-yourself booklet contains 20 self-adhesive 41c stamps

Serpentine Die Cut 10¾ on 2, 3 or 4 Sides

2007, June 27 **Litho.**

Self-Adhesive

4151a A3161 41c pane of 20, no P# 17.00

No. 4151a is a complete booklet (BC234). The peelable backing, which has a plate number (P11111), serves as a booklet cover.

4156d, BC235 — A3163-A3166

Serpentine Die Cut 11 on 2 or 3 Sides

2007, June 29 **Litho.**

Self-Adhesive

4156d A3163 41c pane of 20, 3 each #4153-4156, 2 each #4153a-4156a, P#P1111 17.00

No. 4156d is a complete double-sided booklet with 12 stamps (2 each #4153-4156, 1 each 4153a-4156a) on one side of the peelable backing and eight stamps plus P# and the label that serves as a booklet cover (BC235) on the other side of the backing.

4165a, BC236 — A3173

Serpentine Die Cut 10¾ on 2 or 3 Sides

2007, Aug. 9 **Litho.**

Self-Adhesive

4165a A3173 41c pane of 20, #P11111 17.00

No. 4165a is a complete double-sided booklet with 12 stamps on one side and eight stamps plus P# and a label that serves as the booklet cover (BC236) on the other side.

4185a, BC237 — A3174-A3183

Serpentine Die Cut 11¼x11½ on 2 or 3 Sides

2007, Aug. 10 **Photo.**

Self-Adhesive

4185a 41c pane of 20, 2 each #4176-4185, P#V1111 17.00

No. 4185a is a complete double-sided booklet with 12 stamps (2 each #4176-4177, and 1 each #4178-4185) plus P# on one side and eight stamps (#4178-4185) plus a label (BC237) that serves as the booklet cover on the other side.

4190a—A3184

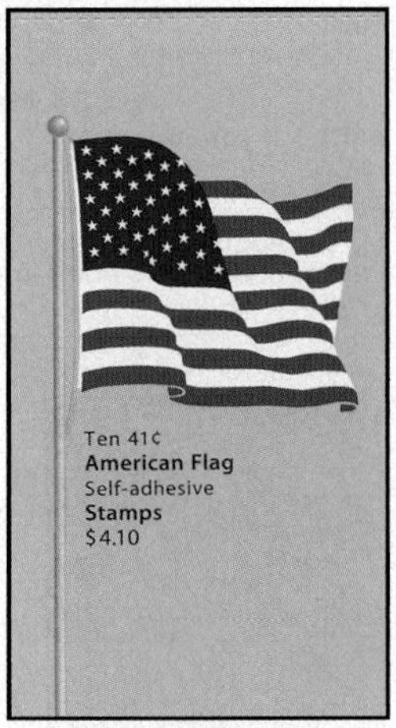

4190a — BC238

2007

$4.10 fold-it-yourself booklet contains 10 self-adhesive 41c stamps

Serpentine Die Cut 11¼x10¾ on 3 Sides

2007, Aug. 15 **Litho.**

Self-Adhesive

With "USPS" Microprinted on Right Side of Flagpole

4190a 41c pane of 10, P#P11111 8.50

By its nature, No. 4190a is a complete booklet (BC238). The peelable backing serves as a booklet cover.

4191a, BC239 — A3184

Serpentine Die Cut 11¼x10¾ on 2 or 3 Sides

With "USPS" Microprinted on Left Side of Flagpole

4191a 41c pane of 20, P#S11111 17.00

No. 4191a is a complete double-sided booklet with 12 stamps plus P# on one side and eight stamps plus a label (BC239) that serves as the booklet cover on the other side.

4206a, BC240 — A3198

Serpentine Die Cut 10¾x11 on 2 or 3 Sides

2007, Oct. 25 **Litho.**

Self-Adhesive

4206a A3198 41c pane of 20, P#P1111 17.00

No. 4206a is a complete double-sided booklet with 12 stamps on one side of the peelable backing and eight stamps plus P# and the label that serves as a booklet cover (BC240) on the other side of the backing.

4210b, BC241 — A3199-A3202

Serpentine Die Cut 10¾ on 2 or 3 Sides

4210b 41c pane of 20, P#S1111 17.00

No. 4210b is a complete double-sided booklet. Eight stamps (two each #4207-4210) plus P# and the label that serves as a booklet cover (BC241) are on one side of the peelable backing and 12 stamps (three each #4207-4210) are on the other side of the backing.

4214b, 4214c, 4214d — A3203-A3206

Serpentine Die Cut 11¼x11 on 2 or 3 Sides

4214b 41c pane of 4, #4211-4214, no P# 3.40

4214c 41c pane of 6, #4213-4214, 2 each #4211-4212, no P# 5.10

4214d 41c pane of 6, #4211-4212, 2 each #42131-4214, no P# 5.10

4214b, 4214c, 4214d — BC242

2007

$8.20 booklet contains 20 self-adhesive 41c stamps

COMBINATION BOOKLET

BK305 BC242 $8.20 **multi,** #4214c, 4214d, 2 #4214b, P#S1111 17.00

On No. BK305, plate number appears on the backing of the lower example of No. 4214b.

4218b — A3203-A3206

4218b — BC243

2007

$7.38 fold-it-yourself booklet contains 18 self-adhesive 41c stamps

Serpentine Die Cut 8 on 2, 3 or 4 Sides

Photo.

4218b 41c pane of 18, 4 each #4215, 4218, 5 each #4216, 4217, P#V1111 15.50

No. 4218b is a complete booklet (BC243). The peelable backing serves as a booklet cover.

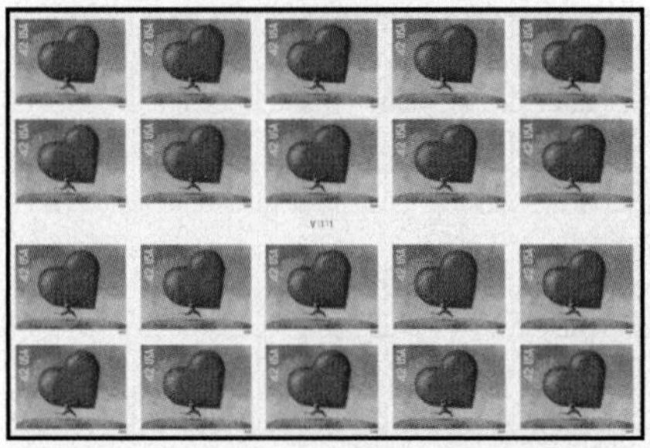

4270a — A3233

4270a — BC244

2008

$8.40 fold-it-yourself booklet contains 20 self-adhesive 42c stamps

Serpentine Die Cut 10¾ on 2, 3 or 4 Sides

2008, June 10 **Photo.**

Self-Adhesive

4270a A3233 42c pane of 20, P#V1111 17.00

No. 4270a is a complete booklet (BC244). The peelable backing serves as a booklet cover.

4271a — A3234

4271a — BC245

2008

$8.40 fold-it-yourself booklet contains 20 self-adhesive 42c stamps

Serpentine Die Cut 10¾ on 2, 3 or 4 Sides

2008, June 10 **Litho.**

Self-Adhesive

4271a A3234 42c pane of 20, no P# 17.00

No. 4271a is a complete booklet (BC245). The peelable backing, which has a plate number (P1111), serves as a booklet cover.

AIR POST BOOKLET PANES

C10a — AP6

FLAT PLATE PRINTING

1928 ***Perf. 11***

C10a AP6 10c **dark blue,** *May 26* 80.00 *65.00*

Never hinged 130.00

Tab at bottom —

No. C10a was printed from specially designed 180-subject plates arranged exactly as a 360-subject plate-each pane of three occupying the relative position of a pane of six in a 360-subject plate. Plate numbers appear at the sides, therefore Position D does not exist except partially on panes which have been trimmed off center. All other plate positions common to a 360-subject plate are known.

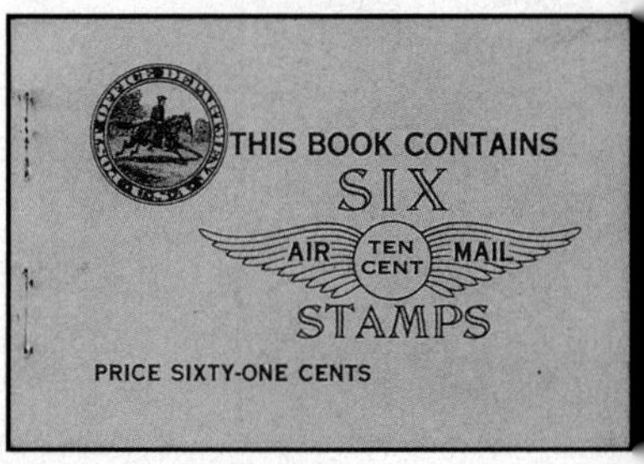

C10a BC8

1928 **Postrider and Wings**

61c booklet contains 2 panes of three 10c stamps.

Booklet

BKC1 BC8 61c **blue** 275.00

Tab at bottom, one pane in complete booklet *13,500.*

Catalogue values for unused panes in this section, from this point to the end, are for Never Hinged items.

C25a — AP17

ROTARY PRESS PRINTINGS

1943

C25a AP17 6c **carmine,** *Mar. 18* 5.00 1.50

180-Subject Plates Electric Eye Convertible.

C25a — BC10

Large background numerals

1943 **Postrider and Wings**

37c booklet contains 2 panes of three 6c stamps.
73c booklet contains 4 panes of three 6c stamps.

Booklets

BKC2	BC10	37c **red**	11.00
BKC3	BC10	73c **red**	22.50

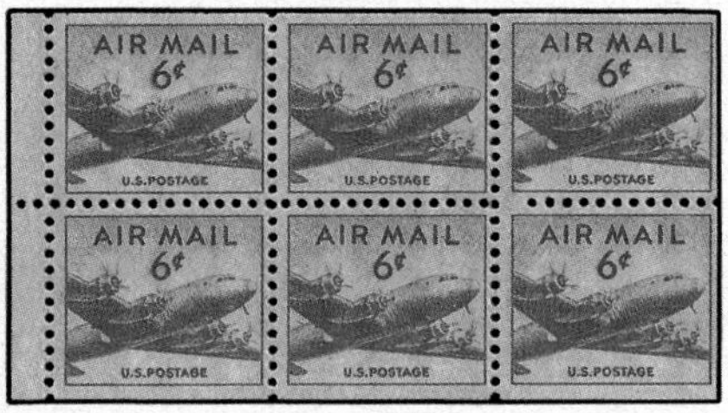

C39a — AP19

1949 ***Perf. 10½x11***

C39a	AP19	6c **carmine,** *Nov. 18*	10.00	5.00
C39c		Dry printing	25.00	—

C39a — BC11A

1949 **U.S. Airmail Wings**

The 73c and 85c booklets were the last sold for 1c over face value.

73c booklet contains 2 panes of six 6c stamps.

Booklets

BKC4	BC11A	73c **red,** with #C39a (4)	25.00
BKC4a	BC11A	73c **red,** with #C39c	60.00

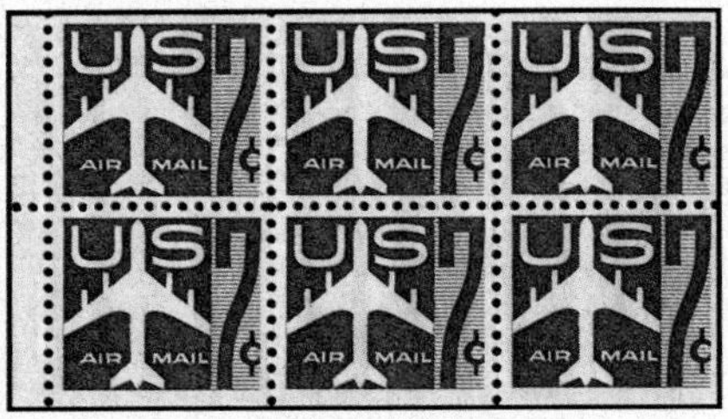

C51a — AP33

1958

C51a	AP33	7c **blue,** *July 31*	9.00	7.00

C51a — BC11B

C51a, C60a — BC11C

1958-60 **U.S. Airmail Wings**

The 73c and 85c booklets were the last sold for 1c over face value.

85c booklet contains 2 panes of six 7c stamps.

Booklets

BKC5	BC11B	85c on 73c **red**	22.50
BKC6	BC11C	85c **blue**	19.00

1960

C60a	AP33	7c **carmine,** *Aug. 19*	10.00	8.00

Booklets

BKC7	BC11C	85c **blue**	21.00
BKC8	BC11C	85c **red**	25.00

C64b — AP42

1962-64

C64b	AP42	8c **carmine,** pane of 5 + label, slogan 1, *Dec. 5, 1962*	7.00	3.00
		With slogan 2, *1963*	60.00	5.00
		With slogan 3, *1964*	13.00	2.50

C64b, C64c — BC11D

1962-64 **U.S. Airmail Wings**

80c booklet contains 2 panes of five 8c stamps.
$2 booklet contains 5 panes of five 8c stamps.

C64b, C64c — BC13B

1963-64 **Mr. Zip**

$2 booklet contains 5 panes of five 8c stamps.

Booklets (No. C64b)

BKC9	BC11D	80c **black,** *pink,* slogan 1	22.50
BKC10	BC11D	$2 **red,** *pink,* slogan 1	35.00
BKC11	BC11D	80c **black,** *pink,* slogan 3 (2)	30.00
BKC12	BC11D	$2 **red,** *pink,* slogan 2	300.00
BKC13	BC13B	$2 **red,** *pink,* slogan 2	350.00
BKC14	BC13B	$2 **red,** slogan 3	*3,500.*
BKC15	BC13B	$2 **red,** *pink,* slogan 3	100.00

The existence of a genuine example of No. BKC14 has been questioned by specialists. Fake examples are known in the marketplace. The editors would like to see evidence of a genuine example of this booklet.

C64c	AP42	As No. C64b, tagged, slogan 3, *1964*	2.00	.75

Plate of 360 subjects (300 stamps, 60 labels).

Booklets (No. C64c)

BKC16	BC11D	80c **black** (2)	50.00
BKC17	BC11D	80c **black,** *pink*	*700.00*
BKC18	BC13B	$2 **red,** *pink*	*325.00*
BKC19	BC13B	$2 **red** (3)	13.00

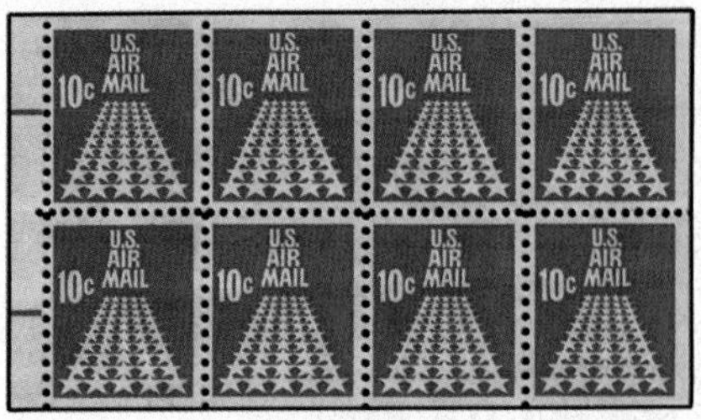

C72b — AP49

1968-73 ***Perf. 11x10½***

C72b	AP49	10c **carmine,** pane of 8, *Jan. 5, 1968*	2.00	.75

C72b — BC14B

1968

$4 booklet contains 5 panes of eight 10c stamps.

Booklet

BKC20	BC14B	$4 **red** (2)	12.00

C72c — AP49

C72c	AP49	10c **carmine,** pane of 5 + label, slogan 4, *Jan. 6, 1968*	3.75	.75
		With slogan 5	3.75	.75

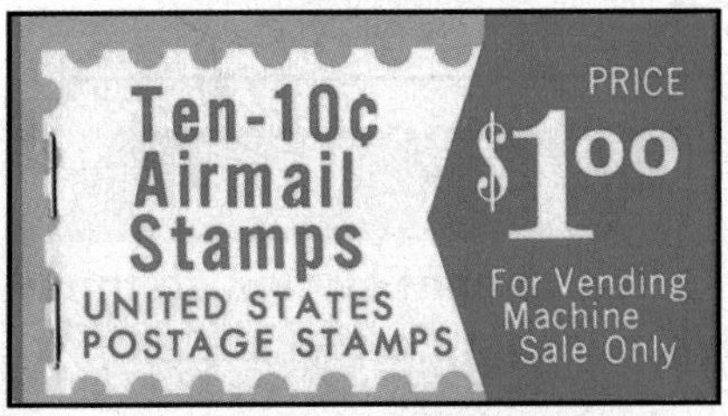

C72c — BC15A

1968

$1 booklet contains 2 panes of five 10c stamps.

Booklet

BKC21	BC15A	$1 **red** (2)	8.00

Variety

C72f	As "b," tagging omitted	—

C78a — AP54

C78a AP54 11c **carmine,** pane of 4 + 2 labels, slogans 5 & 4, *May 7, 1971* 1.25 .75

C78a, 1280c — BC15B

1971

$1 booklet contains 2 panes of four 11c stamps and 1 pane of six 2c stamps.

Combination Booklet

BKC22 BC15B $1 **red,** 2 #C78a + 1 #1280c (2) 3.75

C79a — AP55

C79a AP55 13c **carmine,** pane of 5 + label, slogan 8, *Dec. 27, 1973* 1.50 .75

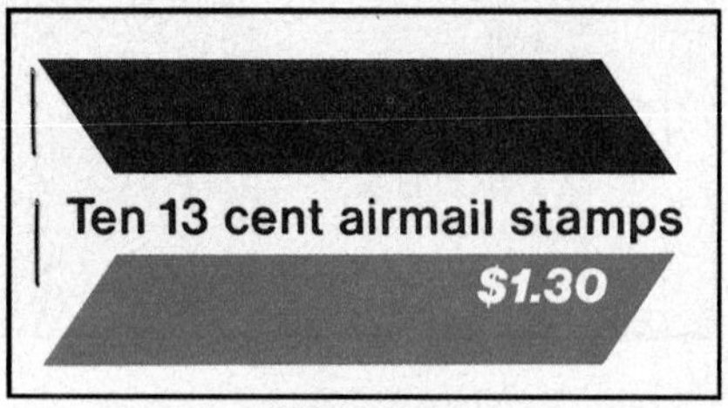

C79a — BC18

1973

$1.30 booklet contains 2 panes of five 13c stamps.

Booklet

BKC23 BC18 $1.30 **blue & red** (2) 3.25

Combination Booklet

See No. BK126.

No. C72b, the 8-stamp pane, was printed from 320-subject plate and from 400-subject plate; No. C72c, C78a and C79a from 360-subject plates.

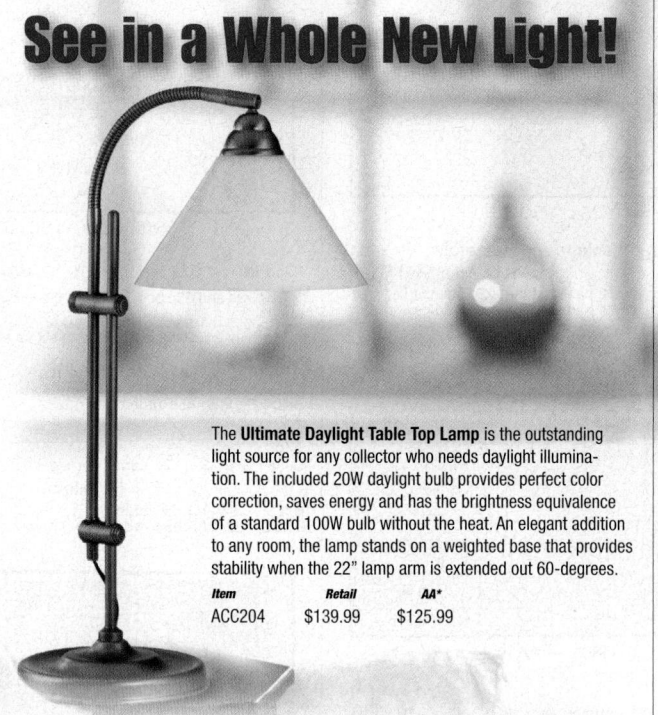

COMPUTER VENDED POSTAGE STAMPS

Unlike meters, except for the limits of the service requested, computer vended postage stamps are usable from any post office at any date.

Self-service user-interactive mailing system machines which vended computer-printed postage were in service and available to the general public at the Martin Luther King, Jr., Station of the Washington, DC, Post Office, and at the White Flint Mall in Kensington, MD, until May 7, 1990.

Machines were also available for use by delegates to the 20th Universal Postal Congress at the Washington Convention Center between Nov. 13 and Dec. 14, 1989. These machines, Washington Nos. 11 and 12, were not readily accessible by the general public.

A variety of services were available by using the machines, which could weigh items to be sent, determine postage rates through the connected computer, permit the customer to cancel the transaction or continue with it and generate a postage stamp, a label and a receipt. The stamps produced were valid only for domestic postage.

A tagged orange strip runs along the left side of the stamp. The requested mail service is in a double line box.

The denomination is in the upper box at right under "U.S. Postage." The date of the transaction is below the denomination. Next to the date is a number which indicates the item number within the transaction. The maximum number of items per transaction may be five.

Above the post office location is a box at right which gives the machine number, followed by the transaction or serial number. Stamps from the same transaction, which are generated and printed at the same time, will have the same transaction number, but different item numbers, even if different mail services are requested. Transaction numbers go back to 00001 every time the machine is reset. Below this is the weight of the item to be mailed.

Along with each stamp generated came an unattached label with one of three slogan types: "We Deliver. . .," used from September to November, "We Deliver. . . / United States Postal Service," used thereafter, and "Developed by / Technology Resource Department," used only on Machine 11 during its limited use.

Listings and values are for the basic denominations of the five postal services, though others are known or possible (45c, 65c, 85c for first class over 1 oz., $1.10 for certified first class, $3.25 for priority mail, $8.50 for express mail to post office boxes, parcel post weight and zone variations, etc.). Values for used copies are for those with a regular cancellation.

A total of 3,000 unused sets of five different service stamps and unused sets of two 25c (Nos. 02501-12500) first class stamps furnished to the Philatelic Agency have a first day date and serial numbers with the final three digits matching. First day dates Nos. 00101-02500 were sold over the counter at post offices.

Stamps were intended to be dispensed individually. The height of the stamps produced differs from machine to machine. Unsevered strips of stamps are known, as are unsevered strips of a slogan and one or more stamps. Printing varieties such as squeezes (more than one impression condensed on to one stamp) and stretches (impression stretched out so that a complete impression will not fit on the paper) also are known.

Issues starting with No. 31 will be explained with the listings.

CVP1

CVP2

1989, Aug. 23 Tagged *Guillotined*

Self-Adhesive

Washington, DC, Machine 82

CVP1	CVP1	25c **First Class,** any date other than first day	6.00	—
	a.	First day dated, serial Nos. 12501-15500	4.50	—
	b.	First day dated, serial Nos. 00001-12500	4.50	—
		On cover with first day cancel		*150.00*
	c.	First day dated, over No. 27500	—	—
		On cover with first day cancel		*150.00*
CVP2	CVP1	$1 **Third Class,** any date other than first day	—	—
	a.	First day dated, serial Nos. 24501-27500	—	—
	b.	First day dated, over No. 27500	—	—
CVP3	CVP2	$1.69 **Parcel Post,** any date other than first day	—	—
	a.	First day dated, serial Nos. 21501-24500	—	—
	b.	First day dated, over No. 27500	—	—
CVP4	CVP1	$2.40 **Priority Mail,** any date other than first day	—	—
	a.	First day dated, serial Nos. 18501-21500	—	—
	b.	Priority Mail ($2.74), with bar code (CVP2)	*100.00*	
	c.	First day dated, over No. 27500	—	—
		On cover with first day cancel or verifying receipt		*500.00*
CVP5	CVP1	$8.75 **Express Mail,** any date other than first day	—	—
	a.	First day dated, serial Nos. 15501-18500	—	—
	b.	First day dated, over No. 27500	—	—
		On cover with first day cancel or verifying receipt		—
		Nos. 1a-5a (5)	82.50	—

Washington, DC, Machine 83

CVP6	CVP1	25c **First Class,** any date other than first day	6.00	—
	a.	First day dated, serial Nos. 12501-15500	4.50	—
	b.	First day dated, serial Nos. 00001-12500	4.50	—
		On cover with first day cancel		*150.00*
	c.	First day dated, over No. 27500	—	—
		On cover with first day cancel		*150.00*

Error dates 11/17/90 and 11/18/90 exist.

CVP7	CVP1	$1 **Third Class,** any date other than first day	—	—
	a.	First day dated, serial Nos. 24501-27500	—	—
	b.	First day dated, over No. 27500	—	—
CVP8	CVP2	$1.69 **Parcel Post,** any date other than first day	—	—
	a.	First day dated, serial Nos. 21501-24500	—	—
	b.	First day dated, over No. 27500	—	—
CVP9	CVP1	$2.40 **Priority Mail,** any date other than first day	—	—
	a.	First day dated, serial Nos. 18501-21500	—	—
	b.	First day dated, over No. 27500	—	—
		On cover with first day cancel or verifying receipt		*500.00*

Error date 11/17/90 exists.

	c.	Priority Mail ($2.74), with bar code (CVP2)	*100.00*	

Error date 11/18/90 exists.

CVP10	CVP1	$8.75 **Express Mail,** any date other than first day	—	—
	a.	First day dated, serial Nos. 15501-18500	—	—
	b.	First day dated, over No. 27500	—	—
		On cover with first day cancel or verifying receipt		—
		Nos. 6a-10a (5)	57.50	—

Error date 11/17/90 exists.

1989, Sept. 1

Kensington, MD, Machine 82

CVP11	CVP1	25c **First Class,** any date other than first day	6.00	—
	a.	First day dated, serial Nos. 12501-15500	4.50	—
	b.	First day dated, serial Nos. 00001-12500	4.50	—
		On cover with first day cancel		*100.00*
	c.	First day dated, over No. 27500	—	—
		On cover with first day cancel		*100.00*
CVP12	CVP1	$1 **Third Class,** any date other than first day	—	—
	a.	First day dated, serial Nos. 24501-27500	—	—
	b.	First day dated, over No. 27500	—	—
CVP13	CVP2	$1.69 **Parcel Post,** any date other than first day	—	—
	a.	First day dated, serial Nos. 21501-24500	—	—
	b.	First day dated, over No. 27500	—	—
CVP14	CVP1	$2.40 **Priority Mail,** any date other than first day	—	—
	a.	First day dated, serial Nos. 18501-21500	—	—
	b.	First day dated, over No. 27500	—	—
	c.	Priority Mail ($2.74), with bar code (CVP2)	*100.00*	
CVP15	CVP1	$8.75 **Express Mail,** any date other than first day	—	—
	a.	First day dated, serial Nos. 15501-18500	—	—
	b.	First day dated, over No. 27500	—	—
		Nos. 11a-15a (5)	57.50	—
		Nos. 1b, 11b (2)	9.00	—

Kensington, MD, Machine 83

CVP16	CVP1	25c **First Class,** any date other than first day	6.00	—
	a.	First day dated, serial Nos. 12501-15500	4.50	—
	b.	First day dated, serial Nos. 00001-12500	4.50	—
	c.	First day dated, over No. 27500	—	—
		On cover with first day cancel		*100.00*
CVP17	CVP1	$1 **Third Class,** any date other than first day	—	—
	a.	First day dated, serial Nos. 24501-27500	—	—
	b.	First day dated, over No. 27500	—	—
CVP18	CVP2	$1.69 **Parcel Post,** any date other than first day	—	—
	a.	First day dated, serial Nos. 21501-24500	—	—
	b.	First day dated, over No. 27500	—	—
CVP19	CVP1	$2.40 **Priority Mail,** any date other than first day	—	—
	a.	First day dated, serial Nos. 18501-21500	—	—
	b.	First day dated, over No. 27500	—	—
	c.	Priority Mail ($2.74), with bar code (CVP2)	100.00	
CVP20	CVP1	$8.75 **Express Mail,** any date other than first day	—	—
	a.	First day dated, serial Nos. 15501-18500	—	—
	b.	First day dated, over No. 27500	—	—
		Nos. 16a-20a (5)	57.50	—
		Nos. 6b, 16b (2)	9.00	—

Unsevered pairs and single with advertising label exist for most, if not all, of the machine vended items from Kensington machine #83. Other combinations also exist.

1989, Nov.

Washington, DC, Machine 11

CVP21	CVP1	25c **First Class**	*150.00*	
	a.	First Class, with bar code (CVP2)		—

Stamps in CVP1 design with $1.10 denominations exist (certified first class).

CVP22	CVP1	$1 **Third Class**	*500.00*	
CVP23	CVP2	$1.69 **Parcel Post**	*500.00*	

CVP24 CVP1 $2.40 **Priority Mail** *500.00*
a. Priority Mail ($2.74), with bar code (CVP2) —
CVP25 CVP1 $8.75 **Express Mail** *500.00*

No. 21 dated Nov. 30 known on cover, Nos. 24-25 known dated Dec. 2.

Washington, DC, Machine 12

CVP26 CVP1 25c **First Class** *150.00*

A $1.10 certified First Class stamp, dated Nov. 20, exists on cover.

CVP27 CVP1 $1 **Third Class** —

A $1.40 Third Class stamp of type CVP2, dated Dec. 1 is known on a Dec. 2 cover.

CVP28 CVP2 $1.69 **Parcel Post** —
CVP29 CVP1 $2.40 **Priority Mail** —
a. Priority Mail ($2.74), with bar code (CVP2) —
CVP30 CVP1 $8.75 **Express Mail** —

Nos. 29-30 known dated Dec. 1. An $8.50 Express Mail stamp, dated Dec. 2, exists on cover.

CVP3 — Type I

CVP3 — Type II

Denomination printed by ECA GARD Postage and Mailing Center machines.

COIL STAMPS

1992, Aug. 20 Engr. Tagged *Perf. 10 Horiz.*

CVP31 CVP3 29c **red & blue**, type I, prephosphored paper (solid tagging), dull gum .70 .25
Pair 1.40
P# strip of 5, P#1 8.50
P# single, #1 5.50
a. 29c Type I, prephosphored paper (mottled tagging), shiny gum .70 .25
Pair 1.40 —
P# strip of 5, P#1 8.50 —
P# single, #1 5.50
First day cover, Oklahoma City, OK 1.25
b. 32c Type II, prephosphored paper (solid tagging), dull gum, *Nov. 1994* .90 .40
Pair 1.80
P# strip of 5, P#1 60.00
P# single, #1 *5.50*
c. 32c Type II, prephosphored paper (mottled tagging), shiny gum 1.00 .40
Pair 2.00
P# strip of 5, P#1 8.75
P# single, #1 *8.00*

Types I and II differ in style of asterisk, period between dollar and cent figures and font used for figures, as shown in illustrations.

No. 31 was available at five test sites in the Southern Maryland, Miami, Oklahoma City, Detroit and Santa Ana, CA, divisions. They were produced for use in ECA GARD Postage and Mailing Center (PMC) machines which can produce denominations from 1c through $99.99.

For Nos. 31-31a, the 29c value is listed because it was the current first class rate and was the only value available through the USPS Philatelic Sales Division. The most common denomination available other than 29c is 1c (value 20c) because these were made in quantity, by collectors and dealers, between plate number strips. Later the machines were adjusted to provide only 19c and higher value stamps.

For Nos. 31b-31c, the 32c value is listed because it was the first class rate in effect for the majority of the period the stamps were in use.

CVP4

Denominations printed by Unisys PMC machines.

1994, Feb. 19 Photo. Tagged *Perf. 9.9 Vert.*

CVP32 CVP4 29c **dark red & dark blue** .70 .35
Pair 1.40 —
P# strip of 5, #A11 8.00 —
P# single, #A11 5.50
First day cover, Merrifield, VA *(26,390)* 1.25

No. 32 was available at six test sites in northern Virginia. It was produced for use in machines which can produce values from 19c to $99.99. See note following No. 31.

For No. 32, the 29c value has been listed because it was the first class rate in effect at the time the stamp was issued.

1996, Jan. 26 Photo. Tagged *Perf. 9.9 Vert.*

CVP33 CVP4 32c **bright red & blue,** "1996" below design .70 .25
Pair 1.40 —
P# strip of 5, same, #11 8.00 —
P# single, #11 6.00

Letters in "USA" on No. 33 are thicker than on No. 32. Numerous other design differences exist in the moire pattern and in the bunting. No. 33 has "1996" in the lower left corner; No. 32 has no date.

For No. 33, the 32c value has been listed because it was the first class rate in effect at the time the stamp was issued.

CVP5

Illustration reduced.

1999 Tagged *Die Cut*
Self-Adhesive

CVP34 CVP5 33c **black** *50.00* —
On cover *75.00*
a. "Priority Mail" under encryption at LL — —
b. "Express Mail" under encryption at LL — —

No. CVP34 was available from 15 NCR Automated Postal Center machines located in central Florida. Machines could produce values in any denomination required. The backing paper is taller and wider than the stamp.

Sales of No. CVP34 were discontinued in 2000 or 2001.

CVP6

Illustration reduced.

1999, May 7 Tagged *Die Cut*
Self-Adhesive
Size: 77½x39mm

Microprinting Above Red Orange Line

CVP35 CVP6 33c **black & red orange,** control numbers only at LL, square corners 190.00 —
Round corners 13.50 —
a. "Priority Mail" at LL, square corners 150.00 —
Round corners — —
b. "Priority Mail AS" and text string at LL, square corners 150.00 —
Round corners — —

No Microprinting Above Red Orange Line

CVP36 CVP6 33c **black & red orange,** control numbers only at LL, square corners 190.00 —
Round corners 10.00 —
a. "Priority Mail" at LL, square corners 125.00 —
Round corners — —
b. "Priority Mail AS" and text string at LL, square corners 125.00 —
Round corners — —

Size: 73½x42mm

CVP37 CVP6 33c **black & pink,** control numbers only at LL 3.75 —
a. "Priority Mail" at LL 5.00 —
b. "Priority Mail AS" and text string at LL 5.00 —

Nos. CVP35-CVP37 were available from 18 IBM Neopost machines located in central Florida. The backing paper is taller than the stamp. Any denomination could be printed up to $99.99.

CVP7

Simplypostage.com — CVP8

2000-01 *Serpentine Die Cut*
Self-Adhesive

CVP38 CVP7 33c **black, yellow & pink** — —
On cover
Pane of 10 — —

Serpentine Die Cut 8 at Right
Eagle and Stars Background

CVP39 CVP8 34c **black, blue & orange,** *2001* — —
On cover 75.00
Pane of 4 — —
CVP40 CVP8 34c **black, blue & orange,** with control number at UL, *2001* — —
On cover 75.00
Pane of 4 — —

Flag Background

CVP41 CVP8 34c **black, blue & orange,** with control number at UL, *2001* — —
On cover 150.00
Pane of 4 — —
CVP42 CVP8 34c **black, blue & orange,** with control number at LL, *2001* — 20.00
On cover 150.00
Pane of 4 — 80.00

Customers could print up to five panes of Nos. CVP39-CVP42 in each transaction. Panes were consecutively numbered identifying the total number of stamps and panes in each transaction.

Neopostage.com — CVP9

2002, June -2003 *Serpentine Die Cut 8¾ at Right*
Self-Adhesive

CVP43 CVP9 21c **black, blue & orange,** *June 2002* — —
On cover —
a. Booklet pane of 10 —
CVP44 CVP9 23c **black, blue & orange,** *June 2002* — —
On cover —
a. Booklet pane of 10 —
CVP45 CVP9 34c **black, blue & orange,** *June 2002* — —
On cover —
a. Booklet pane of 10 —
CVP46 CVP9 37c **black, blue & orange,** *July 1, 2003* — —
On cover —
a. Booklet pane of 10 —
CVP47 CVP9 50c **black, blue & orange,** *July 1, 2003* — —
On cover —
a. Booklet pane of 10 —
CVP48 CVP9 60c **black, blue & orange,** *July 1, 2003* — —
On cover —
a. Booklet pane of 10 —
CVP49 CVP9 70c **black, blue & orange,** *July 1, 2003* — —
On cover —
a. Booklet pane of 10 —
CVP50 CVP9 80c **black, blue & orange,** *July 1, 2003* — —
On cover —
a. Booklet pane of 10 —
CVP51 CVP9 $3.50 **black, blue & orange,** *June 2002* — —
On cover —
a. Booklet pane of 1 —
b. Booklet pane of 2 —
c. Booklet pane of 5 —
d. Booklet pane of 10 —
CVP52 CVP9 $3.85 **black, blue & orange,** *July 1, 2003* — —
On cover —
a. Booklet pane of 1 —
b. Booklet pane of 2 —
c. Booklet pane of 5 —
d. Booklet pane of 10 —
CVP53 CVP9 $13.65 **black, blue & orange,** *July 1, 2003* — —

	On cover		—
a.	Booklet pane of 1		—
b.	Booklet pane of 2		—
c.	Booklet pane of 5		—
d.	Booklet pane of 10		—

Nos. CVP43-CVP53 were printed only with the stated values.

A 57c denomination (pane of 10) and $12.45 denomination (pane of 1) exist, but may have been produced at a site not accessible by the public.

While the name on Nos. CVP38-CVP42 reads simplypostage.com and the name on Nos. CVP43-CVP53 reads neopostage.com, both were products of Neopost.

CVP10

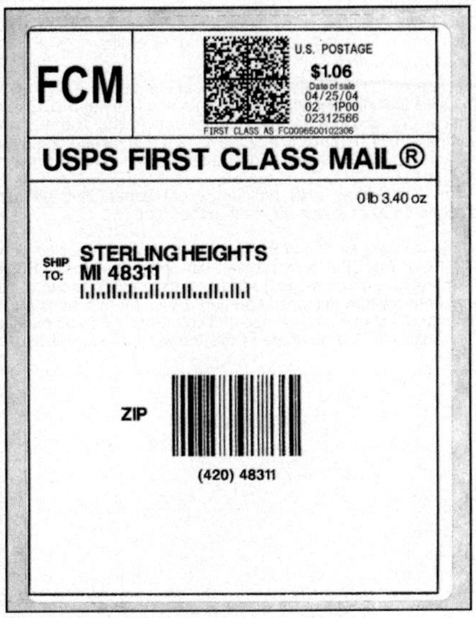

IBM Pitney Bowes — CVP11

Illustrations reduced.

2004, Apr. 14 ***Die Cut***

Self-Adhesive

CVP54	CVP10	37c **black & pink**	5.75	—
a.		"First Class Mail" under encryption at LL	2.50	—
b.		"Priority Mail" under encryption at LL	2.50	—
c.		"Parcel Post" under encryption at LL	2.50	—
d.		"International" under encryption at LL	2.50	—
CVP55	CVP11	37c **black,** "US Postage" under encryption at LL	2.50	—
a.		"First Class Mail" under encryption at LL	—	—
b.		"Priority Mail" under encryption at LL	—	—
c.		"Parcel Post" under encryption at LL	—	—
d.		"International" under encryption at LL	—	—

Nos. CVP54-CVP55 could be printed in any denomination up to $99.99.

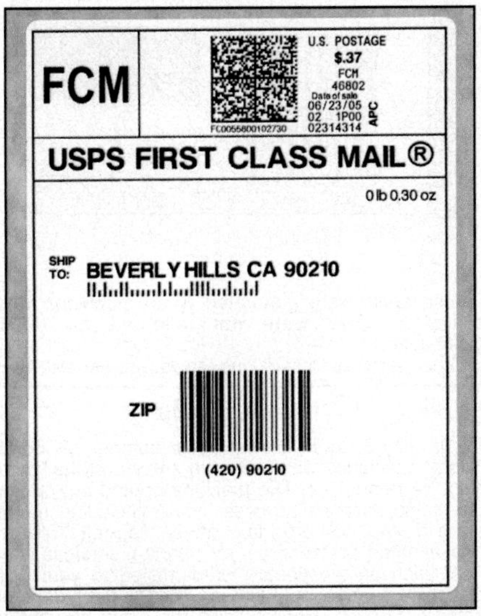

CVP12

IBM Pitney Bowes — CVP13

Illustrations reduced.

2004, Nov. 19 ***Die Cut***

Self-Adhesive

CVP56	CVP12	37c **black & pink**	2.50	.25
a.		"Priority" under denomination	3.00	—
b.		"Parcel Post" under denomination	3.00	—
c.		"Express" under denomination	3.00	—
CVP57	CVP13	37c **black & pink**	1.00	.25
a.		"Priority" under denomination	1.25	—
b.		"Parcel Post" under denomination	1.25	—
c.		"Express" under denomination	1.25	—
d.		"Int Air LP" under denomination	1.25	—
e.		"FCM Letter" under denomination	1.25	—
f.		"FCM Flat" under denomination	1.25	—
g.		"FCM Parcel" under denomination	1.25	—
h.		"FCM Intl" under denomination, "IM" and numbers under encryption	1.25	—
i.		"FCM Lg Env" under denomination	1.25	—
j.		"PM Fr Env" under denomination, "PM" and numbers under encryption	1.25	—
k.		"PM Fr Box" under denomination, "PM" and numbers under encryption	1.25	—
l.		"PM Lfr Box" under denomination, "PM" and numbers under encryption	1.25	—
m.		"Exp Fr Env" under denomination, "EM" and numbers under encryption	1.25	—
n.		"FCMI Ltr" under denomination, "IM" and numbers under encryption	1.25	—
o.		"FCMI L Env" under denomination, "IM" and numbers under encryption	1.25	—

Nos. CVP56-CVP57 could be printed in any denomination. Cataogue values for CVP56a-CVP56c and CVP57a-CVP57o are for stamps with low denominations. Stamps with denominations appropriate to the service described are valued correspondingly higher.

Nos. CVP57e-CVP57h issued May 2007; No. CVP57i issued Sept. 2007; Nos. CVP57j-CVP57m issued 2008; Nos. CVP57n-CVP57o, May 2008.

Under the encryption No. CVP57 has "FC" and numbers; on No. CVP57a, "PM" and numbers; on No. CVP57b,"PP" and numbers; on No. CVP57c, "EM" and numbers; and on No. CVP57d, "IM" and numbers.

Blank Under Denomination

"IM" and Numbers Under Encryption

CVP58	CVP13	60c **black & pink**	3.00	.50
CVP59	CVP13	80c **black & pink**	3.75	.50

"PM" and Numbers Under Encryption

CVP60	CVP13	$3.85 **black & pink**	15.00	.50

"EM" and Numbers Under Encryption

CVP61	CVP13	$13.65 **black & pink**	42.50	1.00

"IB" and Numbers Under Encryption

CVP62	CVP13	$1 **black & pink**	4.00	.25

Nos. CVP58-CVP61 could only be printed in denominations listed. No. CVP62 could be printed in any denomination above 99c. As of May 12, 2008, it was possible to create stamps with "IB" and numbers under encryption in any denomination. The computer software was later changed to once again only permit stamps of certain denominations to be created with "IB" and numbers under the encryption.

IBM Pitney Bowes Type of 2004

2006 ? ***Die Cut***

Self-Adhesive

Blank Under Denomination

"IM" and Numbers Under Encryption

CVP63	CVP13	48c **black & pink**	1.25	.40
CVP64	CVP13	63c **black & pink**	1.50	.50
CVP65	CVP13	84c **black & pink**	2.00	.50

"PM" and Numbers Under Encryption

CVP66	CVP13	$4.05 **black & pink**	9.50	.50
CVP66A	CVP13	$8.10 **black & pink**	16.50	1.00

"EM" and Numbers Under Encryption

CVP67	CVP13	$14.40 **black & pink**	30.00	1.00

Nos. CVP63-CVP67 could only be printed in denominations listed.

IBM Pitney Bowes — CVP14

Illustration reduced.

2006 ***Die Cut***

Self-Adhesive

No Inscription Under Encryption

Serial Number to Right of "APC"

"Ship To:" Above Destination City

CVP69	CVP14	39c **black**	2.25	.25
a.		"Priority" under denomination	2.25	—
b.		"Parcel Post" under denomination	2.25	—
c.		"Express" under denomination	2.25	—
d.		"FCM Flat" under denomination	1.25	—
e.		"FCM Parcel" under denomination	1.25	—
f.		"FCM Lg Env" under denomination	1.25	—
g.		"PM Fr Env" under denomination	1.25	—
h.		"PM Fr Box" under denomination	1.25	—
i.		"PM Lfr Box" under denomination	1.25	—
j.		"Exp Fr Env" under denomination	1.25	—

Nos. CVP69-CVP69j could be printed in any denomination. Catalogue values are for stamps with low denominations. Stamps with denominations appropriate to the service described are valued correspondingly higher.

Nos. CVP69d-CVP69e issued May 2007; No. CVP69f issued Sept. 2007; Nos. CVP69g-CVP69j issued 2008.

IBM Pitney Bowes Type of 2004

2006(?)-07 ***Die Cut***

Self-Adhesive

Blank Under Denomination

"IB" and Numbers Under Encryption

CVP70	CVP13	39c **black & pink**	1.00	.50
CVP71	CVP13	41c **black & pink**	1.00	.50
CVP72	CVP13	69c **black & pink**	1.40	.70

"IM" and Numbers Under Encryption

CVP73	CVP13	61c **black & pink**	1.25	.50
CVP74	CVP13	90c **black & pink**	1.90	.95

Nos. CVP70-CVP74 could only be printed in the denominations listed.

Nos. CVP71-CVP74 issued May, 2007. No. CVP70 was issued before the May rate change. As of May 12, 2008, it was possible to create stamps with "IB" and numbers under encryption in any denomination. The computer software was later changed to once again only permit stamps of certain denominations to be created with "IB" and numbers under the encryption. No. CVP70 was available for sale from Nov. 2006 to May 13, 2007. Nos. CVP71-CVP72 were available for sale from May 14, 2007 to May 11, 2008.

Pitney Bowes — CVP15

Illustration reduced.

2006, Dec. *Die Cut*

Self-Adhesive

CVP75	CVP15	41c **black & pink**		—	—
	a.	"Mailed From Zip Code ..." on bottom line		.20	—
	b.	"Postcard" on bottom line		.55	—
	c.	"First Class Mail Intl" on bottom line		1.25	—
	d.	"Parcel Post" on bottom line		7.50	—
	e.	"Priority" on bottom line		9.25	—
	f.	"Express Mail" on bottom line		33.00	—

No. CVP75 was put into service at large companies and universities in Dec. 2006, with the majority of the machines not being available to the general public. Information about this stamp was not made available until 2007. Other rates and inscriptions might be available.

Nos. CVP75a could be printed in any denomination. Nos. CVP75b-CVP75f could be printed only in pre-programmed denominations based on the current rates for the service, or in any denominations at or above the minimum rates for the service. Values are for stamps with low denominations. A stamp with "First Class" on the bottom line has been reported but has not been seen by the editors. Inscriptions generated by the software may vary from machine to machine depending on when the software was installed.

IBM Pitney Bowes Type of 2004

2008, May *Die Cut*

Self-Adhesive

Blank Under Denomination

"IM" and Numbers Under Encryption

CVP76	CVP13	94c **black & pink**	2.00	.60
CVP77	CVP13	$1.20 **black & pink**	2.40	1.25

Nos. CVP76-CVP77 could only be printed in the denominations listed.

Machine Set-up Test Labels

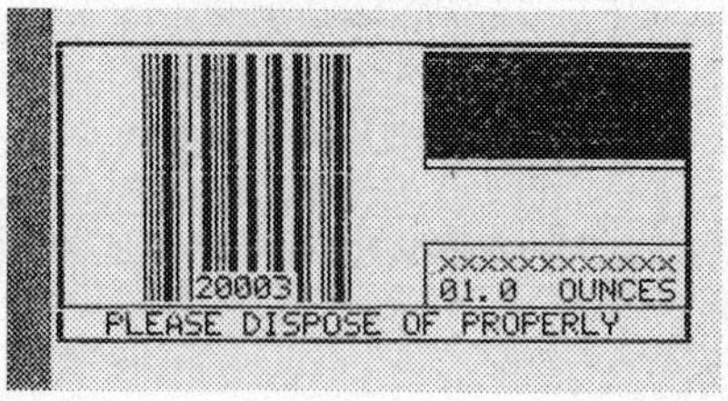

Test labels were generated when machines were activated. They were not intended for public distribution.

Other samples, advertizing labels, proofs, etc. exist.

POSTAL CARDS

On July 5, 1990 the first of a number of "Postal Buddy" machines was placed in service at the Merrifield, VA post office. The machine printed out numerous items such as address labels (including monogram if you wished), fax labels, "penalty" cards, denominated postal cards, etc. Certain services were free, such as the penalty card mailed to your post office for change of address. The 15-cent denominated card cost 33-cents each and could be used to notify others of address change, meeting notices, customized messages, etc. Borders, messages, backs are different. The cards also came in sheets of 4.

These machines were tested in at least 30 locations in Virginia, including 16 post offices.

Denominated Postal Cards

Number under design includes machine number, year, date (1 through 366) and transaction number.

1990, July 5

CVUX1	15c	6.00	*10.00*
	First day cancel, Merrifield, VA *(6,500)*		5.00

1991, Feb. 3

CVUX2	19c	3.00	*8.00*
	First day cancel, any location		35.00

Number under design includes ZIP Code of the originating machine (22033 in illustration), machine number (101), last digit of year, numbers of month and day (21203 for Dec. 3, 1992) and transaction number (041).

1992, Nov. 13

CVUX3	19c	6.00	*15.00*
	First day dated, Reston or Chantilly, VA		25.00

A total of 171 machines were used in the greater Washington, DC area including locations in Virginia and Maryland (109), the greater San Diego area (59), and in Denver (3). The machine numbers (011, 012, 021, 101, 111, 121, 131) when combined with the zip code created unique identification numbers for each machine.

No. 3 is known also on fluorescent paper. Two different designs on back known for each paper type.

The contract for Postal Buddy machines was canceled Sept. 16, 1993. After the contract was canceled, the Postal Buddy Corporation sold remaining stocks of card stock to the public with both reverse designs imprinted. By using this stock and a high quality copier, very dangerous counterfeits can be created. The duplication of numbers in the transaction line will be one indicator.

PERSONAL COMPUTER POSTAGE

Personal computer postage, approved by the US Postal Service, was created by subscribing to Stamps.com, an internet website. Customers ordered self-adhesive labels showing vignettes, but lacking any franking value. The franking value portion of the stamps could be printed at the customer's convenience at any computer with an internet connection, using the customer's access codes. Any postage printed would be charged against the customer's account.

Stamps with major listings could be printed in any denomination up to $999.99. Stamps with minor listings could only be printed in denominations calculated by the weight of the piece being mailed. Denominations for minor listings can range from 23c to $133.20. Customers could print the franking value portion of the stamps on whatever they put into their printer, be it envelopes, plain gummed labels or regular paper, but these listings are limited to items on the self-adhesive labels shown, which have tagging that allows the mail the stamp is on to go through the mail stream smoothly.

Stamps.com

Flag and Star — CVPA1

2002 *Serpentine Die Cut 5¾ at Left*

"Stamps.com" in Lower Case Letters

Identification Code Above Zip Code

1CVP1	CVPA1	37c **black, blue & orange**		4.00	3.00
		On cover			3.50
		Sheet of 25		100.00	
	a.	"First Class" below "US Postage"		2.75	2.00
	b.	"Priority" below "US Postage"		8.25	2.50
	c.	"Express" below "US Postage"		25.00	5.00
	d.	"Media Mail" below "US Postage"		7.75	2.50
	e.	"Parcel Post" below "US Postage"		7.75	2.50
	f.	"Bound Printed Matter" below "US Postage"		7.75	2.50
	g.	"BPM" below "US Postage"		7.75	2.50

Identification Code Below Zip Code

1CVP2	CVPA1	37c **black, blue & orange**		7.00	3.00
		On cover			4.00
		Sheet of 25		175.00	
	a.	"First Class" below zip code		2.75	2.00
	b.	"Priority" below zip code		8.25	2.50
	c.	"Express" below zip code		25.00	5.00
	d.	"Media Mail" below zip code		7.75	2.50
	e.	"Parcel Post" below zip code		7.75	2.50

See Nos. 1CVP9, 1CVP21.

Later versions of the Stamps.com software allow any denomination to be printed, as well as additional or different mail-class inscriptions, on any basic stamp except for No. 1CVP2.

Values for Nos. 1CVP1 and 1CVP3-1CVP42 are for items appropriate to the service described. Stamps with denominations far lower than those appropriate to the service are valued correspondingly lower.

The software changes allow Nos. 1CVP1 and 1CVP3-1CVP37 to be printed with the mail-class inscriptions described for Nos. 1CVP38f-1CVP38p.

Later software changes allow Nos. 1CVP1, 1CVP3-1CVP42 and 1CVP51-1CVP58 to be printed with mail-class inscriptions "Library Mail," "Intl. First Class," "Intl Priority," "Intl Express," and "M-Bag" with any denomination.

Love — CVPA2

2002 ***Serpentine Die Cut 5¾ at Left***

1CVP3	CVPA2 37c **black, blue & orange**	4.00	4.00
	On cover		5.00
	Sheet of 25	100.00	
a.	"First Class" below "US Postage"	2.75	2.00
b.	"Priority" below "US Postage"	8.25	2.50
c.	"Express" below "US Postage"	25.00	5.00
d.	"Media Mail" below "US Postage"	7.75	2.50
e.	"Parcel Post" below "US Postage"	7.75	2.50
f.	"Bound Printed Matter" below "US Postage"	7.75	2.50
g.	"BPM" below "US Postage"	7.75	2.50

Statue of Liberty and Flag — CVPA3

Liberty Bell and Flag — CVPA4

Eagle and Flag — CVPA5

George Washington and Flag — CVPA6

Capitol Building and Flag — CVPA7

2003, June ***Serpentine Die Cut 5¾ at Left***

1CVP4	CVPA3 37c **black, blue & orange**	3.50	2.00
	On cover		3.00
a.	"First Class" below "US Postage"	3.25	2.00
b.	"Priority" below "US Postage"	8.00	1.00
c.	"Express" below "US Postage"	25.00	3.00
d.	"Media Mail" below "US Postage"	7.50	1.00
e.	"Parcel Post" below "US Postage"	7.50	1.00
f.	"Bound Printed Matter" below "US Postage"	7.50	1.00
g.	"BPM" below "US Postage"	7.50	1.00
1CVP5	CVPA4 37c **black, blue & orange**	3.50	2.00
	On cover		3.00
a.	"First Class" below "US Postage"	3.25	2.00
b.	"Priority" below "US Postage"	8.00	1.00
c.	"Express" below "US Postage"	25.00	3.00
d.	"Media Mail" below "US Postage"	7.50	1.00
e.	"Parcel Post" below "US Postage"	7.50	1.00
f.	"Bound Printed Matter" below "US Postage"	7.50	1.00
g.	"BPM" below "US Postage"	7.50	1.00
1CVP6	CVPA5 37c **black, blue & orange**	3.50	2.00
	On cover		3.00
a.	"First Class" below "US Postage"	3.25	2.00
b.	"Priority" below "US Postage"	8.00	1.00
c.	"Express" below "US Postage"	25.00	3.00
d.	"Media Mail" below "US Postage"	7.50	1.00
e.	"Parcel Post" below "US Postage"	7.50	1.00
f.	"Bound Printed Matter" below "US Postage"	7.50	1.00
g.	"BPM" below "US Postage"	7.50	1.00
1CVP7	CVPA6 37c **black, blue & orange**	3.50	2.00
	On cover		3.00
a.	"First Class" below "US Postage"	3.25	.20
b.	"Priority" below "US Postage"	8.00	1.00
c.	"Express" below "US Postage"	25.00	3.00
d.	"Media Mail" below "US Postage"	7.50	1.00
e.	"Parcel Post" below "US Postage"	7.50	1.00
f.	"Bound Printed Matter" below "US Postage"	7.50	1.00
g.	"BPM" below "US Postage"	7.50	1.00
1CVP8	CVPA7 37c **black, blue & orange**	3.50	2.00
	On cover		3.00
a.	"First Class" below "US Postage"	3.25	.20
b.	"Priority" below "US Postage"	8.00	1.00
c.	"Express" below "US Postage"	25.00	3.00
d.	"Media Mail" below "US Postage"	7.50	1.00
e.	"Parcel Post" below "US Postage"	7.50	1.00
f.	"Bound Printed Matter" below "US Postage"	7.50	1.00
g.	"BPM" below "US Postage"	7.50	1.00
h.	Strip of 5, #1CVP4-1CVP8	17.50	

Flag and Star Type of 2002 Redrawn With "Stamps.com" in Upper Case Letters

2003, June ***Serpentine Die Cut 5¾ at Left***

Identification Code Above Zip Code

1CVP9	CVPA1 37c **black, blue & orange**	2.50	1.50
	On cover		2.50
	Sheet of 25	62.50	
a.	"First Class" below "US Postage"	.75	.20
b.	"Priority" below "US Postage"	8.00	1.00
c.	"Express" below "US Postage"	25.00	3.00
d.	"Media Mail" below "US Postage"	7.50	1.00
e.	"Parcel Post" below "US Postage"	7.50	1.00
f.	"Bound Printed Matter" below "US Postage"	7.50	1.00
g.	"BPM" below "US Postage"	7.50	1.00

Snowman — CVPA8

Snowflakes CVPA9

Holly — CVPA10

Dove — CVPA11

Gingerbread Man and Candy — CVPA12

2003, Dec. ***Serpentine Die Cut 4½ at Left***

1CVP10	CVPA8 37c **black, blue & orange**	3.00	1.50
	On cover		2.50
a.	"First Class" below "US Postage"	2.00	1.00
b.	"Priority" below "US Postage"	8.00	1.00
c.	"Express" below "US Postage"	25.00	3.00
d.	"Media Mail" below "US Postage"	7.50	1.00
e.	"Parcel Post" below "US Postage"	7.50	1.00
f.	"Bound Printed Matter" below "US Postage"	7.50	1.00
g.	"BPM" below "US Postage"	7.50	1.00
1CVP11	CVPA9 37c **black, blue & orange**	3.00	1.50
	On cover		2.50
a.	"First Class" below "US Postage"	2.00	1.00
b.	"Priority" below "US Postage"	8.00	1.00
c.	"Express" below "US Postage"	25.00	3.00
d.	"Media Mail" below "US Postage"	7.50	1.00
e.	"Parcel Post" below "US Postage"	7.50	1.00
f.	"Bound Printed Matter" below "US Postage"	7.50	1.00
g.	"BPM" below "US Postage"	7.50	1.00
1CVP12	CVPA10 37c **black, blue & orange**	3.00	1.50
	On cover		2.50
a.	"First Class" below "US Postage"	2.00	1.00
b.	"Priority" below "US Postage"	8.00	1.00
c.	"Express" below "US Postage"	25.00	3.00
d.	"Media Mail" below "US Postage"	7.50	1.00
e.	"Parcel Post" below "US Postage"	7.50	1.00
f.	"Bound Printed Matter" below "US Postage"	7.50	1.00
g.	"BPM" below "US Postage"	7.50	1.00
1CVP13	CVPA11 37c **black, blue & orange**	3.00	1.50
	On cover		2.50
a.	"First Class" below "US Postage"	2.00	1.00
b.	"Priority" below "US Postage"	8.00	1.00
c.	"Express" below "US Postage"	25.00	3.00
d.	"Media Mail" below "US Postage"	7.50	1.00
e.	"Parcel Post" below "US Postage"	7.50	1.00
f.	"Bound Printed Matter" below "US Postage"	7.50	1.00
g.	"BPM" below "US Postage"	7.50	1.00
1CVP14	CVPA12 37c **black, blue & orange**	3.00	1.50
	On cover		2.50
a.	"First Class" below "US Postage"	2.00	1.00
b.	"Priority" below "US Postage"	8.00	1.00
c.	"Express" below "US Postage"	25.00	3.00
d.	"Media Mail" below "US Postage"	7.50	1.00
e.	"Parcel Post" below "US Postage"	7.50	1.00
f.	"Bound Printed Matter" below "US Postage"	7.50	1.00
g.	"BPM" below "US Postage"	7.50	1.00
h.	Strip of 5, #1CVP10-1CVP14	12.50	

Mailbox — CVPA13

2004, Mar. ***Serpentine Die Cut 6½ at Left***

1CVP15	CVPA13 37c **black, blue & orange**	25.00	15.00
	On cover		35.00
a.	"First Class" below "US Postage"	25.00	15.00
b.	"Priority" below "US Postage"	—	—
c.	"Express" below "US Postage"	—	—
d.	"Media Mail" below "US Postage"	—	—
e.	"Parcel Post" below "US Postage"	—	—
f.	"Bound Printed Matter" below "US Postage"	—	—
g.	"BPM" below "US Postage"	—	—

Blank sheets of No. 1CVP15 were sent free of charge to those who responded to special Stamps.com promotions which offered a fixed amount of free postage as an enticement to new subscribers. The franking portion of the stamps could only be applied after subscribing.

George Washington CVPA14

Thomas Jefferson — CVPA15

Abraham Lincoln — CVPA16

Theodore Roosevelt — CVPA17

John F. Kennedy — CVPA18

2004, Apr. ***Serpentine Die Cut 6½ at Left***

1CVP16	CVPA14 37c **black, blue & orange**	2.00	1.00
	On cover		2.50
a.	"First Class" below "US Postage"	1.10	.75
b.	"Priority" below "US Postage"	5.00	2.50
c.	"Express" below "US Postage"	20.00	5.00
d.	"Media Mail" below "US Postage"	5.00	2.50
e.	"Parcel Post" below "US Postage"	5.00	2.50
f.	"Bound Printed Matter" below "US Postage"	5.00	2.50
g.	"BPM" below "US Postage"	5.00	2.50
1CVP17	CVPA15 37c **black, blue & orange**	2.00	1.00
	On cover		2.50
a.	"First Class" below "US Postage"	1.10	.75
b.	"Priority" below "US Postage"	5.00	2.50
c.	"Express" below "US Postage"	20.00	5.00
d.	"Media Mail" below "US Postage"	5.00	2.50
e.	"Parcel Post" below "US Postage"	5.00	2.50
f.	"Bound Printed Matter" below "US Postage"	5.00	2.50
g.	"BPM" below "US Postage"	5.00	2.50
1CVP18	CVPA16 37c **black, blue & orange**	2.00	1.00
	On cover		2.50
a.	"First Class" below "US Postage"	1.10	.75
b.	"Priority" below "US Postage"	5.00	2.50
c.	"Express" below "US Postage"	20.00	5.00
d.	"Media Mail" below "US Postage"	5.00	2.50
e.	"Parcel Post" below "US Postage"	5.00	2.50
f.	"Bound Printed Matter" below "US Postage"	5.00	2.50
g.	"BPM" below "US Postage"	5.00	2.50
1CVP19	CVPA17 37c **black, blue & orange**	2.00	1.00
	On cover		2.50
a.	"First Class" below "US Postage"	1.10	.75
b.	"Priority" below "US Postage"	5.00	2.50
c.	"Express" below "US Postage"	20.00	5.00
d.	"Media Mail" below "US Postage"	5.00	2.50
e.	"Parcel Post" below "US Postage"	5.00	2.50
f.	"Bound Printed Matter" below "US Postage"	5.00	2.50
g.	"BPM" below "US Postage"	5.00	2.50
1CVP20	CVPA18 37c **black, blue & orange**	2.00	1.00
	On cover		2.50
a.	"First Class" below "US Postage"	1.10	.75
b.	"Priority" below "US Postage"	5.00	2.50
c.	"Express" below "US Postage"	20.00	5.00
d.	"Media Mail" below "US Postage"	5.00	2.50
e.	"Parcel Post" below "US Postage"	5.00	2.50
f.	"Bound Printed Matter" below "US Postage"	5.00	2.50
g.	"BPM" below "US Postage"	5.00	2.50
h.	Horiz. strip of 5, #1CVP16-1CVP20	10.00	

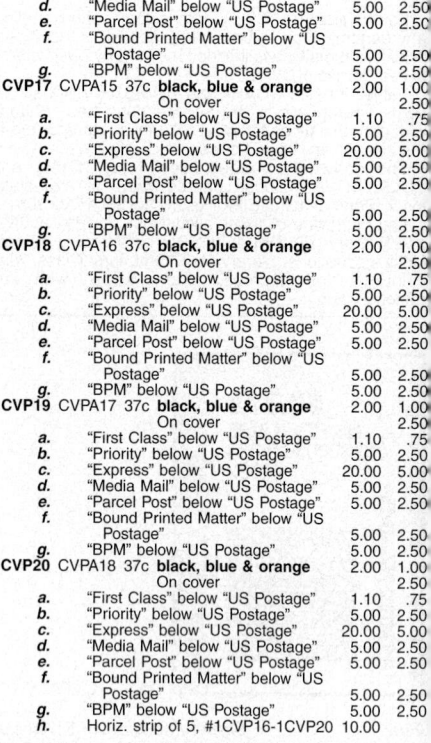

Flag and Star Type of 2002 Redrawn With Orange Stars and Text at Left

2004, Apr. ***Serpentine Die Cut 6½ at Left***

"Stamps.com" in Upper Case Letters

Identification Code Above Zip Code

1CVP21	CVPA1 37c **black, blue & orange**	2.00	1.00
	On cover		2.50
	Sheet of 25	50.00	
a.	"First Class" below "US Postage"	1.35	.75
b.	"Priority" below "US Postage"	6.00	2.50
c.	"Express" below "US Postage"	22.50	5.00
d.	"Media Mail" below "US Postage"	6.00	2.50
e.	"Parcel Post" below "US Postage"	6.00	2.50
f.	"Bound Printed Matter" below "US Postage"	6.00	2.50
g.	"BPM" below "US Postage"	6.00	2.50

Bicycling — CVPA19

Running — CVPA20

Swimming
CVPA21

Boxing — CVPA22

Equestrian
CVPA23

Basketball
CVPA24

Judo — CVPA25

Soccer — CVPA26

Gymnastics
CVPA27

Tennis — CVPA28

2004, Apr. ***Serpentine Die Cut 6½ at Left***

1CVP22	CVPA19 37c **black, blue & orange**		3.00	2.00
		On cover		3.00
	a.	"First Class" below "US Postage"	2.50	1.50
	b.	"Priority" below "US Postage"	8.00	1.00
	c.	"Express" below "US Postage"	25.00	3.00
	d.	"Media Mail" below "US Postage"	7.50	1.00
	e.	"Parcel Post" below "US Postage"	7.50	1.00
	f.	"Bound Printed Matter" below "US Postage"	7.50	1.00
	g.	"BPM" below "US Postage"	7.50	1.00
1CVP23	CVPA20 37c **black, blue & orange**		3.00	2.00
		On cover		3.00
	a.	"First Class" below "US Postage"	2.50	1.50
	b.	"Priority" below "US Postage"	8.00	1.00
	c.	"Express" below "US Postage"	25.00	3.00
	d.	"Media Mail" below "US Postage"	7.50	1.00
	e.	"Parcel Post" below "US Postage"	7.50	1.00
	f.	"Bound Printed Matter" below "US Postage"	7.50	1.00
	g.	"BPM" below "US Postage"	7.50	1.00
1CVP24	CVPA21 37c **black, blue & orange**		3.00	2.00
		On cover		3.00
	a.	"First Class" below "US Postage"	2.50	1.50
	b.	"Priority" below "US Postage"	8.00	1.00
	c.	"Express" below "US Postage"	25.00	3.00
	d.	"Media Mail" below "US Postage"	7.50	1.00
	e.	"Parcel Post" below "US Postage"	7.50	1.00
	f.	"Bound Printed Matter" below "US Postage"	7.50	1.00
	g.	"BPM" below "US Postage"	7.50	1.00
1CVP25	CVPA22 37c **black, blue & orange**		3.00	2.00
		On cover		3.00
	a.	"First Class" below "US Postage"	2.50	1.50
	b.	"Priority" below "US Postage"	8.00	1.00
	c.	"Express" below "US Postage"	25.00	3.00
	d.	"Media Mail" below "US Postage"	7.50	1.00
	e.	"Parcel Post" below "US Postage"	7.50	1.00
	f.	"Bound Printed Matter" below "US Postage"	7.50	1.00
	g.	"BPM" below "US Postage"	7.50	1.00
1CVP26	CVPA23 37c **black, blue & orange**		3.00	2.00
		On cover		3.00
	a.	"First Class" below "US Postage"	2.50	1.50
	b.	"Priority" below "US Postage"	8.00	1.00
	c.	"Express" below "US Postage"	25.00	3.00
	d.	"Media Mail" below "US Postage"	7.50	1.00
	e.	"Parcel Post" below "US Postage"	7.50	1.00
	f.	"Bound Printed Matter" below "US Postage"	7.50	1.00
	g.	"BPM" below "US Postage"	7.50	1.00
	h.	Horiz. strip of 5, #1CVP22-1CVP26	15.00	
1CVP27	CVPA24 37c **black, blue & orange**		3.00	2.00
		On cover		3.00
	a.	"First Class" below "US Postage"	2.50	1.50
	b.	"Priority" below "US Postage"	8.00	1.00
	c.	"Express" below "US Postage"	25.00	3.00
	d.	"Media Mail" below "US Postage"	7.50	1.00
	e.	"Parcel Post" below "US Postage"	7.50	1.00
	f.	"Bound Printed Matter" below "US Postage"	7.50	1.00
	g.	"BPM" below "US Postage"	7.50	1.00
1CVP28	CVPA25 37c **black, blue & orange**		3.00	2.00
		On cover		3.00
	a.	"First Class" below "US Postage"	2.50	1.50
	b.	"Priority" below "US Postage"	8.00	1.00
	c.	"Express" below "US Postage"	25.00	3.00
	d.	"Media Mail" below "US Postage"	7.50	1.00
	e.	"Parcel Post" below "US Postage"	7.50	1.00
	f.	"Bound Printed Matter" below "US Postage"	7.50	1.00
	g.	"BPM" below "US Postage"	7.50	1.00
1CVP29	CVPA26 37c **black, blue & orange**		3.00	2.00
		On cover		3.00
	a.	"First Class" below "US Postage"	2.50	1.50
	b.	"Priority" below "US Postage"	8.00	1.00
	c.	"Express" below "US Postage"	25.00	3.00
	d.	"Media Mail" below "US Postage"	7.50	1.00
	e.	"Parcel Post" below "US Postage"	7.50	1.00
	f.	"Bound Printed Matter" below "US Postage"	7.50	1.00
	g.	"BPM" below "US Postage"	7.50	1.00
1CVP30	CVPA27 37c **black, blue & orange**		3.00	2.00
		On cover		3.00
	a.	"First Class" below "US Postage"	2.50	1.50
	b.	"Priority" below "US Postage"	8.00	1.00
	c.	"Express" below "US Postage"	25.00	3.00
	d.	"Media Mail" below "US Postage"	7.50	1.00
	e.	"Parcel Post" below "US Postage"	7.50	1.00
	f.	"Bound Printed Matter" below "US Postage"	7.50	1.00
	g.	"BPM" below "US Postage"	7.50	1.00
1CVP31	CVPA28 37c **black, blue & orange**		3.00	2.00
		On cover		3.00
	a.	"First Class" below "US Postage"	2.50	1.50
	b.	"Priority" below "US Postage"	8.00	1.00
	c.	"Express" below "US Postage"	25.00	3.00
	d.	"Media Mail" below "US Postage"	7.50	1.00
	e.	"Parcel Post" below "US Postage"	7.50	1.00
	f.	"Bound Printed Matter" below "US Postage"	7.50	1.00
	g.	"BPM" below "US Postage"	7.50	1.00
	h.	Horiz. strip of 5, #1CVP27-1CVP31	15.00	

The item pictured above was produced by Stamps.com for a special promotional mailing of its own and was not made available unused to customers.

Leaning Tower of
Pisa — CVPA29

Sphinx and Pyramids — CVPA30

Sydney Opera House — CVPA31

Mayan Pyramid — CVPA32

Asian Temple — CVPA33

2004, July *Serpentine Die Cut 6½ at Left*

1CVP32	CVPA29 37c **black, blue & orange**	3.00	2.00
	On cover		3.00
a.	"First Class" below "US Postage"	2.30	1.50
b.	"Priority" below "US Postage"	8.00	1.00
c.	"Express" below "US Postage"	25.00	3.00
d.	"Media Mail" below "US Postage"	7.50	1.00
e.	"Parcel Post" below "US Postage"	7.50	1.00
f.	"Bound Printed Matter" below "US Postage"	7.50	1.00
g.	"BPM" below "US Postage"	7.50	1.00
1CVP33	CVPA30 37c **black, blue & orange**	3.00	2.00
	On cover		3.00
a.	"First Class" below "US Postage"	2.30	1.50
b.	"Priority" below "US Postage"	8.00	1.00
c.	"Express" below "US Postage"	25.00	3.00
d.	"Media Mail" below "US Postage"	7.50	1.00
e.	"Parcel Post" below "US Postage"	7.50	1.00
f.	"Bound Printed Matter" below "US Postage"	7.50	1.00
g.	"BPM" below "US Postage"	7.50	1.00
1CVP34	CVPA31 37c **black, blue & orange**	3.00	2.00
	On cover		3.00
a.	"First Class" below "US Postage"	2.30	1.50
b.	"Priority" below "US Postage"	8.00	1.00
c.	"Express" below "US Postage"	25.00	3.00
d.	"Media Mail" below "US Postage"	7.50	1.00
e.	"Parcel Post" below "US Postage"	7.50	1.00
f.	"Bound Printed Matter" below "US Postage"	7.50	1.00
g.	"BPM" below "US Postage"	7.50	1.00
1CVP35	CVPA32 37c **black, blue & orange**	3.00	2.00
	On cover		3.00
a.	"First Class" below "US Postage"	2.30	1.50
b.	"Priority" below "US Postage"	8.00	1.00
c.	"Express" below "US Postage"	25.00	3.00
d.	"Media Mail" below "US Postage"	7.50	1.00
e.	"Parcel Post" below "US Postage"	7.50	1.00
f.	"Bound Printed Matter" below "US Postage"	7.50	1.00
g.	"BPM" below "US Postage"	7.50	1.00
1CVP36	CVPA33 37c **black, blue & orange**	3.00	2.00
	On cover		3.00
a.	"First Class" below "US Postage"	2.30	1.50
b.	"Priority" below "US Postage"	8.00	1.00
c.	"Express" below "US Postage"	25.00	3.00
d.	"Media Mail" below "US Postage"	7.50	1.00
e.	"Parcel Post" below "US Postage"	7.50	1.00
f.	"Bound Printed Matter" below "US Postage"	7.50	1.00
g.	"BPM" below "US Postage"	7.50	1.00
h.	Strip of 5, #1CVP32-1CVP36	15.00	

Computer and Letters — CVPA34

2005, Mar. *Serpentine Die Cut 6½ at Left*

1CVP37	CVPA34 37c **black, blue & orange**	25.00	15.00
	On cover		75.00
a.	"First Class" below "US Postage"	25.00	15.00
b.	"Priority" below "US Postage"	—	—
c.	"Express" below "US Postage"	—	—
d.	"Media Mail" below "US Postage"	—	—
e.	"Parcel Post" below "US Postage"	—	—
f.	"Bound Printed Matter" below "US Postage"	—	—
g.	"BPM" below "US Postage"	—	—

Blank sheets of No. 1CVP37 were sent free of charge to those who responded to special Stamps.com promotions which offered a fixed amount of free postage as an enticement to new subscribers. The franking portion of the stamps could only be applied after subscribing.

Logo — CVPA35

2005, Aug. *Die Cut Perf. 6½ at Left*

1CVP38	CVPA35 37c **black, blue & orange**	1.00	.30
	On cover		2.50
a.	"Priority" below "US Postage"	8.00	1.00
b.	"Express" below "US Postage"	25.00	3.00
c.	"Media Mail" below "US Postage"	7.50	1.00
d.	"Parcel Post" below "US Postage"	7.50	1.00
e.	"BPM" below "US Postage"	7.50	1.00
f.	"Aerogramme" below "US Postage"	1.40	1.00
g.	"Intl Air Letter" below "US Postage"	1.25	1.00
h.	"Intl Eco Letter" (Economy Letter Mail) below "US Postage"	5.50	1.00
i.	"GXG" (Global Express Guaranteed) below "US Postage"	50.00	6.00
j.	"EMS" (Global Express Mail) below "US Postage"	32.50	4.00
k.	"GPM" (Global Priority Mail) below "US Postage"	8.00	1.00
l.	"Intl Air Parcel" (Air Parcel Post) below "US Postage"	26.00	3.00
m.	"Intl Eco Parcel" (Economy Parcel Post) below "US Postage"	32.50	4.00
n.	"M-Bag (Air)" below "US Postage"	35.00	5.00
o.	"M-Bag (Economy)" below "US Postage"	18.00	3.00
p.	"Mat for Blind" below "US Postage"	.20	—

Values for lettered varieties on Nos. 1CVP38 are based on the prices set as the minimum values for each service classification in the software available at the time the stamps were issued. In mid-December 2005, the software was changed to allow for a 1c minimum value for any of these lettered varieties.
In 2006, No. 1CVP38 was made available on a coil roll.

Snowman — CVPA36

Candy Cane — CVPA37

Dove — CVPA38

Stylized Christmas Tree and Window — CVPA39

2005, Nov. *Die Cut Perf. 6 at Right*

1CVP39	CVPA36 37c **multicolored**	1.60	.20
	On cover		2.50
a.	"Priority" below "US Postage"	8.00	1.00
b.	"Express" below "US Postage"	25.00	3.00
c.	"Media Mail" below "US Postage"	7.50	1.00
d.	"Parcel Post" below "US Postage"	7.50	1.00
e.	"BPM" below "US Postage"	7.50	1.00
f.	"Aerogramme" below "US Postage"	1.40	1.00
g.	"Intl Air Letter" below "US Postage"	1.25	1.00
h.	"Intl Eco Letter" (Economy Letter Mail) below "US Postage"	5.50	1.00
i.	"GXG" (Global Express Guaranteed) below "US Postage"	50.00	6.00
j.	"EMS" (Global Express Mail) below "US Postage"	32.50	4.00
k.	"GPM" (Global Priority Mail) below "US Postage"	8.00	1.00
l.	"Intl Air Parcel" (Air Parcel Post) below "US Postage"	26.00	3.00
m.	"Intl Eco Parcel" (Economy Parcel Post) below "US Postage"	32.50	4.00
n.	"M-Bag (Air)" below "US Postage"	35.00	5.00
o.	"M-Bag (Economy)" below "US Postage"	18.00	3.00
p.	"Mat for Blind" below "US Postage"	.20	—
1CVP40	CVPA37 37c **multicolored**	1.60	.20
	On cover		2.50
a.	"Priority" below "US Postage"	8.00	1.00
b.	"Express" below "US Postage"	25.00	3.00
c.	"Media Mail" below "US Postage"	7.50	1.00
d.	"Parcel Post" below "US Postage"	7.50	1.00
e.	"BPM" below "US Postage"	7.50	1.00
f.	"Aerogramme" below "US Postage"	1.40	1.00
g.	"Intl Air Letter" below "US Postage"	1.25	1.00
h.	"Intl Eco Letter" (Economy Letter Mail) below "US Postage"	5.50	1.00
i.	"GXG" (Global Express Guaranteed) below "US Postage"	50.00	6.00
j.	"EMS" (Global Express Mail) below "US Postage"	32.50	4.00
k.	"GPM" (Global Priority Mail) below "US Postage"	8.00	1.00
l.	"Intl Air Parcel" (Air Parcel Post) below "US Postage"	26.00	3.00
m.	"Intl Eco Parcel" (Economy Parcel Post) below "US Postage"	32.50	4.00
n.	"M-Bag (Air)" below "US Postage"	35.00	5.00
o.	"M-Bag (Economy)" below "US Postage"	18.00	3.00
p.	"Mat for Blind" below "US Postage"	.20	—

1CVP41 CVPA38 37c **multicolored** 1.60 .20
On cover 2.50
a. "Priority" below "US Postage" 8.00 1.00
b. "Express" below "US Postage" 25.00 3.00
c. "Media Mail" below "US Postage" 7.50 1.00
d. "Parcel Post" below "US Postage" 7.50 1.00
e. "BPM" below "US Postage" 7.50 1.00
f. "Aerogramme" below "US Postage" 1.40 1.00
g. "Intl Air Letter" below "US Postage" 1.25 1.00
h. "Intl Eco Letter" (Economy Letter Mail) below "US Postage" 5.50 1.00
i. "GXG" (Global Express Guaranteed) below "US Postage" 50.00 6.00
j. "EMS" (Global Express Mail) below "US Postage" 32.50 4.00
k. "GPM" (Global Priority Mail) below "US Postage" 8.00 1.00
l. "Intl Air Parcel" (Air Parcel Post) below "US Postage" 26.00 3.00
m. "Intl Eco Parcel" (Economy Parcel Post) below "US Postage" 32.50 4.00
n. "M-Bag (Air)" below "US Postage" 35.00 5.00
o. "M-Bag (Economy)" below "US Postage" 18.00 3.00
p. "Mat for Blind" below "US Postage" .20 —

1CVP42 CVPA39 37c **multicolored** 1.60 .20
On cover 2.50
a. "Priority" below "US Postage" 8.00 1.00
b. "Express" below "US Postage" 25.00 3.00
c. "Media Mail" below "US Postage" 7.50 1.00
d. "Parcel Post" below "US Postage" 7.50 1.00
e. "BPM" below "US Postage" 7.50 1.00
f. "Aerogramme" below "US Postage" 1.40 1.00
g. "Intl Air Letter" below "US Postage" 1.25 1.00
h. "Intl Eco Letter" (Economy Letter Mail) below "US Postage" 5.50 1.00
i. "GXG" (Global Express Guaranteed) below "US Postage" 50.00 6.00
j. "EMS" (Global Express Mail) below "US Postage" 32.50 4.00
k. "GPM" (Global Priority Mail) below "US Postage" 8.00 1.00
l. "Intl Air Parcel" (Air Parcel Post) below "US Postage" 26.00 3.00
m. "Intl Eco Parcel" (Economy Parcel Post) below "US Postage" 32.50 4.00
n. "M-Bag (Air)" below "US Postage" 35.00 5.00
o. "M-Bag (Economy)" below "US Postage" 18.00 3.00
p. "Mat for Blind" below "US Postage" .20 —
q. Vert. strip, 2 each #1CVP39-1CVP42 6.00

Values for lettered varieties on Nos. 1CVP39-1CVP42 are based on the prices set as the minimum values for each service classification in the software available at the time the stamps were issued. In mid-December 2005, the software was changed to allow for a 1c minimum value for any of these lettered varieties.

Endicia.com

CVPA40

CVPA41

2005-06 ***Serpentine Die Cut 10¼***

1CVP43 CVPA40 24c **black & bright rose** 10.00 4.00
a. 39c "First Class" under "US Postage" 2.00 .50
b. 63c "Intl. Mail" under "US Postage" 3.25 2.50
c. $4.05 "Priority Mail" under "US Postage" 12.00 2.50

Coil Stamps

Serpentine Die Cut 10½x10¼ on 2 Sides

1CVP44 CVPA41 24c **black & pink** 11.00 4.00
a. 39c "First Class" under "US Postage" 2.25 .50
b. 63c "Intl. Mail" under "US Postage" 3.50 2.50
c. $4.05 "Priority Mail" under "US Postage" 12.50 2.50

Issued: Nos. 1CVP43, Nov. 2005; Nos. 1CVP44, Jan. 2006.

Originally, face values of 2c, 52c, 63c, 87c, $1.11, $1.35, $1.59, $1.83, $2.07, $2.31, $2.55, $2.79, $3.03, and $3.27 could also be printed on stamps with the "First class" inscription. Additionally, an 84c face value could be printed on stamps with the "Intl. Mail" inscription, and a $8.10 face value could be printed on stamps with the "Priority Mail" inscription. Values for Nos. 1CVP43-1CVP44 are for stamps with the listed face values and mail-class inscription. Values for stamps with lower or higher face values are correspondingly lower or higher.

In 2007, software changes permitted Nos. 1CVP43 and 1CVP44 to be printed with mail class inscriptions "Media Mail," "BPM," "Parcel Post," "Library Mail," and "Express Mail," as well as any face value for any mail-class inscription.

Nos. 1CVP43 and 1CVP44 printed after the software changes are inscribed "First Class" under "US Postage" and sell for considerably less than the values shown. Stamps printed before the software changes are inscribed "Postcard" under "US Postage," as shown in the illustrations.

Stamps.com

Flag and Mount Rushmore — CVPA42

Flag and Eagle — CVPA43

Flag and Statue of Liberty — CVPA44

Flag and Liberty Bell — CVPA45

2006, Mar. ***Die Cut Perf. 6 at Right***

1CVP51 CVPA42 39c **multicolored** .80 .20
On cover 2.50
1CVP52 CVPA43 39c **multicolored** .80 .20
On cover 2.50
1CVP53 CVPA44 39c **multicolored** .80 .20
On cover 2.50
1CVP54 CVPA45 39c **multicolored** .80 .20
On cover 2.50
a. Vert. strip of 8, 2 each #1CVP51-1CVP54 8.00

Other service inscriptions with any possible face value can be printed on Nos. 1CVP51-1CVP54.

Stamps.com

Leaning Tower of Pisa — CVPA46

Taj Mahal — CVPA47

Eiffel Tower — CVPA48

Parthenon — CVPA49

2006 ***Die Cut Perf 6 at Right***

1CVP55 CVPA46 39c **black** .80 .20
On cover 2.50

Serial Number Under Encryption

APC

1CVP56 CVPA47 39c **black** .80 .20
On cover 2.50
1CVP57 CVPA48 39c **multicolored** .80 .20
On cover 2.50
1CVP58 CVPA49 39c **multicolored** .80 .20
On cover 2.50
a. Vert. strip, 2 each #1CVP55-1CVP58 8.00

With the introduction of the new software in December 2005, any stamp could have any denomination above 1c, and any service classification.

Pitney Bowes Stamp Expressions

CVPA50

Illustration reduced.

2006 ***Die Cut Perf. 6 Horiz.***

Inscribed "pitneybowes.com/se" at Right

1CVP59 CVPA50 39c **black** + label 1.35 .80
On cover 4.00

The stamp and label are separated by vertical roulettes. Users could create their own label images on the Pitney Bowes Stamp Expressions website (which required approval of the image from Pitney Bowes before it could be used), or download various pre-approved label images from the website into their personal computers. Stamps could be printed without label images. Stamps were printed on rolls of tagged thermal paper from a device that could be operated without a direct connection to the personal computer. See No. 1CVT1.

Stamps.com

CVPA51

Personalizable Images — CVPA52

Illustration CVPA51 is reduced.

2006, Sept. ***Die Cut Perf. 6 at Right***

1CVP60	CVPA51	39c	**multicolored**	1.50	.95
			On cover		4.50
1CVP61	CVPA52	39c	**multicolored**	1.50	.95
			On cover		4.50

Users could requisition sheets of Nos. 1CVP60 and 1CVP61 with images of their choice from Stamps.com at $4.99 per sheet of 24. Priority and Express service classifications could also be printed on Nos. 1CVP60-1CVP61 with any denomination. Stamps exist with slightly larger die cutting (60x30mm and 30x60mm) in both squared and rounded corners. The denomination type shown on Nos. 1CVP60-1CVP61 can be placed on label types CVPA36-CVPA39, CVPA42-CVPA49, CVPA53-CVPA60 and any later stamps.com labels of this size.

Autumn Leaves — CVPA53

Pumpkins — CVPA54

Basket of Apples, Sheaf of Wheat, Falling Leaves and Pumpkins — CVPA55

Leaves and Carved Pumpkin — CVPA56

2006 ***Die Cut Perf. 6 at Right***

1CVP62	CVPA53	39c	**multicolored**	1.25	.20
			On cover		2.50
1CVP63	CVPA54	39c	**multicolored**	1.25	.20
			On cover		2.50
1CVP64	CVPA55	39c	**multicolored**	1.25	.20
			On cover		2.50
1CVP65	CVPA56	39c	**multicolored**	1.25	.20
			On cover		2.50
a.			Vert. strip, 2 each #1CVP62-1CVP65	10.00	

See note after No. 1CVP58.

"Season's Greetings" — CVPA57

Christmas Trees — CVPA58

Snowman — CVPA59

Dove — CVPA60

2006 ***Die Cut Perf. 6 at Righ***

1CVP66	CVPA57	39c	**multicolored**	1.25	.20
			On cover		2.50
1CVP67	CVPA58	39c	**multicolored**	1.25	.20
			On cover		2.50
1CVP68	CVPA59	39c	**multicolored**	1.25	.20
			On cover		2.50
1CVP69	CVPA60	39c	**multicolored**	1.25	.20
			On cover		2.50
a.			Vert. strip, 2 each #1CVP66-1CVP69	10.00	

See note after No. 1CVP58.

COMPUTER VENDED POSTAGE TEST STAMPS
Pitney Bowes Stamp Expressions

CVT1

Illustration reduced.

2006 ***Die Cut Perf. 6 Horiz***
Inscribed "pbstampexpressions.com" at Right

1CVT1	CVT1	39c	**black** + label	5.00	—
			On cover		—

No. 1CVT1 were produced only by beta testers of the Pitney Bowes Stamp Expressions system, and as such were not available to normal subscribers to the system. Examples are known to have passed through the mail. Notes concerning No 1CVP59 apply to No. 1CVT1.

NON-PERSONALIZABLE POSTAGE

These stamps, approved by the USPS, were non-personalizable stamps that could be purchased directly from private manufacturers, which shipped them to the customer. Other non-personalizable stamps have been created by a variety of companies, all sold at excessive amounts over face value as "collectibles". Such items are not listed here. Most items created that sold for excessive amounts over face value have vignettes that are licensed images, usually depicting sport team emblems or other sports-related themes, or celebrities.

Personalized postage stamps, first available in 2004, created by a variety of different companies, and heretofore listed with Scott numbers having a "2CVP" prefix, are no longer listed. Personalized stamps, though valid for postage, are not sold at any U.S. Postal Service post office. They are available only by on-line ordering through the company's website. Stamps are only available from the companies in full panes of 20. Each pane is sold at a significant premium above the stated face value to cover the costs of personalization, shipping and handling.

In recent years, there has been a steadily increasing number of private companies, either directly licensed by the USPS or created as spinoff companies of these licensees, creating distinctly different personalized stamps. None of the companies has issued fewer than seven stamps for each rate change, with one issuing as many as 42 different stamps. Because mailing rates set by the USPS are expected to change yearly, the collective output of distinctly different, rate-based stamps from these various companies likely will increase. There are no restrictions in place to prevent more firms from bringing personalized stamps to the marketplace, or to keep stamp producers from offering even more customer options. Some personalized stamps do not differ in any appreciable manner from some of the non-personalizable stamps sold as collectibles and not listed here.

Stamps.com

CVPC1

CVPC2

2007, May ***Die Cut***

Self-Adhesive

3CVP1	CVPC1 2c **black & gray**	.20	.20
	a. Inscribed "US Postag"	—	—

Die Cut Perf. 5¼ at Right

3CVP2	CVPC2 2c **multicolored**	.20	.20
	a. Tagged	*1.40*	*1.40*

2008 ***Die Cut***

3CVP3	CVPC1 1c **black & gray**	.20	.20

VENDING & AFFIXING MACHINE PERFORATIONS

Imperforate sheets of 400 were first issued in 1906 on the request of several makers of vending and affixing machines. The machine manufacturers made coils from the imperforate sheets and applied various perforations to suit the particular needs of their machines. These privately applied perforations were used for many years and form a chapter of postal history.

Unused values are for pairs, used values for singles. Used multiples are highly valued, with prices often equalling or exceeding those for unused pairs or strips. "On cover" values are for single stamps used commercially in the proper period when known that way. Several, primarily the Alaska-Yukon and Hudson-Fulton commemoratives, are known almost exclusively on covers from contemporaneous stamp collectors and stamp dealers. Virtually all are rare and highly prized by specialists.

The 2mm and 3mm spacings refer only to the 1908-10 issues. (See note following No. 330 in the Postage section.) Values for intermediate spacings would roughly correspond to the lower-valued of the two listed spacings. Guide line pairs of 1906-10 issues have 2mm spacing except the Alaska-Yukon and Hudson-Fulton issues, which have 3mm spacing. Scott Nos. 408-611 have 3mm spacing, except the "A" plates which have 2¾mm spacing and Scott No. 577, which has both 2¾mm and 3mm spacing. (All spacing measurements are approximate.)

Spacing on paste-up pairs is not a factor in valuing them. Because they were joined together by hand, many different spacings can occur, from less than 2mm to more than 3mm.

Perfins listed here are punched into the stamp just before being affixed to an envelope. The most common pattern consisted of a 7mm square made up of nine holes. Pins would be removed to create special perfins for each company using the machines. The catalogue value is for the most common perfin pattern on each stamp.

* — Many varieties are suspected or known to have been perforated for philatelic purposes and not actually used in machines. These are indicated by an asterisk before the number. Several of these privately applied perforation varieties exist in blocks, which were not produced in the regular course of business. They are generally valued at a premium over the multiple of the coil pairs contained, with an additional premium for plate numbers attached.

Counterfeits are prevalent, especially of items having a basic imperf. variety valued far lower than the vending machine coil.

The Vending and Affixing Machine Perforations Committee of the Bureau Issues Association (now the United States Stamp Society) and William R. Weiss, Jr., compiled these listings.

The Attleboro Stamp Co.
See following U.S. Automatic Vending Company.

THE BRINKERHOFF COMPANY
Sedalia, Mo., Clinton, Iowa
Manufacturers of Vending Machines

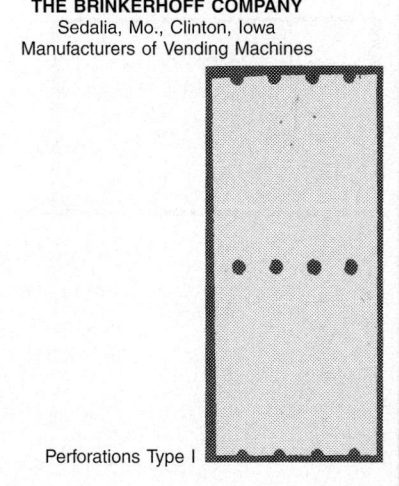

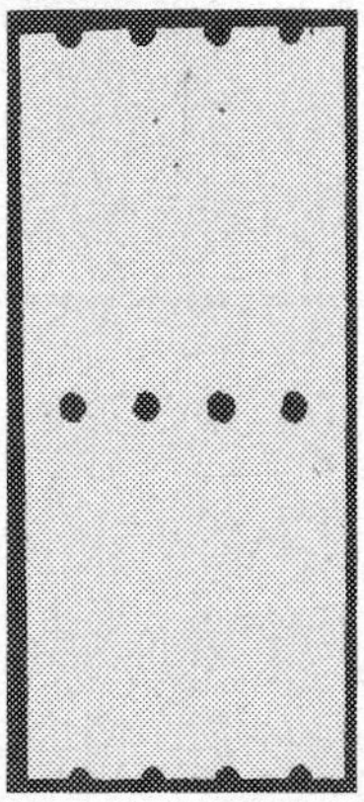

Perforations Type I

Stamps were cut into strips and joined before being perforated.

			Unused Pair	Used Single
		On Issue of 1906-08		
314	1c	**blue green**	200.00	30.00
		Guide line pair	375.00	
320	2c	**carmine**	225.00	30.00
		Guide line pair	425.00	
		Pasteup pair	320.00	
***320a**	2c	**lake**	170.00	25.00
		Guide line pair	325.00	
		Pasteup pair	240.00	
		On Issue of 1908-09		
***343**	1c	**green**	120.00	20.00
		Guide line pair	290.00	
		Pasteup pair	230.00	
***344**	2c	**carmine**	105.00	20.00
		On cover		*1,650.*
		Guide line pair	210.00	—
		Pasteup pair	185.00	
***345**	3c	**deep violet**	140.00	—
		Guide line pair	275.00	
***346**	4c	**orange brown**	160.00	120.00
		Guide line pair	285.00	
		Pasteup pair	210.00	
***347**	5c	**blue**	300.00	80.00
		On cover		*3,250.*
		Guide line pair	500.00	

			Unused Pair	Used Single
		On Lincoln Issue of 1909		
*368	2c	**carmine,** coiled endwise	170.00	*175.00*
		Guide line pair	320.00	
		On Alaska-Yukon Issue of 1909		
*371	2c	**carmine,** coiled sideways	*575.00*	—
		Guide line pair	*1,000.*	
		On Issue of 1910		
*383	1c	**green**	*200.00*	
		Guide line pair	—	
		On Issue of 1912		
*408	1c	**green**	32.50	15.00
		On cover		*800.00*
		Guide line pair	65.00	
		Pasteup pair	52.50	
*409	2c	**carmine**	32.50	15.00
		On cover		*1,100.*
		Guide line pair	65.00	
		Pasteup pair	52.50	

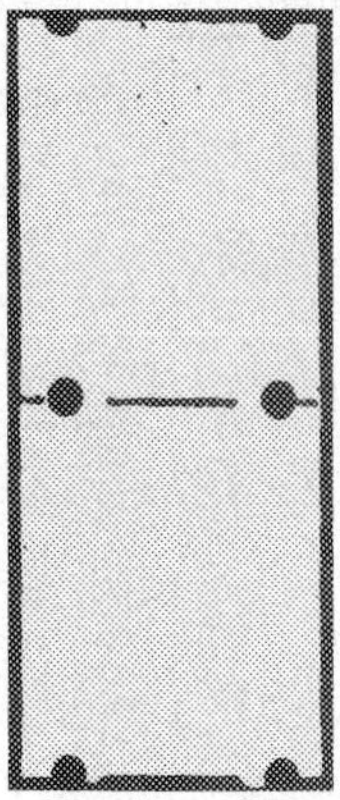
Type IIa — One knife cut.

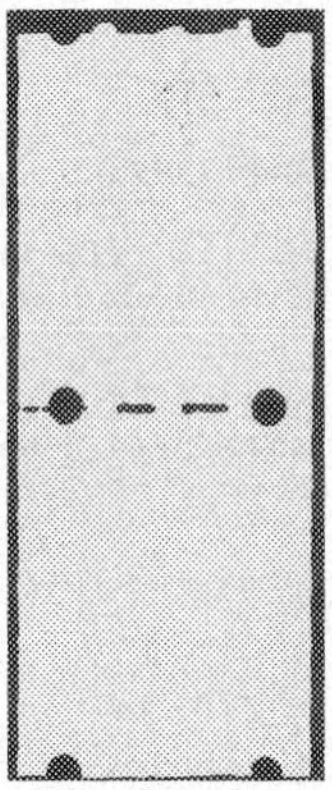
Type IIb — Two knife cuts.

Perforations Type II, 2 Holes

The Type II items listed below are without knife cuts and did not pass through the vending machine. Types IIa and IIb (illustrated above) have knife cuts, applied by the vending machine, to help separate the stamps.

	Type			Unused Pair	Used Single
			On Issue of 1906-08		
314	*II	1c	**blue green**	95.00	12.50
			On cover		*850.00*
	IIa	1c	**blue green**	80.00	12.50
			Guide line pair	160.00	
	*IIb	1c	**blue green**	425.00	—
			Pasteup pair	725.00	
320	*II	2c	**carmine**	200.00	*65.00*
			Pasteup pair	320.00	
	IIa	2c	**carmine**	40.00	12.50
			On cover		*575.00*
			Guide line pair	115.00	
320a	*II	2c	**lake**	200.00	*65.00*
			On cover		*575.00*
	IIa	2c	**lake**	85.00	12.50
			On cover		*575.00*
			Guide line pair	170.00	
			Pasteup pair	95.00	
	*IIb	2c	**lake**	340.00	*75.00*
			On Issue of 1908-09		
343	*II	1c	**green**	65.00	
			On cover		*700.00*
			Guide line pair	110.00	
	IIa	1c	**green**	19.00	3.25
			On cover		700.00
			Pasteup pair	32.50	
	IIb	1c	**green**	32.50	
			On cover		*850.00*
			Pasteup pair	55.00	
344	*II	2c	**carmine**	75.00	
			On cover, pair		*700.00*
			Guide line pair	160.00	
			Pasteup pair	125.00	
	IIa	2c	**carmine**	19.00	3.25
			Guide line pair	37.50	
			On cover		*800.00*
	IIb	2c	**carmine**	26.00	6.50
			Guide line pair	75.00	
			Pasteup pair	57.50	
345	*II	3c	**deep violet**	105.00	12.50
			Guide line pair	260.00	
	*IIa	3c	**deep violet**	85.00	12.50
			On cover		*1,650.*
			Guide line pair	170.00	
	*IIb	3c	**deep violet**	275.00	
346	*II	4c	**orange brown**	150.00	
			Guide line pair	275.00	
	*IIa	4c	**orange brown**	130.00	*50.00*
			On cover		*1,350.*
			Guide line pair	240.00	
			Pasteup pair	200.00	
	*IIb	4c	**orange brown**	150.00	*50.00*
			On cover		*1,650.*
347	*II	5c	**blue**	240.00	
			Guide line pair	400.00	

	Type			Unused Pair	Used Single
	*IIa	5c	**blue**	140.00	*100.00*
			On cover		*3,500.*
			Pasteup pair	210.00	
	*IIb	5c	**blue**	180.00	
			Pasteup pair	350.00	
			On Lincoln Issue of 1909		
368	*II	2c	**carmine**	75.00	
			On cover		*1,150.*
			Guide line pair	150.00	
	IIa	2c	**carmine**	75.00	14.00
			On cover		*1,350.*
			Guide line pair	210.00	
	IIb	2c	**carmine**	210.00	22.50
			On cover		*1,700.*
			Guide line pair	425.00	
			On Alaska-Yukon Issue of 1909		
371	*II	2c	**carmine,** coiled sideways	160.00	*100.00*
			On cover		*1,150.*
			Guide line or pasteup pair	325.00	
	II	2c	**carmine,** coiled endwise	*650.00*	
			Guide line pair	*1,275.*	
	IIa	2c	**carmine,** coiled sideways	170.00	*45.00*
			On cover		*850.00*
			Guide line pair	325.00	
			Pasteup pair	260.00	
			On Hudson-Fulton Issue of 1909		
373	*II	2c	**carmine,** coiled sidewise	*260.00*	
			Guide line or pasteup pair	*475.00*	
			On Issue of 1910		
383	*II	1c	**green**	37.50	
			Guide line pair	75.00	
	IIa	1c	**green**	45.00	9.00
			On cover		*925.00*
	IIb	1c	**green**	90.00	*50.00*
			On cover		*1,150.*
			Guide line pair	170.00	
384	*II	2c	**carmine**	37.50	
			On cover		*850.00*
			Guide line pair	70.00	
	IIa	2c	**carmine**	115.00	
			On cover		*1,150.*
			Pasteup pair	185.00	
	IIb	2c	**carmine**	65.00	9.00
			On cover		*1,700.*
			Guide line pair	185.00	
			Pasteup pair	130.00	
			On Issue of 1912		
408	*II	1c	**green**	95.00	—
			On cover		*925.00*
			Guide line pair	150.00	
			Pasteup pair	115.00	
	*IIa	1c	**green**	115.00	
			Guide line pair	210.00	
	IIb	1c	**green**	24.00	5.50
			On cover		925.00
			Guide line pair	47.50	
409	*II	2c	**carmine**	70.00	
			On cover		*925.00*
			Guide line pair	140.00	
			Pasteup pair	130.00	
	*IIa	2c	**carmine**	270.00	—
			On cover		*925.00*
			Guide line pair	475.00	
	IIb	2c	**carmine**	32.50	5.50
			On cover		*700.00*
			Guide line pair	57.50	

THE FARWELL COMPANY

Chicago, Ill.

A wholesale dry goods firm using Schermack (Mailometer) affixing machines. In 1911 the Farwell Company began to make and perforate their own coils. These were sometimes wrongly called "Chambers" perforations.

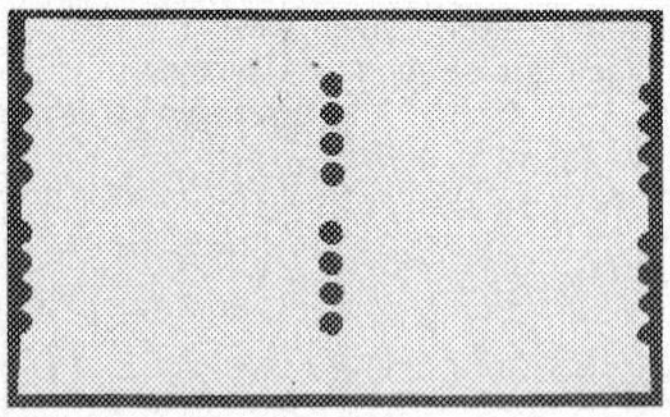
Type A

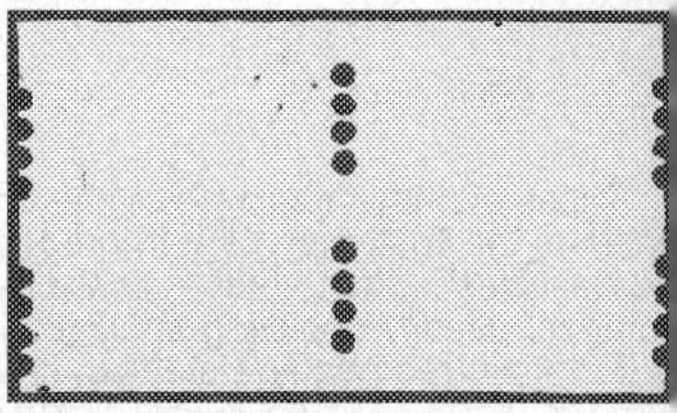
Type B

Stamps were perforated in sheets, then cut into strips and coiled. Blocks exist.

The following listings are grouped according to the number of holes, further divided into two types of spacing, narrow and wide.

The type symbols (3A2) indicate 3 holes over 2 holes with narrow, type A, spacing between groups.

Types A and B occurred in different rows on the same sheet. Left margin or pasteup stamps sometimes show different perforation type on the two sides.

Commercial usages of Farwell perforations are generally, but not always, on printed Farwell Co. corner card covers.

	Type			Unused Pair Spacing 2mm	3mm	Used Single
			Group I, no spacing			
			On Issue of 1910			
384		2c	**carmine,** 7 holes	*2,650.*	*2,650.*	*950.00*
			On cover			*5,000*
384		2c	**carmine,** 6 holes	*4,250.*	*4,250.*	*2,250.*
			On cover			*5,000.*
			Group 2, two and three holes			
			On Issue of 1910			
383	2B3	1c	**green**	*400.00*	*650.00*	*200.00*
	3A2	1c	**green**	*400.00*	*650.00*	
			On cover			—
			Guide line pair	*700.00*		
384	2A3	2c	**carmine**	*290.00*	*500.00*	*200.00*
			On cover			*1,100*
			Guide line pair	1,000.	1,050.	
			Pasteup pair		850.00	
	2B3	2c	**carmine**	*650.00*	*725.00*	*225.00*
			On cover			—
			Pasteup pair		*1,050.*	
	3A2	2c	**carmine**	*450.00*	*500.00*	*210.00*
			On cover			*1,700*
			Guide line pair	*800.00*		
	3B2	2c	**carmine**	*400.00*	*400.00*	*300.00*
			Guide line pair	*850.00*		
			Group 3, three and four holes			
			On Issue of 1910			
383	3B4	1c	**green**	*325.00*	*325.00*	*200.00*
			Pasteup pair	*650.00*		
	4B3	1c	**green**	*400.00*	*400.00*	*200.00*
384	3B4	2c	**carmine**	*525.00*	*525.00*	*260.00*
			On cover			—
			Guide line pair	*850.00*		
	4B3	2c	**carmine**	*850.00*	*850.00*	*400.00*
			On cover			*800.00*
			Guide line pair	—		
	4A3	2c	Carmine			—
			Group 4, four and four holes			
			On Issue of 1908-09			
343	*A	1c	**green**	*240.00*		
	*B	1c	**green**	*240.00*		
			On cover			*575.00*
344	*A	2c	**carmine**	*240.00*	*375.00*	
	*B	2c	**carmine**	*185.00*	*170.00*	*115.00*
			On Lincoln Issue of 1909			
368	*A	2c	**carmine**	*850.00*	*850.00*	
	*B	2c	**carmine**	*850.00*	*850.00*	
			On Issue of 1910			
383	A	1c	**green**	67.50	62.50	*60.00*
			Guide line pair	140.00		
	B	1c	**green**	67.50	57.50	—
			On cover			*290.00*
			Guide line pair	140.00		
384	A	2c	**carmine**	75.00	67.50	25.00
			Guide line pair	150.00		
	B	2c	**carmine**	75.00	67.50	17.50
			On cover			*350.00*
			Guide line pair	150.00		
			Pasteup pair	160.00		
			On Issue of 1912			
408	A	1c	**green**		37.50	2.75
			On cover			450.00
			Guide line pair		67.50	
	B	1c	**green**		37.50	2.75
			On cover			225.00
			Guide line pair		67.50	
409	A	2c	**carmine**		32.50	2.75
			On cover			65.00
	B	2c	**carmine**		32.50	2.75
			On cover			65.00
			Guide line pair		62.50	
			On Issue of 1916-17			
482	A	2c	**carmine**		*425.00*	*60.00*
			On cover			*1,250.*

Type						
			Guide line pair		*750.00*	
			Pasteup pair		*650.00*	
B		2c	**carmine**		*450.00*	*60.00*
			On cover			*1,250.*
			Guide line pair		*800.00*	

Group 5, four and five holes

On Issue of 1910

383	4A5	1c	**green**	*700.00*	650.00	—
			Guide line pair	*1,250.*		
384	4A5	2c	**carmine**	*850.00*	750.00	—
			Guide line pair	*1,600.*		

On Issue of 1912

408	4A5	1c	**green**		1,150.	
			Guide line pair		*2,100.*	
	*5A4	1c	**green**		1,150.	
			Guide line pair		*2,100.*	
409	*4A5	2c	**carmine**		1,150.	—
			Guide line or pasteup pair		*2,100.*	
	*5A4	2c	**carmine**		1,150.	
			Guide line pair		*2,100.*	

INTERNATIONAL VENDING MACHINE CO.

Baltimore, Md.

Similar to the Government Coil stamp #322, but approximately perf. 12½ with somewhat inconsistent spacing.

On Issue of 1906-08

320	2c	**carmine**	*2,600.*
320b	2c	**scarlet**	*2,600.*

On Issue of 1908-09

343	1c	**green**	*2,900.*
344	2c	**carmine**	*1,150.*
345	3c	**deep violet**	*1,150.*
346	4c	**orange brown**	—
347	5c	**blue**	*6,000.*

THE MAILOMETER COMPANY

Detroit, Mich.

Formerly the Schermack Mailing Machine Co., then Mail-om-eter Co., and later the Mail-O-Meter Co. Their round-hole perforations were developed in an attempt to get the Bureau of Engraving and Printing to adopt a larger perforation for coil stamps.

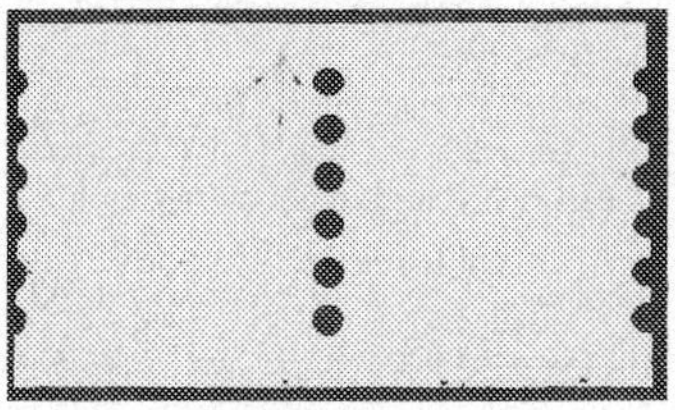

Perforations Type I

Used experimentally in Detroit and Chicago in August, 1909. Later used regularly in the St. Louis branch.

Two varieties exist: six holes 1.95mm in diameter spaced an average 1.2mm apart with an overall length of 17.7mm, and six holes 1.95mm in diameter spaced an average 1.15mm apart with an overall length of 17.45mm.

To date, only the 17.7mm length perfs. have been found on commercial covers.

On Issue of 1906-08

			Unused Pair Spacing 2mm	3mm	Used Single
***320**	2c	**carmine**	475.00		
***320a**	2c	**lake**	375.00		
		Guide line pair	850.00		
***320b**	2c	**scarlet**	350.00		

On Issue of 1908-09

			2mm	3mm	Used Single
343	1c	**green**	47.50	52.50	25.00
		On cover			*575.00*
		Guide line pair	75.00		
344	2c	**carmine**	42.50	47.50	5.00
		On cover, St. Louis			*80.00*
		On cover, Detroit or Chicago			*1,400.*
		On cover, Washington, D.C.			*2,000.*
		Guide line pair	90.00		
		With perforated control mark, single			*100.00*
		Same, on cover			*450.00*
345	3c	**deep violet**	67.50		20.00
		Guide line pair	135.00		
346	4c	**orange brown**	135.00	95.00	40.00
		Guide line pair	260.00		
347	5c	**blue**	150.00		40.00
		Guide line pair	260.00		

On Lincoln Issue of 1909

			2mm	3mm	Used Single
***368**	2c	**carmine**	190.00	135.00	*110.00*
		Guide line or pasteup pair	375.00		

On Alaska-Yukon Issue of 1909

			2mm	3mm	Used Single
***371**	2c	**carmine**		230.00	*110.00*
		Guide line pair		425.00	

On Hudson-Fulton Issue of 1909

			2mm	3mm	Used Single
***373**	2c	**carmine**		220.00	*100.00*
		Guide line pair		425.00	

On Issue of 1910

			2mm	3mm	Used Single
383	1c	**green**	45.00	40.00	3.50
		On cover			—
		Guide line pair	85.00		
384	2c	**carmine**	57.50	47.50	5.00
		On cover			80.00
		Guide line pair	105.00		

On Issue of 1912

			2mm	3mm	Used Single
***408**	1c	**green**		26.00	4.50
		Guide line pair		50.00	
***409**	2c	**carmine**		26.00	4.50
		Guide line pair		50.00	

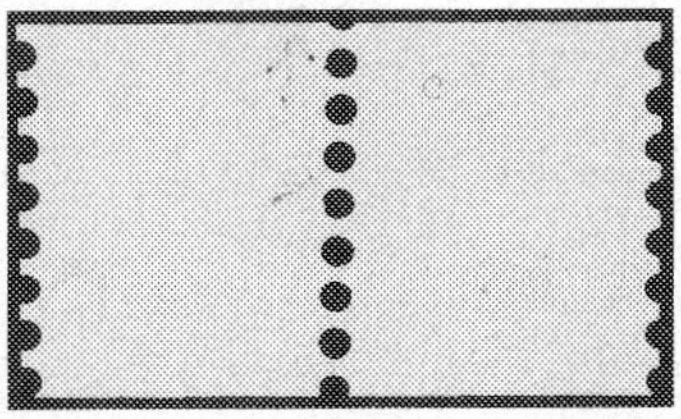

Perforations Type II

Used experimentally: Chicago, 1909; Detroit, 1911. Perforation holes 1.95mm in diameter.

On Issue of 1906-08

			2mm	3mm	Used Single
***320**	2c	**carmine**	750.00		
***320b**	2c	**scarlet**	1,050.		
		Guide line pair	1,500.		

On Issue of 1908-09

			2mm	3mm	Used Single
343	1c	**green**	67.50	67.50	15.00
		Guide line pair	135.00		
344	2c	**carmine**	80.00	80.00	15.00
		On cover			*5,750.*
		Guide line pair	160.00		
***345**	3c	**deep violet**	290.00		*70.00*
		Pasteup pair	425.00		
***346**	4c	**orange brown**	425.00	320.00	
***347**	5c	**blue**	650.00		

On Lincoln Issue of 1909

			2mm	3mm	Used Single
***368**	2c	**carmine**	650.00	600.00	

On Alaska-Yukon Issue of 1909

			2mm	3mm	Used Single
***371**	2c	**carmine**		700.00	

On Hudson-Fulton Issue of 1909

			2mm	3mm	Used Single
***373**	2c	**carmine**		400.00	
		Guide line or pasteup pair		700.00	

On Issue of 1910

			2mm	3mm	Used Single
383	1c	**green**	160.00	160.00	27.50
		Guide line or pasteup pair	320.00		
384	2c	**carmine**	170.00	160.00	*55.00*
		On cover			*4,500.*

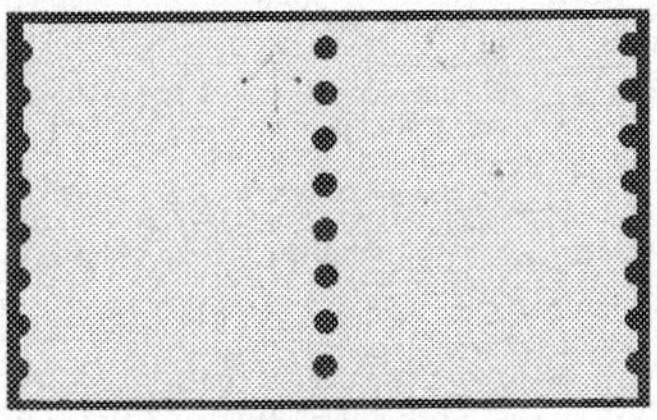

Perforations Type III

Used experimentally in Detroit in 1910. Perforation holes 1.8mm in diameter.

On Issue of 1906-08

			2mm	3mm	Used Single
***320**	2c	**carmine**	850.00		
***320b**	2c	**scarlet**	950.00		

On Issue of 1908-09

			2mm	3mm	Used Single
343	1c	**green**	180.00	180.00	
		Guide line pair	360.00		
344	2c	**carmine**	230.00	230.00	
		Guide line pair		475.00	
		Pasteup pair		*425.00*	
***345**	3c	**deep violet**	320.00		
		Guide line pair	575.00		
***346**	4c	**orange brown**	450.00	375.00	
		Pasteup pair	650.00		
***347**	5c	**blue**	*750.00*		
		Pasteup pair		*1,150.*	

On Lincoln Issue of 1909

			2mm	3mm	Used Single
***368**	2c	**carmine**	340.00	290.00	*100.00*
		Pasteup pair		500.00	

On Alaska-Yukon Issue of 1909

			2mm	3mm	Used Single
***371**	2c	**carmine**		800.00	

On Hudson-Fulton Issue of 1909

			2mm	3mm	Used Single
***373**	2c	**carmine**		750.00	
		Guide line pair		*1,475.*	
		Pasteup pair		—	

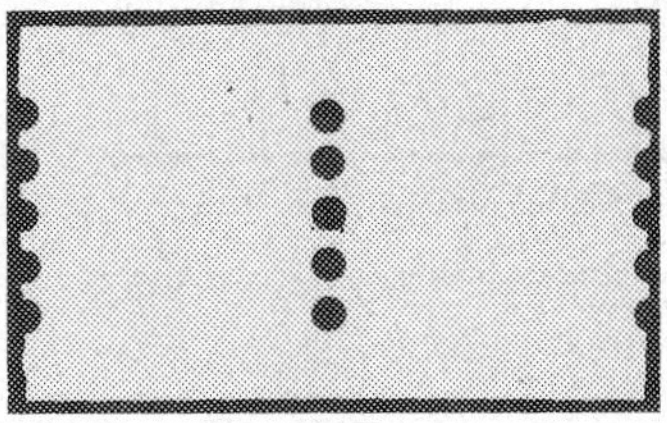

Perforations Type IV

Used in St. Louis branch office. Blocks exist but were not regularly produced or issued.

On Issue of 1906-08

			2mm	3mm	Used Single
***320**	2c	**carmine**	230.00		*80.00*
		Guide line pair	475.00		
		Pasteup pair	425.00		
***320b**	2c	**scarlet**	160.00		*65.00*
		Guide line pair	525.00		

On Issue of 1908-09

			2mm	3mm	Used Single
343	1c	**green**	47.50	42.50	9.00
		Guide line pair	100.00		
		Pasteup pair	95.00		
344	2c	**carmine**	57.50	47.50	9.00
		On cover			—
		Guide line or pasteup pair	105.00		
345	3c	**deep violet**	110.00		
		Guide line or pasteup pair	225.00		
346	4c	**orange brown**	175.00	150.00	
		Guide line pair	340.00		
347	5c	**blue**	210.00		*55.00*
		Guide line pair	400.00		

On Lincoln Issue of 1909

			2mm	3mm	Used Single
***368**	2c	**carmine**	110.00	110.00	27.50
		Guide line or pasteup pair	210.00		

On Alaska-Yukon Issue of 1909

			2mm	3mm	Used Single
***371**	2c	**carmine**		*340.00*	
		Guide line pair		*600.00*	
		Pasteup pair		600.00	

On Hudson-Fulton Issue of 1909

			2mm	3mm	Used Single
***373**	2c	**carmine**		*340.00*	
		On cover		—	
		Guide line pair		*550.00*	

On Issue of 1910

			2mm	3mm	Used Single
383	1c	**green**	15.00	10.50	2.25
		On cover			*225.00*
		Guide line pair	24.00		
384	2c	**carmine**	26.50	24.00	1.25
		On cover			*90.00*
		Guide line pair	42.50		

On Issue of 1912

			2mm	3mm	Used Single
408	1c	**green**		7.50	1.25
		On cover			65.00
		Guide line or pasteup pair		11.50	
409	2c	**carmine**		8.50	.75
		On cover			35.00
		Guide line pair		15.00	
		Pasteup pair		14.00	

On Issue of 1916-17

			2mm	3mm	Used Single
481	1c	**green**			—
482	2c	**carmine**		*115.00*	*65.00*
		On cover			*300.00*
		Guide line pair		*210.00*	
		Pasteup pair		*240.00*	
483	3c	**violet,** type I		*160.00*	*65.00*
		On cover			*425.00*
		Guide line pair		*320.00*	
		Pasteup pair		*240.00*	

THE SCHERMACK COMPANY

Detroit, Mich.

These perforations were developed by the Schermack Mailing Machine Co. before it became the Mailometer Co. The Type III perforation was used in the company's affixing machines from 1908 through 1927 or 1928.

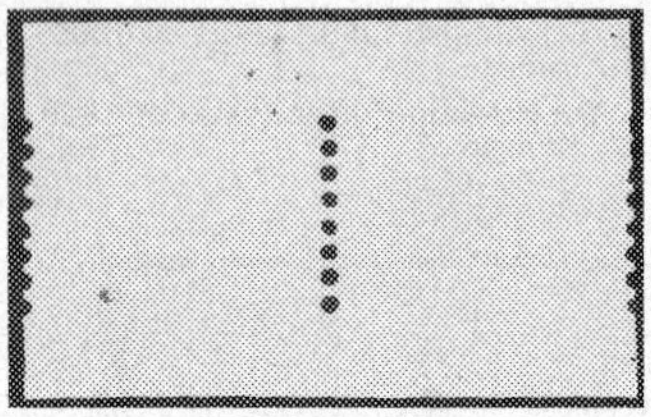

Perforations Type I. Eight Holes

Perforated in sheets, then cut into strips and coiled.

On Issue of 1906-08

No.			Unused Pair Spacing 2mm	3mm	Used Single
314	1c	**blue green**	160.00		*100.00*
		Guide line pair	320.00		
		*Seven holes	1,050.		
		*Pasteup pair	*1,400.*		
		*Six holes	950.00		
		Guide line pair	2,400.		
320	2c	**carmine**	135.00		*55.00*
		On cover			*2,250.*
		Guide line pair	250.00		
		Seven holes	1,150.		*300.00*
		On cover			*8,750.*
		Guide line pair	1,600.		
		Pasteup pair	1,150.		
		*Six holes	1,050.		
		Guide line pair	*2,350.*		
*320a	2c	**lake**	375.00		*110.00*
		*Seven holes	650.00		
		Guide line pair	*1,600.*		
		*Six holes	*1,300.*		
*320b	2c	**scarlet,** six holes			
		Guide line pair	*1,600.*		
*315	5c	**blue**	—		

On Issue of 1908-09

No.			2mm	3mm	Used Single
*343	1c	**green**	260.00	—	80.00
		Guide line pair	—		
*344	2c	**carmine**	1,050.	—	
		Guide line pair	*1,500.*		
*345	3c	**deep violet**	*1,500.*		
		Guide line pair	*1,850.*		
*346	4c	**orange brown**	650.00	—	
		Guide line pair	—		
*347	5c	**blue**	650.00		
		Guide line pair	—		

On Lincoln Issue of 1909

No.			2mm	3mm	Used Single
*368	2c	**carmine**	210.00	240.00	*80.00*
		Guide line pair	375.00		
		*Seven holes	925.00	—	
		*Six holes	1,050.	—	
		Guide line pair		*1,600.*	

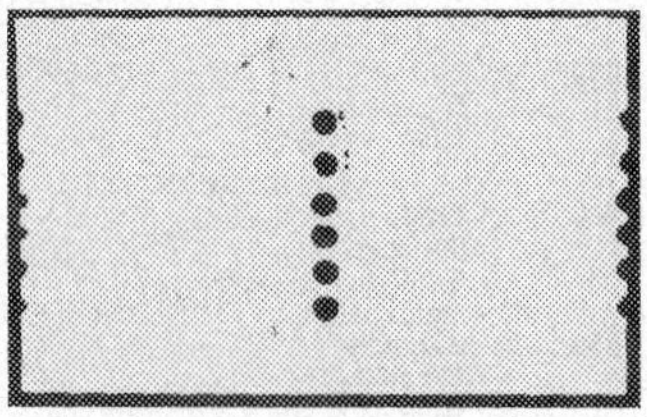

Perforations Type II

Cut into strips and joined before being perforated.

On Issue of 1906-08

No.			2mm	3mm	Used Single
314	1c	**blue green**	320.00		*80.00*
		On cover			*2,000.*
		Guide line pair	525.00		
320	2c	**carmine**	160.00		*55.00*
		Guide line pair	290.00		
*320a	2c	**lake**	275.00		*100.00*
		Guide line pair	475.00		
*315	5c	**blue**	*13,000.*		*1,750.*
		Guide line pair	—		

On Issue of 1908-09

No.			2mm	3mm	Used Single
*343	1c	**green**	*650.00*	*675.00*	
		Guide line pair	*1,100.*		
*344	2c	**carmine**	*650.00*	*625.00*	
		Guide line pair	*1,150.*		
*345	3c	**deep violet**	*650.00*		
		Guide line pair	*1,150.*		
*346	4c	**orange brown**	*850.00*	—	
		Guide line pair	*1,500.*		
*347	5c	**blue**	*800.00*		
		Guide line pair	*1,600.*		

On Lincoln Issue of 1909

No.			2mm	3mm	Used Single
*368	2c	**carmine**	160.00	140.00	*65.00*
		Guide line pair	290.00		

On Issue of 1910

No.			2mm	3mm	Used Single
*383	1c	**green**	—	—	
		Guide line or pasteup pair	—		
*384	2c	**carmine**	—	—	

Existance of genuine copies of Nos. 383-384 has been questioned.

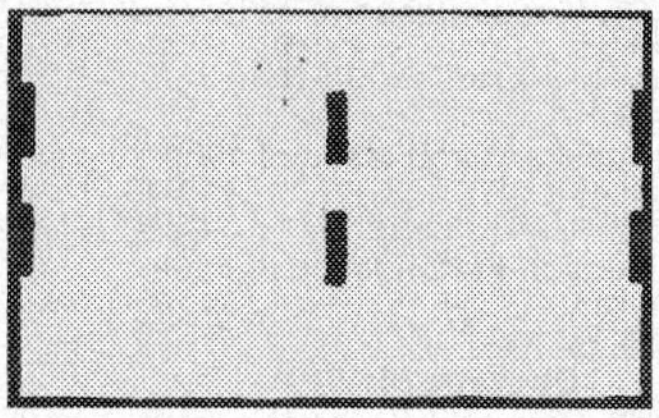

Perforations Type III

Blocks exist but were not regularly produced or issued.

On Issue of 1906-08

No.			Unused Pair Spacing 2mm	3mm	Used Single
314	1c	**blue green**	11.50		2.25
		On cover			*140.00*
		Guide line pair	24.00		
		Pasteup pair	20.00		
		With both Type I (eight holes) and Type III perfs			—
320	2c	**carmine,** type I	17.00		5.50
		On cover			90.00
		Guide line pair	32.50		
		With both Type I (eight holes) and Type III perfs			—
320a	2c	**lake,** type II	24.00		2.75
		On cover			*80.00*
		Guide line pair	47.50		
		Pasteup pair	42.50		
		With perforated control mark, single			—
		With both Type I (seven holes) and Type III perfs			—
*320b	2c	**scarlet,** type I	24.00		5.50
		On cover			—
		Guide line pair	42.50		
320c	2c	**carmine rose,** type I	57.50		
320d	2c	**carmine,** type II, single	130.00		
		On cover			675.00
		Pair	240.00		
		Guide line pair	*475.00*		
314A	4c	**brown,** single	*90,000.*		*50,000.*
		Pair	*225,000.*		
		On cover			*140,000.*
		Guide line pair	*375,000.*		
*315	5c	**blue**	*4,750.*		

On Issue of 1908-09

No.			2mm	3mm	Used Single
343	1c	**green**	5.75	6.75	1.25
		On cover			27.50
		Guide line or pasteup pair	10.50		
		With perforated control mark, single			*50.00*
		Same, on cover			*500.00*
344	2c	**carmine**	5.75	6.75	1.25
		On cover			20.00
		Guide line or pasteup pair	10.50		
		With perforated control mark, single			50.00
		Same, on cover			*500.00*
345	3c	**deep violet**	24.00	*160.00*	12.50
		On cover			—
		Guide line pair	52.50		
		Pasteup pair	52.50		
		With perforated control mark, single			*900.00*
		Same, on cover			*8,000.*
346	4c	**orange brown**	35.00	22.50	17.50
		On cover			*3,250.*
		Guide line or pasteup pair	57.50		
		With perforated control mark, single			*1,500.*
		On cover			*10,000.*
347	5c	**blue**	57.50		17.50
		On cover			*2,500.*
		Guide line pair	105.00		

On Lincoln Issue of 1909

No.			2mm	3mm	Used Single
368	2c	**carmine**	67.50	52.50	12.50
		On cover			*190.00*
		Guide line or pasteup pair	135.00		

On Alaska-Yukon Issue of 1909

No.			2mm	3mm	Used Single
*371	2c	**carmine**		90.00	
		On cover			*4,500.*
		Guide line or pasteup pair		170.00	

On Hudson-Fulton Issue of 1909

No.			2mm	3mm	Used Single
*373	2c	**carmine**		110.00	
		Guide line or pasteup pair		210.00	

On Issue of 1910

No.			Unused Pair Spacing 2mm	3mm	Used Single
383	1c	**green**	4.75	3.40	1.25
		On cover			22.50
		Guide line or pasteup pair	9.25		
		With perforated control mark, single			*40.00*
		Same, on cover			*400.00*

Earliest documented use: Feb. 8, 1911.

No.			2mm	3mm	Used Single
384	2c	**carmine**	10.50	8.25	1.25
		On cover			22.50
		Guide line pair	17.00		
		With perforated control mark, single			*40.00*
		Same, on cover			*400.00*

On Issue of 1912

No.			2mm	3mm	Used Single
408	1c	**green**		2.40	.60
		On cover			22.50
		Guide line or pasteup pair		4.75	
		With perforated control mark, single			*47.50*
		Same, on cover			*350.00*
409	2c	**carmine**		2.40	.50
		On cover			22.50
		Guide line or pasteup pair		4.75	
		Aniline ink ("pink back")		—	
		With perforated control mark, single			*47.50*
		Same, on cover			*350.00*
		Single stamp in pasteup with strip of three No. TD14a test stamps		*6,000.*	

Earliest documented use: Mar. 21, 1912.

On Issue of 1916-17

No.			2mm	3mm	Used Single
481	1c	**green**		3.50	.40
		On cover			22.50
		Guide line or pasteup pair		6.75	
482	2c	**carmine,** type I		4.25	.60
		On cover			20.00
		Guide line or pasteup pair		9.00	
		Aniline ink ("pink back")		—	

Earliest documented use: Dec. 16, 1916.

No.			2mm	3mm	Used Single
482A	2c	**deep rose,** type Ia, single			*65,000.*
		Pair			*140,000.*
		On cover			*70,000.*
483	3c	**violet,** type I		11.50	2.75
		On cover			100.00
		Guide line or pasteup pair		20.00	

Earliest documented use: Nov 2, 1917.

No.			2mm	3mm	Used Single
484	3c	**violet,** type II		17.00	4.50
		On cover			100.00
		Guide line or pasteup pair		32.50	

Earliest documented use: April 5, 1918.

On Issue of 1918-20

No.			2mm	3mm	Used Single
531	1c	**green**		16.00	4.50
		On cover			110.00
		Guide line or pasteup pair		32.50	
532	2c	**carmine,** type IV		42.50	3.50
		On cover			80.00
		Guide line or pasteup pair		85.00	
		Pasteup strip of 4, left pair No. 532, right pair No. 482		*2,000.*	

Earliest documented use: April 28, 1920.

No.			2mm	3mm	Used Single
533	2c	**carmine,** type V		*375.00*	*45.00*
		On cover			*275.00*
		Guide line or pasteup pair		*1,050.*	
534	2c	**carmine,** type Va		27.50	2.25
		On cover			100.00
		Guide line or pasteup pair		57.50	
534A	2c	**carmine,** type VI		47.50	4.50
		On cover			80.00
		Guide line or pasteup pair		95.00	

Earliest documented use: Aug. 31, 1920.

No.			2mm	3mm	Used Single
534B	2c	**carmine,** type VII		*1,275.*	85.00
		On cover			*450.00*
		Guide line or pasteup pair		*2,100.*	
535	3c	**violet,** type IV		21.00	3.50
		On cover			80.00
		Guide line or pasteup pair		42.50	

On Issue of 1923-26

No.			2mm	3mm	Used Single
575	1c	**green**		*210.00*	6.75
		Unused single		25.00	
		On cover			*425.00*
		Guide line or pasteup pair		*400.00*	
		Precanceled		4.75	1.25
		On cover, precanceled			*115.00*
576	1½c	**yellow brown**		24.00	4.50
		On cover			*225.00*

		Guide line or pasteup pair		42.50	
		Precanceled		4.75	1.00
		On cover, precanceled			*85.00*
577	2c	**carmine**	29.00	24.00	1.25
		On cover			22.50
		Guide line or pasteup pair	52.50	42.50	

On Harding Issue of 1923

611	2c	**black**	100.00	17.50
		On cover		*8,250.*
		Guide line or pasteup pair	170.00	

U.S. AUTOMATIC VENDING COMPANY

New York, N.Y.

Separations Type I

Cut into strips and joined before being perforated.

Two varieties exist: 15½ and 16mm between notches of the perforations.

			Unused Pair	Used Single

On Issue of 1906-08

Coiled Endwise

			Unused Pair	Used Single
314	1c	**blue green**	52.50	12.50
		On cover		*2,100.*
		Guide line or pasteup pair	100.00	
320	2c	**carmine**	47.50	9.00
		On cover		*4,000.*
		Guide line pair	95.00	
		Pasteup pair	85.00	
***320a**	2c	**lake**	105.00	9.00
		Guide line or pasteup pair	210.00	
320b	2c	**scarlet**	57.50	8.00
		On cover		*4,000.*
		Guide line pair	115.00	
315	5c	**blue**	800.00	*2,000.*
		On cover		*11,500.*
		Guide line pair	*2,650.*	
		Pasteup pair	*2,900.*	

On Issue of 1908-09

Coiled Endwise

			Unused Pair	Used Single
343	1c	**green**	11.50	1.75
		On cover		110.00
		On postcard		50.00
		Guide line or pasteup pair	23.50	
344	2c	**carmine**	9.50	1.75
		On cover		110.00
		Guide line or pasteup pair	19.00	
***345**	3c	**deep violet**	35.00	9.00
		On cover		*575.00*
		Guide line or pasteup pair	67.50	
***346**	4c	**orange brown**	52.50	10.00
		Guide line or pasteup pair	110.00	
347	5c	**blue**	95.00	45.00
		On cover		*2,500.*
		On cover (pair) with No. 373 USAV type II pair		*7,500.*
		Guide line or pasteup pair	185.00	

On Lincoln Issue of 1909

			Unused Pair	Used Single
368	2c	**carmine,** coiled endwise	42.50	8.00
		On cover		*575.00*
		First day cover, *Feb. 12, 1909*		*14,500.*
		Guide line or pasteup pair	85.00	

On Alaska-Yukon Issue of 1909

			Unused Pair	Used Single
***371**	2c	**carmine,** coiled sideways	85.00	12.50
		On cover		*575.00*
		Guide line pair	160.00	

			Unused Pair	Used Single
		Type Ia, No T. and B. margins	150.00	17.50
		Type Ia, Guide line or pasteup pair	240.00	

Type Ia stamps are a deep shade and have a misplaced position dot in the "S" of "Postage." Beware of trimmed copies of No. 371 type I.

On Issue of 1910

			Unused Pair	Used Single
383	1c	**green**	6.75	2.75
		On cover		110.00
		On postcard		40.00
		Guide line or pasteup pair	11.50	
***384**	2c	**carmine**	24.00	5.00
		Guide line or pasteup pair	42.50	

On Issue of 1912

			Unused Pair	Used Single
***408**	1c	**green**	11.50	2.25
		Guide line pair	20.00	
***409**	2c	**carmine**	15.00	4.50
		Guide line or pasteup pair	24.00	

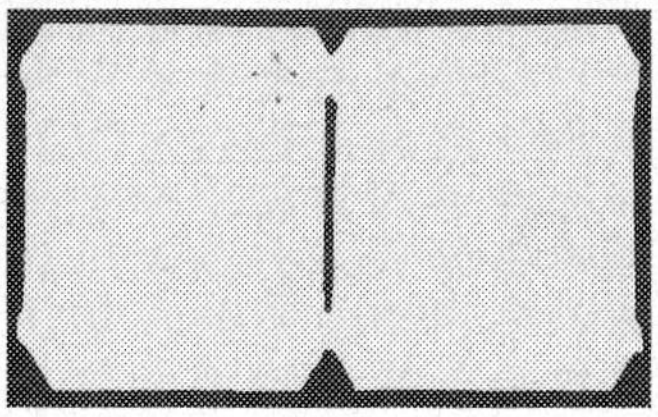

Separations Type II

Similar to Type I but with notches farther apart and a longer slit. Cut into strips and joined before being perforated.

On Issue of 1906-08

Coiled Sideways

			Unused Pair Spacing 2mm	3mm	Used Single
***314**	1c	**blue green**	52.50		9.00
		On cover			—
		Guide line or pasteup pair	87.50		
***320**	2c	**carmine**	92.50		
		Guide line pair	130.00		
***320b**	2c	**scarlet**	62.50		5.50
		Guide line pair	105.00		
***315**	5c	**blue**	1,500.		
		Guide line pair	*2,650.*		

On Issue of 1908-09

			Unused Pair Spacing 2mm	3mm	Used Single
343	1c	**green**	15.00		3.50
		On cover			*1,150.*
		Guide line or pasteup pair	24.00		
344	2c	**carmine**	17.00		
		On cover			*2,800.*
		Guide line pair	27.50		
***345**	3c	**deep violet**	67.50	—	
		Guide line pair	115.00		
***346**	4c	**orange brown**	100.00	87.50	
		Guide line pair	170.00		
***347**	5c	**blue**	200.00		
		Guide line pair	320.00		

On Lincoln Issue of 1909

			Unused Pair Spacing 2mm	3mm	Used Single
368	2c	**carmine**	105.00	92.50	22.50
		Guide line pair	185.00		

On Alaska-Yukon Issue of 1909

			Unused Pair Spacing 2mm	3mm	Used Single
***371**	2c	**carmine**		80.00	40.00
		On cover			*575.00*
		Guide line or pasteup pair		140.00	

On Hudson-Fulton Issue of 1909

			Unused Pair Spacing 2mm	3mm	Used Single
***373**	2c	**carmine**		85.00	*17.50*
		On cover			*2,250.*
		Guide line or pasteup pair		160.00	

See No. 347 USAV type I for combination cover.

On Issue of 1910

			Unused Pair Spacing 2mm	3mm	Used Single
383	1c	**green**	17.00	13.00	
		On cover			*1,150.*
		Guide line pair	29.00		
384	2c	**carmine**	24.00	17.00	
		On cover			*2,750.*
		Guide line pair	42.50		

On Issue of 1912

			Unused Pair Spacing 2mm	3mm	Used Single
408	1c	**green**		11.50	2.25
		On cover			*1,700.*
		Guide line pair		20.00	
409	2c	**carmine**		17.00	4.50

			Unused Pair Spacing 2mm	3mm	Used Single
		Guide line pair		27.50	

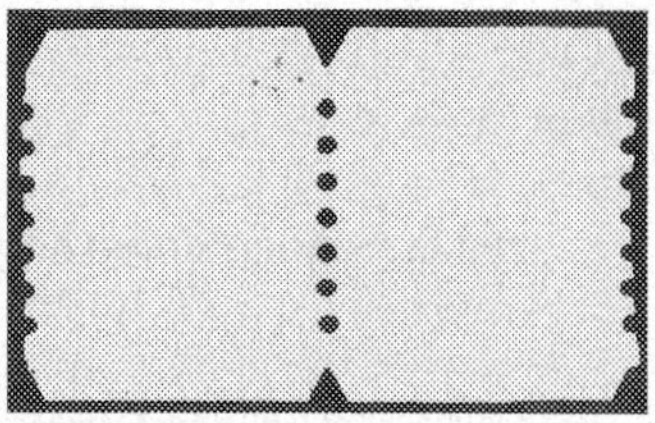

Perforations Type III

Cut into strips and joined before being perforated.

On Issue of 1906-08

			Unused Pair Spacing 2mm	3mm	Used Single
***314**	1c	**blue green**	57.50		12.50
		Guide line pair	105.00		
***320**	2c	**carmine**	105.00		
***320b**	2c	**scarlet**	67.50		12.50
		Guide line pair	115.00		
***315**	5c	**blue**	1,275.		
		Guide line or pasteup pair	*2,650.*		

On Issue of 1908-09

			Unused Pair Spacing 2mm	3mm	Used Single
343	1c	**green**	29.00	26.50	5.50
		Guide line or pasteup pair	47.50		
344	2c	**carmine**	29.00	37.50	5.50
		Guide line pair	47.50		
***345**	3c	**deep violet**	115.00		
		Guide line pair	200.00		
***346**	4c	**orange brown**	115.00	105.00	14.00
		Guide line pair	200.00		
***347**	5c	**blue**	150.00		
		Guide line pair	270.00		

On Lincoln Issue of 1909

			Unused Pair Spacing 2mm	3mm	Used Single
***368**	2c	**carmine**	75.00	62.50	19.00
		Guide line pair	130.00		
		Experimental perf. 12.3	*3,400.*		
		Guide line pair	*5,750.*		

On Alaska-Yukon Issue of 1909

			Unused Pair Spacing 2mm	3mm	Used Single
***371**	2c	**carmine**		95.00	19.00
		On cover			—
		Guide line or pasteup pair		150.00	

On Hudson-Fulton Issue of 1909

			Unused Pair Spacing 2mm	3mm	Used Single
***373**	2c	**carmine**		105.00	19.00
		On cover			—
		Guide line or pasteup pair		150.00	

On Issue of 1910

			Unused Pair Spacing 2mm	3mm	Used Single
383	1c	**green**	16.00	14.00	2.75
		Guide line pair	26.50		
384	2c	**carmine**	19.00	16.00	2.75
		Guide line pair	29.00		

On Issue of 1912

			Unused Pair Spacing 2mm	3mm	Used Single
408	1c	**green**		10.50	
		Guide line pair		17.00	
409	2c	**carmine**		19.00	
		Guide line pair		26.50	
		Pasteup pair		26.50	

On 1914 Rotary Press Coil

			Unused Pair Spacing 2mm	3mm	Used Single
459	2c	**carmine**		*27,500.*	*11,500.*

This firm also produced coil strips of manila paper, folded so as to form small "pockets", each "pocket" containing one 1c stamp and two 2c stamps, usually imperforate but occasionally with either government or U.S.A.V. private perforations. The manila "pockets" were perforated type II, coiled sideways. They fit U.S.A.V. ticket vending machines. Multiples exist.

Values are for "pockets" with known combinations of stamps, listed by basic Scott Number. Other combinations exist, but are not listed due to the fact that the stamps may have been added at a later date.

Pocket Type 1 (1908)
("Patents Pending" on front and green advertising on reverse)

Type 1-1	314 + 320	*2,900.*
Type 1-2	314 + 320b	*2,900.*

Pocket Type 2 (1909)
("Patents Applied For" Handstamped in greenish blue)

Type 2-1	343 + 371	1,600.
Type 2-2	343 + 372	950.
Type 2-3	343 (USAV Type I) + 371	2,100.
Type 2-4	343 + 375	950.

Pocket Type 3 (1909)
("Patents Pending" printed in red)

Type 3-1	347 + 371	1,050.
Type 3-1A	343 + 372	1,050.
Type 3-2	343 + 373	850.
Type 3-3	343 + 375	850.
Type 3-4	383 + 406	850.

Pocket Type 4 (1909)
(No printing on front, serial number on back)

Type 4-1	343 + 344	320.
Type 4-2	343 + 368	320.
Type 4-3	343 + 371	320.
Type 4-4	383 + 344	320.
Type 4-5	383 (USAV Type II) + 344	320.
Type 4-6	383 + 384	320.
Type 4-7	383 + 406	320.

THE ATTLEBORO STAMP COMPANY

Attleboro, Mass.

This Company used an affixing machine to stamp its newsletters during the summer and fall of 1909.

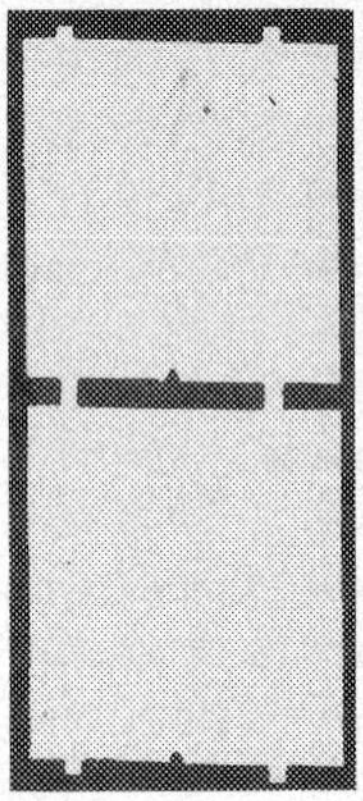

Nos. 343-344

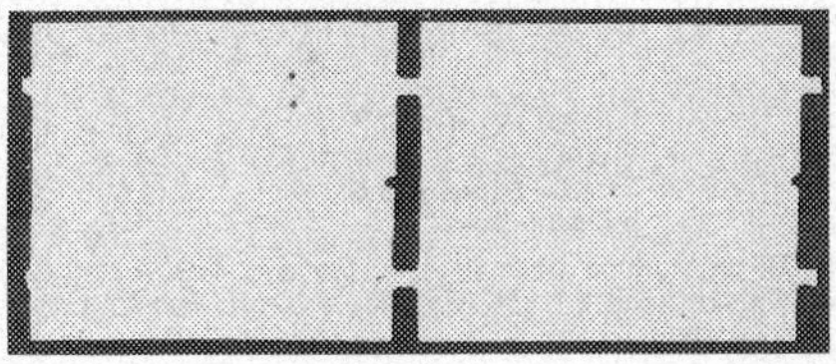

No. 371

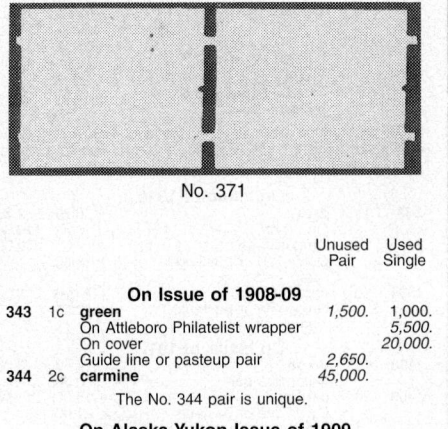

			Unused Pair	Used Single
		On Issue of 1908-09		
343	1c	**green**	*1,500.*	1,000.
		On Attleboro Philatelist wrapper		*5,500.*
		On cover		*20,000.*
		Guide line or pasteup pair	*2,650.*	
344	2c	**carmine**	*45,000.*	

The No. 344 pair is unique.

		On Alaska-Yukon Issue of 1909		
371	2c	**carmine**, coiled sidewise	*3,650.*	*1,100.*
		Guide line or pasteup pair	*5,750.*	—
		On wrapper or cover		*9,000.*

IMPERFORATE FLAT PLATE COIL STAMPS

These flat plate imperforate coil stamps were made from imperforate sheets of the regular issues, and were issued in coils of 500 or 1,000. The numbers assigned below are those of the regularly issued imperforate sheet stamps to which "H" or "V" has been added to indicate that the stamps are coiled horizontally (side by side), or vertically (top to bottom). These coil stamps are virtually indistinguishable from the corresponding imperforate sheet stamps, although they can be authenticated, particularly when in strips of four or longer. Many genuine imperforate coil stamps bear authenticating signatures of contemporaneous experts.

Values for stamps on cover are for single stamps.

FLAT PLATE PRINTING

1908 Wmk. 191 ***Imperf.***

314V	A115	1c	**blue green,** pair, never hinged	—	—
			Strip of 4	—	—
			Guide line pair	—	
			Guide line strip of 4	—	

The Philatelic Foundation has certified one unused No. 314V pair (with coil leader strip attached). The existence of any of the other listed items has been questioned by specialists. The editors would like to see certified evidence of the other listings.

314H	A115	1c	**blue green,** pair	*2,100.*	—
			Never hinged	*3,750.*	
			On cover		*1,300.*
			Pair on cover		*2,000.*
			Strip of 4	—	—
			Never hinged	*8,000.*	
			Guide line pair	*5,000.*	
			Guide line strip of 4	8,000.	
			Pasteup pair	*3,500.*	
			Never hinged	*5,500.*	
			Pasteup strip of 4	*5,000.*	
			Never hinged	*8,000.*	

Earliest documented use: Mar. 9, 1908.

320V	A129	2c	**carmine,** pair	*1,500.*	—
			On cover		—
			Strip of 4	—	—
			Guide line pair	—	
			Guide line strip of 4	—	

Earliest documented use: Apr. 9, 1908.

320H	A129	2c	**carmine,** pair	500.00	—
			Strip of 4	—	—
			Guide line pair	—	
			Guide line strip of 4	—	

Earliest documented use: Sept. 17, 1908.

1908-10 ***Imperf.***

343V	A138	1c	**green,** pair	25.00	8.50
			Never hinged	40.00	
			On cover		10.00
			Strip of 4	60.00	—
			Guide line pair	60.00	—
			Guide line strip of 4	85.00	
			Pasteup pair	50.00	

Earliest documented use: May 24, 1910.

343H	A138	1c	**green,** pair	50.00	—
			Never hinged	80.00	
			Strip of 4	120.00	—
			Guide line pair	100.00	—
			Guide line strip of 4	250.00	
			Pasteup pair	80.00	
344V	A139	2c	**carmine,** pair	30.00	25.00
			Never hinged	50.00	
			On cover		15.00
			Strip of 4	75.00	—
			Guide line pair	60.00	—
			Guide line strip of 4	105.00	
			Pasteup pair	60.00	
			Foreign entry, design of 1c	*2,500.*	*3,000.*
			Never hinged	*3,500.*	

Earliest documented use: Oct. 13, 1909.

344H	A139	2c	**carmine,** pair (2mm spacing)	35.00	25.00
			Never hinged	55.00	
			On cover		—
			Strip of 4	90.00	
			Guide line pair	80.00	
			Guide line strip of 4	140.00	
			Pasteup pair	60.00	
			Pair (3mm spacing)	40.00	—
			Strip of 4	100.00	
			Guide line pair	85.00	—
			Guide line strip of 4	150.00	

Earliest documented use: March 23, 1909.

345H	A140	3c	**deep violet,** type I, pair	—	
346V	A140	4c	**orange brown,** pair	160.00	
			Never hinged	250.00	
			Strip of 4	375.00	—
			Never hinged	650.00	
			Guide line pair	325.00	75.00
			Guide line strip of 4	700.00	
			Pasteup pair	250.00	

Earliest documented use: Feb. 18, 1911.

347V	A140	5c	**blue,** pair	175.00	—
			Never hinged	275.00	
			On cover		—
			Strip of 4	425.00	—
			Never hinged	700.00	
			Guide line pair	375.00	—
			Guide line strip of 4	600.00	

Earliest documented use: April 17, 1909.

1909 ***Imperf.***

368V	A141	2c	**carmine,** *Lincoln,* pair	200.00	—
			Never hinged	300.00	
			On cover		—
			Strip of 4	500.00	—
			Never hinged	750.00	
			Guide line pair	400.00	—
			Never hinged	650.00	
			Guide line strip of 4	800.00	—
			Never hinged	1,250.	
			Pasteup pair	300.00	
			Never hinged	475.00	

Earliest documented use: Feb. 12, 1909.

368H	A141	2c	**carmine,** *Lincoln,* pair	275.00	—
			Never hinged	450.00	
			On cover		—
			Strip of 4	700.00	
			Never hinged	1,050.	
			Guide line pair	525.00	
			Never hinged	900.00	
			Guide line strip of 4	900.00	
			Pasteup pair	425.00	
			Never hinged	650.00	

Earliest documented use: Dec. 9, 1909.

1910 Wmk. 190 ***Imperf.***

383V	A138	1c	**green,** pair	12.00	—
			Never hinged	20.00	
			On cover		6.00
			Strip of 4	27.50	—
			Guide line pair	25.00	—
			Never hinged	40.00	
			Guide line strip of 4	60.00	—
			Never hinged	95.00	
			Pasteup pair	20.00	
			Never hinged	35.00	
			Double transfer	—	—

Earliest documented use: Apr. 13, 1911.

383H	A138	1c	**green,** pair (2mm spacing)	17.50	—
			Never hinged	28.00	
			Strip of 4	42.50	—
			Never hinged	65.00	
			Guide line pair	35.00	—
			Never hinged	55.00	
			Guide line strip of 4	65.00	—
			Never hinged	110.00	
			Pasteup pair	30.00	
			Pair (3mm spacing)	17.50	—

Never hinged	28.00	
Strip of 4	42.50	—
Never hinged	65.00	
Guide line pair	35.00	—
Never hinged	55.00	
Guide line strip of 4	65.00	—
Never hinged	110.00	
384V A139 2c **carmine,** pair	14.00	—
Never hinged	24.00	
On cover		7.00
Strip of 4	30.00	—
Guide line pair	30.00	—
Guide line strip of 4	55.00	—
Pasteup pair	22.50	
Foreign entry, design of 1c	*1,500.*	—

Earliest documented use: Oct. 21, 1910.

384H A139 2c **carmine,** pair (2mm spacing)	27.50	—
Never hinged	45.00	
Strip of 4	70.00	
Guide line pair	60.00	—
Guide line strip of 4	105.00	—
Pasteup pair	50.00	
Pair (3mm spacing)	25.00	—
Strip of 4	70.00	—
Guide line pair	55.00	—
Guide line strip of 4	100.00	—

Earliest documented use: Mar. 9, 1912.

1912 Wmk. 190 ***Imperf.***

408V A140 1c **green,** pair	4.00	
Never hinged	7.00	
On cover		—
Strip of 4	8.50	
Guide line pair	9.00	
Guide line strip of 4	14.00	
Pasteup pair	7.00	

Earliest documented use: May 17, 1912.

408H A140 1c **green,** pair	5.00	
Never hinged	8.00	
Strip of 4	12.00	
Guide line pair	10.00	
Guide line strip of 4	17.50	

409V A140 2c **carmine,** pair	4.00
Never hinged	7.00
Strip of 4	9.00
Never hinged	15.00
Guide line pair	8.00
Never hinged	15.00
Guide line strip of 4	14.00
Pasteup pair	7.00

Earliest documented use: May 29, 1912.

409H A140 2c **carmine,** pair	6.00
Never hinged	10.00
Strip of 4	14.00
Guide line pair	9.00
Never hinged	16.00
Guide line strip of 4	15.00
Pasteup pair	7.00
Double transfer	7.00

Earliest documented use: Dec. 17, 1914.

COMMEMORATIVE STAMPS, QUANTITIES ISSUED

Quantities issued fall into four categories. First are stamps where reasonably accurate counts are made of the number of stamps sold.

Second are stamps where the counts are approximations of the number sold.

Third are stamps where the count is of quantities shipped to post offices and philatelic sales units, but no adjustments are made for returned or destroyed stamps.

Fourth are stamps for which the quantity printed is furnished but no other adjustments are made.

Occasionally more accurate figures are determined. In these cases the quantities here will be adjusted. For example, it is now known that while 2,000,000 sets of the Voyages of Columbus souvenir sheets were printed, the number sold was 1,185,170 sets.

Scott No.		Quantity
230		449,195,550
231		1,464,588,750
232		11,501,250
233		19,181,550
234		35,248,250
235		4,707,550
236		10,656,550
237		16,516,950
238		1,576,950
239		617,250
240		243,750
241		55,050
242		45,550
243		27,650
244		26,350
245		27,350
285		70,993,400
286		159,720,800
287		4,924,500
288		7,694,180
289		2,927,200
290		4,629,760
291		530,400
292		56,900
293		56,200
294		91,401,500
295		209,759,700
296		5,737,100
297		7,201,300
298		4,921,700
299		5,043,700
323		79,779,200
324		192,732,400
325		4,542,600
326		6,926,700
327		4,011,200
328		77,728,794
329		149,497,994
330		7,980,594
367		148,387,191
368		1,273,900
369		637,000
370		152,887,311
371		525,400
372		72,634,631
373		216,480
397 & 401		334,796,926
398 & 402		503,713,086
399 & 403		29,088,726
400 & 404		16,968,365
537		99,585,200
548		137,978,207
549		196,037,327
550		11,321,607
610		1,459,487,085
611		770,000
612		99,950,300
614		51,378,023
615		77,753,423
616		5,659,023
617		15,615,000
618		26,596,600
619		5,348,800
620		9,104,983
621		1,900,983
627		307,731,900
628		20,280,500
629		40,639,485
630	(sheet of 25)	107,398
643		39,974,900
644		25,628,450
645		101,330,328
646		9,779,896
647		5,519,897
648		1,459,897
649		51,342,273
650		10,319,700
651		16,684,674
654		31,679,200
655		210,119,474
656		133,530,000
657		51,451,880
658		13,390,000
659		8,240,000
660		87,410,000
661		2,540,000
662		2,290,000
663		2,700,000
664		1,450,000
665		1,320,000
666		1,530,000
667		1,130,000
668		2,860,000
669		8,220,000
670		8,990,000
671		73,220,000
672		2,110,000
673		1,600,000
674		1,860,000
675		980,000
676		850,000
677		1,480,000
678		530,000
679		1,890,000
680		29,338,274
681		32,680,900
682		74,000,774
683		25,215,574
688		25,609,470
689		66,487,000
690		96,559,400
702		99,074,600
703		25,006,400
704		87,969,700
705		1,265,555,100
706		304,926,800
707		4,222,198,300
708		456,198,500
709		151,201,300
710		170,565,100
711		111,739,400
712		83,257,400
713		96,506,100
714		75,709,200
715		147,216,000
716		51,102,800
717		100,869,300
718		168,885,300
719		52,376,100
724		49,949,000
725		49,538,500
726		61,719,200
727		73,382,400
728		348,266,800
729		480,239,300
730	(sheet of 25)	456,704
730a		11,417,600
731	(sheet of 25)	441,172
731a		11,029,300
732		1,978,707,300
733		5,735,944
734		45,137,700
735	(sheet of 6)	811,404
735a		4,868,424
736		46,258,300
737		193,239,100
738		15,432,200
739		64,525,400
740		84,896,350
741		74,400,200
742		95,089,000
743		19,178,650
744		30,980,100
745		16,923,350
746		15,988,250
747		15,288,700
748		17,472,600
749		18,874,300
750	(sheet of 6)	511,391
750a		3,068,346
751	(sheet of 6)	793,551
751a		4,761,306
752		3,274,556
753		2,040,760
754		2,389,288
755		2,294,948
756		3,217,636
757		2,746,640
758		2,168,088
759		1,822,684
760		1,724,576
761		1,647,696
762		1,682,948
763		1,638,644
764		1,625,224
765		1,644,900
766	(pane of 25)	98,712
766a		2,467,800
767	(pane of 25)	85,914
767a		2,147,850
768	(pane of 6)	267,200
768a		1,603,200
769	(pane of 6)	279,960
769a		1,679,760
770	(pane of 6)	215,920
770a		1,295,520
771		1,370,560
772		70,726,800
773		100,839,600
774		73,610,650
775		75,823,900
776		124,324,500
777		67,127,650
778	(sheet of 4)	2,809,039
778a		2,809,039
778b		2,809,039
778c		2,809,039
778d		2,809,039
782		72,992,650
783		74,407,450
784		269,522,200
785		105,196,150
786		93,848,500
787		87,741,150
788		35,794,150
789		36,839,250
790		104,773,450
791		92,054,550
792		93,291,650
793		34,552,950
794		36,819,050
795		84,825,250
796		25,040,400
797		5,277,445
798		99,882,300

Scott No.	Quantity	Scott No.	Quantity	Scott No.	Quantity
799	78,454,450	965	53,958,100	1115	114,860,200
800	77,004,200	966	61,120,010	1116	126,500,000
801	81,292,450	967	57,823,000	1117	120,561,280
802	76,474,550	968	52,975,000	1118	44,064,576
835	73,043,650	969	77,149,000	1119	118,390,200
836	58,564,368	970	58,332,000	1120	125,770,200
837	65,939,500	971	56,228,000	1121	114,114,280
838	47,064,300	972	57,832,000	1122	156,600,200
852	114,439,600	973	53,875,000	1123	124,200,200
853	101,699,550	974	63,834,000	1124	120,740,200
854	72,764,550	975	67,162,200	1125	133,623,280
855	81,269,600	976	64,561,000	1126	45,569,088
856	67,813,350	977	64,079,500	1127	122,493,280
857	71,394,750	978	63,388,000	1128	131,260,200
858	66,835,000	979	62,285,000	1129	47,125,200
859	56,348,320	980	57,492,610	1130	123,105,000
860	53,177,110	981	99,190,000	1131	126,105,050
861	53,260,270	982	104,790,000	1132	209,170,000
862	22,104,950	983	108,805,000	1133	120,835,000
863	13,201,270	984	107,340,000	1134	115,715,000
864	51,603,580	985	117,020,000	1135	118,445,000
865	52,100,510	986	122,633,000	1136	111,685,000
866	51,666,580	987	130,960,000	1137	43,099,200
867	22,207,780	988	128,478,000	1138	115,444,000
868	11,835,530	989	132,090,000	1139	126,470,000
869	52,471,160	990	130,050,000	1140	124,560,000
870	52,366,440	991	131,350,000	1141	115,455,000
871	51,636,270	992	129,980,000	1142	122,060,000
872	20,729,030	993	122,315,000	1143	120,540,000
873	14,125,580	994	122,170,000	1144	113,075,000
874	59,409,000	995	131,635,000	1145	139,325,000
875	57,888,600	996	121,860,000	1146	124,445,000
876	58,273,180	997	121,120,000	1147	113,792,000
877	23,779,000	998	119,120,000	1148	44,215,200
878	15,112,580	999	112,125,000	1149	113,195,000
879	57,322,790	1000	114,140,000	1150	121,805,000
880	58,281,580	1001	114,490,000	1151	115,353,000
881	56,398,790	1002	117,200,000	1152	111,080,000
882	21,147,000	1003	116,130,000	1153	153,025,000
883	13,328,000	1004	116,175,000	1154	119,665,000
884	54,389,510	1005	115,945,000	1155	117,855,000
885	53,636,580	1006	112,540,000	1156	118,185,000
886	55,313,230	1007	117,415,000	1157	112,260,000
887	21,720,580	1008	2,899,580,000	1158	125,010,000
888	13,600,580	1009	114,540,000	1159	119,798,000
889	47,599,580	1010	113,135,000	1160	42,696,000
890	53,766,510	1011	116,255,000	1161	106,610,000
891	54,193,580	1012	113,860,000	1162	109,695,000
892	20,264,580	1013	124,260,000	1163	123,690,000
893	13,726,580	1014	115,735,000	1164	123,970,000
894	46,497,400	1015	115,430,000	1165	124,796,000
895	47,700,000	1016	136,220,000	1166	42,076,800
896	50,618,150	1017	114,894,600	1167	116,210,000
897	50,034,400	1018	118,706,000	1168	126,252,000
898	60,943,700	1019	114,190,000	1169	42,746,400
902	44,389,550	1020	113,990,000	1170	124,117,000
903	54,574,550	1021	89,289,600	1171	119,840,000
904	63,558,400	1022	114,865,000	1172	117,187,000
906	21,272,800	1023	115,780,000	1173	124,390,000
907	1,671,564,200	1024	115,244,600	1174	112,966,000
908	1,227,334,200	1025	123,709,600	1175	41,644,200
909	19,999,646	1026	114,789,600	1176	110,850,000
910	19,999,646	1027	115,759,600	1177	98,616,000
911	19,999,646	1028	116,134,600	1178	101,125,000
912	19,999,646	1029	118,540,000	1179	124,865,000
913	19,999,646	1060	115,810,000	1180	79,905,000
914	19,999,646	1061	113,603,700	1181	125,410,000
915	19,999,646	1062	128,002,000	1182	112,845,000
916	14,999,646	1063	116,078,150	1183	106,210,000
917	14,999,646	1064	116,139,800	1184	110,810,000
918	14,999,646	1065	120,484,800	1185	116,995,000
919	14,999,646	1066	53,854,750	1186	121,015,000
920	14,999,646	1067	176,075,000	1187	111,600,000
921	14,999,646	1068	125,944,400	1188	110,620,000
922	61,303,000	1069	122,284,600	1189	109,110,000
923	61,001,450	1070	133,638,850	1190	145,350,000
924	60,605,000	1071	118,664,600	1191	112,870,000
925	50,129,350	1072	112,434,000	1192	121,820,000
926	53,479,400	1073	129,384,550	1193	289,240,000
927	61,617,350	1074	121,184,600	1194	120,155,000
928	75,500,000	1075	2,900,731	1195	124,595,000
929	137,321,000	1076	119,784,200	1196	147,310,000
930	128,140,000	1077	123,159,400	1197	118,690,000
931	67,255,000	1078	123,138,800	1198	122,730,000
932	133,870,000	1079	109,275,000	1199	126,515,000
933	76,455,400	1080	112,932,200	1200	130,960,000
934	128,357,750	1081	125,475,000	1201	120,055,000
935	138,863,000	1082	117,855,000	1202	120,715,000
936	111,616,700	1083	122,100,000	1203	121,440,000
937	308,587,700	1084	118,180,000	1204	40,270,000
938	170,640,000	1085	100,975,000	1205	861,970,000
939	135,927,000	1086	115,299,450	1206	120,035,000
940	260,339,100	1087	186,949,627	1207	117,870,000
941	132,274,500	1088	115,235,000	1230	129,945,000
942	132,430,000	1089	106,647,500	1231	135,620,000
943	139,209,500	1090	112,010,000	1232	137,540,000
944	114,684,450	1091	118,470,000	1233	132,435,000
945	156,540,510	1092	102,230,000	1234	135,520,000
946	120,452,600	1093	102,410,000	1235	131,420,000
947	127,104,300	1094	84,054,400	1236	133,170,000
948	10,299,600	1095	126,266,000	1237	130,195,000
949	132,902,000	1096	39,489,600	1238	128,450,000
950	131,968,000	1097	122,990,000	1239	118,665,000
951	131,488,000	1098	174,372,800	1240	1,291,250,000
952	122,362,000	1099	114,365,000	1241	175,175,000
953	121,548,000	1100	122,765,200	1242	125,995,000
954	131,109,500	1104	113,660,200	1243	128,025,000
955	122,650,500	1105	120,196,580	1244	145,700,000
956	121,953,500	1106	120,805,200	1245	120,310,000
957	115,250,000	1107	125,815,200	1246	511,750,000
958	64,198,500	1108	108,415,200	1247	123,845,000
959	117,642,500	1109	107,195,200	1248	122,825,000
960	77,649,600	1110	115,745,280	1249	453,090,000
961	113,474,500	1111	39,743,640	1250	123,245,000
962	120,868,500	1112	114,570,200	1251	123,355,000
963	77,800,500	1113	120,400,200	1252	126,970,000
964	52,214,000	1114	91,160,200	1253	121,250,000

Scott No.	Quantity
1254-1257	1,407,760,000
1258	120,005,000
1259	125,800,000
1260	122,230,000
1261	115,695,000
1262	115,095,000
1263	119,560,000
1264	125,180,000
1265	120,135,000
1266	115,405,000
1267	115,855,000
1268	115,340,000
1269	114,840,000
1270	116,140,000
1271	116,900,000
1272	114,085,000
1273	114,880,000
1274	26,995,000
1275	128,495,000
1276	1,139,930,000
1306	116,835,000
1307	117,470,000
1308	123,770,000
1309	131,270,000
1310	122,285,000
1311	14,680,000
1312	114,160,000
1313	128,475,000
1314	119,535,000
1315	125,110,000
1316	114,853,200
1317	124,290,000
1318	128,460,000
1319	127,585,000
1320	115,875,000
1321	1,173,547,420
1322	114,015,000
1323	121,105,000
1324	132,045,000
1325	118,780,000
1326	121,985,000
1327	111,850,000
1328	117,225,000
1329	111,515,000
1330	114,270,000
1331-1332	120,865,000
1333	110,675,000
1334	110,670,000
1335	113,825,000
1336	1,208,700,000
1337	113,330,000
1339	141,350,000
1340	144,345,000
1342	147,120,000
1343	130,125,000
1344	158,700,000
1345-1354	228,040,000
1355	153,015,000
1356	132,560,000
1357	130,385,000
1358	132,265,000
1359	128,710,000
1360	124,775,000
1361	128,295,000
1362	142,245,000
1363	1,410,580,000
1364	125,100,000
1365-1368	192,570,000
1369	148,770,000
1370	139,475,000
1371	187,165,000
1372	125,555,000
1373	144,425,000
1374	135,875,000
1375	151,110,000
1376-1379	159,195,000
1380	129,540,000
1381	130,925,000
1382	139,055,000
1383	150,611,200
1384	1,709,795,000
1385	127,545,000
1386	145,788,800
1387-1390	201,794,200
1391	171,850,000
1392	142,205,000
1405	137,660,000
1406	135,125,000
1407	135,895,000
1408	132,675,000
1409	134,795,000
1410-1413	161,600,000
1414-1414a	683,730,000
1415-1418, 1415a-1418a	489,255,000
1419	127,610,000
1420	129,785,000
1421-1422	134,380,000
1423	136,305,000
1424	134,840,000
1425	130,975,000
1426	161,235,000
1427-1430	175,679,600
1431	138,700,000
1432	138,165,000
1433	152,125,000
1434-1435	176,295,000
1436	142,845,000
1437	148,755,000
1438	139,080,000
1439	130,755,000
1440-1443	170,208,000
1444	1,074,350,000
1445	979,540,000
1446	137,355,000
1447	150,400,000
1448-1451	172,730,000
1452	104,090,000
1453	164,096,000
1454	53,920,000
1455	153,025,000
1456-1459	201,890,000
1460	67,335,000
1461	179,675,000
1462	46,340,000
1463	180,155,000
1464-1467	198,364,800
1468	185,490,000
1469	162,335,000
1470	162,789,950
1471	1,003,475,000
1472	1,017,025,000
1473	165,895,000
1474	166,508,000
1475	320,055,000
1476	166,005,000
1477	163,050,000
1478	159,005,000
1479	147,295,000
1480-1483	196,275,000
1484	139,152,000
1485	128,048,000
1486	146,008,000
1487	139,608,000
1488	159,475,000
1489-1498	486,020,000
1499	157,052,800
1500	53,005,000
1501	159,775,000
1502	39,005,000
1503	152,624,000
1504	145,840,000
1505	151,335,000
1506	141,085,000
1507	885,160,000
1508	939,835,000
1525	143,930,000
1526	145,235,000
1527	135,052,000
1528	156,750,000
1529	164,670,000
1530-1537	190,156,800
1538-1541	167,212,800
1542	156,265,000
1543-1546	195,585,000
1547	148,850,000
1548	157,270,000
1549	150,245,000
1550	835,180,000
1551	882,520,000
1552	213,155,000
1553	156,995,000
1554	146,365,000
1555	148,805,000
1556	173,685,000
1557	158,600,000
1558	153,355,000
1559	63,205,000
1560	157,865,000
1561	166,810,000
1562	44,825,000
1563	144,028,000
1564	139,928,000
1565-1568	179,855,000
1569-1570	161,863,200
1571	145,640,000
1572-1575	168,655,000
1576	146,615,000
1577-1578	146,196,000
1579	739,430,000
1580	878,690,000
1629-1631	219,455,000
1632	157,825,000
1633-1682	436,005,000
1683	159,915,000
1684	156,960,000
1685	158,470,000
1686	1,990,000
1687	1,983,000
1688	1,953,000
1689	1,903,000
1690	164,890,000
1691-1694	208,035,000
1695-1698	185,715,000
1699	130,592,000
1700	158,332,800
1701	809,955,000
1702-1703	963,370,000
1704	150,328,000
1705	176,830,000
1706-1709	195,976,000
1710	208,820,000
1711	192,250,000
1712-1715	219,830,000
1716	159,852,000
1717-1720	188,310,000
1721	163,625,000
1722	156,296,000
1723-1724	158,676,000
1725	154,495,000
1726	168,050,000
1727	156,810,000
1728	153,736,000
1729	882,260,000
1730	921,530,000
1731	156,560,000
1732-1733	202,155,000
1744	156,525,000
1745-1748	165,182,400
1749-1752	157,598,400
1753	102,856,000
1754	152,270,000
1755	94,600,000
1756	151,570,000
1757	15,170,400
1758	161,228,000
1759	158,880,000
1760-1763	186,550,000
1764-1767	168,136,000
1768	963,120,000
1769	916,800,000
1770	159,297,600
1771	166,435,000
1772	162,535,000
1773	155,000,000
1774	157,310,000
1775-1778	174,096,000
1779-1782	164,793,600
1783-1786	163,055,000
1787	161,860,000
1788	165,775,000
1789	160,000,000
1790	67,195,000
1791-1794	186,905,000
1795-1798	208,295,000
1799	873,710,000
1800	931,880,000
1801	161,290,000
1802	172,740,000
1803	168,995,000
1804	160,000,000
1805-1810	232,134,000
1821	163,510,000
1822	256,620,000
1823	95,695,000
1824	153,975,000
1825	160,000,000
1826	103,850,000
1827-1830	204,715,000
1831	166,545,000
1832	163,310,000
1833	160,000,000
1834-1837	152,404,000
1838-1841	152,420,000
1842	692,500,000
1843	718,715,000
1874	160,155,000
1875	159,505,000
1876-1879	210,633,000
1910	165,175,000
1911	107,240,000
1912-1919	337,819,000
1920	99,420,000
1921-1924	178,930,000
1925	100,265,000
1926	99,615,000
1927	97,535,000
1928-1931	167,308,000
1932	101,625,000
1922	99,170,000
1934	101,155,000
1935	101,200,000
1936	167,360,000
1937-1938	162,420,000
1939	597,720,000
1940	792,600,000
1941	167,130,000
1942-1945	191,560,000
1950	163,939,200
1952	180,700,000
1953-2002	666,950,000
2003	109,245,000
2004	112,535,000
2006-2009	124,640,000
2010	107,605,000
2011	173,160,000
2012	107,285,000
2013	109,040,000
2014	183,270,000
2015	169,495,000
2016	164,235,000
2017	110,130,000
2018	110,995,000
2019-2022	165,340,000
2023	174,180,000
2024	110,261,000
2026	703,295,000
2027-2030	788,880,000
2031	118,555,000
2032-2035	226,128,000
2036	118,225,000
2037	114,290,000
2038	165,000,000
2039	120,430,000
2040	117,025,000
2041	181,700,000
2042	114,250,000
2043	111,775,000
2044	115,200,000
2045	108,820,000
2046	184,950,000
2047	110,925,000
2048-2051	395,424,000
2052	104,340,000
2053	114,725,000
2054	112,525,000
2055-2058	193,055,000
2059-2062	207,725,000
2063	715,975,000
2064	848,525,000
2065	165,000,000
2066	120,000,000
2067-2070	319,675,000
2071	103,975,000
2072	554,675,000
2073	120,000,000
2074	106,975,000
2075	107,325,000
2076-2079	306,912,000
2080	120,000,000
2081	108,000,000

Scott No.	Quantity
2082-2085	313,350,000
2086	130,320,000
2087	120,000,000
2088	117,050,000
2089	115,725,000
2090	116,600,000
2091	120,000,000
2092	123,575,000
2093	120,000,000
2094	117,125,000
2095	117,225,000
2096	95,525,000
2097	119,125,000
2098-2101	216,260,000
2102	120,000,000
2103	108,140,000
2104	117,625,000
2105	112,896,000
2106	116,500,000
2107	751,300,000
2108	786,225,000
2109	105,300,000
2110	124,500,000
2137	120,000,000
2138-2141	300,000,000
2142	120,580,000
2143	729,700,000
2144	124,750,000
2145	203,496,000
2146	126,325,000
2147	130,000,000
2152	119,975,000
2153	120,000,000
2154	119,975,000
2155-2158	147,940,000
2159	120,000,000
2160-2163	130,000,000
2164	120,000,000
2165	759,200,000
2166	757,600,000
2198-2201	67,996,800
2202	947,450,000
2203	130,000,000
2204	136,500,000
2205-2209	219,990,000
2210	130,000,000
2211	130,000,000
2216	5,825,050
2217	5,825,050
2218	5,825,050
2219	5,825,050
2220-2223	130,000,000
2224	220,725,000
2235-2238	240,525,000
2239	131,700,000
2240-2243	240,000,000
2244	690,100,000
2245	882,150,000
2246	167,430,000
2247	166,555,000
2248	811,560,000
2249	142,905,000
2250	130,000,000
2251	149,980,000
2267-2274	610,425,000
2275	156,995,000
2286-2335	645,975,000
2336	166,725,000
2337	186,575,000
2338	184,325,000
2339	165,845,000
2340	155,170,000
2341	102,100,000
2342	103,325,000
2343	162,045,000
2344	153,295,000
2345	160,245,000
2346	183,290,000
2347	179,800,000
2348	164,130,000
2349	157,475,000
2350	156,225,000
2351-2354	163,980,000
2355-2359	584,340,000
2360	168,995,000
2361	163,120,000
2362-2366	394,776,000
2367	528,790,000
2368	978,340,000
2369	158,870,000
2370	145,560,000
2371	97,300,000
2372-2375	158,556,000
2376	97,300,000
2377	153,045,000
2378	841,240,000
2379	169,765,000
2380	157,215,000
2381-2385	635,238,000
2386-2389	162,142,500
2390-2393	305,015,000
2395-2398	480,000,000
2399	821,285,000
2400	1,030,850,000
2401	165,495,000
2402	151,675,000
2403	163,000,000
2404	264,625,000
2405-2409	204,984,000
2410	103,835,000
2411	152,250,000
2412	138,760,000
2413	137,985,000
2414	138,580,000
2415	150,545,000
2416	164,680,000
2417	262,755,000
2418	191,755,000
2420	188,400,000
2421	191,860,000
2422-2425	406,988,000
2426	137,410,000
2427	913,335,000
2428	900,000,000
2429	399,243,000
2433	2,017,225
2434-2437	163,824,000
2438	2,047,200
2439	173,000,000
2440	886,220,000
2441	995,178,000
2442	153,125,000
2444	169,495,000
2445-2448	176,808,000
2449	150,000,000
2470-2474	733,608,000
2496-2500	178,587,500
2501-2505	619,128,000
2506-2507	151,430,000
2508-2511	278,264,000
2512	143,995,000
2513	142,692,000
2514	728,919,000
2515	599,400,000
2516	320,304,000
2532	103,648,000
2533	179,990,000
2534	150,560,000
2538	161,498,000
2545-2549	744,918,000
2550	149,848,000
2551	200,003,000
2552	200,000,000
2553-2557	170,025,600
2558	150,310,000
2560	149,810,000
2561	149,260,000
2562-2566	699,978,000
2567	148,973,000
2577a	33,394,800
2615a	32,000,000
2616	148,665,000
2617	149,990,000
2618	835,000,000
2619	160,000,000
2623a	40,005,000
2624	1,185,170
2625	1,185,170
2626	1,185,170
2627	1,185,170
2628	1,185,170
2629	1,185,170
2630	148,000,000
2634a	37,315,000
2635	146,610,000
2636	160,000,000
2641a	32,000,000
2646a	87,728,000
2696a	11,000,000
2697	12,000,000
2698	105,000,000
2699	142,500,000
2703a	36,831,000
2704	85,000,000
2709a	80,000,000
2721	517,000,000
2722	150,000,000
2723	152,000,000
2730a	14,285,715
2731	98,841,000
2732	32,947,000
2733	32,947,000
2734	32,947,000
2735	65,894,000
2736	65,894,000
2737	65,894,000
2745a	140,000,000
2746	105,000,000
2747	110,000,000
2748	110,000,000
2749	172,870,000
2753a	65,625,000
2754	110,000,000
2755	115,870,000
2759a	40,000,000
2764a	199,784,500
2765	120,000,000
2766	160,000,000
2770a	128,735,000
2774a	25,000,000
2778a	170,000,000
2782a	37,500,000
2784a	41,840,000
2788a	37,550,000
2804	88,300,000
2805	105,000,000
2806	100,000,000
2806a	250,000,000
2811a	35,800,000
2812	150,500,000
2813	357,949,584
2814	830,000,000
2814C	300,000,000
2815	274,800,000
2816	155,500,000
2817	105,000,000
2818	185,500,000
2828a	18,600,000
2833a	166,000,000
2834	201,000,000
2835	300,000,000
2836	269,370,000
2837	60,000,000
2838	120,600,000
2839	209,000,000
2840	20,000,000
2841	12,958,000
2842	100,500,000
2847a	159,200,000
2848	150,500,000
2853a	35,436,000
2854	24,986,000
2855	24,986,000
2856	24,986,000
2857	19,988,800
2858	19,988,800
2859	19,988,800
2860	19,988,800
2861	19,988,800
2862	150,750,000
2866a	56,475,000
2868a	77,748,000
2869	20,000,000
2870	150,186
2871	518,500,000
2872	602,500,000
2873	236,997,600
2874	45,000,000
2875	5,000,000
2876	80,000,000
2948	214,700,000
2949	1,220,970,000
2950	94,500,000
2954a	50,000,000
2955	80,000,000
2956	97,000,000
2957	315,000,000
2958	300,000,000
2965a	30,000,000
2966	125,000,000
2967	400,000,000
2968	99,424,000
2973a	120,240,000
2974	60,000,000
2975	300,000,000
2979a	62,500,000
2980	105,000,000
2981	100,000,000
2982	150,000,000
2983-2992	15,000,000
2992	15,000,000
2997a	200,000,000
2998	300,000,000
2999	85,000,000
3000	300,000,000
3001	80,000,000
3002	80,000,000
3003	300,000,000
3007a	75,000,000
3008	350,495,000
3009	350,495,000
3010	350,495,000
3011	350,495,000
3013	90,000,000
3023a	30,000,000
3024	120,000,000
3029a	160,000,000
3030	2,550,000,000
3058	92,100,000
3059	115,600,000
3060	93,150,000
3064a	23,292,500
3065	111,000,000
3066	314,175,000
3067	209,450,000
3068	16,207,500
3069	156,300,000
3070	100,000,000
3071	60,120,000
3076a	27,850,000
3080a	22,218,000
3081	95,600,000
3082	300,000,000
3086a	23,681,250
3087	133,613,000
3088	103,400,000
3089	60,000,000
3090	134,000,000
3095a	32,000,000
3099a	23,025,000
3103a	23,025,000
3104	300,000,000
3105	14,910,000
3106	93,612,000
3107	243,575,000
3111a	56,479,000
3112	847,750,000
3116a	451,312,500
3117	495,504,000
3118	103,520,000
3120	106,000,000
3121	112,000,000
3123	1,660,000,000
3124	814,000,000
3125	122,000,000
3131a	65,000,000
3134	97,500,000
3135	96,000,000
3136	14,600,000
3137	37,800,000
3138	118,000
3139	593,775
3140	592,849
3141	45,250,000
3142	8,050,000
3146a	22,500,000
3147	20,000,000
3148	20,000,000
3149	10,000,000
3150	10,000,000
3151	7,000,000

Scott No.	Quantity
3152	195,000,000
3153	323,000,000
3157a	21,500,000
3158-3161	12,900,000
3162-3165	8,600,000
3166	25,250,000
3167	45,250,000
3172a	36,250,000
3173	173,000,000
3174	37,000,000
3175	133,000,000
3176	882,500,000
3177	1,621,465,000
3178	15,000,000
3179	51,000,000
3180	80,000,000
3181	45,000,000
3182	12,533,000
3183	12,533,000
3184	12,533,000
3185	12,533,000
3186	12,533,000
3187	12,533,000
3188	8,000,000
3189	6,000,000
3190	6,000,000
3191	8,250,000
3192	30,000,000
3193-3197	250,000,000
3198-3202	80,000,000
3203	85,000,000
3204	39,600,000
3205	650,000
3206	32,000,000
3209	2,200,000
3210	2,200,000
3211	30,000,000
3212-3215	45,000,000
3216-3219	45,000,000
3220	46,300,000
3221	30,000,000
3222-3225	70,000,000
3226	65,000,000
3227	50,000,000
3230-3234	180,000,000
3235	28,000,000
3236	4,000,000
3237	130,750,000
3238-3242	185,000,000
3243	50,000,000
3244	925,200,000
3245-3248	116,760,000
3249-3252	991,750,000
3272	51,000,000
3273	100,000,000
3274	1,000,000,000
3275	
3276	100,000,000
3286	40,400,000
3287	42,500,000
3288-3292	73,155,000
3293a-j	100,000,000
3306	42,700,000
3307	500,000
3308	42,500,000
3309	105,000,000
3310-3313	1,500,000,000
3314	145,375,000
3315	78,100,000
3316	89,270,000
3317-3320	141,175,000
3321-3324	151,976,000
3325-3328	116,083,500
3329	75,500,000
3330	100,750,000
3331	101,800,000
3332	43,150,000
3333-3337	120,000,000
3338	42,500,000
3339-3344	42,500,000
3345-3350	42,500,000
3351	4,235,000
3352	65,000,000
3354	44,600,000
3355	1,555,560,000
3356-3359	116,500,000
3360-3363	1,785,060,000
3364-3367	118,125,000
3368	95,000,000
3369	120,000,000

Quantities for Nos. 3370-on, and for Nos. 3190, 3191 and 3236, are for Quantities ordered.

Scott No.	Quantity
3370	56,000,000
3371	150,000,000
3372	65,150,000
3373-3377	15,000,000
3378a-j	100,000,000
3379-3383	55,000,000
3384-3388	105,350,000
3389	16,000,000
3390	55,000,000
3391	30,000,000
3392	236,000
3393-3396	55,000,000
3397	90,600,000
3398	200,000,000
3399-3402	88,000,000
3403	4,000,000
3408	11,250,000
3409	1,695,000
3410	1,695,000
3411	1,695,000
3412	1,695,000
3413	1,695,000
3414-3417	100,000,000

Scott No.	Quantity
3438	53,000,000
3439-3443	85,000,000
3444	53,000,000
3445	125,000,000
3446	52,000,000
3496	500,000,000
3497	1,500,000,000
3498	80,000,000
3499	180,000,000
3500	55,000,000
3501	200,000,000
3502	125,000,000
3503	100,000,000
3504	35,000,000
3505	1,598,000
3506a-j	89,600,000
3507	125,000,000
3508	200,000,000
3509	55,000,000
3510-3519	125,000,000
3521	55,000,000
3523	110,000,000
3524-3527	96,000,000
3528-3531	100,000,000
3532	75,000,000
3533	30,000,000
3534a	275,000,000
3535	236,000
3536	800,000,000
3537-3540	125,000,000
3537a-3540a	1,500,000,000
3541-3544	201,000,000
3545	32,000,000
3546	69,000,000
3547	49,000,000
3548	40,000,000
3551	100,000,000
3552-3555	80,000,000
3556	125,000,000
3557	120,000,000
3558	75,000,000
3559	70,000,000
3560	55,000,000
3561-3610	200,000,000
3611a-j	70,000,000
3649a-t	60,000,000
3650	70,000,000
3651	61,000,000
3652	61,000,000
3653-3656	200,000,000
3657	1,500,000,000
3658	150,000,000
3659	75,000,000
3660	62,800,000
3661-3664	111,000,000
3665-3668	61,000,000
3669	61,000,000
3670-3671	200,000,000
3672	35,000,000
3673	40,000,000
3674	35,000,000
3675	739,200,000
3676-3679	125,000,000
3680-3683	300,000,000
3684-3687	1,705,000,000
3688-3691	200,000,000
3692	80,000,000
3694	1,610,000
3695	50,000,000
3696-3745	200,000,000
3746	150,000,000
3747	70,000,000
3748	70,000,000
3771	60,000,000
3772a-j	70,000,000
3773	50,000,000
3774	55,000,000
3776-3780	60,000,000
3781	75,000,000
3782	54,000,000
3783	85,000,000
3786	80,000,000
3787-3791	125,000,000
3802a-j	60,000,000
3803	86,800,000
3804-3807	778,800,000
3808-3811	70,000,000
3812	52,000,000
3813	72,000,000
3814-3818	80,000,000
3820	700,000,000
3821-3824	1,875,000,000
3825-3828	200,990,000
3831a-j	76,000,000
3832	80,000,000
3833	750,000,000
3834	130,000,000
3835	172,000,000
3836	750,000,000
3837	150,000,000
3838	60,000,000
3839	80,000,000
3840-3843	57,000,000
3854	62,200,000
3855-3856	20,000,000
3857-3861	57,000,000
3862	96,400,000
3863	71,800,000
3865-3868	284,000,000
3869	45,800,000
3870	60,000,000
3871	50,000,000
3872	794,000,000
3873a-j	87,000,000
3876	100,000,000
3877	96,400,000
3878a-o	125,040,000

Scott No.	Quantity
3879	776,400,000
3881	60,000,000
3882	45,000,000
3883-3886	125,000,000
3887-3890	200,990,000
3891-3894	270,000,000
3895a-l	108,000,000
3896	150,000,000
3897	170,000,000
3898	1,500,000,000
3899a-j	56,000,000
3900-3903	790,000,000
3904	45,000,000
3905	40,000,000
3906-3909	50,000,000
3910a-l	60,000,000
3911	65,000,000
3912-3915	215,000,000
3916-3925	110,000,000
3926-3929	420,000,000
3930	40,000,000
3931-3935	640,000,000
3936	75,000,000
3937a-j	50,000,000
3938	65,000,000
3939-3942	70,000,000
3943	40,000,000
3944a-k	231,000,000
3945-3948	70,000,000
3949-3952	200,000,000
3953-3956	800,000,000
3957-3960	100,000,000
3961-3964	60,000,000
3976	600,000,000
3987-3994	192,000,000
3995	60,000,000
3996	150,000,000
3997a-l	60,000,000
3998-3999	200,000,000
4020	100,000,000
4021-4024	40,000,000
4025-4028	175,000,000
4029	400,000,000
4030	30,000,000
4031	80,000,000
4032	50,000,000
4033-4072	204,000,000
4073	40,000,000
4074	1,000,000
4075a-c	3,000,000
4076a-f	18,000,000
4077	75,000,000
4078	50,000,000
4079	60,000,000
4080-4083	200,000,000
4084a-t	250,000,000
4085-4088	85,000,000
4089-4098	500,000,000
4099a-j	50,000,000
4100	700,000,000
4101-4104	200,000,000
4105-4108	1,515,000,000
4109-4112	100,000,000
4113-4116	54,000,000
4117	35,000,000
4118	40,000,000
4119	40,000,000

AIR POST STAMPS

Cat. No.	Quantity
C1	3,395,854
C2	3,793,887
C3	2,134,888
C4	6,414,576
C5	5,309,275
C6	5,285,775
C7	42,092,800
C8	15,597,307
C9	17,616,350
C10	20,379,179
C11	106,887,675
C12	97,641,200
C13	93,536
C14	72,428
C15	61,296
C16	57,340,050
C17	76,648,803
C18	324,070
C19	302,205,100
C20	10,205,400
C21	12,794,600
C22	9,285,300
C23	349,946,500
C24	19,768,150
C25	4,746,527,700
C26	1,744,878,650
C27	67,117,400
C28	78,434,800
C29	42,359,850
C30	59,880,850
C31	11,160,600
C32	864,753,100
C33	971,903,700
C34	207,976,550
C35	756,186,350
C36	132,956,100
C37	33,244,500
C38	38,449,100
C39	5,070,095,200
C40	75,085,000
C41	260,307,500

Cat. No.	Quantity
C42	21,061,300
C43	36,613,100
C44	16,217,100
C45	80,405,000
C46	18,876,800
C47	78,415,000
C48	50,483,977
C49	63,185,000
C50	72,480,000
C51	1,326,960,000
C52	157,035,000
C53	90,055,200
C54	79,290,000
C55	84,815,000
C56	38,770,000
C57	39,960,000
C58	98,160,000
C59	
C60	1,289,460,000
C61	87,140,000
C62	
C63	
C64	
C65	
C66	42,245,000
C67	
C68	63,890,000
C69	62,255,000
C70	55,710,000

Cat. No.	Quantity
C71	+ 50,000,000
C72	
C73	
C74	+ 60,000,000
C75	
C76	152,364,800
C77	
C78	
C79	
C80	
C81	
C82	
C83	
C84	78,210,000
C85	96,240,000
C86	58,705,000
C87	
C88	
C89	
C90	
C91-C92	
C93-C94	
C95-C96	
C97	
C101-C104	+ 165,000,000
C105-C108	+ 165,000,000
C109-C112	+ 175,000,000
C113	98,600,000

Cat. No.	Quantity
C114	110,475,000
C115	167,625,000
C116	45,700,000
C117	22,975,000
C118	201,150,000
C119	111,550,000
C120	38,532,000
C121	39,325,000
C122-C125	106,360,000
C126	1,944,000
C127	48,000,000
C128	250,000,000
C129	182,400,000
C130	113,000,000
C131	15,260,000
C132	100,000,000
C133	100,750,000
C134	100,750,000
C135	+ 100,800,000
C136	85,000,000
C137	85,000,000
C138	100,000,000
C139	145,000,000
C140	100,000,000
C141	100,000,000

\+ Quantity ordered printed.

CARRIERS' STAMPS

The term "Carriers' Stamps" is applied to certain stamps of the United States used to defray delivery to a post office on letters going to another post office, and for collection and delivery in the same city (local letters handled only by the carrier department). A less common usage was for a collection fee from the addressee at the post office ("drop letters"). During the period when these were in use, the ordinary postage fee defrayed the carriage of mail matter from post office to post office only.

In many of the larger cities the private ("Local") posts delivered mail to the post office or to an addressee in the city direct for a fee of 1 or 2 cents (seldom more), and adhesive stamps were often employed to indicate payment. (See introduction to "Local Stamps" section.)

Carrier service dates back at least to 1689 when the postmaster of Boston was instructed "to receive all letters and deliver them at 1d." In 1794, the law allowed a penny post to collect 2 cents for the delivery of a letter. As these early fees were paid in cash, little evidence survives.

In 1851 the Federal Government, under the acts of 1825 and 1836, began to deliver letters in many cities and so issued Carriers' stamps for local delivery service. This Act of Congress of March 3, 1851, effective July 1, 1851 (succeeding Act of 1836), provided for the collecting and delivering of letters to the post office by carriers, "for which not exceeding 1 or 2 cents shall be charged."

Carriers' stamps were issued under the authority of, or derived from, the postmaster general. The "General Issues" (Nos. LO1-LO2) were general issues of which No. LO2 was valid for postage at face value, and No. LO1 at the value set upon sale, in any post office. They were issued under the direct authority of the postmaster general. The "City Carrier Department" were valid in the city in which they were issued either directly by or sanctioned by the local postmaster under authority derived from the postmaster general.

These "General" and "City Carrier Department" Carriers' stamps prepaid the fees of official letter carriers who were appointed by the postmaster general and were under heavy bond to the United States for the faithful performance of their duties. Some of the letter carriers received fixed salaries from the government. Others were paid from the fees received for the delivery and collection of letters carried by them. After discontinuance of carrier fees on June 30, 1863, all carriers of the United States Post Office were government employees, paid by salary at a yearly rate.

Some Carriers' stamps are often found on cover with the regular government stamps and have the official post office cancellation applied to them as well. Honour's City Express and the other Charleston, S.C., Carrier stamps almost always have the stamp uncanceled or canceled with pen, or less frequently pencil.

Unless indicated otherwise, values for Carriers' stamps on cover are for covers having the stamp tied by a handstamped cancellation. Carriers' stamps, either uncanceled or pen-canceled, **on covers to which they apparently belong**, also are valued where possible. For covers with stamps canceled by pen or pencil with initials or name of carrier, as sometimes seen on No. LO2 from Washington, and on Baltimore carrier stamps, the premium is 75% of the on-cover value.

All Carriers' stamps are imperforate and on wove paper, either white or colored through, unless otherwise stated.

Counterfeits exist of many Carriers' stamps.

GENERAL ISSUE CARRIER STAMPS

Franklin — OC1

Eagle — OC2

Engraved and printed by Toppan, Carpenter, Casilear & Co. Plate of 200 subjects divided into two panes of 100 each, one left, one right

1851, Sept. Unwmk. *Imperf.*

LO1 OC1 (1c) **dull blue** (shades), *rose*	*6,250.*	*6,750.*
On cover from Philadelphia		*17,500.*
On cover from New York		*30,000.*
On cover from New Orleans with 3c #10 (a 2nd #LO1 removed)		*30,000.*
Pair	*17,500.*	*18,000.*
Strip of 3	*25,000.*	*26,000.*
Major plate crack	—	
Major plate crack, on cover		*60,000.*
Corner plate cracks (91L)	—	—
Double transfer	—	—
Double transfer, on cover		*30,000.*

Earliest known use: Oct. 28, 1851.

Cancellations

Red star (Philadelphia)	*6,750.*
Blue town (Philadelphia)	+1,000.
Red town (New York)	+1,000.
Black town (New York), unique	+4,000.
Blue grid (New York)	—
Black grid (New York)	—
Black grid (New Orleans)	+4,000.
Green grid (New Orleans)	—

Of the entire issue of 310,000 stamps, 250,000 were sent to New York, 50,000 to New Orleans, 10,000 to Philadelphia. However, the quantity sent to each city is not indicative of proportionate use. More appear to have been used in Philadelphia than in the other two cities. The use in all three cities was notably limited.

No. LO1, major plate crack on cover, is unique. The double transfer on cover also is unique, as is the unused pair.

U.S.P.O. Despatch

Engraved and printed by Toppan, Carpenter, Casilear & Co. Plate of 200 subjects divided into two panes of 100 each, one upper, one lower

1851, Nov. 17 Unwmk. *Imperf.*

LO2 OC2 1c **blue** (shades)	35.00	*65.00*
On cover, used alone		500.00
On cover, precanceled		600.00
On cover, pair or 2 singles		*1,500.*
On cover with block of 3, 1c #9		*4,500.*
On cover with 3c #11		400.
On cover with 3c #25		—
On cover with 3c #26		*600.*
On cover with strip of 3, 3c #26		—
On cover with 5c #30A and 10c #32		*33,000.*
On cover, tied by town handstamp, with 3c #65 (Washington, D.C.)		*4,500.*
On 3c envelope #U1, #LO2 pen canceled		—
On 3c envelope #U2, tied by handstamp		—
On 3c envelope #U2, #LO2 pen canceled		—
Pair	80.00	
On 3c envelope #U10, not canceled, with certicate		—
Pair on cover (Cincinnati)		*1,000.*
Block of 4	300.00	
Margin block of 8, imprint	*850.00*	
Double transfer	—	—
Double transfer on cover		—

Earliest known use: Jan. 3, 1852.

Cancellations

Red star	*65.*
Philadelphia	+50.
Cincinnati	+200.
Black grid	—
Blue grid	+300.
Red grid	+300.
Black town	+5.
Blue town	+100.
Red town	+300.
Kensington, Pa. (red)	—
Kensington, Pa. red "3c"	—

Washington, D.C. +1,000.
Blue squared target —
Red squared target —
Railroad —
Black carrier (Type C32) —
Red carrier (Type C32) —
Carrier's initial, manuscript —

Earliest known use: Jan. 3, 1852. Used principally in Philadelphia, Cincinnati, Washington, D.C., and Kensington, Pa.

GOVERNMENT REPRINTS

Printed by the Continental Bank Note Co. (first and second printings) and American Bank Note Co. (third printing).

First reprinting-10,000 stamps of each design, on May 19, 1875 (all sold).

Second reprinting-10,000 stamps of each design, on Dec. 22, 1875 (all sold).

Third reprinting of Franklin stamp - 1881 (2,110 sold).

Third reprinting of Easle stamp - 1881 (9,680 sold).

The first reprinting of the Franklin stamp was on the rose paper of the original, obtained from Toppan, Carpenter, Casilear & Co. Two batches of ink were used, both darker than the original. The second reprinting was on rose paper using ink that fluoresces green. The third reprinting was on much thicker, paler paper in an indigo color. All of these differ under ultraviolet light. The design of the reprints is not as distinct as the original design and may appear a bit "muddy" in the lathework above the vignette.

Most of the reprints of the Eagle stamp are on the same hard white paper used for special printings of the postage issue. Stamps from the second reprinting were printed with ink that fluoresces green. Stamps from the third reprinting are on thick wove paper using ink that does not fluoresce. Reprints may be differentiated from the originals under ultraviolet light by the whiteness of the paper. Nos. LO3-LO6 are ungummed, Nos. LO1-LO2 have brown gum.

1875

Franklin Reprints

Imperf

LO3 OC1 (1c) **blue,** *rose* 50.
indigo, *rose* 70.
Block of 4 225.
Margin block of 4, imprint —
Corner plate cracks (91L) 100.
Short transfer —

Perf. 12

LO4 OC1 (1c) **blue** *16,000.*
Pair *35,000.*

No. LO4 is valued in the grade of average to fine.

Eagle Reprints

Imperf.

LO5 OC2 1c **blue** 25.
Block of 4 125.
Margin block of 8, imprint & Pl.# —

Perf. 12

LO6 OC2 1c **blue** 175.
Block of 4 1,000.
Margin block of 8, imprint & Pl.# *12,500.*

CITY CARRIER DEPARTMENT STAMPS

All are imperforate.

Baltimore, Md.

C1

1850-55 Typo. Settings of 10 (2x5) varieties

1LB1 C1 1c **red** (shades), *bluish* 180. 160.
On cover, tied by handstamp *1,000.*
On cover with 1c #9 —
On cover (tied) with 3c #11 *500.*
1LB2 C1 1c **blue** (shades), *bluish* 200. 150.
On cover, tied *1,000.*
a. Bluish laid paper — —
1LB3 C1 1c **blue** (shades) 160. 100.
On cover, tied by handstamp *1,000.*
On cover, tied by ms. *250.*
Block of 4 *1,000.*
a. Laid paper 200. 150.
On cover, tied by handstamp *1,000.*
b. Block of 14 containing three tete-beche gutter pairs (unique) *7,500.*
1LB4 C1 1c **green** — 1,000.
On cover, tied by handstamp *3,500.*
On cover, not tied *1,200.*
On cover with 1c #7, tied by handstamp *2,250.*
On cover with 3c #11, ms. tied —
On 3c envelope #U10 *3,500.*
Pair *5,000.*
1LB5 C1 1c **red** 2,250. 1,750.
On cover, tied by handstamp *4,500.*
On cover, not tied *3,000.*
On cover (tied) with 3c #11 *5,000.*

The No. 1LB4 pair is the unique multiple of this stamp.

Cancellations on Nos. 1LB1-1LB5:

Black grid —
Blue grid —
Black cross —
Black town —
Blue town +100.
Black numeral —
Blue numeral —
Black pen —

C2

1856 Typo.

1LB6 C2 1c **blue** (shades) 130. 90.
On cover 400.
On cover with 3c #11 *1,000.*
On cover with 3c #25 (both tied) *1,350.*
On cover with 3c #26 *1,250.*
1LB7 C2 1c **red** (shades) 130. 90.
On cover *300.*
On cover (tied) with 3c #25 *350.*
On cover (tied) with 3c #26 *350.*
On 3c envelope #U9, tied *300.*
On 3c envelope #U10, tied *350.*
Block of 4 *850.*

C3

Plate of 10 (2x5); 10 Varieties

The sheet consisted of at least four panes of 10 placed horizontally, the two center panes tete beche. This makes possible five horizontal tete beche gutter pairs.

1857 Typo.

1LB8 C3 1c **black** (shades) 65. 50.
On cover, tied by handstamp *125.*
On cover, tied by handstamp, to Germany *3,750.*
On cover (tied) with 3c #26 175.
On 3c envelope #U9, tied *225.*
On 3c envelope #U10 *225.*
On 3c envelope #U27, tied *250.*
Strip of 3 (not tied), on cover *4,000.*
Block of 4 275.
Pane of 10 *1,000.*
Tete beche gutter pair *650.*
a. "SENT," Pos. 7 100. 75.
On cover, tied by handstamp *175.*
On cover with 3c #26 *250.*
On 3c envelope #U9, tied *250.*
On 3c envelope #U10, tied *250.*
b. Short rays, Pos. 2 100. 75.
On cover (tied) with 3c #26 *600.*

Cancellations

Black pen (or pencil) 20.00
Blue town +2.50
Black town +2.50
Black Steamship —

1LB9 C3 1c **red** (shades) 100. 90.
On cover *175.*
On cover with 3c #26 *300.*
On 3c envelope #U9 *325.*
On 3c envelope #U10 *325.*
Block of 6 *2,750.*
a. "SENT," Pos. 7 140. 110.
On cover (tied) with 3c #26 *500.*
b. Short rays, Pos. 2 140. 110.
c. As "b," double impression *800.*

The block of 6 of No. 1LB9 is the only recorded multiple of this stamp.

Cancellations on Nos. 1LB6-1LB7, 1LB9:

Black town —
Blue town —
Blue numeral —
Black pen —
Carrier's initial, manuscript +25.

Boston, Mass.

C6

Several Varieties

1849-50 Pelure Paper Typeset

3LB1 C6 1c **blue** 375. 180.
On cover, tied by handstamp 275.
On cover with 5c #1 *4,000.*
On cover with two 5c #1 *8,750.*
On cover with 3c #10 *450.*
a. Wrong ornament at left *400.*
On cover, not tied —

Cancellations

Red town —
Red grid —
Black ornate double oval —
Black "Penny Post Paid" in 3-bar circle —

C7

1851 Typeset

Several Varieties

Wove Paper Colored Through

3LB2 C7 1c **blue** (shades), *slate* 190. 100.
On cover 220.
On cover with 5c #1 *12,500.*
On cover with 3c #10 500.
On cover with 3c #11 325.
On 3c envelope #U2, #U5 or #U9 350.
Tete beche gutter pair *600.*

Cancellations on Nos. 3LB2:

Black small fancy circle —
Black diamond grid +100.00
Red town —
Black grid —
Black PAID —
Black crayon —
Red small fancy circle +50.00
Red diamond grid +100.00
Black railroad —
Black hollow star —
Black pencil —
Red crayon —
Black "Penny Post Paid" in 3-bar circle —
Red "Penny Post Paid" in 3-bar circle —

Charleston, S. C.

John H. Honour was appointed a letter carrier at Charleston, in 1849, and engaged his brother-in-law, E. J. Kingman, to assist him. They separated in 1851, dividing the carrier business of the city between them. At the same time Kingman was appointed a letter carrier. In March, 1858, Kingman retired, being replaced by Joseph G. Martin. In the summer of 1858, John F. Steinmeyer, Jr., was added to the carrier force. When Honour retired in 1860, John C. Beckman was appointed in his place.

Each of these carriers had stamps prepared. These stamps were sold by the carriers. The Federal Government apparently encouraged their use.

Honour's City Express

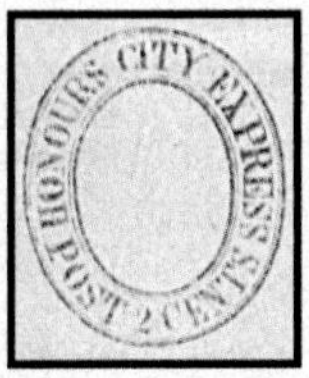

C8

1849 Typo. Wove Paper Colored Through

4LB1 C8 2c **black,** *brown rose* *10,000.*
Cut to shape *4,000.* *4,000.*
On cover, not canceled, with certificate *17,000.*
On cover, cut to shape, tied, with 10c #2 *40,000.*
4LB2 C8 2c **black,** *yellow,* cut to shape —
On cover, not tied, with certificate *12,500.*

On cover, cut to shape, uncanceled —
On cover , rectangular-cut, tied, with 10c #2 —

Cancellations on Nos. 4LB1-4LB2: Red grid, red town, red crayon.

No. 4LB1 unused is a unique uncanceled stamp on piece. The used cut-to-shape stamp is also unique. Additionally, each of the listed covers bearing No. 4LB1 is unique.

Four examples of No. 4LB2 are recorded, each listing above being unique.

C10

1854 Wove Paper Typeset

4LB3 C10 2c **black** *1,500.*
On cover, tied by pen cancel *3,000.*
On cover with 3c #11, tied *4,500.*
On cover with 3c #11, not tied *3,250.*

Cancellations

Black town —
Blue town —
Black pen —
Black pencil —
Brown "PAID" —
Initial "H" —

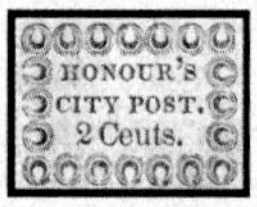

C11

Several Varieties

1849-50 Typeset

Wove Paper Colored Through

4LB5 C11 2c **black,** *bluish,* pelure *750.* *500.*
On cover with pair 5c #1b —
On cover with two 5c #1b —
On cover (tied) with 3c #11 *4,000.*
a. "Ceuts" *5,750.*
4LB7 C11 2c **black,** *yellow* *750.* *1,000.*
On cover, tied by handstamp *9,000.*
a. "Ccnts," ms. tied on cover *14,500.*

No. 4LB5a is unique. It is without gum and is valued thus. No. 4LB7a also is unique.

The varieties of type C11 on bluish wove (thicker) paper and pink, pelure paper are not believed genuine.

Cancellation Nos. 4LB5, 4LB7:

Red town —
Black pen —
Red pen —
Red crayon —

C13

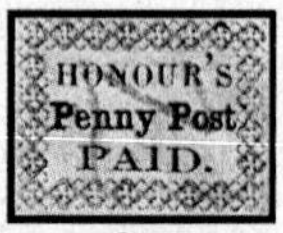

C14

C15

Several varieties of each type

1851-58 Typeset

Wove Paper Colored Through

4LB8 C13 2c **black,** *bluish* 350. 175.
On cover, tied by handstamp *700.*
On cover, not tied *300.*
On cover, tied, with 3c #10 *1,500.*
On cover, tied, with 3c #11 *1,500.*
On cover, tied, with 3c #26 *1,500.*
Pair *1,500.*
a. Period after "PAID" 500. 250.
On cover *650.*
On cover, ms. tied, with 3c #11 *750.*
b. "Cens" 700. 900.
On cover, ms. tied, with 3c #11 *3,250.*
c. "Conours" and "Bents" —
4LB9 C13 2c **black,** *bluish,* pelure *850.* *950.*
4LB11 C14 (2c) **black,** *bluish* — *375.*
On cover, tied by handstamp, with 3c #11 *12,500.*
On cover, ms. tied, with 3c #11 *3,000.*
4LB12 C14 (2c) **black,** *bluish,* pelure — —
4LB13 C15 (2c) **black,** *bluish* ('58) 750. 400.
On cover with 3c #11, Aiken, S.C. postmark, tied by handstamp (unique) *6,000.*
On cover with 3c #26, tied by pen cancel *4,000.*
Horiz. pair *3,500.*
a. Comma after "PAID" *1,100.*
b. No period after "Post" *1,400.*

The pair of No. 4LB13 is the unique multiple of this stamp.

A 2c of design C13 exists on pink pelure paper. It is believed not to have been issued by the post, but to have been created later and perhaps accidentally.

Cancellations on Nos. 4LB8-4LB13

Black town —
Blue town —
Red town —
Black pen —
Black pencil —
Red crayon —
Brown cork initial "H"

Kingman's City Post

C16

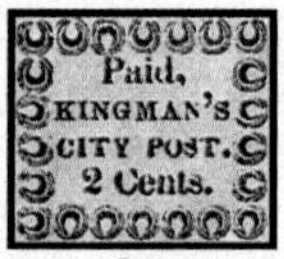

C17

Several varieties of each

1851(?)-58(?) Typeset

Wove Paper Colored Through

4LB14 C16 2c **black,** *bluish* *1,400.* 900.
Vert. pair, ms. tied, on Valentine cover *6,000.*
On cover with 3c #11 *7,500.*
On cover with 3c #26 *6,000.*
a. "Kingman's" erased *5,000.*
4LB15 C17 2c **black,** *bluish* *800.* 800.
On cover —
Vertical pair —
Horiz. pair, not tied, on Valentine cover *8,750.*
Vertical strip of 3 uncanceled, on cover *22,500.*
a. "Kingman's" erased, on cover with 3c #11, tied by pen cancel (unique) *4,500.*

The No. 4LB14 pair on cover is the only recorded multiple of this stamp.

The 4LB15 pair and strip of 3 actually are uncanceled on covers and are valued thus. The horiz. pair on cover is ms. canceled.

Cancellations on Nos. 4LB14-4LB15: Black town, black pen.

Martin's City Post

C18

Several varieties

1858 Wove Paper Colored Through Typeset

4LB16 C18 2c **black,** *bluish* *8,000.*

Beckman's City Post

Same as C19, but inscribed "Beckmann's City Post."

1860

4LB17 C19 2c **black,** on cover —

No. 4LB17 is unique. It is on cover with 3c No. 26, both tied by black circle townmark: "CHARLESTON, S.C. JUN 18, 1860".

Steinmeyer's City Post

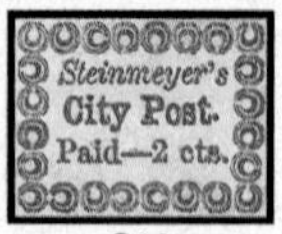

C19

C20

Several varieties of Type C19

Type C20 printed from plate of 10 (2x5) varieties

1859 Wove Paper Colored Through Typeset

4LB18 C19 2c **black,** *bluish* *21,000.*
On cover, uncanceled —
4LB19 C20 2c **black,** *bluish* *4,500.* —
4LB20 C20 2c **black,** *pink* *200.* —
Block of 4 *850.*
Sheet of 10 *2,250.*
4LB21 C20 2c **black,** *yellow* 200.
Block of 4 850.
Sheet of 10 *2,250.*

Sheets of 10 of Nos. 4LB20-4LB21 exist signed by J.F. Steinmeyer Jr. These sell for about 50% more than the unsigned sheets.

Two examples of No. 4LB18 are known on cover, both uncanceled.

Cancellation on Nos. 4LB19-4LB21: Black pen.

Cincinnati, Ohio

Williams' City Post

Organized by C. C. Williams, who was appointed and commissioned by the Postmaster General.

C20a

1854 Wove Paper Litho.

9LB1 C20a 2c **brown** — *4,000.*
On cover, tied by handstamp —
On cover, tied by pen cancel *4,500.*
On cover with 1c #9 *10,000.*
Pair *7,500.*

Cancellations

Red squared target —
Black pen —
Blue company circle —

Fraser & Co.

Local stamps of designs L146-L147 were carrier stamps when used on cover between Feb. 3, 1848 and June 30, 1849.

Cleveland, Ohio

Bishop's City Post.

Organized by Henry S. Bishop, "Penny Postman" who was appointed and commissioned by the Postmaster General.

C20b

C20c

1854 Wove Paper Litho.

10LB1 C20b **blue** *5,000.* *4,000.*
On cover, tied by handstamp *15,000.*
Pair on cover, canceled by pencil, with 3c #11, with certificate *17,000.*

Vertically Laid Paper

10LB2 C20c 2c **black,** *bluish* *7,000.* *7,000.*
On cover —
Pair —

Cancellations on #10LB1-10LB2

Red town —
Red boxed numeral —
Black pencil —
Black pen —

Louisville, Ky.

Carrier Service was first established by the Louisville Post Office about 1854, with one carrier. David B. Wharton, appointed a carrier in 1856, issued an adhesive stamp in 1857, but as he was soon thereafter replaced in the service, it is believed that few, if any, of these stamps were used. Brown & McGill, carriers who succeeded Wharton, issued stamps in April, 1858.

Wharton's U.S.P.O. Despatch

C21

Sheet of 50 subjects in two panes of 25 (5x5) each, one upper, one lower

1857 **Lithographed by Robyn & Co.**

5LB1 C21 (2c) **bluish green** (shades) 125.
Block of 4 *650.*
Pane of 25 *3,250.*
Sheet of 50 *7,000.*

Brown & McGill's U. S. P. O. Despatch

C22

1858 **Litho. by Hart & Maypother**

5LB2 C22 (2c) **blue** (shades) 250. *750.*
On cover, not tied, with 3c #26 *750.00*
On cover with 3c #26, tied by handstamp *6,250.*
Block of 4 *1,250.*
5LB3 C22 (2c) **black** *4,500.* *15,000.*

The value for No. 5LB3 used refers to the finer of the two known used (canceled) examples; it is on a piece with a 3c #26.

Cancellations on Nos. 5LB2-5LB3: Blue town, black pencil.

New York, N. Y.

UNITED STATES CITY DESPATCH POST

By an order made on August 1, 1842, the Postmaster General established a carrier service in New York known as the "United States City Despatch Post." Local delivery service had been authorized by the Act of Congress of July 2, 1836.

Greig's City Despatch Post was sold to the U. S. P. O. Department and on August 16, 1842, began operation as the "United States City Despatch Post" under the superintendence of Alexander M. Greig who was appointed a U. S. letter carrier for that purpose.

The Greig circular introducing this service stated that letter boxes had been placed throughout the city, that letters might be sent prepaid or collect, and that registry service was available for an extra 3 cents.

The City Despatch Post stamps were accepted for the service of the United States City Despatch Post. The stamps thus used bear the cancellation of the New York Post Office, usually "U.S." in an octagon which served to indicate that the carrier service was now a government operation (no longer a private local post) as well as a cancellation.

Some examples are canceled by a circular date stamp reading "U.S. CITY DESPATCH POST" or, infrequently, a New York town postmark. When canceled "FREE" in frame they were used as local stamps. See No. 40L1 in Locals section.

No. 6LB3 was the first stamp issued by authority of the U.S.P.O. Department. The 3c denomination included 1 cent in lieu of drop letter postage until June 30, 1845, and the maximum legal carrier fee of 2 cents. Service was discontinued late in November, 1846.

C23

C24

Engraved and printed by Rawdon, Wright & Hatch.

Plate of 42 (6x7) subjects
Wove Paper Colored Through

1842

6LB1 C23 3c **black,** *grayish* *2,000.*
On cover, tied by handstamp *11,500.*
On cover, not tied *10,000.*
On cover, not tied, with Aug. 16 (1842) cancel, First day of government carrier service *100,000.*

Cancellations

Red "U.S" in octagon *2,000.*
Red circle "U.S. City Despatch Post" —
Red town —

Used examples which do not bear the official cancellation of the New York Post Office and unused examplesd are classed as Local stamps. See No. 40L1.

Wove Paper (unsurfaced) Colored Through

Engraved plate of 50 in two panes of 25

1842-45

6LB2 C24 3c **black,** *rosy buff* *2,500.*
6LB3 C24 3c **black,** *light blue* *550.* 500.
On cover, tied by handstamp *1,750.*
On cover, not tied *750.00*
Pair *2,250.*
6LB4 C24 3c **black,** *green* *11,500.*

Some authorities consider No. 6LB2 to be an essay, and No. 6LB4 a color changeling.

Glazed Paper, Surface Colored

6LB5 C24 3c **black,** *blue green* (shades) 200. 175.
On cover, tied by handstamp 600.
Five on cover *20,000.*
Pair — 400.
Strip of 3 *650.*
Strip of 4 800.
Strip of 5 —
Ribbed paper — —
Double transfer —
a. Double impression *1,500.*
b. 3c **black,** *blue* 650. *300.*
On cover *750.*
Strip of 3 + single on cover *14,000.*
Strip of 3 *2,500.* —
Block of 12 *23,000.* —
c. As "b," double impression *850.*
d. 3c **black,** *green* 1,000. *900.*
On cover —
Strip of 4 + single on cover *36,000.*
e. As "d," double impression —
On cover —

Cancellations

Red curved PAID —
Red "U.S City Despatch Post" —
Red "U.S" in octagon —
Red New York —
Red double line circle "U.S. City Despatch Post" —

No. 6LB5 has been noted on cover with the 5c New York signed "R.H.M.," No. 9X1d.

6LB6 C24 3c **black,** *pink,* on cover front *14,500.*

No. 6LB6 is unique.

C25

1846

No. 6LB5 Surcharged in Red

6LB7 C25 2c on 3c **black,** *bluish green,* on cover, not tied, with certificate *70,000.*

The City Dispatch 2c red formerly listed as No. 6LB8 is now listed under Local Stamps as No. 160L1.

U.S. MAIL

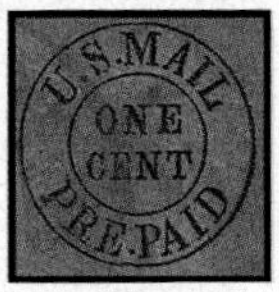

C27

Issued by the Postmaster at New York, N.Y.

1849 **Wove Paper, Colored Through** **Typo.**

6LB9 C27 1c **black,** *rose* 100. 100.
On cover, tied by handstamp *250.*
On cover with 5c #1 *2,000.*
Pair *250.*
Block of 4 *600.*

1849-50

Glazed Surface Paper

6LB10 C27 1c **black,** *yellow* 100. 100.
On cover, tied by handstamp *250.*
On cover with 5c #1 *1,500.*
Pair *250.*
Block of 4 *600.*
6LB11 C27 1c **black,** *buff* 100. 100.
On cover *250.*
On cover, not tied, with 5c #1, with certificate *3,000.*
a. Pair, one stamp sideways *2,850.*

Cancellations on #6LB9-6LB11

Red town —
Red grid —
Red "PAID" +50.
Black numeral in circle —
Red "N.Y. U.S. CITY MAIL" in circle +150.
Black pen —
Black pencil —

Philadelphia, Pa.

C28

Several Varieties
Thick Wove Paper Colored Through

1849-50 **Typeset**

7LB1 C28 1c **black,** *rose* (with "L P") 450.
On cover, tied by handstamp *3,000.*
On cover, not canceled *2,000.*
On cover with 5c #1 —
7LB2 C28 1c **black,** *rose* (with "S") *3,000.*
On cover, not canceled *4,500.*
7LB3 C28 1c **black,** *rose* (with "H") 275.
On cover, tied by handstamp *3,750.*
On cover, not canceled *1,000.*
On cover with 5c #1 —
7LB4 C28 1c **black,** *rose* (with "L S") 400. *500.*
On cover, not canceled *3,000.*
7LB5 C28 1c **black,** *rose* (with "J J") *7,500.*
On cover with 5c #1, uncanceled *70,000.*

The unique used No. 7LB5 in an uncanceled stamp on a cover front.

C29

Several Varieties

7LB6 C29 1c **black,** *rose* 300. 250.
On cover, tied by handstamp *2,500.*
On cover, uncanceled *500.00*
7LB7 C29 1c **black,** *blue,* glazed *1,000.*
On cover, tied by handstamp *6,500.*
On cover, uncanceled *1,500.*
On cover with 5c #1 —
7LB8 C29 1c **black,** *vermilion,* glazed *700.*
On cover, tied by handstamp *1,500.*
On cover with 5c dark brown #1a, uncanceled *12,500.*
On cover with 5c orange brown #1b, uncanceled *21,000.*
7LB9 C29 1c **black,** *yellow,* glazed *2,750.* *2,250.*
On cover, not canceled *4,000.*
On cover with 3c #10, uncanceled *2,000.*

Cancellations on Nos. 7LB1-7LB9: Normally these stamps were left uncanceled on the letter, but occasionally were accidentally tied by the Philadelphia town postmark which was normally struck in blue ink.

A 1c black on buff (unglazed) of type C29 is believed to be a color changeling.

C30

Settings of 25 (5x5) varieties (Five basic types)

1850-52 **Litho.**

7LB11 C30 1c **gold,** *black,* glazed 175. 110.
On cover, tied by handstamp *600.*
On cover (tied) with 5c #1 *3,500.*
On cover (tied) with 3c #10 *800.*
On cover (uncanceled) with 3c #10 *250.*
Block of 19 *8,250.*
7LB12 C30 1c **blue** 400. 275.
On cover, tied by handstamp *1,250.*
On cover (tied) with 3c #10 *1,750.*
On cover (tied) with 3c #11 *1,250.*
Pair 1,600.
7LB13 C30 1c **black** *750.* 550.
On cover, tied by handstamp 2,500.
On cover (tied) with 3c #10 —

On cover (not tied) with 3c #11 — *3,250.*

Cancellations on #7LB11-7LB13

Red star —
Red town —
Blue town —

C31

Handstamped

7LB14 C31 1c **blue,** *buff* 3,250.

No. 7LB14 was handstamped on coarse dark buff paper on which rectangles in the approximate size of the type C31 handstamp had been ruled in pencil. The stamps so produced were later cut out and show traces of the adjoining handstamp markings as well as parts of the penciled rectangle. Some uncanceled examples exist on covers.

1855(?)

7LB16 C31 1c **black** *5,000.*
On cover with strip of 3, 1c #9 —
On cover with 3c 1851 stamp removed, tied by handstamp *7,000.*

C32

1856(?) **Handstamped**

7LB18 C32 1c **black** *1,250. 2,000.*
Paper showing blue plate imprint *4,000.*

On cover (cut diamond-shaped) with pair 1c #7 and single 1c #9 —
On cover with strip of 3, 1c #7 *17,000.*
On cover with 3c #11 *9,500.*
On 3c envelope #U5 —
On 3c envelope #U10, not canceled *9,000.*

Cancellations on #7LB16, 7LB18

Black circled grid —
Black town —

Nos. 7LB16 and 7LB18 were handstamped on the sheet margins of U.S. 1851 1c stamps, cut out and used as adhesives. The paper therefore has some surface bluing, and some stamps show parts of the plate imprint.

Values are for stamps cut square unless otherwise mentioned.

ENVELOPES

Handstamps of types C31 and C32 were also used to make stamped envelopes and letter sheets or circulars. These same types were also used as postmarks or cancellations in the same period.

A handstamp similar to C32, but with "U.S.P. DESPATCH" in serif capitals, is believed to have been used only as a postmark.

Type C31 exists struck in blue or red, type C32 in blue, black or red. When found on cover, on various papers, struck alone, they are probably postmarks and not prepaid stamped envelopes. As such, these entire covers, depending upon the clarity of the handstamp and the general attractiveness of the letter are valued between $400 and $800.

When found on envelopes with the Carrier stamp canceled by a handstamp (such as type C31 struck in blue on a buff envelope canceled by the red solid star cancellation) they can be regarded as probably having been sold as prepaid envelopes. Value approximately $3,000.

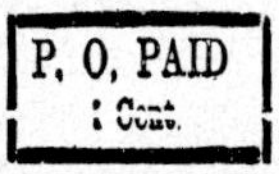

Labels of these designs are believed by most specialists not to be carrier stamps. Those seen are uncanceled, either off cover or affixed to stampless covers of the early 1850s. Some students believe they should be given carrier status.

St. Louis, Mo.

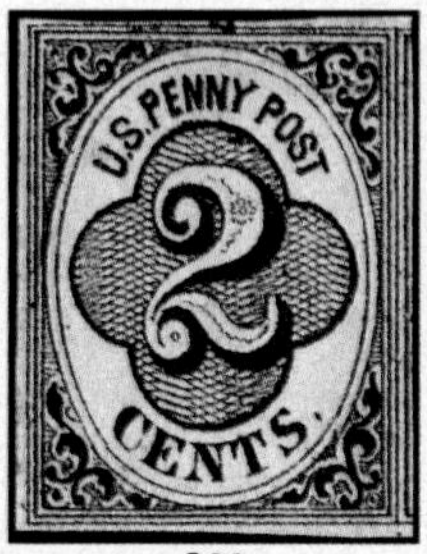

C36

C37

Illustrations enlarged to show details of the two types (note upper corners especially). Sizes of actual designs are 17 1/2x22mm.

1849 **White Wove Paper Two Types** **Litho.**

8LB1 C36 2c **black** *7,000. 3,000.*
8LB2 C37 2c **black** *6,000.* —

Cancellation on Nos. 8LB1-8LB2: Black town.

C38

1857 **Litho.**

8LB3 C38 2c **blue** *22,500.*
On cover, tied by handstamp *55,000.*
On Valentine cover, ms. cancel, not tied *35,000.*

The used example off cover is unique. Four covers are recorded.

Cancellations on No. 8LB3: Black boxed "1ct," "Paid" in arc, black pen.

LOCAL STAMPS

This listing of Local stamps includes stamps issued by Local Posts (city delivery), Independent Mail Routes and Services, Express Companies and other private posts which competed with, or supplemented, official services.

The Independent Mail Routes began using stamps early in 1844 and were put out of business by an Act of March, 1845, which became effective July 1, 1845. By this Act, the Government reduced the zones to two, reduced the rates to 5c and 10c and applied them to weight instead of the number of sheets of paper which composed a letter.

Most of the Local Posts still in business were forced to discontinue service by an Act of 1861, except Boyd's and Hussey's which were able to continue about 20 years longer because of the particular nature of their business. Other posts appeared illegally and sporadically after 1861 and were quickly suppressed.

City posts generally charged 1c to deliver a letter to the Post Office (usually the letter bore a government stamp as well) and 2c for intracity delivery (such letters naturally bore only local stamps). These usages are not catalogued separately because the value of a cover is determined as much by its attractiveness as its franking, rarity being the basic criterion.

Only a few Local Posts used special handstamps for canceling. The stamps frequently were left uncanceled, were canceled by pen, or less often by pencil. **Unless indicated otherwise, values for stamps on cover are for covers having the stamp tied by a handstamped cancellation, either private or governmental.** Local stamps, either uncanceled or pen canceled, **on covers to which they apparently belong**, also are valued where possible.

The absence of any specific cancellation listed indicates that no company handstamp is known so used, and that the canceling, if any, was done by pen, pencil or government handstamp. Local stamps used on letters directed out of town (and consequently bearing government stamps) sometimes, because of their position, are tied together with the government stamp by the cancellation used to cancel the latter.

Values for envelopes are for entires unless specifically mentioned.

All Local stamps are imperforate and on wove paper, either white or colored through, unless otherwise stated.

Counterfeits exist of many Local stamps, but most of these are crude reproductions and would deceive only the novice.

Adams & Co.'s Express, California

This post started in September, 1849, operating only on the Pacific Coast.

D. H. Haskell, Manager

L1 L2

Nos. 1L2-1L5 Printed in Sheets of 40 (8x5).

1854 **Litho.**

1L1 L1 25c	**black,** *blue*		*2,750.*	—
	On cover			—
1L2 L2 25c	**black** (initials in black)		75.00	—
	Block of 4		375.00	
	Sheet of 40		—	
a.	Initials in red			—
b.	Without initials			—

Cancellation (1L1-1L2): Black Express Co.

Nos. 1L1-1L2 were the earliest adhesive franks issued west of the Mississippi River.

No. 1L2 usually bear manuscript control markings "LR" for Louis Reed or less commonly "ICW" for Isaiah C. Wood.

Glazed Surface Cardboard

1L3 L2 25c	**black,** *pink*	30.00	
	Block of 4	160.00	
	Sheet of 40	2,000.	
	Retouched flaw above LR "25"	100.00	

No. 1L3 was probably never placed in use as a postage stamp.

L3

Overprinted in red "Over our California lines only"

1L4 L3 25c	**black** (with initials "LR" or "ICW")	750.00	—

L4 L5

1L5 L4 25c	**black** (black surcharge)	*4,000.*	—
1L6 L5 25c	**black**	*3,000.*	
	Pair	*7,500.*	

The pair of No. 1L6 is unique.

NEWSPAPER STAMP

L6

1LP1 L6	**black,** *claret*	—	*2,000.*

Cancellation: Blue company oval.

ENVELOPES

L6a L6b

Typo.

1LU1 L6a 25c	**blue** (cut square)			*15,000.*
1LU2 L6a 25c	**black,** on U.S. #U9		—	—
1LU3 L6b 50c	**black,** on U.S. #U9		*2,500.*	*2,500.*
1LU4 L6b 50c	**black,** *buff*			*15,000.*

Nos. 1LU2 and 1LU3 exist cut out and apparently used as adhesives.

Cancellation: Blue company oval.

Adams' City Express Post, New York, N.Y.

L7 L7a

L8

1850-51 **Typo.**

2L2 L7 2c **black,** *buff* 5,000. 2,250.
On cover, canceled, not tied, with certificate *10,000.*
2L3 L7a 1c **black,** *gray* — —
2L4 L8 2c **black,** *gray* *450.00 450.00*
On cover, tied by handstamp *5,500.*
2L5 L8 2c **blue,** —
On cover, pen cancel —

Nos. 2L3-2L4 were reprinted in black on white wove paper. Some students claim that a 1c in blue on white wove paper exists as originals.

Allen's City Dispatch, Chicago, Ill.

Established by Edwin Allen for intracity delivery of letters and circulars. The price of the stamps is believed to have been determined on a quantity basis. Uncanceled and canceled remainders were sold to collectors after suppression of the post in February, 1883.

L9

1882 **Typo.** ***Perf. 10***

Sheet of 100 (10x10)

3L1 L9 **pink** 7.50 *25.00*
On cover *900.00*
Block of 4 *40.00*
a. Horizontal pair, imperf. between —
3L2 L9 **black** 12.50 *100.00*
On cover —
Block of 4 55.00
a. Horizontal pair, imperf. between —
3L3 L9 **red,** *yellow* .75 *20.00*
On cover *800.00*
Block of 4 *3.25*
a. Imperf., pair *150.00*
b. Horizontal pair, imperf. between —
3L4 L9 **blackish purple** 120.00

Cancellations: Violet company oval, violet "eagle."

American Express Co., New York, N.Y.

Believed by some researchers to have been established by Smith & Dobson in 1856, and short-lived.

L10

Typeset
Glazed Surface Paper

4L1 L10 2c **black,** *green* *9,000.*

American Letter Mail Co.

Lysander Spooner established this independent mail line operating to and from New York, Philadelphia and Boston.

L12

L13

1844 **Engr.**

Sheet of 20 (5x4)

5L1 L12 5c **black,** thin paper (2nd printing) 7.50 *35.00*
Thick paper (1st printing) 35.00 *50.00*
On cover *850.00*
Pair on cover —
Block of 4, thin paper 40.00
Sheet of 20, thin paper 225.00

No. 5L1 has been extensively reprinted in several colors, distinguishable by the rust marks on the plate, which were mostly removed from the margins and gutters between stamps but remain within the stamp designs. Cancellations: Red dotted star (2 types). Red "PAID," black brush, red brush.

Engr.

5L2 L13 **black,** *gray* 150.00 *250.00*
On cover, tied by handstamp *1,000.*
On cover, ms. tied *500.00*
On cover, not tied *350.00*
Pair on cover, tied by ms. 1,200.
Vertical strip of 4 *3,000.*
Block of 4 *4,000.*
5L3 L13 **blue,** *gray* *2,000. 1,750.*
On cover, uncanceled, with certificate *11,500.*
On cover, tied by ms. *12,500.*

Cancellations: Red "PAID," red company oval.

A. W. Auner's Despatch Post, Philadelphia, Pa.

L13a

1851 **Typeset**

Cut to shape

154L1 L13a **black,** *grayish* *9,000.*
On cover, not tied, with certificate *16,500.*

Nos. 154L1 unused and on cover are each unique.

Baker's City Express Post, Cincinnati, Ohio

L14

1849

6L1 L14 2c **black,** *pink* *2,250.*
On cover, uncanceled, with certificate *12,500.*

Bank & Insurance Delivery Office or City Post
See Hussey's Post.

Barnard's Cariboo Express, British Columbia

The adhesives were used on British Columbia mail and the post did not operate in the United States, so the formerly listed PAID and COLLECT types are omitted. This company had an arrangement with Wells, Fargo & Co. to exchange mail at San Francisco.

Barnard's City Letter Express, Boston, Mass.

Established by Moses Barnard

L19

1845

7L1 L19 **black,** *yellow,* glazed paper *1,250. 1,000.*
On cover, not canceled *3,000.*
7L2 L19 **red** *1,000.*
On cover, ms. cancel, not tied, with certificate *5,000.*

No. 7L2 unused and on cover are each unique.

Barr's Penny Dispatch, Lancaster, Pa.

Established by Elias Barr.

L19a

L20

1855 **Typeset**

Five varieties of each

8L1 L19a **red** 1,000. 1,000.
On cover, ms. cancel, not tied, with certificate *2,000.*
8L2 L20 **black,** *green* 250. 200.00
On cover with 3c #11 —
Pair *650.*

Bayonne City Dispatch, Bayonne City, N.J.

Organized April 1, 1883, to carry mail, with three daily deliveries. Stamps sold at 80 cents per 100.

L21

1883 **Electrotyped**

Sheet of 10

9L1 L21 1c **black** 200. 275.
On cover *750.*
On cover with 1c & 2c #183, 206 *2,750.*
On cover with 3c #207 *1,600.*

Cancellation: Purple concentric circles.

ENVELOPE

1883, May 15 **Handstamped**

9LU1 L21 1c **purple,** *amber* 175. *1,000.*

Bentley's Dispatch, New York, N.Y.

Established by H. W. Bentley, who acquired Cornwell's Madison Square Post Office, operating until 1856, when the business was sold to Lockwood. Bentley's postmark was double circle handstamp.

L22

L22a

1856(?) **Glazed Surface Paper**

10L1 L22 **gold** *9,000. 9,000.*
10L2 L22a **gold** *7,500.*
Pair *10,000.*

Two unused examples of No. 10L1 are known, while the used example is unique.

Cancellation: Black "PAID."

Berford & Co.'s Express, New York, N.Y.

Organized by Richard G. Berford and Loring L. Lombard. Carried letters, newspapers and packages by steamer to Panama and points on the West Coast, North and South America. Agencies in West Indies, West Coast of South America, Panama, Hawaii, etc.

L23

1851

11L1 L23 3c **black** *5,000. 7,000.*
On cover, not canceled —
11L2 L23 6c **green** — —
On cover, tied —
11L3 L23 10c **violet** *5,000.*
On cover, not canceled —

Four cut to shape on cover — 15,000.
Pair
a. Horiz. tete beche pair
On cover with normal pair 67,500.
Two tete beche pair on cover 75,000.
11L4 L23 25c **red** 17,000.
On cover with #11L1 & 2 #11L2 75,000.

Values of cut to shape stamps are about half of those quoted.
No. 11L4 unused and on cover are each unique.
Cancellation: Red "B & Co. Paid" (sometimes impressed without ink). Dangerous counterfeits exist of Nos. 11L1-11L4.

Bicycle Mail Route, California

During the American Railway Union strike, Arthur C. Banta, Fresno agent for Victor bicycles, established this post to carry mail from Fresno to San Francisco and return, employing messengers on bicycles. The first trip was made from Fresno on July 6, 1894. Service was discontinued on July 18 when the strike ended. In all, 380 letters were carried. Stamps were used on covers with U.S. Government adhesive stamps and on stamped envelopes.

L24

Printed from single die. Sheet of six.
Error of spelling "SAN FRANSISCO"

1894 **Typo.** ***Rouletted 10***
12L1 L24 25c **green** 150. 200.
On cover 2,750.
Block of 4 700.
Pane of 6 1,750.

L25

Retouched die. Spelling error corrected.
12L2 L25 25c **green** 30. 75.
On cover 1,500.
On cover with No. 220, both tied 2,000.
Block of 4 125.
Pane of 6 250.
a. "Horiz." pair, imperf. "vert" 75.
As "a," pane of 6 —

ENVELOPES
12LU1 L25 25c **brown,** on 2c No. U311 200. 1,850.
12LU2 L25 25c **brown,** on 2c No. U312 200. 1,850.

Cancellation: Two black parallel bars 2mm apart.
Stamps and envelopes were reprinted from the defaced die.

Bigelow's Express, Boston, Mass.

Authorities consider items of this design to be express company labels rather than stamps.

Bishop's City Post, Cleveland, Ohio

See Carriers' Stamps, Nos. 10LB1-10LB2.

Blizzard Mail

Organized March, 1888, to carry mail to New York City during the interruption of U.S. mail by the Blizzard of 1888. Used March 12-16.

L27

1888, Mar. 12 **Quadrille Paper** **Typo.**
163L1 L27 5c **black** 3,750.
a. "CETNS" instead of "CENTS" —

D.O. Blood & Co., Philadelphia, Pa.
I. Philadelphia Despatch Post

Operated by Robertson & Co., predecessor of D.O. Blood & Co.

L28

L29

Initialed "R & Co."

1842 **Handstamped**
Cut to Shape
15L1 L28 3c **red,** *bluish* 1,500.
On cover, not tied 8,500.
15L2 L28 3c **black** 1,500.
On cover, not tied, with certificate 15,000.

Cancellations on Nos. 15L1-15L2: Red "3," red pattern of segments.

With or without shading in background.
Initialed "R & Co"

1843 **Litho.**
15L3 L29 (3c) **black,** *grayish* 750.
On cover, tied by handstamp 12,500.
On cover, tied by ms. cancel 5,000.
On cover, not tied, with certificate 3,500.
a. Double impression —

Cancellation on No. 15L3: Red "3"
The design shows a messenger stepping over the Merchants' Exchange Building, which then housed the Government Post Office, implying that the private post gave faster service.
See illustration L161 for similar design.

II. D.O. Blood & Co.

Formed by Daniel Otis Blood and Walter H. Blood in 1845. Successor to Philadelphia Despatch Post which issued Nos. 15L1-15L3.

L30

Initialed "Dob & Cos" or "D.O.B. & Co."

1845
Shading in background
15L4 L30 (3c) **black,** *grayish* 600.
On cover, tied by handstamp 6,000.
On cover, not tied 1,500.

L31

L32

1846
15L5 L31 (2c) **black** 125. 250.
On cover —
On cover, not tied, with certificate 800.
Block of 4 475.
Pane of 12 5,500.

1847
15L6 L32 (2c) **black** — 200.
On cover —
On cover, not tied, with certificate 1,250.
On cover, not tied, with 5c #1 —

Cancellations on Nos. 15L4-15L6: Black dot pattern, black cross, red "PAID."
Dangerous counterfeits exist of Nos. 15L3-15L6.

L33

L34

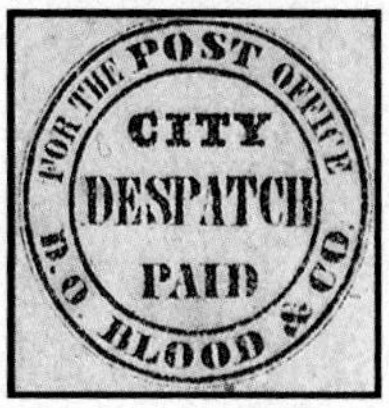

L35

1846-47
15L7 L33 (2c) **black** 175.00 350.00
On cover, tied by handstamp 1,750.
On cover, cut to shape, tied by handstamp 1,100.
On cover, not tied 750.00
15L8 L34 (2c) **black** 110.00 75.00
On cover, tied by handstamp 950.00
On cover, uncanceled 500.00
15L9 L35 (2c) **black** 100.00 60.00
On cover, tied by handstamp 1,500.
On cover, with 5c #1 —
On cover, not tied 500.00
Block of 4 —

Values for Nos. 15L7-15L9 cut to shape are half of those quoted.
"On cover" listings of Nos. 15L7-15L9 are for stamps tied by government town postmarks, either Philadelphia, or rarely Baltimore.

L36

L37

1848

15L10 L36 (2c) **black & blue**	350.00	*500.00*
On cover, tied by handstamp		*1,250.*
On cover, not canceled		*1,000.*
On cover, with 5c #1		—
Pair	*1,300.*	
15L11 L37 (2c) **black,** *pale green*	300.00	300.00
On cover, tied by handstamp		*1,250.*
On cover, not tied		*800.00*

Cancellation: Black grid.

L38

L39

L40

L41

1848-54

15L12 L38 (2c) **gold,** *black,* glazed	*110.00*	100.00
On cover, tied by handstamp		*500.00*
On cover, acid tied		200.00
On cover with 5c #1		—
15L13 L39 1c **bronze,** *black,* glazed ('50)	25.00	12.50
On cover, tied by handstamp		*225.00*
On cover, acid tied		75.00
On cover, acid tied, with 5c #1		*1,500.*
On cover, acid tied, with pair of 5c #1b		—
On cover with 10c #2		—
On cover, acid tied, with three 1c #7		*1,100.*
On cover with, tied by handstamp, 3c #10		*250.00*
Block of 4	150.00	
Pane of 24	*1,250.*	
15L14 L40 (1c) **bronze,** *lilac* ('54)	4.25	2.50
On cover, tied by handstamp		*200.00*
On cover, acid tied		30.00
On cover, acid tied, with 1c #9		*300.00*
On cover with 3c #11		*375.00*
On cover, tied by handstamp, with 3c #26		*200.00*
On cover, acid tied, with 3c #64b		*250.00*
Block of 4	50.00	
Pane of 25	*750.00*	
a. Laid paper	—	—
b. Tete beche pair	—	
15L15 L40 (1c) **blue & pink,** *bluish* ('53)	22.50	12.50
On cover, tied by handstamp		*200.00*
On cover, acid tied		50.00
Block of 4	80.00	
Pane of 25	*1,250.*	
a. Laid paper	—	—
Block of 4	—	
15L16 L40 (1c) **bronze,** *black,* glazed ('54)	30.00	25.00
On cover, tied by handstamp		*225.00*
On cover, acid tied		75.00
On cover, tied by handstamp, with 3c #11		*275.00*
15L17 L41 (2c) **bronze,** *black,* glazed	35.00	20.00
On cover, tied by handstamp		*225.00*
On cover, acid tied		75.00
On cover, acid tied, with 5c #1		*1,250.*
On cover, not tied, with 5c #1		*750.*
On cover, handstamp tied, with pair of 5c #1a		*11,000.*
On cover, tied by handstamp and acid, with 10c #2		*4,500.*

D.O. Blood & Co. reduced the cost for mailing letters from 2c to 1c as of Jan. 8, 1849, in anticipation of the government carrier rate reduction. As a result, Nos. 15L12 and 15L17 could be purchased for 1c after this date.

Cancellations: Black grid (No. 15L12, 15L17). Nos. 15L13-15L16 were almost always canceled with an acid which discolored both stamp and cover.

III. Blood's Penny Post

Blood's Penny Post was acquired by the general manager, Charles Kochersperger, in 1855, when Daniel O. Blood died.

Henry Clay — L42

1855 **Engr. by Draper, Welsh & Co.**

15L18 L42 (1c) **black**	35.00	10.00
On cover		150.00
On cover, tied by handstamp, with 3c #11		*400.00*
On cover, tied by handstamp, with 3c #26		*350.00*
On 3c entire #U9		300.00
Block of 4	175.00	

Cancellations: Black or red circular "Blood's Penny Post," black "1" in frame, red "1" in frame.

ENVELOPES

L42A

L43

L44

1848-60 **Embossed**

15LU1 L42A **albino embossing,** *white*	—	
15LU1A L42A **albino embossing,** *buff*	—	4,500.
15LU1B L43 **red,** *white*	75.00	*100.00*
a. **Pink,** *white*		*100.00*
b. Impressed on US Env. #U9		225.00
15LU2 L43 **red,** *buff*	—	150.00
15LU3 L44 **red,** *white*	75.00	160.00
15LU4 L44 **red,** *buff*	75.00	125.00

One example of No. 15LU1 is recorded, uncanceled, with the embossed stamp cut out and reattached. Two examples of No. 15LU1A are recorded, canceled by the "Blood's Despatch/28 So. Sixth" handstamp.

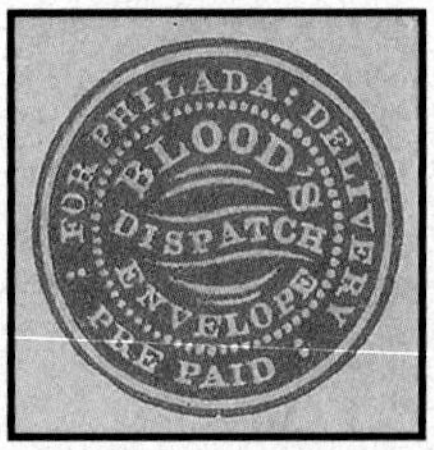

L45

15LU5 L45 **red,** *white*	35.00	75.00
Used with 3c #11		350.00
Used with 3c #26		*350.00*
a. Impressed on US Env. #U7		*250.00*
b. Impressed on US Env. #U9		*250.00*
c. Impressed on US Env. #U1		*300.00*
d. Impressed on US Env. #U3		*500.00*
e. Impressed on US Env. #U2		*275.00*
15LU6 L45 **red,** *amber*	35.00	100.00
15LU6A L45 **red,** *buff*		*350.00*
On cover with 10c #2		—
On cover with three 1c #9		—

Laid Paper

15LU7 L45 **red,** *white*	35.00	125.00
Used with acid tied #15L14		*200.00*
a. Impressed on US env. #U9		350.00
15LU8 L45 **red,** *amber*	35.00	125.00
Used with 3c No. 25		200.00
15LU9 L45 **red,** *buff*	35.00	250.00
15LU10 L45 **red,** *blue*		*6,500.*

Nos. 15LU1-15LU9 exist in several envelope sizes. No. 15LU6A exists in many shades, from buff to brown, as a result of various printings and changes over time.

Cancellations: Black grid (Nos. 15LU1-15LU4), black company circle (2 sizes and types). When on government envelope, the Blood stamp was often left uncanceled.

Bouton's Post, New York, N.Y.
I. Franklin City Despatch Post

Organized by John R. Bouton

L46

1847 **Glazed Surface Paper** **Typo.**

16L1 L46 (2c) **black,** *green*	*7,500.*	
a. "Bouton" in blk. ms. vert. at side	*7,000.*	
On cover		*14,000.*

II. Bouton's Manhattan Express

Acquired from William V. Barr

L47

1847 **Typo.**

17L1 L47 2c **black,** *pink*	*4,000.*	
Cut to shape	*900.*	
On cover, uncanceled		*4,500.*

III. Bouton's City Dispatch Post

(Sold to Swarts' in 1849.)

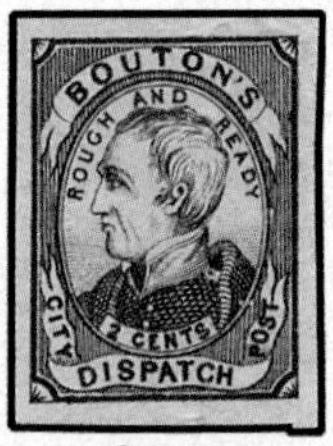

Corner Leaves — L48

Corner Dots — L49

Design: Zachary Taylor

1848 **Litho.**

18L1 L48 2c **black**	—	600.
On cover		*2,000.*
On cover with 5c #1		*27,500.*
On cover with 10c #2		*50,000.*
18L2 L49 2c **black,** *gray blue*	—	250.
On cover, tied by handstamp		600.
On cover tied by Swarts' handstamp		*1,000.*
On cover with 5c #1		*25,000.*
On cover with 10c #2		*7,500.*

Cancellations on Nos. 18L1-18L2: Red "PAID BOUTON."

Boyce's City Express Post, New York, N.Y.

L50

Center background has 17 parallel lines

1852 **Glazed Surface Paper** **Typo.**

19L1 L50 2c **black,** *green*	*1,500.*	*1,000.*
Cut to shape	*850.00*	
On cover, tied by manuscript cancel		*4,000.*

Boyd's City Express, New York, N.Y.

Boyd's City Express, as a post, was established by John T. Boyd, on June 17, 1844. In 1860 the post was briefly operated by John T. Boyd, Jr., under whose management No. 20L15 was issued.

For about six months in 1860 the post was suspended. It was then sold to William and Mary Blackham who resumed operation on Dec. 24, 1860.

The Blackham issues began with No. 20L16. Boyd's had arrangements to handle local delivery mail for Pomeroy, Letter Express, Brooklyn City Express Post, Staten Island Express Post and possibly others.

L51

Designs L51-L56, L59-L60 have a rectangular frame of fine lines surrounding the design.

1844 **Glazed Surface Paper** **Litho.**

20L1 L51 2c **black,** *green* *1,000.*
On cover *4,000.*
On cover, not tied, with #117L4 *7,000.*

Cancellation: Red "FREE."

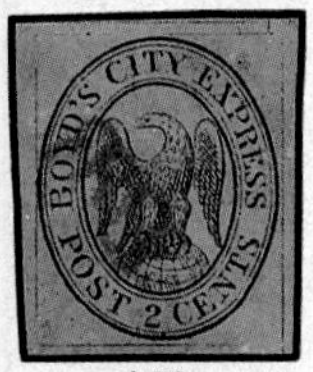

L52

L53

L54

Plain background. Map on globe.

1844 **Litho.**

20L2 L52 2c **black,** *yellow green* 175.00
On cover *450.00*

Cancellation: Red "FREE."

Plain background. Only globe shaded.

1845 **Engr.**

20L3 L53 2c **black,** *bluish green* — 250.00
On cover *500.00*

Cancellation: Red "FREE."

Inner oval frame of two thin lines. Netted background, showing but faintly on late impressions.

1845 **Engr.**

20L4 L54 2c **black,** *green* — 15.00
On cover, tied by handstamp 250.00
On cover, not tied 75.00
On cover, tied, with 5c U.S. Postmaster Provisional #9X1, on cover front —
On cover, tied, with 5c #1 *5,000.*
On cover, not tied, with 5c #1 *1,500.*
Double transfer 35.00
a. Diagonal half used as 1c on cover *2,300.*

Cancellations: Red "FREE." Black grid.

The 20L4 and 9X1 on cover front is the only recorded usage of a local stamp and a Postmaster Provisional.

1848

20L5 L54 2c **gold,** *cream* *600.00* *600.00*
On cover *1,750.*

Designs L54-L59 (except No. 20L23) were also obtainable die cut. An extra charge was made for such stamps. In general, genuine Boyd die-cuts sell for 75% of rectangular cut stamps. Stamps hand cut to shape are worth much less.

L55

L56

L57

No period after "CENTS." Inner oval frame has heavy inner line.

1848 **Engr.**

20L7 L55 2c **black,** *green* (glazed) 10.00 15.00
On cover, tied by handstamp 175.00
On cover, tied by handstamp, with 5c #1 *3,250.*
On cover, tied, with 3c #11 *275.00*
Block of 4 40.00
Partially erased transfer —
On cover —
a. 2c **black,** *yellow green* 15.00
On cover 135.00

Cancellation: Black grid.

No. 20L7a is on unglazed surface-colored paper.

1852 **Litho.**

Period after "CENTS." Inner frame as in L55.

20L8 L56 2c **black,** *green* 25.00 35.00
On cover *150.00*
Vert. strip of 3 on cover *300.00*
20L9 L56 2c **gold,** 12.50 80.00
On cover, tied by handstamp *750.00*
On cover with 3c #11 *1,250.*
Block of 4 80.00

Cancellations on Nos. 20L8-20L9: Black cork. Black "PAID J.T.B."

No. 20L8 was reprinted in 1862 on unglazed paper, and about 1880 on glazed paper without rectangular frame.

1854

Period after "CENTS." Inner oval frame has heavy outer line. Eagle's tail pointed. Upper part of "2" open, with heavy downstroke at left shorter than one at right. "2C" closer than "T2."

20L10 L57 2c **black,** *green* 32.50 25.00
On cover, tied by handstamp 200.00

Cancellation: Black "PAID J.T.B."

L58

L59

1855 **Unglazed Paper Colored Through** **Typo.**

Outer oval frame of three lines, outermost heavy. Solid background.

20L11 L58 2c **black,** *olive green* *65.00* 90.00
On cover, tied by handstamp *350.00*

1856

20L12 L58 2c **brick red,** *white* 50.00 45.00
On cover, tied by handstamp *500.00*
20L13 L58 2c **dull orange,** *white* 50.00 45.00
On cover *400.00*
a. Printed on both sides —

Cancellation on Nos. 20L11-20L13: Black "PAID J.T.B."

Nos. 20L11-20L13 were reprinted in the 1880's for sale to collectors. They were printed from a new small plate of 25 on lighter weight paper and in colors of ink and paper lighter than the originals.

1857 **Glazed Surface Paper** **Litho.**

Similar to No. 20L10, but eagle's tail square. Upper part of "2" closed (in well printed specimens) forming a symmetrical "o" with downstrokes equal. "T2" closer than "2C."

20L14 L59 2c **black,** *green* 12.50 *25.00*
On cover 125.00
On cover, tied by handstamp, with 3c #26 —
Pair on cover —
Block of 4 65.00
a. Serrate perf. —

The serrate perf. is probably of private origin.

No. 20L15 was made by altering the stone of No. 20L14, and many traces of the "S" of "CENTS" remain.

1860

20L15 L59 1c **black,** *green* 1.00 *50.00*
On cover, tied by handstamp *400.00*
Block of 4 7.50
a. "CENTS" instead of "CENT" — —
On cover *450.00*

Cancellation on Nos. 20L14-20L15: Black "PAID J.T.B."

L60

L61

Center dots before "POST" and after "CENTS."

1861

20L16 L60 2c **black,** *red* 7.50 20.00
On cover, tied by handstamp 200.00
Block of 4 37.50
a. Tete beche pair 45.00
20L17 L60 1c **black,** *lilac* 12.50 17.50
On cover, tied by handstamp 250.00
On cover, tied by handstamp, with 3c #26 *200.00*
On cover, tied by handstamp, with 3c #65 *500.00*
Block of 4 50.00
a. "CENTS" instead of "CENT" 50.00 *75.00*
Two on cover (No. 20L17a) —
b. "1" inverted —
20L18 L60 1c **black,** *blue gray* 22.50 35.00
On cover, tied by handstamp *250.00*
On cover, tied by handstamp, with 3c #26 *225.00*
On cover, tied by handstamp, with 3c #65 *225.00*
Block of 4 90.00
a. "CENTS" instead of "CENT" 75.00 90.00
On cover 250.00
On cover, tied by handstamp, with 1c #24 and three 3c #26 *2,000.*
b. "1" inverted —

Cancellations on Nos. 20L16-20L18: Black or blue company oval, black company circle, black or blue "PAID" in circle.

1861

20L19 L60 2c **gold,** *250.00*
Block of 4 —
a. Tete beche pair —
20L20 L60 2c **gold,** *green* 20.00
Block of 4 —
a. Tete beche pair —
20L21 L60 2c **gold,** *dark blue* 12.50
On cover, tied by handstamp *150.00*
Block of 4 —
a. Tete beche pair —
20L22 L60 2c **gold,** *crimson* 25.00
Block of 4 —
a. Tete beche pair —

1866 **Typo.**

20L23 L58 2c **black,** *red* 7.50 25.00
On cover, tied by handstamp 250.00
Block of 4 37.50
a. Tete beche pair 55.00

Cancellations: Black company, black "PAID" in circle.

No. 20L23 was reprinted from a new stone on paper of normal color. See note after No. 20L13.

1866 **Typo.**

No period or center dots.

20L24 L61 1c **black,** *lilac* *30.00* *65.00*
On cover, tied by handstamp *500.00*
Block of 4 —
20L25 L61 1c **black,** *blue* 6.00 *50.00*
On cover, tied by handstamp *500.00*
Block of 4 30.00

Cancellation on Nos. 20L24-20L25: Black company.

Reprints exist of Nos. 20L24 and 20L25. Originals of No. 20L24 are grayish black on glazed paper, while the reprints are deep black on unglazed paper. Reprints of No. 20L25 are identical to the originals, and it is customary to regard stamps with original gum as originals and those without gum as reprints.

Boyd's City Dispatch

(Change in Name)

L62

1874 Glazed Surface Paper Litho.

20L26	L62	2c **light blue**	35.00	40.00
		On cover		—
		Block of 4	—	

A unique sheet of 100 exists. It demonstrates 10 transfer types (2x5) repeated ten times to produce the printing stone. The same stone was modified to produce Nos. 20L30-20L36.

The 2c black on wove paper, type L62, is a cut-out from the Bank Notices Nos. 20LUX1, 20LUX2, or 20LUX3.

Surface Colored Paper

20L28	L62	2c **black,** *red*	—	
20L29	L62	2c **blue,** *red*	250.00	

The adhesives of type L62 were made from the third state of the envelope die.

Nos. 20L28 and 20L29 are color trials, possibly used postally.

L63

L64

1877 Litho.

20L30	L63	2c **lilac,** *roseate*		—

Laid Paper

20L31	L63	2c **lilac,** *roseate*		—

Perf 12½, Wove Paper

20L32	L63	2c **lilac,** *roseate*	27.50	25.00
		On cover		*200.00*
a.		2c **lilac,** *grayish*	27.50	25.00

Laid Paper

20L33	L63	2c **lilac,** *roseate*		25.00
a.		2c **lilac,** *grayish*		—

Glazed Surface Paper

20L34	L63	2c **brown,** *yellow*	35.00	35.00
		On cover, tied by handstamp		—
a.		Imperf. horizontally	—	

1877 Laid Paper *Perf. 11, 12, 12½*

20L35	L64	(1c) **violet,** *lilac*	15.00	17.50
		On cover, tied by handstamp		*350.00*
a.		(1c) **red lilac,** *lilac*	27.50	27.50
b.		(1c) **gray lilac,** *lilac*	17.50	17.50
c.		Vert. pair, imperf. horiz.	*400.00*	
20L36	L64	(1c) **gray,** *roseate*	15.00	15.00
		On cover, tied by handstamp		*250.00*
a.		(1c) **gray,** *grayish*		15.00

Cancellations on Nos. 20L30-20L36: Black "PAID" in circle. Purple company oval.

Boyd's Dispatch

(Change in Name)

Mercury Series — Type I — L65

Printed in sheets of 100.
Inner frame line at bottom broken below foot of Mercury.
Printed by C.O. Jones.

1878 Litho. Wove Paper *Imperf.*

20L37	L65	**black,** *pink*	*400.00*	*300.00*

Surface Colored Wove Paper

20L38	L65	**black,** *orange red*	*750.00*	*500.00*
20L39	L65	**black,** *crimson*	*450.00*	*300.00*

Laid Paper

20L40	L65	**black,** *salmon*	*450.00*	
20L41	L65	**black,** *lemon*	*450.00*	*400.00*
20L42	L65	**black,** *lilac pink*	*450.00*	

Nos. 20L37-20L42 are color trials, some of which may have been used postally.

Surface Colored Paper

Perf. 12

20L43	L65	**black,** *crimson*	60.00	50.00
		On cover, tied by handstamp		*300.00*
a.		**black,** *dull brown red*	40.00	40.00
		On cover, tied by handstamp		*300.00*
20L43A	L65	**black,** *orange red*	150.00	150.00
		On cover, tied by handstamp		*1,000.*

Cancellations on Nos. 20L37-20L43A: Black "PAID" in circle. Purple company oval.

Wove Paper

Perf. 11, 11½, 12, 12½ and Compound

20L44	L65	**black,** *pink*	1.50	2.50
		On cover		*200.00*
a.		Horizontal pair, imperf. between	—	—

1879 *Perf. 11, 11½, 12*

20L45	L65	**black,** *blue*	10.00	15.00
		On cover, tied by handstamp		200.00
20L46	L65	**blue,** *blue*	27.50	32.50
		On cover, tied by handstamp		*400.00*

1880 *Perf. 11, 12, 13½*

20L47	L65	**black,** *lavender*	8.00	20.00
		On cover, tied by handstamp		*300.00*
		Block of 4	50.00	
a.		Horizontal pair, imperf. between	*400.00*	
20L48	L65	**blue,** *lavender*	—	—

1881 Laid Paper *Perf. 12, 12½, 14*

20L49	L65	**black,** *pink*	*350.00*	
		On cover, tied by handstamp		*600.00*
20L50	L65	**black,** *lilac pink*	7.00	25.00
		On cover, tied by handstamp		*325.00*

Mercury Series — Type II — L65a — 20L51

Mercury Series — Type III — L65b — 20L55

No break in frame, the great toe raised, other toes touching line.
Printed by J. Gibson

1881 Wove Paper *Perf. 12, 16 & Compound.*

20L51	L65a	**black,** *blue*	35.00	30.00
20L52	L65a	**black,** *pink*	75.00	75.00
		On cover, tied by handstamp		*400.00*

Laid Paper

20L53	L65a	**black,** *pink*	7.50	7.50
		On cover, tied by handstamp		125.00
20L54	L65a	**black,** *lilac pink*	12.50	10.00
		On cover		*200.00*

No break in frame, the great toe touching.
Printed by the "Evening Post"

Perf. 10, 11½, 12, 16 & Compound

1882 Wove Paper

20L55	L65b	**black,** *blue*	4.00	10.00
		On cover, tied by handstamp		*225.00*
		Pair on cover		225.00
20L56	L65b	**black,** *pink*	.40	*1.50*
		On cover, tied by handstamp		100.00
		Block of 4	2.00	

Cancellations on Nos. 20L44-20L56: black or purple company ovals of various types, purple company circle, purple "SPECIAL," purple Maltese cross.

ENVELOPES

Boyd's City Post

L66

Imprinted in upper right corner.

Used envelopes show Boyd's handstamps.

1864 Diagonally Laid Paper Embossed

20LU1	L66	**red**	*175.00*	
20LU2	L66	**red,** *amber*	*90.00*	
20LU3	L66	**red,** *yellow*	—	—
20LU4	L66	**blue**	*175.00*	—
20LU5	L66	**blue,** *amber*	*175.00*	
20LU6	L66	**blue,** *yellow*	—	—

Several shades of red and blue.

20LU7	L66	**deep blue,** *orange,* cut square	*600.00*	
		Entire		*5,500.*

Reprinted on pieces of white, fawn and oriental buff papers, vertically, horizontally or diagonally laid.

Wove Paper

20LU8	L66	**red,** *cream*	*175.00*	
20LU9	L66	**red,** *orange*	—	*2,500.*
20LU10	L66	**blue,** *cream*	—	
20LU11	L66	**blue,** *orange*	—	
		Impression at upper left		*4,000.*
20LU11A	L66	**blue,** *amber*	—	—

Boyd's City Dispatch

L67a

L67b

L67a. Lines and letters sharp and clear. Trefoils at sides pointed and blotchy, middle leaf at right long and thick at end.

L67b. Lines and letters thick and rough. Lobes of trefoils rounded and definitely outlined. Stamp impressed normally in upper right corner of envelope; L67b rarely in upper left.

1867 Diagonally Laid Paper Typo.

20LU12	L67	2c **red** (a) (b)	—	*800.00*
20LU13	L67	2c **red,** *amber* (b)	—	*300.00*
20LU14	L67	2c **red,** *cream* (b)	—	*300.00*
a.		On horiz. laid paper		—
20LU15	L67	2c **red,** *yellow* (a) (b)	—	*300.00*
20LU16	L67	2c **red,** *orange* (b)	—	*300.00*
a.		Stamp impressed at upper left		—

Wove Paper

20LU17	L67	2c **red** (a) (b)	—	*300.00*
20LU18	L67	2c **red,** *cream* (a) (b)	—	*300.00*
20LU19	L67	2c **red,** *yellow* (a)	—	—
20LU20	L67	2c **red,** *orange* (a) (b)	—	—
20LU21	L67	2c **red,** *blue* (a) (b)	500.00	*400.00*

Design as Type L62

First state of die, showing traces of old address.

1874

Diagonally Laid Paper

20LU22	L62	2c **red,** *amber*		*200.00*
20LU23	L62	2c **red,** *cream*	—	*200.00*

Wove Paper

20LU24	L62	2c **red,** *amber*		*200.00*
20LU25	L62	2c **red,** *yellow*		*200.00*

Second state of die, no traces of address.

1875

Diagonally Laid Paper

20LU26	L62	2c **red,** *amber*		*1,250.*
20LU27	L62	2c **red,** *cream*	—	*375.00*

Wove Paper

20LU28	L62	2c **red,** *amber*		*450.00*

L68

L69

1877

Laid Paper

20LU29	L68	2c **red,** *amber*		*800.00*

Stamp usually impressed in upper left corner of envelope.

1878

Diagonally Laid Paper

20LU30	L69	(1c) **red,** *amber*	—	*650.00*

Wove Paper

20LU31 L69 (1c) **red,** *cream* —
20LU32 L69 (1c) **red,** *yellow* —

Boyd's Dispatch

Mercury Series — Type IV — L70

Mercury Series — Type V — L71

Mercury Series-Type IV

Shading omitted in banner. No period after "Dispatch." Short line extends to left from great toe.

1878

Diagonally Laid Paper

20LU33	L70	**black**	40.00	*100.00*
20LU34	L70	**black,** *amber*		*80.00*
20LU35	L70	**black,** *cream*	50.00	*100.00*
20LU36	L70	**red**		*50.00*
20LU37	L70	**red,** *amber*	35.00	*45.00*
20LU38	L70	**red,** *cream*	35.00	*80.00*
20LU39	L70	**red,** *yellow green*		—
20LU40	L70	**red,** *orange*		*350.00*
20LU41	L70	**red,** *fawn*		—

Wove Paper

20LU42 L70 **red** — *800.00*

Mercury Series-Type V

Colorless crosshatching lines in frame work. Very little shading on arms and legs.

1878

Diagonally Laid Paper

20LU43	L71	**red**	—	*450.00*
20LU44	L71	**red,** *cream*	25.00	*50.00*

Wove Paper

20LU44A L71 **red** *1,000.*

Boyd's Bank Notices

IMPORTERS' AND TRADERS' NATIONAL BANK OF NEW YORK

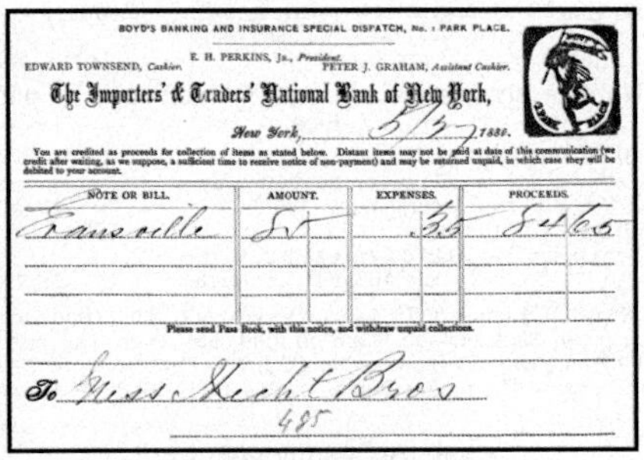
BOYD'S BANKING AND INSURANCE SPECIAL DISPATCH, No. 1 PARK PLACE.
E. H. PERKINS, Jr., President.
EDWARD TOWNSEND, Cashier. PETER J. GRAHAM, Assistant Cashier.
The Importers' & Traders' National Bank of New York,
New York, 5/5/7 188
NOTE OR BILL.	AMOUNT.	EXPENSES.	PROCEEDS.
Evansville	5.00	35	4.65
Please send Pass Book, with this notice, and withdraw unpaid collections.
To Messrs Hecht Bros
485

No. 20LUX9a

1874-83

Incomplete Year Date ("187 "), Card Stock

20LUX1 L62 (2c) **black,** 155x100mm *250.00*

Complete Year Date, Medium Wove Paper

20LUX2 L62 2c **black,** 157x104mm (1875) —
20LUX3 L62 2c **black,** 152x104mm (1876 *250.00*
20LUX4 L68 2c **black,** 154x105mm (1876) —
20LUX5 L68 2c **black,** 156x108mm (1877) *400.00*
20LUX6 L69 (1c) **black,** 156x108mm (1878) —
a. Four officers in masthead instead of three —
20LUX7 L70 (1c) **black,** 158x110mm (1879) *250.00*
20LUX8 L70 (1c) **black,** large year date and city, 158x110mm (1879) *250.00*
20LUX9 L70 (1c) **black,** 149x102mm (1880) *75.00* —
a. Three officers in masthead instead of four, 156x112mm *400.00*
20LUX10 L70 (1c) **black,** 149x102mm (1881) —
a. Four officers in masthead instead of three —
20LUX11 L71 (1c) **black,** 152x106mm (1883) —

Sizes of these cards may vary by up to two millimeters in either dimension from the measurements shown.

Nos. 20LUX5 and 20LUX9 exist on paper with a papermaker's watermark. Nos. 20LUX6, 20LUX9 and 20LUX10 may be found with either three or four bank officers listed in the masthead. The major number is the card that was issued first. No. 20LUX11 is known only unused, and may be a remainder that was printed but not used.

NATIONAL PARK BANK

Medium Wove Paper

1881 (?)
20LUX12 L71 (1c) **black,** 122x63mm ('83) *300.00*

No postmarks or cancellations were used on Bank Notices. Boyd's sometimes added the recipient's address in pencil.

FLEISCHMANN'S MODEL BAKERY

Card Stock

1879
20LUX13 L69 (1c) **black,** 130x75mm *3,000.*

This card is imprinted "Fleischmann's Model Bakery."

Bradway's Despatch, Millville, N.J.

Operated by Isaac Bradway

L72

1857 **Typo.**

21L1 L72 **gold,** *lilac,* on cover, not tied, with certificate *9,250.*
On cover, not tied, with 3c #11, with certificate *12,000.*

Brady & Co., New York, N.Y.

Operated by Abner S. Brady at 97 Duane St. Successor to Clark & Co.

L73

1857 **Typo.**

22L1 L73 1c **red,** *yellow* *1,000.* *1,000.*
On cover, tied by company handstamp *22,000.*
On cover, tied by "PAID" handstamp *10,000.*

Cancellations: Blue boxed "PAID," blue company oval.
Reprints exist.
No. 22L1 tied on corner by company handstamp is unique. Three covers recorded with stamp tied by "PAID."

Brady & Co.'s Penny Post, Chicago, Ill.

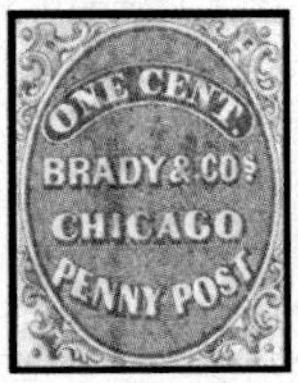

L74

1860(?) **Litho.**

23L1 L74 1c **violet** *650.00* —

The authenticity of this stamp has not been fully established.

Brainard & Co.

Established by Charles H. Brainard in 1844, operating between New York, Albany and Troy, Exchanged mail with Hale & Co. by whom Brainard had been employed.

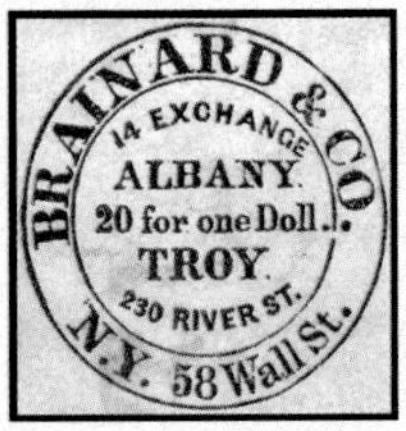

L75

1844 **Typo.**

24L1 L75 **black** *1,000.* *1,250.*
On cover, two stamps tied —
On cover, not tied *2,000.*
On cover, cut to shape, not tied *1,750.*
24L2 L75 **blue** *1,000.* *1,250.*
On cover, not tied *4,500.*

Nos. 21L1-24L2 cut to shape are one half of values quoted.

Brigg's Despatch, Philadelphia, Pa.

Established by George W. Briggs

L76

L77

1847

25L1 L76 (2c) **black,** *yellow buff* *1,000.*
On cover, not tied, with certificate *11,500.*
25L2 L76 (2c) **black,** *blue,* cut to shape *7,500.*

No. 25L2 is unique. It is on cover, manuscript "X" cancel, genuine, but Philatelic Foundation has declined to give an opinion as to whether the stamp originated on the cover.

1848

25L4 L77 (2c) **gold,** *yellow,* glazed *5,500.*
On cover, not tied —
25L5 L77 (2c) **gold,** *black,* glazed *4,000.*
On cover —
25L6 L77 (2c) **gold,** *pink* —

No. 25L4 used and on cover are each unique.

Handstamps formerly illustrated as types L78 and L79 are included in the section "Local Handstamped Covers" at the end of the Local Stamp listings. They were used as postmarks and there is no evidence that any prepaid handstamped envelopes or letter sheets were ever sold.

Broadway Post Office, New York, N.Y.

Started by James C. Harriott in 1848. Sold to Dunham & Lockwood in 1855.

L80

1849(?) **Typo.**

26L1 L80 (1c) **gold,** *black,* glazed *1,000.* *1,250.*
Cut to shape 250.
On cover —
Pair on cover —

1851(?)

26L2 L80 (1c) **black** 250. *400.*
On cover *1,500.*
On cover with 3c #11 *2,750.*
Pair *1,000.* *1,000.*
Pair on part of cover *1,500.*
Block of 4 1,750.

Cancellation: Black oval "Broadway City Express Post-Office 2 Cts."

Bronson & Forbes' City Express Post, Chicago, Ill.

Operated by W.H. Bronson and G.F. Forbes.

L81

1855 **Typo.**

27L1 L81 **black,** *green* *600.* *2,000.*
On cover —
On cover, tied by handstamp, with 3c #11 *14,000.*
27L2 L81 **black,** *lilac* *3,500.*

Cancellation: Black circle "Bronson & Forbes' City Express Post" (2 types).
No. 27L2 is unique.

Brooklyn City Express Post, Brooklyn, N.Y.

According to the foremost students of local stamps, when this concern was organized its main asset was the business of Kidder's City Express Post, of which Isaac C. Snedeker was the proprietor.

L82

L83

1855-64 Glazed Surface Paper Typo.

28L1	L82	1c	**black,** *blue* (shades)	25.00	*80.00*
			On cover, tied by handstamp		*400.00*
			Block of 4	125.00	
a.			Tete beche pair	*80.00*	
28L2	L82	1c	**black,** *green*	20.00	50.00
			On cover, tied by handstamp		*350.00*
			On cover, tied by handstamp, with 3c #65		*1,250.*
			Block of 4	100.00	
a.			Tete beche pair	*125.00*	
28L3	L83	2c	**black,** *crimson*	60.00	70.00
			On cover, tied by handstamp		*400.00*
			Block of 4	*300.00*	
28L4	L83	2c	**black,** *pink*	17.50	*100.00*
			On cover, tied by handstamp		*550.00*
			On cover, tied by handstamp, with 3c #65		*1,750.*
			Block of 4	100.00	
a.			Tete beche pair	60.00	
28L5	L83	2c	**black,** *dark blue*	50.00	*90.00*
			On cover, tied by handstamp		*500.00*
			On cover, tied by handstamp, with 3c #11		*500.00*
			Block of 4	*250.00*	

No. 28L5 has frame (dividing) lines around design.

28L6	L83	2c	**black,** *orange*	—	—
			On cover		—
a.			Tete beche pair	—	

Unsurfaced Paper Colored Through

28L7	L83	2c	**black,** *pink*	*300.00*	*750.00*

Cancellations: Black ring, red "PAID."
Reprints exist of Nos. 28L1-28L4, 28L6.

Browne & Co.'s City Post Office, Cincinnati, Ohio

Operated by John W.S. Browne

L84

L85

1852-55 Litho.

29L1	L84	1c	**black** (Brown & Co.)	175.	150.
			On cover		*1,000.*
			On cover with 3c #11		*2,750.*
			Pair	*450.*	
29L2	L85	2c	**black** (Browne & Co.)	175.	175.
			On cover, tied by handstamp		*5,000.*
			On cover with 3c #11A		*4,500.*
			Pair	*575.*	

Cancellations: Black, blue or red circle "City Post"," red, bright blue or dull blue circle "Browne & Co. City Post Paid."

Browne's Easton Despatch, Easton, Pa.

Established by William J. Browne

L87

L88

1857 Glazed Surface Paper Typeset

30L1	L87	2c	**black,** *red*	—	*5,000.*
30L2	L88	2c	**black,** *red*	—	—

George Washington — L89

Wove Paper Engr.

30L3	L89	2c	**black**	*750.*	*1,000.*
			Pair	*1,600.*	
			Block of 6	*5,750.*	

The No. 30L3 block of 6 is the only reported block of this stamp. Three pairs are reported.

Cancellation on No. 30L3: Black oval "Browne's Despatch Easton Pa."

Brown's City Post, New York, N.Y.

Established by stamp dealer William P. Brown for philatelic purposes.

L86

1877 Glazed Surface Paper Typo.

31L1	L86	1c	**black,** *bright red*	200.00	*275.00*
			On cover		*1,500.*
31L2	L86	1c	**black,** *yellow*	200.00	*275.00*
			On cover		*1,000.*
31L3	L86	1c	**black,** *green*	200.00	*275.00*
			On cover		*1,000.*
31L4	L86	1c	**black,** *violet*	200.00	*275.00*
			On cover		*1,500.*
31L5	L86	1c	**black,** *vermilion*	200.00	*275.00*
			On cover		*500.00*

Cancellation: Black and purple circle "Brown's Despatch Paid."

Bury's City Post, New York, N.Y.

L90

L91

1857 Embossed without color

32L1	L90	1c	*blue*	*8,000.*	

Handstamped

32L2	L91		**black,** *blue*	—	

Bush's Brooklyn City Express, Brooklyn, N.Y.

L91a

1848(?) Cut to shape Handstamped

157L1	L91a	2c	**red,** *green,* glazed	*27,500.*	

No. 157L1 is unique. It is uncanceled on a large piece.
See Bush handstamp in Local Handstamped Covers section.

California City Letter Express Co., San Francisco, Calif.

Organized by J.W. Hoag, proprietor of the Contra-Costa Express, for local delivery. Known also as the California Letter Express Co.

L92

L93

L93a

1862-66 Typeset

33L1	L92	10c	**red**	—	—
			On cover, not tied, with 10c #68, with certificate		*23,000.*
33L2	L92	10c	**blue**		—
			On cover, not tied, with certificate		*16,500.*
33L3	L92	10c	**green**	5,500.	
			On cover, uncanceled, with certificate		*18,000.*
33L4	L93	10c	**red**	—	—
33L5	L93	10c	**blue**		*14,000.*
33L6	L93	10c	**green**	*19,000.*	
			On cover, not tied, with certificate		*31,000.*

No side ornaments, "Hoogs & Madison's" in one line

33L7a	L93a	10c	**red**		*1,200.*
			On cover, not tied, with certificate		*19,000.*
33L8a	L93a	10c	**blue**	*4,000.*	
			On cover, not tied, with 10c #68, with certificate		*60,000.*

Nos. 33L1 unused, 33L1 on cover with #68, 33L3 used, 33L3 on cover, 33L6 unused, 33L6 on (patriotic) cover, 33L7 used, 33L7 on cover, 33L8 unused and 33L8 on cover with #68 each are unique. The other varieties of Nos. 33L1-33L8 are all rare.

California Penny Post Co.

Established in 1855 by J. P. Goodwin and partners. At first confined its operations to San Francisco, Sacramento, Stockton and Marysville, but branches were soon established at Benicia, Coloma, Nevada, Grass Valley and Mokelumne Hill. Operation was principally that of a city delivery post, as it transported mail to the General Post Office and received mail for local delivery. Most of the business of this post was done by means of prepaid envelopes.

L94

L94a

L95

L95a

1855 **Litho.**

34L1	L94	2c	**blue**	700.	*750.*
			On cover		*20,000.*
			Block of 4	*3,000.*	
34L1A	L94a	3c	**blue**	*850.*	
34L2	L95	5c	**blue**	*250.*	*425.*
			On cover		*1,250.*
			Block of 4	750.	
34L3	L95a	10c	**blue**	475.	—
			On cover		*3,000.*

Cancellation: Blue circle "Penny Post Co."

Only one example of No. 34L1 on cover is recorded. The stamp is tied by manuscript cancel. Three examples of No. 34L1A are recorded, each uncanceled on cover.

L96

34L4	L96	5c	**blue**	*600.*	*1,750.*
			On cover		*3,000.*
			Strip of 3	*3,500.*	

The strip of 3 of No. 34L4 has faults but is unique. Value is for strip in faulty condition.

ENVELOPES

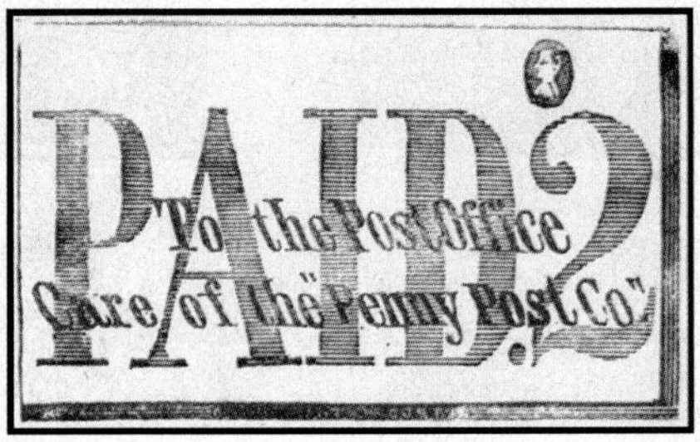

L97

1855-59

34LU1	L97	2c	**black,** *white*	200.	*900.*
			With 1c #9		—
			With 3c #11		*9,000.*
			With 10c #14		*11,000.*
a.			Impressed on 3c US env. #U10	250.	*1,000.*
34LU2	L97	5c	**blue,** *blue*	200.	*900.*
34LU3	L97	5c	**black,** *buff*	200.	*900.*
a.			Impressed on 3c US env. #U10		*1,500.*
34LU4	L97	7c	**black,** *orange buff*	—	
a.			Impressed on 3c US env. #U10	—	

L98

34LU6	L98	7c	**vermilion** on 3c US env. #U9	200.00	*1,000.*
34LU7	L98	7c	**vermilion** on 3c US env. #U10	225.00	*1,750.*

L98A

34LU8	L98A	5c	**black,** *white*	150.	*1,200.*
34LU9	L98A	5c	**black,** *buff*	150.	*1,200.*
			On cover, with 3c #11		—
a.			Impressed on 3c US env. #U10		*1,250.*
34LU10	L98A	7c	**black,** *white*	150.	*1,000.*
			On cover, with 3c #11		—
a.			Impressed on 3c US env. #U9		*1,750.*
34LU11	L98A	7c	**black,** *buff*	150.00	*1,100.*
a.			Impressed on 3c US env. #U10		*1,500.*
34LU11C	L98A		**black,** *buff,* "Collect Penny Postage" (no denomination)	250.	*1,500.*
			On cover, with 3c #11		—

L98B

34LU11B	L98B	7c	**black** on 3c US env. #U10	250.	*1,400.*
34LU12	L98B	7c	**black** on 3c US env. #U9	250.	*4,500.*

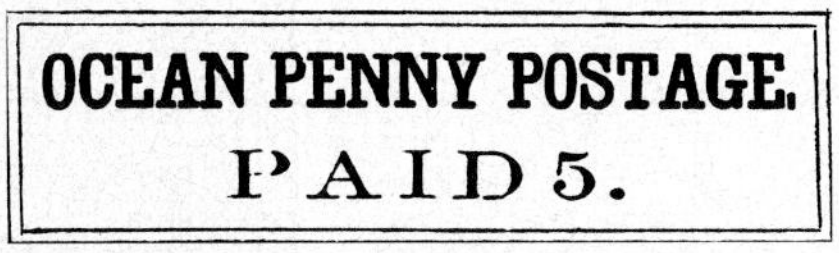

L98C

34LU13	L98C	5c	**black,** *buff*	—	—

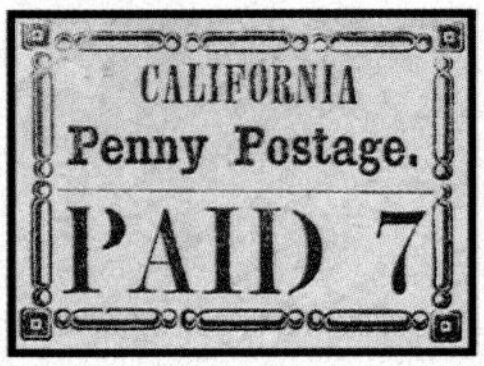

L98D

34LU13A	L98D	5c	**black,** *buff*		—
34LU14	L98D	7c	**black,** *buff*	300.	*3,000.*
			With 3c #11		*5,000.*
34LU15	L98D	7c	**black** on 3c US env. #U9	350.	*2,500.*
34LU16	L98D	7c	**black** on 3c US env. #U10	—	—

The non-government envelopes of types L97, L98A, L98C and L98D bear either 1c No. 9 or 3c No. 11 adhesives. These adhesives are normally canceled with the government postmark of the town of original mailing. Values are for covers of this kind. The U.S. adhesives are seldom canceled with the Penny Post cancellation. When they are, the cover sells for more.

At least eight different varieties of the 34LU14 are known with different printed instructions/addresses, some with room to add U.S. postage.

Carnes' City Letter Express, San Francisco, Calif.

Established by George A. Carnes, former P.O. clerk.

L99

L100

1864 **Typo.**

35L1	L99	(5c)	**rose**	175.	300.
			On cover, tied		*17,500.*
			Block of 4	*750.*	

Cancellations: Black dots. Blue dots. Blue "Paid." Blue oval "Wm. A. Frey."

See illustration L206

Overprinted "X" in Blue

35L2	L99	10c	**rose**	200.00

Litho.

35L3	L100	5c	**bronze**	125.00
a.			Tete beche pair	300.00
35L4	L100	5c	**gold**	125.00
a.			Tete beche pair	300.00
35L5	L100	5c	**silver**	125.00
a.			Tete beche pair	300.00
35L6	L100	5c	**black**	125.00
a.			Tete beche pair	300.00
35L7	L100	5c	**blue**	100.00
a.			Tete beche pair	250.00
35L8	L100	5c	**red**	125.00
a.			Tete beche pair	300.00

Printed in panes of 18 (3x6) from three settings of 6 (3x2), with the bottom setting inverted, creating three tete-beche pairs.

G. Carter's Despatch, Philadelphia, Pa.

Operated by George Carter

L101

1849-51

36L1	L101	2c	**black**	—	100.00
			On cover, tied by pen cancel		*225.00*
			On cover, with 5c #1		—
a.			Ribbed paper	—	140.00
			On cover, tied by pen cancel		*300.00*

No. 36L1 exists on paper with a blue, red or maroon wash. The origin and status are unclear.

Cancellation: Black circle "Carter's Despatch."

ENVELOPE

L102

36LU1	L102		**blue,** *buff*		*1,000.*
			Cut to shape		*150.*
			On cover with 3c No. 10		*3,250.*
			On cover with 3c No. 11		*1,750.*

Cheever & Towle, Boston, Mass.

Sold to George H. Barker in 1851

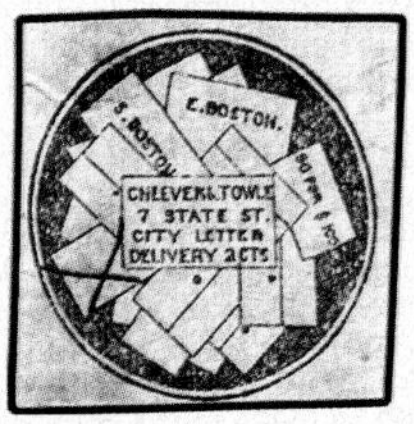

L104

1849(?)

37L1	L104	2c	**blue**	*600.*	*350.*
			Cut to shape		125.
			On cover, tied by handstamp		*7,000.*
			On cover, not tied		*1,500.*
			On cover, not tied, cut to shape		*500.*

Cancellation: Red oval "Towle's City Despatch Post 7 State Street."

Chicago Penny Post, Chicago, Ill.

L105

1862 **Typo.**

38L1	L105	(1c)	**orange brown**	800.	1,250.
			On cover, serrated perforations		*5,000.*

Reprints exist.

Cancellation: Black circle "Chicago Penny Post A. E. Cooke Sup't."

Cincinnati City Delivery, Cincinnati, Ohio

Operated by J. Staley, who also conducted the St. Louis City Delivery Co. He established the Cincinnati post in January, 1883. The government suppressed both posts after a few weeks. Of the 25,000 Cincinnati City Delivery stamps printed, about 5,000 were sold for postal use. The remainders, both canceled and uncanceled, were sold to collectors.

L106

1883 **Typo.** ***Perf. 11***

39L1	L106 (1c) **carmine**		2.50	*12.50*
	On cover			*300.00*
a.	Imperf., pair		—	—

Cancellation: Purple target.

City Despatch Post, New York, N.Y.

The City Despatch Post was started Feb. 1, 1842, by Alexander M. Greig and Henry T. Windsor. Greig's Post extended to 23rd St. Its operations were explained in a circular which throws light on the operations of all Local Posts:

New York City Despatch Post, Principal Office, 46 William Street.

"The necessity of a medium of communication by letter from one part of the city to another being universally admitted, and the Penny Post, lately existing having been relinquished, the opportunity has been embraced to reorganize it under an entirely new proprietory and management, and upon a much more comprehensive basis, by which Despatch, Punctuality and Security-those essential elements of success-may at once be attained, and the inconvenience now experienced be entirely removed."

"*** Branch Offices-Letter boxes are placed throughout every part of the city in conspicuous places; and all letters deposited therein not exceeding two ounces in weight, will be punctually delivered three times a day *** at three cents each."

"*** Post-Paid Letters.-Letters which the writers desire to send free, must have a free stamp affixed to them. An ornamental stamp has been prepared for this purpose *** 36 cents per dozen or 2 dolls. 50c per hundred. ***"

"No money must be put in boxes. All letters intended to be sent forward to the General Post Office for the inland mails must have a free stamp affixed to them."

"Unpaid Letters.-Letters not having a free stamp will be charged three cents, payable by the party to whom they are addressed, on delivery."

"Registry and Despatch.-A Registry will be kept for letters which it may be wished to place under special charge. Free stamps must be affixed for such letters for the ordinary postage, and three cents additional be paid (or an additional fee stamp be affixed), for the Registration."

NOTE: The word "Free," as used in this circular, should be read as "Prepaid." Likewise, the octagonal "FREE" cancellation should be taken to mean "Prepaid" (that is, "Free" of further charge).

The City Despatch Post was purchased by the United States Government and ceased to operate as a private carrier on August 15, 1842. It was replaced by the "United States City Despatch Post" which began operation on August 16, 1842, as a Government carrier.

No. 40L1 was issued by Alexander M. Greig; No. 40L2 and possibly No. 40L3 by Abraham Mead; Nos. 40L4-40L8 probably by Charles Cole.

L106a

Cancellation

Plate of 42 (6x7) subjects

This was the first adhesive stamp used in the United States. This stamp was also used as a carrier stamp. See No. 6LB1.

1842, Feb. 1

40L1	L106a 3c **black,** *grayish*	375.	275.
	On cover, tied by handstamp		*2,500.*
	First day cover		*25,000.*
	Pair	850.	
	Block of 4	1,900.	
	Sheet of 42	*27,500.*	

No. 40L1 was used until Aug. 16, 1842, the first day of operation of the U.S. City Despatch Post. The latest recorded No. 40L1 cover is dated Aug. 13, 1842.

Cancellations: Red framed "FREE" (see illustration above), red circle "City Despatch Post" (2 types).

Die reprints of No. 40L1 were made in 1892 on grayish white, orange, red and green surface-colored papers. It is believed that only four sets were made. Value, each reprint $500.

1846

Glazed Surface Paper

40L2	L106a 2c **black,** *green*	*200.00*	150.00
	On cover, tied by handstamp		*600.00*
	On cover, not tied		*400.00*

1847

40L3	L106a 2c **black,** *pink*		*2,250.*
	On cover, not tied, with certificate		*9,000.*

Cancellations: Red framed "FREE," black framed "FREE," red circle "City Despatch Post."

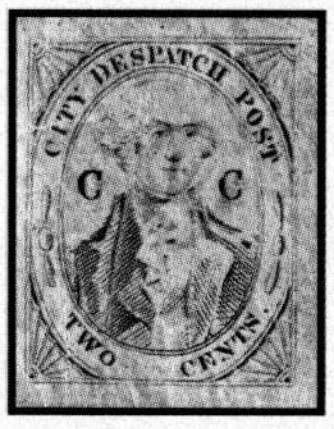
L107

Similar to L106a with "CC" at sides.

1847-52

40L4	L107 2c **black,** *green glazed*	350.00	200.00
	On cover, tied by handstamp		1,500.
a.	"C" at right inverted		—
b.	"C" at left sideways		—
	On cover, tied by handstamp		—
c.	"C" at right only		—

Some students think No. 40L4c may have just a badly worn sideways "C" at left.

40L5	L107 2c **black,** *grayish*		500.00
	On cover, tied by handstamp		850.00
a.	"C" at right inverted		—
b.	"C" at left sideways		—
c.	"C" in ms. between "Two" and "Cents"		*1,000.*
d.	"C" at left sideways plus "C" in ms. between "Two" and "Cents"		*1,900.*
	On cover, tied by handstamp		*4,000.*
40L6	L107 2c **black,** *vermilion glazed*	450.00	300.00
	On cover, tied by handstamp		*1,000.*
a.	"C" at right inverted		—
b.	"C" at left sideways		*4,500.*
	On cover, tied by handstamp		4,000.
	On cover, not tied		2,750.
40L8	L107 2c **black,** *yellowish buff* ('52)	—	—
a.	"C" at right inverted		—
b.	"C" at left sideways		*4,500.*

An uncanceled copy of No. 40L8 exists on cover.

Cancellations: Red framed "FREE," black framed "FREE," black "PAID," red "PAID," red circle company, black grid of 4 short parallel bars.

Each of the No. 40L6b covers are unique as listed.

City Dispatch, New York, N.Y.

L107a

1846 **Typo.**

160L1	L107a 2c **red**	*3,000.*	*4,000.*
	On cover		—
	Vertical pair	*19,000.*	

The unique vertical pair is the only reported multiple of No. 160L1.

Cancellation: Red "PAID."

City Dispatch, Philadelphia, Pa.

Justice — L108

1860 **Thick to Thin Wove Paper** **Litho.**

41L1	L108 1c **black**	7.50	50.00
	On cover, tied by handstamp		*500.00*
	Block of 4	55.00	

Cancellations: Black circle "Penny Post Philada.," black circled grid of X's.

City Dispatch, St. Louis, Mo.

L109

Initials in black ms.

1851 **Litho.**

42L1	L109 2c **black,** *blue*	*40,000.*

No. 42L1 used is unique. A second example, on cover, is recorded.

City Dispatch Post Office, New Orleans, La.

Stamps sold at 5c each, or 30 for $1.

L110

1847 **Glazed Surface Paper** **Typeset**

43L1	L110 (5c) **black,** *green*	*6,000.*	
	On cover		—
43L2	L110 (5c) **black,** *pink*	*6,000.*	
	On cover, not canceled		—

City Express Post, Philadelphia, Pa.

L111

L112

184-(?) **Typeset**

44L1	L111 2c **black,** on cover, uncanceled, with certificate		*11,000.*
44L2	L112 (2c) **black,** *pink*	*10,000.*	
	On cover, uncanceled, with certificate		*20,000.*
44L3	L112 (2c) **red,** *yellow,* on cover, uncanceled		*30,000.*

One example recorded of Nos. 44L1 and 44L3. Six No. 44L2 recorded, five of these uncanceled on covers.

See illustration L8.

City Letter Express Mail, Newark, N.J.

Began business under the management of Augustus Peck at a time when there was no free city delivery in Newark.

L113

1856 **Litho.**

45L1	L113 1c **red**	*350.00*	*500.00*
	Cut to shape	100.00	
	On cover		—
	On cover, cut to shape, tied by handstamp, with 3c #11		*17,000.*
45L2	L113 2c **red,** on cover, cut to shape, uncanceled, with certificate		*11,000.*

On No. 45L2, the inscription reads "City Letter/Express/City Delivery" in three lines across the top. The example on cover is unique.

City Mail Co., New York, N.Y.

There is evidence that Overton & Co. owned this post.

L114

1845

46L1 L114 (2c) **black,** *grayish* *1,500.* *1,500.*
On cover, not tied, with certificate *8,000.*

Cancellation: Red "PAID."

City One Cent Dispatch, Baltimore, Md.

L115

1851

47L1 L115 1c **black,** *pink* (on cover) —

Clark & Co., New York, N.Y.

(See Brady & Co.)

L116

1857 **Typo.**

48L1 L116 1c **red,** *yellow* 600. *900.*
On cover *2,500.*

Cancellation: Blue boxed "PAID."

Clark & Hall, St. Louis, Mo.

Established by William J. Clark and Charles F. Hall.

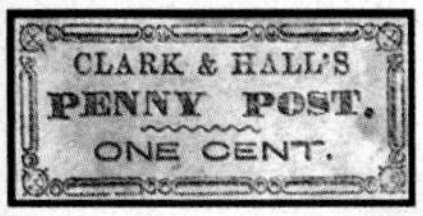

L117

Several varieties

1851 **Typeset**

49L1 L117 1c **black,** *pink,* on cover, uncanceled, with certificate 19,000.

Clarke's Circular Express, New York, N.Y.

Established by Marion M. Clarke

George Washington — L118

Impression handstamped through inked ribbon. Cut squares from envelopes or wrappers.

1865-68(?)

50LU1 L118 **blue,** wove paper *5,750.*
a. Diagonally laid paper *4,500.*
50LU2 L118 **black,** diag. laid paper *5,750.*

No. 50LU1 unused is unique.

Cancellation: Blue dated company circle.

Clinton's Penny Post, Philadelphia, Pa.

L118a

Typo.

161L1 L188a (1c) **black** *22,500.*

Cook's Dispatch, Baltimore, Md.

Established by Isaac Cook

L119

1853

51L1 L119 (1c) **green,** *white* *4,000.* *3,000.*
Cut to shape *1,500.*
On cover —

Cancellation: Red straight-line "I cook."

Cornwell's Madison Square Post Office, New York, N.Y.

Established by Daniel H. Cornwell. Sold to H.W. Bentley.

L120

1856 **Typo.**

52L1 L120 (1c) **red,** *blue* *1,500.* —
52L2 L120 (1c) **red** 250. *600.*
On cover, tied by handstamp — *10,000.*
Pair —

Cancellation: Black oval "Cornwall's Madison Square Post Office." Covers also bear black boxed "Paid Swarts."

Cressman & Co.'s Penny Post, Philadelphia, Pa.

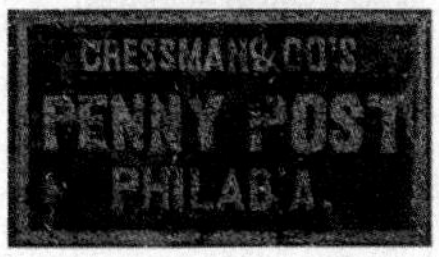

L121

1856

Glazed Surface Paper

53L1 L121 (1c) **gold,** *black* *350.* *350.*
Pair *1,200.*
53L2 L121 (1c) **gold,** *lilac,* on cover, acid tied *25,000.*

The vertical pair of No. 53L1 is unique. No. 53L2 also is unique.

Cancellation: Acid. (See D.O. Blood & Co. Nos. 15L13-15L16.)

Crosby's City Post, New York, N.Y.

Established by Oliver H. Crosby. Stamps printed by J.W. Scott & Co.

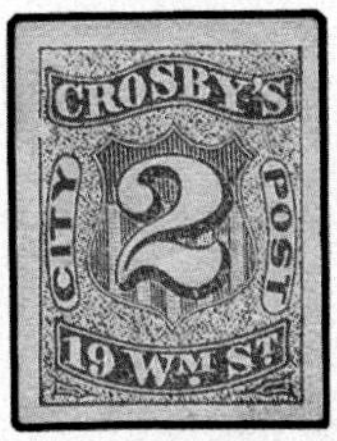

L123

1870 **Typo.**

Printed in sheets 25 (5x5), imprint at left.

54L1 L123 2c **carmine** (shades) 1.00 *50.00*
On cover *750.00*
Pair —
Sheet of 25 50.00

Cancellation: Black oval "Crosby's City Post."

Cummings' City Post, New York, N.Y.

Established by A. H. Cummings.

L124

1844 **Glazed Surface Paper** **Typo.**

55L1 L124 2c **black,** *rose* *1,000.*
On cover, tied, with certificate *5,750.*
On cover, not tied, with certificate —
55L2 L124 2c **black,** *green* *650.*
On cover *2,500.*
55L3 L124 2c **black,** *yellow* *750.*
On cover, tied by handstamp *2,000.*
On cover, not tied, with certificate *1,250.*

Cancellations: Red boxed "FREE," red boxed "PAID AHC," black cork (3 types).

L125

55L4 L125 2c **black,** *green* *750.00* *750.00*
55L5 L125 2c **black,** *olive* *750.00* *750.00*

L126

55L7 L126 2c **black,** *vermilion* *8,250.*
On cover, uncanceled, with certificate *22,000.*

As L124, but "Cummings" erased on cliche

55L8 L124 2c **black,** *vermilion* —

Nos. 55L7 on cover and 55L8 each are unique.

Cutting's Despatch Post, Buffalo, N.Y.

Established by Thomas S. Cutting

L127

Cut to shape

1847

Glazed Surface Paper

56L1 L127 2c **black,** *vermilion* —
On cover, cut to shape, uncanceled, with certificate *22,000.*

Davis's Penny Post, Baltimore, Md.

Established by William D. Davis and brother.

L128

1856 **Typeset**

Several varieties

57L1 L128 (1c) **black,** *lilac* *2,750.*
On cover, tied by handstamp *11,000.*
a. "Pennq," pos. 2 *8,250.* *8,250.*

Cancellation: Red company circle.

Deming's Penny Post, Frankford, Pa.

Established by Sidney Deming

L129

1854 **Litho.**

58L1 L129 (1c) **black,** *grayish* *5,750.*
On cover, with 3c #11 *18,000.*

Douglas' City Despatch, New York, N.Y.

Established by George H. Douglas

L130

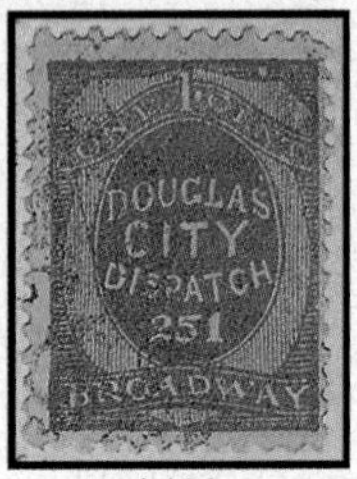

L131

Printed in sheets of 25

1879 **Typo.** ***Perf. 11***

59L1 L130 (1c) **pink** 10.00 *15.00*
On cover *300.00*
a. Imperf. 30.00 —
59L2 L130 (2c) **blue** 10.00 *15.00*
On cover, tied by handstamp *500.00*
a. Imperf. 50.00 —
b. Printed on both sides —

Printed in sheets of 50 (10x5).

Perf. 11, 12 & Compound

59L3 L131 1c **vermilion** 15.00 *35.00*
On cover *325.00*
a. Imperf. 1.00 —
59L4 L131 1c **orange** 25.00 *50.00*
On cover, tied by handstamp *600.00*
59L5 L131 1c **blue** 30.00 *50.00*
On cover *300.00*
a. Imperf. 1.00 —
59L6 L131 1c **slate blue** 20.00 25.00
a. Imperf. 7.50 —

Cancellations on Nos. 59L1-59L6: Ornate purple design, purple circular design composed of bars and wedges.

Imperforates are believed to be remainders sold by the printer.

Dupuy & Schenck, New York, N.Y.

Established by Henry J. Dupuy and Jacob H. Schenck, formerly carriers for City Despatch Post and U. S. City Despatch Post.

Beehive — L132

1846-47 **Engr.**

60L1 L132 (1c) **black,** glazed paper 175. *300.*
On cover, tied by handstamp *1,750.*
On cover, tied by ms. *1,250.*
60L2 L132 (1c) **black,** *gray* 175. *300.*
On cover, tied by handstamp *1,600.*

Cancellation: Red "PAID."

Eagle City Post, Philadelphia, Pa.

Established by W. Stait, an employee of Adams' Express Co.

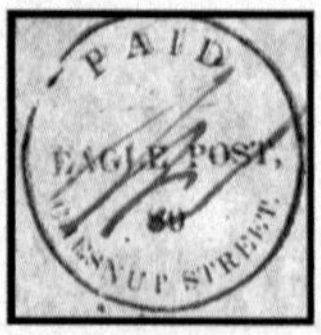

L133

Black manuscript "WS" on used examples

1847 **Pelure Paper** **Typeset**

61L1 L133 (2c) **black,** *grayish* *14,000. 10,000.*
Cut to shape, on cover —

No. 61L1 unused is unique. Value reflects a 1997 auction sale.

L134

L135

Two types: 39 and 46 points around circle

1846 **Litho.**

61L2 L134 (2c) **black** 125.00 *250.00*
On cover, tied by handstamp *1,500.*
On cover, not tied *1,000.*
Block of 4 600.00
a. Tete beche pair 500.00
Block of 18, containing 4 tete beche pairs *4,000.*

Paper varies in thickness.
Five types identified of Nos. 61L3-61L4.

1850

61L3 L135 (1c) **red,** *bluish* 225.00 225.00
On cover, not tied, with certificate *2,250.*
61L4 L135 (1c) **blue,** *bluish* 175.00 250.00
On cover, tied by handstamp *6,500.*
On cover, not tied *400.00*
Block of 4 *1,150.*

Cancellations on Nos. 61L2-61L4: Red "PAID" in large box, red circular "Stait's at Adams Express."

East River Post Office, New York, N. Y.

Established by Jacob D. Clark and Henry Wilson in 1850, and sold to Sigmund Adler in 1852.

L136

1852 **Typo.**

62L1 L136 (1c) **black,** *rose* (on cover) —

L137

L138

1852-54 **Litho.**

62L3 L137 (1c) **black,** *green,* glazed *1,000.* —
On cover, not tied —

1855

62L4 L138 (1c) **black,** *green,* glazed 250.00 250.00
On cover *800.00*
On cover, not tied *400.00*
Vertical pair *2,500.*

The unique No. 62L4 pair is the only recorded multiple of any of the East River Post Office stamps.

Eighth Avenue Post Office, New York, N.Y.

L139

1852 **Typo.**

63L1 L139 **red,** on cover *19,000.*

One example known, uncanceled on cover.

Empire City Dispatch, New York, N.Y.

Established by J. Bevan & Son and almost immediately suppressed by the Government.

L140

1881 **Typo.** **Laid Paper** ***Perf. 12***

64L1 L140 **black,** *green* 1.50
Block of 4 7.50
a. Imperf. —
b. Horiz. pair, imperf. btwn. 85.00
c. Vert. pair, imperf. btwn. 85.00

Essex Letter Express, New York, N.Y.

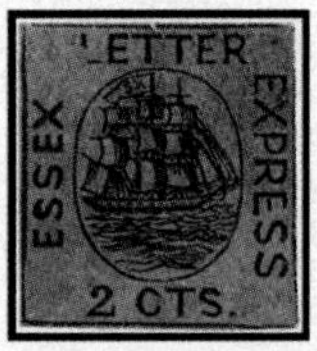

L141

1856 **Glazed Surface Paper** **Typo.**

65L1 L141 2c **black,** *red* *1,250.*

Though uncanceled examples exist affixed to covers, some authorities doubt that No. 65L1 was placed in use.

Faunce's Penny Post, Atlantic City, N.J.

Established in 1884 by Ancil Faunce to provide local delivery of letters to and from the post office. Discontinued in 1887.

L141a

1885 **Die cut**

152L1 L141a (1c) **black,** *red* 225. 350.
On cover *1,500.*

Jabez Fearey & Co.'s Mustang Express, Newark, N.J.

Established by Jabez Fearey, Local Agent of the Pacific & Atlantic Telegraph Co.

L142

1887 (?) **Glazed Surface Paper** **Typeset**

66L1 L142 **black,** *red* *275.00*
On cover —

Some authorities consider this item to be an express company label rather than a stamp.

Fiske & Rice

Authorities consider items of this design to be express company labels rather than stamps.

Floyd's Penny Post, Chicago, Ill.

Established by John R. Floyd early in 1860, operated by him until June 20, 1861, then continued by Charles W. Mappa.

John R. Floyd — L144

1860 **Typo.**

68L1 L144 (1c) **blue** (shades) — 125.
On cover, tied by handstamp *1,000.*
On cover with 3c #26 —
On cover with 3c #65 *1,500.*
Pair 275.
Strip of 4 *1,250.*
68L2 L144 (1c) **brown** *500.* *1,000.*
On cover *4,250.*

68L3 L144 (1c) **green** 4,500. 3,250.
On cover —
On 3c pink entire 27,500.

Cancellations: Black circle "Floyd's Penny Post Chicago," black circle "Floyd's Penny Post" and sunburst, black or blue oval "Floyd's Penny Post Chicago."

Franklin City Despatch Post, N.Y.

(See Bouton's Manhattan Express.)

Frazer & Co., Cincinnati, Ohio.

Established by Hiram Frazer. Stamps used while he was a Cincinnati letter carrier. Stamps of designs L146 and L147 were carrier stamps when used on cover betweeen Feb, 3, 1848 and June 30, 1849.

L145

Cut to shape

1845

Glazed Surface Paper

69L1 L145 2c **black,** *green,* on cover —

L146

L147

1845-51 **Wove Paper** **Litho.**

69L2 L146 2c **black,** *pink* — 3,500.
On cover, ms. tied 6,750.
69L3 L146 2c **black,** *green* 2,500. 2,750.
On 1847 cover, tied by handstamp 11,000.
On cover, not tied 3,500.
69L4 L146 2c **black,** *yellow* 2,500. 2,500.
69L5 L146 2c **black,** *grayish* 2,500. 2,500.
On cover, tied by handstamp 7,000.

Two stamps of type L146 show manual ms. erasure of "& Co."

1848-51

69L6 L147 2c **black,** *rose* 2,750.
On 1848 cover, not tied, with certificate 6,500.
69L7 L147 2c **black,** *blue* (shades) 3,500. —
69L8 L147 2c **black,** *yellow* 2,750.
On 1848 part-printed notice 7,500.

Hiram Frazer was a government letter carrier until June 5, 1849. Therefore, any usage before that date is a government-carrier usage, not a local-post usage.

Freeman & Co.'s Express, New York, N.Y.

L147a

1855 (?) **Litho.**

164L1 L147a (25c) **blue** 3,500.
On cover, not tied, with certificate —

Friend's Boarding School, Barnesville, Ohio.

(Barclay W. Stratton, Supt.)

On Nov. 6, 1877 the school committee decided to charge the students one cent for each letter carried to or from the post office, one and a half miles away. Adhesive labels were prepared and sold for one cent each. Their sale and use continued until 1884.

L147b — Type I

L147b — Type II

L147b — Type III

Three main types and sizes of frame

1877 **Typo.**

151L1 L147b (1c) **black** 175.00 —
On cover, uncanceled, affixed to backflap 400.00
On cover, tied by handstamp, with 3c #158 2,400.
On cover, tied by handstamp, with 2c #210 2,750.

No. 151L1 was usually affixed to the back of the envelope and left uncanceled.

Gahagan & Howe City Express, San Francisco, Calif.

Established by Dennis Gahagan and C. E. B. Howe, as successors to John C. Robinson, proprietor of the San Francisco Letter Express. Sold in 1865 to William E. Loomis, who later purchased the G. A. Carnes business. Loomis used the adhesive stamps and handstamps of these posts, changing the Carnes stamp by erasing his name.

L148

L149

1849-70 **Typeset**

70L1 L148 5c **light blue** 1,200. 800.
70L2 L149 (5c) **blue** 150. 400.
a. Tete beche pair 450.
Sheet of 20, with 4 tete beche pairs —

Sheets of No. 70L2 contain five vertical rows of 4, the first two rows being reversed against the others, making horizontal tete beche pairs with wide margins between. The pairs were not evenly locked up in the form. There are five different types of No. 70L2.

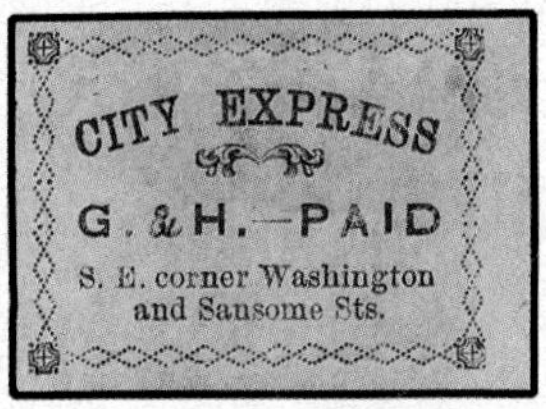

L150

70L3 L150 (5c) **black** 40.00 45.00
Pair 100.00
Strip of 3 175.00

Overprinted "X" in Blue

70L4 L150 10c **black** 1,500.

Cancellations: Blue or black oval "Gahagan & Howe," blue or black oval "San Francisco Letter Express" and horseman (Robinson), blue or black oval "PAID" (Loomis).

Glen Haven Daily Mail, Glen Haven, N.Y.

Glen Haven was located at the head of Skaneateles Lake, Cayuga County, N.Y., until 1910 when the City of Syracuse, having purchased the land for reservoir purposes, razed all the buildings.

Glen Haven, by 1848, had become a famous Water Cure resort, with many sanitariums conducted there. The hamlet had a large summer colony interested in dress reform under the leadership of Amelia Jenks Bloomer; also antislavery, and other reform movements.

A local post was established by the hotel and sanitarium managements for their guests' convenience to deliver mail to the U.S. post offices at Homer or Scott, N.Y. The local stamps were occasionally pen canceled. They are known tied to cover with the Homer or Scott town postmark when the local stamp was placed adjacent to the government stamp and received the cancellation accidentally. The local stamps are only known used in conjunction with government stamps.

L151

L152

1854-58 **Typeset**

Several varieties of each

71L1 L151 1c **black,** *dark green* 1,000.
a. "Gien" instead of "Glen" 3,500.
On cover, uncanceled, with 3c #26, with certificate 6,250.

No. 71L1a unused (actually uncanceled on piece) and on cover with #26 each are unique.

Glazed Surface Paper

71L2 L152 1c **black,** *green* 500. 500.
On cover 2,000.
On cover, tied by handstamp. with 3c #11 3,750.

Links at corners — L153

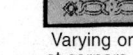

Varying ornaments at corners — L153a

Several varieties of each

Glazed Surface Paper

71L3 L153 1c **black,** *green* 200. 225.
On cover 2,000.
On cover, tied by handstamp, with 3c #11 1,750.
On cover, not tied, with 3c #11 500.
Pair 700.
71L4 L153a 1c **black,** *green* 300. 350.
On cover 1,000.
On 3c entire #U9, tied by handstamp 1,000.
"Block" of 3 900.00

The strip of 3 of No. 71L4 is the only known multiple of any Glen Haven stamp. It has faults and is valued thus.

Gordon's City Express, New York, N. Y.

Established by Samuel B. Gordon

L154

1848-52 **Typo.** **Surface Colored Paper**

72L1 L154 2c **black,** *vermilion* 7,000.
On cover, uncanceled, with certificate 15,000.
72L2 L154 2c **black,** *green* 150. 175.
On cover 650.

Glazed Surface Paper

72L3 L154 2c **black,** *green* 125. 200.
On cover 650.

Cancellation: Small black or red "PAID."

Grafflin's Baltimore Despatch, Baltimore, Md.

Established by Joseph Grafflin; operated from Apr. 1, 1855, until June 30, 1863

L155

Printed in sheets of 49

1856				Litho.
73L1	L155	1c **black**	200.	*350.*
		On cover, tied by handstamp		*4,000.*
		On cover, tied by handstamp, with 3c #11		*5,000.*
		Block of 4	*1,050.*	

Originals show traces of a fine horizontal line through tops of most of the letters in "BALTIMORE."

Guy's City Despatch, Philadelphia, Pa.

Established by F. A. Guy, who employed 8 carriers.

L156

Sheets of 25 (5x5)

1879		Typo.	*Perf. 11, 12, 12½*	
74L1	L156	(1c) **pink**	30.00	35.00
		On cover, tied by handstamp		800.00
		Block of 4	150.00	
a.		Imperf., pair	—	
74L2	L156	(1c) **blue**	45.00	60.00
		On cover, tied by handstamp		1,500.
		Block of 4	225.00	
a.		Imperf., pair	—	
b.		(1c) **Ultramarine**	*75.00*	*100.00*

Cancellation: Purple company oval.

Guy's City Despatch was in operation from April to June, 1879. When Guy's was suppressed, the remainders were sold to a New York stamp dealer.

Hackney & Bolte Penny Post, Atlantic City, N.J.

Established in 1886 by Evan Hackney and Charles Bolte to provide delivery of mail to and from the post office. Discontinued in 1887.

L156a

Die cut

153L1	L156a	(1c) **black,** *red*	250.	375.
		On cover		*1,500.*
		On cover, tied by handstamp, with 2c #210		*5,000.*

Hale & Co.

Established by James W. Hale at New York, N.Y., to carry mail to points in New England, New York State, Philadelphia and Baltimore. Stamps sold at 6 cents each or "20 for $1.00."

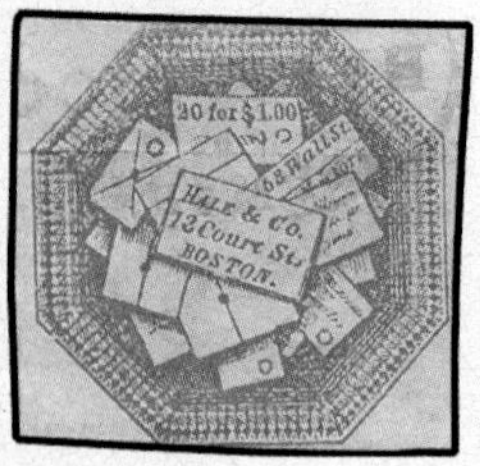

L157

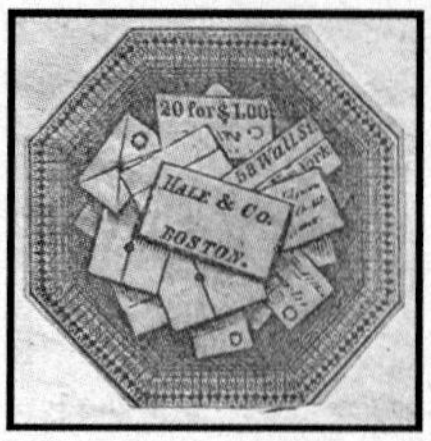

L158

Printed in sheets of 20 (5x4)

Pelure paper was used for initial printings, with medium wove paper used subsequently.

1844				Typo.
75L1	L157	(6c) **light blue** (shades)	65.00	40.00
		Cut to shape		17.50
		On cover, tied by handstamp		500.00
		Cut to shape on cover, tied by handstamp		200.00
		Strip of 3 on cover, tied by handstamp		*7,000.*
		Strip of 3 on cover, not tied		*2,750.*
a.		Pelure paper		—
75L2	L157	(6c) **red,** *bluish*	*300.00*	*300.00*
		Cut to shape		75.00
		On cover, tied by handstamp		*2,500.*
		On cover, not tied		*500.00*
		Cut to shape on cover, tied by handstamp		*1,000.*
		Pair on cover		—
		Ms. "23 State," cut to shape		*1,900.*
		On cover		*4,000.*
a.		Pelure paper		—

Two covers recorded showing the manuscript change of address.

Same Handstamped in Black or Red, "City Despatch Office, 23 State St."

75L3	L157	(6c) **red,** *bluish* (Bk), cut to shape	*2,000.*	
		Pair, partly cut to shape	*44,000.*	
75L4	L157	(6c) **blue** (R), cut to shape	*2,000.*	

No. 75L3 single and pair each are unique.

No. 75L3 and 75L4 represent the first handstamped overprints in philately.

Same as Type L157 but street address omitted

75L5	L158	(6c) **blue** (shades)	40.00	20.00
		Cut to shape		5.00
		On cover, tied by handstamp		450.00
		Cut to shape on cover, tied by handstamp		200.00
		Pair on cover		700.00
		Strip of 3 on cover, not tied		—
		Pair	*500.00*	
		Block of 9	—	
		Block of 15	*9,500.*	
		Sheet of 20 (5x4)	*17,000.*	
		Ms. "23 State St.," on cover, tied by handstamp		*7,500.*

Cancellations on Nos. 75L1-75L5: Large red "PAID," red, black or blue oval "Hale & Co." (several types and cities), small red ornamental framed box (several types), red negative monogram "WE," magenta ms. "NB" (New Bedford).

The No. 75L5 sheet of 20 is unique.

Same as Type L158 Handstamped in Red "Office / 23 State St"

75L6	L158	(6c) **blue,** on cover		—

No. 75L6 is unique.

Hall & Mills' Despatch Post, New York, N.Y.

Established by Gustavus A. Mills and A. C. Hall.

L159

Several Varieties

1847		Glazed Surface Paper		Typeset
76L1	L159	(2c) **black,** *green*	*300.*	*300.*
		On cover, tied by handstamp		*2,500.*
		On cover with 5c #1		*2,500.*

T.A. Hampton City Despatch, Philadelphia, Pa.

L159a

L159b

Several Varieties of L159a

1847		Cut to shape		Typeset
77L1	L159a	(2c) **black**	*1,500.*	
		On cover, tied by handstamp		*14,000.*
		On cover, uncanceled, with certificate		*5,000.*
77L2	L159b	**black,** on cover		*13,000.*

Only one cover known with No. 77L1 tied by handstamp. Five or six covers are known with stamp uncanceled.

Two covers known with No. 77L2, each with stamp canceled, not tied. May 23 cover with certificate is valued above. Second cover is undated Valentine cover.

A handstamp similar to type L159b with denomination "2cts" or "3c" instead of "PAID." in center has been used as a postmark.

Hanford's Pony Express, New York, N.Y.

Established by John W. Hanford.

L160

1845		Glazed Surface Paper		Typo.
78L1	L160	2c **black,** *orange yellow* (shades)	400.	400.
		Cut to shape		60.
		On cover, tied by handstamp		*2,250.*
		On cover, not tied		*1,500.*

Cancellation: Small red "PAID."

The handstamp in black or red formerly listed as Nos. 78LU1-78LU6 is illustrated in the Local Handstamped Covers section. It was used as a postmark and there is no evidence that any prepaid handstamped envelopes or lettersheets were ever sold.

George S. Harris City Despatch Post, Philadelphia, Pa.

L160a

L160b

1847 (?) **Typeset**

79L1 L160a (2c) **black,** on cover —
79L2 L160b **black,** on cover *30,000.*

One example each known of Nos. 79L1-79L2, each uncanceled on cover, No. 79L2 with certificate.

Hartford, Conn. Mail Route

L161

Plate of 12 (6x2) varieties

1844 **Glazed Surface Paper** **Engr.**

80L1 L161 (5c) **black,** *yellow* *1,250.* *2,000.*
On cover, not canceled *11,000.*
Pair *5,000.*
Pair on cover, not canceled *32,500.*
80L3 L161 **black,** *pink* *3,500.*

Chemically affected examples of No. 80L1 appear as buff, and of No. 80L3 as salmon.

Cancellations are usually initials or words ("S," "W," "South," etc.) in black ms. This may indicate destination or routing.

Hill's Post, Boston, Mass.

Established by Oliver B. Hill

L162

1849 **Typo.**

81L1 L162 1c **black,** *rose,* on cover, tied by handstamp *7,500.*
On cover, canceled but not tied, with certificate *6,500.*

Only one No. 81L1 tied to cover recorded. Six covers recorded bearing No. 80L1 not tied, all but one of those also uncanceled.

A. M. Hinkley's Express Co., New York, N.Y.

Organized by Abraham M. Hinkley, Hiram Dixon and Hiram M. Dixon, in 1855, and business transferred to the Metropolitan Errand & Carrier Express Co. in same year.

L163

Sheets of 64 (8x8)

1855 **Litho.**

82L1 L163 1c **red,** *bluish* *650.00*
Block of 4 —
a. Tete-beche pair —

It is doubtful that No. 82L1 was ever placed in use.

Only one example of No. 82L1a is recorded. It is contained in a block of 16 of No. 82L1.

Reprints exist on white paper somewhat thicker than the originals.

Homan's Empire Express, New York, N.Y.

Established by Richard S. Homan

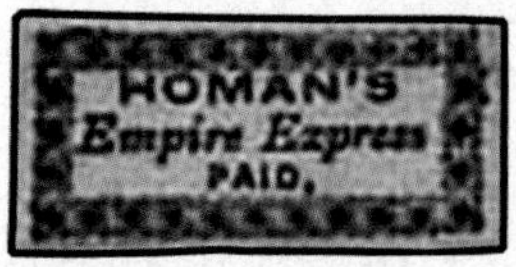

L164

Several varieties

1852 **Typeset**

83L1 L164 **black,** *yellow* — —
a. "1" for "I" in "PAID" *9,750.*

No. 83L1a is unique. It is affixed to a cover front, uncanceled, with certificate.

Hopedale Penny Post, Milford, Mass.

Hopedale was a large farm community southwest of Milford, Mass. The community meeting of Feb. 2, 1849, voted to arrange for regular transportation of mail to the nearest post office, which was at Milford, a mile and a half distant, at a charge of 1c a letter. A complete history of this community may be found in "The Hopedale Community," published in 1897.

Rayed asterisks in corners — L165

Plain asterisks in corners — L166

Several varieties of Types L165-L166

1849 **Glazed Surface Paper** **Typeset**

84L1 L165 (1c) **black,** *pink* *800.00* *800.00*
On cover with 3c #11, handstamp tied *3,750.*
On cover with 3c #11, not canceled *1,250.*
84L2 L166 (1c) **black,** *pink* *1,000.* *1,000.*

Types L165 and L166 probably were printed together in a single small plate.

L167

Wove Paper **Typo.**

84L3 L167 (1c) **black,** *yellow* — *2,400.*
Cut to shape *900.*
On cover —
84L4 L167 (1c) **black,** *pink* *600.* *600.*
Pair *4,500.*

The No. 84L4 pair is unique, defective at top. It is the only recorded multiple of any Hopedale Penny Post issue.

J. A. Howell's City Despatch, Philadelphia, Pa.

L167a

184? **Typo.**

165L1 L167a **black** —

Hoyt's Letter Express, Rochester, N.Y.

David Hoyt, agent at Rochester for the express company of Livingston, Wells & Pomeroy, operated a letter and package express by boats on the Genesee Canal between Dansville, N.Y., and Rochester, where connection was also made with Pomeroy's Letter Express.

L168

Several varieties

1844 **Glazed Surface Paper** **Typeset**

85L1 L168 (5c) **black,** *vermilion* *4,000.* —
a. "Lettcr" instead of "Letter" —
Pair, #85L1, 85L1a, on cover front —

Humboldt Express, Nevada

A branch of Langton's Pioneer Express, connecting with the main line of Pioneer Express at Carson City, Nevada, and making tri-weekly trips to adjacent points.

L169

1863 **Litho.**

86L1 L169 25c **brown** *1,750.* *1,250.*
Pair *2,750.*
On cover (U.S. Envelopes Nos. U34 or U35) *40,000.*
On cover with 3c #65 —

Cancellations: Blue oval "Langton's Pioneer Express Unionville." Red "Langton & Co."

Hussey's Post, New York, N.Y.

Established by George Hussey.

Reprints available for postage are so described.

L170

L171

1854 **Litho.**

87L1 L170 (1c) **blue** *500.*
On cover, tied by handstamp *2,750.*
On cover, with U.S. 3c (#11) —

1856

87L2 L171 (1c) **black** *300.* *200.*
On cover, tied by handstamp *1,850.*
87L3 L171 (1c) **red** *200.*
On cover, tied by handstamp *750.*

Cancellation on Nos. 87L1-87L3: Black "FREE."

L172

L173

1858

87L4 L172 1c **brown red** 45. *125.*
On cover, tied by handstamp *450.*
Pair on cover *1,000.*
87L5 L172 1c **black** *175.* —
On cover —
Block of 4 —
Strip of 7 —

Cancellation on Nos. 87L4-87L5: Black circle "1ct PAID HUSSEY 50 Wm. ST," date in center.

The No. 87L5 block of 4 and strip of 7 are unique.

1858

87L6 L173 (1c) **black** 5.00 —
On cover —
87L7 L173 (1c) **rose red** 5.00 —
On cover —
Sheet of 46 *350.00*
87L8 L173 (1c) **red** 60.00 —
On cover —
Sheet of 46 —

Type L173 was printed in sheets of 46: 5 horizontal rows of 8, one row of 6 sideways at botton. Type L173 saw little, if any, commercial use and was probably issued mainly for collectors. Covers exist, many with apparently contemporaneous corner cards. On-cover stamps bear a black HUSSEY'S POST handstamp, but most if not all of Nos. 87L6-87L8 were canceled after the post ceased to operate.

L174

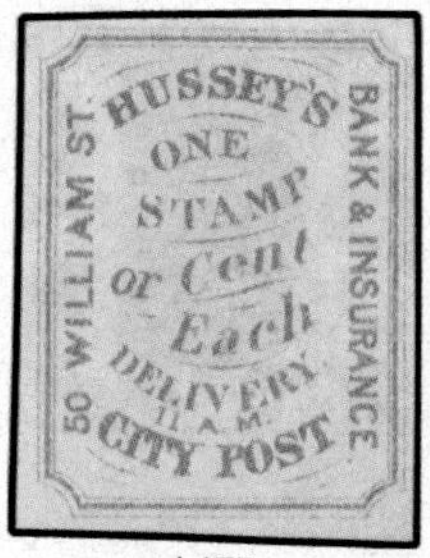

L175

1858 **Typo.**

87L9 L174 (1c) **blue** 5.00

1859 **Litho.**

87L10 L175 1c **rose red** 15.00 *40.00*
On cover *400.00*

No. 87L10 in orange red is not known to have been placed in use.

Cancellations: Black "FREE," black company circle "1 CT PAID HUSSEY 50 WM ST.," no date in center (smaller than cancel on Nos. 87L4-87L5).

87L11 L175 1c **lake** —
87L12 L175 1c **black** —

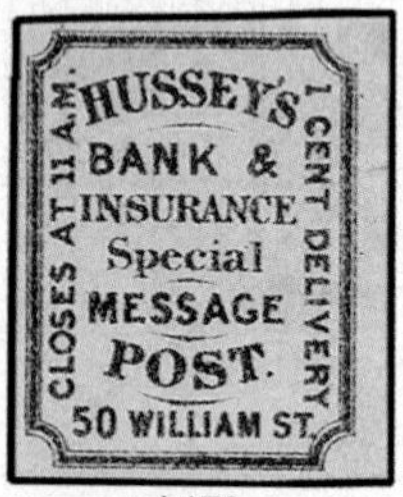

L176

L177

1862

87L13 L176 1c **black** 25.00
87L14 L176 1c **blue** 15.00 *25.00*
On cover *450.00*
87L15 L176 1c **green** 20.00
On cover *450.00*
87L16 L176 1c **red** 30.00
87L17 L176 1c **red brown** 30.00
87L18 L176 1c **brown** 30.00
87L19 L176 1c **lake** —
87L20 L176 1c **purple** 30.00
87L21 L176 1c **yellow** 30.00

Similar to L174 but has condensed "50" and shows a short flourish line over the "I" of "DELIVERY."

Printed in sheets of 49

1862

87L22 L177 (1c) **blue** 3.00 *25.00*
On cover —

L178

Similar to L171, but no dots in corners — L179

Printed in sheets of 30

1863

87L23 L178 (1c) **blue** 7.50
87L24 L179 (1c) **black** 5.00
Sheet of 30 225.00
87L25 L179 (1c) **red** 6.50
Sheet of 30 250.00
On cover with 6c #115 *17,500.*

See No. 87L52.

L180

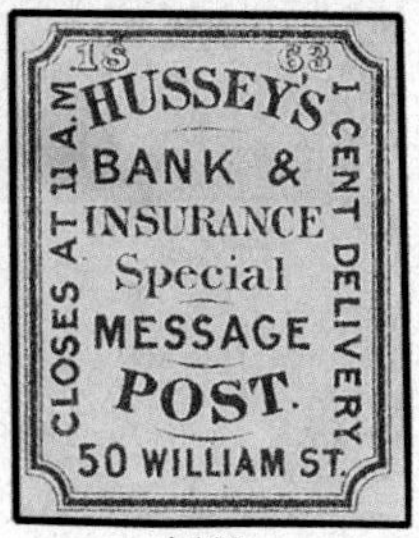

L182

87L26 L180 1c **brown red** 5.00 *25.00*
Block of 4 25.00
On cover, tied by handstamp *450.00*

A so-called "reprint" of No. 87L26, made for J. W. Scott, has a colored flaw extending diagonally upward from the "I" in "CITY."

Reprints of types L173, L174, L178, L179 and L180 were made in 1875-76 on thicker paper in approximately normal colors and were available for postage.

1863

Dated 1863

87L27 L182 1c **blue** 20.00
Cut to shape 12.50
On cover, tied by handstamp *500.00*
87L28 L182 1c **green** 27.50 —
Cut to shape 14.00
On cover, tied by handstamp *550.00*
87L29 L182 1c **yellow** 25.00 —
Cut to shape 12.50
On cover, tied by handstamp *500.00*
87L30 L182 1c **brown** 27.50
Cut to shape 14.00
87L31 L182 1c **red brown** 30.00
Cut to shape 15.00
87L32 L182 1c **red** 27.50
Cut to shape 14.00
87L33 L182 1c **black** 40.00
Cut to shape 20.00
87L34 L182 1c **violet** 40.00
Cut to shape 20.00
87L35 L182 2c **brown** 40.00 *75.00*
Cut to shape 20.00
On cover, tied by handstamp *650.00*

The 2c blue dated 1863 exists only as a counterfeit.

1865

Dated 1865

87L38 L182 2c **blue** 35.00 *45.00*
On cover, tied by handstamp *475.00*

1867

Dated 1867

87L39 L182 2c **blue** 45.00 40.00
On cover, tied by handstamp *450.00*

1868

Dated 1868

87L40 L182 2c **blue** 40.00 *65.00*
On cover, tied by handstamp *500.00*

1869

Dated 1870

87L41 L182 2c **blue** 45.00 *70.00*
On cover, tied by handstamp *500.00*

1871

Dated 1871

87L42 L182 2c **blue** 40.00 *65.00*
On cover, tied by handstamp *750.00*

L183

L184

1872

Wove Paper

87L43 L183 **black** 5.00 *20.0*
On cover, tied by handstamp *300.0*
Pair on cover, tied by handstamp *1,500*
87L44 L183 **red lilac** 9.00 *40.0*
On cover, tied by handstamp *300.0*
87L45 L183 **blue** 6.00 *40.0*
On cover, tied by handstamp *300.0*
Pair on cover, tied by handstamp *750.0*
87L46 L183 **green** 10.00 *45.0*
On cover, tied by handstamp *300.0*

Sheets contain four panes of 28 each. Double periods afte "A.M." on two stamps in two panes, and on four stamps in the other two panes.

Covers show postmark reading: "HUSSEY'S SPECIAL-MES SENGER EXPRESS-PAID-54 PINE ST."

1872

Thick Laid paper

87L47 L184 **black** 10.00 *35.0*
On cover —
Block of 4 45.00
87L48 L184 **yellow** 17.50 *65.0*
87L49 L184 **red brown** 17.50 *50.0*
On cover *200.0*
87L50 L184 **red** 17.50 *40.0*
On cover —

L185

L186

1873

Thin Wove Paper

87L51 L185 2c **black** 75.00 *150.0*
On cover *500.0*

A reprint of No. 87L51, believed to have been made for J. W. Scott, shows a 4mm break in the bottom frameline under "54."

Type of 1863

1875

Thick Wove Paper

87L52 L179 (1c) **blue** *750.00*

1875

L186 in imitation of L180, but no corner dots, "S" for "$," etc.

87L53 L186 1c **black** 2.00

Some authorities believe Nos. 87L52-87L53 are imitations made from new stones. Attributed to J. W. Scott.

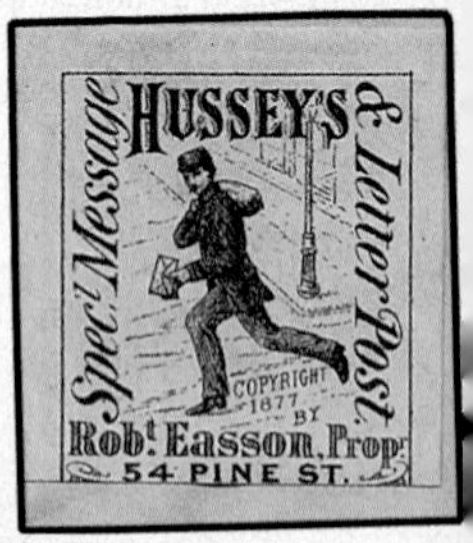

"Copyright 1877" — L188

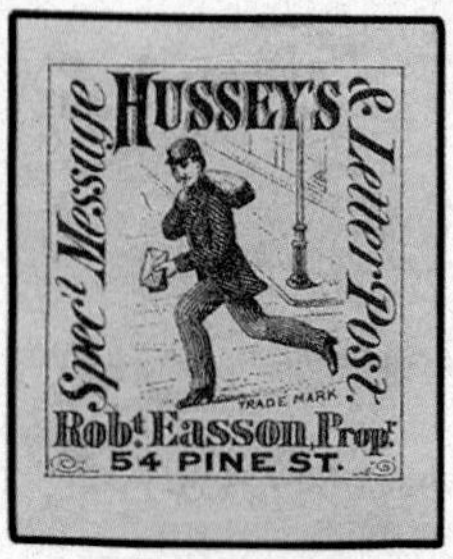

L188a

1877

Thick Wove Paper

87L55 L188 **black** *175.00* —
On cover *600.00*

Error of design, used provisionally. Stamp was never copyrighted. Printed singly.

87L56 L188a **black** *350.00*

Thin Wove Paper

87L57 L188a **blue** 45.00
87L58 L188a **rose** 30.00
On cover —

Perf. 12½

87L59 L188a **blue** 3.00 *10.00*
On cover *250.00*
a. Imperf. horizontally, pair —
87L60 L188a **rose** 3.00 *10.00*
On cover *250.00*

"TRADE MARK" small — L189

"TRADE MARK" medium — L190

"TRADE MARK" larger, touching "s" of "Easson." — L191

1878 **Wove Paper** ***Perf. 11, 11½, 11x12, 12***

87L61 L189 **blue** 15.00 *50.00*
On cover, tied by handstamp *150.00*
87L62 L189 **carmine** 12.50 *40.00*
On cover, tied by handstamp *200.00*
87L63 L189 **black** 100.00

Nos. 87L61-87L63 exist imperforate.

Perf. 11, 12, 12½, 14, 16 and Compound

87L64 L190 **blue** 5.00 *17.50*
On cover, tied by handstamp *200.00*
87L65 L190 **red** 5.00 *10.00*
On cover, tied by handstamp *150.00*
87L66 L190 **black** —

The existence of No. 87L66 either perforated or as an imperf reprint has been questioned by specialists. The editors would like to see authenticated evidence of its existence.

Nos. 87L64-87L65 imperf. are reprints.

1879 ***Perf. 11, 12, and Compound***

87L67 L191 **blue** 3.00 *10.00*
On cover, tied by handstamp *300.00*

1880 ***Imperf.***

87L70 L191 **blue** 4.00 *50.00*
On cover, tied by handstamp *450.00*
87L71 L191 **red** 5.00 *75.00*
87L72 L191 **black** 4.00

The authenticity of Nos. 87L70-87L72 has not been fully established.

L192

Two types of L192:
I. Imprint "N. F. Seebeck, 97 Wall St. N. Y." is in lower tablet below "R Easson, etc."
II. Imprint in margin below stamp.

1880 **Glazed Surface Wove Paper** ***Perf. 12***

87L73 L192 **brown,** type I 10.00 *20.00*
On cover, tied by handstamp *250.00*
Block of 4 —
a. Type II 3.00 *5.00*
On cover, tied by handstamp *250.00*
b. Horiz. pair, imperf. between 50.00
c. Imperf., pair, type I 50.00
87L74 L192 **ultramarine,** type I 12.50 *25.00*
On cover, tied by handstamp *350.00*
a. Imperf., pair —
Imperf (single) on cover *135.00*
b. Deep blue, type II 40.00
87L75 L192 **red,** type II 1.50 *3.50*
On cover, tied by handstamp *175.00*
Block of 4 6.50
a. Imperf, single on cover *150.00*
b. Horiz. pair, imperf between —

1882 ***Perf. 16, 12x16***

87L76 L192 **brown,** type I 12.50 *30.00*
On cover, tied by handstamp *125.00*
87L77 L192 **ultramarine,** type I 10.00 *20.00*
On cover, tied by handstamp *125.00*

Cancellations: Violet 3-ring target, violet ornamental "T." Imperf. impressions of Type I in various colors, on horizontally laid paper, ungummed, are color trials.

SPECIAL DELIVERY STAMPS

L181

Typographed; Numerals Inserted Separately

1863 **Glazed Surface Paper**

87LE1 L181 5c **black,** *vermilion* 2.00 *17.50*
On cover *350.00*
87LE2 L181 10c **gold,** *green* 2.50 *20.00*
On cover *350.00*
87LE3 L181 15c **gold,** *black* 3.50 *27.50*
On cover *400.00*
On cover with 1c #87L10, tied by handstamps —
87LE4 L181 20c **black** 2.00 *17.50*
On cover *400.00*
87LE5 L181 25c **gold,** *blue* 4.00 *40.00*
On cover *400.00*
87LE6 L181 30c **black,** *vermilion* —
87LE7 L181 50c **black,** *green* —

Nos. 87LE1-87LE7 on cover show Hussey handstamp cancellations in various types.

Nos. 87LE4 and 87LE5 are on unglazed paper, the latter surface colored. Ten minor varieties of each value, except the 30c and 50c, which have the figures in manuscript. Printed in two panes of 10, certain values exist in horizontal cross-gutter tete beche pairs.

Originals of the 5c to 20c have large figures of value. The 25c has condensed figures with decimal point. Reprints exist with both large and condensed figures. Reprints of the 25c also exist with serifs on large figures.

Most of the Hussey adhesives are known on cover, tied with Hussey Express postmarks. Many of these were canceled after the post ceased to operate as a mail carrier. "On cover" values are for original stamps used while the post was operating.

LETTERSHEETS AND WRAPPERS (No. 87LUP2)

L192a

L192b

1856 **Handstamped** **Inscribed: "82 Broadway"**

87LUP1 L192a **black** — *500.*

1858 **Inscribed: "50 William St. Basement"**

87LUP2 L192b **black,** *manila* — *600.*
With 1c #87L3, tied by handstamp *1,250.*
87LUP3 L192b **black** — *650.*
With 1c #87L2, tied by handstamp *2,750.*
With 1c #87L3, tied by handstamp *1,750.*

Nos. 87LUP1 and 87LUP3 appear on papers of various colors.

Jefferson Market P. O., New York, N. Y.

Established by Godfrey Schmidt

L193

1850 **Glazed Surface Paper** **Litho.**

88L1 L193 (2c) **black,** *pink* 9,750.
88L2 L193 (2c) **black,** *blue* —
On cover, tied by handstamp —
On cover, not tied *3,500.*

Four examples recorded of No. 88L1, all unused. Five No. 88L2 recorded, all on covers (two with stamp tied by handstamp).

Jenkins' Camden Dispatch, Camden, N. J.

Established by Samuel H. Jenkins and continued by William H. Jenkins.

George Washington — L194

There are two types of design L194.

1853-54 **Litho.**

89L1 L194 **black** (fine impression) (1854) 350.00 *450.00*
Block of 9 7,500.
On cover, not tied *1,000.*
On cover, tied by ms., with certificate *3,500.*

George Washington — L194a

Typo. from Woodcut

89L2 L194a **black,** *yellow* (coarse impression) (1853) *3,000.*
On cover, tied by ms., with certificate *6,500.*

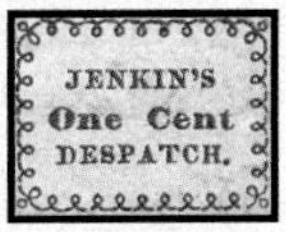

L195

Typeset

89L3 L195 1c **black,** *grayish* (1853) —
On cover, tied by ms. *17,500.*

No. 89L3 was probably the first stamp issued by Jenkins. Each of the four known examples is of a different type. One exampled is unused; three are recorded on cover (one of which is uncanceled).

Johnson & Co.'s City Despatch Post, Baltimore, Md.

Operated by Ezekiel C. Johnson, letter carrier

L196

1848 **Typeset**

90L1 L196 2c **black,** *lavender,* on cover, uncanceled *22,500.*

Two recorded examples of No. 90L1, each uncanceled on cover.

Jones' City Express, Brooklyn, N. Y.

George Washington — L197

1845 **Glazed Surface Paper** **Engr.**
91L1 L197 2c **black,** *pink* *1,000.* *1,500.*
On cover, not tied, with certificate *3,500.*

Cancellation: Red oval "Boyd's City Express Post."

Kellogg's Penny Post & City Despatch, Cleveland, Ohio

L198

1853 **Typo.**
92L1 L198 (1c) **vermilion** *1,750.*
On cover, tied by handstamp —
On cover, tied by handstamp, with 3c #11, with certificate *42,500.*
On cover, not tied, with 3c #11, with certificate *15,000.*
On 3c entire #U2, tied by handstamp *9,000.*

Cancellation: Black grid.

Kidder's City Express Post, Brooklyn, N.Y.

In 1847, Henry A. Kidder took over the post of Walton & Co., and with the brothers Isaac C. Snedeker and George H. Snedeker increased its scope. In 1851, the business was sold to the Snedekers. It was operated under the old name until 1853 when the Brooklyn City Express Post was founded.

L199

Stamps bear black manuscript "I S" control in two styles.

1847 **Glazed Surface Paper** **Typo.**
93L1 L199 2c **black,** *pale blue* *750.* 500.
On cover, tied by handstamp *6,000.*
On cover, not tied *4,500.*
Block of 4 3,500.

Cancellation: Red "PAID."

Reprinted on green paper.

Kurtz Union Despatch Post, New York, N.Y.

L200

Typeset; "T" in Black Ms.

1853
Glazed Surface Paper
94L1 L200 2c **black,** *green* *3,500.*

Langton & Co.
(See Humboldt Express.)

Ledger Dispatch, Brooklyn, N.Y.

Established by Edwin Pidgeon. Stamps reported to have been sold at 80 cents per 100. Suppressed after a few months.

L201

1882 **Typo.** ***Rouletted 12 in color***
95L1 L201 **rose** (shades) 300. *600.*
Block of 4 *1,500.*

Letter Express

Established by Henry Wells. Carried mail for points in Western New York, Chicago, Detroit and Duluth.

L202

L203

1844 **Glazed Surface Paper** **Typo.**
96L1 L202 5c **black,** *pink* 300.00 200.00
On cover, tied by ms. cancel *1,000.*
On cover, not tied *500.00*
Pair on cover, tied by ms. cancel *2,000.*
Pair on cover, not tied *1,000.*
Pair 700.00 450.00
Block of 10 *28,500.*
96L2 L202 5c **black,** *green* — 500.00
On cover, tied by ms. cancel *5,000.*
On cover, not tied *3,500.*
Pair *1,500.*
96L3 L203 10c **black,** *pink* — 500.00
On cover, tied by ms. cancel *1,500.*
On cover, not tied *750.00*
Pair *1,500.* *1,500.*
Strip of 3 *9,250.*
a. Bisect on cover, tied by ms. cancel —

No. 96L3a was sold as a horizontal or vertical bisect. It is known used singly for 5c (rare), or as two bisects for 10c (extremely rare). Stamps are known almost exclusively tied with black ms. "X" covering the cut, and can be authenticated by experts.

The block of 10 of No. 96L1 is the only block recorded of any Letter Express issue. Value represents actual auction sale price in 1999.

L204

96L4 L204 10c **black,** *scarlet* — *2,500.*
On cover, tied by ms. cancel, with certificate *9,250.*
a. Tete beche pair, one stamp a horiz. bisect, on piece *8,750.*

Cancellations: Red large partly boxed "PAID," red boxed "Boyd's City Express Post."

Locomotive Express Post

L205

1847 (?) **Handstamped**
97L1 L205 **black** —

Wm. E. Loomis Letter Express, San Francisco, Calif.

William E. Loomis established this post as the suc cessor to the Gahagan & Howe City Express, which he bought in 1865. He continued to use the Gahagan & Howe stamps unchanged. Later Loomis bough Carnes' City Letter Express. He altered the Carnes stamp by erasing "CARNES}" from the plate anc adding the address below the oval: "S.E. cor. Sans'e & Wash'n."

L206

1868 **Typo.**
98L1 L206 (5c) **rose** 300.00 *650.0*
On cover, tied by ms. *4,250*

Cancellation: Blue "PAID."

McGreely's Express, Alaska

Established in 1898 by S. C. Marcuse to carry letters and packages by motorboat between Dyea and Skagway, Alaska.

L208

1898 **Typo.** ***Perf. 14***
155L1 L208 25c **blue** 50.00
Block of 4 *250.00*

The status of No. 155L1 is questioned.

McIntire's City Express Post, New York, N.Y.

Established by William H. McIntire

Mercury — L207

1859 **Litho.**
99L1 L207 2c **pink** 10.00 *100.00*
Block of 4 75.00
On cover, tied by handstamp *3,250.*
a. Period after CENTS omitted —

Cancellation: Black oval "McIntire's City Express Post Paid."

McMillan's City Dispatch Post, Chicago, Ill.

L208a

1855 **Typeset**
100L1 L208a **black,** *rose* *25,000.*

No. 100L1 is unique.

Mac & Co's Dispatch, Fallsington-Morrisville, Pa.

L208b

Typo.
166L1 L208b 1c **black,** on 3c entire #U1, uncanceled, with certificate *17,500.*

No. 166L1 is unique.

Magic Letter Express, Richmond, Va.

Established by Evans, Porter & Co.

L209

L209a

1865 **Typo.**
101L1 L209 1c **black,** on cover, not tied by cancel 40,000.
101L2 L209a 2c **black,** *brown* 14,000.
101L3 L209a 5c **black,** *brown* — 8,000.

Nos. 101L1-101L2 each are unique.

Mason's New Orleans City Express, New Orleans, La.

J. Mason, proprietor

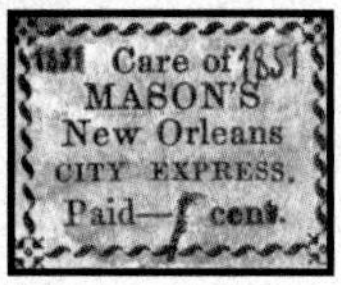

L210

1850-57 **Typeset**
102L1 L210 ½c **black,** *blue* (value changed to "1" in black ms.) 12,500.
On cover, tied —
102L2 L210 2c **black,** *yellow* — 3,000.
On cover, tied by handstamp 10,000.

Cancellations: Red grid, small red circle "Mason's City Express."

Mearis' City Despatch Post, Baltimore, Md.

Established by Malcom W. Mearis

L211

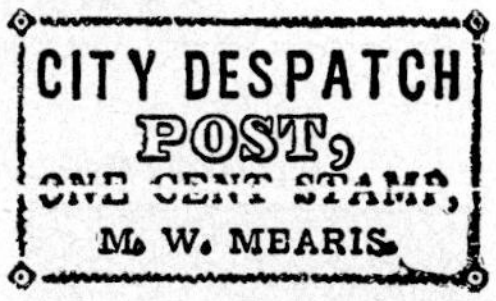

L212

Black ms. initials "M W M" control on all stamps

1846 **Typeset**
103L1 L211 1c **black,** *gray* — —
On cover, tied by handstamp 22,000.
103L2 L212 1c **black,** *gray* —
103L3 L212 2c **black,** *gray* —
On cover, uncancelled, with certificate 16,500.
a. Horiz. pair, #103L2-103L3 —

Two types of No. 103L3.

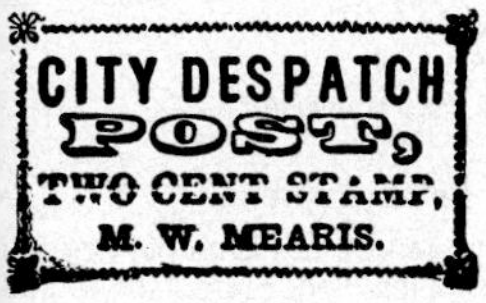

L213

Two types of each.
103L4 L213 1c **black,** *gray* —
103L5 L213 2c **black,** *gray* —
a. Horiz. pair, #103L4-103L5 —

L214

103L6 L214 1c **black,** *gray* 11,000.

No. 103L6 is unique; tied on small piece by handstamp.
Corner ornaments of Nos. 103L1-103L6 differ on each stamp. All varieties of Nos. 103L1-103L6 contained in one plate.

Menant & Co.'s Express, New Orleans, La.

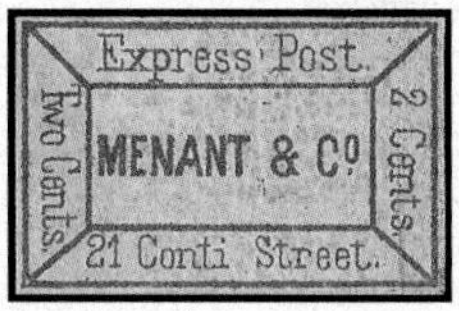

L215

1853 (?) **Typo.**
104L1 L215 2c **dark red** 15,000.

Only four examples are known. Two have Philatelic Foundation Certificates. All four have faults, and the stamp is valued thus.
Reprints are fairly common and are orange red, not dark red.

Mercantile Library Association, New York, N.Y.

Stamps paid for special delivery service of books ordered from the library, and of forms especially provided to subscribers. The forms bore a government stamp on the outside, a library stamp inside.

L216

1870-75 **Litho.**
105L1 L216 5c **black,** *maroon* 250. 350.
105L2 L216 5c **black,** *yellow* 350. 500.
a. With delivery check attached at right 1,150.
105L3 L216 5c **blue** 350. 500.
Pair, on postal card 1,400.
105L5 L216 6c **black,** *maroon* 2,250.
105L6 L216 10c **black,** *yellow* 500. 750.

No. 105L5 is slightly larger than the 5c and 10c stamps.
The stamps "on cover" are affixed to cutouts from order blanks showing order number, title of book desired, and subscriber's name and address. When canceled, the stamps and order blanks show a dull blue double-lined oval inscribed "MERCANTILE LIBRARY ASSOCIATION" and date in center. The stamps are really more a form of receipt for a prepaid parcel delivery service than postage stamps.

POSTAL CARD

Printed on U.S. Postal Card, First Issue
105LUX1 L216 10c **yellow** 3,500.

No. 105LUX1 is unique.

Messenkope's Union Square Post Office, New York, N.Y.

Established by Charles F. Messenkope in 1849 and sold to Joseph E. Dunham in 1850.

L217

1849 **Glazed Surface Paper** **Litho.**
106L1 L217 (1c) **black,** *green* 90. 90.
On cover, tied by handstamp 500.
Two singles on cover (2c rate), tied by handstamp 3,000.
Pair on cover (2c rate), tied by handstamp 3,000.
On cover with 5c #1 3,000.
On cover, tied by handstamp, with 3c #10 1,500.
On cover, tied by handstamp, with 3c #11 2,000.
On cover with 3c #26 1,000.
Strip of 3 400.
106L2 L217 (2c) **black,** *pink* — —
On cover —

Some examples of No. 106L1 are found with "MESSENKOPES" crossed through in black ms. in an apparent attempt (by Dunham?) to obliterate it.
Cancellations: Red "PAID," red oval "DUNHAMS UNION SQUARE POST OFFICE," red grid of dots.

Metropolitan Errand and Carrier Express Co., New York, N.Y.

Organized Aug. 1, 1855, by Abraham M. Hinkley, Hiram Dixon, and others.

L218

L219

Printed in sheets of 100 (10x10), each stamp separated by thin ruled lines.

1855 **Thin to Medium Wove Paper** **Engr.**
107L1 L218 1c **red orange** (shades) 20.00 25.00
Cut to shape 5.00 4.00
On cover, tied by handstamp 600.00
On cover, cut to shape, tied by handstamp 150.00
On cover, cut to shape, tied by handstamp, with 3c #11 900.00
Pair 35.00
Pair on cover, tied by handstamp —
Pair on cover, uncanceled 1,000.
Block of 4 90.00
107L2 L218 5c **red orange** 225.00
Cut to shape 60.00
107L3 L218 10c **red orange** 300.00
Cut to shape 60.00
107L4 L218 20c **red orange** 325.00
Cut to shape 60.00

Cancellations: Black, blue or green boxed "PAID."
The imprint "Baldwin, Bald & Cousland New York" appears in the bottom margin of the two stamps at the bottom right of the sheets.
Nos. 107L1-107L4 have been extensively reprinted in brown and in blue on paper much thicker than the originals.

ENVELOPE
Embossed
Wide Diagonally Laid Paper

107LU1 L219 2c **red,** *amber,* entire 125.00 —

No. 107LU1 has been reprinted on amber wove, diagonally laid or horizontally laid paper with narrow lines. The embossing is sharper than on the original.

Metropolitan Post Office, New York, N.Y.

Established by Lemuel Williams who later took William H. Laws as a partner.

L220

L221

L222

L223

Nos. 108L1-108L5 were issued die cut.

1852-53 Glazed Surface Paper Embossed

108L1	L220	(2c)	**red** (L. Williams)	*550.*	*550.*
			On cover, tied by pencil, with certificate		—
			On cover, tied by blue ms., with two 3c #11 and strip of 3 12c #17		—
108L2	L221	(2c)	**red** (address and name erased)	*1,000.*	*1,000.*
			On cover, uncanceled, with certificate		*5,500.*
108L3	L222	(2c)	**red**	*275.*	*350.*
			On cover, tied by handstamp		*4,000.*
108L3A	L222	(2c)	**blue**	*600.*	*700.*
			On cover, tied by handstamp		*7,500.*
			On cover, tied by handstamp, with 3c #11		*8,250.*

Wove Paper

108L4	L223	1c	**red**	75.	*90.*
			On cover		300.
			On cover, tied by handstamp, with 3c #11		*1,500.*
108L5	L223	1c	**blue**	600.	*100.*
			Cut to shape	400.	
			On cover		350.
			On cover, tied by handstamp, with 3c #26		*700.*

Cancellations: Black circle "METROPOLITAN P. O.," black boxed "PAID W. H. LAWS," black smudge.

G. A. Mills' Despatch Post, New York, N.Y.

Established by Gustavus A. Mills at 6 Wall St., succeeding Hall & Mills.

L224

Several varieties

1847 Glazed Surface Paper Typeset

109L1	L224	(2c)	**black,** *green*	*500.*	*500.*
			On cover, uncanceled		*1,400.*

Moody's Penny Dispatch, Chicago, Ill.

Robert J. Moody, proprietor

"CHICAGO" 8mm — L225

Several varieties

1856 Glazed Surface Paper Typeset

110L1	L225	(1c)	**black,** *red,*	*1,750.*	*1,750.*
			On cover, tied by handstamp, with 3c #11		*16,000.*
			On cover with three 1c #9		*70,000.*
			Vert. strip of 3 showing 3 varieties: period, colon, comma after "Dispatch"	*18,000.*	6,000.
a.			"CHICAGO" sans serif and 12½mm		*2,750.*
b.			"Henny" instead of "Penny," on cover, tied by handstamp, with 3c #11		*40,000.*

Cancellations: Blue circle "Moody's Despatch."

The vertical strip of 3, the cover with the three 1c stamps and No. 110L1b, are each unique.

Morton's Post, Philadelphia, Pa.

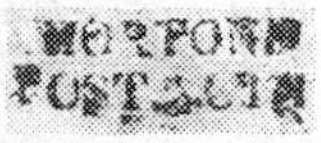

L225a

167L1	L225a	2c	**black,** *grayish,* on cover, uncanceled, with certiificate	*13,000.*

No. 167L1 is unique.

New York City Express Post, New York, N.Y.

L226

Several varieties

1847 Glazed Surface Paper Engr.

111L1	L226	2c	**black,** *green*	*1,200.*	*1,500.*
			Cut to shape	*400.*	*450.*
			On cover, not tied		—
			On cover, tied by handstamp		*4,000.*
			On cover, cut to shape, tied by handstamp		*1,750.*

Wove Paper

111L2	L226	2c	**orange**	—	—
			On cover		*8,000.*

One Cent Despatch, Baltimore, Md., Washington, D.C.

Established by J.H. Wiley to deliver mail in Washington, Georgetown and Baltimore. Made as many as five deliveries daily at 1 cent if prepaid, or 2 cents payable on delivery.

L227

L228

Two types:
I. Courier's letter points to "O" of "ONE."
II. Letter points to "N" of "ONE."

1856 Washington, D.C. Litho.

Inscribed at bottom "Washington City"

112L1	L227	1c	**violet**	*225.*	150.
			On cover, tied by handstamp		*750.*
			On cover, tied by handstamp, with 3c #11		*1,500.*
			On 3c entire #U1, tied by handstamp		*750.*
			Horiz. pair, types I & II		*1,250.*

Baltimore, Maryland

No name at bottom

112L2	L228	1c	**red**	450.	250.
			On cover, tied by handstamp		*2,000.*
			On cover with 3c #11		*2,250.*

The No. 112L1 pair is the unique multiple of either One Cent Despatch stamp.

Cancellation on Nos. 112L1-112L2: Black circle "City Despatch."

Overton & Co.

Carried mail principally between New York and Boston; also to Albany. Stamps sold for 6c each, 20 for $1.

L229

1844

113L1	L229	(6c)	**black,** *greenish*	*400.*	*400.*
			On cover, tied by ms.		*5,000.*
			On cover, not tied		*2,250.*
			Pair		*850.*
a.			"FREE" printed below design		*1,750.*

On cover		*4,000*
Pair on cover, not tied, with certificate		*18,500*

Cancellation: Black "PAID." Red "Cd."

Penny Express Co.

Little information is available on this post, but a sheet is known carrying the ms. initials of Henry Reed of the Holladay staff. The post was part of the Holladay Overland Mail and Express Co. system.

In 1866 in the West the "short-bit" or 10 cents was the smallest currency generally used. The word "penny" is believed to refer to the "half-bit" or 5 cents (nickel).

L230

Printed in sheets of 32 (8x4)

1866 Litho.

114L1	L230	5c	**black**	400.00
			Pair	*850.00*
a.			Sheet of 32 initialed "HR," black ms., original gum	*7,000.*
114L2	L230	5c	**blue**	15.00
			Block of 4	65.00
			Sheet of 32, no gum	650.00
114L3	L230	5c	**red**	15.00
			Block of 4	65.00
			Sheet of 32, no gum	650.00

Nos. 114L1-114L3 lack gum and probably were never placed in use.

Philadelphia Despatch Post, Philadelphia, Pa.

See D.O. Blood & Co.

Pinkney's Express Post, New York, N.Y.

L231

1851 Glazed Surface Paper Typo.

115L1	L231	2c	**black,** *green*	*1,400.*	
			Cut to shape	*800.*	
			On cover, tied by ms., with certificate		*5,750.*
			On cover, not canceled, with certificate		*9,000.*
			On cover, cut to shape, with certificate		*4,500.*

On the cover with No. 115L1 tied, the stamp is faulty. It is valued thus.

Pips Daily Mail, Brooklyn, N.Y.

L232

1862 (?) Litho.

116L1	L232	1c	**black**	400.	
116L2	L232	1c	**black,** *buff*	375.	*2,250.*
116L3	L232	1c	**black,** *yellow*	250.	
116L4	L232	1c	**black,** *dark blue*	800.	
116L5	L232	1c	**black,** *rose*	300.	
			Block of 4	—	

No. 116L2 used is unique.

Pomeroy's Letter Express.

Established in 1844 by George E. Pomeroy. Carried mail principally to points in New York State. Connected with Letter Express for Western points.

L233

Engraved by John E. Gavit, Albany, N.Y. (Seen as GAVIT" in bottom part of stamp). Sheets of 40 (8x5).

1844

Surface Colored Wove Paper

Value Complete ("20 for $1")

117L1 L233 5c **black,** *greenish yellow, dull yellow* 6.50 *65.00*
On cover, tied by ms. *1,000.*
On cover, handstamp cancel *1,000.*
Pair *250.00*
Pair on cover *3,500.*
Block of 4 40.00

Value Incomplete ("20 for $-")

117L2 L233 **black,** *greenish yellow, dull yellow* *750.* *1,500.*
On cover, tied by ms. *5,000.*
On cover, ms. cancel, not tied *3,500.*
On cover, woth No. 117L1 —

Value Complete ("20 for $1")

Thick Wove Paper

117L2A L233 5c **black,** *buff,* without gum —
117L2B L233 5c **black,** *yellow, buff tint on back,* without gum 5.00
Sheet of 40 300.00
117L2C L233 6c **black,** *yellow (colored through),* without gum 5.00
a.. 5c **black,** orange yellow (colored through), with gum 10.00

No. 117L2A may be a proof impression. Mos. 117L2B-117L2Ca may be remainders or reprints.

Thin Bond Paper

117L3 L233 5c **blue (shades)** 150.00 *500.00*
On cover, not tied 2,500.
Pair on cover, not tied *6,000.*
117L4 L233 5c **black** 5.00 *150.00*
On cover *1,500.*
Pair on cover, red "Paid" cancel *7,500.*
Strip of 4 on cover *5,000.*
Block of 4 30.00
Sheet of 40, without gum 300.00
117L5 L233 5c **red (shades)** 5.00 *300.00*
On cover, not tied 3,500.
Strip of 3 on cover *8,500.*
Block of 4 25.00
Sheet of 40 300.00
117L6 L233 5c **lake** — *750.00*
On cover, tied by ms. *1,500.*
Pair on cover —
On cover, tied by handstamp *6,000.*
Block of 4 —

Cancellations: Large red partly boxed "PAID" (Nos. 117L1, 117L6), red "Cd" (Nos. 117L1-117L2, 117L4); stamps are considered "tied to cover" by this "Cd" when the impression shows through the letter paper.

Remainders of Nos. 117L1, 117L3, 117L4 and 117L5 are plentiful in unused condition, including multiples and sheets. A 5c chocolate brown and a 5c bright yellow were prepared but not issued. No. 117L2 was never remaindered.

Thin Pelure Paper

117L7 L233 5c **deep blue (shades)** — —
117L8 L233 5c **black** — —
Pair — —
117L9 L233 5c **chocolate brown** — —

5c stamps on a medium, fibrous paper in orange, deep blue, black, red and brown exist. It is believe that stamps on this paper come from remainders of a printing that was prepared but never issued. They may also be reprints.

P. O. Paid, Philadelphia, Pa.

See note in Carriers' Stamps Section.

Price's City Express, New York, N.Y.

L235

L236

1857-58 Glazed Surface Paper Litho.

119L1 L235 2c **black,** *vermilion* 275.
On cover, tied by handstamp *5,000.*
On cover, ms. tied *1,000.*
On cover, not tied, with certificate *750.00*
On cover, tied by handstamp, with 3c #26 —
119L2 L235 2c **black,** *green* 250.
Cut to shape 85.

1858

Sheets of 108 (12x9)

119L3 L236 2c **black,** *green* 5.00 *150.00*
On cover —
Block of 4 27.50

Cancellation on #119L3: Black oval "Price's City Express."

Price's Eighth Avenue Post Office, New York, N.Y.

Established by James Price at 350 Eighth Avenue, in 1854, and sold to Russell in the same year.

L237

1854 Litho.

120L1 L237 (2c) **red,** *bluish* *600.00*
On cover, uncanceled, with certificate *7,500.*

Priest's Despatch, Philadelphia, Pa.

Established by Solomon Priest

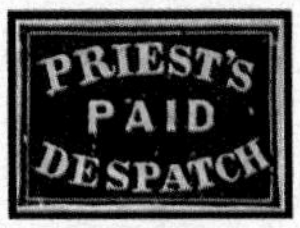
L238

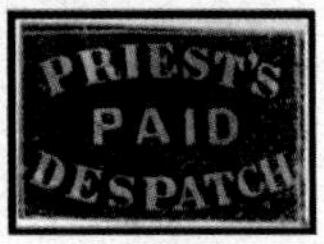
L239

1851 Glazed Surface Paper Typo.

121L1 L238 (2c) **silver,** *vermilion* *2,250.* —
121L2 L238 (2c) **gold,** *dark blue* *500.*

Wove Paper

121L2A L238 (2c) **bronze,** *bluish* *500.* *1,000.*
121L3 L238 (2c) **black,** *yellow* *500.*
On cover, uncanceled, with 3c #11, with certificate *5,500.*
121L4 L238 (2c) **black,** *rose* *500.*
On cover, uncanceled, with certificate *2,500.*
121L5 L238 (2c) **black,** *blue* *1,000.*
121L6 L239 (2c) **black,** *yellow* *500.*
On cover, uncanceled, with 3c #11, with certificate *4,500.*
121L7 L239 (2c) **black,** *blue* *750.*
On cover, uncanceled, with certificate *3,250.*
121L8 L239 (2c) **black,** *rose* *500.*
121L9 L239 (2c) **black,** *emerald,* uncanceled, on cover *6,500.*

No. 121L9 is believed to be unique.

Prince's Letter Dispatch, Portland, Maine

Established by J. H. Prince of Portland. Mail carried nightly by messenger travelling by steamer to Boston. Stamp engraved by Lowell of Lowell & Brett, Boston, his name appearing in the design below the steamship.

L240

Printed in sheets of 40 (5x8)

1861 Litho.

122L1 L240 **black** 7.50 *125.00*
On cover, tied by handstamp *5,000.*
On cover, tied by handstamp, with 3c #65 *8,000.*

On cover, tied by handstamp, with 3c #94 *4,750.*
Block of 4 40.00
Sheet of 40 550.00

Cancellations: Black, blue or red Boston datestamps, blue company serrated oval, black "Boston & Portland/Express/11 State Street, Boston/34 Exchange Street, Portland" framed ribbon-marker handstamp.

Private Post Office, San Francisco, Calif.
ENVELOPES

L241

(Illustration reduced size.)

Impressed on U.S. Envelopes, 1863-64 Issue

1864 Typo.

123LU1 L241 15c **blue,** *orange* (on US #U56) *600.00*
123LU2 L241 15c **blue,** *buff* (on US #U54) *600.00*
a. 15c **blue** (on US #U58) *700.00* *4,750.*
b. 15c **blue,** *buff* (on US #U59) *600.00*
123LU3 L241 25c **blue,** *buff* (on US #U54) *600.00*

Providence Despatch, Providence, R.I.

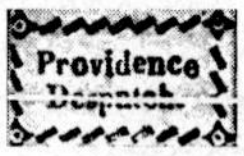
L242

1849 Typeset

124L1 L242 **black** *2,000.*

Public Letter Office, San Francisco, Calif.
ENVELOPES

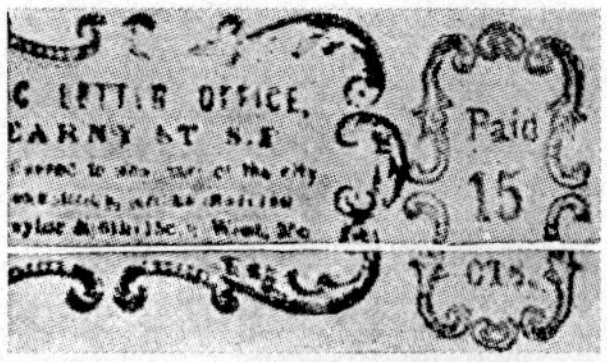
L243

Illustration reduced.

Impressed on U.S. Envelopes, 1863-64 Issue

1864 Typeset

125LU1 L243 **black** *350.00*
125LU2 L243 **blue** *350.00*
125LU3 L243 15c **blue** *400.00* *5,000.*
125LU4 L243 25c **blue** *400.00*

The Private Post Office of San Francisco changed its name to Public Post Office sometime in 1864. The office address was the same for both, 5 Kearny St.

Reed's City Despatch Post, San Francisco, Calif.

Pioneer San Francisco private post. Also serving Adams & Co. for city delivery.

L244

1853-54 Glazed Surface Paper Litho.

126L1 L244 **black,** *green,* on cover, tied by handstamp —
126L2 L244 **black,** *blue,* on cover, uncanceled *27,500.*

No. 126L1 is unique. Two No. 126L2 recorded, each uncanceled on cover.

Cancellation: Blue double-circle "Adams & Co. San Francisco."

Ricketts & Hall, Baltimore, Md.

L244a

1857 Cut to shape Typo.
127L1 L244a 1c **red,** *bluish* — *9,000.*
On cover —

Of the seven recorded examples of No. 127L1, three have been cut to shape removing the outer address circle, including the unique unused stamp. One of the three examples on cover has had the outer address circle removed.

Robison & Co., Brooklyn, N.Y.

L245

1855-56 Typo.
128L1 L245 1c **black,** *blue* *4,750.* *4,750.*
On cover, tied *7,000.*

Cancellation: Blue "PAID."

Roche's City Dispatch, Wilmington, Del.

L246

1850 Glazed Surface Paper Typo.
129L1 L246 (2c) **black,** *green* *2,250.*
Cut to shape *1,750.*
On cover, uncanceled, with certificate *8,250.*
On cover, cut to shape, uncanceled, with certificate *3,500.*

A black negative handstamp similar to type L246 served solely as a postmark and no evidence exists that any prepaid handstamped envelopes or lettersheets were ever sold.

Rogers' Penny Post, Newark, N.J.

Established by Alfred H. Rogers, bookseller, at 194 Broad St., Newark, N.J.

L246a

Cut to shape
1856 Glazed Surface Paper Handstamped
162L1 L246a (1c) **black,** *green* *30,000.*

No. 162L1 is unique. It is on a tiny piece. Value represents 2000 auction sale price.

See Rogers' handstamp in Local Handstamp Covers section.

Russell 8th Ave. Post Office, New York, N.Y.

(See Price's Eighth Avenue Post Office.)

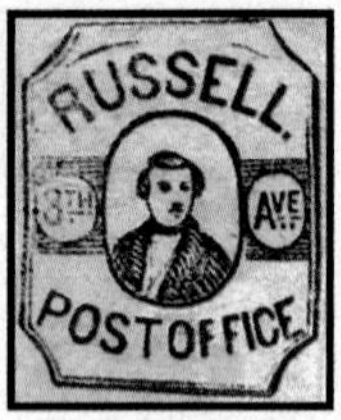

L247

1854-58 Wood Engraving
130L1 L247 (2c) **blue,** *rose* *600.* *500.*
On cover, not tied —
On cover, tied —
130L2 L247 (2c) **black,** *yellow* *750.* *650.*
On cover, tied *5,000.*
On cover, uncanceled, with 3c #11, with certificate *9,250.*
130L3 L247 (2c) **red,** *bluish* *900.* *750.*
On cover, tied by handstamp *8,750.*
On cover, not tied, with 3c #11, with certificate *5,750.*
130L4 L247 (2c) **blue green,** *green* —

No. 130L4 used is unique.

St. Louis City Delivery Company, St. Louis, Mo.

(See Cincinnati City Delivery.)

L249

1883 Typo. *Perf. 12*
131L1 L249 (1c) **red** 4.00 7.50
Block of 4 17.50
On cover, tied by handstamp *2,750.*
a. Imperf., pair —
b. Horiz. pair, imperf between *350.00*

Cancellation: Purple target.

Smith & Stephens' City Delivery, St. Louis, Mo.

L284

Typeset
158L1 L284 1c **black,** *pale rose,* on cover, tied by ms. cancel 25,000.

No. 158L1 is unique.

Smith's City Express Post, New York, N.Y.

Successor to the American Express Co.

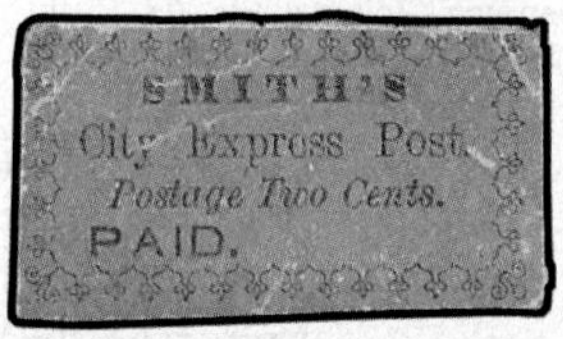

L284a

Typeset
Glazed Surface Paper
168L1 L284a 2c **black,** *green* —

Spaulding's Penny Post, Buffalo, N.Y.

L283

L283a

1848-49
156L1 L283 2c **vermilion** *40,000.*
156L2 L283a 2c **carmine** *40,000.*
On cover —

Nos. 156L1 unused, 156L2 unused and 156L2 on cover each are unique.

A No. 156L1 on cover, uncanceled, was reported but has not been seen.

Spence & Brown Express Post, Philadelphia, Pa.

L285

L286

(Illustrations reduced size.)

1847 (?) Typeset
159L1 L285 2c **black,** *bluish* *10,000.* *11,500.*

One each recorded of No. 159L1 unused and used.

1848 Litho.
159L2 L286 (2c) **black** *1,500.* —
On cover, tied by ms. *33,000.*
Block of 4 *6,500.*

No. 159L2 on cover is unique.

Squier & Co. City Letter Dispatch, St. Louis, Mo. (Jordan & Co.)

This post began to operate as a local carrier on July 6, 1859 and was discontinued in the early part of 1860. Squier & Co. used imperforate stamps; their successors (Jordan & Co.) about Jan. 1 1860, used the roulettes.

L248

1859 Litho. *Imperf.*
132L1 L248 1c **green** *150.* *175.*
On cover *1,500.*
On cover, tied by handstamp, with 3c #26 *3,500.*
On cover, tied by ms., with 3c #26 *1,000.*
On cover, uncanceled, with 3c #26 *600.*
Block of 4 *750.*

1860 *Rouletted 19*
132L2 L248 1c **rose brown** *280.* *280.*
On cover *1,000.*
On cover, with 3c #26, each tied by handstamps (unique) *11,500.*
132L3 L248 1c **brownish purple** *280.* *280.*
On cover *1,000.*
132L4 L248 1c **green** *280.* *350.*
On cover *1,000.*
On cover, tied by handstamp, with 3c #26 *5,000.*

Cancellation: Black circle "Jordan's Penny Post Saint Louis."

Staten Island Express Post, Staten Island, N. Y.

Established by Hagadorn & Co., with office at Stapleton, Staten Island. Connected with Boyd for delivery in New York City.

L250

1849 Typo.
133L1 L250 3c **vermilion** *1,400.* *1,100.*
On cover, tied by ms. *4,750.*
On cover, not tied *3,500.*
On cover, uncanceled, with certificate *3,250.*
133L2 L250 6c **vermilion,** on cover —

Stringer & Morton's City Despatch, Baltimore, Md.

According to an advertisement in the Baltimore newspapers, dated October 19, 1850, this post aimed to emulate the successful posts of other cities, and divided the city into six districts, with a carrier in each district. Stamps were made available throughout the city.

L251

1850 Glazed Surface Paper

134L1 L251 (1c) **gold,** *black* 500. —
On cover, uncanceled 700.

Cancellation: Black circle "Baltimore City Despatch & Express Paid."

Sullivan's Dispatch Post, Cincinnati, Ohio

L252

1853 Glazed Surface Paper Litho.

135L1 L252 (2c) **black,** *green,* uncanceled, on cover —

Wove Paper

135L2 L252 (2c) **bluish black,** uncanceled, on magazine, with certificate 40,000.
135L3 L252 (2c) **green** 60,000.
On cover —

Nos. 135L1-135L2 are either die cut octagonally or cut round. They do not exist cut square.
Each listed Sullivan Post item is unique. Additionally, a second No. 135L2 on magazine is in the Smithsonian Institution collection.

Swarts' City Dispatch Post, New York, N.Y.

Established by Aaron Swarts, at Chatham Square, in 1847, becoming one of the largest local posts in the city.
The postmarks of Swarts' Post Office are often found on stampless covers, as this post carried large quantities of mail without using adhesive stamps.

Zachary Taylor
L253

George Washington
L254

1849-53 Glazed Surface Paper Litho.

136L1 L253 (2c) **black,** *light green* — *175.00*
On cover, tied by handstamp *450.00*
On cover, not tied *300.00*
On cover with 3c #10 *450.00*
136L2 L253 (2c) **black,** *dark green* — 135.00
On cover, tied by handstamp *375.00*

Wove Paper

136L3 L253 (2c) **pink** — 35.00
On cover, tied by handstamp *500.00*
On cover with 5c #1 —
136L4 L253 (2c) **red** (shades) 20.00 20.00
On cover, tied by handstamp *425.00*
On cover with 5c #1 *5,000.*
On cover, tied by handstamp, with 3c #11 *650.00*
Block of 4 85.00
Sheet of 25 *600.00*
136L5 L253 (2c) **pink,** *blue* 60.00
On cover, tied by handstamp *375.00*
136L6 L253 (2c) **red,** *blue* 60.00
On cover, tied by handstamp *400.00*
136L7 L253 (2c) **black,** *blue gray* 200.00 150.00
On cover, tied by handstamp *400.00*
136L8 L253 (2c) **blue** 200.00
On cover, tied by handstamp *1,250.*
136L9 L254 (1c) **red** — 40.00
On cover, tied by handstamp *400.00*
On cover with 3c #11 —
136L10 L254 (1c) **pink** — 30.00
On cover, tied by handstamp *250.00*
On cover, tied by handstamp, with 3c #11 *800.00*
136L11 L254 (1c) **red,** *bluish* — 100.00
On cover *500.00*
136L12 L254 (1c) **pink,** *bluish* — 100.00
On cover *450.00*

Bouton's Stamp with Red ms. "Swarts" at Top

136L13 L49 2c **black,** *gray blue* *500.* *550.*
On cover, tied by handstamp *1,500.*
On cover, not tied *600.*

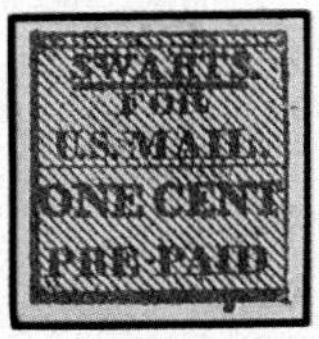

L255

Printed in sheets of 25 (5x5). Five minor varieties, the stamps in each vertical row being identical.

136L14 L255 1c **blue** 15. 60.
On cover, tied by handstamp 175.
On cover, tied by handstamp, with 3c #11 *225.*
Block of 4 *65.*
a. Thin paper 8.00
Block of 4 35.
Sheet of 25 *225.00*
136L15 L255 1c **red** — *500.*
On cover, tied by handstamp *1,000.*
On cover with 3c #10 *1,650.*
On cover, tied by handstamp, with 3c #11 *3,500.*
136L16 L255 1c **red,** *bluish* — 135.
On cover, tied by handstamp *1,000.*
136L17 L255 1c **black,** on cover *36,000.*

Nos. 136L3-136L4, 136L9-136L10, 136L14-136L15 have been reprinted.
Cancellations: Red boxed "PAID" (mostly on Nos. 136L1-136L8, 136L13), black boxed "PAID SWARTS" (mostly on Nos. 136L9-136L12), black oval "Swarts Post Office Chatham Square" (Nos. 136L9-136L12), black oval "Swarts B Post Chatham Square," black grids (5-bar rectangle, 6-bar circle, solid star, hollow star, star in circle, etc). Other handstamp postmarks of the post have been found as cancellations. Government town postmarks exist on almost all Swarts stamps.

Teese & Co. Penny Post, Philadelphia, Pa.

L256

Printed in sheet of 200 divided into two panes of 100. Each pane includes setting of 20, repeated 5 times. Vertical or horizontal tete beche pairs appear twice in each setting. Twenty varieties.

1852 Wove Paper Litho.

137L1 L256 (1c) **blue,** *bluish* 20.00 125.00
On cover, tied by handstamp *3,000.*
On cover, tied by handstamp, with 3c #11 —
Block of 4 90.00
a. Tete beche pair 100.00

Telegraph Despatch P. O., Philadelphia, Pa.

L257

1848

138L1 L257 1c **black,** *yellowish* *2,750.*
On cover, tied by ms., with certificate *15,000.*
On cover, not tied, with certificate *5,500.*
138L2 L257 2c **black,** *yellowish,* on cover with 5c #1 *21,000.*

The 2c differs in design, including the address, "Office No. 6 Sth 8 St" at bottom.
One example known of No. 138L2.

Third Avenue Post Office, New York, N.Y.

Established by S. Rothenheim, a former carrier for Boyd's City Express. All stamps were cut to shape by hand before being sold and exist only in that form.

L258

1855 Glazed Surface Paper Handstamped

139L1 L258 2c **black,** *green* *500.* *500.*
On cover, uncanceled *1,250.*
On cover, uncanceled, with 3c #11, with certificate *1,600.*
139L1A L258 2c **blue,** *green,* on cover, uncanceled, with certificate *2,250.*
139L2 L258 2c **black,** *maroon* *3,250.* *2,250.*

Unsurfaced Paper colored through

139L3 L258 2c **black,** *yellow* *2,250.*
On cover, uncanceled, with 3c #11, with certificate *3,000.*
139L4 L258 2c **black,** *blue* —
On cover, uncanceled, with 3c #11, with certificate *11,000.*
139L5 L258 2c **black,** *brown* *2,250.*
139L6 L258 2c **black,** *buff* *2,500.*
139L7 L258 2c **black,** *pink* *5,250.*
On cover, uncanceled, with 3c #11 *6,500.*
139L8 L258 2c **black,** *green* *4,150.* *2,200.*

Nos. 139L1A, 139L2, 139L4 on cover, 139L7-139L8 unused and 139L8 used are each unique.

Cancellation on No. 139L1: Black "PAID."

Union Post, New York, N.Y.

L259

1846 Handstamped

Thick Glazed Surface Paper

140L3 L259 **blue,** *green* ("UNOIN") *3,000.*
140L4 L259 **red,** *blue* ("UNION") *2,000.*
On cover —

Type L259 was used also as a postmark, usually struck in blue.

Union Square Post Office, New York, N.Y.

Established by Joseph E. Dunham about 1850. In 1851 Dunham acquired Messenkope's Union Square Post Office, operating the combined posts until 1854 or 1855. The business was sold in 1855 to Phineas C. Godfrey.

L259a

L260

Printed in sheets of 120 (6x20)

1852 Typo.

141L1 L259a 1c **black,** *dark green* 9.00 *45.00*
On cover, tied by handstamp *900.00*
On cover, tied by handstamp, with 3c #11 *1,500.*
Block of 4 45.00
141L2 L259a 1c **black,** *light apple green* 40.00 *75.00*
On cover, tied by handstamp *700.00*
On cover, tied by handstamp, with 3c #11 *1,500.*
On cover, cut to shape, tied by handstamp, with 3c #11 *200.00*
141L3 L260 2c **black,** *rose* 3.50 *3,000.*
On cover *3,500.*
Block of 4 17.50

Used stamps must bear handstamp cancels.

Walton & Co.'s City Express, Brooklyn, N.Y.

Operated by Wellington Walton.

L261

1846 Glazed Surface Paper Litho.

142L1	L261	2c	**black,** *pink*	700.	900.
			On cover, tied by ms.		—
			On cover, ms. cancel, not tied, with certificate		15,000.
			On cover, handstamp cancel, not tied		—
			On cover, cut to shape, tied by handstamp, with certificate		4,500.
			On cover, cut to shape, handstamp cancel, not tied, with certificate		6,000.

Cancellations: Black "PAID / W. W." Black oblong quad (ties stamp "through" to cover).

Wells, Fargo and Co.

Wells, Fargo & Company entered the Western field about July 1, 1852, to engage in business on the Pacific Coast, and soon began to acquire other express businesses, eventually becoming the most important express company in its territory.

The Central Overland, California and Pikes Peak Express Company, inaugurated in 1860, was the pioneer Pony Express system and was developed to bring about quicker communication between the extreme portions of the United States. Via water the time was 28 to 30 days, with two monthly sailings, and by the overland route the time was 28 days. In 1860 the pioneer Pony Express carried letters only, reducing the time for the 2,100 miles (St. Joseph to San Francisco) to about 12 days. The postage rate was originally $5 the half-ounce.

About April 1, 1861, Wells, Fargo & Company became agents for the Central Overland, California and Pikes Peak Express Company and issued $2 red and $4 green stamps.

During the July 1 to Oct. 24, 1861, period of use of Nos. 143L3-143L6, Wells, Fargo & Co. was under contract with the U.S. government, so stamps used during this period are technically official issues authorized by Congress.

The rates were cut in half about July 1, 1861, and new stamps were issued: the $1 red, $2 green and $4 black, and the $1 garter design.

The revival of the Pony Express in 1862, known as the "Virginia City Pony" resulted in the appearance of the "cents" values, first rate.

Advertisement in the Placerville newspaper, Aug. 7, 1862: "Wells, Fargo & Co.'s Pony Express. On and after Monday, the 11th inst., we will run a Pony Express Daily between Sacramento and Virginia City, carrying letters and exchange papers, through from San Francisco in 24 hours, Sacramento in 15 hours and Placerville in 10 hours. Rates: All letters to be enclosed in our franks, and TEN CENTS PREPAID, in addition, for each letter weighing half an ounce or less, and ten cents for each additional half-ounce."

Wells, Fargo & Company used various handstamps to indicate mail transit. These are illustrated and described in the handbook, "Wells, Fargo & Co.'s Handstamps and Franks" by V. M. Berthold, published by Scott Stamp & Coin Co., Ltd. (out of print). The history of the Pony Express, a study of the stamps and reprints, and a survey of existing covers are covered in "The Pony Express," by M. C. Nathan and Winthrop S. Boggs, published by the Collectors Club, 22 E. 35th., New York, N.Y. 10016.

Wells Fargo stamps of types L262 and L264 were lithographed by Britton & Rey, San Francisco. Type L263 was printed by George F. Nesbitt, New York.

L262

Front hoof missing

The $2 and $4 stamps were printed from plates of 20 (5x4), while the $1 was printed from a plate of 40 (8x5), and divided into two panes of 20 (4x5) each.

1861 (April to July 1) Litho.

143L1	L262	$2	**red**	175.	800.
			On US envelope #U10		—
			On US envelope #U16		12,500.
			On US envelope #U17		12,500.
			On US envelope #U18		12,500.
			On US envelope #U32 (patriotic cover)		100,000.
			On US envelope #U33		15,000.
			On US envelope #U65		—
143L2	L262	$4	**green**	300.	1,250.
			Block of 4	9,000.	
			On US envelope #U33		—

The No. 143L2 block is the only recorded $4 block.

1861

(July 1 to Nov.)

143L3	L262	$1	**red**	90.	750.
			Block of 4	750.	
			Sheet of 40	7,000.	
			On US envelope #U11		—
			On US envelope #U15		8,500.
			On US envelope #U17		8,500.
			On US envelope #U32		9,000.
			On US envelope #U33		9,000.
			On US envelope #U35		8,500.
			On US envelope #U40		9,000.
			On US envelope #U41		8,500.
			Front hoof missing (9R)	1,250.	6,000.
143L4	L262	$2	**green**	250.	1,750.
			Block of 4	1,200.	
			On US envelope #U41		50,000.
143L5	L262	$4	**black**	175.	6,000.
			Block of 4	—	
			On cover to Wash., D.C., tied by handstamp		350,000.

Cancellations: Blue, black or magenta express company.

Nos. 143L1-143L5 and 143L7-143L9 were reprinted in 1897. The reprints are retouched. Shades vary from originals. Originals and reprints are fully described in "The Pony Express," by M. C. Nathan and W. S. Boggs (Collectors Club).

L263

Printed in sheets of 20 (5x4). One example recorded with Nesbitt imprint (pos. 18).

1861

Thin Wove Paper

143L6	L263	$1	**blue**	750.	1,250.
			Strip of 3	—	
			On 10c US env. #U40		75,000.

No. 143L6 apparently used only from east to west.

Most counterfeits have a horizontal line bisecting the shield. Some genuine stamps have a similar line drawn in with blue or red ink. Value for genuine, $300.

L264

Printed in sheets of 40 (8x5), four panes of 10, each pane 2x5.

1862-64

143L7	L264	10c	**brown** (shades)	50.	150.
			Pair	125.	500.
			Block of 4	500.	
			On US envelope #U26		5,000.
			On US envelope #U32		3,500.
			On US envelope #U34		4,500.
			On US envelope #U35		3,500.
			On cover with 3c #65		—
143L8	L264	25c	**blue**	75.	140.
			Pair	175.	
			Block of 4	500.	
			On plain cover		2,250.
			Strip of 3 on cover		—
			On US envelope #U10		—
			On US envelope #U26		2,000.
			On US envelope #U34		4,000.
			On US envelope #U35		4,000.
143L9	L264	25c	**red**	30.	80.
			Pair	80.	
			Block of 4	225.	
			Sheet of 40	4,500.	
			On US envelope #U9		—
			On US envelope #U10		4,000.
			On US envelope #U34		4,000.
			On US envelope #U35		4,000.
			Pair on US envelope #U35		9,000.
			On US envelope #U59		2,750.

Cancellations on Nos. 143L7-143L9: Blue or black express company, black town.

NEWSPAPER STAMPS

L265

L266

L267

L268

L269

L270

1861-70

143LP1	L265	**black**	1,250.	—
		On cover, uncanceled, with certificate		11,000.
143LP2	L266	**blue**	1,250	
143LP3	L267	**blue**	20.00	75.00
		Pair	100.00	
		Block of 4	—	
		Sheet of 50	—	
a.		Thin paper	40.00	100.00
143LP4	L268	**blue**	50.00	

Rouletted 10

143LP5	L267	**blue**	25.00	125.00
		On wrapper		1,500.
		Pair	55.00	
		Block of 4	125.00	
a.		Thin paper	—	
143LP6	L268	**blue**	22.50	
a.		Tete beche pair	350.00	

Design L267 was printed in sheets of 50 (5x10).

1883-88 ***Perf. 11, 12, 12½***

143LP7	L268	**blue**	12.50	25.00
143LP8	L269	**blue**	25.00	35.00
143LP9	L270	**blue**	3.50	5.00
		Double transfer	—	
		On wrapper		2,400.
		Strip of 3 on wrapper		—
a.		Vertical pair, imperf. between	125.00	
b.		Horiz. pair, imperf. vert.	350.00	

FOR PUBLISHERS' USE

L271

1876 **Typo.**

143LP10	L271		**blue**	8.50	*25.00*
			Pair	17.50	*60.00*
			Block of 4	45.00	
			Sheet of 50	—	
			On wrapper		*1,750.*
			On wrapper with #143LP9		—

Cancellation: Blue company.

ENVELOPES

1862

143LU1	L264	10c	**red**	—	*1,250.*
			On US envelope #U34		*3,000.*
143LU2	L264	10c	**blue**	—	—
			On US envelope #U34		*9,500.*
143LU3	L264	25c	**red**	700.	
			On "Gould & Curry" overall advertising env.	700.	
			On US envelope #U34	950.00	

Westervelt's Post, Chester, N.Y.

Operated by Charles H. Westervelt. Rate was 1 cent for letters and 2 cents for packages carried to the post office. Local and government postage required prepayment.

L273

Several varieties

1863 (?) **Typeset**

144L1	L273	(1c)	**black,** *buff*	35.00	—
			On cover		*650.00*
			On cover, tied by handstamp, with 3c #65		*1,000.*
			Sheet of 6	*675.00*	
144L2	L273		**black,** *lavender*	40.00	—
			On cover		—

Indian Chief — L274

General U. S. Grant — L275

Six varieties

1864 (?) **Typeset**

144L9	L274	(1c)	**red,** *pink*	75.00	—
			On cover		*650.00*
			On cover, tied by handstamp, with 3c #65		*2,000.*

Six varieties

1865 **Typo.**

144L29	L275	2c	**black,** *yellow*	35.00	—
144L30	L275	2c	**black,** *gray green*	40.00	—
144L40	L275	2c	**red,** *pink*	40.00	—

All of the Westervelt stamps are believed to have a philatelic flavor, although it is possible that Nos. 144L1-144L2 were originally issued primarily for postal purposes. It is possible that Nos. 144L9, 144L29-144L30 and 144L40 were used in the regular course of business, particularly No. 144L9.

However, the large number of varieties on various colors of paper, which exist both as originals as well as contemporaneous and near-contemporaneous reprints, are believed to have been produced solely for sale to collectors. Design L275 was certainly issued primarily for sale to collectors. Many of the unlisted colors in all three types exist only as reprints. Forgeries of all three designs also exist.

L276

ENVELOPES

Impressed at top left

1865 **Typo.**

144LU1	L276	**red,** *white*	—	
144LU2	L276	**red brown,** *orange*	—	*250.00*
144LU3	L276	**black,** *bluish*	—	
144LU4	L276	**black,** *buff*	—	
144LU5	L276	**black,** *white*	—	

It is possible that Nos. 114LU1-144LU5 were corner cards and had no franking value.

Westtown, Westtown, Pa.

The Westtown School at Westtown, Pa., is the oldest of the secondary schools in America, managed by the Society of Friends. It was established in 1799. In 1853 the school authorities decided that all outgoing letters carried by stage should pay a fee of 2 cents. Prepaid stamps were placed on sale at the school. Stamps were usually affixed to the reverse of the letter sheets or envelopes.

At first, letters were usually mailed at West Chester, Pa. After March 4, 1859, letters were sent from Street Road Post Office, located at the railroad station. Later this became the Westtown Post Office. The larger stamp was the first used. The smaller stamp came into use about 1867.

L277 — Type I

L277 — Type II

L277 — Type III

L277 — Type IV

L277a — Type V

L277a — Type VI

L277a — Type VII

1853-67(?) **Litho.**

145L1	L277	(2c)	**gold**	45.	—
			On front of cover, tied with 3c #11		*4,500.*
			On front of cover, uncanceled, with 1c #9		*1,000.*
			On front of cover, uncanceled, with 3c #11		*150.*
			On front of cover, uncanceled, with 3c #26a		*200.*
145L2	L277a	(2c)	**gold**	30.	—
			On cover		*400.*
			On cover, tied by handstamp, with 3c #158		*2,250.*
			Block of 4	*400.*	
			Block of 6	*1,000.*	
a.			Tete beche pair	*300.*	

No. 145L1 in red brown is a fake.

Whittelsey's Express, Chicago, Ill.

Operated by Edmund A. and Samuel M. Whittelsey

George Washington — L278

1857 **Typo.**

146L1	L278	2c	**red**	*2,000.*	*6,000.*
			Block of 11	*20,000.*	

Cancellation: Blue oval "Whittelsey's Express."

Williams' City Post, Cincinnati, Ohio.
See Carriers' Stamps, No. 9LB1.

Wood & Co. City Despatch, Baltimore, Md.

Operated by W. Wood

L280

1856 **Typeset**

148L1	L280	(1c)	**black,** *yellow,* on cover, ms. cancel, not tied, with certificate	*11,000.*
			On printed matter, tied by ms.	*7,500.*
			On 3c red entire #U10, tied by ms., with certificate	*14,500.*

W. Wyman, Boston, Mass.

Established to carry mail between Boston and New York

L281

1844 **Litho.**

149L1	L281	5c	**black**	—	*750.00*
			On cover, tied by ms., Wyman handstamp		*3,850.*
			On cover, tied by ms., Overton handtsamp		*10,000.*
			On cover, not tied		*2,000.*

No. 149L1 may have been sold singly at 6 cents each.

Zieber's One Cent Dispatch, Pittsburgh, Pa.

L282

1851 **Typeset**

150L1	L282	1c	**black,** *gray blue*	*20,000.*
			On cover, acid cancel, with 3c #10	—

No. 150L1 used and on cover are each unique.

Cancellation: Acid

For Local #151L1 see **Friend's Boarding School.**
For Local #152L1 see **Faunce's Penny Post.**
For Local #153L1 see **Hackney & Bolte Penny Post.**
For Local #154L1 see **A. W. Auner's Despatch Post.**
For Local #155L1 see **McGreely's Express.**
For Local #156L1-156L2 see **Spaulding's Penny Post.**
For Local #157L1 see **Bush's Brooklyn City Express.**
For Local #158L1 see **Smith & Stephens City Delivery.**
For Local #159L1-159L2 see **Spence & Brown Express Post.**
For Local #160L1 see **City Dispatch, New York City.**
For Local #161L1 see **Clinton's Penny Post.**
For Local #162L1 see **Rogers' Penny Post.**
For Local #163L1 see **Blizzard Mail.**
For Local #164L1 see **Freeman & Co.'s Express, New York City.**
For Local #165L1 see **J. A. Howell's City Despatch.**
For Local #166L1 see **Mac & Co's Dispatch.**
For Local #167L1 see **Morton's Post.**
For Local #168L1 see **Smith's City Express Post.**

LOCAL HANDSTAMPED COVERS

In 1835-1860 when private companies carried mail, many of them used handstamps on the covers they carried. Examples of these handstamps are shown on this and following pages.

Accessory Transit Co. of Nicaragua

Blue or Black

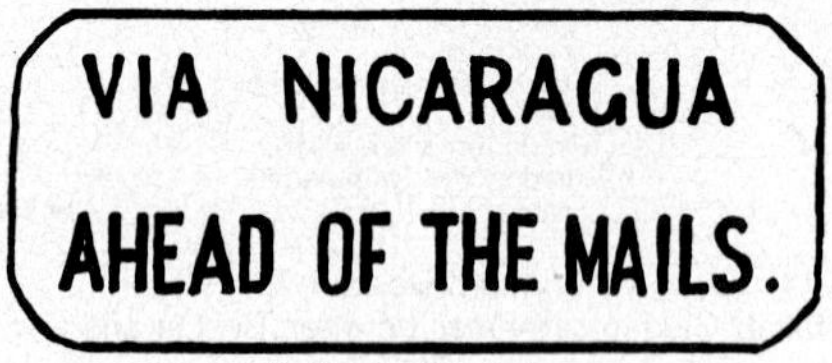

Red, Black or Blue

A sub-variety shows "Leland" below "MAILS" in lower right corner.

Red or Blue

1853

Barker's City Post, Boston, Mass.

Black

1855-59

Also known with "10" instead of "34" Court Square.

E. N. Barry's Despatch Post, New York, N.Y.

Black

1852

Bates & Co., New Bedford, Mass.
(Agent for Hale & Co. at New Bedford)

Red

1845

Branch Post Office, New York, N. Y.
(Swarts' Chatham Square Post Office)

Red

1847

Brigg's Despatch, Philadelphia, Pa.

Black

1848

Bush's Brooklyn City Express, Brooklyn, N. Y.

Red

1848

Cover shows red PAID.

Central Post Office, New York, N.Y.

Black

1856

Cover shows black PAID.

City Despatch Post, New York, N. Y.
(Used by Mead, successor to United States City Despatch Post.)

Black

1848

City Dispatch Post, Baltimore, Md.

Red

1846-47

City Despatch & Express, Baltimore, Md.

Black

1850

Cole's City Despatch P. O., New York, N. Y.
(Used by Cole with some of the City Despatch Post stamps.)

Black or Red

1848-50

Dunhams Post Office, New York, N. Y.
(See Union Square Post Office).

Red

1850-52

Gay, Kinsley & Co., Boston, Mass.
(A package express)

Red

Hanford's Pony Express Post, New York, N.Y.

Black or Red

1845-51

Hartford Penny Post, Hartford, Conn.

Black

1852-61

Hudson Street Post Office, New York, N. Y.

Red

1850

Cover shows red PAID.

Jones & Russell's Pikes Peak Express Co., Denver, Colo.

Black

1859-60

Kenyon's Letter Office, 91 Wall St., New York City

Red

1846-60

Letter Express, San Francisco, Cal.
(See Gahagan & Howe, San Francisco, Cal.)

Blue

1865-66

Libbey & Co.'s City Post, Boston, Mass.

LIBBEY & CO'S
CITY POST.
10 COURT SQUARE

Black or Red

1852

Cover has 3c 1851 postmarked Boston, Mass.

Manhattan Express, New York, N. Y.
(W. V. Barr. See Bouton's Manhattan Express.)

Red

1847

New York Penny Post, New York, N. Y.

Black or Red

1840-41

Also known with hour indicated.

Noisy Carriers, San Francisco, Cal.

Blue or Green

Blue

Black or Red

Black, Blue or Green

Black

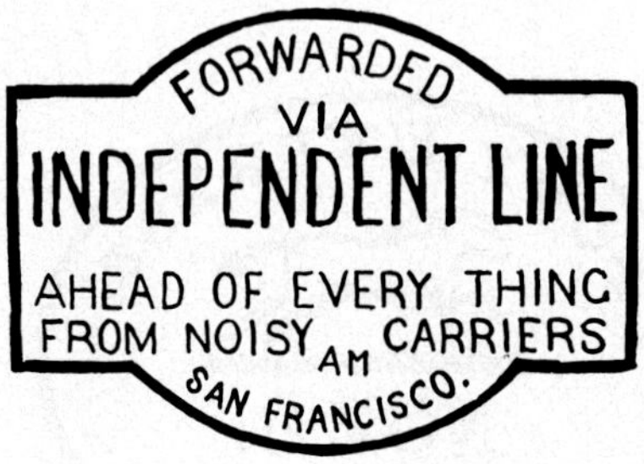

Black or Blue

1853-56

Northern Liberties News Rooms, Philadelphia, Pa.
(Actually a carrier marking mechanically applied.)

Black

Black

1835-36

Overton & Co.'s City Mail, New York, N. Y.

Red

1844-45

Pony Express

Blue or Red

1860

Blue (Enlarged)

1861

Black or Carmine

1860-61

Blue or Red

1853-56

from

St. Joseph, Mo.	Black or Green
Denver City, K. T.	Black
Leavenworth City, K. T.	Black
San Francisco, Cal.	Blue

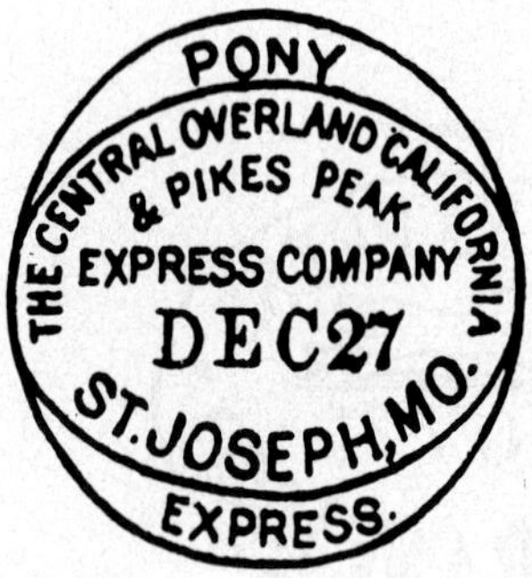

Black or Green

1860-61

Red

Blue

1860

Rogers' Penny Post, Newark, N. J.

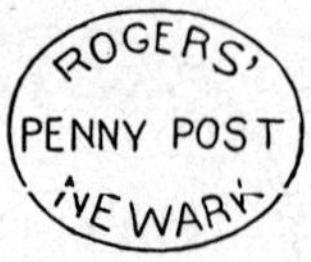

Black

1856

Spark's Post Office, New York, N. Y.

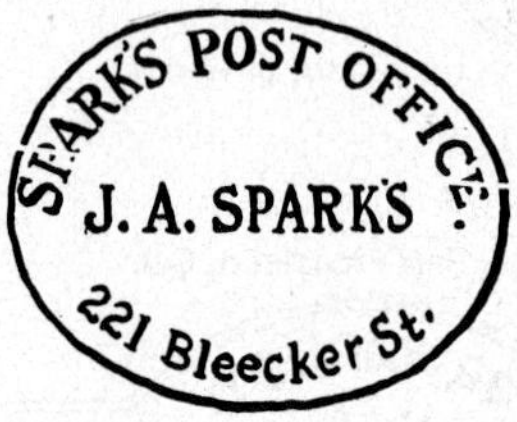

Red, Green, Blue or Black

1848

Spaulding's Penny Post, Buffalo, N. Y.

Black

1848

Spence & Brown Express Post, Philadelphia, Pa.

Black

1848

Stait's Despatch Post, Philadelphia, Pa.
(Eagle City Post)

Red or Black

1850-51

Red

1850-55

Stone's City Post, New York, N. Y.

Red

1858-59

J. W. Sullivan's Newspaper Office,
San Francisco, Cal.

Black or Red

1854-55

Towle & Co. Letter Delivery, Boston, Mass.

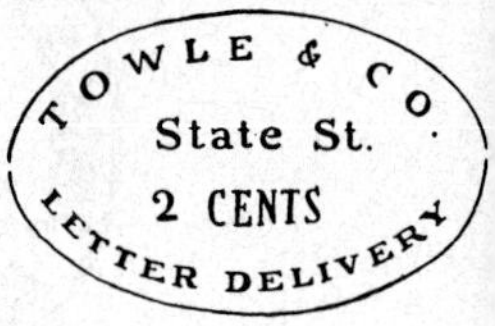

Red

1847

Towle's City Dispatch Post, Boston, Mass.

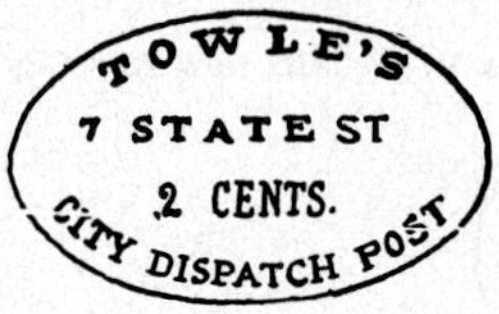

Red

1849

Towle's City Post, Boston, Mass.

(Also 10 Court Sq.)
Red

1849-50

Cover shows PAID.

STAMPED ENVELOPES AND WRAPPERS

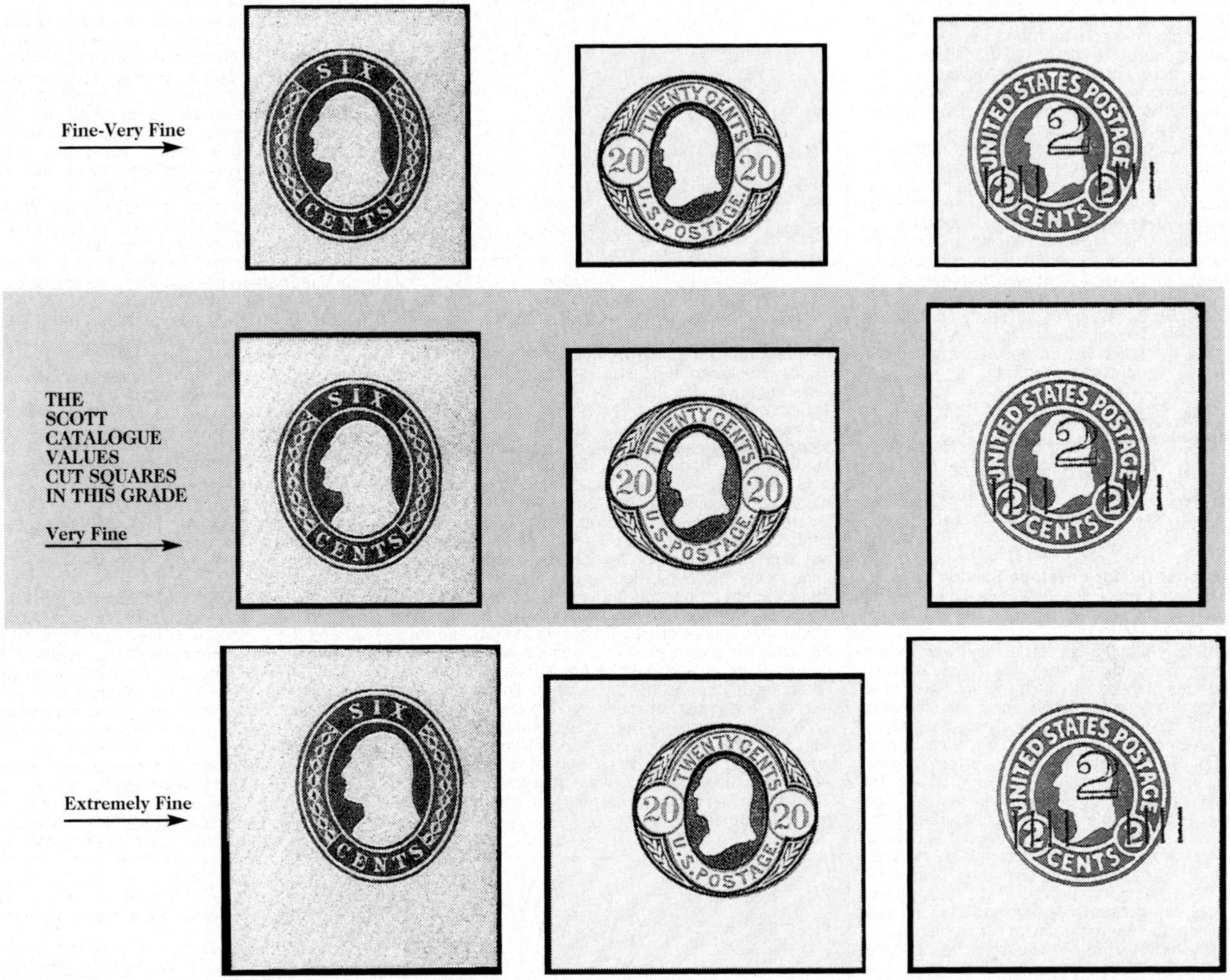

VALUES

Values for cut squares and most entires are for examples in the grade of very fine. Very fine cut squares will have the design well centered within moderately large margins. The margins on 20th century cut squares should be at least ¼ inch on the cut sides unless indicated otherwise. Cut squares of modern issues should show full tagging bars when they exist. An illustrated grading guide is shown above. These examples are computer-manipulated images made from single digitized master illustrations. Selected issues from both the 19th and 20th centuries are shown in the grades of fine-very fine, very fine and extremely fine. In addition to margin size, collectors are reminded that very fine cut squares (and entires) also will possess a fresh appearance and be free from defects.

Precanceled cut squares must include the entire precancellation. Values for unused entires are for those without printed or manuscript address, and for the most popular sizes. In a number of cases the larger envelopes are less expensive than the values shown here, for example, Nos. U348-U351. Values for letter sheets and wrappers are for folded entires. Unfolded examples sell for more.

"Full corner" cut squares include both back and side flaps. These items generally command a premium of 25% or more above the cut square values shown here, which are not for "full corners."

A plus sign (+) before a Catalogue number indicates that the item was not regularly issued and is not known used.

Envelopes are not available before the First day of issue so most cachets are applied after the envelope has been canceled. First day covers are valued uncacheted. First day covers prior to Nos. U532, UC18 and UO73 are addressed. Minimum values are $1 through 1986, and $1.25 after.

PRECANCELED CUT SQUARES

Precanceled envelopes do not normally receive another cancellation. Since the lack of a cancellation makes it impossible to distinguish between cut squares from used and unused envelopes, they are valued here as used only. Precanceled entires are valued mint and used since entires will show evidence of usage.

HISTORY

STAMPED ENVELOPES were first issued on July 1, 1853. They have always been made by private contractors, after public bidding, usually at four-year intervals. They have always been sold to the public at postage value plus cost of manufacture. They have appeared in many sizes and shapes, made of a variety of papers, with a number of modifications.

George F. Nesbitt & Co. made the government envelopes during the 1853-70 period. The Nesbitt seal or crest on the tip of the top flap was officially ordered discontinued July 7, 1853.

Watermarks in envelope paper, illustrated in this introduction, were mandatory from their first appearance in 1853. One important exception started in 1919 and lasted until the manila newspaper wrappers were discontinued in October 1934. The envelope contractor, due to inability to obtain watermarked Manila paper, was permitted to buy unwatermarked stock in the open market, a procedure that accounts for the wide range of shades and weights in this paper, including glazed and unglazed brown (kraft) paper. No. U615, and other unwatermarked envelopes that follow will be so noted in the listings. Diagonally laid paper has been used for some envelopes beginning with Scott U571.

A few stamped envelopes, in addition to the Manila items noted above, have been found without watermarks or with unauthorized watermarks. Such unusual watermarks or lack of watermarks are errors, bidders' samples or "specimen" envelopes, and most of them are quite rare.

Watermarks usually have been changed with every four-year contract, and thus serve to identify the envelope contractor, and since 1911, the manufacturer of the paper.

Envelope paper watermarks can be seen by spreading the envelope open and holding it against the light.

COLORS IN ENVELOPE PAPER

Stamped envelopes usually have been supplied in several colors and qualities of paper, some of which blend into each other and require study for identification. The following are the principal colors and their approximate years of use for stamped envelopes and wrappers:

Amber: 1870-1920 and 1929-1943; in two qualities; a pale yellow color; its intentional use in the Nesbitt series is doubtful.

Amber-Manila: 1886-98; same as Manila-amber.

Blue: 1874-1943; usually in two qualities; light and dark shades.

Buff: 1853-70; called cream, 1870-78; and oriental buff, 1886-1920; varies widely in shades.

Canary: 1873-78; another designation given to lemon.

Cream: 1870-78; see buff; second quality in 1c and 2c envelopes.

Fawn: 1874-86; very dark buff, almost light chocolate.

Lemon: 1873-78; Post Office official envelopes only, same as canary.

Manila: 1861-1934; second quality envelopes 1886-1928, and most wrappers; light and dark shades 1920-34; also kraft colored paper in later years.

Manila-Amber: 1886-98; amber shade of Manila quality.

Orange: 1861-83; second and third qualities only.

Oriental Buff: 1886-1920; see buff.

White: 1853-date; two qualities 1915-date; three qualities 1915-25; many shades including ivory, light gray, and bluish; far more common than any other color of paper. Envelopes that have no paper color given are white.

Laid paper was used almost exclusively from 1853 to 1915, but there were a few exceptions, mostly in the Manila papers. Wove paper has been the rule since 1915.

EMBOSSING AND PRINTING DIES

Until the modern era, stamped envelopes were always embossed, with the colorless areas slightly raised above the colored (or printed) flat background. While this process was not made mandatory in the original act, custom and tradition firmly established this policy. In 1977, No. U584 became the first envelope to have no embossing. Since 1977, most envelopes are not embossed. Embossing is an unusual procedure, seldom seen in other printed matter. Embossed impressions without color and those where lines are raised are not unusual. The method of making envelope embossings has few counterparts in the typographic industries, and hence is not well understood, even by stamp collectors.

Three types of dies are used, closely interrelated in their derivation, MASTER dies, HUB dies and WORKING (or PRINTING) dies. These types and the ways in which they are made, have undergone many changes with the years, and some of the earlier techniques are unrecorded and rather vague. No attempt will be made to describe other than the present day-methods. As an aid to clarity, the design illustrated herewith is the interlocked monogram "US," within a single circular border. Dies with curved faces for rotary printing are used extensively, as well as with straight faces for flat printing; only the latter will be described, since the basic principles are the same for both.

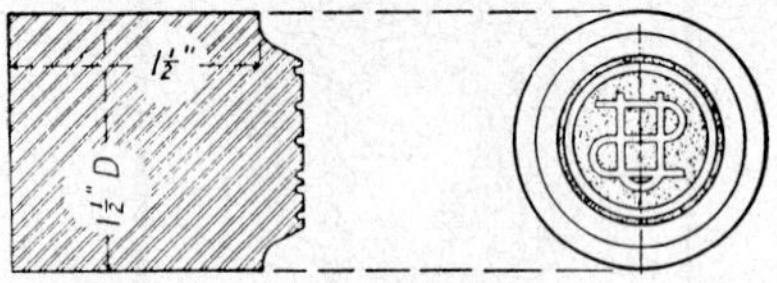

Figure 1

Master Die for Envelope Stamps

Colorless Lines are Recessed Below the Printing Surface.

It Reads Backward.

The MASTER die (Figure 1) is engraved on the squared end of a small soft steel cylinder, before hardening. The lines that are to remain colorless are cut or engraved into the face of this die, leaving the flat area of the face to carry the printing ink. The monogram is reversed, reading backward, as with any printing type or plate. Instead of engraving, a master die may be made by transfer under heavy pressure, usually for some modification in design, in which case it is called a sub-master or supplementary-master die. Sub-master dies are sometimes made without figures of value, when the balance of the design is as desired, and only the figures of value engraved by hand. Various other combinations of transfer and engraving are known, always resulting in a reversed design, with recessed lines and figures, from which proofs can be pulled, and which accurately represents the printing surface that is desired in the eventual working die. The soft steel of a master die, after engraving and transferring is completed, is hardened by heat treatments before it can be used for making hubs.

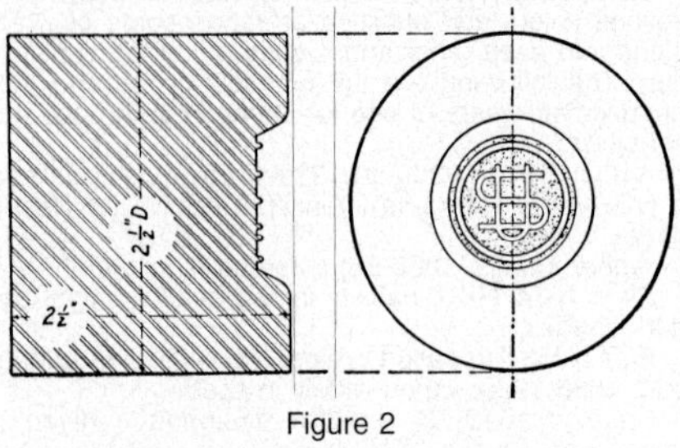

Figure 2

Hub Die for Envelope Stamps

Colorless Lines Protrude above the Surface.

The Monogram Reads Forward.

The HUB die (Figure 2), also called HOB die, is made from soft steel by transfer under pressure from the hardened master or sub-master die, which serves as a matrix or pattern. Since it is a transfer from the master die, the colorless lines protrude from the surface and it reads forward. This transfer impression of the hub die is made in a depression at the end of a sturdy cylinder, as it is subject to extremely hard service in making many working dies.

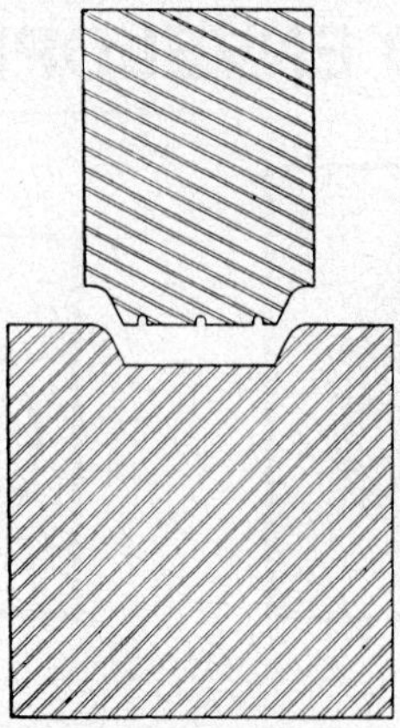

Figure 3

Pressure Transfer From Master Die to Hub Die

Above, Hardened Steel Master Die with Recessed Monogram.

Below, Soft Steel Hub Die Blank.

Figure 3 shows the relative position of the hardened steel master die as it enters the depression in the soft steel hub die blank. Some surplus metal may be squeezed out as the master die is forced into the hub blank, and require removal, leading to possible minor differences between the hub and master dies. At the completion of the pressure transfer the engraver may need to touch up the protruding surfaces to eliminate imperfections, to make letters and figures more symmetrical, and to improve the facial lines of the bust.

A hub die may be made by normal transfer, as above, the figures of value then ground off, and thus be ready for use in making a sub-master die without figures of value, and in which the figures of value may be engraved or punched. Since a hub die may be used to make a hundred or more working dies, it must be exceedingly sturdy and withstand terrific punishment without damage. Duplicate hub dies are frequently made from master dies, as stand-bys or reserves. After completion, hub dies are hardened. Hub dies cannot be engraved, nor can proof impressions be taken from them.

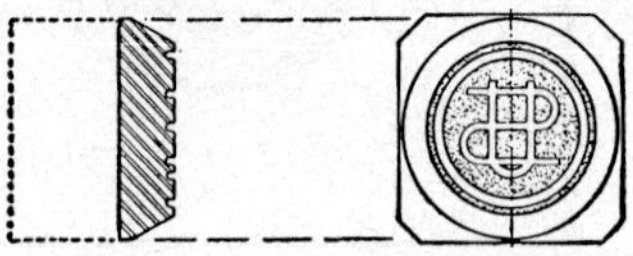

Figure 4

Working or Printing Die for Envelope Stamps

An exact Replica of the Master Die, except for size and shape of shank, which is designed for Printers} lock-up.

It Reads Backward.

The WORKING, or PRINTING, die (Figure 4) is like the type or plate that printers use, and may be thin to clamp to a base block, or type-high with square sides to lock in a printer's form. Its face reads backward, i.e., in reverse, and it is an exact replica of the master die as well as an exact matrix of the hub die.

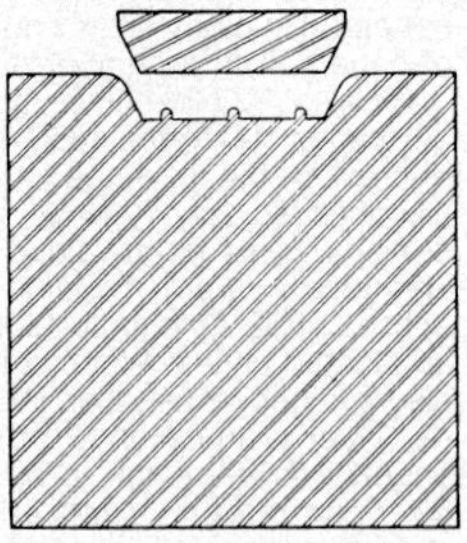

Figure 5

Pressure Transfer from Hub to Working Die

Above, Soft Steel Blank for Working Die.

Below, Hardened Steel Hub Die with Protruding Lines.

The process of pressure transfer is shown in Figure 5. where the soft steel blank of the working die is entering the depression on the top end of the hardened hub die, In fact the pressure transfer of working dies from hub dies closely resembles that of minting coins, and many of these envelope stamp dies are made at the United States Mint in Philadelphia.

In some cases even working dies may be made without figures of value, and the figures of value individually engraved thereon. This is known to be the case in Die B of the 6c orange airmail stamped envelope die, where the size and position of the "6" has eleven variations.

There are some known instances, as in the case of the 4c and 5c envelopes dies of 1903 and 1907, where the engraved master dies were used as printing dies, since the anticipated demand did not justify the expense of making hub dies.

While working envelope dies are heat treated to the hardest temper known, they do wear down eventually to a point where impressions deteriorate and are unsatisfactory, due to shallow recesses or to broken areas, and such dies are destroyed. In many cases these printing dies can be reworked, or deepened, by annealing the steel, touching up the lines or busts by hand engraving to restore the letters or renew the facial contour lines, and then rehardened for subsequent use. This recutting is the principal cause for minor die varieties in envelope stamps. When working dies are no longer useful, they are mutilated and eventually melted down into scrap metal.

The average "life" (in number of good impressions obtained) of a hardened steel working die, as used in envelope printing and embossing machines is around 30,000,000 on flat bed presses, and 43,000,000 on rotary presses. With a production of stamped envelopes of approximately 2 billion annually, 60 to 75 working dies are worn out each year, and require replacement with new dies or a reworking of old dies. Some 200 to 250 working dies can be in constant use, since most envelope printing presses are set up for a special size, type or value, and few can be operated continuously at maximum capacity.

Master and hub dies of obsolete envelope issues are kept in the vaults of the Bureau of Engraving and printing in Washington, as are the original dies of adhesive stamps, revenue paper, government securities and paper currency.

PRINTING ENVELOPE STAMPS

Embossed envelope stamps are not printed against a rigid flat platen, as is the normal printed page, but against a somewhat flexible or resilient platen or make-ready (Figure 6). This resilient platen is hard enough to produce a clear full impression from the ink on the face of the working die, and soft enough to push the paper into the uninked recesses that correspond to the engraved lines cut into the master die. The normal result is raised lines or embossments without ink or color, standing out in relief against an inked or colored background. The method differs from the usual embossing technique, where rigid dies are used on both sides of the paper, as in notarial seals. The use of the resilient platen in envelope embossing permits far higher operating speeds than can be obtained with rigid embossing dies, without the need of such accurate register between the printing surface and the platen.

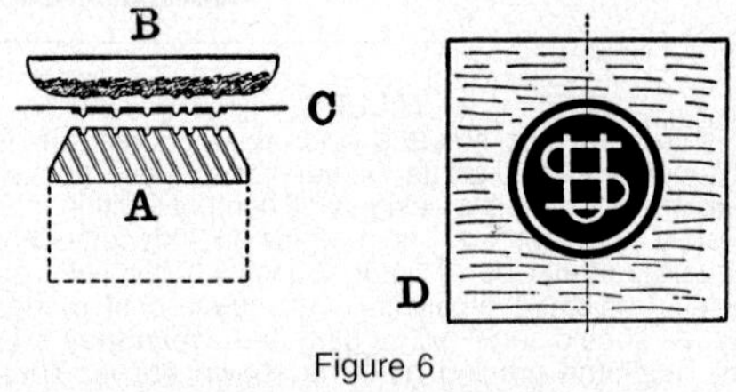

Figure 6

Printing Process for Embossed

A. Working Die, Carrying ink on its surface.

B. Resilient Platen, or Make-ready, Pushing Paper into uninked recesses, so that lines of Embossed Monogram receive no color.

C. Paper of Envelope Blank, after Printing and Embossing. Heavy line shows deposit of ink on surface of paper, but Embossed Lines are not inked.

D. Front view of Embossed impression.

When these recessed lines in a working die become filled with ink or other foreign material, the paper is not pushed in, the plugged area receives ink, and the corresponding colorless line does not appear on the stamp. This accounts for missing letters, lines or figures, and is a printing error, not a die variety.

An ALBINO impression is where two or more envelope blanks are fed into the printing press. The one adjacent to the printing die receives the color and the embossing, while the others are embossed only. Albinos are printing errors and are sometimes worth more than normal, inked impressions. Because of the nature of the printing process, many albinos were produced, and most collectors will not pay much, or any, premium for most of them. Albinos of earlier issues, canceled while current, are scarce.

Before January 1, 1965, stamped envelopes were printed by two processes: (1.) The rotary, with curved dies, on Huckins and Harris presses. (2.) The flat process, with straight dies, as illustrated, on the O'Connell-type press, which is a redesigned Hartford press. The flat bed presses include a gumming and folding attachment, while the rotary presses, running at higher speeds, require separate folding machines.

Different master dies in every denomination are required for Huckins, Harris and flat bed presses. This difference gives rise to most of the major die varieties in envelope stamps.

Web-fed equipment which converts paper from a roll into finished envelopes in a continuous operation has produced envelopes starting with Nos. U547 and UC37. Albino impressions do not occur on envelopes produced by web-fed equipment.

Some authorities claim that Scott U37, U48, U49, U110, U124, U125, U130, U133A, U137A, U137B, U137C, W138, U140A, U145, U162, U178A, U185, U220, U285, U286, U298, U299, UO3, UO32, UO38, UO45 and UO45A (with plus sign + before number), were not regularly issued and are not known to have been used.

Wrappers are listed with envelopes of corresponding design, and are numbered with the prefix "W" instead of "U."

ENVELOPE WATERMARKS

Watermark Illustrations 5, 6, 17 and 18 are condensed. Watermark 4 was used only on Officials. Watermarks 9 and 10 are found on Specimens and Errors. Watermarks 17-18 were the last laid paper watermarks; watermarks 19-21 the first wove paper watermarks. Beginning with No. U615, unwatermarked paper was used for some issues. Beginning with No. U625, unwatermarked paper was used for all issues.

Wmks. 1 (1853-70) & 2 (1870-78)

Wmk. 3 (1876)

Wmk. 4 (1877-82)

Wmk. 5 (1878-82)

Wmk. 6 (1882-86)

Wmks. 7 (1886-90) & 8 (1890-94)

Wmks. 9 (1886-87) & 10 (1886-99)

Wmk. 11 (1893)

Wmks. 12 (1894-98) & 13 (1899-1902)

Wmks. 14 (1903-07) & 15 (1907-11)

Wmks. 15A (1907-11) & 16 (1911-15)

USSE US-SE
1911 1911

Wmks. 17 & 18 (1911-15)

Wmk. 19, 20 & 21 (1915-19)

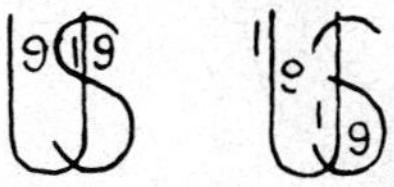

Wmks. 22 & 23 (1919-20)

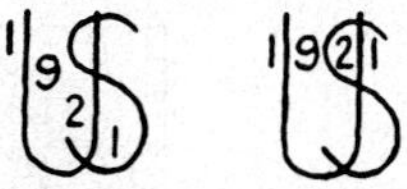

Wmks. 24 & 25 (1921-24)

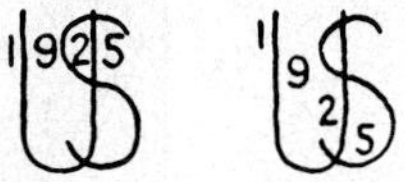

Wmks. 26 & 27 (1925-28)

Wmks. 28 & 28A (1929-32)

Wmks. 29, 30 & 30A (1929-32)

Wmks. 31, 32, 33 (1933-36)

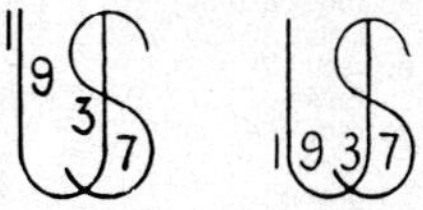

Wmks. 35 & 36 (1937-40)

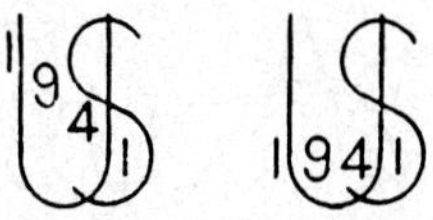

Wmks. 38 & 39 (1941-44)

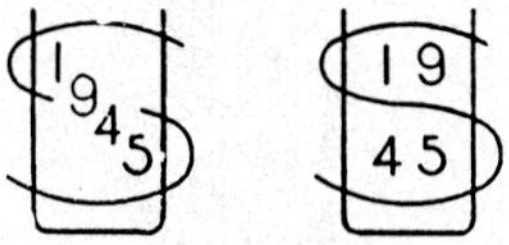

Wmks. 40 & 41 (1945-48)

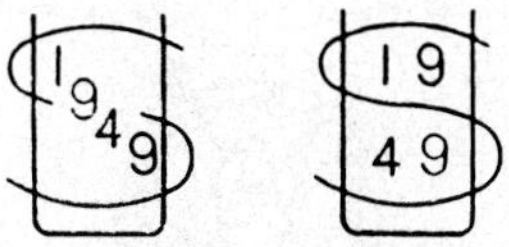

Wmks. 42 & 43 (1949-52)

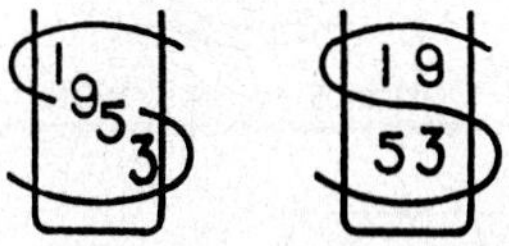

Wmks. 44 & 45 (1953-56)

Wmk. 46 (1957-60)

☆USA USA☆

Wmks. 47 & 48 (1961-88)

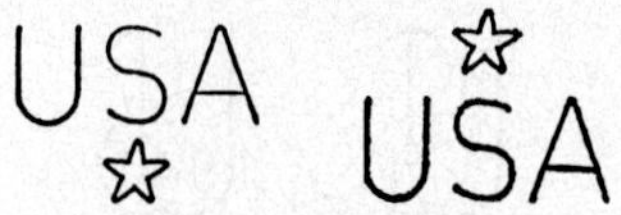

Wmks. 49 & 50 (1965-92)

Letter Sheet (1886-94)

Official Envelopes (1991)

Washington — U1

"THREE" in short label with curved ends; 13mm wide at top. Twelve varieties.

U2

"THREE" in short label with straight ends; 15½mm wide at top. Three varieties.

U3

"THREE" in short label with octagonal ends. Two varieties.

U4

"THREE" in wide label with straight ends; 20mm wide at top.

U5

"THREE" in medium wide label with curved ends; 14½mm wide at top. Ten varieties. A sub-variety shows curved lines at either end of label omitted; both T's have longer cross stroke; R is smaller (20 varieties).

U6

Four varieties.

U7

"TEN" in short label; 15½mm wide at top.

U8

"TEN" in wide label; 20mm wide at top.

Printed by George F. Nesbitt & Co., New York, N.Y.

1853-55

On Diagonally Laid Paper (Early printings of No. U1 on Horizontally Laid Paper)

U1	U1	3c **red**	400.00	35.00
		Entire	1,500.	45.00
U2	U1	3c **red,** *buff*	100.00	25.00
		Entire	1,000.	30.00
U3	U2	3c **red**	900.00	40.00
		Entire	6,000.	100.00
U4	U2	3c **red,** *buff*	350.00	40.00
		Entire	2,500.	75.00
U5	U3	3c **red** ('54)	5,500.	550.00
		Entire	*37,500.*	900.00
U6	U3	3c **red,** *buff* ('54)	4,750.	75.00
		Entire	—	150.00
U7	U4	3c **red**	5,500.	150.00
		Entire	—	300.00
U8	U4	3c **red,** *buff*	*8,750.*	175.00
		Entire	—	300.00
U9	U5	3c **red** ('54)	40.00	4.00
		Entire	150.00	9.00
U10	U5	3c **red,** *buff* ('54)	22.50	4.00
		Entire	72.50	6.00
U11	U6	6c **red**	175.00	90.00
		Entire	350.00	175.00
U12	U6	6c **red,** *buff*	175.00	90.00
		Entire	275.00	200.00
U13	U6	6c **green**	300.00	125.00
		Entire	700.00	225.00
U14	U6	6c **green,** *buff*	225.00	100.00
		Entire	450.00	225.00
U15	U7	10c **green** ('55)	550.00	100.00
		Entire	950.00	150.00
U16	U7	10c **green,** *buff* ('55)	190.00	75.00
		Entire	500.00	150.00
a.		10c **pale green,** *buff*	150.00	65.00
		Entire	425.00	125.00
U17	U8	10c **green** ('55)	475.00	140.00
		Entire	700.00	225.00
a.		10c **pale green**	350.00	125.00
		Entire	700.00	200.00
U18	U8	10c **green,** *buff* ('55)	250.00	90.00
		Entire	600.00	175.00
a.		10c **pale green,** *buff*	240.00	90.00
		Entire	650.00	175.00

Nos. U9, U10, U11, U12, U13, U14, U17, and U18 have been reprinted on white and buff papers, wove or vertically laid, and are not known entire. The originals are on diagonally laid paper. Value, set of 8 reprints on laid, $225. Reprints on wove sell for more.

Franklin — U9

Period after "POSTAGE." (Eleven varieties.)

Franklin — U10

Bust touches inner frame-line at front and back.

Franklin — U11

No period after "POSTAGE." (Two varieties.)

Washington — U12

Nine varieties of type U12.

Envelopes are on diagonally laid paper.
Wrappers on vertically or horizontally laid paper, or on unwatermarked wove paper (Nos. W22, W25)

Wrappers of the 1 cent denomination were authorized by an Act of Congress, February 27, 1861, and were issued in October, 1861. These were suspended in 1863, and their use resumed in June, 1864.

1860-61

W18B	U9	1c **blue** ('61)	*5,750.*	
U19	U9	1c **blue,** *buff*	40.00	15.00
		Entire	90.00	32.50
W20	U9	1c **blue,** *buff* ('61)	70.00	50.00
		Entire	125.00	75.00
W21	U9	1c **blue,** *manila* ('61)	60.00	45.00
		Entire	125.00	100.00
U21A	U9	1c **blue,** *orange,* entire	*2,750.*	
W22	U9	1c **blue,** *orange* ('61)	*4,250.*	
		Entire	*8,000.*	
U23	U10	1c **blue,** *orange*	600.00	350.00
		Entire	900.00	500.00
U24	U11	1c **blue,** *amber*	200.00	100.00
		Entire	500.00	225.00
W25	U11	1c **blue,** *manila* ('61)	*7,500.*	*2,000.*
		Entire	*20,000.*	*5,750.*
U26	U12	3c **red**	35.00	20.00
		Entire	60.00	32.50
U27	U12	3c **red,** *buff*	26.00	13.00
		Entire	45.00	22.50
U28	U12 + U9	3c + 1c **red & blue**	300.00	225.00
		Entire	700.00	400.00
U29	U12 + U9	3c + 1c **red & blue,** *buff*	300.00	250.00
		Entire	700.00	450.00
U30	U12	6c **red**	1,750.	1,250.
		Entire	*3,500.*	

U31	U12	6c	**red,** *buff*	2,500.	1,250.
			Entire	*6,000.*	*15,000.*
U32	U12	10c	**green**	1,000.	400.00
			Entire	*14,000.*	650.00
U33	U12	10c	**green,** *buff*	1,100.	350.00
			Entire	*4,500.*	550.00

Nos. U26, U27, U30 to U33 have been reprinted on the same vertically laid paper as the reprints of the 1853-55 issue, and are not known entire. Value, Nos. U26-U27, $160; Nos. U30-U33, $100.

Washington — U13

17 varieties for Nos. U34-U35; 2 varieties for No. U36.

Washington — U14

Washington — U15

Washington — U16

Envelopes are on diagonally laid paper.

U36 and U45 come on vertically or horizontally laid paper. U36 appeared in August, 1861, and was withdrawn in 1864. Total issue 211,800.

1861

U34	U13	3c	**pink**	32.50	6.00
			Entire	62.50	13.00
U35	U13	3c	**pink,** *buff*	32.50	6.00
			Entire	62.50	13.00
U36	U13	3c	**pink,** *blue* (Letter Sheet)	75.00	60.00
			Entire	225.00	140.00
+U37	U13	3c	**pink,** *orange*	*3,000.*	
			Entire	*6,500.*	
U38	U14	6c	**pink**	125.00	80.00
			Entire	210.00	190.00
U39	U14	6c	**pink,** *buff*	70.00	62.50
			Entire	225.00	160.00
U40	U15	10c	**yellow green**	47.50	30.00
			Entire	82.50	60.00
a.		10c	**blue green**	47.50	30.00
			Entire	82.50	60.00
U41	U15	10c	**yellow green,** *buff*	47.50	30.00
			Entire	82.50	52.50
a.		10c	**blue green,** *buff*	47.50	30.00
			Entire	82.50	52.50
U42	U16	12c	**red & brown,** *buff*	225.00	175.00
			Entire	550.00	*650.00*
a.		12c	**lake & brown,** *buff*	*1,400.*	
U43	U16	20c	**red & blue,** *buff*	250.00	200.00
			Entire	550.00	*1,250.*
U44	U16	24c	**red & green,** *buff*	240.00	200.00
			Entire	700.00	*1,500.*
a.		24c	**lake & green,** *salmon*	325.00	225.00
			Entire	850.00	*1,750.*
U45	U16	40c	**black & red,** *buff*	375.00	350.00
			Entire	850.00	*4,500.*

Nos. U38 and U39 have been reprinted on the same papers as the reprints of the 1853-55 issue, and are not known entire. Value, set of 2 reprints, $60.

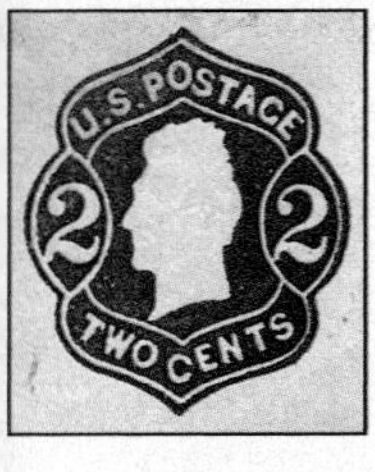
Jackson — U17

"U.S. POSTAGE" above. Downstroke and tail of "2" unite near the point (seven varieties).

Jackson — U18

"U.S. POSTAGE" above. The downstroke and tail of the "2" touch but do not merge.

Jackson — U19

"U.S. POST" above. Stamp 24-25mm wide (Sixteen varieties).

Jackson — U20

"U.S. POST" above. Stamp 25½-26¼mm wide. (Twenty-five varieties.)

Envelopes are on diagonally laid paper.
Wrappers on vertically or horizontally laid paper.

1863-64

U46	U17	2c	**black,** *buff*	55.00	21.00
			Entire	85.00	37.50
W47	U17	2c	**black,** *dark manila*	85.00	50.00
			Entire	105.00	80.00
+U48	U18	2c	**black,** *buff*	*2,500.*	
			Entire	*6,000.*	
+U49	U18	2c	**black,** *orange*	2,750.	
			Entire	5,500.	
U50	U19	2c	**black,** *buff* ('64)	19.00	9.50
			Entire	42.50	21.00
W51	U19	2c	**black,** *buff* ('64)	400.00	200.00
			Entire	650.00	350.00
U52	U19	2c	**black,** *orange* ('64)	19.00	9.50
			Entire	37.50	18.00
W53	U19	2c	**black,** *dark manila* ('64)	52.50	40.00
			Entire	175.00	140.00
U54	U20	2c	**black,** *buff* ('64)	19.00	9.50
			Entire	39.00	16.00
W55	U20	2c	**black,** *buff* ('64)	105.00	65.00
			Entire	160.00	120.00
U56	U20	2c	**black,** *orange* ('64)	22.00	8.50
			Entire	34.00	16.00
W57	U20	2c	**black,** *light manila* ('64)	24.00	14.00
			Entire	37.50	24.00

Washington — U21

79 varieties for Nos. U58-U61; 2 varieties for Nos. U63-U65.

Washington — U22

1864-65

U58	U21	3c	**pink**	12.00	1.60
			Entire	20.00	3.25
U59	U21	3c	**pink,** *buff*	12.00	1.25
			Entire	20.00	3.00
U60	U21	3c	**brown** ('65)	75.00	40.00
			Entire	140.00	125.00
U61	U21	3c	**brown,** *buff* ('65)	60.00	30.00
			Entire	125.00	80.00
U62	U21	6c	**pink**	110.00	29.00
			Entire	190.00	85.00
U63	U21	6c	**pink,** *buff*	55.00	27.50
			Entire	110.00	50.00
U64	U21	6c	**purple** ('65)	70.00	26.00
			Entire	100.00	55.00
U65	U21	6c	**purple,** *buff* ('65)	60.00	20.00
			Entire	80.00	55.00
U66	U22	9c	**lemon,** *buff* ('65)	450.00	250.00
			Entire	625.00	*1,000.*
U67	U22	9c	**orange,** *buff* ('65)	160.00	90.00
			Entire	225.00	275.00
a.		9c	**orange yellow,** *buff*	160.00	90.00
			Entire	225.00	275.00
U68	U22	12c	**brown,** *buff* ('65)	275.00	275.00
			Entire	600.00	*1,200.*
U69	U22	12c	**red brown,** *buff* ('65)	150.00	55.00
			Entire	200.00	360.00
U70	U22	18c	**red,** *buff* ('65)	95.00	95.00
			Entire	200.00	*800.00*
U71	U22	24c	**blue,** *buff* ('65)	100.00	95.00
			entire	200.00	*750.00*
U72	U22	30c	**green,** *buff* ('65)	125.00	80.00
			Entire	200.00	*1,500.*
a.		30c	**yellow green,** *buff*	125.00	*80.00*
			Entire	200.00	*1,500.*
U73	U22	40c	**rose,** *buff* ('65)	125.00	*250.00*
			Entire	350.00	*2,000.*

Printed by George H. Reay, Brooklyn, N. Y.

The engravings in this issue are finely executed.

Franklin — U23

Bust points to the end of the "N" of "ONE."

Jackson — U24

Bust narrow at back. Small, thick figures of value.

Washington — U25

Queue projects below bust.

Lincoln — U26

Neck very long at the back.

Stanton — U27

Bust pointed at the back; figures "7" are normal.

Jefferson — U28

Queue forms straight line with the bust.

Clay — U29

Ear partly concealed by hair, mouth large, chin prominent.

Webster — U30

Has side whiskers.

Scott — U31

Straggling locks of hair at top of head; ornaments around the inner oval end in squares.

Hamilton — U32

Back of bust very narrow, chin almost straight; labels containing figures of value are exactly parallel.

Perry — U33

Front of bust very narrow and pointed; inner lines of shields project very slightly beyond the oval.

1870-71

U74	U23	1c	**blue**	45.00	30.00
			Entire	80.00	45.00
a.		1c	**ultramarine**	72.50	35.00
			Entire	140.00	60.00
U75	U23	1c	**blue,** *amber*	37.50	27.50
			Entire	60.00	40.00
a.		1c	**ultramarine,** *amber*	70.00	30.00
			Entire	100.00	55.00
U76	U23	1c	**blue,** *orange*	20.00	15.00
			Entire	35.00	22.50
W77	U23	1c	**blue,** *manila*	45.00	37.50
			Entire	82.50	70.00
U78	U24	2c	**brown**	40.00	16.00
			Entire	60.00	22.50
U79	U24	2c	**brown,** *amber*	22.50	10.00
			Entire	40.00	17.50
U80	U24	2c	**brown,** *orange*	12.00	6.50
			Entire	17.50	11.00
W81	U24	2c	**brown,** *manila*	29.00	22.50
			Entire	62.50	57.50
U82	U25	3c	**green**	8.50	1.00
			Entire	17.00	4.00
a.		3c	**brown** (error), entire	*9,000.*	
U83	U25	3c	**green,** *amber*	7.25	2.0
			Entire	18.00	5.0
U84	U25	3c	**green,** *cream*	11.00	4.5
			Entire	17.00	10.0
U85	U26	6c	**dark red**	32.50	16.0
			Entire	60.00	21.0
a.		6c	**vermilion**	32.50	16.0
			Entire	75.00	20.0
U86	U26	6c	**dark red,** *amber*	40.00	20.0
			Entire	75.00	30.0
a.		6c	**vermilion,** *amber*	40.00	20.0
			Entire	75.00	30.0
U87	U26	6c	**dark red,** *cream*	40.00	20.0
			Entire	80.00	30.0
a.		6c	**vermilion,** *cream*	40.00	20.0
			Entire	80.00	30.0
U88	U27	7c	**vermilion,** *amber* ('71)	55.00	*190.0*
			Entire	82.50	*900.0*
U89	U28	10c	**olive black**	800.00	900.0
			Entire	1,350.	1,250
U90	U28	10c	**olive black,** *amber*	950.00	900.0
			Entire	1,350.	*1,25*
U91	U28	10c	**brown**	92.50	72.5
			Entire	140.00	125.0
U92	U28	10c	**brown,** *amber*	110.00	52.5
			Entire	140.00	125.0
a.		10c	**dark brown,** *amber*	110.00	75.0
			Entire	140.00	125.0
U93	U29	12c	**plum**	125.00	82.5
			Entire	240.00	*450.0*
U94	U29	12c	**plum,** *amber*	140.00	110.0
			Entire	240.00	*650.0*
U95	U29	12c	**plum,** *cream*	225.00	225.0
			Entire	350.00	
U96	U30	15c	**red orange**	85.00	85.0
			Entire	175.00	
a.		15c	**orange**	85.00	
			Entire	175.00	
U97	U30	15c	**red orange,** *amber*	150.00	*300.0*
			Entire	375.00	
a.		15c	**orange,** *amber*	150.00	
			Entire	375.00	
U98	U30	15c	**red orange,** *cream*	350.00	350.0
			Entire	450.00	
a.		15c	**orange,** *cream*	350.00	
			Entire	450.00	
U99	U31	24c	**purple**	150.00	150.0
			Entire	200.00	
U100	U31	24c	**purple,** *amber*	200.00	*325.0*
			Entire	375.00	
U101	U31	24c	**purple,** *cream*	275.00	*500.0*
			Entire	475.00	
U102	U32	30c	**black**	80.00	*110.0*
			Entire	300.00	*750.0*
U103	U32	30c	**black,** *amber*	250.00	*500.0*
			Entire	650.00	
U104	U32	30c	**black,** *cream*	250.00	*500.0*
			Entire	400.00	
U105	U33	90c	**carmine**	175.00	*350.0*
			Entire	250.00	
U106	U33	90c	**carmine,** *amber*	325.00	*450.0*
			Entire	800.00	*4,500*
U107	U33	90c	**carmine,** *cream*	200.00	*2,500*
			Entire	500.00	*5,000*

Printed by Plimpton Manufacturing Co.

U34

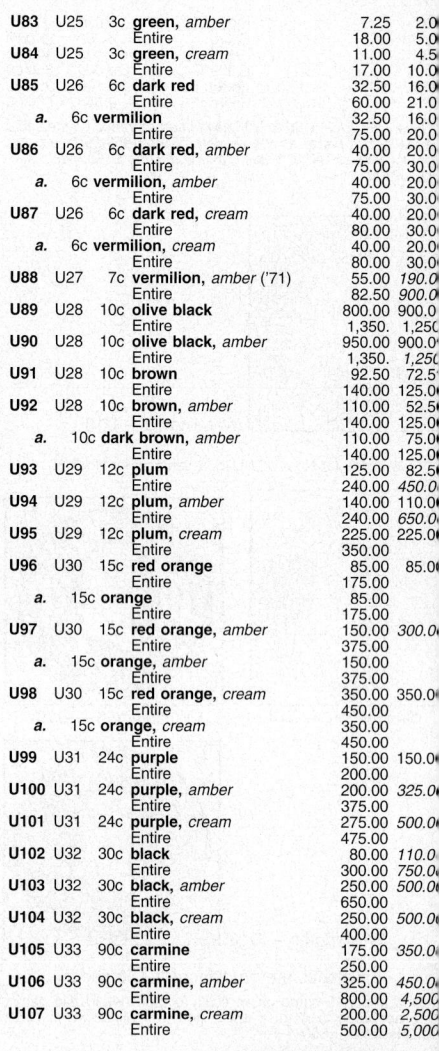

Bust forms an angle at the back near the frame. Lettering poorly executed. Distinct circle in "O" of "Postage."

U35

Lower part of bust points to the end of the "E" in "ONE." Head inclined downward.

U36

Bust narrow at back. Thin numerals. Head of "P" narrow. Bust broad at front, ending in sharp corners.

U37

Bust broad. Figures of value in long ovals.

U38

Similar to U37 but the figure "2" at the left touches the oval.

U39

Similar to U37 but the "O" of "TWO" has the center netted instead of plain and the "G" of "POSTAGE" and the "C" of "CENTS" have diagonal crossline.

U40

Bust broad: numerals in ovals short and thick.

U41

Similar to U40 but the ovals containing the numerals are much heavier. A diagonal line runs from the upper part of the "U" to the white frame-line.

U42

Similar to U40 but the middle stroke of "N" in "CENTS" is as thin as the vertical strokes.

U43

Bottom of bust cut almost semi-circularly.

U44

Thin lettering, long thin figures of value.

U45

Thick lettering, well-formed figures of value, queue does not project below bust.

U46

Top of head egg-shaped; knot of queue well marked and projects triangularly.

Taylor — U47

Die 1 — Figures of value with thick, curved tops.

Die 2 — Figures of value with long, thin tops.

U48

Neck short at back.

U49

Figures of value turned up at the ends.

U50

Very large head.

U51

Knot of queue stands out prominently.

U52

Ear prominent, chin receding.

U53

No side whiskers, forelock projects above head.

U54

Hair does not project; ornaments around the inner oval end in points.

U55

Back of bust rather broad, chin slopes considerably; labels containing figures of value are not exactly parallel.

U56

Front of bust sloping; inner lines of shields project considerably into the inner oval.

1874-86

U108	U34	1c **dark blue**	210.00	70.00
		Entire	275.00	110.00
a.		1c **light blue**	210.00	70.00
		Entire	275.00	125.00
U109	U34	1c **dark blue,** *amber*	190.00	75.00
		Entire	210.00	140.00
+U110	U34	1c **dark blue,** *cream*	1,000.	
U111	U34	1c **dark blue,** *orange*	25.00	17.50
		Entire	35.00	25.00
a.		1c **light blue,** *orange*	25.00	17.50
		Entire	35.00	25.00
W112	U34	1c **dark blue,** *manila*	72.50	42.50
		Entire	110.00	75.00
U113	U35	1c **light blue**	1.50	1.00
		Entire	3.00	1.10
a.		1c **dark blue**	9.00	7.50
		Entire	29.00	20.00
U114	U35	1c **light blue,** *amber*	4.00	4.00
		Entire	8.25	6.00
a.		1c **dark blue,** *amber*	20.00	10.00
		Entire	30.00	20.00
U115	U35	1c **blue,** *cream*	5.25	4.50
		Entire	10.50	6.50
a.		1c **dark blue,** *cream*	20.00	8.50
		Entire	32.50	20.00
U116	U35	1c **light blue,** *orange*	.80	.40
		Entire	1.25	1.00
a.		1c **dark blue,** *orange*	4.50	2.50
		Entire	16.00	8.00
U117	U35	1c **light blue,** *blue* ('80)	8.50	5.25
		Entire	13.50	9.00
U118	U35	1c **light blue,** *fawn* ('79)	8.50	5.25
		Entire	15.00	10.00
U119	U35	1c **light blue,** *manila* ('86)	9.00	3.25
		Entire	17.00	5.00
W120	U35	1c **light blue,** *manila*	1.60	1.10
		Entire	2.75	1.75
a.		1c **dark blue,** *manila*	9.00	8.00
		Entire	16.00	15.00
U121	U35	1c **light blue,** *amber manila* ('86)	19.00	10.00
		Entire	29.00	20.00
U122	U36	2c **brown**	150.00	50.00
		Entire	175.00	85.00
U123	U36	2c **brown,** *amber*	72.50	40.00
		Entire	125.00	70.00
+U124	U36	2c **brown,** *cream*	1,000.	
+U125	U36	2c **brown,** *orange*	*25,000.*	
		Entire	*45,000.*	
W126	U36	2c **brown,** *manila*	175.00	85.00
		Entire	300.00	160.00
W127	U36	2c **vermilion,** *manila*	3,250.	250.00
		Entire	4,750.	*5,000.*
U128	U37	2c **brown**	60.00	35.00
		Entire	110.00	75.00
U129	U37	2c **brown,** *amber*	85.00	45.00
		Entire	125.00	77.50
+U130	U37	2c **brown,** *cream*	*50,000.*	
W131	U37	2c **brown,** *manila*	20.00	17.00
		Entire	29.00	26.00
U132	U38	2c **brown**	82.50	29.00
		Entire	125.00	80.00
U133	U38	2c **brown,** *amber*	525.00	70.00
		Entire	675.00	140.00
+U133A	U38	2c **brown,** *cream*	*100,000.*	
U134	U39	2c **brown**	1,500.	160.00
		Entire	2,250.	300.00
U135	U39	2c **brown,** *amber*	375.00	125.00
		Entire	650.00	160.00
U136	U39	2c **brown,** *orange*	57.50	29.00
		Entire	87.50	37.50
W137	U39	2c **brown,** *manila*	80.00	40.00
		Entire	125.00	55.00
+U137A	U39	2c **vermilion**	*40,000.*	
+U137B	U39	2c **vermilion,** *amber*	*40,000.*	
		Entire	—	
+U137C	U39	2c **vermilion,** *orange*	*100,000.*	
+W138	U39	2c **vermilion,** *manila*	*32,500.*	
U139	U40	2c **brown** ('75)	62.50	37.50
		Entire	82.50	47.50
U140	U40	2c **brown,** *amber* ('75)	97.50	62.50
		Entire	140.00	77.50
+U140A	U40	2c **reddish brown,** *orange* ('75)	*25,000.*	
		Entire	*40,000.*	
W141	U40	2c **brown,** *manila* ('75)	37.50	27.50
		Entire	45.00	32.50
U142	U40	2c **vermilion** ('75)	10.00	5.00
		Entire	13.00	7.50
a.		2c **pink**	10.00	5.00
		Entire	13.00	7.50
U143	U40	2c **vermilion,** *amber* ('75)	10.00	4.50
		Entire	13.00	5.75
U144	U40	2c **vermilion,** *cream* ('75)	21.00	7.50
		Entire	26.00	12.50
+U145	U40	2c **vermilion,** *orange* ('75)	*50,000.*	
U146	U40	2c **vermilion,** *blue* ('80)	140.00	40.00
		Entire	*200.00*	140.00
U147	U40	2c **vermilion,** *fawn* ('75)	11.00	5.00
		Entire	17.00	7.00
W148	U40	2c **vermilion,** *manila* ('75)	4.75	3.75
		Entire	9.00	6.50
U149	U41	2c **vermilion** ('78)	62.50	32.50
		Entire	95.00	45.00
a.		2c **pink**	62.50	35.00
		Entire	95.00	45.00
U150	U41	2c **vermilion,** *amber* ('78)	42.50	17.50
		Entire	62.50	22.50
U151	U41	2c **vermilion,** *blue* ('80)	14.00	10.00
		Entire	21.00	15.00
a.		2c **pink,** *blue*	15.00	10.00
		Entire	17.50	12.50
U152	U41	2c **vermilion,** *fawn* ('78)	15.00	4.75
		Entire	20.00	9.50
U153	U42	2c **vermilion** ('76)	77.50	27.50
		Entire	110.00	37.50
U154	U42	2c **vermilion,** *amber* ('76)	350.00	90.00
		Entire	450.00	175.00
W155	U42	2c **vermilion,** *manila* ('76)	24.00	11.00
		Entire	47.50	20.00
U156	U43	2c **vermilion** ('81)	1,200.	175.00
		Entire	3,750.	*500.00*
U157	U43	2c **vermilion,** *amber* ('81)	*57,500.*	*35,000.*
		Entire	*110,000.*	
W158	U43	2c **vermilion,** *manila* ('81)	110.00	62.50
		Entire	190.00	175.00
U159	U44	3c **green**	40.00	11.50
		Entire	62.50	17.50
U160	U44	3c **green,** *amber*	37.50	10.50
		Entire	65.00	20.00
U161	U44	3c **green,** *cream*	42.50	15.00
		Entire	70.00	30.00
+U162	U44	3c **green,** *blue*	*125,000.*	
U163	U45	3c **green**	1.50	.30
		Entire	4.25	2.25
U164	U45	3c **green,** *amber*	1.60	.70
		Entire	4.25	2.00
U165	U45	3c **green,** *cream*	9.50	6.50
		Entire	19.00	9.00
U166	U45	3c **green,** *blue*	8.50	6.25
		Entire	17.00	11.00
U167	U45	3c **green,** *fawn* ('75)	5.25	3.50
		Entire	9.25	5.00
U168	U46	3c **green** ('81)	1,500.	80.00
		Entire	5,000.	275.00
U169	U46	3c **green,** *amber*	625.00	110.00
		Entire	975.00	300.00
U170	U46	3c **green,** *blue* ('81)	*12,500.*	*3,250.*
		Entire	*20,000.*	*4,750.*
U171	U46	3c **green,** *fawn* ('81)	*45,000.*	*3,250.*
		Entire		*14,000.*
U172	U47	5c **blue,** die 1 ('75)	15.00	11.00
		Entire	21.00	16.00
U173	U47	5c **blue,** die 1, *amber* ('75)	15.00	12.50
		Entire	21.00	17.00
U174	U47	5c **blue,** die 1, *cream* ('75)	125.00	47.50
		Entire	190.00	95.00
U175	U47	5c **blue,** die 1, *blue* ('75)	40.00	19.00
		Entire	57.50	27.50
U176	U47	5c **blue,** die 1, *fawn* ('75)	160.00	70.00
		Entire	300.00	
U177	U47	5c **blue,** die 2 ('75)	14.00	10.00
		Entire	20.00	18.00
U178	U47	5c **blue,** die 2, *amber* ('75)	12.00	10.00
		Entire	21.00	19.00
+U178A	U47	5c **blue,** die 2, *cream* ('76)	*14,000.*	
		Entire	*22,500.*	
U179	U47	5c **blue,** die 2, *blue* ('75)	32.50	13.50
		Entire	47.50	30.00
U180	U47	5c **blue,** die 2, *fawn* ('75)	140.00	47.50
		Entire	240.00	140.00
U181	U48	6c **red**	10.00	6.75
		Entire	15.00	12.50
a.		6c **vermilion**	10.00	6.75
		Entire	15.00	12.50
U182	U48	6c **red,** *amber*	15.00	6.75
		Entire	24.00	15.00
a.		6c **vermilion,** *amber*	15.00	6.75
		Entire	24.00	15.00
U183	U48	6c **red,** *cream*	55.00	17.50
		Entire	87.50	40.00
a.		6c **vermilion,** *cream*	55.00	17.50
		Entire	87.50	40.00
U184	U48	6c **red,** *fawn* ('75)	24.00	13.50
		Entire	35.00	29.00
+U185	U49	7c **vermilion**	*1,250.*	
U186	U49	7c **vermilion,** *amber*	160.00	75.00
		Entire	200.00	
U187	U50	10c **brown**	45.00	22.50
		Entire	65.00	
U188	U50	10c **brown,** *amber*	82.50	35.00
		Entire	160.00	
U189	U51	10c **chocolate** ('75)	8.00	4.25
		Entire	13.00	9.25
a.		10c **bister brown**	9.00	5.25
		Entire	13.00	10.50
b.		10c **yellow ocher**	*4,500.*	
		Entire	*8,500.*	
U190	U51	10c **chocolate,** *amber* ('75)	9.00	7.25
		Entire	14.50	11.50
a.		10c **bister brown,** *amber*	9.00	7.75
		Entire	14.50	11.50
b.		10c **yellow ocher** *amber*	*3,500.*	
		Entire	*6,500.*	
U191	U51	10c **brown,** *oriental buff* ('86)	20.00	8.75
		Entire	22.50	11.50
U192	U51	10c **brown,** *blue* ('86)	20.00	8.75
		Entire	22.50	15.00
a.		10c **gray black,** *blue*	18.00	8.25
		Entire	21.00	15.00
b.		10c **red brown,** *blue*	18.00	8.25
		Entire	21.00	15.00
U193	U51	10c **brown,** *manila* ('86)	19.00	10.00
		Entire	24.00	16.00
a.		10c **red brown,** *manila*	19.00	10.00
		Entire	24.00	16.00
U194	U51	10c **brown,** *amber manila* ('86)	21.00	9.00
		Entire	27.50	17.50
a.		10c **red brown,** *amber manila*	21.00	9.00
		Entire	27.50	17.50
U195	U52	12c **plum**	275.00	100.00
		Entire	650.00	
U196	U52	12c **plum,** *amber*	275.00	175.00
		Entire	350.00	
U197	U52	12c **plum,** *cream*	225.00	150.00
		Entire	950.00	
U198	U53	15c **orange**	55.00	40.00
		Entire	92.50	55.00
U199	U53	15c **orange,** *amber*	160.00	100.00
		Entire	300.00	
U200	U53	15c **orange,** *cream*	400.00	350.00
		Entire	1,000.	
U201	U54	24c **purple**	175.00	150.00
		Entire	250.00	
U202	U54	24c **purple,** *amber*	200.00	125.00
		Entire	260.00	
U203	U54	24c **purple,** *cream*	190.00	125.00
		Entire	750.00	
U204	U55	30c **black**	65.00	27.50
		Entire	90.00	65.00
U205	U55	30c **black,** *amber*	75.00	60.00
		Entire	140.00	*250.00*
U206	U55	30c **black,** *cream* ('75)	250.00	375.00
		Entire	700.00	
U207	U55	30c **black,** *oriental buff* ('81)	100.00	82.50
		Entire	160.00	
U208	U55	30c **black,** *blue* ('81)	110.00	82.50
		Entire	200.00	
U209	U55	30c **black,** *manila* ('81)	95.00	80.00
		Entire	160.00	
U210	U55	30c **black,** *amber manila* ('86)	175.00	85.00

			Entire	210.00	
U211	U56	90c	**carmine** ('75)	110.00	85.00
			Entire	160.00	95.00
U212	U56	90c	**carmine,** *amber* ('75)	225.00	300.00
			Entire	275.00	
U213	U56	90c	**carmine,** *cream* ('75)	1,400.	
			Entire	3,000.	
U214	U56	90c	**carmine,** *oriental buff* ('86)	200.00	275.00
			Entire	400.00	300.00
U215	U56	90c	**carmine,** *blue* ('86)	200.00	250.00
			Entire	275.00	275.00
U216	U56	90c	**carmine,** *manila* ('86)	175.00	250.00
			Entire	275.00	275.00
U217	U56	90c	**carmine,** *amber manila* ('86)	150.00	200.00
			Entire	225.00	275.00

Note: No. U206 has watermark #2; No. U207 watermark #6 or #7. No U213 has watermark #2; No. U214 watermark #7. These envelopes cannot be positively identified except by the watermark.

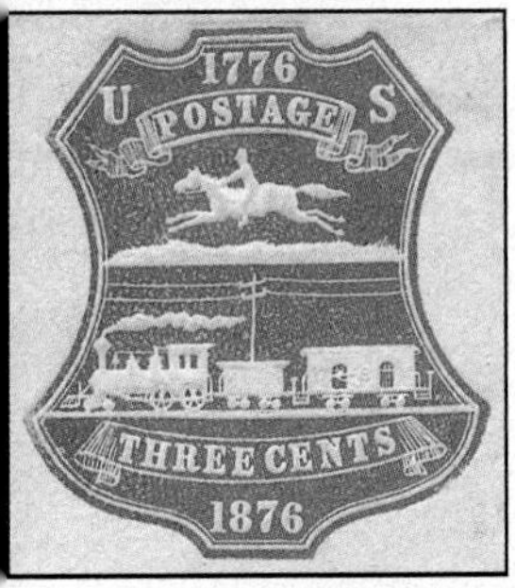

U57

Single line under "POSTAGE."

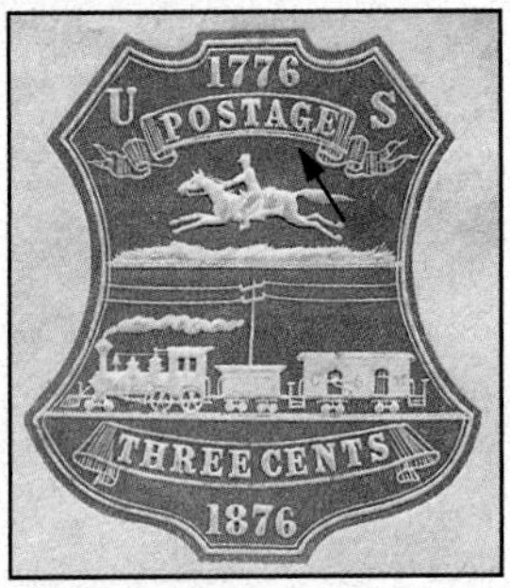

U58

Double line under "POSTAGE."

1876

Printed by Plimpton Manufacturing Co.

U218	U57	3c	**red**	52.50	25.00
			Entire	77.50	50.00
U219	U57	3c	**green**	45.00	17.50
			Entire	65.00	40.00
U220	U58	3c	**red**	*42,500.*	
			Entire	*60,000.*	
U221	U58	3c	**green**	52.50	25.00
			Entire	85.00	50.00

Garfield — U59

1882-86

Printed by Plimpton Manufacturing Co. and Morgan Envelope Co.

U222	U59	5c	**brown**	5.75	3.00
			Entire	10.50	7.00
U223	U59	5c	**brown,** *amber*	6.00	3.50
			Entire	11.00	8.50
U224	U59	5c	**brown,** *oriental buff* ('86)	140.00	75.00
			Entire	200.00	
U225	U59	5c	**brown,** *blue*	82.50	35.00
			Entire	125.00	75.00
U226	U59	5c	**brown,** *fawn*	375.00	
			Entire	525.00	

Washington — U60

1883, October

U227	U60	2c	**red**	4.50	2.25
			Entire	10.00	3.00
	a.	2c	**brown** (error), entire	*10,000.*	
U228	U60	2c	**red,** *amber*	5.75	2.75
			Entire	10.50	6.00
U229	U60	2c	**red,** *blue*	8.50	5.00
			Entire	13.00	8.00
U230	U60	2c	**red,** *fawn*	9.25	5.25
			Entire	15.00	7.00

Washington — U61

Wavy lines fine and clear.

1883, November

Four Wavy Lines in Oval

U231	U61	2c	**red**	5.50	2.50
			Entire	10.00	4.00
U232	U61	2c	**red,** *amber*	6.50	3.75
			Entire	12.00	5.75
U233	U61	2c	**red,** *blue*	11.00	7.50
			Entire	19.00	10.00
U234	U61	2c	**red,** *fawn*	8.00	4.75
			Entire	12.00	6.00
W235	U61	2c	**red,** *manila*	22.50	6.25
			Entire	32.50	12.50

U62

Retouched die. Wavy lines thick and blurred.

1884, June

U236	U62	2c	**red**	14.50	4.00
			Entire	22.50	7.75
U237	U62	2c	**red,** *amber*	17.50	10.00
			Entire	27.50	11.00
U238	U62	2c	**red,** *blue*	29.00	12.00
			Entire	40.00	15.00
U239	U62	2c	**red,** *fawn*	25.00	11.00
			Entire	35.00	12.50

U63

3½ links over left "2."

U240	U63	2c	**red**	100.00	47.50
			Entire	160.00	72.50
U241	U63	2c	**red,** *amber*	1,000.	325.00
			Entire	2,750.	750.00
U242	U63	2c	**red,** *fawn*		*37,500.*
			Entire		*55,000.*

U64

2 links below right "2."

U243	U64	2c	**red**	140.00	75.00
			Entire	175.00	100.00
U244	U64	2c	**red,** *amber*	350.00	100.00
			Entire	500.00	125.00
U245	U64	2c	**red,** *blue*	350.00	210.00
			Entire	650.00	225.00
U246	U64	2c	**red,** *fawn*	300.00	170.00
			Entire	700.00	275.00

U65

Round "O" in "TWO." White lines above "WO" of "TWO" joined to form thick white dash.

U247	U65	2c	**red**	3,500.	500.00
			Entire	4,500.	*1,250.*
U248	U65	2c	**red,** *amber*	5,250.	750.00
			Entire	8,000.	*1,650.*
U249	U65	2c	**red,** *fawn*	1,100.	500.00
			Entire	2,250.	*750.00*

Jackson, Die 1 — U66

Die 1 — Numeral at left is 2¾mm wide.

Die 2 — Numeral at left is 3¼mm wide.

1883-86

U250	U66	4c	**green,** die 1	4.00	3.50
			Entire	6.50	6.00
U251	U66	4c	**green,** die 1, *amber*	5.00	3.50
			Entire	7.50	5.25
U252	U66	4c	**green,** die 1, *oriental buff* ('86)	13.00	9.00
			Entire	18.00	12.50
U253	U66	4c	**green,** die 1, *blue* ('86)	13.00	6.50
			Entire	18.00	8.00
U254	U66	4c	**green,** die 1, *manila* ('86)	16.00	7.50
			Entire	21.00	15.00
U255	U66	4c	**green,** die 1, *amber manila* ('86)	24.00	10.00
			Entire	32.50	15.00
U256	U66	4c	**green,** die 2	11.00	5.00
			Entire	19.00	6.75
U257	U66	4c	**green,** die 2, *amber*	15.00	7.00
			Entire	25.00	10.00
U258	U66	4c	**green,** die 2, *manila* ('86)	15.00	7.50
			Entire	25.00	12.50
U259	U66	4c	**green,** die 2, *amber manila* ('86)	15.00	7.50
			Entire	25.00	12.50

1884, May

U260	U61	2c	**brown**	19.00	5.75
			Entire	21.00	9.00
U261	U61	2c	**brown,** *amber*	19.00	6.50
			Entire	21.00	7.50
U262	U61	2c	**brown,** *blue*	23.00	10.00
			Entire	29.00	14.00
U263	U61	2c	**brown,** *fawn*	18.50	9.25
			Entire	20.00	12.50
W264	U61	2c	**brown,** *manila*	19.00	11.50
			Entire	26.00	19.00

1884, June

Retouched Die

U265	U62	2c	**brown**	20.00	6.50
			Entire	27.50	12.00
U266	U62	2c	**brown,** *amber*	67.50	40.00
			Entire	75.00	50.00
U267	U62	2c	**brown,** *blue*	25.00	9.00
			Entire	32.50	15.00
U268	U62	2c	**brown,** *fawn*	18.00	11.00
			Entire	22.50	15.00
W269	U62	2c	**brown,** *manila*	30.00	15.00
			Entire	35.00	24.00

2 Links Below Right "2"

U270	U64	2c	**brown**	140.00	50.00
			Entire	175.00	110.00
U271	U64	2c	**brown,** *amber*	500.00	110.00
			Entire	600.00	350.00
U272	U64	2c	**brown,** *fawn*	*10,000.*	*3,000.*
			Entire	*12,000.*	*4,000.*

Round "O" in "Two"

U273	U65	2c	**brown**	225.00	110.00
			Entire	400.00	200.00
U274	U65	2c	**brown,** *amber*	225.00	110.00
			Entire	400.00	190.00
U275	U65	2c	**brown,** *blue*		*20,000.*
			Entire		*47,500.*
U276	U65	2c	**brown,** *fawn*	900.00	700.00
			Entire	1,550.	*900.00*

Washington — U67

Extremity of bust below the queue forms a point.

U68

Extremity of bust is rounded. Similar to U61. Two wavy lines in oval.

1884-86

U277	U67	2c	**brown**	.50	.20
			Entire	1.00	.40
a.		2c	**brown lake,** die 1	22.50	21.00
			Entire	27.50	26.00
U278	U67	2c	**brown,** *amber*	.65	.50
			Entire	1.75	.75
a.		2c	**brown lake,** *amber*	35.00	25.00
			Entire	42.50	32.50
U279	U67	2c	**brown,** *oriental buff* ('86)	5.00	2.10
			Entire	7.50	3.00
U280	U67	2c	**brown,** *blue*	3.00	2.10
			Entire	4.50	3.50
U281	U67	2c	**brown,** *fawn*	3.75	2.40
			Entire	5.75	4.00
U282	U67	2c	**brown,** *manila* ('86)	13.00	4.00
			Entire	17.50	6.50
W283	U67	2c	**brown,** *manila*	7.50	5.00
			Entire	11.00	6.50
U284	U67	2c	**brown,** *amber manila* ('86)	9.00	5.75
			Entire	15.00	7.00
+U285	U67	2c	**red**	775.00	
			Entire	1,650.	
+U286	U67	2c	**red,** *blue*	325.00	
			Entire	375.00	
W287	U67	2c	**red,** *manila*	150.00	
			Entire	210.00	
U288	U68	2c	**brown**	325.00	50.00
			Entire	825.00	150.00
U289	U68	2c	**brown,** *amber*	18.00	13.00
			Entire	24.00	17.00
U290	U68	2c	**brown,** *blue*	1,250.	300.00
			Entire	2,400.	450.00
U291	U68	2c	**brown,** *fawn*	35.00	22.50
			Entire	45.00	27.50
W292	U68	2c	**brown,** *manila*	25.00	19.00
			Entire	35.00	22.50

Gen. U.S. Grant — US1

1886

Printed by American Bank Note Co.

Issued August 18, 1886. Withdrawn June 30, 1894.

Letter Sheet, 160x271mm

Stamp in upper right corner

Creamy White Paper

U293	US1	2c	**green,** entire	30.00	20.00

Perforation varieties:

83 perforations at top	30.00	20.00
42 perforations at top	65.00	30.00
33 perforations at top	65.00	30.00

All with 41 perforations at top

Inscribed: Series 1	30.00	20.00
Inscribed: Series 2	30.00	20.00
Inscribed: Series 3	30.00	20.00
Inscribed: Series 4	30.00	20.00
Inscribed: Series 5	30.00	20.00
Inscribed: Series 6	30.00	20.00
Inscribed: Series 7	30.00	20.00
No inscription, continuous side perforations	30.00	20.00
No inscription, interrupted side perforations	30.00	20.00

Franklin — U69

Washington — U70

Bust points between third and fourth notches of inner oval "G" of "POSTAGE" has no bar.

U71

Bust points between second and third notches of inner oval; "G" of "POSTAGE" has a bar; ear is indicated by one heavy line; one vertical line at corner of mouth.

U72

Frame same as U71; upper part of head more rounded; ea indicated by two curved lines with two locks of hair in front; tw vertical lines at corner of mouth.

Jackson — U73

Grant — U74

There is a space between the beard and the collar of the coat. A button is on the collar.

U75

The collar touches the beard and there is no button.

1887-94

Printed by Plimpton Manufacturing Co. and Morgan Envelope Co., Hartford, Conn.; James Purcell, Holyoke, Mass.

U294	U69	1c	**blue**	.55	.20
			Entire	1.00	.50
U295	U69	1c	**dark blue** ('94)	7.50	2.50
			Entire	10.50	6.50
U296	U69	1c	**blue,** *amber*	3.50	1.25
			Entire	6.00	3.50
U297	U69	1c	**dark blue,** *amber* ('94)	47.50	22.50
			Entire	57.50	27.50
+U298	U69	1c	**blue,** *oriental buff*	*15,000.*	
			Entire	*20,000.*	
+U299	U69	1c	**blue,** *blue*	*20,000.*	
			Entire	*30,000.*	
U300	U69	1c	**blue,** *manila*	.65	.35
			Entire	1.25	.75
W301	U69	1c	**blue,** *manila*	.45	.30
			Entire	1.25	.60
U302	U69	1c	**dark blue,** *manila* ('94)	30.00	12.50
			Entire	37.50	20.00
W303	U69	1c	**dark blue,** *manila* ('94)	17.50	10.00
			Entire	25.00	15.00
U304	U69	1c	**blue,** *amber manila*	12.50	5.00
			Entire	17.50	7.50
U305	U70	2c	**green**	19.00	10.50
			Entire	35.00	15.00
U306	U70	2c	**green,** *amber*	45.00	17.50
			Entire	55.00	22.50
U307	U70	2c	**green,** *oriental buff*	97.50	35.00
			Entire	125.00	50.00
U308	U70	2c	**green,** *blue*	*20,000.*	1,250.
			Entire		*22,000.*
U309	U70	2c	**green,** *manila*	*17,500.*	750.00
			Entire	*25,000.*	1,050.
U310	U70	2c	**green,** *amber manila*	40,000.	1,250.
			Entire	—	*3,500.*
U311	U71	2c	**green**	.35	.20
			Entire	.75	.25
a.		2c	**dark green** ('94)	.50	.30
			Entire	1.10	.85
U312	U71	2c	**green,** *amber*	.45	.20
			Entire	.80	.30
a.			Double impression	—	
b.		2c	**dark green,** *amber* ('94)	.60	.35
			Entire	1.10	.85
U313	U71	2c	**green,** *oriental buff*	.60	.25
			Entire	1.20	.40
a.		2c	**dark green,** *oriental buff* ('94)	2.00	1.00
			Entire	4.00	4.00
U314	U71	2c	**green,** *blue*	.65	.30
			Entire	1.25	.40
a.		2c	**dark green** *blue* ('94)	.85	.40
			Entire	1.75	1.50
U315	U71	2c	**green,** *manila*	1.75	.50
			Entire	2.75	1.00
a.		2c	**dark green** *manila* ('94)	2.75	.75
			Entire	4.00	1.50
W316	U71	2c	**green,** *manila*	4.00	2.50
			Entire	11.00	7.00
U317	U71	2c	**green,** *amber manila*	2.75	1.90
			Entire	6.00	3.00
a.		2c	**dark green,** *amber manila* ('94)	4.00	3.00
			Entire	7.50	4.00
U318	U72	2c	**green**	150.00	12.50

		Entire	200.00	45.00
U319	U72	2c **green,** *amber*	190.00	25.00
		Entire	275.00	50.00
U320	U72	2c **green,** *oriental buff*	175.00	40.00
		Entire	240.00	70.00
U321	U72	2c **green,** *blue*	190.00	65.00
		Entire	300.00	82.50
U322	U72	2c **green,** *manila*	275.00	65.00
		Entire	325.00	110.00
U323	U72	2c **green,** *amber manila*	375.00	100.00
		Entire	700.00	175.00
U324	U73	4c **carmine**	3.25	2.00
		Entire	6.00	2.10
a.		4c **lake**	3.50	2.00
		Entire	7.00	3.75
b.		4c **scarlet** ('94)	3.50	2.00
		Entire	7.00	3.75
U325	U73	4c **carmine,** *amber*	3.75	3.50
		Entire	7.50	4.00
a.		4c **lake,** *amber*	3.75	3.50
		Entire	7.75	4.00
b.		4c **scarlet,** *amber* ('94)	4.00	3.75
		Entire	8.00	4.25
U326	U73	4c **carmine,** *oriental buff*	8.00	3.50
		Entire	16.00	6.25
a.		4c **lake,** *oriental buff*	8.00	3.50
		Entire	16.00	6.25
U327	U73	4c **carmine,** *blue*	6.50	4.00
		Entire	13.00	7.00
a.		4c **lake,** *blue*	6.50	4.00
		Entire	13.00	6.00
U328	U73	4c **carmine,** *manila*	9.00	7.00
		Entire	13.00	7.50
a.		4c **lake,** *manila*	9.00	6.00
		Entire	13.00	7.50
b.		4c **pink,** *manila*	15.00	10.00
		Entire	21.00	12.50
U329	U73	4c **carmine,** *amber manila*	7.50	3.25
		Entire	13.50	5.00
a.		4c **lake,** *amber manila*	7.50	3.25
		Entire	13.50	5.00
b.		4c **pink,** *amber manila*	16.00	10.00
		Entire	22.50	12.50
U330	U74	5c **blue**	4.00	4.00
		Entire	8.00	11.00
U331	U74	5c **blue,** *amber*	5.50	2.50
		Entire	10.50	14.00
U332	U74	5c **blue,** *oriental buff*	6.00	4.00
		Entire	17.00	18.00
U333	U74	5c **blue,** *blue*	10.50	6.00
		Entire	17.00	15.00
U334	U75	5c **blue** ('94)	27.50	12.50
		Entire	42.50	22.50
U335	U75	5c **blue,** *amber* ('94)	15.00	7.50
		Entire	20.00	40.00
U336	U55	30c **red brown**	60.00	47.50
		Entire	70.00	*475.00*
a.		30c **yellow brown**	60.00	47.50
		Entire	70.00	*475.00*
b.		30c **chocolate**	60.00	47.50
		Entire	70.00	*475.00*
U337	U55	30c **red brown,** *amber*	60.00	47.50
		Entire	70.00	*475.00*
a.		30c **yellow brown,** *amber*	60.00	47.50
		Entire	70.00	*475.00*
b.		30c **chocolate,** *amber*	60.00	47.50
		Entire	70.00	*475.00*
U338	U55	30c **red brown,** *oriental buff*	60.00	47.50
		Entire	70.00	*475.00*
a.		30c **yellow brown,** *oriental buff*	60.00	47.50
		Entire	70.00	*475.00*
U339	U55	30c **red brown,** *blue*	60.00	47.50
		Entire	70.00	*475.00*
a.		30c **yellow brown,** *blue*	60.00	47.50
		Entire	70.00	*475.00*
U340	U55	30c **red brown,** *manila*	60.00	47.50
		Entire	70.00	*475.00*
a.		30c **brown,** *manila*	60.00	47.50
		Entire	70.00	*475.00*
U341	U55	30c **red brown,** *amber manila*	60.00	47.50
		Entire	70.00	*475.00*
a.		30c **yellow brown,** *amber manila*	60.00	47.50
		Entire	70.00	*475.00*
U342	U56	90c **purple**	77.50	*90.00*
		Entire	110.00	*1,050.*
U343	U56	90c **purple,** *amber*	92.50	90.00
		Entire	140.00	*1,050.*
U344	U56	90c **purple,** *oriental buff*	92.50	90.00
		Entire	150.00	*1,050.*
U345	U56	90c **purple,** *blue*	92.50	*90.00*
		Entire	150.00	*1,050.*
U346	U56	90c **purple,** *manila*	100.00	*92.50*
		Entire	150.00	*1,050.*
U347	U56	90c **purple,** *amber manila*	100.00	*92.50*
		Entire	150.00	*1,050.*

Columbus and Liberty — U76

Four dies were used for the 1c, 2c and 5c:
1 — Meridian behind Columbus' head. Period after "CENTS" and "AMERICA" appears on 1c, 2c and 5c.
2 — No meridian. With periods. Appears on 1c, 2c and 5c.
3 — With meridian. No periods. Appears on 1c, 2c and 10c.
4 — No meridian. No periods. Appears on 2c.

1893

U348	U76	1c **deep blue**	2.25	1.25
		Entire	3.00	1.50
		Entire, Expo. station machine cancel		100.00
		Entire, Expo. station duplex handstamp cancel		250.00
U349	U76	2c **violet**	1.75	.50
		Entire	3.50	.60
		Entire, Expo. station machine cancel		40.00
		Entire, Expo. station duplex handstamp cancel		85.00
a.		2c **dark slate** (error)	*2,500.*	
		Entire	*5,000.*	
U350	U76	5c **chocolate**	8.50	7.50
		Entire	13.00	10.00
		Entire, Expo. station machine cancel		150.00
		Entire, Expo. station duplex handstamp cancel		250.00
a.		5c **slate brown** (error)	*850.00*	*950.00*
		Entire	*1,200.*	*1,400.*
U351	U76	10c **slate brown**	35.00	30.00
		Entire	70.00	60.00
		Entire, Expo. station machine cancel		250.00
		Entire, Expo. station duplex handstamp cancel		450.00

Franklin — U77

Washington — U78

Bust points to first notch of inner oval and is only slightly concave below.

U79

Bust points to middle of second notch of inner oval and is quite hollow below. Queue has ribbon around it.

U80

Same as die 2, but hair flowing. No ribbon on queue.

Lincoln — U81

Bust pointed but not draped.

U82

Bust broad and draped.

U83

Head larger, inner oval has no notches.

Grant — U84

Similar to design of 1887-95 but smaller.

1899

U352	U77	1c **green**	1.10	.20
		Entire	2.75	.50
U353	U77	1c **green,** *amber*	5.50	1.50
		Entire	8.75	2.75
U354	U77	1c **green,** *oriental buff*	14.50	2.75
		Entire	19.00	3.75
U355	U77	1c **green,** *blue*	14.50	7.50
		Entire	19.00	12.50
U356	U77	1c **green,** *manila*	2.40	.95
		Entire	6.50	2.00
W357	U77	1c **green,** *manila*	2.50	1.10
		Entire	9.00	4.00
U358	U78	2c **carmine**	3.00	1.75
		Entire	8.00	3.25
U359	U78	2c **carmine,** *amber*	25.00	15.00
		Entire	32.50	21.00
U360	U78	2c **carmine,** *oriental buff*	24.00	12.50
		Entire	35.00	15.00
U361	U78	2c **carmine,** *blue*	65.00	35.00
		Entire	77.50	50.00
U362	U79	2c **carmine**	.35	.20
		Entire	.65	.30
a.		2c **dark lake**	30.00	30.00
		Entire	37.50	35.00
U363	U79	2c **carmine,** *amber*	1.40	.20
		Entire	3.00	.60
U364	U79	2c **carmine,** *oriental buff*	1.20	.20
		Entire	3.00	.60
U365	U79	2c **carmine,** *blue*	1.50	.55
		Entire	3.50	2.00
W366	U79	2c **carmine,** *manila*	8.00	3.25
		Entire	12.00	7.50
U367	U80	2c **carmine**	6.00	2.75
		Entire	11.00	6.75
U368	U80	2c **carmine,** *amber*	9.00	6.75
		Entire	15.00	12.00
U369	U80	2c **carmine,** *oriental buff*	25.00	12.50
		Entire	32.50	20.00
U370	U80	2c **carmine,** *blue*	12.50	10.00

			Entire	25.00	15.00
U371	U81	4c	**brown**	20.00	13.00
			Entire	30.00	18.00
U372	U81	4c	**brown,** *amber*	20.00	13.00
			Entire	32.50	24.00
U373	U82	4c	**brown**	*13,500.*	1,250.
			Entire	*20,000.*	
U374	U83	4c	**brown**	15.00	8.00
			Entire	27.50	12.50
U375	U83	4c	**brown,** *amber*	65.00	25.00
			Entire	80.00	40.00
W376	U83	4c	**brown,** *manila*	20.00	10.00
			Entire	35.00	25.00
U377	U84	5c	**blue**	13.00	10.00
			Entire	18.00	17.00
U378	U84	5c	**blue,** *amber*	17.00	10.50
			Entire	25.00	18.00

Franklin — U85

Washington — U86

"D" of "UNITED" contains vertical line at right that parallels the left vertical line. One short and two long vertical lines at the right of "CENTS."

Grant — U87

Lincoln — U88

1903

Printed by Hartford Manufacturing Co., Hartford, Conn.

U379	U85	1c	**green**	.80	.20
			Entire	1.25	.35
U380	U85	1c	**green,** *amber*	16.00	2.00
			Entire	22.50	2.50
U381	U85	1c	**green,** *oriental buff*	19.00	2.50
			Entire	26.00	3.00
U382	U85	1c	**green,** *blue*	24.00	2.50
			Entire	35.00	3.00
U383	U85	1c	**green,** *manila*	4.50	.90
			Entire	6.00	1.25
W384	U85	1c	**green,** *manila*	3.00	.40
			Entire	5.00	.80
U385	U86	2c	**carmine**	.50	.20
			Entire	.95	.35
a.		2c	**pink**	2.00	1.50
			Entire	3.00	2.00
b.		2c	**red**	2.00	1.50
			Entire	3.00	2.00
U386	U86	2c	**carmine,** *amber*	2.50	.20
			Entire	4.00	.80
a.		2c	**pink,** *amber*	5.50	3.00
			Entire	7.50	4.00
b.		2c	**red,** *amber*	14.00	7.00
			Entire	20.00	10.00
U387	U86	2c	**carmine,** *oriental buff*	2.25	.30
			Entire	3.50	.35
a.		2c	**pink,** *oriental buff*	3.50	2.00
			Entire	5.00	3.00
b.		2c	**red,** *oriental buff*	4.00	2.25
			Entire	5.50	3.25
U388	U86	2c	**carmine,** *blue*	2.00	.50
			Entire	3.00	.60
a.		2c	**pink,** *blue*	22.50	14.00
			Entire	30.00	18.00
b.		2c	**red,** *blue*	22.50	14.00
			Entire	30.00	18.00
W389	U86	2c	**carmine,** *manila*	21.00	10.00
			Entire	27.50	15.00
U390	U87	4c	**chocolate**	22.50	12.50
			Entire	32.50	15.00
U391	U87	4c	**chocolate,** *amber*	24.00	12.50
			Entire	35.00	15.00
W392	U87	4c	**chocolate,** *manila*	25.00	12.50
			Entire	50.00	40.00
U393	U88	5c	**blue**	24.00	12.50
			Entire	35.00	17.50
U394	U88	5c	**blue,** *amber*	24.00	12.50
			Entire	35.00	20.00

U89

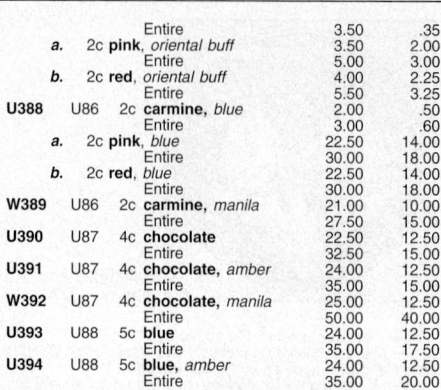

Re-cut die — "D" of "UNITED" is well rounded at right. The three lines at the right of "CENTS" and at the left of "TWO" are usually all short; the lettering is heavier and the ends of the ribbons slightly changed.

1904

Re-cut Die

U395	U89	2c	**carmine**	.75	.20
			Entire	1.75	.45
a.		2c	pink	5.50	2.50
U396	U89	2c	**carmine,** *amber*	9.00	1.00
			Entire	14.00	2.00
a.		2c	pink, *amber*	11.00	3.00
U397	U89	2c	**carmine,** *oriental buff*	6.00	1.10
			Entire	8.50	1.50
a.		2c	pink, *oriental buff*	7.50	2.75
U398	U89	2c	**carmine,** *blue*	4.50	.90
			Entire	6.00	1.40
a.		2c	pink, *blue*	6.00	2.50
W399	U89	2c	**carmine,** *manila*	16.00	10.00
			Entire	35.00	25.00
a.		2c	pink, *manila*	27.50	17.50
			Entire	70.00	85.00

Franklin — U90

U90 Die 1

U90 Die 2

U90 Die 3

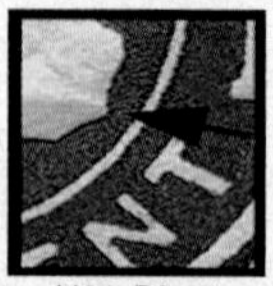
U90 Die 4

Die 1 — Wide "D" in "UNITED."
Die 2 — Narrow "D" in "UNITED."
Die 3 — Wide "S-S" in "STATES" (1910).
Die 4 — Sharp angle at back of bust, "N" and "E" of "ONE" are parallel (1912).

1907-16

Printed by Mercantile Corp. and Middle West Supply Co., Dayton, Ohio

U400	U90	1c	**green,** die 1	.35	.20
			Entire	.60	.30
a.	Die 2			.85	.25
			Entire	1.25	.45
b.	Die 3			.85	.35
			Entire	1.40	.65
c.	Die 4			.90	.30
			Entire	1.40	.45
U401	U90	1c	**green,** *amber,* die 1	2.10	.40
			Entire	2.75	.60
a.	Die 2			2.60	.70
			Entire	3.50	.80
b.	Die 3			3.25	.75
			Entire	4.00	.80
c.	Die 4			2.10	.65
			Entire	3.00	.75
U402	U90	1c	**green,** *oriental buff,* die 1	10.50	1.00
			Entire	13.50	1.75
a.	Die 2			13.00	1.50
			Entire	18.50	1.75
b.	Die 3			15.50	1.50
			Entire	21.00	2.50
c.	Die 4			10.50	1.50
			Entire	13.50	2.25
U403	U90	1c	**green,** *blue,* die 1	10.50	1.50
			Entire	13.50	2.25
a.	Die 2			13.00	3.00
			Entire	16.50	4.00
b.	Die 3			12.50	3.00
			Entire	16.00	3.25
c.	Die 4			9.50	1.25
			Entire	13.50	3.00
U404	U90	1c	**green,** *manila,* die 1	3.50	1.90
			Entire	6.00	2.75
a.	Die 3			4.50	3.00
			Entire	7.00	4.50
W405	U90	1c	**green,** *manila,* die 1	1.00	.25
			Entire	2.25	1.00
a.	Die 2			65.00	25.00
			Entire	90.00	30.00
b.	Die 3			12.00	4.00
			Entire	36.00	25.00
c.	Die 4			90.00	—
			Entire	—	—

Washington — U91 — brown red

U91 Die 1 — carmine

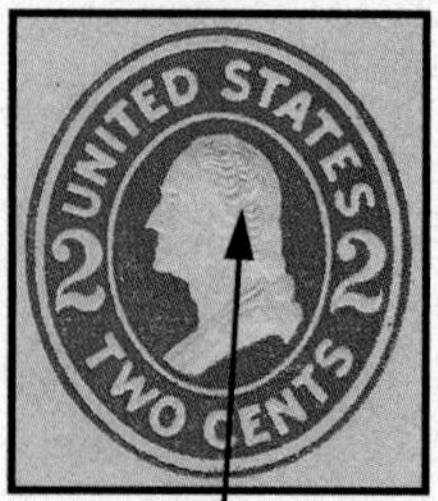
U91 Die 2

U91 Die 3

U91 Die 4

U91 Die 5

U91 Die 6

U91 Die 7

U91 Die 8

Die 1 — Oval "O" in "TWO" and "C" in "CENTS." Front of bust broad.
Die 2 — Similar to 1 but hair re-cut in two distinct locks at top of head.
Die 3 — Round "O" in "TWO" and "C" in "CENTS," coarse lettering.
Die 4 — Similar to 3 but lettering fine and clear, hair lines clearly embossed. Inner oval thin and clear.
Die 5 — All "S's" wide (1910).
Die 6 — Similar to 1 but front of bust narrow (1913).
Die 7 — Similar to 6 but upper corner of front of bust cut away (1916).
Die 8 — Similar to 7 but lower stroke of "S" in "CENTS" is a straight line. Hair as in Die 2 (1916).

U406	U91	2c	**brown red,** die 1	1.00	.20
			Entire	2.75	.30
a.			Die 2	45.00	7.00
			Entire	100.00	50.00
b.			Die 3	.90	.20
			Entire	2.75	1.00
U407	U91	2c	**brown red,** *amber,* die 1	6.50	2.00
			Entire	9.00	5.00
a.			Die 2	375.00	65.00
			Entire	600.00	200.00
b.			Die 3	4.50	1.25
			Entire	7.00	1.90
U408	U91	2c	**brown red,** *oriental buff,* die 1	8.75	1.50
			Entire	12.00	3.75
a.			Die 2	390.00	125.00
			Entire	600.00	300.00
b.			Die 3	7.50	2.50
			Entire	11.00	5.00
U409	U91	2c	**brown red,** *blue,* die 1	5.75	2.00
			Entire	8.00	3.75
a.			Die 2	390.00	200.00
			Entire	750.00	500.00
b.			Die 3	5.75	1.75
			Entire	8.00	3.50
W410	U91	2c	**brown red,** *manila,* die 1	42.50	32.50
			Entire	55.00	42.50
U411	U91	2c	**carmine,** die 1	.35	.20
			Entire	1.25	.35
a.			Die 2	.90	.20
			Entire	2.25	1.50
b.			Die 3	.80	.35
			Entire	1.50	.50
c.			Die 4	.65	.20
			Entire	1.25	.35
d.			Die 5	.65	.30
			Entire	1.75	.50
e.			Die 6	.60	.20
			Entire	1.50	.30
f.			Die 7	42.50	25.00
			Entire	55.00	30.00
g.			Die 8	42.50	25.00
			Entire	55.00	30.00
h.			#U411 with added impression of #U400, entire	475.00	
i.			#U411 with added impression of #U416a, entire	475.00	
U412	U91	2c	**carmine,** *amber,* die 1	.30	.20
			Entire	1.10	.20
a.			Die 2	2.10	.25
			Entire	5.00	3.00
b.			Die 3	2.25	.45
			Entire	3.00	.75
c.			Die 4	.55	.25
			Entire	1.25	.40
d.			Die 5	.90	.35
			Entire	1.50	.55
e.			Die 6	.70	.35
			Entire	1.10	.50
f.			Die 7	37.50	25.00
			Entire	50.00	32.50
U413	U91	2c	**carmine,** *oriental buff,* die 1	.55	.20
			Entire	.75	.25
a.			Die 2	2.25	.45
			Entire	5.00	3.75
b.			Die 3	9.00	3.00
			Entire	15.00	5.50
c.			Die 4	.55	.20
			Entire	1.25	.40
d.			Die 5	3.50	1.25
			Entire	5.00	3.25
e.			Die 6	.70	.35
			Entire	1.25	.55
f.			Die 7	105.00	45.00
			Entire	135.00	62.50
g.			Die 8	32.50	22.50
			Entire	50.00	27.50
U414	U91	2c	**carmine,** *blue,* die 1	.60	.20
			Entire	1.40	.25
a.			Die 2	2.25	.35
			Entire	5.50	5.00
b.			Die 3	2.75	.60
			Entire	4.00	.70
c.			Die 4	.70	.25
			Entire	1.25	.45
d.			Die 5	2.25	.30
			Entire	3.00	.40
e.			Die 6	.65	.30
			Entire	1.10	.40
f.			Die 7	42.50	25.00
			Entire	50.00	35.00
g.			Die 8	42.50	25.00
			Entire	50.00	35.00
W415	U91	2c	**carmine,** *manila,* die 1	5.00	2.00
			Entire	8.00	4.75
a.			Die 2	5.50	1.25
			Entire	8.00	4.50
b.			Die 5	5.50	2.50
			Entire	8.00	3.00
c.			Die 7	130.00	97.50
			Entire	175.00	125.00

U90 4c Die 1

U90 4c Die 2

Die 1 — "F" close to (1mm) left "4."
Die 2 — "F" far from (1¾mm) left "4."

U416	U90	4c	**black,** die 2	6.00	3.00
			Entire	11.00	5.00
a.			Die 1	6.00	3.00
			Entire	11.00	5.00
U417	U90	4c	**black,** *amber,* die 2	7.50	2.50
			Entire	12.00	4.00
a.			Die 1	7.50	2.50
			Entire	12.00	4.00

Die 1 — Tall "F" in "FIVE"

Die 2 — Short "F" in "FIVE"

Die 1 — Tall "F" in "FIVE."
Die 2 — Short "F" in "FIVE."

U418	U91	5c	**blue,** die 2	7.00	2.25
			Entire	13.50	6.50
a.			Die 1	7.00	2.25
			Entire	13.50	6.50
b.			5c **blue,** *buff,* die 2 (error)	*3,000.*	
c.			5c **blue,** *blue,* die 2 (error)	*3,000.*	
d.			As "c," die 1 (error), entire	*6,500.*	
U419	U91	5c	**blue,** *amber,* die 2	16.50	11.00
			Entire	22.50	13.00
a.			Die 1	16.50	11.00
			Entire	22.50	13.00

On July 1, 1915 the use of laid paper was discontinued and wove paper was substituted. Nos. U400 to W405 and U411 to U419 exist on both papers: U406 to W410 come on laid only. Nos. U429 and U430 exist on laid paper.

Franklin — U92

Die 1

Die 2

Die 3

Die 4

Die 5

(The 1c and 4c dies are the same except for figures of value.)
Die 1 — UNITED nearer inner circle than outer circle.
Die 2 — Large U; large NT closely spaced.
Die 3 — Knob of hair at back of neck. Large NT widely spaced.
Die 4 — UNITED nearer outer circle than inner circle.
Die 5 — Narrow oval C, (also O and G).

Printed by Middle West Supply Co. and International Envelope Corp., Dayton, Ohio.

1915-32

U420	U92	1c	**green,** die 1 ('17)	.25	.20
			Entire	.40	.20
a.			Die 2	150.00	55.00
			Entire, size 8	200.00	70.00
b.			Die 3	.35	.20
			Entire	.50	.25
c.			Die 4	.55	.40
			Entire	.80	.50
d.			Die 5	.45	.35
			Entire	.75	.45
U421	U92	1c	**green,***amber,*die 1 ('17)	.55	.30
			Entire	.80	.45
a.			Die 2	500.00	175.00
			Entire, size 8	700.00	200.00
b.			Die 3	1.40	.65
			Entire	2.00	.95
c.			Die 4	1.90	.85
			Entire	2.50	1.25
d.			Die 5	1.10	.55
			Entire	1.75	.80
U422	U92	1c	**green,** *oriental buff,* die 1 ('17)	2.40	.90
			Entire	3.25	1.40
a.			Die 4	5.50	1.25
			Entire	8.00	2.75
U423	U92	1c	**green,** *blue,* die 1 ('17)	.50	.35
			Entire	.90	.50
a.			Die 3	.80	.45
			Entire	1.25	.70
b.			Die 4	1.40	.65
			Entire	2.50	.95
c.			Die 5	.85	.35
			Entire	1.60	.65
U424	U92	1c	**grn,** *manila* (unglazed), die 1 ('16)	7.00	4.00
			Entire	9.00	5.00
W425	U92	1c	**grn,** *manila* (unglazed), die 1 ('16)	.25	.20
			Entire	.85	.20
a.			Die 3	190.00	125.00
			Entire	250.00	140.00
U426	U92	1c	**green,** (glazed) *brown,* die 1 ('20)	45.00	15.00
			Entire	55.00	17.50
W427	U92	1c	**green,** (glazed) *brown,* die 1 ('20)	65.00	30.00
			Entire	75.00	*40.00*
U428	U92	1c	**green,** (unglazed) *brown,* die 1 ('20)	16.50	7.50
			Entire	24.00	9.00
W428A	U92	1c	**green,** (unglazed) *brown,* die 1 ('20), entire		*3,000.*

All manila envelopes of circular dies are unwatermarked. Manila paper, including that of Nos. U424 and W425, exists in many shades.

Washington — 93U

Die 1

Die 2

Die 3

Die 4

Die 5

Die 6

Die 7

Die 8

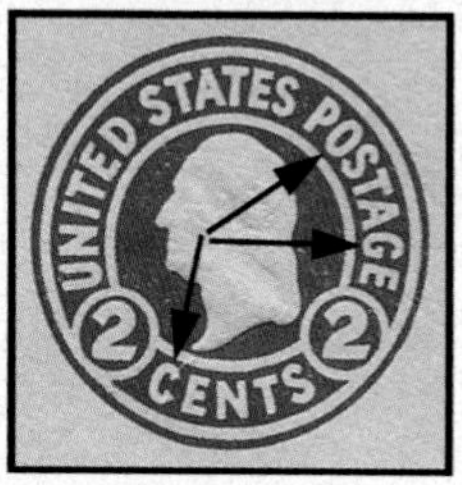
Die 9

(The 1½c, 2c, 3c, 5c, and 6c dies are the same except for figures of value.)

Die 1 — Letters broad. Numerals vertical. Large head (9¼mm). from tip of nose to back of neck. E closer to inner circle than N of cents.

Die 2 — Similar to 1; but U far from left circle.

Die 3 — Similar to 2; but all inner circles very thin (Rejected die).

Die 4 — Large head as in Die 1. C of CENTS close to circle. Baseline of right numeral "2" slants downward to right. Left numeral "2" is larger.

Die 5 — Small head (8¾mm) from tip of nose to back of neck. T and S of CENTS close at bottom.

Die 6 — Similar to 5; but T and S of CENTS far apart at bottom. Left numeral slopes to right.

Die 7 — Large head. Both numerals slope to right. Clean cut lettering. All letters T have short top strokes.

Die 8 — Similar to 7; but all letters T have long top strokes.

Die 9 — Narrow oval C (also O and G).

U429	U93	2c **carmine,** die 1, *Dec. 20, 1915*	.25	.20
		Entire	.40	.20
a.		Die 2	16.00	7.00
		Entire	25.00	10.00
b.		Die 3	47.50	*50.00*
		Entire	100.00	*200.00*
c.		Die 4	32.50	15.00
		Entire	45.00	20.00
d.		Die 5	.55	.35
		Entire	1.00	.45
e.		Die 6	.65	.30
		Entire	1.25	.60
f.		Die 7	.70	.25
		Entire	1.25	.75
g.		Die 8	.50	.20
		Entire	1.00	.50
h.		Die 9	.50	.20
		Entire	1.00	.45
i.		2c **green** (error), die 1, entire	*14,000.*	
j.		#U429 with added impression of #U420	1,100.	
		Entire	1,500.	
k.		#U429 with added impression of #U416a, entire	1,000.	
l.		#U429 with added impression of #U400, entire	1,000.	
m.		#U429, double impression, entire	1,750.	
U430	U93	2c **carmine,** *amber,* die 1 ('16)	.30	.20
		Entire	.50	.20
a.		Die 2	21.00	12.50
		Entire	30.00	15.00
b.		Die 4	52.50	25.00
		Entire	70.00	30.00
c.		Die 5	1.60	.35
		Entire	2.25	.60
d.		Die 6	1.25	.40
		Entire	2.25	.75
e.		Die 7	.75	.35
		Entire	1.75	.95
f.		Die 8	.70	.30
		Entire	1.10	.45
g.		Die 9	.65	.20
		Entire	1.10	.35
U431	U93	2c **carmine,** *oriental buff,* die 1 ('16)	2.25	.65
		Entire	4.50	1.40
a.		Die 2	210.00	75.00
		Entire	275.00	*100.00*
b.		Die 4	77.50	60.00
		Entire	100.00	75.00
c.		Die 5	3.50	2.00
		Entire	6.00	2.75
d.		Die 6	3.50	2.00
		Entire	7.00	2.75
e.		Die 7	3.50	2.00
		Entire	6.00	3.25
U432	U93	2c **carmine,** *blue,* die 1 ('16)	.30	.20
		Entire	.60	.20
b.		Die 2	42.50	25.00
		Entire	60.00	35.00
c.		Die 3	165.00	90.00
		Entire	225.00	*300.00*
d.		Die 4	67.50	50.00
		Entire	100.00	55.00
e.		Die 5	1.10	.30
		Entire	2.00	.75
f.		Die 6	1.10	.40
		Entire	2.00	.60
g.		Die 7	.85	.35
		Entire	1.75	.65
h.		Die 8	.65	.25
		Entire	1.50	.50
i.		Die 9	1.00	.30
		Entire	2.75	.55
j.		2c purple (error), die 9	—	
U432A	U93	2c **car,** *manila,* die 7, unwatermarked, entire	*55,000.*	
W433	U93	2c **carmine,** *manila,* die 1 ('16)	.25	.20
		Entire	.50	.30
W434	U93	2c **carmine,** (glazed) *brown* ('20), die 1	97.50	50.00
		Entire	125.00	60.00
W435	U93	2c **carmine,** (unglazed) *brown,* die 1 ('20)	97.50	50.00
		Entire	125.00	60.00
U436	U93	3c **purple,** die 1 ('32)	.30	.20
		Entire	.55	.25
a.		3c **dark violet,** die 1 ('17)	.60	.20
		Entire	1.00	.25
b.		3c **dark violet,** die 5 ('17)	1.75	.75
		Entire	3.25	.90
c.		3c **dark violet,** die 6 ('17)	2.10	1.40
		Entire	3.25	1.50
d.		3c **dark violet,** die 7 ('17)	1.50	.95
		Entire	3.00	1.00
e.		3c **purple,** die 7 ('32)	.70	.30
		Entire	1.75	.75
f.		3c **purple,** die 9 ('32)	.45	.20
		Entire	.60	.30
g.		3c **carmine** (error), die 1	42.50	30.00
		Entire	65.00	45.00
h.		3c **carmine** (error), die 5	37.50	30.00
		Entire	60.00	45.00
i.		#U436 with added impression of #U420, entire	900.00	
j.		#U436 with added impression of #U429, entire	900.00	950.00
U437	U93	3c **purple,** *amber,* die 1 ('32)	.35	.20
		Entire	.60	.35
a.		3c **dark violet,** die 1 ('17)	5.50	1.25
		Entire	9.00	2.25
b.		3c **dark violet,** die 5 ('17)	8.50	2.50
		Entire	12.00	3.00
c.		3c **dark violet,** die 6 ('17)	8.50	2.50
		Entire	12.00	3.00
d.		3c **dark violet,** die 7 ('17)	8.50	2.25
		Entire	12.00	2.50
e.		3c **purple,** die 7 ('32)	.75	.20
		Entire	1.25	.50
f.		3c **purple,** die 9 ('32)	.55	.20
		Entire	1.00	.30
g.		3c **carmine** (error), die 5	500.00	350.00
		Entire	525.00	*325.00*
h.		3c **black** (error), die 1	200.00	—
		Entire	275.00	—
U438	U93	3c **dark violet,** *oriental buff,* die 1 ('17)	27.50	1.65
		Entire	35.00	2.00
a.		Die 5	27.50	1.65
		Entire	35.00	2.00
b.		Die 6	37.50	3.50
		Entire	50.00	4.50
c.		Die 7	37.50	3.50
		Entire	50.00	7.75
U439	U93	3c **purple,** *blue,* die 1 ('32)	.35	.20
		Entire	.75	.25
a.		3c **dark violet,** die 1 ('17)	8.50	2.00
		Entire	15.00	6.00
b.		3c **dark violet,** die 5 ('17)	9.50	6.00
		Entire	15.00	7.50
c.		3c **dark violet,** die 6 ('17)	9.50	6.00
		Entire	15.00	7.50
d.		3c **dark violet,** die 7 ('17)	12.50	6.00
		Entire	18.50	7.50
e.		3c **purple,** die 7 ('32)	.75	.25
		Entire	1.50	.50
f.		3c **purple,** die 9 ('32)	.60	.20
		Entire	1.50	.45
g.		3c **carmine** (error), die 5	375.00	300.00
		Entire	475.00	*725.00*
U440	U92	4c **black,** die 1 ('18)	1.75	.60
		Entire	3.00	2.00
a.		With added impression of 2c carmine (#U429), die 1, entire	450.00	
U441	U92	4c **black,** *amber,* die 1 ('18)	3.00	.85
		Entire	5.00	2.00

U442	U92	4c **black,** *blue,* die 1 ('21)	3.50	.85
		Entire	6.00	1.75
U443	U93	5c **blue,** die 1 ('18)	3.50	2.75
		Entire	6.00	3.25
U444	U93	5c **blue,** *amber,* die 1 ('18)	4.00	1.60
		Entire	7.00	3.50
U445	U93	5c **blue,** *blue,* die 1 ('21)	4.25	3.25
		Entire	8.50	4.25

For 1½c and 6c see Nos. U481-W485, U529-U531.

Surcharged Envelopes

The provisional 2c surcharges of 1920-21 were made at central post offices with canceling machines using slugs provided by the Post Office Department.

Double or triple surcharge listings of 1920-25 are for specimens with surcharge directly or partly upon the stamp.

Surcharged on 1874-1920 Envelopes indicated by Numbers in Parentheses

Surcharged

Type 1

1920-21

Surcharged in Black

U446	U93	2c on 3c **dark vio** (U436, die 1)	16.00	10.00
		Entire	25.00	12.50
a.		On No. U436b (die 5)	16.00	10.00
		Entire	25.00	12.50

Surcharged

Type 2

Rose Surcharge

U447	U93	2c on 3c **dark vio** (U436, die 1)	10.00	6.50
		Entire	17.50	8.50
b.		On No. U436c (die 6)	13.00	8.50
		Entire	27.50	10.00

Black Surcharge

U447A	U92	2c on 1c **green** (U420, die 1) Entire	*1,500.*	
U447C	U93	2c on 2c **carmine** (U429, die 1)	*50,000.*	
U447D	U93	2c on 2c **carmine,** *amber* (U430, die 1)	—	
U448	U93	2c on 3c **dark vio** (U436, die 1)	2.75	2.00
		Entire	4.00	2.50
a.		On No. U436b (die 5)	2.75	2.00
		Entire	4.00	2.50
b.		On No. U436c (die 6)	3.50	2.00
		Entire	5.00	2.50
c.		On No. U436d (die 7)	2.75	2.00
		Entire	4.00	2.50
U449	U93	2c on 3c **dark violet,** *amber* (U437, die 1)	7.50	6.00
		Entire	10.00	7.50
a.		On No. U437b (die 5)	13.00	7.50
		Entire	17.50	10.00
b.		On No. U437c (die 6)	9.50	6.00
		Entire	13.50	7.50
c.		On No. U437d (die 7)	8.50	6.50
		Entire	12.00	8.00
U450	U93	2c on 3c **dark violet,** *oriental buff* (U438, die 1)	20.00	15.00
		Entire	25.00	18.00
a.		On No. U438a (die 5)	20.00	15.00
		Entire	25.00	18.00
b.		On No. U438b (die 6)	20.00	15.00
		Entire	25.00	18.00
c.		On No. U438c (die 7)	135.00	90.00
		Entire	175.00	125.00
U451	U93	2c on 3c **dark violet,** *blue* (U439, die 1)	16.00	10.50
		Entire	22.50	11.50
b.		On No. U439b (die 5)	16.00	10.50
		Entire	22.50	11.50
c.		On No. U439c (die 6)	16.00	10.50
		Entire	22.50	11.50
d.		On No. U439d (die 7)	29.00	22.50
		Entire	42.50	27.50

Type 2 exists in three city sub-types.

Surcharged

Type 3

Bars 2mm apart, 25 to 26mm in length

U451A	U90	2c on 1c **green** (U400, die 1)	*30,000.*	
		Entire	—	
U452	U92	2c on 1c **green** (U420, die 1)	3,750.	
		Entire	4,250.	
a.		On No. U420b (die 3)	3,750.	
		Entire	4,250.	
b.		As No. U452, double surcharge	4,500.	
		Entire	5,000.	
U453	U91	2c on 2c **car** (U411b, die 3)	5,000.	
		Entire	8,000.	
a.		On No. U411 (die 1)	5,000.	
		Entire	8,000.	
U453B	U91	2c on 2c **carmine,** *blue* (U414e, die 6)	2,500.	
		Entire	3,000.	
U453C	U91	2c on 2c **carmine,** *oriental buff* (U413e, die 6)	2,250.	*750.00*
		Entire	2,750.	
d.		On No. U413 (die 1)	2,250.	
		Entire	2,750.	
U454	U93	2c on 2c **car** (U429e, die 6)	150.00	
		Entire	200.00	
a.		On No. U429 (die 1)	350.00	
		Entire	400.00	
b.		On No. U429d (die 5)	500.00	
		Entire	650.00	
c.		On No. U429f (die 7)	150.00	
		Entire	200.00	
U455	U93	2c on 2c **carmine,** *amber* (U430, die 1)	1,750.	
		Entire	4,250.	
a.		On No. U430d (die 6)	2,250.	
		Entire	4,250.	
b.		On No. U430e (die 7)	2,250.	
		Entire	4,250.	
U456	U93	2c on 2c **carmine,** *oriental buff* (U431a, die 2)	300.00	
		Entire	375.00	
a.		On No. U431c (die 5)	350.00	
		Entire	500.00	
b.		On No. U431e (die 7)	800.00	
		Entire	850.00	
c.		As No. U456, double surcharge	750.00	
U457	U93	2c on 2c **carmine,** *blue* (U432f, die 6)	250.00	
		Entire	450.00	
a.		On No. U432e (die 5)	325.00	
		Entire	500.00	
b.		On No. U432g (die 7)	800.00	
		Entire	850.00	
U458	U93	2c on 3c **dark vio** (U436, die 1)	.55	.35
		Entire	.80	.45
a.		On No. U436b (die 5)	.55	.40
		Entire	.80	.50
b.		On No. U436c (die 6)	.55	.35
		Entire	.80	.45
c.		On No. U436d (die 7)	.55	.35
		Entire	.80	.45
d.		As #U458, double surcharge	25.00	7.50
		Entire	35.00	10.00
e.		As #U458, triple surcharge	110.00	
		Entire	160.00	
f.		As #U458, dbl. surch., 1 in **magenta**	110.00	
		Entire	150.00	
g.		As #U458, dbl. surch., types 2 & 3	140.00	
		Entire	190.00	
h.		As "a," double surcharge	27.50	15.00
		Entire	37.50	20.00
i.		As "a," triple surcharge	110.00	
		Entire	160.00	
j.		As "a," double surch., both **magenta**	110.00	
		Entire	150.00	
k.		As "b," double surcharge	25.00	8.00
		Entire	35.00	11.00
l.		As "c," double surcharge	25.00	8.00
		Entire	35.00	11.00
m.		As "c," triple surcharge	110.00	
		Entire	150.00	
n.		Double impression of indicia, single surcharge, entire	—	
U459	U93	2c on 3c **dark violet,** *amber* (U437c, die 6)	3.25	1.00
		Entire	5.00	1.75
a.		On No. U437 (die 1)	4.25	1.00
		Entire	6.00	1.75
b.		On No. U437b (die 5)	4.25	1.00
		Entire	6.00	1.75
c.		On No. U437d (die 7)	3.25	1.00
		Entire	6.00	1.75
d.		As #U459, double surcharge	35.00	
		Entire	50.00	
e.		As "a," double surcharge	35.00	
		Entire	50.00	
f.		As "b," double surcharge	35.00	
		Entire	50.00	
g.		As "b," double surcharge, types 2 & 3	125.00	
		Entire	175.00	
h.		As "c," double surcharge	35.00	
		Entire	50.00	
U460	U93	2c on 3c **dark violet,** *oriental buff* (U438a, die 5)	4.00	2.00
		Entire	5.00	2.50
a.		On No. U438 (die 1)	4.25	2.00
		Entire	5.00	2.50
b.		On No. U438b (die 6)	4.25	2.00
		Entire	6.00	2.50
c.		As #U460, double surcharge	20.00	
		Entire	30.00	
d.		As "a," double surcharge	20.00	
		Entire	30.00	
e.		As "b," double surcharge	20.00	
		Entire	30.00	
f.		As "b," triple surcharge	150.00	
		Entire	250.00	
U461	U93	2c on 3c **dark violet,** *blue* (U439, die 1)	6.50	1.00
		Entire	9.00	1.50
a.		On No. U439b (die 5)	6.50	1.00
		Entire	9.00	1.50
b.		On No. U439c (die 6)	6.50	1.00
		Entire	9.00	1.50
c.		On No. U439d (die 7)	13.50	2.00
		Entire	20.00	3.00
d.		As #U461, double surcharge	20.00	
		Entire	30.00	
e.		As "a," double surcharge	20.00	
		Entire	30.00	
f.		As "b," double surcharge	20.00	
		Entire	30.00	
g.		As "c," double surcharge	20.00	
		Entire	30.00	
U462	U87	2c on 4c **chocolate** (U390)	350.00	260.00
		Entire	900.00	500.00
U463	U87	2c on 4c **chocolate,** *amber* (U391)	550.00	350.00
		Entire	1,600.	500.00
U463A	U90	2c on 4c **black** (U416, die 2)	1,200.	400.00
		Entire	2,000.	
U464	U93	2c on 5c **blue** (U443)	1,200.	
		Entire	2,000.	

Type 3 exists in 11 city sub-types.

Surcharged

Type 4

Bars 1 mm apart, 21 to 23 mm in length

U465	U92	2c on 1c **green** (U420, die 1)	1,400.	
		Entire	2,250.	
a.		On No. U420b (die 3)	1,750.	
		Entire	2,500.	
U466	U91	2c on 2c **car** (U411e, die 6)	*15,000.*	
		Entire	*27,500.*	

The existence of No. U466 as a cut square has been questioned by specialists.

U466A	U93	2c on 2c **carmine** (U429, die 1)	900.00	
		Entire	1,600.	
c.		On No. U429d (die 5)	1,000.	
		Entire	1,750.	
d.		On No. U429e (die 6)	1,000.	
		Entire	1,750.	
e.		On No. U429f (die 7)	1,000.	
		Entire	1,750.	
U466B	U93	2c on 2c **carmine,** *amber* (U430)	*15,000.*	
		Entire	*27,500.*	
U466C	U93	2c on 2c **carmine,** *oriental buff* (U431), entire	—	
U466D	U25	2c on 3c **green,** die 2 (U82)	*7,500.*	
U467	U45	2c on 3c **green,** die 2 (U163)	425.00	
		Entire	550.00	
U468	U93	2c on 3c **dark vio** (U436, die 1)	.70	.45
		Entire	1.00	.75
a.		On No. U436b (die 5)	.70	.50
		Entire	1.00	.75
b.		On No. U436c (die 6)	.70	.50

		Entire	1.00	.75
c.		On No. U436d (die 7)	.70	.50
		Entire	1.00	.75
d.		As #U468, double surcharge	20.00	
		Entire	30.00	
e.		As #U468, triple surcharge	100.00	
		Entire	150.00	
f.		As #U468, dbl. surch., types 2 & 4	125.00	
		Entire	175.00	
g.		As "a," double surcharge	20.00	
		Entire	30.00	
h.		As "b," double surcharge	20.00	
		Entire	30.00	
i.		As "c," double surcharge	20.00	
		Entire	30.00	
j.		As "c," triple surcharge	100.00	
		Entire	150.00	
k.		As "c," inverted surcharge	75.00	
		Entire	125.00	
l.		2c on 3c **carmine** (error), (U436h)	650.00	
		Entire	800.00	
m.		As #U468, triple surcharge, one inverted, entire		*900.00*
U469	U93	2c on 3c **dark violet,** *amber* (U437, die 1)	3.75	2.25
		Entire	5.00	2.75
a.		On No. U437b (die 5)	3.75	2.25
		Entire	5.00	2.75
b.		On No. U437c (die 6)	3.75	2.25
		Entire	5.00	2.75
c.		On No. U437d (die 7)	3.75	2.25
		Entire	5.00	2.75
d.		As #U469, double surcharge	30.00	
		Entire	40.00	
e.		As "a," double surcharge	30.00	
		Entire	40.00	
f.		As "a," double surcharge, types 2 & 4	100.00	
		Entire	150.00	
g.		As "b," double surcharge	30.00	
		Entire	40.00	
h.		As "c," double surcharge	30.00	
		Entire	40.00	
U470	U93	2c on 3c **dark violet,** *oriental buff* (U438, die 1)	6.00	2.50
		Entire	10.00	4.00
a.		On No. U438a (die 5)	6.00	2.50
		Entire	10.00	4.00
b.		On No. U438b (die 6)	6.00	2.50
		Entire	10.00	4.00
c.		On No. U438c (die 7)	42.50	32.50
		Entire	70.00	45.00
d.		As #U470, double surcharge	25.00	
		Entire	35.00	
e.		As #U470, double surch., types 2 & 4	100.00	
		Entire	150.00	
f.		As "a," double surcharge	25.00	
		Entire	35.00	
g.		As "b," double surcharge	25.00	
		Entire	35.00	
U471	U93	2c on 3c **dark violet,** *blue* (U439, die 1)	7.50	1.75
		Entire	13.00	3.50
a.		On No. U439b (die 5)	7.50	1.75
		Entire	13.00	3.50
b.		On No. U439c (die 6)	7.50	1.75
		Entire	13.00	3.50
c.		On No. U439d (die 7)	10.50	6.00
		Entire	22.50	10.00
d.		As #U471, double surcharge	30.00	
		Entire	40.00	
e.		As #U471, double surch., types 2 & 4	175.00	
		Entire	250.00	
f.		As "a," double surcharge	30.00	
		Entire	40.00	
g.		As "b," double surcharge	30.00	
		Entire	40.00	
U472	U87	2c on 4c **chocolate** (U390)	15.00	8.00
		Entire	27.50	14.00
a.		Double surcharge	150.00	
U473	U87	2c on 4c **chocolate,** *amber* (U391)	16.50	10.00
		Entire	27.50	13.50

Type 4 exists in 30 city sub-types.

Surcharged

Double Surcharge, Type 4 and 1c as above

U474	U93	2c on 1c on 3c **dark violet** (U436, die.1)	300.	
		Entire	400.	
a.		On No. U436b (die 5)	400.	
		Entire	575.	
b.		On No. U436d (die 7)	900.	
		Entire	1,150.	
U475	U93	2c on 1c on 3c **dark violet,** *amber* (U437, die 1)	150.	
		Entire	475.	

Surcharged

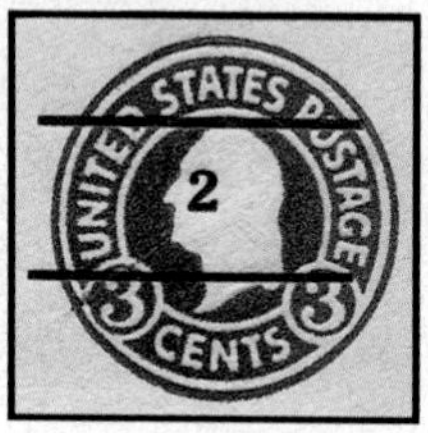

U476	U93	2c on 3c **dark violet,** *amber* (U437, die 1)	300.	
		Entire	475.	
a.		On No. U437c (die 6)	750.	
		Entire	1,000.	
b.		As #U476, double surcharge	—	

Surcharged at Duncan, OK.

Surcharged

U477	U93	2c on 3c **dark vio** (U436, die 1)	140.	
		Entire	190.	
a.		On No. U436b (die 5)	275.	
		Entire	325.	
b.		On No. U436c (die 6)	275.	
		Entire	325.	
c.		On No. U436d (die 7)	275.	
		Entire	325.	
U478	U93	2c on 3c **dark violet,** *amber* (U437, die 1)	350.	
		Entire	450.	

Surcharged at Frederick, OK.

Handstamped Surcharged in Black or Violet

U479	U93	2c on 3c **dark violet** (Bk) (U436, die 1)	300.	—
		Entire	550.	
a.		On No. U436b (die 5)	750.	
		Entire	1,100.	
b.		On No. U436d (die 7)	450.	
		Entire	550.	
U480	U93	2c on 3c **dark violet** (V) (U436d, die 7)	*6,000.*	
		Entire	*8,000.*	
a.		Double overprint	—	

Expertization by competent authorities is required for Nos. U476-U480.

Surcharged at Daytona, FL (#U479) and Orlando Beach, FL (#U480).

1925

Type of 1916-32 Issue

U481	U93	1½c **brown,** die 1, *Mar. 19*	.25	.20
		Entire	.60	.20
		Entire, 1st day cancel		60.00
a.		Die 8	.70	.25
		Entire	1.00	.50
b.		1½c purple, die 1 (error) ('34)	95.00	
		Entire	125.00	—
U482	U93	1½c **brown,** die 1, *amber*	.95	.40
		Entire	1.50	.60
a.		Die 8	1.90	.75
		Entire	2.50	.80
U483	U93	1½c **brown,** die 1, *blue*	1.60	.95
		Entire	2.50	1.25
a.		Die 8	2.40	1.25
		Entire	3.25	1.40
U484	U93	1½c **brown,** die 1, *manila*	6.50	3.00
		Entire	12.00	6.00
W485	U93	1½c **brown,** die 1, *manila*	.85	.20
		Entire	1.40	.45
a.		With added impression of #W433	120.00	—

The manufacture of newspaper wrappers was discontinued in 1934.

New rates on printed matter effective Apr. 15, 1925, resulted in revaluing some of the current envelopes.

Under the caption "Revaluation of Surplus Stocks of the 1 cent envelopes," W. Irving Glover, Third Assistant Postmaster-General, distributed through the Postal Bulletin a notice to postmasters authorizing the surcharging of envelopes under stipulated conditions.

Surcharging was permitted "at certain offices where the excessive quantities of 1 cent stamped envelopes remained in stock on April 15, 1925."

Envelopes were revalued by means of post office canceling machines equipped with special dies designed to imprint "1 ½" in the center of the embossed stamp and four vertical bars over the original numerals "1" in the lower corners.

Postmasters were notified that the revaluing dies would be available for use only in the International and "Universal" Model G machines and that the overprinting of surplus envelopes would be restricted to post offices having such canceling equipment available.

Envelopes of Preceding Issues Surcharged

Provisional surcharges exist for California cities Santa Rosa and Santa Ana. These were unauthorized but served postal duty. All are scarce. Expertization recommended.

1925

On Envelopes of 1887

U486	U71	1½c on 2c **green** (U311)	800.	
		Entire	1,300.	
U487	U71	1½c on 2c **green,** *amber* (U312)	1,000.	
		Entire	1,850.	

On Envelopes of 1899

U488	U77	1½c on 1c **green** (U352)	400.	
		Entire	1,000.	
U489	U77	1½c on 1c **green,** *amber* (U353)	125.	60.
		Entire	200.	90.

On Envelopes of 1907-16

U490	U90	1½c on 1c **green** (U400, die 1)	6.75	3.50
		Entire	11.00	5.50
a.		On No. U400a (die 2)	18.00	9.00
		Entire	22.50	12.00
b.		On No. U400b (die 3)	42.50	17.50
		Entire	55.00	22.50
c.		On No. U400c (die 4)	10.00	2.50
		Entire	14.00	4.00
U491	U90	1½c on 1c **green,** *amber* (U401c, die 4)	8.00	2.25
		Entire	12.50	4.50
a.		On No. U401 (die 1)	12.50	2.50
		Entire	17.50	6.00
b.		On No. U401a (die 2)	120.00	65.00
		Entire	140.00	95.00
c.		On No. U401b (die 3)	52.50	30.00
		Entire	70.00	40.00
U492	U90	1½c on 1c **green,** *oriental buff* (U402a, die 2)	500.00	150.00
		Entire	700.00	175.00
a.		On No. U402c (die 4)	800.00	250.00
		Entire	1,500.	300.00
U493	U90	1½c on 1c **grn,** *blue* (U403c, die 4)	125.00	65.00
		Entire	160.00	70.00
a.		On No. U403a (die 2)	125.00	67.50
		Entire	160.00	90.00
U494	U90	1½c on 1c **grn,** *manila* (U404, die 1)	275.00	100.00
		Entire	550.00	150.00
a.		On No. U404a (die 3)	1,250.	
		Entire	1,500.	

On Envelopes of 1916-20

U495	U92	1½c on 1c **green** (U420, die 1)	.80	.25
		Entire	1.10	.45
a.		On No. U420a (die 2)	85.00	52.50
		Entire	125.00	90.00
b.		On No. U420b (die 3)	2.10	.70
		Entire	3.00	.85
c.		On No. U420c (die 4)	2.10	.85

Entire 3.00 1.15
d. As #U495, double surcharge 10.00 3.00
Entire 15.00 5.00
e. As "b," double surcharge 10.00 3.00
Entire 15.00 5.00
f. As "c," double surcharge 10.00 3.00
Entire 15.00 5.00
U496 U92 1½c on 1c **grn,** *amber* (U421, die 1) 21.00 12.50
Entire 30.00 15.00
a. On No. U421b (die 3) 600.00
Entire 700.00
b. On No. U421c (die 4) 21.00 12.50
Entire 30.00 15.00
U497 U92 1½c on 1c **green,** *oriental buff* (U422, die 1) 3.75 1.90
Entire 7.00 2.25
a. On No. U422b (die 4) 67.50
Entire 100.00
U498 U92 1½c on 1c **grn,** *blue* (U423c, die 4) 1.60 .75
Entire 2.50 1.00
a. On No. U423 (die 1) 2.75 1.50
Entire 4.50 2.00
b. On No. U423b (die 3) 2.10 1.50
Entire 3.50 2.00
U499 U92 1½c on 1c **green,** *manila* (U424) 13.00 6.00
Entire 20.00 7.00
U500 U92 1½c on 1c **green,** *brown* (unglazed) (U428) 85.00 30.00
Entire 100.00 35.00
U501 U92 1½c on 1c **green,** *brown* (glazed) (U426) 85.00 30.00
Entire 100.00 35.00
U502 U93 1½c on 2c **carmine** (U429, die 1) 300.00 —
Entire 500.00 —
a. On No. U429d (die 5) 400.00
Entire 575.00
b. On No. U429f (die 7) 400.00
Entire 575.00
c. On No. U429e (die 6) 425.00
Entire —
d. On No. U429g (die 8) 550.00
U503 U93 1½c on 2c **carmine,** *oriental buff* (U431c, die 5) 300.00 —
Entire 525.00 —
a. Double surcharge —
b. Double surcharge, one inverted *700.00*
U504 U93 1½c on 2c **car,** *blue* (U432, die 1) 300.00 —
Entire 525.00 —
a. On No. U432g (die 7) 300.00
Entire 525.00

On Envelopes of 1925

U505 U93 1½c on 1½c **brown** (U481, die 1) 500.00
Entire 650.00
a. On No. U481a (die 8) 500.00
Entire 650.00
b. As No. U505, double surcharge, entire —
U506 U93 1½c on 1½c **brown,** *blue* (U483a, die 8) 300.00
Entire 650.00
a. On No. U483 (die 1) 500.00

The paper of No. U500 is not glazed and appears to be the same as that used for the wrappers of 1920.
Type 8 exists in 20 city sub-types.

Surcharged

Black Surcharge

On Envelopes of 1887

U507 U69 1½c on 1c **blue** (U294) 2,250.
Entire 2,750.
U507A U69 1½c on 1c **blue,** *amber* (U296) —
U507B U69 1½c on 1c **blue,** *manila* (U300) 5,000.
Entire 6,500.

On Envelope of 1899

U508 U77 1½c on 1c **green,** *amber* (U353) 70.00
Entire 100.00

On Envelopes of 1903

U508A U85 1½c on 1c **green** (U379) 3,000.
Entire 4,000.
U509 U85 1½c on 1c **green,** *amber* (U380) 16.00 10.00
Entire 30.00 15.00
a. Double surcharge 75.00
Entire 100.00
U509B U85 1½c on 1c **green,** *oriental buff* (U381) 60.00 40.00
Entire 75.00 50.00

On Envelopes of 1907-16

U510 U90 1½c on 1c **green** (U400, die 1) 2.90 1.25
Entire 5.00 1.50
b. On No. U400a (die 2) 9.50 4.00
Entire 13.50 6.00
c. On No. U400b (die 3) 37.50 8.00
Entire 50.00 11.00
d. On No. U400c (die 4) 4.25 1.25
Entire 8.00 2.00
e. As No. U510, double surcharge 25.00
Entire 50.00
U511 U90 1½c on 1c **green,** *amber* (U401, die 1) 250.00 100.00
Entire 375.00 150.00
U512 U90 1½c on 1c **green,** *oriental buff* (U402, die 1) 9.00 4.00
Entire 16.50 6.50
a. On No. U402c (die 4) 21.00 14.00
Entire 30.00 17.00
U513 U90 1½c on 1c **grn,** *blue* (U403, die 1) 6.50 4.00
Entire 10.00 5.00
a. On No. U403c (die 4) 6.50 4.00
Entire 10.00 5.00
U514 U90 1½c on 1c **green,** *manila* (U404, die 1)) 34.00 9.00
Entire 45.00 22.50
a. On No. U404a (die 3) 77.50 37.50
Entire 100.00 45.00

On Envelopes of 1916-20

U515 U92 1½c on 1c **green** (U420, die 1) .40 .20
Entire .75 .30
a. On No. U420a (die 2) 21.00 15.00
Entire 30.00 20.00
b. On No. U420b (die 3) .40 .20
Entire .75 .30
c. On No. U420c (die 4) .40 .20
Entire .75 .30
d. As #U515, double surcharge 10.00
Entire 15.00
e. As #U515, inverted surcharge 20.00
Entire 30.00
f. As #U515, triple surcharge 20.00
Entire 30.00
g. As #U515, dbl. surch., one invtd., entire —
h. As "b," double surcharge 10.00
Entire 15.00
i. As "b," inverted surcharge 20.00
Entire 30.00
j. As "b," triple surcharge 30.00
Entire 40.00
k. As "c," double surcharge 10.00
Entire 15.00
l. As "c," inverted surcharge 20.00
Entire 30.00
U516 U92 1½c on 1c **green,** *amber* (U421c, die 4) 50.00 25.00
Entire 65.00 35.00
a. On No. U421 (die 1) 55.00 30.00
Entire 70.00 40.00
U517 U92 1½c on 1c **green,** *oriental buff* (U422, die 1)) 6.25 1.25
Entire 9.00 1.50
a. On No. U422a (die 4) 7.25 1.50
Entire 10.00 2.00
U518 U92 1½c on 1c **green,** *blue* (U423b, die 4) 5.50 1.25
Entire 8.00 1.50
a. On No. U423 (die 1) 7.75 2.50
Entire 11.00 3.00
b. On No. U423a (die 3) 27.50 7.50
Entire 40.00 9.00
c. As "a," double surcharge 30.00
Entire 42.50
U519 U92 1½c on 1c **green,** *manila* (U424, die 1) 32.50 10.00
Entire 45.00 12.50
a. Double surcharge 100.00
U520 U93 1½c on 2c **car** (U429, die 1) 350.00 —
Entire 500.00 —
a. On No. U429d (die 5) 350.00
Entire 500.00
b. On No. U429e (die 6) 350.00
Entire 500.00
c. On No. U429f (die 7) 400.00
Entire 550.00
U520D U93 1½c on 2c **car,** *amber* (U430c, die 5), entire —
U520E U92 1½c on 4c **black,** (U440, die 1), entire —

Magenta Surcharge

U521 U92 1½c on 1c **green** (U420b, die 3), *Oct. 22, 1925* 4.75 3.50
Entire 7.00 5.50
Entire, 1st day cancel, Washington, D.C. 100.00
a. Double surcharge 75.00
Entire 125.00

Sesquicentennial Exposition Issue

150th anniversary of the Declaration of Independence.

Liberty Bell — U94

Die 1. The center bar of "E" of "postage" is shorter than top bar.
Die 2. The center bar of "E" of "postage" is of same length as top bar.

1926, July 27

U522 U94 2c **carmine,** die 1 1.10 .50
Entire 1.60 .95
a. Die 2 6.50 3.75
Entire 11.00 5.50
Entire, die 2, 1st day cancel, Washington, D.C. 32.50
Entire, die 2, 1st day cancel, Philadelphia 27.50

Washington Bicentennial Issue

200th anniversary of the birth of George Washington.

Mount Vernon — U95

2c Die 1 — "S" of "Postage" normal.
2c Die 2 — "S" of "Postage" raised.

1932

U523 U95 1c **olive green,** *Jan. 1* 1.00 .80
Entire 1.50 1.75
Entire, 1st day cancel 18.00
U524 U95 1½c **chocolate,** *Jan. 1* 2.00 1.50
Entire 2.75 2.50
Entire, 1st day cancel 18.00
U525 U95 2c **carmine,** die 1, *Jan. 1* .40 .20
Entire .50 .25
Entire, 1st day cancel 16.00
a. 2c **carmine,** die 2 65.00 20.00
Entire 85.00 27.50
b. 2c **carmine,** *blue,* die 1 (error) entire *40,000.*
U526 U95 3c **violet,** *June 16* 2.00 .35
Entire 2.50 .40
Entire, 1st day cancel 18.00
U527 U95 4c **black,** *Jan. 1* 16.50 *20.00*
Entire 22.50 *35.00*
Entire, 1st day cancel 30.00
U528 U95 5c **dark blue,** *Jan. 1* 4.00 3.50
Entire 4.75 4.75
Entire, 1st day cancel 20.00
Nos. U523-U528 (6) 25.90 26.35

1932, Aug. 18

Type of 1916-32 Issue

U529 U93 6c **orange,** die 7 5.50 4.00
Entire 9.50 7.50
Entire, 1st day cancel, Los Angeles 20.00
U530 U93 6c **orange,** *amber,* die 7 11.00 10.00
Entire 15.00 12.50
Entire, 1st day cancel, Los Angeles 20.00
U531 U93 6c **orange,** *blue,* die 7 11.00 10.00
Entire 15.00 12.50
Entire, 1st day cancel 20.00

Franklin — U96

Die 1

Die 2

Die 3

Die 1 — Short (3½mm) and thick "1" in thick circle.
Die 2 — Tall (4½mm) and thin "1" in thin circle; upper and lower bars of E in ONE long and 1mm from circle.
Die 3 — As in Die 2, but E normal and 1½mm from circle.

Printed by International Envelope Corp.

1950

U532	U96	1c **green,** die 1, *Nov. 16*	4.75	1.75
		Entire	8.00	2.25
		Entire, 1st day cancel, NY, NY		1.00
a.		Die 2	6.50	3.00
		Entire	11.00	3.75
b.		Die 3	6.50	3.00
		Entire	11.00	3.75
		Precanceled, die 3		1.25
		Entire, precanceled, die 3	2.50	1.50

Washington — U97

Die 1

Die 2

Die 3

Die 4

Die 1 — Thick "2" in thick circle; toe of "2" is acute angle.
Die 2 — Thin "2" in thin circle; toe of "2" is almost right angle; line through left stand of "N" in UNITED and stand of "E" in POSTAGE goes considerably below tip of chin; "N" of UNITED is tall; "O" of TWO is high.
Die 3 — Figure "2" as in Die 2. Short UN in UNITED thin crossbar in A of STATES.
Die 4 — Tall UN in UNITED; thick crossbar in A of STATES; otherwise like Die 3.

U533	U97	2c **carmine,** die 3	.75	.25
		Entire	1.25	.35
a.		Die 1, *Nov. 17*	.85	.30
		Entire	1.50	.45
		Entire, 1st day cancel, NY, NY		1.00
b.		Die 2	1.50	.85
		Entire	2.00	.95
c.		Die 4	1.40	.60
		Entire	1.60	.65

Die 1

Die 2

Die 3

Die 4

Die 5

Die 1 — Thick and tall (4½mm) "3" in thick circle; long top bars and short stems in T's of STATES.
Die 2 — Thin and tall (4½mm) "3" in medium circle; short top bars and long stems in T's of STATES.
Die 3 — Thin and short (4mm) "3" in thin circle; lettering wider than Dies 1 and 2; line from left stand of N to stand of E is distinctly below tip of chin.
Die 4 — Figure and letters as in Die 3. Line hits tip of chin; short N in UNITED and thin crossbar in A of STATES.
Die 5 — Figure, letter and chin line as in Die 4; but tall N in UNITED and thick crossbar in A of STATES.

U534	U97	3c **dark violet,** die 4	.40	.20
		Entire	.50	.25
a.		Die 1, *Nov. 18*	2.00	.70
		Entire	2.50	1.20
		Entire, 1st day cancel, NY, NY		1.00
b.		Die 2, *Nov. 19*	.80	.50
		Entire	1.60	.55
		Entire, 1st day cancel, NY, NY		4.00
c.		Die 3	.60	.25
		Entire	1.10	.45
d.		Die 5	.80	.45
		Entire	1.25	.65

Washington — U98

1952

U535	U98	1½c **brown**	4.75	3.50
		Entire	6.00	4.25
		Precanceled		1.25
		Entire, precanceled	2.50	1.50

Die 1

Die 2

Die 3

Die 1 — Head high in oval (2mm below T of STATES). Circle near (1mm) bottom of colored oval.
Die 2 — Head low in oval (3mm). Circle 1½mm from edge of oval. Right leg of A in POSTAGE shorter than left. Short leg on P.
Die 3 — Head centered in oval (2½mm). Circle as in Die 2. Legs of A of POSTAGE about equal. Long leg on P.

1958

U536	U96	4c **red violet,** die 1, *July 31*	.80	.20
		Entire	.95	.25
		Entire, 1st day cancel, Montpelier, Vt. *(163,746)*		1.00
a.		Die 2	1.00	.20
		Entire	1.30	.25
b.		Die 3	1.00	.20
		Entire	1.30	.25

Nos. U429, U429f, U429h, U533, U533a-U533c Surcharged in Red at Left of Stamp

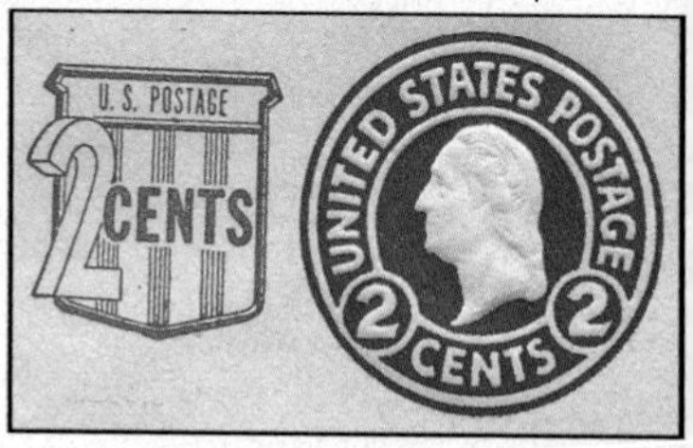

b

1958

U537	U93	2c + 2c **carmine,** die 1	3.00	1.50
		Entire	4.50	*15.00*
a.		Die 7	10.00	7.00
		Entire	14.00	*15.00*
b.		Die 9	5.00	5.00
		Entire	7.50	*15.00*
U538	U97	2c + 2c **carmine,** die 1	.75	*1.25*
		Entire	1.25	*25.00*
a.		Die 2	.80	*1.25*
		Entire	2.00	*25.00*
b.		Die 3	.70	*1.25*
		Entire	2.00	*25.00*
c.		Die 4	.80	*1.25*
		Entire	1.50	*25.00*

Nos. U436a, U436e-U436f, U534, U534b-U534d Surcharged in Green at Left of Stamp

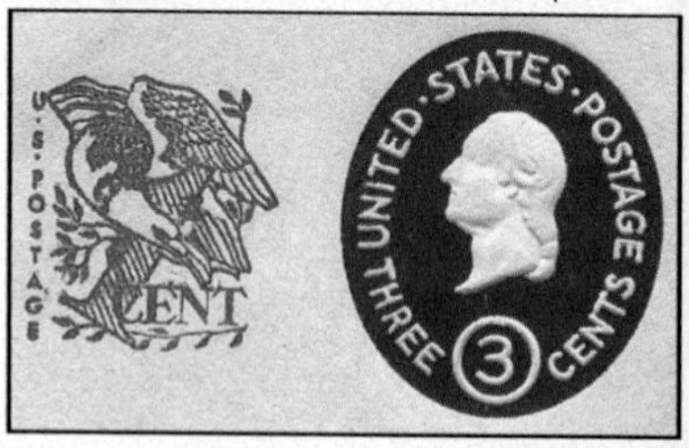

a

U539	U93	3c + 1c **purple,** die 1	14.00	11.00
		Entire	17.50	—
a.		Die 7	11.00	9.00
		Entire	15.00	—
b.		Die 9	25.00	15.00
		Entire	35.00	—
U540	U97	3c + 1c **dark violet,** die 3	.50	*1.00*
		Entire	.60	*2.00*
a.		Die 2	—	—
		Entire	*3,500.*	—
b.		Die 4	.75	*1.00*
		Entire	.90	*2.00*
c.		Die 5	.75	*1.00*
		Entire	1.00	*2.00*

Benjamin Franklin — U99

George Washington — U100

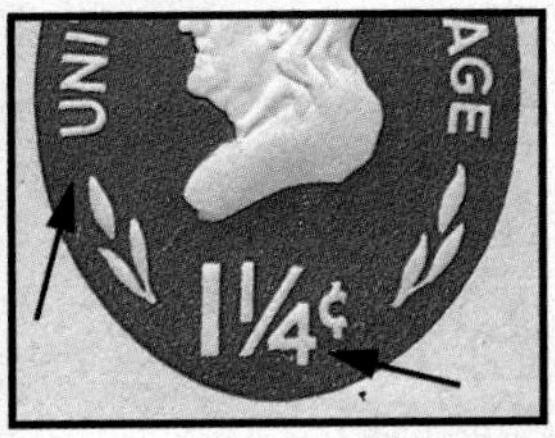
Die 1

Die 2

Dies of 1 ¼c
Die 1 — The "4" is 3mm high. Upper leaf in left cluster is 2mm from "U."
Die 2 — The "4" is 3½mm high. Leaf clusters are larger. Upper leaf at left is 1mm from "U."

1960

U541	U99	1¼c	**turquoise,** die 1, *June 25, 1960*	.75	.50
			Entire	.90	.55
			Entire, 1st day cancel, Birmingham, Ala. *(211,500)*		1.00
			Precanceled		.20
			Entire, precanceled	.45	.45
a.			Die 2, precanceled		1.00
			Entire, precanceled	2.00	2.00
U542	U100	2½c	**dull blue,** *May 28, 1960*	.85	.50
			Entire	1.00	.60
			Entire, 1st day cancel, Chicago, Ill. *(196,977)*		1.00
			Precanceled		.25
			Entire, precanceled	.55	.55

Pony Express Centennial Issue

Pony Express Rider — U101

White Outside, Blue Inside.

1960

U543	U101	4c	**brown,** *July 19, 1960*	.60	.30
			Entire	.75	.40
			Entire, 1st day cancel, St. Joseph, Mo. *(407,160)*		1.00

Abraham Lincoln — U102

Die 1

Die 2

Die 3

Die 1 — Center bar of E of POSTAGE is above the middle. Center bar of E of STATES slants slightly upward. Nose sharper, more pointed. No offset ink specks inside envelope on back of die impression.
Die 2 — Center bar of E of POSTAGE in middle. P of POSTAGE has short stem. Ink specks on back of die impression.
Die 3 — FI of FIVE closer than Die 1 or 2. Second T of STATES seems taller than ES. Ink specks on back of die impression.

1962

U544	U102	5c	**dark blue,** die 2, *Nov. 19, 1962*	.85	.20
			Entire	1.10	.30
			Entire, 1st day cancel, Springfield, Ill. *(163,258)*		1.50
a.			Die 1	.85	.25
			Entire	1.10	.30
b.			Die 3	.90	.35
			Entire	1.20	.40
c.			Die 2 with albino impression of 4c (#U536), entire	85.00	—
d.			Die 3 with albino impression of 4c (#U536), entire	85.00	—
e.			Die 3 on complete impression of 4c (#U536), cut square	60.00	

No. U536 Surcharged in Green at left of Stamp

a

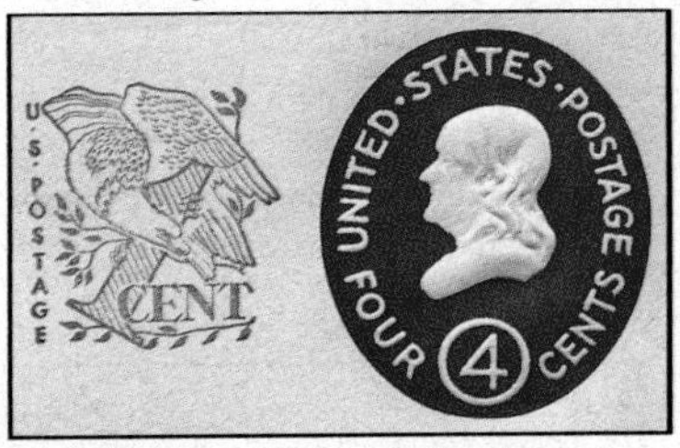

Two types of surcharge:
Type I — "U.S. POSTAGE" 18½mm high. Serifs on cross of T both diagonal. Two lines of shading in C of CENT.
Type II — "U.S. POSTAGE" 17½mm high. Right serif on cross of T is vertical. Three shading lines in C.

1962

U545	U96	4c + 1c	**red vio.,** die 1, type I, *Nov. 1962*	1.40	*1.25*
			Entire	1.60	*2.50*
a.			Type II	1.40	*1.25*
			Entire	1.60	*2.50*

New York World's Fair Issue

Issued to publicize the New York World's Fair, 1964-65.

Globe with Satellite Orbit — U103

1964

U546	U103	5c	**maroon,** *Apr. 22, 1964*	.60	.40
			Entire	.75	.50
			Entire, 1st day cancel World's Fair, N.Y. *(466,422)*		1.00

Precanceled cut squares

Precanceled envelopes do not normally receive another cancellation. Since the lack of a cancellation makes it impossible to distinguish between cut squares from used and unused envelopes, they are valued here as used only.

Liberty Bell — U104

Old Ironsides — U105

Eagle — U106

Head of Statue of Liberty — U107

Printed by the United States Envelope Company, Williamsburg, Pa. Designed (6c) by Howard C. Mildner and (others) by Robert J. Jones.

1965-69

U547	U104	1¼c	**brown,** *Jan. 6, 1965*		.20
			Entire	.90	*2.00*
			Entire, 1st day cancel, Washington, D.C.		1.00
U548	U104	1 4/10c	**brown,** *Mar. 26, 1968*		.20
			Entire	1.00	*2.00*
			Entire, 1st day cancel, Springfield, Mass. *(134,832)*		1.00
U548A	U104	1 6/10c	**orange,** *June 16, 1969*		.20
			Entire	.85	*2.00*
			Entire, 1st day cancel, Washington, D.C.		1.00
b.		1 6/10c	**brown (error), entire**		—
U549	U105	4c	**bright blue,** *Jan. 6, 1965*	.75	.20
			Entire	.95	.20
			Entire, 1st day cancel, Washington, D.C.		1.00
U550	U106	5c	**bright purple,** *Jan. 5, 1965*	.75	.20
			Entire	.85	.25
			Entire, 1st day cancel, Williamsburg, Pa. *(246,496)*		1.00
a.			Bar tagged, *Aug. 15, 1967*	3.00	1.00
			Entire	3.50	*5.00*
			Entire, tagged, 1st day cancel		3.50
b.			orange-red (air post) instead of yellow-green tagging, entire		—

Tagged

U551	U107	6c	**light green,** *Jan. 4, 1968*	.70	.20
			Entire	.80	.25
			Entire, 1st day cancel, New York, N.Y. *(184,784)*		1.25

First day covers of the 1¼c and 4c total 451,960.

Nos. U549-U550 Surcharged Types "b" and "a" in Red or Green at Left of Stamp

1968, Feb. 5

U552	U105	4c + 2c	**bright blue** (R)	3.25	2.00
			Entire	4.00	2.50
			Entire, 1st day cancel		6.00
U553	U106	5c + 1c	**bright purple** (G)	3.00	2.75
			Entire	4.00	3.25
			Entire, 1st day cancel		6.00
a.			Tagged	3.00	2.75
			Entire	4.00	3.25
			Entire, 1st day cancel		6.00

Tagged

Envelopes from No. U554 onward are tagged, except for bulk-rate and non-profit envelopes, which are untagged. The tagging element is in the ink through No. 608 unless otherwise noted. From No. 611 on, envelopes have bar or block tagging unless otherwise noted.

Herman Melville Issue

Issued to honor Herman Melville (1819-1891), writer, and the whaling industry.

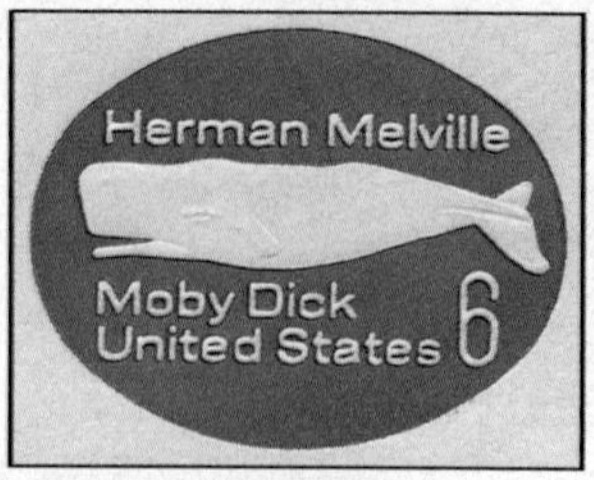

Moby Dick — U108

1970, Mar. 7

U554 U108 6c **blue** .50 .20
Entire .60 .25
Entire, 1st day cancel, New Bedford, Mass. *(433,777)* 1.50

Youth Conference Issue

Issued to publicize the White House Conference on Youth, Estes Park, Colo., Apr. 18-22.

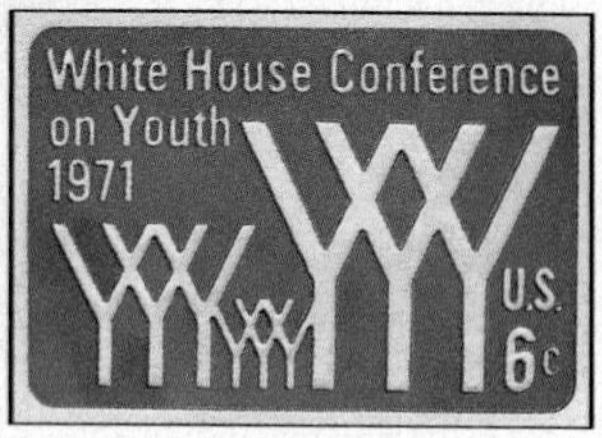

Conference Emblem Symbolic of Man's Expectant Soul and of Universal Brotherhood U109

Printed by United States Envelope Company, Williamsburg, Pa. Designed by Chermayeff and Geismar Associates.

1971, Feb. 24

U555 U109 6c **light blue** .75 .20
Entire .85 .40
Entire, 1st day cancel, Washington, D.C. *(264,559)* 1.00

Liberty Bell Type of 1965 and U110

Eagle — U110

Printed by the United States Envelope Co., Williamsburg, Pa. Designed (8c) by Bradbury Thompson.

1971

U556 U104 1 7/10c **deep lilac,** untagged, *May 10* .20
Entire .30 .20
Entire, 1st day cancel, Baltimore, Md. *(150,767)* 1.00

U557 U110 8c **ultramarine,** *May 6* .40 .20
Entire .50 .25
Entire, 1st day cancel, Williamsburg, Pa. *(193,000)* 1.00

Nos. U551 and U555 Surcharged in Green at Left of Stamp

c

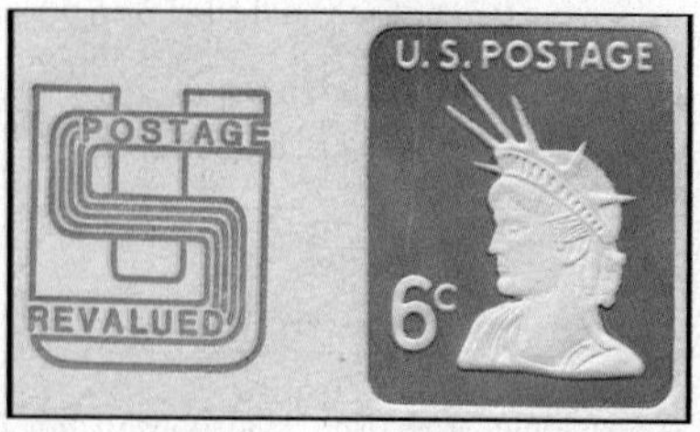

1971, May 16

U561 U107 6c + (2c) **light green** 1.00 1.25
Entire 1.10 2.50
Entire, 1st day cancel, Washington, D.C. 2.50

U562 U109 6c + (2c) **light blue** 2.00 2.50
Entire 2.50 3.00
Entire, 1st day cancel, Washington, D.C. 3.00

Bowling Issue

Issued as a salute to bowling and in connection with the 7th World Tournament of the International Bowling Federation, Milwaukee, Wis.

Bowling Ball and Pin — U111

Designed by George Giusti.

1971, Aug. 21

U563 U111 8c **rose red** .70 .20
Entire .80 .20
Entire, 1st day cancel, Milwaukee, Wis. *(281,242)* 1.00

Aging Conference Issue

White House Conference on Aging, Washington, D.C., Nov. 28-Dec. 2, 1971.

Conference Symbol — U112

Designed by Thomas H. Geismar.

1971, Nov. 15

U564 U112 8c **light blue** .50 .20
Entire .65 .20
Entire, 1st day cancel, Washington, D.C. *(125,000)* 1.00

International Transportation Exhibition Issue

U.S. International Transportation Exhibition, Dulles International Airport, Washington, D.C., May 27-June 4.

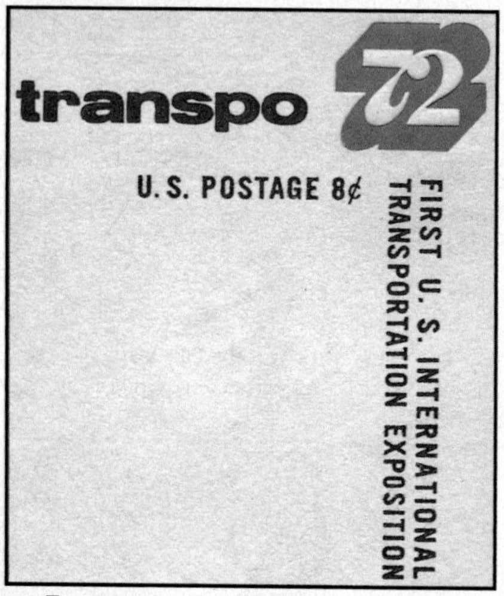

Transportation Exhibition Emblem — U113

Emblem designed by Toshihiki Sakow.

1972, May 2

U565 U113 8c **ultramarine & rose red** .50 .20
Entire .75 .25
Entire, 1st day cancel, Washington, D.C. 1.00

No. U557 Surcharged Type "b" (like Nos. U537-U538) in Ultramarine at Left of Stamp

1973, Dec. 1

U566 U110 8c + 2c **brt. ultramarine** .40 *1.25*
Entire .50 *2.50*
Entire, 1st day cancel, Washington, D.C. 1.50

Liberty Bell — U114

1973, Dec. 5

U567 U114 10c **emerald** .40 .20
Entire .50 .20
Entire, 1st day cancel, Philadelphia, Pa. *(142,141)* 1.00

"Volunteer Yourself" — U115

Designed by Norman Ives.

1974, Aug. 23

Untagged

U568 U115 1 8/10c **blue green** .20
Entire .30 *2.00*
Entire, 1st day cancel, Cincinnati, Ohio 1.00

Tennis Centenary Issue

Centenary of tennis in the United States.

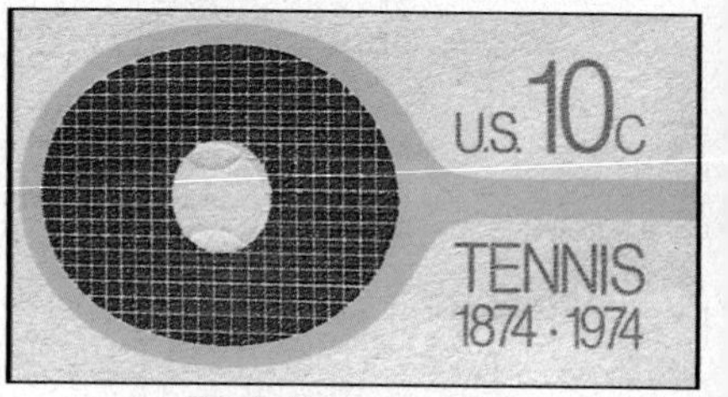

Tennis Racquet — U116

Designed by Donald Moss.

1974, Aug. 31 **Block Tagged**

U569 U116 10c **yellow, brt. blue & light green** .65 .20
Entire .75 .25
Entire, 1st day cancel, Forest Hills, N.Y. *(245,000)* 1.25

Bicentennial Era Issue

The Seafaring Tradition — Compass Rose U118

The American Homemaker — Quilt Pattern — U119

The American Farmer — Sheaf of Wheat U120

The American Doctor — Mortar U121

The American Craftsman — Tools, c. 1750 U122

Designs (in brown on left side of envelope): 10c, Norwegian sloop Restaurationen. No. U572, Spinning wheel. No. U573, Plow. No. U574, Colonial era medical instruments and bottle. No. U575, Shaker rocking chair.
Designed by Arthur Congdon.

1975-76 **Embossed**

Diagonally Laid Paper

U571 U118 10c **brown & blue,** *light brown, Oct. 13, 1975* .30 .20
Entire .45 .20
Entire, 1st day cancel, Minneapolis, Minn. *(255,304)* 1.00
a. Brown ("10c/USA," etc.) omitted, entire *150.00*
U572 U119 13c **brown & blue green,** *light brown, Feb. 2, 1976* .35 .20
Entire .50 .20
Entire, 1st day cancel, Biloxi, Miss. *(196,647)* 1.00
a. Brown ("13c/USA," etc.) omitted, entire *150.00*
U573 U120 13c **brown & bright green,** *light brown, Mar. 15, 1976* .35 .20
Entire .50 .20
Entire, 1st day cancel, New Orleans, La. *(214,563)* 1.00
a. Brown ("13c/USA," etc.) omitted, entire *150.00*
U574 U121 13c **brown & orange,** *light brown, June 30, 1976* .35 .20
Entire .50 .20
Entire, 1st day cancel, Dallas, Texas 1.50
a. Brown ("13c/USA," etc.) omitted, entire *150.00*
U575 U122 13c **brown & carmine,** *lt. brown, Aug. 6, 1976* .35 .20
Entire .50 .20
Entire, 1st day cancel, Hancock, Mass. 1.00
a. Brown ("13c/USA," etc.) omitted, entire *150.00*
Nos. U571-U575 (5) 1.70 1.00

Liberty Tree, Boston, 1646 — U123

Designed by Leonard Everett Fisher.

1975, Nov. 8 **Embossed**

U576 U123 13c **orange brown** .30 .20
Entire .40 .20
Entire, 1st day cancel, Memphis, Tenn. *(226,824)* 1.00

Star and Pinwheel — U124

U125

U126

Eagle — U127

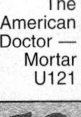

Uncle Sam — U128

Designers: 2c, Rudolph de Harak. 2.1c, Norman Ives. 2.7c, Ann Sforza Clementino. 15c, George Mercer.

1976-78 **Embossed**

U577 U124 2c **red,** untagged, *Sept. 10, 1976* .20
Entire .30 *1.50*
Entire, 1st day cancel, Hempstead, N.Y. *(81,388)* 1.00
U578 U125 2.1c **green,** untagged, *June 3, 1977* .20
Entire .30 *2.00*
Entire, 1st day cancel, Houston, Tex. *(120,280)* 1.00
U579 U126 2.7c **green,** untagged, *July 5, 1978* .20
Entire .35 *1.50*
Entire, 1st day cancel, Raleigh, N.C. *(92,687)* 1.00
U580 U127 (15c) **orange,** *May 22, 1978* .40 .20
Entire .55 *.75*
Entire, 1st day cancel, Memphis, Tenn. 1.00
U581 U128 15c **red,** ink tagged, *June 3, 1978* .40 .20
Entire .55 *.60*
Entire, 1st day cancel, Williamsburg, Pa. *(176,000)* 1.00
a. Bar tagged *6.00* —

Bicentennial Issue

Centennial Envelope, 1876 — U129

1976, Oct. 15 **Embossed**

U582 U129 13c **emerald** .35 .20
Entire .45 .20
Entire, 1st day cancel, Los Angeles, Cal. *(277,222)* 1.00

Golf Issue

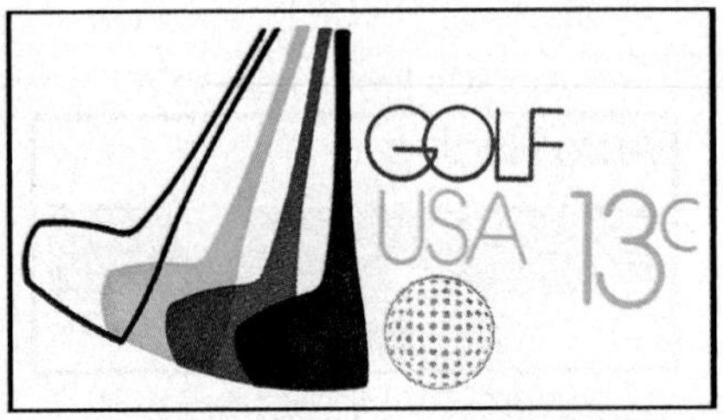

Golf Club in Motion and Golf Ball — U130

Designed by Guy Salvato.

1977, Apr. 7 **Photogravure and Embossed**

U583 U130 13c **black, blue & yellow green** .65 .20
Entire .75 *1.00*
Entire, 1st day cancel, Augusta, Ga. *(252,000)* 1.50
a. Black omitted, entire *650.00*
b. Black & blue omitted, entire *650.00*
c. Black, blue & yellow green omitted, entire *600.00*

On No. U583c, the embossing is present.

Energy Issue

Conservation and development of national resources.

"Conservation" U131

"Development" U132

Designed by Terrance W. McCaffrey.

1977, Oct. 20 **Embossed**

Bar Tagged

U584 U131 13c **black, red & yellow** .40 .20
Entire .50 .20
Entire, 1st day cancel, Ridley Park, Pa. 1.00
a. Red & yellow omitted, entire *250.00*
b. Yellow omitted, entire *175.00*
c. Black omitted, entire *175.00*
d. Black & red omitted, entire *400.00*
U585 U132 13c **black, red & yellow** .40 .20
Entire .50 .20
Entire, 1st day cancel, Ridley Park, Pa. 1.00

First day cancellation applied to 353,515 of Nos. U584 and U585.

Olive Branch and Star — U133

Designed by George Mercer.

1978, July 28 **Embossed**

Black Surcharge

U586 U133 15c on 16c **blue** .35 .20
Entire .50 *1.00*
Entire, 1st day cancel, Williamsburg, Pa. *(193,153)* 1.00
a. Surcharge omitted, entire 375.00 *1,000.*
b. Surcharge on No. U581, entire 100.00 *260.00*
c. As "a," with surcharge printed on envelope flap 175.00 —
d. Surcharge inverted (in lower left corner), entire 450.00 —

Auto Racing Issue

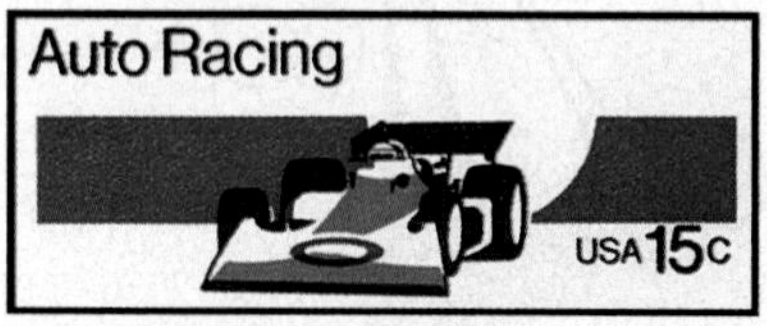

Indianapolis 500 Racing Car — U134

Designed by Robert Peak.

1978, Sept. 2 **Embossed**

U587 U134 15c **red, blue & black** .35 .20
Entire .50 *1.00*
Entire, 1st day cancel, Ontario, Cal. *(209,147)* 1.75
a. Black omitted, entire 120.00
b. Black & blue omitted, entire *450.00*
c. Red omitted, entire 120.00
d. Red & blue omitted, entire *550.00*

No. U576 Surcharged Like No. U586

1978, Nov. 28 **Embossed**

U588 U123 15c on 13c **orange brown** .35 .20
Entire .50 .20
Entire, 1st day cancel, Williamsburg, Pa. *(137,500)* 1.00
a. Surcharge inverted (in lower left corner), entire —

U135

Weaver Violins — U136

U137

Eagle — U138

U139

Eagle — U140

1979, May 18 **Untagged** **Embossed**

U589 U135 3.1c **ultramarine** .50
Entire .25 *1.50*
Entire, 1st day cancel, Denver, Colo. *(117,575)* 1.00

1980, June 23 **Untagged** **Embossed**

U590 U136 3.5c **purple** .50
Entire .30 *1.50*
Entire, 1st day cancel, Williamsburg, Pa. 1.00
a. 3.5c **violet**, tagged (in ink) error of color and tagging using ink intended for No. U592 — —

1982, Feb. 17 **Untagged** **Embossed**

U591 U137 5.9c **brown** .50
Entire .30 *1.50*
Entire, 1st day cancel, Wheeling, WV 1.00

1981, Mar. 15 **Embossed**

U592 U138 (18c) **violet** .45 .25
Entire .55 .30
Entire, 1st day cancel, Memphis, TN *(179,171)* 1.00

1981, Apr. 2 **Embossed**

U593 U139 18c **dark blue** .45 .25
Entire .55 .30
Entire, 1st day cancel, Star City, IN *(160,439)* 1.00

1981, Oct. 11 **Embossed**

U594 U140 (20c) **brown** .45 .25
Entire .55 .30
Entire, 1st day cancel, Memphis, TN *(304,404)* 2.00

Veterinary Medicine Issue

Seal of Veterinarians U141

Design at left side of envelope shows 5 animals and bird in brown, "Veterinary Medicine" in gray.
Designed by Guy Salvato.

1979, July 24 **Embossed**

U595 U141 15c **brown & gray** .50 .20
Entire .60 *1.00*
Entire, 1st day cancel, Seattle, WA *(209,658)* 1.00
a. Gray omitted, entire *1,000.*
b. Brown omitted, entire *1,000.*
c. Gray & brown omitted, entire *450.00*

On No. 595c, the embossing of the seal is present.

Olympic Games Issue

22nd Olympic Games, Moscow, July 19-Aug. 3, 1980.

U142

Design (multicolored on left side of envelope) shows two soccer players with ball.
Designed by Robert M. Cunningham.

1979, Dec. 10 **Embossed**

U596 U142 15c **red, green & black** .60 .20
Entire .70 *1.00*
Entire, 1st day cancel, East Rutherford, NJ *(179,336)* 1.00
a. Red & green omitted, tagging omitted, entire *225.00*
b. Black omitted, tagging omitted, entire *225.00*
c. Black & green omitted, entire *225.00*
d. Red omitted, tagging omitted, entire *400.00*

Highwheeler Bicycle — U143

Design (blue on left side of envelope) shows racing bicycle.
Designed by Robert Hallock.

1980, May 16 **Embossed**

U597 U143 15c **blue & rose claret** .40 .20
Entire .55 .20
Entire, 1st day cancel, Baltimore, MD *(173,978)* 1.25
a. Blue ("15c USA") omitted, entire 100.00

Yacht — U144

Designed by Cal Sachs.

1980, Sept. 15 **Embossed**

U598 U144 15c **blue & red** .40 .20
Entire .55 .20
Entire, 1st day cancel, Newport, RI *(192,220)* 1.00

Italian Honeybee and Orange Blossoms U145

Bee and petals colorless embossed.

Designed by Jerry Pinkney.

1980, Oct. 10 **Photogravure and Embossed**

U599 U145 15c **brown, green & yellow** .35 .20
Entire .50 .20
Entire, 1st day cancel, Paris, IL *(202,050)* 1.00
a. Brown ("USA 15c") omitted, entire *125.00*
b. Green omitted, entire —

No. U599b also has almost all of the brown color missing.

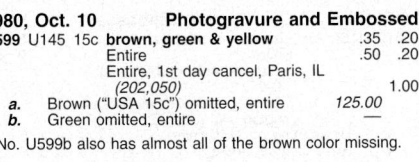

Hand and Braille U146

Hand and braille colorless embossed.

Designed by John Boyd.

1981, Aug. 13 **Embossed**

U600 U146 18c **blue & red** .45 .20
Entire .55 .25
Entire, 1st day cancel, Arlington, VA *(175,966)* 1.00
a. Blue omitted, entire *350.00*
b. Red omitted, entire *250.00*

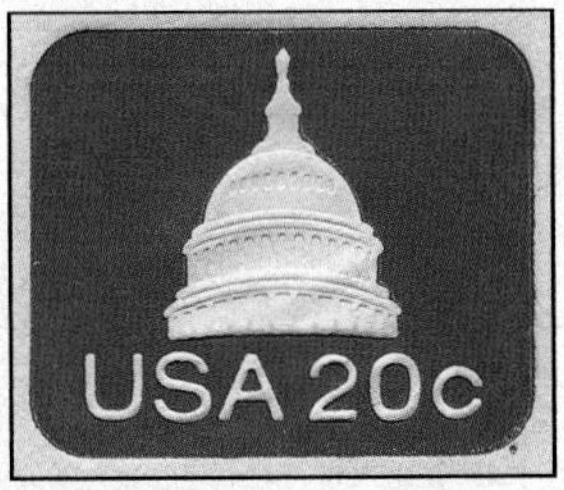

Capitol Dome — U147

1981, Nov. 13 **Embossed**

U601 U147 20c **deep magenta, ink** tagged .45 .20
Entire .55 .20
Entire, 1st day cancel, Los Angeles, CA 1.00
a. Bar tagged 2.50 1.50

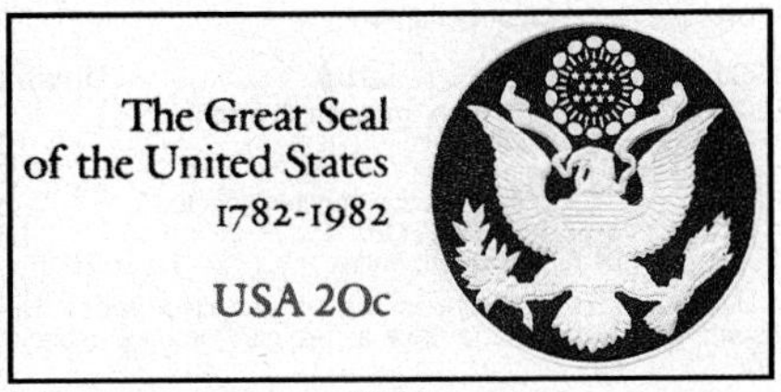

U148

Designed by Bradbury Thompson.

1982, June 15 **Embossed**

U602 U148 20c **dark blue, black & magenta** .45 .20
Entire .55 .20
Entire, 1st day cancel, Washington, DC *(163,905)* 1.00
a. Dark blue omitted, entire *150.00*
b. Dark blue & magenta omitted, entire —

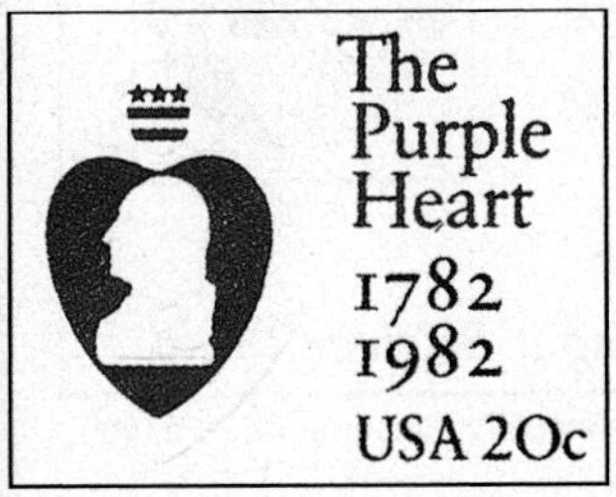

U149

Designed by John Boyd.

1982, Aug. 6 **Embossed**

U603 U149 20c **purple & black** .65 .20
Entire .75 .20
Entire, 1st day cancel, Washington, DC *(110,679)* 1.25
a. Black omitted, entire —
b. Purple omitted, entire *425.00*

U150

1983, Mar. 21 **Untagged** **Embossed**

U604 U150 5.2c **orange** .20
Entire .40 *1.00*
Entire, 1st day cancel, Memphis, TN *(141,979)* 1.00

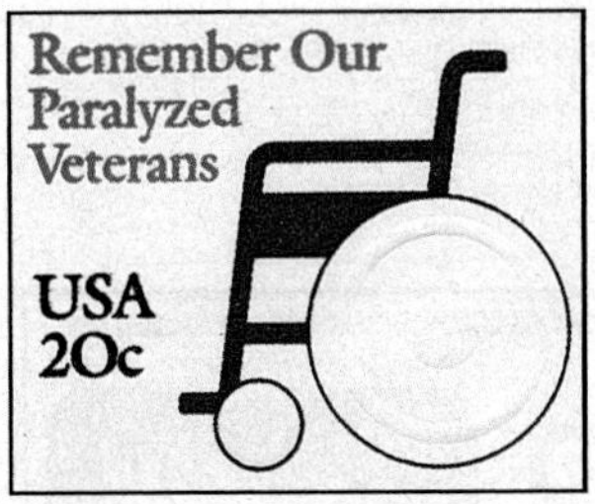

U151

1983, Aug. 3 **Embossed**

U605 U151 20c **red, blue & black** .45 .20
Entire .55 .20
Entire, 1st day cancel, Portland, OR *(21,500)* 1.00
a. Red omitted, entire *350.00*
b. Blue omitted, entire *350.00*
c. Red & black omitted, entire *150.00*
d. Blue & black omitted, entire *150.00*
e. Black omitted, entire *375.00*

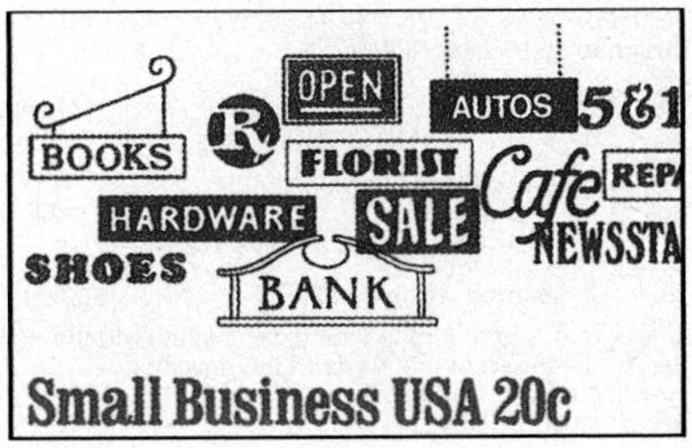

U152

Designed by Peter Spier and Pat Taylor.

Design shows storefronts at lower left. Stamp and design continue on back of envelope.

1984, May 7

U606 U152 20c **multi** .50 .20
Entire .60 .20
Entire, 1st day cancel, Washington, DC *(77,665)* 1.00

U153

Designed by Bradbury Thompson.

1985, Feb. 1 **Embossed**

U607 U153 (22c) **deep green** .55 .30
Entire .65 .40
Entire, 1st day cancel, Los Angeles, CA 1.00

American Buffalo — U154

Designed by George Mercer.

1985, Feb. 25 **Embossed**

U608 U154 22c **violet brown**, ink tagged .55 .20
Entire .65 .20
Entire, 1st day cancel, Bison, SD *(105,271)* 1.00
a. Untagged, 3 precancel lines, unwatermarked, *Nov. 1, 1986* .20
Entire .60 .20
b. Bar tagged 2.00 1.00
Entire 3.00 1.25
c. As "b," tagging omitted — —

Original printings of No. U608 were printed with luminescent ink. later printings have a luminescent vertical bar to the left of the stamp.

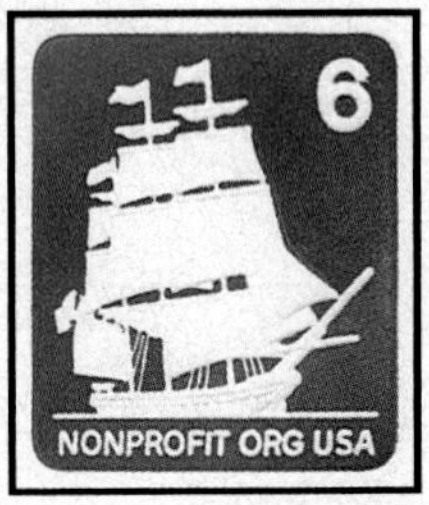

Frigate U.S.S. Constitution — U155

Designed by Cal Sacks.

1985, May 3 **Untagged** **Embossed**

U609 U155 6c **green blue** .20
Entire .25 *1.00*
Entire, 1st day cancel, Boston, MA *(170,425)* 1.25

The Mayflower — U156

Designed by Robert Brangwynne.

1986, Dec. 4 **Untagged Precanceled** **Embossed**

U610 U156 8.5c **black & gray** .20
Entire .30 .30
Entire, 1st day cancel, Plymouth, MA *(105,164)* 1.00

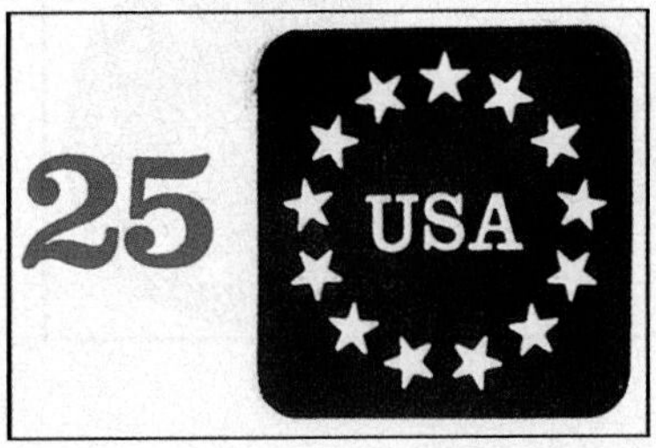

Stars U157

Designed by Joe Brockert.

1988, Mar. 26 **Typo. & Embossed**

U611 U157 25c **dark red & deep blue** .60 .20
Entire .70 .25
Entire, 1st day cancel, Star, MS *(29,393)* 1.25
a. Dark red (25) omitted, tagging omitted, entire 65.00 —
b. Tagging omitted, entire 14.00
c. Dark red (25) omitted, tagging not omitted —

U.S. Frigate Constellation — U158

Designed by Jerry Dadds.

1988, Apr. 12 Untagged Typo. & Embossed
Precanceled

U612 U158 8.4c **black & bright blue** .20
Entire .30 *1.00*
Entire, 1st day cancel, Baltimore, MD *(41,420)* 1.25
a. Black omitted, entire *800.00*

Snowflake — U159

Designed by Randall McDougall. "Holiday Greetings!" inscribed in lower left.

1988, Sept. 8 Typo.

U613 U159 25c **dark red & green** 1.00 *20.00*
Entire 1.25 *50.00*
Entire, 1st day cancel, Snowflake, AZ *(32,601)* 1.25

Stars U160

Designed by Joe Brockert. "Philatelic Mail" and asterisks in dark red below vignette; continuous across envelope face and partly on reverse.

1989, Mar. 10 Typo.

U614 U160 25c **dark red & deep blue** .50 .25
Entire .60 .30
Entire, 1st day cancel, Cleveland, OH 1.25
a. Tagging omitted, entire —

No. U614 was issued only in No. 9 size.

Stars — U161

Designed by Joe Brockert.

1989, July 10 Typo. Unwmk.

U615 U161 25c **dark red & deep blue** .50 .25
Entire .60 .30
Entire, 1st day cancel, Washington, DC *(33,461)* 1.25
a. Dark red omitted, entire —

Lined with a blue design to provide security for enclosures. Issued only in No. 9 size.

Love! U162

Designed by Tim Girvin. Light blue lines printed diagonally over the entire surface of the envelope.

1989, Sept. 22 Litho. & Typo. Unwmk.

U616 U162 25c **dark red & bright blue** .50 *.75*
Entire .60 *.85*
Entire, 1st day cancel, McLean, VA *(69,498)* 1.25
a. Dark red and bright blue omitted, entire 175.00
b. Bright blue omitted, entire —

No. U616 has light blue lines printed over the entire surface of the envelope. Issued only in No. 9 size.

Shuttle Docking at Space Station — U163

Designed by Richard Sheaff.

1989, Dec. 3 Typo. Unwmk.
Die Cut

U617 U163 25c **ultramarine** .90 .60
Entire 1.00 1.00
Entire, 1st day cancel, Washington, DC 1.25
a. Ultramarine omitted, entire *550.00*

A hologram, visible through the die cut window to the right of "USA 25," is affixed to the inside of the envelope.
Available only in No. 9 size.
See Nos. U625, U639.

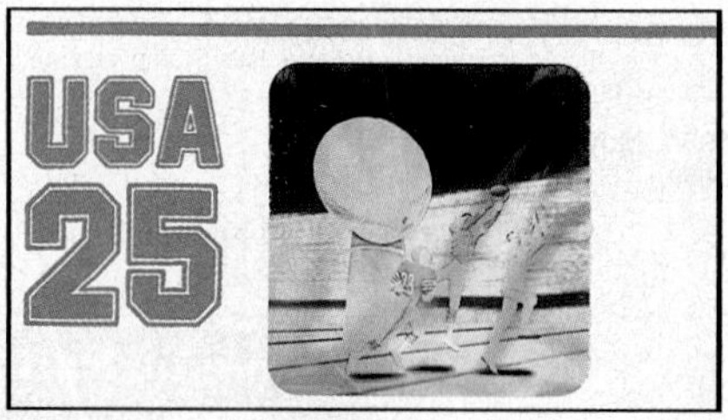

Vince Lombardi Trophy, Football Players — U164

Designed by Bruce Harman.

1990, Sept. 9 Typo. Unwmk. *Die Cut*

U618 U164 25c **vermilion** .90 .60
Entire 1.00 .70
Entire, 1st day cancel, Green Bay, WI *(54,589)* 1.25

A hologram, visible through the die cut window to the right of "USA 25," is affixed to the inside of the envelope.
Issued only in No. 10 size.

Star — U165

Designed by Richard Sheaff.

1991, Jan. 24 Typo. & Embossed Wmk.

U619 U165 29c **ultramarine & rose** .60 .30
Entire .70 .35
Entire, unwatermarked, *May 1, 1992* .70 .35
Entire, 1st day cancel, Washington, DC *(33,025)* 1.25
a. Ultramarine omitted, entire *600.00*
b. Rose omitted, entire *375.00*

Unwatermarked envelopes are on recycled paper, were issued May 1, 1992, and have a "recycled" imprint under the flap.
See No. U623.

Birds — U166

Designed by Richard Sheaff
Stamp and design continue on back of envelope. Illustration reduced.

1991, May 3 Typo. Wmk.
Untagged, Precanceled

U620 U166 11.1c **blue & red** .50
Entire .55 *1.00*
Entire, 1st day cancel, Boxborough, MA *(20,720)* 1.25
Entire, unwatermarked, *May 1, 1992* .60 .25

Unwatermarked envelopes are on recycled paper, were issued May 1, 1992, and have a "recycled" imprint under the flap.

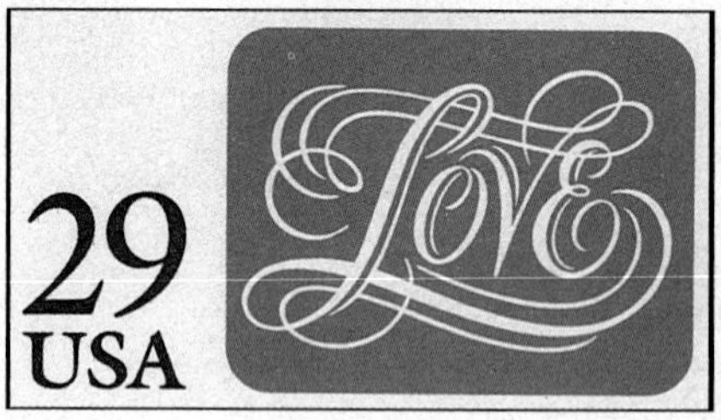

Love — U167

Designed by Salahattin Kanidinc.

1991, May 9 Litho. Unwmk.

U621 U167 29c **light blue, maroon & bright rose** .60 .60
Entire .70 .70
Entire, 1st day cancel, Honolulu, HI *(40,110)* 1.25
a. Bright rose omitted, entire *500.00*

Unwatermarked envelopes are on recycled paper, were issued May 1, 1992, and have a "recycled" imprint under the flap.

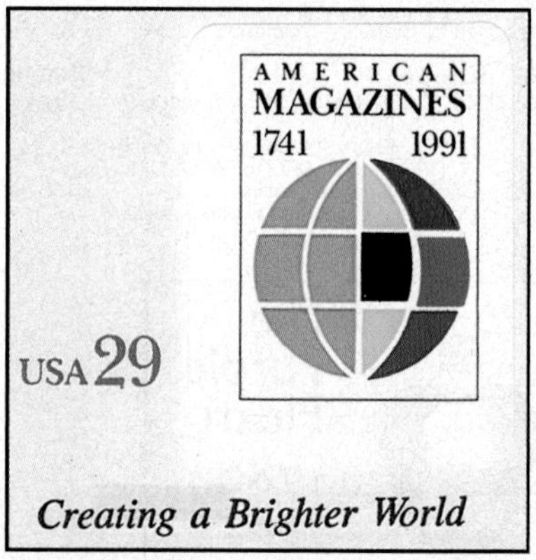

Magazine Industry, 250th Anniv. — U168

Designed by Bradbury Thompson.

1991, Oct. 7 Photo. & Typo. Unwmk.

U622 U168 29c **multicolored** .60 .50
Entire .70 *1.50*
Entire, 1st day cancel, Naples, FL *(26,020)* 1.25

The photogravure vignette, visible through the die cut window to the right of "USA 29", is affixed to the inside of the envelope. Issued only in No. 10 size.

Star
U169

Designed by Richard Sheaff.
Stamp and design continue on back of envelope.

1991, July 20 **Typo.**

U623	U169	29c	**ultra & rose**	.60	.30
			Entire	.70	.35
			Entire, 1st day cancel, Washington, DC *(16,038)*		1.25
a.			Ultra omitted, entire	*575.00*	
b.			Rose omitted, entire	*250.00*	

Lined with a blue design to provide security for enclosures. Unwatermarked envelopes are on recycled paper, were issued May 1, 1992, and have a "recycled" imprint under the flap. Issued only in No. 9 size. Value $1.

Country
Geese
U170

Designed by Marc Zaref.

1991, Nov. 8 **Litho. & Typo.** **Wmk.**

U624	U170	29c	**blue gray & yellow**	.60	.60
			Entire	.70	.70
			Entire, 1st day cancel, Virginia Beach, VA *(21,031)*		1.25
			Entire, unwatermarked, *May 1, 1992*	1.00	.70

Unwatermarked envelopes are on recycled paper were issued May 1, 1992, and have a "recycled" imprint under the flap.

Space Shuttle Type of 1989

Designed by Richard Sheaff.

1992, Jan. 21 **Typo.** **Unwmk.** ***Die Cut***

U625	U163	29c	**yellow green**	.90	.50
			Entire	1.00	.60
			Entire, 1st day cancel, Virginia Beach, VA *(37,646)*		1.25

A hologram, visible through the die cut window to the right of "USA 29," is affixed to the inside of the envelope. Examples on recycled paper were issued May 1, 1992 and have a "recycled" imprint under the flap. Issued only in No. 10 size. Value $1.25.

U171

Designed by Harry Zelenko.

1992, Apr. 10 **Typo. & Litho.** ***Die Cut***

U626	U171	29c	**multicolored**	.60	*.90*
			Entire	.70	*1.75*
			Entire, 1st day cancel, Dodge City, KS *(34,258)*		1.25

The lithographed vignette, visible through the die cut window to the right of "USA 29," is affixed to the inside of the envelope. Issued only in the No. 10 size.

Hillebrandia — U172

Designed by Joseph Brockert. Illustration reduced.

1992, Apr. 22

U627	U172	29c	**multicolored**	.60	.30
			Entire	.70	*1.75*
			Entire, 1st day cancel, Chicago, IL *(29,432)*		1.25

The lithographed vignette, visible through the die cut window to the right of "29 USA," is affixed to the inside of the envelope. Inscribed "Save the Rain Forests" in the lower left. Issued only in the No. 10 size.

Star — U173

Designed by Joseph Brockert.

1992, May 19 **Typo. & Embossed** **Precanceled**
Untagged

U628	U173	19.8c	**red & blue**		.40
			Entire	.50	*1.00*
			Entire, 1st day cancel, Las Vegas, NV *(18,478)*		1.25

Issued only in No. 10 size.

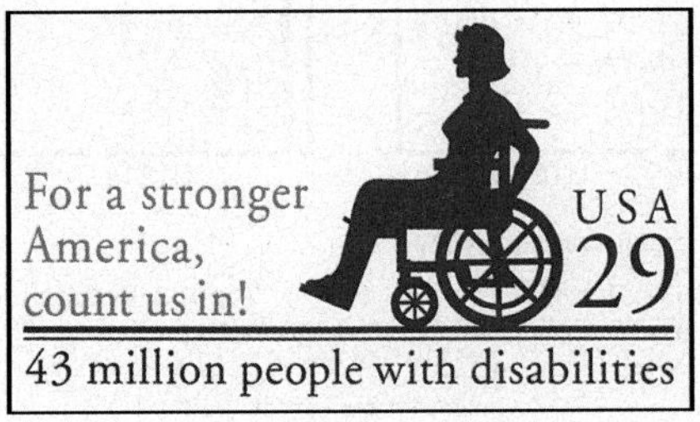

U174

Designed by Richard Sheaff. Illustration reduced.

1992, July 22 **Typo.**

U629	U174	29c	**red & blue**	.60	.30
			Entire	.70	.35
			Entire, 1st day cancel, Washington, DC *(28,218)*		1.25

U175

Designed by Nancy Krause. Illustration reduced.

1993, Oct. 2 **Typo. & Litho.** ***Die Cut***

U630	U175	29c	**multicolored**	.90	*1.00*
			Entire	1.00	*1.75*
			Entire, 1st day cancel, King of Prussia, PA *(6,511)*		1.25

The lithographed vignette, visible through the die cut window to the right of "USA 29," is affixed to the inside of the envelope. Issued only in the No. 10 size.

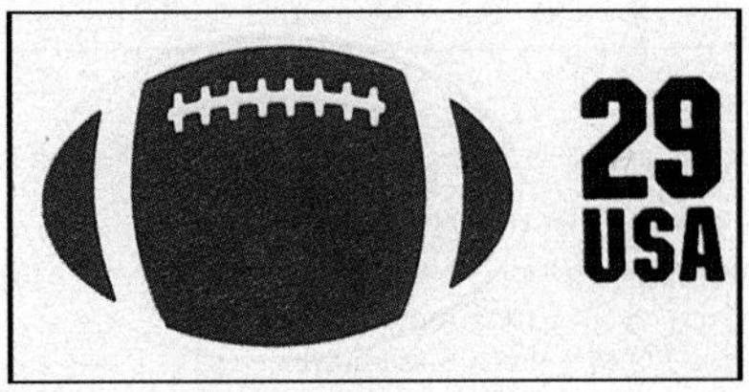

U176

Designed by Richard Sheaff.

1994, Sept. 17 **Typo. & Embossed**

U631	U176	29c	**brown & black**	.60	*.90*
			Entire	.70	*1.50*
			Entire, 1st day cancel, Canton, OH *(28,977)*		1.25
a.			Black ("29/USA") omitted, entire	*375.00*	

Issued only in No. 10 size.

Liberty Bell — U177

Designed by Richard Sheaff.

1995, Jan. 3 **Typo. & Embossed**

U632	U177	32c	**greenish blue & blue**	.65	.30
			Entire	.75	.40
			Entire, 1st day cancel, Williamsburg, PA		1.25
a.			Greenish blue omitted, entire	*450.00*	
b.			Blue ("USA 32") omitted, entire	125.00	

First day cancellation was applied to 54,102 of Nos. U632, UX198.
See No. U638.

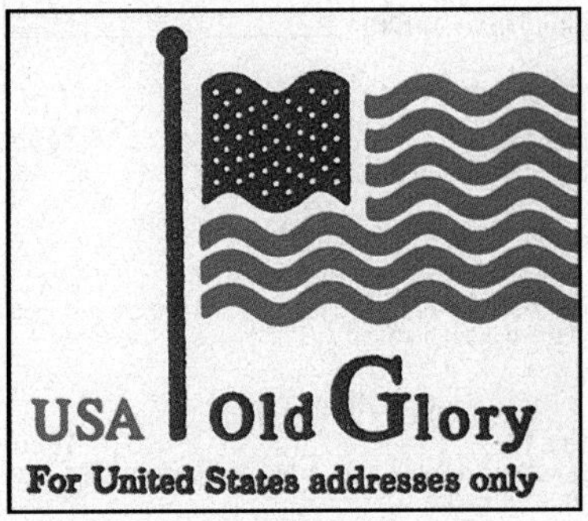

U178

Design sizes: 49x38mm (#U633), 53x44mm (U634). Stamp and design continue on back of envelope.

1995 **Typo.**

U633	U178	(32c)	**blue & red**	.75	*.90*
			Entire, #6¾	1.00	1.00
U634	U178	(32c)	**blue & red**	.75	*.90*
			Entire, #10	1.00	1.00
a.			Red & tagging omitted, entire	*500.00*	
b.			Blue omitted, entire	*500.00*	

Originally, Nos. U633-U634 were only available through the Philatelic Fullfillment Center after their announcement 1/12/95. Envelopes submitted for first day cancels received a 12/13/94 cancel, even though they were not available on that date.

U179

Design size: 58x25mm. Stamp and design continue on back of envelope.
Designed by Douglas Smith.

1995, Mar. 10 **Typo.**

Precanceled, Untagged

U635 U179 (5c) **green & red brown** .50
Entire .55 *1.00*
Entire, 1st day cancel, State College, PA 1.25

Graphic Eagle — U180

Designed by Uldis Purins.

1995, Mar. 10 **Typo.**

Precanceled, Untagged

U636 U180 (10c) **dark carmine & blue** .20
Entire .30 *1.50*
Entire, 1st day cancel, State College, PA 1.25

Issued only in No. 10 size.

Spiral Heart — U181

Designed by Uldis Purins.

1995, May 12 **Typo.**

U637 U181 32c **red,** *light blue* .65 .30
Entire .75 .60
Entire, 1st day cancel, Lakeville, PA 1.25
a. Red omitted, entire —

On No. U637a, the red "RECYCLED" and recycling symbol appear on the bottom backflap.

Liberty Bell Type

1995, May 16 **Typo.**

U638 U177 32c **greenish blue & blue** .65 .30
Entire .70 .35
Entire, 1st day cancel, Washington, DC 1.25
a. Greenish blue omitted, entire —

No. U638 was printed on security paper and was issued only in No. 9 size.

Space Shuttle Type of 1989

Designed by Richard Sheaff.

1995, Sept. 22 **Typo.** ***Die Cut***

U639 U163 32c **carmine rose** .65 .35
Entire .70 .40
Entire, 1st day cancel, Milwaukee, WI 1.25

A hologram, visible through the die cut window to the right of "USA 32," is affixed to the inside of the envelope. No. U639 was issued only in No. 10 size.

U182

Designed by Richard Sheaff.

1996, Apr. 20 **Typo. & Litho.** ***Die Cut***

U640 U182 32c **multicolored** .60 .30
Entire .70 .35
Entire, 1st day cancel, Chicago, IL *(9,921)* 1.25

The lithographed vignette, visible through the die cut window to the right of "USA 32c," is affixed to the inside of the envelope. Issued only in the No. 10 size.

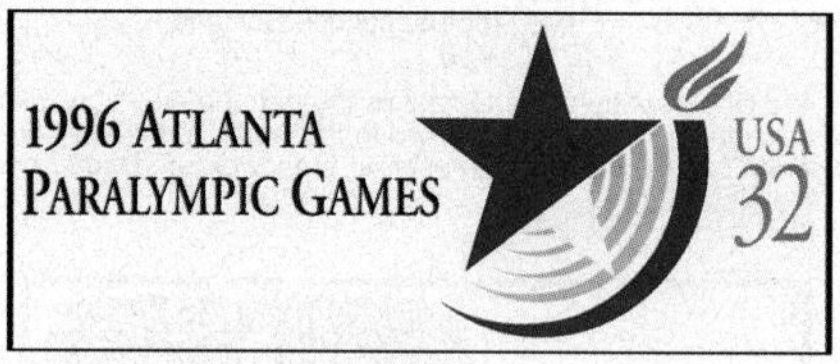

U183

Designed by Brad Copeland. Illustration reduced.

1996, May 2

U641 U183 32c **multicolored** .60 .30
Entire .70 .35
Entire, 1st day cancel, Washington, DC 1.25
a. Blue & red omitted, entire —
b. Blue & gold omitted, entire *675.00*
c. Red omitted, entire —
d. Black & red omitted, entire *450.00*
e. Blue omitted, entire —

U184

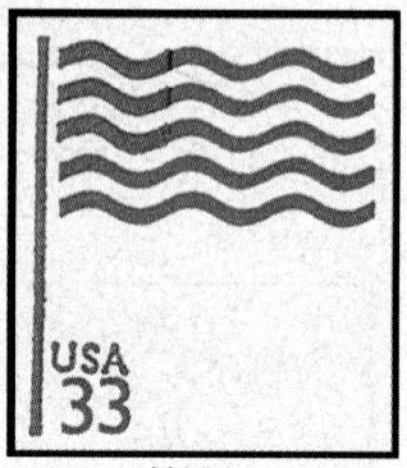

U184a

Designer by Richard Sheaff.

1999, Jan. 11 **Typo. & Embossed**

U642 U184 33c **yellow, blue & red,** tagging bar to left of design .65 .30
Entire .80 .40
Entire, 1st day cancel, Washington, DC 1.25
a. Tagging bar to right of design 3.00 .30
Entire 3.50 .40
b. As "a," blue omitted, entire —
c. As "a," yellow omitted, entire —
d. As "a," yellow and blue omitted, entire —
e. As "a," blue and red omitted, entire —
f. As "a," all colors omitted, entire —

Earliest documented use of No. U642a, 10/12/99.
On No. U642f, the distinctive tagging bar is present. Expertization is required.

1999, Jan. 11 **Typo.**

U643 U184a 33c **blue & red** .65 .30
Entire .80 .40
Entire, 1st day cancel, Washington, DC 1.25
a. Tagging bar to right of design .65 .30
Entire .80 .40

Issued only in No. 9 size.

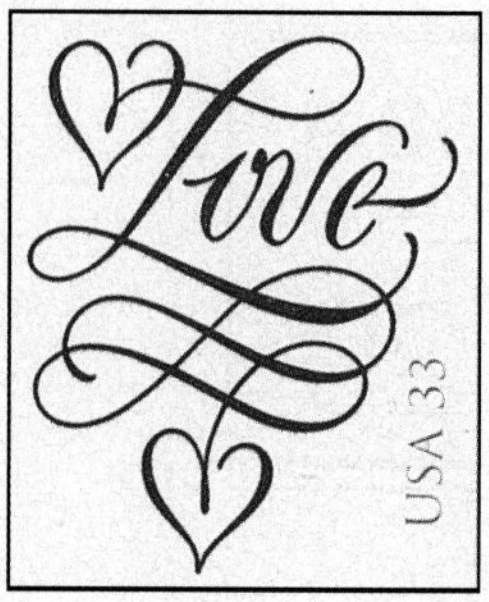

U185

Designed by Julian Waters.

1999, Jan. 28 **Litho.**

U644 U185 33c **violet** .65 .30
Entire .80 .40
Entire, 1st day cancel, Loveland, CO 1.25
a. Tagging bar to right of design .65 .30
Entire .80 .40

Lincoln — U186

Designed by Richard Sheaff.

1999, June 5 **Typo. & Litho.**

U645 U186 33c **blue & black** .65 .30
Entire .80 .40
Entire, 1st day cancel, Springfield, IL 1.25

Eagle — U187

Designed by Michael Doret.

2001, Jan. 7 **Typo.**

U646 U187 34c **blue gray & gray** .65 .30
Entire .85 .40
Entire, 1st day cancel, Washington, DC 1.25
a. Blue gray omitted, entire 275.00

Many color shades known.
All No. U646 were printed on recycled paper. It was also produced using a different blue-gray recycled paper starting in 2002.

Lovebirds U188

Designed by Robert Brangwynne.

2001, Feb. 14 **Litho.**

U647 U188 34c **rose & dull violet** .65 .30
Entire .85 .40
Entire, 1st day cancel, Lovejoy, GA 1.25

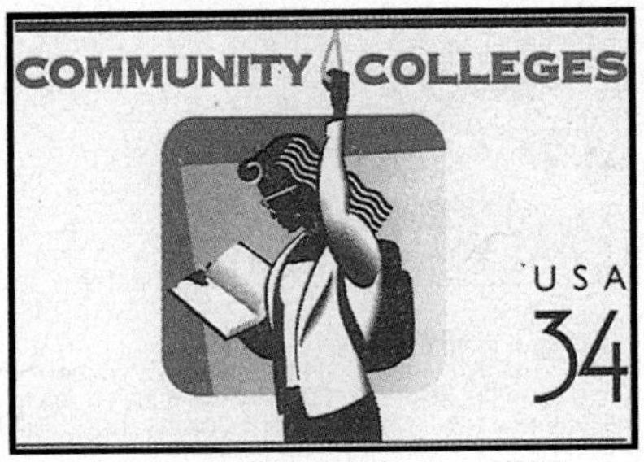

Community Colleges, Cent. — U189

Designed by Howard Paine.

2001, Feb. 20 **Typo.**
U648 U189 34c **dark blue & orange brown** .65 .30
Entire .85 .40
Entire, 1st day cancel, Joliet, IL 1.25

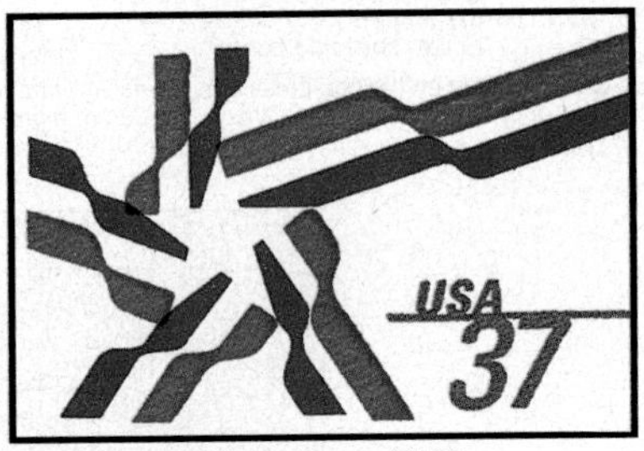

Ribbon Star — U190

Designed by Terrence W. McCaffrey.

2002, June 7 **Typo.**
U649 U190 37c **red, blue & gray** .75 .35
Entire .90 .45
Entire, 1st day cancel, Washington, DC 1.25
Entire, 1st day cancel, any other city 1.25
a. Gray omitted, entire —
b. Blue and gray omitted, entire —

All No. U649 were printed on recycled paper. It was also produced using a different blue-gray recycled paper starting in 2002.

Type of 1995 Inscribed "USA / Presorted / Standard"

Designed by Uldis Purins.

2002, Aug. 8 **Typo.** **Untagged**
Precanceled
U650 U180 (10c) **dark carmine & blue** .20
Entire .35 1.50
Entire, 1st day cancel, Washington, DC 1.25

Issued only in No. 10 size.

Nurturing Love — U191

Designed by Craig Frazier.

2003, Jan. 25 **Typo.**
U651 U191 37c **olive green & yellow orange** .75 .35
Entire .90 .45
Entire, 1st day cancel, Tucson, AZ 1.25
a. Tagging omitted, entire —

Jefferson Memorial Type

Designed by Derry Noyes.

2003, Dec. 29 **Typo.**
U652 A2818 $3.85 **multicolored** 7.75 6.25
Entire 7.75 7.00
Entire, 1st day cancel, Washington, DC 5.75

On No. U652, the stamp indicia is printed on the flap of the envelope.

Disney Type of 2004

Designed by David Pacheco.

2004, June 23 **Litho.**
U653 A2949 37c **multicolored** 2.50 2.10
Entire 2.50 2.50
Entire, 1st day cancel, Anaheim, CA 2.50
U654 A2950 37c **multicolored** 2.50 2.10
Entire 2.50 2.50
Entire, 1st day cancel, Anaheim, CA 2.50
U655 A2951 37c **multicolored** 2.50 2.10
Entire 2.50 2.50
Entire, 1st day cancel, Anaheim, CA 2.50
a. All color missing on reverse, entire —
U656 A2952 37c **multicolored** 2.50 2.10
Entire 2.50 2.50
Entire, 1st day cancel, Anaheim, CA 2.50
a. Booklet of 12 letter sheets, 3 each #U653-U656 30.00

No. U656a sold for $14.95.

White Lilacs and Pink Roses Type of 2004

Designed by Richard Sheaff.

2005, Mar. 3 **Litho.**
U657 A2931 37c **multicolored** 2.50 2.50
First day cancel, New York, NY 2.50

No. U657 was sold in pads of 12 for $14.95.

Computer-generated Study of an X-Plane — U192

2006, Jan. 5 **Typo.** **Unwmk.**
U658 U192 $4.05 **multicolored** 8.25 6.50
Entire 8.25 7.25
Entire, 1st day cancel, Kansas City, MO 6.50

Benjamin Franklin — U193

Designed by Richard Sheaff.

2006, Jan. 9 **Typo.** **Unwmk.**
U659 U193 39c **blue green & black** .80 .40
Entire .95 .50
Entire, 1st day cancel, Washington, DC 1.25
Entire, 1st day cancel, any other city 1.25
a. All color omitted, entire —

On No. 659a, the tagging bar and the blue green printing on the reverse are present.

Air Force One — U194

Designed by Phil Jordan.

2007, May 6 **Typo.** **Unwmk.**
U660 U194 $4.60 **multicolored** 9.25 7.00
Entire 9.25 7.50
Entire, 1st day cancel, Kansas City, MO 9.25

No. U660 was sold only in packs of 5, 10 or 25 envelopes.

Marine One — U195

Designed by Phil Jordan.

2007, May 6 **Typo.** **Unwmk.**
U661 U195 $16.25 **multicolored** 33.00 17.00
Entire 33.00 19.00
Entire, 1st day cancel, Kansas City, MO 33.00

No. U661 was sold only in packs of three envelopes, with each envelope having a different Star Wars character (Darth Vader, Yoda, or Obi-wan Kenobi) on the back of the envelope. Values for entires are for any envelope back.

Horses — U196

illustration reduced. Designed by Tom Engeman.

2007, May 12 **Typo.** **Unwmk.**
U662 U196 41c **reddish brown & black** .85 .40
Entire 1.00 .50
Entire, 1st day cancel, Washington, DC 2.10

Elk U197

Designed by Carl T. Herrman.

2008, May 2 **Typo.** **Unwmk.**
U663 U197 42c **green & black**, tagging bar 20mm takk .85 .40
a. Tagging bar 26mm tall .85 .40
Entire, Westvaco printing 1.00 .50
Entire, Ashton-Potter printing 1.00 .50
Entire, 1st day cancel, Washington, DC 2.10

No. U663 was printed National Envelope for Ashton-Potter (USA) Ltd. No. U663a was printed by Westvaco. Envelopes printed by Westvaco have copyright and recycled content text, found on the envelope's back, in black. These features are in green on Ashton-Potter envelopes. All Westvaco envelopes have pointed flaps, while the Ashton-Potter envelopes have flaps with curved ends.

Mount Rushmore U198

Designed by Carl T. Herrman.

2008, May 12 **Typo.** **Unwmk.**

U664 U198 $4.80 **multicolored**	9.75	7.00
Entire	9.75	7.00
Entire, 1st day cancel, Kansas City, MO		9.75

No. U664 was sold only in packs of 5, 10 or 25 envelopes.

AIR POST STAMPED ENVELOPES AND AIR LETTER SHEETS

All envelopes have carmine and blue borders, unless noted. There are seven types of borders:

Carmine Diamond in Upper Right Corner.

a — Diamonds measure 9 to 10mm paralled to edge of envelope and 11 to 12mm along oblique side (with top flap open). Sizes 5 and 13 only.

b — Like "a" except diamonds measure 7 to 8mm along oblique side (with top flap open). Sizes 5 and 13 only.

c — Diamonds measure 11 to 12mm parallel to edge of envelope. Size 8 only.

Blue Diamond in Upper Right Corner.

d — Lower points of top row of diamonds point to left. Size 8 only.

e — Lower points of top row of diamonds point to right. Size 8 only.

Diamonds Omitted in Upper Right Corner (1965 Onward)

f — Blue diamond above at left of stamp.

g — Red diamond above at left of stamp.

UC1

5c — Vertical rudder is not semi-circular but slopes down to the left. The tail of the plane projects into the G of POSTAGE. Border types a, b, c, d and e.

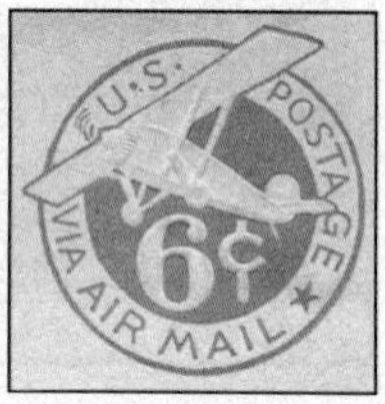

UC2

Die 2 (5c and 8c): Vertical rudder is semi-circular. The tail of the plane touches but does not project into the G of POSTAGE. Border types b, d, and e for the 5c; b and d for the 8c.

Die 2 (6c) — Same as UC2 except three types of numeral.
2a — The numeral "6" is 6½mm wide.
2b — The numeral "6" is 6mm wide.
2c — The numeral "6" is 5½mm wide.

Eleven working dies were used in printing the 6c. On each, the numeral "6" was engraved by hand, producing several variations in position, size and thickness.

Nos. UC1 and UC2 occur with varying size blue blobs, caused by a shallow printing die. They are not constant.

Border types b and d for dies 2a and 2b; also without border (June 1944 to Sept. 1945) for dies 2a, 2b and 2c.

Die 3 (6c): Vertical rudder leans forward. S closer to O than to T of POSTAGE. E of POSTAGE has short center bar. Border types b and d, also without border.

No. UC1 with 1933 and 1937 watermarks and No. UC2 with 1933 watermark were issued in Puerto Rico.

No. UC1 in blue black, with 1925 watermark #26 and border type a, is a proof.

1929-44

UC1 UC1 5c **blue,** *Jan. 12, 1929*	3.50	2.00
Entire, border a or b	4.75	2.25
Entire, border c, d or e	8.50	5.75
First day cancel, border a, entire		40.00
1933 wmk. #33, border d, entire	*750.00*	*750.00*
1933 wmk. #33, border b, entire	—	—
1937 wmk. #36, border d, entire	—	*2,500.*
1937 wmk. #36, border b, entire	—	—
Bicolored border omitted, entire	1,300.	
a. Orange and blue border, type b	375.00	*450.00*
UC2 UC2 5c **blue,** die 2	11.50	5.00
Entire, border b	13.50	6.50
Entire, border e	21.00	12.50
1929 wmk. #28, border d, entire	—	*1,500.*
1933 wmk. #33, border b, entire	*650.00*	—
1933 wmk. #33, border d, entire	325.00	—
UC3 UC2 6c **orange,** die 2a, *July 1, 1934*	1.50	.40
Entire, bicolored border	1.75	.60
Entire, without border	2.50	1.25
Entire, 1st day cancel		14.00
a. With added impression of 3c purple (#U436a), entire without border	*4,000.*	
UC4 UC2 6c **orange,** die 2b ('42)	3.00	2.00
Entire, bicolored border, 1941 wmk. #39	60.00	20.00
Entire, without border	4.50	2.00
UC5 UC2 6c **orange,** die 2c ('44)	.75	.30
Entire, without border	1.00	.45
UC6 UC2 6c **orange,** die 3 ('42)	1.00	.35
Entire, bicolored border	1.50	.75
Entire, without border	2.50	.90
Entire, carmine of border omitted	*4,000.*	
Double impression, entire	400.00	
a. 6c orange, *blue,* die 3 (error) Entire, without border	*3,500.*	*2,400.*
UC7 UC2 8c **olive green,** die 2, *Sept. 26, 1932*	12.00	3.50
Entire, bicolored border	17.50	15.00
Entire, 1st day cancel		11.00

Surcharged in black on envelopes indicated by number in parenthesis

1945

UC8 U93 6c on 2c **carmine** (U429, die 1)	1.25	.65
Entire	1.60	1.00
a. On U429f, die 7	2.25	1.50
Entire	3.00	2.00
b. On U429g, die 8	1.90	1.10
Entire	3.00	1.75
c. On U429h, die 9	11.00	7.50
Entire	16.00	11.00
d. 6c on 1c green (error) (U420)	*1,750.*	
Entire	*2,500.*	
e. 6c on 3c dk violet (error) (U436a)	*2,000.*	
Entire	*4,000.*	
f. 6c on 3c dk violet (error), *amber* (U437a)	*3,000.*	
Entire	*3,500.*	
g. 6c on 3c violet (error) (U526)	*3,000.*	
Entire	*7,000.*	
UC9 U95 6c on 2c **carmine** (U525)	65.00	35.00
Entire	90.00	45.00

Ten surcharge varieties are found on Nos. UC8-UC9.

Surcharged in Black on 6c Air Post Envelopes without borders

1946

UC10 UC2 5c on 6c **orange,** die 2a	2.75	1.50
Entire	3.50	2.50
First day of rate, *Oct. 1, 1946,* entire		100.00
a. Double surcharge	75.00	
UC11 UC2 5c on 6c **orange,** die 2b	9.00	5.50
Entire	11.00	7.00
First day of rate, *Oct. 1, 1946,* entire		150.00
UC12 UC2 5c on 6c **orange,** die 2c	.75	.50
Entire	1.25	.60
First day of rate, *Oct. 1, 1946,* entire		75.00
a. Double surcharge	75.00	*300.00*
UC13 UC2 5c on 6c **orange,** die 3	.80	.60
Entire	1.00	.75
First day of rate, *Oct. 1, 1946,* entire		75.00
a. Double surcharge	75.00	

The 6c borderless envelopes and the revalued envelopes were issued primarily for use to and from members of the armed forces. The 5c rate came into effect Oct. 1, 1946.

Ten surcharge varieties are found on Nos. UC10-UC13.

DC-4 Skymaster — UC3

Envelopes with borders types b and d.

Die 1 — The end of the wing at the right is a smooth curve. The juncture of the front end of the plane and the engine forms an acute angle. The first T of STATES and the E's of UNITED STATES lean to the left.

Die 2 — The end of the wing at the right is a straight line. The juncture of the front end of the plane and the engine is wide open. The first T of STATES and the E's of UNITED STATES lean to the right.

1946

UC14 UC3 5c **carmine,** die 1, *Sept. 25, 1946*	.85	.25
Entire, bicolored border	1.10	.40
Entire, 1st day cancel		1.50
Entire, bicolored border omitted	—	
UC15 UC3 5c **carmine,** die 2	.85	.25
Entire, bicolored border	1.10	.40

No. UC14, printed on flat bed press, measures 21½mm high. No. UC15, printed on rotary press, measures 22mm high. See No. UC18.

DC-4 Skymaster — UC4

1947-55 **Typographed, Without Embossing**

Letter Sheets for Foreign Postage

UC16 UC4 10c **bright red,** *pale blue,* "Air Letter" on face, 2-line inscription on back, entire	8.50	*10.00*
Entire, 1st day cancel, *Apr. 29, 1947*		2.00
Die cutting reversed, entire	110.00	
UC16a UC4 10c **bright red,** *pale blue, Sept. 1951,* "Air Letter" on face, 4-line inscription on back, entire	17.50	14.00
Die cutting reversed, entire	275.00	
b. 10c **chocolate,** *pale blue,* entire	450.00	
UC16c UC4 10c **bright red,** *pale blue, Nov. 1953,* "Air Letter" and "Aerogramme" on face, 4-line inscription on back, entire	45.00	12.50
Die cutting reversed, entire	150.00	
UC16d UC4 10c **bright red,** *pale blue, 1955,* "Air Letter" and "Aerogramme" on face, 3-line inscription on back, entire	9.00	8.00
Die cutting reversed, entire	60.00	
Dark blue (inscriptions & border diamonds) omitted	—	

Printed on protective tinted paper containing colorless inscription,

UNITED STATES FOREIGN AIR MAIL multiple, repeated in parallel vertical or horizontal lines.

Postage Stamp Centenary Issue

Centenary of the first postage stamps issued by the United States Government.

Washington and Franklin, Early and Modern Mail-carrying Methods — UC5

Two dies: Rotary, design measures 22¼mm high; and flat bed press, design 21¾mm high.

1947, May 21 **Embossed**

For Domestic Postage

UC17 UC5 5c **carmine** (rotary)	.50	.30
Entire, bicolored border b	.60	.40
Entire, 1st day cancel, NY, NY		1.25
a. Flat plate printing	.50	.30
Entire	.60	.40

Type of 1946

Type I: 6's lean to right.
Type II: 6's upright.

1950

UC18 UC3 6c **carmine,** type I, *Sept. 22, 1950* .40 .25
Entire, bicolored border .60 .30
Entire, 1st day cancel, Philadelphia 1.00
a. Type II .75 .25
Entire 1.00 .30

Several other types differ slightly from the two listed.

Nos. UC14, UC15, UC18 Surcharged in Red at Left of Stamp

1951

UC19 UC3 6c on 5c **carmine,** die 1 .85 1.00
Entire 1.25 *1.25*
UC20 UC3 6c on 5c **carmine,** die 2 .85 1.00
Entire 1.25 *1.25*
a. 6c on 6c **carmine** (error) entire *1,500.*
b. Double surcharge *975.00* —

Nos. UC14 and UC15 Surcharged in Red at Left of Stamp

1952

UC21 UC3 6c on 5c **carmine,** die 1 27.50 17.50
Entire 35.00 22.50
UC22 UC3 6c on 5c **carmine,** die 2, *Aug. 29, 1952* 4.25 2.50
Entire 6.00 4.25
Entire, 1st day cancel, Norfolk, Va. 25.00
a. Double surcharge 200.00
b. Triple surcharge, entire —

Same Surcharge in Red on No. UC17

UC23 UC5 6c on 5c **carmine** 900.00
Entire 2,000.

The 6c on 4c black (No. U440) is believed to be a favor printing.

Fifth International Philatelic Exhibition Issue

FIPEX, the Fifth International Philatelic Exhibition, New York, N.Y., Apr. 28-May 6, 1956.

Eagle in Flight — UC6

1956, May 2

UC25 UC6 6c **red** .75 .50
Entire 1.00 .80
Entire, 1st day cancel, New York, N.Y. *(363,239)* 1.25

Two types exist, differing slightly in the clouds at top.

Skymaster Type of 1946

1958, July 31

UC26 UC3 7c **blue** .65 .50
Entire 1.00 .55
Entire, 1st day cancel, Dayton, O. *(143,428)* 1.00

Nos. UC3-UC5, UC18 and UC25 Surcharged in Green at Left of Stamp

1958

UC27 UC2 6c + 1c **orange,** die 2a 325.00 250.00
Entire, without border 375.00 *600.00*
Entire, with border 8,000.
UC28 UC2 6c + 1c **orange,** die 2b 80.00 80.00
Entire, without border 110.00 *250.00*
UC29 UC2 6c + 1c **orange,** die 2c 40.00 50.00
Entire 50.00 *110.00*
UC30 UC3 6c + 1c **carmine,** type I 1.00 .50
Entire 1.25 .65
a. Type II 1.00 .50
Entire 1.25 .65
UC31 UC6 6c + 1c **red** 1.00 .50
Entire 1.40 .85

Jet Airliner — UC7

Letter Sheet for Foreign Postage

Type I: Back inscription in 3 lines.
Type II: Back inscription in 2 lines.

1958-59 **Typographed, Without Embossing**

UC32 UC7 10c **blue & red,** *blue,* II, *May, 1959,* entire 6.00 5.00
b. Red omitted, II, entire *850.00*
c. Blue omitted, II, entire *850.00*
UC32a UC7 10c **blue & red,** *blue,* I, *Sept. 12, 1958,* entire 10.00 5.00
Entire, 1st day cancel, St. Louis, Mo. *(92,400)* 1.25
Die cutting reversed, entire 75.00
d. Red omitted, I, entire *1,000.*

Silhouette of Jet Airliner — UC8

1958, Nov. 21 **Embossed**

UC33 UC8 7c **blue** .60 .25
Entire .70 .30
Entire, 1st day cancel, New York, N.Y. *(208,980)* 1.00

1960, Aug. 18

UC34 UC8 7c **carmine** .60 .25
Entire .70 .30
Entire, 1st day cancel, Portland, Ore. *(196,851)* 1.00

Jet Airliner and Globe — UC9

Letter Sheet for Foreign Postage

Typographed, Without Embossing

1961, June 16

UC35 UC9 11c **red & blue,** *blue,* entire 2.75 *3.50*
Entire, 1st day cancel, Johnstown, Pa. *(163,460)* 1.00
Die cutting reversed, entire 35.00
a. Red omitted, entire *1,150.*
b. Blue omitted, entire *1,100.*

Jet Airliner — UC10

1962, Nov. 17 **Embossed**

UC36 UC10 8c **red** .55 .20
Entire .75 .30
Entire, 1st day cancel, Chantilly, Va. *(194,810)* 1.00

Jet Airliner — UC11

1965-67

UC37 UC11 8c **red,** *Jan. 7* .45 .20
Entire, border "f" .60 .30
Entire, border "g" *22.50*
Entire, 1st day cancel, Chicago, Ill. *(226,178)* 1.00
a. Tagged, *Aug. 15, 1967* 3.75 .30
Entire 5.50 .75
Tagged, 1st day cancel 3.50

No. UC37a has a 8x24mm panel at left of stamp that glows orange red under ultraviolet light.

Pres. John F. Kennedy and Jet Plane UC12

Letter Sheets for Foreign Postage

Typographed, Without Embossing

1965, May 29

UC38 UC12 11c **red & dark blue,** *blue,* entire 3.25 *4.00*
Entire, 1st day cancel, Boston, Mass. *(337,422)* 1.50
Die cutting reversed, entire 40.00

1967, May 29

UC39 UC12 13c **red & dark blue,** *blue,* entire 3.25 *4.00*
Entire, 1st day cancel, Chicago, Ill. *(211,387)* 1.50
Die cutting reversed, entire *100.00*
a. Red omitted, entire *750.00*
b. Dark blue omitted, entire *500.00*

Jet Liner — UC13

Designed by Robert J. Jones.

1968, Jan. 8 **Tagged** **Embossed**

UC40 UC13 10c **red** .50 .20
Entire .80 .20
Entire, 1st day cancel, Chicago, Ill. *(157,553)* 1.00

No. UC37 Surcharged in Red at Left of Stamp

1968, Feb. 5

UC41 UC11 8c + 2c **red** .65 .20
Entire .90 .50
Entire, 1st day cancel, Washington, D.C. 8.00

Human Rights Year Issue

Issued for International Human Rights Year, and to commemorate the 20th anniversary of the United Nations' Declaration of Human Rights.

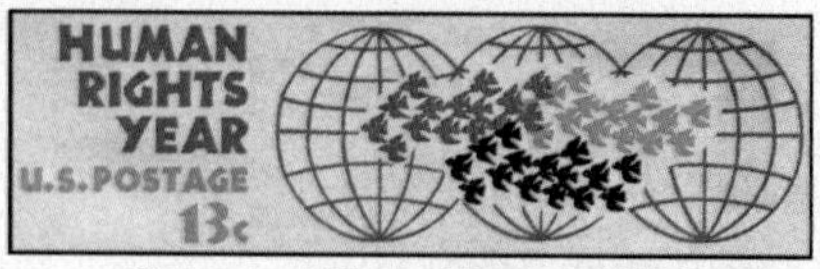

Globes and Flock of Birds — UC14

Printed by Acrovure Division of Union-Camp Corporation, Englewood, N.J. Designed by Antonio Frasconi.

Letter Sheet for Foreign Postage

1968, Dec. 3 **Tagged** **Photo.**

UC42 UC14 13c **gray, brown, orange & black,** *blue,* entire 8.00 5.00
Entire, 1st day cancel, Washington, D.C. *(145,898)* 1.25
Die cutting reversed, entire 75.00
a. Orange omitted, entire *1,000.*
b. Brown omitted, entire *375.00*
c. Black omitted, entire —

No. UC42 has a luminescent panel ⅜x1 inch on the right globe. The panel glows orange red under ultraviolet light.

Jet Plane — UC15

Printed by United States Envelope Co., Williamsburg, Pa. Designed by Robert Geissmann.

1971, May 6 **Embossed (Plane)**
Center Circle Luminescent

UC43 UC15 11c **red & blue** .50 *.90*
Entire .60 *1.00*
Entire, 1st day cancel, Williamsburg, Pa. *(187,000)* 1.00

Birds in Flight — UC16

Printed by Bureau of Engraving and Printing. Designed by Soren Noring.

Letter Sheet for Foreign Postage

1971 **Tagged** **Photo.**

UC44 UC16 15c **gray, red, white & blue,** *blue,* entire, *May 28* 1.50 *3.00*
Entire, 1st day cancel, Chicago, Ill. *(130,669)* 1.25
Die cutting reversed, entire 30.00
a. "AEROGRAMME" added to inscription, entire, *Dec. 13* 1.50 *3.00*
Entire, 1st day cancel, Philadelphia, Pa. 1.25
Die cutting reversed, entire 30.00

Folding instructions (2 steps) in capitals on No. C44; (4 steps) in upper and lower case on No. UC44a.

On Nos. UC44-UC44a the white rhomboid background of "USA postage 15c" is luminescent. No. UC44 is inscribed: "VIA AIR MAIL-PAR AVION". "postage 15c" is in gray. See No. UC46.

No. UC40 Surcharged in Green at Left of Stamp

1971, June 28 **Embossed**

UC45 UC13 10c + (1c) **red** 1.50 .20
Entire 1.90 .50
Entire, 1st day cancel, Washington, D.C. 8.00

HOT AIR BALLOONING CHAMPIONSHIPS ISSUE

Hot Air Ballooning World Championships, Albuquerque, N.M., Feb. 10-17, 1973.

"usa" Type of 1971

Design: Three balloons and cloud at left in address section; no birds beside stamp. Inscribed "INTERNATIONAL HOT AIR BALLOONING." "postage 15c" in blue.

Printed by Bureau of Engraving and Printing. Designed by Soren Noring (vignette) and Esther Porter (balloons).

Letter Sheet for Foreign Postage

1973, Feb. 10 **Tagged** **Photo.**

UC46 UC16 15c **red, white & blue,** *blue,* entire 1.00 .40
Entire, 1st day cancel, Albuquerque, N.M. *(210,000)* 1.00

Folding instructions as on No. UC44a. See notes after No. UC44.

Bird in Flight — UC17

1973, Dec. 1 **Luminescent Ink**

UC47 UC17 13c **rose red** .30 .20
Entire .40 .20
Entire, 1st day cancel, Memphis, Tenn. *(132,658)* 1.00

UC18

Printed by the Bureau of Engraving and Printing. Designed by Bill Hyde.

Letter Sheet for Foreign Postage.

1974, Jan. 4 **Tagged** **Photo.**

UC48 UC18 18c **red & blue,** *blue,* entire 1.00 *2.00*
Entire, 1st day cancel, Atlanta, Ga. *(119,615)* 1.00
Die cutting reversed, entire —
a. Red omitted, entire —

25TH ANNIVERSARY OF NATO ISSUE

UC19

Design: "NATO" and NATO emblem at left in address section.

Printed by Bureau of Engraving and Printing. Designed by Soren Noring.

Letter Sheet for Foreign Postage

1974, Apr. 4 **Tagged** **Photo.**

UC49 UC19 18c **red & blue,** *blue,* entire 1.00 .40
Entire, 1st day cancel, Washington, D.C. 1.00

UC20

Printed by Bureau of Engraving and Printing. Designed by Robert Geissmann.

Letter Sheet for Foreign Postage

1976, Jan. 16 **Tagged** **Photo.**

UC50 UC20 22c **red & blue,** *blue,* entire *.95* *1.50*
Entire, 1st day cancel, Tempe, Ariz. *(118,303)* 1.00
Die cutting reversed, entire 15.00
a. Red color missing due to foldover and die cutting —

"USA" — UC21

Printed by Bureau of Engraving and Printing. Designed by Soren Noring.

Letter Sheet for Foreign Postage

1978, Nov. 3 **Tagged** **Photo.**

UC51 UC21 22c **blue,** *blue,* entire .90 .25
Entire, 1st day cancel, St. Petersburg, Fla. *(86,099)* 1.00
Die cutting reversed, entire 25.00

22nd OLYMPIC GAMES, MOSCOW, JULY 19-AUG. 3, 1980.

UC22

Design (multicolored in bottom left corner) shows discus thrower.

Printed by Bureau of Engraving and Printing. Designed by Robert M. Cunningham.

Letter Sheet for Foreign Postage

1979, Dec. 5 **Tagged** **Photo.**

UC52 UC22 22c **red, black & green,** *bluish,* entire 1.50 .25
Entire, 1st day cancel, Bay Shore, N.Y. 1.00

"USA" — UC23

Design (brown on No. UC53, green and brown on No. UC54): lower left, Statue of Liberty. Inscribed "Tour the United States." Folding area shows tourist attractions.

Printed by Bureau of Engraving and Printing. Designed by Frank J. Waslick.

Letter Sheet for Foreign Postage

1980, Dec. 29 **Tagged** **Photo.**

UC53 UC23 30c **blue, red & brown,** *blue,* entire .85 *1.50*
Entire, 1st day cancel, San Francisco, CA 1.25
Die cutting reversed, entire 20.00
a. Red (30) omitted, entire 70.00

1981, Sept. 21 **Tagged** **Photo.**

UC54 UC23 30c **yellow, magenta, blue & black,** *blue,* entire .65 *1.00*
Entire, 1st day cancel, Honolulu, HI 1.25
Die cutting reversed, entire 20.00

UC24

Design: "Made in USA . . . world's best buys!" on flap, ship, tractor in lower left. Reverse folding area shows chemicals, jet silhouette, wheat, typewriter and computer tape disks. Printed by Bureau of Engraving and Printing.

Designed by Frank J. Waslick.

Letter Sheet for Foreign Postage

1982, Sept. 16 **Tagged** **Photo.**

UC55 UC24 30c **multi,** *blue,* entire .80 *2.75*
Entire, 1st day cancel, Seattle, WA 1.25
Die cutting reversed, entire —

WORLD COMMUNICATIONS YEAR

World Map Showing Locations of Satellite Tracking Stations — UC25

Design: Reverse folding area shows satellite, tracking station.
Printed by Bureau of Engraving and Printing.
Designed by Esther Porter.

Letter Sheet for Foreign Postage

1983, Jan. 7 **Tagged** **Photo.**

UC56 UC25 30c **multi,** *blue,* entire .90 *3.00*
Entire, 1st day cancel, Anaheim, CA 1.25
Die cutting reversed, entire 25.00

1984 OLYMPICS

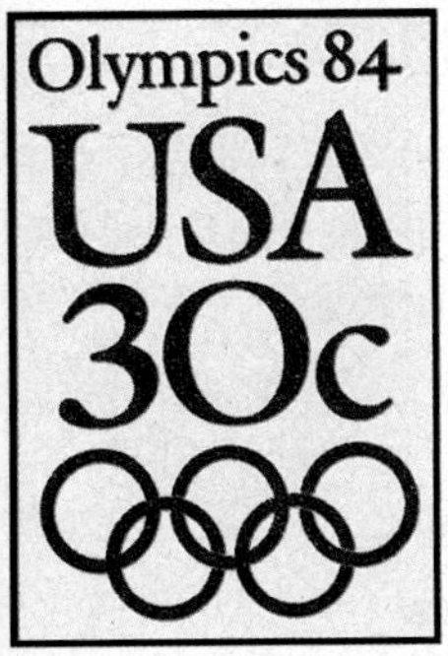

UC26

Indicia in black, multicolor design of woman equestrian at lower left with montage of competitive events on reverse folding area.
Printed by the Bureau of Engraving & Printing.
Designed by Bob Peak.

Letter Sheet for Foreign Postage

1983, Oct. 14 **Tagged** **Photo.**

UC57 UC26 30c **black & multi,** *light blue,* entire .85 *3.00*
Entire, 1st day cancel, Los Angeles, CA 1.25
Die cutting reversed, entire —

WEATHER SATELLITES, 25TH ANNIV.

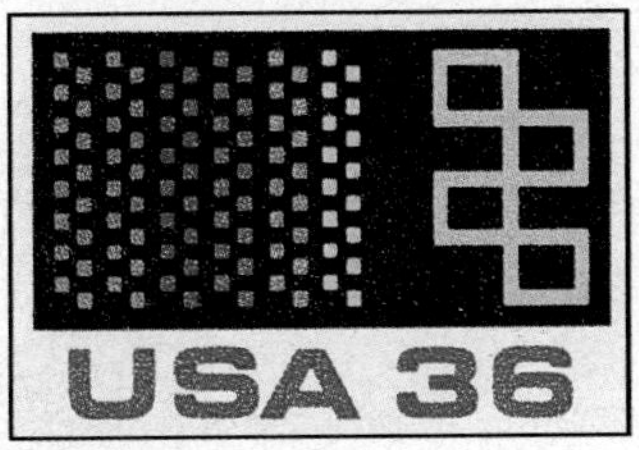

Landsat Infrared and Thermal Mapping Bands UC27

Design: Landsat orbiting the earth at lower left with three Landsat photographs on reverse folding area. Inscribed: "Landsat views the Earth."
Printed by the Bureau of Engraving & Printing.
Designed by Esther Porter.

Letter Sheet for Foreign Postage

1985, Feb. 14 **Tagged** **Photo.**

UC58 UC27 36c **multi,** *blue,* entire .85 *3.00*
Entire, 1st day cancel, Goddard Flight Center, MD 1.40
Die cutting reversed, entire 30.00

NATIONAL TOURISM WEEK

Urban Skyline — UC28

Design: Inscribed "Celebrate America" at lower left and "Travel. . . the perfect freedom" on folding area. Skier, Indian chief, cowboy, jazz trumpeter and pilgrims on reverse folding area.
Printed by the Bureau of Engraving & Printing.
Designed by Dennis Luzak.

Letter Sheet for Foreign Postage

1985, May 21 **Tagged** **Photo.**

UC59 UC28 36c **multi,** *blue,* entire .85 *3.00*
Entire, 1st day cancel, Washington, DC 1.40
Die cutting reversed, entire 25.00
a. Black omitted, entire *950.00* —

MARK TWAIN AND HALLEY'S COMET

Comet Tail Viewed from Space — UC29

Design: Portrait of Twain at lower left and inscribed "I came in with Halley's Comet in 1835. It is coming again next year, and I expect to go out with it. It will be the greatest disappointment of my life if I don't go out with Halley's Comet." "1835 . Mark Twain . 1910 . Halley's Comet . 1985" and Twain, Huckleberry Finn, steamboat and comet on reverse folding areas.
Printed by the Bureau of Engraving & Printing.
Designed by Dennis Luzak.

Letter Sheet for Foreign Postage

1985, Dec. 4 **Tagged** **Photo.**

UC60 UC29 36c **multi,** entire 1.00 *4.00*
Entire, 1st day cancel, Hannibal, MO 2.00
Die cutting reversed, entire 25.00

UC30

Printed by the Bureau of Engraving & Printing.

Letter Sheet for Foreign Postage

1988, May 9 **Litho.** **Tagged**

UC61 UC30 39c **multi,** entire .95 *2.25*
Entire, 1st day cancel, Miami, FL *(27,446)* 1.60
a. Tagging bar to left of design ('89) .95 *1.50*

On No. UC61, the tagging bar is between "USA" and "39."

MONTGOMERY BLAIR, POSTMASTER GENERAL 1861-64

Blair and Pres. Abraham Lincoln — UC31

Design: Mail bags and "Free city delivery," "Railway mail service" and "Money order system" at lower left. Globe, locomotive, bust of Blair, UPU emblem and "The Paris conference of 1863, initiated by Postmaster General Blair, led, in 1874, to the founding of the Universal Postal Union" contained on reverse folding area.
Printed by the Bureau of Engraving & Printing.
Designed by Ned Seidler.

Letter Sheet for Foreign Postage

1989, Nov. 20 **Litho.** **Tagged**

UC62 UC31 39c **multicolored,** entire .95 *2.25*
Entire, 1st day cancel, Washington, DC 1.75
a. Double impression —
b. Triple impression —
c. Quadruple impression —

UC32

Designed by Bradbury Thompson.
Printed by the Bureau of Engraving and Printing.

Letter Sheet for Foreign Postage

1991, May 17 **Litho.** **Tagged**

UC63 UC32 45c **gray, red & blue,** *blue,* entire .95 *1.50*
a. White paper .95 *1.50*
Entire, 1st day cancel, Denver, CO *(19,941)* 1.40

Thaddeus Lowe (1832-1913), Balloonist — UC33

Designed by Davis Meltzer.
Printed by the Bureau of Engraving & Printing.

Letter Sheet for Foreign Postage

1995, Sept. 23 **Litho.** **Tagged**

UC64 UC33 50c **multicolored,** *blue,* entire 1.25 *2.25*
Entire, 1st day cancel, Tampa, FL 1.25

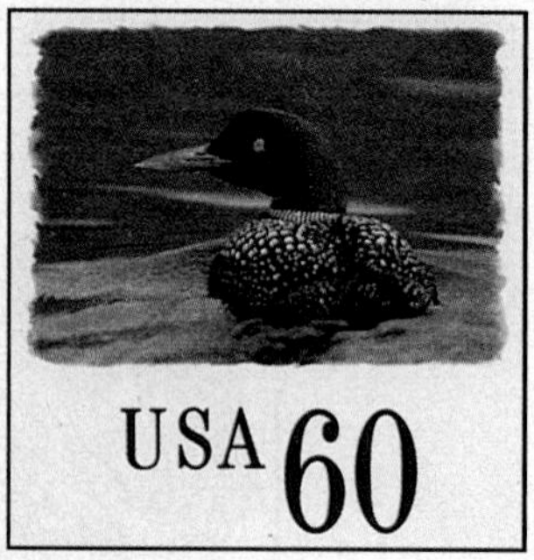

Voyageurs Natl. Park, Minnesota UC34

Designed by Phil Jordan.

Printed by Burean of Engraving & Printing.

Letter Sheet for Foreign Postage

1999, May 15 **Litho.** **Tagged**

UC65	UC34	60c	**multicolored,** *blue,* entire	1.25	*2.25*
			Entire, 1st day cancel, Denver, CO		1.50

OFFICIAL ENVELOPES & WRAPPERS

By the Act of Congress, January 31, 1873, the franking privilege of officials was abolished as of July 1, 1873 and the Postmaster General was authorized to prepare official envelopes. At the same time official stamps were prepared for all Departments. Department envelopes became obsolete July 5, 1884. After that, government offices began to use franked envelopes of varied design. These indicate no denomination and lie beyond the scope of this Catalogue.

Post Office Department

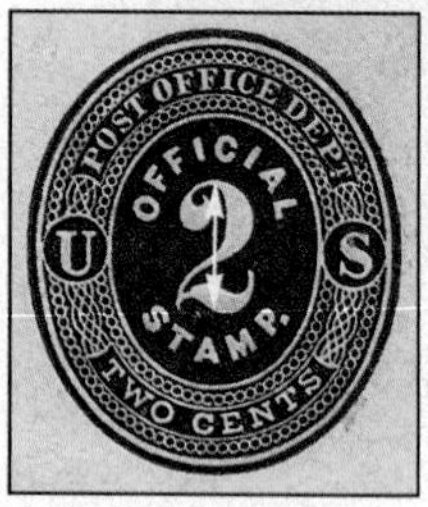

UO1

Numeral 9mm high.

UO2

Numeral 9mm high.

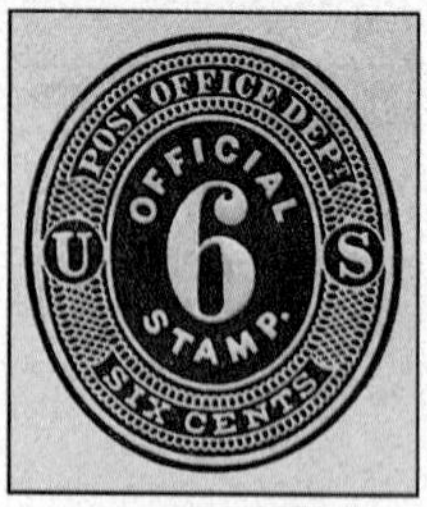

UO3

Numeral 9½mm high.

Printed by George H. Reay, Brooklyn, N.Y.

1873

UO1	UO1	2c	**black,** *lemon*	24.00	10.00
			Entire	35.00	15.00
UO2	UO2	3c	**black,** *lemon*	16.00	6.50
			Entire	29.00	11.00
+UO3	UO2	3c	**black**	*42,500.*	
			Entire	*57,000.*	
UO4	UO3	6c	**black,** *lemon*	26.00	16.00
			Entire	35.00	22.50

The No. UO3 entire is unique. It has a tear through the stamp that has been professionally repaired. Value based on auction sale in 1999.

UO4

Numeral 9¼mm high.

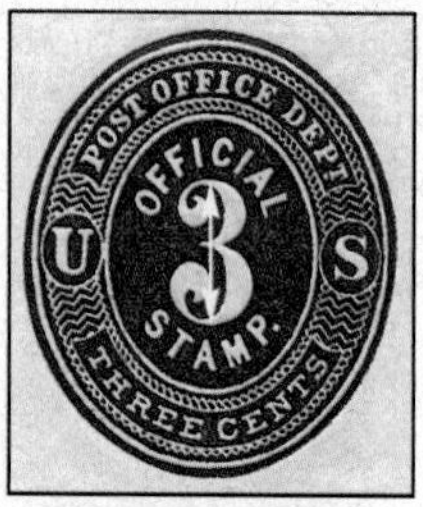

UO5

Numeral 9¼mm high.

UO6

Numeral 10½mm high.

Printed by Plimpton Manufacturing Co., Hartford, Conn.

1874-79

UO5	UO4	2c	**black,** *lemon*	10.50	4.25
			Entire	15.00	7.00
UO6	UO4	2c	**black**	140.00	35.00
			Entire	190.00	55.00
UO7	UO5	3c	**black,** *lemon*	3.25	.85
			Entire	4.25	1.50
UO8	UO5	3c	**black**	1,500.	1,200.
			Entire	5,750.	
UO9	UO5	3c	**black,** *amber*	150.00	40.00
			Entire	175.00	60.00
UO10	UO5	3c	**black,** *blue*	*45,000.*	
			Entire	*50,000.*	
UO11	UO5	3c	**blue,** *blue* ('75)	*45,000.*	
			Entire	*50,000.*	
UO12	UO6	6c	**black,** *lemon*	16.00	6.50
			Entire	26.00	12.50
UO13	UO6	6c	**black**	1,750.	1,750.
			Entire	5,750.	

Fakes exist of Nos. UO3, UO8 and UO13.

Postal Service

UO7

1877

UO14	UO7	**black**	7.00	4.50
		Entire	11.50	6.00
UO15	UO7	**black,** *amber*	225.00	40.00
		Entire	900.00	65.00
UO16	UO7	**blue,** *amber*	210.00	40.00
		Entire	900.00	65.00
UO17	UO7	**blue,** *blue*	9.00	6.75
		Entire	13.50	10.50

War Department

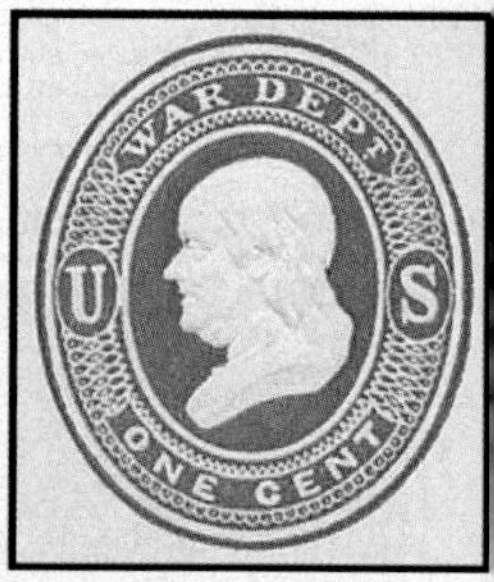

Franklin — UO8

Bust points to the end of "N" of "ONE".

Jackson — UO9

Bust narrow at the back.

Washington — UO10

Queue projects below the bust.

Lincoln — UO11

Neck very long at the back.

Jefferson — UO12

Queue forms straight line with bust.

Clay — UO13

Ear partly concealed by hair, mouth large, chin prominent.

Webster — UO14

Has side whiskers.

Scott — UO15

Hamilton — UO16

Back of bust very narrow; chin almost straight; the labels containing the letters "U S" are exactly parallel.

Printed by George H. Reay.

1873

UO18	UO8	1c	**dark red**	700.00	300.00
			Entire	1,200.	325.00
WO18A	UO8	1c	**dark red**, *manila*		—
UO19	UO9	2c	**dark red**	1,000.	400.00
			Entire	2,000.	
UO20	UO10	3c	**dark red**	72.50	42.50
			Entire	100.00	70.00
UO21	UO10	3c	**dark red,** *amber*	*40,000.*	
			Entire	*50,000.*	
UO22	UO10	3c	**dark red,** *cream*	800.00	300.00
			Entire	1,200.	350.00
UO23	UO11	6c	**dark red**	325.00	100.00
			Entire	425.00	250.00
UO24	UO11	6c	**dark red,** *cream*	9,250.	425.00
			Entire	11,000.	*2,000.*
UO25	UO12	10c	**dark red**	*17,500.*	2,250.
			Entire	*27,500.*	*4,000.*
UO26	UO13	12c	**dark red**	175.00	50.00
			Entire	250.00	—
UO27	UO14	15c	**dark red**	160.00	55.00
			Entire	210.00	*375.00*
UO28	UO15	24c	**dark red**	175.00	50.00
			Entire	225.00	*1,250.*
UO29	UO16	30c	**dark red**	550.00	150.00
			Entire	725.00	500.00

1873

UO30	UO8	1c	**vermilion**	100.00	
			Entire	350.00	
WO31	UO8	1c	**vermilion,** *manila*	20.00	14.00
			Entire	35.00	25.00
+UO32	UO9	2c	**vermilion**	375.00	
			Entire	*25,000.*	
WO33	UO9	2c	**vermilion,** *manila*	225.00	
			Entire	375.00	
UO34	UO10	3c	**vermilion**	100.00	40.00
			Entire	175.00	125.00
UO35	UO10	3c	**vermilion,** *amber*	125.00	
			Entire	375.00	
UO36	UO10	3c	**vermilion,** *cream*	17.00	12.50
			Entire	40.00	26.00
UO37	UO11	6c	**vermilion**	100.00	
			Entire	175.00	
+UO38	UO11	6c	**vermilion,** *cream*	425.00	
			Entire	*27,500.*	
UO39	UO12	10c	**vermilion**	200.00	
			Entire	450.00	
UO40	UO13	12c	**vermilion**	175.00	
			Entire	225.00	
UO41	UO14	15c	**vermilion**	250.00	
			Entire	3,000.	
UO42	UO15	24c	**vermilion**	400.00	
			Entire	650.00	
UO43	UO16	30c	**vermilion**	475.00	
			Entire	625.00	

UO17

Bottom serif on "S" is thick and short; bust at bottom below hair forms a sharp point.

UO18

Bottom serif on "S" is thick and short; front part of bust is rounded.

UO19

Bottom serif on "S" is short; queue does not project below bust.

UO20

Neck very short at the back.

UO21

Knot of queue stands out prominently.

UO22

Ear prominent, chin receding.

UO23

Has no side whiskers; forelock projects above head.

UO24

Back of bust rather broad; chin slopes considerably; the label containing letters "U S" are not exactly parallel.

Printed by Plimpton Manufacturing Co.

1875

UO44	UO17	1c	**red**	190.00	85.00
			Entire	250.00	175.00
+UO45	UO17	1c	**red,** *amber*	600.00	
+UO45A	UO17	1c	**red,** *orange*	*37,500.*	
WO46	UO17	1c	**red,** *manila*	4.50	2.75
			Entire	9.50	6.50
UO47	UO18	2c	**red**	140.00	—
			Entire	190.00	
UO48	UO18	2c	**red,** *amber*	37.50	17.50
			Entire	45.00	27.50
UO49	UO18	2c	**red,** *orange*	70.00	17.50
			Entire	80.00	30.00
WO50	UO18	2c	**red,** *manila*	100.00	50.00
			Entire	225.00	—
UO51	UO19	3c	**red**	17.50	10.00
			Entire	22.50	17.50
UO52	UO19	3c	**red,** *amber*	22.50	10.00
			Entire	30.00	16.00
UO53	UO19	3c	**red,** *cream*	6.00	3.75
			Entire	10.00	6.50
UO54	UO19	3c	**red,** *blue*	4.00	2.75
			Entire	6.00	4.50
UO55	UO19	3c	**red,** *fawn*	6.50	2.75
			Entire	11.50	4.00
UO56	UO20	6c	**red**	65.00	30.00
			Entire	100.00	—
UO57	UO20	6c	**red,** *amber*	95.00	40.00
			Entire	125.00	—
UO58	UO20	6c	**red,** *cream*	225.00	85.00
			Entire	275.00	
UO59	UO21	10c	**red**	250.00	80.00
			Entire	300.00	—
UO60	UO21	10c	**red,** *amber*	800.00	
			Entire	1,650.	
UO61	UO22	12c	**red**	65.00	40.00
			Entire	190.00	*250.00*
UO62	UO22	12c	**red,** *amber*	775.00	
			Entire	950.00	
UO63	UO22	12c	**red,** *cream*	700.00	
			Entire	950.00	
UO64	UO23	15c	**red**	250.00	140.00
			Entire	300.00	—
UO65	UO23	15c	**red,** *amber*	925.00	
			Entire	1,200.	
UO66	UO23	15c	**red,** *cream*	775.00	
			Entire	1,000.	
UO67	UO24	30c	**red**	190.00	140.00
			Entire	225.00	—
UO68	UO24	30c	**red,** *amber*	925.00	
			Entire	2,400.	
UO69	UO24	30c	**red,** *cream*	950.00	
			Entire	1,350.	

POSTAL SAVINGS ENVELOPES

Issued under the Act of Congress, approved June 25, 1910, in lieu of penalty or franked envelopes. Unused remainders, after mid-October 1914, were overprinted with the Penalty Clause. Regular stamped envelopes, redeemed by the Government, were also overprinted for official use.

UO25

1911

UO70	UO25	1c **green**		77.50	25.00
			Entire	110.00	42.50
UO71	UO25	1c **green,** *oriental buff*		200.00	75.00
			Entire	250.00	90.00
UO72	UO25	2c **carmine**		13.50	4.00
			Entire	22.50	12.00
a.		2c **carmine,** *manila* (error)		*1,750.*	*1,000.*
			Entire	*2,500.*	*1,400.*

Tagged

Envelopes from No. UO73 onward are tagged unless otherwise noted.

OFFICIAL MAIL

Great Seal — UO26

1983, Jan. 12 **Embossed**

UO73 UO26 20c **blue,** entire 1.25 *30.00*
First day cancel, Washington, DC 1.00

UO27

1985, Feb. 26 **Embossed**

UO74 UO27 22c **blue,** entire .90 *30.00*
First day cancel, Washington, DC 1.00

UO28

1987, Mar. 2 **Typo.**

UO75 UO28 22c **blue,** entire 1.25 *35.00*
First day cancel, Washington, DC 1.00

Used exclusively to mail U.S. Savings Bonds.

UO29

1988, Mar. 22 **Typo.**

UO76 UO29 (25c) **black & blue,** entire 1.25 *35.00*
First day cancel, Washington, DC 1.25

Used exclusively to mail U.S. Savings Bonds.

UO30

UO31

1988, Apr. 11 **Typo. & Embossed**

UO77 UO30 25c **black & blue,** entire .80 *25.00*
First day cancel, Washington, DC 1.25
a. Denomination & lettering as on No. UO78, entire *5.00* *20.00*

Typo.

UO78 UO31 25c **black & blue,** entire .90 *35.00*
First day cancel, Washington, DC *(12,017)* 1.25
a. Denomination & lettering as on No. UO77, entire 1.00 *35.00*

No. UO78 used exclusively to mail U.S. Savings Bonds.
First day cancellations applied to 12,017 of Nos. UO77, UO78.

Used Values

Postally used examples of Nos. UO79-UO80 have not appeared in the marketplace and thus cannot be valued. The editors would like to see examples of these used envelopes.

1990, Mar. 17 **Typo.**

Stars and "E Pluribus Unum" illegible. "Official" is 13mm, "USA" is 16mm long.

UO79 UO31 45c **black & blue,** entire 1.25 —
First day cancel, Springfield, VA *(5,956)* 1.50
UO80 UO31 65c **black & blue,** entire 1.75 —
First day cancel, Springfield, VA *(6,922)* 2.25

Used exclusively to mail U.S. passports.

UO32

Stars and "E Pluribus Unum" clear and sharply printed. "Official" is 14½mm, "USA" is 17mm long.

1990, Aug. 10 **Litho.**

UO81 UO32 45c **black & blue,** entire 1.25 *100.00*
First day cancel, Washington, DC *(7,160)* 1.50
UO82 UO32 65c **black & blue,** entire 1.60 *150.00*
First day cancel, Washington, DC *(6,759)* 2.25

Used exclusively to mail U.S. passports.

UO33

1991, Jan. 22 **Typo.** **Wmk.**

UO83 UO33 (29c) **black & blue,** entire 1.25 *35.00*
First day cancel, Washington, DC *(30,549)* 1.25

Used exclusively to mail U.S. Savings Bonds.

UO34

1991, Apr. 6 **Wmk.** **Litho. & Embossed**

UO84 UO34 29c **black & blue,** entire .75 *20.00*
First day cancel, Oklahoma City, OK *(27,841)* 1.25
Entire, unwatermarked, *May 1, 1992* .75 —

Unwatermarked envelopes on recycled paper were issued May 1, 1992, and have a "recycled" imprint under the flap.

UO35

1991, Apr. 17 **Typo.** **Wmk.**

UO85 UO35 29c **black & blue,** entire .70 *20.00*
First day cancel, Washington, DC *(25,563)* 1.25
Entire, unwatermarked, *May 1, 1992* .70 —

Used exclusively to mail U.S. Savings Bonds. Unwatermarked envelopes on recycled paper were issued May 1, 1992, and have a "recycled" imprint under the flap.

Consular Service, Bicent. — UO36

Designed by Zebulon Rogers. Quotation from O. Henry on flap.

1992, July 10 **Litho.** **Unwmk.**

UO86 UO36 52c **blue & red,** entire 5.00 *125.00*
First day cancel, Washington, DC *(30,374)* 2.25
a. 52c blue & red, *blue-white,* entire 1.50 *125.00*
UO87 UO36 75c **blue & red,** entire 10.00 *125.00*
First day cancel, Washington, DC *(25,995)* 3.25
a. 75c blue & red, *blue-white,* entire 2.50 *125.00*

Used exclusively to mail U.S. passports.
Available only in 4⅝ inch x 8⅞ inch size with self-adhesive flap.
Original issues have "USPS copyright" on left under flap. Reissues (Nos. UO86a and UO87a) have it at right.

UO37

1995-99 Typo. & Embossed Unwmk.

UO88	UO37 32c	**blue & red,** entire, *May 9, 1995*	.80	*20.00*
		First day cancel, Washington, DC		1.25
UO89	UO37 33c	**blue & red,** entire, *Feb. 22, 1999*	.70	*20.00*
		First day cancel, Washington, DC		1.25

Type of 1995

2001, Feb. 27 Typo. & Embossed Unwmk.

UO90	UO37 34c	**blue & red,** entire	.85	*20.00*
		First day cancel, Washington, DC		1.25

Type of 1995

2002, Aug. 2 Typo. & Embossed Unwmk.

UO91	UO37 37c	**blue & red,** type I, entire	.90	—
		First day cancel, Washington, DC		1.25
		First day cancel, any other city		1.25
a.		Type II, entire, *Aug. 2, 2002*	.90	—

Type I has 29x28mm blue panel, top of "USA" even with the bottom of the eagle's neck and is made with "100% recycled paper" as noted on reverse. Type II has a 27½x27½mm blue panel, top of "USA" even with the highest arrow, and has no mention of "100% recycled paper" on reverse.

Type of 1995

2006, Jan. 9 Typo. & Embossed Unwmk.

UO92	UO37 39c	**blue & red, entire**	.95	—
		Entire, 1st day cancel, Washington, DC		1.25
		Entire, 1st day cancel, any other city		1.25

Type of 1995

2007, May 12 Typo. & Embossed Unwmk.

UO93	UO37 41c	**blue & red,** entire	1.00	.50
		Entire, 1st day cancel, Washington, DC		2.10

Type of 1995

2008, June 20 Typo. Unwmk.

UO94	UO37 42c	**blue & red,** entire	1.00	.50
		Entire, 1st day cancel, Washington, DC		2.10

POSTAL CARDS

Values are for unused cards as sold by the Post Office, without printed or written address or message, and used cards with Post Office cancellation, when current. Used cards with postage added to meet higher rates sell for less. Used cards for international rates are for proper usage. Those used domestically sell for less.

The "Preprinted" values are for unused cards with printed or written address or message.

Starting with No. UX21, all postal cards have been printed by the Government Printing Office.

Nos. UX1-UX48 are typographed; others are lithographed (offset) unless otherwise stated.

Numerous printing varieties exist. Varieties of surcharged cards include (a) inverted surcharge at lower left, (b) double surcharge, one inverted at lower left, (c) surcharge in other abnormal positions, including back of card. Such surcharge varieties command a premium.

Colored cancellations sell for more than black in some instances. **All values are for entire cards.**

As of Jan. 1, 1999, postal cards were sold individually for 1c over face value. Currently, they are sold for 2c over face value.

See Computer Vended Postage section for "Postal Buddy" cards.

Since 1875 it has been possible to purchase some postal cards in sheets for multiple printing, hence pairs, strips and blocks are available. Some sheets have been cut up so that cards exist with stamp inverted, in center of card, two on one card, in another corner, etc. These are only curiosities and of minimal value.

Liberty — PC1

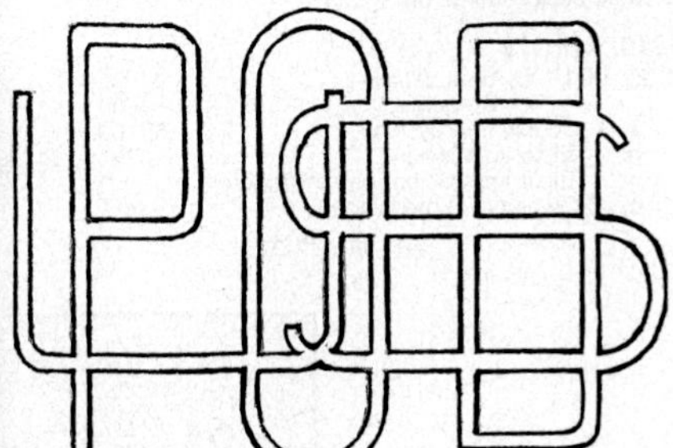

Wmk. Large "U S P O D" in Monogram, (90x60mm)

1873, May Size: 130x76mm

UX1	PC1 1c	**brown,**	375.00	25.00
		Preprinted	70.00	
		First day cancel, Boston, New York or Washington		*12,000.*

One card is documented canceled May 10 in Owensboro, Ky.; another May 11 in Providence, R.I.; and another May 12 in Springfield, Mass.

Wmk. Small "U S P O D" in Monogram, (53x36mm)

1873, July 6

UX3	PC1 1c	**brown,** *buff*	80.00	2.50
		Preprinted	20.00	
a.		Without watermark		800.00

The watermarks on Nos. UX1, UX3 and UX4 are found in normal position, inverted, reversed, and inverted and reversed. They are often dim, especially on No. UX4. Values listed are for clear watermarks.

No. UX3a is not known unused. Cards offered as such are either unwatermarked proofs, or have partial or vague watermarks. See No. UX65.

Liberty — PC2

Inscribed: "WRITE THE ADDRESS . . ."

1875 Wmk. Small "U S P O D" in Monogram

UX4	PC2 1c	**black,** *buff, Sept. 28*	3,500.	350.
		Preprinted	750.	

Unwmk.

UX5	PC2 1c	**black,** *buff, Sept. 30*	82.50	.45
		Preprinted	7.00	

For other postal card of type PC2 see No. UX7.

Liberty — PC3

For International Use

1879, Dec. 1

UX6	PC3 2c	**blue,** *buff*	35.00	25.00
		Preprinted	11.50	
a.		2c **dark blue,** *buff*	35.00	25.00
		Preprinted	11.50	

See Nos. UX13 and UX16.

Design of PC2, Inscribed "NOTHING BUT THE ADDRESS."

1881, Oct. 17 (?)

UX7	PC2 1c	**black,** *buff*	70.00	.40
		Preprinted	6.50	
a.		23 teeth below "ONE CENT"	1,350.	65.00
		Preprinted	225.00	
b.		Printed on both sides	*1,000.*	*750.00*

Jefferson — PC4

1885, Aug. 24

UX8	PC4 1c	**brown,** *buff*	55.00	1.25
		Preprinted	10.00	
c.		1c **dark chocolate,** *buff*	300.00	40.00
		Preprinted	75.00	
d.		Double impression		*7,500.*
e.		Double impression, one inverted	*9,500.*	
f.		Printed on both sides	—	

Card was printed in many shades of brown ink. Earliest documented use: Aug. 29, 1885.

PC5

Head of Jefferson facing right, centered on card.

1886, Dec 1

UX9	PC5 1c **black,** *buff*	25.00	.55
	Preprinted	1.75	
a.	1c **black,** *dark buff*	75.00	5.00
	Preprinted	20.00	
b.	Double impression	—	
c.	Double impression, one inverted	*8,500.*	
d.	**1c black,** *salmon pink*	*2,000.*	*3,250.*
e.	Triple impression	*3,000.*	

Grant — PC6

1891, Dec. 16 **Size: 155x95mm**

UX10	PC6 1c **black,** *buff*	45.00	1.50
	Preprinted	6.50	
a.	Double impression, one inverted	*5,750.*	
b.	Double impression	*1,250.*	
c.	Triple impression, one inverted	5,750.	
d.	Quintuple impression, three inverted	5,750.	

Two types exist of No. UX10.
Earliest documented use: Dec. 23, 1891.

Size: 117x75mm

UX11	PC6 1c **blue,** *grayish white*	22.50	3.00
	Preprinted	5.00	
b.	Double impression, one inverted	*6,750.*	

Cards printed in black instead of blue are invariably proofs.
Earliest documented use: Dec. 21, 1891.

PC7

Head of Jefferson facing left.
Small wreath and name below.
Size: 140x89mm

1894, Jan. 2

UX12	PC7 1c **black,** *buff*	45.00	.65
	Preprinted	2.25	
a.	Double impression	—	

Two types exist of No. UX12: flat bed printing and rotary press printing.

For International Use

1897, Jan. 25 **Design of PC3**

Size: 140x89mm

UX13	PC3 2c **blue,** *cream*	225.00	85.00
	Preprinted	85.00	

Earliest documented use: Apr. 17, 1897.

PC8

Head same as PC7. Large wreath and name below.

1897, Dec. 1

Size: 139x82mm

UX14	PC8 1c **black,** *buff*	40.00	.45
	Preprinted	2.75	
a.	Double impression, one inverted	*10,000.*	*8,750.*
	Preprinted	—	
b.	Printed both sides		—
	Preprinted	*3,000.*	
c.	Double impression	—	—
	Preprinted	—	
d.	**Black,** *salmon pink,* preprinted	1,500.	

John Adams — PC9

1898

Size: 126x74mm

UX15	PC9 1c **black,** *buff, Mar. 31*	47.50	15.00
	Preprinted	12.50	

Design same as PC3, without frame around card.
For International Use
Size: 140x82mm

UX16	PC3 2c **black,** *buff*	15.00	*17.00*
	Preprinted	5.00	

McKinley — PC10

1902

UX17	PC10 1c **black,** *buff*	*9,000.*	
	Preprinted	*3,000.*	*3,750.*

Earliest documented use; May 27, 1902.

McKinley — PC11

1902

UX18	PC11 1c **black,** *buff*	17.50	.35
	Preprinted	1.75	

Earliest documented use; July 14, 1902.
Two types exist of Nos. UX18-UX20.

McKinley — PC12

1907

UX19	PC12 1c **black,** *buff*	45.00	.50
	Preprinted	2.25	

Earliest documented use; June 28, 1907.

Same design, correspondence space at left

1908, Jan. 2

UX20	PC12 1c **black,** *buff*	57.50	4.25
	Preprinted	8.50	

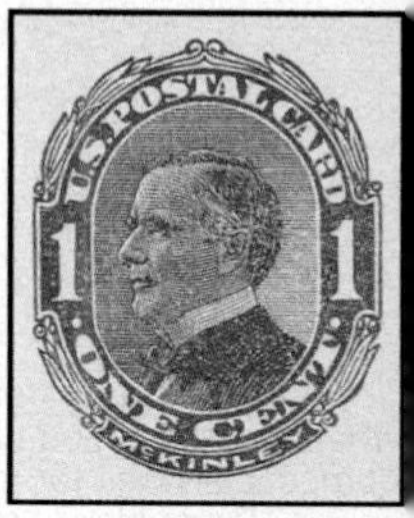

PC13

McKinley, background shaded.

1910

UX21	PC13 1c **blue,** *bluish*	105.00	13.00
	Preprinted	17.50	
a.	1c **bronze blue,** *bluish*	400.00	100.00
	Preprinted	150.00	
b.	Double impression	*1,200.*	
	Preprinted	—	
c.	Triple impression	*2,500.*	
d.	Double impression, one inverted	—	
e.	Four arcs above and below "IS" of inscription to left of stamp impression are pointed	*2,250.*	*600.00*
	Preprinted	*900.00*	

A No. UX21 card exists with Philippines No. UX11 printed on the back.

PC14

Same design, white background.

1910, Apr. 13

UX22	PC14 1c **blue,** *bluish*	20.00	.35
	Preprinted	2.00	
a.	Double impression	*750.00*	
b.	Triple impression	*2,750.*	*2,250.*
c.	Triple impression, one inverted	—	
d.	Quintuple impression	*6,000.*	

See No. UX24.

PC15

Head of Lincoln, solid background.

1911, Jan. 21

Size: 127x76mm

UX23	PC15 1c **red,** *cream*	10.00	5.50
	Preprinted	3.00	
a.	Triple impression	—	
b.	Double impression	*7,250.*	

See No. UX26.

Design same as PC14

1911, Aug. 10 **Size: 140x82mm**

UX24 PC14 1c **red,** *cream* 11.00 .35
Preprinted 1.25
a. Double impression —
b. Triple impression —

Copies with 1920 2-line surcharge are considered favor items.

Grant — PC16

1911, Oct. 27

For International Use

Size: 140x82mm

UX25 PC16 2c **red,** *cream* 1.50 *20.00*
Preprinted .65
a. Double impression —

For surcharge see No. UX36.

1913, July 29

Size: 127x76mm

UX26 PC15 1c **green,** *cream* 13.00 7.50
Preprinted 2.50

Jefferson — PC17

Die I — End of queue small, sloping sharply downward to right.

Die II (re-cut) — End of queue large and rounded.

1914-16

Size: 140x82mm

UX27 PC17 1c **green,** *buff,* die I, *June 4* .25 .25
Preprinted .20
a. 1c **green,** *cream* 5.00 .65
Preprinted 1.25
b. Double impression *2,500.*
e. Triple impression *5,500.*
f. Quadruple impression *6,500.*

On gray, rough surfaced card

UX27C PC17 1c **green,** die I, *1916* *4,000.* 250.00
Preprinted *400.00*
UX27D PC17 1c **dark green,** die II, *Dec. 22, 1916* *24,000.* 160.00
Preprinted 375.00

For surcharges see Nos. UX39 and UX41.

Lincoln — PC19

1917, Mar. 14 **Size: 127x76mm**

UX28 PC19 1c **green,** *cream* .60 .30
Preprinted .30
a. 1c **green,** *dark buff* 1.50 .60
Preprinted .50
b. Double impression —
Preprinted *2,250.*

No. UX28 was printed also on light buff and canary. See No. UX43. For surcharges see Nos. UX40 and UX42.

Jefferson — PC20

Die I — Rough, coarse impression. End of queue slopes sharply downward to right. Left basal ends of "2" form sharp points.

Size: 140x82mm

Die II — Clear fine lines in hair. Left basal ends of "2" form balls.

1917-18

UX29 PC20 2c **red,** *buff,* die I, *Oct. 22* 42.50 2.10
Preprinted 6.50
a. 2c **lake,** *cream,* die I 50.00 4.00
Preprinted 9.00
c. 2c **vermilion,** *buff,* die I 925.00 75.00
Preprinted 70.00
UX30 PC20 2c **red,** *cream,* die II, *Jan. 23, 1918* 30.00 1.60
Preprinted 4.50

2c Postal Cards of 1917-18 Revalued

Surcharged in one line by canceling machine at Washington, DC

1 CENT

1920, Apr.

UX31 PC20 1c on 2c **red,** *cream,* die II *3,750.* *4,250.*
Preprinted *2,600.*

Surcharged in two lines by canceling machine (46 Types)

1
CENT

UX32 PC20 1c on 2c **red,** *buff,* die I 52.50 12.50
Preprinted 15.00
a. 1c on 2c **vermilion,** *buff* 150.00 60.00
Preprinted 60.00
b. Double surcharge 150.00 100.00
Preprinted 100.00 —
c. Double surcharge, one inverted, both in normal position on stamp — —
Preprinted —
d. Double surcharge, one inverted at lower left 65.00 30.00
Preprinted 30.00
e. Triple surcharge — —
Preprinted —
f. Inverted surcharge at lower left 65.00 30.00
Preprinted 30.00
UX33 PC20 1c on 2c **red,** *cream,* die II 13.00 2.00
Preprinted 2.50
a. Inverted surcharge, on stamp 150.00 *200.00*
Preprinted — —
b. Double surcharge 150.00 *175.00*
Preprinted 50.00
c. Double surcharge, one inverted, both in normal position on stamp 350.00
Preprinted —
d. Triple surcharge 375.00
e. Double surcharge, one inverted at lower left 30.00 25.00
Preprinted 20.00
f. Inverted surcharge at lower left 30.00 30.00
Preprinted 20.00
g. Triple surcharge, one inverted at lower left — —
Preprinted —

Double and triple surcharges on Nos. UX32 and UX33 generally sell for less than above values if one or more of the surcharges is not on the stamp.

Surcharged in Two Lines by Press Printing

1920

UX34 PC20 1c on 2c **red,** *buff,* die I 800.00 52.50
Preprinted 125.00
a. Double surcharge 1,000.
UX35 PC20 1c 2c **red,** *cream,* die II 225.00 37.50
Preprinted 55.00
a. Double surcharge, one inverted at lower left —

Surcharges were prepared from (a) special dies fitting International and Universal post office canceling machines (Nos. UX31-UX33), and (b) printing press dies (Nos. UX34-UX35). There are 38 canceling machine types on Die I, and 44 on Die II. There are two printing press types of each die.

UX36 PC16 1c on 2c **red,** *cream* (#UX25) *57,500.*

Unused examples of No. UX36 (New York surcharge) were probably made by favor. Used examples of No. UX36 (Los Angeles surcharge, three to four examples used in Long Beach are recorded) are unquestionably authentic. Surcharges on other numbers exist, but their validity is doubtful.

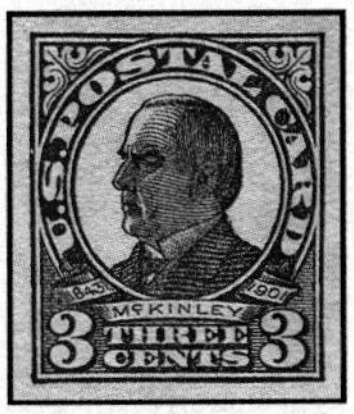

McKinley — PC21

1926, Feb. 1

For International Use

UX37 PC21 3c **red,** *buff* 4.50 *15.00*
Preprinted 1.75
First day cancel, Washington, DC 200.00
a. 3c **red,** *yellow* 6.00 *15.00*
Preprinted 1.75
b. Double impression *5,000.*

Franklin — PC22

1951, Nov. 16

UX38 PC22 2c **carmine rose,** *buff* .35 .25
Preprinted .25
First day cancel 1.00
a. Double impression 500.00
b. 2c **carmine rose,** *dark buff,* (error) 700.00
c. 2c **lake,** *buff,* 35.00 25.00
d. Indicia omitted (inscriptions normal) *1,000.*

No. UX38b was printed on spacer paper used for counting.
For surcharge see No. UX47.

Nos. UX27 and UX28 Surcharged by Canceling Machine at Left of Stamp in Light Green

1952

UX39 PC17 2c on 1c **green,** *buff, Jan. 1* .50 .35
Preprinted .25
First day cancel, any city 12.00
a. Surcharged vertically, reading down 8.00 *10.00*

Preprinted 3.00
b. Double surcharge 20.00 *25.00*
c. Double surcharge, one inverted at lower left 20.00 25.00
d. Inverted surcharge at lower left 12.00 12.00
e. Triple surcharge — —
f. Triple surcharge, one inverted at lower left — —
g. Surcharge black (error), entire *3,000.*

UX40 PC19 2c on 1c **green,** *cream, Mar. 22* .65 .45
Preprinted .40
First day cancel, Washington, D.C. 22.50
a. Surcharged vertically, reading down 7.00 5.50
Preprinted 4.00
b. Double surcharge 240.00
c. Double surcharge, one inverted at lower left 275.00
d. Inverted surcharge at lower left 200.00

Nos. UX27 and UX28 with Similar Surcharge Typographed at Left of Stamp in Dark Green.

1952

UX41 PC17 2c on 1c **green,** *buff* 4.50 2.00
Preprinted 1.75
a. Inverted surcharge at lower left 60.00 125.00
Preprinted 40.00
b. Double surcharge — —

UX42 PC19 2c on 1c **green,** *cream* 5.00 2.50
Preprinted 3.00
a. Surcharged by offset lithography 5.00 2.50
b. Surcharged on back 300.00

Type of 1917

1952, July 31 **Size: 127x76mm**

UX43 PC19 2c **carmine,** *buff* .30 *1.00*
Preprinted .20
First day cancel 1.00

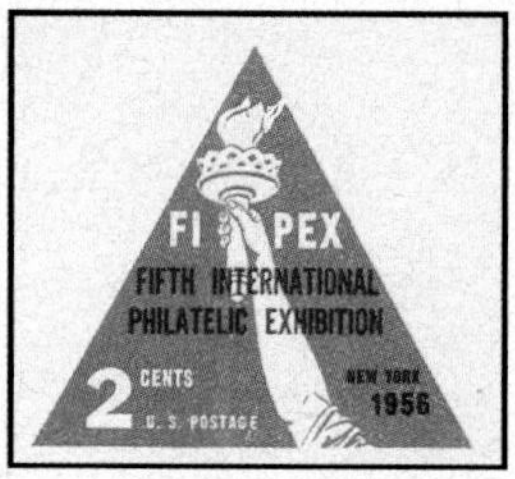

Torch and Arm of Statue of Liberty — PC23

Fifth International Philatelic Exhibition (FIPEX), New York City, Apr. 28-May 6, 1956.

1956, May 4

UX44 PC23 2c **deep carmine & dark violet blue,** *buff* .25 *1.00*
First day cancel, New York, NY *(537,474)* 1.00
a. Dark violet blue omitted 525.00 *600.00*
b. Double impression of dark violet blue 40.00 —
c. Double impression of deep carmine 40.00 30.00
d. Double impression of deep carmine & dark violet blue *650.00*
e. Double impression of deep carmine, dark violet blue omitted —
f. 2c **rose pink & dark violet blue,** *buff* 100.00 75.00
g. As "f," dark violet blue omitted *750.00*
h. 2c **pink & dark violet blue,** *buff* *750.00 750.00*
i. As "h," double impression of dark violet blue —

Statue of Liberty
PC24 PC25

For International Use

1956, Nov. 16

UX45 PC24 4c **deep red & ultramarine,** *buff* 1.50 *90.00*
First day cancel, New York, NY *(129,841)* 1.00

See No. UY16.

1958, Aug. 1

UX46 PC25 3c **purple,** *buff* .50 .20
First day cancel, Philadelphia, Pa. *(180,610)* 1.00
a. "N GOD WE TRUST" 12.00 *25.00*
First day cancel, Philadelphia, Pa. *175.00*
b. Double impression *250.00*
c. Double impression one inverted *4,500.*
d. Precanceled with 3 printed purple lines, *1961* 4.25 2.50
e. Indicia omitted (inscription normal) *1,000.*
f. 3c **purple,** *dark buff* (error) *900.00*

On No. UX46d, the precanceling lines are incorporated with the design. The earliest documented postmark on this experimental card is Oct. 31, 1961. UX46f was printed on spacer paper used for counting.

See No. UY17.

No. UX38 Surcharged by Canceling Machine at Left of Stamp in Black

ONE CENT
ADDITIONAL
PAID

1958

UX47 PC22 2c + 1c **carmine rose,** *buff* 235.00 *700.00*
a. Surcharge inverted at lower left 500.00

The surcharge was applied to 750,000 cards for the use of the General Electric Co., Owensboro, Ky. A variety of the surcharge shows the D of PAID beneath the N of ADDITIONAL. All known examples of No. UX47 have a printed advertisement on the back and a small punch hole near lower left corner.

Used value is for commercially used card.

Lincoln PC26

1962, Nov. 19

Precanceled with 3 printed red violet lines

UX48 PC26 4c **red violet** .50 .20
First day cancel, Springfield, IL *(162,939)* 1.25
a. Tagged, *June 25, 1966* .60 .20
b. Inscription omitted —
First day cancel, Bellevue, OH 30.00

No. UX48a was printed with luminescent ink.

See note on Luminescence in "Information for Collectors."

See No. UY18.

Used values are for contemporaneous usage without additional postage applied. Used values for international-rate cards are for proper usage.

Map of Continental United States — PC27

Designed by Suren H. Ermoyan

For International Use

1963, Aug. 30

UX49 PC27 7c **blue & red** 4.00 *65.00*
First day cancel, New York, NY 1.00
a. Blue omitted *7,500.*

First day cancellation was applied to 270,464 of Nos. UX49 and UY19. See Nos. UX54, UX59, UY19-UY20.

Flags and Map of U.S. PC28

175th anniv. of the U.S. Customs Service.

Designed by Gerald N. Kurtz

1964, Feb. 22

Precanceled with 3 printed blue lines

UX50 PC28 4c **red & blue** .50 *1.00*
First day cancel, Washington, DC *(313,275)* 1.00
a. Blue omitted 650.00
b. Red omitted —
c. Double red impression *650.00*

Americans "Moving Forward" (Street Scene) — PC29

Issued to publicize the need to strengthen the US Social Security system. Released in connection with the 15th conf. of the Intl. Social Security Association at Washington, DC.

Designed by Gerald N. Kurtz

1964, Sept. 26

Precanceled with a blue and 2 red printed lines

UX51 PC29 4c **dull blue & red** .40 *1.00*
First day cancel, Washington, D.C. *(293,650)* 1.00
a. Red omitted —
b. Dull blue omitted *650.00 650.00*

Coast Guard Flag — PC30

175th anniv. of the U.S. Coast Guard.

Designed by Muriel R. Chamberlain

1965, Aug. 4

Precanceled with 3 printed red lines

UX52 PC30 4c **blue & red** .30 *1.00*
First day cancel, Newburyport, Mass. *(338,225)* 1.25
a. Blue omitted *450.00*

Crowd and Census Bureau Punch Card — PC31

Designed by Emilio Grossi

1965, Oct. 21

Precanceled with 3 bright blue printed lines

UX53 PC31 4c **bright blue & black** .30 *1.00*
First day cancel, Philadelphia, Pa. *(275,100)* 1.00

Map Type of 1963

For International Use

1967, Dec. 4

UX54 PC27 8c **blue & red** 4.00 *65.00*
First day cancel, Washington, DC 1.00

First day cancellation was applied to 268,077 of Nos. UX54 and UY20.

Lincoln PC33

Designed by Robert J. Jones

Luminescent Ink

1968, Jan. 4

Precanceled with 3 printed green lines

UX55 PC33 5c **emerald** .30 *.60*
First day cancel, Hodgenville, Ky. 1.25
a. Double impression —

First day cancellation was applied to 274,000 of Nos. UX55 and UY21.

Woman Marine, 1968, and Marines of Earlier Wars — PC34

25th anniv. of the Women Marines.

Designed by Muriel R. Chamberlain

1968, July 26

UX56 PC34 5c **rose red & green** .35 *1.00*
First day cancel, San Francisco, Cal. *(203,714)* 1.25

Tagged

Postal cards from No. UX57 onward are either tagged or printed with luminescent ink unless otherwise noted.

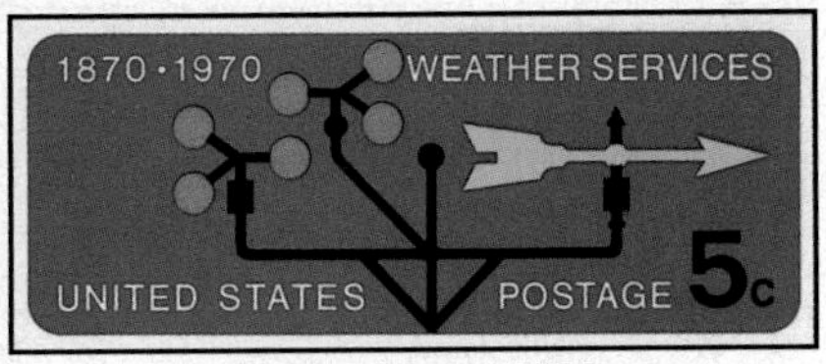

Weather Vane — PC35

Centenary of the Army's Signal Service, the Weather Services (Weather Bureau).

Designed by Robert Geissmann

1970, Sept. 1

UX57 PC35 5c **blue, yellow, red & black** .30 *1.00*
First day cancel, Fort Myer, Va. *(285,800)* 1.00
a. Yellow & black omitted *1,000.* *900.00*
b. Blue omitted *1,000.* *5,000.*
c. Black omitted *1,000.* *850.00*

Paul Revere PC36

Issued to honor Paul Revere, Revolutionary War patriot.

Designed by Howard C. Mildner after statue near Old North Church, Boston

1971, May 15

Precanceled with 3 printed brown lines

UX58 PC36 6c **brown** .30 *1.00*
First day cancel, Boston, Mass. 1.00
a. Double impression *300.00*

First day cancellation was applied to 340,000 of Nos. UX58 and UY22.

Map Type of 1963

For International Use

1971, June 10

UX59 PC27 10c **blue & red** 4.50 *65.00*
First day cancel, New York, NY 1.00

First day cancellation was applied to 297,000 of Nos. UX59 and UXC11.

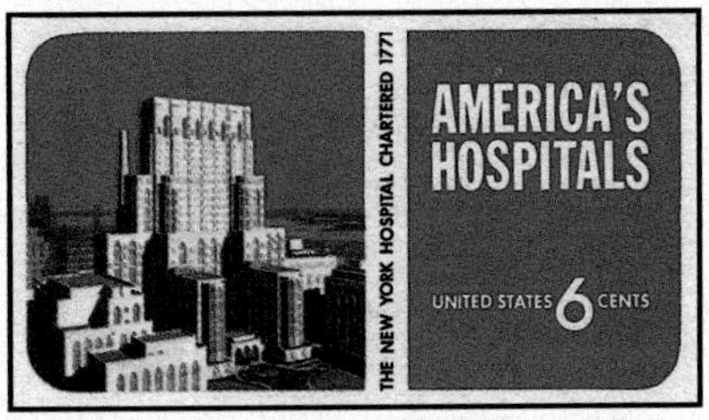

New York Hospital, New York City — PC37

Issued as a tribute to America's hospitals in connection with the 200th anniversary of New York Hospital.

Designed by Dean Ellis

1971, Sept. 16

UX60 PC37 6c **blue & multicolored** .30 *1.00*
First day cancel, New York, NY *(218,200)* 1.00
a. Blue & yellow omitted *1,000.*
b. Yellow omitted *500.00*
c. Red & black omitted —
d. Red omitted —
e. Tagging omitted 150.00
f. Black omitted *3,500.*

No. UX60f is significantly miscut, with only a small portion of the indicia present at the center top. The black vertical inscription line at the center is missing.

U.S.F. Constellation — PC38

Monument Valley — PC39

Gloucester, Mass. — PC40

Tourism Year of the Americas.

Designed by Melbourne Brindle

1972, June 29

Size: 152½x108½mm

UX61 PC38 6c **black,** U.S.F. Constellation, *buff* (Yosemite, Mt. Rushmore, Niagara Falls, Williamsburg on back) .85 *10.00*
First day cancel, any city 1.25
a. Address side blank *300.00*
b. Reverse blank — *750.00*
c. Tagging omitted 200.00
UX62 PC39 6c **black,** Monument Valley, *buff* (Monterey, Redwoods, Gloucester, U.S.F. Constellation on back) .40 *10.00*
First day cancel, any city 1.25
a. Black omitted on back —
b. Orange omitted on back —
c. Reverse blank 350.00
d. Tagging omitted 200.00
UX63 PC40 6c **black,** Gloucester, *buff* (Rodeo, Mississippi Riverboat, Grand Canyon, Monument Valley on back) .40 *6.00*
First day cancel, any city 1.25
a. Black inverted —
b. Reverse blank 500.00
c. Tagging omitted 200.00
Nos. UX61-UX63,UXC12-UXC13 (5) 3.15 *176.00*

Nos. UX61-UX63, UXC12-UXC13 went on sale throughout the United States. They were sold as souvenirs without postal validity at Belgica Philatelic Exhibition in Brussels and were displayed at the American Embassies in Paris and Rome. This is reflected in the first day cancel.

Varieties of the pictorial back printing include: black omitted (UX62), black and pale salmon omitted (UX63), and back inverted in relation to address side (UX63).

Used value for No. UX61b is for a copy that is canceled but unaddressed.

John Hanson — PC41

Designed by Thomas Kronen after statue by Richard Edwin Brooks in Maryland Capitol

1972, Sept. 1

Precanceled with 3 printed blue lines.

UX64 PC41 6c **blue** .50 *1.00*
First day cancel, Baltimore, MD 1.00
a. Coarse paper .75 *1.25*

Liberty Type of 1873

Centenary of first U.S. postal card.

1973, Sept. 14

UX65 PC1 6c **magenta** .25 *1.00*
First day cancel, Washington, D.C. *(289,950)* 1.00
a. Tagging omitted —

Samuel Adams — PC42

Designed by Howard C. Mildner

1973, Dec. 16

Precanceled with 3 printed orange lines

UX66 PC42 8c **orange** .50 *1.00*
First day cancel, Boston, Mass. *(147,522)* 1.00
a. Coarse paper .75 *1.00*
b. Double impression *1,200.*

Ship's Figurehead, 1883 — PC43

Design is after a watercolor by Elizabeth Moutal of the oak figurehead by John Rogerson from the barque Edinburgh.

1974, Jan. 4

For International Use

UX67 PC43 12c **multicolored** .35 *50.00*
First day cancel, Miami, Fla. *(138,500)* 1.00
a. Yellow omitted *650.00*
b. Tagging omitted *300.00*

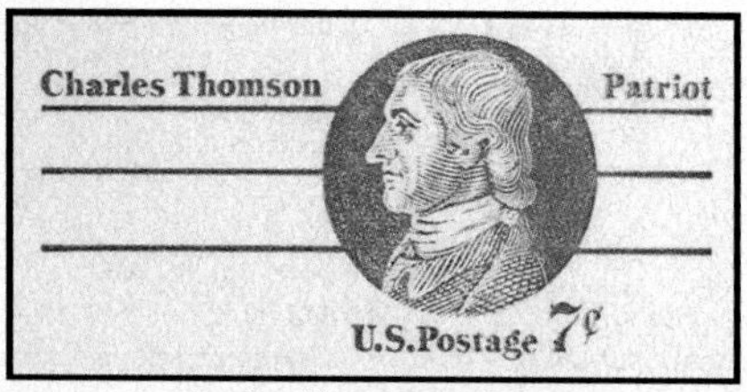

Charles Thomson — PC44

John Witherspoon — PC45

Caesar Rodney — PC46

Designed by Howard C. Mildner

1975-76

Precanceled with 3 printed emerald lines

UX68 PC44 7c **emerald,** *Sept. 14, 1975* .30 *10.00*
First day cancel, Bryn Mawr, Pa. 1.00

Precanceled with 3 printed brown lines

UX69 PC45 9c **yellow brown,** *Nov. 10, 1975* .30 *1.00*
First day cancel, Princeton, N.J. 1.00

Precanceled with 3 printed blue lines

UX70 PC46 9c **blue,** *July 1, 1976* .30 *1.00*
First day cancel, Dover, Del. 1.00
a. Double impression *4,500.*

First day cancellation applied to 231,919 of Nos. UX68 and UY25; 254,239 of Nos. UX69 and UY26; 304,061 of Nos. UX70 and UY27.

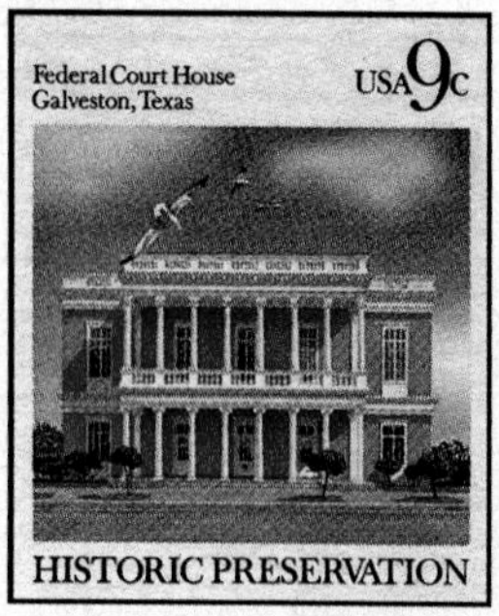

Federal Court House, Galveston, Texas — PC47

The Court House, completed in 1861, is on the National Register of Historic Places.

Designed by Donald Moss

1977, July 20

UX71 PC47 9c **multicolored** .25 *1.00*
First day cancel, Galveston, Tex. *(245,535)* 1.00
a. Black Omitted *6,000.*
b. Tagging omitted 150.00

Nathan Hale PC48

Designed by Howard C. Mildner

1977, Oct. 14

Precanceled with 3 printed green lines

UX72 PC48 9c **green** .25 *1.00*
First day cancel, Coventry, Conn. 1.00
a. Cent sign missing after "9" 125.00
b. Double impression 275.00

First day cancellation applied to 304,592 of Nos. UX72 and UY28.

Approximately 400 examples are recorded of No. UX72a. The variety also exists on fluorescent stock (18 recorded). Value thus is 7 times the listed value.

Cincinnati Music Hall — PC49

Centenary of Cincinnati Music Hall, Cincinnati, Ohio.

Designed by Clinton Orlemann

1978, May 12

UX73 PC49 10c **multicolored** .30 *1.00*
First day cancel, Cincinnati, O. *(300,000)* 1.75

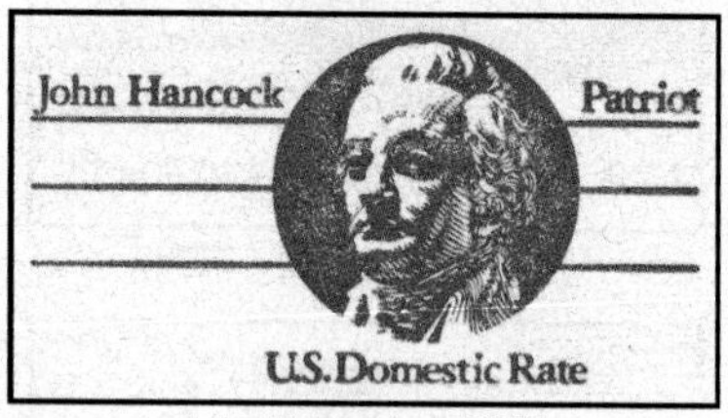

John Hancock — PC50

Designed by Howard Behrens

1978

Precanceled with 3 printed brown orange lines.

UX74 PC50 (10c) **brown orange,** *May 19* .30 *1.00*
First day cancel, Quincy, Mass. *(299,623)* 1.00

Inscribed "U.S. Postage 10¢"

UX75 PC50 10c **brown orange,** *June 20* .30 1.00
First day cancel, Quincy, Mass. *(187,120)* 1.00

Coast Guard Cutter Eagle — PC51

Designed by Carl G. Evers

For International Use

1978, Aug. 4

UX76 PC51 14c **multicolored** .40 *35.00*
First day cancel, Seattle, Wash. *(196,400)* 1.00

Molly Pitcher Firing Cannon at Monmouth — PC52

Bicentennial of Battle of Monmouth, June 28, 1778, and to honor Molly Pitcher (Mary Ludwig Hays).

Designed by David Blossom

1978, Sept. 8 **Litho.**

UX77 PC52 10c **multicolored** .30 *1.60*
First day cancel, Freehold, N.J. *(180,280)* 1.00

Clark and his Frontiersmen Approaching Fort Sackville — PC53

Bicentenary of capture of Fort Sackville from the British by George Rogers Clark.

Designed by David Blossom

1979, Feb. 23 **Litho.**

UX78 PC53 10c **multicolored** .30 *1.50*
First day cancel, Vincennes, Ind. 1.00
a. Yellow omitted —

Gen. Casimir Pulaski — PC54

Bicentenary of the death of Gen. Casimir Pulaski (1748-1779), Polish nobleman who served in American Revolutionary Army.

1979, Oct. 11 **Litho.**

UX79 PC54 10c **multicolored** .30 *1.50*
First day cancel, Savannah. GA *(210,000)* 1.00

Olympic Games Issue

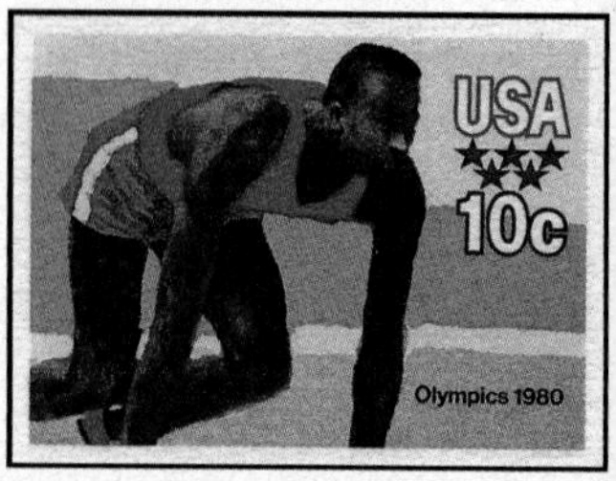

Sprinter PC55

22nd Olympic Games, Moscow, July 19-Aug. 3, 1980.

Designed by Robert M. Cunningham

1979, Sept. 17 **Litho.**

UX80 PC55 10c **multicolored** .60 *1.50*
First day cancel, Eugene, Ore. 1.00
a. Tagging omitted 200.00 *300.00*

Iolani Palace, Honolulu — PC56

1979, Oct. 1 **Litho.**

UX81 PC56 10c **multicolored** .30 *1.50*
First day cancel, Honolulu, HI *(242,804)* 1.00
a. Tagging omitted — —

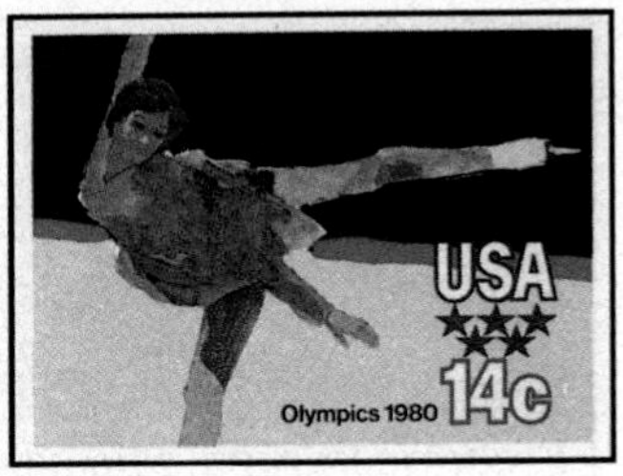

Women's Figure Skating PC57

13th Winter Olympic Games, Lake Placid, N.Y., Feb. 12-24.

Designed by Robert M. Cunningham

For International Use

1980, Jan. 15 **Litho.**

UX82 PC57 14c **multicolored** .60 *25.00*
a. Double impression of tagging bar, one at left —
First day cancel, Atlanta, GA *(160,977)* 1.00

Salt Lake Temple, Salt Lake City — PC58

1980, Apr. 5 **Litho.**

UX83 PC58 10c **multicolored** .25 *1.50*
First day cancel, Salt Lake City, UT *(325,260)* 1.00
a. Tagging omitted 300.00

Rochambeau's Fleet — PC59

Count Jean-Baptiste de Rochambeau's landing at Newport, R.I. (American Revolution) bicentenary.

Designed by David Blossom

1980, July 11 **Litho.**

UX84 PC59 10c **multicolored** .25 *1.50*
First day cancel, Newport, R.I. *(180,567)* 1.00
a. Front normal, black & yellow on back *4,000.*
b. Magenta & blue omitted —

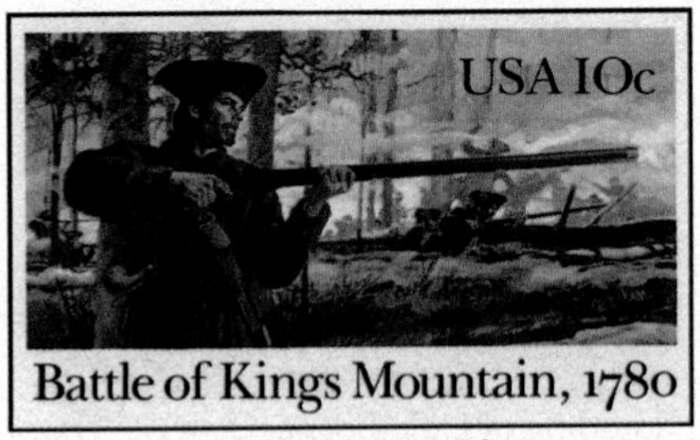

Whig Infantrymen — PC60

Bicentenary of the Battle of Kings Mountain (American Revolution).

Designed by David Blossom

1980, Oct. 7 **Litho.**

UX85 PC60 10c **multicolored** .25 *1.50*
First day cancel, Kings Mountain, NC *(136,130)* 1.00

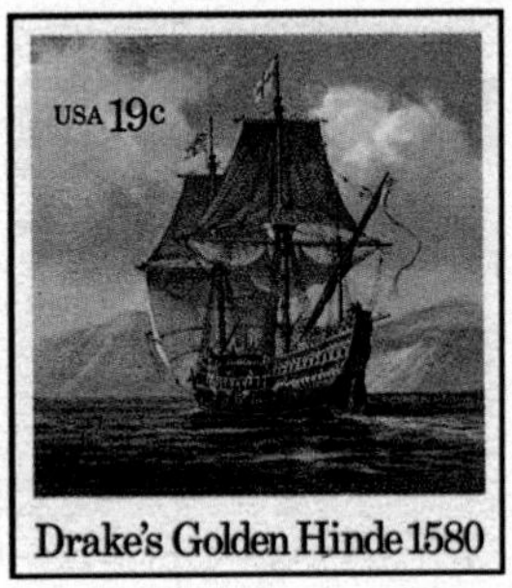

Golden Hinde — PC61

300th anniv. of Sir Francis Drake's circumnavigation (1578-1580).

Designed by Charles J. Lundgren

For International Use

1980, Nov. 21

UX86 PC61 19c **multicolored** .70 *35.00*
First day cancel, San Rafael, CA *(290,547)* 1.00

Cols. Washington and Tarleton — PC62

Bicentenary of the Battle of Cowpens (American Revolution).

Designed by David Blossom

1981, Jan. 17

UX87 PC62 10c **multicolored** .25 *17.50*
First day cancel, Cowpens, SC *(160,000)* 1.00

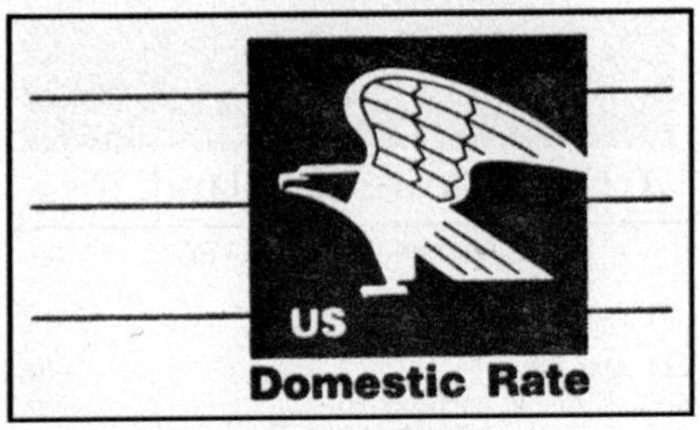

Eagle — PC63

1981, Mar. 15

Precanceled with 3 printed violet lines

UX88 PC63 (12c) **violet** .30 *.65*
First day cancel, Memphis, TN 1.00

See No. 1818, FDC section.

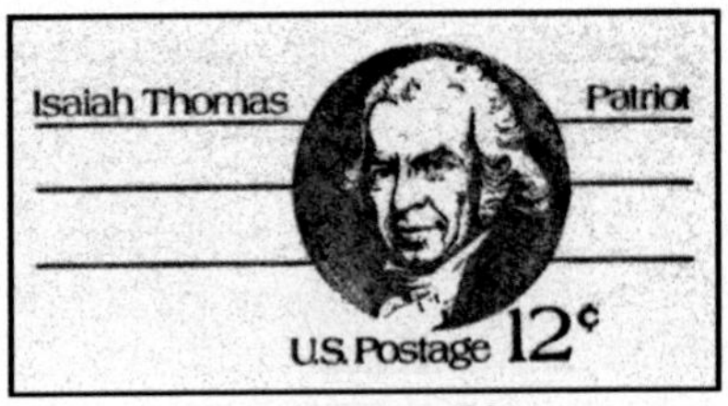

Isaiah Thomas — PC64

Designed by Chet Jezierski

1981, May 5 **Precanceled with 3 printed lines**

UX89 PC64 12c **light blue** .30 *.75*
First day cancel, Worcester, MA *(185,610)* 1.00

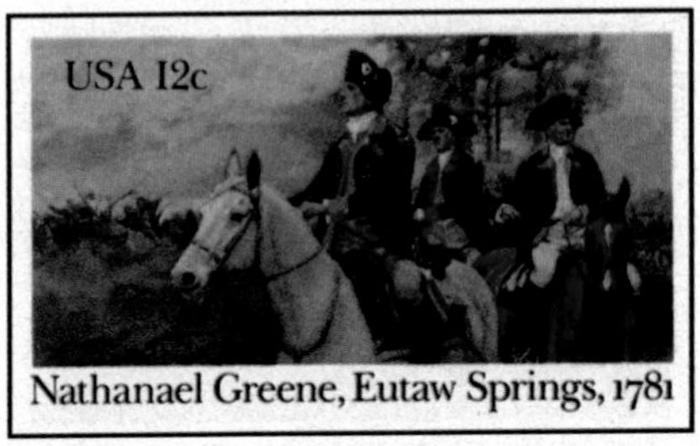

PC65

Bicentenary of the Battle at Eutaw Springs (American Revolution)

Designed by David Blossom

1981, Sept. 8 **Litho.**

UX90 PC65 12c **multicolored** .30 *22.50*
First day cancel, Eutaw Springs, SC *(115,755)* 1.00
a. Red & yellow omitted *2,900.*

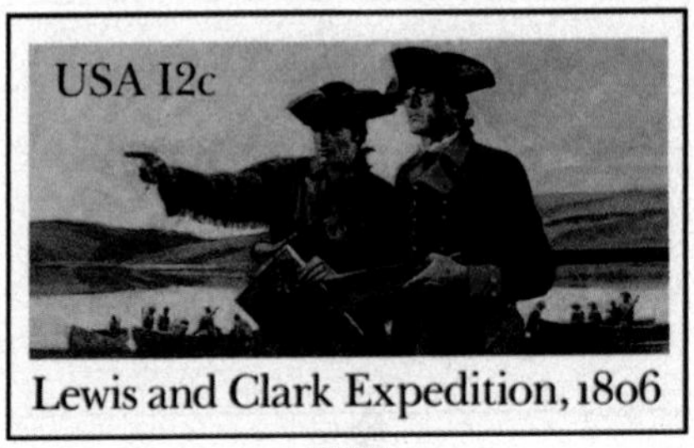

PC66

Designed by David Blossom

1981, Sept. 23

UX91 PC66 12c **multicolored** .30 *30.00*
First day cancel, Saint Louis, MO 1.00

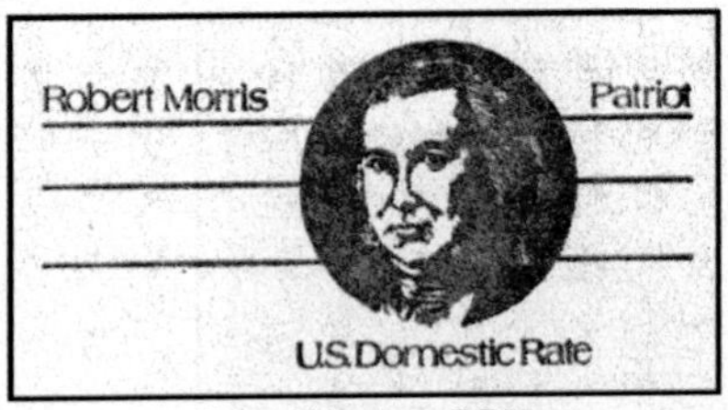

Robert Morris — PC67

1981

Precanceled with 3 printed lines

UX92 PC67 (13c) **buff,** *Oct. 11* .30 *.60*
First day cancel, Memphis, TN 1.00

See No. 1946, FDC section.

Inscribed: U.S. Postage 13¢

UX93 PC67 13c **buff,** *Nov. 10* .30 *.60*
First day cancel, Philadelphia, PA 1.00
a. Buff omitted 500.00

On No. UX93a, the copyright symbol and "1981" in buff is present at the lower left corner of the card.

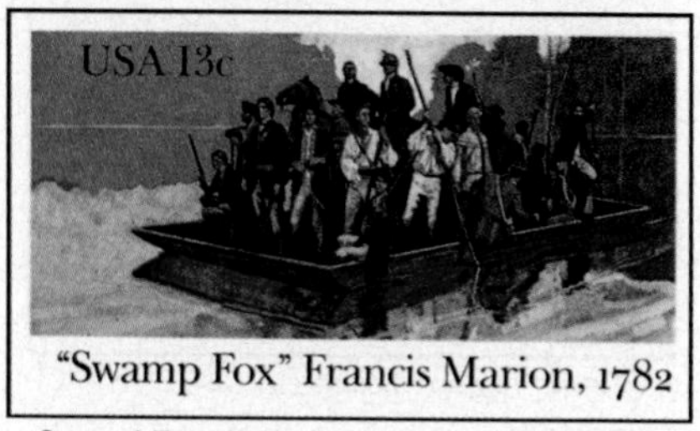

General Francis Marion (1732?-1795) — PC68

Designed by David Blossom

1982, Apr. 3 **Litho.**
UX94 PC68 13c **multicolored** .30 *1.00*
First day cancel, Marion, SC *(141,162)* 1.00

Rene Robert Cavelier, Sieur de la Salle (1643-1687) — PC69

Designed by David Blossom

1982, Apr. 7 **Litho.**
UX95 PC69 13c **multicolored** .30 *1.00*
First day cancel, New Orleans, LA 1.00

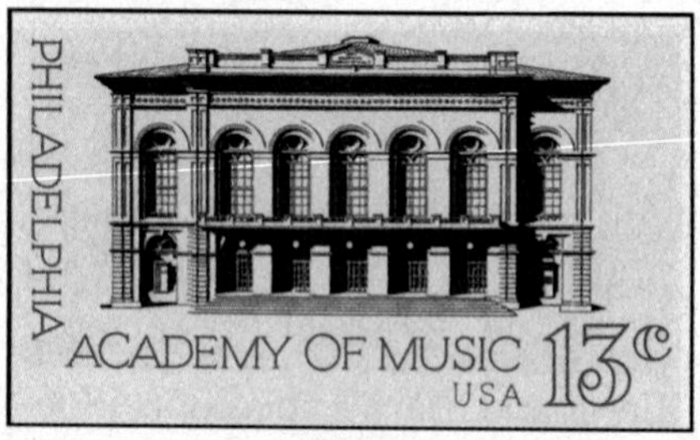

PC70

Designed by Melbourne Brindle

1982, June 18 **Litho.**
UX96 PC70 13c brown, red & cream, *buff* .30 *1.00*
First day cancel, Philadelphia, PA 1.00
a. Brown & cream omitted *750.00*

PC71

Designed by Clint Orlemann

1982, Oct. 14 **Litho.**
UX97 PC71 13c **multicolored** .30 *1.00*
First day cancel, St. Louis, MO 1.00

Gen. Oglethorpe Meeting Chief Tomo-Chi-Chi of the Yamacraw — PC72

Designed by David Blossom

1983, Feb. 12 **Litho.**
UX98 PC72 13c **multicolored** .30 *1.00*
First day cancel, Savannah, GA *(165,750)* 1.00

PC73

Designed by Walter Brooks

1983, Apr. 19 **Litho.**
UX99 PC73 13c **multicolored** .30 *1.00*
First day cancel, Washington, DC *(125,056)* 1.00

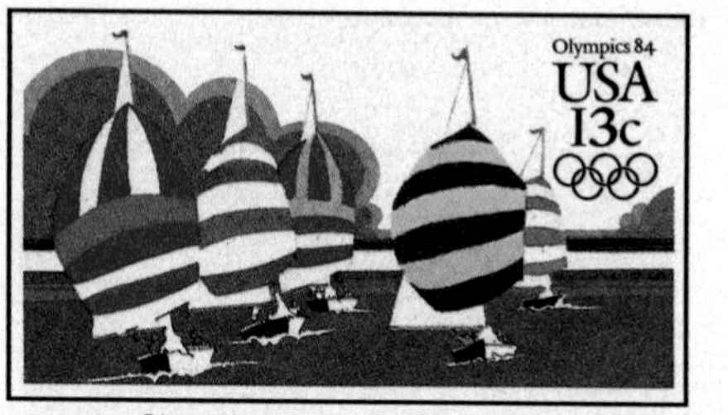

Olympics 84, Yachting — PC74

Designed by Bob Peak

1983, Aug. 5 **Litho.**
UX100 PC74 13c **multicolored** .30 *1.00*
First day cancel, Long Beach, CA *(132,232)* 1.00
a. Yellow & red omitted *5,500.* —
Preprinted *5,000.*

The Ark and the Dove — PC75

Designed by David Blossom

1984, Mar. 25 **Litho.**
UX101 PC75 13c **multicolored** .30 *1.00*
First day cancel, St. Clement's Island, MD *(131,222)* 1.00

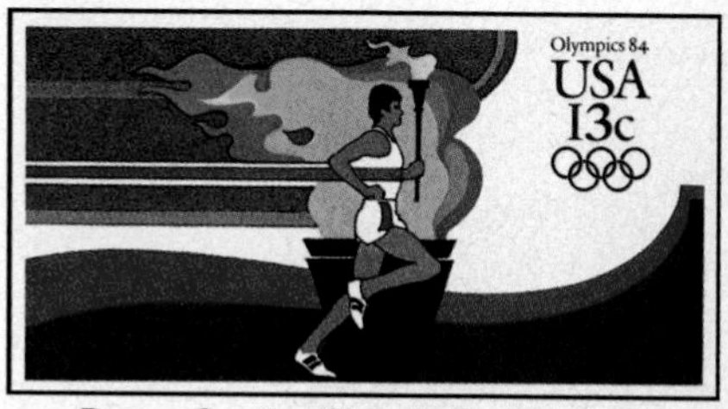

Runner Carrying Olympic Torch — PC76

Designed by Robert Peak

1984, Apr. 30 **Litho.**
UX102 PC76 13c **multicolored** .30 *1.25*
First day cancel, Los Angeles, CA *(110,627)* 1.00
a. Black & yellow inverted —
b. Tagging omitted 350.00

Father Baraga and Indian Guide in Canoe — PC77

Designed by David Blossom

1984, June 29 **Litho.**
UX103 PC77 13c **multicolored** .30 *1.00*
First day cancel, Marquette, MI *(100,156)* 1.00

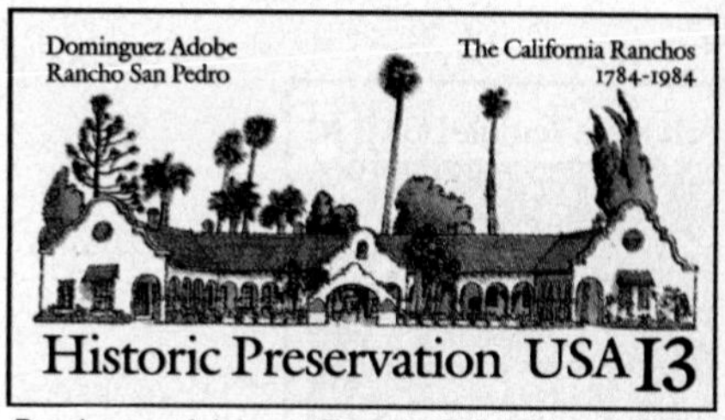

Dominguez Adobe at Rancho San Pedro — PC78

Designed by Earl Thollander

1984, Sept. 16 **Litho.**
UX104 PC78 13c **multicolored** .30 *1.00*
First day cancel, Compton, CA *(100,545)* 1.00
a. Black & blue omitted *1,500.*
b. Tagging omitted —

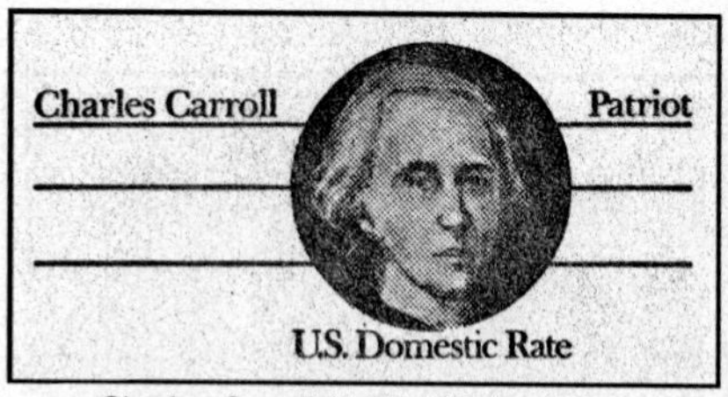

Charles Carroll (1737-1832) — PC79

Designed by Richard Sparks

1985

Precanceled with 3 printed lines

UX105 PC79 (14c) **pale green,** *Feb. 1* .45 *.65*
First day cancel, New Carrollton, MD *(135,642)* 1.00

Inscribed: USA 14

UX106 PC79 14c **pale green,** *Mar. 6* .45 *.55*
First day cancel, Annapolis, MD *(111,122)* 1.00

Clipper Flying Cloud — PC80

Designed by Richard Schlecht

For International Use

1985, Feb. 27 **Litho.**

UX107 PC80 25c **multicolored** .70 *22.50*
First day cancel, Salem, MA *(95,559)* 1.25

No. UX107 was sold by the USPS at CUP-PEX 87, Perth, Western Australia, with a cachet honoring CUP-PEX 87 and the America's Cup race. Value $2.

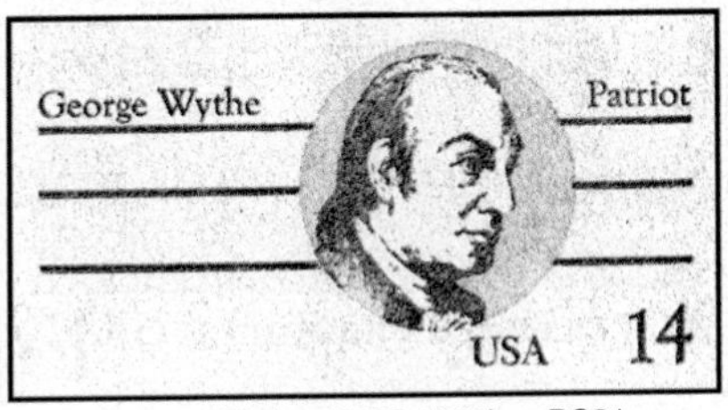

George Wythe (1726-1806) — PC81

Designed by Chet Jezierski from a portrait by John Fergusson.

1985, June 20

Precanceled with 3 printed lines

UX108 PC81 14c **bright apple green** .30 *.75*
First day cancel, Williamsburg, VA *(133,334)* 1.00
a. Indicia missing —

On No. UX108a, the left precancel, "George Wythe" and the copyright symbol are normal.

Arrival of Thomas Hooker and Hartford Congregation — PC82

Settlement of Connecticut, 350th Anniv.

Designed by David Blossom

1986, Apr. 18 **Litho.**

UX109 PC82 14c **multicolored** .30 *1.50*
First day cancel, Hartford, CT *(76,875)* 1.00

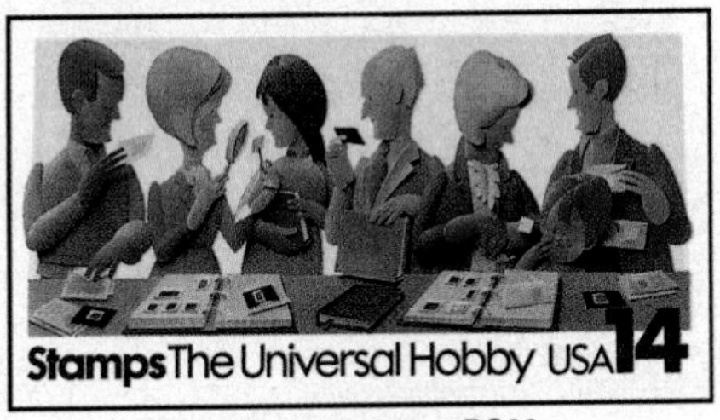

Stamp Collecting — PC83

Designed by Ray Ameijide

1986, May 23 **Litho.**

UX110 PC83 14c **multicolored** .30 *1.25*
First day cancel, Chicago, IL *(75,548)* 1.00

No. UX110 was sold by the USPS at "najubria 86" with a show cachet. Value: unused, $6; used, $20.

Francis Vigo (1747-1836) — PC84

Designed by David Blossom

1986, May 24 **Litho.**

UX111 PC84 14c **multicolored** .30 *1.25*
First day cancel, Vincennes, IN *(100,141)* 1.00

Roger Williams (1603-1683), Clergyman, Landing at Providence — PC85

Settling of Rhode Island, 350th Anniv.

Designed by David Blossom

1986, June 26 **Litho.**

UX112 PC85 14c **multicolored** .30 *1.50*
First day cancel, Providence, RI *(54,559)* 1.00

Miners, Shake Rag Street Housing — PC86

Wisconsin Territory Sesquicentennial.

Designed by David Blossom

1986, July 3 **Litho.**

UX113 PC86 14c **multicolored** .30 *1.00*
First day cancel, Mineral Point, WI *(41,224)* 1.00
a. Tagging omitted 200.00

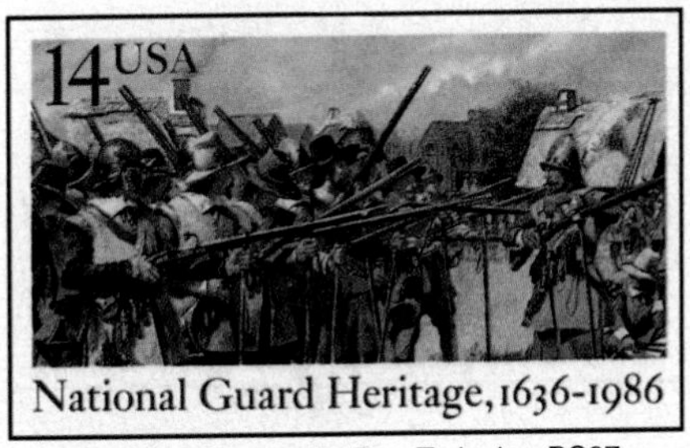

The First Muster, by Don Troiani — PC87

Designed by Bradbury Thompson

1986, Dec. 12 **Litho.**

UX114 PC87 14c **multicolored** .30 *1.25*
First day cancel, Boston, MA *(72,316)* 1.00

PC88

The self-scouring steel plow invented by blacksmith John Deere in 1837 pictured at lower left.

Designed by William H. Bond

1987, May 22 **Litho.**

UX115 PC88 14c **multicolored** .30 *1.25*
First day cancel, Moline, IL *(160,009)* 1.00

Convening of the Constitutional Convention, 1787 — PC89

George Mason, Gouverneur Morris, James Madison, Alexander Hamilton and Charles C. Pinckney are listed in the lower left corner of the card.

Designed by David K. Stone

1987, May 25 **Litho.**

UX116 PC89 14c **multicolored** .30 *.75*
First day cancel, Philadelphia, PA *(138,207)* 1.00
a. Double black and blue, with first day cancel *650.00*

Stars and Stripes — PC90

Designed by Steven Dohanos

1987, June 14 **Litho.**

UX117 PC90 14c **black, blue & red** .30 *.60*
First day cancel, Baltimore, MD 1.00
a. Double impression of tagging bar *175.00*

No. UX117 was sold by the USPS at Cologne, Germany, with a cachet for Philatelia'87. Value $2.

Take Pride in America — PC91

Designed by Lou Nolan

1987, Sept. 22 **Litho.**

UX118 PC91 14c **multicolored** .30 *1.25*
First day cancel, Jackson, WY *(47,281)* 1.00

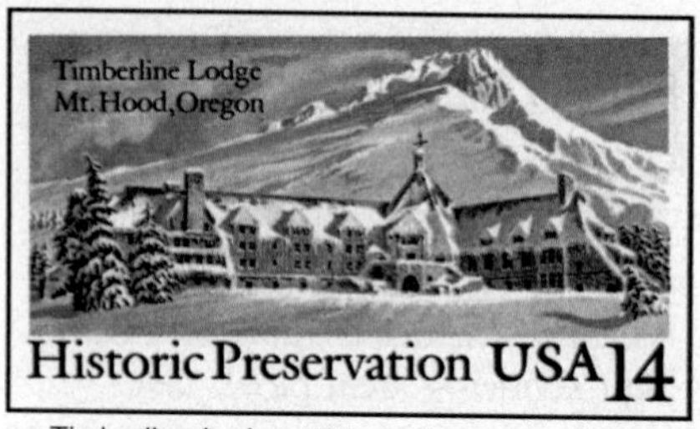

Timberline Lodge, 50th Anniversary — PC92

Designed by Walter DuBois Richards

1987, Sept. 28 **Litho.**

UX119 PC92 14c **multicolored** .30 *1.25*
First day cancel, Timberline, OR *(63,595)* 1.25

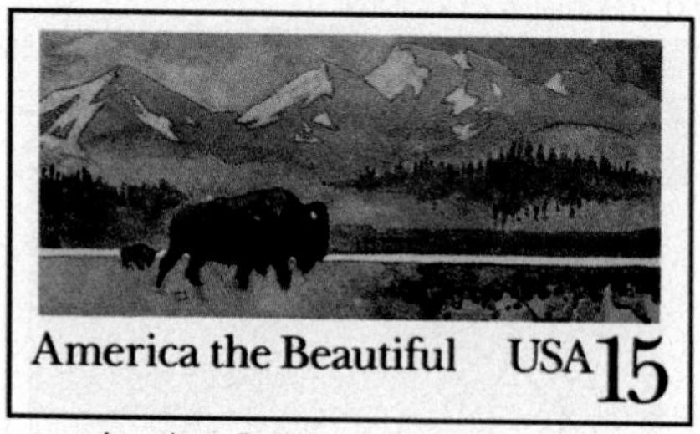

American Buffalo and Prairie — PC93

Designed by Bart Forbes

1988, Mar. 28 **Litho.**

UX120 PC93 15c **multicolored** .30 *.60*
First day cancel, Buffalo, WY *(52,075)* 1.00

a. Black omitted 1,750.
b. Printed on both sides *475.00*
c. Front normal, blue & black on back *600.00*
d. Black & magenta omitted *1,500.*
e. Black, yellow, blue & tagging omitted *1,000.*
f. Black, blue & tagging omitted *1,250.*
g. Black, magenta, yellow & tagging omitted *1,250.*
h. Double black impression —
i. Triple black impression —
j. Double black and blue impression —
k. Double magenta & blue, and triple black impression —

Tagged

Postal cards from No. UX57 onward are either tagged or printed with luminescent ink unless otherwise noted.

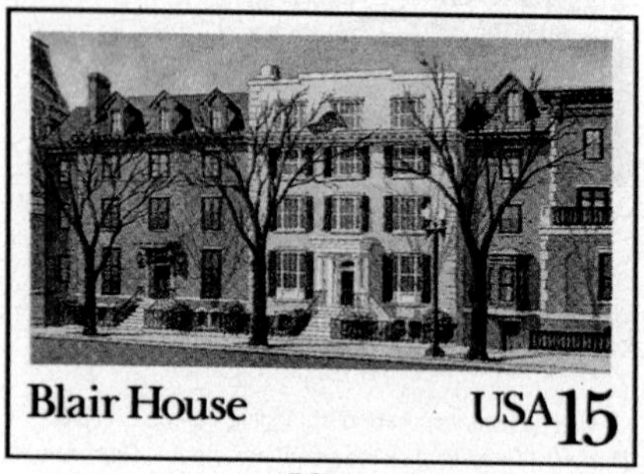

PC94

Designed by Pierre Mion

1988, May 4 **Litho.**

UX121 PC94 15c **multicolored** .30 *1.00*
First day cancel, Washington, DC *(52,188)* 1.00

Yorkshire, Squarerigged Packet — PC95

Inscribed: Yorkshire, Black Ball Line, Packet Ship, circa 1850 at lower left.

Designed by Richard Schlect

For International Use

1988, June 29 **Litho.**

UX122 PC95 28c **multicolored** .60 *20.00*
First day cancel, Mystic, CT *(46,505)* 1.00

a. Black & blue omitted *850.00*
b. Black, blue, yellow & tagging omitted *1,250.*
c. Black, magenta & tagging omitted *1,000.*
d. Black, magenta, yellow & tagging omitted *1,000.*
e. Black & tagging omitted *2,000.*

Harvesting Corn Fields — PC96

Iowa Territory Sesquicentennial.

Designed by Greg Hargreaves

1988, July 2 **Litho.**

UX123 PC96 15c **multicolored** .30 *1.00*
First day cancel, Burlington, IA *(45,565)* 1.00

Flatboat Ferry Transporting Settlers Down the Ohio River — PC97

Bicentenary of the settlement of Ohio, the Northwest Territory. Design at lower left shows map of the eastern United States with Northwest Territory highlighted.

Designed by James M. Gurney and Susan Sanford

1988, July 15 **Litho.**

UX124 PC97 15c **multicolored** .30 *1.00*
First day cancel, Marietta, OH *(28,778)* 1.00

a. Black, blue, yellow & tagging omitted *1,150.*
b. Black, magenta & tagging omitted *750.00*
c. Blue, black & tagging omitted *900.00*
d. Black & tagging omitted *2,000.*
e. Black, magenta, yellow & tagging omitted *1,500.*

PC98

Designed by Robert Reynolds

1988, Sept. 20 **Litho.**

UX125 PC98 15c **multicolored** .30 *1.00*
First day cancel, San Simeon, CA *(84,786)* 1.00

a. Black, magenta & tagging omitted *750.00*
b. Black, blue, yellow & tagging omitted *2,000.*
c. Black, magenta, yellow & tagging omitted *1,000.*
d. Black & tagging omitted *2,000.*
e. Black, blue & tagging omitted —

Pressman, New Yorker Reading Newspaper, 1787 — PC99

Designed by Roy Andersen

1988, Oct. 27 **Litho.**

UX126 PC99 15c **multicolored** .30 *1.00*
First day cancel, New York, NY *(37,661)* 1.00

Red-tailed Hawk and Sonora Desert at Sunset — PC100

Designed by Bart Forbes

1989, Jan. 13 **Litho.**

UX127 PC100 15c **multicolored** .30 *1.00*
First day cancel, Tucson, AZ *(51,891)* 1.00

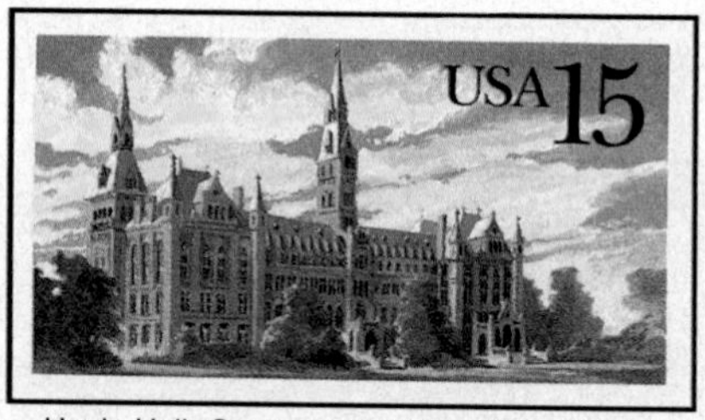

Healy Hall, Georgetown University — PC101

Designed by John Morrell. Inscription at lower left: "Healy Hall / Georgetown / Washington, DC / HISTORIC PRESERVATION."

1989, Jan. 23 **Litho.**

UX128 PC101 15c **multicolored** .30 *1.00*
First day cancel, Washington, DC *(54,897)* 1.00

Great Blue Heron, Marsh — PC102

Designed by Bart Forbes

1989, Mar. 17 **Litho.**

UX129 PC102 15c **multicolored** .30 *1.00*
First day cancel, Okefenokee, GA *(58,208)* 1.25

Settling of Oklahoma — PC103

Designed by Bradbury Thompson

1989, Apr. 22 **Litho.**
UX130 PC103 15c **multicolored** .30 *1.00*
First day cancel, Guthrie, OK *(68,689)* 1.00

Used values are for contemporaneous usage without additional postage applied. Used values for international-rate cards are for proper usage.

Canada Geese and Mountains — PC104

Designed by Bart Forbes

1989, May 5 **Litho.** **For Use to Canada**
UX131 PC104 21c **multicolored** .40 *20.00*
First day cancel, Denver, CO *(59,303)* 1.25

Seashore — PC105

Designed by Bart Forbes

1989, June 17 **Litho.**
UX132 PC105 15c **multicolored** .30 *1.00*
First day cancel, Cape Hatteras, NC *(67,073)* 1.25

PC106

Designed by Bart Forbes

1989, Aug. 26 **Litho.**
UX133 PC106 15c **multicolored** .30 *1.00*
First day cancel, Cherokee, NC *(67,878)* 1.25

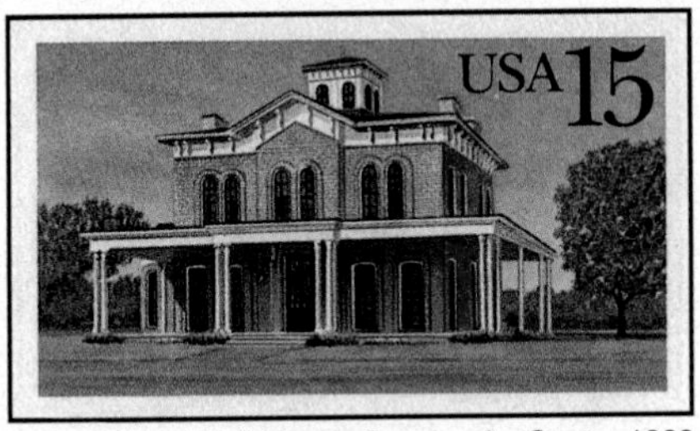

Jane Addams' Hull House Community Center 1889, Chicago — PC107

Designed by Michael Hagel

1989, Sept. 16 **Litho.**
UX134 PC107 15c **multicolored** .30 *1.00*
First day cancel, Chicago, IL *(53,773)* 1.00

Aerial View of Independence Hall, Philadelphia — PC108

Designed by Bart Forbes

1989, Sept. 25 **Litho.**
UX135 PC108 15c **multicolored** .30 *1.00*
First day cancel, Philadelphia, PA *(61,659)* 1.00

See No. UX139.

Inner Harbor, Baltimore — PC109

Designed by Bart Forbes

1989, Oct. 7 **Litho.**
UX136 PC109 15c **multicolored** .30 *1.00*
First day cancel, Baltimore, MD *(58,746)* 1.00

See No. UX140.

59th Street Bridge, New York City — PC110

Designed by Bart Forbes

1989, Nov. 8 **Litho.**
UX137 PC110 15c **multicolored** .30 *1.00*
First day cancel, New York, NY *(48,044)* 1.00

See No. UX141.

West Face of the Capitol, Washington D.C. — PC111

Designed by Bart Forbes

1989, Nov. 26 **Litho.**
UX138 PC111 15c **multicolored** .30 *1.00*
First day cancel, Washington, DC 1.00

See No. UX142.

1989, Dec. 1 **Litho.**

Designed by Bart Forbes. Issued in sheets of 4 + 2 inscribed labels picturing 20th UPU Congress or World Stamp Expo '89 emblems, and rouletted 9½ on 2 or 3 sides.

UX139 PC108 15c **multicolored** 3.25 *4.00*
First day cancel, Washington, DC 1.00
UX140 PC109 15c **multicolored** 3.25 *4.00*
First day cancel, Washington, DC 1.00
UX141 PC110 15c **multicolored** 3.25 *4.00*
First day cancel, Washington, DC 1.00
UX142 PC111 15c **multicolored** 3.25 *4.00*
First day cancel, Washington, DC 1.00
a. Sheet of 4, #UX139-UX142 14.00
Nos. UX135-UX142 (8) 14.20 *20.00*

Unlike Nos. UX135-UX138, Nos. UX139-UX142 do not contain inscription and copyright symbol at lower left. Order on sheet is Nos. UX140, UX139, UX142, UX141.

Most copies of No. UX142a and UX139 are bent at the upper right corner.

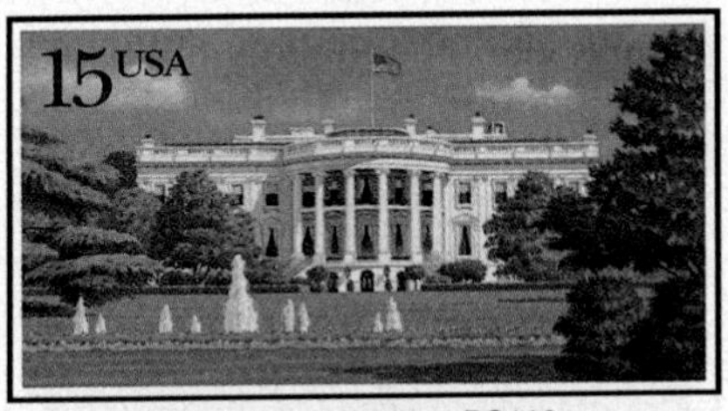

The White House — PC112

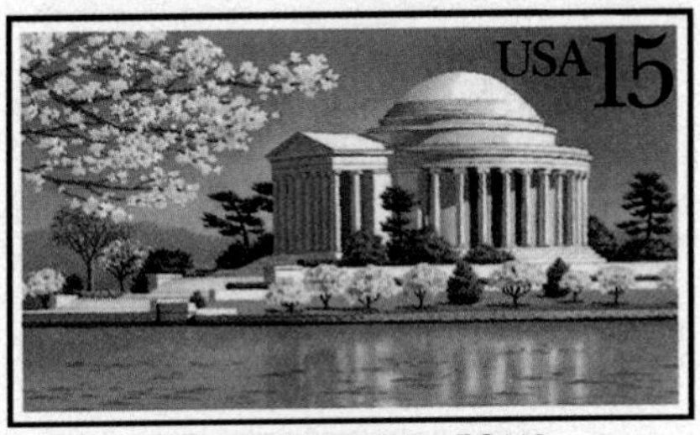

Jefferson Memorial — PC113

Designed by Pierre Mion. Space for message at left.

1989 **Litho.**
UX143 PC112 15c **multicolored**, *Nov. 30* 1.50 *2.50*
First day cancel, Washington, DC 2.00
UX144 PC113 15c **multicolored**, *Dec. 2* 1.50 *2.00*
First day cancel, Washington, DC 2.00

Nos. UX143-UX144 sold for 50c each. Illustrations of the buildings without denominations are shown on the back of the card

Rittenhouse Paper Mill, Germantown, PA — PC114

Designed by Harry Devlin.

1990, Mar. 13 **Litho.**
UX145 PC114 15c **multicolored** .30 *1.00*
First day cancel, New York, NY *(9,866)* 1.00

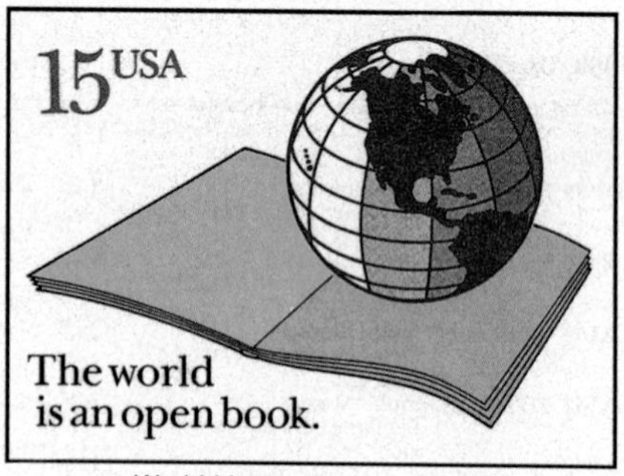

World Literacy Year — PC115

Designed by Joe Brockert.

1990, Mar. 22 **Litho.**
UX146 PC115 15c **multicolored** .30 *.90*
First day cancel, Washington, DC *(11,163)* 1.00

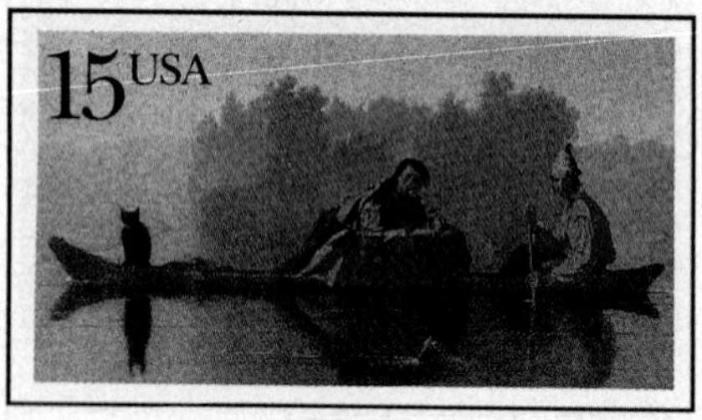

PC116

Designed by Bradbury Thompson. Inscription in upper left corner: "Fur Traders Descending the Missouri / George Caleb Bingham, 1845 / Metropolitan Museum of Art".

1990, May 4 **Litho.**
UX147 PC116 15c **multicolored** 1.50 *2.50*
First day cancel, St. Louis, MO *(13,632)* 2.00

No. UX147 sold for 50c and shows more of the painting without the denomination on the back.

PC117

Designed by Frank Constantino. Inscription at lower left: "HISTORIC PRESERVATION SERIES / Isaac Royall House, 1700s / Medford, Massachusetts / National Historic Landmark".

1990, June 16 **Litho.**
UX148 PC117 15c **multicolored** .30 *1.00*
First day cancel, Medford, MA *(21,708)* 1.00

Quadrangle, Stanford University — PC119

Designed by Jim M'Guinness.

1990, Sept. 30 **Litho.**
UX150 PC119 15c **multicolored** .30 *1.00*
First day cancel, Stanford, CA *(28,430)* 1.00

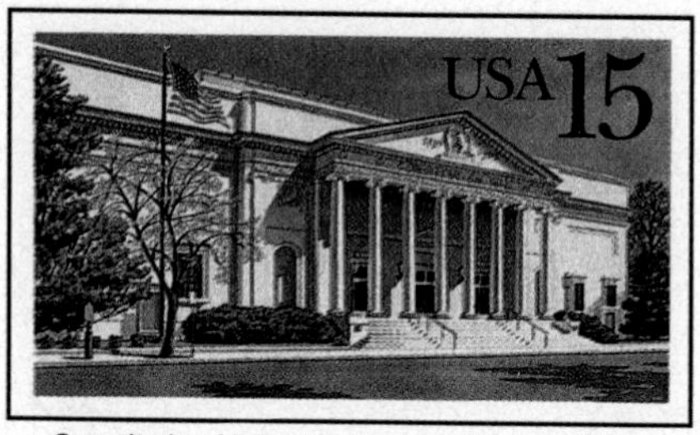

Constitution Hall, Washington, DC — PC120

Designed by Pierre Mion. Inscription at upper left: "Washington: Constitution Hall (at right)/ Memorial Continental Hall (reverse side) / Centennial, Daughters of the American Revolution".

1990, Oct. 11 **Litho.**
UX151 PC120 15c **multicolored** 1.50 *2.00*
First day cancel, Washington, DC *(33,254)* 2.00

No. UX151 sold for 50c.

Chicago Orchestra Hall — PC121

Designed by Michael Hagel. Inscription at lower left: "Chicago: Orchestra Hall / HISTORIC PRESERVATION / Chicago Symphony Orchestra / Centennial, 1891-1991".

1990, Oct. 19 **Litho.**
UX152 PC121 15c **multicolored** .30 *1.00*
First day cancel, Chicago, IL *(28,546)* 1.00

PC122

Designed by Richard Sheaff.

1991, Jan. 24 **Litho.**
UX153 PC122 19c **rose, ultramarine & black** .40 *.75*
First day cancel, Washington, DC *(26,690)* 1.00

PC123

Designed by Howard Koslow.

1991, Apr. 1 **Litho.**
UX154 PC123 19c **multicolored** .40 *1.00*
First day cancel, New York, NY *(27,063)* 1.00

Old Red, University of Texas Medical Branch, Galveston, Cent. — PC124

Designed by Don Adair.

1991, June 14 **Litho.**
UX155 PC124 19c **multicolored** .40 *1.00*
First day cancel, Galveston, TX *(24,308)* 1.00

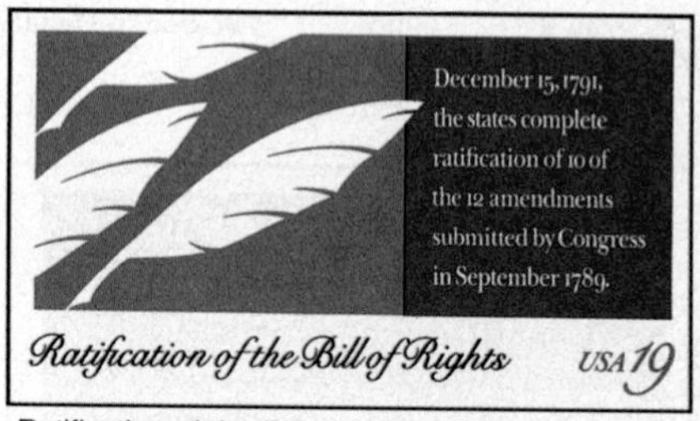

Ratification of the Bill of Rights, Bicent. — PC125

Designed by Mark Zaref.

1991, Sept. 25 **Litho.**
UX156 PC125 19c **red, blue & black** .40 *.90*
First day cancel, Richmond, VA *(27,457)* 1.00

Main Building, University of Notre Dame PC126

Designed by Frank Costantino. Inscription at lower left: Notre Dame / Sesquicentennial / 1842-1992.

1991, Oct. 15 **Litho.**
UX157 PC126 19c **multicolored** .40 *1.00*
First day cancel, Notre Dame, IN *(34,325)* 1.00

Niagara Falls — PC127

Designed by Wendell Minor.

1991, Aug. 21 **Litho.**

For Use to Canada & Mexico

UX158 PC127 30c **multicolored** .75 *13.00*
First day cover, Niagara Falls, NY *(29,762)* 1.25

Tagged

Postal cards from No. UX57 onward are either tagged or printed with luminescent ink unless otherwise noted.

The Old Mill — PC128

Designed by Harry Devlin. Inscription at lower left: The Old Mill / University of Vermont / Bicentennial.

1991, Oct. 29 **Litho.**

UX159 PC128 19c **multicolored** .40 *1.00*
First day cancel, Burlington, VT *(23,965)* 1.00

Wadsworth Atheneum, Hartford, CT — PC129

Designed by Frank Costantino. Inscription at lower left: Wadsworth Atheneum / Hartford, Connecticut / 150th Anniversary / 1842-1992.

1992, Jan. 16 **Litho.**

UX160 PC129 19c **multicolored** .40 *1.00*
First day cancel, Hartford, CT *(41,499)* 1.00

Cobb Hall, University of Chicago — PC130

Designed by Michael P. Hagel. Inscription at lower left: Cobb Hall / The University of Chicago / Centennial Year, 1991-1992.

1992, Jan. 23 **Litho.**

UX161 PC130 19c **multicolored** .40 *1.00*
First day cancel, Chicago, IL *(27,150)* 1.00

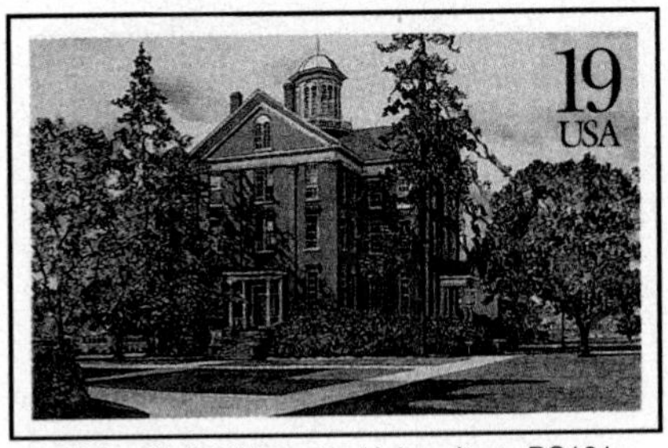

Waller Hall, Willamette University — PC131

Designed by Bradbury Thompson. Inscription at lower left: Waller Hall / Salem, Oregon / Willamette University / Sesquicentennial / 1842-1992.

1992, Feb. 1 **Litho.**

UX162 PC131 19c **multicolored** .40 *1.00*
First day cancel, Salem, OR *(28,463)* 1.00

PC132

Designed by Dennis Simon. Space for message at left. Inscription at upper left: "At right: The Reliance, USA 1903 / Reverse: The Ranger, USA 1937."

1992, May 6 **Litho.**

UX163 PC132 19c **multicolored** 1.75 *3.00*
First day cancel, San Diego, CA *(19,944)* 2.00

No. UX163 sold for 50 cents.

PC133

Designed by Ken Hodges.

1992, May 9 **Litho.**

UX164 PC133 19c **multicolored** .40 *1.00*
First day cancel, Stevenson, WA *(32,344)* 1.00

Ellis Island Immigration Museum — PC134

Designed by Howard Koslow. Inscription at lower left: "Ellis Island / Centennial 1992."

1992, May 11 **Litho.**

UX165 PC134 19c **multicolored** .40 *1.00*
First day cancel, Ellis Island, NY *(38,482)* 1.00

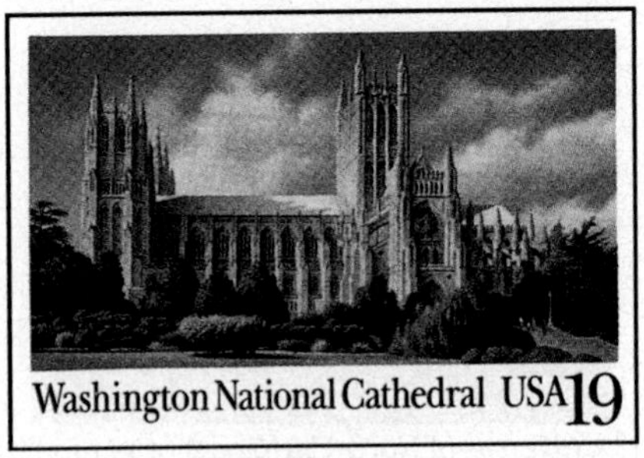

PC135

Designed by Howard Koslow.

1993, Jan. 6 **Litho.**

UX166 PC135 19c **multicolored** .40 *1.00*
First day cancel, Washington, DC *(8,315)* 1.00

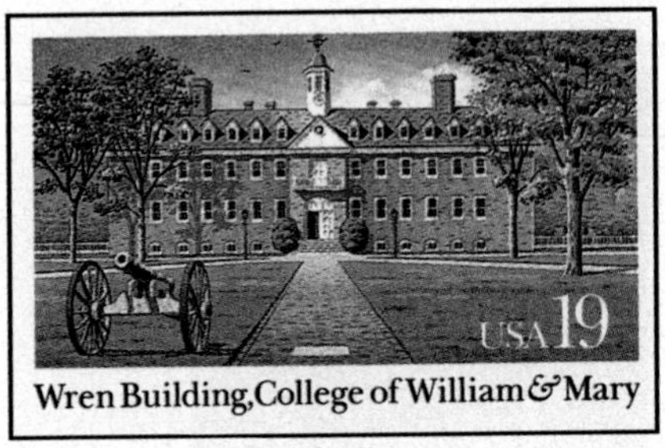

PC136

Designed by Pierre Mion.

1993, Feb. 8 **Litho.**

UX167 PC136 19c **multicolored** .40 *1.00*
First day cancel, Williamsburg, VA *(9,758)* 1.00

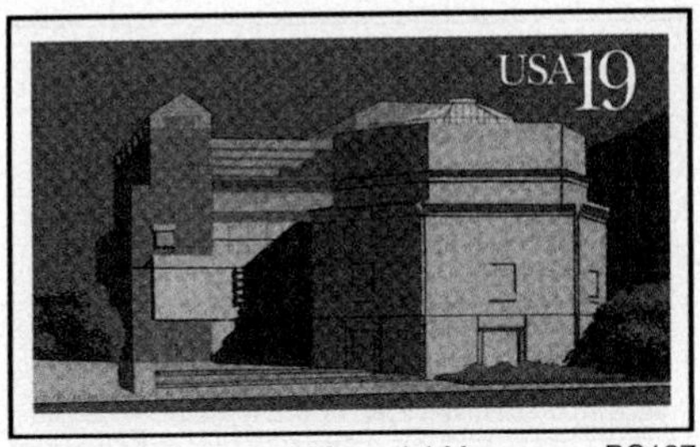

Opening of Holocaust Memorial Museum — PC137

Designed by Tom Engeman. Space for message at left. Inscription at upper left: "Washington, DC: / United States / Holocaust Memorial Museum."

1993, Mar. 23 **Litho.**

UX168 PC137 19c **multicolored** 1.75 *3.00*
First day cancel, Washington, DC *(8,234)* 2.00

No. UX168 sold for 50c, and shows aerial view of museum on the back.

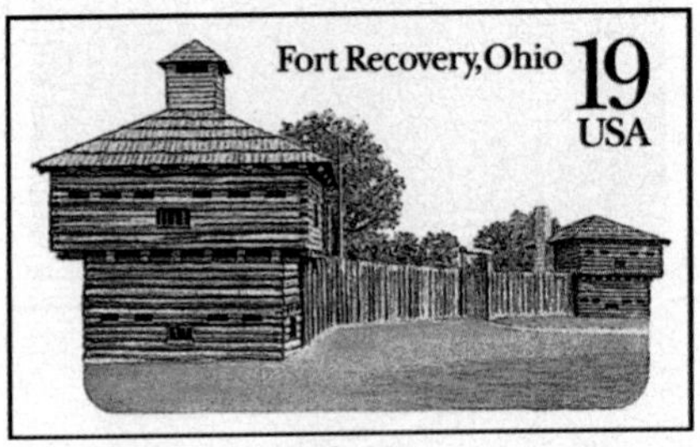

PC138

Designed by Michael Hagel.

1993, June 13 **Litho.**

UX169 PC138 19c **multicolored** .40 *.90*
First day cancel, Fort Recovery, OH *(8,254)* 1.00

PC139

Designed by Robert Timberlake.

1993, Sept. 14 **Litho.**
UX170 PC139 19c **multicolored** .40 *1.00*
First day cancel, Chapel Hill, NC *(7,796)* 1.00

PC140

Designed by Frank Constantino.

1993, Sept. 17 **Litho.**
UX171 PC140 19c **multicolored** .40 *.90*
First day cancel, Worcester, MA *(4,680)* 1.00

PC141

Designed by Michael Hagel.

1993, Oct. 9 **Litho.**
UX172 PC141 19c **multicolored** .40 *.90*
First day cancel, Jacksonville, IL *(5,269)* 1.00

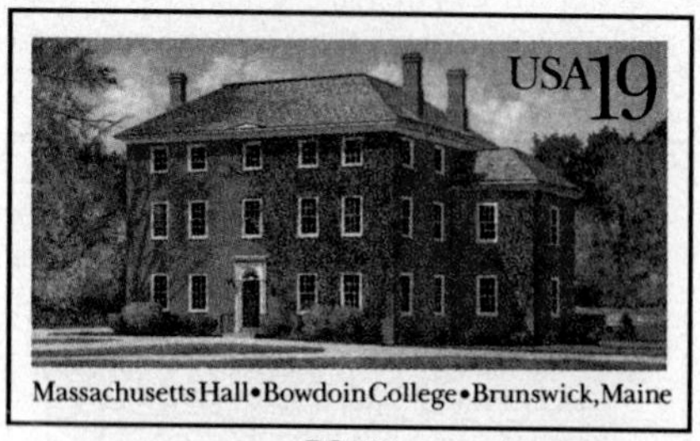

PC142

Designed by Harry Devlin.

1993, Oct. 14 **Litho.**
UX173 PC142 19c **multicolored** .40 *.90*
First day cancel, Brunswick, ME *(33,750 est.)* 1.00

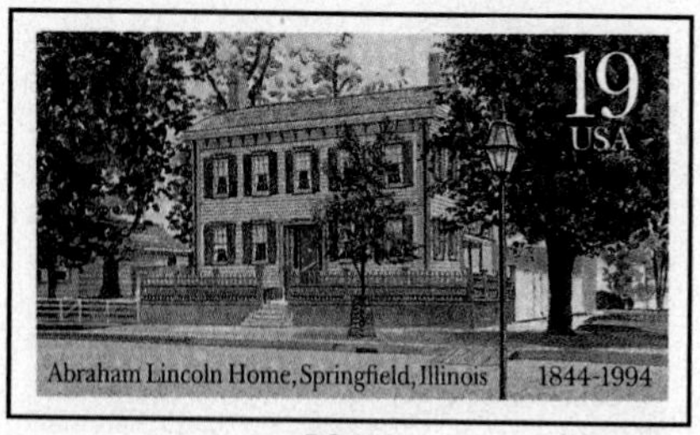

PC143

Designed by Michael Hagel.

1994, Feb. 12 **Litho.**
UX174 PC143 19c **multicolored** .40 *.90*
First day cancel, Springfield, IL *(26,164)* 1.00

PC144

Designed by Michael Hagel.

1994, Mar. 11 **Litho.**
UX175 PC144 19c **multicolored** .40 *.90*
First day cancel, Springfield, OH *(20,230)* 1.00

PC145

Designed by William Matthews.

1994, Aug. 11 **Litho.**
UX176 PC145 19c **multicolored** .40 *1.00*
First day cancel, Chinle, AZ *(19,826)* 1.00

St. Louis Union Station — PC146

Designed by Harry Devlin.

1994, Sept. 3 **Litho.**
UX177 PC146 19c **multicolored** .40 *1.00*
First day cancel, St. Louis, MO *(38,881)* 1.00

Legends of the West Type

Designed by Mark Hess.

1994, Oct. 18 **Litho.**
UX178 A2197 19c Home on the Range 1.10 *3.00*
UX179 A2197 19c Buffalo Bill 1.10 *3.00*
UX180 A2197 19c Jim Bridger 1.10 *3.00*
UX181 A2197 19c Annie Oakley 1.10 *3.00*
UX182 A2197 19c Native American Culture 1.10 *3.00*
UX183 A2197 19c Chief Joseph 1.10 *3.00*
UX184 A2197 19c Bill Pickett (revised) 1.10 *3.00*
UX185 A2197 19c Bat Masterson 1.10 *3.00*
UX186 A2197 19c John Fremont 1.10 *3.00*
UX187 A2197 19c Wyatt Earp 1.10 *3.00*
UX188 A2197 19c Nellie Cashman 1.10 *3.00*
UX189 A2197 19c Charles Goodnight 1.10 *3.00*
UX190 A2197 19c Geronimo 1.10 *3.00*
UX191 A2197 19c Kit Carson 1.10 *3.00*
UX192 A2197 19c Wild Bill Hickok 1.10 *3.00*
UX193 A2197 19c Western Wildlife 1.10 *3.00*
UX194 A2197 19c Jim Beckwourth 1.10 *3.00*
UX195 A2197 19c Bill Tilghman 1.10 *3.00*
UX196 A2197 19c Sacagawea 1.10 *3.00*
UX197 A2197 19c Overland Mail 1.10 *3.00*
Nos. UX178-UX197 (20) 22.00
First day cancel, #UX178-UX197, any card, Tucson, AZ, Lawton, OK or Laramie, WY *(10,000 USPS est.)* 1.50

Nos. UX178-UX197 sold in packages of 20 different for $7.95.

Red Barn — PC147

Designed by Wendell Minor.

1995, Jan. 3 **Litho.**
UX198 PC147 20c **multicolored** .40 *.60*
First day cancel, Williamsburg, PA 1.00

First day cancellation was applied to 54,102 of Nos. U632, UX198.

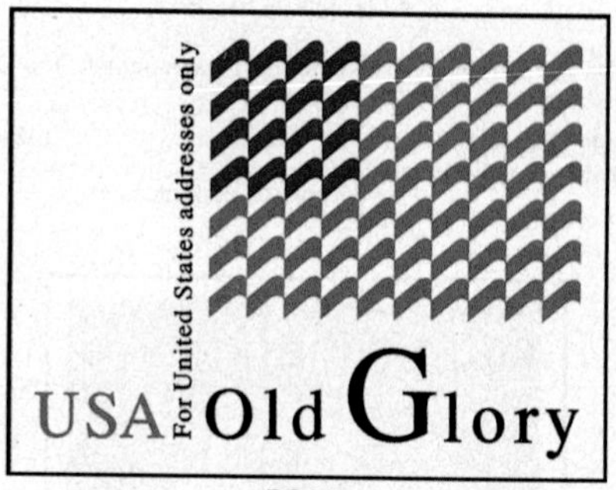

PC148

1995 **Litho.**
UX199 PC148 (20c) **black, blue & red** 3.25 2.50

No. UX199 was only available through the Philatelic Fulfillment Center after its announcement 1/12/95. Cards submitted for first day cancels received a 12/13/94 cancel, even though they were not available on that date.

Civil War Types

Designed by Mark Hess.

1995, June 29 **Litho.**
UX200 A2289 20c Monitor & Virginia 1.75 *3.00*
UX201 A2289 20c Robert E. Lee 1.75 *3.00*
UX202 A2289 20c Clara Barton 1.75 *3.00*
UX203 A2289 20c Ulysses S. Grant 1.75 *3.00*
UX204 A2289 20c Battle of Shiloh 1.75 *3.00*
UX205 A2289 20c Jefferson Davis 1.75 *3.00*
UX206 A2289 20c David Farragut 1.75 *3.00*
UX207 A2289 20c Frederick Douglass 1.75 *3.00*
UX208 A2289 20c Raphael Semmes 1.75 *3.00*
UX209 A2289 20c Abraham Lincoln 1.75 *3.00*
UX210 A2289 20c Harriet Tubman 1.75 *3.00*
UX211 A2289 20c Stand Watie 1.75 *3.00*
UX212 A2289 20c Joseph E. Johnston 1.75 *3.00*
UX213 A2289 20c Winfield Hancock 1.75 *3.00*
UX214 A2289 20c Mary Chesnut 1.75 *3.00*
UX215 A2289 20c Battle of Chancellorsville 1.75 *3.00*
UX216 A2289 20c William T. Sherman 1.75 *3.00*
UX217 A2289 20c Phoebe Pember 1.75 *3.00*
UX218 A2289 20c Stonewall Jackson 1.75 *3.00*
UX219 A2289 20c Battle of Gettysburg 1.75 *3.00*
Nos. UX200-UX219 (20) 35.00
First day cancel, any card, Gettysburg, PA 1.50
First day cancel, any card, any other city 1.50

Nos. UX200-UX219 sold in packages of 20 different for $7.95.

PC148a

For International Use

1995, Aug. 24 **Litho.**

UX219A PC148a 50c **multicolored** 1.25 *9.00*
First day cancel, St. Louis, MO *(6,008)* 1.25

PC149

Designed by Richard Sheaff.

1995, Sept. 3 **Litho.**

UX220 PC149 20c **multicolored** .40 *.75*
First day cancel, Hunt Valley, MD *(5,281)* 1.00

Comic Strip Types

Designed by Carl Herrman.

1995, Oct. 1 **Litho.**

UX221	A2313	20c	The Yellow Kid	2.50	*3.00*
UX222	A2313	20c	Katzenjammer Kids	2.50	*3.00*
UX223	A2313	20c	Little Nemo in Slumberland	2.50	*3.00*
UX224	A2313	20c	Bringing Up Father	2.50	*3.00*
UX225	A2313	20c	Krazy Kat	2.50	*3.00*
UX226	A2313	20c	Rube Goldberg's Inventions	2.50	*3.00*
UX227	A2313	20c	Toonerville Folks	2.50	*3.00*
UX228	A2313	20c	Gasoline Alley	2.50	*3.00*
UX229	A2313	20c	Barney Google	2.50	*3.00*
UX230	A2313	20c	Little Orphan Annie	2.50	*3.00*
UX231	A2313	20c	Popeye	2.50	*3.00*
UX232	A2313	20c	Blondie	2.50	*3.00*
UX233	A2313	20c	Dick Tracy	2.50	*3.00*
UX234	A2313	20c	Alley Oop	2.50	*3.00*
UX235	A2313	20c	Nancy	2.50	*3.00*
UX236	A2313	20c	Flash Gordon	2.50	*3.00*
UX237	A2313	20c	Li'l Abner	2.50	*3.00*
UX238	A2313	20c	Terry and the Pirates	2.50	*3.00*
UX239	A2313	20c	Prince Valiant	2.50	*3.00*
UX240	A2313	20c	Brenda Starr Reporter	2.50	*3.00*
			Nos. UX221-UX240 (20)	50.00	
			First day cancel, any card, Boca Raton, FL		1.50

Nos. UX221-UX240 sold in packages of 20 different for $7.95.

Winter Scene — PC150

1996, Feb. 23 **Litho.**

UX241 PC150 20c **multicolored** .40 .40
First day cancel, Watertown, NY *(11,764)* 1.00

Summer Olympics Type

Designed by Richard Waldrep.

1996, May 2 **Litho.**

Size: 150x108mm

UX242	A2368	20c	Men's cycling	2.75	*3.00*
UX243	A2368	20c	Women's diving	2.75	*3.00*
UX244	A2368	20c	Women's running	2.75	*3.00*
UX245	A2368	20c	Men's canoeing	2.75	*3.00*
a.			Tagging omitted	—	
UX246	A2368	20c	Decathlon (javelin)	2.75	*3.00*
a.			Inverted impression of entire address side, men's cycling picture on reverse	500.00	
UX247	A2368	20c	Women's soccer	2.75	*3.00*
UX248	A2368	20c	Men's shot put	2.75	*3.00*
UX249	A2368	20c	Women's sailboarding	2.75	*3.00*
UX250	A2368	20c	Women's gymnastics	2.75	*3.00*
UX251	A2368	20c	Freestyle wrestling	2.75	*3.00*
UX252	A2368	20c	Women's softball	2.75	*3.00*
UX253	A2368	20c	Women's swimming	2.75	*3.00*
UX254	A2368	20c	Men's sprints	2.75	*3.00*
UX255	A2368	20c	Men's rowing	2.75	*3.00*
UX256	A2368	20c	Beach volleyball	2.75	*3.00*
UX257	A2368	20c	Men's basketball	2.75	*3.00*
UX258	A2368	20c	Equestrian	2.75	*3.00*
UX259	A2368	20c	Men's gymnastics	2.75	*3.00*
UX260	A2368	20c	Men's swimming	2.75	*3.00*
UX261	A2368	20c	Men's hurdles	2.75	*3.00*
a.			Booklet of 20 postal cards, #UX242-UX261	55.00	
			First day cancel, any card, Washington, DC		1.50

First day cancels of Nos. UX242-UX261 were available as sets from the US Postal Service. Unused sets of Nos. UX242-UX261 were not available from the US Philatelic Fullfillment Center for several months after the "official" first day.

PC151

Designed by Harry Devlin.

1996, June 1 **Litho.**

UX262 PC151 20c **multicolored** .50 *.75*
First day cancel, Annapolis, MD *(8,793)* 1.00

PC152

Designed by Howard Koslow.

1996, Sept. 20 **Litho.**

UX263 PC152 20c **multicolored** .50 *.75*
First day cancel, Princeton, NJ *(11,621)* 1.00

Endangered Species Type

Designed by James Balog.

1996, Oct. 2 **Litho.**

UX264	A2403	20c	Florida panther	3.50	1.75
UX265	A2403	20c	Black-footed ferret	3.50	1.75
UX266	A2403	20c	American crocodile	3.50	1.75
UX267	A2403	20c	Piping plover	3.50	1.75
UX268	A2403	20c	Gila trout	3.50	1.75
UX269	A2403	20c	Florida manatee	3.50	1.75
UX270	A2403	20c	Schaus swallowtail butterfly	3.50	1.75
UX271	A2403	20c	Woodland caribou	3.50	1.75
UX272	A2403	20c	Thick-billed parrot	3.50	1.75
UX273	A2403	20c	San Francisco garter snake	3.50	1.75
UX274	A2403	20c	Ocelot	3.50	1.75
UX275	A2403	20c	Wyoming toad	3.50	1.75
UX276	A2403	20c	California condor	3.50	1.75
UX277	A2403	20c	Hawaiian monk seal	3.50	1.75
UX278	A2403	20c	Brown pelican	3.50	1.75
a.			Booklet of 15 cards, #UX264-UX278	55.00	
			First day cancel, #UX264-UX278, any card, San Diego, CA *(5,000)*		1.75

Nos. UX264-UX278 were issued bound three-to-a-page in a souvenir booklet that was sold for $11.95.

Love (Swans) Type

Designed by Supon Design.

1997, Feb. 4 **Litho.**

UX279 A2415 20c multicolored .80 1.10

Stamp Designs Depicted on Reverse of Card

Scott 2814	2.50	1.10
Scott 2815	2.50	1.10
Scott 3123	2.50	1.10
Scott 3124	2.50	1.10
Sheet of 4, #2814-2815, 3123-3124	10.00	
Scott 2202	7.50	1.10
Scott 2248	7.50	1.10
Scott 2440	7.50	1.10
Scott 2813	7.50	1.10
Sheet of 4, #2202, 2248, 2440, 2813	30.00	

No. UX279 was sold in sets of 3 sheets of 4 picture postal cards with 8 different designs for $6.95 (two sheets of #2814-2815, 3123-3124 and one sheet of #2202, 2248, 2440, 2813). The cards are separated by microperfs. The picture side of each card depicted a previously released Love stamp design without the inscriptions and value.

First day cancels were not available on Feb. 4. It was announced after Feb. 4 that collectors could purchase the cards and send them to the U.S.P.S. for First Day cancels.

PC153

Designed by Howard Koslow.

1997, May 7 **Litho.**

UX280 PC153 20c **multicolored** .50 *.75*
First day cancel, New York, NY *(9,576)* 1.00

Bugs Bunny Type

Designed by Warner Bros.

1997, May 22 **Litho.**

UX281 A2425 20c **multicolored** 1.25 *2.00*
First day cancel, Burbank, CA 1.75
a. Booklet of 10 cards 12.50

No. UX281a sold for $5.95.

First day cancellations applied to 378,142 of Nos. UX281 and 3138.

Golden Gate in Daylight — PC154

Golden Gate at Sunset — PC155

Designed by Carol Simowitz.

1997, June 2 **Litho.**

UX282 PC154 20c **multicolored,** *June 2* .40 *.80*
First day cancel, San Francisco, CA 1.25

For International Use

UX283 PC155 50c **multicolored,** *June 3* 1.10 5.00
First day cancel, San Francisco, CA 2.00

First day cancellation was applied to 21,189 of Nos. UX282-UX283.

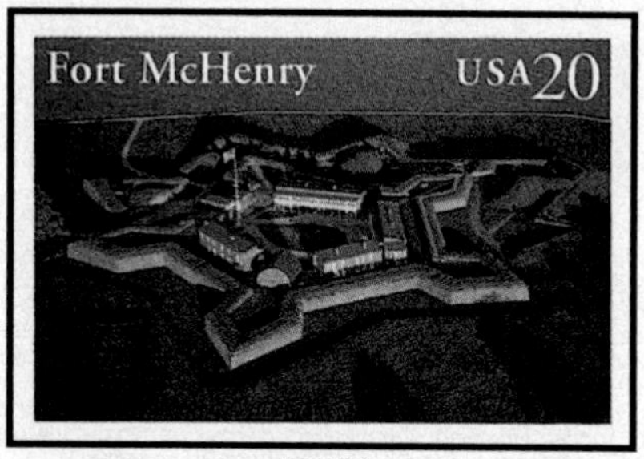

PC156

Designed by Richard Sheaff.

1997, Sept. 7 **Litho.**

UX284 PC156 20c **multicolored** .40 *.75*
First day cancel, Baltimore, MD *(9,611)* 1.00

Similar to Classic Movie Monsters with 20c Denomination

Designed by Derry Noyes.

1997, Sept. 30 **Litho.**

UX285 A2451 20c Phantom of the Opera 1.50 1.40
UX286 A2452 20c Dracula 1.50 1.40
UX287 A2453 20c Frankenstein's Monster 1.50 1.40
UX288 A2454 20c The Mummy 1.50 1.40
UX289 A2455 20c The Wolf Man 1.50 1.40
a. Booklet of 20 cards, 4 each #UX285-UX289 30.00
First day cancel, #UX285-UX289, any card, Universal City, CA 1.75

Nos. UX285-UX289 were issued bound in a booklet of 20 cards containing four of each card. Booklet was sold in package for $5.95.

PC157

Designed by Howard Paine.

1998, Apr. 20 **Litho.**

UX290 PC157 20c **multicolored** .50 *.75*
First day cancel, University, MS *(22,276)* 1.00

Similar to Sylvester & Tweety with 20c Denomination

Designed by Brenda Guttman.

1998, Apr. 27 **Litho.**

UX291 A2487 20c **multicolored** 1.40 *2.00*
First day cancel, New York, NY 1.75
a. Booklet of 10 cards 14.00

No. UX291a sold for $5.95.

First day cancellations applied to 231,839 of Nos. UX291, 3204 and 3205.

PC158

Designed by Phil Jordan.

1998, May 1 **Litho.**

UX292 PC158 20c **multicolored** .50 *.75*
First day cancel, Philadelphia, PA *(13,853)* 1.00

Similar to Tropical Birds with 20c Denomination and No Inscription

Designed by Phil Jordan.

1998, July 29 **Litho.**

UX293 A2503 20c Antillean euphonia 1.00 1.75
UX294 A2504 20c Green-throated carib 1.00 1.75
UX295 A2505 20c Crested honeycreeper 1.00 1.75
UX296 A2506 20c Cardinal honeyeater 1.00 1.75
a. Booklet of 20 cards, 5 ea #UX293-UX296 20.00
First day cancel, #UX293-UX296, any card, Ponce PR 1.75

Nos. UX293-UX296 were issued bound in a booklet of 20 cards containing five of each card. Illustration of the stamp without denomination is shown on the back of each card. Booklet was sold in packages for $6.95.

American Ballet Type

Designed by Derry Noyes.

1998, Sept. 16 **Litho.**

UX297 A2517 20c **multicolored** 1.25 *1.40*
a. Booklet of 10 cards 12.50
First day cancel, New York, NY 1.75

No. UX297a was sold for $5.95.

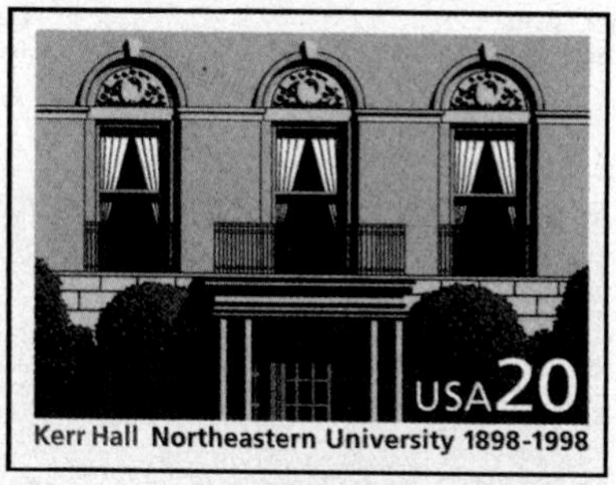

PC159

Designed by Richard Sheaff.

1998, Oct. 3 **Litho.**

UX298 PC159 20c **multicolored** .50 *.75*
First day cancel, Boston, MA *(14,812)* 1.00

PC160

Designed by Richard Sheaff.

1998, Oct. 17 **Litho.**

UX299 PC160 20c **multicolored** .50 *.75*
First day cancel, Waltham, MA *(14,137)* 1.00

Love Type

Designed by John Grossman, Holly Sudduth

1999, Jan. 28 **Litho.**

UX300 A2537 20c **multicolored** 1.25 1.50
First day cancel, Loveland, CO 1.00

No. UX300 was sold in packs containing 5 sheets of 4 cards for $6.95.

PC161

Designed by Carl Herrman.

1999, Feb. 5 **Litho.**

UX301 PC161 20c **multicolored** .50 .50
First day cancel, Madison, WI *(12,582)* 1.00

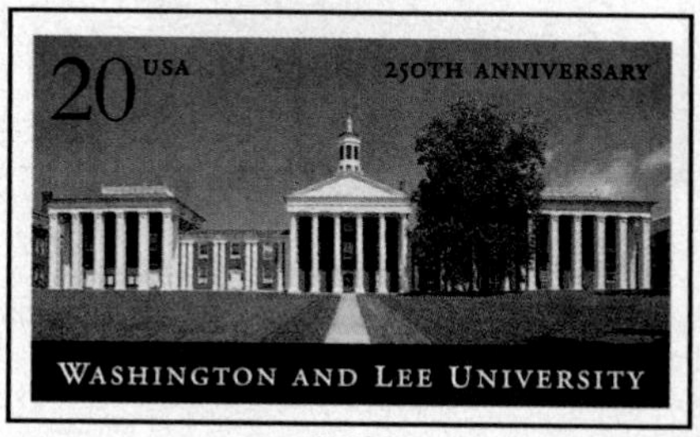

PC162

Designed by Derry Noyes.

1999, Feb. 11

UX302 PC162 20c **multicolored** .50 .50
First day cancel, Lexington, VA *(17,556)* 1.00

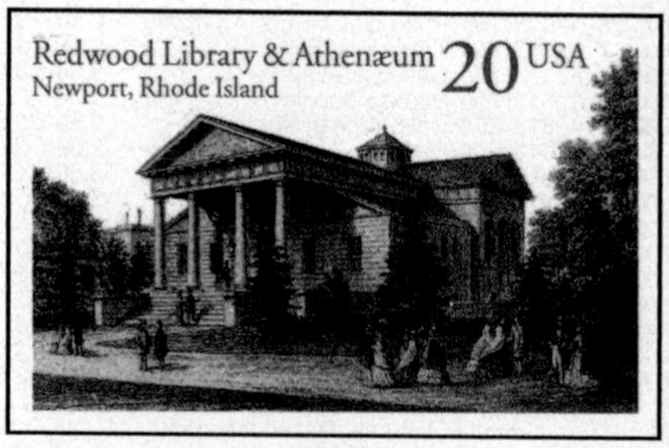

PC163

Designed by Richard Sheaff.

1999, Mar. 11

UX303 PC163 20c **red & black** .50 .50
First day cancel, Newport, RI *(13,649)* 1.00

Daffy Duck Type

Designed by Ed Wieczyk.

1999, Apr. 16 **Litho.**

UX304 A2554 20c **multicolored** 1.40 1.40
First day cancel, Los Angeles, CA 1.40
a. Booklet of 10 cards 14.00

No. UX304a sold for $6.95.

First day cancellation was applied to 177,988 of UX304, 3306 and 3307.

PC164

Designed by Richard Sheaff.

1999, May 14 **Litho.**

UX305 PC164 20c **multicolored** .50 *.50*
First day cancel, Mount Vernon, VA *(14,642)* 1.00

Block Island Lighthouse — PC165

Designed by Derry Noyes.

1999, July 24 **Litho.**

UX306 PC165 20c **multicolored** .40 *.50*
First day cancel, Block Island, RI *(12,694)* 1.25

Famous Trains Type

Designed by Howard Paine.

1999, Aug. 26 **Litho.**

UX307 A2583 20c Super Chief 1.50 1.50
UX308 A2582 20c Hiawatha 1.50 1.50
UX309 A2579 20c Daylight 1.50 1.50
UX310 A2580 20c Congressional 1.50 1.50
UX311 A2581 20c 20th Century Limited 1.50 1.50
a. Booklet of 20 cards, 4 ea #UX307-UX311 25.00
First day cancel, #UX307-UX311, any card, Cleveland, OH 1.75
First day cancel, #UX307-UX311, any card, any other city 1.75

Nos. UX307-UX311 were issued bound in a booklet of 20 cards containing four of each card. Booklet sold for $6.95.

PC166

Designed by Ethel Kessler.

2000, Feb. 28 **Litho.**

UX312 PC166 20c **multicolored** .40 *.50*
First day cancel, Salt Lake City, UT *(14,230)* 1.00

PC167

Designed by Richard Sheaff.

2000, Mar. 18 **Litho.**

UX313 PC167 20c **multicolored** .40 *.50*
First day cancel, Nashville, TN *(12,690)* 1.00

Road Runner & Wile E. Coyote Type

Designed by Ed Wleczyk, Warner Bros.

2000, Apr. 26 **Litho.**

UX314 A2622 20c **multicolored** 1.40 1.40
First day cancel, Phoenix, AZ 1.40
a. Booklet of 10 cards 14.00

No. UX314a sold for $6.95.

First day cancellation was applied to 154,903 of UX314 and 3391.

Adoption Type

Designed by Greg Berger.

2000, May 10 **Litho.**

UX315 A2628 20c **multicolored** 1.40 1.50
First day cancel, Beverly Hills, CA 1.40
a. Booklet of 10 cards 14.00

No. UX315a sold for $6.95. The design, without denominations, is shown on the back of the card.

First day cancellation was applied to 137,903 of UX315 and 3398.

PC168

Designed by Howard Paine.

2000, May 19 **Litho.**

UX316 PC168 20c **multicolored** .40 *.50*
First day cancel, Middlebury, VT *(13,586)* 1.00

Stars and Stripes Type

Designed by Richard Sheaff.

2000, June 14 **Litho.**

UX317 A2633 20c Sons of Liberty Flag, 1775 2.00 2.00
UX318 A2633 20c New England Flag, 1775 2.00 2.00
UX319 A2633 20c Forster Flag, 1775 2.00 2.00
UX320 A2633 20c Continental Colors, 1776 2.00 2.00
a. Sheet of 4 cards, #UX317-UX320 8.00
UX321 A2633 20c Francis Hopkinson Flag, 1777 2.00 2.00
UX322 A2633 20c Brandywine Flag, 1777 2.00 2.00
UX323 A2633 20c John Paul Jones Flag, 1779 2.00 2.00
UX324 A2633 20c Pierre L'Enfant Flag, 1783 2.00 2.00
a. Sheet of 4 cards, #UX321-UX324 8.00
UX325 A2633 20c Indian Peace Flag, 1803 2.00 2.00
UX326 A2633 20c Easton Flag, 1814 2.00 2.00
UX327 A2633 20c Star-Spangled Banner, 1814 2.00 2.00
UX328 A2633 20c Bennington Flag, c. 1820 2.00 2.00
a. Sheet of 4 cards, #UX325-UX328 8.00
UX329 A2633 20c Great Star Flag, 1837 2.00 2.00
UX330 A2633 20c 29-Star Flag, 1847 2.00 2.00
UX331 A2633 20c Fort Sumter Flag, 1861 2.00 2.00
UX332 A2633 20c Centennial Flag, 1876 2.00 2.00
a. Sheet of 4 cards, #UX329-UX332 8.00
UX333 A2633 20c 38-Star Flag, 1877 2.00 2.00
UX334 A2633 20c Peace Flag, 1891 2.00 2.00
UX335 A2633 20c 48-Star Flag, 1912 2.00 2.00
UX336 A2633 20c 50-Star Flag, 1960 2.00 2.00
a. Sheet of 4 cards, #UX333-UX336 8.00
First day cancel, any card, Baltimore, MD .90
Nos. UX317-UX336 (20) 40.00 40.00

Nos. UX320a, UX324a, UX328a, UX332a and UX336a were sold together in a package for $8.95. Microperforations are between individual cards on each sheet. Illustrations of the flags, without denominations, are shown on the back of the cards.

Legends of Baseball Type

Designed by Phil Jordan.

2000, July 6 **Litho.**

UX337 A2638 20c Jackie Robinson 1.50 1.50
UX338 A2638 20c Eddie Collins 1.50 1.50
UX339 A2638 20c Christy Mathewson 1.50 1.50
UX340 A2638 20c Ty Cobb 1.50 1.50
UX341 A2638 20c George Sisler 1.50 1.50
UX342 A2638 20c Rogers Hornsby 1.50 1.50
UX343 A2638 20c Mickey Cochrane 1.50 1.50
UX344 A2638 20c Babe Ruth 1.50 1.50
UX345 A2638 20c Walter Johnson 1.50 1.50
UX346 A2638 20c Roberto Clemente 1.50 1.50
UX347 A2638 20c Lefty Grove 1.50 1.50
UX348 A2638 20c Tris Speaker 1.50 1.50
UX349 A2638 20c Cy Young 1.50 1.50
UX350 A2638 20c Jimmie Foxx 1.50 1.50
UX351 A2638 20c Pie Traynor 1.50 1.50
UX352 A2638 20c Satchel Paige 1.50 1.50
UX353 A2638 20c Honus Wagner 1.50 1.50
UX354 A2638 20c Josh Gibson 1.50 1.50
UX355 A2638 20c Dizzy Dean 1.50 1.50
UX356 A2638 20c Lou Gehrig 1.50 1.50
a. Booklet of 20 cards, #UX337-UX356 30.00
First day cancel, any card, Atlanta, GA .90

No. UX356a sold for $8.95.

Christmas Deer Type of 1999

Designed by Tom Nikosey.

2000, Oct. 12 **Litho.** ***Rouletted on 2 sides***

UX357 A2600 20c **gold & blue** 1.25 1.25
UX358 A2600 20c **gold & red** 1.25 1.25
UX359 A2600 20c **gold & purple** 1.25 1.25
UX360 A2600 20c **gold & green** 1.25 1.25
a. Sheet of 4, #UX357-UX360 5.00
First day cancel, any card, Rudolph, WI 1.75

Nos. UX357-UX360 were sold in packs containing five No. UX360a for $8.95.

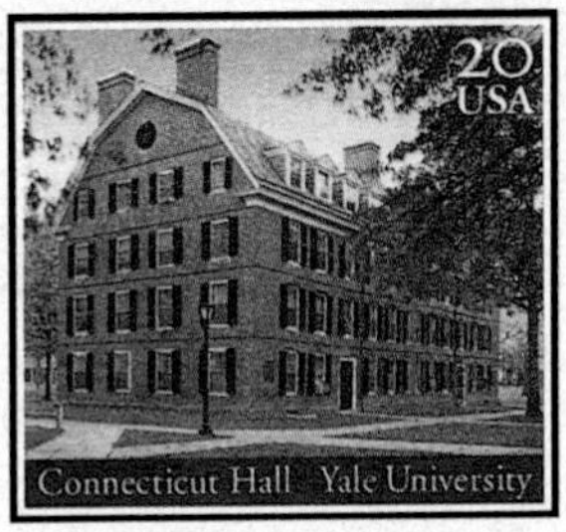

PC169

Designed by Derry Noyes.

2001, Mar. 30 **Litho.**

UX361 PC169 20c **multicolored** .40 .60
First day cancel, New Haven, CT 1.00

PC170

Designed by Ethel Kessler.

2001, Apr. 26 **Litho.**

UX362 PC170 20c **multicolored** .40 *.75*
First day cancel, Columbia, SC 1.00

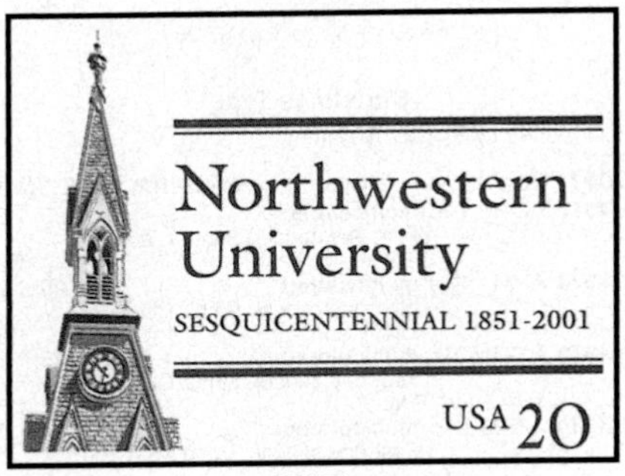

PC171

Designed by Howard Paine.

2001, Apr. 28 **Litho.**

UX363 PC171 20c **multicolored** .40 *.75*
First day cancel, Evanston, IL 1.00

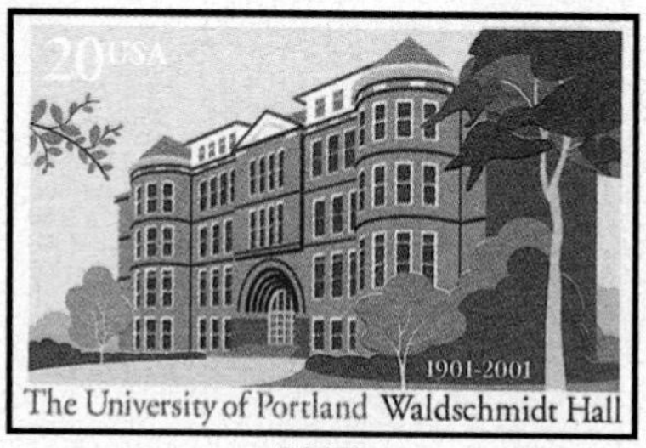

PC172

Designed by Richard Sheaff.

2001, May 1 **Litho.**
UX364 PC172 20c **multicolored** .40 *.65*
First day cancel, Portland, OR 1.00

Legendary Playing Fields Type with 21c Denomination

Designed by Phil Jordan.

2001, June 27 **Litho.**
UX365 A2712 21c Ebbets Field 2.00 2.00
UX366 A2713 21c Tiger Stadium 2.00 2.00
UX367 A2714 21c Crosley Field 2.00 2.00
UX368 A2715 21c Yankee Stadium 2.00 2.00
UX369 A2716 21c Polo Grounds 2.00 2.00
UX370 A2717 21c Forbes Field 2.00 2.00
UX371 A2718 21c Fenway Park 2.00 2.00
UX372 A2719 21c Comiskey Park 2.00 2.00
UX373 A2720 21c Shibe Park 2.00 2.00
UX374 A2721 21c Wrigley Field 2.00 2.00
a. Booklet of 10 cards, #UX365-UX374 22.50
First day cancel, any card, New York, NY, Boston, MA, Chicago, IL, or Detroit MI 1.00

No. UX374a sold for $6.95.

White Barn — PC173

Designed by Derry Noyes.

2001, Sept. 20 **Litho.**
UX375 PC173 21c **multicolored** .45 .45
First day cancel, Washington, DC 1.00

That's All Folks! Type

Designed by Ed Wleczyk, Warner Bros.

2001, Oct. 1 **Litho.**
UX376 A2736 21c **multicolored** 1.50 1.50
First day cancel, Beverly Hills, CA 1.50
a. Booklet of 10 cards 15.00

No. UX376a sold for $7.25.

Christmas Type

Designed by Richard Sheaff.

2001, Oct. 10 **Litho.** ***Rouletted on 2 Sides***
UX377 A2740 21c **multicolored** 1.25 1.25
First day cancel, Santa Claus, IN 1.25
UX378 A2741 21c **multicolored** 1.25 1.25
First day cancel, Santa Claus, IN 1.25
UX379 A2738 21c **multicolored** 1.25 1.25
First day cancel, Santa Claus, IN 1.25
UX380 A2739 21c **multicolored** 1.25 1.25
First day cancel, Santa Claus, IN 1.25
a. Sheet of 4, #UX377-UX380 5.00

Packages of 5 No. UX380a sold for $9.25.

Carlsbad Caverns National Park — PC174

Designed by Carl Herrman.

2002, June 7 **Litho.**
UX381 PC174 23c **multicolored** .50 .50
First day cancel, Carlsbad, NM 1.00
First day cancel, any other city 1.00

Teddy Bears Type

Designed by Margaret Bauer.

2002, Aug. 15 **Litho.** ***Rouletted on 2 Sides***
UX382 A2827 23c Ideal Bear, c. 1905 1.25 1.25
First day cancel, Atlantic City, NJ 1.25
UX383 A2826 23c Gund Bear, c. 1948 1.25 1.25
First day cancel, Atlantic City, NJ 1.25
UX384 A2824 23c Bruin Bear, c. 1907 1.25 1.25
First day cancel, Atlantic City, NJ 1.25
UX385 A2825 23c "Stick" Bear, 1920s 1.25 1.25
First day cancel, Atlantic City, NJ 1.25
a. Sheet of 4, #UX382-UX385 5.50

Packages of 5 No. UX385a sold for $9.25.

Christmas Snowmen Type

Designed by Derry Noyes.

2002, Oct. 28 **Litho.** ***Rouletted on 2 Sides***
Design Size: 28x38mm
UX386 A2844 23c **multicolored** 1.25 1.25
First day cancel, Houghton, MI 1.00
UX387 A2845 23c **multicolored** 1.25 1.25
First day cancel, Houghton, MI 1.00
UX388 A2846 23c **multicolored** 1.25 1.25
First day cancel, Houghton, MI 1.00
UX389 A2847 23c **multicolored** 1.25 1.25
First day cancel, Houghton, MI 1.00
a. Sheet of 4, #UX386-UX389 5.00

Packages of 5 #UX389a sold for $9.75.

Old Glory Type

Designed by Richard Sheaff.

2003, Apr. 3 **Litho.** ***Rouletted on 1 Side***
UX390 A2883 23c **multicolored** 1.25 1.25
First day cancel, New York, NY 1.00
UX391 A2884 23c **multicolored** 1.25 1.25
First day cancel, New York, NY 1.00
UX392 A2885 23c **multicolored** 1.25 1.25
First day cancel, New York, NY 1.00
UX393 A2886 23c **multicolored** 1.25 1.25
First day cancel, New York, NY 1.00
UX394 A2887 23c **multicolored** 1.25 1.25
First day cancel, New York, NY 1.00
a. Booklet of 20 cards, 4 each #UX390-UX394 25.00

No. UX394a sold for $9.75.

Southeastern Lighthouses Type

Designed by Howard E. Paine.

2003, June 13 **Litho.** ***Rouletted on 1 Side***
UX395 A2893 23c **multicolored** 1.10 1.10
First day cancel, Tybee Island, GA 1.00
UX396 A2894 23c **multicolored** 1.10 1.10
First day cancel, Tybee Island, GA 1.00
UX397 A2895 23c **multicolored** 1.10 1.10
First day cancel, Tybee Island, GA 1.00
UX398 A2896 23c **multicolored** 1.10 1.10
First day cancel, Tybee Island, GA 1.00
UX399 A2897 23c **multicolored** 1.10 1.10
First day cancel, Tybee Island, GA 1.00
a. Booklet of 20 cards, 4 each #UX395-UX399 22.50

No. UX399a sold for $9.75.

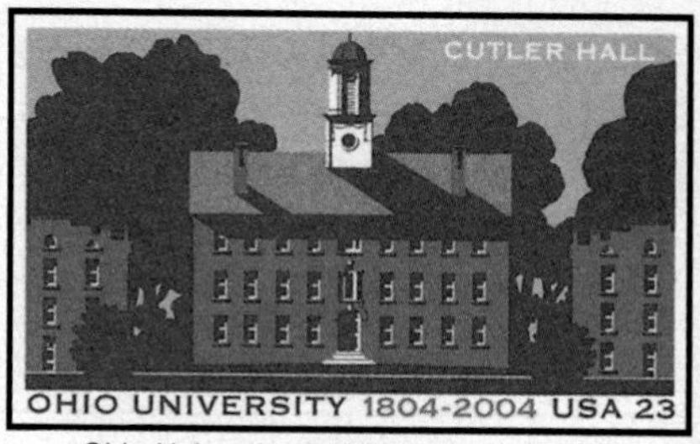

Ohio University, 200th Anniv. — PC175

Designed by Tom Engemann.

2003, Oct. 10 **Litho.**
UX400 PC175 23c **multicolored** .50 .50
First day cancel, Athens, OH 1.00

Christmas Music Makers Type

Designed by Ethel Kessler.

2003, Oct. 23 **Litho.** ***Rouletted on 2 Sides***
UX401 A2917 23c **multicolored** 1.10 1.10
First day cancel, New York, NY 1.00
UX402 A2918 23c **multicolored** 1.10 1.10
First day cancel, New York, NY 1.00
UX403 A2919 23c **multicolored** 1.10 1.10
First day cancel, New York, NY 1.00
UX404 A2920 23c **multicolored** 1.10 1.10
First day cancel, New York, NY 1.00
a. Sheet of 4, #UX401-UX404 4.50

Packages of 5 #UX404a sold for $9.75.

Columbia University, 250th Anniv. — PC176

Designed by Tom Engeman.

2004, Mar. 25 **Litho.**
UX405 PC176 23c **multicolored** .50 .50
First day cancel, New York, NY 1.00

Harriton House, Bryn Mawr, PA, Bicent. PC177

Designed by Carl T. Herrman.

2004, June 10 **Litho.**
UX406 PC177 23c **multicolored** .50 .50
First day cancel, Bryn Mawr, PA 1.00

Disney Type of 2004

Designed by David Pacheco.

2004, June 23 **Litho.**
UX407 A2950 23c **multicolored** 1.25 1.25
First day cancel, Anaheim, CA 1.00
UX408 A2951 23c **multicolored** 1.25 1.25
First day cancel, Anaheim, CA 1.00
UX409 A2949 23c **multicolored** 1.25 1.25
First day cancel, Anaheim, CA 1.00
UX410 A2952 23c **multicolored** 1.25 1.25
First day cancel, Anaheim, CA 1.00
a. Booklet of 20 cards, 5 each #UX407-UX410 25.00

No. UX410a sold for $9.75.

Art of the American Indian Type of 2003

Designed by Richard Sheaff.

2004, Aug. 21 **Litho.** ***Rouletted on 1 Side***

UX411 A2957 23c Mimbres bowl 1.25 1.25
First day cancel, Santa Fe, NM 1.00
UX412 A2957 23c Kutenai parfleche 1.25 1.25
First day cancel, Santa Fe, NM 1.00
UX413 A2957 23c Tlingit sculptures 1.25 1.25
First day cancel, Santa Fe, NM 1.00
UX414 A2957 23c Ho-Chunk bag 1.25 1.25
First day cancel, Santa Fe, NM 1.00
UX415 A2957 23c Seminole doll 1.25 1.25
First day cancel, Santa Fe, NM 1.00
UX416 A2957 23c Mississippian effigy 1.25 1.25
First day cancel, Santa Fe, NM 1.00
UX417 A2957 23c Acoma pot 1.25 1.25
First day cancel, Santa Fe, NM 1.00
UX418 A2957 23c Navajo weaving 1.25 1.25
First day cancel, Santa Fe, NM 1.00
UX419 A2957 23c Seneca carving 1.25 1.25
First day cancel, Santa Fe, NM 1.00
UX420 A2957 23c Luiseño basket 1.25 1.25
First day cancel, Santa Fe, NM 1.00
a. Booklet of 20 cards, 2 each #UX411-UX420 25.00

No. UX420a sold for $9.75.

Cloudscapes Type

Designed by Howard E. Paine.

2004, Oct. 4 **Litho.** ***Rouletted at Left***

UX421 A2960 23c Cirrus radiatus 1.25 1.25
First day cancel, Milton, MA 1.00
UX422 A2960 23c Cirrostratus fibratus 1.25 1.25
First day cancel, Milton, MA 1.00
UX423 A2960 23c Cirrocumulus undulatus 1.25 1.25
First day cancel, Milton, MA 1.00
UX424 A2960 23c Cumulonimbus mammatus 1.25 1.25
First day cancel, Milton, MA 1.00
UX425 A2960 23c Cumulonimbus incus 1.25 1.25
First day cancel, Milton, MA 1.00
UX426 A2960 23c Altocumulus stratiformis 1.25 1.25
First day cancel, Milton, MA 1.00
UX427 A2960 23c Altostratus translucidus 1.25 1.25
First day cancel, Milton, MA 1.00
UX428 A2960 23c Altocumulus undulatus 1.25 1.25
First day cancel, Milton, MA 1.00
UX429 A2960 23c Altocumulus castellanus 1.25 1.25
First day cancel, Milton, MA 1.00
UX430 A2960 23c Altocumulus lenticularis 1.25 1.25
First day cancel, Milton, MA 1.00
UX431 A2960 23c Stratocumulus undulatus 1.25 1.25
First day cancel, Milton, MA 1.00
UX432 A2960 23c Stratus opacus 1.25 1.25
First day cancel, Milton, MA 1.00
UX433 A2960 23c Cumulus humilis 1.25 1.25
First day cancel, Milton, MA 1.00
UX434 A2960 23c Cumulus congestus 1.25 1.25
First day cancel, Milton, MA 1.00
UX435 A2960 23c Cumulonimbus with tornado 1.25 1.25
First day cancel, Milton, MA 1.00
a. Booklet of 20, #UX421-UX422, UX425, UX427, UX429, UX431-UX435, 2 each #UX423-UX424, UX426, UX428, UX430 25.00

No. UX435a sold for $9.75.

Disney Type of 2005

Designed by David Pacheco.

2005, June 30 **Litho.**

UX436 A2989 23c **multicolored** 1.10 1.10
First day cancel, Anaheim, CA 1.00
UX437 A2990 23c **multicolored** 1.10 1.10
First day cancel, Anaheim, CA 1.00
UX438 A2991 23c **multicolored** 1.10 1.10
First day cancel, Anaheim, CA 1.00
UX439 A2992 23c **multicolored** 1.10 1.10
First day cancel, Anaheim, CA 1.00
a. Booklet of 20 cards, 5 each #UX436-UX439 22.50

No. UX439a sold for $9.75.

Sporty Cars Type of 2005

Designed by Art M. Fitzpatrick.

2005, Aug. 20 **Litho.** ***Rouletted at Left***

UX440 A3012 23c 1955 Ford Thunderbird 1.00 1.00
First day cancel, Detroit, MI 1.75
UX441 A3011 23c 1952 Nash Healey 1.00 1.00
First day cancel, Detroit, MI 1.75
UX442 A3010 23c 1953 Chevrolet Corvette 1.00 1.00
First day cancel, Detroit, MI 1.75
UX443 A3008 23c 1953 Studebaker Starliner 1.00 1.00
First day cancel, Detroit, MI 1.75
UX444 A3009 23c 1954 Kaiser Darrin 1.00 1.00
First day cancel, Detroit, MI 1.75
a. Booklet of 20 cards, 4 each #UX440-UX444 20.00

No. UX444a sold for $9.75.

Let's Dance Type

Designed by Ethel Kessler.

2005, Sept. 17 **Litho.** ***Rouletted at Left***

UX445 A3018 23c Cha cha cha 1.00 1.00
First day cancel, New York, NY 1.75
First day cancel, Miami, FL 1.75
UX446 A3019 23c Mambo 1.00 1.00
First day cancel, New York, NY 1.75
First day cancel, Miami, FL 1.75
UX447 A3017 23c Salsa 1.00 1.00
First day cancel, New York, NY 1.75
First day cancel, Miami, FL 1.75
UX448 A3016 23c Merengue 1.00 1.00
First day cancel, New York, NY 1.75
First day cancel, Miami, FL 1.75
a. Booklet of 20, 5 each #UX445-UX448 20.00

No. UX448a sold for $9.75.

Zebulon Pike Expedition at Pikes Peak, Bicent. PC178

Designed by Carl Herrman.

2006, Jan. 9 **Litho.**

UX449 PC178 24c **multicolored** .55 .55
First day cancel, Washington, DC 1.75
First day cancel, any other city 1.75

Disney Type of 2006

Designed by David Pacheco.

2006, Apr. 21 **Litho.** ***Rouletted at Left***

UX450 A3066 24c **multicolored** 1.00 1.00
First day cancel, Orlando, FL 1.75
UX451 A3067 24c **multicolored** 1.00 1.00
First day cancel, Orlando, FL 1.75
UX452 A3069 24c **multicolored** 1.00 1.00
First day cancel, Orlando, FL 1.75
UX453 A3068 24c **multicolored** 1.00 1.00
First day cancel, Orlando, FL 1.75
a. Booklet of 20, 5 each #UX450-UX4538 20.00

No. UX453a sold for $9.75.

Baseball Sluggers Type of 2006

Designed by Phil Jordan.

2006, July 15 **Litho.** ***Rouletted at Left***

UX454 A3121 24c Mickey Mantle 1.25 1.25
First day cancel, Bronx, NY 1.75
UX455 A3118 24c Roy Campanella 1.25 1.25
First day cancel, Bronx, NY 1.75
UX456 A3119 24c Hank Greenberg 1.25 1.25
First day cancel, Bronx, NY 1.75
UX457 A3120 24c Mel Ott 1.25 1.25
First day cancel, Bronx, NY 1.75
a. Booklet of 20 cards, 5 each #UX454-UX457 25.00

No. UX457a sold for $9.95.

DC Comics Superheroes Type of 2006

Designed by Carl T. Herrman.

2006, July 20 **Litho.** ***Rouletted at Left***

UX458 A3122 24c Superman cover 1.50 1.50
First day cancel, San Diego, CA 1.75
UX459 A3122 24c Superman 1.50 1.50
First day cancel, San Diego, CA 1.75
UX460 A3122 24c Batman cover 1.50 1.50
First day cancel, San Diego, CA 1.75
UX461 A3122 24c Batman 1.50 1.50
First day cancel, San Diego, CA 1.75
UX462 A3122 24c Wonder Woman cover 1.50 1.50
First day cancel, San Diego, CA 1.75
UX463 A3122 24c Wonder Woman 1.50 1.50
First day cancel, San Diego, CA 1.75
UX464 A3122 24c Green Lantern cover 1.50 1.50
First day cancel, San Diego, CA 1.75
UX465 A3122 24c Green Lantern 1.50 1.50
First day cancel, San Diego, CA 1.75
UX466 A3122 24c Green Arrow cover 1.50 1.50
First day cancel, San Diego, CA 1.75
UX467 A3122 24c Green Arrow 1.50 1.50
First day cancel, San Diego, CA 1.75
UX468 A3122 24c The Flash cover 1.50 1.50
First day cancel, San Diego, CA 1.75
UX469 A3122 24c The Flash 1.50 1.50
First day cancel, San Diego, CA 1.75
UX470 A3122 24c Plastic Man cover 1.50 1.50
First day cancel, San Diego, CA 1.75
UX471 A3122 24c Plastic Man 1.50 1.50
First day cancel, San Diego, CA 1.75
UX472 A3122 24c Aquaman cover 1.50 1.50
First day cancel, San Diego, CA 1.75
UX473 A3122 24c Aquaman 1.50 1.50
First day cancel, San Diego, CA 1.75
UX474 A3122 24c Supergirl cover 1.50 1.50
First day cancel, San Diego, CA 1.75
UX475 A3122 24c Supergirl 1.50 1.50
First day cancel, San Diego, CA 1.75
UX476 A3122 24c Hawkman cover 1.50 1.50
First day cancel, San Diego, CA 1.75
UX477 A3122 24c Hawkman 1.50 1.50
First day cancel, San Diego, CA 1.75
a. Booklet of 20 cards, #UX458-UX477 30.00

No. UX477a sold for $9.95.

Southern Florida Wetland Type of 2006

Designed by Ethel Kessler.

2006, Oct. 4 **Litho.** ***Rouletted on 1 Side***

UX478 A3137 39c Snail kite 3.50 3.50
First day cancel, Naples, FL 2.00
UX479 A3137 39c Cape Sable seaside sparrow 3.50 3.50
First day cancel, Naples, FL 2.00
a. Sheet of 2, #UX478-UX479 7.00
UX480 A3137 39c Wood storks 3.50 3.50
First day cancel, Naples, FL 2.00
UX481 A3137 39c Florida panther 3.50 3.50
First day cancel, Naples, FL 2.00
a. Sheet of 2, #UX480-UX481 7.00
UX482 A3137 39c Bald eagle 3.50 3.50
First day cancel, Naples, FL 2.00
UX483 A3137 39c White ibis 3.50 3.50
First day cancel, Naples, FL 2.00
a. Sheet of 2, #UX482-UX483 7.00
UX484 A3137 39c American crocodile 3.50 3.50
First day cancel, Naples, FL 2.00
UX485 A3137 39c Everglades mink 3.50 3.50
First day cancel, Naples, FL 2.00
a. Sheet of 2, #UX484-UX485 7.00
UX486 A3137 39c Roseate spoonbills 3.50 3.50
First day cancel, Naples, FL 2.00
UX487 A3137 39c American alligator 3.50 3.50
First day cancel, Naples, FL 2.00
a. Sheet of 2, #UX486-UX487 7.00
Nos. UX478-UX487 (10) 35.00 35.00

Packet of 10 cards sold for $7.95.

Pineapple — PC179

Designed by Ethel Kessler.

2007, May 12 **Litho.**

UX488 PC179 26c **multicolored** .60 .60
First day cancel, Washington, DC 1.75

Star Wars Type of 2007

Designed by Terrence McCaffrey and William J. Gicker, Jr..

2007, May 27 **Litho.** ***Rouletted at Left***

UX489 A3153 26c Darth Vader 1.75 1.75
First day cancel, Los Angeles, CA 3.00
UX490 A3153 26c Luke Skywalker 1.75 1.75
First day cancel, Los Angeles, CA 3.00
UX491 A3153 26c C-3PO 1.75 1.75
First day cancel, Los Angeles, CA 3.00
UX492 A3153 26c Queen Padmé Amidala 1.75 1.75
First day cancel, Los Angeles, CA 3.00
UX493 A3153 26c Millennium Falcon 1.75 1.75

First day cancel, Los Angeles, CA — 3.00
UX494 A3153 26c Emperor Palpatine 1.75 1.75
First day cancel, Los Angeles, CA — 3.00
UX495 A3153 26c Anakin Skywalker and Obi-Wan Kenobi 1.75 1.75
First day cancel, Los Angeles, CA — 3.00
UX496 A3153 26c Obi-Wan Kenobi 1.75 1.75
First day cancel, Los Angeles, CA — 3.00
UX497 A3153 26c Boba Fett 1.75 1.75
First day cancel, Los Angeles, CA — 3.00
UX498 A3153 26c Darth Maul 1.75 1.75
First day cancel, Los Angeles, CA — 3.00
UX499 A3153 26c Yoda 1.75 1.75
First day cancel, Los Angeles, CA — 3.00
UX500 A3153 26c Princess Leia and R2-D2 1.75 1.75
First day cancel, Los Angeles, CA — 3.00
UX501 A3153 26c Chewbacca and Han Solo 1.75 1.75
First day cancel, Los Angeles, CA — 3.00
UX502 A3153 26c X-wing Starfighter 1.75 1.75
First day cancel, Los Angeles, CA — 3.00
UX503 A3153 26c Stormtroopers 1.75 1.75
First day cancel, Los Angeles, CA — 3.00
a. Booklet of 15, #UX489-UX503 26.00

No. UX503a sold for $12.95.

Pacific Lighthouses Type of 2007

Designed by Howard E. Paine.

2007, June 21 Litho. *Rouletted at Left*

UX504 A3158 26c Grays Harbor Lighthouse 1.25 1.25
First day cancel, Westport, WA — 2.50
UX505 A3157 26c Five Finger Lighthouse 1.25 1.25
First day cancel, Westport, WA — 2.50
UX506 A3159 26c Umpqua River Lighthouse 1.25 1.25
First day cancel, Westport, WA — 2.50
UX507 A3156 26c Diamond Head Lighthouse 1.25 1.25
First day cancel, Westport, WA — 2.50
UX508 A3160 26c St. George Reef Lighthouse 1.25 1.25
First day cancel, Westport, WA — 2.50
a. Booklet of 20, 4 each #UX504-UX508 26.00

No. UX503a sold for $12.95.

Marvel Comics Superheroes Type of 2006

Designed by Carl T. Herrman.

2007, July 26 Litho. *Rouletted at Left*

UX509 A3168 26c Spider-Man 1.25 1.25
First day cancel, San Diego, CA — 1.75
UX510 A3168 26c The Hulk 1.25 1.25
First day cancel, San Diego, CA — 1.75
UX511 A3168 26c Sub-Mariner 1.25 1.25
First day cancel, San Diego, CA — 1.75
UX512 A3168 26c The Thing 1.25 1.25
First day cancel, San Diego, CA — 1.75
UX513 A3168 26c Captain America 1.25 1.25
First day cancel, San Diego, CA — 1.75
UX514 A3168 26c Silver Surfer 1.25 1.25
First day cancel, San Diego, CA — 1.75
UX515 A3168 26c Spider-Woman 1.25 1.25
First day cancel, San Diego, CA — 1.75
UX516 A3168 26c Iron Man 1.25 1.25
First day cancel, San Diego, CA — 1.75
UX517 A3168 26c Elektra 1.25 1.25
First day cancel, San Diego, CA — 1.75
UX518 A3168 26c Wolverine 1.25 1.25
First day cancel, San Diego, CA — 1.75
UX519 A3168 26c Spider-Man cover 1.25 1.25
First day cancel, San Diego, CA — 1.75
UX520 A3168 26c Incredible Hulk cover 1.25 1.25
First day cancel, San Diego, CA — 1.75
UX521 A3168 26c Sub-Mariner cover 1.25 1.25
First day cancel, San Diego, CA — 1.75
UX522 A3168 26c Fantastic Four cover 1.25 1.25
First day cancel, San Diego, CA — 1.75
UX523 A3168 26c Captain America cover 1.25 1.25
First day cancel, San Diego, CA — 1.75
UX524 A3168 26c Silver Surfer cover 1.25 1.25
First day cancel, San Diego, CA — 1.75
UX525 A3168 26c Spider-Woman cover 1.25 1.25
First day cancel, San Diego, CA — 1.75
UX526 A3168 26c Iron Man cover 1.25 1.25
First day cancel, San Diego, CA — 1.75
UX527 A3168 26c Elektra cover 1.25 1.25
First day cancel, San Diego, CA — 1.75
UX528 A3168 26c X-Men cover 1.25 1.25
First day cancel, San Diego, CA — 1.75
a. Booklet of 20 cards, #UX509-UX528 26.00

No. UX528a sold for $12.95.

Disney Characters Type of 2007

Designed by David Pacheco.

2007, Aug. 16 Litho. *Rouletted at Left*

UX529 A3185 26c Mickey Mouse 1.25 1.25
First day cancel, Orlando, FL — 2.50
UX530 A3186 26c Peter Pan and Tinker Bell 1.25 1.25
First day cancel, Orlando, FL — 2.50
UX531 A3187 26c Dumbo and Timothy Mouse 1.25 1.25
First day cancel, Orlando, FL — 2.50
UX532 A3188 26c Aladdin and Genie 1.25 1.25
First day cancel, Orlando, FL — 2.50
a. Booklet of 20, 5 each #UX529-UX532 26.00

No. UX503a sold for $12.95.

Mount St. Mary's University, Bicent. PC180

Designed by Richard Sheaff.

2008, Apr. 26 Litho.

UX533 PC180 27c **multicolored** .60 .60
First day cancel, Emmitsburg, MD — 1.75

Corinthian Column From Capitol Building — PC181

Designed by Gerald Gallo.

2008, May 12 Litho.

UX534 PC181 27c **multicolored** .60 .60
First day cancel, Washington, DC — 1.75

PAID REPLY POSTAL CARDS

These are sold to the public as two unsevered cards, one for message and one for reply. These are listed first as unsevered cards and then as severed cards. Values are for:

Unused cards (both unsevered and severed) without printed or written address or message.

Unsevered cards sell for a premium if never folded.

Used unsevered cards, Message Card with Post Office cancellation and Reply Card uncanceled (from 1968 value is for a single used severed card); and used severed cards with cancellation when current.

Used values for International Paid Reply Cards are for proper usage. Those domestically used or with postage added sell for less than the unused value.

"Preprinted," unused cards (both unsevered and severed) with printed or written address or message. Used value applies after 1952.

First day cancel values are for cards without cachets.

PM1

Head of Grant, card framed.
PR1 inscribed "REPLY CARD."

1892, Oct. 25 Size: 140x89mm

UY1 PM1+PR1 1c +1c **black**, *buff*, unsevered 40.00 9.00
Preprinted 15.00
a. Message card printed on both sides, reply card blank 250.00 *750.00*
b. Message card blank, reply card printed on both sides 300.00
c. Cards joined at bottom 200.00 100.00
Preprinted 100.00
m. PM1 Message card detached 6.00 1.75
Preprinted 3.00
r. PR1 Reply card detached 6.00 1.75
Preprinted 3.00

For other postal cards of types PM1 and PR1 see No. UY3.

Liberty — PM2

PR2 inscribed "REPLY CARD."

1893, Mar. 1 For International Use

UY2 PM2+PR2 2c +2c **blue**, *grayish white*, unsevered 22.50 20.00
Preprinted 12.50
a. 2c+2c **dark blue**, *grayish white*, unsevered 22.50 20.00
Preprinted 12.50
b. Message card printed on both sides, reply card blank 500.00
c. Message card blank, reply card printed on both sides —
d. Message card normal, reply card blank 300.00
m. PM2 Message card detached 5.00 *6.00*
Preprinted 2.50
r. PR2 Reply card detached 5.00 *6.00*
Preprinted 2.50

For other postal cards of types PM2 and PR2 see No. UY11.

Design same as PM1 and PR1, without frame around card

1898, Sept.

Size: 140x82mm

UY3 PM1+PR1 1c +1c **black**, *buff*, unsevered 67.50 12.50
Preprinted 12.50
a. Message card normal, reply card blank 400.00
b. Message card printed on both sides, reply card blank 450.00
c. Message card blank, reply card printed on both sides 400.00
d. Message card without "Detach annexed card/for answer" 250.00 150.00
Preprinted —
e. Message card blank, reply card normal 250.00
f. Message card normal, reply card double impression, preprinted *825.00*
m. PM1 Message card detached 12.50 2.50
Preprinted 6.00
r. PR1 Reply card detached 12.50 2.50
Preprinted 6.00

PR3

PM3 pictures Sherman.

1904, Mar, 31

UY4	PM3+PR3 1c +1c **black,** *buff,* unsevered	57.50	6.50
	Preprinted	10.00	
a.	Message card normal, reply card blank	275.00	
b.	Message card printed on both sides, reply card blank	*950.00*	
c.	Message card blank, reply card normal	275.00	
d.	Message card blank, reply card printed on both sides	—	175.00
	Preprinted	200.00	
m.	PM3 Message card detached	9.00	1.10
	Preprinted	4.00	
r.	PR3 Reply card detached	9.00	1.10
	Preprinted	4.00	

PM4

PR4 pictures Martha Washington.

Double frame line around instructions

1910, Sept. 14

UY5	PM4+PR4 1c +1c **blue,** *bluish,* unsevered	175.00	25.00
	Preprinted	40.00	
a.	Message card normal, reply card blank	325.00	*750.00*
m.	PM4 Message card detached	15.00	3.75
	Preprinted	9.00	
r.	PR4 Reply card detached	15.00	3.75
	Preprinted	9.00	

1911, Oct. 27

UY6	PM4+PR4 1c +1c **green,** *cream,* unsevered	175.00	25.00
	Preprinted	60.00	
a.	Message card normal, reply card blank	—	
m.	PM4 Message card detached	22.50	6.50
	Preprinted	12.50	
r.	PR4 Reply card detached	22.50	6.50
	Preprinted	12.50	

Single frame line around instructions

1915, Sept. 18

UY7	PM4+PR4 1c +1c **green,** *cream,* unsevered	1.25	.50
	Preprinted	.60	
a.	1c+1c **dark green,** *buff,* unsevered	1.25	.50
	Preprinted	.60	
b.	Message card normal, reply card blank	—	
m.	PM4 Message card detached	.30	.20
	Preprinted	.20	
r.	PR4 Reply card detached	.30	.20
	Preprinted	.20	
s.	As "a," missing Reply indicia	*2,000.*	

See No. UY13.

PR5

PM5 pictures George Washington.

1918, Aug. 2

UY8	PM5+PR5 2c +2c **red,** *buff,* unsevered	90.00	40.00
	Preprinted	30.00	
m.	PM5 Message card detached	20.00	7.50
	Preprinted	10.00	
r.	PR5 Reply card detached	20.00	7.50
	Preprinted	10.00	

Same Surcharged

Fifteen canceling machine types

1920, Apr.

UY9	PM5+PR5 1c on 2c+1c on 2c **red,** *buff,* unsevered	22.50	11.00
	Preprinted	10.00	
a.	Message card normal, reply card no surcharge	85.00	—
	Preprinted	—	
b.	Message card normal, reply card double surcharge	85.00	—
	Preprinted	—	
c.	Message card double surcharge, reply card normal	85.00	—
	Preprinted	—	
d.	Message card no surcharge, reply card normal	85.00	—
	Preprinted	—	
e.	Message card no surcharge, reply card double surcharge	85.00	
m.	PM5 Message card detached	5.00	4.00
	Preprinted	3.00	
r.	PR5 Reply card detached	5.00	4.00
	Preprinted	3.00	

One press printed type

UY10	PM5+PR5 1c on 2c+1c on 2c **red,** *buff,* unsevered	375.00	200.00
	Preprinted	150.00	
a.	Message card no surcharge, reply card normal	*1,100.*	—
	Preprinted	—	
b.	Surcharge double on message card, reply card normal	*950.00*	
m.	PM5 Message card detached	75.00	45.00
	Preprinted	40.00	
r.	PR5 Reply card detached	75.00	45.00
	Preprinted	40.00	

Designs same as PM2 and PR2

1924, Mar. 18 **For International Use**

Size: 139x89mm

UY11	PM2+PR2 2c +2c **red,** *cream,* unsevered	2.50	*50.00*
	Preprinted	1.50	
m.	PM2 Message card detached	.50	*14.00*
	Preprinted	.40	
r.	PR2 Reply card detached	.50	*20.00*
	Preprinted	.40	

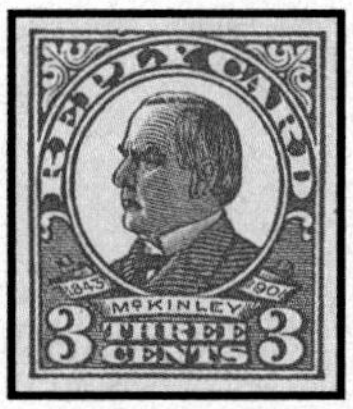

PM6

PR6 inscribed "REPLY CARD."

For International Use

1926, Feb. 1

UY12	PM6+PR6 3c +3c **red,** *buff,* unsevered	12.00	*27.50*
	Preprinted	6.00	
a.	3c +3c **red,** *yellow,* unsevered	12.00	*27.50*
	Preprinted	6.00	
	First day cancel		—
m.	PM6 Message card detached	3.00	*7.50*
	Preprinted	1.50	
r.	PR6 Reply card detached	3.00	*10.00*
	Preprinted	1.50	

Type of 1910

Single frame line around instructions

1951, Dec. 29

UY13	PM4+PR4 2c +2c **carmine,** *buff,* unsevered	1.25	*2.00*
	Preprinted	.65	
	First day cancel, Washington, D.C.		1.25
m.	PM4 Message card detached	.35	*1.00*
	Preprinted	.25	
r.	PR4 Reply card detached	.35	*1.00*
	Preprinted	.25	

No. UY7a Surcharged Below Stamp in Green by Canceling Machine

1952, Jan. 1

UY14	PM4+PR4 2c on 1c+2c on 1c **green,** *buff,* unsevered	1.25	*2.00*
	Preprinted	.50	
a.	Surcharge vertical at left of stamps	12.50	7.50
	Preprinted	7.50	
b.	Surcharge horizontal at left of stamps	15.00	12.50
	Preprinted	8.50	
c.	Inverted surcharge horizontal at left of stamps	140.00	90.00
	Preprinted	75.00	
d.	Message card normal, reply card no surcharge	40.00	40.00
	Preprinted	—	
e.	Message card normal, reply card double surcharge	40.00	40.00
	Preprinted	—	
f.	Message card no surcharge, reply card normal	40.00	40.00
	Preprinted	—	
g.	Message card double surcharge, reply card normal	40.00	40.00
	Preprinted	—	
h.	Both cards, dbl. surch.	50.00	50.00
	Preprinted	—	
m.	PM4 Message card detached	.40	*1.00*
	Preprinted	.30	
r.	PR4 Reply card detached	.40	*1.00*
	Preprinted	.30	

No. UY7a with Similar Surcharge (horizontal) Typographed at Left of Stamp in Dark Green

1952

UY15	PM4+PR4 2c on 1c+2c on 1c **green,** *buff,* unsevered	115.00	45.00
	Preprinted	35.00	
a.	Surcharge on message card only	175.00	
m.	PM4 Message card detached	17.50	10.00
	Preprinted	9.00	
r.	PR4 Reply card detached	17.50	10.00
	Preprinted	9.00	

On No. UY15a, the surcharge also appears on blank side of card.

Liberty Type

For International Use

1956, Nov. 16

UY16	PC24 4c +4c **carmine & dark violet blue,** *buff,* unsevered	1.25	*75.00*
	First day cancel, New York, N. Y. *(127,874)*		1.00
a.	Message card printed on both halves	125.00	—
b.	Reply card printed on both halves	125.00	—
c.	Double scarlet on reply side	200.00	—
	First day cancel		350.00
d.	Double scarlet on message side	200.00	
e.	Double violet blue on message side	—	
f.	Double violet blue on both sides	—	
g.	Message side blank, reply side normal		—
m.	Message card detached	.40	*45.00*
r.	Reply card detached	.40	*45.00*

Liberty Type of 1956

1958, July 31

UY17	PC25 3c +3c **purple,** *buff,* unsevered	3.00	*2.00*
	First day cancel, Boise, Idaho *(136,768)*		1.00
a.	One card blank	500.00	
b.	Double impression on one card, preprinted		—

Both halves of No. UY17 are identical, inscribed as No. UX46, "This side of card is for address."

Lincoln Type

1962, Nov. 19

Precanceled with 3 printed red violet lines

UY18	PC26 4c +4c **red violet,** unsevered	3.00	*2.50*
	First day cancel, Springfield, Ill. *(107,746)*		1.00
a.	Tagged, *Mar. 7, 1967*	6.50	3.00
	First day cancel, Dayton, OH		30.00

Both halves of No. UY18 are identical, inscribed as No. UX48, "This side of card is for address."

No. UY18a was printed with luminescent ink.

Map Type

1963, Aug. 30 **For International Use**

UY19	PC27 7c +7c **blue & red,** unsevered	2.50	*60.00*
	First day cancel, New York		1.00
a.	Message card normal, reply card blank	400.00	100.00
b.	Message card blank, reply card normal	400.00	—

c. Additional message card on back of reply card 550.00
d. Double red on message side —
e. Double red & blue on message side —
m. Message card detached .85 *40.00*
r. Reply card detached .85 *40.00*

Message card inscribed "Postal Card With Paid Reply" in English and French. Reply card inscribed "Reply Postal Card Carte Postale Résponse."

Map Type of 1963

1967, Dec. 4 For International Use

UY20 PC27 8c +8c **blue & red,** unsevered 2.50 *60.00*
First day cancel, Washington, D.C. 1.00
m. Message card detached .85 *40.00*
r. Reply card detached .85 *40.00*
s. Message card normal, reply card blank —

Message card inscribed "Postal Card With Paid Reply" in English and French. Reply card inscribed "Reply Postal Card Carte Postale Résponse."

Tagged

Paid Reply Postal cards from No. UY21 onward are either tagged or printed with luminescent ink unless otherwise noted.

Lincoln Type

1968, Jan. 4

UY21 PC33 5c +5c **emerald,** unsevered 1.25 *2.00*
First day cancel, Hodgenville, Ky. 1.50
a. Printed on one side only —

Paul Revere Type

1971, May 15

Precanceled with 3 printed brown lines.

UY22 PC36 6c +6c **brown,** unsevered .85 *2.00*
First day cancel, Boston, Mass. 1.00

John Hanson Type

1972, Sept. 1

Precanceled with 3 printed blue lines.

UY23 PC41 6c +6c **blue,** unsevered 1.00 *2.00*
First day cancel, Baltimore, Md. 1.00

Samuel Adams Type

1973, Dec. 16

Precanceled with 3 printed orange lines

UY24 PC42 8c +8c **orange,** unsevered .75 *2.00*
First day cancel, Boston, Mass. *(105,369)* 1.00
a. Coarse paper 1.25 *2.00*
b. Printed on one side only, preprinted 750.00

Thomson, Witherspoon, Rodney, Hale & Hancock Types

1975-78

Precanceled with 3 printed emerald lines

UY25 PC44 7c +7c **emerald,** unsevered, *Sept. 14, 1975* .75 *8.00*
First day cancel, Bryn Mawr, Pa. 1.00

Precanceled with 3 printed yellow brown lines

UY26 PC45 9c +9c **yellow brown,** unsevered, *Nov. 10, 1975* .75 *2.00*
First day cancel, Princeton, N.J. 1.00

Precanceled with 3 printed blue lines

UY27 PC46 9c +9c **blue,** unsevered, *July 1, 1976* 1.00 *2.00*
First day cancel, Dover, Del. 1.00

Precanceled with 3 printed green lines

UY28 PC48 9c +9c **green,** unsevered, *Oct. 14, 1977* 1.00 *2.00*
First day cancel, Coventry, Conn. 1.00

Inscribed "U.S. Domestic Rate"

Precanceled with 3 printed brown orange lines

UY29 PC50 (10c +10c) **brown orange,** unsevered, *May 19, 1978* 7.50 *9.00*
First day cancel, Quincy, Mass. 1.75

Precanceled with 3 printed brown orange lines

UY30 PC50 10c +10c **brown orange,** unsevered, *June 20, 1978* 1.00 .25
First day cancel, Quincy, Mass. 1.00
a. One card "Domestic Rate," other "Postage 10¢" —
b. Printed on one side only *800.00*
Nos. UY25-UY30 (6) 12.00

Eagle Type

Inscribed "U. S. Domestic Rate"

1981, Mar. 15

Precanceled with 3 printed violet lines

UY31 PC63 (12c +12) **violet,** unsevered 1.00 *2.00*
First day cancel, Memphis, TN 1.00

Isaiah Thomas Type

1981, May 5

Precanceled with 3 printed lines

UY32 PC64 12c +12c **light blue,** unsevered 5.00 *2.00*
First day cancel, Worcester, MA 1.00
a. Small die on one side 3.00 —

Morris Type

Inscribed "U.S. Domestic Rate"

1981

Precanceled with 3 printed lines

UY33 PC67 (13c +13c) **buff,** *Oct. 11,* unsevered 1.50 *2.00*
First day cancel, Memphis, TN 1.25

Inscribed "U.S. Postage 13¢"

UY34 PC67 13c +13c **buff,** *Nov. 10,* unsevered .85 .20
First day cancel, Philadelphia, PA 1.25
a. Message card normal, reply card blank 200.00
b. Extra copyright symbol and "USPS 1981" on back of reply card —

Charles Carroll Type

Inscribed: U.S. Domestic Rate

1985

Precanceled with 3 printed lines

UY35 PC79 (14c +14c) **pale green,** *Feb. 1,* unsevered 2.50 *2.00*
First day cancel, New Carrollton, MD 1.25

Inscribed: USA

UY36 PC79 14c +14c **pale green,** *Mar. 6,* unsevered 1.00 *2.00*
First day cancel, Annapolis, MD 1.25
a. One card blank *425.00*

George Wythe Type

1985, June 20

Precanceled with 3 printed lines

UY37 PC81 14c +14c **bright apple green,** unsevered .75 *2.00*
First day cancel, Williamsburg, VA 1.25
a. One card blank, preprinted 300.00

Flag Type

1987, Sept. 1

UY38 PC90 14c +14c **black, blue & red,** unsevered .75 *2.00*
First day cancel, Washington, DC *(22,314)* 1.25

America the Beautiful Type

1988, July 11

UY39 PC93 15c +15c **multicolored,** unsevered .75 *1.50*
First day cancel, Buffalo, WY *(24,338)* 1.25

Flag Type

1991, Mar. 27

UY40 PC122 19c +19c **rose, ultramarine & black,** unsevered .80 *1.50*
First day cancel, Washington, DC *(25,562)* 1.25
a. Printed on one side only *750.00*

Red Barn Type

1995, Feb. 1 Litho.

UY41 PC147 20c +20c **multi,** unsevered .80 *1.50*
First day cancel, Williamsburg, PA 1.50
a. One card blank —

Block Island Lighthouse Type

1999, Nov. 10 Litho.

UY42 PC165 20c +20c **multi,** unsevered .85 *1.50*
First day cancel, Block Island, RI 1.75

White Barn Type

2001, Sept. 20 Litho.

UY43 PC173 21c +21c **multi,** unsevered .90 *1.50*
First day cancel, Washington, DC 1.50

Carlsbad Caverns Type

2002, June 7 Litho.

UY44 PC174 23c+23c **multi,** unsevered 1.00 *1.25*
First day cancel, Carlsbad, NM 1.50
First day cancel, any other city 1.50

Pikes Peak Type of 2006

2006, Jan. 9 Litho.

UY45 PC178 24c+24c **multicolored,** unsevered 1.10 *1.25*
First day cancel, Washington, DC 1.50
First day cancel, any other city 1.50

Pineapple Type of 2007

2007, May 12 Litho

UY46 PC179 26c+26c **multicolored,** unsevered 1.25 *1.40*
First day cancel, Washington, DC 2.40

Corinthian Column Type of 2008

2008, May 12 Litho

UY47 PC181 27c+27c **multicolored,** unsevered 1.25 *1.40*
First day cancel, Washington, DC 2.40

AIR POST POSTAL CARDS

Eagle in Flight — APC1

1949, Jan.10 Typo

UXC1 APC1 4c **red orange,** *buff* .50 .75
Preprinted .35
First day cancel, Washington, D.C. *(236,620)* 3.00
a. 4c **deep red,** *buff* 600.00 450.00
First day cancel, Washington, D.C. *250.00*

Expertization is recommended for No. UXC1a.

Type of Air Post Stamp, 1954

1958, July 31

UXC2 AP31 5c **red,** *buff* 1.75 .75
First day cancel, Wichita, Kans. *(156,474)* 1.00

Type of 1958 Redrawn

1960, June 18 Lithographed (Offset)

UXC3 AP31 5c **red,** *buff,* bicolored border 6.50 2.00
First day cancel, Minneapolis, Minn. *(228,500)* 1.50
a. Red omitted —

Size of stamp of No. UXC3: 18½x21mm; on No. UXC2 19x22mm. White cloud around eagle enlarged and finer detail of design on No. UXC3. Inscription "AIR MAIL-POSTAL CARD" has been omitted and blue and red border added on No. UXC3.

Bald Eagle — APC2

1963, Feb. 15

Precanceled with 3 printed red lines

UXC4 APC2 6c **red,** bicolored border 1.10 *2.50*
First day cancel, Maitland, Fla. *(216,203)* 1.50

Emblem of Commerce Department's Travel Service — APC3

Issued at the Sixth International Philatelic Exhibition (SIPEX) Washington, D.C., May 21-30.

1966, May 27 **For International Use**

UXC5 APC3 11c **blue & red** .65 *25.00*
First day cancel, Washington, D.C. *(272,813)* 1.00

Four photographs at left on address side show: Mt. Rainier, New York skyline, Indian on horseback and Miami Beach. The card has blue and red border.

See Nos. UXC8, UXC11.

Virgin Islands and Territorial Flag — APC4

50th anniv. of the purchase of the Virgin Islands.

Designed by Burt Pringle

1967, Mar. 31 **Litho.**

UXC6 APC4 6c **multicolored** .75 *10.00*
First day cancel, Charlotte Amalie, V. I. *(346,906)* 1.00
a. Red & yellow omitted *1,700.*
b. Orange red (instead of red) 6.00

The orange red in No. UXC6b is most easily seen in the two lines at the bottom of the card.

Borah Peak, Lost River Range, Idaho, and Scout Emblem — APC5

12th Boy Scout World Jamboree, Farragut State Park, Idaho, Aug. 1-9.

Designed by Stevan Dohanos

1967, Aug. 4 **Litho.**

UXC7 APC5 6c **blue, yellow, black & red** .75 *15.00*
First day cancel, Farragut State Park, ID *(471,585)* 1.00
a. Blue omitted —
b. Blue & black omitted *11,000.*
c. Red & yellow omitted *11,000.*

Travel Service Type of 1966

Issued in connection with the American Air Mail Society Convention, Detroit, Mich.

1967, Sept. 8 **For International Use**

UXC8 APC3 13c **blue & red** 1.50 *30.00*
First day cancel, Detroit, Mich. *(178,189)* 1.00

Stylized Eagle APC6

Designed by Muriel R. Chamberlain

1968, Mar. 1

Precanceled with 3 printed red lines

UXC9 APC6 8c **blue & red** .75 2.50
First day cancel, New York, N.Y. *(179,923)* 1.00
a. Tagged, *Mar. 19, 1969* 2.50 3.00
Tagged, first day cancel 15.00
b. **Blue & pale pink**, tagged *1,250.*

No. UXC9a is known with tagging omitted. It can be distinguished from No. UXC9, as No. UXC9a was printed on fluorescent stock. Believed to be unique. Value $2,500.

Tagged

Air Post Postal Cards from No. UXC10 onward are either tagged or printed with luminescent ink unless otherwise noted.

1971, May 15

Precanceled with 3 printed blue lines

UXC10 APC6 9c **red & blue** .50 *1.25*
First day cancel, Kitty Hawk, N.C. 1.00

Travel Service Type of 1966

1971, June 10

For International Use

UXC11 APC3 15c **blue & red** 1.75 *45.00*
First day cancel, New York, N.Y. 1.00

Grand Canyon APC7

Niagara Falls APC8

Tourism Year of the Americas 1972.

Designed by Melbourne Brindle

1972, June 29 **Litho.**

Size: 152½x108½mm

UXC12 APC7 9c **black,** Grand Canyon, *buff* (Statue of Liberty, Hawaii, Alaska, San Francisco on back) .75 *75.00*
First day cancel, any city 1.50
a. Red and blue lozenges omitted *2,250.*
b. Red lozenges omitted —
c. Tagging omitted —

For International Use

UXC13 APC8 15c **black,** Niagara Falls, *buff* (Mt. Vernon, Washington, D.C., Lincoln, Liberty Bell on back) .75 *75.00*
First day cancel, any city 1.50
a. Address side blank *400.00*
b. Double blue lozenges *6,000.*
c. Tagging omitted *2,500.*
d. Red and blue lozenges omitted —

See note after No. UX63.

Stylized Eagle — APC9

Eagle Weather Vane — APC10

Designed by David G. Foote (11c) & Stevan Dohanos (18c)

1974, Jan. 4 **Litho.**

UXC14 APC9 11c **ultramarine & red** 1.10 *25.00*
First day cancel, State College, Pa. *(160,500)* 1.00
a. Double tagging *500.00*
b. Tagging omitted *500.00*

For International Use

UXC15 APC10 18c **multicolored** 1.10 *25.00*
First day cancel, Miami, Fla. *(132,114)* 1.00
a. Tagging omitted 350.00
b. Black and yellow omitted *7,500.*

All following issues are for international use.

Angel Gabriel Weather Vane — APC11

Designed by Stevan Dohanos

1975, Dec. 17 **Litho.**

UXC16 APC11 21c **multicolored** .85 *22.50*
First day cancel, Kitty Hawk, N.C. 1.00
a. Blue & red omitted *7,500.*
b. Tagging omitted 250.00 —

Curtiss (JN4H) Jenny — APC12

Designed by Keith Ferris

1978, Sept. 16 **Litho.**

UXC17 APC12 21c **multicolored** 1.00 *22.50*
First day cancel, San Diego, Cal. *(174,886)* 1.25

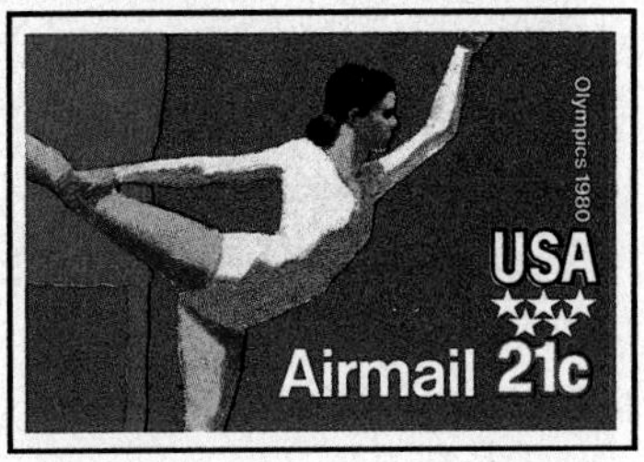

Gymnast APC13

22nd Olympic Games, Moscow, July 19-Aug. 3, 1980.

Designed by Robert M. Cunningham

1979, Dec. 1 **Litho.**

UXC18 APC13 21c **multicolored** 1.25 *20.00*
First day cancel, Fort Worth, Tex. 1.00

Pangborn, Herndon and Miss Veedol — APC14

First non-stop transpacific flight by Clyde Pangborn and Hugh Herndon, Jr., 50th anniv.

Designed by Ken Dallison

1981, Jan. 2 **Litho.**
UXC19 APC14 28c **multicolored** 1.00 *22.50*
First day cancel, Wenatchee, WA 1.25

Gliders — APC15

Designed by Robert E. Cunningham

1982, Mar. 5 **Litho.**
UXC20 APC15 28c **magenta, yellow, blue & black** 1.00 *22.50*
First day cancel, Houston, TX *(106,932)* 1.25

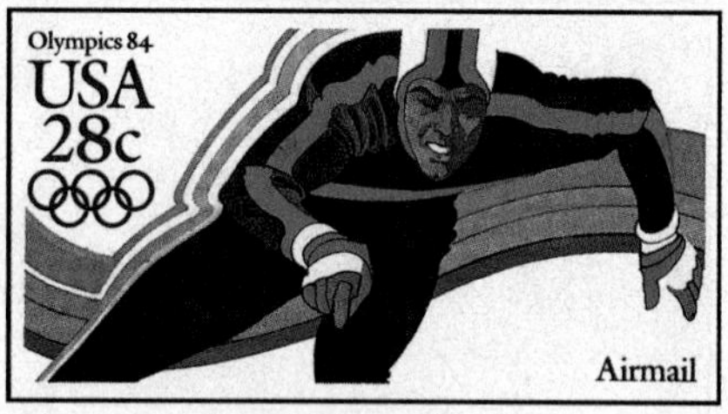

Speedskater — APC16

Designed by Robert Peak

1983, Dec. 29 **Litho.**
UXC21 APC16 28c **multicolored** 1.00 *22.50*
First day cancel, Milwaukee, WI *(108,397)* 1.25

Martin M-130 China Clipper Seaplane — APC17

Designed by Chuck Hodgson

1985, Feb. 15 **Litho.**
UXC22 APC17 33c **multicolored** 1.00 *22.50*
First day cancel, San Francisco, CA 1.50

First day cancellation was applied to 269,229 of Nos. UXC22 and C115.

Chicago Skyline — APC18

AMERIPEX '86, Chicago, May 22-June 1.

Designed by Ray Ameijide

1986, Feb. 1 **Litho.**
UXC23 APC18 33c **multicolored** 1.00 *22.50*
First day cancel, Chicago, IL *(84,480)* 1.25

No. UXC23 was sold at Sudposta '87 by the U.S.P.S. with a show cachet.

DC-3 — APC19

Designed by Chuck Hodgson

1988, May 14 **Litho.**
UXC24 APC19 36c **multicolored** .85 *22.50*
First day cancel, San Diego, CA 1.25

No. UXC24 was sold at SYDPEX '88 by the USPS with a cachet for Australia's bicentennial and SYDPEX '88.
First day cancellations applied to 167,575 of Nos. UXC24 and C118.

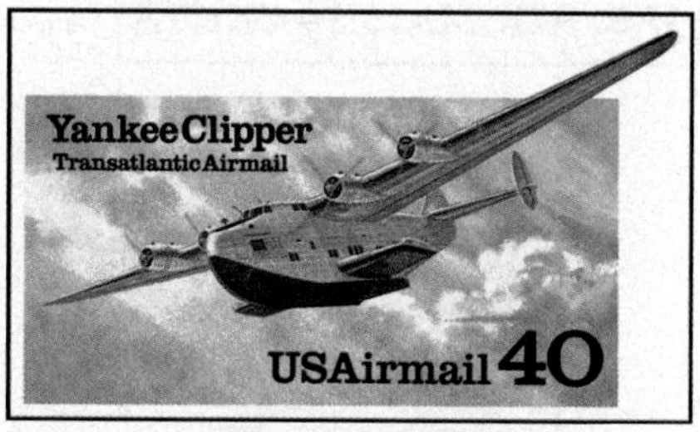

Yankee Clipper — APC20

Designed by Chuck Hodgson.

1991, June 28 **Litho.**
UXC25 APC20 40c **multicolored** .90 *22.50*
First day cancel, Flushing, NY *(24,865)* 1.50

Mt. Rainier — APC22

Designed by Ethel Kessler.

1999, May 15 **Litho.**
UXC27 APC22 55c **multicolored** 1.25 *20.00*
First day cancel, Denver, CO 1.50

First day cancellation was applied to 19,658 of Nos. UXC27 and UC65.
See note before No. C133.

Badlands Natl. Park, South Dakota — APC23

Designed by Ethel Kessler.

2001, Feb. 22 **Litho.**
UXC28 APC23 70c **multicolored** 1.40 *10.00*
First day cancel, Wall, SD 1.50

OFFICIAL POSTAL CARDS

PO1

1913, July
Size: 126x76mm
UZ1 PO1 1c **black** 700.00 475.00

All No. UZ1 cards have printed address and printed form on message side.

Used values are for contemporaneous usage without additional postage applied.

Great Seal — PO2

1983-85
UZ2 PO2 13c **blue,** *Jan. 12* .75 *100.00*
First day cancel, Washington, DC 1.00
UZ3 PO2 14c **blue,** *Feb. 26, 1985* .80 *80.00*
First day cancel, Washington, DC *(62,396)* 1.25

Official postal cards from No. UZ4 onward are tagged unless otherwise noted.

PO3

Designed by Bradbury Thompson

1988, June 10 **Litho.**
UZ4 PO3 15c **multicolored** .80 *90.00*
First day cancel, New York *(133,498)* 1.25

PO4

Designed by Bradbury Thompson

1991, May 24 **Litho.**
UZ5 PO4 19c **multicolored** .80 *90.00*
First day cancel, Seattle, WA *(23,097)* 1.25

PO5

1995, May 9		**Litho.**
UZ6 PO5 20c	**multicolored**	.90 *90.00*
	First day cancel, Washington, DC	1.25

REVENUE STAMPS

The Commissioner of Internal Revenue advertised for bids for revenue stamps in August, 1862, and the contract was awarded to Butler & Carpenter of Philadelphia.

Nos. R1-R102 were used to pay taxes on documents and proprietary articles including playing cards. Until December 25, 1862, the law stated that a stamp could be used only for payment of the tax upon the particular instrument or article specified on its face. After that date, stamps, except the Proprietary, could be used indiscriminately.

Most stamps of the first issue appeared in the latter part of 1862 or early in 1863. The 5c and 10c Proprietary were issued in the fall of 1864, and the 6c Proprietary on April 13, 1871.

Plate numbers and imprints are usually found at the bottom of the plate on all denominations except 25c and $1 to $3.50. On these it is nearly always at the left of the plate. The imprint reads "Engraved by Butler & Carpenter, Philadelphia" or "Jos. R. Carpenter."

Plates were of various sizes: 1c and 2c, 210 subjects (14x15); 3c to 20c, 170 subjects (17x10); 25c to 30c, 102 subjects (17x6); 50c to 70c, 85 subjects (17x5); $1 to $1.90, 90 subjects (15x6); $2 to $10, 72 subjects (12x6); $15 to $50, 54 subjects (9x6); $200, 8 subjects (2x4). No. R132, one subject.

The paper varies, the first employed being thin, hard and brittle until September, 1869, from which time it acquired a softer texture and varied from medium to very thick. Early printings of some revenue stamps occur on paper which appears to have laid lines. Some are found on experimental silk paper, first employed about August, 1870.

Some of the stamps were in use eight years and were printed several times. Many color variations occurred, particularly if unstable pigments were used and the color was intended to be purple or violet, such as the 4c Proprietary, 30c and $2.50 stamps. Before 1868 dull colors predominate on these and the early red stamps. In later printings of the 4c Proprietary, 30c and $2.50 stamps, red predominates in the mixture and on the dollar values of red is brighter. The early $1.90 stamp is dull purple, imperforate or perforated. In a later printing, perforated only, the purple is darker.

In the first issue, canceling usually was done with pen and ink and all values quoted are for stamps canceled in that way. Handstamped cancellations as a rule sell for more than pen. Printed cancellations are scarce and command much higher prices. Herringbone, punched or other types of cancellation which break the surface of the paper adversely affect prices.

Many, but not all, of the pre-1898 revenue stamps exist unused with original gum. These are not valued in the listings, but they sell for more than used examples in the marketplace.

1862-72 revenue stamps from the first three issues were often used on large folded documents. As a result, multiples (blocks and strips of four or more) are not often found in sound condition. In addition, part perforate pairs of all but the most common varieties generally are off center. Catalogue values of the noted multiples are for items in fine condition or for very fine appearing examples with small faults. Examples of such multiples in a true very fine grade without any faults are scarce to rare and will sell for well above catalogue value.

Where a stamp is known in a given form or variety but insufficient information is available on which to base a value, its existence is indicated by a dash.

Part perforate stamps are understood to be imperforate horizontally unless otherwise stated.

Part perforate stamps with an asterisk (*) exist imperforate horizontally or vertically.

Part perforate PAIRS should be imperforate between the stamps as well as imperforate at opposite ends. See illustration **Type A** under "Information For Collectors-Perforations."

All imperforate or part perforate stamps listed are known in pairs or larger multiples. Certain unlisted varieties of this nature exist as singles and specialists believe them genuine. Exceptions are Nos. R13a, R22a and R60b, which have not been reported in multiples but are regarded as legitimate by most students.

Documentary revenue stamps were no longer required after December 31, 1967.

First Issue

George Washington
R1 R2

1862-71 **Engr.** ***Perf. 12***

				a. Imperf.	b. Part Perf.	Perforated c. Old Paper	Perforated d. Silk Paper
R1	R1	1c	**Express, red**	70.00	40.00*	1.40	140.00
			Pair	160.00	180.00	3.25	
			Block of 4	650.00	600.00	12.50	
			Dble. transfer			45.00	
			Short transfer, No. 156	—	—	85.00	
		e.	Vert. pair, imperf. btwn.			*200.00*	
R2	R1	1c	**Playing Cards, red**	1,800.	1,500.	160.00	
			Pair	*3,800.*	*3,600.*	350.00	
			Block of 4			900.00	
			Cracked plate	—		225.00	
R3	R1	1c	**Proprietary, red**	1,000.	250.00*	.50	50.00
			Pair	*2,100.*	700.00	1.25	125.00
			Block of 4		*3,000.*	3.25	*300.00*
R4	R1	1c	**Telegraph, red**	600.00		17.50	
			Pair	1,700.		37.50	
			Block of 4			110.00	

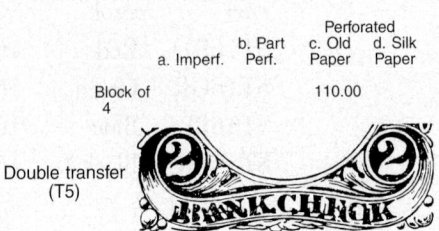

Double transfer (T5)

				a. Imperf.	b. Part Perf.	Perforated c. Old Paper	Perforated d. Silk Paper
R5	R2	2c	**Bank Check, blue**	1.25	5.00*	.50	
			Pair	19.00	17.00	2.00	
			Block of 4	190.00	140.00	8.00	
			Double transfer (T5)	100.00	140.00	50.00	
			Cracked plate		22.50	10.00	
		e.	Double impression			800.00	
		f.	Vert. pair, imperf. btwn.			400.00	
R6	R2	2c	**Bank Check, orange**		55.00*	.25	275.00
			Pair		—	.50	
			Block of 4			1.40	
			Double transfer (T5)			300.00	
		e.	2c **orange,** *green*			700.00	
		f.	Vert. half used as 1c on document			—	

Double transfer (T7)

				a. Imperf.	b. Part Perf.	Perforated c. Old Paper	Perforated d. Silk Paper
R7	R2	2c	**Certificate, blue**	14.00		30.00	
			Pair	45.00		75.00	
			Block of 4	200.00		300.00	
			Double transfer (T7)	400.00		350.00	
			Cracked plate			37.50	
R8	R2	2c	**Certificate, orange**			40.00	
			Pair			190.00	
			Block of 4			*850.00*	
			Double transfer (T7)			450.00	
R9	R2	2c	**Express, blue**	14.00	30.00*	.40	
			Pair	50.00	140.00	1.25	
			Block of 4	160.00	350.00	4.25	
			Dble. transfer	60.00		17.50	
			Cracked plate			20.00	
R10	R2	2c	**Express, orange**		*750.00*	12.50	150.00
			Pair			29.00	
			Block of 4			60.00	
			Dble. transfer			22.50	
R11	R2	2c	**Playing Cards, blue**		250.00	4.00	
			Pair		600.00	13.00	
			Block of 4			50.00	
			Cracked plate			30.00	
R12	R2	2c	**Playing Cards, orange**			50.00	
			Pair			*450.00*	

Double transfer (T13)

Double transfer (T13a)

No.	Design	Denom.	Description	a. Imperf.	b. Part Perf.	c. Old Paper	d. Silk Paper
					Perforated		
R13	R2	2c	**Proprietary, blue**	700.	250.	.40	125.00
			Pair		700.	.90	
			Block of 4		*1,600.*	5.00	
			Double transfer (T13)			150.00	
			Complete double transfer (T13a)			200.00	
			Cracked plate			25.00	
		e.	2c **ultra**			300.00	
			Pair			650.00	
			Block of 4			—	
			Dble. transfer (T13)			—	
			Complete dble. transfer (T13a)			*750.00*	
		f.	Horiz. half used as 1c on document			—	
R14	R2	2c	**Proprietary, orange**			60.00	
			Pair			350.00	
			Block of 4			—	
			Double transfer (T13)			250.00	
			Complete double transfer (T13a)			500.00	

Double transfer (T15)

Double transfer (T15a)

No.	Design	Denom.	Description	a. Imperf.	b. Part Perf.	c. Old Paper	d. Silk Paper
R15	R2	2c	**U. S. Internal Revenue, orange** ('64)	—		.35	.35
			Pair	—	—	.80	1.00
			Block of 4			.70	
			Double transfer (T15)			65.00	
			Double transfer (T15a)			50.00	
			Dble. transfer			12.00	
			Triple transfer			40.00	
			Cracked plate			10.00	
		e.	2c **orange,** *green*			700.00	
		f.	Half used as 1c on document			—	

R3

No.	Design	Denom.	Description	a. Imperf.	b. Part Perf.	c. Old Paper	d. Silk Paper
R16	R3	3c	**Foreign Exchange, green**		550.00	4.50	110.00
			Pair		*1,500.*	10.50	
			Block of 4			75.00	
			Dble. transfer			—	
R17	R3	3c	**Playing Cards, green** ('63)	*25,000.*		150.00	
			Pair	*60,000.*		350.00	
			Block of 4			*900.00*	
R18	R3	3c	**Proprietary, green**		550.00	7.50	80.00
			Pair		*1,200.*	17.00	175.00
			Block of 4		—	42.50	
			Dble. transfer			11.50	
			Cracked plate			—	
		e.	Double impression			*1,000.*	
		f.	Printed on both sides			*3,500.*	
R19	R3	3c	**Telegraph, green**	80.00	27.50	2.75	
			Pair	500.00	82.50	8.75	
			Block of 4	1,200.	300.00	80.00	
			Sewing machine perf, unofficial	*700.00*			
R20	R3	4c	**Inland Exchange, brown** ('63)			2.00	125.00
			Pair			5.25	
			Block of 4			22.50	
			Double transfer at top			7.50	
R21	R3	4c	**Playing Cards, slate** ('63)			600.00	
			Pair			*1,250.*	
			Block of 4			*2,600.*	
R22	R3	4c	**Proprietary, purple**	—	475.00	7.50	160.00
			Pair		1,000.	17.50	*350.00*
			Block of 4		2,100.	55.00	—
			Double transfer at top			17.50	
			Double transfer at bottom			12.50	

There are shade and color variations of Nos. R21-R22. See foreword of Revenue Stamps section.

No.	Design	Denom.	Description	a. Imperf.	b. Part Perf.	c. Old Paper	d. Silk Paper
R23	R3	5c	**Agreement, red**			.50	2.25
			Pair			1.00	4.75
			Block of 4			2.10	20.00
			Dble. transfer in numerals			25.00	
R24	R3	5c	**Certificate, red**	3.50	13.00	.50	.55
			Pair	35.00	150.00	1.25	1.25
			Block of 4	250.00	400.00	3.00	6.00
			Double transfer in upper label			10.00	
			Dble. transfer throughout			200.00	
			Triple transfer (No. 121)			35.00	
		e.	Half used as 2c on document			—	
		f.	Impression of #R3 on back				*2,750.*
R25	R3	5c	**Express, red**	7.00	7.00*	.40	
			Pair	22.50	100.00	.90	
			Block of 4	210.00	300.00	2.25	
			Double transfer			5.00	
R26	R3	5c	**Foreign Exchange, red**		—	.50	425.00
			Pair		—	1.25	
			Block of 4			15.00	
			Double transfer at top			20.00	
			Double transfer at bottom			10.00	

No.	Type	Denom.	Description	a. Imperf.	b. Part Perf.	c. Old Paper	d. Silk Paper
R27	R3	5c	**Inland Exchange, red**	8.25	6.00	.50	17.50
			Pair	37.50	42.50	1.25	40.00
			Block of 4	120.00	110.00	3.00	
			Double transfer at top	77.50	47.50	27.50	
			Cracked plate	95.00	90.00	32.50	
		e.	Double impression			—	
R28	R3	5c	**Playing Cards, red** ('63)			35.00	
			Pair			75.00	
			Block of 4			150.00	
		e.	Double impression			*1,000.*	
R29	R3	5c	**Proprietary, red** ('64)			27.50	250.00
			Pair			60.00	
			Block of 4			160.00	
R30	R3	6c	**Inland Exchange, orange** ('63)			2.00	150.00
			Pair			18.50	
			Block of 4			100.00	
R31	R3	6c	**Proprietary, orange** ('71)			*2,000.*	

Nearly all examples of No. R31 are faulty and poorly centered. The Catalogue value is for a fine centered stamp with minor faults which do not detract from its appearance.

No.	Type	Denom.	Description	a. Imperf.	b. Part Perf.	c. Old Paper	d. Silk Paper
R32	R3	10c	**Bill of Lading, blue**	50.00	425.00	1.50	
			Pair	300.00	900.00	4.00	
			Block of 4	750.00		10.00	
			Dble. transfer (#33 & 143)			—	
		e.	Half used as 5c on document			*200.00*	
R33	R3	10c	**Certificate, blue**	250.00	750.00*	.35	6.00
			Pair	650.00	1,600.	.75	17.50
			Block of 4	*1,600.*	—	2.25	90.00
			Dble. transfer			7.50	
			Cracked plate			15.00	
		e.	Half used as 5c on document			*200.00*	
R34	R3	10c	**Contract, blue**		475.00	.50	2.25
			Pair		1,250.	1.25	6.00
			Block of 4		—	4.75	60.00
			Complete double transfer			70.00	
		e.	10c **ultra**		650.00	1.00	
			Pair			2.50	
			Block of 4			17.50	
		f.	Vertical half used as 5c on document			*200.00*	
R35	R3	10c	**Foreign Exchange, blue**			12.50	—
			Pair			27.50	
			Block of 4			92.50	
		e.	10c **ultra**			18.00	
			Pair			55.00	
			Block of 4			125.00	
R36	R3	10c	**Inland Exchange, blue**	350.00	4.00*	.30	80.00
			Pair	900.00	15.00	.60	160.00
			Block of 4	*3,250.*	80.00	1.75	—
		e.	Half used as 5c on document			*200.00*	
R37	R3	10c	**Power of Attorney, blue**	850.00	27.50	1.00	
			Pair	2,250.	100.00	2.25	
			Block of 4	*5,000.*	300.00	8.00	
		e.	Half used as 5c on document			*200.00*	
R38	R3	10c	**Proprietary, blue** ('64)			17.50	
			Pair			40.00	
			Block of 4			110.00	
R39	R3	15c	**Foreign Exchange, brown** ('63)			15.00	
			Pair			50.00	
			Block of 4			250.00	
		e.	Double impression			*1,000.*	
R40	R3	15c	**Inland Exchange, brown**	37.50	12.50	1.75	
			Pair	250.00	50.00	3.50	
			Block of 4	900.00	450.00	11.50	
			Dble. transfer			6.25	
			Cracked plate	60.00	37.50	14.00	
		e.	Double impression		*1,200.*	*550.00*	
R41	R3	20c	**Foreign Exchange, red**	75.00		60.00	
			Pair	350.00		150.00	
			Block of 4	1,000.		350.00	
R42	R3	20c	**Inland Exchange, red**	15.00	20.00	.45	—
			Pair	50.00	60.00	1.00	
			Block of 4	300.00	300.00	14.00	
		e.	Half used as 10c on document			*200.00*	

R4

R5

				a. Imperf.	b. Part Perf.	c. Old Paper (Perforated)	d. Silk Paper (Perforated)
R43	R4	25c	**Bond, red**	250.00	6.00	3.50	
			Pair	675.00	60.00	8.00	
			Block of 4	*5,000.*	400.00	60.00	
R44	R4	25c	**Certificate, red**	10.00	6.00*	.50	2.75
			Pair	50.00	40.00	1.10	8.25
			Block of 4	500.00	250.00	8.00	27.50
			Double transfer, top or bottom			2.00	
			Triple transfer			—	
		e.	Printed on both sides			*4,500*	
		f.	Impression of No. R48 on back			—	
R45	R4	25c	**Entry of Goods, red**	20.00	125.00*	1.25	70.00
			Pair	70.00	*800.00*	50.00	
			Block of 4	500.00		140.00	
			Top frame line double	72.50	105.00	11.00	
R46	R4	25c	**Insurance, red**	11.00	17.00	.30	5.50
			Pair	42.50	35.00	.75	13.00
			Block of 4	*750.00*	250.00	5.50	
			Cracked plate			17.50	
		e.	Double impression			*500.00*	
R47	R4	25c	**Life Insurance, red**	45.00	475.00	9.50	
			Pair	150.00	1,200.	50.00	
			Block of 4	650.00		240.00	
R48	R4	25c	**Power of Attorney, red**	8.00	40.00	1.00	
			Pair	50.00	125.00	2.25	
			Block of 4	500.00	*600.00*	12.50	
			Dble. transfer			1.10	
			Bottom frame line double			5.50	
R49	R4	25c	**Protest, red**	30.00	800.00	7.50	
			Pair	200.00	1,600.	29.00	
			Block of 4	750.00		115.00	
R50	R4	25c	**Warehouse Receipt, red**	47.50	600.00	40.00	
			Pair	250.00	1,200.	95.00	
			Block of 4	*1,200.*		325.00	
R51	R4	30c	**Foreign Exchange, lilac**	120.00	2,000.	55.00	*500.00*
			Pair	600.00	*4,500.*	225.00	
			Block of 4	*3,500.*		—	
			Dble. transfer			100.00	

No.	Design	Denom.	Description	a. Imperf.	b. Part Perf.	c. Old Paper	d. Silk Paper
			Top frame line double			—	
R52	R4	30c	**Inland Exchange, lilac**	65.00	80.00	8.00	—
			Pair	350.00	425.00	40.00	
			Block of 4	1,000.	—	140.00	
			Dble. transfer			30.00	

There are shade and color variations of Nos. R51-R52. See foreword of "Revenues" section.

No.	Design	Denom.	Description	a. Imperf.	b. Part Perf.	c. Old Paper	d. Silk Paper
R53	R4	40c	**Inland Exchange, brown**	1,300.	8.00	7.50	—
			Pair	*5,250.*	50.00	16.00	
			Block of 4		210.00	140.00	
			Dble. transfer		50.00	30.00	
f.			Double impression			—	
R54	R5	50c	**Conveyance, blue**	17.00	3.00	.35	3.00
			Pair	100.00	45.00	.70	6.50
			Block of 4	600.00	160.00	2.50	
			Dble. transfer			6.00	
			Cracked plate			15.00	
			Scatched plate			—	
e.			50c **ultra**			.50	—
			Pair			1.25	
			Block of 4			10.00	
R55	R5	50c	**Entry of Goods, blue**		15.00	.45	85.00
			Pair		300.00	1.75	200.00
			Block of 4		650.00	25.00	
			Dble. transfer			5.00	
			Cracked plate			20.00	
R56	R5	50c	**Foreign Exchange, blue**	60.00	110.00	7.00	
			Pair	200.00	550.00	42.50	
			Block of 4			140.00	
			Double transfer at left			11.00	
e.			Double impression			*500.00*	
f.			Half used as 25c on document			*200.00*	
R57	R5	50c	**Lease, blue**	27.50	150.00	9.00	
			Pair	200.00	550.00	67.50	
			Block of 4	*1,000.*	1,300.	225.00	
R58	R5	50c	**Life Insurance, blue**	40.00	90.00	1.50	
			Pair	160.00		10.00	
			Block of 4	850.00		50.00	
			Dble. transfer	47.50		11.00	
e.			Double impression			*800.00*	

Cracked Plate (C59)

No.	Design	Denom.	Description	a. Imperf	b. Part Perf.	c. Old Paper	d. Silk Paper
R59	R5	50c	**Mortgage, blue**	20.00	4.50	.65	—
			Pair	100.00	225.00	1.50	
			Block of 4	400.00	500.00	7.50	
			Cracked plate (C59)		37.50	12.50	
			Scratched plate, diagonal	35.00	25.00	12.50	
			Dble. transfer			3.50	
e.			Double impression	—		—	

Scratch is across three stamps. Value is for a single.

No.	Design	Denom.	Description	a. Imperf	b. Part Perf.	c. Old Paper	d. Silk Paper
R60	R5	50c	**Original Process, blue**	5.00	*600.00*	1.00	4.00
			Pair	77.50		2.75	15.00
			Block of 4	*1,000.*		7.50	125.00
			Double transfer at top			5.00	
			Double transfer at bottom			8.00	
			Scratched plate			10.00	
e.			Half used as 25c on document			—	
R61	R5	50c	**Passage Ticket, blue**	100.00	300.00	2.00	
			Pair	300.00	1,300.	12.50	
			Block of 4	*1,250.*		225.00	
			Cracked plate			—	
R62	R5	50c	**Probate of Will, blue**	50.00	160.00	20.00	
			Pair	200.00	750.00	50.00	
			Block of 4	850.00	1,500.	350.00	
			Scratched plate		—		
R63	R5	50c	**Surety Bond, blue**	275.00	2.50	.30	
			Pair	*1,200.*	15.00	1.75	
			Block of 4		100.00	10.00	
e.			50c **ultra**			.75	
			Pair			5.50	
			Block of 4			55.00	
R64	R5	60c	**Inland Exchange, orange**	100.00	75.00	8.00	60.00
			Pair	300.00	225.00	17.50	140.00
			Block of 4	*750.00*	550.00	100.00	
R65	R5	70c	**Foreign Exchange, green**	600.00	175.00	12.00	100.00
			Pair	2,500.	950.00	40.00	200.00
			Block of 4		*2,000.*	250.00	
			Cracked plate		—	30.00	

Pairs and blocks of No. R65b are valued in the grade of fine.

R6

R7

No.	Design	Denom.	Description	a. Imperf	b. Part Perf.	c. Old Paper	d. Silk Paper
R66	R6	$1	**Conveyance, red**	25.00	900.00	25.00	125.00
			Pair	90.00	*3,500.*	65.00	
			Block of 4	650.00		160.00	
			Dble. transfer	35.00		37.50	
			Right frame line double	90.00		77.50	
			Top frame line double	—		60.00	
R67	R6	$1	**Entry of Goods, red**	42.50		2.50	110.00
			Pair	150.00		6.50	
			Block of 4	500.00		55.00	
R68	R6	$1	**Foreign Exchange, red**	80.00		.75	100.00
			Pair	250.00		1.75	
			Block of 4	*1,475.*		11.00	
			Dble. transfer			5.50	
			Left frame line double	180.00		19.00	
e.			Diagonal half used as 50c on document				*200.00*

			.0				
			.00				
			Block of 4				
			Right frame line double	275.00		20.00	
e.			Half used as 50c on document			—	
R72	R6	$1	**Manifest, red**	42.50		35.00	
			Pair	120.00		85.00	
			Block of 4	450.00		210.00	
R73	R6	$1	**Mortgage, red**	25.00		200.00	
			Pair	85.00		400.00	
			Block of 4	600.00		825.00	
			Double transfer at left	—		230.00	
			Bottom frame line double	60.00		350.00	
R74	R6	$1	**Passage Ticket, red**	300.00		275.00	
			Pair	650.00		600.00	
			Block of 4	*1,325.*		1,550.	
R75	R6	$1	**Power of Attorney, red**	90.00		2.50	
			Pair	225.00		6.00	
			Block of 4	500.00		26.00	
			Dble. transfer			9.50	
			Recut			11.50	
R76	R6	$1	**Probate of Will, red**	90.00		50.00	
			Pair	275.00		125.00	
			Block of 4	*800.00*		325.00	
			Right frame line double	160.00		72.50	
R77	R7	$1.30	**Foreign Exchange, orange** ('63)	*6,500.*		75.00	
			Pair			190.00	
			Block of 4			—	

R78	R7	$1.50	**Inland Exchange, blue**	27.50		6.00	
			Pair	140.00		75.00	
			Block of 4	500.00		400.00	
			Double transfer (T78)			12.50	
R79	R7	$1.60	**Foreign Exchange, green** ('63)	1,300.		120.00	
			Pair	*5,500.*		375.00	
R80	R7	$1.90	**Foreign Exchange, purple** ('63)	*10,000.*		110.00	—
			Pair			300.00	
			Block of 4			700.00	

There are many shade and color variations of No. R80. See foreword of "Revenues" section.

R8

R81	R8	$2	**Conveyance, red**	180.00	2,250.	3.50	40.00
			Pair	400.00	*6,250.*	10.00	90.00
			Block of 4	1,000.		65.00	200.00
			Cracked plate			32.50	
e.			Half used as $1 on document			*600.00*	
R82	R8	$2	**Mortgage, red**	135.00		6.00	60.00
			Pair	300.00		14.00	125.00
			Block of 4	700.00		60.00	
			Dble. transfer			12.50	

e.			Half used as $1 on document			—	
R83	R8	$2	**Probate of Will, red** ('63)	*5,500.*		80.00	
			Pair	*11,500.*		200.00	
			Block of 4			425.00	
			Dble. transfer			90.00	
e.			Horiz. half used as $1 on document			*750.00*	
R84	R8	$2.50	**Inland Exchange, purple** ('63)	7,000.		20.00	30.00
			Pair	*22,500.*		40.00	75.00
			Block of 4			325.00	425.00
e.			Double impression			*1,400.*	

There are many shade and color variations of Nos. R84c and R84d. See foreword of "Revenues" section.

R85	R8	$3	**Charter Party, green**	175.00		10.00	150.00
			Pair	400.00		65.00	325.00
			Block of 4	2,000.		250.00	
			Double transfer at top			—	
			Double transfer at bottom			12.00	
e.			Printed on both sides			*4,500.*	
f.			Half used as $1.50 on document			—	
g.			Impression of No. RS208 on back			*10,000.*	
R86	R8	$3	**Manifest, green**	175.00		50.00	
			Pair	400.00		125.00	
			Block of 4	*3,500.*		300.00	
			Dble. transfer			210.00	
R87	R8	$3.50	**Inland Exchange, blue** ('63)	*7,000.*		65.00	
			Pair	*25,000.*		180.00	
			Block of 4			450.00	
e.			Printed on both sides			*4,000.*	

R9

R10

				a. Imperf	b. Part Perf.	Perforated c. Old Paper	d. Silk Paper
R88	R9	$5	**Charter Party, red**	300.00		9.00	90.00
			Pair	625.00		65.00	
			Block of 4	*1,400.*		200.00	
			Right frame line double	325.00		70.00	
			Top frame line double	325.00		60.00	
R89	R9	$5	**Conveyance, red**	40.00		10.00	140.00
			Pair	200.00		22.50	300.00
			Block of 4	*900.00*		110.00	
R90	R9	$5	**Manifest, red**	185.00		90.00	
			Pair	450.00		250.00	
			Block of 4	*1,100.*		550.00	
			Left frame line double	210.00		150.00	
R91	R9	$5	**Mortgage, red**	175.00		22.50	
			Pair	800.00		87.50	
			Block of 4	—		—	
R92	R9	$5	**Probate of Will, red**	700.00		25.00	
			Pair	1,450.		100.00	
			Block of 4	*3,000.*		375.00	
R93	R9	$10	**Charter Party, green**	750.00		32.50	
			Pair	*1,600.*		95.00	
			Block of 4	—		450.00	
			Dble. transfer			85.00	
R94	R9	$10	**Conveyance, green**	125.00		70.00	
			Pair	350.00		175.00	
			Block of 4	900.00		700.00	
			Double transfer at top	150.00		125.00	
			Right frame line double			150.00	
R95	R9	$10	**Mortgage, green**	650.00		35.00	
			Pair	1,600.		120.00	
			Block of 4	*4,500.*		—	
			Top frame line double	675.00		52.50	
R96	R9	$10	**Probate of Will, green**	2,000.		40.00	
			Pair	*6,000.*		87.50	
			Block of 4			400.00	

				a. Imperf	b. Part Perf.	Perforated c. Old Paper	d. Silk Paper
			Double transfer at top			57.50	
R97	R10	$15	**Mortgage, blue**	2,700.		225.00	
			Pair	*6,500.*		500.00	
			Block of 4	*15,000.*		*2,750.*	
	e.		$15 **ultra**			250.00	
			Pair			750.00	
			Block of 4			*4,000.*	
	f.		$15 **milky blue**			275.00	
			Pair			1,500.	
R98	R10	$20	**Conveyance, orange**	150.00		110.00	175.00
			Pair	400.00		250.00	350.00
			Block of 4	1,000.		800.00	
R99	R10	$20	**Probate of Will, orange**	2,000.		2,000.	
			Pair	*4,250.*		*4,250.*	
			Block of 4	*9,000.*		*9,000.*	
R100	R10	$25	**Mortgage, red** ('63)	1,500.		200.00	250.00
			Pair	*3,250.*		400.00	
			Block of 4	*9,000.*		*1,250.*	
	e.		Horiz. pair, imperf. between			*2,500.*	
R101	R10	$50	**U.S. Internal Revenue, green** ('63)	250.00		150.00	
			Pair	600.00		325.00	
			Block of 4	2,300.		675.00	
			Cracked plate			160.00	

R11

				a. Imperf	b. Part Perf.	c. Old Paper	d. Silk Paper
R102	R11	$200	**U.S. Internal Revenue, grn & red** ('64)	2,500.		900.00	
			Pair	*5,500.*		*2,000.*	
			Block of 4	*12,500.*		*6,000.*	

DOCUMENTARY STAMPS

Second Issue

After release of the First Issue revenue stamps, the Bureau of Internal Revenue received many reports of fraudulent cleaning and re-use. The Bureau ordered a Second Issue with new designs and colors, using a patented "chameleon" paper which is usually violet or pinkish, with silk fibers.

While designs are different from those of the first issue, stamp sizes and make up of the plates are the same as for corresponding denominations.

George Washington

R12 R12a

Engraved and printed by Jos. R. Carpenter, Philadelphia.

Various Frames and Numeral Arrangements

1871 ***Perf. 12***

R103	R12	1c	**blue & black**	65.00
			Cut cancel	22.50
			Pair	160.00
			Block of 4	400.00
	a.		Inverted center	*1,500.*
			Pair	*3,100.*
			Block of 4	—
R104	R12	2c	**blue & black**	2.75
			Cut cancel	.20
			Pair	6.25
			Block of 4	40.00
	a.		Inverted center	*6,000.*
R105	R12a	3c	**blue & black**	40.00
			Cut cancel	15.00
			Pair	90.00
			Block of 4	275.00
R106	R12a	4c	**blue & black**	100.00
			Cut cancel	35.00
			Pair	225.00
			Block of 4	400.00
	a.		Horiz. half used as 2c on document	*500.00*
	b.		Vert. half used as 2c on document	*925.00*
R107	R12a	5c	**blue & black**	2.00
			Cut cancel	.50
			Pair	6.00
			Block of 4	22.50
	a.		Inverted center	*4,500.*
R108	R12a	6c	**blue & black**	160.00
			Cut cancel	55.00
			Pair	325.00
			Block of 4	850.00
R109	R12a	10c	**blue & black**	1.50
			Cut cancel	.20
			Pair	9.50
			Block of 4	25.00
	a.		Inverted center	*2,500.*
			Pair	*5,750.*
	b.		Double impression of center	—
	c.		Half used as 5c on document	*250.00*

No. R109a is valued in the grade of fine.

R110	R12a	15c	**blue & black**	60.00
			Cut cancel	20.00
			Pair	120.00
			Block of 4	225.00
R111	R12a	20c	**blue & black**	7.50
			Cut cancel	2.75
			Pair	22.50
			Block of 4	87.50
	a.		Inverted center	*12,500.*
			Pair	—

Nos. R109a and R111a are valued in the grade of fine.

R13

R13a

R112	R13	25c	**blue & black**	1.50
			Cut cancel	.25
			Pair	3.25
			Block of 4	11.00
			Double transfer, position 57	25.00
	a.		Inverted center	*11,000.*
	b.		Sewing machine perf.	110.00
			Cut cancel	65.00
			Pair	300.00
			Block of 4	1,500.
	c.		Perf. 8	400.00
R113	R13	30c	**blue & black**	110.00
			Cut cancel	42.50
			Pair	225.00
			Block of 4	575.00
R114	R13	40c	**blue & black**	100.00
			Cut cancel	
			Pair	
R115	R13a	50c	**blue & black**	
			Cut cancel	
			Pair	
			Block of 4	
			Double transf	
	a.		Sewing mac	
			Pair	
			Block of	
	b.		Inverted	

	Pair	*4,500.*
	Inverted center, punch cancellation	300.00
	Pair	700.00
R116	R13a 60c **blue & black**	150.00
	Cut cancel	50.00
	Pair	325.00
	Foreign entry, design of 70c	185.00
R117	R13a 70c **blue & black**	70.00
	Cut cancel	22.50
	Pair	150.00
a.	Inverted center	*4,000.*
	Cut cancel	*2,000.*

R13b

R13c

R118	R13b $1 **blue & black**	8.00
	Cut cancel	1.75
	Pair	20.00
	Block of 4	50.00
a.	Inverted center	*5,000.*
	Punch cancel	*900.00*
R119	R13b $1.30 **blue & black**	550.00
	Cut cancel	150.00
	Pair	1,150.
R120	R13b $1.50 **blue & black**	19.00
	Cut cancel	8.00
	Pair	65.00
	Block of 4	—
	Foreign entry, design of $1	350.00
a.	Sewing machine perf.	1,000.
	Pair	—
R121	R13b $1.60 **blue & black**	575.00
	Cut cancel	300.00
	Pair	1,200.
R122	R13b $1.90 **blue & black**	400.00
	Cut cancel	120.00
	Pair	850.00
	Block of 4	—
R123	R13c $2 **blue & black**	20.00
	Cut cancel	7.50
	Pair	55.00
	Block of 4	180.00
	Double transfer	20.00
R124	R13c $2.50 **blue & black**	35.00
	Cut cancel	16.00
	Pair	95.00
	Block of 4	750.00
R125	R13c $3 **blue & black**	45.00
	Cut cancel	17.50
	Pair	110.00
	Block of 4	550.00
	Double transfer	—
R126	R13c $3.50 **blue & black**	300.00
	Cut cancel	100.00
	Pair	700.00

R13d

R13e

R127	R13d $5 **blue & black**	27.50
	Cut cancel	9.00
	Pair	100.00
	Block of 4	275.00
a.	Inverted center	*3,750.*
	Punch cancel	*1,100.*
R128	R13d $10 **blue & black**	210.00
	Cut cancel	75.00
	Pair	475.00
	Block of 4	*1,000.*
R129	R13e $20 **blue & black**	800.00
	Cut cancel	290.00
	Pair	1,750.
	Block of 4	*10,000.*
R130	R13e $25 **blue & black**	900.00
	Cut cancel	325.00
	Pair	2,000.
R131	R13e $50 **blue & black**	1,000.
	Cut cancel	375.00
	Pair	2,250.

R13f

R132	R13f $200 **red, blue & black**	*7,500.*
	Cut cancel	*3,250.*

Printed in sheets of one.

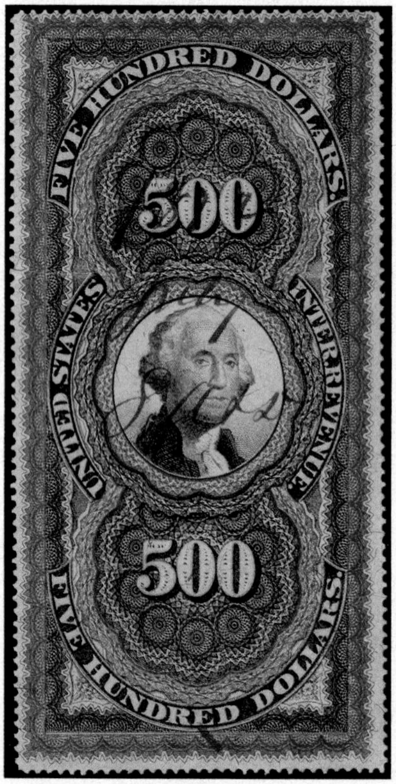

R13g

R133	R13g $500 **red orange, green & black**	*14,000.*

Printed in sheets of one.

Value for No. R133 is for a very fine appearing example with a light circular cut cancel or with minor flaws.

Inverted Centers: Fraudulently produced inverted centers exist, some excellently made.

Confusion resulting from the fact that all 1c through $50 denominations of the Second Issue were uniform in color, caused the ordering of a new printing with values in distinctive colors.

Plates used were those of the preceding issue.

Third Issue

Engraved and printed by Jos. R. Carpenter, Philadelphia.

Various Frames and Numeral Arrangements.

Violet "Chameleon" Paper with Silk Fibers.

1871-72 ***Perf. 12***

R134	R12 1c **claret & black** ('72)	47.50
	Cut cancel	21.00
	Pair	110.00
	Block of 4	350.00

No.	Type	Description	Value
R135	R12	2c **orange & black**	.40
		Cut cancel	.20
		Pair	.80
		Block of 4	1.75
		Double transfer	—
		Double impression of frame	*1,500.*
		Frame printed on both sides	*1,600.*
		Double impression of center	*150.00*
a.		2c vermilion & black (error)	*700.00*
b.		Inverted center	750.00
		Pair	*2,250.*
		Block of 4	—
c.		Imperf., pair	—
R136	R12a	4c **brown & black** ('72)	75.00
		Cut cancel	22.50
		Pair	175.00
R137	R12a	5c **orange & black**	.35
		Cut cancel	.20
		Pair	.75
		Block of 4	1.60
a.		Inverted center	*6,000.*
		"Block" of 3	—

No. R137a is valued in the grade of fine.

No.	Type	Description	Value
R138	R12a	6c **orange & black** ('72)	85.00
		Cut cancel	27.50
		Pair	190.00
		Block of 4	525.00
R139	R12a	15c **brown & black** ('72)	22.50
		Cut cancel	5.75
		Pair	50.00
		Block of 4	160.00
a.		Inverted center	*22,500.*
		Pair	—
R140	R13	30c **orange & black** ('72)	32.50
		Cut cancel	8.25
		Pair	75.00
		Block of 4	300.00
		Double transfer	—
a.		Inverted center	*3,250.*
		Cut cancel	*1,850.*
R141	R13	40c **brown & black** ('72)	70.00
		Cut cancel	21.00
		Pair	160.00
		Block of 4	375.00
R142	R13a	60c **orange & black** ('72)	100.00
		Cut cancel	35.00
		Pair	300.00
		Block of 4	650.00
		Foreign entry, design of 70c	125.00
R143	R13a	70c **green & black** ('72)	80.00
		Cut cancel	25.00
		Pair	190.00
		Block of 4	475.00
R144	R13b	$1 **green & black** ('72)	2.00
		Cut cancel	.55
		Pair	8.50
		Block of 4	75.00
a.		Inverted center	*9,000.*
R145	R13c	$2 **vermilion & black** ('72)	35.00
		Cut cancel	15.00
		Pair	75.00
		Block of 4	175.00
		Double transfer	50.00
R146	R13c	$2.50 **claret & black** ('72)	65.00
		Cut cancel	24.00
		Pair	140.00
		Block of 4	300.00
a.		Inverted center	*25,000.*
R147	R13c	$3 **green & black** ('72)	65.00
		Cut cancel	22.50
		Pair	140.00
		Block of 4	300.00
		Double transfer	—
R148	R13d	$5 **vermilion & black** ('72)	37.50
		Cut cancel	13.50
		Pair	80.00
		Block of 4	160.00
R149	R13d	$10 **green & black** ('72)	225.00
		Cut cancel	50.00
		Pair	475.00
		Block of 4	1,100.
R150	R13e	$20 **orange & black** ('72)	625.00
		Cut cancel	260.00
		Pair	1,300.
		Block of 4	*3,000.*
a.		$20 vermilion & black (error)	1,000.

(See note on Inverted Centers after No. R133.)

1874 *Perf. 12*

No.	Type	Description	Value
R151	R12	2c **orange & black,** *green*	.20
		Cut cancel	.20
		Pair	.40
		Block of 4	.90
a.		Inverted center	500.00

Liberty — R14

1875-78

No.		Description	Silk Paper a. Perf.	Wmkd. 191R b. Perf.	c. Roul. 6
R152	R14 2c	**blue,** *blue*	.45	.35	32.50
		Pair	.90	.70	125.00
		"L" shaped strip of 3			600.00
		Block of 4	1.90	2.10	
		Double transfer	5.50	5.50	
d.		Vert. pair, imperf. horiz.	525.00	350.00	
e.		Imperf., pair		*350.00*	

The watermarked paper came into use in 1878.

Nos. 279, 267a, 267, 279Bg, 279B, 272-274 Overprinted in Red or Blue:

I. R.

a — Rectangular Periods

I. R.

a — Square Periods

I.R.

b

I.R.

b — Small Period

Overprint "a" exists in two (or possibly more) settings, with upright rectangular periods or with changed leg of "R" and square periods, both illustrated. Overprint "b" has 4 stamps with small period in each pane of 100 (pos. 41, 46, 91 & 96).

1898 **Wmk. 191** *Perf. 12*

For Nos. R153-R160, values in the first column are for unused examples, values in the second column are for used.

No.	Type	Description	Unused	Used
R153	A87 (a)	1c **green,** red overprint	5.00	2.75
		Block of 4	29.00	12.00
		P# strip of 3, Impt.	35.00	
		P# block of 6, Impt.	95.00	
R154	A87 (b)	1c **green,** red overprint	.35	.35
		Block of 4	1.50	1.50
		P# strip of 3, Impt.	10.50	
		P# block of 6, Impt.	57.50	
a.		Overprint inverted	30.00	18.00
		Block of 4	150.00	—
		P# strip of 3, Impt.	160.00	
		P# block of 6, Impt.	350.00	
b.		Overprint on back instead of face, inverted	—	
c.		Pair, one without overprint	*10,000.*	
R155	A88 (b)	2c **pink,** type III, blue overprint, *July 1, 1898*	.30	.25
		Block of 4	1.25	1.10
		P# strip of 3, Impt.	11.50	
		P# block of 6, Impt.	55.00	
		Dot in "S" of "CENTS"	1.10	
		P# strip of 3, Impt.	18.00	
b.		2c **carmine,** type III, blue overprint, *July 1, 1898*	.35	.25
		Block of 4	1.40	1.10
		P# strip of 3, Impt.	13.00	
		P# block of 6, Impt.	57.50	
		Dot in "S" of "CENTS"	1.40	
		P# strip of 3, Impt.	24.00	
c.		As No. R155, overprint inverted, *July 1898*	5.00	4.00
		Block of 4	21.00	17.50
		P# strip of 3, Impt.	52.50	
		P# block of 6, Impt.	130.00	
d.		Vertical pair, one without overprint	*1,750.*	
e.		Horiz. pair, one without overprint	—	
f.		As No. R155, overprint on back instead of face, inverted	—	

NOTE: Old No. R155 is now Nos. R155b, R155Ag; old No. R155a is Nos. R155c, R155Ah; old No. R155b is Nos. R155d, R155e; old No. R155c is No. R155f.

No.	Type	Description	Unused	Used
R155A	A88 (b)	2c **pink,** type IV, blue overprint *July 1, 1898*	.25	.25
		Block of 4	1.25	1.10
		P# strip of 3, Impt.	10.50	
		P# block of 6, Impt.	52.50	
g.		2c **carmine,** type IV, blue overprint, *July 1, 1898*	.25	.25
		Block of 4	1.40	1.10
		P# strip of 3, Impt.	11.50	
		P# block of 6, Impt.	55.00	
h.		As No. R155A, overprint inverted, *July 1898*	2.75	2.00
		Block of 4	13.00	9.25
		P# strip of 3, Impt.	32.50	
		P# block of 6, Impt.	77.50	

Handstamped Type "b" in Magenta

No.	Type	Description	Unused	Used
R156	A93	8c **violet brown**		*5,250.*
R157	A94	10c **dark green**		*4,000.*
		Block of 6	—	
R158	A95	15c **dark blue**		*6,500.*

Nos. R156-R158 were emergency provisionals, privately prepared, not officially issued.

Privately Prepared Provisionals

No. 285 Overprinted in Red

I. R.
L. H. C.

1898 **Wmk. 191** *Perf. 12*

No.	Type	Description	Unused	Used
R158A	A100	1c **dark yellow green**	*12,500.*	*10,000.*

Same Overprinted "I.R./P.I.D. & Son" in Red

No.	Type	Description	Unused	Used
R158B	A100	1c **dark yellow green**	*35,000.*	*32,500.*

No. R158B is valued with small faults as each of the four recorded examples have faults.

Nos. R158A-R158B were overprinted with federal government permission by the Purvis Printing Co. upon order of Capt. L. H. Chapman of the Chapman Steamboat Line. Both the Chapman Line and P. I. Daprix & Son operated freight-carrying steamboats on the Erie Canal. The Chapman Line touched at Syracuse, Utica, Little Falls and Fort Plain; the Daprix boat ran between Utica and Rome. Overprintings of 250 of each stamp were made.

Dr. Kilmer & Co. provisional overprints and St. Louis provisional proprietary stamps are listed under "Private Die Medicine Stamps," Nos. RS307-RS315 and RS320-395.

Newspaper Stamp No. PR121 Surcharged in Red

1898 *Perf. 12*

No.	Type	Description	Unused	Used
R159	N18	$5 **dark blue,** surcharge reading down	500.00	200.00
		Block of 4	2,100.	950.00
		P# strip of 3, Impt.	*2,500.*	
R160	N18	$5 **dark blue,** surcharge reading up	140.00	110.00
		Block of 4	550.00	*750.00*
		P# strip of 3, Impt.	2,000.	

Battleship — R15

There are two styles of rouletting for the proprietary and documentary stamps of the 1898 issue, an ordinary rouletting 5½ and one by which small rectangles of the paper are cut out, usually called hyphen-hole perforation 7. Several stamps are known with an apparent roulette 14 caused by slippage of a hyphen-hole 7 rouletting wheel.

1898 **Wmk. 191R**

Rouletted 5½, Hyphen Hole Perf 7

No.	Type	Description	Roul. 5½ Unused	Used	*p.* Hyphen Hole Perf. 7 Unused	Used
R161	R15 ½c	**orange**	4.00	*17.50*		
		Block of 4	18.00	*140.00*		
R162	R15 ½c	**dark gray**	.30	.25		
		Block of 4	1.60	1.10		
		Double transfer		7.75		
a.		Vert. pair, imperf. horiz.	100.00			
R163	R15 1c	**pale blue**	.20	.20	.30	.25
		Block of 4	.40	.25	1.60	1.50
		Double transfer	10.00			
a.		Vert. pair, imperf. horiz.	8.00			
b.		Imperf., pair	*500.00*			
R164	R15 2c	**carmine rose**	.30	.30	.35	.25
		Block of 4	1.50	1.50	2.75	1.10
		Double transfer	1.10	.30		

				Roul. 5½ Unused	Roul. 5½ Used	p. Hyphen Hole Perf. 7 Unused	p. Hyphen Hole Perf. 7 Used
a.			Vert. pair, imperf. horiz.	100.00			
b.			Imperf., pair	300.00			
c.			Horiz. pair, imperf. vert.	—			
R165	R15	3c	**dark blue**	4.00	.35	35.00	1.40
			Block of 4	15.00	1.40	150.00	6.25
			Double transfer	—			
R166	R15	4c	**pale rose**	2.50	.35	13.00	1.60
			Block of 4	11.50	1.40	55.00	7.75
a.			Vert. pair, imperf. horiz.	175.00			
R167	R15	5c	**lilac**	.65	.25	13.00	.35
			Block of 4	3.25	1.25	55.00	1.60
a.			Pair, imperf. horiz. or vert.	275.00	175.00		
b.			Horiz. pair, imperf. between		*650.00*		
R168	R15	10c	**dark brown**	2.00	.25	7.50	.25
			Block of 4	12.00	1.25	32.50	1.25
a.			Vert. pair, imperf. horiz.	40.00	35.00		
b.			Horiz. pair, imperf. vert.	—			
R169	R15	25c	**purple brown**	5.00	.50	15.00	.50
			Block of 4	21.00	2.25	65.00	1.75
			Double transfer	—			
R170	R15	40c	**blue lilac**	125.00	1.25	175.00	30.00
			Block of 4	600.00	52.50	875.00	225.00
			Cut cancel		.35		12.50
R171	R15	50c	**slate violet**	30.00	.25	60.00	1.00
			Block of 4	130.00	2.25	275.00	6.75
a.			Imperf., pair	*300.00*			
b.			Horiz. pair, imperf. between			—	*250.00*
R172	R15	80c	**bister**	110.00	.50	210.00	50.00
			Block of 4	525.00	32.50	1,050.	240.00
			Cut cancel		.20		20.00

Numerous double transfers exist on this issue.

Commerce — R16

				Roul. 5½ Unused	Roul. 5½ Used	p. Hyphen Hole Perf. 7 Unused	p. Hyphen Hole Perf. 7 Used
R173	R16	$1	**dark green**	20.00	.25	30.00	2.00
			Block of 4	82.50	.60		10.00
			Cut cancel		.25		.75
a.			Vert. pair, imperf. horiz.	—			
b.			Horiz. pair, imperf. vert.	—	325.00		
R174	R16	$3	**dark brown**	40.00	1.00	67.50	3.50
			Block of 4	—	5.25		15.00
			Cut cancel		.25		.30
a.			Horiz. pair, imperf. vert.		500.00		
R175	R16	$5	**orange red**	70.00	1.90		
			Block of 4	—	9.50		
			Cut cancel		.25		
R176	R16	$10	**black**	150.00	3.25		
			Block of 4		16.00		
			Cut cancel		.55		
a.			Horiz. pair, imperf. vert.		—		
R177	R16	$30	**red**	475.00	160.00		
			Block of 4		700.00		
			Cut cancel		47.50		
R178	R16	$50	**gray brown**	250.00	5.75		
			Block of 4		29.00		
			Cut cancel		2.10		

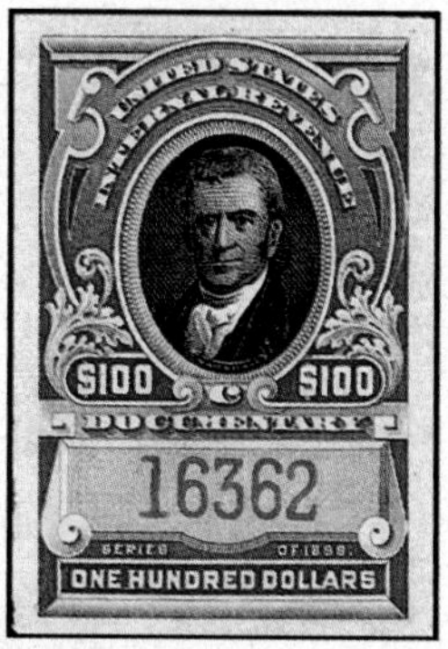
John Marshall — R17

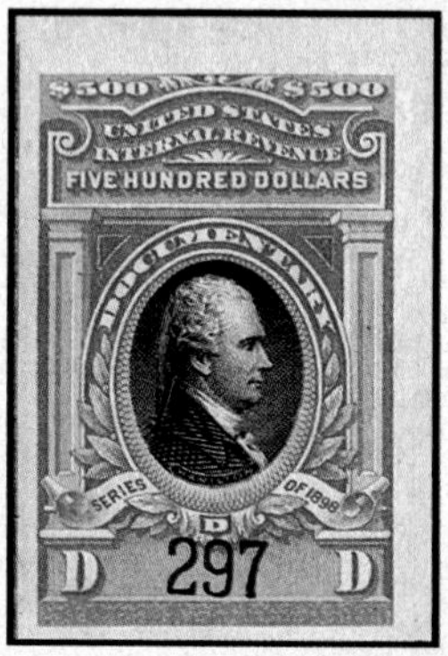
Alexander Hamilton — R18

James Madison — R19

Various Portraits in Various Frames, Each Inscribed "Series of 1898"

1899 ***Imperf.***

Without Gum

R179	R17	$100	**yellow brown & black**	275.00	37.50
			Cut cancel		21.00
			Vertical strip of 4	—	175.00
			Vertical strip of 4, cut cancel		90.00
R180	R18	$500	**carmine lake & black**	1,500.	800.00
			Cut cancel		300.
			Vertical strip of 4	—	2,250.
			Vertical strip of 4, cut cancel		1,000.
R181	R19	$1000	**green & black**	1,250.	375.00
			Cut cancel		150.00
			Vertical strip of 4	—	1,750.
			Vertical strip of 4, cut cancel		600.00

1900 ***Hyphen-hole perf. 7***

Allegorical Figure of Commerce

R182	R16	$1	**carmine**	37.50	.55
			Cut cancel		.30
			Block of 4	160.00	2.50
			Block of 4, cut cancel		1.25
R183	R16	$3	**lake** (fugitive ink)	250.00	52.50
			Cut cancel		9.00
			Block of 4	1,000.	275.00
			Block of 4, cut cancel		40.00

Warning: The ink on No. R183 will run in water.

Surcharged in Black with Open Numerals of Value

R184	R16	$1	**gray**	30.00	.40
			Cut cancel		.25
			Block of 4	—	1.40
			Block of 4, cut cancel		1.10
a.			Horiz. pair, imperf. vert		—
b.			Surcharge omitted	125.00	
			Surcharge omitted, cut cancel		82.50
R185	R16	$2	**gray**	30.00	.35
			Cut cancel		.25
			Block of 4	125.00	1.40
			Block of 4, cut cancel		1.10
R186	R16	$3	**gray**	125.00	11.50
			Cut cancel		4.25
			Block of 4	—	50.00
			Block of 4, cut cancel		18.00
R187	R16	$5	**gray**	75.00	9.00
			Cut cancel		1.40
			Block of 4	—	35.00
			Block of 4, cut cancel		7.00
R188	R16	$10	**gray**	160.00	20.00
			Cut cancel		3.25
			Block of 4	—	92.50
			Block of 4, cut cancel		15.00
R189	R16	$50	**gray**	2,000.	550.00
			Cut cancel		140.00
			Block of 4		2,450.
			Block of 4, cut cancel		550.00

Surcharged in Black with Ornamental Numerals of Value

Warning: If Nos. R190-R194 are soaked, the center part of the surcharged numeral may wash off. Before the surcharging, a square of soluble varnish was applied to the middle of some stamps.

1902

R190	R16	$1	**green**	42.50	3.50
			Cut cancel		.30
			Block of 4	—	15.00
			Block of 4, cut cancel		1.25
a.			Inverted surcharge		*190.00*
R191	R16	$2	**green**	42.50	1.75
			Cut cancel		.30
			Block of 4	—	7.50
			Block of 4, cut cancel		1.40
a.			Surcharged as No. R185	110.00	75.00
b.			Surcharged as No. R185, in violet	*2,000.*	—
c.			As "a," double surcharge	*150.00*	
d.			As "a," triple surcharge	*850.00*	
e.			Pair, Nos. R191c and R191d	*1,650.*	
R192	R16	$5	**green**	225.00	37.50
			Cut cancel		4.50
			Block of 4	—	160.00
			Block of 4, cut cancel		22.50
a.			Surcharge omitted	250.00	
b.			Pair, one without surcharge	*400.00*	

R193 R16 $10 **green**	450.00	140.00
Cut cancel		52.50
Block of 4		600.00
Block of 4, cut cancel		225.00
R194 R16 $50 **green**	2,000.	1,000.
Cut cancel		250.00
Block of 4	—	—
Block of 4, cut cancel		1,050.

R20

Wmk. 190

Inscribed "Series of 1914"

1914 Wmk. 190 Offset Printing *Perf. 10*

R195 R20 ½c **rose**	14.00	4.50
Block of 4	52.50	19.00
R196 R20 1c **rose**	2.50	.30
Block of 4	11.00	1.25
R197 R20 2c **rose**	3.50	.30
Block of 4	15.00	1.25
Double impression	—	
R198 R20 3c **rose**	75.00	30.00
Block of 4	325.00	40.00
R199 R20 4c **rose**	25.00	2.25
Block of 4	100.00	9.50
Recut U. L. corner	*300.00*	
R200 R20 5c **rose**	9.00	.35
Block of 4	37.50	1.50
R201 R20 10c **rose**	7.00	.25
Block of 4	29.00	.45
R202 R20 25c **rose**	47.50	.55
Block of 4	210.00	2.25
R203 R20 40c **rose**	30.00	2.50
Block of 4	125.00	11.00
R204 R20 50c **rose**	12.00	.35
Block of 4	50.00	1.10
R205 R20 80c **rose**	200.00	15.00
Block of 4	825.00	65.00

Wmk. 191R

R206 R20 ½c **rose**	1.60	.50
Block of 4	7.00	2.50
R207 R20 1c **rose**	.25	.20
Block of 4	.70	.25
Double impression	*300.00*	—
R208 R20 2c **rose**	.30	.25
Block of 4	1.25	1.10
R209 R20 3c **rose**	1.50	.25
Block of 4	6.50	1.10
R210 R20 4c **rose**	4.00	.50
Block of 4	19.00	2.25
R211 R20 5c **rose**	1.75	.30
Block of 4	8.00	1.25
R212 R20 10c **rose**	.80	.20
Block of 4	3.75	.35
R213 R20 25c **rose**	7.00	1.50
Block of 4	29.00	7.00
R214 R20 40c **rose**	110.00	14.00
Cut cancel		.45
Block of 4	525.00	57.50
R215 R20 50c **rose**	25.00	.25
Cut cancel		.20
Block of 4	110.00	1.10
R216 R20 80c **rose**	175.00	30.00
Cut cancel		1.10
Block of 4	750.00	225.00

Liberty — R21

Inscribed "Series 1914"

Engr.

R217 R21 $1 **green**	65.00	.55
Cut cancel		.25
Block of 4	—	3.00
Block of 4, cut cancel		1.10
a. $1 **yellow green**	45.00	.25
R218 R21 $2 **carmine**	90.00	.75
Cut cancel		.20
Block of 4	375.00	3.25
Block of 4, cut cancel		.25
R219 R21 $3 **purple**	125.00	3.75
Cut cancel		.50
Block of 4	525.00	13.50
Block of 4, cut cancel		2.10
R220 R21 $5 **blue**	95.00	4.00
Cut cancel		.55
Block of 4	400.00	17.00
Block of 4, cut cancel		2.75
R221 R21 $10 **yellow orange**	225.00	5.25
Cut cancel		.80
Block of 4	—	24.00
Block of 4, cut cancel		3.75
R222 R21 $30 **vermilion**	650.00	19.00
Cut cancel		2.10
Block of 4	—	67.50
Block of 4, cut cancel		10.50
R223 R21 $50 **violet**	1,900.	1,000.
Cut cancel		350.00
Block of 4		*4,250.*

Portrait Types of 1899 Inscribed "Series of 1915" (#R224), or "Series of 1914"

1914-15 Without Gum *Perf. 12*

R224 R19 $60 **brown** *(Lincoln)*	225.00	140.00
Vertical strip of 4		750.00
Cut cancel		67.50
Vertical strip of 4, cut cancel		300.00
R225 R17 $100 **green** *(Washington)*	72.50	45.00
Vertical strip of 4		190.00
Cut cancel		16.00
Vertical strip of 4, cut cancel		70.00
R226 R18 $500 **blue** *(Hamilton)*	—	600.00
Cut cancel		250.00
Vertical strip of 4, cut cancel		1,000.
R227 R19 $1000 **orange** *(Madison)*	—	600.00
Cut cancel		300.00
Vert. strip of 4, cut cancel		1,300.

The stamps of types R17, R18 and R19 in this and subsequent issues were issued in vertical strips of 4 which are imperforate at the top, bottom and right side; therefore, single stamps are always imperforate on one or two sides.

R22

Two types of design R22 are known.
Type I — With dot in centers of periods before and after "CENTS."
Type II — Without such dots.
First printings were done by commercial companies, later printings by the Bureau of Engraving and Printing.

1917 Offset Printing Wmk. 191R *Perf. 11*

R228 R22 1c **carmine rose**	.35	.20
Block of 4	1.50	.50
Double impression	20.00	4.00
R229 R22 2c **carmine rose**	.25	.20
Block of 4	1.10	.35
Double impression	20.00	5.00
R230 R22 3c **carmine rose**	1.75	.40
Block of 4	7.25	1.75
Double impression	—	—
R231 R22 4c **carmine rose**	.75	.25
Block of 4	3.50	1.10
Double impression	—	—
R232 R22 5c **carmine rose**	.30	.20
Block of 4	1.25	.35
R233 R22 8c **carmine rose**	2.50	.35
Block of 4	11.50	1.60
R234 R22 10c **carmine rose**	.40	.20
Block of 4	1.90	.35
Double impression		5.25
R235 R22 20c **carmine rose**	.75	.25
Block of 4	3.50	1.10
Double impression		—
R236 R22 25c **carmine rose**	1.50	.25
Block of 4	6.25	1.10
Double impression	—	—
R237 R22 40c **carmine rose**	2.25	.50
Block of 4	10.50	2.25
Double impression	8.00	5.00
R238 R22 50c **carmine rose**	2.50	.20
Block of 4	10.50	.35
Double impression	—	—
R239 R22 80c **carmine rose**	7.50	.25
Block of 4	32.50	1.10
Double impression	40.00	—

No. R234 is known used provisionally as a playing card revenue stamp in August 1932. Value for this use, authenticated, $300.

Liberty Type of 1914 without "Series 1914"

1917-33 Engr.

R240 R21 $1 **yellow green**	9.00	.30
Block of 4	40.00	1.25
a. $1 green	7.25	.20
R241 R21 $2 **rose**	15.00	.25
Block of 4	65.00	1.10
R242 R21 $3 **violet**	55.00	1.10
Cut cancel		.25
Block of 4	—	4.50
R243 R21 $4 **yellow brown**('33)	35.00	1.90
Cut cancel		.25
Block of 4	—	8.75
Block of 4, cut cancel		1.00
R244 R21 $5 **dark blue**	25.00	.35
Cut cancel		.25
Block of 4	—	1.50
R245 R21 $10 **orange**	50.00	1.40
Cut cancel		.30
Block of 4	—	7.00
Block of 4, cut cancel		1.25

Portrait Types of 1899 without "Series of" and Date

1917 Without Gum *Perf. 12*

R246 R17 $30 **deep orange, green numerals** *(Grant)*	50.00	13.00
Cut cancel		2.25
Vertical strip of 4		—
Cut cancel		3.50
a. As "b," imperf. pair		*750.00*
b. Numerals in blue	80.00	2.25
Cut cancel		1.40
R247 R19 $60 **brown** *(Lincoln)*	60.00	8.00
Cut cancel		.85
Vertical strip of 4		—
Cut cancel		5.00
R248 R17 $100 **green** *(Washington)*	37.50	1.25
Cut cancel		.40
Vertical strip of 4		—
Cut cancel		2.50
R249 R18 $500 **blue, red numerals** *(Hamilton)*	325.00	40.00
Cut cancel		12.50
Vertical strip of 4		*200.00*
Cut cancel		57.50
Double transfer	—	52.50
a. Numerals in orange	375.00	52.50
Double transfer		—
R250 R19 $1000 **orange** *(Madison)*	150.00	12.50
Cut cancel		4.25
Vertical strip of 4		75.00
Cut cancel		17.50
a. Imperf., pair		*2,000.*

See note after No. R227.

1928-29 Offset Printing *Perf. 10*

R251 R22 1c **carmine rose**	2.10	1.60
Block of 4	9.50	7.50
R252 R22 2c **carmine rose**	.60	.30
Block of 4	3.00	1.50
R253 R22 4c **carmine rose**	7.00	4.00
Block of 4	32.50	19.00
R254 R22 5c **carmine rose**	1.60	.55
Block of 4	7.75	2.50
R255 R22 10c **carmine rose**	2.40	1.25
Block of 4	11.00	5.50
R256 R22 20c **carmine rose**	5.50	4.50
Block of 4	25.00	20.00
Double impression		—

Engr.

R257 R21 $1 **green**	175.00	45.00
Block of 4	—	—
Cut cancel		5.00
R258 R21 $2 **rose**	80.00	5.00
Block of 4	—	20.00
R259 R21 $10 **orange**	250.00	65.00
Block of 4	—	—
Cut cancel		27.50

1929 Offset Printing *Perf. 11x10*

R260 R22 2c **carmine rose**('30)	3.00	2.75
Block of 4	13.00	12.00
Double impression	—	—
R261 R22 5c **carmine rose**('30)	2.00	1.90
Block of 4	10.00	8.75
R262 R22 10c **carmine rose**	9.25	6.75
Block of 4	45.00	32.50
R263 R22 20c **carmine rose**	15.00	8.25
Block of 4	70.00	42.50

Types of 1917-33 Overprinted in Black

SERIES 1940

1940 Wmk. 191R Offset Printing *Perf. 11*

R264 R22 1c **rose pink**	3.50	2.40
Cut cancel		.35
Perf. initial		.25
R265 R22 2c **rose pink**	4.00	1.90
Cut cancel		.40
Perf. initial		.35
R266 R22 3c **rose pink**	10.00	4.25
Cut cancel		.75
Perf. initial		.50
R267 R22 4c **rose pink**	4.50	.60
Cut cancel		.20
Perf. initial		.25
R268 R22 5c **rose pink**	4.50	.95
Cut cancel		.30
Perf. initial		.20
R269 R22 8c **rose pink**	20.00	16.00
Cut cancel		3.00
Perf. initial		2.00
R270 R22 10c **rose pink**	2.25	.65
Cut cancel		.25
Perf. initial		.25
R271 R22 20c **rose pink**	3.00	.70
Cut cancel		.20
Perf. initial		.25
R272 R22 25c **rose pink**	7.50	1.40
Cut cancel		.25
Perf. initial		.25
R273 R22 40c **rose pink**	6.25	.90
Cut cancel		.25
Perf. initial		.25
R274 R22 50c **rose pink**	10.00	.55
Cut cancel		.25
Perf. initial		.25
R275 R22 80c **rose pink**	13.00	1.50
Cut cancel		.25
Perf. initial		.25

Engr.

No.	Type	Description	Unused	Used
R276	R21	$1 **green**	72.50	1.00
		Cut cancel		.25
		Perf. initial		.25
R277	R21	$2 **rose**	72.50	1.75
		Cut cancel		.25
		Perf. initial		.25
R278	R21	$3 **violet**	95.00	37.50
		Cut cancel		4.25
		Perf. initial		2.00
R279	R21	$4 **yellow brown**	160.00	35.00
		Cut cancel		5.50
		Perf. initial		2.10
R280	R21	$5 **dark blue**	80.00	20.00
		Cut cancel		1.60
		Perf. initial		.75
R281	R21	$10 **orange**	200.00	45.00
		Cut cancel		3.00
		Perf. initial		.60

Types of 1917 Handstamped "Series 1940" like R264-R281 in Green (Nos. R282-R284, R286) or Violet (No. R285)

1940 **Wmk. 191R** ***Perf. 12***

Without Gum

No.	Type	Description	Unused	Used
R282	R17	$30 **vermilion**		1,000.
		Cut cancel		425.
		Perf. initial		325.
a.		With black 2-line handstamp in larger type		*12,500.*
R283	R19	$60 **brown**		1,750.
		Cut cancel		775.
		Perf. initial		550.
a.		As #R282a, cut cancel		—
R284	R17	$100 **green**		3,000.
		Cut cancel		1,250.
		Perf. initial		800.
R285	R18	$500 **blue**		2,000.
		Cut cancel		1,250.
		Perf. initial		1,000.
		Double transfer		—
a.		As #R282a	*3,250.*	*3,850.*
		Cut cancel		*2,750.*
		Double transfer	—	—
b.		Blue handstamp; double transfer	—	
R286	R19	$1000 **orange**		825.
		Cut cancel		475.
		Perf. initial		325.
a.		Double overprint, cut cancel		—

Alexander Hamilton — R23

Levi Woodbury — R24

Overprinted in Black SERIES 1940

Various Portraits: 2c, Oliver Wolcott, Jr. 3c, Samuel Dexter. 4c, Albert Gallatin. 5c. G. W. Campbell. 8c, Alexander Dallas. 10c, William H. Crawford. 20c, Richard Rush. 25c, S. D. Ingham. 40c. Louis McLane. 50c, William J. Duane. 80c, Roger B. Taney. $2, Thomas Ewing. $3, Walter Forward. $4, J. C. Spencer. $5, G. M. Bibb. $10, R. J. Walker. $20, William M. Meredith.

The "sensitive ink" varieties are in a bluish-purple overprint showing minute flecks of gold.

1940 **Engr.** **Wmk. 191R** ***Perf. 11***

Plates of 400 subjects, issued in panes of 100

No.	Type	Description	Unused	Used
R288	R23	1c **carmine**	5.50	4.50
		Cut cancel		1.75
		Perf. initial		.90
		Sensitive ink	8.25	4.25
a.		Imperf, pair, without gum	*250.00*	
		Block of 4	*500.00*	
R289	R23	2c **carmine**	8.00	4.00
		Cut cancel		1.75
		Perf. initial		1.00
		Sensitive ink	8.25	4.25
a.		Imperf, pair, without gum	*250.00*	
		Block of 4	*500.00*	
R290	R23	3c **carmine**	25.00	10.50
		Cut cancel		3.50
		Perf. initial		2.40
		Sensitive ink	24.00	9.25
a.		Imperf, pair, without gum	*250.00*	
		Block of 4	*500.00*	
R291	R23	4c **carmine**	57.50	25.00
		Cut cancel		4.75
		Perf. initial		4.00
a.		Imperf, pair, without gum	*250.00*	
		Block of 4	*500.00*	
R292	R23	5c **carmine**	4.50	.70
		Cut cancel		.30
		Perf. initial		.25
a.		Imperf, pair, without gum	*250.00*	
		Block of 4	*500.00*	
R293	R23	8c **carmine**	80.00	60.00
		Cut cancel		18.00
		Perf. initial		13.00
a.		Imperf, pair, without gum	*250.00*	
		Block of 4	*500.00*	
R294	R23	10c **carmine**	4.00	.55
		Cut cancel		.25
		Perf. initial		.25
a.		Imperf, pair, without gum	*250.00*	
		Block of 4	*500.00*	
R295	R23	20c **carmine**	5.00	3.75
		Cut cancel		1.10
		Perf. initial		.80
a.		Imperf, pair, without gum	*250.00*	
		Block of 4	*500.00*	
R296	R23	25c **carmine**	4.25	.60
		Cut cancel		.25
		Perf. initial		.25
a.		Imperf, pair, without gum	*250.00*	
		Block of 4	*500.00*	
R297	R23	40c **carmine**	65.00	30.00
		Cut cancel		6.50
		Perf. initial		2.75
a.		Imperf, pair, without gum	*250.00*	
		Block of 4	*500.00*	
R298	R23	50c **carmine**	7.00	.60
		Cut cancel		.30
		Perf. initial		.25
a.		Imperf, pair, without gum	*250.00*	
		Block of 4	*500.00*	
R299	R23	80c **carmine**	160.00	100.00
		Cut cancel		29.00
		Perf. initial		20.00
a.		Imperf, pair, without gum	*475.00*	
		Block of 4	*1,400.*	

Plates of 200 subjects, issued in panes of 50

No.	Type	Description	Unused	Used
R300	R24	$1 **carmine**	40.00	.55
		Cut cancel		.25
		Perf. initial		.25
		Sensitive ink	52.50	21.00
a.		Imperf, pair, without gum	*250.00*	
		Block of 4	*550.00*	
R301	R24	$2 **carmine**	75.00	.75
		Cut cancel		.25
		Perf. initial		.25
		Sensitive ink	55.00	10.50
R302	R24	$3 **carmine**	175.00	95.00
		Cut cancel		11.50
		Perf. initial		8.00
		Sensitive ink	160.00	87.50
a.		Imperf, pair, without gum	*1,400.*	
		Block of 4	*3,000.*	
R303	R24	$4 **carmine**	95.00	32.50
		Cut cancel		6.25
		Perf. initial		1.60
R304	R24	$5 **carmine**	65.00	2.75
		Cut cancel		.50
		Perf. initial		.30
R305	R24	$10 **carmine**	110.00	6.25
		Cut cancel		1.00
		Perf. initial		.40
R305A	R24	$20 **carmine**	*2,500.*	950.00
		Cut cancel		575.00
		Perf. initial		450.00
b.		Imperf, pair, without gum	*700.00*	
		Block of 4	*1,500.*	

Thomas Corwin — R25

Overprint: "SERIES 1940"

Various Frames and Portraits: $50, James Guthrie. $60, Howell Cobb. $100, P. F. Thomas. $500, J. A. Dix, $1,000, S. P. Chase.

Perf. 12

Plates of 16 subjects, issued in strips of 4

Without Gum

No.	Type	Description	Unused	Used
R306	R25	$30 **carmine**	175.00	55.00
		Cut cancel		18.00
		Perf. initial		13.50
R306A	R25	$50 **carmine**	—	*10,000.*
		Cut cancel		2,000.
		Perf. initial		800.00
R307	R25	$60 **carmine**	350.00	70.00
		Cut cancel		45.00
		Perf. initial		22.50
a.		Vert. pair, imperf. btwn.	*2,750.*	*1,450.*
R308	R25	$100 **carmine**	250.00	75.00
		Cut cancel		42.50
		Perf. initial		14.00
R309	R25	$500 **carmine**	—	5,000
		Cut cancel		2,000
		Perf. initial		800.00
R310	R25	$1000 **carmine**	—	475.00
		Cut cancel		225.00
		Perf. initial		160.00

The $30 to $1,000 denominations in this and following similar issues, and the $2,500, $5,000 and $10,000 stamps of 1952-58 have straight edges on one or two sides. They were issued without gum through No. R723.

Nos. R288-R310 Overprinted: SERIES 1941

1941 **Wmk. 191R** ***Perf. 11***

No.	Type	Description	Unused	Used
R311	R23	1c **carmine**	5.00	2.40
		Cut cancel		.75
		Perf. initial		.65
R312	R23	2c **carmine**	5.25	.95
		Cut cancel		.45
		Perf. initial		.40
R313	R23	3c **carmine**	10.00	3.75
		Cut cancel		1.40
		Perf. initial		.90
R314	R23	4c **carmine**	7.50	1.40
		Cut cancel		.35
		Perf. initial		.25
R315	R23	5c **carmine**	1.50	.35
		Cut cancel		.25
		Perf. initial		.30
R316	R23	8c **carmine**	21.00	7.75
		Cut cancel		3.25
		Perf. initial		2.75
R317	R23	10c **carmine**	2.00	.25
		Cut cancel		.25
		Perf. initial		.25
R318	R23	20c **carmine**	4.75	.50
		Cut cancel		.25
		Perf. initial		.30
R319	R23	25c **carmine**	2.40	.55
		Cut cancel		.25
		Perf. initial		.25
R320	R23	40c **carmine**	16.00	2.75
		Cut cancel		1.10
		Perf. initial		.65
R321	R23	50c **carmine**	3.50	.25
		Cut cancel		.25
		Perf. initial		.25
R322	R23	80c **carmine**	65.00	10.50
		Cut cancel		3.00
		Perf. initial		2.40
R323	R24	$1 **carmine**	15.00	.25
		Cut cancel		.20
		Perf. initial		.20
R324	R24	$2 **carmine**	20.00	.45
		Cut cancel		.25
		Perf. initial		.25
R325	R24	$3 **carmine**	32.50	2.75
		Cut cancel		.35
		Perf. initial		.30
R326	R24	$4 **carmine**	47.50	27.50
		Cut cancel		.90
		Perf. initial		.70
R327	R24	$5 **carmine**	60.00	.95
		Cut cancel		.20
		Perf. initial		.20
R328	R24	$10 **carmine**	100.00	6.00
		Cut cancel		.30
		Perf. initial		.25
R329	R24	$20 **carmine**	800.00	325.00
		Cut cancel		70.00
		Perf. initial		45.00

Without Gum ***Perf. 12***

No.	Type	Description	Unused	Used
R330	R25	$30 **carmine**	160.00	50.00
		Cut cancel		16.00
		Perf. initial		10.50
R331	R25	$50 **carmine**	500.00	425.00
		Cut cancel		100.00
		Perf. initial		52.50
R332	R25	$60 **carmine**	225.00	80.00
		Cut cancel		26.00
		Perf. initial		13.00
R333	R25	$100 **carmine**	110.00	37.50
		Cut cancel		7.75
		Perf. initial		5.00
R334	R25	$500 **carmine**	—	325.00
		Cut cancel		160.00
		Perf. initial		55.00
R335	R25	$1000 **carmine**	—	200.00
		Cut cancel		55.00
		Perf. initial		29.00

Nos. R288-R310 Overprinted: SERIES 1942

1942 **Wmk. 191R** ***Perf. 11***

No.	Type	Description	Unused	Used
R336	R23	1c **carmine**	.65	.50
		Cut cancel		.25
		Perf. initial		.25
R337	R23	2c **carmine**	.60	.50
		Cut cancel		.25
		Perf. initial		.25
R338	R23	3c **carmine**	.90	.65
		Cut cancel		.30
		Perf. initial		.25
R339	R23	4c **carmine**	1.75	.95
		Cut cancel		.30
		Perf. initial		.25
R340	R23	5c **carmine**	.60	.25
		Cut cancel		.25
		Perf. initial		.20
R341	R23	8c **carmine**	9.50	4.50
		Cut cancel		1.25
		Perf. initial		1.10

R342 R23 10c **carmine**	1.75	.25
Cut cancel		.25
Perf. initial		.25
R343 R23 20c **carmine**	1.75	.50
Cut cancel		.25
Perf. initial		.25
R344 R23 25c **carmine**	3.00	.45
Cut cancel		.25
Perf. initial		.20
R345 R23 40c **carmine**	6.50	1.40
Cut cancel		.55
Perf. initial		.35
R346 R23 50c **carmine**	4.00	.25
Cut cancel		.20
Perf. initial		.20
R347 R23 80c **carmine**	27.50	13.00
Cut cancel		3.00
Perf. initial		2.00
R348 R24 $1 **carmine**	12.50	.25
Cut cancel		.20
Perf. initial		.20
R349 R24 $2 **carmine**	15.00	.25
Cut cancel		.20
Perf. initial		.20
R350 R24 $3 **carmine**	27.50	2.75
Cut cancel		.35
Perf. initial		.20
R351 R24 $4 **carmine**	35.00	6.00
Cut cancel		.50
Perf. initial		.30
R352 R24 $5 **carmine**	37.50	1.25
Cut cancel		.25
Perf. initial		.20
R353 R24 $10 **carmine**	85.00	2.75
Cut cancel		.25
Perf. initial		.20
R354 R24 $20 **carmine**	160.00	45.00
Cut cancel		20.00
Perf. initial		11.50

Without Gum *Perf. 12*

R355 R25 $30 **carmine**	85.00	42.50
Cut cancel		14.00
Perf. initial		6.50
R356 R25 $50 **carmine**	1,400.	1,000.
Cut cancel		300.00
Perf. initial		160.00
R357 R25 $60 **carmine**	2,500.	1,850.
Cut cancel		450.00
Perf. initial		150.00
R358 R25 $100 **carmine**	210.00	140.00
Cut cancel		55.00
Perf. initial		42.50
R359 R25 $500 **carmine**	*1,600.*	275.00
Cut cancel		160.00
Perf. initial		87.50
R360 R25 $1000 **carmine**	—	120.00
Cut cancel		52.50
Perf. initial		42.50

Nos. R288-R310 Overprinted: **SERIES 1943**

1943 **Wmk. 191R** *Perf. 11*

R361 R23 1c **carmine**	.70	.55
Cut cancel		.25
Perf. initial		.25
R362 R23 2c **carmine**	.55	.45
Cut cancel		.25
Perf. initial		.25
R363 R23 3c **carmine**	3.75	3.50
Cut cancel		.70
Perf. initial		.40
R364 R23 4c **carmine**	1.60	1.50
Cut cancel		.40
Perf. initial		.35
R365 R23 5c **carmine**	.60	.35
Cut cancel		.25
Perf. initial		.25
R366 R23 8c **carmine**	6.00	4.00
Cut cancel		1.90
Perf. initial		1.25
R367 R23 10c **carmine**	.85	.25
Cut cancel		.25
Perf. initial		.20
R368 R23 20c **carmine**	2.50	.80
Cut cancel		.40
Perf. initial		.35
R369 R23 25c **carmine**	2.75	.50
Cut cancel		.30
Perf. initial		.30
R370 R23 40c **carmine**	7.50	4.00
Cut cancel		1.75
Perf. initial		.90
R371 R23 50c **carmine**	2.00	.25
Cut cancel		.25
Perf. initial		.25
R372 R23 80c **carmine**	27.50	8.00
Cut cancel		3.00
Perf. initial		1.50
R373 R24 $1 **carmine**	9.00	.35
Cut cancel		.25
Perf. initial		.25
R374 R24 $2 **carmine**	18.00	.25
Cut cancel		.25
Perf. initial		.20
R375 R24 $3 **carmine**	30.00	3.00
Cut cancel		.45
Perf. initial		.30
R376 R24 $4 **carmine**	45.00	7.50
Cut cancel		.65
Perf. initial		.50
R377 R24 $5 **carmine**	52.50	.65
Cut cancel		.35
Perf. initial		.20
R378 R24 $10 **carmine**	80.00	4.75
Cut cancel		1.75
Perf. initial		.70
R379 R24 $20 **carmine**	160.00	40.00
Cut cancel		6.00
Perf. initial		3.75

Without Gum *Perf. 12*

R380 R25 $30 **carmine**	80.00	22.50
Cut cancel		5.50
Perf. initial		4.75
R381 R25 $50 **carmine**	160.00	40.00
Cut cancel		14.00
Perf. initial		5.75
R382 R25 $60 **carmine**	325.00	125.00
Cut cancel		42.50
Perf. initial		14.00
R383 R25 $100 **carmine**	35.00	22.50
Cut cancel		6.75
Perf. initial		4.25
R384 R25 $500 **carmine**	*375.00*	250.00
Cut cancel		125.00
Perf. initial		87.50
R385 R25 $1000 **carmine**	*350.00*	200.00
Cut cancel		60.00
Perf. initial		40.00

Nos. R288-R310 Overprinted: **Series 1944**

1944 **Wmk. 191R** *Perf. 11*

R386 R23 1c **carmine**	.50	.40
Cut cancel		.25
Perf. initial		.25
R387 R23 2c **carmine**	.60	.50
Cut cancel		.25
Perf. initial		.25
R388 R23 3c **carmine**	.65	.35
Cut cancel		.25
Perf. initial		.25
R389 R23 4c **carmine**	.75	.60
Cut cancel		.25
Perf. initial		.25
R390 R23 5c **carmine**	.40	.25
Cut cancel		.25
Perf. initial		.25
R391 R23 8c **carmine**	2.25	1.75
Cut cancel		.50
Perf. initial		.45
R392 R23 10c **carmine**	.50	.25
Cut cancel		.20
Perf. initial		.25
R393 R23 20c **carmine**	1.10	.35
Cut cancel		.25
Perf. initial		.25
R394 R23 25c **carmine**	2.00	.25
Cut cancel		.25
Perf. initial		.25
R395 R23 40c **carmine**	3.50	.80
Cut cancel		.40
Perf. initial		.30
R396 R23 50c **carmine**	4.00	.30
Cut cancel		.30
Perf. initial		.30
R397 R23 80c **carmine**	21.00	4.75
Cut cancel		1.40
Perf. initial		.85
R398 R24 $1 **carmine**	10.00	.25
Cut cancel		.25
Perf. initial		.25
R399 R24 $2 **carmine**	15.00	.40
Cut cancel		.30
Perf. initial		.25
R400 R24 $3 **carmine**	22.50	2.10
Cut cancel		.55
Perf. initial		.25
R401 R24 $4 **carmine**	30.00	11.50
Cut cancel		1.40
Perf. initial		1.10
R402 R24 $5 **carmine**	32.50	.40
Cut cancel		.20
Perf. initial		.30
R403 R24 $10 **carmine**	65.00	1.40
Cut cancel		.30
Perf. initial		.30
R404 R24 $20 **carmine**	140.00	17.50
Cut cancel		3.50
Perf. initial		2.25

Without Gum *Perf. 12*

R405 R25 $30 **carmine**	95.00	35.00
Cut cancel		9.00
Perf. initial		7.00
R406 R25 $50 **carmine**	42.50	22.50
Cut cancel		7.00
Perf. initial		4.75
R407 R25 $60 **carmine**	275.00	75.00
Cut cancel		29.00
Perf. initial		10.50
R408 R25 $100 **carmine**	52.50	12.50
Cut cancel		5.25
Perf. initial		3.25
R409 R25 $500 **carmine**	—	*2,600.*
Cut cancel		1,200.
Perf. initial		750.00
R410 R25 $1000 **carmine**	—	375.00
Cut cancel		125.00
Perf. initial		65.00

Nos. R288-R310 Overprinted: **Series 1945**

1945 **Wmk. 191R** *Perf. 11*

R411 R23 1c **carmine**	.35	.25
Cut cancel		.25
Perf. initial		.25
R412 R23 2c **carmine**	.35	.25
Cut cancel		.25
Perf. initial		.25
R413 R23 3c **carmine**	.65	.45
Cut cancel		.25
Perf. initial		.25
R414 R23 4c **carmine**	.40	.30
Cut cancel		.30
Perf. initial		.25
R415 R23 5c **carmine**	.45	.25
Cut cancel		.20
Perf. initial		.25
R416 R23 8c **carmine**	6.25	2.50
Cut cancel		.65
Perf. initial		.35
R417 R23 10c **carmine**	1.25	.25
Cut cancel		.25
Perf. initial		.25
R418 R23 20c **carmine**	8.00	1.50
Cut cancel		.60
Perf. initial		.35
R419 R23 25c **carmine**	1.75	.30
Cut cancel		.25
Perf. initial		.20
R420 R23 40c **carmine**	9.00	1.10
Cut cancel		.45
Perf. initial		.40
R421 R23 50c **carmine**	4.00	.25
Cut cancel		.20
Perf. initial		.25
R422 R23 80c **carmine**	26.00	14.00
Cut cancel		4.00
Perf. initial		2.75
R423 R24 $1 **carmine**	13.50	.25
Cut cancel		.20
Perf. initial		.20
R424 R24 $2 **carmine**	13.50	.35
Cut cancel		.20
Perf. initial		.25
R425 R24 $3 **carmine**	27.50	3.00
Cut cancel		1.00
Perf. initial		.75
R426 R24 $4 **carmine**	35.00	4.25
Cut cancel		.70
Perf. initial		.45
R427 R24 $5 **carmine**	35.00	.45
Cut cancel		.25
Perf. initial		.25
R428 R24 $10 **carmine**	65.00	2.50
Cut cancel		.40
Perf. initial		.30
R429 R24 $20 **carmine**	140.00	16.00
Cut cancel		3.75
Perf. initial		3.00

Without Gum *Perf. 12*

R430 R25 $30 **carmine**	175.00	40.00
Cut cancel		10.00
Perf. initial		5.75
R431 R25 $50 **carmine**	200.00	45.00
Cut cancel		20.00
Perf. initial		10.50
R432 R25 $60 **carmine**	375.00	80.00
Cut cancel		32.50
Perf. initial		13.00
R433 R25 $100 **carmine**	35.00	20.00
Cut cancel		9.00
Perf. initial		5.50
R434 R25 $500 **carmine**	425.00	225.00
Cut cancel		80.00
Perf. initial		52.50
R435 R25 $1000 **carmine**	275.00	110.00
Cut cancel		32.50
Perf. initial		17.50

Nos. R288-R310 Overprinted: **Series 1946**

1946 **Wmk. 191R** *Perf. 11*

R436 R23 1c **carmine**	.30	.30
Cut cancel		.25
Perf. initial		.25
R437 R23 2c **carmine**	.45	.35
Cut cancel		.25
Perf. initial		.25
R438 R23 3c **carmine**	.45	.35
Cut cancel		.25
Perf. initial		.25
R439 R23 4c **carmine**	.70	.55
Cut cancel		.25
Perf. initial		.25
R440 R23 5c **carmine**	.45	.25
Cut cancel		.25
Perf. initial		.25
R441 R23 8c **carmine**	2.50	2.00
Cut cancel		.40
Perf. initial		.35
R442 R23 10c **carmine**	1.10	.25
Cut cancel		.25
Perf. initial		.25
R443 R23 20c **carmine**	1.60	.45
Cut cancel		.25
Perf. initial		.25
R444 R23 25c **carmine**	6.00	.30
Cut cancel		.20
Perf. initial		.20
R445 R23 40c **carmine**	4.00	.75
Cut cancel		.35
Perf. initial		.25
R446 R23 50c **carmine**	6.00	.25
Cut cancel		.20
Perf. initial		.20
R447 R23 80c **carmine**	17.50	4.50
Cut cancel		.65
Perf. initial		.50
R448 R24 $1 **carmine**	16.00	.25
Cut cancel		.20
Perf. initial		.20
R449 R24 $2 **carmine**	19.00	.25
Cut cancel		.20
Perf. initial		.20

No.	Type	Description	Unused	Used
R450	R24	$3 **carmine**	27.50	5.00
		Cut cancel		.90
		Perf. initial		.40
R451	R24	$4 **carmine**	40.00	10.50
		Cut cancel		2.10
		Perf. initial		1.00
R452	R24	$5 **carmine**	40.00	.45
		Cut cancel		.25
		Perf. initial		.25
R453	R24	$10 **carmine**	72.50	1.60
		Cut cancel		.35
		Perf. initial		.30
R454	R24	$20 **carmine**	140.00	16.00
		Cut cancel		3.50
		Perf. initial		1.60

Without Gum — ***Perf. 12***

No.	Type	Description	Unused	Used
R455	R25	$30 **carmine**	60.00	17.50
		Cut cancel		5.25
		Perf. initial		3.25
R456	R25	$50 **carmine**	50.00	12.50
		Cut cancel		5.00
		Perf. initial		2.75
R457	R25	$60 **carmine**	95.00	22.50
		Cut cancel		14.00
		Perf. initial		7.75
R458	R25	$100 **carmine**	70.00	12.50
		Cut cancel		4.25
		Perf. initial		3.00
R459	R25	$500 **carmine**	*325.00*	150.00
		Cut cancel		47.50
		Perf. initial		26.00
R460	R25	$1000 **carmine**	*375.00*	160.00
		Cut cancel		37.50
		Perf. initial		18.00

Nos. R288-R310 Overprinted: **Series 1947**

1947 — **Wmk. 191R** — ***Perf. 11***

No.	Type	Description	Unused	Used
R461	R23	1c **carmine**	.85	.50
		Cut cancel		.25
		Perf. initial		.25
R462	R23	2c **carmine**	.75	.55
		Cut cancel		.25
		Perf. initial		.25
R463	R23	3c **carmine**	.85	.50
		Cut cancel		.25
		Perf. initial		.25
R464	R23	4c **carmine**	.85	.65
		Cut cancel		.25
		Perf. initial		.25
R465	R23	5c **carmine**	.50	.35
		Cut cancel		.25
		Perf. initial		.25
R466	R23	8c **carmine**	1.60	.75
		Cut cancel		.25
		Perf. initial		.25
R467	R23	10c **carmine**	1.40	.25
		Cut cancel		.25
		Perf. initial		.25
R468	R23	20c **carmine**	2.25	.50
		Cut cancel		.25
		Perf. initial		.25
R469	R23	25c **carmine**	3.00	.65
		Cut cancel		.25
		Perf. initial		.25
R470	R23	40c **carmine**	5.00	.95
		Cut cancel		.25
		Perf. initial		.25
R471	R23	50c **carmine**	3.75	.35
		Cut cancel		.25
		Perf. initial		.25
R472	R23	80c **carmine**	12.00	8.00
		Cut cancel		.85
		Perf. initial		.35
R473	R24	$1 **carmine**	8.25	.30
		Cut cancel		.25
		Perf. initial		.25
R474	R24	$2 **carmine**	14.00	.60
		Cut cancel		.25
		Perf. initial		.20
R475	R24	$3 **carmine**	17.50	6.00
		Cut cancel		1.25
		Perf. initial		.90
R476	R24	$4 **carmine**	19.00	5.00
		Cut cancel		.55
		Perf. initial		.40
R477	R24	$5 **carmine**	27.50	.55
		Cut cancel		.25
		Perf. initial		.25
R478	R24	$10 **carmine**	67.50	3.00
		Cut cancel		.80
		Perf. initial		.30
R479	R24	$20 **carmine**	110.00	14.00
		Cut cancel		1.40
		Perf. initial		.90

Without Gum — ***Perf. 12***

No.	Type	Description	Unused	Used
R480	R25	$30 **carmine**	140.00	27.50
		Cut cancel		6.00
		Perf. initial		2.75
R481	R25	$50 **carmine**	72.50	17.50
		Cut cancel		5.50
		Perf. initial		3.25
R482	R25	$60 **carmine**	175.00	60.00
		Cut cancel		25.00
		Perf. initial		9.25
R483	R25	$100 **carmine**	65.00	15.00
		Cut cancel		6.00
		Perf. initial		2.10
R484	R25	$500 **carmine**	*500.00*	175.00
		Cut cancel		67.50
		Perf. initial		37.50
R485	R25	$1000 **carmine**	*275.00*	100.00
		Cut cancel		40.00
		Perf. initial		24.00

Nos. R288-R310 Overprinted: **Series 1948**

1948 — **Wmk. 191R** — ***Perf. 11***

No.	Type	Description	Unused	Used
R486	R23	1c **carmine**	.35	.30
		Cut cancel		.25
		Perf. initial		.25
R487	R23	2c **carmine**	.50	.40
		Cut cancel		.25
		Perf. initial		.25
R488	R23	3c **carmine**	.60	.35
		Cut cancel		.25
		Perf. initial		.25
R489	R23	4c **carmine**	.55	.35
		Cut cancel		.25
		Perf. initial		.25
R490	R23	5c **carmine**	.50	.25
		Cut cancel		.25
		Perf. initial		.20
R491	R23	8c **carmine**	1.00	.50
		Cut cancel		.30
		Perf. initial		.30
R492	R23	10c **carmine**	1.00	.25
		Cut cancel		.25
		Perf. initial		.20
R493	R23	20c **carmine**	2.50	.35
		Cut cancel		.25
		Perf. initial		.25
R494	R23	25c **carmine**	2.25	.25
		Cut cancel		.25
		Perf. initial		.25
R495	R23	40c **carmine**	7.00	1.75
		Cut cancel		.35
		Perf. initial		.25
R496	R23	50c **carmine**	2.50	.25
		Cut cancel		.20
		Perf. initial		.25
R497	R23	80c **carmine**	12.00	8.00
		Cut cancel		3.25
		Perf. initial		.80
R498	R24	$1 **carmine**	10.50	.25
		Cut cancel		.25
		Perf. initial		.25
R499	R24	$2 **carmine**	18.00	.30
		Cut cancel		.25
		Perf. initial		.25
R500	R24	$3 **carmine**	24.00	3.50
		Cut cancel		.60
		Perf. initial		.40
R501	R24	$4 **carmine**	35.00	4.00
		Cut cancel		1.00
		Perf. initial		.70
R502	R24	$5 **carmine**	30.00	.50
		Cut cancel		.30
		Perf. initial		.25
R503	R24	$10 **carmine**	70.00	1.50
		Cut cancel		.30
		Perf. initial		.30
a.		Pair, one dated "1946"		—
R504	R24	$20 **carmine**	140.00	18.00
		Cut cancel		5.00
		Perf. initial		2.25

Without Gum — ***Perf. 12***

No.	Type	Description	Unused	Used
R505	R25	$30 **carmine**	100.00	27.50
		Cut cancel		7.00
		Perf. initial		4.00
R506	R25	$50 **carmine**	125.00	27.50
		Cut cancel		12.00
		Perf. initial		3.75
a.		Vert. pair, imperf. btwn.	*2,750.*	
R507	R25	$60 **carmine**	200.00	50.00
		Cut cancel		22.50
		Perf. initial		8.00
a.		Vert. pair, imperf. btwn.	*2,750.*	
R508	R25	$100 **carmine**	75.00	12.00
		Cut cancel		5.50
		Perf. initial		3.50
a.		Vert. pair, imperf. btwn.	*2,000.*	
R509	R25	$500 **carmine**	500.00	160.00
		Cut cancel		60.00
		Perf. initial		32.50
R510	R25	$1000 **carmine**	275.00	90.00
		Cut cancel		40.00
		Perf. initial		22.50

Nos. R288-R310 Overprinted: **Series 1949**

1949 — **Wmk. 191R** — ***Perf. 11***

No.	Type	Description	Unused	Used
R511	R23	1c **carmine**	.40	.30
		Cut cancel		.25
		Perf. initial		.25
R512	R23	2c **carmine**	.75	.40
		Cut cancel		.25
		Perf. initial		.25
R513	R23	3c **carmine**	.60	.40
		Cut cancel		.25
		Perf. initial		.25
R514	R23	4c **carmine**	.80	.55
		Cut cancel		.25
		Perf. initial		.25
R515	R23	5c **carmine**	.55	.25
		Cut cancel		.25
		Perf. initial		.25
R516	R23	8c **carmine**	.90	.65
		Cut cancel		.25
		Perf. initial		.25
R517	R23	10c **carmine**	.60	.30
		Cut cancel		.25
		Perf. initial		.25
R518	R23	20c **carmine**	1.60	.65
		Cut cancel		.35
		Perf. initial		.30
R519	R23	25c **carmine**	2.25	.75
		Cut cancel		.30
		Perf. initial		.30
R520	R23	40c **carmine**	6.50	2.50
		Cut cancel		.45
		Perf. initial		.35
R521	R23	50c **carmine**	5.00	.35
		Cut cancel		.25
		Perf. initial		.25
R522	R23	80c **carmine**	15.00	6.00
		Cut cancel		1.60
		Perf. initial		.80
R523	R24	$1 **carmine**	13.50	.75
		Cut cancel		.25
		Perf. initial		.30
R524	R24	$2 **carmine**	17.00	2.25
		Cut cancel		.45
		Perf. initial		.30
R525	R24	$3 **carmine**	27.50	7.00
		Cut cancel		2.75
		Perf. initial		1.10
R526	R24	$4 **carmine**	30.00	7.00
		Cut cancel		3.00
		Perf. initial		1.60
R527	R24	$5 **carmine**	32.50	3.75
		Cut cancel		.65
		Perf. initial		.45
R528	R24	$10 **carmine**	72.50	4.75
		Cut cancel		1.10
		Perf. initial		.90
R529	R24	$20 **carmine**	150.00	15.00
		Cut cancel		2.50
		Perf. initial		1.60

Without Gum — ***Perf. 12***

No.	Type	Description	Unused	Used
R530	R25	$30 **carmine**	125.00	35.00
		Cut cancel		8.00
		Perf. initial		4.25
R531	R25	$50 **carmine**	140.00	60.00
		Cut cancel		16.00
		Perf. initial		7.50
R532	R25	$60 **carmine**	250.00	70.00
		Cut cancel		27.50
		Perf. initial		11.50
R533	R25	$100 **carmine**	70.00	21.00
		Cut cancel		4.50
		Perf. initial		2.75
R534	R25	$500 **carmine**	*500.00*	250.00
		Cut cancel		125.00
		Perf. initial		57.50
R535	R25	$1000 **carmine**	*375.00*	160.00
		Cut cancel		47.50
		Perf. initial		22.50

Nos. R288-R310 Overprinted: Series 1950

1950 — **Wmk. 191R** — ***Perf. 11***

No.	Type	Description	Unused	Used
R536	R23	1c **carmine**	.40	.25
		Cut cancel		.25
		Perf. initial		.25
R537	R23	2c **carmine**	.40	.30
		Cut cancel		.25
		Perf. initial		.25
R538	R23	3c **carmine**	.50	.35
		Cut cancel		.25
		Perf. initial		.25
R539	R23	4c **carmine**	.65	.45
		Cut cancel		.25
		Perf. initial		.25
R540	R23	5c **carmine**	.40	.25
		Cut cancel		.25
		Perf. initial		.25
R541	R23	8c **carmine**	1.75	.70
		Cut cancel		.25
		Perf. initial		.25
R542	R23	10c **carmine**	.75	.25
		Cut cancel		.25
		Perf. initial		.25
R543	R23	20c **carmine**	1.40	.40
		Cut cancel		.30
		Perf. initial		.30
R544	R23	25c **carmine**	2.00	.40
		Cut cancel		.30
		Perf. initial		.30
R545	R23	40c **carmine**	6.00	1.90
		Cut cancel		.45
		Perf. initial		.30
R546	R23	50c **carmine**	8.00	.25
		Cut cancel		.25
		Perf. initial		.25
R547	R23	80c **carmine**	15.00	8.00
		Cut cancel		.90
		Perf. initial		.55
R548	R24	$1 **carmine**	15.00	.35
		Cut cancel		.30
		Perf. initial		.25
R549	R24	$2 **carmine**	17.50	2.50
		Cut cancel		.40
		Perf. initial		.20
R550	R24	$3 **carmine**	20.00	6.00
		Cut cancel		1.40
		Perf. initial		.80
R551	R24	$4 **carmine**	27.50	7.50
		Cut cancel		2.75
		Perf. initial		1.40
R552	R24	$5 **carmine**	35.00	1.00
		Cut cancel		.30
		Perf. initial		.25
R553	R24	$10 **carmine**	70.00	10.00
		Cut cancel		.85
		Perf. initial		.55
R554	R24	$20 **carmine**	150.00	15.00
		Cut cancel		3.50
		Perf. initial		1.90

Without Gum — ***Perf. 12***

No.	Type	Description	Unused	Used
R555	R25	$30 **carmine**	125.00	70.00
		Cut cancel		17.50
		Perf. initial		10.50

R556 R25 $50 **carmine**	100.00	22.50
Cut cancel		10.00
Perf. initial		5.75
a. Vert. pair, imperf. horiz.		—
R557 R25 $60 **carmine**	210.00	75.00
Cut cancel		25.00
Perf. initial		9.75
R558 R25 $100 **carmine**	85.00	22.50
Cut cancel		6.00
Perf. initial		3.25
R559 R25 $500 **carmine**	*300.00*	125.00
Cut cancel		55.00
Perf. initial		32.50
R560 R25 $1000 **carmine**	*300.00*	95.00
Cut cancel		30.00
Perf. initial		19.00

Nos. R288-R310 Overprinted: **Series 1951**

1951 **Wmk. 191R** ***Perf. 11***

R561 R23 1c **carmine**	.30	.25
Cut cancel		.20
Perf. initial		.20
R562 R23 2c **carmine**	.30	.35
Cut cancel		.25
Perf. initial		.25
R563 R23 3c **carmine**	.30	.35
Cut cancel		.25
Perf. initial		.25
R564 R23 4c **carmine**	.30	.35
Cut cancel		.25
Perf. initial		.25
R565 R23 5c **carmine**	.30	.35
Cut cancel		.25
Perf. initial		.25
R566 R23 8c **carmine**	1.25	.45
Cut cancel		.25
Perf. initial		.25
R567 R23 10c **carmine**	.30	.35
Cut cancel		.25
Perf. initial		.25
R568 R23 20c **carmine**	.30	.55
Cut cancel		.30
Perf. initial		.25
R569 R23 25c **carmine**	.30	.50
Cut cancel		.30
Perf. initial		.25
R570 R23 40c **carmine**	3.75	1.50
Cut cancel		.45
Perf. initial		.30
R571 R23 50c **carmine**	3.00	.60
Cut cancel		.25
Perf. initial		.25
R572 R23 80c **carmine**	10.00	3.25
Cut cancel		2.00
Perf. initial		1.00
R573 R24 $1 **carmine**	16.00	.25
Cut cancel		.20
Perf. initial		.20
R574 R24 $2 **carmine**	21.00	.50
Cut cancel		.25
Perf. initial		.30
R575 R24 $3 **carmine**	16.00	4.00
Cut cancel		2.10
Perf. initial		1.25
R576 R24 $4 **carmine**	16.00	8.00
Cut cancel		3.00
Perf. initial		1.50
R577 R24 $5 **carmine**	10.00	.70
Cut cancel		.35
Perf. initial		.25
R578 R24 $10 **carmine**	18.00	2.25
Cut cancel		1.10
Perf. initial		.80
R579 R24 $20 **carmine**	55.00	16.00
Cut cancel		5.00
Perf. initial		3.25

Without Gum ***Perf. 12***

R580 R25 $30 **carmine**	100.00	17.50
Cut cancel		6.00
Perf. initial		3.75
a. Imperf., pair	*2,000.*	*775.00*
R581 R25 $50 **carmine**	125.00	30.00
Cut cancel		9.00
Perf. initial		4.50
R582 R25 $60 **carmine**	175.00	62.50
Cut cancel		24.00
Perf. initial		16.00
R583 R25 $100 **carmine**	70.00	15.00
Cut cancel		7.50
Perf. initial		5.00
R584 R25 $500 **carmine**	*400.00*	140.00
Cut cancel		60.00
Perf. initial		26.00
R585 R25 $1000 **carmine**	*375.00*	125.00
Cut cancel		45.00
Perf. initial		29.00

No. R583 is known imperf horizontally. It exists as a reconstructed used vertical strip of 4 that was separated into single stamps.

Documentary Stamps and Types of 1940 Overprinted in Black

Series 1952

Designs: 55c, $1.10, $1.65, $2.20, $2.75, $3.30, L. J. Gage; $2500, William Windom; $5000, C. J. Folger; $10,000, W. Q. Gresham.

1952 **Wmk. 191R** ***Perf. 11***

R586 R23 1c **carmine**	.35	.30
Cut cancel		.25
Perf. initial		.25
R587 R23 2c **carmine**	.45	.30
Cut cancel		.25
Perf. initial		.25
R588 R23 3c **carmine**	.40	.30
Cut cancel		.25
Perf. initial		.25
R589 R23 4c **carmine**	.45	.30
Cut cancel		.25
Perf. initial		.25
R590 R23 5c **carmine**	.35	.30
Cut cancel		.25
Perf. initial		.25
R591 R23 8c **carmine**	.90	.50
Cut cancel		.25
Perf. initial		.25
R592 R23 10c **carmine**	.50	.25
Cut cancel		.25
Perf. initial		.20
R593 R23 20c **carmine**	1.25	.40
Cut cancel		.30
Perf. initial		.25
R594 R23 25c **carmine**	2.50	.45
Cut cancel		.30
Perf. initial		.30
R595 R23 40c **carmine**	6.00	1.75
Cut cancel		.55
Perf. initial		.45
R596 R23 50c **carmine**	3.50	.30
Cut cancel		.25
Perf. initial		.25
R597 R23 55c **carmine**	.30	15.00
Cut cancel		2.00
Perf. initial		1.10
R598 R23 80c **carmine**	19.00	4.00
Cut cancel		.80
Perf. initial		.75
R599 R24 $1 **carmine**	7.00	1.50
Cut cancel		.75
Perf. initial		.40
R600 R24 $1.10 **carmine**	25.00	30.00
Cut cancel		14.00
Perf. initial		6.25
R601 R24 $1.65 **carmine**	175.00	62.50
Cut cancel		37.50
Perf. initial		21.00
R602 R24 $2 **carmine**	17.00	.85
Cut cancel		.25
Perf. initial		.25
R603 R24 $2.20 **carmine**	150.00	70.00
Cut cancel		35.00
Perf. initial		16.00
R604 R24 $2.75 **carmine**	190.00	70.00
Cut cancel		35.00
Perf. initial		16.00
R605 R24 $3 **carmine**	32.50	6.00
Cut cancel		1.60
Perf. initial		1.40
a. Horiz. pair, imperf. btwn.	*1,300.*	
R606 R24 $3.30 **carmine**	160.00	70.00
Cut cancel		35.00
Perf. initial		16.00
R607 R24 $4 **carmine**	37.50	6.00
Cut cancel		2.10
Perf. initial		1.60
R608 R24 $5 **carmine**	32.50	1.25
Cut cancel		.45
Perf. initial		.40
R609 R24 $10 **carmine**	60.00	1.25
Cut cancel		.45
Perf. initial		.35
R610 R24 $20 **carmine**	92.50	16.00
Cut cancel		4.50
Perf. initial		3.00

Without Gum ***Perf. 12***

R611 R25 $30 **carmine**	70.00	27.50
Cut cancel		6.00
Perf. initial		4.25
R612 R25 $50 **carmine**	60.00	25.00
Cut cancel		7.00
Perf. initial		5.25
R613 R25 $60 **carmine**	425.00	70.00
Cut cancel		19.00
Perf. initial		10.50
R614 R25 $100 **carmine**	55.00	10.00
Cut cancel		4.00
Perf. initial		2.10
R615 R25 $500 **carmine**	*750.00*	125.00
Cut cancel		70.00
Perf. initial		35.00
R616 R25 $1000 **carmine**	*250.00*	40.00
Cut cancel		16.00
Perf. initial		10.50
R617 R25 $2500 **carmine**	*375.00*	225.00
Cut cancel		160.00
Perf. initial		125.00
R618 R25 $5000 **carmine**	—	*4,000.*
Cut cancel		1,750.
Perf. initial		1,250.
R619 R25 $10,000 **carmine**	—	*1,400.*
Cut cancel		900.00
Perf. initial		750.00

Documentary Stamps and Types of 1940 Overprinted in Black

Series 1953

1953 **Wmk. 191R** ***Perf. 11***

R620 R23 1c **carmine**	.40	.30
Cut cancel		.25
Perf. initial		.25
R621 R23 2c **carmine**	.40	.30
Cut cancel		.25
Perf. initial		.25
R622 R23 3c **carmine**	.45	.30
Cut cancel		.25
Perf. initial		.25
R623 R23 4c **carmine**	.60	.40
Cut cancel		.25
Perf. initial		.25
R624 R23 5c **carmine**	.50	.25
Cut cancel		.25
Perf. initial		.25
a. Vert. pair, imperf. horiz.		*650.00*
R625 R23 8c **carmine**	1.10	.75
Cut cancel		.25
Perf. initial		.25
R626 R23 10c **carmine**	.65	.30
Cut cancel		.25
Perf. initial		.25
R627 R23 20c **carmine**	1.50	.45
Cut cancel		.25
Perf. initial		.25
R628 R23 25c **carmine**	1.75	.55
Cut cancel		.30
Perf. initial		.25
R629 R23 40c **carmine**	2.50	.80
Cut cancel		.45
Perf. initial		.35
R630 R23 50c **carmine**	3.00	.30
Cut cancel		.25
Perf. initial		.25
R631 R23 55c **carmine**	7.00	2.00
Cut cancel		.80
Perf. initial		.55
a. Horiz. pair, imperf. vert.	*375.00*	
R632 R23 80c **carmine**	10.00	2.10
Cut cancel		1.50
Perf. initial		1.40
R633 R24 $1 **carmine**	5.25	.30
Cut cancel		.25
Perf. initial		.25
R634 R24 $1.10 **carmine**	12.00	2.50
Cut cancel		2.10
Perf. initial		1.60
a. Horiz. pair, imperf. vert.	*700.00*	
b. Imperf. pair	*600.00*	
R635 R24 $1.65 **carmine**	12.00	4.50
Cut cancel		3.25
Perf. initial		2.10
R636 R24 $2 **carmine**	9.00	.70
Cut cancel		.30
Perf. initial		.25
R637 R24 $2.20 **carmine**	20.00	6.00
Cut cancel		2.75
Perf. initial		2.10
R638 R24 $2.75 **carmine**	1.75	7.00
Cut cancel		3.75
Perf. initial		2.75
R639 R24 $3 **carmine**	17.00	3.50
Cut cancel		1.60
Perf. initial		1.40
R640 R24 $3.30 **carmine**	35.00	8.00
Cut cancel		5.25
Perf. initial		3.50
R641 R24 $4 **carmine**	32.50	9.00
Cut cancel		2.40
Perf. initial		2.10
R642 R24 $5 **carmine**	27.50	1.25
Cut cancel		.55
Perf. initial		.35
R643 R24 $10 **carmine**	60.00	2.25
Cut cancel		1.10
Perf. initial		.90
R644 R24 $20 **carmine**	125.00	22.50
Cut cancel		4.50
Perf. initial		2.40

Without Gum ***Perf. 12***

R645 R25 $30 **carmine**	100.00	20.00
Cut cancel		8.00
Perf. initial		4.25
R646 R25 $50 **carmine**	160.00	42.50
Cut cancel		15.00
Perf. initial		6.25
R647 R25 $60 **carmine**	625.00	350.00
Cut cancel		150.00
Perf. initial		67.50
With complete receipt tab	*2,000.*	
R648 R25 $100 **carmine**	55.00	15.00
Cut cancel		5.75
Perf. initial		3.75
R649 R25 $500 **carmine**	725.00	175.00
Cut cancel		70.00
Perf. initial		29.00
R650 R25 $1000 **carmine**	475.00	80.00
Cut cancel		27.50
Perf. initial		16.00
R651 R25 $2500 **carmine**	2,000.	1,250.
Cut cancel		525.00
Perf. initial		350.00
R652 R25 $5000 **carmine**	—	*4,500.*
Cut cancel		*2,500.*
Perf. initial		1,500.
R653 R25 $10,000 **carmine**	—	*3,500.*
Cut cancel		1,750.
Perf. initial		800.00

Types of 1940
Without Overprint

1954 **Wmk. 191R** ***Perf. 11***

R654 R23 1c **carmine**	.25	.25
Cut cancel		.25
Perf. initial		.20
a. Horiz. pair, imperf. vert.	*1,500.*	
R655 R23 2c **carmine**	.25	.30
Cut cancel		.25
Perf. initial		.20

R656 R23 3c **carmine**		.25	.30
Cut cancel			.25
Perf. initial			.20
R657 R23 4c **carmine**		.25	.30
Cut cancel			.25
Perf. initial			.20
R658 R23 5c **carmine**		.25	.25
Cut cancel			.20
Perf. initial			.20
R659 R23 8c **carmine**		.25	.25
Cut cancel			.25
Perf. initial			.20
R660 R23 10c **carmine**		.25	.25
Cut cancel			.25
Perf. initial			.20
R661 R23 20c **carmine**		.30	.40
Cut cancel			.30
Perf. initial			.25
R662 R23 25c **carmine**		.35	.45
Cut cancel			.30
Perf. initial			.25
R663 R23 40c **carmine**		.75	.60
Cut cancel			.45
Perf. initial			.35
R664 R23 50c **carmine**		1.00	.25
Cut cancel			.20
Perf. initial			.20
a.	Horiz. pair, imperf. vert.	250.00	
R665 R23 55c **carmine**		.90	1.25
Cut cancel			.55
Perf. initial			.45
R666 R23 80c **carmine**		1.50	1.90
Cut cancel			1.25
Perf. initial			1.10
R667 R24 $1 **carmine**		.90	.30
Cut cancel			.30
Perf. initial			.25
R668 R24 $1.10 **carmine**		2.00	2.50
Cut cancel			1.60
Perf. initial			1.10
R669 R24 $1.65 **carmine**		25.00	10.00
Cut cancel			5.00
Perf. initial			1.00
R670 R24 $2 **carmine**		1.00	.45
Cut cancel			.25
Perf. initial			.25
R671 R24 $2.20 **carmine**		2.25	3.75
Cut cancel			2.75
Perf. initial			1.60
R672 R24 $2.75 **carmine**		25.00	65.00
Cut cancel			37.50
Perf. initial			21.00
R673 R24 $3 **carmine**		2.00	3.00
Cut cancel			1.10
Perf. initial			.80
R674 R24 $3.30 **carmine**		3.50	5.00
Cut cancel			3.25
Perf. initial			2.10
R675 R24 $4 **carmine**		2.75	4.00
Cut cancel			2.10
Perf. initial			1.60
R676 R24 $5 **carmine**		3.25	.50
Cut cancel			.35
Perf. initial			.20
R677 R24 $10 **carmine**		5.00	1.50
Cut cancel			.85
Perf. initial			.70
R678 R24 $20 **carmine**		10.00	6.50
Cut cancel			3.25
Perf. initial			1.90

Documentary Stamps and Type of 1940 Overprinted in Black

Series 1954

1954 Wmk. 191R *Perf. 12*
Without Gum

R679 R25 $30 **carmine**		55.00	17.50
Cut cancel			4.75
Perf. initial			3.25
With complete receipt tab		55.00	
a.	Booklet pane of 4	225.00	
	Complete booklet, 10 #R679a	2,250.	
R680 R25 $50 **carmine**		55.00	29.00
Cut cancel			9.25
Perf. initial			5.75
With complete receipt tab		55.00	
a.	Booklet pane of 4	225.00	
	Complete booklet, 10 #R680a	2,250.	
R681 R25 $60 **carmine**		55.00	30.00
Cut cancel			13.00
Perf. initial			9.25
With complete receipt tab		55.00	
a.	Booklet pane of 4	225.00	
	Complete booklet, 10 #R681a	2,250.	
R682 R25 $100 **carmine**		55.00	7.50
Cut cancel			5.25
Perf. initial			4.00
With complete receipt tab		55.00	
a.	Booklet pane of 4	225.00	
	Complete booklet, 10 #R682a	2,250.	
R683 R25 $500 **carmine**		150.00	87.50
Cut cancel			30.00
Perf. initial			25.00
With complete receipt tab		150.00	
a.	Booklet pane of 4	600.00	
	Complete booklet, 2 #R683a	1,200.	
R684 R25 $1000 **carmine**		300.00	65.00
Cut cancel			19.00
Perf. initial			16.00
With complete receipt tab		300.00	
a.	Booklet pane of 4	800.00	
	Complete booklet, 1 #R684a	800.00	
R685 R25 $2500 **carmine**		350.00	250.00
Cut cancel			97.50
Perf. initial			62.50
With complete receipt tab		350.00	
a.	Booklet pane of 4	1,300.	
	Complete booklet, 10 #R685a	13,000.	
R686 R25 $5000 **carmine**		1,750.	1,250.
Cut cancel			550.00
Perf. initial			475.00
With complete receipt tab		1,750.	
a.	Booklet pane of 4	7,000.	
R687 R25 $10,000 **carmine**		1,750.	1,500.
Cut cancel			350.00
Perf. initial			210.00
With complete receipt tab		1,750.	
a.	Booklet pane of 4	7,000.	

Documentary Stamps and Type of 1940 Overprinted in Black

Series 1955

1955 Wmk. 191R *Perf. 12*
Without Gum

R688 R25 $30 **carmine**	90.00	17.50
Cut cancel		7.00
Perf. initial		3.75
R689 R25 $50 **carmine**	100.00	22.50
Cut cancel		10.00
Perf. initial		6.50
R690 R25 $60 **carmine**	160.00	45.00
Cut cancel		17.50
Perf. initial		5.25
R691 R25 $100 **carmine**	80.00	9.50
Cut cancel		5.50
Perf. initial		3.75
R692 R25 $500 **carmine**	750.00	160.00
Cut cancel		45.00
Perf. initial		21.00
R693 R25 $1000 **carmine**	275.00	50.00
Cut cancel		20.00
Perf. initial		13.00
R694 R25 $2500 **carmine**	500.00	190.00
Cut cancel		90.00
Perf. initial		52.50
R695 R25 $5000 **carmine**	2,500.	1,500.
Cut cancel		600.00
Perf. initial		400.00
R696 R25 $10,000 **carmine**	—	1,100.
Cut cancel		500.00
Perf. initial		190.00

Documentary Stamps and Type of 1940 Overprinted in Black "Series 1956"

1956 Wmk. 191R Without Gum *Perf. 12*

R697 R25 $30 **carmine**	125.00	20.00
Cut cancel		10.50
Perf. initial		4.75
R698 R25 $50 **carmine**	140.00	27.50
Cut cancel		15.00
Perf. initial		6.25
R699 R25 $60 **carmine**	175.00	60.00
Cut cancel		20.00
Perf. initial		7.25
R700 R25 $100 **carmine**	110.00	15.00
Cut cancel		6.00
Perf. initial		5.00
R701 R25 $500 **carmine**	375.00	110.00
Cut cancel		27.50
Perf. initial		16.00
R702 R25 $1000 **carmine**	600.00	90.00
Cut cancel		25.00
Perf. initial		13.00
R703 R25 $2500 **carmine**	—	800.00
Cut cancel		260.00
Perf. initial		150.00
R704 R25 $5000 **carmine**	—	2,200.
Cut cancel		1,100.
Perf. initial		725.00
R705 R25 $10,000 **carmine**	—	750.00
Cut cancel		250.00
Perf. initial		150.00

Documentary Stamps and Type of 1940 Overprinted in Black "Series 1957"

1957 Wmk. 191R *Perf. 12*
Without Gum

R706 R25 $30 **carmine**	150.00	42.50
Cut cancel		14.00
Perf. initial		6.25
R707 R25 $50 **carmine**	125.00	47.50
Cut cancel		14.00
Perf. initial		5.75
R708 R25 $60 **carmine**	500.00	275.00
Cut cancel		125.00
Perf. initial		55.00
R709 R25 $100 **carmine**	110.00	20.00
Cut cancel		9.00
Perf. initial		4.50
R710 R25 $500 **carmine**	450.00	140.00
Cut cancel		65.00
Perf. initial		35.00
R711 R25 $1000 **carmine**	300.00	100.00
Cut cancel		35.00
Perf. initial		21.00
R712 R25 $2500 **carmine**	—	1,200.
Cut cancel		450.00
Perf. initial		300.00
R713 R25 $5000 **carmine**	2,250.	1,800.
Cut cancel		600.00
Perf. initial		210.00
R714 R25 $10,000 **carmine**	—	500.00
Cut cancel		175.00
Perf. initial		150.00

Documentary Stamps and Type of 1940 Overprinted in Black "Series 1958"

1958 Wmk. 191R *Perf. 12*
Without Gum

R715 R25 $30 **carmine**	110.00	27.50
Cut cancel		17.50
Perf. initial		8.25
R716 R25 $50 **carmine**	90.00	27.50
Cut cancel		16.00
Perf. initial		6.25
R717 R25 $60 **carmine**	160.00	42.50
Cut cancel		20.00
Perf. initial		10.50
R718 R25 $100 **carmine**	80.00	15.00
Cut cancel		6.50
Perf. initial		2.10
R719 R25 $500 **carmine**	350.00	95.00
Cut cancel		42.50
Perf. initial		21.00
R720 R25 $1000 **carmine**	425.00	90.00
Cut cancel		35.00
Perf. initial		25.00
R721 R25 $2500 **carmine**	—	1,100.
Cut cancel		575.00
Perf. initial		400.00
R722 R25 $5000 **carmine**	—	3,500.
Cut cancel		2,250.
Perf. initial		2,000.
R723 R25 $10,000 **carmine**	—	2,000.
Cut cancel		1,250.
Perf. initial		700.00

Documentary Stamps and Type of 1940 Without Overprint

1958 Wmk. 191R *Perf. 12*
With Gum

R724 R25 $30 **carmine**		11.00	7.00
Cut cancel			6.00
Perf. initial			4.25
With complete receipt tab		14.00	
a.	Booklet pane of 4	57.50	
	Complete booklet, 10 #R724a	575.00	
b.	Vert. pair, imperf. horiz.	2,250.	
R725 R25 $50 **carmine**		12.00	7.00
Cut cancel			4.00
Perf. initial			3.25
With complete receipt tab		15.00	
a.	Booklet pane of 4	60.00	
	Complete booklet, 10 #R725a	600.00	
b.	Vert. pair, imperf. horiz.		3,500.
R726 R25 $60 **carmine**		17.50	21.00
Cut cancel			10.50
Perf. initial			5.25
With complete receipt tab		22.00	
a.	Booklet pane of 4	90.00	
	Complete booklet, 10 #R726a	900.00	
R727 R25 $100 **carmine**		13.00	4.75
Cut cancel			3.25
Perf. initial			2.00
With complete receipt tab		16.00	
a.	Booklet pane of 4	65.00	
	Complete booklet, 10 #R727a	650.00	
R728 R25 $500 **carmine**		17.50	26.00
Cut cancel			10.50
Perf. initial			7.75
With complete receipt tab		22.00	
a.	Booklet pane of 4	90.00	
	Complete booklet, 10 #R728a	900.00	
R729 R25 $1000 **carmine**		16.00	21.00
Cut cancel			10.50
Perf. initial			7.75
With complete receipt tab		20.00	
a.	Booklet pane of 4	80.00	
	Complete booklet, 10 #R729a	800.00	
b.	Vert. pair, imperf. horiz.		1,750.
R730 R25 $2500 **carmine**		175.00	175.00
Cut cancel			90.00
Perf. initial			55.00
With complete receipt tab		—	
a.	Booklet pane of 4	800.00	
	Complete booklet, 10 #R730a	—	
R731 R25 $5000 **carmine**		275.00	175.00
Cut cancel			90.00
Perf. initial			65.00
With complete receipt tab		—	
a.	Booklet pane of 4	1,200.	
	Complete booklet, 10 #R731a	—	
R732 R25 $10,000 **carmine**		275.00	140.00
Cut cancel			55.00
Perf. initial			25.00
With complete receipt tab		—	
a.	Booklet pane of 4	1,200.	
	Complete booklet, 10 #R732a	—	

Internal Revenue Building, Washington, D.C. — R26

Centenary of the Internal Revenue Service.

Giori Press Printing

1962, July 2 Unwmk. *Perf. 11*

R733 R26 10c **violet blue & bright green**	1.00	.40
Never hinged	1.25	
Cut cancel		.20
Perf. initial		.25
P# block of 4	15.00	
Cross gutter block of 4	*2,500.*	
Horiz. pair with vert. gutter	*200.00*	
Vert. pair with horiz. gutter	*400.00*	

1963

"Established 1862" Removed

R734 R26 10c **violet blue & bright green**	3.00	.70
Never hinged	5.00	
Cut cancel		.25
Perf. initial		.25
P# block of 4	30.00	

Documentary revenue stamps were no longer required after Dec. 31, 1967.

PROPRIETARY STAMPS

Stamps for use on proprietary articles were included in the first general issue of 1862-71. They are R3, R13, R14, R18, R22, R29, R31 and R38.

Several varieties of "violet" paper were used in printing Nos. RB1-RB10. One is grayish with a slight greenish tinge, called "intermediate" paper by specialists. It should not be confused with the "green" paper, which is truly green.

All values prior to 1898 are for used examples. Printed cancellations on proprietary stamps command sizable premiums.

George Washington — RB1a

RB1

Engraved and printed by Jos. R. Carpenter, Philadelphia.

1871-74 ***Perf. 12***

				a. Violet Paper (1871)	b. Green Paper (1874)
RB1	RB1	1c	**green & black**	8.00	14.00
			Pair	17.00	35.00
			Block of 4	37.50	85.00
		c.	Imperf.	80.00	
			Imperf. pair	175.00	
			Imperf. block of 4	475.00	
		d.	Inverted center	*4,500.*	
RB2	RB1	2c	**green & black**	8.75	30.00
			Pair	19.00	67.50
			Block of 4	42.50	160.00
			Double transfer	20.00	
		c.	Inverted center	*50,000.*	*9,000.*
		d.	Vert. half used as 1c on document		—

No. RB2bc is valued with fine centering and small faults.

Only two examples recorded of the inverted center on violet paper, No. RB2ac.

RB3	RB1a	3c	**green & black**	27.50	67.50
			Pair	65.00	150.00
			Block of 4	140.00	325.00
			Double transfer	—	
		c.	Sewing machine perf.	650.00	
		d.	Inverted center	*16,000.*	

No. RB3ad is valued with small faults as 6 of the 7 recorded examples have faults.

RB4	RB1a	4c	**green & black**	16.00	25.00
			Pair	37.50	60.00
			Block of 4	100.00	130.00
			Double transfer	—	
		c.	Inverted center	*19,000.*	
		d.	Vert. half used as 2c on document		—

No. RB4ac is valued with small faults as 6 of the 7 recorded examples have faults.

RB5	RB1a	5c	**green & black**	160.00	175.00
			Pair	350.00	400.00
			Block of 4	750.00	875.00
		c.	Inverted center	*130,000.*	

No. RB5ac is unique. Value represents price realized in 2000 auction sale.

				a. Violet Paper (1871)	b. Green Paper (1874)
RB6	RB1a	6c	**green & black**	57.50	140.00
			Pair	125.00	325.00
			Block of 4	350.00	725.00
			Double transfer	—	
RB7	RB1a	10c	**green & black** ('73)	250.00	65.00
			Pair	600.00	150.00
			Block of 4	—	350.00
			Double transfer	—	

(See note on Inverted Centers after No. R133.)

RB1b

				a. Violet Paper	b. Green Paper (1874)
RB8	RB1b	50c	**green & black** ('73)	725.	1,300.
			Pair	*1,500.*	
RB9	RB1b	$1	**green & black** ('73)	*2,750.*	*12,000.*
			Pair	—	

RB1c

				a. Violet Paper	b. Green Paper (1874)
RB10	RB1c	$5	**green & black** ('73)	*9,000.*	*90,000.*
			Pair	*22,500.*	

No. RB10b is valued with small faults.

When the Carpenter contract expired Aug. 31, 1875, the proprietary stamps remaining unissued were delivered to the Bureau of Internal Revenue. Until the taxes expired, June 30, 1883, the B.I.R. issued 34,315 of the 50c, 6,585 of the $1 and 2,109 of the $5, Nos. RB8-RB10. No. RB19, the 10c blue, replaced No. RB7b, the 10c on green paper, after 336,000 stamps were issued, exhausting the supply in 1881.

RB2

George Washington — RB2a

Plates prepared and printed by both the National Bank Note Co. and the Bureau of Engraving and Printing. No. RB11, and possibly others, also printed by the American Bank Note Co. All silk paper printings were by National, plus early printings of Nos. RB11b-RB14b, RB16b, RB17b. All rouletted stamps printed by the BEP plus Nos. RB15b, RB18b, RB19b. Otherwise, which company printed the stamps can be told only by guide lines (BEP) or full marginal inscriptions. ABN used National plates with A. B. Co. added on the second stamp to the left of the National inscription.

1875-81

				Silk Paper a. Perf.	Wmkd. 191R b. Perf.	c. Roul. 6
RB11	RB2	1c	**green**	2.25	.50	150.00
			Pair	5.00	1.25	350.00
			Block of 4	12.50	3.00	825.00
			Double transfer	—		
		d.	Vert. pair, imperf between		*300.00*	
RB12	RB2	2c	**brown**	3.25	2.00	160.00
			Pair	7.00	4.50	350.00
			Block of 4	65.00	11.00	850.00
RB13	RB2a	3c	**orange**	14.00	4.00	140.00
			Pair	30.00	9.00	325.00
			Block of 4	70.00	21.00	750.00
		d.	Horizontal pair, imperf. between			—
		e.	Vertical pair, imperf. between			*2,000.*
RB14	RB2a	4c	**red brown**	10.00	9.00	
			Pair	25.00	21.00	
			Block of 4	55.00	45.00	
RB15	RB2a	4c	**red**		6.00	275.00
			Pair		15.00	600.00
			Block of 4		35.00	
RB16	RB2a	5c	**black**	175.00	125.00	*1,850.*
			Pair	350.00	275.00	—
			Block of 4	—	—	—
RB17	RB2a	6c	**violet blue**	35.00	25.00	425.00
			Pair	75.00	60.00	*950.00*
			Block of 4	200.00	150.00	
RB18	RB2a	6c	**violet**		35.00	*400.00*
			Pair		85.00	
			Block of 4		225.00	
RB19	RB2a	10c	**blue** ('81)		350.00	
			Pair		750.00	
			Block of 4		—	

Many fraudulent roulettes exist.

Battleship — RB3

Inscribed "Series of 1898." and "Proprietary."
See note on rouletting preceding No. R161.

1898 **Wmk. 191R** **Engr.**

			Roul. 5½ Unused	Used	*p.* Hyphen Hole Perf. 7 Unused	Used
RB20	⅛c	**yellow green**	.25	.25	.30	.25
		Block of 4	.50	.50	.75	.70
		Double transfer	—			
	a.	Vert. pair, imperf. horiz.	—			
RB21	¼c	**brown**	.25	.25	.25	.25
	a.	¼c **red brown**	.20	.20		
	b.	¼c **yellow brown**	.20	.20	.20	.20
	c.	¼c **orange brown**	.20	.20	.20	.20
	d.	¼c **bister**	.20	.20		
		Block of 4	.50	.25	.55	1.00
		Double transfer	—	—		
	e.	Vert. pair, imperf. horiz.	—	—		
	f.	Printed on both sides	—			
RB22	⅜c	**deep orange**	.30	.30	.50	.35
		Block of 4	1.40	1.90	2.25	—
	a.	Horiz. pair, imperf. vert.	12.50			
	b.	Vert. pair, imperf. horiz.	—			
RB23	⅝c	**deep ultra**	.25	.25	.30	.25
		Block of 4	1.25	1.10	1.50	1.25
		Double transfer	1.50			
	a.	Vert. pair, imperf. horiz.	85.00	—		
	b.	Horiz. pair, imperf. vert.	*350.00*			
RB24	1c	**dark green**	2.25	.40	30.00	15.00
		Block of 4	11.00	1.75	140.00	67.50
	a.	Vert. pair, imperf. horiz.	*325.00*			
RB25	1¼c	**violet**	.35	.25	.30	.30
		Block of 4	1.50	1.00	1.40	1.25
	a.	1¼c **brown violet**	.35	.20	.25	.30
	b.	Vertical pair, imperf. between	—			
RB26	1⅞c	**dull blue**	15.00	2.00	35.00	9.00
		Block of 4	65.00	—	175.00	—
		Double transfer	—			
RB27	2c	**violet brown**	1.40	.35	7.25	1.00
		Block of 4	6.75	—	27.50	—
		Double transfer		—		
	a.	Horiz. pair, imperf. vert.	60.00			
RB28	2½c	**lake**	5.00	.35	6.00	.40
		Block of 4	25.00	1.50	32.50	—
	a.	Vert. pair, imperf. horiz.	225.00			
RB29	3¾c	**olive gray**	42.50	15.00	90.00	27.50
		Block of 4	210.00	—	425.00	140.00
RB30	4c	**purple**	16.00	1.50	62.50	22.50
		Block of 4	75.00	7.50	325.00	100.00
		Double transfer	—			
RB31	5c	**brown orange**	15.00	1.50	75.00	25.00
		Block of 4	70.00	7.00	375.00	190.00
	a.	Vert. pair, imperf. horiz.	—	*325.00*		
	b.	Horiz. pair, imperf. vert.	—	*425.00*		

See note after No. RS315 regarding St. Louis Provisional Labels of 1898.

RB4

Inscribed "Series of 1914"

1914 **Wmk. 190** **Offset Printing** ***Perf. 10***

				Unused	Used
RB32	RB4	⅛c	**black**	.25	.35
			Block of 4	1.25	1.60
RB33	RB4	¼c	**black**	3.75	1.50
			Block of 4	17.00	
RB34	RB4	⅜c	**black**	.35	.35
			Block of 4	1.50	1.50
RB35	RB4	⅝c	**black**	7.25	3.00
			Block of 4	32.50	
RB36	RB4	1⅛c	**black**	5.00	1.75
			Block of 4	22.50	
RB37	RB4	1⅞c	**black**	62.50	22.50
			Block of 4	275.00	
RB38	RB4	2½c	**black**	15.00	3.50
			Block of 4	62.50	15.00
RB39	RB4	3⅛c	**black**	140.00	67.50
			Block of 4	600.00	
RB40	RB4	3¾c	**black**	60.00	27.50
			Block of 4	325.00	
RB41	RB4	4c	**black**	85.00	45.00
			Block of 4	400.00	
RB42	RB4	4⅜c	**black**	*3,000.*	—
			Block of 4	*13,000.*	
RB43	RB4	5c	**black**	160.00	110.00
			Block of 4	—	
			Wmk. 191R		
RB44	RB4	⅛c	**black**	.35	.30
			Block of 4	1.50	1.50
RB45	RB4	¼c	**black**	.25	.25
			Block of 4	1.25	1.10
			Double impression	30.00	
RB46	RB4	⅜c	**black**	.75	.45
			Block of 4	3.50	2.00
RB47	RB4	½c	**black**	4.25	3.75
			Block of 4	17.50	
RB48	RB4	⅝c	**black**	.30	.25
			Block of 4	1.50	1.10
RB49	RB4	1c	**black**	5.50	5.50
			Block of 4	25.00	25.00
RB50	RB4	1¼c	**black**	.65	.40
			Block of 4	3.00	1.75
RB51	RB4	1½c	**black**	4.25	3.00
			Block of 4	17.50	14.00
RB52	RB4	1⅞c	**black**	1.35	.90
			Block of 4	6.00	4.00
RB53	RB4	2c	**black**	7.50	6.00
			Block of 4	32.50	
RB54	RB4	2½c	**black**	1.75	1.40
			Block of 4	8.00	7.50
RB55	RB4	3c	**black**	6.00	4.00
			Block of 4	27.50	
RB56	RB4	3⅛c	**black**	8.00	5.00
			Block of 4	35.00	
RB57	RB4	3¾c	**black**	17.50	11.00
			Block of 4	77.50	
RB58	RB4	4c	**black**	.50	.30
			Block of 4	2.25	1.50
			Double impression	—	
RB59	RB4	4⅜c	**black**	20.00	11.00
			Block of 4	85.00	
RB60	RB4	5c	**black**	4.50	3.75
			Block of 4	20.00	
RB61	RB4	6c	**black**	80.00	52.50
			Block of 4	375.00	
RB62	RB4	8c	**black**	25.00	16.00
			Block of 4	110.00	
RB63	RB4	10c	**black**	18.00	11.00
			Block of 4	87.50	
RB64	RB4	20c	**black**	35.00	24.00
			Block of 4	160.00	

RB5

1919 **Offset Printing** ***Perf. 11***

RB65	RB5	1c	**dark blue**	.25	.25
			Block of 4	1.25	1.10
			Double impression	30.00	20.00
RB66	RB5	2c	**dark blue**	.35	.25
			Block of 4	1.50	1.10
			Double impression	70.00	
RB67	RB5	3c	**dark blue**	1.50	.75
			Block of 4	6.00	3.50
			Double impression	70.00	
RB68	RB5	4c	**dark blue**	2.25	.75
			Block of 4	10.00	
RB69	RB5	5c	**dark blue**	3.00	1.25
			Block of 4	13.50	5.75
RB70	RB5	8c	**dark blue**	22.50	16.00
			Block of 4	100.00	
RB71	RB5	10c	**dark blue**	11.00	4.25
			Block of 4	52.50	15.00
RB72	RB5	20c	**dark blue**	17.50	6.00
			Block of 4	87.50	
RB73	RB5	40c	**dark blue**	65.00	20.00
			Block of 4	300.00	

FUTURE DELIVERY STAMPS

Issued to facilitate the collection of a tax upon each sale, agreement of sale or agreement to sell any products or merchandise at any exchange or board of trade, or other similar place for future delivery.

Documentary Stamps of 1917 Overprinted in Black or Red

Type I

1918-34 Wmk. 191R Offset Printing *Perf. 11*

Overprint Horizontal (Lines 8mm apart)

Left Value — Unused

Right Value — Used

RC1	R22	2c **carmine rose**	8.25	.25
		Block of 4	35.00	1.10
RC2	R22	3c **carmine rose** ('34)	45.00	37.50
		Cut cancel		20.00
RC3	R22	4c **carmine rose**	14.00	.25
		Cut cancel		.20
		Block of 4	65.00	1.10
b.		Double impression of stamp		10.00
RC3A	R22	5c **carmine rose** ('33)	85.00	7.50
		Block of 4	—	37.50
RC4	R22	10c **carmine rose**	22.50	.35
		Block of 4	100.00	1.50
a.		Double overprint	—	5.25
b.		"FUTURE" omitted	—	*325.00*
c.		"DELIVERY FUTURE"		37.50
RC5	R22	20c **carmine rose**	32.50	.25
		Cut cancel		.20
		Block of 4	160.00	1.10
a.		Double overprint		21.00
RC6	R22	25c **carmine rose**	70.00	.60
		Cut cancel		.30
		Block of 4	325.00	3.00
		Block of 4, cut cancel		1.50
RC7	R22	40c **carmine rose**	80.00	1.25
		Cut cancel		.35
		Block of 4	350.00	5.75
		Block of 4, cut cancel		1.50
RC8	R22	50c **carmine rose**	20.00	.35
		Cut cancel		.20
		Block of 4	97.50	1.50
a.		"DELIVERY" omitted	—	*110.00*
RC9	R22	80c **carmine rose**	160.00	13.50
		Cut cancel		3.50
		Block of 4	750.00	67.50
		Block of 4, cut cancel		16.00
a.		Double overprint		37.50
		Double overprint, cut cancel		6.25

Engr.

Overprint Vertical, Reading Up (Lines 2mm apart)

RC10	R21	$1 **green** (R)	60.00	.35
		Cut cancel		.20
		Block of 4	250.00	1.60
a.		Overprint reading down		*300.00*
b.		Black overprint		—
		Cut cancel		125.00
RC11	R21	$2 **rose**	70.00	.45
		Cut cancel		.25
		Block of 4	325.00	2.00
RC12	R21	$3 **violet** (R)	200.00	3.50
		Cut cancel		.30
		Block of 4	—	16.00
		Block of 4, cut cancel		1.50
a.		Overprint reading down	—	52.50
RC13	R21	$5 **dark blue** (R)	110.00	.60
		Cut cancel		.25
		Block of 4	—	2.75
		Block of 4, cut cancel		1.10
RC14	R21	$10 **orange**	140.00	1.35
		Cut cancel		.30
		Block of 4	625.00	5.00
		Block of 4, cut cancel		1.40
a.		"DELIVERY FUTURE"		*110.00*
RC15	R21	$20 **olive bister**	275.00	9.00
		Cut cancel		.80
		Perf initial		.35
		Block of 4		47.50
		Block of 4, cut cancel		3.50

Overprint Horizontal (Lines 11⅔mm apart)

Perf. 12

Without Gum

RC16	R17	$30 **vermilion,** green numerals	110.00	5.50
		Cut cancel		1.75
		Perf initial		1.25
		Vertical strip of 4		30.00
		Vertical strip of 4, cut cancel		8.25
a.		Numerals in blue	100.00	4.75
		Cut cancel		2.00
		Perf initial		1.50
b.		Imperf., blue numerals		*110.00*
RC17	R19	$50 **olive green** *(Cleveland)*	90.00	3.00
		Cut cancel		.90
		Vertical strip of 4		15.00
		Vertical strip of 4, cut cancel		3.50
a.		$50 olive bister	90.00	2.75
		Cut cancel		.25
		Perf initial		.50
RC18	R19	$60 **brown**	125.00	8.00
		Cut cancel		1.00
		Perf initial		.80
		Vertical strip of 4		35.00
		Vertical strip of 4, cut cancel		4.75
a.		Vert. pair, imperf. horiz.		*425.00*
RC19	R17	$100 **yellow green** ('34)	210.00	37.50
		Cut cancel		9.00
		Perf initial		7.00
		Vertical strip of 4	—	*200.00*
		Vertical strip of 4, cut cancel		37.50
RC20	R18	$500 **blue,** red numerals (R)	160.00	15.00
		Cut cancel		6.50
		Perf initial		5.00
		Vertical strip of 4		72.50
		Vertical strip of 4, cut cancel		25.00
		Double transfer		25.00
a.		Numerals in orange	—	60.00
		Cut cancel		12.50
		Perf initial		10.00
		Double transfer		90.00
RC21	R19	$1000 **orange**	190.00	7.50
		Cut cancel		2.00
		Perf initial		1.50
		Vertical strip of 4		32.50
		Vertical strip of 4, cut cancel		9.00
a.		Vert. pair, imperf. horiz.		*1,350.*

See note after No. R227.

1923-24 Offset Printing *Perf. 11*

Overprint Horizontal (Lines 2mm apart)

RC22	R22	1c **carmine rose**	1.25	.25
		Block of 4	6.00	1.25
RC23	R22	80c **carmine rose**	160.00	3.50
		Cut cancel		.70
		Block of 4	—	18.00
		Block of 4, cut cancel		3.50

Type II

1925-34 Engr.

RC25	R21	$1 **green** (R)	80.00	2.00
		Cut cancel		.45
		Block of 4	—	8.00
		Block of 4, cut cancel		1.50
RC26	R21	$10 **orange** (Bk) ('34)	200.00	27.50
		Cut cancel		17.50
		Perf initial		11.00

Overprint Type I

1928-29 Offset Printing *Perf. 10*

RC27	R22	10c **carmine rose**		*5,000.*
RC28	R22	20c **carmine rose**		*5,000.*

STOCK TRANSFER STAMPS

Issued to facilitate the collection of a tax on all sales or agreements to sell, or memoranda of sales or delivery of, or transfers of legal title to shares or certificates of stock.

Documentary Stamps of 1917 Overprinted in Black or Red

1918-22 Offset Printing Wmk. 191R *Perf. 11*

Overprint Horizontal (Lines 8mm apart)

RD1	R22	1c **carmine rose**	1.00	.25
		Block of 4	4.25	1.10
a.		Double overprint	—	—
RD2	R22	2c **carmine rose**	.25	.25
		Block of 4	1.10	1.10
a.		Double overprint	—	5.00
		Double overprint, cut cancel		2.50
		Double impression of stamp	—	
RD3	R22	4c **carmine rose**	.25	.25
		Block of 4	1.25	1.10
a.		Double overprint	—	4.25
		Double overprint, cut cancel		2.10
b.		"STOCK" omitted		10.50
d.		Ovpt. lines 10mm apart		—
		Double impression of stamp		6.00
RD4	R22	5c **carmine rose**	.30	.25
		Block of 4	1.40	1.10
RD5	R22	10c **carmine rose**	.30	.25
		Block of 4	1.40	1.10
a.		Double overprint	—	5.25
		Double overprint, cut cancel		2.75
b.		"STOCK" omitted		—
		Double impression of stamp		—
RD6	R22	20c **carmine rose**	.55	.25
		Perf initial		.20
		Block of 4	2.25	1.10
a.		Double overprint		6.25
b.		"STOCK" double		—
		Double impression of stamp		6.00
RD7	R22	25c **carmine rose**	2.25	.25
		Cut cancel		.20
		Block of 4	10.50	1.10
RD8	R22	40c **carmine rose** ('22)	2.25	.25
		Block of 4	10.50	1.10
RD9	R22	50c **carmine rose**	.80	.25
		Block of 4	3.75	1.10
a.		Double overprint	—	
		Double impression of stamp		—
RD10	R22	80c **carmine rose**	9.00	.45
		Cut cancel		.25
		Block of 4	42.50	2.00

Engr.

Overprint Vertical, Reading Up (Lines 2mm apart)

RD11	R21	$1 **green** (R)	160.00	30.00
		Cut cancel		7.00
		Block of 4	—	—
		Block of 4, cut cancel		14.00
a.		Overprint reading down	210.00	30.00
		Overprint reading down, cut cancel		9.00
RD12	R21	$1 **green** (Bk)	3.00	.30
		Block of 4	13.00	1.40
a.		Pair, one without overprint	—	*160.00*
b.		Overprinted on back instead of face, inverted	—	*110.00*
c.		Overprint reading down	—	7.50
d.		$1 yellow green	3.00	.25
RD13	R21	$2 **rose**	3.00	.25
		Perf initial		.20
		Block of 4	13.00	1.10
a.		Overprint reading down		11.50
		Overprint reading down, cut cancel		1.50
b.		Vert. pair, imperf. horiz.	*500.00*	
RD14	R21	$3 **violet** (R)	27.50	6.00
		Cut cancel		.30
		Perf initial		.20
		Block of 4	125.00	—
		Block of 4, cut cancel		1.50

RD15 R21 $4 **yellow brown** 12.00 .25
Cut cancel .20
Block of 4 52.50 1.10
RD16 R21 $5 **dark blue** (R) 8.00 .25
Cut cancel .20
Block of 4 40.00 1.10
Block of 4, cut cancel .20
a. Overprint reading down 42.50 1.35
Overprint reading down, cut cancel .25
RD17 R21 $10 **orange** 30.00 .45
Cut cancel .20
Block of 4 125.00 1.50
Block of 4, cut cancel .20
RD18 R21 $20 **olive bister** ('21) 125.00 18.00
Cut cancel 5.00
Perf initial 2.50
Block of 4 500.00 82.50
Block of 4, cut cancel 25.00

Shifted overprints on the $2, and $10 result in "TRANSFER STOCK," "TRANSFER" omitted, and possibly other varieties.

Overprint Horizontal (Lines 11½mm apart)

1918 Without Gum *Perf. 12*

RD19 R17 $30 **vermilion,** green numerals 42.50 5.75
Cut cancel 2.00
Perf initial 1.25
Vertical strip of 4 26.00
Vertical strip of 4, cut cancel 7.75
a. Numerals in blue 150.00 60.00
RD20 R19 $50 **olive green** *(Cleveland)* 140.00 62.50
Cut cancel 26.00
Perf initial 25.00
Vertical strip of 4 300.00
Vertical strip of 4, cut cancel 110.00
RD21 R19 $60 **brown** 250.00 25.00
Cut cancel 10.50
Perf initial 7.25
Vertical strip of 4 100.00
Vertical strip of 4, cut cancel 47.50
RD22 R17 $100 **green** 45.00 6.50
Cut cancel 3.00
Perf initial 2.25
Vertical strip of 4 30.00
Vertical strip of 4, cut cancel 13.00
RD23 R18 $500 **blue** (R) 425.00 150.00
Cut cancel 75.00
Perf initial 55.00
Vertical strip of 4 —
Vertical strip of 4, cut cancel 325.00
Double transfer *625.00* 200.00
a. Numerals in orange 150.00
Numerals in orange, double transfer 250.00
RD24 R19 $1,000 **orange** 275.00 95.00
Cut cancel 32.50
Perf initial 22.50
Vertical strip of 4 400.00
Vertical strip of 4, cut cancel 150.00

See note after No. R227.

1928 Offset Printing *Perf. 10*

Overprint Horizontal (Lines 8mm apart)

RD25 R22 2c **carmine rose** 5.50 .30
Block of 4 24.00 1.40
RD26 R22 4c **carmine rose** 5.50 .30
Block of 4 24.00 1.40
RD27 R22 10c **carmine rose** 5.50 .30
Block of 4 24.00 1.40
a. Inverted overprint *1,250.*
RD28 R22 20c **carmine rose** 6.50 .35
Perf initial .20
Block of 4 29.00 1.50
Double impression of stamp —
RD29 R22 50c **carmine rose** 10.00 .50
Block of 4 47.50 2.25

Engr.

Overprint Vertical, Reading Up (Lines 2mm apart)

RD30 R21 $1 **green** 45.00 .35
Cut cancel .25
Block of 4 — 1.60
a. $1 yellow green 45.00 .50
RD31 R21 $2 **carmine rose** 40.00 .35
Perf initial .20
Block of 4 — 1.50
a. Pair, one without overprint *225.00 190.00*
RD32 R21 $10 **orange** 40.00 .50
Cut cancel .25
Perf initial .20
Block of 4 — 2.25
Perf. 11 at top or bottom —

Overprinted Horizontally in Black

1920 Offset Printing *Perf. 11*

RD33 R22 2c **carmine rose** 12.50 1.00
Block of 4 60.00 4.25
RD34 R22 10c **carmine rose** 3.00 .35
Block of 4 14.00 1.50
b. Inverted overprint *1,550. 1,000.*
RD35 R22 20c **carmine rose** 5.75 .25
Block of 4 26.00 1.10
a. Horiz. pair, one without overprint 175.00
d. Inverted overprint (perf. initials) —
RD36 R22 50c **carmine rose** 5.00 .30
Block of 4 24.00 1.25

Shifted overprints on the 10c, 20c and 50c result in "TRANSFER STOCK," "TRANFSER" omitted, "STOCK" omitted, pairs, and other varieties.

Engr.

RD37 R21 $1 **green** 60.00 13.50
Cut cancel 2.50
Block of 4 275.00 62.50
Block of 4, cut cancel 11.50
RD38 R21 $2 **rose** 65.00 13.50
Cut cancel 2.50
Block of 4 300.00 70.00
Block of 4, cut cancel 11.50

Offset Printing

Perf. 10

RD39 R22 2c **carmine rose** 13.00 1.10
Block of 4 67.50 5.00
Double impression of stamp —
RD40 R22 10c **carmine rose** 5.25 .55
Block of 4 26.00 2.50
RD41 R22 20c **carmine rose** 6.00 .25
Cut cancel .20
Block of 4 30.00 1.10

Documentary Stamps of 1917-33 Overprinted in Black

1940 Offset Printing Wmk. 191R *Perf. 11*

RD42 R22 1c **rose pink** 4.50 .65
Cut cancel .25
Perf. initial .25
a. "Series 1940" inverted *600.00* 325.00
Cut cancel 125.00

No. RD42a always comes with a natural straight edge at left.

RD43 R22 2c **rose pink** 4.50 .65
Cut cancel .25
Perf. initial .25
RD45 R22 4c **rose pink** 5.25 .35
Cut cancel .25
Perf. initial .25
RD46 R22 5c **rose pink** 5.75 .25
Cut cancel .20
Perf. initial .20
RD48 R22 10c **rose pink** 10.00 .35
Cut cancel .25
Perf. initial .20
RD49 R22 20c **rose pink** 11.50 .35
Cut cancel .25
Perf. initial .20
RD50 R22 25c **rose pink** 11.50 1.10
Cut cancel .35
Perf. initial .25
RD51 R22 40c **rose pink** 8.75 1.00
Cut cancel .35
Perf. initial .25
RD52 R22 50c **rose pink** 9.75 .35
Cut cancel .25
Perf. initial .25
RD53 R22 80c **rose pink** 125.00 80.00
Cut cancel 45.00
Perf. initial 26.00

Engr.

RD54 R21 $1 **green** 40.00 .60
Cut cancel .35
Perf. initial .25
RD55 R21 $2 **rose** 45.00 1.00
Cut cancel .40
Perf. initial .25
RD56 R21 $3 **violet** 250.00 18.00
Cut cancel .75
Perf. initial .50
RD57 R21 $4 **yellow brown** 100.00 1.60
Cut cancel .50
Perf. initial .30
RD58 R21 $5 **dark blue** 80.00 2.00
Cut cancel .55
Perf. initial .35
RD59 R21 $10 **orange** 225.00 10.00
Cut cancel 1.10
Perf. initial .75
RD60 R21 $20 **olive bister** 375.00 150.00
Cut cancel 25.00
Perf. initial 11.50

Nos. RD19-RD24 Handstamped in Blue "Series 1940"

1940 Wmk. 191R *Perf. 12*

Without Gum

RD61 R17 $30 **vermilion** *1,000.* *750.*
Cut cancel *375.*
Perf. initial *200.*
RD62 R19 $50 **olive green** *1,750.* *2,250.*
Cut cancel *1,000.*
Perf. initial *450.*
a. Double ovpt., perf. initial *1,000.*
RD63 R19 $60 **brown** *2,400.* *2,200.*
Cut cancel *675.*
Perf. initial *350.*
RD64 R17 $100 **green** *1,500.* *700.*
Cut cancel *250.*
Perf. initial *100.*
RD65 R18 $500 **blue** *2,250.*
Cut cancel *1,400.*
Perf. initial *775.*
Double transfer *2,500.*
RD66 R19 $1,000 **orange** *3,000.*
Cut cancel *2,250.*
Perf. initial *1,750.*

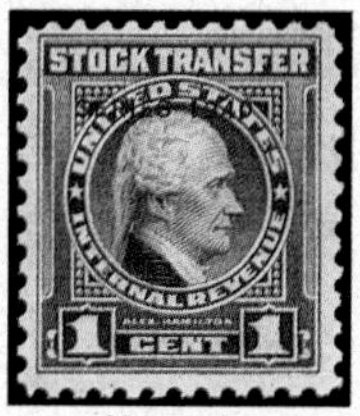

Alexander Hamilton — ST1

Levi Woodbury — ST2

Overprinted in Black **SERIES 1940**

Same Portraits as Nos. R288-R310.

1940 Engr. Wmk. 191R *Perf. 11*

RD67 ST1 1c **bright green** 13.00 3.25
Cut cancel .65
Perf. initial .40
RD68 ST1 2c **bright green** 8.50 1.75
Cut cancel .30
Perf. initial .30
RD70 ST1 4c **bright green** 15.00 4.50
Cut cancel .65
Perf. initial .35
RD71 ST1 5c **bright green** 9.50 1.75
Cut cancel .25
Perf. initial .25
a. Without overprint, cut cancel *400.00*
RD73 ST1 10c **bright green** 13.00 2.10
Cut cancel .25
Perf. initial .25
RD74 ST1 20c **bright green** 15.00 2.40
Cut cancel .25
Perf. initial .25
RD75 ST1 25c **bright green** 50.00 10.50
Cut cancel .90
Perf. initial .45
RD76 ST1 40c **bright green** 100.00 40.00
Cut cancel 3.00
Perf. initial 1.00
RD77 ST1 50c **bright green** 13.00 2.10
Cut cancel .45
Perf. initial .30
RD78 ST1 80c **bright green** 150.00 65.00
Cut cancel 27.50
Perf. initial 3.50
RD79 ST2 $1 **bright green** 55.00 4.25
Cut cancel .55
Perf. initial .30
a. Without overprint, perf. initial *400.00*
RD80 ST2 $2 **bright green** 60.00 12.00
Cut cancel .75
Perf. initial .30
RD81 ST2 $3 **bright green** 85.00 15.00
Cut cancel .90
Perf. initial .25
RD82 ST2 $4 **bright green** 375.00 240.00
Cut cancel 110.00
Perf. initial 50.00
RD83 ST2 $5 **bright green** 85.00 16.00
Cut cancel 2.00
Perf. initial .30
RD84 ST2 $10 **bright green** 210.00 50.00
Cut cancel 6.00
Perf. initial 3.00
RD85 ST2 $20 **bright green** 1,000. 95.00
Cut cancel 15.00
Perf. initial 5.75

Nos. RD67-RD85 exist imperforate, without overprint. Value, set of pairs, $1,100.

Thomas Corwin — ST3

Overprinted "SERIES 1940"

Various frames and portraits as Nos. R306-R310.

Without Gum *Perf. 12*

RD86	ST3	$30	**bright green**	750.00	175.00
			Cut cancel		82.50
			Perf. initial		37.50
RD87	ST3	$50	**bright green**	800.00	500.00
			Cut cancel		225.00
			Perf. initial		92.50
RD88	ST3	$60	**bright green**	*3,000.*	1,100.
			Cut cancel		450.00
			Perf. initial		120.00
RD89	ST3	$100	**bright green**	—	375.00
			Cut cancel		150.00
			Perf. initial		67.50
RD90	ST3	$500	**bright green**	—	*2,000.*
			Cut cancel		1,250.
			Perf. initial		700.
RD91	ST3	$1,000	**bright green**	—	*2,500.*
			Cut cancel		1,500.
			Perf. initial		650.00

Nos. RD86-RD91 exist as unfinished imperforates with complete receipt tabs, without overprints or serial numbers. Known in singles, pairs (Nos. RD86-RD88 and Nos. RD90-RD91, value $450 per pair; No. RD89, value $150 per pair), panes of four with plate number, uncut sheets of four panes (with two plate numbers), cross gutter blocks of eight, and blocks of four with vertical gutter between and plate number.

Nos. RD67-RD91 Overprint Instead: **SERIES 1941**

1941 **Wmk. 191R** ***Perf. 11***

RD92	ST1	1c	**bright green**	.80	.55
			Cut cancel		.25
			Perf. initial		.25
RD93	ST1	2c	**bright green**	.60	.30
			Cut cancel		.25
			Perf. initial		.25
RD95	ST1	4c	**bright green**	.65	.25
			Cut cancel		.20
			Perf. initial		.20
RD96	ST1	5c	**bright green**	.60	.25
			Cut cancel		.20
			Perf. initial		.20
RD98	ST1	10c	**bright green**	1.10	.25
			Cut cancel		.20
			Perf. initial		.20
RD99	ST1	20c	**bright green**	2.40	.30
			Cut cancel		.25
			Perf. initial		.20
RD100	ST1	25c	**bright green**	2.40	.45
			Cut cancel		.30
			Perf. initial		.30
RD101	ST1	40c	**bright green**	3.75	.75
			Cut cancel		.30
			Perf. initial		.20
RD102	ST1	50c	**bright green**	5.00	.35
			Cut cancel		.25
			Perf. initial		.25
RD103	ST1	80c	**bright green**	30.00	8.50
			Cut cancel		.75
			Perf. initial		.50
RD104	ST2	$1	**bright green**	21.00	.20
			Cut cancel		.20
			Perf. initial		.20
RD105	ST2	$2	**bright green**	22.50	.30
			Cut cancel		.20
			Perf. initial		.20
RD106	ST2	$3	**bright green**	32.50	1.50
			Cut cancel		.35
			Perf. initial		.25
RD107	ST2	$4	**bright green**	57.50	8.50
			Cut cancel		.60
			Perf. initial		.30
RD108	ST2	$5	**bright green**	57.50	.65
			Cut cancel		.30
			Perf. initial		.25
RD109	ST2	$10	**bright green**	125.00	5.50
			Cut cancel		1.00
			Perf. initial		.25
RD110	ST2	$20	**bright green**	350.00	80.00
			Cut cancel		21.00
			Perf. initial		4.25

Perf. 12

Without Gum

RD111	ST3	$30	**bright green**	325.00	275.00
			Cut cancel		85.00
			Perf. initial		29.00
RD112	ST3	$50	**bright green**	1,000.	475.00
			Cut cancel		150.00
			Perf. initial		65.00
RD113	ST3	$60	**bright green**	*1,350.*	350.00
			Cut cancel		210.00
			Perf. initial		125.00
RD114	ST3	$100	**bright green**	—	190.00
			Cut cancel		65.00
			Perf. initial		45.00
RD115	ST3	$500	**bright green**	1,900.	*1,650.*
			Cut cancel		1,000.
			Perf. initial		750.00
RD116	ST3	$1,000	**bright green**	—	*1,500.*
			Cut cancel		850.00
			Perf. initial		750.00

Nos. RD67-RD91 Overprint Instead: **SERIES 1942**

1942 **Wmk. 191R** ***Perf. 11***

RD117	ST1	1c	**bright green**	.75	.30
			Cut cancel		.25
			Perf. initial		.25
RD118	ST1	2c	**bright green**	.65	.35
			Cut cancel		.25
			Perf. initial		.25
RD119	ST1	4c	**bright green**	3.50	1.10
			Cut cancel		.55
			Perf. initial		.45
RD120	ST1	5c	**bright green**	.70	.20
			Cut cancel		.20
			Perf. initial		.20
a.			Overprint inverted, cut cancel		*240.00*
			Perf. initial		*200.00*
RD121	ST1	10c	**bright green**	2.25	.20
			Cut cancel		.20
			Perf. initial		.20
RD122	ST1	20c	**bright green**	2.75	.20
			Cut cancel		.20
			Perf. initial		.20
RD123	ST1	25c	**bright green**	2.50	.20
			Cut cancel		.20
			Perf. initial		.20
RD124	ST1	40c	**bright green**	5.75	.40
			Cut cancel		.25
			Perf. initial		.20
RD125	ST1	50c	**bright green**	6.50	.20
			Cut cancel		.20
			Perf. initial		.20
RD126	ST1	80c	**bright green**	27.50	6.00
			Cut cancel		1.50
			Perf. initial		.35
RD127	ST2	$1	**bright green**	24.00	.40
			Cut cancel		.25
			Perf. initial		.20
RD128	ST2	$2	**bright green**	37.50	.40
			Cut cancel		.25
			Perf. initial		.20
RD129	ST2	$3	**bright green**	42.50	1.10
			Cut cancel		.30
			Perf. initial		.20
RD130	ST2	$4	**bright green**	57.50	24.00
			Cut cancel		.65
			Perf. initial		.25
RD131	ST2	$5	**bright green**	50.00	.40
			Cut cancel		.25
			Perf. initial		.25
a.			Double overprint, perf. initial		*1,250.*
RD132	ST2	$10	**bright green**	110.00	9.50
			Cut cancel		2.00
			Perf. initial		1.10
RD133	ST2	$20	**bright green**	225.00	50.00
			Cut cancel		9.50
			Perf. initial		3.50

Perf. 12

Without Gum

RD134	ST3	$30	**bright green**	275.00	72.50
			Cut cancel		26.00
			Perf. initial		20.00
RD135	ST3	$50	**bright green**	425.00	175.00
			Cut cancel		55.00
			Perf. initial		27.50
RD136	ST3	$60	**bright green**	500.00	240.00
			Cut cancel		95.00
			Perf. initial		62.50
RD137	ST3	$100	**bright green**	*625.00*	100.00
			Cut cancel		35.00
			Perf. initial		21.00
RD138	ST3	$500	**bright green**	—	*13,000.*
			Cut cancel		*10,000.*
			Perf. initial		*8,000.*
RD139	ST3	$1,000	**bright green**	—	700.00
			Cut cancel		325.00
			Perf. initial		190.00

Nos. RD67-RD91 Overprint Instead: **SERIES 1943**

1943 **Wmk. 191R** ***Perf. 11***

RD140	ST1	1c	**bright green**	.55	.30
			Cut cancel		.25
			Perf. initial		.25
RD141	ST1	2c	**bright green**	.60	.40
			Cut cancel		.20
			Perf. initial		.20
RD142	ST1	4c	**bright green**	2.10	.20
			Cut cancel		.20
			Perf. initial		.20
RD143	ST1	5c	**bright green**	.60	.20
			Cut cancel		.20
			Perf. initial		.20
RD144	ST1	10c	**bright green**	1.40	.20
			Cut cancel		.20
			Perf. initial		.20
RD145	ST1	20c	**bright green**	2.10	.20
			Cut cancel		.20
			Perf. initial		.20
RD146	ST1	25c	**bright green**	6.50	.35
			Cut cancel		.25
			Perf. initial		.20
RD147	ST1	40c	**bright green**	6.00	.30
			Cut cancel		.25
			Perf. initial		.20
RD148	ST1	50c	**bright green**	5.00	.30
			Cut cancel		.25
			Perf. initial		.20
RD149	ST1	80c	**bright green**	25.00	7.50
			Cut cancel		2.50
			Perf. initial		1.25
RD150	ST2	$1	**bright green**	22.50	.25
			Cut cancel		.20
			Perf. initial		.20
RD151	ST2	$2	**bright green**	25.00	.50
			Cut cancel		.25
			Perf. initial		.25
RD152	ST2	$3	**bright green**	30.00	2.00
			Cut cancel		.35
			Perf. initial		.30
RD153	ST2	$4	**bright green**	60.00	20.00
			Cut cancel		1.50
			Perf. initial		.90
RD154	ST2	$5	**bright green**	80.00	.60
			Cut cancel		.30
			Perf. initial		.25
RD155	ST2	$10	**bright green**	125.00	6.50
			Cut cancel		1.00
			Perf. initial		.35
RD156	ST2	$20	**bright green**	225.00	60.00
			Cut cancel		20.00
			Perf. initial		4.75

Perf. 12

Without Gum

RD157	ST3	$30	**bright green**	500.00	225.00
			Cut cancel		70.00
			Perf. initial		32.50
RD158	ST3	$50	**bright green**	800.00	210.00
			Cut cancel		42.50
			Perf. initial		20.00
RD159	ST3	$60	**bright green**	—	1,500.
			Cut cancel		500.00
			Perf. initial		200.00
RD160	ST3	$100	**bright green**	225.00	80.00
			Cut cancel		22.50
			Perf. initial		20.00
RD161	ST3	$500	**bright green**	—	1,500.
			Cut cancel		575.00
			Perf. initial		225.00
RD162	ST3	$1,000	**bright green**	—	525.00
			Cut cancel		250.00
			Perf. initial		175.00

Nos. RD67-RD91 Overprint Instead: **Series 1944**

1944 **Wmk. 191R** ***Perf. 11***

RD163	ST1	1c	**bright green**	.90	.75
			Cut cancel		.35
			Perf. initial		.25
RD164	ST1	2c	**bright green**	.70	.25
			Cut cancel		.20
			Perf. initial		.20
RD165	ST1	4c	**bright green**	.70	.35
			Cut cancel		.25
			Perf. initial		.20
RD166	ST1	5c	**bright green**	.65	.25
			Cut cancel		.20
			Perf. initial		.20
RD167	ST1	10c	**bright green**	1.00	.30
			Cut cancel		.20
			Perf. initial		.20
RD168	ST1	20c	**bright green**	2.25	.25
			Cut cancel		.20
			Perf. initial		.20
RD169	ST1	25c	**bright green**	3.25	.90
			Cut cancel		.25
			Perf. initial		.25
RD170	ST1	40c	**bright green**	15.00	8.00
			Cut cancel		3.25
			Perf. initial		1.75
RD171	ST1	50c	**bright green**	5.50	.30
			Cut cancel		.25
			Perf. initial		.20
RD172	ST1	80c	**bright green**	14.50	6.25
			Cut cancel		2.75
			Perf. initial		1.75
RD173	ST2	$1	**bright green**	13.50	.50
			Cut cancel		.30
			Perf. initial		.25
RD174	ST2	$2	**bright green**	50.00	.75
			Cut cancel		.35
			Perf. initial		.25
RD175	ST2	$3	**bright green**	47.50	2.00
			Cut cancel		.35
			Perf. initial		.25
RD176	ST2	$4	**bright green**	65.00	9.00
			Cut cancel		.50
			Perf. initial		.30
RD177	ST2	$5	**bright green**	50.00	1.75
			Cut cancel		.40
			Perf. initial		.25
RD178	ST2	$10	**bright green**	125.00	7.25
			Cut cancel		1.00
			Perf. initial		.45
RD179	ST2	$20	**bright green**	210.00	12.00
			Cut cancel		5.25
			Perf. initial		3.75

Perf. 12

Without Gum

Designs: $2,500, William Windom. $5,000, C. J. Folger. $10,000, W. Q. Gresham.

RD180	ST3	$30	**bright green**	350.00	110.00
			Cut cancel		42.50
			Perf. initial		16.00
RD181	ST3	$50	**bright green**	250.00	85.00
			Cut cancel		21.00
			Perf. initial		13.00
RD182	ST3	$60	**bright green**	350.00	225.00
			Cut cancel		80.00
			Perf. initial		60.00
RD183	ST3	$100	**bright green**	325.00	80.00
			Cut cancel		30.00
			Perf. initial		13.00
RD184	ST3	$500	**bright green**	—	725.00
			Cut cancel		400.00
			Perf. initial		240.00
RD185	ST3	$1,000	**bright green**	*2,500.*	1,000.
			Cut cancel		400.00
			Perf. initial		190.00
RD185A	ST3	$2,500	**bright green**		—
RD185B	ST3	$5,000	**bright green**		—
RD185C	ST3	$10,000	**bright green,** cut cancel		*27,500.*

Nos. RD185A-R185C exist as unfinished imperforates with complete receipt tabs, without overprints or serial numbers. Known in singles, pairs, panes of four with plate number, uncut sheets of four panes (with two plate numbers), cross gutter blocks of eight, and blocks of four with vertical gutter between and plate number. Value, pairs $450 each.

Nos. RD67-RD91 Overprint Instead: **Series 1945**

1945 **Wmk. 191R** *Perf. 11*

RD186	ST1	1c	**bright green**	.45	.25
			Cut cancel		.20
			Perf. initial		.20
RD187	ST1	2c	**bright green**	.45	.35
			Cut cancel		.20
			Perf. initial		.20
RD188	ST1	4c	**bright green**	.50	.35
			Cut cancel		.20
			Perf. initial		.20
RD189	ST1	5c	**bright green**	.45	.25
			Cut cancel		.20
			Perf. initial		.20
RD190	ST1	10c	**bright green**	1.25	.35
			Cut cancel		.25
			Perf. initial		.25
RD191	ST1	20c	**bright green**	2.10	.45
			Cut cancel		.25
			Perf. initial		.25
RD192	ST1	25c	**bright green**	3.00	.40
			Cut cancel		.30
			Perf. initial		.25
RD193	ST1	40c	**bright green**	4.50	.25
			Cut cancel		.20
			Perf. initial		.20
RD194	ST1	50c	**bright green**	9.50	.45
			Cut cancel		.30
			Perf. initial		.25
RD195	ST1	80c	**bright green**	12.50	4.75
			Cut cancel		1.00
			Perf. initial		.70
RD196	ST2	$1	**bright green**	17.50	.30
			Cut cancel		.25
			Perf. initial		.25
RD197	ST2	$2	**bright green**	30.00	.75
			Cut cancel		.30
			Perf. initial		.25
RD198	ST2	$3	**bright green**	55.00	1.75
			Cut cancel		.50
			Perf. initial		.25
RD199	ST2	$4	**bright green**	55.00	4.25
			Cut cancel		1.10
			Perf. initial		.65
RD200	ST2	$5	**bright green**	35.00	1.00
			Cut cancel		.30
			Perf. initial		.25
RD201	ST2	$10	**bright green**	85.00	10.50
			Cut cancel		1.25
			Perf. initial		.90
RD202	ST2	$20	**bright green**	210.00	20.00
			Cut cancel		3.00
			Perf. initial		1.40

Perf. 12

Without Gum

RD203	ST3	$30	**bright green**	225.00	90.00
			Cut cancel		40.00
			Perf. initial		22.50
RD204	ST3	$50	**bright green**	125.00	40.00
			Cut cancel		9.50
			Perf. initial		6.00
RD205	ST3	$60	**bright green**	350.00	225.00
			Cut cancel		85.00
			Perf. initial		37.50
RD206	ST3	$100	**bright green**	150.00	65.00
			Cut cancel		20.00
			Perf. initial		10.50
RD207	ST3	$500	**bright green**	—	1,250.
			Cut cancel		475.00
			Perf. initial		300.00
RD208	ST3	$1,000	**bright green**	*1,650.*	1,400.
			Cut cancel		575.00
			Perf. initial		300.00
RD208A	ST3	$2,500	**bright green**		
			Cut cancel		*30,000.*
			Perf. initial		*20,000.*
RD208B	ST3	$5,000	**bright green**		*22,250.*
RD208C	ST3	$10,000	**bright green**		
			Cut cancel		*22,250.*

Stock Transfer Stamps and Type of 1940 Overprinted in Black

Series 1946

1946 **Wmk. 191R** *Perf. 11*

RD209	ST1	1c	**bright green**	.50	.35
			Cut cancel		.25
			Perf. initial		.20
	a.		Pair, one dated "1945"	*550.00*	
RD210	ST1	2c	**bright green**	.50	.25
			Cut cancel		.20
			Perf. initial		.20
RD211	ST1	4c	**bright green**	.50	.25
			Cut cancel		.20
			Perf. initial		.20
RD212	ST1	5c	**bright green**	.55	.25
			Cut cancel		.20
			Perf. initial		.20
RD213	ST1	10c	**bright green**	1.25	.25
			Cut cancel		.20
			Perf. initial		.20
RD214	ST1	20c	**bright green**	2.50	.30
			Cut cancel		.25
			Perf. initial		.20
RD215	ST1	25c	**bright green**	2.75	.40
			Cut cancel		.30
			Perf. initial		.25
RD216	ST1	40c	**bright green**	5.50	1.25
			Cut cancel		.40
			Perf. initial		.25
RD217	ST1	50c	**bright green**	6.75	.25
			Cut cancel		.20
			Perf. initial		.20
RD218	ST1	80c	**bright green**	17.50	9.50
			Cut cancel		3.25
			Perf. initial		1.60
RD219	ST2	$1	**bright green**	14.50	.75
			Cut cancel		.35
			Perf. initial		.25
RD220	ST2	$2	**bright green**	16.00	.80
			Cut cancel		.35
			Perf. initial		.25
RD221	ST2	$3	**bright green**	30.00	2.25
			Cut cancel		.45
			Perf. initial		.25
RD222	ST2	$4	**bright green**	30.00	9.00
			Cut cancel		3.50
			Perf. initial		1.25
RD223	ST2	$5	**bright green**	50.00	2.25
			Cut cancel		.35
			Perf. initial		.25
RD224	ST2	$10	**bright green**	87.50	3.75
			Cut cancel		1.00
			Perf. initial		.30
RD225	ST2	$20	**bright green**	225.00	62.50
			Cut cancel		16.00
			Perf. initial		8.75

Without Gum *Perf. 12*

RD226	ST3	$30	**bright green**	250.00	62.50
			Cut cancel		25.00
			Perf. initial		18.00
RD227	ST3	$50	**bright green**	190.00	75.00
			Cut cancel		27.50
			Perf. initial		15.00
RD228	ST3	$60	**bright green**	300.00	150.00
			Cut cancel		50.00
			Perf. initial		16.00
RD229	ST3	$100	**bright green**	225.00	90.00
			Cut cancel		27.50
			Perf. initial		17.00
RD230	ST3	$500	**bright green**	*700.00*	225.00
			Cut cancel		150.00
			Perf. initial		100.00
RD231	ST3	$1,000	**bright green**	—	250.00
			Cut cancel		175.00
			Perf. initial		95.00
RD232	ST3	$2,500	**bright green**		*22,250.*
			Cut cancel		*15,000.*
RD233	ST3	$5,000	**bright green**		
			Cut cancel		*20,000.*
RD234	ST3	$10,000	**bright green**		
			Cut cancel		*16,500.*

Stock Transfer Stamps and Type of 1940 Overprinted in Black

Series 1947

1947 **Wmk. 191R** *Perf. 11*

RD235	ST1	1c	**bright green**	2.25	.75
			Cut cancel		.35
			Perf. initial		.25
RD236	ST1	2c	**bright green**	2.25	.75
			Cut cancel		.35
			Perf. initial		.25
RD237	ST1	4c	**bright green**	1.60	.60
			Cut cancel		.35
			Perf. initial		.25
RD238	ST1	5c	**bright green**	1.60	.50
			Cut cancel		.35
			Perf. initial		.25
RD239	ST1	10c	**bright green**	1.75	.75
			Cut cancel		.35
			Perf. initial		.25
RD240	ST1	20c	**bright green**	3.25	.75
			Cut cancel		.30
			Perf. initial		.25
RD241	ST1	25c	**bright green**	4.00	.90
			Cut cancel		.35
			Perf. initial		.25
RD242	ST1	40c	**bright green**	4.50	1.40
			Cut cancel		.35
			Perf. initial		.25
RD243	ST1	50c	**bright green**	5.00	.35
			Cut cancel		.25
			Perf. initial		.20
RD244	ST1	80c	**bright green**	25.00	14.00
			Cut cancel		5.50
			Perf. initial		3.75
RD245	ST2	$1	**bright green**	16.00	1.00
			Cut cancel		.35
			Perf. initial		.25
RD246	ST2	$2	**bright green**	27.50	1.25
			Cut cancel		.35
			Perf. initial		.25
RD247	ST2	$3	**bright green**	45.00	2.25
			Cut cancel		.50
			Perf. initial		.35
RD248	ST2	$4	**bright green**	62.50	9.50
			Cut cancel		1.60
			Perf. initial		.90
RD249	ST2	$5	**bright green**	45.00	2.50
			Cut cancel		.50
			Perf. initial		.25
RD250	ST2	$10	**bright green**	82.50	7.75
			Cut cancel		2.75
			Perf. initial		1.60
RD251	ST2	$20	**bright green**	160.00	42.50
			Cut cancel		9.75
			Perf. initial		6.75

Without Gum *Perf. 12*

RD252	ST3	$30	**bright green**	160.00	67.50
			Cut cancel		20.00
			Perf. initial		13.00
RD253	ST3	$50	**bright green**	350.00	190.00
			Cut cancel		57.50
			Perf. initial		22.50
RD254	ST3	$60	**bright green**	450.00	175.00
			Cut cancel		67.50
			Perf. initial		42.50
RD255	ST3	$100	**bright green**	175.00	62.50
			Cut cancel		22.50
			Perf. initial		17.00
RD256	ST3	$500	**bright green**	—	525.00
			Cut cancel		225.00
			Perf. initial		125.00
RD257	ST3	$1,000	**bright green**	—	140.00
			Cut cancel		67.50
			Perf. initial		37.50
RD258	ST3	$2,500	**bright green**		—
			Cut cancel		475.00
			Perf. initial		—
RD259	ST3	$5,000	**bright green**		—
			Cut cancel		375.00
			Perf. initial		—
RD260	ST3	$10,000	**bright green**		—
			Cut cancel		55.00
			Perf. initial		—
	a.		Vert. pair, imperf. horiz., cut cancel		—

Nos. RD67-RD91 Overprint Instead: **Series 1948**

1948 **Wmk. 191R** *Perf. 11*

RD261	ST1	1c	**bright green**	.45	.35
			Cut cancel		.25
			Perf. initial		.20
RD262	ST1	2c	**bright green**	.45	.35
			Cut cancel		.25
			Perf. initial		.20
RD263	ST1	4c	**bright green**	.80	.45
			Cut cancel		.30
			Perf. initial		.25
RD264	ST1	5c	**bright green**	.45	.25
			Cut cancel		.20
			Perf. initial		.20
RD265	ST1	10c	**bright green**	.55	.35
			Cut cancel		.25
			Perf. initial		.20
RD266	ST1	20c	**bright green**	1.60	.40
			Cut cancel		.25
			Perf. initial		.20
RD267	ST1	25c	**bright green**	1.90	.55
			Cut cancel		.30
			Perf. initial		.25
RD268	ST1	40c	**bright green**	3.50	1.00
			Cut cancel		.35
			Perf. initial		.25
RD269	ST1	50c	**bright green**	5.75	.35
			Cut cancel		.25
			Perf. initial		.20
RD270	ST1	80c	**bright green**	26.00	9.50
			Cut cancel		3.50
			Perf. initial		2.25
RD271	ST2	$1	**bright green**	14.00	.45
			Cut cancel		.30
			Perf. initial		.20
RD272	ST2	$2	**bright green**	27.50	1.00
			Cut cancel		.30
			Perf. initial		.25
RD273	ST2	$3	**bright green**	40.00	6.00
			Cut cancel		3.00
			Perf. initial		1.60
RD274	ST2	$4	**bright green**	45.00	14.00
			Cut cancel		3.75
			Perf. initial		2.25
RD275	ST2	$5	**bright green**	47.50	3.75
			Cut cancel		.45
			Perf. initial		.25
RD276	ST2	$10	**bright green**	80.00	7.25
			Cut cancel		1.00
			Perf. initial		.75
RD277	ST2	$20	**bright green**	160.00	25.00
			Cut cancel		7.00
			Perf. initial		4.75

Perf. 12
Without Gum

RD278	ST3 $30 **bright green**	225.00	90.00
	Cut cancel		35.00
	Perf. initial		18.00
RD279	ST3 $50 **bright green**	175.00	85.00
	Cut cancel		32.50
	Perf. initial		16.00
RD280	ST3 $60 **bright green**	350.00	225.00
	Cut cancel		75.00
	Perf. initial		27.50
RD281	ST3 $100 **bright green**	140.00	30.00
	Cut cancel		10.00
	Perf. initial		7.00
RD282	ST3 $500 **bright green**	—	300.00
	Cut cancel		175.00
	Perf. initial		52.50
RD283	ST3 $1,000 **bright green**	—	175.00
	Cut cancel		62.50
	Perf. initial		32.50
RD284	ST3 $2,500 **bright green**	850.00	500.00
	Cut cancel		250.00
	Perf. initial		160.00
RD285	ST3 $5,000 **bright green**	—	425.00
	Cut cancel		225.00
	Perf. initial		150.00
RD286	ST3 $10,000 **bright green**	—	
	Cut cancel		52.50
	Perf. initial		—

Nos. RD67-RD91 Overprint Instead: **Series 1949**

1949 Wmk. 191R *Perf. 11*

RD287	ST1 1c **bright green**	2.25	.70
	Cut cancel		.35
	Perf. initial		.25
RD288	ST1 2c **bright green**	2.25	.75
	Cut cancel		.35
	Perf. initial		.25
RD289	ST1 4c **bright green**	2.50	.75
	Cut cancel		.35
	Perf. initial		.25
RD290	ST1 5c **bright green**	2.50	.75
	Cut cancel		.35
	Perf. initial		.25
RD291	ST1 10c **bright green**	5.00	1.00
	Cut cancel		.35
	Perf. initial		.25
RD292	ST1 20c **bright green**	8.00	1.00
	Cut cancel		.35
	Perf. initial		.25
RD293	ST1 25c **bright green**	9.50	1.25
	Cut cancel		.40
	Perf. initial		.25
RD294	ST1 40c **bright green**	25.00	3.25
	Cut cancel		.50
	Perf. initial		.30
RD295	ST1 50c **bright green**	27.50	.45
	Cut cancel		.35
	Perf. initial		.25
RD296	ST1 80c **bright green**	32.50	10.00
	Cut cancel		4.25
	Perf. initial		3.00
RD297	ST2 $1 **bright green**	27.50	1.00
	Cut cancel		.35
	Perf. initial		.25
RD298	ST2 $2 **bright green**	50.00	1.40
	Cut cancel		.45
	Perf. initial		.30
RD299	ST2 $3 **bright green**	67.50	7.50
	Cut cancel		2.25
	Perf. initial		1.10
RD300	ST2 $4 **bright green**	65.00	12.00
	Cut cancel		3.00
	Perf. initial		1.75
RD301	ST2 $5 **bright green**	72.50	3.00
	Cut cancel		.30
	Perf. initial		.25
RD302	ST2 $10 **bright green**	110.00	8.00
	Cut cancel		2.50
	Perf. initial		1.25
RD303	ST2 $20 **bright green**	250.00	22.50
	Cut cancel		10.00
	Perf. initial		6.25

Perf. 12
Without Gum

RD304	ST3 $30 **bright green**	325.00	125.00
	Cut cancel		45.00
	Perf. initial		18.00
RD305	ST3 $50 **bright green**	375.00	225.00
	Cut cancel		62.50
	Perf. initial		27.50
RD306	ST3 $60 **bright green**	525.00	325.00
	Cut cancel		140.00
	Perf. initial		50.00
RD307	ST3 $100 **bright green**	225.00	80.00
	Cut cancel		35.00
	Perf. initial		18.00
RD308	ST3 $500 **bright green**	*700.00*	300.00
	Cut cancel		100.00
	Perf. initial		60.00
RD309	ST3 $1,000 **bright green**	*450.00*	125.00
	Cut cancel		52.50
	Perf. initial		32.50
RD310	ST3 $2,500 **bright green**	—	
	Cut cancel		*500.00*
	Perf. initial		—
RD311	ST3 $5,000 **bright green**	—	
	Cut cancel		*500.00*
	Perf. initial		*350.00*
RD312	ST3 $10,000 **bright green**	—	475.00
	Cut cancel		45.00
	Perf. initial		—
a.	Pair, one without ovpt., cut cancel		*8,000.*

No. RD312a is unique.

Nos. RD67-RD91 Overprint Instead: **Series 1950**

1950 Wmk. 191R *Perf. 11*

RD313	ST1 1c **bright green**	.80	.40
	Cut cancel		.30
	Perf. initial		.25
RD314	ST1 2c **bright green**	.70	.35
	Cut cancel		.25
	Perf. initial		.20
RD315	ST1 4c **bright green**	.65	.40
	Cut cancel		.25
	Perf. initial		.20
RD316	ST1 5c **bright green**	.75	.25
	Cut cancel		.20
	Perf. initial		.20
RD317	ST1 10c **bright green**	3.25	.30
	Cut cancel		.25
	Perf. initial		.25
RD318	ST1 20c **bright green**	5.00	.80
	Cut cancel		.35
	Perf. initial		.20
RD319	ST1 25c **bright green**	8.00	1.00
	Cut cancel		.25
	Perf. initial		.20
RD320	ST1 40c **bright green**	11.00	1.50
	Cut cancel		.35
	Perf. initial		.25
RD321	ST1 50c **bright green**	13.00	.50
	Cut cancel		.30
	Perf. initial		.25
RD322	ST1 80c **bright green**	22.50	7.25
	Cut cancel		2.40
	Perf. initial		1.50
RD323	ST2 $1 **bright green**	22.50	.55
	Cut cancel		.25
	Perf. initial		.20
RD324	ST2 $2 **bright green**	35.00	1.25
	Cut cancel		.35
	Perf. initial		.25
RD325	ST2 $3 **bright green**	47.50	5.75
	Cut cancel		.90
	Perf. initial		.60
RD326	ST2 $4 **bright green**	60.00	12.50
	Cut cancel		5.00
	Perf. initial		2.75
RD327	ST2 $5 **bright green**	60.00	2.75
	Cut cancel		.35
	Perf. initial		.25
RD328	ST2 $10 **bright green**	175.00	7.50
	Cut cancel		2.25
	Perf. initial		1.00
RD329	ST2 $20 **bright green**	175.00	32.50
	Cut cancel		21.00
	Perf. initial		5.75

Perf. 12
Without Gum

RD330	ST3 $30 **bright green**	225.00	125.00
	Cut cancel		45.00
	Perf. initial		18.00
a.	Booklet pane of 4	*3,300.*	
RD331	ST3 $50 **bright green**	275.00	150.00
	Cut cancel		60.00
	Perf. initial		29.00
a.	Booklet pane of 4	*3,300.*	
RD332	ST3 $60 **bright green**	325.00	200.00
	Cut cancel		85.00
	Perf. initial		47.50
a.	Booklet pane of 4	*4,750.*	
RD333	ST3 $100 **bright green**	125.00	55.00
	Cut cancel		30.00
	Perf. initial		15.00
a.	Vert. pair, imperf. btwn.	2,500.	*1,750.*
RD334	ST3 $500 **bright green**	—	300.00
	Cut cancel		150.00
	Perf. initial		95.00
RD335	ST3 $1,000 **bright green**	—	85.00
	Cut cancel		35.00
	Perf. initial		22.50
RD336	ST3 $2,500 **bright green**	—	*1,500.*
	Cut cancel		1,000.
	Perf. initial		—
a.	Booklet pane of 4	*10,000.*	
RD337	ST3 $5,000 **bright green**	—	950.00
	Cut cancel		600.00
	Perf. initial		—
a.	Booklet pane of 4	*10,000.*	
RD338	ST3 $10,000 **bright green**	—	1,100.
	Cut cancel		97.50
	Perf. initial		—
a.	Booklet pane of 4	*10,000.*	

Nos. RD67-RD91 Overprint Instead: **Series 1951**

1951 Wmk. 191R *Perf. 11*

RD339	ST1 1c **bright green**	3.00	.75
	Cut cancel		.40
	Perf. initial		.25
RD340	ST1 2c **bright green**	2.50	.50
	Cut cancel		.30
	Perf. initial		.25
RD341	ST1 4c **bright green**	3.00	.75
	Cut cancel		.35
	Perf. initial		.25
RD342	ST1 5c **bright green**	2.25	.55
	Cut cancel		.25
	Perf. initial		.20
RD343	ST1 10c **bright green**	3.00	.35
	Cut cancel		.25
	Perf. initial		.20
RD344	ST1 20c **bright green**	7.50	1.25
	Cut cancel		.35
	Perf. initial		.25
RD345	ST1 25c **bright green**	10.00	1.50
	Cut cancel		.35
	Perf. initial		.25
RD346	ST1 40c **bright green**	42.50	12.50
	Cut cancel		4.00
	Perf. initial		2.00
RD347	ST1 50c **bright green**	17.00	1.50
	Cut cancel		.30
	Perf. initial		.25
RD348	ST1 80c **bright green**	35.00	14.00
	Cut cancel		5.25
	Perf. initial		2.25
RD349	ST2 $1 **bright green**	32.50	1.25
	Cut cancel		.35
	Perf. initial		.25
RD350	ST2 $2 **bright green**	45.00	1.75
	Cut cancel		.35
	Perf. initial		.25
RD351	ST2 $3 **bright green**	60.00	14.00
	Cut cancel		4.50
	Perf. initial		2.00
RD352	ST2 $4 **bright green**	72.50	16.00
	Cut cancel		6.00
	Perf. initial		2.25
RD353	ST2 $5 **bright green**	75.00	4.00
	Cut cancel		.35
	Perf. initial		.25
RD354	ST2 $10 **bright green**	150.00	11.00
	Cut cancel		3.00
	Perf. initial		1.75
RD355	ST2 $20 **bright green**	250.00	30.00
	Cut cancel		10.00
	Perf. initial		5.75

Perf. 12
Without Gum

RD356	ST3 $30 **bright green**	325.00	150.00
	Cut cancel		45.00
	Perf. initial		20.00
RD357	ST3 $50 **bright green**	325.00	125.00
	Cut cancel		32.50
	Perf. initial		20.00
RD358	ST3 $60 **bright green**	—	*1,600.*
	Cut cancel		600.00
	Perf. initial		300.00
RD359	ST3 $100 **bright green**	210.00	90.00
	Cut cancel		30.00
	Perf. initial		13.00
RD360	ST3 $500 **bright green**	—	450.00
	Cut cancel		210.00
	Perf. initial		125.00
RD361	ST3 $1,000 **bright green**	—	125.00
	Cut cancel		85.00
	Perf. initial		57.50
RD362	ST3 $2,500 **bright green**	—	*4,000.*
	Cut cancel		1,350.
	Perf. initial		600.00
RD363	ST3 $5,000 **bright green**	—	*1,600.*
	Cut cancel		925.00
	Perf. initial		700.00
RD364	ST3 $10,000 **bright green**	*1,650.*	175.00
	Cut cancel		80.00
	Perf. initial		52.50

Nos. RD67-RD91 Overprint Instead: **Series 1952**

1952 Wmk. 191R *Perf. 11*

RD365	ST1 1c **bright green**	42.50	27.50
	Cut cancel		7.00
	Perf. initial		3.00
RD366	ST1 10c **bright green**	45.00	27.50
	Cut cancel		7.00
	Perf. initial		3.00
RD367	ST1 20c **bright green**	500.00	—
	Cut cancel		—
	Perf. initial		—
RD368	ST1 25c **bright green**	650.00	—
	Cut cancel		—
	Perf. initial		—
RD369	ST1 40c **bright green**	140.00	55.00
	Cut cancel		18.00
	Perf. initial		12.00
RD370	ST2 $4 **bright green**	*1,750.*	575.00
	Perf. initial		—
RD371	ST2 $10 **bright green**	*3,500.*	—
	Cut cancel		—
	Perf. initial		—
RD372	ST2 $20 **bright green**	*6,000.*	—
	Cut cancel		—
	Perf. initial		—

Stock Transfer Stamps were discontinued in 1952.

CORDIALS, WINES, ETC. STAMPS

RE1

Inscribed "Series of 1914"

1914 Wmk. 190 Offset Printing ***Perf. 10***

RE1	RE1	¼c	**green**	1.25	.60
RE2	RE1	½c	**green**	.60	.55
RE3	RE1	1c	**green**	.65	.35
RE4	RE1	1½c	**green**	3.25	1.90
RE5	RE1	2c	**green**	5.25	4.25
RE6	RE1	3c	**green**	4.25	1.60
RE7	RE1	4c	**green**	3.25	1.90
RE8	RE1	5c	**green**	1.75	1.00
RE9	RE1	6c	**green**	9.50	4.00
a.	Double impression				—
RE10	RE1	8c	**green**	7.25	1.90
RE11	RE1	10c	**green**	4.50	3.75
RE12	RE1	20c	**green**	6.00	2.40
RE13	RE1	24c	**green**	19.00	10.00
RE14	RE1	40c	**green**	4.50	.90

RE1a

Without Gum ***Imperf.***

RE15	RE1a	$2	**green**	12.50	.25
a.	Double impression				125.00

1914 Wmk. 191R ***Perf. 10***

RE16	RE1	¼c	**green**	8.50	6.50
RE17	RE1	½c	**green**	7.50	4.00
RE18	RE1	1c	**green**	.30	.25
RE19	RE1	1½c	**green**	95.00	50.00
RE20	RE1	2c	**green**	.30	.25
a.	Double impression				—
RE21	RE1	3c	**green**	3.75	2.50
RE22	RE1	4c	**green**	1.25	1.10
RE23	RE1	5c	**green**	20.00	13.00
a.	Double impression				—
RE24	RE1	6c	**green**	.90	.40
RE25	RE1	8c	**green**	2.75	.65
RE26	RE1	10c	**green**	.90	.35
RE27	RE1	20c	**green**	1.10	.55
RE28	RE1	24c	**green**	17.50	1.00
RE29	RE1	40c	**green**	45.00	14.00

Imperf

Without Gum

RE30	RE1a	$2	**green**	55.00	3.75

Perf. 11

RE31	RE1	2c	**green**	125.00	110.00

WINE STAMPS

Issued Without Gum

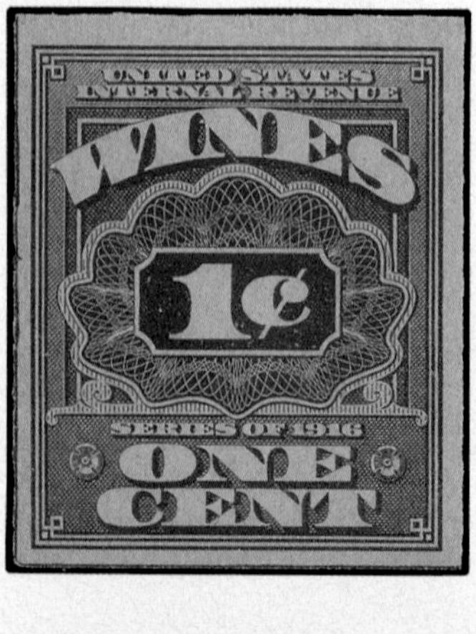

RE2

Inscribed: "Series of 1916"

1916 Wmk. 191R Offset Printing ***Rouletted 3½***

Plates of 100 subjects

RE32	RE2	1c	**green**	.50	.45
a.	Double impression			200.00	
RE33	RE2	3c	**green**	6.50	5.25
RE34	RE2	4c	**green**	.40	.50
a.	Double impression				—
RE35	RE2	6c	**green**	2.75	1.10
RE36	RE2	7½c	**green**	7.75	4.25
RE37	RE2	10c	**green**	1.50	.45
RE38	RE2	12c	**green**	5.25	4.75
RE39	RE2	15c	**green**	1.75	1.90
RE40	RE2	18c	**green**	30.00	32.50
RE41	RE2	20c	**green**	.35	.30
RE42	RE2	24c	**green**	6.00	4.00
a.	Double impression			200.00	
RE43	RE2	30c	**green**	3.50	3.75
a.	Double impression				—
RE44	RE2	36c	**green**	30.00	18.00
RE45	RE2	50c	**green**	1.00	.50
RE46	RE2	60c	**green**	7.00	3.00
RE47	RE2	72c	**green**	40.00	37.50
RE48	RE2	80c	**green**	1.50	.90
RE49	RE2	$1.20	**green**	9.00	7.25
RE50	RE2	$1.44	**green**	13.00	3.75
RE51	RE2	$1.60	**green**	35.00	30.00
RE52	RE2	$2	**green**	1.75	1.60

For rouletted 7 see Nos. RE60-RE80, RE102-RE105.

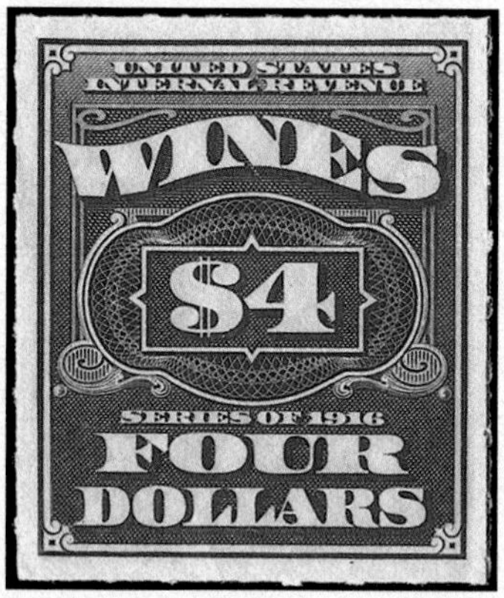

RE3

Engr.

Plates of 50 subjects

RE53	RE3	$4	**green**	1.10	.30
RE54	RE3	$4.80	**green**	4.50	4.00
RE55	RE3	$9.60	**green**	1.60	.45

Nos. RE32-RE55 exist in many shades. Size variations of 1c-$2 are believed due to offset printing. For rouletted 7 see Nos. RE81-RE83, RE106-RE107.

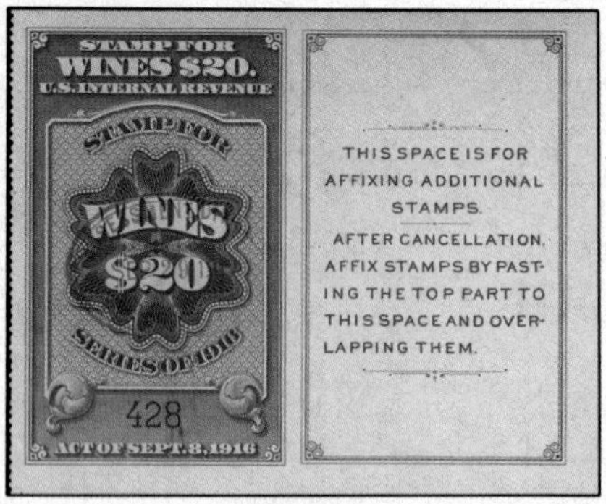

RE4

Illustration reduced.

Plates of 6 subjects

Perf. 12 at left

RE56	RE4	$20	**green**	110.00	60.00
RE57	RE4	$40	**green**	250.00	70.00
RE58	RE4	$50	**green**	80.00	57.50
RE59	RE4	$100	**green**	325.00	200.00

Stamps of design RE4 have an adjoining tablet at right for affixing additional stamps. Values are for examples with the tablets attached. Examples with the tablets removed sell for much less. Used stamps with additional stamps tied on the tablet with cancels sell for about ten times the values given. See Nos. RE107A-RE107D.

Same designs as Issue of 1916

1933 Wmk. 191R Offset Printing ***Rouletted 7***

RE60	RE2	1c	**light green**	3.25	.50
a.	Double impression				—
RE61	RE2	3c	**light green**	7.50	2.75
RE62	RE2	4c	**light green**	2.25	.55
RE63	RE2	6c	**light green**	13.00	7.50
RE64	RE2	7½c	**light green**	6.75	1.40
RE65	RE2	10c	**light green**	2.75	.25
a.	Double impression				—
RE66	RE2	12c	**light green**	13.00	6.00
RE67	RE2	15c	**light green**	5.00	.40
RE69	RE2	20c	**light green**	7.50	.25
a.	Double impression			—	—
RE70	RE2	24c	**light green**	5.75	.25
a.	Double impression			—	*160.00*
RE71	RE2	30c	**light green**	6.00	.25
a.	Double impression				—
RE72	RE2	36c	**light green**	14.00	1.25
RE73	RE2	50c	**light green**	4.75	.30
RE74	RE2	60c	**light green**	10.00	.25
RE75	RE2	72c	**light green**	17.50	.40
RE76	RE2	80c	**light green**	17.50	.40
RE77	RE2	$1.20	**light green**	17.00	1.75
RE78	RE2	$1.44	**light green**	15.00	5.25
RE79	RE2	$1.60	**light green**	450.00	200.00
RE80	RE2	$2	**light green**	40.00	4.50

Engr.

RE81	RE3	$4	**light green**	42.50	8.75
RE82	RE3	$4.80	**light green**	47.50	17.50
RE83	RE3	$9.60	**light green**	190.00	100.00

RE5

Offset Printing

1934-40 Wmk. 191R ***Rouletted 7***

Inscribed: "Series of 1934"

Plates of 200 and 224 subjects

Issued With and Without Gum

RE83A	RE5	⅕c	**green** ('40)	.75	.25
RE84	RE5	½c	**green**	.55	.65
RE85	RE5	1c	**green**	.70	.25
RE86	RE5	1¼c	**green**	1.10	1.00
RE87	RE5	1½c	**green**	7.50	*8.75*
RE88	RE5	2c	**green**	2.25	1.00
RE89	RE5	2½c	**green**	2.00	.70
RE90	RE5	3c	**green**	5.25	4.25
RE91	RE5	4c	**green**	3.00	.30
RE92	RE5	5c	**green**	.70	.25
RE93	RE5	6c	**green**	2.00	.60
RE94	RE5	7½c	**green**	3.25	.25
RE95	RE5	10c	**green**	.50	.70
RE96	RE5	12c	**green**	2.10	.25
RE96A	RE5	14⅖c	**green** ('40)	190.00	3.50
b.	Imperf, pair, without gum			*5,000.*	
RE97	RE5	15c	**green**	.90	.25
RE98	RE5	18c	**green**	1.75	.25
RE99	RE5	20c	**green**	1.40	.25
RE100	RE5	24c	**green**	2.75	.25
RE101	RE5	30c	**green**	2.00	.25

Nos. RE83A-RE101 unused are valued without gum. Examples with gum sell for substantially more.

Nos. RE83A, RE86, RE96A were printed from plates of 200 only and all were issued without gum.

Plates of 100 subjects

Issued Without Gum

RE102	RE2	40c	**green**	4.75	.25
RE102A	RE2	43⅕c	**green** ('40)	21.00	2.75
RE103	RE2	48c	**green**	24.00	2.10
RE104	RE2	$1	**green**	29.00	11.50
RE105	RE2	$1.50	**green**	45.00	17.00
	Perforated initials				5.75

Engr.

Plates of 50 subjects.

RE106	RE3	$2.50	**green**	52.50	18.00
	Perforated initials				9.00
RE107	RE3	$5	**green**	45.00	7.50
	Perforated initials				3.25

Stamps of types RE5 and RE2 overprinted "Rectified Spirits / Puerto Rico" are listed under Puerto Rico.

Nos. RE102-RE204 issued without gum.

Inscribed: "Series of 1916"

Plates of 6 subjects

1934 ***Perf. 12 at left***

RE107A	RE4	$20	**yellow green**	1,800.	
RE107B	RE4	$40	**yellow green**	*8,000.*	

Perf. 12 or 12½ at left

RE107C	RE4	$50	**yellow green**	—	*3,500.*
RE107D	RE4	$100	**yellow green**	*1,750.*	500.00

The serial numbers of Nos. RE107A-RE107D are much thinner than on Nos. RE56-RE59. See valuing note after No. RE59.

RE6

Offset Printing
Inscribed "Series of 1941"

1942 **Wmk. 191R** ***Rouletted 7***

RE108	RE6	1/5c	**green & black**	.80	.55
RE109	RE6	1/4c	**green & black**	2.50	2.50
RE110	RE6	1/2c	**green & black**	3.25	2.10
a.	Horiz. pair, imperf. vertically			200.00	
RE111	RE6	1c	**green & black**	1.25	1.25
RE112	RE6	2c	**green & black**	6.00	5.25
RE113	RE6	3c	**green & black**	6.00	4.50
RE114	RE6	3 1/2c	**green & black**	—	*12,750.*
RE115	RE6	3 3/4c	**green & black**	11.50	7.25
RE116	RE6	4c	**green & black**	4.25	3.25
RE117	RE6	5c	**green & black**	3.00	2.40
RE118	RE6	6c	**green & black**	3.75	2.75
RE119	RE6	7c	**green & black**	7.50	5.50
RE120	RE6	7 1/2c	**green & black**	11.00	6.00
RE121	RE6	8c	**green & black**	5.50	4.25
RE122	RE6	9c	**green & black**	15.00	9.50
RE123	RE6	10c	**green & black**	5.50	1.10
RE124	RE6	11 1/4c	**green & black**	6.00	6.00
RE125	RE6	12c	**green & black**	8.50	6.00
RE126	RE6	14c	**green & black**	37.50	26.00
RE127	RE6	15c	**green & black**	6.00	3.00
a.	Horiz. pair, imperf. vertically				*925.00*
RE128	RE6	16c	**green & black**	14.00	9.00
RE129	RE6	19 1/5c	**green & black**	175.00	7.75
RE130	RE6	20c	**green & black**	7.50	2.10
RE131	RE6	24c	**green & black**	5.50	.25
RE132	RE6	28c	**green & black**	*2,100.*	*1,500.*
RE133	RE6	30c	**green & black**	1.50	.20
RE134	RE6	32c	**green & black**	175.00	7.50
RE135	RE6	36c	**green & black**	3.50	.25
RE136	RE6	40c	**green & black**	3.00	.20
RE137	RE6	45c	**green & black**	8.75	.25
RE138	RE6	48c	**green & black**	21.00	9.25
RE139	RE6	50c	**green & black**	12.00	7.50
RE140	RE6	60c	**green & black**	4.25	.20
RE141	RE6	72c	**green & black**	12.50	1.50
RE142	RE6	80c	**green & black**	*300.00*	10.50
RE143	RE6	84c	**green & black**	—	77.50
RE144	RE6	90c	**green & black**	25.00	.20
RE145	RE6	96c	**green & black**	15.00	.30

See Nos. RE182D-RE194.

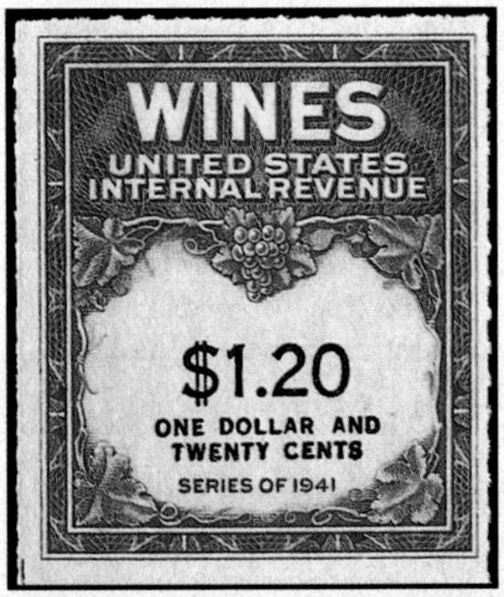

Denomination Spelled Out in Two Lines — RE7

Engraved, Offset (denominations)

1942

RE146	RE7	$1.20	**yel grn & blk**	10.00	.25
RE147	RE7	$1.44	**yel grn & blk**	1.75	.30
a.	Denomination missing (FO)			—	—
	Pair, one with denomination missing (FO)			—	—
RE148	RE7	$1.50	**yel grn & blk**	150.00	67.50
RE149	RE7	$1.60	**yel grn & blk**	12.00	1.40
RE150	RE7	$1.68	**yel grn & blk**	120.00	50.00
	Perforated initials				35.00
RE151	RE7	$1.80	**yel grn & blk**	4.00	.20
a.	Pair, one with denomination missing (FO)			—	—

No. RE151a may be collected as a vertical pair or a horizontal pair.

RE152	RE7	$1.92	**yel grn & blk**	80.00	72.50
RE153	RE7	$2.40	**yel grn & blk**	12.50	1.25
RE154	RE7	$3	**yel grn & blk**	100.00	42.50
RE155	RE7	$3.36	**yel grn & blk**	92.50	29.00
RE156	RE7	$3.60	**yel grn & blk**	*160.00*	6.25
RE157	RE7	$4	**yel grn & blk**	32.50	5.25
RE158	RE7	$4.80	**yel grn & blk**	*175.00*	3.75
RE159	RE7	$5	**yel grn & blk**	17.50	10.50
RE159A	RE7	$7.14	**yel grn & blk**	*175.00*	
RE160	RE7	$7.20	**yel grn & blk**	20.00	.50
RE161	RE7	$10	**yel grn & blk**	240.00	200.00
RE162	RE7	$20	**yel grn & blk**	130.00	77.50
RE163	RE7	$50	**yel grn & blk**	125.00	77.50
	Perforated initials				21.00
RE164	RE7	$100	**yel grn & blk**	375.00	30.00
	Perforated initials				21.00
RE165	RE7	$200	**yel grn & blk**	190.00	24.00
	Perforated initials				8.75
RE165A	RE7	$300	**yel grn & blk**	*175.00*	
RE165B	RE7	$400	**yel grn & blk**	*8,000.*	*12,000.*
RE166	RE7	$500	**yel grn & blk**	*175.00*	150.00
	Perforated initials				35.00
RE167	RE7	$600	**yel grn & blk**	*200.00*	125.00
RE167A	RE7	$700	**yel grn & blk**	*175.00*	
RE167B	RE7	$800	**yel grn & blk**	*175.00*	
RE168	RE7	$900	**yel grn & blk**	*3,250.*	*4,000.*
	Perforated initials				*1,500.*
RE169	RE7	$1,000	**yel grn & blk**	*150.00*	200.00
RE170	RE7	$2,000	**yel grn & blk**	*4,000.*	*2,250.*
RE171	RE7	$3,000	**yel grn & blk**	*175.00*	200.00
RE172	RE7	$4,000	**yel grn & blk**	*1,250.*	800.00

Denomination Repeated, Spelled Out in One Line

1949

RE173	RE7	$1	**yellow green & black**	5.00	1.60
RE174	RE7	$2	**yellow green & black**	9.50	2.10
RE175	RE7	$4	**yellow green & black**	925.00	425.00
	Perforated initials				175.00
RE176	RE7	$5	**yellow green & black**	*100.00*	82.50
RE177	RE7	$6	**yellow green & black**	700.00	500.00
RE178	RE7	$7	**yellow green & black**	*100.00*	47.50
RE179	RE7	$8	**yellow green & black**	1,250.	450.00
	Perforated initials				85.00
RE179A	RE7	$9	**yel grn & blk**	*175.00*	
RE180	RE7	$10	**yellow green & black**	10.00	5.25
	Perforated initials				2.10
RE180A	RE7	$12	**yel grn & blk**	*175.00*	
RE181	RE7	$20	**yellow green & black**	25.00	5.25
	Perforated initials				1.90
RE182	RE7	$30	**yellow green & black**	*1,750.*	1,000.
RE182A	RE7	$40	**yel grn & blk**	*175.00*	
RE182B	RE7	$60	**yel grn & blk**	*175.00*	
RE182C	RE7	$70	**yel grn & blk**	*175.00*	
RE182D	RE7	$80	**yel grn & blk**	*175.00*	
RE182E	RE7	$90	**yel grn & blk**	*175.00*	

The $90 denomination, No. RE182E, was printed but was not delivered to the Internal Revenue Service for use.

Types of 1942-49

1951-54 **Offset Printing**

RE182F	RE6	1 7/10c	**green & black**	*22,500.*	*25,000.*
RE183	RE6	3 2/5c	**green & black**	55.00	52.50
RE183A	RE6	6 7/10c	**green & black**	—	
RE184	RE6	8 1/2c	**green & black**	30.00	20.00
RE184A	RE6	10 1/5c	**green & black**	—	
RE185	RE6	13 2/5c	**green & black**	100.00	82.50
RE186	RE6	17c	**green & black**	16.00	15.00
RE187	RE6	20 2/5c	**green & black**	110.00	62.50
RE188	RE6	33 1/2c	**green & black**	90.00	92.50
RE189	RE6	38 1/4c	**green & black**	150.00	90.00
RE190	RE6	40 4/5c	**green & black**	3.75	.80
RE191	RE6	51c	**green & black**	4.00	1.40
RE192	RE6	67c	**green & black**	12.50	4.25
RE193	RE6	68c	**green & black**	3.75	.70
RE194	RE6	80 2/5c	**green & black**	175.00	110.00

The 6 7/10c and 10 1/5c denominations, Nos. RE183A and RE184A, were printed but were not delivered to the Internal Revenue Service for use.

Engr.

Denomination Spelled Out in Two Lines in Small Letters

Two types of $1.60 4/5:

I — The "4" slants sharply. Loop of "5" almost closes to form oval. Each numeral 2mm high.

II — The "4" is less slanted. Loop of "5" more open and nearly circular. Each numeral 2 1/2mm high.

RE195	RE7	$1.50 3/4	**yel grn & blk**	50.00	47.50
RE196	RE7	$1.60 4/5	**yel grn & blk** (I)	4.25	1.00
a.	"DOLLLAR"			52.50	15.00
	Perforated initials				10.00
b.	As "a," horiz. pair, one with denomination missing			*4,000.*	
c.	Type II			1,000.	250.00
RE197	RE7	$1.88 3/10	**yel grn & blk**	325.00	85.00
	Perforated initials				35.00

Denomination Spelled Out in Two Lines in Slightly Larger Letters Same as Nos. RE146-RE172

RE198	RE7	$1.60 4/5	**yel grn & blk** (II)	35.00	6.25
a.	First line larger letters, second line small letters			*14,000.*	*3,000.*
b.	Type I ('53)			75.00	25.00
RE199	RE7	$2.01	**yel grn & blk**	3.50	1.00
RE200	RE7	$2.68	**yel grn & blk**	3.50	1.40
RE201	RE7	$4.08	**yel grn & blk**	95.00	35.00
RE202	RE7	$5.76	**yel grn & blk**	300.00	225.00
RE203	RE7	$8.16	**yel grn & blk**	17.50	7.00
RE204	RE7	$9.60	**yel grn & blk**	*1,750.*	*5,000.*

No. RE198a unused is unique.

Wine stamps were discontinued on Dec. 31, 1954.

BEER STAMPS

Basic stamps were printed by the Bureau of Engraving and Printing, unless otherwise noted.

All stamps are imperforate, unless otherwise noted.

Values for Nos. REA1-REA13 are for stamps with small faults, due to the fragile nature of the thin paper. Used values for Nos. REA14-REA199 are for canceled stamps with small faults.

All examples of Nos. REA1-REA13 contain a circular pattern of 31 perforations in the design, 27 or 28 1/2mm in diameter, often poorly punched.

Values for cut squares of Nos. REA1-REA13 are for margins clear of the design. Die cut and cut to shape stamps are valued for margins clear to slightly cutting into the design.

Eric Jackson, Michael Aldrich, Henry Tolman II and Thomas W. Priester helped the editors extensively in compiling the listings.

An excellent study of beer stamps by Frank Applegate appeared in *Weekly Philatelic Gossip* from Oct. 1-Nov. 26, 1927.

A List of the Beer Stamps of the United States of America by Ernest R. Vanderhoof appeared in the *American Philatelist* in June 1934. This was reprinted in pamphlet form.

United States Beer Stamps by Thomas W. Priester, published in 1979, comprised an illustrated and priced catalogue, illustrations of all known provisional surcharges, background notes on the stamps and tax laws, and a census of over 27,500 stamps. The catalogue and census sections were updated in the 1990 edition.

Printed by the Treasury Department. Tax rate $1 per barrel (bbl.).

12½c = ⅛ barrel	$1 = 1 barrel
16⅔c = ⅙ barrel	$2 = 1 hogshead
25c = ¼ barrel	$5 = 5 barrels
33⅓c = ⅓ barrel	$10 = 10 barrels
50c = ½ barrel	$25 = 25 barrels

1866 **Engr.**

REA1	12½c **orange**	400.	600.
	Cut to shape		110.
a.	Die cut	300.	300.
b.	Silk paper		*1,500.*
REA2	16⅔c **dark green**	200.	250.
	Cut to shape		30.
a.	Die cut		85.
REA3	25c **blue**	75.	135.
	Cut to shape		25.
a.	Die cut		50.
b.	Silk paper		*2,000.*
	Double transfer		—
REA4	50c **orange brown**	35.	50.
	Printed cancellation, "A.S. 1869"		150.
	Cut to shape		10.
a.	Die cut		75.
REA5	$1 **black**	375.	275.
	Cut to shape		75.
a.	Die cut		225.
REA6	$2 **red**	1,200.	1,500.
	Cut to shape		190.
a.	Die cut		500.

Printed by the Treasury Department. See individual rates before No. REA1.

1867 **Engr.**

REA7	12½c **orange**	*2,400.*	1,850.
	Cut to shape		750.
a.	Die cut		1,250.
REA8	16⅔c **dark green**	*2,600.*	*2,500.*
	Cut to shape		525.
a.	Die cut		1,500.
REA9	25c **blue**	250.	300.
	Cut to shape		50.
a.	Die cut		250.
REA10	33⅓c **violet brown**		*5,500.*
	Cut to shape		*2,500.*
b.	Silk paper		*3,500.*
c.	33⅓c **ocher red,** cut to shape		*3,500.*
d.	33⅓c **ocher red,** die cut		*14,500.*
REA11	50c **orange brown**	75.	125.
	Printed cancellation, "A.S. 1869"		350.
	Cut to shape		35.
a.	Die cut		150.
REA12	$1 **black**		1,350.
	Cut to shape		350.
a.	Die cut		750.
REA13	$2 **red**	*2,000.*	*1,350.*
	Cut to shape		500.
a.	Die cut		1,100.

See individual rates before No. REA1.

Silk Paper

1870 **Engr.** **Lilac Security Lines**

REA14	12½c **brown**	*350.00*	250.
a.	Yellow security lines		1,750.
REA15	16⅔c **yellow orange**		300.
a.	Yellow security lines		*1,100.*
b.	Gray-green and yellow security lines		*1,750.*
c.	16⅔c **yellow ocher,** lilac security lines		1,000.
REA16	25c **green**		100.
a.	Yellow security lines		225.
b.	Gray-green & yellow security lines	*1,000.*	
REA17	50c **red**	300.	125.
a.	Yellow security lines		500.
b.	Gray-green and yellow security lines		1,400.
c.	50c **brick red,** lilac security lines		800.
d.	50c **brick red,** yellow security lines		*2,500.*
REA18	$1 **blue**	*2,000.*	850.
a.	Yellow security lines		350.
b.	Gray-green and yellow security lines		*1,500.*
REA19	$2 **black**	*1,000.*	875.
a.	Yellow security lines		*2,500.*
b.	Gray-green and yellow security lines		*3,250.*

The security lines were printed across the center of the stamp where the cancel was to be placed.

Andrew Jackson

Designs: 16⅔c, Abraham Lincoln. 25c, Daniel Webster. 33⅓c, David G. Farragut. 50c, William T. Sherman. $1, Hugh McCulloch. $2, Alexander Hamilton.

Centers printed by the Bureau of Engraving and Printing. Frames printed by the National Bank Note Co.

See individual rates before No. REA1.

1871 **Engr.**

Centers, Plate Letters and Position Numbers in Black

REA20	12½c **blue,** white silk paper		125.
a.	Pinkish gray silk paper		200.
b.	Gray silk paper		65.
c.	Green silk paper		150.
REA21	16⅔c **vermilion,** white silk paper		325.
a.	Pinkish gray silk paper		350.
b.	Gray silk paper		350.
c.	Green silk paper		350.
REA22	25c **green,** white silk paper		25.
a.	Pinkish gray silk paper		125.
b.	Gray silk paper		30.
c.	Green silk paper		30.
REA23	33⅓c **orange,** green silk paper		*5,000.*
b.	Gray silk paper		*11,000.*
REA24	33⅓c **violet brown,** white silk paper		6,250.
REA25	50c **brown,** gray silk paper		20.
a.	Pinkish gray silk paper		60.
c.	Green silk paper		75.
REA26	50c **red,** white silk paper		55.
REA27	$1 **yellow orange,** white silk paper		250.
a.	Pinkish gray silk paper		1,100.
b.	Gray silk paper		150.
REA28	$1 **scarlet,** gray silk paper		175.
a.	Pinkish gray silk paper		750.
c.	Green silk paper		300.
REA29	$2 **red brown,** white silk paper		200.
a.	Pinkish gray silk paper		*1,450.*
b.	Gray silk paper		350.
c.	Green silk paper		1,000.

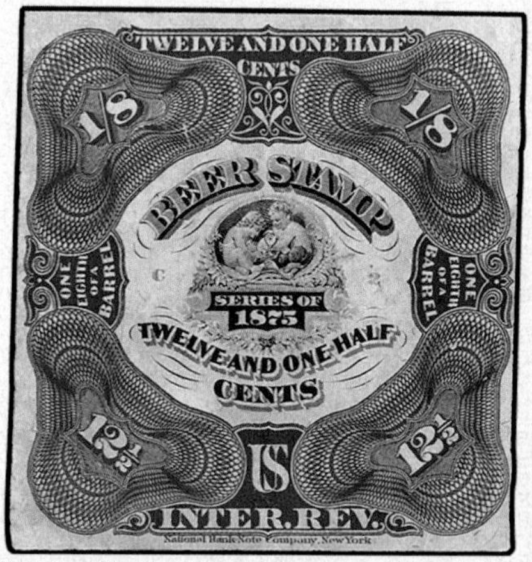

Bacchus Serving the First Fermented Brew to Man

Printed by the National Bank Note Co. See individual rates before No. REA1.

1875 **Typo. & Engr.**

Center in Black

REA30	12½c **blue**	25.00
REA31	16⅔c **red brown**	150.00
REA32	25c **green**	20.00
a.	Inverted center	—
REA33	33⅓c **violet**	1,250.
REA34	50c **orange**	100.00
REA35	$1 **red**	225.00
REA36	$2 **brown**	400.00
a.	Inverted center	—

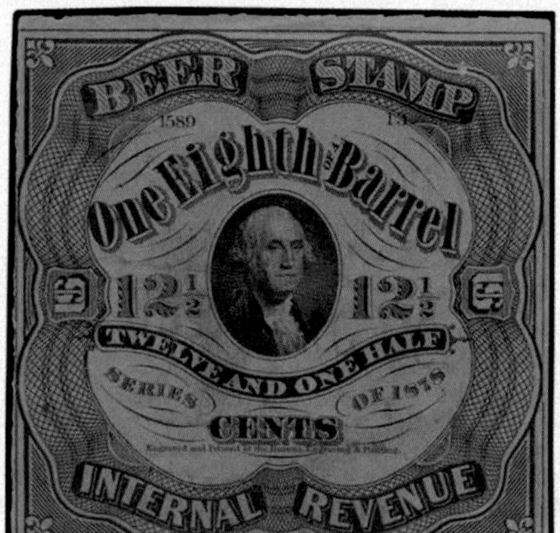

Designs: 12½c, Washington. 16⅔c, Corwin. 25c, Benton. 33⅓c, Thomas. 50c, Jefferson. $1, Johnson. $2, Wright.

Stamps on pale green paper have short greenish blue fibers. Plate designations for center consist of plate letter or number at left and position number at right.

See individual rates before No. REA1.

1878 Typo. & Engr. Wmk. USIR

Center, Plate Letters and Position Numbers in Black

REA37 12½c **blue**, *green* 7.50
b. Green silk paper, unwmkd. 1,250.
c. Pale green paper 200.00
With plate number and position number *1,250.*
d. Light blue paper, with plate number (and position number) 35.00
e. Blue paper, no plate letter or number or position number 30.00
f. Dark blue paper, no plate letter or number or position number 45.00
REA38 16⅔c **light brown**, *green* 7.50
One line under Cents 75.00
b. Green silk paper, unwmkd., one line under Cents 125.00
c. Pale green paper 75.00
With plate number 500.00
d. Light blue paper, with plate number (and position number) 40.00
e. Blue paper, no plate letter or number or position number 150.00
With plate number 1979 250.00
f. Dark blue paper, no plate letter or number or position number 75.00
REA39 25c **green**, *green* 5.00
a. Inverted center —
b. Green silk paper, unwmkd. 200.00
c. Pale green paper 90.00
With plate number 35.00
d. Light blue paper, with plate number (and position number) 7.50
e. Blue paper, no plate letter or number or position number 25.00
f. Dark blue paper, no plate letter or number or position number 27.50
REA40 33⅓c **violet**, *green* 85.00
b. Green silk paper, unwmkd. *2,000.*
c. Pale green paper 1,250.
d. Light blue paper, with plate number (and position number) 110.00
e. Blue paper, no plate letter or number or position number 120.00
f. Dark blue paper, no plate letter or number or position number 250.00
REA41 50c **orange**, *green* 11.00
One line under Cents 100.00
b. Green silk paper, unwmkd. 210.00
c. Pale green paper 90.00
With plate number 350.00
d. Light blue paper, with plate number (and position number) 30.00
e. Blue paper, no plate letter or number or position number 17.50
f. Dark blue paper, no plate letter or number or position number 20.00
REA42 $1 **red**, *green* 27.50
One line under Dollar 85.00
c. Pale green paper 200.00
One line under Dollar 400.00
d. Light blue paper, with plate number (and position number) 175.00
e. Blue paper, no plate letter or number or position number 125.00
One line under Dollar 200.00
f. Dark blue paper, no plate letter or number or position number 100.00
REA43 $2 **brown**, *green* 85.00
One line under Dollars 100.00
b. Green silk paper, unwmkd. 500.00
One line under dollars —
c. Pale green paper 900.00
One line under dollars *1,000.*
e. Blue paper, no plate letter or number or position number 175.00
f. Dark blue paper, no plate letter or number or position number 150.00

See Nos. REA58-REA64, REA65-REA71, REA75-REA81.

Stamps of 1878 Surcharged in Various Ways

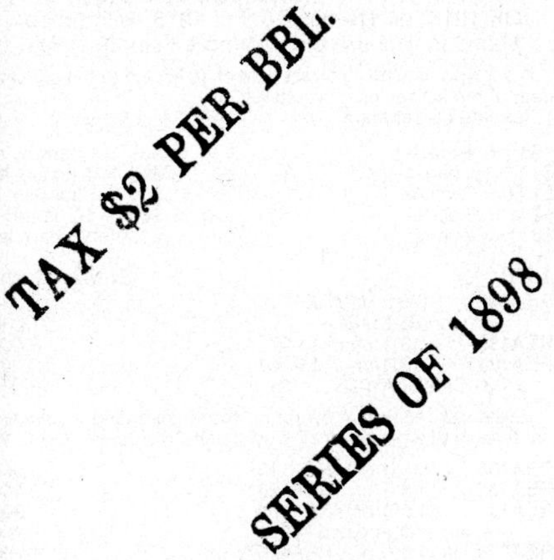

Type A

Four general surcharge types:
A — Bureau of Engraving and Printing surcharge "TAX $2 PER BBL./SERIES OF 1898" printed diagonally in red, letters 4¼mm high.
B — same, but letters 5½mm high.
C — handstamped provisional surcharge with similiar wording in 1-3 lines, more than 30 styles.
D — printed provisional 2-line surcharges, horizontal in various colors.

Tax rate $2 per bbl.

25c = ⅛ barrel $1 = ½ barrel
33⅓c = ⅙ barrel $2 = 1 barrel
50c = ¼ barrel $4 = 1 hogshead
66⅔c = ⅓ barrel

1898 Type A

REA44 (25c) on 12½c #REA37f 350.00
a. Type C surcharge 250.00
b. Type D surcharge 750.00
REA45 (33⅓c) on 16⅔c #REA38e 75.00
a. on #REA38f 175.00
b. As "a," type C surcharge 250.00
c. As "a," type D surcharge 400.00
d. on #REA38d 750.00
REA46 (50c) on 25c #REA39f 90.00
a. Type C surcharge 150.00
b. Type D surcharge 750.00
c. on #REA39e 175.00
d. on #REA39, type C surcharge *4,000.*
REA47 (66⅔c) on 33⅓c #REA40 500.00
REA48 ($1) on 50c #REA41f 35.00
a. Type C surcharge 150.00
b. Type D surcharge 450.00
REA49 ($2) on $1 #REA42f 125.00
a. Type C surcharge 175.00
b. Type D surcharge *1,750.*
c. on #REA42e, type C surcharge 1,250.
REA50 ($4) on $2 #REA43f 500.00
a. Type C surcharge 500.00
b. Type D surcharge *2,500.*
c. on #REA43e, type C surcharge *2,500.*

Type B

REA51 (25c) on 12½c #REA37f 95.00
a. on #REA37e 100.00
b. As "a," type C surcharge *2,000.*
REA52 (33⅓c) on 16⅔c #REA38d 700.00
a. on #REA38f 700.00
b. on #REA38e 700.00
REA53 (50c) on 25c #REA39f 25.00
a. on #REA39e 25.00
REA54 (66⅔c) on 33⅓c #REA40f *9,000.*
a. Type D surcharge *7,500.*
b. On #REA40 *6,000.*
REA55 ($1) on 50c #REA41f 12.50
REA56 ($2) on $1 #REA42f 50.00
REA57 ($4) on $2 #REA43f 275.00

Counterfeit type C and D overprints exist.

Designs: 25c, Washington. 33⅓c, Corwin. 50c, Benton. 66⅔c, Thomas. $1, Jefferson. $2, Johnson. $4, Wright.
See individual rates before No. REA44.

1898 Typo. & Engr. Wmk. USIR

Center in Black, Dark Blue Paper

REA58 25c **blue** 110.
REA59 33⅓c **brown** 85.
REA60 50c **green** 25.
REA61 66⅔c **violet** *10,500.*
REA62 $1 **yellow** 20.
REA63 $2 **red** 25.
REA64 $4 **dark brown** 225.

Used values for 1901-51 issues are for stamps canceled by perforated company name (or abbreviation) and date.

Designs: 20c, Washington. 26⅔c, Corwin. 40c, Benton. 53⅓c, Thomas. 80c, Jefferson. $1.60, Johnson. $3.20, Wright.
Tax rate $1.60 per bbl.

20c = ⅛ barrel 80c = ½ barrel
26⅔c = ⅙ barrel $1.60 = 1 barrel
40c = ¼ barrel $3.20 = 1 hogshead
53⅓c = ⅓ barrel

Engr. (center) & Typo. (frame)

1901 Wmk. USIR

Dark Blue Paper

REA65 20c **blue** 75.
REA66 26⅔c **yellow orange** 75.
REA67 40c **green** 17.50
REA68 53⅓c **violet** 7,000.
REA69 80c **brown** 17.50
REA70 $1.60 **red** 75.
REA71 $3.20 **dark brown** 275.

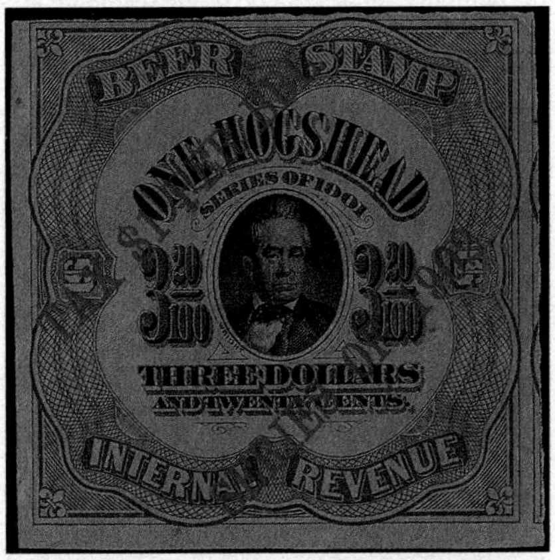

Stamps of 1901 Provisionally Surcharged by Bureau of Engraving & Printing diagonally in red "TAX $1 PER BBL./SERIES OF 1902."

1902

REA72 (16⅔c) on 26⅔c #REA66 150.
REA73 (33⅓c) on 53⅓c #REA68 *4,500.*
REA74 ($2) on $3.20 #REA71 750.

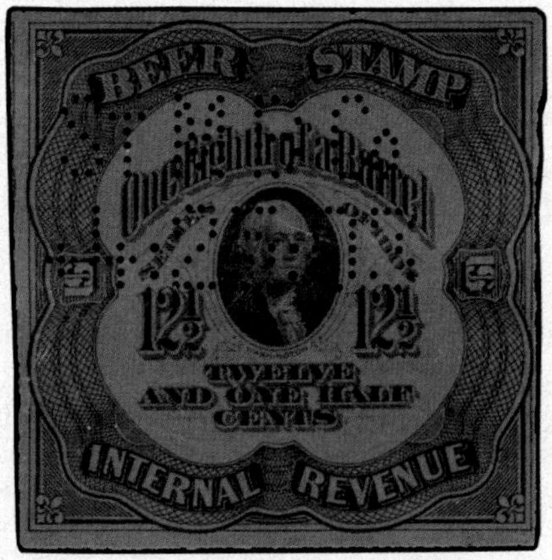

Designs: 12½c, Washington. 16⅔c, Corwin. 25c, Benton. 33⅓c, Thomas. 50c, Jefferson. $1, Johnson. $2, Wright.
Stamps on pale green paper have short greenish blue fibers.
See individual rates before No. REA1.

1902 Typo. & Engr. Wmk. USIR

Center in Black

REA75 12½c **blue**
a. Dark blue paper 75.00
b. Pale green paper 350.00
c. Light blue paper 110.00
d. Bright blue paper 50.00
REA76 16⅔c **yellow orange**
a. Dark blue paper 250.00
b. Pale green paper 350.00
c. Light blue paper 200.00
d. Bright blue paper 400.00
REA77 25c **green**
a. Dark blue paper 25.00
b. Pale green paper 80.00
c. Light blue paper 25.00
d. Bright blue paper 30.00
REA78 33⅓c **violet**
a. Dark blue paper 225.00
c. Light blue paper 450.00
d. Bright blue paper 450.00
REA79 50c **brown**
a. Dark blue paper 20.00
b. Pale green paper 30.00
c. Light blue paper 25.00
d. Bright blue paper 20.00
REA80 $1 **red**
a. Dark blue paper 125.00
b. Pale green paper 300.00
c. Light blue paper 75.00
d. Bright blue paper 75.00

REA81	$2 **dark brown**		
a.	Dark blue paper		750.00
b.	Pale green paper		900.00
c.	Light blue paper		500.00
d.	Bright blue paper		600.00

For surcharges see Nos. REA99a, REA100a, REA100b, REA141.

In the 1911-33 issues, the 5-25 barrel sizes were generally available only as center cutouts of the stamp. Values for these are for cutout portions that show enough of the denomination (or surcharge) to identify the item.

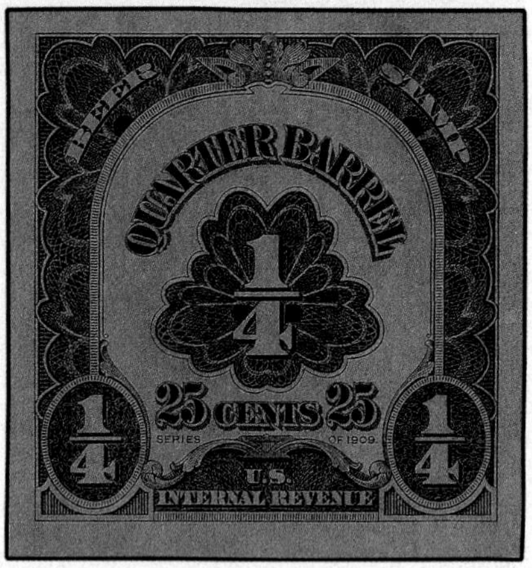

See individual rates before No. REA1.

1909-11 Engr. Wmk. USIR

Paper of Various Shades of Blue

REA82	12½c **black**		500.00
REA83	16⅔c **black**	175.00	90.00
REA84	25c **black**	550.00	450.00
REA85	33⅓c **black**		*20,000.*
REA86	50c **black**	45.00	6.00
REA87	$1 **black**	1,000.	750.00
REA88	$2 **black**		*4,500.*

Center Cutout Only

REA89	$5 **black,** *1911*		*150.00*
REA90	$10 **black,** *1911*		*125.00*
REA91	$25 **black,** *1911*		*100.00*

For surcharges see Nos. REA97, REA99-REA100, REA103-REA105, REA128.

1910 Engr. Wmk. USIR

Paper of Various Shades of Blue

REA92	12½c **red brown**		75.00
REA93	25c **green**		10.00
REA94	$1 **carmine**		75.00
REA95	$2 **orange**		125.00

For surcharges see Nos. REA96, REA98, REA101-REA102, REA126.

1914 Provisional Issue

Stamps of of 1902-11 with printed provisional BEP diagonal surcharge "EMERGENCY/TAX/UNDER ACT OF 1914" in red, black or yellow, or handstamped surcharge of value spelled out in full and separate "Roscoe Irwin" handstamped facsimile signature.

Tax rate $1.50 per bbl.

18¾c = ⅛ barrel	$1.50 = 1 barrel
25c = ⅙ barrel	$3 = 1 hogshead
37½c = ¼ barrel	$7.5 = 5 barrels
50c = ⅓ barrel	$15 = 10 barrels
75c = ½ barrel	$37.50 = 25 barrels

1914 Entire Stamps

REA96	(18¾c) on 12½ #REA92		65.00
REA97	(25c) on 16⅔c #REA83		60.00
REA98	(37½c) on 25c #REA93		7.50
a.	37½c handstamped; 50mm signature		700.00
REA99	(50c) on 33⅓c #REA85		225.00
a.	(50c) on 33⅓c #REA78d		900.00
REA100	(75c) on 50c #REA86		7.50
a.	(75c) On 50c #REA79c		1,000.
b.	(75c) On 50c #REA79b		*5,500.*
c.	75c handstamped on #REA86; 50mm signature		175.00
d.	As "c," 65mm signature		325.00
REA101	($1.50) on $1 #REA94		50.00
a.	$1.50 handstamped; 50mm signature		700.00
b.	As "a," 65mm signature		*9,000.*
REA102	($3.00) on $2 #REA95		75.00
a.	$3 handstamped; 76mm signature		*2,750.*

Center Cutout Only

REA103	($7.50) on $5 #REA89		17.50
REA104	($15) on $10 #REA90		150.00
REA105	($37.50) on $25 #REA91		225.00

For surcharges see Nos. REA119, REA123, REA133, REA140, REA140a.

See individual rates before No. REA96.

1914 Engr. Wmk. USIR

Paper of Various Shades of Blue

Entire Stamp

REA106	18¾c **red brown**		85.00
REA107	25c **black**		175.00
a.	25c **violet blue**		*2,500.*
REA108	37½c **green**		17.50
a.	37½c **black**		*32,500.*
REA108B	50c **black**		—
REA109	75c **black**		6.00
REA110	$1.50 **red orange**		30.00
REA111	$3 **orange**		200.00

Center Cutout Only

REA112	$7.50 **black**		10.00
REA113	$15 **black**		15.00
REA114	$37.50 **black**		7.50

For surcharges see Nos. REA118, REA120, REA120a, REA121, REA124-REA125, REA127, REA129-REA131, REA134, REA134a, REA137, REA144, REA146-REA149.

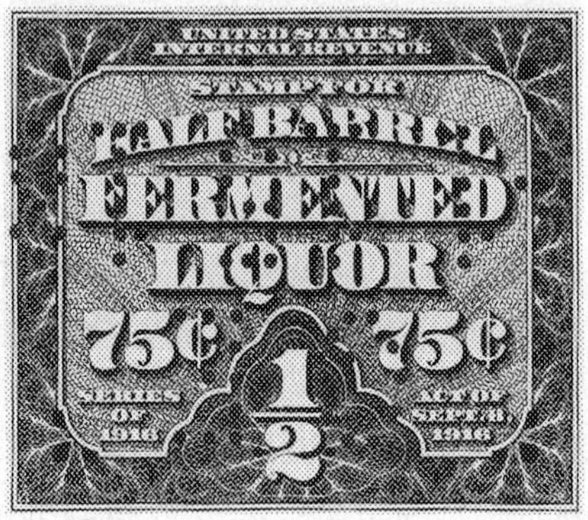

See individual rates before No. REA96.

1916 Engr. Wmk. USIR

Paper of Various Shades of Greenish Blue

Entire Stamp

REA115	37½c **green**		110.00
REA116	75c **black**		40.00

For surcharges see Nos. REA122, REA124, REA138. Surcharge also exists in manuscript on No. REA115.

Stamps of 1914-16 Provisionally Surcharged Types A, B & C

Type C

Surcharge types:

A — "ACT OF 1917" handstamped in 1-3 lines in more than 30 styles.

B — "ACT OF 1917" locally printed horizontally in black or red.

C — "ACT OF 1917" printed in black or red by BEP, horizontally on ⅛ bbl-1 hhd and reading down on 5-25 bbl.

Surcharge also exists in manuscript on some values. Tax rate $3 per bbl.

37½c = ⅛ barrel	$3 = 1 barrel
50c = ⅙ barrel	$6 = 1 hogshead
75c = ¼ barrel	$15 = 5 barrels
$1 = ⅓ barrel	$30 = 10 barrels
$1.50 = ½ barrel	$75 = 25 barrels

1917 Type A Surcharge

Entire Stamp

REA117	(37½c) on #REA96		*17,500.*
REA118	(37½c) on #REA106		300.00
b.	Type B surcharge		—
c.	Type C surcharge		500.00
REA119	(50c) on #REA97		150.00
REA120	(50c) on #REA107a		600.00
a.	On #107		500.00
REA121	(75c) on #REA108		110.00
REA122	(75c) on #REA115		50.00
b.	Type B surcharge		5,500.
c.	Type C surcharge		90.00
REA123	($1) on #REA99		175.00
REA124	($1.50) on #REA116		40.00
b.	Type B surcharge		*6,000.*
c.	Type C surcharge	35.00	7.50
d.	As "c," inverted surcharge	1,000.	

$1.50 surcharge exists in manuscript on #REA109.

REA125	($3) on #REA110		100.00
c.	Type C surcharge		40.00
REA126	($6) on #REA102		2,750.
REA127	($6) on #REA111		500.00

Center Cutout Only

REA128	($15) on #REA103		500.00
REA129	($15) on #REA112, entire stamp, type C surcharge		*6,000.*
REA130	($30) on #REA113		100.00
c.	Type C surcharge		45.00
REA131	($75) on #REA114		225.00
c.	Type C surcharge		12.50

For surcharges see Nos. REA132, REA132a, REA135-REA136, REA139-REA139b, REA142-REA143, REA145, REA150-REA151.

Stamps of 1914-17 provisionally surcharged "ACT OF 1918" or "Revenue Act of 1918" with rubber stamp in various colors in more than 20 styles.

A subtype has the incorrect date of 1919 due to the effective date of the act (at least five styles).

Tax rate $6 per bbl.

75c = ⅛ barrel	$6 = 1 barrel
$1 = ⅙ barrel	$12 = 1 hogshead
$1.50 = ¼ barrel	$30 = 5 barrels
$2 = ⅓ barrel	$60 = 10 barrels
$3 = ½ barrel	$150 = 25 barrels

1918 Entire Stamp

REA132	(75c) on #REA118		600.
a.	On #REA118c		1,200.
REA133	($1) on #REA97		*3,000.*
REA134	($1) on #REA107		*3,000.*
a.	On #REA107a		*10,000.*

Exists with additional overprint "Non-Intoxicating, containing not to/exceed 2¾% of Alcohol by weight." Value, *$1,750.*

REA135	($1) on #REA119		*8,000.*
REA136	($1) on #REA120		*2,500.*
REA137	($1.50) on #REA108		600.
a.	Surcharge dated "1919"		2,250.
REA138	($1.50) on #REA115		1,250.
REA139	($1.50) on #REA122c		75.
a.	Surcharge dated "1919"		60.
b.	On #REA122		350.

REA140	($2) on #REA99		1,000.
	a. On #REA99a		1,500.
REA141	($2) on #REA99a		3,500.

No. REA141 bears additional 1917 provisional surcharge, as well as the 1914 surcharge, but was not issued in that form without 1918 surcharge.

REA142	($2) on #REA123		*10,000.*
REA143	($3) on #REA124c	175.	75.
	a. Surcharge dated "1919"		600.
REA144	($6) on #REA110		750.
REA145	($6) on #REA125c		50.
	a. Surcharge dated "1919"		500.
REA146	($12) on #REA111		700.
REA147	($12) on #REA111		75.

No. REA147 bears additional 1917 Type C provisional surcharge but was not issued in that form without 1918 surcharge.

Center Cutout Only

REA148	($30) on #REA112		75.
REA149	($60) on #REA113		75.
REA150	($60) on #REA130c		300.
	a. Entire stamp		*3,500.*
REA151	($150) on #REA131c		35.
	a. Entire stamp		*4,000.*

REA152-REA158

REA159-REA161

Tax rate $5 per barrel through Jan. 11, 1934. $6 rate also effective Dec. 5, 1933. Provisional handstamp "Surcharged $6.00 Rate" in 1-3 lines (seven styles).

1933 Engr. Wmk. USIR

Paper of Various Shades of Greenish Blue to Blue

Type A

Entire Stamp

REA152	⅛ bbl., **violet red**		17.50
	a. Provisional surcharge, $6 rate		1,500.
REA153	⅙ bbl., **purple**		450.00
REA154	¼ bbl., **green**		6.00
REA155	⅓ bbl., **brown orange**		2,750.
REA156	½ bbl., **orange**	60.00	5.00
	a. Provisional surcharge, $6 rate		*1,500.*
REA157	1 bbl., **blue**		25.00
	a. Provisional surcharge, $6 rate		*3,000.*
REA158	1 hhd., **black**		*7,500.*
REA159	5 bbl., **black**, center cutout only		250.00
REA160	10 bbl., **black**, with cut-out center, rouletted 7 at left		*7,500.*
	a. Center cutout only		250.00
REA161	25 bbl., **black**, with cut-out center, rouletted 7 at left		7,500.
	a. Center cutout only		250.00

Center cutout portions of Nos. REA159-REA161 are on greenish blue paper. See Nos. REA177-REA178A for examples on bright blue paper.

Nos. REA152-REA159, REA161 Surcharged in Black

Type B

A — additional provisional handstamped surcharge.
B — additional manuscript and handstamped surcharges.
Tax rate same as Nos. REA152-REA161.

1933 Engr. Wmk. USIR

Entire Stamp

REA162	⅛ bbl., **violet red**		8.00
REA163	⅙ bbl., **purple**		175.00
REA164	¼ bbl., **green**		15.00
	a. With 1918 provisional handstamped surcharge, $6 rate		*2,250.*
	b. Type A surcharge, $6 rate		*2,750.*
REA165	⅓ bbl., **brown orange**		*6,000.*
REA166	½ bbl., **orange**		15.00
	a. Type A surcharge, $6 rate		*3,000.*
	b. Type B surcharge, $6 rate		*1,500.*
REA167	1 bbl., **blue**		25.00
REA168	1 hhd., **black**		*16,000.*
REA169	5 bbl., **black**		*6,000.*
	a. Center cutout only		500.00
REA170	25 bbl., **black,** center cutout only		450.00

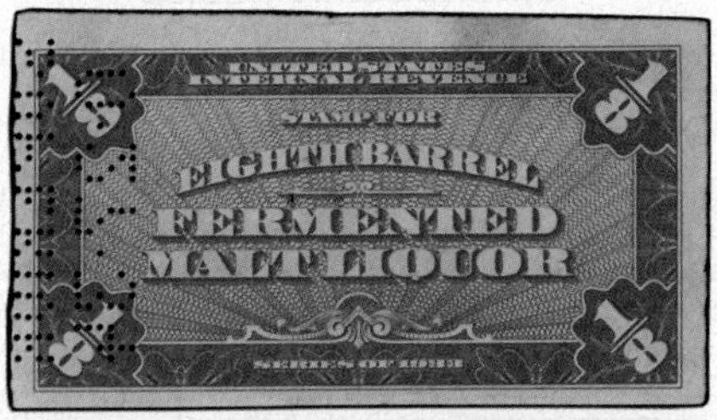

REA171-REA176

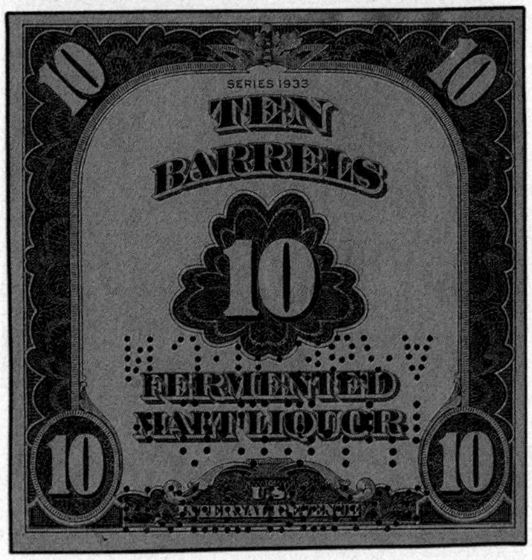

REA177-REA178A

Tax rate same as previous issue. Provisional handstamp reads "SOLD AT $5.00 RATE" or "$5.00 RATE."

1933 Engr. Wmk. USIR

Entire Stamp

REA171	⅛ bbl., **violet red**		35.00
REA172	⅙ bbl., **purple**		500.00
REA173	¼ bbl., **green**	75.00	8.00
	a. Provisional surcharge, $5 rate		*7,500.*
REA174	½ bbl., **brown orange**	100.00	5.00
	a. Provisional surcharge, $5 rate		800.00
REA175	1 bbl., **blue**		100.00
REA176	1 hhd., **black**		*6,500.*

Bright Blue Paper

REA177	5 bbl., **black**		1,000.
	a. Entire stamp with cut-out center		7.50
	b. Center cutout only		1.00
REA178	10 bbl., **black**	750.00	500.00
	a. Entire stamp with cut-out center		10.00
	b. Center cutout only		1.00
REA178A	25 bbl., **black**		500.00
	b. Entire stamp with cut-out center		4.50
	c. Center cutout only		1.00
	d. Rouletted 7 at left		—

For surcharge see No. REA199.

Nos. REA173-REA174 with BEP Printed Surcharge, "Act of March 22, 1933"

Additional provisional handstamped surcharge, $6 rate as previous issue.

1933-40

Entire Stamp

REA179	¼ bbl., **green**		27.50
	a. Handstamped "Surcharged $6 rate," *1940*		2,500.
REA180	½ bbl., **brown orange**		12.50
	a. Handstamped "Surcharged $6 rate," *1940*		2,500.

No. REA178 with handstamp surcharge, "Value increased under Revenue Act of 1940."

1940

Entire Stamp

REA180B	10 bbl., **black**		—

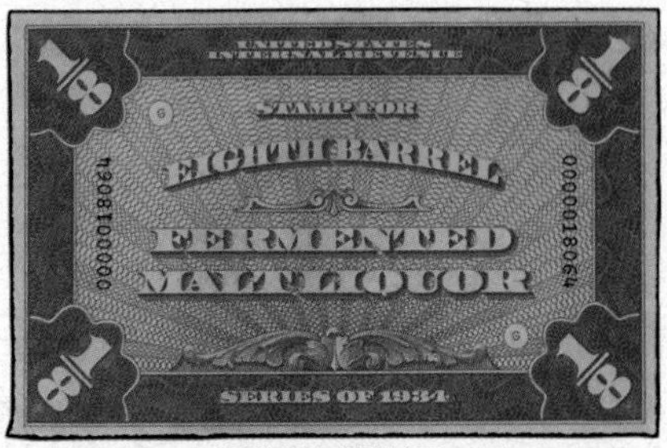

REA181-REA187

REA188-REA189

Tax rates $5 per bbl; $6 from July 1, 1940; $7 from Nov. 1, 1942; $8 from Apr. 1, 1944.

1934-45 Engr. Wmk. USIR

With Black Control Numbers

REA181	⅛ bbl., **violet red**	125.00	7.50
	a. With cutout center		2.00
	b. Ovptd. "NOT LESS THAN 3⅝ GALLONS," uncut		—
REA182	⅙ bbl., **purple**		150.00
	a. With cutout center		100.00
	b. Ovptd. "NOT LESS THAN 4⅚ GALLONS," uncut		—
REA183	¼ bbl., **green**		4.00
	a. With cutout center		2.50
	b. Ovptd. "NOT LESS THAN 7¼ GALLONS," uncut		—
REA184	⅓ bbl., **brown orange**		*20,000.*
REA185	½ bbl., **orange**		3.00
	a. With cutout center		2.00
REA186	1 bbl., **blue**		7.50
	a. With cutout center		7.50
REA187	1 hhd., **black**		500.00
REA188	100 bbl., **carmine**, *1942*		200.00
	a. With cutout center		10.00
REA189	500 bbl., **dark brown**, with cut-out center, *1945*		500.00

Most values also exist as center cutout portions only.

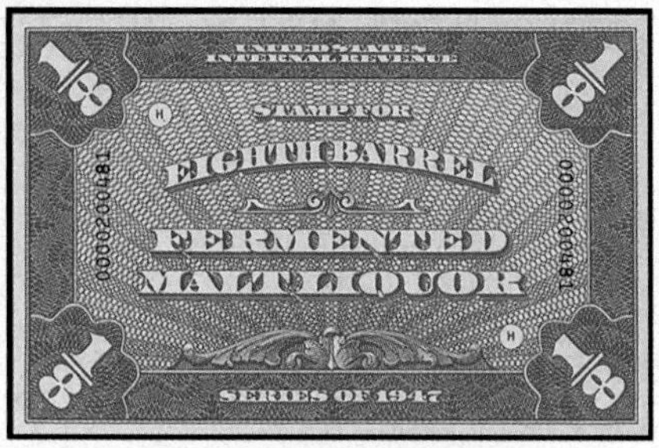

REA190-REA193

REA194-REA198

Tax rates $8 per bbl, $9 from Nov. 1, 1951.

1947 **Litho.**

Black Control Numbers

REA190	⅛ bbl., **carmine**	125.00	60.00
a.	With cutout center		15.00
REA190B	⅛ bbl., **purple**	200.00	
REA191	¼ bbl., **green**	90.00	20.00
a.	With cutout center		22.50
REA192	½ bbl., **orange**	30.00	10.00
a.	With cutout center		12.50
REA193	1 bbl., **blue**	100.00	150.00
a.	With cutout center		15.00

Blue Paper

REA194	5 bbl., **black**	100.00	200.00
a.	With cutout center		12.50
REA195	10 bbl., **black**	200.00	300.00
a.	With cutout center		27.50
REA196	25 bbl., **black**	*1,250.*	*3,200.*
a.	With cutout center		*3,000.*

White Paper

REA197	100 bbl., **carmine**	150.00	250.00
a.	With cutout center		10.00
REA198	500 bbl., **dark brown**	500.00	600.00
a.	With cutout center		60.00

All values except No. REA190B also exist as center cutouts only.

No. REA190B was not officially issued.

No. REA158 Provisionally Handstamp Surcharged "Value increased under / Revenue Act of 1951" in black or purple.

Tax rate $9 per bbl.

1951

REA199	($225) on 25 bbl., #REA178A, uncut	*20,000.*

Also exists as center cutout only, showing portion of handstamped surcharge. Value, $150.

FERMENTED FRUIT JUICE STAMPS

Fermented fruit juice stamps were issued pending the ratification of the Repeal Amendment (Dec. 5, 1933) that made full-strength beer and wine legal again.

Congress, as a temporary measure, redefined intoxicating beverages by changing the legal definition from .5% to 3.2%, thus permitting the sale of 3.2 beer and wine beginning April 7, 1933.

Regular wine stamps were available to pay the Internal Revenue taxes. However, these Fermented Fruit Juice stamps were authorized for placement on individual bottles or containers of fermented fruit juice. Use was discontinued at the end of 1933.

Stamps are valued in the grade of very fine. Most stamps are found in average to fine condition. Unused stamps are valued with original gum.

REF1

Plates of 220 subjects in two panes of 110.

1933 **Wmk. USIR** **Engr.** ***Perf. 11***

REF1	REF1	4 oz **gray**		125.00
REF3	REF1	8 oz **light green**	125.00	100.00
REF4	REF1	12 oz **light blue**	22.50	8.00
REF5	REF1	13 oz **olive green**		70.00
REF6	REF1	16 oz **lavender**	550.00	175.00
REF7	REF1	24 oz **orange**		110.00
REF8	REF1	29 oz **brown**	225.00	175.00
REF9	REF1	32 oz **red**	95.00	75.00

A dark blue 7-ounce stamp was issued, but the only recorded examples currently are in the National Postal Museum collection.

No. REF4 stamps canceled "H. B. Co." (Hoffman Beverage Company) or "M. D. C." (Mission Dry Corporation) command a premium of 10-100 percent. Specialists collect them by date (H. B. Co. and M. D. C.) and control number (M. D. C.).

Earliest known use: May 28, 1933.

Beer Stamp No. REA154 Overprinted "WINE OR FERMENTED FRUIT JUICE" in Red

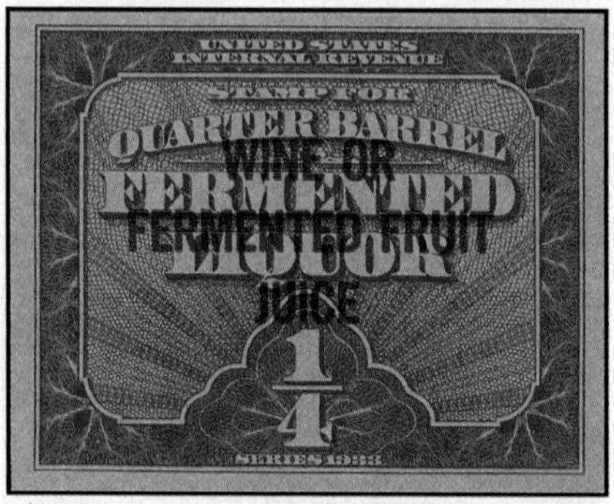

REF10

1933 **Engr.** ***Imperf.***

REF10	¼ bbl., **green**, *blue*	*30,000.*

The ½ barrel and 1 barrel stamps Beer Stamps, Nos. REA156-REA157, also were issued with this overprint, but no examples are currently recorded.

PLAYING CARDS

Stamps for use on packs of playing cards were included in the first general issue of 1862-71. They are Nos. R2, R11, R12, R17, R21 and R28. The tax on playing cards was repealed effective June 22, 1965.

"ON HAND . . ." — RF1

"ACT OF . . ." — RF2

1894 **Engr.** **Unwmk.** ***Rouletted 5½***

RF1	RF1	2c **lake**	.90	.60
a.		Horizontal pair, imperf. between	*600.00*	—
b.		Horiz. pair, imperf. vert.	—	
RF2	RF2	2c **ultramarine**	27.50	2.75
a.		2c **blue**	35.00	3.75
b.		Imperf., pair	600.00	
c.		Imperf. horizontally	160.00	160.00
d.		Rouletted 12½	100.00	100.00
e.		Imperf. horizontally, rouletted 12½ vertically, pair	225.00	225.00

No vertical pairs of No. RF2e are known. Pairs will be horizontal. Singles are valued at 50% of the pair value.

Rouletted 5½, 7; Hyphen Hole 7

1896-99 **Wmk. 191R**

RF3	RF2	2c **blue**	10.00	.65
a.		2c **ultramarine** ('99)	10.00	2.00
b.		Imperf., pair	125.00	

No. RF3 surcharged " VIRGIN / ISLANDS / 4 CTS" are listed under Danish West Indies.

1902 ***Perf. 12***

RF4	RF2	2c **deep blue**	65.00

No. RF4 is known with cancel date "1899" but that is due to the use of an old canceling plate. The stamp was first used in 1902.

Stamp of 1899 Surcharged in Rose

1917 **Wmk. 191R** ***Rouletted 7***

RF5	RF2	7c on 2c **ultramarine**	*850.00*	700.00
a.		Inverted surcharge		—

The surcharge on No. RF5 was handstamped at the Internal Revenue Office in New York City. Different handstamps were used at other Internal Revenue Offices as well, values $350 to $400.

Surcharged in Black

1917

RF6	RF2	(7c) on 2c **blue**	62.50
a.		Inverted surcharge	62.50

The "17" indicated that the 7 cent tax had been paid according to the Act of 1917.
Used by N. Y. Consolidated Card Co.
Cancellations are in red.

Surcharged in Black

RF7	RF2	7c on 2c **blue**	1,100.
a.		Inverted surcharge	600.00

Used by Standard Playing Card Co.

The surcharges on Nos. RF7-RF10, RF13, RF15, RF18 were applied by the manufacturers, together with their initials, dates, etc., thus forming a combination of surcharge and precancellation. The surcharge on No. RF16 was made by the Bureau of Engraving and Printing. After it appeared the use of some combinations was continued but only as cancellations.

Surcharged Vertically Reading Up in Red or Violet

RF8	RF2	7c on 2c **blue**	1,350.
a.		Double surcharge	2,000.
b.		Reading down	2,250.

Used by Russell Playing Card Co.

Surcharged Vertically, Reading Up in Black, Violet or Red

RF9	RF2	7c on 2c **blue**	9.75
a.		Double surcharge (violet)	100.00
b.		Numeral omitted (black)	90.00
c.		Surcharge reading down	11.50
d.		As "c," numeral omitted (black)	77.50
e.		As "c," double surcharge (violet)	275.00
f.		Double surcharge, one down (red)	300.00
g.		Surcharge and "A.D." in violet	375.00
h.		Surcharge and "A.D." in red, "U.S.P.C. Co." in black	*1,050.*
i.		Surcharge and "A.D." in red reading up, "U.S.P.C. Co." in black reading down	*775.00*
j.		As "g," reading down	—
k.		Double surcharge (black)	*1,000.*
l.		Double surcharge (red)	*400.00*
m.		Double surcharge and "A.D.," both reading down (red)	—
n.		Double surcharge and "U.S. P.C. Co.," both reading down (black)	*2,500.*

"A.D." (Andrew Dougherty Co.) printed in red, "S. P. C. Co." (Standard Playing Card Co.) printed in violet, "U.S.P.C. Co." printed in black. The first two became divisions of United States Playing Card Co.
See No. RF13.

Surcharged in Carmine

RF10	RF2	7c on 2c **blue**	85.00
a.		Inverted surcharge	47.50
b.		Double surcharge	550.00
c.		Double surcharge, inverted	550.00
d.		Triple surcharge	—

Used by Russell Playing Card Co.

RF3

1918 **Size: 21x40mm** ***Imperf.***

RF11	RF3	**blue**	50.00	32.50
		Block of 4	190.00	150.00

Private Roulette 14

RF12	RF3	**blue**	300.
a.		Rouletted 13 in red	*1,650.*
b.		Rouletted 6½	425.
c.		Perf. 12 horiz., imperf. vert.	300.
d.		Perf. 12 on 4 sides	*1,600.*

Nos. RF11-RF12 served as 7c stamps when used before April 1, 1919, and as 8c stamps when used after that date.
No. RF11 is known handstamped "7" or "8," or both "7" and "8," as well as "Act of 1918" in black or magenta, either by the user to indicate the value when applied to the pack or by the IRS district offices at the time of sale.
No. RF12 was used by N. Y. Consolidated Card Co., Nos. RF12a, RF12b were used by Russell Playing Card Co., Nos. RF12, RF12d were used by Logan Printing House.

Surcharged like No. RF9 (but somewhat smaller) in Violet, Red or Black

Private Roulette 9½

RF13	RF3	7c **blue**	52.50
a.		Inverted surcharge	52.50
b.		Double surcharge	450.00
c.		Double surcharge, inverted	500.00
d.		Surcharge omitted	—

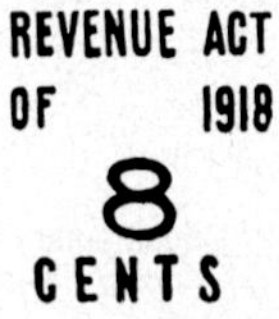

Stamp of 1899 Surcharged in Magenta or Rose

1919 ***Rouletted 7***

RF14	RF2	8c on 2c **ultramarine**	125.00
a.		Double surcharge	300.00
b.		Inverted surcharge	325.00

The surcharge on No. RF14 was handstamped at the Internal Revenue Office in New York City. A handstamp in black is known.
Exists in pair, one double surcharge, also in pair, one with inverted surcharge.

Inverted Surcharge in Carmine 

RF15 RF2 8c on 2c **blue** 625.00
a. Double surcharge *1,500.*

No. RF15 is surcharged only with large "8c" inverted, and overprinted with date and initials (also inverted). No. RF16 is often found with additional impression of large "8c," as on No. RF15, but in this usage the large "8c" is a cancellation.
Used by Russell Playing Card Co.

Surcharged in Carmine or Vermilion

RF16 RF2 8c on 2c **blue** 200.00 .90
a. Inverted surcharge *3,000.*

See note after No. RF15.

RF4

1922 **Size: 19x22mm** ***Rouletted 7***
RF17 RF4 (8c) **blue** 27.50 1.50
Block of 4 125.00 —

No. RF17, rouletted 7 and perforated 11, surcharged " VIRGIN / ISLANDS / 4 cts." are listed under Danish West Indies.

Surcharged in Carmine, Blue or Black

RF18 RF4 8c on (8c) **blue** 65.00
a. Inverted surcharge 65.00

Used by Pyramid Playing Card Co.

RF5

1924 ***Rouletted 7***
RF19 RF5 10c **blue** 20.00 .45
Block of 4 90.00

ROTARY PRESS COIL STAMP

1926 ***Perf. 10 Vertically***
RF20 RF5 10c **blue** .30
Pair 3.25
Joint line pair 6.50

No. RF20 exists only precanceled. **Bureau precancels:** 11 different.

FLAT PLATE PRINTING

1927 ***Perf. 11***
RF21 RF5 10c **blue** 35.00 5.25
Block of 4 160.00

1929 ***Perf. 10***
RF22 RF5 10c **blue** 25.00 4.25
Block of 4 100.00 —

RF6

ROTARY PRESS COIL STAMP

1929 ***Perf. 10 Horizontally***
RF23 RF6 10c **light blue** .25
Pair 2.50
Joint line pair 5.00

No. RF23 exists only precanceled. **Bureau precancels:** 16 different.

FLAT PLATE PRINTING

1930 ***Perf. 10***
RF24 RF6 10c **blue** 22.50 1.40
Block of 4 100.00 11.00
a. Horiz. pair, imperf. vert. 175.00

1931 ***Perf. 11***
RF25 RF6 10c **blue** 20.00 1.40
Block of 4 95.00 —

No. R234 is known used provisionally as a playing card revenue stamp August 6 and 8, 1932. Value for this use, authenticated, $400.

RF7

ROTARY PRESS COIL STAMP

1940 **Wmk. 191R** ***Perf. 10 Vertically***
RF26 RF7 **blue,** wet printing — .45
Pair 2.25
Joint line pair 4.50

Unwmk.

RF26A RF7 **blue,** dry printing 25.00 .40

See note after No. 1029.
Bureau precancels: 11 different.

RF8

ROTARY PRESS COIL STAMP

1940 **Wmk. 191R** ***Perf. 10 Horizontally***
RF27 RF8 **blue,** wet printing 3.00 .25
Pair 7.50
Joint line pair 12.50

Unwmk.

RF27A RF8 **blue,** dry printing 3.25

Bureau precancels: 10 different.

FLAT PLATE PRINTING

Wmk. 191R ***Perf. 11***
RF28 RF8 **blue,** wet printing 5.25 .80
Block of 4 26.00 —
a. Dry printing 5.25 4.25

Unwmk.

RF28B RF8 **blue,** dry printing 5.25
Block of 4 —

ROTARY PRESS PRINTING

Wmk. 191R ***Perf. 10x11***
RF29 RF8 **blue** 200.00 92.50
Block of 4 850.00 —
a. Imperforate (P.C. Co.) 1,000.

SILVER TAX STAMPS

The Silver Purchase Act of 1934 imposed a 50 per cent tax on the net profit realized on a transfer of silver bullion occurring after May 15, 1934. The tax was paid by affixing stamps to the transfer memorandum. Congress authorized the Silver Tax stamps on June 19, 1934. They were discontinued on June 4, 1963.

Documentary Stamps of 1917 Overprinted

1934 **Offset Printing** **Wmk. 191R** ***Perf. 11***

RG1	R22	1c	**carmine rose**	1.60	.95
RG2	R22	2c	**carmine rose**	1.75	.65
			Double impression of stamp	—	
RG3	R22	3c	**carmine rose**	2.00	.80
RG4	R22	4c	**carmine rose**	2.10	1.60
RG5	R22	5c	**carmine rose**	3.25	1.40
RG6	R22	8c	**carmine rose**	4.50	3.25
RG7	R22	10c	**carmine rose**	4.75	3.00
RG8	R22	20c	**carmine rose**	6.75	3.75
RG9	R22	25c	**carmine rose**	6.25	4.25
RG10	R22	40c	**carmine rose**	7.25	6.00
RG11	R22	50c	**carmine rose**	11.00	7.50
RG12	R22	80c	**carmine rose**	19.00	10.50

Engr.

RG13	R21	$1	**green**	40.00	16.00
RG14	R21	$2	**rose**	47.50	25.00
RG15	R21	$3	**violet**	85.00	35.00
RG16	R21	$4	**yellow brown**	67.50	24.00
RG17	R21	$5	**dark blue**	85.00	27.50
RG18	R21	$10	**orange**	125.00	22.50

Perf. 12

Without Gum

RG19	R17	$30	**vermilion**	250.00	55.00
			Cut cancel		20.00
RG20	R19	$60	**brown**	275.00	82.50
			Cut cancel		27.50
			Vertical strip of 4		375.00
RG21	R17	$100	**green**	325.00	35.00
			Vertical strip of 4		150.00
RG22	R18	$500	**blue**	600.00	275.00
			Cut cancel		110.00
			Vertical strip of 4		—
RG23	R19	$1000	**orange**	—	110.00
			Cut cancel		60.00
			Vertical strip of 4		—

See note after No. R227.

Same Overprint, spacing 11mm between words "SILVER TAX"
Without Gum

1936 ***Perf. 12***

RG26	R17	$100	**green**	575.00	90.00
			Vertical strip of 4		—
RG27	R19	$1000	**orange**		1,750.

Documentary Stamps of 1917 Handstamped "SILVER TAX" in Violet, Large Block Letters, in Two Lines

1939 **Wmk. 191R** **Offset Printing** ***Perf. 10***
RG28 R22 1c **rose pink** *30,000.*

Perf. 11

RG29	R22	3c	**rose pink**	*30,000.*
RG30	R22	5c	**rose pink**	*30,000.*
RG31	R22	10c	**rose pink**	*30,000.*
RG32	R22	80c	**rose pink**	*30,000.*

Other handstamps exist on various values. One has letters 4mm high, 2mm wide with "SILVER" and "TAX" applied in separate operations. Another has "Silver Tax" in two lines in a box, but it is believed this handstamp was privately applied.

Overprint Typewritten in Black ($2, $3) or Red ($5)

1934-35		Engr.	Perf. 11
RG34	R21	$2 **carmine**	—
RG35	R21	$3 **violet**	*25,000.*
RG36	R21	$5 **dark blue**	—

No. RG35 is unique.

Typewritten overprints also exist on 2c, 3c, 4c, 20c and 50c.

Type of Documentary Stamps 1917, Overprinted in Black

1940		Offset Printing	Perf. 11	
RG37	R22	1c **rose pink**	30.00	—
RG38	R22	2c **rose pink**	30.00	—
RG39	R22	3c **rose pink**	30.00	—
RG40	R22	4c **rose pink**	35.00	—
RG41	R22	5c **rose pink**	21.00	—
RG42	R22	8c **rose pink**	35.00	—
RG43	R22	10c **rose pink**	30.00	—
RG44	R22	20c **rose pink**	35.00	—
RG45	R22	25c **rose pink**	30.00	—
RG46	R22	40c **rose pink**	52.50	—
RG47	R22	50c **rose pink**	52.50	—
RG48	R22	80c **rose pink**	52.50	—
		Engr.		
RG49	R21	$1 **green**	200.00	—
RG50	R21	$2 **rose**	325.00	—
RG51	R21	$3 **violet**	400.00	—
RG52	R21	$4 **yellow brown**	750.00	—
RG53	R21	$5 **dark blue**	900.00	—
RG54	R21	$10 **orange**	1,100.	—

Nos. RG19-RG20, RG26 Handstamped in Blue "Series 1940"

1940		Without Gum	Perf. 12	
RG55	R17	$30 **vermilion**	—	*7,000.*
RG56	R19	$60 **brown**	—	*22,500.*
RG57	R17	$100 **green**	—	*6,000.*

Nos. RG47, RG51, RG53-RG54, RG57 Handstamped in Black "Silver Tax"

1940			Perf. 11	
RG57A	R22	50c **rose pink**		*3,600.*
RG57B	R21	$3 **violet**	—	*3,600.*
RG57C	R21	$5 **dark blue**	—	*3,600.*
RG57D	R21	$10 **orange**		*2,450.*
RG57E	R17	$100 **carmine**	—	*3,600.*

Additional denominations bearing the provisional "Silver Tax" handstamp might exist.

Alexander Hamilton — RG1

Levi Woodbury — RG2

Thomas Corwin — RG3

Overprinted in Black **SERIES 1941**

1941		Wmk. 191R Engr.	Perf. 11	
RG58	RG1	1c **gray**	7.00	2.40
a.		Imperf, pair, without gum	*75.00*	
RG59	RG1	2c **gray** *(Oliver Wolcott, Jr.)*	7.00	3.00
a.		Imperf, pair, without gum	*75.00*	
RG60	RG1	3c **gray** *(Samuel Dexter)*	7.00	3.00
a.		Imperf, pair, without gum	*75.00*	
RG61	RG1	4c **gray** *(Albert Gallatin)*	10.00	5.25
a.		Imperf, pair, without gum	*75.00*	
RG62	RG1	5c **gray** *(G.W. Campbell)*	15.00	9.25
a.		Imperf, pair, without gum	*75.00*	
RG63	RG1	8c **gray** *(A.J. Dallas)*	15.00	—
a.		Imperf, pair, without gum	*75.00*	
RG64	RG1	10c **gray** *(Wm. H. Crawford)*	17.50	8.50
a.		Imperf, pair, without gum	*75.00*	
RG65	RG1	20c **gray** *(Richard Rush)*	30.00	7.75
a.		Imperf, pair, without gum	*75.00*	
RG66	RG1	25c **gray** *(S.D. Ingham)*	35.00	—
a.		Imperf, pair, without gum	*75.00*	
RG67	RG1	40c **gray** *(Louis McLane)*	60.00	37.50
a.		Imperf, pair, without gum	*75.00*	
RG68	RG1	50c **gray** *(Wm. J. Duane)*	60.00	32.50
a.		Imperf, pair, without gum	*75.00*	
RG69	RG1	80c **gray** *(Roger B. Taney)*	100.00	32.50
a.		Imperf, pair, without gum	*125.00*	
RG70	RG2	$1 **gray**	125.00	45.00
a.		Imperf, pair, without gum	*600.00*	
RG71	RG2	$2 **gray** *(Thomas Ewing)*	300.00	72.50
a.		Imperf, pair, without gum	*600.00*	
RG72	RG2	$3 **gray** *(Walter Forward)*	300.00	97.50
a.		Imperf, pair, without gum	*600.00*	
RG73	RG2	$4 **gray** *(J.C. Spencer)*	375.00	80.00
a.		Imperf, pair, without gum	*600.00*	
RG74	RG2	$5 **gray** *(G.M. Bibb)*	300.00	95.00
a.		Imperf, pair, without gum	*600.00*	
RG75	RG2	$10 **gray** *(R.J. Walker)*	575.00	97.50
a.		Imperf, pair, without gum	*650.00*	
RG76	RG2	$20 **gray** *(Wm. M. Meredith)*	1,000.	300.00
a.		Imperf, pair, without gum	*2,000.*	

Perf. 12

Without Gum

RG77	RG3	$30 **gray**	*3,500.*	300.
		Cut cancel		125.
a.		Imperf, pair, without gum	—	
RG78	RG3	$50 **gray** *(James Guthrie)*	*6,000.*	*4,000.*
a.		Imperf, pair, without gum	—	
RG79	RG3	$60 **gray** *(Howell Cobb)*	*4,500.*	325.
		Cut cancel		150.
a.		Imperf, pair, without gum	—	
RG80	RG3	$100 **gray** *(P.F. Thomas)*	*7,500.*	500.
		Cut cancel		175.
		Vertical strip of 4		—
a.		Imperf, pair, without gum	—	
RG81	RG3	$500 **gray** *(J.A. Dix)*	—	*37,500.*
a.		Imperf, pair, without gum	—	
RG82	RG3	$1000 **gray** *(S.P. Chase)*	*5,000.*	*2,500.*
		Cut cancel		*1,000.*
a.		Imperf, pair, without gum	—	

Nos. RG58-RG82 Overprinted Instead: **SERIES 1942**

1942		Wmk. 191R	Perf. 11	
RG83	RG1	1c **gray**	3.25	—
RG84	RG1	2c **gray**	3.25	—
RG85	RG1	3c **gray**	3.25	—
RG86	RG1	4c **gray**	3.25	—
RG87	RG1	5c **gray**	3.25	—
RG88	RG1	8c **gray**	8.00	—
RG89	RG1	10c **gray**	8.00	—
RG90	RG1	20c **gray**	15.00	—
RG91	RG1	25c **gray**	26.00	—
RG92	RG1	40c **gray**	35.00	—
RG93	RG1	50c **gray**	40.00	—
RG94	RG1	80c **gray**	100.00	—
RG95	RG2	$1 **gray**	150.00	72.50
a.		Overprint "SERIES 5942"	650.00	
RG96	RG2	$2 **gray**	150.00	72.50
a.		Overprint "SERIES 5942"	1,350.	
RG97	RG2	$3 **gray**	275.00	140.00
a.		Overprint "SERIES 5942"	1,450.	
RG98	RG2	$4 **gray**	300.00	140.00
a.		Overprint "SERIES 5942"	1,450.	
RG99	RG2	$5 **gray**	300.00	175.00
a.		Overprint "SERIES 5942"	1,350.	
RG100	RG2	$10 **gray**	725.00	425.00
RG101	RG2	$20 **gray**	1,000.	—
a.		Overprint "SERIES 5942"	*10,000.*	

Perf. 12

Without Gum

RG102	RG3	$30 **gray**	—	—
		Cut cancel		*2,250.*
RG103	RG3	$50 **gray**	*45,000.*	—
RG104	RG3	$60 **gray**	*7,500.*	*1,750.*
		Cut cancel		750.
RG105	RG3	$100 **gray**	—	2,000.
		Cut cancel		750.
RG106	RG3	$500 **gray**	—	*6,000.*
		Cut cancel		*3,500.*
RG107	RG3	$1000 **gray**	—	*7,500.*
		Cut cancel		*4,000.*

Silver Purchase Stamps of 1941 without Overprint

1944		Wmk. 191R	Perf. 11	
RG108	RG1	1c **gray**	1.00	.30
RG109	RG1	2c **gray**	1.00	.65
RG110	RG1	3c **gray**	1.40	1.00
RG111	RG1	4c **gray**	1.60	1.25
RG112	RG1	5c **gray**	3.25	2.75
RG113	RG1	8c **gray**	5.00	2.75
RG114	RG1	10c **gray**	6.50	3.25
RG115	RG1	20c **gray**	10.00	5.50
RG116	RG1	25c **gray**	16.00	6.00
RG117	RG1	40c **gray**	24.00	11.50
RG118	RG1	50c **gray**	25.00	14.00
RG119	RG1	80c **gray**	32.50	20.00
RG120	RG2	$1 **gray**	67.50	21.00
RG121	RG2	$2 **gray**	95.00	47.50
RG122	RG2	$3 **gray**	125.00	37.50
RG123	RG2	$4 **gray**	150.00	85.00
RG124	RG2	$5 **gray**	150.00	47.50
RG125	RG2	$10 **gray**	225.00	35.00
		Cut cancel		19.00
RG126	RG2	$20 **gray**	800.00	500.00
		Cut cancel		250.00

Perf. 12

Without Gum

RG127	RG3	$30 **gray**	400.00	175.00
		Cut cancel		80.00
		Vertical strip of 4		—
a.		Booklet pane of 4	*7,250.*	
RG128	RG3	$50 **gray**	825.00	675.00
		Cut cancel		350.00
		Vertical strip of 4		—
a.		Booklet pane of 4	*9,500.*	
RG129	RG3	$60 **gray**	*1,500.*	575.00
		Cut cancel		250.00
a.		Booklet pane of 4	*10,000.*	
RG130	RG3	$100 **gray**	—	35.00
		Cut cancel		15.00
		Vertical strip of 4		—
RG131	RG3	$500 **gray**	—	500.00
		Cut cancel		250.00
		With complete receipt tab	*1,050.*	
a.		Booklet pane of 4	*5,500.*	
		Complete booklet, 2 #RG131a	*11,500.*	
RG132	RG3	$1000 **gray**	—	160.00
		Cut cancel		80.00
		Vertical strip of 4		—
		With complete receipt tab	800.00	
a.		Booklet pane of 4	—	
		Complete booklet, 1 #RG132a	*5,000.*	

CIGARETTE TUBES STAMPS

These stamps were for a tax on the hollow tubes of cigarette paper, with or without thin cardboard mouthpieces attached. They were sold i packages so buyers could add loose tobacco to make cigarettes.

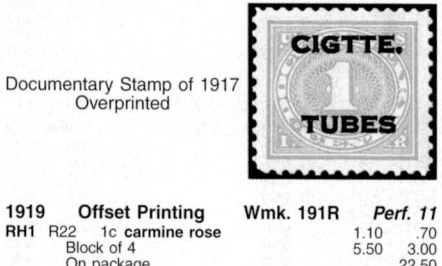

Documentary Stamp of 1917 Overprinted

1919 Offset Printing	**Wmk. 191R**	***Perf. 11***	
RH1 R22 1c **carmine rose**		1.10	.70
Block of 4		5.50	3.00
On package			22.50
Pair on package			45.00
a. Without period		20.00	10.00
On package			—
1929		***Perf. 10***	
RH2 R22 1c **carmine rose**		65.00	11.00
On package			—

RH1

1933 Without Gum	**Wmk. 191R**	***Perf. 11***	
RH3 RH1 1c **rose** (shades)		4.50	2.50
Block of 4		20.00	12.00
On package			22.50
RH4 RH1 2c **rose** (shades)		13.50	5.5
Pair			13.5
On package			110.0

Cigarette tube on-package values for Nos. RH1 and RH3 ar for fine undamaged stamps affixed to an empty package c Himyar Tobacco cigarette tubes manufactured by the Axton Fisher Tobacco Co. Unopened packages containing cigarett tubes command a 50 to 100 percent premium. No. RH1 pair are unseparated stamps. The listing for No. RH1 pair on pack age is not on a Himyar package.

Specialists have questioned whether Nos. RH1a or RH2 ar known on packages. The editors would like to see evidence c the existence of these listings.

POTATO TAX STAMPS

These stamps were required by the Potato Act of 1935, an amendment to the Agricultural Adjustment Act that became effective Dec. 1, 1935.

Potato growers were given allotments for which they were provided Tax Exempt Potato stamps. Growers exceeding their allotments would have paic for the excess with Tax Paid Potato stamps at the rate of ¾ cent per pound.

On Jan. 6, 1936, the U. S. Supreme Court declared the Agricultural Adjustment Act unconstitutional. Officially the Potato Act was in effect until Feb 10, 1936, when it was repealed by Congress but, in essence, the law was ignored once the Supreme Court ruling was issued.

Because of the Act's short life, Tax Paid stamps were never used.

Young Woman from *The Bouquet* — RI1

RI2

Tax Paid Potatoes

1935	**Engr.**	**Unwmk.**	***Perf. 11***
RI1 RI1	¾c **carmine rose**		.50
RI2 RI1	1½c **black brown**		.70
RI3 RI1	2¼c **yellow green**		.75
RI4 RI1	3c **light violet**		.80
RI5 RI1	3¾c **olive bister**		.95
RI6 RI1	7½c **orange brown**		2.75
RI7 RI1	11¼c **deep orange**		3.00
RI8 RI1	18¾c **violet brown**		7.50
RI9 RI1	37½c **red orange**		8.00
RI10 RI1	75c **blue**		8.50
RI11 RI1	93¾c **rose lake**		10.00
RI12 RI1	$1.12½ **green**		17.50
RI13 RI1	$1.50 **yellow brown**		20.00
	Nos. RI1-RI13 (13)		80.95

Tax Exempt Potatoes

1935 Engr.	**Unwmk.**	***Perf. 11x10½***	
RI14 RI2 2 lb **black brown**		1.00	*10.50*
a. Booklet pane of 12		14.00	*250.00*
Provisional booklet of 24, purple on pink cover		35.00	
Provisional booklet of 96, purple on buff cover		100.00	
Provisional booklet of 192, purple on white cover		300.00	
Definitive booklet of 96, black on buff cover		100.00	
Definitive booklet of 192, black on white cover		200.00	
RI15 RI2 5 lb **black brown**		22.50	
a. Booklet pane of 12		*500.00*	
Provisional booklet of 192, purple on white cover		*5,000.*	
RI16 RI2 10 lb **black brown**		22.50	
a. Booklet pane of 12		*450.00*	
Provisional booklet of 192, purple on white cover		*5,000.*	
RI17 RI2 25 lb **black brown**		*600.00*	
a. Booklet pane of 12		*7,000.*	
Provisional booklet of 24, purple on pink cover		*5,000.*	
RI18 RI2 50 lb **black brown**		1.10	*50.00*
a. Booklet pane of 12		25.00	
Provisional booklet of 24, purple on pink cover		50.00	
Provisional booklet of 96, purple on buff cover		150.00	
Provisional booklet of 192, purple on white cover		300.00	
Definitive booklet of 96, black on buff cover		100.00	
Definitive booklet of 192, black on white cover		200.00	
Nos. RI14-RI16,RI18 (4)		*47.10*	

The booklet panes are arranged 4x3 with a tab at top. Edges are imperforate at left, right and bottom, yielding four stamps fully perforated, six stamps imperf. on one side and two stamps imperf. on two sides per pane.

These stamps were printed from 360-subject rotary booklet plates and cut into 30 panes of 12. The panes were stapled into booklets of 24 (2 panes, pink covers), 96 (8 panes, buff covers) and 196 (16 panes, white covers), with handstamped covers (provisionals) and later with covers printed with the Dept. of Agriculture seal in the center (definitives). Both types of cover were prepared by the Bureau of Engraving and Printing.

Values for booklets are for examples containing panes that have very good to fine centering, because the overwhelming majority of booklets are in this grade. It should be noted that Scott values for individual panes (listed above) are for very fine panes. For this reason, individual panes are valued higher than the per-pane value of panes in booklets. For example, a pane of No. RI14a is valued at $14, but the No. RI14 definitive booklet of 96 (8 panes) is valued at $100, or $12.50 per pane, which is a little more than what a collector would pay for an individual very good to fine pane. Booklets containing very fine panes will command a premium over the values given.

All recorded examples of No. RI17 were in three unbroken panes of 12 and two intact booklets. One pane has been broken up and sold. A 100 lb Tax Exempt stamp was printed, but all are believed to have been destroyed.

TOBACCO SALE TAX STAMPS

These stamps were required to pay the tax on the sale of tobacco in excess of quotas set by the Secretary of Agriculture. The tax was 25 per cent of the price for which the excess tobacco was sold. It was intended to affect tobacco harvested after June 28, 1934 and sold before May 1, 1936. The tax was stopped when the Agricultural Adjustment Act was declared unconstitutional by the Supreme Court on Dec. 1, 1935.

Values for unused stamps are for examples with original gum.

Stamps and Types of 1917 Documentary Issue Overprinted

1934 Offset Printing Wmk. 191R *Perf. 11*

RJ1	R22	1c **carmine rose**	.30	.20
RJ2	R22	2c **carmine rose**	.40	.20
RJ3	R22	5c **carmine rose**	1.25	.45
RJ4	R22	10c **carmine rose**	1.60	.40
a.		Inverted overprint	15.00	*22.50*
RJ5	R22	25c **carmine rose**	4.25	1.60
RJ6	R22	50c **carmine rose**	4.25	1.60

Engr.

RJ7	R21	$1 **green**	10.00	1.75
RJ8	R21	$2 **rose**	19.00	1.90
RJ9	R21	$5 **dark blue**	24.00	4.25
RJ10	R21	$10 **orange**	37.50	10.00
RJ11	R21	$20 **olive bister**	90.00	12.50
		Nos. RJ1-RJ11 (11)	192.55	34.85

On No. RJ11 the overprint is vertical, reading up.

The right serif on the "T" of "TOBACCO" exists both normal and split. Both varieties exist within the same sheet, and the quantities of each type are approximately equal.

No. RJ2 is known with a counterfeit inverted overprint.

NARCOTIC TAX STAMPS

The Revenue Act of 1918 imposed a tax of 1 cent per ounce or fraction thereof on opium, coca leaves and their derivatives. The tax was paid by affixing Narcotic stamps to the drug containers. The tax lasted from Feb. 25, 1919, through Apr. 30, 1971.

Members of the American Revenue Association helped compile the listings in this section.

Documentary Stamps of 1914 Handstamped "NARCOTIC" in Magenta or Black

1919 Wmk. 191R Offset Printing *Perf. 10*

RJA1	R20	1c **rose**	95.00	80.00

The overprint was applied by District Collectors of Internal Revenue.

It is always in capital letters and exists in various type faces and sizes, including: 21½x2½mm, serif; 21x2¼mm, sans-serif boldface; 15½x 2½mm, sans-serif; 13x2mm, sans-serif.

The ½c, 2c, 3c, 4c, 5c, 10c, 25c and 50c with similar handstamp in serif capitals measuring about 20x2¼mm are bogus.

Documentary Stamps of 1917 Handstamped "NARCOTIC," "Narcotic," "NARCOTICS" or "ACT/NARCOTIC/1918" in Magenta, Black, Blue, Violet or Red

1919 Wmk. 191R Offset Printing *Perf. 11*

RJA9	R22	1c **carmine rose**	3.00	1.90
RJA10	R22	2c **carmine rose**	6.00	4.00
RJA11	R22	3c **carmine rose**	35.00	37.50
RJA12	R22	4c **carmine rose**	13.00	10.00
RJA13	R22	5c **carmine rose**	20.00	16.00
RJA14	R22	8c **carmine rose**	16.00	12.50
RJA15	R22	10c **carmine rose**	52.50	20.00
RJA16	R22	20c **carmine rose**	*77.50*	*60.00*
RJA17	R22	25c **carmine rose**	47.50	32.50
RJA18	R22	40c **carmine rose**	*150.00*	*110.00*
RJA19	R22	50c **carmine rose**	20.00	*22.50*
RJA20	R22	80c **carmine rose**	*125.00*	*110.00*

Engr.

RJA21	R21	$1 **green**	110.00	60.00
RJA22	R21	$2 **rose**		*1,000.*
RJA23	R21	$3 **violet**		*1,200.*
RJA24	R21	$5 **dark blue**		*1,000.*
RJA25	R21	$10 **orange**		*1,200.*

Drug manufacturer cancels have enabled experts to identify conclusively the origin of only six of the handstamped overprints. Four of these read simply "Narcotic." A 3-line handstamp, "Act / Narcotic / 1918," was used in Seattle; "Narcotics" in Kansas City, Missouri. Perhaps as many as 20 other styles and sizes have been recorded, although these occur only on mint stamps.

Many fake overprints exist.

No. R228 Overprinted in Black: "NARCOTIC / E.L. CO. / 3-19-19"

1919 Wmk. 191R *Perf. 11*

"NARCOTIC" 14½mm wide

RJA26	R22	1c **carmine rose**	*3,750.*

Overprinted by Eli Lilly Co., Indianapolis, for that firm's use.

No. R228 Overprinted in Black: "J W & B / NARCOTIC"

1919 Wmk. 191R *Perf. 11*

"NARCOTIC" 14½mm wide

RJA27	R22	1c **carmine rose**	*2,000.*
RJA27A	R22	2c **carmine rose**	*3,250.*

Overprinted by John Wyeth & Brother, Philadelphia, for that firm's use.

Nos. R228, R231-R232 Handstamped in Blue: "P-W-R-Co. / NARCOTIC"

1919 Wmk. 191R *Perf. 11*

RJA28	R22	1c **carmine rose**	*750.00*
RJA28A	R22	4c **carmine rose**	*1,200.*
RJA29	R22	5c **carmine rose**	—
RJA29A	R22	25c **carmine rose**	—
RJA29B	R21	$1 **green** (violet handstamp)	—

The handstamp was applied by the Powers-Weightmann-Rosengarten Co., Philadelphia, for that firm's use.

Proprietary Stamps of 1919 Handstamped "NARCOTIC" in Blue

1919 Wmk. 191R Offset Printing *Perf. 11*

RJA30	RB5	1c **dark blue**	—	—
RJA31	RB5	2c **dark blue**	—	
RJA32	RB5	4c **dark blue**	—	

No. RB65 is known with "Narcotic" applied in red ms.

Documentary Stamps of 1917 Overprinted in Black, "Narcotic" 17½mm wide

1919 Wmk. 191R Offset Printing *Perf. 11*

RJA33	R22	1c **carmine rose** *(6,900,000)*	1.25	.80
RJA34	R22	2c **carmine rose** *(3,650,000)*	2.50	1.10
RJA35	R22	3c **carmine rose** *(388,400)*	40.00	21.00
RJA36	R22	4c **carmine rose** *(2,400,000)*	6.00	4.75
RJA37	R22	5c **carmine rose** *(2,400,000)*	15.00	10.50
RJA38	R22	8c **carmine rose** *(1,200,000)*	25.00	18.00
RJA39	R22	10c **carmine rose** *(3,400,000)*	3.75	2.75
RJA40	R22	25c **carmine rose** *(700,000)*	25.00	16.00

Overprint Reading Up

Engr.

RJA41	R21	$1 **green** *(270,000)*	47.50	19.00

The overprint on Nos. RJA33-RJA41 was produced by the Bureau of Engraving & Printing. Fake overprints exist on Nos. RJA33-RJA41. In the genuine the C's are not slanted.

NT1

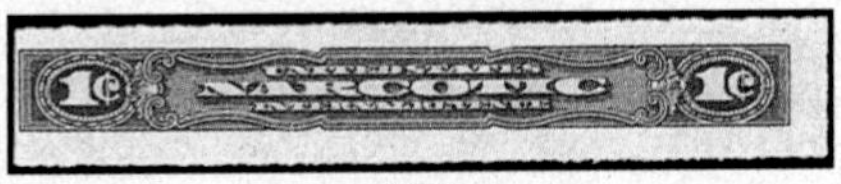

NT2

Imperf., Roulette d

1919-64 Offset Printing Wmk. 191R

Left Value — "a" Imperf.

Right Value — "b" Rouletted 7

RJA42	NT1	1c **violet**	5.25	.25
d.		1c purple	—	7.50
RJA43	NT2	1c **violet**	.55	.30
d.		1c purple	5.00	5.25
RJA44	NT2	2c **violet**	1.40	.55
d.		2c purple		5.25
RJA45	NT2	3c **violet** ('64)		125.00

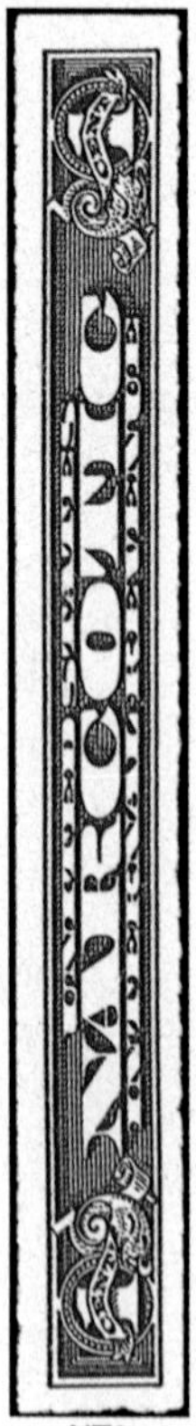
NT3

NT4

Left Value — "a" Imperf.
Right Value — "b" Rouletted 7

RJA46	NT3	1c	**violet**	2.75	.70
d.		1c	**purple**		9.00
RJA47	NT3	2c	**violet**	1.60	.70
d.		2c	**purple**		8.25
RJA48	NT3	3c	**violet**	750.00	
RJA49	NT3	4c	**violet** ('42)	—	10.00
d.		4c	**purple**	—	30.00
RJA50	NT3	5c	**violet**	42.50	3.50
d.		5c	**purple**		13.00
RJA51	NT3	6c	**violet**		.90
d.		6c	**purple**		9.25
RJA52	NT3	8c	**violet**	57.50	4.00
d.		8c	**purple**		26.00
RJA53	NT3	9c	**violet** ('53)	67.50	21.00
RJA54	NT3	10c	**violet**	32.50	.50
d.		10c	**purple**		7.00
RJA55	NT3	16c	**violet**	52.50	4.00
d.		16c	**purple**		14.50
RJA56	NT3	18c	**violet** ('61)	110.00	10.50
RJA57	NT3	19c	**violet** ('61)	125.00	26.00
RJA58	NT3	20c	**violet**	375.00	250.00

Nos. RJA47-RJA58 have "CENTS" below the value.

Left Value — "a" Imperf.
Right Value — "b" Rouletted 7

RJA59	NT4	1c	**violet**	47.50	10.50
c.			Rouletted 3½		4.25
RJA60	NT4	2c	**violet**	50.00	20.00
RJA61	NT4	3c	**violet**	52.50	350.00
RJA62	NT4	5c	**violet**		26.00
RJA63	NT4	6c	**violet**	62.50	21.00
RJA64	NT4	8c	**violet**		47.50
RJA65	NT4	9c	**violet** ('61)	26.00	21.00
RJA66	NT4	10c	**violet**	15.00	15.00
RJA67	NT4	16c	**violet**	16.00	10.00
RJA68	NT4	18c	**violet** ('61)	250.00	425.00
RJA69	NT4	19c	**violet**	16.00	190.00
RJA70	NT4	20c	**violet**	150.00	240.00
RJA71	NT4	25c	**violet**	—	21.00
c.			Rouletted 3½		4.25
RJA72	NT4	40c	**violet**	800.00	*2,500.*
c.			Rouletted 3½		67.50
RJA73	NT4	$1	**green**		1.60
RJA74	NT4	$1.28	**green**	32.50	10.50
c.			As "a," measuring ¾ inch by 8 inches with wide side margins	*200.00*	
d.			As "b," measuring ¾ inch by 8 inches with wide side margins	*100.00*	

On Nos. RJA60-RJA74 the value tablet is solid.

1963(?)-70 Offset Printing ***Imperf., Rouletted***
Unwatermarked
Left Value — "a" Imperf.
Right Value — "b" Rouletted 7

RJA75	NT1	1c	**violet**	7.75	2.10+
RJA76	NT2	1c	**violet**	1.10	1.10
RJA77	NT2	2c	**violet**	5.25	2.10+
RJA78	NT2	3c	**violet**		125.00
RJA79	NT3	1c	**violet**	5.25	2.10
RJA80	NT3	2c	**violet**	375.00+	2.00
RJA81	NT3	4c	**violet**		10.00
RJA82	NT3	5c	**violet**	72.50	
RJA83	NT3	6c	**violet**	—	20.00+
RJA84	NT3	8c	**violet**		5.25
RJA85	NT3	9c	**violet**	—	50.00
RJA86	NT3	10c	**violet**	—	20.00+
RJA87	NT3	16c	**violet**	150.00	4.25
RJA88	NT3	18c	**violet**	—	52.50+
RJA89	NT3	20c	**violet**		325.00+

Nos. RJA80-RJA89 have "CENTS" below the value.
+ Items so marked currently are only known unused with original gum and are valued thus.

Unwatermarked
Left Value — "a" Imperf.
Right Value — "b" Rouletted 7

RJA91	NT4	1c	**violet**	67.50	15.00
RJA92	NT4	2c	**violet**		75.00+
RJA93	NT4	3c	**violet**	85.00	150.00+
RJA94	NT4	6c	**violet**	100.00	75.00+
RJA94C	NT4	8c	**violet**		225.00+
RJA95	NT4	9c	**violet**		200.00+
RJA96	NT4	10c	**violet**		100.00+
RJA97	NT4	16c	**violet**	40.00	21.00
RJA98	NT4	19c	**violet**	26.00	400.00
RJA99	NT4	20c	**violet**	—	500.00+
RJA100	NT4	25c	**violet**		250.00
RJA101	NT4	40c	**violet**	*1,000.*	
RJA102	NT4	$1	**green**		37.50+
RJA103	NT4	$1.28	**green**		60.00+
d.			As "b," measuring ¾ inch by 8 inches with wide side margins	125.00+	
RJA104	NT4	$4	**green** ('70)	*1,000.*	

On Nos. RJA92-RJA104 the value tablet is solid.
+ Items so marked currently are only known unused with original gum and are valued thus.

NT5

Denomination added in black by rubber plate in an operation similar to precanceling.

1963 Engr. Unwmk. ***Imperf.***
Left Value — Unused
Right Value — Used

RJA105	NT5	1c	**violet,** type 2	110.00	85.00
a.			Type 1	*140.00*	*140.00*

Type 1 was produced with four electric eye markings, one in each corner. Type 2 was produced later and has two electric eye markings, one in each corner on the left side of the stamp. Type 2 is the more common of the two varieties and, therefore, is listed as the major number.

Nos. RAJ105 and RAJ105a were issued in vertical coil strips.

Denomination on Stamp Plate

1964 Offset Printing ***Imperf.***

RJA106	NT5	1c	**violet**	90.00	5.25

RJA106 was issued in sheet of 80 stamps.

MARIHUANA TAX STAMPS

Act of Congress, 1937, to enforce uniform regulation of cannabis.

Nos. R240, R244, R245 overprinted

1937 Engr. ***Perf. 10***

RJM1	R21	$1	**yellow green**	*550.*	*15,000.*
			On document		—
			P# block of 6	*3,750.*	
a.			Imperf, pair	*1,200.*	
RJM2	R21	$5	**blue**	*550.*	
			P# block of 6	*3,750.*	
a.			Imperf, pair	*1,200.*	
RJM3	R21	$10	**yellow orange**	*550.*	
			P# block of 6	*3,750.*	
a.			Imperf, pair	*1,200.*	

Same overprint on No. R248

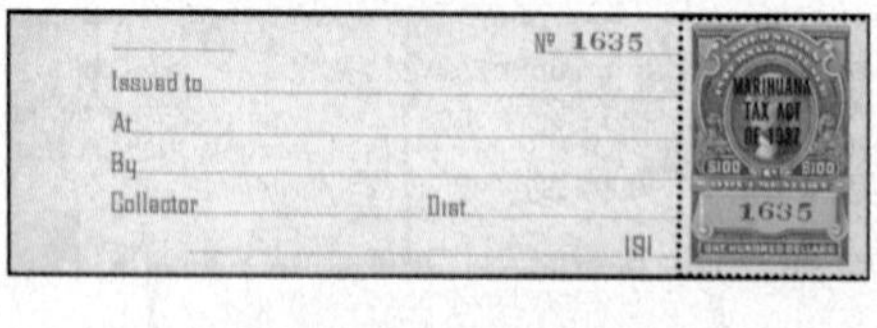

(Illustration reduced)

Without Gum ***Perf. 12***
Control Number in Red

RJM4	R17	$100	**green,** with complete receipt tab	*750.*
a.			Booklet pane of 4	*3,000.*
			Complete booklet, 4 #RJM4a	*12,500.*

Nos. R300, R304, R305 without date inscription overprinted:

1962 ***Perf. 11***

RJM5	R24	$1	**carmine**	*550.00*
RJM6	R24	$5	**carmine**	*550.00*
RJM7	R24	$10	**carmine**	*550.00*

No. R306A without date inscription overprinted:

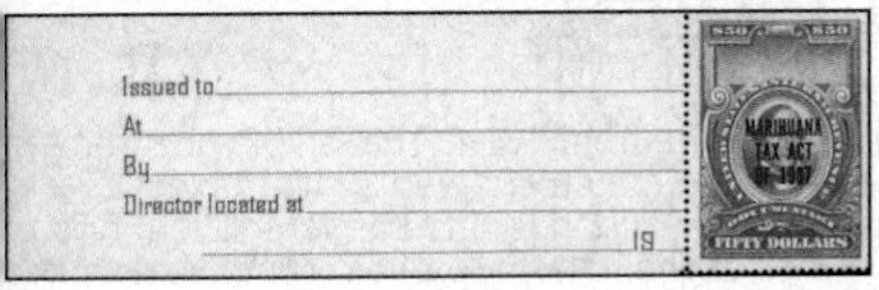

(Illustration reduced)

RJM8	R25	$50 **carmine,** with complete receipt tab, no serial #	*1,500.*
a.		Booklet pane of 4	*6,000.*

CONSULAR SERVICE FEE STAMPS

Act of Congress, April 5, 1906, effective June 1, 1906, provided that every consular officer should be provided with special adhesive stamps printed in denominations determined by the Department of State.

Every document for which a fee was prescribed had to have attached a stamp or stamps representing the amount collected, and such stamps were used to show payment of these prescribed fees.

These stamps were usually affixed close to the signature, or at the lower left corner of the document. If no document was issued, the stamp or stamps were attached to a receipt for the amount of the fee and canceled either with pen and ink or rubber stamp showing the date of cancellation and bearing the initials of the canceling officer or name of the Consular Office. These stamps were not sold to the public uncanceled. Their use was discontinued Sept. 30, 1955.

CSF1

CSF2

1906 **Unwmk.** **Engr.** *Perf. 12*

RK1	CSF1	25c **dark green**	100.00
RK2	CSF1	50c **carmine**	125.00
RK3	CSF1	$1 **dark violet**	11.00
a.		Diagonal half used as 50c with 2 #RK3, paying $2.50 fee, on document	*325.00*
RK4	CSF1	$2 **brown**	6.00
RK5	CSF1	$2.50 **dark blue**	1.90
RK6	CSF1	$5 **brown red**	35.00
a.		Horizontal or diagonal half used as $2.50, on document	*250.00*
RK7	CSF1	$10 **orange**	110.00

Perf. 10

RK8	CSF1	25c **dark green**	100.00
RK9	CSF1	50c **carmine**	125.00
RK10	CSF1	$1 **dark violet**	575.00
RK11	CSF1	$2 **brown**	140.00
a.		Diagonal half used as $1, on document	—
RK12	CSF1	$2.50 **dark blue**	30.00
RK13	CSF1	$5 **brown red**	225.00

Perf. 11

RK14	CSF1	25c **dark green**	110.00
RK15	CSF1	50c **carmine**	175.00
RK16	CSF1	$1 **dark violet**	2.00
a.		Diagonal half used as 50c, on document	*375.00*
RK17	CSF1	$2 **brown**	2.40
RK18	CSF1	$2.50 **dark blue**	.95
RK19	CSF1	$5 **brown red**	5.00
a.		Diagonal half used as $2.50, on document	50.00
RK20	CSF1	$9 **gray**	27.50
RK21	CSF1	$10 **orange**	55.00
a.		Diagonal half used as $5, on document	90.00

1924 *Perf. 11*

RK22	CSF2	$1 **violet**	140.00
RK23	CSF2	$2 **brown**	160.00
RK24	CSF2	$2.50 **blue**	25.00
RK25	CSF2	$5 **brown red**	110.00
RK26	CSF2	$9 **gray**	450.00
		Nos. RK22-RK26 (5)	885.00

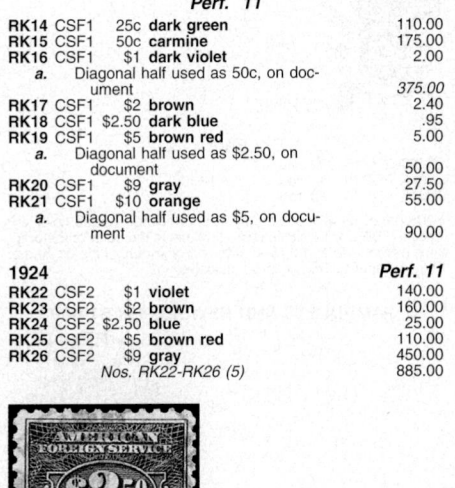

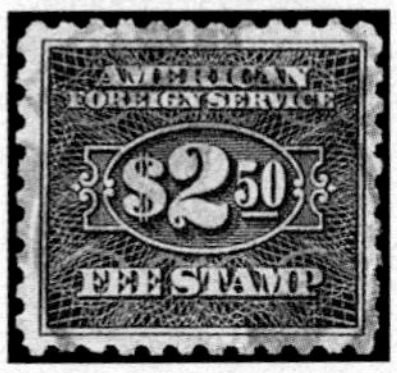

CSF3

1925-52 *Perf. 10*

RK27	CSF3	$1 **violet**	40.00
RK28	CSF3	$2 **brown**	100.00
RK29	CSF3	$2.50 **ultramarine**	2.75
RK30	CSF3	$5 **carmine**	22.50
RK31	CSF3	$9 **gray**	67.50

Perf. 11

RK32	CSF3	25c **green** ('37)	110.00
RK33	CSF3	50c **orange** ('34)	110.00
RK34	CSF3	$1 **violet**	3.75
a.		Diagonal half used as 50c, on document	—
RK35	CSF3	$2 **brown**	5.00
RK36	CSF3	$2.50 **blue**	.45
a.		$2.50 ultramarine	.40
RK37	CSF3	$5 **carmine**	3.25
RK38	CSF3	$9 **gray**	30.00
RK39	CSF3	$10 **blue gray** ('37)	150.00
RK40	CSF3	$20 **violet** ('52)	160.00
		Nos. RK27-RK40 (14)	805.20

Consular Fee

The "Consular Fee stamp" on revenue stamped paper (previously listed as No. RN-Y1 but since deleted) was found to be nothing more than an illustration. Two identical copies are known.

CUSTOMS FEE STAMPS

New York Custom House

Issued to indicate the collection of miscellaneous customs fees. Use was discontinued on February 28, 1918. The stamps were not utilized in the collection of customs duties.

Silas Wright CF1

Size: 48x34mm

1887 **Engr.** *Rouletted 5½*

RL1	CF1	20c **dull rose**	125.00	1.00
a.		20c **red,** perf. 10		*7,500.*
b.		Vert. half used as 10c, on document		*250.00*
c.		20c **red,** rouletted 7		*450.00*
RL2	CF1	30c **orange**	175.00	2.50
RL3	CF1	40c **green**	200.00	4.25
RL4	CF1	50c **dark blue**	200.00	6.00
RL5	CF1	60c **red violet**	150.00	2.50
RL6	CF1	70c **brown violet**	160.00	35.00
RL7	CF1	80c **brown**	225.00	85.00
RL8	CF1	90c **black**	275.00	100.00
		Nos. RL1-RL8 (8)	1,510.	236.25

Each of these stamps has its own distinctive background.

EMBOSSED REVENUE STAMPED PAPER

Some of the American colonies of Great Britain used embossed stamps in raising revenue, as Britain had done from 1694. The British government also imposed stamp taxes on the colonies, and in the early 19th century the U.S. government and some of the states enacted similar taxes.

Under one statute or another, these stamps were required on such documents as promissory notes, bills of exchange, insurance policies, bills of lading, bonds, protests, powers of attorney, stock certificates, letters patent, writs, conveyances, leases, mortgages, charter parties, commissions and liquor licenses.

A few of these stamps were printed, but most were colorless impressions resembling a notary public's seal.

The scant literature of these stamps includes E.B. Sterling's revenue catalogue of 1888, *The Stamps that Caused the American Revolution: The Stamps of the British Stamp Act for America,* by Adolph Koeppel, published in 1976 by the Town of North Hempstead (New York) American Revolution Bicentennial Commission, *New Discovery from British Archives on the 1765 Tax Stamps for America,* edited by Adolph Koeppel and published in 1962 by the American Revenue Association, *First Federal Issue 1798-1801 U.S. Embossed Revenue Stamped Paper,* by W.V. Combs, published in 1979 by the American Philatelic Society, *Second Federal Issue, 1801-1802,* by W.V. Combs, published in 1988 by the American Revenue Association, and *Third Federal Issue, 1814-1817,* by W.V. Combs, published in 1993 by the American Revenue Association.

Values are for stamps of clear impression on entire documents of the most common usage in good condition. The document may be folded. Unusual or rare usages may sell for much more. Parts of documents, cut squares or poor impressions sell for much less.

Colin MacR. Makepeace originally compiled the listings in this section.

INCLUDING COLONIAL EMBOSSED REVENUES

I. COLONIAL ISSUES

A. MASSACHUSETTS

Act of January 8, 1755
In effect May 1, 1755-April 30, 1757

ERP1

ERP2

ERP3

ERP4

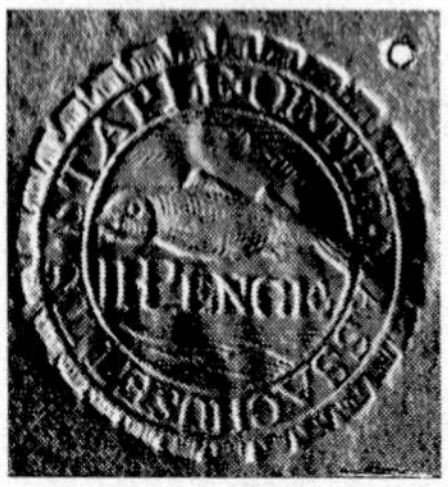
Die 2 — ERP2

Typo.

RM1	ERP1	½p	**red**	*2,300.*

Embossed

RM2	ERP2	2p	400.
RM3	ERP3	3p	200.
RM4	ERP4	4p	800.

A second die of ERP2 with no fin on the under side of the codfish has been seen. There were at least two dies of the ½p.

B. NEW YORK

Act of December 1, 1756
In effect January 1, 1757-December 31, 1760

ERP9

Typo.

RM9	ERP9	½p	**red**	*2,250.*

Embossed

RM10	ERP9	1p	525.
RM11	ERP9	2p	300.
RM12	ERP9	3p	450.
RM13	ERP9	4p	375.

II. BRITISH REVENUES FOR USE IN AMERICA

Act of March 22, 1765
In effect November 1, 1765-May 1, 1766.

A. ALMANAC STAMPS

ERP15

Engr.

RM15	ERP15	2p	**red**	
RM16	ERP15	4p	**red**	—
RM17	ERP15	8p	**red**	

Proofs of all of these stamps printed in the issued color are known. Full size facsimile reproductions in the color of the originals were made about 1876 of the proof sheets of the 8p stamp, Plates 1 and 2, Dies 1 to 50 inclusive.

B. PAMPHLETS AND NEWSPAPER STAMPS

ERP18

Engr.

RM18	ERP18	½p	**red**	*2,000.*
RM19	ERP18	1p	**red**	—
RM20	ERP18	2p	**red**	

Proofs of all of these stamps printed in the issued color are known. Full size facsimile reproductions in the color of the originals were made about 1876 of the proof sheets of the 1p stamp, Plates 3 and 4, Dies 51 to 100 inclusive.

C. GENERAL ISSUE

ERP24

ERP25

ERP26

ERP27

ERP28

ERP29

ERP30

ERP31

ERP33

ERP34

ERP35

Embossed

RM24	ERP24	3p	*3,000.*
RM25	ERP25	4p	*3,000.*
RM26	ERP26	6p	*3,000.*
RM27	ERP27	1sh	*1,750.*
RM28	ERP28	1sh6p	*1,250.*
RM29	ERP29	2sh	*3,000.*
RM30	ERP30	2sh3p	*1,800.*
RM31	ERP31	2sh6p	*2,000.*
a.		Not on document	450.
RM33	ERP33	4sh	*1,750.*
RM34	ERP34	5sh	*2,500.*
RM35	ERP35	10sh	*3,250.*

Proofs exist of similar 1sh, 1sh6p and 2sh6p stamps inscribed "AMERICA CONT.& c."

Various Similar Designs

RM36	£1	
RM37	£2	—
RM38	£3	—
RM39	£4	
RM40	£6	—
RM41	£10	—

The £1 to £10 denominations probably exist only as proofs.

D. PLAYING CARDS STAMP

Type similar to EP29, with Arms of George III Encircled by Garter.

RM42	1sh	—

All of these were embossed without color and most of them were embossed directly on the document except the 2sh 6p which was general embossed on a rectangular piece of bluish or brownish stiff paper or cardboard only slightly larger than the stamp which was attached to the document by a small piece of metal. Three dies exist of the 3p; two of the 4p, 6p, 1sh, 1sh 6p, 2sh and 2sh 3p.

All of these stamps have the word "America" somewhere in the design and this is the feature which distinguishes them from the other British revenues. The stamps of the general issue are occasionally found with a design of a British revenue stamp struck over the American design, as a number of them were afterwards re-struck and used elsewhere as British revenues.

These stamps are sometimes called the "Teaparty" or "Tax on Tea" stamps. This, however, is a misnomer, as the act under which these stamps were issued laid no tax on tea. The tax on tea was levied by an act passed two years later, and the duties imposed by that act were not collected by stamps.

It must be remembered that these stamps were issued under an act applicable to all of the British colonies in America which included many which are not now part of the United States. Examples have been seen which were used in Quebec, Nova Scotia and in the West Indies. So great was the popular clamor against taxation by a body in which the colonists had no representation that ships bringing the stamps from England were not allowed to land them in some of the colonies, the stamps were destroyed in others, and in practically all of those which are now a part of the United States the "Stamp Masters" who were to administer the act were forced to resign and to take oath that they would never carry out the duties of the offices. Notwithstanding the very general feeling about these stamps there is evidence that a very small number of them were actually used on ships' documents for one vessel clearing from New York and for a very small number of vessels clearing from the Savannah River. Florida was at this time under British authority and the only known examples of these stamps used in what is now the United States, a 4p (#RM25), a 1sh (#RM27), and two examples of the 5sh (#RM34) were used there.

III. ISSUES OF THE UNITED STATES

A. FIRST FEDERAL ISSUE

Act of July 6, 1797

In effect July 1, 1798-February 28, 1801

The distinguishing feature of the stamps of this issue is the name of a state in the design. These stamps were issued by the Federal Government, however, and not by the states. The design, with the exception of the name of the state, was the same for each denomination; but different denominations had the shield and the eagle in different positions. The design of only one denomination of these stamps is illustrated.

In addition to the eagle and shield design on the values from four cents to ten dollars there are two other stamps for each state, similar in design to one another, one of which is illustrated. All of these stamps are embossed without color.

Values are for clearly impressed examples.

RM45	4c	Connecticut	45.00
RM46	10c	Connecticut	125.00
RM47	20c	Connecticut	300.00
RM48	25c	Connecticut	45.00
RM49	30c	Connecticut	*2,750.*
RM50	50c	Connecticut	135.00
RM51	75c	Connecticut	—
RM52	$1	Connecticut	*1,750.*
RM54	$4	Connecticut	*1,250.*
RM58	4c	Delaware	350.00
RM59	10c	Delaware	350.00
RM60	20c	Delaware	500.00
RM61	25c	Delaware	450.00
RM62	30c	Delaware	—
RM63	50c	Delaware	550.00
RM64	75c	Delaware	700.00
RM65	$1	Delaware	—
RM71	4c	Georgia	250.00
RM72	10c	Georgia	250.00
RM73	20c	Georgia	—
RM74	25c	Georgia	250.00
RM75	30c	Georgia	*3,000.*
RM76	50c	Georgia	400.00
RM77	75c	Georgia	*1,750.*
RM78	$1	Georgia	—
RM84	4c	Kentucky	20.00
RM85	10c	Kentucky	75.00
RM86	20c	Kentucky	250.00
RM87	25c	Kentucky	40.00
RM88	30c	Kentucky	275.00
RM89	50c	Kentucky	50.00
RM90	75c	Kentucky	125.00
RM91	$1	Kentucky	—
RM97	4c	Maryland	75.00
RM98	10c	Maryland	50.00
RM99	20c	Maryland	700.00
RM100	25c	Maryland	75.00
RM101	30c	Maryland	600.00
RM102	50c	Maryland	125.00
RM103	75c	Maryland	50.00
RM104	$1	Maryland	—
RM106	$4	Maryland	—
RM110	4c	Massachusetts	20.00
RM111	10c	Massachusetts	50.00
RM112	20c	Massachusetts	100.00
RM113	25c	Massachusetts	35.00
RM114	30c	Massachusetts	950.00
RM115	50c	Massachusetts	125.00
RM116	75c	Massachusetts	400.00
RM117	$1	Massachusetts	200.00
RM123	4c	New Hampshire	25.00
RM124	10c	New Hampshire	25.00
RM125	20c	New Hampshire	350.00
RM126	25c	New Hampshire	70.00
RM127	30c	New Hampshire	425.00
RM128	50c	New Hampshire	80.00
RM129	75c	New Hampshire	75.00
RM130	$1	New Hampshire	*2,500.*
RM136	4c	New Jersey	400.00
RM137	10c	New Jersey	175.00
RM138	20c	New Jersey	—
RM139	25c	New Jersey	110.00
RM140	30c	New Jersey	750.00
RM141	50c	New Jersey	200.00
RM142	75c	New Jersey	—
RM143	$1	New Jersey	—
RM147	$10	New Jersey	*4,750.*
RM149	4c	New York	35.00
RM150	10c	New York	20.00
RM151	20c	New York	25.00
RM152	25c	New York	40.00
RM153	30c	New York	25.00
RM154	50c	New York	30.00
RM155	75c	New York	35.00
RM156	$1	New York	350.00
RM157	$2	New York	—
RM159	$5	New York	—
RM160	$10	New York	—
RM162	4c	North Carolina	45.00
RM163	10c	North Carolina	50.00
RM164	20c	North Carolina	950.00
RM165	25c	North Carolina	55.00
RM166	30c	North Carolina	2,500.
RM167	50c	North Carolina	175.00
RM168	75c	North Carolina	325.00
RM169	$1	North Carolina	*3,750.*
RM175	4c	Pennsylvania	30.00
RM176	10c	Pennsylvania	20.00
RM177	20c	Pennsylvania	27.50
RM178	25c	Pennsylvania	15.00
RM179	30c	Pennsylvania	30.00
RM180	50c	Pennsylvania	25.00
RM181	75c	Pennsylvania	75.00
RM182	$1	Pennsylvania	300.00
RM184	$4	Pennsylvania	13,000.
RM187		Pennsylvania, "Ten cents per centum"	—
RM188	4c	Rhode Island	35.00
RM189	10c	Rhode Island	50.00
RM190	20c	Rhode Island	200.00
RM191	25c	Rhode Island	65.00
RM192	30c	Rhode Island	1,500.
RM193	50c	Rhode Island	150.00
RM194	75c	Rhode Island	*1,000.*
RM195	$1	Rhode Island	*1,750.*
RM201	4c	South Carolina	90.00
RM202	10c	South Carolina	200.00
RM203	20c	South Carolina	350.00
RM204	25c	South Carolina	125.00
RM205	30c	South Carolina	—
RM206	50c	South Carolina	175.00
RM207	75c	South Carolina	*4,000.*
RM208	$1	South Carolina	*6,000.*
RM211	$5	South Carolina	—
RM214	4c	Tennessee	350.00
RM215	10c	Tennessee	200.00
RM216	20c	Tennessee	—
RM217	25c	Tennessee	275.00
RM218	30c	Tennessee	—
RM219	50c	Tennessee	*900.00*
RM220	75c	Tennessee	—
RM221	$1	Tennessee	—
RM227	4c	Vermont	75.00
RM228	10c	Vermont	35.00
RM229	20c	Vermont	350.00
RM230	25c	Vermont	100.00
RM231	30c	Vermont	*1,350.*
RM232	50c	Vermont	130.00
RM233	75c	Vermont	*3,000.*
RM234	$1	Vermont	—
RM238	$10	Vermont	—
RM240	4c	Virginia	15.00
RM241	10c	Virginia	20.00
RM242	20c	Virginia	125.00
RM243	25c	Virginia	20.00
RM244	30c	Virginia	500.00
RM245	50c	Virginia	25.00
RM246	75c	Virginia	50.00
RM247	$1	Virginia	*1,000.*

The Act called for a $2, $4, $5 and $10 stamp for each state; only the listed ones have been seen.

The Act also called for a "Ten cents per centum" and a "Six mills per dollar" stamp for each state, none of which has been seen except No. RM187.

A press and a set of dies, one die for each denomination, were prepared and sent to each state where it was the duty of the Supervisors of the Revenue to stamp all documents presented to them upon payment of the proper tax. The Supervisors were also to have on hand for sale blank paper stamped with the different rates of duty to be sold to the public upon which the purchaser would later write or print the proper type of instrument corresponding with the value of the stamp impressed thereon. So far as is now known there was no distinctive watermark for the paper sold by the government. The Vermont set of dies is in the Vermont Historical Society at Montpelier.

B. SECOND FEDERAL ISSUE

Act of April 23, 1800

In effect March 1, 1801-June 30, 1802

RM260

RM261

		(a)Government watermark in italics; laid paper	(b)Government watermark in Roman; wove paper	(c)No Government watermark
RM260	4c	15.00	15.00	50.00
RM261	10c	20.00	20.00	50.00
RM262	20c	65.00	75.00	85.00
RM263	25c	15.00	15.00	17.50
RM264	30c	75.00	75.00	400.00
RM265	50c	65.00	45.00	85.00
RM266	75c	30.00	50.00	100.00
RM267	$1	200.00	150.00	175.00
RM269	$4			*500.00*
RM271	$10		*3,250.*	

The distinguishing feature of the stamps of this issue is the counter stamp, the left stamp shown in the illustration which usually appears on a document below the other stamp. In the right stamp the design of the eagle and the shield are similar to their design in the same denomination of the First Federal Issue but the name of the state is omitted and the denomination appears below instead of above the eagle and the shield. All of these stamps were embossed without color.

All the paper which was furnished by the government contained the watermark vertically along the edge of the sheet, "GEN STAMP OFFICE," either in Roman capitals on wove paper or in italic capitals on laid paper. The wove paper also had in the center of each half sheet either the watermark "W. Y. & Co." or "Delaware." William Young & Co. who owned the Delaware Mills made the government paper. The laid paper omitted the watermark "Delaware." The two stamps were separately impressed. The design of the eagle and shield differed in each value.

All the stamping was done in Washington, the right stamp being put on in the General Stamp Office and the left one or counter stamp in the office of the Commissioner of the Revenue as a check on the stamping done in the General Stamp Office. The "Com. Rev. C. S." in the design of the counter stamp stands for "Commissioner of the Revenue, Counter Stamp."

The Second Federal issue was intended to include $2 and $5 stamps, but these denominations have not been seen.

C. THIRD FEDERAL ISSUE

Act of August 2, 1813
In effect January 1, 1814-December 31, 1817

RM276

		a. Watermark	b. Unwmkd.
RM275	5c	10.00	15.00
RM276	10c	10.00	10.00
RM277	25c	15.00	15.00
RM278	50c	10.00	10.00
RM279	75c	13.00	17.50
RM280	$1	13.00	27.50
RM281	$1.50	15.00	70.00
RM282	$2	30.00	55.00
RM283	$2.50	27.50	110.00
RM284	$3.50	175.00	100.00
RM285	$4		*350.00*
RM286	$5	100.00	*125.00*

The distinguishing features of the stamps of this issue are the absence of the name of a state in the design and the absence of the counter stamp. Different values show different positions of the eagle.

All stamps of this issue were embossed without color at Washington. The paper with the watermark "Stamp U. S." was sold by the government. Unwatermarked paper may be either wove or laid.

IV. ISSUES BY VARIOUS STATES

DELAWARE

Act of June 19, 1793
In effect October 1, 1793-February 7, 1794

ERP50

ERP51

ERP53

RM291	EP50	5c	*1,700.*
RM292	EP51	20c	*1,350.*
RM294	EP53	50c	—

In some cases a reddish ink was used in impressing the stamp and in other cases the impressions are colorless.

Besides the denominations listed, 3c, 33c, and $1 stamps were called for by the taxing act. Stamps of these denominations have not been seen.

VIRGINIA

Act of February 20, 1813
In effect May 1, 1813-April 30, 1815
Act of December 21, 1814
In effect May 1, 1815-February 27, 1816

ERP60

ERP61

			a. Die cut	b. On Document
RM305	EP61	4c	17.50	90.00
RM306	EP60	6c	17.50	200.00
RM307	EP61	10c		200.00
RM308	EP60	12c	25.00	200.00
RM309	EP61	20c	40.00	500.00
RM310	EP61	25c	17.50	225.00
RM311	EP61	37c	17.50	300.00
RM312	EP61	45c	40.00	200.00
RM313	EP61	50c	17.50	225.00
RM314	EP61	70c	40.00	
RM315	EP61	75c	22.50	90.00
RM316	EP61	95c	40.00	300.00
RM317	EP61	100c	40.00	300.00
RM318	EP61	120c		225.00
RM319	EP61	125c	17.50	
RM323	EP60	175c	17.50	
RM325	EP61	200c	17.50	475.00

All of these stamps are colorless impressions and with some exceptions as noted below those issued under the 1813 Act cannot be distinguished from those issued under the 1814 Act. The 10c, 20c, 45c, 70c, 95c, 120c, 145c, 150c, 170c and 190c were issued only under the 1813 Act, the 6c, 12c, and 37c only under the 1814 Act.

No. RM311 has the large lettering of EP60 but the 37 is to the left and the XXXVII to the right as in EP61. The design of the dogwood branch and berries is similar but not identical in all values.

When the tax on the document exceeded "two hundred cents," two or more stamps were impressed or attached to the document. For instance a document has been seen with 45c and 200c to make up the $2.45 rate, and another with 75c and 200c.

Since both the Virginia and the Third Federal Acts to some extent taxed the same kind of document, and since during the period from Jan. 1, 1814 to Feb. 27, 1816, both Acts were in effect in Virginia, some instruments have both stamps on them.

The circular die cut Virginia stamps about 29mm in diameter were cut out of previously stamped paper which after the Act was repealed, was presented for redemption at the office of the Auditor of Public Accounts. They were threaded on fine twine and until about 1940 preserved in his office as required by law. Watermarked die cut Virginia stamps are all cut out of Third Federal watermarked paper.

Not seen yet, the 145c, 150c, and 170c stamps were called for by the 1813 Act, and 195c by both the 1813 and 1814 Acts.

MARYLAND

1. Act of February 11, 1818
In effect May 1, 1818-March 7, 1819

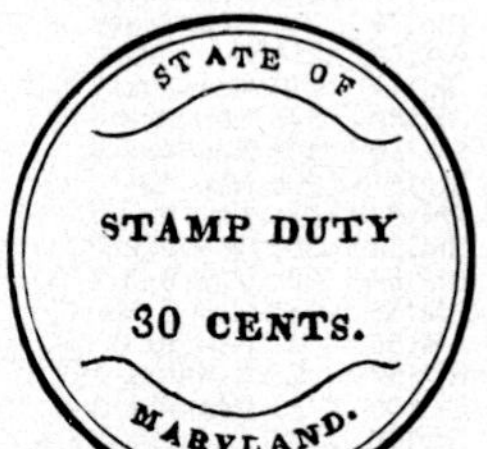

ERP70

RM362	EP70	30c **red** (printed), unused	400.
		Sheet of 4, unused	2,500.

The Act called for six other denominations, none of which has been seen. The Act imposing this tax was held unconstitutional by the United States Supreme Court in the case of McCulloch vs. Maryland.

2. Act of March 10, 1845
In effect May 10, 1845-March 10, 1856

ERP71

RM370	EP71	10c	12.50
RM371	EP71	15c	10.00
RM372	EP71	25c	10.00
RM373	EP71	50c	12.50
RM374	EP71	75c	10.00
RM375	EP71	$1	10.00
RM376	EP71	$1.50	12.50
RM377	EP71	$2	45.00
RM378	EP71	$2.50	17.50
RM379	EP71	$3.50	55.00
RM380	EP71	$4	90.00
RM381	EP71	$5.50	50.00
RM382	EP71	$6	100.00

Nos. RM370-RM382 are embossed without color with a similar design for each value. They vary in size from 20mm in diameter for the 10c to 33mm for the $6.

V. FEDERAL LICENSES TO SELL LIQUOR, ETC.

1. Act of June 5, 1794
In effect September 30, 1794-June 30, 1802

ERP80

RM400	EP80	$5	550.00

Provisionals are in existence using the second issue Connecticut Supervisors' stamp with the words "Five Dollars" written or printed over it or the second issue of the New Hampshire Supervisors' stamp without the words "Five Dollars."

2. Act of August 2, 1813
In effect January 1, 1814-December 31, 1817

ERP81

RM451	EP81	$10	725.00
RM452	EP81	$12	750.00
RM453	EP81	$15	425.00
RM454	EP81	$18	900.00
RM455	EP81	$20	*1,400.*
RM456	EP81	$22.50	650.00
RM457	EP81	$25	550.00
RM458	EP81	$30	*1,500.*
RM459	EP81	$37.50	550.00

The Act of December 23, 1814, increased the basic rates on $10, $12, $15, $20 and $25 by 50 per cent, effective February 1, 1815. This increase applied to the unexpired portions of the year so far as licenses then in effect were concerned and these licenses were required to be brought in and to have the payment of the additional tax endorsed on them.

VI. FEDERAL LICENSES TO WORK A STILL

Act of July 24, 1813
In effect January 1, 1814-December 31, 1817

(Embossed)
ERP82

(Printed)
ERP83

		a. Embossed	b. Printed
RM466	4½c		*2,000.*
RM468	9c	*1,250.*	*1,800.*
RM471	18c	—	*1,400.*
RM477	36c		*2,100.*
RM478	42c		*2,000.*
RM480	52c	*2,000.*	
RM484	70c	*2,100.*	
RM488	$1.08	*2,000.*	

The statute under which these were issued provided for additional rates of 2½c, 5c, 10c, 16c, 21c, 25c, 26c, 32c, 35c, 42c, 50c, 54c, 60c, 64c, 84c, $1.04, $1.05, $1.20, $1.35, $1.40, $2.10, $2.16 and $2.70 per gallon of the capacity of the still. Stamps of these denominations have not been seen.

VII. SUPERVISORS' AND CUSTOM HOUSE SEALS

1. Seals came into use on required certificates, as follows: April 1, 1791, domestic and imported distilled spirits; July 1, 1792, imported wine.

ERP90

Check Letter			State	
RM501	EP90	"B"	South Carolina	50.00
RM503	EP90	"D"	Virginia	*1,350.*
RM505	EP90	"F"	Delaware	—
RM506	EP90	"G"	Pennsylvania	75.00
RM508	EP90	"I"	New York	22.50
RM509	EP90	"K"	Connecticut	30.00
RM510	EP90	"L"	Rhode Island	90.00
RM511	EP90	"M"	Massachusetts	22.50
RM512	EP90	"N"	New Hampshire	700.00
RM514	EP90	"P"	Kentucky	—

Use of RM501-RM514 on certificates for domestic distilled spirits shows payment of the tax that was being resisted in the Whiskey Rebellion. All such reported uses are from the New England states. Nos. RM501-RM514 were removed from service in late 1799. In Connecticut and Massachusetts, they were returned to service after July1, 1802.

2. Use from October 2, 1799

ERP91

RM552	EP91	North Carolina	500.00
RM553	EP91	Virginia	—
RM554	EP91	Maryland	200.00
RM556	EP91	Pennsylvania	250.00
RM558	EP91	New York	20.00
RM559	EP91	Connecticut	30.00
RM560	EP91	Rhode Island	35.00
RM561	EP91	Massachusetts	25.00
RM562	EP91	New Hampshire	90.00

Nos. RM552-RM562 were necessitated by excessive wear on Nos. RM501-RM514.

3. Custom House Seals

ERP92

RM575	EP92	Custom House, Philadelphia	50.00
RM576	EP92	Custom House, Perth Amboy, N.J.	35.00

Although no value is expressed in the Supervisors' and Custom House seals, and they do not evidence the payment of a tax in the same way that the other stamps do, some collectors of stamped paper include them in their collections if they are on instruments evidencing the payment of a tax.

They were all embossed without color and, as to Supervisors' seals issued under the Act of 1791, the only difference in design is that at the left of the eagle there was a different check letter for each state. Custom House seals used in the other cities are in existence, but, in view of the doubtful status of Custom House seals as revenue stamps, it is not proposed to list them.

REVENUE STAMPED PAPER

These stamps were printed in various denominations and designs on a variety of financial documents, including checks, drafts, receipts, specie clerk statements, insurance policies, bonds and stock certificates.

They were authorized by Act of Congress of July 1, 1862, effective October 1, 1862, although regular delivery of stamped paper did not begin until July 1, 1865. The 2-cent tax on receipts ended Oct. 1, 1870. The 2-cent tax on checks and sight drafts ended July 1, 1883. All other taxes ended Oct. 1, 1872. The use of stamped paper was revived by the War Revenue Act of 1898, approved June 13, 1898. Type X was used July 1, 1898 through June 30, 1902.

Most of these stamps were typographed; some, types H, I and J, were engraved. They were printed by private firms under supervision of government representatives from dies loaned by the Bureau of Internal Revenue. Types A-F, P-W were printed by the American Phototype Co., New York (1865-75); type G, Graphic Co., New York (1875-83); types H-L, Joseph R. Carpenter, Philadelphia (1866-75); types M-N, A. Trochsler, Boston (1873-75); type O, Morey and Sherwood, Chicago (1874). Type X was printed by numerous regional printers under contract with the government.

Samples of these stamps are known for types B-G, P and Q with a section of the design removed and replaced by the word "Sample." Types G, P-Q, U-W exist with a redemption clause added by typography or rubber stamp. Redeemed type X's have a 5mm punched hole.

Multiples or single impressions on various plain papers are usually considered proofs or printers' waste.

For further information see "Handbook for United States Revenue Stamped Paper," published (1979) by the American Revenue Association.

Illustration size varies, with actual size quoted for each type.

Values for types A-O are for clear impressions on plain entire checks and receipts. Attractive documents with vignettes sell for more. The value of individual examples is also affected by the place of use. For example, territorial usage generally sells for more than a similar item from New York City.

Values for types P-W are for stamps on documents with attractive engravings, usually stock certificates, bonds and insurance policies. Examples on plain documents and cut squares sell for less.

Type A

Size: 22x25mm

RN-A1	2c **black**		90.	75.
	a. Printed on both sides			30.
RN-A2	2c **orange**			125.
RN-A3	2c **gray**			—
RN-A4	2c **blue**			*8,000.*
RN-A5	2c **brown**			—
RN-A8	2c **purple**			*2,000.*
RN-A9	2c **green**			*1,250.*
	a. Inverted			—

No. RN-A4 is unique. The unique example of No. RN-A9a is on a partial document. The catalogue value for RN-A8 is for an impression on William Moller & Son stationery; a second more violet shade is on Carter, Kirkland & Co. receipts. Value of latter is $3,250.

Same Type with 1 Entire and 53 or 56 Partial Impressions in Vertical Format ("Tapeworm")
Left Col. — Full Document
Right Col. — Strip with Bank Names

RN-A10	2c **orange**, 1 full plus 56 partial impressions	750.	100.
	Cut square (full strip without bank names)		45.
RN-A11	2c **orange**, 1 full plus 53 partial impressions	*1,250.*	250.

Nos. RN-A10 and RN-A11 were used by the Mechanics' National Bank of New York on a bank specie clerk's statement. It was designed so that the full stamp or one of the repeated bottom segments fell on each line opposite the name of a bank.

The three additional banks were added at the bottom of the form. No. RN-A11 must show white space below the "First National Bank" line.

Eagle Type B

Size: 31x48mm

RN-B1	2c **orange**	5.00	3.00
	yellow orange	5.00	3.00
	deep orange	5.00	3.00
	a. Printed on both sides	200.00	20.00
	b. Double impression	350.00	
	c. Printed on back		—

	d. With 10 centimes blue French handstamp, right	400.00	
	e. Inverted		*600.00*

The unique example of No. RN-B1e is on a partial document.

All examples of the previously-listed "yellow" have some red in them.

RN-B2	2c **black**		40.00
RN-B3	2c **blue**		40.00
	light blue		40.00
RN-B4	2c **brown**	125.00	40.00
RN-B5	2c **bronze**		40.00
RN-B6	2c **green** (shades)	110.00	15.00
RN-B10	2c **red** (shades)	200.00	22.50
RN-B11	2c **purple**		125.00
RN-B13	2c **violet** (shades)	125.00	40.00
	a. 2c **violet brown**		45.00

"Good only for checks and drafts payable at sight." in Rectangular Tablet at Base

RN-B16	2c **orange**	45.00	12.50
	a. With 2c orange red Nevada	325.00	225.00

"Good only for checks and drafts payable at sight." in Octagonal Tablet at Base

RN-B17	2c **orange**	42.50	10.00
	a. Tablet inverted		1,250.
	b. With 2c orange red Nevada		35.00
	c. With 2c green Nevada		35.00
	d. With 2c dull violet Nevada		*1,500.*
	e. With 2c brownish violet Nevada		*2,500.*

"Good when issued for the payment of money." in Octagonal Tablet at Base

RN-B20	2c **orange**	70.00	12.50
	a. Printed on both sides	30.00	10.00
	b. As "a," one stamp inverted		*1,500.*
	c. Tablet inverted		*3,750.*

"Good when issued for the payment of money" in two lines at base in orange

RN-B23	2c **orange**		900.00

"Good when the amount does not exceed $100." in Octagonal Tablet at Base

RN-B24	2c **orange**	200.00	90.00

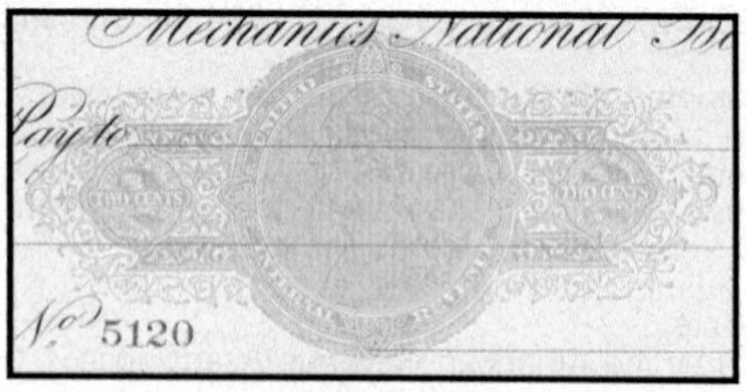

Washington Type C

Size: 108x49mm

RN-C1	2c **orange**	7.00	4.00
	red orange	7.00	4.00
	yellow orange	7.00	4.00
	salmon	8.00	4.00
	brown orange	8.00	4.00
	a. "Good when used..." vert. at left black		*2,250.*

All examples of the previously-listed "yellow" have some red in them.

RN-C2	2c **brown**	30.00	12.00
	a. 2c **buff**	30.00	12.00
RN-C5	2c **pale red** (shades)	50.00	25.00
RN-C8	2c **green**	—	

"Good only for Sight Draft" in two lines in color of stamp

RN-C9	2c **orange,** legend at lower right	85.00	50.00
RN-C11	2c **brown,** legend at lower left		110.00
RN-C13	2c **orange,** legend at lower left	45.00	20.00

"Good only for Receipt for Money Paid" in two lines in color of stamp

RN-C15	2c **orange,** legend at lower right	*2,500.*	—
RN-C16	2c **orange,** legend at lower left		350.00

"Good when issued for the payment of money" in one line at base in color of stamp

RN-C17	2c **orange** (shades)		600.00

"Good when issued for the/Payment of Money" in two tablets at lower left and right

RN-C19	2c **orange**		550.00
	a. Printed on both sides		35.00

"Good/only for Bank/Check" in 3-part Band

RN-C21	2c **orange**	50.00	12.50
	salmon		12.50
	yellow orange		20.00
	a. Inverted		550.00
	b. With 2c red orange Nevada	140.00	65.00
	c. Printed on back		*2,900.*
RN-C22	2c **brown**	300.00	25.00
	a. Printed on back		1,800.

"Good when the amount does not exceed $100" in tablet at lower right

RN-C26	2c **orange**		200.00

Franklin Type D

Size: 80x43mm

RN-D1	2c **orange** (shades)	5.00	2.00
	a. Double impression		—
	b. Printed on back	700.00	400.00
	c. Inverted		425.00

All examples of the previously-listed "yellow" have some red in them and are included in the "shades."

RN-D3	2c **brown**	—	*500.00*
RN-D4	2c **buff** (shades)	9.00	5.00
RN-D5	2c **red**		*2,000.*

"Good only for/Bank Check" in panels within circles at left and right

RN-D7	2c **orange**	25.00	10.00
	a. Printed on back		2,100.

"Good only for/Bank Check" in two lines at lower right in color of stamp

RN-D8	2c **orange**		750.00

"Good only for Sight Draft" in two lines at lower left in color of stamp

RN-D9	2c **orange**	175.00	75.00

Franklin Type E

Size: 28x50mm

RN-E2	2c **brown**		*1,200.*
RN-E4	2c **orange**	12.50	5.00
	Broken die, lower right or left	40.00	20.00
	a. Double impression		*925.00*

"Good only for sight draft" in two lines at base in orange

RN-E5	2c **orange**	75.00	30.00

"Good only for Bank / Check" in two lines at base in orange

RN-E6	2c **orange**	—	

"Good only for / Bank Check" in colorless letters in two lines above and below portrait

RN-E7	2c **orange**	75.00	17.50
	a. Double impression		—

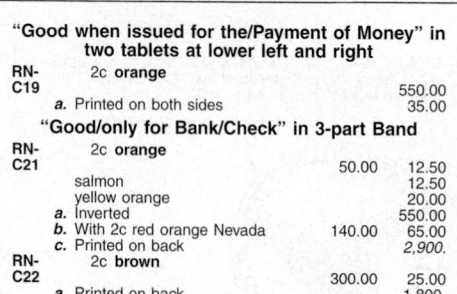

Franklin Type F

Size: 56x34mm

RN-F1	2c **orange**	10.00	5.00
	a. Inverted		—

All examples of the previously-listed "yellow" have some red in them

Liberty Type G

Size: 80x48mm

RN-G1	2c **orange**	2.00	1.00
	a. Printed on back	65.00	40.00
	b. Printed on back, inverted	125.00	50.00

All examples of the previously-listed "yellow" have some red in them

Imprint: "Graphic Co., New York" at left and right in minute type

RN-G3	2c **orange**	110.00	100.00

Eagle Type H

Size: 32x50mm

RN-H3	2c **orange**	15.00	5.00
	a. Inverted		—
	b. Double impression		600.00
	c. "Good when used for payment of money," black		*750.00*
	d. "Good when used as a receipt for payment of money," black		*750.00*
	e. As "d," upward at left		*1,600.*
	f. As "d," legend in red		*1,500.*
	g. "Good when used as a receipt for the payment of money," black		*400.00*
	h. As "g," inverted legend		*7,500.*
	i. As "g," legend in two lines		*700.00*
	j. As "g," legend in violet		*700.00*
	k. As "g," legend in yellow		*2,000.*
	l. "Good only when used as a receipt for the payment of moneys," black		*750.00*

"Good for check or sight draft only" at left and right in color of stamp

RN-H5	2c **orange**		

Experts claim that No. RN-H5 exists only as a proof.

"Good for bank check or sight draft only" in black

RN-H6	2c **orange**		150.00

Type I
Design R2 of 1862-72 adhesive revenues
Size: 20x23mm
"BANK CHECK"

RN-I1	2c **orange**		225.00

"U.S. INTER. REV."

RN-I2	2c **orange**	650.00	350.00

Washington Type J

Size: 105x40mm
Background of medallion crosshatched, filling oval except for bust

RN-J4	2c **orange**	20.00	10.00
	pale orange	20.00	10.00
	deep orange	50.00	12.50
	a. Double impression		—
	b. "Good only for . . ." added vertically at left in red orange		750.00
RN-J5	2c **red**	50.00	12.00
	a. Double impression		—

"Good for check or sight draft only" curved, below

RN-J9	2c **red**	—	*2,000.*

Background shaded below bust and at left.

RN-J11	2c **orange**	60.00	15.00

Washington Type K

Size: 84x33mm

RN-K1	2c **blue**		—
RN-K4	2c **gray**	45.00	15.00
	pale gray	45.00	10.00
RN-K5	2c **brown**	175.00	125.00
RN-K6	2c **orange**	15.00	7.50
RN-K8	2c **red** (shades)	600.00	350.00
RN-K11	2c **olive**	200.00	175.00
	pale olive		110.00

Washington Type L

Size: 50x33mm

RN-L1	2c **blue** (shades)	200.00	—
RN-L2	2c **turquoise**	250.00	200.00
RN-L3	2c **gray**	35.00	20.00
	pale gray	35.00	20.00
RN-L4	2c **green**	900.00	600.00
	light green	600.00	400.00
RN-L5	2c **orange**	15.00	10.00
RN-L6	2c **olive**		55.00
	gray olive		30.00
RN-L10	2c **red**	15.00	10.00
	a. 2c **violet red**	15.00	10.00
RN-L13	2c **brown**	—	300.00

Washington Type M

Size: 68x37mm

RN-M2	2c **orange**	50.00	10.00
	a. Printed on back, inverted		*1,600.*

All examples of the previously-listed "yellow" have some red in them.

RN-M3	2c **green**		475.00
RN-M4	2c **gray**		1,250.

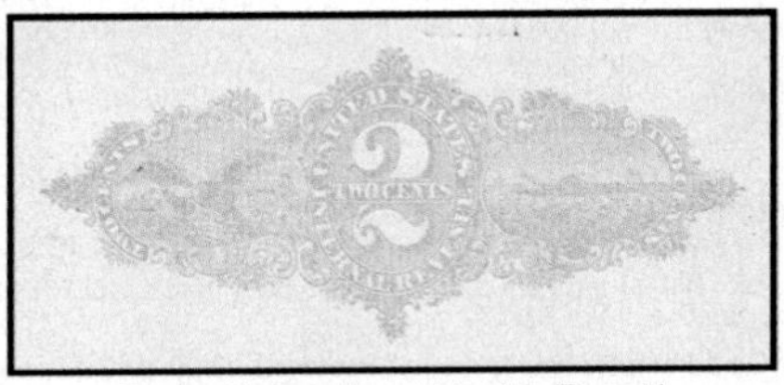

Eagle, Numeral and Monitor Type N

Size: 107x48mm

RN-N3	2c **orange**	60.00	15.00
	a. Printed on back	300.00	225.00
	b. Inverted		900.00
RN-N4	2c **light brown**		150.00

Liberty Type O

Size: 75x35mm

RN-O2	2c **orange**	1,750.	600.

Values for types P-W
are for stamps on documents with attractive engravings, usually stock certificates, bonds and insurance policies. Examples on plain documents sell for less.

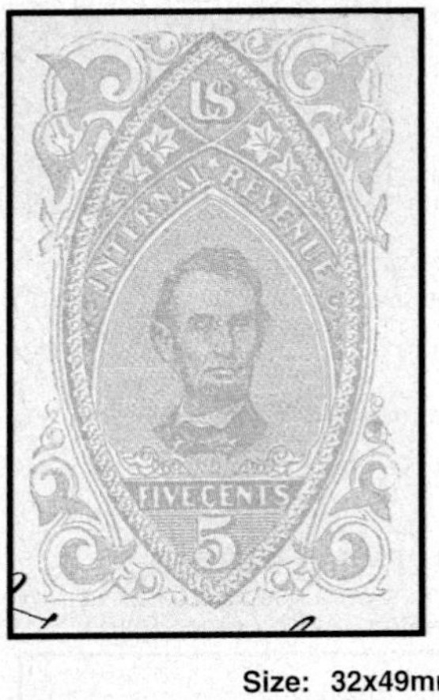

Lincoln Type P

Size: 32x49mm

RN-P2	5c **brown**		350.00
	Cut square		90.00
RN-P3	5c **green**		—
RN-P4	5c **pink**		—
RN-P5	5c **orange**	55.00	40.00
	Cut square		7.00

All examples of the previously listed "yellow" have some orange in them.

RN-P6	5c **red** (shades)	—	225.00
	Cut square		40.00

No. RN-P3 only exists in combination with a 25c green or 50c green. No. RN-P4 is unique and only exists in combination with a $1 pink. See Nos. RN-T2, RN-V1, RN-W6.

Madison Type Q (See note before No. RN-P2)

Size: 28x56mm

RN-Q1	5c **orange**	175.	150.
	Cut square		20.
	brownish orange	175.	150.
RN-Q2	5c **brown**		*2,750.*
	Cut square		500.

Type R
Frame as Type B, Lincoln in center
Size: 32x49mm

RN-R1	10c **brown**		*2,500.*
RN-R2	10c **pale red**	—	675.
	Cut square		100.
RN-R3	10c **orange**		500.
	Cut square		50.

"Good when the premium does not exceed $10" in tablet at base

RN-R6	10c **orange**	—	400.
	Cut square		50.

Motto Without Tablet

RN-R7	10c **orange**		
	Cut square		500.

Washington Type S (See note before No. RN-P2)

Size: 33x54mm

RN-S1	10c **orange**		*3,750.*

"Good when the premium does not exceed $10" in tablet at base

RN-S2	10c **orange**		*4,750.*
	Cut square		500.

Eagle Type T (See note before No. RN-P2)

For type T design with Lincoln in center see type V, Nos. RN-V1 to RN-V10.

Size: 33x40mm

RN-T1	25c **black**	—	
	Cut square		—
RN-T2	25c **green**		*7,500.*
RN-T3	25c **red**	175.00	*100.00*
	Cut square		9.00
RN-T4	25c **orange**	150.00	75.00
	Cut square		7.50
	light orange	150.00	75.00
	light orange, cut square		7.50
	brown orange		75.00
	brown orange, cut square		8.00

No. RN-T2 includes No. RN-P3, and a 25c green, type T, obliterating a No. RN-V4.

"Good when the premium does not exceed $50" in tablet at base

RN-T6	25c **orange**	450.	350.
	Cut square		50.
RN-T7	25c **orange,** motto without tablet		1,500.
	Cut square		400.

"Good when the amount insured shall not exceed $1000" in tablet at base

RN-T8	25c **deep orange**	800.	700.
	Cut square		75.
RN-T9	25c **orange,** motto without tablet		
	Cut square		600.

Franklin Type U (See note before No. RN-P2)

Size: 126x65mm

RN-U1	25c **orange**	35.00	35.00
	Cut square		5.00
RN-U2	25c **brown**	45.00	35.00
	Cut square		5.00

"Good when the premium does not exceed $50" in tablet at lower right

RN-U3	25c **orange**		*2,500.*
	Cut square		400.

Tablet at lower left

RN-U5	25c **red**	800.	
	Cut square		250.
RN-U6	25c **orange**	500.	450.
	Cut square		65.

All examples of the previously-listed "yellow" have some red in them.

Tablet at base

RN-U7	25c **brown**		*1,750.*
	Cut square		300.
RN-U9	25c **orange**		*1,000.*
	Cut square		400.

Lincoln Type V

Size: 32x41mm

RN-V1	50c **green**		175.00
	Cut square		52.50
RN-V2	50c **brown**	—	400.00
	Cut square		125.00
RN-V4	50c **orange**	175.00	90.00
	Cut square		17.50
	deep orange	175.00	90.00
	deep orange, cut square		17.50
RN-V5	50c **red**	700.00	
	Cut square		250.00

No. RN-V1 includes a 50c green, type V, and a No. RN-P3, obliterating a No. RN-W2.

"Good when the amount insured shall not exceed $5000" in tablet at base

RN-V6	50c **orange**	450.00	400.00
	Cut square		60.00
RN-V9	50c **red**		—
	Cut square		550.00

Motto Without Tablet

RN-V10	50c **orange**		
	Cut square		550.00

Washington Type W (See note before No. RN-P2)

Size: 34x73mm

RN-W2	$1 **orange**(shades)	150.00	90.00
	Cut square		15.00
RN-W5	$1 **brown**		*4,500.*
RN-W6	$1 **pink**		*3,750.*

The former light brown is now included with the orange shades.

No. RN-W6 used with No. RN-P4 is unique. Two examples of No. RN-W6 exist used alone.

SPANISH-AMERICAN WAR SERIES

Many of these stamps were used for parlor car tax and often were torn in two or more parts.

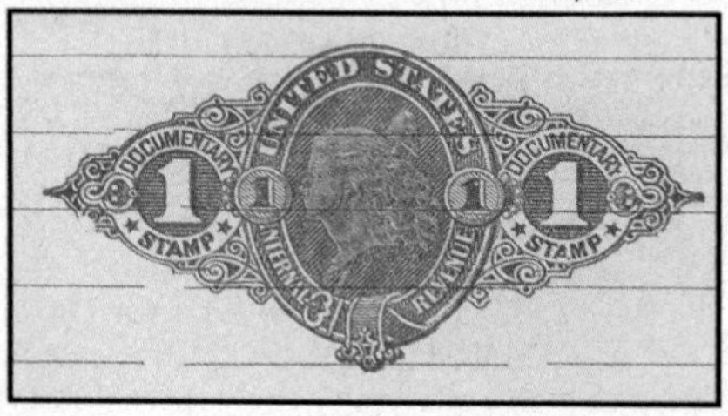

Liberty Type X

1898 **Size: 68x38mm**

RN-X1	1c **rose**	800.00	—
	Partial		65.00
	dark red, partial		65.00
RN-X4	1c **orange**	165.00	
	a. On pullman ticket	600.00	—
	Partial		25.00
	b. As "a," printed on back		
	As "a," printed on back, partial		65.00
RN-X5	1c **green**	65.00	30.00
	Partial		25.00
	a. On parlor car ticket	65.00	15.00
	b. On pullman ticket	500.00	
	On pullman ticket, partial		15.00
RN-X6	2c **yellow**	2.00	1.00
	pale olive		*900.00*
RN-X7	2c **orange**	1.50	1.00
	pale orange	1.50	1.00
	a. Printed on back only	400.00	400.00
	c. Printed on front and back	—	—
	d. Vertical		85.00
	e. Double impression		—
	f. On pullman ticket	1,000.	200.00
	g. Inverted		550.00

No. RN-X1 exists only as a four-part unused pullman ticket used as an unsevered auditor's and passenger's parts of the four-part ticket, or partial as a used half of a two-part ticket. Nos. RN-X4a and RN-X5b exist as unused two-part tickets and as used half portions. No. RN-X7f exists as an unused four-part ticket and as a used two-piece portion with nearly complete stamp design.

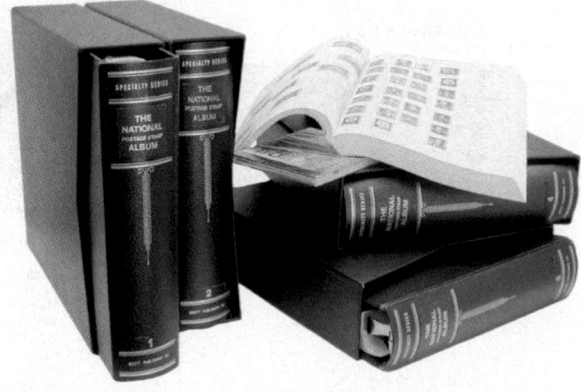

PRIVATE DIE PROPRIETARY STAMPS

The extraordinary demands of the Civil War upon the Federal Treasury resulted in Congress devising and passing the Revenue Act of 1862. The Government provided revenue stamps to be affixed to boxes or packages of matches, and to proprietary medicines, perfumery, playing cards — as well as to documents, etc.

But manufacturers were permitted, at their expense, to have dies engraved and plates made for their exclusive use. Many were only too willing to do this because a discount or premium of from 5% to 10% was allowed on orders from the die which often made it possible for them to undersell their competitors. Also, the considerable advertising value of the stamps could not be overlooked. These are now known as Private Die Proprietary stamps.

The face value of the stamp used on matches was determined by the number, i.e., 1c for each 100 matches or fraction thereof. Medicines and perfumery were taxed at the rate of 1c for each 25 cents of the retail value or fraction thereof up to $1 and 2c for each 50 cents or fraction above that amount. Playing cards were first taxed at the same rate but subsequently the tax was 5c for a deck of 52 cards and 10c for a greater number of cards or double decks.

The stamp tax was repealed on March 3, 1883, effective July 1, 1883.

The various papers were:

a. Old paper, 1862-71. First Issue. Hard and brittle varying from thick to thin.
b. Silk paper, 1871-77. Second Issue. Soft and porous with threads of silk, mostly red, blue and black, up to ¼inch in length.
c. Pink paper, 1877-78. Third Issue. Soft paper colored pink ranging from pale to deep shades.
d. Watermarked paper, 1878-83. Fourth Issue. Soft porous paper showing part of "USIR." Roulettes on watermarked paper are rouletted 6.
e. Experimental silk paper. Medium smooth paper, containing minute fragments of silk threads either blue alone or blue and red (infrequent), widely scattered, sometimes but a single fiber on a stamp.

Early printings of some private die revenue stamps are on paper which appears to have laid lines.

These stamps were usually torn in opening the box or container. **Values quoted are for examples which are somewhat faulty but reasonably attractive, with the faults usually not readily apparent on the face.** Nos. RS278-RS306 are valued in the grade of very fine. Sound examples of these stamps (other than Nos. RS278-RS306) at a grade of fine-very fine can sell for 50% to 300% more than catalogue value. Outstanding examples of stamps in this section with a lower catalogue value can bring many multiples of catalogue value.

PRIVATE DIE MATCH STAMPS

1864 *Perf. 12*

A

Akron Match Company — RO1

Akron Match Company

			a. Old Paper	b. Silk Paper	c. Pink Paper	d. Wmkd. USIR (191R)
RO1	1c	blue	275.00			

Alexander's Matches — RO2

J.J. Allen's Sons — RO4

Alexander's Matches

			a.	b.	c.	d.
RO2	1c	orange	30.00	125.00		
RO3	1c	blue		*5,000.*		

J. J. Allen's Sons

			a.	b.	c.	d.
RO4	1c	blue				16.00

Thos. Allen — RO5

Thos. Allen

			a.	b.	c.	d.
RO5	1c	green	175.00			

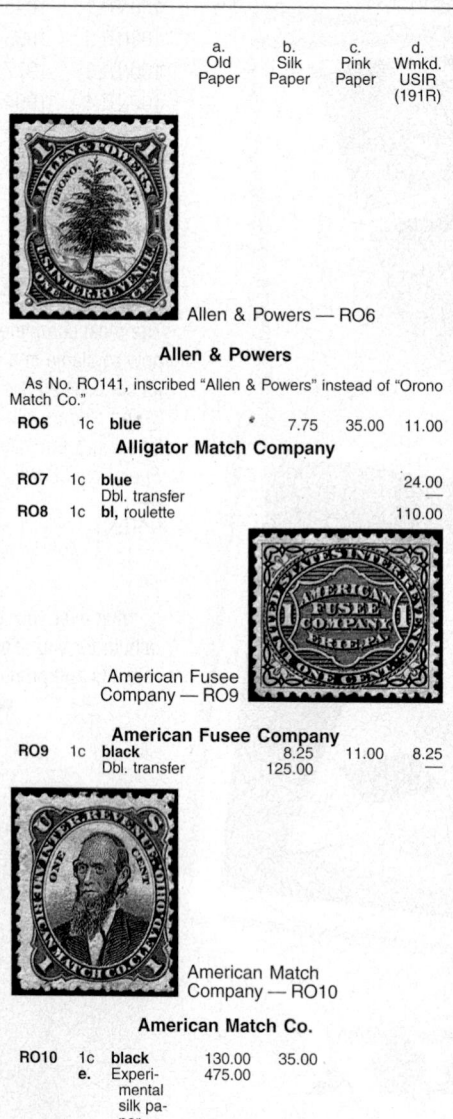

Allen & Powers — RO6

Allen & Powers

As No. RO141, inscribed "Allen & Powers" instead of "Orono Match Co."

			a. Old Paper	b. Silk Paper	c. Pink Paper	d. Wmkd. USIR (191R)
RO6	1c	blue		7.75	35.00	11.00

Alligator Match Company

			a.	b.	c.	d.
RO7	1c	blue				24.00
		Dbl. transfer				—
RO8	1c	bl, roulette				110.00

American Fusee Company — RO9

American Fusee Company

			a.	b.	c.	d.
RO9	1c	black		8.25	11.00	8.25
		Dbl. transfer		125.00		—

American Match Company — RO10

American Match Co.

			a.	b.	c.	d.
RO10	1c	black	130.00	35.00		
	e.	Experimental silk paper	475.00			
RO11	3c	black	550.00	140.00		
		Dbl. transfer		275.00		
	e.	Experimental silk paper	1,500.			

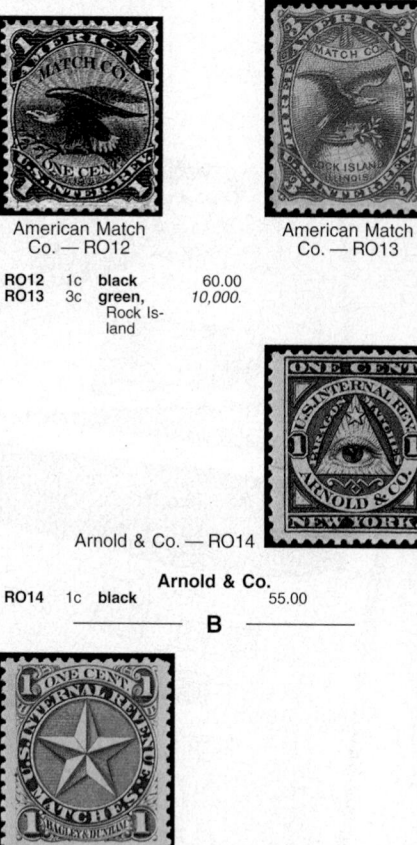

American Match Co. — RO12

American Match Co. — RO13

			a.	b.	c.	d.
RO12	1c	black	60.00			
RO13	3c	green, Rock Island	*10,000.*			

Arnold & Co. — RO14

Arnold & Co.

			a.	b.	c.	d.
RO14	1c	black		55.00		

B

Bagley & Dunham — RO15

Bagley & Dunham

			a.	b.	c.	d.
RO15	1c	green				32.50

Geo. & O. C. Barber

As No. RO17, inscribed "Geo. & O. C. Barber" instead of "Barber Match Co."

			a.	b.	c.	d.
RO16	1c	blue	72.50			

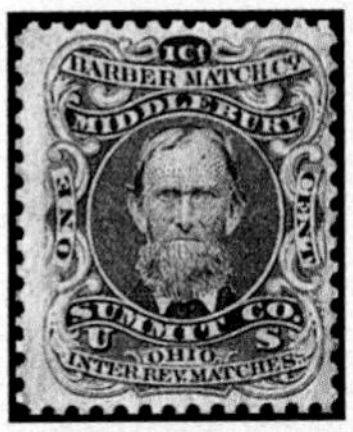

Barber Match Co. — RO17

Barber Match Co.

RO17	1c	**blue**	25.00	1.25	18.00	1.75
		Dbl. transfer	85.00	35.00	85.00	35.00
	e.	Experimental silk paper	125.00			
	u.	1c **ultra**	450.00			
RO18	1c	**bl,** roulette				5,000.
RO19	3c	**black**	200.00	140.00		
	e.	Experimental silk paper	*550.00*			

Barber & Peckham — RO20

Barber & Peckham

RO20	1c	**blue**	67.50			
RO21	3c	**black**	275.00			

Bauer & Beudel

RO22	1c	**blue**	72.50	160.00		
	u.	1c **ultra**	275.00			

A.B. & S. (A. Beecher & Son) — RO23

A. B. & S. (A. Beecher & Son)

As No. RO175, inscribed "A. B. & S." instead of "C. B. C. S." in the four corners.

RO23	1c	**orange**	17.00	62.50		
		Dbl. transfer	—	—		
	e.	Experimental silk paper	160.00			
		As "e," dbl. transfer	200.00			

B. Bendel & Co. — RO25

Illustration reduced.

B. Bendel & Co.

RO24	1c	**brown**		2.75		725.00
		Dbl. transfer		—		
RO25	12c	**brown**		275.00		

H. Bendel — RO26

H. Bendel

Nos. RO26-RO27 are RO24-RO25 altered to read "H. Bendel doing business as B. Bendel & Co."

RO26	1c	**brown**		5.00	2.50	2.00
RO27	12c	**brown**		500.00		

H. & M. Bentz — RO28

Bent & Lea — RO29

H. & M. Bentz

RO28	1c	**blue**	42.50			

Bent & Lea

RO29	1c	**black**	40.00			
		Double transfer at left	125.00			
	e.	Experimental silk paper	50.00			
		Double transfer	600.00			

B. J. & Co. — RO30

Bock, Schneider & Co. — RO31

B. J. & Co. (Barber, Jones & Co.)

As No. RO100 with "B. J. & Co." added above eagle.

RO30	1c	**green**		125.00		
		Dbl. transfer		160.00		

Bock, Schneider & Co.

RO31	1c	**black**		20.00		

Wm. Bond & Co. — RO32/RO33

Bousfield & Poole — RO34/RO35

Wm. Bond & Co.

RO32	4c	**black**		275.00		
RO33	4c	**green**		175.00	200.00	18.00

Bousfield & Poole

RO34	1c	**lilac**	225.00			
		Dbl. transfer	250.00			
RO35	1c	**black**	18.00	11.00		
		Dbl. transfer	70.00	90.00		
	e.	Experimental silk paper	85.00			
RO36	3c	**lilac**	3,000.			

For illustration of No. RO37, see large stamp illustration pages.

RO37	3c	**black**	200.00	150.00		
		Dbl. transfer		175.00		

		Experimental silk paper	500.00			

Boutell & Maynard — RO38

Boutell & Maynard

RO38	1c	**black**		350.00		

Bowers & Dunham

As No. RO15, inscribed "Bowers & Dunham" instead of "Bagley & Dunham."

RO39	1c	**green**				275.00
RO40	1c	**blue**				95.00

B. & N. (Brocket & Newton)

RO41	1c	**lake,** die I		45.00		
RO42	1c	**lake,** die II		8.25		

The initials "B. & N." measure 5¼mm across the top in Die I, and 4¾mm in Die II.

Brown & Durling

RO43

RO43	1c	**black**	2,500.			
RO44	1c	**green**	82.50			

L. W. Buck & Co. — RO45

L. W. Buck & Co.

RO45	1c	**black**	*3,250.*			
	e.	Experimental silk paper	2,100.			

D. Burhans & Co. — RO46

D. Burhans & Co.

RO46	1c	**black**	160.00	*12,500.*		
		Dbl. transfer	275.00			
e.		Experimental silk paper	900.00			

Charles Busch — RO47

Charles Busch

RO47	1c	**black**				35.00

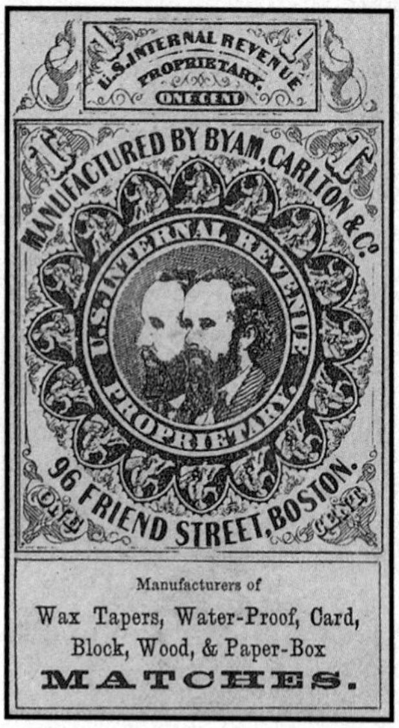

Byam, Carlton & Co. — RO48

2 heads to left, 41x75mm.

Byam, Carlton & Co.

RO48	1c	**black,** imperf	*5,500.*			

Byam, Carlton & Co. — RO49

RO49	1c	**black,** 19x23mm	27.50	7.75		1.40
		Dbl. transfer				140.00
e.		Experimental silk paper	125.00			
i.		Vert. pair, imperf horiz.				140.00
RO50	1c	**black**	2,750.			

2 heads to left, buff wrapper, 131x99mm.

For illustrations of Nos. RO51, RO52, RO54, RO55 and RO56, see large stamp illustration pages.

RO51	1c	**black**	250.00			

As #RO50, 131x89mm.

RO52	1c	**black**	65.00			

1 head to right, white wrapper, 94x54mm.

RO53	1c	**black**	175.00			

As #RO52, buff wrapper.

RO54	1c	**black**	11.00			
h.		Up	60.00			

2 heads to right, buff wrapper, 81x50mm. #RO54h has right block reading up.

RO55	1c	**black**	35.00			

1 head to left, white wrapper, 94x56mm.

RO56	1c	**black**	9.00			

As #RO50, 95x57mm.

C

Cannon Match Co. — RO57

Cannon Match Co.

As No. RO68, "Cannon Match Co." instead of "W. D. Curtis."

RO57	1c	**green**			55.00	

Cardinal Match Co. — RO58

Cardinal Match Co.

RO58	1c	**lake**				32.50

F. E. C. (Frank E. Clark)

As No. RO41, "F.E.C." instead of "B. & N."

RO59	1c	**lake**	110.00	110.00		
e.		Experimental silk paper	140.00			

Chicago Match Co. — RO60

Henry A. Clark — RO61

Chicago Match Co.

RO60	3c	**black**	600.00			

Henry A. Clark

RO61	1c	**green**		110.00		

Jas. L. Clark — RO62/RO63

Clark Match Co. — RO64

Jas. L. Clark

RO62	1c	**green**		2.75	27.50	1.75
		Dbl. transfer				67.50
RO63	1c	**green,** rouletted				1,000.

The Clark Match Co.

RO64	1c	**lake**		10.00		

Cramer & Kemp — RO65/RO66

Crown Match Co. — RO67

Cramer & Kemp

RO65	1c	**black**	72.50			
RO66	1c	**blue,**	125.00	7.75		
e.		Experimental silk paper	300.00			
u.		1c **ultra**	500.00			

Crown Match Co.

RO67	1c	**black**		25.00		

W. D. Curtis Matches — RO68

W. D. Curtis Matches

RO68	1c	**green**	160.00	140.00		
e.		Experimental silk paper	240.00			

D

G. W. H. Davis — RO69/RO70

G. W. H. Davis

RO69	1c	**black**		52.50		
RO70	1c	**carmine**				90.00

W.E. Doolittle — RO71

W. E. Doolittle

RO71	1c	**blue**	450.00			

E. P. Dunham

RO72	1c	**green**				90.00

E

Jas. Eaton — RO73

Jas. Eaton — RO74

Jas. Eaton

RO73	1c	**black**	55.00	1.50	20.00	1.75
e.		Experimental silk paper	200.00			

RO74	1c	**black,** rouletted			72.50

E.B. Eddy — RO75

E.B. Eddy — RO75A

E. B. Eddy

RO75	1c	**car,** die I			25.00
RO75A	1c	**car,** die II			40.00

Die II shows eagle strongly recut; ribbon across bottom is narrower; color is deeper.

Aug. Eichele

Aug. Eichele — RO76

RO76	1c	**black**	160.00		

P. Eichele & Co. — RO77

P. Eichele & Co.

As No. RO78, "P. Eichele & Co." at top.

RO77	1c	**blue**	67.50	8.25	
e.		Experimental silk paper	200.00		
u.		1c **ultra**	500.00		

Eichele & Co. — RO78/RO79

J.W. Eisenhart's — RO80

Eichele & Co.

RO78	1c	**blue**	5.00	20.00	4.50
RO79	1c	**blue,** rouletted			350.00

J. W. Eisenhart's Matches

RO80	1c	**blue**	55.00	125.00	42.50

Excelsior Match Co. (Watertown) — RO81/RO82

Excelsior Match Co.

RO81	1c	**black,** Watertown, N.Y.	110.00		
RO82	1c	**black,** Syracuse, N.Y.	10.00	17.50	10.00
		Dbl. transfer			52.50

Excelsior Match, Baltimore — RO83

Excelsior Match, Baltimore, Md.

RO83	1c	**blue**	95.00	125.00
u.		1c **ultra**	850.00	

F

G. Farr & Co. — RO84

L. Frank — RO85

G. Farr & Co.

RO84	1c	**black**	140.00	

L. Frank

RO85	1c	**brown**		110.00

G

Gardner, Beer & Co. — RO86

Wm. Gates — RO88

Gardner, Beer & Co.

RO86	1c	**black**			400.00

Wm. Gates

RO87	1c	**black,** die I	9.00	6.00	
RO88	1c	**black,** die II	50.00	5.50	
		Dbl. transfer		35.00	
e.		Experimental silk paper	200.00		

The shirt collar is colorless in Die I and shaded in Die II. The colorless circle surrounding the portrait appears about twice as wide on Die I as it does on Die II.

For illustration of No. RO89, see large stamp illustration pages.

RO89	3c	**black**	60.00	52.50	
		Dbl. transfer	92.50	90.00	—
e.		Experimental silk paper	200.00		
RO90	6c	**black**	200.00		
RO91	3c	**black,** 3 1c stamps		160.00	

William Gates' Sons — RO92

William Gates' Sons

The 1c is as No. RO87, 3c as No. RO91, "William Gates' Sons" replaces "Wm. Gates."

For illustration of No. RO94, see large stamp illustration pages.

RO92	1c	**black**	35.00	11.00	2.25
RO93	1c	**black,** rouletted			*3,250.*
RO94	3c	**black,** 3 1c stamps	140.00	200.00	95.00

A. Goldback & Co. — RO95

A. Goldback & Co.

RO95	1c	**green**	55.00		

A. Goldback

As No. RO95, "A. Goldback" instead of "A. Goldback & Co."

RO96	1c	**green**	200.00	13,000.	

T. Gorman & Bro.

As No. RO99, "T. Gorham & Bro." instead of "Thomas Gorham."

RO97	1c	**black**	900.00		
		Dbl. transfer	—		
RO98	1c	**green**	35.00	40.00	
		Dbl. transfer	—		

Thomas Gorman

RO99	1c	**green**	4.50	40.00	82.50

Greenleaf & Co. — RO101/RO102

Griggs & Goodwill — RO103/RO104

Greenleaf & Co.

RO100	1c	**green**	100.00	140.00
e.		Experimental silk paper	650.00	
RO101	3c	**carmine**	95.00	175.00
e.		Experimental silk paper	1,100.	
RO102	5c	**orange**	175.00	4,500.
e.		Experimental silk paper	450.00	

Griggs & Goodwill

RO103	1c	**black**		60.00
RO104	1c	**green**		35.00
		Dbl. transfer		160.00

Griggs & Scott

As No. RO69, inscribed "Griggs & Scott" instead of "G. W. H. Davis."

RO105	1c	**black**	12.00	42.50
e.		Experimental silk paper	75.00	

Bousfield & Poole – RO37

Byam, Carlton & Co. – RO51

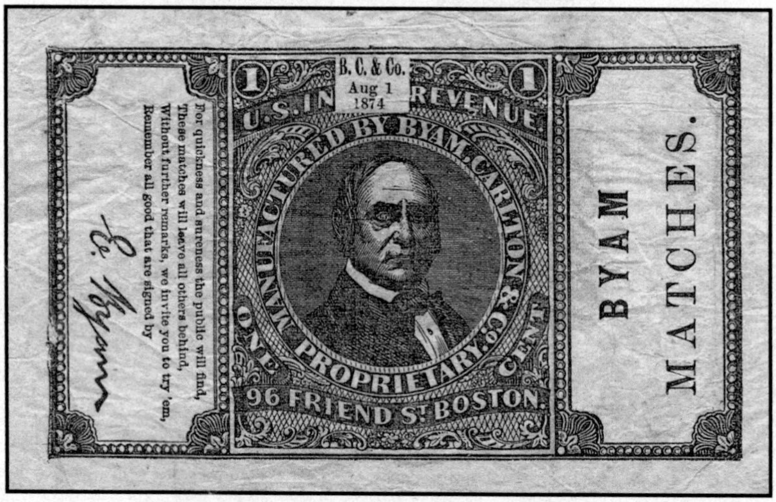

Byam, Carlton & Co. – RO52

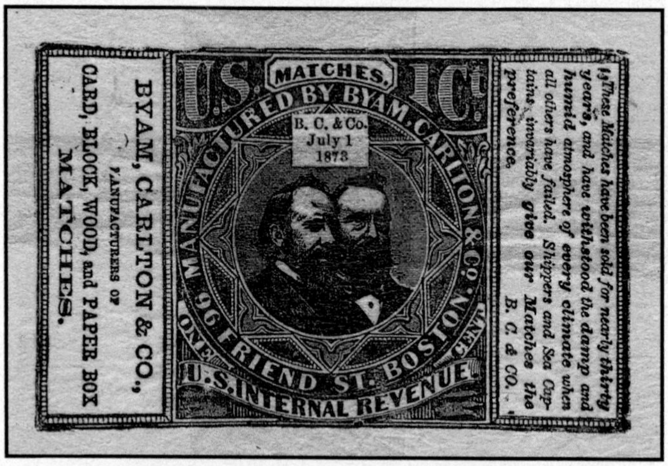

Byam, Carlton & Co. – RO54

Byam, Carlton & Co. – RO55

Byam, Carlton & Co. – RO56

Wm. Gates – RO89

William Gates' Sons – RO94

P.T. Ives – RO118

H

Charles S. Hale — RO106

Charles S. Hale

RO106 1c **green** 300.00

Henning & Bonhack

RO107 1c **blue** 350.00

W. E. Henry & Co. — RO108

W. E. Henry & Co.

RO108 1c **red** 35.00
RO109 1c **black** 17.00

J. G. Hotchkiss — RO110

L. G. Hunt — RO113

The J. G. Hotchkiss Match Co.

RO110 1c **green** 17.00 50.00 12.00

B. & H. D. Howard

RO111 1c **lake** 125.00
RO112 1c **blue** 12.00
u. 1c **ultra** 350.00

L. G. Hunt

RO113 1c **black** 400.00 1,650.
e. Experimental silk paper 425.00

D. F. Hutchinson Jr.

RO114 1c **lake** 22.50

I

Ives Matches

As No. RO116, "Ives Matches" instead of "P. T. Ives."

RO115 1c **blue** 7.75 6.75
Dbl. transfer —
u. 1c **ultra** 400.00

P. T. Ives — RO116/RO117

Ives & Judd — RO119

P. T. Ives

For illustration of No. RO118, see large stamp illustration pages.

RO116 1c **blue** 7.75 45.00 5.00
RO117 1c **blue,** rouletted 550.00

RO118 8c **blue** 240.00
e. Experimental silk paper 1,100.
u. 8c **ultra** 3,250.

Ives & Judd

RO119 1c **green** 27.50 67.50 160.00

Ives & Judd Match Co. — RO120

The Ives & Judd Match Co.

RO120 1c **green** 140.00
Dbl. transfer 325.00

K

Kirby & Sons

Kirby & Sons — RO121

RO121 1c **green** 77.50

W. S. Kyle

RO122 1c **black** 22.50 17.00
Dbl. transfer 82.50
e. Experimental silk paper —

L

Lacour's Matches

RO123 1c **black** 20.00 60.00
Dbl. transfer 110.00
e. Experimental silk paper 125.00

Leeds, Robinson & Co. — RO124

Leeds, Robinson & Co.

RO124 1c **green** 82.50

H. Leigh

RO125 1c **blue** 11.00

Leigh & Palmer

As No. RO125, "Leigh & Palmer" replaces "H. Leigh."

RO126 1c **black** 25.00 77.50 47.50

John Loehr — RO127

John Loehr

RO127 1c **blue** 27.50

Joseph Loehr

As No. RO127, "Joseph" replaces "John."

RO128 1c **blue** 3.50 22.50 5.50

M

John J. Macklin & Co. — RO129

John J. Macklin & Co.

RO129 1c **blk,** roulette *10,000.*

F. Mansfield & Co. — RO130

Maryland Match Co. — RO131

F. Mansfield & Co.

RO130 1c **blue** 7.25 14.00 14.00

Maryland Match Co.

RO131 1c **blue** 140.00 *25,000.*

"Matches" — RO132

A. Messinger — RO133

"Matches"

RO132 1c **blue** 7.75 5.50
Dbl. transfer 110.00
e. Experimental silk paper 160.00
u. 1c **ultra** *1,250.*

See Nos. RO168-RO169.

A. Messinger

RO133 1c **black** 4.50 18.00 4.00

N

National Match Co. — RO134

F. P. Newton — RO135

National Match Co.

RO134	1c	**blue**		82.50

Newbauer & Co. (N. & C.) follows No. RO139.

National Union Match Co. items are bogus.

F. P. Newton

RO135	1c	**lake**	3.50	13.50	4.50

See No. RO64 for another "The Clark Match Co." design.

New York Match Co. — RO136

New York Match Co.

No. RO136 is as No. RO22, "New York Match Co." instead of "Bauer & Beudel."

RO136	1c	**blue,** shield	775.00	9.00

No. RO137 is as No. RO111, "New York Match Co." instead of "B. & H. D. Howard."

RO137	1c	**ver,** eagle	100.00	11,000.
	e.	Experimental silk paper	175.00	
		As "e," dbl. transfer	275.00	

RO139

RO138	1c	**green,** 22x60mm	60.00	11.00	
	e.	Experimental silk paper	100.00		
RO139	5c	**blue,** 22x60mm		3,500.	

N. & C. (Newbauer & Co.)

RO140	4c	**green**	5.50	140.00	6.75

O

Orono Match Co.

RO141	1c	**blue**	40.00	40.00
	e.	Experimental silk paper	375.00	
	u.	1c **ultra**	675.00	

P

Park City Match Co. — RO142

Park City Match Co.

RO142	1c	**green**	55.00	52.50
	e.	Experimental silk paper	375.00	
RO143	3c	**orange**	60.00	
	e.	Experimental silk paper	—	

Penn Match Co. Limited

RO144	1c	**blue**	50.00

Pierce Match Co. — RO145

Pierce Match Co.

RO145	1c	**green**	4,000.

P. M. Co. (Portland M. Co.)

RO146	1c	**black**	27.50

Portland Match Co.

RO147	1c	**black,** wrapper	110.00

The value of No. RO147 applies to commonest date (Dec. 1866); all others are much rarer.

RO148

V.R. Powell — RO149-RO151

V. R. Powell

RO148	1c	**blue**	9.00	12.00
		Dbl. transfer	110.00	
	e.	Experimental silk paper	160.00	
	u.	1c **ultra**	925.00	
RO149	1c	**black**	*7,000.*	

Buff wrapper, uncut.

RO150	1c	**black**	2,750.

Buff wrapper, cut to shape.

RO151	1c	**black**	4,500.

White wrapper, cut to shape.

R

Reading Match Company

RO152	1c	**black**	10.00

Reed & Thompson — RO153

Reed & Thompson

RO153	1c	**black**	22.50

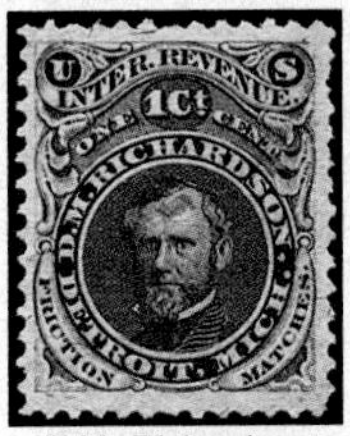

D.M. Richardson RO155

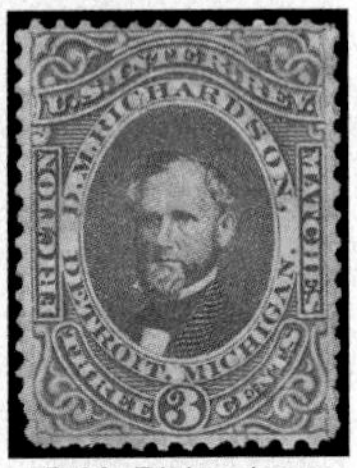

D.M. Richardson RO156

D. M. Richardson

RO154	1c	**red**	160.00	
RO155	1c	**black**	4.00	3.25
		Dbl. transfer		45.00
	e.	Experimental silk paper	75.00	
RO156	3c	**ver**	190.00	
RO157	3c	**blue**	7.75	5.00
		Dbl. transfer		30.00
	e.	Experimental silk paper	87.50	

The Richardson Match Co. — RO158

H. & W. Roeber — RO160

The Richardson Match Co.

The 1c is as No. RO154, 3c as No. RO156, inscribed "The Richardson Match Co." instead of "D. M. Richardson."

RO158	1c	**black**	2.25	6.75	9.00
RO159	3c	**blue**	95.00		

H. & W. Roeber

RO160	1c	**blue**	8.00	3.00
		Dbl. transfer	200.00	
	e.	Experimental silk paper	*450.00*	
	u.	1c **ultra**	300.00	

J.C. Ayer & Co. – RS4

Barham Pile Cure Co. – RS14

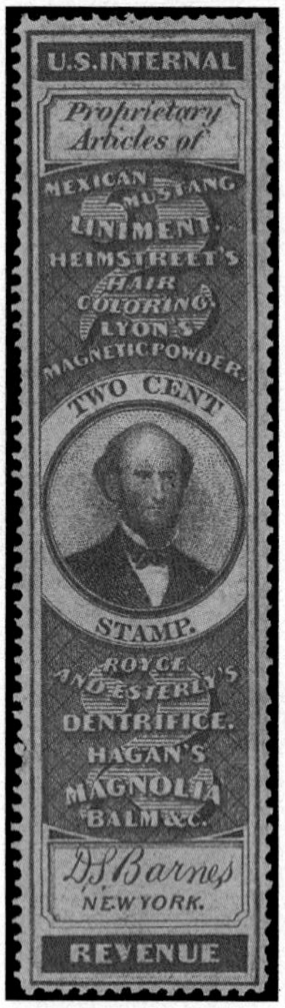

D.S. Barnes RS16

D.S. Barnes RS17

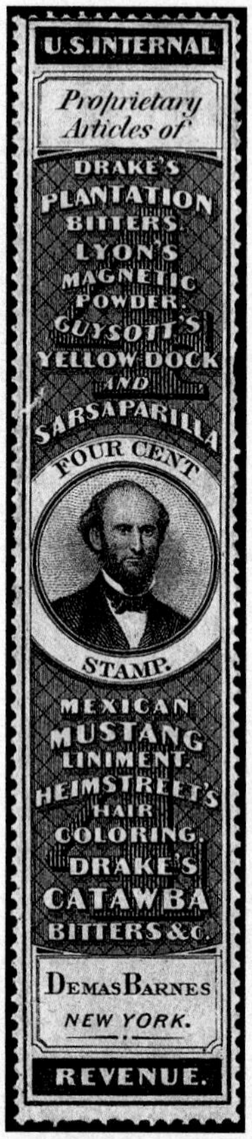

Demas Barnes RS23

Demas Barnes & Co. – RS24

T.H. Barr & Co. – RS27

Dr. John Bull RS42

John I. Brown & Son – RS39

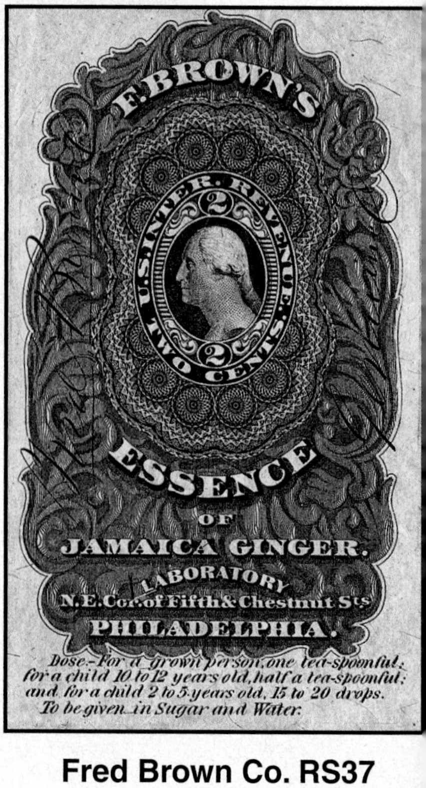

Fred Brown Co. RS37

J.W. Campion & Co. – RS47

Cannon & Co. – RS49

Dr. A.W. Chase, Son & Co. – RS55

Oliver Crook & Co. – RS65

Jeremiah Curtis & Son – RS67

Curtis & Brown – RS72

Dalley's Galvanic Horse Salve – RS73

Dalley's Magical Pain Extractor – RS74

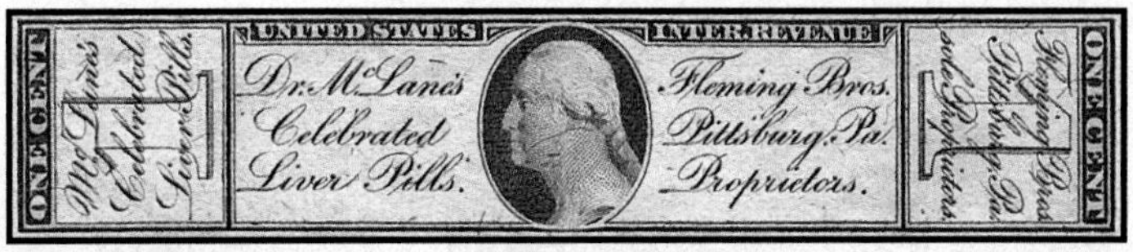

L. Pills – RS90

(Dr.) S.B. Hartman & Co. RS99

The Father Mathew Temperance & Manufacturing Company – RS85

(Dr.) S.B. Hartman & Co. – RS100

John F. Henry RS114

Hiscox & Co. RS123

Herrick's Pills RS117

William Roeber — RO161

William Roeber

As No. RO160, "William Roeber" instead of "H. & W. Roeber."

RO161	1c	**blue**	2.75	9.00	4.00
RO162	1c	**bl,** roulette			125.00

E. T. Russell — RO163

E. T. Russell

RO163	1c	**black**	9.50	20.00
e.		Experimental silk paper	65.00	

R. C. & W. (Ryder, Crouse & Welch)

RO164	1c	**lake**	110.00

S

San Francisco Match Co. — RO165

Illustration reduced.

San Francisco Match Company

RO165	12c	**blue**	550.00

Schmitt & Schmittdiel — RO166/RO167

Schmitt & Schmittdiel

RO166	1c	**ver**	5.50	100.00	5.50
RO167	3c	**blue**	67.50		

E. K. Smith — RO168/RO169

Standard Match Co. — RO170

E. K. Smith

RO168	1c	**blue**	14.00	55.00	20.00
RO169	1c	**blue,** roulette			*7,000.*

See No. RO132.

The Standard Match Company

RO170	1c	**black**	37.50

H. Stanton — RO171

H. Stanton

RO171	1c	**black**	17.00	11.00	22.50	10.00
e.		Experimental silk paper	110.00			

Star Match — RO172

Star Match

RO172	1c	**black**	5.50	1.10	2.00	85
		Dbl. transfer		—		20.00
e.		Experimental silk paper	80.00			

Swift & Courtney — RO173

Swift & Courtney

As No. RO174, "Swift & Courtney" in one line.

RO173	1c	**blue**	3.50	3.50
		Dbl. transfer		—
e.		Experimental silk paper	45.00	
u.		1c **ultra**	100.00	

RO174 Swift & Courtney & Beecher Co.

RO175 Swift & Courtney & Beecher

Swift & Courtney & Beecher Co.

RO174	1c	**blue**	3.50	5.50	2.25
		Dbl. transfer			—
RO175	1c	**black**			140.00

T

Trenton Match Co. — RO176

Trenton Match Co.

RO176	1c	**blue**	12.00

E. R. T. (E. R. Tyler)

As No. RO120, inscribed "E. R. T." instead of "The Ives & Judd Match Co."

RO177	1c	**green**	17.00	4.50
		Dbl. transfer		—
e.		Experimental silk paper	110.00	

U

Alex. Underwood & Co.

RO178	1c	**green**	95.00	160.00
e.		Experimental silk paper	475.00	

Union Match Co. — RO179

U.S.M. Co. — RO180

Union Match Co.

RO179	1c	**black**	60.00

U. S. M. Co. (Universal Safety Match Co.)

RO180	1c	**black**	4.50	30.00
e.		Experimental silk paper	100.00	

W

Washington Match Co. — RO181

Wilmington Parlor Match Co. — RO182

Washington Match Co.

RO181	1c	**black**	55.00

Wilmington Parlor Match Co.

RO182	1c	**black**	175.00	*12,500.*
e.		Experimental silk paper	475.00	

Wise & Co. — RO183

Wise & Co.

RO183	1c	**black**	1,900.

Z

F. Zaiss & Co. — RO184

F. Zaiss & Co.

RO184	1c	**black**	2.25	9.00	2.75

Zisemann, Griesheim & Co.

RO185	1c	**green**	2,500.	
RO186	1c	**blue**	160.00	25.00
u.		1c **ultra**	1,750.	

PRIVATE DIE CANNED FRUIT STAMP

T. Kensett & Co. — RP1

1867 *Perf. 12*

T. Kensett & Co.

			a. Old Paper	b. Silk Paper	c. Pink Paper	d. Wmkd. USIR (191R)
RP1	1c	**green**	2,500.			

PRIVATE DIE MEDICINE STAMPS

1862 *Perf. 12*

A

Anglo American Drug Co. — RS1

Anglo American Drug Co.

			a. Old Paper	b. Silk Paper	c. Pink Paper	d. Wmkd. USIR (191R)
RS1	1c	**black**				70.00

J. C. Ayer & Co.

For illustration of No. RS4, see large stamp illustration pages.

			a. Old Paper	b. Silk Paper	c. Pink Paper	d. Wmkd. USIR (191R)
RS2	1c	**brn car,** imperf	*10,000.*			
RS3	1c	**green,** imperf	*17,500.*			
RS4	1c	**black,** imperf, type 1	160.00	140.00		82.50
		Type 2	160.00	140.00	2,750.	77.50
		Dbl. transfer		—		
	e.	Experimental silk paper	—			

Type 1: long, full-pointed "y" in "Ayers;" Type 2: short, truncated "y" in "Ayers."

			a.	b.	c.	d.
RS5	1c	**blue,** imperf	*10,000.*			
RS6	1c	**org,** imperf	*17,500.*			
RS6F	1c	**red,** imperf	—			
RS7	1c	**gray lilac,** imperf	*17,500.*			

J.C. Ayer & Co. — RS8, RS9, RS11/RS13

J.C. Ayer & Co. RS10

			a. Old Paper	b. Silk Paper	c. Pink Paper	d. Wmkd. USIR (191R)
RS8	4c	**red,** die cut	*10,000.*			
RS9	4c	**blue,** die cut	9.50	9.50		9.50
	e.	Experimental silk paper	—			
	u.	4c **ultra** (die cut)	725.00			
RS10	4c	**blue,** imperf	400.00	275.00		350.00
RS11	4c	**purple,** die cut	*17,500.*			
RS12	4c	**green,** die cut	*15,000.*			
RS13	4c	**ver,** die cut	*10,000.*			

The 4c in black was printed and sent to Ayer & Co. It may exist but has not been seen by collectors.

B

Barham Pile Cure Co.

For illustration of No. RS14, see large stamp illustration pages.

			a.	b.	c.	d.
RS14	4c	**green,** wmkd. lozenges				90.00

D. S. Barnes

The 1c, 2c and 4c are about 184mm, 242mm and 304mm tall. The products mentioned differ. "D. S. Barnes" is in manscript.

For illustration of No. RS16 and RS17, see larger stamp illustration pages.

			a.	b.	c.	d.
RS15	1c	**ver**	525.00			
RS16	2c	**ver**	725.00			
RS17	4c	**ver**	1,400.			
RS18	1c	**black**	30.00			
RS19	2c	**black**	60.00			
RS20	4c	**black**	82.50			

Demas Barnes

Same as above but with "Demas Barnes" in serifed letters.

RS22 Foreign entry

For illustration of No. RS23, see large stamp illustration pages.

			a.	b.	c.	d.
RS21	1c	**black**	27.50			
RS22	2c	**black**	75.00			
		Foreign entry of 1c (No. RS15 or RS21)	*2,750.*			
RS23	4c	**black**	35.00			

Demas Barnes & Co.

For illustration of No. RS24, see large stamp illustration pages.

			a.	b.	c.	d.
RS24	1c	**black**	20.00	675.00		
	e.	Experimental silk paper	*2,000.*			
RS25	2c	**black**	20.00	500.00		
	e.	Experimental silk paper	300.00			
RS26	4c	**black**	20.00			

T. H. Barr & Co.

For illustration of No. RS27, see larger stamp illustration pages.

			a.	b.	c.	d.
RS27	4c	**black**	30.00			
		Dbl. transfer	225.00			
	e.	Experimental silk paper	450.00			

Barry's — RS28/RS29

Barry's

			a.	b.	c.	d.
RS28	2c	**green,** Tricopherous	12.00	22.50		
RS29	2c	**grn,** Proprietary		6.75	275.00	6.00
		Dbl. transfer		275.00		

D. M. Bennett — RS30

D. M. Bennett

			a.	b.	c.	d.
RS30	1c	**lake**	20.00			
	e.	Experiment. silk paper	150.00			

W. T. Blow — RS31

W. T. Blow

			a.	b.	c.	d.
RS31	1c	**green**	325.00	77.50	450.00	95.00
	e.	Experimental silk paper	1,900.			

B. Brandreth — RS33

R. Brandreth — RS35

B. Brandreth

			a.	b.	c.	d.
RS32	1c	**black,** perf	725.00	775.00		
RS33	1c	**black,** imperf	2.75	1.75		
	e.	Experimental silk paper	40.00			

Nos. RS32-RS33 inscribed "United States Certificate of Genuineness" around vignette.

			a.	b.	c.	d.
RS34	1c	**blk,** 41x50mm, imperf		275.00		
RS35	1c	**blk,** 24x30mm, imperf		2.00	11.00	2.25
	p.	Perf				550.00

The Home Bitters Co. – RS128

S.D. Howe – RS137

T.J. Husband – RS140

James A. Jackson & Co. – RS143

Dr. D. Jayne & Son – RS149

Lyon Manufg. Co. – RS167

Dr. Jas. C. Kerr – RS159

Jacob Lippman & Bro. – RS163

J.B. Kelly & Co.
RS153

T.W. Marsden – RS175

T.W. Marsden – RS176

Mercado & Seully – RS177

Mette & Kanne – RS180

Mishler Herb Bitters Co. – RS181

Moody, Michel & Co. – RS182

Morehead's – RS186

New York Pharmacal Association RS187

R. V. Pierce RS190

Dr. M. Perl & Co. – RS188

Bennett Pieters & Co. – RS191

Bennett Pieters & Co. – RS192

Radway & Co. – RS193

M., P.J. & H.M. Sands – RS209

Dr. C.F. Brown — RS36

Dr. C. F. Brown

RS36	1c	**blue**	500.00	87.50		100.00

Fred Brown Co.

For illustration of No. RS37, see larger stamp illustration pages.

RS37	2c	**black,** imperf, die I	140.00	47.50	3,750.	40.00
e.		Experimental silk paper	550.00			
RS38	2c	**black,** imperf, die II	82.50			

Die I has "E" of "Fred" incomplete. Die II shows recutting in the "E" of "Fred" and "Genuine."

John I. Brown & Son.

For illustration of No. RS39, see larger stamp illustration pages.

RS39	1c	**black**	11.00	45.00		10.00
RS40	2c	**green**	11.00	20.00	400.00	400.00
		Dbl. transfer	—			
e.		Experimental silk paper	190.00			
RS41	4c	**brown**	550.00	140.00		2,250.

Dr. John Bull

For illustration of No. RS42, see larger stamp illustration pages.

RS42	1c	**black**	210.00	22.50	825.00	22.50
e.		Experimental silk paper	425.00			
RS43	4c	**blue**	225.00	13.50	600.00	12.00
e.		Experimental silk paper	750.00			
u.		4c **ultra**	*2,750.*			

J. S. Burdsal & Co.

"J. S. Burdsal & Co./Sole Proprietors" added under United States Proprietary Medicine Co. design, as on Nos. RS245-RS247.

RS44	1c	**blk,** wrapper, white paper		60.00		40.00
RS45	1c	**blk,** wrapper, orange paper		*4,250.*		1,650.
RS45A	1c	**blk,** wrapper, yellow paper		*4,000.*		

Joseph Burnett & Co. — RS46

Joseph Burnett & Co.

RS46	4c	**black**	110.00	16.00	400.00	7.75

C

J. W. Campion & Co.

For illustration of No. RS47, see large stamp illustration pages.

RS47	4c	**black,** imperf		550.00		425.00
p.		Pair, perf horiz.				2,750.
RS48	4c	**black,** die cut		160.00	550.00	125.00

Cannon & Co.

For illustration of No. RS49, see larger stamp illustration pages.

RS49	4c	**green,** imperf		140.00	300.00	77.50

The Centaur Co. — RS50/RS52

The Centaur Co.

RS50	1c	**ver**			72.50	11.00
RS51	2c	**black**			16.00	4.00
RS52	4c	**black**				67.50

Dr. A. W. Chase, Son & Co.

For illustration of No. RS55, see large stamp illustration pages.

RS53	1c	**black**		160.00		5,500.
RS54	2c	**black**		160.00		
RS55	4c	**black**		225.00		

Wm. E. Clarke

RS56 RS57

Wm. E Clarke

RS56	3c	**blue**				225.00
RS57	6c	**black**				110.00

R. C. & C. S. Clark — RS58

R. C. & C. S. Clark

RS58	4c	**black**		22.50		27.50

Collins Bros. — RS59

W. H. Comstock — RS60

Collins Bros.

RS59	1c	**black**	29.00	550.00		

W. H. Comstock

RS60	1c	**black**				5.50

Cook & Bernheimer

RS61	4c	**blue**				125.00

Charles N. Crittenton — RS62/RS64

Charles N. Crittenton

RS62	1c	**black**		11.00		
RS63	1c	**blue**			14.00	7.25
RS64	2c	**black**		95.00	55.00	5.50

Oliver Crook & Co.

For illustration of No. RS65, see larger stamp illustration pages.

RS65	4c	**black**	140.00	27.50		
e.		Experimental silk paper	125.00			

Jeremiah Curtis & Son

For illustration of No. RS67, see larger stamp illustration pages.

RS66	1c	**black**	140.00			
		Die I, small "1s."				
RS67	1c	**black**				125.00
		Die II, large "1s."				
RS68	2c	**black**	11.00	11.00	175.00	400.00
		Dbl. transfer		—		

Die II numerals nearly fill the circles.

Curtis & Brown RS69

Curtis & Brown

RS69	1c	**black**	6.25	4.50		
e.		Experimental silk paper	*3,250.*			
RS70	2c	**black**		200.00		

Curtis & Brown Mfg. Co. RS71

Curtis & Brown Mfg. Co.

These are identical to RS69-RS70 with "Mfg. Co. Limtd." instead of the right hand "TWO CENTS."

RS71	1c	**black**			275.00	10.00
RS72	2c	**black**		2,450.		1,100.

D

Dalley's Galvanic Horse Salve

For illustration of No. RS73, see larger stamp illustration pages.

RS73	2c	**green**	125.00	225.00		300.00

Dalley's Magical Pain Extractor

For illustration of No. RS74, see larger stamp illustration pages.

RS74	1c	**black**	16.00	12.00		9.25
h.		$100	500.00			20.00

#RS74h reads "$100" instead of "$1.00."

Perry Davis & Son — RS75/RS81

Perry Davis & Son

RS75	1c	**blue**	10.00	4.00	400.00	2.75
e.		Experimental silk paper	200.00			
u.		1c **ultra**	300.00			
RS76	2c	**brown red**	200.00			
RS77	2c	**black**	90.00			
RS78	2c	**dull pur**		11.00		
RS78A	2c	**slate**		14.00		7.25
RS79	2c	**dull red**		110.00		
RS80	2c	**brown**		*6,000.*		
RS81	4c	**brown**	14.50	4.50		3.25

P.H. Drake & Co. — RS82/RS83

P. H. Drake & Co.

RS82	2c	**black**	*5,000.*			
RS83	4c	**black**	67.50	77.50		
e.		Experimental silk paper	250.00			

F

B. A. Fahnestock — RS84

B. A. Fahnestock

RS84	1c	**lake,** imperf	175.00	140.00		

The Father Mathew Temperance & Manufacturing Company

For illustration of No. RS85, see large stamp illustration pages.

RS85	4c	**black**				11.00

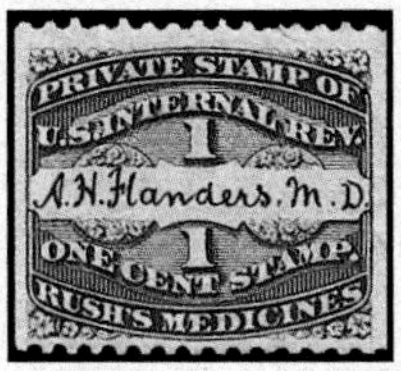

A. H. Flanders, M.D. — RS87

A. H. Flanders, M. D.

RS86	1c	**green,** perf		16.00		14.50
RS87	1c	**green,** part perf	27.50	2.25	45.00	3.25

Fleming Bros. — RS88/RS90

Fleming Bros. Vermifuge

RS88	1c	**black,** imperf	16.00	25.00		67.50
e.		Experimental silk paper	125.00			

L. Pills

For illustration of No. RS90, see large stamp illustration pages.

RS89	1c	**black,** imperf	*8,000.*			
RS90	1c	**blue,** imperf	7.75	9.00		11.00
		Dbl. transfer		77.50		77.50
e.		Experimental silk paper	—			
u.		1c **ultra**	2,400.			

Seth W. Fowle & Son — RS91

Seth W. Fowle & Son, J. P. Dinsmore

RS91	4c	**black**	22.50	3.25		3.25

G

G. G. Green — RS92/RS93

G. G. Green

RS92	3c	**black**				7.75
h.		Tete beche pair				825.00
RS93	3c	**blk,** rouletted				250.00

H

Reuben P. Hall & Co.

RS94	4c	**black**	22.50	22.50		25.00
e.		Experimental silk paper	*550.*			

Hall & Ruckel — RS95

Hall & Ruckel — RS96

Hall & Ruckel as agents for Xavier Bazin — RS95h/RS96h

Hall & Ruckel

RS95	1c	**green**	2.00	2.00	35.00	2.00
e.		Experimental silk paper	35.00			
h.		Handstamped "X.B." (Xavier Bazin) and obliteration				5.00
RS96	3c	**black**	3.50	3.25	67.50	3.25
h.		Handstamped "X.B." (Xavier Bazin) and obliteration				7.50

Dr. Harter & Co.

RS97	1c	**black**	27.50	18.00		
e.		Experimental silk paper	250.00			

Dr. Harter — RS98

Dr. Harter

As No. RS97, inscribed "Dr. Harter" instead of "Dr. Harter & Co."

RS98	1c	**black**		4.50	16.00	5.50
		Dbl. impression		*4,500.*		

(Dr.) S. B. Hartman & Co.

For illustration of No. RS100, see large stamp illustration pages.

RS99	4c	**black**	2,250.	87.50	1,400.	1,900.
RS100	6c	**black**	775.00	400.00		

E. T. Hazeltine — RS101/RS103

E. T. Hazeltine

RS101	1c	**black**				21.00
RS102	2c	**blue**		42.50		
RS103	4c	**black**	900.00	27.50		20.00
e.		Experimental silk paper	3,750.			
i.		Imperf, pair	1,100.			

E. H. (Edward Heaton) — RS105

E. H. (Edward Heaton)

RS104	3c	**black**				55.00
RS105	3c	**brown**				20.00

Helmbold's — RS106/RS109

Helmbold's

RS106	2c	**blue**	1.75	400.00		
		Dbl. transfer	—			
RS107	3c	**green**	55.00	40.00		
RS108	4c	**black**	5.00	225.00		
		Dbl. transfer	175.00			
RS109	6c	**black**	2.25	4.00		
e.		Experimental silk paper	55.00			

Scheetz's Celebrated Bitter Cordial – RS210

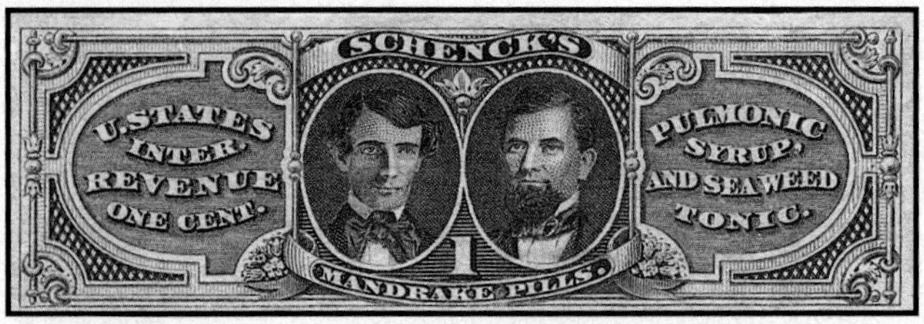

Schenck's Mandrake Pills – RS212

Schenck's Pulmonic Syrup – RS213

J.E. Schwartz & Co. – RS215

Dr. D.H. Seelye & Co. – RS222

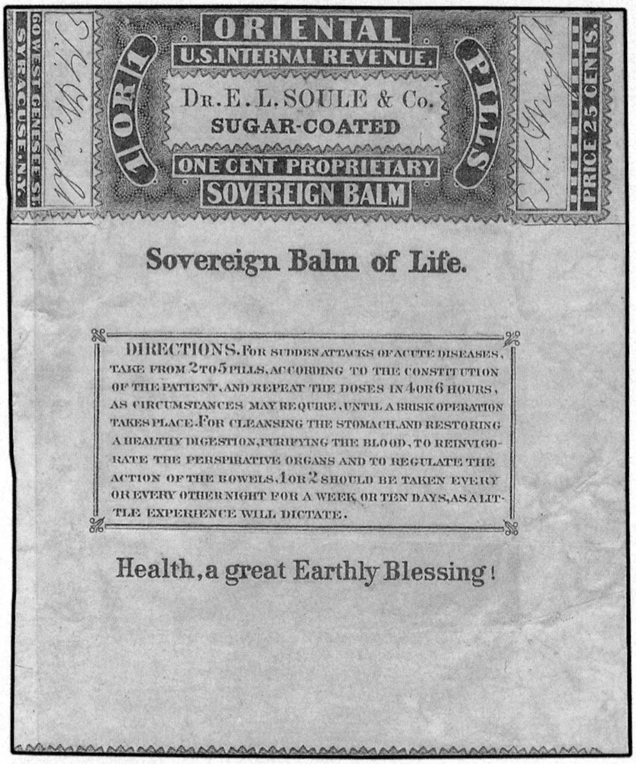

Dr. E.L. Soule & Co. – RS227

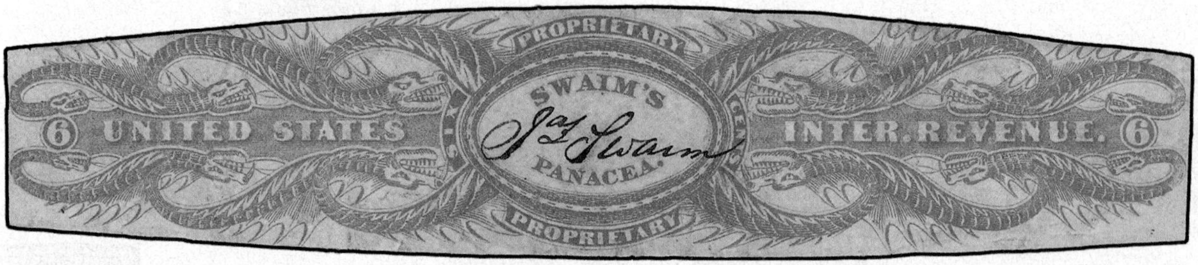

Jas. Swaim RS231

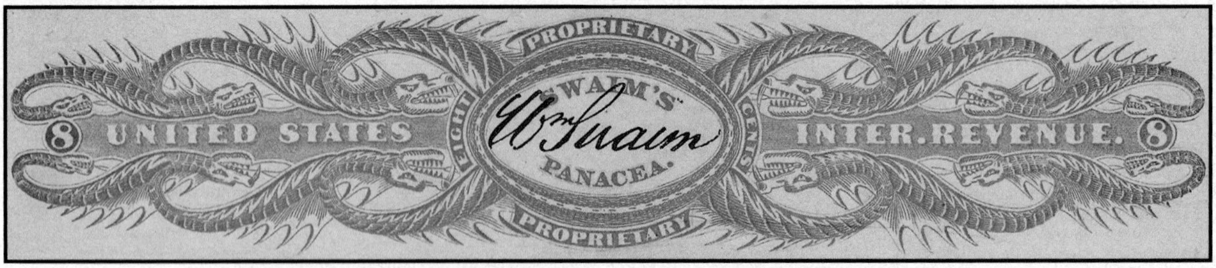

Wm. Swaim RS234

George Tallcot RS240

United States Proprietary Medicine Co. – RS243

S.R. Van Duzer – RS249

United States Proprietary Medicine Co. – RS247

World's Dispensary Medical Association RS272

World's Dispensary Medical Association RS273

West India Manufacturing Co. – RS264

Hostetter Co. – RS285

X. Bazin RT1

E.W. Hoyt & Co. RT7

E.W. Hoyt & Co. RT8

E.W. Hoyt & Co. – RT11

A. L. Helmbold's

Same as "Helmbold's" but inscribed "A. L. Helmbold's."

RS110	2c	**blue**		140.00	200.00	110.00
RS111	4c	**black**		30.00	210.00	11.00

RS112

John F. Henry

RS112	2c	**violet**	900.00			
RS113	4c	**bister**	2,000.			

For illustration of No. RS114, see large stamp illustration pages.

RS114	1c	**black**	67.50	1.10	11.00	1.75
	e.	Experimental silk paper	210.00			

Horiz. pairs imperf between were issued of No. RS114d. All known pairs were originally separated, and some have been matched and rejoined. Three rejoined pairs are reported.

RS115	2c	**blue**	40.00	7.25	160.00	6.75
	u.	**ultra**	600.00			
RS116	4c	**red**	200.00	1.75	40.00	2.75
	e.	Experimental silk paper	110.00			

Herrick's Pills

For illustration of No. RS117, see large stamp illustration pages.

RS117	1c	**black**	100.00	45.00	160.00	50.00
	e.	Experimental silk paper	225.00			
	i.	Imperf, pair	*3,000.*			

No. RS117i is valued in sound condition. Most pairs are faulty and sell for much less.

Herrick's Pills & Plasters — RS118

Herrick's Pills & Plasters

RS118	1c	**red**	2.75	5.50	82.50	2.75
	e.	Experimental silk paper	—			

J.E. Hetherington — RS121

J. E. Hetherington

RS119	1c	**black**				20.00
RS120	2c	**black**				825.00
RS121	3c	**black**				25.00

	i.	Imperf, pair				2,250.

Hiscox & Co.

For illustration of No. RS123, see large stamp illustration pages.

RS122	2c	**black**				17.00
RS123	4c	**black**		125.00	650.00	2,250.

Holloway's Pills and Ointment — RS124/RS125

Holloway's Pills and Ointment

RS124	1c	**blue,** perf	11.00			
RS125	1c	**blue,** imperf	450.00			

Holman Liver Pad Co. — RS126/RS127

Holman Liver Pad Co.

RS126	1c	**green**				22.50
RS127	4c	**green**				11.00

The Home Bitters Co.

For illustration of No. RS128, see large stamp illustration pages.

RS128	2c	**blue**				250.00
		Dbl. transfer				—
RS129	3c	**green**		140.00	175.00	110.00
RS130	4c	**green**		275.00		400.00

Hop Bitters Co. — RS131

Hop Bitters Co.

RS131	4c	**black**				7.75

Hostetter & Smith

RS132	4c	**blk,** imperf	82.50	45.00	110.00	35.00
		Dbl. transfer	—	55.00	125.00	42.50
	e.	Experimental silk paper	400.00			
RS133	6c	**blk,** imperf	100.00			
	e.	Experimental silk paper	500.00			

S. D. Howe

For illustration of No. RS137, see large stamp illustration pages.

RS134	4c	**black,** Duponco's Pills	140.00	400.00		
RS135	4c	**red,** Duponco's Pills		475.00		
RS136	4c	**green,** Duponco's Pills		475.00		

Nos. RS135 and RS136 were never used.

RS137	4c	**blue,** Arabian Milk		9.00		175.00

C.E. Hull & Co. — RS138

C. E. Hull & Co.

RS138	1c	**black**	140.00	6.25	60.00	6.25

T. J. Husband

For illustration of No. RS140, see large stamp illustration pages.

RS139	2c	**vio,** imperf	2,250.			
RS140	2c	**ver,** imperf	17.00	11.00		10.00

Hutchings & Hillyer

RS141	4c	**grn,** imperf	22.50	35.00		
	e.	Experimental silk paper	225.00			

I

H. A. Ingham & Co.

RS142	1c	**black**				60.00

J

James A. Jackson & Co.

For illustration of No. RS143, see large stamp illustration pages.

RS143	4c	**green**	2,250.	400.00		
		Dbl. transfer		—		

Dr. D. Jayne & Son

For illustration of No. RS149, see large stamp illustration pages.

RS144	1c	**blue,** imperf	—	3,750.		600.00
	p.	Perf	900.00			*3,500.*
RS145	2c	**blk,** imperf	*8,750.*	2,750.		1,500.
	p.	Perf	*3,750.*			—
RS146	4c	**grn,** imperf	*4,500.*	2,400.	1,500.	650.00
	p.	Perf	*4,500.*			—
RS146F	4c	**red,** imperf	—			
RS146G	4c	**org,** imperf	—			
RS147	1c	**bl,** die cut	6.75	5.50	250.00	5.50
	e.	Experimental silk paper	—			
	p.	Perf and die cut	160.00	275.00	275.00	550.00
		On horiz. laid paper	62.50			
RS148	2c	**blk,** die cut	11.00	9.00	110.00	5.50
		Dbl. transfer	60.00	60.00	125.00	82.50
	e.	Experimental silk paper	200.00			
	p.	Perf & die cut	45.00	250.00	400.00	
RS149	4c	**grn,** die cut	7.75	5.50	100.00	9.25
		Dbl. transfer		—		
	e.	Experimental silk paper	175.			
	p.	Perf & die cut	50.00	240.00		300.00
		On vertically laid paper	35.00			

I. S. Johnson & Co. — RS150

Johnston Holloway & Co. — RS151/RS152

I. S. Johnson & Co.

RS150	1c	ver		1.50	16.00	1.00
		Dbl. transfer		22.50	60.00	27.50

Johnston Holloway & Co.

RS151	1c	**black**		4.00		3.00
RS152	2c	**green**		4.00		3.25

K

J. B. Kelly & Co.

For illustration of No. RS153, see large stamp illustration pages.

RS153	4c	**blk,** imperf	2,250.			
	e.	Experimental silk paper	2,500.			

B. J. Kendall & Co.

RS154	4c	**blue**				35.00

Dr. Kennedy — RS155

Dr. Kennedy — RS156

Dr. Kennedy

RS155	2c	**green**	60.00	9.00	40.00	6.75
		Dbl. transfer				—
	e.	Experimental silk paper	*1,650.*			
RS156	6c	**black**		9.00	82.50	9.00

Kennedy & Co. RS157

Kennedy & Co.

RS157	2c	**black**		7.75	125.00	9.25

K & Co. (Kennedy & Co.)

RS158	1c	**green**				8.25

Dr. Jas. C. Kerr

For illustration of No. RS159, see large stamp illustration pages.

RS159	4c	**blue**	*8,750.*	375.00		200.00
RS160	6c	**black**	825.00			

L

Lawrence & Martin

RS161	4c	**black**				50.00

Lee & Osgood

RS162	1c	**blue**	16.00	22.50		17.00

Jacob Lippman & Bro.

For illustration of No. RS163, see large stamp illustration pages.

RS163	4c	**blue**	2,000.	2,500.		
	e.	Experimental silk paper	3,750.			

Alvah Littlefield — RS165

Alvah Littlefield

RS164	1c	**black**	1.75	1.10		22.50
		Dbl. transfer	100.00	82.50		
	e.	Experimental silk paper	160.00			
		On horiz. laid paper	*600.00*			
RS165	4c	**green**	2,000.	250.00		

Prof. Low — RS166

Prof. Low

RS166	1c	**black**		3.50	20.00	3.50
		Dbl. transfer		—	60.00	45.00

Lyon Manufg. Co.

As No. RS24, inscribed "Lyon Manufg. Co." instead of "Demas Barnes & Co."

For illustration of No. RS167, see large stamp illustration pages.

RS167	1c	**black**		22.50	400.00	16.00
RS168	2c	**black**		10.00	200.00	10.00
	i.	Vert. pair, imperf btwn.				2,250.

M

J. McCullough

As No. RS137, inscribed "J. McCullough" instead of "S. D. Howe."

RS169	4c	**black**		140.00		125.00

J. H. McLean — RS170

Manhattan Medicine Co. — RS171/RS172

Dr. J. H. McLean

RS170	1c	**black**	2.75	1.75	17.00	1.75
		Dbl. transfer	55.00	72.50	—	40.00
	e.	Experimental silk paper	125.00			
	i.	Vert. pair, imperf horiz.	—			

Manhattan Medicine Co.

RS171	1c	**violet**				42.50
	u.	1c **purple**				67.50
RS172	2c	**black**		30.00	42.50	16.00

Mansfield & Higbee

As No. RS174, inscribed "Mansfield & Higbee Memphis, Tenn."

RS173	1c	**blue**		18.00		
	i.	Pair, imperf btwn.		175.00		
	j.	Block of 4, imperf btwn.		200.00		

S. Mansfield & Co. — RS174

Merchant's Gargling Oil — RS178/RS179

S. Mansfield & Co.

RS174	1c	**blue**		30.00	210.00	17.00
	i.	Pair, imperf btwn.		300.00	750.00	375.00
	j.	Block of 4, imperf btwn.		500.00	1,000.	275.00

Nos. RS173-RS174 are perf on 4 sides. The i. and j. varieties served as 2c or 4c stamps. Straight-edged stamps from severed pairs or blocks are worth much less.

T. W. Marsden

For illustrations of No. RS175-RS176, see large stamp illustration pages.

RS175	2c	**blue**	*10,000.*			
RS176	4c	**black**	525.00			

Mercado & Seully

For illustration of No. RS177, see large stamp illustration pages.

RS177	2c	**blk,** imperf	*8,000.*			

Merchant's Gargling Oil

RS178	1c	**black**	275.00	45.00	1,250.	35.00
	e.	Experimental silk paper	*3,250.*			
RS179	2c	**green**	275.00	35.00	1,500.	27.50
		Foreign entry		*3,000.*		*3,750.*
	e.	Experimental silk paper	3,250.			

Foreign entry is over design of #RO11.

Mette & Kanne

For illustration of No. RS180, see large stamp illustration pages.

RS180	3c	**black**				400.00

Mishler Herb Bitters Co.

For illustration of No. RS181, see large stamp illustration pages.

RS181	4c	**black**				175.00
	p.	Imperf at ends				225.00

Moody, Michel & Co.

For illustration of No. RS182, see large stamp illustration pages.

RS182	4c	**blk,** imperf		200.00		

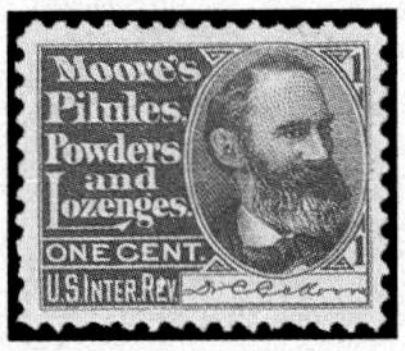

Dr. C. C. Moore — RS183

Dr. C. C. Moore

RS183	1c	**ver,** Pilules				6.75
RS184	2c	**black,** Sure Cure		82.50	*15,000.*	30.00

Morehead's

For illustration of No. RS186, see large stamp illustration pages.

RS185	1c	**black,** Magetic Plaster	30.00			

RS186	4c	**black,** Neurodyne	3,250.			

N

New York Pharmacal Association

For illustration of No. RS187, see larger stamp illustration pages.

RS187	4c	**black**		17.00	40.00	10.00

P

Dr. M. Perl & Co.

For illustration of No. RS188, see large stamp illustration pages.

RS188	6c	**black,** cut to shape	1,650.			

R. V. Pierce — RS189/RS190

R. V. Pierce

For illustration of No. RS190, see large stamp illustration pages.

RS189	1c	**green**		25.00	200.00	27.50
RS190	2c	**black**	30.00	8.25	35.00	7.75
		Dbl. transfer		—		
	e.	Experimental silk paper	150.00			

Bennett Pieters & Co.

For illustration of No. RS191, see large stamp illustration pages.

RS191	4c	**black**	600.00	6,000.		
	e.	Experimental silk paper	2,750.			
RS192	6c	**black**	1,750.			
	i.	Imperf	*1,600.*			

R

Radway & Co.

For illustration of No. RS193, see large stamp illustration pages.

RS193	2c	**black**	5.00	3.25	12.00	5.50
		Dbl. transfer		72.50	110.00	82.50
	e.	Experimental silk paper	85.00			

D. Ransom & Co.

RS194	1c	**blue**	5.00	3.00		
		Dbl. transfer		—		
	e.	Experimental silk paper	160.00			
RS195	2c	**black**	27.50	35.00		
	e.	Experimental silk paper	160.00			

D. Ransom, Son & Co. — RS197

D. Ransom, Son & Co.

As Nos. RS194-RS195 with "Son" added.

RS196	1c	**blue**		4.50	17.00	6.75
		Dbl. transfer		—		
RS197	2c	**black**		18.00	82.50	11.00

Redding's Russia Salve — RS198

Redding's Russia Salve

RS198	1c	**black**		9.00		9.00
		Dbl. transfer		140.00		

Ring's Vegetable Ambrosia — RS199/RS200

Ring's Vegetable Ambrosia

RS199	2c	**blue,** imperf		4,250.		
	p.	Perf		*3,500.*		
RS200	4c	**blk,** imperf	5,000.	5,500.		

Ring's Vegetable Ambrosia — RS201/RS202

RS203

RS201	2c	**bl,** die cut		25.00		
RS202	4c	**black,** die cut	17.00	17.00		25.00
	e.	Experimental silk paper	160.00			
RS203	4c	**black,** perf		2,000.		3,250.
	k.	Perf & die cut				1,100.
	p.	Part perf		3,750.		—

J. B. Rose & Co. — RS204/RS205

J. B. Rose & Co.

RS204	2c	**black**		6.75	35.00	
		Dbl. transfer		160.00	225.00	
RS205	4c	**black**	*8,750.*	160.00		
		Dbl. transfer		—		

Rumford Chemical Works

RS206	2c	**green**				5.00
RS207	2c	**grn,** imperf				27.50

S

A. B. & D. Sands

RS208	1c	**green**	11.00	22.50		
	e.	Experimental silk paper	100.00			

M., P. J. & H. M. Sands

The #RS208 die was altered to make #RS209.

For illustration of No. RS209, see large stamp illustration pages.

RS209	2c	**green**		20.00	125.00	17.00

Scheetz's Celebrated Bitter Cordial

For illustration of No. RS210, see large stamp illustration pages.

RS210	4c	**black,** perf		1,100.		
RS211	4c	**blk,** imperf		*8,000.*		

Schenck's Mandrake Pills

For illustration of No. RS212, see large stamp illustration pages.

RS212	1c	**grn,** imperf	5.50	11.00	140.00	5.50
		Dbl. transfer		3.50		—
	e.	Experimental silk paper	375.			
	p.	Perf				*2,500.*

Schenck's Pulmonic Syrup

For illustration of No. RS213, see larger stamp illustration pages.

RS213	6c	**blk,** imperf	8.25	5.50	110.00	160.00
		Dbl. transfer		62.50		—
	e.	Experimental silk paper	200.00			
	p.	Perf	240.00			

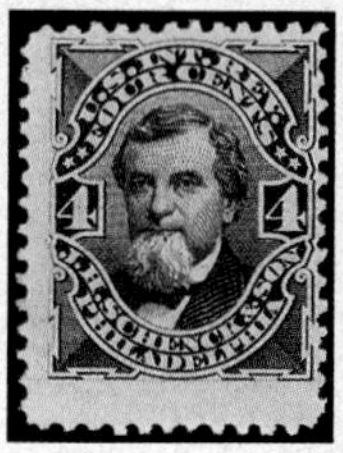

J. H. Schenck & Son — RS214

J. H. Schenck & Son

RS214	4c	**black**				11.00

J. E. Schwartz & Co.

As No. RS84, inscribed "J. E. Schwartz & Co." instead of "B. A. Fahnestock."

For illustration of No. RS215, see large stamp illustration pages.

RS215	1c	**lake,** imperf		160.00	1,100.	125.00

"A. L. Scovill" follows No. RS219.

Seabury & Johnson — RS216

Seabury & Johnson — RS218

Seabury & Johnson

RS216 1c **black** 82.50
RS217 1c **black,** printed obliteration over "porous" 5.50
h. "Porous" obliterated by pen 5.50
RS218 1c **lake** *3,500.*

"Dr. D. H. Seelye & Co." follows No. RS221.

Dr. S. Brown Sigesmond

RS219 4c **blue** 125.00

A. L. Scovill & Co. — RS220/RS221

A. L. Scovill & Co.

RS220 1c **black** 2.00 2.75
Dbl. transfer — —
e. Experimental silk paper 75.00
r. Printed on both sides *2,500.*
RS221 4c **green** 2.25 5.50
e. Experimental silk paper 175.00

Dr. D. H. Seelye & Co.

For illustration of No. RS222, see larger stamp illustration pages.

RS222 8c **blk,** imperf 27.50

Dr. M. A. Simmons

RS223 1c **black,** Iuka, Miss. 125.00 *15,000.*
RS224 1c **black,** St. Louis, Mo. 125.00

S. N. Smith & Co.

As No. RS65, inscribed "S. N. Smith & Co." instead of "Oliver Crook & Co."

For illustration of No. RS225, see large stamp illustration pages.

RS225 4c **black** 55.00 55.00

Dr. E. L. Soule & Co.

For illustration of No. RS227, see large stamp illustration pages.

N.Y. Wrapper

RS226 1c **blue** 82.50
For. entry —

Syracuse Wrapper

RS227 1c **blue** 82.50 40.00
For. entry 400.00 *1,250.*
u. **ultra** 925.00
For. entry —

For Nos. RS226, RS227, the foreign entry is the design of No. RT1 (pos. 1).

H. R. Stevens — RS228/RS229

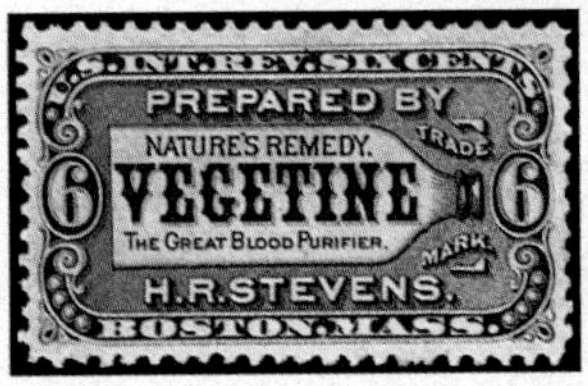

H.R. Stevens — RS230

H. R. Stevens

RS228 1c **brown** 18.00
RS229 2c **choc** 6.75
RS230 6c **black** 125.00 6.75

Jas. Swaim

For illustration of No. RS231, see large stamp illustration pages.

RS231 6c **org** *6,500.*

Die cut, ms signature.

RS232 8c **org,** imperf 3,000.
h. Ms. *10,000.* *10,000.*
RS233 8c **org,** die cut 400.00
e. Experimental silk paper —
h. Ms. 4,500. —

No. RS232h, RS233h have manuscript signature.

Wm. Swaim

For illustration of No. RS234, see large stamp illustration pages.

RS234 8c **org,** imperf *9,000.* *6,000.* 2,650.
k. None *10,000.* *10,000.*

No. RS234k is without signature. No. RS234d is found with signature "Suaim" or "Swaim." Also, No. RS234b is found with a period under the raised "m" of "Wm" and the right leg of "w" of "Swaim" retouched, both by pen.

RS235 8c **org,** die cut *1,650.* 210.00 250.00
h. Ms. *25,000.*
k. Invt. *10,000.*

Nos. RS235h has manuscript signature and is unique. No. RS235k has signature inverted.

RS237

Dr. G. W. Swett

RS236 4c **blk,** die cut 17.00
RS237 4c **green,** perf 250.00 *3,250.*
RS238 4c **green,** perf and die cut 450.00 *3,750.*

T

George Tallcot

For illustration of No. RS240, see large stamp illustration pages.

RS239 2c **ver** 17.00
RS240 4c **black** 95.00 *12,000.* 22.50

Tarrant & Co. RS241

John L. Thompson RS242

Tarrant & Company

RS241 4c **red** 3.25 100.00 2.25

John L. Thompson

RS242 1c **black** 6.75 8.25 6.75
Dbl. transfer —
e. Experimental silk paper 150.00

U

United States Proprietary Medicine Co.

For illustration of No. RS243, see large stamp illustration pages.

RS243 4c **black** 50.00 110.00
e. Experimental silk paper 225.00
RS244 6c **black** *2,500.*

U. S. Proprietary Medicine Co. Wrappers

For illustration of No. RS247, see larger stamp illustration pages.

RS245 1c **black,** *white* 50.00 50.00
e. Experimental silk paper *500.00*
RS246 1c **black,** *yel* 140.00 250.00
RS247 1c **black,** *org* 275.00 *7,000.*
RS248 1c **black,** *org red* *3,750.* *12,000.*

V

S. R. Van Duzer

For illustration of No. RS249, see large stamp illustration pages.

RS249 4c **black** 45.00 40.00 210.00
RS250 6c **black** 82.50

A. Vogeler & Co. — RS251

Vogeler, Meyer & Co. — RS252

A. Vogeler & Co.

RS251 1c **black** 1.75 2.25

Vogeler, Meyer & Co.

RS252 1c **ver** 4.50 1.50

W

Dr. J. Walker

RS253 4c **black** 45.00 22.50 22.50
Dbl. transfer 55.00 45.00
e. Experimental silk paper 300.00

H. H. Warner & Co. — RS254/RS255

H. H. W. & Co. (H. H. Warner & Co.)

RS254 1c **brown** 6.75
RS255 6c **brown,** 19x26mm 90.00

RS256	2c	**brown,** 88x11mm				35.00
RS257	4c	**brown,** 95x18mm				35.00
RS258	6c	**brown**				7.75
		Dbl. transfer				52.50

Weeks & Potter — RS259

RS261

RS262

Weeks & Potter

RS259	1c	**black**		7.75		5.50
RS260	2c	**black**		110.00		
RS261	4c	**black**		30.00	30.00	7.75
RS262	2c	**red**			40.00	7.75

Wells, Richardson & Co. — RS263

Edward Wilder — RS265/RS269

Wells, Richardson & Co.

RS263	4c	**black**				30.00

West India Manufacturing Co.

For illustration of No. RS264, see large stamp illustration pages.

RS264	4c	**blk,** die I		250.00	400.00	550.00
RS264A	4c	**blk,** die II				675.00

Die II shows evidence of retouching, particularly in the central disk.

Edward Wilder

RS265	1c	**grn,** imperf	*2,250.*	350.00		300.00
	e.	Experimental silk paper	*7,500.*			
RS266	1c	**grn,** die cut	55.00	50.00		25.00
	e.	Experimental silk paper	300.			
RS266A	4c	**ver,** imperf				
	e.	Experimental silk paper	*8,000.*			
RS267	4c	**ver,** die cut	200.00	*2,250.*		
	e.	Experimental silk paper	140.			
RS268	4c	**lake,** imperf		275.00		2,250.

RS269	4c	**lake,** die cut	*2,000.*	14.00		14.00

Rev. E. A. Wilson

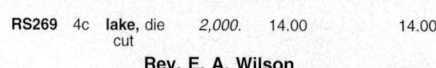

RS270	12c	**blue**		82.50		550.00

Thos. E. Wilson, M.D. RS271

Thos. E. Wilson, M. D.

RS271	4c	**black**	*25,000.*			

World's Dispensary Medical Assocn.

For illustration of No. RS273, see larger stamp illustration pages.

RS272	1c	**green**				27.50
RS273	2c	**black,** 56x256mm				9.00

Wright's Indian Vegetable Pills — RS274

Wright's Indian Vegetable Pills

RS274	1c	**green**	2.25	1.75	40.00	3.50
		Dbl. transfer				—
	e.	Experimental silk paper	150.			

Z

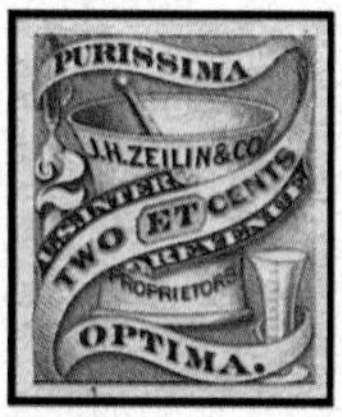

J.H. Zeilin & Co. — RS275/RS277

J.H. Zeilin & Co.

RS275	2c	**red**		1,100.		
RS276	2c	**green,** perf		45.00		—
RS277	2c	**grn,** imperf	200.00	8.25	140.00	5.50

			Roul. 5½ Unused	Used	p. Hyphen Hole Perf. 7 Unused	Used

1898-1900

See rouletting note preceding No. R161.

The Antikamnia Chemical Co. — RS278

The Antikamnia Chemical Co.

RS278	2½c	**car**			4.00	4.00

Fernet Branca (Branca Bros.) — RS279

Fernet Branca (Branca Bros.)

RS279	4c	**black**	9.50	9.50	9.50	9.50

			Roul. 5½ Unused	Used	p. Hyphen Hole Perf. 7 Unused	Used

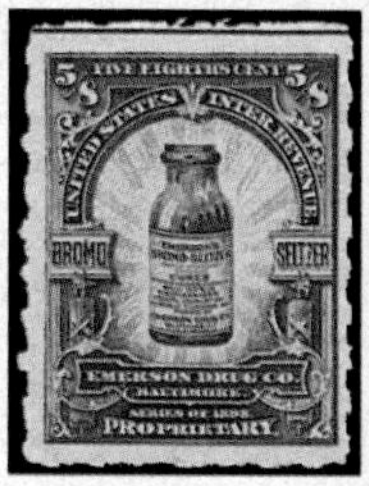

Emerson Drug Co. — RS281

Emerson Drug Co.

RS280	¼c	**car**			7.00	3.00
RS281	⅝c	**green**			7.00	3.50
RS282	1¼c	**vio brn**			9.00	7.00
RS283	2½c	**brn org**			8.50	5.00

Chas. H. Fletcher — RS284

Chas. H. Fletcher

RS284	1¼c	**black**	.50	.50	.50	.50

Hostetter Co.

For illustration of No. RS285, see large stamp illustration pages.

RS285	2½c	**black,** imperf	.60	.60		

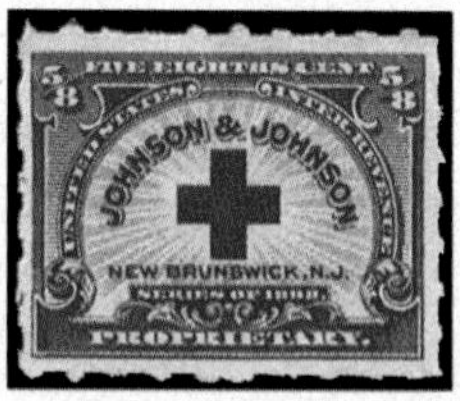

Johnson & Johnson — RS286

Johnson & Johnson

RS286	⅝c	**car**	.50	.50	.50	.50

Lanman & Kemp — RS287

Lanman & Kemp

RS287	⅝c	**green**	8.50	6.00	11.00	4.50
RS288	1¼c	**brown**	11.00	6.50	16.00	12.00
RS289	1⅞c	**blue**	11.00	8.00	21.00	11.00

J. Ellwood Lee Co. — RS290

J. Ellwood Lee Co.

RS290	⅛c	**dk bl**			3.00	3.00
RS291	⅝c	**car**			2.50	2.00
RS292	1¼c	**dk grn**			2.00	2.00
RS293	2½c	**org**			2.50	2.50
RS294	5c	**chocolate**			2.75	2.75

Charles Marchand — RS295

Charles Marchand

RS295	⅝c	black	8.50	8.50	9.00	9.00
RS296	1¼c	black	1.75	1.75	1.75	1.75
RS297	1⅞c	black	2.50	2.50	3.00	3.00
RS298	2½c	black	3.00	3.00	3.00	3.00
RS299	3⅛c	black	8.50	8.50	8.50	8.50
RS300	4⅜c	black	16.00	16.00	16.00	16.00
RS301	7½c	black	11.00	11.00	11.00	11.00

RS302

Od Chem. Co.

RS302	2½c	car	—	2.50

The Piso Company — RS303

The Piso Company (E. T. Hazletine)

RS303	⅝c	blue	.50	.50	.50	.50

Radway & Co. — RS304

Radway & Co.

RS304	⅝c	blue	1.25	1.25	1.25	1.25

Warner's Safe Cure Co. — RS305

Warner's Safe Cure Co.

RS305	3⅛c	brown	1.25	1.25	1.25	1.25

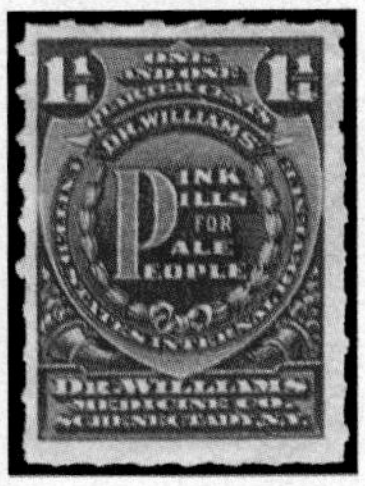

Dr. Williams Medicine Co. — RS306

Dr. Williams Medicine Co.

RS306	1¼c	pink	3.00	3.00

DR. KILMER & CO., PROVISIONAL PROPRIETARY STAMPS

Postage Stamps of 1895, 1897-1903, Nos. 267a, 279, 279Bg and 268, Precancel Overprinted in Black:

Dr. K. & Co.
I. R.
7–5–'98.
a

b

c

1898 **Wmk. 191** ***Perf. 12***

Overprint "a," Large "I.R." Dated July 5, 1898.

RS307	A87	1c **deep green**	175.00	—
a.		Red (trial) plus black ovpts.		
RS308	A88	2c **pink,** type III	160.00	
RS308A	A88	2c **pink,** type IV	175.00	—
b.		Dark blue (trial) ovpt.		
RS309	A89	3c **purple**	160.00	—
a.		Red (trial) ovpt.		
b.		Inverted ovpt.		—

A trial overprint in dark blue on the 2c stamp is known used on July 5.

Overprint "b," Small "I.R," "Dr. K. & Co." with Serifs Dated July 6, 7, 9, 11 to 14, 1898

RS310	A87	1c **deep green**	140.00	
RS311	A88	2c **pink,** type III	150.00	
RS311A	A88	2c **pink,** type IV	77.50	
RS312	A89	3c **purple**	67.50	—
a.		Inverted ovpt.		

Overprint "c," Small "I.R." "Dr. K. & Co." without Serifs Dated July 7, 9, 11 to 14, 1898

RS313	A87	1c **deep green**	150.00	
RS314	A88	2c **pink,** type III	150.00	
RS314A	A88	2c **pink,** type IV	100.00	
RS315	A89	3c **purple**	125.00	—
a.		Inverted ovpt.		

Nos. RS307a, RS308Ab and RS309a were all overprinted on July 5, the first day of overprinting. Though called "trials," there is every reason to believe they were used in the regular course of business, as they represented money spent by Dr. Kilmer & Co. and there was no reason not to use them. Four examples are recorded of No. RS307a, three of No. RS308Ab and one of No. RS309a. For the inverted overprints, four examples are recorded of No. RS309b, 16 of No. RS312a and three of No. RS315a. Forgeries exist of No. RS312a, all dated July 6. The height of "I.R." is shorter on the forgeries, and the periods after these letters are circular rather than diamond shaped. Many varieties of the Kilmer overprints exist. For the complete listing see "The Case of Dr. Kilmer's," by Morton Dean Joyce, 1954 (also serialized in "The Bureau Specialist," Mar.-Nov. 1957).

ST. LOUIS PROVISIONAL PROPRIETARY STAMPS

U.S. "Battleship" revenue stamps (Nos. RB20-RB31) not being available to meet the July 1, 1898, effective date of new taxes on proprietary medicines, eleven proprietary drug companies (10 in St. Louis, Missouri, and one in Macon, Georgia) struck agreements with local collectors of internal revenue to print their own revenue stamps for temporary use and pay their taxes by sworn returns until the government-issued stamps were available. Even though one company that used such stamps was from Macon, Georgia, these stamps are commonly referred to as the St. Louis Provisionals.

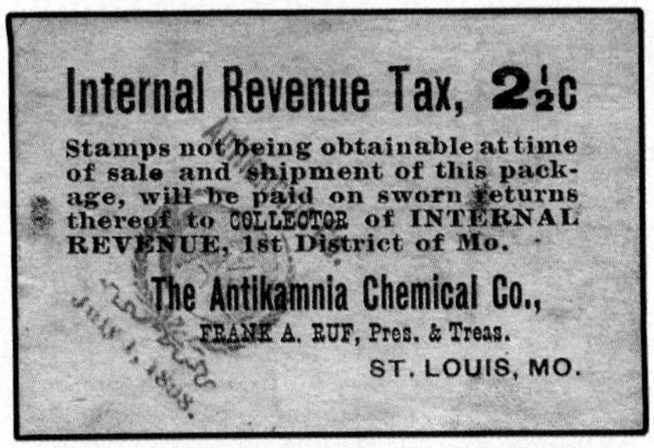

The Antikamnia Chemical Co. — RS320/RS321

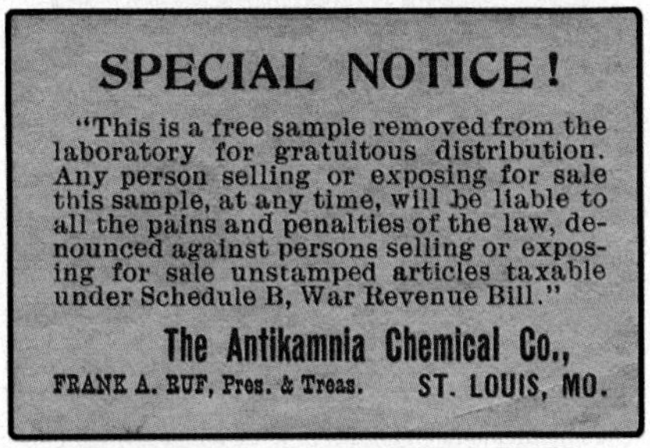

The Antikamnia Chemical Co. — RS323

Antikamnia Chemical Co., St. Louis

1898 ***Imperf.***

RS320	⅛c	**black**, *yellow*	550.00
RS321	2½c	**black**	175.00
RS323	No value,	**black**, *yellow*	350.00

No. RS323 was for use on free samples not subject to tax.

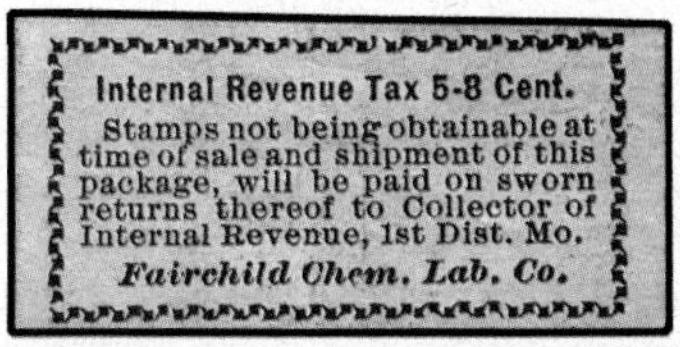

Fairchild Chemical Laboratory Co. — RS325

Fairchild Chemical Laboratory Co., St. Louis
Imperf

RS325	⅝c	**black**	*2,750.*

W.R. Holmes — RS330

W.R. Holmes, Macon, Georgia
Rouletted 9½ Horiz. in Green, Imperf Vert.

RS330	2½c	**green**	*2,750.*

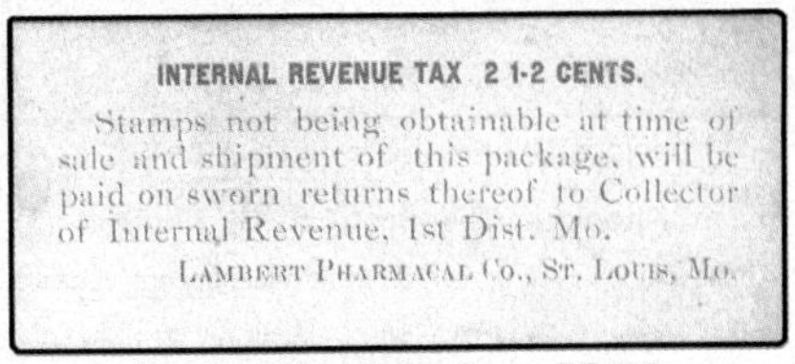

Lambert Pharmacal Co. — RS335

Lambert Pharmacal Co., St. Louis
Imperf

RS335	2½c	**red**	275.00

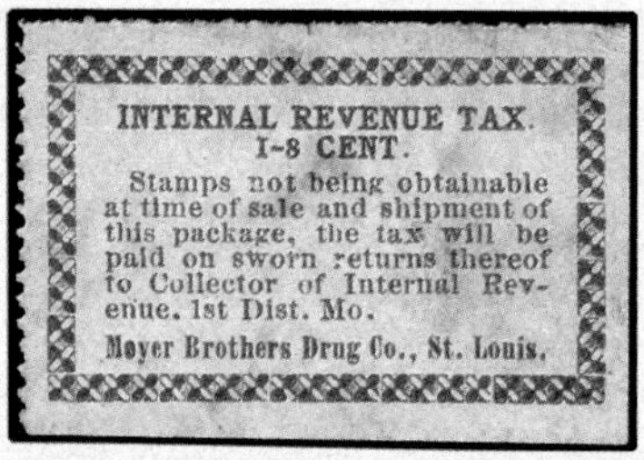

Meyer Brothers Drug Co. — RS340/RS350

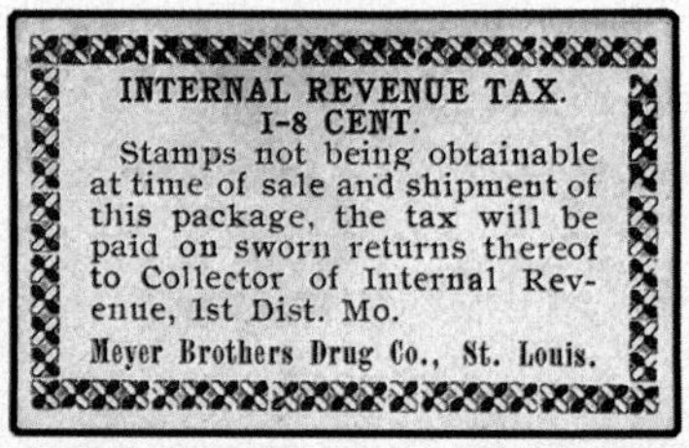

Meyer Brothers Drug Co. — RS351/RS361

Meyer Brothers Drug Co., St. Louis

These stamps were printed on at least three distinct papers: white, buff and rough manila.

Rouletted 9½ Horiz. in Green, Perf 12 and/or Imperf Vert.

				a. White Paper	b. Buff Paper	c. Rough Manila Paper
RS340	⅛c	**green**		*2,750.*		
RS343	⅝c	**green**			*2,250.*	
RS345	1¼c	**green**				*2,750.*
RS349	5c	**green**		*2,750.*		
RS350	11¼c	**green**			*2,750.*	

Imperf

			a. White Paper
RS351	⅛c	**black**	110.00
RS352	¼c	**black**	110.00
RS353	⅜c	**black**	110.00
RS354	⅝c	**black**	110.00
RS355	1c	**black**	110.00
RS357	2c	**black**	110.00
RS358	3c	**black**	110.00
RS359	4c	**black**	110.00
RS360	5c	**black**	110.00
RS361	11¼c	**black**	110.00

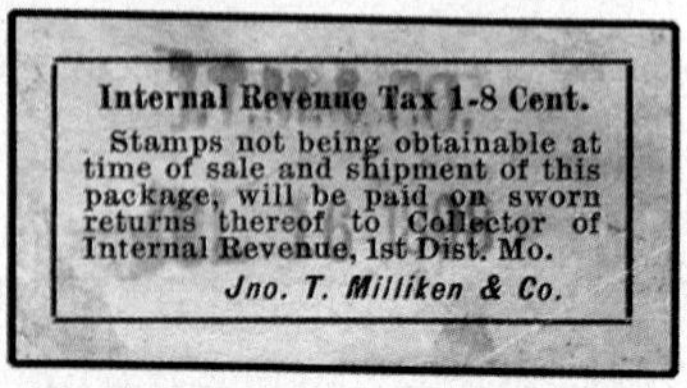

John T. Milliken & Co. — RS365/RS366

John T. Milliken & Co., St. Louis

Imperf

RS365	⅛c	**black**	550.00
RS366	⅝c	**black**	675.00

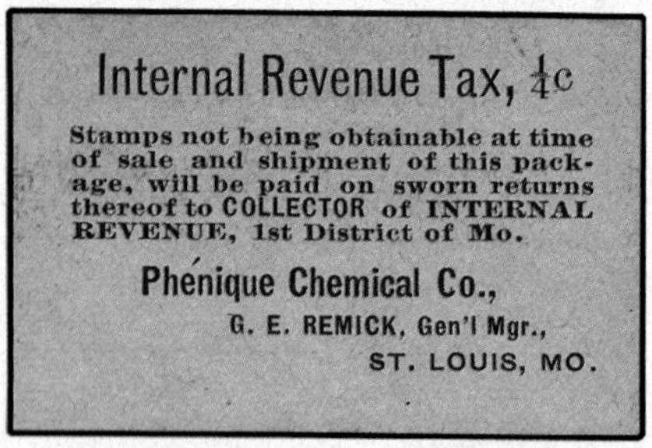

Phenique Chemical Co. — RS370/RS377

Phenique Chemical Co., St. Louis

These stamps were printed on two distinct papers: yellow and buff.

Imperf

			a. Yellow Paper	b. Buff Paper
RS370	⅛c	**black**		*2,750.*
RS371	¼c	**black**	*2,750.*	
RS372	⅝c	**black**	*1,650.*	*2,750.*
RS375	2½c	**black**	*2,750.*	
RS376	3⅛c	**black**		*2,750.*
RS377	3¾c	**black**		*2,750.*

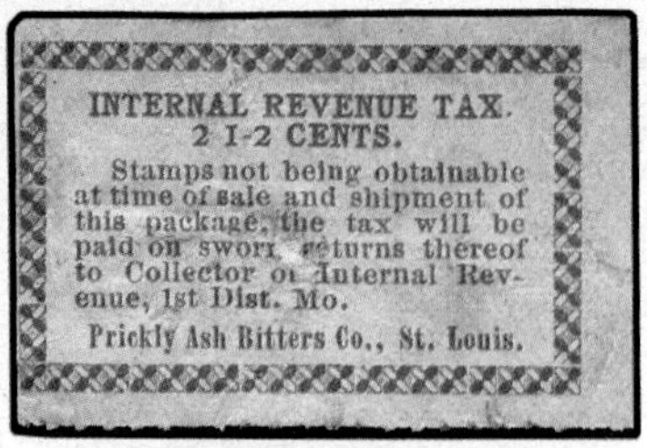

Prickly Ash Bitters Co. — RS381

Prickly Ash Bitters Co., St. Louis

Rouletted 9½ Horiz. in Green, Imperf Vert.

RS381	2½c	**green**	*1,650.*

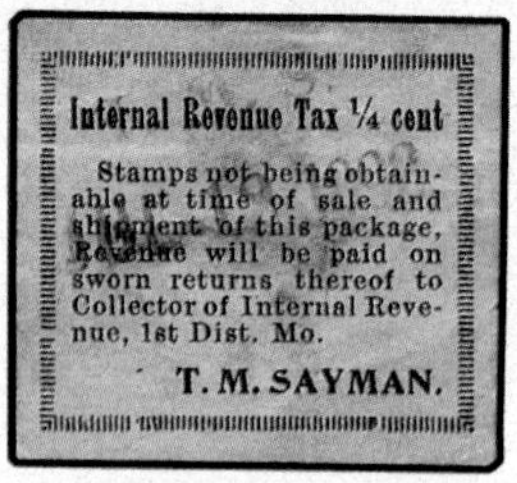

T.M. Sayman — RS385/RS387

T.M. Sayman, St. Louis

Imperf

RS385	¼c	**dark blue**	*2,750.*
RS386	⅝c	**dark blue**	*2,250.*
RS387	1¼c	**dark blue**	*2,750.*

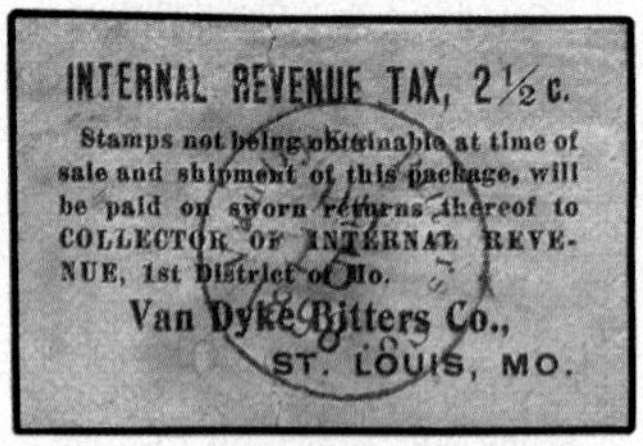

Van Dyke Bitters Co. — RS390

Van Dyke Bitters Co., St. Louis

Imperf

RS390	2½c	**blue**, *bluish glazed*	1,100.

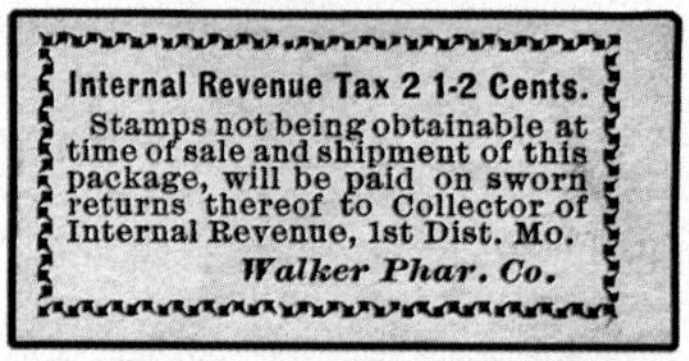

Walker Pharmacal Co. — RS395

Walker Pharmacal Co., St. Louis

Imperf

RS395	2½c	**black**	*2,750.*

PRIVATE DIE PERFUMERY STAMPS

1864 ***Perf. 12***

X. Bazin

For illustration of No. RT1, see large stamp illustration pages.

			a. Old Paper	b. Silk Paper	c. Pink Paper	d. Wmkd. USIR (191R)
RT1	2c	**blue,** die cut	1,400.			

This stamp was never placed in use.

a. Old Paper	b. Silk Paper	c. Pink Paper	d. Wmkd. USIR (191R)

Corning & Tappan — RT2/RT4

Corning & Tappan

RT2	1c	**black,** imperf	2,750.
	h.	Die cut, 19mm diameter	125.00
	k.	Die cut, 21mm diameter	175.00
RT3	1c	**black,** perf	825.00
RT4	1c	**blue,** perf	4.50

Fetridge & Co. — RT5

Fetridge & Co.

RT5	2c	**ver,** cut to shape	125.00

E. W. Hoyt & Co. — RT6

E. W. Hoyt & Co.

For illustrations of Nos. RT7, RT8 and RT11, see large stamp illustration pages.

RT6	1c	**black,** imperf	*6,500.*	5,000.	160.00
RT7	1c	**black,** die cut	35.00	35.00	17.00
RT8	2c	**black,** imperf			1,000.
RT9	2c	**black,** die cut			100.00
RT10	4c	**black,** imperf	2,750.	350.00	2,250.
RT11	4c	**black,** die cut	110.00	77.50	77.50

The 2c is larger than the 1c, 4c larger than 2c.

Kidder & Laird

RT12	1c	**vermilion**	17.00
RT13	2c	**vermilion**	17.00

George W. Laird — RT14/RT15

George W. Laird

RT14	3c	**blk,** imperf		1,000.	1,250.	1,000.
		Double transfer		1,250.	2,250.	1,250.
	p.	Perf	3,250.	*4,000.*		
		As "p," double transfer	*4,250.*			

			a. Old Paper	b. Silk Paper	c. Pink Paper	d. Wmkd. USIR (191R)
RT15	3c	**black,** die cut	3,000.	110.00	3,250.	110.00
		Double transfer		275.00	*6,500.*	325.00
	e.	Experimental silk paper, double transfer	—			
	p.	Perf and die cut	1,250.			

Lanman & Kemp — RT16/RT18

Tetlow's Perfumery — RT19

Lanman & Kemp

No.	Denom.	Color	a.	b.	c.	d.
RT16	1c	**black**		8.25	550.00	8.25
		Dbl. transfer		—		
RT17	2c	**brown**		35.00		11.00
RT18	3c	**green**		9.00		8.25
		Dbl. transfer		175.00		77.50

Tetlow's Perfumery

No.	Denom.	Color	a.	b.	c.	d.
RT19	1c	**vermilion**				3.75

C. B. Woodworth & Son — RT20/RT21

R. & G. A. Wright — RT22/RT25

C. B. Woodworth & Son

No.	Denom.	Color	a.	b.	c.	d.
RT20	1c	**green**		6.00	20.00	7.75
		Dbl. transfer		67.50	82.50	67.50
RT21	2c	**blue**		180.00	3,750.	10.00

R. & G. A. Wright

No.	Denom.	Color	a.	b.	c.	d.
RT22	1c	**blue**	6.75	9.00		67.50
	e.	Experimental silk paper	125.00			
RT23	2c	**black**	13.00	25.00		375.00
RT24	3c	**lake**	35.00	125.00		525.00
RT25	4c	**green**	110.00	140.00		400.00

Young, Ladd & Coffin — RT26/RT33

Young, Ladd & Coffin

			a. Old Paper	b. Silk Paper	c. Pink Paper	d. Wmkd. USIR (191R)
RT26	1c	**green,** imperf		110.00	100.00	110.00
RT27	1c	**green,** perf		25.00	17.00	17.00
RT28	2c	**blue,** imperf		150.00	130.00	90.00
RT29	2c	**blue,** perf		60.00	95.00	17.00
RT30	3c	**ver,** imperf		130.00	150.00	95.00
RT31	3c	**ver,** perf		40.00	8.25	7.75
RT32	4c	**brown,** imperf		6,500.	160.00	110.00
RT33	4c	**brown,** perf		45.00	14.00	5.50

PRIVATE DIE PLAYING CARD STAMPS

1864

Caterson Brotz & Co.

No.	Denom.	Color	a.	b.	c.	d.
RU1	5c	**brown**				*10,000.*

This stamp was never placed in use.

A. Dougherty — RU2/RU6

A. Dougherty — RU5

A. Dougherty

No.	Denom.	Color	a.	b.	c.	d.
RU2	2c	**orange**	77.50			
RU3	4c	**black**	50.00			
RU4	5c	**blue,** 20x26mm	2.00	2.00	14.00	
		Double transfer		—		
	e.	Experimental silk paper	—			
		As "e," inverted dbl. transfer	—			
	u.	5c **ultra**	175.00			
RU5	5c	**blue,** 18x23mm				1.75
RU6	10c	**blue**	45.00			

The 2c, 4c and 5c have numerals in all four corners.

Eagle Card Co. — RU7

Eagle Card Co.

No.	Denom.	Color	a.	b.	c.	d.
RU7	5c	**black**				95.00

Goodall — RU8

Samuel Hart & Co. — RU9

Goodall (London, New York)

As No. RU13, "London Goodall New York" replaces both "American Playing Cards" and Victor E. Mauger and Petrie New York."

No.	Denom.	Color	a.	b.	c.	d.
RU8	5c	**black**	175.00	4.50		
	e.	Experimental silk paper	2,750.			

Samuel Hart & Co.

No.	Denom.	Color	a.	b.	c.	d.
RU9	5c	**black**	6.75	6.75		
	e.	Experimental silk paper	2,750.			

Lawrence & Cohen — RU10/RU11

Lawrence & Cohen

No.	Denom.	Color	a.	b.	c.	d.
RU10	2c	**blue**	90.00			
RU11	5c	**green**	5.50	7.75		
	e.	Experimental silk paper	125.00			

Jn. J. Levy

No.	Denom.	Color	a.	b.	c.	d.
RU12	5c	**black**	27.50	30.00		
	e.	Experimental silk paper	125.00			

Victor E. Mauger & Petrie — RU13

New York Consolidated Card Co. — RU14

Victor E. Mauger and Petrie

No.	Denom.	Color	a.	b.	c.	d.
RU13	5c	**blue**		2.25	2.25	1.25

New York Consolidated Card Co.

No.	Denom.	Color	a.	b.	c.	d.
RU14	5c	**black**		5.50	17.00	5.00

Paper Fabrique — RU15

Russell, Morgan & Co. — RU16

Paper Fabrique Company

No.	Denom.	Color	a.	b.	c.	d.
RU15	5c	**black**		10.00	22.50	10.00

Russell, Morgan & Co.

No.	Denom.	Color	a.	b.	c.	d.
RU16	5c	**black**				22.50

MOTOR VEHICLE USE REVENUE STAMPS

When affixed to a motor vehicle, permitted use of that vehicle for a stated period.

RV1

1942 Wmk. 191R OFFSET PRINTING *Perf. 11*

With Gum on Back

RV1	RV1 $2.09 **light green** *(February)*	1.75	.50

With Gum on Face

Inscriptions on Back

RV2	RV1 $1.67 **light green** *(March)*	30.00	8.50
RV3	RV1 $1.25 **light green** *(April)*	22.50	7.50
RV4	RV1 84c **light green** *(May)*	25.00	7.25
RV5	RV1 42c **light green** *(June)*	25.00	7.25

With Gum and Control Number on Face

Inscriptions on Back

RV6	RV1 $5 **rose red** *(July)*	3.25	1.50
RV7	RV1 $4.59 **rose red** *(August)*	55.00	13.00
RV8	RV1 $4.17 **rose red** *(September)*	60.00	16.00
RV9	RV1 $3.75 **rose red** *(October)*	55.00	12.50
RV10	RV1 $3.34 **rose red** *(November)*	55.00	12.50
RV11	RV1 $2.92 **rose red** *(December)*	55.00	12.50
	Nos. RV1-RV11 (11)	387.50	99.00

1943

RV12	RV1 $2.50 **rose red** *(January)*	62.50	16.00
RV13	RV1 $2.09 **rose red** *(February)*	42.50	11.00
RV14	RV1 $1.67 **rose red** *(March)*	37.50	12.50
RV15	RV1 $1.25 **rose red** *(April)*	37.50	9.00
RV16	RV1 84c **rose red** *(May)*	37.50	9.00
RV17	RV1 42c **rose red** *(June)*	37.50	10.00
RV18	RV1 $5 **yellow** *(July)*	3.75	1.00
RV19	RV1 $4.59 **yellow** *(August)*	65.00	17.00
RV20	RV1 $4.17 **yellow** *(September)*	82.50	21.00
RV21	RV1 $3.75 **yellow** *(October)*	82.50	21.00
RV22	RV1 $3.34 **yellow** *(November)*	90.00	22.00
RV23	RV1 $2.92 **yellow** *(December)*	110.00	25.00
	Nos. RV12-RV23 (12)	688.75	174.50

1944

RV24	RV1 $2.50 **yellow** *(January)*	125.00	25.00
RV25	RV1 $2.09 **yellow** *(February)*	72.50	19.00
RV26	RV1 $1.67 **yellow** *(March)*	62.50	16.00
RV27	RV1 $1.25 **yellow** *(April)*	62.50	17.00
RV28	RV1 84c **yellow** *(May)*	55.00	16.00
RV29	RV1 42c **yellow** *(June)*	55.00	16.00

Gum on Face

Control Number and Inscriptions on Back

RV30	RV1 $5 **violet** *(July)*	2.40	1.75
RV31	RV1 $4.59 **violet** *(August)*	92.50	21.00
RV32	RV1 $4.17 **violet** *(September)*	67.50	19.00
RV33	RV1 $3.75 **violet** *(October)*	67.50	19.00
RV34	RV1 $3.34 **violet** *(November)*	62.50	12.50
RV35	RV1 $2.92 **violet** *(December)*	62.50	12.50
	Nos. RV24-RV35 (12)	787.40	194.75

1945

RV36	RV1 $2.50 **violet** *(January)*	55.00	12.00
RV37	RV1 $2.09 **violet** *(February)*	47.50	12.00
RV38	RV1 $1.67 **violet** *(March)*	47.50	10.50
RV39	RV1 $1.25 **violet** *(April)*	47.50	10.50
RV40	RV1 84c **violet** *(May)*	37.50	9.00
RV41	RV1 42c **violet** *(June)*	28.50	7.25

Daniel Manning — RV2

Gum on Face

Control Number and Inscriptions on Back

1945 Wmk. 191R Offset Printing *Perf. 11*

Bright Blue Green & Yellow Green

RV42	RV2 $5 *(July)*	3.25	1.00
RV43	RV2 $4.59 *(August)*	67.50	19.00
RV44	RV2 $4.17 *(Sept.)*	67.50	19.50
RV45	RV2 $3.75 *(October)*	62.50	12.50
RV46	RV2 $3.34 *(November)*	50.00	12.00
RV47	RV2 $2.92 *(December)*	45.00	9.00
	Nos. RV36-RV47 (12)	559.25	134.25

1946

Bright Blue Green & Yellow Green

RV48	RV2 $2.50 *(January)*	47.50	12.50
RV49	RV2 $2.09 *(February)*	47.50	12.00
RV50	RV2 $1.67 *(March)*	37.50	9.00
RV51	RV2 $1.25 *(April)*	30.00	9.00
RV52	RV2 84c *(May)*	30.00	9.00
RV53	RV2 42c *(June)*	22.50	1.20
	Nos. RV48-RV53 (6)	215.00	52.70

BOATING STAMPS

Required on applications for the certificate of number for motorboats of more than 10 horsepower, starting April 1, 1960. The pictorial upper part of the $3 stamp was attached to the temporary certificate and kept by the boat owner. The lower part (stub), showing number only, was affixed to the application and sent by the post office to the U.S. Coast Guard, which issued permanent certificates. The $3 fee was for three years. The $1 stamp covered charges for reissue of a lost or destroyed certificate of number. These stamps were used in the 12 states and the District of Columbia that had not passed laws in conformity with the Boating Act of 1958.

Catalogue value for unused stamps in this section are for Never Hinged items.

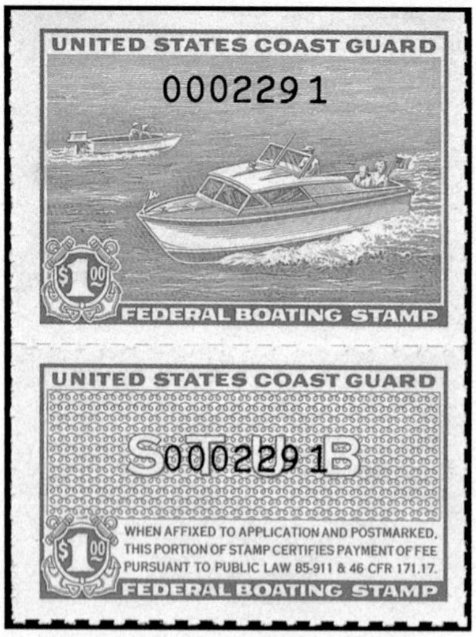

Outboard and Inboard Motorboats — RVB1

Offset Printing, Number Typographed

1960, Apr. 1 Unwmk. *Rouletted*

RVB1	RVB1 $1 **rose red, black number**	37.50	*750.00*
	P# block of 4	160.00	
	On license		—
RVB2	RVB1 $3 **blue, red number**	45.00	27.50
	P# block of 4	190.00	
	On license		40.00
	First day license		*700.00*

Nos. RVB1 and RVB2 unused stamp values are for MNH complete two-part stamps. Used values are for stamps, without the stubs, bearing a complete cancel dated between April 1, 1960, and January 31, 1964. On-license values are for clean licenses with undamaged stamps and a complete cancel. A license fold can be expected. Mute oval cancels are usually favor cancels.

CAMP STAMPS

The Camp Stamp program of the Department of Agriculture's National Forest Service was introduced in 1985. The public was offered the option of prepaying their recreation fees through the purchase of camp stamps. The fees varied but were typically $3 to $4.

The stamps were supplied in rolls with the backing rouletted 9 horizontally. The letter preceding the serial number indicated the face value and printer (A-D, Denver; E-J, Washington). The stamps were designed so that any attempt to remove them from the fee envelope would cause them to come apart.

The program ended in the summer of 1988. The envelopes containing the stamps were destroyed by the National Forerst Service after use. No used examples have been reported.

Catalogue value for unused stamps in this section are for Never Hinged items.

National Forest Service Logo — RVC1

Printed in Denver, CO.

1985 Typo. *Die Cut*
Self-Adhesive, Coated Paper

RVC1	RVC1	50c	**black,** *pink,* "A"	*60.00*
RVC2	RVC1	$1	**black,** *red,* "B"	*60.00*
RVC3	RVC1	$2	**black,** *yellow,* "C"	*60.00*
RVC4	RVC1	$3	**black,** *green,* "D"	*60.00*

RVC2

Printed by the Government Printing Office, Washington, DC (?).

1986 Typo. *Die Cut*
Self-Adhesive, Coated Paper

RVC5	RVC2	50c	**black,** *pink,* "E"	140.00
RVC6	RVC2	$1	**black,** *red,* "F"	150.00
RVC7	RVC2	$2	**black,** *yellow,* "G"	160.00
RVC8	RVC2	$3	**black,** *green,* "H"	110.00
RVC9	RVC2	$5	**black,** *silver,* "I"	350.00
RVC10	RVC2	$10	**black,** *bronze,* "J"	—

TRAILER PERMIT STAMPS

Issued by the National Park Service of the Department of the Interior. Required to be affixed to "License to Operate Motor Vehicle" starting July 1, 1939, when a house trailer was attached to a motor vehicle entering a national park or national monument.

Issued to rangers in booklets of 50 (five 2x5 panes).

Use was continued at least until 1952.

Unused stamps may have a ranger's handwritten control number.

Trailer and Automobile RVT1

1939 Unwmk. Offset Printing *Perf. 11*

RVT1	RVT1	50c	**bright blue**	*2,750.*	*1,250.*
			On license		*2,750.*
RVT2	RVT1	$1	**carmine**	*500.00*	250.00
			On license		*700.00*

Earliest known use: July 1939.

DISTILLED SPIRITS EXCISE TAX STAMPS

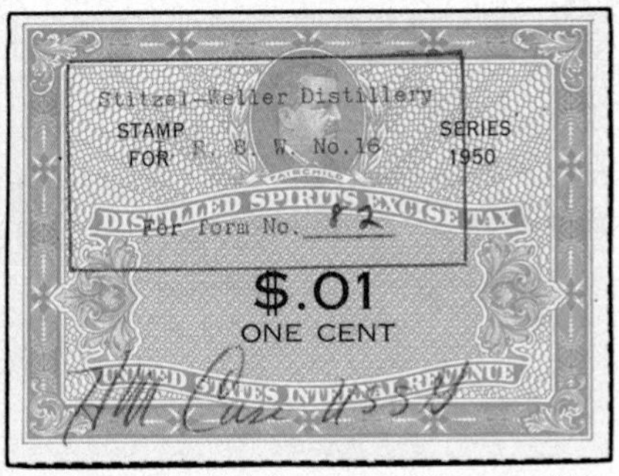

Charles S. Fairchild, Secretary of Treasury 1887-89 — DS1

Actual size: 89½x63½mm

Inscribed "STAMP FOR SERIES 1950"

1950 Wmk. 191R Offset Printing *Rouletted 7*
Left Value — Unused
Right Value — Used

RX1	DS1	1c	**yellow green & black**	50.00	27.50
			Punched cancel		21.00
RX2	DS1	3c	**yellow green & black**	140.00	100.00
			Punched cancel		92.50
RX3	DS1	5c	**yellow green & black**	27.50	20.00
			Punched cancel		17.50
RX4	DS1	10c	**yellow green & black**	25.00	17.50
			Punched cancel		15.00
RX5	DS1	25c	**yellow green & black**	40.00	11.00
			Punched cancel		9.00
RX6	DS1	50c	**yellow green & black**	25.00	11.00
			Punched cancel		8.00
RX7	DS1	$1	**yellow green & black**	30.00	3.00
			Punched cancel		1.75
RX8	DS1	$3	**yellow green & black**	40.00	20.00
			Punched cancel		15.00
RX9	DS1	$5	**yellow green & black**	30.00	6.50
			Punched cancel		4.50
RX10	DS1	$10	**yellow green & black**	15.00	3.00
			Punched cancel		1.75
RX11	DS1	$25	**yellow green & black**	25.00	12.50
			Punched cancel		9.25
RX12	DS1	$50	**yellow green & black**	25.00	8.75
			Punched cancel		5.00
RX13	DS1	$100	**yellow green & black**	15.00	4.00
			Punched cancel		3.00
RX14	DS1	$300	**yellow green & black**	45.00	25.00
			Punched cancel		21.00
RX15	DS1	$500	**yellow green & black**	30.00	15.00
			Punched cancel		10.00
RX16	DS1	$1,000	**yellow green & black**	25.00	11.00
			Punched cancel		8.00
RX17	DS1	$1,500	**yellow green & black**	70.00	50.00
			Punched cancel		40.00
RX18	DS1	$2,000	**yellow green & black**	12.50	5.00
			Punched cancel		4.00
RX19	DS1	$3,000	**yellow green & black**	35.00	25.00
			Punched cancel		15.00
RX20	DS1	$5,000	**yellow green & black**	35.00	25.00
			Punched cancel		17.50
RX21	DS1	$10,000	**yellow green & black**	45.00	27.50
			Punched cancel		22.50
RX22	DS1	$20,000	**yellow green & black**	55.00	35.00
			Punched cancel		30.00
RX23	DS1	$30,000	**yellow green & black**	90.00	70.00
			Punched cancel		50.00
RX24	DS1	$40,000	**yellow green & black**	1,200.	950.00
			Punched cancel		600.00
RX25	DS1	$50,000	**yellow green & black**	200.00	95.00
			Punched cancel		75.00

Inscription "STAMP FOR SERIES 1950" omitted

1952
Left Value — Unused
Right Value — Used

RX27	DS1	3c	**yellow green & black**	*900.00*	
RX28	DS1	5c	**yellow green & black**	300.00	
			Punched cancel		40.00
RX29	DS1	10c	**yellow green & black**	35.00	90.00
			Punched cancel		5.00
RX30	DS1	25c	**yellow green & black**	45.00	90.00
			Punched cancel		15.00
RX31	DS1	50c	**yellow green & black**	45.00	90.00
			Punched cancel		15.00
RX32	DS1	$1	**yellow green & black**	30.00	90.00
			Punched cancel		2.50
RX33	DS1	$3	**yellow green & black**	55.00	90.00
			Punched cancel		22.50
RX34	DS1	$5	**yellow green & black**	55.00	90.00
			Punched cancel		25.00
RX35	DS1	$10	**yellow green & black**	30.00	90.00
			Punched cancel		2.50
RX36	DS1	$25	**yellow green & black**	40.00	90.00
			Punched cancel		10.00

RX37 DS1 $50 **yellow green & black** 90.00 90.00
Punched cancel 25.00
RX38 DS1 $100 **yellow green & black** 30.00 90.00
Punched cancel 2.50
RX39 DS1 $300 **yellow green & black** 40.00 90.00
Punched cancel 7.50
RX40 DS1 $500 **yellow green & black** 450.00
Punched cancel 30.00
RX41 DS1 $1,000 **yellow green & black** 140.00 75.00
Punched cancel 6.00
RX42 DS1 $1,500 **yellow green & black** *900.00*
RX43 DS1 $2,000 **yellow green & black** 700.00
Punched cancel 75.00
RX44 DS1 $3,000 **yellow green & black** 1,200.
Punched cancel 700.00
RX45 DS1 $5,000 **yellow green & black** 600.00
Punched cancel 50.00
RX46 DS1 $10,000 **yellow green & black** 700.00
Punched cancel 90.00

Five other denominations with "Stamp for Series 1950" omitted were prepared but are not known to have been put into use: 1c, $20,000, $30,000, $40,000 and $50,000.
Stamps listed as used have staple holes.
Distilled Spirits Excise Tax stamps were discontinued in 1959.

FIREARMS TRANSFER TAX STAMPS

Documentary Stamp of 1917 Overprinted Vertically in Black. Reading Up

1934 **Engr.** **Wmk. 191R** ***Perf. 11***
Without Gum
RY1 R21 $1 **green** 450.00 —
On license —

RY1

RY2

Eagle, Shield and Stars from U.S. Seal

Two types of $200:
I — Serial number with serifs, not preceded by zeros. Tips of 6 lines project into left margin.
II — Gothic serial number preceded by zeros. Five line tips in left margin.

1934 **Wmk. 191R** ***Perf. 12***
Size: 28x42mm
Without Gum
RY2 RY1 $200 **dark blue & red,** type I, #1-1500 1,350. 750.00
On license *900.00*

Issued in vertical strips of 4 which are imperforate at top, bottom and right side.
See Nos. RY4, RY6-RY8.

1938 **Size: 28x33½mm** ***Perf. 11***
RY3 RY2 $1 **green** 85.00 —
On license —

See No. RY5.

1950 (?) **Wmk. 191R** ***Perf. 12***
Size: 29x43mm
RY4 RY1 $200 **dull blue & red,** type II, #1501-3000 750.00 450.00
On license 500.00

No. RY4 has a clear impression and is printed on white paper. No. RY2 has a "muddy" impression in much darker blue ink and is printed on off-white paper.

1960, July 1 **Size: 29x34mm** ***Perf. 11***
RY5 RY2 $5 **red** 25.00 *40.00*
On license 200.00

No. RY5 was issued in sheets of 50 (10x5) with straight edge on four sides of sheet.
The watermark is hard to see on many examples of #RY2-RY5.

1974 **Unwmk.** ***Perf. 12***
Size: 29x43mm
RY6 RY1 $200 **dull blue & red,** type II, #3001-up 225.00 110.00
On license 125.00

Panes of 32

1990(?) **Litho.** **Without Gum** ***Imperf.***
RY7 RY1 $200 **dull blue** *500.00*
On license *750.00*

1990 ***Perf. 12½***
RY8 RY1 $200 **dull blue** 325.00 125.00
On license 160.00
RY9 RY2 $5 **red,** *1994* 125.00
On license 200.00

Nos. RY7 and RY8 do not have a printed serial number or the tabs at left. Because the stamps do not have a serial number mint stamps were not sold to the public.
WARNING: Nos. RY7-RY9 are usually taped or glued to the transfer of title documents. The glue used is NOT water soluble. Attempts to soak the stamps may result in damage.

2001(?) ***Serpentine Die Cut 11.5***
Self-Adhesive
RY10 RY2 $5 **dull red** —
On license *250.00*

RECTIFICATION TAX STAMPS

Used to indicate payment of the tax on distilled spirits that were condensed and purified for additional blending through repeated distillations.

RZ1

Actual size: 89½x64mm

1946 **Offset Printing** **Wmk. 191R** ***Rouletted 7***
RZ1 RZ1 1c **blue & black** 6.75 4.00
Punched cancel 2.00
RZ2 RZ1 3c **blue & black** 22.50 8.00
Punched cancel 7.50
RZ3 RZ1 5c **blue & black** 12.50 2.50
Punched cancel 1.25
RZ4 RZ1 10c **blue & black** 12.50 3.00
Punched cancel 1.25
RZ5 RZ1 25c **blue & black** 12.50 3.00
Punched cancel 2.00
RZ6 RZ1 50c **blue & black** 17.50 5.00
Punched cancel 3.50
RZ7 RZ1 $1 **blue & black** 17.50 4.00
Punched cancel 2.50
RZ8 RZ1 $3 **blue & black** 90.00 18.00
Punched cancel 9.00
RZ9 RZ1 $5 **blue & black** 30.00 10.00
Punched cancel 6.00
RZ10 RZ1 $10 **blue & black** 22.50 3.00
Punched cancel 1.25
RZ11 RZ1 $25 **blue & black** 90.00 10.00
Punched cancel 3.00
RZ12 RZ1 $50 **blue & black** 90.00 7.50
Punched cancel 3.00
RZ13 RZ1 $100 **blue & black** *175.00* 9.50
Punched cancel 3.50
RZ14 RZ1 $300 **blue & black** *220.00* 10.00
Punched cancel 7.50
RZ15 RZ1 $500 **blue & black** *240.00* 10.00
Punched cancel 7.00
RZ16 RZ1 $1000 **blue & black** *240.00* 18.00
Punched cancel 15.00
RZ17 RZ1 $1500 **blue & black** *260.00* 60.00
Punched cancel 45.00
RZ18 RZ1 $2000 **blue & black** *260.00* 80.00
Punched cancel 60.00

Stamps listed as used have staple holes.

HUNTING PERMIT STAMPS

Authorized by an Act of Congress, approved March 16, 1934, to license hunters. Receipts go to maintain waterfowl life in the United States. Sales to collectors were made legal June 15, 1935.

No. RW1 used is valued with handstamp or manuscript cancel, though technically it was against postal regulations to deface the stamp or to apply a postal cancellation. Beginning with No. RW2, the used values are for stamps with signatures.

Plate number blocks of six have selvage on two sides.

Hunting permit stamps are valid from July 1 - June 30. Stamps have been made available prior to the date of validity, and stamps are sold through the philatelic agency after the period of validity has passed.

All hunting permit stamps through No. RW68A were printed by the Bureau of Engraving & Printing.

Catalogue values for all unused stamps in this section are for stamps with never-hinged original gum. Minor natural gum skips and bends are normal on Nos. RW1-RW20. No-gum stamps are without signature or other cancel.

Department of Agriculture

Mallards Alighting — HP1

Engraved: Flat Plate Printing
Issued in panes of 28 subjects.

1934 **Unwmk.** ***Perf. 11***

Inscribed "Void after June 30, 1935"

RW1 HP1 $1 **blue**	800.	140.
Hinged	400.	
No gum	150.	
P# block of 6	16,500.	
a. Imperf., vertical pair	—	
b. Vert. pair, imperf. horiz.	—	

Used value is for stamp with handstamp or manuscript cancel.

It is almost certain that No. RW1a is No. RW1b with vertical perfs trimmed off. No horizontal pairs of No. RW1a are known. All recorded pairs are vertical, with narrow side margins. Both varieties probably are printer's waste since copies exist with gum on front or without gum.

Canvasbacks Taking to Flight — HP2

1935 **Inscribed "Void after June 30, 1936"**

RW2 HP2 $1 **rose lake**	750.	160.
Hinged	350.	
No gum	200.	
P# block of 6	11,500.	

Canada Geese in Flight — HP3

1936 **Inscribed "Void after June 30, 1937"**

RW3 HP3 $1 **brown black**	350.	75.00
Hinged	175.	
No gum	115.	
P# block of 6	4,000.	

Scaup Ducks Taking to Flight — HP4

1937 **Inscribed "Void after June 30, 1938"**

RW4 HP4 $1 **light green**	375.	60.00
Hinged	160.	
No gum	75.	
P# block of 6	3,250.	

Pintail Drake and Hen Alighting — HP5

1938 **Inscribed "Void after June 30, 1939"**

RW5 HP5 $1 **light violet**	475.	60.00
Hinged	225.	
No gum	80.	
P# block of 6	4,500.	

Department of the Interior

Green-winged Teal — HP6

1939 **Inscribed "Void after June 30, 1940"**

RW6 HP6 $1 **chocolate**	275.	45.00
Hinged	125.	
No gum	60.	
P# block of 6	2,900.	

Black Mallards — HP7

1940 **Inscribed "Void after June 30, 1941"**

RW7 HP7 $1 **sepia**	250.	45.00
Hinged	120.	
No gum	60.	
P# block of 6	2,900.	

Family of Ruddy Ducks — HP8

1941 **Inscribed "Void after June 30, 1942"**

RW8	HP8	$1 **brown carmine**	250.	45.00
		Hinged	110.	
		No gum	60.	
		P# block of 6	2,900.	

Baldpates — HP9

1942 **Inscribed "Void after June 30, 1943"**

RW9	HP9	$1 **violet brown**	250.	45.00
		Hinged	110.	
		No gum	60.	
		P# block of 6	2,900.	

Wood Ducks — HP10

1943 **Inscribed "Void After June 30, 1944"**

RW10	HP10	$1 **deep rose**	125.00	35.00
		Hinged	50.00	
		No gum	40.00	
		P# block of 6	700.00	

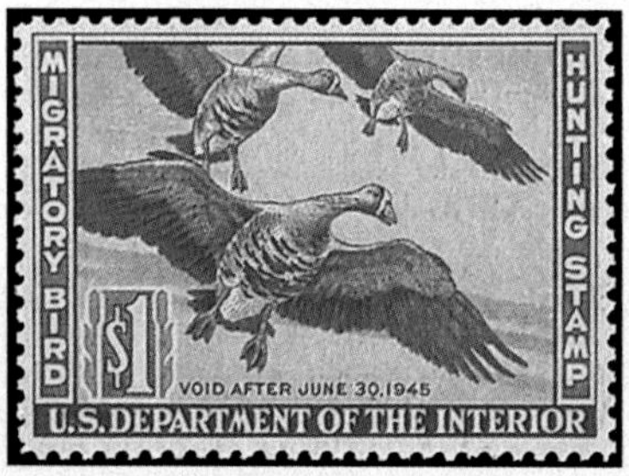

White-fronted Geese — HP11

1944 **Inscribed "Void after June 30, 1945"**

RW11	HP11	$1 **red orange**	135.00	45.00
		Hinged	57.50	
		No gum	50.00	
		P# block of 6	750.00	

Shoveller Ducks in Flight — HP12

1945 **Inscribed "Void after June 30, 1946"**

RW12	HP12	$1 **black**	110.00	25.00
		Hinged	50.00	
		No gum	30.00	
		P# block of 6	475.00	

Beginning with No. RW13, there is a message printed on the back of the sheet stamps telling hunters to sign their names on the face of the stamp. On Nos. RW13-RW17, offset plate no. 47510 for the printing on the backs of the stamps appears on the back of the selvage opposite the stamp in position 24 on the upper right panes. These are collected as plate blocks of six with side and bottom selvage bearing the plate number on the back of the selvage opposite the center margin stamp. Value, mint never hinged $550 each for Nos. RW13-RW16, $1,500 for No. RW17.

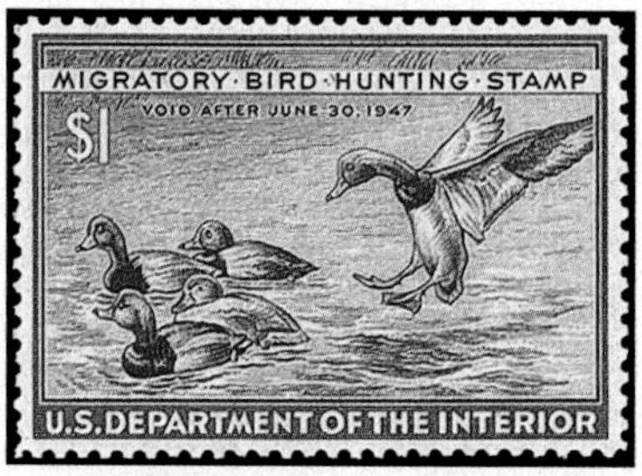

Redhead Ducks — HP13

1946 **Inscribed "Void after June 30, 1947"**

RW13	HP13	$1 **red brown**	55.00	16.00
		No gum	18.00	
		P# block of 6	325.00	
a.		$1 **bright rose pink**	*35,000.*	

Snow Geese — HP14

1947 **Inscribed "Void after June 30, 1948"**

RW14	HP14	$1 **black**	57.50	17.50
		No gum	20.00	
		P# block of 6	350.00	

Buffleheads in Flight — HP15

1948 **Inscribed "Void after June 30, 1949"**

RW15	HP15	$1 **bright blue**	60.00	16.00
		No gum	21.00	
		P# block of 6	425.00	

Goldeneye Ducks — HP16

1949 **Inscribed "Void after June 30, 1950"**

RW16	HP16	$2 **bright green**	70.00	15.00
		No gum	25.00	
		P# block of 6	450.00	

Trumpeter Swans in Flight — HP17

1950 **Inscribed "Void after June 30, 1951"**

RW17	HP17	$2 **violet**	95.00	12.00
		No gum	22.50	
		P# block of 6	575.00	

Gadwall Ducks — HP18

1951 **Inscribed "Void after June 30, 1952"**

RW18	HP18	$2 **gray black**	95.00	12.00
		No gum	22.50	
		P# block of 6	575.00	

Harlequin Ducks — HP19

1952 **Inscribed "Void after June 30, 1953"**

RW19	HP19	$2 **deep ultramarine**	95.00	12.00
		No gum	22.50	
		P# block of 6	575.00	

Blue-winged Teal — HP20

1953 Inscribed "Void after June 30, 1954"

RW20 HP20 $2 **deep brown rose** 95.00 12.00
No gum 22.50
P# block of 6 600.00

No. RW21 and following issues are printed on dry, pregummed paper and the back inscription is printed on top of the gum, except for the self-adhesive stamp issues starting in 1998.

Ring-necked Ducks — HP21

1954 Inscribed "Void after June 30, 1955"

RW21 HP21 $2 **black** 85.00 10.50
No gum 22.50
P# block of 6 600.00

Blue Geese — HP22

1955 Inscribed "Void after June 30, 1956"

RW22 HP22 $2 **dark blue** 85.00 10.50
No gum 22.50
P# block of 6 600.00

a. Back inscription inverted *5,500.* *4,500.*

American Merganser — HP23

1956 Inscribed "Void after June 30, 1957"

RW23 HP23 $2 **black** 85.00 10.50
No gum 22.50
P# block of 6 625.00

American Eiders — HP24

1957 Inscribed "Void after June 30, 1958"

RW24 HP24 $2 **emerald** 85.00 10.50
No gum 22.50
P# block of 6 600.00

a. Back inscription inverted *5,000.*

Canada Geese — HP25

1958 Inscribed "Void after June 30, 1959"

RW25 HP25 $2 **black** 85.00 10.50
No gum 22.50
P# block of 6 600.00

Labrador Retriever Carrying Mallard Drake — HP26

Giori Press Printing
Issued in panes of 30 subjects

1959 Inscribed "Void after June 30, 1960"

RW26 HP26 $3 **blue, ocher & black** 125.00 11.00
No gum 40.00
P# block of 4 575.00

a. Back inscription inverted 35,000. —

Redhead Ducks — HP27

1960 Inscribed "Void after June 30, 1961"

RW27 HP27 $3 **red brown, dark blue & bister** 95.00 10.50
No gum 37.50
P# block of 4 475.00

Mallard Hen and Ducklings — HP28

1961 Inscribed "Void after June 30, 1962"

RW28 HP28 $3 **multicolored** 110.00 10.50
No gum 50.00
P# block of 4 525.00

Pintail Drakes Coming in for Landing
HP29

1962 **Inscribed "Void after June 30, 1963"**

RW29	HP29	$3	**dark blue, dark red brown & black**	125.00	12.50
			No gum	60.00	
			P# block of 4	600.00	
a.			Back inscription omitted	—	

Pair of Brant Landing — HP30

1963 **Inscribed "Void after June 30, 1964"**

RW30	HP30	$3	**multicolored**	120.00	12.50
			No gum	57.50	
			P# block of 4	500.00	

Hawaiian Nene Geese — HP31

1964 **Inscribed "Void after June 30, 1965"**

RW31	HP31	$3	**multicolored**	110.00	12.50
			No gum	55.00	
			P# block of 6	2,300.	

Three Canvasback Drakes — HP32

1965 **Inscribed "Void after June 30, 1966"**

RW32	HP32	$3	**multicolored**	110.00	12.50
			No gum	55.00	
			P# block of 4	550.00	

Whistling Swans — HP33

1966 **Inscribed "Void after June 30, 1967"**

RW33	HP33	$3	**multicolored**	110.00	12.50
			No gum	55.00	
			P# block of 4	550.00	

Old Squaw Ducks — HP34

1967 **Inscribed "Void after June 30, 1968"**

RW34	HP34	$3	**multicolored**	125.00	12.50
			No gum	60.00	
			P# block of 4	600.00	

Hooded Mergansers — HP35

1968 **Inscribed "Void after June 30, 1969"**

RW35	HP35	$3	**multicolored**	70.00	10.50
			No gum	27.50	
			P# block of 4	325.00	
a.			Back inscription omitted	—	

White-winged Scoters — HP36

1969 **Inscribed "Void after June 30, 1970"**

RW36	HP36	$3	**multicolored**	65.00	8.00
			No gum	25.00	
			P# block of 4	300.00	

Ross's Geese — HP37

1970 **Engraved & Lithographed**
Inscribed "Void after June 30, 1971"

RW37	HP37	$3	**multicolored**	70.00	8.00
			No gum	27.50	
			P# block of 4	300.00	

Three Cinnamon Teal — HP38

1971 **Inscribed "Void after June 30, 1972"**

RW38	HP38	$3	**multicolored**	45.00	7.75
			No gum	22.00	
			P# block of 4	200.00	

Emperor Geese — HP39

1972 **Inscribed "Void after June 30, 1973"**

RW39	HP39	$5	**multicolored**	25.00	7.00
			No gum	12.50	
			P# block of 4	110.00	

Steller's Eiders — HP40

1973 **Inscribed "Void after June 30, 1974"**

RW40	HP40	$5	**multicolored**	20.00	7.00
			No gum	11.50	
			P# block of 4	95.00	

Wood Ducks — HP41

1974 **Inscribed "Void after June 30, 1975"**

RW41	HP41	$5	**multicolored**	18.00	6.00
			No gum	9.50	
			P# block of 4	80.00	

Canvasback Ducks and Decoy — HP42

1975 **Inscribed "Void after June 30, 1976"**

RW42	HP42	$5 **multicolored**		17.50	6.00
			No gum	9.00	
			P# block of 4	65.00	

Family of Canada Geese — HP43

1976 **Engr.**

Inscribed "Void after June 30, 1977"

RW43	HP43	$5 **green & black**		17.50	6.00
			No gum	9.00	
			P# block of 4	65.00	

Pair of Ross's Geese — HP44

1977 **Litho. & Engr.**

Inscribed "Void after June 30, 1978"

RW44	HP44	$5 **multicolored**		17.50	6.00
			No gum	9.00	
			P# block of 4	65.00	

Hooded Merganser Drake — HP45

1978 **Inscribed "Void after June 30, 1979"**

RW45	HP45	$5 **multicolored**		15.00	6.00
			No gum	7.50	
			P# block of 4	57.50	

Green-winged Teal — HP46

1979 **Inscribed "Void after June 30, 1980"**

RW46	HP46	$7.50 **multicolored**		17.50	7.00
			No gum	9.00	
			P# block of 4	75.00	

Mallards — HP47

1980 **Inscribed "Void after June 30, 1981"**

RW47	HP47	$7.50 **multicolored**		17.50	7.00
			No gum	9.00	
			P# block of 4	75.00	

Ruddy Ducks — HP48

1981 **Inscribed "Void after June 30, 1982"**

RW48	HP48	$7.50 **multicolored**		17.50	7.00
			No gum	9.00	
			P# block of 4	75.00	

Canvasbacks — HP49

1982 **Inscribed "Void after June 30, 1983"**

RW49	HP49	$7.50 **multicolored**		17.50	7.00
			No gum	9.00	
			P# block of 4	75.00	
	a.	Orange and violet omitted		*7,500.*	

A certificate from a recognized expertization committee is required for No. RW49a.

Pintails — HP50

1983 **Inscribed "Void after June 30, 1984"**

RW50	HP50	$7.50 **multicolored**		17.50	7.00
			No gum	9.00	
			P# block of 4	75.00	

Widgeons — HP51

1984 **Inscribed "Void after June 30, 1985"**

RW51	HP51	$7.50 **multicolored**		17.50	7.00
			No gum	9.00	
			P# block of 4	75.00	

See Special Printings section that follows.

Cinnamon Teal — HP52

1985 **Inscribed "Void after June 30, 1986"**

RW52	HP52	$7.50 **multicolored**		17.50	8.00
			No gum	9.00	
			P# block of 4	75.00	
	a.	Light blue (litho.) omitted		*22,500.*	

The omitted color on No. RW52a coincides with a double paper splice affecting the top row of five stamps from the sheet and top ⅓ of stamps in the second row. There is also a color changeling of the brownish red ducks and their reflections in the water to yellow and yellow orange, respectively, on the error stamps. This error currently exists as three vertical strips of 6 (top stamp the error) and a plate number block of 12 (2x6, top two stamps the error).

Fulvous Whistling Duck — HP53

1986 **Inscribed "Void after June 30, 1987"**

RW53	HP53	$7.50 **multicolored**		17.50	7.00
			No gum	9.50	
			P# block of 4	75.00	
	a.	Black omitted		*3,750.*	

Redheads — HP54

1987 ***Perf. 11½x11***

Inscribed "Void after June 30, 1988"

RW54	HP54	$10 **multicolored**		17.50	9.50
			No gum	10.00	
			P# block of 4	75.00	

Snow Goose — HP55

1988 **Inscribed "Void after June 30, 1989"**

RW55 HP55 $10 **multicolored** 17.50 10.00
No gum 11.00
P# block of 4 75.00

Lesser Scaup — HP56

1989 **Inscribed "Void after June 30, 1990"**

RW56 HP56 $12.50 **multicolored** 20.00 10.00
No gum 12.00
P# block of 4 85.00

Black Bellied Whistling Duck — HP57

1990 **Inscribed "Void after June 30, 1991"**

RW57 HP57 $12.50 **multicolored** 20.00 10.00
No gum 12.00
P# block of 4 85.00
a. Back inscription omitted *375.00*
b. Black inscription printed on the stamp paper rather than the gum *3,500.*
No gum *3,500.*

The back inscription is normally on top of the gum so beware of copies with gum removed offered as No. RW57a. Full original gum must be intact on No. RW57a. Used examples of No. RW57a cannot exist.

All known examples of No. RW57b are used or have no gum. Expertization is recommended.

King Eiders HP58

1991 **Inscribed "Void after June 30, 1992"**

RW58 HP58 $15 **multicolored** 30.00 11.00
No gum 16.00
P# block of 4 140.00
a. Black (engr.) omitted *20,000.*

Spectacled Eider — HP59

1992 **Inscribed "Void after June 30, 1993"**

RW59 HP59 $15 **multicolored** 30.00 11.00
No gum 16.00
P# block of 4 140.00

Canvasbacks — HP60

1993 **Inscribed "Void after June 30, 1994"**

RW60 HP60 $15 **multicolored** 27.50 11.00
No gum 16.00
P# block of 4 130.00
a. Black (engr.) omitted *3,000.*

Red-breasted Mergansers — HP61

1994 ***Perf. 11¼x11***

Inscribed "Void after June 30, 1995"

RW61 HP61 $15 **multicolored** 30.00 11.00
No gum 16.00
P# block of 4 140.00

Mallards — HP62

1995 **Inscribed "Void after June 30, 1996"**

RW62 HP62 $15 **multicolored** 30.00 11.00
No gum 15.00
P# block of 4 140.00

Surf Scoters — HP63

1996 **Inscribed "Void after June 30, 1997"**

RW63 HP63 $15 **multicolored** 30.00 11.00
No gum 15.00
P# block of 4 140.00

Canada Goose — HP64

"Long breast feather" plate flaw

"Short breast feather" plate flaw

1997 **Inscribed "Void after June 30, 1998"**

RW64 HP64 $15 **multicolored** 30.00 11.00
No gum 16.00
P# block of 4 125.00
"Long breast feather" plate flaw, pos. 28 85.00 —
In pair with normal stamp 125.00
"Short breast feather" plate flaw, pos. 28 65.00 —
In pair with normal stamp 100.00

Barrow's Goldeneye — HP65

998 *Perf. 11¼*

Inscribed "Void after June 30, 1999"

W65 HP65 $15 **multicolored** 45.00 20.00
No gum 25.00
P# block of 4 190.00

Self-Adhesive

Die Cut Perf. 10

W65A HP65 $15 *Barrow's Goldeneye* 25.00 15.00
No gum 15.00

Nos. RW65 and later issues were sold in panes of 30 (RW65 and RW66) or 20 (RW67 and later issues), with four plate numbers per pane. The self-adhesives starting with No. RW65A were sold in panes of 1. The self-adhesives are valued unused as complete panes and used as single stamps.

Greater Scaup — HP66

999 *Perf. 11¼*

Inscribed "Void after June 30, 2000"

W66 HP66 $15 **multicolored** 40.00 15.00
No gum 22.50
P# block of 4 170.00

Self-Adhesive

Die Cut Perf. 10

W66A HP66 $15 **multicolored** 25.00 12.00
No gum 15.00

Mottled Duck — HP67

2000 *Perf. 11¼*

Inscribed "Void after June 30, 2001"

W67 HP67 $15 **multicolored** 30.00 14.00
No gum 17.50
P# block of 4 130.00

Self-Adhesive

Die Cut 10

W67A HP67 $15 **multicolored** 22.50 14.00
No gum 17.50

Northern Pintail — HP68

2001 *Perf. 11¼*

Inscribed "Void after June 30, 2002"

RW68 HP68 $15 **multicolored** 27.50 15.00
No gum 16.00
P# block of 4 110.00

Self-Adhesive

Die Cut Perf. 10

RW68A HP68 $15 **multicolored** 25.00 10.00
No gum 15.00

Black Scoters — HP69

Printed by Banknote Corporation of America.

2002 *Perf. 11¼*

Inscribed "Void after June 30, 2003"

RW69 HP69 $15 **multicolored** 27.50 15.00
No gum 16.00
P# block of 4 110.00

Self-Adhesive

Serpentine Die Cut 11x10¾

RW69A HP69 $15 **multicolored** 25.00 10.00
No gum 15.00

Snow Geese — HP70

Printed by Ashton-Potter (USA) Ltd.

2003 *Perf. 11*

Inscribed "Void after June 30, 2004"

RW70 HP70 $15 **multicolored** 27.50 15.00
No gum 16.00
P# block of 4 120.00
b. Imperf, pair *7,500.*
c. Back inscription omitted *4,500.*

Self-Adhesive

Serpentine Die Cut 11x10¾

RW70A HP70 $15 **multicolored** 25.00 10.00
No gum 15.00

Redheads — HP71

Printed by Banknote Corporation of America for Sennett Security Products.

2004 *Perf. 11*

Inscribed "Void after June 30, 2005"

RW71 $15 **multicolored** 27.50 11.00
No gum 16.00
P# block of 4 100.00

Self-Adhesive

Serpentine Die Cut 11x10¾

RW71A HP71 $15 25.00 10.00
No gum 15.00

Hooded Mergansers — HP72

Printed by Banknote Corporation of America for Sennett Security Products

Two types of RW72: I, No framelines at top, right or bottom (from left two panes of the press sheet); II, Gray framelines at top, right and bottom (from right two panes of the press sheet).

2005 **Litho. & Engr.** *Perf. 11*

Inscribed "Void after June 30, 2006"

RW72 HP72 $15 **multicolored,** type I 22.50 11.00
No gum 16.00
P# block of 4 100.00
b. Souvenir sheet of 1 *2,000.*
c. Type II 22.50 11.00
No gum 16.00
P# block of 4 100.00

Self-Adhesive

Litho. & Debossed

Serpentine Die Cut 11x10¾

RW72A HP72 $15 **multicolored** 22.50 11.00
No gum 15.00

One hundred press sheets containing four panes of 20 of No. RW72 and one hundred press sheets containing 18 of No. RW72A were offered for sale by the U.S. Fish and Wildlife Service.

No. RW72b sold for $20. 1,000 No. RW72b were issued. Approximately 750 were signed by the artist in black, value $2,000 as shown. Approximately 150 were signed in blue ink, value $2,500. Approximately 100 were signed in gold ink, value $3,000. Most examples of No. RW72b are in the grade of F-VF. Catalogue values are for Very Fine examples.

The Duck Stamp Office never announced the existence of No. RW72b to the public through a press release or a website announcement during the time the sheet was on sale, apparently because it was not clear beforehand that the souvenir sheet could be produced successfully and on time. No. RW72b sold out before a public announcement of the item's existence could be made.

Ross's Goose — HP73

Printed by Banknote Corporation of America for Sennett Security Products

2006 **Litho. & Engr.** ***Perf. 11***

Inscribed "Void after June 30, 2007"

RW73	HP73 $15 **multicolored**		22.50	11.00
	No gum		15.00	
	P# block of 4		100.00	
b.	Souvenir sheet of 1		*160.00*	—
c.	As "b," without artist's signature (error)		*4,500.*	

Self-Adhesive

Serpentine Die Cut 11x10¾

RW73A	HP73 $15 **multicolored**	22.50	11.00
	No gum	15.00	

Two hundred fifty press sheets containing four panes of 20 of No. RW73 and two hundred fifty press sheets containing 18 of No. RW73A were offered for sale by the U.S. Fish and Wildlife Service.

No. RW73b sold for $25. All examples of No. RW73b have a black signature of the artist on a designated line in the sheet margin. Ten thousand were issued.

The sheet margin has a line designated for the signature of the engraver, Piotr Naszarkowski, but no sheets were sold with his signature. Naszarkowski signed approximately 2,500 sheets during three days at the Washington 2006 World Philatelic Exhibition, and he signed another 2,500 or more after the conclusion of the exhibition. Value $225.

Ring-necked Ducks — HP74

Designed by Richard C. Clifton. Printed by Banknote Corporation of America for Sennett Security Products.

2007 **Litho.** ***Perf. 11***

Inscribed "Void after June 30, 2008"

RW74	HP74 $15 **multicolored**	22.50	11.00
	No gum	15.00	
	P# block of 4	100.00	
b.	Souvenir sheet of 1	*150.00*	
c.	As "b", without artist's signature (error)	*3,500.*	

Self-Adhesive

Serpentine Die Cut 11x10¾

RW74A	HP74 $15 **multicolored**	22.50	11.00
	No gum	15.00	

No. RW74b sold for $25 plus a shipping fee. Ten thousand were issued.

Five hundred press sheets containing four panes of 20 of No. RW74 and 500 press sheets containing 18 of No. RW74A were offered for sale by the Fish and Wildlife Service.

Northern Pintails — HP75

Designed by Joe Hautman. Printed by Ashton-Potter (USA) Ltd.

2008 **Litho.** ***Perf. 13¼***

Inscribed "Void after June 30, 2009"

RW75	HP75 $15 **multicolored**	22.50	11.00
	No gum	15.00	
	Inscription block of 4	100.00	
b.	Souvenir sheet of 1	*85.00*	—
c.	As "b," without artist's signature (error)	—	

Self-Adhesive

Serpentine Die Cut 10¾

RW75A	HP75 $15 **multicolored**	22.50	11.00
	No gum	20.00	

No. RW75 was sold in panes of 20. No. RW75A was sold in panes of 1. No. RW75A is valued unused as a complete pane and used as a single stamp. A sheet commemorating the 75th anniversary of Hunting Permit stamps containing one example of No. RW75 and a label with the vignette of No. RW1 sold for $50. Value, $90.

No. RW75b sold for $30 plus a shipping fee. Ten thousand were prepared.

SPECIAL PRINTING

After No. RW51 became void, fifteen uncut sheets of 120 (4 panes of 30 separated by gutters) were overprinted "1934-84" and "50th ANNIVERSARY" in the margins and auctioned by the U.S. Fish and Wildlife Service.

Bids were accepted from September 1 through November 1, 1985. Minimum bid for each sheet was $2,000. The face value of each sheet, had they still been valid, was $900. Each sheet also had the sheet number and pane position printed in the corner of each pane ("01 of 15-1," "01 of 15-2," etc.). Fourteen of the sheets were sold at this and one subsequent auction and one was donated to the Smithsonian.

An individual sheet could be broken up to create these identifiable collectibles: 4 margin overprint blocks of 10; cross gutter block of 4; 6 horizontal pairs with gutter between; 8 vertical pairs with gutter between.

Single stamps from the sheet cannot be distinguished from No. RW51. No used examples can exist.

RW51x $7.50 *Widgeons*

DESIGNERS

1934 — *RW1* *J.N. Darling*
1935 — *RW2* *Frank W. Benson*
1936 — *RW3* *Richard E. Bishop*
1937 — *RW4* *J.D. Knap*
1938 — *RW5* *Roland Clark*
1939 — *RW6* *Lynn Bogue Hunt*
1940 — *RW7* *Francis L. Jaques*
1941 — *RW8* *E.R. Kalmbach*
1942 — *RW9* *A. Lassell Ripley*
1943 — *RW10* *Walter E. Bohl*
1944 — *RW11* *Walter A. Weber*
1945 — *RW12* *Owen J. Bromme*
1946 — *RW13* *Robert W. Hines*
1947 — *RW14* *Jack Murray*
1948 — *RW15* *Maynard Reece*
1949 — *RW16* *"Roge" E. Preuss*
1950 — *RW17* *Walter A. Weber*
1951 — *RW18* *Maynard Reece*
1952 — *RW19* *John H. Dick*
1953 — *RW20* *Clayton B. Seagears*
1954 — *RW21* *Harvey D. Sandstrom*
1955 — *RW22* *Stanley Stearns*
1956 — *RW23* *Edward J. Bierly*
1957 — *RW24* *Jackson Miles Abbott,*
1958 — *RW25* *Leslie C. Kouba*
1959 — *RW26* *Maynard Reece*
1960 — *RW27* *John A. Ruthven,*
1961 — *RW28* *Edward A. Morris*
1962 — *RW29* *Edward A. Morris*
1963 — *RW30* *Edward J. Bierly*
1964 — *RW31* *Stanley Stearns*
1965 — *RW32* *Ron Jenkins*
1966 — *RW33* *Stanley Stearns*
1967 — *RW34* *Leslie C. Kouba*
1968 — *RW35* *C.G. Pritchard*
1969 — *RW36* *Maynard Reece*
1970 — *RW37* *Edward J. Bierly*
1971 — *RW38* *Maynard Reece*
1972 — *RW39* *Arthur M. Cook*
1973 — *RW40* *Lee LeBlanc*
1974 — *RW41* *David A. Maass*
1975 — *RW42* *James L. Fisher*
1976 — *RW43* *Alderson Magee*
1977 — *RW44* *Martin R. Murk*
1978 — *RW45* *Albert Earl Gilbert*
1979 — *RW46* *Kenneth L. Michaelsen*
1980 — *RW47* *Richard W. Plasschaert*
1981 — *RW48* *John S. Wilson*
1982 — *RW49* *David A. Maass*
1983 — *RW50* *Phil Scholer*
1984 — *RW51* *William C. Morris*
1985 — *RW52* *Gerald Mobley*
1986 — *RW53* *Burton E. Moore, Jr.*
1987 — *RW54* *Arthur G. Anderson*
1988 — *RW55* *Daniel Smith*
1989 — *RW56* *Neal R. Anderson*
1990 — *RW57* *Jim Hautman*
1991 — *RW58* *Nancy Howe*
1992 — *RW59* *Joe Hautman*
1993 — *RW60* *Bruce Miller*
1994 — *RW61* *Neal R. Anderson*
1995 — *RW62* *Jim Hautman*
1996 — *RW63* *Wilhelm Goebel*
1997 — *RW64* *Robert Hautman*
1998 — *RW65* *Robert Steiner*
1999 — *RW66* *Jim Hautman*
2000 — *RW67* *Adam Grimm*
2001 — *RW68* *Robert Hautman*
2002 — *RW69* *Joe Hautman*
2003 — *RW70* *Ron Louque*
2004 — *RW71* *Scot Storm*
2005 — *RW72* *Mark Anderson*
2006 — *RW73* *Sherrie Russell Meline*
2007 — *RW74* *Richard Clifton*
2008 — *RW75* *Joe Hautman*

QUANTITIES SOLD

(Quantities from No. RW65 on are quantities ordered. Quantities sold of these numbers were much less.)

RW1	**635,001**	*RW43*	**2,170,194**
RW2	**448,204**	*RW44*	**2,196,774**
RW3	**603,623**	*RW45*	**2,216,621**
RW4	**783,039**	*RW46*	**2,090,155**
RW5	**1,002,715**	*RW47*	**2,045,114**
RW6	**1,111,561**	*RW48*	**1,907,120**
RW7	**1,260,810**	*RW49*	**1,926,253**
RW8	**1,439,967**	*RW50*	**1,867,998**
RW9	**1,383,629**	*RW51*	**1,913,861**
RW10	**1,169,352**	*RW52*	**1,780,636**
RW11	**1,487,029**	*RW53*	**1,794,484**
RW12	**1,725,505**	*RW54*	**1,663,270**
RW13	**2,016,841**	*RW55*	**1,402,096**
RW14	**1,722,677**	*RW56*	**1,415,882**
RW15	**2,127,603**	*RW57*	**1,408,373**
RW16	**1,954,734**	*RW58*	**1,423,374**
RW17	**1,903,644**	*RW59*	**1,347,393**
RW18	**2,167,767**	*RW60*	**1,402,569**
RW19	**2,296,628**	*RW61*	**1,471,751**
RW20	**2,268,446**	*RW62*	**1,539,622**
RW21	**2,184,550**	*RW63*	**1,560,123**
RW22	**2,369,940**	*RW64*	**1,697,590**
RW23	**2,332,014**	*RW65*	**1,195,000**
RW24	**2,355,190**	*RW65A*	**2,805,000**
RW25	**2,176,425**	*RW66*	**1,194,000**
RW26	**1,626,115**	*RW66A*	**2,799,600**
RW27	**1,725,634**	*RW67*	**1,200,000**
RW28	**1,344,236**	*RW67A*	**2,800,000**
RW29	**1,147,212**	*RW68*	**1,194,000**
RW30	**1,448,191**	*RW68A*	**2,806,000**
RW31	**1,573,155**	*RW69*	**1,194,000**
RW32	**1,558,197**	*RW69A*	**2,806,000**
RW33	**1,805,341**	*RW70*	**1,000,000**
RW34	**1,934,697**	*RW70A*	**3,000,000**
RW35	**1,837,139**	*RW71*	**1,000,000**
RW36	**2,072,108**	*RW71A*	**3,000,000**
RW37	**2,420,244**		
RW38	**2,445,977**		
RW39	**2,184,343**		
RW40	**2,094,414**		
RW41	**2,214,056**		
RW42	**2,237,126**		

JUNIOR DUCK STAMPS

As a courtesy to Duck stamp collectors, we list here the Duck stamps issued under the Federal Junior Duck Stamp program run by the U.S. Fish and Wildlife Service branch of the Department of the Interior and the Federal Duck Stamp Office. The purpose of this program is to teach youth through the medium of art the importance of conserving wetlands and migratory birds.

Students in kindergarden to 12th grade from all 50 states, the District of Columbia, American Samoa and the U.S. Virgin Islands are invited to participate in an annual art competition.

The winning entry from each state, district or territory competes for the national championship. The national winner's art appears on that year's Junior Duck stamp, which is sold to raise funds to support the Junior Duck Stamp art and educational program. The United States Postal Service, through its Stamp Fulfillment Services unit, acts as a sales agent for these stamps.

These stamps are not valid for hunting, nor is it required that hunters buy the stamps in order to hunt.

A precursor sheet of nine stamps was released in 1992 as a part of a pilot program instituted before the formal, annual Junior Duck Stamp art competition was begun. The sheet shows stamps from Arkansas, California (2), Florida (2), Illinois (2), Kansas and Vermont. Value, $30.

All issues were printed in panes of 30 with four control/plate numbers. Imperforate examples of Nos. JDS1, JDS2 and JDS3 exist and are believed to be printer's waste.

Catalogue values for all stamps in this section are for stamps with never-hinged original gum.

JD1

1993 **Artist: Jason Parsons (IL)**
JDS1 JD1 $5 *Redhead* 75.00

1994 **Artist: Clark Weaver (PA)**
JDS2 JD1 $5 *Hooded mergansers* 175.00

1995 **Artist: Jie Huang (MT)**
JDS3 JD1 $5 *Pintail* 350.00
a. Imperf, pair *3,000.*

1996 **Artist: Clark Weaver (PA)**
JDS4 JD1 $5 *Canvasbacks* 400.00

1997 **Artist: Scott Russell (CA)**
JDS5 JD1 $5 *Canada geese* 400.00

1998 **Artist: Eric Peterson (MI)**
JDS6 JD1 $5 *Black ducks* 425.00

1999 **Artist: Ryan Kirby (IL)**
JDS7 JD1 $5 *Wood ducks* 450.00

2000 **Artist: Bonnie Latham (MN)**
JDS8 JD1 $5 *Pintails* 800.00

2001 **Artist: Aremy McCann (MN)**
JDS9 JD1 $5 *Trumpeter swan* 85.00

2002 **Artist: Nathan Closson (MT)**
JDS10 JD1 $5 *Mallards* 50.00

2003 **Artist: Nathan Bauman (PA)**
JDS11 JD1 $5 *Green-winged teals* 30.00

2004 **Artist: Adam Nisbett (MO)**
JDS12 JD1 $5 *Fulvous whistling ducks* 25.00

2005 **Artist: Kerissa Nelson (WI)**
JDS13 JD1 $5 *Ring-necked ducks* 15.00

2006 **Artist: Rebekah Nastav (MO)**
JDS14 JD1 $5 *Redhead* 15.00

2007 **Artist: Paul Willey (AR)**
JDS15 JD1 $5 *Wigeons* 12.00

Type of 1993

2008 **Artist: Seokkyun Hong (TX)**
JDS16 JD1 $5 *Hawaiian Nene Geese* 10.00

STATE HUNTING PERMIT STAMPS

These stamps are used on licenses for hunting waterfowl (ducks, geese, swans) by states and Indian reservations. Stamps which include waterfow along with a variety of other animals are listed here. Stamps for hunting birds that exclude waterfowl are not listed.

A number of states print stamps in sheets as well as in booklets. The booklets are sent to agents for issuing to hunters. Both varieties are listed. The major listing is given to the sheet stamp since it generally is available in larger quantities and has been the more popularly collected item. In some cases the stamp removed from a booklet, with no tabs or selvage, is identical to a single sheet stamp (see Rhode Island). In these cases the identifiable booklet stamp with tabs and selvage receives an unlettered listing. If the single booklet stamp can be identified by type of perforation or the existence of one or more straight edges, the item receives a lettered listing (see Oregon).

Governor's editions are sold at a premium over the license fee with proceeds intended to help waterfowl habitats. Only those which differ from the regular stamp are listed.

After the period of validity, a number of these stamps were sold at less than face value. This explains the low values on stamps such as Montana Nos. 30, 33, and Flathead Indian Reservation Nos. 2-10.

When used, most stamps are affixed to licenses and signed by the hunter. Values for used stamps are for examples off licenses and without tabs. Although used examples may be extremely scarce, they will always sell for somewhat less than unused examples (two-thirds of the unused value would be the upper limit).

ALABAMA

Printed in sheets of 10.
Stamps are numbered serially.

Catalogue values for all unused stamps in this section are for Never Hinged items.

Artists: Barbara Keel, #1; Wayne Spradley, #2; Jack Deloney, #3; Joe Michelet, #4; John Lee, #5, 25; William Morris, #6, 14; Larry Martin, #7; Danny W. Dorning, #8; Robert C. Knutson, #9, 16, 20; John Warr, #10; Elaine Byrd, #11; Steven Garst, #12; Larry Chandler, #13, 24; James Brantley, #15; Neil Blackwell, #17; Judith Huey, #18; E. Hatcher, #19; Eddie LeRoy, #21; David Sellers, #22, 26, 27; H. Andrew McNeely, #23. Clarence Stewart, #28. David Nix, #29.

1979-2007

1	$5 Wood ducks, rouletted	12.00	3.00
2	$5 Mallards, *1980*	12.00	3.00
3	$5 Canada geese, *1981*	12.00	3.00
4	$5 Green-winged teal, *1982*	12.00	3.00
5	$5 Widgeons, *1983*	12.00	3.00
6	$5 Buffleheads, *1984*	12.00	3.00
7	$5 Wood ducks, *1985*	12.00	3.00
8	$5 Canada geese, *1986*	12.00	3.00
9	$5 Pintails, *1987*	12.00	3.00
10	$5 Canvasbacks, *1988*	10.00	3.00
11	$5 Hooded mergansers, *1989*	12.00	3.00
12	$5 Wood ducks, *1990*	10.00	2.50
13	$5 Redheads, *1991*	10.00	2.50
14	$5 Cinnamon teal, *1992*	10.00	2.50
15	$5 Green-winged teal, *1993*	10.00	2.50
16	$5 Canvasbacks, *1994*	10.00	2.50
17	$5 Canada geese, *1995*	10.00	2.50
18	$5 Wood ducks, *1996*	12.00	2.50
19	$5 Snow goose, *1997*	10.00	2.50
20	$5 Barrow's goldeneye, *1998*	10.00	2.50
21	$5 Redheads, *1999*	10.00	2.50
22	$5 Buffleheads, *2000*	9.00	2.50
23	$5 Ruddy duck, *2001*	9.00	2.50
24	$5 Pintail, *2002*	9.00	2.50
25	$5 Wood ducks, *2003*	9.00	2.50
26	$5 Ring-necked ducks, *2004*	9.00	2.50
27	$5 Canada geese, *2005*	9.00	2.50
28	$5 Canvasback, *2006*	9.00	2.50
29	$5 Blue-winged teal, *2007*	8.00	2.50

ALASKA

Printed in sheets of 30.
Stamps are numbered serially on reverse. Booklet pane stamps printed in panes of 5.

Catalogue values for all unused stamps in this section are for Never Hinged items.

Artist: Daniel Smith, #1; James Meger, #2; Carl Branson, #3; Jim Beaudoin, #4; Richard Timm, #5; Louis Frisino, #6; Ronald Louque, #7; Fred Thomas, #8; Ed Tussey, #9; George Lockwood, #10, 13, 23; Cynthia Fisher, #11, 20; Wilhelm Goebel, #12; Robert Steiner, #14, 18, 22; Sherrie Russell Meline, #15; Adam Grimm, #16, 19; Greg Alexander, #17; Don Moore, #21.

1985-2007

1	$5 Emperor geese	10.00	3.00
2	$5 Steller's eiders, *1986*	10.00	3.00
3	$5 Spectacled eiders, perforated, *1987*	10.00	
a.	Bklt. single, rouletted, with tab	10.00	2.50
4	$5 Trumpeter swans, perforated, *1988*	10.00	
a.	Bklt. single, rouletted, with tab	10.00	2.50
5	$5 Barrow's goldeneyes, perforated, *1989*	10.00	
a.	Bklt. single, rouletted, with tab	10.00	2.50
b.	Governor's edition	*140.00*	

No. 5b was sold in full panes through a sealed bid auction.

6	$5 Old squaws, perforated, *1990*	9.50	
a.	Bklt. single, rouletted, with tab	9.50	2.50
7	$5 Snow geese, perforated, *1991*	9.50	
a.	Bklt. single, rouletted, with tab	9.50	2.50
8	$5 Canvasbacks, perforated, *1992*	9.50	
a.	Bklt. single, rouletted, with tab	9.50	2.50
9	$5 Tule white front geese, perforated, *1993*	14.00	
a.	Bklt. single, rouletted, with tab	14.00	2.50
10	$5 Harlequin ducks, perforated, *1994*	20.00	
a.	Bklt. single, rouletted, with tab	15.00	2.50
b.	Governor's edition	*90.00*	
11	$5 Pacific brant, perforated, *1995*	22.00	
a.	Bklt. single, rouletted, with tab	20.00	2.50
12	$5 Canada geese, *1996*	25.00	
a.	Bklt. single, rouletted, with tab	20.00	2.50
13	$5 King eiders, *1997*	20.00	
a.	Bklt. single, rouletted, with tab	16.00	2.50
14	$5 Barrow's goldeneye, *1998*	12.00	
a.	Bklt. single, with tab	12.00	2.50
15	$5 Pintail, *1999*	11.00	
a.	Bklt. single, with tab	11.00	2.50
16	$5 Common eider, *2000*	10.00	
a.	Bklt. single, with tab	10.00	2.50
17	$5 American wigeon, *2001*	10.00	
a.	Bklt. single, with tab	10.00	2.50
18	$5 Black scoters, *2002*	10.00	
a.	Bklt. single, with tab	10.00	2.50
19	$5 Lesser Canada geese, *2003*	12.00	
a.	Bklt. single, with tab	12.00	2.50
20	$5 Lesser scaup, *2004*	10.00	
a.	Bklt. single, with tab	10.00	2.50
21	$5 Hooded merganser, *2005*	8.00	
a.	Bklt. single, with tab	8.50	2.50
22	$5 Pintails, mallard, green-winged teal, *2006*	8.00	
a.	Bklt. single, with tab	8.50	2.50
23	$5 Northern shovelers, *2007*	7.50	
a.	Bklt. single, with tab	8.50	2.50

ARIZONA

Printed in booklet panes of 5 with tab and in sheets of 30.
Stamps are numbered serially.

Catalogue values for all unused stamps in this section are for Never Hinged items.

Artists: Daniel Smith, #1; Sherrie Russell Meline, #2, 6-7, 9, 11-18, 21; Robert Steiner, #3; Ted Blaylock, #4; Brian Jarvi, #5; Harry Adamson, #8, Larry Hayden, #10; Tom Finley, #19, 20.

1987-2007

1	$5.50 Pintails, perf. 4 sides	11.00	
a.	Bklt. single, perf. 3 sides, with tab	11.00	3.00
2	$5.50 Green-winged teal, perf. 4 sides, *1988*	12.00	
a.	Bklt. single, perf. 3 sides, with tab	12.00	3.00
3	$5.50 Cinnamon teal, perf. 4 sides, *1989*	11.00	
a.	Bklt. single, perf. 3 sides, with tab	11.00	2.50
b.	$5.50 +$50 Governor's edition	75.00	
4	$5.50 Canada geese, perf. 4 sides, *1990*	12.00	
a.	Bklt. single, perf. 3 sides, with tab	12.00	2.50
b.	$5.50 +$50 Governor's edition	75.00	
5	$5.50 Blue-winged teal, perf. 4 sides, *1991*	10.00	
a.	Bklt. single, perf. 3 sides, with tab	11.00	2.50
b.	$55.50 Governor's edition	75.00	
6	$5.50 Buffleheads, perf. 4 sides, *1992*	10.00	
a.	Bklt. single, perf. 3 sides, with tab	11.00	2.50
b.	$55.50 Governor's edition	75.00	
7	$5.50 Mexican ducks, perf. 4 sides, *1993*	12.00	
a.	Bklt. single, perf. 3 sides, with tab	12.00	2.50
b.	$55.50 Governor's edition	75.00	
8	$5.50 Mallards, perf. 4 sides, *1994*	12.00	
a.	Bklt. single, perf. 3 sides, with tab	12.00	2.50
b.	$55.50 Governor's edition	75.00	
9	$5.50 Widgeon, perf. 4 sides, *1995*	12.00	
a.	Bklt. single, perf. 3 sides, with tab	12.00	2.50
b.	$55.50 Governor's edition	75.00	
10	$5.50 Canvasbacks, perf. 4 sides, *1996*	11.00	
a.	Bklt. single, perf 3 sides, with tab	11.00	2.50
b.	$55.50 Governor's edition	75.00	
11	$5.50 Gadwalls, *1997*	12.00	
a.	Bklt. single, perf 3 sides, with tab	12.00	2.50
b.	$55.50 Governor's edition	75.00	
12	$5.50 Wood duck, *1998*	12.00	
a.	Bklt. single, perf 3 sides, with tab	12.00	2.50
b.	$55.50 Governor's edition	—	
13	$5.50 Snow goose, *1999*	12.00	
a.	Blkt. single, perf. 3 sides, with tab	12.00	2.50
b.	$55.50 Governor's edition	75.00	
14	$7.50 Ruddy duck, *2000*	14.00	
a.	Bklt. single, perf. 3 sides, with tab	14.00	2.50
b.	$55.50 Governor's edition	75.00	
15	$7.50 Redheads, *2001*	14.00	
a.	Bklt. single, perf. 3 sides, with tab	14.00	2.50
b.	$55.50 Governor's edition	75.00	
16	$7.50 Ring-necked ducks, *2002*	14.00	
a.	Bklt. single, perf. 2 sides, with tabs	14.00	2.50
b.	$55.50 Governor's edition	75.00	
17	$7.50 Northern shovelers, *2003*	14.00	
a.	Bklt. single, perf. 2 sides, with tabs	14.00	2.50
b.	$55.50 Governor's edition	75.00	
18	$7.50 Lesser scaup, *2004*	12.00	
a.	Bklt. single, perf. 2 sides, with tabs	12.00	2.50
b.	$55.50 Governor's edition	75.00	—
19	$7.50 Pintails, *2005*	9.50	
a.	Bklt. single, perf. 3 sides, with tabs	10.50	2.50
20	$7.50 Canada geese, *2006*	9.50	
a.	Bklt. single, perf. 3 sides, with tabs	10.50	2.50
b.	$55 Governor's edition	75.00	
21	$8.75 Wood ducks, *2007*	11.00	
a.	Bklt. single, perf. 2 or 3 sides, with tabs	12.00	2.50
b.	$55 Governor's edition	75.00	

ARKANSAS

Imperforate varieties of these stamps exist in large quantities. Imperforate copies of Nos. 1 and 2 were sold by the state for $1 each.

No. 1 printed in sheets and booklet panes of 30, others in sheets and booklet panes of 10.

Stamps are numbered serially on reverse.

Catalogue values for all unused stamps in this section are for Never Hinged items.

Artists: Lee LeBlanc, #1; Maynard Reece, #2, 8; David Maass, #3, 10, 21; Larry Hayden, #4, 15; Ken Carlson, #5, 13; John P. Cowan, #6; Robert Bateman. #7; Phillip Crowe, #9, 16, 22, 30, 31; Daniel Smith, #11, 14; Jim Hautman, #12, 19; L. Chandler, #17, 20, 26, 27; John Dearman, #18; Zettie Jones, #23; Ralph McDonald, #24-25. Scot Storm, #28-29.

1981-2007

1	$5.50 Mallards	55.00	12.00
	Booklet single with top tab, Nos. 110,001-200,000 on back	60.00	
2	$5.50 Wood ducks, *1982*	45.00	9.00
3	$5.50 Green-winged teal, *1983*	65.00	12.00
4	$5.50 Pintails, *1984*	22.50	5.00
5	$5.50 Mallards, *1985*	13.00	2.50
6	$5.50 Black swamp mallards, *1986*	11.00	2.50
7	$7 Wood ducks, *1987*	11.00	2.50

Stamps like Nos. 7 and 8 with $5.50 face values were sold following an order of the state Supreme Court restoring the fee level of 1986. The stamps were sold after the 1988 season had ended. Value, $11 each.

8	$7 Pintails, *1988*	10.00	2.50

See footnote following No. 7.

9	$7 Mallards, *1989*	10.00	2.50
10	$7 Black ducks & mallards, *1990*	12.00	2.50
11	$7 Sulphur river widgeons, *1991*	10.00	2.50
12	$7 Shirey Bay shovelers, *1992*	12.00	2.50
13	$7 Grand prairie mallards, *1993*	12.00	2.50
14	$7 Canada goose, *1994*	14.00	2.50
15	$7 White River mallards, *1995*	14.00	2.50
16	$7 Mallards, black labrador, *1996*	14.00	2.00
17	$7 Labrador retriever, mallards, *1997*	15.00	2.00
18	$7 Labrador retriever, mallards, *1998*	12.00	2.00
19	$7 Wood duck, *1999*	12.00	2.00
20	$7 Mallards and golden retriever, *2000*	11.00	2.00
21	$7 Canvasbacks, *2001*	11.00	2.00
22	$7 Mallards, *2002*	11.00	2.00
23	$7 Mallards & Chesapeake retriever, *2003*	14.00	2.00
24	$7 Mallards, *2004*	11.00	2.00
25	$20 Mallards, *2004*	26.00	2.00
26	$7 Mallards, Labrador retriever *2005*	9.00	2.00
27	$20 Mallards, Labrador retriever *2005*	26.00	2.00
28	$7 Mallards, *2006*	9.00	2.00
29	$20 Mallards, *2006*	26.00	2.00
30	$7 Mallards, Labrador retriever *2007*	9.00	2.00
31	$20 Mallards, Labrador retriever *2007*	25.00	2.00

Resident and non-resident fees begin in 2004.

CALIFORNIA

Honey Lake Waterfowl Stamps

Required to hunt waterfowl at Honey Lake. Valid for a full season. Stamps are rouletted. Used values are for signed copies. Unsigned stamps without gum probably were used. Values for these stamps are higher than used values, but lower than values shown for gummed unused stamps.

1956-86

A1	$5 black, *1956-1957*		—
A2	$5 black, *blue green, 1957-1958*		—
A3	$5 black, *dark yellow, 1958-1959*		—
A4	$5 black, *dark yellow, 1959-1960*	*1,100.*	*550.00*
A5	$5 black, *1960-1961*		*1,250.*
A6	$5 black, *bluish green, 1961-1962*	—	*1,200.*
A7	$5 black, *dark yellow, 1962-1963*		*700.00*
A8	$5 black, *1963-1964*		*400.00*
A9	$6.50 black, *pink, 1964-1965*	*1,250.*	*400.00*
A10	$6.50 black, *1965-1966*		*350.00*
A11	$6.50 black, *yellow,* Nos. 1-700, printer's information at bottom right, *1966-1967*		*375.00*
a.	Serial Nos. 701-1050, no printer's information		*8,500.*
A12	$10 black, *pink, 1967-1968*	—	*350.00*
A13	$10 black, *blue, 1968-1969*		*450.00*
A14	$10 black, *green, 1969-1970*	—	*500.00*
A15	$15 black, *dark yellow, 1970-1971*	—	*600.00*
A16	$15 black, *pink, 1971-1972*		*1,950.*
A17	$15 black, *blue, 1972-1973*		*2,950.*
A18	$15 black, *blue, 1973-1974*	—	—
A19	$15 black, *pink, 1974-1975*	40.00	*25.00*
A20	$15 black, *green, 1975-1976*	*140.00*	*35.00*
A21	$15 black, *light yellow, 1976-1977*	*140.00*	*35.00*
A22	$20 black, *blue, 1977-1978*	*140.00*	*35.00*
A23	$20 blk, *light yel brown, 1978-1979*	*140.00*	*35.00*
A24	$20 black, *light yellow, 1979-1980*	*140.00*	*35.00*
A25	$15 black, *light blue, 1980-1981*	*100.00*	*30.00*
A26	$20 black, *light yellow, 1981-1982*		—
A27	$20 black, *pink, 1982-1983*	*90.00*	*30.00*
A28	$20 black, *light green, 1983-1984*	45.00	*25.00*
A29	$20 black, *dark yellow, 1984-1985*	42.50	*25.00*
A30	$20 black, *light blue, 1985-1986*	37.50	*20.00*

Eighteen $5 black on dark yellow permit stamps were sold for hunting at the state-owned and operated Madeline Plains waterfowl management area for the 1956-57 season. No examples have been recorded.

Statewide Hunting License Validation Stamps

Fees are for resident, junior and non-resident hunters. "No fee" stamps were for disabled veterans. Stamps with special serial numbers for state officials are known for some years. Nos. 2A1-2A3 imperf on 3 sides, rouletted at top. Others die cut.

Stamps are numbered serially.

Used values are for written-upon stamps. Starting with No. 2A4, unused values are for stamps on backing paper.

1962-1963

2A1	$4 black	*450.00*	7.00
a.	Ovptd. "NO FEE"	*425.00*	*300.00*
2A2	$1 black, *yellow*	*1,500.*	*75.00*
2A3	$25 black, *green*	*2,950.*	*150.00*

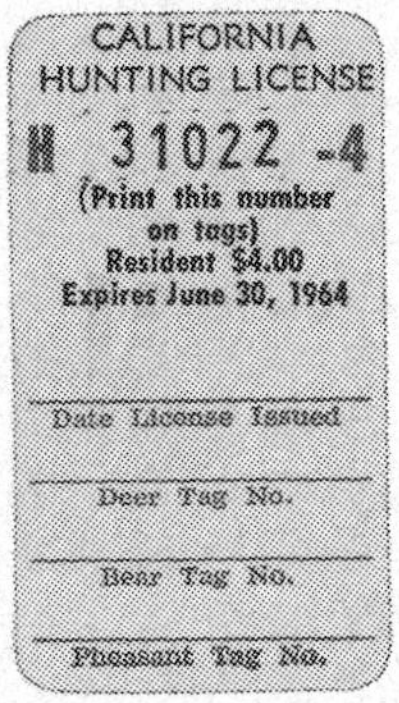

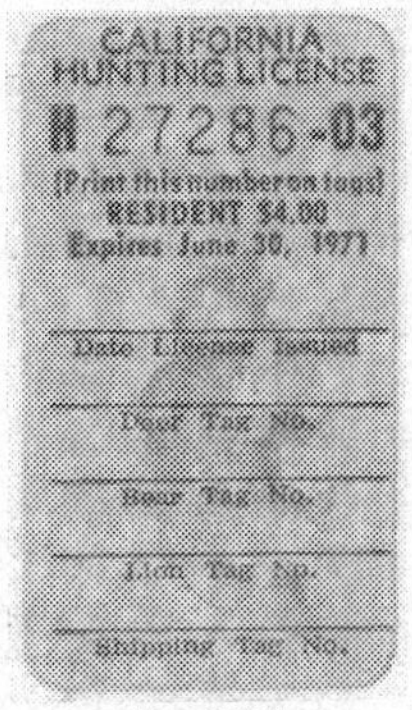

No. 2A25

1963-1964

2A4	$4 black, *green*		3.00
a.	Ovptd. "NO FEE"	—	—
2A5	$1 black, *gray*	—	20.00
2A6	$25 black, *yellow orange*		*450.00*

1964-1965

2A7	$4 black, *pink*	30.00	1.00
a.	Ovptd. "NO FEE"	*450.00*	*225.00*
2A8	$1 black, *yellow brown*	*225.00*	25.00
2A9	$25 black, *dark gray*		*70.00*

1965-1966

2A10	$4 black, *gray*	25.00	1.00
a.	Ovptd. "NO FEE"		—
2A11	$1 black, *yellow gray*		25.00
2A12	$25 black, *ivory*		*75.00*

1966-1967

2A13	$4 black, *salmon*	25.00	1.00
a.	Ovptd. "NO FEE"		*550.00*
2A14	$1 black, *lt blue*	75.00	10.00
2A15	$25 black, *burgundy*		*65.00*

1967-1968

2A16	$4 black, *yellow*	20.00	1.00
a.	Ovptd. "NO FEE"		*500.00*
2A17	$1 black, *green*	45.00	5.00
a.	black, *yellow gray*		—
2A18	$25 black, *brown*	75.00	25.00

1968-1969

2A19	$4 black, *pink*	55.00	1.00
a.	Ovptd. "NO FEE"		*550.00*
2A20	$1 black, *blue gray*	*175.00*	20.00
2A21	$25 black, *light orange*		*85.00*

1969-1970

2A22	$4 black	55.00	1.00
a.	Ovptd. "NO FEE"		*500.00*
2A23	$1 black, *dark pink*	*175.00*	20.00
2A24	$25 black, *light yellow*	70.00	25.00

1970-1971

2A25	$4 black, *manila*	70.00	2.00
a.	Ovptd. "NO FEE"	*1,500.*	*1,000.*
2A26	$1 black, *blue gray*	75.00	10.00
2A27	$25 black, *gray brown*	100.00	25.00

1971-1972

2A28	$4 black, *green*	45.00	1.00
a.	Ovptd. "NO FEE"		*500.00*
b.	Ovptd. "DISABLED VETERANS/NO FEE"		*650.00*
2A29	$1 black, *lavender*		20.00
2A30	$25 black, *peach*	*275.00*	*35.00*

1972-1973

2A31	$6 black, *pink*		1.00
a.	Ovptd. "DISABLED VETERANS/NO FEE"		*650.00*
2A32	$2 black, *light yellow*		30.00
2A33	$35 black, *lavender*	*225.00*	

1973-1974

2A34	$6 black, *blue*		1.00
a.	Ovptd. "DISABLED VETERANS/NO FEE"		*650.00*
2A35	$2 black, *lavender*	*175.00*	20.00
2A36	$35 black, *gray*	*275.00*	*35.00*

1974-1975

2A37	$6 black, *green*	35.00	1.00
a.	Ovptd. "DISABLED VETERANS/NO FEE"		*700.00*
2A38	$2 black, *orange*		20.00
2A39	$35 black, *reddish purple*	175.00	*25.00*

1975-1976

2A40	$10 red brown, *brown*	40.00	1.00
a.	Ovptd. "DISABLED VETERANS/NO FEE"	—	*800.00*
2A41	$2 black, *dark red*	80.00	20.00
2A42	$35 black, *yellow*	85.00	25.00

1976-1977

2A43	$10 black, *blue*	30.00	1.00
a.	Ovptd. "DISABLED VETERANS/NO FEE"		*900.00*
2A44	$2 black, *gray violet*	*100.00*	20.00
a.	Inscibed "Deer Tag No." instead of "Bear Tag No."	—	
2A45	$35 black, *lavender*	85.00	25.00

1977-1978

2A46	$10 black, *red orange*	30.00	1.00
a.	Ovptd. "DISABLED VETERANS/NO FEE"		*750.00*
2A47	$2 black, *yellow green*	95.00	25.00
2A48	$35 black, *pink*	*95.00*	

1978-1979

2A49	$10 black, *yellow*	40.00	1.50
a.	Ovptd. "DISABLED VETERANS/NO FEE"		*700.00*
2A50	$2 black, *red*	80.00	20.00
2A51	$35 black, *light brown*	85.00	

1979-1980

2A52	$10 black, *red*	30.00	1.00
a.	Ovptd. "DISABLED VETERANS/NO FEE"		*800.00*
2A53	$2 black, *yellow green*	80.00	20.00
2A54	$35 black, *dark blue*	85.00	

1980-1981

2A55	$10.25 black, *blue*	30.00	1.00
a.	Ovptd. "DISABLED VETERANS/NO FEE"		*1,250.*
2A56	$2 black, *light brown*	75.00	15.00
2A57	$36.25 black, *tan*	75.00	25.00

1981-1982

2A58	$11.50 black, *dark green*	30.00	1.00
2A59	$2.25 black, *blue*	75.00	20.00
2A60	$40 black, *gray*	*200.00*	

1982-1983

2A61	$12.50 black, *pink*	30.00	1.00
2A62	$2.50 black, *brown*	75.00	20.00
2A63	$43.50 black, *orange*	*140.00*	

1983-1984

2A64	$13.25 black, *blue*	50.00	1.00
2A65	$2.75 black, *purple*	*150.00*	20.00
2A66	$46.50 black, *green*	*175.00*	

1984-1985

2A67	$13.25 black, *yellow*	*50.00*	1.00
2A68	$2.75 black, *green*	*150.00*	20.00
2A69	$49.25 black, *brown*	*175.00*	

1985-1986

2A70	$14 black, *blue*	*50.00*	1.00
2A71	$3.50 black, *yellow*	*150.00*	20.00
2A72	$51.75 black, *purple*	*175.00*	

1986-1987

2A73	$18.50 black, *green*		1.00
2A74	$4.50 black, *dark blue*		*15.00*

1987-1988

2A76	$17.50 black, *dark blue*		1.00
2A77	$4.50 black, *purple*		*15.00*

1988-1989

2A79	$19.25 black, *tan*		1.00
2A80	$5 black, *yellow*		*15.00*

1989-1990

2A82	$19.75 black, *blue gray*		1.00
2A83	$5 black, *dark green*		*15.00*

1990-1991

2A85	$21.50 black, *reddish gray*		1.00
2A86	$5.50 black, *yellow*		*15.00*
2A87	$73 black, *pink*		*25.00*

1991-1992

2A88	$23.10 black, *lime green*		*1.00*
2A89	$5.50 black, *bluish purple*		*15.00*
2A90	$79.80 black, *brown*		*25.00*

1992-1993

2A91	$24.15 black, *yellow*	—	1.00
2A92	$5.80 black, *greenish gold*		*15.00*
2A93	$83.75 black, *mauve*	—	*25.00*

1993-1994

2A94	$24.40 black & white, *green*	1.00
2A95	$5.80 black & white, *light blue*	*15.00*

1994-1995

2A97	$24.95 black & white, *pale yellow*	1.00
2A98	$6.05 black & white, *lavender*	*15.00*
2A99	$86.90 black & white, *gray*	*25.00*

1996-1997

2A100	$25.45 black, *gray brown*	1.00
2A101	$6.30 black, *pink*	*15.00*
2A102	$88.70 black, *pale blue*	*25.00*

Statewide Waterfowl Issues

Nos. 1-24 printed in booklet panes of five, No. 25 in pane of 4.

Issues through 1978 are die cut and self-adhesive. Starting with the 1979 issue, stamps are rouletted. Stamps are numbered serially.

Catalogue values for all unused stamps in this section are for Never Hinged items.

Artists: Paul Johnson, #1-8, 38; Ken Michaelson, #9; Walter Wolfe, #10-11; Robert Steiner, #12, 18-20, 26-35; Robert Richert, #13; Charles Allen, #14; Robert Montanucci, #15; Richard Wilson, #16; Sherrie Russell Meline, #17, 23, 37; Ronald Louque, #21; Larry Hayden, #22; Richard Clifton, #24-25; Richard Radigonda, #36.

Stamps valued with original backing paper. Caution should be used when buying especially Nos. 1 and 2. Both these issues have wider roulletting on the backing paper than Nos. 3-9.

1971-2007

1	$1 Pintails	600.00	65.00
2	$1 Canvasbacks, *1972*	2,000.	150.00
3	$1 Mallards, *1973*	14.50	2.50
4	$1 White-fronted geese, *1974*	3.00	2.50
5	$1 Green-winged teal, backing paper with red wavy lines, *1975*	35.00	8.00
	Waxy backing paper without lines	150.00	

The gum bleeds through the stamp with red wavy lines resulting in a spotted or blotchy effect. Little or no gum bleeds through on stamps with waxy backing paper.

6	$1 Widgeons, *1976*	22.50	2.50
7	$1 Cinnamon teal, *1977*	45.00	9.00
8	$5 Cinnamon teal, *1978*	12.50	2.50
9	$5 Hooded mergansers, *1978*	110.00	15.00
10	$5 Wood ducks, *1979*	9.00	2.50
11	$5 Pintails, *1980*	9.00	2.50
12	$5 Canvasabacks, *1981*	9.00	2.50
13	$5 Widgeons, *1982*	9.00	2.50
14	$5 Green-winged teal, *1983*	12.00	2.50
15	$7.50 Mallard decoy, *1984*	11.00	2.50
16	$7.50 Ring-necked ducks, *1985*	11.00	2.50
17	$7.50 Canada goose, *1986*	11.00	3.00
18	$7.50 Redheads, *1987*	11.00	3.00
19	$7.50 Mallards, *1988*	11.00	3.00
20	$7.50 Cinnamon teal, *1989*	11.00	3.00
21	$7.50 Canada goose, *1990*	11.00	3.00
22	$7.50 Gadwalls, *1991*	11.00	3.00
23	$7.90 White-fronted goose, *1992*	13.00	3.00
24	$10.50 Pintails, *1993*	16.00	4.00

Rouletted Horiz.

25	$10.50 Wood duck, *1994*	15.00	4.00

Perf. Vertically

Birds in flight, denomination at: b, UL. c, UR. d, LL. e, LR.

26	$10.50 Snow geese, booklet pane of 4, #b.-e., *1995*	60.00	
a.	Souvenir sheet of 4, #b.-e. (decorative border)	*150.00*	
b.-e.	Booklet single, each	15.00	4.00

Stamps in No. 26a are perfed on all four sides.

Perf. Horizontally

27	$10.50 Mallards, *1996*	16.00	2.50

Issued in panes of 4.

28	$10.50 Pintails, *1997*	16.00	2.50
29	$10.50 Green-winged teal, pair, *1998*	32.50	
a.-b.	a, Female, b, Male, each	15.00	2.50

No. 29 issued in strips of 4 stamps.

30	$10.50 Wood duck, pair, *1999*	32.50	
a.-b.	a, Male, b, Male and female, each	14.00	2.50

No. 30 issued in strips of 2 pairs.

31	$10.50 Canada geese, mallard, widgeon *2000*	16.00	2.50
32	$10.50 Canvasbacks, *2001*	16.00	2.50
33	$10.50 Pintails, *2002*	16.00	2.50
34	$10.50 Mallards, *2003*	16.00	2.50
35	$13.90 Cinnamon teal, *2004*	17.00	2.50

Perf. Vertically

36	$14.20 Pintails, *2005*	17.50	2.50
37	$14.95 White-fronted goose, *2006*	18.50	2.50
38	$16 Pintails, *2007*	20.00	2.50

COLORADO

North Central Goose Stamp

Used in an area extending from Ft. Collins to approximately 50 miles east of the city.

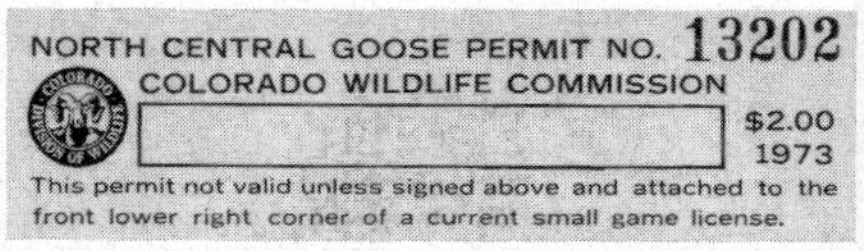

Illustration reduced.

1973

A1	$2 black	—	—

No. A1 is die cut and self-adhesive. Unused stamps have glassine backing.

Statewide Issues

Printed in booklet panes of 5 and panes of 30.

Stamps are numbered serially.

Imperforate varieties of these stamps are printer's proofs.

Catalogue values for all unused stamps in this section are for Never Hinged items.

Artists: Robert Steiner, #1-2; Charles Allen, #3; Dan Andrews, #4; Sarah Woods, #5; Cynthie Fisher, #6, 9-14; Bill Border, #7; Gerald G. Putt, #8; Jeffrey Klinefelter, #15-16, 18. Michael Ashman, #17.

1990-2007

1	$5 Canada geese	12.00	
	Bklt. single, with tab, Nos. 80,001-150,000	12.50	3.00
a.	$5 +$50 Governor's edition	60.00	
2	$5 Mallards, *1991*	17.50	
	Bklt. single, with tab, Nos. 80,001-150,000	16.00	3.00
a.	$5 +$50 Governor's edition	60.00	
3	$5 Pintails, *1992*	10.00	
	Bklt. single, with tab, Nos. 80,001-150,000	10.00	3.00
a.	$5 +$50 Governor's edition	60.00	
4	$5 Green-winged teal, *1993*	12.00	
	Bklt. single, with tab, Nos. 80,001-150,000	12.00	3.00
a.	$5 +$50 Governor's edition	60.00	
5	$5 Wood ducks, *1994*	12.00	
	Bklt. single, with tab	12.00	2.50
6	$5 Buffleheads, *1995*	12.00	
	Bklt. single, with tab	12.00	2.50

7	$5 Cinnamon teal, *1996*	12.00	
	Bklt. single, with tab and top selvage	12.00	2.50
8	$5 Widgeons, gold text, *1997*	10.00	
a.	Bklt. single, with tab and top selvage, text in black & white	12.00	2.50
9	$5 Redheads, *1998*	10.00	
	Bklt. single, with tab and top selvage	10.00	2.50
10	$5 Blue-winged teal, *1999*	10.00	
a.	Bklt. single, with tab and top selvage	10.00	2.50
11	$5 Gadwalls, *2000*	10.00	
a.	Bklt. single, with tab and top selvage	10.00	2.50
12	$5 Ruddy ducks, *2001*	10.00	2.50
13	$5 Common goldeneyes, *2002*	10.00	2.50
14	$5 Canvasbacks, *2003*	10.00	2.50
15	$5 Snow geese, *2004*	10.00	2.50
16	$5 Shovelers, *2005*	10.00	2.50
17	$5 Ring-necked ducks, *2006*	7.50	2.50
18	$5 Hooded mergansers, *2007*	7.50	2.50

CONNECTICUT

Printed in booklet panes of 10 and sheets of 30.
Stamps are numbered serially.
Imperforate varieties are proofs.

Catalogue values for all unused stamps in this section are for Never Hinged items.

Artists: Thomas Hirata, #1; Robert Leslie, #2, 9; Phillip Crowe, #3; Keith Mueller, #4, 7, 15; Robert Steiner, #5; Joe Hautman, #6; George Lockwood, #8; Robert Richert, #10; Paul Fusco, #11-14.

1993-2007

1	$5 Black ducks	12.00	3.00
	Booklet pane pair with L & R selvage, Nos. 51,001-81,000	24.00	
a.	Sheet of 4	80.00	
b.	$5 +$50 Governor's edition	75.00	
2	$5 Canvasbacks, *1994*	11.00	3.00
	Booklet pair with L & R selvage, Nos. 53,000-up	22.50	
a.	Sheet of 4	47.50	
3	$5 Mallards, *1995*	15.00	3.00
	Booklet pair with L & R selvage	30.00	
4	$5 Old squaw ducks, *1996*	16.00	3.00
	Booklet pair with L & R selvage	32.50	
5	$5 Green-winged teal, *1997*	11.00	3.00
a.	$5 +$50 Governor's edition	*150.00*	
6	$5 Mallards, *1998*	10.00	3.00
7	$5 Canada geese, *1999*	15.00	3.00
a.	$5 +$50 Governor's edition	*450.00*	
8	$5 Wood duck, *2000*	10.00	3.00
a.	$5 +$50 Governor's edition	*425.00*	
9	$5 Buffleheads, *2001*	9.00	3.00
a.	$5 +$50 Governor's edition	*425.00*	
10	$5 Greater scaups, *2002*	12.00	3.00
a.	$5 +$50 Governor's edition	*450.00*	

11	$5 Black Duck, *2003*	10.00	3.00
12	$5 Wood duck, *2004*	10.00	3.00
13	$10 Mallards, *2005*	16.00	3.00
14	$10 Buffleheads, *2006*	16.00	3.00
15	$10 Black duck decoy, *2007*	16.00	3.00

DELAWARE

Printed in sheets of 10.
Starting in 1991, a portion of the printing is numbered serially on the reverse.

Catalogue values for all unused stamps in this section are for Never Hinged items.

Artists: Ned Mayne, #1; Charles Rowe, #2; Lois Butler, #3; John Green, #4; Nolan Haan, #5; Don Breyfogle, #6; Robert Leslie, #7, 10; Bruce Langton, #8; Jim Hautman, #9; Francis Sweet, #11; Ronald Louque, #12; Richard Clifton, #13, 17, 19, 26; Robert Metropulos, #14; Louis Frisino, #15; Michael Ashman, #16, 21; Jeffrey Klinefelter, #18, 24; Russ Duerksen, #20; Brian Blight, #22; George Lockwood, #23, 28; Bonnie Field, #25; Joanna Rivera, #26.

1980-2007

1	$5 Black ducks	90.00	20.00
2	$5 Snow geese, *1981*	70.00	20.00
3	$5 Canada geese, *1982*	70.00	20.00
4	$5 Canvasbacks, *1983*	40.00	10.00
5	$5 Mallards, *1984*	15.00	5.00
6	$5 Pintail, *1985*	12.00	3.00
7	$5 Widgeons, *1986*	11.00	3.00
8	$5 Redheads, *1987*	11.00	3.00
9	$5 Wood ducks, *1988*	9.00	3.00
10	$5 Buffleheads, *1989*	9.00	3.00
11	$5 Green-winged teal, *1990*	10.00	3.00
a.	$5 +$50 Governor's edition	85.00	
12	$5 Hooded merganser, no serial number on reverse, *1991*	10.00	
	With serial number on reverse	11.00	3.00
13	$5 Blue-winged teal, no serial number on reverse, *1992*	10.00	
	With serial number on reverse	10.00	2.50
14	$5 Goldeneye, no serial number on reverse, *1993*	10.00	
	With serial number on reverse	10.00	2.50
15	$5 Blue goose, no serial number on reverse, *1994*	12.00	
	With serial number on reverse	12.00	2.50
16	($6) Scaup, no serial number on reverse, *1995*	11.00	
	With serial number on reverse	11.00	2.50
17	$6 Gadwall, no serial number on reverse, *1996*	12.00	
	With serial number on reverse	12.00	2.50
18	$6 White-winged scoter, no serial number on reverse, *1997*	12.00	
	With serial number on reverse	12.00	2.50
19	$6 Blue-winged teal, *1998*	11.00	2.50
20	$6 Tundra swan, *1999*	11.00	
21	$6 American brant, *2000*	12.00	2.50
22	$6 Oldsquaw, *2001*	11.00	2.50
23	$6 Ruddy ducks, *2002*	11.00	2.50
24	$9 Ring-necked ducks, *2003*	12.00	3.00
25	$9 Black scoters and lighthouse, *2004*	12.00	3.00
a.	$9 +$50 Governor's edition	95.00	
26	$9 Common mergansers and lighthouse, *2005*	12.00	3.00
a.	$9 +$50 Governor's edition	75.00	
27	$9 Red-breasted mergansers, *2006*	12.00	3.00
28	$9 Surf scoters, lighthouse *2007*	12.00	3.00

FLORIDA

#1-7 issued in booklet panes of 5. Nos. 8-19 in sheets of 10. No. 20 in sheet of 12.
Stamps are numbered serially and rouletted. Serial numbers for stamps with survey tabs attached end in -04.

Catalogue values for all unused stamps in this section are for Never Hinged items.

Illustration reduced.

Artists: Bob Binks, #1, 7; Ernest Simmons, #2; Clark Sullivan, #3; Lee Cable, #4; Heiner Hertling, #5; John Taylor, #6; Robert Steiner, #8; Ronald Louque, #9-10; J. Byron Test, #11; Ben Test, #12; Richard Hansen, #13; Richard Clifton, #14; John Mogus, #15; Antonie Rossini, #16; Kenneth Nanney, #17; Wally Makuchal, #18; M. Frase, #19; Brian Blight, #20; John Harris, #21, 23; Jeffrey Klinefelter, #22; John Nelson Harris, #24.

1979-2003

1	$3.25 Green-winged teal	175.00	20.00
	With tab	210.00	
2	$3.25 Pintails, *1980*	15.00	5.00
	With tab	20.00	

3	$3.25 Widgeon, *1981*	15.00	5.00
	With tab	40.00	
4	$3.25 Ring-necked ducks, *1982*	22.50	5.00
	With tab	30.00	
5	$3.25 Buffleheads, *1983*	45.00	5.00
	With tab	60.00	
6	$3.25 Hooded merganser, *1984*	11.00	3.50
	With tab	35.00	
7	$3.25 Wood ducks, *1985*	11.00	3.50
	With tab	30.00	
8	$3 Canvasbacks, *1986*	11.00	3.50
	With small tab at top	11.00	
	With larger survey tab at side and small tab at top	25.00	
9	$3.50 Mallards, *1987*	9.00	3.50
	With small tab at top	9.00	
	With larger survey tab at side and small tab at top	25.00	
10	$3.50 Redheads, *1988*	8.00	2.50
	With small tab at top	8.00	
	With larger survey tab at side and small tab at top	20.00	

11	$3.50 Blue-winged teal, *1989*	8.00	2.50
	With small tab at top	8.00	
	With larger survey tab at side and small tab at top	35.00	
12	$3.50 Wood ducks, *1990*	8.00	2.50
	With small tab at top	8.00	
	With larger survey tab at side and small tab at top	35.00	
13	$3.50 Northern Pintails, *1991*	9.00	2.50
	With small tab at top	9.00	
	With larger survey tab at side and small tab at top	30.00	
14	$3.50 Ruddy duck, *1992*	8.00	2.50
	With small tab at top	7.00	
	With larger survey tab at side and small tab at top	12.00	
15	$3.50 American widgeon, *1993*	8.00	2.50
	With small tab at top	8.00	
	With larger survey tab at side and small tab at top	27.50	
16	$3.50 Mottled duck, *1994*	9.00	2.50
	With small tab at top	9.00	
	With larger survey tab at side and small tab at top	27.50	
17	$3.50 Fulvous whistling duck, *1995*	9.00	2.50
	With small tab at top	9.00	
	With larger survey tab at side and small tab at top	27.50	
18	$3.50 Goldeneyes, *1996*	15.00	2.50
	With small tab at top	15.00	
	With larger survey tab at side and small tab at top	27.50	
19	($3.00) Hooded merganser, *1997*	11.00	2.50
	With small tab at top	11.00	
	With larger survey tab at side and small tab at top	27.50	

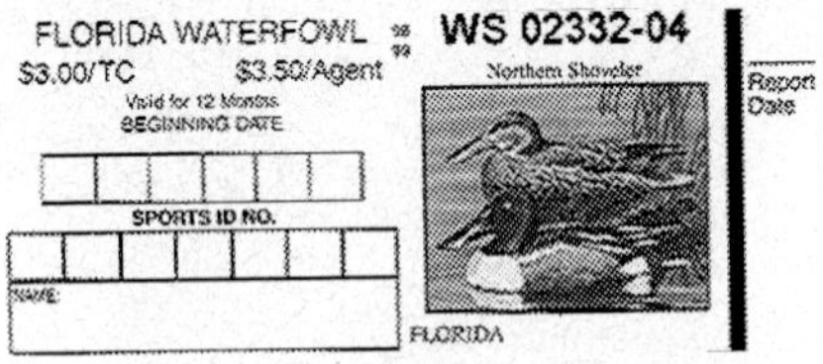

Self-Adhesive

20	$3 Shoveler, *1998*	20.00	2.50
	Sold for $3.50 through agents.		
21	$3 Pintail, *1999*	12.00	2.50
	Sold for $3.50 through agents.		
22	$3 Ring-necked duck, *2000*	9.00	2.50
	Sold for $3.50 through agents.		
23	$3 Canvasback, *2001*	9.00	2.50
	Sold for $3.50 through agents.		
24	$3 Mottled duck, *2002*	9.00	2.50

Sold for $3.50 through agents. No. 24 with rouletting and with duck facing right come from a special limited reprinting demanded by the artist to correct the appearance of his work. Value, $50.

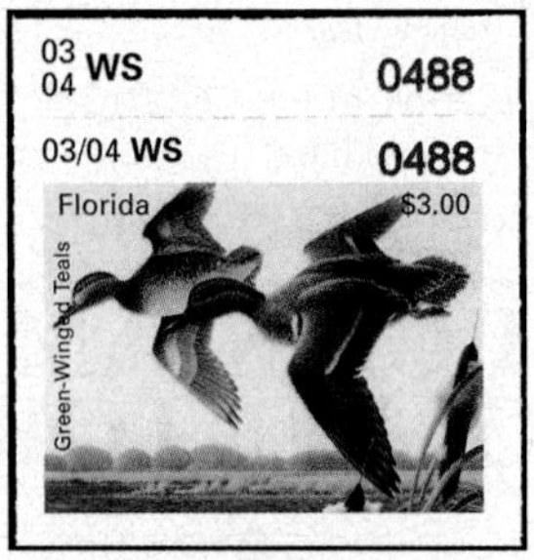

The 2003 stamp was sold by Florida officials only to the stamp's artist. Values: $110; with small tab at top, $150.

GEORGIA

Not required to hunt waterfowl until 1989.

Nos. 1-4 printed in sheets of 30, others in sheets of 20.

Starting with No 5, stamps are numbered serially.

Catalogue values for all unused stamps in this section are for Never Hinged items.

Artists: Daniel Smith, #1; Jim Killen, #2, 14; James Partee, Jr., #3; Paul Bridgeford, #4; Ralph J. McDonald, #5; Guy Coheleach, #6; Phillip Crowe, #7-8, 11; Jerry Raedeke, #9, 13, 15; Herb Booth, #10; David Lanier, #12.

1985-99

1	$5.50 Wood ducks	15.00	
2	$5.50 Mallards, *1986*	9.00	
3	$5.50 Canada geese, *1987*	9.00	
4	$5.50 Ring-necked ducks, *1988*	9.00	
5	$5.50 Duckling & golden retriever puppy, *1989*	14.00	2.50
6	$5.50 Wood ducks, *1990*	9.00	2.50
7	$5.50 Green-winged teal, *1991*	9.50	2.50
8	$5.50 Buffleheads, *1992*	15.00	2.50
9	$5.50 Mallards, *1993*	15.00	2.50
10	$5.50 Ring-necked ducks, *1994*	15.00	2.50
11	$5.50 Widgeons, Labrador retreiver, *1995*	32.50	2.50
12	$5.50 Black ducks, *1996*	25.00	2.50
13	$5.50 Lesser scaup, Cockspur Island lighthouse, *1997*	40.00	2.50
14	$5.50 Labrador retreiver, ring-necked ducks, *1998*	27.50	2.50
15	$5.50 Pintails, *1999*	22.50	2.50

HAWAII

Required for the hunting of small game. Hunting birds was illegal in Hawaii until 2003. Game bird hunting was permitted beginning July 1, 2003. Game birds that can be hunted include pheasants, francolins, partridges, quail, sand grouses, doves and wild turkeys.

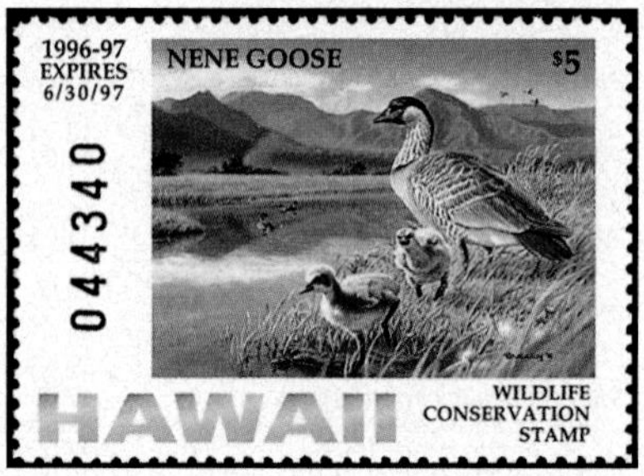

Artists: Patrick Ching, #1, D. Van Zyle, #2; Michael Furuya, #3; Norman Nagai, #4, 7, 10; Marion Berger, #5; Daniel Wang, #6; Joy Keown, #8, 9. Shane Hamamoto, #11. Dan Hoyes, #12.

1996-2007

1	$5 Nene goose	5.00	
a.	$5 +$50 Governor's edition	75.00	
b.	As No. 1, sheet of 4	45.00	
	No. 1b exists imperf.		
2	$5 Hawaiian duck, *1997*	5.00	
	With tab	10.00	
a.	As No. 2, sheet of 4	45.00	
	No. 2a exists imperf.		
3	$5 Wild turkey, *1998*	5.00	
	With tab	10.00	
4	$5 Ring-necked pheasant, *1999*	5.00	
	With tab	14.00	
5	$5 Erckel's francolin, *2000*	5.00	
	With tab	12.00	
6	$5 Green pheasant, *2001*	5.00	
	With tab	12.00	5.00
7	$10 Chukar partridge, *2002*	5.00	
8	$10 Nene geese, *2003*	5.00	
9	$10 Nene geese, *2004*	5.00	
10	$10 California quail, *2005*	5.00	
11	$10 Black francolin, *2006*	5.00	
12	$10 Gray francolin, *2007*	15.00	

IDAHO

Printed in booklet panes of 5 and sheets of 30, except No. 5, which was issued in booklets of 10. Numbered serially except for No. 11.

Catalogue values for all unused stamps in this section are for Never Hinged items.

Artists: Robert Leslie, #1; Jim Killen, #2; Daniel Smith, #3 Francis E. Sweet, #4, Richard Clifton, #6, 11; Richard Plasschaert, #7; Sherrie Russell Meline, #8; Bill Moore, #9; Davi Gressard, #10; T. Smith, #12; Maynard Reece, #13.

1987-98

1	$5.50 Cinnamon teal, perforated	15.00	
a.	Bklt. single, rouletted, with 2-part tab	12.00	3.0
2	$5.50 Green-winged teal, perforated, *1988*	13.00	
a.	Bklt. single, rouletted, with 2-part tab	13.00	3.0
3	$6 Blue-winged teal, perforated, *1989*	10.00	
a.	Bklt. single, rouletted, with 2-part tab	11.00	3.0
4	$6 Trumpeter swans, perforated, *1990*	21.00	
a.	Bklt. single, rouletted, with 2-part tab	21.00	3.0

Die cut self-adhesive

5	$6 green, *1991*	175.00	*35.0*

No. 5 was used provisionally in 1991 when the regula stamps were delayed. Unused value is for stamp, remittanc tab and selvage pieces on backing paper.

Designs like No. 1

6	$6 Widgeons, perforated, *1991*	10.00	
a.	Bklt. single, rouletted, with 2-part tab	10.00	2.5
7	$6 Canada geese, perforated, *1992*	10.00	
a.	Bklt. single, rouletted, with 2-part tab	10.00	2.5
8	$6.00 Common goldeneye, perforated, *1993*	12.00	
a.	Bklt. single, rouletted, with 2-part tab	12.00	2.5
9	$6 Harlequin ducks, perforated, *1994*	12.00	
a.	Bklt. single, rouletted, with 2-part tab	12.00	2.5
10	$6 Wood ducks, perforated, *1995*	12.00	
a.	Bklt. single, rouletted, with 2-part tab	12.00	2.5
11	$6.50 Mallard, *1996*	16.00	2.5
12	$6.50 Shovelers, *1997*	22.50	2.5
13	$6.50 Canada geese, *1998*	15.00	2.5

ILLINOIS

Daily Usage Stamps for State-operated Waterfowl Areas.

Date and fee overprinted in black. $2 and $3 stamps were for hunting ducks, $5 stamps for hunting geese and pheasants. 1953-58 had separate pheasant stamps. No duck stamp was printed in 1971.

Some unused stamps have dry gum.

Used stamps have no gum or have staple holes.

Black printing.

Stamps are numbered serially.

1953-1972

A1	$2 orange, *blue*	—	—
A4	$2 green, *manila, 1956*	—	—
A5	$2 orange, *light blue green, 1957*	*950.*	*400.*
A6	$2 green, *manila, 1958*	*850.*	*400.*
A7	$3 green, *manila, 1959*	*675.*	*300.*
A8	$5 red brown, *light blue green, 1959*	*675.*	*300.*
A9	$3 red brown, *light blue green, 1960*	*675.*	*300.*
A10	$5 green, *manila, 1960*	*675.*	*300.*
A11	$3 green, *manila, 1961*	*675.*	*300.*
A12	$5 red brown, *light blue green, 1961*	*675.*	*300.*
A15	$3 green, *manila, 1962*	*675.*	*300.*
A14	$5 red brown, *light blue green, 1962*	*675.*	*300.*
A15	$3 orange, *light blue green, 1963*	*675.*	*300.*
A16	$5 green, *manila, 1963*	*675.*	*300.*
A17	$3 green, *manila, 1964*	*675.*	*300.*
A18	$5 red, *light blue green, 1964*	*675.*	*250.*
A19	$3 orange, *light blue green, 1965*	*675.*	*300.*
A20	$5 green, *manila, 1965*	*675.*	*300.*
A21	$3 green, *manila, 1966*	*675.*	*300.*
A22	$5 orange, *light blue green, 1966*	*675.*	*300.*
A23	$3 orange, *light blue green, 1967*	*675.*	*300.*
A24	$5 green, *yellow, 1967*	*675.*	*300.*
A25	$3 green, *yellow, 1968*	*675.*	*300.*
A26	$5 orange, *light blue, 1968*	*675.*	*300.*
A27	$3 orange, *light blue, 1969*	*675.*	*300.*
A28	$5 green, *manila, 1969*	*675.*	*300.*
A29	$3 green, *manila, 1970*	*1,500.*	*900.*
A30	$5 orange, *light blue, 1970*	*1,750.*	*900.*
A31	$5 green, *manila, 1971*	*1,950.*	*1,000.*
A32	$3 orange, *light blue green, 1972*	*5,500.*	
A33	$5 orange, *light blue green, 1972*	*5,500.*	*2,250.*

Catalogue values for unused stamps in this section, from this point to the end, are for Never Hinged items.

No. A34

No. A35

1977-91(?)

A34	black, *light blue,* duck, *1991*	—	—
A35	black, *manila,* goose	—	—

Nos. A34-A35 do not show year or denomination and were used until 1994. No. A34 used before 1991 should exist but has not been reported yet. Separate pheasant and controlled quail and pheasant stamps of a similar design have also been used.

No. A36

No. A37

1996

A36	black, *light blue,* duck	—	—
A37	black, *manila,* goose	—	—

Nos. A36-A37 do not show year or denomination.

Statewide Issues

Nos. 1-10 in sheets of 10. Starting with No. 11, in booklet panes of 5; starting with No. 22, in panes of 10.

Stamps are numbered serially and rouletted.

Catalogue values for all unused stamps in this section are for Never Hinged items.

Artists: Robert Eschenfeldt, #1; Robert G. Larson, #2; Richard Lynch, #3; Everett Staffeldt, #4; John Eggert, #5; Bart Kassabaum, #6, 9, 11, 13; Jim Trindel, #7; Arthur Sinden, #8, 12, 14; George Kieffer, #10; Charles McKay Freeman, #15; John Henson, #16; Phillip Crowe, #17-21; Thomas Hirata, #22-24; Jim Killen, #25-29; Gerald Putt, #30-32. Christina Van Dellen, #33.

1975-2007

1	$5 Mallard	*575.00*	85.00
2	$5 Wood ducks, *1976*	*250.00*	50.00
3	$5 Canada goose, *1977*	150.00	35.00
4	$5 Canvasbacks, *1978*	125.00	22.50
5	$5 Pintail, *1979*	115.00	16.00
6	$5 Green-winged teal, *1980*	100.00	16.00
7	$5 Widgeons, *1981*	115.00	16.00
a.	"Green-winged teal"	*500.00*	
8	$5 Black ducks, *1982*	60.00	12.50
9	$5 Lesser scaup, *1983*	75.00	10.00
10	$5 Blue-winged teal, *1984*	60.00	10.00
11	$5 Redheads, *1985*	16.00	3.00
	With 2-part tab	22.50	
12	$5 Gadwalls, *1986*	12.00	3.00
	With 2-part tab	20.00	
13	$5 Buffleheads, *1987*	12.00	3.00
	With 2-part tab	15.00	
14	$5 Common goldeneyes, *1988*	12.00	2.50
	With 2-part tab	15.00	
15	$5 Ring-necked ducks, *1989*	10.00	2.50
	With 2-part tab	10.00	
16	$10 Lesser snow geese, *1990*	16.00	3.00
	With 2-part tab	17.00	
17	$10 Labrador retriever & Canada goose, *1991*	16.00	3.00
	With 2-part tab	16.00	
a.	Governor's edition with tab	*85.00*	
18	$10 Retriever & mallards, *1992*	25.00	3.00
	With 2-part tab	27.50	
19	$10 Pintail decoys and puppy, *1993*	32.50	3.00
	With 2-part tab	35.00	
20	$10 Canvasbacks & retrievers, *1994*	32.50	3.00
	With 2-part tab	35.00	
21	$10 Retriever, green-winged teal, decoys, *1995*	32.50	3.00
	With 2-part tab	35.00	
22	$10 Wood ducks, *1996*	20.00	2.50
23	$10 Canvasbacks, *1997*	17.50	2.50
24	$10 Canada geese, *1998*	17.50	2.50
25	$10 Canada geese, black Labrador retriever, *1999*	22.50	2.50
a.	Anniversary edition, perforated	*92.50*	
b.	Governor's edition, perforated	*92.50*	
c.	Silver edition, perforated	*92.50*	

Nos. 25a-25c were sold as a set of three.

26	$10 Mallards, golden retriever, *2000*	22.50	2.50
27	$10 Pintails, yellow Labrador retriever, *2001*	22.50	2.50
28	$10 Canvasbacks, Chesapeake retriever, *2002*	22.50	2.50
29	$10 Green-winged teal, Labrador retriever, *2003*	15.00	2.50
30	$10 Wood ducks, *2004*	15.00	2.50
31	$10 Green-winged teals, *2005*	15.00	2.50
32	$10 Northern pintails, *2006*	14.00	2.50
33	$10 Bufflehead, *2007*	14.00	2.50

INDIANA

Issued in booklet panes of 4 (Nos. 1-10) and booklet panes of 2, starting with No. 11.

Stamps are numbered serially and rouletted.

Catalogue values for all unused stamps in this section are for Never Hinged items.

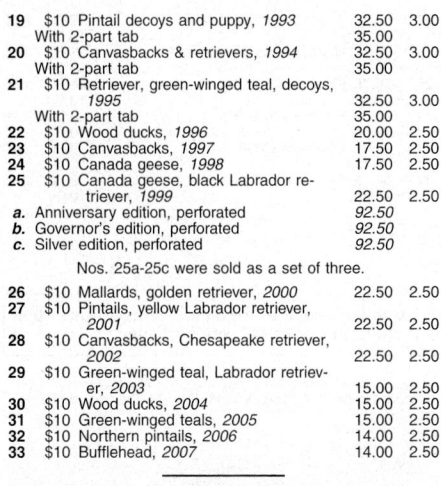

Artists: Justin H. (Sonny) Bashore, #1-2; Carl (Spike) Knuth, #3; Daniel Renn Pierce, #4; Dean Barrick, #5; Rodney Crossman, #6; George Metz, #7; Kieth Freeman, #8; Lyn Briggs, #9; Rick Pas, #10; Ronald Louque, #11; Susan Hastings Bates, #12.

Bruce Langton, #13, 17; Ann Dahoney, #14; Ken Bucklew, #15, 20, 22, 24, 29, 32; Richard Hansen, #16; Jeffrey Klinefelter, #18, 26, 28, 30; Jeffrey Mobley. #19; Charles Riggles, #21, 23, 31; George Lockwood, #25; Biran Blight, 27.

1976-2007

1	$5 Green-winged teal	12.00	2.50
2	$5 Pintail, *1977*	10.00	2.50
3	$5 Canada geese, *1978*	8.00	2.50
4	$5 Canvasbacks, *1979*	8.00	2.50
5	$5 Mallard ducklings, *1980*	8.00	2.50
6	$5 Hooded mergansers, *1981*	8.00	2.50
7	$5 Blue-winged teal, *1982*	8.00	2.50
8	$5 Snow geese, *1983*	8.00	2.50
9	$5 Redheads, *1984*	8.00	2.50
10	$5 Pintail, *1985*	10.00	2.50
	With tab	10.50	
11	$5 Wood duck, *1986*	8.00	2.50
	With tab	10.00	
12	$5 Canvasbacks, *1987*	8.00	2.50
	With tab	10.00	
13	$6.75 Redheads, *1988*	10.00	2.50
	With tab	10.50	
14	$6.75 Canada goose, *1989*	10.00	2.50
	With tab	10.50	
15	$6.75 Blue-winged teal, *1990*	10.00	2.50
	With tab	10.50	
16	$6.75 Mallards, *1991*	10.00	2.50
	With tab	10.50	
17	$6.75 Green-winged teal, *1992*	10.00	2.50
	With tab	10.50	
18	$6.75 Wood ducks, *1993*	10.00	2.50
	With tab	10.50	
19	$6.75 Pintail, *1994*	10.00	2.50
	With tab	10.50	
20	$6.75 Goldeneyes, *1995*	10.00	2.50
	With tab	10.50	
21	$6.75 Black ducks, *1996*	10.00	2.50
	With tab	10.50	
22	$6.75 Canada geese, *1997*	10.00	2.50
	With tab	10.50	
23	$6.75 Widgeon, *1998*	10.00	2.50
	With tab	10.50	
24	$6.75 Bluebills, *1999*	9.00	2.50
	With tab	10.00	
25	$6.75 Ring-necked duck, *2000*	9.00	2.50
	With tab	10.00	
26	$6.75 Hooded mergansers, *2001*	9.00	2.50
	With tab	10.00	

27	$6.75 Green-winged teal, *2002*	9.00	2.50
	With tab	10.00	
28	$6.75 Northern shovelers, *2003*	9.00	2.50
	With tab	10.00	
29	$6.75 Wood duck, *2004*	9.00	2.50
	With tab	10.00	
30	$6.75 Buffleheads, *2005*	9.00	2.50
	With tab	10.00	
31	$6.75 Gadwalls, *2006*	9.00	2.50
	With tab	10.00	
32	$6.75 Pintails, *2007*	9.00	2.50
	With tab	10.00	

IOWA

Catalogue values for all unused stamps in this section are for Never Hinged items.

Issued in booklet pane of 5 (No. 1), 10 (others) and sheets of 10 (No. 19).

Artists: Maynard Reece, #1, 6, 22; Thomas Murphy, #2; James Landenberger, #3; Mark Reece, #4; Nick Klepinger, #5, 7; Andrew Peters, #8; Paul Brigford, #9, 12, 15; Brad Reece, #10; Tom Walker, #11; Larry Zach, #13.

Jack C. Hahn, #14, 18; John Heidersbach, #16; Mark Cary, #17; Patrick Murillo, #19; Jerry Raedeke, #20; Charlotte Edwards, #21, 26; Dietmar Krumrey, #23, 25, 33; Cynthia Fisher, #24; Sherrie Russell Meline, #27, 29, 35; Mark Anderson, #28; Darren Maurer, #30, 31, 36; Neal Anderson, #32, 34.

1972-98

1	$1 Mallards	150.00	25.00
2	$1 Pintails, *1973*	35.00	7.50
3	$1 Gadwalls, rouletted, *1974*	85.00	7.00
4	$1 Canada geese, *1975*	95.00	9.00
5	$1 Canvasbacks, *1976*	25.00	2.50
6	$1 Lesser scaup, rouletted, *1977*	21.00	2.50
7	$1 Wood ducks, rouletted, *1978*	50.00	5.00
8	$5 Buffleheads, *1979*	375.00	25.00
9	$5 Redheads, *1980*	27.50	6.00
10	$5 Green-winged teal, rouletted, *1981*	27.50	4.00
11	$5 Snow geese, rouletted, *1982*	18.00	2.50
12	$5 Widgeons, *1983*	18.00	2.75
13	$5 Wood ducks, *1984*	35.00	3.00
14	$5 Mallard & mallard decoy, *1985*	20.00	2.50
15	$5 Blue-winged teal, *1986*	15.00	2.50
16	$5 Canada goose, *1987*	15.00	2.50
17	$5 Pintails, *1988*	15.00	2.50
18	$5 Blue-winged teal, *1989*	15.00	2.50
19	$5 Canvasbacks, *1990*	10.00	2.50
20	$5 Mallards, *1991*	10.00	2.50
21	$5 Labrador retriever & ducks, *1992*	10.00	2.50
22	$5 Mallards, *1993*	10.00	2.50
23	$5 Green-winged teal, *1994*	10.00	2.50
24	$5 Canada geese, *1995*	10.00	2.50
25	$5 Canvasbacks, *1996*	10.00	2.50
26	$5 Canada geese, *1997*	10.00	2.50
27	$5 Pintails, *1998*	12.00	2.50

1999

28	Trumpeter swan, *1999*	12.00	2.50

No. 28 not required for hunting. The Department of Natural Resources sent customers No. 28 upon receipt of a postcard given to the customer after paying license fee of $5.

2000

29	Hooded merganser, *2000*	10.00	2.50

No. 29 not required for hunting. The Department of Natural Resources sent customers No. 29 upon receipt of a postcard given to the customer after paying license fee of $5.

2001

30	Snow goose, *2001*	11.00	2.50

No. 30 not required for hunting. The Department of Natural Resources sent customers No. 30 upon receipt of a postcard given to the customer after paying license fee of $5.

2002

31	Shovelers, *2002*	17.50	4.00

No. 31 not required for hunting. The Department of Natural Resources sent customers No. 31 upon receipt of a postcard given to the customer after paying license fee of $8.50.

2003

32	Ruddy duck, *2003*	15.00	4.00

No. 32 not required for hunting. The Department of Natural Resources sent customers No. 32 upon receipt of a postcard given to the customer after paying license fee of $8.50.

2004

33	Wood ducks, *2004*	14.00	4.00

No. 33 not required for hunting. The Department of Natural Resources sent customers No. 33 upon receipt of a postcard given to the customer after paying license fee of $8.50.

2005

34	Green-winged teals, *2005*	14.00	4.00

No. 34 not required for hunting. The Department of Natural Resources sent customers No. 34 upon receipt of a postcard given to the customer after paying license fee of $8.50.

2006

35	Ring-necked duck, *2006*	13.00	4.00

No. 35 not required for hunting. The Department of Natural Resources sent customers No. 34 upon receipt of a postcard given to the customer after paying license fee of $8.50.

36	Wigeon, *2007*	13.00	4.00

No. 36 not required for hunting. The Department of Natural Resources sent customers No. 36 upon receipt of a postcard given to the customer after paying license fee of $8.50.

KANSAS

Marion County Resident Duck Stamps

Wording, type face, border and perforation/roulette differs.

Used values are for stamps without gum.

1941-42

A1	25c black	—
A2	25c black, *1942*	—

Remainders from 1941 were rubber stamped "1942" in purple and initialed "J.E.M." by the Park and Lake Supervisor.

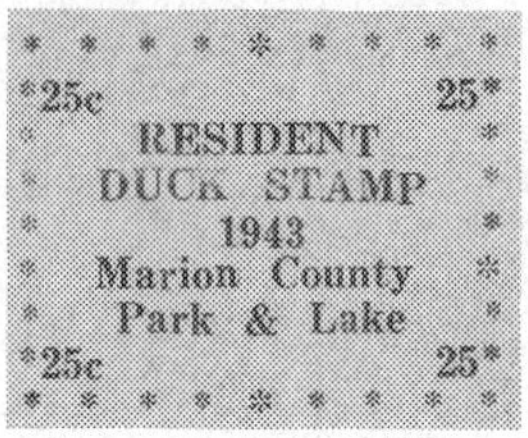

1943-73

A3	25c black, *pink*		—
A4	25c black, *green, 1944*		—
A5	25c green, *1945*		—
A6	25c black, *yellow, 1946*		*16,500*
A7	25c black, *pink, 1947*		*8,500*
A8	50c black, *blue, 1948*		*18,500*
A9	50c black, *1949*		—
A10	50c black, *blue, 1950*		—
A11	50c black, *1951*		—
A13	50c black, *blue, 1953*		—
A14	50c black, *pink, 1954*	100.	*65*
A15	50c black, *green, 1955*	100.	*65*
A16	50c black, *1956*	125.	*100*
A17	50c black, *blue, 1957*	95.	*65*
a.	"1" instead of "I" in "RESIDENT," pos. 3	*1,950.*	*1,350*
b.	1st 2 lines reversed, pos. 6	*2,750.*	*1,900*
A18	50c black, *light yellow, 1958*	450.	*725*
A19	50c black, *1959*	75.	*55*
A20	50c black, *pink, 1960*	100.	*75*
a.	Missing ornamental ball, pos. 9	*2,750.*	
A21	50c black, *1961*	150.	*100*
A22	50c black, *1962*	225.	*150*
A23	50c black, *pink, 1963*	700.	*450*
A24	50c black, *pink, 1964*	700.	*450*
a.	2nd & 3rd lines reversed, pos. 10	*15,000.*	
A25	50c black, *green, 1965*	500.	*400*
A26	50c black, *yellow, 1966*	—	*11,500*
A27	50c black, *green, 1967*	*4,500.*	*2,750*
A28	50c black, *pink, 1968*	300.	*250*
A29	50c black, *yellow, 1969*	300.	*200*
a.	"Dusk" instead of "Duck," pos. 8	*17,000.*	
A30	50c black, *1970*	450.	*350*
A31	50c black, *pink, 1971*	*3,250.*	*2,500*
A32	50c black, *blue, 1972*	*3,250.*	*2,500*
A33	50c black, *pink, 1973*	*9,500.*	*6,500*

Statewide Issues

Issued in booklet panes of 10 (Nos. 1-5) and sheets of 30 (starting with No. 2). Starting with No. 11, issued in sheets of 10. No. 1 issued in booklets with one pane of 10 (serial number has prefix "DD") and booklets with two panes of 10 (serial number has prefix "SS").

Nos. 1-4 numbered serially.

Catalogue values for all unused stamps in this section are for Never Hinged items.

Artists: Guy Coheleach, #1; Ann Dahoney, #2, 8; Leon Parson, #3; Wes Dewey, #4; J. Byron Test, #5; Jerry Thomas, #6, 10; Jerry Roedeke, #7; Neal Anderson, #9; Dustin Teasley, #14-18.

1987-96

1	$3 Green-winged teal	10.00	2.50
	Pair from booklet pane with L & R selvage	20.00	
2	$3 Canada geese, *1988*	8.00	2.50
	Pair from booklet pane with L & R selvage	16.00	
a.	Serial number missing	—	
3	$3 Mallards, *1989*	8.00	2.50
	Pair from booklet pane with L & R selvage	16.00	
4	$3 Wood ducks, *1990*	8.00	2.50
	Pair from booklet pane with L & R selvage	16.00	
5	$3 Pintail, rouletted, *1991*	8.00	2.50
	Pair from booklet pane with selvage at L & straight edge at R	16.00	
6	$3 Canvasbacks, *1992*	8.00	2.50
7	$3 Mallards, *1993*	9.00	2.50
8	$3 Blue-winged teal, *1994*	9.00	2.50
9	$3 Barrow's goldeneye, *1995*	9.00	2.50
10	$3 American widgeon, *1996*	10.00	2.50

No. 2a resulted from a drastic misregistration of the serial numbers during printing. Only one example is documented.

Artist: Dustin Teasley.

1997-2004 **Self-Adhesive** ***Die Cut***

11	$3 blue	9.00	2.50
12	$3 green, *1998*	9.00	2.50
13	$3 red, *1999*	8.50	2.50
14	$3 red lilac, *2000*	8.50	2.50
15	$3 orange, *2001*	8.50	2.50
16	$5 blue, *2002*	8.75	2.50
17	$5 green, *2003*	9.50	2.50
18	$5 red, *2004*	9.50	2.50

KENTUCKY

Printed in booklet panes of 5, starting with No. 12 in panes of 30.
Stamps are numbered serially.

Catalogue values for all unused stamps in this section are for Never Hinged items.

Artists: Ray Harm, #1, 7; David Chapple, #2; Ralph J. McDonald, #3, 10; Lynn Kaatz, #4, 15; Phillip Crowe, #5, 9; Jim Oliver, #6; Phillip Powell, #8, 13; Jim Killen, #11; Laurie Parsons Yarnes, #12; Harold Roe, #14, 17; Tim Donovan, #16; Larry Chandler, #18; Ben Burney, #19; Chris Walden, #20-23.

1985-2007

1	$5.25 Mallards, rouletted	15.00	3.00
	With tab	15.00	
2	$5.25 Wood ducks, rouletted, *1986*	10.00	2.50
	With tab	10.00	
3	$5.25 Black ducks, *1987*	9.00	2.50
	With tab	10.00	
4	$5.25 Canada geese, *1988*	9.00	2.50
	With tab	10.00	
5	$5.25 Retriever & canvasbacks, *1989*	15.00	2.50
	With tab	16.00	
6	$5.25 Widgeons, *1990*	9.00	2.50
	With tab	11.00	
7	$5.25 Pintails, *1991*	9.00	2.50
	With tab	11.00	
8	$5.25 Green-winged teal, *1992*	13.00	2.50
	With tab	15.00	
9	$5.25 Canvasback & decoy, *1993*	20.00	2.50
	With tab	22.50	
10	$5.25 Canada goose, *1994*	16.00	2.50
	With tab	19.00	
11	$7.50 Retriever, decoy, ringnecks, *1995*	25.00	3.00
	With tab	27.50	
12	$7.50 Blue-winged teal, *1996*	13.00	3.00
13	$7.50 Shovelers, *1997*	13.00	3.00
14	$7.50 Gadwalls, *1998*	15.00	3.00
15	$7.50 Common goldeneyes, *1999*	14.00	3.00
16	$7.50 Hooded mergansers, *2000*	16.00	3.00
17	$7.50 Mallards, *2001*	12.00	3.00
18	$7.50 Pintails, *2002*	12.00	3.00
19	$7.50 Snow geese, *2003*	12.00	3.00
20	$7.50 Black ducks, *2004*	12.00	3.00
21	$7.50 Canada geese, *2005*	12.00	3.00
22	$7.50 Mallards, *2006*	12.00	3.00
23	$7.50 Green-winged teal, *2007*	9.50	3.00

Nos. 19-23 not required for hunting.

LOUISIANA

Printed in sheets of 30.
Stamps are numbered serially. Stamps without numbers are artist presentation copies.
Two fees: resident and non-resident.

Catalogue values for all unused stamps in this section are for Never Hinged items.

Artists: David Noll, #1-2; Elton Louviere, #3-4; Brett J. Smith, #5-6; Bruce Heard, #7-8; Ronald Louque, #9-10, 15-16, 21-22; Don Edwards, #11-12; John Bertrand, #13-14; R. Hall, #17-18; R. C. Davis, #19-20; Jude Brunet, #23-24; Edward Butler, #25-26; Reggie McLeroy, #27-28; Dale Pousson, #29-30; Jeffrey Klinefelter, #31-32; Ken Michaelsen, #33-34. Edward Suthoff, #35-36. Tony Bernard, #37-38.

1989-2007

1	$5 Blue-winged teal	12.00	2.50
a.	Governor's edition	*100.00*	
2	$7.50 Blue-winged teal	14.00	2.50
a.	Governor's edition	*150.00*	

Nos. 1a and 2a were available only through a sealed bid auction where sheets of 30 of each denomination with matching serial numbers were sold as a unit.

3	$5 Green-winged teal, *1990*	9.50	2.50
4	$7.50 Green-winged teal, *1990*	12.00	2.50
5	$5 Wood ducks, *1991*	9.00	2.50
6	$7.50 Wood ducks, *1991*	13.00	2.50
7	$5 Pintails, *1992*	9.00	2.50
8	$7.50 Pintails, *1992*	13.00	2.50
9	$5 American widgeon, *1993*	12.00	2.50
10	$7.50 American widgeon, *1993*	13.00	2.50
11	$5 Mottled duck, *1994*	12.00	2.50
12	$7.50 Mottled duck, *1994*	13.00	2.50
13	$5 Speckle bellied goose, *1995*	12.00	2.50
14	$7.50 Speckle bellied goose, *1995*	13.00	2.50
15	$5 Gadwall, *1996*	12.00	2.50
16	$7.50 Gadwall, *1996*	13.00	2.50
17	$5 Ring-necked ducks, *1997*	10.00	2.50
18	$13.50 Ring-necked ducks, *1997*	22.50	2.50
19	$5.50 Mallards, *1998*	11.00	2.50
a.	Governor's edition	*150.00*	
20	$13.50 Mallards, *1998*	22.50	2.50
a.	Governor's edition	*200.00*	
21	$5.50 Snow geese, *1999*	11.00	2.50
22	$13.50 Snow geese, *1999*	22.50	2.50
23	$5.50 Lesser scaup, *2000*	11.00	2.50
24	$13.50 Lesser scaup, *2000*	35.00	2.50

No. 24 sold for $25 as stamps were printed before fee increase was finalized.

25	$5.50 Shovelers, *2001*	11.00	2.50
26	$25 Shovelers, *2001*	35.00	2.50
27	$5.50 Canvasbacks, *2002*	11.00	2.50
28	$25 Canvasbacks, *2002*	35.00	2.50
29	$5.50 Redheads, *2003*	11.00	2.50
30	$25 Redheads, *2003*	35.00	2.50
31	$5.50 Hooded mergansers, *2004*	10.00	2.50
32	$25 Hooded mergansers, *2004*	35.00	2.50
33	$5.50 Pintails, Labrador retriever, *2005*	9.00	2.50
34	$25 Pintails, Labrador retriever, *2005*	32.50	2.50
35	$5.50 Mallards, Labrador retriever, *2006*	9.00	2.50
36	$25 Mallards, Labrador retriever, *2006*	32.50	2.50
37	$5.50 Mallards, Labrador retriever, *2007*	8.00	2.50
38	$25 Mallards, Labrador retriever, *2007*	30.00	2.50

Nos. 29-38 not required for hunting.

MAINE

Printed in sheets of 10. Nos. 1-10 are numbered serially.

Catalogue values for all unused stamps in this section are for Never Hinged items.

Artists: David Maass, #1-3; Ron Van Gilder, #4; Rick Allen, #5; Jeannine Staples, #6, 10, 15, 18, 20, 23; Thea Flanagan, #7; Patricia D. Carter, #8; Persis Weirs, #9; Susan Jordan, #11; Richard Alley, #12, 19, 16, 21, 24; Paul Fillion, #13; T. Kemp, #14; Darby Mumford, #17; Daniel Cake, #22.

1984-2007

1	$2.50 Black ducks	22.50	5.00
2	$2.50 Common eiders, *1985*	45.00	5.00
3	$2.50 Wood ducks, *1986*	9.00	2.50
4	$2.50 Buffleheads, *1987*	8.00	2.50
5	$2.50 Green-winged teal, *1988*	8.00	2.50
6	$2.50 Common goldeneyes, *1989*	8.00	2.50
7	$2.50 Canada geese, *1990*	8.00	2.50
8	$2.50 Ring-necked duck, *1991*	8.00	2.50
9	$2.50 Old squaw, *1992*	8.00	2.50
10	$2.50 Hooded merganser, *1993*	8.00	2.50
11	$2.50 Mallards, *1994*	9.00	2.50
12	$2.50 White-winged scoters, *1995*	12.00	2.50
13	$2.50 Blue-winged teal, *1996*	12.00	2.50
14	$2.50 Greater scaup, *1997*	12.00	2.50
15	$2.50 Surf scoters, *1998*	8.00	2.50
16	$2.50 Black duck, *1999*	9.00	2.50
17	$2.50 Common eider, *2000*	8.00	2.50
18	$2.50 Wood duck, *2001*	8.00	2.50
19	$2.50 Buffleheads, *2002*	8.00	2.50
20	$5.50 Green-winged teal, *2003*	10.00	2.50
21	$8.50 Barrow's goldeneye, *2004*	12.50	2.50
22	$8.50 Canada goose, *2005*	12.50	2.50
23	$7.50 Ring-necked ducks, *2006*	11.50	2.50
24	$7.50 Long-tailed ducks, *2007*	11.50	2.50

MARYLAND

Nos. 1-19 printed in sheets of 10. Starting with No. 20, printed in sheets of 5 with numbered tab at bottom and selvage at top.
Each stamp has tab. Unused value is for stamp with tab. Many used copies have tab attached.

Catalogue values for all unused stamps in this section are for Never Hinged items.

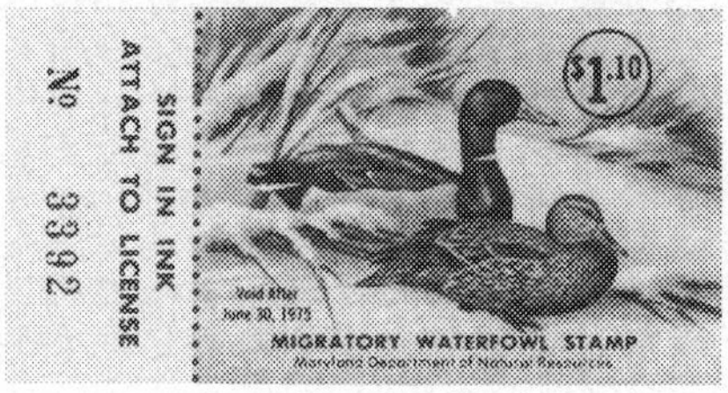

Artists: John Taylor, #1, 6, 24; Stanley Stearns, #2, 5; Louis Frisino, #3, 13, 20; Jack Schroeder, #4, 7; Arthur Eakin, #8; Roger Bucklin, #9; Roger Lent, #10, 16; Carla Huber, #11, 17; David Turnbaugh, #12, 18, 23, 27, 31; Francis Sweet, #14; Christopher White, #15; Will Wilson, #19; Robert Bealle, #21, 30; Charles Schauck, #22; Paul Makuchal, #25, 33; Wally

Makuchal, #26; Wilhelm Goebel, #28, 32; James Kinnett, #29. Jim Taylor, #34.

1974-2007

1	$1.10 Mallards	11.00	2.50
2	$1.10 Canada geese, rouletted, *1975*	10.00	2.50
3	$1.10 Canvasbacks, rouletted, *1976*	10.00	2.50
4	$1.10 Greater scaup, *1977*	10.00	2.50
5	$1.10 Redheads, *1978*	10.00	2.50
6	$1.10 Wood ducks, rouletted, *1979*	10.00	2.50
7	$1.10 Pintail decoy, rouletted, *1980*	10.00	2.50
8	$3 Widgeon, rouletted, *1981*	9.00	2.50
9	$3 Canvasback, *1982*	8.00	2.50
10	$3 Wood duck, *1983*	12.00	2.50
11	$6 Black ducks, *1984*	14.00	2.50
12	$6 Canada geese, *1985*	12.00	2.50
13	$6 Hooded mergansers, *1986*	12.00	2.50
14	$6 Redheads, *1987*	13.00	2.50
15	$6 Ruddy ducks, *1988*	12.00	2.50
16	$6 Blue-winged teal, *1989*	12.00	2.50
17	$6 Lesser scaup, *1990*	12.00	2.50
18	$6 Shovelers, *1991*	12.00	2.50
19	$6 Bufflehead, *1992*	12.00	2.50
20	$6 Canvasbacks, *1993*	12.00	2.50
21	$6 Redheads, *1994*	12.00	2.50
22	$6 Mallards, *1995*	22.50	2.50
23	$6 Canada geese, *1996*	27.50	2.50
24	$6 Canvasbacks, *1997*	12.00	2.50
25	$6 Pintails, *1998*	12.00	2.50
26	$6 Wood ducks, *1999*	12.00	2.50
27	$6 Oldsquaws, *2000*	20.00	2.50
28	$6 Wigeons, *2001*	11.00	2.50
29	$9 Black scoters, *2002*	13.00	2.50
30	$9 Lesser scaup, *2003*	13.00	2.50
31	$9 Pintails, *2004*	13.00	2.50
32	$9 Ruddy duck, *2005*	13.00	2.50
33	$9 Canada geese, *2006*	13.00	2.50
34	$9 Wood ducks, *2007*	12.00	2.50

Public Lands Hunting Stamps

Required to hunt waterfowl in state-managed wildlife areas.

Issued in booklet panes of 10.

1975-79

A1	$2 purple	*1,750.*	75.
A2	$2 black, *pink, 1976*	*1,250.*	45.
A3	$2 black, *yellow, 1977*	*1,100.*	45.
A4	$2 black, *1978*	*2,950.*	125.
A5	$2 black, *yellow, 1979*	*950.*	35.

MASSACHUSETTS

Printed in sheets of 12.

Catalogue values for all unused stamps in this section are for Never Hinged items.

Artists: Milton Weiler, #1; Tom Hennessey, #2; William Tyner, #3-5; Randy Julius, #6, 8, 10, 12, 19, 27; John Eggert, #7, 9, 24; Joseph Cibula, #11; Robert Piscatori, #13, 15, 25, 30; Peter Baedita, #14, 29; Lou Barnicle, #16; Warren Racket Shreve, #17; Benjamin Smith, #18; Donald Little, #20, 32; Sergio Roffo, #21; David Brega, #22; Christine Wilkinson, #23; Stephen Badlam; Barry Julius, #28; Larry Denton, #31. Randy Julius, #33. Matthew Schulz, #34.

1974-2007

1	$1.25 Wood duck decoy, rouletted	15.00	3.00
2	$1.25 Pintail decoy, *1975*	13.00	3.00
3	$1.25 Canada goose decoy, *1976*	13.00	3.00
4	$1.25 Goldeneye decoy, *1977*	13.00	3.00
5	$1.25 Black duck decoy, *1978*	13.00	3.00
6	$1.25 Ruddy turnstone duck decoy, *1979*	15.00	3.00
a.	Imperf, pair	160.00	
7	$1.25 Old squaw decoy, *1980*	15.00	3.00
8	$1.25 Red-breasted merganser decoy, *1981*	15.00	3.00
9	$1.25 Greater yellowlegs decoy, *1982*	15.00	3.00
10	$1.25 Redhead decoy, *1983*	15.00	3.00
11	$1.25 White-winged scoter decoy, *1984*	15.00	3.00
12	$1.25 Ruddy duck decoy, *1985*	12.00	3.00
13	$1.25 Preening bluebill decoy, *1986*	12.00	2.50
14	$1.25 American widgeon decoy, *1987*	12.00	2.50
15	$1.25 Mallard decoy, *1988*	12.00	2.50
16	$1.25 Brant decoy, *1989*	10.00	2.50
17	$1.25 Whistler hen decoy, *1990*	10.00	2.50
18	$5 Canvasback decoy, *1991*	10.00	2.50
19	$5 Black-bellied plover decoy, *1992*	10.00	2.50
20	$5 Red-breasted merganser decoy, *1993*	10.00	2.50
21	$5 White-winged scoter decoy, *1994*	10.00	2.50
22	$5 Female hooded merganser decoy, *1995*	10.00	2.50
23	$5 Eider decoy, *1996*	10.00	2.50
24	$5 Curlew decoy, *1997*	10.00	2.50
25	$5 Canada goose decoy, *1998*	10.00	2.50
26	$5 Oldsquaw decoy, *1999*	10.00	2.50
27	$5 Merganser hen decoy, *2000*	10.00	2.50
28	$5 Black duck decoy, *2001*	10.00	2.50
29	$5 Bufflehead decoy, *2002*	10.00	2.50
30	$5 Greenwing teal decoy, *2003*	10.00	2.50
31	$5 Wood duck drake decoy, *2004*	8.00	2.50
32	$5 Oldsquaw drake decoy, *2005*	8.00	2.50
33	$5 Long-billed curlew decoy, *2006*	8.00	2.50
34	$5 Goldeneye decoy, *2007*	8.00	2.50

MICHIGAN

Nos. 1-5 printed in sheets of 10 with center gutter, rouletted. Printed in sheets of 10 die cut self-adhesives on backing paper (Nos. 6-19), or sheets of 15 (starting with No. 20).

Nos. 1, 3-19 are serially numbered.

Catalogue values for all unused stamps in this section are for Never Hinged items.

Artist: Oscar Warbach.

1976

1	$2.10 Wood duck	5.00	2.50

Artists: Larry Hayden, #2, 5, 12; Richard Timm, #3; Andrew Kurzmann, #4; Dietmar Krumrey, #6, 14, 23-24; Gjisbert van Frankenhuyzen, #7; Rod Lawrence, #8, 15, 20, 25, 27, 32; Larry Cory, #9, 16; Robert Steiner, #10; Russell Cobane, #11; John Martens, #13; Heiner Hertling, #17; Clark Sullivan, #18; David Bollman, #19; Rusty Fretner, #21; M. Monroe, #22; Kim Diment, #26; Dietmar Krumrey, #28; Tim McDonald, #29; Christopher Smith, #30; Peter Mathios, #31.

1977-2007

2	$2.10 Canvasbacks	275.00	35.00
	With numbered tab	400.00	
3	$2.10 Mallards, *1978*	20.00	5.00
	With tab	47.50	
4	$2.10 Canada geese, *1979*	60.00	5.00
	With tab	75.00	
5	$3.75 Lesser scaup, *1980*	17.50	4.0
	With tab	25.00	
6	$3.75 Buffleheads, *1981*	25.00	4.0
7	$3.75 Redheads, *1982*	25.00	4.0

Unused value is for stamp with sufficient margin to sho printed spaces for date and time the stamp was sold.

8	$3.75 Wood ducks, *1983*	25.00	4.0
9	$3.75 on $3.25 Pintails, *1984*	25.00	3.0

No. 9 not issued without surcharge.

10	$3.75 Ring-necked ducks, *1985*	25.00	3.0
11	$3.75 Common goldeneyes, *1986*	22.00	2.5
12	$3.85 Green-winged teal, *1987*	11.00	2.5
13	$3.85 Canada geese, *1988*	10.00	2.5
14	$3.85 Widgeons, *1989*	10.00	2.5
15	$3.85 Wood ducks, *1990*	10.00	2.5
16	$3.85 Blue-winged teal, *1991*	9.00	2.5
17	$3.85 Red-breasted merganser, *1992*	9.00	2.5
18	$3.85 Hooded merganser, *1993*	9.00	2.5
19	$3.85 Black duck, *1994*	9.00	2.5
20	$4.35 Blue winged teal, *1995*	9.00	3.0
21	$4.35 Canada geese, *1996*	9.00	3.0
22	$5 Canvasbacks, *1997*	20.00	3.0
23	$5 Pintail, *1998*	9.00	3.0
24	$5 Shoveler, *1999*	9.00	3.0
25	$5 Mallards, *2000*	30.00	3.0

Self-Adhesive Die Cut

26	$5 Ruddy ducks, *2001*	10.00	3.0
27	$5 Wigeons, *2002*	9.00	3.0
28	$5 Redheads, *2003*	9.00	3.0

Rouletted

29	$5 Wood duck, *2004*	9.00	3.0
30	$5 Blue-winged teals, *2005*	9.00	3.0
31	$5 Widgeon, *2006*	9.00	3.0
32	$5 Pintails, *2007*	8.00	3.0

Nos. 24-32 not required for hunting.

MINNESOTA

License Surcharge Stamps

No. A1 printed in sheets of 10. These stamps served as a $ surcharge to cover the cost of a license increase.

Nos. A1-A2 issued to raise funds for acquisition and develop ment of wildlife lands.

1957 *Perf. 12*

A1	$1 Mallards & Pheasant	100.00	6.0

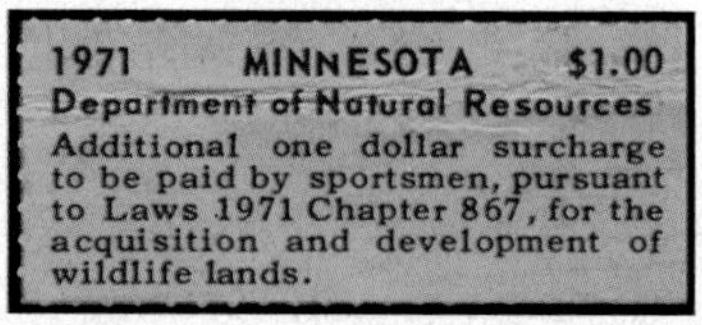

1971 *Rouletted 9*

A2	$1 black, *dark yellow*	*3,950.*	20.0

Regular Issues

Printed in sheets of 10.

Catalogue values for all unused stamps in this section are for Never Hinged items.

Artists: David Maass, #1, 3; Leslie Kouba, #2; James Meger, #4; Terry Redlin, #5, 9, Phil Scholer, #6, 17; Gary Moss, #7; Thomas Gross, #8; Brian Jarvi, #10; Ron Van Gilder, #11; Robert Hautman, #12, 16, 25; Jim Hautman, #13, 20; Kevin Daniel, #14, 21; Daniel Smith, #15; Edward DuRose, #18; Bruce Miller, #19; Thomas Moen, #22, 31; John House, #23; Kim Norlien, #24; John Freiberg, #26; Mark Kness, #27; Scot Storm, #28; David Chapman, #29; Joe Hautman, #30.

1977-2007

1	$3 Mallards	15.00	2.50
2	$3 Lesser scaup, *1978*	12.00	2.50
3	$3 Pintails, *1979*	12.00	2.50
4	$3 Canvasbacks, *1980*	12.00	2.50
5	$3 Canada geese, *1981*	9.50	2.50
6	$3 Redheads, *1982*	12.00	2.50
7	$3 Blue geese & snow goose, *1983*	12.00	2.50
8	$3 Wood ducks, *1984*	12.00	2.50
9	$3 White-fronted geese, *1985*	9.00	2.50
10	$5 Lesser scaup, *1986*	10.00	2.50

Beginning with this issue, left side of sheet has an agent's tab, detachable from the numbered tab.

11	$5 Common goldeneyes, *1987*	11.00	2.50
	With numbered tab	11.00	
	With agent's and numbered tabs	16.00	
12	$5 Buffleheads, *1988*	11.00	2.50
	With numbered tab	11.00	
	With agent's and numbered tabs	17.50	
13	$5 Widgeons, *1989*	11.00	2.50
	With numbered tab	11.00	
	With agent's and numbered tabs	17.50	
14	$5 Hooded mergansers, *1990*	25.00	2.50
	With numbered tab	25.00	
	With agent's and numbered tabs	40.00	
15	$5 Ross's geese, *1991*	10.00	2.50
	With numbered tab	10.00	
	With agent's and numbered tabs	14.00	
16	$5 Barrow's goldeneyes, *1992*	10.00	2.50
	With numbered tab	10.00	
	With agent's and numbered tabs	14.00	
17	$5 Blue-winged teal, *1993*	10.00	2.50
	With numbered tab	10.00	
	With agent's and numbered tabs	14.00	
18	$5 Ringneck duck, *1994*	10.00	2.50
	With numbered tab	10.00	
	With agent's and numbered tabs	13.00	
19	$5 Gadwall, *1995*	10.00	2.50
	With numbered tab	10.00	
	With agent's and numbered tabs	13.00	
20	$5 Greater scaup, *1996*	12.00	2.50
	With numbered tab	12.00	
	With agent's and numbered tabs	18.00	
21	$5 Shovelers, *1997*	11.00	2.50
	With numbered tab	11.00	
	With agent's and numbered tabs	15.00	
22	$5 Harlequins, *1998*	13.00	2.50
	With numbered tab	13.00	
	With agent's and numbered tabs	19.00	
23	$5 Green-winged teal, *1999*	11.00	2.50
	With numbered tab	11.00	
	With agent's and numbered tabs	15.00	

Self- Adhesive Die Cut

24	$5 Red-breasted merganser, *2000*	10.00	2.50

No. 24 is on backing paper affixed to back of license form.

25	$5 Black duck, *2001*	12.50	2.50

No. 25 is on backing paper affixed to back of license form.

26	$5 Ruddy duck, *2002*	12.50	2.50
27	$5 Oldsquaws, *2003*	12.50	2.50
28	$7.50 Common mergansers, *2004*	11.50	2.50
29	$7.50 White-winged scoters, lighthouse, *2005*	11.50	2.50
30	$7.50 Mallard, *2006*	11.50	2.50
31	$7.50 Lesser scaups, *2007*	11.50	2.50

Nos. 26-31 are on backing paper affixed to mailing envelopes.

MISSISSIPPI

Starting with No. 2, stamps are printed in sheets of 10. Nos. 2-14 are rouletted. All stamps are numbered serially.

Catalogue values for all unused stamps in this section are for Never Hinged items.

LICENSE NUMBER
TYPE
AGENT
CO.
PRICE
EXPIRATION DATE
TYPE 23
STATE OF MISSISSIPPI
STATE WATERFOWL STAMP
STATE WATERFOWL—WOOD DUCK
GAME AND FISH COMMISSION
AVERY WOOD
DIRECTOR OF WILDLIFE CONSERVATION
77
NOT VALID UNLESS SIGNED IN INK ACROSS THE FACE OF THIS LICENSE
NOT VALID UNLESS PUNCHED

Illustration reduced.

Artists: Carroll & Gwen Perkins, #1; Allen Hughes, #2; John C. A. Reimers, #3, 6; Carole Pigott Hardy, #4; Bob Tompkins, #5, 13; Jerry Johnson, #7; Jerrie Glasper, #8; Tommy Goodman, #9; Lottie Fulton, #10; Joe Lattl, #11, 17, 22-23; Robert Garner, #12; Debra Aven Swartzendruber, #14; Kathy Dickson, #15; Phillip Crowe, #16; Eddie Suthoff, #18; Emitt Thames, #19-20; James Josey, #21; John Mac Hudspeth, #24, 25; Joe Mac Hudspeth, #26-35.

1976 **Without Gum**

1	$2 Wood duck	18.00	5.00
a.	Complete 2-part data processing card	25.00	

1977-2007

2	$2 Mallards	10.00	2.50
3	$2 Green-winged teal, *1978*	10.00	2.50
4	$2 Canvasbacks, *1979*	10.00	2.50
5	$2 Pintails, *1980*	10.00	2.50
6	$2 Redheads, *1981*	10.00	2.50
7	$2 Canada geese, *1982*	10.00	2.50
8	$2 Lesser scaup, *1983*	10.00	2.50
9	$2 Black ducks, *1984*	10.00	2.50
10	$2 Mallards, *1985*	10.00	2.50
a.	Vert. serial No., imperf btwn. serial No. and stamp	150.00	
b.	Horiz. serial No., no vert. silver bar	700.00	
11	$2 Widgeons, *1986*	10.00	2.50
12	$2 Ring-necked ducks, *1987*	10.00	2.50
13	$2 Snow geese, *1988*	10.00	2.50
14	$2 Wood ducks, *1989*	7.00	2.50
15	$2 Snow geese, *1990*	12.50	2.50
16	$2 Labrador retriever & canvasbacks, *1991*	7.50	2.50
17	$2 Green-winged teal, *1992*	7.50	2.50
18	$5 Mallards, *1993*	9.00	2.50
19	$5 Canvasbacks, *1994*	10.00	2.50
20	$5 Blue-winged teal, *1995*	15.00	2.50
21	$5 Hooded merganser, *1996*	17.00	2.50
22	$5 Pintail, *1997*	22.50	2.50
23	$5 Pintails, *1998*	13.00	2.50
24	$5 Ring-necked duck, *1999*	10.00	2.50
25	$5 Mallards, *2000*	10.00	2.50
26	$5 Gadwall, *2001*	15.00	2.50
27	$10 Wood duck, *2002*	15.00	2.50
28	$10 Pintail, *2003*	15.00	2.50
29	$10 Wood ducks, *2004*	15.00	2.50
30	$10 Blue-winged teal, *2005*	15.00	2.50
31	$10 Wood duck, *2006*	15.00	2.50
32	$15 Wood duck, self-adhesive, die cut, *2006*	15.00	2.50
33	$10 Wood ducks, perf., *2007*	14.00	2.50
34	$10 Wood ducks, self-adhesive, die cut, *2007*	14.00	2.50
35	$15 Wood ducks, self-adhesive, die cut, *2007*	21.00	2.50

MISSOURI

Issued in booklet panes of five with tab. Nos. 1-8 are rouletted. No. 18 issued in pane of 30.

Catalogue values for all unused stamps in this section are for Never Hinged items.

Artists: Charles Schwartz, #1; David Plank, #2; Tom Crain, #3, 8; Gary Lucy, #4; Doug Ross, #5; Glenn Chambers, #6; Ron Clayton, #7; Ron Ferkol, #9, 13, 18; Bruce Bollman, #10; Kathy Dickson, #11; Eileen Melton, #12; Kevin Guinn, #14; Thomas Bates, #15; Keith Alexander, #16; Ryan Peterson, #17.

1979-96

1	$3.40 Canada geese	*525.00*	75.00
	With tab	*650.00*	
2	$3.40 Wood ducks, *1980*	*110.00*	18.00
	With tab	*150.00*	
3	$3 Lesser scaup, *1981*	60.00	9.00
	With tab	75.00	
4	$3 Buffleheads, *1982*	60.00	8.00
	With tab	75.00	
5	$3 Blue-winged teal, *1983*	45.00	8.00
	With tab	55.00	
6	$3 Mallards, *1984*	40.00	7.00
	With tab	50.00	
7	$3 American widgeons, *1985*	22.50	3.00
	With tab	25.00	
8	$3 Hooded mergansers, *1986*	12.00	3.00
	With tab	15.00	
9	$3 Pintails, *1987*	9.00	3.00
	With tab	13.00	
10	$3 Canvasback, *1988*	8.00	2.50
	With tab	11.00	
11	$3 Ring-necked ducks, *1989*	8.00	2.50
	With tab	9.25	

All examples of Nos. 12b, 13b, 14b, 15b, 16b, 17b are signed by the governor.

12	$5 Redheads, *1990*	8.00	2.50
	With two part tab	10.00	
a.	$50 Governor's edition with tab	75.00	
b.	$100 Governor's edition with tab	—	
13	$5 Snow geese, *1991*	8.00	2.50
	With two part tab	9.00	
a.	$50 Governor's edition with tab	72.50	
b.	$100 Governor's edition with tab	—	
14	$5 Gadwalls, *1992*	8.00	2.50
	With tab	9.00	
a.	$50 Governor's edition with tab	75.00	
b.	$100 Governor's edition with tab	—	
15	$5 Green-winged teal, *1993*	8.00	2.50
	With tab	9.00	
a.	$50 Governor's edition with tab	75.00	
b.	$100 Governor's edition with tab	—	
16	$5 White-fronted goose, *1994*	8.00	2.50
	With 2-part tab	9.00	
a.	$50 Governor's edition with tab	75.00	
b.	$100 Governor's edition with tab	—	
17	$5 Goldeneyes, *1995*	8.00	2.50
	With 2-part tab	9.00	
a.	$50 Governor's edition with tab	75.00	
b.	$100 Governor's edition with tab	—	
18	$5 Black ducks, *1996*	8.00	2.50

MONTANA

Bird License Stamps

Required to hunt waterfowl.

Resident ($2, $4, $6), youth ($1, $2), and non-resident ($25, $30, $53) bird licenses. Licenses were no longer produced for youth, beginning in 1985, and non-resident, beginning in 1989.

Nos. 1-33 rouletted.

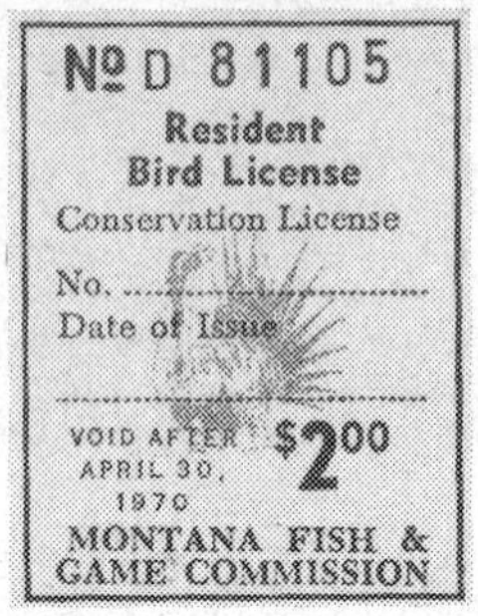

1969

A1	$2	Sage grouse	600.00	15.00
A2	$1	Sage grouse	600.00	50.00
A3	$25	Sage grouse	600.00	75.00

1970

A4	$2	Sage grouse	650.00	10.00
a.		Missing "1" in "1971," pos. 10		*500.00*
A5	$1	Sage grouse	*1,750.*	150.00
A6	$25	Sage grouse	—	275.00

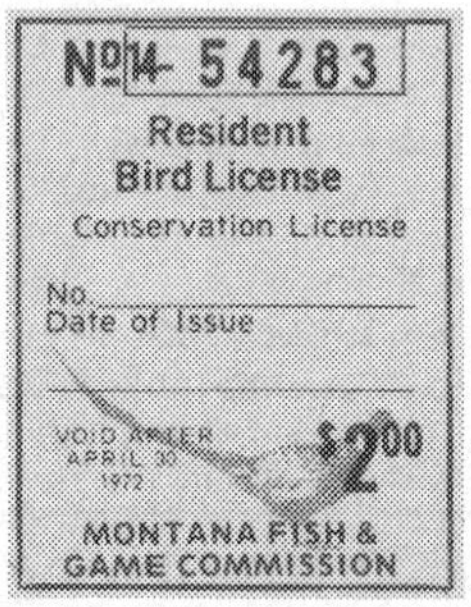

1971

A7	$2	Pheasant	650.00	10.00
A8	$1	Pheasant	650.00	35.00
A9	$25	Pheasant	650.00	50.00

1972

A10	$2	Pheasant	650.00	10.00
A11	$1	Pheasant	650.00	35.00
A12	$25	Pheasant	650.00	50.00

1973

A13	$2	Pheasant	650.00	10.00
A14	$1	Pheasant	650.00	35.00
A15	$25	Pheasant	650.00	50.00

1974

A16	$2	Pheasant	650.00	10.00
A17	$1	Pheasant	650.00	35.00
A18	$25	Pheasant	650.00	50.00

1975

A19	$2	Pheasant	650.00	10.00
A20	$1	Pheasant	650.00	35.00
A21	$25	Pheasant	650.00	50.00

1976

A22	$4	Pheasant	650.00	10.00
A23	$2	Pheasant	650.00	35.00
A24	$30	Pheasant	650.00	50.00

1977

A25	$4	Pheasant	650.00	10.00
A26	$2	Pheasant	650.00	35.00
A27	$30	Pheasant	650.00	50.00

1978

A28	$4	Sage grouse	8.00	2.00
A29	$2	Sage grouse	8.00	5.00
A30	$30	Sage grouse	8.00	5.50

1979

A31	$4	Snow geese	8.00	2.00
A32	$2	Snow geese	8.00	5.00
A33	$30	Snow geese	8.00	5.50

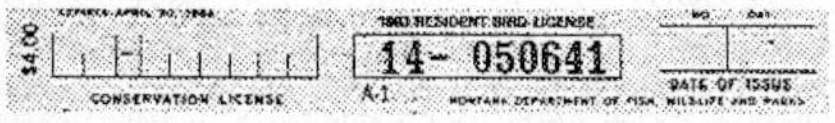

1980

A36	$30	black, *gray green*		*35.00*

1982

A40	$4	black, *yellow*		5.00

1983

A43	$4	black, *yellow gray*	*550.00*	5.00
A44	$2	black, *gray*	*550.00*	
A45	$30	black, *light blue*	*550.00*	

1984

A46	$4	black, *light blue green*	*250.00*	5.00
A47	$2	black, *light violet*	*350.00*	
A48	$30	black, *gray*	*250.00*	

1985

A49	$4	black, *light blue*	*350.00*	5.00
A50	$30	black, *lavender*	*250.00*	

1986

A51	$4	black, *orange*	*350.00*	5.00
A52	$30	black, *light blue*	*350.00*	

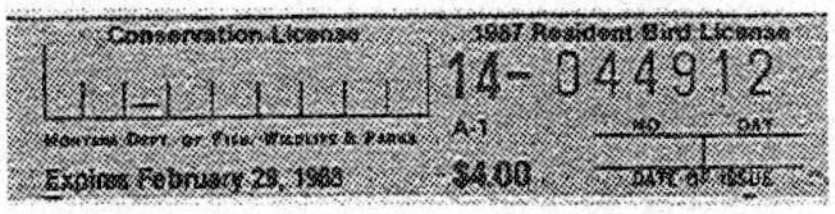

1987

A53	$4	black, *orange brown*	*200.00*	3.00
A54	$30	black, *tan*	*275.00*	

1988

A55	$6	black, *light blue*	*200.00*	3.00
A56	$53	black, *purple*	*275.00*	

1989-99

A57	$6	black, *rose*	150.00	2.00
A58	$6	black, *lavender, 1990*	125.00	2.00
A59	$6	black, *pale blue, 1991*	100.00	2.00
A60	$6	black, *brown, 1992*	70.00	2.00
A61	$6	black, *blue, 1993*	60.00	1.50
A62	$6	black, *red orange, 1994*	55.00	1.50
A63	$6	black, *blue, 1995*	42.50	1.50
A64	$6	black, *purple, 1996*	25.00	1.00
A65	$6	black, *mauve, 1997*	15.00	1.00
A66	$6	black, *gray, 1998*	13.00	1.00
A67	$6	black, *green, 1999*	13.00	1.00

Waterfowl Stamps

Issued in booklet panes of 10 and sheets of 30. Stamps are numbered serially.

Stamps with serial numbers above 31,000 (1986) and above 21,000 (other years) are from booklet panes.

Catalogue values for all unused stamps in this section are for Never Hinged items.

Artist: Joe Thornbrugh, #34, 38, 39, 45, 46, 48; Roger Cruwys, #35, 37, 42; Dave Samuelson, #36; Craig Philips, #40; Darrell Davis, #41; Wayne Dowdy, #43; Jim Borgreen, #44, 50, 51; Cliff Rossberg, #47, 49.

1986-2003

34	$5 Canada geese	12.00	3.00
	Pair from booklet pane with L & R selvage	*1,850.*	
	Top pair from booklet pane with agent tabs and L & R selvage	—	
35	$5 Redheads, *1987*	15.00	3.00
	Pair from booklet pane with L & R selvage	30.00	
	Top pair from booklet pane with agent tabs and L & R selvage	55.00	
36	$5 Mallards, *1988*	11.00	3.00
	Pair from booklet pane with L & R selvage	25.00	
	Top pair from booklet pane with agent tabs and L & R selvage	40.00	
37	$5 Black Labrador retriever & pintail, *1989*	11.00	3.00
	Pair from booklet pane with L & R selvage	25.00	
	Top pair from booklet pane with agent tabs and L & R selvage	40.00	
a.	Governor's edition	*140.00*	

No. 37a was available only in full sheets only through a sealed bid auction.

38	$5 Blue-winged & cinnamon teal, *1990*	10.00	2.50
	Pair from booklet pane with L & R selvage	20.00	
	Top pair from booklet pane with agent tabs and L & R selvage	25.00	
39	$5 Snow geese, *1991*	10.00	2.50
	Pair from booklet pane with L & R selvage	20.00	
	Top pair from booklet pane with agent tabs and L & R selvage	25.00	
40	$5 Wood ducks, *1992*	10.00	2.50
	Pair from booklet pane with L & R selvage	20.00	
	Top pair from booklet pane with agent tabs and L & R selvage	25.00	
41	$5 Harlequin ducks, *1993*	10.00	2.50
	Pair from booklet pane with L & R selvage	22.00	
	Top pair from booklet pane with agent tabs and L & R selvage	25.00	
42	$5 Widgeons, *1994*	11.00	2.50
	Pair from booklet pane with L & R selvage	25.00	
	Top pair from booklet pane with agent tabs and L & R selvage	25.00	
43	$5 Tundra swans, *1995*	11.00	2.50
	Pair from booklet pane with L & R selvage	25.00	
	Top pair from booklet pane with agent tabs and L & R selvage	25.00	
44	$5 Canvasbacks, *1996*	11.00	2.50
	Pair from booklet pane with L & R selvage	25.00	
	Top pair from booklet pane with agent tabs and L & R selvage	30.00	
45	$5 Golden retriever, mallard, *1997*	11.00	2.50
	Pair from booklet pane with L & R selvage	25.00	
	Top pair from booklet pane with agent tabs and L & R selvage	30.00	
46	$5 Gadwalls, *1998*	11.00	2.50
	Pair from booklet pane with L & R selvage	25.00	
	Top pair from booklet pane with agent tabs and L & R selvage	30.00	
47	$5 Barrow's goldeneye, *1999*	11.00	2.50
	Pair from booklet pane with L & R selvage	25.00	
	Top pair from booklet pane with agent tabs and L & R selvage	30.00	
48	$5 Mallard decoy, Chesapeake retriever, *2000*	12.00	2.50
	Pair from booklet pane with L & R selvage	25.00	
	Top pair from booklet pane with agent tabs and L & R selvage	30.00	

49	$5 Canada geese, *2001*	11.00	2.50
	Pair from booklet pane with L & R selvage	25.00	
	Top pair from booklet pane with agent tabs and L & R selvage	30.00	
50	($5) Sandhill crane, *2002*	11.00	2.50
51	$5 Mallards, *2003*	11.00	2.50

No. 51 is not required for hunting.

NEBRASKA

Habitat Stamps

Required to hunt waterfowl.
Printed in sheets of 20.

Catalogue values for all unused stamps in this section are for Never Hinged items.

1977-98

A1	$7.50 Ring-necked pheasant	12.00	1.50
A2	$7.50 White-tailed deer, *1978*	12.00	1.50
A3	$7.50 Bobwhite quail, *1979*	12.00	1.50
A4	$7.50 Pheasant, *1980*	12.00	1.50
A5	$7.50 Cottontail rabbit, *1981*	12.00	1.50
A6	$7.50 Coyote, *1982*	12.00	1.50
A7	$7.50 Wild turkey, *1983*	12.00	1.50
A8	$7.50 Canada goose, *1984*	12.00	1.50
A9	$7.50 Cardinal, *1985*	12.00	1.50
A10	$7.50 Sharp-tailed grouse, *1986*	12.00	1.50
A11	$7.50 Sandhill crane, *1987*	12.00	1.50
A12	$7.50 Snow geese, *1988*	12.00	1.50
A13	$7.50 Mallards, *1989*	12.00	1.50
A14	$7.50 Pheasants, *1990*	12.00	1.50
A15	$7.50 Canada geese, *1991*	12.00	1.50
A16	$10.00 Raccoon, *1992*	15.00	1.50
A17	$10.00 Fox squirrel, *1993*	15.00	1.50
A18	$10.00 Hungarian partridge, *1994*	15.00	1.50
A19	$10.00 Prairie pronghorns, *1995*	15.00	1.50
A20	$10.00 Ring-necked pheasant, *1996*	15.00	1.50
A21	$10.00 White-tailed deer, *1997*	15.00	1.50
A22	$10.00 Mourning doves, *1998*	15.00	1.50

Pictorial Labels

These stamps are not valid for any hunting fees.
Printed in sheets of 10.
Stamps are numbered serially.

Catalogue values for all unused stamps in this section are for Never Hinged items.

Artist: Neal Anderson.

1991-95

Artist: Neal Anderson

1	$6 Canada geese	11.00
2	$6 Pintails, *1992*	11.00
3	$6 Canvasbacks, *1993*	11.00
4	$6 Mallards, *1994*	11.00
5	$6 Wood ducks, *1995*	11.00

Waterfowl Stamp

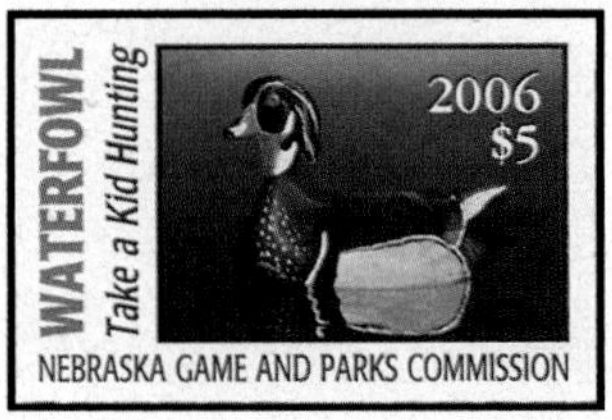

Artist: Brett Cooper

2006-07 ***Rouletted***

6	$5 Wood duck	10.00	2.50
7	$5 Canvasbacks, *2007*	10.00	2.50

Nos. 6-7 are required for hunting.

NEVADA

Printed in booklet panes of 4.
Stamps are rouletted and selvage is found above and below stamps on the pane. The tab portion of the panes in imperforate.
Starting with No. 4 stamps are numbered serially.

Catalogue values for all unused stamps in this section are for Never Hinged items.

Artists: Larry Hayden, #1; Dick Mcrill, #2; Phil Scholer, #3; Richard Timm, #4; Charles Allen, #5; Robert Steiner, #6; Richard Wilson, #7; Nolan Haan. #8, 12; Sherrie Russell Meline, #9, 21; Jim Hautman, #10; Robert Hautman, #11; Tak Nakamura, #13, 17; Richard Clifton, #14, 22; Steve Hopkins, #15; Mark Mueller, #16; Jeffrey Klinefelter, #18, 23, 28; B. Blight, #19; Janie Kreutzjans, #20; Jeff Hoff, #24; David Brevick, #25; Louis Frisino, #26; Adam Oswald, #27. Ken Michaelsen, #29.

1979-2007

1	$2 Canvasbacks and decoy	45.00	12.00
	With numbered tab	55.00	

Stamps with tabs without numbers are printer's waste.

2	$2 Cinnamon teal, *1980*	8.00	3.00
	With tab	10.00	
3	$2 Whistling swans, *1981*	10.00	3.00
	With tab	12.00	
4	$2 Shovelers, *1982*	10.00	3.00
	With tab	12.00	
5	$2 Gadwalls, *1983*	10.50	3.00
	With tab	11.00	
6	$2 Pintails, *1984*	11.00	3.00
	With tab	12.00	
7	$2 Canada geese, *1985*	20.00	3.00
	With tab	25.00	
8	$2 Redheads, *1986*	17.50	2.50
	With tab	25.00	
9	$2 Buffleheads, *1987*	15.00	2.50
	With tab	20.00	
10	$2 Canvasbacks, *1988*	11.00	2.50
	With tab	13.00	
11	$2 Ross's geese, *1989*	12.00	2.50
	With tab	15.00	
12	$5 Green-winged teal, *1990*	11.00	2.50
	With tab	13.00	
13	$5 White-faced ibis, *1991*	11.00	2.50
	With tab	13.00	
14	$5 American widgeon, *1992*	10.00	2.50
	With tab	11.00	
15	$5 Common goldeneye, *1993*	10.00	2.50
	With tab	11.00	
16	$5 Mallards, *1994*	10.00	2.50
	With tab	11.00	
17	$5 Wood duck, *1995*	10.00	2.50
	With tab	11.00	
18	$5 Ring-necked ducks, *1996*	15.00	2.50
	With tab	20.00	
19	$5 Ruddy ducks, *1997*	11.00	2.50
	With tab	13.00	
20	$5 Hooded merganser, *1998*	12.00	2.50
	With tab	15.00	
21	$5 Canvasback decoy, *1999*	11.00	2.50
	With tab	13.00	
22	$5 Canvasbacks, *2000*	15.00	2.50
	With tab	18.00	
23	$5 Lesser Scaups, *2001*	12.00	2.50
	With tab	15.00	
24	$5 Cinnamon teal, *2002*	11.00	2.50
25	$5 Green-winged teal, *2003*	11.00	2.50
	With tab	11.00	
26	$10 Redheads, *2004*	14.00	2.50
	With tab	16.00	
27	$10 Gadwalls, *2005*	14.00	2.50
	With tab	16.00	
28	$10 Tundra swans, *2006*	14.00	2.50
	With tab	16.00	
29	$10 Wood ducks, *2007*	15.00	2.50
	With tab	16.00	

NEW HAMPSHIRE

Printed in booklet panes of 1 with 2-part tab and in sheets of 30. Sheet stamps are perf on four sides. Stamps are numbered serially.

Catalogue values for all unused stamps in this section are for Never Hinged items.

Artists: Richard Plasschaert, #1; Phillip Crowe, #2; Thomas Hirata, #3; Durrant Bell, #4; Robert Steiner, #5-9; Richard Clifton, #10-11, 15; Louis Frisino, #12; Matthew Scharle, #13; Jeffrey Klinefelter, #14; Jim Collins, #16, 20, 23, 24; Bruce Holloway, #17, 21; Susan Knowles Jordan, #18; Charles Freeman, #19; Lindsey Rothe, #22. Kate Kotulak, #25.

1983-2007

1	$4 Wood ducks	135.00	
a.	Booklet single with 2-part tab	95.00	25.00
2	$4 Mallards, *1984*	90.00	
a.	Booklet single with 2-part tab	175.00	20.00
3	$4 Blue-winged teal, *1985*	80.00	
a.	Booklet single with 2-part tab	100.00	20.00
4	$4 Hooded mergansers, *1986*	20.00	
a.	Booklet single with 2-part tab	30.00	6.00
5	$4 Canada geese, *1987*	12.00	
a.	Booklet single with 2-part tab	14.00	4.00
b.	$50 Governor's edition	*325.00*	
6	$4 Buffleheads, *1988*	12.00	
a.	Booklet single with 2-part tab	14.00	3.00
b.	$4 +$46 Governor's edition	60.00	
7	$4 Black ducks, *1989*	11.00	
a.	Booklet single with 2-part tab	12.00	3.00
b.	$4 +$50 Governor's edition	67.50	
8	$4 Green-winged teal, *1990*	11.00	
a.	Booklet single with 2-part tab	12.00	3.00
b.	$4 +$50 Governor's edition	62.50	
9	$4 Golden retriever & mallards, *1991*	15.00	
a.	Booklet single with 2-part tab	17.00	3.00
b.	$4 +$50 Governor's edition	80.00	

Governor's Editions that follow are so inscribed.

10	$4 Ring-necked ducks, *1992*	10.00	
a.	Booklet single with 2-part tab	12.00	3.00
b.	Governor's edition	*500.00*	
11	$4 Hooded mergansers, *1993*	10.00	
a.	Booklet single with 2-part tab	12.00	3.00
b.	Governor's edition	*500.00*	
12	$4 Common goldeneyes, *1994*	10.00	
a.	Bklt. single with 2-part tab	12.00	2.50
b.	Governor's edition	*175.00*	
13	$4 Northern pintails, *1995*	10.00	
a.	Bklt. single with 2-part tab	12.00	2.50
b.	Governor's edition	*150.00*	
14	$4 Surf scooters, *1996*	10.00	
a.	Bklt. single with 2-part tab	12.00	2.50
b.	Governor's edition	150.00	
15	$4 Wood ducks, *1997*	10.00	
a.	Bklt. single with 2-part tab	12.00	2.50
b.	Governor's edition	*125.00*	
16	$4 Canada geese, *1998*	10.00	
a.	Bklt. single with 2-part tab	12.00	2.50
b.	Governor's edition	*130.00*	
17	$4 Mallards, *1999*	11.00	
a.	Bklt. single with 2-part tab	12.00	2.50
b.	Governor's edition	*130.00*	
18	$4 Black ducks, *2000*	11.00	
a.	Bklt. single with 2-part tab	12.00	2.50
b.	Governor's edition	—	
19	$4 Blue-winged teal, *2001*	11.00	
a.	Bklt. single with 2-part tab	12.00	2.50
b.	Governor's edition	—	
20	$4 Pintails, *2002*	8.00	
a.	Bklt. single with 2-part tab	10.00	2.50
b.	Governor's edition	*150.00*	

21	$4 Wood ducks, *2003*	8.00	
a.	Bklt. single with 2-part tab	10.00	2.50
b.	Governor's edition	*125.00*	
22	$4 Wood duck, *2004*	8.00	
a.	Bklt. single with 2-part tab	10.00	2.50
b.	Governor's edition	*125.00*	
23	$4 Oldsquaw, lighthouse, *2005*	8.00	
a.	Bklt. single with 2-part tab	10.00	
b.	Governor's edition	*125.00*	
24	$4 Common eiders, *2006*	8.00	
a.	Bklt. single with 2-part tab	10.00	2.50
b.	Governor's edition	*125.00*	
25	$4 Black ducks, *2007*	6.00	
a.	Bklt. single with 2-part tab	8.00	2.50
b.	Governor's edition	*125.00*	

NEW JERSEY

Resident and non-resident fees.
Printed in sheets of 30 (starting with No. 1) and booklet panes of 10 (all but Nos. 2, 4, 6, 17b, 18b).
Sheet stamps are perf on 4 sides.
Stamps are numbered serially.

Catalogue values for all unused stamps in this section are for Never Hinged items.

Artists: Thomas Hirata, #1-2, 17-18; David Maass, #3-4; Ronald Louque, #5-6; Louis Frisino, #7-8; Robert Leslie, #9-10, 19-20, 29-30; Daniel Smith, #11-12; Richard Plasschaert, #13-14; Bruce Miller, #21-22; Wilhelm Goebel, #23-24, 27-28; Joe Hautman, #25-26, 35-36; Phillip Crowe, #31-32, 43-46; Richard Clifton, #33-34; Bob Hautman, #37-40; Jim Killen, #41-42; Roger Cruwys, #47-50.

1984-2007

1	$2.50 Canvasbacks	45.00	
a.	Booklet single, #51,000-102,000	70.00	10.00
2	$5 Canvasbacks	60.00	10.00
3	$2.50 Mallards, *1985*	15.00	
a.	Booklet single, #51,000-102,000	25.00	6.00
4	$5 Mallards, *1985*	18.00	5.00
5	$2.50 Pintails, *1986*	15.00	
a.	Booklet single, #51,000-102,000	15.00	3.00
6	$5 Pintails, *1986*	13.00	3.00
7	$2.50 Canada geese, *1987*	17.00	
a.	Booklet single, #51,000-102,000	17.00	3.00
8	$5 Canada geese, *1987*	17.00	
a.	Booklet single, #45,001-60,000	17.00	3.00
9	$2.50 Green-winged teal, *1988*	12.00	
a.	Booklet single, #51,000-102,000	12.00	3.00
10	$5 Green-winged teal, *1988*	12.00	
a.	Booklet single, #45,001-60,000	12.00	3.00
11	$2.50 Snow geese, *1989*	11.00	
a.	Booklet single, #45,001-60,000	11.00	3.00
b.	Governor's edition	*72.50*	
12	$5 Snow geese, *1989*	11.00	
a.	Booklet single, #45,001-60,000	11.00	3.00
b.	Governor's edition	*140.00*	

Nos. 11b and 12b were available only in sets of sheets of 30 stamps with matching serial numbers through a sealed bid auction.

13	$2.50 Wood ducks, *1990*	12.00	
a.	Booklet single, #45,001-60,000	12.00	3.00
14	$5 Wood ducks, *1990*	12.00	
a.	Booklet single, #45,001-60,000	12.00	3.00
17	$2.50 Atlantic brant, *1991*	9.00	
a.	Booklet single, #45,001-60,000	9.00	3.00
b.	Atlantic "brandt"	32.50	
18	$5 Atlantic brant, *1991*	12.00	
a.	Booklet single, #45,001-60,000	12.00	3.00
b.	Atlantic "brandt"	37.50	

Matching serial number sets of Nos. 17b and 18b were available for sale only with the purchase of matching serial number sets of Nos. 17 and 18.

19	$2.50 Bluebills, *1992*	10.00	
a.	Booklet single, #27,691-78,690	10.00	2.50
20	$5 Bluebills, *1992*	10.00	
a.	Booklet single, #27,691-57,690	10.00	2.50
21	$2.50 Buffleheads, *1993*	10.00	
a.	Booklet single, #27,691-78,690	10.00	2.50
b.	Sheet of 4	*75.00*	
c.	Governor's edition, signed by Florio or Whitman	42.50	
22	$5 Buffleheads, *1993*	10.00	
a.	Booklet single, #27,691-57,690	10.00	2.50
b.	Sheet of 4	*75.00*	
c.	Governor's edition, signed by Florio or Whitman	82.50	

Nos. 21b and 22b were available only in sets of sheets with matching serial numbers. The set of sheets sold for $35.

Nos. 21c and 22c were available only in sets with matching serial numbers.

23	$2.50 Black ducks, *1994*	12.00	
a.	Bklt. single, perf. 2 or 3 sides	12.00	2.50
24	$5 Black ducks, *1994*	14.00	
a.	Bklt. single, perf. 2 or 3 sides	14.00	2.50
25	$2.50 Widgeon, lighthouse, *1995*	12.00	
a.	Bklt. single, perf. 3 sides	12.00	2.50
26	$5 Widgeon, lighthouse, *1995*	14.00	
a.	Bklt. single, perf. 3 sides	14.00	2.50
27	$5 Goldeneyes, lighthouse, *1996*	14.00	
a.	Bklt. single, perf. 2 or 3 sides	14.00	2.50
28	$10 Goldeneyes, lighthouse, *1996*	16.00	
a.	Bklt. single, perf. 2 or 3 sides	16.00	2.50

The $2.50 was printed but not used as the rate no longer existed. Later they were sold to collectors. Value, unused $10.

29	$5 Old squaws, schooner, *1997*	12.00	
a.	Bklt. single, perf. 2 or 3 sides	12.00	2.50
30	$10 Old squaws, schooner, *1997*	16.00	
a.	Bklt. single, perf. 2 or 3 sides	16.00	2.50
31	$5 Mallards, *1998*	12.00	
a.	Bklt. single, perf. 2 or 3 sides	12.00	2.50
32	$10 Mallards, *1998*	15.00	
a.	Bklt. single, perf. 2 or 3 sides	15.00	2.50
33	$5 Redheads, perf. 4 sides, *1999*	12.00	
a.	Bklt. single, perf. 2 or 3 sides	12.00	2.50
34	$10 Redheads, perf. 4 sides, *1999*	15.00	
a.	Bklt. single, perf. 2 or 3 sides	15.00	2.50
35	$5 Canvasbacks, perf. 4 sides, *2000*	13.00	
a.	Bklt. single, perf. 2 or 3 sides	13.00	2.50
36	$10 Canvasbacks, perf. 4 sides, *2000*	15.00	
a.	Bklt. single, perf. 2 or 3 sides	15.00	2.50
37	$5 Tundra swans, perf. 4 sides, *2001*	11.00	
a.	Bklt. single, perf. 2 or 3 sides	11.00	2.50
38	$10 Tundra swans, perf. 4 sides, *2001*	14.00	
a.	Bklt. single, perf. 2 or 3 sides	14.00	2.50
39	$5 Wood ducks, perf. 4 sides, *2002*	11.00	
a.	Bklt. single, perf. 2 or 3 sides	11.00	2.50
40	$10 Wood ducks, perf. 4 sides, *2002*	14.00	
a.	Bklt. single, perf. 2 or 3 sides	14.00	2.50
41	$5 Pintails, Labrador retriever perf. 4 sides, *2003*	11.00	
a.	Bklt. single, perf. 2 or 3 sides	11.00	2.50
42	$10 Pintails, Labrador retriever, perf. 4 sides, *2003*	14.00	
a.	Bklt. single, perf. 2 or 3 sides	14.00	2.50
43	$5 Hooded merganser decoy, Labrador retriever, perf. 4 sides, *2004*	10.00	
a.	Bklt. single, perf. 2 or 3 sides	10.00	2.50
44	$10 Hooded merganser decoy, Labrador retriever, perf. 4 sides, *2004*	14.00	
a.	Bklt. single, perf. 2 or 3 sides	14.00	2.50
45	$5 Canvasback decoys, Chesapeake Bay retriever, perf. 4 sides, *2005*	10.00	
a.	Bklt. single, perf. 2 or 3 sides	10.00	2.50
46	$10 Canvasback decoys, Chesapeake Bay retriever, perf. 4 sides, *2005*	14.00	
a.	Bklt. single, perf. 2 or 3 sides	14.00	2.50
47	$5 Wood duck decoy, Golden retriever, perf. 4 sides, *2006*	10.00	
a.	Bklt. single, perf. 2 or 3 sides	10.00	2.50
48	$10 Wood duck decoy, Golden retriever, perf. 4 sides, *2006*	14.00	
a.	Bklt. single, perf. 2 or 3 sides	14.00	2.50
49	$5 Green-winged teal, Labrador retriever, perf. 4 sides, *2007*	7.50	
a.	Bklt. single, perf. 2 or 3 sides	7.50	2.50
50	$10 Green-winged teal, Labrador retriever, perf. 4 sides, *2007*	12.50	
a.	Bklt. single, perf. 2 or 3 sides	13.00	2.50

NEW MEXICO

Printed in booklet panes of 5 and sheets of 30.
Stamps are numbered serially.

Catalogue values for all unused stamps in this section are for Never Hinged items.

Artist: Robert Steiner.

1991-94

1	$7.50 Pintails	14.00	
	Booklet single, with large tab and selvage	14.00	5.00
a.	$7.50 +$50 Governor's edition	72.50	
2	$7.50 American widgeon, *1992*	14.00	
	Booklet single, with large tab and selvage	14.00	4.00
a.	$7.50 +$50 Governor's edition	65.00	
3	$7.50 Mallard, *1993*	14.00	
	Booklet single, with large tab and selvage	14.00	4.00
a.	Sheet of 4	60.00	
b.	$7.50 +$50 Governor's edition	65.00	

No. 3a exists imperf. Value, $100.

No. 4: b, Three birds in flight. c, Two birds in flight. d, Two birds flying over land. e, Bird's head close-up.

4	$7.50 Green-winged teal, sheet of 4, #b.-e., *1994*	85.00	
a.	Souvenir sheet of 4, #b.-e. (decorative border)	85.00	
b.-e.	Bklt. single with large tab and selvage, each	15.00	4.00
f.	Bklt. pane of 4, #b.-e.	85.00	

Stamps in Nos. 4-4a are printed with continuous design and have serial numbers reading down. Stamps in No. 4f have framelines around each design, inscriptions at the top and serial numbers reading up.

NEW YORK

Not required to hunt. Printed in sheets of 30.

Catalogue values for all unused stamps in this section are for Never Hinged items.

Artists: Larry Barton, #1; David Maass, #2; Lee LeBlanc, #3; Richard Plasschaert, #4; Robert Bateman, #5; John Seerey Lester, #6; Terry Isaac, #7; Anton Ashak, #8; Ron Kleiber, #9; Jerome Hageman, #10; Frederick Szatkowski, #11; Len Rusin, #12; R. Easton, #13; Barbara Woods, #14; Richard Clifton, #15; Rob Leslie, #16; Bruce Miller, #17; Adam Grimm, #18.

1985-2002

1	$5.50 Canada geese	13.00	
2	$5.50 Mallards, *1986*	9.00	
3	$5.50 Wood ducks, *1987*	9.00	
4	$5.50 Pintails, *1988*	9.00	
5	$5.50 Greater scaup, *1989*	9.00	
6	$5.50 Canvasbacks, *1990*	9.00	
7	$5.50 Redheads, *1991*	11.00	
8	$5.50 Wood ducks, *1992*	11.00	
9	$5.50 Blue-winged teal, *1993*	10.00	
10	$5.50 Canada geese, *1994*	12.00	
11	$5.50 Common goldeneye, *1995*	12.00	
12	$5.50 Common loon, *1996*	11.00	
13	$5.50 Hooded merganser, *1997*	9.00	
14	$5.50 Osprey, *1998*	9.00	
15	$5.50 Buffleheads, *1999*	14.00	
16	$5.50 Wood ducks, *2000*	17.00	
17	$5.50 Pintails, *2001*	9.00	
18	$5.50 Canvasbacks, *2002*	9.00	3.00

NORTH CAROLINA

Not required to hunt until 1988. Printed in sheets of 30. Starting with No. 6, stamps are numbered serially.

Catalogue values for all unused stamps in this section are for Never Hinged items.

Artists: Richard Plasschaert, #1, 10; Jim Killen, #2, 13; Thomas Hirata, #3-4, 17-18; Larry Barton, #5; Ronald Louque, #6, 21-22, 23-26; Louis Frisino, #7; Robert Leslie, #8, 14; Phillip rowe, #9, 12; Bruce Miller, #11; Wilhelm Goebel, #15-16, 27-8; Robert Flowers, #19-20; Gerald Putt, #29-36.

983-2007

$5.50 Mallards 65.00
$5.50 Wood ducks, *1984* 45.00
$5.50 Canvasbacks, *1985* 25.00
$5.50 Canada geese, *1986* 20.00
$5.50 Pintails, *1987* 15.00
$5 Green-winged teal, *1988* 10.00 3.00
$5 Snow geese, *1989* 16.00 3.00
$5 Redheads, *1990* 16.00 3.00
$5 Blue-winged teal, *1991* 16.00 3.00
0 $5 American widgeon, *1992* 16.00 3.00
1 $5 Tundra swans, *1993* 16.00 3.00
2 $5 Buffleheads, *1994* 16.00 3.00
3 $5 Brant, lighthouse, *1995* 16.00 3.00
4 $5 Pintails, *1996* 16.00 3.00
5 $5 Wood ducks, perf., *1997* 12.00 3.00
6 $5 As #15,, self-adhesive, die cut, *1997* 35.00
7 $5 Canada geese, perf., *1998* 12.00 3.00
8 $5 As #17, self-adhesive, die cut, *1998* 25.00
9 $5 Green-winged teal, perf., *1999* 12.00 3.00
0 $5 As #19, self-adhesive, die cut, *1999* 20.00
1 $10 Green-winged teal, perf., *2000* 25.00 3.00
2 $10 Green-winged teal, self-adhesive, die cut, *2000* 20.00
3 $10 Black duck, perf., *2001* 17.00 3.00
4 $10 Black duck, self-adhesive, die cut, *2001* 20.00
5 $10 Pintails, hunters, dog, perf., *2002* 17.00 3.00
6 $10 Pintails, hunters, dog, self-adhesive, die cut, *2002* 25.00
7 $10 Ring-necked ducks, hunters, dog, perf., *2003* 17.00 3.00
8 $10 Ring-necked ducks, hunters, dog, self-adhesive, die cut, *2003* 20.00
9 $10 Mallards, perf., *2004* 14.00 3.00
0 $10 Mallards, self-adhesive, die cut, *2004* 20.00
1 $10 Green-winged teals, perf., *2005* 14.00 3.00
2 $10 Green-winged teals, self-adhesive, die cut, *2005* 14.00
3 $10 Lesser scaups, perf., *2006* 14.00 3.00
4 $10 Lesser scaups, self-adhesive, die cut, *2006* 14.00
5 $10 Wood ducks, perf., *2007* 14.00 3.00
6 $10 Wood ducks, self-adhesive, die cut, *2007* 14.00

Nos. 27-36 not required for hunting.

NORTH DAKOTA

Small Game Stamps

Required to hunt small game and waterfowl statewide. Resident and non-resident fees.

Values for 1967-70 non-resident stamps are for examples with staple holes.

Used values are for signed stamps. Unused values for Nos. 12, 16, 18, 20, 22, 24, 26 and 28 are for stamps on backing.

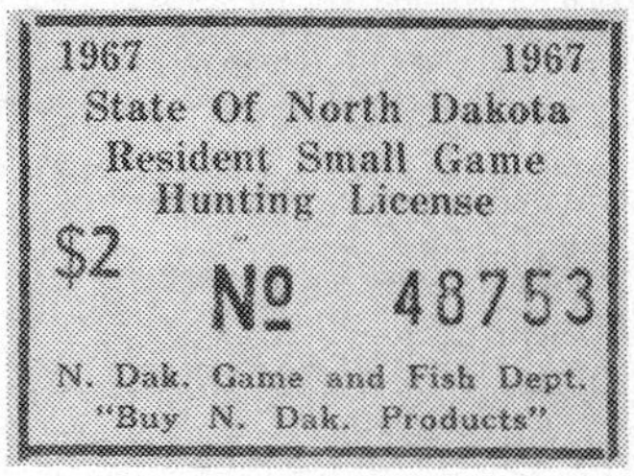

1967-80

$2 black, *green* *850.00* 60.00
$25 black, *green* *3,750.* *350.00*
$2 black, *pink, 1968* 200.00 20.00
$25 black, *yellow, 1968* *450.00*
$2 black, *green, 1969* 190.00 20.00
$35 black, *1969* *400.00*
$2 blue, *1970* 160.00 15.00
$35 black, *pink, 1970* *250.00* *50.00*
$2 black, *yellow, 1971* 125.00 10.00
10 $35 black, *1971* *150.00*
11 $3 black, *pink, 1972* 65.00 5.00
12 $35 red, *1972* *400.00* *75.00*
13 $3 black, *yellow, 1973* 65.00 5.00
14 $35 green, *1973* *1,950.* *175.00*
15 $3 black, *blue, 1974* 125.00 15.00
16 $35 red, *1974* *350.00* *50.00*
17 $3 black, *1975* 95.00 10.00
18 $35 green, *1975* *275.00* *40.00*
19 $3 black, *dark yellow, 1976* 55.00 5.00
20 $35 red, *1976* *125.00* 25.00
21 $3 black, *1977* 90.00 10.00
22 $35 red, *1977* *100.00* 25.00
23 $5 black, *1978* 45.00 5.00
24 $40 red, *1978* 85.00 20.00
25 $5 black, *1979* 35.00 5.00
26 $40 red, *1979* 45.00 15.00
27 $5 black, *1980* 35.00 5.00
28 $40 green, *1980* 45.00 15.00

Small Game and Habitat Stamps

Required to hunt small game and waterfowl statewide.

Resident ($9), youth ($6) and non-resident ($53) fees.

Resident stamps issued in booklet panes of 5 numbered 20,001-150,000 (1982-86 issues) or 20,001-140,000 (starting with 1987 issue) or sheets of 30 numbered 150,001 and up (1982-86 issues) or 140,001 and up (starting with 1987 issue).

Starting with 1984, resident booklet stamps have straight edges at sides.

Nos. 31, 34, 37, 40 are die cut self adhesives.

Unused values are for stamps on backing.

All youth stamps were issued in booklet panes of 5. Non-resident stamps for 1981, 1982, 1996 and following years were issued in booklet panes of 5.

The 1984-95 non-resident stamps were issued se-tenant with non-resident waterfowl and non-resident general game stamps (rouletted on three sides). The 1994 and 1995 non-resident stamps also were issued se-tenant with only the non-resident general game stamp (rouletted at sides), as well as in booklet panes of 5 (rouletted top and bottom).

Catalogue values for all unused stamps in this section, from this point to the end, are for Never Hinged items.

A1

1981

29 A1 $9 black 35.00 3.00
30 A1 $6 black, *blue green* *175.00* 25.00
31 A1 $53 blue 110.00 20.00

A2

Artists: Richard Plaschaert, #32, 73; Terry Radlin, #35; David Maass, #38; Leslie Kouba, #41; Mario Fernandez, #44; Ronald Louque, #47, 75; Louis Frisino, #50; Robert Leslie, #53; Roger Cruwys, #56; Thomas Hirata, #59; Phillip Crowe, #62, 77, 81; Bruce Miller, #65; Darrell Davis, #67; Richard Clifton, #69; Wilhelm Goebel, #71; Jeffrey Klinefelter, #79.

1982

32 A2 $9 Canada geese 125.00
Booklet single with L & R selvage *950.00* 25.00

Serial numbers 1-20,000 are from sheets of 10. Stamps without selvage from booklets sell for considerably less.

33 A1 $6 black, *blue* *175.00* 25.00
34 A1 $53 black 35.00 15.00

1983

35 A2 $9 Mallards 75.00
Booklet single with L & R selvage *2,250.* 25.00

Serial numbers 1-20,000 are from sheets. Stamps without selvage from booklets sell for considerably less.

36 A1 $6 black, *orange* 25.00
37 A1 $53 black *40.00*

1984

38 A2 $9 Canvasbacks 40.00
a. Booklet single, perforated horiz. on 1 or 2 sides *2,500.* 25.00
39 A1 $6 black, *light blue* 25.00
40 A1 $53 black *40.00*

1985

41 A2 $9 Bluebills 20.00
a. Booklet single, perforated horiz. on 1 or 2 sides *3,750.* 25.00
42 A1 $6 black, *light blue* 25.00
43 A1 $53 black *40.00*

1986

44 A2 $9 Pintails 20.00
a. Booklet single, perforated horiz. on 1 or 2 sides *500.00* 20.00
45 A1 $6 black, *light blue* 20.00
46 A1 $53 black *35.00*

1987

47 A2 $9 Snow geese 18.00
a. Booklet single, perforated horiz. on 1 or 2 sides *60.00* 18.00
48 A1 $6 black, *light blue* — 25.00
49 A1 $53 black *30.00*

1988

50 A2 $9 White-winged scoters 14.00
a. Booklet single, perforated horiz. on 1 or 2 sides 30.00 12.00
51 A1 $6 black, *light blue* — 25.00
52 A1 $53 black *30.00*

Stamps Inscribed "Small Game"

Resident ($6), youth ($3) and non-resident ($50, $75) fees.

1989

53 A2 $6 Redheads 12.00
a. Booklet single, perforated horiz. on 1 or 2 sides 15.00 8.00
54 A1 $3 black, *light blue* — 25.00
55 A1 $50 black 30.00

1990

56 A2 $6 Labrador retriever & mallard 15.00
a. Booklet single, perforated horiz. on 1 or 2 sides 15.00 8.00
57 A1 $3 black, *light blue* 200.00 25.00
58 A1 $50 black 25.00

1991

59 A2 $6 Green-winged teal 12.50
a. Booklet single, perforated horiz. on 1 or 2 sides 13.00 6.00
60 A1 $3 black, *light blue* 200.00 25.00
61 A1 $50 black *350.00* 25.00

1992

62 A2 $6 Blue-winged teal 12.50
a. Booklet single, perforated horiz. on 1 or 2 sides 13.00 6.00
63 A1 $3 black, *light blue* 325.00
64 A1 $50 black 25.00

When supplies of No. 64 ran out, No. 58 was used with the date changed by hand. Unused examples exist. Value, $300.

1993

65 A2 $6 Wood ducks 12.50
a. Booklet single, perforated horiz. on 1 or 2 sides 13.00 6.00
66 A1 $50 black *550.00* 25.00

1994

67 A2 $6 Canada geese 10.00
a. Booklet single, perforated horiz. on 1 or 2 sides 10.00 6.00
68 A1 $75 black, rouletted on 2 adjacent sides *400.00* 20.00
a. Booklet single, rouletted top and bottom —

1995

69 A2 $6 Widgeon 10.00
a. Booklet single, perforated horiz. on 1 or 2 sides 10.00 5.00
70 A1 $75 black, rouletted on 2 adjacent sides *350.00* 20.00
a. Booklet single, rouletted top and bottom —

1996

71 A2 $6 Mallards 10.00
a. Booklet single, perforated horiz. on 1 or 2 sides 10.00 2.50
72 A1 $75 black, rouletted at top and bottom —

1997

73 A2 $6 White-fronted geese 10.00
a. Booklet single, perforated horiz. on 1 or 2 sides 10.00 2.50
74 A1 $75 black, rouletted at top and bottom —

1998

75 A2 $6 Blue-winged teal 10.00
a. Bklt. single, perforated horiz. on 1 or 2 sides 10.00 2.50
76 A1 $75 black, rouletted at top and bottom —

1999

77 A2 $6 Gadwalls 10.00
a. Bklt. single, perforated horiz. on 1 or 2 sides 10.00 2.50
78 A1 $75 black, rouletted at top and bottom —

2000-01

79 $6 Pintails, *2000* 10.00
a. Bklt. single, perforated horiz. on 1 or 2 sides 10.00 2.50
81 A2 $6 Canada geese, *2001* 10.00
a. Bklt. single, perforated horiz. on 1 or 2 sides 10.00 2.50

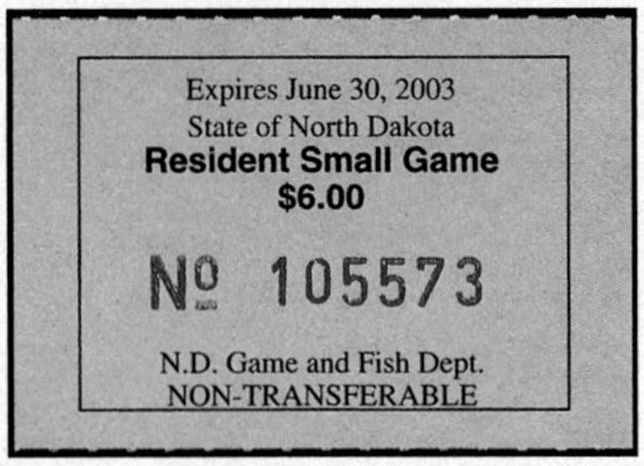
Expires June 30, 2003
State of North Dakota
Resident Small Game
$6.00
Nº 105573
N.D. Game and Fish Dept.
NON-TRANSFERABLE

A3

2002-07

83	A3	$6 black, *green, 2002*	12.00
84	A3	$6 black, *green, 2003*	12.00
85	A3	$6 black, *green, 2004*	12.00
86	A3	$6 black, *green, 2005*	12.00
87	A3	$6 black, *green, 2006*	9.00
88	A3	$6 black, *green, 2007*	8.00

Non-Resident Waterfowl Stamps

Required by non-residents to hunt waterfowl only.

Unused examples of Nos. A1a, A13a-A19a have no serial number. Used stamps have number written in. Nos. A1-A10 are self-adhesive, die cut. Others are rouletted.

Catalogue values for all unused stamps in this section are for Never Hinged items.

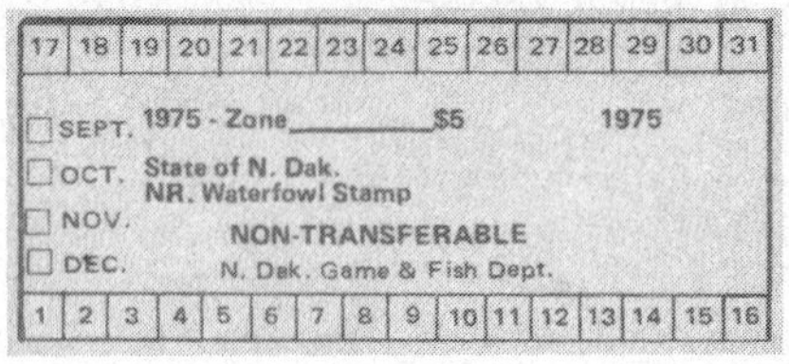
17 18 19 20 21 22 23 24 25 26 27 28 29 30 31
SEPT. 1975 - Zone $5 1975
OCT. State of N. Dak.
NR. Waterfowl Stamp
NOV.
NON-TRANSFERABLE
DEC. N. Dak. Game & Fish Dept.
1 2 3 4 5 6 7 8 9 10 11 12 13 14 15 16

Illustration reduced.

1975-99

A1	$5 green		*150.00*
a.	No serial number	160.00	—
A2	$5 red, *1976*	*475.00*	*100.00*
A3	$5 red, *1977*	*275.00*	*75.00*
A4	$5 red, *1978*	110.00	25.00
A5	$5 red, *1979*	85.00	20.00
A6	$5 green, *1980*	90.00	20.00
A7	$8 blue, *1981*	175.00	25.00
A8	$8 black, *1982*	27.50	15.00
A9	$8 black, *1983*		*55.00*
A10	$8 black, *1984*		*50.00*
A11	$8 black, *1985*		*45.00*
A12	$8 black, *1986*		*45.00*
A13	$8 black, *1987*		*40.00*
a.	No serial number	*400.00*	*50.00*
A14	$8 black, *1988*		35.00
a.	No serial number	*350.00*	*50.00*
A15	$8 black, *1989*		25.00
a.	No serial number, light green paper	*350.00*	*50.00*
A16	$8 black, *1990*		25.00
a.	No serial number	*300.00*	*50.00*
A17	$8 black, *1991*	*400.00*	25.00
a.	No serial number	250.00	*35.00*
A18	$8 black, *1992*		20.00
a.	No serial number	*200.00*	35.00

When supplies of No. A18 ran out, No. A16 was used with the date changed by hand. Values, unused $200, used $50.

A19	$10 black, *1993*	*275.00*	20.00
a.	No serial number	*175.00*	30.00
A20	$10 black, rouletted on 2 adjacent sides, *1994*	*250.00*	20.00
a.	No serial number, rouletted top and bottom	175.00	30.00
A21	$10 black, rouletted on 2 adjacent sides, *1995*	*225.00*	20.00
a.	No serial number, rouletted top and bottom	100.00	25.00
A22	$10 black, rouletted top and bottom, *1996*	*95.00*	20.00
A23	$10 black, rouletted top and bottom, *1997*	*85.00*	14.00
A24	$10 black, rouletted top and bottom, *1998*	*75.00*	12.00
A25	$10 black, rouletted top and bottom, *1999*	*65.00*	12.00

Resident Sportsmen's Stamps

Required to hunt a variety of game, including waterfowl.

Catalogue values for all unused stamps in this section are for Never Hinged items.

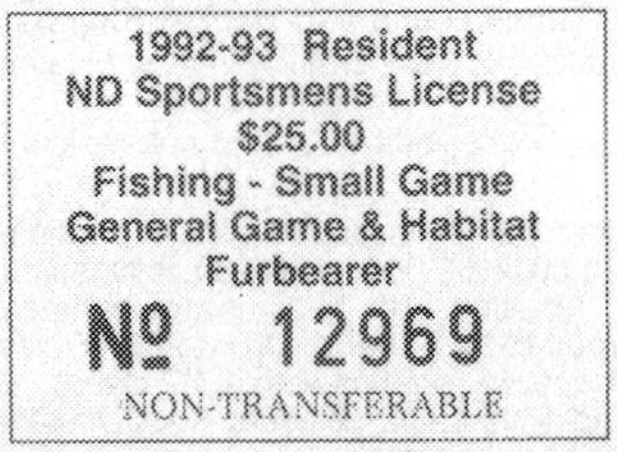
1992-93 Resident
ND Sportsmens License
$25.00
Fishing - Small Game
General Game & Habitat
Furbearer
Nº 12969
NON-TRANSFERABLE

1992-98

2A1	$25 black & purple, *1992-1993*	*3,250.*	*75.00*
2A2	$25 black & purple, *1993-1994*	*1,650.*	*35.00*
2A3	$25 black & purple, *1994-1995*	*375.00*	*25.00*
2A4	$25 black & purple, *1995-1996*	*250.00*	*20.00*
2A5	$25 black & purple, *1996-1997*	*200.00*	*15.00*
2A6	$27 black & purple, *1997-1998*	*125.00*	*12.00*

OHIO

Pymatuning Lake Waterfowl Hunting Stamps

Pymatuning Hunting License
Valid when attached
to Resident Hunters and
Trappers License.
Authority H. B. 668.
YEAR
1938
$1.00
NO FEE

1938-45

A1	$1 black, *light yellow*	—
A2	$1 black, *gray, 1939*	—
A3	$1 black, *blue, 1940*	—
A4	$1 black, *pink, 1941*	—
A5	$1 black, *green, 1942*	—
A6	$1 black, *1943*	—
A7	$1 black, *manila, 1944*	—
A8	$1 black, *manila, 1945*	—

Statewide Issues

Nos. 1-18 printed in sheets of 16. Starting with No. 19, stamps are printed in souvenir sheets of 1.

Catalogue values for all unused stamps in this section are for Never Hinged items.

OHIO WETLANDS HABITAT STAMP
WOOD
DUCK
$5.75
VOID AFTER AUGUST 31, 1983

Artists: John Ruthven, #1; Harry Antis, #2; Harold Roe, #3, 6, 15, 17; Ronald Louque, #4; Lynn Kaatz, #5, 8; Cynthia Fisher, #7; Jon Henson, #9; Gregory Clair, #10, 25; Samuel Timm, #11; Kenneth Nanney, #12; Richard Clifton, #13, 26; Ron Kleiber, #14; D. J. Cleland-Hura, #16: Timothy Donovan, #18; Mark Anderson, #19; Brian Bright, #20, 22; Jeffrey Klinefelter, #21; Robert Mertopulos, #23; Adam Grimm, #24.

1982-2007

1	$5.75 Wood ducks	80.00	10.00
2	$5.75 Mallards, *1983*	70.00	10.00
3	$5.75 Green-winged teal, *1984*	70.00	8.00
4	$5.75 Redheads, *1985*	35.00	6.00
5	$5.75 Canvasback, *1986*	35.00	5.00
6	$6 Blue-winged teal, *1987*	12.00	4.00
7	$6 Common goldeneyes, *1988*	12.00	4.00
8	$6 Canada geese, *1989*	12.00	3.00
9	$9 Black ducks, *1990*	16.00	3.00
10	$9 Lesser scaup, *1991*	16.00	3.00
11	$9 Wood duck, *1992*	16.00	3.00
12	$9 Buffleheads, *1993*	16.00	3.00
13	$11 Mallards, *1994*	21.00	2.50
14	$11 Pintails, *1995*	22.50	2.50
15	$11 Hooded mergansers, *1996*	24.00	2.50
16	$11 Widgeons, *1997*	20.00	2.50
17	$11 Gadwall, *1998*	20.00	2.50
18	$11 Mallard, *1999*	18.00	2.50

Souvenir Sheet

Rouletted

19	$11 Buffleheads, *2000*	18.00	2.5
20	$11 Canvasback, *2001*	18.00	2.5
21	$11 Ring-necked ducks, *2002*	17.00	2.5
22	$11 Hooded mergansers, *2003*	17.00	2.5
23	$15 Tundra swans, *2004*	20.00	2.5
24	$15 Wood duck, *2005*	20.00	2.5
25	$15 Pintail, *2006*	20.00	2.5
26	$15 Canada goose, *2007*	19.00	2.5

Nos. 19-26 not required for hunting.

OKLAHOMA

Printed in booklet panes of 10 (Nos. 1-3) and booklet panes of 5 (Starting with No. 4). No. 10 was the first to be printed in a sheet of 30, No. 17 in a sheet of 24.

Catalogue values for all unused stamps in this section are for Never Hinged items.

Artists: Patrick Sawyer, #1; Hoyt Smith, #2, 5, 7, 20; Jeffre Frey, #3; Gerald Mobley, #4, 6; Rayburn Foster, #8, 12; Ji Gaar, #9; Wanda Mumm, #10; Ronald Louque, #11; Jeffre Mobley, #13; Jerome Hageman, #14; Richard Kirkman, #1 Richard Clifton, #16; Greg Everhart, #17; M. Anderson, #18, 2 Jeffrey Klinefelter, #19, 26; Paul Makuchal, #21; Daniel Brevic #22; Brian Blight, #23; Scot Storm, #25; James Hublick, #2 Jeffrey Hoff, #28.

1980-2007

1	$4 Pintails	55.00	10.0
2	$4 Canada goose, *1981*	25.00	8.0
3	$4 Green-winged teal, *1982*	10.00	4.0
4	$4 Wood ducks, *1983*	10.00	10.0
5	$4 Ring-necked ducks, *1984*	10.00	3.0
	With tab	10.00	
6	$4 Mallards, *1985*	8.00	3.0
	With tab	10.00	
7	$4 Snow geese, *1986*	10.00	3.0
	With tab	10.00	
8	$4 Canvasbacks, *1987*	8.00	3.0
	With tab	9.00	
9	$4 Widgeons, *1988*	8.00	3.0
	With tab	9.00	
10	$4 Redheads, *1989*	8.00	3.0
	Booklet single, with tab & selvage at L, selvage at R	9.00	
a.	Governor's edition	*125.00*	

No. 10a was available only in sheets of 30 through a seale bid auction.

11	$4 Hooded merganser, *1990*	7.50	3.0
	Booklet single, with tab & selvage at L, selvage at R	8.50	
12	$4 Gadwalls, *1991*	7.50	3.0
	Booklet single, with tab & selvage at L, selvage at R	8.50	
13	$4 Lesser scaup, *1992*	7.50	3.0
	Booklet single, with tab & selvage at L, selvage at R	8.50	
14	$4 White-fronted geese, *1993*	7.50	3.0
	Booklet single, with tab & selvage at L, selvage at R	8.50	
15	$4 Blue-winged teal, *1994*	7.50	3.0
	Booklet single, with tab & selvage at L, selvage at R	8.50	
16	$4 Ruddy ducks, *1995*	7.50	3.0
	Booklet single, with tab & selvage at L, selvage at R	8.50	
17	$4 Bufflehead, *1996*	7.50	3.0
	Booklet single, with selvage at L & R	8.50	
18	$4 Goldeneyes, *1997*	7.50	3.0
	Bklt. single, with selvage at L & R	8.50	
19	$4 Shovelers, *1998*	7.50	3.0
	Bklt. single, with selvage at L & R	8.50	
20	$4 Canvasbacks, *1999*	8.00	3.0
21	$4 Pintails, *2000*	8.00	3.0
22	$4 Canada goose, *2001*	8.00	3.0
23	$4 Green-winged teal, *2002*	8.00	3.0
24	$10 Wood duck, *2003*	15.00	3.0
25	$10 Mallard, *2004*	15.00	3.0
26	$10 Snow geese, *2005*	15.00	3.0
27	$10 Widgeons, *2006*	15.00	3.0
28	$10 Redheads, *2007*	14.00	3.0

OREGON

Non-resident fees begin in 1994.

Issued in sheets of 30, except for No. 6. Nos. 2-4 also exist from booklet panes of 5.

Stamps are numbered serially. Nos. 11b, 11c have serial numbers on sheet selvage.

Nos. 10 and 11 were issued on computer form. Unused values are for stamps on form.

Catalogue values for all unused stamps in this section are for Never Hinged items.

Artists: Michael Sieve, #1-3; Dorothy M. Smith, #4; Darrell Davis, #5; Phillip Crowe, #7; Roger Cruwys, #8; Louis Frisino, #9; Kip Richmond, #10; R. Bruce Horsfall, #11; Richard Plasschaert, #12-13; Robert Steiner, #14-31.

1984-88

1	$5 Canada geese	22.50	7.00
2	$5 Lesser snow goose, *1985*	35.00	10.00
	Booklet single, with 3 tabs (2 at left)	*500.00*	
3	$5 Pacific brant, perf. 4 sides, *1986*	15.00	
a.	Booklet single, with 2-part tab	15.00	4.00
4	$5 White-fronted geese, perf. 4 sides, *1987*	15.00	
a.	Booklet single, with 2-part tab	15.00	3.00
5	$5 Great Basin Canada geese, *1988*	15.00	3.00
a.	Booklet pane of 1	15.00	

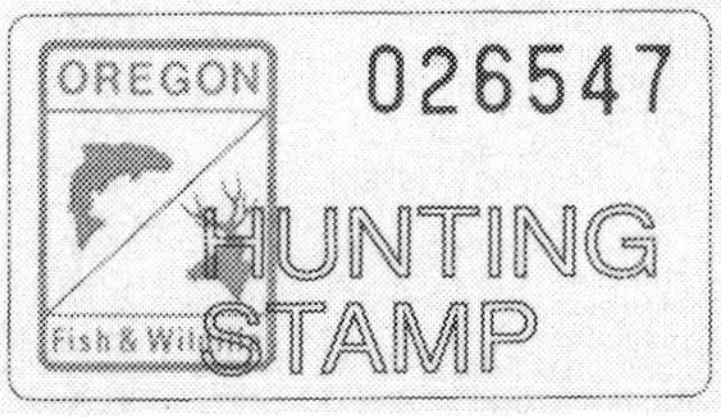

1989-2007 **Die cut self-adhesive**

6	($5) Red Nos., 16,001 and up	15.00	*6.00*
a.	Black Nos., 001-16,000	30.00	*12.50*

This provisional stamp was used in early 1989, when the regular stamps were delayed. Unused value is for stamp and adjacent label with serial number on backing paper.

Designs like No. 1

7	$5 Black Labrador retriever & pintails, *1989*	15.00	2.50
a.	Booklet pane of 1	15.00	
8	$5 Mallards & golden retriever, *1990*	15.00	2.50
a.	Booklet pane of 1	15.00	
9	$5 Buffleheads & Chesapeake Bay retriever, perf, *1991*	15.00	
a.	Rouletted at L	15.00	2.50

No. 9a is straight edged on 3 sides and stamp is attached to paper by selvage. Unused value is for stamp attached to paper.

10	$5 Green-winged teal, *1992*	15.00	
a.	Die cut, self-adhesive	15.00	2.50
11	$5 Mallards, vert., *1993*	15.00	
a.	Die cut self-adhesive	15.00	2.50
b.	Sheet of 2	22.50	
c.	$50 Governor's edition sheet of 1	75.00	

No. 11b contains No. 11 and the Oregon upland bird stamp. Nos. 11b, 11c exist imperf.

12	$5 Pintails, perf. 4 sides, *1994*	15.00	
a.	Die cut self-adhesive	15.00	2.50
13	$25 Pintails, diff., die cut self-adhesive, *1994*	40.00	—
14	$5 Wood ducks, *1995*	15.00	
a.	Booklet pane of 1	15.00	2.50
15	$25 Columbian sharp-tailed grouse, bklt. pane of 1, *1995*	160.00	—
16	$5 Mallards, *1996*	20.00	
a.	Booklet pane of 1	15.00	2.50
17	$25 Common snipe, booklet pane of 1, *1996*	140.00	—
18	$5 Canvasbacks, *1997*	20.00	
a.	Booklet pane of 1	15.00	2.50
19	$25 Canvasbacks, booklet pane of 1, *1997*	140.00	
20	$5 Pintails, *1998*	20.00	
a.	Booklet pane of 1	15.00	2.50
21	$25 Pintails, booklet pane of 1, *1998*	37.50	
22	$5 Canada geese, *1999*	17.50	
a.	Booklet pane of 1	15.00	2.50
23	$25 Canada geese, booklet pane of 1, *1999*	65.00	
24	$7.50 Canada geese, mallard, widgeon, *2000*	15.00	2.50
a.	Booklet pane of 1, no cover	—	
25	$7.50 Redheads, *2001*	15.00	2.50
a.	Booklet pane of 1, no cover	20.00	
26	$7.50 American wigeon, *2002*	14.00	2.50
a.	Booklet pane of 1, no cover	14.00	
27	$7.50 Wood duck, *2003*	14.00	2.50
a.	Booklet pane of 1, no cover	14.00	
28	$7.50 Ross's goose, *2004*	13.00	2.50
a.	Booklet pane of 1, no cover	13.00	
29	$7.50 Hooded merganser, *2005*	13.00	2.50
a.	Booklet pane of 1, no cover	13.00	
30	$7.50 Pintail, mallard, *2006*	12.00	2.50
a.	Booklet pane of 1, no cover	12.00	
31	$7.50 Wood ducks, *2007*	12.00	2.50

Nos. 27-31 not required for hunting.

PENNSYLVANIA

Not required to hunt.

Printed in sheets of 10.

Catalogue values for all unused stamps in this section are for Never Hinged items.

Artists: Ned Smith, #1, 3; Jim Killen, #2; Robert Knutson, #4; Robert Leslie, #5; John Heldersbach, #6; Ronald Louque, #7; Thomas Hirata, #8, 12; Gerald W. Putt, #9, 14, 16, 18, 20, 23, 25; Robert Sopchick, #10; Glen Reichard, #11; Mark Bray, #13; Clark Weaver, #15, 17, 19; Jocelyn Beatty, #21; Carl Clark, #22; Kerry Holzman, #24.

1983-2007

1	$5.50 Wood ducks	15.00	
2	$5.50 Canada geese, *1984*	12.00	
3	$5.50 Mallards, *1985*	12.00	
4	$5.50 Blue-winged teal, *1986*	12.00	
5	$5.50 Pintails, *1987*	12.00	
6	$5.50 Wood ducks, *1988*	12.00	
7	$5.50 Hooded mergansers, *1989*	9.00	
8	$5.50 Canvasbacks, *1990*	9.00	
9	$5.50 Widgeons, *1991*	9.00	
10	$5.50 Canada geese, *1992*	9.00	
11	$5.50 Northern shovelers, *1993*	9.00	
12	$5.50 Pintails, *1994*	9.00	
13	$5.50 Buffleheads, *1995*	9.00	
14	$5.50 Black ducks, *1996*	9.00	
15	$5.50 Hooded merganser, *1997*	9.00	
16	$5.50 Wood ducks, *1998*	9.00	
17	$5.50 Ring-necked ducks, *1999*	9.00	
18	$5.50 Green-winged teal, *2000*	9.00	
19	($5.50) Pintails, *2001*	9.00	
20	$5.50 Snow geese, *2002*	9.00	2.50
21	$5.50 Canvasbacks, *2003*	9.00	2.50
22	$5.50 Hooded mergansers, *2004*	9.00	2.50
23	$5.50 Red-breasted mergansers, *2005*	8.00	2.50
24	$5.50 Pintails, *2006*	8.00	2.50
25	$5.50 Wood ducks, *2007*	7.50	2.50

RHODE ISLAND

Issued in booklet panes of 5 and sheets of 30. Starting with No. 8, the spacing of the reverse text of the booklet stamp differs from the sheet stamp. Stamps are numbered serially.

Catalogue values for all unused stamps in this section are for Never Hinged items.

Artists: Robert Steiner, #1-7, 9-10, 16; Charles Allen, #8; Keith Mueller, #11-15, 17-19.

1989-2007

1	$7.50 Canvasbacks	12.00	3.00
	Booklet single, with tab	16.00	
a.	$7.50 +$50 Governor's edition	92.50	

No. 1a exists without serial number.

2	$7.50 Canada geese, *1990*	12.00	3.00
	Booklet single, with tab	15.00	
a.	$7.50 +$50 Governor's edition	72.50	

No. 2a exists without serial number.

3	$7.50 Wood ducks & Labrador retriever, *1991*	20.00	3.00
	Booklet single, with tab	22.50	
a.	$7.50 +$50 Governor's edition	60.00	

No. 3a exists without serial number.

4	$7.50 Blue-winged teal, *1992*	15.00	3.00
	Booklet single, with tab	15.00	
a.	$7.50 +$50 Governor's edition	60.00	

No. 4a exists without serial number.

5	$7.50 Pintails, *1993*	13.00	3.00
	Booklet single, with tab	13.00	
a.	Sheet of 4	65.00	

No. 5a imperf. is printer's waste.

6	$7.50 Wood ducks, *1994*	17.00	2.50
	Booklet single, with tab and selvage	17.00	
7	$7.50 Hooded mergansers, *1995*	13.00	2.50
	Booklet single, with tab and selvage	13.00	
a.	Governor's edition	*110.00*	

No. 7a inscribed "Governor's edition."

8	$7.50 Harlequin, *1996*	22.50	2.50
	Booklet single, with tab and selvage	22.50	
a.	Governor's edition	*125.00*	

No. 8a inscribed "Governor's edition" and has serial number with "G" prefix.

9	$7.50 Greater scaup, *1997*	13.00	2.50
	Booklet single, with tab and selvage	14.00	
a.	Governor's edition	*110.00*	

No. 9a inscribed "Governor's edition" and has serial number with "G" prefix.

10	$7.50 Black ducks, *1998*	13.00	2.50
	Booklet single, with tab and selvage	14.00	
a.	Governor's edition	*125.00*	

No. 11-14 do not have a serial number.

Rouletted

11	$7.50 Common eiders, *1999*	17.00	2.50
	Horiz. pair from booklet pane	60.00	

Booklet pane contains 10 stamps.

12	$7.50 Canvasbacks, *2000*	16.00	2.50
a.	Inscribed "Hunter"	18.00	
a.	Governor's edition	—	
13	$7.50 Mallard, black duck, *2001*	15.00	2.50
a.	Inscribed "Hunter"	16.00	
a.	Governor's edition	*125.00*	
14	$7.50 White-winged scoter, lighthouse, *2002*	13.00	2.50
a.	Inscribed "Hunter"	13.00	
b.	Governor's edition	130.00	—
15	$7.50 Oldsquaws, *2003*	12.00	2.50
a.	Inscribed "Hunter"	13.00	
b.	Governor's edition	130.00	—
16	$7.50 Canvasbacks, *2004*	11.00	2.50
a.	Inscribed "Hunter"	12.00	
b.	Governor's edition	130.00	—
17	$7.50 Black ducks, lighthouse, *2005*	11.00	2.50
a.	Inscribed "Hunter"	11.00	
18	$7.50 Canvasbacks, lighthouse, *2006*	11.00	2.50
a.	Inscribed "Hunter"	11.00	
b.	Governor's edition	*130.00*	—
19	$7.50 Harlequin decoy, *2007*	9.50	2.50
a.	Inscribed "Hunter"	9.50	
b.	Governor's edition	*130.00*	—

Nos. 15-19 have no serial number.

SOUTH CAROLINA

Issued in sheets of 30. Stamps with serial numbers were to be issued to hunters.

Catalogue values for all unused stamps in this section are for Never Hinged items.

Artists: Lee LeBlanc, #1; Bob Binks, #2; Jim Killen, #3, 8, 11, 27; Al Dornish, #4; Rosemary Millette, #5; Daniel Smith, #6; Steve Dillard, #7; Lee Cable, #9; John Wilson, #10; Russell Cobane, #12; Bob Bolin, #13; Joe Hautman, #14; Rodney Huckaby, #15, 17, 22, 25; D. J. Cleland-Hura, #16, 18; Denise Nelson, #19; Mark Constantine, #20; Jeffrey Klinefelter, #21; James Hublick, #23; Eddie LeRoy, #24; Richard D. Benson, #26.

1981-2007

1	$5.50 Wood ducks	60.00	15.00

No. 2-22 do not have a serial number.

2	$5.50 Mallards, *1982*	95.00	
a.	Serial number on reverse	*495.00*	25.00
3	$5.50 Pintails, *1983*	95.00	
a.	Serial number on reverse	*450.00*	25.00
4	$5.50 Canada geese, *1984*	65.00	
a.	Serial number on reverse	*190.00*	15.00
5	$5.50 Green-winged teal, *1985*	60.00	
a.	Serial number on reverse	100.00	15.00
6	$5.50 Canvasbacks, *1986*	25.00	
a.	Serial number on reverse	42.50	10.00
7	$5.50 Black ducks, *1987*	20.00	
a.	Serial number on reverse	22.50	5.00
8	$5.50 Widgeon & spaniel, *1988*	20.00	
a.	Serial number on reverse	30.00	5.00
9	$5.50 Blue-winged teal, *1989*	11.00	
a.	Serial number on reverse	14.00	4.00
10	$5.50 Wood ducks, *1990*	10.00	
a.	Serial number on reverse	10.00	4.00
b.	$5.50 +$44.50 Governor's edition	82.50	
c.	$5.50 +$94.50 Governor's edition	225.00	

All copies of No. 10c are signed by the governor.

11	$5.50 Labrador retriever, pintails & decoy, *1991*	11.00	
a.	Serial number on reverse	11.00	4.00
12	$5.50 Buffleheads, *1992*	14.00	
a.	Serial number on front	14.00	3.00
13	$5.50 Lesser scaup, *1993*	14.00	
a.	Serial number on front	14.00	3.00
14	$5.50 Canvasbacks, *1994*	14.00	
a.	Serial number on front	14.00	2.50
15	$5.50 Shovelers, lighthouse, *1995*	14.00	
a.	Serial number on front	14.00	2.50
16	$5.50 Redheads, lighthouse, *1996*	17.50	
a.	Serial number on front	17.50	2.50
17	$5.50 Old squaws, *1997*	17.50	
a.	Serial number on front	17.50	2.50
18	$5.50 Green-winged teal, *1998*	17.50	
a.	Serial number on front	17.50	2.50
19	$5.50 Barrow's goldeneye, *1999*	17.50	
20	$5.50 Wood ducks, boykin spaniel, *2000*	13.00	2.50
21	$5.50 Mallard, decoy, yellow Labrador retriever, *2001*	13.00	2.50
22	$5.50 Wigeons, chocolate Labrador retriever, *2002*	11.00	2.50
23	$5.50 Green-winged teal, *2003*	11.00	2.50
24	$5.50 Pintails, Labrador retriever, *2004*	11.00	2.50
25	$5.50 Canvasbacks, *2005*	9.00	2.50
26	$5.50 Black ducks, *2006*	9.00	2.50
27	$5.50 Redheads, Golden retriever, *2007*	8.00	2.50

Nos. 23-27 have no serial number.

SOUTH DAKOTA

Resident Waterfowl Stamps

Vertical safety paper (words read up)

1949-50

1	$1 blk, *grn,* vert. safety paper	*1,350.*	85.00
a.	Horizontal safety paper	—	*150.00*
2	$1 blk, *lt brn,* vert. safety paper	*1,000.*	65.00
a.	Horizontal safety paper	—	*175.00*

Safety paper design of Nos. 1 and 2 washes out if stamp is soaked. Washed out examples sell for considerably less. Used values are for stamps showing safety paper design.

Printed in booklet panes of 5.
Stamps are numbered serially.

Catalogue values for all unused stamps in this section, from this point to the end of the Resident Waterfowl stamps, are for Never Hinged items.

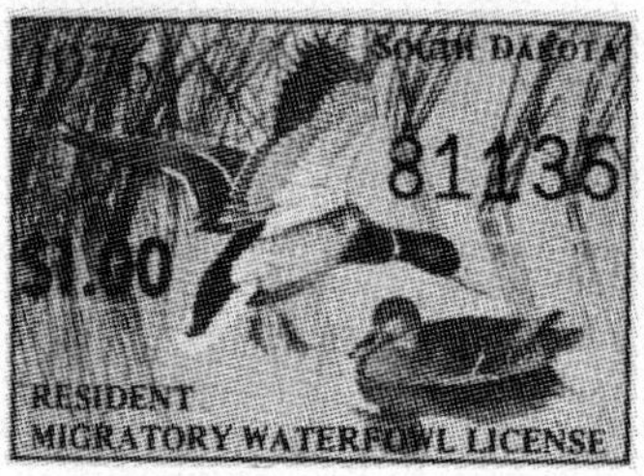

Artists: Robert Kusserow, #3; Don Steinbeck, #4; John Moisan, #5; John Wilson, #6, 12; Rosemary Millett, #7, 9; Marion Toillion, #8; John Green, #10, 17; Russell Duerksen, #11, 15-16, 19-20; Mark Anderson, #13, 18, 21, 22; Jeff Reuter, #14; Joshua Spies. #23.

1976-2003

3	$1 Mallards	35.00	3.00
a.	Serial number 4mm high	65.00	10.00
4	$1 Pintails, *1977*	27.50	2.50
5	$1 Canvasbacks, *1978*	13.00	2.50
6	$2 Canada geese, *1988*	8.50	2.50
7	$2 Blue geese, *1987*	7.00	2.50
8	$2 White-fronted geese, *1988*	6.00	2.50
9	$2 Mallards, *1989*	6.00	2.50
10	$2 Blue-winged teal, *1990*	6.00	2.50
11	$2 Pintails, *1991*	6.00	2.50
12	$2 Canvasbacks, *1992*	6.00	2.50
13	$2 Lesser scaup, *1993*	6.00	2.50
14	$2 Redheads, *1994*	6.00	2.50
15	$2 Wood ducks, *1995*	6.00	2.50
16	$2 Canada geese, *1996*	6.00	2.50
17	$2 Widgeons, *1997*	6.00	2.50
18	$2 Green-winged teal, *1998*	6.00	2.50

Migratory Bird Certification Stamps

19	$3 Tundra swan, *1999*	9.00	2.50
20	$3 Buffleheads, *2000*	9.00	2.50
21	$3 Mallards, *2001*	9.00	2.50
22	$3 Canvasbacks, *2002*	9.00	2.50
23	$3 Pintails, *2003*	9.00	2.50

2004-07

24	$3 purple	9.00	2.50
25	$5 magenta, *2005*	9.00	2.50
26	$5 brown orange, *2006*	9.00	2.50
27	$5 brown, *2007*	9.00	2.50

Non-resident Waterfowl Stamps

Nos. A1-A7, A9 have serial No. in red. Nos. A1-A18 issued in booklet panes of 5. Type faces and designs of Nos. A1-A18 vary.

Unused values are for unpunched stamps. Used values are for signed and punched stamps.

Illustration reduced.

1970-86

A1	$30 black, *pink*	20.00	
a.	Missing serial number	*6,500.*	
A2	$30 black, *pink, 1971*	9.00	
a.	Overprinted "3"		*350.00*
A3	$30 black, *1972*	3.75	
A4	$30 black, *blue, 1973*	8.00	
a.	Overprinted "2"	*2,950.*	
A5	$30 black, *green, 1974*	5.50	
a.	Overprinted "1"	*25.00*	
b.	Overprinted "2"	*30.00*	
c.	Overprinted "4"	*30.00*	
A6	$30 black, *yellow, 1975*	6.50	
a.	Overprinted "UNIT 1"	*45.00*	
b.	Overprinted "UNIT 4"	*35.00*	
c.	Overprinted "UNIT 3"		—
A7	$30 black, *yellow, 1976*	5.00	
a.	Overprinted "1"	18.00	
b.	Overprinted "2"	30.00	*20.00*
c.	Serial No. 4mm high	*18.00*	
d.	As "c," overprinted "1"	*35.00*	
e.	As "c," overprinted "2"	*85.00*	
A8	$30 black, *red, 1977*	7.00	
a.	Overprinted "1"	*20.00*	
b.	Overprinted "2"	*30.00*	
c.	Overprinted "3"	*35.00*	
d.	Overprinted "4"	*30.00*	
e.	Overprinted "5"	*200.00*	
A9	$30 black, *yellow, 1978*	7.00	
a.	Overprinted "1" and 3 strikes of "UNIT 2"	*150.00*	
b.	Overprinted "1"	*175.00*	
A10	$30 black, *red, 1979*	2.50	
A11	$30 black, *light manila, 1980*	4.50	
a.	Overprinted "1"	6.00	
b.	Overprinted "2"	10.00	
A12	$30 black, *light yellow, 1981*	4.50	
a.	Overprinted "UNIT 1"	6.00	
b.	Overprinted "UNIT 2"	10.00	5.00
A13	$30 black, *blue, 1982*	6.50	
A14	$50 black, *dark yellow, 1982*	7.00	
a.	Overprinted "UNIT 2"		—
A15	$50 black, *red, 1983*	8.00	
a.	Overprinted "AREA 1"	*50.00*	
b.	Overprinted "AREA 2"	*65.00*	
c.	Serial No. with serifs	*650.00*	
A16	$50 black, *light manila, 1984*	16.00	
a.	Overprinted "A"	*325.00*	
b.	Overprinted "B"	*125.00*	
A17	$50 black, *red, 1985*	*3,500.*	*750.00*
A18	$50 black, *1986*	*9.00*	5.00

Bennett County Canada Goose Stamps

Type faces and designs vary. Nos. 2A1-2A2 imperf. Nos. 2A3-2A12 printed in booklet panes of 5, perforated horizontally. Some show vertical perforations.

Nos. 2A1-2A4 were free. No. 2A5 cost $5. Stamps were issued to hunters by means of a drawing.

Used values are for signed stamps.

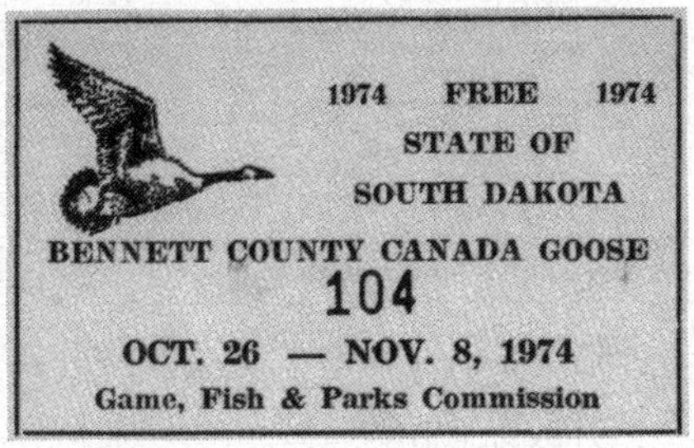

Illustration reduced.

1974-78

2A1	black	75.00	35.00
2A2	black, *pink, 1975*	*250.00*	

2A3	black, *blue, 1976*	47.50	25.00
2A4	black, *yellow, 1977*	42.50	25.00
2A5	black, *greenish blue, 1978*	*750.00*	

West River Unit Canada Goose

Counties handstamped.

Used values are for signed stamps.

1979

2A6	$2 black, *yellow*	*450.00*	
a.	Bennett County	*650.00*	275.00
b.	Haakon County	*275.00*	
c.	Jackson County	*275.00*	
d.	Pennington County	*225.00*	100.00

Stamps overprinted for Perkins County exist but may not have been regularly issued.

1980

2A7	$2 black, *blue*	75.00	
a.	Bennett County	200.00	*75.00*
b.	Haakon County	100.00	
c.	Jackson County	110.00	
d.	As "c," missing serial number	*7,500.*	
e.	Pennington County	90.00	*45.00*
f.	Perkins County	110.00	

Prairie Canada Geese

Counties or Units handstamped.

Used values are for signed stamps.

1981

Perf. 12

2A8	$2 black, *red*	8.00	
a.	Bennett County	80.00	*35.00*
b.	Haakon County	60.00	*20.00*
c.	Jackson County	60.00	*20.00*
d.	Pennington County	60.00	
e.	Perkins County	60.00	

1982

2A9	$2 black, *blue*	125.00	
a.	Bennett County	*950.00*	*350.00*
b.	Haakon County	*650.00*	
c.	Jackson County	*650.00*	
d.	Pennington County	*650.00*	
e.	Perkins County	*650.00*	

1983

Perf. 12

2A10	$2 black, *yellow*	60.00	
a.	UNIT 2A	70.00	
b.	UNIT 31	70.00	*35.00*
c.	UNIT 39	70.00	*35.00*
d.	UNIT 49	70.00	*35.00*
e.	UNIT 53	70.00	*35.00*
f.	UNIT 11, 3mm type	100.00	*50.00*
g.	UNIT 23	100.00	

Rouletted top and bottom

2A11	$2 black, *yellow*	11.00	
a.	UNIT 2A	65.00	
b.	UNIT 6	45.00	
c.	UNIT 11, 3mm type	60.00	
d.	UNIT 11, 4½mm type	45.00	
e.	UNIT 23	45.00	
f.	UNIT 31	65.00	
g.	UNIT 32	45.00	
h.	UNIT 39	65.00	
i.	UNIT 42	45.00	
j.	UNIT 49	65.00	
k.	UNIT 53, 3mm type	45.00	
l.	UNIT 53, 4½mm type	50.00	

1984

Perf. 12

2A12	$2 black, *green*	45.00	
a.	UNIT 6	75.00	
b.	UNIT 11, 3mm type	85.00	
c.	UNIT 11, 4½mm type	75.00	
d.	UNIT 23, 3mm type	85.00	
e.	UNIT 23, 4½mm type	75.00	*30.00*
f.	UNIT 32	85.00	
g.	UNIT 42	75.00	
h.	UNIT 47, 3mm type	85.00	
i.	UNIT 53, 3mm type	75.00	
j.	UNIT 47, 4½mm type		*65.00*
k.	UNIT 53, 4½mm type		*65.00*

1985

Rouletted two adjacent sides

2A13	$2 black, *red*		
a.	UNIT 47		*100.00*
b.	UNIT 53		*100.00*
c.	UNIT 23		*125.00*
d.	UNIT 32		*175.00*
e.	UNIT 42		*125.00*
f.	UNIT 11		*175.00*

1986

No fee printed on stamp

Imperf. on 3 sides, rouletted at top

2A14	black		
a.	UNIT 11		*110.00*
b.	UNIT 47		*110.00*
c.	UNIT 53		*110.00*
d.	UNIT 23		*150.00*

105 stamps for hunting whistling swans during the 1984 season exist. The season was canceled. Value, unused $375.

Pheasant Restoration Stamps

Required to hunt all small game, including waterfowl. Printed in booklet panes of 5. No. 3A4 rouletted, others perforated. Stamps are numbered serially.

Catalogue values for all unused stamps in this section, from this point to the end of the Wildlife Habitat stamps, are for Never Hinged items.

1977-88

3A1	$5 Pheasants	13.00	2.50
a.	Rubber-stamped serial number		—
3A2	$5 Pheasants, *1978*	13.00	1.50
3A3	$5 Pheasants, *1979*	13.00	1.50
3A4	$5 Pheasants, *1980*	13.00	2.00
a.	Serial number omitted	—	
3A5	$5 Pheasants, *1981*	13.00	1.50
3A6	$5 Pheasants, *1982*	13.00	1.50
a.	Pair, imperf. between	—	
3A7	$5 Pheasant, *1983*	13.00	1.00
3A8	$5 Pheasant, *1984*	13.00	2.00
3A9	$5 Pheasant, *1985*	13.00	2.00
3A10	$5 Pheasants, *1986*	13.00	2.50
3A11	$5 Pheasants, *1987*	15.00	2.00
3A12	$5 Pheasants, *1988*	13.00	2.00

Wildlife Habitat Stamps

Required to hunt all small game, including waterfowl. Printed in booklet panes of 5. Starting with No. 3A18 stamps are rouletted, others are perforated. Stamps are numbered serially.

1989-99

3A13	$8 Pheasants	13.00	2.00
3A14	$8 White-tailed deer, *1990*	13.00	2.00
3A15	$8 Greater prairie chicken, *1991*	13.00	2.00
3A16	$8 Mule Deer, *1992*	13.00	2.50
3A17	$8 Sharp-tailed grouse, *1993*	13.00	2.00
a.	Pair, imperf. between	—	
3A18	$8 Turkey, *1994*	13.00	2.00
3A19	$8 Elk, *1995*	13.00	2.00
3A20	$8 Pheasants, *1996*	13.00	2.00
3A21	$8 Antelope, *1997*	13.00	2.00
3A22	$8 Buffalo, *1998*	13.00	2.00
3A23	$8 Buffalo, *1999*	13.00	2.00

Resident Small Game Stamps

Required by residents wishing to hunt small game, including waterfowl. Nos. 4A1, 4A2 issued panes of 10. Others issued in booklet panes of 5. Stamps are numbered serially in red from 1960 to 1967 and 1978. Non-resident small game stamps were not required for hunting.

Catalogue values for all unused stamps in this section are for Never Hinged items.

1960-79

4A1	$2 black, *pink*	12.00	2.00
4A2	$2 black, *blue, 1961*	25.00	3.00
4A3	$2 black, *dark yellow, 1962*	35.00	3.00
4A4	$2 black, *light yellow, 1963*	25.00	3.00
4A5	$2 black, *green, 1964*	25.00	3.00
4A6	$2 black, *1965*	25.00	3.00
4A7	$2 black, *yellow, 1966*	10.00	2.00
4A8	$2 black, *light green, 1967*	25.00	2.00
4A9	$2 black, *light yellow, 1968*	10.00	2.00
4A10	$3 black, *blue, 1969*	25.00	2.00
4A11	$3 black, *light yellow, 1970*	10.00	2.00
4A12	$3 black, *green, 1971*		3.00
4A13	$3 black, *light yellow, 1972*	10.00	2.00
4A14	$3 black, *light yellow, 1973*	9.00	2.00
4A15	$3 black, *1974*	10.00	2.00
4A16	$3 black, *pink, 1975*	8.00	2.00
4A17	$3 black, *gray, 1976*	6.00	1.00
4A18	$3 black, *red, 1977*	5.00	1.00
4A19	$3 black, *1978*	6.00	1.00
4A20	$3 black, *red, 1979*	7.00	1.00

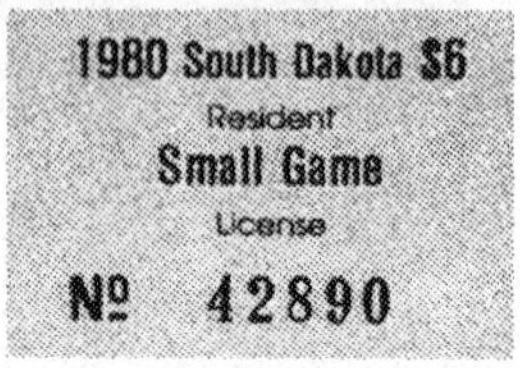

1980-98

4A21	$6 black	8.00	1.00
4A22	$6 black, *light yellow, 1981*	9.00	1.00
4A23	$6 black, *blue, 1982*	5.00	.50
4A24	$6 black, *green, 1983*	10.00	1.00
4A25	$6 black, *light blue, 1984*	*20.00*	1.00
4A26	$6 black, *light blue, 1985*	12.00	1.00
4A27	$6 black, *light blue green, 1986*		2.00
4A28	$6 black, *1987*		2.00
4A29	$6 black, *light green, 1988*	5.00	.50
4A30	$6 black, *1989*		1.00
4A31	$6 black, *light green, 1990*	8.00	.50
4A32	$6 black, *light blue green, 1991*	5.00	.50
4A33	$6 black, *light green, 1992*		1.00
4A34	$6 black, *light pink, 1993*	5.00	.50
4A35	$6 black, *light blue, 1994*	5.00	.50
4A36	$6 black, *yellow, 1995*		1.00
4A37	$6 black, *pink, 1996*	5.00	.50
4A38	$6 black, *light blue, 1997*		.50
4A39	$6 black, *pink, 1998*	8.00	.50

TENNESSEE

Stamps are die cut self-adhesives and are numbered serially.

Cards include both license cost and a fee of 30c (Nos. 1-5), 50c (Nos. 6-13) or $1 (starting with No. 14).

Nos. 3, 5, 7-15 come as 3-part card.

Starting with No. 12, cards come in four parts as well.

1979 and 1980 issues are for resident and non-resident fees.

Unused values are for stamps on original computer card stub.

Catalogue values for all unused stamps in this section are for Never Hinged items.

Artists: Dick Elliott, #1-2; Phillip Crowe, #3-4, 7, 17; Bob Gillespie, #5; Ken Schulz, #6; Allen Hughes, #8; Jimmy Stewart, #9; Ralph J. McDonald, #10, 18; Thomas Hirata, #11, 16; Jim Lamb, #12; Roger Cruwys, #13; Tom Freeman, #14; Richard Clifton, #15, 19; Bob Leslie, #20; Bethany Carter, #21; Beth Ann McMurray, #22; Nick Williamson, #23, 24.; J. Mefford, #25; Joshua Lester, #26-27; Lauren Pollard, #28; Kaydee Hankes, #29.

1979-2007

1	$2 Mallards	140.00	25.00
2	$5 Mallards	*750.00*	*150.00*
3	$2 Canvasbacks, *1980*	60.00	15.00
	3-part card	725.00	
4	$5 Canvasbacks, *1980*	*300.00*	75.00
5	$2 Wood ducks, *1981*	45.00	10.00
	3-part card	—	
6	$6 Canada geese, *1982*	55.00	15.00
7	$6 Pintails, *1983*	50.00	15.00
	3-part card	75.00	
8	$6 Black ducks, *1984*	50.00	12.00
	3-part card	75.00	
9	$6 Blue-winged teal, *1985*	20.00	7.00
	3-part card	50.00	
10	$6 Mallard, *1986*	15.00	5.00
	3-part card	60.00	
11	$6 Canada geese, *1987*	12.00	5.00
	3-part card	25.00	

Card exists with 2/28/88 expiration date rather than correct 2/29 date.

12	$6 Canvasbacks, *1988*	12.00	4.00
	3-part card	20.00	
	4-part card	20.00	
13	$6 Green-winged teal, *1989*	12.00	4.00
	3-part card	20.00	
	4-part card	20.00	
14	$12 Redheads, *1990*	18.00	4.00
	3-part card	25.00	
	4-part card	25.00	
15	$12 Mergansers, *1991*	18.00	4.00
	3-part card	22.00	
	4-part card	22.00	
16	$13 Wood ducks, *1992*	18.00	4.00
	4-part card	22.00	
17	$13 Pintails & decoy, *1993*	20.00	4.00
	4-part card	25.00	
18	$15 Mallard, *1994*	25.00	5.00
	4-part card	30.00	
19	$16 Ring-necked duck, *1995*	25.00	5.00
	4-part card	30.00	
20	$17 Black ducks, *1996*	35.00	5.00
	4-part card	40.00	

Starting with No. 21 stamps are perforated. Not required for hunting.

21	$10 Mallard, *1999*	15.00	2.50
22	$10 Bufflehead, *2000*	15.00	2.50
23	$10 Wood ducks, *2001*	15.00	2.50
24	$10 Green-winged teal, *2002*	13.50	2.50
25	$10 Canada geese, *2003*	13.50	2.50
26	$10 Wood ducks, *2004*	13.50	2.50
27	$10 Mallards, *2005*	13.50	2.50
28	$10 Canada goose, *2006*	13.50	2.50
29	$10 Harlequin, *2007*	12.00	2.50

TEXAS

Printed in sheets of 10.

Nos. 1-4 are rouletted.

Stamps are numbered serially.

Catalogue values for all unused stamps in this section are for Never Hinged items.

Artists: Larry Hayden, #1, 12; Ken Carlson, #2, 14; Maynard Reece, #3; David Maass, #4, 9, 15, 26; John Cowan, #5, 8; Herb Booth, #6, 25; Gary Moss, #7; Robert Bateman, #10; Daniel Smith, #11, 16; Jim Hautman, #13, 17, 22; Phillip Crowe, #18; Robert Hautman, #19; Sherrie Russell Meline, #20, 23; John Dearman, #21; Scott and Stuart Gentling, #24; Bruce Miller, #27.

1981-2007

1	$5 Mallards	40.00	8.00
2	$5 Pintails, *1982*	25.00	5.00
3	$5 Widgeons, *1983*	140.00	18.00
4	$5 Wood ducks, *1984*	25.00	5.00
5	$5 Snow geese, *1985*	10.00	3.00
6	$5 Green-winged teal, *1986*	10.00	2.50
7	$5 White-fronted geese, *1987*	10.00	2.50
8	$5 Pintails, *1988*	10.00	2.50
9	$5 Mallards, *1989*	10.00	2.50
10	$5 American widgeons, *1990*	10.00	2.50
11	$7 Wood duck, *1991*	11.00	2.50
12	$7 Canada geese, *1992*	11.00	2.50
13	$7 Blue-winged teal, *1993*	11.00	2.50
14	$7 Shovelers, *1994*	11.00	2.50
15	$7 Buffleheads, *1995*	11.00	2.50

Beginning with No. 16, these stamps were sold only in booklets with seven other wildlife stamps and were not valid for hunting.

16	$3 Gadwalls, *1996*	75.00
17	$3 Cinnamon teal, *1997*	65.00
18	$3 Pintail, labrador retreiver, *1998*	55.00
19	$3 Canvasbacks, *1999*	40.00
20	$3 Hooded merganser, *2000*	30.00
21	$3 Snow geese, *2001*	20.00
22	$3 Redheads, *2002*	20.00
23	$3 Mottled duck, *2003*	20.00
24	$3 American goldeneye, *2004*	15.00
25	$7 Mallards, *2005*	15.00
26	$7 Green-winged teals, *2006*	15.00
27	$7 Wood duck, *2007*	13.00

No. 23 was issued in booklets with seven other wildlife stamps and was not valid for hunting.

Nos. 25-27 were issued in booklets with five other wildlife stamps and was not valid for hunting.

UTAH

Game Bird Stamps

For hunting game birds, including waterfowl. In 1951 No. A1 or No. 2A1 were required, in 1952 No. A3 or 2A2. No. A1 printed in booklet panes of 25, others in booklet panes of 10. Perforated.

A1

A2

1951

A1	A1	$3 brown, resident	*35.00*	*7.00*
A2	A1	$15 red, non-resident	*150.00*	50.00

1952

A3	A2	$3 red, resident	*110.00*	
A4	A2	$15 blue, non-resident	*300.00*	*50.00*

Resident Fishing and Hunting Stamps

For hunting game birds, including waterfowl. Printed in sheets of 40. No. 2A1 printed on linen.

Unused values are for stamps with deer tags attached at left.

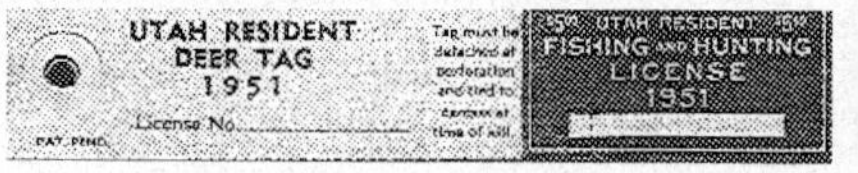

No. 2A1 — UT-2A1

No. 2A2 — UT-2A2

1951-52

2A1	$5 blue	4.50	1.50
2A2	$5 green, *1952*	4.50	1.50

Waterfowl Issues

Printed in sheets of 30 or in booklet panes of 5 (starting in 1990). No. 11 issued in sheets of 9.

Stamps are numbered serially.

Catalogue values for all unused stamps in this section are for Never Hinged items.

Artists: Leon Parsons, #1; Arthur Anderson, #2; David Chapple, #3; Jim Morgan, #4; Daniel Smith, #5; Robert Steiner, #6-12.

1986-97

1	$3.30 Whistling swans	10.00	3.00
2	$3.30 Pintails, *1987*	8.00	3.00
3	$3.30 Mallards, *1988*	8.00	2.50
4	$3.30 Canada geese, *1989*	8.00	2.50
5	$3.30 Canvasbacks, perf. 4 sides, *1990*	8.00	
a.	Booklet single, with 2-part tab	8.00	2.50
6	$3.30 Tundra swans, perf. 4 sides, *1991*	12.00	
a.	Booklet single, with 2-part tab	12.00	2.50
7	$3.30 Pintails, perf. 4 sides, *1992*	10.00	
a.	Booklet single, with 2-part tab	10.00	2.50
8	$3.30 Canvasbacks, perf. 4 sides, *1993*	10.00	
a.	Booklet single, with 2-part tab	10.00	2.50
9	$3.30 Chesapeake Retriever and ducks, perf. 4 sides, *1994*	*85.00*	
a.	Booklet single, with 2-part tab	*85.00*	2.50
10	$3.30 Green-winged teal, *1995*	12.00	
a.	Booklet single, with 2-part tab	12.00	2.50
b.	Governor's edition	130.00	
11	$7.50 White-fronted goose, *1996*	15.00	2.50
a.	$97.50 Governor's edition	125.00	

Redheads: a, Male, serial # at UL. b, Female, serial # at LL.

12	Pair, *1997*	40.00	
a.-b.	$7.50 Any single	14.00	2.50
c.	$97.50 Governor's Edition	110.00	

No. 12c is No. 12 without the central perforations. The denomination appears only in the upper right corner. The bottom inscription has Governor's Edition plus a serial number.

VERMONT

Printed in sheets of 30.

Catalogue values for all unused stamps in this section are for Never Hinged items.

Artists: Jim Killen, #1-4; Richard Plasschaert, #5-8; Reed Prescott, #9, 11; Robert Mullen, #10; J. Collins, #12; George Lockwood, #13-17; Richard E. Bishop, #18-21; Heather Forcier, #22..

1986-2007

1	$5 Wood ducks	12.00	4.00
2	$5 Common goldeneyes, *1987*	12.00	3.00
3	$5 Black ducks, *1988*	12.00	2.50
4	$5 Canada geese, *1989*	12.00	2.50
5	$5 Green-winged teal, *1990*	12.00	2.50
6	$5 Hooded mergansers, *1991*	12.00	2.50
7	$5 Snow geese, *1992*	12.00	2.50
8	$5 Mallards, *1993*	12.00	2.50
9	$5 Ring-necked duck, *1994*	12.00	2.50
10	$5 Bufflehead, *1995*	12.00	2.50
11	$5 Lesser scaup, *1996*	12.00	2.50
12	$5 Pintails, *1997*	12.00	2.50
13	$5 Blue-winged teal, *1998*	12.00	2.50
14	$5 Canvasbacks, *1999*	12.00	2.50
15	$5 Widgeons, *2000*	10.00	2.50
16	$5 Oldsquaws, *2001*	10.00	2.50
17	$5 Greater scaups, *2002*	10.00	2.50
18	$5 Mallards, *2003*	10.00	2.50
19	$5 Pintails, *2004*	10.00	2.50
20	$5 Canvasbacks, *2005*	10.00	2.50
21	$5 Canada goose, *2006*	10.00	2.50
22	$5 Ring-necked duck, *2007*	7.00	2.50

VIRGINIA

Printed in booklet panes of 10 and/or sheets of 30. Stamps are numbered serially.

Catalogue values for all unused stamps in this section are for Never Hinged items.

Artists: Ronald Louque, #1; Arthur LeMay, #2; Louis Frisino, #3; Robert Leslie, #4, 11; Carl Knuth, #5, 12, 17; Bruce Miller, #6; Francis Sweet, #7; Richard Clifton, #8; Wilhelm Goebel, #9; Roger Cruwys, #10; Tim Donovan, #13-14, 21-22; Jim Wilson, #15-16; Guy Crittenden, #18-20, 23-24.

1988-2007

1	$5 Mallards, serial Nos. 1-40,000	13.00	2.50
	Booklet pair with L & R selvage, serial Nos. above 40,000	27.50	
2	$5 Canada geese, serial Nos. 1-40,000, *1989*	12.00	2.50
	Booklet pair with L & R selvage, serial Nos. above 40,000	25.00	
3	$5 Wood ducks, serial Nos. 1-20,000, *1990*	12.00	2.50
	Booklet pair with L & R selvage, serial Nos. above 20,000	24.00	
4	$5 Canvasbacks, serial Nos. 1-20,000, *1991*	12.00	2.50
	Booklet pair with L & R selvage, serial Nos. above 20,000	24.00	
5	$5 Buffleheads, serial Nos. 1-20,000, *1992*	12.00	2.50
	Booklet pair with L & R selvage, serial Nos. above 20,000	24.00	
6	$5 Black ducks, serial Nos. 1-20,000, *1993*	12.00	2.50
	Booklet pair with L & R selvage, serial Nos. above 20,000	24.00	
7	$5 Lesser scaup, *1994*	12.00	2.50
	Booklet pair with L & R selvage	24.00	
8	$5 Snow geese, *1995*	12.00	2.50
	Booklet pair with L & R selvage	24.00	
9	$5 Hooded mergansers, *1996*	12.00	2.50
10	($5) Pintail, Labrador retriever, *1997*	12.00	2.50
11	$5 Mallards, *1998*	12.00	2.50
12	$5 Green-winged teal, *1999*	12.00	2.50
13	$5 Mallards, *2000*	12.00	2.50
14	$5 Blue-winged teal, *2001*	10.00	2.50
15	$5 Canvasbacks, *2002*	10.00	2.50
16	$5 Tundra Swan, *2003*	10.00	2.50
17	$5 American goldeneye, *2004*	10.00	2.50
18	$9.75 Wood ducks, perf. *2005*	13.00	2.50
19	$9.75 Wood ducks, rouletted, with tab *2005*	13.00	2.50
20	$9.75 Wood ducks, self-adhesive, die cut *2005*	14.00	2.50
21	$9.75 Black ducks, perf. *2006*	13.00	2.50
22	$9.75 Black ducks, self-adhesive, die cut *2006*	14.00	2.50
23	$10 Canada geese, perf. *2007*	13.50	2.50
24	$10 Canada geese, self-adhesive, die cut *2007*	13.50	2.50

Starting with 2005, Virginia stamps are mandatory for hunting.

WASHINGTON

Printed in booklet panes of 1 and sheets of 30. Stamps are numbered serially. Booklet panes starting with No. 7 without staple holes were sold to collectors.

Catalogue values for all unused stamps in this section are for Never Hinged items.

Artists: Keith Warrick, #1; Ray Nichol, #2; Robert Bateman, #3; Maynard Reece, #4; Thomas Quinn, #5; Ronald Louque, #6-7; Phillip Crowe, #8; Fred Thomas, #9; David Hagenbaumer, #10; Cynthie Fisher, #11; Greg Beecham, #12; A. Young, #13; Robert Steiner, #14-16, 22-23; Adam Grimm, #17; Don Nicholson Miller, #18-19; Dan Smith, #20-21.

1986-2007

1	$5 Mallards, Nos. 1-60,000	9.00	
	Booklet pane of 1, Nos. 60,001-160,000	12.50	4.00
2	$5 Canvasbacks, Nos. 1-24,000, *1987*	12.00	
	Booklet pane of 1, Nos. 24,001-124,000	12.00	3.00
3	$5 Harlequin, Nos. 1-60,000, *1988*	9.00	
	Booklet pane of 1, Nos. 60,001-160,000	10.00	3.00
4	$5 American widgeons, Nos. 1-60,000, *1989*	9.00	
	Booklet pane of 1, Nos. 60,001-160,000	10.00	2.50
5	$5 Pintails & sour duck, Nos. 1-60,000, *1990*	9.00	
	Booklet pane of 1, Nos. 60,001-160,000	10.00	2.50
6	$5 Wood duck, Nos. 1-30,000, *1991*	12.00	
	Booklet pane of 1, Nos. above 30,000	12.00	4.00
7	$6 Wood duck, Nos. 100,000-130,000, *1991*	10.00	
	Booklet pane of 1, Nos. above 130,000	10.00	2.50
8	$6 Labrador puppy & Canada geese, Nos. 1-30,000, *1992*	14.00	
	Booklet pane of 1, Nos. above 30,000	14.00	2.50
9	$6 Snow geese, Nos. 1-30,000, *1993*	10.00	
	Booklet pane of 1, Nos. above 30,000	10.00	2.50
10	$6 Black brant, Nos. 1-30,000, *1994*	14.00	
	Booklet pane of 1, Nos. above 30,000	14.00	2.50
11	$6 Mallards, Nos. 1-30,000, *1995*	12.00	
	Booklet pane of 1, Nos. above 30,000	12.00	2.50
12	$6 Redheads, Nos. 1-25,050, *1996*	22.50	
	Booklet pane of 1, Nos. above 25,050	22.50	2.50
13	$6 Canada geese, Nos. 9600001-9625050, *1997*	12.00	
	Bklt. pane of 1, Nos. above 9625050	12.00	2.50
14	$6 Barrow's goldeneye Nos. 1-25,050, *1998*	15.00	
	Bklt. pane of 1, Nos. 25,051-27,050	15.00	2.50
15	$6 Bufflehead, *1999*	15.00	
a.	Bklt. pane of 1	15.00	2.50
16	$6 Canada geese, mallard, widgeon, *2000*	25.00	
a.	Bklt. pane of 1	25.00	2.50
17	$6 Mallards, *2001*	15.00	
a.	Bklt. pane of 1	15.00	2.50
18	$10 Green-winged teal, *2002*	17.50	
a.	Souvenir sheet of 1	17.50	2.50
19	$10 Pintails, *2003*	20.00	
a.	Souvenir sheet of 1	20.00	2.50
20	$10 Canada goose, *2004*	15.00	
a.	Souvenir sheet of 1	15.00	2.50
21	$10 Barrow's goldeneyes, *2005*	15.00	
a.	Souvenir sheet of 1	15.00	2.50
22	$10 Widgeons, mallard, *2006*	14.00	
a.	Souvenir sheet of 1	15.00	2.50
23	$10 Ross's goose, *2007*	13.50	
a.	Souvenir sheet of 1	15.00	2.50

Nos. 19-23 not required for hunting.

WEST VIRGINIA

Printed in sheets of 30 and booklet panes of 5. All booklet stamps have straight edges at sides. Starting in 1990, booklet stamps are numbered serially. Some, but not all, of the 1988 booklet stamps are numbered serially. Stamps from sheets are not numbered serially.

Catalogue values for all unused stamps in this section are for Never Hinged items.

Artists: Daniel Smith, #1-2; Steven Dillard, #3-4; Ronald Louque, #5-6; Louis Frisino, #7-8; Robert Leslie, #9-10; Thomas Hirata, #11-12; Phillip Crowe, #13-14; Richard Clifton, #15-16; Fran Sweet, #17-18; Karl Badgley, #19-20.

1987-96

1	$5 Canada geese, resident	17.50	8.00
	Booklet single with tab at top	75.00	
2	$5 Canada geese, non-resident	16.00	8.00
	Booklet single with tab at top	75.00	
3	$5 Wood ducks, resident, *1988*	10.00	4.00
	Booklet single with tab at top, no serial number	40.00	
a.	Booklet single with serial number on reverse	60.00	4.00
4	$5 Wood ducks, non-resident, *1988*	12.00	4.00
	Booklet single with tab at top, no serial number	40.00	
a.	Booklet single with serial number on reverse	60.00	4.00
5	$5 Decoys, resident, *1989*	13.00	3.00
	Booklet single with tab at top	35.00	
a.	Governor's edition	*80.00*	
6	$5 Decoys, non-resident, *1989*	18.00	3.00
	Booklet single with tab at top	35.00	
a.	Governor's edition	*80.00*	

Nos. 5a and 6a were available only in sheets of 30 through a sealed bid auction.

7	$5 Labrador retriever & decoy, resident, *1990*	20.00	
a.	Booklet single	15.00	3.00
8	$5 Labrador retriever & decoy, non-resident, *1990*	22.00	
a.	Booklet single	15.00	3.00
9	$5 Mallards, resident, *1991*	12.00	
a.	Booklet single	12.00	2.50
10	$5 Mallards, non-resident, *1991*	12.00	
a.	Booklet single	12.00	2.50
b.	Sheet, 3 each #9-10	50.00	

No. 10b is numbered serially; exists imperf. without serial numbers.

11	$5 Canada geese, resident, *1992*	12.00	
a.	Booklet single	12.00	2.50
12	$5 Canada geese, non-resident, *1992*	12.00	
a.	Booklet single	12.00	2.50
13	$5 Pintails, resident, *1993*	12.00	
a.	Booklet single	12.00	2.50
14	$5 Pintails, non-resident, *1993*	12.00	
a.	Booklet single	12.00	2.50
15	$5 Green-winged teal, resident, *1994*	12.00	
a.	Booklet single	12.00	2.50
16	$5 Green-winged teal, non-resident, *1994*	12.00	
a.	Booklet single	12.00	2.50
17	$5 Mallards, resident, *1995*	12.00	
a.	Booklet single	12.00	2.50
18	$5 Mallards, non-resident, *1995*	12.00	
a.	Booklet single	12.00	2.50
19	$5 Widgeons, resident, *1996*	12.00	
a.	Booklet single	12.00	2.50
20	$5 Widgeons, non-resident, *1996*	12.00	
a.	Booklet single	12.00	2.50

WISCONSIN

Printed in sheets of 10. Starting in 1980 the left side of the sheet has an agent tab and a numbered tab, the right side a numbered tab.

Catalogue values for all unused stamps in this section are for Never Hinged items.

Artists: Owen Gromme, #1; Rockne (Rocky) Knuth, #2, 6; Martin Murk, #3; Timothy Schultz, #4, 29; William Koelpin, #5; Michael James Riddet, #7, 15, 26; Greg Alexander, #8, 20; Don Moore, #9, 17, 23; Al Kraayvanger, #10; Richard Timm, #11; Rick Kelley, #12; Daniel Renn Pierce, #13; Terry Doughty, #14, 25, 28; Frank Middlestadt, #16, 22; Les Didler, #18, 21, 24; Sam Timm, #19; Arthur Anderson, #27, 30.

1978-2007

1	$3.25 Wood ducks	100.00	9.00
2	$3.25 Buffleheads, rouletted, *1979*	20.00	6.00
3	$3.25 Widgeons, *1980*	12.00	2.50
	With tab	15.00	
4	$3.25 Lesser Scaup, *1981*	10.00	2.50
	With tab	13.00	
5	$3.25 Pintails, *1982*	9.00	2.50
	With numbered tab	9.00	
	With agent's and numbered tab	10.00	
6	$3.25 Blue-winged teal, *1983*	9.00	2.50
	With numbered tab	9.00	
	With agent's and numbered tab	10.00	
7	$3.25 Hooded merganser, *1984*	9.00	2.50
	With numbered tab	9.00	
	With agent's and numbered tab	10.00	
8	$3.25 Lesser scaup, *1985*	12.00	2.50
	With numbered tab	12.00	
	With agent's and numbered tab	15.00	
9	$3.25 Canvasbacks, *1986*	15.00	2.50
	With numbered tab	15.00	
	With agent's and numbered tab	21.00	
10	$3.25 Canada geese, *1987*	9.00	2.50
	With numbered tab	9.00	
	With agent's and numbered tab	10.00	
11	$3.25 Hooded merganser, *1988*	9.00	2.50
	With numbered tab	9.00	
	With agent's and numbered tab	10.00	
12	$3.25 Common goldeneye, *1989*	9.00	2.50
	With numbered tab	9.00	
	With agent's and numbered tab	10.00	
13	$3.25 Redheads, *1990*	9.00	2.50
	With numbered tab	9.00	
	With agent's and numbered tab	10.00	
14	$5.25 Green-winged teal, *1991*	9.00	2.50
	With numbered tab	9.00	
	With agent's and numbered tab	10.00	
15	$5.25 Tundra swans, *1992*	10.00	2.50
	With numbered tab	10.00	
	With agent's and numbered tab	12.00	
16	$5.25 Wood ducks, *1993*	10.00	2.50
	With numbered tab	10.00	
	With agent's and numbered tab	12.00	
17	$5.25 Pintails, *1994*	10.00	2.50
	With numbered tab	10.00	
	With agent's and numbered tabs	12.00	
18	$5.25 Mallards, *1995*	10.00	2.50
	With numbered tab	10.00	
	With agent's and numbered tabs	12.00	
19	($5.25) Green-winged teal, *1996*	10.00	2.50
	With numbered tab	10.00	
	With agent's and numbered tabs	12.00	
20	($7) Canada geese, *1997*	15.00	2.50
	With numbered tab	15.00	
	With agent's and numbered tabs	17.00	
21	$7 Snow goose, *1998*	15.00	2.50
	With numbered tab	15.00	
	With agent's and numbered tabs	17.00	
22	$7 Greater scaups, *1999*	12.00	2.50
23	$7 Canvasbacks, *2000*	12.00	2.50
24	$7 Common goldeneyes, *2001*	14.00	2.50
25	$7 Shovelers, *2002*	11.00	2.50
26	$7 Ring-necked ducks, *2003*	11.00	2.50
27	$7 Pintail, *2004*	11.00	2.50
28	$7 Wood ducks, *2005*	11.00	2.50
29	$7 Green-winged teals, *2006*	9.00	2.50
30	$7 Redheads, *2007*	9.00	2.50

Nos. 26-30 not required for hunting.

WYOMING

Issued in panes of 5. Required to fish as well as to hunt all small and big game, including waterfowl. Stamps are numbered serially.

Catalogue values for all unused stamps in this section are for Never Hinged items.

Artists: From photo by Luroy Parker, #1; Robert Kusserow #2; Dan Andrews, #3; Ted Feeley, #4; Clark Ostergaard, #5 Dave Wade, #6, 8, 10, 13, 17; Connie J. Robinson, #7; Sarah Rogers, #9; James Brooks, #11; Peter Eades, #12; D. Enright #14; Garth Hegeson, #15; Nick Reitzel, #16; Brent Todd, #18 Paul Kay, #19; R. Piskorski, #20; Dustin Van Wechel, #21; Ror Staker, #22; Scott Greenig, #23; Art Biro, #24.

No. 1 is in vertical format. All others are horizontal.

1984-2007

1	$5 Meadowlark	60.00	6.00
2	$5 Canada geese, *1985*	50.00	5.00
3	$5 Antelope, *1986*	90.00	8.00
4	$5 Grouse, *1987*	85.00	8.00
5	$5 Trout, *1988*	100.00	12.00
6	$5 Mule deer, *1989*	175.00	15.00
7	$5 Bear, *1990*	50.00	5.00
8	$5 Rams, *1991*	45.00	3.50
9	$5 Bald eagle, *1992*	35.00	3.50
10	$5 Elk, *1993*	25.00	3.50
11	$5 Bobcat, *1994*	22.00	3.50
12	$5 Moose, *1995*	22.00	3.50
13	$5 Turkey, *1996*	22.00	3.00
14	$5 Mountain goats, *1997*	22.00	3.00
15	$5 Trumpeter swan, *1998*	20.00	3.00
16	$5 Brown trout, *1999*	20.00	3.00
17	$5 Buffalo, *2000*	20.00	3.00
18	$10 White-tailed deer, *2001*	20.00	5.00
19	$10 River otters, *2002*	20.00	5.00
20	$10 Mountain bluebirds, *2003*	17.50	5.00
21	$10 Mountain lion, *2004*	16.00	5.00
22	$10.50 Burrowing owls, *2005*	16.00	5.00
23	$10.50 Cut-throat trout, *2006*	16.00	5.00
24	$10.50 Blue grouses, *2007*	20.00	5.00

INDIAN RESERVATIONS

Stamps for other reservations exist and will be listed after more information is received about them.

CHEYENNE RIVER INDIAN RESERVATION

South Dakota
Birds and Small Game Stamps

Nos. A1-A2 issued in booklet panes of 6, rouletted. Nos. A3-A4 issued in booklet panes of 5, perforated, self-adhesive. Nos. A5-A6 issued in booklet panes of 5, perforated.

A1

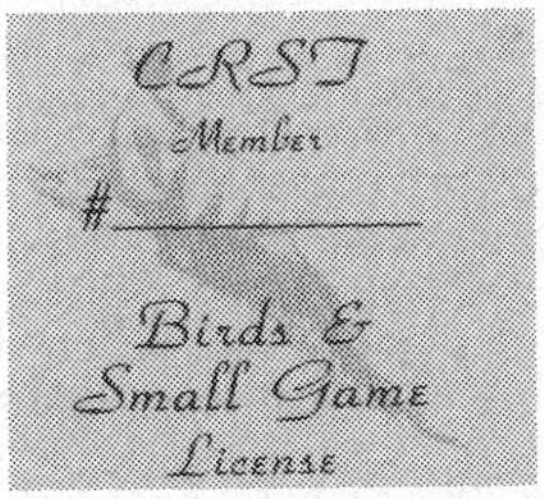

A2

A1	A1	black, *light yellow,* member	*3,500.*	*350.*
A2	A1	black, *yellow,* non-member	*1,250.*	*150.00*

Nos. A1-A2 probably issued starting in 1984.

Catalogue values for all unused stamps in this section, from this point to the end, are for Never Hinged items.

A3	A2	black, *yellow,* member	25.00	10.00
A4	A2	black, *yellow,* non-member	45.00	15.00
A5	A2	black, *light yellow,* member	13.00	5.00
A6	A2	black, *light yellow,* non-member	27.50	10.00

Nos. A3-A4 issued starting in 1989. Nos. A5-A6 issued starting in 1992.

Waterfowl Stamps

Issued starting in 1993 in panes of 5. Perforated.

Catalogue values for all unused stamps in this section are for Never Hinged items.

1	black, *light yellow,* member	15.00	5.00
2	black *light yellow,* non-member	27.50	10.00

COLVILLE INDIAN RESERVATION

Washington
Bird Stamps

Required by non-tribal members to hunt birds, including waterfowl. Stamps are die cut, self-adhesive. No. 2 is numbered serially in red.

Catalogue values for all unused stamps in this section are for Never Hinged items.

A1

A2

1990-91

1	A1		black, *yellow*	—
2	A2	$20	black, *yellow, 1992*	—

CROW INDIAN RESERVATION

Montana
Waterfowl Stamps

Issued in panes of 5 stamps (4 each No. 1, 1 No. 1a). Die cut, self-adhesive. Numbered serially in red.

Catalogue values for all unused stamps in this section are for Never Hinged items.

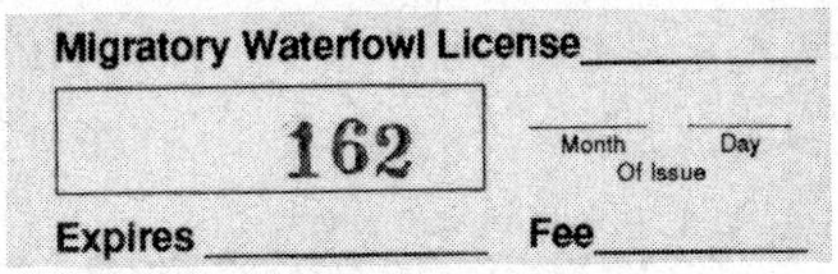

1992

1	blue	*110.00*	*40.00*
a.	Inscribed "Apr. 30, 199_"	*300.00*	*75.00*

Stamps without serial numbers exist. Some may have been issue to hunters during an abbreviated 1993 season.

CROW CREEK SIOUX INDIAN RESERVATION

South Dakota
Non-Indian Small Game Hunting Stamps

Issued 1961-64. The 1961 fee was $2.50. No example is recorded. The 1962 stamps were changed by hand for use in 1963 and 1964. No example of the 1964 stamp is recorded.

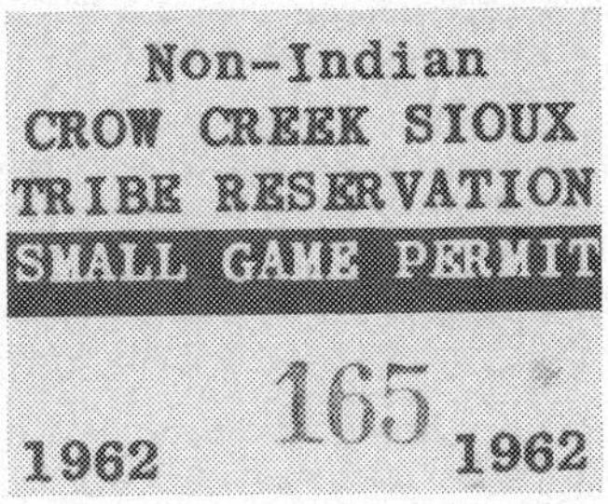

1962-63

2	$5 black	*22,500.*	—
3	$5 black, *1963*	—	—

Waterfowl Stamps

Fees: $10, reservation resident, non-tribal member; $30, South Dakota resident; $65, non-South Dakota resident.

Catalogue values for all unused stamps in this section, from this point to the end, are for Never Hinged items.

	1989		
5	$10 black	400.	*150.*
6	$30 black	*9,000.*	*1,000.*
7	$65 black	*1,250.*	*350.*
	1990		
8	$10 black	250.	*100.*
9	$30 black	150.	
10	$65 black	850.	*300.*

Fees: $5, tribal member; $15, affiliate, reservation resident; $30 ($35), South Dakota resident/non-resident daily use; $75 ($100), South Dakota resident/non-resident season.

1994

11	$5 green	95.00	15.00
12	$15 blue	125.00	
13	$30 red	150.00	
a.	$25 red (error)	—	
14	$75 red	225.00	65.00

1995

15	$5 green	50.00	10.00
16	$15 blue	75.00	
17	$30 red	110.00	
18	$75 red	125.00	40.00

1996

19	$5 green	27.50	10.00
20	$15 blue	45.00	
21	$35 red	75.00	
22	$100 red	125.00	35.00

1997

23	$5 green	12.00	
24	$15 blue	35.00	
25	$35 red	85.00	
26	$75 red	190.00	

No. 25 is inscribed $75, but sold for $35.

1998

27	$5 green	12.00	
28	$15 blue	35.00	
29	$35 red	85.00	
30	$75 red	190.00	

1999

31	$5 green	12.00	
32	$15 blue	35.00	
33	$35 red	85.00	
34	$75 red	190.00	

Waterfowl Stamps

Fees: $5, tribal member; $15, $20, $30, affiliate; $35, $40, non-resident daily use; $75, $100, non-resident season.

2000

35	$5 green	*75.00*	—
36	$15 blue	*75.00*	—
37	$35 red	*75.00*	—
38	$75 red	*75.00*	—

2001

39	$5 green	*100.00*	—
40	$20 blue	*100.00*	—
41	$40 red	*100.00*	—
42	$100 red	*100.00*	—

2002

43	$5 green	*125.00*	—
44	$20 blue	*125.00*	—
45	$40 red	*125.00*	—
46	$100 red	*125.00*	—

2003

47	$5 green	—	—
48	$30 blue	—	—
49	$40 red	—	—
50	$100 red	—	—

2004

52	$30 blue	—	—
53	$40 red	—	—
54	$100 red	—	—

In 2001, $15 affiliate, $35 non-resident daily use and $75 non-resident season stamps were printed. It is not known whether these stamps with incorrect fees were sold. Value, set $200.

A $5 tribal stamp was printed in 2004 but no examples are known. Four stamps for 2005 were printed but no examples are known.

Fees: $10, tribal member; $25, affiliate; $40, non-resident daily use; $100, non-resident season.

2006

59	$10 blue	—	—
60	$25 green	—	—
61	$40 red	—	—
62	$100 red	—	—

Sportsmen's Stamps

For hunting game including waterfowl.

Fees: $10, tribal member; $25, reservation resident, non-tribal member; $100, South Dakota resident; $250, non-South Dakota resident.

Used values are for signed stamps.

Catalogue values for all unused stamps in this section are for Never Hinged items.

1989

A1	$10 black	450.	*100.*
A2	$25 black	1,150.	*300.*
A3	$100 black	450.	*75.*
A4	$250 black	450.	*150.*

1990

A5	$10 black	500.	*100.*
A6	$25 black	650.	*150.*
A7	$100 black	275.	*125.*
A8	$250 black	400.	*150.*

Goose Stamps

Fees: $5, tribal member; $10, $15, $20, affiliate; $50, non-resident.

1998

2A1	$5 green	—	—
2A2	$10 blue	—	—
2A3	$50 red	—	—

1999

2A4	$5 green	*100.00*	—
2A5	$10 blue	*100.00*	—
2A6	$50 red	*100.00*	—

2000

2A7	$5 green	*60.00*	—
2A8	$10 blue	*60.00*	—
2A9	$50 red	*60.00*	—

2001

2A10	$5 green	*60.00*	—
2A11	$10 blue	*60.00*	—
2A12	$50 red	*60.00*	—

2002

2A13	$5 green	*150.00*	—
2A14	$15 blue	*150.00*	—
2A15	$50 red	*150.00*	—

2003

2A16	$5 green	*150.00*	—
2A17	$20 blue	*150.00*	—
2A18	$50 red	*150.00*	—

2004

2A21	$50 red	—	—

In 1997, $5 tribal member, $10 affiliate, and $50 non-resident stamps were printed, but the season was canceled. Value, set $400.

Tribal member and affiliate stamps were printed for 2004 but no examples are known. In 2005, three stamps were printed but no examples are known.

Fees: $10, tribal member; $25, affiliate; $75, non-resident.

2006

2A25	$10 blue	—	—
2A26	$25 green	—	—
2A27	$75 red	—	—

FLATHEAD INDIAN RESERVATION

Montana
Bird or Fish Stamps

The 1988 stamp was printed in booklet panes of 10. Starting in 1989, printed in booklet panes of 5 stamps se-tenant with 5 stamps marked "Duplicate." Numbered serially in red. Rouletted.

Catalogue values for all unused stamps in this section are for Never Hinged items.

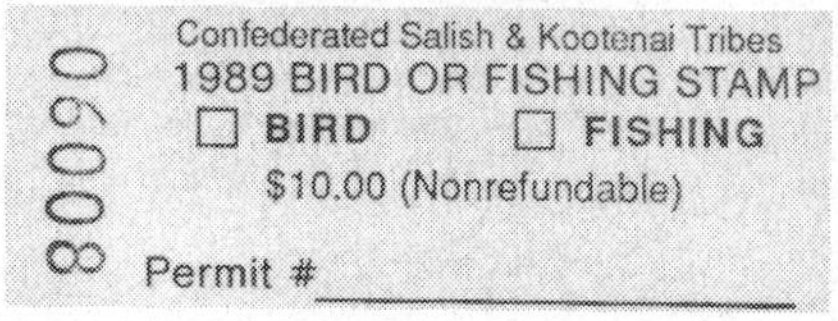

1987-90

1	$10 black	*1,200.*	*350.00*
1A	$10 black, *1988*	*950.00*	*275.00*
2	$10 blue, *1989*	16.00	5.00
3	$10 blue, *1990*	16.00	5.00

Joint Bird License Stamps

Printed in booklet panes of 10. Die cut, self-adhesive. Numbered serially.

1991

4	$10 black, *green*	10.50	5.00

Bird License Stamps

Printed in booklet panes of 10. Die cut, self-adhesive. Numbered serially.

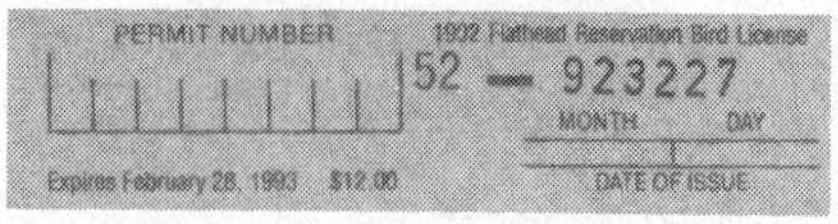

1992-2000

5	$12 black, *rose,* season	10.50	5.00
6	$12 black, *salmon,* 3-day	9.50	5.00
7	$12 black, *dark green,* season, *1993*	8.00	4.00
8	$12 black, *dark blue,* 3-day, *1993*	7.50	4.00
9	$12 black, *blue,* season, *1994*	8.00	4.00
10	$12 black, *orange,* 3-day, *1994*	7.00	3.00
11	$12 black, *yellow,* resident, *1995*	8.00	3.00
12	$55 black, *pale blue green,* non-resident, *1995*	*17.50*	*9.00*
13	$12 black, *turquoise,* resident, *1996*	11.00	3.00
14	$55 black, *pale orange,* non-resident, *1996*	*18.00*	*15.00*
15	$12 black, *pale yellow,* resident, *1997*	10.00	3.00
16	$55 black, *pale blue green,* non-resident, *1997*	*11.00*	
17	$13 black, *turquoise,* resident, *1998*	12.00	3.00
18	$56 black, *blue,* non-resident, *1998*	*12.00*	*3.00*
19	$13 black, *orange,* resident, *1999*	10.00	3.00
20	$56 black, *red,* non-resident, *1999*	*10.00*	*3.00*
21	$13 black, *yellow,* reservation, *2000*	12.00	3.00
22	$14 black, *green,* resident, *2000*	12.00	3.00
23	$110 black, *pink,* out-of-state, *2000*	*12.00*	*3.00*

FORT BERTHOLD INDIAN RESERVATION

North Dakota
Small Game Stamps

Stamps issued before 1990 may exist.

Issued in booklet panes of 6 stamps and 6 tabs. Required for hunting small game including waterfowl.

Values are for stamps with tabs. Fees varied, usually $6 for tribe members and $20-$30 for non-members.

Stamps are numbered serially.

Catalogue values for all unused stamps in this section are for Never Hinged items.

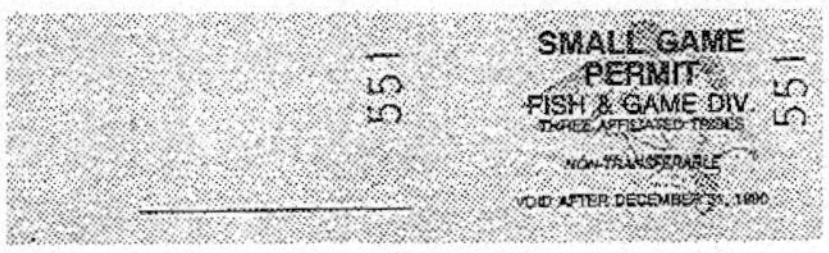

1990-98

Rouletted

A6	black, *pink*	*85.00*	*25.00*
A7	black, *green, 1991*	*80.00*	
A8	black, *pink, 1992*	*80.00*	
A9	black, *blue, 1993*	*175.00*	
A10	black, *pink, 1994*	70.00	
A11	black, *pink, 1995*	*100.00*	*25.00*
A12	black, *green, 1996*	57.50	
A13	black, *light green, 1997*	50.00	*12.00*
A14	black, *green,* 1998	30.00	

Waterfowl Stamps

Stamps issued before 1990 may exist.

Issued in booklet panes of 6 stamps and 6 tabs.

Required for non-member waterfowl hunters only.

Values are for stamps with tabs.

Fees varied, usually $20-$30.

Stamps are numbered serially.

Catalogue values for all unused stamps in this section are for Never Hinged items.

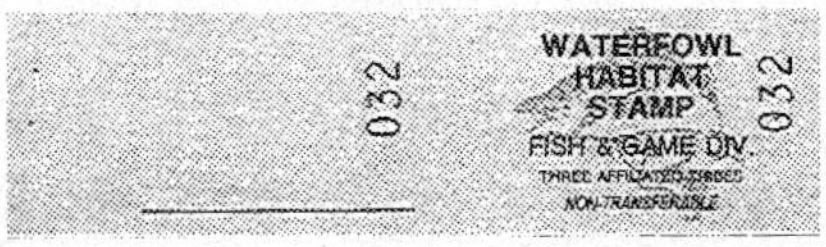

1990-2000

Rouletted

2A6	black	*2,500.*	
2A7	black, *blue, 1991*	*850.00*	
2A8	black, *yellow*, #1-60, *1992*	*3,600.*	
2A9	black, *yellow*, #61-120, *1993*	*650.00*	
2A10	black, *green*, #1-60, *1994*	*625.00*	
2A11	black, *green*, #61-120, *1995*	*275.00*	*50.00*
2A12	black, *green*, #121-198, *1996*	*225.00*	
2A13	black, *light green*, #199-276, *1997*	*250.00*	
2A14	black, *light green*, #277-, *1998*	*300.00*	
2A15	black, *light green*, #355-432, *1999*	*300.00*	
2A16	black, *light green*, #433-588, *2000*	*250.00*	

FORT PECK INDIAN RESERVATION

Montana

Stamps issued before 1975 may exist.

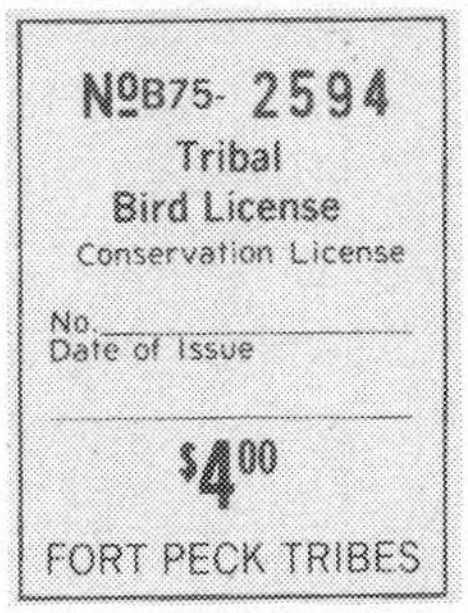

1975-78

Rouletted

2	$4 black	*1,500.*	
3	$4 black, *1976*	100.	
a.	Double impression	*9,500.*	
4	$4 black, *1977*	*17,500.*	
5	$5 black, *orange, 1978*	250.	

JICARILLA APACHE INDIAN RESERVATION

New Mexico
Wildlife Stamp

Believed to have been issued starting in 1988. Issued in booklet panes of 4. Numbered serially. Rouletted.

Catalogue values for all unused stamps in this section are for Never Hinged items.

1	$5 black & gold, *blue*	12.00

LAKE TRAVERSE (SISSETON-WAHPETON) INDIAN RESERVATION

South Dakota-North Dakota
Waterfowl Stamps

No examples are recorded of stamps from 1987-1990. No. 1 is die cut. Nos. 6, 8-9 are die cut, self-adhesive. No. 7 issued in booklet panes of 5, rouletted, numbered serially in red.

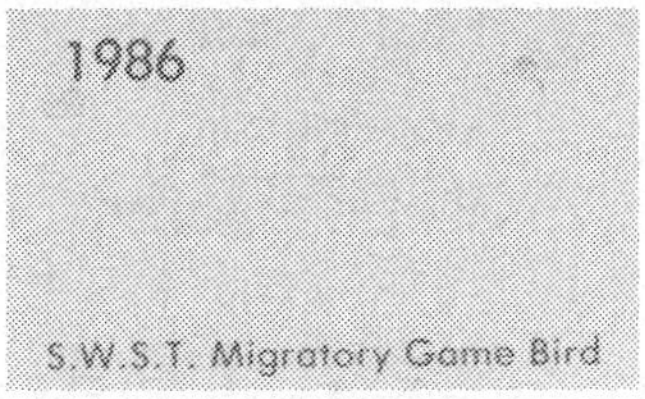

A1

A2

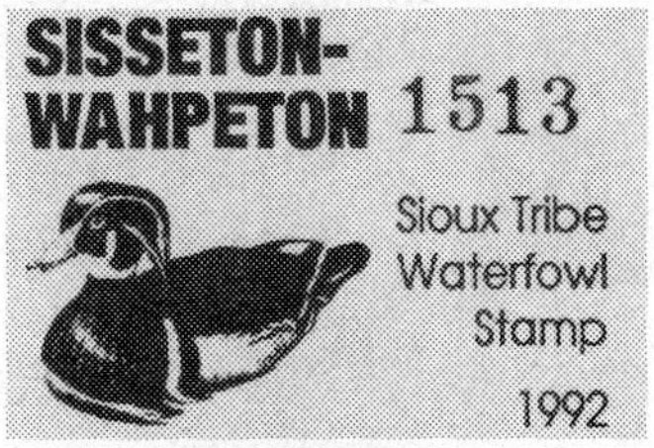

A3

A4

1986-2000

1	A1	green	*250.00*	*75.00*

Catalogue values for all unused stamps in this section, from this point to the end, are for Never Hinged items.

6	A2	black, *bright green, 1991*	*125.00*	
7	A3	Wood duck, *1992*	15.00	
8	A2	black, *bright red, 1993*	25.00	
9	A4	black, *yellow orange, 1994*	7.50	4.00

Inscribed SWST

10	A4	black, *red orange, 1995*	12.00	4.00
11	A4	black, *blue, 1996*	10.00	4.00
12	A4	black, *bright green, 1997*	11.00	3.00
13	A4	black, *red, 1998*	40.00	
14	A4	black, *orange, 1999*	10.00	
15	A4	black, *orange, 2000*	35.00	

LOWER BRULE INDIAN RESERVATION

South Dakota
Waterfowl Stamps

Serial Nos. are in red. Year and fee are written by hand or typewritten on each stamp. The $5 fee was for for non-members and non-Indians. There was a $2.50 fee for tribal members but no examples of these stamps are recorded.

Numbers have been reserved for the $2.50 stamps.

Since no year is on an unused stamp, they are listed under the first year only.

1962-70

2	$5 black		—
4	$5 black, *1963*		—
6	$5 black, *1964*		*3,250.*
8	$5 black, *1965*		*3,250.*
10	$5 black, *1966*		*2,950.*
12	$5 black, *1967*		*2,750.*
14	$5 black, *1968*		*2,600.*
18	$5 black, *1969*		*4,750.*

1969-71

20	$5 black		*5,500.*
24	$5 black, *1971*		—
26	$5 black, *1972*		—

Migratory Bird Hunting and Conservation Stamps

Issued in panes of 20.

All stamps have serial number on reverse.

Catalogue values for all unused stamps in this section, from this point to the end, are for Never Hinged items.

1995

27	$5	green, tribal member	7.00
28	$5	orange brown, resident deeded land owner / operator	7.00
29	$5	blue, resident government employee	7.00
30	$10	red, non-tribal S.D. resident	12.00
31	$10	purple, non-resident, out of state	12.00

1996

32	$5	multi, tribal / resident	7.00
33	$10	multi, non-tribal S.D. resident	12.00
34	$10	multi, non-resident, out of state	12.00

1997

35	$5 multi, tribal / resident	7.00	
36	$10 multi, non-tribal S.D. resident	12.00	
37	$10 multi, non-resident, out of state	12.00	

Nos. 38-40 have been reserved for 1998 stamps which were printed, but use of which has not yet been verified.

1999

41	$5 multi, tribal / resident	7.00	
42	$10 multi, non-tribal S. D. resident	14.00	
43	$10 multi, non-resident, out of state	14.00	

PINE RIDGE (OGLALA SIOUX) INDIAN RESERVATION

South Dakota Waterfowl Stamps

Nos. 1-3 issued in booklet panes of 5, numbered serially in red.

No. 2 perforated, others rouletted.

A1

A2

A3

1	A1 $4 black	*350.00*	

Earliest known use of No. 1 is 1988.

Catalogue values for all unused stamps in this section, from this point to the end, are for Never Hinged items.

2	A2 $4 black, perforated	15.00	
3	A3 $4 Canada geese, *1992*	11.00	

$6 stamps picturing Canada geese were produced and sold for the 1993 season. The same stamp was rubber hand-stamped for the 1994 season. However, there was no hunting season those years. Value, each $15.

ROSEBUD INDIAN RESERVATION

South Dakota Tribal Game Bird Stamps

Nos. 1, 3-4 have red serial number. Stamps for 1960, 1963-69 may exist.

Since no year is on an unused stamp, they are listed under the first year only.

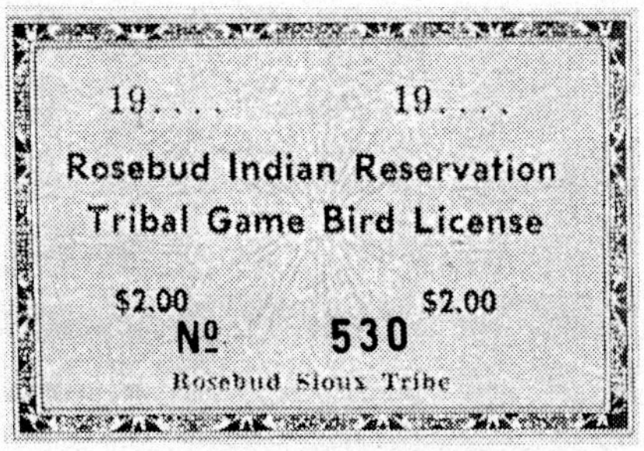

1959-62

1	$2 green	—	
3	$2 green, *1961*	*7,500.*	
4	$2 green, *1962*	*8,500.*	

Small Game Stamps

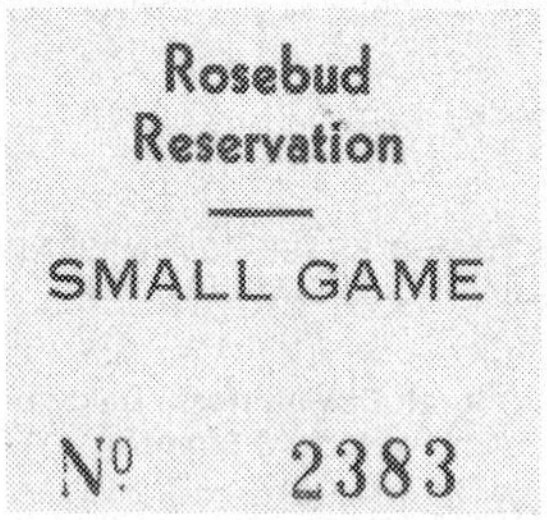

No. 12

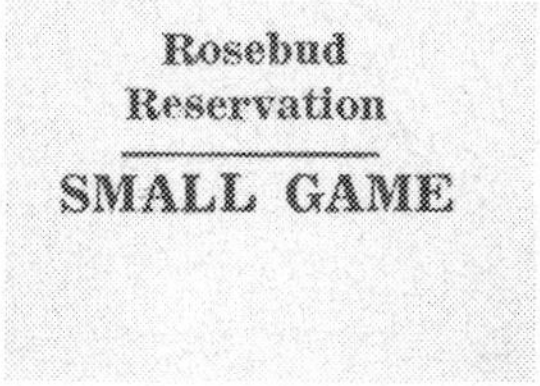

No. 13

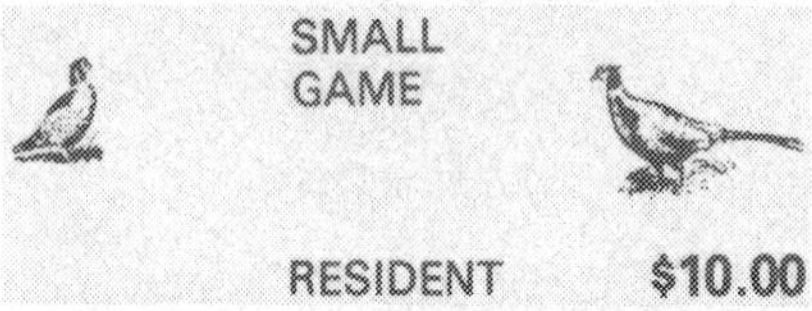

Nos. 14, 15

Nos. 16, 17

12	black	*2,200.*	
13	black	*250.00*	
14	$10 black	25.00	*20.00*
15	$45 black	150.00	

Die cut self-adhesive

16	$10 black (resident)	125.00	*15.00*
a.	Overprinted "RESIDENT" over "Non-resident"	*6,500.*	*1,500.*
17	$45 black	450.00	*50.00*

No. 12 was used in the 1970s, No. 13 in the early 1980s, Nos. 14 (resident) and 15 (non-resident) in the late 1980s, and Nos. 16 (resident) and 17 (non-resident) starting in 1990. Unused values for Nos. 16-17 are for never hinged stamps.

STANDING ROCK INDIAN RESERVATION

South Dakota-North Dakota Waterfowl Stamps

Die cut, self-adhesive.

Catalogue values for all unused stamps in this section are for Never Hinged items.

1992-98

1	black	16.00	5.0
2	black, *1993*	10.00	4.0
3	black, inscribed "SRST," *1994*	8.50	3.0
4	black, *1995*	15.00	5.0
5	black, *1996*	13.00	4.0
6	black, *1997*	9.00	4.0
7	black, *1998*	15.00	4.0

SAVINGS STAMPS

"Savings Stamps" is a general philatelic category that includes four slightly different types of stamps issued at different times by either the U.S. Post Office Department or the U.S. Treasury Department. Their common feature was that they all effectively acted as a means for ordinary citizens to save and/or invest incrementally, a little bit at a time. At the same time, the investments effectively were loans to the federal government.

The four types of Savings Stamps are Postal Savings Stamps (issued from 1911-41) and Savings Stamps (1954-61), both issued by the Post Office Department; and War Savings Stamps (1917-45) and a Treasury Savings Stamp (1920), both issued by the Treasury Department.

Postal Savings Stamps were issued in 10c to $5.00 denominations and were redeemable in the form of credits to postal savings accounts. The 1911 10c stamps were available either as stamps or as a stamp imprint on a card to which other stamps could be added. The postal savings system was discontinued March 28, 1966.

Savings Stamps, also issued in 10c to $5.00 denominations, are the savings stamps most familiar to older philatelists. These collectors may remember buying these stamps at school and placing them in booklets. When full, the booklets were redeemable in the form of United States savings bonds. Sale of Savings Stamps was discontinued June 30, 1970.

War Savings Stamps were issued in 25c and $5 denominations (1917-20) and 10c to $5 denominations (1942-45). They were redeemable in the form of United States treasury war certificates, defense bonds or war bonds.

One Treasury Savings Stamp with a $1.00 denomination was issued in 1920. These stamps were redeemable in the form of either war savings stamps or treasury savings certificates.

POSTAL SAVINGS STAMPS

PS1

Plates of 400 subjects in four panes of 100 each
FLAT PLATE PRINTING

1911, Jan. 3 Wmk. 191 Engr. *Perf. 12*
Size of design: 18x21½mm

PS1 PS1 10c **orange** 8.50 1.40
Never hinged 17.50
Block of 4, 2mm spacing 37.50
Block of 4, 3mm spacing 40.00
P# strip of 3, Impt. open star 57.50
P# block of 6, Impt. open star 550.00

Plate Nos. 5504-5507.

1911, Jan. 3 Unwmk.
Imprinted on Deposit Card
Size of design: 137x79mm

PS2 PS1 10c **orange** 210.00 55.00

A 10c deep blue with head of Washington in circle imprinted on deposit card (design 136x79mm) exists, but there is no evidence that it was ever placed in use.

1911, Aug. 14 Wmk. 190 *Perf. 12*

PS4 PS1 10c **deep blue** 5.00 1.00
Never hinged 8.50
Block of 4, 2mm spacing 22.50
Block of 4, 3mm spacing 25.00
P# strip of 3, Impt. open star 30.00
P# block of 6, Impt. open star 200.00
Never hinged 375.00

Plate Nos. 5504-5507.

1911 Unwmk.
Imprinted on Deposit Card
Size of design: 133x78mm

PS5 PS1 10c **deep blue** 160.00 25.00

Catalogue values for unused stamps in this section, from this point to the end, are for Never Hinged items.

1936 Unwmk. *Perf. 11*

PS6 PS1 10c **deep blue** 5.50 1.25
violet blue 5.50 1.25
Block of 4 25.00
P# block of 6, Impt. solid star 150.00

Plate Nos. 21485, 21486.

PS2

Plates of 400 subjects in four panes of 100 each
FLAT PLATE PRINTING

1940 Unwmk. Engr. *Perf. 11*
Size of design: 19x22mm

PS7 PS2 10c **deep ultramarine,** *Apr. 3* 27.50 6.00
Block of 4 115.00
P# block of 6 300.00

Plate Nos. 22540, 22541.

PS8 PS2 25c **dark car rose,** *Apr. 1* 32.50 9.00
Block of 4 135.00
P# block of 6 340.00

Plate Nos. 22542, 22543.

PS9 PS2 50c **dark blue green,** *Apr. 1* 80.00 17.50
Block of 4 340.00
P# block of 6 1,125.

Plate No. 22544.

PS10 PS2 $1 **gray black,** *Apr. 1* 225.00 17.50
Block of 4 950.00
P# block of 6 2,400.

Plate No. 22545.

Nos. PS11-PS15 redeemable in the form of United States Treasury Defense, War or Savings Bonds.

Minute Man — PS3

E.E. Plates of 400 subjects in four panes of 100 each
ROTARY PRESS PRINTING

1941, May 1 Unwmk. *Perf. 11x10½*
Size of design: 19x22½mm

PS11 PS3 10c **rose red** .60
a. 10c **carmine rose** .60
Block of 4 2.40
P# block of 4 7.25
b. Bklt. pane of 10, *July 30,* trimmed horizontal edges 50.00
As "b," with Electric Eye marks at left 55.00
c. Booklet pane of 10, perf. horizontal edges 100.00
As "c," with Electric Eye marks at left 115.00

Plate Nos., sheet stamps, 22714-22715, 22722-22723, 148245-148246.
Plate Nos., booklet panes, 147084, 147086, 148241-148242.

PS12 PS3 25c **blue green** 2.00
Block of 4 8.25
P# block of 4 22.50
b. Bklt. pane of 10, *July 30* 60.00
Booklet pane with Electric Eye marks at left 65.00

Plate Nos., sheet stamps, 22716-22717, 22724-22725, 148247-148248.
Plate Nos., booklet panes, 147087-147088, 148243-148244.

PS13 PS3 50c **ultramarine** 7.50
Block of 4 32.50
P# block of 4 50.00

Plate Nos. 22718-22719, 22726-22727.

PS14 PS3 $1 **gray black** 12.50
Block of 4 52.50
P# block of 4 75.00

Plate Nos. 22720, 22728.

FLAT PLATE PRINTING
Plates of 100 subjects in four panes of 25 each
Size: 36x46mm *Perf. 11*

PS15 PS3 $5 **sepia** 42.50
Block of 4 175.00
P# block of 6 at top or bottom 475.00

Plate Nos. 22730-22737, 22740.

SAVINGS STAMPS

Catalogue values for unused stamps in this section are for Never Hinged items.

Minute Man — S1

E.E. Plates of 400 subjects in four panes of 100 each
ROTARY PRESS PRINTING

1954-57 Unwmk. *Perf. 11x10½*
Size of design: 19x22½mm

S1 S1 10c **rose red,** wet printing, *Nov. 30, 1954* .50
Block of 4 2.00
P# block of 4 3.50
a. Booklet pane of 10, *Apr. 22, 1955* 150.00
Booklet pane with Electric Eye marks at left 165.00
b. Dry printing .50
Block of 4 2.00
P# block of 4 3.50
c. As "b," booklet pane of 10 150.00
Booklet pane with Electric Eye marks at left 165.00

Plate Nos., sheet stamps, 164991-164992 (wet), 165917-165918, 166643-166644, 167089-167090, 168765-168766 (dry).
Plate Nos., booklet panes, 165218-165219 (wet), 165954-165955, 167001-167002 (dry).

S2 S1 25c **blue green,** wet printing, *Dec. 30, 1954* 7.50
Block of 4 30.00
P# block of 4 35.00
a. Booklet pane of 10, *Apr. 15, 1955* 800.00
Booklet pane with Electric Eye marks at left 825.00
b. Dry printing 7.50

			Block of 4	30.00	
			P# block of 4	35.00	
c.			As "b," booklet pane of 10	800.00	
			Booklet pane with Electric Eye marks at left	825.00	

Plate Nos., sheet stamps, 165007-165008 (wet), 165919-165920 (dry), booklet panes, 165220-165221 (wet), 165956-165957 (dry).

S3	S1	50c	**ultramarine,** wet printing, *Dec. 31, 1956*	9.00	
			Block of 4	37.50	
			P# block of 4	50.00	
a.			Dry printing	9.00	
			Block of 4	37.50	
			P# block of 4	50.00	

Plate Nos. 165050-165051 (wet), 166741-166742, 166941-166942 (dry).

S4	S1	$1	**gray black,** *Mar. 13, 1957*	25.00	
			Block of 4	100.00	
			P# block of 4	125.00	

Plate Nos. 166097-166098, 166683-166684.

FLAT PLATE PRINTING

Plates of 100 subjects in four panes of 25 each

Size: 36x46mm ***Perf. 11***

S5	S1	$5	**sepia,** *Nov. 30, 1956*	95.00	
			Block of 4	400.00	
			P# block of 6 at top or bottom	725.00	

Plate No. 166068.

Minute Man and 48-Star Flag — S2

GIORI PRESS PRINTING

Plates of 400 subjects in four panes of 100 each

1958, Nov. 18 **Unwmk.** ***Perf. 11***

S6	S2	25c	**dark blue & carmine**	2.00	
			Block of 4	8.00	
			P# block of 4	10.00	
a.			Booklet pane of 10	75.00	

Plate Nos.: sheet stamps, 166921, 166925, 166946; booklet panes, 166913, 166916.

Minute Man and 50-Star Flag — S3

Plates of 400 subjects in four panes of 100 each.

1961 **Unwmk.** ***Perf. 11***

S7	S3	25c	**dark blue & carmine**	1.50	
			Block of 4	6.00	
			P# block of 4	11.00	
a.			Booklet pane of 10	300.00	

Plate Nos.: sheet stamps, 167473, 167476, 167486, 167489, 169089; booklet panes, 167495, 167502, 167508, 167516.

WAR SAVINGS STAMPS

Unused values of War Savings stamps are for copies with full original gum. Used values are for stamps without gum that generally have been removed from savings certificates or booklets. **Caution:** beware of used stamps that have been regummed to appear unused.

WS1

Plates of 300 subjects in six panes of 50 each

FLAT PLATE PRINTING

1917, Dec. 1 **Unwmk.** **Engr.** ***Perf. 11***

Size of design: 28x18½mm

WS1	WS1	25c	**deep green**	16.00	2.25
			Never hinged	30.00	
			Block of 4	70.00	
			Margin strip of 3, P#	80.00	
			P# block of 6	1,200.	

Plate Nos. 56800, 56810-56811, 56817, 57074-57077, 57149-57152, 57336, 57382, 57395-57396, 57399, 57443, 58801-58804, 59044-59045, 59156, 61207-61210.

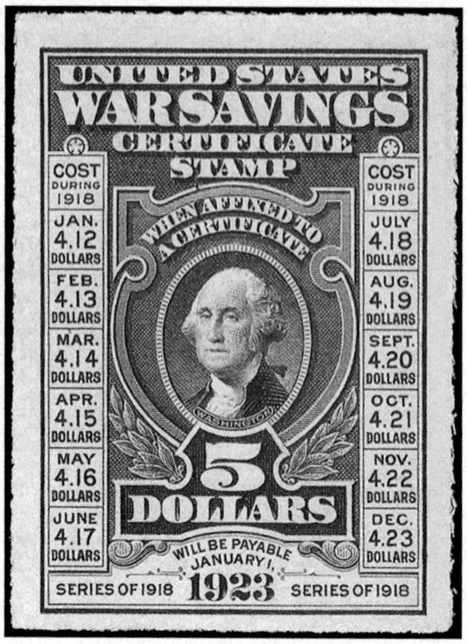

George Washington — WS2

Plates of 80 subjects in four panes of 20 each

FLAT PLATE PRINTING

1917 **Unwmk.** **Engr.** ***Perf. 11***

Size of design: 39x55mm

WS2	WS2	$5	**deep green,** *Nov. 17*	85.00	35.00
			Never hinged	175.00	
			No gum	30.00	
			Block of 4	325.00	
			Margin stamp with P#	90.00	
			P# block of 6	*1,600.*	
b.			Vert. pair, imperf. horiz.	—	

Plate Nos. 56914-56917, 57066-57073, 57145-57148, 57169-57176, 57333-57334, 57343-57348, 58431, 58433-58438, 58726-58729, 59071, 60257-60260, 60659-60662, 60665-60668, 60846-60852, 60899, 61203-61206, 61265-61268, 61360-61367, 61388, 61435, 61502.

Rouletted 7

WS3	WS2	$5	**deep green**	1,200.	650.
			Never hinged	*2,500.*	
			No gum	600.	
			Block of 4	5,000.	
			Margin copy with P#	1,500.	

Benjamin Franklin — WS3

Plates of 150 subjects in six panes of 25 each

FLAT PLATE PRINTING

1919, July 3 **Unwmk.** **Engr.** ***Perf. 11***

Size of design: 27x36mm

WS4	WS3	$5	**deep blue**	325.	160.
			Never hinged	650.	
			No gum	150.	
			Block of 4	1,350.	
			Margin stamp with P#	350.	
			Margin stamp with inverted P#	375.	

Plate Nos. 61882-61885, 61910-61913, 61970-61972, 61997-61998, 62007-62013.

George Washington WS4

Plates of 100 subjects in four panes of 25 each

FLAT PLATE PRINTING

1919, Dec. 11 **Unwmk.** **Engr.** ***Perf. 11***

Size of design: 36x41½mm

WS5	WS4	$5	**carmine**	800.	350.
			Never hinged	1,650.	
			No gum	500.	
			Block of 4	*3,500.*	
			Margin stamp with P#	850.	

Plate Nos. 67545-67552, 69349-69352, 69673-69675, 69677-69680, 69829.

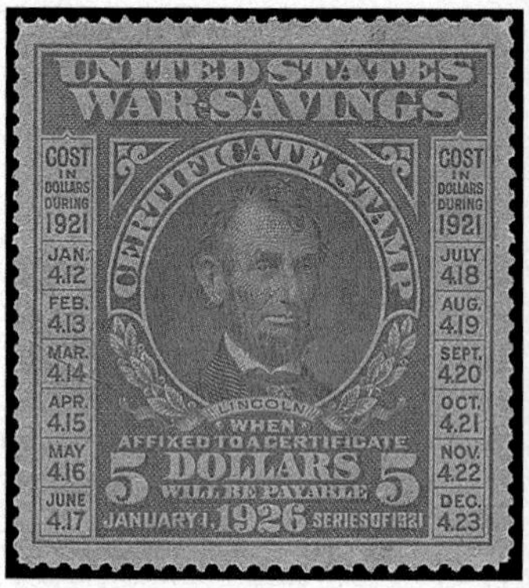

Abraham Lincoln WS5

Plates of 100 subjects in four panes of 25 each

FLAT PLATE PRINTING

1920, Dec. 21 **Unwmk.** **Engr.** ***Perf. 11***

Size of design: 39½x42mm

WS6	WS5	$5	**orange,** *green*	3,500.	1,350.
			Never hinged	*7,000.*	
			No gum	1,500.	
			Block of 4	*15,000.*	
			Margin stamp with P#	3,750.	

Plate Nos. 73129-73136.

Catalogue values for unused stamps in this section, from this point to the end, are for Never Hinged items.

Minute Man — WS6

Plates of 400 subjects in four panes of 100 each

ROTARY PRESS PRINTING

1942 **Unwmk.** ***Perf. 11x10½***

Size of design: 19x22½mm

WS7	WS6	10c	**rose red,** *Oct. 29*	.50	.20
a.			10c carmine rose	.50	
			Block of 4	2.00	
			P# block of 4	5.00	
b.			Booklet pane of 10, *Oct. 27*	50.00	
			Booklet pane with Electric Eye marks at left	55.00	

Plate Nos., sheet stamps, 149492-149495, 150206-150207, 150706-150707, 155311-155312.

Plate Nos., booklet panes, 149655-149657, 150664.

WS8	WS6	25c **dark blue green,** *Oct. 15*	1.10	.25
		Block of 4	5.00	
		P# block of 4	8.25	
b.		Booklet pane of 10, *Nov. 6*	50.00	
		Booklet pane with Electric Eye marks at left	55.00	

Plate Nos., sheet stamps, 149587-149590, 150320-150321, 150708-150709, 155313-155314, 155812-155813, 156517-156518, booklet panes, 149658-149660, 150666.

WS9	WS6	50c **deep ultra,** *Nov. 12*	4.00	1.25
		Block of 4	16.00	
		P# block of 4	22.50	

Plate Nos. 149591-149594.

WS10	WS6	$1 **gray black,** *Nov. 17*	12.50	3.50
		Block of 4	52.50	
		P# block of 4	70.00	

Plate Nos. 149595-149598.

Type of 1942
FLAT PLATE PRINTING
Plates of 100 subjects in four panes of 25 each

1945 Unwmk. Size: 36x46mm *Perf. 11*

WS11	WS6	$5 **violet brown**	55.00	17.50
		Block of 4	240.00	
		P# block of 6 at top or bottom	500.00	

Plate Nos. 150131-150134, 150291.

Type of 1942
Coil Stamps

1943, Aug. 5 Unwmk. *Perf. 10 Vertically*

WS12	WS6	10c **rose red**	2.75	.90
		Pair	6.00	
		Line pair	10.50	

Plate Nos. 153286-153287.

WS13	WS6	25c **dark blue green**	5.00	1.75
		Pair	10.50	
		Line pair	22.50	

Plate Nos. 153289-153290.

TREASURY SAVINGS STAMP

Alexander Hamilton — TS1

FLAT PLATE PRINTING

1920, Dec. 21 Unwmk. Engr. *Perf. 11*
Size of design: 33½x33½mm

TS1	TS1	$1 **red,** *green*	3,500.	1,250.
		Never hinged	*7,500.*	
		No gum	*1,750.*	
		Block of 4	*15,000.*	
		Margin stamp with P#	3,750.	

Plate Nos. 73196-73203.

TELEGRAPH STAMPS

These stamps were issued by the individual companies for use on their own telegrams, and can usually be divided into three classes: Free franking privileges issued to various railroad, newspaper and express company officials, etc., whose companies were large users of the lines; those issued at part cost to the lesser officials of the same type companies; and those bearing values which were usually sold to the general public. Occasionally, some of the companies granted the franking privilege to stockholders and minor State (not Federal) officials. Most Telegraph Stamps were issued in booklet form and will be found with one or more straight edges.

Serial numbers may show evidence of doubling, often of a different number. Such doubling is not scarce.

American Rapid Telegraph Company

Organized Feb. 21, 1879, in New York State. Its wires extended as far north as Boston, Mass., and west to Cleveland, Ohio. It was amalgamated with the Bankers and Merchants Telegraph Co., but when that company was unable to pay the fixed charges, the properties of the American Rapid Telegraph Company were sold on Mar. 11, 1891, to a purchasing committee comprised of James W. Converse and others. This purchasing committee deeded the property and franchise of the American Rapid Telegraph Company to the Western Union Telegraph Company on June 25, 1894. Issued three types of stamps: Telegram, Collect and Duplicate. Telegram stamps were issued in sheets of 100 and were used to prepay messages which could be dropped in convenient boxes for collection. Collect and duplicate stamps were issued in alternate rows on the same sheet of 100 subjects. Collect stamps were attached to telegrams sent collect, the receiver of which paid the amount shown by the stamps, while the Duplicate stamps were retained by the Company as vouchers. **Remainders with punched cancellations were bought up by a New York dealer.**

T1

T2

"Prepaid Telegram" Stamps

Engraved and Printed by the American Bank Note Co.

1881 *Perf. 12*

1T1	T1	1c **black**	12.50	3.00
		Punched		.20
		Block of 4	55.00	
		Punched		1.00
1T2	T1	3c **orange**	50.00	32.50
		Punched		1.50
		Block of 4, punched		10.00
1T3	T1	5c **bister brown**	3.00	.80
		Punched		.25
		Block of 4	13.00	
		Punched		1.10
a.		5c **brown**	3.00	.90
		Punched		.20
		Block of 4	13.00	
		Punched		1.00
1T4	T1	10c **purple**	17.50	5.00
		Punched		.20
		Block of 4	75.00	
		Punched		1.00
1T5	T1	15c **green**	5.50	1.60
		Punched		.20
		Block of 4	25.00	
		Punched		1.00
1T6	T1	20c **red**	5.50	1.60
		Punched		.20
		Block of 4, punched		.80
1T7	T1	25c **rose**	7.50	1.10
		Punched		.20
		Block of 4	32.50	
		Punched		1.00
1T8	T1	50c **blue**	32.50	12.50
		Punched		1.50
		Block of 4, punched		8.00

"Collect" Stamps

1T9	T2	1c **brown**	5.00	3.50
		Punched		.20
1T10	T2	5c **blue**	4.00	2.50
		Punched		.20
1T11	T2	15c **red brown**	4.25	2.00
		Punched		.25
1T12	T2	20c **olive green**	4.00	2.50
		Punched		.20

T3

"Office Coupon" Stamps

1T13	T3	1c **brown**	9.00	2.75
		Punched		.20
a.		Pair, #1T9, 1T13, punched		2.00
		As "a," block of 4, punched		4.50
1T14	T3	5c **blue**	7.50	3.25
		Punched		.20
a.		Pair, #1T10, 1T14	40.00	
		Punched		3.00
		As "a," block of 4	90.00	
		Punched		7.00
1T15	T3	15c **red brown**	13.50	3.00
		Punched		.25
a.		Pair, #1T11, 1T15	35.00	
		Punched		2.50
		As "a," block of 4	75.00	
		Punched		5.50
1T16	T3	20c **olive green**	13.50	3.00
		Punched		.20
a.		Pair, #1T12, 1T16, punched		2.75
		As "a," block of 4, punched		6.00

Atlantic Telegraph Company

Organized 1884 at Portland, Maine. Its lines extended from Portland, Me., to Boston, Mass., and terminated in the office of the Baltimore and Ohio Telegraph Company at Boston. Later bought out by the Baltimore and Ohio Telegraph Co. Stamps issued by the Atlantic Telegraph Company could also be used for messages destined to any point on the Baltimore and Ohio system. Stamps were printed in panes of six and a full book sold for $10. **Remainders of these stamps, without control numbers, were purchased by a Boston dealer and put on the market about 1932.**

T4

1888 *Perf. 13*

2T1	T4	1c **green**	5.00	—
		Remainders		2.25
		Pane of 6	—	
		Remainders		14.00
2T2	T4	5c **blue**	7.50	—
		Remainders		2.25
		Pane of 6	—	
		Remainders		14.00
a.		Horiz. pair, imperf. vert.	—	
b.		Vert. pair, imperf. horiz.	25.00	—
2T3	T4	10c **purple brown**	9.00	—
		Remainders		2.25
		Pane of 6	—	
		Remainders		14.00
a.		Horiz. pair, imperf. between	40.00	—
2T4	T4	25c **carmine**	6.00	—
		Remainders		2.25
		Pane of 6, remainders		16.00
a.		Vert. pair, imperf. horiz., remainders	—	

Baltimore & Ohio Telegraph Companies

"The Baltimore & Ohio Telegraph Co. of the State of New York" was incorporated May 17, 1882. Organization took place under similar charter in 26 other states. It absorbed the National Telegraph Co. and several others. Extended generally along the lines of the Baltimore & Ohio Railroad, but acquired interests in other states. Company absorbed in 1887 by the Western Union Telegraph Co. Stamps were issued in booklet form and sold for $5 and $10, containing all denominations.

T5

T6

Engraved by the American Bank Note Co.

1885 *Perf. 12*

3T1	T5	1c **vermilion**	90.00	25.00
		Pane of 6	600.00	
3T2	T5	5c **blue**	90.00	35.00
3T3	T5	10c **red brown**	45.00	12.50
		Pane of 6	300.00	
3T4	T5	25c **orange**	75.00	25.00
3T5	T6	**brown**	1.75	
		Pane of 4	12.50	

1886

3T6	T6	**black**	2.00	*25.00*
		Pane of 4	22.50	

Imprint of Kendall Bank Note Co.
Thin Paper

1886 *Perf. 14*

3T7	T5	1c **green**	7.00	3.00
a.		Thick paper	12.00	.85
b.		Imperf., pair	90.00	
3T8	T5	5c **blue**	5.00	1.25
a.		Thick paper	10.00	4.00
b.		Imperf., pair		55.00
3T9	T5	10c **brown**	7.00	.75
a.		Thick paper	11.50	1.50
3T10	T5	25c **deep orange**	47.50	.75
a.		Thick paper	50.00	1.50

Used examples of Nos. 3T7-3T20 normally have heavy grid cancellations. Lightly canceled stamps command a premium.

Litho. by A. Hoen & Co.

1886 **Imprint of firm** *Perf. 12*

3T11	T5	1c **green**	3.00	.65
		Pane of 6	22.50	—
3T12	T5	5c **blue**	7.50	.65
		Pane of 6	50.00	—
a.		Imperf., pair	90.00	
3T13	T5	10c **dark brown**	7.50	.75
		Pane of 6	45.00	—
a.		Vert. pair, imperf. between	60.00	

Wmk. "A HOEN AND CO. BALTIMORE" in double lined capitals in sheet

Perf. 12

3T14	T5	1c **green**	15.00	1.25
		Pane of 6	90.00	—
3T15	T5	5c **blue**	25.00	1.50
		Pane of 6	160.00	—
a.		Imperf., pair	52.50	—
3T16	T5	10c **dark brown**	17.50	1.25
		Pane of 6	115.00	—

Lithographed by Forbes Co., Boston

1887 **Imprint of firm** *Perf. 12½*

3T17	T5	1c **green**	45.00	2.75
3T18	T5	5c **blue**	70.00	6.00
3T19	T5	10c **brown**	70.00	5.50
3T20	T5	25c **yellow**	70.00	8.25
a.		25c **orange**	70.00	5.50

Baltimore & Ohio-Connecticut River Telegraph Companies

The Connecticut River Telegraph Co. ran from New Haven to Hartford. An agreement was entered wherein the Baltimore & Ohio System had mutual use of their lines. This agreement terminated when the Baltimore & Ohio System was absorbed by the Western Union. The Connecticut River Telegraph Company then joined the United Lines. In 1885 stamps (black on yellow) were issued and sold in booklets for $10. In 1887 the Connecticut River Telegraph Co. had extended its lines to New Boston, Mass., and new books of stamps (black on blue) were issued for use on this extension. **Remainders were canceled with bars and sold to a New York dealer.**

T7

1885-87 *Perf. 11*

4T1	T7	1c **black,** *yellow*	7.50	6.00
		Remainders		1.25
		Pane of 10	75.00	
		Remainders		6.00
a.		Imperf., pair	40.00	
b.		Vert. pair, imperf. horiz., remainders		—
4T2	T7	5c **black,** *yellow*	5.00	10.00
		Remainders		1.00
		Pane of 10	50.00	
		Remainders		6.00
a.		Horizontal pair, imperf. between, remainders		—
b.		Vert. pair, imperf. between, remainders		35.00
c.		Imperf., pair, remainders		35.00
4T3	T7	1c **black,** *blue* ('87)	12.50	—
		Remainders		4.00
		Pane of 10	125.00	
		Remainders		35.00
4T4	T7	5c **black,** *blue* ('87)	15.00	9.00
		Remainders		4.00
		Pane of 10	160.00	
		Remainders		52.50

California State Telegraph Company

Incorporated June 17, 1854 as the California Telegraph Company and constructed a line from Nevada through Grass Valley to Auburn. Extended to run from San Francisco to Marysville via San Jose and Stockton. Later absorbed Northern Telegraph Co. and thus extended to Eureka. It was incorporated as the California State Telegraph Company on April 6, 1861. At the time of its lease to the Western Union on May 16, 1867 the California State consisted of the following companies which had been previously absorbed:

Alta California Telegraph Co., Atlantic and Pacific States Telegraph Co., National Telegraph Co., Northern California Telegraph Co., Overland Telegraph Co., Placerville and Humboldt Telegraph Co., Tuolumne Telegraph Co. Stamps were issued in booklets, six to a pane. **Remainders of Nos. 5T1 and 5T4 are without frank numbers.**

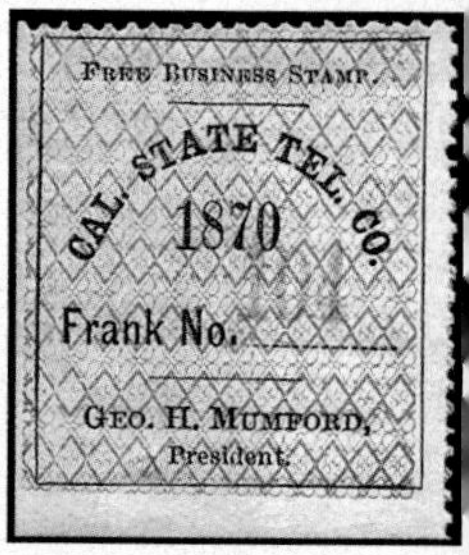

T8

1870 *Perf. 13½*

5T1	T8	**black & blue**	700.	—
		Pane of 6	4,500.	
		Without number	275.	

T9

T10

1870 *Perf. 12, 13*

5T2	T9	**black & red,** without number	350.00	200.00

1871 **Dated "1871"**

5T3	T9	**black & red,** without number	800.00	
a.		Imperf., pair	—	—
5T4	T10	**black & salmon,** blue number	850.00	275.00
		Pane of 6	*5,500.*	
		Without number	260.00	

1872

5T5	T10	**green & red,** red number (no year date)	400.00	—
		Pane of 6	—	

1873 **Dated "1873"**

5T6	T10	**red & salmon,** blue number	525.00	350.00

1874 **Dated "1874"**

5T7	T10	**blue & salmon,** black number	600.00	—
		Pane of 6	—	

1875 **Dated "1875"**

5T8	T10	**brown & green,** black number	500.00	—
		Pane of 6	—	

City & Suburban Telegraph Company (New York City and Suburban Printing Telegraph Company)

Organized 1855. Extended only through New York City and Brooklyn. Sold out to the American Telegraph Co. Stamps were sold to the public for prepayment of messages, which could be dropped in convenient boxes for collection. Stamps were issued in sheets of 60 having a face value of $1. These were arranged in six vertical rows of ten, the horizontal rows having the following denominations: 2c, 1c, 1c, 1c, 2c, 3c.

Counterfeits are known both in black and blue, mostly on pelure or hard white paper. Originals are on soft wove paper, somewhat yellowish. Scalloped edge is more sharply etched on the counterfeits.

T11

Typo. *Imperf.*

6T1	T11	1c **black**	500.	275.
		Pair	—	
		Block of 4	—	
6T2	T11	2c **black**	650.	350.
		Pair	—	
		Pair, 2c + 1c	1,400.	
6T3	T11	3c **black**	825.	475.
		Pair	—	
		Strip of 3, 1c, 2c & 3c	*3,750.*	

Colusa, Lake & Mendocino Telegraph Company

Was organized in California early in 1873. First known as the Princeton, Colusa and Grand Island Telegraph Co. In May, 1873 they completed their line from Princeton through Colusa, at which point it was connected with the Western Union office, to Grand Island. On Feb. 10, 1875 it was incorporated as the Colusa, Lake & Mendocino Telegraph Co. Its lines were extended into the counties of Colusa, Lake, Mendocino and Napa. Eventually reached a length of 260 miles. Went out of business in 1892. Stamps were issued for prepayment of messages and were sold in books. When sold they were stamped "P.L.W." (the superintendent's initials) in blue. The 5c value was printed 10 to a pane, being two horizontal rows of five. Of the 10c and 25c nothing definite is known about the settings.

T11a

1876 *Perf. 12*

7T1	T11a	5c	**black**	*900.*	—
			Block of 4	*4,000.*	
			Pane of 10	*10,000.*	
			Without "P.L.W."	*1,000.*	
7T2	T11a	10c	**black**	*9,000.*	—
7T3	T11a	25c	**red**	*9,000.*	—

Commercial Union Telegraph Company

Incorporated in New York State on March 31, 1886. Its lines ran from Albany through Troy to Berlin, N.Y., thence to North Adams, Mass. The lines of this Company, which was controlled by the Postal Telegraph Company, were later extended throughout Northern New York and the States of Massachusetts, Vermont, New Hampshire and Maine. Stamps issued in panes of four.

T12

T13

T14

1891 **Lithographed by A. C. Goodwin** *Perf. 12*

8T1	T12	25c	**yellow**	25.00	—
			Pane of 4	105.00	
8T2	T13	25c	**green**	25.00	10.00
			Pane of 4	105.00	
	a.		Horiz. pair, imperf. vert.	90.00	
8T3	T14		**lilac rose**	60.00	—

Mutual Union Telegraph Company

Incorporated October 4, 1880. Extended over 22 states. Absorbed about 1883 by the Western Union Telegraph Co. Franks issued for use of stockholders, in books, four to a pane.

T15

Engr. by Van Campen Engraving Co., New York

1882-83 *Perf. 14*

9T1	T15	**blue**		50.00	20.00
		Pane of 4		225.00	
	a.	Vert. pair, imperf. horizontal		140.00	—
	b.	Imperf., pair		150.00	
9T2	T15	**carmine**		50.00	—
		Pane of 4		225.00	

North American Telegraph Company

Incorporated October 15, 1885 to run from Chicago to Minneapolis, later being extended into North and South Dakota. Absorbed in 1929 by the Postal System.

Apparently these stamps were not canceled when used.

Issued in panes of four.

T15a

1899-1907 *Perf. 12*

10T1	T15a	**violet** (1899)	300.00
		Pane of 4	1,250.
10T2	T15a	**green** (1901)	300.00
10T3	T15a	**dark brown** (1902)	525.00
10T4	T15a	**blue** (1903)	525.00
10T5	T15a	**violet** (1904)	190.00
		Pane of 4	800.00
	a.	Horiz. pair, imperf. vertically	500.00
10T6	T15a	**red brown** (1905)	325.00
10T7	T15a	**rose** (1906)	375.00
10T8	T15a	**green** (1907)	2,100.

Nos. 10T1 to 10T8 are known imperforate.

Northern Mutual Telegraph Company

Incorporated in New York State as the Northern Mutual Telegraph and Telephone Company on June 20, 1882. Its line, which consisted of a single wire, extended from Syracuse to Ogdensburg via Oswego, Watertown and Clayton, a distance of 170 miles. It was sold to the Bankers and Merchants Telegraph Company in 1883. Stamps were in use for a few days only in April, 1883. Issued in panes of 35 having a face value of $5. Seven horizontal rows of five covering all denominations as follows: 2 rows of 25c, 1 of 20c, 2 of 10c, 2 of 5c. **The remainders and plates were purchased by a New York dealer in 1887.**

T16

1883 *Perf. 14*

11T1	T16	5c	**yellow brown**	6.50	—
			Block of 4	30.00	
11T2	T16	10c	**yellow brown**	8.50	—
			Block of 4	37.50	
11T3	T16	20c	**yellow brown**	20.00	—
			Horizontal pair	45.00	
11T4	T16	25c	**yellow brown**	5.50	—
			Block of 4	30.00	
			Pane of 35	375.00	

The first reprints are lighter in color than the originals, perf. 14 and the gum is yellowish instead of white. The pane makeup differs in the reprints. The second reprints are darker than the original, perf. 12. Value $1 each.

Northern New York Telegraph Company

Organized about 1892. Extended from Malone, N.Y. to Massena, N.Y. Re-incorporated as the New York Union Telegraph Co. on April 2, 1896.

T16a

Typo. by Charles H. Smith, Brushton, N.Y.

1894-95 ***Rouletted***

12T1	T16a		**green** (overprinted in red "Frank 1894")	45.
			Pane of 6	290.
	a.		Imperf., pair	50.
12T2	T16a		**red** (overprinted in black "Frank 1895")	160.
			Pane of 6	1,500.
	a.		Imperf., pair	50.
12T3	T16a	1c	**yellow** (overprinted in black "One")	80.
			Pane of 6	525.
	a.		Imperf., pair	50.
12T4	T16a	10c	**blue** (overprinted in red "10")	150.
			Pane of 6	950.
	a.		Imperf., pair	50.

Some specialists believe that Nos. 12T1-12T4 were not issued and probably are essays. However, one Northern New York stamp is recorded tied to a piece of a telegraph form by a punch cancel.

Pacific Mutual Telegraph Company

Incorporated in Missouri on June 21, 1883. Operated between St. Louis and Kansas City, Mo., during the years 1884 and 1885. It had 15 offices, 425 miles of poles and 850 miles of wire. The controlling interests were held by the Bankers and Merchants Telegraph Company. The name was changed on Sept. 10, 1910 to Postal Telegraph-Cable Company of Missouri. Stamps were issued in booklets having a face value of $10 and containing 131 stamps as follows: 50-1c, 20-5c, 45-10c, 16-25c. They are not known used.

T17

1883 *Perf. 12*

13T1	T17	1c	**black**	25.00
13T2	T17	1c	**slate**	.35
			Block of 4	1.50
	a.		1c gray	.35

		Block of 4	1.50	
13T3	T17	5c **black,** *buff*	1.00	
		Block of 4	4.50	
13T4	T17	10c **black,** *green*	.35	
		Block of 4	1.75	
a.		Horiz. pair, imperf. between	—	
13T5	T17	25c **black,** *salmon buff*	1.00	
		Block of 4	4.50	

Pacific Postal Telegraph-Cable Company

The Pacific Postal Telegraph-Cable Company was the Pacific Coast Department of the Postal Telegraph-Cable Company, and was organized in 1886. Its first wire ran from San Francisco to New Westminster, B.C., where it touched the lines of the Canadian Pacific Railway Company, then the only connection between the Eastern and Western Postal systems. Later the Postal's own wires spanned the continent and the two companies were united.

Stamps issued in booklet form in vertical panes of five.

T17a

Perf. 12 Horiz.

14T1	T17a	10c **brown**	85.00	60.00
		Pane of 5	450.00	
14T2	T17a	15c **black**	90.00	55.00
		Pane of 5	475.00	
14T3	T17a	25c **rose red**	90.00	55.00
		Pane of 5	475.00	
14T4	T17a	40c **green**	85.00	65.00
		Pane of 5	450.00	
14T5	T17a	50c **blue**	75.00	60.00
		Pane of 5	400.00	

These stamps were issued with three sizes of frank numbers; large closely spaced, small closely spaced and small widely spaced figures. They also exist without frank numbers.

Postal Telegraph Company

Organized in New York in 1881. Reorganized in 1891 as the Postal Telegraph-Cable Co. The Postal Telegraph Co stamps of 1885 were issued in sheets of 100. **Some years after the reorganization a New York dealer purchased the remainders which were canceled with a purple star.** The Postal Telegraph-Cable Co. issued frank stamps in booklets, usually four stamps to a pane. This company was merged with the Western Union Telegraph Company in 1943.

T18

T19

T20

T21

Engraved by Hamilton Bank Note Co.

1885 *Perf. 14*

15T1	T18	10c **green**	3.50	—
		Remainders		.25
		Block of 4	15.00	
		Remainders		1.25
a.		Horiz. pair, imperf. btwn., remainders		20.00
b.		10c **deep green**	3.50	—
		Remainders		.25
		Block of 4	15.00	—
		Remainders		1.25
15T2	T19	15c **orange red**	3.50	—
		Remainders		.60
		Block of 4	15.00	—
		Remainders		3.00
a.		Horizontal pair, imperf. between	37.50	
15T3	T20	25c **blue**	2.00	5.00
		Remainders		.20
		Block of 4	9.00	
		Remainders		.75
a.		Horizontal pair, imperf. between	37.50	
15T4	T21	50c **brown**	1.75	—
		Remainders		.60
		Block of 4	8.00	
		Remainders		3.00

The 25c in ultramarine and the 50c in black were printed and perforated 16 but are not known to have been issued. Value about $7.50 each.

T22

T22a

Typographed by Moss Engraving Co.

1892-1920 *Perf. 14*

Signature of A.B. Chandler

15T5	T22	**blue gray** (1892)	45.00	
a.		Imperf., pair	120.00	

Perf. 13 to 14½ and Compound

15T6	T22	**gray lilac** (1892)	50.00	
15T7	T22	**red** (1893)	20.00	10.00
		Pane of 4	85.00	
15T8	T22	**red brown** (1893)	6.00	4.00

Perf. 12

15T9	T22	**violet brown** (1894)	6.75	
15T10	T22	**gray green** (1894)	4.50	
a.		Imperf., pair	10.00	
15T11	T22	**blue** (1895)	45.00	
15T12	T22	**rose** (1895)	350.00	

Nos. 15T11 and 15T12 are from a new die resembling T22 but without shading under "Postal Telegraph Co."

15T13	T22a	**slate green** (1896)	5.50	
		Pane of 4	25.00	
15T14	T22a	**brown** (1896)	300.00	

Signature of Albert B. Chandler

15T15	T22a	**lilac brown** (1897)	1.50	*10.00*
		Pane of 4	6.50	
15T16	T22a	**orange** (1897)	240.00	

Typographed by Knapp & Co.

15T17	T22a	**pale blue** (1898)	2.25	
		Pane of 4	10.00	
15T18	T22a	**rose** (1898)	300.00	

Typographed by Moss Engraving Co.

Perf. 12

15T19	T22a	**orange brown** (1899)	1.75	
		Pane of 4	8.25	

Perf. 11

15T20	T22a	**blue** (1900)	3.00	3.00
a.		"I" of "Complimentary" omitted	.75	1.00
		Pane of 4	3.25	

The variety 15T20a represents a different die with many variations in the design.

Perf. 14

15T21	T22a	**sea green** (1901)	.60	.60
		Pane of 4	2.50	
a.		Horiz. pair, imperf. between	—	

Signature of John W. Mackay

15T22	T22a	**chocolate** (1902)	1.25	.65
		Pane of 4	5.50	
a.		Horiz. pair, imperf. vert.	—	

Signature of Clarence H. Mackay

15T23	T22a	**blue** (1903)	2.75	2.50
		Pane of 4	12.50	

Perf. 12

15T24	T22a	**blue,** *blue* (1904)	4.00	3.00
		Pane of 4	17.50	
15T25	T22a	**blue,** *yellow* (1905)	5.00	
		Pane of 4	22.50	
15T26	T22a	**blue,** *light blue* (1906)	5.00	5.00
		Pane of 4	22.50	
a.		Horiz. pair, imperf. vert.	—	

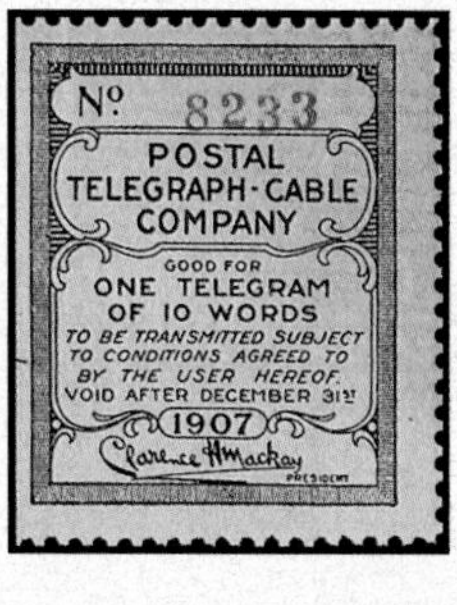

T22b

T22c

Perf. 12

15T27	T22b	**black,** *yellow* (laid paper) (1907)	70.00
		Pane of 4	290.00
15T28	T22b	**blue,** *pink* (laid paper) (1907)	40.00
		Pane of 4	190.00

"One Telegram of 10 Words"

15T29	T22c	**blue** (1908)	60.00
		Pane of 4	250.00
15T30	T22c	**yellow** (1908)	275.00
		Pane of 4	1,150.
15T31	T22c	**black** (1908)	50.00
		Pane of 4	210.00
15T32	T22c	**brown** (1909)	40.00
		Pane of 4	170.00
a.		Date reads "1908"	*2,000.*
15T33	T22c	**olive green** (1909)	22.50
		Pane of 4	95.00
15T34	T22c	**dark blue** (1910)	35.00
15T35	T22c	**dark brown** (1910)	35.00
		Pane of 4	150.00
15T36	T22c	**violet** (1911)	375.00
15T37	T22c	**blue** (1912)	650.00
15T38	T22c	**violet** (1913)	800.00

Perf. 14

15T39	T22c	**violet** (not dated) (1914)	225.00
a.		Red violet	200.00
		Pane of 4	950.00

"One Telegram"

Perf. 12

15T40	T22c	**blue** (1908)	55.00
		Pane of 4	240.00
a.		Horiz. pair, imperf. between	350.00
15T41	T22c	**lilac** (1909)	22.50
		Pane of 4	97.50
15T42	T22c	**black,** *yellow* (laid paper) (1910)	700.00
a.		Date reads "1909"	—
15T43	T22c	**violet** (1910)	15.00
a.		**Red violet**	15.00
		Pane of 4	—
		Pane of 8	140.00
15T44	T22c	**dark blue** (1911)	55.00
		Pane of 4	240.00
a.		Vert. pair, imperf between	*400.00*
15T45	T22c	**light violet** (1912)	37.50
		Pane of 4	170.00

Perf. 14

15T46	T22c	**dark blue** (1913)	160.00
		Pane of 8	1,350.
a.		Imperf. vertically, pair	260.00
b.		Perf. 12	90.00
		Pane of 4	375.00
15T47	T22c	**dark blue** (not dated) (1914)	.25
		Pane of 4	2.50
		Pane of 8	5.00

In panes of four the stamps are 4½mm apart horizontally, panes of eight 5½mm. There are two types of design T22c, one with and one without spurs on colored curved lines above "O" of "Postal" and below "M" of "Company". No. 15T47 comes in both types.

Nos. 15T39 and 15T47 handstamped with date in double line numerals, all four numerals complete on each stamp.

15T47A	T22c	**violet** (1916)	*2,750.*
15T48	T22c	**dark blue** (1917)	*1,500.*
15T49	T22c	**dark blue** (1918)	*2,000.*
15T49A	T22c	**dark blue** (1919)	90.00
		Pane of 8	800.00
15T49B	T22c	**dark blue** (1920)	70.00
		Pane of 8	650.00

No. 15T49B is handstamped "1920" in small single line numerals.

T22d

T22e

1907 *Perf. 12*

15T50 T22d 1c **dark brown** 30.00 20.00
Pane of 4 125.00
15T51 T22d 2c **dull violet** 25.00 20.00
Pane of 4 110.00
15T52 T22d 5c **green** 30.00 22.50
Pane of 4 125.00
15T53 T22d 25c **light red** 32.50 20.00
Pane of 4 140.00

1931 *Perf. 14*

15T54 T22e 25c **gray blue** (1931) .25
Pane of 6 2.00

1932

No. 15T54 overprinted "1932" and control number in red

15T55 T22e 25c **gray blue** 90.00
Pane of 6 600.00

Many varieties between Nos. 15T5 and 15T55 are known without frank numbers.

OFFICIAL

1900-14 **Inscribed "Supts."** *Perf. 11, 12*

15TO1 T22c **black,** *magenta* 2.00 2.00

For Use of Railroad Superintendents

Perf. 12

"C. G. W." (Chicago, Great Western Railroad) at top

15TO2 T22c **carmine** (1908) 50.00
Pane of 4 240.00
15TO3 T22c **carmine** (1909) 200.00
15TO4 T22c **carmine** (1910) 160.00
15TO5 T22c **carmine** (1911) 125.00
15TO6 T22c **carmine** (1912) 140.00

Perf. 14

15TO7 T22c **carmine** (1913) 200.00
a. Perf. 12 —
15TO8 T22c **dull red** (not dated) (1914) .50
Pane of 8 5.00

Perf. 12

"E. P." (El Paso and Northeastern Railroad) at top

15TO9 T22c **orange** (1908) 250.00

"I. C." (Illinois Central Railroad) at top

15TO10 T22c **green** (1908) 60.00
Pane of 4 270.00
15TO11 T22c **yellow green** (1909) 15.00
Pane of 4 —
Pane of 8 130.00
15TO12 T22c **dark green** (1910) 160.00
15TO13 T22c **dark green** (1911) 95.00
Pane of 4 410.00
Pane of 8 825.00
15TO14 T22c **dark green** (1912) 1,250.
15TO15 T22c **dark green** (1913) 1,250.

Perf. 14

15TO16 T22c **dark green** (not dated) (1914) 2.50
Pane of 4 11.00
Pane of 8 22.50
a. **Green** (spurs) 1.25
Pane of 4 7.50
b. Line under "PRESIDENT" (no spurs) 1.00
Pane of 8 12.50

(See note after No. 15T47.)
Both types of design T22c are known of 15TO16.

Perf. 12

"O. D." (Old Dominion Steamship Co.) at top

15TO17 T22c **violet** (1908) 2,100.

"P. R." (Pennsylvania Railroad) at top

15TO18 T22c **orange brown** (1908) 35.00
Pane of 4 150.00
Pane of 8 300.00
15TO19 T22c **orange brown** (1909) 40.00
Pane of 4 175.00
Pane of 8 375.00
15TO20 T22c **orange brown** (1910) 40.00
Pane of 4 175.00
Pane of 8 375.00
15TO21 T22c **orange brown** (1911) 140.00
15TO22 T22c **orange brown** (1912) 85.00
Pane of 4 *550.00*

Perf. 14

15TO23 T22c **orange brown** (1913) 40.00
Pane of 8 350.00
a. Perf. 12 150.00

"P. R. R." (Pennsylvania Rail Road) at top

15TO24 T22c **orange** (not dated) (1914) 27.50
Pane of 4 125.00
Pane of 8 250.00

Perf. 12

"S. W." (El Paso Southwestern Railroad) at top

15TO25 T22c **yellow** (1909) 375.00
15TO26 T22c **yellow** (1910) 1,600.
15TO27 T22c **yellow** (1911) 500.00
15TO28 T22c **yellow** (1912) 500.00
Pane of 4 1,500.

Nos. 15TO1-15TO17 and 15TO25-15TO28 are without frank numbers.

TO1

1942 **Litho.** **Unwmk.**

15TO29 TO1 5c **pink** 6.50 3.00
Pane of 8 55.00
15TO30 TO1 25c **pale blue** 7.75 4.00
Pane of 8 65.00

The stamps were issued in booklets to all Postal Telegraph employees in the Armed Forces for use in the United States. They were discontinued Oct. 8, 1943. Used stamps normally bear manuscript cancellations.

Western Union Telegraph Company

Organized by consolidation in 1856. Now extends throughout the United States. Frank stamps have been issued regularly since 1871 in booklet form. The large size, early issues, were in panes of four, 1871-1913; the medium size, later issues, were in panes of six, 1914-32; and the recent small size issues are in panes of nine, 1933 to 1946.

T23

T24

Engraved by the National Bank Note Co.

1871-94 *Perf. 12*

Signature of William Orton

16T1 T23 **green** (not dated) (1871) 35.00 22.50
16T2 T23 **red** (not dated) (1872) 40.00 20.00
Pane of 4 175.00
16T3 T23 **blue** (not dated) (1873) 45.00 22.50
Pane of 4 200.00
16T4 T23 **brown** (not dated) (1874) 35.00 22.50
Pane of 4 160.00
16T5 T24 **deep green** (1875) 37.50 21.00
16T6 T24 **red** (1876) 40.00
Pane of 4 180.00
16T7 T24 **violet** (1877) 42.50 28.00
16T8 T24 **gray brown** (1878) 40.00

Signature of Norvin Green

16T9 T24 **blue** (1879) 40.00 28.00
Pane of 4 180.00

Engraved by the American Bank Note Co.

16T10 T24 **lilac rose** (1880) 27.50
Pane of 4 120.00
16T11 T24 **green** (1881) 25.00
Pane of 4 110.00
16T12 T24 **blue** (1882) 15.00
Pane of 4 70.00
16T13 T24 **yellow brown** (1883) 27.50
Pane of 4 120.00
16T14 T24 **gray violet** (1884) .60 .30
Pane of 4 3.00
16T15 T24 **green** (1885) 3.25 1.75
Pane of 4 15.00
16T16 T24 **brown violet** (1886) 3.25 2.00
Pane of 4 15.00
a. Imperf pair, without frank numbers —
16T17 T24 **red brown** (1887) 4.50
Pane of 4 22.50
16T18 T24 **blue** (1888) 3.25
Pane of 4 15.00
16T19 T24 **olive green** (1889) 1.75 .80
Pane of 4 8.00
16T20 T24 **purple** (1890) .75 .40
Pane of 4 3.25
16T21 T24 **brown** (1891) 1.50
Pane of 4 6.50
16T22 T24 **vermilion** (1892) 1.75
Pane of 4 8.00
16T23 T24 **blue** (1893) 1.40 .40
Pane of 4 6.25

Signature of Thos. T. Eckert

16T24 T24 **green** (1894) .60 .40
Pane of 4 3.00

T25

Engraved by the International Bank Note Co.

1895-1913 *Perf. 14*

Signature of Thos. T. Eckert

16T25 T25 **dark brown** (1895) .50 .40
Pane of 4 2.50
16T26 T25 **violet** (1896) .50 .40
Pane of 4 2.50
16T27 T25 **rose red** (1897) .50 .40
Pane of 4 2.50
16T28 T25 **yellow green** (1898) .50 .40
Pane of 4 2.50
a. Vertical pair, imperf. between —
16T29 T25 **olive green** (1899) .50 .40
Pane of 4 2.25
16T30 T25 **red violet,** perf. 13 (1900) .50 .45
Pane of 4 3.00
16T31 T25 **brown,** perf. 13 (1901) .50 .40
Pane of 4 2.50
16T32 T25 **blue** (1902) 8.00
Pane of 4 40.00

Signature of R.C. Clowry

16T33 T25 **blue** (1902) 8.00
Pane of 4 40.00
16T34 T25 **green** (1903) .60 .40
Pane of 4 4.00
16T35 T25 **red violet** (1904) .60
Pane of 4 2.75
16T36 T25 **carmine rose** (1905) .60 .50
Pane of 4 2.75
16T37 T25 **blue** (1906) .80 .40
Pane of 4 4.00
a. Vertical pair, imperf. between *200.00*
16T38 T25 **orange brown** (1907) 1.75 .90
Pane of 4 10.00
16T39 T25 **violet** (1908) 2.00 1.00
Pane of 4 9.00
16T40 T25 **olive green** (1909) 2.00
Pane of 4 10.00

Perf. 12

16T41 T25 **buff** (1910) .75 .50
Pane of 4 3.25

Engraved by the American Bank Note Co.

Signature of Theo. N. Vail

16T42 T24 **green** (1911) 14.00
Pane of 4 65.00
16T43 T24 **violet** (1912) 9.00
Pane of 4 42.50

Imprint of Kihn Brothers Bank Note Company

Perf. 14

16T44 T24 **brown** (1913) 10.00
Pane of 4 50.00
a. Vert. pair, imperf. between 35.00
b. Horiz. pair, imperf. between 40.00

T26

T27

Engraved by the E.A. Wright Bank Note Co.

1914-15 **Signature of Theo. N. Vail** *Perf. 12*

16T45 T26 5c **brown** (1914) 1.10
Pane of 6 8.00
a. Vert. pair, imperf. between —
b. Horiz. pair, imperf. between —
16T46 T26 25c **slate** (1914) 7.00 5.00
Pane of 6 45.00

Signature of Newcomb Carlton

16T47	T26	5c	**orange** (1915)	1.50	
			Pane of 6	10.00	
			orange yellow	5.00	
16T48	T26	25c	**olive green** (1915)	4.00	
			Pane of 6	30.00	
a.			Vert. pair, imperf. horizontally	45.00	

Engraved by the American Bank Note Co.

1916-32

16T49	T27	5c	**light blue** (1916)	1.50	
			Pane of 6	11.00	
16T50	T27	25c	**carmine lake** (1916)	1.75	
			Pane of 6	11.00	

Engraved by the Security Bank Note Co.

Perf. 11

16T51	T27	5c	**yellow brown** (1917)	1.00	
			Pane of 6	7.50	
16T52	T27	25c	**deep green** (1917)	3.00	
			Pane of 6	20.00	
16T53	T27	5c	**olive green** (1918)	.60	
			Pane of 6	4.50	
16T54	T27	25c	**dark violet** (1918)	1.75	
			Pane of 6	14.00	
16T55	T27	5c	**brown** (1919)	1.25	
			Pane of 6	9.00	
16T56	T27	25c	**blue** (1919)	3.25	
			Pane of 6	22.50	

Engraved by the E.A. Wright Bank Note Co.

Perf. 12

16T57	T27	5c	**dark green** (1920)	.65	
			Pane of 6	4.25	
a.			Vert. pair, imperf. between	*300.00*	
16T58	T27	25c	**olive green** (1920)	.75	
			Pane of 6	5.00	

Engraved by the Security Bank Note Co.

16T59	T27	5c	**carmine rose** (1921)	.55	
			Pane of 6	4.25	
16T60	T27	25c	**deep blue** (1921)	1.30	
			Pane of 6	8.50	
16T61	T27	5c	**yellow brown** (1922)	.55	
			Pane of 6	3.75	
a.			Horizontal pair, imperf. between	16.00	
16T62	T27	25c	**claret** (1922)	1.65	
			Pane of 6	11.50	
16T63	T27	5c	**olive green** (1923)	.65	
			Pane of 6	4.25	
16T64	T27	25c	**dull violet** (1923)	1.35	
			Pane of 6	9.00	
16T65	T27	5c	**brown** (1924)	1.75	
			Pane of 6	12.00	
16T66	T27	25c	**ultramarine** (1924)	4.00	
			Pane of 6	30.00	
16T67	T27	5c	**olive green** (1925)	.65	
			Pane of 6	4.25	
16T68	T27	25c	**carmine rose** (1925)	1.10	
			Pane of 6	7.00	
16T69	T27	5c	**blue** (1926)	1.00	
			Pane of 6	6.50	
16T70	T27	25c	**light brown** (1926)	2.25	
			Pane of 6	14.00	
16T71	T27	5c	**carmine** (1927)	.85	
			Pane of 6	5.75	
16T72	T27	25c	**green** (1927)	7.25	
			Pane of 6	47.50	

Engraved by the E. A. Wright Bank Note Co.

Without Imprint

16T73	T27	5c	**yellow brown** (1928)	.75	
			Pane of 6	4.50	
16T74	T27	25c	**dark blue** (1928)	1.00	
			Pane of 6	6.25	

Engraved by the Security Bank Note Co.

Without Imprint

16T75	T27	5c	**dark green** (1929)	.30	.25
			Pane of 6	2.00	
16T76	T27	25c	**red violet** (1929)	.85	.50
			Pane of 6	5.50	
16T77	T27	5c	**olive green** (1930)	.25	.20
			Pane of 6	1.75	
16T78	T27	25c	**carmine** (1930)	.25	.25
			Pane of 6	2.00	
a.			Horiz. pair, imperf. vertically	35.00	
16T79	T27	5c	**brown** (1931)	.20	.20
			Pane of 6	1.25	
16T80	T27	25c	**blue** (1931)	.20	.20
			Pane of 6	1.50	
16T81	T27	5c	**green** (1932)	.20	.20
			Pane of 6	1.50	
16T82	T27	25c	**rose carmine** (1932)	.20	.20
			Pane of 6	1.50	

T28

1933-40

Lithographed by Oberly & Newell Co.

Without Imprint

Perf. 14x12½

16T83	T28	5c	**pale brown** (1933)	.25	
			Pane of 9	3.25	
16T84	T28	25c	**green** (1933)	.25	
			Pane of 9	3.25	

Lithographed by Security Bank Note Co.

Without Imprint

Perf. 12, 12½

Signature of R. B. White

16T85	T28	5c	**lake** (1934)	.20	
			Pane of 9	2.00	
16T86	T28	25c	**dark blue** (1934)	.20	
			Pane of 9	2.50	
16T87	T28	5c	**yellow brown** (1935)	.20	
			Pane of 9	2.00	
16T88	T28	25c	**lake** (1935)	.20	
			Pane of 9	2.00	
16T89	T28	5c	**blue** (1936)	.25	.20
			Pane of 9	2.75	
16T90	T28	25c	**apple green** (1936)	.20	.20
			Pane of 9	2.50	
16T91	T28	5c	**bister brown** (1937)	.20	
			Pane of 9	2.50	
16T92	T28	25c	**carmine rose** (1937)	.20	
			Pane of 9	2.00	
16T93	T28	5c	**green** (1938)	.25	.20
			Pane of 9	3.00	
16T94	T28	25c	**blue** (1938)	.30	.20
			Pane of 9	3.50	
16T95	T28	5c	**dull vermilion** (1939)	1.00	
			Pane of 9	11.50	
a.			Horiz. pair, imperf. between	—	
16T96	T28	25c	**bright violet** (1939)	.50	
			Pane of 9	6.00	
16T97	T28	5c	**light blue** (1940)	.55	
			Pane of 9	5.75	
16T98	T28	25c	**bright green** (1940)	.50	
			Pane of 9	5.50	

Samuel F. B. Morse T29

Plates of 90 stamps.
Stamp designed by Nathaniel Yontiff.
Unlike the frank stamps, Nos. 16T99 to 16T103 were sold to the public in booklet form for use in prepayment of telegraph services.

Engraved by Security Bank Note Co. of Philadelphia

1940 Unwmk. *Perf. 12, 12½x12, 12x12½*

16T99	T29	1c	**yellow green**	1.25	
			Pane of 5	6.50	
a.			Imperf., pair	50.00	
16T100	T29	2c	**chestnut**	1.75	1.00
			Pane of 5	15.00	
a.			Imperf., pair	50.00	
16T101	T29	5c	**deep blue**	3.00	
			Pane of 5	18.00	
a.			Vert. pair, imperf. btwn.	65.00	
b.			Imperf., pair	50.00	
16T102	T29	10c	**orange**	5.00	
			Pane of 5	27.50	
a.			Imperf., pair	50.00	
16T103	T29	25c	**bright carmine**	4.00	
			Pane of 5	24.00	
a.			Imperf., pair	50.00	

Type of 1933-40

1941 Litho. *Perf. 12½*

Without Imprint

Signature of R.B. White

16T104	T28	5c	**dull rose lilac**	.25	
			Pane of 9	2.50	
16T105	T28	25c	**vermilion**	.60	
			Pane of 9	6.00	

1942 Signature of A.N. Williams

16T106	T28	5c	**brown**	.30	
			Pane of 9	3.50	
16T107	T28	25c	**ultramarine**	.30	
			Pane of 9	3.50	

1943

16T108	T28	5c	**salmon**	.30	
			Pane of 9	3.50	
16T109	T28	25c	**red violet**	.30	
			Pane of 9	3.50	

1944

16T110	T28	5c	**light green**	.65	
			Pane of 9	7.25	
16T111	T28	25c	**buff**	.35	
			Pane of 9	3.75	

1945

16T112	T28	5c	**light blue**	.40	
			Pane of 9	5.00	
a.			Pair, imperf. between	—	
16T113	T28	25c	**light green**	.35	
			Pane of 9	3.75	

1946

16T114	T28	5c	**light bister brown**	1.25	
			Pane of 9	15.00	
16T115	T28	25c	**rose pink**	1.00	
			Pane of 9	12.00	

Many of the stamps between 16T1 and 16T98 and 16T104 to 16T115 are known without frank numbers. Several of them are also known with more than one color used in the frank number and with handstamped and manuscript numbers. The numbers are also found in combination with various letters: O, A, B, C, D, etc.

Western Union discontinued the use of Telegraph stamps with the 1946 issue.

United States Telegraph-Cable-Radio Carriers

Booklets issued to accredited representatives to the World Telecommunications Conferences, Atlantic City, New Jersey, 1947. Valid for messages to points outside the United States. Issued by All America Cables & Radio, Inc., The Commercial Cable Company, Globe Wireless, Limited, Mackay Radio and Telegraph Company, Inc., R C A Communications, Inc., Tropical Radio Telegraph Company and The Western Union Telegraph Company.

TX1

1947 Litho. Unwmk. *Perf. 12½*

17T1	TX1	5c	**olive bister**	7.00	
			Pane of 9	70.00	
			Pane of 9, 8 5c + 1 10c	700.00	
17T2	TX1	10c	**olive bister**	750.00	
17T3	TX1	50c	**olive bister**	9.00	
			Pane of 9	90.00	

UNLISTED ISSUES

Several telegraph or wireless companies other than those listed above have issued stamps or franks, but as evidence of actual use is lacking, they are not listed. Among these are:

American District Telegraph Co.
American Telegraph Typewriter Co.
Continental Telegraph Co.
Los Angeles and San Gabriel Valley Railroad
Marconi Wireless Telegraph Co.
Mercantile Telegraph Co.
Telepost Co.
Tropical Radio Telegraph Co.
United Fruit Co. Wireless Service.
United Wireless Telegraph Co.

ESSAYS

An essay is a proposed design that differs in some way from the issued stamp.

During approximately 1845-1890, when private banknote engravers competed for contracts to print U.S. postage stamps, essays were produced primarily as examples of the quality of the firms' work and as suggestions as to what their finished product would look like. In most cases, dies were prepared, often with stock vignettes used in making banknotes. These dies were used to print essays for the Post Office Department. Rarely did the competitors go so far as to have essay plates made.

From 1894 onward, virtually all stamps were engraved and printed by the Bureau of Engraving and Printing (BEP). This usually required two types of essays. The first was a model design which was approved — or disapproved — by the Postmaster General. Sometimes preliminary drawings were made by the BEP designers, often in an enlarged size, subsequently photographically reduced to stamp size. An accepted stamp design usually became the engraver's model.

Occasionally during the course of engraving the die, a "progressive proof" was pulled to check the progress of the engraver's work. Because these were produced from an incompletely engraved die, they differ from the final design and are listed here as essays.

During approximately 1867-1870, various experiments were conducted to prevent the reuse of postage stamps. These included experimental grill types, safety papers, water-sensitive papers and inks, coupon essays, and others. These also differed in some way from issued stamps, even if the design was identical. A preliminary listing has been made here.

Because the essays in all their various colors have not been examined by the editors, traditional color names have been retained. Some color names have been taken from *Color Standards and Color Nomenclature,* by Robert Ridgway.

Only essays in private hands have been listed. Others exist but are not available to collectors. Some essays were produced after the respective stamps were issued. Year dates are given where information is available.

Essay papers and cards are white, unless described otherwise.

Values are for full-size essays, where they are known. Measurements are given where such information is available. Essays are valued in the grade of very fine, where such exist. Cut-down or faulty examples sell for less, often much less. A number of essays are unique or are reported in very limited quantities. Such items are valued in the conditions in which they exist.

The listings are by manufacturer. Basic stamps may appear in two or more places.

This listing is not complete. Other designs, papers and colors exist. The editors would appreciate reports of unlisted items, as well as photos of items listed herein without illustrations.

POSTMASTERS' PROVISIONALS

NON-CONTIGUOUS LISTINGS

Because many listings are grouped by manufacturer, some catalogue numbers are separated.

No. 5-E1 to 5-E2	**follow 11-E16**
No. 11-E17 to 72-E5	**follow 5-E2**
No. 65-E5 to 72-E8	**follow 72-E5**
No. 63-E13 to 113-E2	**follow 72-E8**
No. 112-E2 to 129-E2	**follow 113-E2**
No. 120-E1 to 122-E5	**follow 129-E2**
No. 115-E3a to 129-E6	**follow 122-E5**
No. 115-E11 to 116-E8	**follow 129-E6**
No. 115-E17 to 148-E1	**follow 116-E8**
No. 145-E2 to 179-E3	**follow 148-E1**
No. 156-E2 to 191-E2	**follow 179-E3**
No. 184-E8	**follows 191-E2**
No. 182-E4 to 190-E3	**follow 184-E8**
No. 184-E17 to 293-E11	**follow 190-E3**
No. 285-E10 to 856-E2	**follow 293-E11**

Albany, N.Y.
Gavit & Co.

1Xa-E1

Design size: 23½x25½mm
Die size: 58x48mm

Benjamin Franklin. With crosshatching about 2mm outside border (usually cut off).

1847

1Xa-E1 5c

a. Die on India die sunk on large card, printed through a mat to eliminate crosshatching

brownish black	*600.*
scarlet	*600.*
red brown	*600.*
blue	*600.*
green	*600.*

b. Die on India; some mounted on small card

bluish black	325.
scarlet	325.
brown	325.
yellow green	325.
gray blue	325.

c. Die on India cut close

black	250.
blue	250.
red brown	250.
scarlet	250.
green	250.
yellow green	250.
brown violet	250.
rose red	250.

d. Die on bond (1858)

bluish black	375.
scarlet	375.
brown	375.
blue	375.
blue green	375.
violet	375.

e. Die on ivory glazed paper (1905)

black	900.
dark brown	900.
scarlet	900.
blue	900.

New York, N.Y.
Rawdon, Wright & Hatch

9X1-E1

Design 22mm wide
Die size: 50x102mm

Vignette of Washington. Two transfers laid down vertically on the die 22mm apart; top one retouched, with frame around it (this is a proof). Values are for combined transfers. Vignette essay exists cut apart from proof, value $200 each.

1845

9X1-E1 5c

a. Die on India (1879)

black	450.
violet black	450.
gray black	450.
scarlet	450.
dull scarlet	450.
orange	450.
brown	450.
dull brown	450.
green	450.
dull green	450.
ultramarine	450.
dull blue	450.
red violet	450.

b. Die on white bond (1879)

gray black	550.
dull scarlet	550.
dull brown	550.
dull green	550.
dull blue	550.

c. Die on white glazed paper, die sunk (1879)

gray black	700.

POSTAGE STAMPS

1847 ISSUE
Rawdon, Wright, Hatch & Edson

The original model for No. 1 exists, engraved vignette of Franklin mounted on frame, part of frame engraved, rest in pencil, ink and a gray wash. Formerly No. 1-E1, now in the National Postal Museum collection.

Engraved vignette only, matted.

1-E2 5c Die on India (1895), brown *2,500.*

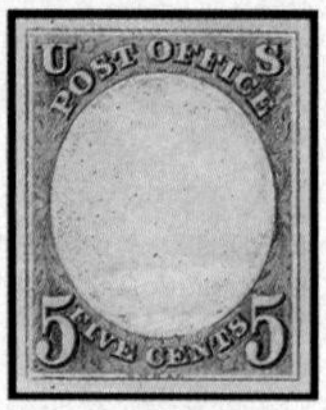

1-E3

Engraved frame only, matted from complete die.

1-E3 5c Die on India (1895), brown 2,500.

The 1895 dates are suppositional.

The original model for No. 2 exists, engraved vignette of Washington mounted (replaced) on frame, "POST OFFICE" and "FIVE CENTS" engraved on former No. 1-E1, "U" and "S" at top and "X" in bottom corners in black ink, rest in pencil and a gray wash. Formerly No. 2-E1, now in the National Postal Museum collection.

2-E2

2-E3

Engraved vignette only.

2-E2 10c Die on India (1895)
black *2,500.*
brownish black *2,500.*
brown *2,500.*

Engraved frame only.

2-E3 10c Die on India (1895)
black *2,500.*
brown orange *2,500.*

The 1895 dates are in suppositional.

1851 ISSUE
Attributed to Rawdon, Wright, Hatch & Edson

11-E1

11-E2

Design size: 18½x23mm
Large 3 in vignette.

11-E1 3c Die on India
black *3,000.*
blue *10,000.*

Design size: 19x24mm
Vignette of Washington.

11-E2 3c
a. Die on India
black *4,500.*
b. Die on proof paper, die sunk on 40x51mm card
black *4,500.*

Attributed to Gavit & Co.

11-E3

11-E4

Design size: 19x23mm

Vignette of Franklin. Three states of die. Second state has double line dash above P of POSTAGE, third state has single dash above P and dot in O of POSTAGE.

11-E3 3c
a. Die on India, die sunk on card
warm black *750.*
scarlet *750.*
red brown *750.*
blue green *750.*
b. Die on India, 41x43mm or smaller
black 300.
greenish black 300.
carmine 300.
scarlet 300.
yellow green 300.
brown 300.
blue green 300.
dull blue 300.
dark blue 300.
c. Die on India, cut to shape
warm black 225.
cool black 225.
black 225.
carmine 225.
orange 225.
brown 225.
dark green 225.
yellow green 225.
olive 225.
light blue 225.
dark blue 225.
violet 225.
scarlet 225.
d. Die on bond
cool black 225.
scarlet 225.
orange brown 225.
brown 225.
green 225.
blue 225.
e. Die on ivory glazed paper
black *750.*
dark brown *750.*
scarlet *750.*
blue *750.*
f. Die on thin card, dusky blue, cut to shape *200.*
g. Die on Francis Patent experimental paper with trial cancel
black *1,250.*
dark blue *1,250.*
brown *1,250.*

Design size: 19x22mm
Die size: 47x75mm
Vignette of Washington. Two states of die. Second state has small diagonal dash in top of left vertical border below arch.

11-E4 3c
a. Die on India, die sunk on card
black *750.*
scarlet *750.*
brown red *750.*
blue green *750.*
b. Die on India, about 30x40mm or smaller
orange 400.
orange brown 400.
brown 400.
dusky yellow brown 400.
yellow green 400.
blue green 400.
dull blue 400.
red violet 400.
deep red orange 400.
black 400.
c. Die on bond (1858)
black 400.
scarlet 400.
brown 400.
green 400.
blue 400.
d. Die on ivory glazed paper (1858)
black *750.*
dark brown *750.*
scarlet *750.*
blue *750.*
e. Die on proof paper (1858)
cool black *475.*
dull red *475.*
dull brown *475.*
dull blue green *475.*
dull blue *475.*

Bradbury, Wilkinson & Co., England

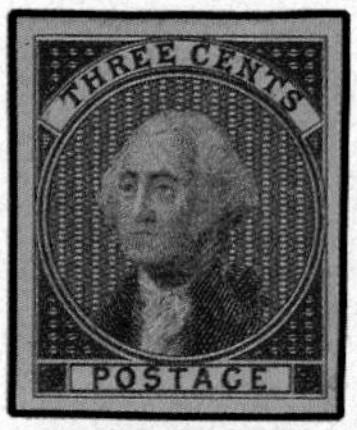

11-E5

Design size: 20½x23½mm
Vignette of Washington.

11-E5 3c
a. On stiff stamp paper about stamp size
black *1,250.*
violet red *1,250.*
deep carmine *1,250.*
dusky carmine *1,250.*
deep scarlet *1,250.*
orange brown *1,250.*
deep green *1,250.*
blue *1,250.*
ultramarine *1,250.*
brown *1,250.*
b. On card
violet black *1,250.*
dull scarlet *1,250.*
blue *1,250.*
green *1,250.*
brown *1,250.*
c. On stiff bond
brown *1,250.*
blue *1,250.*
violet black *1,250.*

Draper, Welsh & Co.

11-E6

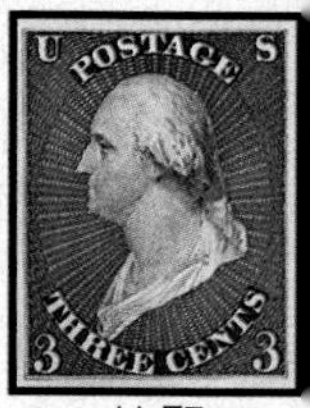

11-E7

Design size: 18x23mm
Vignette of Washington.

11-E6 3c Surface printed on card, black *750.*

Design size: 17½x24mm
Die size: 44x106mm
Engraved vignette of Washington.

11-E7 3c
a. Die on India, about 44x105mm, die sunk on card, in vert. pair with No. 11-E8
black *1,500.*
scarlet *1,500.*
brown red *1,500.*
green *1,500.*
b. Die on India, about 40x45mm or smaller
warm black *400.*
cool black *400.*
dark carmine *400.*
scarlet *400.*
brown red *400.*
orange brown *400.*
brown *400.*
yellow green *400.*
blue green *400.*
blue *400.*
dull blue *400.*
brown violet *400.*
c. Die on India, stamp size
rose 350.
scarlet 350.
red brown 350.
brown 350.
green 350.
cool black 350.
warm black 350.
yellow green 350.
brown violet 350.
ultramarine blue 350.
d. Die on bond
black 400.
scarlet 400.
brown 400.
blue green 400.
blue 400.
e. Die on ivory glazed paper
black *750.*
dark brown *750.*
scarlet *750.*
blue *750.*

11-E8

Design size: 19½x24mm
Die size: 44x106mm
On same die 30mm below No. 11-E7
Vignette of Washington.

11-E8 3c
a. Die on India, 28x32mm or smaller
black *300.*
dark carmine *300.*
scarlet *300.*
brown red *300.*
red brown *300.*
orange brown *300.*
brown *300.*
yellow green *300.*
green *300.*
blue green *300.*
blue *300.*

b. Die on bond, about 32x40mm
black 225.
scarlet 225.
brown 225.
green 225.
blue 225.
c. Die on ivory glazed paper
black *750.*
dark brown *750.*
scarlet *750.*
blue *750.*

11-E8D

11-E9

Design size: 18x23mm
Vignette of Washington.
Washington vignette only. Same head as No. 11-E6 through 11-E8, but with more bust. No gridwork in background.

11-E8D 3c Die on proof paper, mounted on card, black *750.*

Design size (No. 11-E9a): 18x33mm
Vignette design size (Nos. 11-E9b, 11-E9c): 18x22mm
As No. 11-E8D, gridwork added to background oval.

11-E9 3c
a. Die on India
black 350.
scarlet 350.
b. Die on India, single line frame
black 300.
blue 300.
dark carmine 300.
orange red 300.
lilac 300.
brown 300.
scarlet 300.
rose violet 300.
deep yellow green 300.
c. Die on India, imprint of Jocelyn, Draper, Welsh & Co., New York
black 300.
blue 300.
dark carmine 300.
orange red 300.
lilac 300.
brown 300.
scarlet 300.
rose violet 300.
deep yellow green 300.

Danforth, Bald & Co.

11-E10

11-E11

Vignette size: 18x22mm
Design size: 20x26mm
Die size: 57x74mm
Vignette of Washington. Double line frame.

11-E10 3c
a. Die on India, die sunk on card
black *750.*
scarlet *750.*
red brown *750.*
green *750.*
b. Die on India, off card, about 33x38mm
black *175.*
scarlet *175.*
brown *175.*
blue *175.*
green *175.*
dull violet *175.*
dull blue *175.*
red brown *175.*
rose *175.*
c. Die on bond, black *350.*
d. Die on ivory glazed paper
black *750.*
dark brown *750.*
scarlet *750.*
blue *750.*

Washington vignette only.

11-E11 3c Die on India
black 325.
dull rose 325.
scarlet 325.
orange 325.
brown orange 325.
brown 325.
green 325.
dark blue 325.
dull violet 325.
rose violet 325.

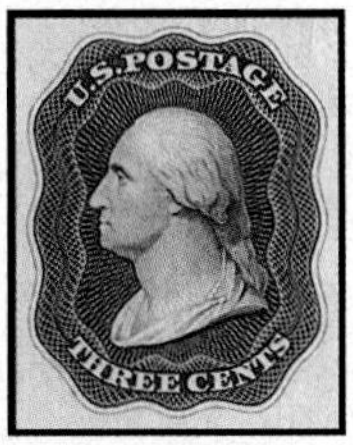
11-E12

Design size: 20x26mm
Die size: 62x66mm
Vignette of Washington. Single line frame. Two states of die. Second state shows scars in lathe lines in front of neck over T, and small dot below design. A third printing has more scars in front of neck.

11-E12 3c
a. Die on India, die sunk on card
black *750.*
scarlet *750.*
brown red *750.*
dusky brown yellow *750.*
brown *750.*
green *750.*
blue *750.*
dull blue *750.*
b. Die on India, about 43x45mm
black *300.*
scarlet *300.*
deep scarlet *300.*
brown *300.*
yellow brown *300.*
green *300.*
yellow green *300.*
blue *300.*
dull blue *300.*
dark blue *300.*
ultramarine blue *300.*
orange *300.*
red *300.*
c. Die on bond
dusky brown yellow *275.*
blue *275.*
d. Die on ivory glazed paper
black *750.*
dark brown *750.*
scarlet *750.*
blue *750.*
e. Plate on thick buff wove
rose 125.
violet brown 125.
orange 125.
dark orange 125.
pink orange 125.
f. Plate on India, dark red orange 150.
g. Plate on ivory wove (head more completely engraved, ruled lines between designs)
black 125.
dark carmine 125.
yellow 125.
blue 125.

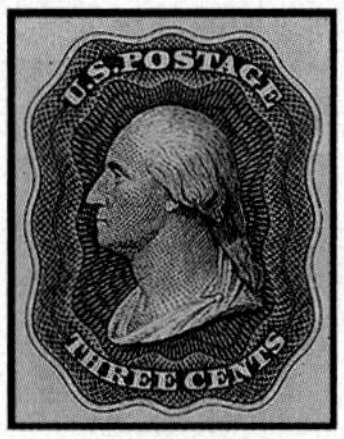
11-E13

Design size: 20x26mm
Die size: 62x66mm
Vignette of Washington. No. 11-E12 reengraved: more dark dots in forehead next to hair, thus line between forehead and hair more distinct.

11-E13 3c
a. Die on India, die sunk on card
black *750.*
scarlet *750.*
brown red *750.*
brown *750.*
green *750.*
b. Die on ivory glazed paper
black *750.*
dark brown *750.*
scarlet *750.*
blue *750.*

Bald, Cousland & Co.

11-E14

11-E15

Design size: 22x28mm
Die size: 95x43mm
Vignette of Washington. On same die with Nos. 11-E16 and incomplete 11-E14.

11-E14 3c
a. Die on India
black *450.*
scarlet *450.*
red brown *450.*
brown *450.*
yellow green *450.*
green *450.*
blue green *450.*
orange brown *450.*
rose pink *450.*
dull blue *450.*
violet *450.*
b. Die on bond
black 250.
scarlet 250.
brown 250.
blue green 250.
blue 250.

Design size: 28x22½mm
POSTAGE / 3 / CENTS in scalloped frame.

11-E15 3c
a. Die on India, die sunk on card
black *750.*
scarlet *750.*
red brown *750.*
green *750.*
slate *750.*
b. Die on bond, about 40x30mm
black 175.
scarlet 175.
brown 175.
green 175.
blue 175.
slate 275.
c. Die on ivory glazed paper
black *750.*
dark brown *750.*
scarlet *750.*
blue *750.*

11-E16

Design size: 28x22½mm
U.S. at sides of 3.

11-E16 3c
a. Die on India, cut small
black *275.*
light red *275.*
red brown *275.*
brown *275.*
yellow green *275.*
blue green *275.*
green *275.*
blue *275.*
red violet *275.*
b. Die on bond, about 40x30mm
black 175.
scarlet 175.
brown 175.
red brown 175.
green 175.
blue green 175.
blue 175.
violet 175.
slate 175.
c. Die on India, Nos. 11-E14 and 11-E16 with albino 11-E14
black *1,000.*
scarlet *1,000.*
brown *1,000.*
green *1,000.*
blue *1,000.*
red violet *1,000.*
d. Die on bond
black *225.*
scarlet *225.*
brown *225.*
green *225.*
blue green *225.*
gray blue *225.*
e. Die on ivory glazed paper, 64x78mm, black *650.*
f. Die on India, die sunk on card
black *900.*
scarlet *900.*

Toppan, Carpenter, Casilear & Co.

5-E1

5-E1E

5-E1Ef

Design size: 20½x26mm
Franklin vignette.

5-E1 1c
a. Die on old proof paper, master die shortened to 18½x22½mm, black *1,500.*
b. Die on thick old proof paper, black *1,500.*
c. Pair, Nos. 5-E1b, 11-E23, black *2,000.*

Design size: 20x24mm
Similar to No. 5-E1 but with no additional shaded oval border.

5-E1E 1c Die on thin card, black blue —
f. Block of 4 in combination with pair of No. 11-E23, on old proof paper, black *3,500.*

5-E2

Complete design, but with SIX CENTS in value tablet.

5-E2 1c Die on India, black, cut to shape 2,750.

11-E17

11-E18

Design size: 21½x25mm
Die size: 50½x60mm
Vignette of Washington.

11-E17 3c
a. Die on India, 22x26mm, rose carmine 2,500.
b. Die on old ivory paper, rose carmine 2,500.
c. Die on proof paper, printed through a mat (1903)
black 175.
bright carmine 175.
dull carmine 175.
dark violet red 175
dull scarlet 175
dull violet 175
dull red violet 175
deep yellow 175
deep orange 175
orange brown 175
dull brown olive 175
deep green 175
dark blue green 175
ultramarine 175
dark blue 175
brown 175
d. Die on colored card (1903)
deep orange, *ivory* 300
dark blue, *pale green* 300
orange brown, *light blue* 300

See note above No. 63-E1.

Design size: 20½x22½mm
Washington. Vignette has solid color background. Crack between N and T of CENTS.

11-E18 3c Die on India, card mounted, 24½x25mm
black *2,000*
carmine *2,000*

Design size: 20½x22½mm
Washington. Like No. 11-E18 except background of vignette is clearly engraved horizontal and vertical lines. Crack between N and T of CENTS.

11-E18A 3c Die on India, die sunk on 60x50mm card, carmine *7,000.*
b. As No. 11-E18A, cut down to stamp's size, black *2,000.*
c. As No. 11-E18A, on old ivory paper, cut down to stamp size, rose carmine *2,000.*

11-E19

11-E20

No. 11-E19
Design size: 20½x22½mm
Similar to No. 11-E18, with a slightly modified design, vignette background engraved horiz. and vert. lines. In pair with No. 11-E20.

No. 11-E20
Design size: 20x22½mm
Blank curved top and bottom labels. In pair with 11-E19. Also found in pair with 11-E21.

11-E19 3c Die on India, Nos. 11-E19, 11-E20 mounted on card, black *6,000.*

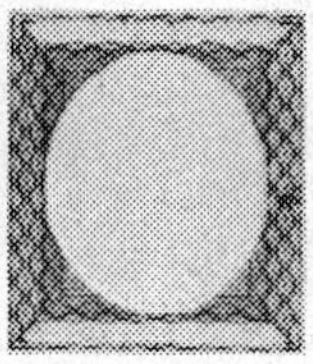
11-E21

Straight labels. Similar to No. 11-E19 but labels erased and vignette cut out. In pair with No. 11-E20.

11-E21 3c Die on India, Nos. 11-E20, 11-E21 mounted on card, black *4,500.*

11-E22

11-E23

Die size: 37½x46mm
Similar to issued stamp except lathework impinges on colorless oval.

11-E22 3c Die on India
dusky blue *5,000*
black *5,000*

Some students consider No. 11-E22 to be proof strikes of the die used to make the "Roosevelt" and Panama-Pacific small die proofs, as the lathework impinges on the colorless oval of Nos. 11P2 and 11P2a as well.

Design size: 18x22mm
Washington vignette only. From master die (21½mm high) with more robe and dark background.

11-E23 3c
a. Master die impression, old proof paper, black *900.*
b. Block of 4, 2mm between ovals, thick old ivory paper, black *3,000.*

13-E1

13-E2

Design as adopted but top label has pencil lettering only, also no lines in leaf ornaments around Xs in top corners.

13-E1 10c Die on India, black *3,000.*

Similar to No. 13-E1 but vert. shading around Xs and lines added in leaf ornaments. No lettering in top label.

13-E2 10c Die on India, black *3,000.*

17-E1

17-E2

Design size: 19x21½mm
Block sinkage size: 57x49mm
Engine engraved frame without labels or interior shadow lines from straight bands and left side rosettes. No small equilateral crosses in central row of diamonds. Original vignette cut out and replaced by engraved vignette of Washington as adopted.

17-E1 12c Die on India, cut close, mounted on block sunk card, 77x57mm, black *10,000.*

Similar to adopted design but no small vertical equilateral crosses in center rows of diamond networks at top, sides and bottom.

17-E2 12c Die on India, brown violet, cut close *900.*
17-E3 12c As No. 17-E2, die on wove, brown violet, cut close *750.*

37-E1

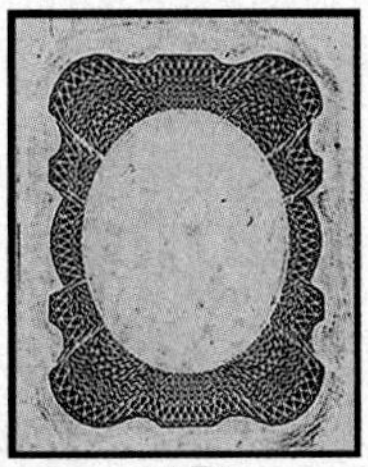
37-E2

Design size: 19½x25½mm
Die size: 46x49mm or larger
Probably not the die used to make the plates. No exterior layout lines. Oval outline recut at bottom of jabot and vignette background etched much darker. Light horizontal lines on stock below chin.

37-E1 24c Die on India, black *2,500.*

Incomplete essay for frame only as adopted: no outer frame-line and lathework not retouched. Also known with 37TC1 struck above it on same piece.

37-E2 24c Die on India, black —

38-E1

Design size: 19x24mm

Incomplete engraving of entire design. Scrolls at each side of 30 have only one outer shading line.

38-E1 30c Die on India, black, cut to stamp size, black *2,500.*

1861 ISSUE
Toppan, Carpenter & Co.

Examples on 1861 paper and in 1861 colors are rare. Most of the following listed on proof paper, colored card and bond paper are 1903 reprints. Ten sets of reprints on proof paper (and fewer on colored card, bond and pelure papers) supposedly were made for Ernest Schernikow, who bought the original dies about 1903. Similar reprints in similar colors on the same papers also were made of Nos. LO1-E2, 11-E18 and the Philadelphia sanitary fair stamps, plus several master dies of vignettes.

63-E1b

63-E2b

Vignette size: 18½x21½mm
Die size: 49x51mm
Franklin vignette only.

63-E1 1c
a. Die on proof paper (1903)
black 75.
carmine 75.
dark carmine 75.
scarlet 75.
red brown 75.
orange 75.
yellow brown 75.
dark brown 75.
violet brown 75.
light green 75.
green 75.
dark blue 75.
ultramarine 75.
red violet 75.
dark violet 75.
dusky olive green 75.
b. Die on colored card (1903)
orange red, *pale yellow* *125.*
orange, *pale pink* *125.*
yellow brown, *buff* *125.*
dark blue, *pink* *125.*
dark violet, *pale olive* *125.*
dull violet, *blue* *125.*
deep green, *pale blue* *125.*
violet, *light green* *125.*
c. Die on green bond (1903)
black *125.*
dismal red *125.*
green *125.*

Franklin vignette with U S POSTAGE at top and ONE CENT at bottom.

63-E2 1c
a. Die on proof paper (1903)
black 100.
carmine 100.
dark carmine 100.
scarlet 100.
red brown 100.
orange 100.
yellow brown 100.
violet brown 100.
gray brown 100.
light green 100.
green 100.
blue 100.
red violet 100.
ultramarine 100.
dusky olive 100.
b. Die on old proof paper, outer line at sides of oval missing (1861), black *1,000.*
c. Die on green bond (1903)
orange *150.*
orange brown *150.*
violet *150.*
d. Die on colored card (1903)
deep green, *pale blue* *150.*
violet, *light green* *150.*
dark orange red, *pale dull green* *150.*
olive, *ivory* *150.*
brown, *pink* *150.*
scarlet, *yellow* *150.*

63-E3

Side ornaments added.

63-E3 1c
a. Die on old proof paper (1861)
black *1,250.*
blue *1,250.*
b. Die on stiff old ivory paper (1861)
black *1,250.*
blue *1,750.*
c. Die on colored card (1903)
black, *ivory* *150.*
brown, *pale pink* *150.*
blue, *blue* *150.*
orange brown, *pale pink* *150.*
gray olive, *ivory* *150.*
gray olive, *buff* *150.*
scarlet, *pale yellow* *150.*
d. Die on proof paper (1903)
black 85.
carmine 85.
dark carmine 85.
scarlet 85.
red brown 85.
orange 85.
yellow brown 85.
violet brown 85.
light green 85.
green 85.
blue 85.
violet 85.
red violet 85.
orange brown 85.
dusky olive 85.
ultramarine 85.
e. Die on green bond (1903)
carmine *150.*
orange *150.*
violet *150.*
f. Die on glazed card, black —

63-E4

63-E4E

With upper and lower right corners incomplete. Serifs of 1s point to right.

63-E4 1c Die on old proof paper (1861), black *2,250.*

As No. 63-E4 but with pencil shading in upper right corner.

63-E4E 1c Die on old proof paper (1861), black *3,500.*

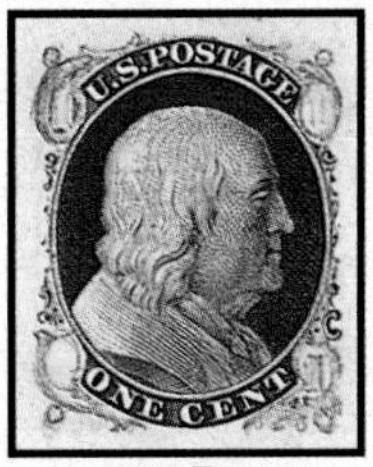

63-E5

63-E6

With four corners and numerals in pencil (ornaments differ in each corner).

63-E5 1c Die on old proof paper (1861), blue *2,750.*

As No. 63-E5 but ornaments different.

63-E6 1c Die on old proof paper (1861), blue *3,500.*

63-E7

As Nos. 63-E5 and 63-E6 but ornaments different.

63-E7 1c Die on old proof paper (1861), blue *3,250.*

Die proof of No. 5 with lower corners cut out of India paper and resketched in pencil on card beneath.

63-E8 1c Die on India, on card (1861), black *2,000.*

63-E9

Completely engraved design.

63-E9 1c
a. Die on India, cut to shape (1861)
black, on brown toned paper *1,000.*
blue *600.*
b. Die on India, about 58x57mm, die sunk on card (1861)
blue *2,000.*
c. Die on old proof paper, about 48x55mm (1861)
black *2,000.*
d. Die on large old white ivory paper (1861)
black *2,000.*
blue *2,000.*
e. Die on proof paper, printed through mat (1903)
black 100.
carmine 100.
dark carmine 100.
scarlet 100.
orange 100.
orange brown 100.
yellow brown 100.
light green 100.
green 100.
black blue 100.
violet 100.
red violet 100.
violet brown 100.
gray 100.
blue 100.
ultramarine 100.
f. Die on bond (1903)
orange *125.*
dismal blue green *125.*
g. Die on bond, Walls of Troy wmk. (1903)
carmine *200.*
orange red *200.*
orange *200.*
orange brown *200.*
dark green *200.*
light ultramarine *200.*
h. Die on bond, double line of scallops wmk. (1903)
orange red *200.*
dark green *200.*
i. Die on green bond (1903)
dismal carmine *125.*
dismal violet brown *125.*
dull dark green *125.*
j. Die on pinkish pelure (1903)
orange red *300.*
brown red *300.*
brown orange *300.*
dull blue green *300.*
violet *300.*
k. Die on colored card (1903)
black, *pale blue* *225.*
carmine, *pale yellow* *225.*
carmine, *pale pink* *225.*
brown red, *pale pink* *225.*
chestnut, *pale olive* *225.*
dismal olive, *buff* *225.*
ultramarine, *ivory* *225.*
l. Die on stiff card (1903), green *250.*

65-E1

65-E2

Vignette size: 16½x19mm
Die size: 49x50mm
1851 master die of Washington vignette only.

65-E1 3c
a. Die on proof paper (1903)
black 75.
carmine 75.
dark carmine 75.
scarlet 75.
red brown 75.
orange 75.
brown orange 75.
violet brown 75.
dusky olive 75.
light green 75.
green 75.
dark blue 75.
ultramarine 75.
lilac 75.
red violet 75.
b. Die on green bond (1903)
red *125.*
brown *125.*
blue *125.*
olive *125.*
c. Die on colored card (1903)
carmine, *pale green* *125.*
scarlet, *yellow* *125.*
orange, *ivory* *125.*
olive brown, *blue* *125.*
dark blue, *pink* *125.*
violet, *buff* *125.*
dark green, *pink* *125.*

With tessellated frame, bottom label and diamond blocks. Without rosettes, top label and diamond blocks.

65-E2 3c
a. Die on old proof paper (1861)
black *1,000.*
red *1,000.*
b. Die on proof paper, printed through a mat (1903)
black *85.*
carmine *85.*
dark carmine *85.*
scarlet *85.*
orange *85.*
yellow *85.*
yellow brown *85.*
dusky gray *85.*
light green *85.*
green *85.*
black blue *85.*
ultramarine *85.*
lilac *85.*
dark lilac *85.*
red violet *85.*
c. Die on green bond (1903)
black *150.*
dull orange red *150.*
orange *150.*
orange brown *150.*
blue violet *150.*
black blue *150.*
dusky green *150.*
d. Die on dull pale gray blue thin wove (1903)
dull red *300.*
orange *300.*
yellow brown *300.*
dusky green *300.*
black blue *300.*
e. Die on colored card (1903)
black, *light blue* *150.*
orange red, *yellow* *150.*
red brown, *ivory* *150.*
light green, *pink* *150.*
green, *light green* *150.*
blue, *buff* *150.*
f. Die on India
black —
rose —

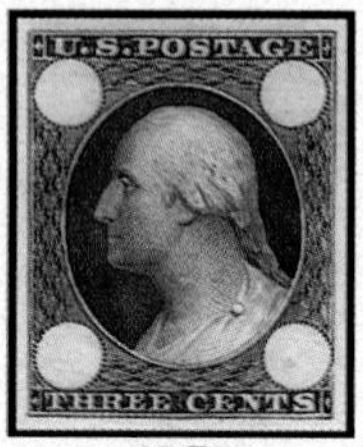

65-E3

65-E4

With top label and diamond blocks.

65-E3 3c
a. Die on old proof paper (1861)
brown red *1,500.*
black *1,500.*
b. Same as No. 65-E3 with numerals in pencil, Die on old proof paper (1861), black *3,500.*
c. Die on proof paper, no numerals, printed through a mat (1903)
black 90.
carmine 90.
dark carmine 90.
scarlet 90.
orange 90.
yellow 90.
yellow brown 90.
dusky olive 90.
light green 90.
green 90.
black blue 90.
violet blue 90.
violet brown 90.
lilac 90.
red violet 90.
d. Die on green bond (1903)
dull scarlet *150.*
dim red *150.*
orange *150.*
yellow brown *150.*
green *150.*
dusky blue *150.*
violet *150.*
black *150.*
e. Die on colored card (1903)
black, *buff* *150.*
scarlet, *ivory* *150.*
orange, *light yellow* *150.*
brown, *light blue* *150.*
violet blue, *light pink* *150.*
violet, *light green* *150.*
f. Die on pink thin wove (1903)
dull yellow *300.*
dismal red *300.*
yellow brown *300.*
dusky blue green *300.*
dusky blue *300.*

Complete die, with numerals in rosette circles.

65-E4 3c
a. Die on India, 75x76mm die sinkage (1861)
black *1,500.*
carmine *1,500.*
b. Die on old proof paper (1861)
black *1,500.*
dark red *1,500.*
c. Die on India, cut to shape (1861)
black *1,000.*
carmine *1,000.*

67-E1a — Die I 67-E1b — Die II

Vignette size: 13½x16mm
Jefferson vignette only. Two dies: die I incomplete, light background in vignette; die II background essentially complete.

67-E1 5c
a. Die I on proof paper, black *650.*
b. Die II on proof paper (1903)
black 75.
carmine 75.
dark carmine 75.
scarlet 75.
red brown 75.
orange brown 75.
brown 75.
dusky olive 75.
green 75.
dark green 75.
black blue 75.
ultramarine 75.
violet brown 75.
red violet 75.
lilac 75.
c. Die II on colored card (1903)
olive, *buff* *150.*
carmine, *pale yellow* *150.*
scarlet, *green* *150.*
brown, *pink* *150.*
black, *ivory* *150.*
ultramarine, *pale blue* *150.*
d. Die II on green bond (1903)
orange brown *150.*
dismal red brown *150.*
dark green *150.*
violet *150.*
black blue *150.*
e. Die II on old thin ivory paper (1903)
green 175.
dark carmine 175.
f. Die I on old thin ivory paper (1861), dark blue *1,000.*
g. Die I on old proof paper (1861)
black *750.*
dusky ultramarine *1,500.*
h. Die II on old ivory paper (1861), navy blue *750.*

67-E2

Vignette die II framed, with spaces for numerals.

67-E2 5c
a. Die II on proof paper (1903)
black 95.
carmine 95.
dark carmine 95.
scarlet 95.
red brown 95.
orange 95.
yellow brown 95.
dusky olive 95.
violet brown 95.
light green 95.
green 95.
blue 95.
ultramarine 95.
red violet 95.
lilac 95.
b. Die II on colored card (1903)
orange brown, *light yellow* *175.*
deep blue, *light pink* *175.*
dusky olive, *light buff* *175.*

dark green, *pale blue* 175.
red violet, *ivory* 175.
c. Die II on green bond (1903)
orange brown 160.
olive green 160.
violet 160.
blue 160.
ultramarine 160.

67-E3

67-E4

With numerals.

67-E3 5c
a. Die I on proof paper, printed through a mat (1903)
black 125.
carmine 125.
dark carmine 125.
scarlet 125.
red brown 125.
yellow brown 125.
dark brown 125.
violet brown 125.
light green 125.
green 125.
dark blue 125.
lilac 125.
ultramarine 125.
red violet 125.
dusky olive 125.
b. Die I on soft laid paper (1861)
black 750.
dark brown 750.
orange brown 750.
c. Die I on old proof paper, pencil designs drawn in corners (1861), black 1,500.
d. Die I on old proof paper, outer lines on corner curves missing (1861), black 500.
e. Die I on colored card (1903)
orange red, *buff* 175.
orange red, *light yellow* 175.
olive green, *pale green* 175.
deep green, *ivory* 175.
dark blue, *light pink* 175.
violet brown, *light blue* 175.
f. Die I on green bond (1903)
black 160.
scarlet 160.
brown 160.
green 160.
g. Die I on yellow pelure (1903)
scarlet 350.
brown red 350.
brown 350.
dark green 350.
violet 350.
blue 350.
h. Die I on bond, Walls of Troy wmk. (1903)
dark orange 250.
blue 250.
carmine 250.
i. Die I on bond, two line scalloped border wmk. (1903)
dark blue green 250.
scarlet 250.

Complete die II design with corner ornaments.

67-E4 5c
a. Die II on India, cut to shape (1861), black 500.
b. Die II on brown toned paper (1861)
black 1,000.
brown 1,000.
c. Die II on old proof paper (1861)
orange brown 1,000.
black 1,000.
d. Die II on old ivory paper (1861), black 1,000.
e. Die II on old proof paper, additional frameline drawn on curved corners and small circle drawn in each corner (1861), black 1,500.
f. Die II on proof paper, printed through a mat (1903)
black 125.
carmine 125.
dark carmine 125.
scarlet 125.
orange 125.
brown 125.
yellow brown 125.
dusky olive 125.
light green 125.
green 125.
blue 125.
black blue 125.
violet brown 125.
red violet 125.
lilac 125.
ultramarine 125.
g. Die II on colored card (1903)
red, *light yellow* 150.
brown, *buff* 150.
olive green, *light pink* 150.
dark violet 150.
violet brown, *pale green* 150.
dusky yellow green, *dull pale blue green* 150.
brown, *ivory* 150.
h. Die II on green bond (1903)
black 125.
dull dark orange 125.
violet 125.
i. Die II on bond, Walls of Troy wmk. (1903)
scarlet 250.
deep red 250.
dark green 250.
j. Die II on bond, two-line scalloped border wmk. (1903)
deep orange 250.
blue 250.
k. Die II on greenish pelure (1903)
orange 350.
olive brown 350.
dark green 350.
l. Die II on bluish pelure (1903), red brown 450.

69-E1

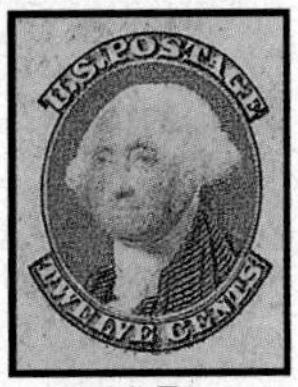
69-E2

Vignette size: 15x17mm
Washington vignette only. Two dies: die I incomplete, horiz. background lines irregularly spaced, space occurring about every 2mm; die II more engraving on face, horiz. background lines regularly spaced, outer oval border smudged. Die II known only as 1851 master die.

69-E1 12c
a. Die II on old proof paper (1851), black 650.
b. Die I on proof paper (1903)
black 60.
carmine 60.
dark carmine 60.
scarlet 60.
red brown 60.
orange 60.
yellow brown 60.
violet brown 60.
gray brown 60.
light green 60.
green 60.
blue 60.
black blue 60.
red violet 60.
lilac 60.
ultramarine 60.
c. Die I on green bond (1903)
black 150.
red brown 150.
brown 150.
d. Die I on colored card (1903)
dark carmine, *ivory* 150.
dark carmine, *light blue* 150.
dark olive, *buff* 150.
dark green, *light yellow* 150.
dark blue, *pale green* 150.
violet brown, *light pink* 150.

Die II with curved labels at top and bottom.

69-E2 12c
a. Die II on proof paper, some printed through a mat (1903)
black 75.
carmine 75.
dark carmine 75.
scarlet 75.
orange 75.
yellow 75.
yellow brown 75.
violet brown 75.
gray brown 75.
light green 75.
green 75.
light blue 75.
black blue 75.
red violet 75.
lilac 75.
ultramarine 75.
b. Die I on old proof paper (1861)
dim red violet 500.
red violet 500.
c. Die I on dull light green bond (1903)
black 150.
dull red 150.
dim orange 150.
yellow brown 150.
dusky green 150.
dusky blue 150.
red violet 150.
d. Die I on pale yellow thin wove (1903)
dim red 200.
deep orange red 200.
yellow brown 200.
dusky blue 200.
red violet 200.
e. Die I on colored card (1903)
dull red, *light pink* 150.
orange red, *buff* 150.
brown, *light blue* 150.
dark olive, *light yellow* 150.
dull dark blue, *ivory* 150.
violet, *pale green* 150.

69-E3

Frame incomplete: all four rosettes blank.

69-E3 12c
a. Die on proof paper (1903)
black 125.
carmine 125.
dark carmine 125.
scarlet 125.
red brown 125.
orange 125.
orange brown 125.
violet brown 125.
light green 125.
green 125.
light blue 125.
black blue 125.
red violet 125.
lilac 125.
ultramarine 125.
b. Die on old proof paper (1861)
black 800.
olive gray 800.
c. Die on old ivory, top border and half of rosettes missing (1861), black 800.
d. Die on stiff old ivory, top border missing (1861), bluish black 800.
e. Die on colored card, top border missing (1903)
orange brown, *light blue* 175.
deep green, *light yellow* 175.
deep blue, *light pink* 175.
violet, *ivory* 175.
deep yellow orange, *pale yellow green* 175.
brown, *buff* 175.
f. Die on green bond, top border missing (1903)
orange 175.
green 175.
violet 175.
g. Die on old proof paper, 1851 die with border lines complete, upper right rosette blank (1861)
orange 800.
dark green 800.
ultramarine 800.
violet 800.
h. Die I on old proof paper, vignette background incomplete or worn, stock on neck unfinished (1861) —
i. Die I on old proof paper, as 69-E3h but both upper rosettes blank (1861), ultramarine 1,000.

69-E3j

69-E3k

j. Die I on old proof paper, as No. 69-E3h but both upper plus lower left rosettes blank (1861), ultramarine 1,000.
k. Die I on old proof paper, as No. 69-E3h but both lower plus upper left rosettes blank, corner borders removed around blank rosettes (1861), ultramarine 1,000.
l. Die I on old proof paper, as No. 69-E3h but all rosettes blank, border lines complete (1861)
dim scarlet 750.
orange 750.
green 750.
ultramarine 750.
violet 750.
m. Die I on white wove, as No. 69-E3l (1861), scarlet 750.
n. Die I on old proof paper, complete design (1861)
orange 750.
dark red 750.
orange red 750.
ultramarine 750.
o. Die I on pale yellow thin wove (1903), dark red 750.
p. Die I on pink thin wove (1903), blue 750.
q. Die I on pale pink (1903), blue 750.

69-E4

Original complete design with numerals in corners.

69-E4 12c
- *a.* Die on India, card mounted (1861)
  - black 800.
  - gray black 800.
- *b.* Die on India, cut to shape (1861), black 500.
- *c.* Die on old proof paper (1861), black 500.
- *d.* Die on old proof paper, corners drawn in pencil (1861), black 1,500.
- *e.* Die on old proof paper, as No. 69-E3a but numerals sketched in diagonally and vert. (1861), black 3,000.
- *f.* Die on stiff old ivory paper, as No. 69-E4e but without top border (1861), bluish black 1,500.
- *g.* Die on thin card, black —

70-E1

70-E2c

Vignette size: 7x16mm
Washington die II vignette only.

70-E1 24c
- *a.* Die II on proof paper (1903)
  - black 60.
  - carmine 60.
  - dark carmine 60.
  - scarlet 60.
  - orange 60.
  - yellow 60.
  - yellow brown 60.
  - violet brown 60.
  - gray olive 60.
  - light green 60.
  - green 60.
  - light blue 60.
  - black blue 60.
  - red violet 60.
  - lilac 60.
- *b.* Die II on green bond (1903)
  - black 150.
  - red brown 150.
  - violet 150.
  - orange 150.
- *c.* Die II on colored card (1903)
  - dull red, *ivory* 150.
  - brown red, *buff* 150.
  - brown orange, *light pink* 150.
  - dark green, *light yellow* 150.
  - blue, *pale green* 150.
  - violet, *blue* 150.

Washington vignette with oval label. Background complete, eyes retouched.

70-E2 24c
- *a.* Die II on proof paper (1903)
  - black 60.
  - carmine 60.
  - dark carmine 60.
  - scarlet 60.
  - orange 60.
  - yellow 60.
  - yellow brown 60.
  - violet brown 60.
  - light green 60.
  - green 60.
  - light blue 60.
  - black blue 60.
  - red violet 60.
  - lilac 60.
  - gray olive 60.
  - ultramarine 60.
- *b.* Die I on old proof paper, background lines incomplete (1861)
  - black 750.
  - dim red violet 750.
- *c.* Die I on colored card (1903)
  - black, *light pink* 150.
  - orange, *buff* 150.
  - orange, *light blue* 150.
  - dark green, *pale green* 150.
  - violet blue, *light yellow* 150.
  - violet, *ivory* 150.
- *d.* Die I on green bond (1903), brown 150.
- *e.* Die I on dull light blue green bond (1903)
  - black 150.
  - orange red 150.
  - orange 150.
  - yellow brown 150.
  - dusky green 150.
  - dull blue 150.
  - red violet 150.
- *f.* Die I on dull pale green blue thin wove (1903)
  - orange red 300.
  - orange 300.
  - yellow brown 300.
  - dusky green 300.
  - dull blue 300.

70-E3

70-E4

With frame. Blank areas in corners for numerals.

70-E3 24c
- *a.* Die on proof paper (1903)
  - black 100.
  - carmine 100.
  - dark carmine 100.
  - scarlet 100.
  - orange 100.
  - yellow brown 100.
  - orange brown 100.
  - violet brown 100.
  - gray olive 100.
  - light green 100.
  - green 100.
  - light blue 100.
  - black blue 100.
  - red violet 100.
  - lilac 100.
  - ultramarine 100.
- *b.* Die on old proof paper (1861), dusky red violet 1,000.
- *c.* Die on colored card (1903)
  - carmine, *light blue* 175.
  - blue, *pale green* 175.
  - scarlet, *buff* 175.
  - yellow brown, *cream* 175.
  - dull violet, *pink* 175.
  - dusky green, *light yellow* 175.
  - gray olive, *ivory* 175.
- *d.* Die on green bond (1903)
  - black 175.
  - orange brown 175.
  - green 175.

Complete design with numerals in corners.

70-E4 24c
- *a.* Die on old proof paper, cut to shape (1861)
  - lilac 400.
  - black 400.
  - red violet 400.
- *b.* Die on India, cut close (1861)
  - black 400.
  - lilac 400.
  - brown lilac 400.
- *c.* Die on India (1861), dark blue 750.
- *d.* Die on India, mounted on 80x115mm card (1861), lilac 750.
- *e.* On stiff old ivory paper (1861)
  - black 1,000.
  - lilac 1,000.
- *f.* Die on proof paper, printed through a mat (1903)
  - black 125.
  - carmine 125.
  - dark carmine 125.
  - scarlet 125.
  - red borwn 125.
  - yellow brown 125.
  - brown 125.
  - violet brown 125.
  - gray olive 125.
  - light green 125.
  - green 125.
  - light blue 125.
  - black blue 125.
  - red violet 125.
  - lilac 125.
  - ultramarine 125.
- *g.* Die on blue pelure (1903)
  - dark carmine 300.
  - scarlet 300.
  - orange 300.
  - brown 300.
  - dusky green 300.
- *h.* Die on bond (1903)
  - black 175.
  - scarlet 175.
  - orange 175.
  - dark green 175.
  - blue 175.
- *i.* Die on green bond (1903)
  - black 250.
  - dark red 250.
  - green 250.
- *j.* Die on bond, Walls of Troy wmk. (1903), dark green 300.
- *k.* Die on bond, double line of scallops wmk. (1903)
  - deep orange red 300.
  - scarlet 300.
  - orange 300.
  - light blue 300.
- *l.* Die on colored card, printed through a mat
  - dark orange, *ivory* 150.
  - dark orange, *light pink* 150.
  - brown, *light blue* 150.
  - dull dark blue, *pale green* 150.
  - violet, *light yellow* 150.
  - violet brown, *buff* 150.

72-E1

72-E2

Vignette size: 16x17½mm
Washington vignette only.

72-E1 90c
- *a.* Die on proof paper (1903)
  - black 100.
  - carmine 100.
  - dark carmine 100.
  - scarlet 100.
  - red brown 100.
  - orange 100.
  - orange brown 100.
  - violet brown 100.
  - gray olive 100.
  - light green 100.
  - green 100.
  - dark blue 100.
  - lilac 100.
  - red violet 100.
  - yellow brown 100.
  - ultramarine 100.
- *b.* Die on colored card (1903)
  - black, *light yellow* 165.
  - red brown, *light pink* 165.
  - carmine, *buff* 165.
  - brown, *pale green* 165.
  - dark brown, *light blue* 165.
  - ultramarine, *ivory* 165.
- *c.* Die on dull light blue green bond (1903)
  - violet brown 165.
  - dusky green 165.
  - dusky blue 165.
  - red violet 165.

Vignette with blank top and bottom labels.

72-E2 90c
- *a.* Die on proof paper (1903)
  - black 100.
  - carmine 100.
  - dark carmine 100.
  - scarlet 100.
  - orange 100.
  - yellow brown 100.
  - brown 100.
  - violet brown 100.
  - gray olive 100.
  - light green 100.
  - green 100.
  - dark blue 100.
  - red violet 100.
  - lilac 100.
  - ultramarine 100.
- *b.* Die on green bond (1903)
  - dull orange 150.
  - dull orange brown 150.
  - red violet 150.
- *c.* Die on colored card (1903)
  - black, *buff* 185.
  - orange red, *light yellow* 185.
  - brown, *ivory* 185.
  - olive green, *light pink* 185.
  - green, *light blue* 185.
  - violet brown, *pale green* 185.

72-E3

72-E5

U.S. POSTAGE in top label.

72-E3 90c
- *a.* Die on proof paper (1903)
  - black 125.

carmine 125.
dark carmine 125.
scarlet 125.
yellow 125.
yellow brown 125.
brown 125.
violet brown 125.
gray olive 125.
light green 125.
green 125.
dark blue 125.
lilac 125.
red violet 125.
ultramarine 125.
b. Die on colored card (1903)
orange, *light blue* *185.*
orange red, *light yellow* *185.*
dark blue, *buff* *185.*
violet, *pale green* *185.*
violet brown, *ivory* *185.*
orange brown, *pale pink* *185.*
c. Die on green bond (1903)
black *175.*
brown *175.*
green *175.*

Lower corners of vignette cut out, "NINETY 90 CENTS" in pencil in bottom label.

72-E4 90c Die on India (1861), black *2,000.*

Complete design.

72-E5 90c
a. Die on India, cut to shape (1861)
black *300.*
dark blue *300.*
b. Die on India, die sunk on card (1861), blue *2,000.*
c. Die on India, cut close (1861)
black *300.*
blue *300.*
d. Die on proof paper, printed through a mat (1903)
black 175.
carmine 175.
dark carmine 175.
scarlet 175.
orange 175.
yellow brown 175.
brown 175.
violet brown 175.
gray olive 175.
light green 175.
green 175.
dark blue 175.
lilac 175.
red violet 175.
ultramarine 175.
e. Die on colored card (1903)
carmine, *light blue* *250.*
dismal brown, *light pink* *250.*
orange brown, *buff* *250.*
blue, *ivory* *250.*
violet, *pale green* *250.*
green, *pale yellow* *250.*
f. Die on green bond (1903)
dark carmine *225.*
red brown *225.*
green *225.*
g. Die on bond (1903), orange brown *250.*
h. Die on bond, "Bond No. 1" wmk. (1903), orange brown *350.*
i. Die on bond, "Bond No 2" wmk. (1903), orange brown *350.*
j. Die on bond, Walls of Troy wmk. (1903)
carmine *300.*
scarlet *300.*
orange *300.*
dark green *300.*
ultramarine *300.*
k. Die on pink pelure (1903)
brown red *350.*
dull yellow *350.*
very dark green *350.*
dark blue *350.*
dull violet *350.*

American Bank Note Co.

65-E5

65-E6

Design size: 19x23½mm
Engraved frame with pencil border, center cut out, mounted over 22x27mm engraved vignette of Washington.

65-E5 3c Die on India, black *2,500.*

Design size: 19x24½mm
Engraved frame with pencil border, center cut out, mounted over engraved ruled background with engraved Washington vignette mounted on it.

65-E6 Three Cents Die on India, on card about 23x27½mm, black *2,500.*

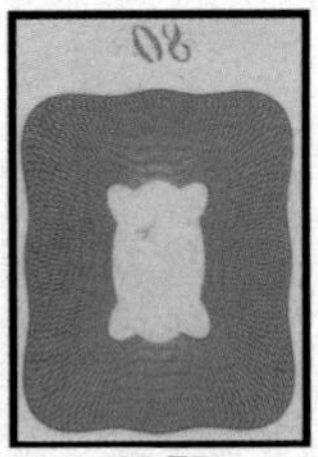

65-E7

65-E8

Master die No. 80 of frame only.

65-E7 3c Die on India, card mounted
deep orange *2,000.*
dark brown *2,000.*
green *2,000.*
dark blue *2,000.*
black *2,000.*

Design size: 19½x24½mm
Engraved lathework frame with Bald, Cousland & Co. engraved Washington vignette and engraved lettered labels and numerals mounted on it.

65-E8 3c Die on India, on 22x27mm card, black *11,000.*

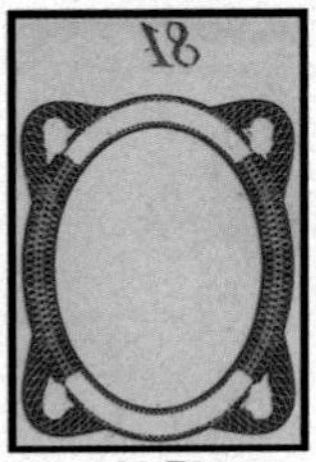

65-E9

65-E10

Master die No. 81 of frame only.

65-E9 3c Die on India
black *2,750.*
brown yellow *2,750.*
dark green *2,750.*
orange red *2,750.*

Engraved lathework frame with Bald, Cousland & Co. engraved Washington vignette and engraved lettered labels and numerals mounted on it.

65-E10 3c Die on India, on 28x35mm card, black *7,000.*

67-E5

Design size: 21x25mm
Engraved frame used for the 1860 Nova Scotia 5c stamp cut to shape, with engraved lettered labels and Washington vignette No. 209-E7 mounted on it.

67-E5 Five Cents Die on India, on 23x27mm card, black *2,500.*

67-E6

67-E7

Design size: 19x24
Engraved lathework background with Bald, Cousland & Co. engraved Washington vignette and engraved lettered labels and numerals mounted on it.

67-E6 5c Die on India, mounted on 22x26mm card, black *7,000.*

Design size: 19x24mm
Engraved lathework background with Bald, Cousland & Co. engraved Washington vignette and engraved lettered labels and numerals mounted on it.

67-E7 5c Die on India, mounted on 21x26½mm card, black *7,000.*

National Bank Note Co.

The following essays include those formerly listed as Nos. 55-57, 59 and 62 in the Postage section, and the corresponding die and plate essays formerly listed in the Proof section. Former No. 58 is now No. 62B. Former Nos. 60 and 61 are now Nos. 70eTC and 71bTC in the Trial Color Proofs section.

63-E10

Frame essay with blank areas for Franklin vignette, labels, numerals, U and S.

63-E10 1c Die on India, black 2,000.

63-E11

63-E12

Die size: 58x56mm
"Premiere Gravure" die No. 440.

63-E11 1c
a. "Premiere Gravure" die essay on India (formerly Nos. 55P1, 55TC1)
black *4,000.*
indigo *1,500.*
ultramarine *2,250.*
b. "Premiere Gravure" small die essay on white wove, 28x31mm (**formerly No. 55P2**), indigo *325.*
c. "Premiere Gravure" plate essay on India (**formerly Nos. 55P3, 55TC3**)
indigo *300.*
blue —
ultramarine *300.*
violet ultramarine —
d. "Premiere Gravure" plate essay on semitransparent stamp paper (**formerly No. 55TC4**), ultramarine *400.*
e. Finished "Premiere Gravure" plate essay on semitransparent stamp paper, perf. 12, gummed (**formerly No. 55**), indigo *30,000.*

No. 63-E11e is valued with perfs cutting slightly into design at top.

Die size: 47x55mm
Apparently complete die except value numerals have been cut out.

63-E12 1c Die on India, die sunk on card, black *1,500.*

65-E11

65-E12

Die size: 64x76½mm
Incomplete engraving of Washington head only.

65-E11 3c
a. Die on India, on card, carmine *750.*
b. Die on white glazed paper
black *750.*
scarlet *750.*
brown violet *750.*

Die size: 78x55mm
Incomplete engraved design, no scrolls outside framelines, no silhouette under chin, no ornaments on 3s, U and S.

65-E12 3c Die on India, die sunk on card
black *1,000.*
blue *1,000.*

65-E13

65-E14

As No. 65-E12 but ornaments on 3s, U and S. Shows traces of first border design erased. With imprint and No. 441 below design.

65-E13 3c Die on India, card mounted
- scarlet *1,000.*
- brown red *1,000.*
- ultramarine *1,000.*

Die size: 59x55mm
As No. 65-E13 but with ornaments outside frame.

65-E14 3c Die on India, die sunk on card
- black *750.*
- scarlet *750.*
- pink *1,250.*
- brown orange *750.*
- deep orange red *750.*
- deep red *750.*

As No. 65-E14 but top of head silhouetted, lines added or strengthened in hair at top of head, around eye, on chin, in hair behind ear. The three lines on bottom edge of bust extended to back. No imprint or die number.

65-E15

65-E15 3c
- ***a.*** Die on India, card mounted, deep orange red *1,000.*
- ***b.*** "Premiere Gravure" die essay on semi-transparent stamp paper, 20x25mm-30x37mm
  - deep orange red *750.*
  - deep red orange *750.*
  - dim red *750.*
  - dim deep red *750.*
  - dim orange red *750.*
  - dull pink *750.*
  - dull violet red *750.*
- ***c.*** "Premiere Gravure" die essay on India (**formerly Nos. 56P1, 56TC1**)
  - red *1,350.*
  - black *2,000.*
  - scarlet *2,000.*
  - pink *2,850.*
  - orange red *2,000.*
  - dark orange red *2,000.*
- ***d.*** Small die essay on white wove, 28x31mm altered laydown die of complete design but with outer scrolls removed and replaced by ones similar to "Premiere Gravure" design (1903) (**formerly No. 56P2**), dim deep red *325.*
- ***e.*** As "c," small die essay on pale cream soft wove, 24x29mm (1915) (**formerly No. 56P2a**), deep red *1,250.*
- ***f.*** "Premiere Gravure" plate No. 2 essay on India (**formerly Nos. 56P3, 56TC3**)
  - red *250.*
  - scarlet *350.*
- ***g.*** "Premiere Gravure" plate essay on semitransparent stamp paper (**formerly Nos. 56aP4, 56TC4**)
  - red, pair with gum *1,750.*
  - black *400.*
- ***h.*** Finished "Premiere Gravure" plate essay on semitransparent stamp paper, perf. 12, gummed (**formerly No. 56**)
  - brown rose *550.*
  - P# block of 8, Impt. *20,000.*
  - orange red *475.*
  - bright orange red *475.*
  - dark orange red *475.*
  - dim deep red *475.*
  - pink *475.*
  - deep pink *475.*

67-E8

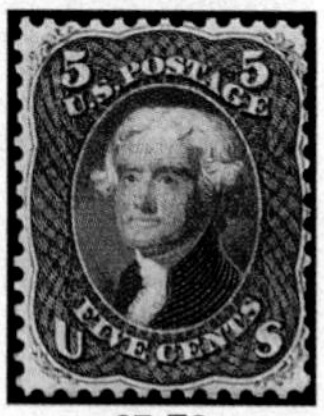

67-E9

Incomplete impression from die No. 442, border lines and corner scrolls missing.

67-E8 5c Die on India, mounted on 34x50mm card, black *1,750.*

Size of die: 58x59mm
"Premiere Gravure" design, with corner scrolls but without leaflets.

67-E9 5c
- ***a.*** "Premiere Gravure" die essay on India, card mounted (formerly No. 57TC1)
  - black *2,500.*
  - scarlet *2,500.*
- ***b.*** Small die essay on white wove, 28x31mm, altered laydown die of complete design but with scrolls removed from corners to resemble "Premiere Gravure" (1903) (**formerly No. 57P2), brown** 325.
- ***c.*** As "b," die essay on pale cream soft wove, 24x29mm (1915) (**formerly No. 57P2a**), brown *1,750.*
- ***d.*** "Premiere Gravure" plate No. 3 essay on India (**formerly Nos. 57P3, 57TC3)**
  - brown *250.*
  - light brown *300.*
  - dark brown *300.*
  - red brown *300.*
- ***e.*** Finished "Premiere Gravure" plate essay on semitransparent stamp paper, perf. 12, gummed (**formerly No. 57**), brown *25,000.*

68-E1

68-E2

Design size: 14x17½mm
Die size: 26x31mm
Washington vignette only.

68-E1 10c
- ***a.*** Die on ivory paper, black *1,000.*
- ***b.*** Die on India *1,000.*

Incomplete die No. 443.

68-E2 10c Die on India, 22x26mm, dark green *2,500.*

Incomplete die of No. 68P1, thin lines missing on top of frame

68-E3

68-E3 10c Die on India
- yellowish green *1,000.*
- dark green *1,000.*

69-E5

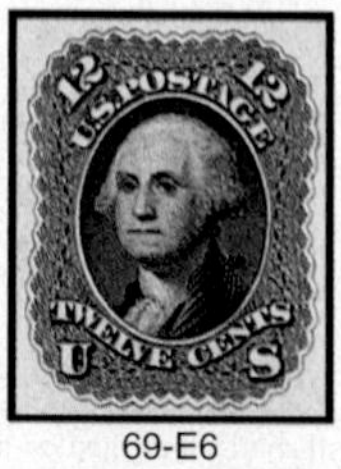

69-E6

Design size: 12½x16mm

Die size: about 62x65mm
Washington vignette only.

69-E5 12c
- ***a.*** Die on India, die sunk on card
  - black *400*
  - dark red *400*
  - orange red *400*
- ***b.*** Die on ivory paper, about 24x28mm
  - black *500*
  - scarlet *500*
  - black brown *500*
  - blue *500*

Incomplete die No. 444, without corner ornaments.

69-E6 12c
- ***a.*** "Premiere Gravure" die essay on India, mounted on card (**formerly Nos. 59P1, 59TC1**)
  - black *2,500*
  - scarlet *2,500*
  - dark green *2,500*
- ***b.*** "Premiere Gravure" small die essay on white wove, 28x31mm (1903) (**formerly No. 59P2**), black *450*
- ***c.*** "Premiere Gravure" small die essay on pale cream soft wove, 24x29mm (1915) (**formerly No. 59P2a**), black *1,750*
- ***d.*** "Premiere Gravure" plate No. 5 essay on India (**formerly No. 59P3**), black *350*
- ***e.*** Finished "Premiere Gravure" plate essay on semitransparent stamp paper, perf. 12, gummed (**formerly No. 59**), black *75,000*

70-E5

70-E6

Washington vignette in incomplete frame.

70-E5 24c Die on India, black *3,250*

Die size: 56½x56mm
Incomplete die (No. 445): silhouette unfinished, especially scrolls around numerals; shadows over numerals not acic etched.

70-E6 24c Die on India, die sunk on card
- black *900*
- violet *900*
- gray violet *900*
- dark violet *900*
- scarlet *900*
- green *900*
- orange *900*
- red brown *900*
- orange brown *900*
- orange yellow *900*
- rose red *900*
- gray *900*
- steel blue *900*
- blue *900*

For finished "Premiere Gravure" trial color plate proof on semitransparent stamp paper, perf 12, gummed (formerly No. 60), see 70eTC in the Trial Color Proof section.

71-E1

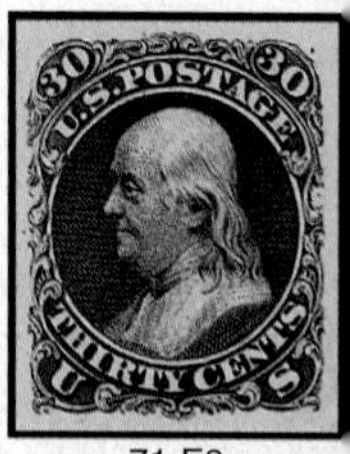

71-E2

Die size: 46x60mm
Incomplete die (No. 446): additional ornaments at top and bottom in pencil, as later engraved.

71-E1 30c Die on India, black *1,750*

"Premiere Gravure" die: left side of frame and silhouette at lower right unfinished.

71-E2 30c
- ***a.*** "Premiere Gravure" die essay on India, die sunk on card (**formerly No. 61TC1**)
  - black *1,750*
  - green *1,750*
  - dull gray blue *1,750*
  - violet brown *1,750*
  - scarlet *1,750*
  - dull rose *1,750*
- ***b.*** "Premiere Gravure" plate essay on India (**formerly No. 61P3**), deep red orange *500*
- ***c.*** "Premiere Gravure" plate essay on card
  - black (split thin) *500*
  - blue *750*

d. "Premiere Gravure" plate essay on card, black 12x2mm SPECIMEN overprint, blue 750.
e. "Premiere Gravure" plate essay on semi-transparent stamp paper
deep red orange 1,250.
yellow orange 1,250.
lemon yellow 1,250.
dark orange yellow 1,250.
dull orange yellow 1,250.

For finished "Premiere Gravure" trial color proof on semi-transparent stamp paper, perf 12, gummed (formerly No. 61), see No. 71bTC in the Trial Color Proof section.

72-E6

72-E7

Die size: 54x63mm
Incomplete die: without thin lines at bottom of frame and in upper left triangle between label and frame, and without leaves at left of U and right of S.

72-E6 90c Die on India, blue (shades) 1,000.

Similar to 72-E6 but lines added in upper left triangle, leaves added at left of U and at right of S. Exists with and without imprint and Die No. 447 added below design.

72-E7 90c
a. Die on India, die sunk on card, black 1,750.
b. "Premiere Gravure" die essay on India, thin line under bottom center frame (**formerly Nos. 62P1, 62TC1**)
blue 1,350.
black 1,750.
c. "Premiere Gravure" small die essay on white wove, 28x31mm (1903) (**formerly No. 62P2**), blue 500.
d. "Premiere Gravure" small die essay on pale cream soft wove, 24x29mm (1915) (**formerly No. 62P2a**), blue 1,750.
e. "Premiere Gravure" plate essay on India, blue 500.
f. "Premiere Gravure" plate essay on card, black (split thin) 500.
g. "Premiere Gravure" plate essay on semi-transparent stamp paper (**formerly Nos. 62aP4, 62TC4**)
blue, pair, gummed 5,500.
blue green 275.
h. Finished "Premiere Gravure" plate essay on semitransparent stamp paper, perf. 12, gummed (**formerly No. 62**), blue 50,000.

Die size: 54x63mm
Similar to Nos. 72-E6 and 72-E7 but leaf at left of "U" only, no shading around "U" and "S," leaf and some shading missing at bottom right above "S," shading missing in top label, etc., faint ms. "8" at bottom of backing card.

72-E8 90c Die on India, die sunk on 3¼x3½-inch card, dark blue —

63-E13

Design size: 20x47mm
Die size: 57x95mm
Bowlsby patent coupon at top of 1c stamp design.

63-E13 1c
a. Die on India, die sunk on card
black 1,750.
red 1,750.
scarlet 1,750.
orange 1,750.
orange brown 1,750.
brown 1,750.
yellow brown 1,750.
blue green 1,750.
blue 1,750.
violet 1,750.
red violet 1,750.
gray 1,750.
gray brown 1,750.
dull orange yellow 1,750.
b. Die on white glazed paper
black 1,750.
dark brown 1,750.
scarlet 1,750.
blue 1,750.
c. Plate on pelure paper, gummed, red 300.
d. Plate on white paper, red 250.
e. Plate on white paper, with 13x16mm points-up grill, red 350.
Split grill 600.
f. Plate on white paper, perf. all around and between stamp and coupon
red 175.
blue 175.
g. Plate on white paper, perf. all around, imperf. between stamp and coupon
red 175.
blue 175.
h. Plate on white paper, perf. all around, rouletted between stamp and coupon
red 300.
blue 300.

1861-66 Essays
Authors Unknown

73-E2

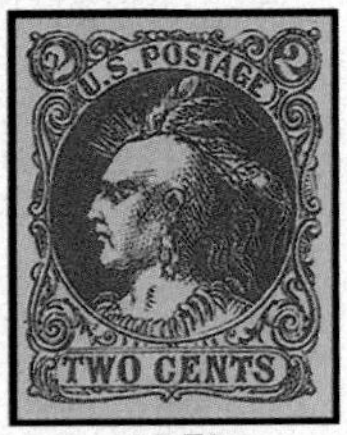

73-E3

Design size: 21x26mm

73-E2 2c Pencil and watercolor on thick card, bright green 3,750.

Design size: 21x26mm
Indian vignette. Typographed printings from woodcuts. Plates of three rows of three, one row each of Nos. 73-E3, 73-E4, 73-E5. Listings are of singles.

73-E3 2c
a. Plate on white wove
red 30.
scarlet 30.
violet 30.
black 30.
blue 30.
green 30.
b. Plate on mauve wove
red 50.
violet 50.
black 50.
blue 50.
green 50.
c. Plate on yellow wove
red 50.
violet 50.
black 50.
blue 50.
green 50.
d. Plate on yellow laid
red 50.
violet 50.
black 50.
blue 50.
green 50.
e. Plate on pink laid
red 50.
violet 50.
black 50.
blue 50.
green 50.
f. Plate on green laid
red 50.
violet 50.
black 50.
blue 50.
green 50.
g. Plate on cream laid
red 50.
violet 50.
black 50.
blue 50.
green 50.
h. Plate on pale yellow wove
red 50.
green 50.
blue 50.
i. Plate on yellow-surfaced card, violet 50.

73-E4

73-E5

Design size: 23x26½mm
Small head of Liberty in shield. Typographed printings from woodcuts. On plate with Nos. 73-E3 and 73-E5. Listings are of singles.

73-E4 3c
a. Plate on white wove
red 30.
scarlet 30.
violet 30.
black 30.
blue 30.
green 30.
b. Plate on mauve wove, violet 50.
c. Plate on yellow wove
red 50.
violet 50.
black 50.
blue 50.
green 50.
d. Plate on yellow laid
red 50.
violet 50.
black 50.
blue 50.
green 50.
e. Plate on pink laid
carmine 50.
violet 50.
black 50.
blue 50.
green 50.
f. Plate on green laid
carmine 50.
green 50.
dull violet 50.
blue 50.
g. Plate on cream laid
red 50.
violet 50.
black 50.
blue 50.
green 50.
h. Plate on pale yellow wove
red 50.
green 50.
blue 50.
i. Plate on yellow-surfaced card, violet 50.
j. Plate on fawn wove, green 50.

Design size: 22½x25½mm
Large head of Liberty. Typographed impressions from woodcut. On plate with Nos. 73-E3 and 73-E4. Listings are of singles.

73-E5 5c
a. Plate on white wove
red 30.
scarlet 30.
violet 30.
black 30.
blue 30.
green 30.
b. Plate on mauve wove, violet 50.
c. Plate on yellow wove
red 50.
violet 50.
black 50.
blue 50.
green 50.
d. Plate on yellow laid
red 50.
violet 50.
black 50.
blue 50.
green 50.
e. Plate on pink laid
red 50.
black 50.
blue 50.
green 50.
f. Plate on green laid
red 50.
violet 50.
black 50.
blue 50.
green 50.
g. Plate on cream laid
red 50.
black 50.
blue 50.
green 50.
h. Plate on pale yellow wove
red 50.
blue 50.
green 50.
i. Plate on yellow-surfaced card, violet 50.

73-E6

Size of design: 21x27mm
Indian vignette. Typographed impressions from woodcut.

73-E6 10c
a. Die on proof paper
black 200.
gray black 200.
carmine 200.
dusky red 200.
brown 200.
green 200.
blue 200.
violet 200.
b. Plate on white paper (pane of 4)
red 600.
violet 600.
brown 600.
black 600.
blue 600.
green 600.
c. Plate on soft cream card (pane of 4)
black 600.
red 600.
blue 600.
green 600.
red violet 600.

1867 Essays
Re-use Prevention
Authors Unknown

Unfolded — 79-E1

Folded — 79-E1

Design size (folded): 18x23mm
Design size (unfolded): 18x58mm
Folded and scored four times, horiz. crease at center. Bronze overprint U 2 S, (2 punched out). Lower ⅔ gummed below second fold so top ⅓ could be torn off for canceling.

79-E1 2c On white paper, dull red violet 5,000.

79-E2

Similar to No. 79-E1 but larger and not folded. Pierced with S-shaped cuts as well as punched out 2.

79-E2 2c
a. On white paper, US 7½mm high, bronze, US in dull black 5,000.
b. On white paper, US 10mm high, bronze, US in violet 5,000.

79-E3

Cuts as on back

U.S. No. 73 as issued but pierced with S-shaped cuts, ovptd. in metallic color.

79-E3 2c Essay on 2c stamp, gold overprint 7,500.

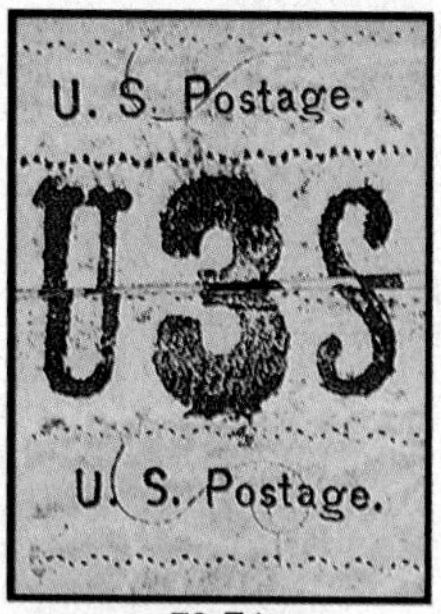

79-E4

79-E6

Similar to No. 79-E1 but with punched out 3.

79-E4 3c
a. On white paper, U 3 S black above, bronze below and on face beneath folds 5,000.
b. On green paper, 3 not punched out, 3 black, POSTAGE blue 5,000.

Similar to No. 79-E4, with "3 U.S. 3 / Three Cents / Void if detached."

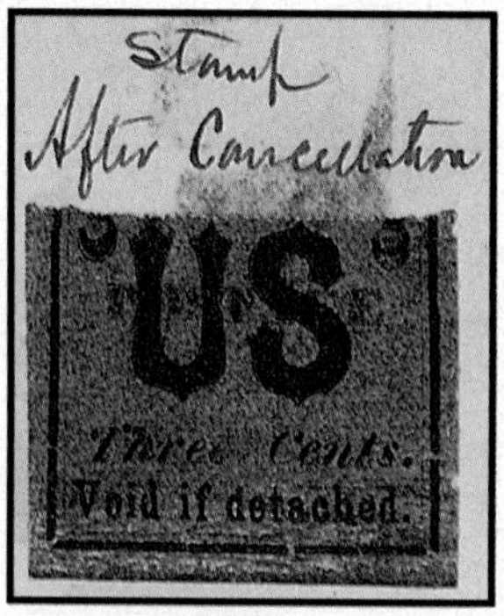

79-E5

79-E5 3c On green paper, black 3,000.

Similar to No. 79-E2 but with punched out 3, gummed.

79-E6 3c
a. On white paper, bronze over violet 3,000.
b. On white paper, U S black, rest bronze 3,000.

79-E7

Vignette map of U.S.

79-E7 3c On thick white paper, rouletted, green, gold 3 on map 2,500.

1867 Essays
Henry Lowenberg

79-E8

79-E9

Washington vignette. Printed in reverse on back of transparent paper, reads correctly from front. Plate essays from sheets of 25.

79-E8 3c
a. Plate on onionskin paper, imperf., gummed
brown 10
orange brown 10
deep orange brown 10
orange 10
green 10
light green 10
blue green 10
pale green 10
red 10
light red 10
dark red 10
violet red 10
violet 10
light violet 10
dull pale violet 10
blue 10
dark blue 10
deep blue 10
pale blue 10
dull blue 10
gold 50
gray 7
black 7
carmine 7
b. Plate on onionskin paper, perf. 12, gummed
gray black 25
gray 25
gray violet 25
dull violet 25
brown red 25
c. Plate on more opaque onionskin paper, imperf.
black 25
red violet 25
dull violet 25
d. Plate on thick transparent paper
gray 25
black 25

Washington vignette. Printed with design reversed on front of various opaque papers, Plate essays are from sheets of 25.

79-E9 3c
a. Plate on white wove, imperf., gummed
blue 10.
red 10.
gray 10.
brown 10.
orange 10.
green 10
yellow green 10
b. Plate on clear white paper, imperf.
orange 10
blue 10.
gray 10.
dark gray 10.
c. Plate on thick wove, fugitive ink, perf., gummed
carmine 10
violet carmine 10
pale dull red 10
gray 10
pale gray 10
pale dull tan 10
green 10
d. As "c," strip of 3, signed Henry Lowenberg, pale tan 400.
e. Plate on white chemically treated paper (turns blue if wet), imperf.
carmine 10.
Prussian blue 10.
orange 10.
green 10.
brown 10.
black 10.
f. As "e," perf.
carmine 10.
scarlet 10.
orange 10.
blue 10.
green 10.
brown 10.
g. Plate on India
violet brown 10.
green 10.
blue 10.
dark blue 10.
h. Plate on India, signed D.H. Craig, red 350.
i. On white card, 62x72mm, design deeply indented, green 15.
j. On blue wove, red 15.

k. On orange laid
black 15.
gray 15.
l. On blue laid, scarlet 15.
m. On white laid, blue 15.
n. On pink laid, blue 15.
o. On linen cloth
green 50.
red 50.
blue 50.
p. On glazed white paper, blue 20.

1867 Essays
John M. Sturgeon

79-E10

Liberty vignette. Curved labels top and bottom. Self-canceling: CANCELLED in colorless sensitive ink, becomes colored when wet. Patented 1867, 1868.

79-E10 10c
a. Die on stiff card, cut close, clearly engraved, not canceled, both labels completely blank, dark carmine 350.
b. Die on wove, rough impression, CANCELLED diagonally each way, dark carmine 450.
c. Die on thick white or tinted paper, gummed, rough impression, about 21x26mm, two lines in upper label, one line in lower label
carmine 200.
dark carmine 200.
very dark carmine 200.
green 200.
dark green 200.
dull red violet 200.
d. As "c," on thick pinkish paper, dark green 250.
g. Single centered in 6-inch wide strip of thick white paper, almost always cut in at top and bottom, dark carmine 400.
h. Horiz. row of five designs on thick white paper, 10mm apart
dark carmine 1,200.
dark purple 1,200.
black 1,200.
i. Single on blue card, ovptd. seal BRITISH CONSULATE, V.R. in center, black 1,250.

American Bank Note Co.

79-E11

Design size: 18x21mm
Vignette of Columbia. Probably submitted by Charles F. Steel.

79-E11 2c and 3c
a. Engraved plate on thick yellowish wove, imperf. (usually found in upper left margin blocks)
rose scarlet 300.
Block of 4 1,250.
blue green 300.
Block of 4 1,250.
b. Engraved plate on stamp paper, perf. 12, gummed
black 175.
rose scarlet 175.
blue green 175.
blue 175.

Author Unknown

79-E12

Design size: 20x26mm
Vignette of Liberty in circle of stars. Vertical color lines outside design to 24x28mm. Curved labels blank. Lithographed.

79-E12 No denomination
a. Die on white paper, dull violet 2,750.
b. Die on bluish paper, blue 2,750.

1867 Grill Essays
National Bank Note Co.

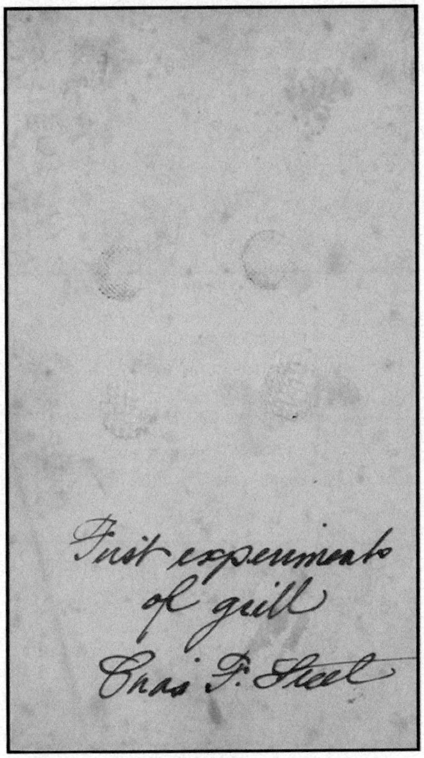

79-E13

Grill essays patented by Charles F. Steel.

79-E13
a. Wove paper, 80x140mm, impressed with four diff. seals, crossed lines and square dots down, circles 11 or 12mm 9,000.

79-E13b

b. Grills in odd shapes on white wove, each about 20x25mm
cross 1,500.
star in square 1,500.
horizontal lined oval in square 1,500.
diagonal lined oval in square 1,500.
c. White wove, gummed, 15mm circle with points down grill, surrounded by 24 perforated holes 1,000.
d. White wove, quadrille batonne watermark, 12mm colored circle with points down grill around 3, roughly grilled colorless 3 below, carmine 1,250.

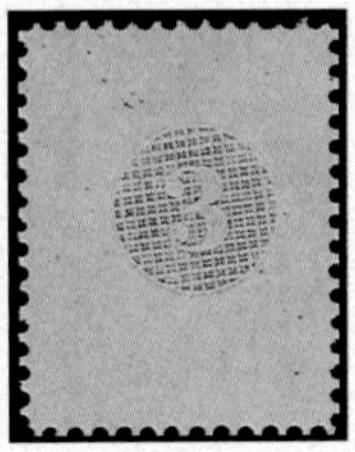
79-E13e

e. Colorless 12mm grilled circle as on "d," on tan wove, perf. 12 200.
f. As "e," yellow wove 200.
g. As "e," white wove, block of 6 with ms. "Subject to a half hour pressure after embossing" 3,500.
h. Colorless 15mm points down grilled circle on white wove, perf. 12 200.

79-E14a

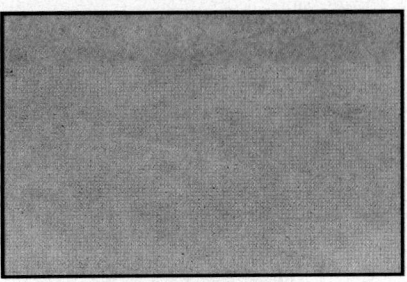

79-E14b

Allover grill.

79-E14
a. White wove, about 55x30mm, points down grill, stamped with red 6-digit number 450.
b. Wove paper in various colors, about 85x40mm, points up grill as adopted
white 200.
pale pink 200.
salmon 200.
light yellow 200.
light gray green 200.
light blue 200.
pale lilac 200.
light gray 200.

79-E15

Experimental grills on perf. or imperf. stamps or stamp-size pieces of paper.

79-E15
a. Allover grill of small squares, points down (points do not break paper as on issued stamp, No. 79)
on 3c rose, gummed (No. 65) 250.
on 3c lake, imperf. pair, gummed (No. 66aP4) 250.
b. As "a" but points up, on 3c stamp, perf. 12, gummed
black 200.
rose 200.
c. As "a" but points up, imperf pair, gummed
3c rose (**formerly No. 79P4**) 500.
3c lake (**formerly No. 66aP4**) 500.

79-E15d

d. Allover pinpoint grill (so-called "Music Box" grill), points up, on No. 65 (plates 11, 34, 52) 75.
e. As "d" but points down, on 3c rose (plate 11) 125.
f. 15x16mm grill on stamp size white wove paper, perf. 12, gummed 125.
g. C grill, 13x16mm, points down on stamp size wove paper, perf. 12, gummed
white 100.
yellowish 100.
pinkish 100.
h. As "g" but points up, on white wove 100.
i. C grill on 1c stamp (No. 63), points down 4,000.
j. C grill on 3c stamp (No. 65)
points up 4,000.
points down 4,000.

The 3c C grill essay is almost identical to the issued stamp. There are slight differences in the essay grill which match those on No. 79-E15i and Nos. 79-E15k through 79-E15n.

k. C grill on 5c stamp (No. 76)
points up 4,000.
points down 4,000.
l. C grill on 10c stamp (No. 68)
points up 4,000.
points down 4,000.
m. C grill on 12c stamp (No. 69)
points up 4,000.
points down 4,000.
n. C grill on 30c stamp (No. 71)
points up 4,000.
points down 4,000.
o. E grill, 11x13mm, points up, on stamp size white wove paper, perf. 12, gummed 100.
p. As "o," points down 100.

79-E15q

q. Z grill, 11x14mm, points down on stamp size wove paper, perf. 12, partly gummed
white 200.
salmon 200.
yellow 200.
greenish 200.
dull violet 200.
pale lilac 200.

These were made on fully perforated sheet selvage from other essays.

79-E15r

r. As "q," in sheet of white wove stamp paper, imperf., gummed 175.

Continental Bank Note Co.

White wove paper about 6x9 inches with 7x9½mm grills spaced as they would fall on centers of stamps in a sheet.

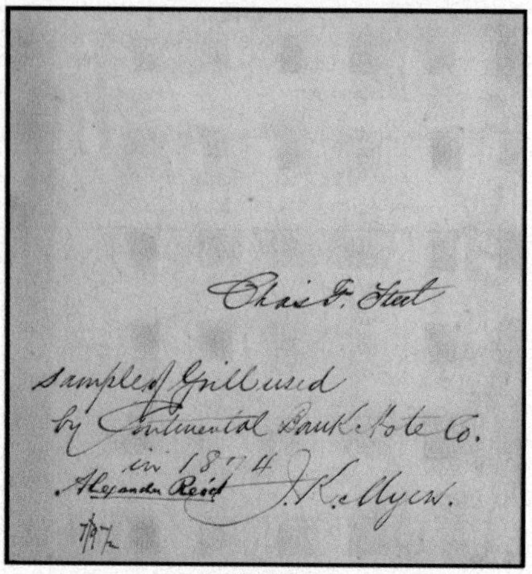

79-E16

79-E16
a. End roller grill at left, ms. "Chas. F. Steel-Sample of Grill used by Continental Bank Note Co. in 1874. Alexander Reid. J.K. Myers." 1,250.
b. Without end roller grill, ms. "Grill of Continental Bank Note Co. Chas. F. Steel." 1,750.
c. End roller grill at right, same inscription as "b" 250.
d. On soft card, six grills 450.

Wilbur I. Trafton

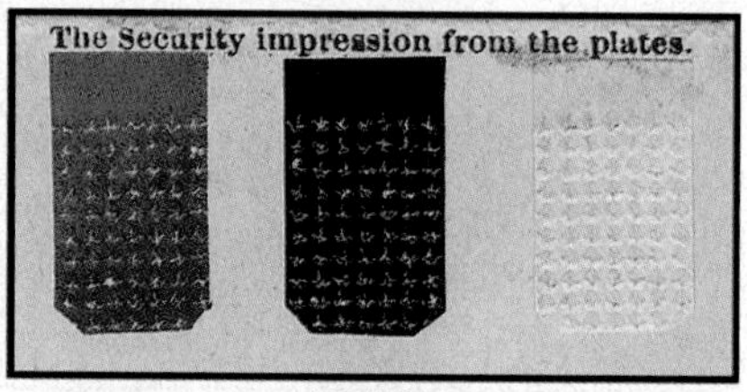

79-E17

Coarse grill in 15mm circle with 7 points up in 11mm, found on 1873 1c, some with 18mm circular cancel, stuck down on printed ad circular along with black, red and albino grill impressions (two each) on paper labeled "The Security Impression from the plates."

79-E17 Entire ad circular with grill examples 750.

Natonal Bank Note Co.

79-E18

Albino 3 in points down shield-shaped grill in lithographed frame of 3c 1861 stamp.

79-E18 3c
a. Die on thick white paper, gummed
black 1,000.
deep pink 1,000.
b. As "a," with Washington, D.C. Feb. 21 pmk.
black 1,750.
deep pink 1,750.

79-E18c

c. As "a" but grill with points up, black 1,000.
d. As "a," perf. 12, gummed, black 1,000.
e. Die on yellow wove, gummed
black 1,000
red 1,000
f. Die on orange wove
black 1,000
carmine 1,000
g. Die on yellow laid, black 1,000
h. Numeral handcolored, dull carmine 1,500
i. Frame only, no grill, on grayish wove with pencil "McDonald P.O. Dept. Steel Nature(?)", pale orange brown 1,500

79-E18j

79-E18k

Albino 3 in 13x14mm shield made up of embossed narrow spaced horiz. lines.

j. White wove stamp paper, 22x27mm, perf. 12, gummed 450

Albino 3 in 13x14mm shield slightly different from No. 79-E18j.

k. As "j," different shield 350

79-E19

Illustration reduced.

Typographed impression of frame, lettering and numerals of 3c 1861 stamp with 3 in double lined shield in center. In strip of three about 20mm apart, impression of 3 and shield progressively lighter on impressions two and three.

79-E19 3c
a. Engraved (die No. 1570), green 3,000
b. Typographed in color on white paper
blue green 2,750
dark red brown 2,750
c. As "b," colored and colorless parts interchanged, on thick paper
blue green 2,750
dark red brown 2,750

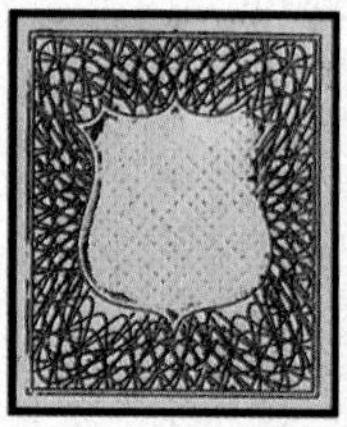

79-E21

Lathework frame with shield shaped vignette cut out, albino 3 in circular grill in center.

79-E21 3c
a. Thick paper, perf. 12
blue 500
carmine 500
b. At left in strip of 3 with 2 No. 79-E13f, latter black cancels, blue 3,500
c. Lathework frame on thin wove, allover diagonal grill, imperf., gummed, blue 500

Lathework frame similar to No. 79-E21 but vignette of 6 horiz bars with 3 in center printed in glossy ink.

79-E22

79-E22 3c On pink lilac paper, blue 3,000

79-E23

Design of 3c 1861 stamp typographed in relief for surface printing. Single impression lightly block sunk 63x62mm in color. Design has 21x26½mm border inside 23x28½mm colorless rectangle.

79-E23 3c
- ***a.*** Die on 64x75mm ivory paper, black *325.*
- ***b.*** Die on India, dull violet-red red *325.*
- ***c.*** Die on 59x54mm stiff white card, color about 40mm wide (not extending to edges)
  - light red violet *325.*
  - carmine *325.*
  - blue *325.*
- ***d.*** Washington head only, lines on face around eye, on soft card
  - dim blue-green blue *250.*
  - dim orange-orange red *250.*

On 17x21mm plain colored rectangle printed through a mat, surrounded by 55x62mm colorless rectangle, vert. 4½mm wide color bands at sides inside 64x62mm die sinkage.

- ***e.*** Washington head with dots around eye, on 17x42mm solid color, on 77x45mm stiff white paper, dull violet-red *250.*
- ***f.*** India paper on soft white card block sunk 63x62mm, dull violet-red-red with solid color margins *250.*

Colored India generally cut away outside colorless rectangle 23x28½mm, design heavily embossed through to card beneath.

- ***g.*** As "f," trimmed to shape
  - dark carmine *350.*
  - orange *350.*
  - blue green *350.*
  - red violet *350.*
- ***h.*** Complete design on India, sunk on card, trimmed to shape
  - blue *100.*
  - dull green blue *100.*
- ***i.*** Plate typographed on white wove, imperf., gummed
  - dim red *50.*
  - dim light orange red *50.*
  - dim blue green *50.*
  - dim pale blue *50.*
  - dim dark blue *50.*
  - dusky violet red *50.*

Color outside design generally fills rectangle, design impression shows on back.

- ***j.*** Complete design on glossy sticky paper, deep violet red *150.*
- ***k.*** As "j," on pelure, perf. 12, gummed, rose *175.*
- ***l.*** As "k," allover grill, dim red *150.*
- ***m.*** As "k," 13x16mm grill, gray black *150.*

79-E24

79-E24c

Block sinkage: 65x76mm
Washington head only.

79-E24 3c
- ***a.*** Lithographed, face dotted, on 65x76mm solid color background
  - black *750.*
  - red violet *750.*
  - olive black *750.*
- ***b.*** Typographed, background irregular edge, on card, gray black *750.*
- ***c.*** Face lined, on 64x72mm solid color background
  - black *750.*
  - scarlet *750.*

79-E25

Plate essays of complete 1861 3c design.

79-E25 3c
- ***a.*** Plate on hard white transparent wove, dark red *50.*
- ***b.*** Plate on more opaque white wove, dim red *50.*
- ***c.*** Plate on Gibson patent starch coated opaque white paper, generally crinkled, lathework design usually poorly printed
  - orange red *25.*
  - deep orange red *25.*
  - pink *25.*
  - dull yellow *25.*
  - yellow orange *25.*
  - dull yellow orange *25.*
  - brown yellow *25.*
  - brown *25.*
  - green *25.*
  - blue green *25.*
  - blue *25.*
  - light blue *25.*
- ***d.*** Plate on semitransparent white wove
  - dull pale blue *20.*
  - green *20.*
  - dull yellow orange *20.*
- ***e.*** Plate on pale green paper, clearly printed, dark g-b green *40.*
- ***f.*** Plate on white wove, 13x16mm points down grill, gummed, dark blue *40.*
- ***g.*** Plate on lilac gray paper, 13x16mm grill, gummed
  - dark blue *40.*
  - dull red *40.*
  - black *40.*
- ***h.*** Plate on white paper (ungrilled), perf. 12, gummed
  - red *25.*
  - light red *25.*
  - pale red *25.*
  - light orange red *25.*
  - deep yellow orange *25.*
  - brown *25.*
  - dark green *25.*
  - deep blue *25.*
  - dull g-b blue *25.*
  - gray black *25.*
- ***i.*** As "h," ms. A or B in UL corner, red *50.*
- ***j.*** Plate on white paper, 13x16mm points down grill, perf. 12, gummed
  - black *25.*
  - gray black *25.*
  - pale red *25.*
  - light red *25.*
  - orange red *25.*
  - deep orange yellow *25.*
  - brown *25.*
  - dark brown *25.*
  - green *25.*
  - blue *25.*
  - dark blue *25.*
- ***k.*** As "j," ms. "s No. 6" on back
  - red *50.*
  - gray black *50.*
  - dark blue *50.*
- ***l.*** As "j," but grill points up
  - red *40.*
  - pink *40.*
  - pale rose *40.*
  - brown *40.*
  - orange yellow *40.*
  - deep red orange *40.*
  - green *40.*
  - dull blue *40.*
  - dull light blue *40.*
- ***m.*** As "l," pair with blue oval "American Bank Note Co. April 17, '79", pink *150.*
- ***n.*** Plate on greenish gray chemical paper, 13x16mm grill, perf. 12
  - black *50.*
  - green *50.*
  - dark blue *50.*
  - orange red *50.*
  - light yellow gray *50.*
  - light red gray *50.*
- ***o.*** As "n," without grill
  - red *50.*
  - rose *50.*
- ***p.*** Plate on pelure, without grill, imperf., gummed, dim red *50.*
- ***q.*** As "p," perf. 12, dim red *50.*

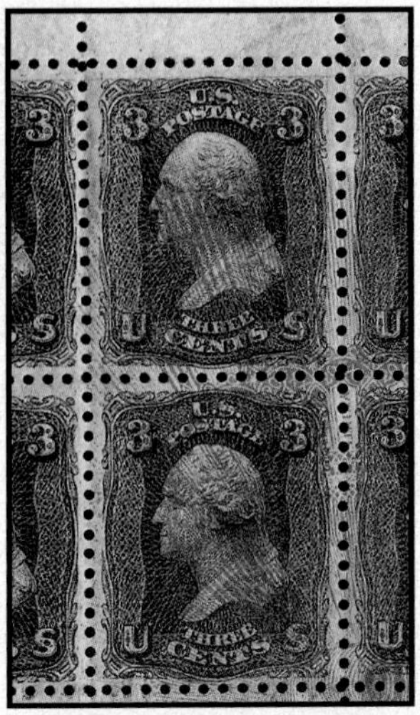

79-E26

Plate impressions of 1861 3c stamp overprinted with various safety network designs. Inks probably fugitive.

79-E26 3c
- ***a.*** Vert. pair on 58x80mm India, overprint die 54x71mm or more, small ONE repeated in 41 vert. lines per 40mm, rose pink, overprint deep orange yellow *2,000.*
- ***b.*** As "a," block of 6 inscribed "J. Sangster Pat. 190376, Jan. 6, 1877" *3,500.*
- ***c.*** 65TC3, "VEINTE" overprint, in miniature sheet of 12, perf. 12, black, overprint orange *7,500.*

3c 1861 printed in various colors in miniature sheets of 12 with safety ovpts. (Apparently only one sheet printed of each color combination, except two Type D combinations known both perf. and imperf.)

- ***d.*** Type A
  - perf. 12, dull violet, overprint gray *425.*
  - perf. 12, rose red, overprint gray blue *425.*
  - perf. 12, violet, overprint gray tan *425.*
  - imperf., pale olive, overprint pale tan *425.*
  - imperf., green, overprint gray tan *425.*
- ***e.*** Type B
  - perf. 12, green, overprint pale tan *425.*
  - perf. 12, violet, overprint gray tan *425.*
  - perf. 12, dull red brown, ovpt. pale brown *425.*
  - perf. 12, dark dull red brown, overprint pale brown *425.*

Type C

Type D

- ***f.*** Type C
  - perf. 12, dull violet, overprint gray tan *550.*
  - perf. 12, dull red, overprint gray blue *550.*
  - perf. 12, rose red, overprint gray blue *550.*
  - perf. 12, green, overprint gray tan *550.*
  - imperf., rose red, overprint pale tan *550.*
  - imperf., pale rose red, overprint pale tan *550.*
  - imperf., yellow brown, overprint tan *550.*
- ***g.*** Type D
  - perf. 12, dull violet, overprint gray blue *550.*
  - perf. 12, rose red, overprint gray blue *550.*
  - perf. 12, light red brown, overprint pale brown *550.*
  - perf. 12, dark green, overprint dull blue *550.*
  - imperf., pale olive, overprint tan *550.*
  - imperf., ultramarine, overprint tan *550.*
  - imperf., dull violet, overprint gray blue *550.*
  - imperf., dull violet, overprint pale green *550.*
  - imperf., dark green, overprint dull blue *550.*

79-E27

Design size: 20½x26½mm
Engraved in relief for surface printing, large 2 vignette, on same die with No. 79-E28, 20mm apart. Also essayed for envelopes on thick papers.

79-E27 2c
a. Untrimmed die, 30x42mm, on paper with "US" monogram, pale rose *850.*
b. Die on stiff glazed paper, 63x50mm, black *600.*
c. Trimmed die on India, on thick soft card, colorless parts in relief
black *450.*
red *450.*
orange *450.*
violet red *450.*
d. Die on 35x40mm white wove, imperf., gummed
blue *450.*
albino *450.*
e. Die on white wove, perf. 12, gummed, smoky violet red *450.*
f. Untrimmed die on white wove, 61x42mm, black *550.*

79-E28

79-E28g

Design size: 21x25½mm
Engraved in relief for surface printing, large 3 in shield vignette, on same die with No. 79-E27, 20mm apart. Also essayed for envelopes on thick papers.

79-E28 3c
a. Untrimmed die on stiff ivory paper, showing color 30x42mm
black *700.*
rose *700.*
orange *700.*
blue *700.*
b. Untrimmed die on India with No. 79-E27, both embossed, yellow orange *1,000.*
c. Trimmed die heavily struck on India, card mounted, colorless parts in relief
black *500.*
red *500.*
orange *500.*
d. Die on wide laid paper, "US" monogram, perf. 12, gummed
pale rose *250.*
dull brown yellow *250.*
e. Die on greenish wove, 10x12mm points down grill, imperf., gummed, dull brown *250.*
f. Die on white paper, perf. 12, gummed
smoky violet red *250.*
green *250.*
g. Underprinted design only on thin white wove
light blue *350.*
albino *350.*

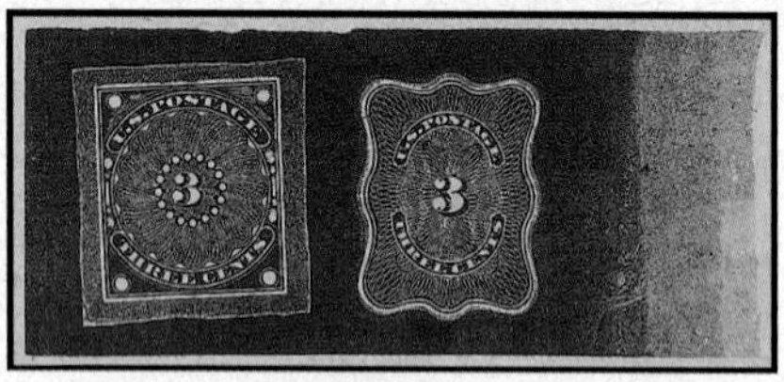

79-E28H

Illustration reduced.
Design size: 68x38mm
Two compound surface-printed designs, "3" within ornate frame.

79-E28H 3c Untrimmed die on wove paper, green *1,250.*

79-E29

1861 1c frame only.

79-E29 1c
a. Die on thin crisp paper, safety design underprint, black on dull olive green *2,750.*
b. Die on pink paper, 18x13mm points down grill, imperf., gummed, red brown *1,250.*
c. Die on pink "laid" paper, red *1,250.*
d. Die on pale pink paper, red brown *1,250.*
e. Die on transparent white paper, red brown *1,250.*
f. Die on thick yellow paper, red brown *1,250.*
g. Die on thin transparent white paper, 11x13mm points down grill, perf. 12, gummed, red brown *1,250.*
h. As "g," imperf. *2,000.*

79-E29i

As No. 79-E29 but with monogram in vignette.
i. Die on transparent white stamp paper, perf. 12, gummed, red brown *11,000.*

79-E30

Design size: 20x26mm
Block size: 64x76½mm
Vignette of Liberty. Typographed.

79-E30 3c
a. Head only on solid color (die size: 67x76mm), on 32x37mm stiff yellowish wove
black *750.*
blue green *750.*
b. Vignette only, on 66x100mm card
black *750.*
blue green *750.*
blue *750.*
c. Vignette only, on proof paper
bright blue *600.*
black *600.*
d. Complete design, untrimmed block, colorless 22x27 rectangle around design, broad outer edge in color, on stiff yellowish wove
black *750.*
blue green *750.*
violet brown *750.*
bright violet red *750.*
red violet *750.*
buff *750.*
e. As "d," on proof paper
buff *750.*
deep blue green *750.*
red brown *750.*
carmine *750.*
black *750.*
f. Die on proof paper, perf. 12, vignette oval perf. 16, carmine *200.*
g. Die on stiff ivory paper about 28x32mm
black *150.*
carmine *150.*
yellow *150.*
dark blue green *150.*
rose violet *150.*
h. Die on stiff ivory paper, no color outside design, block of 4, carmine *500.*
Block of 8 with vert. pairs in orange, dull yellow green, dark green and dark violet *900.*
i. Die on deep orange-surfaced white paper, carmine *150.*
j. As "i," perf. 12, gummed, carmine *150.*
k. Die on yellow-surfaced wove, carmine *150.*

79-E30l

l. Die with outer color removed, on 64x90mm white wove stamp paper with imprint below, imperf., gummed
carmine *150.*
scarlet *150.*
dim orange red *150.*
orange *150.*
dull yellow orange *150.*
pale dull yellow *150.*
brown *150.*
lemon *150.*
yellow green *150.*
dull olive green *150.*
dull greenish gray *150.*
dim blue green *150.*
dull blue *150.*
dull red violet *150.*
pale red violet *150.*
m. As "l," tete-beche pairs, each with imprint
carmine, orange *350.*
buff, pale lilac *350.*
dark orange brown, yellow *350.*
dull green gray *350.*

79-E30n

n. As "l," perf. 12, vignette oval perf. 16 (also found without paper outside perfs.
carmine *150.*
pale rose *150.*
dim scarlet *150.*
dull scarlet *150.*
dim orange red *150.*
light red brown *150.*
dark brown *150.*
orange *150.*
dull orange *150.*
dismal orange *150.*
dull brown orange *150.*
pale dull yellow *150.*
dull brown *150.*
yellow brown *150.*
dull olive green *150.*
dim dark yellow orange *150.*
light yellow green *150.*
green *150.*
dim blue green *150.*
dark blue green *150.*
dull greenish gray *150.*
dull yellowish gray *150.*
dull blue *150.*
dim red violet *150.*
dull red violet *150.*
pale red violet *150.*
red violet *150.*

79-E30o

o. Plate essay on wove, vertical pair of designs 7mm apart, in two colors shading into each other, imperf.
red brown to dark orange 150.
dark orange to brown red 150.
brown olive to red brown 150.
red brown to yellow green 150.
yellow green to dull carmine 150.
dull carmine to yellow green 150.
blue green to dull carmine 150.
brown olive to dull carmine 150.
dull carmine to orange 150.
orange to deep blue 150.
deep blue to orange brown 150.
orange brown to dull orange 150.
dull carmine to deep blue 150.

79-E30p Block

Illustration reduced.

p. As "o," on transparent wove, imperf.
red violet to deep violet 150.
deep violet to carmine 150.
dull scarlet to gold 150.
gold to carmine 150.
dark violet to blue green 150.
blue green to dark violet red 150.
violet to yellow green 150.
yellow green to red violet 150.
q. As "o," plate on stiff yellowish wove, imperf.
dull carmine to orange 150.
orange to deep blue 150.
brown olive to brown red 150.
brown red to yellow green 150.
blue green to dull carmine 150.
dull carmine to deep blue 150.
deep blue to dark brown 150.
dark brown to orange 150.
r. As "q," outside edge perf. 12
blue green to dull carmine 150.
dull carmine to deep blue 150.
deep blue to dark brown 150.
dark brown to dull orange 150.
dull carmine to dull orange 150.
dull orange to deep blue 150.
yellow green to dull carmine 150.
dull carmine to yellow green 150.
brown olive to brown red 150.
brown red to yellow green 150.
s. As "r," plate in single color, outside edge perf. 12, gummed
carmine 150.
dull orange 150.
orange brown 150.
dark brown 150.
brown olive 150.
dark blue green 150.
violet 150.
t. As "s," imperf., gummed
brown 125.
brown orange 125.
dull blue green 125.
deep blue 125.
carmine 125.
u. As "t," one color directly over another (gives effect of one color), black on scarlet 275.
v. As "b," heavily stamped on white card, only faint traces of vignette, albino 125.
w. As "v," printed design at right, very dark blue green 250.

79-E31a

79-E31b

79-E31d

79-E31e

79-E13f

79-E31g

Same design as No. 79-E30, black green on white wove safety paper, underprinted with different designs in various colors, imperf.

79-E31 3c
a. Red horiz. diamonds 1,400.
b. Dull yellow green with ONE repeated 1,400.
c. Red with 2 in circles 1,400.
d. Red with 2 in circular stars 1,400.
e. Red with 2 in ovals 1,400.
f. Red with 3 in diamonds 1,400.
g. Black with 5 in hexagons 1,400.
h. Red with X repeated 1,400.

79-E32

Similar to No. 79-E30f, but perf. vignette removed and frame mounted over 18x23mm Washington vignette.

79-E32 3c Die on 34x40mm white wove, black vignette, blue frame 8,000.

1868 Essays
Experiments for bicolor printing

1c 1861 design, color reversed as adopted. Typographed frame with 43x60mm solid color border.

79-E33 1c Die on thin white paper, frame pink, vignette dark blue over pink 750.

79-E35a

79-E35c

Frame lithographed, colored and colorless parts interchanged, vignette engraved and printed in another color.
Die I: colorless vignette oval (Nos. 79-E35a, 79-E35b)
Die II: vignette with horiz. lines (Nos. 79-E35d through 79-E35f)

79-E35 5c
a. Untrimmed die on thin white paper, 40x60mm (values for cut to stamp size)
frame buff, vignette black 2,000.
frame buff, vignette blue 2,000.
frame buff, vignette red brown 2,000.
frame buff, vignette dark brown 2,000.
frame buff, vignette orange 2,000.
frame buff, vignette carmine 2,000.
frame blue green, vignette dark brown 2,000.
frame blue green, vignette red brown 2,000.
frame blue green, vignette orange 2,000.
frame carmine, vignette blue 2,000.
frame carmine, vignette red brown 2,000.
frame violet, vignette orange 2,000.
frame light red, vignette deep orange red 2,000.
frame light red, vignette yellow orange 2,000.
b. Die on stiff wove, frame brown, vignette scarlet 2,000.
c. 45x65mm die impression of lithographed frame only, on ivory paper
black 2,000.
blue green 2,000.
d. Die on thin white paper
frame violet, vignette carmine 2,000.
frame violet, vignette brown 2,000.
frame violet, vignette red brown 2,000.
frame carmine, vignette black 2,000.
e. Vignette only on white glazed paper
black 2,000.
blue 2,000.
scarlet 2,000.
dark brown 2,000.
f. As "e," without thin outer frameline, on India
lake 2,000.
red 2,000.
deep red orange 2,000.
scarlet 2,000.
deep green 2,000.
ultramarine 2,000.

79-E36

Die II vignette as No. 79-E35e, with gothic "United States" above.

79-E36 5c
a. Die on white glazed paper
black 450.
scarlet 450.
dark brown 450.
green 450.
blue 450.

79-E37

Die size: 51x63½
5c 1861 design, color reversed as adopted, vignette mounted on typographed frame.

79-E37 5c
a. Die on white card, frame light blue, vignette black 1,000.
b. Vignette only, die on India, black 350.
c. Vignette only, die on white glazed paper
blue 350.
black 350.
green 350.

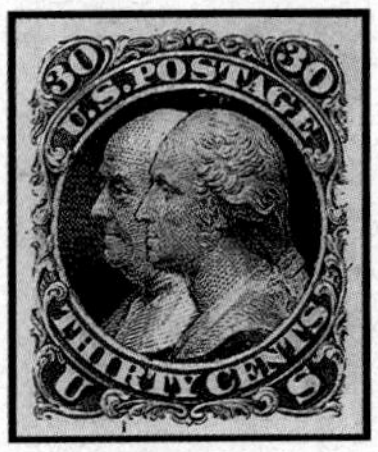

100-E1

Design size: 20½x24½mm

Engraved circular Franklin vignette mounted on 43x75mm white card, engraved Washington head mounted thereon; background, silhouette, etc., retouched in black ink. With engraved frame of No. 71-E1 (vignette cut out) mounted over the double vignette.

100-E1 30c Die on India, 30x34mm, black *6,000.*

1869 ISSUE
George T. Jones

112-E1

113-E1

Design size: 24x30mm
U.S. Grant vignette in frame with blank labels, ovals, etc. Paper overprinted with network of fine colored wavy lines in fugitive inks as on beer stamps.

112-E1 No Denomination
- ***a.*** Die on India cut to stamp size, 1 color
  - black *2,250.*
  - blue *2,250.*
- ***b.*** Die on India cut to stamp size, 2 colors (head in black)
  - blue, light gray overprint *3,250.*
  - red, light gray overprint *3,250.*
  - black, light violet overprint *3,250.*
  - black brown, pale red violet ovpt. *3,250.*
  - carmine, gray overprint *3,250.*
  - blue, yellow overprint *3,250.*

Design size: 24x30mm
U.S. Treasury Dept. seal in vignette oval.

113-E1 2c
- ***a.*** Die on India cut to stamp size, 1 color
  - carmine *2,500.*
  - blue *2,500.*
- ***b.*** Die on India cut to stamp size, 3 colors, black on pale red violet wavy lines and blue green lined vignette *3,750.*

Frame as 112-E1 but with Washington vignette and 2c denomination. Another Washington vignette below but in horiz. lined oval frame.

113-E2 2c Die on 1⅝x3½inch India, black *5,000.*

National Bank Note Co.

All values originally essayed with numerals smaller than adopted. All designs are same size as issued stamps. Sheets of 150 of 1c-12c, sheets of 50 of 24c-90c. Many colors of plate essays exist from one sheet only, some colors from two sheets and a few from three. Some plate essays exist privately perforated.

112-E2

112-E3

Die size: 40x65mm
Vignette size: 17mm diameter
Vignette of Franklin.

112-E2 1c Die of vignette only on India
- orange *900.*
- violet brown *900.*
- black *900.*

Circle of pearls added to vignette, suggestion for frame and 1 in circle at bottom penciled in.

112-E3 1c Die on India, black *1,500.*

112-E4

112-E5

Complete design as issued but with small value numeral.

112-E4 1c
- ***a.*** Die on India, die sunk on card
  - black *1,250.*
  - violet brown *1,250.*
  - dark brown *1,250.*
  - yellow brown *1,250.*
  - scarlet *1,250.*
  - carmine *1,250.*
  - deep violet *1,250.*
  - blue *1,250.*
  - green *1,250.*
  - yellow *1,250.*
- ***b.*** Plate on stamp paper, imperf., gummed
  - buff *100.*
  - deep orange brown *100.*
  - orange brown *100.*
- ***c.*** Plate on stamp paper, perf. 12, gummed
  - buff *100.*
  - orange brown *100.*
  - orange *125.*
- ***d.*** As "c," with 9x9mm grill
  - buff *110.*
  - orange brown *85.*
  - red brown *85.*
  - chocolate *85.*
  - black brown *85.*
  - dull red *85.*
  - violet *110.*
  - dark violet *110.*
  - blue *110.*
  - deep blue *110.*
  - green *110.*
  - yellow *110.*
  - orange *110.*
  - rose red *110.*
- ***e.*** Horiz. pair, one #112-E4c, one #112-E4d *400.*

Design size: 23x31mm
Die size: 51x55mm
Design as issued but surrounded by fancy frame with flags and shield. Also essayed for envelopes and wrappers on thick paper.

112-E5 1c
- ***a.*** Die on stamp paper, perf. 12, gummed, gray *3,000.*
- ***b.*** Die on white ivory paper
  - black *2,000.*
  - black brown *2,000.*
  - scarlet *2,000.*
  - blue *2,000.*
- ***c.*** Die on India
  - blue *2,000.*
  - blue green *2,000.*
- ***d.*** Die on India, cut to shape
  - carmine *750.*
  - yellow *750.*

113-E3

Die size: 41x50mm
Design as issued but with small value numeral. Nos. 113-E3a and 113-Eb have incomplete shading around "UNITED STATES."

113-E3 2c
- ***a.*** Die on India, die sunk on card
  - black *1,500.*
  - yellow *1,500.*
  - red orange *1,500.*
  - deep scarlet *1,500.*
  - brown *1,500.*
  - green *1,500.*
  - dusky blue *1,500.*
  - deep blue *1,500.*
- ***b.*** Die on India, cut to stamp size
  - deep orange red *400.*
  - deep orange yellow *400.*
  - blue green *400.*
  - gray black *400.*
  - light blue *400.*
  - rose *400.*
- ***c.*** Complete die on India, die sunk on card
  - brown *1,500.*
  - rose *1,500.*
  - mauve *1,500.*
  - green *1,500.*
  - dark chocolate *1,500.*
  - red brown *1,500.*
- ***d.*** Plate on stamp paper, perf. 12, gummed
  - brown *425.*
  - dark brown *425.*
  - yellow *425.*
- ***e.*** As "d," with 9x9mm grill
  - brown *80.*
  - dark brown *80.*
  - orange brown *80.*
  - dark orange brown *80.*
  - rose *80.*
  - brown rose *80.*
  - copper red *80.*
  - deep copper red *80.*
  - green *80.*
  - deep green *80.*
  - blue green *80.*
  - yellow *80.*
  - orange *80.*
  - dull yellow orange *80.*
  - blue *80.*
  - light violet *80.*
  - violet *80.*
  - dark violet *80.*
- ***f.*** As "e," double grill, orange *300.*
- ***g.*** Horiz. pair, one #113-E3d, one #113-E3e *1,000.*

113-E4

Original sketch of postrider, printed "NATIONAL BANK NOTE COMPANY. BUSINESS DEPARTMENT. 1868" at top, pencil instructions at bottom, "Reduce to this length" and "2 copies on one plate. Daguerrotype."

113-E4 2c Drawing on paper, black —

114-E3

114-E4

Die size: 53x47mm
Design nearly as issued: larger motive above and below "POSTAGE" erased, no shading on numeral shield, top leaves and corner leaves do not touch, no dots in lower corners or scrolls beside bottom of shield, no vert. shading lines in "POSTAGE" label. Small value numeral.

114-E3 3c Die on 30x30mm ivory paper, black *1,500.*

Similar to 114-E3, but smaller motive around "POSTAGE," shield shaded.

114-E4 3c
- ***a.*** Die on India, die sunk on card
  - black *1,500.*
  - carmine *1,500.*
  - scarlet *1,500.*
  - orange red *1,500.*
  - yellow orange *1,500.*
  - dull yellow *1,500.*
  - red sepia *1,500.*
  - blue green *1,500.*
  - blue *1,500.*
  - dull red *1,500.*
  - orange brown *1,500.*
- ***b.*** Die on India, cut to stamp size
  - black *500.*
  - rose *500.*
  - scarlet *500.*
  - chocolate *500.*
  - dull dusky orange *500.*
  - red violet *500.*
  - blackish slate *500.*

Similar to No. 114-E4 but vert. shading lines added to "POSTAGE" frame.

114-E5 3c Die on India, dusky yellow orange *1,750.*

114-E6

114-E7

Completed small numeral die essay: leaves at top and sides touch, dots in lower corners added, vert. shading lines in frame around "POSTAGE," shield shaded darker at bottom, scrolls added to bottom of shield.

114-E6 3c
- ***a.*** Die on India, card mounted
  - black *1,750.*
  - blue *1,750.*
  - deep orange red *1,750.*
- ***b.*** Plate on stamp paper, imperf., gummed
  - ultramarine *125.*
  - dark ultramarine *125.*
  - light brown *85.*
  - red brown *85.*
  - dark red brown *85.*
  - pale rose *85.*

rose 85.
brown rose 85.
c. Plate on stamp paper, perf. 12, gummed
ultramarine 500.
dark ultramarine 500.
d. As "c," with 9x9mm grill
blue 80.
deep blue 80.
orange brown 80.
black brown 80.
deep black brown 80.
rose red 80.
green 80.
yellow 80.
orange 80.
deep orange 80.
dull violet 80.
deep violet 80.
red violet 80.

Same design and color as issued stamp, but with allover essay grill of squares up.

114-E7 3c
a. Imperf., gummed, ultramarine 700.
b. As "a," 23mm "NATIONAL BANK NOTE CO. N.Y. SEP 27, 1869" circular pmk., ultramarine 1,100.
c. On thick paper, imperf., gummed, horiz. line defacement, ultramarine 700.
d. Perf. 12, horiz. line defacement, ultramarine 700.

115-E1

115-E2

Die size: 40x60mm
Vignette of Washington. Design as issued 6c stamp but with 5c denomination. Large lettering, large U and S in corners. Also essayed for envelopes on thick paper.

115-E1 6c
a. Die on India, no frameline, solid vignette background, corner spandrels short at centers
black 700.
carmine 700.
dismal red brown 700.
smoky dusky brown 700.
gray violet 700.
b. Completed die on India, die sunk on card
black 600.
carmine 600.
deep rose 600.
red violet 600.
red brown 600.
deep yellow brown 600.
black brown 600.
dull yellow 600.
orange 600.
dusky blue 600.
dusky slate blue 600.
green 600.
blue green 600.
scarlet 600.
c. Die on proof paper, about 40x65mm
black 600.
carmine 600.
scarlet 600.
red orange 600.
orange 600.
dull yellow 600.
orange brown 600.
olive brown 600.
dusky green 600.
dusky yellow green 600.
light blue 600.
deep blue 600.
red violet 600.
d. Die on pink bond
orange 600.
brown 600.
blue 600.
e. Die on light yellow green bond, black 600.
f. Die on pale olive buff bond
black 600.
carmine 600.
orange 600.
red orange 600.
brown 600.
g. Die on cream wove
black 600.
orange 600.
brown 600.
blue 600.
h. Die on clear white bond
black 600.
blue 600.
orange 600.
red orange brown 600.
i. Die on thick cloudy bond
black 600.
red 600.
orange 600.
orange brown 600.
blue 600.

reddish brown 600.
j. Die on pale lilac bond
dark red orange 700.
orange 700.
blue 700.
k. Die on glazed paper
black 550.
scarlet 550.
yellow 550.
dark brown 550.
blue 550.
l. Die on marbled white card
green on red violet veined 1,750.
black on green veined 1,750.
red violet on green veined 1,750.
m. Die on ivory card
black 1,500.
blue 1,500.
n. Die on white card, cut to stamp size, red orange 250.

Die size: 43x63mm
Similar to No. 115-E1 but lettering, U and S smaller.

115-E2 6c
a. Incomplete die on India (incomplete spandrel points, hair on top of head, etc.)
black 750.
dull red brown 750.
b. Complete die on India, die sunk on card
black 750.
blue 750.
dull dusky violet 750.
scarlet 750.
dark orange red 750.
dim dusky red orange 750.
dusky green 750.
dusky green blue green 750.
dusky blue green 750.
c. Plate essay on wove, imperf., gummed
deep ultramarine 150.
orange 150.
dull red violet 80.
deep red violet 80.
red brown 80.
dull red brown 80.
buff 80.
green 80.
d. Plate essay on wove, perf. 12, gummed
orange 200.
blue 200.

115-E3

Vignette of Washington as used on stamp but with longer shirt front.

115-E3E 6c Die on india, affixed to card, 35x37mm, black —

116-E1

Die size: 14x18mm

Vignette of Lincoln as on No. 77.

116-E1 10c Die on India, on card, black —

116-E1a

Design size:14x14½mm
Vignette of Lincoln as on No. 77, reduced.

116-E1a Die on India, on card, black 1,500.

116-E1b

Design size: about 19½x19½mm
Die size: 64x68½mm
Head as on No. 77 but less bust, large unshaded collar, no cross shading in triangles between labels and fasces, no shading on diamonds at end of value label.

116-E1b Incomplete die on India, on card, black 5,750.

116-E1c

Small collar, shading on diamonds at end of value label. Also essayed for envelopes on yellow laid paper.

116-E1c Complete die on India, die sunk on card
black 1,000.
brown black 1,000.
gray black 1,000.
carmine 1,000.
scarlet 1,000.
brown red 1,000.
orange 1,000.
deep orange 1,000.
deep red 1,000.
yellow brown 1,000.
yellow 1,000.
green 1,000.
blue green 1,000.
deep blue 1,000.
red violet 1,000.
brown 1,000.
d. Die on proof paper
black 1,000.
carmine 1,000.
bright red 1,000.
orange red 1,000.
orange 1,000.
dark chocolate 1,000.
dusky yellow brown 1,000.
green 1,000.
blue 1,000.
red violet 1,000.
e. Die on ivory paper
black 1,000.
scarlet 1,000.
black brown 1,000.
blue 1,000.
f. Die on clear white thin bond, about 30x35mm
black 1,000.
red orange 1,000.
red brown 1,000.
orange 1,000.
yellow 1,000.
blue 1,000.
g. Die on cloudy cream bond, about 30x35mm
black 1,000.
light red brown 1,000.
red orange 1,000.
blue 1,000.
h. Die on pink bond, about 39x45mm
red orange 1,000.
red brown 1,000.
yellow 1,000.
i. Die on pale greenish gray bond, about 33x37mm
black 1,000.
deep carmine 1,000.
dull scarlet 1,000.
dark brown 1,000.
blue 1,000.
j. Die on marbled white ivory card, about 38x62mm
black on green veined 1,900.
orange red on green veined 1,900.
red orange on green veined 1,900.
dark orange brown on red violet veined 1,900.
k. Plate on stamp paper, imperf., gummed
deep green 150.
blue 125.
ultramarine 125.
dark ultramarine 125.
light ultramarine 125.
l. Plate on stamp paper, perf. 12, gummed, orange 200.

116-E2

Die size: 101x62mm
Vignette of signing the Declaration of Independence as adopted for 24c.

116-E2 10c
a. Die on India, die sunk on card
black 3,750.
carmine 3,750.
dim rose 3,750.
dull scarlet 3,750.
red orange 3,750.
orange yellow 3,750.
red brown 3,750.
orange brown 3,750.
green 3,750.
blue 3,750.
gray 3,750.
b. Die on India, cut to stamp size
black 1,500.
red orange 1,500.
blue green 1,500.
dim rose 1,500.
brown 1,500.
buff 1,500.
dull scarlet 1,500.

Other colors reported to exist.

116-E3

116-E4

Die size: 63x75mm
Design as adopted for issued stamp, but incomplete shading on bottom ribbon, thin shading lines behind "States," and center of "0" of "10" not filled in.

116-E3 10c Die on India on 61x53mm card, black 2,500.

Similar to No. 116-E3 except shading lines added behind "Ten Cents" and center of "0" of "10" filled in.

116-E4 10c Die on India, die sunk on card
black 2,500.
orange 2,500.
blue 2,500.

117-E1

117-E2

Die size: 47x51mm
Design as issued but with smaller value numerals.

117-E1 12c
a. Die on card, black 1,600.
b. Vignette die on India, pencil "Adriatic", black 1,600.
c. Complete die on India, die sunk on card
black 1,350.
rose 1,350.
yellow 1,350.
scarlet 1,350.
dark red brown 1,350.
blue green 1,350.
blue 1,350.
dull violet 1,350.
gray black 1,350.
orange brown 1,350.
yellow brown 1,350.
dull orange red 1,350.
d. Die on India, cut to stamp size
black 600.
dusky red orange 600.
deep orange red 600.
dim blue 600.
e. Plate on stamp paper, 9x9mm grill, perf. 12, gummed
green 125.
rose red 125.
pale rose red 125.
yellow brown 125.
red brown 125.
orange 125.
blue 125.
dull violet 125.
dull red violet 125.
yellow orange 125.

Similar to No. 117-E1, but small numeral not printed, large 12 drawn in pencil.

117-E2 12c Die on India, black 2,750.

117-E3

117-E4

Typographed small numeral design similar to No. 117-E1, relief engraved for surface printing. Heavier lines, upper label with solid background, letters of "UNITED STATES POSTAGE" colorless. Nos. 117-E3a through 117-E3c from untrimmed die, heavily struck with uncolored areas in relief, color covering borders beyond white line exterior of frame. Untrimmed die size: 58x45mm.

117-E3 12c
a. Untrimmed die on card
brown red 750.
green 750.
black 750.
red brown 750.
b. Untrimmed die on thin pinkish wove
gray black 450.
dull deep red orange 450.
dark red orange 450.
c. Untrimmed die on thick white wove
carmine 600.
green 600.
d. Die on white paper, stamp size
carmine 400.
orange 400.
brown 400.
lilac 400.
green 400.
e. Die on thin white wove
carmine 400.
gray black 400.
dull deep red orange 400.
deep orange red 400.
g. Die on pinkish wove, perf. 12, gummed, red brown 400.
h. Die on yellow wove, imperf.
gray black 400.
carmine 400.
red brown 400.
dark red violet 400.
i. Die on yellow wove, 11x13mm grill, imperf., red brown 400.
j. Die on white laid
gray 400.
gray black 400.
brown 400.
red brown 400.
k. Die on yellow laid
red brown 400.
brown 400.
dull red violet 400.
carmine 400.
l. Die on salmon laid, red brown 400.
m. Die on pinkish laid
red brown 400.
gray 400.
n. Die on pinkish laid, 11x13mm grill, gummed, red brown 400.
o. Die on dull red violet laid, gray 400.

Vignette size: 15x11mm
Untrimmed die size: 63x32mm
Vignette only, similar to No. 117-E3 but lithographed instead of typographed.

117-E4 12c
a. Die on white ivory paper, black 1,000.
b. Complete impression from untrimmed stone in solid color about 63x63mm, on white ivory paper, black 750.
c. Die on glossy-surfaced thin white wove, trimmed to stamp size
carmine 750.
rose pink 750.
yellow 750.
blue green 750.
dim red violet 750.
pale red violet 750.
deep red orange 750.
dull dark red orange 750.
dull dark yellow orange 750.
dark violet red 750.
pale gray 750.
d. Die on thick white wove
yellow 750.
violet red 750.
deep red violet 750.

118-E1a

Die size: 62x49mm
Type I design as issued but with smaller value numerals.

118-E1 15c
a. Die of vignette only on India, mounted on 62x62mm India, die sunk on card, dark blue 3,500
b. Incomplete die (no outer frameline or shading outside frame scrolls) on India, black 4,500

118-E1c

c. Complete die on India, die sunk on card
black 5,000
scarlet 5,000
orange brown 5,000
green 5,000
dull violet 5,000
red brown 5,000

119-E1a

Type II design with large value numerals as issued.

119-E1 15c
a. Type II frame only, die on India
black 3,000.
red brown 3,000.
b. Vignette only, die on India, blue —

119-E1c

c. Type II frame with vignette mounted in place, die on India, red brown frame, blue vignette 7,500.
d. Type II frame with vignette mounted at right, die on India, red brown frame, blue vignette —

129-E1

129-E2

Die size: 65x49
Type III design as adopted, except in various single colors, large "15" overprint in diff. color.

129-E1 15c
a. Die on India, die sunk on card
orange brown, red overprint 3,500.
blue green, red overprint 3,500.
ultramarine, red overprint 3,500.
violet, red overprint 3,500.
red brown, red overprint 3,500.
b. Die on India, die sunk on card
rose red, ultramarine overprint 3,500.
dull scarlet, ultramarine overprint 3,500.
dark red brown, ultramarine ovpt. 3,500.
c. Die on India, die sunk on card
scarlet, blue green overprint 3,500.
orange brown, blue green overprint 3,500.
dark red brown, blue green overprint 3,500.

Type III frame only.

129-E2 15c
a. Die on India, red brown 2,750.
b. Die on India, with vignette mounted in place, blue frame, yellow vignette 3,500.

120-E1

120-E2

Die size: 102x63mm
Design nearly as issued, but shading under leaves at top of frame and ribbon over "TWENTY" are unfinished. Small value numerals. Single color.

120-E1 24c Die on India, black *4,000.*

Completed small numeral design in single color. No. 120-E2a has 8mm-high bands of shaded colored lines 31mm long overprinted above and below vignette, printed in various single colors with bands in contrasting color.

120-E2 24c
a. Die on India
black with carmine bands *4,000.*
black with violet brown bands *4,000.*
black with brown orange bands *4,000.*
orange brown with deep dull violet bands *4,000.*
orange brown with blue green bands *4,000.*
b. Die on India
black *2,250.*
scarlet *2,250.*
dark red brown *2,250.*
blue *2,250.*
violet *2,250.*
c. Plate on red salmon tinted paper, black *200.*
d. Plate on orange buff tinted paper, black *250.*
e. Plate on dull yellowish tinted paper, black *250.*
f. Plate on blue tinted paper, black *250.*
g. Plate on gray tinted paper, black *500.*
h. Plate on India, black *300.*
j. Plate on card, imperf., black *250.*

120-E3a

120-E3b

No. 120-E3a bicolor design as issued, except vignette printed separately and mounted in place; No. 120-E3b frame only with 3 border lines around vignette space; No. 120-E3c frame only with 2 border lines around vignette space as issued.

120-E3 24c
a. Die on India, card mounted
dull violet frame, green vignette *2,500.*
violet frame, red vignette *2,500.*
green frame, violet vignette *2,500.*
rose frame, green vignette *2,500.*
b. Frame die on India, card mounted
black *5,000.*
light green *2,500.*
dark green *2,500.*
c. Frame die on India, block sunk on India, green *2,500.*

121-E1

Design size: 21½x22mm
Die Size: 71x51mm
Vignette of Surrender of Gen. Burgoyne in ornate frame.

121-E1 30c
a. Die on India, die sunk on card
black *800.*
carmine *800.*
rose red *800.*
light brown red *800.*
red brown *800.*
brown orange *800.*
orange *800.*
red orange *800.*
yellow green *800.*
blue *800.*
dull dark violet *800.*
yellow brown *800.*
scarlet *800.*
b. Die on stiff ivory paper
black *650.*
c. Die on India, cut to stamp size
dim deep orange red *250.*
deep yellow orange *250.*
dim deep blue green *250.*
dim dusky blue *250.*
d. Die on India die sunk on 78x58mm white card
dusky blue *1,000.*
e. Die on white card, cut to stamp size
dim orange *500.*
f. Die on proof paper, about 70x50mm
black *500.*
carmine *500.*
scarlet *500.*
red orange *500.*
green *500.*
violet *500.*
g. Die on ivory paper, about 64x50mm
black *750.*
dark brown *750.*
scarlet *750.*
blue *750.*
h. Die on ivory card
black *1,000.*
carmine *1.000.*
i. Die on clear white bond, about 33x33mm
black *600.*
blue *600.*
light red brown *600.*
orange *600.*
j. Die on yellowish cloudy bond, about 34x34mm
black *600.*
orange *600.*
light red brown *600.*
blue *600.*
k. Die on smoky yellow greenish bond
black *600.*
carmine *600.*
orange *600.*
l. Die on pink bond, about 40x40mm
blue *600.*
dim orange red *600.*
orange *600.*
m. Die on pale olive buff paper
black *600.*
dim orange red *600.*
orange *600.*
n. Die on thick yellowish wove, dim green blue *600.*
o. Die on marbled white ivory card, about 40x60mm
black on green veined *2,500.*
black on red violet veined *2,500.*
p. Plate essay in black on thin surface-tinted paper
pale gray *275.*
salmon red *175.*
yellow *175.*
orange *275.*
orange buff *275.*
pink *275.*
pale pink *275.*
blue *275.*
light blue *275.*
pale green *275.*
brown violet *275.*
q. Plate essay in black on India *300.*
r. Plate on thick rough pitted card, black *300.*

121-E1s

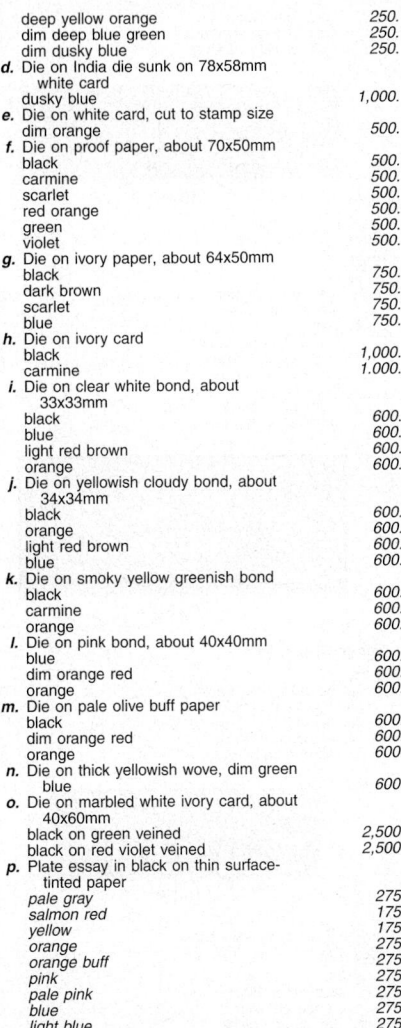

s. Plate on bond, red bands overprinted top and bottom as on No. 120-E2a, dull red violet *350.*

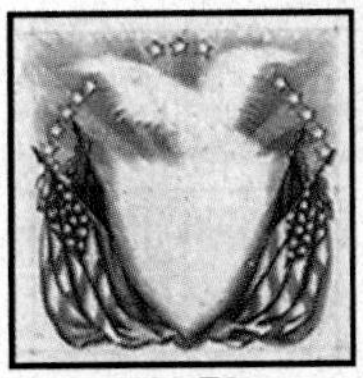
121-E2

121-E3

Flags, stars and rays only as adopted for issued stamp. Black essay shows traces of vignette also.

121-E2 30c Die on India, mounted on India, block sunk on card
black *7,500.*
light ultramarine *6,000.*
dark blue *6,000.*

Eagle, shield and value only as adopted for issued stamp.

121-E3 30c Die on India, card mounted, black *8,500.*

122-E1

Die size: 62x69mm
Vignette of Washington in frame similar to that of issued stamp but no shading over U and S in lower corners, small value numerals.

122-E1 90c Die on India, black *3,250.*

Similar to No. 122-E1 but shading over U and S.

122-E2

122-E2 90c
a. Die on India, die sunk on card
black *2,500.*
carmine *2,500.*
scarlet *2,500.*
red brown *2,500.*
blue green *2,500.*
violet *2,500.*
b. Plate essay with black vignette on stamp paper, imperf.
dull violet *275.*
red brown *275.*
orange red *275.*
pale orange red *275.*
blue *275.*

122-E3

122-E4

Frame as No. 122-E2, vignette oval with narrow-spaced horiz. lines in same color as frame, but no head.

122-E3 90c Plate on medium India paper, imperf.
red brown *225.*
blue *225.*
dark blue *225.*
red violet *225.*
dull violet *225.*
dark violet *225.*
rose red *225.*
deep rose red *225.*
yellow *225.*
orange brown *225.*
dark navy blue *225.*
blue green *225.*
deep blue green *225.*
dark blue green *225.*
orange *225.*

Small numeral frame but with black Lincoln vignette on India from No. 77 mounted in place.

122-E4 90c
a. Die on medium India
yellow *2,000.*
red brown *2,000.*
rose red *2,000.*
deep blue green *2,000.*
dark navy blue *2,000.*
b. Plate of Lincoln vignette only, on rough pitted thick gray paper, black *600.*
Block of 4 *2,500.*
c. Die on India, Lincoln vignette as used on No. 77, black *2,500.*

122-E5

Similar to No. 122-E1, with Washington vignette but with large numerals as on issued stamp.

122-E5 90c
- ***a.*** Die on India, die sunk on card
  - black *5,000.*
  - carmine *5,000.*
- ***b.*** Plate of frame only, 2 lines at top, 3 lines at bottom, on India, mounted on block sunk card, rose red *1,250.*
- ***c.*** As "b," 3 lines at top, 2 lines at bottom
  - rose red *4,500.*
  - red brown *1,250.*

Safety essays: die essays on thin wove, underprinted with various engraved safety paper designs in another color, probably with fugitive ink.

Found on 5c (No. 115-E1), 10c (No. 116-E1), 15c (No. 129-E1 without overprint) and 30c (No. 121-E1). Stamp color given first.

115-E3a

Design 1: wavy lines

115-E3
- ***a.*** 5c
  - carmine on scarlet *3,250.*
  - orange on scarlet *3,250.*
- ***b.*** 10c blue on scarlet *5,000.*
- ***c.*** 30c carmine on scarlet *3,500.*

115-E4

Design 2: banknote type

115-E4
- ***a.*** 5c
  - carmine on violet *3,250.*
  - orange on violet *3,250.*
- ***b.*** 10c carmine on violet *5,000.*
- ***c.*** 30c
  - carmine on violet *3,500.*
  - orange on violet *3,500.*
  - orange on gray *3,500.*

115-E5

Design 3: banknote type

115-E5
- ***a.*** 5c
  - carmine on orange and red *3,250.*
  - carmine on brown *3,250.*
  - orange on brown *3,250.*
- ***b.*** 10c
  - carmine on orange and red *5,000.*
  - blue on orange and red *5,000.*
- ***c.*** 30c
  - carmine on orange and red *3,500.*
  - orange on brown *3,500.*

115-E6

Design 4: continuous wavy lines

115-E6
- ***a.*** 5c orange on scarlet 3,250.
- ***b.*** 10c
  - blue on scarlet *5,000.*
  - carmine on scarlet *5,000.*
- ***c.*** 30c black on scarlet *3,500.*

115-E7

Design 5: wavy lines

115-E7
- ***a.*** 5c
  - orange on scarlet *3,250.*
  - orange on black *3,250.*
- ***b.*** 10c
  - dark brown on black *5,000.*
  - orange red on black *5,000.*
  - carmine on scarlet *5,000.*
- ***c.*** 30c
  - carmine on black *3,500.*
  - carmine on scarlet *3,500.*

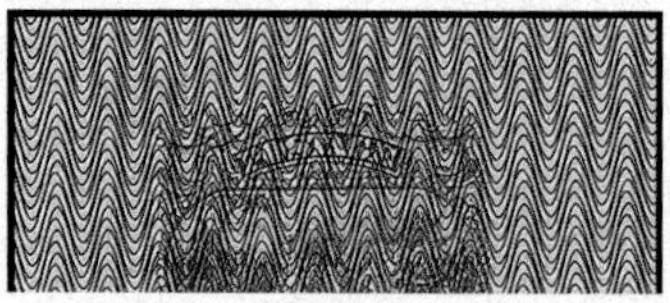
115-E8

Design 6: wavy lines

115-E8
- ***a.*** 5c orange on black *3,250.*
- ***b.*** 10c blue on black *5,000.*
- ***c.*** 30c
  - carmine on black *3,500.*
  - orange on black *3,500.*

115-E9

Design 7: crossed wavy lines

115-E9
- ***a.*** 5c
  - carmine on black *3,250.*
  - orange on black *3,250.*
- ***b.*** 10c blue on black *5,000.*
- ***c.*** 30c orange on black *3,500.*

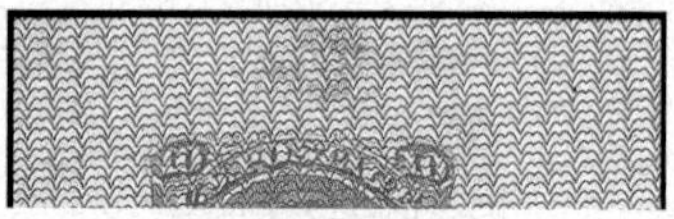
115-E10

Design 8: wavy lines

115-E10
- ***a.*** 5c carmine on scarlet *3,250.*
- ***b.*** 10c
  - blue on scarlet *5,000.*
  - carmine on scarlet *5,000.*
  - orange red on scarlet *5,000.*

129-E3

Design 9: wavy lines

129-E3 15c
- orange brown on orange, vert. *3,500.*
- blue green on orange, horiz. *3,500.*
- dark blue on orange, horiz. *3,500.*

129-E4

Design 10: banknote type

129-E4 15c
- orange brown on scarlet *3,500.*
- blue green on scarlet *3,500.*
- dark blue on scarlet *3,500.*

129-E5

Design 11: banknote type

129-E5 15c
- orange brown on light scarlet *3,500.*
- blue green on light scarlet, vert. *3,500.*
- dark blue on light scarlet *3,500.*

129-E6

Design 12: banknote type

129-E6 15c
- orange brown on deep scarlet *3,500.*
- blue green on deep scarlet *3,500.*
- dark blue on deep scarlet *3,500.*

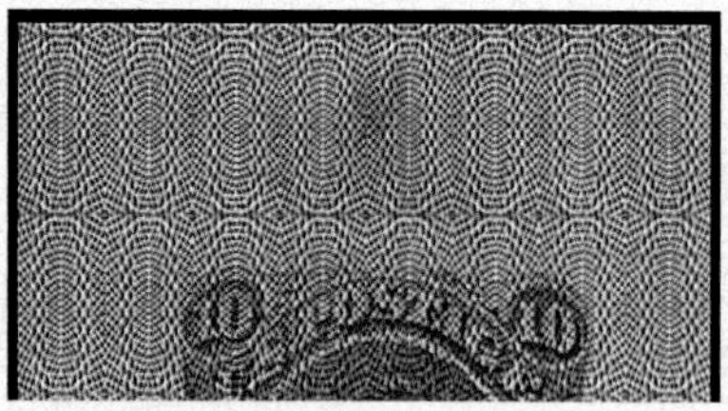
115-E11

Design 13: banknote type

115-E11
- ***a.*** 5c orange on brown *3,250.*
- ***b.*** 10c
  - carmine on brown *5,500.*
  - orange red on brown *5,500.*
  - blue on brown (horiz. underprinting) *5,500.*
  - blue on brown (vert. underprinting) *5,500.*
- ***c.*** 30c carmine on brown *3,500.*

115-E12

Design 14: banknote type

115-E12
- ***a.*** 5c
  - carmine on scarlet (horiz.) *4,000.*
  - black on scarlet (vert.) *4,000.*
- ***b.*** 10c
  - carmine on scarlet *5,500.*
  - orange on scarlet *5,500.*
  - sepia on scarlet *5,500.*
  - blue on scarlet *5,500.*
- ***c.*** 30c black on scarlet *3,500.*

115-E13

Design 15: banknote type

115-E13
a. 5c carmine on orange brown *3,250.*
b. 30c carmine on deep orange *3,500.*

115-E14

Design 16: multiple rosettes

115-E14
a. 5c orange on scarlet *3,250.*
b. 10c
carmine on scarlet *5,500.*
orange red on scarlet *5,500.*
sepia on scarlet *5,500.*
blue on scarlet *5,500.*

115-E15

Design 17: multiple oval rosettes

115-E15
a. 5c carmine on scarlet *3,250.*
b. 30c
carmine on scarlet *3,500.*
orange on scarlet *3,500.*

115-E16

Design 18: negative stars in diagonal lines

115-E16
a. 5c
black on scarlet *3,250.*
carmine on scarlet *3,250.*
b. 10c
carmine on scarlet *5,500.*
sepia on scarlet *5,500.*
c. 30c carmine on scarlet *3,500.*

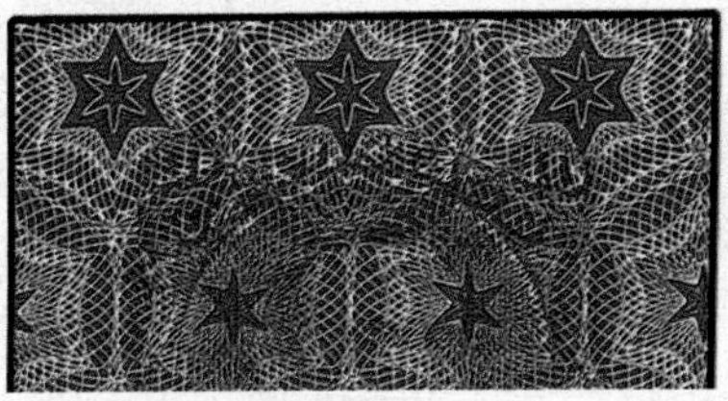

116-E6a

Design 19: multiple 6-point stars in lathework

116-E6
a. 10c blue on blue green *5,500.*
b. 30c carmine on blue green *3,500.*

116-E7

Design 20: banknote type

116-E7
a. 10c
brown on orange *5,500.*
blue on orange *5,500.*
b. 30c carmine on orange *3,500.*

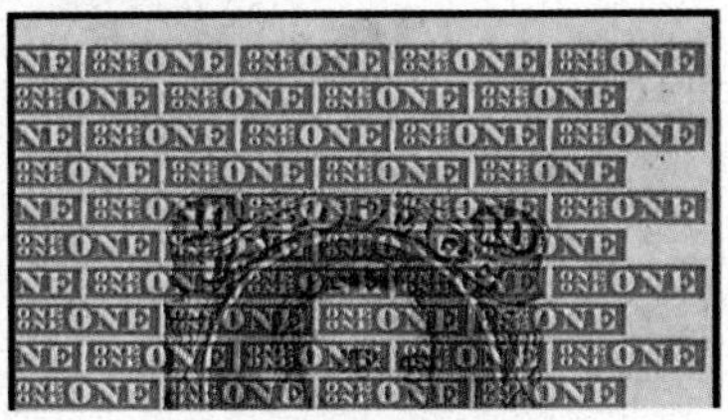

116-E8

Design 21: multiple "ONE"

116-E8 10c blue on scarlet *5,500.*

115-E17

Design 22: multiple "TWO"

115-E17
a. 5c orange on scarlet *3,250.*
b. 10c carmine on scarlet *5,500.*

115-E18

Design 23: multiple "5"s in oval rosettes

115-E18 5c black on carmine *3,250.*

115-E19

Design 24: multiple "TEN 10"

115-E19
a. 5c
orange on scarlet *3,250.*
carmine on scarlet *3,250.*
b. 10c
carmine on scarlet *5,500.*
orange red on scarlet *5,500.*
brown on scarlet *5,500.*
blue on scarlet *5,500.*
c. 30c
carmine on scarlet *3,500.*
orange red on scarlet *3,500.*
brown on scarlet *3,500.*
blue on scarlet *3,500.*

115-E20

Design 25: multiple "50"

115-E20 5c
black on black *3,250.*
orange on black *3,250.*

1870 ISSUE

Continental Banknote Co.

145-E1

Vignette of Washington in large ornate "1." Labels and side ornaments not yet engraved.

145-E1 1c engraved die on India, black —

145-E1C

Vignette of Washington in large ornate "1."

145-E1C One Cent
a. Die on India, die sunk on card
black *1,500.*
scarlet *1,500.*
green *1,500.*
ultramarine *1,500.*
blue *1,500.*
b. On proof paper, about 25x30mm
black *1,000.*
green *1,000.*

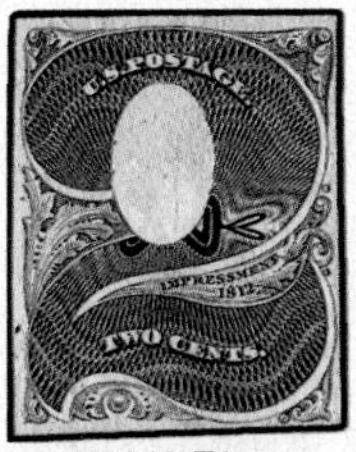

146-E1

147-E1

Blank vignette in large ornate "2."

146-E1 2c Engraved die on India, die sunk on card
black *1,500.*
scarlet *1,500.*
ultramarine *1,500.*
blue *1,500.*
green *1,500.*

Design size: 20x25mm
Die size: 43x48mm
Vignette of Lincoln in large ornate "3" with rounded top.

147-E1 3c Engraved die on proof paper
black *2,250.*
scarlet *1,750.*
ultramarine *1,750.*
green *1,750.*

147-E1A

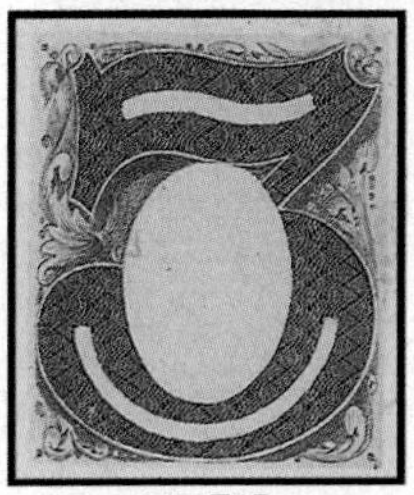

147-E1B

Design size: 11½x15½mm
Die size: 25x32mm
Vignette only of Columbia. Imprint and die number below design.

147-E1A 3c Engraved die on India, black —

Design size: 21x25mm

Blank vignette in frame of large ornate "3" with upper and lower labels not yet engraved.

147-E1B 3c Engraved die on India, die sunk on card
black 2,250.
green 2,000.

147-E1C

Design size: 21x25mm
No. 147-E1A cut to shape and mounted in frame of large ornate "3" with upper and lower labels not yet engraved.

147-E1C 3c Engraved die on India, die sunk on card
black 2,250.
green 2,000.

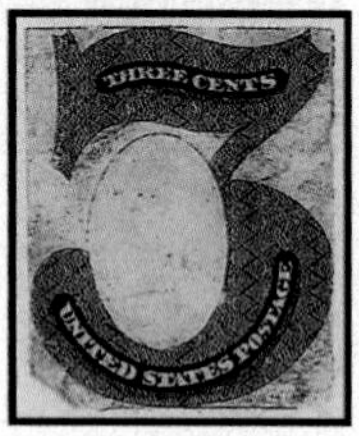

147-E2

Design size: 21x25mm
Blank vignette in frame only as No. 147-E1B but with upper and lower labels engraved.

147-E2 3c Engraved die on India, die sunk on card
black 2,250.
green 2,000.

Vignette of Columbia mounted in place on No. 147-E2.

147-E3 3c Engraved die on India, die sunk on card
black 2,250.
green 2,000.

147-E4

Complete design with Columbia vignette in large ornate "3" surrounded by foliate ornamentation.

147-E4 3c Engraved die on India, die sunk on card
black 2,250.
green 2,000.

147-E5

Design size: 22x27mm
Blank vignette in large ornate "3" surrounded by scrolled ornamentation.

147-E5 3c Engraved die on India, die sunk on card
black 2,250.
green 2,000.

147-E6

Vignette of Columbia mounted in place on No. 147-E5B.

147-E6 3c Engraved die on India, die sunk on card
black 2,250.
green 2,000.

148-E1

Blank vignette in large ornate "6."

148-E1 6c
a. Engraved die on India, die sunk on card
black 2,000.
scarlet 2,000.
green 2,000.
dark green 2,000.
ultramarine 2,000.
b. Engraved die on India, cut close
black 1,750.
scarlet 1,750.
blue 1,750.
green 1,750.

National Banknote Co.

145-E2

145-E3

Die size: 64x74mm
Engraved vignette of Franklin facing right.

145-E2 1c Die on India, die sunk on card
black (with pencil lines on bust 700.
dull dark orange 700.

Engraved incomplete Franklin vignette facing right mounted over pencil sketch of frame.

145-E3 1c Die on thin white card, 55x66mm, black 2,850.

145-E4

145-E5

Incomplete Franklin vignette mounted on more complete pencil sketch of frame.

145-E4 1c Die on thin white card, orange brown 2,000.

Design size: 20x26mm
Engraved vignette mounted on pencil and watercolor frame design.

145-E5 1c Die on thin white card, 45x51mm, dull dark orange 2,000.

145-E6

Incomplete engraving of entire design; lower edge of bust vert. shading only.

145-E6 1c
a. Die on 64x71mm India, die sunk on card
ultramarine 475
red 475
orange brown 475
red brown 475
blue green 475
mauve 475
dull lilac 475
black 475
gray 475
carmine 475
carmine rose 475
dull rose 475
dull yellow brown 475
brown violet 475
light green 475
green 475
gray olive 475
yellow 475
b. Die on bond, die sunk on card, dark yellow 750

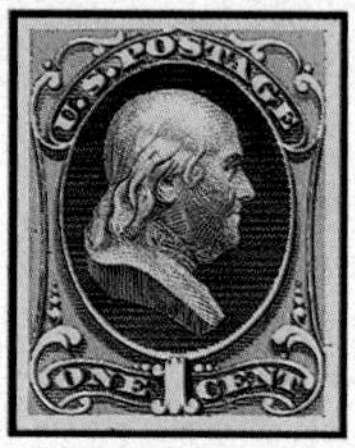

145-E8

Completed die: additional shading lines in background, four horiz. shading lines at top of lower edge of bust.

145-E8 1c
a. Die on India, die sunk on card
black 475
blue green 475
carmine 475
yellow 475
orange brown 475
orange 475
gray green 475
dull red violet 475
dark blue 475
b. Die on ivory glazed paper, 65x72mm
black 425
black brown 425
scarlet 425
blue 425
c. Completed die on thick wove, dismal dusky yellow 425

145-E9

145-E10

Die size: 50½x64mm
Engraved vignette of Franklin facing left, no shading lines at top of bust, etc.

145-E9 1c
a. Die on white glazed paper, black 475.
b. Die on India, mounted on card stamped "J.I. PEASE.", black 450.

Engraved Franklin vignette with 1 and value label.

145-E10 1c Die on India, on card (1873), black 2,000.

This is an essay for Official stamps.

146-E2

146-E3

Die size: 62x76mm
Vignette only of Jackson in high stiff collar.

146-E2 2c Die on India, die sunk on card
black *900.*
orange brown *900.*
dull violet *900.*

Engraved Jackson vignette mounted on watercolor frame.

146-E3 2c Die on thin white card, 46x89mm, black vignette, dark gray frame *5,000.*

146-E4

146-E5

Engraved Jackson vignette, mounted on watercolor frame (diff. from No. 146-E3).

146-E4 2c Die on thin white card, 46x89mm, black vignette, gray frame *5,000.*

Similar to No. 146-E4 but with pencil border around frame.

146-E5 2c Die on thin white card, 45x50mm, dark orange *5,000.*

Incomplete die: without shading lines under value ribbon, vert. lines in colorless strips, and broken horiz. lines at top and bottom of frame.

146-E6

146-E6 2c Die on thin white card, dark orange *1,250.*

146-E7

Die size: 64½x73mm
Completed die of unadopted design.

146-E7 2c
a. Die on India
carmine *1,000.*
deep rose *1,000.*
scarlet *1,000.*
dim dusky orange orange red *1,000.*
deep yellow orange *1,000.*
bone brown *1,000.*
orange brown *1,000.*
brown *1,000.*
canary yellow *1,000.*
yellow brown *1,000.*
dark olive green *1,000.*
green *1,000.*
dim dusky blue green *1,000.*
dark blue *1,000.*
deep ultramarine *1,000.*
bright blue *1,000.*
dull violet *1,000.*
smoky deep red violet red *1,000.*
gray *1,000.*
black *1,000.*
b. Die on ivory glazed paper, about 64x77mm
black *1,000.*
brown black *1,000.*
scarlet *1,000.*
blue *1,000.*
c. Die on thin wove, dark yellow *1,000.*

146-E8

Die size: 62x76mm
Incomplete vignette of Jackson as on issued stamp: incomplete shading in eye and hair in front of ear, right neck tendon on chest not shaded.

146-E8 2c
a. Die on India, on 55x66mm card
black *750.*
orange *750.*
deep yellow orange *750.*
red brown *750.*
orange brown *750.*
dark blue green *750.*
red violet *750.*

Also known on 87x143mm card showing full die sinkage, pencil inscribed "2c" above and "Jackson" below sinkage area. Value, *$750.*

b. Die on glazed paper, die sinkage 50x63mm, black *1,000.*

Completed Jackson vignette.

146-E9

146-E9 2c Die on glazed paper, black *750.*

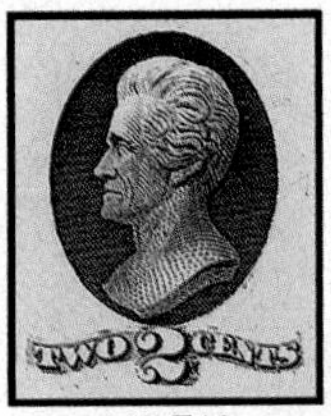
146-E10

146-E11

Engraved Jackson vignette with 2 and value label.

146-E10 2c Die on glazed paper (1873), black *1,750.*

This is an essay for Official stamps.

Engraved vignette with pencil and watercolor frame design, labels blank.

146-E11 2c Die on thin white card, 50x60mm, dim dusky bright blue green vignette, dark green frame *6,250.*

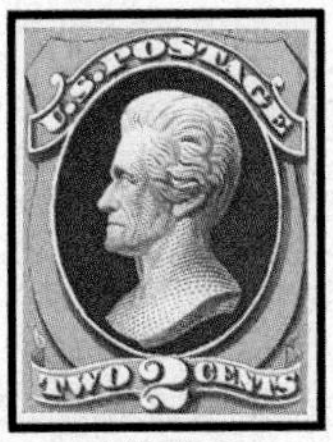
146-E12

Die size: 62x75mm
Incomplete engraving of entire design: no leaves on wide bands at sides below vignette, neck tendon and hair in front of ear changed, top of head incomplete, ear hole too dark. This design essayed for envelopes on thick papers.

146-E12 2c Die on India, die sunk on card
carmine *1,250.*
orange *1,250.*
brown orange *1,250.*
brown *1,250.*
blue *1,250.*
violet *1,250.*
green *1,250.*

147-E7

Incomplete engraved vignette of Lincoln (horiz. line background), mounted on pencil and watercolor frame design.

147-E7 3c Die on thin white card, black vignette, gray black frame *3,500.*

147-E8

147-E9

Design size: 20x25mm
Die Size: 62x72½mm
Incomplete engraving of head only of Washington.

147-E8 3c Die on white glazed paper, black *550.*

Engraved Washington vignette only as adopted.

147-E9 3c Die on white glazed paper, black *650.*

Nos. 147-E8 and 147-E9 may have been made from completed dies of No. 147 to produce Nos. 184-E9 and 184-E10.

147-E10

147-E11

Washington vignette, 3 and value label.

147-E10 3c Die on India, card mounted (1873), black *1,600.*

This is an essay for Official stamps.

Design size: 20x25½mm
Incomplete engraved vignette (horiz. lined background), mounted on pencil and watercolor frame design.

147-E11 3c Die on thin white card, 45x54mm, carmine vignette, dim light red violet red frame *5,000.*

Incomplete engraving of entire design: no horizontal lines on nose, parts of hair, chin, collar, forehead unfinished.

147-E12

147-E12 3c Die on India, die sunk on card
black *575.*
deep red *575.*
carmine *575.*
yellow orange *575.*
brown *575.*
red brown *575.*
dark red brown *575.*
yellow brown *575.*
ultramarine *575.*
dark blue *575.*
dark violet blue *575.*
blue green *575.*
dark red violet *575.*

Issued stamp, No. 147, in trial colors, underprinted network in fugitive ink.

147-E13 3c
- ***a.*** On thick paper, perf. 12, gummed
  - gray blue, underprinting gray brown *150.*
  - gray blue, underprinting olive gray *150.*
  - green, underprinting olive gray *150.*
  - dim red, underprinting olive gray *150.*
  - dull orange, underprinting olive gray *150.*
  - brown, underprinting olive gray *150.*
- ***b.*** As "a," faint 6mm-high horiz. bar trial cancel
  - dim red *450.*
  - dull orange *450.*
- ***c.*** As "a," underprinting omitted
  - gray blue —
  - dim red —
  - dull orange —
  - brown —
- ***d.*** As "a," imperf, green, underprinting olive gray *325.*
  - Pair *700.*
- ***e.*** As "d," underprinting omitted *325.*
  - Pair *700.*
  - P# block of 10 —

Multiples of the No. 147-E13 varieties can be found with fully or partially underprinted stamps in conjunction with underprinting-omitted stamps.

148-E2

148-E3

Design size: 19½x25½mm
Die size: 63x76mm
Engraved Lincoln vignette only, hair brushed back, horiz. line background.

148-E2 6c Die on India, die sunk on card
- black *700.*
- blue *700.*

Incomplete engraved Lincoln vignette (horiz. lined background) mounted on pencil and watercolor frame with blank labels.

148-E3 6c Die on thin white card, 45x52mm, dim blue vignette, dim dark blue frame *4,000.*

148-E4

Incomplete engraving of entire design: horiz. line background in vignette, lines on cheek and hair unfinished.

148-E4 6c Die on India, on card, about 50x52mm
- carmine *600.*
- rose *600.*
- dull rose *600.*
- red violet *600.*
- dull violet *600.*
- deep ultramarine *600.*
- dark black blue *600.*
- yellow *600.*
- green *600.*
- dark green *600.*
- dark red brown *600.*
- deep yellow brown *600.*
- yellow brown *600.*
- orange brown *600.*

Incomplete engraving of entire design: horiz. line background in vignette, no shading directly under value label, shadows on "SIX CENTS" and shading on ornaments in upper corners unfinished.

148-E5 6c Die on India, on card, ultramarine *900.*

148-E6

Similar to No. 148-E5 but with diagonal lines added to vignette background. (Essay in orange brown has pencil notations for changes.)

148-E6 6c Die on India, die sunk on card
- black *1,000.*
- dull carmine *1,000.*
- dark rose *1,000.*
- yellowish black *1,000.*
- brown *1,000.*
- gray brown *1,000.*
- black brown *1,000.*
- yellow *1,000.*
- gray olive green *1,000.*
- dark green *1,000.*
- ultramarine *1,000.*
- deep ultramarine *1,000.*
- dull ultramarine *1,000.*
- violet *1,000.*
- dark violet *1,000.*
- red violet *1,000.*
- orange brown *1,000.*

148-E7

Similar to No. 148-E6 but with dots added to top of hair.

148-E7 6c Die on India, on card
- dark carmine *1,000.*
- dull rose *1,000.*
- orange *1,000.*
- yellow brown *1,000.*
- dark brown *1,000.*
- black brown *1,000.*
- yellow green *1,000.*
- blue green *1,000.*
- ultramarine *1,000.*
- dark red violet *1,000.*

Completed die with lines on cheek softened to dots only.

148-E8

148-E8 6c Die on India
- yellow green *250.*
- brown *250.*
- rose *250.*

All known examples are much reduced.

Incomplete engraving of entire design, similar to No. 148-E10 but with hair brushed forward as on adopted design but shadow under hair in front of ear is round at bottom, not pointed as on approved design. Shading on cheek behind nostril is dotted instead of lined on completed design.

148-E9

148-E9 6c Die on India, on card, red violet *750.*

148-E10

Die size: 64x75mm
Frame as adopted, vignette similar to No. 148-E6 but with hair brushed back; lines on cheek.

148-E10 6c
- ***a.*** Die on India, die sunk on card, deep blue *850.*
- ***b.*** Die on India, about 30x35mm, carmine *600.*
- ***c.*** As "a," but no panels above top label, carmine *850.*

Similar to No. 148-E10a but dots (not lines) on cheek and on lower lip. Shadow under hair in front of ear is rounded at bottom, not pointed as on approved design.

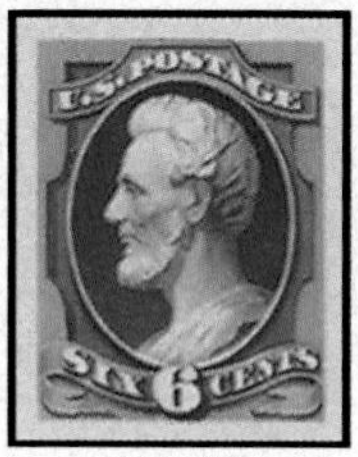

148-E11

148-E11 6c Die on India, on card
- rose pink *700.*
- deep rose *700.*
- pale rose *700.*
- brown rose *700.*
- rose carmine *700.*
- deep carmine *700.*
- brown *700.*
- yellow brown *700.*
- blue *700.*
- red violet *700.*

Die of completed vignette only with hair brushed forward.

148-E12 6c Die on white glazed paper, black *1,500.*

148-E13

Completed vignette with 6 and value label.

148-E13 6c Die on India, on card (1873), black *1,500.*

This is an essay for Official stamps.

149-E4

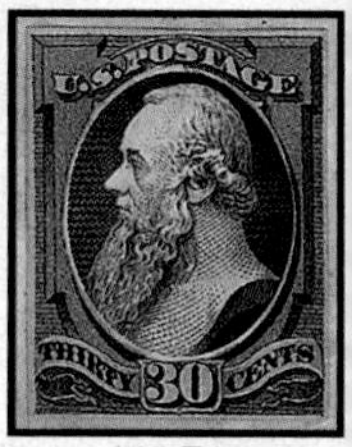

149-E4a

Die size: 62x75mm
Vignette of Stanton.

149-E4 7c Die on India, on card, black *1,000.*

Engraved frame of adopted 30c design but with vignette cut out and mounted over Stanton vignette on India No. 149-E4.

149-E4a Stanton vignette with 30c frame on thin, stiff paper mounted on top, black *500.*

The status of No. 149-E4a has been questioned.

149-E5

Die size: 62x76mm
Completed vignette with 7 and value label.

149-E5 7c
a. Die on India, on card (1873), black 1,000.
b. Die on white glazed paper, black 1,000.

This is an essay for Official stamps.

149-E6

Design as issued but shading under ear incomplete.

149-E6 7c Die on India, die sunk on card

black	500.
dark red	500.
light red	500.
gray green	500.
gray black	500.
yellow brown	500.
dark brown	500.
dull yellow brown	500.
dull red brown	500.
blue green	500.
ultramarine	500.
dim blue	500.
lilac	500.
red orange	500.
yellow orange	500.

Similar to No. 149-E6 but with dots added on forehead.

149-E7 7c Die on India, brown 1,250.

150-E1

150-E2

Design size: 20x25½mm
Incomplete engraved vignette of Jefferson (horiz. line background) mounted on pencil and watercolor frame design with blank labels.

150-E1 10c Die on thin white card, 45x51mm, black vignette, gray frame 3,000.

Design size: 19½x25½mm
Die size: 62x75mm
Jefferson vignette with incomplete engraving of frame: unfinished shading under "TEN" ribbon, under oval at ends of "U.S. POSTAGE," and under shield over ends of value label ribbons.

150-E2 10c Die on India, on card, deep blue green 2,500.

Similar to No. 150-E2 but showing horizontal shading lines only.

150-E2A 10c Die on India, die sunk on 152x225mm card

blue green	750.
red violet	750.

150-E3

Completed engraving of unadopted design.

150-E3 10c
a. Die on India, die sunk on card

carmine	750.
rose	750.
gray brown rose	750.
yellow	750.
yellow brown	750.
orange	750.
orange brown	750.
brown	750.
chocolate	750.
green	750.
blue green	750.
greenish gray	750.
blue	750.
dull violet	750.
dull red violet	750.
dark navy blue	750.
ultramarine	750.
deep ultramarine	750.
dull dusky blue	750.
navy blue	750.
slate	750.

b. Die on bond

dull dusky brown	500.
brown gray	500.

All known examples of No. 153-E3b are reduced.

150-E4

150-E5

Three separate designs. Left one dark blue green, similar to No. 150-E3 but shows engraved attempt to remove coat collar to obtain nude neck (some coat still shows under chin). Middle one brown orange (No. 150-E2) with coat collar and top of hair cut out, neck and bust drawn in. Right one black vignette of head finally adopted (No. 150-E7).

150-E4 10c Dies on India, on card 2,500.

Design size: 19½x25½mm
Same frame as No. 150-E2, but Jefferson vignette has hair arranged differently and bust has no clothing.

150-E5 10c
a. Die on India, die sunk on card

black	600.
scarlet	600.
brown	600.
blue	600.
green	600.

b. Die on ivory glazed paper, 66x75mm

black	500.
black brown	500.
scarlet	500.
blue	500.

c. Die on thin wove, dark yellow 500.

150-E6

150-E7

Frame of No. 150-E5 with vignette cut out and replaced by black vignette as adopted.

150-E6 10c Die on India

deep orange brown	1,500.
black	1,500.

Die size: 62x76mm
Vignette of Jefferson as adopted.

150-E7 10c Die on India, die sunk on card

dark ultramarine	700.
yellow	700.
brown	700.

151-E1

151-E2

Design size: 20x25½mm
Engraved vignette of Washington (No. 79-E37b) mounted on incomplete pencil drawing of frame design.

151-E1 12c Die on India, on 38x47½mm card, black vignette, pencil frame 2,500.

Design size: 20x25½mm
Engraved vignette of Washington (No. 79-E37b) mounted on pencil and watercolor frame design with blank labels.

151-E2 12c Die on card, 46x89mm, black vignette, gray frame 3,000.

151-E3

151-E4

Design size: 20x25½mm
Engraved vignette of Washington (No. 79-E37b) mounted on pencil and watercolor frame design with ribbons and blank labels.

151-E3 12c Die on card, 46x89mm, black vignette, gray frame 3,000.

Design size: 20x25½mm
Engraved vignette of Washington (No. 79-E37b) mounted on pencil and watercolor frame design with "U, S, 12" and blank labels.

151-E4 12c Die on card, 46x89mm, black vignette, gray frame 3,000.

151-E5

151-E6

Design size: 19½x25½mm
Die size: 62x74mm
Vignette of Henry Clay only.

151-E5 12c Die on India, die sunk on card

black	600.
deep carmine	600.
yellow	600.
yellow brown	600.
brown orange	600.
dark orange brown	600.
black brown	600.
ultramarine	600.
dark blue green	600.
red violet	600.

Incomplete Clay vignette mounted on watercolor shield-like frame design on gray background, pencil notation "background of stars to be gray."

151-E6 12c Die on card, 53x75mm, blue black vignette, blue frame 3,250.

151-E7

Die sinkage size: 63x77mm

Completed die of unadopted design similar to No. 151-E6. This design essayed for envelopes on thick paper.

151-E7 12c

a. Die on India, on card

deep orange brown	*900.*
green	*900.*
deep ultramarine	*900.*
violet	*900.*
deep red	*900.*
deep orange red	*900.*
orange	*900.*
dusky red	*900.*

b. Die on wove

carmine	*700.*
orange	*700.*
brown	*700.*
orange brown	*700.*
ultramarine	*700.*

c. Die on card colored yellow, black *700.*

Engraved vignette of Washington mounted on partly complete pencil drawing of frame, pencil notation "new border for clay 12c."

151-E8

151-E8 12c Die on card, black, pencil frame *2,750.*

151-E9

151-E10

Die size: 55x63mm
Incomplete engraving of entire adopted design, without 3 vert. shading lines at left side of lower triangle.

151-E9 12c

a. Die on India, die sunk on card

black	*650.*
carmine	*650.*
blue green	*650.*
blue	*650.*
light blue	*650.*
orange	*650.*
orange brown	*650.*
dull red	*650.*
brown red	*650.*

b. Die on proof paper, about 38x45mm

carmine	*650.*
dull carmine	*650.*
orange brown	*650.*
dull red	*650.*
ultramarine	*650.*

c. Die on India, on card, about 30x35mm, dark blue *650.*

Completed Clay vignette with 12 and value label.

151-E10 12c Die on white glazed paper (1873), black *1,250.*

This is an essay for Official stamps.

152-E1

152-E2

Design size: 19 ½x25mm
Incomplete vignette of Webster with side whiskers bolder than as adopted, mounted on watercolor frame design with 15 and blank labels.

152-E1 15c Die on white card, 40x61mm, dim red vignette, light red violet frame *2,250.*

Design size: 19 ½x25mm
Die size: 63x76mm

Incomplete engraving of vignette only: missing shading under ear and at back of neck.

152-E2 15c Die on India, die sunk on card, black *750.*

152-E3

152-E4

Vignette similar to No. 152-E2 but with shading under ear, more shading at back of neck.

152-E3 15c Die on India, die sunk on card

black	*700.*
dark orange	*700.*
orange	*700.*
yellow	*700.*
red violet	*700.*
ultramarine	*700.*
brown	*700.*

Vignette of Webster with 15 below.

152-E4 15c Die on white glazed paper (1873), black *1,000.*

This is an essay for Official stamps.

152-E5

Incomplete engraved design: shading on corner panel bevels incomplete, side whiskers bolder than as adopted. Also essayed for envelopes on thick paper.

152-E5 15c Die on India, die sunk on card, orange brown *750.*

Similar to No. 152-E5 but with pencil marks suggesting shading on corner panels.

152-E6 15c Die on India, orange brown *750.*

Similar to No. 152-E5 with engraved shading added to corner panels but white areas incomplete.

152-E7

152-E7 15c Die on India

orange	*650.*
orange yellow	*650.*
orange brown	*650.*
green	*650.*
red violet	*650.*
rose carmine	*650.*

Similar to No. 152-E7 but shading on corner panels complete.

152-E8

152-E8 15c Die on India, on card, black *1,000.*

153-E1

153-E2

Design size: 18x23mm
Incomplete engraved vignette of Scott mounted on pencil sketch of partial frame design.

153-E1 24c Die on white card, 33x39mm, dull red violet vignette, pencil frame *1,750.*

Design size: 19 ½x25mm
Complete engraved vignette mounted on pencil and watercolor frame design with "U.S. POSTAGE" in ink.

153-E2 24c Die on white card, 73x110mm, dim blue green *3,250.*

153-E3

153-E4

Die size: 62x76mm
Incomplete engraved vignette only.

153-E3 24c Die on India, die sunk on card

black	*600.*
yellow	*600.*
yellow brown	*600.*
dark orange brown	*600.*
ultramarine	*600.*
dark ultramarine	*600.*
red violet	*600.*

Die size: 62x77mm
Incomplete design as adopted: upper corners not squared outside scrolls, no periods after U and S in stars.

153-E4 24c Die on India, die sunk on card

carmine	*650.*
orange	*650.*
brown orange	*650.*
yellow brown	*650.*
deep brown	*650.*
ultramarine	*650.*
dark red violet	*650.*
green	*650.*

Value off card, cut down, $275.

Previous No. 154-E1 is now No. 149-E4a.

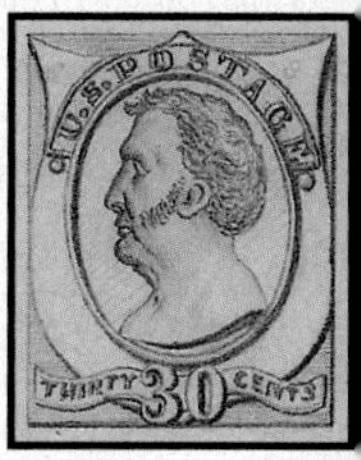

154-E2

Pencil drawing of entire design, labeled "Scott."

154-E2 30c Pencil drawing on white card, 53x92mm *2,400.*

Engraved vignette of Hamilton mounted on pencil drawing of frame.

154-E3 30c Die on card, yellow brown vignette, pencil frame *1,500.*

154-E4

Incomplete engraved vignette of Hamilton.

154-E4 30c Die on India, die sunk on card

yellow brown	*700.*
dark ultramarine blue	*700.*
orange	*700.*

Vignette of Hamilton with more engraving on forehead, nose, neck, etc.

154-E5

154-E5 30c Die on India, die sunk on card

dark red brown	*700.*
dull carmine	*700.*
ultramarine	*700.*

154-E6

Completed vignette with 30 below.

154-E6 30c Die on white glazed paper (1873), black *1,750.*

This is an essay for Official stamps.

155-E1

155-E2

Pencil drawing of entire design, labeled "Perry."

155-E1 90c Pencil drawing on white card, 53x92mm *2,000.*

Design size: 19½x25mm
Engraved vignette of Perry mounted on pencil and watercolor frame design.

155-E2 90c Die on white card, 73x110mm, dull dark violet vignette, dull red violet frame *3,250.*

155-E3

Die size: 58x79mm
Incomplete engraving of Perry vignette as adopted.

155-E3 90c

a. Die on India, die sunk on card

deep yellow orange	*600.*
orange brown	*600.*
dark brown	*600.*
dull carmine	*600.*
ultramarine blue	*600.*
dark blue green	*600.*
dark red violet	*600.*

b. Die on white ivory paper, black *600.*

Similar to No. 155-E3 but more lines in hair above forehead.

155-E4

155-E4 90c Die on India, on card, black *600.*

155-E5

Incomplete engraving of design as adopted: rope above vignette unfinished. Also essayed for envelopes on thick paper.

155-E5 90c Die on India, die sunk on card

black	*750.*
carmine, off card	*325.*
orange	*750.*
dark orange	*750.*
yellow brown	*750.*
brown	*750.*
deep orange brown	*750.*
deep ultramarine	*750.*
blue green	*750.*
red violet	*750.*

Value off card, cut down, $250.

1873 ISSUE
Continental Bank Note Co.

179-E1

179-E2

Die size: 20x25mm
Vignette of Taylor by Bureau of Engraving and Printing, in engraved frame.

179-E1 Five Cents, Die on India

black	*4,500.*
blue	*4,500.*

Design size: 24x29mm
Vignette of Taylor by Bureau of Engraving and Printing, in ornate wash drawing of frame ("FIVE CENTS" black, on shaded ribbon).

179-E2 5c Die on card, black *4,000.*

Incomplete vignette: hair, coat, background, etc., unfinished.

179-E3

179-E3 5c Die on India, violet *2,000.*

George W. Bowlsby 1873 essay similar in concept to his No. 63-E13 but without coupon attached. It consisted of an unused 1c stamp (No. 156) with horiz. sewing machine perfs. through center, gummed on upper half only, as described in his Dec. 26, 1865 patent. Stamp was meant to be torn in half by postal clerk as cancellation, to prevent reuse.

156-E1 1c blue *250.*

1876 Experimental Ink and Paper Essays

Plate designs of 1873-75 issues in normal colors, printed on paper tinted with sensitive inks and on heavily laid (horiz.) colored papers (unless otherwise noted).

156-E2 1c Blue on:

carmine	*150.*
pale rose	*150.*
deep yellow	*150.*
pale violet	*150.*

158-E1 3c Green on:

pale rose	*150.*
deep yellow	*150.*
pale violet	*150.*

158-E2 3c Green on paper covered with pink varnish which vanishes with the color *100.*

158-E3 3c Green on thick white blotting paper which absorbs canceling ink *100.*

161-E1 10c Brown on:

pale rose	*150.*
deep yellow	*150.*
pale violet	*150.*

163-E1 15c Yellow orange on:

pale rose	*200.*
deep yellow	*200.*
pale violet	*200.*

165-E1 30c Gray black on:

pale rose	*200.*
deep yellow	*200.*
pale violet	*200.*

166-E1 90c Rose carmine on:

pale rose	*200.*
deep yellow	*200.*
pale violet	*200.*

178-E1 2c Vermilion on:

pale rose	*150.*
deep yellow	*150.*
pale violet	*150.*

179-E4

179-E4 5c Blue on:

pale rose	*300.*
deep yellow	*300.*
pale violet	*300.*

See No. 147-E13.

1877 Essays
Philadelphia Bank Note Co.

Die essays for this section were all engraved. The frame-only dies for all values of this series were engraved with two values appearing per die, except the 3c (No. 184-E1) which was engraved alone. In each case the listing is under the lower denomination. The Washington vignette associated with each value of the frames is from engraved master die No. 14. (No. 182-E1).

Except as noted, plate essays in this section are all lithographed from a composite stone plate of two panes. The left pane ("plate 1") consists of horiz. rows of four of the 1c, 3c, 7c, 24c and 90c. The right pane ("plate 2") consists of horiz. rows of four 2c, 6c, 12c and 30c. "Printed by Philadelphia Bank Note Co. Patented June 16, 1876" imprint below 2nd and 3rd designs on each row.

See note above No. 63-E1.

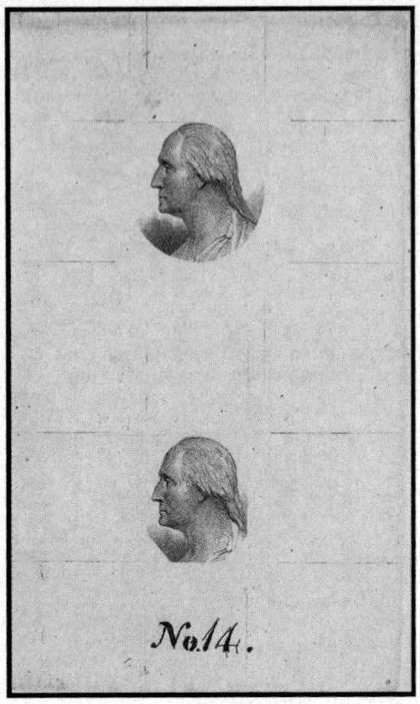

182-E1

Vignette master die "No. 14": two slightly diff. vignettes of Washington, one above the other, bottom one with truncated queue, bust and shading in front of neck.

182-E1
a. Die on old white glazed paper, black *500.*
b. Die on proof paper (1903)
black *100.*
carmine *100.*
dull carmine *100.*
dusky carmine *100.*
yellow *100.*
dull scarlet *100.*
dull orange *100.*
brown orange *100.*
brown *100.*
gray olive *100.*
blue green *100.*
dark green *100.*
black blue *100.*
ultramarine *100.*
violet *100.*
red violet *100.*

182-E2b

Design size: 20x25mm
Die size: 98x53mm
Frames of 1c and 2c side by side.

182-E2 1c + 2c
a. Die on white pelure
dark carmine *250.*
orange *250.*
brown *250.*
blue green *250.*
blue *250.*
b. Die with vertical line between designs (die size 85x54mm), on India, die sunk on card
dusky red *400.*
deep orange *400.*
orange brown *400.*
dark green *400.*
dark blue *400.*
c. Die on stiff glazed paper, black *400.*
d. Die on proof paper, printed through a mat (1903)
black *100.*
bright carmine *100.*
dull carmine *100.*
dim scarlet *100.*
dark orange *100.*
dull yellow *100.*
dark orange brown *100.*
black olive *100.*
dark blue green *100.*
dark blue *100.*
ultramarine *100.*
dark navy blue *100.*
blue violet *100.*
dull violet *100.*
red violet *100.*
e. Plate sheet of 1c, 2c, 3c, 12c, 24c, 30c, 90c frames only, on card, pale green blue *1,500.*

182-E3b

Complete 1c design, lithographed.

182-E3 1c
a. Plate on stamp paper, imperf., gummed
black *75.*
blue green *75.*
bright ultramarine *75.*
yellow *75.*
b. Plate on stamp paper, perf. 12, gummed
dark red orange *50.*
orange brown *50.*
red brown *50.*
red violet *50.*
violet blue *50.*
ultramarine *50.*
c. Plate 1 "sheet" of 20, complete designs, without imprint, on old glazed paper, imperf., deep brown orange *800.*
d. As "c," with imprint, on old glazed paper, imperf., gummed
dull deep violet red *800.*
ultramarine *800.*
scarlet *800.*
orange *800.*
carmine *800.*
dark carmine *800.*
green *800.*
bluish green *800.*
e. As "d," perf. 12, gummed
dull deep violet red *700.*
ultramarine *700.*
red brown *700.*
violet blue *700.*

Concerning plate 1 sheets of 20, note that composite stone plates also contained the plate 2 sheets of 16 listed as Nos. 183-E2c to 183-E2e. Many such composite sheets remain intact. All separated plate 1 or plate 2 sheets originally were part of a composite sheet.

183-E2b

Complete 2c design, lithographed.

183-E2 2c
a. Plate on stamp paper, imperf.
blue green *60.*
bright ultramarine *60.*
brown *60.*
b. Plate on stamp paper, perf. 12, gummed
bright red orange *35.*
dull red orange *35.*
dark red orange *35.*
red brown *35.*
dark red brown *35.*
dark orange brown *35.*
yellow brown *35.*
dull yellow green *35.*
green *35.*
dull ultramarine *35.*
bright ultramarine *35.*
blue violet *35.*
red violet *35.*
light red violet *35.*
violet red *35.*
c. Plate 2 "sheet" of 16, complete designs, without imprint, on old glazed paper, imperf., deep brown orange *600.*
d. As "c," with imprint, on old glazed paper, imperf., gummed, dull deep violet red *600.*
e. As "d," perf. 12, gummed, dull deep violet red *500.*

See note following No. 182-E3e.

Design size: 20x25mm
Die size: 54x55mm
Engraved frame of 3c alone on die.

184-E1 3c
a. Die on pelure paper
dark carmine *250.*
dark orange *250.*
orange brown *250.*
bright blue *250.*
green *250.*
dark green *250.*
b. Die on proof paper (1903)
black *100.*
bright carmine *100.*
dull carmine *100.*
dim scarlet *100.*
dark orange *100.*
dull yellow *100.*
dark orange brown *100.*
black olive *100.*
dark rose *100.*
green *100.*
yellow green *100.*
dark blue green *100.*
dark blue *100.*
deep ultramarine *100.*
dark navy blue *100.*
blue violet *100.*
dull violet *100.*
red violet *100.*

Built-up model of engraved frame cut to shape inside and out, mounted atop engraved vignette of the same color. Warning: fraudulent models combining engraved and lithographed materials exist.

184-E2 3c
a. Die on proof paper, cut close
dark scarlet *250.*
blue green *250.*
deep blue *250.*
b. Four examples mounted 2½mm apart on stiff white card, 80x87mm
red *1,000.*
orange brown *1,000.*
green *1,000.*
blue *1,000.*
violet *1,000.*
green frame, light blue vignette *1,000.*

Built-up model as No. 184-E2, vignette as No. 184-E5 with dark background.

184-E3 3c Die on proof paper, scarlet *250.*

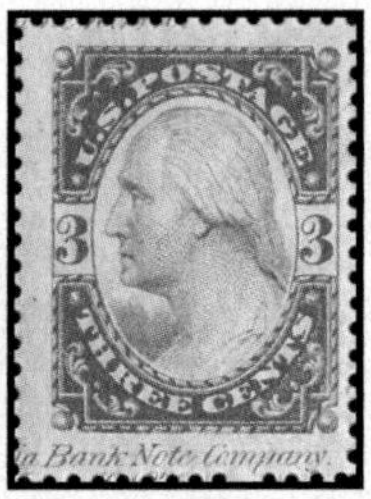

184-E4d

Complete 3c design, vignette with light background.

184-E4 3c
c. Plate lithographed on stamp paper, imperf.
black *75.*
green *75.*
dark green *75.*
bright ultramarine *75.*
orange *75.*

No. 184-E4c exists in two plates of 9 tete-beche, in diff. colors, on same piece of paper. Value, $800 sheet of 18.

d. Plate lithographed on stamp paper, perf. 12, gummed
dark red orange *50.*
red brown *50.*
red voilet *50.*
brown orange *50.*
ultramarine *50.*
violet blue *50.*
e. Plate sheet of 9 (3x3), imprint below, on stiff white wove
carmine *300.*
blue green *300.*
f. Plate sheet of 9 (3x3), on glazed thin wove
carmine *300.*
blue green *300.*
blue *300.*
orange *300.*
g. Plate sheet of 9 (3x3), on yellowish wove
carmine *300.*
blue green *300.*
blue *300.*
h. Die of complete design on old stiff glazed paper (die size: 55x66mm), black *350.*
i. Complete die on glazed wove
deep carmine *200.*
scarlet *200.*
ultramarine *200.*
j. Complete die on India, light orange red *200.*
k. Complete die on proof paper (1903)
black *75.*
bright carmine *75.*
dull carmine *75.*
dim scarlet *75.*
dark orange *75.*
dull yellow *75.*
dark orange brown *75.*
black olive *75.*
green *75.*
dark blue green *75.*

deep ultramarine 75.
dark navy blue 75.
blue violet 75.
dull violet 75.
red violet 75.
l. Complete die on large colored card (1903)
black, *light green* 150.
deep scarlet, *ivory* 150.
red violet, *light blue* 150.
carmine, *pink* 150.

184-E5

Design size: 19x24½mm
Die No. 1 size: about 63x94mm Vignette of Washington slightly diff. from rest of series but with quite diff. frame design.

184-E5 3c
a. Die on glazed paper, about 50x75mm, black 350.
b. Die on proof paper (with and without printing through mats) (1903)
black 100.
dark carmine 100.
carmine 100.
bright carmine 100.
brown 100.
red brown 100.
yellow 100.
orange 100.
violet 100.
red violet 100.
violet brown 100.
blue 100.
steel blue 100.
light green 100.
dark green 100.
dull olive 100.
c. Die on colored card, 61x93mm (1903)
scarlet, *yellow* 150.
olive gray, *pale pink* 150.
dull violet, *buff* 150.

Plate proofs printed in sheets of 25 (plate size: 140x164mm). A horiz. crack extends through upper 3s from 2mm back of head on position 11 to vignette on position 12.
All plate essay items valued as singles except No. 184-E5d.

d. Engraved plate of 25 on India, mounted on large card, red brown 750.
e. Plate on proof paper (1903)
black 15.
blue black 15.
greenish black 15.
dull red violet 15.
dark red violet 15.
dull violet 15.
violet brown 15.
light red brown 15.
orange brown 15.
brown carmine 15.
brown 15.
dim orange 15.
yellow 15.
dull yellow 15.
carmine 15.
light carmine 15.
dark carmine 15.
dull carmine 15.
dull scarlet 15.
dark green 15.
light green 15.
dull olive green 15.
deep ultramarine 15.
f. Plate on proof paper, perf. 12, lithographed
carmine 100.
rose lilac 100.
red orange 100.
g. Plate on green bond, "Crane & Co. 1887" wmk. (1903)
black 25.
carmine 25.
dull carmine 25.
scarlet 25.
brown 25.
brown red 25.
orange brown 25.
red violet 25.
yellow 25.
orange 25.
dark green 25.
light green 25.
yellow green 25.
deep ultramarine 25.
dark navy blue 25.
h. Plate (printed before plate crack developed) on semiglazed yellowish wove, laid watermark
carmine 30.
dull red 30.
bright orange red 30.
deep orange red 30.
scarlet 30.
deep orange 30.
yellow orange 30.
orange brown 30.
orange yellow 30.
dark yellow green 30.
dusky blue green 30.
dull green blue 30.
violet blue 30.
red violet 30.
black 30.
i. Plate single from sheets of 100 with imprint on yellowish glazed chemically prepared wove, lithographed
black 20.
brown 20.
scarlet 20.
light red 20.
rose pink 20.
carmine 20.
deep carmine 20.
violet rose 20.
deep violet rose 20.
violet red 20.
red violet 20.
violet 20.
blue 20.
pale blue 20.
pale dull blue 20.
yellow 20.
dull brown yellow 20.
orange 20.
red orange 20.

184-E6

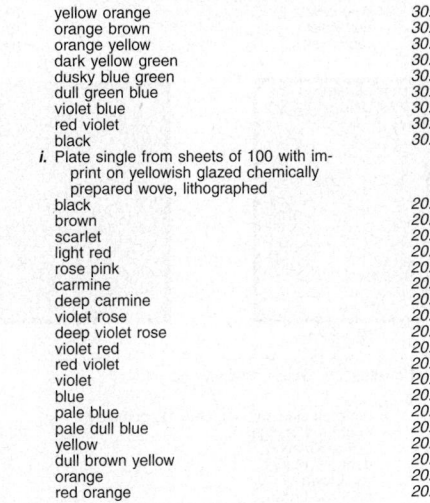

Illustration with card margins reduced.
Similar to No. 184-E1 but engraved vignette of Lincoln on India facing ¾ to right. Each design has vignette attached to frame from behind.

184-E6 3c Four examples mounted on 80x89mm card to resemble block of 4
blue 3,500.
green 3,500.

Frame of No. 184-E5 with engraved vignette of Lincoln mounted in place.

184-E7 3c Die on card, brown —

There is some doubt whether No. 184-E7 exists as a genuine essay. The editors would like to see authenticated evidence of its existence.

186-E1a

Design size: 20x25mm
Die size: 92x50mm
Frames of 6c and 7c side by side (6c at right).

186-E1 6c + 7c
a. Die on white pelure, orange 375.
b. Die on proof paper, printed through a mat (1903)
black 100.
bright carmine 100.
dull carmine 100.
dim scarlet 100.
dark orange 100.
dull yellow 100.
dark orange brown 100.
black olive 100.
green 100.
dark blue green 100.
dark blue 100.
deep ultramarine 100.
dark navy blue 100.
blue violet 100.
dull violet 100.
red violet 100.
c. Die on white pelure, both 7s reversed on 7c frame, orange 750.
d. Die on old stiff glazed, black 400.

186-E2a

Complete 6c design, lithographed.

186-E2 6c
a. Plate on stamp paper, perf. 12, gummed
bright red orange 35.
dull red orange 35.
dark red orange 35.
red brown 35.
dark red brown 35.
dark orange brown 35.
yellow brown 35.
dull yellow green 35.
green 35.
dull ultramarine 35.
bright ultramarine 35.
blue violet 35.
red violet 35.
light violet red 35.
violet red 35.
b. Plate on stamp paper, gummed
ultramarine 60.
lilac 60.
scarlet 60.
orange 60.
carmine 60.
dark carmine 60.
blue green 60.

186a-E2b

Complete 7c design, lithographed.

186a-E2 7c
a. Plate on stamp paper, imperf.
black 75.
carmine 75.
red orange 75.
yellow orange 75.
green 75.
dark green 75.
dark blue 75.
b. Plate on stamp paper, perf. 12, gummed
red brown 50.
dark red orange 50.
brown orange 50.
red violet 50.
ultramarine 50.
violet blue 50.

Design size: 20x25mm
Die size: 78½x64mm
Frames of 12c and 24c side by side (12c on right).

188a-E1 12c + 24c
a. Die on white pelure
deep carmine 300.
brown orange 300.
orange brown 300.
blue green 300.
blue 300.
b. Die on proof paper, printed through a mat (1903)
black 100.
bright carmine 100.
dull carmine 100.
dim scarlet 100.
dark orange 100.
dull yellow 100.
dark orange brown 100.
black olive 100.
green 100.
dark blue green 100.
dark blue 100.
deep ultramarine 100.
dark navy blue 100.
blue violet 100.

dull violet 100.
red violet 100.
c. Die on old stiff glazed, black 400.

188a-E2a

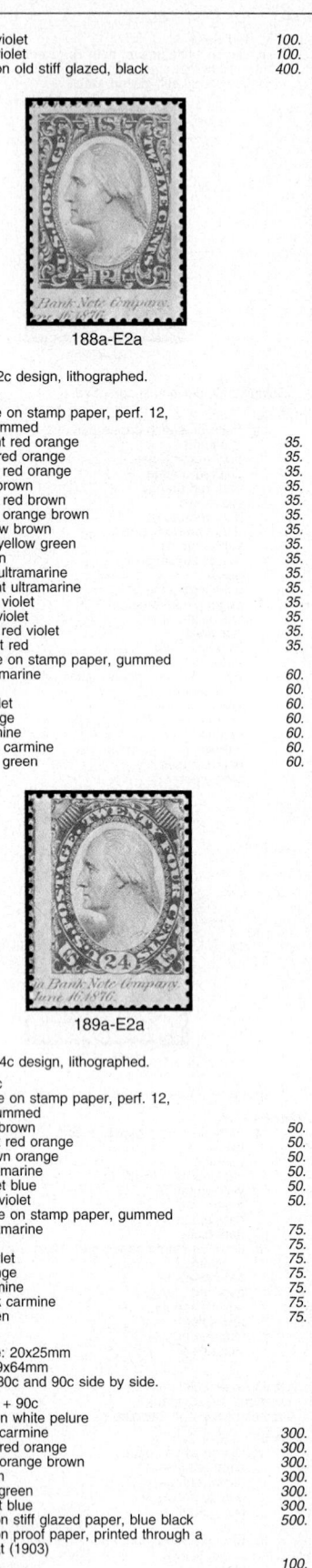

Complete 12c design, lithographed.

188a-E2 12c
a. Plate on stamp paper, perf. 12, gummed
bright red orange 35.
dull red orange 35.
dark red orange 35.
red brown 35.
dark red brown 35.
dark orange brown 35.
yellow brown 35.
dull yellow green 35.
green 35.
dull ultramarine 35.
bright ultramarine 35.
blue violet 35.
red violet 35.
light red violet 35.
violet red 35.
b. Plate on stamp paper, gummed
ultramarine 60.
lilac 60.
scarlet 60.
orange 60.
carmine 60.
dark carmine 60.
blue green 60.

189a-E2a

Complete 24c design, lithographed.

189a-E2 24c
a. Plate on stamp paper, perf. 12, gummed
red brown 50.
dark red orange 50.
brown orange 50.
ultramarine 50.
violet blue 50.
red violet 50.
b. Plate on stamp paper, gummed
ultramarine 75.
lilac 75.
scarlet 75.
orange 75.
carmine 75.
dark carmine 75.
green 75.

Design size: 20x25mm
Die size: 79x64mm
Frames of 30c and 90c side by side.

190-E1 30c + 90c
a. Die on white pelure
dark carmine 300.
dark red orange 300.
dark orange brown 300.
brown 300.
blue green 300.
bright blue 300.
b. Die on stiff glazed paper, blue black 500.
c. Die on proof paper, printed through a mat (1903)
black 100.
bright carmine 100.
dull carmine 100.
dim scarlet 100.
dark orange 100.
dull yellow 100.
dark orange brown 100.
black olive 100.
green 100.
dark blue green 100.
dark blue 100.
deep ultramarine 100.
dark navy blue 100.

blue violet 100.
dull violet 100.
red violet 100.

190-E2a

191-E2

Complete 30c design, lithographed.

190-E2 30c
a. Plate on stamp paper, perf. 12, gummed
bright red orange 35.
dull red orange 35.
dark red orange 35.
red brown 35.
dark red brown 35.
dark orange brown 35.
yellow brown 35.
dull yellow green 35.
green 35.
dull ultramarine 35.
bright ultramarine 35.
blue violet 35.
red violet 35.
light red violet 35.
violet red 35.
b. Plate on stamp paper, gummed
ultramarine 60.
lilac 60.
scarlet 60.
orange 60.
carmine 60.
dark carmine 60.
blue green 60.

Complete 90c design, lithographed.

191-E2 90c
a. Plate on stamp paper, perf. 12, gummed
black 50.
red brown 50.
dark red orange 50.
brown orange 50.
ultramarine 50.
violet blue 50.
red violet 50.
violet red 50.
dark blue green 50.
orange brown 50.
b. Plate on stamp paper, gummed
ultramarine 75.
lilac 75.
scarlet 75.
orange 75.
carmine 75.
dark carmine 75.
green 75.

1879 Coupon Essay
Azariah B. Harris

184-E8a

Size of coupon design: 25x7½mm
A proposed $300 30-year Postal Revenue Bond with 3.65% interest. Daily coupons 3c each, "Receivable for Postage in all parts of the U.S." after date thereon. Entire bond contained six pages of coupons with 16 rows of four (one for each day of two months); 20% bear month and day, others blank.

184-E8 3c
a. Coupon on bond (dated Jan. or Feb.), imperf., black 350.
b. Engraved die on old ivory paper (undated), black 900.
c. Single coupon on bond (dated), perf. 12, gummed, blue green 125.
d. Single coupon on bond (undated), perf. 12, gummed, blue green 50.

Continental Bank Note Co.

182-E4

Design size: 18x22mm
Die size: 59x67mm
Engraved vignette of Franklin on white background in unadopted frame.

182-E4 1c
a. Die on India, blue 575.
b. Die on proof paper
black 500.
dull scarlet 500.
dull brown 500.
dull green 500.
dull blue 500.
c. Die on ivory glazed paper
black 750.
black brown 750.
scarlet 750.
blue 750.

All known examples of "b" have reduced margins.

184-E9

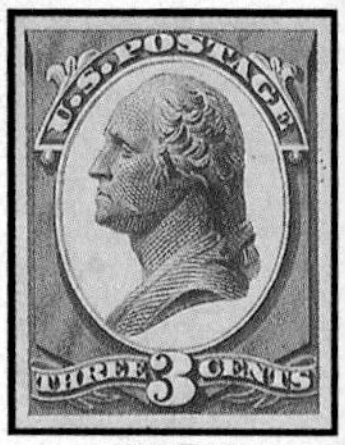
184-E10

Die size: 61½x76½mm
Vignette of Washington on white background in incomplete frame as adopted: no veins in trifoliate ornaments in upper corners.

184-E9 3c Die on India, on card
black 750.
green 750.

Similar to No. 184-E9 but completed frame with veins in trifoliate ornaments.

184-E10 3c
a. Die on India, die sunk on card, green 750.
b. Die on proof paper, about 35x40mm
gray black 350.
dull red 350.
dull blue 350.
dull green 350.
dull brown 350.
c. Die on ivory glazed paper
black 600.
black brown 600.
scarlet 600.
blue 600.

Nos. 147-E8 and 147-E9 may have been made from completed dies of No. 147 to produce Nos. 184-E9 and 184-E10.

184-E11

Design size: 17½x21½mm
Die size: 60x75mm
Complete unadopted design with vignette of Liberty on white background.

184-E11 3c
a. Die on India
black 350.
brown red 350.
orange 350.
green 350.
blue 350.
scarlet 350.
b. Die on proof paper
brown 350.
green 350.
gray black 350.
dull red 350.
dull blue 350.
c. Die on ivory glazed paper
black 750.
black brown 750.
scarlet 750.
blue 750.

All known examples of Nos. 184-E11a, 184-E11b have reduced margins.

184-E12

Design size: 19½x24½mm
Die size: 61x71mm
Complete unadopted design with vignette of Washington on white background in frame similar to No. 184-E11 but with numerals of value.

184-E12 3c
a. Die on India, die sunk on card
black *650.*
dull scarlet *650.*
brown *650.*
green *650.*
b. Die on white glazed paper
black *500.*
black brown *500.*
scarlet *500.*
blue *500.*
c. Plate on India (some adhering to original card backing), imperf.
black *100.*
scarlet *100.*
orange red *100.*
green *100.*
d. Plate on white paper, perf. 12, gummed
black *75.*
green *75.*
blue *75.*
brown *75.*
red brown *75.*
orange *75.*
dull scarlet *75.*
orange brown *75.*
e. Plate on Francis Patent bluish chemical paper, perf. 12, gummed
black *150.*
scarlet *150.*
red brown *150.*
brown *150.*
yellow *150.*
green *150.*
gray *150.*
f. Plate on brown chemical paper, perf. 12, gummed
blue *150.*
ultramarine *150.*
g. Hybrid die on India, mounted on India, block sunk on card, green *400.*

184-E13

184-E14

Design size: 18x22mm
Die size: about 61x62mm
Similar to No. 184-E12 but slightly different frame.

184-E13 3c
a. Die on India, die sunk on card
black *650.*
scarlet *650.*
green *650.*
blue *650.*
black brown *650.*
blue green *650.*
b. Die on ivory glazed paper
black *750.*
black brown *750.*
scarlet *750.*
blue *750.*
c. Plate on India, imperf.
black *100.*
deep scarlet *100.*
green *100.*
dark green *100.*
dark yellow brown *100.*
olive brown *100.*
violet brown *100.*
orange *100.*
d. Plate on stamp paper, perf. 12, gummed
black *75.*
dull scarlet *75.*
blue green *75.*
brown *75.*
red brown *75.*
dull blue *75.*
dark blue *75.*
orange *75.*
yellow *75.*
yellow brown *75.*
gray *75.*

Design size: 19x24½mm
Die size: about 67x71mm
Similar to No. 184-E13 but value label with "THREE" above "CENTS."

184-E14 3c
a. Hybrid die on India mounted on India, block sunk on card
brown red *400.*
green *400.*
b. Die on ivory glazed paper
black 500.
black brown *500.*
scarlet *500.*
blue *500.*
c. Die on proof paper, about 35x35mm
black *300.*
dull scarlet *300.*
dull brown *300.*
dull green *300.*
dull blue *300.*
brown red *300.*
red brown *300.*

184-E15

184-E16

Design size: 20x25½mm
Die size: 60x73mm
Vignette of Indian maiden in headdress, "PORTAGE" error in top label.

184-E15 3c
a. Hybrid die on India, cut close, mounted on India, block sunk on card
black *900.*
dark green *900.*
b. Die on proof paper, about 28x35mm
black *600.*
dull scarlet *500.*
dull brown *500.*
dull blue *500.*
dull green *500.*
c. Die on ivory glazed paper
black *750.*
black brown *750.*
scarlet *750.*
blue *750.*
d. Die on India, scarlet —

Similar to No. 184-E15 but with spelling corrected to "POSTAGE."

184-E16 3c Die on India, cut close, mounted on India, block sunk on card
black *1,250.*
blue *1,250.*
steel blue *1,250.*
carmine *1,250.*
scarlet *1,250.*
brown *1,250.*
dark green *1,250.*

190-E3

Die size: 44½x71½mm
Vignette of Hamilton on white background in frame as adopted.

190-E3 30c
a. Die on proof paper, about 35x48mm
gray black *500.*
dull red *500.*
dull green *500.*
dull brown *500.*
dull blue *500.*
b. Die on ivory glazed paper
black *750.*
black brown *750.*
scarlet *750.*
blue *750.*

American Bank Note Co.

184-E17

Design size: 22x30mm
Silver photo print of engraved vignette of Washington mounted on pencil and ink frame design.

184-E17 3c
a. Die on white card, 38x49mm
light brown vignette, black frame *1,250.*
b. Die on white card, 38x50mm
light brown vignette, black frame *1,250.*

Frame ornaments extend beyond framelines, lettering less complete than on No. 184-E17a.

1881-82 ISSUE
American Bank Note Co.

205-E1

Die size: 59x74mm
Vignette of Garfield in lined oval.

205-E1 5c Die on India, die sunk on card, black *500.*

205-E2

205-E3

Die No. C-47 size: 70x83mm
Vignette of Garfield in beaded oval, in plain border of horiz. lines. Found with and without imprint and die number.

205-E2 5c Die on India, die sunk on card
gray brown *250.*
gray black *250.*

No. 205-E2 may not be a stamp essay.

Die size: 78x78mm
Vignette of Garfield in beaded oval with cutout at bottom for top of star.

205-E3 5c
a. Die on India, die sunk on card
black *750.*
deep red orange *750.*
red brown *750.*
blue *750.*
green *750.*
b. Die on ivory glazed paper
black *750.*
green *750.*
blue *750.*
scarlet *750.*
red brown *750.*
c. Negative impression, solid color outside design, die on India, bright red orange *1,000.*

205-E4

Vignette of Garfield as No. 205-E1 in lined oval and finished frame as adopted.

205-E4 5c Die on India, 24x30mm, black *900.*

E206-E1

Image of unadopted frame, printed on 40x60mm India paper with text and right "1" cut out.

206-E1 1c Black on India *2,500.*

206-E1B

Image of frame with "DOS CENTAVOS" in upper label and "ONE CENT" pasted on bottom label, affixed to 57x71mm card with additional pencil sketch at right.

206-E1B 1c Black image affixed to card *2,500.*

206-E1C

206-E2

Design size: 21x26mm
Engraved frame of unadopted design.

206-E1C 1c
- ***a.*** Die on white glazed paper, 42x74mm, black *1,000.*
- ***b.*** Die on surface-tinted glazed paper, cut close
  - green, *buff* *600.*
  - black, *orange* *600.*
  - brown orange, *blue* *600.*

Engraved frame almost identical to No. 206-E1C with small typographed vignette of Peace.

206-E2 1c Die on blue surface-tinted ivory paper, cut close, buff vignette, carmine frame *800.*

206-E3

Vignette of Peace only.

206-E3 1c
- ***a.*** Engraved vignette
  - black *350.*
  - dull red violet *350.*
- ***b.*** Typographed vignette *350.*

206-E4

Engraved frame (No. 206-E1) with typographed vignette of Lincoln mounted on it. Four diff. colors (dull carmine, dull scarlet, dark brown, green) on cream white ivory paper, 22x27mm each, mounted together on 92x114mm thick white card, ms. "American Bank Note Co. N.Y." at lower right.

206-E4 1c Four designs on cream white ivory on card *2,500.*

Design size: 18x23½mm
Typographed vignette of Lincoln only.

206-E5

206-E5 1c Die on white ivory paper
- dull carmine *400.*
- dark yellowish brown *400.*
- dull purple *400.*
- dull dark blue *400.*
- orange *400.*

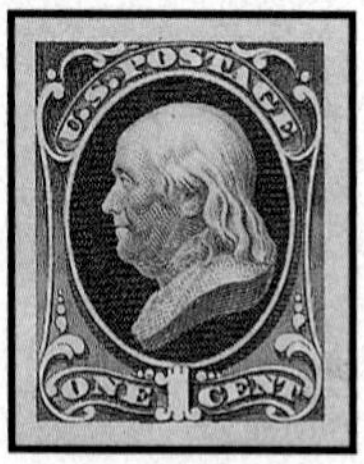

206-E6

Incomplete engraving of complete design as issued: no shading in upper arabesques.

206-E6 1c
- ***a.*** Die on India
  - gray blue *750.*
  - green blue *750.*
- ***b.*** Die on India, cut close, on India block sunk on card, deep gray blue *350.*

207-E1

207-E2

207-E3

Design size: 20½x25½mm
Die size: 49x54½mm
Engraved unadopted frame design with 3's at sides and large 3 at top.

207-E1 3c
- ***a.*** Die on India
  - yellow brown *750.*
  - dull brown *750.*
  - dull blue *750.*
  - green *750.*
- ***b.*** Die on white glazed paper, 32x38mm
  - black *650.*
  - dull dark yellow *650.*
- ***c.*** Die on surface-tinted ivory paper, cut close
  - black, *orange* *500.*
  - green, *buff* *500.*
  - violet blue, *orange* *500.*

Engraved frame as No. 207-E1, with typographed vignette of Peace.

207-E2 3c Die on blue surface-tinted ivory paper, cut close, buff vignette, carmine frame *850.*

Engraved frame (No. 207-E1) with typographed vignette of Peace mounted on it. Four diff. color combinations (orange red vignette, dull carmine frame; dull carmine vignette, dull red brown frame; yellow brown vignette and frame; blue green vignette and frame) on cream white ivory paper, 22x27mm each, mounted together on 92x114mm thick white card, ms. "American Bank Note Co. N.Y." at lower right.

207-E3 3c 4 designs on cream white ivory on card *2,500.*

208-E1

Incomplete engraving of design as adopted: unfinished shading on top label and bottom ribbon, four lines between frame sinkage at right and left edges, horiz. line at bottom.

208-E1 6c Die on India, on card, black *1,500.*

This is a new die engraved by the Bureau of Engraving & Printing for "Roosevelt" proof albums.

209-E1

Design size: 20x25mm
Die size: 58x76mm
Engraving of unadopted frame only, no horiz. lines in background.

209-E1 10c Die on thick white card, about 25x33mm
- blue *800.*
- green *800.*

Similar to No. 209-E1 but with horiz. lines added to background.

209-E2

209-E2 10c
- ***a.*** Die on thick white card
  - black *700.*
  - red *700.*
  - green *700.*
  - blue *700.*
- ***b.*** Die on India, on 50x70mm card, black *800.*
- ***c.*** Die on white glazed paper, black *800.*

209-E3

Engraved frame similar to No. 209-E2 with typographed vignette of Peace.

209-E3 10c
  a. Die on blue surface-tinted glazed paper, cut close, buff vignette, carmine frame *650.*
  b. Die on orange surface-tinted glazed paper
  dull carmine vignette, violet frame *650.*
  dull yellow vignette, violet frame *650.*
  yellow vignette, green frame *650.*

209-E4

209-E5

Vignette diameter: 17mm
Engraved Franklin vignette.

209-E4 10c
  a. Die on India
  black *575.*
  dusky carmine *575.*
  dull scarlet *575.*
  dim orange *575.*
  orange brown *575.*
  yellow green *575.*
  dim blue green *575.*
  deep blue *575.*
  red brown on blue ground *575.*
  dark red violet *575.*
  b. Die sunk on glazed paper, approx. 51x69mm
  dusky carmine *775.*
  dim scarlet *775.*
  dim orange *775.*
  deep blue *775.*
  dim blue green *775.*

Design size: 21x26mm
Engraved frame with typographed vignette mounted on it. Four diff. color combinations (dull scarlet vignette, dull carmine frame; dull orange vignette, brown orange frame; yellow brown vignette, dark brown frame; blue green vignette and frame) on cream white ivory paper, 22x27mm each, mounted together on 92x114mm thick white card, ms. "American Bank Note Co. N.Y." at lower right.

209-E5 10c Four designs on cream white ivory on card *2,500.*

209-E6

209-E7a

Vignette diameter: 18mm
Engraved Washington vignette.

209-E6 10c
  a. Die on India
  black *600.*
  dim deep carmine *600.*
  dim deep scarlet *600.*
  dull orange *600.*
  dull brown *600.*
  dim blue green *600.*
  blue *600.*
  dusky red violet *600.*
  b. Die sunk on white ivory paper, 55x67mm
  dusky carmine *800.*
  dull orange *800.*
  dull blue green *800.*
  scarlet *800.*
  dull brown *800.*
  red violet *800.*

Design size: 21x26mm
Engraved frame with typographed vignette mounted on it. Four diff. color combinations (dull carmine vignette and frame; dull orange vignette, brown orange frame; yellow brown vignette, dark brown frame; blue green vignette and frame) on cream white ivory paper, 22x27mm each, mounted together on 92x114mm thick white card, ms. "American Bank Note Co. N.Y." at lower right.

209-E7 10c
  a. Four designs on cream white ivory on card *2,500.*
  b. Single composite off card, dull carmine vignette, blue green frame *400.*

Issued stamp, No. 209, in trial color, overprinted network in fugitive ink.

209-E8 10c On thick paper, perf. 12, gummed, sepia, overprint olive gray *150.*

1883 ISSUE
American Bank Note Co.

210-E1

210-E2

Design size: 20x25½mm
Engraved vignette of Washington (from proof on India of No. 207) with watercolor frame design nearly as adopted but with "TWO" and "CENTS" at an angle, rubber stamp "Feb. 17, 1883" on back.

210-E1 2c Die on white card, 80x90mm, black vignette, gray and white frame *3,000.*

Design size: 20x25mm
Engraved vignette of Washington (from proof on India of No. 207) mounted on unadopted watercolor and ink frame design. backstamped "American Bank Note Co. Feb. 27, 1883."

210-E2 2c Die on thick white card, 87x100mm, black and white *3,000.*

210-E3

210-E4

Design size: 20x25½mm
Engraved vignette of Washington (from proof on India of No. 207) mounted on watercolor frame design as adopted, ms. "2 March 1883 No. 1."

210-E3 2c Die on white card, 80x90mm, black vignette, gray & white frame *3,000.*

Design size: 20x25mm
Engraved vignette of Washington on white background mounted on a brush and pen watercolor drawing of unadopted fancy frame design, backstamped "American Bank Note Co. Mar. 2, 1883" and pencil "No. 2."

210-E4 2c Die on white card, 88x101mm, dusky blue green *3,000.*

210-E5

Design size: 20x25mm
Engraved vignette of Washington (from revenue stamp No. RB17) mounted on wash drawing of unadopted ornate frame design, backstamped "American Bank Note Co. Mar. 2, 1883" and pencil "No. 3."

210-E5 2c Die on white card, 88x101mm, blue violet vignette, black frame *2,500.*

211-E1

Design size: 20x25½mm
Engraved vignette of Jackson mounted on unadopted watercolor frame design.

211-E1 4c Die on white card, 70x70mm, blue green vignette and frame *3,500.*

211-E2

Engraved head of Jackson only.

211-E2 4c Die on India, die sunk on card, black *1,000.*

211-E3

Incomplete engraved vignette of Jackson: lower edge of bust incomplete.

211-E3 4c Die on India, die sunk on card
  black *2,500.*
  green *2,500.*
  red brown *2,500.*

Complete engraved vignette of Jackson.

211-E4 4c Die on India, die sunk on card, blue green *2,500.*

211-E6

Die size: 60x62mm

Complete design as adopted but with pencil sketch of pedestal top under bust.

211-E5 4c Die on India, die sunk on card, gray black *5,750.*

Similar to No. 211-E5 but with incomplete shading engraved on pedestal.

211-E6 4c Die on India, die sunk on card, blue green *2,500.*

1887 ISSUE
American Bank Note Co.

212-E1

Die size: 55x63mm

Incomplete engraved vignette of Franklin facing right: horiz. background lines only.

212-E1 1c Die on 32½x35mm card, India mounted, die sunk on card

black	*600.*
ultramarine	*600.*

Die size: 62x62mm

Franklin vignette similar to No. 212-E1 but diagonal lines (in one direction only) added to background.

212-E2

212-E2 1c Die on India, die sunk on card

black	*600.*
ultramarine	*600.*

Die size: 55x64mm

Similar to No. 212-E2 but diagonal lines in both directions.

212-E3 1c Die on India, die sunk on card, black *500.*

212-E4

Complete design as issued except Franklin facing right.

212-E4 1c

a. Die on India, die sunk on card

black	*600.*
ultramarine	*600.*

b. Die on ivory glazed paper, about 64x76mm

black	*750.*
black brown	*750.*
scarlet	*750.*
blue	*750.*

Die size: 62x62mm

Incomplete vignette of Franklin facing left as adopted.

212-E5 1c Die on India, die sunk on card, ultramarine *450.*

212-E6

212-E7

Die size: 56x64½mm

Incomplete design as adopted except three lines below value label and taller numeral, shadow on edge of bust and in background below chin too dark.

212-E6 1c Die on India, die sunk on card

ultramarine	*750.*
green	*750.*

Similar to No. 212-E6 but with shadows lightened.

212-E7 1c Die on India, die sunk on card, ultramarine *750.*

1890 ISSUE
American Bank Note Co.

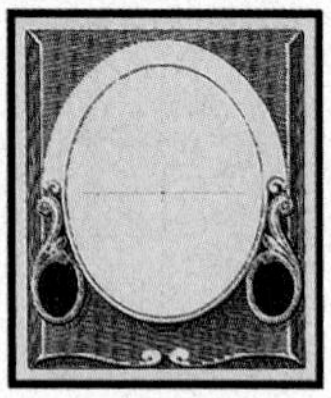

219-E1

Design size: 19x22½mm
Die size: 58x64mm

Engraved die of frame only with blank labels quite similar to adopted design.

219-E1 1c Die on ivory paper, 64x72mm, black *700.*

219-E2

219-E3

Design size: 19x22mm

Engraved Franklin vignette cut down from 1887 1c stamp (No. 212) mounted on watercolor frame design.

219-E2 1c Die on thick light buff card, ultramarine frame *3,500.*

Die size: 62x62mm

Engraved Franklin vignette with lettered label above.

219-E3 1c Die on India, die sunk on card, blue *800.*

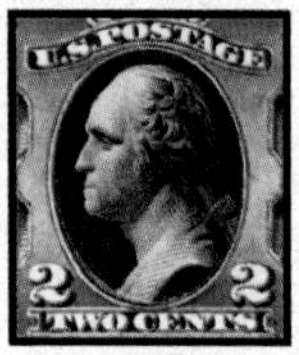

220-E1

220-E2

Design size: 19x22mm

Engraved Washington vignette from 3c stamp (from proof on India of No. 184) mounted on watercolor frame design.

220-E1 2c Die on thick white card, 62x66mm, light carmine frame *3,750.*

Design size: 19x23mm

Engraved Washington vignette cut from 1887 2c stamp (No. 213) mounted on shield-like watercolor frame design.

220-E2 2c Die on thick light buff card, gray frame *3,000.*

220-E3

220-E4

Design size: 19x23mm

Engraved Washington vignette cut from 1887 2c stamp (No. 213) mounted on watercolor frame design.

220-E3 2c Die on white card, 105x135mm, gray black frame *3,000.*

Design size: 19x22mm
Die size: 56x63mm

Engraved unadopted frame only.

220-E4 2c Die on white ivory paper, black *1,250.*

220-E5

220-E6

Die size: 62x62mm

Engraved vignette of Washington in oval line frame.

220-E5 2c Die on India, die sunk on card, dark carmine *800.*

Engraved Washington vignette with lettered label above.

220-E6 2c Die on India, dusky carmine *1,250.*

220-E7

220-E8

Design size: 19x22½mm

Engraved Washington vignette and lettered top label mounted on pencil drawing of frame design adopted, ms. "J.J.M. — engraved background only without figures or words;" backstamped "Nov. 15, 1889 American Bank Note Co."

220-E7 2c Die on 50x55mm white card, mounted on thick white card, 119x122mm, black vignette, pencil frame *3,000.*

Design size: 19x22mm
Die size: 56x63mm

Engraved frame only as adopted with numerals, blank curved top label.

220-E8 2c

a. Die on ivory paper, 64x71mm, black *900.*

b. Die on India, 51x62mm

black	*700.*
brown black	*700.*
dark brown	*700.*
dull scarlet	*700.*
dark blue green	*700.*
dark blue	*700.*
red violet	*700.*
red orange	*700.*

220-E9

Incomplete engraving of entire design as adopted: no dots in rectangular spaces between shading lines on cheek under hair in front of ear and on back of neck.

220-E9 2c Die on India, die sunk on card, lake *1,250.*

(Probably by) The Times, Philadelphia

220-E11

Surface-printed essay for proposed business advertising on stamps.

220-E11 2c Die on India, on card, bright green blue —

American Bank Note Co.

221-E1

221-E2

Engraved 3c frame as adopted with vignette cut out, mounted over photo of James Madison.

221-E1 3c Die on India, cut close, dark green *2,500.*

Engraved vignette of Jackson with lettered label above.

221-E2 3c Die on India, die sunk on card, purple *750.*

Design size: 19x22mm
Incomplete engraved design as adopted except Lincoln facing ¾ left: unfinished shading under collar.

222-E1 4c Die on India, die sunk on card, black brown *1,250.*

222-E2

222-E3

Die No. C-226 size: 62½x62½mm
Completed design with die no. and impt., Lincoln facing ¾ left.

222-E2 4c Die on India, on 25x32mm card, black brown *1,000.*

Incomplete engraving as adopted: no wart on face, no lines on shirt.

222-E3 4c Die on India, die sunk on card, black brown *1,000.*

223-E1

Design size: 19x21½mm
Photo of Seward vignette mounted on watercolor frame design.

223-E1 5c Gray and white on light buff paper in upper right corner of short envelope *1,750.*

223-E2

223-E3

Design size: 19x26½mm
Die size: 63x62mm
Incomplete engraved design as adopted except Grant facing ¾ left: hair neatly combed.

223-E2 5c Die on India, die sunk on card
black *700.*
orange brown *700.*

Design size: 19x26½mm
Die size: 63x62mm
Incomplete engraving of complete bearded left-facing design: eye pupils not solid color, light shading on right side of face, only one diagonal shading line on left coat shoulder.

223-E3 5c Die on India, die sunk on card, chocolate *700.*

Similar to No. 223-E3 but more complete. Left beard has no diagonal lines and is light at top center.

223-E4 5c Die on India, die sunk on card, chocolate *700.*

Third state of die: no horiz. lines on left moustache or under lower lip.

223-E5 5c Die on India, die sunk on card, chocolate *700.*

223-E6

223-E7

Completed left-facing design: shows lines omitted from No. 223-E5, several diagonal shading lines on left shoulder of coat.

223-E6 5c Die on India, die sunk on card
black *700.*
chocolate *700.*

Design size: 19x26½mm
Die size: 62x62mm
Left-facing design with slightly diff. portrait, hair neatly combed. Horiz. shading lines on left coat shoulder, no wash-etched shadows on coat, beard and tie.

223-E7 5c
a. Die on India, die sunk on card
black *700.*
dark brown *700.*
b. Die on glazed paper, impt. and "ESSAY MARCH 1890"
black *750.*
black brown *750.*
scarlet *750.*
blue *750.*

Design size: 19x26½mm
Die similar to No. 223-E7 but diagonal shading lines on left coat shoulder, wash-etched shadows on coat, beard and tie.

223-E8 5c Die on India, on card, brown *700.*

223-E9

223-E10

Die size: 62x63mm
Engraving of right-facing Grant design diff. than adopted: light oval line around vignette, three diagonal lines on shirtfront under tie. Incomplete engraving: right collar unshaded.

223-E9 5c Die on India, dark orange brown *700.*

Similar to No. 223-E9 but engraving completed: right collar shaded.

223-E10 5c
a. Die on India, die sunk on card, dark orange brown *700.*
b. Die on ivory paper, impt. and "ESSAY MARCH 1890"
black *750.*
black brown *750.*
scarlet *750.*
blue *750.*

Ferrotype plate 39x51mm of Grant facing ¾ right, outlines engraved, filled with red.

223-E11 5c Metal plate *650.*

223-E12

Printing from ferrotype plate, No. 223-E11.

223-E12 5c Die on card, 43x56mm, red *650.*

226-E1

226-E2

Design size: 19x22½mm
Incomplete engraved vignette of Webster with curved label above, mounted on pencil drawing of frame design (includes additional pencil drawings of lower part of frame, value lettering), backstamped "D.S. Ronaldson," frame engraver.

226-E1 10c Die on white card, 51x55mm, black *13,500.*

Design size: 19x22½mm
Engraving of unadopted frame design.

226-E2 10c Die on white glazed paper, black *1,000.*

226-E3

226-E4

Design size: 19x22mm
Engraved 10c frame as adopted, vignette cut out and mounted over photo of John Adams.

226-E3 10c Die on India, cut close, dark green *2,500.*

Design size: 19x22mm
Engraved 10c frame as adopted, vignette cut out and mounted over photo of William T. Sherman.

226-E4 10c Die on India, cut close, dark green *2,500.*

227-E1

Design size: 19x22½mm
Engraved vignette of Henry Clay with curved label above, mounted on wash drawing of frame design (includes additional enlarged pencil and wash drawing of frame).

227-E1 15c Die on white card, mounted at left on light buff card, 110x123mm (frame drawing at right), black *1,750.*

228-E1

Design size: 19x22½mm
Die size: 62x61mm
Incomplete engraved vignette of Jefferson with curved lettered label at top: hair shading incomplete.

228-E1 30c Die on India, die sunk on card, black *750.*

Similar to No. 228-E1 but more shading on hair, vert. shading lines on chin.

228-E2 30c Die on India, die sunk on card, black *750.*

229-E1

Design size: 19x22½mm
Die size: 62x62mm
Engraved vignette of Perry with curved lettered label at top.

229-E1 90c Die on India, die sunk on card, red orange *750.*

COLUMBIAN ISSUE
Lyman H. Bagg

230-E1

237-E1

Design sizes: 22x22mm
Left: No. 230-E1 — pencil drawing of Columbus in armor, on paper. "I do not know whether these designs will be of any use to you or not — they are so rough. L.H.B." written at top, "My idea illustrated" at bottom.
Right: No. 237-E1 — pencil drawing of North American continent, on paper.

230-E1 One Cent, Ten Cents, Drawings on 114x72mm white wove, Nos. 230-E1, 237-E1 *6,000.*

American Bank Note Co.

230-E2

230-E3

230-E4

Design size: 33x22mm

Silver print photo vignette of Columbus head mounted on watercolor drawing of unadopted frame design.

230-E2 1c Red violet on stiff white drawing paper *4,500.*
230-E3 1c Blue green on stiff white drawing paper *4,500.*
230-E4 1c Light red on stiff white drawing paper *4,500.*

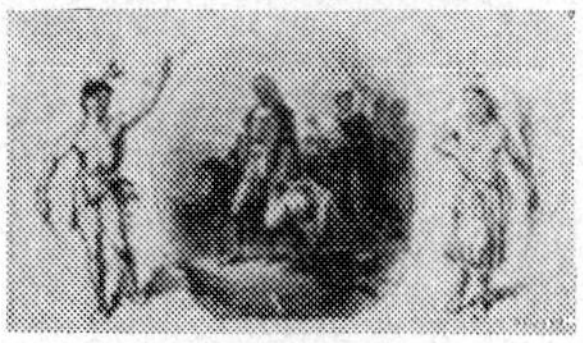

230-E5

Ferrotype metal plate with outline of adopted vignette (reversed) and drawings of Indian man and woman at sides in single line frame 39mm long.

230-E5 1c Metal plate, 57x38mm 1,250.

230-E6

Vignette size: 16x15mm
Engraved vignette only as adopted.

230-E6 1c Die on 53x39mm India, on card
yellow brown *2,000.*
black *2,000.*

230-E7

Incomplete engraving of vignette, lettering, value numerals and tablet as issued: without palm tree, incomplete shading on and behind Indian and maiden, on Columbus' head, no shading on scrollwork, etc.

230-E7 1c Die on 39x28mm stiff wove, deep blue *2,000.*

230-E8

Incomplete engraving of entire design as issued: maiden's skirt only lightly engraved, chief's torso and shoulder incompletely engraved, incomplete shading in frame design at top, etc.

230-E8 1c Die on India, die sunk on 99x84mm card, deep blue *1,500.*

231-E1

Design size: 34x22mm
Silver print photo of vignette as adopted, mounted on watercolor drawing of unadopted frame design.

231-E1 2c Die on stiff white drawing paper, red violet *8,500.*

Die size: 74x61½mm
Incomplete engraving of adopted vignette only.

231-E2 2c Die on India, die sunk on card
black *1,500.*
sepia *1,500.*

231-E3

Design size: 35½x22mm
Engraved vignette of Columbus asking aid of Isabella as adopted for 5c, mounted on watercolor drawing of frame design similar to that adopted for 2c.

231-E3 2c Die on stiff white drawing paper, dark brown *4,000.*

231-E4

Vignette size: 29x15mm
Die size: 74x61½mm
Incomplete engraving of vignette as adopted (probably first state of die): cape on back of central figure incomplete, etc.

231-E4 2c Die on India, die sunk on card, black *2,500.*

231-E5

Incomplete engraving of vignette as adopted (probably second state of die): more shading on top right face, etc.; also pencil sketches for lengthening vignette.

231-E5 2c Die on India, die sunk on card, black *3,250.*

231-E6

Vignette size: 31½x15mm
Die size: 74x61½mm
Incomplete engraving of vignette, longer than Nos. 231-E4 and 231-E5, later shortened as adopted: Columbus' legs, central figure's cape, etc., are incomplete.

231-E6 2c Die on India, die sunk on card, black *2,500.*

231-E7

Design size: 33x22mm
Die size: 74x61½mm
Incomplete engraving of entire design almost as adopted: figures of value narrower, unfinished crosset shadows in lower corners.

Ridgway numbers used for colors of No. 231-E7.

231-E7 2c
a. Die on India, die sunk on card
13m/4 smoky dusky o-yellow-orange *1,250.*
b. Die on thin white wove card
69o/5 black *800.*
1m/0 dusky red *800.*
3k/2 dull dark orange-red *800.*
5i/0 deep o-orange-red *800.*
5j/1 deep v-deep o-orange-red *800.*
6i/0 deep m. red-orange *800.*
9i/0 deep o-yellow-orange *800.*
9m/0 dusky o-red-orange *800.*
9m/3 dismal dusky o-red-orange *800.*
9m/4 smoky dusky o-red-orange *800.*
9n/2 dull v. dusky o-red-orange *800.*
10k/0 m. dark orange *800.*
11i/0 deep orange *800.*
11k/1 dim dark orange *800.*
13m/1 dim dusky o-yellow-orange *800.*

13m/4 smoky dusky o-yellow-orange 800.
33m/2 dull dusky g-yellow-green 800.
37m/1 dim dusky g-blue-green 800.
43m/2 dull dusky green-blue 800.
49m/0 dusky blue 800.
49m/1 dim dusky blue 800.
55m/2 dull dusky blue-violet 800.
59m/2 dull dusky violet 800.
65m/2 dull dusky r-red-violet 800.
70i/0 deep violet-red-red 800.

231-E8

Design size: 33x22mm
Incomplete engraving of entire design as adopted: value numerals same as on issued stamp but without thick shading bars at ends of outer frame rectangles, etc.

231-E8 2c Die on India, card mounted, sepia 1,500.

232-E1

Design size: 33½x22mm
Silver print photo of vignette unadopted for any value (Columbus embarking on voyage of discovery), mounted on watercolor drawing of unadopted frame design.

232-E1 3c Die on stiff white drawing paper, 41x29mm, orange brown 4,000.

Ferrotype metal plate showing 19x15mm outline of *Santa Maria* (reversed) in 33x15mm vignette frame, outline engraved and filled with red ink.

232-E2 3c Metal plate, 51x30mm 1,250.

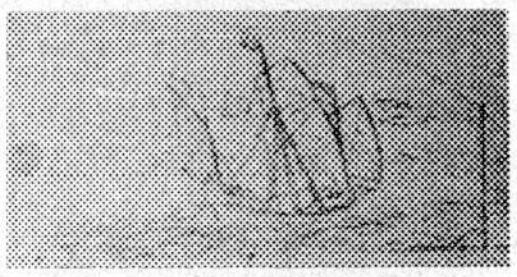

232-E3

Printing from ferrotype plate No. 232-E3.

232-E3 3c Die on stiff white card with rounded corners, 55x42mm, red 1,250.

232-E4

Vignette size: 30x15mm
Die size: 74x61mm
Incomplete engraving of vignette as adopted: sky composed of horiz. ruled lines, no clouds.

232-E4 3c Die on India, die sunk on card
black 1,250.
dark yellow-orange 1,250.
sepia 1,750.

232-E5

Engraved vignette similar to No. 232-E4 but with "1492 UNITED STATES OF AMERICA 1892" and scrolls around numerals engraved in outline only, pencil outline of frame.

232-E5 3c Die on thick artist's card with beveled edges, 50x38mm, dark yellow orange 3,000.

233-E1

Design size: 33½x22mm
Silver print photo of wash drawing of vignette as adopted, mounted on watercolor drawing of frame design as adopted but titled "COLUMBUS ON VOYAGE OF DISCOVERY. SHIPS AT SEA."

233-E1 4c Die on stiff white drawing paper, 41x29mm, brown red 4,750.

233-E2

Design size: 33x22mm
Die size: 74x61½mm
Incomplete engraving of complete design as adopted: unfinished crosset shadows in lower corners.

Ridgway numbers used for some colors of No. 233-E2.

233-E2 4c
a. Die on India, die sunk on card
black 1,250.
dark yellow orange 1,250.
b. Die on thin white wove card, die sunk on card
1m/0 dusky red 800.
3i/1 dim deep orange-red 800.
3k/2 dull dark orange-red 800.
5i/0 deep o-orange-red 800.
9i/0 deep o-red-orange 800.
9m/1 dim dusky o-red-orange 800.
11i/0 deep orange 800.
11k/1 dim dark orange 800.
11m/2 dull dusky orange 800.
13k/1 dim dark o-yellow-orange 800.
13m/2 dull dusky o-yellow-orange 800.
13k/3 dismal dark o-yellow-orange 800.
13k/4 smoky dark o-yellow-orange 800.
13m/4 smoky dusky o-yellow-orange 800.
15m/2 dull dusky yellow-orange 800.
33m/2 dull dusky g-yellow-green 800.
35m/5 gloomy dusky green 800.
37m/1 dim dusky g-blue-green 800.
39m/1 dim dusky blue-green 800.
41m/1 dim dusky b-blue-green 800.
47m/0 dusky green-blue-blue 800.
55m/2 dull dusky blue-violet 800.
63m/2 dull dusky red-violet 800.
69m/1 dull dusky red-violet-red 800.
69k/3 dismal dark red-violet-red 800.
71i/0 deep violet-red-red 800.
71m/0 dusky violet-red-red 800.
71o/5 black 800.
ultramarine 800.
violet 800.
red violet 800.
brown violet 800.
orange brown 800.
dark brown 800.

234-E1

Design size: 38½x22mm
Engraved vignette as adopted, mounted on watercolor drawing of frame design similar to but longer than adopted. Vignette also used on No. 231-E3.

234-E1 5c Die on thick artist's card, block sunk as die essay, black brown 4,000.

234-E2

Design size: 34x22½mm
Die size: 67x63mm
Engraved vignette as adopted, mounted on watercolor drawing of frame design as adopted, pencil "Oct. 5/92," approval monogram of J.D. Macdonough and ⅞x1 1/32 inches. Vignette also used on No. 231-E3.

234-E2 5c Die on thick artist's card, die sunk, black brown & white 4,000.

234-E3

Vignette size: 29½x15mm
Die size: 74x61½mm
Engraved vignette only as adopted.

234-E3 5c Die on India, die sunk on card, sepia 1,250.

234-E4

Incomplete engraving of entire design: bench at left has horiz. shading only, incomplete shading in Columbus' face, etc.

234-E4 5c Die on 74x60mm India, on card
sepia 1,000.
blue 1,000.

Ferrotype metal plate with engraved outline design (reversed) of vignette as used on 6c, engraved lines filled with red ink.

235-E1 6c Metal plate, 38x38mm 1,100.

235-E2

Printing from ferrotype plate No. 235-E1.

235-E2 6c Die on stiff white card with rounded corners, 55x42mm, red 1,250.

235-E3

Incomplete engraving of frame as adopted: unfinished crosset shadows in lower corners.

235-E3 6c Die on India, black 2,000.

235-E4

Design size: 34x22mm
Die size: 73x60mm
Incomplete engraving of entire design as adopted: neck and shoulder of horse, side figures in niches, crosset shadows in lower corners all unfinished.

235-E4 6c Die on India, die sunk on card, blue violet *1,500.*

236-E1

Design size: 33½x22mm
Die size: 73x62mm
Design as adopted but frame incompletely engraved: unfinished crosset shadows in lower corners.

236-E1 8c Die on India, on card, black *2,500.*

236-E2

Design as adopted but frame incompletely engraved: unfinished crosset shadows in lower corners, incomplete gown at left and faces at right.

236-E2 8c Die on India, on card, black *1,000.*

237-E2

Ferrotype metal plate with engraved outline design (reversed) of vignette as used on 10c, engraved lines filled with red ink.

237-E2 10c Metal plate, 43x28mm *1,000.*

237-E3

Printing from ferrotype plate No. 237-E2.

237-E3 10c Die on stiff white card with rounded corners, 55x42mm, red *1,000.*

237-E4

Design size: 33x22mm
Die size: 74x62mm
Incomplete engraving of entire design as adopted: surroundings of Columbus, floor, etc., three figures behind King Ferdinand, crosset shadows in lower corners all unfinished.

237-E4 10c Die on India, card mounted
black brown *1,000.*
rose carmine *1,000.*

Similar to No. 237-E4 but more completely engraved: missing lines on ankle bracelet of Indian, many details in vignette and crosset shadows in lower corners.

237-E5 10c Die on India, die sunk on card
black brown *1,500.*
carmine *1,500.*

238-E1

Design size: 33½x22mm
Silver print photo of vignette unadopted for any value (Columbus relating incidents of voyage to Ferdinand and Isabella), mounted on watercolor drawing of frame design similar to that adopted.

238-E1 15c Die on stiff white drawing paper, 42x30mm, bright ultramarine *5,000.*

238-E2

Vignette size: 30x15mm
Die size: 71x59mm
Incomplete engraving of vignette only as adopted: shading on Columbus' tunic and arms, Isabella's sholder, Ferdinand's robe, seated Indian's robe, robe of kneeling figure in lower left corner, etc., all unfinished.

238-E2 15c Die on India, die sunk on card, black brown *1,500.*

Complete engraving of vignette adopted.

238-E3 15c Die on India, black brown *1,500.*

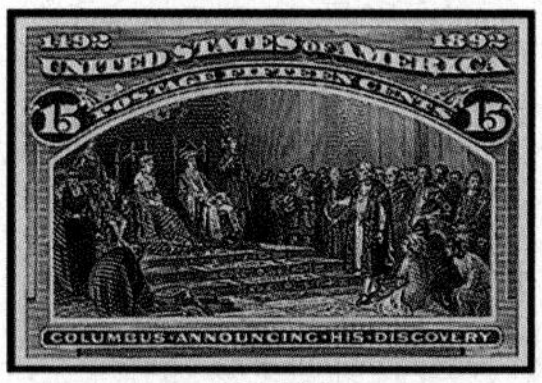

238-E4

Design size: 33½x22mm
Die size: 73½x62mm
Incomplete engraving of complete design as adopted: shading on Isabella's shoulder, Ferdinand's robe, seated Indian's blanket and crosset shadows in lower corners all unfinished.

238-E4 15c Die on India, on card
black brown *1,500.*
blue green *1,500.*

239-E1

Design size: 34½x22½mm
Silver print photo of vignette adopted for 15c, mounted on watercolor and ink drawing of unadopted frame design, titled "COLUMBUS PRESENTING NATIVES TO FERDINAND AND ISABELLA."

239-E1 30c Bluish gray on stiff white drawing paper, 42x30mm *5,000.*

239-E2

Ferrotype metal plate with engraved outline design (reversed) of vignette as used on 30c, engraved lines filled with red ink.

239-E2 30c Metal plate, 39x29mm *1,000.*

239-E3

Printing from ferrotype plate No. 239-E2.

239-E3 30c Die on stiff white card with rounded corners, 55x43mm, red *1,000.*

239-E4

Vignette size: 30x15mm
Die size: 74x62mm
Incomplete engraving of adopted vignette only: table cloth dark at top; horiz. lines on front edge of octagonal footstool, horiz. dots in shadow below windowsill at left, dots on top of head of man standing next to Columbus, etc., all missing.

239-E4 30c Die on India, die sunk on card, black *1,750.*

Similar to No. 239-E4 but further engraved: has horiz. lines on front of footstool, etc. Eight pencil instructions for finishing vignette engraving written on large card backing, e.g., "Too much color on table cloth near top."

239-E5 30c Die on India, die sunk on 177x117mm card
black *2,000.*
black brown *2,000.*

239-E6

Design size: 33½x22mm
Die size: 74x63mm
Incomplete engraving of entire design as adopted: table cloth dark at top, diagonal dashes in one direction only between horiz. lines at lower left of vignette, etc.

239-E6 30c Die on India, die sunk on card
black *2,000.*
black brown *2,000.*

Similar to No. 239-E6 but diagonal dashes in two directions, more dots on head and hand of man seated at near end of table.

239-E7 30c Die on India, die sunk on card
black brown *1,750.*
orange *1,750.*

Incomplete engraving of entire design: window frame, horiz. shading lines on shoulder of man at right, vert. lines on front of table cloth below Columbus all missing. Lighter shading at top of table cloth as on issued stamp.

239-E8 30c Die on India, on card, orange *2,500.*

240-E1

Design size: 34x22mm
Die size: Incomplete engraving of entire design as adopted: unfinished shadows between right arm and body of man on donkey, distant object in front of bowing man's head darker than on issued stamp.

240-E1 50c Die on India, on card, slate blue *1,500.*

240-E2

Incomplete engraving of entire design: missing dots on donkey's flank and long lines on wrist of bowing man, no etching on two riders or their mounts.

240-E2 50c Die on India, on card, slate blue *1,500.*

240-E3

Incomplete engraving of entire design: additional engraving on donkey's hindquarters and face of figure to left of Columbus.

240-E3 50c Die on India, on card, slate blue *1,500.*

241-E1

Ferrotype metal plate with engraved outline design (reversed) of vignette as used on $1, engraved lines filled with red ink.

241-E1 $1 Metal plate, 45x29mm *1,000.*

241-E2

Printing from ferrotype plate No. 241-E1.

241-E2 $1 Die on stiff white card with rounded corners, 55½x43mm, red *1,000.*

241-E3

Vignette size: 31x15mm
Die size: 72x59mm
Incomplete engraving of vignette only as adopted (very early state of die): very little shading on Isabella, floor, walls, etc.

241-E3 $1 Die on India, die sunk on card, black brown *2,000.*

241-E4

Incomplete engraving of entire design as adopted: shadow on table cloth, woman in front of table, crosslet shadows at lower corners all unfinished.

241-E4 $1 Die on India, on card, black brown *2,000.*

241-E5

Later state of complete design: horiz. lines in rectangle above Isabella missing.

241-E5 $1 Die on India, die sunk on 86x69mm card, black brown *2,000.*

242-E1

Design size: 33½x22mm
Die size: 75x62mm
Incomplete engraving of entire design as adopted: about 12 horiz. lines missing on back of cape of tall man at right, some vert. dashes missing on corselet of soldier at right, incomplete foliage over "C" of "COLUMBUS," etc.

242-E1 $2 Die on India, die sunk on card
dull yellow orange *2,000.*
olive brown *2,000.*

243-E1

Ferrotype metal plate with engraved outline design (reversed) of vignette as used on $3, engraved lines filled with red wax.

243-E1 $3 Metal plate, 45x29mm *1,250.*

243-E2

Printing from ferrotype plate No. 243-E1.

243-E2 $3 Die on stiff white card with rounded corners, 55x43mm, red *1,250.*

243-E3

Design size: 33½x22mm
Incomplete engraving of entire design as adopted: unshaded crossets in lower corners, shading lines on crossets and frame above title label too light. Pencil marks correct these.

243-E3 $3 Die on India, die sunk on card, dark yellow green *1,500.*

243-E4

Incomplete engraving of entire design as adopted, before etching of shadows on Columbus, Ferdinand, backs of chairs, etc.

243-E4 $3 Die on India, on card, dark red *2,000.*

Ferrotype metal plate with engraved outline design (reversed) of Queen Isabella vignette as used on $4, engraved lines filled with red wax.

244-E1 $4 Metal plate, 33x44mm *1,500.*

244-E2

Printing from ferrotype plate No. 244-E1.

244-E2 $4 Die on stiff white card with rounded corners, 43x55mm, red *1,500.*

244-E3

Vignette diameter: 14mm
Incomplete engraving of Isabella head with background of uniform ruled horiz. lines only, blank circle for Columbus vignette at right adjoining.

244-E3 $4 Die on India, on card, black *3,000.*

Similar to No. 244-E3 but background has diagonal shading also.

244-E4 $4 Die on India, on card, black *3,000.*

244-E5

Design size: about 34x21½mm
Die size: 74½x61½mm
Incomplete engraving of vignettes and lettering only: no diagonal shading lines in background of Columbus vignette.

244-E5 $4 Die on India, die sunk on card
black *3,500.*
dark red *4,000.*

244-E6

Design size: 34x22mm
Same engraving as No. 244-E5 but with wash drawing of frame design as adopted.

244-E6 $4 Die on thick artist's card with beveled edges, 50x39mm, gray black *3,000.*

244-E7

Incomplete engraving of entire design as adopted: shadow at top of vert. bar and lines on leaves at bottom between vignettes unfinished; no circular line bordering vignette at Isabella's right shoulder.

244-E7 $4 Die on India, on card, black brown *2,000.*

244-E8

More complete engraving than No. 244-E7 but still missing circular line at Isabella's shoulder; only light shading on Columbus' collar.

244-E8 $4 Die on India, on card
black brown *2,000.*
dark red —

245-E1

Design size: 34½x22½mm
Incomplete engraved vignette as adopted for 1c: missing sky, etc., with pencil drawing of part of frame design.

245-E1 $5 Die on 50x38mm artist's cardboard, on thicker card, 55x43mm, black *4,000.*

Design size: 34x22½mm
Die size: 74½x61½mm
Incomplete engraving of vignette, lettering and frame as adopted (side panels blank): shading unfinished on Columbus' neck, hair and background, and with white and black wash touches.

245-E2 $5 Die on India, die sunk on card, black *3,000.*

245-E3

Similar to No. 245-E2 but further engraved: shading lines on neck, diagonal lines in background, etc.

245-E3 $5 Die on India, on card, 49x38mm, black *3,000.*

Model with photos of female figures mounted each side of vignette, pencil "Design approved subject to inspection of engraved proof, color to be black. A.D.H. Dec. 6 '92" (A.D. Hazen, 3rd asst. PMG).

245-E4 $5 Die on thick white card, on 117x116mm card, black *3,000.*

245-E5

Engraving of No. 245-E3 with retouched photos of side subjects mounted in place.

245-E5 $5 Die on white artist's cardboard, 56½x46mm, die sunk on card, black *2,000.*

Design size: 33½x22mm
Incomplete engraving of entire design: one line under "POSTAGE FIVE DOLLARS", no lines outside and no diagonal lines in sky to upper right and upper left of vignette, etc.

245-E6 $5 Die on India, on card, black *2,000.*

245-E7

Similar to No. 245-E2 but with pencil marks to show engraver where to place diagonal shading lines behind head and in front of bust.

245-E7 $5 Die on 65x55mm India, card mounted, black *3,000.*

245-E8

Similar to No. 245-E6 but with pencil marks and white ink suggestions for further engraving.

245-E8 $5 Die on India, die sunk on 83x68mm card, black *2,000.*

245-E9

Similar to No. 245-E6 but further engraved: with diagonal shading above side figures, below numerals and around vignette circle, but still incomplete in arched band above vignette.

245-E9 $5 Die on India, die sunk on 110x83mm card, black *2,000.*

245-E10

Similar to No. 245-E9 but further engraved: with shading lines in arched band above vignette but no shading on pole of liberty cap, object below shield has dotted shading only, spear tip shading incomplete.

245-E10 $5 Die on India, die sunk on 85x70mm card, black *2,000.*

1894 ISSUE
Bureau of Engraving and Printing

The 1c-15c designs of the 1890 issue engraved by the American Bank Note Co. were worked over by the BEP, including the addition of triangles in the upper corners. The 1890 30c was changed to a 50c and the 90c to a $1. Some 1894 essays have American Bank Note Co. imprints below the design.

247-E1

Design size: 18½x22mm
Die size: 61x62mm
Large die engraving of 1890 1c with pencil drawing of UL triangle 3½mm high with straight side next to curved upper label, freehand horiz. ink line at UR.

247-E1 1c Die on India, die sunk on card, black *2,000.*

247-E2

Experimental laydown die with 1890 1c proof 4mm to left of similar design with 15-line high type I triangle in UR corner. Same laydown die also contains two 2c designs 18mm below, 5½mm apart, either uninked or lightly inked in color of 1c (sometimes found separated from 1c designs). No. 247-E2b nearly always found cracked horiz. through designs.

247-E2 1c
a. Die on semiglazed white wove with pencil notations
blue *1,850.*
ultramarine *1,850.*
b. Die on white card with pencil notations re color
"1-1 Antwerp, 4 Ultra." *1,500.*
"2--little lighter--" *1,500.*
"1 Antwerp blue, 1 Ultra." (not cracked) *1,750.*
"4 Cobalt and Indigo" *1,500.*
"No 5" *1,500.*
"No. 6--Antwerp blue" *1,500.*
"No. 6--with little Antwerp blue" *1,500.*

Die impression of 1890 1c with 15-line high type I triangle in UR corner.

247-E3 1c Die on India, 50x52mm, dusky green *2,000.*

Experimental die impression of single 1890 1c with 2c 18mm below, triangles added in ink to upper corners of both designs, ms. "Approved" notations.

247-E4 1c +2c, Die on India, mounted on 57x102mm card, mounted on another card, 144x195mm
green *2,500.*
dull violet (without added triangles) *2,400.*

247-E5

247-E6

Large die engraving of 1890 1c with 18-line high triangle in UL corner (inner lines very thick).

247-E5 1c Die on India, die sunk on card, dusky blue green *1,250.*

Similar to No. 247-E5 but inner line of triangle almost as thin as outer line.

247-E6 1c Die on India, die sunk on card, dusky blue green *1,250.*

247-E7

Similar to No. 247-E6 but inner line of triangle same thickness as adopted.

247-E7 1c Die on India, die sunk on card, dusky blue green *1,250.*

Incomplete engraving of entire design as adopted including triangles: coat collar, scroll under "U," horiz. lines on frame, oval line of vignette, etc., all unfinished; vignette background not re-etched.

247-E8 1c Die on India, die sunk on card
ultramarine *1,000.*
blue ("Cobalt 2--Indigo 4") *1,250.*

Design size: 18½x22mm
Die size: 61x62½mm
Large die engraving of 1890 2c with pencil drawing of UL triangle 2½mm high.

250-E1 2c Die on India, die sunk on card,
black *2,250.*

Die width: 92mm
Experimental laydown die with 1890 2c proof 5½mm to left of similar design with 14-line high type I triangles in upper corners (found cut apart from No. 247-E2 and used for trial colors as noted thereon in pencil).

250-E2 2c Die on white card
"1 R&D Lake, 1½P. white" *2,000.*
"M3 1 white, 7 Gem Lake, ¼ Car. Lake" *2,000.*
"2 White, 4 Ger. Lake No. 1, ½ R&D Lake" *2,000.*
"Opal Red" *2,000.*
"Opal Orange" *2,000.*
"Opal Maroon" *2,000.*

250-E3

Die size: 61½x62½mm
American Banknote Co. die No. C-224 annealed, with 18-line high type I triangles engraved in upper corners, ms "No. 1" at lower left of card backing.

250-E3 2c Die on India, die sunk on card
medium deep red *1,000.*
deep red *1,000.*
dusky red *1,000.*
dim red *1,000.*
medium deep orange-red *1,000.*
deep o-orange-red *1,000.*
dusky g-blue-green *1,000.*
dark medium violet-red-red *1,000.*

Incomplete engraving of entire design: shadows on frame not etched; lines on foliage, front collar and oval line at vignette bottom not recut; dots instead of lines over corner of eye; only one line on truncated scroll at left of right 2 and no line on similar scroll at right of left 2; shadows of TWO CENTS not etched.

250-E4 2c Die on India, die sunk on card
bright red *1,000.*
light red *1,000.*
dark red *1,000.*
deep orange red *1,000.*

Similar to No. 250-E4 but line added to scroll at right of left 2, ms. "A.B.N.Co. Die worked over and ornaments put in" at top, ms. "No. 1" at lower left.

250-E5 2c medium deep red *1,250.*

Incomplete engraving of entire design: two lines on truncated scroll at left of right 2 (one later removed), scroll at left of right 2 unfinished, profile of nose and forehead darker than on issued stamp, shadows of "TWO CENTS" not etched, short dashes on inside of outer edge of white oval at lower right, veins on scrolls around 2s not recut. Pencil notations incl. "Old A.B.N.Co. annealed & triangles engraved and rehardened to take up roll for plate."

250-E6 2c Die on India, die sunk on card, medium deep red *1,250.*

Incomplete engraving of entire design: bottom of ear still angular and not yet rounded, dots on lobe not yet gathered into two lines, dot shading under corner of eye not yet gathered into four lines, shadows of "TWO CENTS" have been etched.

250-E7 2c Die on India, die sunk on card,
medium deep red *1,000.*

Die size: 57x76mm
Incomplete engraving of entire design with type II triangles: top of head not silhouetted. Pencil notation "2/ Transfer from roll taken from No. 1 so as to change portrait and make cameo effect. Unfinished."

251-E1 2c Die on India, die sunk on card,
dark violet red *1,250.*

Similar to No. 251-E1 but hair in front of ear unfinished, forehead and hair lightened.

251-E2 2c Die on India, die sunk on card,
dusky gray *1,500.*

252-E1

Die size: 57x81mm
Incomplete engraving of entire design with type III triangles: top of head not silhouetted, unfinished shadow over eye, etc.

252-E1 2c Die on India, die sunk on card,
medium deep red *1,000.*

Incomplete engraving of entire design with type III triangles: unfinished shadow over eye, etc.

252-E2 2c Die on India, die sunk on card
dusky blue green *1,500.*
dark violet red *1,000.*

252-E3

Design size: 19x22mm
Die size: 56x80½mm
Discarded die, vignette overengraved: too much shading on front hair, cheek, nose, below eye; background too dark; hair in front of ear very prominent.

252-E3 2c Die on India, die sunk on card
light carmine *2,000.*
green *2,250.*

253-E1

Die size: 60x63mm
Complete engraved design as adopted but with type II triangles.

253-E1 3c
a. Die on India, die sunk on card
dusky blue green *1,500.*
dark red violet *1,000.*
dusky red violet *1,000.*
b. Die printed directly on card, die sunk on card, violet *1,250.*

254-E1

Design size: about 19x22mm
Die size: 61x63mm
Incomplete engraving of entire design: line under collar wings missing, oval line around vignette not recut; hair, beard, forehead, neck, collar, shirt, etc., all incomplete.

254-E1 4c Die on India, die sunk on card,
dark yellow brown *1,500.*

Entire design engraved further than No. 254-E1 but still incomplete: shadows in lettering, etc., not etched, faint lines under collar incomplete, oval around vignette not recut.

254-E2 4c Die on India, die sunk on card,
dark yellow brown *1,500.*

Entire design engraved further than No. 254-E2 but still incomplete: beard, collar and necktie, etc., unfinished. Some veins recut on foliage under oval label.

254-E3 4c Die on India, die sunk on card,
dark brown *1,250.*

255-E1

Design size: 19x22mm
Engraved frame of American Bank Note Co. die No. C-227 with triangles, vignette cut out, mounted over engraved vignette of Washington.

255-E1 5c Die on 41x53mm India, on white wove, 48x75mm, black *3,500.*

Washington vignette only as on No. 255-E1.

255-E2 5c Die on India, green *2,000.*

255-E3

255-E4

Design size: 19x22mm
Engraved frame as adopted with William H. Seward photo mounted on it.

255-E3 5c Die on India, cut close, mounted on 74x84mm white card, black *3,500.*

Design size: about 19x22mm
Die size: 62½x75mm
Incomplete engraving of entire design as adopted: no oval border line around vignette.

255-E4 5c Die on India, die sunk on card, orange brown *1,250.*

256-E1

Design size: about 19x22mm
Die size: 62x61½mm
Incomplete engraving of entire design as adopted: white spot on eye and shadows not darkened, diagonal lines missing on beard under mouth, lines on coat unfinished.

256-E1 6c Die on India, die sunk on card,
dark red *1,250.*

256-E2

Entire design engraved further than No. 256-E1 but still incomplete: diagonal lines on beard under mouth incomplete, lines on coat not as dark as on issued stamp.

256-E2 6c Die on India, die sunk on card,
dim dusky red *1,000.*

257-E1

Design size: about 19x22mm
Die size: 58½x60mm

Incomplete engraving of entire design as adopted: lines on coat not recut darker, vignette background not etched darker.

257-E1 8c Die on India, die sunk on card, dusky red violet *1,000.*

258-E1

Design size: about 19x22mm
Die size: 61½x61½mm
Incomplete engraving of entire design as adopted: shading unfinished on cheek, in ear, etc.

258-E1 10c Die on India, die sunk on card, dark brown *1,500.*

Entire design engraved further than No. 258-E1 but still incomplete: unfinished shading on cheek under eye.

258-E2 10c Die on India, die sunk on card, red brown *1,500.*

261-E1

Design size: 19x22mm
Die size: 50x101mm
Large die engraving of 1890 90c with value label and figure circles blank, no triangles.

261-E1 $1 Die on India, die sunk on card, black *3,500.*

Similar to No. 261-E1 but head further re-engraved and background shadows etched deeper.

261-E2 $1 Die on India, die sunk on card, blue green *3,750.*

261-E3

261-E4

Design size: 19x22mm
Model of engraved Perry vignette mounted on 1890 engraved frame with penciled in triangles, values painted in white and black. Ms. "O.K. July 14/94 TFM" below.

261-E3 $1 Die on India, cut close, mounted on 63x101mm white card, green vignette, black frame *4,000.*

Similar to No. 261-E3 but with value lettering and circles added, background of circles unfinished, no triangles.

261-E4 $1 Die on India, die sunk on card, dark indigo blue *3,500.*

Incomplete engraving of entire design: hair on top and back of head, whiskers and back of neck, and shading in value circles all unfinished. Triangles are engraved.

261-E5 $1 Die on India, die sunk on card, black *1,750.*

261-E6

Similar to No. 261-E5 but hair at back of head and whiskers darker, face in front of whiskers darker as on issued stamp. Circular lines extend into colorless vignette oval.

261-E6 $1 Die on India, die sunk on card
black *1,500.*
blue green *2,000.*

261-E7

Design size: 19x21½mm
Die size: 49x100mm
Incomplete engraving of unadopted dollar value design with portrait of Sen. James B. Beck: value label and numerals blank.

261-E7 $1 Die on India, die sunk on card, black *4,000.*

262-E1

262-E2

Design size: 19x22mm
Die size: 50x101mm
Incomplete engraving of frame only nearly as adopted: smaller $2's.

262-E1 $2 Die on India, die sunk on card, blue green *3,500.*

Design size: 19x22mm
Die size: 51x112mm
Incomplete engraving of entire design: left value circle blank, right circle engraved $2 outline only.

262-E2 $2 Die on India, die sunk on card, black *3,250.*

Die size: 51x112mm
Incomplete engraving of entire design: vignette shading unfinished, no veins in leaves around value circles.

262-E3 $2 Die on India, die sunk on card, black *2,850.*

262-E4

Incomplete engraving of entire design: inside of right border line above $2 unfinished.

262-E4 $2 Die on India, die sunk on card, black *2,750.*

Similar to No. 262-E4 but border line complete.

262-E5 $2 Die on India, die sunk on card, black *2,500.*

263-E1

Die size: 50x112½mm
Incomplete engraving of entire design: only one line in each scroll at right and left of $5, inner line of right border above $5 unfinished, etc., veins on leaves around right value circle unfinished.

263-E1 $5 Die on India, die sunk on card, black *2,750.*

Similar to No. 263-E1 but horiz. lines cut into oval line at top and inner oval line above L and R of DOLLARS required retouching as indicated by pencil instructions. Two lines in scrolls around value circles as adopted.

263-E2 $5 Die on India, die sunk on card, black *3,250.*

The bicolored essays commonly offered as No. 285-293 bicolored proofs can be found under the following listings: Nos. 285-E8, 286-E8, 287-E9, 288-E5, 289-E4, 290-E4, 291-E8, 292-E6, 293-E7. Values are for full-size cards (approximately 8x6 inches).

TRANS-MISSISSIPPI ISSUE

Die size: 79x68mm
Incomplete engraving of vignette only: initial state of die, no lines in sky or water.

285-E1 1c Die on India, die sunk on card, black *2,500.*

Vignette further engraved: lines in sky and water.

285-E2 1c Die on India, die sunk on card, black *2,500.*

Vignette further engraved: more background lines added.

285-E3 1c Die on India, die sunk on card, black *2,500.*

285-E4

Vignette further engraved: Indian at right darker, robe shadow etched.

285-E4 1c Die on India, die sunk on card, black *2,500.*

Vignette further engraved: rock in water more complete.

285-E5 1c Die on India, die sunk on card, black *2,500.*

Design size: 34x22mm
Die size: 73x62mm
Incomplete bicolor engraving of entire design: no second inner line in numerals.

285-E6 1c Die on India, die sunk on card, orange red & black *2,500.*

Die size: 83x68mm
Incomplete engraving of entire design: vignette unfinished and unetched, frame has second inner line in numerals.

285-E7 1c Die on India, die sunk on card, black *3,500.*

285-E8

Die size: 63x51mm
Complete bicolor engraving of entire design.

285-E8 1c Die with black vignette on India, die sunk on card
dark yellow green ("normal" bicolor) *300.*
dusky green *2,000.*
dusky blue green *2,000.*
brown *2,000.*

Incomplete engraving of entire design: corn husks and panels in ends of cartouche unfinished, lines under MARQUETTE and MISSISSIPPI not as thick as on completed die.

285-E9 1c Die on India, die sunk on card, dusky green *2,500.*

285-E10

Unfinished frame in red brown missing second inner line in numerals, with black unfinished "Cattle in the Storm" vignette as used on the $1 value, foreground snow at left incomplete.

285-E10 1c Die on India, red brown & black 3,500.

Die size: 78x68mm
Incomplete engraving of Mississippi River Bridge vignette (originally intended for 2c but eventually used on $2): initial state of die, very lightly engraved.

286-E1 2c Die on India, die sunk on card, black *3,750.*

Vignette further engraved but no lines on bridge beside two trolley cars.

286-E2 2c Die on India, die sunk on card, black *5,000.*

286-E3

Vignette further engraved but foreground between bridge and boat and foretopdeck incomplete, horse truck visible (later removed).

286-E3 2c Die on India, die sunk on card, black *3,000.*

Complete engraving of vignette only.

286-E4 2c Die on India, die sunk on card, black *3,000.*

286-E5

Design size: 137x88 ½mm
Pencil sketch by R. Ostrander Smith of 2c frame design as adopted except titled "ST. LOUIS BRIDGE."

286-E5 2c Sketch on tracing paper, 120x178mm *1,500.*

286-E6

Complete pencil drawing by R.O. Smith of frame design ("P" of "POSTAGE" in ink), titled "ST. LOUIS BRIDGE."

286-E6 2c Drawing on Whatman drawing board, 1889 wmk., 237x184mm *1,500.*

286-E7

Pencil drawing by R.O. Smith, no title.

286-E7 2c Drawing on 72x61mm tracing paper *1,500.*

286-E7A

Ink and wash drawing of frame, stamp size, similar to adopted design.

286-E7A 2c Drawing on hard, thick paper, black *11,000.*

286-E8

Die size: 63x51mm
Complete bicolor engraving of 2c design but with Mississippi River Bridge vignette as used on $2.

Ridgway numbers used for colors of No. 286-E8.

286-E8 2c Die with black vignette on India, die sunk on card

dark red ("normal" bicolor)	*300.*
3k/0 dark orange red	*2,000.*
5k/0 dark o-orange-red	*2,000.*
5m/1 dim dusky o-orange-red	*2,000.*
7i/0 deep red orange	*2,000.*
7m/0 dusky red orange	*2,000.*
9m/0 dusky o-red-orange	*2,000.*
9k/2 dull dark o-red-orange	*2,000.*
13m/3 dismal dusky o-yellow-orange	*2,000.*
35m/1 dim dusky green	*2,000.*
49m/1 dim v. dusky blue	*2,000.*
63m/1 dim dusky red violet	*2,000.*
71-/0 deep violet-red-red	*2,000.*

286-E10

Die size: 82x68mm
Complete engraving with "FARMING IN THE WEST" vignette as adopted but from a die not used for the stamp: horses at left vignette border engraved dark up to border line which is solid complete line at both left and right.

286-E10 2c Die on India, die sunk on card (marked "Proof from 1st die.")

black	*2,500.*
dark orange red	*2,500.*

Design size: 34x22mm
Die No. 259 size: 63x51mm
Initial state of die, very lightly engraved.

287-E1 4c Die on India, die sunk on card, black *3,000.*

Vignette further engraved: sky lines ruled in.

287-E2 4c Die on India, die sunk on card, black *3,000.*

287-E3

Vignette further engraved: more lines added, no right forefoot on bison.

287-E3 4c Die on India, die sunk on card, black *4,500.*

Shadow under bison incomplete.

287-E4 4c Die on India, die sunk on card, black *3,750.*

Shadow under bison and foreground penciled in.

287-E5 4c Die on India, die sunk on card, black *3,750.*

Vignette further engraved: right forefoot added, shadow under bison engraved but not etched.

287-E6 4c Die on India, die sunk on card, black *3,750.*

287-E7

Die size: 83x67mm
Incomplete engraving of entire design: no lines in sky, frame shadow etching unfinished.

287-E7 4c Die on India, die sunk on card

black	*3,500.*
deep orange	*3,500.*

287-E8

Die size: 63x51mm
Incomplete engraving of entire design: corn husks at lower sides of frame unfinished.

Ridgway numbers used for colors of No. 287-E8.

287-E8 4c Die with black vignette on India, die sunk on card

5k/0 dark o-orange-red	*2,000.*
5m/0 dusky o-orange-red	*2,000.*
7m/0 dusky red orange	*2,000.*
11o/2 dull v. dusky orange	*2,000.*
13m/3 dismal dusky o-yellow-orange	*2,000.*
35m/1 dim dusky green	*2,000.*
39m/1 dim dusky blue green	*2,000.*
49o/1 dim v. dusky blue	*2,000.*
61k/1 dim dark violet-red violet	*2,000.*
63m/1 dim dusky red violet	*2,000.*
71m/0 dusky violet-red-red	*2,000.*

Complete bicolor engraving.

287-E9 4c Die with black vignette on India, die sunk on card

red orange ("normal" bicolor)	*300.*
deep red orange ("normal" bicolor)	*300.*

Die size: 77x69mm
Initial state of die, very lightly engraved.

288-E1 5c Die on India, die sunk on card, black *3,500.*

Vignette further engraved: lower clouds at right darkened.

288-E2

288-E2 5c Die on India, die sunk on card, black *5,500.*

Vignette further engraved: shading penciled in on figures at right, etc.

288-E3 5c Die on India, die sunk on card, black *3,750.*

288-E4

Vignette further engraved but dots in sky at left of flag unfinished.

288-E4 5c Die on India, die sunk on card, black *3,750.*

288-E5

Design size: 34x22mm
Die size: 63x51mm
Incomplete bicolor engraving of entire design: unfinished crosshatching at left of "FREMONT," lines against bottom label and frame unfinished, no etching on flag.

Ridgway numbers used for colors of No. 288-E5.

288-E5 5c Die with black vignette on India, die sunk on card

49m/1 dim dusky blue ("normal" bicolor)	*300.*
49k/1 dim dark blue ("normal" bicolor)	*300.*
3k/0 dark orange red	*2,000.*
3m/0 dusky orange red	*2,000.*
7m/0 dusky red orange	*2,000.*
7m/1 dim dusky red orange	*2,000.*
9m/0 dusky o-red-orange	*2,000.*
11o/2 dull v. dusky orange	*2,000.*
37m/1 dim dusky g-blue-green	*2,000.*
39m/1 dim dusky blue green	*2,000.*
49o/1 dim v. dusky blue	*2,000.*
63m/1 dim dusky red violet	*2,000.*
71n/0 medium deep violet-red-red	*2,000.*
35m/1 dim dusky green	*2,000.*

Die size: 82x68½mm
Incomplete engraving of entire design: cornhusks, panels at ends of cartouche, mountains, foreground at sides of title label, sky, etc., all unfinished, figures and mountains not etched dark.

288-E7 5c Die on India, die sunk on card, black *3,250.*

Incomplete engraving of vignette: no dots on mountain tops next to right border, unfinished crosshatching at left end of title label.

288-E8 5c Die on India, die sunk on card, black *3,750.*

289-E1

Engraved vignette only of mounted Indian, not used for any value.

289-E1 8c Die on India, on card, black *7,500.*

Incomplete engraving of vignette only as adopted: blank area for label wider than completed bicolor vignette, knee of kneeling soldier unfinished, etc.

289-E2 8c Die on India, die sunk on card, black *3,000.*

289-E3

Design size: about 33½x21½mm
Incomplete engraving of frame only: shading of sunken center of cartouche at right of vignette unfinished.

289-E3 8c Die on India, 26x37mm, black *3,000.*

289-E4

Incomplete engraving of entire design: top row of distant shrubbery under "ERICA" missing, crosshatching on distant mountains at left, blades of grass at left end of label, some dots against top label all unfinished.

Ridgway numbers used for colors of No. 289-E4.

289-E4 8c Die with black vignette on India, die sunk on card

dark red ("normal" bicolor)	*375.*
dusky red ("normal" bicolor)	*375.*
3m/0 dusky orange red	*2,750.*
5m/0 dusky o-orange-red	*2,750.*
7i/0 deep red orange	*2,750.*
7m/0 dusky red orange	*2,750.*
9m/0 dusky o-red-orange	*2,750.*
11o/2 dull v. dusky orange	*2,750.*
35m/1 dim dusky green	*2,750.*
39m/1 dim dusky blue-green	*2,750.*
49o/1 dim v. dusky blue	*2,750.*
63m/1 dim dusky red violet	*2,750.*
71-/0 deep violet-red-red	*2,750.*

Die size: 77x64mm
Incomplete engraving of vignette only: two rows of dots in sky over wagon.

290-E1

290-E1 10c Die on India, die sunk on card, black *8,500.*

290-E2

Vignette further engraved: three rows of dots in sky over wagon.

290-E2 10c Die on India, die sunk on card, black *3,750.*

Vignette further engraved: front of wagon canvas crosshatched.

290-E3 10c Die on India, die sunk on card, black *3,750.*

290-E4

Incomplete bicolor engraving of entire design: cornhusks unfinished, blades of grass to right of girl's feet and some to right of dark horse's feet are missing. Five lines of dots in sky over wagon.

Ridgway numbers used for colors of No. 290-E4.

290-E4 10c Die with black vignette on India, die sunk on card

dull dusky violet blue ("normal" bicolor)	*350.*
dusky blue violet ("normal" bicolor)	*350.*
1i/0 deep red	*2,500.*
3k/0 dark orange red	*2,500.*
5k/0 dark o-orange-red	*2,500.*
5m/0 dusky o-orange-red	*2,500.*
7i/0 deep red orange	*2,500.*
9m/0 dusky o-red-orange	*2,500.*
11o/2 dull v. dusky orange	*2,500.*
35m/1 dim dusky green	*2,500.*
39m/1 dim dusky blue green	*2,500.*
49o/1 dim v. dusky blue	*2,500.*
55m/2 smoky dark v.-blue violet	*2,500.*
63m/1 dim dusky red violet	*2,500.*
71-/0 deep violet-red-red	*2,500.*

Incomplete engraving of entire design: cornhusks unfinished, vignette from No. 290-E4 trimmed by engraving to fit frame.

290-E6 10c Die on India, die sunk on card, dark red orange *3,000.*

Incomplete engraving of entire design: cornhusks and panels at ends of cartouche and both sides and botton of vignette next to border unfinished.

290-E7 10c Die on India, die sunk on card, dull red violet *3,000.*

Incomplete engraving of entire design: cornhusks and both sides and bottom of vignette next to border are unfinished, vert. lines on cartouche frame at right of vignette missing.

290-E8 10c Die on India, dull red violet *3,000.*

291-E1

Die size: 62x52mm
Incomplete engraving of vignette only: without sky or mountains.

291-E1 50c Die on India, die sunk on card, black *3,750.*

Vignette further engraved: sky ruled in.

291-E2 50c Die on India, die sunk on card, black *3,750.*

Vignette further engraved but no shading on distant mountains.

291-E3

291-E3 50c Die on India, die sunk on card, black *3,750.*

Vignette further engraved: light shading on distant mountains.

291-E4 50c Die on India, die sunk on card, black *3,750.*

Vignette further engraved: more shading on distant mountains.

291-E5 50c Die on India, die sunk on card, black *3,750.*

291-E6

Vignette further engraved: shadows on miner's hat darker (etched).

291-E6 50c Die on India, die sunk on card, black *3,750.*

291-E7

Vignette further engraved: girth under donkey darkened.

291-E7 50c Die on India, die sunk on card, black *9,000.*

291-E8

Design size: 34x22mm
Die size: 89x71mm
Incomplete bicolor engraving of entire design: shading lines on scroll in LR corner of frame and shrubbery in UL corner of vignette unfinished, sky incomplete.

Ridgway numbers used for colors of No. 291-E8.

291-E8	50c Die with black vignette on India, die sunk on card	
	dull dusky b-blue-green ("normal" bicolor; die size: 63x51mm)	*300.*
	dull dusky g-blue-green ("normal" bicolor; die size: 63x51mm)	*300.*
	1i/0 deep red	*2,500.*
	3k/0 dark orange red	*2,500.*
	5m/0 dusky o-orange-red	*2,500.*
	7m/0 dusky red orange	*2,500.*
	9i/0 deep o-yellow-orange	*2,500.*
	9m/0 dusky o-red-orange	*2,500.*
	11m/2 dull dusky orange	*2,500.*
	13m/3 dismal dusky o-yellow-orange	*2,500.*
	35m/1 dim dusky green	*2,500.*
	39m/1 dim dusky blue green	*2,500.*
	47n/2 dull v. dusky green-blue blue	*2,500.*
	49o/1 dim v. dusky blue	*2,500.*
	61k/1 dim dark violet-red-violet	*2,500.*
	71m/0 dusky violet-red-red	*2,500.*

Incomplete engraving of entire design: vignette against top frame unfinished.

291-E9	50c Die on India, die sunk on card	
	black	*3,000.*
	deep red orange	*3,000.*

Incomplete engraving of entire design: engraving on bottom of miner's pan dots only, not lines as on issued stamp.

291-E10 50c Die on wove, sage green *3,000.*

Incomplete engraving of vignette only: initial state of die, lightly engraved.

292-E1

292-E1 $1 Die on India, die sunk on card, black *4,500.*

292-E2

Vignette further engraved: light shield-shaped vignette outline (later removed.)

292-E2 $1 Die on India, die sunk on card, black *4,500.*

Vignette further engraved: left front hoof of lead bull darker.

292-E3 $1 Die on India, die sunk on card, black *3,750.*

Vignette similar to No. 292-E3 but with penciled modeling in snow and among cattle.

292-E4 $1 Die on India, die sunk on card, black *3,750.*

Vignette further engraved: foreground snow at left darkened, shield outline removed.

292-E5

292-E5 $1 Die on India, die sunk on card, black *10,000.*

292-E6

Incomplete engraving of entire bicolored design: right cornhusk and sky against top of frame unfinished, bull's right forefoot does not touch frame, foreground at right end of label unfinished.

Ridgway numbers used for colors of No. 292-E6, where available.

292-E6	$1 Die with black vignette on India, die sunk on card	
	dull violet blue ("normal" bicolor)	*450.*
	dull blue ("normal" bicolor)	*450.*
	dull violet ("normal" bicolor)	*3,000.*
	3k/0 dark orange red	*3,000.*
	5m/0 dusky-o-orange-red	*3,000.*
	7m/0 dusky red orange	*3,000.*
	9m/0 dusky o-red-orange	*3,000.*
	9n/3 dismal v. dusky o-red-orange	*3,000.*
	13n/3 dismal v. dusky o-yellow-orange	*3,000.*
	35m/1 dim dusky green	*3,000.*
	43m/1 dim dusky green blue	*3,000.*
	49m/1 dim dusky blue	*3,000.*
	57k/4 smoky dark violet-blue violet	*3,000.*
	63m/1 dim dusky red violet	*3,000.*
	71-/0 violet-red-red	*3,000.*
	47n/2 dull dusky green blue	*3,000.*
	dark brown	*3,000.*

Incomplete engraving of entire design: left frameline, cornhusks and shading in frame over cornhusks all unfinished.

292-E7 $1 Die on India, die sunk on card, dusky red orange *3,000.*

293-E1

Design size: 34x22mm
Die size: 73x63mm
Vignette of Western mining prospector as used on 50c, but labeled HARVESTING IN THE WEST, frame shows $ same size as numeral 2.

293-E1 $2 Die on India, on card, dusky violet & black *3,500.*

293-E2

Die size: 77x66mm
Incomplete engraving of Farming in the West vignette (originally intended for $2 but eventually used on 2c): initial state of die, very lightly engraved.

293-E2 $2 Die on India, die sunk on card, black *3,000.*

Vignette further engraved: four horses shaded.

293-E3 $2 Die on India, die sunk on card, black *3,000.*

Vignette further engraved: shading added to background figures and horses, pencil shading above and below half horse at left.

293-E4 $2 Die on India, die sunk on card, black *3,000.*

Vignette further engraved: foreground and shadows under horse teams darkened, no shading dots above half horse at left, etc.

293-E5 $2 Die on India, die sunk on card, black *3,000.*

293-E6

Vignette further engraved but foreground in front of plow wheel still unfinished.

293-E6 $2 Die on India, die sunk on card, black *3,000.*

293-E7

Die size: 62x51mm
Incomlpete engraving of entire bicolor design: only one plowshare shown, label longer, less foreground than on issued stamp.

Ridgway numbers used for colors of No. 293-E7.

293-E7	$2 Die with black vignette on India, die sunk on card	
	dusky orange red ("normal" bicolor; die size: 63x61mm)	*450.*
	dark red orange ("normal" bicolor; die size: 63x61mm)	*450.*
	1-/0 red	*3,000.*
	3k/0 dark orange red	*3,000.*
	7m/0 dusky red orange	*3,000.*
	35m/1 dim dusky green	*3,000.*
	39m/1 dim dusky blue green	*3,000.*
	45o/1 dim v. dusky blue-green blue	*3,000.*
	45m/2 dull dusky blue-green blue	*3,000.*
	63m/1 dim dusky red violet	*3,000.*
	71i/0 deep violet-red-red	*3,000.*
	47n/2 dull dusky green blue	*3,000.*

Incomplete engraving of entire design as adopted: black wash over engraving on side of bridge and foreground (engraving under wash unfinished).

293-E9 $2 Die on India, die sunk on card, black *3,500.*

Complete design, vignette further engraved: engraving completed between title label and steamboat and city next to right frame, near side of bridge and smoke shadow on water lighter than on issued stamp.

293-E10 $2 Die on India, die sunk on card, black *3,500.*

Incomplete engraving of entire design: circles in upper corners of vignette next to value ovals, water next to right end of value label, panels at ends of cartouche all unfinished.

293-E11 $2 Die on India, die sunk on card, black *3,500.*

Edward Rosewater

Rosewater, of St. Louis, was asked by the Post Office Dept. in 1897 to submit proposed designs for the Trans-Mississippi Exposition issue. For that reason, they are listed here.
All are drawings on tracing paper, on 91x142mm buff card.

285-E11

Design size: 62x97mm
Wash drawing of cattle.

285-E11 1c dull orange *12,500.*

286-E11

Design size: 57x98mm
Wash drawing of mounted Indian saluting wagon train.

286-E11 2c deep orange red *12,500.*

288-E9

Design size: 61x100mm
Wash drawing of man plowing field.

288-E9 5c dark yellow *12,500.*

290-E9

Design size: 62x99mm
Wash drawing of train coming around mountain.

290-E9 Ten Cents, dusky blue *12,500.*

292-E9

Design size: 60x98mm
Wash drawing of woman holding light, standing on globe.

292-E9 $1 deep orange yellow *12,500.*

PAN-AMERICAN ISSUE
Bureau of Engraving and Printing

294-E1

Design size: 108x82mm
Preliminary pencil drawing for frame design as adopted.

294-E1 1c Drawing on tracing paper, black *1,500.*

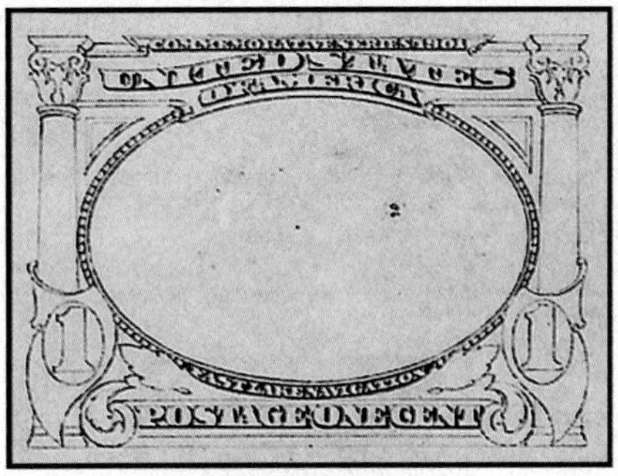

294-E2

Design size: 114x82½mm
Final ink drawing for frame design as adopted.

294-E2 1c Drawing on white card, about 6½x5 inches, black *1,500.*

294-E3

Die size: 87x68½mm
Incomplete engraving of vignette only.

294-E3 1c Die on India, die sunk on card, black *1,500.*

295-E1

Design size: 108x82mm
Preliminary pencil drawing of frame similar to that adopted (side ornaments, etc., different); UR corner, etc., unfinished.

295-E1 2c Drawing on tracing paper, black *1,500.*

295-E2

Design size: 114x83mm
Preliminary pencil drawing of frame similar to No. 295-E1 (minor differences) but with UR corner complete.

295-E2 2c Drawing on tracing paper, black 1,500.

295-E3

Design size: 108x82mm
Preliminary pencil drawing of frame design similar to No. 295-E2 but with minor differences at top, in lettering, etc.

295-E3 2c Drawing on tracing paper, black 1,500.

295-E4

Design size: 95x70mm
Ink and wash drawing model of frame design as adopted, side torchbearers engraved on India as on U.S. Series of 1901 $10 note.

295-E4 2c Die on white card, about 108x82mm, black 1,500.

295-E4A

Design size: 88x69mm
Incomplete engraving of vignette only.

295-E4A 2c Die on India, die sunk on card, black 3,500.

295-E5

295-E6

Design size: 27x19½mm
Die size: 88x68mm
Complete engraving of frame only as adopted.

295-E5 2c Die on India, die sunk on card, carmine 3,750.

Die size: 88½x69mm
Engraving of entire design with vignette incomplete near frame and on cars.

295-E6 2c Die on India, die sunk on card, carmine & black 4,750.

296-E1

Preliminary pencil drawing of unadopted frame design.

296-E1 4c Drawing on tracing paper, black 1,500.

296-E2

Design size: 114x82½mm
Final ink drawing for frame design as adopted.

296-E2 4c Drawing on white card, about 6½x5 inches, black 1,500.

296-E3

Design size: 27x19mm
Die size: 88x67mm
Incomplete engraving of entire design as adopted: lines missing at base of capitol dome, above driver's head.

296-E3 4c Die on India, die sunk on card, deep red brown & black 1,750.

297-E1

Photo reproduction of pencil sketch of unadopted frame design on photosensitive tan paper, reduced to stamp size. Incomplete preliminary pencil drawing of frame design as adopted.

297-E1 5c Photo reproduction on tan paper 1,500.

297-E2

Design size: 114x83mm
Incomplete preliminary pencil drawing of frame design as adopted.

297-E2 5c Drawing on tracing paper, black 1,500.

297-E3

Design size: 114x82½mm
Final ink drawing for frame design as adopted.

297-E3 5c Drawing on white card, about 6½x5 inches, black 1,500.

297-E4

Photo reproduction of sketch of adopted frame design on photosensitive paper, reduced to stamp size.

297-E4 5c Photo reproduction on tan paper 750.

297-E5

297-E6

Die size: 87x68mm
Incomplete engraving of vignette only.

297-E5 5c Die on India, die sunk on card, black 1,500.

Die size: 87x68mm
As No. 297-E5, but more completely engraved.

297-E6 5c Die on India, die sunk on card, black 1,500.

297-E7

Design size: 27x19½mm
Die size: 87x68mm

Incomplete engraving of entire design as adopted: shading at bottom of battleaxes and scrolls at ends of title frame unfinished.

297-E7 5c Die on India, die sunk on card, blue & black *1,750.*

298-E1

Design size:108x82mm
Preliminary pencil drawing of unadopted frame design.

298-E1 8c Drawing on tracing paper, black *1,500.*

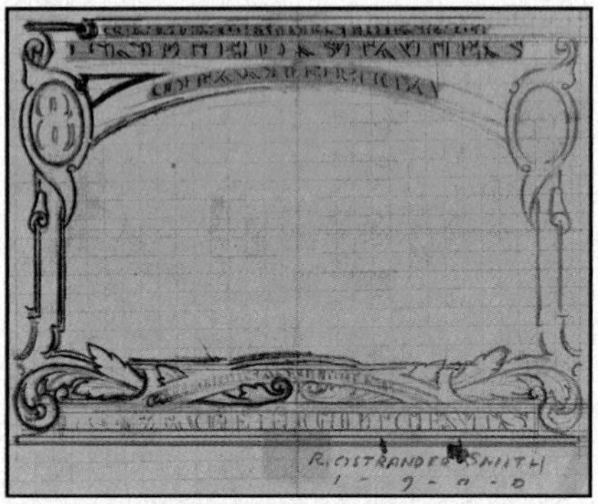

298-E2

Design size: 114x83mm
Incomplete preliminary pencil drawing of unadopted frame design.

298-E2 8c Drawing on tracing paper, black *1,500.*

298-E3

Design size: 114x83mm
Preliminary pencil drawing of unadopted frame design.

298-E3 8c Drawing on tracing paper, black *1,500.*

298-E4

Design size: 114x83mm
Preliminary pencil drawing of frame design as adopted.

298-E4 8c Drawing on tracing paper, black *1,500.*

298-E5

Design size: 114x82½mm
Final ink drawing for frame design as adopted. No. 298-E5 has an example of No. 298 mounted in the vignette area.

298-E5 8c Drawing on white card, about 6½x5 inches, black *1,500.*

298-E6

Photo reproduction of sketch of adopted frame design on photosensitive paper, reduced to stamp size.

298-E6 8c Photo reproduction on tan paper *1,500.*

298-E7

Design size: 27x20mm
Die size: 87x69mm
Incomplete engraving of entire design: shading lines of ornaments, scrolls and ribbons at top unfinished, vignette incomplete at right, no etching on building in left foreground.

298-E7 8c Die on India, die sunk on card, bi-colored *1,750.*

299-E1

Design size: 114x83mm
Preliminary pencil drawing of unadopted frame design (small blank oval at center).

299-E1 10c Drawing on tracing paper, black *1,500.*

299-E2

Design size: 114x82½mm
Similar to No. 299-E1 but with outline of eagle and shield in center oval.

299-E2 10c Drawing on tracing paper, black *1,500.*

299-E3

Design size: 114x83mm
Preliminary pencil drawing for frame design as adopted.

299-E3 10c Drawing on tracing paper, black *1,500*

299-E4

Design size: 114x82½mm
Final ink drawing for frame design as adopted.

299-E4 10c Drawing on white card, about 6½x9 inches, black *1,500.*

299-E5

Photo reproduction of sketch of adopted frame design on photosensitive paper, reduced to stamp size.

299-E5 10c Photo reproduction on tan paper *750.*

299-E6

Die size: 87x68mm
Incomplete engraving of entire design: frame complete but lines later engraved in the mast, smokestack and sky.

299-E6 10c Die on India, die sunk on card, bi-colored *1,750.*

1902 ISSUE

300-E1

300-E2

Incomplete engraving of vignette and lower part of frame.

300-E1 1c Die on India, die sunk on card, black *4,000.*

Design size: 19x22mm
Die size: 74½x88½mm
Incomplete engraving of entire design: vignette background has horiz. lines only, neckpiece, men at sides, etc., all unfinished.

300-E2 1c Die on India, die sunk on card, black *3,500.*

300-E3

Design size: 136x190mm
Preliminary ink drawing for 5c frame design but later adopted for 1c.

300-E3 1c Drawing on manila paper, black & blue green *2,000.*

No. 300-E3 is on the opposite side of the same piece of paper bearing No. 307-E1. Value is for both essays.

300-E4

Design size: 116x135mm
Preliminary pencil and ink drawing for frame design as adopted.

300-E4 1c Drawing on white card, black *3,000.*

301-E1

Design size: 164x181mm
Paper size: 169x214mm
Preliminary pencil drawing of frame design (Raymond Ostrander Smith). Not adopted.

301-E1 2c Drawing on yellowed transparent tracing paper, black *1,500.*

301-E1A

Preliminary pencil and ink drawing of unadopted frame design, on 77x82mm yellowish wove paper, folded vertically and with ink tracing of frame on reverse.

301-E1A 2c Drawing on woven paper, black *2,000.*

301-E1B

Design size: 145x168mm
Preliminary pencil drawing of frame design as adopted.

301-E1B 2c Drawing on tracing paper, black *3,500.*

301-E2

301-E3

Model with vignette of Houdon bust of Washington, on wash drawing over photo reduced to stamp size for approval by PMG.

301-E2 2c Model mounted on card, black *750.*

Design size: 19x22mm
Die size: 75x87½mm
Incomplete engraving of entire design: head unfinished, horiz. background lines only, frame unfinished, lettering either blank or unfinished.

301-E3 2c Die on India, die sunk on card, black *4,000.*

301-E4

Design size: 60x88mm
Preliminary pencil drawing of right numeral 2 design as adopted.

301-E4 2c Drawing on tracing paper, black *500.*

301-E5

Design size: 176x120mm
Preliminary pencil drawing of lower left and upper right design.

301-E5 2c Drawing on tracing paper, black *700.*

301-E6

Design size: 19x22mm
Die size: 74x89mm
Incomplete engraving of entire design: head unfinished, horiz. background lines only, frame almost finished, lettering complete. No. 62057 on back.

301-E6 2c Die on India, die sunk on 153x202mm card, black *3,000.*

302-E1

303-E1

Design size: 19x22mm
Die size: 74½x88mm

Incomplete engraving of entire design: vignette unfinished, horiz. background lines only, atlantes at sides unfinished. No. 66218 on back.

302-E1 3c Die on India, die sunk on card, black *3,250.*

Design size: 19x22mm
Die size: 75x88mm

Incomplete engraving of entire design: vignette unfinished on eyes, hair, beard, etc. No. 58920 on back.

303-E1 4c Die on India, die sunk on card, black *3,250.*

Design size: 19x22mm

Incomplete engraving of entire design, shading lines in top of frame unfinished. No. 60085 on back.

303-E2 4c Die on India, die sunk on card, black *2,000.*

Photograph of unaccepted design, stamp size, with white wash inside vignette and eagles in corners drawn in pen over protions of photo.

303-E3 4c Retouched photo-sensitive paper, black *900.*

Photograph of unaccepted design with additional overlay photo of top portion of frame with eagles similar to those on No. 303-E3.

303-E4 4c Photo-sensitive paper mounted on paper, black *1,100.*

304-E1

Design size: 19x22mm
Die size: 74x87½mm

Rejected die: figure at right poorly draped, blank triangles below "UNITED STATES," no shading in frame around "POSTAGE/FIVE CENTS" except at extreme ends.

304-E1 5c Die on India, die sunk on card, blue *2,300.*

Incomplete engraving of entire design: shading on side figures unfinished.

304-E2 5c Die on India, die sunk on card, blue *1,250.*

304-E3

Design size: 107x110mm
Paper size: 141x128mm

Preliminary pencil and ink drawing of unadopted frame design.

304-E3 5c Drawing on onion skin paper, black —

Incomplete engraving of entire design as adopted.

305-E1 6c Die on India, lake *1,250.*

305-E2

Design size: 123x210mm
Preliminary ink drawing for unadopted frame design.

305-E2 6c Drawing on kraft paper, black & blue green *4,500.*

Nos. 305-E2, 306-E3 and 308-E2, are all on same piece of kraft paper, with No. 306-E3 on one side and the other two on the other side. Value is for the entire unit of three essays.

306-E1

Design size: 7x3½ inches
Preliminary pencil drawing of left side of frame design as adopted.

306-E1 8c Drawing on tracing paper, black *2,200.*

306-E2

Die size: 76x89mm
Incomplete engraving of vignette and numerals only: head drapery unfinished, horiz. background lines only.

306-E2 8c Die on India, die sunk on card, black *5,000.*

306-E3

Design size: 165x175mm
Preliminary ink drawing for unadopted frame design.

306-E3 8c Drawing on kraft paper, black, blue & green *4,500.*

See note after No. 305-E2.

307-E1

Design size: 135x174mm
Preliminary ink drawing for unadopted frame design.

307-E1 10c Drawing on kraft paper, black, blue & green *2,000.*

No. 307-E1 is on the opposite side of the same piece of paper bearing No. 300-E3. Value is for both essays.

308-E1

Design size: 19x22mm
Die size: 69x85½mm
Incomplete engraving of entire design: hair, beard, right cheek, eyes and right shoulder all unfinished, horiz. background lines only, name panel blank, ribbon shading unfinished, etc. No. 57796 on back.

308-E1 13c Die on India, die sunk on card, black *3,750.*

308-E2

Design size: 177x220mm
Preliminary ink drawing of 3c frame design but later adopted for 13c.

308-E2 13c Drawing on kraft paper, black & blue green *4,500.*

See note after No. 305-E2.

310-E1

Design size: 19x22mm
Die size: 74x87½mm
Incomplete engraving of entire design: hair and right cheek unfinished, horiz. background lines only, top of frame and eagles unfinished.

310-E1 50c Die on India, die sunk on card, black *4,000.*

310-E2

Incomplete engraving of entire design, further engraved than No. 310-E1: oval line outside top label thinner at bottom ends than on issued stamp.

310-E2 50c Die on India, die sunk on card, black *4,000.*

312-E1

313-E1

Design size: 19x22mm
Die size: 76x88mm
Incomplete engraving of entire design: hair, neckpiece, etc., unfinished, horiz. background lines only; top of frame, leaves and numeral surrounds all unfinished.

312-E1 $2 Die on India, die sunk on card, black *4,500.*

Design size: 19x22mm
Die size: 75½x87½mm
Incomplete engraving of entire design: eyes, cheeks, hair, neckpiece all unfinished, horiz. background lines only, frame engraved in outlines only.

313-E1 $5 Die on India, die sunk on card, dark green *8,000.*

319-E1

Design size: 19½x22mm
Die size: 75x87½mm
Incomplete engraving of entire design from rejected die (central star between UNITED and STATES, four lines above small lettering, bottom of shield curved): name and date ribbon blank.

319-E1 2c Die on India, die sunk on card, carmine *5,250.*

319-E2

319-E3

Incomplete engraving of entire design from rejected die: shading on leaves and vignette completed, lettering added to bottom ribbon and started on label above vignette. Blue pencil note on card backing, "May 1903. This die was abandoned at this stage because of crowded condition of lettering above portrait. G.F.C.S." No. 83909 on back.

319-E2 2c Die on India, die sunk on card, carmine *5,250.*

Design size: 19½x22mm
Die I size: 75½x88mm
Incomplete engraving of entire design as adopted (no star between UNITED and STATES, bottom of shield straight): small label above vignette is blank.

319-E3 2c Die on India, die sunk on card, black *5,250.*

LOUISIANA PURCHASE ISSUE

324-E1

Incomplete engraving of entire design: head, hair, eyes, chin, coat all unfinished, horiz. background lines only, bottom label and upper corner labels blank, frame shading unfinished.

324-E1 2c Die on India, die sunk on card, black *2,500.*

325-E1

Incomplete engraving of entire design: head only lightly engraved, horiz. background lines only, laurel leaves unshaded, leaves' background and numeral shields blank.

325-E1 3c Die on India, die sunk on card, black *2,500.*

326-E1

Incomplete engraving of entire design: vignette unfinished, horiz. background lines only, much of frame blank or incomplete.

326-E1 5c Die on India, die sunk on card, black blue *2,500.*

JAMESTOWN ISSUE

328-E1

Incomplete engraving of entire design: vignette, shading on heads in upper corners, numerals and numeral shields all unfinished.

328-E1 1c Die on pale cream soft wove, 30x24mm, dusky green *1,250.*

Incomplete engraving of entire design: vignette, shading on heads in upper corners, and value tablets unfinished, pencil note "unfinished" at bottom of card.

328-E2 1c Die on India, die sunk on card, 109x94mm, green *2,500.*

330-E1

330-E2

Incomplete engraving of vignette only: collar, hat, corselet, etc., unfinished. No. 245910 on back.

330-E1 5c Die on India, die sunk on card, 123x132mm, black *2,250.*

Incomplete engraving of entire design: no shading in frame background.

330-E2 5c Die on India, die sunk on card, 109x95mm, blue *6,000.*

330-E3

Incomplete engraving of entire design: shading on corselet and arm of Pocahontas unfinished, horiz. background lines only, shading around date and name ribbon unfinished. No. 247606 on back.

330-E3 5c Die on card, 123x175mm, die sunk, blue *4,250.*

Incomplete engraving of entire design: shading on ribbons unfinished.

330-E4 5c Die on India, die sunk on card, 108x98mm, black *5,000.*

1908 ISSUE

331-E1

Photograph of wash drawing of entire design, head and vignette background retouched with black wash. Ms. "GVLM-Sept. 26th-1908" (PMG) in LR corner of backing card.

331-E1 1c Retouched photo on thick gray cardboard, 83x100mm, black *5,000.*

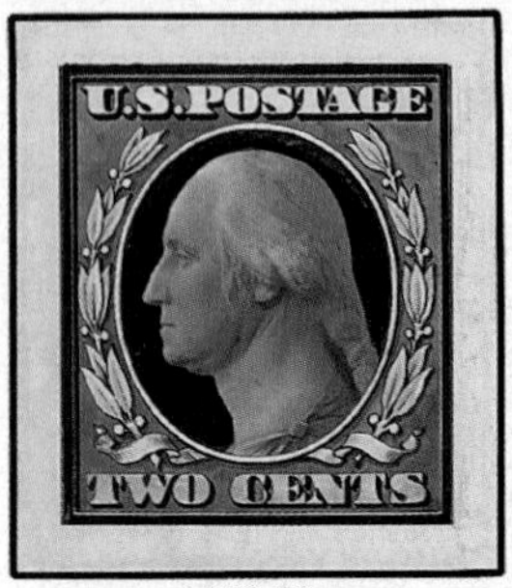
332-E1

332-E2

Design size: 6⅛x7¼ inches
Wash drawing of frame design with vignette cut out, mounted over retouched glossy black photo of Houdon bust of Washington.

332-E1 Two Cents, Design on drawing paper, black *1,250.*

Design size: 19x22mm
Photograph of wash drawing of entire design, almost completely retouched with black ink and wash. Pencil "GVLM" (PMG) at top of backing card.

332-E2 Two Cents, Retouched photo on thick gray cardboard, 81x100mm, black *2,000.*

332-E3

Design size: 19x22mm
Incomplete engraving of entire design: shading on leaves at right unfinished. Pencil "Oct 15 - 1908" at LR of backing card.

332-E3 Two Cents, Die on India, die sunk on card, carmine *1,250.*

333-E1

333-E2

Design size: 18½x22mm
Engraving of design as adopted except "THREE CENTS" at bottom.

333-E1 Three Cents, Die printed directly on card, deep violet *1,250.*

Design size: 19x22mm
Photograph of wash drawing of entire design with "3 CENTS 3" drawn in black and white wash. Ms. "Nov. 24/08. J.E.R." (BEP director) in LR corner of backing card.

333-E2 3c Retouched photo on thick gray cardboard, 80x100mm, black *2,000.*

334-E1

334-E2

Design size: 18½x22mm
Engraving of design as adopted except "FOUR CENTS" at bottom.

334-E1 Four Cents, Die printed directly on card, orange brown *1,250.*

Design size: 19x22mm
Photograph of wash drawing of entire design with "4 CENTS 4" drawn in black and white wash. Ms. "Nov. 24/08. J.E.R." (BEP director) in LR corner of backing card.

334-E2 4c Retouched photo on thick gray cardboard, 80x100mm, black *2,000.*

335-E1

335-E2

Design size: 18½x22mm
Engraving of design as adopted except "FIVE CENTS" at bottom.

335-E1 Five Cents, Die printed directly on card, blue *1,500.*

Design size: 19x22mm
Photograph of wash drawing of entire design with "5 CENTS 5" drawn in black and white wash. Ms. "Nov. 24/08. J.E.R." (BEP director) in LR corner of backing card.

335-E2 5c Retouched photo on thick gray cardboard, 80x100mm, black *2,000.*

Design size: 18½x22mm
Incomplete engraving of design with "SIX CENTS" at bottom.

336-E1 Six Cents, Die on India, on card, red orange *1,250.*

336-E2

Design size: 19x22mm
Photograph of wash drawing of entire design with "6 CENTS 6" drawn in black and white wash. Ms. "Nov. 24/08. J.E.R." (BEP director) in LR corner of backing card.

336-E2 6c Retouched photo on thick gray cardboard, 80x100mm, black *2,000.*

337-E1

338-E1

Design size: 19x22mm
Photograph of wash drawing of entire design with "8 CENTS 8" drawn in black and white wash. Ms. "Nov. 24/08. J.E.R." (BEP director) in LR corner of backing card.

337-E1 8c Retouched photo on thick gray cardboard, 80x100mm, black *2,000.*

Design size: 19x22mm
Photograph of wash drawing of entire design with "10 CENTS 10" drawn in black and white wash. Ms. "Nov. 24/08. J.E.R." (BEP director) in LR corner of backing card.

338-E1 10c Retouched photo on thick gray cardboard, 80x100mm, black *2,000.*

338a-E1

Design size: 18½x22mm
Complete engraving of entire adopted design but a value not issued: "12 CENTS 12" at bottom. Virtually all are stamp size, imperf.

Ridgway numbers used for colors of No. 338a-E1.

338a-E1 12c
a. Die on bluish white wove
41n/1 dim v. dusky b-blue-green *900.*
b. Die on 1f/1 dim pale red wove
c. Die on 7d/1 dim light red orange wove
47m/1 dim dusky g-b. blue *900.*
d. Die on 17b/1 dim bright o-y. yellow wove
1i/0 deep red *900.*
5i/0 deep o-orange-red *900.*
27m/0 dusky green yellow *900.*
37m/0 dusky g-blue-green *900*
41m/0 dusky b-blue-green *900*
55m/1 dim dusky blue violet *900*
59m/1 dim dusky violet *900*
69m/3 dismal dusky r-violet-red *900*
e. Die on 19f/0 pale y-orange yellow wove
1i/0 deep red *900*
15i/1 dim deep yellow orange *900*
35m/0 dusky green *900*
43d/1 dim light green blue *900*
61m/3 dismal dusky v-red-violet *900*
69o/5 black *900*
f. Die on 31f/2 dull pale yellow green wove
69o/5 black *900*
g. Die on 42d/1 dim bright green blue wove
41m/1 dim dusky b-blue-green *900*
h. Die on 44-/1 dim medium green blue wove
9k/2 dull dark o-r-orange *900*
i. Die on 45l/1 dim v. dark b-green-blue wove
5i/0 deep o-orange-red *900*
27m/2 dull dusky green yellow *900*
j. Die on 69g/0 pale r-v. red wove *900*
k. Die on dark blue bond, 69o/5 black *900*

339-E1

340-E1

Design size: 19x22mm
Photograph of wash drawing of entire design with "13 CENTS 13" drawn in black and white wash. Ms. "Oct. 7-08. J.E.R.-GVLM" (BEP director, PMG) in LL corner of backing card.

339-E1 13c Retouched photo on thick gray cardboard, 80x100mm, black *2,000*

Design size: 19x22mm
Photograph of wash drawing of entire design with "15 CENTS 15" drawn in black and white wash. Ms. "Oct. 7-08. J.E.R.-GVLM" (BEP director, PMG) at bottom of backing card.

340-E1 15c Retouched photo on thick gray cardboard, 80x100mm, black *2,000*

341-E1

342-E1

Design size: 19x22mm
Photograph of wash drawing of entire design with "50 CENTS 50" drawn in black and white wash. Ms. "Oct. 7-08. J.E.R.-GVLM" (BEP director, PMG) at bottom of backing card.

341-E1 50c Retouched photo on thick gray cardboard, 80x100mm, black *2,000*

Design size: 19x22mm
Photograph of wash drawing of entire design with "1 DOLLAR 1" drawn in black and white wash. Ms. "Oct. 7-08. J.E.R.-GVLM" (BEP director, PMG) at bottom of backing card.

342-E1 $1 Retouched photo on thick gray cardboard, 80x100mm, black *2,000*

LINCOLN MEMORIAL ISSUE

Design size: 7x8 inches
Photostat of 1980 2c frame design with wash drawing of ribbons and vignette photo of Lincoln's head.

367-E1 Two Cents, Model of Lincoln design, black *1,500*

Photo of No. 367-E1 reduced to stamp size, retouched to highlight hair and beard.

367-E2 Two Cents, Retouched photo, black *1,500.*

367-E3

Design size: 19x22mm

Incomplete engraving of entire design: head, background, ame/date ribbon all unfinished.

67-E3 Two Cents, Die on India, die sunk on card, 148x201mm, carmine *3,500.*

ALASKA-YUKON-PACIFIC EXPOSITION ISSUE

Design size: 18½x22mm
Wash drawing of frame similar to 1908 2c design with photo of wash drawing of seal on ice cake as vignette. Ms. "#1" at UL corner of backing card.

370-E1 2c Model on card, about 3x4 inches, black *1,500.*

370-E2

Design size: 18½x22mm
Engraved frame similar to 1908 2c but with wash drawing of "1870 1909" in ribbons and "2 CENTS 2" at bottom, vignette cut out, mounted over engraved vignette of Wm. H. Seward from snuff stamp. Ms. "#2" at UL corner of backing card.

370-E2 2c Model on card, about 3x4 inches, black *1,500.*

370-E3

Design size: 27½x20½mm
Photo of seal on ice cake vignette as originally approved, mounted on ink and wash drawing of frame design as approved. Ms. "#3" at UL corner of backing card, engraved Seward vignette pasted on at bottom, "Approved April 3, 1909 FH Hitchcock Postmaster-General" at right.

370-E3 2c Model on glazed card, 93x70mm, black, white and gray *2,250.*

370-E4

Design size: 27½x20mm
Photo of wash drawing of frame and arched ribbon as adopted, vignette cut out, mounted over photo of engraved Seward vignette, background retouched with black wash. Ms. "Approved subject to addition of the name Seward, as indicated in letter of Director, Bureau of Engraving and Printing, dated April 24, 1909. F.H. Hitchcock Postmaster General."

370-E4 2c Model on 93x75mm thick gray card, black *2,250.*

370-E5

Design size: 27x20mm
Retouched photo of wash drawing of adopted frame with seal on ice cake vignette but pencil "WILLIAM H. SEWARD" on white wash ribbon below. Ms. "April 26/09 Approved J.E.R." (BEP director) at LR corner of backing card.

370-E5 2c Retouched photo and pencil on 94x66mm thick gray card, black *2,000.*

Incomplete engraving of entire design: no shading on head or vignette background, no shading lines on ribbons.

370-E6 2c Die on India, die sunk on 8x6 inch card, carmine *2,000.*

370-E7

Design size: 26½x19½mm
Similar to No. 370-E6 but further engraved: face and collar lightly engraved, horiz. background lines only, no shading lines on ribbons.

370-E7 2c Die on wove, 32x26½mm, carmine *2,000.*

372-E1

Wash drawing of adopted vignette design.

372-E1 2c Drawing on artist's cardboard, 11¼x6¾ inches, black *1,500.*

372-E2

Wash drawing of frame design as adopted except "HUDSON-FULTON CENTENARY" at top.

372-E2 2c Drawing on artist's cardboard, 7¾x6¾ inches, black *1,500.*

Design size: 33x21½mm
Wash drawing of frame design as adopted with dates "1609-1807" and photo of No. 372-E1 reduced to fit and worked over with wash.

372-E3 2c Model on card, 4x3 inches, black *2,000.*

Design size: 33x21½mm
Wash drawing of frame with vignette cut out, mounted over photo of No. 372-E1. Typed/ms. "Approved August 17, 1909 F.H. Hitchcock Postmaster General" and "August 19, 1909 Amend by substituting word 'Celebration' for 'Centenary.' F.H. Hitchcock Postmaster General." Pencil "P.O. 488" in LR corner.

372-E4 2c Model on white card, 129x103mm, black *2,000.*

372-E5

Incomplete engraving of entire design: lettering on flag at masthead of *Clermont* has "N" reversed and no "T."

372-E5 2c Die on wove, 38x27mm, carmine *2,000.*

PANAMA-PACIFIC ISSUE

397-E1

Design size: 27x20mm
Photo of incomplete frame with overlay of circular photo vignette as adopted, with wash drawing of palm trees on each side and "1 CENT 1" in wash. Ms. "Approved July 16, 1912 Frank H. Hitchcock Postmaster General" on backing card.

397-E1 1c Model on card, about 89x77mm, black *1,500.*

Design size: 27x20mm
Photo of incomplete frame with overlay circular photo vignette as adopted, with wash drawing of palm trees on each side and "1 CENT 1" in wash, with "Approved" and signed by the BEP Director J.E. Ralph, but "Opening of Panama Canal 1913" later changed for stamp to "San Francisco 1913."

397-E2 1c Model on thick gray card, 106x86mm, black *1,500.*

398-E1

Design size: about 29½x20mm
Ink and wash drawing of frame design longer than adopted with photo of wash drawing of Golden Gate as eventually used (reduced) on 5c. Backstamp "STAMP DIVISION FEB. 12, 1912 P.O. DEPT" on backing card.

398-E1 2c Model on card, about 4x3 inches, black *1,500.*

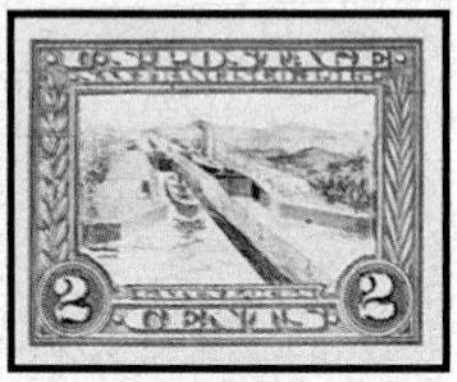

398-E2

Design size: 27x20mm
Photo of incomplete frame with photo of wash drawing of vignette as adopted with title "GATUN LOCKS," wash drawing of value numerals. Ms. "Approved Aug. 27, 1912 Frank H. Hitchcock Postmaster General" on backing card.

398-E2 2c Model on thick gray card, 99x72mm, black *1,500.*

Very similar to No. 398-E2 with slightly different wash touch-up and "2"s, with "Approved" and signed by BEP Director J.E. Ralph.

398-E2A 2c Model on thick gray card, 107x86mm, black *1,500.*

398-E3

Completely engraved design as adopted except titled "GATUN LOCKS" in error (design pictures Pedro Miguel locks).

398-E3 2c
- ***a.*** Large die on India, die sunk on card, 202x152mm, carmine *10,000.*
- ***b.*** Small die on India (formerly #398AP2), carmine *6,000.*

398-E4

Design size: 27x20mm
Photo of incomplete engraving (no sky in vignette) with "GATUN LOCKS" in error, ms. "Approved Dec. 17, 1912 Frank Hitchcock Postmaster General" on backing card.

398-E4 2c Model on thick gray card, 97x74mm, black *1,500.*

399-E1

Design size: 27x20mm
Photo of wash drawing of frame design as adopted with photo of wash drawing of adopted vignette mounted in place, with additional hand touch-up done in wash on vignette, ms. "Approved July 16, 1912 Frank H., Hitchcock Postmaster General" on backing card.

399-E1 5c Model on 30x22mm white paper, mounted on card, 97x73mm, black *1,500.*

Very similar to No. 399-E1 with slightly different wash touch-up and no steamship below sun, with "Approved" and signed by BEP Director J.E. Ralph.

399-E2 5c Model on thick gray card, 106x86mm, black *1,500.*

400-E1

Design size: 27x20mm
Photo of wash drawing of frame design as adopted with photo of painting adopted for vignette mounted in place, ms. printed "Approved" and dated and signed " Aug. 22, 1912, Frank H. Hitchcock Postmaster General" on backing card.

400-E1 10c Model on 31x34mm white paper, on thick gray card, 98x73mm, black *1,500.*

Very similar to No. 400-E1 with more extensive touching-up of the vignette and frame, with "Approved" and signed by BEP Director J.E. Ralph.

400-E1A 10c Model on thick gray card, 107x86mm, black *1,500.*

Design size: 27x20mm
Photo of wash drawing of frame design as adopted with photo of wash drawing of two galleons at anchor in bay, titled "CABRILLO 1542" mounted in place. Backing card marked "II."

400-E2 10c Model on white paper, on 91x85mm thick gray card, black *1,500.*

400-E3

Design size: 27x20mm
Photo of wash drawing of frame design as adopted with photo of Liberty standing among palm fronds, wash touch-up on vignette and "10" denominations drawn in black and white wash, two battleships in bay. Backing card marked "III."

400-E3 10c Model on white paper, on thick gray card, 90x84mm, black *1,500.*

400-E4

Design size: 27x20mm
Similar to No. 400-E3 but steamships replace battleships. Backing card marked "IV."

400-E4 10c Model on white paper, on thick gray card, 90x83mm, black *1,500.*

400-E5

Design size: 27x20mm
Similar to No. 400-E2 but different hand drawn vignette picturing two galleons under full sail in front of snowclad mountains. Backing card marked "V."

400-E5 10c Model on white paper, on thick gray card, 89x83mm, black *1,500.*

1912 ISSUE

Incomplete engraving of entire design: wash drawing of "1 CENT 1" at bottom. Ms. "Approved. July 17, 1911 Frank H. Hitchcock. P.M. Gen." on backing card.

405-E1 1c Model on 3½x3¾-inch card, black *5,750.*

406-E1

Incomplete engraving of , except value tablet area which is "2 CENTS 2" at bottom drawn in wash. Ms. "Approved. July 17, 1911 Frank H. Hitchcock P. M. Gen." on backing card.

406-E1 2c Model on 3⅜x3 11/16-inch card, black —

Wash drawing of design as adopted, worked over partial photo with 8 in lower corners drawn in wash. Ms. "Approved. July 17, 1911 Frank H. Hitchcock Postmaster General" on backing card.

414-E1 8c Model on 3½x3¾-inch card, black —

414-E2

Vignette of head only without background gridwork, control #490311 on back of card.

414-E2 8c Die on India, die sunk on 152x202mm, olive green *2,250.*

416-E1

418-E1

Design size: 19x22mm
Photo of wash drawing of generic design with 10 in lower corners drawn in black ink. Ms. "July 17, 1911. (May, 1911 erased) Approved: Frank H. Hitchcock PM Gen" on backing card, backstamped "STAMP DIVISION P.O. DEPT. MAY 15, 1911."

416-E1 10c Model on 87x113mm thick gray card, black *1,000.*

Design size: 19x22mm
Photo of wash drawing of generic design with background of frame between oval and outer colorless line in dark gray wash and some colorless retouching, 15 in lower corners drawn in black ink. Ms. "July 17, 1911. (May, 1911 erased) Approved: Frank H. Hitchcock PM Gen" on backing card, backstamped "STAMP DIVISION P.O. DEPT. MAY 15, 1911."

418-E1 15c Model on 87x113mm thick gray card, black *1,000.*

421-E1

423-E1

Design size: 19x22mm
Photo of wash drawing of generic design with 50 in lower corners drawn in black ink. Ms. "July 17, 1911. (May, 1911 erased) Approved: Frank H. Hitchcock PM Gen" on backing card, backstamped "STAMP DIVISION P.O. DEPT. MAY 15, 1911."

421-E1 50c Model on 77x112mm thick gray card, black *1,000.*

Design size: 19x22mm
Photo of wash drawing of generic design with entire value label drawn in black ink. Ms. "July 17, 1911. (May, 1911 erased) Approved: Frank H. Hitchcock PM Gen" on backing card, backstamped "STAMP DIVISION P.O. DEPT. MAY 15, 1911."

423-E1 $1 Model on 87x113mm thick gray card, black *1,000.*

1916 PRECANCEL ESSAYS

499-E1

Design size: 19x22mm
Die size: 90x88mm
"NEW YORK/N.Y." precancel engraved directly onto type I die, printed in one color. Ms. "8/16/22 J.S." in LR corner of backing card on No. 499-E1a. Although dated 1922, records indicate an original proof was pulled in 1916.

499-E1 2c
a. Die on India, die sunk on card, lake —
b. Die on bond paper, 33x36mm, dark carmine —

1918 ISSUE

Complete engraving of Franklin head only as on $2 and $5 values, no shading around head, control #834424 on back of card.

523-E2 $2 Die on India, die sunk on 151x103mm card, black *1,750.*

523-E3

Design size: 16x18¾mm
Complete engraving of vignette only including shading. Pencil control # "837660 May 1917" on back of India paper, pencil "Schofield" at bottom of backing card (#523-E3a), or control #837662 (1917) on back of card (No. 523-E3b).

523-E3 $2
a. Die on 32x33mm India, card mounted, black 1,000.
b. Die on wove, die sunk on card, 203x151mm, black 1,000.

PEACE ISSUE

537-E1

537-E2

Design size: 21½x18½mm
Stamp never issued due to World War I.

537-E1 2c
a. Die on India, die sunk on card, deep red 1,500.
b. Die on wove, die sunk on card, 201x138mm, signed on card by Harry S. New 4,000.

Die size: 22x19mm

Stamp never issued due to World War I.

537-E2 5c
a. Die on India, die sunk on card, dim dusky g-b-blue 1,500.
b. Die on wove, die sunk on card, 201x138mm, signed on card by Harry S. New 4,000.

SAMUEL F.B. MORSE ISSUE

537-E3

Design size: 21½x18½mm
Incomplete engraving of entire design: vignette and lettering finished but blank spaces beside vignette. Backstamped "932944" and "Jan. 1, 1919" or "932945" and "Jan. 7, 1919". Frame design subsequently used for 3c Victory issue, No. 537, though lettering and value numerals made slightly smaller.

537-E3 3c Die on India, die sunk on card, 141x173mm (#932944) or 151x202mm (#932945), black *3,000.*

VICTORY ISSUE

537-E4

Design size: 21½x18½mm
Die size: 85½x75½mm
Incomplete engraving of entire design: no shading in border and some flags unfinished. Backstamped "936356 Jan. 25, 1919."

537-E4 3c Die on India, die sunk on card, black *1,500.*

PILGRIM ISSUE

548-E1

Design size: 26x19mm
Incomplete engraving of entire design: sky blank, sails unshaded.

548-E1 1c Die on India, die sunk on card, 201x151mm, green *1,600.*

PILGRIM ISSUE

Almost complete engraving of entire design as adopted, but no crosshatching behind the "1" denominations.

548-E2 1c Die on India, die sunk on card, 203x151mm, green *1,600.*

549-E1

Incomplete engraving of frame only: "CENTS" engraved but numeral circles blank (probably an essay for the 2c and 5c).

549-E1 Die on India, die sunk on card
black *1,600.*
green *1,600.*

549-E2

Design size: 26x19mm
Incomplete engraving of entire design: vignette unfinished, control #1063097 on back of card.

549-E2 2c Die on India, die sunk on card, 202x151mm, black *1,600.*

Incomplete engraving of entire design, virtually complete but no crosshatching behind the numeral "2" denominations.

549-E3 2c
a. Die on India, die sunk on card, 202x151mm, control #1063875 on back, black 1,600.
b. Die on India, die sunk on card, 202x151mm, control #1064174 or #1064271 on back, carmine rose 1,600.

1922 ISSUE

551-E1

Design size: 19x22mm
Incomplete engraving of entire design as adopted: name label blank, vignette unfinished. Ms. "Approved--Harry S. New" on backing card on olive brown essay; others not signed but with notation of denomination of stamp for color used ("1c" for green, etc.)

551-E1 ½c Die on India, die sunk on 151x202mm card

olive brown	*3,000.*
green	*2,500.*
carmine	*2,500.*
orange	*2,500.*
rose	*2,500.*
yellow	*2,500.*
blue green	*2,500.*
yellow green	*2,500.*
carmine rose	*2,500.*

Incomplete engraving of entire design but further engraved than No. 551-E1: no lines in white oval over ends of title ribbon and ribbon foldunders not etched as darkly as on issued stamp.

551-E2 ½c Die on India, die sunk on 149x201mm card, olive brown *1,500.*

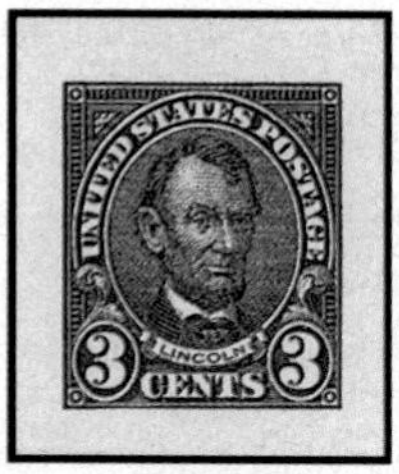

555-E2

Complete engraving with horizontal lines surrounding bust of Lincoln.

555-E2 3c Die on India, affixed to card, 26x30mm, violet *2,750.*

560-E1

Complete engraving with background of cross-hatched lines surrounding slightly larger bust of Grant.

560-E1 8c Die on India, die sunk on 97x111mm card, dark olive green *2,000.*

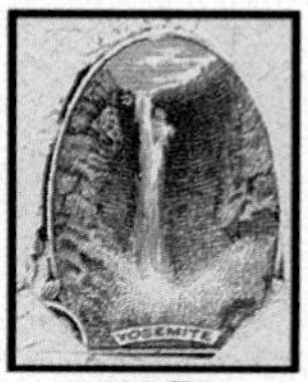

567-E2

568-E2

Design size: 19x22mm
Engraving of unadopted vignette with unadopted engraved frame cut away.

567-E2 20c Die on India, die sunk on 151x201mm card, cobalt blue *1,750.*

Design size: 19x15mm
Die size: 88x75mm
Engraving of adopted vignette with engraved frame cut away.

568-E2 25c Die on India, die sunk on 202x151mm card, green *1,750.*

Pencil drawings for unadopted frame design.

555-E1	3c black	*1,150.*
557-E1	5c black	*1,150.*
557-E2	5c black	*1,150.*
566-E1	15c black	*1,150.*
571-E1	$1 black	*1,150.*

573-E1

Engraving of accepted vignette.

573-E1 $5 Die on India, affixed to card, 73x87mm, blue *3,750.*

HUGUENOT-WALLOON TERCENTENARY ISSUE

614-E1

Design size: 8½x7¼ inches
Preliminary pencil drawing of *Nieu Nederland* in circular frame. Pencil note: "Reverse--Sailing to America, not away from America--J. B. Stoudt" originally on drawing has been removed.

614-E1 1c black *1,000.*

Incomplete engraving of entire design, background of vignette incomplete and central figures only roughed in.

615-E1 2c Die on India, 82x69mm, black *4,500.*

616-E1

Design size: 5½x3⅛ inches
Wash drawing of design adopted for vignette.

616-E1 5c black *1,500.*

Almost complete engraving of entire design, lacking strong shading in the foreground of the vignette.

617-E1 5c Die on India, die sunk on card, 126x115mm, green *1,500.*

618-E1

Design size: 36x21mm
Incomplete engraving of entire design as adopted: spaces between letters of "BIRTH OF LIBERTY" not solid color.

618-E1 2c Die on India, die sunk on card, carmine *1,250.*

Design size: 36x21mm
Incomplete engraving of entire design as adopted: numeral circles blank, many shading lines missing in vignette, no shading around "TWO CENTS," etc.

618-E2 2c Die on India, die sunk on 91x71mm card, black *1,500.*

Design size: 36x21mm
Engraving of frame only, without vignette or value tablets, control #1317765 on back of card.

618-E3 2c Die on India, die sunk on card, 202x118mm, carmine *1,500.*

ERICSSON MEMORIAL ISSUE

Wash drawing of design as adopted, stamp size.

628-E1 5c black *750.*

BATTLE OF WHITE PLAINS ISSUE

629-E1

Design size: 8⅜x9 inches
Preliminary ink and watercolor drawing of entire design quite similar to that adopted.

629-E1 2c black & red *750.*

BURGOYNE CAMPAIGN ISSUE

644-E1

Design size: 22x19mm
Essay size: 25x22mm
Card size: 78x98mm
Photo of wash drawing of unadopted design, on white paper mounted on thick gray card with "Approved" in ink and "May 7, 1927" in pencil subsequently crossed out with "X's."

644-E1 2c black *1,500.*

683-E1

Design size: 13x17 inches
Preliminary ink drawing of design nearly as adopted.

683-E1 2c Drawing on artist's cardboard, black *500.*

American flag and pencil touch-up of outer frame on photo of artist's model with vignette as adopted but entirely different frame.

690-E1 2c black *400.*

702-E1

Engraving of entire design without red cross, engraved cross shows faintly, control #70015 on back of card.

702-E1 2c Die on India, die sunk on 120x142mm card, black *5,000.*

704-E1

Design size: 119x150mm
Preliminary pencil sketch of unadopted ½c design.

704-E1 ½c Drawing on tracing paper, mounted on 195x192mm manila paper, black *1,250.*

718-E1

Design size: 6x7 inches
Watercolor drawing of unadopted design with 2c denomination.

718-E1 2c Drawing on thick artist's card, red *1,250.*

719-E1

Design size: 6x7 inches
Watercolor drawing of entire design similar to that eventually adopted for 5c but with 2c denomination.

719-E1 2c Drawing on thick artist's card, 150x175mm, blue *1,250.*

Engraving of vignette as adopted, within frame, but reversed from final design, without denomination or inscriptions.

742-E1 3c Die on white card, 88x69mm, black *1,750.*

Unadopted engraving of entire design without denomination, portraits as adopted but rest of design different from accepted design, control #70027 on back of card.

786-E1 2c Die on wove, die sunk on card, 202x153mm, carmine *1,500.*

Engravings of Decatur and MacDonough as adopted, widely spaced.

791-E1 2c Die on wove, die sunk on card, 202x153mm, carmine *1,500.*

Engraving of incomplete design without central vignette, control #491747 (1936) on back of card.

791-E2 2c Die on wove, die sunk on card, 198x136mm, carmine *1,500.*

Unfinished engravings of three portraits only, control #70031 on back.

793-E1 4c Die on wove, die sunk on card, 202x153mm, red brown *1,500.*

Engraving of entire design, lacks crosshatching in the shading of background.

899-E1 1c Die on wove, die sunk on card, 140x162mm, green *1,000.*

Engraving of frame as adopted, with "84075" at top and "United States of America" at bottom of die impression, stamped "For Approval" at top of card, signed and dated by four individuals on card.

909-921-E1 5c Die on India, die sunk on card, 227x151mm, violet *3,000.*

Unadopted design showing steamship under sail, without denomination or background shading, handstamp "Engraver's Stock Proof/Authorized by," initials, "Brooks" (the engraver) in pencil and control #818347A all on back of stamp.

923-E1 3c Die on wove, die sunk on card, 201x152mm, violet *1,500.*

Unfinished engraving of adopted design, lacking smoke from the smokestack and background shading. "Modeling" handstamp and control #818995A on back of card.

923-E2 3c Die on wove, die sunk on card, 201x150mm, violet *1,500.*

Engraved vignette as adopted, "Engraver's Stock Proof/Authorized by," initials, "Brooks" (the engraver) in pencil and control #867263A all on back of stamp.

930-933-E2 Die on wove, die sunk on card, 202x151mm, black *1,500.*

PANAMA CANAL ISSUE

856-E1

Design size: 37x21½mm
Essay size: 99x81mm
Card size: 141x117mm
Engraving of unadopted design: "3 CENTS 3" and "25th ANNIVERSARY PANAMA CANAL" changed for final design. "W. O. Marks" at lower right corner, "Engraver's Stock Proof 594256 / Authorized by 'OML'" on reverse.

856-E1 3c Die on India, die sunk on card, deep violet —

1016-E1

Engraving of adopted design, except "c" cut in design at right where cross should be printed (held in place by tape on back); "Engraver's Stock Proof, Authorized by," initials and blue "103120B" control number on back.

1016-E1 3c Die on wove, die sunk on card, 202x152mm, deep blue *2,500.*

1140-E1

Drawing, similar to issued design but with different symbol at left and different signature of Benjamin Franklin, signed by Frank V. Conley (designer of Credo issue).

1140-E1 4c Drawing on tracing paper, 129x81mm, red, blue and white ink *1,000.*

AIR POST STAMPS

1918 ISSUE

Complete engraving of frame only as adopted. Backstamped "626646A ENGRAVER'S STOCK PROOF AUTHORIZED BY" (signature), plus pencil "663" and "Weeks" (?).

C3-E1 24c Die on India, die sunk on card, deep carmine *5,000.*

Incomplete engraving of entire design as adopted: unfinished plumes above value numerals and no serial number on biplane.

C3-E2 24c Die on wove, 40x37mm, black vignette, blue frame —

Engraving of adopted design except without denomination, "C" punch where denominations go, control #722657A (1942) on back of card.

C25-C31-E1 Die on wove, die sunk on card, 201x150mm, black *5,500.*

SPECIAL DELIVERY STAMPS

1885 ISSUE
American Bank Note Co.

E1-E1

Incomplete engraving of entire design as adopted: ornaments missing at each side of "SPECIAL," line under messenger is in pencil, shading on left side of messenger tablet missing, leaves and vert. background lines unfinished (latter shaded over with pencil).

E1-E1 10c Die on India, dim dusky g-b. green *2,500.*

1888 ISSUE

No. E1P1 with "AT ANY OFFICE" drawn in wash on small piece of thin paper and mounted over "AT A SPECIAL / DELIVERY / OFFICE." Pencil "any post office" and ms. "At once O.K. / J.C.M. 14 Aug. 86" (?) on backing card.

E2-E1 10c Die on India, on card, black *2,500.*

1908 ISSUE
Bureau of Engraving and Printing

E7-E1

Design size: about 8½x7⅛ inches
Preliminary ink and pencil drawing of entire design somewhat similar to that adopted: ("V.S." for U.S. and other minor changes).

E7-E1 10c Drawing on vellum, black *750.*

E7-E2

Design size: about 8½x7⅛ inches
Preliminary ink and pencil drawing of entire design nearly as adopted: ("V.S." for U.S.)

E7-E2 10c Drawing on white drawing paper, black *750.*

E7-E3

Design size: 213½x179mm
Similar to No. E7-E2 but with "U.S."

E7-E3 10c Drawing on white drawing paper, black *750.*

E7-E4 E7-E5

Design size: 26x21½mm
Woodblock size: 45x42mm
Woodblock of entire design as adopted with about 5mm colorless border outside design, solid color beyond, engraved on wood by Giraldon of Paris. (One exists with ms. "Wood cut made in Paris by Mr. Whitney Warren — The cuts and the impression therefrom were turned over to the Director of the Bureau of Engraving & Printing, and by him turned over to the Custodian of Dies, Rolls and Plates and given No. 446. They are now held by the Custodian." Another has typewritten "Prints made in Paris, France, from a wood-cut engraving by an unknown engraver from a design made by Mr. Whitney Warren, architect, of New York City." with ms. "Compliments J.E. Ralph" director of B.E.P. and pencil date "9/7/1917.")

Ridgeway numbers used for colors of Nos. E7-E4 and E7-E5.

E7-E4 10c
- ***a.*** Woodcut on 19g/2 yellowish wove
  - 43k/1 dim dark green blue *450.*
  - 44m/2 dull dusky m. g-blue *450.*
  - 45j/1 dim v. dark b-g-blue *450.*
  - 45m/1 dim dusky b-g-blue *450.*
- ***b.*** Woodcut on 19f/2 dull faint y-o-yellow wove
  - 43k/1 dim dark g-blue *450.*
  - 43m/1 dim dusky g-blue *450.*
  - 44k/1 dim dark m. g-blue *450.*
  - 44k/2 dull dark m. g-blue *450.*
  - 45m/1 dim dusky b-g-blue *450.*
  - 45m/2 dull dusky b-g-blue *450.*
- ***c.*** Woodcut on 19g/2 dull v. faint y-o-yellow wove
  - 43k/1 dim dark g-blue *450.*
  - 43m/1 dim dusky g-blue *450.*

Design size: 26x21½mm
Complete engraving of entire design fairly similar to that adopted but with minor differences.

E7-E5 10c
- ***a.*** Die on India, die sunk on card, 37m/0 dusky g-b. green blue *750.*
- ***b.*** Die on soft white wove, 30x35mm, 37m/0 dusky g-blue-green *750.*

REGISTRATION STAMP

F1-E1

Design size: 19x22½mm
Retouched circular photo of vignette mounted on wash drawing of frame design as adopted. Ms. "Approved July 8/11 — Frank H. Hitchcock — Postmaster General" on backing card.

F1-E1 10c Model on white paper, mounted on thick gray cardboard, 81x92mm, black *1,250.*

POSTAGE DUE STAMPS

1879 ISSUE
American Bank Note Co.

J1-E1

Design size: 19½x25½mm
Die size: 54x66½mm
Complete engraving of entire design as adopted except "UNPAID POSTAGE" instead of "POSTAGE DUE" above vignette oval.

J1-E1 1c
a. Die on India, die sunk on card
orange brown *850.*
slate gray *850.*
dark red violet *850.*
dull yellow *850.*
light orange *850.*
red brown *850.*
b. Die on India, cut small (1-4mm)
gray black *400.*
dull red *400.*
dull brown *400.*
dull green *400.*
dull blue *400.*
c. Die on India, cut close (0-1mm)
orange brown *400.*
slate gray *400.*
dark red violet *400.*
dull yellow *400.*
d. Die on ivory glazed paper, die sunk
black *700.*
black brown *700.*
scarlet *700.*
blue *700.*

Design size: 19½x25½mm
Die size: 53½x53½mm
Complete engraving of entire design as adopted except "UNPAID POSTAGE" instead of "POSTAGE DUE" above vignette oval.

J2-E1 2c
a. Die on India, die sunk on card
dark red violet *850.*
black *850.*
b. Die on India, cut small
gray black *400.*
dull red *400.*
dull brown *400.*
dull green *400.*
dull blue *400.*
c. Die on India, cut close
orange brown *400.*
dark red violet *400.*
slate gray *400.*
d. Die on ivory glazed paper, die sunk
black *700.*
black brown *700.*
scarlet *700.*
blue *700.*

Design size: 19½x25½mm
Die size: 53x53mm
Complete engraving of entire design as adopted except "UNPAID POSTAGE" instead of "POSTAGE DUE" above vignette oval.

J3-E1 3c
a. Die on India, die sunk on card, dull yellow *850.*
b. Die on India, cut small
gray black *400.*
dull red *400.*
dull brown *400.*
dull green *400.*
dull blue *400.*
c. Die on India, cut close, dull yellow *400.*
d. Die on ivory glazed paper, die sunk
black *700.*
black brown *700.*
scarlet *700.*
blue *700.*

Design size: 19½x25½mm
Complete engraving of entire design as adopted except "UNPAID POSTAGE" instead of "POSTAGE DUE" above vignette oval.

J4-E1 5c
a. Die on India, die sunk on card, slate gray *850.*
b. Die on India, cut small
gray black *400.*
dull red *400.*
dull brown *400.*
dull green *400.*
dull blue *400.*
c. Die on India, cut close
orange brown *400.*
slate gray *400.*
dark red violet *400.*
dull yellow *400.*
d. Die on ivory glazed paper, die sunk
black *700.*
black brown *700.*
scarlet *700.*
blue *700.*

J4-E2 5c As No. J4-E1 except frame a pencil and wash drawing, vignette engraved numeral and oval lathework numeral cut to shape and pasted over lathework, on thick card (70x88mm) with design notations, brown —

1894 ISSUE
Bureau of Engraving and Printing

J31-E1

J31-E2

Design size: 18½x22½mm
Die size: 50x99mm
Incomplete engraving of entire design: no engraved lines on numeral, lathework unfinished on two inclined spots at each side of numeral.

J31-E1 1c Die on India, die sunk on card, deep claret *1,000.*

Design size: 18½x22½mm
Die size: 50x99mm
Incomplete engraving of entire design: engraved lines on numeral but lathework still unfinished on two inclined spots at each side of numeral.

J31-E2 1c Die on India, die sunk on card, claret *1,000.*

J33-E1

J33-E2

Incomplete engraving of entire design: blank space for numeral with "3" drawn in pencil.

J33-E1 3c Die on India, die sunk on card, black *1,000.*

Incomplete engraving of entire design: no engraved lines on numeral, bottom lettering in pencil only, no hand retouching of lathework around numeral.

J33-E2 3c Die on India, die sunk on card, black *1,000.*

J33-E3

Incomplete engraving of entire design: no engraved lines on numeral.

J33-E3 3c Die on India, die sunk on card, claret *1,000.*

J35-E1

J36-E1

Incomplete engraving of entire design: no engraved lines on numerals.

J35-E1 10c Die on India, die sunk on card, black *1,000.*

Incomplete engraving of entire design: no engraved lines on numerals.

J36-E1 30c Die on India, die sunk on card, claret *1,000.*

J37-E1

J37-E2

Incomplete engraving of entire design: 9x9mm blank space for numerals.

J37-E1 50c Die on India, die sunk on card
black *1,000.*
claret *1,000.*

Incomplete engraving of entire design: numerals engraved but hand engraving to retouch lathework around numerals missing.

J37-E2 50c Die on India, die sunk on card, black *1,000.*

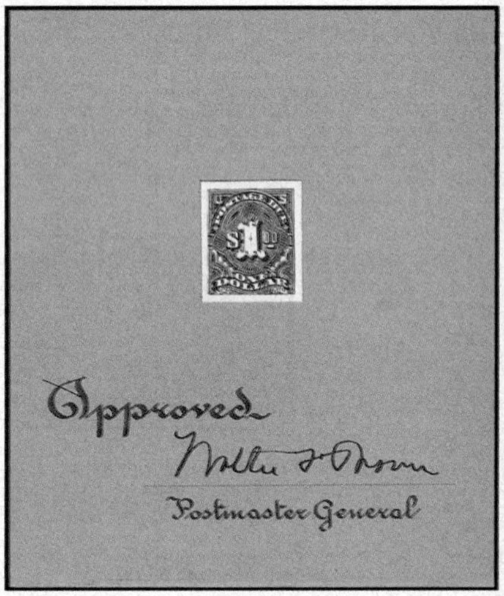

J67-E1

Complete engraving of unissued 1917 denomination, "Approved / Walter F. Brown (signature) / Postmaster General" below design.

J67-E1 $1 Die on white card, mounted on gray card, black *4,500.*

OFFICIAL STAMPS

For additional official essays, see Nos. 145-E10, 146-E10, 147-E10, 148-E13, 149-E5, 151-E10, 152-E4 and 154-E6.

Continental Bank Note Co.
AGRICULTURE

O2-E1

Design size: 20x25mm
Engraved vignette, numeral and value label from 1873 2c (No. 146-E10) mounted on pencil and wash drawing for frame design as adopted for Agriculture set. Pencil signature "J. Claxton" on backing card. Frame differs for each dept.

O2-E1 2c Model on yellowish card, 23x30mm, on 90x118mm white card, black vignette, gray black frame *6,500.*

EXECUTIVE

O12-E1

O12-E2

Design size: 20x25mm
See design note for No. O2-E1.

O12-E1 3c Model on yellowish card, 23x30mm, on 90x118mm white card, black *6,000.*

Design size: 19½x25mm
Die size: 64x76mm
Engraving of complete design of No. O12-E1 with "DEP'T" in op label.

O12-E2 3c
- ***a.*** Die on India, die sunk on card, green *2,750.*
- ***b.*** Die on India, cut close
  - black *2,250.*
  - green *2,250.*

INTERIOR

O17-E1

Design size: 20x25mm
See design note for No. O2-E1.

O17-E1 3c Model on yellowish card, 23x30mm, on 90x118mm white card, black *9,000.*

JUSTICE

O27-E1

Design size: 20x25mm
See design note for No. O2-E1.

O27-E1 3c Model on yellowish card, 23x30mm, on 90x118mm white card, black *10,000.*

NAVY

O37-E1

Design size: 20x25mm
See design note for No. O2-E1.

O37-E1 3c Model on yellowish card, 23x30mm, on 90x118mm white card, black *4,750.*

POST OFFICE

O47-E1

Design size: 19½x25mm
Complete engraving of entire design as adopted except with Franklin vignette instead of large numeral.

O47-E1 1c
- ***a.*** Die on India, mounted on white ivory card
  - blue *1,750.*
- ***b.*** Die on proof paper
  - gray black *1,250.*
  - dull scarlet *1,250.*
  - dull brown *1,250.*
  - dull green *1,250.*
  - dull blue *1,250.*
- ***c.*** Die on ivory glazed paper
  - brown black *1,750.*
  - orange red *1,750.*
  - blue *1,750.*

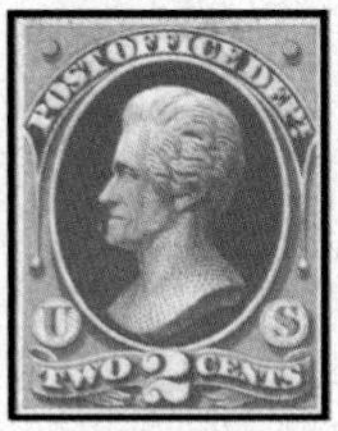

O48-E1

Design size: 19½x25mm
Complete engraving of entire design as adopted except with Jackson vignette instead of large numeral.

O48-E1 2c
- ***a.*** Die on India, mounted on white ivory card
  - orange brown *1,500.*
- ***b.*** Die on proof paper
  - gray black *1,250.*
  - dull scarlet *1,250.*
  - dull brown *1,250.*
  - dull green *1,250.*
  - dull blue *1,250.*
- ***c.*** Die on ivory glazed paper
  - brown black *1,750.*
  - orange red *1,750.*
  - blue *1,750.*

O49-E1

O49-E2

Design size: 20x25mm
Engraved vignette, numeral and value label from 1873 3c (No. 147-E10) mounted on pencil and wash drawing for frame design not adopted for Post Office set.

O49-E1 3c Model on yellowish card, 23x30mm, on 90x118mm white card, black *5,750.*

O49-E2 3c Model on yellowish card, 23x30mm, on 90x118mm white card, black *5,750.*

O49-E3

Design size: 20x25mm
See design note for No. O2-E1.

O49-E3 3c Model on yellowish card, 23x30mm, on 90x118mm white card, black *5,750.*

O49-E4

Design size: 19½x25mm
Complete engraving of entire design as adopted except with Washington vignette instead of large numeral.

O49-E4 3c
- ***a.*** Die on India, mounted on white ivory card
  - green *1,500.*
- ***b.*** Die on proof paper
  - gray black *1,250.*
  - dull scarlet *1,250.*
  - dull brown *1,250.*
  - dull green *1,250.*
  - dull blue *1,250.*
- ***c.*** Die on ivory glazed paper
  - brown black *1,750.*
  - orange red *1,750.*
  - blue *1,750.*

O49-E5

1870 1c stamp (No. 145) with vignette cut out, "OFFICIAL 3 STAMP" drawn in pencil on envelope on which stamp is mounted. Blue pencil notations on backing envelope "1st design of official stamp for POD" and "Design by Mr. J. Barber for P O Official."

O49-E5 1c Stamp frame mounted on envelope, ultramarine frame, black vignette *7,500.*

O49-E6

O49-E8

Model of engraved frame from No. O49-E4 with hollow oval engraved lathework band with "OFFICIAL / STAMP" drawn in wash mounted in place, numeral drawn in pencil and wash. Ms. "No. 1" on backing card.

O49-E6 3c Model on stiff white card, 50x75mm, green 7,500.

Like No. O49-E6, Ms. "No. 3" on backing card.

O49-E8 3c Model on stiff white card, 50x75mm, black *7,500.*

O50-E1

Incomplete engraving of design with Lincoln vignette, without rectangular frame design.

O50-E1 6c Die on white ivory paper, black *4,250.*

O56-E1

Design size: 19½x25mm
Complete engraving of entire design as adopted except with Perry vignette instead of large numeral.

O56-E1 90c
a. Die on India, mounted on white ivory card

brown	*1,500.*
blue	*1,500.*
orange red	*1,500.*

b. Die on proof paper

gray black	*1,500.*
dull scarlet	*1,500.*
dull brown	*1,500.*
dull green	*1,500.*
dull blue	*1,500.*

c. Die on ivory glazed paper

brown black	*1,750.*
orange red	*1,750.*
blue	*1,750.*

STATE

O59-E1

O68-E1

Design size: 20x25mm
Engraved vignette, numeral and value label from 1873 3c (No. 147-E10) mounted on pencil and wash drawing for frame design as adopted for State set. Pencil signature "J. Claxton" on backing card.

O59-E1 3c Model on yellowish card, 23x30mm, on 90x118mm white card, black *4,750.*

Design size: 25½x40mm
Engraved vignette of Seward mounted in watercolor drawing of adopted frame design. Ms. signatures of J. Claxton and Chas. Skinner on backing card.

O68-E1 Two Dollars, Model on 29x43mm grayish white card, mounted on 96x120mm white card, black *7,500.*

O68-E2

Complete engraving of adopted frame only with "TWO DOLLARS." in value label at bottom. With "FIVE DOLLARS." and "TEN DOLLARS." value labels outside design at left and "TWENTY DOLLs." value tablet at right.

O68-E2 Two Dollars, Die on India, black *8,750.*

O68-E3

Plate engraved frame only (three examples in a block of four with complete bicolor plate proof of $2 at upper left in block).

O68-E3 Two Dollars, Plate essay on India, green *10,000.*

O71-E1

Plate engraving of top half of frame only, paired with $20 plate proof.

O71-E1 Die on India, mounted on card, green *9,000.*

WAR

O85-E1

Design size: 20x25mm
Engraved vignette, numeral and value label from 1873 3c (No. 147-E10) mounted on pencil and wash drawing for frame design as adopted for War set. Pencil signature "J. Claxton" on backing card.

O85-E1 3c Model on yellowish card, 23x30mm, on 90x118mm white card, black *2,500.*

NEWSPAPER AND PERIODICALS

1865 ISSUE
National Bank Note Co.

PR1-E1

Design size: 51x89mm
Typographed design somewhat similar to that adopted bu[t] with large Franklin vignette facing left, "PACKAGE" at bottom, other minor differences.

PR1-E1 5c Die on stiff white ivory paper

deep orange red	*2,000*
dusky g-b. blue	*2,000*
bright blue	*2,000*

a. Die on paper with blue ruled lines

deep orange red	*2,000*
carmine	*2,000*

1875 ISSUE
National Bank Note Co.

PR5-E1

Design size: 52x96½mm

Typographed design as issued but lacking "National Bank Note Company, New York" imprint at bottom.

PR5-E1 5c Die on wove paper, blue —

1875 ISSUE
Continental Bank Note Co.

PR9-E1

PR9-E2

Design size: 19½x25mm
Engraved vignette and numerals (25's) with pencil sketch of unadopted frame design.

PR9-E1 25c Die on India, on card, black *2,750.*

Design size: 19½x25mm
Complete engraving of unadopted design with "U S" at top and "25 CENTS 25" at bottom.

PR9-E2 25c
- ***a.*** Die on India, on card
  - black *1,350.*
  - scarlet *1,350.*
  - blue *1,350.*
- ***b.*** Die on white ivory paper
  - black *1,350.*
  - black brown *1,350.*
  - scarlet *1,350.*
  - blue *1,350.*

PR14-E1

PR23-E1

Design size: 25x35mm
Wash drawing of complete design as adopted. Backing card signed by both designers, Chas. Skinner and Jos. Claxton.

PR14-E1 9c Drawing on 26x36mm card, on 56x74mm card, black *900.*

Design size: 24x35½mm
Wash drawing similar to that adopted, backing card signed by designers Skinner and Claxton, also has pencil "$12" and ms. "Continental Bank Note Co."

PR23-E1 96c Drawing on 88x121mm card, black *900.*

PR27-E1

PR28-E1

Design size: 24½x35mm
Incomplete engraving of entire design: unshaded (shading pencilled in) inside left, right and bottom framelines, value label, top of "9." Upper corners unfinished.

PR27-E1 $9 Die on India, die sunk on 76x82mm card, black *1,350.*

Design size: 24½x35mm
Incomplete engraving of entire design: no shading on dollar signs and numerals. No shading on frame around numerals and around value tablet.

PR28-E1 $12 Die on India, die sunk on 66x80mm card, black *1,350.*

Incomplete engraving of entire design, shading pencilled in around bottom value tablet and top right and left dollar signs and numerals.

PR28-E2 $12 Die on India, die sunk on card, 75x90mm, black —

PR29-E1

Design size: 24x35½mm
Wash drawing similar to that adopted but with "U S" in six-pointed stars instead of at top. Backing card signed by designers Skinner and Claxton, also pencil "31/32" and "8 13/32," pencil "Alter" with lines to stars.

PR29-E1 $24 Drawing on 88x121mm card, black *750.*

PR31-E1

PR31-E2

Vignette size: 13½x26mm
Engraved vignette only as adopted.

PR31-E1 $48 Die on India, die sunk on card, black *750.*

Design size: 24x36mm
Wash drawing similar to that adopted, backing card signed by designers Skinner and Claxton, also has pencil "$48" above each value numeral.

PR31-E2 $48 Drawing on 88x121mm card, black *1,350.*

PR32-E1

Design size: 24½x35½mm
Wash drawing similar to that adopted, backing card signed by designers Skinner and Claxton.

PR32-E1 $60 Drawing on 88x121mm card, black *750.*

1885 ISSUE
American Bank Note Co.

PR81-E1

Design size: 23x25mm
Complete engraving of entire design as adopted for 12c-96c.

PR81-E1 1c
- ***a.*** Die on India, die sunk on card
  - black *1,350.*
- ***b.*** Die on white ivory paper
  - black *600.*
  - black brown *600.*
  - scarlet *600.*
  - blue *600.*

1895 ISSUE
Bureau of Engraving and Printing

Incomplete engraving of entire design: background at upper ends of value label, shading on side lettering and numerals missing.

PR102-E2 1c Die on India, die sunk on card
- black *900.*
- green *1,250.*

Incomplete engraving of entire design but further engraved than No. PR102-E2: shading on PA is light, no shading on PE of NEWSPAPERS or IO of PERIODICALS and shading on OD is light.

PR102-E3 1c Die on India, die sunk on card, black *900.*

Incomplete engraving of entire design but further engraved than No. PR102-E3: shading on PERIODICALS is finished but not on PAPE.

PR102-E4 1c Die on India, die sunk on card, black *900.*

PR103-E1

PR103-E2

Design size: 21½x34½mm
Die size: 56x75½mm
Incomplete engraving of entire design: spaces for numerals and value label blank but with pencil outline of lettering.

PR103-E1 2c Die on India, die sunk on card, black *1,750.*

Incomplete engraving of entire design but further engraved than No. PR103-E1: shading on leaves at ends of value label unfinished, numerals unshaded, unfinished shading on APE of NEWSPAPERS and RIO of PERIODICALS.

PR103-E2 2c Die on India, black *1,250.*

Incomplete engraving of entire design but further engraved than No. PR103-E2: no shading on PE of NEWSPAPERS, unfinished shading on PA of NEWSPAPERS and RIO of PERIODICALS.

PR103-E3 2c Die on India, die sunk on card, black *1,250.*

PR104-E1

Design size: 21½x34½mm
Die size: 57x73mm
Incomplete engraving of entire design: spaces for numerals and value label blank but with pencil outline of lettering.

PR104-E1 5c Die on India, die sunk on card, black *1,500.*

PR105-E1

PR105-E2

Design size: 21½x34½mm
Die size: 56x75mm
Incomplete engraving of entire design: spaces for numerals and value label blank but with pencil outline of lettering.

PR105-E1 10c Die on India, die sunk on card, black *1,500.*

Incomplete engraving of entire design but further engraved than No. PR105-E1: numerals unfinished, lower corners blank.

PR105-E2 10c Die on India, die sunk on card, black *1,500.*

Incomplete engraving of entire design but further engraved than No. PR105-E2: lower right corner blank.

PR105-E3 10c Die on India, die sunk on card, black *1,250.*

Incomplete engraving of entire design but further engraved than No. PR105-E3: numerals blank, no inner lines.

PR105-E4 10c Die on India, die sunk on card, black *1,250.*

PR105-E5

Design size: 21½x34½mm
Die size: 56x75mm
Incomplete engraving of entire design (early state of die similar to No. PR105-E1) with "10" pencilled in upper right corner and "TEN CENTS" pencilled in at bottom. Pencil notes on India include "Make top of 1 a little larger and put on spur," "Work up Vignette" and "Use same scrolls as marked on 5c-."

PR105-E5 10c Die on India, die sunk on card, black *2,750.*

PR106-E1

PR106-E2

Vignette size: 13x25½mm
Die size: 56x72mm
Incomplete engraving of vignette only (transfer of Continental Banknote Co. die for 72c with left side cut off): eagle crest faces front and its right wing is not pointed, shading on left thigh near sword hilt incomplete, bottom of vignette straight instead of curved.

PR106-E1 25c Die on India, die sunk on card
black *2,250.*
deep red *2,250.*

Design size: about 21x34½mm
Die size: 57½x75mm
Entire design with frame incompletely engraved: vert. lines around CENTS label missing, no shading on TWENTY FIVE, colorless beads under E and FI of same.

PR106-E2 25c Die on India, die sunk on card
black *2,250.*
deep red *2,250.*

An impression from No. PR106-E2 with pencil shading on TWENTY FIVE and vert. ink lines in spaces around CENTS label, colorless beads also blacked out in ink. Below engraving are three diff. pencil sketches for shape and shading to be engraved.

PR106-E3 25c Die on India, die sunk on card, black *2,250.*

An impression from No. PR106-E2 but with shading suggestions from No. PR106-E3 partly engraved except colorless beads have pencil shading only. Below engraving is pencil sketch for corner of CENTS label.

PR106-E4 25c Die on India, die sunk on card
black *2,250.*
deep red *2,000.*

PR106-E5

Design size: 21½x34½mm
Die size: 55x72mm
Large die proof of PR107 with bottom value label cut out and "TWENTY-FIVE CENTS" pencilled in on backing card.

PR106-E5 25c Die on India, die sunk on card, black *1,500.*

PR107-E1

PR107-E3

Incomplete engraving of entire design: eagle's head and much of bottom of stamp's design unfinished, top of frame unfinished, value lettering sketched in pencil.

PR107-E1 50c Die on India, die sunk on card, black *1,750.*

Incomplete engraving of entire design: top of frame and scrolls below FIFTY CENTS unfinished.

PR107-E3 50c Die on India, die sunk on card, black *1,500.*

PR108-E1

PR108-E2

Design size: 24½x37mm
Die size: 75x76mm
Incomplete engraving of entire design: vignette and spaces around numerals incomplete, pencil sketch instructions for engraver at top and side for these spaces.

PR108-E1 $2 Die on India, die sunk on card, black *1,650.*

Design size: 24½x37mm
Die size: 75x76mm
Incomplete engraving of entire design but further engraved than No. PR108-E1: space for ornaments under POSTAGE blank, numerals unshaded.

PR108-E2 $2 Die on India, die sunk on card, scarlet *1,500.*

Further engraved than No. PR108-E2: scrolls under POSTAGE engraved but unfinished.

PR108-E3 $2 Die on India, die sunk on card, black *1,500.*

Incomplete engraving of design, no frame line under "Postage" and other small differences from final design.

PR110-E1 $10 Die on India, green *1,500.*

PR111-E1

PR112-E1

Design size (incomplete): 24½x30mm
Die size: 75x84mm
Incomplete engraving of partial design: spaces for stars and 0s of numerals blank, design missing below bottom of vignette.

PR111-E1 $20 Die on India, die sunk on card, black *1,850.*

Design size: 24½x35½mm
Die size: 72½x76mm
Incomplete engraving of entire design: upper corners around value numerals unfinished, etc.

PR112-E1 $50 Die on India, on card, black *1,850.*

PR113-E1

Design size: 24½x35½mm
Die size: 75x74mm
Incomplete engraving of entire design: spaces at lower inner corners of value shields blank, shading on numerals and letters at top unfinished.

PR113-E1 $100 Die on India, on card, black *1,350.*

Further engraved than No. PR113-E1: vignette completed but numerals not shaded, shadows on frame not etched dark.

PR113-E2 $100 Die on India
black *1,350.*
red-violet *1,350.*

Further engraved than No. PR113-E2: numerals shaded, shadows on frame not finally etched, especially above POSTAGE.

PR113-E3 $100 Die on India, black *1,350.*

PARCEL POST STAMPS

Q1-E1

Design size: 35½x23mm
Photo of wash drawing of frame design with numerals, CENT and POST OFFICE CLERK in black ink, vignette in black wash. Ms. "Changed from 15c" and "Approved Nov. 15, 1912 — Frank H. Hitchcock — Postmaster General" on backing card.

Q1-E1 1c Model on thick gray card, 106x91mm, black *3,000.*

Q2-E1

Design size: 35x23½mm

Photo of wash drawing of frame only as adopted. Ms. 'Approved Oct. 10, 1912, for border and size of stamps. Engraving to be ⅞ by 1⅜ inches. Frank H. Hitchcock. Postmaster General" on backing card.

Q2-E1 2c Model on thick gray cardboard, 122x110mm, black *1,500.*

Q2-E2

Design size: 35x23mm

Photo of wash drawing of frame design and retouched photo of ship vignette as eventually used for 10c, numerals and STEAMSHIP AND MAIL TENDER in black ink. Ms. "Changed to 10c" and "Approved Oct. 11, 1912. Frank H. Hitchcock. Postmaster General" on backing card.

Q2-E2 2c Model on thick gray cardboard, 110x83mm, black *2,500.*

Q2-E3

Design size: 34x22mm

Photo of wash drawing of entire design with adopted vignette, numerals in white wash and CITY CARRIER in black ink. Ms. "Changed from 5c" and "Approved Nov. 14, 1912. Frank H. Hitchcock. Postmaster General" on backing card.

Q2-E3 2c Model on thick gray cardboard, 111x92mm, black *2,500.*

Design size: 34½x22mm

Engraving of adopted design with blank value tablets and "CITY CARRIER" inscription, mail carrier unfinished.

Q2-E4 2c Die on India, sunk on 118x89mm card, black —

Q3-E1

Design size: 35x23mm

Complete engraving of unadopted design: vignette shows mail truck backing up to railroad mail train with clerk about to handle pouches.

Q3-E1 3c Die on white wove, about 43x31mm, carmine *2,000.*

Q3-E2

Design size: 35x22mm

Photo of wash drawing of entire design with adopted vignette (retouched around door to mail car). Ms. "Approved Feb. 22, 1913. Frank H. Hitchcock. Postmaster General" on backing card.

Q3-E2 3c Model on thick gray cardboard, black *2,500.*

Q3-E3

Design size: 35x22mm

Almost complete engraving of adopted design with subtle differences (most evident in shading on windows), on 100x76mm card, affixed with tape to 125x98mm card, small cutout in design, blue control No. 578444 on back.

Q3-E3 3c Die sunk on card, affixed to card, carmine *2,500.*

Q4-E1

Design size: 33½x22mm

Photo of wash drawing of entire design with adopted vignette, numerals drawn in white and RURAL CARRIER in black ink. Ms. "Changed from 10c" and "Approved Nov. 14, 1912. Frank H. Hitchcock. Postmaster General" on backing card.

Q4-E1 4c Model on thick gray cardboard, 116x92mm, black *2,500.*

Q5-E1

Design size: 35x23mm

Photo of wash drawing of entire design with vignette (retouched) eventually used for 2c, numerals and CITY LETTER CARRIER in black ink and white wash. Ms. "Changed to 2c.--City Carrier" and "Approved Oct. 10, 1912. Frank H. Hitchcock. Postmaster General" on backing card.

Q5-E1 5c Model on thick gray cardboard, 110x84mm, black *2,500.*

Q5-E2

Design size: 33½x21½mm

Photo of wash drawing of entire design with numerals in gray, unadopted vignette with MAIL TRAIN in black ink, first car retouched with wash. Ms. "Approved . . . 1912 / . . . Postmaster General" on backing card.

Q5-E2 5c Model on thick gray cardboard, 104½x92mm, black *2,500.*

Q5-E3

Design size: 33½x22mm

Photo of wash drawing of entire design with numerals in gray, MAIL TRAIN in black ink, first car retouched with wash. Ms. "Approved . . . 1912 / . . . Postmaster General" on backing card.

Q5-E3 5c Model on thick gray cardboard, 104½x92mm, black *2,500.*

Q5-E4

Design size: 33½x22mm

Photo of wash drawing of entire design with numerals in white with black background, MAIL TRAIN and pouch catcher in black ink. Ms. "Approved Nov. 19, 1912 Frank H. Hitchcock Postmaster General" on backing card.

Q5-E4 5c Model on thick gray cardboard, 94x90mm, black *2,500.*

Q6-E1

Design size: 35½x23mm

Photo of wash drawing of entire design with vignette (retouched) eventually used for 4c, numerals and RURAL DELIVERY in black ink and white wash. Ms. "Changed to 4c." and "Approved Oct. 10, 1912. Frank H. Hitchcock. Postmaster General" on backing card.

Q6-E1 10c Model on thick gray cardboard, 111x83mm, black *2,500.*

Q6-E2

Design size: 35x23mm

Photo of wash drawing of entire design with adopted vignette, numerals and STEAMSHIP AND MAIL TENDER in black ink and white wash. Ms. "Changed from 2c." and "Approved Nov. 8, 1912. Frank H. Hitchcock. Postmaster General" on backing card.

Q6-E2 10c Model on thick gray cardboard, 116x92mm, black *2,500.*

Q7-E1

Design size: 33½x22mm

Photo of wash drawing of entire design (redrawn in front of autocar and U S MAIL and STATION A) with AUTOMOBILE SERVICE in black ink. Ms. "Approved . . . 1912 / . . . Postmaster General" on backing card.

Q7-E1 15c Model on thick gray cardboard, 115x93mm, black *1,500.*

Design size:

Complete engraving of entire design with unadopted title label "COLLECTION SERVICE" instead of the adopted "AUTOMOBILE SERVICE."

Q7-E2 15c Die on white wove, card mounted, carmine *1,500.*

Q8-E1

Design size: 35x22mm
Incomplete engraved design nearly as adopted: aviator wears football helmet, head tilted far forward and one leg dangling over edge of plane, mail bag "No. 1" at his right while another sack hangs loosely out of plane.

Q8-E1 20c Die on white wove, about 37x24mm, carmine *1,500.*

Q8-E2

Design size: 35x22mm
Photo of incomplete engraved design as adopted. Ms. "Approved Nov. 19, 1912. Frank H. Hitchcock. Postmaster General" on backing card.

Q8-E2 20c Model on thick gray cardboard, 98x95mm, black *2,500.*

Q9-E1

Design size: 34½x22½mm
Photo of wash drawing of entire design with numerals and smoke at right painted in. Ms. "Changed from $1.00." and "Approved Nov. 14, 1912. Frank H. Hitchcock. Postmaster General" on backing card.

Q9-E1 25c Model on thick gray cardboard, 112x92mm, black *2,500.*

Q10-E1

Design size: 35x23mm
Photo of drawing of entire design with vignette eventually used for 25c with roof, smokestacks and smoke drawn in. Typed label "Stamp Division / Feb / 21 / 1912 / P.O. Dept" on back of backing paper.

Q10-E1 50c Model on thick white paper, black *1,500.*

Q10-E2

Design size: 33x21½mm
Photo of wash drawing of frame design with vignette cut out, mounted over photo of wash drawing of unadopted vignette design, retouched with wash on cows, etc., with DAIRYING in black ink. Pencil "Original" and ms. "Approved . . . 1912 / . . . Postmaster General" on backing card.

Q10-E2 50c Model on thick gray cardboard, 98x93mm, black *1,500.*

Q10-E3

Design size: 35x23mm
Complete engraving of entire design with unadopted vignette: silo and barns placed closer to front of design.

Q10-E3 50c Die on white wove, about 43x31mm, carmine *1,750.*

Q10-E4

Design size: 35x22mm
Photo of incomplete engraved design: no vert. lines on frame around corner foliate spandrels or in numeral circles. Ms. "Approved Jan. 8, 1913. Frank H. Hitchcock. Postmaster General" on backing card.

Q10-E4 50c Model on thick gray cardboard, 99x94mm, black *2,500.*

Q11-E1

Design size: 33½x21½mm
Photo of wash drawing of entire design with central horses and thresher retouched. Ms. "Approved Dec. 12, 1912. Frank H. Hitchcock. Postmaster General" on backing card.

Q11-E1 75c Model on thick gray cardboard, 108x89mm, black *2,500.*

Q12-E1

Photo of wash drawing of entire design with vignette much retouched in black ink, numerals, MANUFACTURING and DOLLAR drawn in black ink and white wash. Ms. "Changed to 25c" and "Approved Oct. 22, 1912. Frank H. Hitchcock. Postmaster General" on backing card.

Q12-E1 $1 Model on thick gray cardboard, 114x86mm, black *2,500.*

Q12-E2

Design size: 35x22mm
Photo of wash drawing of complete design with DOLLAR painted in white and black and FRUIT GROWING in black ink, vignette retouched with wash on fruit pickers. Ms. "Approved . . . 1912 . . . Postmaster General" on backing card.

Q12-E2 $1 Model on thick gray cardboard, 105x94mm, black *1,500.*

Q12-E3

Design size: 36x23½mm
Incomplete engraving of entire design: no shading lines in sky. This may be from a rejected die.

Q12-E3 $1 Die on white wove, about 43x31mm, carmine *1,500.*

Q12a-E1

Engraving of entire design as adopted for 1917 offset Documentary Revenues, etc., but with "U.S. PARCEL POST" around value oval.

Q12a-E1 1c Die on card, green *1,000.*
Q12b-E1 2c Die on card, carmine *1,000.*
Q12c-E1 3c Die on card, deep violet *1,000.*
Q12d-E1 4c Die on card, brown *1,000.*
Q12e-E1 5c Die on card, blue *1,000.*
Q12f-E1 10c Die on card, orange yellow *1,000.*
Q12g-E1 15c Die on card, gray *1,000.*
Q12h-E1 20c Die on wove, carmine rose, affixed to card *1,500.*

PARCEL POST POSTAGE DUE

Retouched photo of design as adopted, officially dated and approved.

QJQ5-E1a 25c Model, black *1,500.*

CARRIER'S STAMPS

Essays by Toppan, Carpenter, Casilear & Co. in 1851

LO1-E1

Unfinished die with lathework impinging on white oval and framelines complete at top and bottom, plus uncleaned horizontal and vertical layout lines.

1851

LO1-E1 (1c) Die on 34x42mm, white bond, black *10,000.*

LO1-E1A

Die size: 57x50mm

Unfinished die distinguished by having top and bottom frame nes, lathework impinging on white oval, and rosettes in lower ight corner.

.O1-E1A (1c) Die on 62x54mm, pale green bond, red *4,000.*

Essays by Schernikow in 1903 from a new soft steel die made from the original 1851 transfer roll.

See note above No. 63-E1.

LO1-E2

LO1-E3

Die size: 50x50mm

Engraving of Franklin vignette only.

1903

LO1-E2 (1c)

a. Die on proof paper	
black	*75.*
carmine	*75.*
red	*75.*
light red	*75.*
orange	*75.*
orange brown	*75.*
yellow	*75.*
olive	*75.*
green	*75.*
dark green	*75.*
dark blue	*75.*
violet	*75.*
violet brown	*75.*
b. Die on colored card, about 75x75mm	
deep red, *pinkish white*	*175.*
yellow brown, *pale blue*	*175.*
violet brown, *pale green*	*175.*
dark green, *pale pink*	*175.*
dark blue, *pale pink*	*175.*
violet, *pale yellow*	*175.*
c. Die on green bond (die size: 49x50mm)	
dull scarlet	*175.*
dull olive	*175.*
dark ultramarine	*175.*

Design size: 19½x25mm

Die size: 50x50mm

Design as No. LO1-E1, but distinguished by addition of left and right inner frame lines.

1903

LO1-E3 (1c)

a. Die on proof paper	
black	*100.*
carmine	*100.*
dark carmine	*100.*
scarlet	*100.*
orange	*100.*
yellow	*100.*
yellow brown	*100.*
olive	*100.*
light green	*100.*
green	*100.*
steel blue	*100.*
violet	*100.*
red violet	*100.*
violet brown	*100.*
ultramarine	*100.*
b. Die on colored card	
dull carmine, *pale olive*	*175.*
brown orange, *pink*	*175.*
brown, *pale buff*	*175.*
brown, *pale blue*	*175.*
gray green, *buff*	*175.*
gray green, *yellow*	*175.*
violet, *ivory*	*175.*
dull carmine, *pale blue*	*175.*
c. Die on blue pelure	
carmine	*200.*
scarlet	*200.*
orange	*200.*
brown	*200.*
dark green	*200.*
d. Die on green bond	
scarlet	*250.*
orange	*250.*
green	*250.*
dull violet	*250.*
e. Die on gummed thick rose paper, cut to stamp size	6,500.

Essays by Clarence Brazer in 1952 using the Schernikow complete die with addition of two diagonal lines in upper right corner.

Die size: 50x50mm

1952

LO1-E4 (1c) Die on glazed card

scarlet	*500.*
brown	*500.*
green	*500.*
red	*500.*

POST OFFICE SEALS

Registry Seals
1872 ISSUE
National Bank Note Co.

Design size: 72x40mm
Block size: 100x56½mm
Typographed design similar to that adopted but inscription STAMP HERE DATE AND PLACE OF MAILING around central circular disk is in colorless capitals, remainder of lettering in solid colors without shading lines. The word REGISTERED obliterates other words where it touches them.

OXF1-E1

a. Block impression on white card, brown	*2,000.*
b. Die on India, dark brown	—

Similar to No. OXF1-E1 except REGISTERED appears to be under other words it touches and does not obliterate them, as in design adopted.

OXF1-E2

a. Block impression on white paper, card mounted, brown	*2,000.*
b. Block impression on large card	
brown	*2,000.*
red	*2,000.*
yellow	*2,000.*

Similar to adopted type but circular disk in center has a ground of concentric circles, REGISTERED without colorless shading and obliterates other words where it touches them.

OXF1-E3 Block impression on white card, red violet —

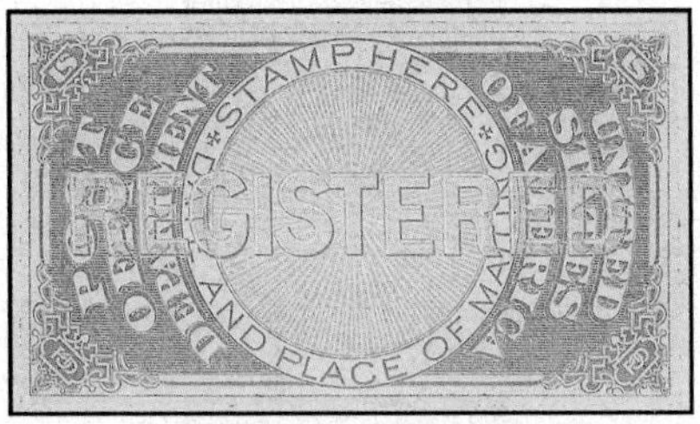

LO1-E4 — OXF1-E4

Similar to adopted design except REGISTERED obliterates other words where it touches them; colored shading as adopted.

OXF1-E4

a. Block on India, on card	
carmine	*1,000.*
yellow	*1,000.*
blue	*1,000.*
green	*1,000.*
red brown	*1,000.*
rose	*1,000.*
brown orange	*1,000.*
b. Block on India, printed in two colors	
top dark green, bottom light green	*1,000.*
left half blue, right half green	*1,000.*
c. Block sunk on white card, colored border around stamp (full size 57x100mm)	
deep carmine	*1,000.*
brown orange	*1,000.*
brown	*1,000.*
light green	*1,000.*
blue	*1,000.*
d. Block sunk on white wove, colorless border, stamp size, imperf., dim dusky blue	*1,000.*
e. As "d," perf. 12, gummed, dim dusky blue	*1,000.*

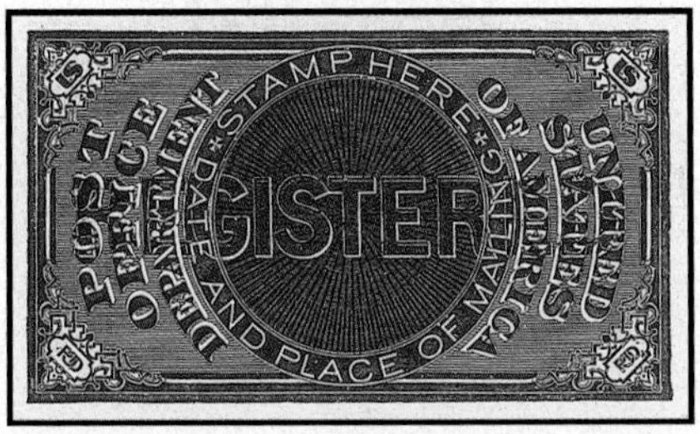

OXF1-E5

Block size: 80x128mm

Engraving of entire design as adopted but in reverse for making typographed block.

OXF1-E5 Die on white wove, chocolate *1,000.*

Post Office Seals
1877 ISSUE

OX1-E3

Design size: 45x27½mm
Incomplete engraving of entire design: no shading lines on 2mm-wide border frame, no cap or background in vignette.

OX1-E3 Die on India, on card, orange brown *1,000.*

1861 FIRST DESIGN ESSAYS AND TRIAL COLOR PROOFS

For the convenience of collectors and dealers, the Scott editors present here in one location the important 1861 First Design Essays and Trial Color Proofs that were at one time listed in the Postage section as Nos. 55-57 and 59-62. These so-called "August" issues or "Premiere Gravure" issues, printed on thin and semitransparent stamp paper, gummed and perforated, were not issued as prepared, but were either engraved further to complete the issued designs (1c, 3c, 5c, 12c and 90c) or issued in slightly revised colors (24c and 30c), and they were therefore appropriately moved to the Essay and Trial Color Proof sections of the U.S. Specialized catalogue in 1991.

The 10c denomination of this First Design series, previously No. 55, was pressed into service as an issued stamp, No. 62B, presumably because the demand for this denomination was greater than could be supplied by the plate or plates in use. Former No. 55 and current No. 62B are the same stamp, and it is listed in the Postage section as No. 62B.

The listings here duplicate the listings in the Essay and Trial Color Proof sections rather than replace them. Their listing here is for the convenience of catalogue users only.

63-E11e

"Premiere Gravure" die No. 440.

63-E11e 1c **indigo,** finished "Premiere Gravure" plate essay on semitransparent stamp paper, gummed, perf. 12 (formerly No. 55) *30,000.*

No. 63-E11e is valued with perfs cutting slightly into design at top.

65-E15h

65-E15h 3c **brown rose,** finished "Premiere Gravure" plate essay on semitransparent stamp paper, gummed, perf. 12 (formerly No. 56) 550.

orange red	475.
bright orange red	475.
dark orange red	475.
dim deep red	475.
pink	475.
deep pink	475.
P# block of 8, Impt. (any shade)	*20,000.*

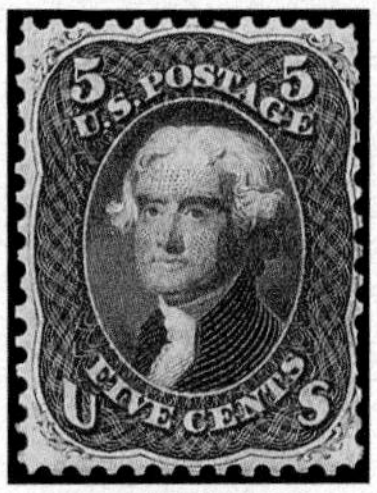

67-E9e

67-E9e 5c **brown,** finished "Premiere Gravure" plate essay on semitransparent stamp paper, gummed, perf. 12 (formerly No. 57) *25,000.*

No. 67-E9e is valued with small faults, as all recorded original-gum examples come thus.

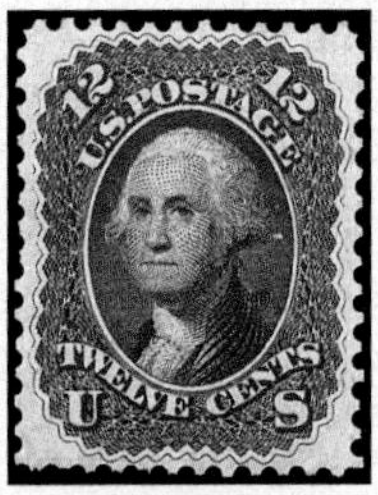

69-E6e

69-E6e 12c **black,** finished "Premiere Gravure" plate essay on semitransparent stamp paper, gummed, perf. 12 (formerly No. 59) *75,000.*

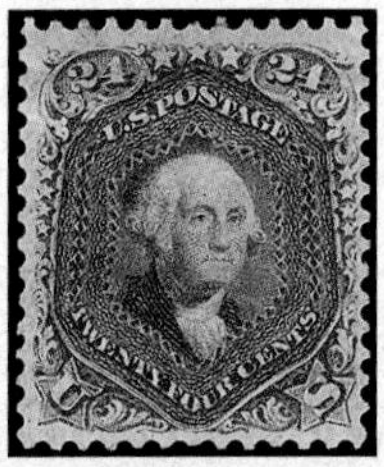

70eTC

70eTC 24c **dark violet,** trial color plate proof on semitransparent stamp paper, gummed, perf. 12 (formerly No. 60) *12,500.*

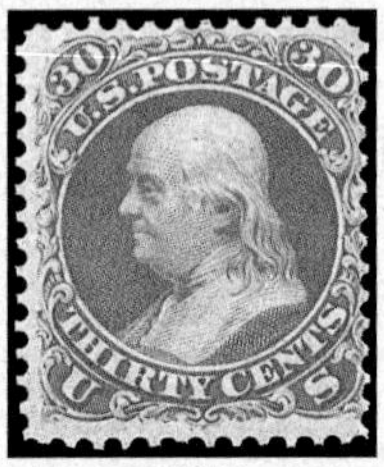

71bTC

71bTC 30c **red orange,** trial color plate proof on semitransparent stamp paper, gummed, perf. 12 (formerly No. 61) *45,000.*

No. 71bTC is valued in the grade of fine.

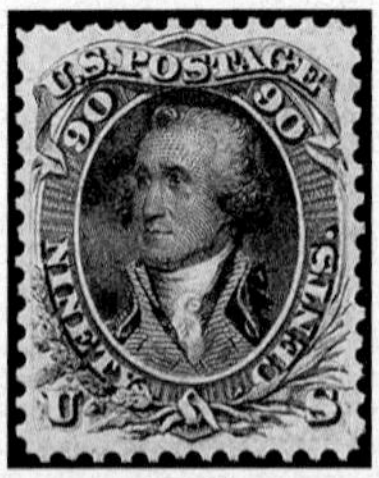

72-E7h

72-E7h 90c **blue,** finished "Premiere Gravure" plate essay on semitransparent stamp paper, gummed, perf. 12 (formerly No. 62) *50,000.*

DIE AND PLATE PROOFS

PROOFS are known in many styles other than those noted in this section. For the present, however, listings are restricted to die proofs, large and small, and plate proofs on India paper and card, and occasionally on stamp paper. The listing of normal color proofs includes several that differ somewhat from the types and colors of the issued stamps.

Large Die Proofs are so termed because of the relatively large piece of paper on which they are printed which is about the size of the die block, 40mm by 50mm or larger. The margins of this group of proofs usually are from 15mm to 20mm in width though abnormal examples prevent the acceptance of these measurements as a complete means of identification.

These proofs were prepared in most cases by the original contracting companies and 19th century issues often show the imprint thereof and letters and numbers of identification. They are listed under "DIE-Large (1)." The India paper on which these proofs are printed is of an uneven texture and in some respects resembles hand-made paper. These large die proofs were usually mounted on cards though many are found removed from the card. Large Die Proofs autographed by the engraver or officially approved are worth much more, except for those of the 1922-29 period, which are generally approved and signed proofs.

Values for Large Die Proofs are for the full die proofs mounted on cards unless noted otherwise. Full large die proofs measure 5-6" x 7-8". Cut-down Large Die Proofs sell for less. Values for die proofs of the bicolored 1869 issue are for examples which are completely printed. Occasionally the vignette has been cut out and affixed to an impression of the border.

Die Proofs of all United States stamps of later issues exist. Only those known outside of government ownership are listed.

Small Die Proofs are so called because of the small piece of paper on which they are printed. Proofs of stamps issued prior to 1904, are reprints, and not in all cases from the same dies as the large die proofs.

Small Die Proofs (Roosevelt Album, "DIE-Small (2)") — These 302 small die proofs are from sets prepared for 85 ("Roosevelt presentation") albums in 1903 by the Bureau of Engraving and Printing but bear no imprint to this effect. The white wove paper on which they are printed is of a fibrous nature. The margins are small, seldom being more than from 3-5mm in width. Values are for proofs affixed to the original gray card backing from the Roosevelt album. Proofs without the card backing sell for less.

Small Die Proofs (Panama-Pacific Issue, "DIE-Small (2a)") — A special printing of 413 different small die proofs was made in 1915 for the Panama-Pacific Exposition. These have small margins (2½-3mm) and are on soft yellowish wove paper. They are extremely scarce as only 3-5 of each are known and a few exist only in this special printing. 6-10 exist of No. E6 in two slightly different colors.

Plate Proofs are, quite obviously, impressions taken from finished plates and differ from the stamps themselves chiefly in their excellence of impression and the paper on which they are printed. Some of the colors vary.

Hybrids are plate proofs of all issues before 1894 which have been cut to shape, mounted and pressed on large cards to resemble large die proofs. These sell for somewhat less than the corresponding large die proofs.

India Paper is a thin, soft, opaque paper which wrinkles when wet. It varies in thickness and shows particles of bamboo.

Card is a plain, clear white card of good quality, which is found in varying thicknesses for different printings. Plate proofs on card were made in five printings in 1879-94. Quantities range from 500 to 3,200 of the card proofs listed between Scott 3P and 245P.

Margin blocks with full imprint and plate number are indicated by the abbreviation "P# blk. of -."

Numbers have been assigned to all proofs consisting of the number of the regular stamp with the suffix letter "P" to denote Proof.

Proofs in other than accepted or approved colors exist in a large variety of shades, colors and papers produced at various times by various people for many different reasons. The field is large. The task of listing has been begun under "Trial Colors" following the regular proofs.

Some proofs are not identical to the issued stamps. Some of these are now listed in the Essay section. Others have been left in the proof section to keep sets together at this time.

Values are for items in very fine condition. Most "Panama-Pacific" small die proofs are toned. Values are for moderately toned examples. **Plate proof pairs on stamp paper are valued with original gum unless otherwise noted.**

NORMAL COLORS

1845 **New York**

		DIE (1) Large	DIE (2) Small	(2a)	PLATE (3) India	PLATE (4) Card
9X1P	5c black on India paper	750.	350.		—	
a.	With scar on neck		300.			
b.	Dot in "P" of "POST" and scar on neck	525.	300.			
c.	As "b," on Bond	525.	300.			—
d.	As "b," on glazed paper	525.				
e.	As "a," on Bond	525.				

The above listed Large Die varieties have an additional impression of the portrait medallion. Some experts question the existance of plate proofs from the sheets of 40. Plate proofs from the sheet of 9 exist on white and bluish bond paper. Value $125.

Providence, R.I.

10X1P	5c black					300.
10X2P	10c black					500.
	Sheet of 12					3,250.

General Issues

1847

1P	5c red brown on India paper	800.			600.	
a.	White bond paper	800.				
b.	Colored bond paper	1,250.				
c.	White laid paper	800.				
d.	Bluish laid paper	800.				
e.	Yellowish wove paper	800.				
f.	Bluish wove paper	800.				
g.	White wove paper	800.				
h.	Card	1,000.				
i.	Glazed paper	1,000.				
2P	10c black on India paper	800.			900.	
	Double transfer (31R1)				—	
a.	White bond paper	800.				
b.	Colored bond paper	1,250.				
c.	White laid paper	800.				
d.	Bluish laid paper	800.				
e.	Yellowish wove paper	800.				
g.	White wove paper	800.				
h.	Card	1,000.				
i.	Glazed paper	1,000.				

Original die proofs are generally found cut to stamp size; full size die proofs sell at higher prices. Reprint proofs with cross-hatching are valued as full size; cut down examples sell for less.

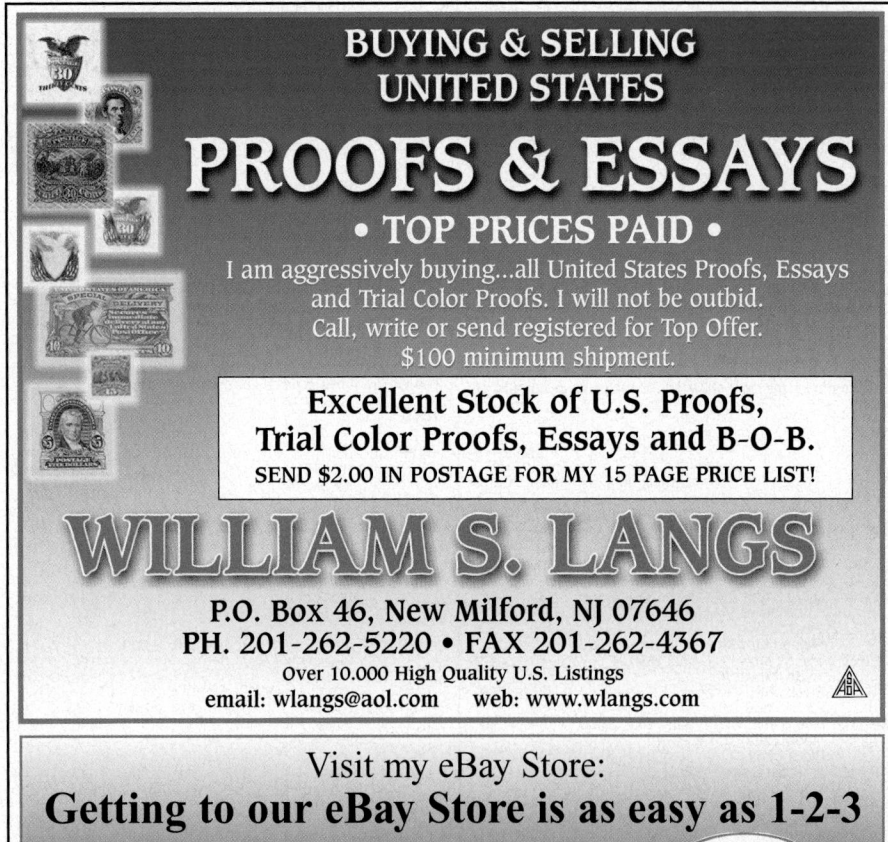

Plate proofs overprinted "Specimen" sell for about half the above figures.

Reproductions of 1847 Issue

Actually, official imitations made about 1875 from new dies and plates by order of the Post Office Department.

3P	5c	red brown	900.	425.	2,750.	250.	200.
		Block of 4				1,300.	900.
a.		On bond paper		650.			
4P	10c	black	900.	425.	2,750.	250.	200.
		Block of 4				1,300.	900.
a.		On bond paper		650.			

1851-60

5P	1c	blue, type I	*5,000.*				
11P	3c	red, type I	*5,000.*				
		brush obliteration				1,000.	
		Block of 4				5,000.	
		P# block of 8				*20,000.*	
12P	5c	brn, type I	*7,000.*		*5,000.*		
13P	10c	grn, type I	*5,000.*				
17P	12c	black	*12,500.*				
24P	1c	blue, type V (pl. 9)				*1,250.*	
		Pair				*3,000.*	
26P	3c	red, type II (pl. 20)				*1,250.*	
		Pair				*3,000.*	
30P	5c	brn, type II				*1,250.*	
35P	10c	grn, type V				*1,250.*	
36BP	12c	black, plate III (broken frame lines)				*1,250.*	
		Block of 4				*5,500.*	
d.		On stamp paper					—
		Pair					—
		Block of 4					—
37P	24c	lilac	—			*1,250.*	
		Pair				*3,000.*	
c.		On stamp paper					*1,500.*
		Pair					*15,500.*
38P	30c	orange	—	—		*1,250.*	
		Pair				*3,000.*	
a.		On stamp paper					*2,500.*
		Pair					*7,750.*
39P	90c	blue	—	—		*1,250.*	
		Pair				*3,000.*	
a.		On stamp paper					*4,500.*
		Pair					*37,500.*

Plate proofs of 24P to 39P are from the original plates. They may be distinguished from the 40P to 47P by the type in the case of the 1c, 3c, 10c and 12c, and by the color in the case of the 5c, 24c, 30c and 90c.

The 3c plate proofs (No. 11) are on proof paper and all known copies have a vertical brush stroke obliteration.

Die proofs of the 30c show full spear point in corners of design.

Reprints of 1857-60 Issue

			DIE (1) Large	DIE (2) Small	(2a)	PLATE (3) India	PLATE (4) Card
40P	1c	bright blue, type I (new plate)	325.	350.	*2,500.*	80.	75.
		Block of 4				400.	300.
a.		On stamp paper					750.
41P	3c	scarlet, type I (new plate)	325.	350.	*2,500.*	80.	50.
		Block of 4				400.	250.
		Orange brown			*2,500.*		
42P	5c	orange brown type II (plate II)	325.	350.		80.	50.
		Block of 4				400.	250.
		P# blk. of 8				1,050.	—
43P	10c	blue green, type I (new plate)	325.	350.	*2,500.*	80.	50.
		Block of 4				400.	250.
44P	12c	greenish black (new plate, frame line complete)	325.	350.	*3,500.*	110.	50.
		Block of 4				550.	250.
45P	24c	blksh vio (pl. I)	325.	350.	*2,500.*	80.	50.
		Block of 4				400.	250.
		P# blk. of 8				1,050.	
46P	30c	yel org (pl. I)	325.	350.	*2,500.*	80.	50.
		Block of 4				400.	250.
		P# blk. of 8				1,050.	—
47P	90c	deep blue (pl. I)	325.	350.	*2,500.*	110.	75.
		Block of 4				550.	375.
		P# blk. of 8				1,150.	1,050.

Nos. 42P2-44P2 were printed from original dies, and the 5c shows type I projections at top and bottom.

Nos. 40P-47P, large die, exist only as hybrids.

SECOND DESIGNS (Regular Issue)

For "First Designs" see Essay section (former Nos. 55-57, 59, 62), Proofs and Trial Color Proofs (former No. 58) and Trial Color Proofs (former Nos. 60-61).

1861

			DIE (1) Large	DIE (2) Small	(2a)	PLATE (3) India	PLATE (4) Card
62BP	10c	dark green		*325.*		*375.*	
63P	1c	blue	700.	225.	2,750.	55.	40.
		Block of 4				225.	250.
		P# blk. of 8				1,100.	—
		Indigo			2,750.		
64P	3c	pink	3,500.	—			
65P	3c	rose	1,000.	—	2,750.	100.	130.
		Block of 4				550.	
		P# blk. of 8				1,400.	
a.		3c dull red				100.	
c.		On stamp paper, pair					*1,000.*
		P# blk. of 8					—
67P	5c	buff	*5,000.*		2,750.		
76P	5c	brown	700.	225.	2,750.	45.	30.
		Block of 4				225.	140.
		P# blk. of 8				875.	—
68P	10c	green	650.	225.	2,750.	65.	30.
		Block of 4				300.	140.
		P# blk. of 8				950.	—
69P	12c	black	700.	225.	2,750.	65.	30.
		Block of 4				300.	140.
		P# blk. of 8				950.	—
70P	24c	red lilac	—		2,750.		500.
78P	24c	lilac		225.	2,750.	80.	75.
		Block of 4				400.	375.
		P# blk. of 8				1,200.	—
71P	30c	orange	500.	225.	2,750.	50.	30.
		Block of 4				250.	140.
		P# blk. of 8				1,100.	—
72P	90c	blue	500.	225.	2,750.	50.	30.
		Block of 4				225.	140.
		P# blk. of 8				1,100.	—

1861-67

			DIE (1) Large	DIE (2) Small	(2a)	PLATE (3) India	PLATE (4) Card
73P	2c	black, die I	10,000.			150.	
		Block of 4				750.	
		P# blk. of 8				2,000.	—
a.		Die II	2,500.	1,350.	8,750.	110.	75.
		Block of 4				550.	400.
		P# blk. of 8				1,500.	—
77P	15c	black	1,250.	500.	2,750.	55.	45.
		Block of 4				250.	200.
		P# blk. of 8				950.	—
79P	3c	rose, A grill, on stamp paper, pair					*1,500.*
		Block of 4					*4,000.*
		P# blk. of 8					*10,000.*
83P	3c	rose, C grill, on stamp paper, pair					*1,850.*
94P	3c	red, F grill, on stamp paper, pair					*1,500.*

The listed plate proofs of the 1c (63P), 5c (76P), 10c (68P) and 12c (69P) are from the 100 subject re-issue plates of 1875. Single proofs of these denominations from the regular issue plates cannot be told apart from the reprints. As the reprint plates had wider spacing between the subjects, multiples can be differentiated. Values are for proofs from the reprint plates. The 2c Die II has a small dot on the left cheek.

1869

			DIE (1) Large	DIE (2) Small	(2a)	PLATE (3) India	PLATE (4) Card
112P	1c	buff	750.	350.	2,000.	55.	65.
		Block of 4				250.	300.
		P# blk. of 10				750.	
113P	2c	brown	750.	350.	2,000.	40.	50.
		Block of 4				175.	225.
		P# blk. of 10				600.	—
114P	3c	ultra.	900.	575.	2,000.	45.	85.
		Block of 4				190.	375.
		P# blk. of 10				800.	—
115P	6c	ultra.	900.	350.	2,000.	45.	85.
		Block of 4				190.	375.
		P# blk. of 10				800.	—
116P	10c	yellow	900.	350.	2,000.	45.	55.
		Block of 4				190.	250.
		P# blk. of 10				1,500.	—
117P	12c	green	900.	350.	2,000.	45.	55.
		Block of 4				190.	265.
		P# blk. of 10				875.	—
119P	15c	brown & blue (type II)	550.	450.	2,000.	120.	
		Block of 4				600.	
		P# blk. of 8				1,450.	
129P	15c	Reissue (type III)	550.	450.	2,000.	350.	140.
		Block of 4				1,600.	725.
		P# blk. of 8				3,500.	—
a.		Center inverted (100)					2,500.
		Block of 4					*11,000.*
		P# blk. of 8					*37,500.*
120P	24c	green & violet	550.	450.	2,000.	140.	140.
		Block of 4				625.	650.
		P# blk. of 8				1,450.	—
a.		Center inverted (100)					2,750.
		Block of 4					*12,000.*
		P# blk. of 8					*37,500.*
121P	30c	ultra & carmine	1,250.	450.	2,000.	140.	170.
		Block of 4				625.	875.
		P# blk. of 8				1,450.	
a.		Flags inverted (100)					2,750.
		Block of 4					*12,000.*
		P# blk. of 8					*37,500.*
122P	90c	carmine & black	550.	450.	2,000.	180.	170.
		Block of 4				825.	875.
		P# blk. of 8				1,750.	—
a.		Center inverted (100)					2,750.
		Block of 4					*14,000.*
		P# blk. of 8					*37,500.*

Large die proofs of Nos. 119, 129, 120 and 122 exist only as hybrids.

1880

			DIE (1) Large	DIE (2) Small	(2a)	PLATE (3) India	PLATE (4) Card
133P	1c	dark buff	1,000.			100.	
		Block of 4				450.	
		P# blk. of 10				1,250.	

1870-71 National Bank Note Co

			DIE (1) Large	DIE (2) Small	(2a)	PLATE (3) India	PLATE (4) Card
136P	3c	green, grill, on stamp paper, pair					*1,200.*
		P# blk. of 12					—
145P	1c	ultra	250.	175.	1,200.	20.	
		Block of 4				90.	
		P# blk. of 12				385.	
146P	2c	red brown	250.			20.	
		Block of 4				90.	
		P# blk. of 12				385.	
147P	3c	green	300.			20.	
		Block of 4				90.	
		P# blk. of 12				400.	

The former No. 147Pc4 is now listed in the Essay section as No. 147-E13e.

			DIE (1) Large	DIE (2) Small	(2a)	PLATE (3) India	PLATE (4) Card
148P	6c	carmine	450.			35.	
		Block of 4				150.	
		P# blk. of 12				900.	
149P	7c	vermilion	250.			15.	
		Block of 4				70.	
		P# blk. of 12				400.	
150P	10c	brown	300.			40.	
		Block of 4				165.	
		P# blk. of 12				2,000.	
151P	12c	violet	250.			16.	
		Block of 4				70.	
		P# blk. of 12				425.	
152P	15c	orange	300.			30.	
		Block of 4				135.	
		P# blk. of 12				750.	
153P	24c	purple	300.			30.	
		Block of 4				135.	
		P# blk. of 12				750.	
154P	30c	black	300.			40.	
		Block of 4				170.	
		P# blk. of 12				2,250.	
155P	90c	carmine	300.			45.	
		Block of 4				195.	
		P# blk. of 12				2,500.	

Secret Marks on 24, 30 and 90c Dies of the Bank Note Issues

National 24c — Rays of lower star normal.

Continental 24c — Rays of lower star strengthened.

National 30c — Lower line does not join point of shield.

Continental and American 30c — Lower line joins point of shield and bottom line of shield thicker.

National 90c — Rays of star in upper right normal.

Continental and American 90c — Rays of star in upper right strengthened.

1873 Continental Bank Note Co.

No.	Denom.	Description	DIE (1) Large	DIE (2) Small	(2a)	PLATE (3) India	PLATE (4) Card
156P	1c	ultra	450.			55.	300.
		Block of 4				250.	
		P# blk. of 14				1,150.	
157P	2c	brown	350.	175.	1,200.	35.	15.
		Block of 4				165.	80.
		P# blk. of 12				650.	—
	a.	On stamp paper					—
158P	3c	green	350.	175.	1,200.	55.	150.
		Block of 4				250.	
		P# blk. of 14				1,150.	
	f.	On stamp paper, pair					*750.*
	g.	On stamp paper, grill, pair					*650.*
159P	6c	pink	750.	250.	1,400.	110.	300.
		Block of 4				525.	
		P# blk. of 12				2,000.	
160P	7c	orange vermilion	250.	175.	1,200.	35.	10.
		Block of 4				165.	50.
		P# blk. of 14				825.	—
161P	10c	brown	450.	200.	1,200.	60.	300.
		Block of 4				300.	
		P# blk. of 14				1,300.	
162P	12c	blackish violet	200.	175.	1,200.	38.	20.
		Block of 4				190.	100.
		P# blk. of 14				975.	—
	a.	On stamp paper					—
163P	15c	yellow orange	400.	175.	1,200.	65.	20.
		Block of 4				250.	100.
		P# blk. of 12				1,000.	—
	a.	On stamp paper					—
164P	24c	violet	400.	175.	1,200.	50.	30.
		Block of 4				225.	140.
		P# blk. of 12				975.	
165P	30c	gray black	400.	175.	1,200.	40.	20.
		Block of 4				200.	90.
		P# blk. of 12				825.	
166P	90c	rose carmine	400.	175.	1,200.	55.	40.
		Block of 4				250.	190.
		P# blk. of 12				1,000.	

Die proofs of the 24c, 30c and 90c show secret marks, as illustrated, but as plates of these denominations were not made from these dies, plate proofs can be identified only by color.

No.	Denom.	Description	(1)	(2)	(2a)	(3)	(4)
178P	2c	vermilion	—				
	a.	On stamp paper, pair					*600.*
		P# blk. of 12					—
179P	5c	blue	—				

1879 American Bank Note Co.

No.	Denom.	Description	(1)	(2)	(2a)	(3)	(4)
182P	1c	gray blue	525.			60.	
		Block of 4				275.	
		P# blk. of 12				1,000.	
183P	2c	vermilion	300.	190.	1,200.	35.	20.
		Block of 4				160.	100.
		P# blk. of 12				600.	—
184P	3c	green on stamp paper, pair					*400.*
		P# blk. of 12					—
185P	5c	blue	450.	225.	1,200.	70.	25.
		Block of 4				325.	110.
		P# blk. of 12				1,300.	—
190P	30c	full black				—	150.
		Block of 4				—	600.
		P# blk. of 12					*2,500.*
191P	90c	carmine on stamp paper, pair					*2,500.*
		P# strip of 5					—

1881-82 American Bank Note Co.

No.	Denom.	Description	(1)	(2)	(2a)	(3)	(4)
205P	5c	yellow brown	250.	200.	1,200.	40.	15.
		Block of 4				175.	75.
		P# blk. of 12				1,000.	—
206P	1c	blue	375.	200.	1,200.	40.	20.
		Block of 4				175.	90.
		P# blk. of 12				1,000.	—
207P	3c	blue green	375.	200.	1,200.	40.	20.
		Block of 4				175.	90.
		P# blk. of 12				1,000.	—
208P	6c	rose	800.	200.	1,200.	90.	60.
		Block of 4				425.	210.
		P# blk. of 12				—	—
	a.	6c brown red			1,200.	100.	50.
209P	10c	brown	800.	200.	1,200.	40.	25.
		Block of 4				170.	110.
		P# blk. of 12				1,000.	—

1883

No.	Denom.	Description	(1)	(2)	(2a)	(3)	(4)
210P	2c	red brown	400.	200.	1,200.	32.	20.
		Block of 4				145.	85.
		P# blk. of 12				950.	—
	a.	On stamp paper, pair					—
211P	4c	green	500.	200.	1,200.	40.	25.
		Block of 4				165.	110.
		P# blk. of 12				1,000.	—
	a.	On stamp paper, pair					—

1887-88

No.	Denom.	Description	(1)	(2)	(2a)	(3)	(4)
212P	1c	ultra	650.	200.	1,200.	125.	*2,000.*
		Block of 4				600.	—
		P# blk. of 12				2,250.	
	a.	On stamp paper, pair					*1,000.*

Examples of No. 212P3 mounted on card are frequently offered as No. 212P4.

No.	Denom.	Description	(1)	(2)	(2a)	(3)	(4)
213P	2c	green	500.	190.	1,200.	75.	50.
		Block of 4				325.	225.
		P# blk. of 12				1,150.	—
	a.	On stamp paper, pair					*750.*
214P	3c	vermilion	500.	190.	1,200.	75.	50.
		Block of 4				325.	225.
		P# blk. of 12				—	—

Nos. 207P1 & 214P1 inscribed: "Worked over by new company, June 29th, 1881."

No.	Denom.	Description	(1)	(2)	(2a)	(3)	(4)
215P	4c	carmine	650.	190.	1,200.	95.	50.
		Block of 4				475.	225.
		P# blk. of 12					—
216P	5c	indigo	650.	190.	1,200.	75.	50.
		Block of 4				325.	225.
		P# blk. of 12					—
	b.	On stamp paper, pair					*1,400.*
217P	30c	organge brown	750.	190.	1,200.	75.	50.
		Block of 4				325.	225.
		P# blk. of 10					—
	a.	On stamp paper, pair					*1,750.*
218P	90c	purple	1,100.	190.	1,200.	90.	50.
		Block of 4				400.	225.
		P# blk. of 10					
	a.	On stamp paper, pair					—

1890-93

No.	Denom.	Description	(1)	(2)	(2a)	(3)	(4)
219P	1c	ultra	225.	190.	1,100.	25.	40.
		Block of 4				110.	180.
		P# blk. of 12				500.	650.
	c.	On stamp paper, pair					*190.*
219DP	2c	lake	550.	190.	1,100.	80.	165.
		Block of 4				385.	700.
		P# blk. of 12				1,650.	3,250.
	e.	On stamp paper, pair					*80.*
220P	2c	carmine	450.	190.		300.	200.
		Block of 4				1,250.	825.
		P# blk. of 12				3,850.	2,500.
	d.	On stamp paper, pair					*80.*
		As "d," without gum					*40.*
		P# blk. of 12					—
221P	3c	purple	225.	190.	1,100.	35.	25.
		Block of 4				160.	110.
		P# blk. of 12				650.	600.
	a.	On stamp paper, pair					*225.*
222P	4c	dark brown	225.	190.	1,100.	35.	25.
		Block of 4				160.	110.
		P# blk. of 12				650.	600.
	a.	On stamp paper, pair					*210.*
223P	5c	chocolate	225.	190.	1,100.	32.	25.
		Block of 4				135.	110.
		P# blk. of 12				600.	625.
	b.	Yellow brown, on stamp paper, pair					*225.*
224P	6c	brown red	225.	190.	1,100.	32.	20.
		Block of 4				135.	85.
		P# blk. of 12				600.	775.
	a.	On stamp paper, pair					*225.*
225P	8c	lilac	600.	190.	1,100.	55.	110.
		Block of 4				250.	500.
		P# blk. of 12				1,100.	2,000.
	a.	On stamp paper, pair					*1,000.*
226P	10c	green	225.	190.	1,100.	45.	40.
		Block of 4				200.	180.
		P# blk. of 12				700.	750.
	a.	On stamp paper, pair					*325.*
227P	15c	indigo	300.	190.	1,100.	45.	40.
		Block of 4				190.	180.
		P# blk. of 12				825.	875.
	a.	On stamp paper, pair					*625.*
228P	30c	black	300.	190.	1,100.	45.	45.
		Block of 4				190.	190.
		P# blk. of 12				825.	875.
	a.	On stamp paper, pair					*1,000.*
229P	90c	orange	300.	190.	1,100.	60.	50.
		Block of 4				275.	225.
		P# blk. of 12				1,100.	1,150.
	a.	On stamp paper, pair					*1,450.*

COLUMBIAN ISSUE

1893

No.	Denom.	Description	(1)	(2)	(2a)	(3)	(4)
230P	1c	blue	700.	325.	1,400.	40.	25.
		Block of 4				175.	125.
		P# blk. of 8				400.	350.
231P	2c	violet	800.	350.	1,750.	225.	65.
		Block of 4				1,000.	280.
		P# blk. of 8				2,250.	825.
	b.	On stamp paper, pair					*1,250.*
	c.	"Broken hat" variety					130.

Almost all examples of No. 231Pb are faulty. Value is for pair with minimal faults.

No.	Denom.	Description	(1)	(2)	(2a)	(3)	(4)
232P	3c	green	700.	325.	2,000.	60.	50.
		Block of 4				260.	225.
		P# blk. of 8				675.	600.
233P	4c	ultra.	700.	325.	2,000.	60.	50.
		Block of 4				260.	225.
		P# blk. of 8				675.	600.
233aP	4c	blue (error) on thin card	2,750.				
234P	5c	chocolate	700.	325.	2,000.	60.	45.
		Block of 4				260.	200.
		P# blk. of 8				675.	550.
235P	6c	purple	700.	325.	2,000.	60.	50.
		Block of 4				260.	225.
		P# blk. of 8				675.	600.
236P	8c	magenta	700.	325.	2,000.	60.	100.
		Block of 4				260.	450.
		P# blk. of 8				675.	1,250.
237P	10c	black brown	700.	325.	2,000.	60.	50.
		Block of 4				260.	225.
		P# blk. of 8				675.	600.
238P	15c	dark green	700.	325.	2,000.	60.	55.
		Block of 4				260.	250.
		P# blk. of 8				675.	1,400.

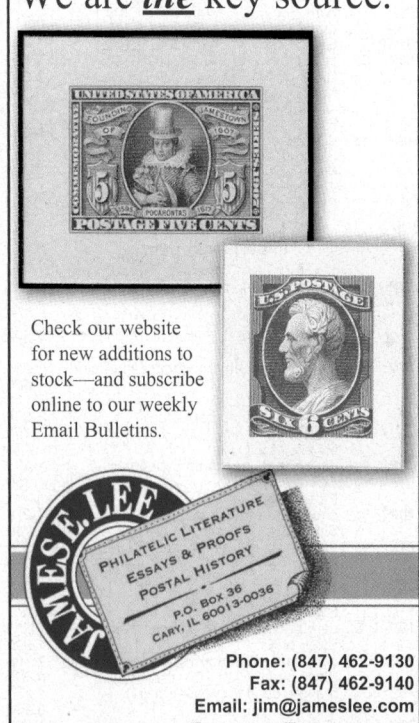

239P	30c	orange brown	700.	325.	2,000.	90.	65.
		Block of 4				400.	300.
		P# blk. of 8				1,250.	1,100.
240P	50c	slate blue	700.	325.	2,000.	135.	75.
		Block of 4				575.	350.
		P# blk. of 8				1,500.	1,100.
241P	$1	salmon	900.	450.	2,000.	160.	130.
		Block of 4				775.	575.
		P# blk. of 8				1,900.	
242P	$2	brown red	900.	450.	2,000.	180.	125.
		Block of 4				750.	550.
		P# blk. of 8				2,050.	1,500.
243P	$3	yellow green	900.	450.	2,000.	225.	150.
		Block of 4				1,000.	675.
		P# blk. of 8				2,700.	1,900.
244P	$4	crimson lake	900.	450.	2,000.	275.	175.
		Block of 4				1,200.	775.
		P# blk. of 8				3,000.	2,500.
245P	$5	black	900.	450.	2,000.	325.	225.
		Block of 4				1,425.	1,000.
		P# blk. of 8				3,500.	3,000.

This set also exists as Large Die proofs, not die sunk, but printed directly on thin card. Set value $4,725. 1c through 50c, $225 each; $1 through $5, $450 each.

Nos. 234P1, 234P2 differ from issued stamp.

Bureau of Engraving and Printing

1894

246P	1c	ultra	450.				
247P	1c	blue	250.	250.	1,100.		100.
		Block of 4					450.
		P# blk. of 6					950.
248P	2c	pink, type I					100.
		Block of 4					475.
		P# blk. of 6					950.
250P	2c	car, type I	250.	250.			
251P	2c	car, type II	250.	—			

The existence of No. 251P2 has been questioned by specialists. The editors would like to see evidence that the item exists.

252P	2c	car, type III				350.	
		Block of 4				1,500.	
253P	3c	purple (triangle I)	750.				
	a.	On stamp paper, pair					*300.*
		Block of 4					*625.*
		P# blk. of 6					*3,500.*
253AP	3c	purple (triangle II)	325.	250.	1,100.		
254P	4c	dark brown	250.	250.	1,100.		
	a.	On stamp paper, pair					*300.*
		Block of 4					*625.*
		P# blk. of 6					*4,000.*
255P	5c	chocolate	250.	250.	1,100.		
	b.	On stamp paper, pair					*300.*
		Block of 4					*625.*
		P# blk. of 6					*4,500.*
256P	6c	brown	250.	250.	1,100.		450.
		Block of 4					1,900.
		P# blk. of 6					*3,750.*
257P	8c	violet brown	275.	250.	1,100.		
258P	10c	green	275.	250.	1,100.		
	a.	On stamp paper, pair					*500.*
		Block of 4					*1,100.*
		P# blk. of 6					*5,000.*
259P	15c	dark blue	300.	250.	1,100.		
260P	50c	orange	450.	210.	1,100.		
261AP	$1	black	475.	350.	1,100.		
262P	$2	dark blue	475.	350.	1,100.		450.
		Block of 4					2,250.
		Margin block of 4, arrow					*2,750.*
		P# blk. of 6					*6,250.*
263P	$5	dark green	650.	375.	1,100.		450.
		Block of 4					2,250.
		Margin block of 4, arrow					*2,750.*
		P# blk. of 6					*6,250.*

1895

Imperf, with gum

264P	1c	blue, on stamp paper, pair	*275.*
		Block of 4	*750.*
		P# blk. of 6	—
	b.	Horiz. P# strip of 3, perf horiz., imperf. vert.	*7,500.*
267P	2c	carmine, type III, on stamp paper, pair	*225.*
		Block of 4	*600.*
		P# blk. of 6	—
268P	3c	purple, on stamp paper, pair	*275.*
		Block of 4	*750.*
		P# blk. of 6	—
269P	4c	dark brown, on stamp paper, pair	*275.*
		Block of 4	*750.*
		P# blk. of 6	—
270P	5c	chocolate, on stamp paper, pair	*275.*
		Block of 4	*750.*
271P	6c	dull brown, on stamp paper, pair	*300.*
		Block of 4	*800.*
272P	8c	violet brown, on stamp paper, pair	*450.*
		Block of 4	*1,250.*
		P# blk. of 6	—
273P	10c	dark green, on stamp paper, pair	*350.*
		Block of 4	*1,000.*
274P	15c	dark blue, on stamp paper, pair	*1,100.*
		Block of 4	*3,000.*
275P	50c	orange, on stamp paper, pair	*1,250.*
		Block of 4	*3,500.*
276P	$1	black, type I, on stamp paper, pair	*1,600.*
		Block of 4	*4,000.*
277P	$2	bright blue, on stamp paper, pair	*3,500.*
		Block of 4	*8,250.*
278P	$5	dark green, on stamp paper, pair	*3,500.*
		Block of 4	*8,250.*

No. 264Pb exists only as a bottom margin P#24 and imprint strip of 3.

1897-1903

279P	1c	green	700.	375.	1,100.
279BdP	2c	orange red, type IV			1,100.
279BfP	2c	car, type IV	400.		1,100.
280P	4c	rose brown	700.		1,100.
281P	5c	blue	700.	375.	1,100.
282P	6c	lake	700.		1,100.
283P	10c	orange brown, type II	800.	375.	1,100.
283aP	10c	brown, type II	800.		
284P	15c	olive green, type II	800.	375.	1,100.

TRANS-MISSISSIPPI ISSUE

1898

285P	1c	green	650.	650.	1,250.	
286P	2c	copper red	650.	650.	1,250.	4,000.
287P	4c	orange	650.	650.	1,250.	
288P	5c	dull blue	650.	650.	1,250.	
289P	8c	violet brown	650.	650.	1,250.	
290P	10c	gray violet	650.	650.	1,250.	
291P	50c	sage green	650.	650.	1,250.	
292P	$1	black	750.	650.	1,250.	
293P	$2	orange brown	750.	650.	1,250.	6,000.
		Block of 4				30,000.
		P# block of 4				35,000.

The bicolored items commonly offered as No. 285-293 bicolored proofs can be found under the following essay listings: No. 285-E8a, 286-E8a, 287-E9a, 288-E5a, 289-E4a, 290-E4a, 291-E8a, 292-E6a, 293-E7a.

PAN-AMERICAN ISSUE

1901

294P	1c	green & black	575.	575.	2,000.
295P	2c	carmine & black	575.	575.	2,000.
	b.	Small die proof on yellowish bond		*1,250.*	
296P	4c	chocolate & black	575.	575.	2,000.
297P	5c	ultra & black	575.	575.	2,000.
298P	8c	brown violet & black	575.	575.	2,000.
299P	10c	yel brn & blk	575.	575.	2,000.

1902-03

300P	1c	green	1,500.	300.	2,500.
301P	2c	carmine	1,500.	300.	2,500.
302P	3c	purple	1,500.	300.	2,500.
303P	4c	orange brown	1,500.	300.	2,500.
304P	5c	blue	1,500.	300.	2,500.
305P	6c	lake	1,500.	300.	2,500.
306P	8c	violet black	1,500.	300.	2,500.
307P	10c	orange brown	1,500.	300.	2,500.
308P	13c	deep vio brn	1,500.	300.	2,500.
309P	15c	olive green	1,500.	300.	2,500.
310P	50c	orange	1,500.	300.	2,500.
311P	$1	black	1,500.	300.	2,500.
312P	$2	blue	2,000.	300.	2,500.
313P	$5	green	2,500.	375.	2,500.

1903

319P	2c	carmine, Type I	1,500.		
319aP	2c	lake, Type I	—		
319iP	2c	carmine, Type II	2,000.	1,000.	3,500.
	b.	Small die proof on yellowish wove		*1,000.*	

LOUISIANA PURCHASE ISSUE

1904

323P	1c	green	1,400.	750.	1,250.
324P	2c	carmine	1,400.	750.	1,250.
325P	3c	violet	1,400.	750.	1,250.
326P	5c	dark blue	1,400.	750.	1,250.
327P	10c	brown	1,400.	750.	1,250.

JAMESTOWN EXPOSITION ISSUE

1907

328P	1c	green	1,000.	900.	1,250.
329P	2c	carmine	1,000.	900.	1,250.
330P	5c	blue	1,000.	900.	1,250.

1908-09

331P	1c	green	1,250.	725.	1,200.
332P	2c	carmine	1,250.	725.	1,200.
		carmine, *amber*	—		
		carmine, *lt blue*	—		
333P	3c	deep violet	1,250.	725.	1,200.
334P	4c	brown	1,250.	725.	1,200.
335P	5c	blue	1,250.	725.	1,200.
		blue, *salmon*	—		
336P	6c	red orange	1,250.	725.	1,200.
337P	8c	olive green	1,250.	725.	1,200.
		olive green, *yellow*	—		
338P	10c	yellow	1,250.	725.	1,200.
339P	13c	blue green	1,250.	725.	1,200.
340P	15c	pale ultramarine	1,250.	725.	1,200.
341P	50c	violet	1,250.	725.	1,200.
		violet, *pale lilac*	—		
		violet, *yellow*	—		
		violet, *greenish*	—		
342P	$1	violet black	1,500.	725.	1,200.

LINCOLN MEMORIAL ISSUE

1909

367P	2c	carmine	1,100.	1,000.	1,750.

ALASKA-YUKON ISSUE

1909

370P	2c	carmine	1,100.	1,000.	1,750.

HUDSON-FULTON ISSUE

1909

372P	2c	carmine	1,250.	1,000.	1,750.

PANAMA-PACIFIC ISSUE

1912-13

397P	1c	green	1,750.	1,500.	1,250.
398P	2c	carmine	1,750.	1,500.	1,250.
399P	5c	blue	1,750.	1,500.	1,250.
400P	10c	org. yellow	1,750.	1,500.	1,250.
400AP	10c	orange	1,750.	1,500.	1,250.

No. 398P inscribed "Gatun Locks" is listed in the Essay section as No. 398-E3.

1912-19

			DIE (1) Large	DIE (2) Small	(2a)
405P	1c	green	1,400.	650.	1,200
406P	2c	carmine	1,400.	650.	1,200
407P	7c	black	1,400.	650.	1,200
414P	8c	olive green	1,400.	650.	1,200
415P	9c	salmon red	1,400.	650.	1,200
416P	10c	orange yellow	1,400.	650.	1,200
434P	11c	dark green	1,500.		
417P	12c	claret brown	1,400.	650.	1,200
513P	13c	apple green	1,500.		
418P	15c	gray	1,400.	650.	1,200
419P	20c	ultramarine	1,400.	650.	1,200
420P	30c	orange red	1,400.	650.	1,200
421P	50c	violet	1,400.	650.	1,200
423P	$1	violet black	1,400.	650.	1,200

1918-20

524P	$5	deep green & black	1,500.	
547P	$2	carmine & black	1,500.	

VICTORY ISSUE

1919

537P	3c	violet	1,100.	850.

PILGRIM ISSUE

1920

548P	1c	green	1,250.	1,200.
549P	2c	carmine rose	1,250.	1,200.
550P	5c	deep blue	1,250.	1,200.

1922-26

			LARGE DIE (1) India	LARGE DIE (1a) White Wove	PLATE (3) White Wove	PLATE (4) Card
551P	½c	olive brown	1,500.	—	—	—
552P	1c	deep green	1,000.	700.	—	
553P	1½c	yel brn	1,500.		—	
554P	2c	carmine	1,000.	700.	—	
555P	3c	violet	1,250.	1,000.	—	
556P	4c	yel brn	1,200.	700.	—	
557P	5c	dark blue	1,000.	700.	—	
558P	6c	red orange	1,000.	700.	—	
559P	7c	black	1,000.	700.	—	
560P	8c	olive green	1,000.	700.	—	
561P	9c	rose	1,000.	700.	—	
562P	10c	orange	1,000.	700.	—	
563P	11c	light blue	1,500.	700.	—	
564P	12c	brn vio	1,000.	700.	—	
622P	13c	green	1,000.	700.	—	
565P	14c	dark blue	1,250.	700.	—	
566P	15c	gray	1,250.	700.	—	
623P	17c	black	1,000.		—	
567P	20c	car rose	1,000.	700.	—	
568P	25c	deep green	1,000.	700.	—	
569P	30c	olive brown	1,000.	700.	—	
570P	50c	lilac	1,250.	700.	—	
571P	$1	vio brn	1,500.	700.	—	
572P	$2	deep blue	2,500.	700.	—	
572P	$2	deep blue, small die on India	—			
573P	$5	carmine & dark blue	*5,000.*			

1923-26

		LARGE DIE (1) India	LARGE DIE (1a) White Wove	SMALL DIE (2) White or Yellowish Wove
610P	Harding, 2c black	1,400.	1,400.	1,000
614P	Huguenot Walloon, 1c	750.	700.	700
615P	Huguenot Walloon, 2c	750.	700.	700
616P	Huguenot Walloon, 5c	750.	700.	700
617P	Lexington Concord, 1c	750.	700.	700

		LARGE DIE		SMALL DIE (2)
		(1) India	(1a) White Wove	White or Yellowish Wove
618P	Lexington Concord, 2c	750.	700.	700.
619P	Lexington Concord, 5c	750.	700.	700.
620P	Norse American, 2c	850.	850.	850.
621P	Norse American, 5c	850.	850.	850.
627P	Sesquicentennial, 2c	800.	750.	850.
628P	Ericsson, 5c	800.	750.	850.
629P	White Plains, 2c	800.	750.	850.

1927-29

643P	Vermont, 2c	800.	750.	850.
644P	Burgoyne, 2c	800.	750.	850.
645P	Valley Forge, 2c	800.	750.	850.
649P	Aeronautics, 2c	1,250.	900.	900.
650P	Aeronautics, 5c	1,250.	900.	900.
651P	Clark, 2c	900.	800.	850.
654P	Edison, 2c	900.	800.	850.
657P	Sullivan, 2c	850.	800.	850.
680P	Fallen Timbers, 2c	850.	800.	850.
681P	Ohio River Canalization, 2c	850.	800.	850.

1930-31

682P	Massachusetts Bay, 2c	850.	800.	750.
683P	Carolina Charleston, 2c	850.	800.	750.
684P	1½c brown	650.		
685P	4c brown	650.		
688P	Braddock's Field, 2c	850.	800.	750.
689P	von Steuben, 2c	850.	800.	750.
690P	Pulaski, 2c	850.	800.	750.
702P	Red Cross, 2c black & red		900.	900.
703P	Yorktown, 2c	1,250.	800.	750.

1932

Washington Bicentennial

704P	½c olive brown	1,000.	800.	750.
705P	1c green	1,000.	800.	750.
706P	1½c brown	1,000.	800.	750.
707P	2c carmine rose	1,000.	800.	750.
708P	3c deep violet	1,000.	800.	750.
709P	4c light brown	1,000.	800.	750.
710P	5c blue	1,000.	800.	750.
711P	6c red orange	1,000.	800.	750.
712P	7c black	1,000.	800.	750.
713P	8c olive bister	1,000.	800.	750.
714P	9c pale red	1,000.	800.	750.
715P	10c orange yellow	1,000.	800.	750.
716P	Winter Games, 2c	1,100.	950.	900.
717P	Arbor Day, 2c	900.	900.	800.
718P	Olympic Games, 3c violet	*10,000.*	950.	900.
719P	Olympic Games, 5c blue	*15,000.*	950.	900.
720P	3c deep violet	1,000.		
724P	Penn, 3c violet	800.	850.	750.
725P	Webster, 3c violet	800.	850.	750.

1933-34

726P	Georgia, 3c violet	700.	800.	650.
727P	Peace, 3c violet	700.	800.	650.
728P	Century of Progress, 1c	700.	800.	650.
729P	Century of Progress, 3c	700.	800.	650.
732P	N.R.A., 3c violet		900.	650.
733P	Byrd Antarctic, 3c	*1,250.*	900.	650.
734P	Kosciuszko, 5c blue	*1,250.*	800.	650.
736P	Maryland, 3c carmine rose	*1,250.*	800.	650.
737P	Mothers Day, 3c	800.	800.	650.
739P	Wisconsin, 3c deep violet		800.	650.
740P	Parks, 1c green		800.	650.
741P	Parks, 2c red			650.
742P	Parks, 3c violet		800.	650.
743P	Parks, 4c brown			650.
744P	Parks, 5c blue			650.
745P	Parks, 6c dark blue			650.
746P	Parks, 7c black		800.	650.
747P	Parks, 8c sage green			650.
748P	Parks, 9c red orange	800.		650.
749P	Parks, 10c gray black			650.

1935-37

772P	Conn., 3c violet	*1,150.*		650.
773P	San Diego, 3c purple			650.
774P	Boulder Dam, 3c purple			650.
775P	Michigan, 3c purple			650.
776P	Texas, 3c purple			650.
777P	Rhode Is., 3c purple			650.
782P	Arkansas, 3c pur.	800.	800.	650.
783P	Oregon, 3c purple	—	800.	650.
784P	Anthony, 3c violet			650.
785P	Army, 1c green		800.	800.
786P	Army, 2c carmine			800.
787P	Army, 3c purple	800.	800.	800.
788P	Army, 4c gray			800.
789P	Army, 5c ultramarine	*1,350.*	800.	800.
790P	Navy, 1c green			800.
791P	Navy, 2c car.	800.		800.
792P	Navy, 3c purple			800.
793P	Navy, 4c gray			800.
794P	Navy, 5c ultramarine			800.
795P	Ordinance, 3c red violet			650.
796P	Virginia Dare, 5c	800.		650.
797P	S.P.A. Sheet, 10c			650.
798P	Constitution, 3c red violet	800.		650.
799P	Hawaii, 3c violet	800.		650.
800P	Alaska, 3c violet			750.
801P	Puerto Rico, 3c	800.		650.
802P	Virgin Is., 3c light violet	—		650.

PRESIDENTIAL ISSUE

1938

803P	½c deep orange	*2,000.*		650.
804P	1c green			650.
805P	1½c bister brown			650.
806P	2c rose carmine		*1,800.*	650.
807P	3c deep violet			650.
a.	On glazed card	—		
808P	4c red violet			650.
809P	4½c dark gray	*1,500.*		650.
810P	5c bright blue	*1,500.*		650.
811P	6c red orange			650.
812P	7c sepia	*1,500.*		650.
813P	8c olive green		*1,800.*	650.
814P	9c olive green	*1,800.*	*1,800.*	650.
815P	10c brown red	*2,500.*		650.
816P	11c ultramarine			650.
817P	12c bright violet	*1,500.*		650.
818P	13c blue green			650.
819P	14c blue			650.
820P	15c blue gray	*1,800.*	*1,800.*	650.
821P	16c black	*1,500.*		650.
822P	17c rose red			650.
823P	18c brown carmine			650.
824P	19c bright violet	*1,800.*	*1,800.*	650.
825P	20c bright blue green	*1,800.*	*1,800.*	650.
826P	21c dull blue			650.
827P	22c vermilion			650.
828P	24c gray black	*1,800.*		650.
829P	25c deep red lilac			650.
830P	30c deep ultramarine			650.
831P	50c light red violet	*1,250.*		650.
832P	$1 purple & black			650.
833P	$2 yellow green & black			800.
834P	$5 carmine & black			800.

1938

835P	Constitution, 3c	—		600.
836P	Swedes & Finns, 3c	—		600.
837P	N.W. Territory, 3c			600.
838P	Iowa, 3c violet	*1,250.*		600.

1939

852P	Golden Gate, 3c	*1,800.*		600.
853P	World's Fair, 3c	*1,250.*		700.
854P	Inauguration, 3c	*1,250.*		650.
855P	Baseball, 3c violet	*1,500.*	*2,000.*	600.
856P	Panama Canal, 3c			600.
857P	Printing, 3c violet			600.
858P	Statehood, 3c rose violet			600.

FAMOUS AMERICANS ISSUE

1940

859P	Authors, 1c bright blue green			800.
860P	Authors, 2c rose carmine			800.
861P	Authors, 3c bright red violet			800.
862P	Authors, 5c ultramarine	*800.*		800.
863P	Authors, 10c dark brown	*2,500.*		800.
864P	Poets, 1c bright blue green	*1,300.*		800.
865P	Poets, 2c rose carmine			800.
866P	Poets, 3c bright red violet			800.
867P	Poets, 5c ultramarine	—		800.
868P	Poets, 10c dark brown	*1,450.*		800.
869P	Educators, 1c bright blue green	—		800.
870P	Educators, 2c rose carmine			800.
871P	Educators, 3c bright red violet			800.
872P	Educators, 5c ultramarine	*800.*		800.
873P	Educators, 10c dark brown	*900.*		800.
874P	Scientists, 1c bright blue green	*1,450.*		800.
875P	Scientists, 2c rose carmine	*800.*		800.
876P	Scientists, 3c bright red violet	*800.*		800.
877P	Scientists, 5c ultramarine			800.
878P	Scientists, 10c dark brown	*1,300.*		800.
879P	Composers, 1c bright blue green			800.
880P	Composers, 2c rose carmine	*900.*		800.
881P	Composers, 3c bright red violet			800.
882P	Composers, 5c ultramarine	*800.*		800.
883P	Composers, 10c dark brown			800.
884P	Artists, 1c bright blue green			800.
885P	Artists, 2c rose carmine			800.
886P	Artists, 3c bright red violet			800.
887P	Artists, 5c ultramarine	*800.*		800.
888P	Artists, 10c dark brown	*800.*		800.
889P	Inventors, 1c bright blue green			800.
890P	Inventors, 2c rose carmine	*1,275.*		800.
891P	Inventors, 3c bright red violet	*800.*		800.
892P	Inventors, 5c ultramarine			800.
893P	Inventors, 10c dark brown			800.

1940

894P	Pony Express, 3c henna brown	*1,100.*		600.
895P	Pan American, 3c light violet			600.
896P	Idaho, 3c bright violet	*800.*		600.
897P	Wyoming, 3c brown violet			600.
898P	Coronado, 3c violet	*1,100.*		600.
899P	Defense, 1c bright blue green	*800.*		600.
900P	Defense, 2c rose carmine	*800.*		600.
901P	Defense, 3c bright violet	*800.*		600.
902P	Emancipation, 3c deep violet	*800.*		750.

1941-44

903P	Vermont, 3c light violet			600.
904P	Kentucky, 3c violet	*750.*		600.
905P	Win the War, 3c violet			600.
906P	China, 5c bright blue			1,700.
907P	Allied Nations, 2c rose carmine			600.
908P	Four Freedoms, 1c br blue green	*800.*		600.
922P	Railroad, 3c violet	*800.*		600.
923P	Steamship, 3c violet	*1,500.*		600.
924P	Telegraph, 3c br red violet	*800.*		600.
925P	Corregidor, 3c deep violet	*1,275.*		600.
926P	Motion Picture, 3c deep violet	*800.*		600.

1945-46

927P	Florida, 3c br red violet	*1,100.*		600.
928P	United Nations, 5c ultramarine			600.
929P	Iwo Jima, 3c yellow green			600.
930P	Roosevelt, 1c blue green			600.
931P	Roosevelt, 2c carmine rose	*800.*		600.
932P	Roosevelt, 3c purple	*1,400.*		600.
933P	Roosevelt, 5c bright blue	—		
934P	Army, 3c olive	*1,250.*		600.
935P	Navy, 3c blue	*800.*		600.
939P	Merchant Marine, 3c blue green	—		
941P	Tennessee, 3c dark violet	*800.*		
942P	Iowa, 3c deep blue	*800.*		
944P	Kearny, 3c brown violet	*800.*		

1947-50

945P	Edison, 3c br red violet	*700.*		
946P	Pulitzer, 3c purple	*1,100.*		
947P	Stamp Centenary, 3c deep blue	—		
949P	Doctors, 3c brown violet	*1,325.*		
951P	Constitution, 3c blue green	*700.*		
955P	Mississippi, 3c brown violet	—		
956P	Four Chaplains, 3c gray black	—		
958P	Wisconsin, 5c deep blue	*700.*		
959P	Women, 3c dark violet	*700.*		
960P	White, 3c br red violet	*900.*		
962P	Key, 3c rose pink	*700.*		
965P	Stone, 3c bright violet	*700.*		
967P	Barton, 3c rose pink	*1,900.*		
971P	Volunteer Firemen, bright rose carmine	—		
972P	Indian Centennial, 3c dark brown	*900.*		
973P	Rough Riders, 3c violet brown	*700.*		
975P	Rogers, 3c br red violet	—		
976P	Fort Bliss, 3c henna brown	—		
977P	Michael, 3c rose pink	*1,150.*		
981P	Minnesota Terr., 3c blue green	*1,500.*	—	
983P	Puerto Rico, 3c green	*1,000.*		
985P	G.A.R., 3c br rose carmine	*1,500.*		
988P	Gompers, 3c br red violet	*1,500.*		
989P	Statue of Freedom, 3c br blue	*1,500.*		
991P	Supreme Court, 3c light violet	*700.*		
992P	Capitol, 3c br red violet	*700.*		

1951-53

999P	Nevada, 3c lt olive green	*1,000.*		
1000P	Cadillac, 3c blue	*800.*		
1001P	Colorado, 3c blue violet	*1,250.*		
1002P	Chemical, 3c violet brown	*700.*		
1003P	Brooklyn, 3c violet	*1,325.*		
1004P	Betsy Ross, 3c carmine rose	*800.*		
1005P	4H Clubs, 3c blue green	*1,250.*		
1006P	B. & O. Railroad, 3c br blue	*1,750.*		
1007P	A.A.A., 3c deep blue	*700.*	—	
1009P	Grand Coulee Dam, 3c blue green	*700.*		
1010P	Lafayette, 3c br blue	*800.*		
1011P	Mt. Rushmore, 3c blue green	*700.*	—	
1012P	Engineering, 3c violet blue	—		
1013P	Service Women, 3c deep blue	*800.*		
1016P	Red Cross, 3c dp blue * carmine	—		
1017P	National Guard, 3c br blue	*700.*		
1018P	Ohio Statehood, 3c chocolate		—	
1019P	Washington, 3c green	*700.*		
1020P	Louisiana, 3c violet brown	*800.*		
1021P	Japan, 5c green	*1,650.*		
1022P	American Bar, 3c rose violet	*700.*		
1025P	Trucking, 3c violet	*1,100.*		
1026P	Gen. Patton, 3c blue violet	*700.*	—	

1954

1029P	Columbia, 3c blue	*700.*		

LIBERTY ISSUE

1030P	Franklin, ½c red orange	*1,250.*		
1031P	Washington, 1c dark green	*700.*		

1032P Mount Vernon, 1 ½c brown carmine 900.
1033P Jefferson, 2c carmine rose — —
1036P Lincoln, 4c red violet 700.
1038P Monroe, 5c dp blue 700.
1039P Roosevelt, 6c carmine — —
1044P Independence Hall, 10c rose lake —
1047P Monticello, 20c ultramarine 1,100.
1049P Lee, 30c black 700.
1050P Marshall, 40c brown red 700.
1051P Anthony, 50c br purple 1,000.
1052P Henry, $1 purple 700.
1053P Hamilton, $5 black 1,200.

1954-61

1060P Nebraska, 3c violet 950.
1062P Eastman, 3c brown orange 900.
1063P Lewis & Clark, 3c violet brown 825.
1064P Academy of Fine Arts, 3c rose brown 800.
1067P Armed Forces Reserve, 3c purple 1,275.
1068P New Hampshire, 3c green 700.
1069P Soo Locks, 3c blue 825.
1071P Fort Ticonderoga, 3c lt brown 825.
1073P Franklin, 3c br carmine 700.
1074P Washington, 3c dp blue 700.
1076P FIPEX, 3c & 8c S/S 700. —
1077P Turkey, 3c rose lake 800.
1078P Antelope, 3c brown 700.
1079P Salmon, 3c bl green 700.
1080P Pure Food & Drug Act, 3c dk bl green 800.
1081P Wheatland, 3c black brown 700.
1082P Labor Day, 3c dp blue 700.
1083P Nassau Hall, 3c black, *orange* 700.
1085P Children, 3c dk blue 800.
1086P Hamilton, 3c rose red 700. —
1087P Polio, 3c red lilac 800.
1088P Coast & Geodetic Survey, 3c dk blue —
1090P Steel, 3c br ultramarine 700.
1092P Oklahoma, 3c dk blue —
1178P Ft. Sumter, lt green 1,500.
1193P Project Mercury, dark blue & yellow —

The following proofs are all from the proof files of the American Bank Note Co. archives that were sold and that are available to collectors. All items listed are on gummed stamp paper and are imperf unless otherwise noted, and they therefore have the appearance of imperf or part-perf stamps, though their source makes clear that they are, in fact, proofs. This group includes progressive proofs in the different colors, plus one variety of No. 2624P and three varieties of No. 2770aP that differ slightly from the issued designs and, therefore, are actually essays. Where single proofs are listed, pairs are worth double the values shown.

1979-93

1789Pg finished design as issued, pair

1789Pd blue color only, pair

1789P 15c John Paul Jones
a. Single, red color ("John Paul Jones") only —
pair with vert. gutter between —
pair with horiz. gutter between —
cross gutter block of four —
b. Single, yellow color only —
pair with vert. gutter between —
pair with horiz. gutter between —
cross gutter block of four —
c. Single, magenta color only —
pair with vert. gutter between —
pair with horiz. gutter between —
cross gutter block of four —
d. Single, blue color only —
pair with vert. gutter between —
pair with horiz. gutter between —
cross gutter block of four —
e. Single, black color only —
pair with vert. gutter between —
pair with horiz. gutter between —
cross gutter block of four —
f. Single, tagging blocks only —
pair with vert. gutter between —
pair with horiz. gutter between —
cross gutter block of four —
g. Single, finished design as issued —
pair 450.
pair with vert. gutter between 700.
pair with horiz. gutter between 600.
cross gutter block of four 3,000.

2418P

2418P 25c Ernest Hemingway, pair —
pair with vert. gutter between —
pair with horiz. gutter between —
cross gutter block of four -

2478Pa cross gutter block

Illustration reduced.

2476P 1c Kestrel, pair 300.
pair with vert. gutter between 450.
pair with horiz. gutter between 450.
cross gutter block of four —
a. Perforated
Pair with vert. gutter between 500.
Pair with horiz. gutter between 500.
Cross gutter block of four —
2478P 3c Bluebird, pair 300.
pair with vert. gutter between 450.
pair with horiz. gutter between 450.
cross gutter block of four —
a. Se-tenants, Nos. 2476P and 2478P
pair, one No. 2476P and one No. 2478P, with vert. gutter between —
cross gutter block of four, two No. 2476P at left and two No. 2478P at right —
b. Perforated
pair with vert. gutter between —
pair with horiz. gutter between —
cross gutter block of four —
c. Perforated se-tenants
pair, one No. 2476Pa and one No. 2478Pb, with vert. gutter between —
cross gutter block of four, two No. 2476Pa at left and two No. 2478Pb at right (unique) —
2500aP 25c Olympics, horiz. strip of five —
two strips of five with vert. gutter between —
two strips of five with horiz. gutter between —
cross gutter block of four strips of five —
2513P 25c Dwight D. Eisenhower, pair —
2517P (29c) "F" stamp, perforated
pair with vert. gutter between —
pair with horiz. gutter between —
cross gutter block of four (unique) —

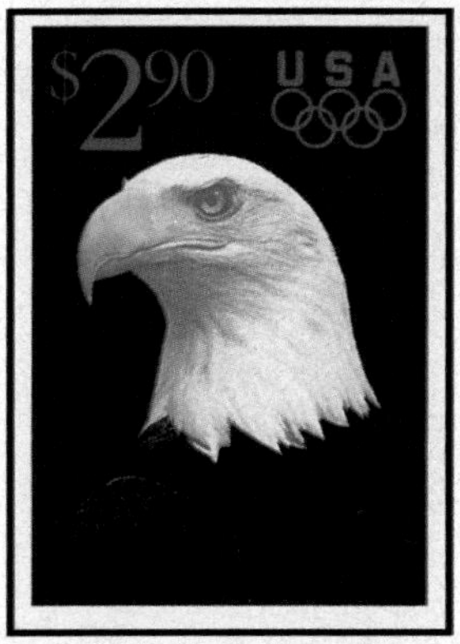

2540Pi with all litho. colors

2540Pf magenta, yellow and blue colors only

2540P $2.90 Eagle
a. Single, magenta color only —
pair with vert. gutter between —
pair with horiz. gutter between —
cross gutter block of four —
b. Single, yellow color only —
pair with vert. gutter between —
pair with horiz. gutter between —
cross gutter block of four —
c. Single, blue color only —
pair with vert. gutter between —
pair with horiz. gutter between —
cross gutter block of four —
d. Single, magenta and yellow colors only —
pair with vert. gutter between —
pair with horiz. gutter between —
cross gutter block of four —
e. Single, yellow and blue colors only —
pair with vert. gutter between —
pair with horiz. gutter between —
cross gutter block of four —
f. Single, magenta, yellow and blue colors only —
pair with vert. gutter between —
pair with horiz. gutter between —
cross gutter block of four —
g. Single, black (litho.) color only —
pair with vert. gutter between —
pair with horiz. gutter between —
cross gutter block of four —
h. Single, black (litho.) and yellow colors only —
pair with vert. gutter between —
pair with horiz. gutter between —
cross gutter block of four —
i. Single, all litho. colors but without black engr. —
pair with vert. gutter between —
pair with horiz. gutter between —
cross gutter block of four —
j. Single, finished design as issued —
pair —
pair with vert. gutter between —
pair with horiz. gutter between —
cross gutter block of four —
k. Perforated, all litho. colors but without black engr. —
pair with vert. gutter between —
pair with horiz. gutter between —
cross gutter block of four —
l. Perforated, finished design as issued —
pair with vert. gutter between —
pair with horiz. gutter between —
cross gutter block of four —

2605P, with plate numbers

2605P 23c Flag Presorted First Class Coil, vert. pair, uncut between — 400.
vert. pair, uncut between, with P#A111 —
2624P 1c, 4c and $1 Columbian souvenir sheet —
pair of sheets —
a. As No. 2624P, but with background of No. 2627P (essay) —
2625P 2c, 3c and $4 Columbian souvenir sheet —
pair of sheets —
2626P 5c, 30c and 50c Columbian souvenir sheet —
pair of sheets —
2627P 6c, 8c and $3 Columbian souvenir sheet —
pair of sheets —
2628P 10c, 15c and $2 Columbian souvenir sheet —
pair of sheets —
2629P $4 Columbian souvenir sheet —
pair of sheets —

2646aPi finished design as issued

2646aPe brown color only

Illustrations reduced.

2646aP 29c Hummingbirds booklet pane
b. Pane of five, yellow color only —
two panes of five with vert. gutter between —
two panes of five with horiz. gutter between —
cross gutter block of four panes of five —
c. Pane of five, magenta color only —
two panes of five with vert. gutter between —
two panes of five with horiz. gutter between —
cross gutter block of four panes of five —
d. Pane of five, blue color only —
two panes of five with vert. gutter between —
two panes of five with horiz. gutter between —
cross gutter block of four panes of five —
e. Pane of five, brown color (birds) only —
two panes of five with vert. gutter between —
two panes of five with horiz. gutter between —
cross gutter block of four panes of five —
f. Pane of five, brown color ("USA/29") only —
two panes of five with vert. gutter between —
two panes of five with horiz. gutter between —
cross gutter block of four panes of five —
g. Pane of five, green color (frames) only —
two panes of five with vert. gutter between —
two panes of five with horiz. gutter between —
cross gutter block of four panes of five —
h. Pane of five, orange color (frames) only —
two panes of five with vert. gutter between —
two panes of five with horiz. gutter between —
cross gutter block of four panes of five —
i. Pane of five, finished design as issued —
two panes of five with vert. gutter between —
two panes of five with horiz. gutter between —
cross gutter block of four panes of five —

2718aPd

2718aPe

Illustrations reduced.

2718aP 29c Christmas Toys booklet pane 800.
horiz. pair of panes of four 1,800.
vert. pair of panes of four 1,800.
b. As No. 2718aP, pane of four with two stamps at top from bottom row of normal pane and two stamps at bottom from top row of normal pane 1,200.
c. As No. 2718aP, perforated, pair of panes, uncut horiz. 2,000.
d. Pane of four with two stamps at top from bottom row of normal pane and two stamps at bottom from top row of normal pane, perforated 1,200.
e. Pane of four without red "Greetings" or green denominations 1,200.
f. As No. 2718aPe, two stamps at top from bottom row of "normal" pane and two stamps at bottom from top row of "normal" pane 1,500.
g. Pane of four without green denominations 1,200.
h. As No. 2718aPg, two stamps at top from bottom row of "normal" pane and two stamps at bottom from top row of "normal" pane 1,500.
2737aP 29c American Music booklet pane of eight —
pair of panes of eight —
c. As No. 2737aP, perforated horiz., uncut vert., pair of panes of eight —
2737bP 29c American Music booklet pane of four —
d. As No. 2737bP, perforated horiz., uncut vert., pair of panes of four —
e. Pair of panes, one No. 2737aP + one 2737bP —
f. Pair of panes, one No. 2737aPc + one 2737bPd —

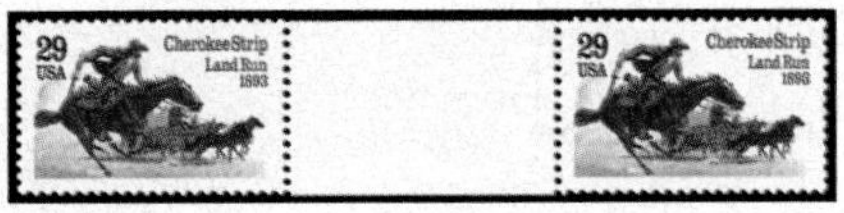

2754Pa

2754Pb

Illustration of No. 2754Pa reduced.

2754P 29c Cherokee Strip Land Run, pair —
pair with vert. gutter between —
pair with horiz. gutter between —
cross gutter block of four —
a. Perforated
pair with vert. gutter between —
pair with horiz. gutter between —
cross gutter block of four —
b. As No. 2754P, without purple inscriptions and black denominations, pair —
pair with vert. gutter between —
pair with horiz. gutter between —
cross gutter block of four —
c. Die proof, signed 11/25/92 for color and/or engraving —
2770aP 29c American Musicals booklet pane of four —
pair of panes —
a. Perforated horiz., uncut vert., pair of panes of four —
b. Pane of four, blue color only, with designs slightly different from issued designs (essay) —
c. Pane of four, blue and magenta colors only, with designs slightly different from issued designs (essay) —
d. Pane of four, blue, magenta and yellow colors only, with designs slightly different from issued designs (essay) —
2778aP 29c American Music booklet pane of four
a. Pane of four, yellow color only —
on approval card (unique) —
b. Pane of four, pink color only —
on approval card (unique) —
c. Pane of four, red color only —
on approval card (unique) —
d. Pane of four, blue color only —
on approval card (unique) —
e. Pane of four, black color (frames and wording) only —
on approval card (unique) —
f. Pane of four, black color (Musicians) only —
on approval card (unique) —
g. Pane of four, finished design as issued —
on approval card (unique) —
h. Pane of four, finished design as issued, on cromalin paper, taped to approval card (unique) —
i. Booklet cover, finished design as issued, on card stock, pair of covers —
j. Booklet cover, finished design as issued, on cromalin paper, taped to approval card (unique) —
k. Perforated horiz., uncut vert., pair of panes of four —

Some of the sets of progressive proofs are in panes that are 2½ to 3½ stamps tall. These sell for somewhat less than the full panes.

About 20 percent of the examples of No. 2778aPk are split into two pieces. From these pieces come horizontal pairs or blocks of booklet stamps imperf vertically.

2788aP 29c Classic Books, block of four —
pair of blocks with vert. gutter between —
pair of blocks with horiz. gutter between —
cross gutter block of four blocks —

AIR POST

1918

			DIE (1) Large	(2) Small
C1P	6c	orange	8,500.	
C2P	16c	green	7,000.	
C3P	24c	carmine rose & blue	8,500.	

1923

			DIE (1) Large	(2) Small
C4P	8c	dark green	4,750.	6,500.
C5P	16c	dark blue	4,750.	6,500.
C6P	24c	carmine	4,750.	6,500.

1926-27

C7P	10c	dark blue	*3,000.*	
C8P	15c	olive brown	*3,000.*	—
C9P	20c	yellow green	*3,000.*	

LINDBERGH ISSUE

1927

C10P	10c	dark blue	*6,000.*	*6,000.*

1928

C11P	5c	carmine & blue	*6,000.*	

1930

C12P	5c	violet	*3,000.*	

ZEPPELIN ISSUE

1930

C13P	65c	green	*15,000.*	*8,250.*
	a.	on wove	*15,000.*	
	b.	on stamp paper, imperf corner margin plate single		—
C14P	$1.30	brown	*15,000.*	*8,500.*
	a.	on wove	*15,000.*	
	b.	on stamp paper, imperf corner margin plate single		—
C15P	$2.60	blue	*15,000.*	*8,500.*
	a.	on wove	*15,000.*	
	b.	on stamp paper, imperf corner margin plate single		—

1932

C17P	8c	olive bister	*4,000.*	

CENTURY OF PROGRESS ISSUE

1933

C18P	50c	green	*12,500.*	*8,250.*

1935-39

C20P	25c	blue on wove		*2,750.*
C21P	20c	green on wove		*2,750.*
C22P	50c	carmine on wove		*2,750.*
C23P	6c	dark blue & carm. on wove		*2,750.*
C24P	30c	dull blue	*3,500.*	*2,750.*

1941-53

C25P	6c	carmine on wove		*3,000.*
C26P	8c	olive green on wove		*3,000.*
C27P	10c	violet on wove	*5,000.*	*3,000.*
C28P	15c	brown carmine on wove		*3,000.*
C29P	20c	bright green on wove		*3,000.*
C30P	30c	blue on wove		*3,000.*
C31P	50c	orange on wove		*3,000.*
C33P	5c	carmine	*5,500.*	
C40P	6c	carmine	*5,000.*	
C44P	25c	rose carmine	*5,000.*	*3,500.*
C45P	6c	magenta	*6,000.*	*5,000.*
C46P	80c	bright red violet	*5,000.*	—
C47P	6c	carmine	*6,000.*	
C48P	4c	bright blue		—

AIR POST SPECIAL DELIVERY

1934

CE1P	16c	dark blue on wove		*3,000.*

1936

CE2P	16c	red & blue on wove		*3,000.*

SPECIAL DELIVERY

1885

			DIE (1) Large	DIE (2) Small	*(2a)*	PLATE (3) India	PLATE (4) Card
E1P	10c	blue	600.	250.	2,250.	35.	30.
		Block of 4				175.	150.
		P# blk. of 8					—

1888

			(1)	(2)	(2a)	(3)	(4)
E2P	10c	blue	750.	250.	2,250.	35.	30.
		Block of 4				200.	150.
		P# blk. of 8				525.	—

1893

			(1)	(2)	(2a)	(3)	(4)
E3P	10c	orange	1,100.	300.	2,250.	65.	70.
		Block of 4				280.	310.
		P# blk. of 8					875.

1894-95

			(1)	(2)	(2a)	(3)	(4)
E4P	10c	blue	500.	250.	2,250.		
	a.	On stamp paper, pair					*5,500.*
E5P	10c	blue, on stamp paper, pair					*4,500.*

1902

			(1)	(2)	(2a)
E6P	10c	ultra	900.	250.	1,250.

1908

			(1)	(2)	(2a)
E7P	10c	green	2,250.	1,500.	2,250.

1922

			LARGE DIE (1) India	LARGE DIE *(1a)* White Wove	DIE (2) Small

1922

			(1)	(1a)	(2)
E12P	10c	deep ultra	1,850.	1,100.	

1925-54

			(1)	(1a)	(2)
E13P	15c	deep orange	1,750.		
E14P	20c	black	1,750.		
E17P	13c	blue			—
E20P	20c	deep blue	1,500.		

REGISTRATION

1911

			DIE (1) Large	DIE (2) Small	*(2a)*	PLATE (3) India	PLATE (4) Card
F1P	10c	ultra	5,000.	1,000.	1,100.		

POSTAGE DUE

1879

			(1)	(2)	(2a)	(3)	(4)
J1P	1c	brown	250.	100.	500.	22.	10.
		Block of 4				105.	65.
		P# blk. of 12				450.	
J2P	2c	brown	250.	100.	500.	20.	10.
		Block of 4				90.	65.
		P# blk. of 12				425.	
		2c dark brown	—				
J3P	3c	brown	250.	100.	500.	20.	10.
		Block of 4				90.	65.
		P# blk. of 12				425.	
		3c dark brown	—	—			
J4P	5c	brown	250.	100.	500.	20.	10.
		Block of 4				90.	65.
		P# blk. of 12				425.	
		5c dark brown	—				
J5P	10c	brown	250.	100.	500.		10.
		10c dark brown	—			32.	
		Block of 4				145.	65.
		P# blk. of 12				675.	
J6P	30c	brown	250.	100.	500.		10.
		30c dark brown	—			32.	
		Block of 4				145.	65.
		P# blk. of 12				675.	
J7P	50c	brown	250.	100.	500.		10.
		50c dark brown	—			32.	
		Block of 4				145.	65.
		P# blk. of 12				675.	

1887

			(1)	(2)	(2a)	(3)	(4)
J15P	1c	red brown			500.		15.
		Block of 4					
		P# blk. of 12					
J16P	2c	red brown			500.		15.
		Block of 4					
		P# blk. of 12					
J17P	3c	red brown			500.		20.
		Block of 4					
		P# blk. of 12					
J18P	5c	red brown			500.		15.
		Block of 4					
		P# blk. of 12					
J19P	10c	red brown			500.	19.	25.
		Block of 4				90.	
		P# blk. of 12				360.	
J20P	30c	red brown			500.	19.	18.
		Block of 4				90.	
		P# blk. of 12				360.	
J21P	50c	red brown			500.	45.	25.
		Block of 4				210.	
		P# blk. of 12				900.	

1891-93

			(1)	(2)	(2a)	(3)	(4)
J22P	1c	bright claret	140.	125.	500.	12.	17.
		Block of 4				65.	80.
		P# blk. of 12					—
	a.	On stamp paper, pair					*425.*
J23P	2c	bright claret	140.	125.	500.	12.	17.
		Block of 4				65.	80.
		P# blk. of 12					—
	a.	On stamp paper, pair					*425.*
J24P	3c	bright claret	140.	125.	500.	12.	17.
		Block of 4				65.	80.
		P# blk. of 12					—
	a.	On stamp paper, pair					*425*
J25P	5c	bright claret	140.	125.	500.	12.	17
		Block of 4				65.	80
		P# blk. of 12					—
	a.	On stamp paper, pair					*425*
J26P	10c	bright claret	140.	125.	500.	12.	17
		Block of 4				65.	80
		P# blk. of 12					—
	a.	On stamp paper, pair					*425*
J27P	30c	bright claret	140.	125.	500.	28.	17
		Block of 4				140.	80
		P# blk. of 12					—
	a.	On stamp paper, pair					*500*
J28P	50c	bright claret	140.	125.	500.	19.	17
		Block of 4				90.	80
		P# blk. of 12					—
	a.	On stamp paper, pair					*500*

Values for J22Pa-J28Pa are for pairs with original gum and minor faults.

1894

			(1)	(2)	(2a)	(3)	(4)
J31P	1c	claret	165.	120.	500.		
	a.	On stamp paper, pair					*225*
		Block of 4					*500*
J32P	2c	claret	165.	120.	500.		100
		Block of 4					475
		P# blk. of 6					3,000
J33P	3c	claret	165.	120.	500.		
J34P	5c	claret	165.	120.	500.		
J35P	10c	claret	165.	120.	500.		
J36P	30c	claret	165.	120.	500.		
J37P	50c	claret	165.	120.	500.		

1925

J68P	½c	dull red	*5,750.*

1930-31

J69P	½c	deep car	450.
J70P	1c	deep car	450.
J71P	2c	deep car	450.
J72P	3c	deep car	450.
J73P	5c	deep car	450.
J74P	10c	deep car	450.
J75P	30c	deep car	450.
J76P	50c	deep car	450.
J77P	$1	deep car	1,400.
J78P	$5	deep car	1,400.

PARCEL POST POSTAGE DUE

1912

			DIE (1) Large	DIE (2) Small	*(2a)*	PLATE (3) India	PLATE (4) Card
JQ1P	1c	dark green	600.	500.	700.		
JQ2P	2c	dark green	600.	500.	700.		
JQ3P	5c	dark green	600.	500.	700.		
JQ4P	10c	dark green	600.	500.	700.		
JQ5P	25c	dark green	600.	500.	700.		

CARRIERS

1851

			(1)	(2)	(2a)	(3)	(4)
LO1P	1c	blue *(Franklin)*	800.	300.	1,500.	50.	30.
		Block of 4				210.	125.
		Cracked plate				—	—
LO2P	1c	blue *(Eagle)*	800.	300.	1,500.	50.	30.
		Block of 4				210.	125.
		P # blk. of 8				675.	

Nos. LO1P (1) and LO2P (1) exist only as hybrids.

OFFICIAL

AGRICULTURE

1873

			(1)	(2)	(2a)	(3)	(4)
O1P	1c	yellow	80.	100.	500.	15.	8.
		Block of 4				65.	50.
		P# blk. of 12					225.
O2P	2c	yellow	80.	100.	500.	15.	8.
		Block of 4				65.	50.
		P# blk. of 10					225.
O3P	3c	yellow	80.	100.	500.	15.	8.
		Block of 4				65.	50.
		P# blk. of 12					225.
O4P	6c	yellow	80.	100.	500.	15.	8.
		Block of 4				65.	50.
		P# blk. of 12					225.
O5P	10c	yellow	80.	100.	500.	15.	8.
		Block of 4				65.	50.
		P# blk. of 12					225.
O6P	12c	yellow	80.	100.	500.	15.	8.
		Block of 4				65.	50.
		P# blk. of 12					225.
O7P	15c	yellow	80.	100.	500.	15.	8.
		Block of 4				65.	50.

		P# blk. of 12					225.
O8P	24c	yellow	80.	100.	500.	15.	8.
		Block of 4				65.	50.
		P# blk. of 12					225.
O9P	30c	yellow	80.	100.	500.	15.	8.
		Block of 4				65.	50.
		P# blk. of 12					225.

EXECUTIVE

O10P	1c	carmine	100.	100.	500.	15.	10.
		Block of 4				65.	50.
		P# blk. of 14					225.
O11P	2c	carmine	100.	100.	500.	15.	10.
		Block of 4				65.	50.
		P# blk. of 12					225.
		Foreign entry of 6c Agriculture					—
O12P	3c	carmine	100.	100.	500.	15.	10.
		Block of 4				65.	50.
		P# blk. of 12					225.
O13P	6c	carmine	100.	100.	500.	25.	15.
		Block of 4				125.	85.
		P# blk. of 10					350.
O14P	10c	carmine	100.	100.	500.	15.	10.
		Block of 4				65.	50.
		P# blk. of 12					225.

INTERIOR

O15P	1c	vermilion	80.	100.	500.	15.	8.
		Block of 4				65.	50.
		P# blk. of 12					225.
O16P	2c	vermilion	80.	100.	500.	15.	8.
		Block of 4				65.	50.
		P# blk. of 10					200.
O17P	3c	vermilion	80.	100.	500.	15.	8.
		Block of 4				65.	50.
		P# blk. of 10					225.
O18P	6c	vermilion	80.	100.	500.	20.	10.
		Block of 4				90.	50.
		P# blk. of 12					250.
O19P	10c	vermilion	80.	100.	500.	15.	8.
		Block of 4				65.	45.
		P# blk. of 12					225.
O20P	12c	vermilion	80.	100.	500.	15.	8.
		Block of 4				65.	45.
		P# blk. of 10					225.
O21P	15c	vermilion	80.	100.	500.	15.	8.
		Block of 4				65.	45.
		P# blk. of 12					225.
O22P	24c	vermilion	80.	100.	500.	15.	8.
		Block of 4				65.	45.
		P# blk. of 12					225.
O23P	30c	vermilion	80.	100.	500.	15.	8.
		Block of 4				65.	45.
		P# blk. of 12					225.
O24P	90c	vermilion	80.	100.	500.	15.	8.
		Block of 4				65.	45.
		P# blk. of 12					225.

JUSTICE

O25P	1c	purple	80.	100.	500.	15.	8.
		Block of 4				65.	50.
		P# blk. of 12					225.
O26P	2c	purple	80.	100.	500.	15.	8.
		Block of 4				65.	50.
		P# blk. of 12					225.
O27P	3c	purple	80.	100.	500.	15.	8.
		Block of 4				65.	50.
		P# blk. of 12					225.
		Plate Scratches					—
O28P	6c	purple	80.	100.	500.	15.	8.
		Block of 4				65.	50.
		P# blk. of 12					225.
O29P	10c	purple	80.	100.	500.	15.	8.
		Block of 4				65.	50.
		P# blk. of 10					225.
O30P	12c	purple	80.	100.	500.	15.	8.
		Block of 4				65.	50.
		P# blk. of 12					225.
O31P	15c	purple	80.	100.	500.	15.	8.
		Block of 4				65.	50.
		P# blk. of 10					225.
O32P	24c	purple	80.	100.	500.	15.	8.
		Block of 4				65.	50.
		P# blk. of 12					225.
		Short transfer (pos. 98)					—
O33P	30c	purple	80.	100.	500.	15.	8.
		Block of 4				65.	50.
		P# blk. of 12					225.
O34P	90c	purple	80.	100.	500.	15.	8.
		Block of 4				65.	50.
		P# blk. of 10					225.

NAVY

O35P	1c	ultramarine	80.	100.	500.	15.	8.
		Block of 4				65.	50.
		P# blk. of 12					225.
O36P	2c	ultramarine	80.	100.	500.	15.	8.
		Block of 4				65.	50.
		P# blk. of 12					225.
O37P	3c	ultramarine	80.	100.	500.	15.	8.
		Block of 4				65.	50.
		P# blk. of 10					225.
O38P	6c	ultramarine	80.	100.	500.	20.	15.
		Block of 4				90.	75.
		P# blk. of 10					350.
O39P	7c	ultramarine	80.	100.	500.	15.	8.
		Block of 4				65.	50.
		P# blk. of 10					225.
O40P	10c	ultramarine	80.	100.	500.	15.	8.
		Block of 4				65.	50.
		P# blk. of 12				—	225.
O41P	12c	ultramarine	80.	100.	500.	15.	8.
		Block of 4				65.	50.
		P# blk. of 12					225.
O42P	15c	ultramarine	80.	100.	500.	15.	8.
		Block of 4				65.	50.
		P# blk. of 12					225.
O43P	24c	ultramarine	80.	100.	500.	15.	8.
		Block of 4				65.	50.
		P# blk. of 12					225.
O44P	30c	ultramarine	80.	100.	500.	15.	8.
		Block of 4				65.	50.
		P# blk. of 12					225.
O45P	90c	ultramarine	80.	100.	500.	15.	8.
		Block of 4				65.	50.
		P# blk. of 12					225.
		Short transfer at upper left (106, pos. 1, 5)					—

POST OFFICE

O47P	1c	black	80.	100.	500.	15.	8.
		Block of 4				65.	50.
		P# blk. of 10					225.
O48P	2c	black	80.	100.	500.	15.	8.
		Block of 4				65.	50.
		P# blk. of 14					225.
O49P	3c	black	80.	100.	500.	15.	8.
		Block of 4				65.	50.
		P# blk. of 12					225.
O50P	6c	black	80.	100.	500.	15.	8.
		Block of 4				65.	50.
		P# blk. of 12					225.
O51P	10c	black	80.	100.	500.	15.	8.
		Block of 4				65.	50.
		P# blk. of 12					225.
O52P	12c	black	80.	100.	500.	15.	8.
		Block of 4				65.	50.
		P# blk. of 12					225.
O53P	15c	black	80.	100.	500.	15.	8.
		Block of 4				65.	50.
		P# blk. of 12					225.
O54P	24c	black	80.	100.	500.	15.	8.
		Block of 4				65.	50.
		P# blk. of 12					225.
O55P	30c	black	80.	100.	500.	15.	8.
		Block of 4				65.	50.
		P# blk. of 12					225.
O56P	90c	black	80.	100.	500.	15.	8.
		Block of 4				65.	50.
		P# blk. of 12					225.

STATE

O57P	1c	green	80.	100.	600.	15.	8.
		Block of 4				65.	50.
		P# blk. of 12					225.
O58P	2c	green	80.	100.	600.	15.	8.
		Block of 4				65.	50.
		P# blk. of 10					225.
O59P	3c	green	80.	100.	600.	15.	8.
		Block of 4				65.	50.
		P# blk. of 10					225.
O60P	6c	green	80.	100.	600.	25.	16.
		Block of 4				120.	85.
		P# blk. of 12					375.
O61P	7c	green	80.	100.	600.	15.	8.
		Block of 4				65.	50.
		P# blk. of 12					225.
O62P	10c	green	80.	100.	600.	15.	8.
		Block of 4				65.	50.
		P# blk. of 12					225.
O63P	12c	green	80.	100.	600.	15.	8.
		Block of 4				65.	50.
		P# blk. of 10					225.
O64P	15c	green	80.	100.	600.	15.	8.
		Block of 4				65.	50.
		P# blk. of 12					225.
O65P	24c	green	80.	100.	600.	15.	8.
		Block of 4				65.	50.
		P# blk. of 12					225.
O66P	30c	green	80.	100.	600.	15.	8.
		Block of 4				65.	50.
		P# blk. of 12					225.
O67P	90c	green	80.	100.	600.	15.	8.
		Block of 4				65.	50.
		P# blk. of 12					225.
O68P	$2	green & black	150.	125.	750.	85.	35.
		Block of 4				375.	175.
		Sheet of 10				—	*5,000.*
	a.	Invtd. center					*7,000.*
		Half sheet of 5					*31,500.*
O69P	$5	green & black	150.	125.	750.	85.	35.
		Block of 4				375.	175.
		Sheet of 10					*5,000.*
	a.	Invtd. center					*7,000.*
		Half sheet of 5					*31,500.*
		Sheet of 10					*75,000.*
O70P	$10	green & black	150.	125.	800.	85.	35.
		Block of 4				375.	—
		Sheet of 10					*5,000.*
O71P	$20	green & black	150.	125.	800.	85.	35.
		Block of 4				375.	175.
		Sheet of 10					*5,000.*
	a.	Invtd. center					*7,000.*
		Block of 4					*30,000.*
		Half sheet of 5					*31,500.*

O68P to O71P Large Dies exist as hybrids only.

TREASURY

O72P	1c	brown	80.	100.	500.	15.	8.
		Block of 4				65.	50.
		P# blk. of 12					225.
O73P	2c	brown	80.	100.	500.	15.	8.
		Block of 4				65.	50.
		P# blk. of 12					225.
O74P	3c	brown	80.	100.	500.	15.	8.
		Block of 4				65.	50.
		P# blk. of 14					225.
O75P	6c	brown	80.	100.	500.	20.	15.
		Block of 4				100.	75.
		P# blk. of 12					375.
O76P	7c	brown	80.	100.	500.	15.	8.
		Block of 4				65.	50.
		P# blk. of 12					225.
O77P	10c	brown	80.	100.	500.	15.	8.
		Block of 4				65.	50.
		P# blk. of 12					225.
O78P	12c	brown	80.	100.	500.	15.	8.
		Block of 4				65.	50.
		P# blk. of 12					225.
O79P	15c	brown	80.	100.	500.	15.	8.
		Block of 4				65.	50.
		P# blk. of 12					275.
O80P	24c	brown	80.	100.	500.	15.	8.
		Block of 4				65.	45.
		P# blk. of 12					225.
O81P	30c	brown	80.	100.	500.	15.	8.
		Block of 4				65.	45.
		P# blk. of 12					225.
O82P	90c	brown	80.	100.	500.	15.	8.
		Block of 4				65.	50.
		P# blk. of 12					225.

WAR

O83P	1c	rose	80.	100.	500.	15.	8.
		Block of 4				65.	50.
		P# blk. of 12					225.
O84P	2c	rose	80.	100.	500.	15.	8.
		Block of 4				65.	50.
O85P	3c	rose	80.	100.	500.	15.	8.
		Block of 4				65.	50.
		Plate flaw at upper left (32R20)					—
O86P	6c	rose	80.	100.	500.	15.	8.
		Block of 4				65.	50.
		P# blk. of 12					225.
O87P	7c	rose	80.	100.	500.	15.	8.
		Block of 4				65.	50.
		P# blk. of 10					225.
O88P	10c	rose	80.	100.	500.	15.	8.
		Block of 4				65.	50.
		P# blk. of 10					225.
O89P	12c	rose	80.	100.	500.	15.	8.
		Block of 4				65.	50.
		P# blk. of 12					225.
O90P	15c	rose	80.	100.	500.	15.	8.
		Block of 4				65.	50.
		P# blk. of 12					225.
O91P	24c	rose	80.	100.	500.	15.	8.
		Block of 4				65.	50.
		P# blk. of 10					225.
O92P	30c	rose	80.	100.	500.	15.	8.
		Block of 4				65.	50.
		P# blk. of 10					225.
O93P	90c	rose	80.	100.	500.	15.	8.
		Block of 4				65.	50.
		P# blk. of 12					225.

O83-O93 exist in a plum shade.

POSTAL SAVINGS MAIL

1911

O124P	1c	dark violet	450.	275.	1,000.
O121P	2c	black	450.	275.	1,000.
O126P	10c	carmine	450.	275.	1,000.
O122P	50c	dark green	450.	275.	1,000.
O123P	$1	ultramarine	450.	275.	1,000.

NEWSPAPERS

1865

			DIE (1) Large	DIE (2) Small	(2a)	PLATE (3) Wove Paper	PLATE (4) Card
PR2P	10c	green	575.	225.		40.	60.
		Block of 4				200.	300.
		P# blk. of 6					—
PR3P	25c	orange red	575.	225.		45.	60.
		Block of 4				225.	300.
		P# blk. of 6					—
PR4P	5c	blue	575.	225.		40.	60.
		Block of 4				200.	300.
		P# blk. of 6					—

1875

PR5P	5c	dark blue			*1,750.*		60.
PR6P	10c	deep green			*1,750.*		60.
PR7P	25c	dark car red			*1,750.*		60.
PR9P	2c	black	100.	50.	250.	15.	12.
		Block of 4				65.	55.
		P# blk. of 8					—
PR10P	3c	black	100.	50.	250.	15.	12.
		Block of 4				65.	55.
		P# blk. of 8					—
PR11P	4c	black	100.	50.	250.	15.	12.
		Block of 4				65.	55.
		P# blk. of 8					—
PR12P	6c	black	100.	50.	250.	15.	12.
		Block of 4				65.	55.
		P# blk. of 8					—
PR13P	8c	black	100.	50.	250.	15.	12.
		Block of 4				65.	55.
		P# blk. of 8					—
PR14P	9c	black	100.	50.	250.	15.	12.
		Block of 4				65.	55.
		P# blk. of 8					—
PR15P	10c	black	100.	50.	250.	15.	12.
		Block of 4				65.	55.
		P# blk. of 8					—
PR16P	12c	rose	100.	50.	250.	15.	12.
		Block of 4				65.	55.
		P# blk. of 8					—
PR17P	24c	rose	100.	50.	250.	15.	12.

		Block of 4				65.	55.
		P# blk. of 8					—
PR18P	36c	rose	100.	50.	250.	15.	12.
		Block of 4				65.	55.
		P# blk. of 8					—
PR19P	48c	rose	100.	50.	250.	15.	12.
		Block of 4				65.	55.
		P# blk. of 8					—
PR20P	60c	rose	100.	50.	250.	15.	12.
		Block of 4				65.	55.
		P# blk. of 8					—
PR21P	72c	rose	100.	50.	250.	15.	12.
		Block of 4				65.	55.
		P# blk. of 8					—
PR22P	84c	rose	100.	50.	250.	15.	12.
		Block of 4				65.	55.
		P# blk. of 8					—
PR23P	96c	rose	100.	50.	250.	15.	12.
		Block of 4				65.	55.
		P# blk. of 8					—
PR24P	$1.92	dark brown	100.	50.	250.	18.	15.
		Block of 4				80.	70.
		P# blk. of 8					—
PR25P	$3	vermilion	100.	50.	250.	18.	15.
		Block of 4				80.	70.
		P# blk. of 8					—
PR26P	$6	ultra	100.	50.	250.	18.	15.
		Block of 4				80.	70.
		P# blk. of 8					—
PR27P	$9	yellow	100.	50.	250.	18.	15.
		Block of 4				80.	70.
		P# blk. of 8					—
PR28P	$12	blue green	100.	50.	250.	18.	15.
		Block of 4				80.	70.
		P# blk. of 8					—
PR29P	$24	dark gray violet	100.	50.	250.	18.	15.
		Block of 4				80.	70.
		P# blk. of 8					—
PR30P	$36	brown rose	100.	50.	250.	21.	15.
		Block of 4				90.	70.
		P# blk. of 8					—
PR31P	$48	red brown	100.	50.	250.	23.	15.
		Block of 4				100.	70.
		P# blk. of 8					—
PR32P	$60	violet	100.	50.	250.	25.	18.
		Block of 4				110.	85.
		P# blk. of 8					—

1879

PR57P	2c	deep black	100.	12.	4.
		Block of 4		60.	24.
a.		On stamp paper, pair			—
PR58P	3c	deep black	100.	12.	4.
		Block of 4		60.	24.
a.		On stamp paper, pair			—
PR59P	4c	deep black	100.	12.	4.
		Block of 4		60.	24.
a.		On stamp paper, pair			—
PR60P	6c	deep black	100.	12.	4.
		Block of 4		60.	24.
a.		On stamp paper, pair			—
PR61P	8c	deep black	100.	12.	4.
		Block of 4		60.	24.
a.		On stamp paper, pair			—
PR62P	10c	deep black	100.	12.	4.
		Block of 4		60.	24.
a.		On stamp paper, pair			—
PR63P	12c	red	100.	12.	6.
		Block of 4		60.	32.
PR64P	24c	red	100.	12.	6.
		Block of 4		60.	32.
PR65P	36c	red	100.	12.	6.
		Block of 4		60.	32.
PR66P	48c	red	100.	12.	6.
		Block of 4		60.	32.
PR67P	60c	red	100.	12.	6.
		Block of 4		60.	32.
PR68P	72c	red	100.	12.	6.
		Block of 4		60.	32.
PR69P	84c	red	100.	12.	6.
		Block of 4		60.	32.
PR70P	96c	red	100.	12.	6.
		Block of 4		60.	32.
PR71P	$1.92	pale brown	100.	15.	8.
		Block of 4		75.	45.
a.		On stamp paper, pair			—
PR72P	$3	red verm.	100.	15.	8.
		Block of 4		75.	45.
a.		On stamp paper, pair			—
PR73P	$6	blue	100.	15.	8.
		Block of 4		75.	45.
a.		On stamp paper, pair			—
PR74P	$9	orange	100.	15.	8.
		Block of 4		75.	45.
a.		On stamp paper, pair			—
PR75P	$12	yel. green	100.	15.	8.
		Block of 4		75.	45.
a.		On stamp paper, pair			—
PR76P	$24	dark violet	100.	18.	8.
		Block of 4		90.	45.
a.		On stamp paper, pair			—
PR77P	$36	Indian red	100.	20.	8.
		Block of 4		100.	45.
a.		On stamp paper, pair			—
PR78P	$48	yellow brown	100.	24.	8.
		Block of 4		120.	45.
a.		On stamp paper, pair			—
PR79P	$60	purple	100.	24.	8.
		Block of 4		120.	45.
a.		On stamp paper, pair			—

1885

PR81P	1c	black	100.	60.	250.	10.	8.
		Block of 4				50.	40.
		P# blk. of 8					200.
a.		On stamp paper, pair					—
PR82P	12c	carmine		80.	250.	17.	8.
		Block of 4				85.	
a.		On stamp paper, pair					—
PR83P	24c	carmine		80.	250.	17.	8.
		Block of 4				85.	
a.		On stamp paper, pair					—
PR84P	36c	carmine		80.	250.	17.	8.
		Block of 4				85.	
a.		On stamp paper, pair					—
PR85P	48c	carmine		80.	250.	17.	8.
		Block of 4				85.	
a.		On stamp paper, pair					—
PR86P	60c	carmine		80.	250.	17.	8.
		Block of 4				85.	
a.		On stamp paper, pair					—
PR87P	72c	carmine		80.	250.	17.	8.
		Block of 4				85.	
a.		On stamp paper, pair					—
PR88P	84c	carmine		80.	250.	17.	8.
		Block of 4				85.	
a.		On stamp paper, pair					—
PR89P	96c	carmine		80.	250.	17.	8.
		Block of 4				85.	
a.		On stamp paper, pair					—

1895

PR102P	1c	black	125.	100.	275.
PR103P	2c	black	125.	100.	275.
PR104P	5c	black	125.	100.	275.
PR105P	10c	black	125.	100.	275.
PR106P	25c	carmine	125.	100.	275.
PR107P	50c	carmine	125.	100.	275.
PR108P	$2	scarlet	125.	100.	275.
PR109P	$5	blue	125.	100.	275.
PR110P	$10	green	125.	100.	275.
PR111P	$20	slate	125.	100.	275.
PR112P	$50	carmine	125.	100.	275.
PR113P	$100	purple	125.	100.	275.

PARCEL POST

1912-13

			DIE ON INDIA			PLATE	
			(1) Large	(2) Small	(2a)	(3) India	(4) Card
Q1P	1c	car rose	1,400.	1,200.	1,200.		
Q2P	2c	car rose	1,400.	1,200.	1,200.		
Q3P	3c	car rose	1,400.	1,200.	1,200.		
Q4P	4c	car rose	1,400.	1,200.	1,200.		
Q5P	5c	car rose	1,400.	1,200.	1,200.		
Q6P	10c	car rose	1,400.	1,200.	1,200.		
Q7P	15c	car rose	1,400.	1,200.	1,200.		
Q8P	20c	car rose	1,400.	1,200.	1,200.		
Q9P	25c	car rose	1,400.	1,200.	1,200.		
Q10P	50c	car rose	1,400.	1,200.	1,200.		
Q11P	75c	car rose	1,400.	1,200.	1,200.		
Q12P	$1	car rose	1,400.	1,200.	1,200.		

SPECIAL HANDLING

1925-28

QE1P	10c	yel grn	*1,500.*
QE2P	15c	yel grn	*1,500.*
QE3P	20c	yel grn	*1,500.*
QE4P	25c	deep grn	*1,500.*
QE4aP	25c	yel grn	*1,500.*

LOCAL

1844

5L1P	5c	black	*3,500.*

TELEGRAPH

AMERICAN RAPID TELEGRAPH CO.

1881

			DIE (2) Small	PLATE (3) India
1T1P	1c	black	80.	32.
		Pair		68.
1T2P	3c	orange		32.
		Pair		68.
1T3P	5c	bister brown	80.	32.
		Pair		68.
1T4P	10c	purple		32.
		Pair		68.
1T5P	15c	green	80.	32.
		Pair		68.
1T6P	20c	red	80.	32.
		Pair		68.
1T7P	25c	rose	80.	32.
		Pair		68.
1T8P	50c	blue		32.
		Pair		68.

"Collect"

1T9P	1c	brown	32.
		Pair, Nos. 1T9P, 1T13P	68.
		Same, block of 4	145.
1T10P	5c	blue	32.
		Pair, Nos. 1T10P, 1T14P	68.
		Same, block of 4	145.
1T11P	15c	red brown	32.
		Pair, Nos. 1T11P, 1T15P	68.
		Same, block of 4	145.
1T12P	20c	olive green	32.
		Pair, Nos. 1T12P, 1T16P	68.
		Same, block of 4	145.

Office Coupon

1T13P	1c	brown	32.
1T14P	5c	blue	32.
1T15P	15c	red brown	32.
1T16P	20c	olive green	32.

BALTIMORE & OHIO TELEGRAPH CO.

1885

3T1P	1c	vermilion	32.
		Pair	68.
3T2P	5c	blue	32.
		Pair	68.
3T3P	10c	red brown	32.
		Pair	68.
3T4P	25c	orange	32.
		Pair	68.

1886

3T6P		black	32.
		Pair	68.
3T7P	1c	green	32.
3T8P	5c	blue	32.
3T9P	10c	brown	32.
3T10P	25c	orange	32.

POSTAL TELEGRAPH CO.

1885

			DIE		PLATE
			(1) Large	(2) Small	(3) India
15T1P	10c	green		55.	32.
15T2P	15c	orange red			32.
15T3P	25c	blue	65.		32.
15T4P	50c	brown		65.	32.

WESTERN UNION TELEGRAPH CO.

16T1P	(1871)	green			17.
		Pair			35.
16T2P	(1872)	red			17.
		Pair			35.
16T3P	(1873)	blue			17.
		Pair			35.
16T4P	(1874)	brown			17.
		Pair			35.
16T5P	(1875)	deep green			17.
16T6P	(1876)	red			17.
16T7P	(1877)	violet			—
16T8P	(1878)	gray brown			20.
16T9P	(1879)	blue			14.
16T10P	(1880)	lilac rose			16.
16T11P	(1881)	green			16.
16T12P	(1882)	blue			20.
16T13P	(1883)	yellow brown			16.
16T14P	(1884)	gray violet			20.
16T15P	(1885)	green			20.
16T16P	(1886)	brown violet			13.
		Pair			28.
16T17P	(1887)	red brown			13.
		Pair			28.
16T18P	(1888)	blue			13.
		Pair			28.
16T19P	(1889)	olive green			16.
16T22P	(1892)	vermilion			16.
16T30P	(1900)	red violet			28.
16T44P	(1913)	brown	—	—	—

REVENUE

NORMAL COLORS

1862-68 by Butler & Carpenter, Philadelphia.

1868-75 by Joseph R. Carpenter, Philadelphia.

In the following listing the so-called small die proofs on India paper may be, in fact probably are, plate proofs. The editors shall consider them die proofs, however, until they see them in pairs or blocks. Many revenue proofs on India are mounted on card.

FIRST ISSUE

1862-71

			DIE ON INDIA (1) Large	DIE ON INDIA (2) Small	PLATE (3) India	PLATE (4) Card
R1P	1c	Express, red			70.	65.
		Block of 4				275.
R2P	1c	Playing Cards, red	600.		60.	65.
		Block of 4			250.	275.
R3P	1c	Proprietary, red			140.	45.
		Block of 4				200.
R4P	1c	Telegraph, red				28.
		Block of 4				125.
R5P	2c	Bank Check, blue		525.		33.
		Block of 4				140.
R6P	2c	Bank Check, orange			60.	
		Block of 4			250.	
R7P	2c	Certificate, blue				28.
		Block of 4				125.
R8P	2c	Certificate, orange			82.	
		Block of 4			350.	
R9P	2c	Express, blue				28.
		Block of 4				125.
R10P	2c	Express, orange	600.		60.	
		Pair			250.	
R11P	2c	Playing Cards, blue				38.
		Block of 4				160.
R13P	2c	Proprietary, blue		400.		28.
		Block of 4				125.
R15P	2c	U.S.I.R., orange			*1,250.*	
R16P	3c	Foreign Exchange, green	600.		225.	38.
		Block of 4				160.
		R16P1 + R19P1 composite	—			
R17P	3c	Playing Cards, green	*700.*	400.		100.
		Block of 4				425.
R18P	3c	Proprietary, green			60.	28.
		Block of 4			250.	125.
R19P	3c	Telegraph, green	600.		225.	28.
		Block of 4				125.
R20P	4c	Inland Exchange, brown			225.	28.
		Block of 4				125.
R21P	4c	Playing Cards, violet		400.		95.
		Block of 4				400.
R22P	4c	Proprietary, violet	600.		110.	60.
		Block of 4			475.	250.
R23P	5c	Agreement, red				33.
		Block of 4				140.
R24P	5c	Certificate, red			95.	110.
		Block of 4			400.	
		R24P1 + R25P1 composite	—			
R25P	5c	Express, red		250.		33.
		Block of 4				145.
R26P	5c	Foreign Exchange, red				300.
R27P	5c	Inland Exchange, red		250.		28.
		Block of 4				125.
R28P	5c	Playing Cards, red		—	105.	325.
		Block of 4			440.	
R29P	5c	Proprietary, red on blue wove, gummed				—
R30P	6c	Inland Exchange, orange			60.	33.
		Block of 4			250.	140.
R32P	10c	Bill of Lading, blue				33.
		Block of 4				140.
R33P	10c	Certificate, blue			140.	33.
		Block of 4				140.
R34P	10c	Contract, blue				33.
		Block of 4				140.
R35P	10c	Foreign Exchange, blue				33.
		Block of 4				140.
R36P	10c	Inland Exchange, blue				33.
		Block of 4				140.
R37P	10c	Power of Attorney, blue				33.
		Block of 4				140.
R38P	10c	Proprietary, blue	*700.*		70.	
		Block of 4			300.	
R39P	15c	Foreign Exchange, brown			90.	325.
		Block of 4			375.	1,600.
R40P	15c	Inland Exchange, brown			120.	33.
		Block of 4				140.
R41P	20c	Foreign Exchange, red	600.		90.	100.
		Block of 4			375.	425.
		R41P1 + R42P1 composite	—			
R42P	20c	Inland Exchange, red	600.	250.	260.	33.
		Block of 4				140.
R43P	25c	Bond, red				500.
		Block of 4				2,500.
R44P	25c	Certificate, red				33.
		Block of 4				140.
R45P	25c	Entry of Goods, red				550.
R46P	25c	Insurance, red			60.	33.
		Block of 4			250.	140.
R47P	25c	Life Insurance, red				33.
		Block of 4				140.
R48P	25c	Power of Attorney, red				33.
		Block of 4				140.
R49P	25c	Protest, red				33.
		Block of 4				140.
R50P	25c	Warehouse Receipt, red				33.
		Block of 4				140.
R51P	30c	Foreign Exchange, lilac			110.	100.
		Block of 4			475.	425.
R52P	30c	Inland Exchange, lilac			65.	55.
		Block of 4			275.	230.
R53P	40c	Inland Exchange, brown			150.	75.
		Block of 4				325.
R54P	50c	Conveyance, blue		250.		33.
		Block of 4				140.
R55P	50c	Entry of Goods, blue			65.	45.
		Block of 4			275.	190.
R56P	50c	Foreign Exchange, blue			65.	45.
		Block of 4			275.	190.
R57P	50c	Lease, blue			65.	38.
		Block of 4			275.	160.
R58P	50c	Life Insurance, blue			65.	38.
		Block of 4			275.	160.
R59P	50c	Mortgage, blue				110.
		Block of 4				475.
R60P	50c	Original Process, blue			65.	38.
		Block of 4			275.	160.
R61P	50c	Passage Ticket, blue				55.
		Block of 4				230.
R62P	50c	Probate of Will, blue			65.	55.
		Block of 4			275.	230.
R63P	50c	Surety Bond, blue				55.
		Block of 4				230.
R64P	60c	Inland Exchange, orange			55.	38.
		Block of 4				160.
R65P	70c	Foreign Exchange, green			120.	55.
		Block of 4				230.
R66P	$1	Conveyance, red				45.
		Block of 4				190.
R67P	$1	Entry of Goods, red	525.			45.
		Block of 4				190.
R68P	$1	Foreign Exchange red				33.
		Block of 4				140.
R69P	$1	Inland Exchange, red				55.
		Block of 4				230.
R70P	$1	Lease, red				*425.*
R71P	$1	Life Insurance, red				33.
		Block of 4				140.
R72P	$1	Manifest, red			55.	33.
		Block of 4			—	140.
R73P	$1	Mortgage, red				55.
		Block of 4				230.
R74P	$1	Passage Ticket, red				*425.*
		Block of 4				*1,850.*
R75P	$1	Power of Attorney, red				100.
		Block of 4				425.
R76P	$1	Probate of Will, red				33.
		Block of 4				140.
R77P	$1.30	Foreign Exchange, orange	*700.*		140.	100.
		Block of 4			575.	425.
R78P	$1.50	Inland Exchange, blue			110.	45.
		Block of 4			475.	190.
R79P	$1.60	Foreign Exchange green			140.	100.
		Block of 4				425.
R80P	$1.90	Foreign Exchange, violet			140.	100.
		Block of 4			575.	425.
R81P	$2	Conveyance, red			120.	33.
		Block of 4				140.
R82P	$2	Mortgage, red			120.	33.
		Block of 4			—	140.
R83P	$2	Probate of Will, red				110.
		Block of 4				—
R84P	$2.50	Inland Exchange, violet			250.	225.
		Block of 4				—
R85P	$3	Charter Party, green			120.	65.
		Block of 4			500.	275.
R86P	$3	Manifest, green	—	350.	180.	65.
		Block of 4				275.
R87P	$3.50	Inland Exchange, blue			180.	140.
		Block of 4				575.
R88P	$5	Charter Party, red			70.	55.
		Block of 4			300.	230.
R89P	$5	Conveyance, red			450.	55.
		Block of 4				230.
R90P	$5	Manifest, red		300.		55.
		Block of 4				230.
R91P	$5	Mortgage, red			650.	55.
		Block of 4				230.
R92P	$5	Probate of Will, red		300.		55.
		Block of 4				230.
R93P	$10	Charter Party, green			120.	55.
		Block of 4				230.
R94P	$10	Conveyance, green				55.
		Block of 4				230.
R95P	$10	Mortgage, green				55.
		Block of 4				230.
R96P	$10	Probate of Will, green	*700.*	300.		75.
		Block of 4				325.
R97P	$15	Mortgage, dark blue		—		180.
		Block of 4				800.
R97eP	$15	Mortgage, ultramarine		—		350.
		Block of 4				—
R97fP	$15	Mortgage, milky blue			290.	
R98P	$20	Conveyance, orange			220.	100.
		Block of 4			900.	425.
R99P	$20	Probate of Will, orange				220.
		Block of 4				—
R100P	$25	Mortgage, red			220.	160.
		Block of 4				675.
R101P	$50	U.S.I.R., green			220.	230.
		Block of 4				950.
R102P	$200	U.S.I.R., green & orange red			1,400.	

SECOND ISSUE

1871-72

			DIE ON INDIA (1) Large	DIE ON INDIA (2) Small	PLATE (3) India	PLATE (4) Card
R105P	3c	blue & black			20.	15.
		Block of 4			90.	65.
R109P	10c	blue & black			20.	15.
		Block of 4			90.	65.
R111P	20c	blue & black			20.	15.
		Block of 4			90.	65.
R112P	25c	blue & black			20.	15.
		Block of 4			90.	65.
R115P	50c	blue & black			50.	15.
		Block of 4			225.	65.

			DIE ON INDIA (1) Large	(2) Small	PLATE (3) India	(4) Card
R119P	$1.30	blue & black			50.	38.
		Block of 4			225.	160.
R120P	$1.50	blue & black			28.	22.
		Block of 4			120.	100.
		Double transfer, design of $1				—
R121P	$1.60	blue & black			60.	60.
		Block of 4			260.	260.
R122P	$1.90	blue & black			50.	38.
		Block of 4			225.	170.
R126P	$3.50	blue & black			90.	100.
		Block of 4			400.	425.
R130P	$25	blue & black			150.	110.
		Block of 4			650.	500.
R131P	$50	blue & black			160.	140.
		Block of 4			700.	625.

The "small die proofs" formerly listed under Nos. R103P-R131P are plate proofs from the sheets listed under "Trial Color Proofs."

			DIE ON INDIA (1) Large	(2) Small	PLATE (3) India	(4) Card
R132P	$200	red, blue & black	3,500.	2,750.	2,500.	
		Red (frame) inverted			—	
R133P	$500	red orange, green & black	3,750.			
R133AP	$5000	red orange, dark green & black	*7,500.*			

No. R133AP was approved in these colors but never issued. Shade differences of the red orange and dark green colors will be found. It comes both with and without manufacturer's imprints to the left and right of the design. One example exists on bond paper mounted on card with "853½" printed on the lower right card margin.

Due to the unusual manufacturing process of printing these tri-color stamps from single impression plates, proofs with imprints could also be considered to be plate proofs. All are extremely scarce or unique, and are valued in the grade, condition and scarcity in which they exist. For other colors see the trial color proofs listings under No. R133ATC.

THIRD ISSUE

1871-72

			PLATE (3) India	(4) Card
R134P	1c	claret & black		15.
		Block of 4		70.
R135P	2c	orange & black	16.	15.
		Block of 4	70.	70.
R136P	4c	brown & black	20.	15.
		Block of 4	85.	70.
R137P	5c	orange & black	20.	15.
		Block of 4	85.	70.
R138P	6c	orange & black	20.	15.
		Block of 4	85.	70.
R139P	15c	brown & black	20.	15.
		Block of 4	85.	70.
R140P	30c	orange & black	25.	18.
		Block of 4	105.	80.
R141P	40c	brown & black	25.	18.
		Block of 4	105.	80.
R142P	60c	orange & black	65.	50.
		Block of 4	270.	225.
		Foreign entry, design of 70c	200.	150.
	a.	Center inverted		*2,250.*
		Block of 4		*10,000.*
		Foreign entry, design of 70c		—
R143P	70c	green & black	45.	38.
		Block of 4	190.	170.
R144P	$1	green & black	40.	38.
		Block of 4	170.	170.
R145P	$2	vermilion & black	80.	105.
		Block of 4	335.	450.
R146P	$2.50	claret & black	50.	40.
		Block of 4	210.	170.
R147P	$3	green & black	65.	70.
		Block of 4	270.	300.
R148P	$5	vermilion & black	65.	55.
		Block of 4	270.	240.
R149P	$10	green & black	80.	55.
		Block of 4	335.	240.
R150P	$20	orange & black	115.	150.
		Block of 4	500.	635.

The "small die proofs" formerly listed under Nos. R134P-R150P are plate proofs from the sheets listed under "Trial Color Proofs."

1875 National Bank Note Co., New York City

			DIE ON INDIA (1) Large	(2) Small	PLATE (3) India
R152P	2c	blue *(Liberty)*	450.		110.
		Block of 4			475.

DOCUMENTARY

1898

R173P	$1	dark green	*600.*
R174P	$3	dark brown	*600.*
R175P	$5	orange red	*600.*
R176P	$10	black	*600.*
R177P	$30	red	*600.*
R178P	$50	gray brown	*600.*

1899

R180P	$500	car lake & blk	*1,650.*

1914

R197P	2c	rose	—

1914-15

R226P	$500	blue	*675.*

1917

R246P	$30	deep orange (without serial No.)	*650.*

1940

R298P	50c	car (without ovpt.)	*700.*
R305P	$10	carmine	*825.*
		Without overprint	—
R306AP	$50	carmine	*825.*
		Without overprint	—

1952

R597P	55c	carmine	*675.*

PROPRIETARY

1871-75 Joseph R. Carpenter, Philadelphia

			DIE ON INDIA (2) Small	(3) India	PLATE (4) Card	(5) Bond
RB1P	1c	grn & blk		—	12.	12.
		Block of 4			52.	52.
		P# block of 10				175.
RB2P	2c	grn & blk		175.	12.	
		Block of 4			52.	
		P# block of 10				175.
RB3P	3c	grn & blk		22.	12.	
		Block of 4		100.	52.	
		P# block of 10				175.
RB4P	4c	grn & blk		22.	12.	
		Block of 4		100.	52.	
		P# block of 10				175.
RB5P	5c	grn & blk		22.	12.	
		Block of 4		100.	52.	
		P# block of 10				175.
RB6P	6c	grn & blk		22.	12.	
		Block of 4		100.	52.	
		P# block of 10				175.
RB7P	10c	grn & blk		22.	12.	
		Block of 4		100.	52.	
		P# block of 10				175.
RB8P	50c	grn & blk	1,000.		1,000.	
RB9P	$1	grn & blk	1,000.		1,250.	
RB10P	$5	grn & blk	6,000.	4,500.	2,000.	

The "small die proofs" formerly listed under Nos. RB1P-RB7P are from the composite plate proofs listed under "Trial Color Proofs."

National Bank Note Co., New York City

1875-83

			DIE ON INDIA (1) Large	(2) Small	PLATE (3) India	(4) Card
RB11P	1c	green	600.		65.	—
		Block of 4			325.	
RB12P	2c	brown	600.		65.	—
		Pair			160.	
RB13P	3c	orange	600.		65.	—
		Pair			160.	—
		Block of 4				—
RB14P	4c	red brown	600.		65.	—
		Pair			160.	—
		Block of 4				—
RB15P	4c	red	600.			
RB16P	5c	black	600.		65.	—
		Pair			160.	—
		Block of 4				—
RB17P	6c	violet blue	600.		65.	
		Pair			160.	
RB18P	6c	blue	600.		175.	
		Pair			400.	
RB19P	10c	blue	600.			

No. RB19P was produced by the Bureau of Engraving and Printing.

Battleship Type

1898

RB20P	⅛c	yellow green	*2,000.*
RB21P	¼c	brown	*2,000.*
RB22P	⅜c	deep orange	*2,000.*
RB23P	⅝c	deep ultramarine	*2,000.*
RB24P	1c	dark green	*2,000.*
RB25P	1¼c	violet	*2,000.*
RB26P	1⅞c	dull blue	*2,000.*
RB27P	2c	violet brown	*2,000.*
RB28P	2½c	lake	*2,000.*
RB29P	3¾c	olive gray	*2,000.*
RB30P	4c	purple	*2,000.*
RB31P	5c	brown orange	*2,000.*

Wines

1916

RE56P	$20	green	*5,000.*

PLAYING CARDS

1896 Bureau of Engraving & Printing

RF2P	2c	ultramarine	*550.*
	a.	2c blue	*1,100.*

PRIVATE DIE PROPRIETARY

The editors are indebted to Eric Jackson and Philip T. Bansner for the compilation of the following listing of Private Die Proprietary die and plate proofs as well as the corrresponding trial color proofs. The large die proofs range in size and format from die impressions on India die sunk on cards generally up to 6x9 inches, through die impressions on India on or off card in medium to stamp size. Many individual listings are known in more than one size and format. Values reflect the size and format most commonly seen.

PRIVATE DIE MATCH STAMPS

1864

			DIE ON INDIA (1) Large	PLATE (3) India	(4) Card
RO1P	1c	blue	225.		
RO2P	1c	orange	500.	90.	
RO3P	1c	blue	225.		
RO4P	1c	blue	500.		
RO5P	1c	green	500.		
RO6P	1c	Blue	175.		
RO7P	1c	blue	175.		
RO9P	1c	black	175.		
RO10P	1c	black	175.		
RO11P	3c	Black	250.		
RO12P	1c	black	225.		
RO12/185P	1c	black	750.		
RO13P	3c	green	1000.		
RO14P	1c	black	175.		
RO15P	1c	green	300.		
RO16P	1c	blue	225.	60.	
RO17P	1c	blue	175.		
RO17/19P	1c/3c	blue	1000.		
RO17/19P	1c/3c	black	750.		
RO19P	3c	black	375.		
RO20P	1c	blue	175.		
RO21P	3c	black	250.		
RO23P	1c	orange	225.		
RO24P	1c	brown	225.		
RO28P	1c	blue	300.	90.	
RO29P	1c	black	175.		
RO30P	1c	green	175.		
RO31P	1c	black	175.		
RO32P	4c	black	300.		
RO33P	4c	green	225.		
RO35P	1c	black	175.		
RO37P	3c	black	225.		
RO38P	1c	black	350.		
RO39P	1c	green	500.		
RO40P	1c	blue	175.		
RO41P	1c	lake	225.		
RO42P	1c	lake	225.		
RO43P	1c	black	225.		
RO44P	1c	green	225.		
RO45P	1c	black	225.		
RO46P	1c	black	300.		
RO47P	1c	black	225.	90.	75.
RO48P	1c	black	500.		
RO49P	1c	black	175.		
RO50P	1c	black	375.		
RO55P	1c	black	250.		
RO56P	1c	black	250.		
RO57P	1c	green	300.		
RO58P	1c	lake	225.	75.	
RO60P	3c	black	300.		
RO61P	1c	green	300.		
RO62P	1c	green	175.		
RO64P	1c	lake	225.		
RO65P	1c	black	225.		
RO66P	1c	blue	175.		
RO67P	1c	black	175.		
RO68P	1c	green	225.		
RO69P	1c	black	175.		
RO72P	1c	green	500.		
RO73P	1c	black	175.		
RO75P	1c	carmine	450.		
RO76P	1c	black	175.		
RO77P	1c	blue	225.		
RO78P	1c	blue	225.		
RO80P	1c	blue	300.		
RO81P	1c	black	175.		
RO82P	1c	black	175.		
RO83P	1c	blue	175.		
RO84P	1c	black	175.		
RO85P	1c	brown	300.	100.	
RO86P	1c	black	250.	125.	
RO87P	1c	black	500.	50.	
RO88P	1c	black	175.		
RO89P	3c	black	175.		

			DIE ON INDIA (1) Large	PLATE (3) India	PLATE (4) Card
RO90P	6c	black	175.	125.	
RO91P	3c	black	225.	125.	
RO92P	1c	black	175.		
RO94P	3c	black	175.	175.	
RO95P	1c	green	225.		
RO96P	1c	green	300.		
RO97P	1c	black	175.		
RO98P	1c	green	225.		
RO99P	1c	green	300.		
RO100P	1c	green	225.	65.	
RO101P	3c	carmine		75.	
RO102P	5c	orange		75.	
RO103P	1c	black	175.		
RO104P	1c	green	175.		
RO105P	1c	black	175.	100.	
RO106P	1c	green	300.		
RO107P	1c	blue	225.		
RO108P	1c	red	750.		
RO109P	1c	black	300.		
RO110P	1c	green	175.		
RO112P	1c	blue	225.	100.	
RO113P	1c	black	175.		
RO114P	1c	lake	750.		
RO115P	1c	blue	175.		
RO116P	1c	blue	175.		
RO118P	8c	blue	500.		
RO119P	1c	green	300.		
RO121P	1c	green	500.		
RO122P	1c	black	175.		
RO123P	1c	black	175.		
RO124P	1c	green	750.		
RO125P	1c	blue	300.		
RO126P	1c	black	175.		
RO127P	1c	blue	175.		
RO128P	1c	blue	225.		
RO130P	1c	blue	500.		
a. On thin card					—
RO131P	1c	blue	300.		
RO132P	1c	blue	225.	125.	
RO133P	1c	black	225.		
RO134P	1c	blue	175.	75.	
RO135P	1c	lake	500.		
RO136P	1c	blue	175.		
RO138P	1c	green	175.		
RO139P	5c	blue	225.		
RO140P	4c	green	225.		
RO141P	1c	blue	175.		
RO142P	1c	green	225.		
RO143P	3c	orange	225.		
RO144P	1c	blue	400.		
RO146P	1c	black	175.		
RO148P	1c	blue	225.	100.	
RO152P	1c	black	175.	75.	
RO153P	1c	black	175.	75.	
RO155P	1c	black	175.	65.	
RO157P	3c	blue	225.	80.	
RO158P	1c	black	175.		
RO159P	3c	blue	175.		
RO160P	1c	blue	175.		
RO161P	1c	blue	500.		
RO163P	1c	black	175.		
RO164P	1c	lake	500.		
RO165P	12c	blue	750.		
RO166P	1c	vermilion	225.		
RO167P	3c	blue	175.		
RO168P	1c	blue	175.		
RO170P	1c	black	450.		
RO171P	1c	black	175.		
RO172P	1c	black	175.		
RO173P	1c	blue	225.	75.	
RO174P	1c	blue	175.		
RO175P	1c	black	225.		
RO176P	1c	blue	500.		
RO177P	1c	green	175.		
RO178P	1c	green	500.		
RO179P	1c	black	175.	75.	75.
RO180P	1c	black	175.	80.	
RO181P	1c	black	175.		
RO182P	1c	black	175.		
RO183P	1c	black	500.		
RO184P	1c	black	175.	75.	
RO186P	1c	blue	225.		

PRIVATE DIE CANNED FRUIT STAMP

RP1P	1c	green	375.

PRIVATE DIE MEDICINE STAMPS

			DIE ON INDIA (1) Large	PLATE (3) India	PLATE (4) Card
RS1P	1c	black	175.	—	
RS4P	1c	black	225.	125.	150.
RS5P	1c	blue	500.		
RS10P	4c	blue	225.	125.	150.
RS14P	4c	green	500.	10.	
RS16P	2c	vermilion	500.		
RS18P	1c	black	500.		125.
RS19P	2c	black			125.
RS20P	4c	black			125.
RS21P	1c	black	175.	125.	
RS22P	2c	black	225.	125.	
RS23P	4c	black	225.	125.	
RS24P	1c	black	175.		
RS25P	2c	black	175.		
RS26P	4c	black	175.		
RS27P	4c	black	175.		
RS28P	2c	green	175.		
RS29P	2c	green	225.		
RS29/RO120P	2c/1c	green	1250.		
RS30P	1c	lake	300.		
RS31P	1c	green	175.	100.	100.
RS33P	1c	black	175.	50.	50.
RS34P	1c	black	225.		
RS35P	1c	black	175.		
RS36P	1c	blue	175.		
RS37P	2c	black	450.		
RS38P	2c	black	300.		
RS39P	1c	black	175.	100.	100.
RS40P	2c	green	500.	100.	100.
RS41P	4c	brown		125.	125.
RS42P	1c	black	175.		
RS43P	4c	blue	225.		
RS44P	1c	black	600.		
RS46P	4c	black	175.		
RS47P	4c	black	175.	125.	
RS49P	4c	green	175.		
RS50P	1c	vermilion	225.		
RS51P	2c	black	175.		
RS52P	4c	black	175.		
RS53P	1c	black	175.	125.	
RS54P	2c	black	175.	125.	
RS55P	4c	black	175.	125.	
RS56P	3c	blue	350.	125.	
RS57P	6c	black	175.	100.	
RS58P	4c	black	175.		
RS59P	1c	black	175.		
RS60P	1c	black	175.	65.	
RS61P	4c	blue	500.		
RS62P	1c	black	225.	125.	
RS63P	1c	blue	175.		
RS64P	2c	black	175.	125.	
RS65P	4c	black	175.		
RS66P	1c	black	500.		85.
RS67P	1c	black	175.		
RS68P	2c	black	175.	90.	
RS69P	1c	black	175.		
RS70P	2c	black	225.		
RS71P	1c	black	175.		
RS72P	2c	black	175.		
RS73P	2c	green	500.		
RS74P	1c	black	225.		
RS74hP	1c	black	175.		
RS75P	1c	blue	175.		
RS77P	2c	black	225.		
RS78P	2c	dull pur	750.		
RS81P	4c	brown	225.		
RS82P	2c	black	175.		
RS83P	4c	black	225.		
RS84P	1c	lake	500.	—	110.
RS85P	4c	black	250.	—	
RS86P	1c	green	175.		
RS88P	1c	black	225.	100.	100.
RS89P	1c	black	500.		
RS90P	1c	blue	225.	125.	125.
RS91P	4c	black	175.		
RS92P	3c	black	175.	—	
RS94P	4c	black	175.		
RS95P	1c	green	225.	90.	
RS96P	3c	black	175.	50.	
RS97P	1c	black	175.		
RS98P	1c	black	175.		
RS99P	4c	black	175.		
RS100P	6c	black	175.		
RS101P	1c	black	175.		
RS102P	2c	blue	175.		
RS103P	4c	black	175.		
RS104P	3c	black	750.		
RS105P	3c	brown	600.		
RS106P	2c	blue	225.	60.	
RS107P	3c	black	225.		
RS107/109P	3c/6c	black	1000.		
RS108P	4c	black	175.	45.	
RS109P	6c	black	225.		
RS110P	2c	blue	175.		
RS111P	4c	black	175.		
RS114P	1c	black	225.		
RS114/115P	1c/2c	black	1000.		
RS115P	2c	blue	225.		
RS116P	4c	red	225.		
RS117P	1c	black	250.		
RS118P	1c	red	300.	55.	50.
RS119P	1c	black	225.		
RS120P	2c	black	175.		
RS121P	3c	black	225.	75.	
RS122P	2c	black	175.	100.	
RS123P	4c	black	175.	125.	
RS124P	1c	blue	300.	90.	65.
RS126P	1c	green	175.		
RS127P	4c	green	175.	65.	
RS128P	2c	blue	275.	150.	
RS130P	4c	green	275.		
RS131P	4c	black	175.	75.	
RS132P	4c	black			75.
RS133P	6c	black	175.	125.	
RS134P	4c	blue	225.		
RS137P	4c	blue	500.		
RS138P	1c	black	175.		
RS141P	4c	green	300.	125.	
RS142P	1c	black	175.		
RS143P	4c	green	225.		
RS144P	1c	blue	175.	100.	100.
RS145P	2c	black	175.	100.	100.
RS146P	4c	green	225.	100.	100.
RS150P	1c	vermilion	225.	100.	
RS151P	1c	black	175.		
RS152P	2c	green	175.		
RS153P	4c	black	450.	175.	150.
RS154P	4c	blue	500.		
RS155P	2c	green	175.		
RS156P	6c	black	175.		
RS157P	2c	black	175.		
RS158P	1c	green	500.		
RS159P	4c	blue	225.		
RS160P	6c	black	225.		
RS161P	4c	black	300.	150.	
RS162P	1c	blue	300.		
RS163P	4c	blue	600.		
RS164P	1c	black	175.		
RS165P	4c	green	500.		
RS166P	1c	black	175.		
RS169P	4c	black	175.		
RS170P	1c	black	175.		
RS171P	1c	violet	175.		
RS171uP	1c	purple	500.		
RS172P	2c	black	175.	100.	
RS173P	1c	blue	175.		
RS174P	1c	blue	175.		
RS176P	4c	black	250.		
RS177P	2c	black	350.		
RS178P	1c	black	225.		
RS179P	2c	green	225.		
RS180P	3c	black	275.	125.	
RS181P	4c	black	225.	—	
RS182P	4c	black	175.		
RS183P	1c	vermilion	225.	85.	
RS184P	2c	black	175.	100.	
RS185P	1c	black	175.	100.	
RS186P	4c	black	175.		
RS187P	4c	black	175.	100.	
RS188P	6c	black	300.		
RS189P	1c	green	225.		
RS190P	2c	black	175.		
RS191P	4c	black	250.		
RS192P	6c	black	250.	125.	
RS193P	2	black	175.		
RS194P	1c	blue	175.		
RS195P	2c	black	175.		
RS196P	1c	blue	175.		
RS197P	2c	black	175.		
RS198P	1c	black	225.		
RS199P	2c	black	175.		
RS204P	2c	black	175.		
RS205P	4c	black	175.		
RS208P	1c	green	175.	100.	95.
RS209P	2c	green	225.		
RS210P	4c	black	225.		
RS212P	1c	green	225.	100.	
RS213P	6c	black	175.	100.	150.
RS214P	4c	black	175.	65.	
RS215P	1c	lake	300.		
RS216P	1c	black	175.	75.	
RS219P	4c	blue	300.		
RS220P	1c	black	175.	50.	
RS221P	4c	green	225.	50.	
RS222P	8c	black	175.		
RS223P	1c	black	175.	—	
RS224P	1c	black	175.	—	
RS225P	4c	black	175.		
RS226P	1c	blue		350.	
RS228P	1c	brown	225.	—	
RS229P	2c	chocolate	175.	75.	
RS230P	6c	black	175.	—	
RS231P	6c	orange	750.		750.
RS232P	8c	orange	750.		
RS236P	4c	black	175.		
RS239P	2c	vermilion	225.	100.	
RS240P	4c	black	175.	125.	50.

"USIR" & "4 cents" obliterated on #RS240P4.

			DIE ON INDIA (1) Large	PLATE (3) India	PLATE (4) Card
RS241P	4	red	225.		
RS242P	1c	black	175.	80.	75.
RS243P	4c	black	175.		
RS244P	6c	black	175.		
RS245P	1c	black	250.		
RS250P	6c	black	175.	100.	
RS251P	1c	black	175.		
RS252P	1c	ver	175.	100.	
RS253P	4c	black	175.		
RS258P	6c	brown	175.		
RS259P	1c	black	175.	90.	
RS260P	2c	black	225.	90.	
RS261P	4c	black	175.	100.	
RS262P	2c	black	175.		
RS263P	4c	black	225.	90.	
RS264P	4c	black	225.		
RS264AP	4c	black	300.		
RS265P	1c	green	225.		
RS267P	4c	lake	225.		
RS270P	12c	blue	175.		
RS271P	4c	black	2500.		
RS272P	1c	green	225.		
RS273P	2c	black	175.		
RS274P	1c	green	225.	65.	60.
RS276P	2c	green	175.		
RS300P	4⅜c	black	*1,000.*		
RS306P	1¼c	pink	*1,000.*		

PRIVATE DIE PERFUMERY STAMPS

			DIE ON INDIA (1) Large	PLATE (3) India	PLATE (4) Card
RT1P	2c	blue		125.	125.
RT2P	1c	black	250.	95.	
RT4P	1c	blue	225.		
RT5P	2c	ver		100.	
RT6P	1c	black	250.	150.	
RT8P	2c	black	500.		
RT10P	4c	black	250.	150.	
RT12P	1c	ver	225.	—	
RT14P	3c	black	500.		
RT16P	1c	black	175.		
RT17P	2c	brown	175.		
RT18P	3c	green	175.		
RT19P	1c	ver	225.		
RT20P	1c	green	225.		
RT21P	2c	blue	175.		
RT22P	1c	blue	225.		
RT23P	2c	black	175.		
RT25P	4c	green	175.		
RT26P	1c	green	175.		

			DIE ON INDIA (1) Large	PLATE (3) India	PLATE (4) Card
RT27P	1c	green		100.	
RT28P	2c	blue	175.		
RT30P	3c	ver	225.		
RT32P	4c	brown	175.		

PRIVATE DIE PLAYING CARD STAMPS

			DIE ON INDIA (1) Large	PLATE (3) India	PLATE (4) Card
RU1P	5c	black	2500.		
RU3P	4c	black	175.	100.	
RU4P	5c	blue	175.		
RU5P	5c	blue	175.		
RU6P	10c	blue	500.	100.	
RU7P	5c	black	250.	100.	
RU8P	5c	black	175.		
RU9P	5c	black	175.		
RU10P	2c	blue	175.		
RU11P	5c	green	225.		
RU12P	5c	black	175.		
RU13P	5c	blue	300.		
RU14P	5c	black	175.	—	
RU15P	5c	black	175.		
RU16P	5c	black	500.		

HUNTING PERMIT

				DIE (Wove) (1) Large	DIE (Wove) (2) Small
RW1P	1934	$1	blue	—	*17,500.*
RW2P	1935	$1	rose lake		*9,500.*
RW3P	1936	$1	brown black	*7,500.*	*7,500.*
RW4P	1937	$1	light green	—	*7,500.*
RW5P	1938	$1	light violet	—	*7,500.*
RW6P	1939	$1	chocolate		*7,500.*
RW7P	1940	$1	sepia		*7,800.*
RW8P	1941	$1	brown carmine	*7,500.*	*7,500.*
RW9P	1942	$1	violet brown		*7,500.*
RW10P	1943	$1	deep rose	*7,500.*	*7,500.*
RW11P	1944	$1	red orange		*7,500.*
RW12P	1945	$1	black	*7,500.*	*6,000.*
RW13P	1946	$1	red brown	*7,500.*	
RW14P	1947	$1	black	*7,500.*	
RW15P	1948	$1	bright blue	*9,500.*	
RW19P	1952	$2	deep ultra.	*7,500.*	
RW23P	1956	$2	black	12,500.	

POSTAL SAVINGS

1911

			DIE (1) Large	DIE (2) Small	(2a)
PS1P	10c	orange	1,000.		750.
PS4P	10c	deep blue			750.

1940

			DIE (1) Large	DIE (2) Small	(2a)
PS7P	10c	deep ultra. on wove		1,200.	
PS8P	25c	dk. car. rose on wove		1,200.	
PS9P	50c	dk. bl. green on wove		1,200.	
PS10P	$1	gray black on wove		1,200.	

1941

			DIE (1) Large	DIE (2) Small	(2a)
PS11P	10c	rose red on wove		1,000.	
PS12P	25c	blue green on wove		1,000.	
PS13P	50c	ultramarine on wove		1,000.	
PS14P	$1	gray black on wove		1,000.	
PS15P	$5	sepia on wove	*4,000.*	1,000.	

WAR SAVINGS STAMP

1942

WS7P	10c	rose red	1,400.

POST OFFICE SEALS

1872

		DIE (1) Large	PLATE (3) India	PLATE (4) Card
OXF1P	green	275.		—
a.	Wove paper	*950.*		*750.*
b.	Glazed paper	190.		

1877

		DIE (1) Large	PLATE (3) India	PLATE (4) Card
OX1P	brown	*1,750.*	125.	
	Block of 4		650.	

1879

		DIE (1) Large	PLATE (3) India	PLATE (4) Card
OX2aP	brown	2,500.	125.	
	Block of 4		650.	

1888-94

		DIE (1) Large	PLATE (3) India	PLATE (4) Card
OX5P	chocolate	*750.*		

1901-03

		DIE (1) Large	PLATE (3) India	PLATE (4) Card
OX11P	red brown	*750.*		

No. OX11P is a hybrid proof sunk on card.

1972

		DIE (1) Large	PLATE (3) India	PLATE (4) Card
OX41P	Pane of 5, blue line proof	—		

TRIAL COLOR PROOFS

Values are for items in very fine condition. The listings of trial color proofs include several that are similar to the colors of the issued stamps.

New York

All on India paper unless otherwise stated.

Original Die

1845

			DIE (1) Lg.	DIE (2) Sm.	PLATE (5) Bond
9X1TC	5c	dull dark violet		300.	
9X1TC	5c	brown violet		300.	
9X1TC	5c	deep rose violet		300.	
9X1TC	5c	deep blue		300.	200.
9X1TC	5c	dark green		300.	200.
9X1TC	5c	orange yellow		300.	
9X1TC	5c	brown		300.	200.
9X1TC	5c	scarlet			200.

With "Scar" on Neck

			DIE (1) Lg.	DIE (2) Sm.	PLATE (5) Bond
9X1TC	5c	dull blue		175.	
9X1TC	5c	vermilion		175.	

With "Scar" and dot in "P" of "POST"

			DIE (1) Lg.	DIE (2) Sm.	PLATE (5) Bond
9X1TC	5c	dull gray blue		300.	
9X1TC	5c	deep blue on Bond		250.	
9X1TC	5c	deep ultramarine on thin glazed card	450.		
9X1TC	5c	deep green		300.	
9X1TC	5c	deep green on Bond		250.	
9X1TC	5c	dull dark green		300.	
9X1TC	5c	orange vermilion on thin glazed card	450.		
9X1TC	5c	dull brown red on Bond		250.	
9X1TC	5c	dark brown red		300.	
9X1TC	5c	dull dark brown		300.	
9X1TC	5c	dull dark brown on Bond		250.	
9X1TC	5c	brown black on thin glazed card	450.		

Large die trial color proofs with additional impression of the portrait medallion are listed in the Essay section as Nos. 9X1-E1.

Plate proofs are from the small sheet of 9.

Providence, R. I.

1846

			Plate on Card
10X1TC	5c	gray blue	250.
10X1TC	5c	green	250.
10X1TC	5c	brown carmine	250.
10X1TC	5c	brown	250.
10X2TC	10c	gray blue	450.
10X2TC	10c	green	450.
10X2TC	10c	brown carmine	450.
10X2TC	10c	brown	450.
		Sheet of 12, any color	3,750.

General Issues

1847

			LARGE DIE India	LARGE DIE Bond	LARGE DIE Wove	LARGE DIE Thin Glazed Card
1TC	5c	violet	1,000.			
1TC	5c	dull blue	1,000.			
1TC	5c	deep blue		800.	800.	
		Small, India				625.
1TC	5c	deep ultra				850.
1TC	5c	blue green	1,000.			
		Small, India				625.
1TC	5c	dull blue green		800.		
1TC	5c	dull green	1,000.			
		Small, bond				600.
1TC	5c	dark green	1,000.			
1TC	5c	yellow green, small India				625.
1TC	5c	orange yellow	1,000.	800.	800.	
		Small, India				625.
1TC	5c	deep yellow			800.	
1TC	5c	orange vermilion	1,000.	800.	800.	
1TC	5c	scarlet vermilion	1,000.	800.		850.
1TC	5c	rose lake	1,000.			
		Small, bond				625.
1TC	5c	black brown		800.		850.
1TC	5c	dull rose lake, small bond				625.
1TC	5c	brown red	1,000.			
1TC	5c	black	1,000.	800.		850.
		Small, India				675.
2TC	10c	violet	1,000.			
2TC	10c	dull blue				
2TC	10c	deep blue	1,000.	800.	800.	850.
		Small, India				675.
2TC	10c	dull gray blue, small bond				625.
2TC	10c	blue green		800.		
2TC	10c	dull blue green		800.		
2TC	10c	dull green		800.		
2TC	10c	dark green	1,000.			
2TC	10c	yel green, small India				675.
2TC	10c	dull yellow			800.	
2TC	10c	orange yellow	1,000.		800.	
2TC	10c	orange vermilion	1,000.	800.	800.	
		Small, India				625.
2TC	10c	scarlet vermilion				850.
2TC	10c	golden brown	1,000.	800.		850.
2TC	10c	light brown	1,000.			
2TC	10c	dark brown	1,000.	800.		
2TC	10c	red brown				675.
2TC	10c	dull red				675.
2TC	10c	rose lake	1,000.			
2TC	10c	dull rose lake, small India				625.
2TC	10c	black brown				850.
2TC	10c	yellow green on blue pelure paper	1,000.			

Original die proofs are often cut down and reduced in size; full-size die proofs sell at higher prices. Reprint proofs with cross-hatching are valued as full-size; cut down examples sell for less.

			DIE (1) Lg.	DIE (2) Sm.	PLATE (3) India	PLATE (4) Card
1TC	5c	orange			600.	
1TC	5c	black			600.	
		Double transfer (80R1)			—	
		Double transfer (90R1)			—	
2TC	10c	orange			600.	
2TC	10c	deep brown			600.	

Nos. 1TC3-2TC3 exist with and without "specimen" overprint. Values are for examples without the overprint. Examples with the overprint are equally as scarce but sell for slightly less.

1875

			DIE (1) Lg.	DIE (2) Sm.	PLATE (3) India	PLATE (4) Card
3TC	5c	dull rose lake				600.
3TC	5c	black	900.			
3TC	5c	green	900.			
4TC	10c	green	900.		750.	

1851-60

			DIE (1) Lg.	DIE (2) Sm.	PLATE (3) India	PLATE (5) Wove Paper
5TC	1c	black	—			
7TC	1c	black on stamp paper				*3,750.*
11TC	3c	black on stamp paper				*3,000.*
12TC	5c	pale brown				300.
12TC	5c	rose brown				300.
12TC	5c	deep red brown				1,500.
12TC	5c	dark olive bister				300.
12TC	5c	olive brown				300.
12TC	5c	olive green				300.
12TC	5c	deep orange				300.
12TC	5c	black	*8,500.*			*5,000.*
13TC	10c	black	*5,000.*			1,500.
15TC	10c	black				*5,000.*
37TC	24c	claret brown				600.
37TC	24c	red brown				600.
37TC	24c	orange				600.

			DIE (1) Lg.	DIE (2) Sm.	PLATE (3) India	PLATE (5) Wove Paper
37TC	24c	deep yellow				600.
37TC	24c	yellow				600.
37TC	24c	deep blue				600.
37TC	24c	black	*7,000.*			—
37TC	24c	violet black				600.
37TC	24c	red lilac on stamp paper, perf. 15½, gummed (formerly No. 37b)				1,000.
		Block of 4				6,000.
38TC	30c	black	*5,000.*	1,250.	1,400.	1,000.
		Block of 4			9,000.	
39TC	90c	rose lake				625.
39TC	90c	henna brown				625.
39TC	90c	orange red				625.
39TC	90c	brown orange	*5,000.*			625.
39TC	90c	sepia				625.
39TC	90c	dark green				625.
39TC	90c	dark violet brown				625.
39TC	90c	black	*5,000.*	1,250.		675.

Former Nos. 55-57, 59, 62 are now in the Essay section. Former Nos. 60-61 will be found below as Nos. 70TCe and 71TCb, respectively.

1875

40TC	1c	orange vermilion	275.
40TC	1c	orange	275.
40TC	1c	yellow orange	275.
40TC	1c	orange brown	275.
40TC	1c	dark brown	275.
40TC	1c	dull violet	275.
40TC	1c	violet	275.
40TC	1c	red violet	275.
40TC	1c	gray	275.
41TC	3c	red	—

1861

			PLATE (5) Wove Paper, Imperf.	PLATE (6) Wove Paper, Perf.
63TC	1c	rose	40.	50.
63TC	1c	deep orange red	40.	50.
63TC	1c	deep red orange	40.	50.
63TC	1c	dark orange	40.	50.
63TC	1c	yellow orange	40.	50.
63TC	1c	orange brown	40.	50.
63TC	1c	dark brown	40.	50.
63TC	1c	yellow green	40.	50.
63TC	1c	green	40.	50.
63TC	1c	blue green	40.	50.
63TC	1c	gray lilac	40.	50.
63TC	1c	gray black	40.	50.
63TC	1c	slate black	40.	50.
63TC	1c	blue	40.	50.
63TC	1c	light blue	40.	50.
63TC	1c	deep blue	100.	50.

The perforated 1861 1c trial colors are valued with perfs cutting the design on two sides. Well centered examples are extremely scarce and sell for more.

There are many trial color impressions of the issues of 1861 to 1883 made for experimentation with various patent papers, grills, etc. Some are fully perforated, gummed and with grill.

1861-62

			DIE (1) Lg.	DIE (2) Sm.	(2a)	PLATE India (3)
62BTC	10c	black	*2,500.*			
62BTC	10c	green				300.
62BTC	10c	light green				300.
63TC	1c	black	*2,500.*	750.		
63TC	1c	red		750.		
63TC	1c	brown		750.		
63TC	1c	green		—		
63TC	1c	orange		—		
64TC	3c	carmine pink on thin stamp paper, perf 12, gummed				—
65TC	3c	black	2,500.			
65TC	3c	black on glazed	2,500.			
65TC	3c	blue green	2,500.			
65TC	3c	orange	2,500.			
65TC	3c	brown	2,500.			
65TC	3c	dark blue	2,500.			
65TC	3c	ocher	2,500.			
65TC	3c	green	2,500.			
65TC	3c	dull red	2,500.			
65TC	3c	slate	2,500.			
65TC	3c	red brown	2,500.			
65TC	3c	deep pink	2,500.			
65TC	3c	rose pink	2,500.			
65TC	3c	dark rose	2,500.			
67TC	5c	black	2,500.	—		
67TC	5c	dark orange	2,500.			
67TC	5c	green	2,500.			
67TC	5c	ultramarine	2,500.			
67TC	5c	gray	2,500.			
67TC	5c	rose brown	—			
68TC	10c	orange	2,500.			
68TC	10c	red brown	2,500.			
68TC	10c	dull pink	2,500.			
68TC	10c	scarlet	2,500.			
68TC	10c	black	2,500.	550.		
69TC	12c	scarlet verm.	2,500.			
69TC	12c	brown	2,500.			
69TC	12c	red brown	2,500.			
69TC	12c	green	2,500.			
69TC	12c	orange yellow	2,500.			
69TC	12c	black		550.		
70TC	24c	scarlet	2,500.			
70TC	24c	green	2,500.			
70TC	24c	orange	2,500.			
70TC	24c	red brown	2,500.			
70TC	24c	orange brown	2,500.			
70TC	24c	orange yellow	2,500.			
70TC	24c	rose red	2,500.			
70TC	24c	gray	2,500.			
70TC	24c	gray on bluish gray stamp paper				—
70TC	24c	steel blue	2,500.			
70TC	24c	blue	2,500.			
70TC	24c	black	2,500.	500.		
70TC	24c	violet	2,500.	375.	2,250.	500.
		Block of 4				2,250.
	e.	dark violet, semitransparent stamp paper, perf. 12, gummed **(formerly #60)**				*12,500.*
71TC	30c	rose	2,500.			
71TC	30c	black		600.		
71TC	30c	red orange	2,500.	375.	1,250.	
		Block of 4				
	b.	red orange, semitransparent stamp paper, perf. 12, gummed **(formerly #61)**				*45,000.*
72TC	90c	black	2,500.	600.		
72TC	90c	ultramarine	2,500.			
72TC	90c	bluish gray	2,500.			
72TC	90c	violet gray	2,500.			
72TC	90c	red brown	2,500.			
72TC	90c	orange	2,500.			
72TC	90c	yellow orange	2,500.			
72TC	90c	scarlet	2,500.			
72TC	90c	green	2,500.			

1861

			STAMP PAPER Unused	STAMP PAPER Used
66TC	3c	lake, perf. 12, gummed	*2,000.*	
		Pair	*4,500.*	
		Block of 4	*9,250.*	
		P# strip of 4	*10,000.*	
		Double transfer	*2,250.*	
	a.	Imperf, pair, gummed	*1,850.*	
		P# blk. of 8	—	

John N. Luff recorded the plate number for No. 66TC as 34.

			STAMP PAPER Unused	STAMP PAPER Used
74TC	3c	scarlet, perf. 12, gummed	*7,000.*	
		Block of 4	*29,000.*	
		With 4 horiz. black pen strokes		*5,000.*
	a.	Imperf, pair, gummed	*4,000.*	

John N. Luff recorded the plate number for No. 74TC as 19.

1861

			DIE (1) Large	DIE (2) Small	(2a)	PLATE (3) India	PLATE (4) Card
66TC	3c	lake		250.	1,100.	150.	
		Block of 4				850.	
		P# blk. of 8				2,250.	
74TC	3c	scarlet	2,250.	375.	1,100.	100.	100.
		Block of 4				500.	450.
		P# blk. of 8					—

1863

			DIE (1) Lg.	DIE (2) Sm.	PLATE (3) India	PLATE (4) Card
73TC	2c	light blue			250.	
73TC	2c	dull chalky blue	*8,000.*		500.	
73TC	2c	green	*8,000.*		250.	
73TC	2c	olive green			250.	
73TC	2c	blue green			*400.*	
73TC	2c	dull yellow	*8,000.*			
73TC	2c	dark orange	*8,000.*			
73TC	2c	vermilion			250.	
73TC	2c	scarlet	*8,000.*		250.	
73TC	2c	dull red			250.	
73TC	2c	dull rose	*8,000.*		250.	
73TC	2c	brown	*8,000.*			
73TC	2c	gray black			250.	
73TC	2c	ultramarine	*8,000.*			

1866

77TC	15c	deep blue	2,500.	335.
		Block of 4		1,650.
77TC	15c	dark red	2,500.	
77TC	15c	orange red	2,500.	
77TC	15c	dark orange	2,500.	
77TC	15c	yellow orange	2,500.	
77TC	15c	yellow		
77TC	15c	sepia		
77TC	15c	orange brown	2,500.	
77TC	15c	red brown	2,500.	
77TC	15c	blue green	2,500.	
77TC	15c	dusky blue	2,500.	
77TC	15c	gray black	2,500.	

1869

112TC	1c	black	2,500.	
113TC	2c	black	2,500.	
114TC	3c	black	2,500.	
115TC	6c	deep dull blue	2,500.	
115TC	6c	black	2,500.	
116TC	10c	black	2,500.	
116TC	10c	dull dark violet	2,500.	
116TC	10c	deep green	2,500.	
116TC	10c	dull dark orange	2,500.	
116TC	10c	dull rose	2,500.	
116TC	10c	copper red	2,500.	
116TC	10c	chocolate	2,500.	
116TC	10c	dk Prussian bl	2,500.	
117TC	12c	black	2,500.	
118TC	15c	dull dark violet	2,500.	
118TC	15c	deep blue	2,500.	
118TC	15c	dull red brown	2,500.	
118TC	15c	black	2,500.	
118TC	15c	dark blue gray	2,500.	
120TC	24c	black	3,500.	
121TC	30c	deep blue & deep green	3,500.	
121TC	30c	deep brown & blue	3,500.	
121TC	30c	golden brown & carmine lake	3,500.	
121TC	30c	carmine lake & dull violet	3,500.	
121TC	30c	car lake & green	3,500.	
121TC	30c	car lake & brown	3,500.	
121TC	30c	car lake & black	3,500.	
121TC	30c	dull orange red & deep green	3,500.	
121TC	30c	deep ocher & golden brown	3,500.	
121TC	30c	dull violet & golden brown	3,500.	
121TC	30c	black & deep green	3,500.	
122TC	90c	brown & deep green	3,500.	
122TC	90c	green & black		1,500.

1870-71

			DIE (1) Lg.	DIE (2) Sm.	PLATE (3) India	PLATE (4) Card
145TC	1c	yellow orange	600.			
145TC	1c	red brown	600.			
145TC	1c	red violet	600.			
145TC	1c	black	—		—	
145TC	1c	green	600.			
146TC	2c	black	600.			
147TC	3c	brown	—		125.	
147TC	3c	dark brown			125.	
147TC	3c	red brown	—		125.	
147TC	3c	orange brown			125.	
147TC	3c	dark red	—		125.	
147TC	3c	deep red brown, wove paper			125.	
147TC	3c	light ultramarine	—		125.	
147TC	3c	yellow brown	—		125.	
147TC	3c	dull red violet	—		125.	
147TC	3c	dull grayish red	—			
147TC	3c	yellow orange	—		125.	
147TC	3c	red violet	—		125.	
147TC	3c	black	600.			

Former Nos. 147aTC and 147bTC are now listed in the Essay section as No. 147-E13c.

			DIE (1) Lg.	DIE (2) Sm.	PLATE (3) India	PLATE (4) Card
148TC	6c	deep magenta	600.			
148TC	6c	ultramarine	600.			
148TC	6c	carmine	600.			
148TC	6c	maroon	600.			
149TC	7c	black	550.			
150TC	10c	blue	550.			
150TC	10c	dull pale blue	550.			
150TC	10c	ultramarine	550.			
150TC	10c	blue green	550.			

			DIE (1) Lg.	DIE (2) Sm.	PLATE (3) India	PLATE (4) Card
150TC	10c	carmine	550.			
150TC	10c	bister	550.			
150TC	10c	dull red	550.			
150TC	10c	red orange	550.			
150TC	10c	yellow brown	550.			
150TC	10c	brown orange	550.			
151TC	12c	orange	550.			
151TC	12c	orange brown	550.			
151TC	12c	brown red	550.			
151TC	12c	dull red	550.			
151TC	12c	carmine	550.			
151TC	12c	blue	550.			
151TC	12c	light blue	550.			
151TC	12c	ultramarine	550.			
151TC	12c	green	550.			
153TC	24c	dark brown	550.			
155TC	90c	carmine	550.			
155TC	90c	ultramarine	550.			
155TC	90c	black	550.			

1873

			(1)	(2)	(3)	(4)
156TC	1c	black			15.	30.
		Block of 4			65.	140.
156TC	1c	scarlet	*1,500.*			
157TC	2c	black	850.		15.	
		Block of 4			65.	
157TC	2c	dull blue	850.			
157TC	2c	rose	850.			
157TC	2c	deep rose	850.			
158TC	3c	black	750.		12.	
		Block of 4			55.	
158TC	3c	orange red	—			
159TC	6c	black		300.	30.	
		Block of 4			150.	
159TC	6c	deep green		300.		
159TC	6c	deep brown		300.		
159TC	6c	dull red		300.		
159TC	6c	dull gray blue		300.		
160TC	7c	black		300.	75.	
		Block of 4			325.	
160TC	7c	deep green		300.		
160TC	7c	deep brown		300.		
160TC	7c	dull gray blue		300.		
160TC	7c	dull red		300.		
161TC	10c	black		300.		
161TC	10c	deep green		300.		
161TC	10c	deep brown		300.		
161TC	10c	dull gray blue		300.		
161TC	10c	dull red		300.		
162TC	12c	black		300.		
162TC	12c	deep green		300.		
162TC	12c	dull gray blue		300.		
162TC	12c	deep brown		300.		
162TC	12c	dull red		300.		
163TC	15c	black		300.		
163TC	15c	deep green		300.		
163TC	15c	dull gray blue		300.		
163TC	15c	deep brown		300.		
163TC	15c	dull red		300.		
164TC	24c	black		300.		
164TC	24c	deep green		300.		
164TC	24c	dull gray blue		300.		
164TC	24c	deep brown		300.		
164TC	24c	dull red		300.		
165TC	30c	black		300.		
165TC	30c	deep green		300.		
165TC	30c	dull gray blue		300.		
165TC	30c	deep brown		300.		
165TC	30c	dull red		300.		
166TC	90c	black		300.		
166TC	90c	deep green		300.		
166TC	90c	dull gray blue		300.		
166TC	90c	deep brown		300.		
166TC	90c	dull red		300.		

1875

			(1)	(2)	(3)	(4)
179TC	5c	black	650.	300.	25.	45.
		Block of 4			125.	200.
179TC	5c	deep green		300.		
179TC	5c	dull gray blue		300.		
179TC	5c	deep brown		300.		
179TC	5c	dull red		300.		
179TC	5c	scarlet	1,000.			

Small die proofs of 1873-75 issues are "Goodall" prints.

1879 **On stamp paper, gummed** ***Perf. 12***

182TC	1c	ultramarine	300.
182TC	1c	green	300.
182TC	1c	deep green	300.
182TC	1c	vermilion	300.
182TC	1c	brown	300.
183TC	2c	ultramarine	300.
183TC	2c	blue	300.
183TC	2c	green	300.
184TC	3c	ultramarine	300.
184TC	3c	blue	300.
184TC	3c	vermilion	300.
		Block of 4	1,100.
184TC	3c	brown	300.
185TC	5c	ultramarine	300.
185TC	5c	green	300.
185TC	5c	vermilion	300.
186TC	6c	ultramarine	300.
186TC	6c	blue	300.
186TC	6c	vermilion	300.
187TC	10c	ultramarine	300.
187TC	10c	blue	300.
187TC	10c	vermilion	300.
187TC	10c	green	300.
189TC	15c	ultramarine	300.
189TC	15c	green	300.
189TC	15c	vermilion	300.
189TC	15c	brown	300.
189TC	15c	dull red	300.
190TC	30c	ultramarine	300.
190TC	30c	blue	300.
190TC	30c	green	300.

See Specimens for No. 189 in deep blue (No. 189S L), No. 209 in green (No. 209S L), No. 210 in pale rose lake (No. 210S L).

1881-82

			(1)	(2)	(3)	(4)
206TC	1c	deep green	600.	125.		
206TC	1c	black	600.		125.	
206TC	1c	ultramarine	600.			
206TC	1c	dark yellow green	600.			

1882-87

			LARGE DIE (1) India	LARGE DIE (2) Card	PLATE (3) India	PLATE (4) Card
212TC	1c	indigo	1,000.			
212TC	1c	carmine	1,000.			
212TC	1c	green	1,000.	450.		
212TC	1c	deep green	1,000.	450.		
212TC	1c	copper brown	1,000.	450.		
212TC	1c	chestnut brown	1,000.			
210TC	2c	brown red	1,000.	450.		
210TC	2c	deep dull orange	1,000.			
210TC	2c	chestnut brown	1,000.	450.		
210TC	2c	violet rose	1,000.	450.		
210TC	2c	indigo	1,000.	450.		
210TC	2c	black	1,000.			
210TC	2c	pale ultramarine	1,000.			
210TC	2c	olive green	1,000.	450.		
210TC	2c	olive brown		450.		
210TC	2c	lake				140.
210TC	2c	rose lake				140.
210TC	2c	dark carmine				140.
210TC	2c	deep red				140.
214TC	3c	green	1,000.	450.		
214TC	3c	dark green				—
214TC	3c	dark brown	1,000.	450.		
214TC	3c	chestnut brown	1,000.	450.		
214TC	3c	dull red brown	1,000.	450.		
214TC	3c	deep dull orange	—	—		

All of 214TC above bear inscription "Worked over by new company, June 29th, 1881."

			(1)	(2)	(3)	(4)
211TC	4c	green	1,000.	450.		
211TC	4c	chestnut brown	1,000.	450.		
211TC	4c	orange brown	1,000.	450.		
211TC	4c	pale ultra.	1,000.	450.		
211TC	4c	dark brown	1,000.			
211TC	4c	black	1,000.	450.		
205TC	5c	chestnut brown	1,000.	—		
205TC	5c	deep dull orange	1,000.			
205TC	5c	pale ultra	1,000.	—		
205TC	5c	deep green	1,000.			
205TC	5c	green	1,000.		200.	
205TC	5c	carmine	1,000.	450.		
205TC	5c	carmine lake	1,000.		225.	
205TC	5c	blue black	1,000.			
205TC	5c	black on glazed	1,000.			
208TC	6c	deep dull orange	1,000.	450.		
208TC	6c	indigo	1,000.			
208TC	6c	orange vermilion	1,000.	450.		
208TC	6c	dark violet	1,000.	450.		
208TC	6c	chestnut brown	1,000.	450.		
208TC	6c	carmine	1,000.			
209TC	10c	carmine	1,000.	450.		
209TC	10c	orange brown	1,000.	450.		125.
209TC	10c	orange	1,000.			
209TC	10c	deep dull orange	1,000.	450.		
209TC	10c	chestnut brown	1,000.	450.		
209TC	10c	indigo	1,000.	450.		
209TC	10c	pale ultra	1,000.	450.		
209TC	10c	green				125.
209TC	10c	black (glazed)	1,000.			
189TC	15c	orange vermilion	1,000.	450.		
189TC	15c	orange brown	1,000.	450.		
189TC	15c	chestnut brown	1,000.	450.		
189TC	15c	dark brown	1,000.	450.		
189TC	15c	deep green	1,000.	450.		
189TC	15c	black	1,000.	450.		
190TC	30c	black	1,000.			
190TC	30c	orange vermilion	1,000.	450.		
190TC	30c	dark brown	1,000.	450.		
190TC	30c	deep green	1,000.	450.		
190TC	30c	dull red brown	1,000.	450.		
190TC	30c	green	1,000.	450.		
191TC	90c	carmine	1,000.	450.		
191TC	90c	dark brown	1,000.	450.		
191TC	90c	deep dull orange	1,000.	450.		
191TC	90c	indigo	1,000.	450.		
191TC	90c	dull red brown	1,000.	450.		
191TC	90c	black	1,000.	450.		

1890-93

			DIE (1) India	DIE (2) Card	PLATE (3) India	PLATE (4) Card
219TC	1c	green	400.			
219TC	1c	dull violet	400.			
220TC	2c	dull violet	400.			
220TC	2c	blue green	400.			
220TC	2c	slate black	400.			
222TC	4c	orange brown on wove				—
222TC	4c	yellow brown on wove				—
222TC	4c	green	400.			
223TC	5c	blue on glossy wove	400.			
223TC	5c	dark brown on glossy wove	400.			
223TC	5c	bister on wove				—
223TC	5c	sepia on wove				—
223TC	5c	blk brown on wove				—
224TC	6c	deep orange red	400.			
224TC	6c	orange red on wove				120.
224TC	6c	vio. blk. on wove				120.
224TC	6c	yellow on wove				120.
224TC	6c	olive grn. on wove				120.
224TC	6c	purple on wove				120.
224TC	6c	red org. on wove				120.
224TC	6c	brown on wove				120.
224TC	6c	red brn. on wove				120.
224TC	6c	org. brn. on wove				120.
224TC	6c	blk. brn. on wove				120.
224TC	6c	slate grn. on wove				120.
224TC	6c	brn. olive on wove				120.
225TC	8c	dark violet red		400.		
225TC	8c	metallic green		400.		
225TC	8c	salmon		400.		
225TC	8c	yellow orange	—			
225TC	8c	orange brown		400.		
225TC	8c	green	—			
225TC	8c	light green		400.		
225TC	8c	blue		400.		
225TC	8c	steel blue		400.		

1893

			(1)	(2)	(3)	(4)
231TC	2c	sepia	850.	850.		
231TC	2c	orange brown		850.		
231TC	2c	deep orange		850.		
231TC	2c	light brown		850.		
231TC	2c	blue green		850.		
231TC	2c	bright rose red		850.		
231TC	2c	rose violet		850.		
232TC	3c	sepia		850.		
232TC	3c	blackish green		850.	800.	
232TC	3c	black		850.		
233TC	4c	sepia		850.		
233TC	4c	deep orange		850.		
233TC	4c	light brown		850.		
233TC	4c	blue green		850.		
233TC	4c	rose red		850.		
233TC	4c	rose violet		850.		
234TC	5c	black	850.			
234TC	5c	dark violet	850.	850.		
234TC	5c	rose violet	850.	850.		
234TC	5c	red violet	850.			
234TC	5c	brown violet	850.			
234TC	5c	deep blue	850.			
234TC	5c	deep ultra	850.			
234TC	5c	green	850.			
234TC	5c	deep green	850.			
234TC	5c	blue green	—	850.		
234TC	5c	dark olive green	850.	—		
234TC	5c	deep orange	850.	—		
234TC	5c	orange red	850.			
234TC	5c	orange brown	850.	850.		
234TC	5c	bright rose red	850.			
234TC	5c	claret	850.	—		
234TC	5c	brown rose	850.			
234TC	5c	dull rose brown		850.		
234TC	5c	sepia	850.	850.		
234TC	5c	black brown	—	—		

The 5c trial color proofs differ from the issued stamp.

			(1)	(2)	(3)	(4)
237TC	10c	bright rose red	1,250.			
237TC	10c	claret	1,250.			
239TC	30c	sepia		1,000.		
239TC	30c	black				350.
240TC	50c	sepia		1,000.		
242TC	$2	blackish brown			1,000.	
242TC	$2	sepia	—			
242TC	$2	red brown	—			

1894

			DIE (1) Lg.	DIE (2) Sm.	PLATE (3) India	PLATE (4) Card
246TC	1c	dusky blue green	—			
246TC	1c	dark blue	—			
253TC	3c	light red violet	—			
253TC	3c	dark red violet	—			
255TC	5c	black	1,250.			
256TC	6c	dark brown	1,000.			
257TC	8c	black	1,250.			
258TC	10c	olive	1,250.			
259TC	15c	red violet	1,250.			
259TC	15c	dark red orange	1,250.			
261ATC	$1	lake	1,500.			
262TC	$2	black	1,500.			
262TC	$2	dull violet	1,500.			
262TC	$2	violet	1,500.			
262TC	$2	turquoise blue	1,500.			
262TC	$2	orange brown	1,500.			
262TC	$2	olive green	1,500.			
262TC	$2	sepia	1,500.			
262TC	$2	greenish black	1,500.			
263TC	$5	black	1,500.			
263TC	$5	dark yellow	1,500.			
263TC	$5	orange brown	1,500.			
263TC	$5	olive green	1,500.			
263TC	$5	dull violet	1,500.			
263TC	$5	sepia	1,500.			
263TC	$5	brown red	1,500.			

1898

			(1)	(2)	(3)	(4)
283TC	10c	orange	1,250.			
283TC	10c	sepia	1,250.			
284TC	15c	yellowish olive	—			
284TC	15c	red violet	*2,000.*			

1898

			(1)	(2)	(3)	(4)
285TC	1c	black	—			
286TC	2c	purple				2,000.
286TC	2c	black	—			2,000.
286TC	2c	blue				2,000.
286TC	2c	brown				2,000.
286TC	2c	deep carmine rose				2,000.
287TC	4c	black	—			
288TC	5c	black	—			
288TC	5c	orange brown	*2,500.*			
289TC	8c	black	—			
290TC	10c	black	1,500.	1,250.		
291TC	50c	black	1,500.	1,250.		
292TC	$1	black	—			
293TC	$2	black	5,000.			

1901

			(1)	(2)	(3)	(4)
298TC	8c	violet & black on wove paper		*2,500.*		

1902-03

			(1)	(2)	(3)	(4)
308TC	13c	gray violet, type I	1,000.			
319TC	2c	black, type I	3,250.			

1904

			(1)	(2)	(3)	(4)
326TC	5c	black on glazed card	—			

1907

			(1)	(2)	(3)	(4)
330TC	5c	ultramarine	1,600.			
330TC	5c	black	1,700.			

1908

			(1)	(2)	(3)	(4)
332TC	2c	dull violet	750.			
332TC	2c	light ultra.	750.			
332TC	2c	bright ultra.	750.			
332TC	2c	light green	750.			
332TC	2c	dark olive green	750.			
332TC	2c	golden yellow	750.			
332TC	2c	dull orange	750.			
332TC	2c	rose carmine	750.			
332TC	2c	ultramarine	750.			
332TC	2c	black	—			
332TC	2c	dark blue	—			
332TC	2c	blue	850.			
332TC	2c	lilac brown	850.			
332TC	2c	lilac	850.			
332TC	2c	blue black	850.			
332TC	2c	sage green	850.			
332TC	2c	lilac black	850.			
332TC	2c	brown	850.			
332TC	2c	brown black	850.			
332TC	2c	purple	—			
332TC	2c	orange brown	850.			
332TC	2c	ultra. on orange brown	750.			
332TC	2c	ultra. on green	750.			
332TC	2c	green on pink	750.			
332TC	2c	green on rose	750.			
332TC	2c	dark green on grn	750.			
332TC	2c	green on orange brown	750.			
332TC	2c	purple on orange brown	750.			
332TC	2c	blue on yellow	750.			
332TC	2c	green on yellow	750.			
332TC	2c	brown on orange brown	750.			
332TC	2c	brown on yellow	750.			
332TC	2c	green on amber yel	—			
335TC	5c	green on pink	—			
336TC	6c	brown	—			
337TC	8c	green (shades) on yellow	—			
337TC	8c	orange (shades) on yellow	—			
337TC	8c	blue on buff	—			
337TC	8c	blue on yellow	—			
338TC	10c	carmine on pale yellow green	—			
338TC	10c	brown on yellow	—			
338TC	10c	green on pink	—			
338TC	10c	orange on greenish blue	—			
338TC	10c	brown on gray lavender	—			
338TC	10c	orange on orange	—			
338TC	10c	black on pink	—			
338TC	10c	orange on yellow	—			
338TC	10c	brown	—			
338TC	10c	carmine	—			
338TC	10c	blue on pink	—			
338TC	10c	brown on pink	—			
338TC	10c	black	—			
339TC	13c	blue on yellow	—			
339TC	13c	sea green on deep yellow	—			
339TC	13c	sea green on pale blue	—			
339TC	13c	deep violet on yellow	—			
340TC	15c	blue on pale lilac	—			
340TC	15c	blue on greenish blue	—			
340TC	15c	blue on pink	—			
340TC	15c	blue on yellow	—			
340TC	15c	dark blue on buff	—			
340TC	15c	orange brown on yellow	—			
340TC	15c	dark purple on yel	—			
340TC	15c	orange on yellow	—			
340TC	15c	violet on yellow	—			
340TC	15c	black on orange	—			
341TC	50c	lilac on light blue	—			
341TC	50c	dark violet on yellow	—			
341TC	50c	violet on yellow	—			
341TC	50c	orange on yellow	—			
341TC	50c	orange brown on yellow	—			
342TC	$1	brown on blue	—			

1909

			(1)	(2)	(3)	(4)
342TC	$1	carmine lake	1,200.	1,100.		
342TC	$1	pink	1,200.	1,100.		
342TC	$1	brown on blue green	—			
342TC	$1	violet brown on pink	—			
342TC	$1	violet brown on gray	—			

1912-13

			(1)	(2)	(3)	(4)
400TC	10c	brown red	1,750.	1,100.		
414TC	8c	black	1,750.			

1918

			(1)	(2)	(3)	(4)
524TC	$5	carmine & black	1,350.			

1919

			(1)	(2)	(3)	(4)
513TC	13c	violet	650.			
513TC	13c	lilac	650.			
513TC	13c	violet brown	650.			
513TC	13c	light ultra	650.			
513TC	13c	ultramarine	650.			
513TC	13c	deep ultra	650.			
513TC	13c	green	650.			
513TC	13c	dark green	650.			
513TC	13c	olive green	650.			
513TC	13c	orange yellow	650.			
513TC	13c	orange	650.			
513TC	13c	red orange	650.			
513TC	13c	ocher	650.			
513TC	13c	salmon red	650.			
513TC	13c	brown carmine	650.			
513TC	13c	claret brown	650.			
513TC	13c	brown	650.			
513TC	13c	black brown	650.			
513TC	13c	gray	650.			
513TC	13c	black	650.			

1920

			(1)	(2)	(3)	(4)
547TC	$2	green & black	1,500.			

1922-25

			(1)	(2)	(3)	(4)
552TC	1c	black (thin glazed card)		—		
554TC	2c	black (bond paper)		1,250.		
561TC	9c	red orange	2,250.			
563TC	11c	deep green	2,250.			
565TC	14c	dark brown	2,250.			
566TC	15c	black	2,250.			

1923

			(1)	(2)	(3)	(4)
610TC	2c	Harding, green	*4,000.*			

1925

			(1)	(2)	(3)	(4)
618TC	2c	Lexington Concord, black	*1,650.*			

1926

			(1)	(2)	(3)	(4)
622TC	13c	black	2,250.			
628TC	5c	Ericsson, dull dusky blue	1,000.			
628TC		gray blue		1,000.		

1932

			(1)	(2)	(3)	(4)
718TC	3c	Olympic, carmine	*10,000.*			
720TC	3c	black (bond paper)		750.		

1935

			(1)	(2)	(3)	(4)
772TC	3c	Connecticut Tercentenary, black (thin glazed card)	*1,500.*			
773TC	3c	San Diego, org. red (yel. glazed card)	*1,500.*			

1936-43

			(1)	(2)	(3)	(4)
785TC	1c	Army, black (bond paper)		750.		
788TC	4c	Army, dark brown	1,000.			
789TC	5c	Army, blue	1,000.			
793TC	4c	Navy, dark brown	1,000.			
798TC	3c	Constitution, black (bond paper)		750.		
799TC	3c	Hawaii, black (bond paper)		750.		
800TC	3c	Alaska, black (bond paper)		750.		
800TC		(India paper)		750.		
801TC	3c	Puerto Rico, black (bond paper)	900.	750.		
801TC		(India paper)	900.			
802TC	3c	Virgin Islands, black (bond paper)		750.		
803TC	½c	black	*3,000.*			
815TC	10c	sepia	900.			
829TC	25c	green	*2,000.*			
836TC	3c	Swedes & Finns, purple	900.			
837TC	3c	Northwest Terr., dark purple	900.			
854TC	3c	Inauguration, purple	900.			
855TC	3c	Baseball, red violet	*2,250.*			
862TC	5c	Authors, dull blue	900.			
866TC	3c	Poets, dark blue violet	900.			
897TC	3c	Wyoming, red violet	—			
929TC	3c	Iwo Jima, bright purple	*2,300.*			
959TC	3c	Progress of Women, brt. violet	*1,500.*			
963TC	3c	Youth, violet	900.			
964TC	3c	Oregon, dull violet	900.			
968TC	3c	Poultry, red brown	900.			

1923-47

AIR POST

			DIE (1) Lg.	(2) Sm.	PLATE (3) India	(4) Card
C5TC	16c	dark green	5,000.			
C8TC	15c	orange	4,750.			
C32TC	5c	blue	4,750.			
C35TC	15c	brown violet	4,750.			

1934

AIR POST SPECIAL DELIVERY

			(1)	(2)	(3)	(4)
CE1TC	16c	black	3,500.			

1885-1902

SPECIAL DELIVERY

			(1)	(2)	(3)	(4)
E1TC	10c	black	2,500.			
E1TC	10c	dark brown	2,500.			
E1TC	10c	org. yellow (wove paper)		*2,000.*		
E2TC	10c	black	2,500.			
E2TC	10c	green	2,500.			
E2TC	10c	olive yellow		800.		
E6TC	10c	orange	2,500.			
E6TC	10c	black	2,500.			
E6TC	10c	rose red	*4,000.*			

1922-25

			(1)	(2)	(3)	(4)
E12TC	10c	black	1,500.			

1911

REGISTRATION

			(1)	(2)	(3)	(4)
F1TC	10c	black (glazed card)	1,500.			

1851

CARRIERS

		(1)	(2)	(3)	(4)
LO1TC	deep green			250.	
	Block of 4			1,250.	
	a. orange (wove paper)				350.
LO2TC	deep green			250.	
	Block of 4			1,250.	
	a. orange (wove paper)				350.

LOCALS

		(1)	(2)	(3)	(4)
15L18TC	(1c) brown			—	
15L18TC	(1c) blue			—	
15L18TC	(1c) green			—	
15L18TC	(1c) reddish brown			—	

1879

POSTAGE DUE

			DIE (1) Lg.	(2) Sm.	PLATE (3) India	(4) Card
J1TC	1c	black	500.			50.
J1TC	1c	gray black	500.			
J1TC	1c	ultramarine	500.			
J1TC	1c	blue	500.			
J1TC	1c	blue green	500.			
J1TC	1c	orange	500.	100.		
J1TC	1c	red orange	500.			
J1TC	1c	olive bister	500.			
J2TC	2c	black	500.			
J2TC	2c	gray black	500.			
J2TC	2c	ultramarine	500.			
J2TC	2c	blue	500.			
J2TC	2c	blue green	500.			
J2TC	2c	orange	500.	100.		
J2TC	2c	red orange	500.			
J2TC	2c	sepia	500.			
J3TC	3c	black	500.			
J3TC	3c	gray black		100.		
J3TC	3c	ultramarine	500.			
J3TC	3c	blue	500.			
J3TC	3c	blue green	500.			
J3TC	3c	orange	500.	100.		
J3TC	3c	red orange	500.			
J3TC	3c	light brown	500.			
J4TC	5c	black	500.			
J4TC	5c	gray black	500.			
J4TC	5c	ultramarine	500.			
J4TC	5c	blue	500.			
J4TC	5c	blue green	500.			
J4TC	5c	orange	500.	100.		
J4TC	5c	red orange	500.			
J5TC	10c	black	500.			
J5TC	10c	gray black	500.			
J5TC	10c	blue	500.			
J5TC	10c	olive yellow	500.			
J5TC	10c	blue green	500.			
J5TC	10c	orange	500.	100.		
J5TC	10c	red orange	500.			
J5TC	10c	olive bister	500.			
J5TC	10c	sepia	500.			
J5TC	10c	gray	500.			
J6TC	30c	black	500.			
J6TC	30c	gray black	500.			
J6TC	30c	blue	500.			
J6TC	30c	olive yellow		100.		
J6TC	30c	blue green	500.			
J6TC	30c	orange	500.	100.		
J6TC	30c	red orange	500.			

			DIE (1) Lg.	DIE (2) Sm.	PLATE (3) India	PLATE (4) Card
J6TC	30c	olive bister	500.			
J6TC	30c	sepia		100.		
J7TC	50c	black	500.			
J7TC	50c	gray black	500.			
J7TC	50c	blue	500.	100.		
J7TC	50c	olive yellow		100.		
J7TC	50c	blue green	500.			
J7TC	50c	orange	500.	100.		
J7TC	50c	red orange	500.			
J7TC	50c	olive bister	500.			
J7TC	50c	sepia	500.			
J7TC	50c	gray	500.			

OFFICIAL

Agriculture

			(1) Lg.	(2) Sm.	(3) India	(4) Card
O1TC	1c	black	500.		75.	
O2TC	2c	black	500.		75.	
O3TC	3c	black	500.			
O3TC	3c	deep green	500.			
O4TC	6c	black	500.		150.	
O5TC	10c	black	500.			
O6TC	12c	black	500.		75.	
O9TC	30c	black	500.			

Executive

			(1) Lg.	(2) Sm.	(3) India	(4) Card
O11TC	2c	black	500.		75.	
O11TC	2c	deep brown	500.			
O11TC	2c	brown carmine				75.
O12TC	3c	black	500.		75.	
O12TC	3c	deep green	500.			
O13TC	6c	black			90.	
O14TC	10c	black			90.	

Interior

			(1) Lg.	(2) Sm.	(3) India	(4) Card
O16TC	2c	black	500.			
O16TC	2c	deep brown	500.			
O17TC	3c	black	500.		90.	
O17TC	3c	deep green	500.			

Justice

			(1) Lg.	(2) Sm.	(3) India	(4) Card
O27TC	3c	black	500.		90.	
O27TC	3c	deep green	500.			
O27TC	3c	bister yellow			90.	
O27TC	3c	dull orange			90.	
O27TC	3c	black violet			90.	

Navy

			(1) Lg.	(2) Sm.	(3) India	(4) Card
O35TC	1c	black			90.	
O36TC	2c	black	500.			
O36TC	2c	deep brown	500.			
O36TC	2c	black on wove paper, perf.				250.
O36TC	2c	deep green on wove paper, perf.				250.
O36TC	2c	deep green on wove paper, imperf.				250.
O37TC	3c	black	500.		90.	
O37TC	3c	deep green	500.			

Post Office

			(1) Lg.	(2) Sm.	(3) India	(4) Card
O48TC	2c	deep brown	500.			
O49TC	3c	deep green	500.			
O50TC	6c	deep brown	500.			
O50TC	6c	brown carmine	500.			

State

			(1) Lg.	(2) Sm.	(3) India	(4) Card
O57TC	1c	black	500.			
O57TC	1c	light ultramarine	500.			
O58TC	2c	black	500.			
O58TC	2c	deep brown	500.			
O59TC	3c	black	500.			
O67TC	90c	black	500.			
O68TC	$2	violet & black	2,500.			
O68TC	$2	brown red & black	2,500.			
O68TC	$2	orange red & slate blue	2,500.			

Treasury

			(1) Lg.	(2) Sm.	(3) India	(4) Card
O72TC	1c	black	500.			
O72TC	1c	light ultramarine	500.			
O73TC	2c	black	500.			
O74TC	3c	black	500.			
O74TC	3c	deep green	500.			
O75TC	6c	black	500.			
O77TC	10c	black	500.			
O78TC	12c	black	500.			
O79TC	15c	black	500.			
O80TC	24c	black	500.			
O81TC	30c	black	500.			
O82TC	90c	black	500.			

War

			(1) Lg.	(2) Sm.	(3) India	(4) Card
O83TC	1c	black	500.		80.	
O83TC	1c	light ultramarine	500.			
O84TC	2c	black	500.		80.	75.
O84TC	2c	deep brown	500.			
O85TC	3c	black	500.			
O85TC	3c	deep green	500.			
O85TC	3c	chocolate	675.			
O86TC	6c	black			80.	
O89TC	12c	black			80.	

1910

POSTAL SAVINGS MAIL

			(1) Lg.	(2) Sm.	(3) India	(4) Card
O121TC	2c	lake	500.			
O126TC	10c	black (on wove)	*1,250.*			

The so-called "Goodall" set of Small Die proofs on India Paper of Official Stamps in five colors

Agriculture

		(a) Black	(b) Deep green	(c) Dull gray blue	(d) Deep brown	(e) Dull red
O1TC	1c	150.	140.	140.	140.	140.
O2TC	2c	150.	140.	140.	140.	140.
O3TC	3c	150.	140.	140.	140.	140.
O4TC	6c	150.	140.	140.	140.	140.
O5TC	10c	150.	140.	140.	140.	140.
O6TC	12c	150.	140.	140.	140.	140.
O7TC	15c	150.	140.	140.	140.	140.
O8TC	24c	150.	140.	140.	140.	140.
O9TC	30c	150.	140.	140.	140.	140.

Executive

		(a)	(b)	(c)	(d)	(e)
O10TC	1c	150.	140.	140.	140.	140.
O11TC	2c	150.	140.	140.	140.	140.
O12TC	3c	150.	140.	140.	140.	140.
O13TC	6c	150.	140.	140.	140.	140.
O14TC	10c	150.	140.	140.	140.	140.

Interior

		(a)	(b)	(c)	(d)	(e)
O15TC	1c	150.	140.	140.	140.	140.
O16TC	2c	150.	140.	140.	140.	140.
O17TC	3c	150.	140.	140.	140.	140.
O18TC	6c	150.	140.	140.	140.	140.
O19TC	10c	150.	140.	140.	140.	140.
O20TC	12c	150.	140.	140.	140.	140.
O21TC	15c	150.	140.	140.	140.	140.
O22TC	24c	150.	140.	140.	140.	140.
O23TC	30c	150.	140.	140.	140.	140.
O24TC	90c	150.	140.	140.	140.	140.

Justice

		(a)	(b)	(c)	(d)	(e)
O25TC	1c	150.	140.	140.	140.	140.
O26TC	2c	150.	140.	140.	140.	140.
O27TC	3c	150.	140.	140.	140.	140.
O28TC	6c	150.	140.	140.	140.	140.
O29TC	10c	150.	140.	140.	140.	140.
O30TC	12c	150.	140.	140.	140.	140.
O31TC	15c	150.	140.	140.	140.	140.
O32TC	24c	150.	140.	140.	140.	140.
O33TC	30c	150.	140.	140.	140.	140.
O34TC	90c	150.	140.	140.	140.	140.

Navy

		(a)	(b)	(c)	(d)	(e)
O35TC	1c	150.	140.	140.	140.	140.
O36TC	2c	150.	140.	140.	140.	140.
O37TC	3c	150.	140.	140.	140.	140.
O38TC	6c	150.	140.	140.	140.	140.
O39TC	7c	150.	140.	140.	140.	140.
O40TC	10c	150.	140.	140.	140.	140.
O41TC	12c	150.	140.	140.	140.	140.
O42TC	15c	150.	140.	140.	140.	140.
O43TC	24c	150.	140.	140.	140.	140.
O44TC	30c	150.	140.	140.	140.	140.
O45TC	90c	150.	140.	140.	140.	140.

Post Office

		(a)	(b)	(c)	(d)	(e)
O47TC	1c	150.	140.	140.	140.	140.
O48TC	2c	150.	140.	140.	140.	140.
O49TC	3c	150.	140.	140.	140.	140.
O50TC	6c	150.	140.	140.	140.	140.
O51TC	10c	150.	140.	140.	140.	140.
O52TC	12c	150.	140.	140.	140.	140.
O53TC	15c	150.	140.	140.	140.	140.
O54TC	24c	150.	140.	140.	140.	140.
O55TC	30c	150.	140.	140.	140.	140.
O56TC	90c	150.	140.	140.	140.	140.

State

		(a)	(b)	(c)	(d)	(e)
O57TC	1c	150.	140.	140.	140.	140.
O58TC	2c	150.	140.	140.	140.	140.
O59TC	3c	150.	140.	140.	140.	140.
O60TC	6c	150.	140.	140.	140.	140.
O61TC	7c	150.	140.	140.	140.	140.
O62TC	10c	150.	140.	140.	140.	140.
O63TC	12c	150.	140.	140.	140.	140.
O64TC	15c	150.	140.	140.	140.	140.
O65TC	24c	150.	140.	140.	140.	140.
O66TC	30c	150.	140.	140.	140.	140.
O67TC	90c	150.	140.	140.	140.	140.

O68TC	$2	scarlet frame, green center	*3,250.*
O68TC	$2	scarlet frame, black center	*3,250.*
O68TC	$2	scarlet frame, blue center	*3,250.*
O68TC	$2	scarlet frame, brown center	*3,250.*
O68TC	$2	violet frame, black center	*3,250.*
O68TC	$2	green frame, brown center	*3,250.*
O68TC	$2	brown frame, green center	*3,250.*
O68TC	$2	brown frame, black center	*3,250.*
O68TC	$2	red brown frame, green center	*3,250.*

Treasury

		(a)	(b)	(c)	(d)	(e)
O72TC	1c	150.	140.	140.	140.	140.
O73TC	2c	150.	140.	140.	140.	140.
O74TC	3c	150.	140.	140.	140.	140.
O75TC	6c	150.	140.	140.	140.	140.
O76TC	7c	150.	140.	140.	140.	140.
O77TC	10c	150.	140.	140.	140.	140.
O78TC	12c	150.	140.	140.	140.	140.
O79TC	15c	150.	140.	140.	140.	140.
O80TC	24c	150.	140.	140.	140.	140.
O81TC	30c	150.	140.	140.	140.	140.
O82TC	90c	150.	140.	140.	140.	140.

War

		(a)	(b)	(c)	(d)	(e)
O83TC	1c	150.	140.	140.	140.	140.
O84TC	2c	150.	140.	140.	140.	140.
O85TC	3c	150.	140.	140.	140.	140.
O86TC	6c	150.	140.	140.	140.	140.
O87TC	7c	150.	140.	140.	140.	140.
O88TC	10c	150.	140.	140.	140.	140.
O89TC	12c	150.	140.	140.	140.	140.
O90TC	15c	150.	140.	140.	140.	140.
O91TC	24c	150.	140.	140.	140.	140.
O92TC	30c	150.	140.	140.	140.	140.
O93TC	90c	150.	140.	140.	140.	140.

OFFICIAL SEALS

1872

OXF1TC	ultra	Die on India	*1,000.*
OXF1TC	blue	Die on card, colored border	*1,000.*
OXF1TC	dp bl	Die on card, colored border	*1,000.*
OXF1TC	green	Die on card, colored border	*1,000.*
OXF1TC	choc	Die on glossy bond	*1,000.*
OXF1TC	choc	Die on card, colored border	*1,000.*
OXF1TC	car	Die on India	*1,000.*
OXF1TC	brown	Die on India	*1,000.*
OXF1TC	red vio	Die on India	*1,000.*

1877

OX1TC	blue	Die on India	500.
OX1TC	green	Die on India	500.
OX1TC	green	Plate on bond	500.
OX1TC	green	Plate on bond, perforated and gummed	—
OX1TC	orange	Die on India	500.
OX1TC	red orange	Die on India	500.
OX1TC	black	Die on India	500.

1879

OX2TC	black	Die on India	—

POSTAL NOTE STAMPS

PN1TC	1c bister	imperf, on white wove	—

NEWSPAPERS

1865

			(1) Die on India	(5) Thick cream wove paper
PR1TC	5c	bright red	500.	
PR1TC	5c	deep reddish brown	2,000.	
PR1TC	5c	dark orange	2,000.	
PR1TC	5c	green	2,000.	
PR2TC	10c	brown	500.	
PR2TC	10c	dull red	500.	
PR2TC	10c	blue	500.	
PR2TC	10c	black		70.
PR2TC	10c	lake		70.
PR2TC	10c	blue green		70.
PR2TC	10c	blue		70.
PR3TC	25c	black		70.
PR3TC	25c	lake		70.
PR3TC	25c	blue green		70.
PR3TC	25c	blue		70.
PR3TC	25c	ocher	500.	
PR3TC	25c	brown	500.	
PR3TC	25c	brick red	500.	
PR4TC	5c	black		70.
PR4TC	5c	lake		70.
PR4TC	5c	blue green		70.
PR4TC	5c	blue		70.

1875

			(1) Die on India	(3) Plate on India
PR9TC	2c	dark carmine		35.
PR9TC	2c	brown rose		35.
PR9TC	2c	scarlet		35.
PR9TC	2c	orange brown	250.	35.
PR9TC	2c	black brown	250.	
PR9TC	2c	sepia		35.
PR9TC	2c	orange yellow		35.
PR9TC	2c	dull orange		35.
PR9TC	2c	green		35.
PR9TC	2c	blue green	250.	
PR9TC	2c	light ultramarine		35.
PR9TC	2c	light blue		35.
PR9TC	2c	dark violet		35.
PR9TC	2c	violet black		35.
PR10TC	3c	rose lake	250.	
PR16TC	12c	dark carmine		35.
PR16TC	12c	brown rose	250.	35.
PR16TC	12c	scarlet	250.	35.
PR16TC	12c	orange brown		35.
PR16TC	12c	sepia	250.	35.
PR16TC	12c	orange yellow		35.
PR16TC	12c	dull orange		35.
PR16TC	12c	green	250.	35.
PR16TC	12c	light ultramarine	250.	35.
PR16TC	12c	light blue		35.
PR16TC	12c	dark violet	250.	35.
PR16TC	12c	violet black	250.	35.
PR16TC	12c	black	250.	35.
PR17TC	24c	sepia		
PR17TC	24c	green	250.	
PR17TC	24c	black	250.	35.
PR18TC	36c	black	250.	35.
PR18TC	36c	sepia	250.	
PR18TC	36c	green	250.	
PR19TC	48c	black	250.	35.
PR19TC	48c	sepia	250.	
PR19TC	48c	green	250.	
PR20TC	60c	black	250.	35.
PR21TC	72c	black	250.	35.
PR22TC	84c	black	250.	35.
PR23TC	96c	black		35.
PR24TC	$1.92	dark carmine		35.
PR24TC	$1.92	brown rose		35.
PR24TC	$1.92	scarlet		35.
PR24TC	$1.92	orange brown	250.	35.

			(1) Die on India	(3) Plate on India
PR24TC	$1.92	sepia		35.
PR24TC	$1.92	orange yellow		35.
PR24TC	$1.92	dull orange		35.
PR24TC	$1.92	green	250.	35.
PR24TC	$1.92	light ultramarine		35.
PR24TC	$1.92	dark violet		35.
PR24TC	$1.92	violet black		35.
PR24TC	$1.92	black		35.
PR25TC	$3	dark carmine	250.	35.
PR25TC	$3	brown rose		35.
PR25TC	$3	scarlet		35.
PR25TC	$3	orange brown		35.
PR25TC	$3	sepia		35.
PR25TC	$3	orange yellow	250.	35.
PR25TC	$3	dull orange	250.	35.
PR25TC	$3	green	250.	35.
PR25TC	$3	light ultramarine	250.	35.
PR25TC	$3	light blue		35.
PR25TC	$3	dark violet	250.	35.
PR25TC	$3	violet black	250.	35.
PR25TC	$3	black	250.	35.
PR26TC	$6	dark carmine	250.	35.
PR26TC	$6	brown rose	250.	35.
PR26TC	$6	scarlet	250.	35.
PR26TC	$6	orange brown		35.
PR26TC	$6	dark brown		35.
PR26TC	$6	sepia	250.	35.
PR26TC	$6	orange yellow	250.	35.
PR26TC	$6	dull orange	250.	35.
PR26TC	$6	green	250.	35.
PR26TC	$6	light ultramarine		35.
PR26TC	$6	light blue	250.	35.
PR26TC	$6	dark violet	250.	35.
PR26TC	$6	violet black	250.	35.
PR26TC	$6	black	250.	35.
PR27TC	$9	dark carmine	250.	35.
PR27TC	$9	brown rose	250.	35.
PR27TC	$9	scarlet	250.	35.
PR27TC	$9	orange brown		35.
PR27TC	$9	sepia	250.	35.
PR27TC	$9	orange yellow	250.	35.
PR27TC	$9	dull orange	250.	35.
PR27TC	$9	green	250.	35.
PR27TC	$9	light ultramarine	250.	35.
PR27TC	$9	light blue		35.
PR27TC	$9	dark violet	250.	35.
PR27TC	$9	violet black	250.	35.
PR27TC	$9	black	250.	35.
PR28TC	$12	black	250.	
PR28TC	$12	sepia	250.	
PR28TC	$12	orange brown	250.	
PR29TC	$24	black	250.	35.
PR29TC	$24	black brown	250.	
PR29TC	$24	orange brown	250.	
PR29TC	$24	green	250.	
PR30TC	$36	dark carmine	250.	
PR30TC	$36	black	250.	35.
PR30TC	$36	black brown	250.	
PR30TC	$36	orange brown	250.	
PR30TC	$36	sepia	250.	
PR30TC	$36	violet	250.	
PR30TC	$36	green	250.	
PR31TC	$48	violet brown	250.	35.
PR31TC	$48	black	250.	35.
PR31TC	$48	sepia	250.	
PR31TC	$48	green	250.	
PR32TC	$60	dark carmine	250.	40.
PR32TC	$60	scarlet	250.	40.
PR32TC	$60	sepia	250.	40.
PR32TC	$60	green	250.	40.
PR32TC	$60	light ultramarine	250.	40.
PR32TC	$60	black	250.	40.
PR32TC	$60	violet black	250.	
PR32TC	$60	orange brown	250.	
PR32TC	$60	orange yellow	250.	
PR32TC	$60	dull orange	250.	
PR32TC	$60	brown rose	250.	

1885

PR81TC	1c	salmon	250.	
PR81TC	1c	scarlet		120.
PR81TC	1c	dark brown		120.
PR81TC	1c	violet brown		120.
PR81TC	1c	dull orange		120.
PR81TC	1c	green		120.
PR81TC	1c	light blue		120.

1894

PR106TC	25c	deep carmine	250.
PR106TC	25c	dark carmine	250.
PR107TC	50c	black	250.
PR108TC	$2	deep scarlet	250.
PR108TC	$2	dark scarlet	250.
PR109TC	$5	light ultramarine	250.
PR109TC	$5	dark ultramarine	250.
PR110TC	$10	black	250.
PR112TC	$50	black	250.
PR112TC	$50	deep rose	250.
PR112TC	$50	dark rose	250.
PR113TC	$100	black	250.

The so-called "Goodall" set of Small Die proofs on India Paper of Newspaper Stamps in five colors

		(a) Black	(b) Deep green	(c) Dull gray blue	(d) Deep brown	(e) Dull red
PR9TC	2c	150.	125.	125.	125.	125.
PR10TC	3c	150.	125.	125.	125.	125.
PR11TC	4c	150.	125.	125.	125.	125.
PR12TC	6c	150.	125.	125.	125.	125.
PR13TC	8c	150.	125.	125.	125.	125.
PR14TC	9c	150.	125.	125.	125.	125.
PR15TC	10c	150.	125.	125.	125.	125.
PR16TC	12c	150.	125.	125.	125.	125.
PR17TC	24c	150.	125.	125.	125.	125.
PR18TC	36c	150.	125.	125.	125.	125.
PR19TC	48c	150.	125.	125.	125.	125.
PR20TC	60c	150.	125.	125.	125.	125.
PR21TC	72c	150.	125.	125.	125.	125.
PR22TC	84c	150.	125.	125.	125.	125.
PR23TC	96c	150.	125.	125.	125.	125.
PR24TC	$1.92	150.	125.	125.	125.	125.
PR25TC	$3	150.	125.	125.	125.	125.
PR26TC	$6	150.	125.	125.	125.	125.
PR27TC	$9	150.	125.	125.	125.	125.
PR28TC	$12	150.	125.	125.	125.	125.
PR29TC	$24	150.	125.	125.	125.	125.
PR30TC	$36	150.	125.	125.	125.	125.
PR31TC	$48	150.	125.	125.	125.	125.
PR32TC	$60	150.	125.	125.	125.	125.

1925

SPECIAL HANDLING

QE4TC	25c	apple green	1,500.
QE4TC	25c	olive green	1,500.
QE4TC	25c	light blue green	1,500.
QE4TC	25c	dark blue	1,500.
QE4TC	25c	orange yellow	1,500.
QE4TC	25c	orange	1,500.
QE4TC	25c	dull rose	1,500.
QE4TC	25c	carmine lake	1,500.
QE4TC	25c	brown	1,500.
QE4TC	25c	gray brown	1,500.
QE4TC	25c	dark violet brown	1,500.
QE4TC	25c	gray black	1,500.
QE4TC	25c	black	1,500.

THE "ATLANTA" SET OF PLATE PROOFS

A set in five colors on thin card reprinted in 1881 for display at the International Cotton Exhibition in Atlanta, Ga.

1847 Designs (Reproductions)

		Black	Scarlet	Brown	Green	Blue
3TC	5c	300.	300.	300.	300.	300.
4TC	10c	300.	300.	300.	300.	300.

1851-60 Designs

40TC	1c	120.	100.	100.	100.	100.
41TC	3c	120.	100.	100.	100.	100.
42TC	5c	120.	100.	100.	100.	100.
43TC	10c	120.	100.	100.	100.	100.
44TC	12c	120.	100.	100.	100.	100.
45TC	24c	120.	100.	100.	100.	100.
46TC	30c	120.	100.	100.	100.	100.
47TC	90c	120.	100.	100.	100.	100.

1861-66 Designs

102TC	1c	100.	90.	90.	90.	90.
103TC	2c	175.	175.	175.	175.	175.
104TC	3c	100.	90.	90.	90.	90.
105TC	5c	100.	90.	90.	90.	90.
106TC	10c	100.	90.	90.	90.	90.
107TC	12c	100.	90.	90.	90.	90.
108TC	15c	100.	90.	90.	90.	90.
109TC	24c	100.	90.	90.	90.	90.
110TC	30c	100.	90.	90.	90.	90.
111TC	90c	100.	90.	90.	90.	90.

1869 Designs

123TC	1c	175.	150.	150.	150.	150.
124TC	2c	175.	150.	150.	150.	150.
125TC	3c	175.	150.	150.	150.	150.
126TC	6c	175.	150.	150.	150.	150.
127TC	10c	175.	150.	150.	150.	150.
128TC	12c	175.	150.	150.	150.	150.

129TC	15c	black frame, scarlet center	375.
129TC	15c	black frame, green center	375.
129TC	15c	scarlet frame, black center	375.
129TC	15c	scarlet frame, blue center	375.
129TC	15c	brown frame, black center	375.
129TC	15c	brown frame, green center	375.
129TC	15c	brown frame, blue center	375.
129TC	15c	green frame, black center	375.
129TC	15c	green frame, blue center	375.
129TC	15c	blue frame, black center	375.
129TC	15c	blue frame, brown center	375.
129TC	15c	blue frame, green center	375.
130TC	24c	black frame, scarlet center	375.
130TC	24c	black frame, green center	375.
130TC	24c	black frame, blue center	375.
130TC	24c	scarlet frame, black center	375.
130TC	24c	scarlet frame, blue center	375.
130TC	24c	brown frame, black center	375.
130TC	24c	brown frame, blue center	375.
130TC	24c	green frame, black center	375.
130TC	24c	green frame, brown center	375.
130TC	24c	green frame, blue center	375.
130TC	24c	blue frame, brown center	375.
130TC	24c	blue frame, green center	375.
131TC	30c	black frame, scarlet center	375.
131TC	30c	black frame, green center	375.
131TC	30c	black frame, blue center	375.
131TC	30c	scarlet frame, black center	375.
131TC	30c	scarlet frame, green center	375.
131TC	30c	scarlet frame, blue center	375.
131TC	30c	brown frame, black center	375.
131TC	30c	brown frame, scarlet center	375.
131TC	30c	brown frame, blue center	375.
131TC	30c	green frame, black center	375.
131TC	30c	green frame, brown center	375.
131TC	30c	blue frame, scarlet center	375.
131TC	30c	blue frame, brown center	375.
131TC	30c	blue frame, green center	375.
132TC	90c	black frame, scarlet center	550.
132TC	90c	black frame, brown center	550.
132TC	90c	black frame, green center	550.
132TC	90c	scarlet frame, blue center	550.
132TC	90c	brown frame, black center	550.
132TC	90c	brown frame, blue center	550.
132TC	90c	green frame, black center	—
132TC	90c	green frame, brown center	550.
132TC	90c	green frame, blue center	550.
132TC	90c	blue frame, brown center	550.
132TC	90c	blue frame, green center	550.

1873-75 Designs

		Black	Scarlet	Brown	Green	Blue
156TC	1c	55.	50.	50.	50.	50.
157TC	2c	55.	50.	50.	50.	50.
158TC	3c	60.	55.	55.	55.	55.
159TC	6c	65.	60.	60.	60.	60.
160TC	7c	55.	50.	50.	50.	50.
161TC	10c	55.	50.	50.	50.	50.
162TC	12c	55.	50.	50.	50.	50.
163TC	15c	55.	50.	50.	50.	50.
164TC	24c	55.	50.	50.	50.	50.
165TC	30c	60.	55.	55.	55.	55.
166TC	90c	55.	50.	50.	50.	50.
179TC	5c	80.	75.	75.	75.	75.

POSTAGE DUE

J1TC	1c	55.	50.	50.	50.	50.
J2TC	2c	55.	50.	50.	50.	50.
J3TC	3c	55.	50.	50.	50.	50.
J4TC	5c	55.	50.	50.	50.	50.
J5TC	10c	55.	50.	50.	50.	50.
J6TC	30c	55.	50.	50.	50.	50.
J7TC	50c	55.	50.	50.	50.	50.

OFFICIALS

Agriculture

O1TC	1c	43.	37.	37.	37.	37.
O2TC	2c	43.	37.	37.	37.	37.
O3TC	3c	43.	37.	37.	37.	37.
O4TC	6c	55.	50.	50.	50.	50.
O5TC	10c	43.	37.	37.	37.	37.
O6TC	12c	43.	37.	37.	37.	37.
O7TC	15c	43.	37.	37.	37.	37.
O8TC	24c	43.	37.	37.	37.	37.
O9TC	30c	43.	37.	37.	37.	37.

Executive

O10TC	1c	43.	37.	37.	37.	37.
O11TC	2c	43.	37.	37.	37.	37.
O12TC	3c	43.	37.	37.	37.	37.
O13TC	6c	55.	50.	50.	50.	50.
O14TC	10c	43.	37.	37.	37.	37.

Interior

O15TC	1c	43.	37.	37.	37.	37.
O16TC	2c	43.	37.	37.	37.	37.
O17TC	3c	43.	37.	37.	37.	37.
O18TC	6c	55.	50.	50.	50.	50.
O19TC	10c	43.	37.	37.	37.	37.
O20TC	12c	43.	37.	37.	37.	37.
O21TC	15c	43.	37.	37.	37.	37.
O22TC	24c	43.	37.	37.	37.	37.
O23TC	30c	60.	55.	55.	55.	55.
O24TC	90c	43.	37.	37.	37.	37.

Justice

O25TC	1c	43.	37.	37.	37.	37.
O26TC	2c	43.	37.	37.	37.	37.
O27TC	3c	43.	37.	37.	37.	37.
O28TC	6c	55.	50.	50.	50.	50.
O29TC	10c	43.	37.	37.	37.	37.
O30TC	12c	43.	37.	37.	37.	37.
O31TC	15c	43.	37.	37.	37.	37.
O32TC	24c	43.	37.	37.	37.	37.
O33TC	30c	60.	55.	55.	55.	55.
O34TC	90c	43.	37.	37.	37.	37.

Navy

O35TC	1c	43.	37.	37.	37.	37.
O36TC	2c	43.	37.	37.	37.	37.
O37TC	3c	43.	37.	37.	37.	37.
O38TC	6c	55.	50.	50.	50.	50.
O39TC	7c	43.	37.	37.	37.	37.
O40TC	10c	43.	37.	37.	37.	37.
O41TC	12c	43.	37.	37.	37.	37.
O42TC	15c	43.	37.	37.	37.	37.
O43TC	24c	43.	37.	37.	37.	37.
O44TC	30c	60.	55.	55.	55.	55.
O45TC	90c	43.	37.	37.	37.	37.

Post Office

O48TC	2c	43.	37.	37.	37.	37.
O49TC	3c	43.	37.	37.	37.	37.
O50TC	6c	43.	37.	37.	37.	37.
O51TC	10c	43.	37.	37.	37.	37.
O52TC	12c	43.	37.	37.	37.	37.
O53TC	15c	43.	37.	37.	37.	37.
O54TC	24c	43.	37.	37.	37.	37.
O55TC	30c	43.	37.	37.	37.	37.
O56TC	90c	43.	37.	37.	37.	37.

State

O57TC	1c	43.	37.	37.	37.	37.
O58TC	2c	43.	37.	37.	37.	37.
O59TC	3c	43.	37.	37.	37.	37.
O60TC	6c	55.	50.	50.	50.	50.

		Black	Scarlet	Brown	Green	Blue
O61TC	7c	43.	37.	37.	37.	37.
O62TC	10c	43.	37.	37.	37.	37.
O63TC	12c	43.	37.	37.	37.	37.
O64TC	15c	43.	37.	37.	37.	37.
O65TC	24c	43.	37.	37.	37.	37.
O66TC	30c	60.	55.	55.	55.	55.
O67TC	90c	43.	37.	37.	37.	37.

O68TC	$2	scarlet frame, black center	1,000.
O68TC	$2	scarlet frame, blue center	1,000.
O68TC	$2	brown frame, black center	1,000.
O68TC	$2	brown frame, blue center	1,000.
O68TC	$2	green frame, brown center	1,000.
O68TC	$2	blue frame, brown center	1,000.
O68TC	$2	blue frame, green center	1,000.
O69TC	$5	scarlet frame, black center	1,000.
O69TC	$5	scarlet frame, blue center	1,000.
O69TC	$5	brown frame, black center	1,000.
O69TC	$5	brown frame, blue center	1,000.
O69TC	$5	green frame, brown center	1,000.
O69TC	$5	blue frame, brown center	1,000.
O69TC	$5	blue frame, green center	1,000.
O70TC	$10	scarlet frame, black center	1,000.
O70TC	$10	scarlet frame, blue center	1,000.
O70TC	$10	brown frame, black center	1,000.
O70TC	$10	brown frame, blue center	1,000.
O70TC	$10	green frame, brown center	1,000.
O70TC	$10	blue frame, brown center	1,000.
O70TC	$10	blue frame, green center	1,000.
O71TC	$20	scarlet frame, black center	1,000.
O71TC	$20	scarlet frame, blue center	1,000.
O71TC	$20	brown frame, black center	1,000.
O71TC	$20	brown frame, blue center	1,000.
O71TC	$20	green frame, brown center	1,000.
O71TC	$20	blue frame, brown center	1,000.
O71TC	$20	blue frame, green center	1,000.

Treasury

		Black	Scarlet	Brown	Green	Blue
O72TC	1c	43.	37.	37.	37.	37.
O73TC	2c	43.	37.	37.	37.	37.
O74TC	3c	43.	37.	37.	37.	37.
O75TC	6c	55.	50.	50.	50.	50.
O76TC	7c	43.	37.	37.	37.	37.
O77TC	10c	43.	37.	37.	37.	37.
O78TC	12c	43.	37.	37.	37.	37.
O79TC	15c	43.	37.	37.	37.	37.
O80TC	24c	43.	37.	37.	37.	37.
O81TC	30c	60.	55.	55.	55.	55.
O82TC	90c	43.	37.	37.	37.	37.

War

		Black	Scarlet	Brown	Green	Blue
O83TC	1c	43.	37.	37.	37.	37.
O84TC	2c	43.	37.	37.	37.	37.
O85TC	3c	43.	37.	37.	37.	37.
	Plate flaw at upper left (32R20)			—		
O86TC	6c	55.	50.	50.	50.	50.
O87TC	7c	43.	37.	37.	37.	37.
O88TC	10c	43.	37.	37.	37.	37.
O89TC	12c	43.	37.	37.	37.	37.
O90TC	15c	43.	37.	37.	37.	37.
O91TC	24c	43.	37.	37.	37.	37.
O92TC	30c	60.	55.	55.	55.	55.
O93TC	90c	43.	37.	37.	37.	37.

NEWSPAPERS

		Black	Scarlet	Brown	Green	Blue
PR9TC	2c	55.	40.	40.	40.	40.
PR10TC	3c	55.	40.	40.	40.	40.
PR11TC	4c	55.	40.	40.	40.	40.
PR12TC	6c	55.	40.	40.	40.	40.
PR13TC	8c	55.	40.	40.	40.	40.
PR14TC	9c	55.	40.	40.	40.	40.
PR15TC	10c	55.	40.	40.	40.	40.
PR16TC	12c	55.	40.	40.	40.	40.
PR17TC	24c	55.	40.	40.	40.	40.
PR18TC	36c	55.	40.	40.	40.	40.
PR19TC	48c	55.	40.	40.	40.	40.
PR20TC	60c	55.	40.	40.	40.	40.
PR21TC	72c	55.	40.	40.	40.	40.
PR22TC	84c	55.	40.	40.	40.	40.
PR23TC	96c	55.	40.	40.	40.	40.
PR24TC	$1.92	55.	40.	40.	40.	40.
PR25TC	$3	55.	40.	40.	40.	40.
PR26TC	$6	55.	40.	40.	40.	40.
PR27TC	$9	55.	40.	40.	40.	40.
PR28TC	$12	55.	40.	40.	40.	40.
PR29TC	$24	55.	40.	40.	40.	40.
PR30TC	$36	55.	40.	40.	40.	40.
PR31TC	$48	55.	40.	40.	40.	40.
PR32TC	$60	55.	40.	40.	40.	40.

CARRIERS

		Black	Scarlet	Brown	Green	Blue
LO1TC	1c Franklin	120.	110.	110.	110.	110.
LO2TC	1c Eagle	120.	110.	110.	110.	110.

TELEGRAPH

American Rapid Telegraph Co.

			DIE (2) Small	PLATE (3) India	PLATE (4) Card
1T1TC	1c	green	55.		
1T1TC	1c	brown	55.		
1T1TC	1c	red	55.		
1T1TC	1c	blue	55.		
1T1TC	1c	bluish green	55.		
1T3TC	5c	green	55.		
1T3TC	5c	black	55.		
1T3TC	5c	red	55.		
1T3TC	5c	blue	55.		
1T3TC	5c	bluish green	55.		
1T5TC	15c	red	55.		
1T5TC	15c	black	55.		
1T5TC	15c	brown	55.		
1T5TC	15c	bluish green	55.		
1T6TC	20c	green	55.		
1T6TC	20c	black	55.		
1T6TC	20c	brown	55.		
1T6TC	20c	blue	55.		
1T6TC	20c	bluish green	55.		

Collect

			DIE (1) Large	DIE (2) Small	PLATE (3) India	PLATE (4) Card
1T10TC	5c	red		55.		
1T10TC	5c	black		55.		
1T10TC	5c	brown		55.		
1T10TC	5c	green		55.		
1T10TC	5c	bluish green		55.		
1T11TC	15c	red		55.		
1T11TC	15c	black		55.		
1T11TC	15c	brown		55.		
1T11TC	15c	green		55.		
1T11TC	15c	blue		55.		
1T11TC	15c	bluish green		55.		

Office Coupon

			DIE (1) Large	DIE (2) Small	PLATE (3) India	PLATE (4) Card
1T14TC	5c	red		55.		
1T14TC	5c	black		55.		
1T14TC	5c	brown		55.		
1T14TC	5c	green		55.		
1T14TC	5c	bluish green		55.		
1T15TC	15c	red		55.		
1T15TC	15c	black		55.		
1T15TC	15c	brown		55.		
1T15TC	15c	green		55.		
1T15TC	15c	blue		55.		
1T15TC	15c	bluish green		55.		

Baltimore & Ohio Telegraph Co.

			DIE (1) Large	DIE (2) Small	PLATE (3) India	PLATE (4) Card
3T2TC	5c	dark olive		65.		
3T4TC	25c	dark olive		65.		

Postal Telegraph Co.

			DIE (1) Large	DIE (2) Small	PLATE (3) India	PLATE (4) Card
15T1TC	10c	brown red		65.		
15T1TC	10c	red	65.			
15T1TC	10c	blue	65.			
15T1TC	10c	black	65.			
15T1TC	10c	orange			65.	
15T2TC	15c	black	65.		55.	
15T2TC	15c	red	65.	55.		
15T2TC	15c	blue	65.	55.		
15T2TC	25c	brown red		65.		
15T3TC	25c	black	65.			
15T3TC	25c	red	65.			
15T3TC	25c	ultramarine			40.	
15T3TC	25c	brown		65.	40.	
15T4TC	50c	dull blue		65.		
15T4TC	50c	black	65.		40.	
15T4TC	50c	red	65.			
15T4TC	50c	blue	65.			
15T6TC		red brown			40.	

Western Union Telegraph Co.

		DIE (1) Large	DIE (2) Small	PLATE (3) India	PLATE (4) Card
16T1TC	lilac (1871)			20.	20.
	Pair			45.	45.
16T1TC	orange			20.	20.
	Pair			45.	45.
16T1TC	black			20.	20.
	Pair			45.	45.
16T1TC	violet brown				20.
	Pair				45.
16T1TC	light olive				20.
	Pair				45.
16T1TC	brown				20.
	Pair				45.
16T1TC	orange brown				20.
	Pair				45.
16T1TC	blue green				20.
	Pair				45.
16T6TC	violet blue (1876)			20.	20.
16T7TC	orange yellow (1877)				20.
	Pair				45.
16T7TC	dark brown				20.
	Pair				45.
16T7TC	black				20.
	Pane of 4				—
16T8TC	dark brown (1878)				—
16T9TC	blue (1879)				—
16T10TC	violet brown (1880)				—
16T10TC	rose				—
16T22TC	black (1892)				—

Die Proof Printed Directly on Card

16T44TC	dull red	—
16T44TC	orange	—
16T44TC	rose red	—
16T44TC	orange brown	—
16T44TC	ocher	—
16T44TC	dark blue	—
16T44TC	dark ultramarine	—
16T44TC	green	—
16T44TC	brown lake	—
16T44TC	reddish brown	—
16T44TC	sepia	—
16T44TC	sepia, unsurfaced card	—
16T44TC	dull violet	—
16T44TC	slate green	—
16T44TC	slate blue	—
16T44TC	black	—
16T44TC	black, unsurfaced card	—

On India

16T44TC	deep rose	—
16T44TC	carmine lake	—
16T44TC	rose lake	—
16T44TC	deep ultramarine	—

Plate Proofs, Sheets of 16 on India or Bond

16T44TC	deep rose, on India	—
16T44TC	deep rose, on Bond	—
16T44TC	orange, on India	—
16T44TC	orange, on Bond	—
16T44TC	dark blue, on India	—
16T44TC	dark blue, on Bond	—
16T44TC	slate green, on India	—
16T44TC	slate green, on Bond	—
16T44TC	rose lake, on India	—
16T44TC	rose lake, on Bond	—
16T44TC	sepia, on Bond	—

REVENUES

Several lists of revenue proofs in trial colors have been published, but the accuracy of some of them is questionable. The following listings are limited to items seen by the editors. The list is not complete.

1862-71 FIRST ISSUE

R3TC	1c	**Proprietary,** black	Plate on India	80.
R3TC		carmine	Plate on Card	125.
R3TC		dull red	Plate on Bond	125.
R3TC		orange red	Plate on Bond	125.
R3TC		dull yel.	Plate on Bond	125.
R3TC		violet rose	Plate on Bond	125.
R3TC		deep blue	Plate on Bond	125.
R3TC		red on blue	Plate on Bond	125.
R3TC		blue, perf. & gum	Plate on Bond	125.
R3TC		green	Plate on buff wove	—
R3TC		black	Die on India	*950.*
R7TC	2c	**Certificate,** ultra.	Plate on Card	65.
R11TC	2c	**Playing Cards,** black	Die on India	500.
R13TC	2c	**Proprietary,** black	Plate on India	75.
R13TC		black	Die on India	650.
R13TC		carmine	Die on India	650.
R15TC	2c	**U.S.I.R.,** violet rose	Plate on Bond	110.
R15TC		light green	Plate on Bond	110.
R15TC		pale blue	Plate on Bond	110.
R15TC		pale rose	Plate on Bond	200.
R15TC		orange	Plate on blue Bond	—
R15TC		black	Plate on India	110.
R15TC		pale orange, perf. & gum	Plate on Bond	110.
R16TC	3c	**Foreign Exchange,** green on blue	Plate on Bond	140.
R16TC		blue	Plate on Goldbeater's Skin	110.
R18TC	3c	**Proprietary,** black	Die on India	300.
R21TC	4c	**Playing Cards,** black	Die (?) on India	300.
R22TC	4c	**Proprietary,** black	Plate on India	110.
R22TC		black	Die on India	350.
R22TC		deep red lilac	Die on India	400.
R22TC		red lilac	Plate on Card	110.
R24TC	5c	**Certificate,** carmine	Plate on India	110.
R25TC	5c	**Express,** pale olive	Plate on Wove	—
R26TC	5c	**Foreign Exchange,** orange	Plate on India	110.
R28TC	5c	**Playing Cards,** black	Die (?) on India	300.
R29TC	5c	**Proprietary,** red	Plate on blue Bond	—
R30TC	6c	**Inland Exchange,** black	Die on India	350.
R31TC	6c	**Proprietary,** black	Die on India	—
R32TC	10c	**Bill of Lading,** greenish blue	Die on India	350.
		R32TC+R37TC composite, dark green	Large Die on India	—
R35TC	10c	**Foreign Exchange,** black	Die (?) on India	350.
R37TC	10c	**Power of Attorney,** greenish blue	Die on India	350.
R38TC	10c	**Proprietary,** black	Die on India	350.
R43TC	25c	**Bond,** carmine	Plate on Card	90.
R44TC	25c	**Certificate,** blue	Plate on Bond	300.
R44TC		green	Plate on Bond	300.
R44TC		orange	Plate on Bond	300.
R45TC	25c	**Entry of Goods,** black	Hybrid Die on India	—
R46TC	25c	**Insurance,** dull red	Plate on Bond	150.
R46TC		dull red	Plate on Goldbeater's Skin	210.

R46TC		vermilion	Plate on Goldbeater's Skin	210.
R46TC		vermilion	Plate on Bond	170.
R46TC		blue	Plate on Bond	170.
R46TC		blue	Plate on Goldbeater's Skin	215.
R46TC		dark blue	Plate on Bond	155.
R46TC		dark blue	Plate on Goldbeater's Skin	215.
R46TC		green	Plate on Goldbeater's Skin	215.
R51TC	30c	**Foreign Exchange,** violet	Plate on India	130.
R51TC		violet gray	Plate on India	130.
R51TC		deep red lilac	Plate on India	155.
R51TC		slate blue	Plate on India	155.
R51TC		black	Plate on India	155.
R51TC		red	Plate on India	155.
R52TC		**Inland Exchange,** deep red lilac	Plate on India	155.
R53TC	40c	**Inland Exchange,** black	Hybrid Die on India	—
R55TC	50c	**Entry of Goods,** orange	Plate on Bond	275.
R55TC		green	Plate on Bond	275.
R55TC		red	Plate on Bond	340.
R55TC		deep blue	Plate on Bond	—
R58TC	50c	**Life Insurance,** ultramarine	Plate on India	85.
R60TC	50c	**Original Process,** black	Die (?) on India	280.
R64TC	60c	**Inland Exchange,** green	Die (?) on India	—
R65TC	70c	**Foreign Exchange,** orange	Die (?) on India	—
R65TC		black	Die (?) on India	285.
R66TC	$1	**Conveyance,** carmine	Plate on India	85.
R67TC	$1	**Entry of Goods,** carmine	Plate on India	60.
R68TC	$1	**Foreign Exchange,** carmine	Plate on India	60.
R69TC	$1	**Inland Exchange,** carmine	Plate on India	60.
R70TC	$1	**Lease,** carmine	Plate on India	130.
R71TC	$1	**Life Insurance,** carmine	Plate on India	75.
R72TC	$1	**Manifest,** carmine	Plate on India	80.
R73TC	$1	**Mortgage,** carmine	Plate on India	85.
R73TC		black	Hybrid Die on India	—
R74TC	$1	**Passage Ticket,** carmine	Plate on India	120.
R75TC	$1	**Power of Attorney,** carmine	Plate on India	120.
R76TC	$1	**Probate of Will,** carmine	Plate on India	60.
R78TC	$1.50	**Inland Exchange,** black	Die on India	475.
R80TC	$1.90	**Foreign Exchange,** black	Plate on India	155.
R81TC	$2	**Conveyance,** carmine	Plate on Card	85.
R82TC	$2	**Mortgage,** carmine	Plate on Card	85.
R83TC	$2	**Probate of Will,** black	Hybrid Die on India	—
R84TC	$2.50	**Inland Exchange,** black	Die (?) on India	120.
R85TC	$3	**Charter Party,** dark green	Plate on Thin Card	—
R87TC	$3.50	**Inland Exchange,** black	Die on India	400.
R88TC	$5	**Charter Party,** carmine	Plate on India	85.
R88TC		black	Hybrid Die on India	—
R89TC	$5	**Conveyance,** carmine	Plate on India	90.
R91TC	$5	**Mortgage,** carmine	Plate on India	90.
R95TC	$10	**Mortgage,** yellow green	Plate on Thin Card	—
R98TC	$20	**Conveyance,** red orange	Plate on Card	120.
R98TC		red orange	Plate on India	220.
R99TC	$20	**Probate of Will,** red orange	Plate on Card	275.
R99TC		black	Plate on Card	275.
R101TC	$50	**U.S.I.R.,** orange	Plate on Bond	275.
R101TC		deep blue	Plate on Bond	275.
		black	Hybrid Die on India	—
R102TC	$200	black & red	Plate on Card	1,600.
R102TC		gray brown & red	Plate on Bond	1,600.
R102TC		green & brown red	Plate on India	1,600.
R102TC		black	Plate on India	—

SECOND ISSUE

R104TC	2c	pale blue & black	Plate on Bond	60.
R132TC	$200	red, green & black	India	2,500.
R132TC		orange (master die)	India	2,500.
R132TC		blue (master die)	India	2,500.
R132TC		green (master die)	India	2,500.
R133TC	$500	black (master die)	India	7,000.
R133TC		yellow, green & black	India	5,000.
R133TC		bright green, orange brown & black	India	5,000.
R133TC		red, green & black	Bond	5,000.
R133TC		light green, light brown & black	Bond	5,000.
R133TC		blue, scarlet & black	Bond	5,000.
R133ATC	$5000	yel org, green & black	India	7,500.
R133ATC		olive brown, green & black	India	8,000.
R133ATC		org red, dark green & black	India	8,000.
R133ATC		org red, dark blue & black	India	20,000.

The master die is the completed stamp design prior to its division into separate color dies.

See note after No. R133AP in Die and Plate Proofs section.

THIRD ISSUE

R134TC	1c	brown & black	Plate on Card	60.

1875 National Bank Note Co., New York City

R152TC	2c	(Liberty), green	Die on India	600.
R152TC		(Liberty), brown	Die on India	600.
R152TC		(Liberty), black	Die on India	600.

1898

R161TC	½c	green	Lg. die on India	750.
R163TC	1c	green	Lg. die on India	750.
R163TC		black	Lg. die on India	750.
R165TC	3c	green	Sm. die on India	650.
R169TC	25c	green	Lg. die on India	650.
R170TC	40c	black	Lg. die on India	650.
R172TC	80c	green	Lg. die on India	650.

1898

R174TC	$3	black	Die on India	650.
R176TC	$10	green	Die on India	650.

1899

R179TC	$100	dark green & black	Die on India	1,250.
R181TC	$1000	dark blue & black	Die on India	1,250.

1914

R195TC	½c	black	Small die on Wove	—
R196TC	1c	blue green	Small die on Wove	—
R198TC	3c	ultramarine	Small die on Wove	—
R199TC	4c	brown	Small die on Wove	—
R200TC	5c	blue	Small die on Wove	—
R201TC	10c	yellow	Small die on Wove	—
R202TC	25c	dull violet	Small die on Wove	—
R203TC	40c	blue green	Small die on Wove	—
R204TC	50c	red brown	Small die on Wove	—
R205TC	80c	orange	Small die on Wove	—

PROPRIETARY

1871-75

RB1TC	1c	blue & black	Plate on Bond	70.
RB1TC		scarlet & black	Plate on Bond	70.
RB1TC		orange & black	Plate on Bond	70.
RB1TC		orange & ultramarine	Plate on Granite Bond	60.
RB3TC	3c	blue & black, with gum	Plate on Bond	60.
RB3TC		blue & black	Plate on Gray Bond	60.
RB3TC		blue & black	Plate on wove	—
RB8TC	50c	green & brown	Die on India	675.
RB8TC		green & purple	Die on India	675.
RB8TC		green & brown red	Die on India	675.
RB8TC		green & violet	Die on India	675.
RB8TC		green & dark carmine	Die on India	675.
RB8TC		ultramarine & red	Die on India	675.
RB9TC	$1	green & brown	Die on India	675.
RB9TC		green & purple	Die on India	675.
RB9TC		green & violet brown	Die on India	675.
RB9TC		green & brown red	Die on India	675.
RB9TC		green & violet	Die on India	675.
RB9TC		green & dark carmine	Die on India	675.

1875-83

RB11TC	1c	brown	Die on India	500.
RB11TC		red brown	Die on India	500.
RB11TC		blue	Die on India	500.
RB11TC		black	Die on India	500.
RB12TC	2c	green	Die on India	500.
RB12TC		black	Die on India	500.
RB12TC		brown	Die on India	500.
RB12TC		orange brown	Die on India	500.
RB12TC		blue	Die on India	500.
RB13TC	3c	brown	Die on India	500.
RB13TC		green	Die on India	500.
RB13TC		blue	Die on India	500.
RB13TC		black	Plate on India	150.
RB14TC	4c	dark brown	Die on India	450.
RB14TC		green	Die on India	450.
RB14TC		black	Die on India	450.
RB14TC		blue	Die on India	450.
RB14TC		black	Plate on India	150.
RB16TC	5c	green	Die on India	450.
RB16TC		dark slate	Die on India	450.
RB16TC		blue	Die on India	450.
RB17TC	6c	green	Plate on India	150.
RB17TC		black	Plate on India	150.
RB17TC		black	Die on India	500.
RB17TC		blue	Die on India	500.
RB17TC		purple	Die on India	500.
RB17TC		dull violet	Die on India	500.
RB17TC		violet	Die on India	500.
RB17TC		violet brown	Die on India	500.
RB17TC		dark brown	Die on India	500.
RB19TC	10c	black	Die on India	550.

SECOND, THIRD AND PROPRIETARY ISSUES

Stamps Nos. R103 to R131, R134 to R150 and RB1 to RB7.

A special composite plate was made and impressions taken in various colors and shades. Although all varieties in all colors must have been made, only those seen by the editors are listed.

PLATE PROOFS ON INDIA PAPER
CENTERS IN BLACK

1871-75

R103TC 1c

a.	dark purple	60.
b.	dull purple	60.
d.	brown	60.
e.	black brown	60.
g.	light blue	60.
h.	dark blue	70.
i.	ultramarine	70.
k.	yellow green	70.
n.	green	65.
o.	dark green	65.
p.	blue green	65.
q.	light orange	65.
r.	dark orange	65.
s.	deep orange	65.
t.	scarlet	65.
u.	carmine	65.
x.	dark brown red	65.
y.	dark brown orange, goldbeater's skin	90.

R104TC 2c

a.	dark purple	60.
b.	dull purple	60.
d.	brown	60.
e.	black brown	60.
g.	light blue	60.
h.	dark blue	70.
i.	ultramarine	70.
k.	yellow green	70.
l.	dark yellow green	70.
n.	green	65.
o.	dark green	65.
p.	blue green	65.
q.	light orange	65.

r. dark orange 65.
s. deep orange 65.
t. scarlet 65.
u. carmine 65.
x. dark brown red 65.
y. dark brown orange, goldbeater's skin 90.

R105TC 3c
a. dark purple 60.
b. dull purple 60.
d. brown 60.
e. black brown 60.
g. light blue 60.
h. dark blue 70.
i. ultramarine 70.
k. yellow green 70.
n. green 65.
o. dark green 65.
p. blue green 65.
q. light orange 65.
r. dark orange 65.
s. deep orange 65.
t. scarlet 65.
u. carmine 65.
x. dark brown red 65.
y. dark brown orange, goldbeater's skin 90.

R106TC 4c
a. dark purple 60.
b. dull purple 60.
d. brown 60.
e. black brown 60.
f. orange brown 65.
g. light blue 60.
h. dark blue 70.
i. ultramarine 70.
k. yellow green 70.
n. green 65.
o. dark green 65.
p. blue green 65.
q. light orange 65.
r. dark orange 65.
s. deep orange 65.
t. scarlet 65.
u. carmine 65.
x. dark brown red 65.
y. dark brown orange, goldbeater's skin 90.

R107TC 5c
a. dark purple 60.
b. dull purple 60.
d. brown 60.
e. black brown 60.
f. orange brown 65.
g. light blue 60.
h. dark blue 70.
i. ultramarine 70.
k. yellow green 70.
n. green 65.
o. dark green 65.
p. blue green 65.
q. light orange 65.
r. dark orange 65.
s. deep orange 65.
t. scarlet 65.
u. carmine 65.
v. dark carmine 65.
w. purplish carmine 65.
x. dark brown red 65.
y. dark brown orange, goldbeater's skin 90.

R108TC 6c
a. dark purple 60.
b. dull purple 60.
d. brown 60.
e. black brown 60.
f. orange brown 65.
g. light blue 60.
h. dark blue 70.
i. ultramarine 70.
k. yellow green 70.
n. green 65.
o. dark green 65.
p. blue green 65.
q. light orange 65.
r. dark orange 65.
s. deep orange 65.
t. scarlet 65.
u. carmine 65.
v. dark carmine 65.
w. purplish carmine 65.
x. dark brown red 65.
y. dark brown orange, goldbeater's skin 90.

R109TC 10c
a. dark purple 60.
b. dull purple 60.
d. brown 60.
e. black brown 60.
g. light blue 60.
h. dark blue 70.
i. ultramarine 70.
k. yellow green 70.
n. green 65.
o. dark green 65.
p. blue green 65.
q. light orange 65.
r. dark orange 65.
s. deep orange 65.
t. scarlet 65.
u. carmine 65.
x. dark brown red 65.

R110TC 15c
a. dark purple 60.
b. dull purple 60.
d. brown 60.
e. black brown 60.
f. orange brown 65.
g. light blue 60.
h. dark blue 70.
i. ultramarine 70.
k. yellow green 70.
n. green 65.
o. dark green 65.
p. blue green 65.
q. light orange 65.
r. dark orange 65.
s. deep orange 65.
t. scarlet 65.
u. carmine 65.
w. purplish carmine 65.
x. dark brown red 65.

R111TC 20c
a. dark purple 60.
b. dull purple 60.
d. brown 60.
e. black brown 60.
g. light blue 60.
h. dark blue 70.
i. ultramarine 70.
k. yellow green 70.
n. green 65.
o. dark green 65.
p. blue green 65.
q. light orange 65.
r. dark orange 65.
s. deep orange 65.
t. scarlet 65.
u. carmine 65.
w. purplish carmine 65.
x. dark brown red 65.
y. dark brown orange, goldbeater's skin 90.

R112TC 25c
a. dark purple 60.
b. dull purple 60.
d. brown 60.
e. black brown 60.
g. light blue 60.
h. dark blue 70.
i. ultramarine 70.
k. yellow green 70.
l. dark yellow green 70.
n. green 65.
o. dark green 65.
p. blue green 65.
q. light orange 65.
r. dark orange 65.
s. deep orange 65.
t. scarlet 65.
u. carmine 65.
x. dark brown red 65.
y. dark brown orange, goldbeater's skin 90.

R113TC 30c
a. dark purple 60.
b. dull purple 60.
d. brown 60.
e. black brown 60.
g. light blue 60.
h. dark blue 70.
i. ultramarine 70.
k. yellow green 70.
n. green 65.
o. dark green 65.
p. blue green 65.
q. light orange 65.
r. dark orange 65.
s. deep orange 65.
t. scarlet 65.
u. carmine 65.
v. dark carmine 65.
w. purplish carmine 65.
x. dark brown red 65.
y. dark brown orange, goldbeater's skin 90.

R114TC 40c
a. dark purple 60.
b. dull purple 60.
d. brown 60.
e. black brown 60.
f. orange brown 65.
g. light blue 60.
h. dark blue 70.
i. ultramarine 70.
k. yellow green 70.
n. green 65.
o. dark green 65.
p. blue green 65.
q. light orange 65.
r. dark orange 65.
s. deep orange 65.
t. scarlet 65.
u. carmine 65.
x. dark brown red 65.

R115TC 50c
a. dark purple 60.
b. dull purple 60.
d. brown 60.
e. black brown 60.
g. light blue 60.
h. dark blue 70.
i. ultramarine 70.
k. yellow green 70.
n. green 65.
o. dark green 65.
p. blue green 65.
q. light orange 65.
r. dark orange 65.
s. deep orange 65.
t. scarlet 65.
u. carmine 65.
x. dark brown red 65.

R116TC 60c
a. dark purple 60.
b. dull purple 60.
d. brown 60.
e. black brown 60.
g. light blue 60.
h. dark blue 70.
i. ultramarine 70.
k. yellow green 70.
n. green 65.
o. dark green 65.
p. blue green 65.
q. light orange 65.
r. dark orange 65.
s. deep orange 65.
t. scarlet 65.
u. carmine 65.
v. dark carmine 65.
x. dark brown red 65.
y. dark brown orange, goldbeater's skin 90.

R117TC 70c
a. dark purple 60.
b. dull purple 60.
d. brown 60.
e. black brown 60.
g. light blue 60.
h. dark blue 70.
i. ultramarine 70.
k. yellow green 70.
n. green 65.
o. dark green 65.
p. blue green 65.
q. light orange 65.
r. dark orange 65.
s. deep orange 65.
t. scarlet 65.
u. carmine 65.
x. dark brown red 65.

R118TC $1
a. dark purple 70.
b. dull purple 70.
d. brown 70.
e. black brown 70.
g. light blue 80.
h. dark blue 85.
i. ultramarine 85.
k. yellow green 80.
n. green 75.
o. dark green 75.
p. blue green 75.
q. light orange 75.
r. dark orange 75.
s. deep orange 75.
t. scarlet 80.
u. carmine 80.
w. purplish carmine 80.
x. dark brown red 80.
y. dark brown orange, goldbeater's skin 90.

R119TC $1.30
a. dark purple 70.
b. dull purple 70.
d. brown 70.
e. black brown 70.
g. light blue 80.
h. dark blue 85.
i. ultramarine 85.
k. yellow green 80.
n. green 75.
o. dark green 75.
p. blue green 75.
q. light orange 75.
r. dark orange 75.
s. deep orange 75.
t. scarlet 80.
u. carmine 80.
x. dark brown red 80.

R120TC $1.50
a. dark purple 70.
b. dull purple 70.
d. brown 70.
e. black brown 70.
g. light blue 80.
h. dark blue 85.
i. ultramarine 85.
j. bright yellow green, on card 75.
k. yellow green 80.
n. green 75.
o. dark green 75.
p. blue green 75.
q. light orange 75.
r. dark orange 75.
s. deep orange 75.
t. scarlet 80.
u. carmine 80.
x. dark brown red 80.

R121TC $1.60
a. dark purple 70.
b. dull purple 70.
d. brown 70.
e. black brown 70.
g. light blue 80.
h. dark blue 85.
i. ultramarine 85.
k. yellow green 80.
n. green 75.
o. dark green 75.
p. blue green 75.
q. light orange 75.
r. dark orange 75.
s. deep orange 75.
t. scarlet 80.
u. carmine 80.
x. dark brown red 80.

R122TC $1.90
a. dark purple 70.
b. dull purple 70.
d. brown 70.
e. black brown 70.
g. light blue 80.
h. dark blue 85.

i. ultramarine 85.
j. bright yellow green, on card 75.
k. yellow green 80.
n. green 75.
o. dark green 75.
p. blue green 75.
q. light orange 75.
r. dark orange 75.
s. deep orange 75.
t. scarlet 80.
u. carmine 80.
x. dark brown red 80.

R123TC $2
a. dark purple 70.
b. dull purple 70.
d. brown 70.
e. black brown 70.
g. light blue 80.
h. dark blue 85.
i. ultramarine 85.
j. bright yellow green, on card 75.
k. yellow green 80.
n. green 75.
o. dark green 75.
p. blue green 75.
q. light orange 75.
r. dark orange 75.
s. deep orange 75.
t. scarlet 80.
u. carmine 80.
w. purplish carmine 80.
x. dark brown red 80.
y. dark brown orange, goldbeater's skin 90.

R124TC $2.50
a. dark purple 70.
b. dull purple 70.
d. brown 70.
e. black brown 70.
g. light blue 80.
h. dark blue 85.
i. ultramarine 85.
k. yellow green 80.
n. green 75.
o. dark green 75.
p. blue green 75.
q. light orange 75.
r. dark orange 75.
s. deep orange 75.
t. scarlet 80.
u. carmine 80.
v. dark carmine 80.
x. dark brown red 80.

R125TC $3
a. dark purple 70.
b. dull purple 70.
d. brown 70.
e. black brown 70.
g. light blue 80.
h. dark blue 85.
i. ultramarine 85.
j. bright yellow green, on card 75.
k. yellow green 80.
n. green 75.
o. dark green 75.
p. blue green 75.
q. light orange 75.
r. dark orange 75.
s. deep orange 75.
t. scarlet 80.
u. carmine 80.
x. dark brown red 80.

R126TC $3.50
a. dark purple 70.
b. dull purple 70.
c. red purple 75.
d. brown 70.
e. black brown 70.
g. light blue 80.
h. dark blue 85.
i. ultramarine 85.
k. yellow green 80.
n. green 75.
o. dark green 75.
p. blue green 75.
q. light orange 75.
r. dark orange 75.
s. deep orange 75.
t. scarlet 90.
u. carmine 80.
x. dark brown red 80.

R127TC $5
a. dark purple 70.
b. dull purple 70.
d. brown 70.
e. black brown 70.
g. light blue 80.
h. dark blue 85.
i. ultramarine 85.
k. yellow green 80.
n. green 75.
o. dark green 75.
p. blue green 75.
q. light orange 75.
r. dark orange 75.
s. deep orange 75.
t. scarlet 75.
u. carmine 75.
w. purplish carmine 75.
x. dark brown red 80.
y. dark brown orange, goldbeater's skin 100.

R128TC $10
a. dark purple 70.
b. dull purple 70.
d. brown 70.
e. black brown 70.
g. light blue 80.
h. dark blue 85.
i. ultramarine 85.
j. bright yellow green, on card 75.
k. yellow green 75.
n. green 75.
o. dark green 75.
p. blue green 75.
q. light orange 75.
r. dark orange 75.
s. deep orange 75.
t. scarlet 75.
u. carmine 80.
x. dark brown red 80.

R129TC $20
a. dark purple 95.
b. dull purple 95.
d. brown 95.
e. black brown 95.
g. light blue 90.
h. dark blue 90.
i. ultramarine 90.
k. yellow green 85.
m. emerald green 85.
n. green 75.
o. dark green 75.
p. blue green 75.
q. light orange 75.
r. dark orange 85.
s. deep orange 85.
t. scarlet 90.
u. carmine 80.
v. dark carmine 90.
x. dark brown red 80.

R130TC $25
a. dark purple 100.
b. dull purple 100.
d. brown 100.
e. black brown 100.
g. light blue 90.
h. dark blue 90.
i. ultramarine 90.
k. yellow green 85.
m. emerald green 85.
n. green 75.
o. dark green 75.
p. blue green 75.
q. light orange 75.
r. dark orange 85.
s. deep orange 85.
t. scarlet 90.
u. carmine 80.
w. purplish carmine 90.
x. dark brown red 300.
y. dark brown orange, goldbeater's skin 100.

R131TC $50
a. dark purple 95.
b. dull purple 95.
d. brown 95.
e. black brown 95.
g. light blue 90.
h. dark blue 90.
i. ultramarine 90.
j. bright yellow green, on card 85.
k. yellow green 85.
m. emerald green 85.
n. green 75.
o. dark green 75.
p. blue green 75.
q. light orange 75.
r. dark orange 85.
s. deep orange 85.
t. scarlet 90.
u. carmine 80.
x. dark brown red 80.

RB1TC 1c
a. dark purple 70.
b. dull purple 70.
d. brown 65.
e. black brown 65.
g. light blue 75.
h. dark blue 75.
i. ultramarine 70.
k. yellow green 70.
l. dark yellow green 70.
n. green 65.
o. dark green 65.
p. blue green 65.
q. light orange 65.
r. dark orange 65.
s. deep orange 65.
t. scarlet 65.
u. carmine 65.
x. dark brown red 65.

RB2TC 2c
a. dark purple 70.
b. dull purple 70.
d. brown 65.
e. black brown 65.
g. light blue 70.
h. dark blue 70.
i. ultramarine 70.
j. bright yellow green, on card 70.
k. yellow green 70.
n. green 65.
o. dark green 65.
p. blue green 65.
q. light orange 65.
r. dark orange 65.
s. deep orange 65.
t. scarlet 65.
u. carmine 65.
x. dark brown red 65.

RB3TC 3c
a. dark purple 70.
b. dull purple 70.
d. brown 65.
e. black brown 65.
g. light blue 70.
h. dark blue 70.
i. ultramarine 70.
k. yellow green 70.
l. dark yellow green 70.
n. green 65.
o. dark green 65.
p. blue green 65.
q. light orange 65.
r. dark orange 65.
s. deep orange 65.
t. scarlet 65.
u. carmine 65.
x. dark brown red 65.

RB4TC 4c
a. dark purple 70.
b. dull purple 70.
d. brown 65.
e. black brown 65.
g. light blue 70.
h. dark blue 70.
i. ultramarine 70.
k. yellow green 70.
n. green 65.
o. dark green 65.
p. blue green 65.
q. light orange 65.
r. dark orange 65.
s. deep orange 65.
t. scarlet 65.
u. carmine 65.
x. dark brown red 65.

RB5TC 5c
a. dark purple 70.
b. dull purple 70.
d. brown 65.
e. black brown 65.
g. light blue 70.
h. dark blue 70.
i. ultramarine 70.
j. bright yellow green, on card 70.
k. yellow green 70.
l. dark yellow green 70.
n. green 65.
o. dark green 65.
p. blue green 65.
q. light orange 65.
r. dark orange 65.
s. deep orange 65.
t. scarlet 65.
u. carmine 65.
x. dark brown red 65.

RB6TC 6c
a. dark purple 70.
b. dull purple 70.
d. brown 65.
e. black brown 65.
g. light blue 70.
h. dark blue 70.
i. ultramarine 70.
k. yellow green 70.
l. dark yellow green 70.
n. green 65.
o. dark green 65.
p. blue green 65.
q. light orange 65.
r. dark orange 65.
s. deep orange 65.
t. scarlet 65.
u. carmine 65.
x. dark brown red 65.

RB7TC 10c
a. dark purple 70.
b. dull purple 70.
d. brown 65.
e. black brown 65.
g. light blue 70.
h. dark blue 70.
i. ultramarine 70.
k. yellow green 70.
l. dark yellow green 70.
n. green 65.
o. dark green 65.
p. blue green 65.
q. light orange 65.
r. dark orange 65.
s. deep orange 65.
t. scarlet 65.
u. carmine 65.
x. dark brown red 65.

1898

RB20TC	⅛c	light blue	Large die on card	*1,000.*
RB21TC	¼c	dull green	Large die on India	1,300.
RB22TC	⅜c	dull green	Large die on India	750.
RB24TC	1c	dull green	Large die on India	750.
RB26TC	1⅞c	dull green	Large die on India	750.
RB26TC	1⅞c	black	Large die on India	750.
RB27TC	2c	dull green	Large die on India	500.
RB31TC	5c	dull green	Large die on India	500.

1918-29

Stock Transfer

RD20TC	$50	black	Die on India	*2,250.*
RD20TC	$50	blue	Die on India	*2,250.*

1894

Playing Cards

RF1TC	2c	black (On hand)	Die on India	*1,500.*
RF2TC	2c	lake (Act of)	Die on India	*1,000.*

PRIVATE DIE MATCH STAMPS

For important valuing information see the note before Private Die Proprietary die and plate proofs.

1864

			DIE ON INDIA (1) Large	PLATE (3) India	(4) Card
RO1TC	1c	black	175.		
RO1TC	1c	green	300.		
RO2TC	1c	black	225.		
RO2TC	1c	green	300.		
RO5TC	1c	black	275.		
RO5TC	1c	blue	500.		
RO6TC	1c	black	300.		
RO6TC	1c	green	500.		
RO7TC	1c	black	300.		
RO7TC	1c	dull green	300.		
RO7TC	1c	green	500.		
RO9TC	1c	blue	225.		
RO9TC	1c	brown	275.		
RO9TC	1c	dark green	500.		
RO9TC	1c	green	300.		
RO10TC	1c	blue	300.		
RO10TC	1c	green	500.		
RO11TC	3c	blue	500.		
RO11TC	3c	green	500.		
RO12TC	1c	blue	225.		
RO12TC	1c	green	500.		
RO13TC	3c	black	500.		
RO13TC	3c	blue	1,000.		
RO14TC	1c	blue	225.		
RO14TC	1c	green	500.		
RO15TC	1c	black	225.		
RO15TC	1c	blue	225.		
RO16TC	1c	black	225.		
RO16TC	1c	green	300.		
RO17/19TC	1c/3c	green	1,250.		
RO17TC	1c	black	225.		
RO17TC	1c	green	500.		
RO19TC	3c	blue	250.		
RO19TC	3c	green	600.		
RO20TC	1c	black	175.		
RO20TC	1c	green	500.		
RO21TC	3c	blue	375.		
RO21TC	3c	green	375.		
RO22TC	1c	black	300.		
RO23TC	1c	black	225.		
RO23TC	1c	blue	225.		
RO23TC	1c	green	500.		
RO24TC	1c	black	225.		
RO24TC	1c	blue	225.		
RO24TC	1c	green	500.		
RO25TC	12c	black	400.		
RO25TC	12c	blue	750.		
RO25TC	12c	green	750.		
RO26TC	1c	black	225.		
RO26TC	1c	blue	225.		
RO26TC	1c	dark brn	225.		
RO26TC	1c	green	300.		
RO26TC	1c	light brn	300.		
RO27TC	12c	black	400.		
RO27TC	12c	blue	500.		
RO27TC	12c	green	750.		
RO28TC	1c	black	175.		
RO28TC	1c	brown	300.		
RO28TC	1c	green	300.		
RO29TC	1c	blue	300.		
RO29TC	1c	green	300.		
RO30TC	1c	black	175.		
RO30TC	1c	blue	225.		
RO30TC	1c	green	300.		
RO30TC	1c	red	500.		
RO31TC	1c	blue	300.		
RO31TC	1c	green	225.		
RO31TC	1c	red	500.		
RO32TC	4c	blue	500.		
RO32TC	4c	brown	500.		
RO32TC	4c	orange	500.		
RO32TC	4c	vermilion	500.		
RO35TC	1c	blue	300.		
RO35TC	1c	green	500.		
RO37TC	3c	blue	400.		
RO37TC	3c	green	400.		
RO38TC	1c	blue	350.		
RO38TC	1c	dk bl	500.		
RO38TC	1c	green	375.		
RO38TC	1c	red	600.		
RO39TC	1c	black	300.		
RO41TC	1c	black	225.		
RO41TC	1c	green	300.		
RO42TC	1c	black	300.		
RO42TC	1c	blue	300.		
RO42TC	1c	green	500.		
RO43TC	1c	blue	500.		
RO45TC	1c	blue	350.		
RO45TC	1c	green	750.		
RO46TC	1c	blue	350.		
RO46TC	1c	dk bl	500.		
RO46TC	1c	green	500.		
RO46TC	1c	orange	300.		
RO47TC	1c	blue	300.		
RO47TC	1c	green	500.		
RO49TC	1c	blue	225.		
RO49TC	1c	brown	500.		
RO49TC	1c	brn red	300.		
RO49TC	1c	dk bl	500.		
RO49TC	1c	green	500.		
RO49TC	1c	red brn	500.		
RO55TC	1c	blue	375.		
RO56TC	1c	blue	750.		
RO56TC	1c	green	300.		
RO57TC	1c	black	175.		
RO57TC	1c	blue	225.		
RO58TC	1c	black	300.		
RO58TC	1c	blue	225.		
RO58TC	1c	dark rose	500.		
RO58TC	1c	green	500.		
RO58TC	1c	rose	300.		
RO59TC	1c	black	225.		
RO60TC	3c	blue	500.		
RO60TC	3c	green	500.		
RO61TC	1c	black	175.		
RO61TC	1c	blue	300.		
RO62TC	1c	black	175.		
RO62TC	1c	blue	175.		
RO64TC	1c	black	225.		
RO64TC	1c	blue	300.		
RO64TC	1c	green	300.		
RO65TC	1c	green	300.		
RO67TC	1c	blue	225.		
RO67TC	1c	green	300.		
RO67TC	1c	red	500.		
RO67TC	1c	rose	500.		
RO68TC	1c	black	225.		
RO68TC	1c	blue	225.		
RO69TC	1c	blue	300.		
RO69TC	1c	green	500.		
RO71TC	1c	black	250.		
RO71TC	1c	green	400.		
RO72TC	1c	black	500.		
RO73TC	1c	blue	225.		
RO73TC	1c	green	300.		
RO73TC	1c	red	500.		
RO73TC	1c	red brn	225.		
RO76TC	1c	blue	500.		
RO76TC	1c	green	300.		
RO77TC	1c	black	225.		
RO77TC	1c	green	300.		
RO78TC	1c	black	225.		
RO78TC	1c	dk bl	500.		
RO78TC	1c	green	500.		
RO80TC	1c	black	225.		
RO80TC	1c	green	500.		
RO81TC	1c	blue	175.		
RO81TC	1c	dark green	500.		
RO81TC	1c	green	225.		
RO81TC	1c	lake	500.		
RO81TC	1c	red	300.		
RO82TC	1c	blue	175.		
RO82TC	1c	green	500.		
RO83TC	1c	black	175.		
RO83TC	1c	green	300.		
RO83TC	1c	red	500.		
RO84TC	1c	blue	300.		
RO84TC	1c	green	500.		
RO85TC	1c	black	250.		
RO85TC	1c	blue	300.		
RO85TC	1c	green	350.		
RO85TC	1c	orange	500.		
RO85TC	1c	vermilion	500.		
RO86TC	1c	blue	500.		
RO86TC	1c	brown	500.		
RO86TC	1c	green	400.		
RO86TC	1c	orange	500.		
RO86TC	1c	red	500.		
RO87TC	1c	dull rose	500.		
RO87TC	1c	orange	500.		
RO88TC	1c	blue	300.		
RO88TC	1c	green	500.		
RO89TC	3c	blue	300.		
RO89TC	3c	green	300.		
RO90TC	6c	blue	225.		
RO90TC	6c	brown	500.		
RO90TC	6c	green	500.		
RO90TC	6c	orange	500.		
RO91TC	3c	blue	225.		
RO91TC	3c	brown	500.		
RO91TC	3c	green	500.		
RO91TC	3c	orange	500.		
RO91TC	3c	red	500.		
RO92TC	1c	blue	300.		
RO92TC	1c	green	500.		
RO94TC	3c	blue	225.		
RO94TC	3c	brown	300.		
RO94TC	3c	green	225.		
RO94TC	3c	orange	300.		
RO94TC	3c	red	500.		
RO94TC	3c	vermilion	500.		
RO95TC	1c	black	175.		
RO95TC	1c	blue	175.		
RO95TC	1c	brown	225.		
RO95TC	1c	dk bl	500.		
RO96TC	1c	black	175.		
RO96TC	1c	blue	225.		
RO97TC	1c	blue	300.		
RO99TC	1c	black	175.		
RO99TC	1c	blue	500.		
RO100TC	1c	blue	500.		
RO101TC	3c	black	175.		
RO101TC	3c	green	300.		
RO101TC	3c	orange		75.	
RO102TC	5c	black	175.		
RO102TC	5c	blue	500.		
RO102TC	5c	green	500.		
RO103TC	1c	blue	225.		
RO103TC	1c	rose	300.		
RO105TC	1c	blue	300.		
RO105TC	1c	green	500.		
RO106TC	1c	black	175.		
RO106TC	1c	blue	225.		
RO107TC	1c	black	175.		
RO107TC	1c	green	300.		
RO110TC	1c	black	175.		
RO110TC	1c	blue	175.		
RO110TC	1c	orange	500.		
RO110TC	1c	red	225.		
RO112TC	1c	black	175.		
RO112TC	1c	green	500.		
RO113TC	1c	blue	300.		
RO113TC	1c	green	500.		
RO113TC	1c	orange	500.		
RO114TC	1c	black	750.		
RO115TC	1c	black	175.		
RO115TC	1c	green	500.		
RO116TC	1c	black	225.		
RO116TC	1c	green	300.		
RO118TC	8c	black	225.		
RO118TC	8c	dk bl	500.		
RO118TC	8c	green	500.		
RO119TC	1c	black	225.		
RO119TC	1c	blue	225.		
RO120TC	1c	black	500.		
RO121TC	1c	black	175.		
RO121TC	1c	blue	300.		
RO122TC	1c	blue	300.		
RO122TC	1c	green	500.		
RO123TC	1c	blue	500.		
RO125TC	1c	black	225.		
RO126TC	1c	blue	300.		
RO126TC	1c	green	500.		
RO127TC	1c	black	300.		
RO127TC	1c	green	225.		
RO128TC	1c	black	225.		
RO128TC	1c	green	500.		
RO130TC	1c	black	225.		
RO130TC	1c	green	300.		
RO131TC	1c	black	175.		
RO131TC	1c	green	225.		
RO131TC	1c	red	225.		
RO132TC	1c	black	225.		
RO132TC	1c	green	500.		
RO133TC	1c	blue	500.		
RO133TC	1c	green	300.		
RO134TC	1c	black	300.	150.	
RO134TC	1c	green	300.		
RO135TC	1c	black	500.		
RO135TC	1c	blue	300.		
RO135TC	1c	green	300.		
RO135TC	1c	rose	225.		
RO136TC	1c	black	225.		
RO136TC	1c	green	300.		
RO137TC	1c	black	175.		
RO137TC	1c	blue	175.		
RO137TC	1c	green	500.		
RO138TC	1c	black	175.		
RO138TC	1c	blue	500.		
RO139TC	5c	black	175.		
RO139TC	5c	green	500.		
RO140TC	4c	black	225.		
RO140TC	4c	blue	300.		
RO141TC	1c	black	175.		
RO141TC	1c	dk bl	300.		
RO141TC	1c	green	500.		
RO141TC	1c	yellow green	300.		
RO141TC	1c	green	500.		
RO142TC	1c	black	175.		
RO142TC	1c	blue	225.		
RO143TC	3c	black	175.		
RO143TC	3c	blue	225.		
RO143TC	3c	green	300.		
RO144TC	1c	black	500.		
RO145TC	1c	black	500.		
RO145TC	1c	blue	500.		
RO146TC	1c	blue	500.		
RO146TC	1c	green	300.		
RO148TC	1c	black	175.		
RO148TC	1c	green	300.		
RO148TC	1c	red	300.		
RO152TC	1c	blue	300.		
RO152TC	1c	green	300.		
RO153TC	1c	blue	225.		
RO153TC	1c	brown	300.		
RO153TC	1c	green	225.		
RO153TC	1c	orange	300.		
RO153TC	1c	red	300.		
RO155TC	1c	blue	225.		
RO155TC	1c	green	500.		
RO157TC	3c	black	175.		
RO157TC	3c	green	300.		
RO158TC	1c	blue	300.		
RO158TC	1c	green	500.		
RO159TC	3c	black	225.		
RO159TC	3c	green	500.		
RO160TC	1c	black	225.		
RO160TC	1c	brown	500.		
RO160TC	1c	green	300.		
RO161TC	1c	black	225.		
RO161TC	1c	green	300.		
RO163TC	1c	blue	300.		
RO163TC	1c	green	500.		
RO164TC	1c	black	500.		
RO165TC	12c	black	750.		
RO165TC	12c	green	1,000.		
RO165TC	12c	red	1,000.		
RO166TC	1c	black	300.		
RO166TC	1c	blue	225.		
RO166TC	1c	green	500.		
RO166TC	1c	red	175.		
RO167TC	3c	black	175.		
RO167TC	3c	green	300.		
RO167TC	3c	red	300.		

			DIE ON INDIA (1) Large	PLATE (3) India	(4) Card
RO167TC	3c	ultramarine	300.		
RO168TC	1c	black	500.		
RO168TC	1c	green	300.		
RO171TC	1c	blue	300.		
RO171TC	1c	green	300.		
RO172TC	1c	blue	225.		
RO172TC	1c	green	500.		
RO173TC	1c	black	225.		
RO173TC	1c	green	300.		
RO174TC	1c	black	300.		
RO174TC	1c	green	300.		
RO175TC	1c	blue	275.		
RO175TC	1c	green	350.		
RO175TC	1c	red	500.		
RO177TC	1c	black	175.		
RO177TC	1c	blue	225.		
RO177TC	1c	green	500.		
RO178TC	1c	black	175.		
RO178TC	1c	blue	300.		
RO179TC	1c	blue	500.		
RO179TC	1c	green	500.		
RO180TC	1c	blue	225.		
RO180TC	1c	green	500.		
RO181TC	1c	blue	500.		
RO181TC	1c	green	300.		
RO182TC	1c	blue	300.		
RO182TC	1c	green	300.		
RO183TC	1c	blue	650.		
RO183TC	1c	green	650.		
RO184TC	1c	blue	225.		
RO184TC	1c	brown	300.		
RO184TC	1c	green	225.		
RO184TC	1c	orange	300.		
RO184TC	1c	red	300.		
RO186TC	1c	black	175.		

PRIVATE DIE CANNED FRUIT STAMP

RP1TC	1c	black	375.		

PRIVATE DIE MEDICINE STAMPS

			DIE ON INDIA (1) Large	PLATE (3) India	(4) Card
RS1TC	1c	blue	300.		
RS4TC	1c	green	500.		
RS10TC	4c	black	300.		
RS14TC	4c	black	300.		
RS14TC	4c	blue	300.		
RS16TC	2c	green	500.		
RS21TC	1c	blue	500.		
RS21TC	1c	green	500.		
RS22TC	2c	blue	500.		
RS22TC	2c	green	500.		
RS23TC	4c	green	500.		
RS24TC	1c	blue	500.		
RS24TC	1c	green	500.		
RS25TC	2c	blue	500.		
RS25TC	2c	green	500.		
RS26TC	4c	blue	500.		
RS26TC	4c	green	500.		
RS27TC	4c	blue	225.		
RS27TC	4c	green	500.		
RS28TC	2c	black	225.		
RS28TC	2c	blue	225.		
RS29TC	1c	black	175.		
RS29/RO120TC	2c/1c	black	750.		
RS29TC	2c	blue	175.		
RS29TC	2c	dk bl	500.		
RS29TC	2c	green	500.		
RS29TC	2c	red	300.		
RS30TC	1c	black	175.		
RS30TC	1c	blue	500.		
RS30TC	1c	green	500.		
RS30TC	1c	red	500.		
RS31TC	1c	black	500.		
RS31TC	1c	blue	225.		
RS31TC	1c	red	500.		
RS33TC	1c	blue	175.		
RS33TC	1c	green	225.		
RS33TC	1c	red	500.		
RS34TC	1c	blue	500.		
RS34TC	1c	green	500.		
RS35TC	1c	blue	300.		
RS35TC	1c	green	500.		
RS36TC	1c	black	500.		
RS36TC	1c	dk bl	500.		
RS36TC	1c	green	500.		
RS36TC	1c	ultramarine	500.		
RS36TC	1c	yellow green	225.		
RS38TC	2c	blue	750.		
RS38TC	2c	green	750.		
RS39TC	1c	blue	300.		
RS39TC	1c	green	300.		
RS39TC	1c	orange	500.		
RS40TC	2c	black	225.		
RS40TC	2c	blue	300.		
RS41TC	4c	black	225.		
RS41TC	4c	blue	500.		
RS41TC	4c	green	500.		
RS42TC	1c	green	500.		
RS43TC	4c	black	225.		
RS43TC	4c	green	500.		
RS44TC	1c	green	750.		
RS46TC	4c	blue	225.		
RS46TC	4c	green	300.		
RS47TC	4c	blue	300.		
RS47TC	4c	brown	500.		
RS47TC	4c	green	300.		
RS47TC	4c	orange	500.		
RS47TC	4c	red	500.		
RS49TC	4c	black	225.		
RS49TC	4c	blue	300.		
RS50TC	1c	black	300.		
RS50TC	1c	blue	300.		
RS50TC	1c	green	500.		
RS51TC	2c	blue	500.		
RS51TC	2c	green	500.		
RS52TC	4c	blue	500.		
RS52TC	4c	green	500.		
RS53TC	1c	blue	225.		
RS53TC	1c	brown	300.		
RS53TC	1c	green	225.		
RS53TC	1c	orange	300.		
RS53TC	1c	red	300.		
RS54TC	2c	blue	225.		
RS54TC	2c	brown	300.		
RS54TC	2c	green	225.		
RS54TC	2c	orange	300.		
RS54TC	2c	red	500.		
RS55TC	4c	blue	225.		
RS55TC	4c	green	225.		
RS55TC	4c	orange	225.		
RS55TC	4c	red	500.		
RS56TC	3c	black	350.		
RS56TC	1c	green	500.		
RS57TC	6c	blue	225.		
RS57TC	6c	brown	300.		
RS57TC	6c	green	225.		
RS57TC	6c	orange	300.		
RS57TC	6c	red	300.		
RS58TC	4c	blue	225.		
RS58TC	4c	blue green	500.		
RS58TC	4c	dk bl	500.		
RS58TC	4c	green	225.		
RS58TC	4c	light blue	500.		
RS58TC	4c	red	225.		
RS59TC	1c	blue	300.		
RS59TC	1c	green	500.		
RS60TC	1c	blue	500.		
RS62TC	1c	brown	300.		
RS62TC	1c	green	225.		
RS62TC	1c	orange	300.		
RS62TC	1c	red	500.		
RS62TC	1c	vermilion	500.		
RS64TC	2c	blue	225.		
RS64TC	2c	brown	300.		
RS64TC	2c	green	225.		
RS64TC	2c	orange	300.		
RS64TC	2c	red	500.		
RS64TC	1c	vermilion	500.		
RS65TC	4c	blue	500.		
RS65TC	4c	green	500.		
RS66TC	1c	blue	300.		
RS66TC	1c	green	500.		
RS66TC	1c	light green	500.		
RS66TC	1c	orange	500.		
RS66TC	1c	rose red	500.		
RS67TC	1c	green	500.		
RS69TC	1c	blue	500.		
RS69TC	1c	green	500.		
RS70TC	2c	blue	500.		
RS70TC	2c	green	500.		
RS71TC	1c	blue	500.		
RS71TC	1c	green	500.		
RS72TC	2c	blue	500.		
RS72TC	2c	green	500.		
RS73TC	2c	black	500.		
RS73TC	2c	blue	750.		
RS73TC	2c	red	1,000.		
RS74TC	1c	blue	500.		
RS74TC	1c	green	500.		
RS74hTC	1c	blue	500.		
RS74hTC	1c	green	500.		
RS75TC	1c	black	300.		
RS75TC	1c	green	500.		
RS76TC	2c	blue	300.		
RS76TC	2c	green	300.		
RS81TC	4c	black	225.		
RS81TC	4c	blue	500.		
RS81TC	4c	green	500.		
RS83TC	4c	blue	500.		
RS83TC	4c	green	500.		
RS84TC	1c	black	250.		
RS84TC	1c	blue	350.		
RS84TC	1c	green	250.		
RS84TC	1c	orange	650.		
RS84TC	1c	red	650.		
RS84TC	1c	slate	650.		
RS85TC	4c	blue	275.		
RS85TC	4c	brown	275.		
RS85TC	4c	green	300.		
RS85TC	4c	orange	375.		
RS86TC	1c	black	225.		
RS86TC	1c	blue	225.		
RS88TC	1c	blue	500.		
RS88TC	1c	green	500.		
RS89TC	1c	green	300.		
RS91TC	4c	blue	225.		
RS91TC	4c	green	500.		
RS92TC	3c	blue	225.		
RS92TC	3c	brown	300.		
RS92TC	3c	green	225.		
RS92TC	3c	orange	300.		
RS92TC	3c	red	500.		
RS92TC	3c	vermilion	500.		
RS94TC	4c	blue	500.		
RS94TC	4c	green	500.		
RS95TC	1c	black	300.		
RS95TC	1c	blue	225.		
RS95TC	1c	dk bl	90.		
RS96TC	3c	blue	225.		
RS96TC	3c	green	500.		
RS97TC	1c	blue	300.		
RS97TC	1c	green	500.		
RS98TC	1c	blue	225.		
RS98TC	1c	green	175.		
RS98TC	1c	red	500.		
RS99TC	4c	blue	500.		
RS100TC	6c	green	500.		
RS101TC	1c	blue	500.		
RS101TC	1c	green	500.		
RS102TC	2c	black	175.		
RS102TC	2c	green	225.		
RS102TC	2c	rose	225.		
RS103TC	4c	blue	500.		
RS103TC	4c	green	500.		
RS106TC	2c	black	500.		
RS106TC	2c	green	300.		
RS107/109TC	3c/6c	green	1,250.		
RS107TC	3c	blue	300.		
RS108TC	4c	blue	300.		
RS108TC	4c	green	500.		
RS109TC	6c	blue	300.		
RS110TC	2c	black	300.		
RS110TC	2c	green	300.		
RS111TC	4c	blue	300.		
RS111TC	4c	green	500.		
RS114TC	1c	green	300.		
RS116TC	4c	black	225.		
RS116TC	4c	blue	300.		
RS116TC	4c	brown	500.		
RS116TC	4c	green	500.		
RS116TC	4c	vermilion	500.		
RS117TC	1c	blue	350.		
RS117TC	1c	green	750.		
RS118TC	1c	black	175.		
RS118TC	1c	blue	225.		
RS118TC	1c	brn red	300.		
RS118TC	1c	green	300.		
RS120TC	2c	blue	225.		
RS120TC	2c	brown	300.		
RS120TC	2c	green	225.		
RS120TC	2c	orange	300.		
RS120TC	2c	red	500.		
RS120TC	2c	vermilion	500.		
RS121TC	3c	blue	500.		
RS121TC	3c	green	500.		
RS122TC	2c	blue	500.		
RS122TC	2c	green	500.		
RS123TC	4c	blue	225.		
RS123TC	4c	brown	300.		
RS123TC	4c	green	225.		
RS123TC	4c	orange	300.		
RS123TC	4c	red	500.		
RS123TC	4c	vermilion	500.		
RS124TC	1c	black	175.		
RS124TC	1c	blue green	300.		
RS124TC	1c	green	500.		
RS124TC	1c	orange	500.		
RS124TC	1c	red	225.		
RS126TC	1c	black	225.		
RS126TC	1c	blue	225.		
RS126TC	1c	brown	300.		
RS126TC	1c	orange	300.		
RS126TC	1c	red	500.		
RS126TC	1c	vermilion	500.		
RS127TC	4c	black	225.		
RS127TC	4c	blue	225.		
RS127TC	4c	brown	225.		
RS127TC	4c	orange	300.		
RS127TC	4c	red	500.		
RS127TC	4c	vermilion	500.		
RS128TC	2c	black	600.		
RS128TC	2c	green	400.		
RS128TC	2c	pale blue	500.		
RS130TC	4c	black	275.		
RS130TC	4c	blue	350.		
RS131TC	4c	blue	225.		
RS131TC	4c	brown	500.		
RS131TC	4c	green	300.		
RS131TC	4c	orange	300.		
RS131TC	4c	red	500.		
RS131TC	4c	vermilion	500.		
RS132TC	4c	blue	500.		
RS132TC	4c	orange	500.		
RS133TC	6c	blue	500.		
RS133TC	6c	green	500.		
RS134TC	4c	black	300.		
RS134TC	4c	green	300.		
RS134TC	4c	red	500.		
RS138TC	1c	blue	300.		
RS138TC	1c	green	500.		
RS138TC	1c	red	500.		
RS138TC	1c	yel grn	500.		
RS139TC	2c	black	225.		
RS139TC	2c	blackish violet			90.
RS139TC	2c	blue	500.		
RS139TC	2c	green	500.		
RS139TC	2c	red	225.		
RS139TC	2c	rose	500.		
RS141TC	4c	black	225.		
RS141TC	4c	blue	300.		
RS142TC	1c	blue	225.		
RS142TC	1c	brown	300.		
RS142TC	1c	green	225.		
RS142TC	1c	orange	300.		
RS142TC	1c	red	500.		
RS142TC	1c	vermilion	500.		
RS143TC	4c	black	225.		
RS143TC	4c	blue	225.		
RS144TC	1c	black	500.		
RS144TC	1c	green	500.		
RS145TC	2c	blue	500.		
RS146TC	4c	black	300.		

			DIE ON INDIA (1) Large	PLATE (3) India	(4) Card
RS146TC	4c	blue	300.		
RS150TC	1c	black	300.		
RS150TC	1c	blue	175.		
RS150TC	1c	carmine	500.		
RS150TC	1c	green	225.		
RS151TC	1c	blue	500.		
RS151TC	1c	green	500.		
RS152TC	2c	black	175.		
RS152TC	2c	blue	300.		
RS153TC	4c	blue	750.		
RS153TC	4c	green	750.		
RS154TC	4c	black	500.		
RS155TC	2c	black	300.		
RS155TC	2c	black	300.		
RS155TC	2c	blue	225.		
RS155TC	2c	red	500.		
RS156TC	6c	blue	225.		
RS156TC	6c	green	225.		
RS156TC	6c	red	225.		
RS157TC	2c	blue	225.		
RS157TC	2c	green	225.		
RS157TC	2c	red	500.		
RS157TC	2c	vermilion	300.		
RS158TC	1c	black	500.		
RS159TC	4c	black	375.		
RS160TC	6c	blue	300.		
RS160TC	6c	green	500.		
RS161TC	4c	blue	500.		
RS161TC	4c	green	750.		
RS162TC	1c	black	175.		
RS162TC	1c	green	300.		
RS162TC	1c	red	500.		
RS163TC	4c	black	300.		
RS163TC	4c	green	600.		
RS163TC	4c	yellow green	600.		
RS164TC	1c	blue	225.		
RS164TC	1c	green	500.		
RS165TC	4c	black	175.		
RS165TC	4c	blue	225.		
RS166TC	1c	blue	300.		
RS166TC	1c	green	500.		
RS169TC	4c	blue	225.		
RS169TC	4c	green	500.		
RS169TC	4c	red	225.		
RS170TC	1c	blue	300.		
RS170TC	1c	green	500.		
RS171TC	1c	black	225.		
RS171TC	1c	blue	225.		
RS171TC	1c	brown	300.		
RS171TC	1c	dull blue	500.		
RS171TC	1c	green	225.		
RS171TC	1c	orange	300.		
RS171TC	1c	red	500.		
RS171TC	1c	vermilion	500.		
RS172TC	2c	blue	225.		
RS172TC	2c	brown	300.		
RS172TC	2c	green	225.		
RS172TC	2c	orange	225.		
RS172TC	2c	red	500.		
RS172TC	2c	vermilion	500.		
RS173TC	1c	black	225.		
RS173TC	1c	green	225.		
RS173TC	1c	red	300.		
RS174TC	1c	black	300.		
RS174TC	1c	dk bl	500.		
RS174TC	1c	green	300.		
RS175TC	2c	black	250.		
RS175TC	2c	blue	500.		
RS175TC	2c	green	500.		
RS176TC	4c	blue	375.		
RS176TC	4c	green	500.		
RS177TC	2c	blue	750.		
RS177TC	2c	green	1,000.		
RS178TC	6c	blue	300.		
RS178TC	6c	green	500.		
RS179TC	2c	black	300.		
RS179TC	2c	blue	375.		
RS180TC	3c	blue	300.		
RS180TC	3c	green	300.		
RS181TC	4c	blue	225.		
RS181TC	4c	green	500.		
RS182TC	4c	blue	225.		
RS182TC	4c	green	225.		
RS182TC	4c	rose	300.		
RS183TC	1c	black	500.		
RS183TC	1c	blue	300.		
RS183TC	1c	green	500.		
RS183TC	1c	red	225.		
RS184TC	2c	blue	300.		
RS184TC	2c	brown	225.		
RS184TC	2c	green	225.		
RS184TC	2c	orange	300.		
RS184TC	2c	vermilion	300.		
RS185TC	1c	blue	300.		
RS186TC	4c	blue	225.		
RS186TC	4c	green	500.		
RS187TC	4c	blue	225.		
RS187TC	4c	brown	300.		
RS187TC	4c	green	300.		
RS187TC	4c	orange	500.		
RS187TC	4c	red	500.		
RS187TC	4c	vermilion	500.		
RS188TC	1c	blue	500.		
RS188TC	1c	green	500.		
RS189TC	1c	black	175.		
RS189TC	1c	blue	225.		
RS189TC	1c	red	225.		
RS190TC	2c	blue	500.		
RS190TC	2c	green	500.		
RS191TC	4c	blue	400.		
RS191TC	4c	green	400.		
RS192TC	6c	blue	400.		
RS192TC	6c	green	400.		

			DIE ON INDIA (1) Large	PLATE (3) India	(4) Card
RS192TC	6c	rose	500.		
RS193TC	2c	blue	500.		
RS193TC	2c	green	500.		
RS194TC	1c	green	175.		
RS195TC	2c	blue	500.		
RS195TC	2c	green	500.		
RS196TC	1c	black	500.		
RS196TC	1c	green	225.		
RS197TC	2c	blue	300.		
RS198TC	1c	green	300.		
RS198TC	1c	red	500.		
RS199TC	2c	blue	225.		
RS199TC	2c	green	500.		
RS204TC	2c	blue	500.		
RS204TC	2c	green	500.		
RS205TC	4c	blue	225.		
RS205TC	4c	green	500.		
RS208TC	1c	black	225.		
RS208TC	1c	blue	225.		
RS208TC	1c	orange	300.		
RS209TC	2c	black	500.		
RS209TC	2c	blue	500.		
RS210TC	4c	blue	225.		
RS210TC	4c	green	225.		
RS210TC	4c	red	225.		
RS212TC	1c	black	225.		
RS212TC	1c	blue	300.		
RS212TC	1c	green	500.		
RS213TC	6c	blue	500.		
RS213TC	6c	green	500.		
RS214TC	4c	blue	300.		
RS214TC	4c	brown	300.		
RS214TC	4c	green	225.		
RS214TC	4c	orange	300.		
RS214TC	4c	red	500.		
RS214TC	4c	vermilion	500.		
RS215TC	1c	black	300.		
RS215TC	1c	blue	450.		
RS215TC	1c	dark red	500.		
RS215TC	1c	green	500.		
RS216TC	1c	blue	500.		
RS216TC	1c	green	500.		
RS220TC	1c	blue	300.		
RS221TC	4c	black	175.		
RS221TC	4c	blue	225.		
RS222TC	8c	green	500.		
RS223TC	1c	blue	300.		
RS223TC	1c	brown	300.		
RS223TC	1c	green	225.		
RS223TC	1c	orange	300.		
RS223TC	1c	vermilion	300.		
RS224TC	1c	blue	500.		
RS224TC	1c	brown	300.		
RS224TC	1c	green	225.		
RS224TC	1c	orange	300.		
RS224TC	1c	red	500.		
RS225TC	4c	blue	500.		
RS225TC	4c	green	500.		
RS226TC	1c	black	350.		
RS228TC	1c	black	175.		
RS228TC	1c	blue	225.		
RS228TC	1c	brown	500.		
RS228TC	1c	green	225.		
RS228TC	1c	orange	500.		
RS228TC	1c	red	500.		
RS228TC	1c	vermilion	500.		
RS229TC	2c	black	225.		
RS229TC	2c	blue	225.		
RS229TC	2c	brown	300.		
RS229TC	2c	green	225.		
RS229TC	2c	orange	225.		
RS229TC	2c	red	300.		
RS229TC	2c	vermilion	500.		
RS230TC	6c	blue	225.		
RS230TC	6c	brown	300.		
RS230TC	6c	green	225.		
RS230TC	6c	orange	300.		
RS230TC	6c	vermilion	225.		
RS231TC	6c	black	1,000.		
RS231TC	6c	blue	1,000.		
RS231TC	6c	green	1,000.		
RS231TC	6c	red	750.		
RS236TC	4c	blue	500.		
RS239TC	2c	black	225.		
RS239TC	2c	blue	300.		
RS239TC	2c	brown	500.		
RS239TC	2c	green	225.		
RS239TC	2c	orange	300.		
RS239TC	2c	vermilion	500.		
RS240TC	4c	red	500.		
RS240TC	4c	blue	175.		
RS240TC	4c	blue green	500.		
RS240TC	4c	brown	500.		
RS240TC	4c	green	225.		
RS240TC	4c	orange	225.		
RS240TC	4c	vermilion	225.		
RS241TC	4c	green	500.		
RS242TC	1c	blue	225.		
RS242TC	1c	green	500.		
RS243TC	4c	blue	500.		
RS243TC	4c	green	500.		
RS244TC	6c	blue	500.		
RS244TC	6c	green	500.		
RS245TC	1c	blue	500.		
RS250TC	6c	blue	500.		
RS250TC	6c	green	500.		
RS251TC	1c	blue	225.		
RS251TC	1c	brown	225.		
RS251TC	1c	green	225.		
RS252TC	1c	black	225.		
RS252TC	1c	blue	225.		
RS252TC	1c	brown	300.		
RS252TC	1c	green	225.		

			DIE ON INDIA (1) Large	PLATE (3) India	(4) Card
RS252TC	1c	orange	500.		
RS252TC	1c	red	500.		
RS252TC	1c	rose	225.		
RS253TC	4c	blue	500.		
RS253TC	4c	green	500.		
RS258TC	6c	black	500.		
RS259TC	1c	blue	225.		
RS259TC	1c	brown	300.		
RS259TC	1c	green	225.		
RS259TC	1c	orange	300.		
RS259TC	1c	red	500.		
RS259TC	1c	vermilion	500.		
RS260TC	2c	blue	175.		
RS260TC	2c	brown	300.		
RS260TC	2c	green	225.		
RS260TC	2c	orange	300.		
RS260TC	2c	red	500.		
RS260TC	2c	rose	500.		
RS260TC	2c	vermilion	225.		
RS261TC	4c	blue	225.		
RS261TC	4c	brown	300.		
RS261TC	4c	green	225.		
RS261TC	4c	orange	300.		
RS261TC	4c	red	500.		
RS261TC	4c	vermilion	500.		
RS262TC	2c	blue	500.		
RS262TC	2c	green	500.		
RS264TC	4c	blue	300.		
RS264TC	4c	green	300.		
RS265TC	1c	black	225.		
RS265TC	1c	blue	500.		
RS267TC	4c	black	225.		
RS267TC	4c	blue	500.		
RS267TC	4c	green	300.		
RS270TC	12c	black	300.		
RS270TC	12c	blue green	500.		
RS270TC	12c	green	300.		
RS270TC	12c	red	225.		
RS271TC	4c	blue	2,500.		
RS272TC	1c	black	300.		
RS272TC	1c	blue	300.		
RS273TC	2c	blue	500.		
RS274TC	1c	black	225.		
RS274TC	2c	blue	300.		
RS276TC	2c	black	225.		
RS276TC	2c	blue	300.		
RS278TC	2½c	black	*1,000.*		
RS280TC	¼c	black	*1,000.*		
RS302TC	2½c	black	*1,000.*		
RS303TC	⅝c	black	*1,000.*		

PRIVATE DIE PERFUMERY STAMPS

			DIE ON INDIA (1) Large	PLATE (3) India	(4) Card
RT2TC	1c	brown	500.		
RT2TC	1c	green	400.		
RT2TC	1c	orange	300.		
RT2TC	1c	red	500.		
RT5TC	2c	black	175.		
RT5TC	2c	blue	225.		
RT5TC	2c	green	500.		
RT5TC	2c	orange	500.	125.	
RT6TC	1c	blue	375.		
RT6TC	1c	brown	500.		
RT6TC	1c	green	375.		
RT6TC	1c	orange	500.		
RT6TC	1c	red	500.		
RT10TC	4c	blue	375.		
RT10TC	4c	brown	500.		
RT10TC	4c	green	400.		
RT10TC	4c	orange	500.		
RT10TC	4c	red	500.		
RT12TC	1c	black	225.		90.
RT12TC	1c	blue	225.		
RT12TC	1c	green	500.		
RT13TC	2c	black	225.	75.	
RT13TC	2c	blue	300.		
RT13TC	2c	green	300.		
RT13TC	2c	red	225.		
RT14TC	3c	blue	1,000.		
RT16TC	1c	blue	175.		
RT16TC	1c	green	225.		
RT17TC	2c	black	300.		
RT17TC	2c	blue	300.		
RT17TC	2c	green	300.		
RT17TC	2c	orange	500.		
RT18TC	3c	black	175.		
RT18TC	3c	blue	175.		
RT18TC	3c	green	500.		
RT18TC	3c	orange	500.		
RT18TC	3c	red	300.		
RT19TC	1c	black	500.		
RT20TC	1c	black	225.		
RT20TC	1c	blue	300.		
RT20TC	1c	green	175.		
RT21TC	2c	black	500.		
RT21TC	2c	green	500.		
RT22TC	1c	black	175.		
RT22TC	1c	blue	300.		
RT22TC	1c	green	300.		
RT22TC	1c	red brn	300.		
RT22TC	1c	ultramarine	500.		
RT23TC	2c	blue	225.		
RT23TC	2c	green	500.		
RT24TC	3c	black	175.		
RT24TC	3c	blue	225.		
RT24TC	3c	green	300.		
RT24TC	3c	red	225.		
RT25TC	4c	black	175.		
RT25TC	4c	blue	225.		
RT26TC	1c	black	175.		

			DIE ON INDIA (1) Large	PLATE (3) India	(4) Card
RT26TC	1c	blue	225.		
RT26TC	1c	brown	300.		
RT26TC	1c	green	500.		
RT26TC	1c	orange	300.		
RT26TC	1c	red	500.		
RT28TC	2c	black	225.		
RT28TC	2c	brown	300.		
RT28TC	2c	green	225.		
RT28TC	2c	orange	300.		
RT28TC	2c	red	300.		
RT30TC	3c	black	225.		
RT30TC	3c	blue	225.		
RT30TC	3c	brown	300.		
RT30TC	3c	green	225.		
RT30TC	3c	orange	300.		
RT30TC	3c	red	175.		
RT32TC	4c	black	225.		
RT32TC	4c	blue	225.		
RT32TC	4c	brown	500.		
RT32TC	4c	green	225.		
RT32TC	4c	orange	225.		
RT32TC	4c	red	300.		

PRIVATE DIE PLAYING CARD STAMPS

			DIE ON INDIA (1) Large	PLATE (3) India	(4) Card
RU2TC	2c	black	175.		
RU2TC	2c	blue	225.		
RU2TC	2c	green	300.		
RU3TC	4c	blue	225.		
RU3TC	4c	green	225.		
RU4TC	5c	black	225.		
RU4TC	5c	green	300.		
RU5TC	5c	black	225.		
RU5TC	5c	brown	300.		
RU5TC	5c	green	300.		
RU5TC	5c	light brn	500.		
RU5TC	5c	orange	500.		
RU5TC	5c	red	500.		
RU6TC	10c	black	175.		
RU6TC	10c	green	300.		
RU7TC	5c	blue	375.		
RU7TC	5c	green	375.		
RU8TC	5c	blue	225.		
RU8TC	5c	green	225.		
RU8TC	5c	orange	300.		
RU9TC	5c	blue	225.		
RU9TC	5c	green	500.		
RU10TC	2c	black	175.		
RU10TC	2c	brown	500.		
RU10TC	2c	green	500.		
RU11TC	5c	black	225.		
RU11TC	5c	blue	225.		
RU11TC	5c	brown	300.		
RU12TC	5c	blue	300.		
RU12TC	5c	green	300.		
RU13TC	5c	green	175.		
RU14TC	5c	blue	225.		
RU14TC	5c	brown	300.		
RU14TC	5c	green	300.		
RU14TC	5c	light brn	500.		
RU14TC	5c	orange	500.		
RU14TC	5c	red	300.		
RU15TC	5c	blue	300.		
RU15TC	5c	green	300.		

HUNTING PERMIT

			DIE ON INDIA (1) Large
RW4TC	$1	light violet	*5,500.*

SPECIMEN STAMPS

These are regular stamps overprinted "Specimen." Each number has a suffix letter "S" to denote "specimen." The Scott number is that of the stamp as shown in the regular listings and the second letter "A," etc., indicates the type of overprint. Values are for items of a grade of fine-very fine, with at least part original gum.

Specimen
Type A; 12mm long

Specimen.
Type B; 15mm long

Specimen.
Type C; 30mm long

SPECIMEN
Type D; Capital Letters

Specimen.
Type E; Initial Capital

Specimen.
Type F; 22mm long

SPECIMEN
Type G; 14mm long

SPECIMEN
Type H; 16mm long

Specimen
Type I; 20mm long

Overprinted in Black — Specimen

1851-56

7S	A	1c **blue,** type II	*2,500.*
11S	A	3c **dull red,** type I	*6,500.*

1857-60

21S	A	1c **blue,** type III	*1,500.*
24S	A	1c **blue,** type V	*1,000.*
26S	A	3c **dull red,** type II	*1,000.*
30S	A	5c **orange brown,** type II	*1,000.*
35S	A	10c **green,** type V	*1,250.*
36BS	A	12c **black**	*3,500.*
37S	A	24c **lilac**	*1,000.*
38S	A	30c **orange**	*1,000.*
26S	F	3c **dull red,** type II	*2,000.*
26S	I	3c **dull red,** type II	*4,000.*

1861

63S	A	1c **blue**	750.
65S	A	3c **rose**	750.
68S	A	10c **dark green**	750.
70S	A	24c **red lilac**	750.
72S	A	90c **blue**	750.
73S	A	2c **black**	1,750.
76S	A	5c **brown**	750.

Specimen.

Overprint Black, Except As Noted

1861-66

63S	B	1c **blue** *(1300)*	120.
		P# block of 8, Impt.	*1,750.*
		Without period	—
65S	B	3c **rose** *(1500)*	120.
68S	B	10c **dark green** *(1600)*	120.
		P# block of 8, Impt.	—
69S	B	12c **black** (orange) *(1300)*	120.
71S	B	30c **orange** *(1400)*	120.
		P# block of 8, Impt.	*15,000.*
72S	B	90c **blue** *(1394)*	120.
		P# block of 8, Impt.	—
73S	B	2c **black** (vermilion) *(1306)*	250.
		Block of 4	*1,100.*
		Without period	*500.*
		Block of 4, one stamp without period	*1,500.*
76S	B	5c **brown** *(1306)*	120.
		P# block of 8, Impt.	—
77S	B	15c **black** (vermilion) *(1208)*	200.
		Block of 4	*900.*
78S	B	24c **lilac** *(1300)*	200.

1867-68

86S	A	1c **blue**	*1,000.*
85ES	A	12c **black**	*1,000.*
93S	A	2c **black**	*1,100.*
94S	A	3c **rose**	*1,000.*
95S	A	5c **brown**	*1,100.*
97S	A	12c **black**	—
98S	A	15c **black**	*1,000.*
99S	A	24c **gray lilac**	*1,250.*
		Split grill	
100S	A	30c **orange**	*1,250.*

1869

112S	A	1c **buff**	*1,750.*
113S	A	2c **brown**	*1,500.*
115S	A	6c **ultramarine**	*1,250.*
116S	A	10c **yellow**	*1,250.*
117S	A	12c **green**	*1,250.*
119S	A	15c **brown & blue**	*1,500.*
120S	A	24c **green & violet**	*1,750.*
		a. Without grill	—
121S	A	30c **blue & carmine**	*1,750.*
		a. Without grill	—
122S	A	90c **carmine & black**	*2,000.*
		a. Without grill	—
123S	B	1c **buff**	*3,500.*
124S	B	2c **brown**	*3,500.*
125S	B	3c **blue** (blue)	*3,500.*
126S	B	6c **blue** (blue)	*3,500.*
127S	B	10c **yellow** (blue)	—
129S	B	10c **brown & blue** (blue)	*5,250.*

1870-71

145S	A	1c **ultramarine**	*600.*
146S	A	2c **red brown**	*600.*
146S	B	2c **red brown**	*600.*
147S	A	3c **green**	*600.*
148S	A	6c **carmine**	*600.*
149S	A	7c **vermilion**	*600.*
150S	A	10c **brown**	*600.*
151S	A	12c **dull violet**	*600.*
152S	A	15c **bright orange**	*600.*
155S	A	90c **carmine**	*600.*
155S	B	90c **carmine** (blue)	*600.*

1873

158S	B	3c **green** (blue)	*750.*
159S	B	6c **dull pink**	*700.*
160S	B	7c **orange vermilion** (blue)	*700.*
162S	B	12c **blackish violet** (blue)	—
165S	B	30c **greenish black** (blue)	*700.*
166S	B	90c **carmine** (blue)	*750.*

Overprinted in Red — SPECIMEN

1879

Type D

189S	D	15c **red orange**	80.
190S	D	30c **full black**	80.
191S	D	90c **carmine**	80.
	a.	Overprint in black brown	80.

1881-82

205S	D	5c **yellow brown**	80.
206S	D	1c **gray blue**	80.
207S	D	3c **blue green**	80.
208S	D	6c **brown red**	80.
209S	D	10c **brown**	80.

1883

210S	D	2c **red brown**	100.
211S	D	4c **blue green**	100.

Handstamped in Dull Purple — Specimen.

1890-93

Type E

219S	E	1c **dull blue**	150.
220S	E	2c **carmine**	150.
221S	E	3c **purple**	150.
222S	E	4c **dark brown**	150.
223S	E	5c **chocolate**	150.
224S	E	6c **dull red**	150.
225S	E	8c **lilac**	150.
226S	E	10c **green**	150.
227S	E	15c **blue**	150.
228S	E	30c **black**	150.
229S	E	90c **orange**	175.

COLUMBIAN ISSUE

1893

230S	E	1c **deep blue**	400.
		Double overprint	—
231S	E	2c **violet**	400.
232S	E	3c **green**	400.
233S	E	4c **ultramarine**	400.
234S	E	5c **chocolate**	400.
235S	E	6c **purple**	400.
236S	E	8c **magenta**	400.
237S	E	10c **black brown**	400.
238S	E	15c **dark green**	400.
239S	E	30c **orange brown**	400.
240S	E	50c **slate blue**	400.
241S	E	$1 **salmon**	500.
242S	E	$2 **brown red**	500.
243S	E	$3 **yellow green**	550.
244S	E	$4 **crimson lake**	575.
245S	E	$5 **black**	675.

Overprinted in Magenta **Specimen.**

Type F

230S	F	1c **deep blue**	550.
232S	F	3c **green**	550.
233S	F	4c **ultramarine**	550.
234S	F	5c **chocolate**	550.
235S	F	6c **purple**	550.
237S	F	10c **black brown**	550.
243S	F	$3 **yellow green**	700.

Overprinted Type H in Black or Red

231S	H	2c **violet** (Bk)	625.
233S	H	4c **ultramarine** (R)	625.
234S	H	5c **chocolate** (R)	625.

Overprinted Type I in Black or Red

231S	I	2c **violet** (R)	625.
232S	I	3c **green** (R)	625.
233S	I	4c **ultramarine** (R)	625.
234S	I	5c **chocolate** (Bk)	625.
235S	I	6c **purple** (R)	625.
236S	I	8c **magenta** (Bk)	625.
237S	I	10c **black brown** (R)	625.
238S	I	15c **dark green** (R)	625.
239S	I	30c **orange brown** (Bk)	625.
240S	I	50c **slate blue** (R)	625.

1895

Handstamped Type E in Purple

264S	E	1c **blue**	90.
267S	E	2c **carmine,** type III	90.
267aS	E	2c **pink,** type III	90.
268S	E	3c **purple**	90.
269S	E	4c **dark brown**	100.
270S	E	5c **chocolate**	90.
271S	E	6c **dull brown**	90.
272S	E	8c **violet brown**	90.
273S	E	10c **dark green**	90.
274S	E	15c **dark blue**	90.
275S	E	50c **orange**	90.
276S	E	$1 **black,** type I	325.
276AS	E	$1 **black,** type II	*2,000.*
277S	E	$2 **dark blue**	300.
278S	E	$5 **dark green**	400.

1897-1903

279S	E	1c **deep green**	90.
279BS	E	2c **light red,** type IV	90.
279BjS	E	2c Booklet pane of 6, **light red,** type IV (Bk)	525.
		Never hinged	750.
		With plate number	1,100.
		Never hinged	1,500.
a.		As No. 279BjS, inverted overprint	—
b.		As No. 279BjS, double impression of overprint on bottom two stamps	—
280S	E	4c **rose brown**	160.
281S	E	5c **dark blue**	80.
282S	E	6c **lake**	80.
282CS	E	10c **brown,** type I	80.
283S	E	10c **brown,** type II	—
284S	E	15c **olive green**	80.

Special Printing

In March 1900 one pane of 100 stamps of each of Nos. 279, 279B, 268, 280-282, 272, 282C, 284 and 275-278 were specially handstamped type E "Specimen" in black for displays at the Paris Exposition (1900) and Pan American Exposition (1901). The 2c pane was light red, type IV.

These examples were handstamped by H. G. Mandel and mounted by him in separate displays for the two Expositions. Examples from the panes in addition to those displayed were handstamped "Specimen," but most were destroyed after the Expositions. Examples of all issues that were handstamped are known.

Additional stamps, not from the mounted display panes, do exist with a black "Specimen" handstamp, but it is believed Mandel applied such handstamps to regularly issued stamps from his personal collection. These include Nos. 267, 267a and 279B in pale red.

TRANS-MISSISSIPPI ISSUE

1898

Type F

285S	F	1c **dark yellow green**	250.

Type E

285S	E	1c **dark yellow green**	250.
286S	E	2c **copper red**	250.
287S	E	4c **orange**	250.
288S	E	5c **dull blue**	250.
289S	E	8c **violet brown**	250.
290S	E	10c **gray violet**	250.
291S	E	50c **sage green**	300.
292S	E	$1 **black**	600.
293S	E	$2 **orange brown**	750.

PAN-AMERICAN ISSUE

1901

294S	E	1c **green & black**	235.
295S	E	2c **carmine**	235.
296S	E	4c **chocolate & black**	235.
a.		Center inverted	*10,000.*
297S	E	5c **ultramarine & black**	235.
298S	E	8c **brown violet & black**	235.
299S	E	10c **yellow brown & black**	235.

1902

300S	E	1c **blue green**	125.
301S	E	2c **carmine**	125.
302S	E	3c **bright violet**	125.
303S	E	4c **brown**	125.
304S	E	5c **blue**	125.
305S	E	6c **claret**	125.
306S	E	8c **violet black**	125.
307S	E	10c **pale red brown**	125.
308S	E	13c **purple black**	125.
309S	E	15c **olive green**	125.
310S	E	50c **orange**	125.
311S	E	$1 **black**	250.
312S	E	$2 **dark blue**	375.
313S	E	$5 **dark green**	500.

1903

319S	E	2c **carmine**	110.

LOUISIANA PURCHASE ISSUE

1904

323S	E	1c **green**	350.
324S	E	2c **carmine**	350.
325S	E	3c **violet**	350.
326S	E	5c **dark blue**	350.
327S	E	10c **red brown**	350.

SPECIAL DELIVERY STAMPS

Overprinted in Red **SPECIMEN**

1885

Type D

E1S	D	10c **blue**	140.

Handstamped in Dull Purple **Specimen.**

1888

Type E

E2S	E	10c **blue**	150.

1893

E3S	E	10c **orange**	200.

1894

E4S	E	10c **blue**	300.

1895

E5S	E	10c **blue**	175.

1902

E6S	E	10c **ultramarine**	175.

POSTAGE DUE STAMPS

Overprinted in Red **SPECIMEN**

1879

Type D

J1S	D	1c **brown**	250.00
J2S	D	2c **brown**	250.00
J3S	D	3c **brown**	250.00
J4S	D	5c **brown**	250.00

1884

J15S	D	1c **red brown**	45.00
J16S	D	2c **red brown**	45.00
J17S	D	3c **red brown**	45.00
J18S	D	5c **red brown**	45.00
J19S	D	10c **red brown**	45.00
J20S	D	30c **red brown**	45.00
J21S	D	50c **red brown**	45.00

Handstamped in Dull Purple **Specimen.**

1895

Type E

J38S	E	1c **deep claret**	85.00
J39S	E	2c **deep claret**	85.00
J40S	E	3c **deep claret**	85.00
J41S	E	5c **deep claret**	85.00
J42S	E	10c **deep claret**	85.00
J43S	E	30c **deep claret**	85.00
J44S	E	50c **deep claret**	85.00

OFFICIAL STAMPS

Special printings of Official stamps were made in 1875 at the time the other Reprints, Re-issues and Special Printings were printed. The Official stamps reprints received specimen overprints, but philatelists believe they most properly should be considered to be part of the special printings. See Official section after No. O120.

NEWSPAPER STAMPS

Overprinted in Red **Specimen.**

1865-75

Type C — Overprint 30mm Long

PR5S	C	5c **dark blue**	400.00
a.		Triple overprint	900.00
PR2S	C	10c **blue green**	400.00
PR3S	C	25c **carmine red**	400.00

Handstamped in Black **Specimen**

1875

Type A

PR9S	A	2c **black**	500.00
PR11S	A	4c **black**	500.00
PR12S	A	6c **black**	500.00
PR16S	A	12c **rose**	500.00

Overprinted in Black, except as noted **Specimen.**

1875

Type B
Overprint 15mm Long

PR9S	B	2c **black**	45.00
PR10S	B	3c **black**	45.00
PR11S	B	4c **black**	45.00
PR12S	B	6c **black**	45.00
PR13S	B	8c **black**	45.00
PR14S	B	9c **black**	45.00
a.		Overprint in blue	—
PR15S	B	10c **black**	45.00
PR16S	B	12c **rose**	45.00
PR17S	B	24c **rose**	45.00
PR18S	B	36c **rose**	45.00
PR19S	B	48c **rose**	45.00
a.		Overprint in blue	65.00
PR20S	B	60c **rose**	45.00
PR21S	B	72c **rose**	45.00
a.		Overprint in blue	65.00
PR22S	B	84c **rose**	45.00
a.		Overprint in blue	—
PR23S	B	96c **rose**	45.00
a.		Overprint in blue	—
PR24S	B	$1.92 **dark brown**	45.00
PR25S	B	$3 **vermilion**	45.00
a.		Overprint in blue	65.00
PR26S	B	$6 **ultramarine**	45.00
a.		Overprint in blue	250.00
PR27S	B	$9 **yellow**	45.00
a.		Overprint in blue	250.00
PR28S	B	$12 **dark green**	45.00
a.		Overprint in blue	250.00
PR29S	B	$24 **dark gray violet**	45.00
a.		Overprint in blue	65.00
PR30S	B	$36 **brown rose**	62.00
PR31S	B	$48 **red brown**	62.00
PR32S	B	$60 **violet**	62.00

Overprinted in Red **SPECIMEN**

1875

Type D

PR14S	D	9c **black**	30.00

1879

PR57S	D	2c **black**	75.00
PR58S	D	3c **black**	75.00
PR59S	D	4c **black**	75.00
PR60S	D	6c **black**	75.00
PR61S	D	8c **black**	75.00
PR62S	D	10c **black**	75.00
a.		Double overprint	*2,000.*
PR63S	D	12c **red**	75.00
PR64S	D	24c **red**	75.00
PR65S	D	36c **red**	75.00
PR66S	D	48c **red**	75.00
PR67S	D	60c **red**	75.00
PR68S	D	72c **red**	75.00
PR69S	D	84c **red**	75.00
PR70S	D	96c **red**	75.00
PR71S	D	$1.92 **pale brown**	75.00
PR72S	D	$3 **red vermilion**	75.00
PR73S	D	$6 **blue**	75.00
PR74S	D	$9 **orange**	75.00
PR75S	D	$12 **yellow green**	75.00
PR76S	D	$24 **dark violet**	75.00

PR77S	D	$36 **Indian red**	75.00
PR78S	D	$48 **yellow brown**	75.00
PR79S	D	$60 **purple**	75.00

1885

PR81S	D	1c **black**	25.00

Handstamped in Dull Purple — Specimen.

1879

Type E

PR57S	E	2c **black**	125.00
PR58S	E	3c **black**	125.00
PR59S	E	4c **black**	125.00
PR60S	E	6c **black**	125.00
PR61S	E	8c **black**	125.00
PR62S	E	10c **black**	125.00
PR63S	E	12c **red**	125.00
PR64S	E	24c **red**	125.00
PR65S	E	36c **red**	125.00
PR66S	E	48c **red**	125.00
PR67S	E	60c **red**	125.00
PR68S	E	72c **red**	125.00
PR69S	E	84c **red**	125.00
PR70S	E	96c **red**	125.00
PR71S	E	$1.92 **pale brown**	125.00
PR72S	E	$3 **red vermilion**	125.00
PR73S	E	$6 **blue**	125.00
PR74S	E	$9 **orange**	125.00
PR75S	E	$12 **yellow green**	125.00
PR76S	E	$24 **dark violet**	125.00
PR77S	E	$36 **Indian red**	125.00
PR78S	E	$48 **yellow brown**	125.00
PR79S	E	$60 **purple**	125.00

1885

PR81S	E	1c **black**	125.00

1895 **Wmk. 191**

PR114S	E	1c **black**	125.00
PR115S	E	2c **black**	125.00
PR116S	E	5c **black**	125.00
PR117S	E	10c **black**	125.00
PR118S	E	25c **carmine**	125.00
PR119S	E	50c **carmine**	125.00
PR120S	E	$2 **scarlet**	125.00
PR121S	E	$5 **dark blue**	125.00
PR122S	E	$10 **green**	125.00
PR123S	E	$20 **slate**	125.00
PR124S	E	$50 **dull rose**	125.00
PR125S	E	$100 **purple**	125.00

REVENUE STAMPS

SPECIMEN

1862

Overprint 14mm Long

R5S	G	2c Bank Check, **blue** (red)	375.00
R15S	A	2c U. S. I. R., **orange**	—

SPECIMEN

Overprint 16mm Long

R23S	H	5c Agreement, **red**	375.00
R34S	H	10c Contract, **blue** (red)	375.00
R35eS	H	10c Foreign Exchange, **ultra** (red)	375.00
R36S	H	10c Inland Exchange, **blue** (red)	375.00
R46S	H	25c Insurance, **red**	375.00
R52S	H	30c Inland Exchange, **lilac** (red)	375.00
R53S	H	40c Inland Exchange, **brown** (red)	375.00
R68S	H	$1 Foreign Exchange, **red**	375.00

Type I — Specimen

1898 **Overprint 20mm Long**

R153S	I	1c **green** (red)	475.00

1875

RB11S	H	1c **green** (red)	300.00

PRIVATE DIE MATCH STAMP

Overprinted with Type G in Red — SPECIMEN

RO133dS	G	1c **black,** A. Messinger	*500.00*

SAVINGS STAMPS

Overprinted Vertically Reading Down in Red — SPECIMEN

1911

PS4S	10c **deep blue**	—

1917-18 Handstamped "SPECIMEN" in Violet

WS1S	25c **deep green**	—
WS2S	$5 **deep green**	—

VARIOUS OVERPRINTS

Overprinted with control numbers in carmine — 7890

1861

Type J

63S	J A24	1c **pale blue** (overprint 9012)	200.00
65S	J A25	3c **brown red** (overprint 7890)	200.00
		Block of 4	*900.*
68S	J A27	10c **green** (overprint 5678)	200.00
69S	J A28	12c **gray black** (overprint 4567)	200.00
71S	J A30	30c **orange** (overprint 2345)	200.00
		Block of 4	*900.*
72S	J A31	90c **pale blue** (overprint 1234)	200.00
a.		Pair, one without overprint	—

1863-66

73S	J A32	2c **black** (overprint 8901)	300.00
		Block of 4	*1,400.*
76S	J A26	5c **brown** (overprint 6789)	200.00
77S	J A33	15c **black** (overprint 235)	250.00
		Block of 4	*1,150.*
78S	J A29	24c **gray lilac** (overprint 3456)	200.00

Special Printings Overprinted in Red or Blue — SAMPLE.

1889

Type K

212S	K A59	1c **ultramarine** (red)	75.00
210S	K A57	2c **red brown** (blue)	75.00
210S	K A57	2c **rose lake** (blue)	75.00
210S	K A57	2c **scarlet** (blue)	75.00
214S	K A46b	3c **vermilion** (blue)	75.00
211S	K A58	4c **blue green** (red)	75.00
205S	K A56	5c **gray brown** (red)	75.00
208S	K A47b	6c **brown red** (blue)	75.00
209S	K A49b	10c **brown** (red)	75.00
		Without overprint	80.00
189S	K A51a	15c **orange** (blue)	75.00
190S	K A53	30c **full black** (red)	75.00
191S	K A54	90c **carmine** (blue)	75.00

Special Printings Overprinted in Red or Blue — SAMPLE A.

Type L

212S	L A59	1c **ultramarine** (red)	75.00
210S	L A57	2c **rose lake** (blue)	75.00
		Without overprint	—
214S	L A46b	3c **purple** (red)	75.00
211S	L A58	4c **dark brown** (red)	75.00
205S	L A56	5c **yellow brown** (blue)	75.00
		Without overprint	—
208S	L A47b	6c **vermilion** (blue)	75.00
209S	L A49b	10c **green** (red)	75.00
		Without overprint	100.00
189S	L A51a	15c **blue** (red)	75.00
		Without overprint	100.00
190S	L A53	30c **full black** (red)	75.00
191S	L A54	90c **orange** (blue)	75.00

Overprinted with Type K Together with "A" in Black Manuscript

191S	M A54	90c **carmine** (blue)	140.00
209S	M A49b	10c **brown** (red)	140.00
211S	M A58	4c **blue green** (red)	140.00

"SAMPLE A" in Manuscript (red or black)

216S	N A56	5c **indigo**	160.00

Regular Issues Overprinted in Blue or Red — UNIVERSAL POSTAL CONGRESS

125 sets were distributed to delegates to the Universal Postal Congress held in Washington, D. C., May 5 to June 15, 1897.

1897 **Type O**

264S	O A87	1c **blue**	110.00
267S	O A88	2c **carmine,** type III	110.00
268S	O A89	3c **purple**	110.00
269S	O A90	4c **dark brown**	110.00
270S	O A91	5c **chestnut**	110.00
271S	O A92	6c **claret brown**	110.00
272S	O A93	8c **violet brown**	110.00
273S	O A94	10c **dark green**	110.00
274S	O A95	15c **dark blue**	110.00
275S	O A96	50c **red orange**	110.00
276S	O A97	$1 **black,** type I	350.00
276AS	O A97	$1 **black,** type II	300.00
277S	O A98	$2 **dark blue**	250.00
278S	O A99	$5 **dark green**	350.00

SPECIAL DELIVERY

E5S	O SD3	10c **blue** (R)	250.00

POSTAGE DUE

J38S	O D2	1c **deep claret**	125.00
J39S	O D2	2c **deep claret**	125.00
J40S	O D2	3c **deep claret**	125.00
J41S	O D2	5c **deep claret**	125.00
J42S	O D2	10c **deep claret**	125.00
J43S	O D2	30c **deep claret**	125.00
J44S	O D2	50c **deep claret**	125.00

NEWSPAPERS

PR114S	O N15	1c **black**	150.00
PR115S	O N15	2c **black**	150.00
PR116S	O N15	5c **black**	150.00
PR117S	O N15	10c **black**	150.00
PR118S	O N16	25c **carmine**	150.00
PR119S	O N16	50c **carmine**	150.00
PR120S	O N17	$2 **scarlet**	150.00
PR121S	O N18	$5 **dark blue**	150.00
PR122S	O N19	$10 **green**	150.00
PR123S	O N20	$20 **slate**	150.00
PR124S	O N21	$50 **dull rose**	150.00
PR125S	O N22	$100 **purple**	150.00

ENVELOPES

Overprinted — UNIVERSAL POSTAL CONGRESS

Type P

U294S	P	1c **blue**	100.00
U296S	P	1c **blue,** *amber*	100.00
U300S	P	1c **blue,** *manila*	100.00
W301S	P	1c **blue,** *manila*	100.00
U304S	P	1c **blue,** *amber manila*	100.00
U311S	P	2c **green,** Die 2	100.00
U312S	P	2c **green,** Die 2, *amber*	100.00
U313S	P	2c **green,** Die 2, *oriental buff*	100.00
U314S	P	2c **green,** Die 2, *blue*	100.00
a.		Double impression of overprint	—
U315S	P	2c **green,** Die 2, *manila*	100.00
W316S	P	2c **green,** Die 2, *manila*	100.00
U317S	P	2c **green,** Die 2, *amber manila*	100.00
U324S	P	4c **carmine**	100.00
U325S	P	4c **carmine,** *amber*	120.00
U330S	P	5c **blue,** Die 1	110.00
U331S	P	5c **blue,** Die 1, *amber*	110.00

Two settings of type P overprint are found.
See the July\August 1949 issue of the Scott Monthly Stamp Journal for others.

POSTAL CARDS

Overprinted — UNIVERSAL POSTAL CONGRESS.

Type Q

UX12S	Q	1c **black,** *buff*	750.00
UX13S	Q	2c **blue,** *cream*	750.00

PAID REPLY POSTAL CARDS

Overprinted with Type Q

UY1S	Q	1c **black,** *buff*	750.00
UY2S	Q	2c **blue,** *grayish white*	750.00

As Nos. UY1S-UY2S were made by overprinting unsevered reply cards, values are for unsevered cards.

SOUVENIR CARDS

These cards were issued as souvenirs of the philatelic and numismatic gatherings at which they were distributed by the United States Postal Service (USPS), its predecessor the United States Post Office Department (POD), or the Bureau of Engraving and Printing (BEP). They were not valid for postage.

Most of the cards bear reproductions of United States stamps with the design enlarged, altered by removal of denomination, country name and "Postage" or "Air Mail" or defaced by diagonal bars. The cards are not perforated.

Numismatic cards are listed following the philatelic cards.

A forerunner of the souvenir cards is the 1939 Philatelic Truck souvenir sheet which the Post Office Department issued and distributed in various cities visited by the Philatelic Truck. It shows the White House, printed in blue on white paper. A total of 730,040 were printed, 173,220 with gum (first printing, many destroyed) and the rest without gum. Value, with gum, $50; without gum, $8. Some of the first printing was made into coil rolls of 500. A joint line pair and a strip of three (both damaged) are known.

Standard abbreviations:
APS — American Philatelic Society
ASDA — American Stamp Dealers Association

No. SC28

1954

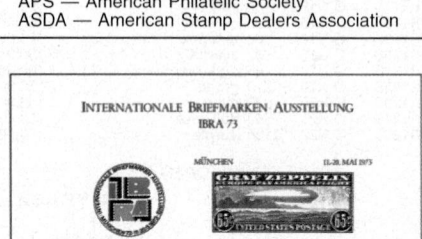

SC1	Postage Stamp Design Exhibition, Natl. Philatelic Museum, Mar. 13, 1954, Philadelphia. Card of 4 monochrome views of Washington. Inscribed: "Souvenir sheet designed, engraved and printed by members, Bureau, Engraving and Printing. Reissued by popular request."	*1,500.*

1960

SC2	Barcelona, 1st Intl. Philatelic Congress, Mar. 26-Apr. 5, 1960. Vignette, Landing of Columbus from #231. (POD)	350.00

1966

SC3	SIPEX, 6th Intl. Philatelic Exhibition, May 21-30, 1966, Washington. Card of 3 multicolored views of Washington.	95.00

1968

SC4	EFIMEX, Intl. Philatelic Exhibition, Nov. 1-9, 1968, Mexico City. #292. Spanish text. (POD)	2.00

1969

SC5	SANDIPEX, San Diego Philatelic Exhibition, July 16-20, 1969, San Diego, Cal. Card of 3 multicolored views of Washington. (BEP)	40.00
SC6	ASDA Natl. Postage Stamp Show, Nov. 21-23, 1969, New York. Card of 4 #E4. (BEP)	18.50

1970

SC7	INTERPEX, Mar. 13-15, 1970, New York. Card of 4, #1027, 1035, C35, C38. (BEP)	42.50
SC8	COMPEX, Combined Philatelic Exhibition of Chicagoland, May 29-31, 1970. Card of 4 #C18. (BEP)	9.00
SC9	PHILYMPIA, London Intl. Stamp Exhibition, Sept. 18-26 1970. Card of 3, #548-550. (POD)	1.25
SC10	HAPEX, APS Convention, Nov. 5-8, 1970, Honolulu. Card of 3, #799, C46, C55. (BEP)	8.00

1971

SC11	INTERPEX, Mar. 12-14, 1971, New York. Card of 4 #1193. Background includes #1331-1332, 1371, C76. (BEP)	1.50
SC12	WESTPEX, Western Philatelic Exhibition, Apr. 23-25, 1971, San Francisco. Card of 4, #740, 852, 966, 997. (BEP)	1.50
SC13	NAPEX 71, Natl. Philatelic Exhibition, May 21-23, 1971, Washington. Card of 3, #990, 991, 992. (BEP)	2.00
SC14	TEXANEX 71, Texas Philatelic Association and APS conventions, Aug. 26-29, 1971, San Antonio, Tex. Card of 3, #938, 1043, 1242. (BEP)	2.00
SC15	EXFILIMA 71, 3rd Inter-American Philatelic Exhibition, Nov. 6-14, 1971, Lima, Peru. Card of 3, #1111, 1126, Peru #360. Spanish text. (USPS)	1.00
SC16	ASDA Natl. Postage Stamp Show, Nov. 19-21, 1971, New York. Card of 3, #C13-C15. (BEP)	2.50
SC17	ANPHILEX '71, Anniv. Philatelic Exhibition, Nov. 26-Dec. 1, 1971, New York. Card of 2, #1-2. (BEP)	1.00

1972

SC18	INTERPEX, Mar. 17-19, 1972, New York. Card of 4 #1173. Background includes #976, 1434-1435, C69. (BEP)	1.25
SC19	NOPEX, Apr. 6-9, 1972, New Orleans. Card of 4 #1020. Background includes #323-327. (BEP)	1.25
SC20	BELGICA 72, Brussels Intl. Philatelic Exhibition, June 24-July 9, 1972, Brussels, Belgium. Card of 3, #914, 1026, 1104. Flemish and French text. (USPS)	1.00
SC21	Olympia Philatelie Munchen 72, Aug. 18-Sept. 10, 1972, Munich, Germany. Card of 4, #1460-1462, C85. German text. (USPS)	1.00
SC22	EXFILBRA 72, 4th Inter-American Philatelic Exhibition, Aug. 26-Sept. 2, 1972, Rio de Janeiro, Brazil. Card of 3 #C14, Brazil #C18-C19. Portuguese text. (USPS)	1.00
SC23	Natl. Postal Forum VI, Aug. 28-30, 1972, Washington. Card of 4 #1396. (USPS)	1.25
SC24	SEPAD '72, Oct. 20-22, 1972, Philadelphia. Card of 4 #1044. (BEP)	1.25
SC25	ASDA Natl. Postage Stamp Show, Nov. 17-19, 1972, New York. Card of 4, #883, 863, 868, 888. (BEP)	1.25
SC26	STAMP EXPO, Nov. 24-26, 1972, San Francisco. Card of 4 #C36. (BEP)	1.50

1973

SC27	INTERPEX, Mar. 9-11, 1973, New York. Card of 4 #976. (BEP)	1.25
SC28	IBRA 73 Intl. Philatelic Exhibition, Munich, May 11-20, 1973. #C13. (USPS)	1.25
SC29	COMPEX 73, May 25-27, 1973, Chicago. Card of 4 #245. (BEP)	2.75
SC30	APEX 73, Intl. Airmail Exhibition, Manchester, England, July 4-7, 1973. Card of 3, #C3a, Newfoundland #C4, Honduras #C12. (USPS)	1.25
SC31	POLSKA 73, World Philatelic Exhibition, Poznan, Poland, Aug. 19-Sept. 2, 1973. Card of 3, #1488, Poland #1944-1945. Polish text. (USPS)	1.25
SC32	NAPEX 73, Sept. 14-16, 1973, Washington. Card of 4 #C3. Background includes montage of #C4-C6. (BEP)	1.75
SC33	ASDA Natl. Postage Stamp Show, Nov. 16-18, 1973, New York. Card of 4 #908. Foreground includes #1139-1144. (BEP)	1.00
SC34	STAMP EXPO NORTH, Dec. 7-9, 1973, San Francisco. Card of 4 #C20. (BEP)	2.00

A card of 10, Nos. 1489-1498, was distributed to postal employees. Not available to public. Size: about 14x11 inches.

1974

SC35	Natl. Hobby Industry Trade Show, Feb. 3-6, 1974, Chicago. Card of 4, #1456-1459. Reproductions of silversmith (#1457) and glassmaker (#1456). (USPS)	1.50
SC36	MILCOPEX 1974, Mar. 8-10, 1974, Milwaukee. Card of 4 #C43. (BEP)	1.25
SC37	INTERNABA 1974, June 6, 1974, Basel, Switzerland. Card of 8, #1530-1537. German, French, and Italian text. (USPS)	2.25
SC38	STOCKHOLMIA 74, Intl. Philatelic Exhibition, Sept. 21-29, 1974, Stockholm. Card of 3, #836, Sweden #300, 767. Swedish text. (USPS)	2.25
SC39	EXFILMEX 74, Interamerican Philatelic Exposition, Oct. 26-Nov. 3, 1974, Mexico City. Card of 2, #1157, Mexico #910. Spanish text. (USPS)	2.25

1975

SC40	ESPANA 75, World Stamp Exhibition, Apr. 4-13, Madrid. Card of 3, #233, #1271, Spain #1312. Spanish text. (USPS)	1.25
SC41	NAPEX 75, May 9-11, 1975, Washington. Card of 4 #708. (BEP)	4.00
SC42	ARPHILA 75, June 6-16, 1975, Paris. Card of 3. Designs of #1187, #1207, France #1117. French text. (USPS)	2.00
SC43	Intl. Women's Year, 1975. Card of 3 #872, 878, 959. Reproduction of 1886 dollar bill. (BEP)	15.00
SC44	ASDA Natl. Postage Stamp Show, Nov. 21-23, 1975. Bicentennial series. Card of 4 #1003. (BEP)	18.00

1976

SC45	WERABA 76, 3rd Intl. Space Stamp Exhibition, Apr. 1-4, 1976, Zurich, Switzerland. Card of 2, #1434-1435. (USPS)	2.25
SC46	INTERPHIL 76, 7th Intl. Philatelic Exhibition, May 29-June 6, 1976. Philadelphia. Bicentennial series. Card of 4 #120. (BEP)	4.00

An Interphil '76 card issued by the American Revolution Bicentennial Administration was bound into the Interphil program. It shows an altered #1044 in black brown, the Bicentennial emblem and a view of Independence Hall. Printed by BEP.

SC48	Bicentennial Exposition on Science and Technology, May 30-Sept. 6, 1976, Kennedy Space Center, Fla. #C76. (USPS)	2.50
SC49	STAMP EXPO 76, June 11-13, 1976, Los Angeles. Bicentennial series. Card of 4, #1351, 1352, 1345, 1348. (BEP)	5.00
SC50	Colorado Statehood Centennial, Aug. 1, 1976. Card of 3, #743, 288, 1670. (USPS)	2.25
SC51	HAFNIA 76, Intl. Stamp Exhibition, Copenhagen. Aug. 20-29, 1976. Card of 2, #5, Denmark #2. Danish and English text. (USPS)	2.25
SC52	ITALIA 76, Intl. Philatelic Exhibition, Oct. 14-24, Milan. Card of 3, #1168, Italy #578, 601. Italian text. (USPS)	2.25
SC53	NORDPOSTA 76, North German Stamp Exhibition, Oct. 30-31, Hamburg. Card of 3, #689, Germany #B366, B417. German text. (USPS)	2.25

1977

SC54	MILCOPEX, Milwaukee Philatelic Society, Mar. 4-6, Milwaukee. Card of 2, #733, 1128. (BEP)	1.75
SC55	ROMPEX 77, Rocky Mountain Philatelic Exhibition, May 20-22, Denver. Card of 4 #1001. (BEP)	1.75
SC56	AMPHILEX 77, Intl. Philatelic Exhibition, May 26-June 5, Amsterdam. Card of 3, #1027, Netherlands #41, 294. Dutch text. (USPS)	2.25

SC57	SAN MARINO 77, Intl. PhilatelicExhibition, San Marino, Aug. 28-Sept. 4. Card of 3, #1-2, San Marino #1. Italian text. (USPS)	2.25
SC58	PURIPEX 77, Silver Anniv. Philatelic Exhibit, Sept. 2-5, San Juan, P. R. Card of 4 #801. (BEP)	2.00
SC59	ASDA Natl. Postage Stamp Show, Nov. 15-20, New York. Card of 4 #C45. (BEP)	2.25

1978

SC60	ROCPEX 78, Intl. Philatelic Exhibition, Mar. 20-29, Taipei. Card of 6, #1706-1709, China #1812, 1816. Chinese text. (USPS)	2.50
SC61	NAPOSTA '78 Philatelic Exhibition, May 20-25, Frankfurt. Card of 3, #555, 563, Germany #1216. German text. (USPS)	2.25
SC62	CENJEX 78, Federated Stamp Clubs of New Jersey, 30th annual exhibition, June 23-25, Freehold, NJ. Card of 9, #646, 680, 689, 1086, 1716, 4 #785. (BEP)	2.00

1979

SC63	BRASILIANA 79, Intl. Philatelic Exhibition, Sept. 15-23, Rio de Janeiro. Card of 3, #C91-C92, Brazil #1295. Portuguese text. (USPS)	3.00
SC64	JAPEX 79, Intl. Philatelic Exhibition, Nov. 2-4, Tokyo. Card of 2, #1158, Japan #1024. Japanese text. (USPS)	3.00

1980

SC65	LONDON 1980, Intl. Philatelic Exhibition, May 6-14, London. #329. (USPS)	3.00
SC66	NORWEX 80, Intl. Stamp Exhibition, June 13-22, Oslo. Card of 3, #620-621, Norway #658. Norwegian text. (USPS)	3.00
SC67	NAPEX 80, July 4-6, Washington. Card of 4 #573. (BEP)	8.50
SC68	ASDA Stamp Festival, Sept. 25-28, 1980, New York. Card of 4 #962. (BEP)	9.50
SC69	ESSEN 80, 3rd Intl. Stamp Fair, Nov. 15-19, Essen. Card of 2, #1014, Germany #723. German text. (USPS)	3.00

1981

SC70	STAMP EXPO '81 SOUTH, Mar. 20-22, Anaheim, Calif. Card of 6, #1331-1332, 4 #1287. (BEP)	11.00
SC71	WIPA 1981, Intl. Stamp Exhibition, May 22-31, Vienna. Card of 2, #1252, Austria #789. German text. (USPS)	3.00
SC72	Natl. Stamp Collecting Month, Oct., 1981. Card of 2, #245, 1918. (USPS)	3.00
SC73	PHILATOKYO '81, Intl. Stamp Exhibition, Oct. 9-18. Tokyo. Card of 2, #1531, Japan #800. Japanese text. (USPS)	3.00
SC74	NORDPOSTA 81, North German Stamp Exhibition, Nov. 7-8. Hamburg. Card of 2, #923, Germany #B538. German text. (USPS)	3.00

1982

SC75	MILCOPEX '82, Milwaukee Philatelic Association Exhibition, Mar. 5-7. Card of 4 #1137. (BEP)	11.00
SC76	CANADA 82, Intl. Philatelic Youth Exhibition, May 20-24, Toronto. Card of 2, #116, Canada #15. French and English text. (USPS)	3.00
SC77	PHILEXFRANCE '82, Intl. Philatelic Exhibition, June 11-21, Paris. Card of 2, #1753, France #1480. French text. (USPS)	3.00
SC78	Natl. Stamp Collecting Month, Oct. #C3a. (USPS)	3.00
SC79	ESPAMER '82, Intl. Philatelic Exhibition, Oct. 12-17, San Juan, P.R. Card of 4 #244. English and Spanish text. (BEP)	24.00
SC80	ESPAMER '82, Intl. Philatelic Exhibition, Oct. 12-17, San Juan, P.R. Card of 3, #801, 1437, 2024. Spanish and English text. (USPS)	3.00

1983

SC81	Joint stamp issues, Sweden and US. Mar. 24. Card of 3, #958, 2036, Sweden #1453. Swedish and English text. (USPS)	3.00
SC82	Joint stamp issues, Germany and US. Apr. 29. Card of 2, #2040, Germany #1397. German and English text. (USPS)	3.00
SC83	TEMBAL 83, Intl. Philatelic Exhibition, Mar. 21-29, Basel. Card of 2, #C71, Basel #3L1. German text. (USPS)	3.00
SC84	TEXANEX-TOPEX '83 Exhibition, June 17-19, San Antonio. Card of 5, #1660, 4 #776. (BEP)	16.00
SC85	BRASILIANA 83, Intl. Philatelic Exhibition, July 29-Aug. 7, Rio de Janeiro. Card of 2, #2, Brazil #1. Portuguese text. (USPS)	3.00
SC86	BANGKOK 83, Intl. Philatelic Exhibition, Aug. 4-13, Bangkok. Card of 2, #210, Thailand #1. Thai text. (USPS)	3.00
SC87	Intl. Philatelic Memento, 1983-84. #1387. (USPS)	3.00
SC88	Natl. Stamp Collecting Month, Oct. #293 bicolored. (USPS)	4.00
SC89	Philatelic Show '83, Boston, Oct. 21-23. Card of 2, #718-719. (BEP)	9.00
SC90	ASDA 1983, Natl. Postage Stamp Show, New York, Nov. 17-20. Card of 4 #881. (BEP)	9.00

1984

SC91	ESPANA 84, World Exhibition of Philately. Madrid, Apr. 27-May 6. Card of 4 #241. Enlarged vignette, Landing of Columbus, from #231. English and Spanish text. (BEP)	15.00
SC92	ESPANA 84, Intl. Philatelic Exhibition, Madrid, Apr. 27-May 6. Card of 2, #233, Spain #428. Spanish text. (USPS)	3.00
SC93	Stamp Expo '84 South, Anaheim, CA, Apr. 27-29. Card of 4, #1791-1794. (BEP)	12.00
SC94	COMPEX '84, Rosemont, IL, May 25-27. Card of 4 #728. (BEP)	15.00
SC95	HAMBURG '84, Intl. Exhibition for 19th UPU Congress, Hamburg, June 19-26. Card of 2, #C66, Germany #669. English, French and German text. (USPS)	3.00
SC96	St. Lawrence Seaway, 25th anniv., June 26. Card of 2, #1131, Canada #387. English and French text. (USPS)	3.25
SC97	AUSIPEX '84, Australia's 1st intl. exhibition, Melbourne, Sept. 21-30. Card of 2, #290, Western Australia #1. (USPS)	3.00
SC98	Natl. Stamp Collecting Month, Oct. #2104, tricolored. (USPS)	3.00
SC99	PHILAKOREA '84, Seoul, Oct. 22-31. Card of 2, #741, Korea #994. Korean and English text. (USPS)	3.00
SC100	ASDA 1984, Natl. Postage Stamp Show, New York, Nov. 15-18. Card of 4 #1470. (BEP)	12.00

1985

SC101	Intl. Philatelic Memento, 1985. #2. (USPS)	3.00
SC102	OLYMPHILEX '85. Intl. Philatelic Exhibition, Lausanne. Mar. 18-24. Card of 2, #C106, Switzerland #746. French and English text. (USPS)	3.00
SC103	ISRAPHIL '85. Intl. Philatelic Exhibition, Tel Aviv, May 14-22. Card of 2, #566, Israel #33. Hebrew and English text. (USPS)	3.00
SC104	LONG BEACH '85, Numismatic and Philatelic Exposition, Long Beach, CA, Jan. 31-Feb. 3. Card of 4 #954, plus a Series 1865 $20 Gold Certificate. (BEP)	10.00
SC105	MILCOPEX '85, Milwaukee Philatelic Society annual stamp show, Mar. 1-3. Card of 4 #880. (BEP)	10.50
SC106	NAPEX '85, Natl. Philatelic Exhibition, Arlington, VA, June 7-9. Card of 4 #2014. (BEP)	9.50
SC107	ARGENTINA '85, Intl. Philatelic Exhibition, Buenos Aires, July 5-14. Card of 2, #1737, Argentina #B27. Spanish text. (USPS)	3.00
SC108	MOPHILA '85, Intl. Philatelic Exhibition, Hamburg, Sept. 11-15. Card of 2, #296, Germany #B595. German text. (USPS)	3.00
SC109	ITALIA '85, Intl. Philatelic Exhibition, Rome, Oct. 25-Nov. 3. Card of 2, #1107, Italy #830. Italian text. (USPS)	3.00

1986

SC110	Statue of Liberty Centennial, Natl. Philatelic Memento, 1986. #C87. (USPS)	5.00
SC111	Garfield Perry Stamp Club, Natl. Stamp Show, Cleveland, Mar. 21-23. Card of 4 #306. (BEP)	9.50
SC112	AMERIPEX '86, Intl. Philatelic Exhibition, Chicago, May 22-June 1. Card of 3, #134, 2052, 1474.(BEP)	9.50
SC113	STOCKHOLMIA '86, Intl. Philatelic Exhibition, Stockholm, Aug. 28-Sept. 7. Card of 2, #113, Sweden #253. Swedish text. (USPS)	4.50
SC114	HOUPEX '86, Natl. Stamp Show, Houston. Sept. 5-7. Card of 3, #1035, 1042, 1044A. (BEP)	11.50
SC115	LOBEX '86, Numismatic and Philatelic Exhibition, Long Beach, CA, Oct. 2-5. Long Beach Stamp Club 60th anniv. Card of 4, #291, plus a series 1907 $10 Gold Certificate. (BEP)	15.00
SC116	DCSE '86, Dallas Coin and Stamp Exhibition, Dallas, Dec. 11-14. Card of 4 #550, plus $10,000 Federal Reserve Note. (BEP)	15.00

1987

SC117	CAPEX '87, Intl. Philatelic Exhibition, Toronto, June 13-21. Card of 2, #569, Canada #883. English and French text. (USPS)	4.50
SC118	HAFNIA '87, Intl. Philatelic Exhibition, Copenhagen, Oct. 16-25. Card of 2, #299, Denmark #B52. English and Danish text. (USPS)	4.50
SC119	SESCAL '87, Stamp Exhibition of Southern California, Los Angeles, Oct. 16-18. #798. (BEP)	11.50
SC120	HSNA '87, Hawaii State Numismatic Association Exhibition, Honolulu, Nov. 12-15. #799 and a Series 1923 $5 Silver Certificate. (BEP)	20.00
SC121	MONTE CARLO, Intl. Philatelic Exhibition, Monte Carlo, Nov. 13-17. Card of 3, #2287, 2300, Monaco #1589. French and English text. (USPS)	4.00

1988

SC122	FINLANDIA '88, Intl. Philatelic Exhibition, Helsinki, June 1-12. Card of 2, #836, Finland #768. English and Finnish text. (USPS)	4.00
SC123	STAMPSHOW '88, APS natl. stamp show, Detroit, Aug. 25-28. #835. (BEP)	9.50
SC124	MIDAPHIL '88, Kansas City, Nov. 18-20. #627. (BEP)	9.50

1989

SC125	PHILEXFRANCE '89 intl. philatelic exhibition, Paris, July 7-17. Card of 2, #C120, France #2144. English and French text. (USPS)	7.75
SC126	STAMPSHOW '89, APS natl. stamp show, Anaheim, CA, Aug. 24-27. #565. Various reproductions of the portrait of Chief Hollow Horn Bear from which the stamp was designed. (BEP)	9.50
SC127	WORLD STAMP EXPO '89, Washington, Nov. 17-Dec. 3. Card of 4, #2433a-2433d. Embossed reproductions of Supreme Court, Washington Monument, Capitol and Jefferson Memorial. (USPS)	8.00

1990

SC128	ARIPEX 90, Arizona Philatelic Exhibition, Phoenix, Apr. 20-22. Card of 2, #285 and #285 with black vignette. (BEP)	9.50
SC129	STAMPSHOW '90, APS natl. stamp show, Cincinnati, Aug. 23-26. Card of 2, #286 and essay with frame of #286 in red with vignette of #293 in black. (BEP)	9.50
SC130	STAMP WORLD LONDON 90, London, England, May 3-13. Card of 2, #1, Great Britain #1. (USPS)	7.00

1991

SC131	STAMPSHOW '91, APS natl. stamp show, Philadelphia, Aug. 22-25. Card of 3, #537, Essays #537a-E1, 537b-E1. Embossed figure of "Freedom." (BEP)	11.00

1992

SC132	World Columbian Stamp Expo, Chicago, May 22-31. Card of 2, #118, 119b. (BEP)	10.00
SC133	Savings Bond, produced as gift to BEP employees, available to public. 1954 Savings stamp, Series E War Savings bond. (BEP)	12.00
SC134	STAMPSHOW '92. Oakland, CA (BEP)	9.50

1993

SC135	Combined Federal Campaign, produced as gift to BEP employees, available to public. #1016. Photos of 6 other stamps. (BEP)	11.00
SC136	ASDA stamp show, New York, May 1993. Card of 7 #859, 864, 869, 874, 879, 884, 889 (BEP)	11.00
SC137	Savings Bonds, produced as gift to BEP employees, available to the public Aug. 1993. $200 War Savings Bond, #WS8 (BEP)	11.50
SC138	Omaha Stamp Show, Sept. 1993. Card of 4, #E7, PR2, JQ5, QE4 (BEP)	11.00
SC139	ASDA New York Show, Oct. 1993. Card of 2, #499-E1a and similar with negative New York precancel (BEP)	11.00

1994

SC140	Sandical, San Diego, CA, Feb. 1994. Card of 4 #E4 (BEP)	10.00
SC140A	Centennial of U.S. Stamp Production, July 1994, BEP Intaglio Print. Card of 13 Types A87-A99 in black	125.00
SC141	Savings Bonds, produced as a gift to BEP employees, available to the public Aug. 1, 1994. #WS7-WS11.	16.00
SC142	STAMPSHOW '94, APS National Stamp Show Pittsburgh, PA. Card of 3, 1c, 2c and 10c Type D2	10.00
SC143	American Stamp Dealers Association, Nov. 1994, New York, NY. Card of 4, 2c, 12c, $3, $6 Types N4-N5, N7-N8	11.00

1995

SC144	Natl. Exhibition of the Columbus Philatelic Club, Apr. 1995, Columbus, OH. Block of 4 of #261.	9.00

No. 144 was issued folded in half.

SC145	Centennial of U.S. Stamp Production, June 1995, BEP Intaglio Print. Card of 13 of Types A87-A99 in blue	85.00
SC146	Savings Bonds, produced as a gift to BEP employees, available to the public Aug. 1, 1995. Card of 3 #905, 907, 940	9.50
SC147	American Stamp Dealers Association, Nov. 1995, New York, NY. Block of 4, #292	11.00

No. SC147 issued folded in half.

1996

SC148	CAPEX '96, Toronto, Canada, June 1996. Block of 4, #291	11.00
SC149	Olymphilex '96, Atlanta, GA, July-August, 1996, Block of 4, #718	11.00

SC150 Billings Stamp Club, Billings, MT, Oct. 1996, Block of 4, #1130 — 11.00

1997

SC151 Long Beach Coin & Collectibles Expo, Feb. 1997, Lock Seal revenue stamp — 11.00
SC152 PACIFIC 97, May 1997, Process or renovated butter revenue stamp — 10.00
SC153 Milcopex, Milwaukee, WI, Sept. 1997, Newspaper Types N15, N16 and N19 — 11.00

1998

SC154 OKPEX 98, Oklahoma City, OK, May 1998, Block of 4, #922 — 11.00
SC155 Centennial of Trans-Mississippi Exposition Issue, Sept. 1998, BEP Engraved Print. Card of 9 die impressions in green of designs A100-A108 — 72.50

1999

SC156 Philadelphia National Stamp Exhibition, Oct. 1999, Card of 4, #RS281, RS284, RS290, RS306 — 12.00

2003

SC157 Georgia Numismatic Association, Dalton, GA (card of one #C45 in blue gray, without denomination and some inscriptions) — 45.00

2005

SC158 ANA Coin, Stamp and Collectibles Show, Las Vegas, Oct. 2005, Card of 7, #999, 1248, RF1, RF11, RF26, 7c essay of #RF11, 5c essay of #RF26 — *40.00*

2006

SC159 ANA World's Fair of Money, Denver, CO, card of #1001 without denomination and some inscriptions, 1908 $10 silver certificate — *40.00*
SC160 Long Beach Coin, Stamp & Collectible Expo, Long Beach, CA, Sept. 2006, Card of #997 in blue, California state shield, Reverse of Series 1923 $10 United States Note — *40.00*

2007

SC161 Whitman Baltimore Coin and Collectibles Convention, Baltimore, MD, Nov. 2007, Card of #962, 1142 in black — 35.00

2008

SC162 Florida United Numismatists, Orlando, FL, Jan. 2008, Card of #Q12, 952 — 35.00

NUMISMATIC SOUVENIR CARDS

Included in this section are cards issued by the Bureau of Engraving and Printing showing fractional currency, paper money or parts thereof, for numismatic shows. Not included are press samples sold or given away only at the shows and other special printings. Cards showing both money and stamps are listed in the preceeding section.

Standard abbreviations:
ANA- American Numismatic Association
IPMS- International Paper Money Show
FUN- Florida United Numismatists

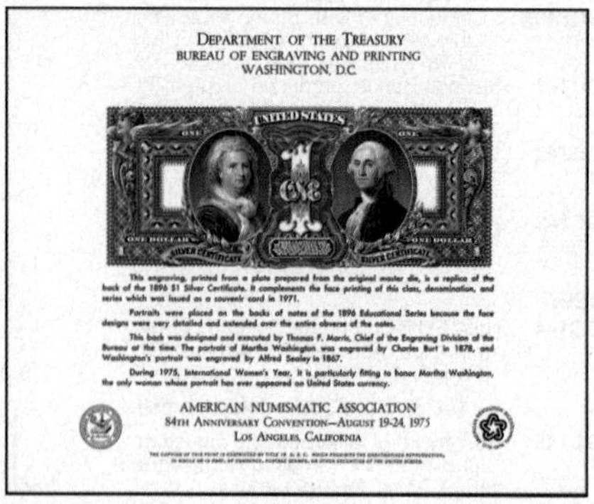

No. NSC8

1969-84

NSC1	ANA	60.00
NSC2	Fresno Numismatic Fair	*275.00*
NSC3	ANA ('70)	75.00
NSC4	ANA ('71)	8.00
NSC5	ANA ('72)	8.00
NSC6	ANA ('73)	10.00
NSC7	ANA ('74)	9.00
NSC8	ANA ('75)	9.50
NSC9	ANA ('76)	8.00
NSC10	ANA ('77)	12.00
NSC11	IPMS ('78)	4.00
NSC12	ANA ('80)	16.00
NSC13	IPMS ('80)	22.00
NSC14	IPMS ('81)	16.00
NSC15	ANA ('81)	12.00
NSC16	IPMS ('82)	13.00
NSC17	ANA ('82)	10.50
NSC18	FUN ('83)	20.00
NSC19	ANA ('83)	16.00
NSC20	FUN ('84)	19.00
NSC21	IPMS ('84)	22.00
NSC22	ANA ('84)	15.00

1985

NSC23	International Coin Club of El Paso	18.00
NSC24	Pacific Northwest Numismatic Assoc.	15.00
NSC25	IPMS	18.00
NSC26	ANA	16.00
NSC27	International Paper Money Convention (IPMC)	15.00

1986

NSC28	FUN	15.00
NSC29	ANA Midwinter	15.00
NSC30	IPMS	13.00
NSC31	ANA	12.00
NSC32	National World Paper Money Convention (NWPMC)	12.00

1987

NSC33	FUN	15.00
NSC34	ANA Midwinter	14.00
NSC35	BEP Fort Worth	20.00
NSC36	IPMS	14.00
NSC37	ANA	12.00
NSC38	Great Eastern Numismatic Association	15.00

1988

NSC39	FUN	12.00
NSC40	ANA Midwinter	16.00
NSC41	IPMS	14.00
NSC42	ANA	20.00
NSC43	Illinois Numismatic Association	13.00

1989

NSC44	FUN	13.50
NSC45	ANA Midwinter	17.50
NSC46	TNA	18.00
NSC47	IPMS	13.00
NSC48	ANA	15.00

1990

NSC49	FUN	14.00
NSC50	ANA Midwinter	12.00
NSC51	Central States Numismatic Society	13.00
NSC52	Dallas Coin and Stamp Exposition	15.00
NSC53	ANA, Seattle, WA	22.00
NSC54	Westex	14.50
NSC55	Honolulu State Numismatic Association	15.00

1991

NSC56	FUN	14.00
NSC57	ANA Midwinter, Dallas, Texas	16.00
NSC58	IPMS	14.00
NSC59	ANA Convention, Chicago, IL	20.00

1992

NSC60	FUN	10.00
NSC61	Central States Numismatics Society	20.00
NSC62	IPMS, Memphis, TN	12.00
NSC63	ANA Convention, Orlando, FL	17.00

1993

NSC64	FUN	17.00
NSC65	ANA Convention, Colorado Springs, CO	16.50
NSC66	Texas Numismatic Association Show	13.00
NSC67	Georgia Numismatic Association Show	15.00
NSC68	ANA Convention, Baltimore, MD	15.00
NSC69	IPMS, Memphis, TN	18.00

1994

NSC70	FUN	12.00
NSC71	ANA Convention, New Orleans, LA	20.00
NSC72	European Paper Money Bourse, Netherlands	16.00
NSC73	IPMS, Memphis, TN	14.00
NSC74	ANA Convention, Detroit, MI	14.00

Nos. NSC75-NSC79 were issued folded in half.

1995

NSC75	FUN	20.00
NSC76	New York Intl. Numismatic Convention	16.00
NSC77	IPMS, Memphis, TN	15.00
NSC78	ANA Convention, Anaheim, CA	17.50
NSC79	Long Beach Numismatic/Philatelic Exposition, Long Beach, CA	14.00

1996

NSC80	FUN	18.00
NSC81	Suburban Washington/Baltimore Coin Show	15.00
NSC82	Central States Numismatic Association	18.00
NSC83	ANA Convention, Denver, CO	18.00

1997

NSC84	FUN	20.00
NSC85	Bay State Coin Show	14.00
NSC86	IPMS, Memphis, TN	14.00
NSC87	ANA Convention, New York, NY	15.00

1998

NSC88	FUN	15.00
NSC89	IPMS, Memphis, TN	14.00
NSC90	ANA Convention, Portland, OR	15.00
NSC91	Long Beach Coin & Collectibles Expo, Long Beach, CA	15.00

1999

NSC92	FUN	18.00
NSC93	Bay State Coin Club	16.00
NSC94	IPMS, Memphis, TN	18.00
NSC95	ANA Convention, Rosemont, IL	17.50

2001

NSC96	FUN	18.00
NSC97	Intl. Paper Money Show, Memphis, TN	16.00
NSC98	ANA Convention, Atlanta, GA	16.00
NSC99	Long Beach Coin & Collectibles Expo, Long Beach, CA	17.50

2002

NSC100	FUN	18.00
NSC101	Texas Numismatic Association, Fort Worth	20.00
NSC102	ANA Convention, New York, NY	18.00
NSC103	Long Beach Coin & Collectibles Expo, Long Beach, CA	18.00

2003

NSC104	FUN	45.00

2002

NSC106	ANA Convention, Baltimore, MD	45.00

2003

NSC107	Natl. & World Paper Money Convention, St. Louis, MO	45.00

2004

NSC108	ANA Convention, Portland, OR	70.00
NSC109	ANA Convention, Pittsburgh, PA	45.00

2005

NSC110	FUN	40.00
NSC111	Money Show of the Southwest, Houston, TX	40.00
NSC112	Long Beach Coin & Stamp Expo, Long Beach, CA	40.00
NSC113	ANA National Money Show, Kansas City, MO	40.00
NSC114	ANA World's Fair of Money, San Francisco, CA	40.00

2006

NSC115	ANA National Money Show, Atlanta, GA	35.00

2007

NSC116	ANA National Money Show, Charlotte, NC	35.00
NSC117	ANA World's Fair of Money, Milwaukee, WI	35.00

2008

NSC118	ANA National Money Show, Phoenix, AZ	35.00

COMMEMORATIVE PANELS

The U.S. Postal Service began issuing commemorative panels September 20, 1972, with the Wildlife Conservation issue (Scott Nos. 1464-1467). Each panel is devoted to a separate issue. It includes unused examples of the stamp or stamps (usually a block of four), reproduction of steel engravings, and background information on the subject of the issue. Values are for panels without protective sleeves. Values for panels with protective sleeves are 10% to 25% higher.

No. CP53

1972

CP1	Wildlife Conservation, #1467a	7.00
CP2	Mail Order, #1468	7.00
CP3	Osteopathic Medicine, #1469	14.00
CP4	Tom Sawyer, #1470	13.00
CP5	Pharmacy, #1473	9.50
CP6	Christmas (angel), #1471	9.50
CP7	Santa Claus, #1472	9.50
CP8	Stamp Collecting, #1474	7.00

1973

CP9	Love, #1475	9.00
CP10	Pamphleteers, #1476	7.00
CP11	George Gershwin, #1484	9.00
CP12	Posting a Broadside, #1477	6.50
CP13	Copernicus, #1488	6.50
CP14	Postal Service Employees, #1489-1498	6.50
CP15	Harry S Truman, #1499	11.00
CP16	Postrider, #1478	9.00
CP17	Boston Tea Party, #1483a	25.00
CP18	Electronics Progress, #1500-1502, C86	11.00
CP19	Robinson Jeffers, #1485	6.50
CP20	Lyndon B. Johnson, #1503	9.00
CP21	Henry O. Tanner, #1486	6.50
CP22	Willa Cather, #1487	6.50
CP23	Drummer, #1479	12.00
CP24	Angus and Longhorn Cattle, #1504	9.00
CP25	Christmas (Madonna), #1507	13.50
CP26	Christmas Tree, needlepoint, #1508	11.50

1974

CP27	Veterans of Foreign Wars, #1525	6.50
CP28	Robert Frost, #1526	7.50
CP29	EXPO '74, #1527	9.50
CP30	Horse Racing, #1528	12.00
CP31	Skylab, #1529	14.00
CP32	Universal Postal Union, #1537a	9.00
CP33	Mineral Heritage, #1541a	12.00
CP34	Kentucky Settlement (Ft. Harrod), #1542	7.00
CP35	First Continental Congress, #1546a	9.00
CP36	Chautauqua, #1505	9.00
CP37	Kansas Wheat, #1506	9.00
CP38	Energy Conservation, #1547	7.00
CP39	Sleepy Hollow Legend, #1548	9.00
CP40	Retarded Children, #1549	6.50
CP41	Christmas (Currier-Ives), #1551	9.50
CP42	Christmas (angel), #1550	9.50

1975

CP43	Benjamin West, #1553	9.00
CP44	Pioneer 10, #1556	15.00
CP45	Collective Bargaining, #1558	7.50
CP46	Contributors to the Cause, #1559-1562	9.00
CP47	Mariner 10, #1557	17.50
CP48	Lexington-Concord Battle, #1563	7.00
CP49	Paul Laurence Dunbar, #1554	9.00
CP50	D. W. Griffith, #1555	12.00
CP51	Battle of Bunker Hill, #1564	9.00
CP52	Military Services (uniforms), #1568a	8.75
CP53	Apollo Soyuz, #1569a	16.00
CP54	World Peace through Law, #1576	7.00
CP55	International Women's Year, #1571	7.00
CP56	Postal Service 200 Years, #1575a	7.00
CP57	Banking and Commerce, #1577a	9.00
CP58	Early Christmas Card, #1580	9.00
CP59	Christmas (Madonna), #1579	9.00

1976

CP60	Spirit of '76, #1631a	12.50
CP61	Interphil '76, #1632	11.00
CP62	State Flags, block of 4 from #1633-1682	25.00
CP63	Telephone Centenary, #1683	9.00
CP64	Commercial Aviation, #1684	11.00
CP65	Chemistry, #1685	9.00
CP66	Benjamin Franklin, #1690	10.00
CP67	Declaration of Independence, #1694a	9.00
CP68	12th Winter Olympics, #1698a	11.50
CP69	Clara Maass, #1699	16.50
CP70	Adolph S. Ochs, #1700	11.00
CP71	Christmas (Currier print), #1702	11.00
CP72	Christmas (Copley Nativity), #1701	13.00

1977

CP73	Washington at Princeton, #1704	14.00
CP74	Sound Recording, #1705	40.00
CP75	Pueblo Art, #1709a	90.00
CP76	Lindbergh Flight, #1710	95.00
CP77	Colorado Statehood, #1711	16.50
CP78	Butterflies, #1715a	19.00
CP79	Lafayette, #1716	16.00
CP80	Skilled Hands for Independence, #1720a	16.00
CP81	Peace Bridge, #1721	16.00
CP82	Battle of Oriskany, #1722	16.00
CP83	Energy Conservation-Development, #1723a	16.00
CP84	Alta California, #1725	16.00
CP85	Articles of Confederation, #1726	24.00
CP86	Talking Pictures, #1727	19.00
CP87	Surrender at Saratoga, #1728	20.00
CP88	Christmas (Washington at Valley Forge), #1729	18.50
CP89	Christmas (rural mailbox), #1730	35.00

1978

CP90	Carl Sandburg, #1731	9.50
CP91	Captain Cook, #1732a	15.50
CP92	Harriet Tubman, #1744	12.00
CP93	American Quilts, #1748a	19.00
CP94	American Dance, #1752a	14.00
CP95	French Alliance, #1753	11.50
CP96	Pap Test, #1754	12.00
CP97	Jimmie Rodgers, #1755	14.50
CP98	Photography, #1758	14.50
CP99	George M. Cohan, #1756	19.00
CP100	Viking Missions, #1759	42.50
CP101	American Owls, #1763a	42.50
CP102	American Trees, #1767a	34.00
CP103	Christmas (Madonna), #1768	16.00
CP104	Christmas (hobby-horse), #1769	16.50

1979

CP105	Robert F. Kennedy, #1770	14.50
CP106	Martin Luther King, Jr., #1771	11.00
CP107	Year of the Child, #1772	9.00
CP108	John Steinbeck, #1773	8.50
CP109	Albert Einstein, #1774	11.50
CP110	Pennsylvania Toleware, #1778a	14.00
CP111	American Architecture, #1782a	11.00
CP112	Endangered Flora, #1786a	11.50
CP113	Seeing Eye Dogs, #1787	9.50
CP114	Special Olympics, #1788	9.00
CP115	John Paul Jones, #1789	11.00
CP116	Olympic Games, #1794a	11.00
CP117	Christmas (Madonna), #1799	12.00
CP118	Christmas (Santa Claus), #1800	12.00
CP119	Will Rogers, #1801	13.00
CP120	Viet Nam Veterans, #1802	11.50
CP121	10c, 31c Olympics, #1790, C97	12.00

1980

CP122	Winter Olympics, #1798a	9.00
CP123	W.C Fields, #1803	16.00
CP124	Benjamin Banneker, #1804	9.00
CP125	Frances Perkins, #1821	7.00
CP126	Emily Bissell, #1823	12.00
CP127	Helen Keller, #1824	7.00
CP128	Veterans Administration, #1825	7.00
CP129	Galvez, #1826	7.00
CP130	Coral Reefs, #1830a	10.00
CP131	Organized Labor, #1831	7.00
CP132	Edith Wharton, #1832	7.00
CP133	Education, #1833	7.00
CP134	Indian Masks, #1837a	17.00
CP135	Architecture, #1841a	9.00
CP136	Christmas Window, #1842	11.50
CP137	Christmas Toys, #1843	12.00

1981

CP138	Dirksen, #1874	8.00
CP139	Young, #1875	12.00
CP140	Flowers, #1879a	12.00
CP141	Red Cross, #1910	9.00
CP142	Savings and Loan, #1911	9.00
CP143	Space Achievements, #1919a	16.50
CP144	Management, #1920	7.00
CP145	Wildlife, #1924a	11.50
CP146	Disabled, #1925	7.00
CP147	Millay, #1926	7.00
CP148	Architecture, #1931a	9.00
CP149	Zaharias, Jones, #1932, 1933	42.50
CP150	Remington, #1934	12.00
CP151	18c, 20c Hoban, #1935, 1936	7.00
CP152	Yorktown, Va. Capes, #1938a	7.00
CP153	Madonna and Child, #1939	10.00
CP154	Teddy Bear, #1940	11.00
CP155	John Hanson, #1941	7.00
CP156	Desert Plants, #1945a	11.50

1982

CP157	FDR, #1950	11.50
CP158	Love, #1951	14.00
CP159	Washington, #1952	15.00
CP160	Birds and Flowers, block of 4 from #1953-2002	42.50
CP161	US-Netherlands, #2003	16.50
CP162	Library of Congress, #2004	14.00
CP163	Knoxville World's Fair, #2009a	12.00
CP164	Horatio Alger, #2010	13.00
CP165	Aging, #2011	13.00
CP166	Barrymores, #2012	16.00
CP167	Dr. Mary Walker, #2013	12.00
CP168	Peace Garden, #2014	13.00
CP169	Libraries, #2015	12.00
CP170	Jackie Robinson, #2016	40.00
CP171	Touro Synagogue, #2017	12.00
CP172	Wolf Trap Farm, #2018	14.00
CP173	Architecture, #2022a	15.00
CP174	Francis of Assisi, #2023	14.00
CP175	Ponce de Leon, #2024	14.00
CP176	Puppy, Kitten, #2025	22.50
CP177	Madonna and Child, #2026	19.00
CP178	Children Playing, #2030a	19.00

1983

CP179	Science, #2031	7.00
CP180	Ballooning, #2035a	9.00
CP181	US-Sweden, #2036	7.00
CP182	CCC, #2037	7.00
CP183	Priestley, #2038	7.00
CP184	Voluntarism, #2039	19.00
CP185	German Immigration, #2040	7.00
CP186	Brooklyn Bridge, #2041	9.50
CP187	TVA, #2042	7.00
CP188	Fitness, #2043	7.00
CP189	Scott Joplin, #2044	9.50
CP190	Medal of Honor, #2045	11.50
CP191	Babe Ruth, #2046	32.50
CP192	Hawthorne, #2047	7.00
CP193	13c Olympics, #2051a	9.00
CP194	28c Olympics, #C104a	9.00
CP195	40c Olympics, #C108a	9.50
CP196	35c Olympics, #C112a	11.50
CP197	Treaty of Paris, #2052	8.00
CP198	Civil Service, #2053	8.00
CP199	Metropolitan Opera, #2054	12.00
CP200	Inventors, #2058a	10.00
CP201	Streetcars, #2062a	12.00
CP202	Madonna and Child, #2063	11.50
CP203	Santa Claus, #2064	11.50
CP204	Martin Luther, #2065	10.00

1984

CP205	Alaska, #2066	7.00
CP206	Winter Olympics, #2070a	9.00
CP207	FDIC, #2071	7.00
CP208	Love, #2072	7.00
CP209	Woodson, #2073	9.00
CP210	Conservation, #2074	7.00
CP211	Credit Union, #2075	6.50
CP212	Orchids, #2079a	9.00
CP213	Hawaii, #2080	9.00
CP214	National Archives, #2081	6.50
CP215	Olympics, #2085a	9.00
CP216	World Expo, #2086	7.00
CP217	Health Research, #2087	6.50
CP218	Fairbanks, #2088	9.00
CP219	Thorpe, #2089	9.00
CP220	McCormack, #2090	9.00
CP221	St. Lawrence Seaway, #2091	9.00
CP222	Waterfowl, #2092	13.50
CP223	Roanoke Voyages, #2093	6.50
CP224	Melville, #2094	9.00
CP225	Horace Moses, #2095	6.50
CP226	Smokey Bear, #2096	32.50
CP227	Roberto Clemente, #2097	42.50
CP228	Dogs, #2101a	12.00
CP229	Crime Prevention, #2102	7.00
CP230	Hispanic Americans, #2103	6.50
CP231	Family Unity, #2104	6.50
CP232	Eleanor Roosevelt, #2105	16.00
CP233	Readers, #2106	6.50
CP234	Madonna and Child, #2107	9.00
CP235	Child's Santa, #2108	9.00
CP236	Vietnam Memorial, #2109	14.50

1985

CP237	Jerome Kern, #2110	9.00
CP238	Bethune, #2137	9.00
CP239	Duck Decoys, #2141a	22.50
CP240	Winter Special Olympics, #2142	6.50
CP241	Love, #2143	7.00
CP242	REA, #2144	6.50
CP243	AMERIPEX '86, #2145	7.50
CP244	Abigail Adams, #2146	6.50
CP245	Bartholdi, #2147	12.00
CP246	Korean Veterans, #2152	12.50
CP247	Social Security, #2153	6.50
CP248	World War I Veterans, #2154	8.00
CP249	Horses, #2158a	17.00

CP250	Education, #2159	7.00
CP251	Youth Year, #2163a	16.00
CP252	Hunger, #2164	6.50
CP253	Madonna and Child, #2165	10.00
CP254	Poinsettias, #2166	10.00

1986

CP255	Arkansas, #2167	7.00
CP256	Stamp Collecting booklet pane, #2201a	9.00
CP257	Love, #2202	11.50
CP258	Sojourner Truth, #2203	11.50
CP259	Texas Republic, #2204	9.00
CP260	Fish booklet pane, #2209a	11.50
CP261	Hospitals, #2210	7.00
CP262	Duke Ellington, #2211	11.00
CP263	Presidents Souvenir Sheet No. 1, #2216	10.00
CP264	Presidents Souvenir Sheet No. 2, #2217	10.00
CP265	Presidents Souvenir Sheet No. 3, #2218	10.00
CP266	Presidents Souvenir Sheet No. 4, #2219	10.00
CP267	Arctic Explorers, #2223a	11.50
CP268	Statue of Liberty, #2224	11.50
CP269	Navajo Art, #2238a	15.00
CP270	T.S. Eliot, #2239	9.00
CP271	Woodcarved Figurines, #2243a	11.50
CP272	Madonna and Child, #2244	8.00
CP273	Village Scene, #2245	8.00

1987

CP274	Michigan, #2246	9.00
CP275	Pan American Games, #2247	6.50
CP276	Love, #2248	9.00
CP277	du Sable, #2249	9.00
CP278	Caruso, #2250	11.50
CP279	Girl Scouts, #2251	14.50
CP280	Special Occasions booklet pane, #2274a	8.00
CP281	United Way, #2275	7.00
CP282	Wildlife, #2286, 2287, 2296, 2297, 2306, 2307, 2316, 2317, 2326, 2327	10.00
CP283	Wildlife, #2288, 2289, 2298, 2299, 2308, 2309, 2318, 2319, 2328, 2329	10.00
CP284	Wildlife, #2290, 2291, 2300, 2301, 2310, 2311, 2320, 2321, 2330, 2331	10.00
CP285	Wildlife, #2292, 2293, 2302, 2303, 2312, 2313, 2322, 2323, 2332, 2333	10.00
CP286	Wildlife, #2294, 2295, 2304, 2305, 2314, 2315, 2324, 2325, 2334, 2335	10.00

1987-90

CP287	Delaware, #2336	12.00
CP288	Pennsylvania, #2337	9.00
CP289	New Jersey, #2338	9.00
CP290	Georgia, #2339	9.00
CP291	Connecticut, #2340	9.00
CP292	Massachusetts, #2341	9.00
CP293	Maryland, #2342	9.00
CP294	South Carolina, #2343	9.00
CP295	New Hampshire, #2344	9.00
CP296	Virginia, #2345	9.00
CP297	New York, #2346	9.00
CP298	North Carolina, #2347	9.00
CP299	Rhode Island, #2348	9.00

1987

CP300	U.S.-Morocco, #2349	7.00
CP301	William Faulkner, #2350	7.00
CP302	Lacemaking, #2354a	12.00
CP303	Drafting of the Constitution booklet pane, #2359a	9.00
CP304	Signing of the Constitution, #2360	9.00
CP305	Certified Public Accounting, #2361	52.50
CP306	Locomotives booklet pane, #2366a	12.00
CP307	Madonna and Child, #2367	8.00
CP308	Christmas Ornaments, #2368	7.00

1988

CP309	Winter Olympics, #2369	9.00
CP310	Australia Bicentennial, #2370	11.50
CP311	James Weldon Johnson, #2371	9.00
CP312	Cats, #2375a	12.00
CP313	Knute Rockne, #2376	18.50
CP314	New Sweden, #C117	9.00
CP315	Francis Ouimet, #2377	27.50
CP316	25c, 45c Love, #2378 and #2379	9.00
CP317	Summer Olympics, #2380	9.00
CP318	Classic Automobiles booklet pane, #2385a	12.00
CP319	Antarctic Explorers, #2389a	9.00
CP320	Carousel Animals, #2393a	12.00
CP321	Special Occasions booklet singles, #2395-2398	9.00
CP322	Madonna and Child, Sleigh, #2399, 2400	9.00

1989

CP323	Montana, #2401	9.00
CP324	A. Philip Randolph, #2402	11.00
CP325	North Dakota, #2403	9.00
CP326	Washington Statehood, #2404	9.00
CP327	Steamboats booklet pane, #2409a	11.50
CP328	World Stamp Expo, #2410	7.00
CP329	Arturo Toscanini, #2411	11.50

1989-90

CP330	House of Representatives, #2412	11.50
CP331	Senate, #2413	11.50
CP332	Executive Branch, #2414	11.50
CP333	Supreme Court, #2415	11.50

1989

CP334	South Dakota, #2416	9.00
CP335	Lou Gehrig, #2417	40.00
CP336	French Revolution, #C120	9.00
CP337	Ernest Hemingway, #2418	16.00
CP338	Letter Carriers, #2420	9.00
CP339	Bill of Rights, #2421	9.00
CP340	Dinosaurs, #2425a	21.00
CP341	Pre-Columbian Artifacts, #2426, C121	9.25
CP342	Madonna, Sleigh with Presents, #2427, 2428	11.00
CP343	Traditional Mail Delivery, #2437a	9.00
CP344	Futuristic Mail Delivery, #C125a	11.00

1990

CP345	Idaho, #2439	9.00
CP346	Love, #2440	9.00
CP347	Ida B. Wells, #2442	15.00
CP348	Wyoming, #2444	9.00
CP349	Classic Films, #2448a	22.00
CP350	Marianne Moore, #2449	6.50
CP351	Lighthouses booklet pane, #2474a	22.00
CP352	Olympians, #2500a	15.00
CP353	Indian Headdresses booklet pane, #2505c	14.00
CP354	Micronesia, Marshall Islands, #2507a	9.00
CP355	Sea Creatures, #2511a	19.00
CP356	Grand Canyon & Tropical Coastline, #2512, C127	11.00
CP357	Eisenhower, #2513	11.50
CP358	Madonna and Child, Christmas Tree, #2514-2515	11.00

1991

CP359	Switzerland, #2532	12.00
CP360	Vermont Statehood, #2533	9.00
CP361	Savings Bonds, #2534	8.00
CP362	Love, #2535-2536	11.00
CP363	William Saroyan, #2538	21.00
CP364	Fishing Flies, #2549a	19.00
CP365	Cole Porter, #2550	9.00
CP366	Antarctic Treaty, C130	9.00
CP367	Operations Desert Shield & Desert Storm, #2551	40.00
CP368	Summer Olympics, #2557a	11.00
CP369	Numismatics, #2558	9.00
CP370	World War II, #2559	17.00
CP371	Basketball, #2560	21.00
CP372	District of Columbia, #2561	9.00
CP373	Comedians, #2566c	17.00
CP374	Jan E. Matzeliger, #2567	11.00
CP375	Space Exploration, #2577a	16.50
CP376	Bering Land Bridge, #C131	9.00
CP377	Madonna and Child, Santa in Chimney, #2578-2579	14.00

1992

CP378	Winter Olympics, #2615a	10.00
CP379	World Columbian Stamp Expo '92, #2616	11.00
CP380	W.E.B. DuBois, #2617	17.00
CP381	Love, #2618	10.00
CP382	Olympic Baseball, #2619	42.50
CP383	Voyages of Columbus, #2623a	13.00
CP384	Columbus, #2624-2625	70.00
CP385	Columbus, #2626, 2629	70.00
CP386	Columbus, #2627-2628	70.00
CP387	New York Stock Exchange, #2630	22.50
CP388	Space Accomplishments, #2634a	17.00
CP389	Alaska Highway, #2635	9.00
CP390	Kentucky Statehood, #2636	9.00
CP391	Summer Olympics, #2641a	11.00
CP392	Hummingbirds, #2646a	17.00
CP393	World War II, #2697	17.00
CP394	Wildflowers, #2647, 2648, 2657, 2658, 2667, 2668, 2677, 2678, 2687, 2688	40.00
CP395	Wildflowers, #2649, 2650, 2659, 2660, 2669, 2670, 2679, 2680, 2689, 2690	40.00
CP396	Wildflowers, #2651, 2652, 2661, 2662, 2671, 2672, 2681, 2682, 2691, 2692	40.00
CP397	Wildflowers, #2653, 2654, 2663, 2664, 2673, 2674, 2683, 2684, 2693, 2694	40.00
CP398	Wildflowers, #2655, 2656, 2665, 2666, 2675, 2676, 2685, 2686, 2695, 2696	40.00
CP399	Dorothy Parker, #2698	9.00
CP400	Dr. Theodore von Karman, #2699	15.00
CP401	Minerals, #2703a	17.00
CP402	Juan Rodriguez Cabrillo, #2704	11.00
CP403	Wild Animals, #2709a	15.00
CP404	Madonna and Child, wheeled toys, #2710, 2714a	15.00
CP405	Chinese New Year, #2720	30.00

1993

CP406	Elvis Presley, #2721	32.50
CP407	Space Fantasy, #2745a	19.00
CP408	Percy Lavon Julian, #2746	15.00
CP409	Oregon Trail, #2747	11.00
CP410	World University Games, #2748	11.00
CP411	Grace Kelly, #2749	28.00
CP412	Oklahoma!, #2722	11.00
CP413	Circus, #2753a	14.50
CP414	Cherokee Strip, #2754	11.00
CP415	Dean Acheson, #2755	15.00
CP416	Sports horses, #2759a	16.00
CP417	Garden flowers, #2764a	11.00
CP418	World War II, #2765	16.00
CP419	Hank Williams, #2723	29.00
CP420	Rock & Roll/Rhythm & Blues, #2737b	32.50
CP421	Joe Louis, #2766	39.00
CP422	Broadway Musicals, #2770a	16.00
CP423	National Postal Museum, #2782a	14.00
CP424	American Sign Language, #2784a	13.00
CP425	Country & Western Music, #2778a	28.50
CP426	Christmas, #2789, 2794a	16.50
CP427	Youth Classics, #2788a	16.50
CP428	Mariana Islands, #2804	13.00
CP429	Columbus' Landing in Puerto Rico, #2805	14.00
CP430	AIDS Awareness, #2806	14.00

Starting with No. CP431, panels are shrink wrapped in plastic with cardboard backing. Values are for items with plastic intact.

1994

CP431	Winter Olympics, #2807-2811	22.50
CP432	Edward R. Murrow, #2812	14.00
CP434	Love, #2814	16.00
CP436	Dr. Allison Davis, #2816	17.50
CP437	Chinese New Year, #2817	20.00
CP438	Buffalo Soldiers, #2818	17.50
CP439	Silent Screen Stars, #2828a	20.00
CP440	Garden Flowers, #2829-2833	16.00
CP441	World Cup Soccer, #2837	17.50
CP442	World War II, #2838	17.50
CP443	Norman Rockwell, #2839	29.50
CP444	Moon Landing, #2841	27.50
CP445	Locomotives, #2843-2847	17.50
CP446	George Meany, #2848	11.00
CP447	Popular Singers, #2853a	17.50
CP448	Jazz/Blues Singers, block of 10, 2854-2861	22.50

Block of 10 on No. CP448 may contain different combination of stamps.

CP449	James Thurber, #2862	11.00
CP450	Wonders of the Sea, #2866a	17.50
CP451	Cranes, block of 2 #2868a	17.50
CP453	Christmas Madonna and Child, #2871	11.00
CP454	Christmas stocking, #2872	11.00
CP455	Chinese New Year, #2876	17.50

1995

CP456	Florida Statehood, #2950	13.00
CP457	Earth Day, #2954a	13.00
CP458	Richard M. Nixon, #2955	22.50
CP459	Bessie Coleman, #2956	18.00
CP460	Love, #2957-2958	18.00
CP461	Recreational Sports, #2965a	18.00
CP462	Prisoners of War/Missing in Action, #2966	16.00
CP463	Marilyn Monroe, #2967	37.50
CP464	Texas Statehood, #2968	16.00
CP465	Great Lakes Lighthouses, #2973a	18.00
CP466	United Nations, #2974	13.00
CP467	Carousel Horses, #2979a	20.00
CP468	Woman Suffrage, #2980	13.00
CP469	World War II, #2981	20.00
CP470	Louis Armstrong, #2982	22.50
CP471	Jazz Musicians, #2992a	22.50
CP472	Garden Flowers, #2993-2997	13.00
CP473	Republic of Palau, #2999	13.00
CP474	Naval Academy, #3001	18.00
CP475	Tennessee Williams, #3002	16.00
CP476	Christmas, Madonna and Child, #3003	18.00
CP477	Santa Claus, Children with toys, #3007a	18.00
CP478	James K. Polk, #2587	13.00
CP479	Antique Automobiles, 3023a	22.50

1996

CP480	Utah Statehood, #3024	13.00
CP481	Garden Flowers, #3029a	13.00
CP482	Ernest E. Just, #3058	18.00
CP483	Smithsonian Institution, #3059	13.00
CP484	Chinese New Year, #3060	22.50
CP485	Pioneers of Communication, #3064a	18.00
CP486	Fulbright Scholarships, #3065	13.00
CP487	Summer Olympic Games, #3068, 2 pages	50.00

Beginning with No. CP487, some items contain two pages. One has text and engraved illustrations, the second has the stamp(s).

CP488	Marathon, #3067	18.00
CP489	Georgia O'Keeffe, #3069	13.00
CP490	Tennessee Statehood, #3070	13.00
CP491	Indian Dances, #3076a	22.50
CP492	Prehistoric Animals, #3080a	22.50
CP493	Breast Cancer Awareness, #3081	13.00
CP494	James Dean, #3082	22.50
CP495	Folk Heroes, #3086a	22.50
CP496	Olympic Games, Cent., #3087	16.00
CP497	Iowa Statehood, #3088	13.00
CP498	Rural Free Delivery, #3090	13.00
CP499	Riverboats, #3095a	22.50
CP500	Big Band Leaders, #3099a	21.00
CP501	Songwriters, #3103a	21.00
CP502	F. Scott Fitzgerald, #3104	22.50
CP503	Endangered Species, #3105, 2 pages	37.50
CP504	Computer Technology, #3106	22.50
CP505	Madonna & Child, #3107	18.00
CP506	Family Scenes, #3111a	18.00
CP507	Hanukkah, #3118	16.00
CP507A	Cycling, #3119	45.00

1997

CP508	Chinese New Year, #3120	24.00
CP509	Benjamin O. Davis, Sr., #3121	21.00
CP510	Love Swans, #3123-3124	16.00
CP511	Helping Children Learn, #3125	13.00
CP512	PACIFIC 97 Stagecoach & Ship, #3131a	20.00
CP513	Thornton Wilder, #3134	18.00
CP514	Raoul Wallenberg, #3135	16.00
CP515	Dinosaurs, #3136	30.00
CP516	Bugs Bunny, #3137c	24.00
CP517	PACIFIC 97 Franklin, #3139	55.00
CP518	PACIFIC 97 Washington, #3140	55.00
CP519	Marshall Plan, #3141	16.00
CP520	Classic American Aircraft, #3142, 2 pages	36.00
CP521	Football Coaches, #3146a	30.00

CP522 American Dolls, #3151 55.00
CP523 Humphrey Bogart, #3152 20.00
CP524 "The Stars & Stripes Forever!," #3153 16.00
CP525 Opera Singers, #3157a 19.00
CP526 Composers & Conductors, #3165a 20.00
CP527 Padre Felix Varela, #3166 16.00
CP528 Department of the Air Force, #3167 20.00
CP529 Movie Monsters, #3172a 22.50
CP530 Supersonic Flight, #3173 22.50
CP531 Women in Military Service, #3174 18.00
CP532 Kwanzaa, #3175 16.00
CP533 Madonna & Child, #3176a 21.00
CP534 Holly, #3177a 21.00

1998

CP535 Chinese New Year, #3179 17.50
CP536 Alpine Skiing, #3180 15.50
CP537 Madam C.J. Walker, #3181 18.00

1998-2000

Celebrate the Century

CP537A 1900s, #3182, 2 pages 27.00
CP537B 1910s, #3183, 2 pages 27.00
CP537C 1920s, #3184, 2 pages 27.00
CP537D 1930s, #3185, 2 pages 30.00
CP537E 1940s, #3186, 2 pages 35.00
CP537F 1950s, #3187, 2 pages 29.00
CP537G 1960s, #3188, 2 pages 32.50
CP537H 1970s, #3189, 2 pages 30.00
CP537I 1980s, #3190, 2 pages 29.00
CP537J 1990s, #3191, 2 pages 29.00

1998

CP538 Remember the Maine,inscribed "Key West, Florida" #3192 16.00
a. Inscribed "Scottsdale, Arizona." 22.50
CP539 Flowering Trees, #3197a 18.00
CP540 Alexander Calder, #3202a 18.00
CP541 Cinco de Mayo, #3203 16.00
CP542 Sylvester & Tweety, #3204c 22.50
CP543 Wisconsin Statehood, #3206 17.50
CP544 Trans-Mississippi, #3209-3210, 2 pages 27.50
CP545 Berlin Airlift, #3211 15.00
CP546 Folk Musicians, #3215a 20.00
CP547 Gospel Singers, #3219a 20.00
CP548 Spanish Settlement, #3220 16.00
CP549 Stephen Vincent Benét, #3221 15.00
CP550 Tropical Birds, #3225a 17.00
CP551 Alfred Hitchcock, #3226 19.00
CP552 Organ & Tissue Donation, #3227 17.00
CP553 Bright Eyes, #3234a 17.00
CP554 Klondike Gold Rush, #3235 15.00
CP555 American Art, #3236 30.00
CP556 American Ballet, #3237 16.00
CP557 Space Discovery, #3242a 20.00
CP558 Giving & Sharing, #3243 15.00
CP559 Madonna & Child, #3244a 20.00
CP560 Wreaths, #3252a 16.00
CP561 Breast Cancer Awareness, #B1 25.00

1999

CP562 Chinese New Year, #3272 17.50
CP563 Malcolm X, #3273 16.00
CP564 Love, #3274a 22.50
CP565 Love, #3275 17.00
CP566 Hospice Care, #3276 16.00
CP567 Irish Immigration, #3286 21.00
CP568 Lunt & Fontanne, #3287 16.00
CP569 Arctic Animals, #3292a 18.00
CP570 Sonoran Desert, #3293, 2 pages 25.00
CP571 Daffy Duck, #3306c 25.00
CP572 Ayn Rand, #3308 32.50
CP573 Cinco de Mayo, #3309 17.00
CP574 John & William Bartram, #3314 18.00
CP575 Prostate Cancer, #3315 18.00
CP576 California Gold Rush, #3316 18.00
CP577 Aquarium Fish, #3320a 18.00
CP578 Extreme Sports, #3324a 18.00
CP579 American Glass, #3328a 18.00
CP580 James Cagney, #3329 18.00
CP581 Honoring Those who Served, #3331 16.00
CP582 Famous Trains, #3337a 22.50
CP583 Frederick Law Olmsted, #3338 18.00
CP584 Hollywood Composers, #3344a 20.00
CP585 Broadway Songwriters, #3350a 20.00
CP586 Insects & Spiders, #3351, 2 pages 30.00
CP587 Hanukkah, #3352 18.00
CP588 NATO, #3354 18.00
CP589 Madonna & Child, #3355 18.00
CP590 Deer, #3359a 18.00
CP591 Kwanzaa, #3368 18.00
CP592 Year 2000, #3369 22.50

2000

CP593 Chinese New Year, #3370 16.00
CP594 Patricia Roberts Harris, #3371 22.50
CP595 Los Angeles Class Submarine, #3372 25.00
CP596 Pacific Coast Rain Forest, #3378, 2 pages 29.00
CP597 Louise Nevelson, #3383a 20.00
CP598 Hubble Space Telescope Images, #3388a 23.00
CP599 American Samoa, #3389 18.00
CP600 Library of Congress, #3390 18.00
CP601 Road Runner & Wile E. Coyote, #3391c 20.00
CP602 Distinguished Soldiers, #3396a 22.00
CP603 Summer Sports, #3397 18.00
CP604 Adoption, #3398 22.00
CP605 Youth Team Sports, #3402a 22.00
CP606 The Stars and Stripes, #3403, 2 pages 34.50
CP607 Legends of Baseball, #3408, 2 pages 40.00
CP608 Stampin' the Future, #3417a 20.00
CP609 California Statehood, #3438 18.00
CP610 Deep Sea Creatures, #3443a 21.00
CP611 Thomas Wolfe, #3444 17.50
CP612 White House, #3445 21.50
CP613 Edward G. Robinson, #3446 10.00

2001

CP614 Non-denominated Love Letters, #3496 19.00
CP615 34c Love, #3497 19.00
CP615A 55c Love, #3499 21.00
CP616 Chinese New Year, #3500 25.00
CP617 Roy Wilkins, #3501 29.00
CP618 Nine-Mile Prairie, #C136 19.00
CP618A American Illustrators, #3502, 2 pages 37.50
CP619 Diabetes Awareness, #3503 19.00
CP620 Nobel Prize, #3504 22.50
CP621 Pan-American Inverts, #3505, 2 pages 40.00
CP622 Mt. McKinley, #C137 20.00
CP623 Great Plains Prairie, #3506, 2 pages 37.50
CP624 Peanuts Comic Strip, #3507 27.50
CP625 Honoring Veterans, #3508 20.00
CP626 Frida Kahlo, #3509 26.00
CP627 Legendary Playing Fields, #3510-3519 45.00

No. CP627 consists of 2 pages. One has text and engraved illustrations. The other consists of the pane of stamps.

CP628 Leonard Bernstein, #3521 22.50
CP629 Lucille Ball, #3523 22.50
CP630 Amish Quilts, #3527a 22.50
CP631 Carnivorous Plants, #3531a 20.00
CP632 Eid, #3532 16.00
CP633 Enrico Fermi, #3533 20.00
CP634 That's All Folks!, #3535c 22.50
CP635 Madonna & Child, #3536 16.50
CP636 Santas, #3540b 19.00
CP637 James Madison, #3545 20.00
CP638 Thanksgiving, #3546 20.00
CP639 Hanukkah, #3547 19.00
CP640 Kwanzaa, #3548 21.00
CP641 57c Love, #3551 19.00
CP648 Greetings from America, #3610a 50.00
CP649 Longleaf Pine Forest, #3611 40.00

Nos. CP648 and CP649 each consist of 2 pages. One has text and engraved illustrations. The other contains the pane of stamps.

2002

CP642 Winter Olympics, #3555a 19.00
CP643 Mentoring a Child, #3556 19.00
CP644 Langston Hughes, #3557 19.00
CP645 Happy Birthday, #3558 19.00
CP646 Chinese New Year, #3559 25.00
CP647 U.S. Military Academy Bicentennial, #3560 21.00
CP650 Heroes of 2001, #B2 25.00
CP651 Masters of American Photography, #3649 45.00

No. CP651 consists of 2 pages. One has text and engraved illustrations. The other consists of the pane of stamps.

CP652 John James Audubon, #3650 21.00
CP653 Harry Houdini, #3651 21.00
CP654 Andy Warhol, #3652 21.00
CP655 Teddy Bears, #3653-3656 16.50
CP656 37c Love, #3657 19.00
CP657 60c Love, #3658 19.00
CP658 Ogden Nash, #3659 20.00
CP659 Duke Kahanamoku, #3660 27.50
CP660 American Bats, #3664a 27.50
CP661 Women in Journalism, #3668a 24.00
CP662 Irving Berlin, #3669 19.00
CP663 Neuter or Spay, #3671a 22.50
CP664 Hanukkah, #3672 20.00
CP665 Kwanzaa, #3673 20.00
CP666 Eid, #3674 16.00
CP667 Madonna & Child, #3675 19.00
CP668 Christmas Snowmen, #3679a 16.50
CP669 Cary Grant, #3692 22.50
CP670 Hawaiian Missionary Stamps, #3694 40.00

No. CP670 consists of 2 pages. One has text and engraved illustrations. The other contains the pane of stamps.

CP671 Happy Birthday, #3695 17.50
CP672 Greetings from America, #3745a 52.50

No. CP672 consists of 2 pages. One has text and engraved illustrations. The other contains the pane of stamps.

2003

CP673 Thurgood Marshall, #3746 19.00
CP674 Chinese New Year, #3747 21.00
CP675 Zora Neale Hurston, #3748 24.00
CP676 Special Olympics, #3771 21.00
CP677 American Filmmaking: Behind the Scenes, #3772 42.50

No. CP677 consists of 2 pages. One has text and engraved illustrations. The other contains the pane of stamps.

CP678 Ohio Statehood, Bicent., #3773 21.00
CP679 Pelican Island National Wildlife Refuge, #3774 21.00
CP680 Old Glory, #3780b 24.00
CP681 Cesar E. Chavez, #3781 21.00
CP682 Louisiana Purchase, #3782 21.00
CP683 First Flight of Wright Brothers, #3783b 21.00
CP684 Audrey Hepburn, #3786 25.00
CP685 Southeastern Lighthouses, #3791a 21.00
CP686 Arctic Tundra, #3802 40.00
CP687 Korean War Veterans Memorial, #3803 21.00
CP688 Mary Cassatt Paintings, #3807a 21.00
CP689 Early Football Heroes, #3811a 27.50
CP690 Roy Acuff, #3812 21.00
CP691 District of Columbia, #3813 21.00
CP692 Reptiles and Amphibians, #3818a 27.50
CP693 Stop Family Violence, #B3 21.00
CP694 Madonna and Child, #3820 21.00
CP695 Christmas Holiday Music Makers, #3824a 21.00

2004

CP696 Pacific Coral Reef, #3831 40.00

No. CP696 consists of 2 pages. One has text and engraved illustrations. The other contains the pane of stamps.

CP697 Chinese New Year, #3832 21.00
CP698 Love, #3833 21.00
CP699 Paul Robeson, #3834 22.50
CP700 Theodor Seuss Geisel (Dr. Seuss), #3835 27.50
CP701 Love (White Lilacs and Pink Roses), #3836 19.00
CP702 Love (Five Varieties of Pink Roses), #3837 19.00
CP703 U.S. Air Force Academy, #3838 21.00
CP704 Henry Mancini, #3839 21.00
CP705 American Choreographers, #3843a 22.50
CP706 Lewis and Clark, #3854 25.00
CP707 Lewis and Clark booklet pane, #3856b 25.00
CP708 Isamu Noguchi, #3861a 19.00
CP709 National World War II Memorial, #3862 22.50
CP710 Summer Olympics, Athens, Greece, #3863 20.00
CP711 Art of Disney, #3868a 24.00
CP712 USS Constellation, #3869 22.50
CP713 R. Buckminster Fuller, #3870 19.00
CP714 James Baldwin, #3871 18.00
CP715 Martin Johnson Heade, #3872 18.00
CP716 Art of the American Indian, #3873 42.50

No. CP716 consists of 2 pages. One has text and engraved illustrations. The other contains the pane of stamps.

CP717 John Wayne, #3876 26.00
CP718 Sickle Cell Disease, #3877 19.00
CP719 Cloudscapes, #3878 40.00

No. CP719 consists of 2 pages. One has text and engraved illustrations. The other contains the pane of stamps.

CP720 Christmas Madonna, #3879 19.00
CP721 Hanukkah, #3880 16.50
CP722 Kwanzaa, #3881 16.50
CP723 Moss Hart, #3882 19.00
CP724 Christmas Ornaments, #3886a 19.00

2005

CP725 Chinese New Year, #3895 35.00

No. CP725 consists of two pages. One has text and engraved illustrations. The other contains the pane of stamps.

CP726 Marian Anderson, #3896 25.00
CP727 Ronald Reagan, #3897 27.50
CP728 Love, #3898 21.00
CP729 Northeast Deciduous Forest, #3899 37.50

No. CP729 consists of two pages. One has text and engraved illustrations. The other contains the pane of stamps.

CP730 Spring Flowers, #3903a 19.00
CP731 Robert Penn Warren, #3904 16.00
CP732 Yip Harburg, #3905 16.00
CP733 American Scientists, #3909a 16.00
CP734 Modern American Architecture, #3910 42.50

No. CP734 consists of two pages. One has text and engraved illustrations. The other contains the pane of stamps.

CP735 Henry Fonda, #3911 17.50
CP736 Disney Characters, #3915a 30.00
CP737 Advances in Aviation, #3916-3925 42.50

No. CP737 consists of two pages. One has text and illustrations. The other contains the pane of stamps.

CP738 Rio Grande Blankets, #3929a 16.00
CP739 Presidential Libraries, #3930 16.00
CP740 Sporty Cars of the 1950s, #3935b 30.00
CP741 Arthur Ashe, #3936 20.00
CP742 To Form a More Perfect Union, #3937 32.50

No. CP742 consists of two pages. One has text and illustrations. The other contains the pane of stamps.

CP743 Child Health, #3938 16.00
CP744 Let's Dance, #3942a 16.00
CP745 Greta Garbo, #3943 25.00
CP746 Jim Henson and the Muppets, #3944 42.50

No. CP746 consists of two pages. One has text and engraved illustrations. The other contains the pane of stamps.

CP747 Constellations, #3948a 29.00
CP748 Christmas, #3952a 15.00
CP749 Distinguished Marines, #3964a 29.00

2006

CP750 Love, #3976 14.00
CP751 Children's Book Animals, #3994a 32.50

No. CP751 consists of two pages. One has text and illustrations. The other contains the pane of stamps.

CP752 2006 Winter Olympics, #3995 15.00
CP753 Hattie McDaniel, #3996 17.50
CP754 Chinese New Year, #3997 30.00

No. CP754 consists of two pages. One has text and illustrations. The other contains the pane of stamps.

CP755 39c Wedding, #3998 14.00
CP756 63c Wedding, #3999 14.00
CP757 Sugar Ray Robinson, #4020 14.00
CP758 Benjamin Franklin, #4024a 14.00
CP759 Disney Characters, #4028a 14.00
CP760 Love Birds, #4029 14.00

CP761	Katherine Anne Porter, #4030	14.00
CP762	Amber Alert, #4031	14.00
CP763	Wonders of America, #4033-4072	37.50

No. CP763 consists of two pages. One has text and illustrations. The other contains the pane of stamps.

CP764	Samuel de Champlain, #4073	14.00
CP765	Washington 2006 World Philatelic Exhibition, #4075	17.50
CP766	Distinguished American Diplomats, #4076	14.00

No. CP766 consists of two pages. One has text and illustrations. The other contains the pane of stamps.

CP767	Judy Garland, #4077	14.00
CP768	Ronald Reagan, #4078	15.00
CP769	Happy Birthday, #4079	14.00
CP770	Baseball Sluggers, #4083a	14.00
CP771	DC Comics Superheroes, #4084	32.50

No. CP771 consists of two panes. One has text and engraved illustrations. The other contains the pane of stamps.

CP772	Motorcycles, #4088a	15.00
CP773	Quilts of Gee's Bend, Alabama, #4098b	16.00
CP774	Southern Florida Wetland, #4099	35.00

No. CP774 consists of two panes. One has text and engraved illustrations. The other contains the pane of stamps.

CP775	Christmas Madonna, #4100	12.00
CP776	Christmas Snowflakes, #4104a	12.00
CP777	Eid, #4117	12.00
CP778	Hanukkah, #4118	12.00
CP779	Kwanzaa, #4119	12.00
CP780	39c Ella Fitzgerald, #4120	12.00
CP781	39c Oklahoma Statehood, #4121	12.00
CP782	39c Love, #4122	12.00
CP783	84c International Polar Year, #4123	12.00
CP784	39c Henry Wadsworth Longfellow, #4124	12.00
CP785	41c Settlement of Jamestown, #4136	30.00

No. CP785 consists of two pages. One has text and illustrations. The other contains the pane of stamps.

CP786	Star Wars, #4143	30.00

No. CP786 consists of two panes. One has text and engraved illustrations. The other contains the pane of stamps.

CP787	Pacific Lighthouses, #4150a	12.00
CP788	41c Wedding Hearts, #4151	12.00
CP789	58c Wedding Hearts, #4152	12.00
CP790	Pollination, #4156d	16.50
CP791	Marvel Comics Super Heroes, #4159	30.00

No. CP791 consists of two panes. One has text and engraved illustrations. The other contains the pane of stamps.

CP792	Vintage Mahogany Speedboats, #4163a	12.00
CP793	Louis Comfort Tiffany, #4165	12.00
CP794	Disney Characters, #4195a	12.00
CP795	Celebrate, #4196	12.00
CP796	James Stewart, #4197	12.00
CP797	Alpine Tundra, #4198	30.00

No. CP796 consists of two panes. One has text and engraved illustrations. The other contains the pane of stamps.

CP798	Gerald R. Ford, #4199	12.00
CP799	Jury Duty, #4200	12.00
CP800	Mendez v. Westminster School District, #4201	12.00
CP801	Eid, #4202	12.00
CP802	Polar Lights, #4204a	12.00
CP803	Yoda, #4205	12.00
CP804	Christmas Madonna, #4206	12.00
CP805	Christmas Holiday Knits #4210a	12.00
CP806	Hanukkah, #4219	12.00
CP807	Kwanzaa, #4220	12.00

2008

CP808	Chinese New Year, #4221	12.00
CP809	Charles W. Chesnutt, #4222	12.00
CP810	Marjorie Kinnan Rawlings, #4223	12.00

SOUVENIR PAGES

These are post office new-issue announcement bulletins, including an illustration of the stamp's design and informative text. They bear a copy of the stamp, tied by a first day of issue cancellation. Varieties of bulletin watermarks and text changes, etc., are beyond the scope of this catalogue.

Values for Scott Nos. SP1-SP295 are for folded copies. Values for Official Souvenir Pages (Nos. SP296 on) are for copies that never have been folded.

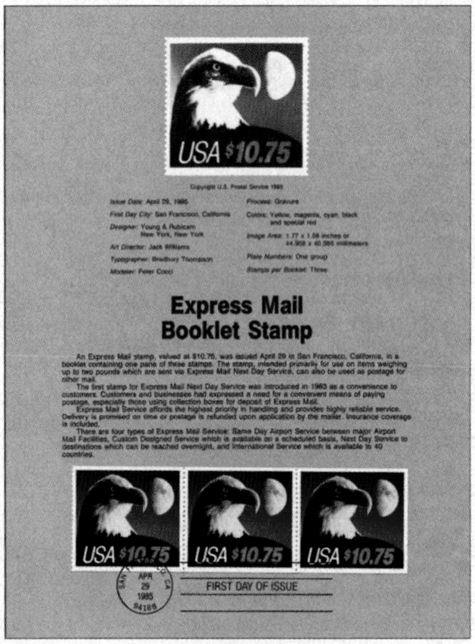

No. SP674a

UNOFFICIAL SOUVENIR PAGES

Liberty Issue

1960-65

SP1	1¼c	Palace of Governors, sheet, coil, #1031A, 1054A	50.00
SP2	8c	Pershing, #1042A	30.00
SP3	11c	Statue of Liberty, #1044A	27.50
SP4	25c	Revere coil, #1059A	10.00

1959

SP5	4c	49 Star Flag, #1132	—
SP6	7c	Hawaii Statehood, #C55	—
SP7	4c	Soil Conservation, #1133	—
SP8	10c	Pan American Games, #C56	—
SP9	4c	Petroleum, #1134	—
SP10	4c	Dental Health, #1135	—
SP11	4c, 8c	Reuter, #1136, 1137	—
SP12	4c	McDowell, #1138	—

1960-61

SP13	4c	Washington Credo, #1139	75.00
SP14	4c	Franklin Credo, #1140	75.00
SP15	4c	Jefferson Credo, #1141	75.00
SP16	4c	F.S. Key Credo, #1142	75.00
SP17	4c	Lincoln Credo, #1143	65.00
SP18	4c	P. Henry Credo, #1144	45.00

1961

SP19	4c	Boy Scout, #1145	75.00
SP20	4c	Winter Olympics, #1146	75.00
SP21	4c, 8c	Masaryk, #1147, 1148	75.00
SP22	4c	Refugee Year, #1149	45.00
SP23	4c	Water Consevation, #1150	30.00
SP24	4c	SEATO, #1151	30.00
SP25	4c	American Women, #1152	30.00
SP26	10c	Liberty Bell, #C57	—
SP27	15c	Statue of Liberty, #C58	—
SP28	25c	Lincoln, #C59	—
SP29	4c	50 Star Flag, #1153	50.00
SP30	4c	Pony Express, #1154	50.00
SP31	7c	Jet, carmine, #C60	25.00
SP32	7c	Booklet pane of 6, #C60a	37.50
SP33	7c	Jet coil, #C61	17.50
SP34	4c	Handicapped, #1155	50.00
SP35	4c	Forestry Congress, #1156	50.00
SP36	4c	Mexican Independence, #1157	35.00
SP37	4c	U.S., Japan Treaty, #1158	25.00
SP38	4c, 8c	Paderewski, #1159-1160	40.00
SP39	4c	Sen. Taft, #1161	45.00
SP40	4c	Wheels of Freedom, #1162	45.00
SP41	4c	Boys' Clubs, #1163	45.00
SP42	4c	Automated Post Office, #1164	45.00
SP43	4c, 8c	Mannerheim, #1165-1166	45.00
SP44	4c	Camp Fire Girls, #1167	45.00
SP45	4c, 8c	Garibaldi, #1168-1169	45.00
SP46	4c	Sen. George, #1170	45.00
SP47	4c	Carnegie, #1171	45.00
SP48	4c	Dulles, #1172	45.00
SP49	4c	Echo I, #1173	25.00

1961

SP50	4c, 8c	Gandhi, #1174-1175	20.00
SP51	4c	Range Conservation, #1176	20.00
SP52	4c	Greeley, #1177	20.00

1961-65

SP53	4c	Ft. Sumter, #1178	20.00
SP54	4c	Shiloh, #1179	27.50
SP55	5c	Gettysburg, #1180	9.00
SP56	5c	Wilderness, #1181	9.50
SP57	5c	Appomattox, #1182	9.50

1961

SP58	4c	Kansas, #1183	15.00
SP59	13c	Liberty Bell, #C62	20.00
SP60	4c	Sen. Norris, #1184	14.00
SP61	4c	Naval Aviation, #1185	20.00
SP62	4c	Workmen's Compensation, #1186	20.00
SP63	4c	Remington, #1187	12.00
SP64	4c	Sun Yat sen, #1188	20.00
SP65	4c	Basketball, #1189	20.00
SP66	4c	Nursing, #1190	25.00

1962

SP67	4c	New Mexico, #1191	12.50
SP68	4c	Arizona, #1192	12.50
SP69	4c	Project Mercury, #1193	10.00
SP70	4c	Malaria, #1194	15.00
SP71	4c	Hughes, #1195	21.00
SP72	4c	Seattle World's Fair, #1196	17.50
SP73	4c	Louisiana, #1197	17.50
SP74	4c	Homestead Act, #1198	17.50
SP75	4c	Girl Scouts, #1199	20.00
SP76	4c	McMahon, #1200	17.50
SP77	4c	Apprenticeship, #1201	17.50
SP78	4c	Rayburn, #1202	17.50
SP79	4c	Hammarskjold, #1203	17.50
SP80	4c	Hammarskjold, yellow inverted, #1204	40.00
SP81	4c	Christmas, #1205	50.00
SP82	4c	Higher Education, #1206	12.00
SP83	8c	Capitol, #C64	15.00
SP83a	8c	Capitol sheet, booklet, coil, #C64, C64b, C65	20.00
SP84	8c	Capitol, tagged, #C64a	37.50
SP85	8c	Capitol booklet single, #C64b	25.00
SP86	8c	Capitol coil, #C65	15.00
SP87	4c	Winslow Homer, #1207	15.00
SP88	5c	Flag, #1208	12.50
SP89	1c	Jackson, #1209	12.50
SP90	5c	Washington, #1213	17.50
SP91	5c	Washington booklet pane of 5 + label, #1213a	30.00
SP92	1c	Jackson coil, #1225	17.50
SP93	5c	Washington coil, #1229	17.50
SP94	15c	Montgomery Blair, #C66	—

1963

SP96	5c	Food for Peace, #1231	7.00
SP97	5c	West Virginia, #1232	10.00
SP97A	6c	Eagle, #C67	8.50
SP97B	8c	Amelia Earhart, #C68	20.00
SP98	5c	Emancipation Proclamation, #1233	12.50
SP99	5c	Alliance for Progress, #1234	8.00
SP100	5c	Cordell Hull, #1235	8.00
SP101	5c	Eleanor Roosevelt, #1236	8.00
SP102	5c	Science, #1237	7.50
SP103	5c	City Mail Delivery, #1238	10.00
SP104	5c	Red Cross, #1239	7.00
SP105	5c	Christmas, #1240	9.00
SP106	5c	Audubon, #1241	8.00

1964

SP107	5c	Sam Houston, #1242	12.00
SP108	5c	C.M. Russell, #1243	10.00
SP109	5c	N.Y. World's Fair, #1244	9.00
SP110	5c	John Muir, #1245	12.00
SP111	5c	Kennedy (Boston, Mass.) (At least 4 other cities known), #1246	15.00
SP112	5c	New Jersey, #1247	9.00
SP113	5c	Nevada, #1248	9.00
SP114	5c	Register and Vote, #1249	7.50
SP115	5c	Shakespeare, #1250	9.00
SP116	5c	Mayo Brothers, #1251	10.00
SP117	8c	Goddard, #C69	9.00
SP118	5c	Music, #1252	9.00
SP119	5c	Homemakers, #1253	9.00
SP120	5c	Christmas Plants, #1257b	20.00
SP121	5c	Christmas, tagged, #1257c	90.00
SP122	5c	Verrazano Narrows Bridge, #1258	9.00
SP123	5c	Fine Arts, #1259	9.00
SP124	5c	Amateur Radio, #1260	8.00

1965

SP125	5c	New Orleans, #1261	8.00
SP126	5c	Sokols, #1262	8.00
SP127	5c	Cancer, #1263	8.00
SP128	5c	Churchill, #1264	8.50
SP129	5c	Magna Carta, #1265	8.00
SP130	5c	I.C.Y., #1266	8.00
SP131	5c	Salvation Army, #1267	8.00
SP132	5c	Dante, #1268	8.00
SP133	5c	Hoover, #1269	8.25
SP134	5c	Fulton, #1270	8.00
SP135	5c	Florida, #1271	8.50
SP136	5c	Traffic Safety, #1272	8.00
SP137	5c	Copley, #1273	8.50
SP138	11c	I.T.U., #1274	8.50
SP139	5c	Stevenson, #1275	8.00
SP140	5c	Christmas, #1276	7.50

Prominent Americans

1965-73

SP141	1c Jefferson, #1278	7.50
SP141a	1c Jefferson sheet, booklet, coil, #1278, 1278a 1299	7.00
SP142	1c Jefferson booklet pane of 8, #1278a	8.25
SP143	1¼c Gallatin, #1279	7.50
SP144	2c Wright, #1280	6.50
SP145	2c Wright booklet pane of 5 + label, #1280a	9.50
SP146	3c Parkman, #1281	7.50
SP147	4c Lincoln, #1282	6.00
SP148	5c Washington, #1283	6.00
SP149	5c Washington, redrawn, #1283B	6.50
SP150	6c Roosevelt, #1284	6.00
SP151	6c Roosevelt booklet pane of 8, #1284b	13.00
SP151a	6c Roosevelt booklet, vert. coil, #1284b, 1298	6.00
SP151b	6c Roosevelt booklet, horiz. coil, #1284b, 1305	6.00
SP152	8c Einstein, #1285	10.00
SP153	10c Jackson, #1286	7.50
SP154	12c Ford, #1286A	11.00
SP155	13c Kennedy, #1287	20.00
SP156	15c Holmes, #1288	10.00
SP157	20c Marshall, #1289	9.00
SP158	25c Douglass, #1290	12.00
SP159	30c Dewey, #1291	30.00
SP160	40c Paine, #1292	40.00
SP161	50c Stone, #1293	35.00
SP162	$1 O'Neill, #1294	65.00
SP163	$5 Moore, #1295	150.00
SP164	6c Roosevelt, vert. coil, #1298	6.00
SP165	1c Jefferson, coil, #1299	6.50
SP166	4c Lincoln, coil, #1303	7.50
SP167	5c Washington, coil, #1304	7.00
SP168	6c Roosevelt, horiz. coil, #1305	6.50

Nos. 1297, 1305C and 1305E are known on unofficial pages. They are not listed here. For official pages of these issues, see Nos. SP296-SP298.

1966

SP169	5c Migratory Bird Treaty, #1306	10.00
SP170	5c ASPCA, #1307	8.00
SP171	5c Indiana, #1308	7.50
SP172	5c Circus, #1309	9.00
SP173	5c SIPEX, #1310	7.00
SP174	5c SIPEX Souvenir Sheet, #1311	7.25
SP175	5c Bill of Rights, #1312	8.00
SP176	5c Poland, #1313	8.00
SP177	5c National Park Service, #1314	7.50
SP178	5c Marine Corps Reserve, #1315	8.50
SP179	5c Women's Clubs, #1316	8.00
SP180	5c Johnny Appleseed, #1317	8.00
SP181	5c Beautifcation of America, #1318	8.50
SP182	5c Great River Road, #1319	7.50
SP183	5c Savings Bonds Servicemen, #1320	8.00
SP184	5c Christmas, #1321	7.00
SP185	5c Mary Cassatt, #1322	7.50

1967

SP186	8c Alaska, #C70	10.00
SP187	5c Grange, #1323	7.00
SP188	20c Audubon, #C71	10.00
SP189	5c Canada, #1324	7.00
SP190	5c Erie Canal, #1325	7.00
SP191	5c Search for Peace, #1326	7.50
SP192	5c Thoreau, #1327	7.00
SP193	5c Nebraska, #1328	7.00
SP194	5c VOA, #1329	7.00
SP195	5c Crockett, #1330	8.00
SP196	5c Space, #1332b	25.00
SP197	5c Urban Planning, #1333	7.00
SP198	5c Finland, #1334	7.50
SP199	5c Eakins, #1335	7.25
SP200	5c Christmas, #1336	7.00
SP201	5c Mississippi, #1337	7.00

1968-71

SP202	6c Flags, Giori Press, #1338	6.50
SP203	6c Flag, Huck Press, #1338D	6.00
SP204	8c Flag, #1338F	6.50
SP205	6c Flag coil, #1338A	6.25

1968

SP206	10c 50 star Runway, #C72	9.00
SP207	10c sheet, coil, booklet pane of 8, #C72, C72b, C73	25.00
SP207a	10c sheet, booklet single, coil, #C72, C72b, C73	9.00
SP208	10c 50 star Runway coil, #C73	9.00
SP209	6c Illinois, #1339	6.00
SP210	6c HemisFair, #1340	7.50
SP211	$1 Airlift, #1341	65.00
SP212	6c Youth, #1342	6.00
SP213	10c Air Mail Service, #C74	8.50
SP214	6c Law and Order, #1343	6.00
SP215	6c Register and Vote, #1344	6.00
SP216	6c Historic Flags, #1345-1354	90.00
SP217	6c Disney, #1355	20.00
SP218	6c Marquette, #1356	8.00
SP219	6c Daniel Boone, #1357	8.00
SP220	6c Arkansas River Navigation, #1358	7.50
SP221	6c Leif Erikson, #1359	15.00
SP222	6c Cherokee Strip, #1360	9.00
SP223	6c John Trumbull, #1361	7.50
SP224	6c Waterfowl, #1362	9.00
SP225	6c Christmas, #1363	7.50
SP226	6c Chief Joseph, #1364	9.00
SP227	20c USA, #C75	12.00

1969

SP228	6c Beautification, #1368a	20.00
SP229	6c American Legion, #1369	7.50
SP230	6c Grandma Moses, #1370	7.00
SP231	6c Apollo 8, #1371	15.00
SP232	6c W.C. Handy, #1372	10.00
SP233	6c California, #1373	7.00
SP234	6c Powell, #1374	7.50
SP235	6c Alabama, #1375	7.50
SP236	6c Botanical Congress, #1379a	20.00
SP237	10c Man on the Moon, #C76	14.00
SP238	6c Dartmouth, #1380	7.50
SP239	6c Baseball, #1381	40.00
SP240	6c Football, #1382	15.00
SP241	6c Eisenhower, #1383	7.50
SP242	6c Christmas, #1384	7.50
SP243	6c Hope, #1385	7.00
SP244	45c Special Delivery, #E22	35.00
SP245	6c Harnett, #1386	7.00

1970

SP246	6c Natural History, #1390a	40.00
SP247	6c Maine, #1391	9.00
SP248	6c Wildlife Conservation, #1392	12.00

Regular Issue

1970-71

SP249	6c Eisenhower, #1393	6.00
SP249a	6c sheet, booklet, coil stamps, #1393, 1393a, 1401	8.50
SP249b	6c sheet, coil stamps, #1393, 1401	8.00
SP250	6c Eisenhower booklet pane of 8, #1393a	12.50
SP250a	6c booklet, coil, #1393a, 1401	6.00
SP251	6c Eisenhower booklet pane of 5 + label, #1393b	6.00
SP252	8c Eisenhower, #1394	6.00
SP252a	8c sheet, booklet, coil, #1394-1395, 1402	6.00
SP253	8c Eisenhower booklet pane of 8, #1395a	15.00
SP254	8c Eisenhower booklet pane of 8, #1395b	15.00
SP255	8c U.S.P.S., #1396	10.00
SP256	16c Pyle, #1398	9.00
SP257	6c Eisenhower coil, #1401	7.00
SP258	8c Eisenhower coil, #1402	6.00

1970

SP259	6c Masters, #1405	7.50
SP260	6c Suffrage, #1406	7.00
SP261	6c So. Carolina, #1407	7.00
SP262	6c Stone Mountain, #1408	9.00
SP263	6c Ft. Snelling, #1409	7.50
SP264	6c Anti pollution, #1413a	22.50
SP265	6c Christmas Nativity, #1414	13.00
SP266	6c Christmas Toys, #1418b	10.00
SP267	6c Toys, precanceled, #1418c	45.00
SP268	6c U.N., #1419	9.00
SP269	6c Mayflower, #1420	7.50
SP270	6c DAV, Servicemen, #1422a	27.50

1971

SP271	6c Wool, #1423	9.00
SP272	6c MacArthur, #1424	10.00
SP273	6c Blood Donors, #1425	7.50
SP274	8c Missouri, #1426	8.00
SP275	9c Delta Wing, #C77	9.00
SP276	11c Jet, #C78	9.00
SP276a	11c sheet, booklet, coil, #C78, C78a, C82	12.50
SP277	11c Jet booklet pane, #C78a	17.50
SP278	60c Special Delivery, #E23	25.00
SP279	8c Wildlife, #1430a	15.00
SP280	8c Antarctic Treaty, #1431	12.00
SP281	8c Bicentennial Emblem, #1432	15.00
SP282	17c Statue of Liberty, #C80	15.00
SP283	21c USA, #C81	20.00
SP284	11c Jet coil, #C82	10.00
SP285	8c Sloan, #1433	11.00
SP286	8c Space, #1435b	20.00
SP287	8c Dickenson, #1436	12.50
SP288	8c San Juan, #1437	17.50
SP289	8c Drug Abuse, #1438	10.00
SP290	8c CARE, #1439	10.00
SP291	8c Historic Preservation, #1443a	12.50
SP292	8c Adoration, #1444	10.00
SP293	8c Patridge, #1445	10.00

1972

SP294	8c Lanier, #1446	10.00
SP295	8c Peace Corps, #1447	10.00

OFFICIAL SOUVENIR PAGES

In 1972 the USPS began issuing "official" Souvenir pages by subscription. A few more "unofficials" were produced.

Prominent Americans

1970-78

SP296	3c Parkman, coil, #1297	4.00
SP297	$1 O'Neill, coil, #1305C	15.00
SP298	15c Holmes, coil, #1305E	4.00
SP299	7c Franklin, #1393D	5.00
SP300	14c LaGuardia, #1397	100.00
SP301	18c Blackwell, #1399	3.50
SP302	21c Giannini, #1400	4.50

1972

SP303	2c Cape Hatteras, #1451a	80.00
SP304	6c Wolf Trap Farm, #1452	32.50
SP305	8c Yellowstone, #1453	110.00
SP306	11c City of Refuge, #C84	95.00
SP307	15c Mt. McKinley, #1454	20.00
SP308	8c Family Planning, #1455	675.00

Unofficials exist, value $150.

SP309	8c Colonial Craftsmen, #1459a	13.00
SP310	Olympics, #1460-1462, C85	10.00
SP311	8c PTA, #1463	6.00
SP312	8c Wildlife, #1467a	7.00
SP313	8c Mail Order, #1468	4.50
SP314	8c Osteopathic, #1469	5.50
SP315	8c Tom Sawyer, #1470	8.00
SP316	8c Christmas, #1471-1472	6.00
SP317	8c Pharmacy, #1473	7.00
SP318	8c Stamp Collecting, #1474	5.00

1973

SP319	8c Love, #1475	7.00
SP320	8c Printing, #1476	5.00
SP321	8c Broadside, #1477	5.00
SP322	8c Postrider, #1478	5.00
SP323	8c Drummer, #1479	3.25
SP324	8c Tea Party, #1483a	6.00
SP325	8c Gershwin, #1484	6.00
SP326	8c Jeffers, #1485	5.25
SP327	8c Tanner, #1486	6.00
SP328	8c Cather, #1487	7.00
SP329	8c Copernicus, #1488	5.75
SP330	8c Postal People, #1489-1498	5.75
SP331	8c Truman, #1499	5.00
SP332	Electronics, #1500-1502, C86	9.00
SP333	8c L.B. Johnson, #1503	4.75

1973-74

SP334	8c Cattle, #1504	3.75
SP335	10c Chautauqua, #1505	3.25
SP336	10c Kansas Winter Wheat, #1506	3.00

1973

SP337	8c Christmas, #1507	6.25

Regular Issues

1973-74

SP338	10c Crossed Flags, #1509	3.50
SP339	10c Jefferson Memorial, #1510	3.50
SP340	10c ZIP, #1511	5.00
SP341	6.3c Liberty Bell coil, #1518	4.00
SP341A	13c Winged Envelope, #C79	4.00
SP341B	13c Airmail, coil, #C83	4.00

1974

SP342	18c Statue of Liberty, #C87	7.50
SP343	26c Mt. Rushmore, #C88	5.25
SP344	10c VFW, #1525	3.25
SP345	10c Robert Frost, #1526	5.25
SP346	10c EXPO '74, #1527	6.00
SP347	10c Horse Racing, #1528	6.00
SP348	10c Skylab, #1529	5.75
SP349	10c UPU, #1537a	6.00
SP350	10c Minerals, #1541a	6.00
SP351	10c Ft. Harrod, #1542	3.25
SP352	10c Continental Congress, #1546a	5.25
SP353	10c Energy, #1547	3.25
SP354	10c Sleepy Hollow, #1548	5.25
SP355	10c Retarded Children, #1549	3.25
SP356	10c Christmas, #1550-1552	5.25

1975

SP357	10c Benjamin West, #1553	3.75
SP358	10c Dunbar, #1554	5.00
SP359	10c D.W. Griffith, #1555	5.25
SP360	10c Pioneer, #1556	6.00
SP361	10c Mariner, #1557	6.00
SP362	10c Collective Bargaining, #1558	3.25
SP363	8c Sybil Ludington, #1559	3.25
SP364	10c Salem Poor, #1560	4.00
SP365	10c Haym Salomon, #1561	3.75
SP366	15c Peter Francisco, #1562	3.75
SP367	10c Lexington & Concord, #1563	3.75
SP368	10c Bunker Hill, #1564	3.75
SP369	10c Military Uniforms, #1568a	6.00
SP370	10c Apollo Soyuz, #1570a	7.50
SP371	10c Women's Year, #1571	3.25
SP372	10c Postal Service, #1575	4.00
SP373	10c Peace through Law, #1576	3.25
SP374	10c Banking and Commerce, #1578a	3.75
SP375	10c Christmas, #1579-1580	4.25

Americana Issue

1975-81

SP376	1c, 2c, 3c, 4c Americana, #1581-1585	4.00
SP377	9c Capitol Dome, #1591	3.25
SP378	10c Justice, #1592	3.25
SP379	11c Printing Press, #1593	3.50
SP380	12c Torch sheet, coil, #1594, 1816	3.50
SP381	13c Eagle and Shield, #1596	5.00
SP382	15c Flag sheet, coil, #1597, 1618C	3.25
SP383	16c Statue of Liberty sheet, coil, #1599, 1619	3.50
SP384	24c Old North Church, #1603	3.50
SP385	28c Ft. Nisqually, #1604	4.00
SP386	29c Lighthouse, #1605	5.00
SP387	30c Schoolhouse, #1606	4.75
SP388	50c "Betty" Lamp, #1608	4.25
SP389	$1 Candle Holder, #1610	4.75
SP390	$2 Kerosene Lamp, #1611	6.00
SP391	$5 R. R. Lantern, #1612	11.00
SP392	1c Inkwell, coil, #1811	3.50
SP393	3.1c Guitar, coil, #1613	6.50
SP394	3.5c Violin, coil, #1813	3.25
SP395	7.7c Saxhorns, coil, #1614	3.25
SP396	7.9c Drum, coil, #1615	3.25
SP397	8.4c Piano, coil, #1615C	4.25
SP398	9c Capitol Dome, coil, #1616	3.25
SP398A	10c Justice, coil, #1617	3.25
SP399	13c Liberty Bell, coil, #1618	3.25

SP400	13c	13 star Flag sheet, coil, #1622, 1625	3.25
SP401	9c, 13c	Booklet pane, perf. 10, #1623Bc	17.50

1976

SP402	13c	Spririt of '76, #1631a	5.00
SP403	25c, 31c	Plane and Globes, #C89-C90	3.50
SP404	13c	Interphil 76, #1632	3.75
SP405	13c	State Flags, #1633-1642	9.00
SP406	13c	State Flags, #1643-1652	9.00
SP407	13c	State Flags, #1653-1662	9.00
SP408	13c	State Flags, #1663-1672	9.00
SP409	13c	State Flags, #1673-1682	9.00
SP410	13c	Telephone, #1683	3.50
SP411	13c	Aviation, #1684	3.50
SP412	13c	Chemistry, #1685	3.50
SP413	13c	Bicentennial Souvenir Sheet, #1686	10.00
SP414	18c	Bicentennial Souvenir Sheet, #1687	10.00
SP415	24c	Bicentennial Souvenir Sheet, #1688	10.00
SP416	31c	Bicentennial Souvenir Sheet, #1689	10.00
SP417	13c	Franklin, #1690	3.00
SP418	13c	Declaration of Independence, #1694a	4.75
SP419	13c	Olympics, #1698a	4.75
SP420	13c	Clara Maass, #1699	6.50
SP421	13c	Adolph Ochs, #1700	3.50
SP422	13c	Christmas, #1701-1703	3.75

1977

SP423	13c	Washington at Princeton, #1704	3.25
SP424	13c	Sound Recording, #1705	4.00
SP425	13c	Pueblo Pottery, #1709a	7.00
SP426	13c	Lindbergh Flight, #1710	4.00
SP427	13c	Colorado, #1711	3.00
SP428	13c	Butterflies, #1715a	5.00
SP429	13c	Lafayette, #1716	3.00
SP430	13c	Skilled Hands, #1720a	4.00
SP431	13c	Peace Bridge, #1721	3.50
SP432	13c	Oriskany, #1722	3.50
SP433	13c	Energy, #1724a	3.50
SP434	13c	Alta California, #1725	3.50
SP435	13c	Articles of Confederation, #1726	4.50
SP436	13c	Talking Pictures, #1727	4.50
SP437	13c	Saratoga, #1728	3.25
SP438	13c	Christmas, #1729-1730	3.25

1978

SP439	13c	Sandburg, #1731	4.00
SP440	13c	Capt. Cook, #1732, 1733	4.50
SP441	13c	Indian Head Penny, #1734	3.25
SP442	15c	A Sheet, coil, #1735, 1743	5.50
SP443	15c	Roses booklet single, #1737	4.25
SP444	15c	Windmills booklet pane of 10, #1742a	9.50
SP445	13c	Tubman, #1744	4.00
SP446	13c	Quilts, #1748a	5.00
SP447	13c	American Dance, #1752a	6.00
SP448	13c	French Alliance, #1753	3.50
SP449	13c	Cancer Detection, #1754	4.50
SP450	13c	Jimmie Rodgers, #1755	4.50
SP451	15c	George M. Cohan, #1756	4.50
SP452	13c	CAPEX '78 Souvenir Sheet, #1757	7.75
SP453	15c	Photography, #1758	5.00
SP454	15c	Viking Missions, #1759	6.25
SP455	15c	Owls, #1763a	5.50
SP456	31c	Wright Brothers, #C92a	4.00
SP457	15c	Trees, #1767a	4.00
SP458	15c	Madonna and Child, #1768	3.50
SP459	15c	Hobby Horse, #1769	3.50

1979

SP460	15c	Robert F. Kennedy, #1770	4.25
SP461	15c	Martin Luther King Jr., #1771	5.00
SP462	15c	Year of the Child, #1772	3.25
SP463	15c	John Steinbeck, #1773	6.50
SP464	15c	Einstein, #1774	6.50
SP465	21c	Chanute, #C94a	4.00
SP466	15c	Toleware, #1778a	5.50
SP467	15c	Architecture, #1782a	4.00
SP468	15c	Endangered Flora, #1786a	4.00
SP469	15c	Seeing Eye Dogs, #1787	3.25
SP470	15c	Special Olympics, #1788	3.25
SP471	15c	John Paul Jones, #1789	3.25
SP472	10c	Olympics, #1790	3.50
SP473	15c	Olympics, #1794a	5.00
SP474	31c	Olympics, #C97	4.50

1980

SP475	15c	Winter Olympics, #1798a	5.25

1979

SP476	15c	Madonna and Child, #1799	3.25
SP477	15c	Santa Claus, #1800	3.25
SP478	15c	Will Rogers, #1801	4.00
SP479	15c	Vietnam Veterans, #1802	5.50
SP480	25c	Wiley Post, #C96a	4.50

1980

SP481	15c	W.C. Fields, #1803	5.00
SP482	15c	Benjamin Banneker, #1804	4.25
SP483	15c	Letter Writing Week, #1805-1810	4.00
SP484	18c	B sheet, coil, #1818, 1820	3.25
SP485	18c	B booklet pane of 8, #1819a	3.25
SP486	15c	Frances Perkins, #1821	3.25
SP487	15c	Dolley Madison, #1822	4.50
SP488	15c	Emily Bissell, #1823	4.50
SP489	15c	Helen Keller, #1824	3.25
SP490	15c	Veterans Administration, #1825	3.25
SP491	15c	Galvez, #1826	3.25
SP492	15c	Coral Reefs, #1830a	5.50
SP493	15c	Organized Labor, #1831	4.00
SP494	15c	Edith Wharton, #1832	4.00
SP495	15c	Education, #1833	3.50
SP496	15c	Indian Masks, #1837a	5.00
SP497	15c	Architecture, #1841a	4.00
SP498	40c	Mazzei, #C98	3.75
SP499	15c	Christmas Window, #1842	3.25
SP500	15c	Christmas Toys, #1843	4.00
SP501	28c	Blanche Stuart Scott, #C99	3.75
SP502	35c	Curtiss, #C100	3.75

Great Americans

1980-85

SP503	1c	Dix, #1844	3.50
SP504	2c	Stravinsky, #1845	3.75
SP505	3c	Clay, #1846	3.50
SP506	4c	Schurz, #1847	4.25
SP507	5c	Buck, #1848	4.00
SP508	6c	Lippmann, #1849	4.25
SP509	7c	Baldwin, #1850	3.25
SP510	8c	Knox, #1851	3.25
SP511	9c	Thayer, #1852	3.25
SP512	10c	Russell, #1853	3.25
SP513	11c	Partridge, #1854	3.25
SP514	13c	Crazy Horse, #1855	4.00
SP515	14c	Lewis, #1856	5.50
SP516	17c	Carson, #1857	3.25
SP517	18c	Mason, #1858	3.25
SP518	19c	Sequoyah, #1859	3.25
SP519	20c	Bunche, #1860	5.25
SP520	20c	Gallaudet, #1861	3.25
SP521	20c	Truman, #1862	3.25
SP522	22c	Audubon, #1863	4.25
SP523	30c	Laubach, #1864	3.25
SP524	35c	Drew, #1865	3.25
SP525	37c	Millikan, #1866	3.25
SP526	39c	Clark, #1867	3.25
SP527	40c	Gilbreth, #1868	3.25
SP528	50c	Nimitz, #1869	4.00

1981

SP529	15c	Dirksen, #1874	3.25
SP530	15c	Young, #1875	5.50
SP531	18c	Flowers, #1879a	4.00
SP532	18c	Animals, #1889a	6.50
SP533	18c	Flag sheet, coil, #1890-1891	3.25
SP534	6c, 18c	Booklet pane, #1893a	3.25
SP535	20c	Flag sheet, coil, #1894-1895	3.25
SP536	20c	Flag booklet pane of 6, #1896a	3.25

1982

SP537	20c	Flag booklet pane of 10, #1896b	4.50

Transportation Coils

1981-84

SP538	1c	Omnibus, #1897	3.25
SP539	2c	Locomotive, #1897A	4.50
SP540	3c	Handcar, #1898	4.00
SP541	4c	Stagecoach, #1898A	4.25
SP542	5c	Motorcycle, #1899	5.75
SP543	5.2c	Sleigh, #1900	4.75
SP544	5.9c	Bicycle, #1901	6.50
SP545	7.4c	Baby Buggy, #1902	4.00
SP546	9.3c	Mail Wagon, #1903	4.25
SP547	10.9c	Hansom Cab, #1904	4.50
SP548	11c	Caboose, #1905	4.25
SP549	17c	Electric Auto, #1906	3.25
SP550	18c	Surrey, #1907	4.75
SP551	20c	Fire Pumper, #1908	5.25

1983

SP552	$9.35	Express Mail single, #1909	80.00
SP552a	$9.35	Express Mail booklet pane of 3, #1909a	195.00

1981

SP553	18c	Red Cross, #1910	3.25
SP554	18c	Savings and Loan, #1911	3.25
SP555	18c	Space Achievements, #1919a	8.00
SP556	18c	Management, #1920	3.25
SP557	18c	Wildlife, #1924a	4.00
SP558	18c	Disabled, #1925	3.25
SP559	18c	Millay, #1926	3.25
SP560	18c	Alcoholism, #1927	3.25
SP561	18c	Architecture, #1931a	4.50
SP562	18c	Zaharias, #1932	17.50
SP563	18c	Jones, #1933	20.00
SP564	18c	Remington, #1934	5.00
SP565	18c, 20c	Hoban, #1935-1936	3.25
SP566	18c	Yorktown, Va. Capes, #1938a	4.00
SP567	20c	Madonna and Child, #1939	3.25
SP568	20c	Teddy Bear, #1940	4.75
SP569	20c	John Hanson, #1941	3.25
SP570	20c	Desert Plants, #1945a	4.50
SP571	20c	C sheet, coil, #1946	4.00
SP572	20c	C Booklet pane of 10, #1948a	3.75

1982

SP573	20c	Bighorn Sheep, #1949a	4.00
SP574	20c	FDR, #1950	3.25
SP575	20c	Love, #1951	3.25
SP576	20c	Washington, #1952	4.00
SP577	20c	Birds and Flowers, #1953-1962	12.00
SP578	20c	Birds and Flowers, #1963-1972	12.00
SP579	20c	Birds and Flowers, #1973-1982	12.00
SP580	20c	Birds and Flowers, #1983-1992	12.00
SP581	20c	Birds and Flowers, #1993-2002	12.00
SP582	20c	US Netherlands, #2003	3.25
SP583	20c	Library of Congress, #2004	3.25
SP584	20c	Consumer Education, #2005	4.25
SP585	20c	Knoxville World's Fair, #2009a	3.25
SP586	20c	Horatio Alger, #2010	3.25
SP587	20c	Aging, #2011	3.25
SP588	20c	Barrymores, #2012	4.25
SP589	20c	Dr. Mary Walker, #2013	3.25
SP590	20c	Peace Garden, #2014	3.25
SP591	20c	Libraries, #2015	3.25
SP592	20c	Jackie Robinson, #2016	14.00
SP593	20c	Touro Synagogue, #2017	3.25
SP594	20c	Wolf Trap Farm, #2018	3.25
SP595	20c	Architecture, #2022a	4.50
SP596	20c	Francis of Assisi, #2023	3.25
SP597	20c	Ponce de Leon, #2024	3.25
SP598	13c	Puppy, Kitten, #2025	4.25
SP599	20c	Madonna and Child, #2026	4.00
SP600	20c	Children Playing, #2030a	4.50

1983

SP601	1c, 4c, 13c	Official Mail, #O127-O129	4.00
SP602	17c	Official Mail, #O130	4.00
SP603	$1	Official Mail, #O132	5.50
SP604	$5	Official Mail, #O133	10.00
SP605	20c	Official Mail coil, #O135	4.00
SP606	20c	Science, #2031	3.25
SP607	20c	Ballooning, #2035a	3.25
SP608	20c	US Sweden, #2036	3.25
SP609	20c	CCC, #2037	3.25
SP610	20c	Priestley, #2038	3.25
SP611	20c	Voluntarism, #2039	3.25
SP612	20c	German Immigration, #2040	3.25
SP613	20c	Brooklyn Bridge, #2041	3.25
SP614	20c	TVA, #2042	3.25
SP615	20c	Fitness, #2043	3.25
SP616	20c	Scott Joplin, #2044	3.25
SP617	20c	Medal of Honor, #2045	6.50
SP618	20c	Babe Ruth, #2046	12.00
SP619	20c	Hawthorne, #2047	3.25
SP620	13c	Olympics, #2051a	4.00
SP621	28c	Olympics, #C104a	4.00
SP622	40c	Olympics, #C108a	4.00
SP623	35c	Olympics, #C112a	4.00
SP624	20c	Treaty of Paris, #2052	3.25
SP625	20c	Civil Service, #2053	3.25
SP626	20c	Metropolitan Opera, #2054	3.75
SP627	20c	Inventors, #2058a	3.75
SP628	20c	Streetcars, #2062a	4.75
SP629	20c	Madonna and Child, #2063	3.25
SP630	20c	Santa Claus, #2064	3.25
SP631	20c	Martin Luther, #2065	5.25

1984-85

SP632	20c	Alaska, #2066	3.25
SP633	20c	Winter Olympics, #2070a	4.00
SP634	20c	FDIC, #2071	3.25
SP635	20c	Love, #2072	3.25
SP636	20c	Woodson, #2073	4.00
SP637	14c, 22c	D sheet, coil, #O138-O139	3.25
SP638	20c	Conservation, #2074	3.25
SP639	20c	Credit Union, #2075	3.25
SP640	20c	Orchids, #2079a	5.25
SP641	20c	Hawaii, #2080	3.75
SP642	20c	National Archives, #2081	3.25
SP643	20c	Olympics, #2085a	4.00
SP644	20c	World Expo, #2086	3.25
SP645	20c	Health Research, #2087	3.25
SP646	20c	Fairbanks, #2088	5.25
SP647	20c	Thorpe, #2089	10.00
SP648	20c	McCormack, #2090	5.25
SP649	20c	St. Lawrence Seaway, #2091	3.25
SP650	20c	Waterfowl, #2092	5.25
SP651	20c	Roanoke Voyages, #2093	3.25
SP652	20c	Melville, #2094	3.50
SP653	20c	Horace Moses, #2095	3.25
SP654	20c	Smokey Bear, #2096	10.00
SP655	20c	Clemente, #2097	13.00
SP656	20c	Dogs, #2101a	5.25
SP657	20c	Crime Prevention, #2102	3.75
SP658	20c	Hispanic Americans, #2103	3.25
SP659	20c	Family Unity, #2104	3.25
SP660	20c	Eleanor Roosevelt, #2105	4.75
SP661	20c	Readers, #2106	3.25
SP662	20c	Madonna and Child, #2107	3.25
SP663	20c	Child's Santa, #2108	3.25
SP664	20c	Vietnam Memorial, #2109	5.25

1985-87

SP665	20c	Jerome Kern, #2110	3.25
SP666	22c	D sheet, coil, #2111-2112	3.25
SP667	22c	D booklet pane of 10, #2113a	4.25
SP668	33c	Verville, #C113	3.25
SP669	39c	Sperry, #C114	3.75
SP670	44c	Transpacific, #C115	3.25
SP671	22c	Flags sheet, coil, #2114-2115	3.25
SP671a	22c	Flag "T" coil, #2115b	3.75
SP672	22c	Flag booklet pane of 5, #2116a	3.25
SP673	22c	Seashells, #2121a	5.50
SP674	$10.75	Express Mail single, #2122	47.50
SP674a	$10.75	Express Mail booklet pane of 3, #2122a	100.00

Transportation Coils

1985-89

SP675	3.4c	School Bus, #2123	4.00
SP676	4.9c	Buckboard, #2124	3.75
SP677	5.5c	Star Route Truck, #2125	4.00
SP678	6c	Tricycle, #2126	3.75

SP679 7.1c Tractor, #2127 3.25
SP679a 7.1c Tractor, Zip+4 precancel, #2127b 3.25
SP680 8.3c Ambulance, #2128 3.25
SP681 8.5c Tow Truck, #2129 3.25
SP682 10.1c Oil Wagon, #2130 3.25
SP682a 10.1c Red precancel, #2130a 3.25
SP683 11c Stutz Bearcat, #2131 3.75
SP684 12c Stanley Steamer, #2132 4.00
SP685 12.5c Pushcart, #2133 3.75
SP686 14c Iceboat, #2134 4.00
SP687 17c Dog Sled, #2135 3.25
SP688 25c Bread Wagon, #2136 4.00

1985

SP689 22c Bethune, #2137 5.25
SP690 22c Duck Decoys, #2141a 6.00
SP691 22c Winter Special Olympics, #2142 3.25
SP692 22c Love, #2143 3.50
SP693 22c REA, #2144 3.25
SP694 14c, 22c Official Mail, #O129A, O136 3.25
SP695 22c AMERIPEX '86, #2145 3.25
SP696 22c Abigail Adams, #2146 3.25
SP697 22c Bartholdi, #2147 3.75
SP698 18c Washington coil, #2149 3.25
SP699 21.1c Letters coil, #2150 3.75
SP700 22c Korean Veterans, #2152 4.00
SP701 22c Social Security, #2153 3.25
SP702 44c Serra, #C116 3.25
SP703 22c World War I Veterans, #2154 5.25
SP704 22c Horses, #2158a 5.75
SP705 22c Education, #2159 3.25
SP706 22c Youth Year, #2163a 5.75
SP707 22c Hunger, #2164 3.25
SP708 22c Madonna and Child, #2165 3.25
SP709 22c Poinsettias, #2166 3.25

1986

SP710 22c Arkansas, #2167 3.25

Great Americans

1986-94

SP711 1c Mitchell, #2168 5.50
SP712 2c Lyon, #2169 3.25
SP713 3c White, #2170 3.25
SP714 4c Flanagan, #2171 3.25
SP715 5c Black, #2172 4.00
SP716 5c Munoz Marin, #2173 3.25
SP717 10c Red Cloud, #2175 5.50
SP718 14c Howe, #2176 3.25
SP719 15c Cody, #2177 3.25
SP720 17c Lockwood, #2178 4.00
SP721 20c Apgar, #2179 4.75
SP722 21c Carlson, #2180 3.25
SP723 23c Cassatt, #2181 3.25
SP724 25c London, #2182 3.25
SP724a 25c London, pane of 10, #2182a 5.75
SP725 28c Sitting Bull, #2183 4.75
SP726 29c Warren, #2184 3.75
SP727 29c Jefferson, #2185 3.25
SP728 35c Chavez, #2186 4.00
SP729 40c Chennault, #2187 4.25
SP730 45c Cushing, #2188 3.25
SP731 52c Humphrey, #2189 3.50
SP732 56c Harvard, #2190 3.50
SP733 65c Arnold, #2191 4.50
SP734 75c Willkie, #2192 4.50
SP735 $1 Revel, #2193 3.75
SP736 $1 Hopkins, #2194 3.75
SP737 $2 Bryan, #2195 5.00
SP739 $5 Harte, #2196 10.00
SP740 25c London, #2197a 3.25

1986

SP741 22c Stamp Collecting, #2201a 4.50
SP742 22c Love, #2202 4.00
SP743 22c Sojourner Truth, #2203 5.50
SP744 22c Texas Republic, #2204 3.25
SP745 22c Fish booklet pane of 5, #2209a 6.00
SP746 22c Hospitals, #2210 2.75
SP747 22c Duke Ellington, #2211 6.00
SP748 22c Presidents Sheet #1, #2216 5.75
SP749 22c Presidents Sheet #2, #2217 5.75
SP750 22c Presidents Sheet #3, #2218 5.75
SP751 22c Presidents Sheet #4, #2219 5.75
SP752 22c Arctic Explorers, #2223a 5.25
SP753 22c Statue of Liberty, #2224 3.75

1987

SP754 2c Locomotive, reengraved, #2226 3.25

1986

SP755 22c Navajo Art, #2238a 5.25
SP756 22c T.S. Eliot, #2239 5.25
SP757 22c Woodcarved Figurines, #2243a 5.50
SP758 22c Madonna and Child, #2244 3.25
SP759 22c Village Scene, #2245 3.25

1987

SP760 22c Michigan, #2246 3.75
SP761 22c Pan American Games, #2247 3.25
SP762 22c Love, #2248 3.25
SP763 22c du Sable, #2249 6.50
SP764 22c Caruso, #2250 3.75
SP765 22c Girl Scouts, #2251 6.00

Transportation Coils

1987-88

SP766 3c Conestoga Wagon, #2252 3.25
SP767 5c, 17.5c Milk Wagon, Racing Car, #2253, 2262 3.25
SP768 5.3c Elevator, #2254 3.50
SP769 7.6c Carreta, #2255 3.50
SP770 8.4c Wheelchair, #2256 3.50
SP771 10c Canal Boat, #2257 3.75
SP772 13c Patrol Wagon, #2258 5.25
SP773 13.2c Coal Car, #2259 5.25
SP774 15c Tugboat, #2260 3.75
SP775 16.7c Popcorn Wagon, #2261 3.75
SP776 20c Cable Car, #2263 3.75
SP777 20.5c Fire Engine, #2264 4.75
SP778 21c Mail Car, #2265 4.75
SP779 24.1c Tandem Bicycle, #2266 3.50

1987

SP780 22c Special Occasions, #2274a 4.50
SP781 22c United Way, #2275 3.25

1987-89

SP782 22c Flag and Fireworks, #2276 3.25
SP783 22c Flag, pair from booklet, #2276a 3.25
SP784 (25c) "E" sheet, coil, #2277, 2279 3.50
SP785 (25c) "E" booklet pane of 10, #2282a 4.00
SP786 25c Flag with Clouds, #2278 3.25
SP787 25c Flag with Clouds booklet pane of 6, #2285c 3.75
SP788 25c Flag over Yosemite coil, block tagging, #2280 3.25
SP788a 25c Flag over Yosemite, prephosphored uncoated paper (mottled tagging), #2280a 3.25
SP789 25c Honeybee coil, #2281 4.75
SP790 25c Pheasant, #2283a 5.25
SP791 25c Owl and Grosbeak, #2285b 4.00
SP792 (25c) "E" Official coil, #O140 3.25
SP793 20c Official coil, #O138B 3.25
SP794 15c, 25c Official coils, #O138A, O141 3.25

1987

SP795 22c Wildlife, #2286-2295 6.50
SP796 22c Wildlife, #2296-2305 6.50
SP797 22c Wildlife, #2306-2315 6.50
SP798 22c Wildlife, #2316-2325 6.50
SP799 22c Wildlife, #2326-2335 6.50

Ratification of the Constitution

1987-90

SP800 22c Delaware, #2336 3.75
SP801 22c Pennsylvania, #2337 3.25
SP802 22c New Jersey, #2338 3.75
SP803 22c Georgia, #2339 3.75
SP804 22c Connecticut, #2340 3.75
SP805 22c Massachusetts, #2341 3.75
SP806 22c Maryland, #2342 3.75
SP807 25c South Carolina, #2343 3.25
SP808 25c New Hampshire, #2344 3.25
SP809 25c Virginia, #2345 3.75
SP810 25c New York, #2346 3.25
SP811 25c North Carolina, #2347 3.75
SP812 25c Rhode Island, #2348 3.25

1987

SP813 22c U.S./Morocco, #2349 3.25
SP814 22c William Faulkner, #2350 6.25
SP815 22c Lacemaking, #2354a 6.75
SP816 22c Constitution, #2359a 4.00
SP817 22c Signing of Constitution, #2360 3.25
SP818 22c Certified Public Accounting, #2361 6.00
SP819 22c Locomotives, #2366a 9.00
SP820 22c Madonna and Child, #2367 3.25
SP821 22c Christmas Ornament, #2368 3.25

1988

SP822 22c Winter Olympics, #2369 3.25
SP823 22c Australia Bicentennial, #2370 4.00
SP824 22c James Weldon Johnson, #2371 3.75
SP825 22c Cats, #2375a 6.50
SP826 22c Knute Rockne, #2376 10.00
SP827 44c New Sweden, #C117 3.25
SP828 45c Samuel P. Langley, #C118 3.25
SP829 25c Francis Ouimet, #2377 12.00
SP830 36c Igor Sikorsky, #C119 3.25
SP831 25c Love, #2378 3.25
SP832 45c Love, #2379 3.25
SP833 25c Summer Olympics, #2380 3.25
SP834 25c Classic Automobiles, #2385a 6.00
SP835 25c Antarctic Explorers, #2389a 3.75
SP836 25c Carousel Animals, #2393a 5.25
SP837 $8.75 Express Mail, #2394 22.00
SP838 25c Special Occasions, #2396a 20.00
SP839 25c Special Occasions, #2398a 20.00
SP840 25c Madonna and Child, #2399 3.25
SP841 25c Village Scene, #2400 3.25

1989

SP842 25c Montana, #2401 3.25
SP843 25c A. Philip Randolph, #2402 4.25
SP844 25c North Dakota, #2403 3.25
SP845 25c Washington Statehood, #2404 3.25
SP846 25c Steamboats, #2409a 6.50
SP847 25c World Stamp Expo, #2410 3.25
SP848 25c Toscanini, #2411 5.25

Branches of Government

1989-90

SP849 25c House of Representatives, #2412 3.25
SP850 25c Senate, #2413 3.25
SP851 25c Executive, #2414 3.25
SP852 25c Supreme Court, #2415 3.25

1989

SP853 25c South Dakota, #2416 3.25
SP854 25c Lou Gehrig, #2417 12.00
SP855 1c Official, litho., #O143 3.25
SP856 45c French Revolution, #C120 5.25
SP857 25c Ernest Hemingway, #2418 6.00
SP858 $2.40 Moon Landing, #2419 20.00
SP859 25c Letter Carriers, #2420 3.25
SP860 25c Bill of Rights, #2421 3.25
SP861 25c Dinosaurs, #2425a 8.00
SP862 25c, 45c Pre-Columbian Artifacts, #2426, C121 3.25
SP863 25c Madonna sheet single, booklet pane of 10, #2427, 2427a 7.25
SP864 25c Sleigh single, booklet pane of 10, #2428, 2429a 7.25
SP865 25c Eagle & Shield, #2431 3.25
SP866 90c World Stamp Expo '89, #2433 12.00
SP867 25c Traditional Mail Delivery, #2437a 5.00
SP868 45c Futuristic Mail Delivery, #C126 6.00
SP869 45c Futuristic Mail Delivery, #C125a 6.00
SP870 25c Traditional Mail Delivery, #2438 6.50

1990

SP871 25c Idaho, #2439 3.25
SP872 25c Love single, booklet pane of 10, #2440, 2441a 5.25
SP873 25c Ida B. Wells, #2442 5.25
SP874 15c Beach Umbrella, #2443a 5.25
SP875 25c Wyoming, #2444 4.00
SP876 25c Classic Films, #2448a 9.00
SP877 25c Marianne Moore, #2449 4.00

Transportation Coils

1990-92

SP879 4c Steam Carriage, #2451 3.50
SP880 5c Circus Wagon, #2452 3.75
SP880A 5c Circus Wagon, #2452B 5.25
SP880B 5c Circus Wagon with cent sign, #2452D 5.00
SP881 5c, 10c Canoe, engr., Tractor Trailer, #2453, 2457 3.50
SP882 5c Canoe, photo., #2454 3.75
SP883 10c Tractor trailer, photo., #2458 5.00
SP891 20c Cog Railway, #2463 4.00
SP892 23c Lunch Wagon, #2464 3.75
SP893 32c Ferry Boat, #2466 4.00
SP895 $1 Seaplane, #2468 6.50

1990-94

SP897 25c Lighthouses, booklet pane of 5, #2474a 9.00
SP898 25c Flag, #2475 3.75

Flora and Fauna Series

SP899 1c, 3c, 30c Kestrel, Bluebird, Cardinal, #2476, 2478, 2480 3.50
SP900 1c Kestrel with cent sign, #2477 3.50
SP901 19c Fawn, #2479 3.50
SP902 45c Pumpkinseed Sunfish, #2481 3.75
SP903 $2 Bobcat, #2482 5.25
SP904 20c Blue jay, #2483 3.50
SP905 29c Wood Ducks booklet panes of 10, #2484a, 2485a 12.00
SP906 29c African Violets bklt. pane of 10, #2486a 5.00
SP907 32c Peach & Pear, #2488b, 2493-2494 5.25
SP908 29c Red Squirrel, #2489 3.75
SP909 29c Red Rose, #2490 3.25
SP910 29c Pine Cone, #2491 3.75
SP911 32c Pink rose, #2492 5.25
SP919 25c Olympians, #2496-2500 5.75
SP920 25c Indian Headdresses, #2505a 6.75
SP921 25c Micronesia, Marshall Islands, #2507a 3.25
SP922 25c Sea Creatures, #2511a 7.00
SP923 25c, 45c Grand Canyon, Tropical Coastline, #2512, C127 3.25
SP924 25c Eisenhower, #2513 3.75
SP925 25c Madonna sheet single, booklet pane of 10, #2514, 2514a 6.00
SP926 25c Christmas Tree sheet single, booklet pane of 10, #2515, 2516a 6.00

1991-95

SP927 (29c) "F" Flower single, coil pair, #2517, 2518 3.25
SP928 (29c) "F" Flower booklet panes of 10, #2519a, 2520a 10.00
SP929 (4c) Make-up Rate, #2521 3.25
SP930 (29c) "F" Flag, #2522 3.75
SP931 (29c) "F" Official coil, #O144 3.25
SP932 29c Mt. Rushmore, #2523 3.75
SP933 29c Mt. Rushmore, photo., #2523A 3.25
SP934 29c Flower single, booklet pane of 10, #2524, 2527a 6.25
SP935 29c Flower coil, #2525 3.25
SP936 29c Flower coil, #2526 3.25
SP937 4c Official, #O146 3.50
SP938 29c Flag, Olympic Rings, #2528a 6.50
SP939 19c Fishing Boat coil, #2529 5.25
SP939A 19c Fishing Boat coil reissue, #2529C 4.00
SP940 19c Ballooning, #2530a 5.25
SP941 29c Flags on Parade, #2531 3.50
SP942 29c Liberty Torch, #2531A 3.50
SP943 50c Switzerland, #2532 3.25
SP944 20c Vermont Statehood, #2533 3.50
SP945 50c Harriet Quimby, #C128 3.75

SP946	29c	Savings Bonds, #2534	3.25
SP947	29c, 52c	Love, #2535, 2536a, 2537	12.00
SP948	40c	William T. Piper, #C129	3.25
SP949	29c	William Saroyan, #2538	6.00
SP950		Official 19c, 23c, 29c, #O145, O147-O148	3.50
SP951	$1.00	USPS/Olympic Rings, #2539	4.00
SP952	$2.90	Eagle, #2540	12.00
SP953	$9.95	Eagle, #2541	32.50
SP954	$14	Eagle, #2542	42.50
SP955	$2.90	Futuristic Space Shuttle, #2543	12.00
SP956	$3	Challenger Shuttle, #2544	14.00
SP956A	$10.75	Endeavour Shuttle, #2544A	25.00
SP957	29c	Fishing Flies, #2549a	19.00
SP958	29c	Cole Porter, #2550	3.75
SP959	50c	Antarctic Treaty, #C130	3.75
SP960	29c	Desert Shield, Desert Storm, #2551	10.00
SP961	29c	1992 Summer Olympics, #2553-2557	7.00
SP962	29c	Numismatics, #2558	5.20
SP963	29c	World War II, #2559	11.00
SP964	29c	Basketball, #2560	8.00
SP965	29c	District of Columbia, #2561	3.25
SP966	29c	Comedians, #2566a	8.75
SP967	29c	Jan E. Matzeliger, #2567	6.00
SP968	29c	Space Exploration, #2577a	11.00
SP969	50c	Bering Land Bridge, #C131	3.25
SP970	29c	Madonna and Child sheet single, booklet pane of 10, #2578, 2578a	11.00
SP971	29c	Santa Claus sheet and booklet singles, #2579, 2580 or 2581, 2582-2585	18.00
SP973	32c	James K. Polk, #2587	7.00
SP976	$1	Surrender of Gen. Burgoyne, #2590	5.00
SP978	$5	Washington and Jackson, #2592	13.00
SP980	29c	Pledge of Allegiance, #2593a	5.00
SP982	29c	Eagle & Shield self-adhesives, #2595-2597	4.50
SP983	29c	Eagle self-adhesive, #2598	3.50
SP984	29c	Statue of Liberty, #2599	3.50
SP990	(10c)	Eagle and Shield coil, #2602	5.25
SP991	(10c)	Eagle and Shield coils, #2603-2604	5.25
SP993	23c	Stars and Stripes coil, #2605	3.25
SP994	23c	USA coil, #2606	4.00
SP994A	23c	USA coil, #2607	3.25
SP994B	23c	USA coil, #2608	3.50
SP995	29c	Flag over White House, #2609	3.50

1992

SP997	29c	Winter Olympics, #2611-2615	5.25
SP998	29c	World Columbian Stamp Expo '92, #2616	4.50
SP999	29c	W.E.B. DuBois, #2617	6.00
SP1000	29c	Love, #2618	3.25
SP1001	29c	Olympic Baseball, #2619	14.00
SP1002	29c	First Voyage of Columbus, #2623a	4.50
SP1003	1c, 4c, $1	First Sighting of Land souvenir sheet, #2624	10.00
SP1004	2c, 3c, $4	Claiming a New World souvenir sheet, #2625	11.00
SP1005	5c, 30c, 50c	Seeking Royal Support souvenir sheet, #2626	9.00
SP1006	6c, 8c, $3	Royal Favor Restored souvenir sheet, #2627	11.00
SP1007	10c, 15c, $2	Reporting Discoveries souvenir sheet, #2628	10.00
SP1008	$5	Columbus souvenir sheet, #2629	12.00
SP1009	29c	New York Stock Exchange, #2630	3.50
SP1010	29c	Space Accomplishments, #2634a	7.50
SP1011	29c	Alaska Highway, #2635	3.75
SP1012	29c	Kentucky Statehood, #2636	3.50
SP1013	29c	Summer Olympics, #2637-2641	5.25
SP1014	29c	Hummingbirds, #2646a	8.00
SP1015	29c	Wildflowers, #2647-2656	8.00
SP1016	29c	Wildflowers, #2657-2666	8.00
SP1017	29c	Wildflowers, #2667-2676	8.00
SP1018	29c	Wildflowers, #2677-2686	8.00
SP1019	29c	Wildflowers, #2687-2696	8.00
SP1020	29c	World War II, #2697	7.75
SP1021	29c	Dorothy Parker, #2698	3.75
SP1022	29c	Dr. Theodore von Karman, #2699	6.00
SP1023	29c	Minerals strip of 4, #2703a	5.75
SP1024	29c	Juan Rodriguez Cabrillo, #2704	3.75
SP1025	29c	Wild Animals, #2709a	7.25
SP1026	29c	Madonna and Child sheet single, booklet pane of 10, #2710, 2710a	10.00
SP1027	29c	Christmas Toys block of 4, booklet pane of 4 and booklet single, #2714a, 2718a, 2719	6.00
SP1028	29c	Chinese New Year, #2720	11.00

1993

SP1029	29c	Elvis Presley, #2721	14.00
SP1030	29c	Oklahoma!, #2722	3.25
SP1030A	29c	Hank Williams sheet stamp, #2723A	6.00
SP1030B	29c	Rock & Roll/Rhythm & Blues sheet single, booklet pane of 8, #2737b	24.00

No. SP1030B exists with any one of #2724-2730 affixed along with #2737b.

SP1034	29c	Space Fantasy, #2745a	10.00
SP1035	29c	Percy Lavon Julian, #2746	5.25
SP1036	29c	Oregon Trail, #2747	3.25
SP1037	29c	World University Games, #2748	3.25
SP1038	29c	Grace Kelly, #2749	9.00
SP1039	29c	Circus, #2753a	6.00
SP1040	29c	Cherokee Strip, #2754	5.00
SP1041	29c	Dean Acheson, #2755	3.25
SP1042	29c	Sporting Horses, #2759a	7.00
SP1043	29c	Garden Flowers, #2764a	5.25
SP1044	29c	World War II, #2765	9.00
SP1045	29c	Joe Louis, #2766	12.00
SP1046	29c	Broadway Musicals, #2770a	6.75
SP1047	29c	National Postal Museum strip of 4, #2782a	4.50
SP1048	29c	American Sign Language, #2784a	3.25
SP1049	29c	Country & Western Music sheet stamp and booklet pane of 4, #2778a	15.00

No. SP1049 exists with any one of #2771-2774 affixed along with #2778a.

SP1050	10c	Official Mail, #O146A	3.50
SP1052	29c	Classic Books strip of 4, #2788a	4.25
SP1053	29c	Traditional Christmas sheet stamp, booklet pane of 4, #2789, 2790a	6.75
SP1054	29c	Contemporary Christmas booklet pane of 10, sheet and self-adhesive single stamps, #2803	18.00

No. SP1054 exists with any one of #2791-2794, 2798a, 2798b, 2799-2802 affixed along with #2803.

SP1055	29c	Mariana Islands, #2804	3.25
SP1056	29c	Columbus' Landing in Puerto Rico, #2805	4.00
SP1057	29c	AIDS Awareness, #2806, 2806b	6.50

1994

SP1058	29c	Winter Olympics, #2811a	6.75
SP1059	29c	Edward R. Murrow, #2812	4.25
SP1060	29c	Love self-adhesive, #2813	4.25
SP1061	29c, 52c	Love booklet pane of 10, single sheet stamp, #2814a, 2815	9.00
SP1062	29c	Love sheet stamp, #2814C	4.00
SP1063	29c	Dr. Allison Davis, #2816	6.50
SP1064	29c	Chinese New Year, #2817	4.75
SP1065	29c	Buffalo Soldiers, #2818	7.00
SP1066	29c	Silent Screen Stars, #2819-2828	8.00
SP1067	29c	Garden Flowers, #2833a	8.00
SP1068	29c, 40c, 50c	World Cup Soccer, #2834-2836	8.00
SP1069		World Cup Soccer, #2837	8.00
SP1070	29c	World War II, #2838	7.25
SP1071	29c, 50c	Norman Rockwell stamp, souvenir sheet, #2839-2840	14.00
SP1072	29c, $9.95	Moon Landing, #2841-2842	25.00
SP1073	29c	Locomotives, #2847a	8.75
SP1074	29c	George Meany, #2848	4.00
SP1075	29c	Popular Singers, #2853a	8.00
SP1076	29c	Jazz and Blues Singers block of 10, #2854-2861	11.00

Block of 10 on No. SP1076 may contain different combinations of stamps.

SP1077	29c	James Thurber, #2862	5.25
SP1078	29c	Wonders of the Sea, #2866a	6.50
SP1079	29c	Cranes, #2868a	4.00
SP1079A		Legends of the West, #2869	21.50
SP1080	29c	Traditional Christmas sheet stamp, booklet pane of 10, #2871, 2871b	9.75
SP1081	29c	Contemporary Christmas sheet stamp, block of 4 from booklet pane, #2872	6.75
SP1082	29c	Contemporary Christmas self-adhesive stamps, #2873--2874	8.00
SP1083	$2	Bureau of Engraving and Printing Souvenir Sheet, #2875	18.00

1995-96

SP1084	29c	Chinese New Year, #2876	6.75
SP1085	G	make-up rate, G stamps, #2877, 2884, 2890, 2893	5.25
SP1086	G	make-up rate, G stamps, #2878, 2880, 2882, 2885, 2888, 2892	5.25
SP1087	G	stamps, official G stamp, #2879, 2881, 2883, 2889, O152	5.25
SP1088	G	self-adhesive stamps, #2886-2887	10.00
SP1091	32c	Flag Over Porch, #2897, 2913, 2915-2916	6.50
SP1096	(5c)	Butte coil, #2902	5.75
SP1097	(5c)	Mountain coil, #2903, 2904	6.50
SP1099		Butte, Mountain, Juke Box, Auto Tail Fin, Auto, Flag over porch, #2902B, 2904A, 2906, 2910, 2912A, 2915B	5.50
SP1099A		Mountain, Juke Box, Flag Over Porch coil and booklet stamps, #2904B, 2912B, 2915D, 2921b	5.50
SP1100	(10c)	Auto coil, #2905	5.25
SP1102		Eagle & shield, Flag over porch, #2907, 2920D, 2921	5.25
SP1103	(15c)	Auto Tail Fin, #2908-2909	5.25
SP1105	(25c)	Juke Box, #2911-2912	4.25
SP1110	32c	Flag over Field self-adhesive, #2919	6.00
SP1114	(32c)	Non-denominated Love, #2948-2949	3.25
SP1115	32c	Florida Statehood, #2950	3.25

Great Americans Series

1995-99

SP1126	32c	Milton Hershey, #2933	3.25
SP1127	32c	Cal Farley, #2934	4.00
SP1128	32c	Henry R. Luce, #2935	7.25
SP1129	32c	Lila & DeWitt Wallace, #2936	5.75
SP1131	46c	Ruth Benedict, #2938	4.00
SP1133	55c	Alice Hamilton, #2940	3.25
SP1134	55c	Justin S. Morrill, #2941	7.25
SP1135	77c	Mary Breckinridge, #2942	6.50
SP1136	78c	Alice Paul, #2943	3.25

1995

SP1141	32c	Kids Care, #2954a	4.00
SP1142	32c	Richard Nixon, #2955	4.00
SP1143	32c	Bessie Coleman, #2956	5.25
SP1144	1-32c	Official, #O153-O156	3.50
SP1145	32c, 55c	Love (with denominations), #2957-2960	4.00
SP1146	32c	Recreational Sports, #2965a	10.00
SP1147	32c	Prisoners of War/Missing in Action, #2966	4.50
SP1148	32c	Marilyn Monroe, #2967	14.00
SP1149	32c	Texas Statehood, #2968	5.00
SP1150	32c	Great Lakes Lighthouses, #2973a	10.00
SP1151	32c	United Nations, #2974	3.25
SP1152	32c	Civil War, #2975	16.00
SP1153	32c	Carousel Horses, #2979a	7.00
SP1154	32c	Woman Suffrage, #2980	3.25
SP1155	32c	World War II, #2981	8.00
SP1156	32c	Louis Armstrong, #2982	5.00
SP1157	32c	Jazz Musicians, #2992a	9.00
SP1158	32c	Garden Flowers, #2997a	8.00
SP1159	60c	Eddie Rickenbacker, #2998	5.00
SP1160	32c	Republic of Palau, #2999	4.00
SP1161	32c	Comic Strip Classics, #3000	16.00
SP1162	32c	Naval Academy, #3001	5.00
SP1163	32c	Tennessee Williams, #3002	5.00
SP1164	32c	Traditional Christmas sheet stamp, booklet pane of 10, #3003, 3003b	7.25
SP1165	32c	Contemporary Christmas block of 4, self-adhesive stamps, #3007a, 3010-3011	6.00

No. SP1165 may include different combinations of Nos. 3008-3011.

SP1166	32c	Midnight Angel, #3012	5.25
SP1167	32c	Children Sledding, #3013	5.25
SP1168	32c	Antique Automobiles, #3023a	7.50

1996

SP1169	32c	Utah Statehood, #3024	4.00
SP1170	32c	Garden Flowers, #3029a	7.25
SP1171	1, 32c	Flag Over Porch, Love self-adhesives, Kestrel coil, #2920e, 3030, 3044	16.00

1996-99

Flora and Fauna Series

SP1171A	1c	Kestrel, self-adhesive, #3031	7.25
SP1172	2c	Woodpecker, #3032	4.00
SP1173	3c	Bluebird, #3033	4.00
SP1184	$1	Red Fox, #3036	9.00
SP1185	2c	Woodpecker coil, #3045	7.25
SP1187	20c	Bluejay self-adhesive coil, booklet stamps, #3048, 3053	5.75
SP1188	32c	Yellow Rose, #3049	6.00
SP1189	20c	Ring-necked Pheasant, #3050, 3055	7.25
SP1191A	33c	Coral Pink Rose, serpentine die cut 10¾x10½, #3052E	7.25
SP1191	33c	Coral Pink Rose, #3052	7.25
SP1192	32c	Yellow Rose coil, #3054	7.25

1996

SP1197	32c	Ernest E. Just, #3058	6.00
SP1198	32c	Smithsonian Institution, #3059	4.00
SP1199	32c	Chinese New Year, #3060	7.25
SP1200	32c	Pioneers of Communication, #3064a	5.50
SP1201	32c	Fulbright Scholarships, #3065	4.00
SP1202	50c	Jacqueline Cochran, #3066	4.00
SP1203	32c	Marathon, #3067	4.00
SP1204	32c	Olympic Games, #3068	17.50
SP1205	32c	Georgia O'Keeffe, #3069	5.25
SP1206	32c	Tennessee Statehood, #3070	4.00
SP1207	32c	American Indian Dances, #3076a	5.25
SP1208	32c	Prehistoric Animals, #3080a	5.25
SP1209	32c	Breast Cancer Awareness, #3081	5.75
SP1210	32c	James Dean, #3082	7.25
SP1211	32c	Folk Heroes, #3086a	6.25

SP1212 32c Centennial Olympic Games, #3087 5.75
SP1213 32c Iowa Statehood, #3088-3089 5.75
SP1214 32c Rural Free Delivery, #3090 4.50
SP1215 32c Riverboats, #3095a 75.00
SP1216 32c Big Band Leaders, #3099a 7.25
SP1217 32c Songwriters, #3103a 7.25
SP1218 23c F. Scott Fitzgerald, #3104 4.50
SP1219 32c Endangered Species, #3105 18.00
SP1220 32c Computer Technology, #3106 4.50
SP1221 32c Madonna & Child sheet & booklet stamps, #3107, 3112 7.25
SP1222 32c Contemporary Christmas block of 4, self-adhesive stamp, #3111a, 3113 7.25

#SP1222 may contain #3114-3116 instead of #3113.

SP1223 32c Skaters, #3117 7.25
SP1224 32c Hanukkah, #3118 5.75
SP1225 32c Cycling souvenir sheet, #3119 7.25

1997

SP1226 32c Chinese New Year, #3120 8.75
SP1227 32c Benjamin O. Davis, Sr., #3121 7.25
SP1228 32c Statue of Liberty, #3122 6.50
SP1229 32, 55c Love Swans, #3123-3124 6.50
SP1230 32c Helping Children Learn, #3125 5.75
SP1231 32c Merian Botanical Prints, #3126-3129 6.50
SP1232 32c PACIFIC 97 Triangles, #3131a 7.25
SP1233 (25c), 32c Flag Over Porch, Juke Box linerless coils, #3132-3133 6.50
SP1234 32c Thornton Wilder, #3134 5.75
SP1235 32c Raoul Wallenberg, #3135 5.75
SP1236 32c Dinosaurs, #3136 18.00
SP1237 32c Bugs Bunny, #3137 18.00
SP1238 50c PACIFIC 97 Franklin, #3139 16.00
SP1239 60c PACIFIC 97 Washington, #3140 16.00
SP1240 32c Marshall Plan, #3141 6.50
SP1241 32c Classic American Aircraft, #3142 18.00
SP1242 32c Football Coaches, #3146a 16.00
SP1242A 32c Vince Lombardi, #3147 11.00
SP1242B 32c Bear Bryant, #3148 11.00
SP1242C 32c Pop Warner, #3149 11.00
SP1242D 32c George Halas, #3150 11.00
SP1243 32c Classic American Dolls, #3151 15.00
SP1244 32c Humphrey Bogart, #3152 7.25
SP1245 32c The Stars and Stripes Forever!, #3153 7.25
SP1246 32c Opera Singers, #3157a 11.00
SP1247 32c Composers & Conductors, #3165a 12.00
SP1248 32c Padre Felix Varela, #3155 7.20
SP1249 32c Department of the Air Force, #3167 11.00
SP1250 32c Movie Monsters, #3172a 14.00
SP1251 32c Supersonic Flight, #3173 11.00
SP1252 32c Women in Military Service, #3174 7.25
SP1253 32c Kwanzaa, #3175 8.00
SP1254 32c Madonna and Child, #3176 9.00
SP1255 32c Holly, #3177 9.00
SP1256 $3 Mars Pathfinder, #3178 18.00

1998

SP1257 32c Chinese New Year, #3179 8.00
SP1258 32c Alpine Skiing, #3180 8.00
SP1259 32c Madam C.J. Walker, #3181 8.00

1998-2000

Celebrate the Century

SP1259A 32c 1900s, #3182 17.50
SP1259B 32c 1910s, #3183 17.50
SP1259C 32c 1920s, #3184 17.50
SP1259D 32c 1930s, #3185 17.50
SP1259E 32c 1940s, #3186 17.50
SP1259F 33c 1950s, #3187 17.50
SP1259G 33c 1960s, #3188 17.50
SP1259H 33c 1970s, #3189 17.50
SP1259I 33c 1980s, #3190 17.50
SP1259J 33c 1990s, #3191 17.50

1998

SP1260 32c "Remember the Maine," #3192 8.00
SP1261 32c Flowering Trees, #3197a 9.75
SP1262 32c Alexander Calder, #3202a 9.75
SP1263 32c Cinco de Mayo, #3203 7.25
SP1264 32c Sylvester & Tweety, #3204a 9.75
SP1265 32c Wisconsin Statehood, #3206 8.00
SP1266 (5c), (25c) Wetlands, Diner Coils, #3207-3208 7.25
SP1266A (25c) Diner coil, #3208A 7.25
SP1267 1c-$2 Trans-Mississippi, #3209 20.00
SP1268 $1 Trans-Mississippi, #3209h 15.00
SP1269 32c Berlin Airlift, #3211 7.25
SP1270 32c Folk Musicians, #3215a 10.00
SP1271 32c Gospel Singers, #3219a 9.00
SP1272 32c Spanish Settlement, #3220 7.25
SP1273 32c Stephen Vincent Benét, #3221 7.25
SP1274 32c Tropical Birds, #3225a 11.00
SP1275 32c Alfred Hitchcock, #3226 8.00
SP1276 32c Organ & Tissue Donation, #3227 7.25
SP1277 (10c) Modern Bicycle, #3229 7.25
SP1278 32c Bright Eyes, #3234a 10.00
SP1279 32c Klondike Gold Rush, #3235 8.00
SP1280 32c American Art, #3236 16.00
SP1281 32c Ballet, #3237 8.00
SP1282 32c Space Discovery, #3242a 9.75
SP1283 32c Giving & Sharing, #3243 7.25
SP1284 32c Madonna & Child, #3244 7.25
SP1285 32c Wreaths, #3248a, 3252a 9.75
SP1286 (32+8c) Breast Cancer Awareness, #B1 8.00
SP1287 (1c), (33c) Weather Vane, Uncle Sam's Hat, #3257-3258, 3260 8.00
SP1288 22c Uncle Sam, #3259, 3263 7.25
SP1289 $3.20 Space Shuttle Landing, #3261 17.50
SP1290 $11.75 Piggyback Space Shuttle, #3262 27.50
SP1291 (33c) Uncle Sam's Hat, #3267-3269 8.50
SP1292 (33c) Uncle Sam's Hat, #3264, 3266 9.00
SP1293 (5c), (10c) Wetlands, Eagle & Shield, #3207A, 3270-3271 8.00

1999

SP1294 33c Chinese New Year, #3272 9.75
SP1295 33x Malcolm X, #3273 13.00
SP1296 33c Love, #3274 8.00
SP1297 55c Love, #3275 8.00
SP1298 33c Hospice Care, #3276 7.25
SP1299 33c Flag and City, #3279-3280, 3282 8.00
SP1300 33c Flag Over Chalkboard, #3283 7.25
SP1301 33c Irish Immigration, #3286 7.25
SP1302 33c Lunt & Fontanne, #3287 7.25
SP1303 33c Arctic Animals, #3292a 9.75
SP1304 33c Sonoran Desert, #3293 16.00
SP1305 33c Berries, #3294-3297 9.00
SP1306 33c Daffy Duck, #3306a 9.75
SP1307 33c Ayn Rand, #3308 8.00
SP1308 33c Cinco de Mayo, #3309 7.25
SP1309 33c Tropical Flowers, #3310-3313 9.00
SP1310 48c Niagara Falls, #C133 8.50
SP1311 33c John & William Bartram, #3314 7.25
SP1312 33c Prostate Cancer, #3315 7.25
SP1313 33c California Gold Rush, #3316 7.25
SP1314 33c Aquarium Fish, #3317-3320 9.00
SP1315 33c Extreme Sports, #3321-3324 8.75
SP1316 33c American Glass, #3328a 9.00
SP1317 33c James Cagney, #3329 9.00
SP1318 55c Billy Mitchell, #3330 8.75
SP1319 40c Rio Grande, #C134 7.25
SP1320 33c Honoring Those Who Served, #3331 7.25
SP1321 45c Universal Postal Union, #3332 7.25
SP1322 33c Famous Trains, #3337a 10.00
SP1323 33c Frederick Law Olmsted, #3338 7.25
SP1324 33c Hollywood Composers, #3344a 15.00
SP1325 33c Broadway Songwriters, #3350a 14.50
SP1326 33c Insects & Spiders, #3351 18.00
SP1327 33c Hanukkah, #3352 7.25
SP1328 22c Uncle Sam, #3353 7.25
SP1329 33c Official coil, #O157 7.25
SP1330 33c NATO, #3354 7.25
SP1331 33c Madonna & Child, #3355 7.25
SP1332 33c Christmas Deer, #3359a 8.75
SP1333 33c Kwanzaa, #3368 7.25
SP1334 33c Year 2000, #3369 7.25

2000

SP1335 33c Chinese New Year, #3370 9.75
SP1336 60c Grand Canyon, #C135 7.25
SP1337 33c Patricia Roberts Harris, #3371 8.00
SP1338 33c Berries, dated 2000, #3294a-3296a, 3297c 8.00
SP1339 33c Los Angeles Class Submarine (sheet stamp), #3372 16.00
SP1340 33c Pacific Coast Rain Forest, #3378 18.50
SP1341 33c Louise Nevelson, #3383a 9.25
SP1342 33c Hubble Space Telescope Images, #3388a 9.25
SP1343 33c American Samoa, #3389 7.25
SP1344 33c Library of Congress, #3390 7.25
SP1345 33c Road Runner & Wile E. Coyote, #3391a 10.00
SP1346 33c Distinguished Soldiers, 3396a 9.75
SP1347 33c Summer Sports, #3397 7.25
SP1348 33c Adoption, #3398 11.00
SP1349 33c Youth Team Sports, #3402a 8.00
SP1350 33c The Stars and Stripes, #3403 16.00
SP1351 33c Legends of Baseball, #3408 20.00
SP1352 33c Stampin' the Future, #3417a 8.00

Distinguished Americans Series

2000-07

SP1355 10c Gen. Joseph W. Stilwell, #3420 7.25
SP1357 23c Wilma Rudolph, #3422, 3436 7.25
SP1361 33c Claude Pepper, #3426 7.25
SP1362 58c Margaret Chase Smith, #3427 7.50
SP1363 63c Dr. Jonas Salk, #3428 7.50
SP1365 75c Harriet Beecher Stowe, #3430 7.50
SP1366 76c Hattie Caraway, #3431 7.25
SP1367 83c Edna Ferber, #3432 7.25
SP1368 87c Dr. Albert Sabin, #3435 7.50

2000

SP1373 33c California Statehood, #3438 7.25
SP1374 33c Deep Sea Creatures, #3443a 9.25
SP1375 33c Thomas Wolfe, #3444 8.00
SP1376 33c White House, #3445 7.25
SP1377 33c Edward G. Robinson, #3446 8.00
SP1378 (10c) New York Public Library Lion, #3447 7.25
SP1379 (34c) Flag Over Farm, #3448-3450 7.25
SP1380 (34c) Statue of Liberty, #3451-3453 7.25
SP1381 (34c) Flowers, #3454-3457 7.25

2001

SP1382 34c Statue of Liberty self-adhesive coil, #3466 6.50
SP1382A 21c American Buffalo, #3467, 3484 6.50
SP1383 21c American Buffalo, #3468, 3475 6.50
SP1383A 23c George Washington, #3468A, 3475A 7.25
SP1384 34c Flag over Farm, #3469 6.50
SP1385 34c Flag over Farm self-adhesive, #3470 6.50
SP1386 55c Eagle, #3471 7.25
SP1386A 57c Eagle, #3471A 7.50
SP1387 $3.50 US Capitol, #3472 13.50
SP1388 $12.25 Washington Monument, #3473 27.50
SP1389 34c Statue of Liberty, #3476, 3477, 3485 7.50
SP1390 34c Flowers, #3478-3481 7.50
SP1391 20c George Washington, #3482 6.50
SP1392 34c Apple and Orange, #3491, 3492 7.25
SP1393 34c Flag over Farm self-adhesive booklet, #3495 8.00
SP1394 (34c) Love, #3496 6.50
SP1395 34c, 55c Love, #3497, 3499 9.00
SP1396 34c Chinese New Year, #3500 8.75
SP1397 34c Roy Wilkins, #3501 10.00
SP1398 34c American Illustrators, #3502 26.00
SP1399 34c Official, #O158 6.50
SP1400 70c Nine-Mile Prairie, #C136 7.25
SP1401 34c Diabetes Awareness, #3503 8.00
SP1402 34c Nobel Prize, #3504 8.00
SP1403 1c-80c Pan-American Inverts, #3505 18.00
SP1404 80c Mt. McKinley, #C137 9.00
SP1405 34c Great Plains Prairie, #3506 17.50
SP1406 34c Peanuts Comic Strip, #3507 12.00
SP1407 34c Honoring Veterans, #3508 9.00
SP1408 60c Acadia National Park, #C138 8.00
SP1409 34c Frida Kahlo, #3509 12.00
SP1410 34c Legendary Playing Fields, #3510-3519 27.50
SP1411 (10c) Atlas Statue, #3520 6.50
SP1412 34c Leonard Bernstein, #3521 8.00
SP1413 (15c) Woody Wagon, #3522 6.50
SP1414 34c Lucille Ball, #3523 10.00
SP1415 34c Amish Quilts, #3524-3527 8.75
SP1416 34c Carnivorous Plants, #3528-3531 8.75
SP1417 34c Eid, #3532 6.50
SP1418 34c Enrico Fermi, #3533 8.00
SP1419 34c That's All Folks!, #3534a 10.00
SP1420 34c Christmas Madonna, #3536 6.50
SP1421 34c Christmas Santas, #3537-3540 8.00
SP1422 34c James Madison, #3545 6.50
SP1423 34c Thanksgiving, #3546 6.50
SP1424 34c Hanukkah, #3547 6.50
SP1425 34c Kwanzaa, #3548 6.50
SP1426 34c United We Stand booklet and coil, #3549, 3550 13.50
SP1427 57c Love, #3551 7.50

2002

SP1428 34c Winter Olympics, #3552-3555 9.75
SP1429 34c Mentoring a Child, #3556 6.50
SP1430 34c Langston Hughes, #3557 9.75
SP1431 34c Happy Birthday, #3558 6.50
SP1432 34c Chinese New Year, #3559 8.00
SP1433 34c US Military Academy, Bicent., #3560 8.00
SP1434 34c Greetings from America, #3561-3610 37.50
SP1435 34c Longleaf Pine Forest, #3611 17.50
SP1436 5c Toleware Coffeepot, #3612 6.50
SP1437 3c Star, #3613-3615 6.50
SP1438 23c George Washington, #3616-3618 7.50
SP1439 (37c) Flag, #3620-3623 8.75
SP1440 (37c) Toy coils, #3626-3629 8.00

2003

SP1440A 37c Flag, perf. 11¼, #3629F 6.50

2002

SP1441 37c Flag, #3630-3631, 3633, 3635 6.50

2003

SP1441A 37c Flag, self-adhesive booklet stamp, #3637 8.00

2002

SP1442	37c	Toy coils, #3638-3641	8.00

2003

SP1442A	37c	Antique Toys booklet stamps, #3642a, 3643a, 3644a, 3644f	8.75

2002

SP1443	60c	Coverlet Eagle, #3646	6.50
SP1444	$3.85	Jefferson Memorial, #3647	12.00
SP1445	$13.65	Capitol Dome, #3648	27.50
SP1446	(34c+11c)	Heroes of 2001, #B2	16.00
SP1447	37c	Masters of American Photography, #3649	25.00
SP1448	37c	John James Audubon, #3650	7.25
SP1449	37c	Harry Houdini, #3651	7.25
SP1450	37c	Official coil, #O159	7.00
SP1451	37c	Andy Warhol, #3652	7.25
SP1452	37c	Teddy Bears, #3653-3656	8.00
SP1453	37c,60c	Love #3657-3658	8.00
SP1454	37c	Ogden Nash, #3659	7.25
SP1455	37c	Duke Kahanamoku, #3660	7.50
SP1456	37c	American Bats, #3661-3664	8.00
SP1457	37c	Women in Journalism, #3665-3668	9.75
SP1458	37c	Irving Berlin, #3669	7.25
SP1459	37c	Neuter and Spay, #3670-3671	7.75
SP1460	37c	Hanukkah, #3672	7.00
SP1461	37c	Kwanzaa, #3673	7.00
SP1462	37c	Eid #3674	7.00
SP1463	37c	Christmas Madonna, #3675	7.25
SP1464	37c	Christmas Snowmen, #3676-3679	8.00
SP1465	37c	Cary Grant, #3692	9.25
SP1466	(5c)	Sea Coast, #3693	7.25
SP1467	37c	Hawaiian Missionary Stamps, #3694	13.00
SP1468	37c	Happy Birthday, #3695	7.25
SP1469	37c	Greetings from America, #3696-3745	37.50

2003

SP1470	37c	Thurgood Marshall, #3746	7.50
SP1471	37c	Chinese New Year, #3747	7.50
SP1472	37c	Zora Neale Hurston, #3748	7.50

2003-06

SP1473	1c	Tiffany Lamp, #3749	7.00
SP1475	10c	American Clock, #3757	7.00
SP1476	2c	Navajo Necklace, #3751-3752, *2005*	7.00
SP1477	2c	Navajo Necklace, #3753	7.00
SP1478	3c	Silver Coffeepot, #3754	7.00
SP1479	4c	Chippendale Chair, #3755	7.00
SP1480	5c	Toleware, #3756	7.00
SP1481	2c	Navajo Necklace, #3750	7.00
SP1482	1c	Tiffany Lamp coil, #3758	7.50
SP1483	3c	Silver Coffeepot coil, #3759	7.00
SP1484	4c	Chippendale Chair coil, #3761	7.00
SP1486	10c	American Clock coil, #3762	7.00
SP1490	$1	Wisdom, #3766	9.00
SP1493	(10c)	New York Public Library Lion, perf. 10 vert, #3769	7.50

2004

SP1494	(10c)	Atlas Statue, #3770	7.00

2003

SP1495	80c	Special Olympics, #3771	8.50
SP1496	37c	American Filmmaking: Behind the Scenes, #3772	13.50
SP1497	37c	Ohio Statehood, Bicent., #3773	7.50
SP1498	37c	Pelican Island National Wildlife Refuge, #3774	7.50
SP1499	(5c)	Sea Coast perforated coil, #3775	7.50
SP1500	37c	Old Glory, #3776-3780	8.00
SP1501	37c	Cesar E. Chavez, #3781	7.50
SP1502	37c	Louisiana Purchase, #3782	7.50
SP1503	37c	First Flight of Wright Brothers, #3783	7.50
SP1504	37c	Purple Heart, #3784	7.50
SP1505	37c	Purple Heart, #3784A	7.50
SP1506	37c	Audrey Hepburn, #3786	8.50
SP1507	37c	Southeastern Lighthouses #3787-3791	9.00
SP1508	(25c)	Eagles, two different stamps from #3792-3801	6.50
SP1508A	(25c)	Eagles, #3792-3801	10.00
SP1508Ab	(25c)	Eagles, dated 2005, #3792a-3801b	10.00
SP1509	37c	Arctic Tundra, #3802	12.50
SP1510	37c	Korean War Veterans Memorial, #3803	7.00
SP1511	37c	Mary Cassatt Paintings, #3804-3807	8.00
SP1512	37c	Early Football Heroes, #3808-3811	10.00
SP1513	37c	Roy Acuff, #3812	7.00
SP1514	37c	District of Columbia, #3813	6.50
SP1515	37c	Reptiles And Amphibians, #3814-3818	9.00
SP1516	(37c+8c)	Stop Family Violence, #B3	7.25
SP1517	37c	Christmas Madonna, #3820	6.50
SP1518	37c	Christmas Holiday Music Makers, 2 sets of #3821-3824	7.50
SP1519	37c	Snowy Egret coil, #3829	6.50

2004

SP1520	37c	Snowy Egret booklet stamp, #3830	6.50
SP1521	37c	Pacific Coral Reef, #3831	17.50
SP1522	37c	Chinese New Year, #3832	7.25
SP1523	37c	Love, #3833	6.50
SP1524	37c	Paul Robeson, #3834	6.00
SP1525	37c	Theodor Seuss Geisel (Dr. Seuss), #3835	8.00
SP1526	37c	Love (White Lilacs and Pink Roses), #3836	6.00
SP1527	60c	Love (Five Varieties of Pink Roses), #3837	6.00
SP1528	37c	US Air Force Academy, #3838	6.50
SP1529	(5c)	Sea Coast coil reprint, serpentine die cut 9½x10, #3785	6.00

A souvenir page containing the original printing of No. 3785 was not prepared as there was no first day cancel applied to that stamp.

SP1530	37c	Henry Mancini, #3839	6.50
SP1531	37c	American Choreographers, #3840-3843	8.00
SP1532	(25c)	Eagles, perforated, #3844-3853	10.00
SP1533	37c	Lewis and Clark sheet stamp, #3854 (11 cancels)	12.00
SP1534	37c	Lewis and Clark booklet stamps, #3855-3856 (11 cancels)	12.00
SP1535	37c	Isamu Noguchi, #3857-3861	7.50
SP1536	37c	National World War II Memorial, #3862	6.00
SP1537	37c	Summer Olympic Games, Athens, #3863	6.00
SP1538	(5c)	Sea Coast coil, perf. 9¾ vert., #3864	6.00
SP1539	37c	Disney Characters, #3865-3868	9.00
SP1540	37c	USS Constellation, #3869	6.00
SP1541	37c	R. Buckminster Fuller, #3870	6.00
SP1542	37c	James Baldwin, #3871	6.00
SP1543	37c	Martin Johnson Heade, #3872	6.00
SP1544	37c	Art of the American Indian, #3873	11.00
SP1547	37c	John Wayne, #3876	9.00
SP1548	37c	Sickle Cell Disease Awareness, #3877	6.00
SP1549	37c	Cloudscapes, #3878	11.00
SP1550	37c	Christmas Madonna, #3879	6.50
SP1551	37c	Hanukkah, #3880	6.00
SP1552	37c	Kwanzaa, #3881	6.00
SP1553	37c	Moss Hart, #3882	6.00
SP1554	37c	Christmas Santa Claus Ornaments, #3883-3894	10.00

2005

SP1555	37c	Chinese New Year double-sided sheet, #3895	20.00

No. SP1555 was sold in a shrink-wrapped package containing the announcement page, a stamp mount, a cardboard backing and one pane of No. 3895 canceled on both sides.

SP1556	37c	Marian Anderson, #3896	6.00
SP1557	37c	Ronald Reagan, #3897	11.00
SP1558	37c	Love, #3898	6.00
SP1559	37c	Northeast Deciduous Forest, #3899	13.50
SP1560	37c	Spring Flowers, #3900-3903	7.50
SP1561	37c	Robert Penn Warren, #3904	6.00
SP1562	37c	Yip Harburg, #3905	6.00
SP1563	37c	American Scientists, #3906-3909	7.50
SP1564	37c	Modern American Architecture, #3910	12.00
SP1565	37c	Henry Fonda, #3911	6.00
SP1566	37c	Disney Characters, #3912-3915	9.00
SP1567	37c	Advances in Aviation, pane of #3916-3925	15.00
SP1568	37c	Rio Grande Blankets, #3926-3929	7.50
SP1568A	37c	Presidential Libraries, #3930	10.00
SP1569	37c	Sporty Cars, #3931-3935	8.75
SP1570	37c	Arthur Ashe, #3936	6.50
SP1571	37c	To Form a More Perfect Union, #3937	10.00
SP1572	37c	Child Health, #3938	6.00
SP1573	37c	Let's Dance, #3939-3942	8.00
SP1574	37c	Greta Garbo, #3943	7.75
SP1575	37c	Jim Henson and the Muppets, #3944	11.00
SP1576	37c	Constellations, #3945-3948	7.50
SP1577	37c	Christmas, #3949-3960	10.00
SP1578	37c	Distinguished Marines, #3961-3964	8.00
SP1579	(37c)	Flag and Statue of Liberty, #3965-3967, 3970, 3972, 3974, 3975	10.00

No. SP1579 consists of two sheets.

2006

SP1580	(39c)	Love, #3976	6.00
SP1582	39c	Flag and Statue of Liberty, #3978, 3981, 3982, 3983, 3985	7.50
SP1583	39c	Flag and Statue of Liberty Coil, perf. 10 vert., #3979	7.50
SP1584	39c	Flag and Statue of Liberty Coil serpentine die cut 11 vert., #3980	6.00
	a.	Like #1584, but dated and canceled 2/8/06, "S" plate number text	6.00
	b.	Like #1584a, but with "V" in plate number text	6.00

No. SP1584 is dated and canceled 1/9/06.

SP1585	39c	Flag and Statue of Liberty, #3985b	6.00
SP1591	39c	Children's Book Animals, #3987-3994	10.00
SP1592	39c	Turin Winter Olympics, #3995	6.00
SP1593	39c	Hattie McDaniel, #3996	6.00
SP1594	39c	Chinese New Year, #3997	10.00
SP1595	63c	Bryce Canyon, #C139	6.00
SP1596	75c	Great Smoky Mountains National Park, #C140	6.00
SP1597	84c	Yosemite National Park, #C141	6.00
SP1598	39c	Official, #O160	6.00
SP1599		Weddings, #3998-3999	7.50
SP1600	24c	Common Buckey Butterfly, #4000-4002	7.50
SP1601	39c	Crops, #4003-4017	12.00
SP1602	$4.05	X-Plane, #4018	10.00
SP1603	$14.40	X-Plane, #4019	22.50
SP1604	39c	Sugar Ray Robinson, #4020	6.00
SP1605	39c	Benjamin Franklin, #4021-4024	7.50
SP1606	39c	Disney Characters, #4025-4028	7.50
SP1607	39c	Love, #4029	6.00
SP1608	39c	Katherine Anne Porter, #4030	6.00
SP1609	39c	Amber Alert, #4031	6.00
SP1610	39c	Purple Heart, #4032	6.00
SP1611	39c	Wonders of America, #4033-4072	40.00
SP1612	39c	Samuel de Champlain, #4073	7.50
SP1613		Samuel de Champlain souvenir sheet, #4074	7.50
SP1614		Washington 2006 World Philatelic Exhibition souvenir sheet, #4075	16.00
SP1615	39c	Distinguished American Diplomats souvenir sheet, #4076	7.50
SP1616	39c	Judy Garland, #4077	6.00
SP1617	39c	Ronald Reagan, #4078	6.00
SP1618	39c	Happy Birthday, #4079	6.00
SP1619	39c	Baseball Sluggers, #4080-4083	7.50
SP1620	39c	DC Comics Superheroes, #4084	15.00
SP1621	39c	Motorcycles, #4085-4088	7.50
SP1622	39c	Quilts of Gee's Bend, Alabama, #4089-4098	10.00
SP1623	39c	Southern Florida Wetland, #4099	10.00
SP1624	$1	Official with solid blue background, #O161	7.50
SP1625	39c	Christmas Madonna, #4100	6.00
SP1626	39c	Christmas Snowflakes, #4101-4116	10.00
SP1627	39c	Eid, #4117	6.00
SP1628	39c	Hanukkah, #4118	6.00
SP1629	39c	Kwanzaa, #4119	6.00

2007

SP1630	39c	Ella Fitzgerald, #4120	6.00
SP1631	39c	Oklahoma Statehood, #4121	

1992

SPCVP1	29c	Postage and Mailing Center (PMC) coil strip of 3, #31	4.00

1994

SPCVP2	29c	Postage and Mailing Center (PMC) horiz. coil strip of 3, #32	4.25

1996

SPCVP3	32c	Postage and Mailing Center (PMC) horiz. strip of 3, #33	5.50

INTERNATIONAL REPLY COUPONS

Coupons produced by the Universal Postal Union for member countries to provide for payment of postage on a return letter from a foreign country. Exchangeable for a stamp representing single-rate ordinary postage (and starting with the use of Type D3, airmail postage) to a foreign country under the terms of contract as printed on the face of the coupon in French and the language of the issuing country and on the reverse in four, five or six other languages.

Postmasters are instructed to apply a postmark indicating date of sale to the left circle on the coupon. When offered for exchange for stamps, the receiving postmaster is instructed to cancel the right circle.

Coupons with no postmark are not valid for exchange. Coupons with two postmarks have been redeemed and normally are kept by the post office making the exchange. **Coupons with one postmark are valued here.** Some coupons with a stamp added to pay an increased rate are listed in footnotes.

The following is a list of all varieties issued by the Universal Postal Union for any or all member countries.

Dates are those when the rate went into effect. The date that any item was put on sale in the United States can be very different.

Type A — Face

Wmk. "25c Union Postale Universelle 25c"

1907-20

A1 Face — Name of country in letters 1½mm high.
Reverse — Printed rules between paragraphs German text contains four lines.

1907-20

A2 Face — Same as A1.
Reverse — Same as A1 but without rules between paragraphs.

1910-20

A3 Face — Same as A1 and A2.
Reverse — Same as A2 except German text has but three lines.

1912-20

A4 Face — Name of country in bold face type; letters 2mm to 2½mm high.
Reverse — Same as A3.

1922-25

A5 Face — French words "le mois d'émission écoulé, deux mois encore."
Reverse — As A3 and A4 but overprinted with new contract in red; last line of red German text has five words.

Wmk. "50c Union Postale Universelle 50c"

1925-26

A6 Face — Same as A5.
Reverse — Four paragraphs of five lines each.

1926-29

A7 Face — French words "il est valable pendant un délai de six mois."
Reverse — As A6 but overprinted with new contract in red; last line of red German text has two words.

Wmk. "40c Union Postale Universelle 40c"

1926-29

A8 Face — Design redrawn. Without lines in hemispheres.
Reverse — Four paragraphs of four lines each.

Type B — Face

1931-35 **Wmk. Double-lined "UPU"**

B1 Face — French words "d'une lettre simple."
Reverse — Four paragraphs of three lines each.

1935-36

B2 Face — French words "d'une lettre ordinaire de port simple."
Reverse — Last line of German text contains two words.

1936-37

B3 Face — Same as B2.
Reverse — Last line of German text contains one word.

1937-40

B4 Face — Same as B2 and B3. "Any Country of the Union."
Reverse — German text is in German Gothic type.

1945

B5 Face — "Any Country of the Universal Postal Union."
Reverse — Each paragraph reads "Universal Postal Union."

Type B5 exists without central printing on face.

1950

B6 Face — Same as B5.
Reverse — Five paragraphs (English, Arabic, Chinese, Spanish, Russian).

1954

B7 Face — Same as B5.
Reverse — Six paragraphs (German, English, Arabic, Chinese, Spanish, Russian.)

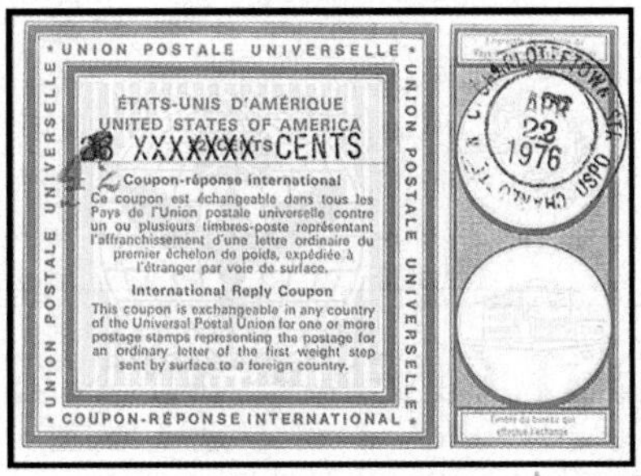

Type C — Face

1968 **Wmk. Single-lined "UPU" Multiple**

C1 Face — French words "d'une lettre ordinaire de port simple."
Reverse — Six paragraphs (German, English, Arabic, Chinese, Spanish, Russian).

Foreign coupons, but not U.S., of type C1 are known with large double-lined "UPU" watermark, as on type B coupons.

1971

C2 Face — French words "d'une lettre ordinaire du premier échelon de poids."
Reverse — Six paragraphs (German, English, Arabic, Chinese, Spanish, Russian).

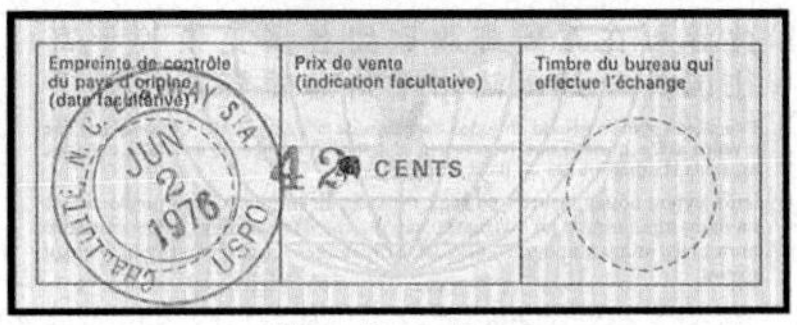

Type D — Face

1975 **Wmk. Single-lined "UPU" Multiple**

D1 Face — French words "d'une lettre ordinaire, expédiée à l'étranger par voie de surface."
Reverse — Six paragraphs (German, English, Arabic, Chinese, Spanish, Russian).

D2 Face — Left box does not have third line of French and dotted circle.
Reverse — Same as D1.

On D1 and D2 the watermark runs horizontally or vertically.

D3 Face — ....aerienne. Left box as D2 with (faculative) added.
Reverse — As D1, all references are to air service.

D4 Face — As D3, "CN 01 / (ancien C22)" replaces "C22."

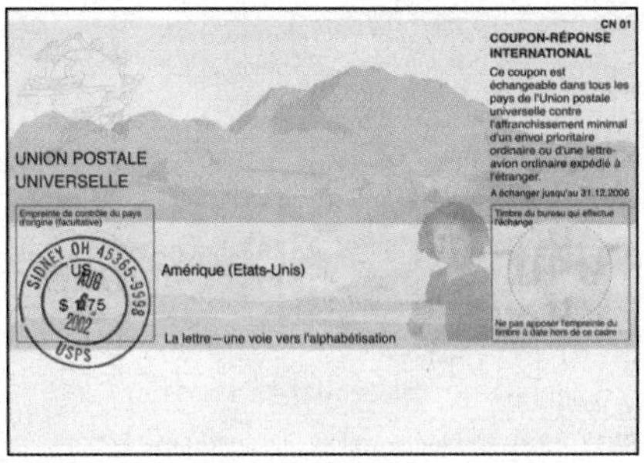

Type E — Face

Wmk. "UPU" in cross & 8-pointed star horiz. across sheet

2002

E1 Face — Shown
Reverse — Six paragraphs (German, English, Arabic, Chinese, Spanish, Russian), repeating expiration date paragraph in same languages, bar code.

Coupons exist without the validating origination markings. Type E coupons have a bar code on the reverse that identifies the originating country and the date of printing.

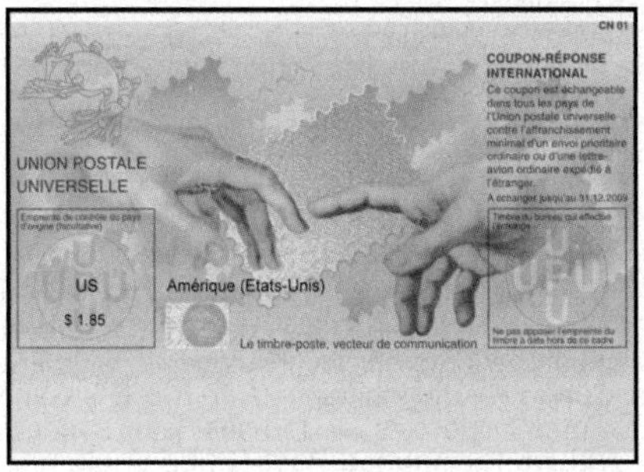

Type F — Face

Wmk. "UPU" in cross & 8-pointed star horiz. across sheet

2006

F1 Face — Shown
Reverse — Six paragraphs (German, English, Arabic, Chinese, Spanish, Russian), repeating expiration date paragraph in same languages, bar code.

UNITED NATIONS (6/07)

REPLY COUPONS ISSUED FOR THE UNITED STATES

1907, Oct. 1

IRC2 A2 6c **slate green & gray green** 27.50

Rules omitted on reverse.
Earliest documented use: Oct. 10, 1907.

1912

IRC3 A4 6c **slate green & gray green** 32.50

Three line English paragraph on face.

1922, Jan. 1

IRC4 A5 11c **slate green & gray green,** name 81 ½mm long 25.00
a. Name 88 ½mm long 25.00

Five line English paragraph on face. Red overprint on reverse.

1925-26

IRC5 A6 11c **slate green & gray green** 22.50

Five line English paragraph on face. No overprint on reverse.

IRC6 A6 9c **slate green & gray green,** *Oct. 1, 1925* 22.50

1926

IRC7 A7 9c **slate green & gray green** 32.50

Four line English paragraph on face. Red overprint on reverse.

IRC8 A8 9c **slate green & gray green** 25.00

Without lines in hemispheres.

1935

IRC9 B2 9c **blue & yellow** 11.00

On reverse, last line of German text contains two words.

1936

IRC10 B3 9c blue and yellow 11.00

On reverse, last line of German text contains one word.

1937

IRC11 B4 9c **blue & yellow** 8.00

On reverse, German text in German Gothic type.

1945

IRC12 B5 9c **blue & yellow,** Italian text on reverse in 4 lines 6.00
a. Italian text on reverse in 3 lines 7.50

1948, Oct. 15

IRC13 B5 11c **blue & yellow** 5.00

On face, "Universal Postal Union" replaces "Union."

1950

IRC14 B6 11c **blue & yellow** 6.00

On reverse, text in English, Arabic, Chinese, Spanish, Russian.

1954, July 1

IRC15 B7 13c **blue & yellow** 6.00

On reverse, text in German, English, Arabic, Chinese, Spanish, Russian.

Varieties: period under "u" of "amount" in English text on reverse, and period under "n" of "amount." Also, country name either 47mm or 50mm long.

No. IRC15 Surcharged in Various Manners

1959, May 2

IRC16 B7 15c on 13c **blue & yellow** 6.00

Individual post offices were instructed to surcharge the 13c coupon, resulting in many types of surcharge in various inks. For example, "REVALUED 15 CENTS," reading vertically; "15," etc.

1959, May 2

IRC17 B7 15c **blue & yellow** 5.00

1964

IRC18 B7 15c **blue & yellow** 5.00
a. Reverse printing 60mm deep instead of 65mm (smaller Arabic characters) 5.00

On face, box at lower left: "Empreinte de contrôle / du Pays d'origine / (date facultative)" replaces "Timbre du / Bureau / d'Emission."

1969

IRC19 C1 15c **blue & yellow** 4.50

1971, July 1

IRC20 C2 22c **blue & yellow** 4.50

No. IRC20 Surcharged in Various Manners

1974, Jan. 5

IRC21 C2 26c on 22c **blue & yellow** 6.50

See note after No. IRC16.

1975, Jan. 2

IRC22 D1 26c **blue & yellow** 4.00

No. IRC22 Surcharged in Various Manners

1976, Jan. 3

IRC23 D1 42c on 26c **blue & yellow** 6.50

See note after No. IRC16. Several post offices are known to have surcharged No. IRC21 (42c on 26c on 22c).

Provisional surcharges on Nos. IRC24-IRC27 were not permitted.

1976, Jan. 3

IRC24 D1 42c **blue & yellow** 4.50

Many foreign countries use non-denominated IRCs. The U.S. has never ordered or used these "generic" items.

1981, July 1

IRC26 D1 65c **blue & yellow** 5.50

1986, Jan. 1

IRC27 D2 80c **blue & yellow** 5.50

1988, Apr. 3

IRC28 D2 95c **blue & yellow** 5.00
IRC29 D3 95c **blue & yellow** 5.00
a. "9.1992" in lower left corner 5.00

Post offices were authorized on July 11, 1995 to revalue remaining stock of 95c IRCs to $1.05 by applying 10c in stamps until new stock (No. 30) arrived. All 95c varieties are known revalued thus.

The date of issue of No. 29 is not known. Earliest documented use: Jan. 2, 1992.

No. 28 exists with inverted watermark (tops of letters facing right).

1995

IRC30 D4 $1.05 **blue & yellow,** "4.95" in lower left corner 3.75
a. "10.98" in lower left corner 3.75
b. As "a," with "United States of America" in left box 8.00

"1.05" comes 1 ½mm or 3mm high. 3mm height has numerals more widely spaced.

Earliest documented use: July 12, 1995.

Post offices were authorized on Jan. 7, 2001, to revalue remaining stock of $1.05 IRCs to $1.75 by applying 70c in stamps until new stock arrived. All $1.05 varieties are known revalued thus. Value $7.

2002, Jan. 1

IRC31 E1 $1.75 **multicolored** 3.50

Effective Jan. 8, 2006, the rate increased to $1.85. Post offices were authorized to revalue remaining stock of $1.75 IRCs to $1.85 by applying 10c in stamps.

2006, Aug. 17

IRC32 F1 $1.85 **multicolored** 3.75

Effective May 14, 2007, the rate increased to $2. Post offices were authorized to revalue remaining stock of $1.85 IRCs to $2 by applying 15c in stamps or postal validation imprinter labels.

POST OFFICE SEALS

Official Seals began to appear in 1872. They do not express any value, having no franking power.

The first seal issued was designed to prevent tampering with registered letters while in transit. It was intended to be affixed over the juncture of the flaps of the large official envelopes in which registered mail letters were enclosed or stamp requisitions were shipped to postmasters and was so used exclusively. Beginning in 1877 (No. OX1 and later), Post Office Seals were used to repair damaged letters, reseal those opened by mistake or by customs inspectors, and to seal letters received by the Post Office unsealed.

Values for unused Post Office Seals are for those without creases. Uncanceled seals without gum will sell for less.

Used Post Office Seals will usually have creases from being applied over the edges of damaged or accidentally opened covers but will have either cancels, precancels or a signature or notation indicating use on the seal. Creased, uncanceled seals without gum are considered used and will sell for less than either an unused or a canceled used seal.

Covers with Post Office Seals are almost always damaged except in cases when the seal was applied to a cover marked "Received Unsealed." The values shown are for covers where the damage is consistent with the application of the seal.

Post Office Seals must be tied or exhibit some auxiliary marking or docketing to qualify for "on cover" values. No. OXF1 must bear a circular date stamp cancel and the cover to which it is affixed must bear the identical cancel to qualify for the "on cover" value.

REGISTRY SEALS

RGS1

National Bank Note Co.
Typographed from a copper plate of 30 subjects (3x10) in two panes of 15 (3x5)

1872 Unwmk. White Wove Paper *Perf. 12*

OXF1	RGS1	**green**	30.00	7.50
		On cover, Barber signature		40.00
		On cover, Terrell signature		75.00
		Block of 4	*500.00*	
		Pane of 15	*2,500.*	
a.		**Yellow green,** pelure paper	75.00	40.00
b.		Imperf., pair	*1,500.*	
c.		Horizontally laid paper	*500.00*	
d.		Printed on both sides	*500.00*	
e.		Printed on both sides, back inverted	*800.00*	
f.		Double impression	*750.00*	—
g.		Double impression, one inverted	—	*750.00*

The second impression of Nos. OXF1d-OXF1g, is very faint.

Also issued as a pane of 9 (3x3) (attributed to Continental Bank Note Co.).

Cancellations

Black	7.50
Blue	+5.00
Red	+15.00
Green	+50.00
Magenta	+50.00
Carrier	+25.00
Panama	—
Shanghai	—

Special Printings

Continental Bank Note Co.
Plate of 30 subjects (5x6)

1875(?) Hard White Wove Paper *Perf. 12*
Without Gum

OXF2 RGS1 **bluish green** *1,000.*

American Bank Note Co.
Plate of 15 subjects (5x3)

1880 (?) **Soft Porous Paper Without Gum** *Perf. 12*

OXF3 RGS1 **bluish green** *1,000.*

POSTAGE STAMP AGENCY SEALS

Used to seal registered pouches containing stamps for distribution to Post Offices.

PSA1

Background size: 102x52mm.

1875-93 **Litho.** **Unwmk.** *Die Cut*

Barber Signature

OXF4 PSA1 **brown & black** 25.00
On cover 60.00

PSA2

Hazen Signature, Text 86mm Wide

OXF5 PSA2 **brown & black,** *1877* 25.00
On cover 60.00

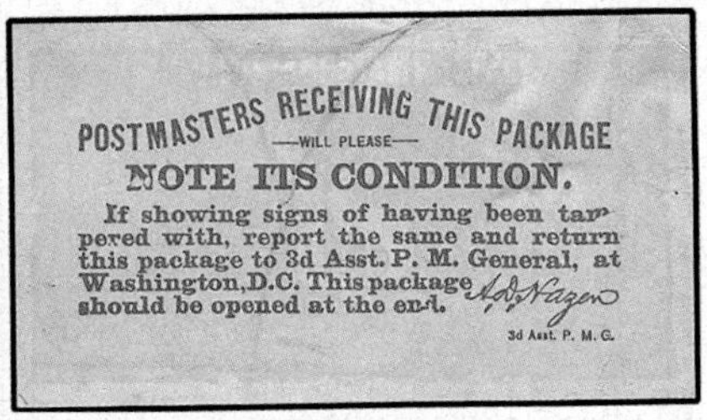

PSA3

Hazen Signature, Text 87mm Wide

OXF6 PSA3 **pink & red,** *1886* 50.00
On cover 350.00
a. **Salmon & red** 60.00
On cover *400.00*

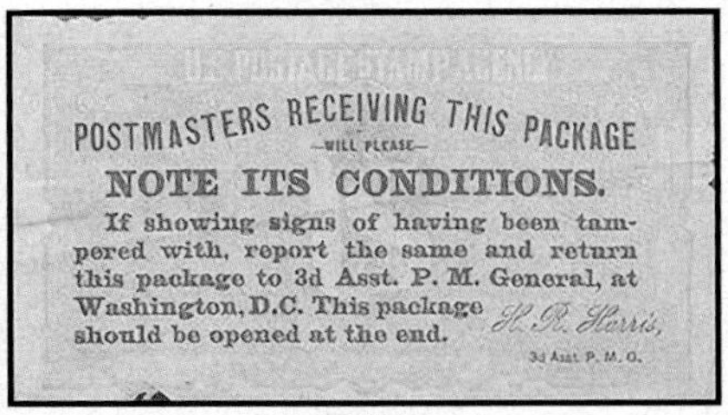

PSA4

Harris Signature

OXF7 PSA4 **pink & red,** *1887* 45.00
On cover 150.00
a. **Salmon & red,** 55.00
On cover 175.00

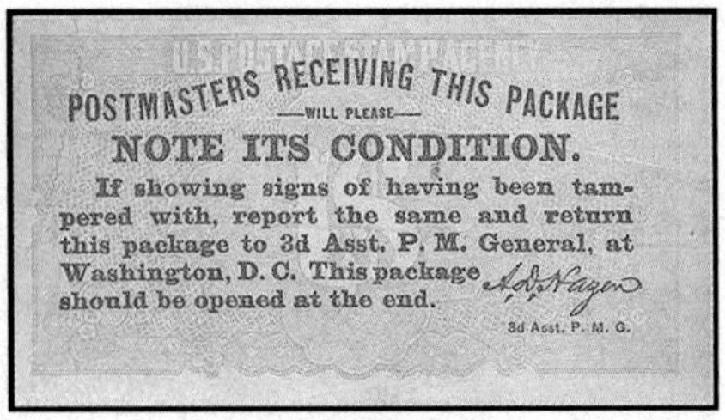

PSA5

Hazen Signature, Text 90½mm Wide

OXF8 PSA5 **pink & red,** *1889* 40.00
On cover 140.00

PSA6

Craige Signature

OXF9 PSA6 **pink & red,** *1893* 45.00
On cover 175.00

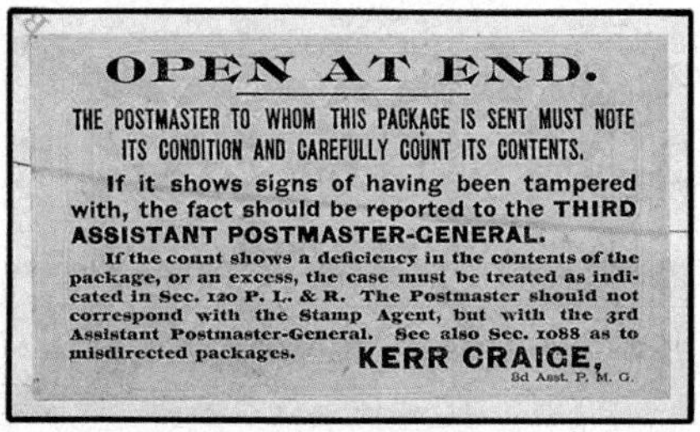

PSA7

Background size: 120½x67mm.

1894 **Litho.** **Unwmk.** *Die Cut*

Craige Signature, "3rd Asst. P.M.G."

OXF10 PSA7 **pink & black** 55.00
On cover 200.00

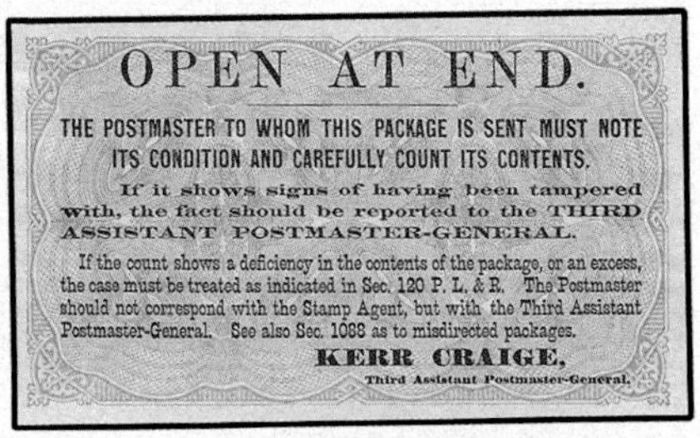

PSA8

Craige Signature, "Third Assistant Postmaster General"

OXF11 PSA8 **pink & black** 35.00
On cover 150.00
a. **Deep pink & black** 35.00
On cover 150.00

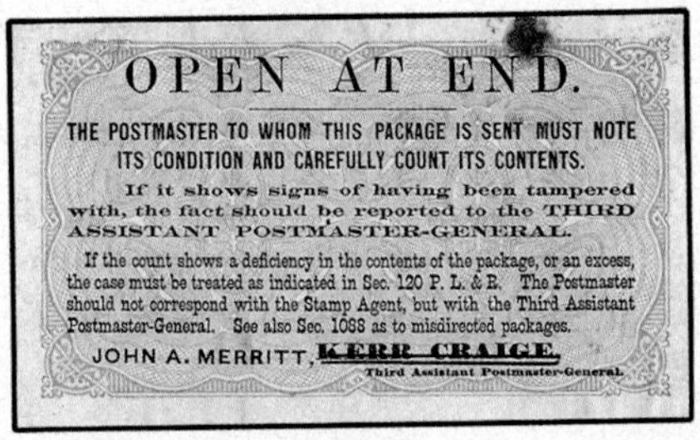

PSA9

"John A. Merritt" in Sans-Serif Capitals at Left. Two Horizontal Lines Obliterating "Kerr Craige."

1897

OXF12 PSA9 **pale pink & black** 100.00
On cover 400.00

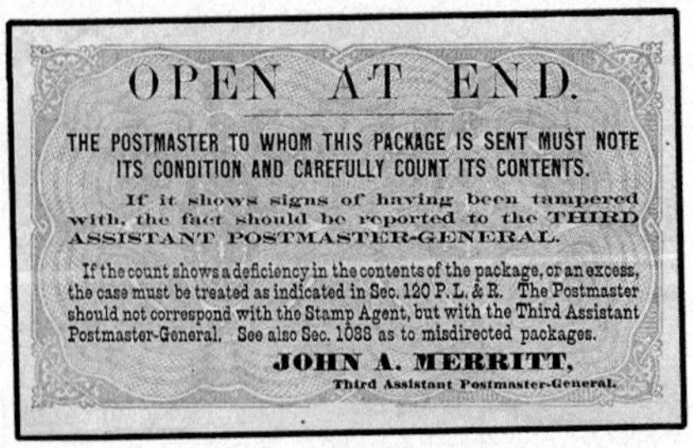

PSA10

1897-1914

Merritt Signature

OXF13 PSA10 **rose & black** 35.00
On cover 130.00

PSA11

Madden Signature

OXF14 PSA11 **rose & black,** *1899* 40.00
On cover 145.00

The first paragraph of text reads: "...MUST NOTE ITS CONDITION AND CAREFULLY COUNT..."

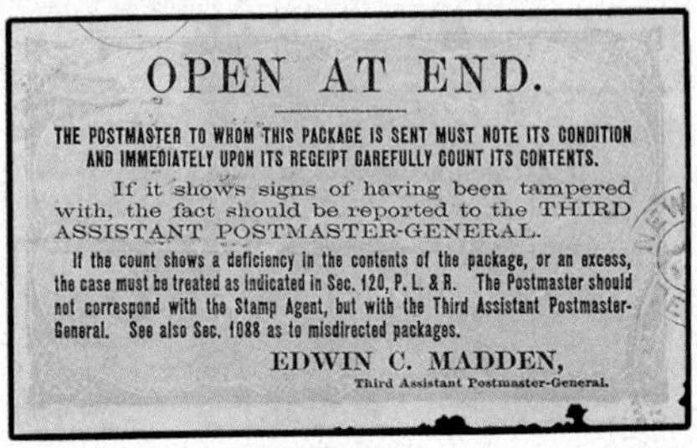

PSA12

OXF14A PSA12 **rose & black,** *1899* —
On cover

The first paragraph of text reads: "...MUST NOTE ITS CONDITION AND IMMEDIATELY UPON.."

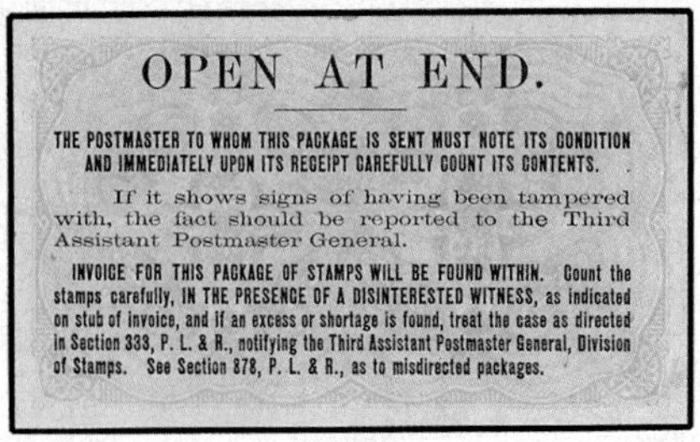

PSA13

"Section 878"

OXF15 PSA13 **rose & black,** *1907* 30.00
On cover 140.00

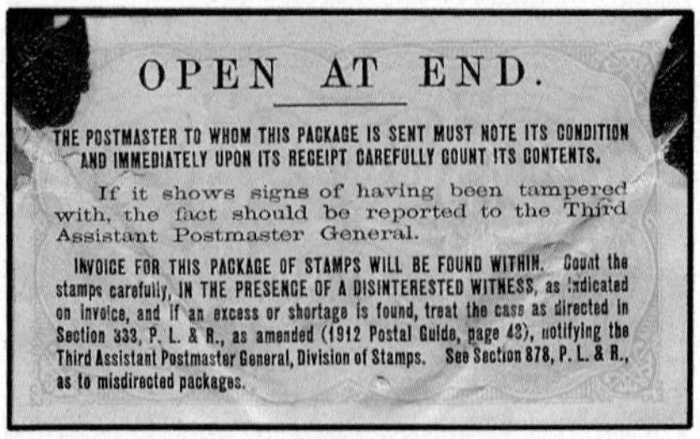

PSA14

OXF15A	PSA14	**rose & black,** *1912*	
		On cover	—

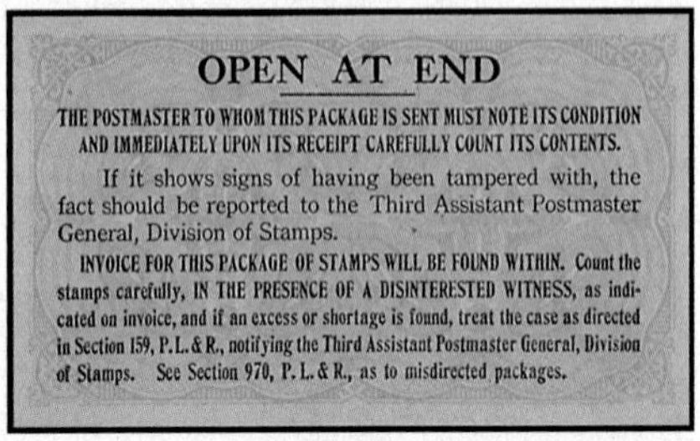

PSA15

"Section 970"

OXF16	PSA15	**rose & black,** *1912*	35.00
		On cover	175.00

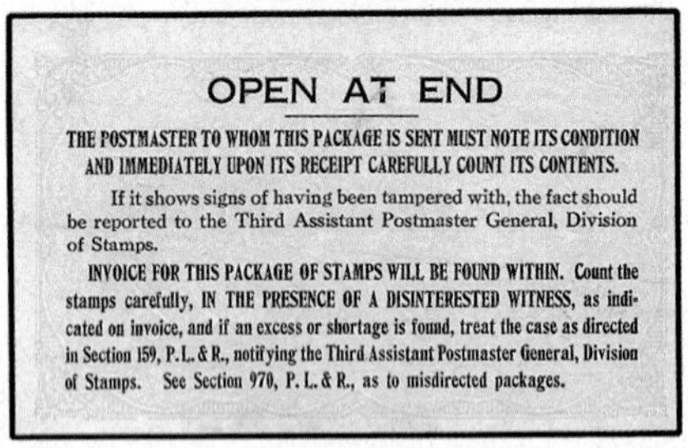

PSA16

OXF17	PSA16	**rose & black,** *1914*	40.00
		On cover	175.00

DEAD LETTER OFFICE SEALS

Nos. OXA1-OXA9 were used only on mail that could be forwarded to the intended recipient, after examination in the Dead Letter Office. Nos. OXB1-OXB5 were used only on mail returned to the originating post office.

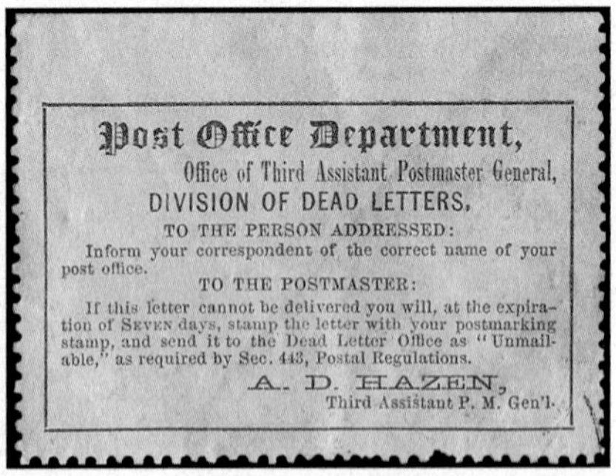

"Hazen" — DLO1

1884 **Litho.** ***Perf. 10½***

OXA1	DLO1	**black**	45.00
		On cover	175.00

Perf. 12

OXA1A	DLO1	**black**	25.00
		On cover	125.00

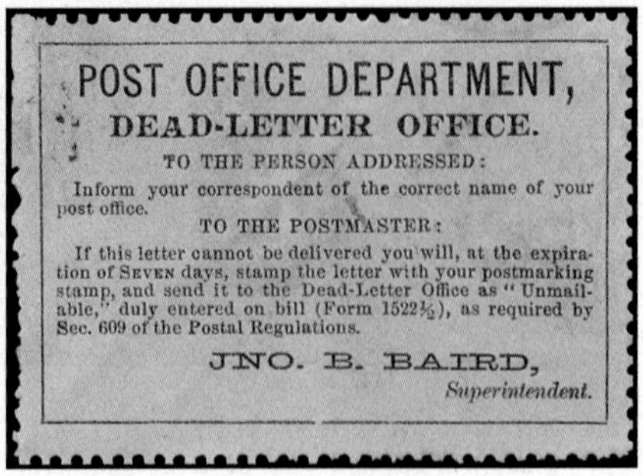

"Baird" — DLO2

1889 ***Perf. 12***

OXA2	DLO2	**black**	45.00
		On cover	*300.00*

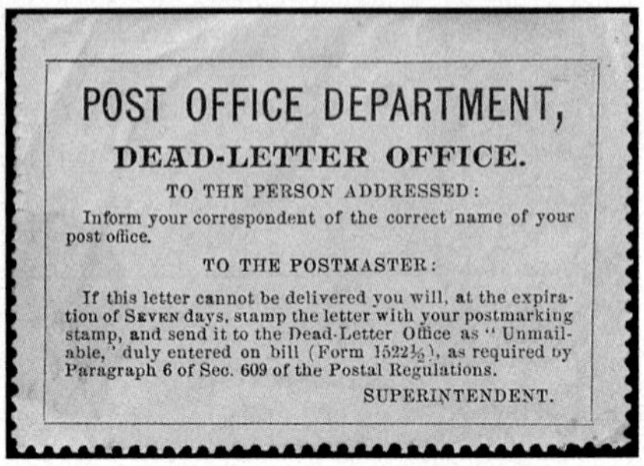

"Superintendent" — DLO3

1891 ***Perf. 10½***

OXA3	DLO3	**black**	35.00
		On cover	175.00

Perf. 12

OXA3A	DLO3	**black**	25.00
		On cover	125.00

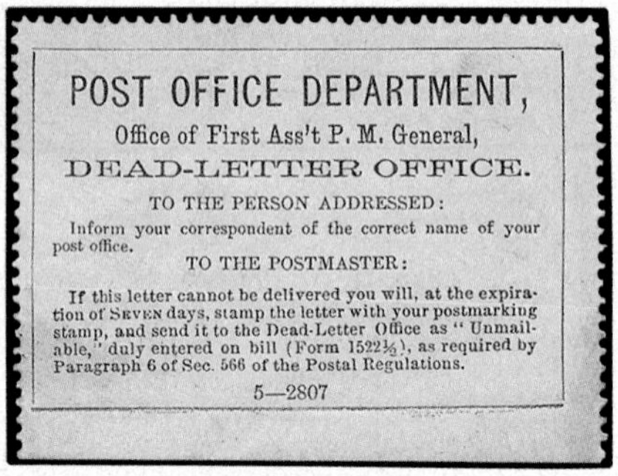

"5-2807" — DLO4

1892 ***Perf. 12***

OXA4	DLO4	**black**	25.00
		On cover	125.00

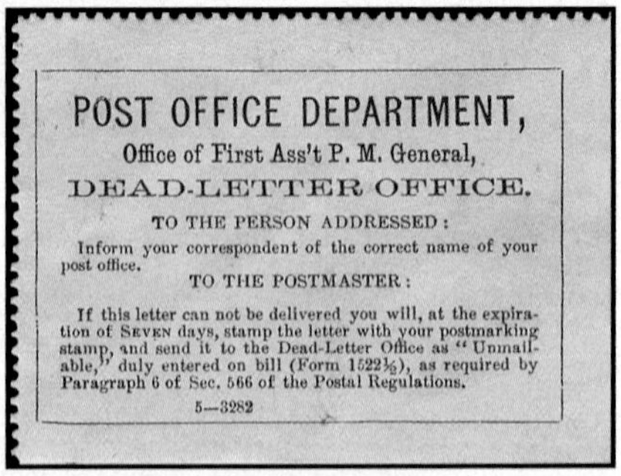

"5-3282" — DLO5

1895 ***Perf. 12***

OXA5	DLO5	**black**	22.50
		On cover	110.00

1898(?) ***Hyphen hole perf. 7***

OXA6	DLO5	**black**	40.00
		On cover	200.00

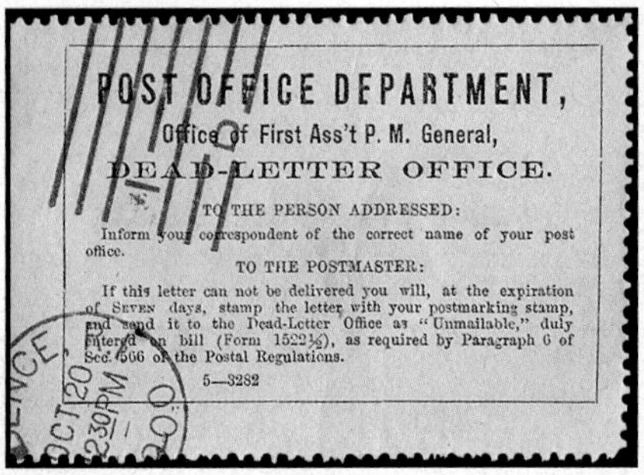

DLO6

Similar to DLO5 but smaller type used for instructions to the postmasters.

1900 ***Perf. 12***

OXA7	DLO6	**black**	20.00
		On cover	100.00

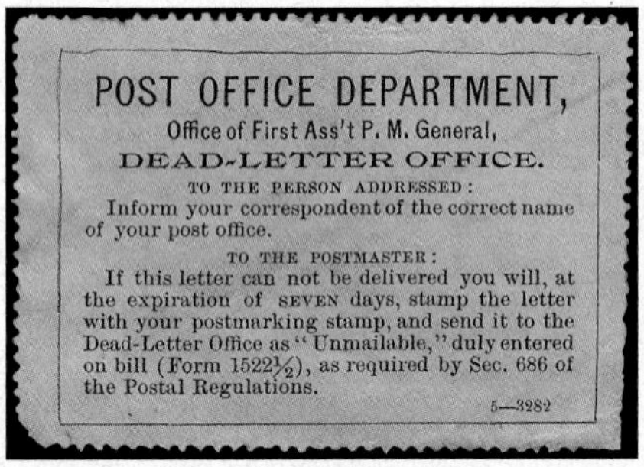

"5-3282" at Right — DLO7

1902(?) 12 ***Perf. 12***

OXA8	DLO7	**black**	25.00
		On cover	125.00

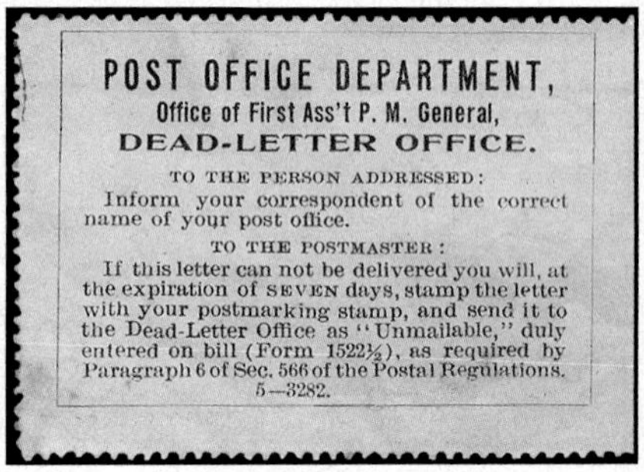

"5-3282" at Center — DLO8

1902(?) ***Perf. 12***

OXA9	DLO8	**black**	25.00
		On cover	125.00

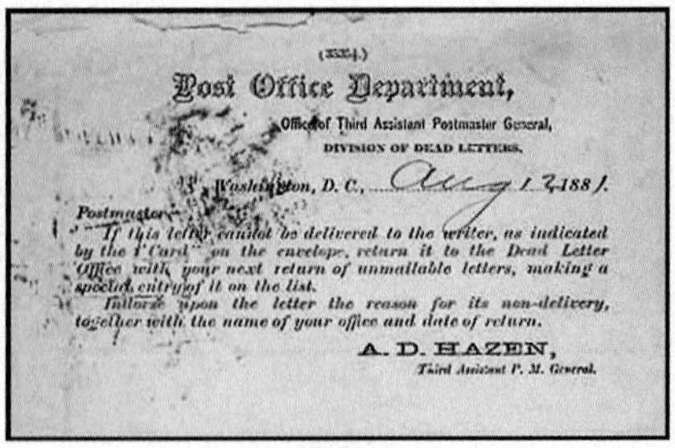

DLO9

1881-91 ***Die Cut***

Incomplete Year Date ("188")

OXB1	DLO9	**black**	—
		On cover	*1,000.*

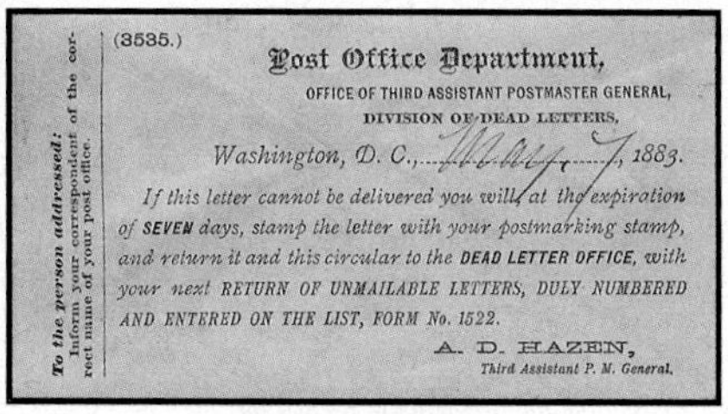

(3535.)

Post Office Department,

OFFICE OF THIRD ASSISTANT POSTMASTER GENERAL,
DIVISION OF DEAD LETTERS,

Washington, D. C., May 7, 1883.

If this letter cannot be delivered you will at the expiration of SEVEN days, stamp the letter with your postmarking stamp, and return it and this circular to the DEAD LETTER OFFICE, with your next RETURN OF UNMAILABLE LETTERS, DULY NUMBERED AND ENTERED ON THE LIST, FORM No. 1522.

A. D. HAZEN,
Third Assistant P. M. General.

To the person addressed: Inform your correspondent of the correct name of your post office.

"1883" — DLO10

Complete Year Date

OXB2	DLO10	**black** (1882)		75.00
		On cover		*400.00*
OXB3	DLO10	**black** (1883)		75.00
		On cover		*400.00*
OXB4	DLO10	**black** (1886)		75.00
		On cover		*400.00*

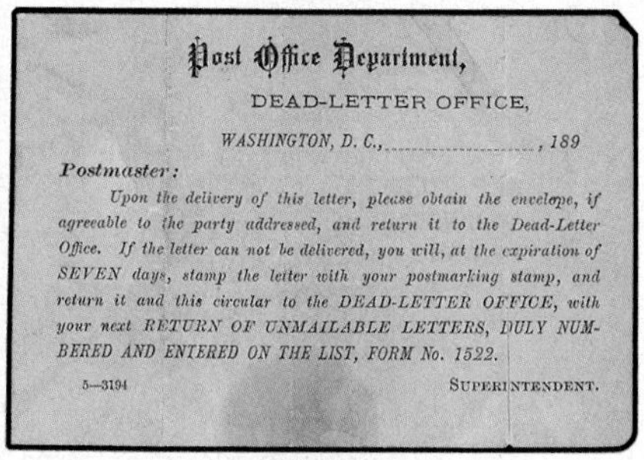

Post Office Department,

DEAD-LETTER OFFICE,

WASHINGTON, D. C., ________, 189

Postmaster:

Upon the delivery of this letter, please obtain the envelope, if agreeable to the party addressed, and return it to the Dead-Letter Office. If the letter can not be delivered, you will, at the expiration of SEVEN days, stamp the letter with your postmarking stamp, and return it and this circular to the DEAD-LETTER OFFICE, with your next RETURN OF UNMAILABLE LETTERS, DULY NUMBERED AND ENTERED ON THE LIST, FORM No. 1522.

5—3194 SUPERINTENDENT.

DLO11

Incomplete Year Date ("189")

OXB5	DLO11	**black** (1891?)		75.00
		On cover		*500.00*

POST OFFICE SEALS

No. OX1 supposedly was issued as a Dead Letter Office Seal. It was prepared for use in the Dead Letter Office but was distributed to other offices and used in the same way as later seals. Most on-cover examples are normal Post Office usages from larger East Coast cities. New York and Philadelphia predominate. Very few examples with Dead Letter Office markings are recorded. For that reason, No. OX1 is listed with the other Post Office Seals.

POS1

("Post Obitum" in background.)
National Bank Note Co.
Plate of 100 subjects (10x10)
Silk Paper

1877 Engr. *Perf. 12*

OX1	POS1	**brown**	45.00	25.00
		On cover		*1,200.*
		Block of 4	*500.00*	

POS2

American Bank Note Co.
Plate of 100 subjects (10x10) in two panes of 50 bearing imprint of American Bank Note Co. in the selvage.
(Also plates of 50 (10x5) subjects)

1879 Engr. *Perf. 12*

Thin, crisp, semi-translucent paper, yellowish gum

OX2	POS2	**red brown**	3.00	1.00
		On cover		85.00
		Block of 4	15.00	
		Margin block with imprint	25.00	
a.		**Brown**	10.00	5.00
		On cover		200.00
		Block of 4	60.00	
		Margin block with imprint	85.00	

Seal impression can be clearly seen when viewed from the back.

Plate of 50 subjects (5x10). Four imprints of the American Bank Note Co. centered on each side of the pane in the selvage, with a reversed "2" to the right of the top imprint.

1879(?)

Thick, opaque paper, clear transparent gum

OX3	POS2	**yellow brown**	*150.00*	*150.00*

1881(?)

Thin, hard porous paper, clear transparent gum

OX4	POS2	**deep brown**	75.00	
		Block of 4	350.00	
		Margin block of 4 with imprint (side)	400.00	
		Margin block of 6 with imprint (bottom)	550.00	
		Margin block of 4 with imprint & reversed "2" (top)	575.00	

No. OX4 is the so-called "Special Printing." It was produced from a new plate prepared from the original die. It received little usage, but at least two full panes are known to have existed.

Colors

Beginning with OX5, many Official Seals exhibit a wide variety of shades. Minimal care was exercised in their printing. It is not uncommon for seals within a single pane to vary in shade from dark to very light. No attempt is being made here to list all of the various shades separately.

POS3

Typographed
Without words in lower label.
Outer frame line at top and left is thick and heavy (compare with POS4).
Plate of 72 subjects (8x9)

1888 *Rough perf. 12*

Medium thick, crisp paper

OX5	POS3	**chocolate** (shades)	.75	.75
		On cover		50.00
		On cover with typeset seal No. LOX8		—
		Block of 4	5.00	
a.		Imperf, pair	50.00	
		Sheet of 72, imperf	—	

Imperforates

Imperforates of Nos. OX6, OX7, OX10 and OX13 are believed to be printer's waste. No seals were issued imperforate, though some may have been sent to post offices.

Plate of 42 subjects (7x6)

1889 *Rough perf. 12*

Thick to extremely thick paper

OX6	POS3	**chocolate** (shades)	.75	.50
		On cover		40.00
		Block of 4	5.00	

1889(?) *Perf. 12*

OX7	POS3	**bister brown** (shades)	.75	.50
		On cover		40.00
		Block of 4	5.00	
a.		**Rose brown**	4.00	2.50
		On cover		65.00
		Block of 4	22.50	
b.		**Yellow brown**	2.00	2.00
		On cover		50.00
		Block of 4	10.00	
c.		Imperf. vertically, pair	25.00	—
d.		Imperf. horizontally, pair	25.00	—
e.		Vertical pair, imperf. between	20.00	
f.		Horizontal pair, imperf. between	75.00	
g.		Double impression		—

Cancellation

Puerto Rico	+75.00

Examples of No. OX7 with multiple impressions widely spaced or at angles to each other, are found on normal paper and various documents. These are printer's waste.

1892 *Rouletted 5½*

OX8	POS3	**light brown** (shades)	20.00	15.00
		On cover		*1,250.*
		Block of 4	300.00	

1895 (?) *Hyphen Hole Perf. 7*

OX9	POS3	**gray brown**	7.50	5.00
		On cover		500.00
		Block of 4	200.00	

Earliest documented use: Feb. 3, 1897.

1898(?) *Perf. 12*

Thin soft paper

OX10	POS3	**brown** (shades)	1.50	1.50
		On cover		250.00
		Block of 4	8.00	

POS4

Plate of 143 (11x13)

Outer frame line at top and left is thin.
Otherwise similar to POS3.

1900 Litho. *Perf. 12*

OX11	POS4	**red brown**	.50	.25
		On cover		30.00
		Block of 4	2.50	
a.		**Gray brown**	2.00	1.25
		On cover		45.00
		Block of 4	15.00	
b.		**Dark brown**	2.50	*4.50*
		On cover		85.00
		Block of 4	15.00	
c.		**Orange brown**	.75	*2.00*
		On cover		75.00
		Block of 4	4.00	

Most imperfs and part perfs are printers waste. Some genuine perforation errors may have been issued to post offices.

Watermarks

Watermarks cover only a portion of the panes. Many stamps in each pane did not receive any of the watermark. Values for watermarked panes are for examples with at least 50% of the watermark present.

Similar to POS4 but smaller.
Design: 38x23mm
Issued in panes of 20 (5x4)

1907 Typo. *Perf. 12*

OX12	POS4	**bright royal blue**	2.00	2.00
		On cover		45.00
		Pane of 20	60.00	

Earliest documented use: June 1, 1907.

OX13	POS4	**blue** (shades)	.20	.20
		On cover		25.00
		Pane of 20	20.00	
a.		Wmkd. Seal of U.S. in sheet (2 types)	1.50	1.50
		Pane of 20	50.00	
b.		Wmkd. "Rolleston Mills" in sheet	1.00	1.00
		Pane of 20	40.00	
c.		Wmkd. "Birchwood Superfine" in sheet	—	—
		Pane of 20	—	
d.		Pelure paper	*20.00*	*20.00*
e.		Toned paper	*25.00*	*25.00*
f.		Printed on both sides	—	

Numerous varieties such as imperf., part perf., tete beche, and double impressions exist. These seem to be from printer's waste. Some genuine perforation errors may have been issued to post offices.

All recorded examples of No. OX13f show the reverse-side impression inverted in relation to the impression on the face.

1912 *Hyphen Hole 6½*

OX14	POS4	**blue**	1.75	1.50
		On cover		75.00
		Pane of 20	45.00	
a.		Wmkd. Seal of U.S. in sheet	10.00	10.00

Pane of 20 300.00
b. Wmkd. "Rolleston Mills" in sheet 2.50 2.50
Pane of 20 80.00

Panes of 10 were made from panes of 20 for use in smaller post offices. Complete booklets with covers exist.

1913 ***Perf. 12 x Hyphen Hole 6½***
OX15 POS4 **blue** 3.50 3.00
On cover 100.00
Pane of 20 110.00
a. Hyphen-hole perf 6½ (right) x Perf. 12 (left, top, bottom) 15.00 —
Pane of 20 150.00
b. Wmkd. Seal of U.S. in sheet 4.50 4.00
Pane of 20 125.00
c. As "a" and "b" 20.00 —

No. OX15a comes from panes that are perfed between the left selvage and the seals.

1913 ***Hyphen Hole 6½ x Perf. 12***
OX16 POS4 **blue** 5.25 5.25
On cover 250.00
Pane of 20 250.00
a. Wmkd. Seal of U.S. in sheet 6.50 6.50
Pane of 20 300.00
b. Wmkd. "Rolleston Mills" in sheet — —
Pane of 20 —

1916 ***Perf. 12***
OX17 POS4 **black,** *pink* 1.25 1.25
On cover 150.00
Pane of 20 75.00
a. Vert. pair, imperf. horizontally —

Three complete panes of No. OX17a have been reported.

1917 ***Perf. 12***
OX18 POS4 **gray black** .40 .40
On cover 27.50
Pane of 20 40.00
a. **Black** .50 .50
On cover 30.00
Pane of 20 45.00
b. Vert. pair, imperf horizontally 25.00
c. Horiz. pair, imperf vertically 20.00
d. Vertical pair, imperf between 60.00
e. Horizontal pair, imperf between 35.00
f. Imperf, pair 50.00

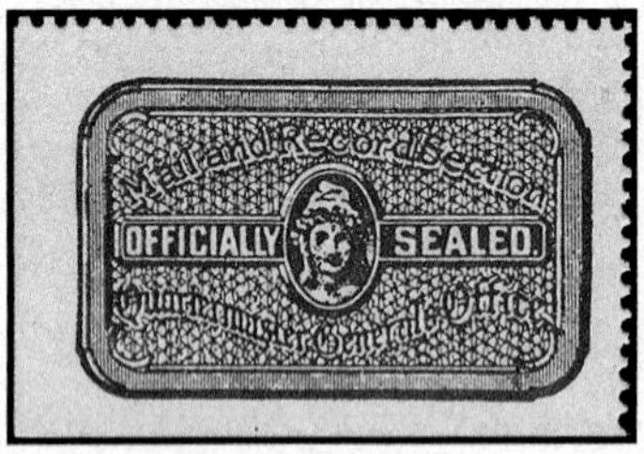

POS5

Quartermaster General's Office
Issued in panes of 10 (2x5) without selvage.

1919 ***Perf. 12***
OX19 POS5 **indigo** 300.
Block of 4 *1,500.*
Pane of 10 *3,600.*

Rouletted 7
OX20 POS5 **indigo** — *3,250.*

The pane format of No. OX20 is not known. One of the few reported examples is rouletted on four sides.

Nos. OX19-OX20 were used on mail to and from the Procurement Division of the Quartermaster General's Office. After five weeks of use the seals were withdrawn when the Mail and Records Section became a full branch of the Quartermaster General's Office.

POS6

Issued in panes of 20 (5x4) and 16 (4x4).

Panes of 10 were made from panes of 20 for use in smaller post offices.

1919 ***Perf. 12 (sometimes rough)***

Thin, white, crisp paper

OX21 POS6 **black** (shades) .20 .20
On cover 10.00
Pane of 20 10.00
a. Imperf, pair 15.00
On cover —
b. Vert. pair, imperf horiz. 10.00
c. Horiz. pair, imperf vert. 10.00
d. Vert. pair, imperf btwn. 25.00
e. Horiz. pair, imperf btwn. 25.00
f. Wmkd. eagle and star in sheet (1936?) 2.00 2.00
Pane of 20 70.00
g. As "f," imperf, pair 35.00
h. As "f," vert. pair, imperf horiz. 27.50
i. As "f," vert. pair, imperf btwn. 27.50
j. Wmkd. "Certificate Bond" in sheet (1936?) 10.00 10.00
Pane of 20 300.00

The paper used for Nos. OX21-OX27 is thin enough to allow reading text on the envelope.

Earliest documented use: 1920.

1936(?) ***Perf. 12x9***
OX22 POS6 **black** (shades) 7.50 7.50
On cover 85.00
Pane of 20 200.00
a. Vert. pair, imperf horiz. 50.00
b. Horiz. pair, imperf vert. 50.00
c. Wmkd. eagle and star in sheet 7.50 7.50
Pane of 20 200.00
d. As "c." vert. pair, imperf horiz. 50.00
e. As "c," horiz. pair, imperf vert. 50.00

Earliest documented use: Oct. 1936 (No. OX22 or OX23.)

1936(?) ***Perf. 12x8½***
OX23 POS6 **black** (shades) 2.50 2.50
On cover 40.00
Pane of 20 75.00
a. Wmkd. eagle and star in sheet 4.00 4.00
Pane of 20 110.00

1936(?) ***Perf. 12½***
OX24 POS6 **gray black,** pane of 20 —

1936(?) ***Perf. 8½***
OX25 POS6 **gray black** —
a. Wmkd. eagle and star in sheet —

1936(?) ***Perf. 12x9½***
OX26 POS6 **gray black,** pane of 20 —

1936(?) ***Perf. 11½***
OX27 POS6 **gray black** —
On cover —

Medium to thick, opaque, egg or cream colored paper

1946(?) ***Perf. 12***
OX28 POS6 **gray black** .40 .40
On cover 25.00
Pane of 20 22.50
a. Vert. pair, imperf btwn. 15.00

1946(?) ***Perf. 12½***
OX29 POS6 **gray black** .50 .50
On cover 25.00
Pane of 20 25.00

1947(?) ***Perf. 12½x8½***
OX30 POS6 **gray black** 1.50 1.50
On cover 45.00
Pane of 20 50.00

1947(?) ***Perf. 8½***
OX31 POS6 **gray black** 1.50 1.50
On cover 45.00
Pane of 20 50.00

1947(?) ***Perf. 8½x12***
OX32 POS6 **gray black** —

1947(?) ***Perf. 8½x8***
OX33 POS6 **gray black,** on cover —

1947(?) ***Perf. 8x8½***
OX33A POS6 **gray black,** on cover —

Thick, gray, very soft paper

1948 ***Perf. 12½ (sometimes rough)***
OX34 POS6 **gray black** 1.00 1.00
On cover 35.00
Pane of 16 45.00

1948(?) ***Perf. 8½***
OX35 POS6 **gray black** 5.00 5.00
On cover 60.00
Pane of 16 —

1948(?) ***Perf. 12½x8½***
OX36 POS6 **gray black** — —
Pane of 10 —
Pane of 20 —

1948(?) ***Perf. 8½x12½***
OX37 POS6 **gray black** — —

1948 ***Hyphen Hole Perf. 9½***
OX38 POS6 **gray black** 15.00 15.00
On cover 100.00
Pane of 5, imperf at sides 200.00
Pane of 16 350.00

Pane of 5, tab inscribed "16-56146-1 GPO."

1950(?) ***Hyphen Hole Perf. 9½ x Imperf***

Medium thick, cream paper

Design width: 37½mm

OX39 POS6 **gray black,** imperf at sides .25 .20
On cover 12.50
Pane of 5, imperf at sides 1.25
a. Vert. pair, imperf between 10.00
b. Pane of 5, imperf 15.00
c. Pane of 5, imperf at top & btwn. rows 2 & 3, 4 & 5 20.00

Pane of 5 tab inscribed, "16-56164-1 GPO."
Earliest documented use: Jan. 23, 1950.

1969(?) ***Hyphen Hole Perf. 9½ x Imperf***

Medium thick, white paper

Design width: 38½mm

OX40 POS6 **gray black** .25 .20
On cover *30.00*
Pane of 5, imperf at sides 2.25
a. Vert. pair, imperf. btwn. 10.00
b. Pane of 5, Imperf 20.00

Tab inscribed, "c43-16-56164-1 GPO"

Earliest documented use: Feb. 11, 1969.

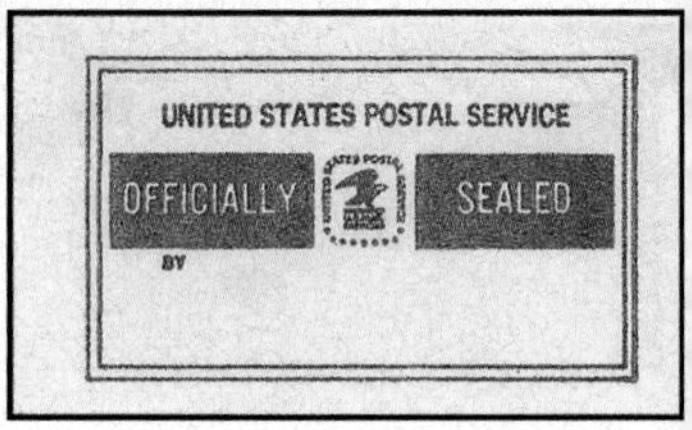

POS7

On Nos. OX41-OX50, tab is inscribed, "LABEL 21, JULY 1971."

1972 **Litho.** ***Rouletted 9½ x Imperf***
OX41 POS7 **black** .20 .20
On cover 12.50
Pane of 5 2.00
a. Imperf, pair 10.00

1972(?) ***Rouletted 6½ x Imperf***
OX42 POS7 **black** .20 .20
On cover 5.00
Pane of 5 2.75

1973(?) **Litho.** ***Hyphen Hole 7 x Imperf***
OX43 POS7 **black** .30 .20
On cover 7.50
Pane of 5 9.00

1976(?) **Litho.** ***Rouletted 8½ x Imperf***
OX44 POS7 **black** .20 .20
On cover 7.50
Pane of 5 2.00

1979(?) **Litho.** ***Perf. 12½ x Imperf***
OX45 POS7 **black** .20 .20
On cover 7.50
Pane of 5 2.25
Small holes .20 .20
On cover 7.50
Pane of 5 2.25

1988(?) **Litho.** ***Die Cut***

Self-Adhesive

OX46 POS7 **black,** 38x21mm, tagged, fluorescent paper .25 .25
On cover *7.50*
Pane of 5 3.50
OX47 POS7 **bluish black,** 38x21mm, untagged, non-fluorescent paper .25 .25
On cover *7.50*
Pane of 5 3.50
OX48 POS7 **gray** (shades), 37x21mm .25 .25
On cover *7.50*
Pane of 5 3.50
OX49 POS7 **black,** 40x21mm .50 .50
On cover *15.00*
Pane of 5 10.00
OX50 POS7 **purple,** 37x21mm — —
On cover —

No. OX47 is on a creamier, thicker paper than No. OX46.

On No. OX49, BY is 2x1mm, P of POSTAL is left of P in POSTAL of Emblem. Tab inscribed as No. OX41, but 1's have no bottom serif.

Earliest documented use: No. OX50, Dec. 12, 1995.

POS8

Tab inscribed "LABEL 21, JAN. 1992."

1992 **Size: 44x22mm** ***Die Cut***

Self-adhesive

OX51 POS8 **black** 1.00 1.00
On cover *25.00*
Pane of 5 10.00

Earliest documented use: Mar. 1992.

1992? ***Die Cut***

Self-Adhesive

Size: 41x21mm

OX52 POS8 **black** .25 .25
On cover *7.50*
Pane of 5 3.50

No. OX52 exists on both white and brown backing paper. Those on brown backing paper are worth more.

POS9

Tab inscribed "LABEL 21, April 1994."

1994 ***Die Cut***

Self-Adhesive

OX53 POS9 **black** .25 .25
On cover *7.50*
Pane of 5 3.50

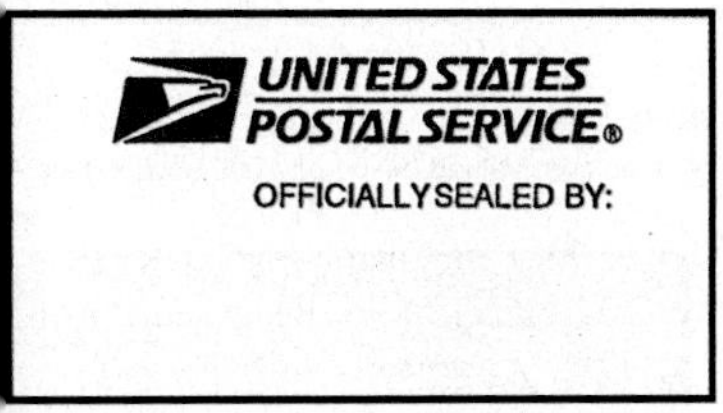

POS10

Tab inscribed "LABEL 21, August 1996."

1996 ***Die Cut***

Self-Adhesive

OX54 POS10 **black** .25 .25
On cover *7.50*
Pane of 5 2.00
a. "OFFICALLY" *1.00* —
On cover 20.00
Pane of 5 *8.00*

POS11

Tab inscribed "LABEL 21, August 1996."

1996 ***Die Cut***

Self-Adhesive

OX55 POS11 **black** .25 .25
On cover 7.50
Pane of 5 3.00

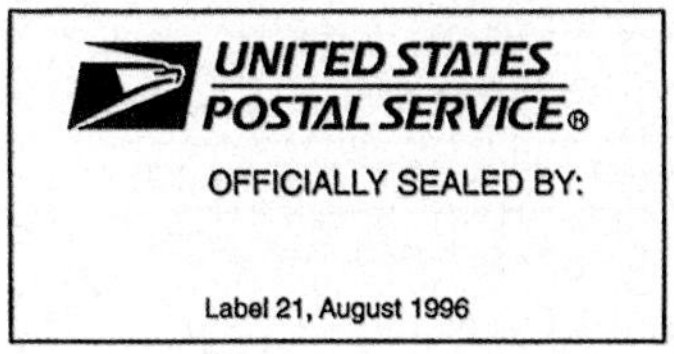

POS12

Seal inscribed "LABEL 21, August 1996."

2006 (?) ***Die Cut***

Self-Adhesive

OX56 POS12 **black** .25 .25
On cover *7.50*
Pane of 5 3.00

Although No. OX56 is inscribed "August 1996," it likely was issued in 2006.

TYPESET SEALS

These seals were privately printed for sale mostly to Fourth Class Post Offices. Many are extremely rare. Unquestioned varieties are listed. Many others exist.

All are imperf or die cut except Nos. LOX7-LOX11 and LOX36.

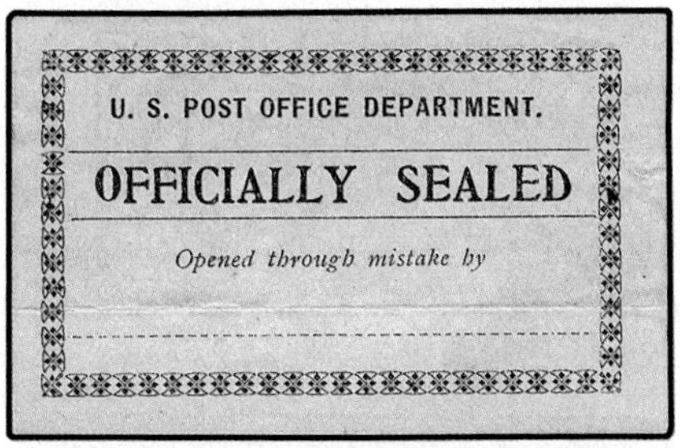

TSS1

LOX1 TSS1 **black** *500.00 500.00*
On cover —

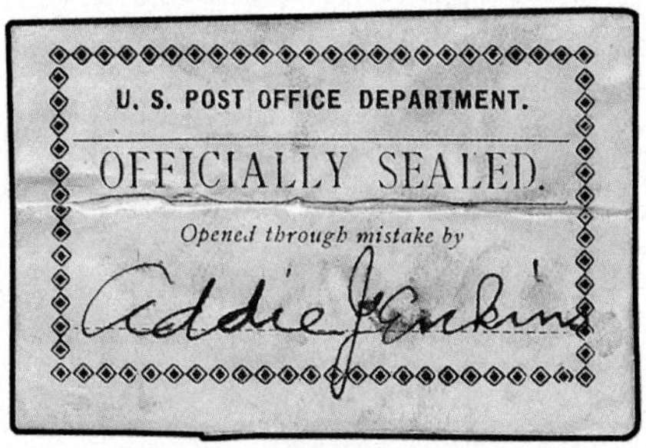

TSS2

LOX2 TSS2 **black,** 15 diamonds vertically in frame *1,500. 1,500.*
a. 14 diamonds vertically *750.*
b. 14 diamonds vertically, no period after "DEPARTMENT" *750.*
c. "OFFICALLY" misspelling, 14 diamonds vertically *1,500.*
On cover —

TSS3

LOX3 TSS3 **black** —
On cover —

TSS4

LOX4 TSS4 **black,** *pink* *1,250.*

No. LOX4 used is valued with minor flaws.

TSS5

LOX5 TSS5 **black** *500.00*
LOX5A TSS5 **black,** *pink* —

TSS6

LOX6 TSS6 **black** —

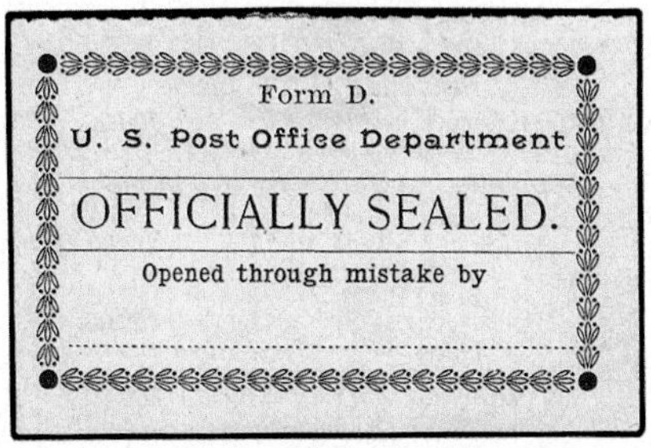

TSS7

Rouletted 9½ horizontally

LOX7 TSS7 **black** *1,000.* —

TSS8

Printed and distributed by Morrill Bros., P.O. Supply Printers, Fulton, N.Y., in panes of 4, two tete beche pairs.

Rouletted 11½, 12½, 16½ in black at top & side

LOX8 TSS8 **black,** rouletted 11½ 100.00 100.00
On cover *1,250.*
a. **black,** rouletted 12½ 100.00 100.00
On cover *1,250.*
b. **black,** rouletted 11½ by 12½ 100.00 100.00
On cover *1,250.*
c. **black,** rouletted 12½ by 11½ 100.00 100.00

On cover 1,250.
Sheet of 4, 1 each Nos. LOX8, LOX8a-LOX8c 1,250.
d. **black,** rouletted 11½ and 12½ compound by 11½ 250.00 150.00
e. **black,** rouletted 11½ and 12½ compound by 12½ 250.00 150.00
Sheet of 4, 1 each Nos. LOX8a, LOX8c, LOX8d-LOX8e 1,500.
f. **black,** rouletted 16½ 300.00 300.00
On cover 1,750.
g. **black,** rouletted 16½ on 3 or 4 sides —

Gauge of rouletting on Nos. LOX8d and LOX8e transitions about one-quarter of way across top edge of seal. A sheet of 4 of No. LOX8f exists and is in the Luff reference collection of the Philatelic Foundation. No. LOX8g is unique.

TSS9

Solid lines above and below "OFFICIALLY SEALED."

Rouletted 12½, 16½ in black between

LOX9 TSS9 **black** 500.00 500.00
On cover —

TSS10

Dotted lines above and below "OFFICIALLY SEALED."

Rouletted 12½ in black

LOX10 TSS10 **black,** *pink* 500.00 750.00
a. Dot after "OFFICIALLY" 1,500.

Rouletted 11½, 12½ or 16½ in black

LOX11 TSS10 **black,** rouletted 12½ at top and side 2.00 75.00
On cover 1,000.
Sheet of 4 15.00
a. Double impression 400.00
Sheet of 4 2,000.
b. Double impression, one inverted 400.00
c. Dot after "OFFICIALLY" 4.00 150.00
On cover 1,500.
Sheet of 4, one seal with dot 12.50
d. **black,** rouletted 11½ at top or bottom 200.00
e. **blue,** rouletted 11½ at top or bottom 2,500.
f. **black,** rouletted 11½ at top and side 100.00
Sheet of 4 1,500.
g. **black,** rouletted 12½ by 11½ —
h. **black,** rouletted 16½ at top or bottom 250.00
Sheet of 2, both seals with dot 1,750.
Sheet of 2, tete beche —
i. **black,** rouletted 16½ at top and side 250.00

Dyed examples of No. LOX11 are frequently misrepresented as No. LOX10.

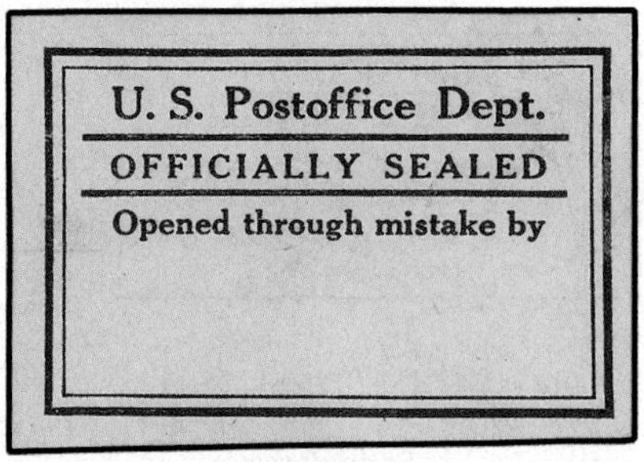

TSS11

Printed and distributed by The Lemoyne Supply Co., Lemoyne, Pa.
Nos. LOX13 and LOX13a have thin lines above and below 37¼mm long "OFFICIALLY SEALED"

LOX12 TSS11 **black** 250.00
On cover —
LOX13 TSS11 **blue** 750.00
a. **black** —

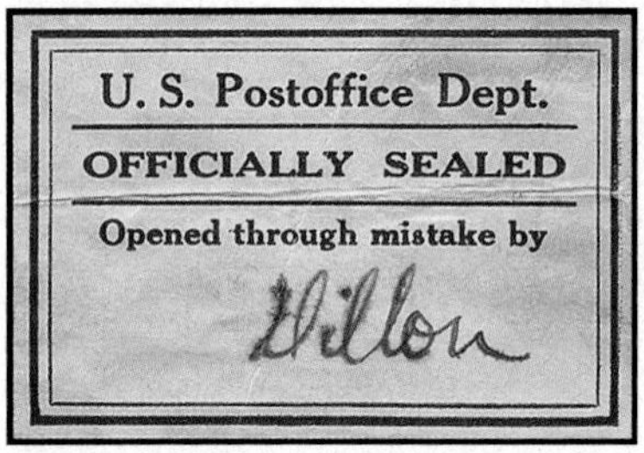

TSS12

LOX14 TSS12 **blue** 1,750. 1,750.

TSS13

LOX15 TSS13 **black** 1,250. —
On cover 2,000.

No. LOX15 unused is valued with small faults and crease. See No. LOX29 for a similar design in blue.

TSS14

LOX16 TSS14 **blue** 1,500. 1,000.

No. LOX16 used is valued with usual crease, thin spots and small tear.

TSS15

LOX17 TSS15 **dark blue** 100.00 200.0
On cover 1,00C
a. Printed on both sides 1,750.
b. 2mm between "y" & "S," no period after "d" 250.00 400.0
LOX18 TSS15 **black** 300.00 —
On cover 1,25C

TSS16

LOX19 TSS16 **black** 600.00 —

TSS16A

LOX19A TSS16a **black** 2,750.

No. LOX19A is unique. Valued based on 2000 auction sale.

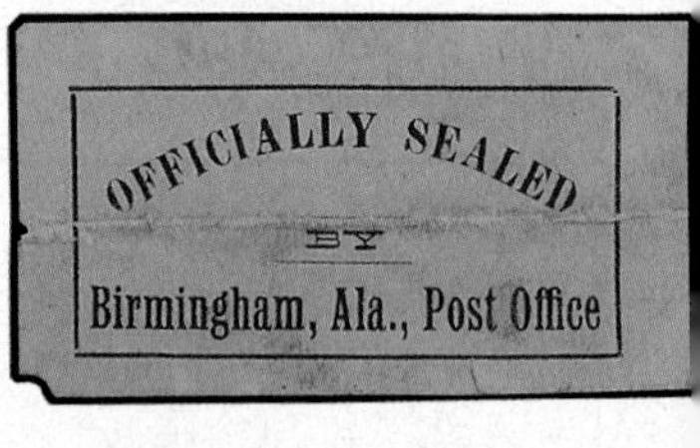

Type I
TSS17

Type II — Bottom line in heavy type face. Period after "Office."

LOX20 TSS17 **black,** *light green* (Type I) — —

At least two different types or settings are known. The illustrated type has a dotted line above "BY" that does not show in the illustration.

LOX20A TSS17 **black,** *light green* (Type II) 2,000.

No. LOX20A is valued with major thin at top center.

TSS18

LOX21 TSS18 **black** 750.00

TSS18a

LOX21A TSS18a **black** — *1,500.*
On cover *1,500.*

No. LOX21A unused is valued with crease and small faults.

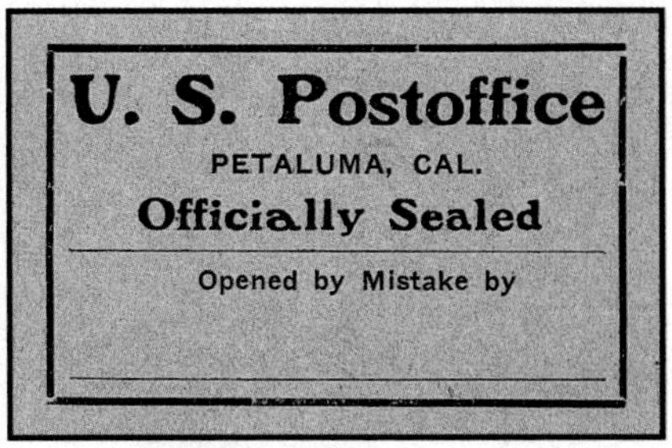

TSS19

LOX22 TSS19 **black,** *blue* *2,000.*

No. LOX22 is unique. It is creased and is valued as such.

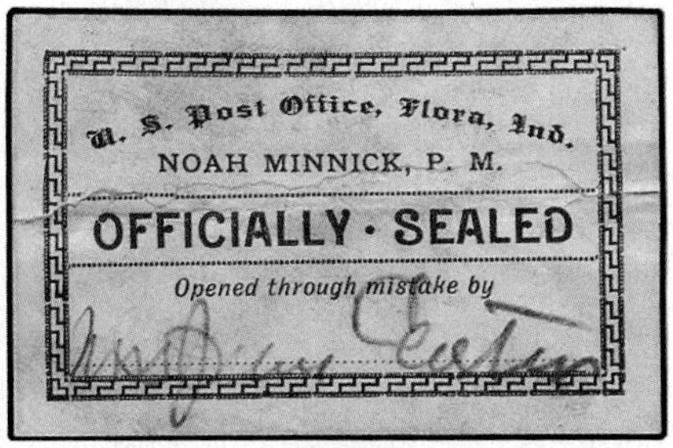

TSS20

LOX23 TSS20 **black** —

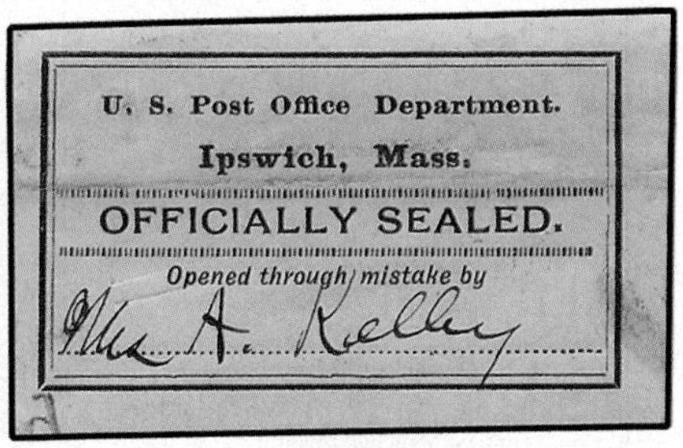

TSS21

LOX24 TSS21 **black,** on cover *3,000.*

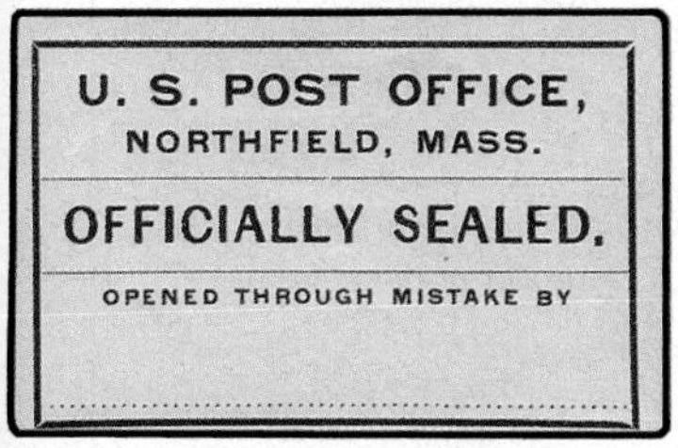

TSS22

LOX25 TSS22 **black** *1,350.*

At least three examples of No. LOX25 exist. All have faults. Value is for the finest example.

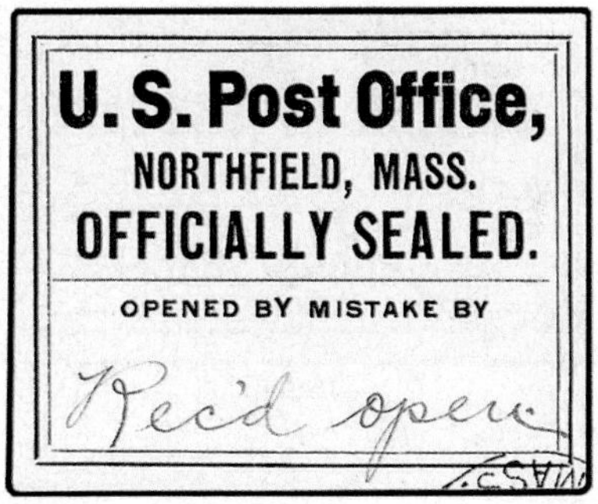

TSS23

LOX26 TSS23 **black** *1,100.*

No. LOX26 used is valued with small fault.

TSS24

LOX27 TSS24 **black,** *dark brown red* *1,250.*

No. LOX27 is valued with crease and small flaws.

TSS25

LOX28 TSS25 **black** —
On cover *2,700.*

The on-cover seal shown was torn in half when the envelope was opened. Value is based on 2007 auction sale.

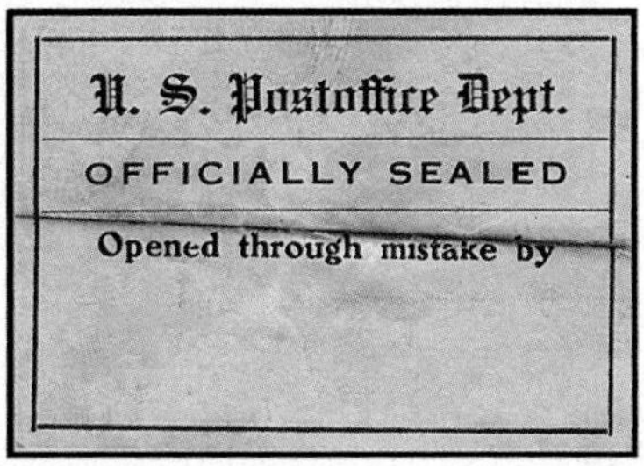

TSS26

LOX29 TSS26 **blue,** on cover *3,750.*

No. LOX29 is unique.

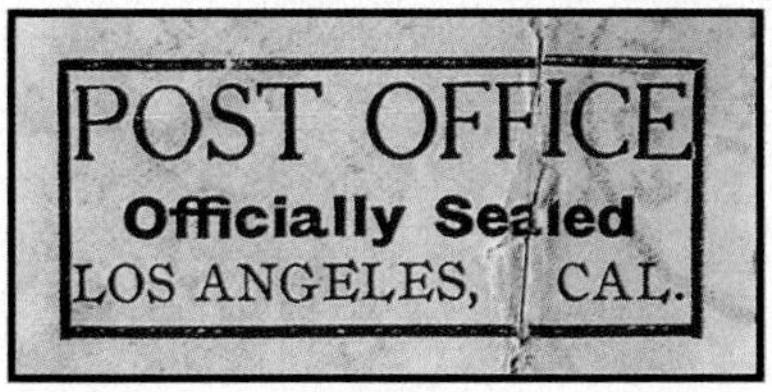

TSS27

LOX30 TSS27 **black,** pair on cover *5,000.*

No. LOX30 is unique. The seals were torn in half when the envelope was opened. Value is based on 2006 auction sale.

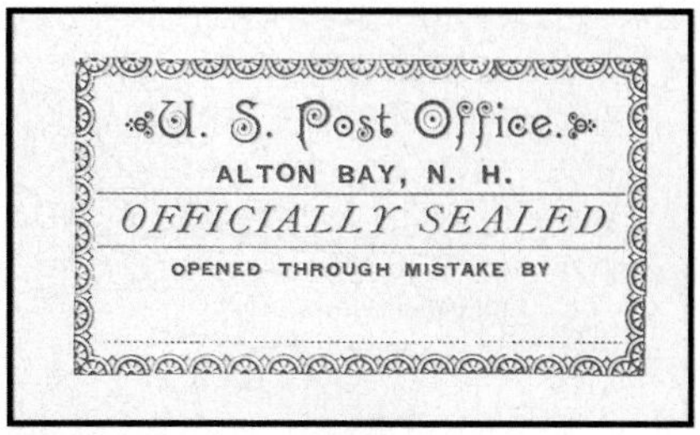

TSS28

LOX31 TSS28 **red,** *cream* *1,000.*

No. LOX31 is unique. It has a thin spot and crease and is valued as such.

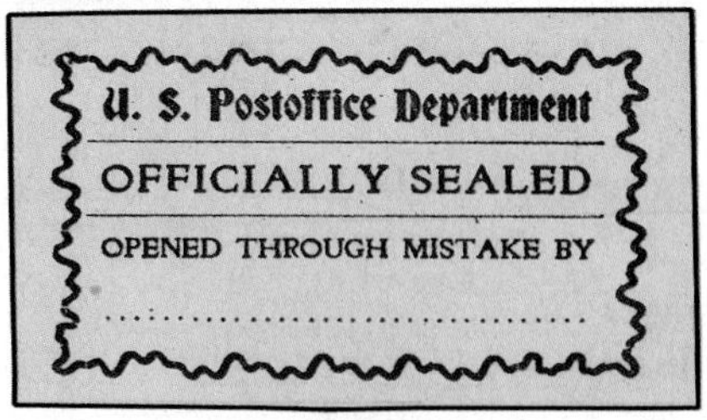

TSS29

LOX32 TSS29 **black** *1,250.*

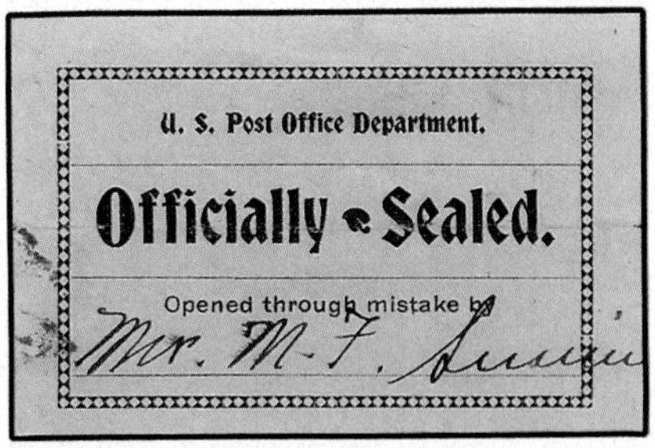

TSS30

LOX33 TSS30 **black** —

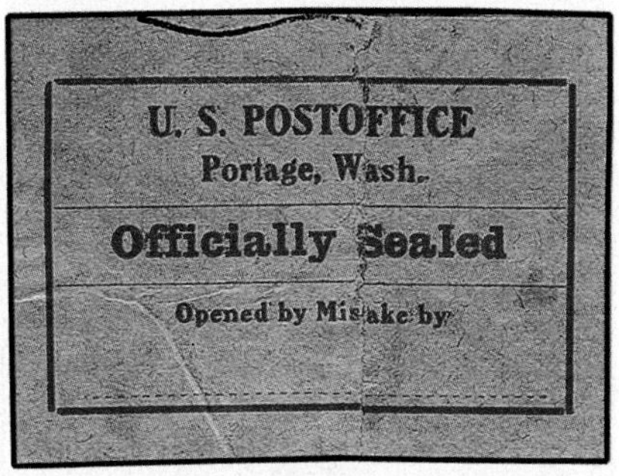

TSS31

LOX34 TSS31 **red,** *rose* *1,250.*
On cover *1,500.*

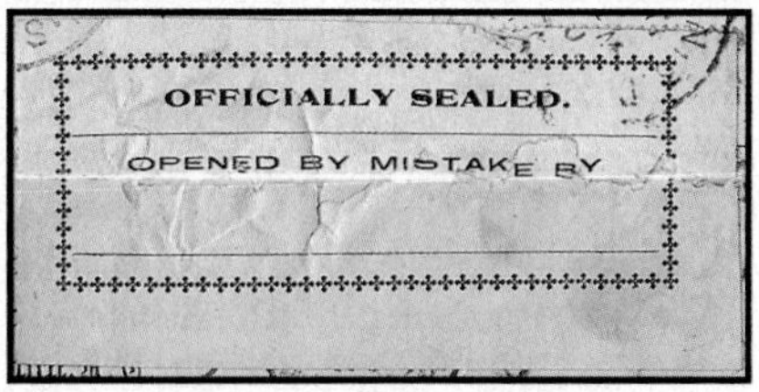

TSS32

LOX35 TSS32 **black,** on cover —

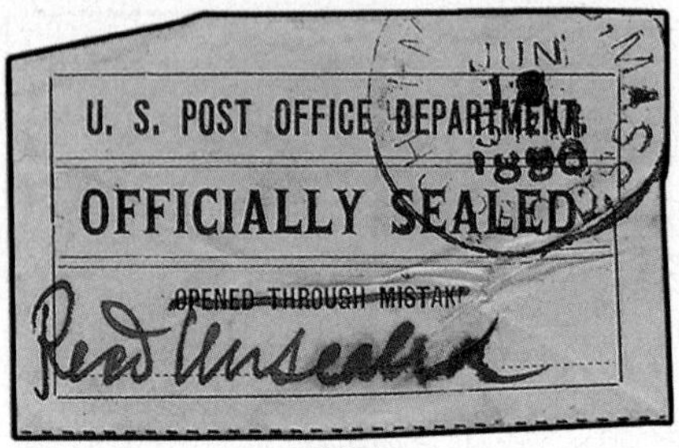

TSS33

Rouletted (at least one side)

LOX36 TSS33 **black** —

TSS34

LOX37 TSS34 **green** —

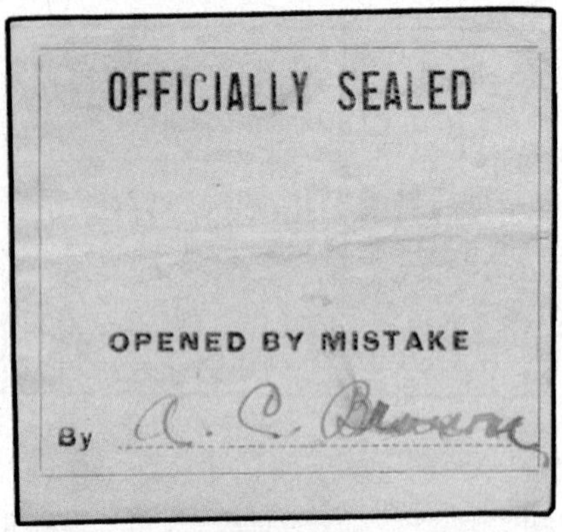

TSS35

LOX38 TSS35 **black,** *tan* *1,250.*

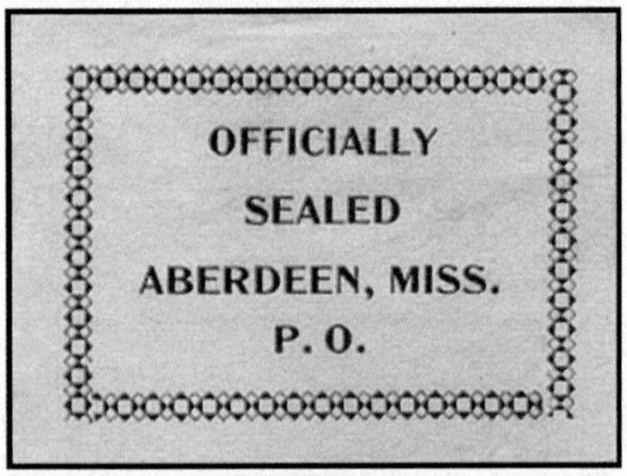

TSS36

LOX39 TSS36 **black,** *tan* *1,750.*

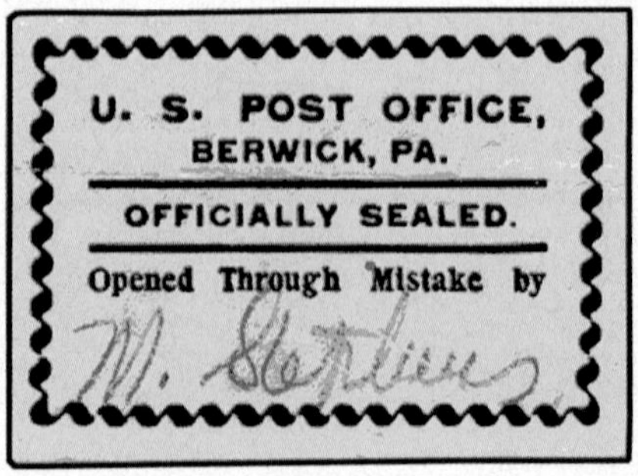

TSS37

LOX40 TSS37 **black,** *tan* *1,750.*

TSS38

LOX41 TSS38 **black** —

TSS39

LOX42 TSS39 **black,** on cover —

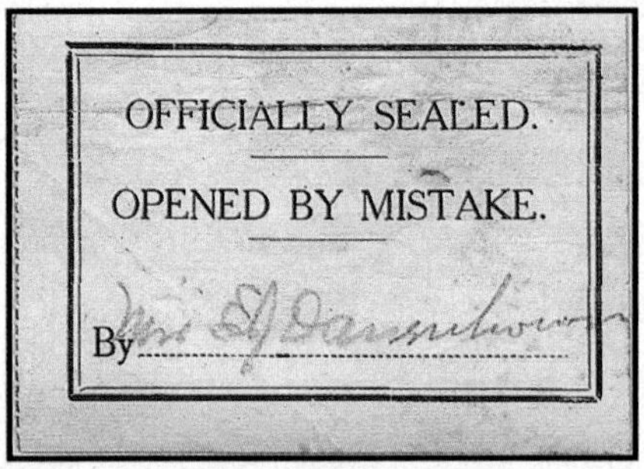

TSS40

LOX43 TSS40 **black** *1,250.*

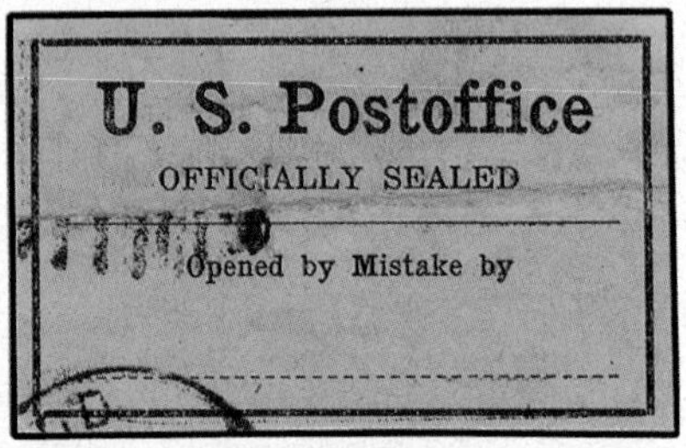

TSS41

LOX44 TSS41 **blue,** *yellow* *1,250.*

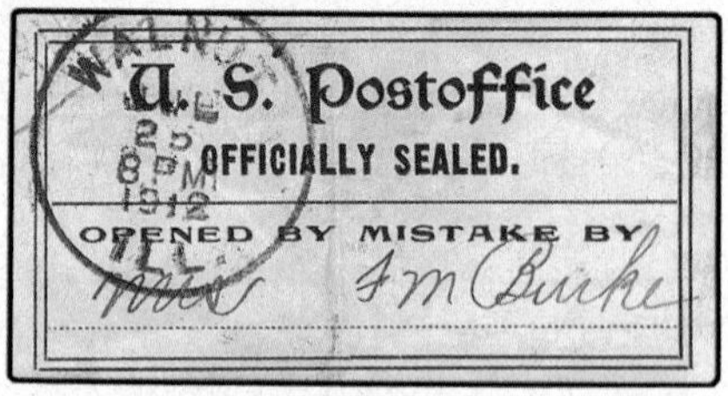

TSS42

LOX45 TSS42 **dark blue** *1,250.*

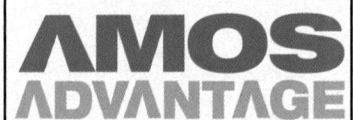

TEST STAMPS

Test stamps, also called "dummy stamps," came into being in the late 19th century, and their production continues to the present. These stamps have been printed by both the Bureau of Engraving and Printing and by private companies for use when the Post Office Department, United States Postal Service and other companies wanted to use test stamps rather than accountable paper (i.e., actual stamps that would have to be accounted for).

With the growth of automation and the development of vending equipment in the 20th century, the production and use of test stamps proliferated. A majority are very scarce, as these items generally were not made available to the general public or philatelists.

The test stamps listed here were produced for several purposes:

1. To develop and test production equipment, including printing presses and stamp and booklet manufacturing equipment.
2. To design stamp vending equipment by private companies.
3. To test, adjust and promote stamp affixing equipment by commercial vendors.
4. To test and adjust stamp vending equipment at dispensing sites by the Postal Service and private companies.

The test stamp listings are arranged into two sections, the first being sheet and coil stamps, and the second being booklets. These listings were formed by Steven R. Unkrich, in consultation with other leading collectors of test stamps. Thanks to Dan Undersander for supplying much of the information in this section's introduction. Those interested in learning more about test (dummy) stamps are invited to join the Dummy Stamps Study Group. Contact Terry Scott at trs@napanet.net.

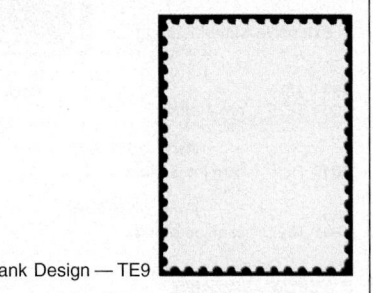

Blank Design — TE9

Produced by Continental Bank Note or American Bank Note Company.

1878-79 **Soft Paper** **Unwmk.** ***Perf. 12***

TD9	TE9	blank	—
		Block of 4	—

See Nos. TD30, TD44-TD50A, TD75-TD76, TD79-TD82, TD83-TD86, TD106, TD113-TD114, TD122 for other blank design stamps.

Burt and Toby's Stamp Battery — TE9a

1890 ***Perf. 12***

TD9A	TE9a	light green	—

Perf. 12¼x12

TD9B	TE9a	lavender	—

Blank Design Type of 1878-79

Produced by Bureau of Engraving and Printing.

1907 **Wmk. 191** ***Perf. 12***

Brownish Gum

TD10	TE9	blank	—

TE10

Schermack Coil — TE11

Mailometer Coil — TE12

1906-09 **Unwmk.** ***Perf. 12***

TD12	TE10	**orange,** on cover	—

Schermack Type III Perforations

TD13	TE11	**red**	—
		Pair	—
		Pasteup pair	—
TD14	TE12	**brown**	—
		On cover	—
		Pair	—
		Guide line pair	—
		Pasteup pair	—
a.		Imperf.	100.00
		Pair	200.00
b.		Pair, No. TD14 + No. TD14a	—

Mailometer Type I Perforations

TD14C	TE11	**red**	—
		Pair	—
TD15	TE12	**brown**	—
		Pair	—
		Pasteup pair	—

Mailometer Type II Perforations

TD15A	TE11	**brown**	—
		Pair	—
TD16	TE12	**red**	—
		Pair	—
		Guide line pair	—
		Pasteup pair	—

Mailometer Type III Perforations

TD17	TE12	**brown**	—
		Pair	—

See Vending and Affixing Machines Perforations section for illustrations of perforation types.

Bureau of Engraving and Printing Test Stamps for Rotary Press Development

Numerals and Oval — TE13

Numerals and Alexander Hamilton — TE14

Nos. TD18-TD23 were the first test stamps used by the BEP during efforts to develop rotary press printing as a less costly method of stamp production than flat plate printing. Experiments were conducted with intaglio (engraving), letterpress (typography) and offest lithography printing. Engraving was the selected technique. The rotary press was developed under the direction of BEP Director Joseph E. Ralph, but is generally named the Stickney Press after its inventor and patent holder, Benjamin F. Stickeny.

1909-10 **Engr.** ***Imperf.***

Design: 19x22mm

Ungummed Soft Wove Paper

TD18	TE13	**deep red**	1,500.
		Block of 4	—
		Block of 12 with pencil inscription on back	*11,000.*

Inscription on block of 12 reads "first impression printed from an experimental press designed by J. E. Ralph & B. F. Stickney from intaglio roll JER."

Design: 19½x22½mm

TD19	TE14	**red**	125.00
		Block of 4	600.00

No. TD19 portrait has facial shading composed of fine lines and dots. Subjects spaced 3½mm horizontally and 2mm vertically. Large die proofs exist with "400894" on back. Value, $2,000.

Coil Stamps (Nos. TD20-TD21, TD23)

Typo.

Design: 19x22½mm

Perf. 12 Vert.

Ungummed Soft Wove Paper

TD20	TE14	**deep red,** *1910*	1,000.

Three different die proofs are known for No. TD20. The first is black on thick glazed card, measuring 73x83mm, with inscription "first die proof impression of experimental surface die from surface print. JER April 25/10," with "420279" on back. Value, $2,000.

The second is deep red on thick glazed card, measuring 73x83mm, with inscription "Sample of surface printing from die: done by Bureau E&P 5/20/1910," with "420270" on back. Value, $1,500.

The third is deep red cut to design size on thick card with number stamps on back. Value, $1,000.

Perf. 12 Horiz.

Soft Wove Paper

TD21	TE14	**deep red,** *1910*	*3,100.*

Perf. 12

TD22	TE14	**deep red,** *1910*	—

The portrait on Nos. TD21-TD22 has facial shading composed of fine lines and small squares, open-centered when large.

Offset (Litho.)

Design: 19x21½mm

Perf. 10½ Horiz.

TD23	TE14	**deep red,** *1910*	100.00
		Pair	200.00
		Pair, on cover	1,000.

The portrait of No. TD23 has facial shading composed of dots and short lines providing a coarse appearance.

Automatic Vending Co. Coil — TE15

1909 ***Imperf.***

TD24	TE15	**dark red**	—
		Horiz. pair	—
a.		Vert. pair, U.S. Automatic Vending Co. Type I separations	—
		On cover	—
b.		Vert. pair, imperf. horiz.	—

Rosback perf 11.75 Vert.

TD24C	TE15	**red**	—
		Horiz. pair	—
d.		Vert. pair, imperf. horiz.	—

Imperf

TD24E	TE15	**green**	—
		Vert. pair	—

Simplex Mfg. Co. — TE16

1909-10 *Imperf.*

Solid Background

TD25	TE16	**red**	60.00

Horizontal Lines in Background

TD26	TE16	**green**	60.00

Simplex Stamp Affixer — TE17

1909-10 *Imperf.*

TD27	TE17	**red**	—

BEP Test Stamps for Offset Printing

Minerva Facing Right — TE18

Minerva Facing Left (Text Reversed) — TE19

Nos. TD28-TD29 were made to test the Harris offset press at the Bureau of Engraving and Printing. The offset method was not adopted in 1910 but several Harris presses were used to print revenue stamps and the offset postage issues of 1918-20.

1910 **Litho.** *Imperf.*

Design: 30½x34mm

Ungummed White Wove Paper

TD28	TE18	**red**	650.00
		Pair	1,300.
		Block of 4	—

Design: 30x33½mm

TD29	TE19	**red**	650.00
		Pair	1,300.
		Block of 4	—

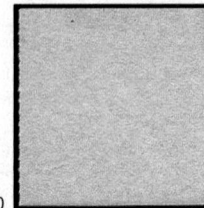

Blank Design — TE20

1910 ? *Rouletted 13¼ Vert.*

Stamp Size: 25.5x25.75mm

Shiny Gum

TD30	TE20	blank, *tan*	20.00
		Pair	40.00

Standard Stamp Affixer Coils

Inscribed "Boston, Mass." — TE21

Inscribed "Everett, Mass." — TE22

Inscribed "Somerville, Mass." — TE23

1910s *Perf. 10½ Vert.*

TD31	TE21	**green**	—
		Pair	—
TD32	TE21	**red**	—
		Pair	—
TD33	TE22	**green**	20.00
		Pair	50.00
TD33A	TE22	**red**	20.00
		Pair	50.00

Alternating Perf. 8¼ and 8½ Vert.

TD34	TE23	**green**	20.00
		Pair	50.00

Perf. 8½ Vert.

TD35	TE23	**light green**	20.00
		Pair	50.00

Perf. 10½ Vert.

TD36	TE23	**green**	20.00
		Pair	50.00

Alternating Perf. 10.9 and 10.2 Vert.

TD36A	TE23	**red**	20.00
		Pair	50.00

Multipost Co. Coil — TE24a

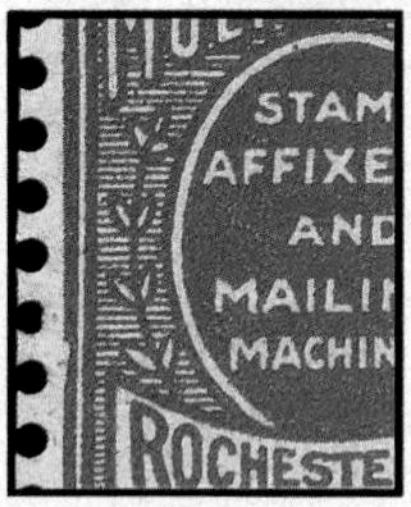

TE24 Detail

TE24a Detail

Midland Supply Co. Coil — TE24b

1910-20 *Perf. 9¾ Vert*

TD37	TE24	**red**	20.0
		Pair	50.0

Perf. 10¼ Vert.

TD38	TE24a	**carmine**	20.0
		Pair	50.0

Perf. 10½ Vert.

TD38A	TE24b	**red**	—
		Pair	—

No. TD37 has full shading lines, and No. TD38 has shorte shading lines.

Extensive Manufacturing Co. Coils — TE25

1911-13 *Perf. 8½ Horiz*

TD39	TE25	**red & blue**	—
		Pair	—

Perf. 10¼ Vert.

TD40	TE25	**carmine & black**	35.0
		Pair	75.0

Perf. 10¾ Vert.

TD41	TE25	**carmine & black**	35.0
		Pair	75.0

Standard Mailing Machine Co Coils — TE26

1913 *Perf. 10½ Vert*

TD42	TE26	**red**	40.0
		Pair	80.0
TD43	TE26	**light purple**	40.0
		Pair	80.0

Blank Designs Type of 1878-79

1910-27 *Imperf*

Smooth Gum

TD44	TE9	blank	—
		Pair	—

Perf. 10½ Vert.

TD45	TE9	blank	—
		Pair	—

Schermack Type III Perforations

TD46	TE9	blank	—
		Pair	—
		Paste up pair	—

Mailometer Type I Perforations

TD47	TE9	blank	200.0
		Pair	—
		Paste up pair	—

Mailometer Type II Perforations

TD48	TE9	blank	—
		Pair	—
		Paste up pair	—

Mailometer Type III Perforations

TD49	TE9	blank	—
		Pair	—
		Paste up pair	—

Perf. 11 Vert. Schermack Type I 7-hole Perforations

TD50	TE9	blank	—
		Pair	—

Perf. 10 Vert. Schermack Type I 7-hole Perforations

TD50A	TE9	blank	—
		Pair	—

Expertization is recommended for No. TD44.

George Washington — TE27

1912 *Imperf.*

Without Gum

TD51	TE27	**brown**	100.00
		Pair	200.00
		Block of 4	450.00

No. TD51 tested a photo-etching process by Bruckmann A. G. of Munich, Germany.

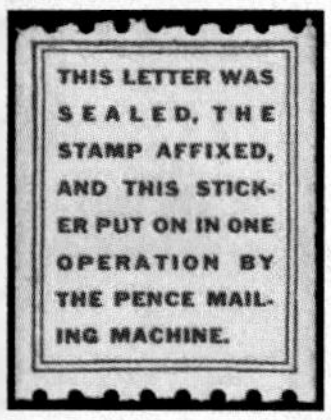

Pence Mailing Machine — TE27a

1914 *Perf 8½ Horiz.*

TD51A	TE27a	**red**	100.00
		Pair	—

New Jersey Vending Machine Co. Coil — TE28

1914-16 *Perf. 10½ Vert.*

TD52	TE28	**red**	—
		Pair	—

National Envelope Sealing and Stamp Manufacturing Coils — TE29

U.S. Stamp Distributing and Sales Corporation Coil — TE29a

1915 *Perf. 8½ Horiz.*

TD53	TE29	**red & blue**	—
		Pair	—
TD54	TE29	**red**	—
		Pair	—

1919 *Perf. Alternating 8.5 and 8.35 Vert.*

TD54A	TE29a	**red**	—
		Pair	—

Mailometer Coils — TE30

1922 *Nine small perforation holes*

TD55	TE30	**red**	—
		Pair	—

Perf. 10¼ Vert. (10 small holes)

TD56	TE30	**deep purple**	—
		Pair	—

Perf. 12 Vert. (8 small holes)

TD57	TE30	**deep purple**	—
		Pair	—

Perf. 12 Vert. (9 small holes)

TD57A	TE30	**deep purple**	—
		Pair	—

Perf. 10¼ Vert.

TD58	TE30	**red**	—
		Pair	—
		On cover	—

Inscribed "10,000 Envelopes Per Hour"

Perf. 10½ Vert.

TD59	TE30	**red**	—
		Pair	—

TE30a

Perf. 10.5 Vert.

TD60	TE30a	**red**	—
		Pair	—

TE30b

Perf. 10.5 Vert.

TD60A	TE30b	**red**	—
		Pair	—

Wizard Label Affixer Coil — TE31

1912-14 *Perf. 10¼ Vert.*

TD61	TE31	**red**	—
		Pair	—

Wizard Label Affixer Coil — TE32

1920s *Schermack Type III Perforations*

TD62	TE32	**red & blue**	—

Wizard Stamp Affixer Coil — TE32a

1920s *Perf. 10 Vert.*

TD62A	TE32a	**red & blue**	—
		Pair	—

Postage Stamp Machine Co. Coil — TE33

1920s *Perf. 8½ Vert.*

TD63	TE33	*red*	—
		Pair	—

Natural Method Stamp Affixer — TE33a

1910-30 *Perf. 11¾ Vert.*

TD63A	TE33a	**red,** *tan*	—
		Pair	—

Security Coil — TE33b

1910-30 *Perf. 8½ Horiz.*

TD63B	TE33b	**red**	—
		Pair	—

Licensed Sanitary Postage Coil — TE34

TE34a

1920s *Perf. 10½ Horiz.*

TD64	TE34	**red**	—
		Pair	—

Perf. 10¾ Vert.

TD65	TE34a	**red**	20.00
		Pair	50.00

Postcraft Stamp Affixer Coil — TE35

1920s *Perf. 10 Vert.*

TD66	TE35	color unknown	—
		Pair	—

Vidaver Mailing Machine Co. Inc. Coil — TE36

1920s *Perf. 10½ Vert.*

TD67	TE36	**red**	90.00
		Pair	180.00

Agnew Auto Mailing — TE37

1920s *Perf.*

TD68	TE37	**red brown**	45.00

Royalty Stamp — TE38

1925 ? *Perf.*
TD69 TE38 **red** —

Molyneaux Automatic Mailing Machine Coil — TE38a

1920s *Perf. 11¾x12*
TD69A TE38a **light blue green** —
TD69B TE38a **orange** —

Stearns-Daniels Co. Coil — TE39

1920s-30s *Perf. 10 Vert.*
TD70 TE39 **green** —
Pair —

RO-TA-RE Stamp Affixer Service Machines Company — TE39a

1910-30 *Perf. Vert.*
TD70A TE39a **blue** —
Pair —

Edison Dictating Machine Coil — TE40

1920s-30s *Perf. 10¼ Vert.*
TD71 TE40 **red** 60.00
Pair 125.00

Schermack Dummy Coil — TE41

1920s-30s *Perf. 10½ Horiz.*
TD72 TE41 **red** —
Pair —

National Postal Meter Co., Inc. Coil — TE42

1920s-30s *Perf. 9¾ Vert.*
TD73 TE42 **red** —
Pair —

Stampmasters Inc. Coil — TE43

1920s-30s *Perf. 9¾ Vert.*
TD74 TE43 **violet** 15.00
Pair 30.00

Blank Design Types of 1878-79

Produced by Bureau of Engraving & Printing.

1927-30 *Perf. 9¾ Vert.*

Horiz. Ribbed Gum

TD75 TE9 blank, *cream* .60
Pair 1.25

With Red Horizontal Lines 13½ mm Apart

TD76 TE9 blank, *1930-40* .60
Pair 1.25
Pair with gap in lines 4.00
Strip of 10 with wide and narrow line gaps 15.00

Gaps appear every six stamps.

Central Machine & Supply Co. Coil — TE44

1930s *Perf. Vert.*
TD77 TE44 **red** —
Pair —

Puritan Mailing Machine Co. Coil — TE45

1930s *Perf. 8½ Vert.*
TD78 TE45 **red & black** —
Pair —

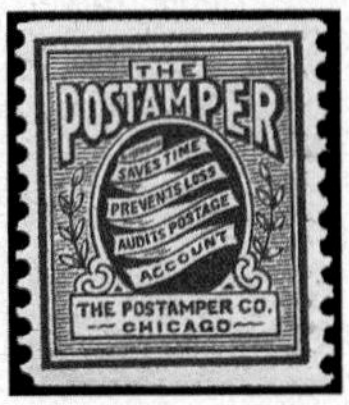

The Postamper Co. Coil — TE45a

1930s *Perf. 10½ Vert.*
TD78A TE45a **red** —
Pair —

Peerless Stamp Affixer Coil — TE45b

1930s *Perf. 10½ Vert.*
TD78B TE45b **red** —
Pair —

Blank Design Types of 1878-79

Produced by Electric Vendors (Zeigle), Inc.

1930s *Perf. 10½ Vert.*

Shiny Smooth Gum

TD79 TE9 blank 15.00
Pair 40.00
TD80 TE9 *blue* 15.00
Pair 40.00
TD81 TE9 *green* 15.00
Pair 40.00
TD82 TE9 *yellow* 15.00
Pair 40.00

Blank Design Types of 1878-79

Produced by Bureau of Engraving & Printing.

1920s-1950s *Perf. 10*

With Gum Breaker Ridges 5½mm Apart

TD83 TE9 blank, *1920s* 25.00
Block of 4 100.00
Vert. pair with horiz. gutter between —

With Gum Breaker Ridges 11mm Apart

Perf. 11x10½

TD84 TE9 blank, *1936* 25.00
Block of 4 100.00
Vert. pair with horiz. gutter between 80.00

With Gum Breaker Ridges

Perf. 11x10½

TD84A TE9 blank, *1956* 12.50
Block of 4 50.00

Genuine examples of No. TD84A are known with blue, green or red defacement markings.

Stamp Size:40x25mm

With Gum Breaker Ridges

Brownish Gum

Perf. 11¼x10½

TD85 TE9 blank 50.00
Block of 4 200.00

Produced by American Bank Note Co.

Perf. 12

TD86 TE9 blank pane of 50 with manuscript marginal markings, *1943* —

No. TD86 was produced as a test for the Overrun Countries stamps.

Multipost Mailing System & Equipment Coil — TE46

1930s-40s *Perf. 9½ Vert.*
TD87 TE46 **red** —
Pair —

Multipost Co. Walter I. Plant Agent Coil — TE46a

1930s *Perf. 11¾ Vert.*
TD87A TE46a **red** —
On cover —
Pair —

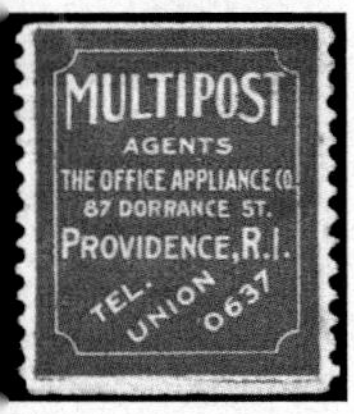

Multipost Agents The Office Appliance Co. Coil — TE46b

1930s ***Perf. 11¾ Vert.***

TD87B TE46b **red** —
Pair —

Multipost Commercial Controls Coil — TE47

1944-49 ***Perf. 9¾ Vert.***

TD88 TE47 **blue** 20.00
Pair 50.00
TD89 TE47 **black** 20.00
Pair 50.00
On cover 75.00
TD90 TE47 **blue black** 20.00
Pair 50.00

Multipost Commercial Controls Multipost Mailmaster Coil — TE48

Multipost Friden Multipost Mailmaster Coil — TE49

1944-49 ***Perf. 9¾ Vert.***

TD91 TE48 **purple** 20.00
Pair 50.00
TD92 TE48 **carmine** 30.00
Pair 80.00
TD93 TE49 **carmine** 20.00
Pair 50.00

Framed Rectangle — TE50

Printed by Bureau of Engraving & Printing.

1954 ***Perf. 11.2x10.5***

TD94 TE50 **carmine** 100.00
Block of 4 400.00
P# block of 4, P#141730 or 141731 800.00

Imperf

TD94A TE50 **carmine** 100.00
Pair 200.00
Block of 4 400.00
P# block of 4, P#141730 or 141731 800.00
Horiz. pair with vert. gutter 300.00

Coil Stamps

Perf. 9¾ Vert.

TD95 TE50 **purple,** large holes 3.00
Pair 8.00
Joint line pair 20.00
On cover with "Parade of Postal Progress" cancel 85.00
Small holes, *1959* 6.00
Pair 15.00
Joint line pair 35.00
a. Imperf., pair 50.00
Joint line pair 200.00

Examples of No. TD95 with poor centering are common and sell for less.

TD96 TE50 **red violet,** small holes 2.00
Pair 5.00
Joint line pair 15.00
Large holes 5.00
Pair 12.50
Joint line pair 125.00
On cover with "Parade of Postal Progress" cancel 85.00
a. Imperf., pair 80.00
Joint line pair —
b. Block of 8 with joint line, sheet margin and P#165939 and 165940, unslit horiz. —

See "large hole" and "small hole" illustrations after No. 1053 in Postage section.

TD97 TE50 **carmine** 200.00
Pair 400.00
Joint line pair 600.00
a. Imperf., horiz. pair 300.00
b. Vert. pair, unslit horiz. —

Expertization is recommended for Nos. TD97, TD97a and TD97b.

Nos. TD97a and TD97b exist as top or bottom P# blocks of 10, unslit horiz. Value, each $1,250. P# blocks of No. TD97b have selvage trimmed so EE marks do not show.

No. TD97a exists as a joint line pair, and No. TD97b also exists as a block of 4 with joint line, unslit horiz.

Kansas Territorial Centennial Experimental TE51

Printed by Bureau of Engraving and Printing.

1954 ***Perf. 12x11¾***

TD98 TE51 **brown, red & yellow** *200.00*
Block of 4 *800.00*

Nebraska Territorial Centennial Experimental — TE52

1954 ***Imperf.***

Size: 25x40mm

TD99 TE52 **brown** *200.00*
Block of 4 *800.00*
a. **brown,** *tan* —
TD100 TE52 **black** *200.00*
Block of 4 *800.00*
TD101 TE52 **blue** *200.00*
Block of 4 *800.00*
a. **blue,** *tan* *800.00*

Pitney Bowes Co. — TE53

1958-59 ***Imperf.***

Helecon Paper

TD102 TE53 **rose carmine** —
a. Lumogen paper —
TD103 TE53 **black** —

Helecon paper glows reddish orange under shortwave UV light. Lumogen paper glows bright yellow-green under shortwave UV light.

Stamp-E-Z Postage Stamp Affixer Coil — TE54

1960s ***Imperf.***

TD104 TE54 **light purple** —
Pair —

Perf. 9¾ Vert.

TD105 TE54 **red** —
Pair —

Blank Design Type of 1878-79

Produced by Bureau of Engraving and Printing

1960-70s **Overall Tagging Dull Gum** ***Perf. 9¾ Vert.***

TD106 TE9 blank 12.50
Pair 25.00
Joint line pair 100.00

No. TD106 was printed on an inked press. The ink was wiped, but some stamps have wiping marks and black joint lines.

For Testing Purposes Only Coil — TE55

Produced by Bureau of Engraving and Printing.

1962-88 **Engr.** ***Perf. 9¾ Vert.***

Design Size: Approximately 19½mm Wide

TD107 TE55 **black,** untagged, shiny gum .50
Pair 1.00
Joint line pair 5.00
a. Tagged, shiny gum .50
Pair 1.00
Joint line pair 5.00
b. Tagged, pebble-surfaced gum 1.50
Pair 3.00
Joint line pair 15.00
c. As "b," imperf. pair 50.00
Joint line pair 200.00
d. Tagged, dull gum 2.00
Pair 4.00
Joint line pair 20.00
e. Untagged, dull gum 1.00
Pair 2.00
Joint line pair 10.00

No. TD107 is known on hi-brite fluorescent paper.

No. TD107b has been found with red, dark red, rose red, blue, blue green, green, orange, violet, brown, black violet, black, gray black, gray and silver defacement lines, which vary in number and thickness and which have been known to have been forged. Some defacement line colors may all be forgeries.

No. TD107e is known on fluorescent and non-fluorescent papers, as well as on papers with diagonal gum striations or wavy, intermittent gum striations.

TD108 TE55 **carmine,** tagged, *1970* 875.00
Pair 1,750.
Joint line pair —

The tagging on Nos. TD108 and TD114 is orange red. All other stamps glow yellow green.

TD109 TE55 **green,** untagged, dull gum, *1970* 90.00
Pair 180.00
Joint line pair 450.00
Block of 12 with joint line, imperf or unslit horiz., P# 36111 and 36112 1,500.
a. Imperf., pair 400.00
Joint line pair 550.00
b. Vert. pair, imperf. horiz. 200.00
c. Tagged, gray paper, shiny gum 160.00
Pair 325.00
Joint line pair —
d. As "c," imperf, pair 150.00
Joint line pair 500.00
e. As "c," vert. pair, imperf. horiz. 175.00

No. TD109 was sent to Germany in large imperf. and part perforate sheets to test coil production equipment.

TD110 TE55 **orange,** *gray,* tagged, *1975* 1,000.
Pair 2,000.
Joint line pair —
TD111 TE55 **brown,** untagged, *1978* 3.00
Pair 10.00
Joint line pair 30.00

Design Size: Approximately 19mm Wide

TD112 TE55 **black,** untagged, dull gum *1978* .50
Pair 1.00

No. TD107 was printed on the Cottrell press. No. TD112 was printed on the B press.

See Nos. TD121, TD126-TD127, TD133, TD136-TD137.

Blank Design Type of 1878-79

Produced by Bureau of Engraving and Printing, with tagging added by Pitney Bowes.

1964 *Perf. 11*

TD113	TE9	blank, yellow green tagging	50.00
		Block of 4	200.00
TD114	TE9	blank, orange red tagging	50.00
		Block of 4	200.00

Nos. TD113-TD114 was produced as a test for Nos. 1254-1257.

Flag — TE56

Produced by Avery Products Corp.

1970s *Die Cut*

Self-Adhesive

TD115	TE56	**blue,** on rouletted backing paper	200.00
a.		On imperforate backing paper	—

Proclaim Liberty TE57

1970s *Perf. 12x11½*

TD116	TE57	**blue, red & green**	75.00

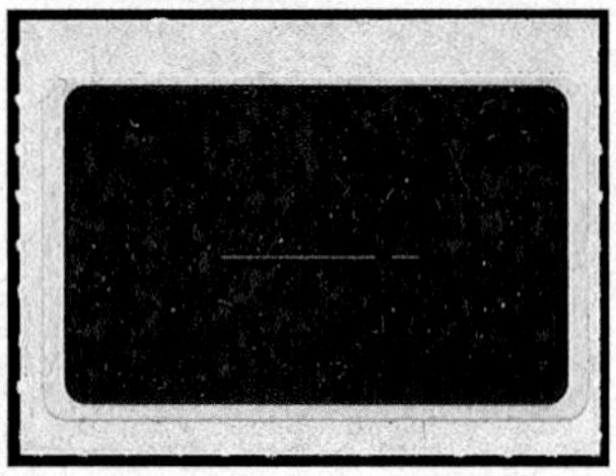
Christmas Test Stamp TE58

Printed by Bureau of Engraving and Printing for Avery Products Corp. to add die cutting.

1973 *Die Cut*

Self-Adhesive

TD117	TE58	**black,** rouletted backing paper	2.50
		Block of 4 with intact matrix	10.00
		Pane of 50	150.00
		Press sheet of 200	750.00
a.		With imperforate backing paper	—

No. TD117 was produced as a test for No. 1552.

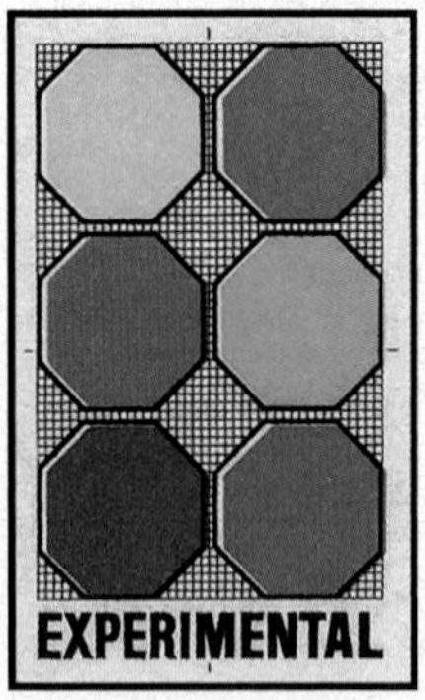

Octagons — TE59

Printed by Bureau of Engraving and Printing.

1980s *Imperf.*

TD118	TE59	**multicolored**	140.00
		Block of 4	600.00
		P# block of 4, P#173404	1,200.

Flag and Eagle Over Trees Coil — TE60

Printed by Stamp Venturers.

1989 *Perf. 10 Vert.*

TD119	TE60	**gray**	.25
		Pair	.50

Rouletted

TD120	TE60	**gray**	.25
		Pair	.50

A similar design, in multicolor, with "Sennett Security Products" at lower left was a souvenir distributed at World Stamp Expo 2000.

For Testing Purposes Only Type of 1962-88

Printed by Martin Marietta Corp.

1990s **Photo.** **Untagged** *Imperf.*

TD121	TE55	**black**	75.00
		Pair	150.00
		Block of 4	400.00

Blank Design Type of 1878-79

Produced by Bureau of Engraving and Printing.

1990s **Untagged** *Perf. 9¾ Vert.*

TD122	TE9	blank, shiny gum	10.00
		Pair	30.00
		Dull gum	10.00
		Pair	30.00

Stylized Eagle Coil — TE61

Printed by 3M Corp.

Linerless Self-Adhesive

1992 *Imperf.*

TD123	TE61	**multicolored**	15.00
		Pair	30.00
		P# strip of 5, #1111	350.00

Stamps have simulated perforations.

Rectangle With Thick Lines Coil — TE62

Printed by Bureau of Engraving and Printing.

1996 *Perf. 9¾ Vert.*

TD124	TE62	**blue,** shiny gum	50.00
		Pair	100.00
		Strip of 5 with one stamp with crudely etched reversed "2"	1,500.
		Strip of 5 with one stamp with crudely etched reversed "12"	1,500.

Reversed numbers appear in the center of every 24th stamp.

TD125	TE62	**gray black,** dull gum	125.00
		Pair	250.00

For Testing Purposes Only Type of 1962-88

Printed by Bureau of Engraving and Printing (#TD126), Avery-Dennison (#TD127).

1996 *Die Cut*

Self-Adhesive

TD126	TE55	**black,** *blue*	.25
		Pair	.50
		P# strip of 5, #1111	5.00

TE55a

Serpentine Die Cut 11.2 Vert.

TD127	TE55a	**black**	.25
		Pair	.50
		P# strip of 5, #V1	15.00

Design T55a has printed perforation "holes" in addition to serpentine die cutting.

Polar Bear Ice Skating — TE62a

Printed by Ashton-Potter (USA) Ltd.

1995 ***Serpentine Die Cut 11x10.5***

Design Size: 21x35mm

Self-Adhesive

TD127A	TE62a	**multicolored**	750.00
		Block of 4	—
		Sheetlet of 25	—

The sheetlet of 20 has vertical and horizontal gutters between the stamps with the matrix removed.

Serpentine Die Cut 11x11.5

TD127B	TE62a	**multicolored**	750.00
		Block of 4	—
		Sheetlet of 25	—

The sheetlet of 20 has no vertical or horizontal gutters between the stamps.

Parrot — TE63

Printed by Banknote Corporation of America.

1996 ***Serpentine Die Cut 11¾x11½***

Design Size: 22x31mm

Self-Adhesive (#TD128)

TD128	TE63	**multicolored**	300.00

Design Size: 25x40mm

Perf. 11½

TD129	TE63	**multicolored**	—

No. TD129 has hidden lettering "c 1995 GSSC" across bottom, and "Scrambled Indicia" vertically up the right side. Used to test luminescent inks.

Flower — TE63a

Printed by Dittler Brothers Inc. and American Bank Note Co.

1997 *Imperf.*

Self-Adhesive

Design Size: 18x18mm

TD129A	TE63a	**multicolored**	375.00

Design Size: 18x21mm

TD129B	TE63a	**multicolored**	250.00

Design Size: 22x31mm

TD129C	TE63a	**multicolored**	375.00
TD129D	TE63a	**multicolored**	375.00

Nos. TD129A and TD129C-TD129D were printed by photogravure and intaglio. No. TD129B was printed by photogravure only. No. TD129D has engraved black lines in the flower. No. TD129C does not have these engraved lines.

Rectangle With Thin Lines Coil — TE64

Printed by Bureau of Engraving and Printing.

1998 ***Serpentine Die Cut 9¾ Vert.***

Self-Adhesive

TD130	TE64	**blue**	125.00
		Pair	250.00
		Strip of 3 with one stamp with "3" printed horizontally	—

Star Spangled Banner/Not for Postage Coil — TE64a

1998 ***Serpentine Die Cut 11¼ Vert.***

Self-Adhesive

TD130A	TE64a	**multicolored**	35.00
		On cover	—

All known examples of No. TD130A were affixed to envelope backs for use in testing.

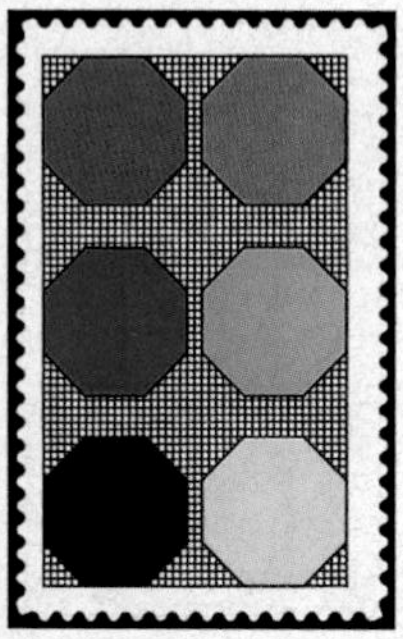

Octagons — TE64b

1998 ***Serpentine Die Cut 12.6***

Self-Adhesive

TD130B	TE64b	**multicolored**	45.00
		On cover	—

All known examples of No. TD130B were affixed to envelope backs for use in testing.

RENA Test Stamp Coil — TE65

1999 ***Die Cut***

Self-Adhesive

TD131	TE65	**blue**	10.00
		Pair	25.00

Mailbox Coil — TE66

Printed by Avery Dennison.

2000 ***Imperf.***

Linerless Self-Adhesive

TD132	TE66	**red**	100.00
		Pair	200.00
	a.	Pair with "xxxx" on one stamp	1,500.

Pairs have 1-2mm slit marks between stamps in right margin.

For Testing Purposes Only Type of 1962-88

Printed by Bureau of Engraving and Printing.

2000 ***Serpentine Die Cut 9¾ Vert.***

Self-Adhesive

TD133	TE55	**black**	.50
		Pair	1.00
		P# strip of 5, #1111	7.50

No. TD133 is printed on white backing paper with 2mm gap between perforation tips. A four digit counting number is on the back of the backing paper on every 20th stamp. Stamps appear to be printed on light blue paper. The blue color is caused by the buildup of white ink with a blue tint, which was applied to white paper.

TD133A	TE55	**black**	15.00
		Pair	30.00
		P# strip of 5, #1111	300.00

No. TD133A is printing on white backing paper with no gap between perforation tips.

South Carolina Flag Coil — TE67

Printed by Avery Dennison.

2000 ***Serpentine Die Cut 8½ Vert.***

Self-Adhesive

TD134	TE67	**dark blue**	—
		Pair	—
		P# strip of 5, #V1	—
TD135	TE67	**light blue**	15.00
		Pair	30.00
		P# strip of 5, #V1	225.00

Plate-number examples of Nos. TD134 and TD135 bear a "2000" year date at lower left.

For Testing Purposes Only Type of 1962-88

Printed by Bureau of Engraving and Printing (#TD136), Sennett Security Products (#TD137).

For Testing Purposes Only Coil with Vertical Line Between "N" and "L" of "Only" — TE55b

1997 ***Serpentine Die Cut 9¾ Vert.***

Self-Adhesive

TD136	TE55b	**black**	.65
		Pair	1.25
		Strip of 5 with white line on left or right margin of center stamp	7.50

Stamps with white lines appear every 21st stamp. Stamps appear to be printed on light blue paper. The blue color is caused by the buildup of white ink with a blue tint, which was applied to white paper.

Serpentine Die Cut 11¼ Vert.

TD137	TE55	**black**	.50
		Pair	1.00
		P# strip of 5, #S1	7.00

SSP Test Void Coil — TE69

Printed by Sennett Security Products.

2005 ***Serpentine Die Cut 10½ Vert.***

Self-Adhesive

TD138	TE69	**black**	2.00
		Pair	4.00

2000 ***Serpentine Die Cut 11.6 Vert.***

Self-Adhesive

TD138A	TE69	**black**	10.00
		Pair	20.00

RENA No Postage Test Stamp Coil — TE70

2006 ***Die Cut***

Self-Adhesive

TD139	TE70	**blue**	2.00
		Pair	4.00

TEST STAMP PROOFS

Bureau of Engraving and Printing

1910

TD28TC	**black,** large die proof, die sunk on card	1,000.
TD28TC	**blue,** large die proof on India, die sunk on card	1,000.
TD28TC	**carmine,** large die proof on India, die sunk on card	1,000.
TD28TC	**dark brown,** large die proof on India, die sunk on card	1,000.
TD28TC	**dark green,** large die proof on India, die sunk on card	1,000.
TD28TC	**dark violet brown,** large die proof on India, die sunk on card	1,000.

TEST BOOKLETS: PANES & COVERS

Test booklets normally are collected as complete booklets, and the major listings are for complete booklets. Very often the booklet panes in different booklets are the same or similar. Booklet panes are presented as lettered minor listings. Where similar booklet panes can be differentiated by gum breaker measurements, size measurements, or other factors, they are given separate minor listings. Single stamps from these booklets are not given minor listings.

This test booklet section is divided into four categories: stapled booklets, folded and glued booklets with water-activated gum, folded and glued booklets with self-adhesive gum, and ATM sheetlets.

STAPLED BOOKLETS

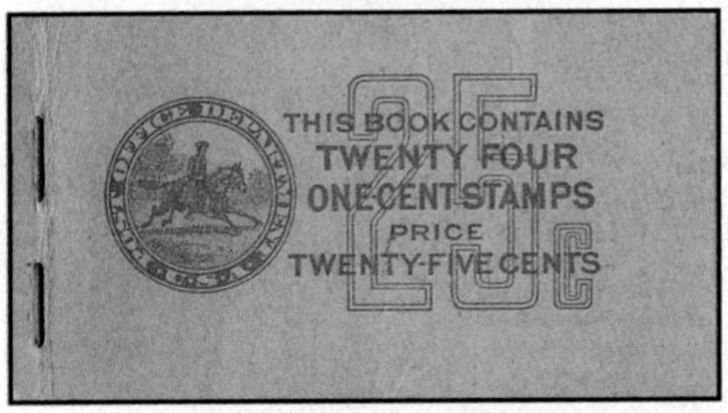

Small Postrider — BC5A

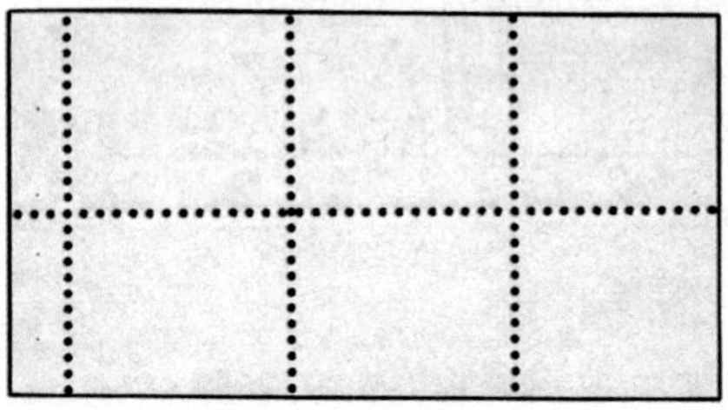

Blank Stamps — TDP1

1927-30 ***Perf. 11¼x10½***

TDB1 BC5A 25c **green,** *green,* 4 #TDB1a —
a. TDP1 Pane of 6 —

Horiz. gum breakers are 22mm apart on No. TDB1a. No. TDB1 has 5 waxed glassine interleaves, 1 in front of the first pane and 1 behind each pane.

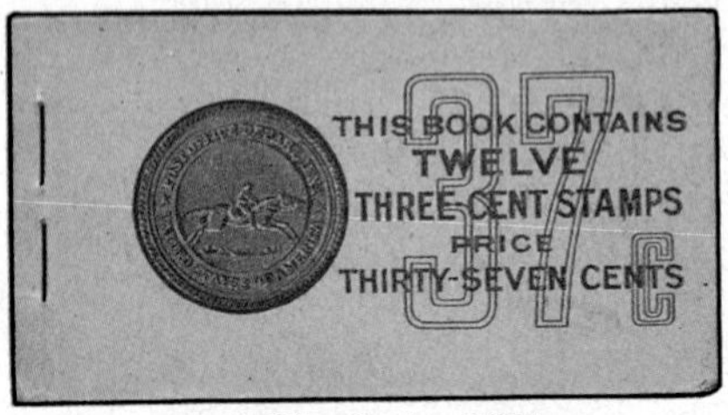

Post Office Seal — BC9A

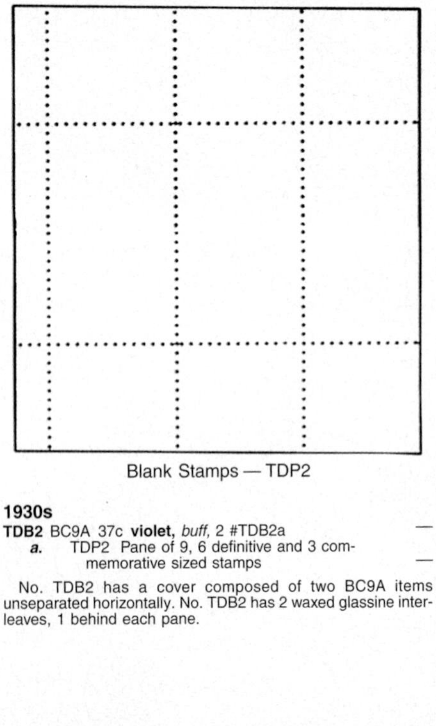

Blank Stamps — TDP2

1930s

TDB2 BC9A 37c **violet,** *buff,* 2 #TDB2a —
a. TDP2 Pane of 9, 6 definitive and 3 commemorative sized stamps —

No. TDB2 has a cover composed of two BC9A items unseparated horizontally. No. TDB2 has 2 waxed glassine interleaves, 1 behind each pane.

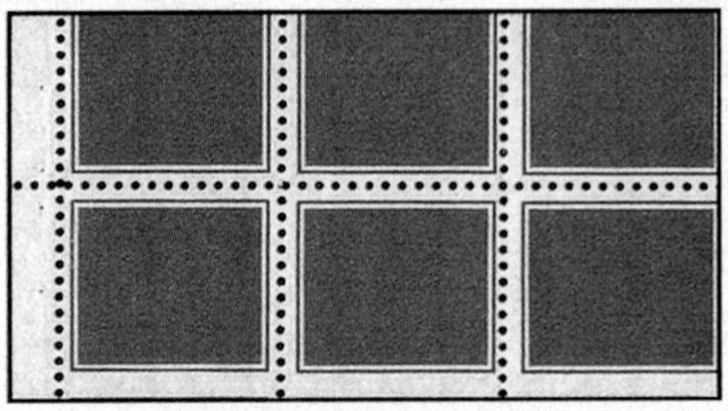

Framed Rectangles — TDP3

1940

TDB3 BC9A 37c **violet,** *buff,* 2 #TDB3a 600.00
a. TDP3 **purple,** pane of 6 250.00

Horiz. gum breakers are 11mm apart on No. TDB3a. No. TDB3 has 2 waxed glassine interleaves, 1 behind each pane.

Type of 1940

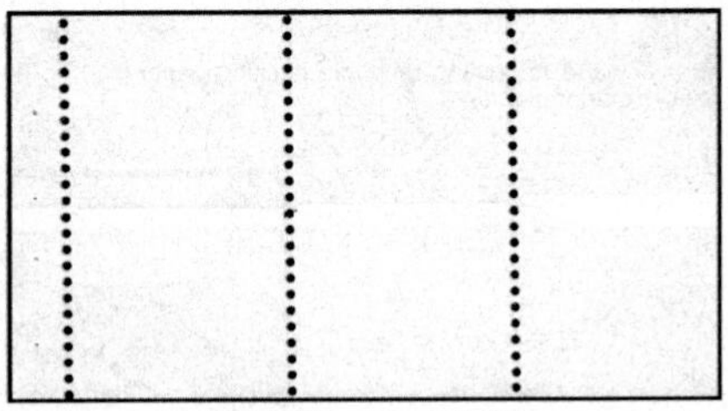

Blank Stamps — TDP4

1940s

TDB4 BC9A 37c **violet,** *buff,* #TDB4a, TDB4b *450.00*
a. TDP1 Pane of 6 —
b. TDP4 Pane of 3, perf. 10 vert.

Horiz. gum breakers are 6mm apart on Nos. TDB4a and TDB4b. No. TDB4 has 2 waxed glassine interleaves, 1 behind each pane.

Post Office Seal — BC9H

1959

TDB5 BC9H 97c **blue,** *pink,* 4 #TDB5a 175.00
a. TDP1 Pane of 6 —
b. As #TDB5, with silicone interleaves 325.00

Horiz. gum breakers are 5½mm apart, and vert. gum breakers are 21mm apart on No. TDB5a. No. TDB5 has 4 waxed glassine interleaves, and No. TDB5a has 4 silicone interleaves, 1 behind each pane. Some panes may show a joint line and/or EE markings.

U.S. Airmail Wings — BC11C

1959

TDB6 BC11C 97c **blue,** 2 #TDB6a 175.00
a. TDP1 Pane of 6 —

Horiz. gum breakers are 5½mm apart on No. TDB6a. Some panes may exhibit faint vertical gum breakers. Nos. TDB6 has 2 waxed glassine interleaves, 1 behind each pane.

Post Office Seal Type of 1959

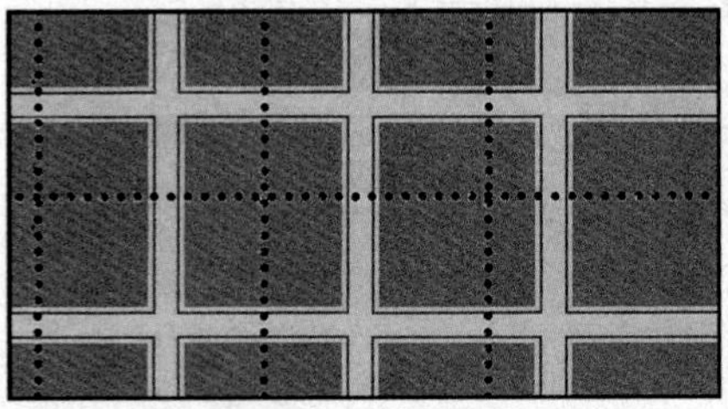

Misperforated and Miscut Framed Rectangles — TDP5

1960-62

TDB7 BC9H 97c **blue,** *pink,* 4 #TDB7a *900.00*
a. TDP5 **red violet,** pane of 6 *200.00*

Horiz. gum breakers are 4½-6½mm apart and vert. gum breakers are 22½mm apart on No. TDB7a. Panes were made from coil sheet stock and therefore are always miscut and misperforated. No. TDB7 has 4 glassine interleaves, 1 behind each pane.

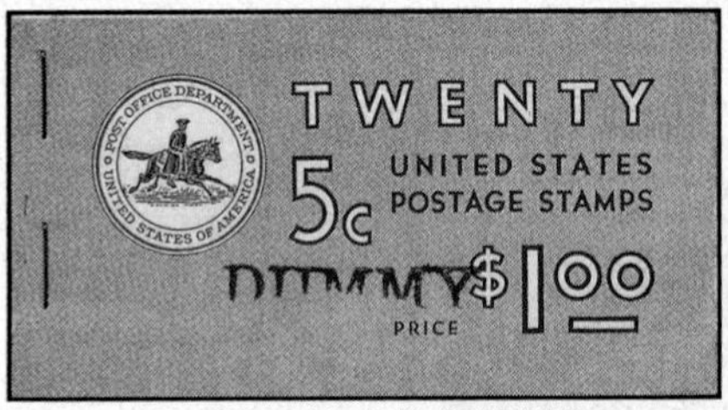

Small Postrider With "DUMMY" Handstamp — TBC12A

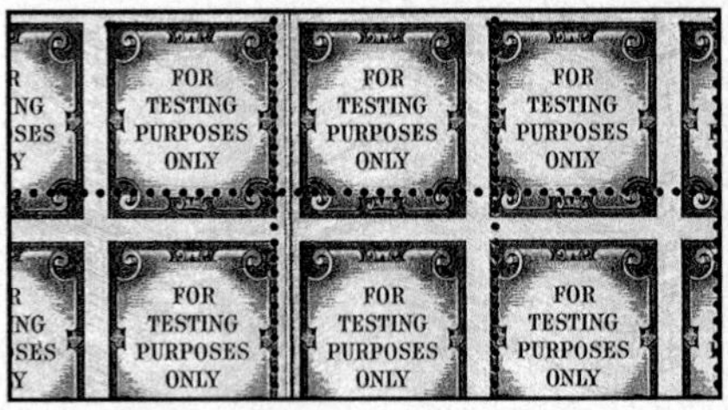

For Testing Purposes Only — TDP6

No. TDP6 panes were made from coil stock and therefore are always miscut and misperforated.

1962-67 **Untagged**

TDB8 TBC12A $1 **blue,** 4 #TDB8a 200.00
a. TDP6 **black,** pane of 6 stamps of type TE55 35.00

Horiz. gum breakers are 5½mm apart and alternating vert. gum breakers are 22½mm and 8½mm apart on No. TDB8a. No. TDB8 has 4 silicone interleaves, 1 behind each pane, and staples at left. Some panes may show a joint line and/or EE markings.

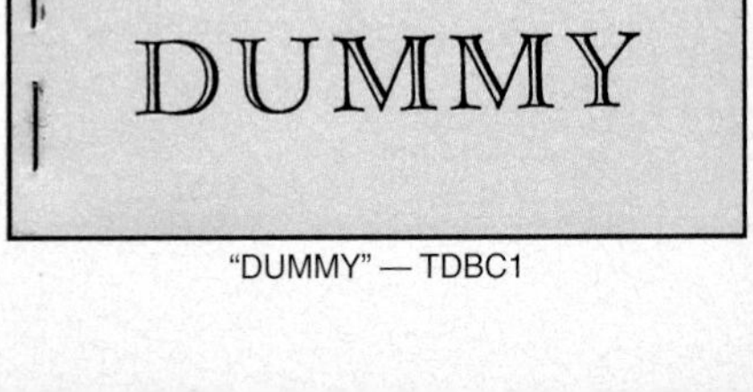

"DUMMY" — TDBC1

1962-67

TDB9 TDBC1 **black** 2 #TDB9a 90.00
a. TDP1 Pane of 6 —
TDB10 TDBC1 **red** 2 #TDB9a *200.00*

Horiz. gum breakers are 11½mm apart, and alternating vert. gum breakers are 14mm and 8½mm apart on No. TDB9a. Nos. TDB9 and TDB10 have 2 glassine interleaves, 1 behind each pane.

Mr. Zip With "DUMMY" — TBC13A

1963-66

Black or Violet "Dummy" Handstamp

TDB11 TBC13A $1 **blue,** 4 #TDB9a 125.00
a. TDP1 Pane of 6 10.00
b. As #TDB11, with 4 #TDB11a 125.00

55x7½mm Red "Dummy" Overprint

TDB12 TBC13A $1 **blue,** 4 #TDB9a 50.00
a. As #TDB12, with different inside front cover 15.00

Alternating horiz. gum breakers are 4½mm and 6½mm apart, and alternating vert. gum breakers are 14mm and 8½mm apart on No. TDB11a.

No. TDB12 has inside front cover reading "Domestic Postage Rates." No. TDB12a has inside front cover reading "Minute Man — Buy — HOLD US Savings Bonds."

Nos. TDB11-TDB12a have 4 silicone interleaves, 1 behind each pane.

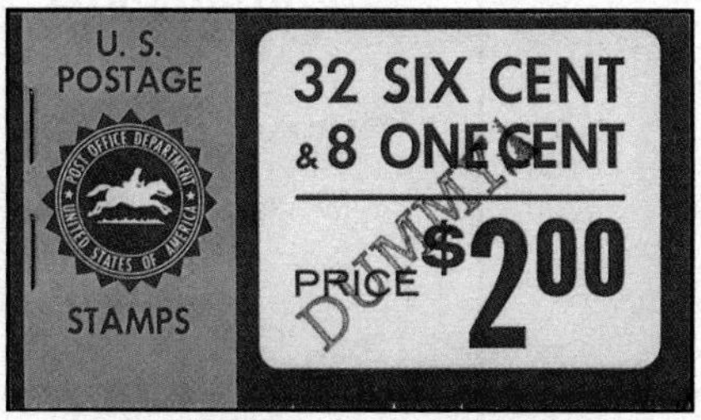

Post Office Seal With Violet "DUMMY" Handstamp — TBC14A

For Testing Purposes Only — TDP7

No. TDP7 panes were made from coil stock and therefore are always miscut and misperforated.

1967-68 **Tagged** ***Perf. 11¼x10½***

TDB13 TBC14A $2 **brown,** 5 #TDB13a 200.00
a. TDP7 **black,** pane of 8 stamps of type TE55 35.00

Horiz. gum breakers are 11mm apart and alternating vert. gum breakers are 14mm and 8½mm apart on No. TDB13a. No. TDB13 has 5 silicone interleaves, 1 behind each pane, and staples at left. Some booklets and panes have felt pen markings along the top and bottom edges placed by the technicians for machine adjustments.

On Nos. TDB14, TDB15, TDB16 and TDB17, the perforation gauge is measured with the staple position at left, and the gum breakers are measured with the staple position at top.

Stamp Silhouette With Violet "DUMMY" Handstamp — TBC15

1960s-72 **Tagged** ***Perf. 10½x11¼***

TDB14 TBC15 $1 **brown,** 4 #TDB14a 150.00
a. TDP6 **black,** pane of 6 stamps of type TE55, staple position at top 35.00

Horiz. gum breakers are 11mm apart and vert. gum breakers are 22mm apart on No. TDB14a. No. TDB14 has 4 silicone interleaves, 1 behind each pane, and staples at left. "Dummy" handstamp is 34½x6½mm. Some booklets and panes have felt pen markings on the front and/or back covers.

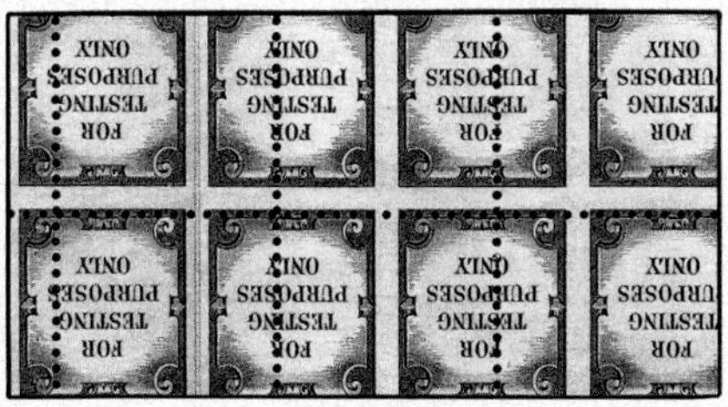

TDP6A

TDB15 TBC15 $1 **blue,** 4 #TDB15a 150.00
a. TDP6A **black,** pane of 6 stamps of type TE55, staple position at top 35.00

Horiz. gum breakers are 11mm apart on No. TDB15a. No. TDB15 has 4 silicone interleaves, 1 behind each pane, and staples at left. "Dummy" handstamp is 34½x6½mm. Panes are upside down relative to covers. Some booklets and panes have felt pen markings on the front and/or back covers.

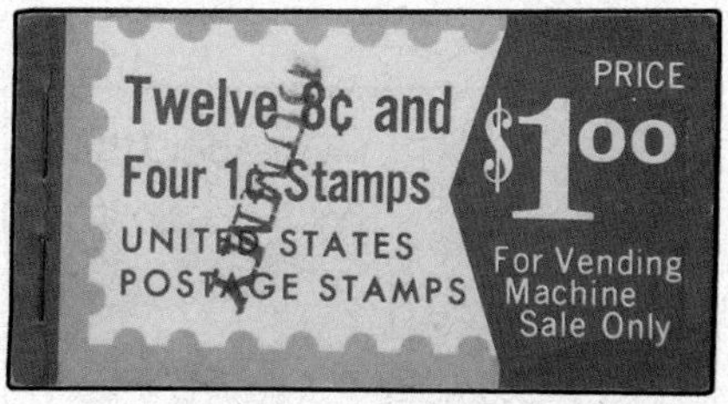

TBC15A

TDB16 TBC15A $1 **claret,** 3 #TDB16a 250.00
a. TDP6A **black,** pane of 6 stamps of type TE55, staple position at top 35.00
b. As #TDB16, with 34½x6½mm "Dummy" handstamp 250.00

Horiz. gum breakers are 11mm apart on No. TDB16a. No. TDB16 has 3 silicone interleaves, 1 behind each pane, and staples at left. "Dummy" handstamp is 29½x4½mm on No. TDB16.

TBC15B

TDB17 TBC15B $1 **red,** 2 #TDB17a 175.00
a. TDP6B or TDP6A **black,** pane of 6 stamps of type TE55, staple position at top 35.00
b. As #TDB17, with 34½x6½mm "Dummy" handstamp 175.00

Horiz. gum breakers are 11mm apart, and alternating vert. gum breakers are 14 and 8½mm apart on No. TDB17a. Some panes do not show vertical gum breakers. No. TDB17 has 2 silicone interleaves, 1 behind each pane, and staples at left. "Dummy" handstamp is 29½x4½mm on No. TDB17. Some booklets and panes have felt pen markings on the front and/or back covers.

Eisenhower With Violet "DUMMY" Handstamp — TBC16

1970-71 **Tagged** ***Perf. 11¼x10½***

TDB18 TBC16 $2 **blue,** 5 #TDB18a 200.00
a. TDP7 **black,** pane of 8 stamps of type TE55 35.00
b. As #TDB18, with 34½x6½mm "Dummy" handstamp 200.00

Horiz. gum breakers are 11mm apart and vert. gum breakers are 22mm apart on No. TDB18a. No. TDB18 has 5 silicone interleaves, 1 behind each pane, and staples at left. "Dummy" handstamp is 29½x4½mm on No. TDB18.

TBC17

With Red "Dummy" Handstamp

TDB19 TBC17 $1.92 **claret,** 3 #TDB13a 150.00
a. TDP7 **black,** pane of 8 stamps of type TE55 35.00
b. As #TDB19, with violet 34½x6½mm "Dummy" handstamp 150.00

No. TDB19 has 3 silicone interleaves, 1 behind each pane, and staples at left. "Dummy" handstamp is 29½x4½mm on No. TDB19.

FOLDED AND GLUED BOOKLETS

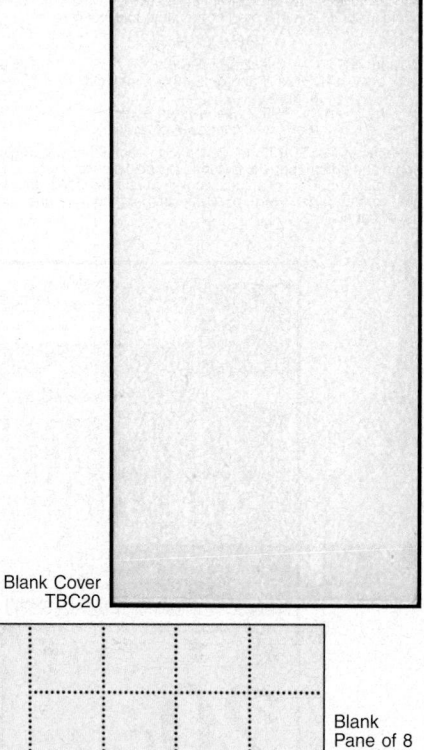

Blank Cover TBC20

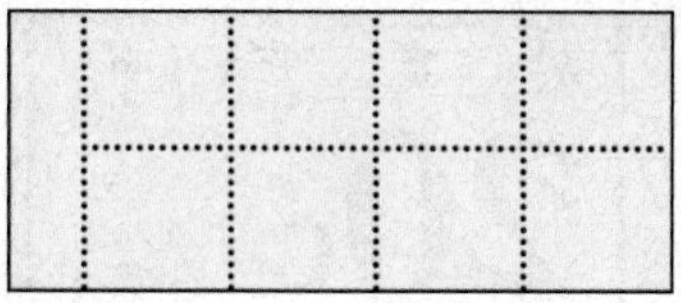

Blank Pane of 8 TDP10

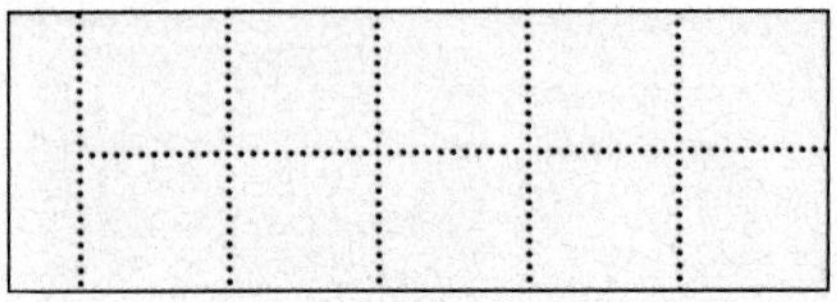

Blank Pane of 10 — TDP11

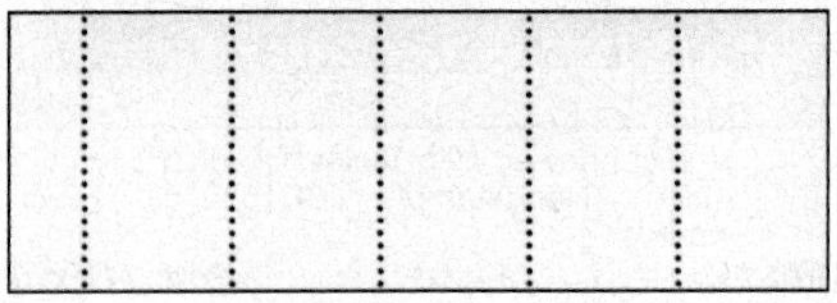

Blank Pane of 5 — TDP12

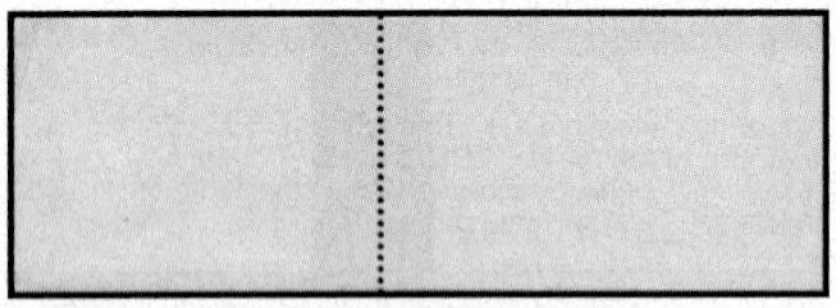

Blank Pane of 2 — TDP12a

Produced by Bureau of Engraving and Printing.

1970s-80s **Untagged** ***Perf. 11x10½***

TDB25 TBC20 blank, #TDB25a 400.00
 a. TDP10 Pane of 8 —

Perf. 10x9¾

TDB26 TBC20 blank, 2 #TDB26a 80.00
 a. TDP11 Pane of 10, 43x137mm —

Perf. 10 Horiz.

TDB27 TBC20 blank, #TDB27a 50.00
 a. TDP12 Pane of 5, 43x137mm, dull gum —
TDB28 TBC20 blank, 2 #TDB28a 30.00
 a. TDP12 Pane of 5, 43x135mm, dull gum —
 b. As #TDB28, with 2 #TDB28a, shiny gum —

Produced by KCS Industries

Imperf

TDB29 TBC20 blank, 2 #TDB29a 50.00
 a. TDP12 Pane of 5, 43x135mm, dull gum —

Panes in No. TDB29 are fastened to each other and to the booklet cover at the top tab with 3 glue spots. The booklet cover of No. TDB29 is not scored at the pane fold location.

Perf. 11 Horiz.

TDB30 TBC20 blank, 2 #TDB30a 125.00
 a. TDP12a Pane of 2, 43x137mm, dull gum —
 b. As #TDB30, with inverted pane (perfs unaligned with cover fold) —

Panes in No. TDB30 are fastened to each other with 3 glue spots and bottom pane is fastened to booklet cover with a 1mm wide glue line. Covers are known with handstamps "A1" (black), "A2" (orange), "B1" (red), or "B2" (violet) on the front and back cover panels.

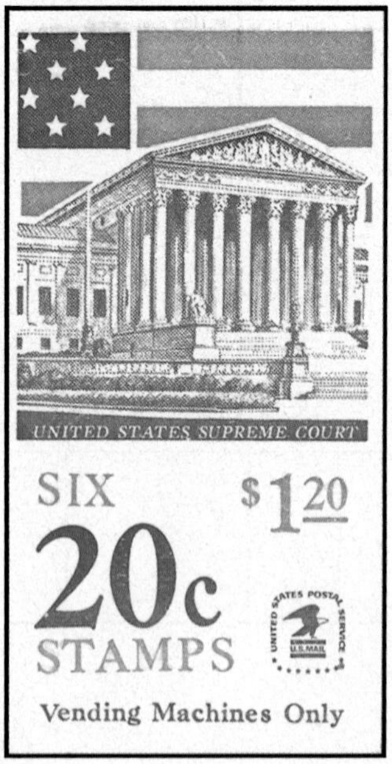

Flag Over Supreme Court BC29

Printed by Bureau of Engraving & Printing.

1985 **Untagged** ***Perf. 10 Horiz.***

TDB31 BC29 $1.20 **red & blue,** #TDB31a *450.00*
 a. TDP12 Pane of 5, 43x133mm, dull gum —

Tab selvage is 9mm high.

Flag Over Capitol BC33C

Printed by Bureau of Engraving & Printing.

1985 **Untagged** ***Perf. 10 Horiz.***

TDB32 BC33C $1.10 **red & blue,** #TDB32a 20.00
 a. TDP12 Pane of 5, 43x130mm, dull gum —

Tab selvage is 9 or 12mm high.

Seashells — BC33A

Seashells Without Text — TBC21

Printed by Bureau of Engraving & Printing.

1985 **Untagged** ***Perf. 10x9¾***

TDB33 BC33A $4.40 **multicolored,** 2 #TDB33a *350.00*
 a. TDP11 Pane of 10, 43x135mm, dull gum —

Tab selvage is 11mm high. Panes are scored at all horizontal perforation rows. Some booklet covers have red felt pen marks on the outside front cover.

TDB34 TBC21 **multicolored,** 2 #TDB33a *350.00*
TDB35 TBC21 **multicolored,** 2 #TDB28a *250.00*

Scoring on No. TDB35 varies. Seven adjacent booklet covers are needed to show the complete design of all 25 seashells for Nos. TDB33-TDB35.

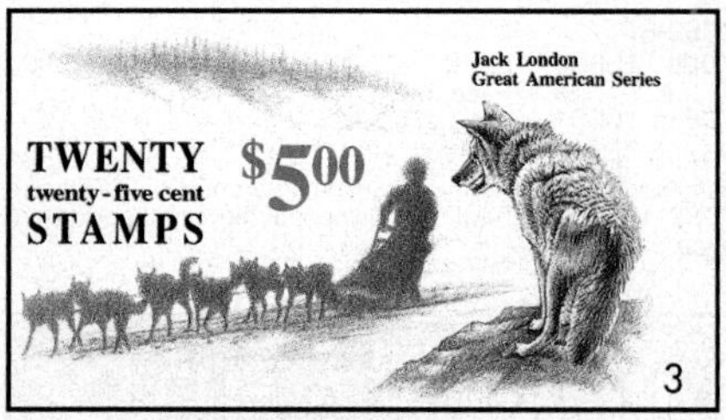

Jack London — TBC22

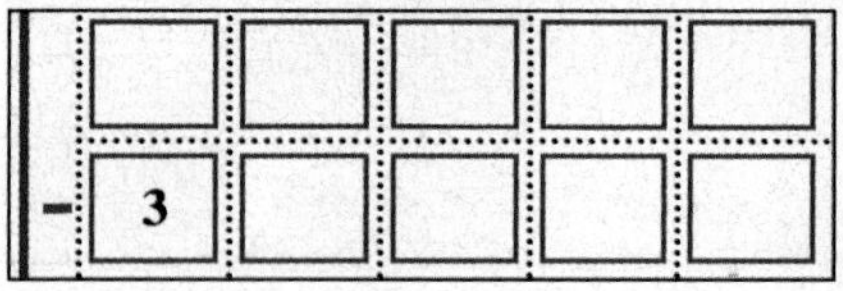

Rectangles and Numeral — TDP13

Printed by Bureau of Engraving & Printing.

1988 **Untagged** ***Perf. 11x9¾***

TDB36 TBC22 $5 **multicolored,** 2 #TDB36a —
 a. TDP13 **blue,** pane of 10, 43x135mm, shiny gum —

Tab selvage is 11½mm high. Panes are scored at all horizontal perforation rows. No. TDB36 booklet covers have a small printed number in the lower right corner that matches the large number on the booklet panes on the inside. Some booklet covers have red felt pen marks on the outside front cover. Numeral on No. TDB36a is "3." An unpublished quote from George Washington is printed on inside front cover and unissued "American Garden" printed on inside back cover.

Hummingbird BC80

Printed by American Bank Note Company.

1994 **Untagged** ***Perf. 11 Horiz.***

TDB37 BC80 $5.80 **multicolored,** 2 #TDB37a —
 a. TDP12 Pane of 5, 41x137mm, glossy gum —

Outside front covers have 2 green felt pen marks.

Flag
BC106

Printed by American Bank Note Company.

1994 **Untagged** *Perf. 10*

TDB38 BC106 G **multicolored,** 2 #TDB38a —
a. TDP12 Pane of 5, 43x137mm, glossy gum —

Front covers have felt pen marks.

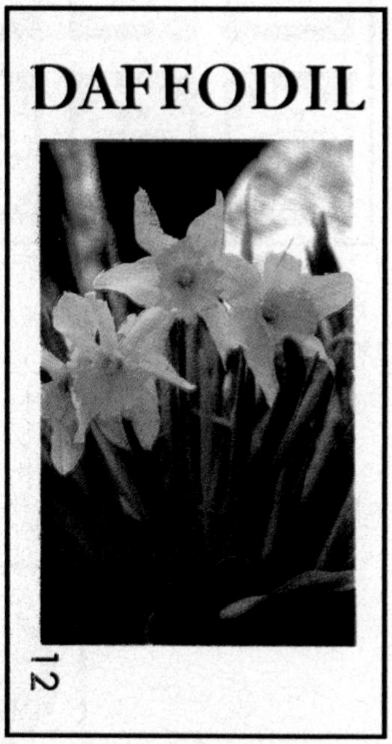

Daffodils — TBC23

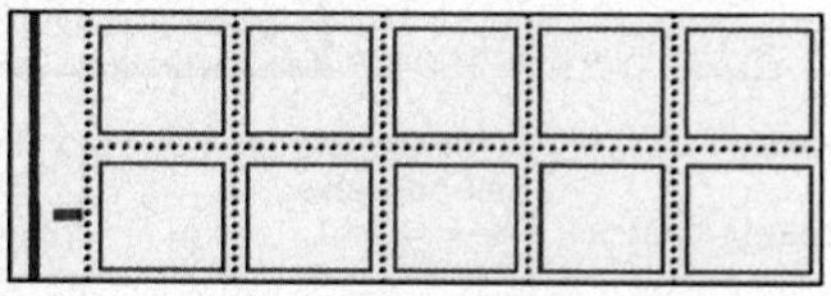
Rectangles — TDP14

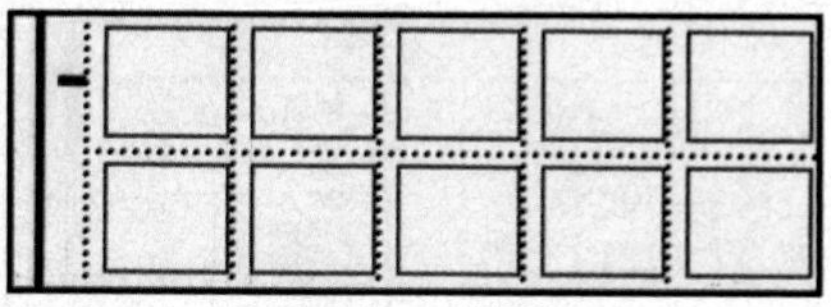
Rectangles — TBP14a

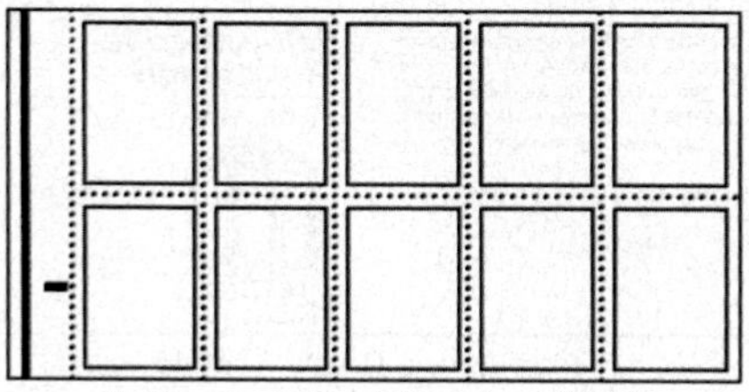
Rectangles (Large Stamps) — TDP15

Printed by Bureau of Engraving and Printing.

1990s **Untagged** *Perf. 11x9¾*

TDB39 TBC23 **multicolored,** 2 #TDB39a —
a. TDP14 **blue,** pane of 10, 43x135mm, shiny gum —
TDB40 TBC23 **multicolored,** 4 #TDB40a —
a. TDP13 **blue,** pane of 10, 43x135mm, shiny gum —
TDB40B TBC23 **multicolored,** 2 #TDB40Bc —
c. TDP13 **blue,** pane of 10, 43x135mm, shiny gum —
TDB41 TBC23 **multicolored,** 4 #TDB41a —
a. TDP14 **dark blue,** pane of 10, 43x135mm, shiny gum —
TDB42 TBC23 **multicolored,** 4 #TDB42a —
a. TDP14a **dark blue,** pane of 10, 43x135mm, shiny gum —
TDB43 TBC23 **multicolored,** 2 #TDB42a —
a. TDP15 **black,** pane of 10, 66x137mm, shiny gum —

Tab selvage is 12mm high on Nos. TDB39-TDB43. Numerals shown on Nos. TDB40a, TDB42a are "11." Numeral shown on No. TDB40Bc is "6." Nos. TDB42 and TDB43 lack printing on inside covers found on Nos. TDB39-TDB41. Booklet cover of No. TDB43 is larger and shows a 3mm tall "6" in the lower right corner of the outside front cover. Other covers of type TBC23 show a 3mm "12" there.

SELF-ADHESIVE FOLDED & GLUED BOOKLETS
Blank Cover and Pane Types

1990s ? **Untagged** *Perf. 11 Horiz.*

TDB60 TBC20 blank, 2 #TDB60a —
a. TDP12 blank, pane of 2, self-adhesive, 44x132mm —

Blank Convertible Booklet Cover TBC30

Serpentine Die Cut 10½x11, 11

1999 **Overall Tagging**

TDB61 TBC30 blank, self-adhesive blank pane of 10 150.00

Stamps in pane have same arrangement as that of the 1999 20c Pheasant booklet, No. BK242A.

ATM TEST SHEETLETS

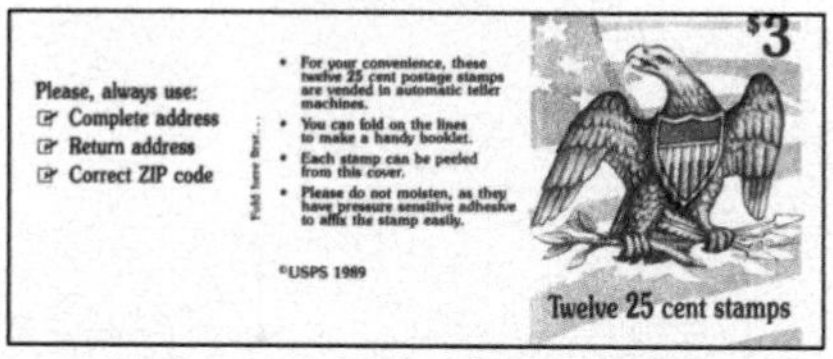

Eagle and Flag Pane Cover — TBC40

Stamp Layout — TBC40R

1989 *Imperf.*

Self-Adhesive

TDB80 TBC40 $3 **multicolored,** *blue,* pane of 12 (TBC40R) *1,500.*
a. With "Paper Corp" handwritten in right margin *2,250.*

Shiny, Water-Activated Gum

TDB81 TBC40R $3 **multicolored,** *blue,* pane of 12 (TBC40R) *2,250.*

The backing paper serves as a booklet cover on No. TDB80. Sizes: No. TDB80, 61x157mm; No. TDB80a, 62½x178mm; No. TDB81, 66x160mm. No. TDB80 exists not fully trimmed, and measuring 62½x159mm. No. TDB81 does not have a cover, and does not require a backing paper.

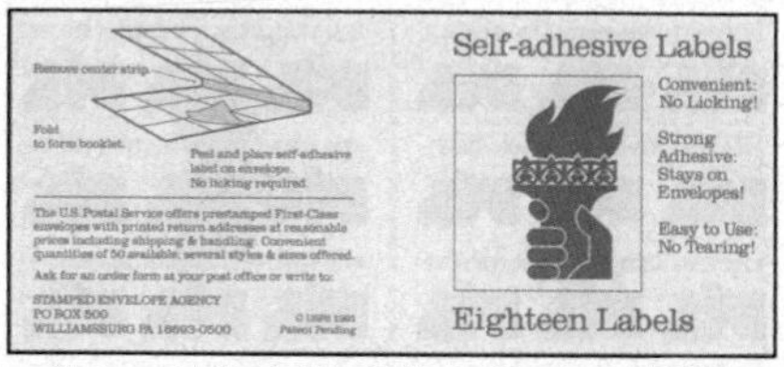

Statue of Liberty Torch Pane Cover — TBC41

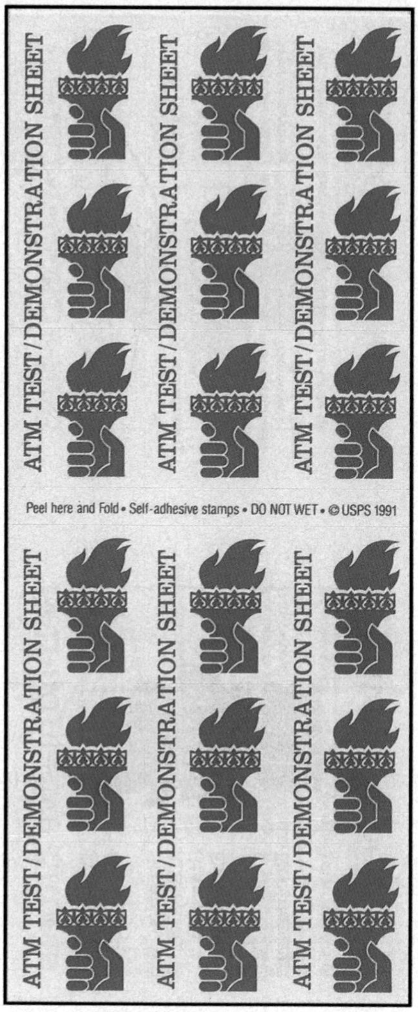

Stamp Layout — TBC41R

Printed by Avery Dennison.

1990 **Untagged** *Die Cut*

Self-Adhesive

TDB82 TBC41 **green,** pane of 18 (TBC41R) 15.00

No. 2475a Overprinted in Black "SPECIMEN / FOR ATM TEST" on Each Stamp

Statue of Liberty Torch Pane Cover — TBC41AR

Printed by Avery Dennison.

1990 **Untagged** ***Die Cut***

Self-Adhesive

Printed on Plastic

TDB83 TBC41AR 25c **dark red & dark blue,** pane of 12 —

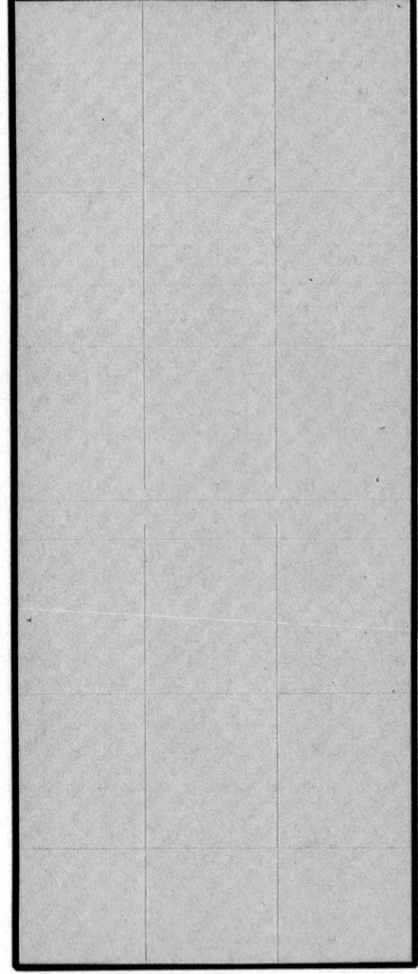

Representation of Stamp Layout — TBC42R

Produced by Dittler Brothers.

1992 **Untagged** ***Misaligned Die Cut***

Self-Adhesive

TDB84 blank, pane of 18 (TBC42R) *500.00*

1992 ***No Die Cuts***

TDB85 **blank,** pane of 18 (TBC42R) *300.00*

Nos. TDB84 and TDB85 were printed on thick paper similar to regular postage No. 2596a and were used for testing Postal Buddy machines. Backing paper of Nos. TDB84 and TDB85 reads "SELF-ADHESIVE * DO NOT WET." A detailed illustration of No. TBC42R is difficult to reproduce.

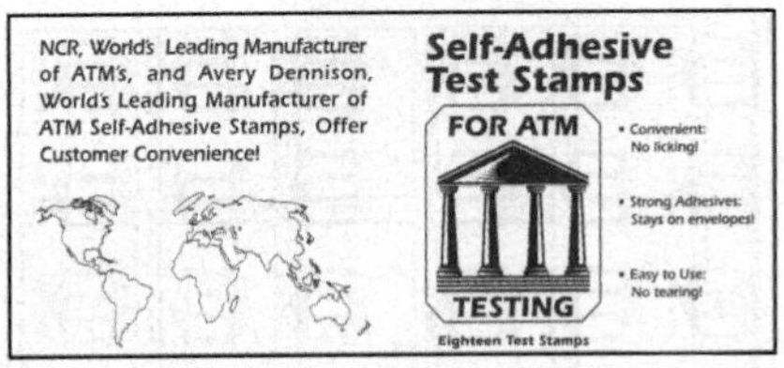

Temple Pane Cover — TBC43

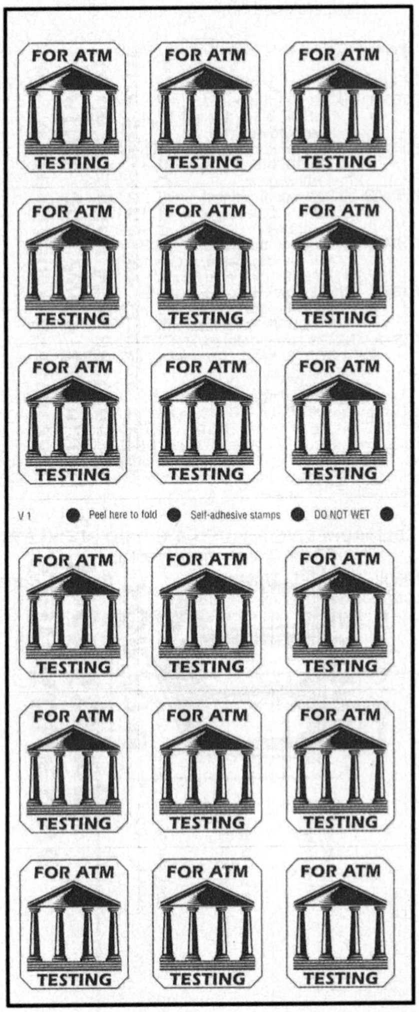

Stamp Layout — TBC43R

Printed by Avery Dennison.

1997 ***Die Cut***

Self-Adhesive

TDB86 TBC43 **dark blue,** pane of 18 (TBC43R), Plate #V1 250.00

For Testing Purposes Only Pane Cover — TBC44

Stamp Layout — TBC44R

Printed by Avery Dennison.

1997 ***Die Cut***

Self-Adhesive

TDB87 TBC44 **black,** pane of 18 black labels (TBC44R), Plate #V1 150.00

Serpentine Die Cut 7¾

TDB88 TBC44 **black,** pane of 18 black labels (TBC44R), Plate #V1 15.00

TDB89 TBC44 **blue,** pane of 18 magenta labels (TBC44R), Plate #V1 250.00

George Clinton — TBC46R

1998 ***Serpentine Die Cut 11.2x11.6***

Self-Adhesive

TDB89A TBC46R **blue gray** 35.00
On cover —

All known examples of No. TDB89A were affixed to envelope backs for use in testing.

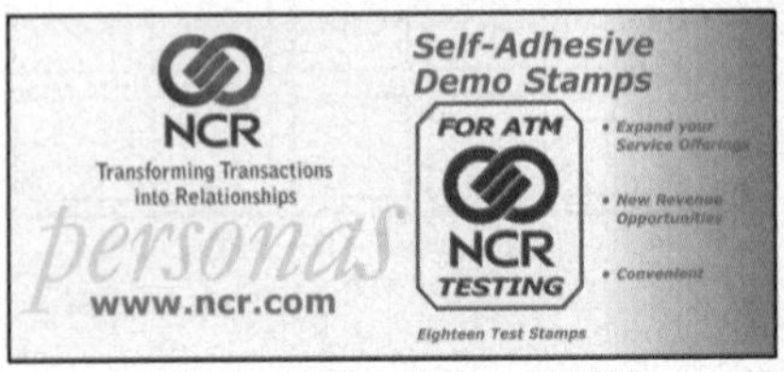

NCR Logo Pane Cover — TBC45

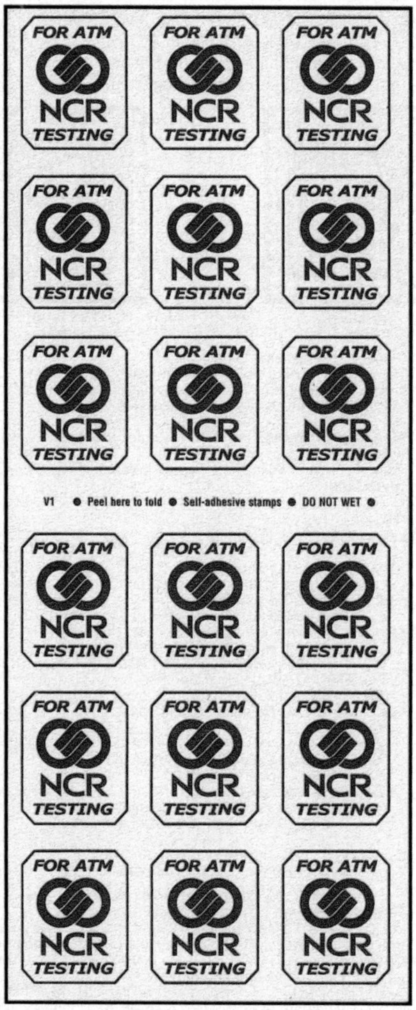

Stamp Layout — TBC45R

Printed by NCR.

2000 *Imperf.*

Without Gum

TDB90 TBC45 **multicolored,** pane of 18 black labels (TBC45R), Plate #V1 50.00

CHRISTMAS SEALS

Issued by the American National Red Cross (1907-1919), the National Tuberculosis Association (1920-1967), the National Tuberculosis and Respiratory Disease Association (1968-1972) and the American Lung Association (1973-).

While the Christmas Seal is not a postage stamp, it has long been associated with the postal service because of its use on letters and packages.

Einar Holboell, an employee of the Danish Post Office, created the Christmas Seal. He believed that seal sales could raise money for charity. The post offices of Denmark, Iceland and Sweden began to sell such seals in the 1904 Christmas season. In the United States, Christmas Seals were first issued in 1907 under the guidance of Emily P. Bissell, following the suggestion of Jacob Riis, social service worker.

Until 1975, all seals (except those of 1907 and 1908 type I) were issued in sheets of 100. The grilled gum (1908) has small square depressions like a waffle. The broken gum (1922), devised to prevent paper curling, consists of depressed lines in the gum, ½mm. apart, forming squares. The vertical and horizontal broken gum (1922, 1923, 1925, 1927-1932) forms diamonds. The perf. 12.00 (1917-1919, 1923, 1925, 1931) has two larger and wider-spaced holes between every 11 smaller holes.

Values are for unused seals with original gum.

SEALS ISSUED BY THE
DELAWARE CHAPTER OF THE
AMERICAN NATIONAL RED CROSS

CS1 (Type II)

Designer — Emily P. Bissell.
Nearly $4,000 worth of seals were sold, $3,000 cleared.

Type I — "Merry Christmas" only.
Type II — "Merry Christmas" and "Happy New Year."

1907 *Perf. 14*

WX1	CS1	Type I	17.50
WX2	CS1	Type II	15.00

Types I and II litho. by Theo. Leonhardt & Son, Philadelphia, Pa. The 1st seals were sold Dec. 7, 1907, in Wilmington, Del. Issued in sheets of 228 (19x12). Type II was issued to extend the sale of seals until New Year's Day, 1908.

Counterfeits of both types exist (perf. 12).

SEALS ISSUED BY THE
AMERICAN NATIONAL RED CROSS

CS2 (Type II)

Designer — Howard Pyle. Sales $135,000.

Type I — frame lines with square corners, small "C" in "Christmas."

Type II — frame lines have rounded corners, large "C" in "Christmas," leaves veined.

1908 ***Perf. 12, 14***

WX3	CS2	Type I, perf. 14, smooth gum	35.00
	a.	Perf. 12, smooth gum	45.00
	c.	Perf. 14, grilled gum	75.00
	d.	Perf. 12, grilled gum	50.00
	e.	As #WX3, bklt. pane of 6	250.00
	f.	As "c," bklt. pane of 6	250.00
	g.	As #WX3, bklt. pane of 3	250.00
WX4	CS2	Type II, perf. 12	30.00
	a.	Booklet pane of 6	175.00
	b.	Booklet pane of 3	125.00

Type I litho. by Theo. Leonhardt & Son. Sheets of 250 (14x18), with the 1st space in the 9th and 18th rows left blank.

Type II litho. by American Bank Note Co., New York, N.Y. in sheets of 100 (10x10).

Two sub-types of Type I, one with horn separated from the "8" (slightly more common) and the other with horn connected to the "8." Booklet panes are of the first sub-type.

Booklet panes have straight edges on 3 sides and perforated on left side where there is a stub, except No. WX4b which is a vert. strip of 3 with stub at top. Panes of 6 were made up in books of 24 and 48 and sold for 25c and 50c, and panes of 3 in books of 9 sold for 10c. The grilled gum has small square depressions like on a waffle.

CS3

CS4

Designer — Carl Wingate. Sales $250,000.

1909 ***Perf. 12***

WX5	CS3	One type only	1.25

Litho. by The Strobridge, Cincinnati, Ohio. Seals with a round punched hole of 3½mm are printers' samples.

1910 ***Perf. 12***

Designer — Frances Thompson. Sales $300,000.

WX6	CS4	One type only	20.00

Lithographed by The Strobridge Lithographing Co.

SEALS ISSUED BY THE AMERICAN NATIONAL RED CROSS (But sold by the National Association for the Study and Prevention of Tuberculosis)

"The Old Home Among the Cedars" — CS5 (Type II)

CS6

Designer — Anton Rudert under directions of F. D. Millet. Sales $320,000.

Type I — diameter of circle 22mm, solid end in house.
Type II — same circle but thinner, lined end to house.
Type III — diameter of circle 20mm, lined end to house.

1911 ***Perf. 12***

WX7	CS5	Type I	50.00
WX8	CS5	Type II	120.00

COIL STAMP

Perf. 8½ Vertically

WX9	CS5	Type III	75.00

Typo. by Eureka, Scranton, Pa. Type I has name and address of printer and union label in red in top margin. Type II has union label only in green on left margin.

1912 ***Perf. 12***

Designer — John H. Zeh. Sales $402,256.

WX10	CS6	One type only	11.00

Lithographed by The Strobridge Lithographing Co.

CS7 (Type I)

Designer — C. J. Budd. Sales $449,505.

Type I — with Poinsettia flowers and green circles around red crosses at either side.
Type II — the Poinsettia flowers have been removed.
Type III — the Poinsettia flowers and green circles have been removed.

1913 ***Perf. 12***

WX11	CS7	Type I	*1,400.*
WX12	CS7	Type II	7.50
WX13	CS7	Type III	8.50

Lithographed by American Bank Note Co.

CS8

CS9

Designer — Benjamin S. Nash. Sales $555,854.

1914 ***Perf. 12***

WX15	CS8	One type only	10.00

Lithographed by The Strobridge Lithographing Co.

1915

Designer — Benjamin S. Nash. Sales $760,000.

WX16	CS9	Perf. 12½	10.00
	a.	Perf. 12	65.00

Lithographed by Andrew B. Graham Co., Washington, D.C.

CS10

CS11

Designer — T. M. Cleland. Sales $1,040,810.

1916

WX18	CS10	Perf. 12	5.00
	a.	Perf. 12x12½	6.00
	b.	Perf. 12½x12	15.00
	c.	Perf. 12½	14.00

Lithographed by the Strobridge Lithographing Co.

Seals of 1917-21 are on coated paper.

1917

Designer — T. M. Cleland. Sales $1,815,110.

WX19	CS11	Perf. 12	2.00
	a.	Perf. 12½	15.00
	b.	Perf. 12x12.00	2.00
	c.	Perf. 12x12½	*20.00*

Typographed by Eureka Specialty Printing Co.

Perf. 12.00 has two larger and wider-spaced holes between every eleven smaller holes.

Sheets come with straight edged margins on all four sides also with perforated margins at either right or left. Perforated margins have the union label imprint in green.

SEALS ISSUED BY THE AMERICAN NATIONAL RED CROSS (Distributed by the National Tuberculosis Association)

CS12

CS13 (Type I)

Designer — Charles A. Winter.

These seals were given to members and others in lots of 10, the Natl. Tuberculosis Assoc. being subsidized by a gift of $2,500,000 from the American National Red Cross.

Type I — "American Red Cross" 15mm long, heavy circles between date.

Type II — "American Red Cross" 15½mm long, periods between date.

1918

WX21	CS12	Type I, perf. 11½x12.00	7.50
	a.	Perf. 12	8.50
	b.	Perf. 12.00, booklet pane of 10	2.00
	c.	Perf. 12x12.00, booklet pane of 10	2.00
	d.	Perf. 12, booklet pane of 10	2.00
	e.	Perf. 12.00x12, booklet pane of 10	65.00
WX22	CS12	Type II, from booklet pane, perf. 12½xRoulette 9½	.60
	a.	Perf. 12½, booklet pane of 10	1.50
	b.	Perf. 12½x12, bklt. pane of 10	—
	d.	Roulette 9½xPerf. 12½, bklt. pane of 10	—
	e.	Perf. 12½xRoulette 9½, bklt. pane of 10	20.00
	f.	Perf. 12½, booklet pane of 10	20.00
	h.	Roulette 9½xPerf. 12½, bklt. pane of 10	20.00
	i.	Roulette 9½xPerf. 12½ and Roulette 12½, booklet pane of 10	—
	j.	Perf. 12½, booklet pane of 10	50.00
	k.	Perf. 12½x12½ and 12, bklt. pane of 10	—
	l.	Roulette 9½xPerf. 12½, booklet pane of 10	—
	m.	Perf. 12½, booklet pane of 10	—
	n.	As "m," stub at bottom, bklt. pane of 10	50.00

For perf 12.00, see note following No. WX19.

Type I typographed by Eureka Specialty Printing Co.

Booklet panes of 10 (2x5) normally have straight edges on all four sides. They were cut from the sheets of 100 and can be plated by certain flaws which occur on both. Sheets have union label imprint on top margin in brown.

Type II lithographed by Strobridge Lithographing Co.

Booklet panes are the same but normally have a perforated margin at top and stub attached. These too can be plated by flaws. One or both vert. sides are rouletted on #WX22e; perforated on #WX22f and WX22h. #WX22i is rouletted 12½ on left, perf. 12½ on right. #WX22j, WX22k and WX22l are panes of 10 (5x2). #WX22m has a perforated margin at left.

Nos. WX21-WX21a are from sheet of 100, no straight edges.

The seal with "American Red Cross" 17¼mm long is believed to be an essay.

1919

Designer — Ernest Hamlin Baker. Sales $3,872,534.
Type I — plume at right side of Santa's cap.
Type II — no plume but a white dot in center of band.

WX24	CS13	Type I, perf. 12	.40
	a.	Perf. 12x12.00	.60
	b.	Perf. 12½x12	.50
	c.	Perf. 12½x12.00	2.75
WX25	CS13	Type II, perf. 12½	.40

For perf 12.00, see note following No. WX19.

This is the first time the double barred cross, the emblem of the National Tuberculosis Association, appeared in the design of the seals. It is also the last time the red cross emblem of the American National Red Cross was used on seals.

Type I typo. by Eureka, and has union label on margin at left in dark blue. Type II litho. by Strobridge.

SEALS ISSUED BY THE NATIONAL TUBERCULOSIS ASSOCIATION

CS14

CS15

Designer — Ernest Hamlin Baker. Sales $3,667,834.

Type I — size of seal 18x22mm.
Type II — seal 18½x23½mm, letters larger & numerals heavier.

1920

WX26	CS14	Type I, perf. 12x12½	.50
a.		Perf. 12	.40
b.		Perf. 12½x12	13.50
c.		Perf. 12½	15.00
WX27	CS14	Type II, perf. 12½	.50

Type I typo. by Eureka, and has union label imprint and rings on margin at left in dark blue. Type II litho. & offset by Strobridge.

1921

Designer — George V. Curtis. Sales $3,520,303.

Type I — dots in the chimney shading and faces are in diagonal lines, dots on chimney are separate except between the 2 top rows of bricks where they are solid.

Type II — dots in the chimney shading and faces are in horiz. lines.

Type III — as Type I except red dots on chimney are mostly joined forming lines, dots between the 2 top rows of bricks are not a solid mass.

WX28	CS15	Type I, perf. 12½	.65
WX29	CS15	Type II, perf. 12½	.40
WX29A	CS15	Type III, perf. 12	.50

Type I typo. by Eureka. Type II offset by Strobridge. Type III typo. by Zeese-Wilkinson Co., Long Island City, N.Y.

CS16

CS17

Designer — T. M. Cleland. Sales $3,857,086.

1922

WX30	CS16	Perf. 12½, broken gum	.80
a.		Perf. 12, broken gum	3.00
b.		Perf. 12x12½, broken gum	7.50
c.		Perf. 12, smooth gum	3.00
d.		Perf. 12½, vertical broken gum	3.00

Typographed by Eureka Specialty Printing Co.

The broken gum, which was devised to prevent curling of paper, consists of depressed lines in the gum ½mm apart, forming squares, or vertical broken gum forming diamonds.

1923

Designer — Rudolph Ruzicka. Sales $4,259,660.

WX31	CS17	Perf. 12½, vertical broken gum	.30
a.		Perf. 12, horizontal broken gum	3.00
b.		Perf. 12x12.00, vertical broken gum	3.50
c.		Perf. 12½x12, vertical broken gum	6.50
d.		Perf. 12, vertical broken gum	.90
e.		Perf. 12.00x12, vertical broken gum	3.00

For perf 12.00, see note following No. WX19.

Typographed by Eureka Specialty Printing Co.

The broken gum on this and issues following printed by Eureka consists of very fine depressed lines forming diamonds.

CS18

CS19 (Type II)

Designer — George V. Curtis. Sales $4,479,656.

1924

WX32	CS18	One type only	.30

Offset by Strobridge, E.&D., and U.S.P.& L.

1925 *Perf. 12½*

Designer — Robert G. Eberhard. Sales $4,937,786.

Type I — red lines at each side of "1925" do not join red tablet below.

Type II — red lines, as in type I, join red tablet below.

Type III — as type I but shorter rays around flames and "ea" of "Health" smaller.

WX35	CS19	Type I, vert. broken gum	.30
a.		Perf. 12, vertical broken gum	3.50
b.		Perf. 12x12½ vertical broken gum	.60
c.		Perf. 12.00x12½ vert. broken gum	—
WX36	CS19	Type II	.30
WX37	CS19	Type III	.75

For perf 12.00, see note following No. WX19.

Type I typo. by Eureka. Type II offset by E.&D. Type III litho. by Gugler Lithographing Co., Milwaukee.

CS20

CS21

Designer — George V. Curtis. Sales $5,121,872.

1926 *Perf. 12½*

WX38	CS20	One type only	.25

Offset by E.&D. and U.S.P.&L.

Printers' marks: E.&D. has a red dot at upper right on seal 91 on some sheets. U.S.P.&L. has a black dot at upper left on seal 56 on some sheets.

1927

Designer — John W. Evans. Sales $5,419,959.

WX39	CS21	Perf. 12, horizontal broken gum	.20
a.		Smooth gum (see footnote)	1.00
WX40	CS21	Perf. 12½, no dot	.20
WX41	CS21	Perf. 12½, one larger red dot in background 1mm above right post of dashboard on sleigh	.20

"Bonne Sante" added to design and #WX39a but with body of sleigh myrtle green instead of green were used in Canada.

Offset: #WX39, WX39a by Eureka. #WX40 by E.&D. #WX41 by U.S.P.&L.

Printer's marks: Eureka has no mark but can be identified by the perf. 12. E.&D. has red dot to left of knee of 1st reindeer on seal 92. U.S.P.&L. has 2 red dots in white gutter, one at lower left of seal 46 (and sometimes 41) and the other at upper right of seal 55. The perforations often strike out one of these dots.

The Gallant Ship "Argosy" — CS22

CS23

Designer — John W. Evans. Sales $5,465,738.

Type I — shading on sails broken, dots in flag regular.
Type II — shading on sails broken, dots in flag spotty.
Type III — shading on sails unbroken, dots in flag regular.

1928 *Perf. 12½*

WX44	CS22	Type I, vertical broken gum	.20
WX45	CS22	Type II	.20
WX46	CS22	Type III	.20

Seals inscribed "Bonne Annee 1929" or the same as type II but green in water, and black lines of ship heavier and deeper color were used in Canada.

Offset: Type I by Eureka, Type II by Strobridge, Type III by E.&D.

Printers' marks: Type I comes with and without a blue dash above seal 10, also with a blue and a black dash. Type II has 2 blue dashes below seal 100. Type III has red dot in crest of 1st wave on seal 92.

1929 *Perf. 12½*

Designer — George V. Curtis. Sales $5,546,147.

WX49	CS23	Vertical broken gum	.20
a.		Perf. 12, vertical broken gum	.50
b.		Perf. 12½x12, vertical broken gum	1.25
WX50	CS23	Smooth gum	.20

Seals inscribed "Bonne Sante 1929" or "Christmas Greetings 1929" were used in Canada.

Offset: #WX49-WX49b by Eureka, #WX50 by E.&D., U.S.P.&L., and R.R. Heywood Co., Inc., New York, N.Y.

Printers' marks: Eureka is without mark but identified by broken gum. E.&D. has a black dot in lower left corner of seal 92. U.S.P.&L. has blue dot above bell on seal 56. Heywood has a blue dot at lower right corner of seal 100.

CS24

CS25

Designer — Ernest Hamlin Baker, and redrawn by John W. Evans. Sales $5,309,352.

1930 *Perf. 12½*

WX55	CS24	Vertical broken gum	.20
a.		Perf. 12, vert. broken gum	.50
b.		Perf. 12.00x12, vert. broken gum	.25
c.		Perf. 12½x12, vertical broken gum	2.50
d.		Perf. 12, booklet pane of 10, horiz. broken gum	.50
WX56	CS24	Smooth gum	.20

Seals inscribed "Bonne Sante" or "Merry Christmas" on red border of seal were used in Canada.

Offset: #WX55-WX55d by Eureka, #WX56 by Strobridge, E.&D. and U.S.P.&L.

Printers' marks: Eureka has a dot between the left foot and middle of "M" of "Merry" on seal 1. Strobridge has 2 dashes below "ALL" on seal 100. E.&D. printed on Nashua paper has dot on coat just under elbow on seal 92, and on Gummed Products Co. paper has the dot on seals 91, 92. U.S.P.&L. has a dash which joins tree to top frame line just under "MA" of "Christmas" on seal 55.

The plate for booklet panes was made up from the left half of the regular plate and can be plated by certain flaws which occur on both.

1931 *Perf. 12½*

Designer — John W. Evans. Sales $4,526,189.

WX61	CS25	Horiz. broken gum (see footnote)	2.00
WX62	CS25	Horizontal broken gum	.20
a.		Perf. 12x12½, horiz. broken gum	.35
b.		Perf. 12.00x12½, horizontal broken gum	2.50
c.		Perf. 12, horizontal broken gum	1.00
g.		Perf. 12, vertical broken gum, booklet pane of 10	.50
h.		Perf. 12x12.00, vertical broken gum, booklet pane of 10	.60
WX63	CS25	Smooth gum	.20

For perf 12.00, see note following No. WX19.

Offset: #WX61-WX62h by Eureka, #WX63 by Strobridge. #WX61 has a green dash across inner green frame line at bottom center on each seal in sheet except those in 1st and last vertical rows and the 2 rows at bottom.

Printers' marks: Eureka has none. Strobridge has the usual 2 dashes under seal 100.

The plate for booklet panes was made up from transfers of 60 seals (12x5). The panes can be plated by minor flaws.

CS26

CS27

Designer — Edward F. Volkmann. Sales $3,470,637.

1932

WX64	CS26	Perf. 12½x12¾	.20
a.		Vertical broken gum	.50
WX65	CS26	Perf. 12	.20
WX66	CS26	Perf. 12½	.20
WX67	CS26	Perf. 12½	.20

Offset: #WX64 by Eureka, #WX65 by E.&D., #WX66 by U.S.P.&L., #WX67 by Columbian Bank Note Co., Chicago. #WX64, WX67 have a little red spur on bottom inner frame line of each seal, at left corner.

Printers' marks: Eureka has a red dash, in each corner of the sheet, which joins the red border to the red inner frame line. E.&D. has a blue dot in snow at lower left on seal 91. U.S.P.&L. has a blue dot on top of post on seal 56. Columbian Bank Note has small "C" in lower part of girl's coat on seal 82.

1933

Designer — Hans Axel Walleen. Sales $3,429,311.

WX68	CS27	Perf. 12	.20
WX69	CS27	Perf. 12½	.20

Offset: #WX68 by Eureka, #WX69 by Strobridge, U.S.P.&L., and the Columbian Bank Note Co.

Printers' marks; Eureka has rope joining elbow of figure to left on seals 11, 20, 91, 100. Strobridge has the usual 2 dashes under seal 100. U.S.P.&L. has green dot on tail of "s" of "Greetings" on seal 55. Columbian has white "c" on margin, under cross, on seal 93.

CS28

CS29

Designer — Herman D. Giesen. Sales $3,701,344.

1934

WX72	CS28	Perf. 12½x12¼	.20
WX73	CS28	Perf. 12½ (see footnote)	.20
WX74	CS28	Perf. 12½ (see footnote)	.20
WX75	CS28	Perf. 12½ (see footnote)	.20

Offset: #WX72 by Eureka, #WX73 by Strobridge, #WX74 by E.&D. and #WX75 by U.S.P.&L.

Cutting of blue plate for the under color: #WX72, WX73 (early printing) and WX74 have lettering and date cut slightly larger than ultramarine color. #WX73 (later printing) has square cutting around letters and date, like top part of letter "T". #WX75 has cutting around letters and date cut slightly larger.

Printers' marks: Eureka has 5 stars to right of cross on seal 10. Strobridge has 2 blue dashes in lower left corner of seal 91 or in lower right corner of seal 100. E.&D. has a red dot in lower left corner of seal 99. U.S.P.&L. has 5 stars to left of cross on seal 56.

Great Britain issued seals of this design which can be distinguished by the thinner and whiter paper. Sheets have perforated margins on all 4 sides but without any lettering on bottom margin, perf. 12½.

1935

Designer — Ernest Hamlin Baker. Sales $3,946,498.

WX76	CS29	Perf. 12½x12¼	.20
WX77	CS29	Perf. 12½	.20

Offset: #WX76 by Eureka, #WX77 by Strobridge, U.S.P.&L. and Columbian Bank Note Co.

Eureka recut their blue plate and eliminated the faint blue shading around cross, girl's head and at both sides of the upper part of post. U.S.P.& L. eliminated the 2 brown spurs which pointed to the base of cross, in all 4 corners of the sheet.

Printers' marks: Eureka has an extra vertical line of shading on girl's skirt on seal 60. Strobridge has 2 brown dashes in lower right corner of position 100 but sheets from an early printing are without this mark. U.S.P.&L. has a blue dot under post on seal 55. Columbian has a blue "c" under post on seal 99.

The corner seals carry slogans: "Help Fight Tuberculosis," "Protect Your Home from Tuberculosis," "Tuberculosis Is Preventable," "Tuberculosis Is Curable."

Printers' marks appear on seal 56 on sheets of 100 unless otherwise noted:

E Eureka Specialty Printing Co.
S Strobridge Lithographing Co. (1930-1958).
S Specialty Printers of America (1975-).
D Edwards & Deutsch Lithographing Co. (E.&D.)
U United States Printing & Lithographing Co. (U.S.P.&L.)
F Fleming-Potter Co., Inc.
W Western Lithograph Co.
B Berlin Lithographing Co. (1956-1969); I. S. Berlin Press (1970-1976); Barton-Cotton (1977-).
R Bradford-Robinson Printing Co.
N Sale-Niagara, Inc.

Seals from 1936 onward are printed by offset.

Seals with tropical gum (dull), starting in 1966, were used in Puerto Rico.

CS30

CS31

Designer — Walter I. Sasse. Sales $4,522,269.

1936 — Pair

WX80	CS30	Perf. 12½x12 (E)	.20
WX81	CS30	Perf. 12½ (S,D,U)	.20

Seals with red background and green cap-band alternate with seals showing green background and red cap-band. The corner seals carry the same slogans as those of 1935.

Two of the three Strobridge printings show vertical green dashes in margin below seal 100, besides "S" on seal 56.

1937

Designer — A. Robert Nelson. Sales $4,985,697.

WX88	CS31	Perf. 12x12½ (E)	.20
WX89	CS31	Perf. 12½ (S,D,U)	.20

Positions 23, 28, 73 and 78, carry slogans: "Health for all," "Protect your home," "Preventable" and "Curable."

The "U" printer's mark of U.S.P.&L. appears on seal 55. It is omitted on some sheets.

CS32

CS33

Designer — Lloyd Coe. Sales $5,239,526.

1938

WX92	CS32	Perf. 12½x12 (E)	.20
WX93	CS32	Perf. 12½ (S,D,U)	.20
a.		Miniature sheet, imperf.	2.50

The corner seals bear portraits of Rene T. H. Laennec, Robert Koch, Edward Livingston Trudeau and Einar Holboll.

No. WX93a contains the 4 corner seals, with the regular seal in the center. It sold for 25 cents.

1939

Designer — Rockwell Kent. Sales $5,593,399.

WX96	CS33	Perf. 12½x12 (E)	.20
a.		Booklet pane of 20, perf. 12	.50
WX97	CS33	Perf. 12½ (S,D,U)	.20

The center seals, positions 45, 46, 55, 56, carry slogans: "Health to All," "Protect Your Home," "Tuberculosis Preventable Curable" and "Holiday Greetings."

Printers' marks appear on seal 57.

CS34

CS35

Designer — Felix L. Martini. Sales $6,305,979.

1940

WX100	CS34	Perf. 12½x12 (E)	.20
WX101	CS34	Perf. 12½x13 (E)	.20
WX103	CS34	Perf. 12½ (S,D,U)	.20

Seals 23, 32 and 34 carry the slogan "Protect Us from Tuberculosis." Each slogan seal shows one of the 3 children.

1941

Designer — Stevan Dohanos. Sales $7,530,496.

WX104	CS35	Perf. 12½x12 (E)	.20
WX105	CS35	Perf. 12½ (S,D,U)	.20

"S" and "U" printers' marks exist on same sheet.

CS36

CS37

Designer — Dale Nichols. Sales $9,390,117.

1942

WX108	CS36	Perf. 12x12½ (E)	.20
WX109	CS36	Perf. 12½ (S,D,U)	.20

1943

Designer — Andre Dugo. Sales $12,521,494.

Pair

WX112	CS37	Perf. 12½x12 (E)	.20
WX113	CS37	Perf. 12½ (S,D,U)	.20

On alternate seals, the vert. frame colors (blue & red) are transposed as are the horiz. frame colors (buff & black).

Seals where "Joyeux Noel" replaces "Greetings 1943" and "1943" added on curtain or the same as #WX113 but darker colors were used in Canada.

CS38

CS39

Designer — Spence Wildey. Sales $14,966,227.

1944

WX118	CS38	Perf. 12½x12 (E)	.20
WX119	CS38	Perf. 12½ (S,D,U)	.20

Seals with "USA" omitted are for Canada.

1945 — "USA" at Lower Right Corner

Designer — Park Phipps. Sales $15,638,755.

WX124	CS39	Perf. 12½x12 (E)	.20
WX125	CS39	Perf. 12½ (S,D,U)	.20

Seals with "USA" omitted are for Canada.

CS40

CS41

Designer — Mary Louise Estes and Lloyd Coe. Sales $17,075,608.

1946 — "USA" at Left of Red Cross

WX130	CS40	Perf. 12½x12 (E)	.20
WX131	CS40	Perf. 12½ (S,D,U)	.20

Seals with "USA" omitted are for Canada and Bermuda.

Printers' marks are on seal 86.

The center seals (45, 46, 55, 56) bear portraits of Jacob Riis, Emily P. Bissell, E. A. Van Valkenburg and Leigh Mitchell Hodges.

1947

Designer — Raymond H. Lufkin. Sales $18,665,523.

WX135	CS41	Perf. 12x12½ (E)	.20
WX136	CS41	Perf. 12½ (S,D,U)	.20

Seals with "USA" omitted are for Canada and Great Britain.

The "U" printer's mark of U.S.P.&L. appears on seal 46.

CS42

CS43

Designer — Jean Barry Bart. Sales $20,153,834.

1948

WX140	CS42	Perf. 12x12½ (E)	.20
WX141	CS42	Perf. 12½ (S,D,U)	.20

Seals with "USA" omitted are for Canada and Great Britain.

1949

Designer — Herbert Meyers. Sales $20,226,794.

WX145	CS43	Perf. 12x12½ (E)	.20
WX146	CS43	Perf. 12½ (S,D,U)	.20

Seals with "USA" omitted are for Canada & Great Britain.

CS44

CS45

Designer — Andre Dugo. Sales $20,981,540.

1950

WX150	CS44	Perf. 12½x12 (E)	.20
WX151	CS44	Perf. 12½ (S,D,U,F)	.20

Seals with "USA" omitted are for Canada & Great Britain.

1951

Designer — Robert K. Stephens. Sales $21,717,953.

WX155	CS45	Perf. 12½x12 (E)	.20
WX156	CS45	Perf. 12½ (S,D,U,F)	.20

Seals with "USA" omitted are for Canada.

CS46

CS47

Designer — Tom Darling. Sales $23,238,148.

1952

WX159	CS46	Perf. 12½x12 (E)	.20
WX160	CS46	Perf. 12½ (S,D,U,F)	.20

For Nos. WX159-WX160 overprinted "Ryukyus" in Japanese characters, see Ryukyu Islands Nos. WX1 and WX1a.

1953

Designers — Elmer Jacobs and E. Willis Jones. Sales $23,889,044.

WX164	CS47	Perf. 13 (E)	.20
WX165	CS47	Perf. 12½ (S,D,U,F)	.20

CS48

Designer — Jorgen Hansen. Sales $24,670,202.

1954 **Block of 4**

WX168	CS48	Perf. 13 (E)	.40
WX169	CS48	Perf. 12½ (S,U,F,W)	.40
WX170	CS48	Perf. 11 (D)	.50

CS49

Designer — Jean Simpson. Sales $25,780,365.

1955 **Pair**

WX173	CS49	Perf. 13 (E)	.25
WX174	CS49	Perf. 12½ (S,U,F,W)	.25
WX175	CS49	Perf. 11 (D)	.25

CS50

Designer — Heidi Brandt. Sales $26,310,491.

1956 **Block of 4**

WX178	CS50	Perf. 12½x12 (E)	.40
WX179	CS50	Perf. 12½ (E,S,U,F,W)	.50
WX180	CS50	Perf. 11 (D,B)	.40
WX183	CS50	"Puerto Rico," perf. 12½	3.00

CS51

Designer — Clinton Bradley. Sales $25,959,998.

1957 **Block of 4**

WX184	CS51	Perf. 13 (E)	.40
WX185	CS51	Perf. 12½ (S,U,F,W,R)	.40
WX186	CS51	Perf. 11 (D,B)	.50
WX187	CS51	Perf. 10½x11 (D)	.75
WX188	CS51	Perf. 10½ (D)	3.00
WX190	CS51	"Puerto Rico," perf. 13	3.00

CS52

Designer — Alfred Guerra. Sales $25,955,390.

1958 **Pair**

WX191	CS52	Perf. 13 (E)	.25
WX192	CS52	Perf. 12½ (S,U,F,W,R)	.25
WX193	CS52	Perf. 10½x11 (B,D)	.50
WX194	CS52	Perf. 11 (B,D)	.35
WX196	CS52	"Puerto Rico," perf. 13	1.50

CS53

Designer — Katherine Rowe. Sales $26,740,906.

1959 **Pair**

WX197	CS53	Perf. 13 (E)	.25
WX198	CS53	Perf. 12½ (F,R,W)	.25
a.		Horiz. pair, imperf. btwn. (D)	1.50
WX199	CS53	Perf. 10½x11 (B)	.40
WX200	CS53	Perf. 11 (B,D)	.25
WX201	CS53	Perf. 10½ (B)	2.00
WX203	CS53	"Puerto Rico," perf. 13	1.25

E.&D. omitted every other vertical row of perforation on a number of sheets which were widely distributed as an experiment. #WX198a (shown above in illustration) is from these sheets.

CS54

Designer — Philip Richard Costigan. Sales $26,259,030.

1960 **Block of 4**

WX204	CS54	Perf. 12½ (E,F,R,W)	.35
WX205	CS54	Perf. 12½x12 (E)	1.00
WX206	CS54	Perf. 11x10½ (B)	.35
WX207	CS54	Perf. 11 (D)	.35

Puerto Rico used No. WX204 (E).

CS55

Designer — Heidi Brandt. Sales $26,529,517.

1961 **Block of 4**

WX209	CS55	Perf. 12½ (E,F,R,W)	.35
WX209A	CS55	Perf. 12½x12 (E)	2.00
WX210	CS55	Perf. 11x10½ (B)	.35
WX211	CS55	Perf. 11 (D)	.35

Puerto Rico used No. WX209 (E).

CS56

Designer — Paul Dohanos. Sales $27,429,202.

1962 **Block of 4**

WX213	CS56	Perf. 12½ (F,R,W)	.35
WX214	CS56	Perf. 13 (E)	.35
WX215	CS56	Perf. 10½x11 (B)	.35
WX216	CS56	Perf. 11 (D,B)	.35

Puerto Rico used No. WX214.

CS57

Designer — Judith Campbell Piussi. Sales $27,411,806.

1963 **Block of 4**

WX218	CS57	Perf. 12½ (E,F,R,W)	.35
WX219	CS57	Perf. 11 (B,D)	.35

Puerto Rico used No. WX218 (E).

CS58

Designer — Gaetano di Palma. Sales $28,784,043.

1964 **Block of 4**

WX220	CS58	Perf. 12½ (E,F,R,W)	.35
WX221	CS58	Perf. 11 (B,D)	.35

Puerto Rico used No. WX221 (B).

CS59

Designer — Frede Salomonsen. Sales $29,721,878.

1965 **Block of 4**

WX222	CS59	Perf. 12½ (F,W)	.35
WX223	CS59	Perf. 11 (B,D)	.35
WX224	CS59	Perf. 13 (E)	.35

Puerto Rico used No. WX223 (B).

CS60

Designer — Heidi Brandt. Sales $30,776,586.

1966 **Block of 8**

WX225	CS60	Perf. 12½ (E,F,W)	.65
WX226	CS60	Perf. 10½x11 (B)	.65
WX227	CS60	Perf. 11 (D)	.65

Blocks of four seals with yellow green and white backgrounds alternate in sheet in checkerboard style.
Puerto Rico used No. WX226.

Holiday Train — CS61

Designer — L. Gerald Snyder. Sales $31,876,773.
The seals come in 10 designs showing a train filled with Christmas gifts and symbols. The direction of the train is reversed in alternating rows as are the inscriptions "Christmas 1967" and "Greetings 1967." The illustration shows first 2 seals of top row.

1967 **Block of 20 (10x2)**

WX228	CS61	Perf. 13 (E)	.65
WX229	CS61	Perf. 12½ (F,W)	.65
WX230	CS61	Perf. 10½ (B)	1.50
WX231	CS61	Perf. 11 (D)	.75
WX232	CS61	Perf. 11x10½ (B)	.75

Puerto Rico used No. WX229 (F).

SEALS ISSUED BY NATIONAL TUBERCULOSIS AND RESPIRATORY DISEASE ASSOCIATION

CS62

Designer — William Eisele. Sales $33,059,107.

1968 **Block of 4**

WX233	CS62	Perf. 13 (E)	.50
WX234	CS62	Perf. 10½x11 (B)	.50
WX234A	CS62	Perf. 10½ (B)	.50
WX235	CS62	Perf. 11 (D)	.50
WX236	CS62	Perf. 12½ (F,W)	.50

Pairs of seals with bluish green and yellow backgrounds alternate in sheet in checkerboard style.
Puerto Rico used No. WX236 (F).

CS63

Designer — Bernice Kochan. Sales $34,437,591.

1969 **Block of 4**

WX237	CS63	Perf. 13 (E)	.35
WX238	CS63	Perf. 12½ (F,W)	.35
WX239	CS63	Perf. 10½x11 (B)	.50
WX240	CS63	Perf. 11 (B)	.50

Puerto Rico used No. WX238 (F).

CS64

Designer — L. Gerald Snyder. Sales $36,237,977.
Sheets contain 100 different designs, Christmas symbols, toys, decorated windows; inscribed alternately "Christmas 1970" and "Greetings 1970." The illustration shows 6 seals from the center of the sheet.

1970 **Sheet of 100 (10x10)**

WX242	CS64	Perf. 12½ (E,F,W)	1.25
WX243	CS64	Perf. 11 (B)	1.25
WX244	CS64	Perf. 11x10½ (B)	1.25

Puerto Rico used No. WX242 (F).

CS65

Designer — James Clarke. Sales $36,120,000.

1971 **Block of 8 (2x4)**

WX245	CS65	Perf. 12½ (E,F)	.50
WX246	CS65	Perf. 11 (B)	.50

The 4 illustrated seals each come in a 2nd design arrangement: cross at left, inscriptions transposed, and reversed bugler, candle and tree ornaments. Each sheet of 100 has 6 horiz. rows as shown and 4 rows with 2nd designs.
Puerto Rico used No. WX245 (F).
Eureka printings are found with large "E," small "E" and without "E."

CS66

Designer — Linda Layman. Sales $38,000,557.
The seals come in 10 designs showing various holiday scenes with decorated country and city houses, carolers, Christmas trees and snowman. Inscribed alternately "1972 Christmas" and "Greetings 1972." Shown are seals from center of row.

1972 **Strip of 10**

WX247	CS66	Perf. 13 (E)	.50
WX248	CS66	Perf. 12½ (F)	.75
WX249	CS66	Perf. 11 (B)	.50

Seal 100 has designer's name. Puerto Rico used No. WX248.

SEALS ISSUED BY AMERICAN LUNG ASSOCIATION

CS67

Designer — Cheri Johnson. Sales $36,902,439.

The seals are in 12 designs representing "The 12 Days of Christmas." Inscribed alternately "Christmas 1973" and "Greetings 1973." Shown is block from center of top 2 rows.

1973			Block of 12
WX250	CS67	Perf. 12½ (F), 18x22mm	.50
a.		Size 16½x20½mm (E)	.50
WX251	CS67	Perf. 11 (B,W)	.50

Seal 100 has designer's name. Puerto Rico used #WX250 (F).

CS68

Designer — Rubidoux. Sales $37,761,745.

1974			Block of 4
WX252	CS68	Perf. 12½ (E,F)	.35
WX253	CS68	Perf. 11 (B)	.35

Seal 99 has designer's name. Puerto Rico used #WX252 (F).

CS69

Children's paintings of holiday scenes. Different design for each state or territory. Paintings by elementary school children were selected in a nationwide campaign ending in Jan., 1974.

Sales $34,710,107.

1975			Sheet of 54 (6x9)
WX254	CS69	Perf. 12½ (S,F)	1.25
WX255	CS69	Perf. 11 (B)	1.25

Printers' marks are on seal 28 (New Mexico). Specialty Printers' seals (S) carry union labels: "Scranton 4," "Scranton 7," "E. Stroudsburg."

Puerto Rico used No. WX254 (F).

CS70

Continuous village picture covers sheet with Christmas activities and Santa crossing the sky with sleigh and reindeer. No inscription on 34 seals. Others inscribed "Christmas 1976," "Greetings 1976," and (on 9 bottom-row seals) "American Lung Association." Illustration shows seals 11-12, 20-21.

Sales $36,489,207.

1976			Sheet of 54 (9x6)
WX256	CS70	Perf. 12½ (F,N)	1.25
WX257	CS70	Perf. 11 (B)	1.25
WX258	CS70	Perf. 13 (S)	1.25

Printers' marks (N, B, S) on seal 32 and (F) on seal 23.

Puerto Rico used No. WX256 (F).

CS71

Children's paintings of holiday scenes. Different design for each state or territory.

Sales $37,583,883.

1977			Sheet of 54 (6x9)
WX259	CS71	Perf. 12½ (F)	1.25
WX260	CS71	Perf. 11 (B)	1.25
WX261	CS71	Perf. 13 (S)	1.50

Printers' marks on seal 28 (Georgia).

Puerto Rico used No. WX259.

CS72

Children's paintings of holiday scenes. Different design for each state or territory.

Sales $37,621,466.

1978			Sheet of 54 (6x9)
WX262	CS72	Perf. 12½ (F)	1.25
WX263	CS72	Perf. 11 (B)	1.25
WX264	CS72	Perf. 13 (S)	1.25

Printers' marks on seal 29 (New Hampshire).

Puerto Rico used No. WX262.

Type of 1978 Inscribed 1979

1979			Sheet of 54 (6x9)
WX265	CS72	Perf. 12½ (F)	1.25
WX266	CS72	Perf. 11 (B)	1.25
WX267	CS72	Perf. 13 (S)	1.25

Printer's marks on seal 22 (Virgin Islands). Puerto Rico used No. WX265.

Beginning in 1979 there is no longer one national issue. Additional designs are issued on a limited basis as test seals to determine the designs to be used the following year.

SANITARY FAIR

The United States Sanitary Commission was authorized by the Secretary of War on June 9, 1861, and approved by President Lincoln on June 13, 1861. It was a committee of inquiry, advice and aid dealing with the health and general comfort of Union troops, supported by public contributions.

Many Sanitary Fairs were held to raise funds for the Commission, and eight issued stamps. The first took place in 1863 at Chicago, where no stamp was issued. Some Sanitary Fairs advertised on envelopes.

Sanitary Fair stamps occupy a position midway between United States semi-official carrier stamps and the private local posts. Although Sanitary Fair stamps were not valid for U.S. postal service, they were prepared for, sold and used at the fair post offices, usually with the approval and participation of the local postmaster.

The Commission undertook to forward soldiers' unpaid and postage due letters. These letters were handstamped "Forwarded by the U.S. Sanitary Commission."

Details about the Sanitary Fair stamps may be found in the following publications:

American Journal of Philately, Jan. 1889, by J. W. Scott
The Collector's Journal, Aug-Sept. 1909, by C. E. Severn
Scott's Monthly Journal, Jan. 1927 (reprint, Apr. 1973), by Elliott Perry
Stamps, April 24th, 1937, by Harry M. Konwiser
Pat Paragraphs, July, 1939, by Elliott Perry
Covers, Aug. 1952, by George B. Wray
Sanitary Fairs, 1992, by Alvin and Marjorie Kantor

The listings were compiled originally by H. M. Konwiser and Dorsey F. Wheless.

SF1

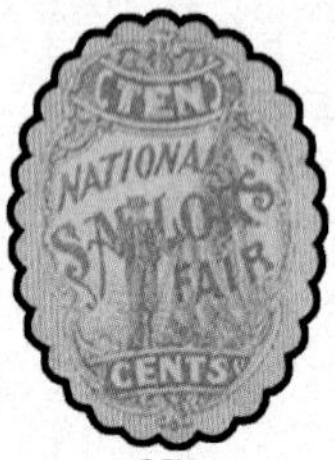

SF2

Albany, New York

Army Relief Bazaar

Setting A: narrow spacing, pane of 12.
Setting B: wider spacing, sheet of 25.

1864, Feb. 22-Mar. 30 — Litho. — *Imperf.*

Thin White Paper

WV1	SF1	10c	**rose**	125.	
			Used on cover (tied "Albany")		*9,500.*
			Block of 4, setting A	1,200.	
			Pane of 12, setting A	*4,800.*	
			Block of 4, setting B	500.	
			Sheet of 25, setting B	*2,500.*	
WV2	SF1	10c	**black**	700.	
			Block of 5, setting A	*4,500.*	
			Vert. pair, setting B	*1,500.*	

The No. WV1 tied by Albany cancel on cover is unique. One other cover exists in private hands with the stamp uncanceled and slightly damaged.

Vert. pair is only setting B multiple of No. WV2.

Imitations are typographed in red, blue, black or green on a thin white or ordinary white paper, also on colored papers and are:

(a) Eagle with topknot, printed in sheets of 30 (6x5).
(b) Eagle without shading around it.
(c) Eagle with shading around it, but with a period instead of a circle in "C" of "Cents," and "Ten Cents" is smaller.

Boston, Mass.

National Sailors' Fair

1864, Nov. 9-22 — Litho.

Die Cut

WV3	SF2	10c	**green**	350.

Brooklyn, N.Y.

Brooklyn Sanitary Fair

Sheets of 25 (WV4)

SF3

1864, Feb. 22-Mar. 8 — Litho. — *Imperf.*

WV4	SF3	(15c)	**green**	1,250.	*3,600.*
			On cover, Fair postmark on envelope		*3,000.*
			Block of 4	*6,500.*	
			Block of 6	*10,000.*	
WV5	SF3	(25c)	**black**	*4,750.*	
			On cover, with 1c local #28L2, Fair postmark on envelope		*36,000.*

No. WV4 used is valued canceled by the Fair postmark. One or more examples also exist with a manuscript cancel. No. WV5 unused is unique as is the usage on cover.

Imitations: *(a)* Typographed and shows "Sanitary" with a heavy cross bar to "T" and second "A" with a long left leg. *(b)* Is a rough typograph print without shading in letters of "Fair."

SF4

SF5

1863, Dec. — Typeset — *Imperf.*

WV6	SF4	5c	**black,** *rosy buff*	750.	*200.*
WV7	SF5	10c	**green**	1,350.	
			Tete beche pair	*9,000.*	

No. WV6 used is believed to be unique. It has a manuscript cancel and is faulty. It is valued thus.

SF6

SF7

New York, N.Y.

Metropolitan Fair

1864, Apr. 4-27 — Engr. — *Imperf.*

Thin White Paper

WV8	SF6	10c	**blue**	250.
			Sheet of 4	1,500.
WV9	SF6	10c	**red**	1,500.
			Pair	3,500.
WV10	SF6	10c	**black**	*14,000.*

Engraved and printed by John E. Gavit of Albany, N.Y. from a steel plate composed of four stamps, 2x2. Can be plated by the positions of scrolls and dots around "Ten Cents."

No. WV10 is unique.

Philadelphia, Pa.

Great Central Fair

1864, June 7-28 — Engr. — *Perf. 12*

Printed by Butler & Carpenter, Philadelphia

Sheets of 126 (14x9)

WV11	SF7	10c	**blue**	40.00	525.00
			On cover tied with Fair postmark		*2,250.*
			On cover with 3c #65, Fair and Philadelphia postmarks		*36,000.*
			On cover with 3c #65, New York postmark		*42,500.*
			Block of 4	250.00	
WV12	SF7	20c	**green**	27.50	500.00
			On cover tied with Fair postmark		*1,500.*
			Block of 4	135.00	
			Block of 12	475.00	
WV13	SF7	30c	**black**	35.00	400.00
			On cover tied with Fair postmark		*1,500.*
			Nos. WV11-WV13 on single cover, Fair postmark		*7,500.*
			Block of 4	160.00	
			Block of 6	240.00	

Imprint "Engraved by Butler & Carpenter, Philadelphia" on right margin adjoining three stamps.

Used examples of Nos. WV11-WV13 have Fair cancellation.

The No. WV11 covers used with 3c #65 are each unique. The New York usage is on a Metropolitan Fair illustrated envelope.

Imitation of No. WV13 comes typographed in blue or green on thick paper.

White and amber envelopes were sold by the fair inscribed "Great Central Fair for the Sanitary Commission," showing picture in several colors of wounded soldier, doctors and ambulance marked "U.S. Sanitary Commission." Same design and inscription are known on U.S. envelope No. U46.

SF8

SF9

Springfield, Mass.

Soldiers' Fair

1864, Dec. 19-24 — Typo. — *Imperf.*

WV14	SF8	10c	**lilac**	210.00	
			On unaddressed cover, Fair postmark on envelope		750.00
			Horizontal strip of 4	950.00	

Design by Thomas Chubbuck, engraver of the postmaster provisional stamp of Brattleboro, Vt.

One cover exists pencil-addressed to Wm. Ingersoll, Springfield Armory; value slightly more than an unaddressed cover.

Imitations: *(a)* Without designer's name in lower right corner, in lilac on laid paper. *(b)* With designer's name, but roughly typographed, in lilac on white wove paper. Originals show 5 buttons on uniform.

Stamford, Conn.

Soldiers' Fair

1864, July 27-29

WV15	SF9	15c	**pale brown**	*2,000.*	*4,500.*

Originals have tassels at ends of ribbon inscribed "SOLDIERS FAIR." Imitations have leaning "S" in "CENTS" and come in lilac, brown, green, also black on white paper, green on pinkish paper and other colors.

ESSAY

Great Central Fair, Philadelphia

1864

WV11-E1	Design as issued but value tablets blank, greenish black on glazed paper (unique)	—

PROOFS

Metropolitan Fair, New York

1864

WV10P	10c **black,** plate on India, mounted on card	900.

Great Central Fair, Philadelphia

1864

WV11P	10c	**blue,** card	32.50
		Block of 4	150.00
WV11TC/WV13TC	10c	and 30c **grnsh blk,** se-tenant, glazed paper, large die	—
WV12P	20c	**green,** card	35.00
		Block of 4	175.00
WV12TC	20c	**carmine,** wove, perf.	35.00
		Block of 4	175.00
WV12TC	20c	**vermilion,** India on card, large die	275.00
WV12TC	20c	**vermilion,** wove, imperf.	22.50
		Block of 4	115.00
WV12TC	20c	**vermilion,** wove, perf.	35.00
		Block of 4	175.00
WV12TC	20c	**orange,** wove, imperf.	22.50
		Block of 4	115.00
WV12TC	20c	**brown orange,** opaque paper	22.50
		Block of 4	115.00
WV12TC	20c	**red brown,** wove, perf.	35.00
		Block of 4	175.00
WV12TC	20c	**black brown,** wove, imperf.	25.00
		Block of 4	125.00
WV12TC	20c	**olive,** wove, imperf.	22.50
		Block of 4	100.00
WV12TC	20c	**yellow green,** wove, imperf.	22.50
		Block of 4	125.00
WV12TC	20c	**light green,** wove, perf.	35.00
		Block of 4	175.00
WV12TC	20c	**blue,** India on card, large die	275.00
WV12TC	20c	**blue,** wove, perf.	175.00
WV12TC	20c	**bright blue,** wove, imperf.	22.50
		Block of 4	125.00
WV12TC	20c	**bright blue,** wove, perf.	35.00
		Block of 4	175.00
WV12TC	20c	**lt. ultramarine,** wove, imperf.	22.50
		Block of 4	125.00
WV12TC	20c	**purple,** wove, imperf.	22.50
		Block of 4	125.00
WV12TC	20c	**claret,** wove, imperf.	35.00
		Block of 4	200.00
WV12TC	20c	**brown black,** wove, perf.	35.00
		Block of 4	175.00
WV12TC	20c	**greenish black,** glazed paper, large die	225.00
WV12TC	20c	**gray black,** opaque paper, wove, imperf.	22.50
		Block of 4	125.00
WV12TC	20c	**gray black,** wove, perf.	35.00
		Block of 4	175.00
WV12TC	20c	**black,** experimental double paper, wove, imperf.	25.00
		Block of 4	140.00
WV13P	30c	**black,** card	35.00
		Block of 4	175.00
WV13TC	30c	**blue,** imperf	35.00

Reprints (1903?) exist of WV11TC-WV13TC, se-tenant vertically, large die on glazed white, pink or yellow card and small die on India paper (mounted se-tenant) in carmine, red carmine, vermilion, orange, brown, yellow brown, olive, yellow green, blue green, gray blue, ultramarine, light violet, violet, claret and gray black.

There also exist large die essay reprints on India paper, green bond paper and glazed cardboard without denomination or with 20c. The 20c value has an added line below the center shield.

ENCASED POSTAGE STAMPS

In early 1862, months after the beginning of the American Civil War, people were conserving resources in anticipation of hard times and shortages ahead. Coins were one of the most hoarded resources, and as a result of this hoarding, coins began to command a premium over paper money. The public was reluctant to spend their coins, fearing the premiums for coins might increase, and a loss might result. Many millions of dollars in gold and silver coins, even copper-nickel cents, disappeared into private hands.

The U.S, Mint began coining copper-nickel cents almost exclusively, but could not meet demand. In response, the public turned to postage stamps to meet small obligations, and shopkeepers were forced to accept stamps as change. Envelopes stating the amount of stamps contained within and cards bearing stamps were sometimes used to keep the stamps from sticking and becoming destroyed, and printers sold advertisements on large numbers of these envelopes. By July 1862, the government had authorized the monetizing of postage stamps and began printing stamp impressions on bank note paper.

On August 12, 1862, John Gault was issued a patent for a "Design for Encasing Government Stamps" to be used as the equivalent of currency. Gault's plans called for a postage stamp to have its corners wrapped around a cardboard circle and show through a thin mica covering. An outer metal frame would hold these items secure, and a heavier brass backing would complete the piece. The brass backing would be suitable for advertising purposes. The resulting piece was about the size of a quarter, but much lighter in weight. The stamps placed in the new encased postage were the 1c, 3c, 5c, 10c, 12c, 24c, 30c and 90c stamps of the 1861 issue. Of course, Gault sold his encased postage at a small markup over the value of the stamp enclosed and the cost of production.

On August 21, 1862, the government issued postage currency in 5c, 10c, 25c and 50c denominations, and fractional currency was issued in 1863. These policies, plus the increased production of brass and copper-nickel coinage in 1863, effectively ended Gault's enterprise. Still, encased postage proved very popular, because it solved the major problems of stamp damage and the necessity of opening stamp envelopes to count the contents. At least 30 companies took advantage of the advertising possibilities and had their ads stamped on the brass backing. Perhaps $50,000 or a little more in encased postage eventually was sold and circulated, not nearly enough by itself to solve the nation's small change crisis. Of the approximately 750,000 pieces sold, only 3,500-7,000 are believed to have survived for collectors.

Values are for very fine examples with mica intact, although signs of circulation and handling are to be expected.

Grading encompasses three areas: 1. Case will show signs of wear or handling and signs of original toning. 2. Mica will be intact with no pieces missing. 3. Stamp will be fresh with no signs of toning or wrinkling.

Examples that came with silvered cases and still have some or all of the original silvering will sell for more than the values shown.

The Eight Stamps of the 1861 Issue Used for Encased Postage

Aerated Bread Co., New York

EP1	1c	*7,000.*
EP1A	5c	*15,000.*

No. EP1A is unique.

Ayer's Cathartic Pills, Lowell, Mass.

Varieties with long and short arrows below legend occur on all denominations.

EP2	1c	500.
EP3	3c	425.
EP4	5c	1,000.
EP5	10c	1,000.
EP6	12c	2,500.
EP7	24c	*3,500.*

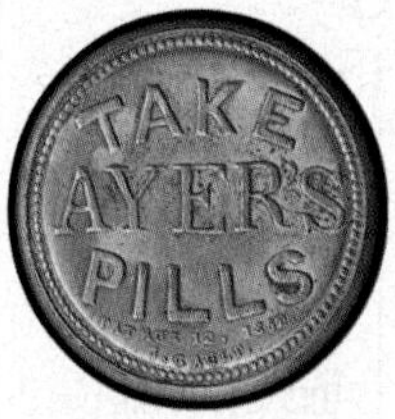

Take Ayer's Pills

EP8	1c	500.
EP9	3c	400.
EP10	5c	1,000.
	a. Ribbed frame	*3,000.*
EP11	10c	1,250.
	a. Ribbed frame	*5,000.*
EP12	12c	2,500.
EP12A	30c	*5,000.*

Nos. EP11a and EP12A each are unique.

Ayer's Sarsaparilla

Three varieties: "AYER'S" small, medium or large. Example illustrated is the medium variety.

EP13	1c medium "Ayer's"	500.
	a. Small	750.
EP15	3c medium "Ayer's"	400.
	a. Small	650.
	b. Large	450.
	c. Ribbed frame, medium	2,000.
EP16	5c medium "Ayer's"	2,000.
	a. Large	1,500.
EP17	10c medium "Ayer's"	550.
	a. Ribbed frame, medium	1,750.
	b. Small	1,250.
	c. Large	1,100.
EP18	12c medium "Ayer's"	2,250.
	a. Small	2,750.
EP19	24c medium "Ayer's"	1,900.
EP20	30c medium "Ayer's"	*4,500.*

Bailey & Co., Philadelphia

EP21	1c	1,100.
EP22	3c	1,200.
EP23	5c	*2,250.*
EP24	10c	*2,250.*
EP25	12c	*3,000.*

"FANCYGOODS" as one word

"FANCY GOODS" as two words

Joseph L. Bates, Boston

EP26	1c one word	450.
a.	Two words	600.
EP27	3c one word	2,000.
a.	Two words	1,000.
EP28	5c two words	1,250.
a.	One word	1,500.
b.	Ribbed frame, one word	*2,750.*
EP29	10c two words	1,750.
a.	One word	1,500.
b.	Ribbed frame, one word	*2,500.*
EP30	12c two words	*4,000.*

Brown's Bronchial Troches

EP31	1c	2,250.
EP32	3c	650.
EP33	5c	450.
EP34	10c	1,000.
EP35	12c	*2,750.*
EP36	24c	*3,250.*
EP37	30c	*4,000.*

F. Buhl & Co., Detroit

EP38	1c	*2,750.*
EP39	3c	*9,000.*
EP40	5c	*2,000.*
EP41	10c	1,750.
EP42	12c	*6,000.*
EP43	24c	*5,750.*

No. EP39 is unique.

Burnett's Cocoaine Kalliston

EP44	1c	750.
EP45	3c	750.
EP46	5c	650.
EP47	10c	700.
EP48	12c	*3,750.*
EP49	24c	*5,000.*
EP50	30c	*4,000.*
EP51	90c	*7,500.*

Burnett's Cooking Extracts

EP52	1c	450.
EP53	3c	500.
EP54	5c	500.
EP55	10c	750.
a.	Ribbed frame	*4,000.*
EP56	12c	*2,000.*
EP57	24c	*5,000.*
EP58	30c	*5,500.*
EP58A	90c	*5,500.*

No. EP58A is unique.

A. M. Claflin, Hopkinton, Mass.

EP59	1c	*11,000.*
EP60	3c	—
EP61	5c	*15,000.*
EP62	10c	*7,500.*
EP63	12c	*16,000.*

No. EP60 is unique.

H. A. Cook, Evansville, Ind.

EP64	5c	*4,000.*
EP65	10c	*3,000.*

Dougan, Hatter, New York

EP66	1c	*2,500.*
EP67	3c	*2,500.*
EP68	5c	*3,750.*
EP69	10c	*3,750.*

Drake's Plantation Bitters

EP70	1c	500.
EP71	3c	500.
EP72	5c	600.
a.	Ribbed frame	*2,500.*
EP73	10c	650.
a.	Ribbed frame	*2,500.*
EP74	12c	*2,000.*
EP75	24c	*3,500.*
EP76	30c	*3,500.*
EP77	90c	*11,000.*

Ellis, McAlpin & Co., Cincinnati

EP78	1c	—
EP79	3c	*2,250.*
EP80	5c	1,250.
EP81	10c	1,100.
EP82	12c	*3,500.*
EP83	24c	*2,750.*

Specialists have questioned the existence of No. EP78. The editors would like to see authenticated evidence of this listing.

G. G. Evans, Philadelphia

EP84	1c	1,250.
EP85	3c	1,500.
EP86	5c	—
EP87	10c	*7,000.*

Gage Bros. & Drake, Tremont House, Chicago

EP88	1c	1,200.
EP89	3c	600.
EP90	5c	750.
EP91	10c	1,100.
a.	Ribbed frame	*4,000.*
EP92	12c	*3,000.*

Only one example of No. EP91a is available to collectors.

J. Gault

EP93	1c	600.
a.	Ribbed frame	—
EP95	3c	600.
a.	Ribbed frame	1,400.
EP96	5c	350.
a.	Ribbed frame	600.
EP97	10c	750.
a.	Ribbed frame	650.
EP98	12c	900.
a.	Ribbed frame	*2,500.*
EP99	24c	1,850.
a.	Ribbed frame	*2,750.*
EP100	30c	*2,750.*
a.	Ribbed frame	*3,750.*
EP101	90c	*9,000.*

L. C. Hopkins & Co., Cincinnati

EP102	1c	*2,500.*
EP103	3c	*5,500.*
EP104	5c	*7,000.*
EP105	10c	*6,000.*

Hunt & Nash, Irving House, New York

EP106	1c	2,000.
EP107	3c	2,000.
a.	Ribbed frame	3,000.
EP108	5c	900.
a.	Ribbed frame	950.
EP109	10c	1,400.
a.	Ribbed frame	1,000.
EP110	12c	2,000.
a.	Ribbed frame	3,000.
EP111	24c	3,750.
a.	Ribbed frame	4,500.
EP112	30c	6,000.

No. EP112 is unique.

Kirkpatrick & Gault, New York

EP113	1c	500.
EP114	3c	700.
EP115	5c	500.
EP116	10c	500.
EP117	12c	1,250.
EP118	24c	*1,750.*
EP119	30c	*2,750.*
EP120	90c	*10,000.*

Lord & Taylor, New York

EP121	1c	1,250.
EP122	3c	1,500.
EP123	5c	1,100.
EP124	10c	1,250.
EP125	12c	*2,500.*
EP126	24c	*2,750.*
EP127	30c	*3,750.*
EP128	90c	*10,000.*

Mendum's Family Wine Emporium, New York

EP129	1c	1,000.
EP130	3c	1,200.
EP131	5c	1,500.
EP132	10c	*3,000.*
a.	Ribbed frame	*2,750.*
EP133	12c	*3,500.*

B. F. Miles, Peoria

EP134	1c	*25,000.*
EP135	5c	*15,000.*

John W. Norris, Chicago

EP136	1c	*3,750.*
EP137	3c	*3,750.*
EP138	5c	*3,250.*
EP139	10c	*3,500.*

"INSURANCE" Curved

"INSURANCE" Straight

North America Life Insurance Co., N. Y.

EP140	1c Curved	475.
a.	Straight	525.
EP141	3c Straight	800.
a.	Curved	1,750.
EP142	5c Straight	675.
a.	Straight, ribbed frame	1,100.
b.	Curved	*3,000.*
EP143	10c Straight	900.
a.	Straight, ribbed frame	*3,250.*
b.	Curved	1,750.
c.	Curved, ribbed frame	*2,250.*
EP144	12c Straight	*2,500.*
a.	Curved	*3,500.*

No. EP142b is unique. Nos. EP143a and EP144a each may be unique.

Pearce, Tolle & Holton, Cincinnati

EP145	1c	*3,250.*
EP146	3c	*3,000.*
EP147	5c	*3,000.*
EP148	10c	*7,000.*
EP149	12c	*4,250.*
EP150	24c	—

No. EP149 is unique.

The existence of No. EP150 has been questioned by specialists. The editors would like to see authenticated evidence of its existence.

Sands Ale

EP151	5c	*3,750*
EP152	10c	*4,500*
EP153	12c	—
EP154	30c	—

No. EP154 is unique. The case of the known example has been opened. It is possible that the 30c stamp has been substituted for the original stamp and/or the mica has been replaced.

Schapker & Bussing, Evansville, Ind.

EP155	1c	2,000
EP156	3c	1,750.
EP157	5c	850
EP158	10c	750.
EP159	12c	*5,000.*

John Shillito & Co., Cincinnati

EP160	1c	3,000.
EP161	3c	1,100.
EP162	5c	600.
EP163	10c	950.
EP164	12c	*5,500.*

S. Steinfeld, New York

EP165	1c	*3,750.*
EP166	5c	*7,000.*
EP167	10c	*6,000.*
EP168	12c	*6,000.*

N. G. Taylor & Co., Philadelphia

EP169	1c	*3,700.*
EP170	3c	*3,500.*
EP171	5c	*3,250.*
EP172	10c	*3,500.*
EP173	12c	*3,750.*

No. EP173 is unique.

Weir and Larminie, Montreal

EP174 1c		*4,000.*
EP175 3c		*15,000.*
EP176 5c		*4,250.*
EP177 10c		*3,000.*

White, the Hatter, New York

EP178 1c		*3,750.*
EP179 3c		*2,750.*
EP180 5c		*5,000.*
EP181 10c		*5,000.*

POSTAGE CURRENCY

Small coins disappeared from circulation in 1861-62 as cash was hoarded. To ease business transactions, merchants issued notes of credit, promises to pay, tokens, store cards, etc. U.S. Treasurer Francis E. Spinner made a substitute for small currency by affixing postage stamps, singly and in multiples, to Treasury paper. He arranged with the Post office to replace worn stamps with new when necessary.

The next step was to print the stamps on Treasury paper. On July 17, 1862, Congress authorized the issue of such "Postage Currency." It remained in use until May 27, 1863. It was not money, but a means of making stamps negotiable.

On Oct. 10, 1863 a second issue was released. These, and the later three issues, did not show stamps and are called Fractional Currency. In 1876 Congress authorized the minting of silver coins to redeem the outstanding fractional currency.

Values quoted are for notes in crisp, new condition, not creased or worn.
Creased or worn notes sell for 25 percent to 75 percent less.
Items valued with a dash are believed to be unique.

Illustrations reduced.

Front Engraved and Printed by the National Bank Note Co.
Back Engraved and Printed in Black by The American Bank Note Co.
"A B Co." on Back

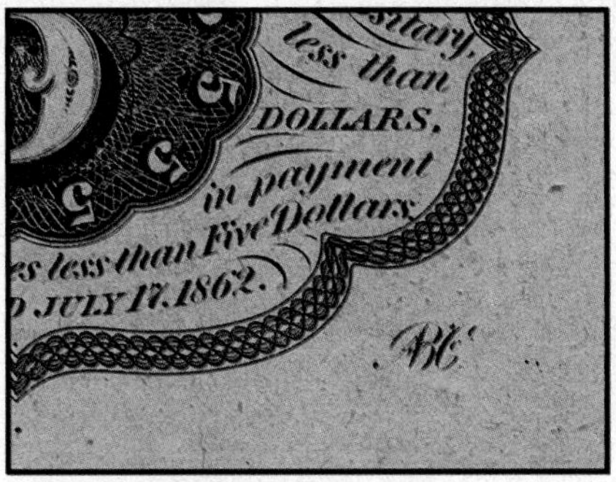

"ABCo." imprint, lower right corner of back (#1-8)

1862, Aug. 21

Perforated Edges-Perf. 12

PC1	5c Bust of Jefferson on 5c stamp, brown	190.00
	a. Inverted back	*950.00*
PC2	10c Bust of Washington on 10c stamp, green	160.00
PC3	25c Five 5c stamps, brown	240.00
PC4	50c Five 10c stamps, green	290.00
	a. Inverted back	*950.00*

Imperforate Edges

PC5	5c Bust of Jefferson on 5c stamp	75.00
	a. Inverted back	*525.00*
PC6	10c Bust of Washington on 10c stamp	75.00
	a. Inverted back	*675.00*
PC7	25c Five 5c stamps	135.00
	a. Inverted back	*600.00*
PC8	50c Five 10c stamps	160.00
	a. Inverted back	*750.00*

No. PC8 exists perforated 14, privately produced.

Front and Back Engraved and Printed by the the National Bank Note Co.

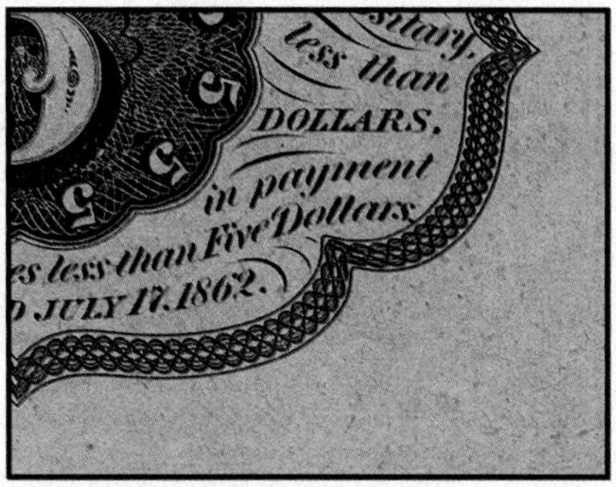

Without "A B Co." on Back

Perforated Edges-Perf. 12

PC9	5c Bust of Jefferson on 5c stamp	230.00
	a. Inverted back	—
PC10	10c Bust of Washington on 10c stamp	250.00
	a. Inverted back	—
PC11	25c Five 5c stamps	340.00
	a. Inverted back	*1,100.*
PC12	50c Five 10c stamps	450.00
	a. Inverted back	—

Imperforate Edges

PC13	5c Bust of Jefferson on 5c stamp	210.00
	a. Inverted back	—
PC14	10c Bust of Washington on 10c stamp	320.00
	a. Inverted back	*1,100.*
PC15	25c Five 5c stamps	425.00
PC16	50c Five 10c stamps	750.00
	a. Inverted back	—

CONFEDERATE STATES OF AMERICA

3¢ 1861 POSTMASTERS' PROVISIONALS

With the secession of South Carolina from the Union on Dec. 20, 1860, a new era began in U.S. history as well as its postal history. Other Southern states quickly followed South Carolina's lead, which in turn led to the formation of the provisional government of the Confederate States of America on Feb. 4, 1861.

President Jefferson Davis' cabinet was completed Mar. 6, 1861, with the acceptance of the position of Postmaster General by John H. Reagan of Texas. The provisional government had already passed regulations that required payment for postage in cash and that effectively carried over the U.S. 3c rate until the new Confederate Post Office Department took over control of the system.

Soon after entering on his duties, Reagan directed the postmasters in the Confederate States and in the newly seceded states to "continue the performance of their duties as such, and render all accounts and pay all moneys (sic) to the order of the Government of the U.S. as they have heretofore done, until the Government of the Confederate States shall be prepared to assume control of its postal affairs."

As coinage was becoming scarce, postal patrons began having problems buying individual stamps or paying for letters individually, especially as stamp stocks started to run short in certain areas. Even though the U.S. Post Office Department was technically in control of the postal system and southern postmasters were operating under Federal authority, the U.S.P.O. was hesitant in re-supplying seceded states with additional stamps and stamped envelopes.

The U.S. government had made the issuance of postmasters' provisionals illegal many years before, but the southern postmasters had to do what they felt was necessary to allow patrons to pay for postage and make the system work. Therefore, a few postmasters took it upon themselves to issue provisional stamps in the 3c rate then in effect. Interestingly, these were stamps and envelopes that the U.S. government did not recognize as legal, but they did do postal duty unchallenged in the Confederate States. Yet the proceeds were to be remitted to the U.S. government in Washington! Six authenticated postmasters' provisionals in the 3c rate have been recorded.

On May 13, 1861, Postmaster General Reagan issued his proclamation "assuming control and direction of postal service within the limits of the Confederate States of America on and after the first day of June," with new postage rates and regulations. The Federal government suspended operations in the Confederate States (except for western Virginia and the seceding state of Tennessee) by a proclamation issued by Postmaster General Montgomery Blair on May 27, 1861, effective from May 31, 1861, and June 10 for western and middle Tennessee. As Tennessee did not join the Confederacy until July 2, 1861, the unissued 3c Nashville provisional was produced in a state that was in the process of seceding, while the other provisionals were used in the Confederacy before the June 1 assumption of control of postal service by the Confederate States of America.

HILLSBORO, N.C.

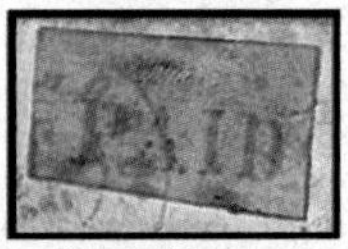

A1

Handstamped Adhesive

1AX1 A1 3c **bluish black,** on cover —

No. 1AX1 is unique. This is the same handstamp as used for No. 39X1. 3c usage is determined from the May 27, 1861 circular date stamp.

Cancellation: black town.

JACKSON, MISS.

E1

Handstamped Envelope

2AXU1 E1 3c **black** *2,500.*

See Nos. 43XU1-43XU4.

MADISON COURT HOUSE, FLA.

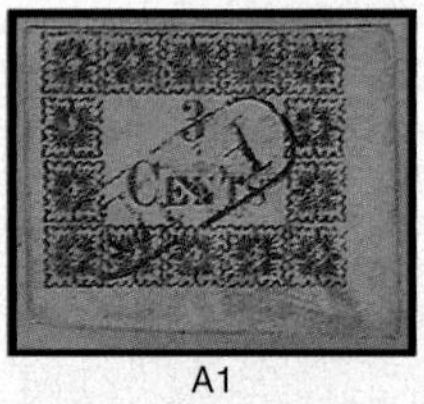

A1

"CNETS"

Typeset Adhesive

3AX1 A1 3c **gold**	—	*10,000.*
On cover		*65,000.*
a. "CNETS"		*14,000.*

No. 3AX1 on cover and No. 3AX1a are each unique.

Cancellations: black town, oblong paid, ms "Paid in Money," manuscript.

See No. 137XU1.

NASHVILLE, TENN.

A1

Typeset Adhesive (5 varieties)

4AX1 A1 3c **carmine**	200.
Horizontal strip of 5 showing all varieties	1,500.

No. 4AX1 was prepared by Postmaster McNish with the U.S. rate, but the stamp was never issued.

Fakes exist of the horizontal strips. Expertization is recommended.

See Nos. 61X2-61XU2.

SELMA, ALA.

E1

Handstamped Envelope

5AXU1 E1 3c **black** *2,500.*

See Nos. 77XU1-77XU3.

TUSCUMBIA, ALA.

E1

Handstamped Envelope, impression at upper right

6AXU1 E1 3c **dull red,** *buff* *17,500.*

No. 6AXU1 also exists with a 3c 1857 stamp affixed at upper right over the provisional handstamp, tied by black circular "TUSCUMBIA, ALA." town postmark. Value $15,000.

See Nos. 84XU1-84XU3.

CONFEDERATE POSTMASTERS' PROVISIONALS

These stamps and envelopes were issued by individual postmasters generally during the interim between June 1, 1861, when the use of United States stamps stopped in the Confederacy, and October 16, 1861, when the first Confederate Government stamps were issued. They were occasionally issued at later periods, especially in Texas, when regular issues of government stamps were unavailable.

Canceling stamps of the post offices were often used to produce envelopes, some of which were supplied in advance by private citizens. These envelopes and other stationery therefore may be found in a wide variety of papers, colors, sizes and shapes, including patriotic and semi-official types. It is often difficult to determine whether the impression made by the canceling stamp indicates provisional usage or merely postage paid at the time the letter was deposited in the post office. Occasionally the same mark was used for both purposes.

The *press-printed* **provisional envelopes are in a different category. They were produced in quantity, using envelopes procured in advance by the postmaster, such as those of Charleston, Lynchburg, Memphis, etc.** *The* **press-printed** *envelopes are listed and valued on all known papers.*

The **handstamped** *provisional envelopes are listed and valued according to type and variety of handstamp, but not according to paper. Many exist on such a variety of papers that they defy accurate, complete listing. The value of a handstamped provisional envelope is determined primarily by the clarity of the markings and its overall condition and attractiveness, rather than the type of paper.*

All handstamped provisional envelopes, when used, should also show the postmark of the town of issue.

Most handstamps are impressed at top right, although they exist from some towns in other positions.

Many illustrations in this section are reduced in size.

Values for envelopes are for entires. Values for stamps of provisional issues are for examples with little or no gum; original gum over a large portion of the stamp will increase the value substantially.

ABERDEEN, MISS.

E1

Handstamped Envelopes

1XU1	E1	5c	**black**		6,000.
a.		10c (ms.) on 5c	**black**		*12,500.*

No. 1XU1a is unique.

ABINGDON, VA.

E1

Handstamped Envelopes

2XU1	E1	2c	**black**		*11,000.*
2XU2	E1	5c	**black**		1,400.
			On patriotic cover		*3,000.*
2XU3	E1	10c	**black**	*2,200.*	*3,500.*

The unused No. 2XU3 is a unique mint example, and the value represents the price realized in a 1997 auction sale. No. 2XU3 used also is unique.

ALBANY, GA.

E1

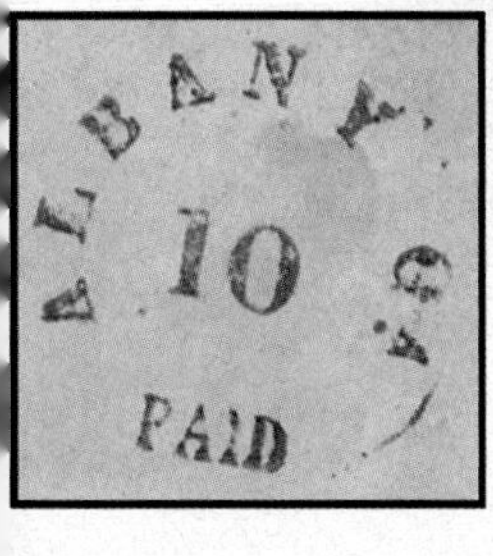

E2

E3

E4

Handstamped Envelopes

3XU1	E1	5c	**greenish blue**		900.
			On patriotic cover		—
3XU2	E2	10c	**greenish blue**		*2,000.*
a.		10c on 5c	**greenish blue**		*3,500.*
3XU5	E3	5c	**greenish blue**		—
3XU6	E4	10c	**greenish blue**		*2,500.*

The "10" in the No. 3XU2 marking is larger than the "10" in the No. 3XU3 marking.

Only one example each recorded of Nos. 3XU2, 3XU2a and 3XU6. No. 3XU2a is the unique Confederate example of one provisional marking revaluing another.

The existence of No. 3XU5 is in question. The editors would like to see an authenticated example of this marking.

ANDERSON COURT HOUSE, S.C.

E1

Handstamped Envelopes

4XU1	E1	5c	**black**	500.	2,250.
4XU2	E1	10c (ms.)	**black**		*3,000.*

ATHENS, GA

A1 (Type I)

A1 (Type II)

Typographed Adhesives
(from woodcuts of two types)

Pairs, both horizontal and vertical, always show one of each type.

5X1	A1	5c	**purple** (shades)	1,000.	1,500.
			Pair	—	4,000.
			On cover		2,500.
			Pair on cover		5,500.
			Strip of 4 on cover (horiz.)		*10,000.*
a.			Tete beche pair (vertical)		*7,500.*
			Tete beche pair on cover		*27,500.*
5X2	A1	5c	**red**	—	4,750.
			On cover		*15,000.*
			Pair on cover		—

Cancellations in black: grid, town, "PAID."

The colorless ornaments in the four corners of No. 5X2 were recut making them wider than those in No. 5X1.

Dangerous fakes exist of Nos. 5X1 and 5X2. Certificates of authenticity from recognized committees are strongly recommended.

The existence of a pair on cover of No. 5X2 is in question. The editors would like to see an example of this usage.

ATLANTA, GA.

E1

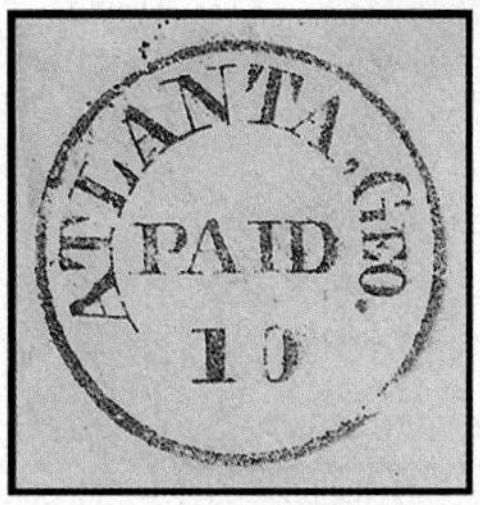

E2

Handstamped Envelopes

6XU1	E1	5c	**red**		*3,500.*
6XU2	E1	5c	**black**	175.	700.
			On patriotic cover		*3,500.*
a.		10c on 5c	**black**		*1,500.*
			On patriotic cover		—
6XU4	E2	2c	**black**		*3,000.*
6XU5	E2	5c	**black**		1,500.
			On patriotic cover		3,500.
a.		10c on 5c	**black**		*2,500.*
6XU6	E2	10c	**black**		950.
			On patriotic cover		—

Only one example recorded of No. 6XU1.

E3

Handstamped Envelopes

6XU8 E3 5c **black** 3,500.
6XU9 E3 10c **black** ("10" upright) 2,750.

Only one example recorded of No. 6XU8.

AUSTIN, MISS.

E1

Press-printed Envelope (typeset)

8XU1 E1 5c **red,** *amber* *75,000.*

One example recorded.

Cancellation: black "Paid."

AUSTIN, TEX.

E1a

Handstamped Adhesive

9X1 E1a 10c **black** —
On cover, uncanceled *1,500.*
On cover, tied —

Only one example of No. 9X1 tied on cover is recorded.

Handstamped Envelope

9XU1 E1a 10c **black** 1,750.

Cancellation on Nos. 9X1 and 9XU1: black town.

AUTAUGAVILLE, ALA.

E1

E2

Handstamped Envelopes

10XU1 E1 5c **black** *10,000.*
10XU2 E2 5c **black** *12,500.*

No. 10XU2 is unique.

BALCONY FALLS, VA.

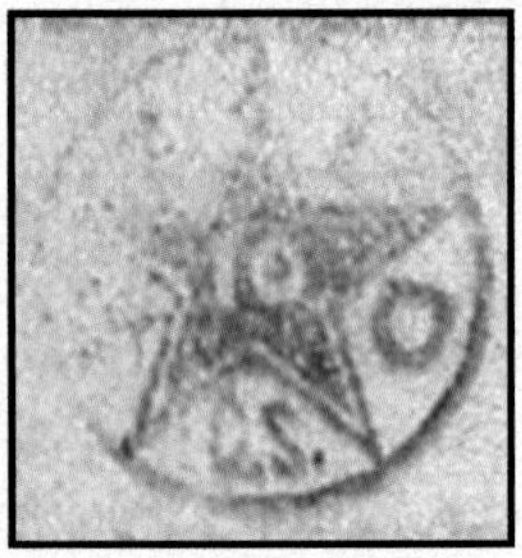

E1

Handstamped Envelope

122XU1 E1 10c **blue** *2,000.*

BARNWELL COURT HOUSE, S. C.

E1

Handstamped Envelope

123XU1 E1 5c **black** *1,750.*

These are two separate handstamps.

BATON ROUGE, LA.

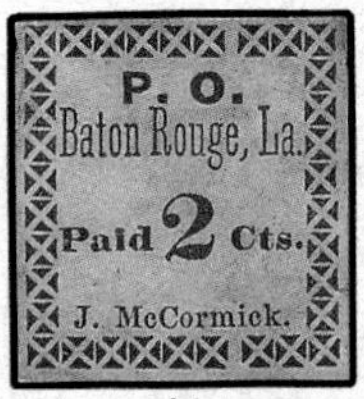

A1

A2

Typeset Adhesives

Ten varieties of each

11X1 A1 2c **green** *8,000.* *5,000.*
On cover *20,000.*
a. "McCcrmick" *37,500.* *35,000.*
On cover —
11X2 A2 5c **green & carmine** (Maltese cross border) 1,500. 1,400.
On cover 3,000.
Strip of 3 *5,000.*
Strip of 5 *22,500.*
Canceled in New Orleans, on cover *20,000.*
a. "McCcrmick" — *2,000.*
On cover *7,000.*

Only one example each is recorded of No. 11X1a unused, used and on cover.

The "Canceled in New Orleans" examples entered the mails in New Orleans after having been placed (uncanceled) on riverboats in Baton Rouge. Two such covers are recorded.

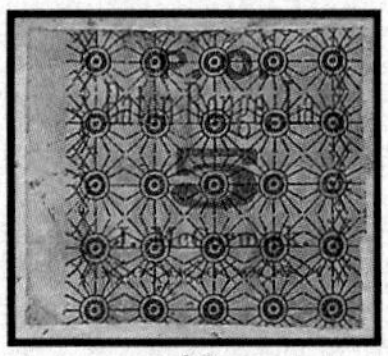

A3

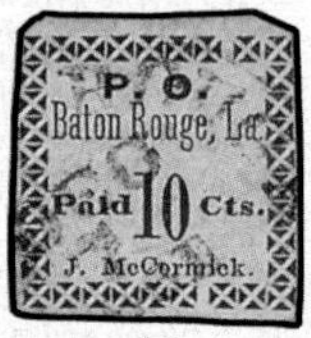

A4

Ten varieties of each

11X3 A3 5c **green & carmine** (crisscross border) *4,500.* *2,750.*
On cover *10,000.*
a. "McCcrmick" *3,500.*
11X4 A4 10c **blue** *14,000.*
On cover *75,000.*

No. 11X4 on cover is unique.

Cancellation on Nos. 11X1-11X4: black town.

BEAUMONT, TEX.

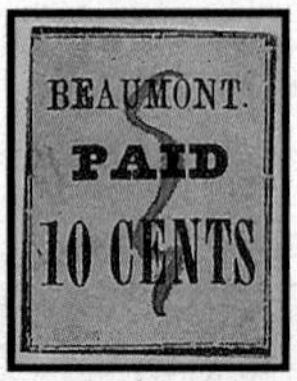

A1

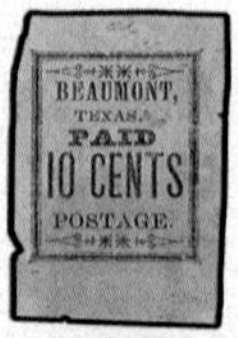

A2

Typeset Adhesives

Several varieties of each

12X1 A1 10c **black,** *yellow* *12,500.*
On cover *55,000.*
12X2 A1 10c **black,** *pink* *12,500.*
On cover *30,000.*
12X3 A2 10c **black,** *yellow,* on cover *90,000.*

One example recorded of No. 12X3.

Cancellations: black pen; black town.

BLUFFTON, S. C.

E1

Handstamped Envelope

124XU1 E1 5c **black** *8,000.*

Only one example recorded of No. 124XU1.

BRIDGEVILLE, ALA.

A1

Handstamped Adhesive in black within red pen-ruled squares

13X1 A1 5c **black & red,** pair on cover *20,000.*

Cancellation is black pen.

CAMDEN, S. C.

E1

E2

Handstamped Envelopes

125XU1 E1 5c **black** *4,500.*
125XU2 E2 10c **black** *450.*

No. 125XU2 unused was privately carried and is addressed but has no postal markings. No. 125XU2 is indistinguishable from a handstamp paid cover when used.

CANTON, MISS.

E1

"P" in star is initial of Postmaster William Priestly.

Handstamped Envelopes

14XU1 E1 5c **black** 2,750.
a. 10c (ms.) on 5c **black** 5,000.

CAROLINA CITY, N. C.

E1

Handstamped Envelope

18XU1	E1	5c **black**	*3,500.*

CARTERSVILLE, GA.

E1

Handstamped Envelope

26XU1	E1	(5c) **red**	*1,250.*

CHAPEL HILL, N. C.

E1

Handstamped Envelope

5XU1	E1	5c **black**	3,250.
		On patriotic cover	5,000.

CHARLESTON, S. C.

A1

E1

E2

Lithographed Adhesive

16X1	A1	5c **blue**	1,200.	850.
		Pair	2,500.	2,200.
		On cover		*2,500.*
		On patriotic cover		*5,000.*
		Pair, on cover		*5,000.*
		On cover with No. 112XU1		—
		Used on cover with C.S.A. 5c #6 to make 10c rate		—

Values are for stamps showing parts of the outer frame lines on at least 3 sides.

Cancellation: black town (two types).

Press-printed Envelopes (typographed from woodcut)

6XU1	E1	5c **blue**	1,250.	*4,000.*
16XU2	E1	5c **blue,** *amber*	1,250.	*4,000.*
16XU3	E1	5c **blue,** *orange*	1,250.	*4,000.*
16XU4	E1	5c **blue,** *buff*	1,250.	*4,000.*
16XU5	E1	5c **blue,** *blue*	1,250.	*4,000.*
16XU6	E2	10c **blue,** *orange*		*77,500.*

The No. 16XU6 used entire is unique; value based on 1997 auction sale.

Beware of fakes of the E1 design.

Handstamped Cut Square

16XU7	E2	10c **black**	*3,000.*

There is only one example of No. 16XU7. It is a cutout, not an entire. It may not have been mailed from Charleston, and it may not have paid postage.

Beware of fakes of the E1 design.

CHARLOTTESVILLE, VA.

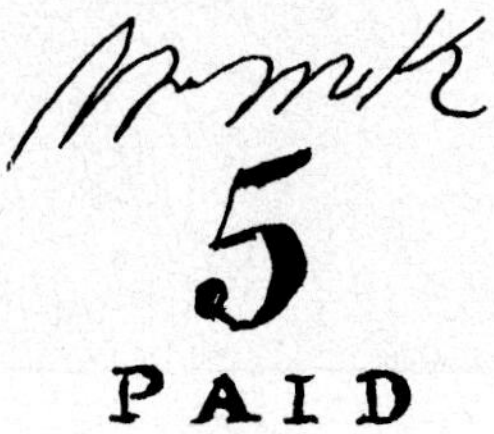

E1

Handstamped Envelopes, Manuscript Initials

127XU1	E1	5c **blue**	—
127XU2	E1	10c **blue**	—

CHATTANOOGA, TENN.

E1

Handstamped Envelopes

17XU2	E1	5c **black**		2,500.
17XU3	E1	5c on 2c **black**	*4,250.*	

CHRISTIANSBURG, VA.

E1

Handstamped Envelopes

Impressed at top right

99XU1	E1	5c **black**	*2,250.*
99XU2	E1	5c **blue**	*2,000.*
99XU4	E1	5c **green** on U.S. envelope No. U27	*4,500.*
99XU5	E1	10c **blue**	*3,500.*

The absence of 5c and 10c handstamped paid markings from this town suggests that Nos. 99XU1-99XU5 were used as both provisional and handstamped paid markings.

COLAPARCHEE, GA.

E1

Control

Handstamped Envelope

119XU1	E1	5c **black**	*3,500.*

There are only two recorded examples of No. 119XU1, and both are used with general issue stamp from Savannah.

COLUMBIA, S. C.

E1

E2

Handstamped Envelopes

18XU1	E1	5c **blue**	550.	900.
		Used on cover with C.S.A. 5c #1 or #1c to make 10c rate		*3,000.*
		Used on cover with C.S.A. 5c #7 to make 10c rate		*7,500.*
18XU2	E1	5c **black**	600.	1,250.
18XU3	E1	10c on 5c **blue**		*3,500.*

Three types of "PAID," one in circle

18XU4	E2	5c **blue,** seal on front	*2,500.*
a.		Seal on back	*1,250.*
18XU5	E2	10c **blue,** seal on back	*2,750.*

Three types of "PAID" for Nos. 18XU4-18XU5, one in circle.

Circular Seal similar to E2, 27mm diameter

18XU6	E2	5c **blue** (seal on back)	*4,000.*

COLUMBIA, TENN.

E1

Handstamped Envelope

113XU1	E1	5c **red**	*7,000.*

One example recorded.

COLUMBUS, GA.

E1

Handstamped Envelopes

19XU1	E1	5c **blue**	800.
19XU2	E1	10c **red**	*2,250.*

COURTLAND, ALA.

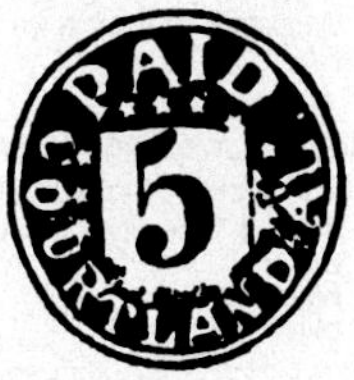

E1

Handstamped Envelopes (from woodcut)

103XU2	E1	5c **red**	*10,000.*

DALTON, GA

E1

Handstamped Envelopes

20XU1	E1	5c **black**	600.
a.		Denomination omitted (5c rate)	*725.*
b.		10c (ms.) on 5c **black**	1,500.
20XU2	E1	10c **black**	800.

DANVILLE, VA.

A1

E1

E2

E3

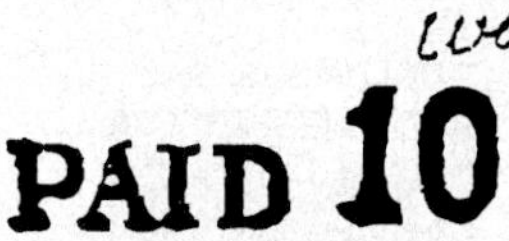

E4

Typeset Adhesive
Wove Paper

21X1	A1	5c	**red**	*5,500.*
			On cover	—
			Cut to shape	*4,000.*
			On cover, cut to shape	*10,000.*

Two varieties known.

Cancellation: blue town.

Laid Paper

21X2	A1	5c	**red**	*10,000.*

Cancellation: black town.
No. 21X2 is unique.

Press-printed Envelopes (typographed)
Two types: "SOUTHERN" in straight or curved line
Impressed (usually) at top left

21XU1	E1	5c	**black**	*6,000.*
21XU2	E1	5c	**black,** *amber*	—
21XU3	E1	5c	**black,** *dark buff*	*6,000.*

The existence of No. 21XU2 is in question. The editors would like to see authenticated evidence of its existence.

Unissued 10c envelopes (type E1, in red) are known. All recorded examples are envelopes on which added stamps paid the postage.

Handstamped Envelopes

21XU3A	E4	5c	**black** (ms "WBP" initials)	*1,000.*
21XU4	E2	10c	**black**	*2,500.*
21XU6	E3	10c	**black**	*2,750.*
21XU7	E4	10c	**black** (ms "WBP" initials)	—

Types E2 and E3 both exist on one cover.

DEMOPOLIS, ALA.

E1

Handstamped Envelopes, Signature in ms.

22XU1	E1	5c	**black** ("Jno. Y. Hall")	*3,500.*
22XU2	E1	5c	**black** ("J. Y. Hall")	*3,500.*
22XU3	E1	5c	(ms.) **black** ("J. Y. Hall")	*4,000.*

EATONTON, GA.

E1

E2

Handstamped Envelopes

23XU1	E1	5c	**black**	*3,000.*
23XU2	E2	5c + 5c	**black**	*5,000.*

EMORY, VA.

A1

Handstamped Adhesives ("PAID" and "5" in circle on selvage of U.S. 1c 1857 issue)
Perf. 15 on three sides

24X1	A1	5c	**blue,** on cover, ms. tied	*15,000.*

Also known with "5" above "PAID."

Cancellation: blue town.

E1

E2

Handstamped Envelopes

24XU1	E1	5c	**blue**	*2,000.*
24XU2	E2	10c	**blue**	*10,000.*

Only one example recorded of No. 24XU2.

FINCASTLE, VA.

E1

Press-printed Envelope (typeset)
Impressed at top right

104XU1	E1	10c	**black**	*20,000.*

One example recorded.

FORSYTH, GA.

E1

Handstamped Envelope

120XU1	E1	10c	**black**	*1,750.*

Only one example recorded of No. 120XU1.

FRANKLIN, N. C.

E1

Press-printed Envelope (typeset)
Impressed at top right

25XU1	E1	5c	**blue,** *buff*	*30,000.*

The one known envelope shows black circular Franklin postmark with manuscript date.

FRAZIERSVILLE, S. C.

E1

Handstamped Envelope, "5" manuscript

128XU1	E1	5c	**black**	*2,250.*

Only one example recorded of No. 128XU1.

FREDERICKSBURG, VA.

A1

Sheets of 20, two panes of 10 varieties each

Typeset Adhesives
Thin bluish paper

26X1	A1	5c	**blue,** *bluish*	450.	*850.*
			Block of 4	2,250.	
			Sheet of 20	12,500.	
			On cover		*5,000.*
			Pair on cover		*12,000.*
26X2	A1	10c	**red,** *bluish*	1,250.	
			Brown red, *bluish*	1,500.	
			Block of 4	—	

Cancellation: black town.

GAINESVILLE, ALA.

E1

E2

Handstamped Envelopes

27XU1	E1	5c	**black**	*4,500.*
27XU2	E2	10c	("01") **black**	*6,000.*

Postmark spells town name "Gainsville."

GALVESTON, TEX.

E1

Handstamped Envelopes

98XU1	E1	5c	**black**	500.	*1,500.*
98XU2	E1	10c	**black**		*2,000.*

E2

Handstamped Envelopes

3XU3	E2	10c	**black**	550.	*2,400.*
8XU4	E2	20c	**black**		*3,500.*

GASTON, N. C.

E1

Handstamped Envelope

29XU1	E1	5c	**black**	4,500.

Only one example recorded of No. 129XU1.

GEORGETOWN, S. C.

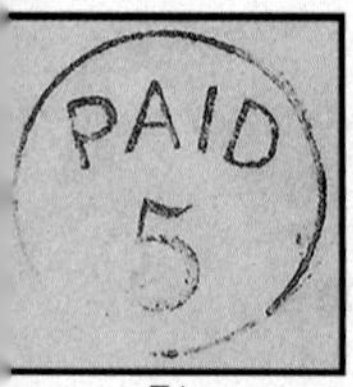

E1 Control

Handstamped Envelope

8XU1	E1	5c	**black**	950.
8XU2	E1	5c	**black**, separate "5" and straightline "PAID" handstamps, control on reverse	*2,000.*

GOLIAD, TEX.

A1 A2

Typeset Adhesives

9X1	A1	5c	**black**		*12,000.*
9X2	A1	5c	**black,** *gray*		*11,500.*
9X3	A1	5c	**black,** *rose*		*12,000.*
			On cover front		*50,000.*
9X4	A1	10c	**black**	—	*12,000.*
9X5	A1	10c	**black,** *rose*		*12,000.*

Type A1 stamps are signed "Clarke-P.M." vertically in black or ed.

9X6	A2	5c	**black,** *gray*	*10,000.*
a.			"GOILAD"	*12,000.*
			Pair, left stamp the error	—
9X7	A2	10c	**black,** *gray*	*12,000.*
			On cover	*25,000.*
a.			"GOILAD"	*15,000.*
			On cover	*30,000.*
9X8	A2	5c	**black,** *dark blue,* on cover	*7,000.*
9X9	A2	10c	**black,** *dark blue*	*20,000.*

Cancellations in black: pen, town, "Paid"

GONZALES, TEX.

Colman & Law were booksellers when John B. Law of the firm) was appointed Postmaster. The firm used small lithographed label on drugs and on the front or ıside of books they sold.

A1

Lithographed Adhesives on colored glazed paper

30X1	A1	(5c)	**gold,** *dark blue,* pair on cover, *1861*	*15,000.*
30X2	A1	(10c)	**gold,** *garnet,* on cover, *1864*	*12,500.*
30X3	A1	(10c)	**gold,** *black,* on cover, *1865*	—

Cancellations: black town, black pen. No. 30X1 must bear double-circle town cancel as validating control. The control was applied to the labels in the sheet before their sale as stamps. When used, the stamps bear an additional Gonzales double-circle postmark.

GREENSBORO, ALA.

E1

E2

Handstamped Envelopes

31XU1	E1	5c	**black**	*3,000.*
31XU2	E1	10c	**black**	*2,750.*
31XU3	E2	10c	**black**	*6,000.*

GREENSBORO, N. C.

E1

Handstamped Envelope

32XU1	E1	10c	**red**	1,250.

GREENVILLE, ALA.

A1 A2

Typeset Adhesives On pinkish surface-colored glazed paper.

33X1	A1	5c	**blue & red**	*25,000.*	
			On cover		*40,000.*
33X2	A2	10c	**red & blue**	—	
			On cover		*40,000.*

Two used examples each are known of Nos. 33X1-33X2, and all are on covers. Covers bear a postmark but it was not used to cancel the stamps.

The former No. 33X1a has been identified as a counterfeit.

GREENVILLE COURT HOUSE, S. C.

E1 

E1a

Control

Handstamped Envelopes (Several types)

34XU1	E1	5c	**black**	*2,000.*
34XU2	E1a	10c	**black**	*2,000.*
a.			20c (ms.) on 10c **black**	*3,000.*

Envelopes must bear the black control on the back.

GREENWOOD DEPOT, VA.

A1

"PAID" Handstamped Adhesive ("PAID" with value and signature in ms.) Laid Paper

35X1	A1	10c	**black,** *gray blue,* uncanceled, on cover	20,000.
			On cover, tied	—

Six examples recorded of No. 35X1, all on covers. One of these is in the British Library collection. Of the remaining five, only one has the stamp tied to the cover.

Cancellation: black town.

GRIFFIN, GA.

E1

Handstamped Envelope

102XU1	E1	5c	**black**	2,250.

GROVE HILL, ALA.

A1

Handstamped Adhesive (from woodcut)

36X1	A1	5c	**black**	—
			On cover, tied	*75,000.*

Two examples are recorded. One is on cover tied by the postmark. The other is canceled by magenta pen on a cover front.

Cancellations: black town, magenta pen.

HALLETTSVILLE, TEX.

A1

Handstamped Adhesive Ruled Letter Paper

37X1	A1	10c	**black,** *gray blue,* on cover	*15,000.*

One example known.

Cancellation: black ms.

HAMBURGH, S. C.

E1

Handstamped Envelope

112XU1 E1 5c **black** *9,000.*
On cover with #16X1 (forwarded) —

HARRISBURGH (Harrisburg), TEX.

E1

Handstamped Envelope

130XU1 E1 5c **black** —

No. 130XU1 is indistinguishable from a handstamp paid cover when used.

HELENA, TEX.

A1

Typeset Adhesives

Several varieties

38X1 A1 5c **black,** *buff* *7,500. 6,000.*
38X2 A1 10c **black,** *gray* *5,000.*

On 10c "Helena" is in upper and lower case italics.
Used examples are valued with small faults or repairs, as all recorded have faults.

Cancellation: black town.

HILLSBORO, N. C.

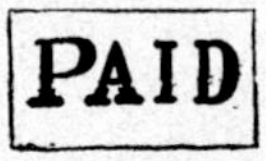

A1

Handstamped Adhesive

39X1 A1 5c **black,** on cover *15,000.*

No. 39X1 is unique.
See 3c 1861 Postmasters' Provisional No. 1AX1.

Cancellation: black town.

Ms./Handstamped Envelope

39XU1 10c "paid 10" in manuscript with undated blue town cancel as control on face —

HOLLANDALE, TEX.

E1

Handstamped Envelope

132XU1 E1 5c **black** —

HOUSTON, TEX.

E1

Handstamped Envelopes

40XU1 E1 5c **red** — 750.
On patriotic cover —
a. 10c (ms.) on 5c **red** *3,000.*
40XU2 E1 10c **red** — *1,500.*
40XU3 E1 10c **black** *2,250.*
40XU4 E1 5c +10c **red** *2,500.*
40XU5 E1 10c +10c **red** *2,500.*

Nos. 40XU2-40XU5 show "TEX" instead of "TXS."

HUNTSVILLE, TEX.

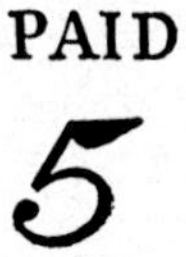

E1

Control

Handstamped Envelope

92XU1 E1 5c **black** *5,000.*

No. 92XU1 exists with "5" outside or within control circle.

INDEPENDENCE, TEX.

A1

Handstamped Adhesives

41X1 A1 10c **black,** *buff,* on cover, uncanceled, cut to shape *20,000.*
41X2 A1 10c **black,** *dull rose,* on cover

With small "10" and "Pd" in manuscript

41X3 A1 10c **black,** *buff,* on cover, uncanceled, cut to shape *32,500.*
On cover, uncanceled, cut square —

No. 41X1 is unique.
All known examples of Nos. 41X1-41X3 are uncanceled on covers with black "INDEPENDANCE TEX." (sic) postmark.
The existence of No. 41X2 has been questioned by specialists. The editors would like to see authenticated evidence of the existence of this item.

ISABELLA, GA.

E1

Handstamped Envelope, "5" Manuscript

133XU1 E1 5c **black** *2,000.*

Only one example recorded of No. 133XU1.

IUKA, MISS.

E1

Handstamped Envelope

42XU1 E1 5c **black** *1,750*
On patriotic cover *4,000*

JACKSON, MISS.

E1a

Handstamped Envelopes

Two types of numeral

43XU1 E1a 5c **black** 750
On patriotic cover 3,000
a. 10c on 5c **black** *2,750*
43XU2 E1a 10c **black** *2,000*
43XU4 E1a 10c on 5c **blue** *2,750*

The 5c also exists on a lettersheet.
See 3c 1861 Postmasters' Provisional No. 2AXU1.

JACKSONVILLE, ALA.

E1

Handstamped Envelope

110XU1 E1 5c **black** — *3,000*

JACKSONVILLE, FLA.

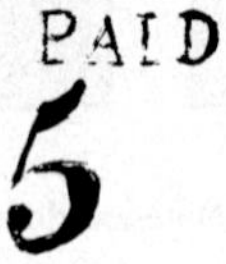

E1

Handstamped Envelope

134XU1 E1 5c **black**

Undated double circle postmark control on reverse.

JETERSVILLE, VA.

A1

Handstamped Adhesive
("5" with ms. "AHA." initials)
Laid Paper

44X1 A1 5c **black,** vertical pair on cover, uncanceled 16,000

Initials are those of Postmaster A. H. Atwood.

Cancellation: black town.

JONESBORO, TENN.

E1

Handstamped Envelopes

45XU1 E1 5c **black** *7,000*
45XU2 E1 5c **dark blue** *7,000*

KINGSTON, GA.

E1

E2

E3

E4

Typeset Envelopes
(design types E1-E2, E4 are handstamps; typeset design E3 probably impressed by hand but possibly press printed)

46XU1 E1 5c **black** 2,250.
46XU2 E2 5c **black** — 3,250.
46XU4 E3 5c **black** —
46XU5 E4 5c **black** *2,000.*

There is only one recorded example of No. 46XU4.

KNOXVILLE, TENN.

A1

Typographed Adhesives
(stereotype from woodcut)
Grayish Laid Paper

47X1 A1 5c **brick red** *1,400.* 1,400.
Manuscript cancel 350.
Horizontal pair *4,000.* *3,000.*
Vertical pair *3,500.*
Vertical strip of 3 *6,500.*
On cover, tied by handstamp *7,000.*
On cover, manuscript cancel *2,100.*
Pair on cover *7,500.*
47X2 A1 5c **carmine** *1,900.* 2,250.
Manuscript cancel 1,000.
Vertical strip of 3 —
On cover, tied by handstamp *7,500.*
On cover, manuscript cancel *2,100.*
47X3 A1 10c **green,** on cover *57,750.*

The #47X3 cover is unique. Value is based on 1997 auction sale.

Cancellations in black: town, bars, pen or pencil.

E1

E2

Press-printed Envelopes (typographed)

47XU1 E1 5c **blue** 750. *2,000.*
47XU2 E1 5c **blue,** *orange* 750. *2,250.*
47XU3 E1 10c **red** (cut to shape) *4,000.*
47XU4 E1 10c **red,** *orange* (cut to shape) *4,000.*

Only one example each recorded of Nos. 47XU3 and 47XU4. Dangerous fakes exist of Nos. 47XU1 and 47XU2.

Handstamped Envelopes

47XU5 E2 5c **black** 750. *1,500.*
On patriotic cover *3,750.*
a. 10c on 5c **black** *3,500.*

Type E2 exists with "5" above or below "PAID."

LA GRANGE, TEX.

E1

Handstamped Envelopes

48XU1 E1 5c **black** — 2,250.
48XU2 E1 10c **black** 3,000.

LAKE CITY, FLA.

E1

Control

Handstamped Envelope

96XU1 E1 10c **black** *2,000.*

Envelopes have black circle control mark, or printed name of E. R. Ives, postmaster, on face or back.

LAURENS COURT HOUSE, S. C.

E1

Handstamped Envelope

116XU1 E1 5c **black** *1,750.*

LENOIR, N. C.

A1

E1

Handstamped Adhesive (from woodcut)
White wove paper with cross-ruled orange lines

49X1 A1 5c **blue & orange** *7,250.* *6,750.*
On cover, pen canceled *12,500.*
On cover, tied by handstamp *25,000.*

Cancellations: blue town, blue "Paid" in circle, black pen.

Handstamped Envelopes

49XU1 A1 5c **blue** *3,500.*
49XU2 A1 10c (5c+5c) **blue** *25,000.*
49XU3 E1 5c **blue** *4,500.*
49XU4 E1 5c **black**

No. 49XU2 is unique. The existence of No. 49XU4 has been questioned. A variety of No. 49XU3 is recorded with two light strikes of the provisional handstamp, one in blue and one in black.

LEXINGTON, MISS.

E1

Handstamped Envelopes

50XU1 E1 5c **black** *5,000.*
50XU2 E1 10c **black** *5,000.*

LEXINGTON, VA.

E1

Handstamped Envelopes

135XU1 E1 5c **blue** *500.*
Used with 5c #6 to make 10c rate *500.*
135XU2 E1 10c **blue** *750.*

Nos. 135XU1-135XU2 by themselves are indistinguishable from a handstamp paid cover when used.

LIBERTY, VA. (and Salem, Va.)

A1

Typeset Adhesive (probably impressed by hand)
Laid Paper

74X1 A1 5c **black,** on cover, uncanceled, with Liberty postmark *35,000.*
On cover, uncanceled, with Salem postmark *40,000.*

Two known on covers with Liberty, Va. postmark; one cover known with the nearby Salem, Va. office postmark.

LIMESTONE SPRINGS, S. C.

A1

Handstamped Adhesive

121X1 A1 5c **black,** *light blue,* on cover *10,000.*
Two on cover *15,000.*
121X2 A1 5c **black,** *white* —
Two on cover *30,000.*

Stamps are cut round or rectangular. Covers are not postmarked.

LIVINGSTON, ALA.

A1

Lithographed Adhesive

51X1 A1 5c **blue**		*14,000.*
On cover		*60,000.*
Pair on cover		*120,000.*

The pair on cover is unique.

Cancellation: black town.

LYNCHBURG, VA.

A1

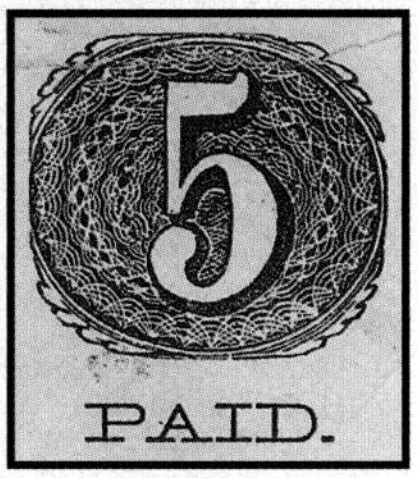

E1

Typographed Adhesive (stereotype from woodcut)

52X1 A1 5c **blue** (shades)	*1,800.*	*1,350.*
Pair		*3,000.*
On cover		*5,000.*
Pair on cover		*20,000.*

Cancellations: black town, blue town.

Press-printed Envelopes (typographed)

Impressed at top right or left

52XU1 E1 5c **black**		*3,000.*
52XU2 E1 5c **black,** *amber*	650.	*3,000.*
52XU3 E1 5c **black,** *buff*		*3,000.*
52XU4 E1 5c **black,** *brown*	900.	*3,000.*
On patriotic cover		—

MACON, GA.

A1

A2

A3

A4

Typeset Adhesives

Several varieties of type A1, 10 of A2, 5 of A3

Wove Paper

53X1 A1 5c **black,** *light blue green* (shades)	900.	700.
On cover		*4,000.*
Pair on cover		*9,000.*
Comma after "OFFICE"	950.	1,100.
Comma after "OFFICE," on cover		*7,500.*

Warning: Dangerous forgeries exist of the normal variety and the Comma after "OFFICE" variety. Certificates of authenticity from recognized committees are strongly recommended.

53X3 A2 5c **black,** *yellow*	2,500.	850.
On cover		*4,750.*
On patriotic cover		*9,000.*
Pair on cover		*8,000.*
53X4 A3 5c **black,** *yellow* (shades)	3,000.	1,400.
On cover		*6,000.*
Pair on cover		*10,000.*
a. Vertical tête bêche pair		—
53X5 A4 2c **black,** *gray green*		—
On cover		*60,000.*

Laid Paper

53X6 A2 5c **black,** *yellow*	*6,000.*	*3,500.*
On cover		*6,000.*
53X7 A3 5c **black,** *yellow*	*6,000.*	
On cover		*9,000.*
53X8 A1 5c **black,** *light blue green*	1,750.	*2,250.*
On cover		*4,500.*

No. 53X4a is unique.

Cancellations: black town, black "PAID" (2 types).

E1

Handstamped Envelope

Two types: "PAID" over "5," "5" over "PAID"

53XU1 E1 5c **black**	250.	575.
On patriotic cover		1,900.

Values are for "PAID" over "5" variety. "5" over "PAID" is much scarcer.

MADISON, GA.

E1

Handstamped Envelope

136XU1 E1 5c **red**	*500.*

No. 136XU1 is indistinguishable from a handstamp paid cover when used.

MADISON COURT HOUSE, FLA.

E1

Typeset Envelope

137XU1 E1 5c **black,** *yellow*	*23,000.*

No. 137XU1 is unique.

See 3c 1861 Postmasters' Provisional No. 3AX1.

MARIETTA, GA.

E1

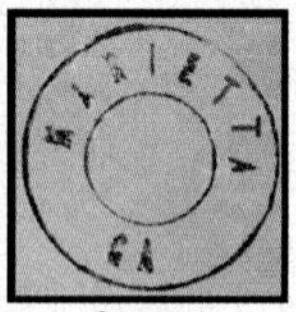

Control

E2

Handstamped Envelopes

54XU1 E1 5c **black**		400.
a. 10c on 5c **black**		*1,750.*

With Double Circle Control

54XU3 E2 10c **black**		
54XU4 E2 5c **black**		*2,000.*

The existence of No. 54XU3 has been questioned by specialists. The editors would like to see authenticated evidence that verifies this listing.

MARION, VA.

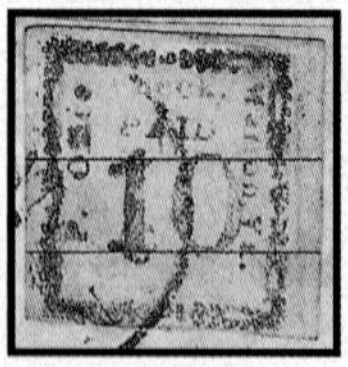

A1

Adhesives with Typeset frame and Handstamped numeral in center

55X1 A1 5c **black**		*7,500.*
On cover		*20,000.*
55X2 A1 10c **black**	*16,500.*	*10,000.*
On cover		*60,000.*
55X3 A1 5c **black,** *bluish,* laid paper	—	—

The 2c, 3c, 15c and 20c are believed to be bogus items printed later using the original typeset frame.

Cancellations: black town, black "PAID."

MEMPHIS, TENN.

A1

A2

Typographed Adhesives (stereotyped from woodcut)

Plate of 50 (5x10) for the 2c. The stereotypes for the 5 stamps were set in 5 vertical rows of 8, with at least 2 rows se sideways to the right (see Thomas H. Pratt's monograph, "Th Postmaster's Provisionals of Memphis").

56X1 A1 2c **blue** (shades)	100.	*1,25*
Block of 4	550.	
On cover		*10,00*
Cracked plate (16, 17, 18)	160.	*1,35*

The "cracking off" (breaking off) of the plate at right edg caused incomplete printing of stamps in positions 5, 10, 15, 2 and 50. Poor make-ready also caused incomplete printing i position 50.

56X2 A2 5c **red** (shades)	150.	19
Pair	*340.*	47
Block of 4	*1,000.*	
On cover		1,75
Pair on cover		*3,50*
Strip of 4 on cover		*7,00*
On patriotic cover		*5,00*
a. Tête bêche pair		1,50
Pair on cover		*10,00*
b. Pair, one sideways	2,500.	
c. Pelure paper	—	—

Cancellation on Nos. 56X1-56X2: black town.

Press-printed Envelopes (typographed)

56XU1 A2 5c **red** (shades)	*2,50*
Used with 5c #56X2 to make 10c rate	*7,50*
56XU2 A2 5c **red,** *amber*	*2,50*
Used with C.S.A. 5c #1 to make 10c rate	*7,50*
56XU3 A2 5c **red,** *orange*	*2,50*
On patriotic cover	—

MICANOPY, FLA.

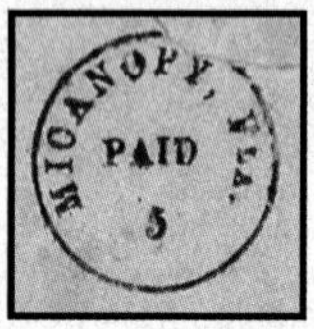

E1

Handstamped Envelope

105XU1 E1 5c **black**	*11,50*

One example recorded.

MILLEDGEVILLE, GA.

E1

E2

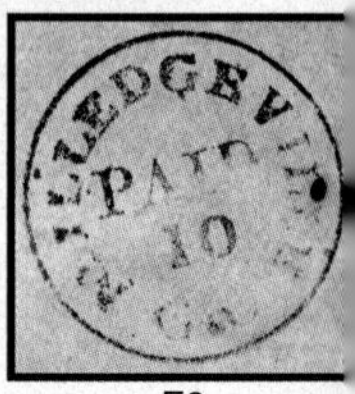

E3

Handstamped Envelopes

Two types of No. 57XU5: Type I, tall, thin "1" and "0" of "10" Type II, short, fat "1" and "0" of "10."

57XU1 E1 5c **black**	37
a. Wide spacing between "I" and "D" of "PAID"	50
b. 10c on 5c **black**	1,00

7XU2	E1	5c **blue**			800.
7XU4	E2	10c **black**		375.	1,000.
	a.	Wide spacing between "I" and "D" of "PAID"			1,000.
7XU5	E3	10c **black**, type I			800.
	a.	Type II			1,500.

On No. 57XU4, the "PAID/10" virtually always falls outside the Milledgeville control marking (as in illustration E1).

The existence of No. 57XU2 as a provisional has been questioned by specialists. The editors would like to see authenticated evidence of provisional use of this marking.

MILTON, N. C.

E1

Handstamped Envelope, "5" Manuscript

38XU1	E1	5c **black**	*2,000.*

MOBILE, ALA.

A1

Lithographed Adhesives

8X1	A1	2c **black**		2,250.	1,100.
			Pair	—	*2,100.*
			On cover		*5,000.*
			Pair on cover		*20,000.*
			Three singles on one cover		*20,000.*
			Five stamps on one cover		*20,000.*
8X2	A1	5c **blue**		350.	400.
			Pair	900.	950.
			On cover		1,800.
			On cover, canceled in Claiborne, Ala.		—
			On cover, canceled in Montgomery, Ala.		—
			Pair on cover		2,400.
			Strip of 3 on cover		*14,000.*
			Strip of 4 on cover		—
			Strip of 5 on cover		—
			Line through "O" of "Office" (plate scratch)		—

Cancellations: black town, express company.

The existence of a strip of 5 of No. 58X2 has been questioned by specialists. The editors would like to see authenticated evidence of the existence of this strip either on or off cover.

MONTGOMERY, ALA.

E1

Handstamped Envelopes

9XU1	E1	5c **red**		1,100.
	a.	10c on 5c **red**		*2,750.*
9XU2	E1	5c **blue**	400.	900.
9XU3	E1	10c **red**		850.
9XU4	E1	10c **blue**		1,500.
9XU5	E1	10c **black**		850.

The 10c design is larger than the 5c.

The absence of 5c and 10c handstamped paid markings from this town suggests that Nos. 59XU1-59XU5 were used as both provisional and handstamped paid markings.

E2

E3

9XU7	E2	2c **red**	*2,500.*
9XU7A	E2	2c **blue**	*3,500.*
9XU8	E2	5c **black**	*2,250.*
9XU9	E3	10c **black**	*3,250.*
9XU10	E3	10c **red**	*1,750.*

MT. LEBANON, LA.

A1

Woodcut Adhesive (mirror image of design)

60X1	A1	5c **red brown,** on cover	*385,000.*

One example known. Value is based on 1999 auction sale.

Cancellation: black pen.

NASHVILLE, TENN.

A2

Typographed Adhesives (stereotyped from woodcut)

Gray Blue Ribbed Paper

61X2	A2	5c **carmine** (shades)		1,000.	600.
			Pair		2,000.
			On cover		3,000.
			On patriotic cover		*4,500.*
			Pair on cover		*6,000.*
			On cover with U.S. 3c 1857 (express)		*25,000.*
	a.	Vertical tête bêche pair			*4,000.*
			On cover		*30,000.*
61X3	A2	5c **brick red** (shades)		1,000.	700.
			Pair		1,750.
			On cover		3,500.
			On patriotic cover		*6,000.*
			Pair on cover		*7,500.*
			On U.S. #U26 (express)		*35,000.*
			On U.S. #U27 with #26 (express)		*25,000.*
61X4	A2	5c **gray** (shades)		1,250.	1,000.
			On cover		*5,750.*
			On patriotic cover		*12,000.*
			Pair on cover		*7,500.*
			Strip of 5 on cover front		*8,750.*
61X5	A2	5c **violet brown** (shades)		1,100.	750.
			Block of 4	—	
			On cover		4,500.
			On patriotic cover		—
			Pair on cover		*6,000.*
	a.	Vertical tete beche pair		*5,000.*	*4,000.*
			Pair on cover		—
61X6	A2	10c **green**			*5,500.*
			On cover		*22,500.*
			On cover with U.S. 3c 1857 (express)		*75,000.*
			On U.S. #U26 (express)		*100,000.*
			On cover with No. 61X2		*27,500.*

Cancellations

Blue "Paid"
Blue "Postage Paid"
Blue town
Blue numeral "5"
Blue numeral "10"
Blue express company
Black express company

For the former 61X1, see No. 4AX1 in the 3c 1861 Postmasters' Provisional section.

E1

Handstamped Envelopes

61XU1	E1	5c **blue**		900.
			On patriotic envelope	1,900.
61XU2	E1	5c +10c **blue**		*2,750.*

NEW ORLEANS, LA.

A1

A2

Typographed Adhesives (stereotyped from woodcut)

Plate of 40

62X1	A1	2c **blue,** *July 14, 1861*		200.	500.
			Pair	600.	1,150.
			Block of 4	*6,500.*	
			On cover		*4,250.*
			On patriotic cover		*8,000.*
			Pair on cover		*10,000.*
			Three singles on one cover		*20,000.*
			Strip of 5 on cover		*30,000.*
	a.	Printed on both sides		—	
			On cover		*7,500.*
62X2	A1	2c **red** (shades), *Jan. 6, 1862*		175.	*1,000.*
			Pair	450.	
			Block of 4	*1,750.*	
			On cover		*25,000.*
62X3	A2	5c **brown,** *white, June 12, 1861*		275.	200.
			Pair	575.	425.
			Block of 4	1,750.	
			On cover		450.
			On cover from town other than N.O.		*5,000.*
			On patriotic cover		*5,500.*
			Pair on cover		850.
			Strip of 5 on cover		*5,000.*
			On cover with U.S. #26 (Southern Letter Unpaid)		*150,000.*
			On cover with U.S. No. 30A		—
	a.	Printed on both sides			*2,250.*
			On cover		*7,500.*
	b.	5c **ocher,** *June 18, 1861*		700.	625.
			Pair		1,500.
			On cover		2,750.
			On patriotic cover		*6,000.*
			Pair on cover		3,500.
	c.	chocolate brown, *white,* June 20, 1861			*1,500.*

The editors would like to see authenticated evidence of the existence of No. 62X3a on cover.

62X4	A2	5c **red brn,** *bluish, Aug. 22, 1861*		300.	200.
			Pair	675.	475.
			Horizontal strip of 6		*3,500.*
			Block of 4		2,200.
			On cover		425.
			On patriotic cover		*5,500.*
			Pair on cover		700.
			Block of 4 on cover		*5,000.*
			Used on cover with C.S.A. 5c #1 to make 10c rate		*27,500.*
	a.	Printed on both sides			*2,750.*
			On cover		*9,000.*
62X5	A2	5c **yel brn,** *off-white, Dec. 3, 1861*		150.	240.
			Pair	325.	525.
			Block of 4	700.	
			On cover		850.
			On patriotic cover		*3,000.*
			Pair on cover		1,000.
			Strip of 5 on cover		—
62X6	A2	5c **red**		—	*7,500.*
62X7	A2	5c **red,** *bluish*			*15,000.*

Cancellations

Black town (single or double circle New Orleans)
Red town (double circle New Orleans)
Town other than New Orleans
Postmaster's handstamp
Black "Paid"
Express Company
Packet boat, cover "STEAM"

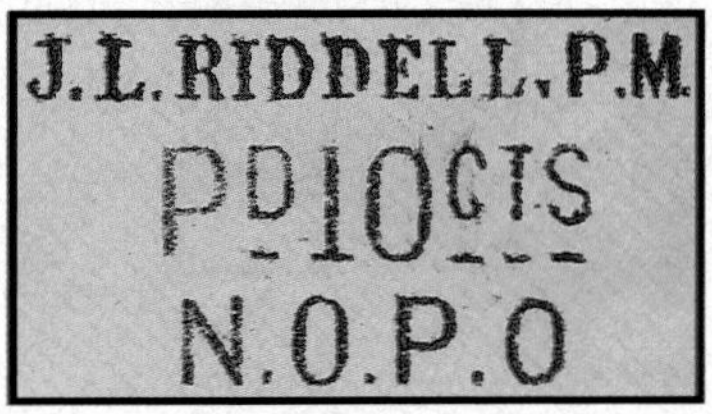

E1

These provisional handstamps were applied at the riverfront postal station.

Handstamped Envelopes

62XU1	E1	5c **black**	4,500.
62XU2	E1	10c **black**	*12,500.*

"J. L. RIDDELL, P. M." omitted

62XU3	E1	2c **black**	*9,500.*

NEW SMYRNA, FLA.

A1

Handstamped Adhesive

On white paper with blue ruled lines

63X1 A1 10c ("O1") on 5c **black** *45,000.*

One example known. It is uncanceled on a postmarked patriotic cover.

NORFOLK, VA.

E1

Handstamped Envelopes

Ms Signature on Front or Back

139XU1	E1	5c **blue**	—	*1,250.*
139XU2	E1	10c **blue**		*1,750.*

OAKWAY, S. C.

A1

Handstamped Adhesive (from woodcut)

115X1 A1 5c **black,** on cover *66,000.*

Two used examples of No. 115X1 are recorded, both on cover. Value represents 1997 auction realization for the cover on which the stamp is tied by manuscript "Paid."

PENSACOLA, FLA.

E1

Handstamped Envelopes

106XU1	E1	5c **black**	*3,750.*
a.		10c (ms.) on 5c **black**	*4,250.*
		On patriotic cover	*13,500.*

PETERSBURG, VA.

A1

Typeset Adhesive

Ten varieties

Thick white paper

65X1	A1	5c **red** (shades)	*2,250.*	750.
		Pair	*5,000.*	*2,000.*
		Block of 4	*11,000.*	
		On cover		2,500.
		On patriotic cover		—
		Pair on cover		*8,000.*
		Used on cover with C.S.A. 5c #1 to make 10c rate		*57,500.*

Cancellation: blue town.

PITTSYLVANIA COURT HOUSE, VA.

A1

Typeset Adhesives

66X1	A1	5c **dull red,** wove paper	*7,000.*	*6,000.*
		Octagonally cut		*5,000.*
		On cover		*55,000.*
		On cover, octagonally cut		*20,000.*
66X2	A1	5c **dull red,** laid paper		*6,500.*
		Octagonally cut		*5,500.*
		On cover		*55,000.*
		On cover, octagonally cut		*40,000.*

Cancellation: black town.

PLAINS OF DURA, GA.

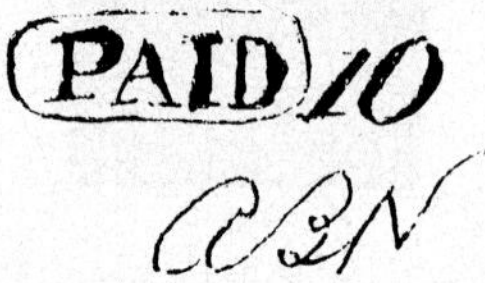

E1

Handstamped Envelopes, Ms. Initials

140XU1	E1	5c **black**	—
140XU2	E1	10c **black**	—

PLEASANT SHADE, VA.

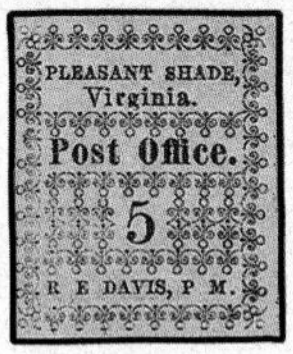

A1

Typeset Adhesive

Five varieties

67X1	A1	5c **blue**	*2,750.*	*20,000.*
		On cover		*27,500.*
		Pair	*8,000.*	
		Pair on cover		*55,000.*
		Block of 6	*25,000.*	

Cancellation: blue town.

PLUM CREEK, TEX.

E1

Manuscript Adhesive

141X1 E1 10c **black,** *blue,* on cover —

The ruled lines and "10" are done by hand. Size and shape of the stamp varies.

PORT GIBSON, MISS.

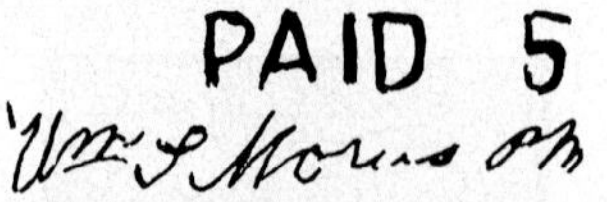

E1

Handstamped Envelope, Ms Signature

142XU1 E1 5c **black** —

PORT LAVACA, TEX.

A1

Typeset Adhesive

107X1 A1 10c **black,** on cover *25,00*

One example known. It is uncanceled on a postmarked cove

RALEIGH, N. C.

E1

Handstamped Envelopes

68XU1	E1	5c **red**	60(
		On patriotic cover	4,00(
68XU2	E1	5c **blue**	*3,00*

RHEATOWN, TENN.

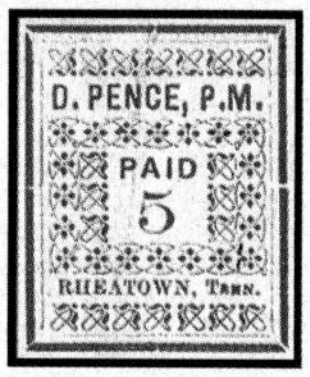

A1

Typeset Adhesive

Three varieties

69X1	A1	5c **red**	*6,000.*	*7,50*
		On cover, ms. cancel		*20,00*
		On cover, tied by handstamp		*37,50*
		Pair	*6,000.*	

Stamps normally were canceled in manuscript. One cover i known with stamp tied by red town postmark.

Cancellations: red town or black pen.

RICHMOND, TEX.

E1

Handstamped Envelopes or Letter Sheets

70XU1	E1	5c **red**	2,50(
a.		10c on 5c **red**	*5,00(*
70XU2	E1	10c **red**	2,00(
a.		15c (ms.) on 10c **red**	*5,00(*

RINGGOLD, GA.

E1

Handstamped Envelope

71XU1 E1 5c **blue black** *3,00(*

RUTHERFORDTON, N. C.

A1

Handstamped Adhesive, Ms. "Paid 5cts"

72X1	A1	5c **black,** cut round, on cover (uncanceled)	*25,000.*

No. 72X1 is unique.

SALEM, N. C.

E1

E2

Handstamped Envelopes

73XU1	E1	5c **black**	1,750.
73XU2	E1	10c **black**	*2,250.*
73XU3	E2	5c **black**	*2,250.*
a.		10c on 5c **black**	*2,800.*

Reprints exist on various papers. They either lack the "Paid" and value or have them counterfeited.

Salem, Va.
See No. 74X1 under Liberty, Va.

SALISBURY, N. C.

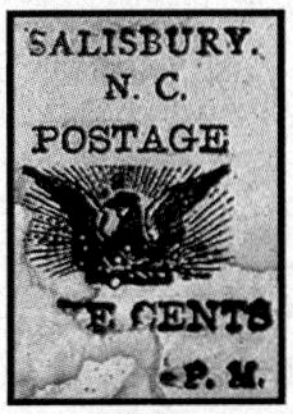
E1

Press-printed Envelope (typeset)

Impressed at top left

75XU1	E1	5c **black,** *greenish*	*5,000.*

One example known. Part of envelope is torn away, leaving part of design missing. Illustration E1 partly suppositional.

SAN ANTONIO, TEX.

E1

E2

Control

Handstamped Envelopes

76XU1	E1	10c **black**	275.	*2,000.*
76XU1A	E2	5c **black**		*1,500.*
76XU2	E2	10c **black**		*2,500.*

Black circle control mark is on front or back.

SAVANNAH, GA.

E1

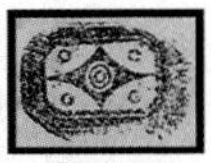
Control

E2

Handstamped Envelopes

101XU1	E1	5c **black**	400.
		On patriotic cover	—
a.		10c on 5c **black**	1,500.
101XU2	E2	5c **black**	600.
a.		20c on 5c **black**	*2,000.*
101XU3	E1	10c **black**	750.
101XU4	E2	10c **black**	750.

Envelopes must have octagonal control mark. One example is known of No.101XU6.

SELMA, ALA.

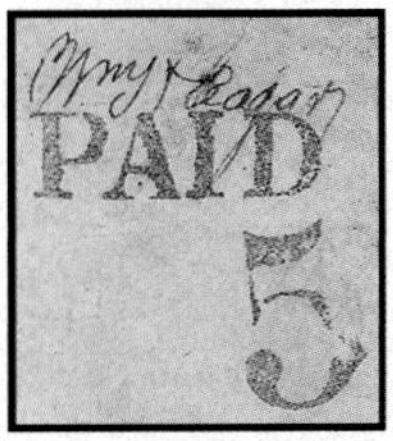
E1

Handstamped Envelopes; Signature in Ms.

77XU1	E1	5c **black**	*1,250.*
a.		10c on 5c **black**	*3,000.*
77XU2	E1	10c **black**	*2,500.*

Signature is that of Postmaster William H. Eagar. See 3c 1861 Postmasters' Provisional No. 5AX1.

SPARTA, GA.

E1a

Handstamped Envelopes

93XU1	E1a	5c **red**	—	1,750.
93XU2	E1a	10c **red**		*2,500.*

Only one example recorded of No. 93XU2.

SPARTANBURG, S. C.

A1

A2

Handstamped Adhesives

(on ruled or plain wove paper)

78X1	A1	5c **black**	*3,500.*
		On cover	*25,000.*
		Pair on cover	*30,000.*
		On patriotic cover	*30,000.*
a.		"5" omitted (on cover)	—
78X2	A2	5c **black,** *bluish*	*4,000.*
		On cover	*15,000.*
78X3	A2	5c **black,** *brown*	*4,000.*
		On cover	*18,000.*

Most examples of Nos. 78X1-78X3 are cut round. Cut square examples in sound condition are worth much more. The only recorded pair of No. 78X1 is on cover. The stamps are cut round, but are still connected.

Cancellations: black "PAID," black town.

STATESVILLE, N. C.

E1

Handstamped Envelopes

79XU1	E1	5c **black**	250.	*675.*
a.		10c on 5c **black**		*2,250.*

Fakes exist of No. 79XU1 unused.

SUMTER, S. C.

E1

Handstamped Envelopes

80XU1	E1	5c **black**	400.	
a.		10c on 5c **black**		*800.*
80XU2	E1	10c **black**	500.	
a.		2c (ms.) on 10c **black**		*1,100.*

Used examples of Nos. 80XU1-80XU2 are indistinguishable from handstamped "Paid" covers.

TALBOTTON, GA.

E1

Handstamped Envelopes

94XU1	E1	5c **black**	1,000.
94XU2	E1	10c **black**	1,000.
a.		10c on 5c **black**	*2,000.*

TALLADEGA, ALA.

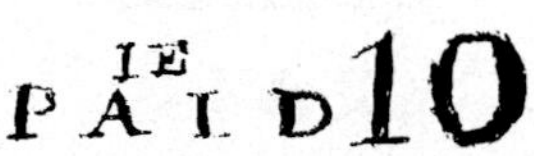
E1

Handstamped Envelopes

143XU1	E1	5c **black**	*1,200.*	—
143XU2	E1	10c **black**	*1,200.*	—

TELLICO PLAINS, TENN.

A1

Typeset Adhesives

Settings of two 5c and one 10c
Laid Paper

81X1	A1	5c	**red**	1,750.	—
			On cover		*50,000.*
81X2	A1	10c	**red**	3,250.	
			Se-tenant with 5c	*5,500.*	
			Strip of 3 (5c+5c+10c)	*9,500.*	

Cancellation: black pen.

THOMASVILLE, GA.

E1

Control

Handstamped Envelopes

82XU1	E1	5c	**black**	575.
			On patriotic cover	—

On No. 82XU1, the control is on the reverse of the cover. The dated control is known with four different dates.

E2

82XU2	E2	5c	**black**	900.

TULLAHOMA, TENN.

E1

Control

Handstamped Envelope

111XU1	E1	10c	**black**	*3,000.*

TUSCALOOSA, ALA.

E1

Handstamped Envelopes

83XU1	E1	5c	**black**	250.
83XU2	E1	10c	**black**	250.

Used examples of Nos. 83XU1-83XU2 are indistinguishable from handstamped "Paid" covers. Some authorities question the use of E1 to produce provisional envelopes.

TUSCUMBIA, ALA.

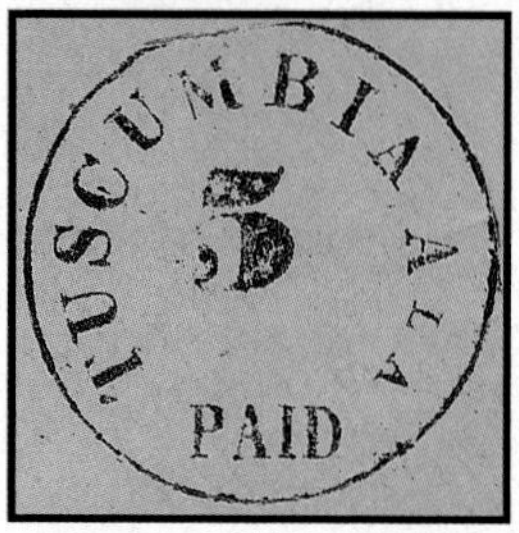

E1

Handstamped Envelopes

84XU1	E1	5c	**black**	2,250.
			On patriotic cover	—
84XU2	E1	5c	**red**	*3,000.*
84XU3	E1	10c	**black**	*3,500.*

See 3c 1861 Postmasters' Provisional No. 6AXU1.

UNIONTOWN, ALA.

A1

Typeset Adhesives

(settings of 4 (2x2), 4 varieties of each value)
Laid Paper

86X1	A1	2c	**dark blue,** *gray blue,* on cover		—
86X2	A1	2c	**dark blue,** sheet of 4	*57,500.*	
86X3	A1	5c	**green,** *gray blue*	*4,000.*	*3,250.*
			Pair	—	
			On cover		*9,000.*
86X4	A1	5c	**green**	*4,000.*	*3,250.*
			On cover		*7,500.*
			Pair on cover		*20,000.*
86X5	A1	10c	**red,** *gray blue*		—
			On cover		*37,500.*

Two examples known of No. 86X1, both on cover (drop letters), one uncanceled and one pen canceled.

The only recorded examples of No. 86X2 are in a unique sheet of 4.

The item listed as No. 86X5 used is an uncanceled stamp on a large piece with part of addressee's name in manuscript.

Cancellation on Nos. 86X3-86X5: black town.

UNIONVILLE, S. C.

A1

Handstamped Adhesive
"PAID" and "5" applied separately

Paper with Blue Ruled Lines

87X1	A1	5c	**black,** *grayish*	—
			On cover, uncanceled	*17,500.*
			On cover, tied	—
			Pair on patriotic cover	*32,500.*

The pair on patriotic cover is the only pair recorded.

Cancellation: black town.

VALDOSTA, GA.

E1

Control

Handstamped Envelopes

100XU1	E1	10c	**black**	*2,00*
100XU2	E1	5c +5c	**black**	—

The black circle control must appear on front of the No 100XU2 envelope and on the back of the No. 100XU envelope.

There is one recorded cover each of Nos. 100XU1-100XU2

VICTORIA, TEX.

A1

A2

Typeset Adhesives

Surface colored paper

88X1	A1	5c	**red brown,** *green*	*17,500.*	
88X2	A1	10c	**red brown,** *green*	*22,500.*	
			On cover		*125,000*
88X3	A2	10c	**red brown,** *green,* pelure paper	*27,500.*	*22,500*

WALTERBOROUGH, S. C.

E1

Handstamped Envelopes

108XU1	E1	10c	**black,** *buff*	—
108XU2	E1	10c	**carmine**	*4,250*

The existence of No. 108XU1 is in question. The editors would like to see authenticated evidence of its existence.

WARRENTON, GA.

E1

Handstamped Envelopes

89XU1	E1	5c	**black**	1,250
a.		10c (ms.) on 5c	**black**	1,000

Fakes of the Warrenton provisional marking based on the illustration shown are known on addressed but postally unused covers.

WASHINGTON, GA.

E1

Handstamped Envelope

117XU1	E1	10c	**black**	*2,000.*

Envelopes must have black circle postmark control on the back. Examples with the undated control on the front are not considered provisional unless a dated postmark is also present.

WEATHERFORD, TEX.

E1

Handstamped Envelopes (woodcut with "PAID" inserted in type)

109XU1	E1	5c	**black**	*2,000.*
109XU2	E1	5c +5c	**black**	*11,000.*

One example is known of No. 109XU2.

WINNSBOROUGH, S. C.

E1

Control

Handstamped Envelopes

97XU1	E1	5c	**black**	*1,750.*
97XU2	E1	10c	**black**	*3,500.*

Envelopes must have black circle control on front or back.

WYTHEVILLE, VA.

E1

Control

Handstamped Envelope

114XU1	E1	5c	**black**	900.

For later additions, listed out of numerical sequence, see:

#74X1, **Liberty, Va.**
#92XU1, **Huntsville, Tex.**
#93XU1, **Sparta, Ga.**
#94XU1, **Talbotton, Ga.**
#96XU1, **Lake City, Fla.**
#97XU1, **Winnsborough, S. C.**
#98XU1, **Galveston, Tex.**
#99XU1, **Christiansburg, Va.**
#100XU1, **Valdosta, Ga.**
#101XU1, **Savannah, Ga.**
#102XU1, **Griffin, Ga.**
#103XU1, **Courtland, Ala.**
#104XU1, **Fincastle, Va.**
#105XU1, **Micanopy, Fla.**
#106XU1, **Pensacola, Fla.**
#107X1, **Port Lavaca, Tex.**
#108XU1, **Walterborough, S. C.**
#109XU1, **Weatherford, Tex.**
#110XU1, **Jacksonville, Ala.**
#111XU1, **Tullahoma, Tenn.**
#112XU1, **Hamburgh, S. C.**
#113XU1, **Columbia, Tenn.**
#114XU1, **Wytheville, Va.**
#115X1, **Oakway, S. C.**
#116XU1, **Laurens Court House, S. C.**
#117XU1, **Washington, Ga.**
#118XU1, **Carolina City, N.C.**
#119XU1, **Colaparchee, Ga.**
#120XU1, **Forsyth, Ga.**
#121XU1, **Limestone Springs, S.C.**
#122XU1, **Balcony Falls, Va.**
#123XU1, **Barnwell Court House, S.C.**
#124XU1, **Bluffton, S.C.**
#125XU1, **Camden, S.C.**
#126XU1, **Cartersville, Ga.**
#127XU1, **Charlottesville, Va.**
#128XU1, **Fraziersville, S.C.**
#129XU1, **Gaston, N.C.**
#130XU1, **Harrisburgh, Tex.**
#132XU1, **Hollandale, Tex.**
#133XU1, **Isabella, Ga.**
#134XU1, **Jacksonville, Fla.**
#135XU1, **Lexington, Va.**
#136XU1, **Madison, Ga.**
#137XU1, **Madison Court House, Fla.**
#138XU1, **Milton, N.C.**
#139XU1, **Norfolk, Va.**
#140XU1, **Plains of Dura, Ga.**
#141X1, **Plum Creek, Tex.**
#142XU1, **Port Gibson, Miss.**
#143XU1, **Talladega, Ala.**

CONFEDERATE STATES OF AMERICA, GENERAL ISSUES

The general issues are valued in the very fine grade, and unused stamps are valued both with and without original gum. As noted in the catalogue introduction, "original gum" for this era is defined as at least a majority part original gum, that is, at least 51% original gum. Stamps with substantially more than 51% original gum may be expected to sell for more than the values given, and stamps with less than a majority part original gum will sell for somewhat less.

For explanations of various terms used see the notes at the end of the postage listings.

Jefferson Davis — A1

1861 Litho. Soft Porous Paper *Imperf.*

All 5c Lithographs were printed by Hoyer & Ludwig, of Richmond, Va.

Stones A or B — First stones used. Earliest dated cancellation October 16, 1861. Plating not completed hence size of sheets unknown. These stones had imprints. Stamps from Stones A or B are nearly all in the olive green shade. Sharp, clear impressions. Distinctive marks are few and minute.

Stone 1 — Earliest dated cancellation October 18, 1861. Plating completed. Sheet consists of four groups of fifty varieties arranged in two panes of one hundred each without imprint. The first small printing was in olive green and later small printings appeared in light and dark green; the typical shade, however, is an intermediate shade of bright green. The impressions are clear though not as sharp as those from Stones A or B. Distinctive marks are discernible.

Stone 2 — Earliest dated cancellation December 2, 1861. Plating completed. Sheet consists of four groups of fifty varieties arranged in two panes of one hundred each without imprint. All shades other than olive green are known from this stone, the most common being a dull green. Poor impressions. Many noticeable distinctive marks.

Stone 2

1	A1	5c	**green** (shades)	275.	175.
			No gum	175.	
			bright green	300.	175.
			dull green	275.	175.
			On cover		300.
			Single on cover (overpaid drop letter)		500.
			On wallpaper cover		*1,500.*
			On prisoner's cover		—
			On prisoner's cover with U.S. #65		—
			On prisoner's cover with U.S. #U34		—
			On patriotic cover		2,500.
			Pair	600.	425.
			Pair on cover		500.
			Block of 4	1,450.	1,300.
			Pair with full horiz. gutter between		—
a.		5c	**light green**	275.	175.
			No gum	175.	
b.		5c	**dark green**	350.	225.
			No gum	210.	

VARIETIES

Spur on upper left scroll (Pos. 21)	425.	275.
Side margin copy showing initials (Pos. 41 or 50)	—	—
Misplaced transfer (clear twin impressions of lower left scrolls — pos. 1 entered over pos. 10)	—	—
Roulettted unofficially	500.	850.
On cover		*1,750.*
Pair on cover		*3,750.*

Cancellations

Blue town	+10.
Red town	+125.
Violet town	+150.
Green town	+175.
Orange town	+225.
Texas town	+35.
Arkansas town	+100.
Florida town	+110.
Kentucky town	+300.
Blue gridiron	+5.
Red gridiron	+50.
Blue concentric	+5.
Star or flowers	+100.
Numeral	+50.
"Paid"	+50.
"Steamboat"	+150.
Express Co.	+350.
Railroad	+300.
Pen	60.

Stone 1

1	A1	5c	**green**	300.	200.
			No gum	200.	
			bright green	300.	200.
			dull green	275.	200.
a.		5c	**light green**	275.	200.
			No gum	175.	
b.		5c	**dark green**	325.	225.
			No gum	210.	
c.		5c	**olive green**	375.	250.
			No gum	225.	
			On cover		300.
			On patriotic cover		2,500.
			Pair	750.	475.
			Pair on cover		600.
			Block of 4	1,650.	1,250.

VARIETIES

Acid flaw	350.	200.
Arrow between panes	600.	325.
Flaw on "at" of "States" (Pos. 38)	325.	225.

Cancellations

Blue town	+10.
Red town	+80.
Green town	+225.
Texas town	+35.
Arkansas town	+90.
Florida town	+110.
Kentucky town	+300.
October, 1861, year date	+40.
Blue gridiron	+5.
Red gridiron	+75.
Blue concentric	+5.
Numeral	+50.
"Paid"	+50.
"Steam"	+150.
"Steamboat"	+150.
Express Company	+350.

Railroad +300.
Pen 70.

Stones A or B

1c	A1	5c	**olive green**	400.	200.
			No gum	250.	
			On cover		400.
			On patriotic cover		1,400.
			Pair	850.	450.
			Pair on cover		700.
			Block of 4	2,250.	1,300.

VARIETIES

White curl back of head	425.	275.
Imprint	775.	475.

Cancellations

Blue town	+10.
Red town	+150.
October, 1861, year date	+50.
Blue gridiron	+5.
Blue concentric	+5.
Numeral	+60.
"Paid"	+50.
"Steam"	+150.
Express Co.	+400.
Pen	100.

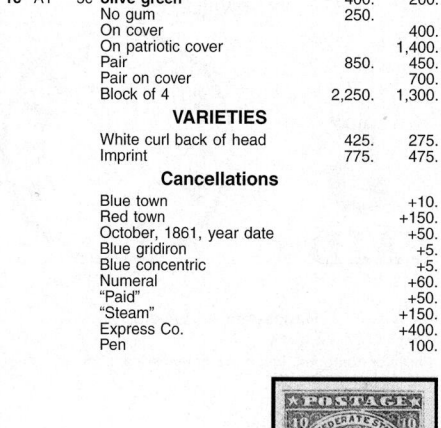

Thomas Jefferson — A2

1861-62 Litho. Soft Porous Paper

Hoyer & Ludwig — First stone used. Earliest dated cancellation November 8, 1861. Sheet believed to consist of four groups of fifty varieties each arranged in two panes of one hundred each with imprint at bottom of each pane. Two different imprints are known. Hoyer & Ludwig printings are always in a uniform shade of dark blue. Impressions are clear and distinct, especially so in the early printings. Plating marks are distinct.

J. T. Paterson & Co. — Earliest dated cancellation July 25, 1862. Sheet consists of four groups of fifty varieties each arranged in two panes of one hundred each with imprint at bottom of each pane. Two different imprints are known and at least one pane is known without an imprint. Wide range of shades. Impressions are less clear than those from the Hoyer & Ludwig stone. Paterson stamps show small vertical colored dash below the lowest point of the upper left triangle.

Stone "Y" — Supposedly made by J. T. Paterson & Co., as it shows the distinctive mark of that firm. Plating not completed hence size of sheet unknown. No imprint found. Color is either a light milky blue or a greenish blue. Impressions are very poor and have a blurred appearance. Stone Y stamps invariably show a large flaw at the back of the head as well as small vertical colored dash beneath the upper left triangle.

Paterson

2	A2	10c	**blue**	300.	200.
			No gum	180.	
			On cover		325.
			On wallpaper cover		1,500.
			On patriotic cover		2,250.
			On prisoner's cover with U.S. #65		—
			Pair	750.	475.
			Pair on cover		950.
			Strip of 3 on cover		—
			Block of 4	1,850.	
			Horiz. pair, gutter btwn.	1,500.	
a.		10c	**light blue**	300.	200.
			No gum	180.	
b.		10c	**dark blue**	700.	275.
			No gum	450.	
c.		10c	**indigo**	*3,000.*	*2,500.*
			No gum	*2,000.*	
d.			Printed on both sides	—	—

VARIETIES

Malformed "O" of "POSTAGE" (Pos. 25)	425.	240.
J. T. Paterson & Co. imprint	1,250.	1,250.

Cancellations

Blue town	+10.
Red town	+100.
Green town	+200.
Violet town	—
Texas town	+125.
Arkansas town	+275.
Florida town	+325.
July, 1862, date	+300.
Straight line town	+500.
Blue gridiron	+10.
Red gridiron	+75.
Blue concentric	+10.
Numeral	+80.
"Paid"	+75.
Star or flower	+150.
Railroad	+350.
Express Co.	+300.
Pen	75.

Hoyer

2b	A2	10c	**dark blue**	700.	27
			No gum	425.	
			On cover		45
			On wallpaper cover		2,00
			On patriotic cover		3,00
			On prisoner's cover with U.S. #65		–
			Pair	1,300.	85
			Pair on cover		1,50
			Strip of 3 on cover		3,50
			Block of 4	2,900.	–
d.			Printed on both sides	—	

VARIETIES

Malformed "T" of "TEN" (Pos. 4)	625.	30
"G" and "E" of "POSTAGE" joined (Pos. 10)	625.	30
Circular flaw, upper left star (Pos. 11)	625.	30
Third spiked ornament at right, white (Pos. 45)	625.	35
Hoyer & Ludwig imprint	875.	82
Rouletted unofficially, on cover		*3,00*

Cancellations

Blue town	+3
Red town	+10
Texas town	+12
Arkansas town	+27
Florida town	+32
Kentucky town	+40
Nov., 1861, date	+30
Straight line town	+50
Blue gridiron	+1
Red gridiron	+7
Blue concentric	+1
Numeral	+7
"Paid"	+5
Railroad	+35
Express Company	+30
Pen	7

Stone Y

2e	A2	10c	**greenish blue**	1,100.	35
			No gum	650.	
			light milky blue	1,100.	35
			No gum	650.	
			On cover		52
			On wallpaper cover		1,00
			On patriotic cover		2,10
			Pair	2,750.	–
			Block of 4	—	2,35

Cancellations

Blue town	+1
Red town	+12
Violet town	+7
Green town	+30
Texas town	+12
Arkansas town	+27
Florida town	–
Straight line town	+50
Blue gridiron	+1
Red gridiron	+7
Blue concentric	+1
Numeral	+10
"Paid"	+10
Pen	10

Andrew Jackson — A3

Sheet consists of four groups of fifty varieties arranged in tw panes of 100 each.

One stone only was used. Printed by Hoyer & Ludwig, o Richmond, Va. Issued to prepay drop letter and circular rates Strips of five used to prepay regular 10c rate, which was changed from 5c on July 1, 1862. Earliest known cancellation March 21, 1862.

1862 (March?) Soft Porous Paper Litho

3	A3	2c	**green**	900.	750
			light green	900.	750
			dark green	900.	800
			No gum	550.	
			dull yellow green	1,300.	900
			No gum	850.	
			On cover		*2,750*
			Pair on cover (double circular rate)		*3,250*
			Strip of 5 on cover		*13,500*
			On patriotic cover		—
			Pair	2,000.	—
			Block of 4	5,500.	5,000
			Block of 5	6,500.	*5,500*
a.		2c	**bright yellow green**	*2,000.*	—
			No gum	*1,300.*	
			On cover		*4,000*
			Pair		—

VARIETIES

Diagonal half used as 1c with unsevered pair, on cover		—
Horiz. pair, vert. gutter between	—	—

Pair, mark between stamps (btwn. Pos. 4 and 5)	2,100.	2,100.
Mark above upper right corner (Pos. 30)	1,000.	850.
Mark above upper left corner (Pos. 31)	1,000.	850.
Acid flaw	1,000.	700.

Cancellations

Blue town	+500.
Red town	+800.
Arkansas town	—
Texas town	+1,250.
Blue gridiron	+250.
"Paid"	—
Express Company	—
Railroad	+3,000.
Pen	400.

1862 Soft Porous Paper Litho.

Stone 2 — First stone used for printing in blue. Plating is the same as Stone 2 in green. Earliest dated cancellation Feb. 26, 1862. Printings from Stone 2 are found in all shades of blue. Rough, coarse impressions are typical of printings from Stone 2.

Stone 3 — A new stone used for printings in blue only. Earliest dated cancellation April 10, 1862. Sheet consists of four groups of fifty varieties each arranged in two panes of one hundred each without imprint. Impressions are clear and sharp, often having a proof-like appearance, especially in the deep blue printing. Plating marks, while not so large as on Stone 2 are distinct and clearly defined.

Stone 2

4 A1 5c **blue**	225.	125.
No gum	130.	
light blue	250.	140.
No gum	150.	
Pair	625.	450.
Block of 4	1,300.	*2,000.*
Horiz. pair, wide gutter between	1,250.	—
Vert. pair, narrow gutter between	—	
On cover		275.
Single on cover (overpaid drop letter)		400.
Pair on cover		450.
On wallpaper cover		1,250.
On patriotic cover		*2,500.*
On prisoner's cover		—
On prisoner's cover with U.S. #65		—
a. 5c **dark blue**	250.	175.
No gum	150.	
b. 5c **light milky blue**	300.	200.
No gum	180.	

VARIETIES

Spur on upper left scroll (Pos. 21)	250.	150.
Thin hard paper	—	140.
Misplaced transfer (faint twin impression of second lower left scroll at left — pos. 2 entered over pos. 10)		—

Cancellations

Blue town	+20.
Red town	+100.
Orange town	+400.
Texas town	+300.
Arkansas town	+325.
Florida town	+200.
Straight line town	+300.
Blue gridiron	+10.
Red gridiron	+85.
Star or Flowers	+125.
Numeral	+85.
Railroad	—
"Paid"	+25.
"Steamboat"	+400.
Express Company	—
"Way"	+250.
Pen	65.

Stone 3

4 A1 5c **blue**	750.	250.
No gum	500.	
a. 5c **dark blue**	800.	275.
No gum	550.	
b. 5c **light milky blue**	750.	250.
No gum	500.	
Pair	1750.	550.
Block of 4	4,500.	*2,000.*
On cover		500.
Pair on cover		625.
On patriotic cover		*2,750.*
Horiz. pair, wide gutter btwn.	—	
Vert. pair, narrow gutter between	—	

Stone 3 stamps can be positively identified by plating only. Color or shade is not a determinant.

VARIETIES

Tops of "C" and "E" of "cents" joined by flaw (Pos. 33)	850.	325.
"Flying bird" above lower left corner ornament (Pos. 19)	850.	325.

Cancellations

Blue town	+40.
Red town	+100.
Texas town	+300.
Arkansas town	+325.
Straight line town	+325.
Blue gridiron	+10.
Star or Flowers	+125.
"Paid"	+50.
Pen	80.

1862 (March?) Soft Porous Paper Litho.

Settings of fifty varieties repeated.

Printed by Hoyer & Ludwig, of Richmond, Va. One stone used, being the same as that used for the Hoyer & Ludwig 10c value in blue. Color change occured probably in March, 1862.

There are many shades of this stamp. The carmine is a very dark, bright color and should not be confused with the deeper shade of rose.

Earliest known cancellation, March 10, 1862. The earliest date of usage of the carmine shade is May 1, 1862.

5 A2 10c **rose** (shades)	1,500.	500.
No gum	900.	
dull rose	1,350.	500.
brown rose	1,850.	1,000.
deep rose	1,600.	650.
carmine rose	1,850.	875.
On cover		800.
On wallpaper cover		*2,000.*
On patriotic cover		*3,000.*
On prisoner's cover		*5,500.*
On prisoner's cover with U.S. #65		—
Pair	3,350.	2,250.
Strip of 3	—	*4,000.*
Block of 4	*11,000.*	*6,500.*
a. 10c **carmine**	*3,500.*	*1,900.*
No gum	*2,100.*	
On cover		*4,500.*

VARIETIES

Malformed "T" of "TEN" (Pos. 4)	1,850.	600.
"G" and "E" of "POSTAGE" joined (Pos. 10)	1,850.	600.
Circular flaw, upper left star (Pos. 11)	1,950.	675.
Third spiked ornament at right, white (Pos. 45)	1,950.	675.
Scratched stone (occurring on Pos. 40, 39, 49 and 48, one pane)	1,950.	925.
Imprint		1,750.
Horiz. pair, vert. gutter between		—
Side margin copy, initials (Pos. 41)		1,500.

Cancellations

Blue town	+50.
Red town	+125.
Green town	+350.
Texas town	+150.
Arkansas town	—
Straight line town	+500.
April, 1862, year date	—
Blue gridiron	+50.
Black concentric	+50.
Blue concentric	+50.
"Paid"	—
Railroad	—
Express Company	—
Pen	200.

Jefferson Davis — A4

Plate of 400 in four panes of 100 each. No imprint.

No. 6 represents London printings from De La Rue & Co., a number of sheets being sent over by blockade runners. Fine clear impressions. The gum is light and evenly distributed. Exact date of issue unknown. Earliest known cancellation, April 16, 1862.

Typographed by De La Rue & Co. in London, England

1862 (April) Hard Medium Paper

6 A4 5c **light blue**	15.00	27.50
No gum	7.50	
Single on cover used before July 1, 1862		150.00
Single on cover (overpaid drop letter)		275.00
Single on patriotic cover used before July 1, 1862		2,000.
Single on prisoner's cover used before July 1, 1862		—
On wallpaper cover		800.00
On patriotic cover		1,200.
On prisoner's cover		—
On prisoner's cover with U.S. #65		—
Pair	35.00	75.00
Pair on cover		100.00
Pair on patriotic cover		*1,300.*
Block of 4	80.00	290.00
Block of 4 on cover		900.00

Cancellations

Blue town	+2.00
Red town	+55.00
Green town	+75.00
Texas town	+65.00
Arkansas town	+100.00
Straight line town	+150.00
Blue gridiron	+2.00
Red gridiron	+35.00
Blue concentric	+2.00

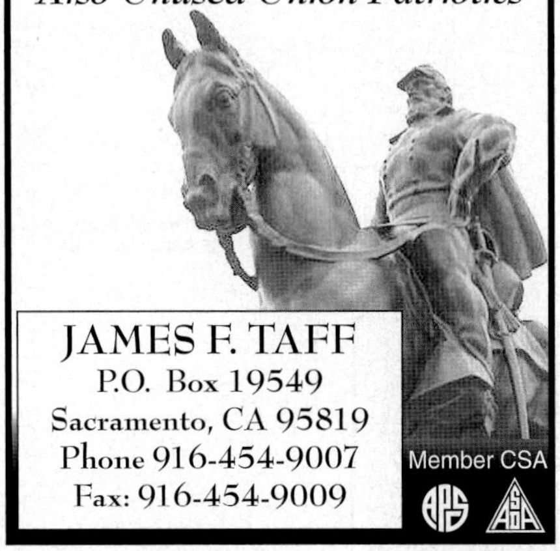

Express Company	+350.00
Railroad	+250.00
"Paid"	+50.00

1862 (August) Typo. Thin to Thick Paper

Plate of 400 in four panes of 100 each. No imprint.

Locally printed by Archer & Daly of Richmond, Va., from plates made in London, England, by De La Rue & Co. Printed on both imported English and local papers. Earliest known cancellation, July 25, 1862.

No. 7 shows coarser impressions than No. 6, and the color is duller and often blurred. Gum is light or dark and unevenly distributed.

7 A4 5c **blue**	18.00	20.00
No gum	9.00	
a. 5c **deep blue**	20.00	35.00
No gum	10.50	
Single on cover (overpaid drop letter)		200.00
On wallpaper cover		800.00
On patriotic cover		1,200.
On prisoner's cover		—
On prisoner's cover with U.S. #65		—
Pair	40.00	47.50
Pair on cover		95.00
Block of 4	90.00	350.00
Block of 4 on cover		800.00
Eight on cover (Trans-Miss. rate)		—
b. Printed on both sides	*2,500.*	*1,500.*
Pair		*3,250.*
Pair on cover		*4,000.*

VARIETIES

White tie (U.R. 30)	150.00	150.00
White tie on cover		350.00
De La Rue paper (thin)	27.50	45.00
No gum	17.50	

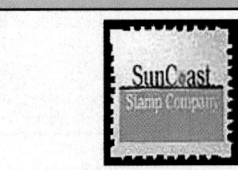

White tie, De La Rue paper 200.00 250.00
Thick paper 22.50 *35.00*
Horiz. pair, vert. gutter between 200.00

Cancellations

Blue town +2.00
Red town +75.00
Brown town +30.00
Violet town +110.00
Green town +150.00
Texas town +90.00
Arkansas town +110.00
Florida town +140.00
Straight line town +140.00
Blue gridiron +2.00
Red gridiron +60.00
Blue concentric +2.00
Railroad +250.00
Express Company +400.00
Design (stars, etc. +75.00
"Paid" +50.00

The unissued 10c design A4 was privately printed in various colors for philatelic purposes. (See note below No. 14.)
Counterfeits of the 10c exist.

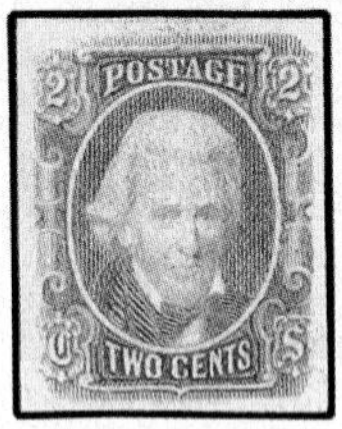

Andrew Jackson — A5

Sheet of 200 (two panes of 100 each).
One plate. Printed by Archer & Daly of Richmond, Va. Earliest known cancellation. Apr. 21, 1863. Issued to prepay drop letter and circular rates. Strips of five used to prepay regular 10c rate.

1863 (April) Soft Porous Paper Engraved

8 A5 2c **brown red** 70. *350.*
No gum 40.
a. 2c **pale red** 90. *450.*
No gum 45.
Single on cover *1,500.*
On prisoner's cover —
On prisoner's cover with U.S. #65 —
Pair 150. *1,000.*
Pair on cover *3,250.*
On wallpaper cover —
Block of 4 350. —
Block of 5 —
Strip of 5 on cover *4,500.*
Strip of 5 on wallpaper cover —
Strip of 10 on cover —
Double transfer 125. *450.*
Horiz. pair, vert. gutter between 325.

Cancellations

Blue town +35.
Red town +225.
Violet town +300.
Army of Tenn. —
Blue gridiron +35.
Black numeral —
Railroad +325.

Jefferson Davis "TEN CENTS" — A6

One plate of 200 subjects all of which were probably recut as every example examined to date shows distinct recutting. Plating not completed.
Printed by Archer & Daly of Richmond, Va. First printings in milky blue. First issued in April, 1863. Earliest known cancellation, April 23, 1863.

1863, Apr. Soft Porous Paper Engraved

9 A6 10c **blue** 900. 550.
No gum 575.
a. 10c **milky blue** (first printing) 900. 550.
No gum 575.
b. 10c **gray blue** 950. 650.
No gum 625.
On cover 1,600.
On wallpaper cover *3,000.*
On patriotic cover *3,500.*
On prisoner's cover —
On prisoner's cover with U.S. #65 —
Pair 2,000. 2,200.
Pair on cover *3,000.*
Block of 4 *5,250.*
Four stamps on one cover (Trans-Mississippi rate) *13,500.*

Curved lines outside the labels at top and bottom are broken in the middle (Pos. 63R) 1,050. 775.
Double transfer 1,100. 1,000.
Damaged plate 1,200. 1,100.

Cancellations

Blue town +25.
Red town +150.
Green town +600.
Violet town —
Straight line town +500.
April, 1863, year date —
Black gridiron +25.
Blue gridiron +50.
Red gridiron +200.
Railroad +400.
Circle of wedges +1,250.
Pen 350.

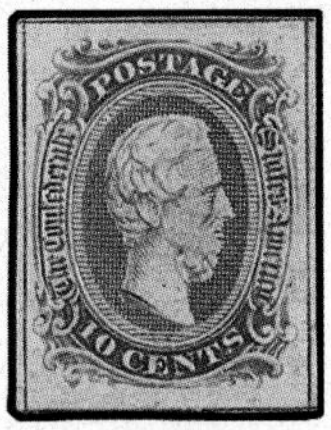

Frame Line "10 CENTS" — A6a

Printed by Archer & Daly of Richmond, Va.
One copper plate of 100 subjects, all but one of which were recut. Earliest known use April 19, 1863.
Stamp design same as Die A (Pos. 11).
Values are for stamps showing parts of lines on at least 3 of 4 sides. Used stamps showing 4 complete lines sell for 200%-300% of the values given. Unused stamps showing 4 complete lines are exceedingly rare (only two recorded), and the sound example is valued at $25,000.

1863, Apr. Soft Porous Paper Engraved

10 A6a 10c **blue** 5,000. 1,800.
No gum 3,500.
a. 10c **milky blue** 5,000. 1,800.
No gum 3,500.
b. 10c **greenish blue** 5,500. 1,900.
No gum 4,000.
c. 10c **dark blue** 5,500. 1,900.
No gum 4,000.
On cover *3,000.*
On wallpaper cover *4,750.*
On patriotic cover *10,000.*
On prisoner's cover *7,000.*
On prisoner's cover with U.S. #65 —
Pair *11,500.* *6,000.*
Pair on cover *7,000.*
Block of 4 *27,500.*
Strip of 4 *26,000.*
Strip of 6 — *20,000.*
Strip of 7 *42,500.*
Double transfer (Pos. 74) 5,500. 1,900.

Cancellations

Blue town +100.
Red town +500.
Straight line town +750.
April, 1863, year date —
Blue gridiron +100.
Pen 800.

No Frame Line "10 CENTS" (Die A) — A7

There are many slight differences between A7 (Die A) and A8 (Die B), the most noticeable being the additional line outside the ornaments at the four corners of A8 (Die B).
Stamps were first printed by Archer & Daly, of Richmond, Va. In 1864 the plates were transferred to the firm of Keatinge & Ball in Columbia, S. C., who made further printings from them. Two plates, each with two panes of 100, numbered 1 and 2. First state shows numbers only, later states show various styles of Archer & Daly imprints, and latest show Keatinge & Ball imprints. Archer & Daly stamps show uniformly clear impressions and a good quality of gum evenly distributed (Earliest known cancellation, April 21, 1863); Keatinge & Ball stamps generally show filled in impressions in a deep blue, and the gum is brown and unevenly distributed. (Earliest known cancellation, Oct. 4, 1864). The so-called laid paper is probably due to thick streaky gum. (These notes also apply to No. 12.)

1863-64 Thick or Thin Paper Engraved

11 A7 10c **blue** 15.00 20.00
No gum 7.50
deep blue, Keatinge & Ball ('64) 15.00 *35.00*
No gum 9.00
On cover 100.00
Single on cover (overpaid drop letter) 200.00
On wallpaper cover 800.00
On patriotic cover 1,000.
On prisoner's cover 750.00
On prisoner's cover with U.S. #65 2,500.
On cover, dp. blue (K. & B.) ('64) 200.00
On wallpaper cover (K. & B.) 1,250.
On prisoner's cover (K. & B.) with U.S. #65 ('64) —
Pair 35.00 45.00
Pair on cover 275.00
Block of 4 80.00 350.00
Strip of 4 on cover (Trans-Mississippi rate) —
Margin block of 12, Archer & Daly impt. & P# 450.00
Margin block of 12, Keatinge & Ball impt. & P# 425.00
Horiz. pair, vert. gutter between 125.00
a. 10c **milky blue** 45.00 47.50
No gum 30.00
b. 10c **dark blue** 22.50 25.00
No gum 13.50
c. 10c **greenish blue** 30.00 20.00
No gum 20.00
d. 10c **green** 60.00 *80.00*
No gum 40.00
e. Officially perforated 12½ (A. & D.) 325.00 275.00
On cover *750.00*
On wallpaper cover —
Pair 650.00 600.00
Pair on cover *2,750.*
Block of 4 1,500. *4,250.*

VARIETIES

Double transfer 75.00 100.00
Rouletted unofficially 500.00
On cover 800.00

Cancellations

Blue town +5.00
Red town +35.00
Orange town +110.00
Brown town +60.00
Green town +175.00
Violet town +100.00
Texas town +60.00
Arkansas town +125.00
Florida town +200.00
Straight line town +350.00
Army of Tenn. +300.00
April, 1863 year date +75.00
"FREE" +250.00
Blue gridiron +5.00
Black concentric circles +10.00
Star +100.00
Crossroads +150.00
"Paid" +100.00
Numeral +100.00
Railroad +175.00
Steamboat +1,500

Jefferson Davis (Die B) — A8

Plates bore Nos. 3 and 4, otherwise notes on No. 11 apply.
Earliest known use: Archer & Daly — May 1, 1863; Keatinge & Ball — Sept. 4, 1864.

1863-64 Thick or Thin Paper Engraved

12 A8 10c **blue** 18.00 20.00
No gum 9.00
deep blue, Keatinge & Ball ('64) 17.50 40.00
No gum 10.00
On cover 90.00
Single on cover (overpaid drop letter) 200.00
On wallpaper cover 800.00
On patriotic cover 1,000
On prisoner's cover 750.00
On prisoner's cover with U.S. #65 2,500
On cover, dp. blue (K. & B.) ('64) 130.00
Pair 40.00 52.50
Pair on cover 200.00
Block of 4 90.00 300.00
Strip of 4 on cover (Trans-Mississippi rate) —
Margin block of 12, Archer & Daly impt. & P# 475.00
Margin block of 12, Keatinge & Ball impt. & P# 425.00
Horiz. pair, vert. gutter between 125.00
a. 10c **milky blue** 45.00 47.50
No gum 30.00
b. 10c **light blue** 17.50 20.00
No gum 9.00
c. 10c **greenish blue** 35.00 *55.00*
No gum 20.00
d. 10c **dark blue** 18.00 22.50
No gum 9.00
e. 10c **green** 125.00 140.00

	No gum	75.00	
f.	Officially perforated 12½ (A. & D.)	350.00	300.00
	On cover		*750.00*
	Pair	750.00	600.00
	Pair on cover		—
	Block of 4	1,900.	

VARIETIES

	Double transfer	95.00	110.00
	Rouletted unofficially	—	375.00
	On cover		850.00

Cancellations

Blue town	+5.00
Red town	+35.00
Brown town	+90.00
Green town	+120.00
Violet town	+85.00
Texas town	+125.00
Arkansas town	+150.00
Florida town	+200.00
Straight line town	+400.00
Army of Tenn.	+350.00
May, 1863, year date	+60.00
Blue gridiron	+5.00
Black concentric circles	+10.00
Railroad	+175.00

George Washington — A9

1863 (June?) Engraved by Archer & Daly

One plate which consisted of two panes of 100 each. First printings were from plates with imprint in Old English type under each pane, which was later removed. Printed on paper of varying thickness and in many shades of green. This stamp was also used as currency. Earliest known cancellation, June 1, 1863. Forged cancellations exist.

13	A9 20c **green**	40.00	*400.*
	No gum	25.00	
	On cover		*1,250.*
	On wallpaper cover		*1,750.*
	On prisoner's cover		*4,000.*
	On prisoner's cover with U.S. #65		*5,000.*
	Pair	85.00	*900.*
	Horizontal pair with gutter between	350.00	
	Pair on cover (non-Trans-Mississippi rate)		*4,500.*
	Pair on cover (Trans-Mississippi rate)		—
	Block of 4	200.00	*3,500.*
	Strip of 4 with imprint	425.00	
	Block of 8 with imprint	1,050.	
a.	20c **yellow green**	70.00	*450.*
	No gum	45.00	
b.	20c **dark green**	65.00	*500.*
	No gum	40.00	
c.	20c **bluish green**	100.00	—
	No gum	65.00	
d.	Diagonal half used as 10c on cover		*2,000.*
	Diagonal half on prisoner's cover		—
e.	Horizontal half used as 10c on cover		*3,500.*

VARIETIES

Double transfer, 20 doubled (Pos. 24L and 35R)	300.	—
"20" on forehead	*3,000.*	—
Rouletted unofficially		*1,100.*
On cover		*3,750.*

Cancellations

Blue town	+50.
Red town	+200.
Violet town	—
Texas town	+100.
Arkansas town	+400.
Tennessee town	+1,000.
Railroad	—

John C. Calhoun — A10

Typographed by De La Rue & Co., London, England

1862

14	A10 1c **orange**	110.00	
	No gum	65.00	
	Pair	230.00	
	Block of 4	475.00	
a.	1c **deep orange**	130.00	
	No gum	80.00	

This stamp was never put in use.

Upon orders from the Confederate Government, De La Rue & Co. of London, England, prepared Two Cents and Ten Cents typographed plates by altering the One Cent (No. 14) and the Five Cents (Nos. 6-7) designs previously made by them. Stamps were never officially printed from these plates although privately made prints exist in various colors.

Explanatory Notes

The following notes by Lawrence L. Shenfield explain the various routes, rates and usages of the general issue Confederate stamps.

"Across the Lines" Letters Carried by Private Express Companies

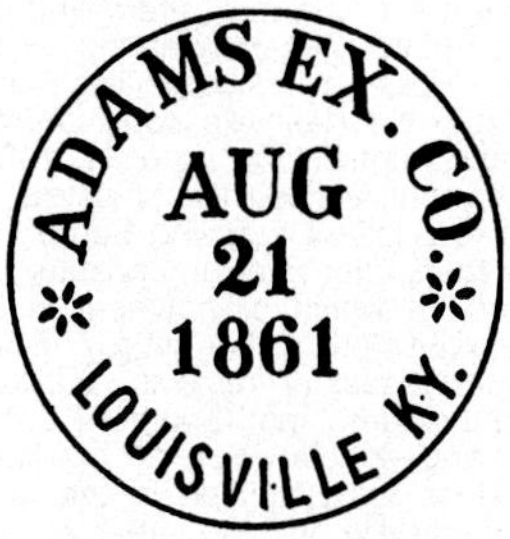

Adams Express Co. and American Letter Express Company Handstamps Used on "Across the Lines" Letters

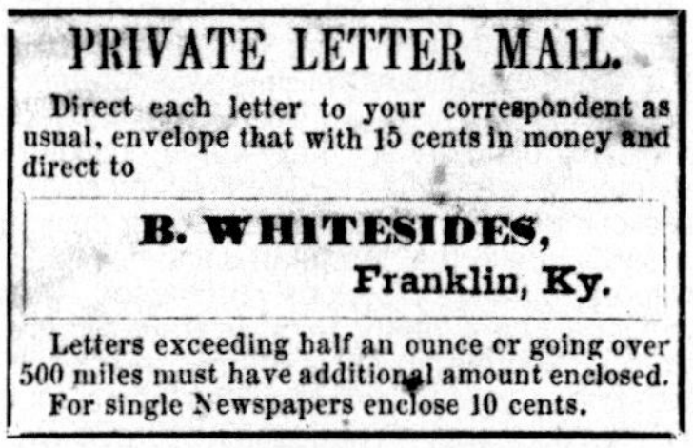

PRIVATE LETTER MAIL.

Direct each letter to your correspondent as usual, envelope that with 15 cents in money and direct to

B. WHITESIDES,
Franklin, Ky.

Letters exceeding half an ounce or going over 500 miles must have additional amount enclosed. For single Newspapers enclose 10 cents.

B. Whitesides Label

About two months after the outbreak of the Civil War, in June, 1861, postal service between North and South and vice versa was carried on largely by Adams Express Company, and the American Letter Express Company. Northern terminus for the traffic was Louisville, Ky.; Southern terminus was Nashville, Tenn. Letters for transmission were delivered to any office of the express company, together with a fee, usually 20c or 25c per ½ ounce to cover carriage. The express company messengers carried letters across the lines and delivered them to their office on the other side, where they were deposited in the Government mail for transmission to addressees, postage paid out of the fee charged. Letters from North to South, always enclosed in 3c U.S. envelopes, usually bear the handstamp of the Louisville office of the express company, and in addition the postmark and "Paid 5" of Nashville, Tenn., indicating its acceptance for delivery at the Nashville Post Office. Letters from South to North sometimes bear the origin postmark of a Southern post office, but more often merely the handstamp of the Louisville express company office applied as the letters cleared through Louisville. The B. Whitesides South to North cover bears a "Private Letter Mail" label. In addition, these covers bear the 3c 1857 U.S. adhesive stamp, cancelled with the postmark and grid of Louisville, Ky., where they went into the Government mail for delivery. Some across-the-lines letters show the handstamp of various express company offices, according to the particular routing the letters followed. On August 26, 1861, the traffic ceased by order of the U.S. Post Office Dept. (Values are for full covers bearing the usual Louisville, Ky., or Nashville, Tenn., handstamps of the express company. Unusual express office markings are rarer and worth more.)

North to South 3c U.S. Envelope, Adams Exp. Co. Louisville, Ky., handstamp	*1,500.*
North to South 3c U.S. Envelope, American Letter Express Co., Ky., handstamp	*2,100.*
South to North 3c 1857, Adams Exp. Co., Louisville, Ky., handstamp	*1,750.*
South to North 3c 1857, American Letter Exp. 250, Nashville, Tenn., handstamp	*2,500.*
South to North 3c 1861, Adams Exp. Co., Louisville, Ky., handstamp	*3,250.*
South to North 3c 1857, B. Whitesides, Franklin, Ky., label	*16,500.*

Blockade-Run Letters from Europe to the Confederate States

Charleston "STEAM-SHIP" in Oval Handstamp

As the Federal Fleet gradually extended its blockade of the Confederate States coastal regions, the South was forced to resort to blockade runners to carry letters to and from outside ports. These letters were all private-ship letters and never bore a foreign stamp if from Europe, nor a Confederate stamp if to Europe. The usual route from Europe was via a West Indies port, Nassau, Bahamas; Hamilton, Bermuda, or Havana, into the Southern ports of Wilmington, N.C. and Charleston, S.C. More rarely such letters came in to Savannah, Mobile and New Orleans. Letters from Europe are the only ones which are surely identified by their markings. They bore either the postmark of Wilmington, N.C., straightline "SHIP" and "12", "22", "32", etc., in manuscript; or the postmark of Charleston, S. C., "STEAMSHIP" in oval, and "12", "22", "32", etc., in manuscript. Very rarely Charleston used a straightline "SHIP" instead of "STEAMSHIP" in oval. All such letters were postage due; the single letter rate of 12c being made up of 2c for the private ship captain plus 10c for the regular single letter Confederate States rate. Over-weight letters were 22c (due), 32c, 42c, etc. A few examples are known on which Confederate General Issue stamps were used, usually as payment for forwarding postage. Covers with such stamps, or with the higher rate markings, 22c, 32, etc., are worth more.

Values are for full covers in fine condition.

Charleston, S.C. "6" handstamp	*2,500.*
Charleston, S.C., postmark, "STEAMSHIP," and "12" in ms.	*3,000.*
Charleston, S.C., postmark, "SHIP," and "12" in ms.	*3,000.*
Wilmington, N.C., postmark, "SHIP," and "12" in ms.	*3,000.*
Savannah, Ga., postmark "SHIP," and "7" in ms. (*)	*4,000.*
New Orleans, La. postmark, "SHIP" and "10" in ms.	*5,000.*

(* 7c rate: 5c postage before July 1, 1862, plus 2c for ship captain.)

Express Company Mail in the Confederacy

Southern Express Company Handstamps

Shortly after the outbreak of war in 1861, the Adams Express Company divisions operating in the South were forced to suspend operations and turned their Southern lines over to a new company organized under the title Southern Express Company. This express did the bulk of the express business in the Confederacy despite the continued opposition of the Post Office Dept. of the C.S.A. and the ravages of the contending armies upon railroads. Other companies operating in the Confederacy were: South Western Express Co. (New Orleans), Pioneer Express Company, White's Southern Express (only one example known) and some local expresses of limited operation.

The first three used handstamps of various designs usually bearing the city name of the office. Postal regulation necessitated the payment of regular Confederate postal rates on letters carried by express companies, express charges being paid in addition. Important letters, particularly money letters, were entrusted to these express companies as well as goods and wares of all kinds. The express rates charged for letters are not known; probably they varied depending upon the difficulty and risk of transmittal. Covers bearing stamps and express company handstamps are very rare.

Prisoner-of-War and Flag-of-Truce Letters

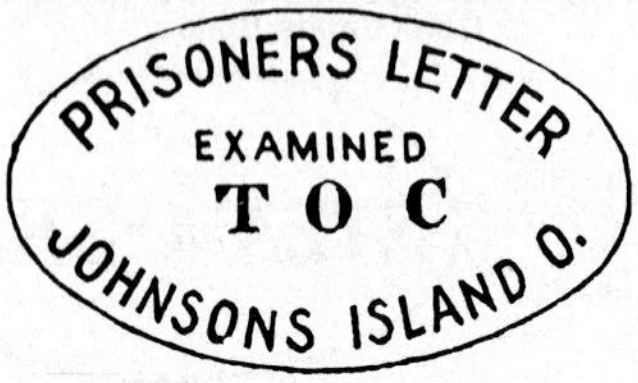

Prison Censor Handstamps

By agreement between the United States and the Confederate States, military prisoners and imprisoned civilians of both sides were permitted to send censored letters to their respective countries. Such letters, if from North to South, usually bore a U.S. 3c 1861 adhesive, postmarked at a city near the prison, to pay the postage to the exchange ground near Old Point Comfort, Va.; and a 10c Confederate stamp, canceled at Richmond, Va. (or "due" handstamp) to pay the Confederate postage to destination. If from South to North, letters usually bore a 10c Confederate stamp canceled at a Southern city (or "paid" handstamp) and a U. S. 3c 1861 adhesive (or "due 3" marking) and the postmark of Old Point Comfort, Va. In addition, prison censor markings, handstamped or manuscript, the name and rank of the soldier, and "Flag of Truce, via Fortress Monroe" in manuscript usually appear on these covers. Federal prison censor handstamps of various designs are known from these prisons:

Camp Chase, Columbus, O.
David's Island, Pelham, N.Y.
Fort Delaware, Delaware City, Del.
Camp Douglas, Chicago, Ill.
Elmira Prison, Elmira, N.Y.
Johnson's Island, Sandusky, O.
Fort McHenry, Baltimore, Md.
Camp Morton, Indianapolis, Ind.
Fort Oglethorpe, Macon, Ga.
Old Capitol Prison, Washington, D.C.
Point Lookout Prison, Point Lookout, Md.
Fort Pulaski, Savannah, Ga.
Rock Island Prison, Rock Island, Ill.
Ship Island, New Orleans, La.
West's Hospital, Baltimore, Md.
U.S. General Hospital, Gettysburg, Pa.

Several other Federal prisons used manuscript censor markings.

Southern prison censor markings are always in manuscript, and do not identify the prison. The principal Southern prisons were at Richmond and Danville, Va.; Andersonville and Savannah, Ga.; Charleston, Columbia and Florence S.C.; Salisbury, N.C.; Hempstead and Tyler, Tex.

Civilians residing in both the North and the South were also, under exceptional circumstances, permitted to send Flag of Truce letters across the lines. Such covers bore no censor marking nor prison markings, but were always endorsed "via Flag of Truce".

Values will be found under various individual stamps for "on prisoner's cover" and are for the larger prisons. Prisoners' letters from the smaller prisons are much rarer. Only a very small percentage of prisoners' covers bore *both* a U.S. stamp and a Confederate stamp.

The "SOUTHERN LETTER UNPAID" Marking On Northbound Letters of Confederate Origin

By mid-May, 1861, correspondence between the North and South was difficult. In the South, postmasters were resigning and closing their accounts with Washington as the Confederacy prepared to organize its own postal system by June 1. From that date on, town marks and "paid" handstamps (and later postmasters' provisional stamps) were used in all post offices of the seceded states. The three most important Southern cities for clearing mail to the North were Memphis, Nashville and Richmond. The Richmond-Washington route was closed in April; Memphis was closed by June 1st, and mail attempting to cross the lines at these points generally ended up at the dead letter office. However, at Louisville, Kentucky, mail from the South via Nashville continued to arrive in June, July and August. On June 24, 1861, the Post Office Department advised the Louisville post office, "You will forward letters from the South for the Loyal States as unpaid, after removing postage stamps, but foreign letters in which prepayment is compulsory must come to the Dead Letter Office." However, Louisville avoided the task of "removing postage stamps," and instead prepared the "Southern Letter Unpaid" handstamp and special "due 3" markers for use. These markings were applied in the greenish-blue color of the Louisville office to letters of Southern origin that had accumulated, in addition to the usual town mark and grid of Louisville. The letters were delivered in the North as unpaid. Probably Louisville continued to forward such unpaid mail until about July 15. The marking is very rare. Other Southern mail was forwarded from Louisville as late as Aug. 27.

For listings see under U.S. 1857-61 issue, Nos. 26, 35-38. Values shown there are generally for this marking on off-cover stamps. Complete covers bearing stamps showing the full markings are valued from $10,000 upward depending upon the stamps, other postal markings and unusual usages, and condition. Fraudulent covers exist.

Trans-Mississippi Express Mail-the 40c Rate

From the fall of New Orleans on April 24, 1862, the entire reach of the Mississippi River was threatened by the Federal fleets. Late in 1862 the Confederacy experienced difficulty in maintaining regular mail routes trans-Mississippi to the Western states. Private express companies began to carry some mail, but by early 1863 when the Meridian-Jackson-Vicksburg-Shreveport route was seriously menaced, the Post Office Department of the Confederate States was forced to inaugurate an express mail service by contracting with a private company the name of which remains undisclosed. The eastern termini were at Meridian and Brandon, Miss.; the western at Shreveport and Alexandria, La. Letters, usually endorsed "via Meridian (or Brandon)" if going West; "via Shreveport (or Alexandria)" if going East were deposited in any Confederate post office. The rate was 40c per ½ ounce or less. Such Trans-Mississippi Express Mail upon arrival at a terminus was carried by couriers in a devious route across the Mississippi and returned to the regular mails at the nearest terminus on the other side of the river. The precise date of the beginning of the Trans-Mississippi service is not known. The earliest date of use so far seen is November 2, 1863 and the latest use February 9, 1865. These covers can be identified by the written endorsement of the route, but particularly by the rate since many bore no route endorsements.

Strips of four of 10c engraved stamps, pairs of the 20c stamp and various combinations of 10c stamps and the 5c London or Local prints are known; also handstamped Paid 40c marking. No identifying handstamps were used, merely the postmark of the office which received the letter originally. Values for Trans-Mississippi Express covers will be found under various stamps of the General Issues.

A 50c Preferred Mail Express rate, announced in April, 1863, preceded the Trans-Mississippi Express Mail 40c rate. One cover showing this rate is known.

Packet and Steamboat Covers and Markings

Letters carried on Confederate packets operating on coastal routes or up and down the inland waterways were usually handstamped with the name of the packet or marked STEAM or STEAMBOAT. Either United States stamps of the 1857 issue or stamped envelopes of the 1853 or 1860 issues have been found so used, as well as Confederate Postmasters' Provisional and General Issue stamps. Some specially designed pictorial or imprinted packet boat covers also exist. All are scarce and command values from $1,000 upward for handstamped United States envelopes and from $1,500 up for covers bearing Confederate stamps.

TABLE OF SECESSION

	Ordinance of Secession	Admitted to Confederacy	Period for Use of U.S. Stamps As Independent State	Total to 5/31/1861*
SC	12/20/1860	2/4/1861	46 days	163 days
MS	1/9/1861	2/4/1861	26 days	143 days
FL	1/10/1861	2/4/1861	25 days	142 days
AL	1/11/1861	2/4/1861	24 days	141 days
GA	1/19/1861	2/4/1861	16 days	133 days
LA	1/26/1861	2/4/1861	9 days	126 days
TX	2/1/1861	3/6/1861	33 days	120 days
VA	4/17/1861	5/7/1861	20 days	45 days
AR	5/6/1861	5/18/1861	12 days	26 days
TN	5/6/1861	7/2/1861	57 days	26 days
NC	5/20/1861	5/27/1861	7 days	12 days

* The use of United States stamps in the seceded States was prohibited after May 31, 1861.

TX — Ordinance of Secession adopted Feb. 1. Popular vote to secede Feb. 23, effective Mar. 2, 1861.

VA — Ordinance of Secession adopted. Admitted to Confederacy May 7. Scheduled election of May 23 ratified the Ordinance of Secession.

TN — Ordinance passed to "submit to vote of the people a Declaration of Independence, and for other purposes." Adopted May 6. Election took place June 8. General Assembly ratified election June 24.

The Confederate postal laws did not provide the franking privilege for any mail except official correspondence of the Post Office Department. Such letters could be sent free only when enclosed in officially imprinted envelopes individually signed by the official using them. These envelopes were prepared and issued for Post Office Department use.

The imprints were on United States envelopes of 1853-61 issue, and also on commercial envelopes of various sizes and colors. When officially signed and mailed, they were postmarked, usually at Richmond Va., with printed or handstamped "FREE". Envelopes are occasionally found unused and unsigned, and more rarely, signed but unused. When such official envelopes were used on other than official Post Office Department business, Confederate stamps were used.

Semi-official envelopes also exist bearing imprints of other government departments, offices, armies, states, etc. Regular postage was required to carry such envelopes through the mails.

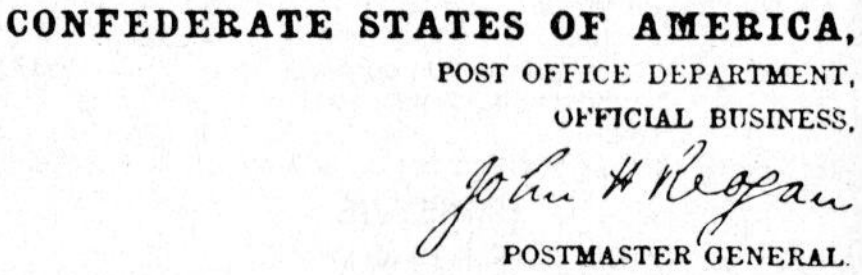

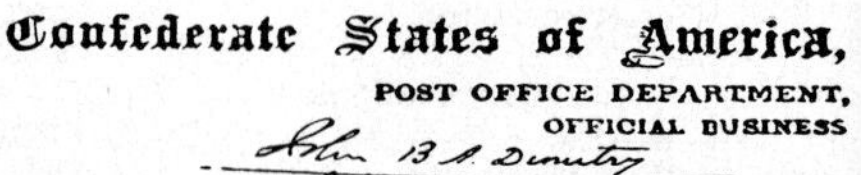

Typical Imprints of Official Envelopes of the Post Office Department. (Many variations of type, style and wording exist.)

Office	Signature
Postmaster General	John H. Reagan
Chief of the Contract Bureau	H. St. Geo. Offutt
Chief of the Appointment Bureau	B. N. Clements
Chief of the Finance Bureau	Jno. L. Harrell
Chief of the Finance Bureau	J. L. Lancaster
Chief of the Finance Bureau	A. Dimitry
Dead Letter Office	A. Dimitry
Dead Letter Office	Jno. L. Harrell
Chief Clerk, P. O. Department	B. Fuller
Chief Clerk	W. D. Miller
Auditor's Office	W. W. Lester
Auditor's Office	B. Baker
Auditor's Office	J. W. Robertson
First Auditor's Office, Treasury Department	J. W. Robertson
First Auditor's Office, Treasury Department	B. Baker
Third Auditor's Office	A. Moise
Third Auditor's Office	I. W. M. Harris
Agency, Post Office Dept. Trans-Miss.	Jas. H. Starr

PROOFS

1861

(1) — Die on Glazed Card
(1a) — Die on Wove Paper
(5) — Plate on Wove Paper
(6) — Plate on Thin Card
(7) — Plate on Thick Ribbed Paper

1P	(5)	5c **green,** plate on wove paper	*1,500.*
2P	(5)	10c **blue,** plate on wove paper	*1,500.*
2TC	(5)	10c **black,** plate on wove paper (stone Y)	*3,000.*

1862

6P	(1)	5c **light blue,** die on glazed card	600.
6P, 14P	(1)	5c **blue** & 1c **orange,** composite die proof, 20x90mm card	*6,000.*
6P	(5)	5c **light blue,** plate on wove paper	150.
		Pair with gutter between	375.
6TC	(1a)	5c **dark blue,** die on woven paper	600.
6TC	(5)	5c **gray blue,** plate on wove paper	600.
6TC	(1)	5c **black,** die on glazed card	900.
6TC	(5)	5c **black,** plate on wove paper	1,000.
6TC	(1)	5c **pink,** die on glazed card	900.
7TC	(5)	5c **carmine,** plate on wove paper	850.
7TC	(6)	5c **carmine,** plate on thin card	750.

1863

8TC	(1a)	2c **black,** die on wove paper	1,750.
9TC	(1a)	10c **black,** die on wove paper	1,500.
11TC	(1a)	10c **black,** die on wove paper	1,100.
12P	(7)	10c **deep blue,** plate on thick ribbed paper	750.
13P	(1a)	20c **green,** die on wove paper	*4,000.*
13TC	(1a)	20c **red brown,** die on wove paper	*4,000.*

1862

14P	(1)	1c **orange,** die on glazed card	*2,000.*
14TC	(1)	1c **black,** die on glazed card	*2,500.*
14TC	(5)	1c **light yellow brown,** plate on wove paper	800.

Essay Die Proofs

In working up the final dies, proofs of incomplete designs in various stages were made. Usually dated in typeset lines, they are very rare. Others, of the 10c (No. 12) and the 20c (No. 13) were proofs made as essays from the dies. They are deeply engraved and printed in deep shades of the issued colors, but show only small differences from the stamps as finally issued. All are very rare.

Specimen Overprints

The De La Rue typographed 5c and 1c are known with "SPECIMEN" overprinted diagonally, also horizontally for 1c.

Counterfeits

In 1935 a set of 12 lithographed imitations, later known as the "Springfield facsimiles," appeared in plate form. They are in approximately normal colors on yellowish soft wove paper of modern manufacture.

CANAL ZONE

The Canal Zone, a strip of territory with an area of about 552 square miles following generally the line of the Canal, was under the jurisdiction of the United States, 1904-1979, and under the joint jurisdiction of the United States and Panama, 1979-1999, when the Canal, in its entirety, reverted to Panama.

The Canal organization underwent two distinct and fundamental changes. The construction of the Canal and the general administration of civil affairs were performed by the Isthmian Canal Commission under the provisions of the Spooner Act. This was supplanted in April, 1914, by the Panama Canal Act which established the organization known as The Panama Canal. This was an independent government agency which included both the operation and maintenance of the waterway and civil government in the Canal Zone. Most of the quasi-business enterprises relating to the Canal operation were conducted by the Panama Railroad, an adjunct of The Panama Canal.

A basic change in the mode of operations took effect July 1, 1951, under provisions of Public Law 841 of the 81st Congress. This in effect transferred the Canal operations to the Panama Railroad Co., which had been made a federal government corporation in 1948, and changed its name to the Panama Canal Co. Simultaneously the civil government functions of The Panama Canal, including the postal service, were renamed the Canal Zone Government. The organization therefore consisted of two units — the Panama Canal Co. and Canal Zone Government — headed by an individual who was president of the company and governor of the Canal Zone. His appointment as governor was made by the president of the United States, subject to confirmation by the Senate, and he was ex-officio president of the company.

The Canal Zone Government functioned as an independent government agency, and was under direct supervision of the president of the United States who delegated this authority to the Secretary of the Army.

The Panama Canal is 50 miles long from deep water in the Atlantic to deep water in the Pacific. It runs from northwest to southeast with the Atlantic entrance being 33.5 miles north and 27 miles west of the Pacific entrance. The airline distance between the two entrances is 43 miles. It requires about eight hours for an average ship to transit the Canal. Transportation between the Atlantic and Pacific sides of the Isthmus is available by railway, highway or air.

The Canal Zone Postal Service began operating June 24, 1904, when nine post offices were opened in connection with the construction of the Panama Canal. It ceased Sept. 30, 1979, and the Panama Postal Service took over.

Italicized numbers in parentheses indicate quantity issued.

100 CENTAVOS = 1 PESO
100 CENTESIMOS = 1 BALBOA
100 CENTS = 1 DOLLAR

Catalogue values for unused stamps are for Never Hinged items beginning with No. 118 in the regular postage section and No. C6 in the airpost section.

Map of Panama — A1

Violet to Violet Blue Handstamp on Panama Nos. 72, 72a-72c, 78, 79.

On the 2c "PANAMA" is normally 13mm long. On the 5c and 10c it measures about 15mm.

On the 2c, "PANAMA" reads up on the upper half of the sheet and down on the lower half. On the 5c and 10c, "PANAMA" reads up at left and down at right on each stamp.

On the 2c only, varieties exist with inverted "V" for "A," accent on "A," inverted "N," etc., in "PANAMA."

1904, June 24 Engr. Unwmk. ***Perf. 12***

1	A1	2c **rose,** both "PANAMA" reading up or down *(2600)*		600.	425.
		Single on post card			*1,650.*
		Strip of 3 on cover			1,500.
		Block of 4		2,750.	2,100.
		"PANAMA" 15mm long *(260)*		650.	600.
		"P NAMA"		650.	600.
a.		"CANAL ZONE" inverted *(100)*		*1,000.*	850.
b.		"CANAL ZONE" double		*3,250.*	2,000.
c.		"CANAL ZONE" double, both inverted		*20,000.*	
d.		"PANAMA" reading down and up *(52)*		750.	650.
e.		As "d," "CANAL ZONE" invtd.		*9,000.*	*7,000.*
f.		Vert. pair, "PANAMA" reading up on top 2c, down on other		*2,100.*	*2,100.*
g.		As "f," "CANAL ZONE" inverted		*20,000.*	
2	A1	5c **blue** *(7800)*		300.	200.
		On cover			250.
		First day cover			*7,500.*
		Block of 4		1,400.	1,000.
		Left "PANAMA" 2 ¼mm below bar *(156)*		575.	500.
		Colon between right "PANA-MA" and bar *(156)*		575.	500.
a.		"CANAL ZONE" inverted		775.	600.
		On cover			*800.*
b.		"CANAL ZONE" double		2,250.	1,500.
c.		Pair, one without "CANAL ZONE" overprint		*5,000.*	*5,000.*
d.		"CANAL ZONE" overprint diagonal, reading down to right		800.	700.
3	A1	10c **yellow** *(4946)*		400.	250.
		On cover			325.
		First day cover			*5,000.*
		Block of 4		1,750.	1,150.
		Left "PANAMA" 2 ¼mm below bar *(100)*		675.	575.
		Colon between right "PANA-MA" and bar *(100)*		650.	550.
a.		"CANAL ZONE" inverted *(200)*		775.	600.
		On cover			*800.*
b.		"CANAL ZONE" double			*15,000.*
c.		Pair, one without "CANAL ZONE" overprint		*6,000.*	5,000.

Cancellations consist of town and/or bars in magenta or black, or a mixture of both colors.

Nos. 1-3 were withdrawn July 17, 1904.

Forgeries of the "Canal Zone" overprint and cancellations are numerous.

United States Nos. 300, 319, 304, 306 and 307 Overprinted in Black

1904, July 18 Wmk. 191

4	A115	1c **blue green** *(43,738)*	40.00	22.50
		green	40.00	22.50
		On cover		75.00
		Block of 4	175.00	140.00
		P# strip of 3, Impt.	160.00	
		P# block of 6, Impt.	925.00	
5	A129	2c **carmine** *(68,414)*	35.00	25.00
		On cover		75.00
		Block of 4	150.00	125.00
		P# strip of 3, Impt.	150.00	
		P# block of 6, Impt.	1,000.	
a.		2c **scarlet**	35.00	30.00
6	A119	5c **blue** *(20,858)*	110.00	65.00
		On cover		275.00
		Block of 4	525.00	325.00
		P# strip of 3, Impt.	475.00	
		P# block of 6, Impt.	1,450.	
7	A121	8c **violet black** *(7932)*	175.00	85.00
		On cover		500.00
		Block of 4	800.00	450.00
		P# strip of 3, Impt.	725.00	
		P# block of 6, Impt.	3,500.	
8	A122	10c **pale red brown** *(7856)*	160.00	90.00
		On cover		500.00
		Block of 4	700.00	475.00
		P# strip of 3, Impt.	675.00	
		P# block of 6, Impt.	2,900.	
		Nos. 4-8 (5)	520.00	287.50

Nos. 4-8 frequently show minor broken letters.

Cancellations consist of circular town and/or bars in black, blue or magenta.

Beware of fake overprints.

A2

A3

CANAL ZONE
Regular Type

CANAL ZONE
Antique Type

The Canal Zone overprint on stamps Nos. 9-15 and 18-20 was made with a plate which had six different stages, each with its peculiar faults and errors. Stage 1: Broken CA-L, broken L, A-L spaced, on Nos. 9, 10, 12-15. Stage 2: broken L, Z, N, E, on Nos. 9, 10, 12-14. Stage 3: same as 2 with additional antique ZONE, on Nos. 9, 11-14, 18. Stage 4: same as 3 with additional antique CANAL on Nos. 9, 12, 13. Stage 5: broken E and letters L, Z, N, and words CANAL and ZONE in antique type on Nos. 12-14, 19, 20. Stage 6: same as 5 except for additional antique Z on stamp which had antique L, on No. 12. The Panama overprints can be distinguished by the different shades of the red overprint, the width of the bar, and the word PANAMA. No. 11 has two different Panama overprints; No. 12 has six; No. 13 five; No. 14 two; and Nos. 15, 18-20, one each. In the "8cts" surcharge of Nos. 14 and 15, there are three varieties of the igure “8.” The bar is sometimes misplaced so that it appears on he bottom of the stamp instead of the top.

1904-06 **Unwmk.**

Black Overprint on Stamps of Panama

9 A2 1c **green** *(319,800) Dec. 12, 1904* 2.75 2.25
On cover 12.50
Block of 4 12.00 12.00
Spaced “A L” in “CANAL” *(700)* 110.00 100.00
“ON” of “ZONE” dropped 300.00 275.00
a. “CANAL” in antique type *(500)* 100.00 100.00
b. “ZONE” in antique type *(1500)* 70.00 70.00
c. Inverted overprint *5,500.* *4,000.*
d. Double overprint *2,750.* *2,000.*
10 A2 2c **rose** *(367,500) Dec. 12, 1904* 4.50 3.00
On cover 17.50
Block of 4 21.00 17.50
Spaced “A L” of “CANAL” *(1700)* 85.00 85.00
“ON” of “ZONE” dropped 400.00 400.00
a. Inverted overprint 225.00 275.00
b. “L” of “CANAL” sideways 2,500. 2,500.

“PANAMA” (15mm long) reading up at left, down at right

Overprint “CANAL ZONE” in Black, “PANAMA” and Bar in Red

11 A3 2c **rose** *(150,000) Dec. 9, 1905* 7.50 5.00
On cover 50.00
Block of 4 35.00 27.50
Inverted “M” in “PANAMA” *(3,000)* 45.00 40.00
“PANAMA” 16mm long *(3000)* 45.00 40.00
a. “ZONE” in antique type *(1500)* 200.00 200.00
b. “PANAMA” overprint inverted, bar at bottom *(200)* 675.00 675.00
12 A3 5c **blue** *(400,000) Dec. 12, 1904* 8.00 3.75
On cover 100.00
Block of 4 35.00 25.00
Spaced “A L” in “CANAL” *(300)* 90.00 80.00
“PAMANA” reading up *(2800)* 75.00 70.00
“PAMANA” reading down *(400)* 200.00 180.00
“PANAMA” 16mm long *(1300)* 40.00 37.50
Inverted “M” in “PANAMA” *(1300)* 40.00 37.50
Right “PANAMA” 5mm below bar *(600)* 75.00 70.00
“PANAM” 70.00 65.00
“PANAAM” at right 950.00 900.00
“PAN MA” 75.00 70.00
“ANAMA” 80.00 75.00
a. “CANAL” in antique type *(2750)* 75.00 65.00
b. “ZONE” in antique type *(2950)* 75.00 65.00
c. “CANAL ZONE” double *(200)* 800.00 800.00
d. “PANAMA” double *(120)* 1,050. 1,000.
e. “PANAMA” inverted, bar at bottom 2,000.
13 A3 10c **yellow** *(64,900) Dec. 12, 1904* 22.50 12.50
On cover 125.00
Block of 4 110.00 62.50
Spaced “A L” in “CANAL” *(200)* 200.00 180.00
“PANAMA” 16mm long *(400)* 75.00 65.00
“PAMANA” reading down *(200)* 200.00 180.00
Invtd. “M” in “PANAMA” *(400)* 100.00 90.00
Right “PANAMA” 5mm below bar *(398)* 150.00 140.00
Left “PANAMA” touches bar *(400)* 200.00 160.00
a. “CANAL” in antique type *(200)* 200.00 200.00
b. “ZONE” in antique type *(400)* 175.00 160.00
c. “PANAMA” ovpt. double *(80)* 650.00 650.00
d. “PANAMA” overprint in red brown *(5000)* 27.50 27.50
“PANAMA” ovpt. in orange red 32.50 32.50

With Added Surcharge in Red

a

There are three varieties of “8” in the surcharge on #14-15.

14 A3 8c on 50c **bister brown** *(27,900) Dec. 12, 1904* 32.50 22.50
On cover 175.00
Block of 4 190.00 140.00
Spaced “A L” in “CANAL” *(194)* 175.00 160.00
Right “PANAMA” 5mm below bar *(438)* 200.00 175.00
a. “ZONE” in antique type *(25)* 1,150. 1,150.
b. “CANAL ZONE” inverted *(200)* 450.00 425.00
c. “PANAMA” overprint in rose brown *(6000)* 40.00 40.00
d. As “c,” “CANAL” in antique type *(10)* 2,000.
e. As “c,” “ZONE” in antique type *(10)* 2,000.
f. As “c,” “8 cts” double *(30)* *1,100.*
g. As “c,” “8” omitted *4,250.*

Nos. 11-14 are overprinted or surcharged on Panama Nos. 77, 77e, 78, 78c, 78d, 78f, 78g, 78h, 79 79c, 79e, 79g and 81 respectively.

Panama No. 74a, 74b Overprinted “CANAL ZONE” in Regular Type in Black and Surcharged Type “a” in Red

Both “PANAMA” (13mm long) Reading Up

15 A3(a) 8c on 50c **bister brown** *(435) Dec. 12, 1904* 2,600. *4,750.*
On cover *10,000.*
Block of 4 *11,500.*
“PANAMA” 15mm long *(50)* 2,750. *5,000.*
“P NAMA” 5,000.
Spaced “A L” in “CANAL” *(5)* 5,000.
a. “PANAMA” reading down and up *(10)* *7,500.* —

On No. 15 with original gum, the gum is almost always disturbed. Unused stamps are valued thus.

Map of Panama — A4

Panama Nos. 19 and 21 Surcharged in Black:

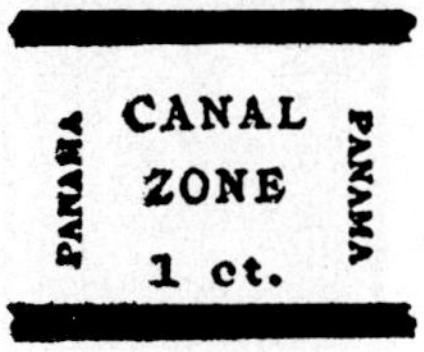

a

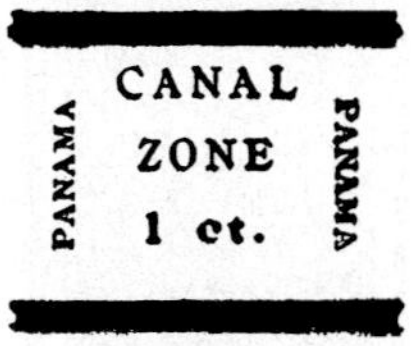

b

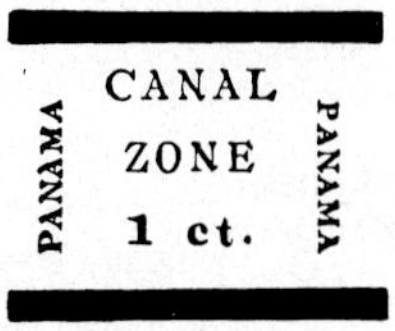

c

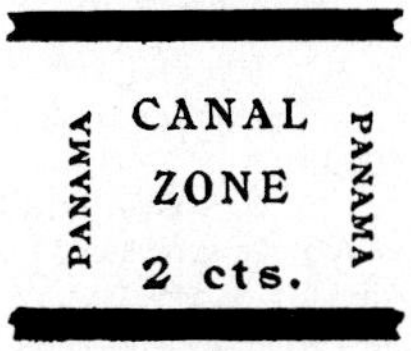

d

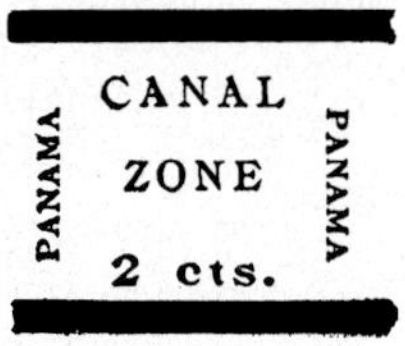

e

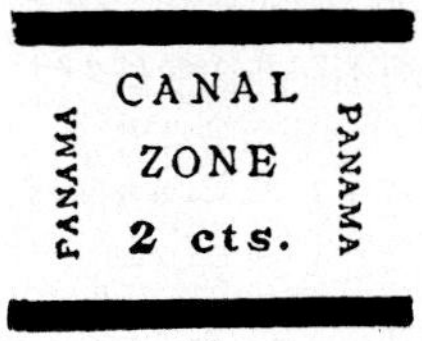

f

1906

There were three printings of each denomination, differing principally in the relative position of the various parts of the surcharges. Varieties occur with inverted “V” for the final “A” in “PANAMA,” “CA” spaced, “ZO” spaced, “2c” spaced, accents in various positions, and with bars shifted so that two bars appear on top or bottom of the stamp (either with or without the corresponding bar on top or bottom) and sometimes with only one bar at top or bottom.

16 A4 1c on 20c **violet,** type a *(100,000) Mar.* 2.00 1.60
On cover 10.00
Block of 4 9.00 7.50
a. Type b *(100,000) May* 2.00 1.60
On cover 10.00
Block of 4 9.00 7.50
b. Type c *(300,000) Sept.* 2.00 1.60
On cover 10.00
Block of 4 10.50 7.50
Spaced C A 13.00 12.00
c. As No. 16, double surcharge *2,000.*
17 A4 2c on 1p **lake,** type d *(200,000) Mar.* 2.75 2.75
On cover 12.00
Block of 4 14.00 12.50
a. Type e *(200,000) May* 2.75 2.75
On cover 12.00
Block of 4 14.00 12.50
b. Type f *(50,000) Sept.* 20.00 20.00
On cover 75.00
Block of 4 90.00 90.00

Panama Nos. 74, 74a and 74b Overprinted “CANAL ZONE” in Regular Type in Black and Surcharged in Red

8 cts.
b

8 cts
c

1905-06

Both “PANAMA” Reading Up

18 A3(b) 8c on 50c **bister brown** *(17,500) Nov. 1905* 55.00 50.00
On cover 225.00
Block of 4 250.00 230.00
“PANAMA” 15mm long *(1750)* 90.00 80.00
“P NAMA” 125.00 110.00
a. “ZONE” in antique type *(175)* 200.00 180.00
b. “PANAMA” reading down and up *(350)* 175.00 160.00
19 A3(c) 8c on 50c **bister brown** *(19,000) Apr. 23, 1906* 55.00 45.00
On cover 250.00
Block of 4 250.00 200.00
“PANAMA” 15mm long *(1900)* 85.00 70.00
“P NAMA” 90.00
a. “CANAL” in antique type *(190)* 210.00 180.00
b. “ZONE” in antique type *(190)* 210.00 180.00
c. “8 cts” double *1,100.* *1,100.*
d. “PANAMA” reading down and up *(380)* 110.00 90.00

On Nos. 18-19 with original gum, the gum is usually disturbed. Unused stamps are valued thus.

Panama No. 81 Overprinted “CANAL ZONE” in Regular Type in Black and Surcharged in Red Type “c” plus Period

“PANAMA” reading up and down

20 A3(c) 8c on 50c **bister brown** *(19,600) Sept. 1906* 45.00 40.00
On cover 200.00
Block of 4 190.00 175.00
“PAMANA” reading up *(392)* 120.00 110.00
a. “CANAL” antique type *(196)* 200.00 180.00
b. “ZONE” in antique type *(196)* 200.00 180.00
c. “8 cts” omitted *(50)* 800.00 800.00
d. “8 cts” double *1,500.*
e. “cts 8” —

Nos. 14 and 18-20 exist without CANAL ZONE overprint but were not regularly issued and are considered printer's waste. Forgeries of the overprint varieties of Nos. 9-15 and 18-20 are known.

Vasco Núñez de Balboa — A5

Fernández de Córdoba — A6

Justo Arosemena — A7

Manuel J. Hurtado — A8

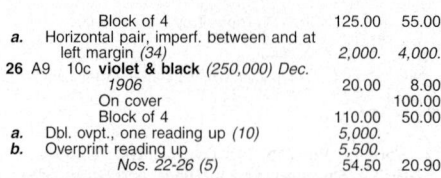

José de Obaldía — A9

Engraved by Hamilton Bank Note Co.

Overprinted in Black by Isthmian Canal Commission Press.

1906-07 Unwmk. *Perf. 12*

Overprint Reading Up

21 A6 2c **red & black** *(50,000) Oct. 29, 1906* 27.50 27.50
On cover 55.00
Block of 4 140.00 190.00
a. "CANAL" only *4,000.*

Overprint Reading Down

22 A5 1c **green & black** *(2,000,000) Jan. 14, 1907* 2.25 1.25
dull green & black 2.25 1.25
On cover 5.00
Block of 4 10.00 8.00
"ANA" for "CANAL" *(1000)* 70.00 70.00
"CAN L" for "CANAL" 80.00 80.00
"ONE" for "ZONE" *(3000)* 80.00 80.00
a. Horiz. pair, imperf. btwn. *(50)* 1,300. 1,300.
b. Vert. pair, imperf. btwn. *(20)* *2,000.* *1,750.*
c. Vert. pair, imperf. horiz. *(20)* *2,250.* *1,750.*
d. Inverted overprint reading up *(100)* 550.00 550.00
e. Double overprint *(300)* 275.00 275.00
f. Double overprint, one inverted 1,750. 1,600.
g. Invtd. center, ovpt. reading up *5,000.* *5,000.*
Pair on cover *12,500.*
h. Horiz. pair, imperf vert. —

23 A6 2c **red & black** *(2,370,000) Nov. 25, 1906* 3.25 1.40
scarlet & black, *1907* 3.25 1.40
On cover 6.00
Block of 4 14.00 9.00
"CAN L" for "CANAL" 45.00
a. Horizontal pair, imperf. between *(20)* 2,000. 1,750.
b. Vertical pair, one without overprint 2,500. 2,500.
c. Double overprint *(100)* 700.00 700.00
d. Double overprint, one diagonal 800.00 800.00
e. Double overprint, one diagonal, in pair with normal 2,500.
f. 2c carmine red & black, *Sept. 9, 1907* 5.00 2.75
g. As "f," inverted center and overprint reading up *6,000.*
On cover *12,000.*
h. As "d," one "ZONE CANAL" *4,000.*
i. "CANAL" double *4,000.*

24 A7 5c **ultramarine & black** *(1,390,000) Dec. 1906* 6.50 2.25
light ultramarine & black 6.50 2.25
blue & black, *Sept. 16, 1907* 6.50 2.25
dark blue & black 6.50 2.25
dull blue & black 6.50 2.25
light blue & black 6.50 2.25
On cover 40.00
Block of 4 27.50 20.00
"CAN L" for "CANAL" 60.00
c. Double overprint *(200)* 500.00 400.00
d. "CANAL" only *(10)* *4,000.*
e. "ZONE CANAL" *4,500.*

25 A8 8c **purple & black** *(170,000) Dec. 1906* 22.50 8.00
On cover 100.00
Block of 4 125.00 55.00
a. Horizontal pair, imperf. between and at left margin *(34)* *2,000.* *4,000.*

26 A9 10c **violet & black** *(250,000) Dec. 1906* 20.00 8.00
On cover 100.00
Block of 4 110.00 50.00
a. Dbl. ovpt., one reading up *(10)* *5,000.*
b. Overprint reading up *5,500.*
Nos. 22-26 (5) 54.50 20.90

The early printings of this series were issued on soft, thick, porous-textured paper, while later printings of all except No. 25 appear on hard, thin, smooth-textured paper.

Normal spacing of the early printings is 7¼mm between the words; later printings, 6¾mm. Nos. 22 and 26 exist imperf. between stamp and sheet margin. Nos. 22-25 occur with "CA" of "CANAL" spaced ½mm further apart on position No. 50 of the setting.

The used pair of No. 25a is unique.

Córdoba — A11

Arosemena — A12

Hurtado — A13

José de Obaldía — A14

Engraved by American Bank Note Co.

1909

Overprint Reading Down

27 A11 2c **vermilion & black** *(500,000) May 11, 1909* 12.50 5.50
On cover 15.00
First day cover 750.00
Block of 4 57.50 30.00
a. Horizontal pair, one without overprint *2,600.*
b. Vert. pair, one without ovpt. *3,500.*

28 A12 5c **deep blue & black** *(200,000) May 28, 1909* 45.00 12.50
On cover 60.00
Block of 4 200.00 60.00

29 A13 8c **violet & black** *(50,000) May 25, 1909* 40.00 14.00
On cover 90.00
Block of 4 200.00 82.50

30 A14 10c **violet & black** *(100,000) Jan. 19, 1909* 40.00 15.00
On cover 85.00
Block of 4 200.00 85.00
a. Horizontal pair, one with "ZONE" omitted *2,400.*
b. Vertical pair, one without overprint *3,000.*

Nos. 27-30 occur with "CA" spaced (position 50).

Do not confuse No. 27 with Nos. 39d or 53a.

On No. 30a, the stamp with "ZONE" omitted is also missing most of "CANAL."

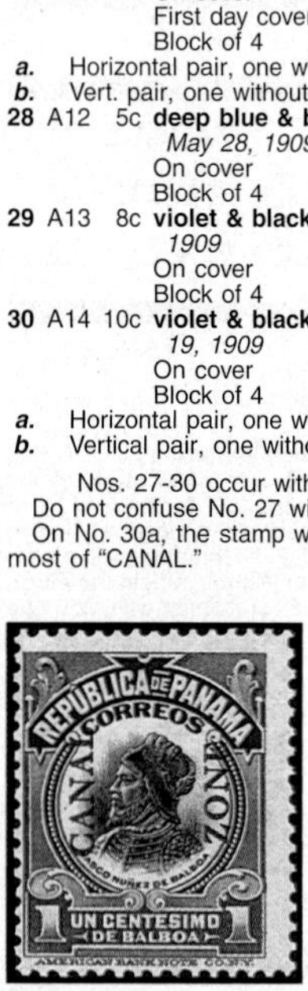
Vasco Núñez de Balboa — A15

Engraved, Printed and Overprinted by American Bank Note Co.

Black Overprint Reading Up

Type I

Type I Overprint: "C" with serifs both top and bottom. "L," "Z" and "E" with slanting serifs.

Compare Type I overprint with Types II to V illustrated before Nos. 38, 46, 52 and 55. Illustrations of Types I to V are considerably enlarged and do not show actual spacing between lines of overprint.

1909-10

31 A15 1c **dark green & black** *(4,000,000) Nov. 8, 1909* 5.00 1.60
On cover 5.00
Block of 4 21.00 8.50
a. Inverted center and overprint reading down *22,500.*
c. Bklt. pane of 6, handmade, perf. margins *575.00*

32 A11 2c **vermilion & black** *(4,000,000) Nov. 8, 1909* 4.50 1.60
On cover 5.00
Block of 4 20.00 8.50
a. Vert. pair, imperf. horiz. 1,000. 1,000.
c. Bklt. pane of 6, handmade, perf. margins *750.00*
d. Double overprint —

33 A12 5c **deep blue & black** *(2,000,000) Nov. 8, 1909* 17.00 4.00
On cover 40.00
Block of 4 80.00 20.00
a. Double overprint *(200)* 375.00 375.00
On cover *1,000.*

34 A13 8c **violet & black** *(200,000) Mar. 18, 1910* 12.00 5.25
On cover 75.00
Block of 4 55.00 27.50
a. Vertical pair, one without overprint *(10)* *1,750.*

35 A14 10c **violet & black** *(100,000) Nov. 8, 1909* 50.00 20.00
On cover 100.00
Block of 4 225.00 100.00
Nos. 31-35 (5) 88.50 32.45

Normal spacing between words of overprint on No. 31 is 10mm and on Nos. 32 to 35, 8½mm. Minor spacing variations are known.

A16

A17

1911, Jan. 14

36 A16 10c on 13c **gray** *(476,700)* 6.00 2.25
On cover 50.00
Block of 4 30.00 15.00
a. "10 cts" inverted 350.00 300.00
b. "10 cts" omitted 350.00

The "10 cts" surcharge was applied by the Isthmian Canal Commission Press after the overprinted stamps were received from the American Bank Note Co.

Many used stamps offered as No. 36b are merely No. 36 from which the surcharge has been removed with chemicals.

1914, Jan. 6

37 A17 10c **gray** *(200,000)* 55.00 12.50
On cover 85.00
Block of 4 230.00 65.00

Black Overprint Reading Up

Type II

Type II Overprint: "C" with serif at top only. "L" and "E" with vertical serifs. "O" tilts to left.

1912-16

38 A15 1c **green & black** *(3,000,000)*
July 1913 11.00 3.00
On cover 5.50
Block of 4 50.00 20.00
a. Vertical pair, one without overprint 1,750. 1,750.
On cover *2,250.*
b. Booklet pane of 6, imperf. margins *(120,000)* 625.00
c. Booklet pane of 6, handmade, perf. margins *1,000.*

39 A11 2c **vermilion & black** *(7,500,000) Dec. 1912* 8.50 1.40
orange vermilion & black, *1916* 8.50 1.40
On cover 5.00
Block of 4 42.50 8.00
a. Horiz. pair, right stamp without overprint (20) *1,500.*
b. Horiz. pair, left stamp without overprint (10) *2,000.*
c. Booklet pane of 6, imperf. margins *(194,868)* 550.00
d. Overprint reading down 200.00
e. As "d," inverted center 600.00 *750.00*
f. As "e," booklet pane of 6, handmade, perf. margins *8,000.*
g. As "c," handmade, perf. margins 1,000.
h. As No. 39, "CANAL" only 1,100.

40 A12 5c **deep blue & black** *(2,300,000) Dec. 1912* 22.50 3.25
On cover 35.00
Block of 4 105.00 15.00
a. With Cordoba portrait of 2c *10,000.*

41 A14 10c **violet & black** *(200,000)*
Feb. 1916 47.50 8.50
On cover 80.00
Block of 4 240.00 40.00

Normal spacing between words of overprint on the first printing of Nos. 38-40 is 8½mm and on the second printing 9¼mm. The spacing of the single printing of No. 41 and the imperf. margin booklet pane printings of Nos. 38 and 39 is 7¾mm. Minor spacing variations are known.

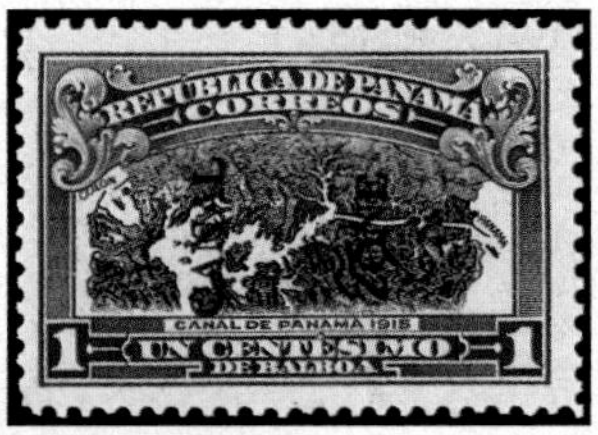

Map of Panama Canal — A18

Balboa Taking Possession of the Pacific Ocean — A19

Gatun Locks — A20

Culebra Cut — A21

Engraved, Printed and Overprinted by American Bank Note Co.

1915, Mar. 1

Blue Overprint, Type II

42 A18 1c **dark green & black** *(100,000)* 9.00 6.50
On cover 17.50
Block of 4 40.00 30.00
First day cover 200.00

43 A19 2c **carmine & black** *(100,000)* 12.00 4.25
vermilion & black 12.00 4.25
On cover 25.00
First day cover 150.00
Block of 4 50.00 21.00

44 A20 5c **blue & black** *(100,000)* 11.00 5.75
On cover 55.00
Block of 4 50.00 29.00
First day cover 500.00

45 A21 10c **orange & black** *(50,000)* 22.50 11.00
On cover 70.00
Block of 4 95.00 55.00
First day cover 500.00

Normal spacing between words of overprint is 9¼mm on all four values except position No. 61 which is 10mm.

Black Overprint Reading Up

Type III

Type III Overprint: Similar to Type I but letters appear thinner, particularly the lower bar of "L," "Z" and "E." Impressions are often light, rough and irregular, and not centered.

Engraved and Printed by American Bank Note Co.
Overprint applied by
Panama Canal Press, Mount Hope, C.Z.

1915-20

46 A15 1c **green & black**, *Dec. 1915* 160.00 125.00
light green & black, *1920* 225.00 180.00
On cover 160.00
Pair on cover *500.00*
Block of 4 725.00 650.00
a. Overprint reading down *(200)* 375.00
b. Double overprint *(180)* 350.00
c. "ZONE" double *(2)* *4,250.*
d. Double overprint, one reads "ZONE CANAL" *(18)* 2,000.

47 A11 2c **orange vermilion & black,** *Aug. 1920* 3,250. 100.00
On cover 375.00
Block of 4 *13,500.* 800.00

48 A12 5c **deep blue & black,** *Dec. 1915* 500.00 175.00
On cover 800.00
Block of 4 *2,400.* 850.00

Normal spacing between words of overprint on Nos. 46-48 is 9¼mm. This should not be confused with an abnormal 9¼mm spacing of the 2c and 5c values of type I, which are fairly common in singles, particularly used. Blocks of the abnormal spacing are rare.

A22

S. S. "Panama" in Culebra Cut — A23

S. S. "Cristobal" in Gatun Locks — A24

Engraved, Printed and Overprinted by American Bank Note Co.

1917, Jan. 23

Blue Overprint, Type II

49 A22 12c **purple & black** *(314,914)* 17.50 5.50
On cover 50.00
First day cover —
Block of 4 87.50 30.00

50 A23 15c **bright blue & black** 55.00 25.00
On cover 135.00
Block of 4 250.00 125.00

51 A24 24c **yellow brown & black** 40.00 15.00
On cover 325.00
Block of 4 190.00 90.00

Normal spacing between words of overprint is 11¼mm.

Black Overprint Reading Up

Type IV

Type IV Overprint: "C" thick at bottom, "E" with center bar same length as top and bottom bars.

Engraved, Printed and Overprinted by American Bank Note Co.

1918-20

52 A15 1c **green & black** *(2,000,000)*
Jan. 1918 32.50 11.00
On cover 12.50
Block of 4 150.00 47.50
a. Overprint reading down 175.00 —
b. Booklet pane of 6 *(60,000)* 650.00
c. Booklet pane of 6, left vertical row of 3 without overprint *7,500.*
d. Booklet pane of 6, right vertical row of 3 with double overprint *7,500.*
e. Horiz. bklt. pair, left stamp without overprint *3,000.*
f. Horiz. bklt. pair, right stamp with double overprint *3,000.*
g. Double overprint, booklet single 3,000.

53 A11 2c **vermilion & black** *(2,000,000)*
Nov. 1918 110.00 7.00
On cover 10.00
Block of 4 500.00 35.00
a. Overprint reading down 150.00 150.00
b. Horiz. pair, right stamp without ovpt. 2,000.
c. Booklet pane of 6 *(34,000)* 1,050.
d. Booklet pane of 6, left vertical row of 3 without overprint *15,000.*
e. Horiz. bklt. pair, left stamp without overprint *3,000.*
On cover (unique) *4,500.*

54 A12 5c **deep blue & black** *(500,000)*
Apr. 1920 150.00 35.00
On cover 200.00
Block of 4 825.00 160.00

Normal spacing between words of overprint on Nos. 52 and 53 is 9¼mm. On No. 54 and the booklet printings of Nos. 52 and 53, the normal spacing is 9mm. Minor spacing varieties are known.

Black Overprint Reading Up

Type V

Type V Overprint: Smaller block type 1¾mm high. "A" with flat top.

1920-21

55 A15 1c **light green & black,** *Apr. 1921* 22.50 3.50
On cover 8.00
Block of 4 100.00 17.50
a. Overprint reading down 300.00 225.00
b. Horiz. pair, right stamp without ovpt. (10) *1,750.*
c. Horiz. pair, left stamp without ovpt. (21) 1,000.
d. "ZONE" only *4,250.* —
e. Booklet pane of 6 *2,250.*
f. As No. 55, "CANAL" double (10) *2,000.*

56 A11 2c **orange vermilion & black,** *Sept. 1920* 8.50 2.25
On cover 7.00
Block of 4 37.50 10.50
a. Double overprint *(100)* 600.00
b. Double overprint, one reading down *(100)* 650.00
c. Horiz. pair, right stamp without overprint (11) 1,500.
d. Horiz. pair, left stamp without overprint (20) 1,250.
e. Vertical pair, one without overprint 1,500.
f. "ZONE" double 1,250.
g. Booklet pane of 6 850.00
h. As No. 56, "CANAL" double 1,000.

57 A12 5c **deep blue & black,** *Apr. 1921* 300.00 55.00
On cover 225.00
Block of 4 1,350. 250.00
a. Horiz. pair, right stamp without overprint *(10)* *2,500.*
b. Horiz. pair, left stamp without overprint *(10)* *2,500.*

Normal spacing between words of overprint on Nos. 55-57 is 9½mm. On booklet printings of Nos. 55 and 56 the normal spacing is 9¼mm.

Drydock at Balboa — A25

U.S.S. "Nereus" in Pedro Miguel Locks — A26

1920, Sept.

Black Overprint Type V

58 A25 50c **orange & black** 275.00 160.00
On cover *1,000.*
Block of 4 1,375. 800.00

59 A26 1b **dark violet & black** *(23,014)* 175.00 65.00
On cover *1,000.*
Block of 4 825.00 325.00

José Vallarino — A27

"Land Gate" — A28

Bolívar's Tribute — A29

Municipal Building in 1821 and 1921 — A30

Statue of Balboa — A31

Tomás Herrera — A32

José de Fábrega — A33

Engraved, Printed and Overprinted by American Bank Note Co.

Type V overprinted in black, reading up, on all values except the 5c which is overprinted with larger type in red

1921, Nov. 13

60 A27 1c **green** 4.00 1.40
On cover 6.00
Block of 4 19.00 6.75
a. "CANAL" double *2,500.*
b. Booklet pane of 6 *1,000.*

61 A28 2c **carmine** 3.00 1.50
On cover 15.00
Block of 4 13.50 6.50
a. Overprint reading down 200.00 *225.00*
b. Double overprint 900.00
c. Vertical pair, one without overprint *3,500.*
d. "CANAL" double *1,900.*
f. Booklet pane of 6 *2,100.*

62 A29 5c **blue** (R) 11.00 4.50
On cover 30.00
Block of 4 50.00 25.00
a. Overprint reading down (R) 60.00

63 A30 10c **violet** 18.00 7.50
On cover 60.00
Block of 4 100.00 35.00
a. Overprint, reading down 90.00

64 A31 15c **light blue** 50.00 17.50
On cover 175.00
Block of 4 240.00 95.00

65 A32 24c **black brown** 70.00 22.50
On cover *600.00*
Block of 4 375.00 125.00

66 A33 50c **black** 150.00 100.00
On cover *600.00*
Block of 4 725.00 475.00
Nos. 60-66 (7) 306.00 154.90

Experts question the status of the 5c with a small type V overprint in red or black.

Type III overprint in black, reading up, applied by the Panama Canal Press, Mount Hope, C. Z.

Engraved and printed by the American Bank Note Co.

1924, Jan. 28

67 A27 1c **green** 500. 200.
On cover 350.
Block of 4 2,250. 900.
a. "ZONE CANAL" reading down 850.
b. "ZONE" only, reading down *1,900.*
c. Se-tenant pair, #67a and 67b *2,750.*

Arms of Panama — A34

1924, Feb.

68 A34 1c **dark green** 11.00 4.5
On cover 12.0
Block of 4 52.50 24.0

69 A34 2c **carmine** 8.25 2.7
carmine rose 8.25 2.7
On cover 15.0
Block of 4 35.00 12.5

The following were prepared for use, but not issued.

A34 5c **dark blue** *(600)* 350.
Block of 4 1,750.
A34 10c **dark violet** *(600)* 350.
Block of 4 1,750.
A34 12c **olive green** *(600)* 350.
Block of 4 1,750.
A34 15c **ultramarine** *(600)* 350.
Block of 4 1,750.
A34 24c **yellow brown** *(600)* 350.
Block of 4 1,750.
A34 50c **orange** *(600)* 350.
Block of 4 1,750.
A34 1b **black** *(600)* 350.
Block of 4 1,750.

The 5c to 1b values were prepared for use but never issue due to abrogation of the Taft Agreement which required th Canal Zone to use overprinted Panama stamps. Six hundred c each denomination were not destroyed, as they were forwarde to the Director General of Posts of Panama for transmission t the UPU which then required about 400 sets. Only a sma number of sets appear to have reached the public market.

All Panama stamps overprinted "CANAL ZONE" were with drawn from sale June 30, 1924, and were no longer valid fc postage after Aug. 31, 1924.

United States Nos. 551-554, 557, 562, 564-566, 569, 570 and 571 Overprinted in Red (No. 70) or Black (all others)

Printed and Overprinted by the U.S. Bureau of Engraving and Printing.

Type A

Letters "A" with Flat Tops

1924-25 **Unwmk.** ***Perf. 1***

70 A154 ½c **olive brown** *(399,500) Apr. 15, 1925* 2.00 .7
Never hinged 3.75
On cover 4.0
First day cover 75.0
Block of 4 8.50 3.5
P# block of 6 27.50

71 A155 1c **deep green** *(1,985,000) July 1, 1924* 1.40 1.0
Never hinged 2.60
On cover 4.0
First day cover 75.0
Block of 4 6.00 4.2
P# block of 6 30.00
a. Inverted overprint 500.00 500.0
b. "ZONE" inverted 350.00 325.0
c. "CANAL" only *(20)* 1,750.
d. "ZONE CANAL" *(180)* 500.00
e. Booklet pane of 6 *(43,152)* 80.00

72 A156 1½c **yellow brown** *(180,599) Apr. 15, 1925* 2.00 1.7
brown 2.00 1.7
Never hinged 3.25
First day cover, Nos. 70, 72 80.0
Block of 4 8.75 9.5
P# block of 6 37.50

73 A157 2c **carmine** *(2,975,000) July 1, 1924* 7.50 1.7
Never hinged 11.00
First day cover 80.0
Block of 4 35.00 8.0
P# block of 6 175.00
a. Booklet pane of 6 *(140,000)* 175.00

74 A160 5c **dark blue** *(500,000) July 1, 1924* 19.00 7.5
Never hinged 29.00
On cover 20.0
Block of 4 80.00 37.5
P# block of 6 325.00

75 A165 10c **orange** *(60,000) July 1, 1924* 42.50 20.0
Never hinged 62.50
On cover 45.0
First day cover 500.0
Block of 4 200.00 105.0
P# block of 6 875.00

76 A167 12c **brown violet** *(80,000) July 1, 1924* 37.50 32.5

Never hinged 67.50
First day cover 750.00
Block of 4 160.00 140.00
P# block of 6 500.00
a. "ZONE" inverted 3,750. 3,000.
77 A168 14c **dark blue** *(100,000) June 27, 1925* 30.00 22.50
Never hinged 45.00
On cover 50.00
Block of 4 130.00 140.00
P# block of 6 425.00
78 A169 15c **gray** *(55,000) July 1, 1924* 50.00 37.50
Never hinged 75.00
On cover 52.50
Block of 4 225.00 190.00
P# block of 6 850.00
79 A172 30c **olive brown** *(40,000) July 1, 1924* 40.00 22.50
Never hinged 60.00
On cover 50.00
Block of 4 175.00 110.00
P# block of 6 625.00
80 A173 50c **lilac** *(25,000) July 1, 1924* 85.00 45.00
Never hinged 150.00
On cover *500.00*
Block of 4 375.00 225.00
P# block of 6 3,000.
81 A174 $1 **violet brown** *(10,000) July 1, 1924* 225.00 95.00
Never hinged 350.00
On cover *1,000.*
Block of 4 1,000. 500.00
Margin block of 4, arrow, top or bottom 1,250.
P# block of 6 *4,250.*
Nos. 70-81 (12) 541.90 287.65

Normal spacing between words of the overprint is 9¼mm. Minor spacing variations are known. The overprint of the early printings used on all values of this series except No. 77 is a sharp, clear impression. The overprint of the late printings, used only on Nos. 70, 71, 73, 76, 77, 78 and 80 is heavy and smudged, with many of the letters, particularly the "A" practically filled.

Booklet panes Nos. 71e, 73a, 84d, 97b, 101a, 106a and 117a were made from 360 subject plates. The handmade booklet panes Nos. 102a, 115c and a provisional lot of 117b were made from Post Office panes from regular 400-subject plates.

United States Nos. 554, 555, 557, 562, 564-567, 569, 570, 571, 623 Overprinted in Red (No. 91) or Black (all others)

Type B
Letters "A" with Sharp Pointed Tops

1925-28 ***Perf. 11***

84 A157 2c **carmine** *(1,110,000) May 1926* 30.00 8.00
Never hinged 45.00
On cover 11.00
Block of 4 125.00 37.50
P# block of 6 375.00
P# block of 6 & large 5 point star, side only *2,000.*
a. "CANAL" only *(20)* *2,750.*
b. "ZONE CANAL" *(180)* 500.00
c. Horizontal pair, one without overprint *3,500.*
d. Booklet pane of 6 *(82,000)* 175.00
e. Vertical pair, "a" and "b" se-tenant *2,750.*
85 A158 3c **violet** *(199,200) June 27, 1925* 4.00 3.25
Never hinged 6.00
On cover 6.00
Block of 4 17.50 13.50
P# block of 6 175.00
a. "ZONE ZONE" 600.00 550.00
86 A160 5c **dark blue** *(1,343,147) Jan. 7, 1926* 4.00 3.00
Never hinged 6.00
On cover 20.00
Block of 4 17.50 13.00
P# block of 6 165.00
Double transfer (15571 UL 86) — —
a. "ZONE ZONE" (LR18) 1,250.
b. "CANAL" inverted (LR7) 950.00
c. Inverted overprint *(80)* 500.00
d. Horizontal pair, one without overprint *3,250.*
e. Overprinted "ZONE CANAL" *(90)* 350.00
f. "ZONE" only *(10)* *2,000.*
g. Vertical pair, one without overprint, other overprint inverted *(10)* *2,500.*
h. "CANAL" only *2,250.*
87 A165 10c **orange** *(99,510) Aug. 1925* 35.00 13.00
Never hinged 52.50
On cover 40.00
Block of 4 160.00 75.00
P# block of 6 500.00
a. "ZONE ZONE" (LR18) *3,000.*
88 A167 12c **brown violet** *(58,062) Feb. 1926* 22.50 14.00
Never hinged 34.00
On cover 45.00
Block of 4 110.00 62.50
P# block of 6 375.00
a. "ZONE ZONE" (LR18) *5,250.*
89 A168 14c **dark blue** *(55,700) Dec. 1928* 27.50 16.00

Never hinged 42.50
On cover 50.00
Block of 4 125.00 75.00
P# block of 6 350.00
90 A169 15c **gray** *(204,138) Nov. 1925* 7.50 4.50
Never hinged 11.50
On cover 15.00
Block of 4 35.00 21.00
P# block of 6 200.00
P# block of 4, large 5 point star, side only *3,000.*
a. "ZONE ZONE" (LR18) *5,500.*

It is believed that the four recorded P# blocks of 4 with large 5-point star are the largest known P# multiples from the plate that shows the star.

91 A187 17c **black** *(199,500) Apr. 5, 1926* 4.50 3.00
Never hinged 7.50
On cover 12.50
Block of 4 19.00 14.00
P# block of 6 190.00
a. "ZONE" only *(20)* 1,200.
b. "CANAL" only 1,700.
c. "ZONE CANAL" *(270)* 300.00
92 A170 20c **carmine rose** *(259,807) Apr. 5, 1926* 7.25 3.25
Never hinged 11.00
On cover 32.50
Block of 4 32.50 14.00
P# block of 6 175.00
a. "CANAL" inverted (UR48) *4,000.*
b. "ZONE" inverted (LL76) *4,250.*
c. "ZONE CANAL" (LL91) *3,600.*
93 A172 30c **olive brown** *(154,700) Dec. 1925* 5.75 4.00
Never hinged 8.50
On cover 60.00
Block of 4 25.00 20.00
P# block of 6 250.00
94 A173 50c **lilac** *(13,533) July 1928* 240.00 165.00
Never hinged 375.00
On cover *500.00*
Block of 4 1,200. 750.00
P# block of 6 2,500.
95 A174 $1 **violet brown** *(20,000) Apr. 1926* 150.00 60.00
Never hinged 275.00
On cover *1,000.*
Block of 4 650.00 265.00
Margin block of 4, arrow, top or bottom 675.00
P# block of 6 2,100.
Nos. 84-95 (12) 538.00 297.00

Nos. 85-88, 90 and 93-95 exist with wrong-font "CANAL" and "ZONE." Positions are: Nos. 85-88 and 90, UL51 (CANAL) and UL82 (ZONE); Nos. 93-95, U51 (CANAL) and U82 (ZONE).

Normal spacing between words of the overprint is 11mm on No. 84; 9mm on Nos. 85-88, 90, first printing of No. 91 and the first, third and fourth printing of No. 92; 7mm on the second printings of Nos. 91-92. Minor spacing varieties exist on Nos. 84-88, 90-92.

Overprint Type B on U.S. Sesquicentennial Stamp No. 627

1926

96 A188 2c **carmine rose** *(300,000) July 6, 1926* 5.00 3.75
Never hinged 7.50
First day cover 60.00
Block of 4 22.50 18.00
P# block of 6 85.00

On this stamp there is a space of 5mm instead of 9mm between the two words of the overprint.

The authorized date, July 4, fell on a Sunday with the next day also a holiday, so No. 96 was not regularly issued until July 6. But the postmaster sold some stamps and canceled some covers on July 4 for a few favored collectors.

Overprint Type B in Black on U.S. Nos. 583, 584, 591

1926-27 **Rotary Press Printings** ***Perf. 10***

97 A157 2c **carmine** *(1,290,000) Dec. 1926* 50.00 11.00
Never hinged 85.00
On cover 14.00
Block of 4 250.00 50.00
P# block of 4 475.00
a. Pair, one without overprint *(10)* *3,250.*
b. Booklet pane of 6 *(58,000)* 525.00
c. "CANAL" only *(10)* *2,000.*
d. "ZONE" only *2,750.*
98 A158 3c **violet** *(239,600) May 9, 1927* 8.00 4.25
Never hinged 12.00
On cover 12.00
Block of 4 35.00 19.00
P# block of 4 120.00
99 A165 10c **orange** *(128,400) May 9, 1927* 18.00 7.50
Never hinged 27.50
On cover 35.00
Block of 4 82.50 40.00
P# block of 4 225.00

No. 97d is valued in the grade of fine. Very fine examples are not known.

Overprint Type B in Black on U.S. Nos. 632, 634 (Type I), 635, 637, 642

1927-31 **Rotary Press Printings** ***Perf. 11x10½***

100 A155 1c **green** *(434,892) June 28, 1927* 2.25 1.40
Never hinged 3.50
On cover 3.00
Block of 4 10.00 6.75

P# block of 4 20.00
a. Vertical pair, one without overprint *(10)* *5,500.*
101 A157 2c **carmine** *(1,628,195) June 28, 1927* 2.50 1.00
Never hinged 3.75
On cover 3.00
Block of 4 11.00 4.75
P# block of 4 24.00
a. Booklet pane of 6 *(82,108)* 160.00
102 A158 3c **violet** *(1,250,000) Feb., 1931* 4.50 2.75
Never hinged 6.75
On cover 5.00
Block of 4 22.50 13.50
P# block of 4 90.00
a. Booklet pane of 6, handmade, perf. margins *6,500.*
103 A160 5c **dark blue** *(60,000) Dec. 13, 1927* 30.00 10.00
Never hinged 50.00
On cover 30.00
Block of 4 130.00 42.50
P# block of 4 200.00
104 A165 10c **orange** *(119,800) July, 1930* 17.50 10.00
Never hinged 26.00
On cover 35.00
Block of 4 77.50 45.00
P# block of 4 190.00
Nos. 100-104 (5) 56.75 25.15

Wet and Dry Printings

Canal Zone stamps printed by both the "wet" and "dry" process are Nos. 105, 108-109, 111-114, 117, 138-140, C21-C24, C26, J25, J27. Starting with Nos. 147 and C27, the Bureau of Engraving and Printing used the "dry" method exclusively, except for Nos. 152, 157 and 164.

See note on Wet and Dry Printings following U.S. No. 1029.

Maj. Gen. William Crawford Gorgas — A35

Maj. Gen. George Washington Goethals — A36

Gaillard Cut — A37

Maj. Gen. Harry Foote Hodges — A38

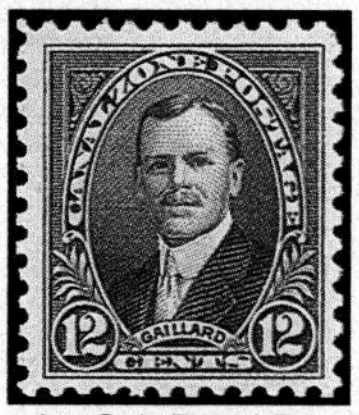

Lt. Col. David Du Bose Gaillard — A39

Maj. Gen. William Luther Sibert — A40

Jackson Smith — A41

Rear Adm. Harry Harwood Rousseau — A42

Col. Sydney Bacon Williamson — A43

Joseph Clay Styles Blackburn — A44

Printed by the U. S. Bureau of Engraving and Printing.

Plates of 400 subjects (except 5c), issued in panes of 100. The 5c was printed from plate of 200 subjects, issued in panes of 50. The 400-subject sheets were originally cut by knife into Post Office panes of 100, but beginning in 1948 they were separated by perforations to eliminate straight edges.

1928-40 Flat Plate Printing Unwmk. *Perf. 11*

105	A35	1c	**green** *(22,392,147)*	.20	.20
			Never hinged	.25	
			P# block of 6	2.50	—
a.			Wet printing, yel grn, *Oct. 3, 1928*	.20	.20
			Never hinged	.25	
			First day cover		17.50
			P# block of 6	4.25	—
106	A36	2c	**carmine** *(7,191,600) Oct. 1, 1928*	.20	.20
			Never hinged	.25	
			First day cover		17.50
			P# block of 6	2.75	—
a.			Booklet pane of 6 *(284,640)*	15.00	*20.00*
			Never hinged	22.50	
107	A37	5c	**blue** *(4,187,028) June 25, 1929*	1.00	.40
			Never hinged	1.30	
			First day cover		5.00
			P# block of 6	13.00	—
108	A38	10c	**orange** *(4,559,788)*	.20	.20
			Never hinged	.25	
			P# block of 6	4.75	—
a.			Wet printing, *Jan. 11, 1932*	.40	.25
			Never hinged	.50	
			First day cover		40.00
			P# block of 6	6.00	—
109	A39	12c	**brown violet** *(844,635)*	.75	.60
			Never hinged	1.00	
			P# block of 6	12.00	—
a.			Wet printing, violet brown, *July 1, 1929*	1.50	1.00
			Never hinged	2.00	
			First day cover		60.00
			P# block of 6	21.00	—
110	A40	14c	**blue** *(406,131) Sept. 27, 1937*	.85	.85
			Never hinged	1.20	
			First day cover		5.00
			P# block of 6	16.00	—
111	A41	15c	**gray black** *(3,356,500)*	.40	.35
			Never hinged	.55	
			P# block of 6	9.00	—
a.			Wet printing, gray, *Jan. 11, 1932*	.80	.50
			Never hinged	1.10	
			First day cover		45.00
			P# block of 6	12.50	5.00
112	A42	20c	**dark brown** *(3,619,080)*	.60	.20
			Never hinged	.80	
			P# block of 6	9.00	—
a.			Wet printing, olive brown, *Jan. 11, 1932*	1.00	.30
			Never hinged	1.30	
			First day cover		45.00
			P# block of 6	16.00	—
113	A43	30c	**black** *(2,376,491)*	.80	.70
			Never hinged	1.10	
			P# block of 6	12.00	—
a.			Wet printing, brn blk, *Apr. 15, 1940*	1.25	1.00
			Never hinged	1.60	
			First day cover		10.00
			P# block of 6	22.50	—
114	A44	50c	**rose lilac**	1.50	.65
			Never hinged	2.00	
			P# block of 6	18.00	—
a.			Wet printing, lilac, *July 1, 1929*	2.50	.85
			Never hinged	3.50	
			First day cover		150.00
			P# block of 6	35.00	—
			Nos. 105-114 (10)	6.50	4.35

Nos. 105, 108, 112, 113 and 114 exist with both shiny gum and dull gum.

Coils are listed as Nos. 160-161.

United States Nos. 720 and 695 Overprinted type B

Rotary Press Printing

1933, Jan. 14 ***Perf. 11x10½***

115	A226	3c	**deep violet** *(3,150,000)*	2.75	.25
			Never hinged	4.00	
			First day cover		12.00
			P# block of 4	35.00	—
b.			"CANAL" only	*2,600.*	
c.			Booklet pane of 6, handmade, perf. margins	175.00	—
116	A168	14c	**dark blue** *(104,800)*	4.50	3.50
			Never hinged	7.00	
			First day cover		20.00
			P# block of 4	60.00	—
a.			"ZONE CANAL" *(16)*	*1,500.*	

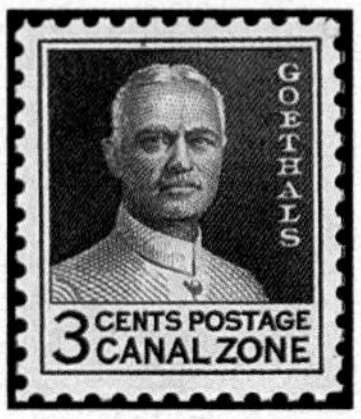

Maj. Gen. George Washington Goethals — A45

20th anniversary of the opening of the Panama Canal.

Flat Plate Printing

1934, Aug. 15 Unwmk. *Perf. 11*

117	A45	3c	**red violet**	.20	.20
			Never hinged	.25	
			First day cover		3.00
			P# block of 6	1.00	—
a.			Booklet pane of 6	45.00	*32.50*
			Never hinged	60.00	
b.			As "a," handmade, perf. margins	160.00	—
c.			Wet printing, violet	.20	.20
			P# block of 6	1.00	—

Coil is listed as No. 153.

Catalogue values for unused stamps in this section, from this point to the end, are for Never Hinged items.

United States Nos. 803 and 805 Overprinted in Black

Rotary Press Printing

1939, Sept. 1 Unwmk. *Perf. 11x10½*

118	A275	½c	**red orange** *(1,030,000)*	.20	.20
			First day cover		1.00
			P# block of 4	2.75	—
119	A277	1½c	**bister brown** *(935,000)*	.20	.20
			brown	.20	.20
			First day cover		1.00
			P# block of 4	2.25	—

Balboa-Before A46

Balboa-After A47

Gaillard Cut-Before A48

Gaillard Cut-After A49

Bas Obispo-Before A50

Bas Obispo-After A51

Gatun Locks-Before A52

Gatun Locks-After A53

Canal Channel-Before A54

Canal Channel-After A55

Gamboa-Before A56

Gamboa-After A57

Pedro Miguel Locks-Before A58

Pedro Miguel Locks-After A59

Gatun Spillway-Before A60

Gatun Spillway-After A61

25th anniversary of the opening of the Panama Canal.
Withdrawn Feb. 28, 1941; remainders burned Apr. 12, 1941.

Flat Plate Printing

1939, Aug. 15 — Unwmk. — *Perf. 11*

120	A46	1c	**yellow green** *(1,019,482)*	.65	.30
			First day cover		2.00
			P# block of 6	17.50	—
121	A47	2c	**rose carmine** *(227,065)*	.75	.35
			First day cover		2.00
			P# block of 6	17.50	—
122	A48	3c	**purple** *(2,523,735)*	.75	.20
			First day cover		2.00
			P# block of 6	17.50	—
123	A49	5c	**dark blue** *(460,213)*	2.50	1.25
			First day cover		2.50
			P# block of 6	30.00	—
124	A50	6c	**red orange** *(68,290)*	5.00	3.00
			First day cover		6.00
			P# block of 6	75.00	—
125	A51	7c	**black** *(71,235)*	5.50	3.00
			First day cover		6.00
			P# block of 6	75.00	—
126	A52	8c	**green** *(41,576)*	7.00	3.50
			First day cover		6.00
			P# block of 6	85.00	—
127	A53	10c	**ultramarine** *(83,571)*	6.00	5.00
			First day cover		6.00
			P# block of 6	85.00	—
128	A54	11c	**blue green** *(34,010)*	11.00	8.00
			First day cover		10.00
			P# block of 6	175.00	—
129	A55	12c	**brown carmine** *(66,735)*	11.00	7.50
			First day cover		10.00
			P# block of 6	150.00	—
130	A56	14c	**dark violet** *(37,365)*	11.00	7.50
			First day cover		10.00
			P# block of 6	175.00	—
131	A57	15c	**olive green** *(105,058)*	15.00	6.00
			First day cover		10.00
			P# block of 6	200.00	—
132	A58	18c	**rose pink** *(39,255)*	16.00	8.50
			First day cover		10.00
			P# block of 6	190.00	—
133	A59	20c	**brown** *(100,244)*	17.50	7.50
			First day cover		10.00
			P# block of 6	225.00	—
134	A60	25c	**orange** *(34,283)*	25.00	17.50
			First day cover		20.00
			P# block of 6	400.00	—
135	A61	50c	**violet brown** *(91,576)*	30.00	6.00
			First day cover		20.00
			P# block of 6	450.00	—
			Nos. 120-135 (16)	164.65	85.10

Maj. Gen. George W. Davis — A62

Gov. Charles E. Magoon — A63

Theodore Roosevelt — A64

John F. Stevens — A65

John F. Wallace — A66

1946-49 — Unwmk. — *Perf. 11*

Size: 19x22mm

136	A62	½c	**bright red** *(1,020,000) Aug. 16, 1948*	.40	.25
			First day cover		1.25
			P# block of 6	2.50	—
137	A63	1½c	**chocolate** *(603,600) Aug. 16, 1948*	.40	.25
			First day cover		1.25
			P# block of 6	2.50	—
138	A64	2c	**light rose carmine** *(6,951,755)*	.20	.20
			P# block of 6	.65	—
a.			Wet printing, rose carmine, *Oct. 27, 1949*	.20	.20
			First day cover		1.00
			P# block of 6	1.00	—
139	A65	5c	**dark blue**	.35	.20
			P# block of 6	2.25	—
a.			Wet printing, deep blue, *Apr. 25, 1946*	.60	.20
			First day cover		1.00
			P# block of 6	4.00	—
140	A66	25c	**green** *(1,520,000)*	.85	.55
			P# block of 6	7.00	—
a.			Wet printing, yel grn, *Aug. 16, 1948*	3.00	1.00
			First day cover		3.50
			P# block of 6	20.00	—
			Nos. 136-140 (5)	2.20	1.45

See Nos. 155, 162, 164.

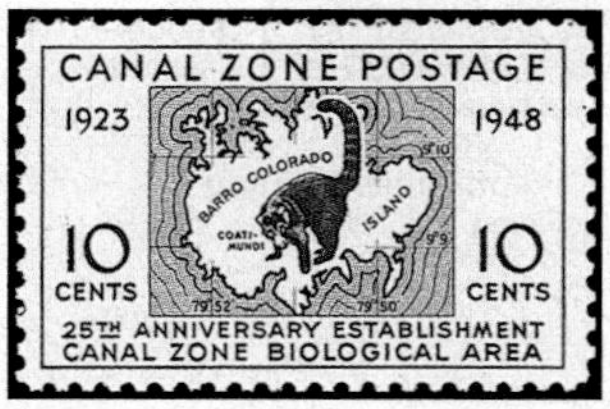

Map of Biological Area and Coati-mundi A67

25th anniversary of the establishment of the Canal Zone Biological Area on Barro Colorado Island.
Withdrawn Mar. 30, 1951, and remainders destroyed Apr. 10, 1951.

1948, Apr. 17 — Unwmk. — *Perf. 11*

141	A67	10c	**black** *(521,200)*	1.75	.80
			First day cover		3.00
			P# block of 6	10.00	—

"Forty-niners" Arriving at Chagres — A68

Journeying in "Bungo" to Las Cruces — A69

Las Cruces Trail to Panama — A70

Departure for San Francisco — A71

Centenary of the California Gold Rush.
Stocks on hand were processed for destruction on Aug. 11, 1952 and destroyed Aug. 13, 1952.

1949, June 1 — Unwmk. — *Perf. 11*

142	A68	3c	**blue** *(500,000)*	.65	.25
			First day cover		1.00
			P# block of 6	6.50	—
143	A69	6c	**violet** *(481,600)*	.65	.30
			First day cover		1.00
			P# block of 6	6.50	—
144	A70	12c	**bright blue green** *(230,200)*	1.75	.90
			First day cover		2.00
			P# block of 6	21.00	—
145	A71	18c	**deep red lilac** *(240,200)*	2.00	1.50
			First day cover		3.25
			P# block of 6	20.00	—
			Nos. 142-145 (4)	5.05	2.95

Workers in Culebra Cut — A72

Early Railroad Scene — A73

Contribution of West Indian laborers in the construction of the Panama Canal.
Entire issue sold, none withdrawn and destroyed.

1951, Aug. 15 — Unwmk. — *Perf. 11*

146	A72	10c	**carmine** *(480,000)*	3.00	1.50
			First day cover		3.00
			P# block of 6	25.00	—

Centenary of the completion of the Panama Railroad and the first transcontinental railroad trip in the Americas.

1955, Jan. 28 — Unwmk. — *Perf. 11*

147	A73	3c	**violet** *(994,000)*	1.00	.60
			First day cover		1.50
			P# block of 6	7.25	—

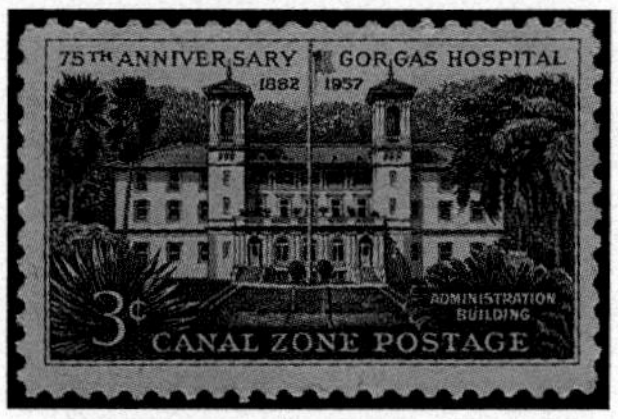

Gorgas Hospital and Ancon Hill — A74

75th anniversary of Gorgas Hospital.

1957, Nov. 17 — Unwmk. — *Perf. 11*

148	A74	3c	**black,** *dull blue green (1,010,000)*	.45	.35
			Light blue green paper	.40	.35
			First day cover		1.00
			P# block of 4	4.25	—

S.S. Ancon — A75

1958, Aug. 30 **Unwmk.** ***Perf. 11***
149 A75 4c **greenish blue** *(1,749,700)* .40 .30
First day cover 1.00
P# block of 4 3.25 —

Roosevelt Medal and Canal Zone Map — A76

Centenary of the birth of Theodore Roosevelt (1858-1919).

1958, Nov. 15 **Unwmk.** ***Perf. 11***
150 A76 4c **brown** *(1,060,000)* .60 .30
First day cover 1.00
P# block of 4 3.50 —

Boy Scout Badge — A77

Administration Building, Balboa Heights — A78

50th anniversary of the Boy Scouts of America.

Giori Press Printing

1960, Feb. 8 **Unwmk.** ***Perf. 11***
151 A77 4c **dark blue, red & bister** *(654,933)* .55 .40
First day cover 1.50
P# block of 4 4.50 —

1960, Nov. 1 **Unwmk.** ***Perf. 11***
152 A78 4c **rose lilac** *(2,486,725)* .20 .20
First day cover 1.00
P# block of 4 .90 —

Types of 1934, 1960 and 1946
Coil Stamps

1960-62 **Unwmk.** ***Perf. 10 Vertically***
153 A45 3c **deep violet** *(3,743,959) Nov. 1, 1960* .20 .20
First day cover 1.00
Pair .40 .25
Joint line pair 1.10 —

Perf. 10 Horizontally
154 A78 4c **dull rose lilac** *(2,776,273) Nov. 1, 1960* .20 .20
First day cover 1.00
Pair .40 .25
Joint line pair 1.10 —

Perf. 10 Vertically
155 A65 5c **deep blue** *(3,288,264) Feb. 10, 1962* .25 .20
First day cover 1.00
Pair .50 .50
Joint line pair 1.25 —
Nos. 153-155 (3) .65 .60

Girl Scout Badge and Camp at Gatun Lake — A79

50th anniversary of the Girl Scouts.

Giori Press Printing

1962, Mar. 12 **Unwmk.** ***Perf. 11***
156 A79 4c **blue, dark green & bister** *(640,000)* .40 .30
First day cover *(83,717)* 1.25
P# block of 4 2.75 —

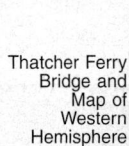

Thatcher Ferry Bridge and Map of Western Hemisphere A80

Opening of the Thatcher Ferry Bridge, spanning the Panama Canal.

Giori Press Printing

1962, Oct. 12 **Unwmk.** ***Perf. 11***
157 A80 4c **black & silver** *(775,000)* .35 .25
First day cover *(65,833)* 1.00
P# block of 4, 2P# 3.75 —
a. Silver (bridge) omitted *(50)* *7,500.*
Hinged *5,500.*
P# block of 6, black P# only *52,500.*

Goethals Memorial, Balboa — A81

Fort San Lorenzo — A82

1968-71 **Giori Press Printing** ***Perf. 11***
158 A81 6c **green & ultra.** *(1,890,000) Mar. 15, 1968* .30 .30
First day cover 1.00
P# block of 4 2.00 —
159 A82 8c **slate green, blue, dark brown & ocher** *(3,460,000) July 14, 1971* .35 .20
First day cover 1.00
P# block of 4 2.75 —

Types of 1928, 1932 and 1948
Coil Stamps

1975, Feb. 14 **Unwmk.** ***Perf. 10 Vertically***
160 A35 1c **green** *(1,090,958)* .20 .20
First day cover 1.00
Pair .40 .30
Joint line pair 1.00 —
161 A38 10c **orange** *(590,658)* .70 .40
First day cover 1.00
Pair 1.40 .80
Joint line pair 5.00 —
162 A66 25c **yellow green** *(129,831)* 2.75 2.75
First day cover 3.00
Pair 5.50 5.50
Joint line pair 20.00 —
Nos. 160-162 (3) 3.65 3.35

Dredge Cascadas A83

1976, Feb. 23 **Giori Press Printing** ***Perf. 11***
163 A83 13c **multicolored** *(3,653,950)* .35 .20
First day cover 1.00
P# block of 4 2.00 —
a. Booklet pane of 4 *(1,032,400) Apr. 19* 3.00 —

Stevens Type of 1946

1977 **Rotary Press Printing** ***Perf. 11x10½***
Size: 19x22½mm
164 A65 5c **deep blue** *(1,009,612)* .60 .85
P# block of 4 3.50 —
a. Tagged, dull gum 12.00 15.00
P# block of 4 125.00 —

No. 164 exists with both shiny gum and dull gum.
No. 164a exists even though there was no equipment in the Canal Zone to detect tagging.

Towing Locomotive, Ship in Lock, by Alwyn Sprague A84

1978, Oct. 25 ***Perf. 1***
165 A84 15c **dp grn & bl grn** *(2,921,083)* .35 .2
First day cover *(81,405)* 1.0
P# block of 4 2.00 –

AIR POST STAMPS

Regular Issue of 1928 Surcharged in Dark Blue

15 Type I — Flag of "5" pointing up

Type II — Flag of "5" curved **1**

1929-31 **Flat Plate Printing** **Unwmk.** ***Perf. 1***
C1 A35 15c on 1c **green,** type I, *Apr. 1, 1929* 8.00 5.5
Never hinged 12.00
First day cover 25.0
Block of 4 35.00 25.0
P# block of 6 120.00 –
C2 A35 15c on 1c **yellow green,** type II, *Mar. 1931* 70.00 47.5
Never hinged 115.00
On cover 175.0
Block of 4 340.00 340.0
P# block of 6 900.00 –
C3 A36 25c on 2c **carmine** *(223,880) Jan. 11, 1929* 3.50 2.0
Never hinged 5.25
First day cover 17.5
Block of 4 15.00 9.0
P# block of 6 115.00 –

Nos. 114 and 106 Surcharged in Black

1929, Dec. 31
C4 A44 10c on 50c **lilac** *(116,666)* 8.00 6.5
Never hinged 12.00
First day cover 25.0
Block of 4 35.00 27.5
P# block of 6 115.00 –
C5 A36 20c on 2c **carmine** *(638,395)* 5.00 1.7
Never hinged 7.50
First day cover 20.0
Block of 4 20.00 8.0
P# block of 6 110.00 –
a. Dropped "2" in surcharge *(7,000)* 80.00 60.0

Catalogue values for unused stamps in this section, from this point to the end, are for Never Hinged items.

Gaillard Cut — AP1

Printed by the U. S. Bureau of Engraving and Printing.

Plates of 200 subjects, issued in panes of 50.

1931-49 Unwmk. *Perf. 11*

C6	AP1	4c **red violet** *(525,000) Jan. 3, 1949*	.75	.70
		First day cover		2.00
		P# block of 6	5.25	—
C7	AP1	5c **yellow green** *(9,935,500) Nov. 18, 1931*	.60	.45
		green	.60	.45
		First day cover		10.00
		P# block of 6	4.50	—
C8	AP1	6c **yellow brown** *(9,399,500) Feb. 15, 1946*	.75	.35
		First day cover		2.00
		P# block of 6	5.25	—
C9	AP1	10c **orange** *(5,079,000) Nov. 18, 1931*	1.00	.35
		First day cover		10.00
		P# block of 6	10.00	—
C10	AP1	15c **blue** *(11,072,700) Nov. 18, 1931*	1.25	.30
		pale blue	1.25	.30
		First day cover		15.00
		P# block of 6	11.00	—
C11	AP1	20c **red violet** *(3,184,100) Nov. 18, 1931*	2.00	.30
		deep violet	2.00	.30
		First day cover		35.00
		P# block of 6	20.00	—
C12	AP1	30c **rose lake** *(1,119,500) July 15, 1941*	4.50	1.00
		dull rose	4.50	1.00
		First day cover		22.50
		P# block of 6	37.50	—
C13	AP1	40c **yellow** *(795,600) Nov. 18, 1931*	3.50	1.10
		lemon	3.50	1.10
		First day cover		75.00
		P# block of 6	32.50	—
C14	AP1	$1 **black** *(372,500) Nov. 18, 1931*	9.00	1.90
		First day cover		150.00
		P# block of 6	85.00	—
		Nos. C6-C14 (9)	23.35	6.45

Douglas Plane over Sosa Hill — AP2

Planes and Map of Central America AP3

Pan American Clipper and Scene near Fort Amador — AP4

Pan American Clipper at Cristobal Harbor — AP5

Pan American Clipper over Gaillard Cut — AP6

Pan American Clipper Landing — AP7

10th anniversary of Air Mail service and the 25th anniversary of the opening of the Panama Canal.

Withdrawn Feb. 28, 1941, remainders burned Apr. 12, 1941.

Flat Plate Printing

1939, July 15 Unwmk. *Perf. 11*

C15	AP2	5c **greenish black** *(86,576)*	4.50	2.25
		First day cover		5.00
		P# block of 6	47.50	—
C16	AP3	10c **dull violet** *(117,644)*	4.00	3.00
		First day cover		5.00
		P# block of 6	50.00	—
C17	AP4	15c **light brown** *(883,742)*	5.50	1.00
		First day cover		3.00
		P# block of 6	57.50	—
C18	AP5	25c **blue** *(82,126)*	16.00	8.00
		First day cover		17.50
		P# block of 6	275.00	—
C19	AP6	30c **rose carmine** *(121,382)*	16.00	7.75
		First day cover		15.00
		P# block of 6	175.00	—
C20	AP7	$1 **green** *(40,051)*	45.00	27.50
		First day cover		60.00
		P# block of 6	550.00	—
		Nos. C15-C20 (6)	91.00	49.50

Globe and Wing — AP8

Flat Plate Printing

1951, July 16 Unwmk. *Perf. 11*

C21	AP8	4c **lt red violet** *(1,315,000)*	.75	.35
		P# block of 6	7.00	—
a.		Wet printing, red violet	1.25	.40
		1st day card, Balboa Heights		1.50
		P# block of 6	10.00	—
C22	AP8	6c **lt brown** *(22,657,625)*	.50	.25
		P# block of 6	5.00	—
a.		Wet printing, brown	.95	.35
		1st day cover, Balboa Heights		1.00
		P# block of 6	7.50	—
C23	AP8	10c **lt red orange** *(1,049,130)*	.90	.35
		P# block of 6	8.00	—
a.		Wet printing, red orange	2.00	.50
		1st day cover, Balboa Heights		2.00
		P# block of 6	16.00	—
C24	AP8	21c **lt blue** *(1,460,000)*	7.50	4.00
		P# block of 6	70.00	—
a.		Wet printing, blue	15.00	5.00
		1st day cover, Balboa Heights		7.50
		P# block of 6	125.00	—
C25	AP8	31c **cerise** *(375,000)*	7.50	3.75
		1st day cover, Balboa Heights		7.50
		P# block of 6	70.00	—
a.		Horiz. pair, imperf. vert. *(98)*	1,250.	—
C26	AP8	80c **lt gray black** *(827,696)*	4.50	1.50
		P# block of 6	35.00	—
a.		Wet printing, gray black	12.50	1.65
		1st day cover, Balboa Heights		12.50
		1st day cover, Balboa Heights, #C21-C26		20.00
		P# block of 6	100.00	—
		Nos. C21-C26 (6)	21.65	10.20

See note after No. 114. Total number of first day covers with one or more of Nos. C21-C26, about 12,000.

Flat Plate Printing

1958, Aug. 16 Unwmk. *Perf. 11*

C27	AP8	5c **yellow green** *(899,923)*	1.00	.60
		First day cover *(2,176)*		4.50
		P# block of 4	6.00	—
C28	AP8	7c **olive** *(9,381,797)*	1.00	.45
		First day cover *(2,815)*		4.50
		P# block of 4	6.00	—
C29	AP8	15c **brown violet** *(359,923)*	5.00	2.75
		First day cover *(2,040)*		6.00
		P# block of 4	40.00	—
C30	AP8	25c **orange yellow** *(600,000)*	12.50	2.75
		First day cover *(2,115)*		9.00
		P# block of 4	125.00	—
C31	AP8	35c **dark blue** *(283,032)*	10.00	2.75
		First day cover *(1,868)*		11.00
		P# block of 4	65.00	—
		Nos. C27-C31 (5)	29.50	9.30
		Nos. C21-C31 (11)	51.15	19.50

Emblem of US Army Caribbean School — AP9

US Army Caribbean School for Latin America at Fort Gulick.

Giori Press Printing

1961, Nov. 21 Unwmk. *Perf. 11*

C32	AP9	15c **red & blue** *(560,000)*	1.75	.75
		First day cover *(25,949)*		1.75
		P# block of 4	10.00	—

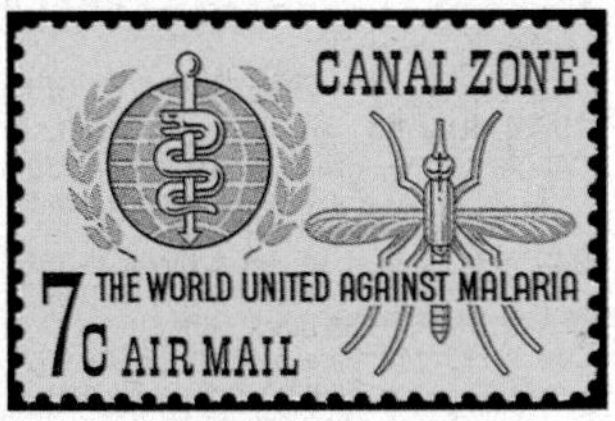

Malaria Eradication Emblem and Mosquito AP10

World Health Organization drive to eradicate malaria.

Giori Press Printing

1962, Sept. 24 Unwmk. *Perf. 11*

C33	AP10	7c **yellow & black** *(862,349)*	.50	.40
		First day cover *(44,433)*		1.00
		P# block of 4	3.00	—

Globe-Wing Type of 1951

Rotary Press Printing

1963, Jan. 7 *Perf. 10½x11*

C34	AP8	8c **carmine** *(5,054,727)*	.75	.30
		First day cover *(19,128)*		1.00
		P# block of 4	4.00	—

Alliance for Progress Emblem AP11

2nd anniv. of the Alliance for Progress, which aims to stimulate economic growth and raise living standards in Latin America.

Giori Press Printing

1963, Aug. 17 Unwmk. *Perf. 11*

C35	AP11	15c **gray, grn & dk ultra** *(405,000)*	1.50	.85
		First day cover *(29,594)*		1.50
		P# block of 4	12.50	—

Jet over Canal Zone Views — AP12

50th anniversary of the opening of the Panama Canal.

Designs: 6c, Cristobal. 8c, Gatun Locks. 15c, Madden Dam. 20c, Gaillard Cut. 30c, Miraflores Locks. 80c, Balboa.

Giori Press Printing

1964, Aug. 15 Unwmk. *Perf. 11*

C36	AP12	6c **green & black** *(257,193)*	.60	.35
		1st day cover, Balboa		1.50
		P# block of 4	3.75	—
C37	AP12	8c **rose red & black** *(3,924,283)*	.60	.35
		1st day cover, Balboa		1.00
		P# block of 4	4.00	—
C38	AP12	15c **blue & black** *(472,666)*	1.25	.75
		1st day cover, Balboa		1.00
		P# block of 4	9.25	—
C39	AP12	20c **rose lilac & black** *(399,784)*	1.60	1.00
		1st day cover, Balboa		2.00
		P# block of 4	10.00	—
C40	AP12	30c **reddish brown & black** *(204,524)*	2.75	2.25
		1st day cover, Balboa		3.00
		P# block of 4	17.50	—
C41	AP12	80c **olive bister & black** *(186,809)*	4.25	3.00

1st day cover, Balboa 4.00
1st day cover, Balboa, #C36-C41 10.00
P# block of 4 24.00 —
Nos. C36-C41 (6) 11.05 7.70

There were 57,822 first day covers with one or more of Nos. C36-C41.
No. C40 exists with dull gum.

Canal Zone Seal and Jet Plane — AP13

Giori Press Printing

1965, July 15 Unwmk. *Perf. 11*

C42 AP13 6c **green & black** *(548,250)* .50 .30
First day cover, Balboa 2.00
P# block of 4 3.25 —
C43 AP13 8c **rose red & black** *(8,357,700)* .45 .20
First day cover, Balboa 1.00
P# block of 4 3.00 —
C44 AP13 15c **blue & black** *(2,385,000)* .75 .20
First day cover, Balboa 1.00
P# block of 4 7.00 —
C45 AP13 20c **lilac & black** *(2,290,699)* .80 .30
First day cover, Balboa 1.25
P# block of 4 4.25 —
C46 AP13 30c **redsh brn & blk** *(2,332,255)* 1.10 .30
First day cover, Balboa 1.25
P# block of 4 4.75 —
C47 AP13 80c **bister & black** *(1,456,596)* 2.50 .75
First day cover, Balboa 2.50
First day cover, Balboa, #C42-C47 7.00
P# block of 4 18.00 —
Nos. C42-C47 (6) 6.10 2.05

There were 35,389 first day covers with one or more of Nos. C42-C47.

1968-76

C48 AP13 10c **dull orange & black** *(10,055,000) Mar. 15, 1968* .35 .20
First day cover, Balboa *(7,779)* 1.00
P# block of 4 3.50 —
a. Booklet pane of 4 *(713,390) Feb. 18, 1970* 4.25 —
First day cover, Balboa *(5,054)* 5.00
C49 AP13 11c **olive & black** *(3,335,000) Sept. 24, 1971* .35 .20
First day cover, Balboa *(10,916)* 1.00
P# block of 4 3.50 —
a. Booklet pane of 4 *(1,277,760) Sept. 24, 1971* 3.50 —
First day cover, Balboa *(2,460)* 5.00
C50 AP13 13c **emerald & black** *(1,865,000) Feb. 11, 1974* .85 .25
First day cover, Balboa *(7,646)* 1.00
P# block of 4 5.00 —
a. Booklet pane of 4 *(619,200) Feb. 11, 1974* 6.00 —
First day cover, Balboa *(3,660)* 5.00
C51 AP13 22c **vio & blk** *(363,720) May 10, 1976* 1.10 *2.00*
First day cover, Balboa 2.50
P# block of 4 6.25 —
C52 AP13 25c **pale yellow green & black** *(1,640,441) Mar. 15, 1968* .80 .70
First day cover, Balboa 1.00
P# block of 4 5.50 —
C53 AP13 35c **salmon & black** *(573,822) May 10, 1976* 1.25 *2.00*
First day cover, Balboa 2.50
P# block of 4 10.00 —
Nos. C48-C53 (6) 4.70 *5.35*

There were 5,047 first day covers with one or more of Nos. C51, C53.

AIR POST OFFICIAL STAMPS

Beginning in March 1915, stamps for use on official mail were identified by a large "P" perforated through each stamp. These were replaced by overprinted issues in 1941. The use of official stamps was discontinued December 31, 1951. During their currency, they were not for sale in mint condition and were sold to the public only when canceled with a parcel post rotary canceler reading "Balboa Heights, Canal Zone" between two wavy lines.

After having been withdrawn from use, mint stamps (except Nos. CO8-CO12 and O3, O8) were made available to the public at face value for three months beginning Jan. 2, 1952. **Values for used examples of Nos. CO1-CO7, CO14, O1-O2, O4-O9, are for canceled-to-order stamps with original gum, postally used stamps being worth more.** Sheet margins were removed to facilitate overprinting and plate numbers are, therefore, unknown.

Air Post Stamps of 1931-41 Overprinted in Black

Two types of overprint.

Type I — "PANAMA CANAL" 19-20mm long

1941-42 Unwmk. *Perf. 11*

CO1 AP1 5c **yellow green** *(42,754) Mar. 31, 1941* 5.50 1.50
green 5.50 1.50
On cover 50.00
Block of 4 25.00 6.00
CO2 AP1 10c **orange** *(49,723) Mar. 31, 1941* 8.50 2.00
On cover 25.00
Block of 4 37.50 9.00
CO3 AP1 15c **blue** *(56,898) Mar. 31, 1941* 11.00 2.00
On cover 25.00
Block of 4 47.50 17.00
CO4 AP1 20c **red violet** *(22,107) Mar. 31, 1941* 12.50 4.00
deep violet 12.50 4.00
On cover 110.00
Block of 4 60.00 22.50
CO5 AP1 30c **rose lake** *(22,100) June, 4, 1942* 17.50 5.00
dull rose 17.50 4.50
On cover 40.00
Block of 4 80.00 22.50
CO6 AP1 40c **yellow** *(22,875) Mar. 31, 1941* 17.50 7.50
lemon yellow 17.50 7.50
On cover 75.00
Block of 4 80.00 37.50
CO7 AP1 $1 **black** *(29,525) Mar. 31, 1941* 20.00 10.00
On cover 150.00
Block of 4 90.00 45.00
Nos. CO1-CO7 (7) 92.50 32.00

Overprint varieties occur on Nos. CO1-CO7 and CO14: "O" of "OFFICIAL" over "N" of "PANAMA" (entire third row). "O" of "OFFICIAL" broken at top (position 31). "O" of "OFFICIAL" over second "A" of "PANAMA" (position 45). First "F" of "OFFICIAL" over second "A" of "PANAMA" (position 50).

1941, Sept. 22

Type II — "PANAMA CANAL" 17mm long

CO8 AP1 5c **yellow green** *(2,000)* — 160.00
On cover 500.00
Block of 4 925.00
CO9 AP1 10c **orange** *(2,000)* — 275.00
On cover 400.00
Block of 4 1,650.
CO10 AP1 20c **red violet** *(2,000)* — 175.00
On cover —
Block of 4 1,050.
CO11 AP1 30c **rose lake** *(5,000)* *1,250.* 65.00
On cover 125.00
Block of 4 325.00
CO12 AP1 40c **yellow** *(2,000)* — 180.00
On cover 500.00
Block of 4 1,100.
Nos. CO8-CO12 (5) 855.00

1947, Nov.

Type I — "PANAMA CANAL" 19-20mm long

CO14 AP1 6c **yellow brown** *(33,450)* 12.50 5.00
On cover 50.00
Block of 4 57.50 25.00
a. Inverted overprint *(50)* *2,750.*

POSTAGE DUE STAMPS

Prior to 1914, many of the postal issues were handstamped "Postage Due" and used as postage due stamps.

Postage Due Stamps of the United States Nos. J45a, J46a, and J49a Overprinted in Black

1914, Mar. Wmk. 190 *Perf. 12*

J1 D2 1c **rose carmine** *(23,533)* 85. 15.
On cover 275.
Block of 4 (2mm spacing) 425. 70.
Block of 4 (3mm spacing) 450. 80.
P# block of 6, impt. & star 1,000. —
J2 D2 2c **rose carmine** *(32,312)* 250. 42.50
On cover 275.
Block of 4 1,250. 200.
P# block of 6 2,000. —
J3 D2 10c **rose carmine** *(92,493)* 1,000. 40.
On cover 900.
Block of 4 (2mm spacing) 4,250. 170.
Block of 4 (3mm spacing) 4,250. 170.
P# block of 6, Impt. & star *8,500.* —

Many examples of Nos. J1-J3 show one or more letters of the overprint out of alignment, principally the "E."

San Geronimo Castle Gate, Portobelo (See footnote) — D1

Statue of Columbus — D2

Pedro J. Sosa — D3

1915, Mar. Unwmk. *Perf. 12*

Blue Overprint, Type II, on Postage Due Stamps of Panama

J4 D1 1c **olive brown** *(50,000)* 12.50 5.00
On cover 150.00
Block of 4 55.00 22.50
J5 D2 2c **olive brown** *(50,000)* 225.00 17.50
On cover 400.00
Block of 4 975.00 90.00
J6 D3 10c **olive brown** *(200,000)* 50.00 10.00
On cover 175.00
Block of 4 225.00 45.00

Type D1 was intended to show a gate of San Lorenzo Castle, Chagres, and is so labeled. By error the stamp actually shows the main gate of San Geronimo Castle, Portobelo.

Surcharged in Red

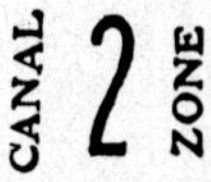

1915, Nov. Unwmk. *Perf. 12*

J7 D1 1c on 1c **olive brown** *(60,614)* 110.00 15.00
On cover 160.00
Block of 4 500.00 70.00
J8 D2 2c on 2c **olive brown** 25.00 7.50
On cover 200.00
Block of 4 110.00 37.50
J9 D3 10c on 10c **olive brown** *(175,548)* 22.50 5.00
On cover 200.00
Block of 4 100.00 25.00

One of the printings of No. J9 shows wider spacing between "1" and "0." Both spacings occur on the same sheet.

D4

Capitol, Panama — D5

1919, Dec.

Surcharged in Carmine at Mount Hope

J10 D4 2c on 2c **olive brown** 30.00 12.50
On cover 110.00
Block of 4 130.00 55.00
J11 D5 4c on 4c **olive brown** *(35,695)* 35.00 15.00
On cover 190.00
Block of 4 160.00 75.00
a. "ZONE" omitted *8,250.*
b. "4" omitted *8,250.*

Blue Overprint, Type V, on Postage Due Stamp of Panama

1922

J11C D1 1c **dark olive brown** — 10.00
d. "CANAL ZONE" reading down 200.00

United States Postage Due Stamps Nos. J61, J62b and J65b Overprinted

Type A
Letters "A" with Flat Tops

1924, July 1 ***Perf. 11***

J12 D2 1c **carmine rose** *(10,000)*		110.00	27.50
	On cover		100.00
	Block of 4	475.00	125.00
	P# block of 6	1,250.	—
J13 D2 2c **deep claret** *(25,000)*		55.00	15.00
	On cover		110.00
	Block of 4	275.00	65.00
	P# block of 6	725.00	—
J14 D2 10c **deep claret** *(30,000)*		250.00	50.00
	On cover		190.00
	Block of 4 (2mm spacing)	1,250.	210.00
	Block of 4 (3mm spacing)	1,250.	210.00
	Margin block of 6, imprint, star and P#	*3,500.*	—

Values for Nos. J12-J29 on cover are for philatelically contrived items. Commercial usages on cover are much more valuable.

United States Nos. 552, 554 and 562 Overprinted Type A and Additionally Overprinted at Mount Hope in Red or Blue

1925, Feb. ***Perf. 11***

J15 A155 1c **deep green** (R) *(15,000)*		90.00	15.00
	On cover		110.00
	Block of 4	400.00	62.50
	P# block of 6	900.00	—
J16 A157 2c **carmine** (Bl) *(21,335)*		22.50	7.00
	On cover		67.50
	Block of 4	100.00	30.00
	P# block of 6	225.00	—
J17 A165 10c **orange** (R) *(39,819)*		50.00	11.00
	On cover		90.00
	Block of 4	250.00	47.50
	P# block of 6	500.00	—
a.	"POSTAGE DUE" double	800.00	
b.	"E" of "POSTAGE" omitted	750.00	
c.	As "b," "POSTAGE DUE" double	*3,250.*	

Overprinted Type B
Letters "A" with Sharp Pointed Tops
On U.S. Postage Due Stamps Nos. J61, J62, J65, J65a

1925, June 24

J18 D2 1c **carmine rose** *(80,000)*		8.00	3.00
	On cover		50.00
	Block of 4	35.00	15.00
	P# block of 6	90.00	—
a.	"ZONE ZONE" (LR18)	1,750.	
J19 D2 2c **carmine rose** *(146,430)*		15.00	4.00
	On cover		47.50
	Block of 4	65.00	17.50
	P# block of 6	160.00	—
a.	"ZONE ZONE" (LR18)	1,750.	
J20 D2 10c **carmine rose** *(153,980)*		150.00	20.00
	On cover		300.00
	Block of 4, 2mm spacing	650.00	85.00
	Block of 4, 3mm spacing	675.00	90.00
	P# block of 6, Impt. & Star	1,250.	—
a.	Vert. pair, one without ovpt. *(10)*	*3,500.*	
	P# block of 6, Impt. & Star	*18,000.*	
b.	10c **rose red**	*250.00*	150.00
	On cover		—
c.	As "b," double overprint	*450.00*	—

Nos. J18-J20 exist with wrong font "CANAL" (UL51) and "ZONE" (UL82).

Regular Issue of 1928-29 Surcharged

1929-30

J21 A37 1c on 5c **blue** *(35,990) Mar. 20, 1930*		4.50	1.75
	Never hinged	9.00	
	On cover		37.50
	P# block of 6	45.00	—
a.	"POSTAGE DUE" omitted *(5)*	*5,500.*	
J22 A37 2c on 5c **blue** *(40,207) Oct. 18, 1930*		7.50	2.50
	Never hinged	15.00	
	On cover		32.50
	P# block of 6	75.00	—
J23 A37 5c on 5c **blue** *(35,464) Dec. 1, 1930*		7.50	2.75
	Never hinged	15.00	
	On cover		32.50
	P# block of 6	75.00	—
J24 A37 10c on 5c **blue** *(90,504) Dec. 16, 1929*		7.50	2.75
	Never hinged	15.00	
	On cover		32.50
	P# block of 6	75.00	—

On No. J23 the three short horizontal bars in the lower corners of the surcharge are omitted.

Canal Zone Seal — D6

Printed by the U.S. Bureau of Engraving and Printing.
Plates of 400 subjects, issued in panes of 100.

1932-41 **Flat Plate Printing**

J25 D6 1c **claret** *(378,300) Jan. 2, 1932*		.20	.20
	Never hinged	.25	
	On cover		30.00
	P# block of 6	2.00	—
a.	Dry printing, red violet	.25	.20
	Never hinged	.30	
	On cover		32.50
	P# block of 6	3.00	—
J26 D6 2c **claret** *(413,800) Jan. 2, 1932*		.20	.20
	Never hinged	.25	
	On cover		22.50
	P# block of 6	3.00	—
J27 D6 5c **claret** *Jan. 2, 1932*		.35	.20
	Never hinged	.40	
	On cover		25.00
	P# block of 6	3.50	—
a.	Dry printing, red violet	1.00	.30
	Never hinged	1.30	
	On cover		22.50
	P# block of 6	10.00	—
J28 D6 10c **claret** *(400,600) Jan. 2, 1932*		1.40	1.50
	Never hinged	2.00	
	On cover		32.50
	P# block of 6	15.00	—
J29 D6 15c **claret** *Apr. 21, 1941*		1.10	1.00
	Never hinged	1.50	
	On cover		37.50
	P# block of 6	12.00	—
	Nos. J25-J29 (5)	3.25	3.10

See note after No. J14.

OFFICIAL STAMPS

See note at beginning of Air Post Official Stamps

Regular Issues of 1928-34 Overprinted in Black by the Panama Canal Press, Mount Hope, C.Z.

Type 1

OFFICIAL
PANAMA CANAL
Type 2

Type 1 — "PANAMA" 10mm long
Type 1a — "PANAMA" 9mm long

1941, Mar. 31 **Unwmk.** ***Perf. 11***

O1 A35 1c **yellow green,** type 1 *(87,198)*		2.25	.40
	Never hinged	3.00	
	On cover		70.00
O2 A45 3c **deep violet,** type 1 *(34,958)*		4.00	.75
	Never hinged	5.25	
	On cover		90.00
O3 A37 5c **blue,** type 2 *(19,105)*		*1,000.*	32.50
	On cover		*110.00*
O4 A38 10c **orange,** type 1 *(18,776)*		7.50	1.90
	Never hinged	10.00	
	On cover		200.00
O5 A41 15c **gray black,** type 1 *(16,888)*		13.00	2.25
	Never hinged	17.50	
	gray		2.25
	On cover		140.00
O6 A42 20c **olive brown,** type 1 *(20,264)*		15.00	2.75
	Never hinged	22.50	
	On cover		100.00
O7 A44 50c **lilac,** type 1 *(19,175)*		37.50	5.50
	Never hinged	52.50	
	rose lilac		5.50
	On cover		—
O8 A44 50c **rose lilac,** type 1a *(1000)*			650.00

No. O3 exists with "O" directly over "N" of "PANAMA."

No. 139 Overprinted in Black

1947, Feb.

O9 A65 5c **deep blue,** type 1 *(21,639)*		9.00	3.50
	Never hinged	13.50	
	On cover		75.00

POST OFFICE SEALS

POS1

Issued in sheets of 8 without gum, imperforate margins.

1907 **Typo.** **Unwmk.** ***Perf. 11½***

OX1 POS1 **blue**		40.00	—
	Block of 4	175.00	
a.	Wmkd. seal of U.S. in sheet	55.00	—

No. OX1 clichés are spaced 3½mm apart.

1910

OX2 POS1 **ultramarine**		70.00	—
	Block of 4, cliches ½mm apart	325.00	
	Block of 4, cliches 1½mm apart horiz., 4mm vert.	800.00	
a.	Wmkd. "Rolleston Mills" in sheet	90.00	—
b.	Wmkd. U.S. Seal in sheet	225.00	—
	Block of 4, cliches 1½mm apart horiz., 4mm vert.	1,400.	

POS2

Printed by the Panama Canal Press, Mount Hope, C.Z.
Issued in sheets of 25, without gum, imperforate margins.

Rouletted 6 horizontally in color of seal, vertically without color

1917, Sept. 22

OX3 POS2 **dark blue**		4.00	—
	Block of 4	17.50	
a.	Wmkd. double lined letters in sheet ("Sylvania")	35.00	

1946 ***Rouletted 6, without color***

Issued in sheets of 20, without gum, imperforate margins.

OX4 POS2 **slate blue**		9.00	—
	Block of 4	40.00	

POS3

Typographed by the Panama Canal Press
Issued in sheets of 32, without gum, imperforate margins
except at top of sheet.

Size: 46x27mm
Seal Diameter: 13mm

1954, Mar. 8 Unwmk. *Perf. 12½*

OX5 POS3 **black** *(16,000)* 5.00 —
a. Wmkd. Seal of U. S. in sheet 20.00 —

Seal Diameter: 11½mm

1961, May 16 *Perf. 12½*

OX6 POS3 **black** (48,000) 3.00 —
b. Wmkd. Seal of U.S. in sheet, perf. 12½ 6.00
c. Double impression 110.00
d. As "b," double impression 125.00

1974, July 1 *Rouletted 5*

OX7 POS3 **black** 3.00 —

ENVELOPES

Values for cut squares are for examples with fine margins on all sides. Values for unused entires are for those without printed or manuscript address. A "full corner" includes back and side flaps and commands a premium.

Vasco Núñez de Balboa — U1

Fernandez de Córdoba — U2

Envelopes of Panama Lithographed and Overprinted by American Bank Note Co.

1916, Apr. 24

On White Paper

U1 U1 1c **green & black** 15.00 10.00
Entire 95.00 35.00
a. Head and overprint only — —
Entire *2,000. 2,000.*
b. Frame only — —
Entire *1,500. 2,500.*
U2 U2 2c **carmine & black** 12.50 5.00
Entire 90.00 25.00
a. 2c **red & black** 12.50 5.00
Entire 85.00 45.00
b. Head and overprint only — —
Entire *1,500. 2,000.*
c. Frame only (red) — —
Entire *1,000. 2,000.*
d. Frame double (carmine) — —
Entire *2,500. 2,250.*

José Vallarino — U3

"The Land Gate" — U4

1921, Nov. 13

On White Paper

U3 U3 1c **green** 140.00 100.00
Entire 700.00 375.00
U4 U4 2c **red** 35.00 20.00
Entire 275.00 125.00

Arms of Panama — U5

Typographed and embossed by American Bank Note Co. with "CANAL ZONE" in color of stamp.

1923, Dec. 15

On White Paper

U5 U5 2c **carmine** 55.00 32.50
Entire 200.00 125.00

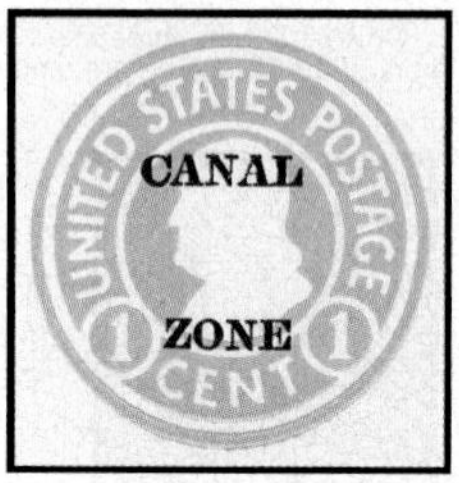

U.S. Nos. U420 and U429 Overprinted in Black by Bureau of Engraving and Printing, Washington, D.C.

1924, July 1

U6 U92 1c **green** *(50,000)* 5.00 3.00
Entire 30.00 19.00
Entire, 1st day cancel 125.00
U7 U93 2c **carmine** *(100,000)* 5.00 3.00
Entire 30.00 19.00
Entire, 1st day cancel 125.00

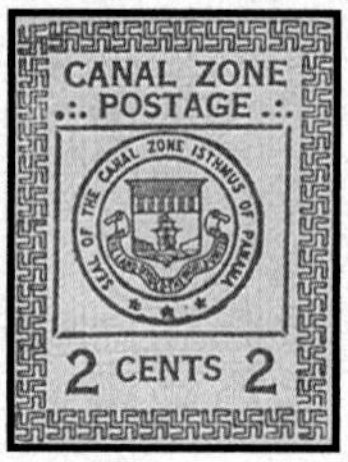

Seal of Canal Zone — U6

Printed by the Panama Canal Press, Mount Hope, C.Z.

1924, Oct.

On White Paper

U8 U6 1c **green** *(205,000)* 2.00 1.00
Entire 24.00 15.00
U9 U6 2c **carmine** *(1,997,658)* .75 .40
Entire 27.50 15.00

Gorgas — U7

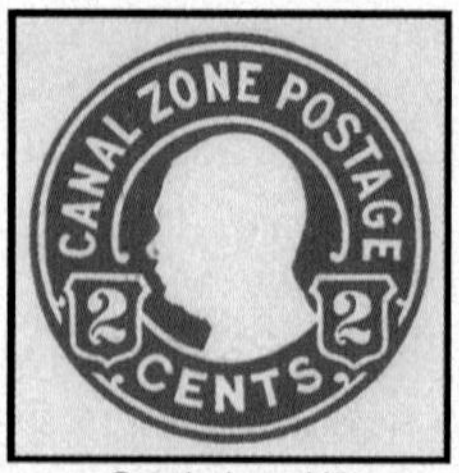

Goethals — U8

Typographed and Embossed by International Envelope Corp., Dayton, O.

1932, Apr. 8

U10 U7 1c **green** *(1,300,000)* .20 .20
Entire 3.00 1.10
Entire, 1st day cancel 35.00
U11 U8 2c **carmine** *(400,250)* .25 .20
Entire 3.50 1.75
Entire, 1st day cancel 35.00

No. U9 Surcharged in Violet by Panama Canal Press, Mount Hope, C.Z. Numerals 3mm high

1932, July 20

U12 U6 3c on 2c **carmine** *(20,000)* 17.50 7.50
Entire 225.00 125.00

No. U11 Surcharged in Violet, Numerals 5mm high

1932, July 20

U13 U8 3c on 2c **carmine** *(320,000)* 2.00 1.00
Entire 25.00 15.00
Entire, 1st day cancel 75.00

1934, Jan. 17

Numerals with Serifs

U14 U6 3c on 2c **carmine** (Numerals 4mm high) *(8,000)* 115.00 60.00
Entire 450.00 525.00
U15 U8 3c on 2c **carmine** (Numerals 5mm high) *(23,000)* 25.00 15.00
Entire 250.00 150.00

Typographed and Embossed by International Envelope Corp., Dayton, O.

1934, June 18

U16 U8 3c **purple** *(2,450,000)* .20 .20
Entire 1.20 1.40

1958, Nov. 1

U17 U8 4c **blue** *(596,725)* .20 .25
Entire 1.25 1.25
Entire, 1st day cancel, Cristobal 2.00

Surcharged at Left of Stamp in Ultra. as No. UX13

1969, Apr. 28

U18 U8 4c +1c **blue** *(93,850)* .20 *.25*
Entire 1.25 *1.60*
Entire, 1st day cancel 1.50
U19 U8 4c +2c **blue** *(23,125)* .50 *.65*
Entire 2.50 *4.00*
Entire, 1st day cancel 1.50

Ship Passing through Gaillard Cut — U9

Typographed and Embossed by United States Envelope Co., Williamsburg, Pa.

1971, Nov. 17

U20 U9 8c **emerald** *(121,500)* .25 *.30*
Entire .75 .65
Entire, 1st day cancel, Balboa *(9,650)* 1.50

Surcharged at Left of Stamp in Emerald as #UX13

1974, Mar. 2

U21 U9 8c +2c **emerald** .30 *.35*
Entire 1.00 *2.00*
Entire, 1st day cancel 1.25

1976, Feb. 23

U22 U9 13c **violet** *(638,350)* .35 *.40*
Entire .85 .85
Entire, 1st day cancel, Balboa *(9,181)* 1.25

Surcharged at Left of Stamp in Violet as No. UX13

1978, July 5

U23 U9 13c +2c **violet** *(245,041)* .35 *.40*
Entire .85 *2.00*
Entire, 1st day cancel 1.25

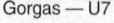

AIR POST ENVELOPES

No. U9 Overprinted with Horizontal Blue and Red Bars Across Entire Face. Overprinted by Panama Canal Press, Mount Hope. Boxed inscription in lower left with nine lines of instructions. Additional adhesives required for air post rate.

1928, May 21

UC1	U6	2c **red,** entire *(15,000)*	135.00	65.00
		First day cancel		175.00

No. U9 with Similar Overprint of Blue and Red Bars, and "VIA AIR MAIL" in Blue, At Left, no box.

1929

UC2	U6	2c **red,** entire *(60,200)*	65.00	27.50
a.		Inscription centered *(10,000) Jan. 11*	325.00	190.00

Earliest known use of No. UC2 is Feb. 6.

DC-4 Skymaster UC1

Typographed and Embossed by International Envelope Corp., Dayton, O.

1949, Jan. 3

UC3	UC1	6c **blue** *(4,400,000)*	.25	.25
		Entire	4.00	3.00
		Entire, 1st day cancel		2.00

1958, Nov. 1

UC4	UC1	7c **carmine** *(1,000,000)*	.25	.20
		Entire	4.00	3.50
		Entire, 1st day cancel		1.50

No. U16 Surcharged at Left of Stamp and Imprinted "VIA AIR MAIL" in Dark Blue

Surcharged by Panama Canal Press, Mount Hope, C.Z.

1963, June 22

UC5	U8	3c + 5c **purple** *(105,000)*	1.00	1.00
		Entire	6.00	*8.00*
		Entire, 1st day cancel		5.00
a.		Double surcharge	*1,250.*	

Jet Liner and Tail Assembly UC2

Typographed and Embossed by International Envelope Corp., Dayton, O.

1964, Jan. 6

UC6	UC2	8c **deep carmine** *(600,000)*	.35	.35
		Entire	2.25	2.50
		Entire, 1st day cancel, Balboa *(3,855)*		2.25

No. U17 Surcharged at Left of Stamp as No. UC5 and Imprinted "VIA AIR MAIL" in Vermilion

Surcharged by Canal Zone Press, La Boca, C.Z.

1965, Oct. 15

UC7	U8	4c + 4c **blue** *(100,000)*	.50	.40
		Entire	4.50	*7.50*
		Entire, 1st day cancel		5.00

Jet Liner and Tail Assembly — UC3

Typographed and Embossed by United States Envelope Co., Williamsburg, Pa.

1966, Feb.

UC8	UC3	8c **carmine** *(224,000)*	.50	.45
		Entire	5.00	5.00

Earliest known use: Feb. 23.

No. UC8 Surcharged at Left of Stamp as No. UX13 in Vermilion

Surcharged by Canal Zone Press, La Boca, C.Z.

1968, Jan. 18

UC9	UC3	8c + 2c **carmine** *(376,000)*	.40	.35
		Entire	2.75	*5.00*
		Entire, 1st day cancel		4.50

No. UC7 with Additional Surcharge at Left of Stamp as No. UX13 and Imprinted "VIA AIR MAIL" in Vermilion

Surcharged by Canal Zone Press, La Boca, C.Z.

1968, Feb. 12

UC10	U8	4c + 4c + 2c **blue** *(224,150)*	.60	.50
		Entire	2.25	*6.00*
		Entire, 1st day cancel		5.00

Type of 1966

Typographed and Engraved by United States Envelope Co., Williamsburg, Pa.

1969, Apr. 1

Luminescent Ink

UC11	UC3	10c **ultramarine** *(448,000)*	.60	.40
		Entire	4.00	*5.00*
		Entire, 1st day cancel, Balboa *(9,583)*		2.00

No. U17 Surcharged at Left of Stamp as Nos. UC5 and UX13, and Imprinted "VIA AIR MAIL" in Vermilion

1971, May 17

UC12	U8	4c + 5c + 2c **blue** *(55,775)*	.75	.50
		Entire	4.00	*6.00*
		Entire, 1st day cancel		5.00

No. UC11 Surcharged in Ultra. at Left of Stamp as No. UX13

1971, May 17

Luminescent Ink

UC13	UC3	10c + 1c **ultramarine** *(152,000)*	.45	.40
		Entire	4.00	*7.00*
		Entire, 1st day cancel		3.50

Type of 1966

Typographed and Engraved by United States Envelope Co., Williamsburg, Pa.

1971, Nov. 17

UC14	UC3	11c **rose red** *(258,000)*	.30	.20
		Entire	1.10	1.25
		Entire, 1st day cancel, Balboa *(3,451)*		1.50
a.		11c **carmine,** stamp tagged, *(395,000)*	.30	.20
		Entire	1.10	1.25
		Entire, 1st day cancel, Balboa *(5,971)*		1.50

The red diamonds around the envelope edges are luminescent on both Nos. UC14 and UC14a. No. UC14 is size 10, No. UC14a size 6¾.

Surcharged at Left of Stamp in Rose Red as No. UX13

1974, Mar. 2

UC15	UC3	11c + 2c **carmine,** tagged *(305,000)*	.35	.30
		Entire	1.50	*3.00*
		Entire, 1st day cancel		1.25
a.		11c + 2c **rose red,** untagged, *(87,000)*	.35	.25
		Entire	1.75	2.00

No. U21 with Additional Surcharge in Vermilion at Left of Stamp as No. UX13 and Imprinted "VIA AIR MAIL" in Vermilion

1975, May 3

UC16	U9	8c + 2c + 3c **emerald** *(75,000)*	.50	.30
		Entire	1.25	*2.50*
		Entire, 1st day cancel		1.50

REGISTRATION ENVELOPES

RE1

Panama Registration Envelope surcharged by Panama Canal Press, Mount Hope, C.Z.

1918, Oct. 8mm between CANAL & ZONE

UF1	RE1	10c on 5c **black & red,** *cream (10,000),* entire	*1,750.*	*2,000.*
a.		9¼mm between CANAL & ZONE *(25,000),* entire ('19)	*1,300.*	*2,000.*

Stamped envelopes inscribed "Diez Centesimos," surcharged with numerals "5" and with solid blocks printed over "Canal Zone," were issued by the Republic of Panama after being rejected by the Canal Zone. Parts of "Canal Zone" are often legible under the surcharge blocks. These envelopes exist without surcharge.

POSTAL CARDS

Values are for Entires

Map of Panama — PC1

Panama Card Lithographed by American Bank Note Co., revalued and surcharged in black by the Isthmian Canal Commission.

1907, Feb. 9

UX1	PC1	1c on 2c **carmine,** "CANAL" 15mm *(50,000)*	40.	25.
a.		Double surcharge	*1,500.*	*2,000.*
b.		Double surcharge, one reading down	*2,750.*	
c.		Triple surcharge, one reading down	*3,300.*	
d.		"CANAL" 13mm *(10,000)*	250.	200.
e.		As "d," double surcharge	*2,400.*	

Balboa — PC2

Panama card lithographed by Hamilton Bank Note Co. Overprinted in black by Isthmian Canal Commission.

At least six types of overprint, reading down.

1908, Mar. 3

UX2	PC2	1c **green & black,** "CANAL" 13mm *(295,000)*	190.	80.
a.		Double overprint	*2,000.*	*2,000.*
b.		Triple overprint	*1,750.*	—
c.		Period after "ZONE" *(40,000)*	200.	125.
d.		"CANAL" 15mm *(30,000)*	200.	125.
e.		"ZONE CANAL", reading up		*4,000.*

Balboa
PC3 PC4

Lithographed by Hamilton Bank Note Co.
Overprinted in Black by Panama Canal Press, Mount Hope, C.Z.

1910, Nov. 10
UX3 PC3 1c **green & black** *(40,000)* 190. 70.
a. Double overprint *4,250.*

This card, with overprint reading up, is actually the fourth of seven settings of UX2.

Lithographed and Overprinted by American Bank Note Co.

1913, Mar. 27
UX4 PC4 1c **green & black** *(634,000)* 160. 60.

Design of Canal Zone Envelopes
Overprinted in black by the American Bank Note Co.

1921, Oct.
UX5 U3 1c **green** 1,100. 450.

Typographed and embossed by American Bank Note Co. with "CANAL ZONE" in color of stamp.

1924, Jan.
UX6 U5 1c **green** 1,050. *1,100.*

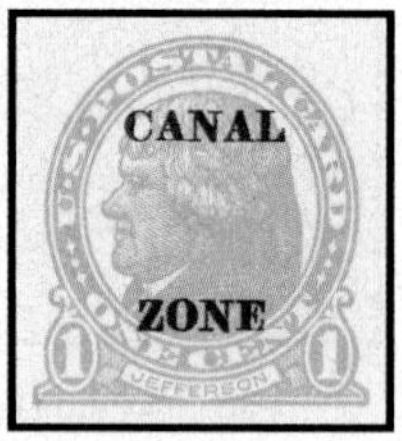

U.S. No. UX27 Overprinted by U.S. Gov't. Printing Office at Washington, D.C.

1924, July 1
UX7 PC17 1c **green,** *buff (Jefferson)*
(50,000) 85. 35.

Design of Canal Zone Envelope
Printed by Panama Canal Press.

1925, Jan.
UX8 U6 1c **green,** *buff (25,000)* 80. 35.
a. Background only *1,800.*

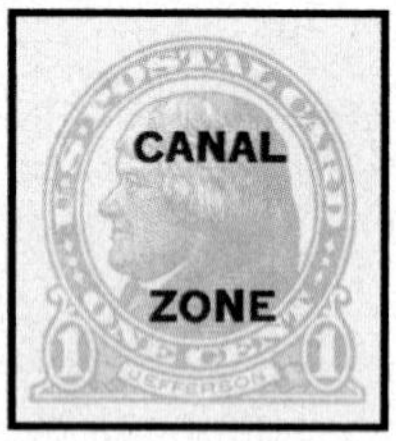

U.S. No. UX27 Overprinted

1925, May
UX9 PC17 1c **green,** *buff (Jefferson)*
(850,000) 8.50 5.00

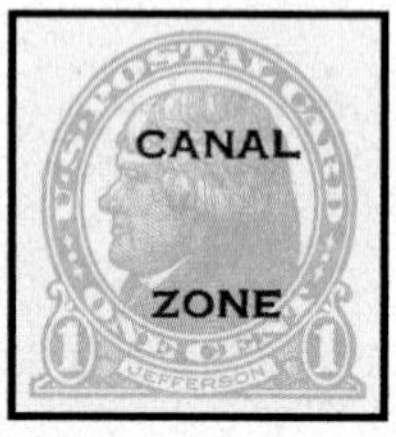

U.S. No. UX27 Overprinted

1935, Oct.
UX10 PC17 1c **green,** *buff (Jefferson)*
(2,900,000) 1.80 1.80
a. Double overprint *1,900.*

Used values are for contemporaneous usage without additional postage applied.

Same on U.S. No. UX38

1952, May 1
UX11 PC22 2c **carmine rose,** *buff (Franklin)*
(800,000) 2.00 2.00
1st day cancel, Balboa Heights 3.50

Ship in Lock — PC5

Printed by Bureau of Engraving & Printing, Washington, D.C.

1958, Nov. 1
UX12 PC5 3c **dark blue,** *buff (335,116)* 1.90 *3.00*
First day cancel, Cristobal 1.25

No. UX12 Surcharged at Left of Stamp in Green by Panama Canal Press, Mount Hope, C.Z.

1963, July 27
UX13 PC5 3c + 1c **dark blue,** *buff (78,000)* 4.00 *6.00*
First day cancel 3.50

Ship Passing through Panama Canal — PC6

Printed by Panama Canal Press, Mount Hope, C.Z.

1964, Dec. 1
UX14 PC6 4c **violet blue,** *buff (74,200)* 3.75 *7.50*
1st day cancel, Cristobal
(19,260) 3.50

Ship in Lock (Towing locomotive at right redrawn) — PC7

Printed by Bureau of Engraving & Printing, Washington, D.C.

1965, Aug. 12
UX15 PC7 4c **emerald** *(95,500)* 1.10 *2.00*
1st day cancel, Cristobal
(20,366) 1.00

No. UX15 Surcharged at Left of Stamp in Green as No. UX13 by Canal Zone Press, La Boca, C.Z.

1968, Feb. 12
UX16 PC7 4c + 1c **emerald** *(94,775)* 1.10 *4.00*
First day cancel 1.00

Ship-in-Lock Type of 1965

1969, Apr. 1
UX17 PC7 5c **light ultramarine** *(63,000)* 1.00 *2.50*
1st day cancel, Balboa *(11,835)* 1.00

No. UX17 Surcharged at Left of Stamp in Light Ultramarine as No. UX13

1971, May 24
UX18 PC7 5c + 1c **light ultramarine** *(100,500)* .90 *3.50*
First day cancel 1.00

Ship-in-Lock Type of 1965
Printed by Bureau of Engraving & Printing, Washington, D.C.

1974, Feb. 11
UX19 PC7 8c **brown** *(90,895)* .90 *2.00*
1st day cancel, Balboa *(10,375)* 1.00

No. UX19 Surcharged at Left of Stamp in Brown as No. UX13

1976, June 1
UX20 PC7 8c + 1c **brown** *(60,249)* .65 *4.00*
First day cancel 1.00

No. UX19 Surcharged at Left of Stamp in Brown as No. UX13

1978, July 5
UX21 PC7 8c + 2c **brown** *(74,847)* .85 *4.00*
First day cancel 1.00

AIR POST POSTAL CARDS

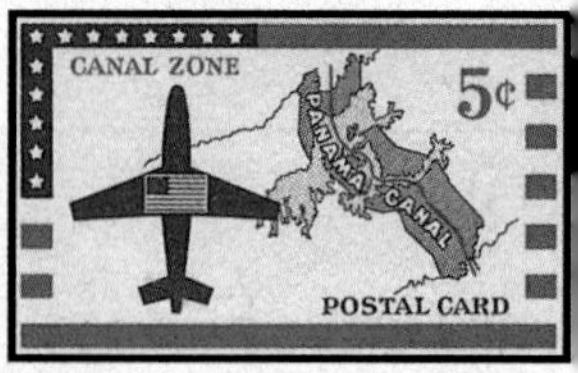

Plane, Flag and Map — APC1

Printed by Bureau of Engraving & Printing, Washington, D.C.

1958, Nov. 1
UXC1 APC1 5c **blue & carmine rose**
(104,957) 3.75 *7.50*
1st day cancel, Balboa 3.75

No. UXC1 Surcharged at Left of Stamp in Green as No. UX13 by Panama Canal Press, Mount Hope, C.Z.

1963, July 27
UXC2 APC1 5c + 1c **blue & carmine rose**
(48,000) 9.50 *18.00*
a. Inverted surcharge *1,500.*
First day cancel 5.00

No. UX15 Surcharged at Left of Stamp as No. UX13 and Imprinted "AIR MAIL" in Vermilion

1965, Aug. 18
UXC3 PC7 4c + 2c **emerald** *(41,700)* 4.00 *20.00*
First day cancel 6.00

No. UX15 Surcharged at Left of Stamp as No. UC5 and Imprinted "AIR MAIL" in Vermilion by Canal Zone Press, La Boca, C.Z.

1968, Feb. 12
UXC4 PC7 4c + 4c **emerald** *(60,100)* 2.75 *16.00*
First day cancel 6.00

No. UX17 Surcharged at Left of Stamp as No. UC5 and Imprinted "AIR MAIL" in Vermilion

1971, May 24
UXC5 PC7 5c + 4c **light ultramarine**
(68,000) 1.00 *15.00*
First day cancel 6.00

PROOFS

1928-40

Column (1) — Large Die
Column (2) — Small Die

			(1)	(2)
106TC	2c	**black**	*1,300.*	
113P	30c	**brown black**		975.

1934

			(1)	(2)
117P	3c	**deep violet** *(8)*		475.

1939

			(1)	(2)
120P	1c	**yellow green**	*1,300.*	875.
121P	2c	**rose carmine**		875.
122P	3c	**purple**	*1,300.*	875.
123P	5c	**dark blue**	*1,300.*	875.
124P	6c	**red orange**		875.
125P	7c	**black**		875.
126P	8c	**green**	*1,300.*	875.
127P	10c	**ultramarine**	*1,300.*	875.
128P	11c	**blue green**	*1,300.*	875.
129P	12c	**brown carmine**	*1,300.*	875.
130P	14c	**dark violet**		875.
131P	15c	**olive green**		875.
132P	18c	**rose pink**		875.
133P	20c	**brown**	*1,300.*	875.
134P	25c	**orange**	*1,300.*	875.
135P	50c	**violet brown**	*1,300.*	875.

1946-48

			(1)	(2)
136P	½c	**bright red**	*1,300.*	
137P	1½c	**chocolate**	*1,300.*	
139P	5c	**deep blue**	*1,300.*	
140P	25c	**yellow green**	*1,300.*	
141P	10c	**black**	*825.*	

1949

142P	3c **blue**	*1,150.*	
143P	6c **violet**	*1,150.*	
144P	12c **bright blue green**	*1,150.*	
145P	18c **deep red lilac**	*1,150.*	

1951

146P	10c **carmine**	*1,500.*	

1955

147P	3c **violet**	*1,500.*	

Air Post

1931-49

C6P	4c **red violet**	*1,600.*	
C7P	5c **light green**	*1,600.*	
C8P	6c **yellow brown**	*1,600.*	
C13TC	40c **orange**	*1,600.*	

1939

C15P	5c **greenish black**		925.
C15TC	5c **scarlet**	*1,300.*	
C16P	10c **dull violet**	*1,300.*	925.
C17P	15c **light brown**	*1,300.*	925.
C18P	25c **blue**		925.
C19P	30c **rose carmine**	*1,300.*	925.
C20P	$1 **green**	*1,300.*	925.

1951

C21P	4c **red violet**	*1,300.*	

The Small Die proofs listed are on soft yellowish wove paper.
Only No. 117P has more than two examples reported in private collections.

CUBA

After the U.S. battleship "Maine" was destroyed in Havana harbor with a loss of 266 lives in February, 1898, the United States demanded the withdrawal of Spanish troops from Cuba. The Spanish-American War followed. With the peace treaty of Dec. 10, 1898, Spain relinquished Cuba to the United States in trust for its inhabitants. On Jan. 1, 1899, Spanish authority was succeeded by U.S. military rule which lasted until May 20, 1902, when Cuba, as a republic, assumed self-government.

The listings in this catalogue cover the U.S. Administration issue of 1899, the Republic's 1899-1902 issues under U.S. military rule and the Puerto Principe issue of provincial provisionals.

Values for Nos. 176-220 are for stamps in the grade of fine and in sound condition where such exist. Values for Nos. 221-UX2b are for very fine examples.

100 CENTS = 1 DOLLAR

Puerto Principe Issue

In December, 1898, Puerto Principe, a provincial capital now called Camagüey, ran short of 1c, 2c, 3c, 5c and 10c stamps. The Postmaster ordered Cuban stamps to be surcharged on Dec. 19, 1898.

The surcharging was done to horizontal strips of five stamps, so vertical pairs and blocks do not exist. Five types are found in each setting, and five printings were made. Counterfeits are plentiful.

First Printing

Black Surcharge, 17½mm high

Surcharge measures 17½mm high and is roughly printed in dull black ink.

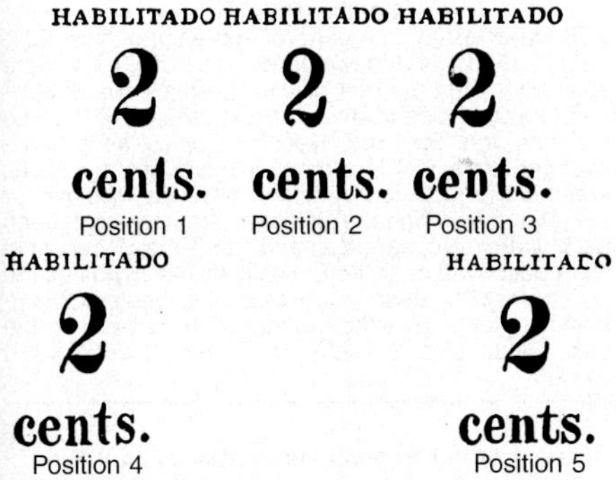

Position 1 Position 2 Position 3
Position 4 Position 5

Position 1	— No serif at right of "t"
Position 2	— Thin numeral except on 1c on 1m No. 176
Position 3	— Broken right foot of "n"
Position 4	— Up-stroke of "t" broken
Position 5	— Broken "DO"

This printing consisted of the following stamps:

176	1c on 1m orange brown, Pos. 1, 2, 3, 4 and 5
178	2c on 2m orange brown, Pos. 1, 3, 4 and 5
179	2c on 2m orange brown, Pos. 2
180	3c on 3m orange brown, Pos. 1, 3, 4 and 5
181	3c on 3m orange brown, Pos. 2
188	5c on 5m orange brown, Pos. 1, 3, 4 and 5
189	5c on 5m orange brown, Pos. 2

Second Printing

Black Surcharge, 17½mm high

This printing was from the same setting as used for the first printing, but the impression is much clearer and the ink quite shiny.

The printing consisted of the following stamps:

179F	3c on 2m orange brown, Pos. 1, 3, 4 and 5
179G	3c on 2m orange brown, Pos. 2
182	5c on 1m orange brown, Pos. 1, 3, 4 and 5
183	5c on 1m orange brown, Pos. 2
184	5c on 2m orange brown, Pos. 1, 3, 4 and 5
185	5c on 2m orange brown, Pos. 2
186	5c on 3m orange brown, Pos. 1, 3, 4 and 5
187	5c on 3m orange brown, Pos. 2
188	5c on 5m orange brown, Pos. 1, 3, 4 and 5
189	5c on 5m orange brown, Pos. 2
190	5c on ½m blue green, Pos. 1, 3, 4 and 5
191	5c on ½m blue green, Pos. 2

Third Printing

Red Surcharge, 20mm high

The same setting as for the first and second was used for the third printing. The 10c denomination first appeared in this printing and position 2 of that value has numerals same as on positions 1, 3, 4 and 5, while position 4 has broken "1" in "10."

The printing consisted of the following stamps:

196	3c on 1c black violet, Pos. 1, 3, 4 and 5
197	3c on 1c black violet, Pos. 2
198	5c on 1c black violet, Pos. 1, 3, 4 and 5
199	5c on 1c black violet, Pos. 2
200	10c on 1c black violet, Pos. 1, 2, 3 and 5
200a	10c on 1c black violet, Pos. 4

Fourth Printing

Black Surcharge, 19½mm high

The same type as before but spaced between so that the surcharge is 2mm taller. Clear impression, shiny ink.

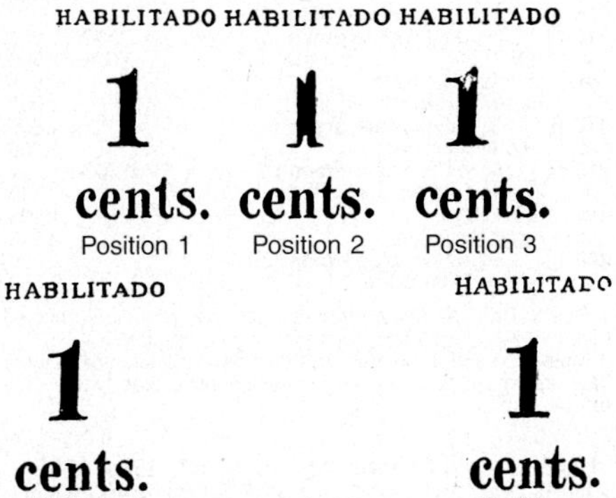

Position 1 Position 2 Position 3
Position 4 Position 5

Position 1	— No serif at right of "t"
Position 2	— Broken "1" on No. 177
Position 2	— Thin numerals on 5c stamps
Position 3	— Broken right foot of "n"
Position 4	— Up-stroke of "t" broken
Position 4	— Thin numeral on 3c stamps
Position 5	— Broken "DO"

This printing consisted of the following stamps:

177	1c on 1m orange brn, Pos. 1, 3, 4 and 5
177a	1c on 1m orange brn, Pos. 2
179B	3c on 1m orange brn, Pos. 1, 2, 3 and 5
179D	3c on 1m orange brn, Pos. 4
183B	5c on 1m orange brn, Pos. 1, 3, 4 and 5
189C	5c on 5m orange brn, Pos. 1, 3, 4 and 5
192	5c on ½m blue green, Pos. 1, 3, 4 and 5
193	5c on ½m blue green, Pos. 2

Fifth Printing

Black Surcharge, 19½mm high

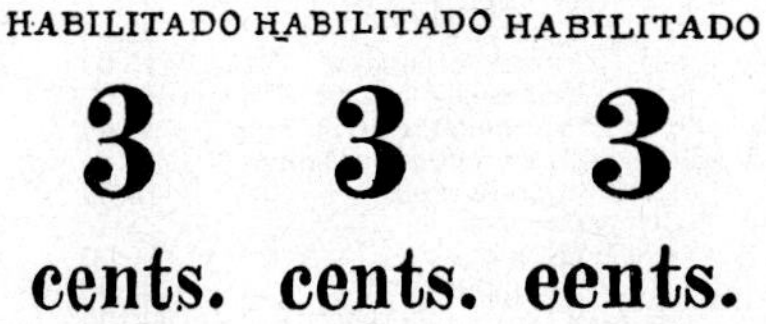

Position 1 Position 2 Position 3

Position 4 Position 5

Position 1	— Nick in bottom of "e"and lower serif of "s"
Position 2	— Normal surcharge
Position 3	— "eents"
Position 4	— Thin numeral
Position 5	— Nick in upper part of right stroke of "n"

This printing consisted of the following stamps:

201	3c on 1m blue green, Pos. 1, 2 and 5
201b	3c on 1m blue green, Pos. 3
202	3c on 1m blue green, Pos. 4
203	3c on 2m blue green, Pos. 4
203a	3c on 2m blue green, Pos. 3
204	3c on 2m blue green, Pos. 4
205	3c on 3m blue green, Pos. 1, 2 and 5
205b	3c on 3m blue green, Pos. 3
206	3c on 3m blue green, Pos. 4
211	5c on 1m blue green, Pos. 1, 2 and 5
211a	5c on 1m blue green, Pos. 3
212	5c on 1m blue green, Pos. 4
213	5c on 2m blue green, Pos. 1, 2 and 5
213a	5c on 2m blue green, Pos. 3
214	5c on 2m blue green, Pos. 4
215	5c on 3m blue green, Pos. 1, 2 and 5
215a	5c on 3m blue green, Pos. 3
216	5c on 3m blue green, Pos. 4
217	5c on 4m blue green, Pos. 1, 2 and 5
217a	5c on 4m blue green, Pos. 3
218	5c on 4m blue green, Pos. 4
219	5c on 8m blue green, Pos. 1, 2 and 5
219b	5c on 8m blue green, Pos. 3
220	5c on 8m blue green, Pos. 4

Counterfeits exist of all Puerto Principe surcharges. Illustrations have been altered to discourage further counterfeiting.

Regular Issues of Cuba of 1896 and 1898 Surcharged:

a b

Numeral in ( ) after color indicates printing.

1898-99

Black Surcharge on Nos. 156-158, 160

176	(a)	1 cent on 1m **orange brn** (1)	50.00	30.00
177	(b)	1 cents on 1m **org brn** (4)	45.00	35.00
a.		Broken figure "1"	75.00	65.00
b.		Inverted surcharge		200.00
d.		Same as "a" inverted		*250.00*

HABILITADO
2
cents.
c

HABILITADO
2
cents.
d

178 (c) 2c on 2m **orange brown** (1) 24.00 20.00
a. Inverted surcharge 250.00 50.00
179 (d) 2c on 2m **orange brown** (1) 40.00 35.00
a. Inverted surcharge 350.00 100.00

HABILITADO
3
cents.
k

HABILITADO
3
cents.
l

179B (k) 3c on 1m **orange brown** (4) 300. 175.
c. Double surcharge 1,500. 750.

An unused copy is known with "cents" omitted.

179D (l) 3c on 1m **orange brown** (4) *1,500.* *750.*
e. Double surcharge — —

HABILITADO
3
cents.
e

HABILITADO
3
cents.
f

179F (e) 3c on 2m **orange brown** (2) *1,500.*

Value is for copy with minor faults.

179G (f) 3c on 2m **orange brown** (2) — *2,000.*

Value is for copy with minor faults.

180 (e) 3c on 3m **orange brown** (1) 30. 30.
a. Inverted surcharge 110.
181 (f) 3c on 3m **orange brown** (1) 75. 75.
a. Inverted surcharge *200.*

HABILITADO
5
cents.
g

HABILITADO
5
cents.
h

HABILITADO
5
cents.
i

HABILITADO
5
cents.
j

182 (g) 5c on 1m **orange brown** (2) 700. 200.
a. Inverted surcharge *500.*
183 (h) 5c on 1m **orange brown** (2) *1,300.* *500.*
a. Inverted surcharge *700.*
184 (g) 5c on 2m **orange brown** (2) 750. 250.
185 (h) 5c on 2m **orange brown** (2) 1,500. 500.
186 (g) 5c on 3m **orange brown** (2) 650. 175.
a. Inverted surcharge 1,200. 700.
187 (h) 5c an 3m **orange brown** (2) 400.
a. Inverted surcharge 1,000.
188 (g) 5c on 5m **orange brown** (1) (2) 80. 60.
a. Inverted surcharge 400. 200.
b. Double surcharge — —
189 (h) 5c on 5m **orange brown** (1) (2) 350. 250.
a. Inverted surcharge 400.
b. Double surcharge — —
189C (i) 5c on 5m **orange brown** (4) *7,500.*

Values for Nos. 188, 189 are for the first printing.

Black Surcharge on No. P25

190 (g) 5c on ½m **blue green** (2) 250. 75.
a. Inverted surcharge 500. 150.
b. Pair, one without surcharge 500.
191 (h) 5c on ½m **blue green** (2) 300. 90.
a. Inverted surcharge 200.
192 (i) 5c on ½m **blue green** (4) 550. 200.
a. Double surcharge, one diagonal *11,500.*

Value for No. 190b is for pair with unsurcharged stamp at right. One pair with unsurcharged stamp at left is known.
No. 192a is unique.

193 (j) 5c on ½m **blue green** (4) 800. 300.

Red Surcharge on No. 161

196 (k) 3c on 1c **black violet** (3) 65. 35.
a. Inverted surcharge 325.
197 (l) 3c on 1c **black violet** (3) 125. 55.
a. Inverted surcharge 400.
198 (i) 5c on 1c **black violet** (3) 25. 30.
a. Inverted surcharge 125.
b. Vertical surcharge *3,500.*
c. Double surcharge *400.* *600.*
d. Double inverted surcharge —
199 (j) 5c on 1c **black violet** (3) 55. 55.
a. Inverted surcharge 250.
b. Vertical surcharge *2,000.*
c. Double surcharge 1,000. 700.

Value for No. 198b is for surcharge reading up. One example is known with surcharge reading down.

HABILITADO
10
cents. m

200 (m) 10c on 1c **black violet** (3) 20. *50.*
a. Broken figure "1" 40. *100.*

Black Surcharge on Nos. P26-P30

201 (k) 3c on 1m **blue green** (5) 350. 350.
a. Inverted surcharge 450.
b. "EENTS" 550. 450.
c. As "b", inverted 850.
202 (l) 3c on 1m **blue green** (5) 550. 400.
a. Inverted surcharge 850.
203 (k) 3c on 2m **blue green** (5) 850. 400.
a. "EENTS" 1,250. 500.
b. Inverted surcharge 850.
c. As "a," inverted 950.
204 (l) 3c on 2m **blue green** (5) 1,250. 600.
a. Inverted surcharge 750.
205 (k) 3c on 3m **blue green** (5) 900. 400.
a. Inverted surcharge 500.
b. "EENTS" 1,250. 450.
c. As "b," inverted 700.
206 (l) 3c on 3m **blue green** (5) 1,200. 550.
a. Inverted surcharge 700.
211 (i) 5c on 1m **blue green** (5) 1,800.
a. "EENTS" — 2,500.
212 (j) 5c on 1m **blue green** (5) 2,250.
213 (i) 5c on 2m **blue green** (5) 1,800.
a. "EENTS" — 1,900.
214 (j) 5c on 2m **blue green** (5) 1,750.
215 (i) 5c on 3m **blue green** (5) 550.
a. "EENTS" 1,000.
216 (j) 5c on 3m **blue green** (5) — 1,000.
217 (i) 5c on 4m **blue green** (5) *2,500.* 900.
a. "EENTS" *3,000.* 1,500.
b. Inverted surcharge *2,000.*
c. As "a," inverted 2,000.
218 (j) 5c on 4m **blue green** (5) *1,500.*
a. Inverted surcharge *2,000.*
219 (i) 5c on 8m **blue green** (5) *2,500.* 1,250.
a. Inverted surcharge 1,500.
b. "EENTS" — 1,800.
c. As "b," inverted 2,500.
220 (j) 5c on 8m **blue green** (5) 2,000.
a. Inverted surcharge 2,500.

Puerto Principe pairs, strips and stamps properly canceled on cover are scarce and command high premiums.
Most copies of all but the most common varieties are faulty or have tropical toning. Values are for sound copies where they exist.

United States Stamps Nos. 279, 267, 267b, 279Bf, 279Bh, 268, 281, 282C and 283 Surcharged in Black

1899 **Wmk. 191** ***Perf. 12***

221 A87 1c on 1c **yellow green** 5.25 .40
On cover 15.00
Block of 4 27.50 4.50
P# strip of 3, Impt. 57.50
P# block of 6, Impt. 300.00
222 A88 2c on 2c **reddish carmine,** type III, *Feb.* 10.00 .75
On cover 22.50
Block of 4 55.00 8.00
P# strip of 3, Impt. 115.00
P# block of 6, Impt. 650.00
b. 2c on 2c **vermilion,** type III, *Feb.* 10.00 .75
222A A88 2c on 2c **reddish carmine,** type IV, *Feb.* 6.00 .40
On cover 12.50
Block of 4 30.00 4.50
P# strip of 3, Impt. 65.00
P# block of 6, Impt. 600.00
"CUBA" at bottom *600.00*
"CUPA" (broken letter. pos. 99) 175.00
c. 2c on 2c **vermilion,** type IV, *Feb.* 6.00 .40
d. As No. 222A, inverted surcharge *5,500.* *5,000.*
223 A88 2½c on 2c **reddish carmine,** type III, *Jan. 2* 5.00 .80
On cover 20.00
Block of 4 27.50 8.00
P# strip of 3, Impt. 90.00
P# block of 6, Impt. 350.00
b. 2½ on 2c **vermilion,** type III, *Jan. 2* 5.00 .80
223A A88 2½c on 2c **reddish carmine,** type IV, *Jan. 2* 3.50 .50
On cover 12.50
Block of 4 20.00 4.50
P# strip of 3, Impt. 62.50
P# block of 6, Impt. 250.00
c. 2½c on 2c **vermilion,** type IV, *Jan. 2* 3.50 .50

All 2½c stamps were sold and used as 2 centavo stamps.

224 A89 3c on 3c **purple** 14.00 1.75
On cover 25.00
Block of 4 65.00 14.00
P# strip of 3, Impt. 110.00
P# block of 6, Impt. 675.00
a. Period between "B" and "A" 40.00 35.00

Two types of surcharge
I — "3" directly over "P"
II — "3" to left over "P"

225 A91 5c on 5c **blue** 14.00 2.00
On cover 30.00
Block of 4 65.00 15.00
P# strip of 3, Impt. 190.00
P# block of 6, Impt. 800.00
"CUBA" at bottom — —
"CUPA" (broken letter) 80.00 40.00
226 A94 10c on 10c **brown,** type I 25.00 6.50
On cover 110.00
Block of 4 115.00 45.00
P# strip of 3, Impt. 260.00
P# block of 6, Impt. 1,000.
"CUBA" at bottom 400.00 550.00
b. "CUBA" omitted *5,500.* *4,000.*
226A A94 10c on 10c **brown,** type II *6,500.*
Block of 4 —
Nos. 221-226 (8) 82.75 13.10

No. 226A exists only in the special printing.
The No. 225 "CUPA" variety always has a straight edge at the right.

Special Printing

In March 1900, one pane of 100 each of Nos. 221-225, 226A, J1-J4 and two panes of 50 of No. E1, were specially overprinted for displays at the Paris Exposition (1900) and Pan American Exposition (1901). The 2c pane was light red, type IV. Copies were handstamped type E "Specimen" in black ink by H. G. Mandel and mounted by him in separate displays for the two Expositions. Additional stamps from each pane were also handstamped "specimen," but most were destroyed after the Expositions. Nearly all examples remaining bear impression of a dealer's handstamp reading "Special Surcharge" in red ink on the back. Value: Nos. 221-225, J1-J4, each $625; No. E1, $1,000.

Issues of the Republic under US Military Rule

Statue of Columbus — A20

Royal Palms — A21

Allegory, "Cuba" — A22

Ocean Liner — A23

Cane Field — A24

Re-engraved

The re-engraved stamps issued by the Republic of Cuba in 1905-07 may be distinguished from the Issue of 1899 as follows:

Nos. 227-231 are watermarked U S-C

The re-engraved stamps are unwatermarked.

1c: The ends of the label inscribed "Centavo" are rounded instead of square.

2c: The foliate ornaments, inside the oval disks bearing the numerals of value, have been removed.

5c: Two lines forming a right angle have been added in the upper corners of the label bearing the word "Cuba."

10c: A small ball has been added to each of the square ends of the label bearing the word "Cuba."

No. 227 Re-engraved

No. 228 Re-engraved

No. 230 Re-engraved

No. 231 Re-engraved

Printed by the U.S. Bureau of Engraving and Printing

1899 Wmk. US-C (191C) *Perf. 12*

227	A20	1c **yellow green**	3.50	.20
		On cover		2.00
		Block of 4	15.00	1.00
		P# block of 10, Impt., type VII	225.00	—
228	A21	2c **carmine**	3.50	.20
		On cover		2.00
		Block of 4	15.00	1.00
		P# block of 10, Impt., type VII	180.00	—
a.		2c **scarlet**	3.50	.20
b.		Booklet pane of 6	*3,750.*	
229	A22	3c **purple**	3.50	.20
		On cover		4.00
		Block of 4	15.00	2.50
		P# block of 10, Impt., type VII	275.00	—
230	A23	5c **blue**	4.50	.20
		On cover		4.00
		Block of 4	21.00	2.50
		P# block of 10, Impt., type VII	450.00	—
231	A24	10c **brown**	11.00	.50
		On cover		6.50
		Block of 4	52.50	5.50
		P# block of 10, Impt., type VII	1,200.	—
		Nos. 227-231 (5)	26.00	1.30

SPECIAL DELIVERY STAMPS

Issued under Administration of the United States

Special Delivery Stamp of the United States No. E5 Surcharged in Red

1899 Wmk. 191 *Perf. 12*

E1	SD3	10c on 10c **blue**	130.	100.
		On cover		450.
		Block of 4	575.	
		Margin block of 4, arrow	650.	
		P# strip of 3, Impt.	1,000.	
		P# block of 6, Impt.	*6,000.*	
		Five dots in curved frame above messenger's head (Pl. 882)	—	
a.		No period after "CUBA"	575.	400.

Issue of the Republic under US Military Rule

Special Delivery Messenger SD2

Printed by the US Bureau of Engraving and Printing

1899 Wmk. US-C (191C)

Inscribed: "Immediata"

E2	SD2	10c **orange**	50.00	15.00
		On cover		150.00
		Block of 4	250.00	—
		P# strip of 3, Impt., type VII	300.00	
		P# block of 6, Impt., type VII	1,000.	

Re-engraved

In 1902 the Republic of Cuba issued a stamp of design SD2 re-engraved with word correctly spelled "Inmediata." The corrected die was made in 1899 (See No. E3P). It was printed by the U.S. Bureau of Engraving and Printing.

POSTAGE DUE STAMPS

Issued under Administration of the United States Postage Due Stamps of the United States Nos. J38, J39, J41 and J42 Surcharged in Black Like Regular Issue of Same Date

1899 Wmk. 191 *Perf. 12*

J1	D2	1c on 1c **deep claret**	45.00	5.25
		Block of 4	210.00	45.00
		P# block of 6, Impt.	*900.00*	
J2	D2	2c on 2c **deep claret**	45.00	5.25
		Block of 4	200.00	30.00
		P# block of 6, Impt.	*900.00*	
a.		Inverted surcharge		*4,000.*
J3	D2	5c on 5c **deep claret**	45.00	5.25
		Block of 4	220.00	45.00
		P# block of 6, Impt.	*900.00*	
		"CUPA" (broken letter)	150.00	140.00
J4	D2	10c on 10c **deep claret**	27.50	2.50
		Block of 4	125.00	27.50
		P# block of 6, Impt.	*800.00*	

The No. J3 "CUPA" variety always has a straight edge at right.

ENVELOPES

Values are for Cut Squares

US Envelopes of 1887-99 Surcharged

a

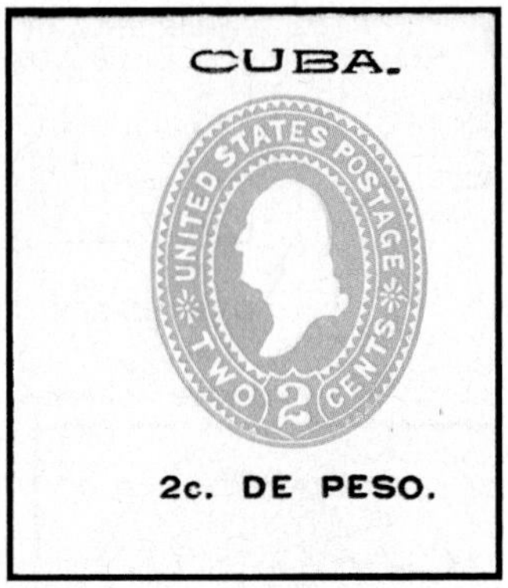

b

1899

U1	U77 (a)	1c on 1c **green,** *oriental buff* (No. U354)	5.00	3.50
		Entire	12.00	15.00
U2	U77 (a)	1c on 1c **green,** *blue* (No. U355)	3.25	2.50
		Entire	5.00	6.50
a.		Double surcharge, entire	*5,250.*	
U3	U71 (b)	2c on 2c **green** (No. U311)	1.50	1.10
		Entire	3.00	3.50
a.		Double surcharge, entire	*4,500.*	*6,500.*
U4	U71 (b)	2c on 2c **green,** *amber* (No. U312)	2.75	1.65
		Entire	5.25	6.00
a.		Double surcharge, entire	*5,250.*	
U5	U71 (a)	2c on 2c **green,** *oriental buff* (No. U313)	17.50	8.00
		Entire	47.50	47.50
U6	U79 (a)	2c on 2c **carmine,** *amber* (No. U363)	17.50	17.50
		Entire	47.50	47.50
U7	U79 (a)	2c on 2c **carmine,** *oriental buff* (No. U364)	25.00	25.00
		Entire	100.00	80.00
U8	U79 (a)	2c on 2c **carmine,** *blue* (No. U365)	3.00	2.00
		Entire	7.00	8.00
a.		Double surcharge, entire		*6,750.*
		Nos. U1-U8 (8)	75.50	61.25

In addition to the envelopes listed above, several others are known but were not regularly issued. They are:

1c on 1c green
1c on 1c green, *manila*
2c on 2c carmine
4c on 4c brown
5c on 5c blue

Issue of the Republic under US Military Rule

Columbus — E1

Similar envelopes without watermark on white and amber papers, were issued by the Republic after Military Rule ended in 1902.

1899 Wmk. "US POD '99" in Monogram

U9	E1	1c **green**	.75	.65
		Entire	4.00	4.00
U10	E1	1c **green,** *amber*	1.00	.65
		Entire	4.00	4.00
U11	E1	1c **green,** *buff*	17.50	13.00
		Entire	85.00	42.50
U12	E1	1c **green,** *blue*	25.00	15.00
		Entire	85.00	42.50
U13	E1	2c **carmine**	1.00	.70
		Entire	3.75	3.00
U14	E1	2c **carmine,** *amber*	1.00	.70
		Entire	3.75	3.00
U15	E1	2c **carmine,** *buff*	9.00	7.75
		Entire	35.00	21.00
U16	E1	2c **carmine,** *blue*	25.00	18.00
		Entire	60.00	52.50
U17	E1	5c **blue**	3.25	2.25
		Entire	5.00	2.75
U18	E1	5c **blue,** *amber*	6.00	4.00
		Entire	9.00	5.75
		Nos. U9-U18 (10)	89.50	62.70

WRAPPERS

Issue of the Republic under US Military Rule

1899

W1	E1	1c **green,** *manila*	4.00	10.00
		Entire	11.00	50.00
W2	E1	2c **carmine,** *manila*	12.00	10.00
		Entire	25.00	50.00

POSTAL CARDS

Values are for Entires

U.S. Postal Cards Nos. UX14, UX16 Surcharged

UX1	PC8	1c on 1c **black,** *buff, Jefferson (1,000,000)*	15.00	16.50
a.		No period after "1c"	40.00	75.00
b.		No period after "Peso"	35.00	
c.		Surcharge "2c" (error)	*6,500.*	
UX2	PC3	2c on 2c **black,** *buff, Liberty (583,000)*	15.00	16.50
a.		No period after "Peso"	40.00	75.00
b.		Double surcharge		—

In 1904 the Republic of Cuba revalued remaining stocks of No. UX2 by means of a perforated numeral "1."

PROOFS

1899

Column (1) — Large Die

Column (2) — Small Die

		(1)	(2)
227P	1c **yellow green**	160.	160.
227TC	1c **blue green**	375.	
227TC	1c **black**	625.	
228P	2c **carmine**	160.	160.
228TC	2c **black**	625.	
229P	3c **purple**	160.	160.
229TC	3c **black**	375.	
230P	5c **blue**	160.	160.
230TC	5c **black**	625.	
231P	10c **brown**	160.	160.
231TC	10c **gray**	625.	
231TC	10c **black**	625.	

Special Delivery

E2TC	10c **blue**	1,500.	
E3P	10c **orange**	375.	325.

SPECIMEN STAMPS

Handstamped U.S. Type E in Purple

1899

221S	E	1c on 1c **yellow green**	200.
222AS	E	2c on 2c **reddish carmine,** type IV	200.
223AS	E	2½c on 2c **reddish carmine,** type IV	200.
224S	E	3c on 3c **purple**	200.
225S	E	5c on 5c **blue**	200.
226S	E	10c on 10c **brown,** type I	200.
226AS	E	10c on 10c **brown,** type II	*4,000.*

See note after No. 226A for Special Printings with black "Specimen" overprints.

1899

227S	E	1c **yellow green**	225.
228S	E	2c **carmine**	225.
229S	E	3c **purple**	225.
230S	E	5c **blue**	225.
231S	E	10c **brown**	225.

Special Delivery

1899

E1S	E	10c on 10c **blue**	550.
a.		Five dots in curved frame above messenger's head	1,750.
E2S	E	10c **orange**	1,000.

Postage Due

1899

J1S	E	1c on 1c **deep claret**	275.
J2S	E	2c on 2c **deep claret**	275.
J3S	E	5c on 5c **deep claret**	275.
J4S	E	10c on 10c **deep claret**	275.

Black "Specimen" overprint known on all stamps of the Special Printing.

DANISH WEST INDIES

Formerly a Danish colony, these islands were purchased by the United States on March 31, 1917 and have since been known as the U.S. Virgin Islands. They lie east of Puerto Rico, have an area of 132 square miles and had a population of 27,086 in 1911. The capital is Charlotte Amalie (also called St. Thomas). Stamps of Danish West Indies were replaced by those of the United States in 1917. However, for the first six months of U.S. ownership, until September 30, 1917, a postal transition period existed. During this period, either U.S., D.W.I. or mixed frankings could be used. The domestic printed matter or postcard rate was 5 bits or 1 cent, and the foreign printed matter or postcard rate was 10 bits, 2 cents, or 5 bits + 1 cent. The domestic minimum weight letter rate was 10 bits, 2 cents, or 5 bits + 1 cent, while the foreign minimum letter rate was 25 bits, 5 cents, or any combination of U.S. and D.W.I. stamps that together totalled 25 bits or 5 cents.

Letters posted to foreign destinations during the transition period are rare because of World War I. Values for covers listed here are for the period before the transition. Transition-period covers, including those with mixed franking, sell for much more.

100 CENTS = 1 DOLLAR
100 BIT = 1 FRANC (1905)

Coat of Arms — A1

Wmk. 111 — Small Crown

1856 **Typo.** **Wmk. 111** ***Imperf.***

Yellowish Paper

Yellow Wavy-line Burelage, UL to LR

1	A1	3c **dark carmine,** brown gum	200.	*275.*
		On cover		3,000.
		Block of 4	1,300.	
a.		3c **dark carmine,** yellow gum	220.	*275.*
		On cover		3,000.
		Block of 4	2,850.	
b.		3c **carmine,** white gum	*4,250.*	—
		On cover		—

The brown and yellow gums were applied locally.

Reprint: 1981, carmine, back-printed across two stamps ("Reprint by Dansk Post og Telegrafmuseum 1978"), value, pair, $10.

1866

White Paper

Yellow Wavy-line Burelage UR to LL

2	A1	3c **rose**	40.	*75.*
		On cover		3,000.
		Block of 4	200.	*350.*
		Rouletted 4½ privately	350.	175.
		On cover, rouletted 4½		—
		Rouletted 9	450.	200.

The value for used blocks is for favor cancel (CTO).

No. 2 reprints, unwatermarked: 1930, carmine, value $100. 1942, rose carmine, back-printed across each row ("Nytryk 1942 G. A. Hagemann Danmark og Dansk Vestindiens Frimaerker Bind 2"), value $50.

1872 ***Perf. 12½***

3	A1	3c **rose**	92.50	*275.*
		On cover		*7,500.*
		Block of 4	525.	

1873

Without Burelage

4	A1	4c **dull blue**	250.	*475.*
		On cover		—
		Block of 4	1,300.	
a.		Imperf., pair	775.	
b.		Horiz. pair, imperf. vert.	575.	

The 1930 reprint of No. 4 is ultramarine, unwatermarked and imperf., value $100.

The 1942 4c reprint is blue, unwatermarked, imperf. and has printing on back (see note below No. 2), value $60.

Numeral of Value — A2

NORMAL FRAME

INVERTED FRAME

The arabesques in the corners have a main stem and a branch. When the frame is in normal position, in the upper left corner the branch leaves the main stem half way between two little leaflets. In the lower right corner the branch starts at the foot of the second leaflet. When the frame is inverted the corner designs are, of course, transposed.

The central element in the fan-shaped scrollwork at the outside of the lower left corner of Nos. 5a, 6a, 7b and 11a looks like an elongated diamond.

Wmk. 112 — Crown

1874-79 **Wmk. 112** ***Perf. 14x13½***

White Wove Paper, Printings 1-3 Thin, 4-7 Medium, 8-9 Thick

1c	Nine printings
3c	Eight printings
4c	Two printings
5c	Six printings
7c	Two printings
10c	Seven printings
12c	Two printings

14c One printing
50c Two printings

Values for inverted frames, covers and blocks are for the cheapest variety.

5 A2 1c **green & brown red** 20.00 *30.00*
On cover 250.00
Block of 4 90.00 *240.00*
a. 1c **green & rose lilac,** thin paper 80.00 *125.00*
b. 1c **green & red violet,** medium paper 45.00 *65.00*
c. 1c **green & claret,** thick paper 20.00 *30.00*
e. As "c," inverted frame 20.00 *30.00*
f. As "a," inverted frame *475.00*

No. 5 exists with "b" surcharge, "10 CENTS 1895." See note below No. 15.

6 A2 3c **blue & carmine** 25.00 20.00
On cover 225.00
Block of 4 110.00 —
White "wedge" flaw 50.00 50.00
a. 3c **light blue & rose carmine,** thin paper 65.00 50.00
b. 3c **deep blue & dark carmine,** medium paper 40.00 17.00
c. 3c **greenish blue & lake,** thick paper 22.50 17.00
d. Imperf., pair 375.00 —
e. Inverted frame, thick paper 24.00 15.00
f. As "a," inverted frame *350.00*
7 A2 4c **brown & dull blue** 16.00 *19.00*
On cover 225.00
Block of 4 75.00 —
b. 4c **brown & ultramarine,** thin paper 190.00 *225.00*
c. Diagonal half used as 2c on cover 140.00
d. As "b," inverted frame *825.00* *1,400.*
8 A2 5c **green & gray** 30.00 25.00
On cover 250.00
Block of 4 130.00 —
a. 5c **yellow green & dark gray,** thin paper 55.00 37.50
b. Inverted frame, thick paper 27.50 25.00
9 A2 7c **lilac & orange** 32.50 *95.00*
On cover 1,100.
Block of 4 160.00 —
a. 7c **lilac & yellow** 90.00 *100.00*
b. Inverted frame 60.00 *150.00*
10 A2 10c **blue & brown** 25.00 *30.00*
On cover 300.00
Block of 4 115.00 —
a. 10c **dark blue & black brown,** thin paper 70.00 45.00
b. Period between "t" & "s" of "cents" 30.00 30.00
c. Inverted frame 27.50 *32.50*
11 A2 12c **red lilac & yellow green** 42.50 *175.00*
On cover 1,750.
Block of 4 230.00 —
a. 12c **lilac & deep green** 150.00 *200.00*
12 A2 14c **lilac & green** 650.00 *1,100.*
On cover
Block of 4 *4,000.*
a. Inverted frame *2,500.* *3,500.*
13 A2 50c **violet,** thin paper 175.00 *300.00*
On cover 2,500.
Block of 4 1,250.
a. 50c **gray violet,** thick paper 225.00 *350.00*

Issue dates: 1c, 3c, 4c, 14c, Jan. 15, 1874. 7c, July 22, 1874. 5c, 10c, 1876; 12c, 1877; 50c, 1879. Colors of major numbers are generally those of the least expensive of two or more shades, and do not indicate the shade of the first printing.

Nos. 9 and 13 Surcharged in Black:

a

b

1887
14 A2 (a) 1c on 7c **lilac & orange** 100.00 *200.00*
On cover 3,000.
Block of 4 450.00 —
a. 1c on 7c **lilac & yellow** 100.00 *225.00*
b. Double surcharge 250.00 *500.00*
c. Inverted frame 110.00 *350.00*

1895
15 A2 (b) 10c on 50c **violet,** thin paper 42.50 *67.50*
On cover 275.00
Block of 4 275.00 —

The "b" surcharge also exists on No. 5, with "10" found in two sizes. These are essays.

1896-1901 ***Perf. 13***
16 A2 1c **green & red violet,** inverted frame ('98) 13.00 *22.50*
On cover 150.00
Block of 4 65.00 —
a. Normal frame 290.00 *425.00*
17 A2 3c **blue & lake,** inverted frame ('98) 12.00 *17.50*
On cover 150.00
Block of 4 55.00 —
White "wedge" flaw 35.00 *45.00*
a. Normal frame 250.00 *425.00*
18 A2 4c **bister & dull blue** ('01) 17.50 15.00
On cover 150.00
Block of 4 77.50 —
a. Diagonal half used as 2c on cover 100.00
b. Inverted frame 55.00 *85.00*
On cover 250.00
c. As "b," diagonal half used as 2c on cover 350.00
19 A2 5c **green & gray,** inverted frame 35.00 35.00
On cover 325.00
Block of 4 160.00 —
a. Normal frame 750.00 *1,100.*
20 A2 10c **blue & brown** ('01) 80.00 *150.00*
On cover 1,150.
Block of 4 475.00 —
a. Inverted frame 925.00 *1,600.*
b. Period between "t" and "s" of "cents" 170.00 160.00
Nos. 16-20 (5) 157.50 *240.00*

Two printings each of Nos. 18-19.

Arms — A5

1900
21 A5 1c **light green** 3.00 3.00
On cover, pair 80.00
On cover, single franking 300.00
Block of 4 12.50 12.50
22 A5 5c **light blue** 17.50 *25.00*
On cover 300.00
Block of 4 80.00 —

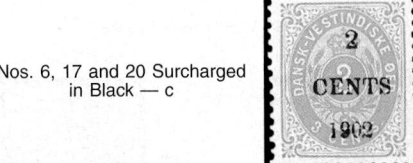

Nos. 6, 17 and 20 Surcharged in Black — c

1902 ***Perf. 14x13½***
23 A2 2c on 3c **blue & carmine,** inverted frame 575.00 725.00
On cover *4,000.*
Block of 4 *3,000.*
a. "2" in date with straight tail 650.00 *800.00*
b. Normal frame 4,000.

Perf. 13
24 A2 2c on 3c **blue & lake,** inverted frame 10.00 *27.50*
On cover 160.00
Block of 4 45.00 —
White "wedge" flaw 55.00 55.00
a. "2" in date with straight tail 12.00 *32.50*
b. Dated "1901" 600.00 *650.00*
c. Normal frame 175.00 *250.00*
d. Dark green surcharge 2,000.
e. As "d" & "a" — —
f. As "d" & "c" —

One example recorded of No. 24f.

25 A2 8c on 10c **blue & brown** 25.00 *42.50*
On cover 225.00
Block of 4 105.00 —
a. "2" with straight tail 30.00 *45.00*
b. On No. 20b 32.50 *45.00*
c. Inverted frame 250.00 *425.00*

Nos. 17 and 20 Surcharged in Black — d

1902 ***Perf. 13***
27 A2 2c on 3c **blue & lake,** inverted frame 12.00 *40.00*
On cover 500.00
Block of 4 52.50
White "wedge" flaw 40.00 *55.00*
a. Normal frame 240.00 *425.00*
28 A2 8c on 10c **blue & brown** 12.00 14.00
On cover 175.00
Block of 4 52.50 —
a. On No. 20b 18.50 *25.00*
b. Inverted frame 225.00 *400.00*

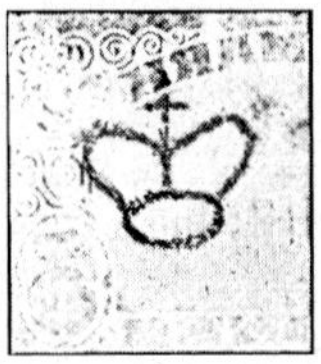
Wmk. 113 — Crown

1903 **Wmk. 113**
29 A5 2c **carmine** 8.00 *22.50*
On cover 125.00
Block of 4 35.00 —
30 A5 8c **brown** 27.50 *30.00*
On cover 250.00
Block of 4 115.00 —

King Christian IX — A8

St. Thomas Harbor — A9

1905 **Typo.** ***Perf. 12½***
31 A8 5b **green** 3.75 3.25
On cover 35.00
Block of 4 17.00 —
32 A8 10b **red** 3.75 3.25
On cover 35.00
Block of 4 16.00 —
33 A8 20b **green & blue** 8.75 8.25
On cover 150.00
Block of 4 40.00 —
34 A8 25b **ultramarine** 8.75 10.50
On cover 85.00
Block of 4 40.00 —
35 A8 40b **red & gray** 8.25 8.25
On cover 225.00
Block of 4 37.50 —
36 A8 50b **yellow & gray** 10.00 12.00
On cover 250.00
Block of 4 42.50 -

Perf. 12

Wmk. Two Crowns (113)

Frame Typographed, Center Engraved

37	A9	1fr **green & blue**	17.50	*45.00*
		On cover		*625.00*
		Block of 4	75.00	—
38	A9	2fr **orange red & brown**	30.00	*60.00*
		On cover		*1,100.*
		Block of 4	150.00	—
39	A9	5fr **yellow & brown**	77.50	*275.00*
		On cover		*1,750.*
		Block of 4	375.00	—
		Nos. 31-39 (9)	168.25	*425.50*

On cover values are for commercial usages, usually parcel address cards. Philatelic covers are valued at approximately 25% of these figures.

Nos. 18, 22 and 30 Surcharged in Black

1905		**Wmk. 112**		***Perf. 13***
40	A2	5b on 4c **bister & dull blue**	16.00	*45.00*
		On cover		*250.00*
		Block of 4	77.50	—
a.		Inverted frame	45.00	*82.50*
41	A5	5b on 5c **light blue**	14.00	*37.50*
		On cover		*250.00*
		Block of 4	65.00	—

Wmk. 113

42	A5	5b on 8c **brown**	14.00	*37.50*
		On cover		*250.00*
		Block of 4	60.00	—

Favor cancels exist on Nos. 40-42. Value 25% less.

King Frederik VIII — A10

Frame Typographed, Center Engraved

1908		**Wmk. 113**		***Perf. 13***
43	A10	5b **green**	1.90	1.90
		On cover		22.50
		Block of 4	9.50	—
		Number block of 6	18.50	
44	A10	10b **red**	1.90	1.90
		On cover		22.50
		Block of 4	9.50	—
		Number block of 6	18.50	
45	A10	15b **violet & brown**	3.75	*4.50*
		On cover		125.00
		Block of 4	19.00	—
		Number block of 6	52.50	
46	A10	20b **green & blue**	30.00	27.50
		On cover		110.00
		Block of 4	130.00	—
		Number block of 6	375.00	
47	A10	25b **blue & dark blue**	1.90	*2.50*
		On cover		35.00
		Block of 4	9.00	—
		Number block of 6	18.50	
48	A10	30b **claret & slate**	50.00	52.50
		On cover		350.00
		Block of 4	220.00	240.00
		Number block of 6	525.00	
49	A10	40b **vermilion & gray**	5.75	*9.50*
		On cover		210.00
		Block of 4	25.00	—
		Number block of 6	55.00	
50	A10	50b **yellow & brown**	5.75	*14.00*
		On cover		210.00
		Block of 4	25.00	—
		Number block of 6	70.00	
		Nos. 43-50 (8)	100.95	114.30

Printing numbers appear in the selvage, once per pane, in Roman or Arabic numerals.

King Christian X — A11

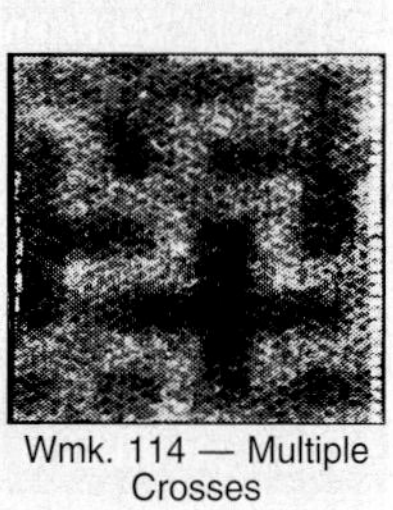

Wmk. 114 — Multiple Crosses

Frame Typographed, Center Engraved

1915		**Wmk. 114**		***Perf. 14x14½***
51	A11	5b **yellow green**	4.00	4.25
		On cover		45.00
		Block of 4	17.50	—
		Number block of 4	40.00	
52	A11	10b **red**	4.00	*42.50*
		On cover		100.00
		Block of 4	17.50	—
		Number block of 4	40.00	
53	A11	15b **lilac & red brown**	4.00	*47.50*
		On cover		300.00
		Block of 4	17.50	—
		Number block of 4	40.00	
54	A11	20b **green & blue**	4.00	*47.50*
		On cover		350.00
		Block of 4	17.50	—
		Number block of 4	40.00	
55	A11	25b **blue & dark blue**	4.00	*12.50*
		On cover		100.00
		Block of 4	17.50	—
		Number block of 4	40.00	
56	A11	30b **claret & black**	4.00	*85.00*
		On cover		900.00
		Block of 4	17.50	—
		Number block of 4	40.00	
57	A11	40b **orange & black**	4.00	*85.00*
		On cover		550.00
		Block of 4	18.50	—
		Number block of 4	40.00	
58	A11	50b **yellow & brown**	4.00	*85.00*
		On cover		650.00
		Block of 4	18.50	—
		Number block of 4	40.00	
		Nos. 51-58 (8)	32.00	*409.25*

Forged and favor cancellations exist.

Plate identifications 11-D, 50-D or 50-O are located in the selvage in all four corners of the pane. The 50-D is on all denominations. 11-D, all but the 50b, 50-O, all but 15b, 20b, 25b.

POSTAGE DUE STAMPS

Royal Cipher "Christian Rex" — D1

Numeral of Value — D2

1902		**Litho.** **Unwmk.**		***Perf. 11½***
J1	D1	1c **dark blue**	4.50	*17.50*
		On cover		400.00
		Block of 4	22.50	
J2	D1	4c **dark blue**	11.50	*22.50*
		On cover		350.00
		Block of 4	50.00	
J3	D1	6c **dark blue**	19.00	*60.00*
		On cover		450.00
		Block of 4	92.50	
J4	D1	10c **dark blue**	18.00	*65.00*
		On cover		400.00
		Block of 4	87.50	

There are five types of each value. On the 4c they may be distinguished by differences in the figure "4"; on the other values differences are minute.

Used values of Nos. J1-J8 are for canceled stamps. Uncanceled stamps without gum have probably been used. Value 60% of unused. On cover values are for stamps tied by cancellation.

Excellent counterfeits of Nos. J1-J4 exist.

1905-13				***Perf. 13***
J5	D2	5b **red & gray**	4.50	*6.75*
		On cover		*450.00*
		Block of 4	20.00	—
J6	D2	20b **red & gray**	7.50	*14.00*
		On cover		*450.00*
		Block of 4	32.50	—
J7	D2	30b **red & gray**	6.75	*14.00*
		On cover		*450.00*
		Block of 4	30.00	—
J8	D2	50b **red & gray**	6.00	*35.00*
		On cover		*900.00*
		Block of 4	27.50	—
a.		Perf. 14x14½ ('13)	37.50	*140.00*
		Block of 4	175.00	—
b.		Perf. 11½	325.00	

Nos. J5-J8 are known imperforate but were not regularly issued. Excellent counterfeits exist.

See notes following No. J4 for canceled stamps.

ENVELOPES

E1

1877-78				**On White Paper**
U1	E1	2c **light blue** ('78)	5.50	*14.00*
		Entire	22.50	*65.00*
a.		2c **ultramarine**	20.00	*200.00*
		Entire	100.00	*800.00*
U2	E1	3c **orange**	5.50	*12.50*
		Entire	22.50	*65.00*
a.		3c **red orange**	5.50	*12.50*
		Entire	22.50	*65.00*

Three different Crown watermarks are found on entires of No. U1, four on entires of No. U2. Envelope watermarks do not show on cut squares.

POSTAL CARDS

Values are for entire cards.

Italicized numbers in parentheses indicate quantities issued.

Designs of Adhesive Stamps

"BREV-KORT" at top

1877

Inscription in Three Lines

UX1	A2	6c **violet**	40.00	*1,400.*

Used value is for card to foreign destination postmarked before April 1, 1879.

1878-85

Inscription in Four Lines

UX2	A2	2c **light blue** *(8,800)*	22.50	*50.00*
UX3	A2	3c **carmine rose** *(17,700)*	17.50	*35.00*

1888

Inscription in Five Lines

UX4	A2	2c **light blue** *(30,500)*	20.00	*32.50*
UX5	A2	3c **red** *(26,500)*	12.50	*22.50*

Card No. UX5 Locally Surcharged with type "c" but with date "1901"

1901

UX6	A2	1c on 3c **red** *(2,000)*	50.00	*200.00*

1902

Card No. UX4 Locally Surcharged with type "c"

UX7	A2	1c on 2c **light blue** *(3,000)*	37.50	*160.00*

Card No. UX5 Surcharged similar to type "c" but heavy letters

1902

UX8	A2	1c on 3c **red** *(7,175)*	12.50	*150.00*

1903

UX9	A5	1c **light green** *(10,000)*	12.50	*30.00*
UX10	A5	2c **carmine** *(10,000)*	19.00	*70.00*

1905

UX11	A8	5b **green** *(16,000)*	12.50	*22.50*
UX12	A8	10b **red** *(14,000)*	12.50	*35.00*

1907-08				**Unwmk.**
UX13	A10	5b **green** ('08) *(30,750)*	9.50	*30.00*
UX14	A10	10b **red** *(19,750)*	12.50	*40.00*

1913				**Wmk. Wood-grain**
UX15	A10	5b **green** *(10,000)*	90.00	*210.00*
UX16	A10	10b **red** *(10,000)*	100.00	*325.00*

1915-16				**Wmk. Wood-grain**
UX17	A11	5b **yellow green** *(8,200)*	80.00	*250.00*
UX18	A11	10b **red** ('16) *(2,000)*	100.00	—

PAID REPLY POSTAL CARDS

Designs similar to Nos. UX2 and UX3 with added inscriptions in Danish and French:

Message Card-Four lines at lower left.

Reply Card-Fifth line centered, "Svar. Réponse."

Italicized numbers in parentheses indicate quantities issued.

1883

UY1	A2	2c +2c **light blue,** unsevered *(2,600)*	25.00	*250.00*
m.		Message card, detached	12.50	*35.00*
r.		Reply card, detached	12.50	*35.00*

UY2 A2 3c +3c **carmine rose,** unsevered 21.00 *150.00*
m. Message card, detached 12.50 *20.00*
r. Reply card, detached 12.50 *25.00*

Designs similar to Nos. UX4 and UX5 with added inscription in fifth line, centered in French:
Message Card-"Carte postale avec réponse payée."
Reply Card-"Carte postale-réponse."

1888

UY3 A2 2c +2c **light blue,** unsevered *(26,000)* 25.00 *125.00*
m. Message card, detached 10.00 *20.00*
r. Reply card, detached 10.00 *100.00*
UY4 A2 3c +3c **carmine rose,** unsevered *(5,000)* 22.50 *175.00*
m. Message card, detached 11.00 *35.00*
r. Reply card, detached 11.00 *125.00*

No. UY4 Locally Surcharged with type "c" but with date "1901"

1902

UY5 A2 1c on 3c+1c on 3c **carmine rose,** unsevered *(1,000)* 35.00 *300.00*
m. Message card, detached 12.50 *50.00*
r. Reply card, detached 14.00 *75.00*

No. UY4 Surcharged in Copenhagen with type similar to "c" but heavy letters

UY6 A2 1c on 3c+1c on 3c **carmine rose,** unsevered *(975)* 50.00 *350.00*
m. Message card, detached 20.00 *60.00*
r. Reply card, detached 20.00 *75.00*

Designs similar to Nos. UX9 and UX10 with added inscriptions in Danish and English

1903

UY7 A5 1c +1c **light green,** unsevered *(5,000)* 35.00 *75.00*
m. Message card, detached 11.00 *20.00*
r. Reply card, detached 11.00 *25.00*
UY8 A5 2c +2c **carmine,** unsevered *(5,000)* 40.00 *400.00*
m. Message card, detached 15.00 *50.00*
r. Reply card, detached 15.00 *75.00*

Designs similar to Nos. UX11 and UX12 with added inscriptions

1905

UY9 A8 5b +5b **green,** unsevered *(5,000)* 21.00 *75.00*
m. Message card, detached 10.00 *20.00*
r. Reply card, detached 10.00 *30.00*
UY10 A8 10b +10b **red,** unsevered *(4,000)* 30.00 *90.00*
m. Message card 12.50 *25.00*
r. Reply card, detached 15.00 *35.00*

Designs similar to Nos. UX13, UX14 and UX15 with added inscriptions

1908 **Unwmk.**

UY11 A10 5b +5b **green,** unsevered *(7,150)* 25.00 *100.00*
m. Message card, detached 11.00 *30.00*
r. Reply card, detached 11.00 *35.00*
UY12 A10 10b +10b **red,** unsevered *(6,750)* 25.00 *100.00*
m. Message card, detached 12.50 *30.00*
r. Reply card, detached 11.00 *40.00*

1913 **Wmk. Wood-grain**

UY13 A10 5b +5b **green,** unsevered *(5,000)* —
m. Message card, detached —
r. Reply card, detached —

The 10b + 10b red type A10 with wood-grain watermark was authorized and possibly printed, but no example is known.

REVENUE STAMPS

PLAYING CARDS

These stamps were overprinted by the Bureau of Engraving and Printing. Shipments of 10,000 each of Nos. RFV1-RFV3 were sent to the Virgin Islands on June 17, 1920, Jan. 16, 1926, and Mar. 5, 1934, respectively.

U.S. Playing Card Stamp No. RF3 Overprinted in Carmine

1920 **Engr.** **Wmk. 191R** ***Rouletted 7***

RFV1 RF2 4c on 2c **blue** 225.00

U.S. Playing Card Stamp No. RF17 Overprinted in Carmine

1926 ***Rouletted 7***

RFV2 RF4 4c on (8c) **blue** 60.00

RFV2 was surcharged with new value in "Bits" for use in collecting a tobacco tax.

Same Overprint on U.S. Type RF4

1934 ***Perf. 11***

RFV3 RF4 4c on (8c) **light blue** 225.00 125.00

The above stamp with perforation 11 was not issued in the United States without the overprint.

GUAM

A former Spanish island possession in the Pacific Ocean, one of the Mariana group, about 1,450 miles east of the Philippines. Captured June 20, 1898, and ceded to the United States by treaty after the Spanish-American War. Stamps overprinted "Guam" were used while the post office was under the jurisdiction of the Navy Department from July 7, 1899, until March 29, 1901, when a Postal Agent was appointed by the Post Office Department and the postal service passed under that Department's control. From this date on Guam was supplied with regular United States postage stamps, although the overprints remained in use for several more years.

Italicized numbers in parentheses indicate quantities issued.

Population 9,000 (est. 1899).

100 CENTS = 1 DOLLAR

United States Nos. 279, 279B, 279Bc, 268, 280a, 281, 282, 272, 282C, 283, 284, 275, 275a, 276 and 276A Overprinted

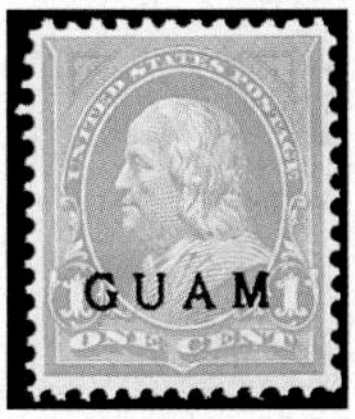

1899 **Wmk. 191** ***Perf. 12***

Black Overprint

1 A87 1c **deep green** *(25,000)* 20.00 *25.00*
Never hinged 40.00
On cover *200.00*
Block of 4 90.00 *140.00*
P# strip of 3, Impt. 90.00
P# block of 6, Impt. 350.00

A bogus inverted overprint exists.

2 A88 2c **red,** type IV, *Dec. (105,000)* 17.50 *25.00*
light red, type IV 17.50 *25.00*
On cover *200.00*
Never hinged 35.00
Block of 4 85.00 *140.00*
P# strip of 3, Impt. 75.00
P# block of 6, Impt. 300.00
a. 2c **rose carmine,** type IV, *Aug. 15* 30.00 30.00
Never hinged 60.00
On cover *225.00*
Block of 4 125.00 *175.00*
P# strip of 3, Impt. 100.00
P# block of 6, Impt. 375.00
3 A89 3c **purple** *(5000)* 140.00 *175.00*
Never hinged 275.00
On cover *400.00*
Block of 4 600.00 *850.00*
P# strip of 3, Impt. 575.00
P# block of 6, Impt. 1,600.
4 A90 4c **lilac brown** *(5000)* 135.00 *175.00*
Never hinged 270.00
On cover *450.00*
Block of 4 600.00 *825.00*
P# strip of 3, Impt. 550.00
P# block of 6, Impt. *2,000.*
Extra frame line at top (Plate 793 R62) —
5 A91 5c **blue** *(20,000)* 32.50 *45.00*
Never hinged 65.00
On cover *200.00*
Block of 4 140.00 *250.00*
P# strip of 3, Impt. 140.00
P# block of 6, Impt. 775.00
6 A92 6c **lake** *(5000)* 125.00 *200.00*
Never hinged 250.00
On cover *450.00*
Block of 4 550.00 *1,000.*
P# strip of 3, Impt. 500.00
P# block of 6, Impt. 1,600.
7 A93 8c **violet brown** *(5000)* 140.00 *200.00*
Never hinged 275.00
On cover *450.00*
Block of 4 600.00 *1,000.*
P# strip of 3, Impt. 600.00
P# block of 6, Impt. 1,700.
8 A94 10c **brown,** type I *(10,000)* 47.50 *55.00*
Never hinged 95.00
On cover *275.00*
Block of 4 210.00 *300.00*
P# strip of 3, Impt. 225.00
P# block of 6, Impt. 1,000.
9 A94 10c **brown,** type II *4,000.* —
Never hinged *7,000.*
Pair —
10 A95 15c **olive green** *(5000)* 150.00 *175.00*
Never hinged 300.00
On cover *900.00*
Block of 4 650.00 *875.00*
P# strip of 3, Impt. 600.00
P# block of 6, Impt. 2,200.
11 A96 50c **orange** *(4000)* 350.00 *425.00*
Never hinged 700.00
On cover *1,500.*
Block of 4 1,600. *2,000.*
P# strip of 3, Impt. 1,600.
P# block of 6, Impt. 4,500.
a. 50c **red orange** 550.00 —
Never hinged 1,100.

Red Overprint

12 A97 $1 **black,** type I *(3000)* 350.00 *400.00*
Never hinged 700.00
On cover *3,500.*
Block of 4 1,750. *1,750.*
P# strip of 3, Impt. 1,750.
P# block of 6, Impt. *16,000.*
13 A97 $1 **black,** type II *4,500.*
Never hinged —
Block of 4 —
Nos. 1-8,10-12 (11) 1,507. *1,900.*

Counterfeits of overprint exist.

No. 13 exists only in the special printing.

Special Printing

In March 1900, one pane of 100 stamps of each of Nos. 1-8, 10-12 and two panes of 50 stamps of No. E1 were specially overprinted for displays at the Paris Exposition (1900) and Pan American Exposition (1901). The 2c pane was light red, type IV.

Stamps were handstamped type E "Specimen" in black ink by H. G. Mandel and mounted by him in separate displays for the two Expositions. Additional stamps from each pane were also handstamped "Specimen" but most were destroyed after the Expositions.

J. M. Bartels, a stamp dealer, signed some stamps from these panes "Special Surcharge" in pencil on the gum to authenticate them as coming from the "Mandel" Special Printing panes. In 1904 or later, he handstamped additional surviving examples "Special Surcharge" in red ink on the back as his guarantee. Some of these guaranteed stamps had Mandel's "Specimen" handstamp on the face while others did not. Value (with or without "Specimen" handstamp): Nos. 1-8, 10, each $1,000; Nos. 11, E1, each $1,250; No. 12, $2,000.

SPECIAL DELIVERY STAMP

Special Delivery Stamp of the United States, No. E5 Overprinted diagonally in Red

1899 **Wmk. 191** *Perf. 12*

E1	SD3	10c	**blue** *(5000)*	150.	*200.*
			Never hinged	275.	
			On cover		*1,500.*
			Block of 4	650.	
			Margin block of 4, arrow	750.	
			P# strip of 3, Impt.	900.	
			P# block of 6, Impt.	*4,000.*	
a.			Dots in curved frame above messenger (Plate 882)	200.	
			Never hinged	400.	
			P# block of 6, Impt. (Plate 882)	*4,250.*	

Counterfeits of overprint exist.

The special stamps for Guam were replaced by the regular issues of the United States.

GUAM GUARD MAIL

LOCAL POSTAL SERVICE

Inaugurated April 8, 1930, by Commander Willis W. Bradley, Jr., U.S.N., Governor of Guam, for the conveyance of mail between Agaña and the other smaller towns.

Philippines Nos. 290 and 291 Overprinted

1930, Apr. 8 **Unwmk.** *Perf. 11*

M1	A40	2c	**green** *(2,000)*	400.	300.
			Never hinged	575.	
			On cover		600.
			Block of 4	1,700.	
			P# block of 6	—	
M2	A40	4c	**carmine** *(3,000)*	225.	150.
			Never hinged	325.	
			On cover		400.
			Block of 4	950.	
			P# block of 6	—	

Counterfeits of overprint exist.

Seal of Guam — A1

1930, July **Unwmk.** *Perf. 12*

Without Gum

M3	A1	1c	**red & black** *(1,000)*	125.00	150.00
			On cover		225.00
			Block of 4	525.00	
M4	A1	2c	**black & red** *(4,000)*	75.00	95.00
			On cover		250.00
			Block of 4	325.00	
a.			Block of 4 with extra impression of vignette covering the intersection of the block	*10,000.*	

Examples are often found showing parts of watermark "CLEVELAND BOND."

Philippines Nos. 290 and 291 Overprinted in Black

1930, Aug. 10 **Unwmk.** *Perf. 11*

M5	A40	2c	**green** *(20,000)*	2.75	4.50
			Never hinged	4.00	
			On cover		75.00
			Block of 4	12.00	
			P# block of 6	*125.00*	
a.			2c **yellow green**	2.50	4.50
M6	A40	4c	**carmine** *(80,000)*	.50	1.75
			Never hinged	.75	
			On cover		75.00
			Block of 4	2.25	
			P# block of 6	*90.00*	

Same Overprint in Red on Philippines Nos. 290, 291, 292, 293a, and 294

1930, Dec.

M7	A40	2c	**green** *(50,000)*	.80	2.00
			Never hinged	1.20	
			On cover		50.00
			Block of 4	3.50	
			P# block of 6	*125.00*	
a.			GRAUD (Pos. 63) *(500)*	425.00	
b.			MIAL (Pos. 84) *(500)*	425.00	
M8	A40	4c	**carmine** *(50,000)*	.85	1.50
			Never hinged	1.30	
			On cover		50.00
			Block of 4	3.50	
			P# block of 6	*90.00*	
M9	A40	6c	**deep violet** *(25,000)*	2.50	4.50
			Never hinged	3.75	
			On cover		60.00
			Block of 4	11.00	
			P# block of 10, Impt.	*250.00*	
M10	A40	8c	**orange brown** *(25,000)*	2.50	4.50
			Never hinged	3.75	
			On cover		60.00
			Block of 4	11.00	
			P# block of 10, Impt.	*300.00*	
M11	A40	10c	**deep blue** *(25,000)*	2.75	4.50
			Never hinged	4.00	
			On cover		60.00
			Block of 4	11.00	
			P# block of 10, Impt.	*350.00*	

The local postal service was discontinued April 8th, 1931, and replaced by the service of the United States Post Office Department.

SPECIMEN STAMPS

Handstamped U.S. Type E in Purple Specimen.

1899

1S	E	1c	**deep green**	175.00
2aS	E	2c	**rose carmine,** type IV	175.00
3S	E	3c	**purple**	175.00
4S	E	4c	**lilac brown**	175.00
5S	E	5c	**blue**	175.00
6S	E	6c	**lake**	175.00
7S	E	8c	**violet brown**	175.00
8S	E	10c	**brown,** type I	175.00
10S	E	15c	**olive green**	175.00
11S	E	50c	**orange**	350.00
12S	E	$1	**black,** type I	350.00
13S	E	$1	**black,** type II	—

Special Delivery

1899

E1S	E	10c	**blue**	500.00

Values for specimen stamps are for fine-very fine appearing examples with minor faults.

See note after No. 13 for Special Printings with black "Specimen" overprints.

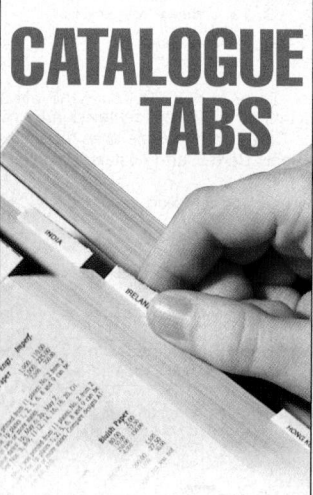

HAWAII

Until 1893, Hawaii was an independent kingdom. From 1893-1898 it was a republic. The United States annexed Hawaii in 1898, and it became a Territory on April 30, 1900. Hawaiian stamps remained in use through June 13, 1900, and were replaced by U.S. stamps on June 14. In 1959 Hawaii became the 50th State of the Union. Hawaii consists of about 20 islands in the mid-Pacific, about 2,300 miles southwest of San Francisco. The area is 6,434 square miles and the population was estimated at 150,000 in 1899. Honolulu is the capital.

100 CENTS = 1 DOLLAR

Values of Hawaii stamps vary considerably according to condition. Quotations for Nos. 5-82 are for very fine examples. Extremely fine to superb stamps sell at much higher prices, and inferior or poor stamps sell at reduced prices, depending on the condition of the individual example.

A1

A2

A3

1851-52 Unwmk. Typeset Pelure Paper *Imperf.*

1	A1	2c	**blue**	*660,000.*	*250,000.*
			On cover		*2,100,000.*
2	A1	5c	**blue**	*55,000.*	*32,500.*
			On cover		*80,000.*
3	A2	13c	**blue**	*32,500.*	*28,000.*
			On cover		*75,000.*
4	A3	13c	**blue**	*52,500.*	*37,500.*
			On cover		*80,000.*

Nos. 1-4 are known as the "Missionaries."

Two varieties of each. Nos. 1-4, off cover, are almost invariably damaged. Values are for examples with minor damage which has been skillfully repaired.

No. 1 unused and on cover are each unique; the on-cover value is based on a 1995 auction sale.

A4

King Kamehameha III — A5

Printed in Sheets of 20 (4x5)

1853 Thick White Wove Paper Engr.

5	A4	5c	**blue**	1,750.	1,600.
			On cover		*4,000.*
			On cover with U.S. #17		*12,000.*
			Pair	*3,750.*	*4,500.*
a.			Line through "Honolulu" (Pos. 2)	*3,000.*	*3,000.*
6	A5	13c	**dark red**	700.	*1,500.*
			On cover		*32,500.*
			On cover with #5		*10,000.*
			On cover with U.S. #11 (pair)		*25,000.*
			On cover with U.S. #17		*35,000.*
			On cover with #5 and U.S. #17		*35,000.*
			On cover with #8 and U.S. #36b		*38,500.*
			Pair	*1,900.*	*4,750.*
			Block of 4	*4,000.*	

Black Manuscript Surcharge on Scott 6

1857

7	A6	5c	on 13c **dark red**	*7,000.*	*10,000.*
			On cover with pair U.S. #7 and 15		*57,500.*
			On cover with pair U.S. #11, 14		*55,000.*
			On cover with U.S. #14		*50,000.*
			On cover with U.S. #17		*40,000.*

1857

Thin White Wove Paper

8	A4	5c	**blue**	650.	*750.*
			On cover		*2,750.*
			On cover with U.S. #11		—
			On cover with U.S. #7, 15		—
			On cover with U.S. #17		*10,000.*
			On cover with U.S. #26		—
			On cover with U.S. #35		*11,000.*
			On cover with U.S. #36		*10,000.*
			On cover with U.S. #69		*12,500.*
			On cover with U.S. #76		—
			Pair	1,600.	
			Pair on cover		*15,000.*
a.			Line through "Honolulu" (Pos. 2)	*1,250.*	*1,250.*
			On cover with U.S. #17		*6,500.*
b.			Double impression	*3,500.*	*4,750.*

1861

Thin Bluish Wove Paper

9	A4	5c	**blue**	350.	375.
			On cover		*4,000.*
			On cover with U.S. #36b		*3,250.*
			On cover with U.S. #65		*3,000.*
			On cover with U.S. #65, 73		*6,500.*
			On cover with U.S. #68		*4,250.*
			On cover with U.S. #76		*7,000.*
			Block of 4	2,000.	—
a.			Line through "Honolulu" (Pos. 2)	*750.*	*1,000.*

1868

RE-ISSUE

Ordinary White Wove Paper

10	A4	5c	**blue**	25.
			Block of 4	125.
a.			Line through "Honolulu" (Pos. 2)	55.
			In pair with #10	350.
11	A5	13c	**dull rose**	300.
			Block of 4	1,400.

Remainders of Nos. 10 and 11 were overprinted "SPECIMEN." See Nos. 10S-11Sb.

Nos. 10 and 11 were never placed in use but stamps (both with and without overprint) were sold at face value at the Honolulu post office.

REPRINTS (Official Imitations) 1889

5c Originals have two small dots near the left side of the square in the upper right corner. These dots are missing in the reprints.

13c The bottom of the 3 of 13 in the upper left corner is flattened in the originals and rounded in the reprints. The "t" of "Cts" on the left side is as tall as the "C" in the reprints, but shorter in the originals.

10R	A4	5c	**blue**	60.
			Block of 4	275.
11R	A5	13c	**orange red**	300.
			Block of 4	1,400.

On August 19, 1892, the remaining supply of reprints was overprinted in black "REPRINT." The reprints (both with and without overprint) were sold at face value.

Quantities sold (including overprints) were 5c-3634 and 13c-1696. See Nos. 10R-S and 11R-S.

Values for the Numeral stamps, Nos. 12-26, are for four-margin examples. Unused values are for stamps without gum.

A7

A8

A9

1859-62 Typeset from settings of 10 varieties

12	A7	1c	**light blue,** *bluish white*	*17,500.*	*15,000.*
			Pair		*37,500.*
a.			"1 Ce" omitted		*22,500.*
b.			"nt" omitted	—	—
13	A7	2c	**light blue,** *bluish white*	*6,250.*	*5,000.*
			On cover		*12,500.*
			Block of 4	*27,500.*	
a.			2c **dark blue,** *grayish white*	*6,750.*	*5,000.*
			On cover		*12,500.*
b.			Comma after "Cents"	—	*6,750.*
			On cover		*12,500.*
c.			No period after "LETA"	—	—
14	A7	2c	**black,** *greenish blue* ('62)	*8,000.*	*5,250.*
			On cover		*10,000.*
a.			"2-Cents."	—	—

1862-63

15	A7	1c	**black,** *grayish* ('63)	650.	*2,750.*
			On cover		—
			Block of 4	3,250.	
a.			Tête bêche pair	*9,000.*	
b.			"NTER"	—	
c.			Period omitted after "Postage"	850.	
16	A7	2c	**black,** *grayish*	1,000.	800.
			On cover		*5,000.*
			Pair	—	—
a.			"2" at top of rectangle	*3,750.*	*3,750.*
			On cover		*13,500.*
b.			Printed on both sides	—	*21,000.*
c.			"NTER"	*3,250.*	*6,500.*
d.			2c **black,** *grayish white*	1,000.	725.
e.			Period omitted after "Cents"	—	
f.			Overlapping impressions	—	—
g.			"TAGE"	—	—
17	A7	2c	**dark blue,** *bluish* ('63)	*12,000.*	*8,750.*
			Pair	*25,000.*	
a.			"ISL"	—	—
18	A7	2c	**black,** *blue gray* ('63)	*3,500.*	*6,000.*
			On cover		*18,000.*
			Pair		*13,500.*
			Thick paper	—	

1864-65

19	A7	1c	**black**	525.	*10,000.*
			Pair	1,100.	
			Block of 4	2,500.	
20	A7	2c	**black**	725.	1,500.
			On cover		*19,000.*
			Pair	1,550.	
			Block of 4	*4,000.*	
21	A8	5c	**blue,** *blue* ('65)	850.	650.
			On cover (pair)		*13,000.*
			On cover with U.S. #65		—
			On cover with U.S. #68		—
			On cover with U.S. #76		*8,250.*
			Block of 4	*3,400.*	—
a.			Tête bêche pair	*10,500.*	
b.			5c **bluish black,** *grayish white*	*12,500.*	*3,500.*

No. 21b unused is unique. Value based on 1995 auction sale. No. 21b used is also unique but defective. Value based on 2007 auction sale.

22	A9	5c	**blue,** *blue* ('65)	550.	*900.*
			On cover with U.S. #76		*9,250.*
			On cover with U.S. #63 and 76		—
			Block of 4	2,500.	
a.			Tête bêche pair	*20,000.*	
b.			5c **blue,** *grayish white*	—	
c.			Overlapping impressions	—	

1864

Laid Paper

23 A7 1c **black** 275. *2,500.*
On cover with U.S. #76 *12,000.*
Block of 4 1,150.
a. "HA" instead of "HAWAIIAN" *3,750.*
b. Tête bêche pair *6,250.*
c. Tête bêche pair, Nos. 23, 23a *18,000.*
24 A7 2c **black** 300. *1,050.*
Block of 4 1,250.
a. "NTER" *3,750.*
b. "S" of "POSTAGE" omitted *1,500.*
c. Tête bêche pair *5,500.*

A10

King Kamehameha IV — A11

1865

Wove Paper

25 A10 1c **dark blue** 350.
Block of 4 1,450.
a. Double impression —
b. With inverted impression of No. 21 on face *18,500.*
26 A10 2c **dark blue** 350.
Block of 4 1,450.

Nos. 12 to 26 were typeset and were printed in sheets of 50 (5 settings of 10 varieties each). The sheets were cut into panes of 25 (5x5) before distribution to the post offices.

1861-63 **Litho.**

Horizontally Laid Paper

27 A11 2c **pale rose** 325. 300.
On cover *1,000.*
Pair —
a. 2c **carmine rose** ('63) 3,000. 2,500.

Vertically Laid Paper

28 A11 2c **pale rose** 325. 300.
On cover *1,500.*
Block of 4 1,750. 1,600.
a. 2c **carmine rose** ('63) 300. *375.*
On cover *2,000.*
Block of 4 1,600.

RE-ISSUE

1869 **Engr.** **Thin Wove Paper**

29 A11 2c **red** 45.00 —
Block of 4 225.00

No. 29 was not issued for postal purposes although canceled examples are known. It was sold only at the Honolulu post office, at first without overprint and later with overprint "CANCELLED." See No. 29S.
See note following No. 51.

Princess Victoria Kamamalu — A12

King Kamehameha IV — A13

King Kamehameha V — A14

Kamehameha V — A15

Mataio Kekuanaoa — A16

1864-86 **Engr.** **Wove Paper** ***Perf. 12***

30 A12 1c **purple** ('86) 11.00 8.00
Never hinged 27.50
On cover 150.00
Block of 4 55.00
a. 1c **mauve** ('71) 60.00 20.00
Never hinged 100.00
Block of 4 300.00
b. 1c **violet** ('78) 20.00 10.00
Never hinged 50.00
Block of 4 160.00 200.00
31 A13 2c **rose vermilion** 65.00 9.00
Never hinged 160.00
On cover 200.00
On cover with U.S. #76 *1,000.*
Block of 4 275.00 *400.00*
a. 2c **vermilion** ('86) 45.00 20.00
Never hinged 110.00
On cover 150.00
b. Half used as 1c on cover with #32 *8,500.*
As "b," with U.S. #117 *18,000.*
32 A14 5c **blue** ('66) 175.00 30.00
Never hinged 400.00
On cover 250.00
On cover with any U.S. issues of 1861-67 *4,000.*
On cover with U.S. #116 *17,500.*
On cover with U.S. #116 and 69 *25,000.*
Block of 4 800.00 175.00
33 A15 6c **yellow green** ('71) 45.00 9.00
Never hinged 110.00
On cover 300.00
a. 6c **bluish green** ('78) 35.00 9.00
Never hinged 87.50
On cover 300.00
On cover with U.S. #179 *1,500.*
On cover with U.S. #183 + #184 *1,750.*
On cover with U.S. #185 *800.00*
Block of 4 160.00 500.00
34 A16 18c **dull rose** ('71) 90.00 35.00
Never hinged 230.00
On cover 350.00
On cover with No. 36 —
On cover with No. 36 and U.S. No. 179 *2,000.*
On cover with U.S. No. 161 —
On cover with U.S. No. 163 —
On cover with U.S. No. 185 *10,000.*
Block of 4 400.00 —
Nos. 30-34 (5) 386.00 91.00
Set, never hinged 927.50

Half of No. 31 was used with a 5c stamp to make up the 6-cent rate to the United States.
No. 32 has traces of rectangular frame lines surrounding the design. Nos. 39 and 52C have no such frame lines.

King David Kalakaua — A17

Prince William Pitt Leleiohoku — A18

1875

35 A17 2c **brown** 8.50 3.00
Never hinged 22.00
On cover 200.00
Block of 4 42.50 40.00
36 A18 12c **black** 65.00 27.50
Never hinged 165.00
On cover 400.00
On cover with U.S. No. 161 —
On cover with U.S. No. 179b —
Block of 4 350.00 —

Princess Likelike — A19

King David Kalakaua — A20

Queen Kapiolani — A21

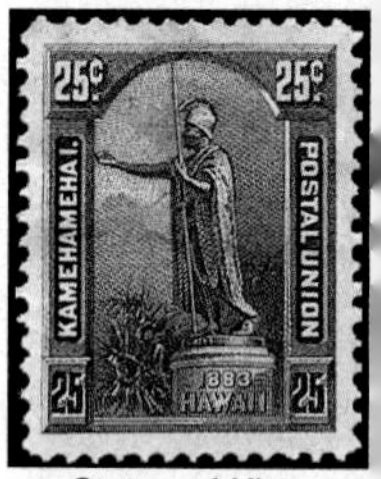

Statue of King Kamehameha I — A22

King William Lunalilo — A23

Queen Emma Kaleleonalani — A24

1882

37 A19 1c **blue** 11.00 6.00
Never hinged 27.50
On cover 60.00
Block of 4 55.00 50.00
38 A17 2c **lilac rose** 125.00 45.00
Never hinged 275.00
On cover 150.00
Block of 4 625.00
39 A14 5c **ultramarine** 15.00 3.25
Never hinged 37.50
On cover 27.50
Block of 4 75.00 60.00
a. Vert. pair, imperf. horiz. *5,000.* *6,000.*
40 A20 10c **black** 45.00 20.00
Never hinged 115.00
On cover 150.00

Block of 4	200.00	130.00
41 A21 15c **red brown**	60.00	25.00
Never hinged	150.00	
On cover		200.00
Block of 4	275.00	200.00
Nos. 37-41 (5)	256.00	99.25
Set, never hinged	605.00	

1883-86

42 A19 1c **green**	3.25	2.00
Never hinged	8.00	
On cover		25.00
Block of 4	15.00	14.00
43 A17 2c **rose** ('86)	4.50	1.00
Never hinged	11.00	
On cover		25.00
Block of 4	22.50	12.50
a. 2c **dull red**	62.50	21.00
Never hinged	140.00	
Block of 4	310.00	
44 A20 10c **red brown** ('84)	37.50	10.00
Never hinged	95.00	
On cover		125.00
Block of 4	175.00	100.00
45 A20 10c **vermilion**	42.50	12.50
Never hinged	105.00	
On cover		125.00
Block of 4	200.00	80.00
46 A18 12c **red lilac**	85.00	32.50
Never hinged	225.00	
On cover		425.00
Block of 4	425.00	240.00
47 A22 25c **dark violet**	140.00	60.00
Never hinged	325.00	
On cover		375.00
Block of 4	650.00	350.00

48 A23 50c **red**	175.00	85.00
Never hinged	400.00	
On cover		525.00
Block of 4	900.00	
49 A24 $1 **rose red**	275.00	250.00
Never hinged	625.00	
On cover		*8,000.*
Block of 4	1,400.	
Maltese cross cancellation		100.00
Nos. 42-49 (8)	762.75	453.00
Set, never hinged	1,794.	

Other fiscal cancellations exist on No. 49.

Nos. 48-49 are valued used with postal cancels. Canceled-to-order cancels exist and are worth less.

REPRODUCTION and REPRINT

Yellowish Wove Paper

1886-89 Engr. *Imperf.*

50 A11 2c **orange vermilion**	160.00	
Never hinged	275.00	
Block of 4	800.00	
51 A11 2c **carmine** ('89)	25.00	
Never hinged	45.00	
Block of 4	125.00	

In 1885 the Postmaster General wished to have on sale complete sets of Hawaii's portrait stamps, but was unable to find either the stone from which Nos. 27 and 28, or the plate from which No. 29 was printed. He therefore sent a copy of No. 29 to the American Bank Note Company, with an order to engrave a new plate like it and print 10,000 stamps therefrom, of which 5000 were overprinted "SPECIMEN" in blue.

The original No. 29 was printed in sheets of fifteen (5x3), but the plate of these "Official Imitations" was made up of fifty stamps (10x5). Later, in 1887, the original die for No. 29 was discovered, and, after retouching, a new plate was made and 37,500 stamps were printed (No. 51). These, like the originals, were printed in sheets of fifteen. They were delivered during 1889 and 1890. In 1892 all remaining unsold in the Post Office were overprinted "Reprint".

No. 29 is red in color, and printed on very thin white wove paper. No. 50 is orange vermilion in color, on medium, white to buff paper. In No. 50 the vertical line on the left side of the portrait touches the horizontal line over the label "Elua Keneta", while in the other two varieties, Nos. 29 and 51, it does not touch the horizontal line by half a millimeter. In No. 51 there are three parallel lines on the left side of the King's nose, while in No. 29 and No. 50 there are no such lines. No. 51 is carmine in color and printed on thick, yellowish to buff, wove paper.

It is claimed that both Nos. 50 and 51 were available for postage, although not made to fill a postal requirement. They exist with favor cancellation. No. 51 also is known postally used. See Nos. 50S-51S.

Queen Liliuokalani — A25

1890-91 *Perf. 12*

52 A25 2c **dull violet** ('91)	5.00	1.50
Never hinged	12.50	
On cover		25.00
Block of 4	25.00	12.00
a. Vert. pair, imperf. horiz.	*4,000.*	
52C A14 5c **deep indigo**	120.00	150.00
Never hinged	275.00	
On cover		500.00
Block of 4	575.00	

Stamps of 1864-91
Overprinted in Red

Three categories of double overprints:
I. Both overprints heavy.
II. One overprint heavy, one of moderate strength.
III. One overprint heavy, one of light or weak strength.

1893

53 A12 1c **purple**	8.50	12.50
Never hinged	21.50	
On cover		35.00
Block of 4	42.50	70.00
a. "189" instead of "1893"	575.00	—
b. No period after "GOVT"	*265.00*	*250.00*
f. Double overprint (III)	*600.00*	
54 A19 1c **blue**	8.50	*12.50*
Never hinged	22.50	
On cover		40.00
Block of 4	45.00	67.50
b. No period after "GOVT"	*140.00*	*140.00*
e. Double overprint (II)	*1,500.*	
f. Double overprint (III)	*400.00*	
55 A19 1c **green**	1.75	*3.00*
Never hinged	4.50	
On cover		25.00
Block of 4	8.00	15.00
d. Double overprint (I)	*625.00*	*450.00*
f. Double overprint (III)	*200.00*	*250.00*
g. Pair, one without ovpt.	*10,000.*	
56 A17 2c **brown**	12.00	*20.00*
Never hinged	28.50	
On cover		60.00
Block of 4	60.00	120.00
b. No period after "GOVT"	*300.00*	—
57 A25 2c **dull violet**	1.50	1.25
Never hinged	3.50	
On cover		25.00
Block of 4	6.50	6.50
a. "18 3" instead of "1893"	*750.00*	*500.00*
d. Double overprint (I)	*1,300.*	*650.00*
f. Double overprint (III)	*175.00*	*175.00*
g. Inverted overprint	*4,000.*	*4,500.*
58 A14 5c **deep indigo**	13.00	*25.00*
Never hinged	32.00	
On cover		100.00
Block of 4	65.00	140.00
b. No period after "GOVT"	*225.00*	*250.00*
f. Double overprint (III)	*1,250.*	*650.00*
59 A14 5c **ultramarine**	6.50	2.50
Never hinged	15.00	
On cover		40.00
Block of 4	32.50	20.00
d. Double overprint (I)	*6,500.*	
e. Double overprint (II)	*4,000.*	*4,000.*
f. Double overprint (III)		*600.00*
g. Inverted overprint	*1,500.*	*1,500.*
60 A15 6c **green**	17.50	*25.00*
Never hinged	40.00	
On cover		140.00
Block of 4	85.00	125.00
e. Double overprint (II)	*1,000.*	
61 A20 10c **black**	12.00	*15.00*
Never hinged	30.00	
On cover		125.00
Block of 4	60.00	82.50
e. Double overprint (II)	*900.00*	*650.00*
f. Double overprint (III)	*200.00*	
61B A20 10c **red brown**	*14,000.*	*29,000.*
Block of 4	*60,000.*	
Strip of 5, plate imprint	*75,000.*	
62 A18 12c **black**	12.00	*17.50*
Never hinged	30.00	
On cover		150.00
Block of 4	62.50	110.00
d. Double overprint (I)	*2,000.*	
e. Double overprint (II)	*1,750.*	
63 A18 12c **red lilac**	165.00	*250.00*
Never hinged	400.00	
On cover		550.00
Block of 4	950.00	—
64 A22 25c **dark violet**	32.00	*40.00*
Never hinged	72.00	
On cover		225.00
Block of 4	150.00	200.00
b. No period after "GOVT"	*325.00*	*325.00*
f. Double overprint (III)	*1,000.*	
Nos. 53-61,62-64 (12)	290.25	424.25
Nos. 53-61, 62-64 never hinged	699.50	

Virtually all known copies of No. 61B are cut in at the top.

Overprinted in Black

65 A13 2c **vermilion**	80.00	*75.00*
Never hinged	200.00	
On cover		*450.00*
Block of 4	*350.00*	*500.00*
b. No period after "GOVT"	*250.00*	*250.00*
66 A17 2c **rose**	1.25	*2.25*
Never hinged	3.00	
On cover		25.00
Block of 4	6.50	*11.00*
b. No period after "GOVT"	50.00	60.00
d. Double overprint (I)	*4,000.*	
e. Double overprint (II)	*2,750.*	
f. Double overprint (III)	*300.00*	
66C A15 6c **green**	*14,000.*	*29,000.*
On cover		—
Block of 4	*60,000.*	
67 A20 10c **vermilion**	20.00	*30.00*
Never hinged	50.00	
On cover		125.00
Block of 4	100.00	180.00
f. Double overprint (III)	*1,250.*	
68 A20 10c **red brown**	10.00	*13.00*
Never hinged	25.00	
On cover		100.00
Block of 4	50.00	75.00
f. Double overprint (III)	*4,000.*	
69 A18 12c **red lilac**	325.00	*500.00*
Never hinged	575.00	
On cover		950.00
Block of 4	1,500.	*2,400.*
70 A21 15c **red brown**	22.50	*30.00*
Never hinged	50.00	
On cover		300.00
Block of 4	110.00	*150.00*
e. Double overprint (II)	*2,000.*	
71 A16 18c **dull rose**	35.00	*35.00*
Never hinged	75.00	
On cover		225.00
Block of 4	160.00	*175.00*
a. "18 3" instead of "1893"	*475.00*	*475.00*
b. No period after "GOVT"	*300.00*	*300.00*
d. Double overprint (I)	*600.00*	
f. Double overprint (III)	*250.00*	—
g. Pair, one without ovpt.	*3,500.*	
h. As "b," double overprint (II)	*1,750.*	

72 A23 50c **red**	75.00	*90.00*
Never hinged	175.00	
On cover		600.00
Block of 4	350.00	*500.00*
b. No period after "GOVT"	*400.00*	*400.00*
Never hinged	675.00	
f. Double overprint (III)	*1,000.*	
73 A24 $1 **rose red**	135.00	*175.00*
Never hinged	300.00	
On cover		775.00
Block of 4	600.00	*875.00*
b. No period after "GOVT"	*450.00*	425.00
Nos. 65-66,67-73 (9)	*703.75*	*950.25*
Nos. 65-66, 67-73 never hinged	1,453.	

Coat of Arms — A26

View of Honolulu — A27

Statue of Kamehameha I — A28

Stars and Palms — A29

S. S. "Arawa" — A30

Pres. Sanford Ballard Dole — A31

"CENTS" Added — A32

1894

74 A26 1c **yellow**	2.25	1.25
Never hinged	5.75	
On cover		25.00
Block of 4	10.00	8.00
75 A27 2c **brown**	2.25	.60
Never hinged	5.75	
On cover		25.00
Block of 4	9.00	7.00
"Flying goose" flaw (48 LR 2)	550.00	400.00
Never hinged	1,400.	
Double transfer	5.00	5.00
76 A28 5c **rose lake**	5.00	2.00
Never hinged	13.00	
On cover		25.00
Block of 4	25.00	15.00
77 A29 10c **yellow green**	7.50	5.00
Never hinged	20.00	
On cover		45.00
Block of 4	35.00	25.00
78 A30 12c **blue**	15.00	*17.50*
Never hinged	40.00	
On cover		150.00
Block of 4	65.00	*80.00*
Double transfer	22.50	25.00
79 A31 25c **deep blue**	20.00	13.50
Never hinged	52.50	
On cover		100.00
Block of 4	100.00	—
Nos. 74-79 (6)	52.00	*39.85*
Set, never hinged	137.00	

Numerous double transfers exist on Nos. 75 and 81.

1899

80 A26 1c **dark green**	1.75	1.25
Never hinged	4.50	
On cover		25.00
Block of 4	8.50	7.00
81 A27 2c **rose**	1.40	1.00
Never hinged	3.50	
On cover		20.00
Block of 4	6.00	6.00
Double transfer	—	—
"Flying goose" flaw (48 LR 2)	325.00	300.00
Never hinged	850.00	
a. 2c **salmon**	1.50	1.25
Never hinged	4.00	
b. Vert. pair, imperf. horiz.	*4,500.*	
82 A32 5c **blue**	7.50	3.25
Never hinged	20.00	
On cover		25.00
Block of 4	37.50	52.50
Set, never hinged	28.00	

OFFICIAL STAMPS

Lorrin Andrews Thurston — O1

1896 **Engr.** **Unwmk.** ***Perf. 12***

O1 O1 2c **green**	40.00	17.50
Never hinged	100.00	
On cover		400.00
Block of 4	175.00	
O2 O1 5c **black brown**	40.00	17.50
Never hinged	100.00	
On cover		450.00
Block of 4	175.00	
O3 O1 6c **deep ultramarine**	40.00	17.50
Never hinged	100.00	
On cover		—
Block of 4	175.00	
O4 O1 10c **bright rose**	40.00	17.50
Never hinged	100.00	
On cover		500.00
Block of 4	175.00	
O5 O1 12c **orange**	50.00	17.50
Never hinged	125.00	
On cover		—
Block of 4	225.00	
O6 O1 25c **gray violet**	57.50	17.50
Never hinged	140.00	
On cover		—
Block of 4	250.00	
Nos. O1-O6 (6)	267.50	105.00
Set, never hinged	665.00	

Used values for Nos. O1-O6 are for stamps canceled-to-order "FOREIGN OFFICE/HONOLULU H.I." in double circle without date. Values of postally used stamps: Nos. O1-O2, O4, $35 each; No. O3, $100; No. O5, $125; No. O6, $150.

ENVELOPES

Italicized numbers in parentheses indicate quantities issued.

All printed by American Bank Note Co., N.Y.

View of Honolulu Harbor — E1

Envelopes of White Paper, Outside and Inside

1884

U1 E1 1c **light green** *(109,000)*	2.50	3.00
Entire	6.00	*15.00*
a. 1c **green** *(10,000)*	6.00	*15.00*
Entire	15.00	*90.00*
b. 1c **dark green**	10.00	*10.00*
Entire	25.00	*75.00*
U2 E1 2c **carmine** *(386,000 including U2a, U2b)*	2.50	4.00
Entire	5.00	*17.50*
a. 2c **red**	2.50	4.00
Entire	5.00	*17.50*
b. 2c **rose**	2.50	4.00
Entire	5.00	*17.50*
c. 2c **pale pink** *(5,000)*	10.00	12.50
Entire	35.00	*60.00*
U3 E1 4c **red** *(18,000)*	14.00	17.50
Entire	30.00	*90.00*
U4 E1 5c **blue** *(90,775)*	6.50	7.50
Entire	17.50	*30.00*
U5 E1 10c **black** *(3,500 plus)*	20.00	25.00
Entire	50.00	*100.00*

Envelopes White Outside, Blue Inside

U6 E1 2c **rose**	150.00	200.00
Entire	400.00	*1,500.*
U7 E1 4c **red**	150.00	200.00
Entire	400.00	—
U8 E1 5c **blue**	150.00	200.00
Entire	400.00	*1,250.*
U9 E1 10c **black**	250.00	400.00
Entire	450.00	—
Nos. U1-U9 (9)	745.50	1,057.

Nos. U1, U2, U4 & U5 Overprinted Locally "Provisional Government 1893" in Red or Black

1893

U10 E1 1c **light green** (R) *(16,000)*	3.50	7.00
Entire	7.00	*20.00*
a. Double overprint	*1,750.*	
Entire	*6,000.*	
U11 E1 2c **carmine** (Bk) *(37,000)*	2.50	3.50
Entire	4.50	*15.00*
a. Double overprint	500.00	
Entire	*1,100.*	*1,250.*
b. Double overprint, one inverted, entire	*1,500.*	

No. U11 is known as an unused entire with a triple overprint, two of the overprints being at the bottom right portion of the envelope. Unique. Value, $9,500.

U12 E1 5c **blue** (R) *(34,891)*	4.25	5.00
Entire	10.00	*15.00*
a. Double overprint	375.00	*400.00*
Entire	600.00	*3,000.*
b. Triple overprint, entire		*7,500.*
U13 E1 10c **black** (R) *(17,707 incl. No. U14)*	12.50	16.00
Entire	20.00	*90.00*
a. Double overprint, entire	*1,800.*	*2,000.*

Envelope No. U9 with same overprint

U14 E1 10c **black** (R)	300.	*725.00*
Entire	1,000.	—

SPECIAL DELIVERY ENVELOPE

Value is for Entire.

Envelope No. U5 with added inscription "Special Despatch Letter" etc. in red at top left corner

1885

UE1 E1 10c **black** *(2,000)*	175.

Envelope No. UE1 was prepared for use but never issued for postal purposes. Postally used examples exist, but no special delivery service was performed. Favor cancellations exist.

POSTAL CARDS

All printed by American Bank Note Co., N.Y.
Values are for entires.

Queen Liliuokalani — PC1

View of Diamond Head — PC2

Royal Emblems — PC3

1882-92 **Engr.**

UX1	PC1	1c **red,** *buff (125,000)*	30.00	*75.00*
UX2	PC2	2c **black** *(45,000)*	50.00	*90.00*
a.		Lithographed ('92)	150.00	250.00
UX3	PC3	3c **blue green** *(21,426)*	60.00	*125.00*

1889 **Litho.**

UX4	PC1	1c **red,** *buff (171,240)*	25.00	*50.00*

Cards Nos. UX4, UX2a and UX3 overprinted locally "Provisional Government 1893" in red or black

1893

UX5	PC1	1c **red,** *buff* (Bk) *(28,760)*	30.00	*75.00*
a.		Double overprint	*4,000.*	*3,500.*
UX6	PC2	2c **black** (R) *(10,000)*	55.00	*95.00*

No. UX6 is known unused with double overprint, one inverted at lower left of card. Unique. Value, $16,000.

UX7	PC3	3c **blue green** (R) *(8,574)*	65.00	*250.00*
a.		Double overprint	*1,750.*	

Iolani Palace — PC4

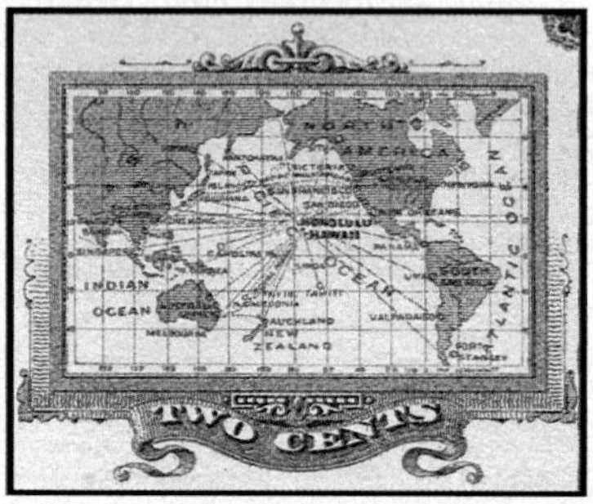

Map of Pacific Ocean, Mercator's Projection — PC5

1894-97 **Litho.**

Border Frame 131½x72½mm

UX8	PC4	1c **red,** *buff (100,000)*	20.00	*40.00*
a.		Border frame 132½x74mm ('97) *(200,000)*	20.00	*40.00*
UX9	PC5	2c **green** *(60,000)*	45.00	*80.00*
a.		Border frame 132½x74mm ('97) *(190,000)*	45.00	*80.00*

PAID REPLY POSTAL CARDS

Double cards, same designs as postal cards with added inscriptions on reply cards.

1883 **Litho.**

UY1	PC1	1c +1c **purple,** *buff,* unsevered *(5,000)*	400.00	*450.00*
m.		Message card, detached	35.00	*100.00*
r.		Reply card, detached	35.00	*100.00*
UY2	PC2	2c +2c **dark blue,** unsevered *(5,000)*	450.00	*500.00*
m.		Message card, detached	55.00	*140.00*
r.		Reply card, detached	55.00	*140.00*

1889

UY3	PC1	1c +1c **gray violet,** *buff,* unsevered *(5,000)*	400.00	*450.00*
m.		Message card, detached	35.00	*100.00*
r.		Reply card, detached	35.00	*100.00*
UY4	PC2	2c +2c **sapphire,** unsevered *(5,000)*	400.00	*450.00*
m.		Message card, detached	35.00	*80.00*
r.		Reply card, detached	35.00	*80.00*

Values for unused unsevered Paid Reply Postal Cards are for cards which have not been folded. Folded cards sell for about 33% of these values.

Detached card used values are for canceled cards with printed messages on the back.

REVENUE STAMPS

R1

R2

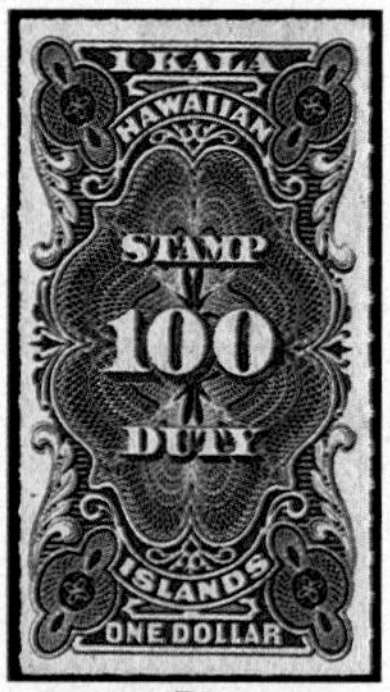

R3

R4

R5

R6

Printed by the American Bank Note Co.
Sheets of 70

1877 **Engr.** **Unwmk.** ***Rouletted 8***

R1	R1	25c **green** *(160,000)*	14.00	15.50
		Never hinged	35.00	
R2	R2	50c **yellow orange** *(190,000)*	34.00	13.25
		Never hinged	85.00	
R3	R3	$1 **black** *(580,000)*	34.00	7.00
		Never hinged	85.00	
a.		$1 gray	34.00	7.00
		Never hinged	85.00	

Denominations Typo.

R4	R4	$5 **vermilion & violet blue** *(21,000)*	145.00	45.00
		Never hinged	350.00	
R5	R5	$10 **reddish brown & green** *(14,000)*	145.00	45.00
		Never hinged	350.00	
R6	R6	$50 **slate blue & carmine** *(3,500)*	*1,050.*	*350.00*

No. R6 unused is valued without gum, as all known examples come thus.

Unused values for all revenues except No. R6 are for stamps with original gum. Apparently unused stamps without gum sell for less.

No. R1 Surcharged in Black or Gold

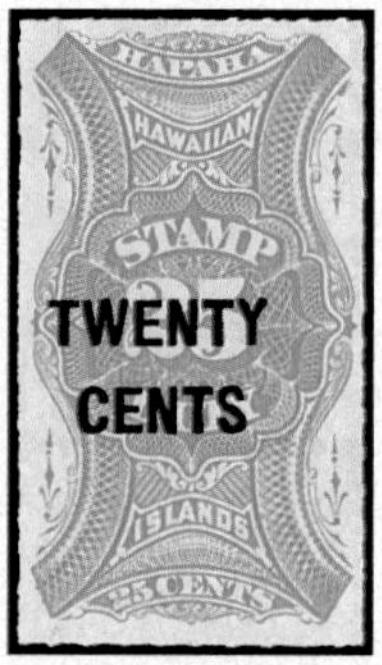

a

b

1893-94

R7	R1 (a)	20c on 25c **green**	33.00	18.50
		Never hinged	75.00	
a.		Inverted surcharge	*1,250.*	*900.00*
R8	R1 (b)	20c on 25c **green** (G)	65.00	52.50
		Never hinged	145.00	
a.		Inverted surcharge		—
b.		Double surcharge	—	—
c.		Double surcharge, one black, one gold	—	*1,500.*
d.		Double surcharge, one gold, one red in different font	—	
e.		Double surcharge, with a single added letter "c"	—	
f.		Double surcharge with two "c" letters added	—	

On No. R8b, one surcharge is always diagonal. On No. R8c, the black surcharge is 20mm wide, while the normal gold surcharge is 15mm wide.

R7

Kamehameha I — R8

Sheets of 50

1894 **Litho.** ***Perf. 14***

R9	R7	20c **red** *(10,000)*	240.00	220.00
		Never hinged	575.00	
a.		Imperf. *(25,000)*	450.00	400.00
		Never hinged	1,100.	
		Pair	1,050.	
		Never hinged	2,400.	

No. R9a is known in an unused pair on paper with "DENNIS" papermaker's watermark.

R10	R7	25c **violet brown**	975.00	850.00
		Never hinged	2,100.	
a.		Imperf.	1,500.	—
		Never hinged	3,200.	
		Pair	3,450.	
		Never hinged	7,350.	
b.		As "a," tete beche pair		—

Printed by the American Bank Note Co.
Sheets of 100

1897 **Engr.** ***Perf. 12***

R11	R8	$1 **dark blue** *(60,000)*	11.00	8.50
		Never hinged	22.00	

R9

1901 *Rouletted 8*

R12 R9 $50 **slate blue & carmine** *(7,000)* 60.00 *65.00*
Never hinged 130.00

Types of 1877
Printed by the American Bank Note Co.
Sheets of 70

1910-13 **Engr.** *Perf. 12*

R13 R2 50c **yellow orange** ('13) *(70,000)* 16.50 *27.50*
Never hinged 36.00
R14 R3 $1 **black** ('13) *(35,000)* 22.50 *32.50*
Never hinged 47.50
R15 R4 $5 **vermilion & violet blue** *(14,000)* 45.00 *55.00*
Never hinged 100.00
a. Denomination inverted —
R16 R5 $10 **reddish brown & green** *(14,000)* 45.00 *55.00*
Never hinged 100.00

PROOFS and TRIAL COLOR PROOFS

The large die proofs range in size and format from die impressions on India die sunk on cards generally up to 6x9 inches, through die impressions on India on or off card in medium to stamp size. Many individual listings are known in more than one size and format. Values reflect the size and format most commonly seen.

1853

			DIE (1) Large	PLATE (3) India	(4) Card
5TC	5c	**black** on wove		*6,000.*	
6TC	13c	**black** on wove		*6,000.*	

1868-89

			DIE (1) Large	PLATE (3) India	(4) Card
10TC	5c	**orange red**	875.		
11TC	13c	**orange red**	875.	475.	
11RP	13c	**orange red**	*2,500.*	575.	

1861-63

			DIE (1) Large	PLATE (3) India	(4) Card
27TC	2c	**black**		875.	

1864-71

			DIE (1) Large	PLATE (3) India	(4) Card
30P	1c	**purple**	650.	190.	
		Block of 4		750.	
31P	2c	**rose vermilion**	650.	190.	225.
		Block of 4		—	
31TC	2c	**green**	*1,700.*		
32P	5c	**blue**	625.	230.	200.
32TC	5c	**black**	1,250.		
32TC	5c	**dark red**		250.	
32TC	5c	**orange red**		250.	
32TC	5c	**orange**		250.	
32TC	5c	**red brown**		250.	
		Block of 4		1,250.	
32TC	5c	**green**		250.	
		Block of 4		1,250.	
32TC	5c	**dark violet**		250.	
		Block of 4		1,250.	
33P	6c	**green**	650.	250.	
		Block of 4		1,250.	
34P	18c	**dull rose**	650.	250.	275.
		Block of 4		1,250.	
34TC	18c	**orange red**	875.	650.	
34TC	18c	**dark orange**	875.		

1875

			DIE (1) Large	PLATE (3) India	(4) Card
35P	2c	**brown**	650.	190.	225.
		Block of 4		800.	
35TC	2c	**black**	*2,600.*		
36P	12c	**black**	650.	190.	225.
36TC	12c	**violet blue**	875.		

1882

			DIE (1) Large	PLATE (3) India	(4) Card
37P	1c	**blue**		190.	
		Block of 4		800.	
37TC	1c	**black**	*3,750.*		
39P	5c	**ultramarine**	575.	190.	
40P	10c	**black**	575.	230.	
		Block of 4		950.	
41P	15c	**red brown**		190.	225.
		Block of 4		800.	

1883-86

			DIE (1) Large	PLATE (3) India	(4) Card
42P	1c	**green**		190.	225.
		Block of 4		800.	
43P	2c	**rose**		150.	225.
		Block of 4		700.	
47P	25c	**dark violet**	550.	190.	
		Block of 4		800.	
47TC	25c	**black**	*875.*		
48P	50c	**red**	550.	230.	
		Block of 4		1,300.	
48TC	50c	**lake**	*1,150.*	*375.*	
49P	$1	**rose red**	*1,750.*	190.	225.
		Block of 4		800.	
49TC	$1	**black**		190.	
49TC	$1	**orange red**	875.	*375.*	
49TC	$1	**carmine**		*375.*	
49TC	$1	**vermilion**		*375.*	
		Block of 4		*1,600.*	

1886-89

			DIE (1) Large	PLATE (3) India	(4) Card
50P	2c	**orange vermilion**	875.	250.	
51P	2c	**carmine**	875.		

1890-91

			DIE (1) Large	PLATE (3) India	(4) Card
52P	2c	**dull violet**	*3,750.*	250.	225.
52CP	5c	**deep indigo**		175.	

1894

			DIE (1) Large	PLATE (3) India	(4) Card
74P	1c	**yellow**	700.	150.	225.
75P	2c	**brown**	700.	150.	
75TC	2c	**dark green**	650.		
76P	5c	**rose lake**	700.	150.	225.
77P	10c	**yellow green**	700.	150.	225.
		Block of 4		625.	
77TC	10c	**deep blue green**	700.		
78P	12c	**blue**	700.	150.	225.
79P	25c	**deep blue**	700.	150.	225.

1899

			DIE (1) Large	PLATE (3) India	(4) Card
82P	5c	**blue**		190.	225.
		Block of 4		800.	

Official

1896

			DIE (1) Large	PLATE (3) India	(4) Card
O1P	2c		875.	300.	190.
O2P	5c	**black brown**	875.	300.	190.
O3P	6c	**deep ultramarine**	875.	300.	190.
O4P	10c	**bright rose**	875.	300.	190.
		Block of 4		—	
O4TC	10c	**black**	875.		
O5P	12c	**orange**	875.	300.	190.
O5TC	12c	**black**	875.		
O6P	25c	**gray violet**	875.	300.	190.
O6TC	25c	**black**	875.		

Envelopes

Uncleared indicia only

1884

			DIE (1) Large	PLATE (3) India	(4) Card
U1P	1c	**green**	*750.*		
U1TC	1c	**black**	*750.*		
U1TC	1c	**orange**	*750.*		
U2P	2c	**carmine**	*750.*		
U2TC	2c	**black**	*750.*		
U2TC	2c	**blue**	*750.*		
U3P	4c	**red**	*750.*		
U3TC	4c	**black**	*750.*		
U4P	5c	**blue**	*750.*		
U4TC	5c	**black**	*750.*		
U5P	10c	**black**	*750.*		

Postal Cards

Large die proofs are of indicia only, India proofs are entire card.

1882-95

			DIE (1) Large	PLATE (3) India	(4) Card
UX1P	1c	**red**	*3,500.*	*1,700.*	
UX1TC	1c	**green**		*1,950.*	
UX2P	2c	**black**		*1,700.*	
UX3P	3c	**blue green**		*3,000.*	
UX8TC	1c	**orange**		*3,000.*	
UX8TC	1c	**brown**		*3,000.*	

Revenues

1877-97

			DIE (1) Large	PLATE (3) India	(4) Card
R1P	25c	**green**		*300.*	*300.*
		Block of 4		*1,300.*	
R1TC	25c	**blue green**	*1,150.*		
R1TC	25c	**black**	*1,150.*		
R1TC	25c	**brown red**	*1,150.*		
R1TC	25c	**brown**	*1,150.*		
R1TC	25c	**grayish blue**	*1,150.*		
R2P	50c	**yellow orange**		*300.*	*350.*
		Block of 4		*1,300.*	
R2TC	50c	**blue green**	*1,150.*		
R2TC	50c	**black**	*1,150.*		
R2TC	50c	**brown red**	*1,150.*		
R2TC	50c	**brown**	*1,150.*		
R2TC	50c	**grayish blue**	*1,150.*		
R3P	$1	**black**	*1,150.*		*350.*
		Block of 4		*1,300.*	
R3TC	$1	**blue green**	*1,150.*		
R3TC	$1	**brown red**	*1,150.*		
R3TC	$1	**brown**	*1,150.*		
R3TC	$1	**grayish blue**	*1,150.*		
R4P	$5	**vermilion & violet blue**			*350.*
		Block of 4		*1,200.*	
R5P	$10	**reddish brown & green**		*300.*	*350.*
		Block of 4		*1,200.*	
R6P	$50	**slate blue & carmine**			*350.*
		Block of 4		*1,200.*	
R11P	$1	**dark blue**	*1,250.*	*300.*	*350.*

SPECIMEN STAMPS

Overprinted in Black or Red — Type A

1868

10S A 5c **blue** (R) 20.
Block of 4 100.
a. Line through "Honolulu" (Pos. 2) 75.
11S A 13c **dull rose** 20.
Block of 4 100.

Overprinted in Black — Type B

11S B 13c **dull rose** 275.
Block of 4 1,250.
a. Double overprint, one as #11S A, one as #11S B *4,000.*
b. Period omitted (Pos. 18, 20) 575.

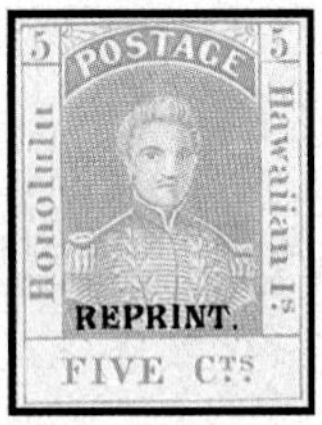

Overprinted in Black — Type C

1889

10RS C 5c **blue** 60.
Block of 4 250.
11RS C 13c **orange red** 225.
Block of 4 950.

Overprinted in Black — Type D

1869

29S D 2c **red** 50.
Block of 4 250.

Overprinted in Blue — Type E

1886

50S E 2c **orange vermilion** 60.
Block of 4 250.

Overprinted in Black — Type C

1889

51S	C	2c **carmine**	25.	
		Block of 4	125.	

PHILIPPINES

Issued under U.S. Administration

Following the American occupation of the Philippines, May 1, 1898, after Admiral Dewey's fleet entered Manila Bay, an order was issued by the U. S. Postmaster General (No. 201, May 24, 1898) establishing postal facilities with rates similar to the domestic rates.

Military postal stations were established as branch post offices, each such station being placed within the jurisdiction of the nearest regular post office. Supplies were issued to these military stations through the regular post office of which they were branches.

Several post office clerks were sent to the Philippines and the San Francisco post office was made the nearest regular office for the early Philippine mail and the postmarks of the period point out this fact.

U.S. stamps overprinted "PHILIPPINES" were placed on sale in Manila June 30, 1899. Regular U.S. stamps had been in use from early March, and at the Manila post office Spanish stamps were also acceptable.

The first regular post office was established at Cavite on July 30, 1898, as a branch of the San Francisco post office. The first cancellation was a dated handstamp with "PHILIPPINE STATION" and "SAN FRANCISCO, CAL."

On May 1, 1899, the entire Philippine postal service was separated from San Francisco and numerous varieties of postmarks resulted. Many of the early used stamps show postmarks and cancellations of the Military Station, Camp or R.P.O. types, together with "Killers" of the types employed in the U.S. at the time.

The Philippines became a commonwealth of the United States on November 15, 1935, the High Commissioner of the United States taking office on the same day. The official name of the government was "Commonwealth of the Philippines" as provided by Article 17 of the Constitution. Upon the final and complete withdrawal of sovereignty of the United States and the proclamation of Philippine independence on July 4, 1946, the Commonwealth of the Philippines became the "Republic of the Philippines."

Italicized numbers in parentheses indicate quantities issued.

Authority for dates of issue, stamps from 1899 to 1911, and some quantities issued-"The Postal Issues of the Philippines," by F. L. Palmer (New York, 1912). Authority for quantities issued — "NAPP's Numbers, Volume 2," by Joseph M. Napp (2001).

100 CENTS = 1 DOLLAR
100 CENTAVOS = 1 PESO (1906)

Regular Issues of the United States Overprinted in Black

Printed and overprinted by the U.S. Bureau of Engraving and Printing.

1899, June 30 **Unwmk.** ***Perf. 12***

On U.S. Stamp No. 260

212	A96	50c **orange**	350.	225.
		Never hinged	800.	
		On cover		—
		Block of 4	1,650.	—
		P# strip of 3, Impt.	1,550.	
		P# block of 6, Impt.	*12,500.*	

On U.S. Stamps
Nos. 279, 279B, 279Bd, 279Be, 279Bf, 279Bc, 268, 281, 282C, 283, 284, 275, 275a

Wmk. Double-lined USPS (191)

213	A87	1c **yellow green** *(5,500,000)*	4.25	.60
		Never hinged	10.00	
		On cover		10.00
		Block of 4	20.00	5.00
		P# strip of 3, Impt.	40.00	
		P# block of 6, Impt.	225.00	
a.		Inverted overprint	*32,500.*	
214	A88	2c **red,** type IV *(6,970,000)*	1.75	.60
		light red	1.75	.60
		Never hinged	4.25	
		On cover		10.00
		Block of 4	7.00	4.00
		P# strip of 3, Impt.	25.00	
		P# block of 6, Impt.	175.00	
a.		2c **orange red,** type IV, *1901*	1.75	.60
		pale orange red	1.75	.60
		deep orange red, *1903*	1.75	.60
		Never hinged	4.25	
b.		Booklet pane of 6, **red,** type IV *1900*	250.00	*300.00*
		orange red, *1901*	250.00	*300.00*
		Never hinged	600.00	
c.		2c **reddish carmine,** type IV	2.50	.90
		Never hinged	6.00	
		On cover		12.50
		Block of 4	11.00	7.50
		P# strip of 3, Impt.	35.00	
		P# block of 6, Impt.	225.00	
d.		2c **rose carmine,** type IV	3.00	1.10
		Never hinged	7.25	
		On cover		15.00
		Block of 4	14.00	8.50
		P# strip of 3, Impt.	40.00	
		P# block of 6, Impt.	260.00	
215	A89	3c **purple** *(673,814)*	9.00	1.25
		Never hinged	21.50	
		On cover		30.00
		Block of 4	42.50	13.50
		P# strip of 3, Impt.	85.00	
		P# block of 6, Impt.	475.00	
216	A91	5c **blue** *(1,700,000)*	9.00	1.00
		Never hinged	21.50	
		On cover		20.00
		Block of 4	42.50	9.00
		P# strip of 3, Impt.	85.00	
		P# block of 6, Impt.	500.00	
a.		Inverted overprint		*3,750.*

No. 216a is valued in the grade of fine.

217	A94	10c **brown,** type I *(750,000)*+	35.00	4.00
		Never hinged	80.00	
		On cover		60.00
		Block of 4	160.00	55.00
		P# strip of 3, Impt.	175.00	
		P# block of 6, Impt.	700.00	

(+ Quantity includes Nos. 217, 217A)

217A	A94	10c **orange brown,** type II	135.00	27.50
		Never hinged	325.00	
		On cover		160.00
		Block of 4	650.00	190.00
		P# strip of 3, Impt.	950.	
		P# block of 6, Impt.	*3,000.*	
218	A95	15c **olive green** *(200,000)*	40.00	8.00
		light olive green	37.50	8.50
		Never hinged	95.00	
		On cover		110.00
		Block of 4	175.00	52.50
		P# strip of 3, Impt.	200.00	
		P# block of 6, Impt.	1,250.	
219	A96	50c **orange** *(50,000)*+	125.00	37.50
		Never hinged	300.00	
		On cover		*400.00*
		Block of 4	575.00	*250.00*
		P# strip of 3, Impt.	575.00	
		P# block of 6, Impt.	*5,000.*	
a.		50 **red orange**	250.00	55.00
		Never hinged	600.00	
		Block of 4	1,700.	
		Nos. 213-219 (8)	359.00	80.45

(+ Quantity includes Nos. 212, 219, 219a)

Special Printing

In March 1900 one pane of 100 stamps of each of Nos. 213-217, 218, 219 and J1-J5 were specially overprinted for displays at the Paris Exposition (1900) and Pan American Exposition (1901). The 2c pane was light red, type IV.

Stamps were handstampd type E "Specimen" in black ink on the face by H. G. Mandel and mounted by him in separate displays for the two Expositions. Additional stamps from each pane were also handstamped "Specimen" but most were destroyed after the Expositions.

J. M. Bartels, a stamp dealer, signed some stamps from these panes "Special Surcharge" in pencil on the gum to authenticate them as coming from the "Mandel" Special Printing panes. In 1904 or later, he handstamped additional surviving examples "Special Surcharge" in red ink on the back as his guarantee. Some of these guaranteed stamps had Mandel's "Specimen" handstamp on the face while others did not. Value, each $775.

Regular Issue

1901, Aug. 30

Same Overprint in Black On U.S. Stamps Nos. 280b, 282 and 272

220	A90	4c **orange brown** *(404,907)*	30.00	5.00
		Never hinged	75.00	
		On cover		50.00
		Block of 4	140.00	50.00
		P# strip of 3, Impt.	160.00	
		P# block of 6, Impt.	725.00	
221	A92	6c **lake** *(223,465)*	35.00	7.00
		Never hinged	90.00	
		On cover		65.00
		Block of 4	175.00	50.00
		P# strip of 3, Impt.	175.00	
		P# block of 6, Impt.	900.00	
222	A93	8c **violet brown** *(248,000)*	37.50	7.50
		Never hinged	90.00	
		On cover		50.00
		Block of 4	190.00	55.00
		P# strip of 3, Impt.	190.00	
		P# block of 6, Impt.	950.00	

Same Overprint in Red On U.S. Stamps Nos. 276, 276A, 277a and 278

223	A97	$1 **black,** type I *(3,000)*+	450.00	250.00
		Never hinged	1,150.	
		On cover		*800.00*
		Block of 4	2,000.	

P# strip of 3, Impt. *2,100.*
P# block of 6, Impt. —
Horiz. pair, types I & II *3,750.*
(+ Quantity includes Nos. 223, 223A)

223A A97 $1 **black,** type II 2,400. 750.00
Never hinged 5,750.
On cover —
Block of 4 *10,500.* —
P# strip of 3, Impt., one stamp No. 223 8,500.
P# block of 6, Impt., two stamps No. 223 —

224 A98 $2 **dark blue** *(1800)* 450.00 325.00
Never hinged 1,150.
On cover 3,250.
Block of 4 2,000. —
P# strip of 3, Impt. *2,600.*
P# block of 6, Impt. —

225 A99 $5 **dark green** *(782)* 775.00 *825.00*
Never hinged 2,000.
On cover *12,500.*
Block of 4 *3,250.* —
P# strip of 3, Impt. *4,000.*
P# block of 6, Impt. —

Special Printing

Special printings exist of Nos. 227, 221, 223-225, made from defaced plates. These were made for display at the St. Louis Exposition. All but a few copies were destroyed. Most of the existing copies have the handstamp "Special Printing" on the back. Value: Nos. 227, 221, each $775; No. 223, $1,200; No. 224, $1,650; No. 225, $2,500.

Regular Issue

1903-04

Same Overprint in Black On U.S. Stamps Nos. 300 to 310 and shades

226 A115 1c **blue green** *(9,631,172)* 7.00 .40
Never hinged 15.50
On cover 8.25
Block of 4 32.50 4.25
P# strip of 3, Impt. 25.00
P# block of 6, Impt. 260.00

227 A116 2c **carmine** *(850,000)* 9.00 1.10
Never hinged 20.00
On cover 10.00
Block of 4 42.50 6.00
P# strip of 3, Impt. 42.50
P# block of 6, Impt. 325.00

228 A117 3c **bright violet** *(14,500)* 67.50 12.50
Never hinged 150.00
On cover 55.00
Block of 4 275.00 85.00
P# strip of 3, Impt. 275.00
P# block of 6, Impt. 1,650.

229 A118 4c **brown** *(13,000)* 75.00 22.50
Never hinged 175.00
a. 4c **orange brown** 80.00 20.00
Never hinged 175.00
On cover 40.00
Block of 4 350.00 150.00
P# strip of 3, Impt. 325.00
P# block of 6, Impt. 1,950.

230 A119 5c **blue** *(1,211,844)* 17.50 1.00
Never hinged 40.00
On cover 22.50
Block of 4 80.00 7.50
P# strip of 3, Impt. 70.00
P# block of 6, Impt. 425.00

231 A120 6c **brownish lake** *(11,500)* 85.00 22.50
Never hinged 190.00
On cover 65.00
Block of 4 350.00 150.00
P# strip of 3, Impt. 350.00
P# block of 6, Impt. 2,100.

232 A121 8c **violet black** *(49,033)* 50.00 15.00
Never hinged 125.00
On cover 300.00
Block of 4 250.00 100.00
P# strip of 3, Impt. 275.00
P# block of 6, Impt. 1,500.

233 A122 10c **pale red brown** *(300,179)* 35.00 2.25
Never hinged 80.00
On cover 27.50
Block of 4 160.00 20.00
P# strip of 3, Impt. 175.00
P# block of 6, Impt. 1,000.
a. 10c **red brown** 30.00 3.00
Never hinged 70.00
On cover 35.00
Block of 4 140.00 32.50
P# strip of 3, Impt. 150.00
P# block of 6, Impt. 1,200.
b. Pair, one without overprint *1,500.*

234 A123 13c **purple black** *(91,341)* 35.00 17.50
Never hinged 80.00
a. 13c **brown violet** 35.00 17.50
Never hinged 80.00
On cover 55.00
Block of 4 150.00 110.00
P# strip of 3, Impt. 175.00
P# block of 6, Impt. 1,350.

235 A124 15c **olive green** *(183,965)* 60.00 15.00
Never hinged 135.00
On cover 100.00
Block of 4 275.00 100.00
P# strip of 3, Impt. 300.00
P# block of 6, Impt. 2,000.

236 A125 50c **orange** *(57,641)* 125.00 35.00
Never hinged 275.00
On cover 300.00
Block of 4 575.00 275.00
P# strip of 3, Impt. 575.00
P# block of 6, Impt. *17,500.*
Nos. 226-236 (11) 566.00 144.75

Same Overprint in Red On U.S. Stamps Nos. 311, 312 and 313

237 A126 $1 **black** *(5617)* 450.00 250.00
Never hinged 1,000.
On cover 750.00
Block of 4 2,100. 1,850.
P# strip of 3, Impt. 2,100.
P# block of 6, Impt. *8,500.*

238 A127 $2 **dark blue** *(695)* 750.00 *800.00*
Never hinged 1,800.
Block of 4 *3,400.* —
P# strip of 3, Impt. *3,600.*
P# block of 6, Impt. *16,000.*

239 A128 $5 **dark green** *(746)* 1,000. *5,000.*
Never hinged 2,250.
Block of 4 *4,250.* —
P# strip of 3, Impt. *4,750.*
P# block of 6, Impt. —

Same Overprint in Black On U.S. Stamp No. 319

240 A129 2c **carmine** *(862,245)* 7.00 2.25
Never hinged 16.00
On cover 3.50
Block of 4 30.00 15.00
P# strip of 3, Impt. 40.00
P# block of 6, Impt. 325.00
a. Booklet pane of 6 *1,100.*
b. 2c **scarlet** 7.50 2.75
Never hinged 18.00
On cover 4.00
Block of 4 32.50 17.50
P# strip of 3, Impt. 42.50
P# block of 6, Impt. 350.00
c. As "b," booklet pane of 6 —

Dates of issue:
Sept. 20, 1903, Nos. 226, 227, 236.
Jan. 4, 1904, Nos. 230, 234, 235, 237, 240a.
Nov. 1, 1904, Nos. 228, 229, 231, 232, 233, 238, 239, 240.
Nos. 212 to 240 became obsolete on Sept. 8, 1906, the remainders being destroyed.

Special Printing

Two sets of special printings exist of the 1903-04 issue. The first consists of Nos. 226, 230, 234, 235, 236, 237 and 240. These were made for display at the St. Louis Exposition. All but a few stamps were destroyed. Most of the existing examples have the handstamp "Special Surcharge" on the back. Value: No. 237, $1,550; others $900; J6, J7, $1,150:

In 1907 the entire set Nos. 226, 228 to 240, J1 to J7 were specially printed for the Bureau of Insular Affairs on very white paper. They are difficult to distinguish from the ordinary stamps except the Special Delivery stamp which is on U.S. No. E6 (see Philippines No. E2A). Value: No. 237, $1,300; No. 238, $2,600; No. 239, $3,500; others, $775.

Regular Issue

José Rizal — A40

Printed by the U.S. Bureau of Engraving and Printing.
Plates of 400 subjects in four panes of 100 each.

Booklet panes Nos. 240a, 241b, 242b, 261a, 262b, 276a, 277a, 285a, 286a, 290e, 291b and 292c were made from plates of 180 subjects. No. 214b came from plates of 360 subjects.

Designs: 4c, McKinley. 6c, Ferdinand Magellan. 8c, Miguel Lopez de Legaspi. 10c, Gen. Henry W. Lawton. 12c, Lincoln. 16c, Adm. William T. Sampson. 20c, Washington. 26c, Francisco Carriedo. 30c, Franklin. 1p-10p, Arms of City of Manila.

Wmk. Double-lined PIPS (191)

1906, Sept. 8 ***Perf. 12***

241 A40 2c **deep green** *(51,000,019)* .40 .20
Never hinged 1.00
Block of 4 1.75 .20
a. 2c **yellow green** ('10) .60 .20
Never hinged 1.50
Double transfer *40.00*
b. Booklet pane of 6 *(720,120)* 750.00 *800.00*
Never hinged *1,500.*

242 A40 4c **carmine** *(11,000,019)* .50 .20
Never hinged 1.25
Block of 4 2.25 .20
a. 4c **carmine lake** ('10) 1.00 .20
Never hinged 2.50
b. Booklet pane of 6*(300,600)* *650.00 700.00*
Never hinged *1,250.*

243 A40 6c **violet** *(1,980,019)* 2.50 .20
Never hinged 6.25
Block of 4 11.00 .85

244 A40 8c **brown** *(770,019)* 4.50 .90
Never hinged 11.00
Block of 4 20.00 6.00

245 A40 10c **blue** *(5,500,019)* 3.50 .30
Never hinged 8.75
a. 10c **dark blue** 3.50 .30
Never hinged 8.75
Block of 4 15.00 1.25

246 A40 12c **brown lake** *(670,019)* 9.00 2.50
Never hinged 22.50
Block of 4 42.50 17.00

247 A40 16c **violet black** *(1,300,019)* 6.00 .35
Never hinged 15.00
Block of 4 30.00 2.00

248 A40 20c **orange brown** *(2,100,019)* 7.00 .35
Never hinged 17.50
Block of 4 35.00 2.25

249 A40 26c **violet brown** *(428,000)* 11.00 3.00
Never hinged 27.50
Block of 4 50.00 20.00

250 A40 30c **olive green** *(1,256,019)* 6.50 1.75
Never hinged 16.00
Block of 4 32.50 8.75

251 A40 1p **orange** *(200,019)* 45.00 7.50
Never hinged 110.00
Block of 4 200.00 40.00

252 A40 2p **black** *(100,000)* 55.00 1.75
Never hinged 140.00
Block of 4 250.00 10.00

253 A40 4p **dark blue** *(10,000)* 160.00 20.00
Never hinged 375.00
Block of 4 700.00 90.00

254 A40 10p **dark green** *(6,019)* 275.00 80.00
Never hinged 675.00
Block of 4 1,250. 400.00
Nos. 241-254 (14) 585.90 119.00

1909

Change of Colors

255 A40 12c **red orange** *(300,000)* 11.00 3.00
Never hinged 27.50
Block of 4 52.50 15.00

256 A40 16c **olive green** *(500,000)* 6.00 .75
Never hinged 15.00
Block of 4 27.50 3.50

257 A40 20c **yellow** *(800,000)* 9.00 1.25
Never hinged 22.50
Block of 4 42.50 7.50

258 A40 26c **blue green** *(250,000)* 3.50 .75
Never hinged 8.75
Block of 4 16.00 4.00

259 A40 30c **ultramarine** *(600,000)* 13.00 3.50
Never hinged 32.50
Block of 4 60.00 22.50

260 A40 1p **pale violet** *(100,000)* 45.00 5.00
Never hinged 110.00
Block of 4 225.00 32.50

260A A40 2p **violet brown** *(50,000)* 100.00 4.00
Never hinged 250.00
Block of 4 475.00 25.00
Nos. 255-260A (7) 187.50 18.25

1911 **Wmk. Single-lined PIPS (190)** ***Perf. 12***

261 A40 2c **green** *(44,000,000)* .75 .20
Never hinged 1.80
Block of 4 5.00 .35
a. Booklet pane of 6 *(896,160)* *800.00 900.00*
Never hinged *1,400.*

262 A40 4c **carmine lake** *(6,000,000)* 3.00 .20
Never hinged 6.75
Block of 4 14.00 .35
a. 4c **carmine** — —
b. Booklet pane of 6 *(100,020)* *600.00 700.00*
Never hinged *1,100.*

263 A40 6c **deep violet** *(3,200,000)* 3.00 .20
Never hinged 6.75
Block of 4 13.00 .30

264 A40 8c **brown** *(1,400,000)* 9.50 .50
Never hinged 21.50
Block of 4 45.00 2.25

265 A40 10c **blue** *(3,700,000)* 4.00 .20
Never hinged 9.00
Block of 4 19.00 .30

266 A40 12c **orange** *(1,320,000)* 4.00 .45
Never hinged 9.00
Block of 4 17.50 2.10

267 A40 16c **olive green** *(1,000,000)* 4.50 .40
Never hinged 10.00
a. 16c **pale olive green** 4.50 .50
Never hinged 10.00
Block of 4 20.00 1.60

268 A40 20c **yellow** *(3,000,000)* 3.50 .20
Never hinged 7.75
Block of 4 15.00 .65
a. 20c **orange** 4.00 .30
Never hinged 9.00
Block of 4 17.00 1.40

269 A40 26c **blue green** *(249,900)* 6.00 .30
Never hinged 13.50
Block of 4 27.50 1.50

270 A40 30c **ultramarine** *(1,000,000)* 6.00 .50
Never hinged 13.50
Block of 4 27.50 2.50

271 A40 1p **pale violet** *(694,000)* 27.50 .60
Never hinged 62.50
Block of 4 140.00 3.00

272 A40 2p **violet brown** *(100,000)* 45.00 1.00
Never hinged 100.00
Block of 4 200.00 6.25

273 A40 4p **deep blue** *(10,000)* 700.00 110.00
Never hinged 1,400.
Block of 4 3,250. 550.00

274 A40 10p **deep green** *(20,000)* 250.00 32.50
Never hinged 500.00
Block of 4 1,100. 160.00
Nos. 261-274 (14) 1,066. 147.25

1914

275 A40 30c **gray** *(700,000)* 12.00 .50
Never hinged 27.50
Block of 4 57.50 3.00

1914 ***Perf. 10***

276 A40 2c **green** *(60,000,000)* 2.00 .20
Never hinged 4.50
Block of 4 8.50 .45
a. Booklet pane of 6 *(400,080)* *750.00 800.00*
Never hinged *1,250.*

277 A40 4c **carmine** *(2,500,000)* 3.50 .30

Never hinged 8.50
Block of 4 15.00 .85
a. Booklet pane of 6 *(56,040)* *750.00*
Never hinged *1,300.*
278 A40 6c **light violet** *(700,000)* 45.00 9.50
Never hinged 100.00
Block of 4 210.00 55.00
a. 6c **deep violet** 50.00 6.25
Never hinged 110.00
Block of 4 220.00 35.00
279 A40 8c **brown** *(200,000)* 50.00 10.50
Never hinged 110.00
Block of 4 220.00 57.50
280 A40 10c **dark blue** *(2,000,000)* 30.00 .20
Never hinged 67.50
Block of 4 130.00 1.00
281 A40 16c **olive green** *(700,000)* 100.00 5.00
Never hinged 225.00
Block of 4 450.00 29.00
282 A40 20c **orange** *(2,000,000)* 32.50 1.00
Never hinged 75.00
Block of 4 150.00 5.75
283 A40 30c **gray** *(1,300,000)* 70.00 4.50
Never hinged 150.00
Block of 4 300.00 17.50
284 A40 1p **pale violet** *(198,000)* 140.00 3.75
Never hinged 300.00
Block of 4 600.00 22.50
Nos. 276-284 (9) 473.00 34.95

1918 ***Perf. 11***
285 A40 2c **green** *(40,000,000)* 21.00 4.25
Never hinged 40.00
Block of 4 92.50 18.00
a. Booklet pane of 6 *(50,040)* *750.00 800.00*
Never hinged *1,300.*
286 A40 4c **carmine** *(3,000,000)* 26.00 2.50
Never hinged 55.00
Block of 4 115.00 12.50
a. Booklet pane of 6 *1,350. 2,000.*
287 A40 6c **deep violet** *(1,000,000)* 40.00 1.75
Never hinged 90.00
Block of 4 175.00 8.50
287A A40 8c **light brown** *(200,000)* 220.00 25.00
Never hinged 400.00
Block of 4 925.00 160.00
288 A40 10c **dark blue** *(2,000,000)* 60.00 1.50
Never hinged 140.00
Block of 4 260.00 8.00
289 A40 16c **olive green** *(700,000)* 110.00 7.50
Never hinged 250.00
Block of 4 525.00 32.50
289A A40 20c **orange** *(1,000,000)* 85.00 8.00
Never hinged 200.00
Block of 4 400.00 42.50
289C A40 30c **gray** *(500,000)* 95.00 13.00
Never hinged 215.00
Block of 4 400.00 62.50
289D A40 1p **pale violet** *(200,000)* 100.00 17.50
Never hinged 225.00
Block of 4 425.00 92.50
Nos. 285-289D (9) 757.00 81.00

1917 **Unwmk.** ***Perf. 11***
290 A40 2c **yellow green** *(444,746,800)* .25 .20
Never hinged .55
Block of 4 1.10 .20
a. 2c **dark green** .30 .20
Never hinged .65
green .20 .20
Double transfer — —
b. Vert. pair, imperf. horiz. *1,500.*
c. Horiz. pair, imperf. between *1,500.* —
d. Vertical pair, imperf. btwn. *1,750. 1,000.*
e. Booklet pane of 6 *(3,251,080)* 27.50 *30.00*
Never hinged 60.00
291 A40 4c **carmine** *(50,579,100)* .30 .20
Never hinged .65
Block of 4 1.35 .30
a. 4c **light rose** .30 .20
Never hinged .65
Block of 4 1.25 .20
b. Booklet pane of 6 *(500,820)* 20.00 *22.50*
Never hinged 35.00
292 A40 6c **deep violet** *(8,803,600)* .35 .20
Never hinged .70
Block of 4 1.50 .30
a. 6c **lilac** .40 .20
Never hinged .80
b. 6c **red violet** .40 .20
Never hinged .70
c. Booklet pane of 6 *(75)* *550.00 800.00*
Never hinged *900.00*
293 A40 8c **yellow brown** *(6,036,700)* .35 .20
Never hinged .45
a. 8c **orange brown** .35 .20
Never hinged .45
Block of 4 1.75 .35
294 A40 10c **deep blue**(15,848,800) .30 .20
Never hinged .65
Block of 4 1.25 .25
295 A40 12c **red orange** *(3,396,500)* .35 .20
Never hinged .75
Block of 4 1.50 .50
296 A40 16c **light olive green** *(3,249,600)* 65.00 .25
Never hinged 130.00
Block of 4 300.00 1.25
a. 16c **olive bister** 65.00 .50
Never hinged 130.00
297 A40 20c **orange yellow** *(10,814,600)* .35 .20
Never hinged .75
Block of 4 2.25 .30
298 A40 26c **green** *(1,595,400)* .50 .45
Never hinged 1.10
Block of 4 2.25 2.10
a. 26c **blue green** .60 .25

Never hinged 1.35
299 A40 30c **gray** *(6,031,300)* .55 .20
Never hinged 1.35
Block of 4 2.60 .35
Dark gray .55 .20
300 A40 1p **pale violet** *(1,173,200)* 40.00 1.00
Never hinged 90.00
Block of 4 175.00 4.50
a. 1p **red lilac** 40.00 1.00
Never hinged 90.00
Block of 4 175.00 4.50
b. 1p **pale rose lilac** 40.00 1.10
Never hinged 90.00
Block of 4 175.00 4.50
301 A40 2p **violet brown** *(475,300)* 35.00 1.00
Never hinged 77.50
Block of 4 160.00 4.75
302 A40 4p **blue** *(541,800)* 32.50 .50
Never hinged 72.50
Block of 4 150.00 2.25
a. 4p **dark blue** 35.00 .55
Never hinged 77.50
Nos. 290-302 (13) 175.80 4.80

1923-26
303 A40 16c **olive bister** *(Adm. George Dewey) (13,524,300)* 1.00 .20
Never hinged 2.25
Block of 4 4.75 .45
a. 16c **olive green** 1.25 .20
Never hinged 2.75
304 A40 10p **deep green** ('26) *(32,400)* 50.00 6.00
Never hinged 110.00
Block of 4 210.00 27.50

Legislative Palace Issue

Issued to commemorate the opening of the Legislative Palace.

Legislative Palace — A42

Printed by the Philippine Bureau of Printing.

1926, Dec. 20 **Unwmk.** ***Perf. 12***
319 A42 2c **green & black** *(502,300)* .50 .25
Never hinged 1.25
First day cover 3.50
Block of 4 2.25 1.10
a. Horiz. pair, imperf. between *300.00*
b. Vert. pair, imperf. between *575.00*
320 A42 4c **carmine & black** *(304,150)* .55 .40
Never hinged 1.20
First day cover 3.50
Block of 4 2.50 1.60
a. Horiz. pair, imperf. between *325.00*
b. Vert. pair, imperf. between *600.00*
321 A42 16c **olive green & black** *(203,500)* 1.00 .65
Never hinged 2.25
First day cover 10.00
Block of 4 5.00 3.00
a. Horiz. pair, imperf. between *350.00*
b. Vert. pair, imperf. between *625.00*
c. Double impression of center *675.00*
322 A42 18c **light brown & black** *(103,700)* 1.10 .50
Never hinged 2.50
First day cover 10.00
Block of 4 5.00 2.25
a. Double impression of center *(150)* *1,250.*
b. Vertical pair, imperf. between *675.00*
323 A42 20c **orange & black** *(103,200)* 2.00 1.00
Never hinged 4.50
Block of 4 8.50 5.00
a. 20c **orange & brown** *(100)* *600.00* —
b. As No. 323, imperf., pair *(50)* *575.00 575.00*
c. As "a," imperf., pair *(100)* *1,750.*
d. Vert. pair, imperf. between *700.00*
324 A42 24c **gray & black** *(103,100)* 1.00 .55
Never hinged 2.25
Block of 4 4.50 2.50
a. Vert. pair, imperf. between *700.00*
325 A42 1p **rose lilac & black** *(10,800)* 47.50 32.50
Never hinged 70.00
Block of 4 200.00 150.00
a. Vert. pair, imperf. between *700.00*
First day cover, #319-325 400.00
Nos. 319-325 (7) 53.65 35.85

No. 322a is valued in the grade of fine.

Coil Stamp
Rizal Type of 1906
Printed by the U.S. Bureau of Engraving and Printing.

1928 **Unwmk.** ***Perf. 11 Vertically***
326 A40 2c **green** *(110,000)* 7.50 *15.00*
Never hinged 18.75
Pair 17.50 *37.50*
Line pair 55.00 *100.00*
Never hinged 140.00

Types of 1906-1923

1925-31 **Unwmk.** ***Imperf.***
340 A40 2c **yellow green** ('31) *(99,986)* .40 .40
Never hinged .90
Block of 4 1.75 1.75
a. 2c **green** ('25) *(51,000)* 1.75 .60
Never hinged 1.80
341 A40 4c **carmine rose** ('31) *(49,855)* .45 .40
Never hinged 1.00
Block of 4 2.00 1.75
a. 4c **carmine** ('25) *(25,500)* 1.20 .60
Never hinged 2.75
Block of 4 5.25 4.00
342 A40 6c **violet** ('31) *(10,000)* 2.00 1.75
Never hinged 4.00
Block of 4 8.50 7.50
a. 6c **deep violet** ('25) *(5,200)* 12.00 6.00
Never hinged 13.50
343 A40 8c **brown** ('31) *(10,000)* 2.00 2.00
Never hinged 4.00
Block of 4 8.50 8.25
a. 8c **yellow brown** ('25) *(5,200)* 12.00 6.00
Never hinged 13.50
344 A40 10c **blue** ('31) *(7,000)* 3.75 3.00
Never hinged 7.50
Block of 4 16.00 11.00
a. 10c **deep blue** ('25) *(2,200)* 45.00 16.00
Never hinged 100.00
345 A40 12c **deep orange** ('31) *(7,000)* 5.00 4.00
Never hinged 11.00
Block of 4 21.00 17.00
a. 12c **red orange** ('25) *(2,200)* 55.00 30.00
Never hinged 125.00
346 A40 16c **olive green** *(Dewey)* ('31) *(7,000)* 3.50 3.00
Never hinged 7.00
Block of 4 15.00 12.50
a. 16c **bister green** ('25) *(2,200)* 40.00 12.50
Never hinged 90.00
347 A40 20c **deep yellow orange** ('31) *(7,000)* 4.00 3.00
Never hinged 8.00
Block of 4 17.00 12.50
a. 20c **yellow orange** ('25) *(2,200)* 42.50 15.00
Never hinged 95.00
348 A40 26c **green** ('31) *(7,000)* 4.00 3.50
Never hinged 8.00
Block of 4 17.00 12.50
a. 26c **blue green** ('25) *(2,200)* 45.00 16.00
Never hinged 100.00
349 A40 30c **light gray** ('31) *(7,000)* 5.00 4.00
Never hinged 10.00
Block of 4 21.00 13.00
a. 30c **gray** ('25) *(2,200)* 45.00 16.00
Never hinged 100.00
350 A40 1p **light violet** ('31) *(6,395)* 7.50 7.00
Never hinged 15.00
Block of 4 35.00 29.00
a. 1p **violet** ('25) *(2,100)* 175.00 85.00
Never hinged 375.00
351 A40 2p **brown violet** ('31) *(3,612)* 18.00 15.00
Never hinged 35.00
Block of 4 75.00 62.50
a. 2p **violet brown** ('25) *(600)* 375.00 200.00
Never hinged 625.00
352 A40 4p **blue** ('31) *(2,570)* 65.00 55.00
Never hinged 125.00
Block of 4 300.00 —
a. 4p **deep blue** ('25) *(300)* 2,000. 875.00
Never hinged 3,350.
353 A40 10p **green** ('31) *(2,208)* 135.00 130.00
Never hinged 220.00
Block of 4 575.00
a. 10p **deep green** ('25) *(200)* 2,875. 1,550.
Never hinged 4,750.
Nos. 340-353 (14) 255.60 232.05

Nos. 340a-353a were the original post office issue. These were reprinted twice in 1931 for sale to collectors (Nos. 340-353).

Mount Mayon, Luzon — A43

Post Office, Manila — A44

Pier No. 7, Manila Bay — A45

Vernal Falls, Yosemite Park, California (See Footnote) — A46

Rice Planting — A47

Rice Terraces — A48

Baguio Zigzag — A49

1932, May 3			Unwmk.	*Perf. 11*	
354	A43	2c	**yellow green**(5,432,000)	.60	.30
			Never hinged	.90	
			First day cover		2.00
			Block of 4	3.00	1.25
355	A44	4c	**rose carmine** *(1,602,800)*	.60	.30
			Never hinged	.90	
			First day cover		2.00
			Block of 4	3.00	1.25
356	A45	12c	**orange** *(483,000)*	.75	.60
			Never hinged	1.10	
			First day cover		6.50
			Block of 4	3.25	2.25
357	A46	18c	**red orange** *(983,400)*	30.00	10.00
			Never hinged	45.00	
			First day cover		16.00
			Block of 4	130.00	45.00
358	A47	20c	**yellow** *(441,000)*	1.00	.65
			Never hinged	1.50	
			First day cover		6.50
			Block of 4	4.25	2.50
359	A48	24c	**deep violet** *(425,000)*	1.50	.80
			Never hinged	2.25	
			First day cover		6.50
			Block of 4	6.25	4.75
360	A49	32c	**olive brown** *(510,600)*	1.40	.80
			Never hinged	2.10	
			First day cover		6.50
			Block of 4	6.00	4.75
			First day cover, #354-360		50.00
			Nos. 354-360 (7)	35.85	13.45

The 18c vignette was intended to show Pagsanjan Falls in Laguna, central Luzon, and is so labeled. Through error the stamp pictures Vernal Falls in Yosemite National Park, California.

Nos. 302, 302a Surcharged in Orange or Red

1932				
368	A40 1p on 4p **blue** (O) *(134,000)*		5.00	.75
		Never hinged	7.75	
		On cover		.60
		Block of 4	22.50	3.50
a.	1p on 4p **dark blue** (O)		5.00	1.50
		Never hinged	7.75	
369	A40 2p on 4p **dark blue** (R) *(80,000)*		7.50	1.00
		Never hinged	11.00	
a.	2p on 4p **blue** (R)		7.50	1.00
		Never hinged	12.00	
		On cover		.90
		Block of 4	35.00	4.75

Far Eastern Championship

Issued in commemoration of the Tenth Far Eastern Championship Games.

Baseball Players — A50

Tennis Player — A51

Basketball Players — A52

Printed by the Philippine Bureau of Printing.

1934, Apr. 14			Unwmk.	*Perf. 11½*	
380	A50	2c	**yellow brown** *(999,985)*	1.50	.80
			brown	1.50	.80
			Never hinged	2.25	
			First day cover		2.00
			"T" of "Eastern" malformed	2.00	1.25
381	A51	6c	**ultramarine** *(800,000)*	.25	.20
			pale ultramarine	.25	.20
			Never hinged	.30	
			First day cover		1.60
a.			Vertical pair, imperf. between	*1,250.*	
382	A52	16c	**violet brown** *(500,000)*	.50	.50
			dark violet	.50	.50
			Never hinged	.75	
			First day cover		2.25
a.			Vert. pair, imperf. horiz.	*1,750.*	
			Nos. 380-382 (3)	2.25	1.50

José Rizal — A53

Woman and Carabao — A54

La Filipina — A55

Pearl Fishing — A56

Fort Santiago — A57

Salt Spring — A58

Magellan's Landing, 1521 — A59

"Juan de la Cruz" — A60

Rice Terraces — A61

Miguel Lopez de Legaspi and Chief Sikatuna Signing "Blood Compact," 1565 — A62

Barasoain Church, Malolos A63

Battle of Manila Bay, 1898 — A64

Montalban Gorge — A65

George Washington — A66

Printed by U.S. Bureau of Engraving and Printing.

1935, Feb. 15 **Unwmk.** ***Perf. 11***

383	A53	2c	**rose** *(62,183,400)*	.20	.20
			Never hinged	.25	
			First day cover		1.00
384	A54	4c	**yellow green** *(14,238,193)*	.20	.20
			Light yellow green	.20	.20
			Never hinged	.25	
			First day cover		1.00
385	A55	6c	**dark brown** *(1,958,928)*	.25	.20
			Never hinged	.35	
			First day cover		1.00
386	A56	8c	**violet** *(792,000)*	.25	.20
			Never hinged	.35	
			First day cover		1.60
387	A57	10c	**rose carmine** *(341,400)*	.30	.20
			Never hinged	.45	
			First day cover		1.60
388	A58	12c	**black** *(319,500)*	.35	.20
			Never hinged	.50	
			First day cover		1.60
389	A59	16c	**dark blue** *(2,422,778)*	.35	.20
			Never hinged	.55	
			First day cover		1.60
390	A60	20c	**light olive green** *(1,061,400)*	.35	.20
			Never hinged	.45	
			First day cover		2.25
391	A61	26c	**indigo** *(212,000)*	.40	.25
			Never hinged	.60	
			First day cover		3.00
392	A62	30c	**orange red** *(171,200)*	.40	.25
			Never hinged	.60	
			First day cover		3.00
393	A63	1p	**red orange & black** *(80,000)*	2.00	1.25
			Never hinged	3.00	
			First day cover		8.25
394	A64	2p	**bister brown & black** *(61,100)*	8.00	1.25
			Never hinged	11.00	
			First day cover		14.00
395	A65	4p	**blue & black** *(59,000)*	7.00	3.50
			Never hinged	10.50	
			First day cover		20.00
396	A66	5p	**green & black** *(54,000)*	20.00	3.50
			Never hinged	30.00	
			First day cover		27.50
			Nos. 383-396 (14)	40.05	11.60

USED VALUES

Used values in italics are for postally used examples with cancels of the proper function during the correct period of use.

Issues of the Commonwealth

Commonwealth Inauguration Issue

Issued to commemorate the inauguration of the Philippine Commonwealth, Nov. 15, 1935.

"The Temples of Human Progress" A67

1935, Nov. 15 **Unwmk.** ***Perf. 11***

397	A67	2c	**carmine rose** *(1,531,000)*	.25	.20
			Never hinged	.30	
			First day cover		1.00
398	A67	6c	**deep violet** *(523,000)*	.25	.20
			Never hinged	.30	
			First day cover		1.00
399	A67	16c	**blue** *(313,500)*	.25	.20
			Never hinged	.35	
			First day cover		1.00
400	A67	36c	**yellow green** *(261,000)*	.40	.30
			Never hinged	.60	
			First day cover		1.40
401	A67	50c	**brown** *(218,500)*	.60	.55
			Never hinged	.90	
			First day cover		2.00
			Nos. 397-401 (5)	1.75	1.45

Jose Rizal Issue

75th anniversary of the birth of Jose Rizal (1861-1896), national hero of the Filipinos.

Jose Rizal — A68

Printed by the Philippine Bureau of Printing.

1936, June 19 **Unwmk.** ***Perf. 12***

402	A68	2c	**yellow brown** *(500,000)*	.20	.20
			light yellow brown	.20	.20
			Never hinged	.25	
			First day cover		1.00
403	A68	6c	**slate blue** *(300,000)*	.20	.20
			light slate green	.20	.20
			Never hinged	.25	
			First day cover		1.00
a.			Imperf. vertically, pair	*1,350.*	
			Never hinged	*1,950.*	
404	A68	36c	**red brown** *(200,000)*	.50	.45
			light red brown	.50	.45
			Never hinged	.75	
			First day cover		2.25
			Nos. 402-404 (3)	.90	.85

Commonwealth Anniversary Issue

Issued in commemoration of the first anniversary of the Commonwealth.

President Manuel L. Quezon — A69

Printed by U.S. Bureau of Engraving and Printing.

1936, Nov. 15 **Unwmk.** ***Perf. 11***

408	A69	2c	**orange brown** *(4,946,816)*	.20	.20
			Never hinged	.30	
			First day cover		1.00
409	A69	6c	**yellow green** *(1,019,900)*	.20	.20
			Never hinged	.30	
			First day cover		1.00
410	A69	12c	**ultramarine** *(527,600)*	.20	.20
			Never hinged	.30	
			First day cover		1.50
			Nos. 408-410 (3)	.60	.60

Stamps of 1935 Overprinted in Black

a

b

1936-37 **Unwmk.** ***Perf. 11***

411	A53(a)	2c	**rose,** *Dec. 28, 1936 (84,092,400)*	.20	.20
			Never hinged	.25	
			First day cover		*35.00*
a.			Bklt. pane of 6, *Jan. 15 1937 (239,492)*	2.50	2.00
			Never hinged	4.00	
			First day cover		*40.00*
412	A54(b)	4c	**yellow green,** *Mar. 29, 1937 (100,000)*	.50	*4.00*
			Never hinged	.75	
413	A55(a)	6c	**dark brown,** *Oct. 7, 1936 (2,230,394)*	.20	.20
			Never hinged	.25	
			On cover		.20
414	A56(b)	8c	**violet,** *Mar. 29, 1937 (627,500)*	.25	.20
			Never hinged	.35	
			On cover		.25
415	A57(b)	10c	**rose carmine,** *Dec. 28, 1936 (1,687,550)*	.20	.20
			Never hinged	.25	
			First day cover		35.00
a.			"COMMONWEALT"	20.00	—
			Never hinged	30.00	
416	A58(b)	12c	**black,** *Mar. 29, 1937 (2,118,600)*	.20	.20
			Never hinged	.30	
			On cover		.20
417	A59(b)	16c	**dark blue,** *Oct. 7, 1936 (597,300)*	.30	.20
			Never hinged	.45	
			On cover		.20
418	A60(a)	20c	**lt olive green,** *Mar. 29, 1937 (100,000)*	1.00	.40
			Never hinged	1.60	
			On cover		.45
419	A61(b)	26c	**indigo,** *Mar. 29, 1937 (100,000)*	.90	.35
			Never hinged	1.50	
			On cover		.40
420	A62(b)	30c	**orange red,** *Dec. 28, 1936 (836,252)*	.50	.20
			Never hinged	.80	
			First day cover		*35.00*
421	A63(b)	1p	**red org & blk,** *Oct. 7, 1936 (319,250)*	1.00	.25
			Never hinged	1.60	
			On cover		.40
422	A64(b)	2p	**bis brn & blk,** *Mar. 29, 1937 (50,000)*	10.00	3.00
			Never hinged	15.00	
			On cover		3.50
423	A65(b)	4p	**blue & blk,** *Mar. 29, 1937 (30,000)*	35.00	6.50
			Never hinged	55.00	
			On cover		*50.00*
424	A66(b)	5p	**green & blk,** *Mar. 29, 1937 (60,500)*	10.00	2.50
			Never hinged	15.00	
			On cover		*35.00*
			Nos. 411-424 (14)	60.25	18.40
			Set, Never hinged	93.10	

Eucharistic Congress Issue

Issued to commemorate the 33rd International Eucharistic Congress held at Manila, Feb. 3-7, 1937.

Map, Symbolical of the Eucharistic Congress Spreading Light of Christianity — A70

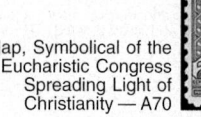

FLAT PLATE PRINTING

Plates of 256 subjects in four panes of 64 each.

1937, Feb. 3 **Unwmk.** ***Perf. 11***

425	A70	2c	**yellow green** *(4,102,848)*	.20	.20
			Never hinged	.25	
			First day cover		1.00
426	A70	6c	**light brown** *(2,626,240)*	.20	.20
			Never hinged	.25	
			First day cover		1.00
427	A70	12c	**sapphire** *(2,165,440)*	.20	.20
			Never hinged	.25	
			First day cover		1.00
428	A70	20c	**deep orange** *(1,640,640)*	.30	.20
			Never hinged	.50	
			First day cover		1.00
429	A70	36c	**deep violet** *(1,115,840)*	.55	.40
			Never hinged	.80	
			First day cover		1.40
430	A70	50c	**carmine** *(1,115,840)*	.70	.35
			Never hinged	1.10	
			First day cover		2.00
			Nos. 425-430 (6)	2.15	1.55
			Set, Never hinged	3.15	

Arms of City of Manila — A71

1937, Aug. 27 **Unwmk.** ***Perf. 11***

431	A71	10p	**gray** *(70,000)*	6.00	2.00
			Never hinged	8.50	
432	A71	20p	**henna brown** *(90,600)*	5.00	1.40
			Never hinged	8.00	
			First day cover, #431-432		50.00

Stamps of 1935 Overprinted in Black:

a

b

1938-40 **Unwmk.** ***Perf. 11***

433	A53(a)	2c	**rose,** *1939 (103,549,959)*	.20	.20
			Never hinged	.25	
a.			Booklet pane of 6 *(157,176)*	3.50	2.50
			Never hinged	5.50	
b.			As "a," lower left-hand stamp overprinted "WEALTH COMMON-" *(24)*	*4,000.*	
c.			Hyphen omitted	—	—
434	A54(b)	4c	**yellow green,** *1940 (72,500)*	3.00	*30.00*
			Never hinged	4.75	
435	A55(a)	6c	**dark brown,** *May 12, 1939 (4,013,440)*	.25	.20
			Never hinged	.40	
			First day cover		*35.00*
a.			6c golden brown	.25	.20
			Never hinged	.40	
436	A56(b)	8c	**violet,** *1939 (1,583,357)*	.20	.20
			Never hinged	.25	
a.			"COMMONWEALT" (LR 31)	90.00	
			Never hinged	140.00	
437	A57(b)	10c	**rose carmine,** *May 12, 1939 (2,695,242)*	.20	.20
			Never hinged	.25	
a.			"COMMONWEALT" (LR 31)	65.00	—
			Never hinged	100.00	
438	A58(b)	12c	**black,** *1940 (3,765,000)*	.20	.20
			Never hinged	.25	
439	A59(b)	16c	**dark blue** *(1,415,700)*	.20	.20
			Never hinged	.25	
440	A60(a)	20c	**light olive green,** *1939 (1,663,799)*	.20	.20
			Never hinged	.25	
441	A61(b)	26c	**indigo,** *1940 (597,500)*	.30	.20
			Never hinged	.45	
442	A62(b)	30c	**orange red,** *May 23, 1939 (643,100)*	2.50	.70
			Never hinged	4.00	
443	A63(b)	1p	**red org & blk,** *Aug. 29, 1938 (1,065,629)*	.50	.20
			Never hinged	.80	
			First day cover		*40.00*
444	A64(b)	2p	**bister brown & black,** *1939 (98,000)*	6.00	.75
			Never hinged	9.00	
445	A65(b)	4p	**blue & black,** *1940 (6,500)*	275.00	300.00
			Never hinged	450.00	
			On cover		500.00
446	A66(b)	5p	**green & black,** *1940 (31,500)*	16.00	4.00
			Never hinged	26.00	
			Nos. 433-446 (14)	304.75	337.25
			Set, Never hinged	496.90	

Overprint *"b"* measures 18½x1¾mm.

No. 433b occurs in booklet pane, No. 433a, position 5; all examples are straight-edged, left and bottom.

First Foreign Trade Week Issue

Nos. 384, 298a and 432 Surcharged in Red, Violet or Black:

a

b c

1939, July 5

449	A54(a)	2c	on 4c **yellow green** (R) *(500,000)*	.20	.20
			Never hinged	.35	
			First day cover		1.40
450	A40(b)	6c	on 26c **blue green** (V) *(166,700)*	.20	.20
			Never hinged	.35	
			First day cover		2.00
a.			6c on 26c **green**	2.00	.30
			Never hinged	2.50	
451	A71(c)	50c	on 20p **henna brown** (Bk) *(60,000)*	1.25	1.00
			Never hinged	2.00	
			First day cover		5.00
			Nos. 449-451 (3)	1.65	1.40
			Set, Never hinged	2.70	

Commonwealth 4th Anniversary Issue (#452-460)

Triumphal Arch — A72

Printed by U.S. Bureau of Engraving and Printing.

1939, Nov. 15 **Unwmk.** ***Perf. 11***

452	A72	2c	**yellow green** *(1,562,352)*	.20	.20
			Never hinged	.25	
			First day cover		1.00
453	A72	6c	**carmine** *(1,267,717)*	.20	.20
			Never hinged	.25	
			First day cover		1.00
454	A72	12c	**bright blue** *(971,724)*	.20	.20
			Never hinged	.25	
			First day cover		1.40
			Nos. 452-454 (3)	.60	.60
			Set, Never hinged	.75	

Malacañan Palace — A73

1939, Nov. 15 **Unwmk.** ***Perf. 11***

455	A73	2c	**green** *(1,578,600)*	.20	.20
			Never hinged	.25	
			First day cover		1.00
456	A73	6c	**orange** *(1,252,859)*	.20	.20
			Never hinged	.25	
			First day cover		1.00
457	A73	12c	**carmine** *(935,800)*	.20	.20
			Never hinged	.25	
			First day cover		1.40
			Nos. 455-457 (3)	.60	.60
			Set, Never hinged	.75	

President Quezon Taking Oath of Office — A74

1940, Feb. 8 **Unwmk.** ***Perf. 11***

458	A74	2c	**dark orange** *(1,572,400)*	.20	.20
			Never hinged	.25	
			First day cover		1.00
459	A74	6c	**dark green** *(1,257,900)*	.20	.20
			Never hinged	.25	
			First day cover		1.00
460	A74	12c	**purple** *(980,779)*	.25	.20
			Never hinged	.30	
			First day cover		1.40
			Nos. 458-460 (3)	.65	.60
			Set, Never hinged	.80	

José Rizal — A75

ROTARY PRESS PRINTING

1941, Apr. 14 **Unwmk.** ***Perf. 11x10½***

Size: 19x22½mm

461	A75	2c	**apple green** *(59,915,600)*	.20	*.50*
			Never hinged	.25	
			First day cover		1.00
			P# block of 4	1.00	

FLAT PLATE PRINTING

1941-43 **Unwmk.** **Size: 18¾x22mm** ***Perf. 11***

462	A75	2c	**apple green**	.20	*5.00*
			Never hinged	.25	
a.			2c **pale apple green** ('41)	.20	*.50*
			Never hinged	.25	
b.			As No. 462, booklet pane of 6 *(24,000)*	1.25	*50.00*
			Never hinged	2.00	
c.			As "a," booklet pane of 6 ('41) *(114,960)*	2.50	*7.50*
			Never hinged	4.00	

This stamp was issued only in booklet panes and all examples have one or two straight edges.

Further printings were made in 1942 and 1943 in different shades from the first supply of stamps sent to the islands.

Stamps of 1935-41 Handstamped in Violet

1944 **Unwmk.** ***Perf. 11, 11x10½***

463	A53	2c	**rose** (On 411), *Dec. 3 (168)*	325.00	160.00
a.			Booklet pane of 6 *(28)*	*12,500.*	
463B	A53	2c	**rose** (On 433), *Dec. 14 (41)*	*2,000.*	*1,750.*
464	A75	2c	**apple green** (On 461), *Nov. 8 (24,400)*	10.00	8.00
			Never hinged	17.50	
			On cover		17.50
465	A54	4c	**yellow green** (On 384), *Nov. 8 (807)*	42.50	*42.50*
			Never hinged	70.00	
			On cover		—
466	A55	6c	**dark brown** (On 385), *Dec. 14 (64)*	*3,500.*	*2,000.*
			On cover		—
467	A69	6c	**yellow green** (On 409), *Dec. 3*	225.00	*150.00*
			Never hinged	*400.00*	
			On cover		—
468	A55	6c	**dark brown** (On 413), *Dec. 28 (206)*	*4,750.*	*825.00*
469	A72	6c	**carmine** (On 453), *Nov. 8 (235)*	*350.00*	*125.00*
			On cover		—
470	A73	6c	**orange** (On 456), *Dec. 14 (141)*	*1,750.*	*725.00*
			On cover		—

471 A74 6c **dark green** (On 459), *Nov. 8* *275.00* *225.00*
On cover —
472 A56 8c **violet** (On 436), *Nov. 8 (1,643)* 17.50 *24.00*
Never hinged 30.00
On cover —
473 A57 10c **carmine rose** (On 415), *Nov. 8 (450)* *300.00* *150.00*
On cover —
474 A57 10c **carmine rose** (On 437), *Nov. 8 (358)* *275.00* *200.00*
Never hinged *475.00*
On cover —
475 A69 12c **ultramarine** (On 410), *Dec. 3* *1,100.* *400.00*
On cover —
476 A72 12c **bright blue** (On 454), *Nov. 8 (36)* *6,000.* *2,500.*
On cover —
477 A74 12c **purple** (On 460), *Nov. 8* *375.00* *275.00*
On cover —
478 A59 16c **dark blue** (On 389), *Dec. 3 (122)* *2,250.*
479 A59 16c **dark blue** (On 417), *Nov. 8 (200)* *1,250.* *1,000.*
On cover —
480 A59 16c **dark blue** (On 439), *Nov. 8 (500)* *500.00* *200.00*
481 A60 20c **light olive green** (On 440), *Nov. 8 (1,401)* 110.00 35.00
Never hinged 185.00
On cover —
482 A62 30c **orange red** (On 420), *Dec. 3 (248)* *450.00* *1,500.*
On cover —
483 A62 30c **orange red** (On 442), *Dec. 3 (200)* *750.00* *375.00*
On cover —
484 A63 1p **red orange & black** (On 443) *Dec. 3 (21)* *6,250.* *4,500.*
On cover —

Nos. 463-484 are valued in the grade of fine to very fine.
No. 463 comes only from the booklet pane. All examples have one or two straight edges.

Types of 1935-37 Overprinted

a

b

c

1945 **Unwmk.** ***Perf. 11***
485 A53(a) 2c **rose,** *Jan. 19 (65,816,000)* .20 .20
Never hinged .20
First day cover 2.50
486 A54(b) 4c **yellow green,** *Jan. 19 (4,986,800)* .20 .20
Never hinged .20
First day cover 2.50
487 A55(a) 6c **golden brown,** *Jan. 19 (4,381,440)* .20 .20
Never hinged .20
First day cover 2.50
488 A56(b) 8c **violet,** *Jan. 19 (535,000)* .20 .20
Never hinged .25
First day cover 3.00
489 A57(b) 10c **rose carmine,** *Jan. 19 (1,060,000)* .20 .20
Never hinged .20
First day cover 3.00
490 A58(b) 12c **black,** *Jan. 19 (3,214,200)* .20 .20
Never hinged .20
First day cover 3.50
491 A59(b) 16c **dark blue,** *Jan. 19 (1,060,000)* .25 .20
Never hinged .30
First day cover 4.00
492 A60(a) 20c **light olive green,** *Jan. 19 (976,800)* .30 .20
Never hinged .40
First day cover 4.25
493 A62(b) 30c **orange red,** *May 1 (535,000)* .50 .35
Never hinged .75
First day cover 2.50
494 A63(b) 1p **red orange & black,** *Jan. 19 (1,434,400)* 1.10 .25
Never hinged 1.60
First day cover 6.50
495 A71(c) 10p **gray,** *May 1 (22,000)* 45.00 13.50
Never hinged 70.00
First day cover 20.00
496 A71(c) 20p **henna brown,** *May 1 (42,500)* 35.00 15.00
Never hinged 55.00
First day cover 25.00
Nos. 485-496 (12) 83.35 30.70
Set, Never hinged 129.30

José Rizal — A76

ROTARY PRESS PRINTING

1946, May 28 **Unwmk.** ***Perf. 11x10½***
497 A76 2c **sepia** *(53,560,000)* .20 .20
Never hinged .20
P# block of 4 .50

Later issues, released by the Philippine Republic on July 4, 1946, and thereafter, are listed in Scott's Standard Postage Stamp Catalogue, Vol. 5.

AIR POST STAMPS

Madrid-Manila Flight Issue

Issued to commemorate the flight of Spanish aviators Gallarza and Loriga from Madrid to Manila.

Regular Issue of 1917-26 Overprinted in Red or Violet by the Philippine Bureau of Printing

1926, May 13 **Unwmk.** ***Perf. 11***
C1 A40 2c **green** (R) *(9,900)* 18.00 15.00
Never hinged 40.00
First day cover 26.00
Block of 4 80.00 67.50
C2 A40 4c **carmine** (V) *(8,900)* 20.00 17.50
Never hinged 45.00
First day cover 26.00
Block of 4 90.00 80.00
a. Inverted overprint *(100)* *4,000.* —
C3 A40 6c **lilac** (R) *(5,000)* 55.00 55.00
Never hinged 125.00
First day cover 40.00
Block of 4 240.00
C4 A40 8c **orange brown** (V) *(5,000)* 57.50 50.00
Never hinged 130.00
First day cover 40.00
Block of 4 250.00
C5 A40 10c **deep blue** (R) *(5,000)* 57.50 50.00
Never hinged 130.00
First day cover 40.00
Block of 4 250.00
C6 A40 12c **red orange** (V) *(4,000)* 65.00 50.00
Never hinged 145.00
First day cover 42.50
Block of 4 275.00
C7 A40 16c **light olive green** *(Sampson)* (V) *(300)* *3,250.* *1,600.*
Block of 4 —
C8 A40 16c **olive bister** *(Sampson)* (R) *(100)* *5,000.* *3,000.*
Block of 4 —
C9 A40 16c **olive green** *(Dewey)* (V) *(3,600)* 70.00 50.00
Never hinged 160.00
First day cover 42.50
Block of 4 325.00
C10 A40 20c **orange yellow** (V) *(4,000)* 70.00 65.00
Never hinged 160.00
First day cover 42.50
Block of 4 325.00
C11 A40 26c **blue green** (V) *(3,900)* 70.00 65.00
Never hinged 155.00
First day cover 45.00
Block of 4 325.00
C12 A40 30c **gray** (V) *(4,000)* 70.00 65.00
Never hinged 155.00
First day cover 45.00
Block of 4 325.00
C13 A40 2p **violet brown** (R) *(900)* 650.00 300.00
Never hinged 1,200.
On cover 350.00
Block of 4 —
C14 A40 4p **dark blue** (R) *(700)* 750.00 500.00
Never hinged 1,300.
On cover *575.00*
Block of 4 —
C15 A40 10p **deep green** (V) *(500)* 1,350. 700.00
On cover *775.00*
Block of 4 —

Same Overprint on No. 269
Wmk. Single-lined PIPS (190)
Perf. 12

C16 A40 26c **blue green** (V) *(100)* *6,250.*
Block of 4 —

Same Overprint on No. 284
Perf. 10

C17 A40 1p **pale violet** (V) *(2,000)* 225.00 175.00
Never hinged 450.00
On cover 200.00
First day cover *225.00*
Block of 4 950.00

Overprintings of Nos. C1-C6, C9-C15 and C17 were made from two plates. Position No. 89 of the first printing shows broken left blade of propeller.

London-Orient Flight Issue

Issued Nov. 9, 1928, to celebrate the arrival of a British squadron of hydroplanes.

Regular Issue of 1917-25 Overprinted in Red

1928, Nov. 9 **Unwmk.** ***Perf. 11***
C18 A40 2c **green** *(101,200)* 1.00 .50
Never hinged 1.75
First day cover 7.75
C19 A40 4c **carmine** *(50,500)* 1.10 .75
Never hinged 2.00
First day cover 9.50
C20 A40 6c **violet** *(12,600)* 3.50 2.25
Never hinged 6.25
On cover 2.50
C21 A40 8c **orange brown** *(10,000)* 4.00 2.50
Never hinged 7.00
On cover 3.00
C22 A40 10c **deep blue** *(10,000)* 4.00 2.50
Never hinged 7.00
On cover 3.00
C23 A40 12c **red orange** *(8,000)* 5.00 3.25
Never hinged 8.75
On cover 3.75
C24 A40 16c **olive green** (No. 303a) *(12,600)* 4.50 2.50
Never hinged 7.75
On cover 3.00
C25 A40 20c **orange yellow** *(8,000)* 6.00 3.25
Never hinged 10.50
On cover 4.00
C26 A40 26c **blue green** *(7,000)* 16.00 7.25
Never hinged 28.00
On cover 9.25
C27 A40 30c **gray** *(7,000)* 16.00 7.25
Never hinged 28.00
On cover 9.25

Same Overprint on No. 271
Wmk. Single-lined PIPS (190)
Perf. 12

C28 A40 1p **pale violet** *(6,000)* 55.00 30.00
Never hinged 90.00
On cover 34.00
Nos. C18-C28 (11) 116.10 62.00
Set, never hinged 197.00

Von Gronau Issue

Issued commemoration of the visit of Capt. Wolfgang von Gronau's airplane on its round-the-world flight.

Nos. 354-360 Overprinted by the Philippine Bureau of Printing

1932, Sept. 27 Unwmk. *Perf. 11*

C29 A43 2c **yellow green** *(100,000)* .90 .30
Never hinged 1.40
First day cover 2.00
C30 A44 4c **rose carmine** *(80,000)* 1.00 .40
Never hinged 1.60
First day cover 2.00
C31 A45 12c **orange** *(55,000)* 1.25 .65
Never hinged 2.00
On cover 1.00
C32 A46 18c **red orange** *(25,305)* 5.00 3.25
Never hinged 8.00
On cover 3.50
C33 A47 20c **yellow** *(30,000)* 4.00 2.00
Never hinged 6.50
On cover 2.25
C34 A48 24c **deep violet** *(30,000)* 4.00 2.00
Never hinged 6.50
On cover 2.25
C35 A49 32c **olive brown** *(30,000)* 3.50 2.00
Never hinged 5.75
On cover 2.25
First day cover, #C29-C35 35.00
Nos. C29-C35 (7) 19.65 10.60
Set, never hinged 31.75

Rein Issue

Commemorating the flight from Madrid to Manila of the Spanish aviator Fernando Rein y Loring.

Regular Issue of 1917-25 Overprinted in Black

1933, Apr. 11

C36 A40 2c **green** *(95,000)* .75 .45
Never hinged 1.10
First day cover 1.60
C37 A40 4c **carmine** *(75,000)* .90 .45
Never hinged 1.40
First day cover —
C38 A40 6c **deep violet** *(65,000)* 1.10 .80
Never hinged 1.75
First day cover 3.00
C39 A40 8c **orange brown** *(35,000)* 3.75 1.75
Never hinged 5.75
C40 A40 10c **dark blue** *(35,000)* 3.75 1.25
Never hinged 5.75
C41 A40 12c **orange** *(35,000)* 3.75 1.25
Never hinged 5.75
C42 A40 16c **olive green** *(Dewey) (35,000)* 3.50 1.25
Never hinged 5.25
C43 A40 20c **yellow** *(35,000)* 3.75 1.25
Never hinged 5.75
C44 A40 26c **green** *(35,000)* 3.75 1.75
Never hinged 5.75
a. 26c **blue green** 4.00 2.00
Never hinged 6.00
C45 A40 30c **gray** *(30,000)* 4.00 2.00
Never hinged 6.00
First day cover, #C36-C45 40.00
Nos. C36-C45 (10) 29.00 12.20
Set, never hinged 44.25

Stamp of 1917 Overprinted by the Philippine Bureau of Printing

1933, May 26 Unwmk. *Perf. 11*

C46 A40 2c **green** *(500,000)* .65 .40
Never hinged 1.00

Regular Issue of 1932 Overprinted

C47 A44 4c **rose carmine** *(799,878)* .30 .20
Never hinged .45
C48 A45 12c **orange** *(500,000)* .60 .20
Never hinged .90
C49 A47 20c **yellow** *(500,000)* .60 .20
Never hinged .90
C50 A48 24c **deep violet** *(500,000)* .65 .25
Never hinged 1.00
C51 A49 32c **olive brown** *(500,000)* .85 .35
Never hinged 1.40
First day cover, #C46-C51 35.00
Nos. C46-C51 (6) 3.65 1.60
Set, never hinged 4.65

Transpacific Issue

Issued to commemorate the China Clipper flight from Manila to San Francisco, Dec. 2-5, 1935.

Nos. 387, 392 Overprinted in Gold

1935, Dec. 2 Unwmk. *Perf. 11*

C52 A57 10c **rose carmine** *(500,000)* .40 .20
Never hinged .60
First day cover 2.00
C53 A62 30c **orange red** *(300,000)* .60 .35
Never hinged .90
First day cover 3.00

Manila-Madrid Flight Issue

Issued to commemorate the Manila-Madrid flight by aviators Antonio Arnaiz and Juan Calvo.

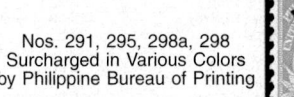

Nos. 291, 295, 298a, 298 Surcharged in Various Colors by Philippine Bureau of Printing

1936, Sept. 6

C54 A40 2c on 4c **carmine** (Bl) *(2,000,000)* .20 .20
Never hinged .25
First day cover 1.00
C55 A40 6c on 12c **red orange** (V) *(500,000)* .20 .20
Never hinged .30
First day cover 3.00
C56 A40 16c on 26c **blue green** (Bk) *(300,000)* .25 .20
Never hinged .40
First day cover 5.00
a. 16c on 26c **green** 2.00 .70
Never hinged 3.00
Nos. C54-C56 (3) .65 .60
Set, never hinged .95

Air Mail Exhibition Issue

Issued to commemorate the first Air Mail Exhibition, held Feb. 17-19, 1939.

Nos. 298a, 298, 431 Surcharged in Black or Red by Philippine Bureau of Printing

1939, Feb. 17

C57 A40 8c on 26c **blue green** (Bk) *(200,000)* 1.00 .40
Never hinged 1.50
First day cover 3.50
a. 8c on 26c **green** (Bk) 3.50 .55
Never hinged 5.25
C58 A71 1p on 10p **gray** (R) *(30,000)* 3.25 2.25
Never hinged 4.75
First day cover 8.00

Moro Vinta and Clipper — AP1

Printed by the US Bureau of Engraving and Printing.

1941, June 30 Unwmk. *Perf. 11*

C59 AP1 8c **carmine** *(210,000)* 2.00 .60
Never hinged 2.75
First day cover 2.00
C60 AP1 20c **ultramarine** *(25,000)* 3.00 .50
Never hinged 4.00
First day cover 2.50
C61 AP1 60c **blue green** *(50,000)* 2.25 1.00
Never hinged 3.00
First day cover 3.50
C62 AP1 1p **sepia** *(1,110,000)* .70 .50
Never hinged 1.00
First day cover 2.25
Nos. C59-C62 (4) 7.95 2.60
Set, never hinged 10.75

No. C47 Handstamped in Violet

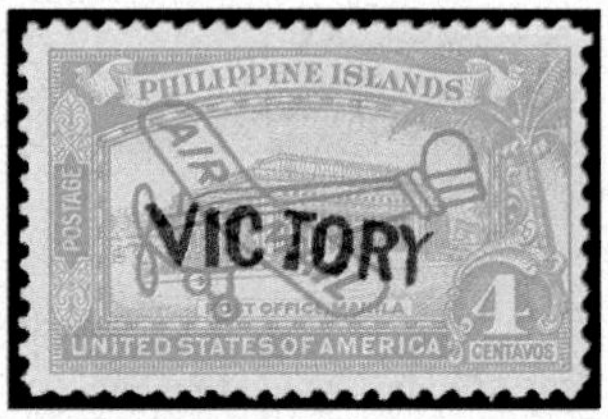

1944, Dec. 3 Unwmk. *Perf. 11*

C63 A44 4c **rose carmine** *(122)* *3,750. 2,750.*
On cover —

SPECIAL DELIVERY STAMPS

U.S. No. E5 Overprinted in Red

a

Printed by U.S. Bureau of Engraving & Printing

Wmk. Double-lined USPS (191)

1901, Oct. 15 *Perf. 12*

E1 SD3 10c **dark blue** *(14,998)* 100. 75.
Never hinged 185.
On cover 350.
Block of 4 500.
P# strip of 3, Impt. 500.
P# block of 6, Impt. *5,000.*
a. Dots in curved frame above messenger (Pl. 882) *175. 160.*
P# block of 6, Impt. (Pl. 882) *5,500.*

Special Delivery Messenger SD2

Wmk. Double-lined PIPS (191)

1906, Sept. 8 *Perf. 12*

E2 SD2 20c **deep ultramarine** *(40,019)* 45.00 8.00
Never hinged 90.00
On cover 17.50
Block of 4 200.00
b. 20c **pale ultramarine** 35.00 8.00
Never hinged 70.00
On cover 17.50
Block of 4 150.00

SPECIAL PRINTING

U.S. No. E6 Overprinted Type "a" in Red

1907 Wmk. Double-lined USPS (191) *Perf. 12*

E2A SD4 10c **ultramarine** *2,750.*
Block of 4 *11,500.*
P# block of 6, Impt. *38,500.*

This stamp was part of the set specially printed for the Bureau of Insular Affairs in 1907. See note following No. 240.

There is only one intact plate block of No. E2A. It is fine and is valued thus.

1911, Apr. Wmk. Single-lined PIPS (190) *Perf. 12*

E3 SD2 20c **deep ultramarine** *(200,000)* 22.00 1.75
Never hinged 42.00
On cover 12.50
Block of 4 90.00

1916 *Perf. 10*

E4 SD2 20c **deep ultramarine** *(200,000)* 175.00 75.00
Never hinged 275.00
On cover 100.00
Block of 4 825.00
pale ultramarine —

Early in 1919 the supply of Special Delivery stamps in the Manila area was exhausted. A Government decree permitted the use of regular issue postage stamps for payment of the special delivery fee when so noted on the cover. This usage was permitted until the new supply of Special Delivery stamps arrived.

1919 **Unwmk.** ***Perf. 11***

E5	SD2 20c **ultramarine** *(4,195,862)*	.60	.20
	Never hinged	.90	
	On cover		5.00
	Block of 4	2.50	
a.	20c **pale blue**	.75	.20
	Never hinged	1.00	
	On cover		5.25
	Block of 4	3.00	
b.	20c **dull violet**	.60	.20
	Never hinged	.90	
	On cover		5.00
	Block of 4	2.50	

Type of 1906 Issue

1925-31 **Unwmk.** ***Imperf.***

E6	SD2 20c **dull violet** ('31) *(6,500)*	30.00	*75.00*
	Never hinged	45.00	
	On cover		250.00
	Block of 4	130.00	
	P# block of 6	400.00	
a.	20c **violet blue** ('25) *(2,100)*	50.00	—
	Never hinged	80.00	
	On cover		—
	Block of 4	250.00	
	P# block of 6	750.00	

Type of 1919 Overprinted in Black

1939, Apr. 27 **Unwmk.** ***Perf. 11***

E7	SD2 20c **blue violet** *(1,253,250)*	.25	.20
	Never hinged	.40	
	First day cover		35.00

Nos. E5b and E7 Handstamped in Violet

1944 **Unwmk.** ***Perf. 11***

E8	SD2 20c **dull violet** (On E5b) *(138)*	*1,400.*	*550.00*
E9	SD2 20c **blue violet** (On E7), *Nov. 8 (600)*	*550.00*	*250.00*
	On cover		—

Type SD2 Overprinted "VICTORY" As No. 486

1945, May 1 **Unwmk.** ***Perf. 11***

E10	SD2 20c **blue violet** *(578,600)*	.70	.55
	Never hinged	1.10	
	First day cover		10.00
a.	"IC" close together	3.25	2.75
	Never hinged	4.75	

SPECIAL DELIVERY OFFICIAL STAMP

Type of 1906 Issue Overprinted

1931 **Unwmk.** ***Perf. 11***

EO1	SD2 20c **dull violet** *(46,750)*	3.00	*75.00*
	Never hinged	4.50	
a.	No period after "B"	35.00	—
	Never hinged	52.50	
b.	Double overprint	—	

It is strongly recommended that expert opinion be acquired for No. EO1 used.

POSTAGE DUE STAMPS

U.S. Nos. J38-J44 Overprinted in Black

Printed by the U.S. Bureau of Engraving and Printing.

Wmk. Double-lined USPS (191)

1899, Aug. 16 ***Perf. 12***

J1	D2 1c **deep claret** *(340,892)*	7.50	2.50
	Never hinged	15.00	
	On cover		30.00
	On cover, used as regular postage		110.00
	P# strip of 3, Impt.	125.00	
	P# block of 6, Impt.	*650.00*	
J2	D2 2c **deep claret** *(306,983)*	7.50	2.50
	Never hinged	15.00	
	On cover		37.50
	P# strip of 3, Impt.	125.00	
	P# block of 6, Impt.	*650.00*	
J3	D2 5c **deep claret** *(34,565)*	15.00	2.50
	Never hinged	30.00	
	On cover		*70.00*
	P# strip of 3, Impt.	200.00	
	P# block of 6, Impt.	*1,500.*	
J4	D2 10c **deep claret** *(15,848)*	19.00	5.50
	Never hinged	37.50	
	On cover		100.00
	P# strip of 3, Impt.	175.00	
	P# block of 6, Impt.	*1,100.*	
J5	D2 50c **deep claret** *(6,168)*	200.00	100.00
	Never hinged	335.00	
	On cover		—
	P# strip of 3, Impt.	1,100.	
	P# block of 6, Impt.	*4,000.*	

No. J1 was used to pay regular postage Sept. 5-19, 1902.

1901, Aug. 31

J6	D2 3c **deep claret** *(14,885)*	17.50	7.00
	Never hinged	35.00	
	On cover		60.00
	P# strip of 3, Impt.	175.00	
	P# block of 6, Impt.	*875.00*	
J7	D2 30c **deep claret** *(2,140)*	250.00	110.00
	Never hinged	415.00	
	On cover		—
	P# strip of 3, Impt.	1,000.	
	P# block of 6, Impt.	*4,000.*	
	Nos. J1-J7 (7)	516.50	230.00
	Set, never hinged	882.50	

Post Office Clerk — D3

1928, Aug. 21 **Unwmk.** ***Perf. 11***

J8	D3 4c **brown red** *(948,054)*	.20	.20
	Never hinged	.25	
J9	D3 6c **brown red** *(255,490)*	.30	.75
	Never hinged	.45	
J10	D3 8c **brown red** *(508,621)*	.25	.75
	Never hinged	.35	
J11	D3 10c **brown red** *(254,195)*	.30	.75
	Never hinged	.45	
J12	D3 12c **brown red** *(407,457)*	.25	.75
	Never hinged	.35	
J13	D3 16c **brown red** *(253,215)*	.30	.75
	Never hinged	.45	
J14	D3 20c **brown red** *(259,665)*	.30	.75
	Never hinged	.45	
	Nos. J8-J14 (7)	1.90	4.70
	Set, never hinged	2.75	

No. J8 Surcharged in Blue

1937, July 29 **Unwmk.** ***Perf. 1***

J15	D3 3c on 4c **brown red**	.25	.2
	Never hinged	.35	
	First day cover		35.0

See note after No. NJ1.

Nos. J8-J14 Handstamped in Violet **VICTORY**

1944, Dec. 3 **Unwmk.** ***Perf. 1***

J16	D3 4c **brown red** *(306)*	*150.00*	—
J17	D3 6c **brown red** *(390)*	*90.00*	—
J18	D3 8c **brown red** *(379)*	*95.00*	—
J19	D3 10c **brown red** *(405)*	*90.00*	—
J20	D3 12c **brown red** *(423)*	*90.00*	—
J21	D3 16c **brown red** *(425)*	*95.00*	—
J22	D3 20c **brown red** *(375)*	*95.00*	—
	Nos. J16-J22 (7)	*705.00*	

OFFICIAL STAMPS

Official Handstamped Overprints

"Officers purchasing stamps for government business may, if they so desire, surcharge them with the letters O.B. either in writing with black ink or by rubber stamps but in such a manner as not to obliterate the stamp that postmasters will be unable to determine whether the stamps have been previously used." C.M. Cotterman, Director of Posts, December 26, 1905.

Beginning January 1, 1906, all branches of the Insular Government used postage stamps to prepay postage instead of franking them as before. Some officials used manuscript, some utilized the typewriting machines but by far the larger number provided themselves with rubber stamps. The majority of these read "O.B." but other forms were: "OFFICIAL BUSINESS" or "OFFICIAL MAIL" in two lines, with variations on many of these.

These "O.B." overprints are known on U.S. 1899-1901 stamps; on 1903-06 stamps in red and blue; on 1906 stamps in red, blue, black, yellow and green.

"O.B." overprints were also made on the centavo and peso stamps of the Philippines, per order of May 25, 1907.

Beginning in 1926 the Bureau of Posts issued press-printed official stamps, but many government offices continued to handstamp ordinary postage stamps "O.B."

During the Japanese occupation period 1942-45, the same system of handstamped official overprints prevailed, but the handstamp usually consisted of "K.P.", initials of the Tagalog words, "Kagamitang Pampamahalaan" (Official Business), and the two Japanese characters used in the printed overprint on Nos. NO1 to NO4.

Legislative Palace Issue of 1926 Overprinted in Red

Printed and overprinted by the Philippine Bureau of Printing.

1926, Dec. 20 **Unwmk.** ***Perf. 12***

O1	A42 2c **green & black** *(90,500)*	3.00	1.00
	Never hinged	4.50	
	On cover		2.00
	Block of 4	13.00	5.50
O2	A42 4c **carmine & black** *(90,450)*	3.00	1.25
	Never hinged	4.50	
	On cover		2.00
	First day cover		10.00
	Block of 4	13.00	5.50
a.	Vertical pair, imperf. between	750.00	
O3	A42 18c **light brown & black** *(70,000)*	8.00	4.00
	Never hinged	12.00	
	On cover		6.50
	Block of 4	36.00	20.00
O4	A42 20c **orange & black** *(70,250)*	7.75	1.75
	Never hinged	11.50	
	On cover		2.25
	Block of 4	36.00	8.25
	First day cover, #O1-O4		50.00
	Nos. O1-O4 (4)	21.75	8.00
	Set, never hinged	32.50	

Regular Issue of 1917-25 Overprinted

Printed and overprinted by the U.S. Bureau of Engraving and Printing.

1931 **Unwmk.** ***Perf. 11***

O5	A40 2c **green** *(22,940,100)*	.40	.20
	Never hinged	.65	
a.	No period after "B"	17.50	5.00

Never hinged 27.50
b. No period after "O" —
O6 A40 4c **carmine** *(5,377,000)* .45 .20
Never hinged .70
a. No period after "B" 20.00 5.00
Never hinged 31.00
O7 A40 6c **deep violet** *(616,500)* .75 .20
Never hinged 1.25
O8 A40 8c **yellow brown** *(706,700)* .75 .20
Never hinged 1.25
O9 A40 10c **deep blue** *(1,006,800)* 1.20 .20
Never hinged 1.90
O10 A40 12c **red orange** *(158,050)* 2.00 .20
Never hinged 3.00
a. No period after "B" 65.00
Never hinged 100.00
O11 A40 16c **light olive green** *(Dewey) (824,400)* 1.00 .20
Never hinged 1.50
a. 16c olive bister 2.00 .20
Never hinged 3.00
O12 A40 20c **orange yellow** *(509,050)* 1.25 .20
Never hinged 1.90
a. No period after "B" 50.00 15.00
Never hinged 77.50
O13 A40 26c **green** *(68,600)* 2.00 .30
Never hinged 3.25
a. 26c blue green 2.50 .65
Never hinged 4.00
O14 A40 30c **gray** *(199,400)* 2.00 .25
Never hinged 3.25
Nos. O5-O14 (10) 11.80 2.15
Set, never hinged 18.65

Regular Issue of 1935 Overprinted in Black

1935 Unwmk. *Perf. 11*
O15 A53 2c **rose** *(7,927,800)* .20 .20
Never hinged .25
a. No period after "B" 15.00 5.00
Never hinged 22.50
O16 A54 4c **yellow green** *(5,079,266)* .20 .20
Never hinged .25
a. No period after "B" 15.00 8.50
Never hinged 52.50
O17 A55 6c **dark brown** *(786,896)* .25 .20
Never hinged .40
a. No period after "B" 35.00 17.50
Never hinged 52.50
O18 A56 8c **violet** *(656,200)* .30 .20
Never hinged .45
O19 A57 10c **rose carmine** *(756,100)* .30 .20
Never hinged .45
O20 A58 12c **black** *(104,500)* .75 .20
Never hinged 1.10
O21 A59 16c **dark blue** *(254,800)* .55 .20
Never hinged .85
O22 A60 20c **light olive green** *(203,079)* .60 .20
Never hinged .90
O23 A61 26c **indigo** *(67,750)* .90 .25
Never hinged 1.50
O24 A62 30c **orange red** *(83,500)* .80 .20
Never hinged 1.20
Nos. O15-O24 (10) 4.85 2.05
Set, never hinged 7.35

Nos. 411 and 418 with Additional Overprint in Black

1937-38 Unwmk. *Perf. 11*
O25 A53 2c **rose,** *Apr. 10, 1937 (11,580,800)* .20 .20
Never hinged .20
First day cover 50.00
a. No period after "B" 15.00 2.25
Never hinged 22.50
b. Period after "B" raised (UL 4) 150.00
O26 A60 20c **light olive green,** *Apr. 26, 1938 (174,929)* .70 .50
Never hinged 1.10

Regular Issue of 1935 Overprinted In Black:

a

b

1938-40 Unwmk. *Perf. 11*
O27 A53(a) 2c **rose** *(23,239,872)* .20 .20
Never hinged .20
a. Hyphen omitted 20.00 20.00
Never hinged 30.00
b. No period after "B" 25.00 25.00
Never hinged 37.50
O28 A54(b) 4c **yellow green** *(85,000)* .75 .25
Never hinged 1.10
O29 A55(a) 6c **dark brown** *(393,549)* .30 .20
Never hinged .45
O30 A56(b) 8c **violet** *(82,000)* .75 .25
Never hinged 1.10
O31 A57(b) 10c **rose carmine** *(1,188,735)* .20 .20
Never hinged .20
a. No period after "O" 40.00 30.00
Never hinged 60.00
O32 A58(b) 12c **black** *(340,000)* .30 .20
Never hinged .45
O33 A59(b) 16c **dark blue** *(490,000)* .30 .20
Never hinged .45
O34 A60(a) 20c **light olive green** ('40) *(162,000)* .55 .25
Never hinged .85
O35 A61(b) 26c **indigo** *(77,000)* .75 .30
Never hinged 1.10
O36 A62(b) 30c **orange red** *(82,000)* .75 .25
Never hinged 1.10
Nos. O27-O36 (10) 4.85 2.30
Set, never hinged 7.00

No. 461 Overprinted in Black

c

ROTARY PRESS PRINTING

1941, Apr. 14 Unwmk. *Perf. 11x10½*
O37 A75 2c **apple green** *(21,087,900)* .20 .20
Never hinged .20
First day cover 3.50
Margin block of 4, P# .25

Nos. O27, O37, O16, O29, O31, O22 and O26 Handstamped in Violet

1944 Unwmk. *Perf. 11, 11x10½*
O38 A53 2c **rose** (On O27) *(128)* *375.00* *150.00*
O39 A75 2c **apple green** (On O37) *(13,100)* 10.00 14.00
Never hinged 15.00
On cover *25.00*
Block of 4 47.50 —
O40 A54 4c **yellow green** (On O16) *(2,634)* *42.50* *30.00*
Never hinged 75.00
Block of 4 *190.00*
O40A A55 6c **dark brown** (On O29) *8,000.* —
O41 A57 10c **rose carmine** (On O31) *(665)* *500.00*
Block of 4 *2,100.*
a. No period after "O" *4,000.*
O42 A60 20c **light olive green** (On O22) *8,000.*
O43 A60 20c **light olive green** (On O26) *1,750.*

No. 497 Overprinted Type "c" in Black

1946, June 19 Unwmk. *Perf. 11x10½*
O44 A76 2c **sepia** *(10,470,000)* .20 .20
Never hinged .20
Margin block of 4, P# .40

POST OFFICE SEALS

POS1

1906 Litho. Unwmk. *Perf. 12*
OX1 POS1 **light brown** 65.00 65.00

Wmk. "PIRS" in Double-lined Capitals
1907 *Perf. 12*
OX2 POS1 **light brown** 85.00 85.00
Hyphen-hole Perf. 7
OX3 POS1 **orange brown** 40.00 *45.00*

1911 *Hyphen-hole Perf. 7*
OX4 POS1 **yellow brown** 37.50 *40.00*
OX5 POS1 **olive bister** 75.00 75.00
a. Unwatermarked —
OX6 POS1 **yellow** 85.00 85.00

1913 Unwmk. *Hyphen-hole Perf. 7*
OX7 POS1 **lemon yellow** 2.00 *3.00*
Perf. 12
OX8 POS1 **yellow** 100.00 50.00

Wmk. "USPS" in Single-lined Capitals
Hyphen-hole Perf. 7
OX9 POS1 **yellow** 100.00 75.00

1934 Unwmk. *Rouletted*
OX10 POS1 **dark blue** 1.00 *1.50*

POS2

OX11 POS2 **dark blue** 1.00 *1.50*

POS3

1938 *Hyphen-hole Perf. 7*
OX12 POS3 **dark blue** 5.50 *5.50*

ENVELOPES

U.S. Envelopes of 1899 Issue Overprinted below stamp in color of the stamp, except where noted

1899-1900

Note: Many envelopes for which there was no obvious need were issued in small quantities. Anyone residing in the Islands could, by depositing with his postmaster the required amount, order any envelopes in quantities of 500, or multiples thereof, provided it was on the schedule of U.S. envelopes.

Such special orders are indicated by a plus sign after the quantity.

U1 U77 1c **green** (#U352) *(370,000)* 3.00 2.00
Entire 8.75 9.50
U2 U77 1c **green,** *amber* (#U353) *(1,000)+* 18.00 14.00
Entire 40.00 40.00
U3 U77 1c **green,** *amber* (#U353) red overprint *(500)+* 22.50 20.00
Entire 60.00 57.50
U4 U77 1c **green,** *oriental buff* (#U354) *(1,000)+* 14.00 14.00
Entire 30.00 30.00
U5 U77 1c **green,** *oriental buff* (#U354) red overprint *(500)+* 35.00 35.00
Entire 72.50 *72.50*
U6 U77 1c **green,** *blue* (#U355) *(1,000)+* 9.00 9.00
Entire 30.00 30.00
U7 U77 1c **green,** *blue* (#U355) red overprint *(500)+* 20.00 19.00
Entire 72.50 67.50
U8 U79 2c **carmine** (#U362) *(1,180,000)* 1.50 1.50
Entire 4.00 3.00
U9 U79 2c **carmine,** *amber* (#U363) *(21,000)* 5.25 5.00
Entire 15.00 12.50
U10 U79 2c **carmine,** *oriental buff* (#U364) *(10,000)* 5.25 4.75
Entire 17.00 13.50
U11 U79 2c **carmine,** *blue* (#U365) *(10,000)* 4.75 6.25
Entire 12.50 12.00
U12 U81 4c **brown,** *amber* (#U372) *(500)+* 40.00 35.00
Entire 85.00 *92.50*
a. Double overprint —
Entire *4,000.*
U13 U83 4c **brown** (#U374) *(10,500)* 12.50 9.00
Entire 30.00 *40.00*
U14 U83 4c **brown,** *amber* (#U375) *(500)+* 55.00 50.00
Entire 175.00 125.00
U15 U84 5c **blue** (#U377) *(20,000)* 6.25 6.00
Entire 13.00 13.00
U16 U84 5c **blue,** *amber* (#U378) *(500)+* 35.00 35.00
Entire 87.50 *110.00*
Nos. U1-U16 (16) 287.00 265.50

1903 Same Overprint on U.S. Issue of 1903

U17 U85 1c **green** (#U379) *(300,000)* 1.50 1.25
Entire 4.25 4.25
U18 U85 1c **green,** *amber* (#U380) *(1,000)+* 12.50 12.00
Entire 22.50 *25.00*
U19 U85 1c **green,** *oriental buff* (#U381) *(1,000)+* 14.50 12.50
Entire 26.00 *24.00*
U20 U85 1c **green,** *blue* (#U382) *(1,500)+* 12.00 11.00
Entire 26.00 *26.00*
U21 U85 1c **green,** *manila* (#U383) *(500)+* 20.00 20.00
Entire 45.00 *47.50*
U22 U86 2c **carmine** (#U385) *(150,500)* 5.00 3.50
Entire 7.50 7.00
U23 U86 2c **carmine,** *amber* (#U386) *(500)+* 17.50 14.00
Entire 35.00 42.50
U24 U86 2c **carmine,** *oriental buff* (#U387) *(500)+* 17.50 *25.00*
Entire 45.00 —
U25 U86 2c **carmine,** *blue* (#U388) *(500)+* 17.50 17.50
Entire 40.00
U26 U87 4c **chocolate,** *amber* (#U391) *(500)+* 55.00 *75.00*
Entire 140.00 *190.00*
a. Double overprint, entire *7,000.*
U27 U88 5c **blue,** *amber* (#U394) *(500)+* 55.00 —
Entire 125.00 125.00
Nos. U17-U27 (11) 228.00 191.75

1906

Same Overprint on Re-cut U.S. issue of 1904

U28 U89 2c **carmine** (#U395) 42.50 27.50
Entire 150.00 125.00
U29 U89 2c **carmine,** *Oriental buff* (#U397) 67.50 *110.00*
Entire 225.00 *275.00*

Rizal — E1

E2, McKinley.

1908

U30 E1 2c **green** .50 .25
Entire .85 1.50
U31 E1 2c **green,** *amber* 4.00 2.25
Entire 9.00 8.00
U32 E1 2c **green,** *oriental buff* 5.00 3.00
Entire 9.00 9.00
U33 E1 2c **green,** *blue* 5.00 3.00
Entire 9.00 9.00
U34 E1 2c **green,** *manila (500)* 7.25 —
Entire 15.00 20.00
U35 E2 4c **carmine** .50 .25
Entire 1.40 1.25
U36 E2 4c **carmine,** *amber* 4.00 2.50
Entire 9.00 7.00
U37 E2 4c **carmine,** *oriental buff* 4.25 3.50
Entire 9.00 17.00
U38 E2 4c **carmine,** *blue* 4.00 3.00
Entire 8.50 8.50
U39 E2 4c **carmine,** *manila (500)* 9.00 —
Entire 20.00 30.00
Nos. U30-U39 (10) 43.50 17.75

Rizal — E3

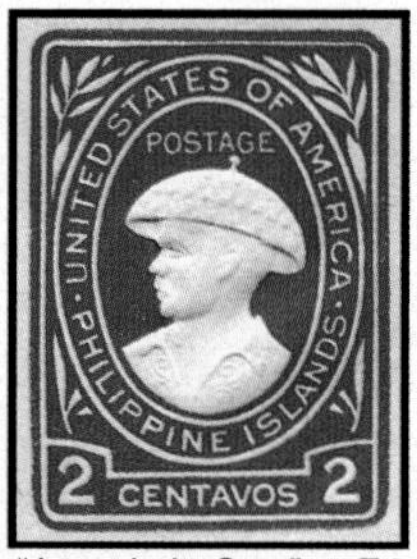

"Juan de la Cruz" — E4

1927, Apr. 5

U40 E3 2c **green** 11.50 9.50
Entire 30.00 25.00
Entire, 1st day cancel *37.50*

1935, June 19

U41 E4 2c **carmine** .35 .25
Entire 1.25 .75
U42 E4 4c **olive green** .50 .30
Entire 1.65 1.10

For surchages see Nos. NU1-NU2.

Nos. U30, U35, U41 and U42 Handstamped in Violet

1944

U42A E1 2c **green** (On U30), Entire —
U43 E4 2c **carmine** (On U41) 17.50 14.00
Entire 47.50 *77.00*
U44 E2 4c **carmine,** *McKinley* (On U35) — —
Entire 950.00 *950.00*
U45 E4 4c **olive green** (On U42) 82.50 70.00
Entire 140.00 175.00

WRAPPERS

U.S. Wrappers Overprinted in Color of Stamp

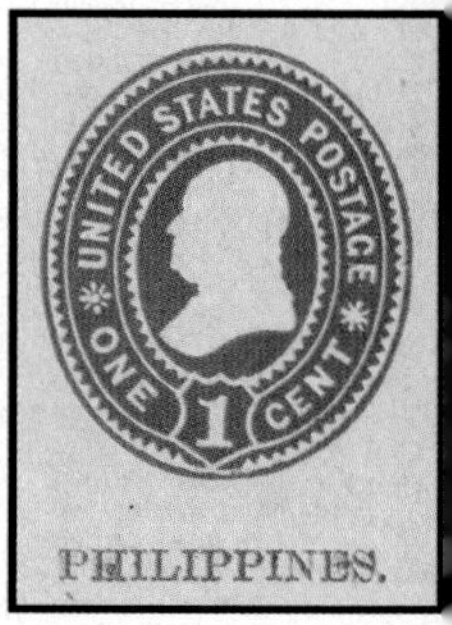

1901

W1 U77 1c **green,** *manila* (No. W357) *(320,000)* 1.50 1.25
Entire 5.00 *10.00*

1905

W2 U85 1c **green,** *manila* (No. W384) 9.00 9.00
Entire 22.50 *25.00*
a. Double overprint, entire *4,500.*
W3 U86 2c **carmine,** *manila* (No. W389) 11.00 10.50
Entire 22.50 *27.50*

Design of Philippine Envelopes

1908

W4 E1 2c **green,** *manila* 2.00 2.00
Entire 11.00 *15.00*

POSTAL CARDS

Values are for Entires.

U.S. Cards Overprinted in Black below Stamp

a **PHILIPPINES.**

1900, Feb.

UX1 (a) 1c **black** (Jefferson) (UX14) *(100,000)* 17.50 15.00
a. Without period 47.50 75.00
UX2 (a) 2c **black** (Liberty) (UX16) *(20,000)* 40.00 30.00
a. With double "PHILIPPINES" overprint *20,000.*

b

1903, Sept. 15

UX3 (b) 1c **black** (McKinley) (UX18) *1,350.* *1,150.*
UX4 (b) 2c **black** (Liberty) (UX16) *800.* *700.*

c PHILIPPINES.

1903, Nov. 10

UX5 (c) 1c **black** (McKinley) (UX18) 47.50 40.00
UX6 (c) 2c **black** (Liberty) (UX16) 60.00 55.00

d **PHILIPPINES**

1906

UX7 (d) 1c **black** (McKinley) (UX18) *275.* *300.*
UX8 (d) 2c **black** (Liberty) (UX16) *2,000.* *1,500.*

Designs same as postage issue of 1906

1907

UX9 A40 2c **black,** *buff* (Rizal) 10.00 8.00
UX10 A40 4c **black,** *buff* (McKinley) 25.00 20.00

Color changes

1911

UX11 A40 2c **blue,** *light blue* (Rizal) 8.00 8.00
a. 2c blue on white 20.00 20.00
UX12 A40 4c **blue,** *light blue* (McKinley) 25.00 25.00

An impression of No. UX11 exists on the back of a U.S. No. UX21.

915
X13 A40 2c **green,** *buff* (Rizal) 3.00 2.00
X14 A40 2c **yellow green,** *amber* 3.50 1.50
X15 A40 4c **green,** *buff* (McKinley) 20.00 15.00

Design of postage issue of 1935

935
JX16 A53 2c **red,** *pale buff* (Rizal) 2.50 1.60

No. UX16 Overprinted at left of Stamp **COMMONWEALTH**

938
X17 A53 2c **red,** *pale buff* 2.50 1.60

No. UX16 Overprinted **COMMONWEALTH**

JX18 A53 2c **red,** *pale buff* 45.00 45.00

No. UX16 Overprinted **COMMONWEALTH**

JX19 A53 2c **red,** *pale buff* 4.00 4.00

Nos. UX13, UX18 and UX19 Handstamped in Violet

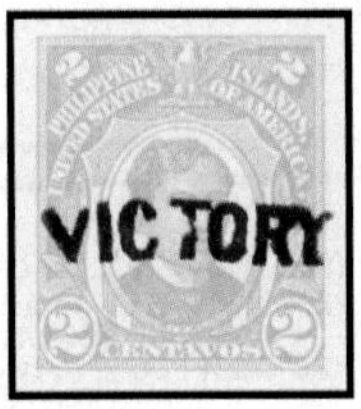

1944
UX20 A40 2c **green,** *buff, Rizal* (On UX13) *180.00* *225.00*
UX21 A53 2c **red,** *pale buff* (On UX18) *650.00* —
UX22 A53 2c **red,** *pale buff* (On UX19) *285.00* *550.00*

Overprinted in Black at left **VICTORY**

1945, Jan. 19
UX23 A76 2c **gray brown,** *pale buff* 1.25 .75
First day cancel 3.25
a. "IC" of "Victory" very close 5.00 3.00

This card was not issued without overprint.

PAID REPLY POSTAL CARDS

U.S. Paid Reply Cards of 1892-93 issues Overprinted with type "a" in blue

1900, Feb.
UY1 2c +2c **blue,** unsevered *(5,000)* *160.00* *500.00*
m. PM2 Message card, detached 27.50 50.00
r. PR2 Reply card, detached 27.50 50.00

Overprinted type "c" in black

1903
UY2 1c + 1c **black,** *buff,* unsevered *(20,000)* *150.00* *375.00*
m. PM1 Message card, detached 22.50 25.00
r. PR1 Reply card, detached 22.50 25.00
UY3 2c + 2c **blue,** unsevered *(20,000)* 300.00 *700.00*
m. PM2, Message card, detached 55.00 50.00
r. PR2, Reply card, detached 55.00 50.00

OFFICIAL CARDS

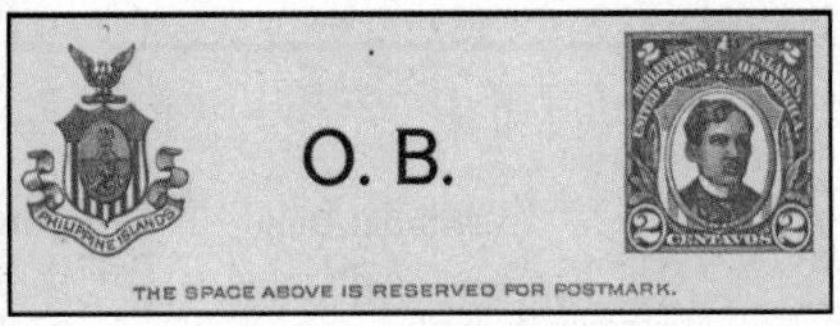

Overprinted at left of stamp

1925 **On postal card No. UX13**
UZ1 A40 2c **green,** *buff* (Rizal) 35.00 35.00

1935 **On postal card No. UX16**
UZ2 A53 2c **red,** *pale buff* 14.00 *17.50*

Overprinted at Left of Stamp **O. B.**

1938 **On postal card No. UX19**
UZ3 A53 2c **red,** *pale buff* 13.00 *17.50*

Overprinted Below Stamp **O. B.**

1941 **Design of postage issue of 1941**
UZ4 A75 2c **light green,** *pale buff* 160.00 *200.00*

This card was not issued without overprint.

Postal Card No. UX19 Overprinted at Left of Stamp **O. B.**

1941
UZ5 A53 2c **red,** *pale buff* 20.00 *25.00*

OCCUPATION STAMPS

Issued Under Japanese Occupation

Nos. 461, 438 and 439 Overprinted with Bars in Black

1942-43 **Unwmk.** ***Perf. 11x10½, 11***
N1 A75 2c **apple green,** *Mar. 4, 1942 (3,000,000)* .20 *1.00*
Never hinged .20
P# block of 4 .25
a. Pair, one without overprint —
N2 A58 12c **black,** *Apr. 30, 1943 (310,000)* .25 *2.00*
Never hinged .40
N3 A59 16c **dark blue,** *Mar. 4, 1942 (160,000)* 5.00 3.75
Never hinged 7.50
Nos. N1-N3 (3) 5.45 6.75
Set, never hinged 8.10

Nos. 435a, 435, 442, 443, and 423 Surcharged in Black

1942-43 ***Perf. 11***
N4 A55(a) 5(c) on 6c **golden brown** *Sept. 1, 1942 (800,000)* .20 *1.00*
Never hinged .30
First day cover, Manila 4.00
a. Top bar shorter and thinner *(200,000)* .20 *1.00*
Never hinged .30
b. 5(c) on 6c **dark brown** .20 *1.00*
Never hinged .30
c. As "b," top bar shorter and thinner .20 *1.00*
Never hinged .30
N5 A62(b) 16(c) on 30c **orange red,** *Jan. 11, 1943 (210,000)* .25 *.60*
Never hinged .45
First day cover 5.00
N6 A63(c) 50c on 1p **red orange & black,** *Apr. 30, 1943 (20,000)* .75 *1.25*
Never hinged 1.10
a. Double surcharge *300.00*
N7 A65(d) 1p on 4p **blue & black,** *Apr. 30, 1943 (19,975)* 100.00 *175.00*
Never hinged 155.00
Inverted "S" in "PESO," position 4 150.00 *225.00*
Nos. N4-N7 (4) 101.20 177.85
Set, never hinged 156.85

On Nos. N4 and N4b, the top bar measures 1½x22½mm. On Nos. N4a and N4c, the top bar measures 1x21mm and the "5" is smaller and thinner.

The used value for No. N7 is for postal cancellation. Used stamps exist with first day cancellations. They are worth somewhat less.

1942, May 18
N8 A54 2(c) on 4c **yellow green** *(100,000)* 6.00 6.00
Never hinged 8.75
First day cover 6.00

Issued to commemorate Japan's capture of Bataan and Corregidor. The American-Filipino forces finally surrendered May 7, 1942. No. N8 exists with "R" for "B" in BATAAN.

No. 384 Surcharged in Black

1942, Dec. 8
N9 A54 5(c) on 4c **yellow green** *(400,000)* .50 *1.00*
Never hinged .75
First day cover 3.00

1st anniversary of the "Greater East Asia War."

Nos. C59 and C62 Surcharged in Black

1943, Jan. 23
N10 AP1 2(c) on 8c **carmine** *(400,000)* .25 *1.00*
Never hinged .35
N11 AP1 5c on 1p **sepia** *(300,000)* .50 *1.50*
Never hinged .75
First day cover, #N10-N11 4.00

1st anniv. of the Philippine Executive Commission.

Nipa Hut — OS1

Rice Planting — OS2

Mt. Mayon and Mt. Fuji — OS3

Moro Vinta — OS4

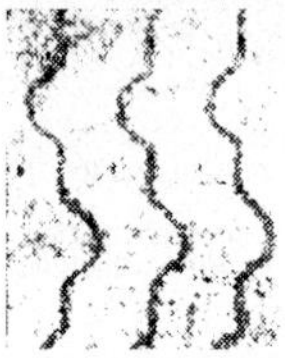

Wmk. 257

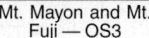

The "c" currency is indicated by four Japanese characters, "p" currency by two.

Engraved; Typographed (2c, 6c, 25c)

1943-44 Wmk. 257 *Perf. 13*

N12	OS1	1c	**deep orange,** *June 7, 1943*	.20	.20
			Never hinged	.25	
N13	OS2	2c	**bright green,** *Apr. 1, 1943*	.20	.20
			Never hinged	.25	
N14	OS1	4c	**slate green,** *June 7, 1943*	.20	.20
			Never hinged	.25	
N15	OS3	5c	**orange brown,** *Apr. 1, 1943*	.20	.20
			Never hinged	.25	
N16	OS2	6c	**red,** *July 14, 1943*	.20	.20
			Never hinged	.25	
N17	OS3	10c	**blue green,** *July 14, 1943*	.20	.20
			Never hinged	.25	
N18	OS4	12c	**steel blue,** *July 14, 1943*	1.00	1.00
			Never hinged	1.50	
N19	OS4	16c	**dark brown,** *July 14, 1943*	.20	.20
			Never hinged	.25	
N20	OS1	20c	**rose violet,** *Aug. 16, 1943*	1.25	1.25
			Never hinged	1.90	
N21	OS3	21c	**violet,** *Aug. 16, 1943*	.25	.20
			Never hinged	.35	
N22	OS2	25c	**pale brown,** *Aug. 16, 1943*	.25	.20
			Never hinged	.35	
N23	OS3	1p	**deep carmine,** *June 7, 1943*	.75	.75
			Never hinged	1.15	
N24	OS4	2p	**dull violet,** *Sept. 16, 1943*	5.50	5.50
			Never hinged	8.25	
			First day cover		*14.00*
N25	OS4	5p	**dark olive,** *Apr. 10, 1944*	14.00	14.00
			Never hinged	21.00	
			First day cover		*14.00*
			Nos. N12-N25 (14)	24.40	24.30
			Set, never hinged	35.25	

Map of Manila Bay Showing Bataan and Corregidor — OS5

1943, May 7 Photo. Unwmk.

N26	OS5	2c	**carmine red**	.20	*.75*
			Never hinged	.25	
N27	OS5	5c	**bright green**	.25	*1.00*
			Never hinged	.35	
			Colorless dot after left "5"	4.00	—
			First day cover, #N26-N27, Manila		4.00

1st anniversary of the fall of Bataan and Corregidor.

No. 440 Surcharged in Black

1943, June 20 Engr. *Perf. 11*

N28	A60	12(c)	on 20c **light olive green** *(350,000)*	.25	*.75*
			Never hinged	.35	
			First day cover		6.00
a.			Double surcharge	—	

350th anniversary of the printing press in the Philippines. "Limbagan" is Tagalog for "printing press."

Rizal Monument, Filipina and Philippine Flag — OS6

1943, Oct. 14 Photo. Unwmk. *Perf. 12*

N29	OS6	5c	**light blue**	.20	*.90*
			Never hinged	.20	
a.			Imperf.	.20	.90
N30	OS6	12c	**orange**	.20	*.90*
			Never hinged	.25	
a.			Imperf.	.20	*.90*
N31	OS6	17c	**rose pink**	.20	*.90*
			Never hinged	.30	
			First day cover, #N29-N31, Manila		3.00
a.			Imperf.	.20	*.90*
			First day cover, #N29a-N31a, Manila		3.00
			Nos. N29-N31 (3)	.60	*2.70*
			Set, never hinged	.75	

"Independence of the Philippines." Japan granted "independence" Oct. 14, 1943, when the puppet republic was founded.
The imperforate stamps were issued without gum.

José Rizal — OS7

Rev. José Burgos — OS8

Apolinario Mabini — OS9

1944, Feb. 17 Litho. Unwmk. *Perf. 12*

N32	OS7	5c	**blue**	.20	*1.00*
			Never hinged	.20	
a.			Imperf.	.20	*1.00*
			Never hinged	.20	
N33	OS8	12c	**carmine**	.20	*1.00*
			Never hinged	.25	
a.			Imperf.	.20	*1.00*
			Never hinged	.25	
N34	OS9	17c	**deep orange**	.20	*1.00*
			Never hinged	.30	
			First day cover, #N32-N34, Manila		1.00
a.			Imperf.	.20	*1.00*
			Never hinged	.30	
			First day cover, #N32a-N34a, *Apr. 17,* Manila		3.00
			Nos. N32-N34 (3)	.60	*3.00*
			Set, never hinged	.75	

Nos. C60 and C61 Surcharged in Black

1944, May 7 Unwmk. *Perf. 11*

N35	AP1	5(c)	on 20c **ultramarine**	.50	1.00
			Never hinged	.75	
N36	AP1	12(c)	on 60c **blue green** *(165,000)*	1.75	1.75
			Never hinged	2.50	
			First day cover, #N35-N36		4.00

2nd anniversary of the fall of Bataan and Corregidor.

José P. Laurel — OS10

1945, Jan. 12 Litho. Unwmk. *Imperf.*
Without Gum

N37	OS10	5c	**dull violet brown**	.20	*.50*
			Never hinged	.20	
N38	OS10	7c	**blue green**	.20	*.50*
			Never hinged	.20	
N39	OS10	20c	**chalky blue**	.20	*.50*
			Never hinged	.20	
			First day cover, #N37-N39		3.00
			Nos. N37-N39 (3)		*1.50*
			Set, never hinged	.60	

Issued belatedly on Jan. 12, 1945, to commemorate the first anniversary of the puppet Philippine Republic, Oct. 14, 1944. "S" stands for "sentimos."

The special cancellation devices prepared for use on Oct. 14, 1944, were employed on "First Day" covers Jan. 12, 1945.

OCCUPATION SEMI-POSTAL STAMPS

Woman, Farming and Cannery — OSP1

1942, Nov. 12 Litho. Unwmk. *Perf. 12*

NB1	OSP1	2c + 1c	**pale violet**	.20	*.85*
			Never hinged	.20	
NB2	OSP1	5c + 1c	**bright green**	.25	*1.00*
			Never hinged	.30	
NB3	OSP1	16c + 2c	**orange**	30.00	*32.50*
			Never hinged	42.00	
			First day cover, #NB1-NB3		37.50
			Nos. NB1-NB3 (3)	30.45	34.35
			Set, never hinged	42.50	

Issued to promote the campaign to produce and conserve food. The surtax aided the Red Cross.

Souvenir Sheet

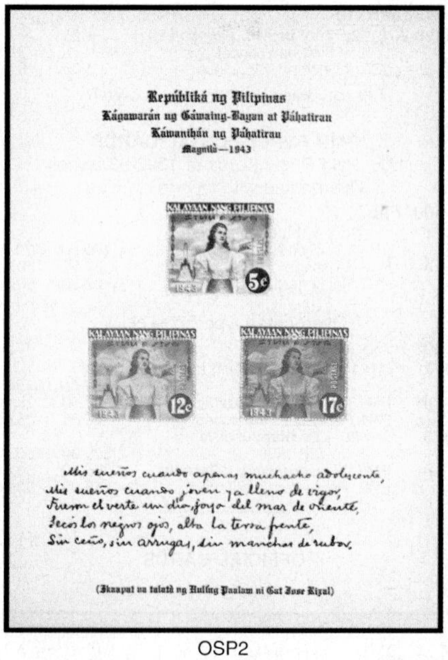

OSP2

Illustration reduced.

1943, Oct. 14 Without Gum *Imperf.*

NB4	OSP2	Sheet of 3	75.00	*17.50*
		Sheet with first day cancel and cachet, Manila		17.50
		First day cover, Manila		—

"Independence of the Philippines."

No. NB4 contains one each of Nos. N29a-N31a. Marginal inscription is from Rizal's "Last Farewell." Sold for 2.50p.

The value of No. NB4 used is for a sheet from a first day cover. Commercially used sheets are extremely scarce and worth much more.

Nos. N18, N20 and N21 Surcharged in Black

1943, Dec. 8 — **Wmk. 257** — *Perf. 13*

NB5	OS4 12c + 21c **steel blue**	.20	*.80*
	Never hinged	.30	
NB6	OS1 20c + 36c **rose violet**	.20	*.80*
	Never hinged	.30	
NB7	OS3 21c + 40c **violet**	.20	*.80*
	Never hinged	.30	
	First day cover, #NB5-NB7		2.50
	Nos. NB5-NB7 (3)	.60	2.40
	Set, never hinged	.90	

The surtax was for the benefit of victims of a Luzon flood. Baha" is Tagalog for "flood."

Souvenir Sheet

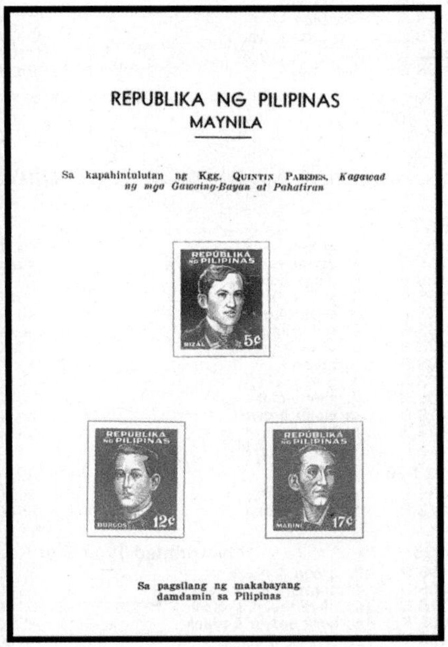

OSP3

Illustration reduced.

1944, Feb. 9 — **Litho.** — **Unwmk.** — *Imperf.*

Without Gum

NB8	OSP3 Sheet of 3	6.50	*3.50*
	First day cover		*4.00*

No. NB8 contains one each of Nos. N32a-N34a.

The sheet sold for 1p, the surtax going to a fund for the care of heroes' monuments. Size: 101x143mm. No. NB8 exists with 5c inverted.

OCCUPATION POSTAGE DUE

No. J15 Overprinted with Bar in Blue

1942, Oct. 14 — **Unwmk.** — *Perf. 11*

NJ1	D3 3c on 4c **brown red** *(40,000)*	30.00	*20.00*
	Never hinged	45.00	
	First day cover		*35.00*
	Double bar	—	—

On examples of No. J15, two lines were drawn in India ink with a ruling pen across "United States of America" by employees of the Short Paid Section of the Manila Post Office to make a provisional 3c postage due stamp which was used from Sept. 1, 1942 (when the letter rate was raised from 2c to 5c) until Oct. 14 when No. NJ1 went on sale. Value on cover, $125.

OCCUPATION OFFICIAL STAMPS

Nos. 461, 413, 435, 435a and 442 Overprinted or Surcharged in Black with Bars and

1943-44 — **Unwmk.** — *Perf. 11x10½, 11*

NO1	A75 2c **apple green,** *Apr. 7, 1943 (200,000)*	.20	.75
	Never hinged	.30	
	P# block of 4	.25	
a.	Double overprint	*400.00*	
	Never hinged	*600.00*	
	On cover (double overprint)		*1,250.*
NO2	A55 5(c) on 6c **dark brown** (On No. 413), *June 26, 1944 (23,049)*	40.00	45.00
	Never hinged	55.00	
	First day cover		*125.00*
NO3	A55 5(c) on 6c **golden brown** (On No. 435a), *Apr. 7, 1943 (250,000)*	.20	.90
	Never hinged	.30	
a.	Narrower spacing between bars *(249,951)*	.20	.90
	Never hinged	.30	
b.	5(c) on 6c dark brown (On No. 435)	.20	.90
	Never hinged	.30	
c.	As "b," narrower spacing between bars	.20	.90
	Never hinged	.30	
d.	Double overprint	—	
NO4	A62 16(c) on 30c **orange red,** *Apr. 7, 1943 (100,000)*	.30	1.25
	Never hinged	.45	
a.	Wider spacing between bars	.30	1.25
	Never hinged	.45	
	First day cover, Nos. NO1, NO3-NO4		*35.00*
	Nos. NO1-NO4 (4)	40.70	47.90
	Set, never hinged	56.05	

On Nos. NO3 and NO3b the bar deleting "United States of America" is 9¾ to 10mm above the bar deleting "Common." On Nos. NO3a and NO3c, the spacing is 8 to 8½mm.

On No. NO4, the center bar is 19mm long, 3½mm below the top bar and 6mm above the Japanese characters. On No. NO4a, the center bar is 20½mm long, 9mm below the top bar and 1mm above the Japanese characters.

"K.P." stands for Kagamitang Pampamahalaan, "Official Business" in Tagalog.

Nos. 435 and 435a Surcharged in Black

1944, Aug. 28 — **Unwmk.** — *Perf. 11*

NO5	A55 (5c) on 6c **golden brown** *(500,000)*	.30	*.40*
	Never hinged	.45	
a.	5(c) on 6c **dark brown**	.30	*.40*
	Never hinged	.45	

Nos. O34 and C62 Overprinted in Black

a

b

NO6	A60(a) 20c **light olive green** *(200,000)*	.40	*.50*
	Never hinged	.60	
NO7	AP1(b) 1p **sepia** *(100,000)*	.90	*1.00*
	Never hinged	1.45	
	First day cover, #NO5-NO7		4.00
	Nos. NO5-NO7 (3)	1.60	1.90
	Set, never hinged	2.50	

OCCUPATION ENVELOPES

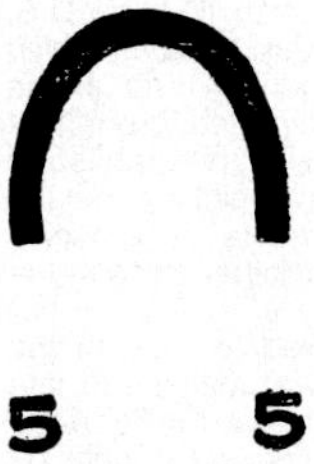

No. U41 Surcharged in Black

1943, Apr. 1

NU1	E4 5c on 2c **carmine**	.50	.30
	Entire	3.00	3.00
	Entire, 1st day cancel		4.00

No. U41 Surcharged in Black

1944, Feb. 17

NU2	E4 5c on 2c **carmine**	.75	.50
	Entire	3.50	*5.00*
	Entire, 1st day cancel		7.50
a.	Inverted surcharged	—	
b.	Double surcharge	—	
c.	Both 5's missing	—	

OCCUPATION POSTAL CARDS

Values are for entire cards.

Nos. UX19 and UZ4 Overprinted with Bars in Black

1942

NUX1	A53 2c **red,** *pale buff, Mar. 4, 1942*	15.00	15.00
	First day cancel		*85.00*
a.	Vertical obliteration bars reversed	*140.00*	
NUX2	A75 2c **light green,** *pale buff, Dec. 12, 1942*	3.00	2.00
	First day cancel		6.00

Rice Planting — A77

1943, May 17

NUX3	A77 2c **green**	1.00	*1.00*
	First day cancel, Manila		2.00

OCCUPATION OFFICIAL CARDS

Nos. UX19, UX17 and UX18 Overprinted in Black with Bars and 公用 (K.P.)

1943, Apr. 7

NUZ1	A53 2c **red,** *pale buff*	5.00	5.00
	First day cancel		100.00
a.	On No. UX17	—	—
b.	On No. UX18	—	—

No. NUX3 Overprinted in Black

REPUBLIKA
NG PILIPINAS
(K. P.)

1944, Aug. 28

NUZ2 A77 2c **green**		1.50	*1.00*
	First day cancel		2.00
a.	Double overprint	—	

FILIPINO REVOLUTIONARY GOVERNMENT

Following the defeat of the Spanish fleet by U.S. Commodore Dewey in Manila on May 1, 1898, which essentially ended the Spanish-American War in the Philippines, postal services were disrupted throughout the Philippines. Postal service was reestablished through U.S. Army military stations, beginning in June 1898 near Manila, continuing province by province until culminating at Zamboanga and other cities in the southern areas in late 1899.

Provisional stamps were prepared for use in the central part of the island of Luzon at Malolos in late 1898 under the leadership of General Emilio Aguinaldo, who had proclaimed the Philippine Republic on June 12, 1898. Later, other provisional stamps were prepared by local Filipino insurgents at Iloilo (Panay Island), Bohol, Cebu and Negros, and Spanish period stamps were overprinted and/or surcharged for use by postal officials at Zamboanga and La Union.

The most familiar of these provisionals were the "Aguinaldo" issues of the Filipino Revolutionary Government in central Luzon near Manila. The letters "KKK," the initials of the revolutionary society, "Kataastaasang, Kagalang-galang Katipunan nang Mañga Anak nang Bayan," meaning "Sovereign Worshipful Association of the Sons of the Country," readily identify the Aguinaldo provisionals. Hostilities broke out between the Aguinaldo regime and the occupying American administration in February 1899, and the Filipino-American War continued until the American capture of Aguinaldo on March 23, 1901.

The Aguinaldo regular postage, registration, revenue, newspaper and telegraph stamps were in use in Luzon as early as November 10, 1898, and continued in use through early 1901. Although the postal regulations specified that these stamps be used for their inscribed purpose, they were commonly used interchangeably.

POSTAGE ISSUES

A1

A2

Coat of Arms — A3

1898-99 Unwmk. *Perf. 11½*

Y1 A1 2c **red**		175.00	125.00
	On cover		*1,500.*
a.	Double impression	*225.00*	
Y2 A2 2c **red**		.20	.25
	On cover		450.00
b.	Double impression	—	
d.	Horiz. pair, imperf. between	—	
e.	Vert. pair, imperf. between	*200.00*	
Y3 A3 2c **red**		150.00	*200.00*
	On cover		*2,000.*

Imperf pairs and pairs, imperf horizontally, have been created from No. Y2e.

RS1

N1

REGISTRATION STAMP

YF1 RS1 8c **green**		3.50	*10.00*
	On cover with #Y2		*3,500.*
a.	Imperf., pair	400.00	
b.	Imperf. vertically, pair	—	

NEWSPAPER STAMP

YP1 N1 1m **black**		1.00
a.	Imperf., pair	1.00

PROOFS

			(1) Large	DIE (2) Small	*(2a)*
1906					
241P	2c	**yellow green**		500.	750.
242P	4c	**carmine lake**	*600.*	500.	750.
243P	6c	**violet**	*600.*	500.	750.
244P	8c	**brown**	*600.*	500.	750.
245P	10c	**dark blue**		500.	750.
246P	12c	**brown lake**		500.	750.
247P	16c	**violet black**	*600.*	500.	750.
248P	20c	**orange brown**		500.	750.
249P	26c	**violet brown**		500.	750.
250P	30c	**olive green**	*600.*	500.	750.
251P	1p	**orange**		500.	750.
252P	2p	**black**		500.	750.
253P	4p	**dark blue**		500.	750.
254P	10p	**dark green**		500.	750.
1909-13					
255P	12c	**red orange**		600.	625.
256P	16c	**olive green**		600.	625.
257P	20c	**yellow**		600.	625.
258P	26c	**blue green**		600.	625.
259P	30c	**ultramarine**		600.	625.
260P	1p	**pale violet**		600.	625.
260AP	2p	**violet brown**		600.	625.
275P	30c	**gray**		600.	625.
1923					
303P	16c	**olive bister**	450.		
303TC	16c	**olive green**	450.		
1926					
322P	18c	**light brown & black,** plate, glazed card			350.
1932					
357P	18c	**red orange**	450.		
357TC	18c	**orange red**	450.		
360TC	32c	**green**	450.		
360TC	18c	**olive green**	450.		
1935					
383P	2c	**rose**	600.		
384P	4c	**yellow green**	600.		
385P	6c	**dark brown**	600.		
386P	8c	**violet**	600.		
387P	10c	**rose carmine**	600.		
388P	12c	**black**	600.		
389P	16c	**dark blue**	600.		
390P	20c	**light olive green**	600.		
390TC	20c	**black**	—		
391P	26c	**indigo**	600.		
392P	30c	**orange red**	600.		
393P	1p	**red orange & black**	600.		
394P	2p	**bister brown & black**	600.		
395P	4p	**blue & black**	600.		
396P	5p	**green & black**	600.		
1936					
408P	2c	**orange brown**	450.		
408TC	2c	**yellow green**	450.		
1937					
425P	2c	**yellow green**		500.	
1939					
452P	2c	**yellow green**		500.	
453P	6c	**carmine**		500.	
454P	12c	**bright blue**		500.	
1939					
455P	2c	**green**	750.	500.	
456P	6c	**orange**		500.	
457P	12c	**carmine**		500.	
1940					
458P	2c	**dark orange**	1,000.	600.	
459P	6c	**dark green**		600.	
460P	12c	**purple**		600.	
1941					
461P	2c	**apple green**	600.		
1946					
497P	2c	**sepia**	—		

AIR POST

1941				
C59P	8c	**carmine**		500.
C60P	20c	**ultramarine**		500.
C61P	60c	**blue green**		500.
C62P	1p	**sepia**		500.

SPECIAL DELIVERY

1906

E2P	20c	**ultramarine**	1,000.	1,000.	850.
E2TC	20c	**green**		1,000.	

POSTAGE DUE

1899			
J1P	1c	**deep claret**	1,100.
J2P	2c	**deep claret**	1,100.
J3P	5c	**deep claret**	1,100.
J4P	10c	**deep claret**	1,100.
J5P	50c	**deep claret**	1,100.
1901			
J6P	3c	**deep claret**	1,100.
J7P	30c	**deep claret**	1,100.

SPECIMEN STAMPS

Handstamped US Type E in Purple **Specimen.**

1899

213S E	1c	**yellow green**	175.00
214dS E	2c	**rose carmine,** type IV	175.00
215S E	3c	**purple**	175.00
216S E	5c	**blue**	175.00
217S E	10c	**brown,** type I	175.00
218S E	15c	**olive brown**	175.00
219S E	50c	**orange**	175.00

See note after No. 219 for Special Printings with black "Specimen" overprints.

Overprinted US Type R in Black ***Specimen***

1917-25			
290S R	2c	**green**	40.00
291S R	4c	**carmine**	40.00
292S R	6c	**deep violet**	40.00
293S R	8c	**yellow brown**	40.00
294S R	10c	**deep blue**	40.00
295S R	12c	**red orange**	40.00
297S R	20c	**orange yellow**	40.00
298S R	26c	**green**	40.00
299S R	30c	**gray**	40.00
300S R	1p	**pale violet**	40.00
301S R	2p	**violet brown**	40.00
302S R	4p	**blue**	40.00
1923-26			
303S R	16c	**olive bister**	25.00
304S R	10p	**deep green**	25.00

1926 **Overprinted Type R in Red**

319S R	2c	**green & black**	65.00
320S R	4c	**carmine & black**	65.00
321S R	16c	**olive green & black**	65.00
322S R	18c	**light brown & black**	65.00
323S R	20c	**orange & black**	65.00
324S R	24c	**gray & black**	65.00
325S R	1p	**rose lilac & black**	65.00

Overprinted US Type S in Red ***Cancelled***

1926

319S S	2c	**green & black**	65.00
320S S	4c	**carmine & black**	65.00
321S S	16c	**olive green & black**	65.00
322S S	18c	**light brown & black**	65.00
323S S	20c	**orange & black**	65.00
324S S	24c	**gray & black**	65.00
325S S	1p	**rose lilac & black**	65.00

Imperforate examples of this set, on glazed cards with centers in brown, are known with the "Cancelled" overprint. Value, $2,250 for set.

Handstamped "SPECIMEN" in Red Capitals, 13x3mm

1925

340S S	2c	**green**	75.00
341S S	4c	**carmine**	75.00
342S S	6c	**deep violet**	75.00
343S S	8c	**yellow brown**	100.00
344S S	10c	**deep blue**	100.00
345S S	12c	**red orange**	100.00
346S S	16c	**olive bister**	100.00
347S S	20c	**yellow**	100.00
348S S	26c	**blue green**	100.00
349S S	30c	**gray**	100.00
350S S	1p	**violet**	100.00
351S S	2p	**violet brown**	100.00
352S S	4p	**deep blue**	150.00
353S S	10p	**deep green**	250.00

SPECIAL DELIVERY

1919 **Overprinted Type R in Black**

E5S R	20c	**ultramarine**	200.00
E5bS R	20c	**dull violet**	—

Handstamped "SPECIMEN" in Red Capitals, 13x3mm

1925

E6aS	20c	**violet blue**	300.00

POSTAGE DUE

1899 Overprinted Type E in Black

J1S E	1c	**deep claret**	225.00
J2S E	2c	**deep claret**	225.00
J3S E	5c	**deep claret**	225.00
J4S E	10c	**deep claret**	225.00
J5S E	50c	**deep claret**	225.00

OFFICIAL

1926 Overprinted Type R in Red

O1S R	2c	**green & black**	30.00
O2S R	4c	**carmine & black**	30.00
O3S R	18c	**light brown & black**	30.00
O4S R	20c	**orange & black**	30.00

1926 Overprinted Type S in Red

O1S S	2c	**green & black**	30.00
O2S S	4c	**carmine & black**	30.00
O3S S	18c	**light brown & black**	30.00
O4S S	20c	**orange & black**	30.00

PUERTO RICO

(Porto Rico)

United States troops landed at Guanica Bay, Puerto Rico, on July 25, 1898, and mail service between various points in Puerto Rico began soon after under the authority of General Wilson, acting governor of the conquered territory, who authorized a provisional service early in August, 1898. The first Military Postal Station was opened at La Playa de Ponce on August 3, 1898. Control of the island passed formally to the United States on October 18, 1898. Twenty-one military stations operating under the administration of the Military Postal Service were authorized in Puerto Rico after the Spanish-American war. After the overprinted provisional issue of 1900, unoverprinted stamps of the United States replaced those of Puerto Rico.

Name changed to Puerto Rico by Act of Congress, approved May 17, 1932.

Italicized numbers in parentheses indicate quantities issued.

100 CENTS = 1 DOLLAR.

PROVISIONAL ISSUES

Ponce Issue

A11

1898 Unwmk. Handstamped *Imperf.*

200 A11	5c	**violet,** *yellowish*	*7,500.*	—

The only way No. 200 is known used is handstamped on envelopes. Both unused stamps and used envelopes have a violet control mark.

Uses on 2c U.S. stamps on cover were strictly as a cancellation, not as provisional postage.

Dangerous counterfeits exist.

Coamo Issue

A12

Types of "5":

I — Curved flag. Pos. 2, 3, 4, 5.
II — Flag turns down at right. Pos. 1, 9, 10.
III — Fancy outlined "5." Pos. 6, 7.
IV — Flag curls into ball at right. Pos. 8.

Typeset, setting of 10

1898, Aug. Unwmk. *Imperf.*

201 A12	5c	**black,** Type I	650.	*1,050.*
		Type II	700.	*1,100.*
		Type III	775.	*1,200.*
		Type IV	850.	*1,350.*
		Irregular "block" of 4 showing one of each type	3,750.	
		Sheet of 10	10,000.	
		On cover		*32,500.*
		Pair on cover		—

Blocks not showing all four types and pairs normally sell for 10-20% over the value of the individual stamps.

The stamps bear the control mark "F. Santiago" in violet. About 500 were issued.

Dangerous counterfeits exist.

Regular Issue

United States Nos. 279, 279Bf, 281, 272 and 282C Overprinted in Black at 36 degree Angle

1899 Wmk. 191 *Perf. 12*

210 A87	1c	**yellow green,** *Mar. 15*	5.00	1.40
		On cover		50.00
		First day cover		—
		Block of 4	25.00	10.00
		P# strip of 3, Impt.	45.00	
		P# block of 6, Impt.	275.00	
a.		Overprint at 25 degree angle	7.50	2.25
		Pair, 36 degree and 25 degree angles	25.00	
		"PORTO RICU"	30.00	—
211 A88	2c	**reddish carmine,** type IV, *Mar. 15*	4.25	1.25
		On cover		50.00
		Block of 4	22.50	10.00
		P# strip of 3, Impt.	37.50	
		P# block of 6, Impt.	350.00	
		"FORTO RICO" (pos. 77)	—	
a.		Overprint at 25 degree angle, *Mar. 15*	5.50	2.25
		On cover		50.00
		First day cover		—
		Block of 4	27.50	17.50
		P# strip of 3, Impt.	45.00	
		P# block of 6, Impt.	275.00	
		Pair, 36 degree and 25 degree angles	25.00	
		P# strip of 3, Impt.	95.00	
		P# block of 6, Impt.	700.00	
		"PORTU RICO" (pos. 46)	50.00	20.00
		"PORTO RICU" (pos. 3)	—	
		"PURTO RICO"	—	
		"FURTU RICO"	—	
212 A91	5c	**blue**	12.50	2.50
		On cover		50.00
		Block of 4	55.00	27.50
		P# strip of 3, Impt.	70.00	
		P# block of 6, Impt.	350.00	
213 A93	8c	**violet brown**	35.00	17.50
		On cover		125.00
		Block of 4	160.00	110.00
		P# strip of 3, Impt.	250.00	
		P# block of 6, Impt.	*2,250.*	
		"FORTO RICO"	90.00	60.00
a.		Overprint at 25 degree angle	40.00	19.00
		Pair, 36 degree and 25 degree angles	100.00	
c.		"PORTO RIC"	150.00	110.00
214 A94	10c	**brown,** type I	25.00	6.00
		On cover		120.00
		Block of 4	110.00	45.00
		P# strip of 3, Impt.	160.00	
		P# block of 6, Impt.	1,250.	
		"FORTO RICO"	85.00	70.00
		Nos. 210-214 (5)	81.75	28.65

Misspellings of the overprint on Nos. 210-214 (PORTO RICU, PORTU RICO, FORTO RICO) are actually broken letters.

United States Nos. 279 and 279B Overprinted in Black

1900

215 A87	1c	**yellow green**	6.50	1.40
		On cover		50.00
		Block of 4	27.50	10.00
		P# strip of 3, Impt.	30.00	
		P# block of 6, Impt.	175.00	
216 A88	2c	**red,** type IV, *Apr. 2*	4.75	2.00
		On cover		50.00
		Block of 4	22.50	15.00
		P# strip of 3, Impt.	32.50	
		P# block of 6, Impt.	175.00	
b.		Inverted overprint		*8,250.*

Special Printing

In March 1900 one pane of 100 stamps of each of the 1c (No. 215), 2c (No. 216) and 5c, 8c and 10c values, as well as 1c, 2c and 10c postage due stamps were specially overprinted for displays at the Paris Exposition (1900) and Pan American Exposition (1901). These last six items were never regularly issued with the PUERTO RICO overprint and therefore have no Scott catalogue number. The 2c pane was light red, type IV.

Stamps were handstampd type E "Specimen" in black ink by H. G. Mandel and mounted by him in separate displays for the two Expositions. Additional stamps from each pane were also handstamped "Specimen," but most were destroyed after the Expositions.

J. M. Bartels, a stamp dealer, signed some stamps from these panes "Special Surcharge" in pencil on the gum to authenticate them as coming from the "Mandel" Special Printing panes. In 1904 or later, he handstamped additional surviving examples "Special Surcharge" in red ink on the back as his guarantee. Some of these guaranteed stamps had Mandel's "Specimen" handstamp on the face while others did not. Value, each $1,750.

No Special Printing panes overprinted "Porto Rico" were produced by the government. Stamps do exist with a black type E "Specimen" handstamp, but it is believed that H. G. Mandel applied such handstamps to regularly issued overprinted "Porto Rico" stamps from his personal collection. Examples are known of the 2c type IV, in reddish carmine, 25 degree angle.

AIR POST

In 1938 a series of eight labels, two of which were surcharged, was offered to the public as "Semi-Official Air Post Stamps", the claim being that they had been authorized by the "Puerto Rican postal officials." These labels, printed by the Ever Ready Label Co. of New York, were a private issue of Aerovias Nacionales Puerto Rico, operating a passenger and air express service. Instead of having been authorized by the postal officials, they were at first forbidden but later tolerated by the Post Office Department at Washington.

In 1941 a further set of eight triangular labels was prepared and offered to collectors, and again the Post Office Department officials at Washington objected and forbade their use after September 16, 1941.

These labels represent only the charge for service rendered by a private enterprise for transporting matter outside the mails by plane. Their use did not and does not eliminate the payment of postage on letters carried by air express, which must in every instance be paid by United States postage stamps.

POSTAGE DUE STAMPS

United States Nos. J38, J39 and J42 Overprinted in Black at 36 degree Angle

1899 Wmk. 191 *Perf. 12*

J1 D2 1c **deep claret** 22.50 5.50
On cover 125.00
Block of 4 100.00 35.00
P# strip of 3, Impt. 120.00
P# block of 6, Impt. *625.00*
a. Overprint at 25 degree angle 22.50 7.50
Pair, 36 degree and 25 degree angles 65.00
P# strip of 3, Impt. 150.00
P# block of 6, Impt. *750.00*
J2 D2 2c **deep claret** 20.00 6.00
On cover 250.00
Block of 4 80.00 37.50
P# strip of 3, Impt. 120.00
P# block of 6, Impt. *800.00*
a. Overprint at 25 degree angle 20.00 7.00
Pair, 36 degree and 25 degree angles 60.00
P# strip of 3, Impt. 140.00
P# block of 6, Impt. *900.00*
J3 D2 10c **deep claret** 190.00 60.00
On cover —
Block of 4 800.00 —
P# strip of 3, Impt. *1,250.*
P# block of 6, Impt. *3,750.*
a. Overprint at 25 degree angle 175.00 85.00
Pair, 36 degree and 25 degree angles 650.00

ENVELOPES

U.S. Envelopes of 1887 Issue Overprinted in Black

PORTO RICO.

20mm long

1899-1900

Note: Some envelopes for which there was no obvious need were issued in small quantities. Anyone residing in Puerto Rico could, by depositing with his postmaster the required amount, order any envelope in quantities of 500, or multiples thereof, provided it was on the schedule of U.S. envelopes. Such special orders are indicated by a plus sign, i. e., Nos. U15 and U18, and half the quantities of Nos. U16 and U17.

U1 U71 2c **green** (No. U311) *(3,000)* 16.00 *20.00*
Entire 40.00 *350.00*
a. Double overprint, entire *3,500.*
U2 U74 5c **blue** (No. U330) *(1,000)* 20.00 20.00
Entire 55.00 *350.00*
a. Double overprint, entire —

U.S. Envelopes of 1899 Overprinted in color of the stamp

PORTO RICO.

21mm long

U3 U79 2c **carmine** (No. U362) *(100,000)* 3.00 3.00
Entire 10.00 *12.00*
U4 U84 5c **blue** (No. U377) *(10,000)* 8.00 *9.00*
Entire 17.50 *32.50*

Overprinted in Black PORTO RICO.

19mm long

U5 U77 1c **green,** *blue* (No. U355) *(1,000)* 750.
Entire 1,900.
U6 U79 2c **carmine,** *amber* (No. U363), Die 2 *(500)* 450. *500.*
Entire 1,100. 1,250.
U7 U79 2c **carmine,** *oriental buff* (No. U364), Die 2 *(500)* 500.
Entire 1,250.
U8 U80 2c **carmine,** *oriental buff* (No. U369), Die 3 *(500)* 600.
Entire 1,300.
U9 U79 2c **carmine,** *blue* (No. U365), Die 2
Entire *4,000.*
U10 U83 4c **brown** (No. U374), Die 3 *(500)* 200. *500.*
Entire 500. *900.*

U.S. Envelopes of 1899 Issue Overprinted

PUERTO RICO.

23mm long

U11 U79 2c **carmine** (No. U362) red overprint *(100,000)* 4.00 3.00
Entire 10.00 *11.00*
U12 U79 2c **carmine,** *oriental buff* (No. U364), Die 2, black overprint *(1,000)* — 325.00
Entire *1,200.* *1,300.*
U13 U80 2c **carmine,** *oriental buff* (No. U369), Die 3, black overprint *(1,000)* 375.00
Entire *1,750.*
U14 U84 5c **blue** (No. U377) blue overprint *(10,000)* 14.00 14.00
Entire 42.50 *50.00*

Overprinted in Black PUERTO RICO.

U15 U77 1c **green,** *oriental buff* (No. U354) *(500)+* 20.00 *50.00*
Entire 75.00 *80.00*
U16 U77 1c **green,** *blue* (No. U355) *(1,000)+* 25.00 *50.00*
Entire 95.00 *125.00*
U17 U79 2c **carmine,** *oriental buff* (No. U364) *(1,000)+* 20.00 *50.00*
Entire 95.00 *135.00*
U18 U79 2c **carmine,** *blue* (No. U365) *(500)+* 20.00 *50.00*
Entire 75.00 *135.00*

There were two settings of the overprint, with minor differences, which are found on Nos. U16 and U17.

WRAPPER

U.S. Wrapper of 1899 Issue Overprinted in Green

PORTO RICO.

21mm long

W1 U77 1c **green,** *manila* (No. W357) *(15,000)* 8.00 *35.00*
Entire 17.00 *110.00*

POSTAL CARDS

Values are for Entires.

Imprinted below stamp PORTO RICO.

1899-1900 U.S. Postal Card No. UX14

UX1 PC8 1c **black,** *buff,* imprint 21mm long 165. *175.*
b. Double imprint *2,250.*

Imprinted below stamp PORTO RICO.

UX1A PC8 1c **black,** *buff,* imprint 20mm long 1,200. *1,300.*

Imprinted below stamp PORTO RICO.

UX2 PC8 1c **black,** *buff,* imprint 26mm long 165. *190.*

Imprinted below stamp PUERTO RICO.

UX3 PC8 1c **black,** *buff* 150. *200.*

REVENUE STAMPS

U.S. Revenue Stamps Nos. R163, R168-R169, R171 and Type of 1898 Surcharged in Black or Dark Blue

PORTO RICO
10 C.
Excise Revenue
a

PORTO RICO
$1
EXCISE REVENUE
b

1901 Wmk. 191R *Hyphen-hole Roulette 7*

R1 R15(a) 1c on 1c **pale blue** (Bk) 10.00 8.75
R2 R15(a) 10c on 10c **dark brown** 12.50 11.00
R3 R15(a) 25c on 25c **purple brown** 15.00 11.00
R4 R15(a) 50c on 50c **slate violet** 25.00 16.50
R5 R16(b) $1 on $1 **pale greenish gray** 62.50 22.50
R6 R16(b) $3 on $3 **pale greenish gray** 70.00 32.50
R7 R16(b) $5 on $5 **pale greenish gray** 85.00 37.50
R8 R16(b) $10 on $10 **pale greenish gray** 120.00 70.00
R9 R16(b) $50 on $50 **pale greenish gray** 325.00 160.00
Nos. R1-R9 (9) 725.00 369.75

Lines of 1c surcharge spaced farther apart; total depth of surcharge 15¾mm instead of 11mm.

RECTIFIED SPIRITS

U.S. Wine Stamps of 1933-34 Overprinted in Red or Carmine

RECTIFIE[D]
SPIRITS

1934 Offset Printing Wmk. 191R *Rouletted*

Overprint Lines 14mm Apart, Second Line 25mm Long

RE1 RE5 2c **green** 15.0
RE2 RE5 3c **green** 55.0
RE3 RE5 4c **green** 17.5
RE4 RE5 5c **green** 15.0
RE5 RE5 6c **green** 17.5

Overprint Lines 21½mm Apart, Second Line 23½mm Long

RE6 RE2 50c **green** 27.5
RE7 RE2 60c **green** 25.0

Handstamped overprints are also found on U.S. Wine stamps of 1933-34.

U.S. Wine Stamps of 1933-34 Overprinted in Black

RECTIFIED
SPIRITS
a

RECTIFIED
SPIRITS
b

1934 Offset Printing Wmk. 191R *Rouletted*

RE8 RE5(a) 1c **green** 22.5
RE9 RE5(a) 2c **green** 12.5
RE10 RE5(a) 3c **green** 60.0
RE11 RE5(a) 5c **green** 12.5
RE12 RE5(a) 6c **green** 15.0
RE13 RE2(b) 50c **green** 17.5
RE14 RE2(b) 60c **green** 15.0
RE15 RE2(b) 72c **green** 75.0
RE16 RE2(b) 80c **green** 40.0

U.S. Wine Stamps of 1933-34 Overprinted in Black

RECTIFIED SPIRITS
PUERTO RICO

1934 Offset Printing Wmk. 191R *Rouletted*

RE17 RE5 ½c **green** 2.5
RE18 RE5 1c **green** 50.00 .6
RE19 RE5 2c **green** 50.00 .5
RE20 RE5 3c **green** 100.00 3.5
RE21 RE5 4c **green** .7
RE22 RE5 5c **green** 50.00 1.0
RE23 RE5 6c **green** 50.00 1.2
RE24 RE5 10c **green** 100.00 3.5
RE25 RE5 30c **green** 30.0

Overprint Lines 12½mm Apart

RE26 RE2 36c **green** 6.0
RE27 RE2 40c **green** 150.00 5.0
RE28 RE2 50c **green** 150.00 2.5
RE29 RE2 60c **green** 125.00 .5
a. Inverted overprint —
RE30 RE2 72c **green** 150.00 4.0
RE31 RE2 80c **green** 150.00 4.0
RE32 RE2 $1 **green** 175.00 7.5

George Sewall Boutwell — R1

Engr. (8c & 58c); Litho.

1942-57 Wmk. 191 *Rouletted 7*

Without Gum

RE33	R1	½c **carmine**	3.50	1.25
RE34	R1	1c **sepia**	8.25	3.50
RE35	R1	2c **bright yellow green**	1.10	.20
RE36	R1	3c **lilac**	70.00	35.00
RE37	R1	4c **olive**	2.25	.50
RE38	R1	5c **orange**	5.50	1.00
RE39	R1	6c **red brown**	4.00	1.25
RE40	R1	8c **bright pink** ('57)	8.25	3.50
RE41	R1	10c **bright purple**	12.50	5.00
RE41A	R1	30c **vermilion**	175.00	
RE42	R1	36c **dull yellow**	250.00	70.00
RE43	R1	40c **deep claret**	20.00	7.00
RE44	R1	50c **green**	11.00	4.00
RE45	R1	58c **red orange**	87.50	7.00
RE46	R1	60c **brown**	1.40	.20
RE47	R1	62c **black**	3.50	.70
RE48	R1	72c **blue**	40.00	1.00
RE49	R1	77½c **olive gray**	11.00	3.50
RE50	R1	80c **brownish black**	14.00	6.00
RE51	R1	$1 **violet**	87.50	25.00
		Nos. RE33-RE51 (20)	816.25	175.60

The 30c is believed not to have been placed in use.

SPECIMEN STAMPS

Handstamped U.S. Type E in Purple **Specimen.**

1899

210S	E	1c **yellow green**	180.00
211S	E	2c **reddish carmine,** type IV	180.00
212S	E	5c **blue**	180.00
213S	E	8c **violet brown**	180.00
214S	E	10c **brown**	180.00

See note after No. 216 for Special Printings with **black** "Specimen" overprint.

Postage Due

1899

J1S	E	1c **deep claret**	225.00
J2S	E	2c **deep claret**	225.00
J3S	E	10c **deep claret**	225.00

Revenue

R1S	E	1c on 1c **pale blue**	40.00
R2S	E	10c on 10c **dark brown**	40.00
R3S	E	25c on 25c **purple brown**	40.00
R4S	E	50c on 50c **state violet**	40.00
R5S	E	$1 on $1 **pale greenish gray**	40.00
R6S	E	$3 on $3 **pale greenish gray**	40.00
R7S	E	$5 on $5 **pale greenish gray**	40.00
R8S	E	$10 on $10 **pale greenish gray**	40.00
R9S	E	$50 on $50 **pale greenish gray**	40.00

RYUKYU ISLANDS

LOCATION — Chain of 63 islands between Japan and Formosa, separating the East China Sea from the Pacific Ocean.
GOVT. — Semi-autonomous under United States administration.
AREA — 848 sq. mi.
POP. — 945,465 (1970)
CAPITAL — Naha, Okinawa

The Ryukyus were part of Japan until American forces occupied them in 1945. The islands reverted to Japan May 15, 1972.

100 Sen = 1 Yen
100 Cents = 1 Dollar (1958).

In the Provisional Issues and Postal Stationery sections, italicized numbers in parentheses indicate quantity sold.

Values for First Day Covers are for unaddressed, cacheted covers. Values are for official cachets for Scott 1-26, C1-C3 and E1; and for commercial cachets for all others. Early cachets from the Japanese Philatelic Society command substantial premiums.

Catalogue values for unused stamps are for Never Hinged items beginning with Scott 1 in the regular postage section, Scott C1 in the air post section, Scott E1 in the special delivery section, Scott R1 in the revenue section, Scott 91S in the specimen section and Scott RQ1 in the unemployment insurance section.

Cycad — A1

Lily — A2

Sailing Ship — A3

Farmer — A4

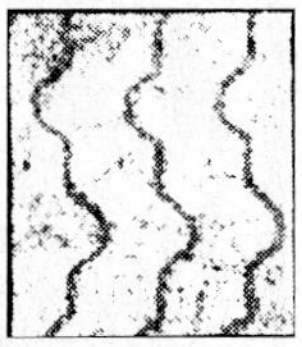
Wmk. 257

1948-49 Typo. Wmk. 257 *Perf. 13*

Second Printing, July 18, 1949

1	A1	5s **magenta**	2.50	2.50
		Imprint block of 10	37.50	
2	A2	10s **yellow green**	6.00	5.50
		Imprint block of 10	90.00	
3	A1	20s **yellow green**	3.50	3.50
		Imprint block of 10	55.00	
4	A3	30s **vermilion**	1.50	1.50
		Imprint block of 10	25.00	
5	A2	40s **magenta**	1.50	1.50
		Imprint block of 10	25.00	
6	A3	50s **ultramarine**	6.00	*4.00*
		Imprint block of 10	90.00	
7	A4	1y **ultramarine**	6.00	5.50
		Imprint block of 10	90.00	
		Nos. 1-7 (7)	27.00	24.00

First Printing, July 1, 1948

1a	A1	5s **magenta**	3.00	*3.50*
		First day cover		250.00
		Imprint block of 10	45.00	
2a	A2	10s **yellow green**	2.00	*2.00*
		First day cover		250.00
		Imprint block of 10	30.00	
3a	A1	20s **yellow green**	2.00	*2.00*
		First day cover		250.00
		Imprint block of 10	30.00	
4a	A3	30s **vermilion**	4.00	*3.50*
		First day cover		250.00
		Imprint block of 10	45.00	
5a	A2	40s **magenta**	60.00	60.00
		First day cover		250.00
		Imprint block of 10	900.00	
6a	A3	50s **ultramarine**	4.00	4.00
		First day cover		250.00
		Imprint block of 10	55.00	
7a	A4	1y **ultramarine**	475.00	350.00
		First day cover		250.00
		Imprint block of 10	*7,000.*	
		Nos. 1a-7a (7)	550.00	425.00

First printing: thick yellow gum, dull colors, rough perforations, grayish paper. Second printing: white gum, sharp colors, cleancut perforations, white paper.

A5

Ryukyu University — A6

Designs: 50s, Tile rooftop & Shishi. 1y, Ryukyu girl. 2y, Shuri Castle. 3y, Guardian dragon. 4y, Two women. 5y, Sea shells.

1950, Jan. 21 Photo. Unwmk. *Perf. 13x13½*

Off-white Paper

8	A5	50s **dark carmine rose**	.20	.20
		First day cover		20.00
		Imprint block of 6	2.00	
a.		White paper, third printing, *Sept. 6, 1958*	.50	.50
		First day cover		27.50
		Imprint block of 10	6.50	
b.		"White Sky" variety (pos. 76)	3.50	3.50
9	A5	1y **deep blue**	4.00	3.00
		First day cover		20.00
		Imprint block of 6	35.00	
10	A5	2y **rose violet**	12.00	6.00
		First day cover		20.00
		Imprint block of 6	100.00	
11	A5	3y **carmine rose**	30.00	11.00

		First day cover		20.00
		Imprint block of 6	275.00	
12	A5	4y **greenish gray**	15.00	11.00
		First day cover		20.00
		Imprint block of 6	110.00	
13	A5	5y **blue green**	8.00	6.00
		First day cover		20.00
		Imprint block of 6	60.00	
		First day cover, #8-13		200.00
		Nos. 8-13 (6)	69.20	37.20

No. 8a has colorless gum and an 8-character imprint in the sheet margin. The original 1950 first two printings on off-white paper have yellowish gum and a 5-character imprint.

For No. 8b, a defect in pos. 76 of the plates used for the first two printings resulted in the sky above the tile roof being predominantly white. A new master negative and plate was made for the third printing, so pos. 76 for this printing does not have the "white sky" variety.

For surcharges see Nos. 16-17.

1951, Feb. 12 ***Perf. 13½x13***

14	A6	3y **red brown**	60.00	25.00
		First day cover		60.00
		Imprint block of 6	450.00	

Opening of Ryukyu University, Feb. 12.

Pine Tree — A7

1951, Feb. 19 ***Perf. 13***

15	A7	3y **dark green**	55.00	25.00
		First day cover		60.00
		Imprint block of 6	450.00	

Reforestation Week, Feb. 18-24.

No. 8 surcharged in Black

16A Type I

16 Type II

16B Type III

There are three types of 10y surcharge:

Type I: narrow-spaced rules, "10" normal spacing, "Kai Tei" characters in 9-point type. First printing, Jan. 1, 1952.

Type II: wide-spaced rules, "10" normal spacing, "Kai Tei" characters in 9-point type. Second printing, June 5, 1952.

Type III: rules and "10" both wide-spaced, "Kai Tei" characters in 8-point type. Third printing, Dec. 8, 1952.

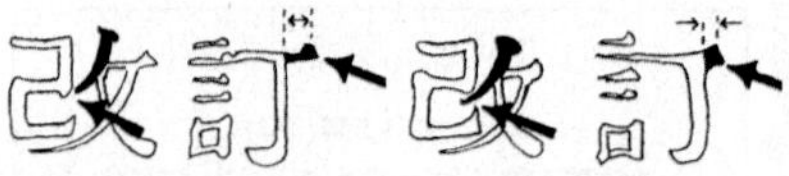

9 Point Kai Tei   8 Point Kai Tei

Both eight and nine point type were used in overprinting Nos. 16-17. In the varieties listed below, the first number indicates the size of the "Kai" character, and the second number is the size of the "Tei" character.

1952 ***Perf. 13½x13***

16	A5	10y on 50s **dark carmine rose** (II)	10.00	10.00
		Imprint block of 6	90.00	
		Top imprint block of 4, *Higa Seal* (pos. 8, 9, 18, 19)	75.00	
c.		8/8 point Kai Tei	10.00	10.00
d.		9/8 point Kai Tei	90.00	90.00
		9/9-9/8-8/8 se-tenant (horiz. strip of all 3 varieties)	150.00	150.00
		8/8-9/9 horiz. se-tenant pair	30.00	30.00
		9/9-8/8 horiz. se-tenant pair	30.00	30.00
e.		Surcharge transposed	900.00	—
f.		Legend of surcharge only (no obliteration bars)	1,200.	
g.		Wrong font for "0" (pos. 59)	150.00	150.00
h.		Wrong font for "Yen" symbol (pos. 69)	150.00	150.00
i.		Surcharge on "white sky" variety (No. 8b) (pos. 76)	150.00	150.00

On No. 16e, the entire obliteration-bars portion of the surcharge normally under the 10 Yen must be visible at the top of the stamp. Ten examples of No. 16e exist (pos. 91-100) with the full obliteration bars also in the bottom selvage.

Forgeries to defraud the Postal Agency of revenue are known, used only, at the Gusikawa Post Office. Two types. Value, $500 each.

16A	A5	10y on 50s **dark carmine rose** (I)	40.00	40.00
		Imprint block of 6	350.00	
a.		8/8 point Kai Tei	40.00	40.00
		8/8-9/9 horiz. se-tenant pair (pos. 23-24)	200.00	250.00
		9/9-8/8 horiz. se-tenant pair	110.00	110.00
b.		Bottom two bars inverted (pos. 17)	150.00	150.00
c.		Wrong font for "0" (pos. 73)	250.00	250.00
d.		Surcharge on "white sky" variety (No. 8b) (pos. 76)	250.00	250.00
e.		Wide spaced obliterating bars (pos. 72)	150.00	150.00
f.		Wide spaced bottom obliterating bars (pos. 86, 95)	80.00	80.00
16B	A5	10y on 50s **dark carmine rose** (III)	50.00	40.00
		Imprint block of 6	450.00	
a.		Wrong font for "Yen" symbol (pos. 25, 35, 85)	200.00	200.00
b.		Wrong font for "Tei" (pos. 26)	350.00	350.00
c.		Asterisk missing (pos. 54)	—	—
d.		"Kai Tei" 1.25mm above asterisk (pos. 54)	350.00	350.00
e.		"Kai" omitted (pos. 71)	—	
f.		Narrow spaced "10" (pos. 96)	350.00	350.00
		Strip of 3, narrow spaced "10" in center (pos. 95-97)	450.00	
g.		Surcharge on "white sky" variety (No. 8b)	350.00	350.00
h.		Extra wide spaced "10" (pos. 60)	200.00	200.00
i.		Asterisk within 2.0mm of "Kai Tei" (pos. 87)	200.00	200.00

The Kai Tei of the third printing measures the same as the 8-point type in the earlier printings but has differing characteristics. The Top curved line of the Kai is shorter and the lower curved line is also much shorter.

No. 10 surcharged 100y in black

17	A5	100y on 2y **rose violet,** Kai Tei characters in 9/9-point type, June 16, 1952	2,200.	1,600.
		Hinged	1,600.	
		Imprint block of 6	18,500.	
		Top imprint block of 4, *Higa Seal* (pos. 7, 8, 17, 18)	10,000.	
a.		8/8 point Kai Tei	2,200.	1,600.
b.		9/8 point Kai Tei	3,500.	3,500.
		9/9-9/8-8/8 se-tenant (horiz. strip of all 3 varieties)	*9,750.*	*9,750.*
		8/8-9/9 horiz. se-tenant pair	*5,000.*	*5,000.*
		9/9-8/8 horiz. se-tenant pair	*7,000.*	*7,000.*
c.		Center "0" in wrong font, stamp with 9/9 Kai Tei (pos. 42)	5,000.	5,000.
d.		Center "0" in wrong font, stamp with 8/8 Kai Tei (pos. 67, 86)	3,500.	3,500.
e.		Center "0" in wrong font, stamp with 9/8 Kai Tei (pos. 53)	5,000.	5,000.
f.		Wrong font for last "0" (pos. 59)	5,000.	5,000.
g.		Wrong font for "yen" symbol (pos. 69)	5,000.	5,000.

Varieties of shifted and damaged surcharge characters exist, most notably a damaged ("clipped") Kai.

See note after 16B to differentiate between 8-point and 9-point charaters.

Surcharge forgeries are known. Authentication by competant experts is recommended.

Dove, Bean Sprout and Map — A8

Madanbashi Bridge — A9

1952, Apr. 1 ***Perf. 13½x13***

18	A8	3y **deep plum**	120.00	40.00
		First day cover		80.00
		Imprint block of 10	1,800.	

Establishment of the Government of the Ryukyu Islands (GRI), April 1, 1952.

1952-53

Designs: 2y, Main Hall, Shuri Castle. 3y, Shurei Gate. 6y Stone Gate, Soenji Temple, Naha. 10y, Benzaiten-do Temple 30y, Sonohan Utaki (altar) at Shuri Castle. 50y, Tamaudu (royal mausoleum). Shuri. 100y, Stone Bridge, Hosho Pon Enkaku Temple.

19	A9	1y **red,** *Nov. 20, 1952*	.30	.3
		Imprint block of 10	4.50	
20	A9	2y **green,** *Nov. 20, 1952*	.40	.4
		Imprint block of 10	6.00	
21	A9	3y **aquamarine,** *Nov. 20, 1952*	.50	.5
		First day cover, #19-21		40.0
		Imprint block of 10	7.50	
22	A9	6y **blue,** *Jan. 20, 1953*	3.00	3.0
		First day cover		27.5
		Imprint block of 10	45.00	
23	A9	10y **crimson rose,** *Jan. 20, 1953*	4.00	1.5
		First day cover		47.5
		Imprint block of 10	60.00	
24	A9	30y **olive green,** *Jan. 20, 1953*	15.00	10.0
		First day cover		75.0
		Imprint block of 10	225.00	
a.		30y **light olive green,** *1958*	60.00	
		Imprint block of 10	850.00	
25	A9	50y **rose violet,** *Jan. 20, 1953*	20.00	12.0
		First day cover		125.0
		Imprint block of 10	275.00	
26	A9	100y **claret,** *Jan. 20, 1953*	25.00	6.5
		First day cover		190.0
		Imprint block of 10	325.00	
		First day cover, #22-26		550.0
		Nos. 19-26 (8)	68.20	34.2

Issued: 1y, 2y and 3y, Nov. 20, 1952. Others, Jan. 20, 1953

Reception at Shu Castle — A10

Perry and American Fleet — A11

1953, May 26 ***Perf. 13½x13, 13x13***

27	A10	3y **deep magenta**	14.00	6.5
		Imprint block of 6	120.00	
28	A11	6y **dull blue**	1.50	1.5
		First day cover, #27-28		15.0
		Imprint block of 6	12.00	

Centenary of the arrival of Commodore Matthew Calbrait Perry at Naha, Okinawa.

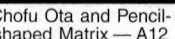

Chofu Ota and Pencil-shaped Matrix — A12

Shigo Toma and Pen — A13

1953, Oct. 1 ***Perf. 13½x1***

29	A12	4y **yellow brown**	12.00	5.0
		First day cover		20.0
		Imprint block of 10	150.00	

Third Newspaper Week.

1954, Oct. 1

30 A13 4y **blue** 14.00 7.50
First day cover 25.00
Imprint block of 10 175.00

Fourth Newspaper Week.

Ryukyu Pottery — A14

Noguni Shrine and Sweet Potato Plant — A15

Designs: 15y, Lacquerware. 20y, Textile design.

1954-55 **Photo.** ***Perf. 13***

31 A14 4y **brown,** *June 25, 1954* 1.00 .60
First day cover 10.00
Imprint block of 10 11.00

32 A14 15y **vermilion,** *June 20, 1955* 5.00 4.00
First day cover 12.50
Imprint block of 10 75.00

33 A14 20y **yellow orange,** *June 20, 1955* 3.00 2.50
First day cover 12.50
Imprint block of 10 45.00
First day cover, #32-33 35.00
Nos. 31-33 (3) 9.00 7.10

For surcharges see Nos. C19, C21, C23.

1955, Nov. 26

34 A15 4y **blue** 14.00 7.00
First day cover 22.50
Imprint block of 10 175.00

350th anniv. of the introduction of the sweet potato to the Ryukyu Islands.

Stylized Trees — A16

Willow Dance — A17

1956, Feb. 18 **Unwmk.**

35 A16 4y **bluish green** 12.00 6.00
First day cover 20.00
Imprint block of 6 100.00

Arbor Week, Feb. 18-24.

1956, May 1 ***Perf. 13***

8y, Straw hat dance. 14y, Dancer in warrior costume with fan.

36 A17 5y **rose lilac** 1.00 .60
First day cover 6.50
Imprint block of 10 15.00

37 A17 8y **violet blue** 2.50 2.00
First day cover 6.50
Imprint block of 10 37.50

38 A17 14y **reddish brown** 4.00 3.00
First day cover 6.50
Imprint block of 10 55.00
First day cover, #36-38 35.00
Nos. 36-38 (3) 7.50 5.60

For surcharges see Nos. C20, C22.

Telephone A18

1956, June 8

39 A18 4y **violet blue** 15.00 8.00
First day cover 20.00
Imprint block of 6 120.00

Establishment of dial telephone system.

Garland of Pine, Bamboo and Plum — A19

Map of Okinawa and Pencil Rocket — A20

1956, Dec. 1 ***Perf. 13½x13***

40 A19 2y **multicolored** 2.00 2.00
First day cover 3.50
Imprint block of 10 27.50

New Year, 1957.

1957, Oct. 1 **Photo.** ***Perf. 13½x13***

41 A20 4y **deep violet blue** 1.00 1.00
First day cover 6.00
Imprint block of 10 12.50

7th annual Newspaper Week, Oct. 1-7.

Phoenix — A21

1957, Dec. 1 **Unwmk.** ***Perf. 13***

42 A21 2y **multicolored** .25 .25
First day cover 1.50
Imprint block of 10 3.50

New Year, 1958.

Ryukyu Stamps — A22

1958, July 1 ***Perf. 13½***

43 A22 4y **multicolored** .80 .80
First day cover 1.25
Imprint block of 4 4.00

10th anniv. of 1st Ryukyu stamps.

Yen Symbol and Dollar Sign — A23

Perf. 10.3, 10.8, 11.1 & Compound

1958, Sept. 16 **Typo.**

Without Gum

44 A23 ½c **orange** .90 .90
Imprint block of 6 8.00
a. Imperf., pair *1,750.*
b. Horiz. pair, imperf. between 150.00
c. Vert. pair, imperf. between 200.00
d. Vert. strip of 4, imperf. between 800.00

45 A23 1c **yellow green** 1.40 1.40
Imprint block of 6 11.00
a. Horiz. pair, imperf. between 200.00
b. Vert. pair, imperf. between 150.00
c. Vert. strip of 3, imperf. between 700.00
d. Vert. strip of 4, imperf. between 800.00
e. Block of 4, imperf. btwn. vert. & horiz. *10,000.*

46 A23 2c **dark blue** 2.25 2.25
Imprint block of 6 17.50
a. Horiz. pair, imperf. between 200.00
b. Vert. pair, imperf. between *2,000.*
c. Horiz. strip of 3, imperf. between 450.00
d. Horiz. strip of 4, imperf. between 800.00

47 A23 3c **deep carmine** 1.75 1.50
Imprint block of 6 14.00
a. Horiz. pair, imperf. between 200.00
b. Vert. pair, imperf. between 150.00
c. Vert. strip of 3, imperf. between 450.00
d. Vert. strip of 4, imperf. between 800.00
e. Block of 4, imperf. btwn. vert. & horiz. *10,000.*

48 A23 4c **bright green** 2.25 2.25
Imprint block of 6 17.50
a. Horiz. pair, imperf. between *500.00*
b. Vert. pair, imperf. between 200.00

49 A23 5c **orange** 4.25 3.75
Imprint block of 6 35.00
a. Horiz. pair, imperf. between 225.00
b. Vert. pair, imperf. between *850.00*

50 A23 10c **aquamarine** 5.75 4.75
Imprint block of 6 42.50
a. Horiz. pair, imperf. between 300.00
b. Vert. pair, imperf. between 200.00
c. Vert. strip of 3, imperf. between 800.00

51 A23 25c **bright violet blue** 8.00 6.00
Imprint block of 6 62.50
a. Gummed paper, perf. 10.3 ('61) 15.00 15.00
Imprint block of 6 95.00
b. Horiz. pair, imperf. between *2,000.*
c. Vert. pair, imperf. between *5,000.*
d. Vert. strip of 3, imperf. between 900.00

52 A23 50c **gray** 17.50 10.00
Imprint block of 6 140.00
a. Gummed paper, perf. 10.3 ('61) 15.00 15.00
Imprint block of 6 150.00
First day cover, #51a-52a 35.00
b. Horiz. pair, imperf. between *1,750.*

53 A23 $1 **rose lilac** 12.50 5.50
Imprint block of 6 100.00
a. Horiz. pair, imperf. between 500.00
b. Vert. pair, imperf. between *2,500.*
Nos. 44-53 (10) 56.55 38.30

Printed locally. Perforation, paper and shade varieties exist. Nos. 51a and 52a are on off-white paper and perf 10.3.

First day covers come with various combinations of stamps: Nos. 44-48, 49-53, 44-53 etc. Values $20 for short set of low values (Nos. 44-48) to $60 for full set on one cover.

Gate of Courtesy — A24

1958, Oct. 15 **Photo.** ***Perf. 13½***

54 A24 3c **multicolored** 1.25 1.25
First day cover 1.50
Imprint block of 4 6.25

Restoration of Shureimon, Gate of Courtesy, on road leading to Shuri City.

Imitations of this stamp were distributed in 1972 to discourage speculation in Ryukyuan stamps. The imitations were printed without gum and have a lengthy message in light blue printed on the back. A second type exists, with printed black perforations and three Japanese characters on the back ("Mozo Hin" — imitation) in black. Value, sheet of 10 $15.

Lion Dance — A25

Trees and Mountains — A26

1958, Dec. 10 **Unwmk.** ***Perf. 13½***

55 A25 1½c **multicolored** .30 .30
First day cover 1.50
Imprint block of 6 2.00

New Year, 1959.

1959, Apr. 30 **Litho.** ***Perf. 13½x13***

56 A26 3c **blue, yellow green, green & red** .70 .60
First day cover 1.00
Imprint block of 6 5.50

"Make the Ryukyus Green" movement.

Yonaguni Moth — A27

1959, July 23 **Photo.** ***Perf. 13***

57 A27 3c **multicolored** 1.20 1.00
First day cover 1.50
Imprint block of 6 9.00

Meeting of the Japanese Biological Education Society in Okinawa.

Hibiscus — A28

Toy (Yakaji) — A29

Designs: 3c, Fish (Moorish idol). 8c, Sea shell (Phalium bandatum). 13c, Butterfly (Kallinia Inachus Eucerca), denomination at left, butterfly going up. 17c, Jellyfish (Dactylometra pacifera Goette).

Inscribed:
琉球郵便

1959, Aug. 10 ***Perf. 13x13½***

58 A28 ½c **multicolored** .25 .20
Imprint block of 10 3.50
59 A28 3c **multicolored** .75 .40
Imprint block of 10 9.00
60 A28 8c **light ultramarine, black & ocher** 15.00 5.50
Imprint block of 10 225.00
61 A28 13c **light blue, gray & orange** 2.50 1.75
Imprint block of 10 32.50
62 A28 17c **violet blue, red & yellow** 25.00 9.00
Imprint block of 10 375.00
First day cover, #58-62 17.50
Nos. 58-62 (5) 43.50 16.85

Four-character inscription measures 10x2mm on ½c; 12x3mm on 3c, 8c; 8½x2mm on 13c, 17c. See Nos. 76-80.

1959, Dec. 1 **Litho.**

63 A29 1½c **gold & multicolored** .55 .45
First day cover 1.50
Imprint block of 10 8.00

New Year, 1960.

University Badge A30

1960, May 22 **Photo.** ***Perf. 1***

64 A30 3c **multicolored** .95 .7
First day cover 1.2
Imprint block of 6 7.25

10th anniv. opening of Ryukyu University.

Dancer — A31

Designs: Various Ryukyu Dances.

1960, Nov. 1 **Photo.** ***Perf. 1***

Dark Gray Background

65 A31 1c **yellow, red & violet** 1.50 .8
Imprint block of 10 18.00
66 A31 2½c **crimson, blue & yellow** 3.00 1.0
Imprint block of 10 37.50
67 A31 5c **dark blue, yellow & red** .70 .5
Imprint block of 10 10.00
68 A31 10c **dark blue, yellow & red** .90 .7
Imprint block of 10 12.00
First day cover, #65-68 5.5
Nos. 65-68 (4) 6.10 3.0

See Nos. 81-87, 220.

Perforation and Paper Varieties of Ryukyu Islands Scott 44-53

Perforation	Perf. ID#	1/2¢ (No. 44) Paper Type 1	2	3	4	1¢ (No. 45) Paper Type 1	2	3	4	2¢ (No. 46) Paper Type 1	2	3	4	3¢ (No. 47) Paper Type 1	2	3	4	4¢ (No. 48) Paper Type 1	2	3	4
11.1 x 11.1	M	*			*	*	*			*			*	*	*		*	*	*		
11.1 x 10.8	N	*			*	*	*			*			*	*	*		*	*	*		∞
11.1 x 10.3	O	*			*	?	*			*			*	*	*			*			
10.8 x 11.1	P	*			*	*	*			*			*	*	*			*	*		
10.8 x 10.8	Q	*			*	*	*			*			*	*	*			*	*		
10.8 x 10.3	R	*			*	*	*			*			*	?	*			*	*		
10.3 x 11.1	S	*				*	*			*			*	*	*		*	?	*		
10.3 x 10.8	T	*			*	*	*			*			*	*	*		*		*		
10.3 x 10.3	U	*				?	*			*			*	?	*						

Perforation	Perf. ID#	5¢ (No. 49) Paper Type 1	2	3	4	10¢ (No. 50) Paper Type 1	2	3	4	25¢ (No. 51) Paper Type 1	2	3	4	50¢ (No. 52) Paper Type 1	2	3	4	$1 (No. 53) Paper Type 1	2	3	4
11.1 x 11.1	M	*	*		*	*	*	*		*		*		*				*		*	
11.1 x 10.8	N	*	?		*	*	*			*		*		*				*		*	
11.1 x 10.3	O	*	*			*				*		*		*				*			
10.8 x 11.1	P	*	*		*	*	*			*		*		*				*		*	
10.8 x 10.8	Q	*			*	*	*			*	*	*		*				*		*	
10.8 x 10.3	R	*				*	*			*				*							
10.3 x 11.1	S	*	*		*		*			*								*			
10.3 x 10.8	T	*	*			?	*	*										*		*	
10.3 x 10.3	U	*	*		*	?	*			\		*		\							

Paper Legend: 1= off-white; 2= white; 3= ivory; 4= thick

Specialists use a shorthand to refer to perf. and paper types: e.g., 50M3 =10¢ stamp, perf. 11.1 x 11.1, ivory paper.

Notes:

* = Verified variety

? = Reported in literature, but unverified variety.

∞ = 48N4 is unknown; however, a single example of 48N exists on a thick white paper unknown used for any other issue.

\ = These particular perf/paper combinations are known only in stamps of the Second (1961) Printing (51a and 52a)

The following are known unused only: 45R1, 45T2, 47O1, 48N4, 53O1.

The following are known used only: 47N4, 47T4, 50M3, 50Q2, 50R2, 50T2, 51P3, 51S1, 53T3.

Chart classifications and data supplied by courtesy of the Ryukyu Philatelic Specialist Society.

Torch and Nago Bay — A32

Runners at Starting Line — A33

1960, Nov. 8

72	A32	3c	**light blue, green & red**	6.00	3.00
			First day cover		3.50
			Imprint block of 6	45.00	
73	A33	8c	**orange & slate green**	1.00	.75
			First day cover		1.50
			Imprint block of 6	7.50	
			First day cover, #72-73		5.00

8th Kyushu Inter-Prefectural Athletic Meet, Nago, Northern Okinawa, Nov. 6-7.

Little Egret and Rising Sun — A34

1960, Dec. 1 Unwmk. *Perf. 13*

74	A34	3c	**reddish brown**	5.50	3.50
			First day cover		4.00
			Imprint block of 6	42.50	

National census.

Okinawa Bull Fight — A35

1960, Dec. 10 *Perf. 13½*

75	A35	1½c	**bister, dark blue & red brown**	1.75	1.50
			First day cover		2.00
			Imprint block of 6	12.50	

New Year, 1961.

Type of 1959 With Japanese Inscription Redrawn:

A28a

1960-61 Photo. *Perf. 13x13½*

76	A28a	½c	**multicolored,** *Oct. 1961*	.45	.45
			Imprint block of 10	5.50	
77	A28a	3c	**multicolored,** *Aug. 23, 1961*	.90	.35
			First day cover		1.50
			Imprint block of 10	12.50	
78	A28a	8c	**light ultramarine, black & ocher,** *July 1, 1960*	.90	.80
			Imprint block of 10	12.50	
79	A28a	13c	**blue, brown & red,** *July 1, 1960*	1.10	.90
			Imprint block of 10	15.00	
80	A28a	17c	**violet blue, red & yellow,** *July 1, 1960*	15.00	6.00
			Imprint block of 10	190.00	
			First day cover, #78-80		15.00
			Nos. 76-80 (5)	18.35	8.50

Size of Japanese inscription on Nos. 78-80 is 10½x1½mm. On No. 79 the denomination is at right, butterfly going down.

Dancer Type of 1960 with "RYUKYUS" Added in English

1961-64 *Perf. 13*

81	A31	1c	**multicolored,** *Dec. 5, 1961*	.20	.20
			First day cover		1.00
			Imprint block of 10	2.00	
82	A31	2½c	**multicolored,** *June 20, 1962*	.20	.20
			Imprint block of 10	2.25	
83	A31	5c	**multicolored,** *June 20, 1962*	.25	.25
			Imprint block of 10	3.00	
84	A31	10c	**multicolored,** *June 20, 1962*	.45	.40
			First day cover, #82-84		1.50
			Imprint block of 10	5.75	
84A	A31	20c	**multicolored,** *Jan. 20, 1964*	3.25	1.40
			First day cover		2.50
			Imprint block of 10	37.50	
85	A31	25c	**multicolored,** *Feb. 1, 1962*	1.00	.90
			First day cover		2.00
			Imprint block of 10	13.00	
86	A31	50c	**multicolored,** *Sept. 1, 1961*	2.50	1.40
			Imprint block of 10	32.50	
87	A31	$1	**multicolored,** *Sept. 1, 1961*	6.00	.25
			Imprint block of 10	70.00	
			First day cover, #86-87		35.00
			Nos. 81-87 (8)	13.85	5.00

Pine Tree — A36

1961, May 1 Photo. *Perf. 13*

88	A36	3c	**yellow green & red**	1.80	1.25
			First day cover		1.50
			Imprint block of 6	15.00	

"Make the Ryukyus Green" movement.

Naha, Steamer and Sailboat A37

1961, May 20

89	A37	3c	**aquamarine**	2.25	1.50
			First day cover		1.75
			Imprint block of 6	18.00	

40th anniv. of Naha.

White Silver Temple — A38

Books and Bird — A39

1961, Oct. 1 Typo. Unwmk. *Perf. 11*

90	A38	3c	**red brown**	2.50	2.00
			First day cover		2.00
			Imprint block of 6	18.00	
a.			Horiz. pair, imperf. between	*1,000.*	
b.			Vert. pair, imperf. between	*700.00*	

Merger of townships Takamine, Kanegushiku and Miwa with Itoman.

A 3-cent stamp to commemorate the merger of two cities, Shimoji-cho and Hirara-shi of Miyako Island, was scheduled to be issued on Oct. 30, 1961. However, the merger was called off and the stamp never issued. It features a white chaplet on Kiyako linen on a blue background.

1961, Nov. 12 Litho. *Perf. 13*

91	A39	3c	**multicolored**	1.10	.90
			First day cover		1.25
			Imprint block of 6	10.00	

Book Week.

Rising Sun and Eagles — A40

Symbolic Steps, Trees and Government Building — A41

1961, Dec. 10 Photo. *Perf. 13½*

92	A40	1½c	**gold, vermilion & black**	2.00	2.00
			First day cover		3.00
			Imprint block of 6	16.00	

New Year, 1962.

1962, Apr. 1 Unwmk. *Perf. 13½*

Design: 3c, Government Building.

93	A41	1½c	**multicolored**	.60	.60
			Imprint block of 6	4.75	
94	A41	3c	**bright green, red & gray**	.80	.80
			Imprint block of 6	6.50	
			First day cover, #93-94		2.00

10th anniv. of the Government of the Ryukyu Islands (GRI).

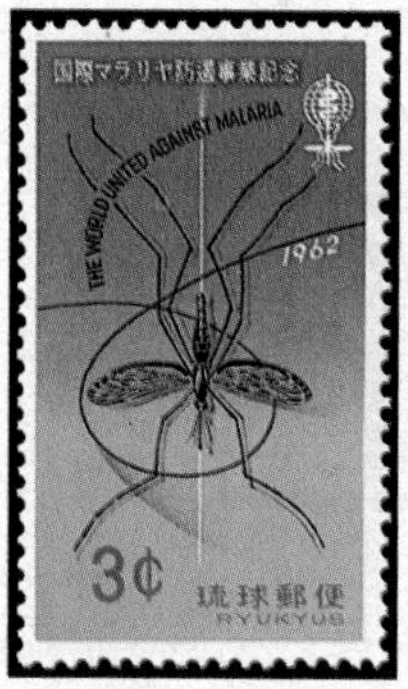

Anopheles Hyrcanus Sinensis — A42

Design: 8c, Malaria eradication emblem and Shurei gate.

1962, Apr. 7 *Perf. 13½x13*

95	A42	3c	**multicolored**	.60	.60
			Imprint block of 6	4.50	
96	A42	8c	**multicolored**	.90	.75
			Imprint block of 6	7.50	
			First day cover, #95-96		2.25

World Health Organization drive to eradicate malaria.

Dolls and Toys — A43

Linden or Sea Hibiscus — A44

1962, May 5 **Litho.** ***Perf. 13½***

97	A43	3c	**red, black, blue & buff**	1.10	1.00
			First day cover		1.50
			Imprint block of 6	9.00	

Children's Day, 1962.

1962, June 1 **Photo.**

Flowers: 3c, Indian coral tree. 8c, Iju (Schima liukiuensis Nakal). 13c, Touch-me-not (garden balsam). 17c, Shell flower (Alpinia speciosa).

98	A44	½c	**multicolored**	.20	.20
			Imprint block of 10	1.75	
99	A44	3c	**multicolored**	.35	.20
			Imprint block of 10	4.75	
100	A44	8c	**multicolored**	.50	.45
			Imprint block of 10	6.50	
101	A44	13c	**multicolored**	.70	.60
			Imprint block of 10	9.00	
102	A44	17c	**multicolored**	1.25	.80
			Imprint block of 10	15.00	
			First day cover, #98-102		3.75
			Nos. 98-102 (5)	3.00	2.25

See Nos. 107 and 114 for 1½c and 15c flower stamps. For surcharge see No. 190.

Earthenware A45

1962, July 5 ***Perf. 13½x13***

103	A45	3c	**multicolored**	3.50	2.50
			First day cover		2.75
			Imprint block of 6	26.00	

Philatelic Week.

Japanese Fencing (Kendo) A46

1962, July 25 ***Perf. 13***

104	A46	3c	**multicolored**	4.00	3.00
			First day cover		3.50
			Imprint block of 6	30.00	

All-Japan Kendo Meeting in Okinawa, July 25, 1962.

Rabbit Playing near Water, Bingata Cloth Design — A47

Young Man and Woman, Stone Relief — A48

1962, Dec. 10 ***Perf. 13x13½***

105	A47	1½c	**gold & multicolored**	1.00	.80
			First day cover		1.50
			Imprint block of 10	12.50	

New Year, 1963.

1963, Jan. 15 **Photo.** ***Perf. 13½***

106	A48	3c	**gold, black & blue**	.90	.80
			First day cover		1.50
			Imprint block of 6	6.75	

Gooseneck Cactus — A49

Trees and Wooded Hills — A50

1963, Apr. 5 ***Perf. 13x13½***

107	A49	1½c	**dark blue green, yellow & pink**	.20	.20
			First day cover		1.25
			Imprint block of 10	1.50	

1963, Mar. 25 ***Perf. 13½x13***

108	A50	3c	**ultramarine, green & red brown**	1.00	.80
			First day cover		1.25
			Imprint block of 6	7.00	

"Make the Ryukyus Green" movement.

Map of Okinawa — A51

Hawks over Islands — A52

1963, Apr. 30 **Unwmk.** ***Perf. 13½***

109	A51	3c	**multicolored**	1.25	1.00
			First day cover		1.50
			Imprint block of 6	9.00	

Opening of the Round Road on Okinawa.

1963, May 10 **Photo.**

110	A52	3c	**multicolored**	1.10	.95
			First day cover		1.50
			Imprint block of 6	9.00	

Bird Day, May 10.

Shioya Bridge — A53

1963, June 5

111	A53	3c	**multicolored**	1.10	.9
			First day cover		1.4
			Imprint block of 6	8.25	

Opening of Shioya Bridge over Shioya Bay.

Tsuikin-wan Lacquerware Bowl — A54

1963, July 1 **Unwmk.** ***Perf. 13***

112	A54	3c	**multicolored**	3.00	2.5
			First day cover		2.7
			Imprint block of 6	22.50	

Map of Far East and JCI Emblem — A55

1963, Sept. 16 **Photo.** ***Perf. 13***

113	A55	3c	**multicolored**	.70	.7
			First day cover		1.2
			Imprint block of 6	6.00	

Meeting of the International Junior Chamber of Commerc (JCI), Naha, Okinawa, Sept. 16-19.

Mamaomoto — A56

Site of Nakagusuku Castle — A57

1963, Oct. 15 ***Perf. 13x13***

114	A56	15c	**multicolored**	2.00	.8
			First day cover		1.2
			Imprint block of 10	25.00	

1963, Nov. 1 ***Perf. 13½x1***

115	A57	3c	**multicolored**	.70	.6
			First day cover		1.2
			Imprint block of 6	5.25	

Protection of national cultural treasures.

Flame — A58

Dragon (Bingata Pattern) — A59

1963, Dec. 10 *Perf. 13½*

116 A58 3c **red, dark blue & yellow** .70 .60
First day cover 1.25
Imprint block of 6 5.25

15th anniv. of the Universal Declaration of Human Rights.

1963, Dec. 10 **Photo.**

117 A59 1½c **multicolored** .60 .50
First day cover 1.50
Imprint block of 10 7.50

New Year, 1964.

Carnation — A60

Pineapples and Sugar Cane — A61

1964, May 10 *Perf. 13½*

118 A60 3c **blue, yellow, black & carmine** .40 .35
First day cover 1.25
Imprint block of 6 3.00

Mothers Day.

1964, June 1

119 A61 3c **multicolored** .40 .35
First day cover 1.25
Imprint block of 6 3.00

Agricultural census.

Minsah Obi (Sash Woven of Kapok) — A62

1964, July 1 **Unwmk.** *Perf. 13½*

120 A62 3c **deep blue, rose pink & ocher** .55 .50
First day cover 2.25
Imprint block of 6 4.50
a. 3c **deep blue, deep carmine & ocher** .70 .65
First day cover 2.75
Imprint block of 6 5.25

Philatelic Week.

Girl Scout and Emblem — A63

1964, Aug. 31 **Photo.**

121 A63 3c **multicolored** .40 .35
First day cover 1.25
Imprint block of 6 3.00

10th anniv. of Ryukyuan Girl Scouts.

Shuri Relay Station — A64

Parabolic Antenna and Map — A65

1964, Sept. 1 **Unwmk.** *Perf. 13½*

Black Overprint

122 A64 3c **deep green** .65 .65
Imprint block of 6 5.50
a. Figure "1" inverted 35.00 35.00
b. Overprint inverted *1,500.*
c. Overprint missing *3,500.*
123 A65 8c **ultramarine** 1.25 1.25
Imprint block of 6 10.00
First day cover, #122-123 4.75
a. Overprint missing *3,500.*

Opening of the Ryukyu Islands-Japan microwave system carrying telephone and telegraph messages. The overprints indicate the system was not actually opened until 1964.

Many of the stamps with overprint errors listed above are damaged. The values listed here are for stamps in very fine condition.

A number of different overprint shifts also exist with the shifts to greater and lesser degrees.

Gate of Courtesy, Olympic Torch and Emblem — A66

1964, Sept. 7 **Photo.** *Perf. 13½x13*

124 A66 3c **ultramarine, yellow & red** .30 .20
First day cover (Sept. 7) 1.25
First day cover (Sept. 6 & 7) 25.00
Imprint block of 6 2.50

Relaying the Olympic torch on Okinawa en route to Tokyo.

Torch arrival was scheduled for Sept. 6. A typhoon delayed arrival until Sept. 7. A small number of covers received both Sept. 6 and 7 cancels.

"Naihanchi," Karate Stance — A67

"Makiwara," Strengthening Hands and Feet — A68

"Kumite," Simulated Combat — A69

1964-65 **Photo.** *Perf. 13½*

125 A67 3c **dull claret, yel & blk,** *Oct. 5, 1964* .50 .45
First day cover 1.25
Imprint block of 6 3.25
126 A68 3c **yel & multi,** *Feb. 5, 1965* .40 .40
First day cover 1.25
Imprint block of 6 3.00
Incomplete vertical stroke in "cent" sign 17.50 17.50
First day cover 25.00
127 A69 3c **gray, red & blk,** *June 5, 1965* .40 .40
First day cover 1.25
Imprint block of 6 3.00
Nos. 125-127 (3) 1.30 1.25

Karate, Ryukyuan self-defense sport.

Miyara Dunchi — A70

Snake and Iris (Bingata) — A71

1964, Nov. 1 *Perf. 13½*

128 A70 3c **multicolored** .30 .25
First day cover 1.25
Imprint block of 6 2.25

Protection of national cultural treasures. Miyara Dunchi was built as a residence by Miyara-pechin Toen in 1819.

1964, Dec. 10 **Photo.**

129 A71 1½c **multicolored** .30 .25
First day cover 2.00
Imprint block of 10 4.00

New Year, 1965.

Boy Scouts — A72

1965, Feb. 6 *Perf. 13½*

130 A72 3c **light blue & multi** .45 .40
First day cover 1.50
Imprint block of 6 4.00

10th anniv. of Ryukyuan Boy Scouts.

Main Stadium, Onoyama A73

1965, July 1 *Perf. 13x13½*
131 A73 3c **multicolored** .25 .25
First day cover 1.00
Imprint block of 6 2.00

Inauguration of the main stadium of the Onoyama athletic facilities.

Samisen of King Shoko — A74

1965, July 1 **Photo.** *Perf. 13½*
132 A74 3c **buff & multicolored** .45 .40
First day cover 1.25
Imprint block of 6 3.25

Philatelic Week.

Kin Power Plant — A75

ICY Emblem, Ryukyu Map — A76

1965, July 1
133 A75 3c **green & multicolored** .25 .25
First day cover 1.00
Imprint block of 6 2.00

Completion of Kin power plant.

1965, Aug. 24 **Photo.** *Perf. 13½*
134 A76 3c **multicolored** .20 .20
First day cover 1.00
Imprint block of 6 1.75

20th anniv. of the UN and International Cooperation Year, 1964-65.

Naha City Hall — A77

1965, Sept. 18 **Unwmk.** *Perf. 13½*
135 A77 3c **blue & multicolored** .20 .20
First day cover 1.00
Imprint block of 6 1.75

Completion of Naha City Hall.

Chinese Box Turtle — A78

Horse (Bingata) — A79

Turtles: No. 137, Hawksbill turtle (denomination at top, country name at bottom). No. 138, Asian terrapin (denomination and country name on top).

1965-66 **Photo.** *Perf. 13½*
136 A78 3c **golden brown & multi,** *Oct. 20, 1965* .30 .30
First day cover 1.00
Imprint block of 6 2.50
137 A78 3c **black, yel & brown,** *Jan. 20, 1966* .30 .30
First day cover 1.00
Imprint block of 6 2.50
138 A78 3c **gray & multicolored,** *Apr. 20, 1966* .30 .30
First day cover 1.00
Imprint block of 6 2.50
Nos. 136-138 (3) .90 .90

1965, Dec. 10 **Photo.** *Perf. 13½*
139 A79 1½c **multicolored** .20 .20
First day cover 1.50
Imprint block of 10 2.25
a. Gold omitted *1,200. 2,000.*

New Year, 1966.

There are 92 unused and 2 used examples of No. 139a known.

NATURE CONSERVATION ISSUE

Noguchi's Okinawa Woodpecker — A80

Sika Deer — A81

Design: No. 142, Dugong.

1966 **Photo.** *Perf. 13½*
140 A80 3c **blue green & multi,** *Feb. 15* .20 .20
First day cover 1.00
Imprint block of 6 1.65
141 A81 3c **blue, red, black, brown & green,** *Mar. 15* .25 .25
First day cover 1.00
Imprint block of 6 1.75
142 A81 3c **blue, yellow green, black & red,** *Apr. 20* .25 .25
First day cover 1.00
Imprint block of 6 1.75
Nos. 140-142 (3) .70 .70

Ryukyu Bungalow Swallow — A82

1966, May 10 **Photo.** *Perf. 13½*
143 A82 3c **sky blue, black & brown** .20 .20
First day cover 1.00
Imprint block of 6 1.10

4th Bird Week, May 10-16.

Lilies and Ruins A83

1966, June 23 *Perf. 13x13½*
144 A83 3c **multicolored** .20 .20
First day cover 1.00
Imprint block of 6 1.00

Memorial Day, end of the Battle of Okinawa, June 23, 1945.

University of the Ryukyus A84

1966, July 1
145 A84 3c **multicolored** .20 .20
First day cover 1.00
Imprint block of 6 1.00

Transfer of the University of the Ryukyus from U.S. authority to the Ryukyu Government.

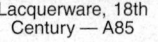

Lacquerware, 18th Century — A85

Tile-Roofed House and UNESCO Emblem — A86

1966, Aug. 1 *Perf. 13½*
146 A85 3c **gray & multicolored** .20 .20
First day cover 1.50
Imprint block of 6 1.30

Philatelic Week.

1966, Sept. 20 **Photo.** *Perf. 13½*
147 A86 3c **multicolored** .20 .20
First day cover 1.00
Imprint block of 6 1.10

20th anniv. of UNESCO.

Government Museum and Dragon Statue — A87

1966, Oct. 6
148 A87 3c **multicolored** .20 .20
First day cover 1.00
Imprint block of 6 1.00

Completion of the GRI (Government of the Ryukyu Islands) Museum, Shuri.

Tomb of Nakasone-Tuimya Genga, Ruler of Miyako — A88

1966, Nov. 1 **Photo.** ***Perf. 13½***

149 A88 3c **multicolored** .20 .20
First day cover 1.00
Imprint block of 6 1.00

Protection of national cultural treasures.

Ram in Iris Wreath — A89

Clown Fish — A90

1966, Dec. 10 **Photo.** ***Perf. 13½***

150 A89 1½c **dark blue & multicolored** .20 .20
First day cover 1.50
Imprint block of 10 1.10

New Year, 1967.

1966-67

Fish: No. 152, Young boxfish (white numeral at lower left). No. 153, Forceps fish (pale buff numeral at lower right). No. 154, Spotted triggerfish (orange numeral). No. 155, Saddleback butterflyfish (carmine numeral, lower left).

151 A90 3c **orange red & multi,** *Dec. 20, 1966* .20 .20
First day cover 1.00
Imprint block of 6 1.75
152 A90 3c **orange yellow & multi,** *Jan. 10, 1967* .25 .20
First day cover 1.00
Imprint block of 6 1.75
153 A90 3c **multicolored,** *Apr. 10, 1967* .40 .25
First day cover 1.00
Imprint block of 6 2.75
154 A90 3c **multicolored,** *May 25, 1967* .35 .25
First day cover 1.00
Imprint block of 6 2.25
155 A90 3c **multicolored,** *June 10, 1967* .30 .25
First day cover 1.00
Imprint block of 6 1.90
Nos. 151-155 (5) 1.50 1.15

A 3-cent stamp to commemorate Japanese-American-Ryukyuan Joint Arbor Day was scheduled for release on March 16, 1967. However, it was not released. The stamp in light blue and white features American and Japanese flags joined by a shield containing a tree.

Tsuboya Urn — A91

Episcopal Miter — A92

1967, Apr. 20

156 A91 3c **yellow & multicolored** .20 .20
First day cover 1.25
Imprint block of 6 1.65

Philatelic Week.

1967-68 **Photo.** ***Perf. 13½***

Seashells: No. 158, Venus comb murex. No. 159, Chiragra spider. No. 160, Green truban. No. 161, Euprotomus bulla.

157 A92 3c **light green & multi,** *July 20, 1967* .20 .20
First day cover 1.00
Imprint block of 6 1.25
158 A92 3c **greenish blue & multi,** *Aug. 30, 1968* .25 .20
First day cover 1.00
Imprint block of 6 1.75
159 A92 3c **emerald & multi,** *Jan. 18, 1968* .25 .20
First day cover 1.00
Imprint block of 6 1.65
160 A92 3c **light blue & multi,** *Feb. 20, 1968* .30 .25
First day cover 1.00
Imprint block of 6 1.65
161 A92 3c **bright blue & multi,** *June 5, 1968* .60 .50
First day cover 1.00
Imprint block of 6 4.00
Nos. 157-161 (5) 1.60 1.35

Red-tiled Roofs and ITY Emblem — A93

1967, Sept. 11 **Photo.** ***Perf. 13½***

162 A93 3c **multicolored** .20 .20
First day cover 1.00
Imprint block of 6 1.25

International Tourist Year.

Mobile TB Clinic — A94

1967, Oct. 13 **Photo.** ***Perf. 13½***

163 A94 3c **lilac & multicolored** .20 .20
First day cover 1.00
Imprint block of 6 1.25

15th anniv. of the Anti-Tuberculosis Society.

Hojo Bridge, Enkaku Temple, 1498 — A95

1967, Nov. 1

164 A95 3c **blue green & multicolored** .20 .20
First day cover 1.00
Imprint block of 6 1.50

Protection of national cultural treasures.

Monkey (Bingata) — A96

TV Tower and Map — A97

1967, Dec. 11 **Photo.** ***Perf. 13½***

165 A96 1½c **silver & multicolored** .25 .20
First day cover 1.50
Imprint block of 10 3.00

New Year, 1968.

1967, Dec. 22

166 A97 3c **multicolored** .25 .25
First day cover 1.00
Imprint block of 6 1.50

Opening of Miyako and Yaeyama television stations.

Dr. Kijin Nakachi and Helper — A98

Pill Box (Inro) — A99

1968, Mar. 15 **Photo.** ***Perf. 13½***

167 A98 3c **multicolored** .30 .25
First day cover 1.00
Imprint block of 6 1.75

120th anniv. of the first vaccination in the Ryukyu Islands, by Dr. Kijin Nakachi.

1968, Apr. 18

168 A99 3c **gray & multicolored** .45 .45
First day cover 1.25
Imprint block of 6 3.50

Philatelic Week.

Young Man, Library, Book and Map of Ryukyu Islands — A100

1968, May 13

169 A100 3c **multicolored** .30 .25
First day cover 1.00
Imprint block of 6 1.75

10th International Library Week.

Mailmen's Uniforms and Stamp of 1948 A101

1968, July 1 **Photo.** ***Perf. 13x13½***

170 A101 3c **multicolored** .30 .25
First day cover 1.00
Imprint block of 6 1.75

First Ryukyuan postage stamps, 20th anniv.

Main Gate, Enkaku Temple — A102

1968, July 15 **Photo. & Engr.** ***Perf. 13½***

171 A102 3c **multicolored**	.30	.25
First day cover		1.00
Imprint block of 6	1.75	

Restoration of the main gate Enkaku Temple, built 1492-1495, destroyed during World War II.

Old Man's Dance — A103

Mictyris Longicarpus — A104

1968, Sept. 15 **Photo.** ***Perf. 13½***

172 A103 3c **gold & multicolored**	.30	.25
First day cover		1.00
Imprint block of 6	2.00	

Old People's Day.

1968-69 **Photo.** ***Perf. 13½***

Crabs: No. 174, Uca dubia stimpson. No. 175, Baptozius vinosus. No. 176, Cardisoma carnifex. No. 177, Ocypode ceratophthalma pallas.

173 A104 3c **blue, ocher & black,** *Oct. 10, 1968*	.30	.25
First day cover		1.25
Imprint block of 6	2.50	
174 A104 3c **light blue green & multi,** *Feb. 5, 1969*	.35	.30
First day cover		1.25
Imprint block of 6	2.75	
175 A104 3c **light green & multi,** *Mar. 5, 1969*	.35	.30
First day cover		1.25
Imprint block of 6	2.75	
176 A104 3c **light ultra & multi,** *May 15, 1969*	.45	.40
First day cover		1.25
Imprint block of 6	3.25	
177 A104 3c **light ultra & multi,** *June 2, 1969*	.45	.40
First day cover		1.25
Imprint block of 6	3.25	
Nos. 173-177 (5)	1.90	1.65

Saraswati Pavilion — A105

1968, Nov. 1 **Photo.** ***Perf. 13½***

178 A105 3c **multicolored**	.30	.25
First day cover		1.00
Imprint block of 6	2.00	

Restoration of the Sarawati Pavilion (in front of Enkaku Temple), destroyed during World War II.

Tennis Player — A106

Cock and Iris (Bingata) — A107

1968, Nov. 23 **Photo.** ***Perf. 13½***

179 A106 3c **green & multicolored**	.40	.35
First day cover		1.00
Imprint block of 6	3.25	

35th All-Japan East-West Men's Soft-ball Tennis Tournament, Naha City, Nov. 23-24.

1968, Dec. 10

180 A107 1½c **orange & multicolored**	.25	.20
First day cover		1.50
Imprint block of 10	3.50	

New Year, 1969.

Boxer — A108

Ink Slab Screen — A109

1969, Jan. 3

181 A108 3c **gray & multicolored**	.40	.30
First day cover		1.00
Imprint block of 6	2.75	

20th All-Japan Amateur Boxing Championships held at the University of the Ryukyus, Jan. 3-5.

1969, Apr. 17 **Photo.** ***Perf. 13½***

182 A109 3c **salmon, indigo & red**	.40	.35
First day cover		1.50
Imprint block of 6	2.75	

Philatelic Week.

Box Antennas and Map of Radio Link — A110

Gate of Courtesy and Emblems — A111

1969, July 1 **Photo.** ***Perf. 13½***

183 A110 3c **multicolored**	.30	.25
First day cover		1.00
Imprint block of 6	2.25	

Opening of the UHF (radio) circuit system between Okinawa and the outlying Miyako-Yaeyama Islands.

1969, Aug. 1 **Photo.** ***Perf. 13½***

184 A111 3c **Prussian blue, gold & vermilion**	.30	.25
First day cover		1.00
Imprint block of 6	2.25	

22nd All-Japan Formative Education Study Conf., Naha, Aug. 1-3.

FOLKLORE ISSUE

Tug of War Festival A112

Hari Boat Race A113

Izaiho Ceremony, Kudaka Island A114

Mortardrum Dance A115

Sea God Dance A116

1969-70 **Photo.** ***Perf. 13***

185 A112 3c **multicolored,** *Aug. 1, 1969*	.30	.25
First day cover		1.50
Imprint block of 6	2.25	
186 A113 3c **multicolored,** *Sept. 5, 1969*	.35	.30
First day cover		1.50
Imprint block of 6	2.25	
187 A114 3c **multicolored,** *Oct. 3, 1969*	.35	.30
First day cover		1.50
Imprint block of 6	2.25	
188 A115 3c **multicolored,** *Jan. 20, 1970*	.50	.45
First day cover		1.50
Imprint block of 6	3.50	
189 A116 3c **multicolored,** *Feb. 27, 1970*	.50	.45
First day cover		1.50
Imprint block of 6	3.50	
Nos. 185-189 (5)	2.00	1.75

No. 99 Surcharged

1969, Oct. 15 **Photo.** ***Perf. 13½***

190 A44 ½c on 3c **multicolored**	1.00	1.00
First day cover		3.00
Imprint block of 10	13.50	
a. "1/2c" only surcharge	950.00	

No. 190a are right margin stamps from a pane with a leftward misregistration of the surcharging plate.

Nakamura-ke Farm House, Built 1713-51 — A117

1969, Nov. 1 **Photo.** ***Perf. 13½***

191 A117	3c **multicolored**		.25	.20
	First day cover			1.00
	Imprint block of 6		1.50	

Protection of national cultural treasures.

Statue of Kyuzo Toyama, Maps of Hawaiian and Ryukyu Islands — A118

1969, Dec. 5 **Photo.** ***Perf. 13½***

192 A118 3c **light ultra & multi**		.50	.50
First day cover			1.50
Imprint block of 6		3.75	
a. Without overprint		*3,000.*	
b. Wide-spaced bars		*750.00*	

70th anniv. of Ryukyu-Hawaii emigration led by Kyuzo Toyama.

The overprint "1969" at lower left and bars across "1970" at upper right was applied before No. 192 was issued.

Dog and Flowers (Bingata) — A119

Sake Flask Made from Coconut — A120

1969, Dec. 10

193 A119 1½c **pink & multicolored**		.20	.20
First day cover			1.50
Imprint block of 10		2.75	

New Year, 1970.

1970, Apr. 15 **Photo.** ***Perf. 13½***

194 A120 3c **multicolored**		.25	.25
First day cover			1.25
Imprint block of 6		1.75	

Philatelic Week, 1970.

CLASSIC OPERA ISSUE

"The Bell" (Shushin Kaneiri) — A121

Child and Kidnapper (Chunusudu) A122

Robe of Feathers (Mekarushi) A123

Vengeance of Two Young Sons (Nidotichiuchi) A124

The Virgin and the Dragon (Kokonomaki) A125

1970 **Photo.** ***Perf. 13½***

195 A121 3c **dull blue & multi,** *Apr. 28*		.40	.40
First day cover			1.75
Imprint block of 6		3.00	
a. Souvenir sheet of 4		5.00	5.00
First day cover			5.00
196 A122 3c **light blue & multi,** *May 29*		.40	.40
First day cover			1.75
Imprint block of 6		3.00	
a. Souvenir sheet of 4		5.00	5.00
First day cover			5.00
197 A123 3c **bluish green & multi,** *June 30*		.40	.40
First day cover			1.75
Imprint block of 6		3.00	
a. Souvenir sheet of 4		5.00	5.00
First day cover			5.00
198 A124 3c **dull blue green & multi,** *July 30*		.40	.40
First day cover			1.75
Imprint block of 6		3.00	
a. Souvenir sheet of 4		5.00	5.00
First day cover			5.00
199 A125 3c **multicolored,** *Aug. 25*		.40	.40
First day cover			1.75
Imprint block of 6		3.00	
a. Souvenir sheet of 4		5.00	5.00
First day cover			5.00
Nos. 195-199 (5)		2.00	2.00
Nos. 195a-199a (5)		25.00	*25.00*

Underwater Observatory and Tropical Fish — A126

1970, May 22

200 A126 3c **blue green & multi**		.30	.25
First day cover			1.25
Imprint block of 6		2.00	

Completion of the underwater observatory of Busena-Misaki, Nago.

Noboru Jahana (1865-1908), Politician — A127

Map of Okinawa and People — A128

Portraits: No. 202, Saion Gushichan Bunjaku (1682-1761), statesman. No. 203, Choho Giwan (1823-1876), regent and poet.

1970-71 **Engr.** ***Perf. 13½***

201 A127 3c **rose claret,** *Sept. 25, 1970*		.50	.45
First day cover			2.50
Imprint block of 6		3.50	
202 A127 3c **dull blue green,** *Dec. 22, 1970*		.75	.65
First day cover			2.50
Imprint block of 6		6.00	
203 A127 3c **black,** *Jan. 22, 1971*		.50	.45
First day cover			2.50
Imprint block of 6		3.50	

1970, Oct. 1 **Photo.**

204 A128 3c **red & multicolored**		.25	.25
First day cover			1.00
Imprint block of 6		1.75	

Oct. 1, 1970 census.

Great Cycad of Une — A129

1970, Nov. 2 **Photo.** ***Perf. 13½***

205 A129 3c **gold & multicolored**		.25	.25
First day cover			1.00
Imprint block of 6		1.75	

Protection of national treasures.

Japanese Flag, Diet and Map of Ryukyus — A130

Wild Boar and Cherry Blossoms (Bingata) — A131

1970, Nov. 15 **Photo.** ***Perf. 13½***

206 A130 3c **ultramarine & multicolored**		.80	.75
First day cover			2.00
Imprint block of 6		6.00	

Citizen's participation in national administration to Japanese law of Apr. 24, 1970.

1970, Dec. 10

207 A131 1½c **multicolored**		.20	.20
First day cover			1.50
Imprint block of 10		2.40	

New Year, 1971.

Low Hand Loom (Jibata) — A132

Farmer Wearing Palm Bark Raincoat and Kuba Leaf Hat — A133

Fisherman's Wooden Box and Scoop — A134

Designs: No. 209, Woman running a filature (reel). No. 211, Woman hulling rice with cylindrical "Shiri-ushi."

1971		Photo.		*Perf. 13½*
208	A132	3c **light blue & multi,** *Feb. 16*	.30	.25
		First day cover		1.25
		Imprint block of 6	2.00	
209	A132	3c **pale green & multi,** *Mar. 16*	.30	.25
		First day cover		1.25
		Imprint block of 6	2.00	
210	A133	3c **light blue & multi,** *Apr. 30*	.35	.30
		First day cover		1.25
		Imprint block of 6	2.25	
211	A132	3c **yellow & multi,** *May 20*	.40	.35
		First day cover		1.25
		Imprint block of 6	3.00	
212	A134	3c **gray & multi,** *June 15*	.35	.30
		First day cover		1.25
		Imprint block of 6	2.25	
		Nos. 208-212 (5)	1.70	1.45

Water Carrier (Taku) — A135

1971, Apr. 15		Photo.		*Perf. 13½*
213	A135	3c **blue green & multicolored**	.35	.30
		First day cover		1.50
		Imprint block of 6	2.75	

Philatelic Week, 1971.

Old and New Naha, and City Emblem A136

1971, May 20				*Perf. 13*
214	A136	3c **ultramarine & multicolored**	.25	.20
		First day cover		1.00
		Imprint block of 6	1.75	

50th anniv. of Naha as a municipality.

Caesalpinia Pulcherrima — A137

Design: 2c, Madder (Sandanka).

1971		Photo.		*Perf. 13*
215	A137	2c **gray & multicolored,** *Sept. 30*	.25	.20
		First day cover		1.00
		Imprint block of 10	3.00	
216	A137	3c **gray & multicolored,** *May 10*	.25	.20
		First day cover		1.00
		Imprint block of 10	3.00	

GOVERNMENT PARK SERIES

View from Mabuni Hill — A138

Mt. Arashi from Haneji Sea — A139

Yabuchi Island from Yakena Port — A140

1971-72				
217	A138	3c **green & multi,** *July 30, 1971*	.20	.20
		First day cover		1.25
		Imprint block of 6	1.50	
218	A139	3c **blue & multi,** *Aug. 30, 1971*	.20	.20
		First day cover		1.25
		Imprint block of 6	1.50	
219	A140	4c **multicolored,** *Jan. 20, 1972*	.25	.20
		First day cover		1.25
		Imprint block of 6	1.75	
		Nos. 217-219 (3)	.65	.60

For the 4-cent unissued "stamp" picturing Iriomote Park, originally planned for issue in 1971 but never released, see the note after No. R31.

Dancer — A141

Deva King, Torinji Temple — A142

1971, Nov. 1		Photo.		*Perf. 13*
220	A141	4c **Prussian blue & multicolored**	.20	.20
		First day cover		1.00
		Imprint block of 10	2.50	

1971, Dec. 1				
221	A142	4c **deep blue & multicolored**	.20	.20
		First day cover		1.00
		Imprint block of 6	1.50	

Protection of national cultural treasures.

Rat and Chrysanthemums A143

Student Nurse A144

1971, Dec. 10				
222	A143	2c **brown orange & multi**	.20	.20
		First day cover		1.50
		Imprint block of 10	2.50	

New Year, 1972.

1971, Dec. 24				
223	A144	4c **lilac & multicolored**	.20	.20
		First day cover		1.00
		Imprint block of 6	1.50	

Nurses' training, 25th anniversary.

A145

A147

Coral Reef — A146

1972		Photo.		*Perf. 13*
224	A145	5c **bright blue & multi,** *Apr. 14*	.40	.35
		First day cover		1.25
		Imprint block of 6	2.75	
225	A146	5c **gray & multi,** *Mar. 30*	.40	.35
		First day cover		1.25
		Imprint block of 6	2.75	
226	A147	5c **ocher & multi,** *Mar. 21*	.40	.35
		First day cover		1.25
		Imprint block of 6	2.75	
		Nos. 224-226 (3)	1.20	1.05

Dove, U.S. and Japanese Flags — A148

1972, Apr. 17		Photo.		*Perf. 13*
227	A148	5c **bright blue & multi**	.80	.80
		First day cover		1.50
		Imprint block of 6	5.50	

Antique Sake Pot (Yushibin) — A149

1972, Apr. 20

228 A149 5c **ultramarine & multicolored** .60 .60
First day cover 1.25
Imprint block of 6 4.50

Ryukyu stamps were replaced by those of Japan after May 15, 1972.

AIR POST STAMPS

Catalogue values for all unused stamps in this section are for Never Hinged items.

Dove and Map of Ryukyus — AP1

1950, Feb. 15 Photo. Unwmk. *Perf. 13x13½*

C1 AP1 8y **bright blue** 150.00 60.00
First day cover 35.00
Imprint block of 6 1,250.
C2 AP1 12y **green** 35.00 30.00
First day cover 35.00
Imprint block of 6 275.00
C3 AP1 16y **rose carmine** 20.00 20.00
First day cover 35.00
Imprint block of 6 125.00
First day cover, #C1-C3 200.00
Nos. C1-C3 (3) 205.00 110.00

Heavenly Maiden AP2

1951-54

C4 AP2 13y **blue,** *Oct. 1, 1951* 3.00 2.00
First day cover 60.00
Imprint block of 6, 5-character 300.00
Imprint block of 6, 8-character 37.50
C5 AP2 18y **green,** *Oct. 1, 1951* 4.00 3.00
First day cover 60.00
Imprint block of 6, 5-character 55.00
Imprint block of 6, 8-character 45.00
C6 AP2 30y **cerise,** *Oct. 1, 1951* 6.00 1.50
First day cover 60.00
First day cover, #C4-C6 250.00
Imprint block of 6, 5-character 70.00
Imprint block of 6, 8-character 150.00
C7 AP2 40y **red violet,** *Aug. 16, 1954* 8.00 7.00
First day cover 35.00
Imprint block of 6 90.00
C8 AP2 50y **yellow orange,** *Aug. 16, 1954* 9.00 8.00
First day cover 35.00
Imprint block of 6 100.00
First day cover, #C7-C8 125.00
Nos. C4-C8 (5) 30.00 21.50

Heavenly Maiden Playing Flute — AP3

1957, Aug. 1 Engr. *Perf. 13½*

C9 AP3 15y **blue green** 9.00 4.00
Imprint block of 6 65.00
C10 AP3 20y **rose carmine** 15.00 7.00
Imprint block of 6 100.00
C11 AP3 35y **yellow green** 17.00 8.00
Imprint block of 6 130.00
a. 35y **light yellow green,** *1958* *150.00*
C12 AP3 45y **reddish brown** 20.00 10.00
Imprint block of 6 150.00
C13 AP3 60y **gray** 24.00 12.00
Imprint block of 6 210.00
First day cover, #C9-C13 45.00
Nos. C9-C13 (5) 85.00 41.00

On one printing of No. C10, position 49 shows an added spur on the right side of the second character from the left. Value unused, $175.

Same Surcharged in Brown Red or Light Ultramarine

1959, Dec. 20

C14 AP3 9c on 15y **blue green** (BrR) 3.00 2.00
Imprint block of 6 22.50
a. Inverted surcharge *950.00*
Imprint block of 6 *6,750.*
C15 AP3 14c on 20y **rose carmine** (L.U.) 4.00 4.00
Imprint block of 6 30.00
C16 AP3 19c on 35y **light yellow green** (BrR) 8.00 6.00
Imprint block of 6 57.50
C17 AP3 27c on 45y **reddish brown** (L.U.) 19.00 6.00
Imprint block of 6 150.00
C18 AP3 35c on 60y **gray** (BrR) 16.00 9.00
Imprint block of 6 125.00
First day cover, #C14-C18 35.00
Nos. C14-C18 (5) 50.00 27.00

No. C15 is found with the variety described below No. C13. Value unused, $125.

Nos. 31-33, 36 and 38 Surcharged in Black, Brown, Red, Blue or Green

1960, Aug. 3 Photo. *Perf. 13*

C19 A14 9c on 4y **brown** 4.00 1.00
Imprint block of 10 50.00
a. Surcharge inverted and transposed *15,000.* *15,000.*
b. Inverted surcharge (legend only) *12,000.*
c. Surcharge transposed *1,500.*
d. Legend of surcharge only *4,000.*
e. Vert. pair, one without surcharge *6,000.*

Nos. C19c and C19d are from a single sheet of 100 with surcharge shifted downward. Ten examples of No. C19c exist with "9c" also in bottom selvage. No. C19d is from the top row of the sheet.

No. C19e is unique, pos. 100, caused by paper foldover.

C20 A17 14c on 5y **rose lilac** (Br) 5.00 3.00
Imprint block of 10 65.00
C21 A14 19c on 15y **vermilion** (R) 3.50 3.00
Imprint block of 10 45.00
C22 A17 27c on 14y **reddish brown** (Bl) 10.50 2.50
Imprint block of 10 150.00
C23 A14 35c on 20y **yellow orange** (G) 7.50 5.00
Imprint block of 10 90.00
First day cover, #C19-C23 25.00
Nos. C19-C23 (5) 30.50 14.50

Wind God — AP4

Designs: 9c, Heavenly Maiden (as on AP2). 14c, Heavenly Maiden (as on AP3). 27c, Wind God at right. 35c, Heavenly Maiden over treetops.

1961, Sept. 21 Unwmk. *Perf. 13½*

C24 AP4 9c **multicolored** .30 .20
Imprint block of 6 2.25
C25 AP4 14c **multicolored** .80 .80
Imprint block of 6 6.00
C26 AP4 19c **multicolored** .90 .90
Imprint block of 6 6.50
C27 AP4 27c **multicolored** 3.50 .60
Imprint block of 6 27.50
C28 AP4 35c **multicolored** 2.50 1.25
Imprint block of 6 20.00
First day cover, #C24-C28 35.00
Nos. C24-C28 (5) 8.00 3.75

AP5

AP6

1963, Aug. 28 *Perf. 13x13½*

C29 AP5 5½c **multicolored** .25 .25
First day cover 1.00
Imprint block of 10 3.00
C30 AP6 7c **multicolored** .30 .30
First day cover 1.00
First day cover, #C29-C30 2.50
Imprint block of 10 3.50

SPECIAL DELIVERY STAMP

Catalogue value for the unused stamp in this section is for a Never Hinged item.

Sea Horse and Map of Ryukyus — SD1

1950, Feb. 15 Unwmk. Photo. *Perf. 13x13½*

E1 SD1 5y **bright blue** 35.00 20.00
First day cover 100.00
Imprint block of 6 350.00

QUANTITIES ISSUED

Regular Postage and Commemorative Stamps

Cat. No.	*Quantity*	*Cat. No.*	*Quantity*
1	90,214	*87*	3,019,000
2	55,901	*88*	298,966
3	94,663	*89*	298,966
4	55,413	*90*	398,901
5	76,387	*91*	398,992
6	117,321	*92*	1,498,970
7	291,403	*93*	598,989
1a	61,000	*94*	398,998
2a-4a	181,000	*95*	398,993
5a	29,936	*96*	298,993
6a	99,300	*97*	398,997
7a	46,000	*98*	9,699,000
8	2,559,000	*99*	10,991,500
8a	300,000	*100*	1,549,000
9	1,198,989	*101*	799,000
10	589,000	*102*	1,299,000
11	479,000	*103*	398,995
12	598,999	*104*	298,892
13	397,855	*105*	1,598,949
14	499,000	*106*	348,989
15	498,960	*107*	10,099,000
16	199,197	*108*	348,865
16A	199,900	*109*	348,937
16B	39,900	*110*	348,962
17	9,800	*111*	348,974
18	299,500	*112*	398,974

Cat. No.	*Quantity*	*Cat. No.*	*Quantity*
19	3,014,427	*113*	398,911
20	3,141,777	*114*	1,199,000
21	2,970,827	*115*	398,948
22	191,917	*116*	398,943
23	1,118,617	*117*	1,698,912
24	276,218	*118*	550,000
24a	ca. 1,300	*119*	549,000
25	231,717	*120*	749,000
26	220,130	*121*	799,000
27	398,993	*122*	389,000
28	386,421	*123*	319,000
29	498,854	*124*	1,999,000
30	298,994	*125-127*	999,000
31	4,768,413	*128*	799,000
32	1,202,297	*129*	1,699,000
33	500,059	*130-131*	799,000
34	298,994	*132*	849,000
35	199,000	*133*	799,000
36	455,896	*134*	1,299,000
37	160,518	*135*	1,099,000
38	198,720	*136*	1,299,000
39	198,199	*137-138*	1,598,000
40	599,000	*139*	3,098,000
41	598,075	*140-142*	1,598,000
42	1,198,179	*143-148*	2,498,000
43	1,625,406	*149*	2,298,000
44	994,880	*150*	3,798,000
45	997,759	*151*	2,298,000
46	996,759	*152-156*	1,998,000
47	2,705,955	*157-158*	1,698,000
48	997,542	*159-160*	1,298,000
49	996,609	*161*	898,000
50	996,928	*162*	1,498,000
51	499,000	*163-164*	1,298,000
52	249,000	*165*	3,998,000
52a	78,415	*166-167*	1,298,000
53	248,700	*168*	998,000
54	1,498,991	*169-179*	898,000
55	2,498,897	*180*	3,198,000
56	1,098,972	*181-189*	898,000
57	998,918	*190*	1,773,050
58	2,699,000	*191*	898,000
59	2,499,000	*192*	864,960
60	199,000	*193*	3,198,000
61	499,000	*194*	898,000
62	199,000	*195-199*	598,000
63	1,498,931	*195a-199a*	124,500
64	798,953	*200-206*	898,000
65-68	999,000	*207*	3,198,000
72	598,912	*208-210*	1,098,000
73	398,990	*211-212*	1,298,000
74	598,936	*213*	1,098,000
75	1,998,992	*214*	1,298,000
76	1,000,000	*215-216*	4,998,000
77	2,000,000	*217*	1,498,000
78	500,000	*218-219*	1,798,000
79-80	400,000	*220*	2,998,000
81	12,599,000	*221*	1,798,000
82	11,979,000	*222*	4,998,000
83	6,850,000	*223*	1,798,000
84	5,099,000	*224-226*	2,498,000
84A	1,699,000	*227*	2,998,000
85	4,749,000	*228*	3,998,000
86	2,099,000		

AIR POST STAMPS

C1-C3	198,000	*C18*	96,650
C4	1,952,348	*C19*	1,033,900
C5	331,360	*C19a*	100
C6	762,530	*C20*	230,000
C7	76,166	*C21*	185,000
C8	122,816	*C22*	191,000
C9	708,319	*C23*	190,000
C10	108,824	*C24*	17,199,000
C11	164,147	*C25*	1,999,000
C12	50,335	*C26*	1,250,000
C13	69,092	*C27*	3,499,000
C14	597,103	*C28*	1,699,000
C15	77,951	*C29*	1,199,000
C16	97,635	*C30*	1,949,000
C17	98,353		

SPECIAL DELIVERY STAMP

E1	198,804

PROVISIONAL ISSUES

Stamps of Japan Overprinted by Postmasters in Four Island Districts

Trading Ship — A82

Rice Harvest — A83

Gen. Maresuke Nogi — A84

Admiral Heihachiro Togo — A86

Garambi Lighthouse, Taiwan — A88

Meiji Shrine, Tokyo — A90

Plane and Map of Japan — A92

Kasuga Shrine, Nara — A93

Mount Fuji and Cherry Blossoms — A94

Horyu Temple, Nara — A95

Miyajima Torii, Itsukushima Shrine — A96

Golden Pavilion, Kyoto — A97

Great Budda, Kamakura — A98

Kamatari Fujiwara — A99

War Factory Girl — A144

Hyuga Monument & Mt. Fuji — A146

War Worker & Planes — A147

Palms and Map of "Greater East Asia" — A148

Aviator Saluting & Japanese Flag — A150

Torii of Yasukuni Shrine — A151

Mt. Fuji and Cherry Blossoms — A152

Torii of Miyajima — A153

Garambi Lighthouse, Taiwan — A154

Sun & Cherry Blossoms — A161

Sunrise at Sea & Plane — A162

Coal Miners — A163

Yasukuni Shrine — A164

"Thunderstorm below Fuji," by Hokusai — A167

KUME ISLAND

Values are for unused stamps. Used stamps sell for considerably more, should be expertized and are preferred on cover or document.

A1

Mimeographed
Seal Handstamped in Vermilion

1945, Oct. 1 Without Gum Unwmk. *Imperf.*

1X1 A1 7s **black,** *cream (2,400)* 3,200. —
On cover —
a. "7" & "SEN" one letter space to left 3,500.

Printed on legal-size U.S. military mimeograph paper and validated by the official seal of the Kume Island postmaster, Norifume Kikuzato. Valid until May 4, 1946.

Cancellations "20.10.1" (Oct. 1, 1945) or "20.10.6" (Oct. 6, 1945) are by favor. See proofs section for stamps on white watermarked U.S. official bond paper.

AMAMI DISTRICT

Inspection Seal ("Ken," abbreviation for *kensa zumi,* inspected or examined; five types and five colors)

Stamps of Japan 1937-46 Handstamped in Black, Blue, Purple, Vermilion or Red

Typographed, Lithographed, Engraved

1947-48 Wmk. 257 *Perf. 13, Imperf*

2X1 A82 ½s **purple,** #257 1,000.
2X2 A83 1s **fawn,** #258 —
2X3 A144 1s **orange brown,** #325 *1,750.*
2X4 A84 2s **crimson,** #259 600.
a. 2s **vermilion,** #259c —
2X5 A84 2s **rose red,** imperf., #351 2,000.
2X6 A85 3s **green,** #260 *1,700.*
2X7 A84 3s **brown,** #329 —
2X8 A161 3s **rose carmine,** imperf., #352 *1,800.*
2X9 A146 4s **emerald,** #330 700.
2X10 A86 5s **brown lake,** #331 700.
2X11 A162 5s **green,** imperf., #353 *1,500.*
2X12 A147 6s **light ultramarine,** #332 —
2X13 A86 7s **orange vermilion,** #333 *1,250.*
2X14 A90 8s **dark purple & pale violet,** #265 *1,500.*
2X15 A148 10s **crimson & dull rose,** #344 600.
2X16 A152 10s **red orange,** imperf., #355 *(48)* *2,500.*
2X17 A93 14s **rose lake & pale rose,** #268 —
2X18 A150 15s **dull blue,** #336 600.
2X19 A151 17s **gray violet,** #337 *1,750.*
2X20 A94 20s **ultramarine,** #269 *1,750.*
2X21 A152 20s **blue,** #338 600.
2X22 A152 20s **ultramarine,** imperf., #356 *(48)* *1,750.*
2X23 A95 25s **dark brown & pale brown,** #270 900.
2X24 A151 27s **rose brown,** #339 —
2X25 A153 30s **bluish green,** #340 —
2X26 A153 30s **bright blue,** imperf., #357 *2,000.*
2X27 A88 40s **dull violet,** #341 *1,750.*
2X28 A154 40s **dark violet,** #342 *1,750.*
2X29 A97 50s **olive & pale olive,** #272 —
2X30 A163 50s **dark brown,** imperf., #358 *(48)* *2,000.*
2X31 A164 1y **deep olive green,** imperf., #359 *2,500.*
2X32 A167 1y **deep ultramarine,** imperf., #364 —
2X33 A99 5y **deep gray green,** #274 —
2X34 A99 5y **deep gray green,** imperf., #360 —

Nos. 2X5, 2X8, 2X11, 2X16, 2X22, 2X26, 2X30, 2X31, 2X32 and 2X34 were issued without gum.

MIYAKO DISTRICT

Personal Seal of Postmaster Jojin Tomiyama

Stamps of Japan 1937-46 Handstamped in Vermilion or Red

Typographed, Lithographed, Engraved

1946-47 Wmk. 257 *Perf. 13*

3X1 A144 1s **orange brown,** #325 175.
3X2 A84 2s **crimson,** #259 125. —
a. 2s **vermilion** #259c ('47) 150.
b. 2s **pink** #259b ('47) 550.
3X3 A84 3s **brown,** #329 100. —
3X4 A86 4s **dark green,** #261 100. —
3X5 A86 5s **brown lake,** #331 550. —
On cover with #3X17 —
3X6 A88 6s **orange,** #263 100. —
3X7 A90 8s **dark purple & pale violet,** #265 100. —
3X8 A148 10s **crimson & dull rose,** #334 100. —
On cover with #3X15 —
3X9 A152 10s **red orange,** imperf., #355 ('47) *(1,000)* 150.
3X10 A92 12s **indigo,** #267 100. —
3X11 A93 14s **rose lake & pale rose,** #268 100. —
3X12 A150 15s **dull blue,** #336 100. —
3X13 A151 17s **gray violet,** #337 100. —
3X14 A94 20s **ultramarine,** #269 —
3X15 A152 20s **blue,** #338 100. —
3X16 A152 20s **ultramarine,** imperf., #356 ('47) 200.
3X17 A95 25s **dark brown & pale brown,** #270 100. —
3X18 A153 30s **bluish green,** #340 100. —
3X19 A88 40s **dull violet,** #341 250.
3X20 A154 40s **dark violet,** #342 100. —
3X21 A97 50s **olive & pale olive,** #272 100. —
3X22 A163 50s **dark brown,** #358 ('47) *(750)* 250. —
3X23 A98 1y **brown & pale brown,** #273 *9,000.*
3X24 A167 1y **deep ultramarine,** #364 ('47) *(500)* *1,500.* *600.*

Nos. 3X9, 3X16, 3X22 and 3X24 were issued without gum.

Nos. 3X22 and 3X24 have sewing machine perf.; No. 3X16 exists with that perf. also.

Nos. 3X1-3X2, 3X2a, 3X3-3X5, 3X8 Handstamp Surcharged with 2 Japanese Characters

1946-47

3X25 A144 1y on 1s **orange brown** 140. —
3X26 A84 1y on 2s **crimson** 3,000.
3X27 A84 1y on 3s **brown** ('47) 3,000.
3X28 A84 2y on 2s **crimson** 175. —
a. 2y on 2s **vermilion** ('47) 175. —
3X29 A86 4y on 4s **dark green** 140. —
3X30 A86 5y on 5s **brown lake** 140. —
3X31 A148 10y on 10s **crimson & dull rose** 140. —

The overwhelming majority of used examples of Miyako District stamps were used on Bulk Mailing Records documents and Letter Content Certification Records documents. Stamps affixed to such documents command a substantial premium above off-document used stamps.

Cancellation: black Miyako cds.

OKINAWA DISTRICT

Personal Seal of Postmaster Shiichi Hirata

R1

Japan Nos. 355-356, 358, 364 Overprinted in Black

1947, Nov. 1 Wmk. 257 Litho. *Imperf.*
Without Gum

4X1 A152 10s **red orange** *(13,997)* 1,200. *1,000.*
On cover, strip of 3 *9,500.*
On cover with #4X2 *7,500.*
4X2 A152 20s **ultramarine** *(13,611)* 600. *1,000.*
4X3 A163 50s **dark brown** *(6,276)* 900. *700.*
4X4 A167 1y **deep ultramarine** *(1,947)* 1,750. *1,000.*

On Revenue Stamp of Japan

4X5 R1 30s **brown** *(14,000)* *3,500.* *3,500.*
On cover *7,500.*

No. 4X5 is on Japan's current 30s revenue stamp. The Hirata seal validated it for postal use.

Nos. 4X1-4X5 are known with rough sewing machine perforations, full or partial.

YAEYAMA DISTRICT

Personal Seal of Postmaster Kenpuku Miyara

Stamps of Japan 1937-46 Handstamped in Black

Typographed, Engraved, Lithographed

1948 Wmk. 257 *Perf. 13*

5X1 A86 4s **dark green,** #261 1,200.
5X2 A86 5s **brown lake,** #331 1,200.
5X3 A86 7s **orange vermilion,** #333 800.
5X4 A148 10s **crimson & dull rose,** #334 *5,000.*
5X5 A94 20s **ultramarine,** #269 150.
On cover with 2 #5X8 —
5X6 A96 30s **peacock blue,** #271 1,000.
5X7 A88 40s **dull violet,** #341 80.
5X8 A97 50s **olive & pale olive,** #272 100.
5X9 A163 50s **dark brown,** imperf., #358 *(250)* 1,350.
5X10 A99 5y **deep gray green,** #274 2,000.

No. 5X9 was issued without gum.

This handstamp exists double, triple, inverted and in pair, one stamp without overprint.

Provisional postal stationery of the four districts also exists.

LETTER SHEETS

Values are for entires.

Stylized Deigo Blossom — US1

Banyan Tree — US2

Typographed by Japan Printing Bureau.
Stamp is in upper left corner.

Designer: Shutaro Higa

1948-49

U1 US1 50s **vermilion,** *cream, July 18, 1949 (250,000)* 50.00 60.00
First day cancel —
a. 50s **orange red,** *gray, July 1, 1948 (1,000)* 1,500. —

Designer: Ken Yabu

1950, Jan. 21

U2 US2 1y **carmine red,** *cream (250,000)* 40.00 50.00
First day cancel —

AIR LETTER SHEETS

DC-4 Skymaster and Shurei Gate — UC1

UC2

Designer: Chosho Ashitomi
"PAR AVION" (Bilingual) below Stamp

Litho. & Typo. by Japan Printing Bureau

1952-53

UC1 UC1 12y **light rose,** *pale blue green, Mar. 9, 1953 (76,000)* 20.00 12.50
a. 12y **dull rose,** *pale blue green, Nov. 1, 1952 (50,000)* 30.00 15.00
First day cancel, No. UC1a 80.00

No. UC1a is on tinted paper with colorless overall inscription "RYUKYU FOREIGN AIRMAIL," repeated in parallel vertical lines, light and indistinct. Dull rose ink of imprinted design and legend "AIR LETTER" appears to bleed. No. UC1 has overall inscription darker and more distinct. Light rose ink of design and legend does not bleed. Model: U.S. No. UC16.

Litho. & Typo. by Nippon Toppan K.K.
"AEROGRAMME" below Stamp

1955, Sept. 10

UC2 UC2 15y **violet blue & bright red,** *pale yellow green (89,300)* 30.00 15.00
First day cancel 60.00
a. 15y **violet blue & dull red,** *pale blue green, Oct. 1957 (33,742)* 45.00 25.00

Printing on the envelope stamp is heavier on No. UC2a than on No. UC2.

No. UC2 surcharged in Red

"13" & "¢" aligned at bot.; 2 thick bars — a

"¢" raised; 2 thick bars — b

"13" & "¢" as in "a"; 4 thin bars — c

"¢" raised; 4 thin bars — d

Printers: Type "a," Nakamura Printing Co., "b" and "d," Okinawa Printing Co., "c," Sun Printing Co.

1958-60

UC3 UC2 13c on 15y type "a," *Sept. 16, 1958 (60,000)* 20.00 18.00
First day cancel 60.00
a. Type "b," on No. UC2, *June 1, 1959 (2,000)* 40.00 30.00
b. Type "b," on No. UC2a *(7,000)* 50.00 30.00
c. Type "c," on No. UC2, *Sept. 22, 1959 (1,000)* 80.00 80.00
d. As "c," small wrong font "¢" sign 1,000. —
e. Type "c," on No. UC2a *(1,000)* 80.00 80.00
f. As "e," double surcharge, one on reverse *2,000.*
g. Type "b" and No. 46 on No. UC2a, *Aug. 22, 1960 (1,000)* 500.00 —
h. Type "d" and Nos. 55, 58 on No. UC2, *Oct. 1, 1960 (1,000)* 450.00 450.00
i. Type "d" and Nos. 55, 58 on No. UC2a *(2,000)* 300.00 300.00

For Nos. UC3g, UC3h and UC3i, additional stamps have been affixed to make up the 15c rate.

UC3

Lithographed by Japan Printing Bureau

1959, Nov. 10

UC4 UC3 15c **dark blue,** *pale blue (560,000)* 4.00 2.50
First day cancel 10.00

POSTAL CARDS

Values are for entire cards.

Nos. UX1-UX9 are typo., others litho.

Printed by Japan Printing Bureau unless otherwise stated.

Quantities in parentheses; "E" means estimated.

Deigo Blossom Type

Designer: Shutaro Higa

1948, July 1

UX1 US1 10s **dull red,** *grayish tan (100,000)* 50.00 *60.00*

1949, July 1

UX2 US1 15s **orange red,** *gray (E 175,000)* 40.00 *70.00*
First day cancel —
a. 15s **vermilion,** *tan (E 50,000)* 110.00 *125.00*

Banyan Tree Type

Designer: Ken Yabu

1950, Jan. 21

UX3 US2 50s **carmine red,** *light tan (E 200,000)* 10.00 10.00
First day cancel 60.00
a. Grayish tan card (E 25,000) 25.00 *50.00*

Nos. UX2, UX2a Handstamp Surcharged in Vermilion

19-21x23-25mm — a

22-23x26-27mm — b

20-21x24-24½mm — c

22-23½x25-26mm — d

1951

UX4 US1 (c) 15s + 85s on #UX2 *(E 35,000)* 100. 100.
a. Type "c" on #UX2a *(E 5,000)* 150. 150.
b. Type "a" on #UX2 *(E 39,000)* 75. *100.*
c. Type "a" on #UX2a 1,000. —
d. Type "b" on #UX2 *1,000.* *1,000.*
e. Type "d" on #UX2 *(E 4,000)* 150. *200.*
f. Type "d" on #UX2a *(E 1,000)* 250. *300.*

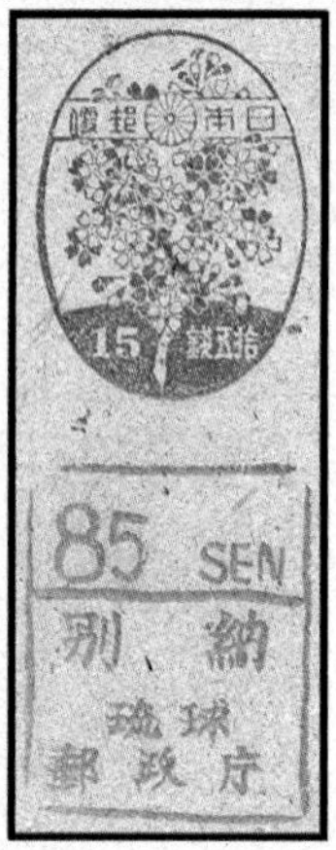

Type "a" exists on the 15s cherry blossom postal card of Japan. Value $100.

Crown, Leaf Ornaments

Naha die 21x22mm
PC3

Tokyo die 18½x19mm
PC4

Designer: Masayoshi Adaniya Koshun Printing Co.

1952

UX5 PC3 1y **vermilion,** *tan, Feb. 8 (400,600)* 50.00 30.00
UX6 PC4 1y **vermilion,** *off-white, Oct. 6 (1,295,000)* 25.00 14.00
a. Tan card, coarse *(50,000)* 30.00 20.00
b. Tan card, smooth *(16,000)* 500.00 150.00

Naminoue Shrine

PC5
Naha die 23x25½mm

PC6
Tokyo die 22x24½mm

Designer: Gensei Agena

1953-57

UX7 PC5 2y **green,** *off-white, Dec. 2, 1953 (1,799,400)* 60.00 20.00
First day cancel 80.00
a. Printed both sides *500.00*
UX8 PC6 2y **green,** *off-white, 1955 (2,799,400)* 15.00 6.00
a. 2y **deep blue green,** *1956 (300,000)* 30.00 16.50
b. 2y **yellow green,** *1957 (2,400,000)* 12.50 3.50
c. As "a," printed on both sides *500.00*
d. As "b," printed on both sides *500.00*

Stylized Pine, Bamboo, Plum Blossoms — PC7

1956 New Year Card

Designer: Koya Oshiro Kotsura and Koshun Printing Companies

1955, Dec. 1

UX9 PC7 2y **red,** *cream* 100.00 45.00
First day cancel 125.00

No. UX9 was printed on rough card (43,400) and smooth-finish card (356,600)

Sun — PC8

Temple Lion — PC9

1957 New Year Card

Designer: Seikichi Tamanaha Kobundo Printing Co.

1956, Dec. 1

UX10 PC8 2y **brown carmine & yellow,** *off-white (600,000)* 6.00 3.75
First day cancel 10.00

1958 New Year Card

Designer: Shin Isagawa Fukuryu Printing Co.

1957, Dec. 1

UX11 PC9 2y **lilac rose,** *off-white (1,000,000)* 1.75 *2.25*
First day cancel 4.00
a. "1" omitted in right date 75.00 75.00
b. Printed on both sides 250.00 *300.00*

Nos. UX8, UX8a and UX8b "Revalued" in Red, Cherry or Pink by Three Naha Printeries

a

b

c

1958-59

UX12 PC6 1½c on 2y **green,** type "a," *Sept. 16 (600,000)* 5.00 5.00
First day cancel 10.00
- *a.* Shrine stamp omitted *750.00 1,000.*
- *b.* Bar of ½ omitted, top of 2 broken 75.00 *100.00*
- *c.* Type "b," *Nov. (1,000,000)* 10.00 *12.50*
- *d.* Type "c," *1959 (200,000)* 15.00 *22.50*
- *e.* Wrong font "¢," type "c" 30.00 *45.00*
- *f.* "¢" omitted, type "c" *1,500.* 1,500.
- *g.* Double surcharge, type "c" *1,000.* —

Multicolor Yarn Ball
PC10

Toy Pony
19½x23mm
PC11

1959 New Year Card

Designer: Masayoshi Adaniya Kobundo Printing Co.

1958, Dec. 10

UX13 PC10 1½c **black, red, yellow & gray blue,** *off-white (1,514,000)* 1.50 *1.90*
First day cancel 2.00
- *a.* Black omitted —

1959, June 20

Designer: Seikichi Tamanaha Kobundo Printing Co.

UX14 PC11 1½c **dark blue & brown** *(1,140,000)* 1.50 1.25
First day cancel 1.50
- *a.* Dark blue omitted 500.00

Toy Carp and
Boy — PC12

Toy Pony
21x25mm — PC13

1960 New Year Card

Designer: Masayoshi Adaniya

1959, Dec. 1

UX15 PC12 1½c **violet blue, red & black,** *cream (2,000,000)* 1.25 *1.50*
First day cancel 1.75

1959, Dec. 30

UX16 PC13 1½c **gray violet & brown,** *cream (3,500,000)* 3.00 .75
First day cancel 2.75

Household
Altar — PC14

Coral Head — PC15

1961 New Year Card

Designer: Shin Isagawa

1960, Nov. 20

UX17 PC14 1½c **gray, carmine, yellow & black,** *off-white (2,647,591)* 1.50 1.50
First day cancel 1.50

Summer Greeting Card

Designer: Shinzan Yamada Kidekuni Printing Co.

1961, July 5

UX18 PC15 1½c **ultramarine & cerise,** *off-white (264,900)* 2.25 *3.75*
First day cancel 4.00

Tiger — PC16

Inscribed
"RYUKYUS" — PC17

1962 New Year Card

Designer: Shin Isagawa

1961, Nov. 15

UX19 PC16 1½c **ocher, black & red,** *off-white (2,891,626)* 1.50 *2.50*
First day cancel 1.65
- *a.* Red omitted 750.00 —
- *b.* Red inverted *500.00* —
- *c.* Red omitted on face, inverted on back *500.00* —
- *d.* Double impression of red, one inverted *500.00* —
- *e.* Double impression of ocher & black, red inverted *500.00* —
- *f.* Double impression of ocher & black, one inverted *500.00* —

1961-67

Designer: Seikichi Tamanaha

UX20 PC17 1½c **gray violet & brown,** *white ('67) (18,600,000)* 1.00 .50
- *a.* Off-white card ('66) *(4,000,000)* 1.50 .75
- *b.* Cream card, *Dec. 23 (12,500,000)* 1.00 .50

First day cancel 1.35

Ie Island — PC18

New Year
Offerings — PC19

Summer Greeting Card

Designer: Shinzan Yamada Sakai Printing Co.

1962, July 10

UX21 PC18 1½c **bright blue, yellow & brown,** *off-white (221,500)* 1.50 *2.50*
First day cancel 3.00
Square notch at left 40.00 *45.00*

1963 New Year Card; Precanceled

Designer: Shin Isagawa Sakai Printing Co.

1962, Nov. 15

UX22 PC19 1½c **olive brown, carmine & black** *(3,000,000)* 1.50 *3.00*
First day cancel 2.25
- *a.* Yellow brown background —
- *b.* Brown ocher background —

Ryukyu Temple
Dog and Wine
Flask Silhouette
PC20

Water Strider — PC21

International Postal Card

Designer: Shin Isagawa

1963, Feb. 15

UX23 PC20 5c **vermilion, emerald & black,** *pale yellow (150,000)* 1.75 *2.75*
First day cancel 1.65
- *a.* Black & emerald omitted 450.00

Summer Greeting Card

Designer: Seikichi Tamanaha

1963, June 20

UX24 PC21 1½c **Prussian green & black,** *off-white (250,000)* 4.00 *4.25*
First day cancel 3.50

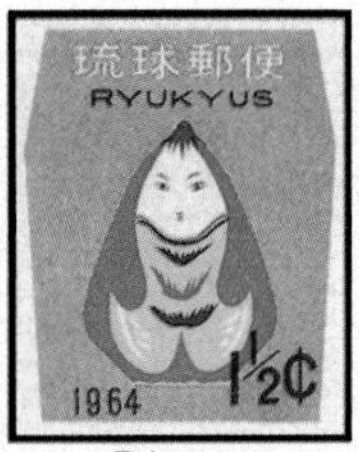

Princess
Doll — PC22

Bitter Melon
Vine — PC23

1964 New Year Card; Precanceled

Designer: Koya Oshiro

1963, Nov. 15

UX25 PC22 1½c **orange red, yellow & ultra,** *off-white (3,200,000)* 2.00 2.00
First day cancel 2.00

Summer Greeting Card

Designer: Shinzan Yamada

1964, June 20

UX26 PC23 1½c **multicolored,** *off-white (285,410)* 1.40 *2.25*
First day cancel 1.75

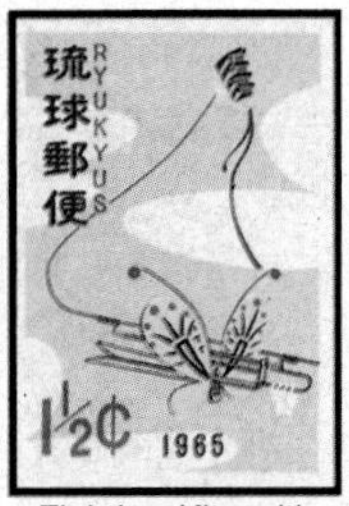

Fighting Kite with
Rider — PC24

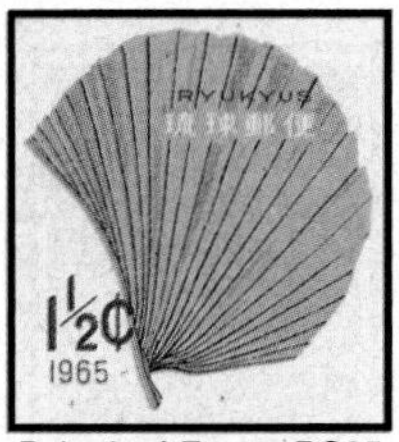

Palm-leaf Fan — PC25

1965 New Year Card; Precanceled

Designer: Koya Oshiro

1964, Nov. 15

UX27 PC24 1½c **multicolored,** *off-white (4,876,618)* 1.25 *1.75*
First day cancel 2.00

Summer Greeting Card

Designer: Koya Oshiro

1965, June 20

UX28 PC25 1½c **multicolored,** *off-white (340,604)* 1.40 *2.50*
First day cancel 1.65

Toy Pony Rider — PC26

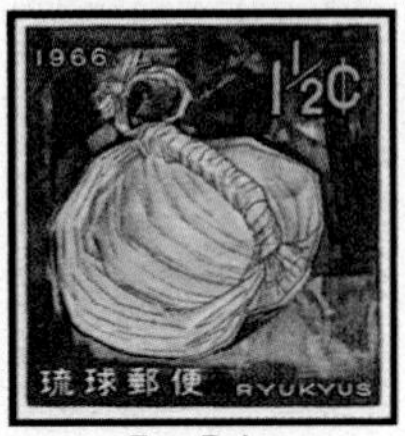

Fan Palm Dipper — PC27

1966 New Year Card; Precanceled

Designer: Seikichi Tamanaha

1965, Nov. 15

UX29 PC26 1½c **multicolored,** *off-white (5,224,622)* 1.25 *1.75*
First day cancel 1.40
a. Silver (background) omitted 250.00

Summer Greeting Card

Designer: Seikichi Tamanaha

1966, June 20

UX30 PC27 1½c **multicolored,** *off-white (339,880)* 1.25 *2.00*
First day cancel 1.40

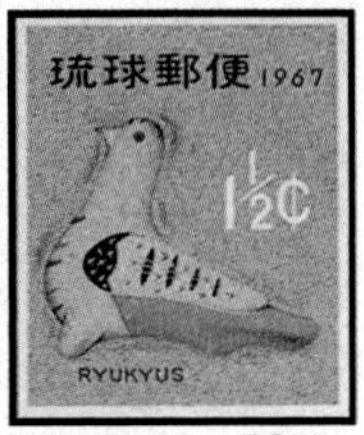

Toy Dove — PC28

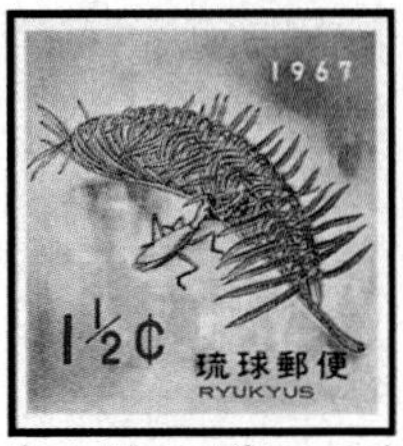

Cycad Insect Cage and Praying Mantis — PC29

1967 New Year Card; Precanceled

Designer: Seikichi Tamanaha

1966, Nov. 15

UX31 PC28 1½c **multicolored,** *off-white (5,500,000)* 1.25 *1.75*
First day cancel 1.65
a. Silver (background) omitted *500.00*
b. Gray blue & green omitted *750.00*

Summer Greeting Card

Designer: Shin Isagawa

1967, June 20

UX32 PC29 1½c **multicolored,** *off-white (350.000)* 1.50 *2.50*
First day cancel 1.75

Paper Doll Royalty — PC30

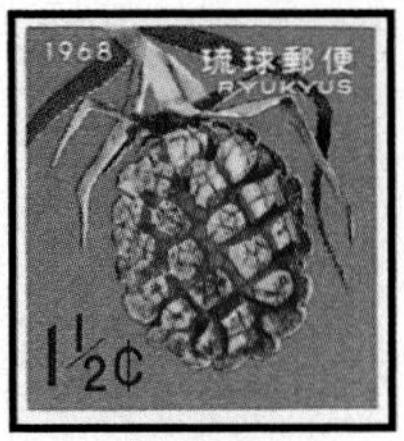

Pandanus Drupe — PC31

1968 New Year Card; Precanceled

Designer: Shin Isagawa

1967, Nov. 15

UX33 PC30 1½c **multicolored,** *off-white (6,200,000)* 1.10 *1.50*
First day cancel 1.75
a. Gold omitted 500.00

Summer Greeting Card

Designer: Seikan Omine

1968, June 20

UX34 PC31 1½c **multicolored,** *off-white (350,000)* 1.25 *2.25*
First day cancel 1.75

Toy Lion — PC32

Ryukyu Trading Ship — PC33

1969 New Year Card; Precanceled

Designer: Teruyoshi Kinjo

1968, Nov. 15

UX35 PC32 1½c **multicolored,** *off-white (7,000,000)* 1.10 *1.50*
First day cancel 1.50

Summer Greeting Card

Designer: Seikichi Tamanaha

1969, June 20

UX36 PC33 1½c **multicolored,** *(349,800)* 1.25 *2.25*
First day cancel 1.75

Toy Devil Mask — PC34

Ripe Litchis — PC35

1970 New Year Card; Precanceled

Designer: Teruyoshi Kinjo

1969, Nov. 15

UX37 PC34 1½c **multicolored** *97,200,000)* 1.10 *1.50*
First day cancel 1.25

Summer Greeting Card

Designer: Kensei Miyagi

1970, June 20

UX38 PC35 1½c **multicolored** *(400,000)* 1.40 *2.25*
First day cancel 1.50

Thread-winding Implements for Dance — PC36

Ripe Guavas — PC37

1971 New Year Card; Precanceled

Designer: Yoshinori Arakai

1970, Nov. 16

UX39 PC36 1½c **multicolored** *(7,500,000)* 1.10 *1.50*
First day cancel 1.25

Summer Greeting Card

Designer: Kensei Miyagi

1971, July 10

UX40 PC37 1½c **multicolored** *(400,000)* 1.25 *2.25*
First day cancel 1.25

Pony Type of 1961

Zip Code Boxes in Vermilion

1971, July 10

UX41 PC17 1½c **gray violet & brown** *(3,000,000)* 1.25 *3.50*
First day cancel 2.00

No. UX41 Surcharged below Stamp in Vermilion

"Revalued 2¢" applied by Nakamura Printing Co.

1971, Sept. 1

UX42 PC17 2c on 1½c **gray violet & brown** *(1,699,569)* 1.10 *2.25*
First day cancel 2.00
a. Inverted surcharge *500.00*
b. Double surcharge *500.00*
c. Surcharge on back *500.00*
e. Surcharge on back, inverted *500.00*

1972 New Year Card; Precanceled

Tasseled Castanets — PC38

Zip Code Boxes in Vermilion

Designer: Yoshinori Arakaki

1971, Nov. 15

UX43 PC38 2c **multicolored** *(8,000,000)* 1.00 *1.50*
First day cancel 1.25

Type of 1961

Zip Code Boxes in Vermilion

1971, Dec. 15

UX44 PC17 2c **gray violet & brown** *(3,500,000)* 1.25 *1.75*
First day cancel 1.65

PAID REPLY POSTAL CARDS

Sold as two attached cards, one for message, one for reply. The major listings are of unsevered cards except Nos. UY4-UY6.

Message

Reply

1948, July 1

UY1 US1 10s + 10s **dull red,** *grayish tan (1,000)* 2,000. —
m. Message card 600. 1,000.
r. Reply card 600. 1,000.

1949, July 18

UY2 US1 15s + 15s **vermilion,** *tan (E 150,000)* 30.00 *40.00*
a. Gray card *(E 75,000)* 75.00 —
First day cancel
m. Message card 8.00 *16.50*
r. Reply card 8.00 *16.50*

1950, Jan. 21

UY3 US2 50s + 50s **carmine red,** *gray cream (E 130,000)* 25.00 *40.00*
a. Double impression of message card — —
b. Light tan card *(E 96,000)* 15.00 —
First day cancel
m. Message card 3.50 *13.50*
r. Reply card 3.50 *13.50*

No. UY2a Handstamp Surcharged in Vermilion

1951

UY4 US1 1y (15s+85s) message, type "b" *(E 3,000)* 350. 350.
a. Reply, type "b" *(E 3,000)* 350. 350.
b. Message, type "a" *(E 300)* 600. —
c. Reply, type "a" *(E 300)* 600. —
d. Message, type "d" *(E 200)* 500. —
e. Reply, type "d" *(E 200)* 500. —
f. Message, UY2, type "a" *(E 3,000)* 150. *225.*
g. Reply, UY2, type "a" *(E 3,000)* 150. *225.*
h. Message, UY2, type "b" *(E 2,500)* 275. 275.
i. Reply, UY2, type "b" *(E 2,500)* 275. 275.
j. Message, UY2, type "d" *(E 2,800)* 150. *250.*
k. Reply, UY2, type "d" *(E 2,800)* 150. *250.*
l. 1y + 1y unsevered, type "b" *850.*
m. 1y + 1y unsevered, type "a" *1,450.*
n. 1y + 1y unsevered, type "d" *1,200.*
o. 1y + 1y unsevered, UY2, type "a" *360.*
p. 1y + 1y unsevered, UY2, type "b" *650.*

q.	1y + 1y unsevered, UY2, type "d"	*360.*	
r.	1y + 1y unsevered, UY2, type "c"	*3, 500.*	
s.	Message, UY2, type "c,"		—
t.	Reply, UY2, type "c"		—
u.	Message, type "c"		—
v.	Reply, type "c"		—

Types are illustrated above No. UX4.

e

f

g

h

Typographed Surcharge in Vermilion on No. UY2a

UY5 US1	1y (15s+85s) message, type "f" *(E 20,000)*	125.	125.
a.	Reply, type "f" *(E 20,000)*	125.	125.
b.	Message, type "e" *(E 12,500)*	225.	225.
c.	Reply, type "e" *(E 12,500)*	225.	225.
d.	Message, type "g" *(E 500)*	*1,000.*	*1,000.*
e.	Reply, type "g" *(E 500)*	*1,000.*	*1,000.*
f.	Message, UY2, type "e" *(E 15,000)*	125.	125.
g.	Reply, UY2, type "e" *(E 15,000)*	125.	125.
h.	Message, UY2, type "f" *(E 9,000)*	125.	125.
i.	Reply, UY2, type "f" *(E 9,000)*	125.	125.
j.	Message, UY2, type "g" *(E 500)*	*1,000.*	*1,000.*
k.	Reply, UY2, type "g" *(E 500)*	*1,000.*	*1,000.*
l.	1y + 1y unsevered, type "e"	*675.*	
m.	1y + 1y unsevered, UY2, type "e"	*375.*	

Typographed Surcharge Type "h" in Vermilion on No. UY3

UY6 US2	1y (50s+50s) message *(E 35,000)*	125.00	*150.00*
a.	Reply *(E 35,000)*	125.00	*150.00*
b.	Message, UY3b *(E 10,000)*	125.00	*150.00*
c.	Reply, UY3b *(E 10,000)*	125.00	*150.00*

No. UY6 is unknown as a joined card.

Smooth or Coarse Card

1952, Feb. 8

UY7 PC3	1y + 1y **vermilion,** *gray tan (60,000)*	120.00	*140.00*
	First day cancel		250.00
m.	Message card	25.00	*50.00*
r.	Reply card	25.00	*50.00*

1953

UY8 PC4	1y + 1y **vermilion,** *tan (22,900)*	30.00	*40.00*
	First day cancel		—
a.	Off-white card *(13,800)*	40.00	*50.00*
m.	Message card	7.50	*19.00*
r.	Reply card	7.50	*26.50*

Off-white or Light Cream Card

1953, Dec. 2

UY9 PC5	2y + 2y **green** *(50,000)*	100.00	90.00
	First day cancel		150.00
m.	Message card	15.00	*25.00*
r.	Reply card	15.00	*35.00*

1955, May

UY10 PC6	2y + 2y **green,** *off-white (280,000)*	10.00	—
a.	Reply card blank	500.00	
m.	Message card	3.25	*11.00*
r.	Reply card	3.25	*15.00*

No. UY10 Surcharged in Red

1958, Sept. 16

UY11 PC6	1½c on 2y, 1½c on 2y *(95,000)*	8.00	—
	First day cancel		22.50
a.	Surcharge on reply card only	*500.00*	—
b.	Surcharge on message card only	*500.00*	—
c.	Reply card double surcharge	*750.00*	—
d.	Reply card stamp omitted (surcharge only)	*1,000.*	
m.	Message card	2.75	*10.00*
r.	Reply card	2.75	*16.50*

Surcharge varieties include: "1" omitted; wrong font "2".

Pony Types

1959, June 20

UY12 PC11	1½c + 1½c **dark blue & brown** *(366,000)*	3.50	—
	First day cancel		4.00
m.	Message card	.65	*3.50*
r.	Reply card	.65	*3.50*

1960, Mar. 10

UY13 PC13	1½c + 1½c **gray violet & brown,** *(150,000)*	7.00	—
	First day cancel		5.00
m.	Message card	1.50	*5.00*
r.	Reply card	1.50	*5.00*

International Type

1963, Feb. 15

UY14 PC20	5c + 5c **vermilion, emerald & black,** *pale yellow (70,000)*	2.50	—
	First day cancel		3.00
m.	Message card	.75	*3.75*
r.	Reply card	.75	*3.75*

Pony ("RYUKYUS") Type

1963-69

UY15 PC17	1½c + 1½c **gray violet & brown,** *cream, Mar. 15, (800,000)*	2.00	—
	First day cancel		2.50
a.	Off-white card, *Mar. 13, 1967 (100,000)*	2.25	—
b.	White card, *Nov. 22, 1969 (700,000)*	1.75	—
m.	Message card detached	.40	*4.00*
r.	Reply card detached	.40	*4.00*

No. UY14 Surcharged below Stamp in Vermilion

1971, Sept. 1

UY16 PC17	2c on 1½c + 2c on 1½c **gray violet & brown** *(80,000)*	2.00	—
	First day cancel		2.25
m.	Message card	.50	*2.50*
r.	Reply card	.50	*2.50*

Pony ("RYUKYUS") Type

Zip Code Boxes in Vermilion

1971, Nov. 1

UY17 PC17	2c + 2c **gray violet & brown** *(150,000)*	2.00	—
	First day cancel		2.50
m.	Message card	.50	*2.50*
r.	Reply card	.50	*2.50*

OFFICIAL STAMPS ELECTION POSTAL CARDS

Official election free-mail postal cards were authorized by the United States Civil Administration of the Ryukyus, Ordinance 57, Dec. 18, 1951, as a measure to ensure equal access to voters for each candidate standing in district or general elections in the islands. Under the terms of the ordinance and the local enabling legislation, each candidate, on request, could receive a fixed number of cards per election, which were serviced with no mailing costs to the candidate.

Until the issuance of No. UZE15 in 1960, cards were processed without canceling; beginning with that issue, they were treated as regular postal cards and canceled.

With the exception of pieces bearing emergency handstamp or machine-cancel indicia, the cards were special-order printings (incorporating the election indicium) of designs and types of postal cards concurrently in use as regular postal cards (though at times in different colors).

ELECTION INDICIA

Type I

Type II

Type I: Typographed, Size: 18x45mm
Type II: Typographed, Size: 17½x48-49mm

Type III

Type IV

Type III: Typographed, Size: 17½x49-51mm
Type IV: Typographed, Size: 16½x62mm

Type IVa

Type V

Type IVa: Like Type IV but with second character from bottom ("SEN") having one stroke at upper left instead of two
Type V: Typographed, Size: 16-17x61-63mm (similar to Type IV, but with different bottom character)

Type VI

Type VII

Type VI: Typographed, Size: 17½x51-52mm
Type VII: Typographed, Size: 17½x51-52mm (similar to Type VI, but with different bottom character)

Type VIII

Type IX

Type VIII: Typographed, Size: 17¼-17½x 52mm (similar to Type VII but with second character from bottom ("SEN") having one stroke at upper left instead of two)
Type IX: Handstamped, Size: 17½x51mm

Type X

Type XI

Type X: Typographed, Size: 17½x51-51½mm (similar to Type VIII, but with different appearance of five smaller characters at top)
Type XI: Typographed, Size: 10x31½mm

Type XII

Type XIII

Type XII: Handstamped, Size: 17½-18x49½-51½mm, Thick characters
Type XIII: Handstamped, Size: 17½-18x50¼-51mm, Thin characters

Type XIIIa

Type XIV

Type XIIIa: Handstamped, Size: 17½-18x50¼x51mm, Thick characters, with shorter lvertical line at lower left.
Type XIV: Typographed, Size: 18x50-50½mm

Type XV

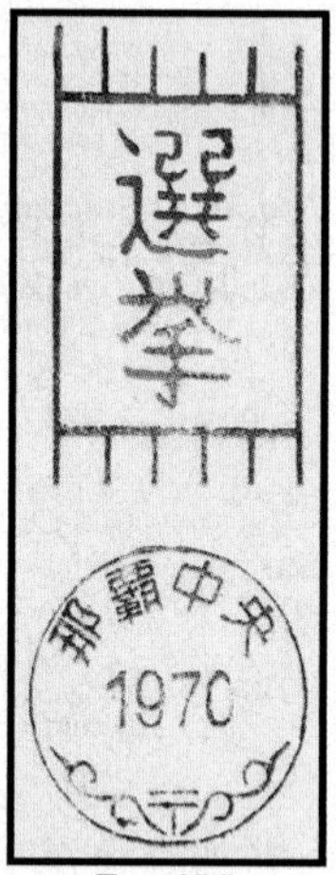

Type XVI

Type XV: Typographed, Size: 18x50-50½mm
Type XVI: Machine cancel, Circle diameter: 20mm, Height of legend box: 23½mm

Type XVIa

Type XVII

Type XVIa: Machine cancel, Circle diameter: 20mm, Height of legend box: 20½-22mm
Type XVII: Typographed, Size: 18½x48½-50mm

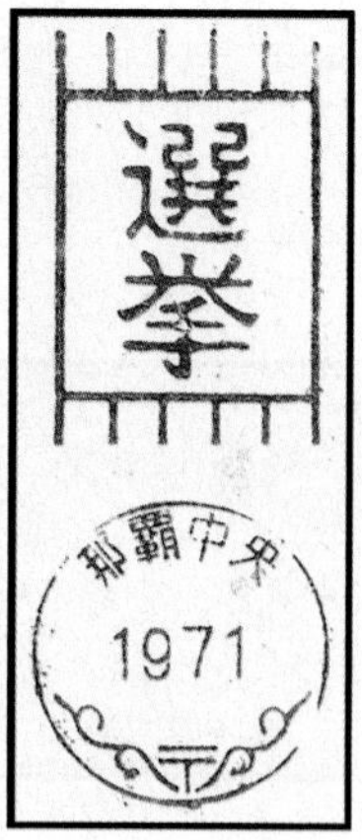

Type XVIII

Type XVIII: Machine cancel, Circle diameter: 20mm, Height of legend box: 20½-22 mm

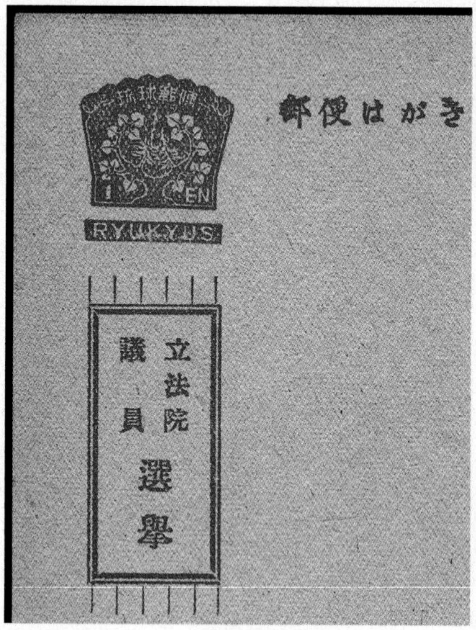

UZE1

1952, Feb. 2 **First General Election**

UZE1 PC3 1y **vermilion,** *tan* coarse (Naha die) + Type I *(345,000)* 300.00 —

a. Postmarked (error) —

1952, July 26 **1st District Special Election**

UZE2 PC3 1y **vermilion,** *tan* coarse (Naha die) + Type II *(est. 25,000)* 50.00 —

a. 2nd character from bottom in indicium (SEN) inverted — —

Used cards or unused with campaign messages must have reference to the 1st District (Kasari, Amami Gunto) election.

1953, Mar. 3 **4th District Special Election**

UZE3 PC4 1y **vermilion,** *tan* coarse (Tokyo die) + Type II *(est. 10,000)* —

a. Postmarked (error) —

Identifiable only when postmarked (in error, with dates between Mar. 3-Mar.31, 1953) and/or with campaign message in reference to 4th District election (Motobu, Okinawa Gunto).

1953, Mar. 27 **3rd District Special Election**

UZE4 PC4 1y **vermilion,** *tan* coarse (Tokyo die) + Type II *(est. 10,000)* —

a. Postmarked (error) —

Identifiable only when postmarked (in error, with dates between Mar. 27-Apr. 1953) and/or with campaign message in reference to 3rd District election (Yagaji, Okinawa Gunto).

UZE5

1954, Feb. 23 **Second General Election**

UZE5 PC5 2y **rose red,** *off white* (Naha die) + Type III *(70,000)* 50.00 —
a. Postmarked (error) —

1954, Nov. 19 **18th District Special Election**

UZE6 PC6 2y **red,** *off white* (Tokyo die) + Type IV 500.00 —
a. Postmarked (error) —
UZE6A PC6 2y **red,** *off white* (Tokyo die) + Type V 500.00 —
a. Postmarked (error) —

Postal records show receipt of 4,000 total cards of Nos. UZE6 and UZE6A, undefined as to type.

1955, Feb. 15 **20th District Special Election**

UZE7 PC6 2y **dark purple,** *off white* (Tokyo die) + Type IV *(2,000)* 500.00 —

1955, Mar. 8 **23rd District Special Election**

UZE8 PC6 2y **turquoise blue,** *off white* (Tokyo die) + Type V *(2,000)* 500.00 —
a. Postmarked (error) —

1955, June 28 **22nd District Special Election**

UZE9 PC6 2y **dull brown,** *gray cream* (Tokyo die) + Type V *(3,030)* 400.00 —
a. Postmarked (error) —

1956, Feb. 20 **Third General Election**

UZE10 PC6 2y **pale blue green,** *off white* (Tokyo die) + Type VI 75.00 150.00
a. Postmarked (error) —
UZE10A PC6 2y **pale blue green,** *off white* (Tokyo die) + Type VII 75.00 150.00
a. Postmarked (error) —

Postal records show receipt of 65,000 total cards of Nos. UZE10 and UZE10A, undefined as to type.

1956, Oct. 26 **25th District Special Election**

UZE11 PC6 2y **brown red,** *off white* (Tokyo die) + Type IV 300.00 —
UZE11A PC6 2y **brown red,** *off white* (Tokyo die) + Type V 180.00 350.00

Postal records show a total quantity of 3,030 examples of Nos. UZE11 and UZE11A prepared, unidentified as to type, of which 2,000 were issued.

1957, Aug. 5 **18th District Special Election**

UZE12 PC6 2y **lilac,** *off white* (Tokyo die) + Type IVa *(3,030)* 250.00 —

1958, Feb. 25 **Fourth General Election**

UZE13 PC6 2y **deep blue,** *off white* (Tokyo die) + Type VI (bold face print) 130.00 70.00
UZE13A PC6 2y **deep blue,** *off white* (Tokyo die) + Type VI (light face print) 130.00 70.00
UZE13B PC6 2y **deep blue,** *off white* (Tokyo die) + Type VII (bold face print) 130.00 70.00
UZE13C PC6 2y **deep blue,** *off white* (Tokyo die) + Type VII (light face print) 90.00 70.00

Postal records show a total of 140,300 cards of Nos. UZE13-UZE13C prepared in two printings, undefined as to types.

UZE14

1959, July 23 **26th District Special Election**

UZE14 PC6 1½c on 2y **lemon,** *white* (Tokyo die) + Type VIII *(4,100)* 450.00 —

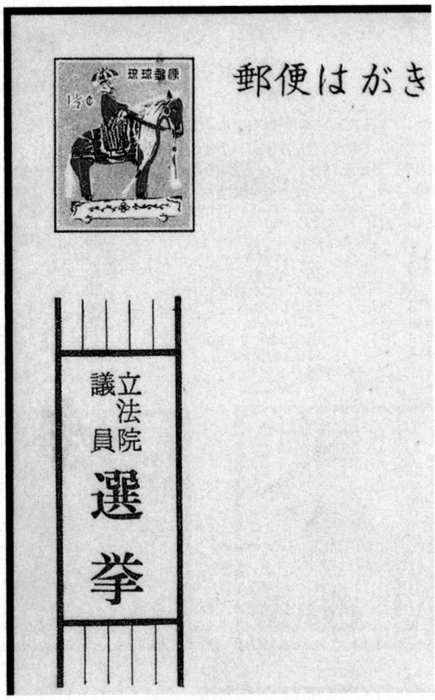

UZE15

1960, Oct. 24 **Fifth General Election**

UZE15 PC11 1½c **indigo & claret brown,** *white* (Naha die) + Type VIII *(150,000)* 70.00 70.00
UZE16 PC13 1½c **violet gray & claret brown,** *cream* (Tokyo die) + Type IX in LL corner *(10,000)* — —

1962, Oct. 22 **Sixth General Election**

UZE17 PC17 1½c **violet gray & claret brown,** *cream* + Type VIII 50.00 —
UZE17A PC17 1½c **violet gray & claret brown,** *cream* + Type X 50.00 —

Postal records show a total of 116,000 cards of Nos. UZE17-UZE17A prepared, undefined as to type.

1962, Oct. 22
Sixth General Election Emergency Issue

UZE18 PC17 1½c **violet gray & claret brown,** *cream* + Type IX *(6,000)* 250.00 —
a. Indicium inverted — —

1965, Oct. 25 **Seventh General Election**

UZE19 PC17 1½c **violet gray & claret brown,** *cream* + Type XI *(134,000)* 20.00 90.00

1966, Aug. 1 **3rd District Special Election**

UZE20 PC17 1½c **violet gray & claret brown,** *cream* + Type XI *(est. 3,800)* —

No. UZE20 is a remainder copy of No. UZE19, identifiable only when canceled at the Nakijin Post Office between Aug. 1-Aug. 20, 1966.

1966, Aug. 11
3rd District Special Election Emergency Issue

UZE21 PC17 1½c **violet gray & claret brown,** *cream* + Type XII *(est. 200)* — —
UZE22 PC17 1½c **violet gray & claret brown,** *cream* + Type XIII 225.00 —

1968, Oct. 21 **First Chief Executive Election**

UZE23 PC17 1½c **violet gray & claret brown,** *white* + Type XIV *(300,000)* 30.00 25.00

1968, Oct. 21 **Eighth General Election**

UZE24 PC17 1½c **violet gray & claret brown,** *white* + Type XV *(142,000)* 30.00 35.00

1970, Oct. 12 **1st District Special Election**

UZE25 PC17 1½c **violet gray & claret brown,** *white* + Type XV *(4,000)* —

No. UZE25 is a remainder card of No. UZE24, identifiable only when canceled at the Higashi, Kunigami, Ogimi or Oku Post Offices between Oct. 12-Oct. 31, 1970.

UZE26A

1970, Oct. 23
First General Election for Coucilors and Representatives to the Japanese Diet

UZE26 PC17 1½c **violet gray & claret brown,** *white* + Type XVI *(300,000)* 250.00 30.00
UZE26A PC17 1½c **violet gray & claret brown,** *white* + Type XVIa *(300,000)* 250.00 30.00

Postal records show a total of 171,000 examples of Nos. UZE26-UZE26A prepared, undefined as to type.

Emergency Commercial Card Issue for First General Japanese Diet Election

UZE27 *white or light gray blue* + Type XVI — 30.00
UZE27A *white or light gray blue* + Type XVIa — 30.00

Postal records show a total of 79,000 commercial cards were acquired for official issue as Nos. UZE27-UZE27A after validating. Some of the cards show an imprinted black square, while others show nothing.

1970, Nov. 16 **21st District Special Election**

UZE28 PC17 1½c **violet gray & claret brown,** *white* + Type XVII *(8,000)* — 180.00

推薦状

島本「ケン」は言う
「政治は相互の理解と協調と和の中にあり、抵抗や反抗の中にはない。抵抗と反抗はいたずらに憎悪の感情を増し、混乱を招くだけである」と、常に現実を踏へて、前向きに誠実で勇気をもつて実践する人、島本「ケン」
島本「ケン」こそは新沖縄建設に必要な人であります。
善意に満ちた、豊かな明るい清らかな新沖縄建設の為に第二十二区から立法院議員に立候補しました
島本「ケン」に絶大なる御支援を賜ります様お願い申し上げると共に絶対自信をもつて「ケン」を推薦致します。

昭和四十五年十一月　日

那覇市古波蔵二四四
島本ケン選挙本部
推薦者

UZE29

1970, Nov. 16 — 22nd District Special Election

UZE29	PC17	1½c	**violet gray & claret brown,** *white* + Type XVII *(2,000)*	—	350.00

No. UZE29 is a remainder card of No. UZE28, identifiable only with the imprinted message shown above of candidate Shimamoto Ken.

UZE30	PC17	1½c	**violet gray & claret brown,** *white* + Type XIII	—	—
UZE30A	PC17	1½c	**violet gray & claret brown,** *white* + Type XIIIa	—	—

Postal records show a total of 2,000 of Nos. UZE30-UZE30A prepared, undefined as to type.

1971, Feb. 15 — 7th District Special Election

UZE31	PC17	1½c	**violet gray & claret brown,** *white* + Type XV *(4,000)*	—	—

1971, June 4

Second General Election for Coucilors and Representatives to the Japanese Diet

UZE32	PC17	1½c	**violet gray & claret brown,** *white* + Type XVIII *(25,000)*	—	45.00

Emergency Commercial Card Issue for Second General Japanese Diet Election

UZE33	*white* + Type XVIII, 100x148mm *(25,000)*	—	20.00
a.	Double strike of election indicia, one inverted in LR corner	—	—
UZE33A	*white* + Type XVIII, 104x150mm *(25,000)*	—	50.00

REVENUE STAMPS

Upon its establishment Apr. 1, 1952, the government of the Ryukyu Islands assumed responsibility for the issuing of and the profit from revenue stamps. The various series served indiscriminately as evidence of payment of the required fees for various legal, realty and general commercial transactions.

1 yen — R1

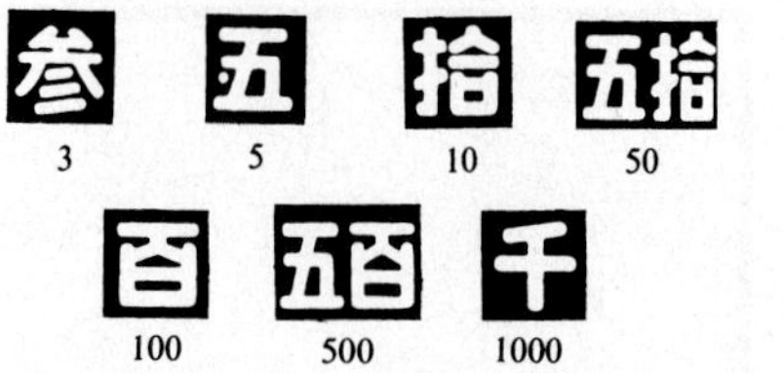

Litho. by Japan Printing Bureau.
Designer: Eizo Yonamine

1952-54 — Wmk. 257 — *Perf. 13x13½*

R1	R1	1y	**brown**	15.00	10.00
R2	R1	3y	**carmine**	20.00	12.00
R3	R1	5y	**green**	25.00	15.00
R4	R1	10y	**blue**	30.00	20.00
R5	R1	50y	**purple**	35.00	25.00
R6	R1	100y	**yellow brown**	80.00	30.00
R7	R1	500y	**dark green**	350.00	100.00
R8	R1	1,000y	**carmine**	300.00	150.00
			Nos. R1-R8 (8)	855.00	362.00

Issued: #R1-R6, July 15, 1952; #R7-R8, Apr. 16, 1954.

Denomination Vertical

"Cent" 

"Dollar" 

Litho. by Kobundo Printing Co., Naha
Perf. 10, 10½, 11 and combinations

1958, Sept. 16 — Without Gum — Unwmk.

R9	R1	1c	**red brown**	30.00	25.00
a.			Horiz. pair, imperf. between	500.00	
R10	R1	3c	**red**	40.00	35.00
a.			Horiz. pair, imperf. between	500.00	
R11	R1	5c	**green**	50.00	45.00
R12	R1	10c	**blue**	70.00	65.00
a.			Horiz. pair, imperf. between	500.00	
R13	R1	50c	**purple**	135.00	120.00
R14	R1	$1	**sepia**	200.00	175.00
R15	R1	$5	**dark green**	400.00	350.00
R16	R1	$10	**carmine**	450.00	400.00
			Nos. R9-R16 (8)	1,375.	1,215.

R2

R3

R4

Litho. by Japan Printing Bureau.

1959-69 — Wmk. 257 — *Perf. 13x13½*

R17	R2	1c	**brown**	3.00	1.90
R18	R2	3c	**red**	3.00	1.10
R19	R2	5c	**purple**	5.50	3.25
R20	R2	10c	**green**	10.00	6.00
R21	R2	20c	**sepia** ('69)	80.00	55.00
R22	R2	30c	**light olive** ('69)	100.00	65.00
R23	R2	50c	**blue**	40.00	14.00

Engr.

R24	R3	$1	**olive**	45.00	12.50
R25	R3	$2	**vermilion** ('69)	250.00	50.00
R26	R3	$3	**purple** ('69)	450.00	60.00
R27	R3	$5	**orange**	120.00	45.00
R28	R3	$10	**dark green**	180.00	60.00
R29	R4	$20	**carmine** ('69)	2,000.	200.00
R30	R4	$30	**blue** ('69)	2,500.	—
R31	R4	$50	**black** ('69)	3,000.	—
			Nos. R17-R28 (12)	1,286.	373.75

UNEMPLOYMENT INSURANCE

These stamps, when affixed in an official booklet and canceled, certified a one-day contract for a day laborer. They were available to employers at certain post offices on various islands.

Dove — RQ1

Shield — RQ2

Lithographed in Naha

1961, Jan. 10 — Without Gum — Unwmk. — *Rouletted*

RQ1	RQ1	2c	**pale red**	800.00	—
RQ2	RQ2	4c	**violet**	60.00	60.00

Redrawn

Lithographed by Japan Printing Bureau

1966, Feb. — Unwmk. — *Perf. 13x13½*

RQ3	RQ1	2c	**pale red**	—	—
RQ4	RQ2	4c	**violet**	30.00	30.00

Redrawn stamps have bolder numerals and inscriptions, and fewer, stronger lines of shading in background.

Cycad — RQ3

Lithographed by Japan Printing Bureau

1968, Apr. 19 — Wmk. 257 — *Perf. 13x13½*

RQ5	RQ3	8c	**brown**	35.00	35.00

Nos. RQ3-RQ4 Surcharged with New Values and 2 Bars

1967-72

RQ6	RQ1	8c on 2c	**pale red**	70.00	70.00
RQ7	RQ2	8c on 4c	**violet** ('72)	35.00	35.00
RQ8	RQ2	12c on 4c	**violet** ('71)	30.00	30.00

A 4-cent "stamp" picturing Iriomote Park was originally planned for postage in 1971. Its use was changed, and it became a label that was used on the "Ryukyu Islands Emergency Conversion Confirmation Certificate." Value, $150 unused, $250 on document.

PROVISIONAL ISSUES MIYAKO

Stamps of Japan 1938-42 Handstamped in Black, Red or Orange

1948 Typo., Litho., Engr. Wmk. 257 *Perf. 13*

3XR1 A84	3s **brown,** #329	75.00	—
3XR2 A86	5s **brown lake,** #331	75.00	—
3XR3 A152	20s **blue,** #338 (R)	60.00	—
3XR4 A95	25s **dark brown & pale brown,** #270 (R)	60.00	—
a.	Black overprint	600.00	—
3XR5 A96	30s **peacock blue,** #271 (R)	60.00	—
3XR6 A154	40s **dark violet,** #342 (R)	60.00	—
3XR7 A97	50s **olive & pale olive,** #272 (R)	135.00	—
a.	Orange overprint	*500.00*	

Doubled handstamps are known on all values and pairs with one stamp without handstamp exist on the 5s and 20s.

PROVISIONAL ISSUES YAEYAMA

In addition to the continued use of the then-current Japanese revenue stamps in stock from the wartime period, the varying authorities of the Yaeyama Gunto issued three district-specific revenue series, with a total of 28 values. Only those values at present verified by surviving examples are indicated. Numbers are reserved for other values believed to have been issued, but as yet not seen and verified.

No. 5XR2 — R5

No. 5XR3 — R6

No. 5XR5 — R7

No. 5XR27 — R8

1946 (?) Without Gum *Imperf.*

Value printed, frame handstamped

5XR1 R5	3s **vermilion & black**	—	
5XR2 R5	10s **vermilion & black**	—	—

Validating handstamp below

5XR3 R6	1y **vermilion & black**	—	—

Civil Administration Issues

1947 (?) Without Gum *Imperf.*

Value printed, frame handstamped

Cream Paper

5XR5 R7	10s **vermilion & black**	—	
5XR6 R7	50s **vermilion & black**	—	—

Gunto Government Issues

1950 (?) Without Gum *Imperf.*

Value printed, frame handstamped

Cream Paper

5XR17 R8	10s **vermilion & black**	—	
5XR18 R8	50s **vermilion & black**	—	
a.	50s **vermilion & blue**	—	
5XR20 R8	1.50y **vermilion & black**	—	
5XR22 R8	5y **vermilion & black**	—	
5XR24 R8	20y **vermilion & black**		—
5XR27 R8	100y **vermilion & black**	—	

Nos. 5XR17-5XR27 are known with rough perforations, full or partial.

SPECIMEN STAMPS

Regular stamps and postal cards of 1958-65 overprinted with three cursive syllabics *mi-ho-n* ("specimen").

Type A

1961-64

Overprinted in Black

91S	3c **multicolored** *(1,000)*	250.00
118S	3c **multicolored** *(1,100)*	450.00
119S	3c **multicolored** *(1,100)*	400.00

Type B

1964-65

Overprinted in Red or Black

120aS	3c **deep blue, deep carmine & ocher** (R) *(1,500)*	200.00
121S	3c **multicolored** (R) *(1,500)*	175.00
124S	3c **ultra, yel & red** (R) *(5,000)*	35.00
125S	3s **dull claret, yel & black** *(1,500)*	70.00
126S	3c **yellow & multi** *(2,000)*	60.00
127S	3c **gray, red & black** *(2,000)*	60.00
128S	3c **multicolored** *(1,500)*	70.00
129S	1½c **multicolored** (R) *(1,500)*	70.00
130S	3c **light blue & multi** (R) *(1,500)*	200.00
131S	3c **multicolored** (R) *(1,500)*	60.00
132S	3c **buff & multicolored** *(2,000)*	60.00
133S	3c **green & multi** (R) *(2,000)*	50.00
134S	3c **multicolored** *(2,000)*	50.00
135S	3c **blue & multicolored** *(2,000)*	50.00
136S	3c **golden brown & multi** *(2,000)*	50.00
139S	1½c **multicolored** (R) *(2,500)*	50.00

Postal Cards

1964-65

Overprinted Type A or B in Black or Red

UX26S A	1½c **multicolored** *(1,000)*	500.00
UX27S B	1½c **multicolored** *(1,000)*	350.00
UX28S A	1½c **multicolored** *(1,000)*	300.00
UX29S A	1½c **multicolored** *(1,100)*	250.00

See also Nos. 46TCS and 48TCS following Proofs and Trial Color Proofs.

PROOFS AND TRIAL COLOR PROOFS

1948

Salmon Paper, Imperf.

1aP	5s **magenta**	—
2aP	10s **yellow green**	—
3aP	20s **yellow green**	—
5aP	40s **magenta**	—
6aP	50s **ultramarine**	—
7aP	1y **ultramarine**	—

Between the printing of Nos. 1a-7a and Nos. 1-7 essay sheets of the series were prepared in Tokyo and overprinted with a swirl-pattern of blue or red dots. These essays sell for about $800 each.

Except for No. 12TC 4y olive, the trial color proofs of Nos. 8-13, 18, C1-C3 and E1 are from blocks of 9.

1950

Soft White Paper, Imperf.

Proofs are Gummed, Trial Color Proofs are Without Gum

8P	50s **dark carmine rose**	1,500.
8TC	50s **rose**	1,750.
8TC	50s **green**	1,750.
9P	1y **deep blue**	1,500.
9TC	1y **rose**	1,750.
9TC	1y **green**	1,750.
10P	2y **rose violet**	1,500.
10TC	2y **rose**	1,750.
10TC	2y **green**	1,750.
11P	3y **carmine rose**	1,500.
11TC	3y **rose**	1,750.
11TC	3y **green**	1,750.
12P	4y **greenish gray**	1,500.
12TC	4y **rose**	1,750.
12TC	4y **olive**	1,750.
13P	5y **blue green**	1,500.
13TC	5y **rose**	1,750.
13TC	5y **green**	1,750.

1951

Soft White Paper, Imperf., Without Gum

14P	3y **red brown**	1,000.
15P	3y **dark green**	800.

1952

Whitish Paper, Imperf., With Gum

18TC	3y **pale salmon**	1,750.
18TC	3y **scarlet**	1,750.
18TC	3y **red orange**	1,900.

Perforated, gummed proof sheets of Nos. 18, 27 and 28 with oversized, untrimmed selvage were printed for display purposes.

1958

Off White Paper, Imperf., Without Gum

46TC	2c **black** (100)	800.
48TC	4c **black** (100)	800.

AIR POST

1950

Soft White Paper, Imperf.

Proofs are Gummed, Trial Color Proofs are Without Gum

C1P	8y **bright blue**	1,500.
C1TC	8y **rose**	1,750.
C1TC	8y **light green**	1,750.
C2P	12y **green**	1,500.
C2TC	12y **rose**	1,750.
C2TC	12y **light green**	1,750.
C3P	16y **rose carmine**	1,500.
C3TC	16y **rose**	1,750.

1951

Soft White Paper, Imperf., Without Gum

C4P	13y **blue**	1,000.
C5P	18y **green**	1,000.
C6P	30y **cerise**	800.

SPECIAL DELIVERY

1950

Soft White Paper, Imperf.

Proofs are Gummed, Trial Color Proofs are Without Gum

E1P	5y **bright blue**	1,500.
E1TC	5y **rose**	1,750.
E1TC	5y **green**	1,750.

Official proof folders contain one each of Nos. 8P-13P, 12TC in olive, C1P-C3P and E1P. The stamps are securely adhered to the folder. Value, $9,000.

Similar folders exist containing photographs of die proofs in black of the same issues and mockups of Nos. U2, UX3 and UY3.

KUME ISLAND

1945

U.S. Official Watermarked White Bond Paper

Seal Handstamped in Vermilion

Without Gum

1X1P	7s **black**	*3,000.*
a.	"7" and "SEN" one letter space to left, pos. 8	*4,000.*

SPECIMEN OVERPRINTS ON TRIAL COLOR PROOFS

1961

Overprinted in Vermillion

46TCS	2c **black** *(100)*	*1,000.*
48TCS	4c **black** *(100)*	*1,000.*

Cursive type used for these two trial color proofs is different from the mihon overprints.

TUBERCULOSIS PREVENTION SEALS

Issued by the Ryukyu Tuberculosis Prevention Association (1952-71) in panes of 100 (Nos. WX1 and WX5) and 20 (Nos. WX2-WX4 and WX6-WX20). The sale of seals provided income beyond government funding for treatment. Seals were sold by the pane for the price of 1 Yen (1952-58) or 1¢ (1959-71) per seal.

Nos. WX1 and WX1a are overprinted U.S. Christmas seals (Nos. WX159-WX160). Nos. WX2-WX20 were printed for the Ryukyu Tuberculosis Prevention Association by the Japan Printing Bureau. Nos. WX2-WX20 bear a year date and the word "GREETINGS." Nos. WX2-WX4 show "RYUKYUS" in kanji, and Nos. WX5-WX20 show "RYUKYUS" in both kanji and English.

Nos. WX1-WX20 were printed on unwatermarked paper. Values are for unused seals with original gum.

Designer — Tom Darling.

1952 *Perf. 12½x12*

Overprinted in Black

WX1	CS46	**green, red, yellow & black** *(600,000)*	4.00
		Pane of 100	450.00
		Imprint single	10.00
		Imprint block of 4	25.00
a.		Perf 12½	4.00
		Pane of 100	450.00
		Imprint single	10.00
		Imprint block of 4	25.00

Lithographed by Eureka Specialty Co. (No. WX1) and United States Printing and Lithographing Co. (No. WX1a).

Panes of the 1952 Christmas seals (U.S. Nos. WX159 and WX160) were donated by the National Tuberculosis Association and overprinted "Ryu-Kyu" in kanji by the Koshun Insatsusho in Naha. Printer's marks appear on seal 56 in each pane of 100: "E" for Eureka Specialty Printing Co.; "U" for United States Printing and Lithographing Co. Panes printed by the Strobridge Lithographing Co. ("S"), Edwards & Deutch Lithographing Co. ("D") and the Fleming-Potter Co., Inc. ("F") may also have been overprinted, but these have not been verified.

Imprint appears in selvage below seal 100; imprint of Union Local No. 41 on No. WX1, and imprint of Union Local No. 1 on No. WX1a.

TBS1

Designer — Adaniya Masayoshi.

1953 *Perf. 13x13¼*

WX2	TBS1	**green, red, & buff** *(780,000)*	2.00
		Pane of 20, perf through top and bottom selvage	30.00
		Imprint single, type I	5.00
		Imprint block of 6	15.00
		Pane of 20, perf through top selvage only	30.00
		Imprint single, type I	5.00
		Imprint block of 6	15.00
a.		Imperf *(20,000)*	100.00
		Pane of 20	2,500.
		Imprint single, type I	150.00
		Imprint block of 6	750.00

Imprint appears in selvage below seal 19.

TBS2

Designer — Adaniya Masayoshi.

1954

WX3	TBS2	**light green, red, & black** *(780,000)*	2.00
		Pane of 20, perf through top and bottom selvage	30.00
		Imprint single, type I	5.00
		Imprint block of 6	15.00
		Pane of 20, perf through top selvage only	30.00
		Imprint single, type I	5.00
		Imprint block of 6	15.00
a.		Imperf *(20,000)*	—
		Pane of 20	—
		Imprint single, type I	—
		Imprint block of 6	—

Imprint appears in selvage below seal 19.

TBS3

Designer — Adaniya Masayoshi.

1955

WX4	TBS3	**carmine red, apple green & black** *(1,180,000)*	2.00
		Pane of 20, perf through top and bottom selvage	20.00
		Imprint single, type I	5.00
		Imprint block of 6	10.00
		Pane of 20, perf through top selvage only	20.00
		Imprint single, type I	5.00
		Imprint block of 6	10.00
a.		Imperf *(20,000)*	3.00
		Pane of 20	50.00
		Imprint single, type I	5.00
		Imprint block of 6	20.00

Imprint appears in selvage below seal 19.

TBS4

Designer — Adaniya Masayoshi.

1956

WX5	TBS4	**cobalt, carmine red, yellow & black** *(1,460,000)*	2.00
		Pane of 100, perf through top and bottom selvage	150.00
		Imprint single, type I	5.00
		Imprint block of 10	40.00
		Control No. strip of 3	15.00
a.		Imperf *(40,000)*	5.00
		Pane of 100	300.00
		Imprint single, type I	20.00
		Imprint block of 10	80.00
		Control No. strip of 3	50.00

Imprint appears in selvage below seal 98. Five-digit control number appear in right selvage next to seals 20 and 30, or 20, 30 and 40.

Two types of Marginal Imprint on Nos. WX6-WX20

Type I

Type II

TBS5

Designer — Yamazato Keiichi.

1957

WX6	TBS5	**orange yellow, black, red & light blue** *(1,750,000)*	1.00
		Pane of 20, perf through top and bottom selvage	15.00
		Imprint single, type I	2.00
		Imprint block of 4, type I	4.00
		Imprint single, type II	2.00
		Imprint block of 4, type II	4.00
a.		Imperf *(50,000)*	2.00
		Pane of 20	20.00
		Imprint single, type I	4.00
		Imprint block of 4, type I	10.00
		Imprint single, type II	4.00
		Imprint block of 4, type II	10.00

Imprint type I appears in selvage below seal 20; imprint type II appears in selvage below seal 17. Legend printed in Japanese in right selvage.

TBS6

Designer — Adaniya Masayoshi.

1958 *Perf. 13¼x13*

WX7	TBS6	**yellow, blue, carmine red & black** *(1,900,000)*	.50
		Pane of 20, perf through left and right selvage	8.00
		Imprint single, type I	2.00
		Imprint block of 4, type I	3.00
		Imprint single, type II	2.00
		Imprint block of 4, type II	3.00
a.		Imperf *(80,000)*	2.00
		Pane of 20	20.00
		Imprint single, type I	4.00
		Imprint block of 4, type I	10.00
		Imprint single, type II	4.00
		Imprint block of 4, type II	10.00
b.		Perf 11*(20,000)*	10.00
		Pane of 20	200.00
		Imprint single, type I	25.00
		Imprint block of 4, type I	75.00
		Imprint single, type II	25.00
		Imprint block of 4, type II	75.00

Imprint type I appears in selvage below seal 20; imprint type II appears in selvage below seal 16. Legend printed in Japanese in top selvage. A total of 1,000 imperforate sheets were later perforated (No. WX7b), by order of the Ryukyu Tuberculosis Prevention Association.

TBS7

Designer — Tamanaha Seikichi.

1959 *Perf. 13x13¼*

WX8	TBS7	**vermilion, mauve, ultramarine & indigo** *(2,100,000)*	.50
		Pane of 20, perf through top and bottom selvage	8.00
		Imprint single, type I	2.00
		Imprint block of 4, type I	3.00
		Imprint single, type II	2.00
		Imprint block of 4, type II	3.00
a.		Imperf *(200,000)*	2.00
		Pane of 20	20.00
		Imprint single, type I	4.00
		Imprint block of 4, type I	10.00
		Imprint single, type II	4.00
		Imprint block of 4, type II	10.00

Imprint type I appears in selvage below seal 20; imprint type II appears in selvage below seal 17. Legend printed in Japanese in right selvage.

TBS8

Designer — Oshiro Kohya.

1960 *Perf. 13¼x13*

WX9	TBS8	**scarlet, orange, cobalt, bright blue & black** *(2,450,000)*	.50
		Pane of 20, perf through left and right selvage	8.00
		Imprint single, type I	2.00
		Imprint block of 4, type I	3.00
		Imprint single, type II	2.00
		Imprint block of 4, type II	3.00
a.		Imperf *(50,000)*	2.00
		Pane of 20	20.00
		Imprint single, type I	4.00
		Imprint block of 4, type I	10.00
		Imprint single, type II	4.00
		Imprint block of 4, type II	10.00

Imprint type I appears in selvage below seal 20; imprint type II appears in selvage below seal 16. Legend printed in Japanese in top selvage.

TBS9

Designer — Omine Seikan.

1961 *Perf. 13x13¼*

WX10	TBS9 **multicolored** *(3,450,000)*	.30
	Pane of 20, perf through top and bottom selvage	6.00
	Imprint single, type I	.80
	Imprint block of 4, type I	2.00
	Imprint single, type II	.80
	Imprint block of 4, type II	2.00
a.	Imperf *(50,000)*	1.00
	Pane of 20	12.00
	Imprint single, type I	3.00
	Imprint block of 4, type I	6.00
	Imprint single, type II	3.00
	Imprint block of 4, type II	6.00

Imprint type I appears in selvage below seal 20; imprint type II appears in selvage below seal 17. Legend printed in Japanese in right selvage.

TBS10

Designer — Kabira Choshin.

1962 *Perf. 13¼*

WX11	TBS10 **multicolored** *(3,450,000)*	.30
	Pane of 20, perf through top and bottom selvage	5.00
	Imprint single, type I	.60
	Imprint block of 6, type I	1.50
	Imprint single, type II	.60
	Imprint block of 6, type II	1.50
a.	Imperf *(50,000)*	.50
	Pane of 20	7.00
	Imprint single, type I	1.00
	Imprint block of 6, type I	2.50
	Imprint single, type II	1.00
	Imprint block of 6, type II	2.50

Imprint type I appears in selvage below seal 19; imprint type II appears in selvage below seal 17. Legend printed in English in left selvage and in Japanese in right selvage.

TBS11

Designer — Kabira Choshin.

1963 *Perf. 13x13¼*

WX12	TBS11 **multicolored** *(3,450,000)*	.30
	Pane of 20, perf through top and bottom selvage	5.00
	Imprint single, type I	.60
	Imprint block of 4, type I	1.50
	Imprint single, type II	.60
	Imprint block of 4, type II	1.50
a.	Imperf *(50,000)*	.50
	Pane of 20	7.00
	Imprint single, type I	1.00
	Imprint block of 4, type I	2.50
	Imprint single, type II	1.00
	Imprint block of 4, type II	2.50

Imprint type I appears in selvage below seal 20; imprint type II appears in selvage below seal 17. Legend printed in Japanese in right selvage.

TBS12

Designer — Kabira Choshin.

1964

WX13	TBS12 **multicolored** *(3,650,000)*	.30
	Pane of 20, perf through top and bottom selvage	5.00
	Imprint single, type I	.60
	Imprint block of 4, type I	1.50
	Imprint single, type II	.60
	Imprint block of 4, type II	1.50
a.	Imperf *(50,000)*	.50
	Pane of 20	7.00
	Imprint single, type I	1.00
	Imprint block of 4, type I	2.50
	Imprint single, type II	1.00
	Imprint block of 4, type II	2.50

Imprint type I appears in selvage below seal 20; imprint type II appears in selvage below seal 17. Legend printed in English in left selvage and in Japanese in right selvage.

TBS13

Designer — Oyama Masaru.

1965 *Perf. 13¼x13*

WX14	TBS13 **dark blue, light green, carmine & pink** *(3,700,000)*	.30
	Pane of 20, perf through left and right selvage	5.00
	Imprint single, type I	.60
	Imprint block of 4, type I	1.50
	Imprint single, type II	.60
	Imprint block of 4, type II	1.50
a.	Imperf *(100,000)*	.50
	Pane of 20	7.00
	Imprint single, type I	1.00
	Imprint block of 4, type I	2.50
	Imprint single, type II	1.00
	Imprint block of 4, type II	2.50

Imprint type I appears in selvage below seal 20; imprint type II appears in selvage below seal 16. Legend printed in English in top selvage and in Japanese in top and bottom selvage.

TBS14

Designer — Kabira Choshin.

1966 *Perf. 13x13¼*

WX15	TBS14 **dark green, yellow & carmine** *(3,700,000)*	.30
	Pane of 20, perf through top and bottom selvage	5.00
	Imprint single, type I	.60
	Imprint block of 4, type I	1.50
	Imprint single, type II	.60
	Imprint block of 4, type II	1.50
a.	Imperf *(100,000)*	.50
	Pane of 20	7.00
	Imprint single, type I	1.00
	Imprint block of 4, type I	2.50
	Imprint single, type II	1.00
	Imprint block of 4, type II	2.50

Imprint type I appears in selvage below seal 20; imprint type II appears in selvage below seal 17. Legend printed in English in left selvage and in Japanese in right selvage.

TBS15

Designer — Kabira Choshin.

1967

WX16	TBS15 **blue, carmine, yellow & black** *(4,100,000)*	.30
	Pane of 20, perf through top and bottom selvage	5.00
	Imprint single, type I	.60
	Imprint block of 4, type I	1.50
	Imprint single, type II	.60
	Imprint block of 4, type II	1.50
a.	Imperf *(100,000)*	.50
	Pane of 20	7.00
	Imprint single, type I	1.00
	Imprint block of 4, type I	2.50
	Imprint single, type II	1.00
	Imprint block of 4, type II	2.50

Imprint type I appears in selvage below seal 20; imprint type II appears in selvage below seal 17. Legend printed in English in left selvage and in Japanese in right selvage.

TBS16

Designer — Kabira Choshin.

1968

WX17	TBS16 **blue, carmine & black** *(4,400,000)*	.30
	Pane of 20, perf through top and bottom selvage	5.00
	Imprint single, type I	.60
	Imprint block of 4, type I	1.50
	Imprint single, type II	.60
	Imprint block of 4, type II	1.50
a.	Imperf *(100,000)*	.50
	Pane of 20	7.00
	Imprint single, type I	1.00
	Imprint block of 4, type I	2.50
	Imprint single, type II	1.00
	Imprint block of 4, type II	2.50

Imprint type I appears in selvage below seal 20; imprint type II appears in selvage below seal 17. Legend printed in English in left selvage and in Japanese in right selvage.

TBS17

Designer — Oshiro Kohya.

1969

WX18	TBS17 **multicolored** *(4,600,000)*	.30
	Pane of 20, perf through top and bottom selvage	5.00
	Imprint single, type I	.60
	Imprint block of 4, type I	1.50
	Imprint single, type II	.60
	Imprint block of 4, type II	1.50
a.	Imperf *(100,000)*	.50
	Pane of 20	7.00
	Imprint single, type I	1.00
	Imprint block of 4, type I	2.50
	Imprint single, type II	1.00
	Imprint block of 4, type II	2.50

Imprint type I appears in selvage below seal 20; imprint type II appears in selvage below seal 17. Legend printed in English in left selvage and in Japanese in right selvage.

TBS18

Designer — Kabira Choshin.

1970

WX19	TBS18 **multicolored** *(4,650,000)*	.30
	Pane of 20, perf through top and bottom selvage	5.00
	Imprint single, type I	.60
	Imprint block of 4, type I	1.50
	Imprint single, type II	.60
	Imprint block of 4, type II	1.50
a.	Imperf *(50,000)*	.50
	Pane of 20	7.00
	Imprint single, type I	1.00

Imprint block of 4, type I	2.50
Imprint single, type II	1.00
Imprint block of 4, type II	2.50

Imprint type I appears in selvage below seal 20; imprint type II appears in selvage below seal 17. Legend printed in English in left selvage and in Japanese in right selvage.

TBS19

Designer — Ashimine Kinsei.

1971

WX20	TBS19 **multicolored** *(4,650,000)*	.30	
	Pane of 20, perf through top and bottom selvage	5.00	
	Imprint single, type I	.60	
	Imprint block of 4, type I	1.50	
	Imprint single, type II	.60	
	Imprint block of 4, type II	1.50	
a.	Imperf *(50,000)*	.50	
	Pane of 20	7.00	
	Imprint single, type I	1.00	
	Imprint block of 4, type I	2.50	
	Imprint single, type II	1.00	
	Imprint block of 4, type II	2.50	

Imprint type I appears in selvage below seal 20; imprint type II appears in selvage below seal 17. Legend printed in English in left selvage and in Japanese in right selvage.

UNITED NATIONS

United Nations stamps are used on UN official mail sent from UN Headquarters in New York City, the UN European Office in Geneva, Switzerland, or from the Donaupark Vienna International Center or Atomic Energy Agency in Vienna, Austria to points throughout the world. They may be used on private correspondence sent through the UN post offices.

UN mail is carried by the US, Swiss and Austrian postal systems.

See Switzerland official stamp listings in the Scott *Standard Postage Stamp Catalogue* for stamps issued by the Swiss Government for official use of the UN European Office and other UN affiliated organizations. See France official stamp listings for stamps issued by the French Government for official use of UNESCO.

+: When following the quantity, this indicates the total printed to date. Unless otherwise noted, these are the initial printing order. Final quantities frequently are not given for definitives and air post stamps. The total printed is shown here.

Blocks of four generally sell for four times the single stamp value.

Values for first day covers are for cacheted and unaddressed covers. Addressed covers sell for much less, and addressed and uncacheted first day covers sell for very little.

For imperforate stamps, see the Proofs section following U.N. Souvenir Cards.

Catalogue values for all unused stamps in this section are for Never Hinged items.

Peoples of the World — A1

UN Headquarters Building — A2

"Peace, Justice, Security" — A3

UN Flag — A4

UN International Children's Emergency Fund — A5

World Unity — A6

Printed by Thomas De La Rue & Co., Ltd., London (1c, 3c, 10c, 15c, 20c, 25c), and Joh. Enschedé and Sons, Haarlem, Netherlands (1½c, 2c, 5c, 50c, $1). The 3c, 15c and 25c have frame engraved, center photogravure; other denominations are engraved. Panes of 50. Designed by O. C. Meronti (A1), Leon Helguera (A2), J. F. Doeve (A3), Ole Hamann (A4), S. L. Hartz (5c) and Hubert Woyty-Wimmer (20c).

Perf. 13x12½, 12½x13

1951 Engr. and Photo. Unwmk.

1	A1	1c	**magenta,** *Oct. 24 (8,000,000)*	.20	.20
			First day cover		1.00
			Margin block of 4, UN seal	.20	—
2	A2	1½c	**blue green,** *Oct. 24 (7,450,000)*	.20	.20
			First day cover		1.00
			Margin block of 4, UN seal	.20	—
			Precanceled *(361,700)*		55.00
3	A3	2c	**purple,** *Nov. 16 (8,470,000)*	.20	.20
			First day cover		1.00
			Margin block of 4, UN seal	.25	—
4	A4	3c	**magenta & blue,** *Oct. 24 (8,250,000)*	.20	.20
			First day cover		1.00
			Margin block of 4, UN seal	.25	—
5	A5	5c	**blue,** *Oct. 24 (6,000,000)*	.20	.20
			First day cover		1.75
			Margin block of 4, UN seal	.40	—
6	A1	10c	**chocolate,** *Nov. 16 (2,600,000)*	.35	.25
			First day cover		2.00
			Margin block of 4, UN seal	1.50	—
7	A4	15c	**violet & blue,** *Nov. 16 (2,300,000)*	.35	.25
			First day cover		2.00
			Margin block of 4, UN seal	1.50	—
8	A6	20c	**dark brown,** *Nov. 16 (2,100,000)*	.55	.30
			First day cover		2.00
			Margin block of 4, UN seal	2.40	—
9	A4	25c	**olive gray & blue,** *Oct. 24 (2,100,000)*	.60	.30
			First day cover		2.00
			Margin block of 4, UN seal	2.75	—
10	A2	50c	**indigo,** *Nov. 16 (1,785,000)*	6.00	2.50
			First day cover		8.00
			Margin block of 4, UN seal	27.50	—
11	A3	$1	**red,** *Oct. 24 (2,252,500)*	2.50	1.50
			First day cover		8.00
			Margin block of 4, UN seal	11.50	—
			Nos. 1-11 (11)	11.35	6.10

First day covers of Nos. 1-11 and C1-C4 total 1,113,216.

The various printings of Nos. 1-11 vary in sheet marginal perforation. Some were perforated through left or right margins, or both; some through all margins.

Sheets of this issue carry a marginal inscription consisting of the UN seal and "First UN/Issue 1951." This inscription appears four times on each sheet. The listing "Margin block of 4, UN seal" or "Inscription block of 4" in this and following issues refers to a corner block.

Sheets of the 1½c, 2c, 50c and $1 have a cut-out of different shape in one margin. The printer trimmed this off entirely on most of the 1½c third printing, and partially on the 1½c fourth printing and $1 fifth and sixth printings.

See UN Offices in Geneva Nos. 4, 14.

Forgeries of the 1½c precancel abound. Examination by a competent authority is necessary.

Veterans' War Memorial Building, San Francisco A7

Issued to mark the 7th anniversary of the signing of the United Nations Charter.

Engraved and printed by the American Bank Note Co., New York. Panes of 50. Designed by Jean Van Noten.

1952, Oct. 24 ***Perf. 12***

12	A7	5c	**blue** *(1,274,670)*	.80	.35
			First day cover *(160,117)*		1.00
			Inscription block of 4	3.75	—

Globe and Encircled Flame — A8

4th anniversary of the adoption of the Universal Declaration of Human Rights.

Engraved and printed by Thomas De La Rue & Co., Ltd., London. Panes of 50. Designed by Hubert Woyty-Wimmer.

1952, Dec. 10			***Perf. 13½x14***	
13	A8	3c **deep green** *(1,554,312)*	.50	.35
		First day cover		1.50
		Inscription block of 4	2.25	—
14	A8	5c **blue** *(1,126,371)*	.60	.40
		First day cover		2.00
		First day cover, #13-14		5.75
		Inscription block of 4	2.50	—

First day covers of Nos. 13 and 14 total 299,309.

Refugee Family — A9

Issued to publicize "Protection for Refugees."
Engraved and printed by Thomas De La Rue & Co., Ltd., London. Panes of 50. Designed by Olav Mathiesen.

1953, Apr. 24			***Perf. 12½x13***	
15	A9	3c **dark red brown & rose brown** *(1,299,793)*	.25	.25
		First day cover		2.25
		Inscription block of 4	1.00	—
16	A9	5c **indigo & blue** *(969,224)*	.50	.40
		First day cover		3.25
		First day cover, #15-16		7.50
		Inscription block of 4	2.75	—

First day covers of Nos. 15 and 16 total 234,082.

Envelope, UN Emblem and Map — A10

Issued to honor the Universal Postal Union.
Engraved and printed by Thomas De La Rue & Co., Ltd., London. Panes of 50. Designed by Hubert Woyty-Wimmer.

1953, June 12			***Perf. 13***	
17	A10	3c **black brown** *(1,259,689)*	.40	.40
		First day cover		5.00
		Inscription block of 4	1.60	—
18	A10	5c **dark blue** *(907,312)*	1.25	1.00
		First day cover		4.50
		First day cover, #17-18		9.50
		Inscription block of 4	5.00	—

First day covers of Nos. 17 and 18 total 231,627.
Plate number ("1A" or "1B") in color of stamp appears below 47th stamp of sheet.

Gearwheels and UN Emblem — A11

Hands Reaching Toward Flame — A12

Issued to publicize United Nations activities in the field of technical assistance.

Engraved and printed by Thomas De La Rue & Co. Ltd. London. Panes of 50. Designed by Olav Mathiesen.

1953, Oct. 24 ***Perf. 13x12½***

19	A11	3c **dark gray** *(1,184,348)*		.30	.25
		First day cover			2.00
		Inscription block of 4		1.25	—
20	A11	5c **dark green** *(968,182)*		.50	.45
		First day cover			5.00
		First day cover, #19-20			9.00
		Inscription block of 4		2.75	—

First day covers of Nos. 19 and 20 total 229,211.

1953, Dec. 10 ***Perf. 12½x13***

Issued to publicize Human Rights Day.

Engraved and printed by Thomas De La Rue & Co., Ltd., London. Panes of 50. Designed by León Helguera.

21	A12	3c **bright blue** *(1,456,928)*		.35	.30
		First day cover			2.00
		Inscription block of 4		1.50	—
22	A12	5c **rose red** *(983,831)*		1.50	1.00
		First day cover			4.00
		First day cover, #21-22			8.00
		Inscription block of 4		6.00	—

First day covers of Nos. 21 and 22 total 265,186.

Ear of Wheat — A13

UN Emblem and Anvil Inscribed "ILO" — A14

Issued to honor the Food and Agriculture Organization and printed by Thomas De La Rue & Co., Ltd., London. Panes of 50. Designed by Dirk Van Gelder.

1954, Feb. 11 ***Perf. 12½x13***

23	A13	3c **dark green & yellow** *(1,250,000)*		.30	.20
		First day cover			2.00
		Inscription block of 4		1.75	—
24	A13	8c **indigo & yellow** *(949,718)*		.75	.50
		First day cover			4.00
		First day cover, #23-24			5.00
		Inscription block of 4		4.00	—

First day covers of Nos. 23 and 24 total 272,312.

1954, May 10 ***Perf. 12½x13***

Design: 8c, inscribed "OIT."

Issued to honor the International Labor Organization.

Engraved and printed by Thomas De La Rue & Co., Ltd., London. Panes of 50. Designed by José Renau.

25	A14	3c **brown** *(1,085,651)*		.20	.20
		First day cover			2.00
		Inscription block of 4		.50	—
26	A14	8c **magenta** *(903,561)*		1.25	.85
		First day cover			4.00
		First day cover, #25-26			4.75
		Inscription block of 4		5.25	—

First day covers of Nos. 25 and 26 total 252,796.

UN European Office, Geneva — A15

Issued on the occasion of United Nations Day.

Engraved and printed by Thomas De La Rue & Co., Ltd., London. Panes of 50. Designed by Earl W. Purdy.

1954, Oct. 25 ***Perf. 14***

27	A15	3c **dark blue violet** *(1,000,000)*		1.75	1.25
		First day cover			1.75
		Inscription block of 4		8.50	—
28	A15	8c **red** *(1,000,000)*		.35	.30
		First day cover			2.25
		First day cover, #27-28			3.50
		Inscription block of 4		1.75	—

First day covers of Nos. 27 and 28 total 233,544.

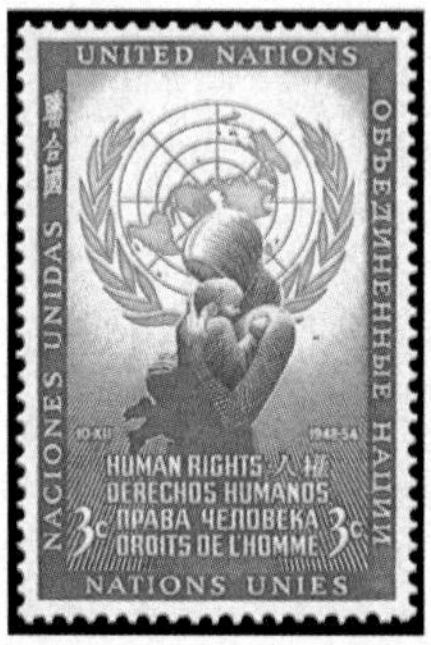

Mother and Child — A16

Issued to publicize Human Rights Day.

Engraved and printed by Thomas De La Rue & Co., Ltd. London. Panes of 50. Designed by Leonard C. Mitchell.

1954, Dec. 10 ***Perf. 14***

29	A16	3c **red orange** *(1,000,000)*		12.00	4.00
		First day cover			2.75
		Inscription block of 4		55.00	—
30	A16	8c **olive green** *(1,000,000)*		.75	.35
		First day cover			3.25
		First day cover, #29-30			7.50
		Inscription block of 4		4.50	—

First day covers of Nos. 29 and 30 total 276,333.

Symbol of Flight — A17

Design: 8c, inscribed "OACI."

Issued to honor the International Civil Aviation Organization.

Engraved and printed by Waterlow & Sons, Ltd., London. Panes of 50. Designed by Angel Medina Medina.

1955, Feb. 9 ***Perf. 13½x14***

31	A17	3c **blue** *(1,000,000)*		1.50	.90
		First day cover			2.00
		Inscription block of 4		7.00	—
32	A17	8c **rose carmine** *(1,000,000)*		.85	.80
		First day cover			3.00
		First day cover, #31-32			5.50
		Inscription block of 4		3.50	—

First day covers of Nos. 31 and 32 total 237,131.

UNESCO Emblem — A18

Issued to honor the UN Educational, Scientific and Cultural Organization.

Engraved and printed by Waterlow & Sons, Ltd., London. Panes of 50. Designed by George Hamori.

1955, May 11 ***Perf. 13½x14***

33	A18	3c **lilac rose** *(1,000,000)*		.45	.35
		First day cover			2.00
		Inscription block of 4		2.50	—
34	A18	8c **light blue** *(1,000,000)*		.40	.35
		First day cover			3.00
		First day cover, #33-34			5.00
		Inscription block of 4		1.75	—

First day covers of Nos. 33 and 34 total 255,326.

United Nations Charter — A19

Design: 4c, Spanish inscription. 8c, French inscription.

10th anniversary of the United Nations.

Engraved and printed by Waterlow & Sons, Ltd., London. Panes of 50. Designed by Claude Bottiau.

1955, Oct. 24 ***Perf. 13½x14***

35	A19	3c **deep plum** *(1,000,000)*		1.00	.60
		First day cover			3.00
		Inscription block of 4		4.00	—
36	A19	4c **dull green** *(1,000,000)*		.55	.40
		First day cover			3.00
		Inscription block of 4		2.75	—
37	A19	8c **bluish black** *(1,000,000)*		.40	.30
		First day cover			4.00
		First day cover, #35-37			11.00
		Inscription block of 4		2.25	—
		Nos. 35-37 (3)		1.95	1.30

Wmk. 309 — Wavy Lines

Souvenir Sheet

1955, Oct. 24 **Wmk. 309** ***Imperf.***

38	A19	Sheet of 3 *(250,000)*		120.00	20.00
		Hinged		65.00	
a.		3c **deep plum**		3.00	.50
b.		4c **dull green**		3.00	.50
c.		8c **bluish black**		3.00	.50
		First day cover			20.00
		Sheet with retouch on 8c		135.00	42.50

No. 38 measures 108x83mm and has marginal inscriptions in deep plum.

Two printings were made of No. 38. The first (200,000) may be distinguished by the broken line of background shading on the 8c. It leaves a small white spot below the left leg of the "n" of "Unies." For the second printing (50,000), the broken line was retouched, eliminating the white spot. The 4c was also retouched.

First day covers of Nos. 35-38 total 455,791.

Examples of No. 38 are known with the 4c and 8c stamps misaligned.

Hand Holding Torch — A20

Issued in honor of Human Rights Day.
Engraved and printed by Waterlow & Sons, Ltd., London. Panes of 50. Designed by Hubert Woyty-Wimmer.

1955, Dec. 9 **Unwmk.** ***Perf. 14x13½***

39	A20	3c **ultramarine** *(1,250,000)*	.30	.30
		First day cover		1.25
		Inscription block of 4	1.25	—
40	A20	8c **green** *(1,000,000)*	.35	.30
		First day cover		1.25
		First day cover, #39-40		2.50
		Inscription block of 4	1.75	—

First day covers of Nos. 39 and 40 total 298,038.

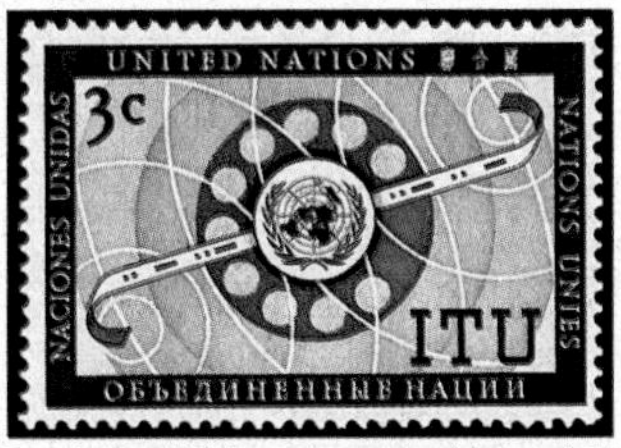

Symbols of Telecommunication — A21

Design: 8c, inscribed "UIT."
Issued in honor of the International Telecommunication Union.
Engraved and printed by Thomas De La Rue & Co., Ltd., London. Panes of 50. Designed by Hubert Woyty-Wimmer.

1956, Feb. 17 ***Perf. 14***

41	A21	3c **turquoise blue** *(1,000,000)*	.35	.25
		First day cover		1.50
		Inscription block of 4	1.10	—
42	A21	8c **deep carmine** *(1,000,000)*	.35	.30
		First day cover		2.25
		First day cover, #41-42		3.50
		Inscription block of 4	1.50	—

Plate number ("1A" or "1B") in color of stamp appears below 47th stamp of sheet.

Globe and Caduceus — A22

Design: 8c, inscribed "OMS."
Issued in honor of the World Health Organization.
Engraved and printed by Thomas De La Rue & Co., Ltd., London. Panes of 50. Designed by Olav Mathiesen.

1956, Apr. 6 ***Perf. 14***

43	A22	3c **bright greenish blue** *(1,250,000)*	.20	.20
		First day cover		1.00
		Inscription block of 4	.50	—
44	A22	8c **golden brown** *(1,000,000)*	.20	.25
		First day cover		1.50
		First day cover, #43-44		14.00
		Inscription block of 4	1.50	—

First day covers of Nos. 43 and 44 total 260,853.

General Assembly A23

Design: 8c, French inscription.
Issued to commemorate United Nations Day.
Engraved and printed by Thomas De La Rue & Co., Ltd., London. Panes of 50. Designed by Kurt Plowitz.

1956, Oct. 24 ***Perf. 14***

45	A23	3c **dark blue** *(2,000,000)*	.20	.20
		First day cover		1.00
		Inscription block of 4	.40	—
46	A23	8c **gray olive** *(1,500,000)*	.20	.20
		First day cover		1.00
		First day cover, #45-46		7.50
		Inscription block of 4	1.25	—

First day covers of Nos. 45 and 46 total 303,560.

Flame and Globe — A24

Issued to publicize Human Rights Day
Engraved and printed by Thomas De La Rue & Co., Ltd., London. Panes of 50. Designed by Rashid-ud Din.

1956, Dec. 10 ***Perf. 14***

47	A24	3c **plum** *(5,000,000)*	.20	.20
		First day cover		1.00
		Inscription block of 4	.40	—
48	A24	8c **dark blue** *(4,000,000)*	.20	.20
		First day cover		1.00
		First day cover, #47-48		2.00
		Inscription block of 4	.90	—

First day covers of Nos. 47 and 48 total 416,120.

Weather Balloon — A25

Badge of UN Emergency Force — A26

Design: 8c, Agency name in French.
Issued to honor the World Meterological Organization.
Engraved and printed by Thomas De La Rue & Co., Ltd., London. Panes of 50. Designed by A. L. Pollock.

1957, Jan. 28 ***Perf. 14***

49	A25	3c **violet blue** *(5,000,000)*	.20	.20
		First day cover		1.00
		Inscription block of 4	.25	—
50	A25	8c **dark carmine rose** *(3,448,985)*	.20	.20
		First day cover		1.00
		First day cover, #49-50		2.25
		Inscription block of 4	.65	—

First day covers of Nos. 49 and 50 total 376,110.

1957, Apr. 8 ***Perf. 14x12½***

Issued in honor of the UN Emergency Force.
Engraved and printed by Thomas De La Rue & Co., Ltd., London. Panes of 50. Designed by Ole Hamann.

51	A26	3c **light blue** *(4,000,000)*	.20	.20
		First day cover		1.00
		Inscription block of 4	.30	—
52	A26	8c **rose carmine** *(3,000,000)*	.20	.20
		First day cover		1.00
		First day cover, #51-52		1.75
		Inscription block of 4	.70	—

First day covers of Nos. 51 and 52 total 461,772.

Nos. 51-52 Re-engraved

1957, Apr.-May ***Perf. 14x12½***

53	A26	3c **blue** *(2,736,206)*	.20	.20
		Inscription block of 4	.60	—
54	A26	8c **rose carmine** *(1,000,000)*	.35	.20
		Inscription block of 4	2.00	—

On Nos. 53-54 the background within and around the circles is shaded lightly, giving a halo effect. The lettering is more distinct with a line around each letter.

UN Emblem and Globe — A27

Design: 8c, French inscription.
Issued to honor the Security Council.
Engraved and printed by Thomas De La Rue & Co., Ltd., London. Panes of 50. Designed by Rashid-ud Din.

1957, Oct. 24 ***Perf. 12½x13***

55	A27	3c **orange brown** *(3,674,968)*	.20	.20
		First day cover		1.00
		Inscription block of 4	.25	—
56	A27	8c **dark blue green** *(2,885,938)*	.20	.20
		First day cover		1.00
		First day cover, #55-56		2.25
		Inscription block of 4	.70	—

First day covers of Nos. 55 and 56 total 460,627.

Flaming Torch — A28

Issued in honor of Human Rights Day.
Engraved and printed by Thomas De La Rue & Co., Ltd., London. Panes of 50. Designed by Olav Mathiesen.

1957, Dec. 10 ***Perf. 14***

57	A28	3c **red brown** *(3,368,405)*	.20	.20
		First day cover		1.00
		Inscription block of 4	.25	—
58	A28	8c **black** *(2,717,310)*	.20	.20
		First day cover		1.00
		First day cover, #57-58		1.25
		Inscription block of 4	.65	—

First day covers of Nos. 57 and 58 total 553,669.

UN Emblem Shedding Light on Atom — A29

Design: 8c, French inscription.
Issued in honor of the International Atomic Energy Agency.
Engraved and printed by the American Bank Note Co., New York. Panes of 50. Designed by Robert Perrot.

1958, Feb. 10 ***Perf. 12***

59	A29	3c **olive** *(3,663,305)*	.20	.20
		First day cover		1.00
		Inscription block of 4	.25	—
60	A29	8c **blue** *(3,043,622)*	.20	.20

First day cover 1.00
First day cover, #59-60 1.00
Inscription block of 4 .85 —

First day covers of Nos. 59 and 60 total 504,832.

Central Hall, Westminster — A30

UN Seal — A31

Design: 8c, French inscription.
Central Hall, Westminster, London, was the site of the first session of the United Nations General Assembly, 1946.
Engraved and printed by the American Bank Note Co., New York. Panes of 50. Designed by Olav Mathiesen.

1958, Apr. 14 *Perf. 12*

61 A30 3c **violet blue** *(3,353,716)* .20 .20
First day cover 1.00
Inscription block of 4 .25 —
62 A30 8c **rose claret** *(2,836,747)* .20 .20
First day cover 1.00
First day cover, #61-62 2.00
Inscription block of 4 .60 —

First day covers of Nos. 61 and 62 total 449,401.

1958, Oct. 24 *Perf. 13½x14*

Engraved and printed by Bradbury, Wilkinson & Co., Ltd., England. Panes of 50. Designed by Herbert M. Sanborn.

63 A31 4c **red orange** *(9,000,000)* .20 .20
First day cover 1.00
First day cover of #63 also bearing #64 *75.00*
Inscription block of 4 .20 —

1958, June 2 *Perf. 13x14*

64 A31 8c **bright blue** *(5,000,000)* .20 .20
First day cover *(219,422)* 1.00
Inscription block of 4 .55 —
Margin block of 4, Bradbury, Wilkinson imprint 3.00 —

Gearwheels — A32

Hands Upholding Globe — A33

Design: 8c, French inscription.
Issued to honor the Economic and Social Council.
Engraved and printed by the American Bank Note Co., New York. Panes of 50. Designed by Ole Hamann.

1958, Oct. 24 **Unwmk.** *Perf. 12*

65 A32 4c **dark blue green** *(2,556,784)* .20 .20
First day cover 1.00
Inscription block of 4 .30 —
66 A32 8c **vermilion** *(2,175,117)* .20 .20
First day cover 1.00
First day cover, #65-66 1.00
Inscription block of 4 .60 —

First day covers of Nos. 63, 65 and 66 total 626,236.

1958, Dec. 10 **Unwmk.** *Perf. 12*

Issued for Human Rights Day and to commemorate the 10th anniversary of the signing of the Universal Declaration of Human Rights.

Engraved and printed by the American Bank Note Co., New York. Panes of 50. Designed by Leonard C. Mitchell.

67 A33 4c **yellow green** *(2,644,340)* .20 .20
First day cover 1.00
Inscription block of 4 .40 —
68 A33 8c **red brown** *(2,216,838)* .20 .20
First day cover 1.00
First day cover, #67-68 1.00
Inscription block of 4 .75 —

First day covers of Nos. 67 and 68 total 618,124.

New York City Building, Flushing Meadows A34

Design: 8c, French inscription.
New York City Building at Flushing Meadows, New York, was the site of many General Assembly meetings, 1946-50.
Engraved and printed by Canadian Bank Note Company, Ltd., Ottawa. Panes of 50. Designed by Robert Perrot.

1959, Mar. 30 **Unwmk.** *Perf. 12*

69 A34 4c **light lilac rose** *(2,035,011)* .20 .20
First day cover 1.00
Inscription block of 4 .30 —
70 A34 8c **aquamarine** *(1,627,281)* .20 .20
First day cover 1.00
First day cover, #69-70 1.75
Inscription block of 4 .70 —

First day covers of Nos. 69 and 70 total 440,955.

A35

A36

Design: UN emblem and symbols of agriculture, industry and trade.
Issued to honor the Economic Commission for Europe.
Engraved and printed by Canadian Bank Note Company, Ltd., Ottawa. Panes of 50. Designed by Ole Hamann.

1959, May 18 **Unwmk.** *Perf. 12*

71 A35 4c **blue** *(1,743,502)* .20 .20
First day cover 1.00
Inscription block of 4 .60 —
72 A35 8c **red orange** *(1,482,898)* .20 .20
First day cover 1.00
First day cover, #71-72 1.25
Inscription block of 4 .75 —

First day covers of Nos. 71 and 72 total 433,549.

1959, Oct. 23 **Unwmk.** *Perf. 12*

Designs: 4c, Figure Adapted from Rodin's "Age of Bronze." 8c, same, French inscription.
Issued to honor the Trusteeship Council.
Engraved and printed by Canadian Bank Note Co., Ltd., Ottawa. Panes of 50. Designed by León Helguera; lettering by Ole Hamann.

73 A36 4c **bright red** *(1,929,677)* .20 .20
First day cover 1.00
Inscription block of 4 .30 —
74 A36 8c **dark olive green** *(1,587,647)* .20 .20
First day cover 1.00
First day cover, #73-74 1.50
Inscription block of 4 1.00 —

First day covers of Nos. 73 and 74 total 466,053.

World Refugee Year Emblem — A37

Chaillot Palace, Paris — A38

Design: 8c, French inscription.
Issued to publicize World Refugee Year, July 1, 1959-June 30, 1960.
Engraved and printed by Canadian Bank Note Co., Ltd., Ottawa. Panes of 50. Designed by Olav Mathiesen.

1959, Dec. 10 **Unwmk.** *Perf. 12*

75 A37 4c **olive & red** *(2,168,963)* .20 .20
First day cover 1.00
Inscription block of 4 .35 —
76 A37 8c **olive & bright greenish blue** *(1,843,886)* .20 .20
First day cover 1.00
First day cover, #75-76 2.00
Inscription block of 4 .75 —

First day covers of Nos. 75 and 76 total 502,262.

1960, Feb. 29 **Unwmk.** *Perf. 14*

Design: 8c, French inscription.
Chaillot Palace in Paris was the site of General Assembly meetings in 1948 and 1951.
Engraved and printed by Thomas De La Rue & Co., Ltd., London. Panes of 50. Designed by Hubert Woyty-Wimmer.

77 A38 4c **rose lilac & blue** *(2,276,678)* .20 .20
First day cover 1.00
Inscription block of 4 .20 —
78 A38 8c **dull green & brown** *(1,930,869)* .20 .20
First day cover 1.00
First day cover, #77-78 2.50
Inscription block of 4 .70 —

First day covers of Nos. 77 and 78 total 446,815.

Map of Far East and Steel Beam — A39

Design: 8c, French inscription.
Issued to honor the Economic Commission for Asia and the Far East (ECAFE).
Printed by the Government Printing Bureau, Tokyo. Panes of 50. Designed by Hubert Woyty-Wimmer.

1960, Apr. 11 **Photo.** **Unwmk.** *Perf. 13x13½*

79 A39 4c **deep claret, blue green & dull yellow** *(2,195,945)* .20 .20
First day cover 1.00
Inscription block of 4 .20 —
80 A39 8c **olive green, blue & rose** *(1,897,902)* .20 .20
First day cover 1.00
First day cover, #79-80 2.00
Inscription block of 4 .75 —

First day covers of Nos. 79 and 80 total 415,127.

Tree, FAO and UN Emblems — A40

UN Headquarters and Preamble to UN Charter — A41

Design: 8c, French inscription.
Issued to commemorate the Fifth World Forestry Congress, Seattle, Washington, Aug. 29-Sept. 10.
Printed by the Government Printing Bureau, Tokyo. Panes of 50. Designed by Ole Hamann.

1960, Aug. 29 Photo. Unwmk. *Perf. 13½*

81 A40 4c **dark blue, green & orange** *(2,188,293)* .20 .20
First day cover 1.00
Inscription block of 4 .35 —
82 A40 8c **yellow green, black & orange** *(1,837,778)* .20 .20
First day cover 1.00
First day cover, #81-82 2.00
Inscription block of 4 .65 —

First day covers of Nos. 81 and 82 total 434,129.

1960, Oct. 24 Unwmk. *Perf. 11*

Design: 8c, French inscription.
Issued to commemorate the 15th anniversary of the United Nations.
Engraved and printed by the British American Bank Note Co., Ltd., Ottawa, Canada. Panes of 50. Designed by Robert Perrot.

83 A41 4c **blue** *(2,631,593)* .20 .20
First day cover 1.00
Inscription block of 4 .35 —
84 A41 8c **gray** *(2,278,022)* .20 .20
First day cover 1.00
First day cover, #83-84 1.50
Inscription block of 4 .65 —

Souvenir Sheet

Imperf

85 Sheet of 2 *(1,000,000)* 1.25 1.25
a. A41 4c **blue** .55 .55
b. A41 8c **gray** .55 .55
First day cover *(256,699)* .50

No. 85 has dark gray marginal inscription. Size: 92x71mm. Broken "I" and "V" flaws occur in "ANNIVERSARY" in marginal inscription. Value $40. Examples are known with the two stamps misaligned.

Block and Tackle — A42

Scales of Justice from Raphael's Stanze — A43

Design: 8c, French inscription.
Issued to honor the International Bank for Reconstruction and Development.
Printed by the Government Printing Bureau, Tokyo. Panes of 50. Designed by Angel Medina Medina.

1960, Dec. 9 Photo. Unwmk. *Perf. 13½x13*

86 A42 4c **multicolored** *(2,286,117)* .20 .20
First day cover 1.00
Inscription block of 4 .35 —
87 A42 8c **multicolored** *(1,882,019)* .20 .20
First day cover 1.00
First day cover, #86-87 1.25
Inscription block of 4 .65 —

First day covers of Nos. 86 and 87 total 559,708.

1961, Feb. 13 Photo. Unwmk. *Perf. 13½x13*

Design: 8c, French inscription.
Issued to honor the International Court of Justice.
Printed by the Government Printing Bureau, Tokyo, Japan. Panes of 50. Designed by Kurt Plowitz.

88 A43 4c **yellow, orange brown & black** *(2,234,588)* .20 .20
First day cover 1.00
Inscription block of 4 .35 —
89 A43 8c **yellow, green & black** *(2,023,968)* .20 .20
First day cover 1.00
First day cover, #88-89 1.00
Inscription block of 4 .65 —

First day covers of Nos. 88 and 89 total 447,467.

Seal of International Monetary Fund — A44

Design: 7c, French inscription.
Issued to honor the International Monetary Fund.
Printed by the Government Printing Bureau, Tokyo, Japan. Panes of 50. Designed by Roy E. Carlson and Hordur Karlsson, Iceland.

1961, Apr. 17 Photo. Unwmk. *Perf. 13x13½*

90 A44 4c **bright bluish green** *(2,305,010)* .20 .20
First day cover 1.00
Inscription block of 4 .35 —
91 A44 7c **terra cotta & yellow** *(2,147,201)* .20 .20
First day cover 1.00
First day cover, #90-91 1.00
Inscription block of 4 .65 —

First day covers of Nos. 90 and 91 total 448,729.

Abstract Group of Flags — A45

Printed by Courvoisier S.A., La Chaux-de-Fonds, Switzerland. Panes of 50. Designed by Herbert M. Sanborn.

1961, June 5 Photo. Unwmk. *Perf. 11½*

92 A45 30c **multicolored** *(3,370,000)* .45 .20
First day cover *(182,949)* 1.00
Inscription block of 4 2.00 —

See UN Offices in Geneva No. 10.

Cogwheel and Map of Latin America — A46

Design: 11c, Spanish inscription.
Issued to honor the Economic Commission for Latin America.
Printed by the Government Printing Bureau, Tokyo. Panes of 50. Designed by Robert Perrot.

1961, Sept. 18 Photo. Unwmk. *Perf. 13½*

93 A46 4c **blue, red & citron** *(2,037,912)* .20 .20
First day cover 1.00
Inscription block of 4 .45 —
94 A46 11c **green, lilac & orange vermilion** *(1,835,097)* .25 .20
First day cover 1.00
First day cover, #93-94 1.00
Inscription block of 4 1.25 —

First day covers of Nos. 93 and 94 total 435,820.

Africa House, Addis Ababa, and Map — A47

Design: 11c, English inscription.
Issued to honor the Economic Commission for Africa.
Printed by Courvoisier S.A., La Chaux-de-Fonds, Switzerland. Panes of 50. Designed by Robert Perrot.

1961, Oct. 24 Photo. Unwmk. *Perf. 11½*

95 A47 4c **ultramarine, orange, yellow & brown** *(2,044,842)* .20 .20
First day cover 1.00
Inscription block of 4 .30 —
96 A47 11c **emerald, orange, yellow & brown** *(1,790,894)* .25 .20
First day cover 1.00
First day cover, #95-96 1.00
Inscription block of 4 1.10 —

First day covers of Nos. 95 and 96 total 435,131.

Mother Bird Feeding Young and UNICEF Seal — A48

Designs: 3c, Spanish inscription. 13c, French inscription.
15th anniversary of the United Nations Children's Fund.
Printed by Courvoisier S.A., La Chaux-de-Fonds, Switzerland. Panes of 50. Designed by Minoru Hisano.

1961, Dec. 4 Photo. Unwmk. *Perf. 11½*

97 A48 3c **brown, gold, orange & yellow** *(2,867,456)* .20 .20
First day cover 1.00
Inscription block of 4 .25 —
98 A48 4c **brown, gold, blue & emerald** *(2,735,899)* .20 .20
First day cover 1.00
Inscription block of 4 .35 —
99 A48 13c **deep green, gold, purple & pink** *(1,951,715)* .20 .20
First day cover 1.00
First day cover, #97-99 1.40
Inscription block of 4 1.25 —
Nos. 97-99 (3) .60 .60

First day covers of Nos. 97-99 total 752,979.

Family and Symbolic Buildings A49

Design: 7c, inscribed "Services Collectifs".
Issued to publicize the UN program for housing and urban development, and in connection with the expert committee meeting at UN headquarters, Feb. 7-21.
Printed by Harrison and Sons, Ltd., London, England. Panes of 50. Designed by Olav Mathiesen.

1962, Feb. 28 Photo. Unwmk. *Perf. 14½x14*

Central design multicolored

100 A49 4c **bright blue** *(2,204,190)* .20 .20
First day cover 1.00
Inscription block of 4 .35 —
a. Black omitted 200.00
b. Yellow omitted —
c. Brown omitted —
101 A49 7c **orange brown** *(1,845,821)* .20 .20
First day cover 1.00
First day cover, #100-101 1.25
Inscription block of 4 .65 —
a. Red omitted —
b. Black omitted —
c. Gold omitted —

First day covers of Nos. 100-101 total 466,178.

"The World Against Malaria" — A50

Issued in honor of the World Health Organization and to call attention to the international campaign to eradicate malaria from the world.

Printed by Harrison and Sons, Ltd., London, England. Panes of 50. Designed by Rashid-ud Din.

1962, Mar. 30 Photo. Unwmk. *Perf. 14x14½*
Word frame in gray

102 A50 4c **orange, yellow, brown, green & black** *(2,047,000)* .20 .20
First day cover 1.00
Inscription block of 4 .35 —
103 A50 11c **green, yellow, brown & indigo** *(1,683,766)* .25 .20
First day cover 1.00
First day cover, #102-103 1.50
Inscription block of 4 1.10 —

First day covers of Nos. 102-103 total 522,450.

"Peace" — A51

UN Flag — A52

Hands Combining "UN" and Globe — A53

UN Emblem over Globe — A54

Printed by Harrison & Sons, Ltd. London, England (1c, 3c and 11c), and by Canadian Bank Note Co., Ltd., Ottawa (5c). Panes of 50. Designed by Kurt Plowitz (1c), Ole Hamann (3c), Renato Ferrini (5c) and Olav Mathiesen (11c).

Photo.; Engr. (5c)
1962, May 25 Unwmk. *Perf. 14x14½*

104 A51 1c **vermilion, blue, black & gray** *(5,000,000)* .20 .20
First day cover 1.00
Inscription block of 4 .25 —
105 A52 3c **light green, Prussian blue, yellow & gray** *(5,000,000)* .20 .20
First day cover 1.00
Inscription block of 4 .25 —

Perf. 12

106 A53 5c **dark carmine rose** *(4,000,000)* .20 .20
First day cover 1.00
Inscription block of 4 .65 —

Perf. 12½

107 A54 11c **dark & light blue & gold** *(4,400,000)* .25 .20
First day cover 1.00
First day cover, #104-107 6.00
Inscription block of 4 1.10 —
Nos. 104-107 (4) .85 .80

First day covers of Nos. 104-107 total 738,985.
Size of 5c, No. 106: 36½x23½mm.
See No. 167. See UN Offices in Geneva Nos. 2 and 6.

Flag at Half-mast and UN Headquarters — A55

World Map Showing Congo — A56

Issued on the 1st anniversary of the death of Dag Hammarskjold, Secretary General of the United Nations 1953-61, in memory of those who died in the service of the United Nations.

Printed by Courvoisier S. A., La Chaux-de-Fonds, Switzerland. Panes of 50. Designed by Ole Hamann.

1962, Sept. 17 Photo. Unwmk. *Perf. 11½*

108 A55 5c **black, light blue & blue** *(2,195,707)* .20 .20
First day cover 1.00
Inscription block of 4 .50 —
109 A55 15c **black, gray olive & blue** *(1,155,047)* .20 .20
First day cover 1.00
First day cover, #108-109 2.00
Inscription block of 4 .85 —

First day covers of Nos. 108-109 total 513,963.

1962, Oct. 24 Photo. Unwmk. *Perf. 11½*

Design: 11c inscribed "Operation des Nations Unies au Congo."

Issued to commemorate the United Nations Operation in the Congo.

Printed by Courvoisier S. A., La Chaux-de-Fonds, Switzerland. Panes of 50. Designed by George Hamori.

110 A56 4c **olive, orange, black & yellow** *(1,477,958)* .20 .20
First day cover 1.00
Inscription block of 4 .50 —
111 A56 11c **blue green, orange, black & yellow** *(1,171,255)* .20 .20
First day cover 1.00
First day cover, #110-111 1.75
Inscription block of 4 .95 —

First day covers of Nos. 110-111 total 460,675.

Globe in Universe and Palm Frond — A57

Development Decade Emblem — A58

Design: 4c, English inscription.

Issued to honor the Committee on Peaceful Uses of Outer Space.

Printed by Bradbury, Wilkinson and Co., Ltd., England. Panes of 50. Designed by Kurt Plowitz.

1962, Dec. 3 Engr. Unwmk. *Perf. 14x13½*

112 A57 4c **violet blue** *(2,263,876)* .20 .20
First day cover 1.00
Inscription block of 4 .35 —
113 A57 11c **rose claret** *(1,681,584)* .25 .20
First day cover 1.00
First day cover, #112-113 2.00
Inscription block of 4 1.25 —

First day covers of Nos. 112-113 total 529,780.

1963, Feb. 4 Photo. Unwmk. *Perf. 11½*

Design: 11c, French inscription.

UN Development Decade and UN Conference on the Application of Science and Technology for the Benefit of the Less Developed Areas, Geneva, Feb. 4-20.

Printed by Courvoisier S. A., La Chaux-de-Fonds, Switzerland. Panes of 50. Designed by Rashid-ud Din.

114 A58 5c **pale green, maroon, dark blue & Prussian blue** *(1,802,406)* .20 .20
First day cover 1.00
Inscription block of 4 .35 —
115 A58 11c **yellow, maroon, dark blue & Prussian blue** *(1,530,190)* .20 .20
First day cover 1.00
First day cover, #114-115 1.50
Inscription block of 4 .90 —

First day covers of Nos. 114-115 total 460,877.

Stalks of Wheat — A59

Design: 11c, French inscription.

Issued for the "Freedom from Hunger" campaign of the Food and Agriculture Organization.

Printed by Courvoisier S. A., La Chaux-de-Fonds, Switzerland. Panes of 50. Designed by Ole Hamann.

1963, Mar. 22 Photo. Unwmk. *Perf. 11½*

116 A59 5c **vermilion, green & yellow** *(1,666,178)* .20 .20
First day cover 1.00
Inscription block of 4 .35 —
117 A59 11c **vermilion, deep claret & yellow** *(1,563,023)* .25 .20
First day cover 1.00
First day cover, #116-117 1.50
Inscription block of 4 1.10 —

First day covers of Nos. 116-117 total 461,868.

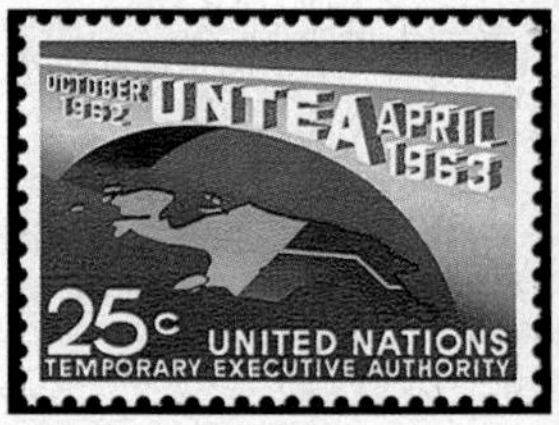

Bridge over Map of New Guinea — A60

1st anniversary of the United Nations Temporary Executive Authority (UNTEA) in West New Guinea (West Irian).

Printed by Courvoisier S.A., La Chaux-de-Fonds, Switzerland. Panes of 50. Designed by Henry Bencsath.

1963, Oct. 1 Photo. Unwmk. *Perf. 11½*

118 A60 25c **blue, green & gray** *(1,427,747)* .50 .30
First day cover *(222,280)* 1.00
Inscription block of 4 2.25 —

General Assembly Building, New York — A61

Design: 11c, French inscription.

Since October 1955 all sessions of the General Assembly have been held in the General Assembly Hall, UN Headquarters, NY.

Printed by the Government Printing Bureau, Tokyo. Panes of 50. Designed by Kurt Plowitz.

1963, Nov. 4 Photo. Unwmk. *Perf. 13*

119 A61 5c **violet blue, blue, yellow green & red** *(1,892,539)* .20 .20
First day cover 1.00
Inscription block of 4 .35 —
120 A61 11c **green, yellow green, blue, yellow & red** *(1,435,079)* .20 .20
First day cover 1.00
First day cover, #119-120 1.25
Inscription block of 4 .85 —

First day covers of Nos. 119-120 total 410,306.

Flame — A62

Design: 11c inscribed "15e Anniversaire."
15th anniversary of the signing of the Universal Declaration of Human Rights.
Printed by the Government Printing Bureau, Tokyo. Panes of 50. Designed by Rashid-ud Din.

1963, Dec. 10 Photo. Unwmk. *Perf. 13*

121 A62 5c **green, gold, red & yellow** *(2,208,008)* .20 .20
First day cover 1.00
Inscription block of 4 .55 —

122 A62 11c **carmine, gold, blue & yellow** *(1,501,125)* .20 .20
First day cover 1.00
First day cover, #121-122 1.00
Inscription block of 4 .70 —

First day covers of Nos. 121-122 total 567,907.

Ships at Sea and IMCO Emblem — A63

Design: 11c, inscribed "OMCI."
Issued to honor the Intergovernmental Maritime Consultative Organization.
Printed by Courvoisier S.A., La Chaux-de-Fonds, Switzerland. Panes of 50. Designed by Henry Bencsath; emblem by Olav Mathiesen.

1964, Jan. 13 Photo. Unwmk. *Perf. 11½*

123 A63 5c **blue, olive, ocher & yellow** *(1,805,750)* .20 .20
First day cover 1.00
Inscription block of 4 .35 —

124 A63 11c **dark blue, dark green, emerald & yellow** *(1,583,848)* .20 .20
First day cover 1.00
First day cover, #123-124 1.00
Inscription block of 4 .85 —

First day covers of Nos. 123-124 total 442,696.

World Map, Sinusoidal Projection — A64

UN Emblem — A65

Three Men United Before Globe — A66

Stylized Globe and Weather Vane — A67

Printed by Thomas De La Rue & Co. Ltd., London (2c) and Courvoisier S.A., La Chaux-de-Fonds, Switzerland (7c, 10c and 50c). Panes of 50.
Designed by Ole Hamann (2c), George Hamori (7c, 10c) and Hatim El Mekki (50c).

1964-71 Photo. Unwmk. *Perf. 14*

125 A64 2c **light & dark blue, orange & yellow green** *(3,800,000)* .20 .20
First day cover 1.00
Inscription block of 4 .20 —
a. Perf. 13x13½, *Feb. 24, 1971 (1,500,000)* .20 .20

Perf. 11½

126 A65 7c **dark blue, orange brown & black** *(2,700,000)* .20 .20
First day cover 1.00
Inscription block of 4 .80 —

127 A66 10c **blue green, olive green & black** *(3,200,000)* .20 .25
First day cover 1.00
First day cover, #125-127 5.00
Inscription block of 4 .80 —

128 A67 50c **multicolored** *(2,520,000)* .75 .45
First day cover *(210,713)* 1.00
Inscription block of 4 3.75 —
Nos. 125-128 (4) 1.35 1.10

Issue dates: 50c, Mar. 6; 2c, 7c, 10c, May 29, 1964.
First day covers of 2c, 7c and 10c total 524,073.
See UN Offices in Geneva Nos. 3 and 12.

Arrows Showing Global Flow of Trade — A68

Design: 5c, English inscription.
Issued to commemorate the UN Conference on Trade and Development, Geneva, Mar. 23-June 15.
Printed by Thomas De La Rue & Co., Ltd., London. Panes of 50. Designed by Herbert M. Sanborn and Ole Hamann.

1964, June 15 Photo. Unwmk. *Perf. 13*

129 A68 5c **black, red & yellow** *(1,791,211)* .20 .20
First day cover 1.00
Inscription block of 4 .35 —

130 A68 11c **black, olive & yellow** *(1,529,526)* .20 .20
First day cover 1.00
First day cover, #129-130 1.50
Inscription block of 4 .85 —

First day covers of Nos. 129-130 total 422,358.

Poppy Capsule and Reaching Hands — A69

Design: 11c, Inscribed "Echec au Stupéfiants."
Issued to honor international efforts and achievements in the control of narcotics.
Printed by the Canadian Bank Note Co., Ottawa. Panes of 50. Designed by Kurt Plowitz.

1964, Sept. 21 Engr. Unwmk. *Perf. 12*

131 A69 5c **rose red & black** *(1,508,999)* .20 .20
First day cover 1.00
Inscription block of 4 .45 —

132 A69 11c **emerald & black** *(1,340,691)* .20 .20
First day cover 1.00
First day cover, #131-132 1.75
Inscription block of 4 1.10 —

First day covers of Nos. 131-132 total 445,274.

Padlocked Atomic Blast — A70

Education for Progress — A71

Signing of the nuclear test ban treaty pledging an end to nuclear explosions in the atmosphere, outer space and under water.
Printed by Artia, Prague, Czechoslovakia. Panes of 50. Designed by Ole Hamann.

Litho. and Engr.

1964, Oct. 23 Unwmk. *Perf. 11x11½*

133 A70 5c **dark red & dark brown** *(2,422,789)* .20 .20
First day cover *(298,652)* 1.00
Inscription block of 4 .45 —

1964, Dec. 7 Photo. Unwmk. *Perf. 12½*

Design: 11c, French inscription.
Issued to publicize the UNESCO world campaign for universal literacy and for free compulsory primary education.
Printed by Courvoisier, S. A., La Chaux-de-Fonds, Switzerland. Panes of 50. Designed by Kurt Plowitz.

134 A71 4c **orange, red, bister, green & blue** *(2,375,181)* .20 .20
First day cover 1.00
Inscription block of 4 .40 —

135 A71 5c **bister, red, dark & light blue** *(2,496,877)* .20 .20
First day cover 1.00
Inscription block of 4 .50 —

136 A71 11c **green, light blue, black & rose** *(1,773,645)* .20 .20
First day cover 1.00
First day cover, #134-136 1.25
Inscription block of 4 1.25 —
Nos. 134-136 (3) .60 .60

First day covers of Nos. 134-136 total 727,875.

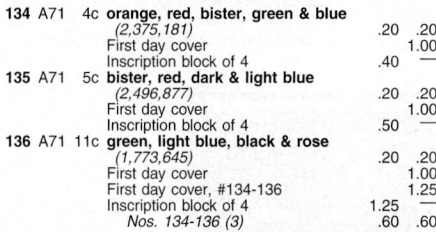

Progress Chart of Special Fund, Key and Globe — A72

UN Emblem, Stylized Leaves and View of Cyprus — A73

Design: 11c, French inscription.
Issued to publicize the Special Fund program to speed economic growth and social advancement in low-income countries.
Printed by the Government Printing Bureau, Tokyo. Panes of 50. Designed by Rashid-ud Din, Pakistan.

1965, Jan. 25 Photo. Unwmk. *Perf. 13½x13*

137 A72 5c **dull blue, dark blue, yellow & red** *(1,949,274)* .20 .20
First day cover 1.00
Inscription block of 4 .40 —

138 A72 11c **yellow green, dark blue, yellow & red** *(1,690,908)* .20 .20
First day cover 1.00
First day cover, #137-138 1.25
Inscription block of 4 .85 —
a. Black omitted (UN emblem on key) —

First day covers of Nos. 137-138 total 490,608.

1965, Mar. 4 Photo. Unwmk. *Perf. 11½*

Design: 11c, French inscription.
Issued to honor the United Nations Peace-keeping Force on Cyprus.
Printed by Courvoisier S.A., Switzerland. Panes of 50. Designed by George Hamori, Australia.

139 A73 5c **orange, olive & black** *(1,887,042)* .20 .20
First day cover 1.00
Inscription block of 4 .40 —

140 A73 11c **yellow green, blue green & black** *(1,691,767)* .20 .20
First day cover 1.00
First day cover, #139-140 1.25
Inscription block of 4 .80 —

First day covers of Nos. 139-140 total 438,059.

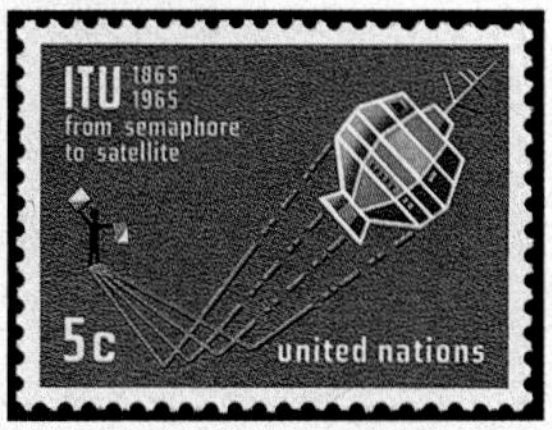

"From Semaphore to Satellite" — A74

Design: 11c, French inscription.
Centenary of the International Telecommunication Union.
Printed by Courvoisier S.A., Switzerland. Panes of 50. Designed by Kurt Plowitz, United States.

1965, May 17 Photo. Unwmk. *Perf. 11½*

141 A74 5c **aquamarine, orange, blue & purple** *(2,432,407)* .20 .20
First day cover 1.00
Inscription block of 4 .40 —

142 A74 11c **light violet, red orange, bister & bright green** *(1,731,070)* .20 .20
First day cover 1.00
First day cover, #141-142 1.25
Inscription block of 4 .80 —

First day covers of Nos. 141-142 total 434,393.

ICY Emblem — A75

Design: 15c, French inscription.
20th anniversary of the United Nations and International Cooperation Year.
Printed by Bradbury, Wilkinson and Co., Ltd., England. Panes of 50. Designed by Olav Mathiesen, Denmark.

1965, June 26 Engr. Unwmk. *Perf. 14x13½*

143 A75 5c **dark blue** *(2,282,452)* .20 .20
First day cover 1.00
Inscription block of 4 .40 —

144 A75 15c **lilac rose** *(1,993,562)* .20 .20
First day cover 1.00
First day cover, #143-144 1.00
Inscription block of 4 1.00 —

Souvenir Sheet

145 A75 Sheet of two *(1,928,366)* .35 .35
First day cover 1.00

No. 145 contains one each of Nos. 143-144 with dark blue and ocher marginal inscription, ocher edging. Size: 92x70mm.
First day covers of Nos. 143-145 total: New York, 748,876; San Francisco, 301,435.

"Peace" — A76

Opening Words, UN Charter — A77

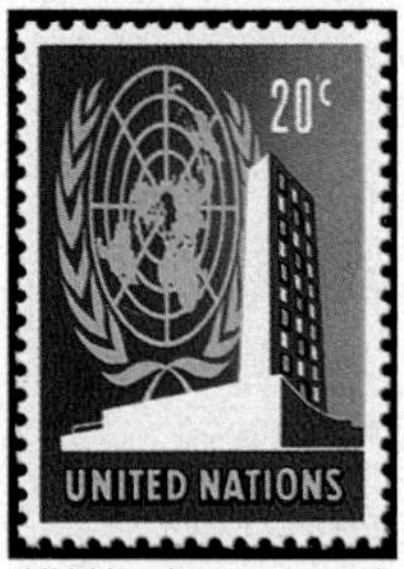

UN Headquarters and Emblem — A78

UN Emblem — A79

UN Emblem Encircled — A80

Printed by Government Printing Bureau, Tokyo (1c); Government Printing Office, Austria (15c, 20c); Government Printing Office (Bundesdruckerei), Berlin (25c), and Courvoisier S.A., Switzerland ($1). Panes of 50.

Designed by Kurt Plowitz US (1c); Olav S. Mathiesen, Denmark (15c); Vergniaud Pierre-Noel, US (20c); Rashid-ud Din, Pakistan (25c), and Ole Hamann, Denmark ($1).

1965-66 Photo. Unwmk. *Perf. 13½x13*

146 A76 1c **vermilion, blue, black & gray** *(7,000,000)* .20 .20
First day cover 1.00
Inscription block of 4 .20 —

Perf. 14

147 A77 15c **olive bister, dull yellow, black & deep claret** *(2,500,000)* .25 .20
First day cover 1.00
Inscription block of 4 1.10 —

Perf. 12

148 A78 20c **dark blue, blue, red & yellow** *(3,000,000)* .30 .25
First day cover 1.00
First day cover, #147-148 1.25
Inscription block of 4 1.25 —
a. Yellow omitted —

Litho. and Embossed

Perf. 14

149 A79 25c **light & dark blue** *(3,200,000)* .35 .30
First day cover 1.25
First day cover, #146, 149 1.50
Inscription block of 4 1.50 —
Inscription block of 6, "Bundesdruckerei Berlin" imprint 20.00
First day cover, "Bundesdruckerei," margin block of 6 32.50
a. Tagged (Berlin printing) 10.00 10.00

Photo.

Perf. 11½

150 A80 $1 **aquamarine & sapphire** *(2,570,000)* 1.75 1.60
First day cover *(181,510)* 2.00
Inscription block of 4 7.75 —
Nos. 146-150 (5) 2.85 2.55

Issued: 1c, 25c, Sept. 20, 1965; 15c, 20c, Oct. 25, 1965; $1, Mar. 25, 1966.
First day covers of Nos. 146 and 149 total 443,964. Those of Nos. 147-148 total 457,596.
The 25c has the marginal inscription (UN emblem and "1965") in two sizes: 1st printing (with Bundesdruckerei imprint), 6mm in diameter; 2nd printing, 8mm. In 1st printing, "halo" of UN emblem is larger, overlapping "25c."
See UN Offices in Geneva Nos. 5, 9 and 11.

Fields and People — A81

Globe and Flags of UN Members — A82

Design: 11c, French inscription.
Issued to emphasize the importance of the world's population growth and its problems and to call attention to population trends and development.
Printed by Government Printing Office, Austria. Panes of 50. Designed by Olav S. Mathiesen, Denmark.

1965, Nov. 29 Photo. Unwmk. *Perf. 12*

151 A81 4c **multicolored** *(1,966,033)* .20 .20
First day cover 1.00
Inscription block of 4 .25 —

152 A81 5c **multicolored** *(2,298,731)* .20 .20
First day cover 1.00
Inscription block of 4 .30 —

153 A81 11c **multicolored** *(1,557,589)* .20 .20
First day cover 1.00
First day cover, #151-153 1.75
Inscription block of 4 .90 —
Nos. 151-153 (3) .60 .60

First day covers of Nos. 151-153 total 710,507.

1966, Jan. 31 Photo. Unwmk. *Perf. 11½*

Design: 15c, French inscription.
Issued to honor the World Federation of United Nations Associations.
Printed by Courvoisier S.A., Switzerland. Panes of 50. Designed by Olav S. Mathiesen, Denmark.

154 A82 5c **multicolored** *(2,462,215)* .20 .20
First day cover 1.00
Inscription block of 4 .35 —

155 A82 15c **multicolored** *(1,643,661)* .20 .20
First day cover 1.00
First day cover, #154-155 1.25
Inscription block of 4 .90 —

First day covers of Nos. 154-155 total 474,154.

WHO Headquarters, Geneva — A83

Design: 11c, French inscription.
Issued to commemorate the opening of the World Health Organization Headquarters, Geneva.
Printed by Courvoisier, S.A., Switzerland. Panes of 50. Designed by Rashid-ud Din.

1966, May 26 Photo. *Perf. 12½x12*

Granite Paper

156 A83 5c **lt & dk blue, orange, green & bister** *(2,079,893)* .20 .20
First day cover 1.00
Inscription block of 4 .45 —

157 A83 11c **orange, lt & dk blue, green & bister** *(1,879,879)* .20 .20
First day cover 1.00
First day cover, #156-157 1.25
Inscription block of 4 .90 —

First day covers of Nos. 156-157 total 466,171.

Coffee — A84

UN Observer — A85

Design: 11c, Spanish inscription.
Issued to commemorate the International Coffee Agreement of 1962.
Printed by the Government Printing Bureau, Tokyo. Panes of 50. Designed by Rashid-ud Din, Pakistan.

1966, Sept. 19 Photo. *Perf. 13½x13*

158 A84 5c **orange, lt blue, green, red & dk brown** *(2,020,308)* .20 .20
First day cover 1.00
Inscription block of 4 .40 —

159 A84 11c **lt blue, yellow, green, red & dk brown** *(1,888,682)* .20 .20
First day cover 1.00
First day cover, #158-159 1.00
Inscription block of 4 .90 —

First day covers of Nos. 158-159 total 435,886.

1966, Oct. 24 Photo. *Perf. 11½*

Issued to honor the Peace Keeping United Nation Observers.
Printed by Courvoisier, S.A. Panes of 50. Designed by Ole S. Hamann.

Granite Paper

160 A85 15c **steel blue, orange, black & green** *(1,889,809)* .25 .20
First day cover *(255,326)* 1.00
Inscription block of 4 1.40 —

Children of Various Races — A86

Designs: 5c, Children riding in locomotive and tender. 11c, ;hildren in open railroad car playing medical team (French ·scription).

20th anniversary of the United Nations Children's Fund JNICEF).

Printed by Thomas De La Rue & Co., Ltd. Panes of 50. ·esigned by Kurt Plowitz.

966, Nov. 28 Litho. *Perf. 13x13½*

61 A86 4c **pink & multi** *(2,334,989)* .20 .20
First day cover 1.00
Inscription block of 4 .30 —
62 A86 5c **pale green & multi** *(2,746,941)* .20 .20
First day cover 1.00
Inscription block of 4 .35 —
a. Yellow omitted — —
63 A86 11c **light ultramarine & multi** *(2,123,841)* .20 .20
First day cover 1.00
First day cover, #161-163 1.00
Inscription block of 4 .85 —
b. Dark blue omitted —
Nos. 161-163 (3) .60 .60

First day covers of Nos. 161-163 total 987,271.

Hand Rolling up Sleeve and Chart Showing Progress — A87

Design: 11c, French inscription.
United Nations Development Program.
Printed by Courvoisier, S.A. Panes of 50. Designed by Olav ;. Mathiesen.

967, Jan. 23 Photo. *Perf. 12½*

64 A87 5c **green, yellow, purple & orange** *(2,204,679)* .20 .20
First day cover 1.00
Inscription block of 4 .35 —
65 A87 11c **blue, chocolate, light green & orange** *(1,946,159)* .20 .20
First day cover 1.00
First day cover, #164-165 1.00
Inscription block of 4 1.00 —

First day covers of Nos. 164-165 total 406,011.

Type of 1962 and

UN Headquarters, NY, and World Map — A88

Printed by Courvoisier, S.A. Panes of 50. Designed by Jozsef /ertel, Hungary (1½c); Renato Ferrini, Italy (5c).

967 Photo. *Perf. 11½*

66 A88 1½c **ultramarine, black, orange & ocher** *(4,000,000)* .20 .20
First day cover *(199,751)* 1.00
Inscription block of 4 .20 —

Size: 33x23mm

67 A53 5c **red brown, brown & orange yellow** *(5,500,000)* .20 .20
First day cover *(212,544)* 1.00
Inscription block of 4 .40 —

Issue dates: 1½c, Mar. 17; 5c, Jan. 23.
For 5c of type A88, see UN Offices in Geneva No. 1.

Fireworks — A89

Design: 11c, French inscription.
Issued to honor all nations which gained independence since 1945.
Printed by Harrison & Sons, Ltd. Panes of 50. Designed by Rashid-ud Din.

1967, Mar. 17 Photo. *Perf. 14x14½*

168 A89 5c **dark blue & multi** *(2,445,955)* .20 .20
First day cover 1.00
Inscription block of 4 .35 —
169 A89 11c **brown lake & multi** *(2,011,004)* .20 .20
First day cover 1.00
First day cover, #168-169 1.00
Inscription block of 4 .85 —

First day covers of Nos. 168-169 total 390,499.

"Peace" — A90

UN Pavilion, EXPO '67 — A91

Designs: 5c, Justice. 10c, Fraternity. 15c, Truth.
EXPO '67, International Exhibition, Montreal, Apr. 28-Oct. 27, 1967.
Under special agreement with the Canadian Government Nos. 170-174 were valid for postage only on mail posted at the UN pavilion during the Fair. The denominations are expressed in Canadian currency.
Printed by British American Bank Note Co., Ltd., Ottawa. The 8c was designed by Olav S. Mathiesen after a photograph by Michael Drummond. The others were adapted by Ole S. Hamann from reliefs by Ernest Cormier on doors of General Assembly Hall, presented to UN by Canada.

1967, Apr. 28 Engr. & Litho. *Perf. 11*

170 A90 4c **red & red brown** *(2,464,813)* .20 .20
First day cover 1.00
Inscription block of 4 .30 —
171 A90 5c **blue & red brown** *(2,177,073)* .20 .20
First day cover 1.00
Inscription block of 4 .30 —

Litho.

172 A91 8c **multicolored** *(2,285,440)* .20 .20
First day cover 1.00
Inscription block of 4 .50 —

Engr. and Litho.

173 A90 10c **green & red brown** *(1,955,352)* .20 .20
First day cover 1.00
Inscription block of 4 .75 —
174 A90 15c **dark brown & red brown** *(1,899,185)* .20 .20
First day cover 1.00
First day cover, #170-174 1.25
Inscription block of 4 .85
Nos. 170-174 (5) 1.00 1.00

First day covers of Nos. 170-174 total 901,625.

Luggage Tags and UN Emblem A92

Issued to publicize International Tourist Year, 1967.
Printed by Government Printing Office, Berlin. Panes of 50. Designed by David Dewhurst.

1967, June 19 Litho. *Perf. 14*

175 A92 5c **reddish brown & multi** *(2,593,782)* .20 .20
First day cover 1.00
Inscription block of 4 .35 —
176 A92 15c **ultramarine & multi** *(1,940,457)* .25 .20
First day cover 1.00
First day cover, #175-176 1.25
Inscription block of 4 1.10 —

First day covers of Nos. 175-176 total 382,886.

Quotation from Isaiah 2:4 — A93

Design: 13c, French inscription.
Issued to publicize the UN General Assembly's resolutions on general and complete disarmament and for suspension of nuclear and thermonuclear tests.
Printed by Heraclio Fournier S.A., Spain. Panes of 50. Designed by Ole Hamann.

1967, Oct. 24 Photo. *Perf. 14*

177 A93 6c **ultramarine, yellow, gray & brown** *(2,462,277)* .20 .20
First day cover 1.00
Inscription block of 4 .45 —
178 A93 13c **magenta, yellow, gray & brown** *(2,055,541)* .20 .20
First day cover 1.00
First day cover, #177-178 1.00
Inscription block of 4 .95 —

First day covers of Nos. 177-178 total 403,414.

Art at UN Issue

Miniature Sheet

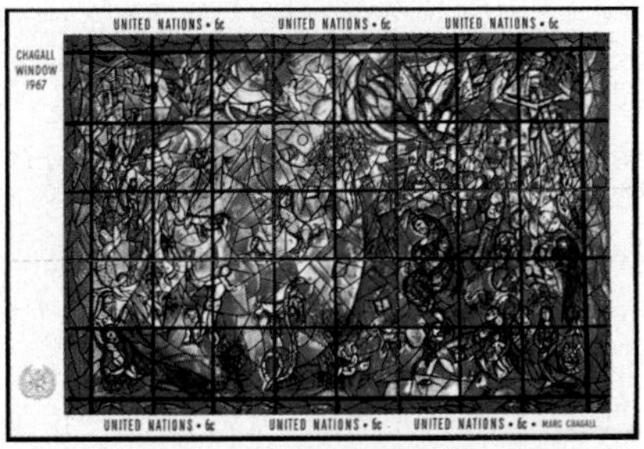

Stained Glass Memorial Window by Marc Chagall, at UN Headquarters — A94

"The Kiss of Peace" by Marc Chagall — A95

Printed by Joh. Enschede and Sons, Netherlands. No. 180 issued in panes of 50. Design adapted by Ole Hamann from photograph by Hans Lippmann.

Sizes: a, 41x46mm. b, 24x46mm. c, 41x33½mm. d, 36x33½mm. e, 29x33½mm. f, 41½x47mm.

1967, Nov. 17 Litho. *Rouletted 9*

179 A94 6c Sheet of 6, #a.-f. *(3,178,656)* .40 .40
First day cover 1.00

Perf. 13x13½

180 A95 6c **multicolored** *(3,438,497)* .20 .20
First day cover 1.00
Inscription block of 4 .50 —

No. 179 contains six 6c stamps, each rouletted on 3 sides, imperf. on fourth side. Size: 124x80mm. On Nos. 179a-179c, "United Nations 6c" appears at top; on Nos. 179d-179f, at bottom. No. 179f includes name "Marc Chagall."

First day covers of Nos. 179-180 total 617,225.

Globe and Major UN Organs — A96

Statue by Henrik Starcke — A97

Design: 13c, French inscriptions.
Issued to honor the United Nations Secretariat.
Printed by Courvoisier, S. A., Switzerland. Panes of 50. Designed by Rashid-ud Din.

1968, Jan. 16 Photo. *Perf. 11½*

181 A96 6c **multicolored** *(2,772,965)* .20 .20
First day cover 1.00
Inscription block of 4 .40 —
182 A96 13c **multicolored** *(2,461,992)* .20 .20
First day cover 1.00
First day cover, #181-182 1.00
Inscription block of 4 1.00 —

First day covers of Nos. 181-182 total 411,119.

Art at UN Issue

The 6c is part of the "Art at the UN" series. The 75c belongs to the regular definitive series. The teakwood Starcke statue, which stands in the Trusteeship Council Chamber, represents mankind's search for freedom and happiness.
Printed by Courvoisier, S.A., Switzerland. Panes of 50.

1968, Mar. 1 Photo. *Perf. 11½*

183 A97 6c **blue & multi** *(2,537,320)* .20 .20
First day cover 1.00
Inscription block of 4 .50 —
184 A97 75c **rose lake & multi** *(2,300,000)* 1.10 .90
First day cover 1.25
First day cover, #183-184 5.00
Inscription block of 4 5.00 —

First day covers of Nos. 183-184 total 413,286.
See UN Offices in Geneva No. 13.

Factories and Chart — A98

UN Headquarters — A99

Design: 13c, French inscription ("ONUDI," etc.).
Issued to publicize the UN Industrial Development Organization.
Printed by Canadian Bank Note Co., Ltd., Ottawa. Panes of 50. Designed by Ole Hamann.

1968, Apr. 18 Litho. *Perf. 12*

185 A98 6c **greenish blue, lt greenish blue, black & dull claret** *(2,439,656)* .20 .20
First day cover 1.00
Inscription block of 4 .35 —
186 A98 13c **dull red brown, light red brown, black & ultra** *(2,192,453)* .20 .20
First day cover 1.00
First day cover, #185-186 1.00
Inscription block of 4 .80 —

First day covers of Nos. 185-186 total 396,447.

1968, May 31 Litho. *Perf. 12x13½*

Printed by Aspioti Elka-Chrome Mines, Ltd., Athens. Panes of 50. Designed by Olav S. Mathiesen.

187 A99 6c **green, blue, black & gray** *(4,000,000)* .20 .20
First day cover *(241,179)* 1.00
Inscription block of 4 .50 —

Radarscope and Globe — A100

Design: 20c, French inscription.
Issued to publicize World Weather Watch, a new weather system directed by the World Meteorological Organization.
Printed by the Government Printing Bureau, Tokyo. Designed by George A. Gundersen and George Fanais, Canada.

1968, Sept. 19 Photo. *Perf. 13x13½*

188 A100 6c **green, black, ocher, red & blue** *(2,245,078)* .20 .20
First day cover 1.00
Inscription block of 4 .40 —
189 A100 20c **lilac, black, ocher, red & blue** *(2,069,966)* .30 .20
First day cover 1.00
First day cover, #188-189 1.25
Inscription block of 4 1.40 —

First day covers of Nos. 188-189 total 620,510.

Human Rights Flame — A101

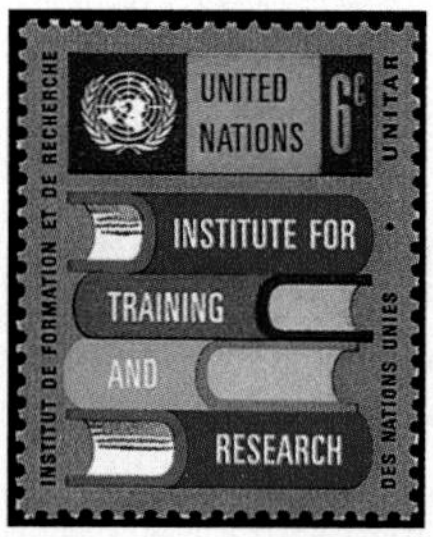

Books and UN Emblem — A102

Design: 13c, French inscription.
Issued for International Human Rights Year, 1968.
Printed by Harrison & Sons, Ltd., England. Designed by Rob ert Perrot, France.

1968, Nov. 22 Photo.; Foil Embossed *Perf. 12½*

190 A101 6c **bright blue, deep ultra & gold** *(2,394,235)* .20 .2
First day cover 1.0
Inscription block of 4 .40 —
191 A101 13c **rose red, dark red & gold** *(2,284,838)* .20 .2
First day cover 1.0
First day cover, #190-191 1.0
Inscription block of 4 .85 —

First day covers of Nos. 190-191 total 519,012.

1969, Feb. 10 Litho. *Perf. 13½*

Design: 13c, French inscription in center, denomination pane at bottom.
United Nations Institute for Training and Research (UNITAR)
Printed by the Government Printing Bureau, Tokyo. Panes of 50. Designed by Olav S. Mathiesen.

192 A102 6c **yellow green & multi** *(2,436,559)* .20 .2
First day cover 1.0
Inscription block of 4 .35 —
193 A102 13c **bluish lilac & multi** *(1,935,151)* .25 .2
First day cover 1.0
First day cover, #192-193 1.0
Inscription block of 4 1.00 —

First day covers of Nos. 192-193 total 439,606.

UN Building, Santiago, Chile A103

Design: 15c, Spanish inscription.
The UN Building in Santiago, Chile, is the seat of the UN Economic Commission for Latin America and of the Latin American Institute for Economic and Social Planning.
Printed by Government Printing Office, Berlin. Panes of 50. Design by Ole Hamann, adapted from a photograph.

1969, Mar. 14 Litho. *Perf. 14*

194 A103 6c **light blue, violet blue & light green** *(2,543,992)* .20 .2
First day cover 1.00
Inscription block of 4 .35 —
195 A103 15c **pink, cream & red brown** *(2,030,733)* .25 .20
First day cover 1.00
First day cover, #194-195 1.00
Inscription block of 4 1.10 —

First day covers of Nos. 194-195 total 398,227.

"UN" and UN Emblem — A104

UN Emblem and Scales of — A105

Printed by Government Printing Bureau, Tokyo. Panes of 50. Designed by Leszek Holdanowicz and Marek Freudenreich, Poland.

969, Mar. 14 Photo. *Perf. 13½*

96 A104 13c **bright blue, black & gold** *(4,000,000)* .20 .20
First day cover *(177,793)* 1.00
Inscription block of 4 .90 —

See UN Offices in Geneva No. 7.

969, Apr. 21 Photo. *Perf. 11½*

Design: 13c, French inscription.
20th anniversary session of the UN International Law Commission.
Printed by Courvoisier S.A., Switzerland. Panes of 50. Designed by Robert Perrot, France.

Granite Paper

97 A105 6c **bright green, ultra & gold** *(2,501,492)* .20 .20
First day cover 1.00
Inscription block of 4 .40 —
98 A105 13c **crimson, lilac & gold** *(1,966,994)* .20 .20
First day cover 1.00
First day cover, #197-198 1.00
Inscription block of 4 .90 —

First day covers of Nos. 197-198 total 439,324.

Allegory of Labor, Emblems of UN and ILO — A106

Design: 20c, French inscription.
Printed by Government Printing Bureau, Tokyo. Panes of 50. Designed by Nejat M. Gur, Turkey.
Issued to publicize "Labor and Development" and to commemorate the 50th anniversary of the International Labor Organization.

1969, June 5 Photo. *Perf. 13*

199 A106 6c **blue, deep blue, yellow & gold** *(2,078,381)* .20 .20
First day cover 1.00
Inscription block of 4 .40 —
200 A106 20c **orange vermilion, magenta, yellow & gold** *(1,751,100)* .25 .20
First day cover 1.00
First day cover, #199-200 1.25
Inscription block of 4 1.40 —

First day covers of Nos. 199-200 total 514,155.

Art at UN Issue

Ostrich, Tunisian Mosaic, 3rd Century — A107

Design: 13c, Pheasant; French inscription.
The mosaic "The Four Seasons and the Genius of the Year" was found at Haidra, Tunisia. It is now at the Delegates' North Lounge, UN Headquarters, New York.
Printed by Heraclio Fournier, S. A., Spain. Panes of 50. Designed by Olav S. Mathiesen.

1969, Nov. 21 Photo. *Perf. 14*

201 A107 6c **blue & multi** *(2,280,702)* .20 .20
First day cover 1.00
Inscription block of 4 .35 —
202 A107 13c **red & multi** *(1,918,554)* .20 .20
First day cover 1.00
First day cover, #201-202 1.00
Inscription block of 4 .90 —

First day covers of Nos. 201-202 total 612,981.

Art at UN Issue

Peace Bell, Gift of Japanese — A108

Design: 25c, French inscription.
The Peace Bell was a gift of the people of Japan in 1954, cast from donated coins and metals. It is housed in a Japanese cypress structure at UN Headquarters, New York.
Printed by Government Printing Bureau, Tokyo. Panes of 50. Designed by Ole Hamann.

1970, Mar. 13 Photo. *Perf. 13½x13*

203 A108 6c **violet blue & multi** *(2,604,253)* .20 .20
First day cover 1.00
Inscription block of 4 .40 —
204 A108 25c **claret & multi** *(2,090,185)* .35 .25
First day cover 1.25
First day cover, #203-204 1.25
Inscription block of 4 1.75 —

First day covers of Nos. 203-204 total 502,384.

Mekong River, Power Lines and Map of Mekong Delta — A109

Design: 13c, French inscription.
Issued to publicize the Lower Mekong Basin Development project under UN auspices.
Printed by Heraclio Fournier, S.A., Spain. Panes of 50. Designed by Ole Hamann.

1970, Mar. 13 *Perf. 14*

205 A109 6c **dark blue & multi** *(2,207,309)* .20 .20
First day cover 1.00
Inscription block of 4 .35 —
206 A109 13c **deep plum & multi** *(1,889,023)* .20 .20
First day cover 1.00
First day cover, #205-206 1.00
Inscription block of 4 .90 —

First day covers of Nos. 205-206 total 522,218.

"Fight Cancer" — A110

Design: 13c, French inscription.
Issued to publicize the fight against cancer in connection with the 10th International Cancer Congress of the International Union Against Cancer, Houston, Texas, May 22-29.
Printed by Government Printing Office, Berlin. Panes of 50. Designed by Leonard Mitchell.

1970, May 22 Litho. *Perf. 14*

207 A110 6c **blue & black** *(2,157,742)* .20 .20
First day cover 1.00
Inscription block of 4 .35 —
208 A110 13c **olive & black** *(1,824,714)* .20 .20
First day cover 1.00
First day cover, #207-208 1.00
Inscription block of 4 .85 —

First day covers of Nos. 207-208 total 444,449.

UN Emblem and Olive Branch — A111

UN Emblem — A112

Design: 13c, French inscription.
25th anniv. of the UN. First day covers were postmarked at UN Headquarters, NY, and at San Francisco.
Printed by Courvoisier, S.A., Switzerland. Designed by Ole Hamann and Olav S. Mathiesen (souvenir sheet).

1970, June 26 Photo. *Perf. 11½*

209 A111 6c **red, gold, dark & light blue** *(2,365,229)* .20 .20
First day cover 1.00
Inscription block of 4 .35 —
210 A111 13c **dark blue, gold, green & red** *(1,861,613)* .20 .20
First day cover 1.00
Inscription block of 4 .80 —

Perf. 12½

211 A112 25c **dark blue, gold & light blue** *(1,844,669)* .35 .25
First day cover 1.25
First day cover, #209-211 1.50
Inscription block of 4 1.50 —
Nos. 209-211 (3) .75 .65

Souvenir Sheet

Imperf

212 Sheet of 3 *(1,923,639)* .75 .75
a. A111 6c **red, gold & multicolored** .20 .20
b. A111 13c **violet blue, gold & multi** .20 .20
c. A112 25c **violet blue, gold & light blue** .35 .35
First day cover 1.25

No. 212 contains 3 imperf. stamps, gold border and violet blue marginal inscription. Size: 94½x78mm.
First day covers of Nos. 209-212 total: New York, 846,389; San Francisco, 471,100.

Scales, Olive Branch and Symbol of Progress — A113

Sea Bed, School of Fish and Underwater Research — A114

Design: 13c, French inscription.
Issued to publicize "Peace, Justice and Progress" in connection with the 25th anniversary of the United Nations.
Printed by Government Printing Bureau, Tokyo. Panes of 50. Designed by Ole Hamann.

1970, Nov. 20 Photo. *Perf. 13½*

213 A113 6c **gold & multi** *(1,921,441)* .20 .20
First day cover 1.00
Inscription block of 4 .40 —
214 A113 13c **silver & multi** *(1,663,669)* .20 .20
First day cover 1.00
First day cover, #213-214 1.00
Inscription block of 4 1.00 —

First day covers of Nos. 213-214 total 521,419.

1971, Jan. 25 Photo. & Engr. *Perf. 13*

Issued to publicize peaceful uses of the sea bed.
Printed by Setelipaino, Finland. Panes of 50. Designed by Pentti Rahikainen, Finland.

215 A114 6c **blue & multi** *(2,354,179)* .20 .20
First day cover *(405,554)* 1.00
Inscription block of 4 .50 —

See UN Offices in Geneva No. 15.

Refugees, Sculpture by Kaare K. Nygaard — A115

Wheat and Globe — A116

International support for refugees.
Printed by Joh. Enschede and Sons, Netherlands. Panes of 50. Designed by Dr. Kaare K. Nygaard and Martin J. Weber.

1971, Mar. 2 **Litho.** ***Perf. 13x12½***

216 A115 6c **brown, ocher & black** *(2,247,232)* .20 .20
First day cover 1.00
Inscription block of 4 .30 —
217 A115 13c **ultramarine, greenish blue & black** *(1,890,048)* .20 .20
First day cover 1.00
First day cover, #216-217 1.00
Inscription block of 4 .90 —

First day covers of Nos. 216-217 total 564,785.
See UN Offices in Geneva No. 16.

1971, Apr. 13 **Photo.** ***Perf. 14***

Publicizing the UN World Food Program.
Printed by Heraclio Fournier, S.A., Spain. Panes of 50. Designed by Olav S. Mathiesen.

218 A116 13c **red & multicolored** *(1,968,542)* .20 .20
First day cover *(409,404)* 1.00
Inscription block of 4 .90 —

See UN Offices in Geneva No. 17.

UPU Headquarters, Bern — A117

Opening of new Universal Postal Union Headquarters, Bern.
Printed by Courvoisier, S.A. Panes of 50. Designed by Olav S. Mathiesen.

1971, May 28 **Photo.** ***Perf. 11½***

219 A117 20c **brown orange & multi** *(1,857,841)* .35 .25
First day cover *(375,119)* 1.00
Inscription block of 4 1.40 —

See UN Offices in Geneva No. 18.

A118

"Eliminate Racial Discrimination" A119

International Year Against Racial Discrimination.
Printed by Government Printing Bureau, Tokyo. Panes of 50. Designers: Daniel Gonzague (8c); Ole Hamann (13c).

1971, Sept. 21 **Photo.** ***Perf. 13½***

220 A118 8c **yellow green & multi** *(2,324,349)* .20 .20
First day cover 1.00
Inscription block of 4 .60 —
221 A119 13c **blue & multi** *(1,852,093)* .20 .20
First day cover 1.00
First day cover, #220-221 1.00
Inscription block of 4 .90 —

First day covers of Nos. 220-221 total 461,103.
See UN Offices in Geneva Nos. 19-20.

UN Headquarters, New York — A120

UN Emblem and Symbolic Flags — A121

No. 222 printed by Heraclio Fournier, S.A., Spain. No. 223 printed by Government Printing Bureau, Tokyo. Panes of 50. Designers: O. S. Mathiesen (8c); Robert Perrot (60c).

1971, Oct. 22 **Photo.** ***Perf. 13½***

222 A120 8c **violet blue & multi** *(5,600,000)* .20 .20
First day cover 1.00
Inscription block of 4 .60 —

Perf. 13

223 A121 60c **ultra & multi** *(3,500,000)+* .80 .80
First day cover 1.25
First day cover, #222-223 3.00
Inscription block of 4 4.00 —

First day covers of Nos. 222-223 total 336,013.

Maia, by Pablo Picasso — A122

To publicize the UN International School.
Printed by Courvoisier, S.A. Panes of 50. Designed by Ole Hamann.

1971, Nov. 19 **Photo.** ***Perf. 11½***

224 A122 8c **olive & multi** *(2,668,214)* .20 .20
First day cover 1.00
Inscription block of 4 .45 —
225 A122 21c **ultra & multi** *(2,040,754)* .30 .20
First day cover 1.00
First day cover, #224-225 1.75
Inscription block of 4 1.50 —

First day covers of Nos. 224-225 total 579,594.
See UN Offices in Geneva No. 21.

Letter Changing Hands A123

Printed by Bundesdruckerei, Berlin. Panes of 50. Designed by Olav S. Mathiesen.

1972, Jan. 5 **Litho.** ***Perf. 14***

226 A123 95c **carmine & multi** *(2,000,000)* 1.30 1.10
First day cover *(188,193)* 1.25
Inscription block of 4 6.00 —

"No More Nuclear Weapons" A124

To promote non-proliferation of nuclear weapons.
Printed by Heraclio Fournier, S. A., Spain. Panes of 50. Designed by Arne Johnson, Norway.

1972, Feb. 14 **Photo.** ***Perf. 13½x14***

227 A124 8c **dull rose, black, blue & gray** *(2,311,515)* .20 .20
First day cover *(268,789)* 1.00
Inscription block of 4 .55 —

See UN Offices in Geneva No. 23.

Proportions of Man, by Leonardo da Vinci — A125

"Human Environment" — A126

World Health Day, Apr. 7.
Printed by Setelipaino, Finland. Panes of 50. Designed by George Hamori.

1972, Apr. 7 **Litho. & Engr.** ***Perf. 13x13½***

228 A125 15c **black & multi** *(1,788,962)* .25 .20
First day cover *(322,724)* 1.00
Inscription block of 4 1.00 —

See UN Offices in Geneva No. 24.

1972, June 5 **Litho. & Embossed** ***Perf. 12½x14***

UN Conf. on Human Environment, Stockholm, June 5-16, 1972.
Printed by Joh. Enschede and Sons, Netherlands. Panes of 50. Designed by Robert Perrot.

229 A126 8c **red, buff, green & blue** *(2,124,604)* .20 .20
First day cover 1.00
Inscription block of 4 .50 —
230 A126 15c **blue green, buff, green & blue** *(1,589,943)* .25 .20
First day cover 1.00
First day cover, #229-230 1.00
Inscription block of 4 1.25 —

First day covers of Nos. 229-230 total 437,222.
See UN Offices in Geneva Nos. 25-26.

"Europe" and UN Emblem — A127

The Five Continents by José Maria Sert — A128

Economic Commission for Europe, 25th anniversary.
Printed by Government Printing Bureau, Tokyo. Panes of 50.
esigned by Angel Medina Medina.

972, Sept. 11 Litho. *Perf. 13x13½*
31 A127 21c **yellow brown & multi** *(1,748,675)* .35 .25
First day cover *(271,128)* 1.00
Inscription block of 4 1.60 —

See UN Offices in Geneva No. 27.

Art at UN Issue

Design shows part of ceiling mural of the Council Hall, Palais es Nations, Geneva. It depicts the five continents joining in pace.
Printed by Courvoisier, S. A. Panes of 50. Designed by Ole lamann.

972, Nov. 17 Photo. *Perf. 12x12½*
32 A128 8c **gold, brown & golden brown** *(2,573,478)* .20 .20
First day cover 1.00
Inscription block of 4 .50 —
33 A128 15c **gold, blue green & brown** *(1,768,432)* .30 .20
First day cover 1.00
First day cover, #232-233 1.00
Inscription block of 4 1.25 —

First day covers of Nos. 232-233 total 589,817.
See UN Offices in Geneva Nos. 28-29.

Olive Branch and Broken Sword — A129

Poppy Capsule and Skull — A130

Disarmament Decade, 1970-79.
Printed by Ajans-Turk, Turkey. Panes of 50. Designed by Kurt lowitz.

1973, Mar. 9 Litho. *Perf. 13½x13*
34 A129 8c **blue & multi** *(2,272,716)* .20 .20
First day cover 1.00
Inscription block of 4 .50 —
35 A129 15c **lilac rose & multi** *(1,643,712)* .35 .20
First day cover 1.00
First day cover, #234-235 1.00
Inscription block of 4 1.50 —

First day covers of Nos. 234-235 total 548,336.
See UN Offices in Geneva Nos. 30-31.

1973, Apr. 13 Photo. *Perf. 13½*

Fight against drug abuse.
Printed by Heraclio Fournier, S.A., Spain. Panes of 50. esigned by George Hamori.

236 A130 8c **deep orange & multi** *(1,846,780)* .20 .20
First day cover 1.00
Inscription block of 4 .60 —
237 A130 15c **pink & multi** *(1,466,806)* .35 .25
First day cover 1.00
First day cover, #236-237 1.00
Inscription block of 4 1.50 —

First day covers of Nos. 236-237 total 394,468.
See UN Offices in Geneva No. 32.

Honeycomb — A131

5th anniversary of the United Nations Volunteer Program.
Printed by Heraclio Fournier, S.A., Spain. Panes of 50. Designed by Courvoisier, S.A.

1973, May 25 Photo. *Perf. 14*
238 A131 8c **olive bister & multi** *(1,868,176)* .20 .20
First day cover 1.00
Inscription block of 4 .50 —
239 A131 21c **gray blue & multi** *(1,530,114)* .35 .25
First day cover 1.00
First day cover, #238-239 1.25
Inscription block of 4 1.50 —

First day covers of Nos. 238-239 total 396,517.
See UN Offices in Geneva No. 33.

Map of Africa with Namibia — A132

To publicize Namibia (South-West Africa) for which the UN General Assembly ended the mandate of South Africa and established the UN Council for Namibia to administer the territory until independence.
Printed by Heraclio Fournier, S.A., Spain. Panes of 50. Designed by George Hamori.

1973, Oct. 1 Photo. *Perf. 14*
240 A132 8c **emerald & multi** *(1,775,260)* .20 .20
First day cover 1.00
Inscription block of 4 .50 —
241 A132 15c **bright rose & multi** *(1,687,782)* .35 .25
First day cover 1.00
First day cover, #240-241 1.00
Inscription block of 4 1.50 —

First day covers of Nos. 240-241 total 385,292.
See UN Offices in Geneva No. 34.

UN Emblem and Human Rights Flame — A133

25th anniversary of the adoption and proclamation of the Universal Declaration of Human Rights.
Printed by Government Printing Bureau, Tokyo. Panes of 50. Designed by Alfred Guerra.

1973, Nov. 16 Photo. *Perf. 13½*
242 A133 8c **deep carmine & multi** *(2,026,245)* .20 .20
First day cover 1.00
Inscription block of 4 .50 —
243 A133 21c **blue green & multi** *(1,558,201)* .35 .25
First day cover 1.00
First day cover, #242-243 1.25
Inscription block of 4 1.50 —

First day covers of Nos. 242-243 total 398,511.
See UN Offices in Geneva Nos. 35-36.

ILO Headquarters, Geneva — A134

New Headquarters of International Labor Organization.
Printed by Heraclio Fournier, S.A., Spain. Panes of 50. Designed by Henry Bencsath.

1974, Jan. 11 Photo. *Perf. 14*
244 A134 10c **ultra & multi** *(1,734,423)* .20 .20
First day cover 1.00
Inscription block of 4 .90 —
245 A134 21c **blue green & multi** *(1,264,447)* .35 .25
First day cover 1.00
First day cover, #244-245 1.25
Inscription block of 4 1.75 —

First day covers of Nos. 244-245 total 282,284.
See UN Offices in Geneva Nos. 37-38.

UPU Emblem and Post Horn Encircling Globe — A135

Centenary of Universal Postal Union.
Printed by Ashton-Potter Ltd., Canada. Panes of 50. Designed by Arne Johnson.

1974, Mar. 22 Litho. *Perf. 12½*
246 A135 10c **gold & multi** *(2,104,919)* .25 .20
First day cover *(342,774)* 1.00
Inscription block of 4 1.10 —

See UN Offices in Geneva Nos. 39-40.

Art at UN Issue

Peace Mural, by Candido Portinari — A136

The mural, a gift of Brazil, is in the Delegates' Lobby, General Assembly Building.
Printed by Heraclio Fournier, S.A., Spain. Panes of 50. Design adapted by Ole Hamann.

1974, May 6 Photo. *Perf. 14*
247 A136 10c **gold & multi** *(1,769,342)* .20 .20
First day cover 1.00
Inscription block of 4 .75 —
248 A136 18c **ultra & multi** *(1,477,500)* .40 .30
First day cover 1.00
First day cover, #247-248 1.25
Inscription block of 4 1.50 —

First day covers of Nos. 247-248 total 271,440.
See UN Offices in Geneva Nos. 41-42.

Dove and UN Emblem — A137

UN Headquarters — A138

Globe, UN Emblem, Flags — A139

Printed by Heraclio Fournier, S.A., Spain. Panes of 50.
Designed by Nejut M. Gur (2c); Olav S. Mathiesen (10c); Henry Bencsath (18c).

1974, June 10 Photo. *Perf. 14*

249	A137	2c	**dark & light blue** *(6,900,000)*	.20	.20
			First day cover		1.00
			Inscription block of 4	.25	—
250	A138	10c	**multicolored** *(4,000,000)*	.20	.20
			First day cover		1.00
			Inscription block of 4	.70	—
251	A139	18c	**multicolored** *(2,300,000)*	.30	.20
			First day cover		1.00
			First day cover, #249-251		1.25
			Inscription block of 4	1.50	—
			Nos. 249-251 (3)	.70	.60

First day covers of Nos. 249-251 total 307,402.
+ Printing orders to Feb. 1990.

Children of the World — A140

Law of the Sea — A141

World Population Year
Printed by Heraclio Fournier, S.A., Spain. Panes of 50. Designed by Henry Bencsath.

1974, Oct. 18 Photo. *Perf. 14*

252	A140	10c	**light blue & multi** *(1,762,595)*	.20	.20
			First day cover		1.00
			Inscription block of 4	1.00	—
253	A140	18c	**lilac & multi** *(1,321,574)*	.40	.25
			First day cover		1.00
			First day cover, #252-253		1.25
			Inscription block of 4	1.75	—

First day covers of Nos. 253-254 total 354,306.
See UN Offices in Geneva Nos. 43-44.

1974, Nov. 22 Photo. *Perf. 14*

Declaration of UN General Assembly that the sea bed is common heritage of mankind, reserved for peaceful purposes.
Printed by Heraclio Fournier, S.A., Spain. Panes of 50. Designed by Asher Kalderon.

254	A141	10c	**green & multi** *(1,621,328)*	.20	.20
			First day cover		1.00
			Inscription block of 4	.80	—
255	A141	26c	**orange red & multi** *(1,293,084)*	.40	.30
			First day cover		1.25
			First day cover, #254-255		1.40
			Inscription block of 4	1.90	—

First day covers of Nos. 254-255 total 280,686.
See UN Offices in Geneva No. 45.

Satellite and Globe — A142

Peaceful uses (meteorology, industry, fishing, communications) of outer space.
Printed by Setelipaino, Finland. Panes of 50. Designed by Henry Bencsath.

1975, Mar. 14 Litho. *Perf. 13*

256	A142	10c	**multicolored** *(1,681,115)*	.20	.20
			First day cover		1.00
			Inscription block of 4	.85	—
257	A142	26c	**multicolored** *(1,463,130)*	.40	.30
			First day cover		1.25
			First day cover, #256-257		1.40
			Inscription block of 4	1.75	—

First day covers of Nos. 256-257 total 330,316.
See UN Offices in Geneva Nos. 46-47.

Equality Between Men and Women — A143

UN Flag and "XXX" — A144

International Women's Year
Printed by Questa Colour Security Printers, Ltd., England. Panes of 50. Designed by Asher Kalderon and Esther Kurti.

1975, May 9 Litho. *Perf. 15*

258	A143	10c	**multicolored** *(1,402,542)*	.20	.20
			First day cover		1.00
			Inscription block of 4	.80	—
259	A143	18c	**multicolored** *(1,182,321)*	.40	.30
			First day cover		1.00
			First day cover, #258-259		1.25
			Inscription block of 4	1.75	—

First day covers of Nos. 258-259 total 285,466.
See UN Offices in Geneva Nos. 48-49.

1975, June 26 Litho. *Perf. 13*

30th anniversary of the United Nations.
Printed by Ashton-Potter, Ltd., Canada. Nos. 260-261 panes of 50. Stamps designed by Asher Calderon, sheets by Olav S. Mathiesen.

260	A144	10c	**olive bister & multi** *(1,904,545)*	.20	.20
			First day cover		1.00
			Inscription block of 4	.70	—
261	A144	26c	**purple & multi** *(1,547,766)*	.50	.35
			First day cover		1.25
			First day cover, #260-261		1.40
			Inscription block of 4	2.25	—

Souvenir Sheet

Imperf

262		Sheet of 2 *(1,196,578)*	.65	.50
a.	A144 10c	**olive bister & multicolored**	.20	.20
b.	A144 26c	**purple & multicolored**	.40	.25
		First day cover		1.25

No. 262 has blue and bister margin with inscription and UN emblem.
First day covers of Nos. 260-262 total: New York 477,912; San Francisco, 237,159.
See Offices in Geneva Nos. 50-52.

Hand Reaching up over Map of Africa and Namibia — A145

Wild Rose Growing from Barbed Wire — A146

"Namibia-United Nations direct responsibility." See note after No. 241.
Printed by Heraclio Fournier S.A., Spain. Panes of 50. Designed by Henry Bencsath.

1975, Sept. 22 Photo. *Perf. 13½*

263	A145	10c	**multicolored** *(1,354,374)*	.20	.20
			First day cover		1.00
			Inscription block of 4	.80	—
264	A145	18c	**multicolored** *(1,243,157)*	.35	.30
			First day cover		1.00
			First day cover, #263-264		1.25
			Inscription block of 4	1.60	—

First day covers of Nos. 263-264 total 281,631.
See UN Offices in Geneva Nos. 53-54.

1975, Nov. 21 Engr. *Perf. 12½*

United Nations Peace-keeping Operations
Printed by Setelipaino, Finland. Panes of 50. Designed by Mrs. Eeva Oivo.

265	A146	13c	**ultramarine** *(1,628,039)*	.25	.20
			First day cover		1.00
			Inscription block of 4	1.00	—
266	A146	26c	**rose carmine** *(1,195,580)*	.50	.40
			First day cover		1.2
			First day cover, #265-266		1.4
			Inscription block of 4	2.00	—

First day covers of Nos. 265-266 total 303,711.
See UN Offices in Geneva Nos. 55-56.

Symbolic Flags Forming Dove — A147

UN Emblem — A149

People of All Races A148

United Nations Flag — A150

Dove and Rainbow — A151

Printed by Ashton-Potter, Ltd., Canada (3c, 4c, 30c, 50c), and Questa Colour Security Printers, Ltd., England (9c). Panes of 50.
Designed by Waldemar Andrzesewski (3c); Arne Johnson (4c); George Hamori (9c, 30c); Arthur Congdon (50c).

1976 Litho. *Perf. 13x13½, 13½x13*

267	A147	3c	**multicolored** *(4,000,000)*	.20	.20
			First day cover		1.00
			Inscription block of 4	.30	—
268	A148	4c	**multicolored** *(4,000,000)*	.20	.20
			First day cover		1.00
			Inscription block of 4	.35	—

Photo.

Perf. 14

269	A149	9c	**multicolored** *(3,270,000)+*	.20	.20
			First day cover		1.00
			Inscription block of 4	.65	—

Litho.

Perf. 13x13½

270	A150	30c	**blue, emerald & black** *(2,500,000)*	.40	.35
			First day cover		2.00
			Inscription block of 4	2.00	—
271	A151	50c	**yellow green & multi** *(2,000,000)*	.70	.65
			First day cover		1.25
			First day cover, #267-268, 270-271		1.50
			Inscription block of 4	3.75	—
			Nos. 267-271 (5)	1.70	1.60

Issue dates: 3c, 4c, 30c, 50c, Jan. 6; 9c, Nov. 19.
First day covers of Nos. 267-268, 270-271 total 355,165; of Nos. 269 and 280 total 366,556.
See UN Offices in Vienna No. 8.

Interlocking Bands and UN Emblem — A152

World Federation of United Nations Associations.
Printed by Heraclio Fournier, S.A., Spain. Panes of 50. Designed by George Hamori.

1976, Mar. 12 Photo. *Perf. 14*

272 A152 13c **blue, green & black** *(1,331,556)* .20 .20
First day cover 1.00
Inscription block of 4 .80 —
273 A152 26c **green & multi** *(1,050,145)* .35 .30
First day cover 1.25
First day cover, #272-273 1.25
Inscription block of 4 1.60 —

First day covers of Nos. 272-273 total 300,775.
See UN Offices in Geneva No. 57.

Cargo, Globe and Graph — A153

Houses Around Globe — A154

UN Conference on Trade and Development (UNCTAD), Nairobi, Kenya, May 1976.
Printed by Courvoisier, S.A. Panes of 50. Designed by Henry Bencsath.

1976, Apr. 23 Photo. *Perf. 11½*

274 A153 13c **deep magenta & multi** *(1,317,900)* .20 .20
First day cover 1.00
Inscription block of 4 .80 —
275 A153 31c **dull blue & multi** *(1,216,959)* .40 .30
First day cover 1.25
First day cover, #274-275 1.40
Inscription block of 4 2.00 —

First day covers of Nos. 274-275 total 234,657.
See UN Offices in Geneva No. 58.

1976, May 28 Photo. *Perf. 14*

Habitat, UN Conference on Human Settlements, Vancouver, Canada, May 31-June 11.
Printed by Heraclio Fournier, S.A., Spain. Panes of 50. Designed by Eliezer Weishoff.

276 A154 13c **red brown & multi** *(1,346,589)* .20 .20
First day cover 1.00
Inscription block of 4 .75 —
277 A154 25c **green & multi** *(1,057,924)* .40 .30
First day cover 1.25
First day cover, #276-277 1.40
Inscription block of 4 1.75 —

First day covers of Nos. 276-277 total 232,754.
See UN Offices in Geneva Nos. 59-60.

Magnifying Glass, Sheet of Stamps, UN Emblem — A155

Grain — A156

United Nations Postal Administration, 25th anniversary.
Printed by Courvoisier, S.A. Designed by Henry Bencsath.

1976, Oct. 8 Photo. *Perf. 11½*

278 A155 13c **blue & multi** *(1,996,309)* .20 .20
First day cover 1.00
Inscription block of 4 .90 —
279 A155 31c **green & multi** *(1,767,465)* 1.40 1.40
First day cover 2.00
First day cover, #278-279 2.50
Inscription block of 4 6.25 —
Panes of 20, #278-279 27.50 —

First day covers of Nos. 278-279 total 366,784.
Upper margin blocks are inscribed "XXV ANNIVERSARY"; lower margin blocks "UNITED NATIONS POSTAL ADMINISTRATIONS."
See UN Offices in Geneva Nos. 61-62.

1976, Nov. 19 Litho. *Perf. 14½*

World Food Council.
Printed by Questa Colour Security Printers, Ltd., England. Panes of 50. Designed by Eliezer Weishoff.

280 A156 13c **multicolored** *(1,515,573)* .25 .20
First day cover 1.00
Inscription block of 4 1.10 —

See UN Offices in Geneva No. 63.

WIPO Headquarters, Geneva A157

World Intellectual Property Organization (WIPO).
Printed by Heraclio Fournier, S. A., Spain. Panes of 50. Designed by Eliezer Weishoff.

1977, Mar. 11 Photo. *Perf. 14*

281 A157 13c **citron & multi** *(1,330,272)* .20 .20
First day cover 1.00
Inscription block of 4 .75 —
282 A157 31c **bright green & multi** *(1,115,406)* .45 .35
First day cover 1.25
First day cover, #281-282 1.25
Inscription block of 4 2.00 —

First day covers of Nos. 281-282 total 364,184.
See UN Offices in Geneva No. 64.

Drops of Water Falling into Funnel — A158

UN Water Conference, Mar del Plata, Argentina, Mar. 14-25.
Printed by Government Printing Bureau, Tokyo. Panes of 50. Designed by Elio Tomei.

1977, Apr. 22 Photo. *Perf. 13½x13*

283 A158 13c **yellow & multi** *(1,317,536)* .20 .20
First day cover 1.00
Inscription block of 4 .75 —
284 A158 25c **salmon & multi** *(1,077,424)* .45 .35
First day cover 1.25
First day cover, #283-284 1.40
Inscription block of 4 2.00 —

First day covers of Nos. 283-284 total 321,585.
See UN Offices in Geneva Nos. 65-66.

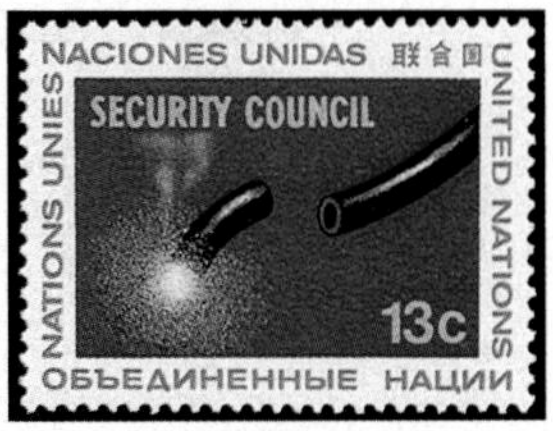

Burning Fuse Severed — A159

UN Security Council.
Printed by Heraclio Fournier, S.A., Spain. Panes of 50. Designed by Witold Janowski and Marek Freudenreich.

1977, May 27 Photo. *Perf. 14*

285 A159 13c **purple & multi** *(1,321,527)* .20 .20
First day cover 1.00
Inscription block of 4 .75 —
286 A159 31c **dark blue & multi** *(1,137,195)* .45 .30
First day cover 1.25
First day cover, #285-286 1.40
Inscription block of 4 2.00 —

First day covers of Nos. 285-286 total 309,610.
See UN Offices in Geneva Nos. 67-68.

"Combat Racism" — A160

Fight against racial discrimination.
Printed by Setelipaino, Finland. Panes of 50. Designed by Bruno K. Wiese.

1977, Sept. 19 Litho. *Perf. 13½x13*

287 A160 13c **black & yellow** *(1,195,739)* .20 .20
First day cover 1.00
Inscription block of 4 .75 —
288 A160 25c **black & vermilion** *(1,074,639)* .40 .30
First day cover 1.25
First day cover, #287-288 1.40
Inscription block of 4 1.75 —

First day covers of Nos. 287-288 total 356,193.
See UN Offices in Geneva Nos. 60-70.

Atom, Grain, Fruit and Factory — A161

Peaceful uses of atomic energy.
Printed by Heraclio Fournier, S.A., Spain. Panes of 50. Designed by Henry Bencsath.

1977, Nov. 18 Photo. *Perf. 14*

289 A161 13c **yellow bister & multi** *(1,316,473)* .20 .20
First day cover 1.00
Inscription block of 4 .90 —
290 A161 18c **dull green & multi** *(1,072,246)* .35 .25
First day cover 1.00
First day cover, #289-290 1.25
Inscription block of 4 1.50 —

First day covers of Nos. 289-290 total 325,348.
See UN Offices in Geneva Nos. 71-72.

Opening Words of UN Charter — A162

"Live Together in Peace" — A163

People of the World — A164

Printed by Questa Colour Security Printers, United Kingdom. Panes of 50. Designed by Salahattin Kanidinc (1c); Elio Tomei (25c); Paula Schmidt ($1).

1978, Jan. 27 Litho. *Perf. 14½*

291 A162 1c **gold, brown & red** *(4,800,000)+* .20 .20
First day cover 1.00
Inscription block of 4 .25 —
292 A163 25c **multicolored** *(3,000,000)+* .35 .30
First day cover 1.25
Inscription block of 4 1.50 —
293 A164 $1 **multicolored** *(3,400,000)+* 1.25 1.25
First day cover 1.50
First day cover, #291-293 1.75
Inscription block of 4 5.50 —
Nos. 291-293 (3) 1.80 1.75

+ Printing orders to Sept. 1989.
First day covers of Nos. 291-293 total 264,782.
See UN Offices in Geneva No. 73.

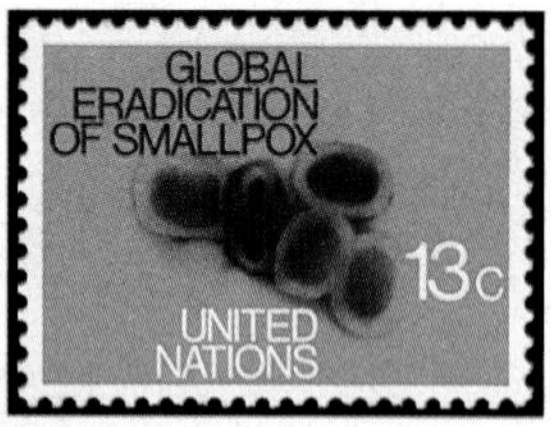

Smallpox Virus — A165

Global eradication of smallpox.
Printed by Courvoisier, S.A. Panes of 50. Designed by Herbert Auchli.

1978, Mar. 31 Photo. *Perf. 12x11½*

294 A165 13c **rose & black** *(1,188,239)* .20 .20
First day cover 1.00
Inscription block of 4 .75 —
295 A165 31c **blue & black** *(1,058,688)* .45 .40
First day cover 1.25
First day cover, #294-295 1.40
Inscription block of 4 2.00 —

First day covers of Nos. 294-295 total 306,626.
See UN Offices in Geneva Nos. 74-75.

Open Handcuff — A166

Multicolored Bands and Clouds — A167

Liberation, justice and cooperation for Namibia.
Printed by Government Printing Office, Austria. Panes of 50. Designed by Cafiro Tomei.

1978, May 5 Photo. *Perf. 12*

296 A166 13c **multicolored** *(1,203,079)* .20 .20
First day cover 1.00
Inscription block of 4 1.00 —
297 A166 18c **multicolored** *(1,066,738)* .30 .25
First day cover 1.00
First day cover, #296-297 1.25
Inscription block of 4 1.40 —

First day covers of Nos. 296-297 total 324,471.
See UN Offices in Geneva No. 76.

1978, June 12 Photo. *Perf. 14*

International Civil Aviation Organization for "Safety in the Air."
Printed by Heraclio Fournier, S.A., Spain. Panes of 50. Designed by Cemalettin Mutver.

298 A167 13c **multicolored** *(1,295,617)* .20 .20
First day cover 1.00
Inscription block of 4 .85 —
299 A167 25c **multicolored** *(1,101,256)* .40 .30
First day cover 1.25
First day cover, #298-299 1.40
Inscription block of 4 1.75 —

First day covers of Nos. 298-299 total 329,995.
See UN Offices in Geneva Nos. 77-78.

General Assembly — A168

Printed by Government Printing Bureau, Tokyo. Panes of 50. Designed by Jozsef Vertel.

1978, Sept. 15 Photo. *Perf. 13½*

300 A168 13c **multicolored** *(1,093,005)* .20 .20
First day cover 1.00
Inscription block of 4 1.00 —
301 A168 18c **multicolored** *(1,065,934)* .35 .30
First day cover 1.00
First day cover, #300-301 1.25
Inscription block of 4 1.50 —

First day covers of Nos. 300-301 total 283,220.
See UN Offices in Geneva Nos. 79-80.

Hemispheres as Cogwheels A169

Technical Cooperation Among Developing Countries Conference, Buenos Aires, Argentina, Sept. 1978.
Printed by Heraclio Fournier, S.A., Spain. Panes of 50. Designed by Simon Keter and David Pesach.

1978, Nov. 17 Photo. *Perf. 14*

302 A169 13c **multicolored** *(1,251,272)* .20 .20
First day cover 1.00
Inscription block of 4 1.00 —
303 A169 31c **multicolored** *(1,185,213)* .50 .40
First day cover 1.25
First day cover, #302-303 1.40
Inscription block of 4 2.25 —

First day covers of Nos. 302-303 total 272,556.
See UN Offices in Geneva No. 81.

Hand Holding Olive Branch — A170

Various Races Tree — A171

Globe, Dove with Olive Branch — A172

Birds and Globe — A173

Printed by Heraclio Fournier, S.A., Spain. Panes of 50. Designed by Raymon Müller (5c); Alrun Fricke (14c); Eliezer Weishoff (15c); Young Sun Hahn (20c).

1979, Jan. 19 Photo. *Perf. 14*

304 A170 5c **multicolored** *(3,000,000)* .20 .20
First day cover 1.00
Inscription block of 4 .35 —
305 A171 14c **multicolored** *(3,000,000)+* .20 .20
First day cover 1.00
Inscription block of 4 .90 —
306 A172 15c **multicolored** *(3,000,000)+* .30 .25
First day cover 1.00
Inscription block of 4 1.40 —
307 A173 20c **multicolored** *(3,400,000)+* .30 .25
First day cover 1.00
First day cover, #304-307 1.75
Inscription block of 4 1.40 —
Nos. 304-307 (4) 1.00 .90

First day covers of Nos. 304-307 total 295,927.
+ Printing orders to June 1990.

UNDRO Against Fire and Water — A174

Office of the UN Disaster Relief Coordinator (UNDRO).
Printed by Heraclio Fournier, S.A., Spain. Panes of 50. Designed by Gidon Sagi.

1979, Mar. 9 Photo. *Perf. 14*

308 A174 15c **multicolored** *(1,448,600)* .25 .20
First day cover 1.00
Inscription block of 4 1.00 —
309 A174 20c **multicolored** *(1,126,295)* .35 .30
First day cover 1.00
First day cover, #308-309 1.25
Inscription block of 4 1.50 —

First day covers of Nos. 308-309 total 266,694.
See UN Offices in Geneva Nos. 82-83.

Child and IYC Emblem — A175

International Year of the Child.
Printed by Heraclio Fournier, S.A., Spain. Panes of 20 (5x4). Designed by Helena Matuszewska (15c) and Krystyna Tarkowska-Gruszecka (31c).

1979, May 4 Photo. *Perf. 14*

310 A175 15c **multicolored** *(2,290,329)* .20 .20
First day cover 1.00
Inscription block of 4 1.00 —
311 A175 31c **multicolored** *(2,192,136)* .35 .35
First day cover 1.25
First day cover, #310-311 2.25
Inscription block of 4 1.60 —
Panes of 20, #310-311 13.00

First day covers of Nos. 310-311 total 380,022.
See UN Offices in Geneva Nos. 84-85.

Map of Namibia, Olive Branch — A176

Scales and Sword of Justice — A177

For a free and independent Namibia.
Printed by Ashton-Potter Ltd., Canada. Panes of 50. Designed by Eliezer Weishoff.

1979, Oct. 5 **Litho.** ***Perf. 13½***

312	A176	15c	**multicolored** *(1,470,231)*	.20	.20
			First day cover		1.00
			Inscription block of 4	.95	—
313	A176	31c	**multicolored** *(1,355,323)*	.40	.35
			First day cover		1.25
			First day cover, #312-313		1.50
			Inscription block of 4	1.75	—

First day covers of Nos. 312-313 total 250,371.
See UN Offices in Geneva No. 86.

1979, Nov. 9 **Litho.** ***Perf. 13x13½***

International Court of Justice, The Hague, Netherlands.
Printed by Setelipaino, Finland. Panes of 50. Designed by Henning Simon.

314	A177	15c	**multicolored** *(1,244,972)*	.20	.20
			First day cover		1.00
			Inscription block of 4	.85	—
315	A177	20c	**multicolored** *(1,084,483)*	.40	.35
			First day cover		1.00
			First day cover, #314-315		1.25
			Inscription block of 4	1.75	—

First day covers of Nos. 314-315 total 322,901.
See UN Offices in Geneva Nos. 87-88.

Graph of Economic Trends — A178

Key — A179

New International Economic Order.
Printed by Questa Colour Security Printers, United Kingdom. Panes of 50. Designed by Cemalettin Mutver (15c), George Hamori (31c)

1980, Jan. 11 **Litho.** ***Perf. 15x14½***

316	A178	15c	**multicolored** *(1,163,801)*	.20	.20
			First day cover		1.00
			Inscription block of 4	.85	—
317	A179	31c	**multicolored** *(1,103,560)*	.50	.35
			First day cover		1.25
			First day cover, #316-317		1.40
			Inscription block of 4	2.25	—

First day covers of Nos. 316-317 total 211,945.
See UN Offices in Geneva No. 89; Vienna No. 7.

Women's Year Emblem — A180

United Nations Decade for Women.
Printed by Questa Colour Security Printers, United Kingdom. Panes of 50. Designed by Susanne Rottenfusser.

1980, Mar. 7 **Litho.** ***Perf. 14½x15***

318	A180	15c	**multicolored** *(1,409,350)*	.20	.20
			First day cover		1.00
			Inscription block of 4	1.00	—
319	A180	20c	**multicolored** *(1,182,016)*	.30	.25
			First day cover		1.00
			First day cover, #318-319		1.25
			Inscription block of 4	2.00	—

First day covers of Nos. 318-319 total 289,314.
See UN Offices in Geneva Nos. 90-91; Vienna Nos. 9-10.

UN Emblem and "UN" on Helmet — A181

Arrows and UN Emblem — A182

United Nations Peace-keeping Operations.
Printed by Joh. Enschede en Zonen, Netherlands. Panes of 50. Designed by Bruno K. Wiese (15c), James Gardiner (31c)

1980, May 16 **Litho.** ***Perf. 14x13***

320	A181	15c	**blue & black** *(1,245,521)*	.25	.20
			First day cover		1.00
			Inscription block of 4	1.00	—
321	A182	31c	**multicolored** *(1,191,009)*	.40	.40
			First day cover		1.25
			First day cover, #320-321		1.40
			Inscription block of 4	2.25	—

First day covers of Nos. 320-321 total 208,442.
See UN Offices in Geneva No. 92; Vienna No. 11.

"35" and Flags — A183

Globe and Laurel — A184

35th Anniversary of the United Nations.
Printed by Ashton-Potter Ltd, Canada. Nos. 322-323, panes of 50. Designed by Cemalettin Matver (15c), Mian Mohammad Saeed (31c).

1980, June 26 **Litho.** ***Perf. 13x13½***

322	A183	15c	**multicolored** *(1,554,514)*	.20	.20
			First day cover		1.00
			Inscription block of 4	1.00	—
323	A184	31c	**multicolored** *(1,389,606)*	.40	.35
			First day cover		1.25
			First day cover, #322-323		1.40
			Inscription block of 4	2.00	—

Souvenir Sheet

Imperf

324			Sheet of 2 *(1,215,505)*	.70	.60
a.	A183	15c	**multicolored**	.20	.20
b.	A184	31c	**multicolored**	.40	.40
			First day cover		1.25

First day covers of Nos. 322-324 total: New York, 369,345; San Francisco, 203,701.
See UN Offices in Geneva Nos. 93-95; Vienna Nos. 12-14.

Flag of Turkey — A185

Printed by Courvoisier, S.A., Switzerland. Panes of 16. Designed by Ole Hamann.

Each pane contains 4 blocks of 4 (Nos. 325-328, 329-332, 333-336, 337-340). A se-tenant block of 4 designs centers each pane.

1980, Sept. 26 **Litho.** ***Perf. 12***

Granite Paper

325	A185	15c	shown *(3,490,725)*	.20	.20
326	A185	15c	Luxembourg *(3,490,725)*	.20	.20
327	A185	15c	Fiji *(3,490,725)*	.20	.20
328	A185	15c	Viet Nam *(3,490,725)*	.20	.20
a.			Se-tenant block of 4, #325-328	.80	.75
329	A185	15c	Guinea *(3,442,633)*	.20	.20
330	A185	15c	Surinam *(3,442,633)*	.20	.20
331	A185	15c	Bangladesh *(3,442,633)*	.20	.20
332	A185	15c	Mali *(3,442,633)*	.20	.20
a.			Se-tenant block of 4, #329-332	.80	.75
333	A185	15c	Yugoslavia *(3,416,292)*	.20	.20
334	A185	15c	France *(3,416,292)*	.20	.20
335	A185	15c	Venezuela *(3,416,292)*	.20	.20
336	A185	15c	El Salvador *(3,416,292)*	.20	.20
a.			Se-tenant block of 4, #333-336	.80	.75
337	A185	15c	Madagascar *(3,442,497)*	.20	.20
338	A185	15c	Cameroon *(3,442,497)*	.20	.20
339	A185	15c	Rwanda *(3,442,497)*	.20	.20
340	A185	15c	Hungary *(3,442,497)*	.20	.20
a.			Se-tenant block of 4, #337-340	.80	.75
			First day covers of Nos. 325-340, each		.60
			Set of 4 diff. panes of 16	8.00	
			Nos. 325-340 (16)	3.20	3.20

First day covers of Nos. 325-340 total 6,145,595.
See Nos. 350-365, 374-389, 399-414, 425-440, 450-465, 477-492, 499-514, 528-543, 554-569, 690-697, 719-726, 744-751.

Symbolic Flowers — A186

Symbols of Progress — A187

Printed by Ashton-Potter Ltd., Canada. Panes of 50. Designed by Eliezer Weishoff (15c), Dietman Kowall (20c).

1980, Nov. 21 **Litho.** ***Perf. 13½x13***

341	A186	15c	**multicolored** *(1,192,165)*	.25	.25
			First day cover		1.00
			Inscription block of 4	1.25	—
342	A187	20c	**multicolored** *(1,011,382)*	.40	.35
			First day cover		1.00
			First day cover, #341-342		1.40
			Inscription block of 4	1.75	—

First day covers of Nos. 341-342 total 232,149.
See UN Offices in Geneva, Nos. 96-97; Vienna Nos. 15-16.

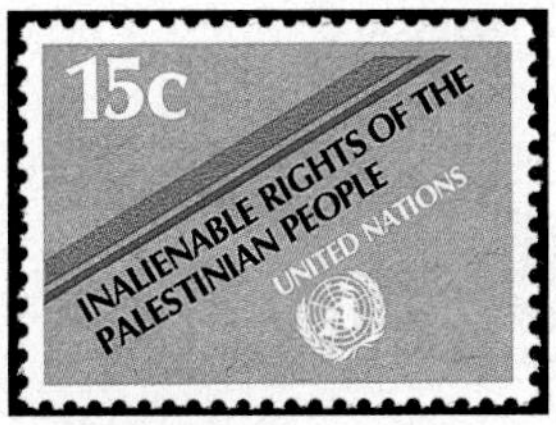

Inalienable Rights of the Palestinian People — A188

Printed by Courvoisier S.A., Switzerland. Panes of 50. Designed by David Dewhurst.

1981, Jan. 30 **Photo.** ***Perf. 12x11½***

343	A188	15c	**multicolored** *(993,489)*	.25	.20
			First day cover *(127,187)*		1.00
			Inscription block of 4	1.25	—

See UN Offices in Geneva No. 98; Vienna No. 17.

Interlocking Puzzle Pieces — A189

Stylized Person — A190

International Year of the Disabled.

Printed by Heraclio Fournier S.A., Spain. Panes of 50. Designed by Sophia Van Heeswijk (20c) and G.P. Van der Hyde (35c).

1981, Mar. 6 **Photo.** ***Perf. 14***

344	A189	20c	**multicolored** *(1,218,371)*	.25	.20
			First day cover		1.00
			Inscription block of 4	1.25	—
345	A190	35c	**black & orange** *(1,107,298)*	.50	.45
			First day cover		1.25
			First day cover, #344-345		1.40
			Inscription block of 4	2.25	—

First day covers of Nos. 344-345 total 204,891.

See UN Offices in Geneva Nos. 99-100; Vienna Nos. 18-19.

Desislava and Sebastocrator Kaloyan, Bulgarian Mural, 1259, Boyana Church, Sofia — A191

Art at UN Issue

Printed by Courvoisier. Panes of 50. Designed by Ole Hamann.

1981, Apr. 15 **Photo.** ***Perf. 11½***

Granite Paper

346	A191	20c	**multicolored** *(1,252,648)*	.25	.25
			First day cover		1.00
			Inscription block of 4	1.40	—
347	A191	31c	**multicolored** *(1,061,056)*	.45	.45
			First day cover		1.25
			First day cover, #346-347		1.40
			Inscription block of 4	2.00	—

First day covers of Nos. 346-347 total 210,978.

See UN Offices in Geneva No. 101; Vienna No. 20.

Solar Energy — A192

Conference Emblem — A193

Conference on New and Renewable Sources of Energy, Nairobi, Aug. 10-21.

Printed by Setelipaino, Finland. Panes of 50. Designed by Ulrike Dreyer (20c); Robert Perrot (40c).

1981, May 29 **Litho.** ***Perf. 13***

348	A192	20c	**multicolored** *(1,132,877)*	.30	.25
			First day cover		1.00
			Inscription block of 4	1.40	—
349	A193	40c	**multicolored** *(1,158,319)*	.55	.50
			First day cover		1.25
			First day cover, #348-349		1.40
			Inscription block of 4	2.50	—

First day covers of Nos. 348-349 total 240,205.

See UN Offices in Geneva No. 102; Vienna No. 21.

Flag Type of 1980

Printed by Courvoisier, S.A., Switzerland. Panes of 16. Designed by Ole Hamann.

Each pane contains 4 blocks of 4 (Nos. 350-353, 354-357, 358-361, 362-365). A se-tenant block of 4 designs centers each pane.

1981, Sept. 25 **Litho.**

Granite Paper

350	A185	20c	Djibouti *(2,342,224)*	.25	.20
351	A185	20c	Sri Lanka *(2,342,224)*	.25	.20
352	A185	20c	Bolivia *(2,342,224)*	.25	.20
353	A185	20c	Equatorial Guinea *(2,342,224)*	.25	.20
a.			Se-tenant block of 4, #350-353	1.50	1.40
354	A185	20c	Malta *(2,360,297)*	.25	.20
355	A185	20c	Czechoslovakia *(2,360,297)*	.25	.20
356	A185	20c	Thailand *(2,360,297)*	.25	.20
357	A185	20c	Trinidad & Tobago *(2,360,297)*	.25	.20
a.			Se-tenant block of 4, #354-357	1.50	1.40
358	A185	20c	Ukrainian SSR *(2,344,755)*	.25	.20
359	A185	20c	Kuwait *(2,344,755)*	.25	.20
360	A185	20c	Sudan *(2,344,755)*	.25	.20
361	A185	20c	Egypt *(2,344,755)*	.25	.20
a.			Se-tenant block of 4, #358-361	1.50	1.40
362	A185	20c	US *(2,450,537)*	.25	.20
363	A185	20c	Singapore *(2,450,537)*	.25	.20
364	A185	20c	Panama *(2,450,537)*	.25	.20
365	A185	20c	Costa Rica *(2,450,537)*	.25	.20
a.			Se-tenant block of 4, #362-365	1.50	1.40
			First day covers, #350-365, each		.60
			Set of 4 diff. panes of 16	11.50	
			Nos. 350-365 (16)	4.00	3.20

First day covers of Nos. 350-365 total 3,961,237.

Seedling and Tree Cross-section A194

"10" and Symbols of Progress — A195

United Nations Volunteers Program, 10th anniv.

Printed by Walsall Security Printers, Ltd., United Kingdom. Pane of 50. Designed by Gabriele Nussgen (18c), Angel Medina Medina (28c).

1981, Nov. 13 **Litho.**

366	A194	18c	**multicolored** *(1,246,833)*	.30	.25
			First day cover		1.00
			Inscription block of 4	1.50	—
367	A195	28c	**multicolored** *(1,282,868)*	.60	.55
			First day cover		1.25
			First day cover, #366-367		1.40
			Inscription block of 4	2.75	—

First day covers of Nos. 366-367 total 221,106.

See UN Offices in Geneva Nos. 103-104; Vienna Nos. 22-23.

A196

A197

A198

Respect for Human Rights (17c), Independence of Colonial Countries and People (28c), Second Disarmament Decade (40c).

Printed by Courvoisier, S.A., Switzerland. Panes of 50. Designed by Rolf Christianson (17c); George Hamori (28c); Marek Kwiatkowski (40c).

1982, Jan. 22 ***Perf. 11½x12***

368	A196	17c	**multicolored** *(3,000,000)+*	.30	.25
			First day cover		1.00
			Inscription block of 4	1.25	—
369	A197	28c	**multicolored** *(3,000,000)+*	.50	.40
			First day cover		1.25
			Inscription block of 4	2.25	—
370	A198	40c	**multicolored** *(3,000,000)*	.80	.70
			First day cover		1.25
			First day cover, #368-370		1.25
			Inscription block of 4	3.50	—
			Nos. 368-370 (3)	1.60	1.35

First day covers of Nos. 368-370 total 243,073.

Sun and Hand Holding Seedling — A199

Sun, Plant Land and Water — A200

10th Anniversary of United Nations Environment Program.

Printed by Joh. Enschede En Zonen, Netherlands. Panes of 50. Designed by Philine Hartert (20c); Peer-Ulrich Bremer (40c).

1982, Mar. 19 **Litho.** ***Perf. 13½x13***

371	A199	20c	**multicolored** *(1,017,117)*	.25	.25
			First day cover		1.00
			Inscription block of 4	1.25	—
372	A200	40c	**multicolored** *(884,798)*	.70	.65
			First day cover		1.25
			First day cover, #371-372		1.40
			Inscription block of 4	3.25	—

First day covers of Nos. 371-372 total 288,721.

See UN Offices in Geneva Nos. 107-108; Vienna Nos. 25-26.

UN Emblem and Olive Branch in Outer Space — A201

Exploration and Peaceful Uses of Outer Space.

Printed By Enschede. Panes of 50. Designed by Wiktor C. Nerwinski.

1982, June 11 **Litho.** ***Perf. 13x13½***

373	A201	20c	**multicolored** *(1,083,426)*	.55	.45
			First day cover *(156,965)*		1.00
			Inscription block of 4	2.40	—

See UN Offices in Geneva Nos. 109-110; Vienna No. 27.

Flag Type of 1980

Printed by Courvoisier. Panes of 16. Designed by Ole Hamann.

Issued in 4 panes of 16. Each pane contains 4 blocks of four (Nos. 374-377, 378-381, 383-385, 386-389). A se-tenant block of 4 designs centers each pane.

1982, Sept. 24 Litho. *Perf. 12*
Granite Paper

374 A185 20c Austria *(2,314,006)* .25 .20
375 A185 20c Malaysia *(2,314,006)* .25 .20
376 A185 20c Seychelles *(2,314,006)* .25 .20
377 A185 20c Ireland *(2,314,006)* .25 .20
a. Se-tenant block of 4, #374-377 1.50 1.40
378 A185 20c Mozambique *(2,300,958)* .25 .20
379 A185 20c Albania *(2,300,958)* .25 .20
380 A185 20c Dominica *(2,300,958)* .25 .20
381 A185 20c Solomon Islnads *(2,300,958)* .25 .20
a. Se-tenant block of 4, #378-381 1.50 1.40
382 A185 20c Philippines *(2,288,589)* .25 .20
383 A185 20c Swaziland *(2,288,589)* .25 .20
384 A185 20c Nicaragua *(2,288,589)* .25 .20
385 A185 20c Burma *(2,288,589)* .25 .20
a. Se-tenant block of 4, #382-385 1.50 1.40
386 A185 20c Cape Verde *(2,285,848)* .25 .20
387 A185 20c Guyana *(2,285,848)* .25 .20
388 A185 20c Belgium *(2,285,848)* .25 .20
389 A185 20c Nigeria *(2,285,848)* .25 .20
a. Se-tenant block of 4, #386-389 1.50 1.40
First day cover, #374-389, each .75
Set of 4 diff. panes of 16 14.00
Nos. 374-389 (16) 4.00 3.20

First day covers of Nos. 374-389 total 3,202,744.

Conservation and Protection of Nature — A202

Printed by Fournier. Panes of 50. Designed by Hamori.

1982, Nov. 19 Photo. *Perf. 14*

390 A202 20c Leaf *(1,110,027)* .35 .30
First day cover 1.00
margin block of 4, inscription 1.75 —
391 A202 28c Butterfly *(848,772)* .60 .50
First day cover 1.25
First day cover, #390-391 1.40
Inscription block of 4 2.50 —

First day covers of Nos. 390-391 total 214,148.
See UN Offices in Geneva Nos. 111-112; Vienna Nos. 28-29.

A203

A204

World Communications Year
Printed by Walsall. Panes of 50. Designed by Hanns Lohrer (A203) and Lorena Berengo (A204).

1983, Jan. 28 Litho. *Perf. 13*

392 A203 20c **multicolored** *(1,282,079)* .25 .25
First day cover 1.00
Inscription block of 4 1.25 —
393 A204 40c **multicolored** *(931,903)* .70 .65
First day cover 1.25
First day cover, #392-393 1.40
Inscription block of 4 3.50 —

First day covers of Nos. 392-393 total 183,499.
See UN Offices in Geneva No. 113; Vienna No. 30.

A205

A206

Safety at Sea.
Printed by Questa. Panes of 50. Designed by Jean-Marie Lenfant (A205), Ari Ron (A206).

1983, Mar. 18 Litho. *Perf. 14½*

394 A205 20c **multicolored** *(1,252,456)* .30 .25
First day cover 1.00
Inscription block of 4 1.50 —
395 A206 37c **multicolored** *(939,910)* .60 .55
First day cover 1.25
First day cover, #394-395 1.40
Inscription block of 4 2.75 —

First day covers of Nos. 394-395 total 199,962.
See UN Offices in Geneva Nos. 114-115; Vienna Nos. 31-32.

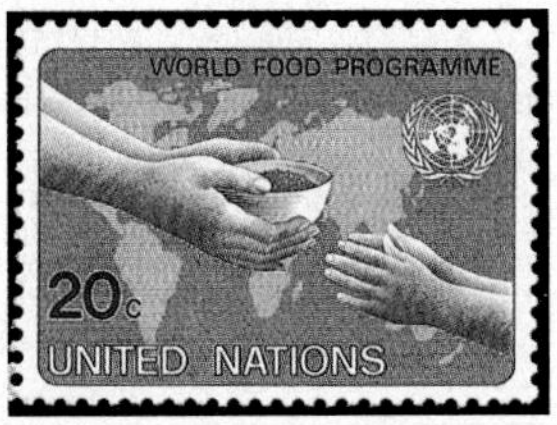

World Food Program — A207

Printed by Government Printers Bureau, Japan. Designed by Marek Kwiatkowski.

1983, Apr. 22 Engr. *Perf. 13½*

396 A207 20c **rose lake** *(1,238,997)* .35 .35
First day cover *(180,704)* 1.00
Inscription block of 4 1.60 —

See UN Offices in Geneva No. 116; Vienna Nos. 33-34.

A208

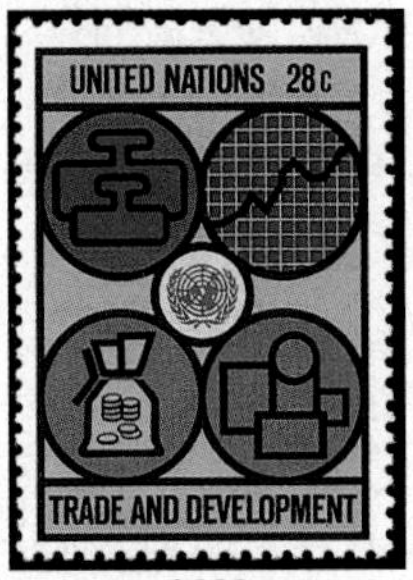

A209

UN Conference on Trade and Development.
Printed by Carl Uberreuter Druck and Verlag M. Salzer, Austria. Panes of 50. Designed by Dietmar Braklow (A208), Gabriel Genz (A209).

1983, June 6 Litho. *Perf. 14*

397 A208 20c **multicolored** *(1,060,053)* .35 .35
First day cover 1.10
Inscription block of 4 1.50 —
398 A209 28c **multicolored** *(948,981)* .70 .65
First day cover 1.40
First day cover, #397-398 1.50
Inscription block of 4 2.90 —

First day covers of Nos. 397-398 total 200,131.
See UN Offices in Geneva Nos. 117-118; Vienna Nos. 35-36.

Flag Type of 1980

Printed by Courvoisier. Panes of 16. Designed by Ole Hamann.
Issued in 4 panes of 16. Each pane contains 4 blocks of four (Nos. 399-402, 403-406, 407-410, 411-414). A se-tenant block of 4 designs centers each pane.

1983, Sept. 23 Photo. *Perf. 12*
Granite Paper

399 A185 20c Great Britain *(2,490,599)* .25 .20
400 A185 20c Barbados *(2,490,599)* .25 .20
401 A185 20c Nepal *(2,490,599)* .25 .20
402 A185 20c Israel *(2,490,599)* .25 .20
a. Se-tenant block of 4, #399-402 1.75 1.50
403 A185 20c Malawi *(2,483,010)* .25 .20
404 A185 20c Byelorussian SSR *(2,483,010)* .25 .20
405 A185 20c Jamaica *(2,483,010)* .25 .20
406 A185 20c Kenya *(2,483,010)* .25 .20
a. Se-tenant block of 4, #403-406 1.75 1.50
407 A185 20c People's Republic of China *(2,474,140)* .25 .20
408 A185 20c Peru *(2,474,140)* .25 .20
409 A185 20c Bulgaria *(2,474,140)* .25 .20
410 A185 20c Canada *(2,474,140)* .25 .20
a. Se-tenant block of 4, #407-410 1.75 1.50
411 A185 20c Somalia *(2,482,070)* .25 .20
412 A185 20c Senegal *(2,482,070)* .25 .20
413 A185 20c Brazil *(2,482,070)* .25 .20
414 A185 20c Sweden *(2,482,070)* .25 .20
a. Se-tenant block of 4, #411-414 1.75 1.50
First day cover, #399-414, each .75
Set of 4 diff. panes of 16 15.00
Nos. 399-414 (16) 4.00 3.20

First day covers of Nos. 399-414 total 2,214,134.

Window Right — A210

Peace Treaty with Nature — A211

35th Anniversary of the Universal Declaration of Human Rights.
Printed by Government Printing Office, Austria. Panes of 16 (4x4). Designed by Friedensreich Hundertwasser, Austria.

1983, Dec. 9 Photo. & Engr. *Perf. 13½*

415 A210 20c **multicolored** *(1,591,102)* .30 .25
First day cover 1.00
Inscription block of 4 1.25 —
416 A211 40c **multicolored** *(1,566,789)* .70 .65
First day cover 1.25
First day cover, #415-416 1.50
Inscription block of 4 3.00 —
Panes of 16, #415-416 16.00

First day covers of Nos. 415-416 total 176,269.
See UN Offices in Geneva Nos. 119-120; Vienna Nos. 37-38.

International Conference on Population — A212

Printed by Bundesdruckerei, Federal Republic of Germany. Panes of 50. Designed by Marina Langer-Rosa and Helmut Langer, Federal Republic of Germany.

1984, Feb. 3 Litho. *Perf. 14*

417 A212 20c **multicolored** *(905,320)* .30 .25
First day cover 1.00
Inscription block of 4 1.40 —
418 A212 40c **multicolored** *(717,084)* .65 .55
First day cover 1.25
First day cover, #417-418 1.40
Inscription block of 4 2.50 —

First day covers of Nos. 417-418 total 118,068.
See UN Offices in Geneva No. 121; Vienna No. 39.

Tractor Plowing
A213

Rice Paddy
A214

World Food Day, Oct. 16

Printed by Walsall Security Printers, Ltd., United Kingdom. Panes of 50. Designed by Adth Vanooijen, Netherlands.

1984, Mar. 15 **Litho.** ***Perf. 14½***

419 A213 20c **multicolored** *(853,641)* .35 .30
First day cover 1.25
Inscription block of 4 1.60 —
420 A214 40c **multicolored** *(727,165)* .65 .65
First day cover 1.50
First day cover, #419-420 1.75
Inscription block of 4 2.75 —

First day covers of Nos. 419-420 total 116,009.

See UN Offices in Geneva Nos. 122-123; Vienna Nos. 40-41.

Grand Canyon — A215

Ancient City of Polonnaruwa, Sri Lanka — A216

World Heritage

Printed by Harrison and Sons, United Kingdom. Panes of 50. Designs adapted by Rocco J. Callari, U.S., and Thomas Lee, China.

1984, Apr. 18 **Litho.** ***Perf. 14***

421 A215 20c **multicolored** *(814,316)* .25 .20
First day cover 1.00
Inscription block of 4 1.10 —
422 A216 50c **multicolored** *(579,136)* .75 .75
First day cover 1.25
First day cover, #421-422 1.40
Inscription block of 4 3.50 —

First day covers of Nos. 421-422 total 112,036.

See Nos. 601-602, UN Offices in Geneva Nos. 124-125, 211-212; Vienna Nos. 42-43, 125-126.

A217

A218

Future for Refugees

Printed by Courvoisier. Panes of 50. Designed by Hans Erni, Switzerland.

1984, May 29 **Photo.** ***Perf. 11½***

423 A217 20c **multicolored** *(956,743)* .35 .35
First day cover 1.00
Inscription block of 4 1.50 —
424 A218 50c **multicolored** *(729,036)* 1.00 .85
First day cover 1.25
First day cover, #423-424 1.40
Inscription block of 4 4.25 —

First day covers of Nos. 423-424 total 115,789.

See UN Offices in Geneva Nos. 126-127; Vienna Nos. 44-45.

Flag Type of 1980

Printed by Courvoisier. Panes of 16. Designed by Ole Hamann.

Issued in 4 panes of 16. Each pane contains 4 blocks of four (Nos. 425-428, 429-432, 433-436, 437-440). A se-tenant block of 4 designs centers each pane.

1984, Sept. 21 **Photo.** ***Perf. 12***

Granite Paper

425 A185 20c Burundi *(1,941,471)* .50 .45
426 A185 20c Pakistan *(1,941,471)* .50 .45
427 A185 20c Benin *(1,941,471)* .50 .45
428 A185 20c Italy *(1,941,471)* .50 .45
a. Se-tenant block of 4, #425-428 2.75 2.50
429 A185 20c Tanzania *(1,969,051)* .50 .45
430 A185 20c United Arab Emirates *(1,969,051)* .50 .45
431 A185 20c Ecuador *(1,969,051)* .50 .45
432 A185 20c Bahamas *(1,969,051)* .50 .45
a. Se-tenant block of 4, #429-432 2.75 2.50
433 A185 20c Poland *(2,001,091)* .50 .45
434 A185 20c Papua New Guinea *(2,001,091)* .50 .45
435 A185 20c Uruguay *(2,001,091)* .50 .45
436 A185 20c Chile *(2,001,091)* .50 .45
a. Se-tenant block of 4, #433-436 2.75 2.50
437 A185 20c Paraguay *(1,969,875)* .50 .45
438 A185 20c Bhutan *(1,969,875)* .50 .45
439 A185 20c Central African Republic *(1,969,875)* .50 .45
440 A185 20c Australia *(1,969,875)* .50 .45
a. Se-tenant block of 4, #437-440 2.75 2.50
First day cover, #425-440, each 1.00
Set of 4 diff. panes of 16 27.50
Nos. 425-440 (16) 8.00 7.20

First day covers of Nos. 425-440 total 1,914,972.

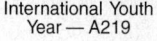

International Youth Year — A219

ILO Turin Center — A220

Printed by Waddingtons Ltd., United Kingdom. Panes of 50. Designed by Ramon Mueller, Federal Republic of Germany.

1984, Nov. 15 **Litho.** ***Perf. 13½***

441 A219 20c **multicolored** *(884,962)* .40 .35
First day cover 1.00
Inscription block of 4 2.00 —
442 A219 35c **multicolored** *(740,023)* 1.25 1.10
First day cover 1.25
First day cover, #441-442 1.40
Inscription block of 4 5.75 —

First day covers of Nos. 441-442 total 125,315.

See UN Offices in Geneva No. 128; Vienna Nos. 46-47.

1985, Feb. 1 **Engr.** ***Perf. 13½***

Printed by the Government Printing Bureau, Japan. Panes of 50. Engraved by Mamoru Iwakuni and Hiroshi Ozaki, Japan.

443 A220 23c **blue** *(612,942)* .55 .45
First day cover *(76,541)* 1.00
Inscription block of 4 2.50 —

See UN Offices in Geneva Nos. 129-130; Vienna No. 48.

UN University
A221

Printed by Helio Courvoiser, Switzerland. Panes of 50. Designed by Moshe Pereg, Israel, and Hinedi Geluda, Brazil.

1985, Mar. 15 **Photo.** ***Perf. 13½***

444 A221 50c Farmer plowing, discussion group *(625,043)* 1.10 1.00
First day cover *(77,271)* 1.25
Inscription block of 4 5.00 —

See UN Offices in Geneva Nos. 131-132; Vienna No. 49.

Peoples of the World United — A222

Painting UN Emblem — A223

Printed by Carl Ueberreuter Druck and Verlag M. Salzer, Austria. Panes of 50. Designed by Fritz Henry Oerter, Federal Republic of Germany (22c), and Rimondi Rino, Italy ($3).

1985, May 10 **Litho.** ***Perf. 14***

445 A222 22c **multicolored** *(2,000,000)+* .35 .30
First day cover 1.00
Inscription block of 4 1.50 —
446 A223 $3 **multicolored** *(2,000,000)+* 4.00 1.00
First day cover 4.50
First day cover, #445-446 6.50
Inscription block of 4 17.00 —

First day covers of Nos. 445-446 total 88,613.

See UN Offices in Geneva Nos. 133-134; Vienna Nos. 50-51.

The Corner, 1947 — A224

Alvaro Raking Hay, 1953 — A225

UN 40th anniversary. Oil paintings (details) by American artist Andrew Wyeth (b. 1917). Printed by Helio Courvoisier, Switzerland. Nos. 447-448 panes of 50. Designed by Rocco J. Callari, U.S., and Thomas Lee, China (#449).

1985, June 26 **Photo.** ***Perf. 12 x 11½***

447 A224 22c **multicolored** *(944,960)* .40 .35
First day cover 1.00
Inscription block of 4 1.25 —
448 A225 45c **multicolored** *(680,079)* 1.10 .85
First day cover 1.25
First day cover, #447-448 1.50
Inscription block of 4 4.25 —

Souvenir Sheet

Imperf

449 Sheet of 2 *(506,004)* 1.50 1.40
a. A224 22c **multicolored** .50 .40
b. A225 45c **multicolored** .75 .90
First day cover .75

First day covers of Nos. 447-449 total; New York, 210,189; San Francisco, 92,804.

See UN Offices in Geneva Nos. 135-137; Vienna Nos. 52-54.

Flag Type of 1980

Printed by Helio Courvoisier, Switzerland. Designed by Ole Hamann.

Issued in panes of 16; each contains 4 blocks of four (Nos. 450-453, 454-457, 458-461, 462-465). A se-tenant block of 4 designs is at the center of each pane.

1985, Sept. 20 Photo. *Perf. 12*

Granite Paper

450 A185 22c Grenada *(1,270,755)* .55 .50
451 A185 22c Federal Republic of Germany *(1,270,755)* .55 .50
452 A185 22c Saudi Arabia *(1,270,755)* .55 .50
453 A185 22c Mexico *(1,270,755)* .55 .50
a. Se-tenant block of 4, #450-453 3.25 2.75
454 A185 22c Uganda *(1,216,878)* .55 .50
455 A185 22c St. Thomas & Prince *(1,216,878)* .55 .50
456 A185 22c USSR *(1,216,878)* .55 .50
457 A185 22c India *(1,216,878)* .55 .50
a. Se-tenant block of 4, #454-457 3.25 2.75
458 A185 22c Liberia *(1,213,231)* .55 .50
459 A185 22c Mauritius *(1,213,231)* .55 .50
460 A185 22c Chad *(1,213,231)* .55 .50
461 A185 22c Dominican Republic *(1,213,231)* .55 .50
a. Se-tenant block of 4, #458-461 3.25 2.75
462 A185 22c Sultanate of Oman *(1,215,533)* .55 .50
463 A185 22c Ghana *(1,215,533)* .55 .50
464 A185 22c Sierra Leone *(1,215,533)* .55 .50
465 A185 22c Finland *(1,215,533)* .55 .50
a. Se-tenant block of 4, #462-465 3.25 2.75
First day covers, #460-465, each 1.00
Set of 4 diff. panes of 16 30.00
Nos. 450-465 (16) 8.80 8.00

First day covers of Nos. 450-465 total 1,774,193.

UNICEF Child Survival Campaign — A226

Africa in Crisis — A227

Printed by the Government Printing Bureau, Japan. Panes of 50. Designed by Mel Harris, United Kingdom (#466) and Dipok Deyi, India (#467).

1985, Nov. 22 Photo. & Engr. *Perf. 13½*

466 A226 22c Asian Toddler *(823,724)* .35 .30
First day cover 1.00
Inscription block of 4 1.50 —
467 A226 33c Breastfeeding *(632,753)* .65 .60
First day cover 1.25
First day cover, #466-467 1.75
Inscription block of 4 3.00 —

First day covers of Nos. 466-467 total 206,923.
See UN Offices in Geneva Nos. 138-139; Vienna Nos. 55-56.

1986, Jan. 31 Photo. *Perf. 11½x12*

Printed by Helio Courvoisier, Switzerland. Pane of 50. Designed by Wosene Kosrof, Ethiopia.

468 A227 22c **multicolored** *(708,169)* .50 .45
First day cover *(80,588)* 1.75
Inscription block of 4 2.50 —

Campaign against hunger. See UN Offices in Geneva No. 140; Vienna No. 57.

Water Resources A228

Printed by the Government Printing Bureau, Japan. Pane of 40, 2 blocks of 4 horizontal by 5 blocks of 4 vertical. Designed by Thomas Lee, China.

1986, Mar. 14 Photo. *Perf. 13½*

469 A228 22c Dam *(525,839)* 1.00 .90
470 A228 22c Irrigation *(525,839)* 1.00 .90
471 A228 22c Hygiene *(525,839)* 1.00 .90
472 A228 22c Well *(525,839)* 1.00 .90
a. Block of 4, #469-472 4.00 4.00
First day cover, #472a 6.50
First day cover, #469-472, each 2.00
Inscription block of 4, #469-472 7.50 —
Pane of 40, #469-472 45.00

UN Development Program. No. 472a has continuous design.
First day covers of Nos. 469-472 total 199,347.
See UN Offices in Geneva Nos. 141-144; Vienna Nos. 58-61.

Human Rights Stamp of 1954 — A229

Stamp collecting: 44c, Engraver. Printed by the Swedish Post Office, Sweden. Panes of 50. Designed by Czeslaw Slania and Ingalill Axelsson, Sweden.

1986, May 22 Engr. *Perf. 12½*

473 A229 22c **dark violet & bright blue** *(825,782)* .30 .25
First day cover 1.00
Inscription block of 4 1.50 —
474 A229 44c **brown & emerald green** *(738,552)* .80 .70
First day cover 1.25
First day cover, #473-474 1.50
Inscription block of 4 3.25 —

First day covers of Nos. 473-474 total: New York, 121,143; Chicago, 89,557.
See UN Offices in Geneva Nos. 146-147; Vienna Nos. 62-63.

Bird's Nest in Tree — A230

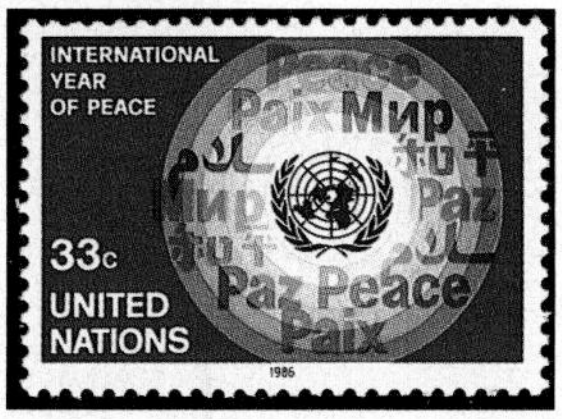

Peace in Seven Languages A231

Printed by the Government Printing Bureau, Japan. Panes of 50. Designed by Akira Iriguchi, Japan (#475), and Henryk Chylinski, Poland (#476).

1986, June 20 Photo. & Embossed *Perf. 13½*

475 A230 22c **multicolored** *(836,160)* .50 .40
First day cover 1.00
Inscription block of 4 2.50 —
476 A231 33c **multicolored** *(663,882)* 1.25 1.25
First day cover 2.00
First day cover, #475-476 4.50
Inscription block of 4 6.50 —

International Peace Year.
First day covers of Nos. 475-476 total 149,976.
See UN Offices in Geneva Nos. 148-149; Vienna Nos. 64-65.

Flag Type of 1980

Printed by Helio Courvoisier, Switzerland. Designed by Ole Hamann. Issued in panes of 16; each contains 4 blocks of four (Nos. 477-480, 481-484, 485-488, 489-492). A se-tenant block of 4 designs centers each pane.

1986, Sept. 19 Photo. *Perf. 12*

Granite Paper

477 A185 22c New Zealand *(1,150,584)* .55 .50
478 A185 22c Lao PDR *(1,150,584)* .55 .50
479 A185 22c Burkina Faso *(1,150,584)* .55 .50
480 A185 22c Gambia *(1,150,584)* .55 .50
a. Se-tenant block of 4, #477-480 3.25 2.75
481 A185 22c Maldives *(1,154,870)* .55 .50
482 A185 22c Ethiopia *(1,154,870)* .55 .50
483 A185 22c Jordan *(1,154,870)* .55 .50
484 A185 22c Zambia *(1,154,870)* .55 .50
a. Se-tenant block of 4, #481-484 3.25 2.75
485 A185 22c Iceland *(1,152,740)* .55 .50
486 A185 22c Antigua & Barbuda *(1,152,740)* .55 .50
487 A185 22c Angola *(1,152,740)* .55 .50
488 A185 22c Botswana *(1,152,740)* .55 .50
a. Se-tenant block of 4, #485-488 3.25 2.75
489 A185 22c Romania *(1,150,412)* .55 .50
490 A185 22c Togo *(1,150,412)* .55 .50
491 A185 22c Mauritania *(1,150,412)* .55 .50
492 A185 22c Colombia *(1,150,412)* .55 .50
a. Se-tenant block of 4, #489-492 3.25 2.75
First day covers, #477-492, each 1.00
Set of 4 diff. panes of 16 31.00
Nos. 477-492 (16) 8.80 8.00

First day covers of Nos. 477-492 total 1,442,284.

World Federation of UN Associations, 40th anniv. — A232

Printed by Johann Enschede and Sons, Netherlands. Designed by Rocco J. Callari, U.S.
Designs: 22c, Mother Earth, by Edna Hibel, U.S. 33c, Watercolor by Salvador Dali (b. 1904), Spain. 39c, New Dawn, by Dong Kingman, U.S. 44c, Watercolor by Chaim Gross, U.S.

1986, Nov. 14 Litho. *Perf. 13x13½*

Souvenir Sheet

493 Sheet of 4 *(433,888)* 3.25 3.25
a. A232 22c **multicolored** .40 .40
b. A232 33c **multicolored** .50 .40
c. A232 39c **multicolored** .75 .50
d. A232 44c **multicolored** 1.10 .75
First day cover *(106,194)* 2.00

No. 493 has inscribed margin picturing UN and WFUNA emblems.
See UN Offices in Geneva No. 150; Vienna No. 66.

Trygve Halvdan Lie (1896-1968), first Secretary-General — A233

1987, Jan. 30 Photo. & Engr. *Perf. 13½*

Printed by the Government Printing Office, Austria. Panes of 50. Designed by Rocco J. Callari, U.S., from a portrait by Harald Dal, Norway.

494 A233 22c **multicolored** *(596,440)* .80 .80
First day cover *(84,819)* 1.75
Inscription block of 4 3.75 —

See Offices in Geneva No. 151; Vienna No. 67.

International Year of Shelter for the Homeless A234

Printed by Johann Enschede and Sons, Netherlands. Panes of 50. Designed by Wladyslaw Brykczynski, Poland.
Designs: 22c, Surveying and blueprinting. 44c, Cutting lumber.

1987, Mar. 13 Litho. *Perf. 13½x12½*

495 A234 22c **multicolored** *(620,627)* .40 .35
First day cover 1.60
Inscription block of 4 1.75 —
496 A234 44c **multicolored** *(538,096)* 1.25 1.25
First day cover 1.90
First day cover, #495-496 2.75
Inscription block of 4 5.50 —

First day covers of Nos. 495-496 total 94,090.
See Offices in Geneva Nos. 154-155; Vienna Nos. 68-69.

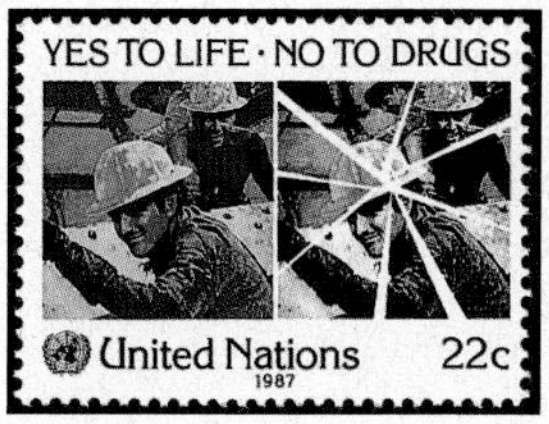

Fight Drug Abuse — A235

Printed by the House of Questa, United Kingdom. Panes of 50. Designed by Susan Borgen and Noel Werrett, U.S.
Designs: 22c, Construction. 33c, Education.

1987, June 12 **Litho.** ***Perf. 14½x15***

497 A235 22c **multicolored** *(674,563)* .65 .50
First day cover 1.75
Inscription block of 4 2.75 —
498 A235 33c **multicolored** *(643,153)* 1.10 1.00
First day cover 2.00
First day cover, #497-498 2.25
Inscription block of 4 5.25 —

First day covers of Nos. 497-498 total 106,941.
See Offices in Geneva Nos. 156-157; Vienna Nos. 70-71.

Flag Type of 1980

Printed by Courvoisier. Designed by Ole Hamann.
Issued in panes of 16; each contains 4 block of four (Nos. 499-502, 503-506, 507-510, 511-514). A se-tenant block of 4 designs centers each pane.

1987, Sept. 18 **Photo.** ***Perf. 12***
Granite Paper

499 A185 22c Comoros *(1,235,828)* .55 .35
500 A185 22c Yemen PDR *(1,235,828)* .55 .35
501 A185 22c Mongolia *(1,235,828)* .55 .35
502 A185 22c Vanuatu *(1,235,828)* .55 .35
a. Se-tenant block of 4, #499-502 3.25 2.75
503 A185 22c Japan *(1,244,534)* .55 .35
504 A185 22c Gabon *(1,244,534)* .55 .35
505 A185 22c Zimbabwe *(1,244,534)* .55 .35
506 A185 22c Iraq *(1,244,534)* .55 .35
a. Se-tenant block of 4, #503-506 3.25 2.75
507 A185 22c Argentina *(1,238,065)* .55 .35
508 A185 22c Congo *(1,238,065)* .55 .35
509 A185 22c Niger *(1,238,065)* .55 .35
510 A185 22c St. Lucia *(1,238,065)* .55 .35
a. Se-tenant block of 4, #507-510 3.25 2.75
511 A185 22c Bahrain *(1,239,323)* .55 .35
512 A185 22c Haiti *(1,239,323)* .55 .35
513 A185 22c Afghanistan *(1,239,323)* .55 .35
514 A185 22c Greece *(1,239,323)* .55 .35
a. Se-tenant block of 4, #511-514 3.25 2.75
First day covers, #499-514, each 1.00
Set of 4 diff. panes of 16 32.50
Nos. 499-514 (16) 8.80 5.60

United Nations Day — A236

Printed by The House of Questa, United Kingdom. Panes of 12. Designed by Elisabeth von Janota-Bzowski (#515) and Fritz Henry Oerter (#516), Federal Republic of Germany.
Designs: Multinational people in various occupations.

1987, Oct. 23 **Litho.** ***Perf. 14½x15***

515 A236 22c **multicolored** *(1,119,286)* .40 .35
First day cover 1.00
Inscription block of 4 2.00 —
516 A236 39c **multicolored** *(1,065,468)* .60 .65
First day cover 2.00
First day cover, #515-516 1.60
Inscription block of 4 2.50 —
Panes of 12, #515-516 12.00

See Offices in Geneva Nos. 158-159; Vienna Nos. 74-75.

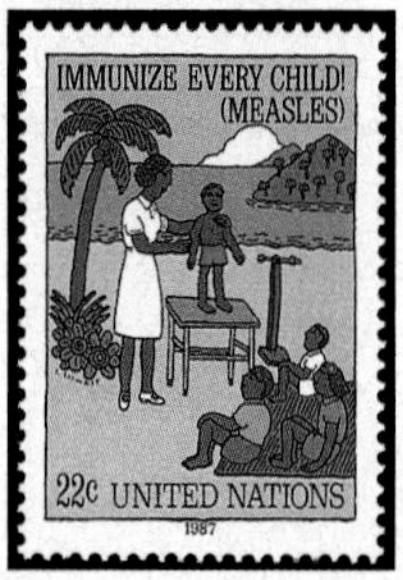

Immunize Every Child — A237

Printed by The House of Questa, United Kingdom. Panes of 50. Designed by Seymour Chwast, U.S.
Designs: 22c, Measles. 44c, Tetanus.

1987, Nov. 20 **Litho.** ***Perf. 15x14½***

517 A237 22c **multicolored** *(660,495)* 1.00 .50
First day cover 2.00
Inscription block of 4 3.00 —
518 A237 44c **multicolored** *(606,049)* 1.75 1.25
First day cover 2.25
First day cover, #517-518 3.50
Inscription block of 4 9.00 —

See Offices in Geneva Nos. 160-161; Vienna Nos. 76-77.

Intl. Fund for Agricultural Development (IFAD) A238

Printed by CPE Australia Ltd., Australia. Panes of 50. Designed by Santiago Arolas, Switzerland.
Designs: 22c, Fishing. 33c, Farming.

1988, Jan. 29 **Litho.** ***Perf. 13½***

519 A238 22c **multicolored** *(392,649)* .45 .40
First day cover 1.00
Inscription block of 4 2.25 —
520 A238 33c **multicolored** *(475,185)* .90 .85
First day cover 1.25
First day cover, #519-520 3.00
Inscription block of 4 4.75 —

See Offices in Geneva Nos. 162-163; Vienna Nos. 78-79.

A239

Printed by Heraclio Fournier, S.A., Spain. Panes of 50. Designed by David Ben-Hador, Israel.

1988, Jan. 29 **Photo.** ***Perf. 13½x14***

521 A239 3c **multicolored** *(3,000,000)+* .20 .20
First day cover 1.00
Inscription block of 4 .75 —

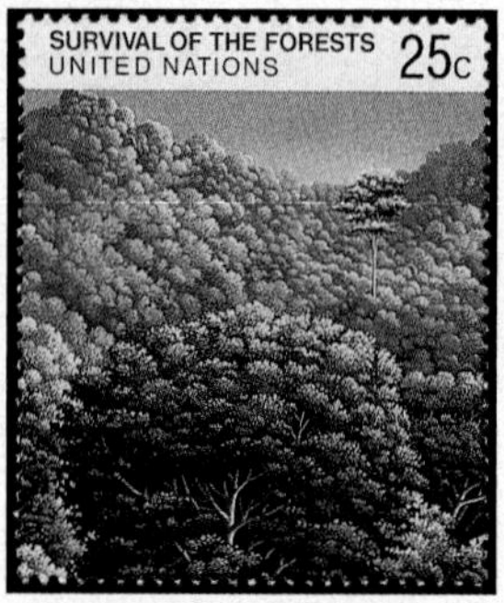

Survival of the Forests — A240

Printed by The House of Questa, United Kingdom. Panes of six se-tenant pairs. Designed by Braldt Bralds, the Netherlands.
Tropical rain forest: 25c, Treetops. 44c, Ground vegetation and tree trunks. Printed se-tenant in a continuous design.

1988, Mar. 18 **Litho.** ***Perf. 14x15***

522 A240 25c **multicolored** *(647,360)* 1.00 1.00
First day cover 3.50
523 A240 44c **multicolored** *(647,360)* 1.75 1.75
First day cover 6.50
a. Pair, #522-523 3.25 3.25
First day cover, #523a 9.50
Inscription block of 4 7.00
Pane of 12, #522-523 22.50

See Offices in Geneva Nos. 165-166; Vienna Nos. 80-81.

Intl. Volunteer Day — A241

Printed by Johann Enschede and Sons, the Netherlands. Panes of 50. Designed by James E. Tennison, U.S.
Designs: 25c, Edurahon. 50c, Vocational training, horiz.

1988, May 6 **Litho.** ***Perf. 13x14, 14x13***

524 A241 25c **multicolored** *(688,444)* .55 .50
First day cover 2.50
Inscription block of 4 2.50 —
525 A241 50c **multicolored** *(447,784)* 1.25 1.00
First day cover 3.00
First day cover, #524-525 3.25
Inscription block of 4 5.00 —

See Offices in Geneva Nos. 167-168; Vienna Nos. 82-83.

Health in Sports A242

Printed by the Government Printing Bureau, Japan. Panes of 50. Paintings by LeRoy Neiman, American sports artist.
Designs: 25c, Cycling, vert. 35c, Marathon.

1988, June 17 **Litho.** ***Perf. 13½x13, 13x13½***

526 A242 25c **multicolored** *(658,991)* .50 .45
First day cover 2.25
Inscription block of 4 2.50 —
527 A242 38c **multicolored** *(420,421)* 1.10 1.10
First day cover 2.50
First day cover, #526-527 3.75
Inscription block of 4 6.50 —

See Offices in Geneva Nos. 169-170; Vienna Nos. 84-85.

Flag Type of 1980

Printed by Helio Courvoisier, Switzerland. Designed by Ole Hamann, Denmark. Issued in panes of 16; each contains 4 blocks of four (Nos. 528-531, 532-535, 536-539 and 540-543). A se-tenant block of 4 centers each pane.

1988, Sept. 15 **Photo.** ***Perf. 12***
Granite Paper

528 A185 25c Spain *(1,029,443)* .60 .50
529 A185 25c St. Vincent & Grenadines *(1,029,443)* .60 .50
530 A185 25c Ivory Coast *(1,029,443)* .60 .50
531 A185 25c Lebanon *(1,029,443)* .60 .50
a. Se-tenant block of 4, #528-531 3.25 2.75
532 A185 25c Yemen (Arab Republic) *(1,010,774)* .60 .50
533 A185 25c Cuba *(1,010,774)* .60 .50
534 A185 25c Denmark *(1,010,774)* .60 .50
535 A185 25c Libya *(1,010,774)* .60 .50
a. Se-tenant block of 4, #532-535 3.25 2.75
536 A185 25c Qatar *(1,016,941)* .60 .50
537 A185 25c Zaire *(1,016,941)* .60 .50
538 A185 25c Norway *(1,016,941)* .60 .50
539 A185 25c German Democratic Republic *(1,016,941)* .60 .50
a. Se-tenant block of 4, #536-539 3.25 2.75
540 A185 25c Iran *(1,009,234)* .60 .50
541 A185 25c Tunisia *(1,009,234)* .60 .50
542 A185 25c Samoa *(1,009,234)* .60 .50
543 A185 25c Belize *(1,009,234)* .60 .50
a. Se-tenant block of 4, #540-543 3.25 2.75
First day covers, #528-543, each 1.25
Set of 4 diff. panes of 16 32.50
Nos. 528-543 (16) 9.60 8.00

Universal Declaration of Human Rights, 40th. Anniv. — A243

Printed by Helio Couvoisier, Switzerland. Panes of 50. Designed by Rocco J. Callari, U.S.

1988, Dec. 9 **Photo. & Engr.** ***Perf. 11x11½***

544 A243 25c **multicolored** *(893,706)* .50 .45
First day cover 2.25
Inscription block of 4 2.40 —

Souvenir Sheet

545 A243 $1 **multicolored** *(411,863)* 1.50 1.50
First day cover 2.75

No. 545 has multicolored decorative margin inscribed with the preamble to the human rights declaration in English.
See Offices in Geneva Nos. 171-172; Vienna Nos. 86-87.

World Bank — A244

A245

Printed by Johann Enschede and Sons, the Netherlands. Panes of 50. Designed by Saturnino Lumboy, Philippines.

1989, Jan. 27 **Litho.** ***Perf. 13x14***

546 A244 25c Energy and nature *(612,114)* .75 .45
First day cover 2.00
Inscription block of 4 3.00 —
547 A244 45c Agriculture *(528,184)* 1.50 1.00
First day cover 2.50
First day cover, #546-547 3.00
Inscription block of 4 7.00 —

First day covers of Nos. 546-547 total 103,087 (NYC), 56,501 (Washington).
See Offices in Geneva Nos. 173-174; Vienna Nos. 88-89.

1989, Mar. 17 **Litho.** ***Perf. 14x13½***

UN Peace-Keeping Force, awarded 1988 Nobel Peace Prize.
Printed by CPE Australia, Ltd., Australia. Panes of 50. Designed by Tom Bland, Australia.

548 A245 25c **multicolored** *(808,842)* .50 .40
First day cover *(52,115)* 2.25
Inscription block of 4 2.25 —

See Offices in Geneva No. 175; Vienna No. 90.

Aerial Photograph of New York Headquarters — A246

Printed by Johann Enschede and Sons, the Netherlands. Panes of 25. Designed by Rocco J. Callari, United States, from a photograph by Simon Nathan.

1989, Mar. 17 **Litho.** ***Perf. 14½x14***

549 A246 45c **multicolored** *(2,000,000)+* .75 .65
First day cover *(41,610)* 2.00
Inscription block of 4 3.00 —

World Weather Watch, 25th Anniv. (in 1988) — A247

Printed by Johann Enschede and Sons, the Netherlands. Panes of 50.
Satellite photographs: 25c, Storm system off the U.S. east coast. 36c, Typhoon Abby in the north-west Pacific.

1989, Apr. 21 **Litho.** ***Perf. 13x14***

550 A247 25c **multicolored** *(849,819)* .70 .60
First day cover 1.75
Inscription block of 4 3.00 —
551 A247 36c **multicolored** *(826,547)* 1.40 1.25
First day cover 2.50
First day cover, #550-551 3.00
Inscription block of 4 7.25 —

First day covers of Nos. 550-551 total 92,013.
See Offices in Geneva Nos. 176-177; Vienna Nos. 91-92.

Offices in Vienna, 10th Anniv.
A248 A249

Printed by the Government Printing Office, Austria. Panes of 25. Designed by Paul Flora (25c) and Rudolf Hausner (90c), Austria.

Photo. & Engr., Photo. (90c)

1989, Aug. 23 ***Perf. 14***

552 A248 25c **multicolored** *(580,663)* 2.25 2.25
First day cover 2.25
Inscription block of 4 11.00 —
553 A249 90c **multicolored** *(505,776)* 2.00 2.00
First day cover 2.25
First day cover, #552-553 8.50
Inscription block of 4 8.00 —
Panes of 25, #552-553 150.00

First day covers of Nos. 552-553 total 89,068.
See Offices in Geneva Nos. 178-179; Vienna Nos. 93-94.

Flag Type of 1980

Printed by Helio Courvoisier, Switzerland. Designed by Ole Hamann, Denmark. Issued in panes of 16; each contains 4 blocks of 4 (Nos. 554-557, 558-561, 562-565, 566-569). A se-tenant block of 4 designs centers each pane.

1989, Sept. 22 **Photo.** ***Perf. 12***
Granite Paper

554 A185 25c Indonesia *(959,076)* .60 .55
555 A185 25c Lesotho *(959,076)* .60 .55
556 A185 25c Guatemala *(959,076)* .60 .55
557 A185 25c Netherlands *(959,076)* .60 .55
a. Se-tenant block of 4, #554-557 3.50 3.00
558 A185 25c South Africa *(960,502)* .60 .55
559 A185 25c Portugal *(960,502)* .60 .55
560 A185 25c Morocco *(960,502)* .60 .55
561 A185 25c Syrian Arab Republic *(960,502)* .60 .55
a. Se-tenant block of 4, #558-561 3.50 3.00
562 A185 25c Honduras *(959,814)* .60 .55
563 A185 25c Kampuchea *(959,814)* .60 .55
564 A185 25c Guinea-Bissau *(959,814)* .60 .55
565 A185 25c Cyprus *(959,814)* .60 .55
a. Se-tenant block of 4, #562-565 3.50 3.00
566 A185 25c Algeria *(959,805)* .60 .55
567 A185 25c Brunei *(959,805)* .60 .55
568 A185 25c St. Kitts and Nevis *(959,805)* .60 .55
569 A185 25c United Nations *(959,805)* .60 .55
a. Se-tenant block of 4, #566-569 3.50 3.00
First day covers, #554-569, each 1.25
Set of 4 diff. panes of 16 35.00
Nos. 554-569 (16) 9.60 8.80

First day covers of Nos. 554-569 total 794,934.

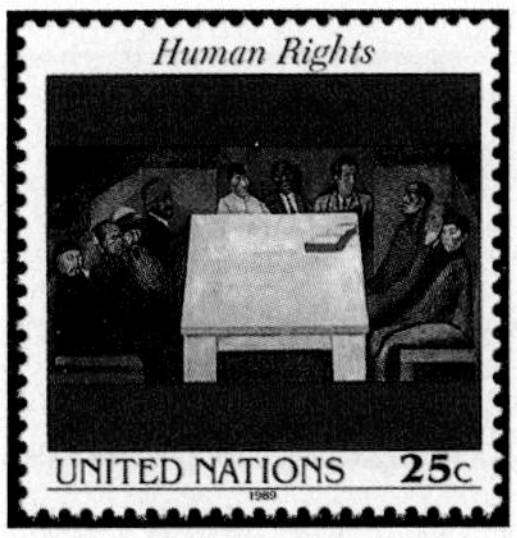

Declaration of Human Rights, 40th Anniv. (in 1988) — A250

Printed by Johann Enschede and Sons, the Netherlands. Panes of 12+12 se-tenant labels containing Articles 1 (25c) or 2 (45c) inscribed in English, French or German. Designed by Rocco J. Callari and Robert Stein, US.
Paintings: 25c, The Table of Universal Brotherhood, by Jose Clemente Orozco. 45c, Study for Composition II, by Vassily Kandinsky.

1989, Nov. 17 **Litho.** ***Perf. 13½***

570 A250 25c **multicolored** *(1,934,135)* .40 .30
First day cover 1.50
Inscription block of 3 + 3 labels 1.25 —
571 A250 45c **multicolored** *(1,922,171)* .90 .80
First day cover 1.75
First day cover, #570-571 2.00
Inscription block of 3 + 3 labels 2.75 —
Panes of 12, #570-571 14.00

First day covers of Nos. 570-571 total 146,489 (NYC), 46,774 (Washington).
See Nos. 582-583, 599-600, 616-617, 627-628; Offices in Geneva Nos. 180-181, 193-194, 209-210, 224-225, 234-235; Vienna Nos. 95-96, 108-109, 123-124, 139-140, 150-151.

Intl. Trade Center — A251

Printed by House of Questa, United Kingdom. Panes of 50. Designed by Richard Bernstein, US.

1990, Feb. 2 **Litho.** ***Perf. 14½x15***

572 A251 25c **multicolored** *(429,081)* 1.60 1.25
First day cover *(52,614)* 2.50
Inscription block of 4 6.50 —

See Offices in Geneva No. 182; Vienna No. 97.

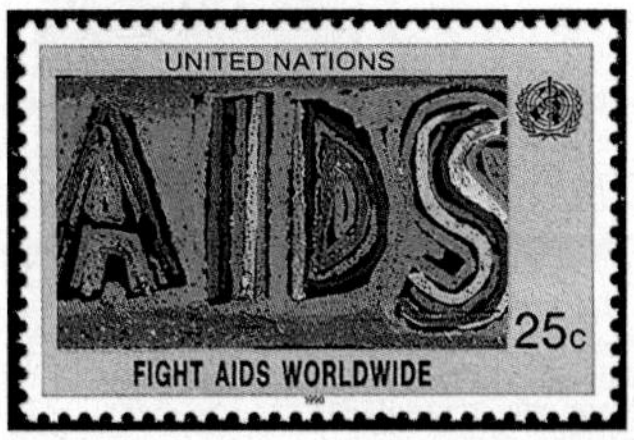

Fight AIDS Worldwide A252

Printed by Johann Enschede and Sons, the Netherlands. Panes of 50. Designed by Jacek Tofil, Poland (25c) and Fritz Henry Oerter, Federal Republic of Germany (40c).
Design: 40c, Shadow over crowd.

1990, Mar. 16 **Litho.** ***Perf. 13½x12½***

573 A252 25c **multicolored** *(492,078)* .50 .40
First day cover 2.00
Inscription block of 4 2.00 —
574 A252 40c **multicolored** *(394,149)* 1.50 1.25
First day cover 3.50
First day cover, #573-574 5.00
Inscription block of 4 6.00 —

First day covers of Nos. 573-574 total 95,854.
See Offices in Geneva Nos. 184-185, Vienna Nos. 99-100.

Medicinal Plants — A253

Printed by Helio Courvoisier, Switzerland. Panes of 50. Designed by Rocco J. Callari & Robert Stein, US from illustrations from "Curtis's Botanical Magazine".

1990, May 4 **Photo.** **Granite Paper** ***Perf. 11½***

575 A253 25c Catharanthus roseus *(796,792)* .75 .65
First day cover 1.50
Inscription block of 4 2.25 —
576 A253 90c Panax quinquefolium *(605,617)* 1.75 1.50
First day cover 2.10
First day cover, #575-576 5.00
Inscription block of 4 7.75 —

First day covers of Nos. 575-576 total 100,548.
See Offices in Geneva Nos. 186-187, Vienna Nos. 101-102.

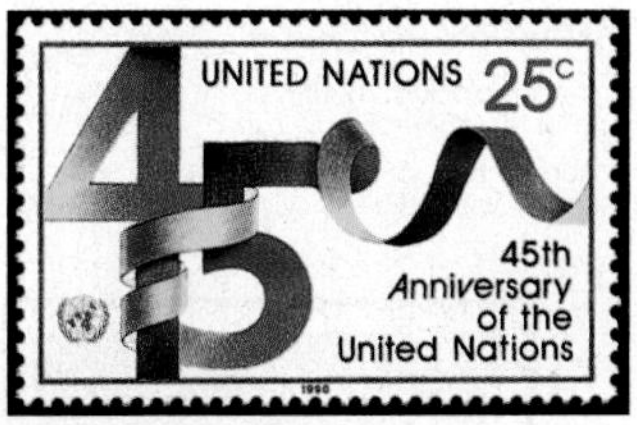

United Nations, 45th Anniv. A254

Printed by Johann Enschede and Sons, the Netherlands. Panes of 50. Designed by Kris Geysen, Belgium (25c), Nejat M. Gur, Turkey (45c), Robert Stein, US (No. 579).
Design: 45c, "45," emblem.

1990, June 26 **Litho.** ***Perf. 14½x13***

577 A254 25c **multicolored** *(581,718)* .75 .70
First day cover 1.25
Inscription block of 4 3.50 —
578 A254 45c **multicolored** *(582,769)* 2.50 2.50
First day cover 1.25

First day cover, #577-578 2.75
Inscription block of 4 11.00 —

Souvenir Sheet

579 Sheet of 2, #577-578 *(315,946)* 5.50 5.50
First day cover 4.00

First day covers of Nos. 577-579 total 129,011.
See Offices in Geneva Nos. 188-190; Vienna Nos. 103-105.

Crime Prevention — A255

Printed by Heraclio Fournier, S.A. Spain. Panes of 50. Designed by Josef Ryzec, Czechoslovakia.

1990, Sept. 13 **Photo.** ***Perf. 14***

580 A255 25c Crimes of youth *(533,089)* 1.00 .80
First day cover 2.00
Inscription block of 4 4.00 —
581 A255 36c Organized crime *(427,215)* 2.00 2.00
First day cover 3.25
First day cover, #580-581 6.00
Inscription block of 4 8.00 —

First day covers of Nos. 580-581 total 68,660.
See Offices in Geneva Nos. 191-192; Vienna Nos. 106-107.

Human Rights Type of 1989

Printed by Johann Enschede and Sons, the Netherlands. Panes of 12+12 se-tenant labels containing Articles 7 (25c) or 8 (45c) inscribed in English, French or German. Designed by Rocco J. Callari and Robert Stein, US.

Artwork: 25c, Fragment from the sarcophagus of Plotinus, c. 270 A.D. 45c, Combined Chambers of the High Court of Appeal by Charles Paul Renouard.

1990, Nov. 16 **Litho.** ***Perf. 13½***

582 A250 25c **black, gray & tan** *(1,492,950)* .45 .35
First day cover 1.50
Inscription block of 3 + 3 labels 1.50 —
583 A250 45c **black & brown** *(1,490,934)* .90 .75
First day cover 2.25
First day cover, #582-583 3.75
Inscription block of 3 + 3 labels 4.00 —
Panes of 12, #582-583 15.00

First day covers of Nos. 582-583 total 108,560.
See Offices in Geneva Nos. 193-194; Vienna Nos. 108-109.

Economic Commission for Europe — A256

Printed by Heraclio Fournier, S.A., Spain. Panes of 40. Designed by Carlos Ochagavia, Argentina.

1991, Mar. 15 **Litho.** ***Perf. 14***

584 A256 30c Two storks *(590,102)* 1.10 .90
585 A256 30c Woodpecker, ibex *(590,102)* 1.10 .90
586 A256 30c Capercaille, plover *(590,102)* 1.10 .90
587 A256 30c Falcon, marmot *(590,102)* 1.10 .90
a. Block of 4, #584-587 4.50 4.50
First day cover, #587a 4.00
First day cover, #584-587, any single 3.00
Inscription block of 4, #587a 5.00 —
Pane of 40, #584-587 45.00

First day covers of Nos. 584-587 total 53,502.
See Offices in Geneva Nos. 195-198; Vienna Nos. 110-113.

Namibian Independence A257

Printed by Heraclio Fournier, S.A., Spain. Designed by Rocco J. Callari, US, from photographs by John Isaac, India.

1991, May 10 **Litho.** ***Perf. 14***

588 A257 30c Dunes, Namib Desert *(360,825)* .75 .65
First day cover 2.00
Inscription block of 4 3.25 —
589 A257 50c Savanna *(415,648)* 1.50 1.25
First day cover 2.75
First day cover, #588-589 4.00
Inscription block of 4 6.50 —

First day covers of Nos. 588-589 total 114,258.
See Offices in Geneva Nos. 199-200; Vienna Nos. 114-115.

A258

The Golden Rule by Norman Rockwell — A259

UN Headquarters, New York — A260

Printed by Johann Enschede and Sons, the Netherlands (30c), Helio Courvoisier, S.A., Switzerland (50c), and by Government Printing Bureau, Japan ($2). Panes of 50. Designed by Rocco J. Callari (30c), Norman Rockwell, US (50c), Rocco J. Callari and Robert Stein, US ($2).

1991 **Litho.** ***Perf. 13½***

590 A258 30c **multi,** *Sept. 11, (2,000,000)+* .75 .65
First day cover 1.25
Inscription block of 4 3.25 —

Photo.

Perf. 12x11½

591 A259 50c **multi,** *Sept. 11, (2,000,000)+* 1.50 1.25
First day cover 2.50
Inscription block of 4 6.25

Engr.

592 A260 $2 **dark blue,** *May 10, (2,000,000)+* 3.00 2.75
First day cover 4.50
Inscription block of 4 11.00 —

First day covers of Nos. 590-591 total 66,016, No. 592, 36,022.
See Offices in Geneva Nos. 199-200; Vienna Nos. 114-115.

Rights of the Child — A261

Printed by The House of Questa, United Kingdom. Panes of 50. Designed by Nicole Delia Legnani, US (30c) and Alissa Duffy, US (70c).

1991, June 14 **Litho.** ***Perf. 14½***

593 A261 30c Children, globe *(440,151)* 1.00 .75
First day cover 1.50
Inscription block of 4 4.50 —
594 A261 70c House, rainbow *(447,803)* 2.00 1.75
First day cover 3.00
First day cover, #593-594 3.00
Inscription block of 4 9.00 —

First day covers of Nos. 593-594 total 96,324.
See Offices in Geneva Nos. 203-204; Vienna Nos. 117-118.

Banning of Chemical Weapons A262

Printed by Heraclio Fournier, S.A., Spain. Panes of 50. Designed by Oscar Asboth, Austria (30c), Michael Granger, France (90c).

Design: 90c, Hand holding back chemical drums.

1991, Sept. 11 **Litho.** ***Perf. 13½***

595 A262 30c **multicolored** *(367,548)* 1.00 .85
First day cover 1.50
Inscription block of 4 4.25 —
596 A262 90c **multicolored** *(346,161)* 3.00 2.50
First day cover 2.50
First day cover, #595-596 2.50
Inscription block of 4 13.00 —

First day covers of Nos. 595-596 total 91,552.
See Offices in Geneva Nos. 205-206; Vienna Nos. 119-120.

UN Postal Administration, 40th Anniv. — A263

Printed by The House of Questa, United Kingdom. Panes of 25. Designed by Rocco J. Callari, US.

1991, Oct. 24 **Litho.** ***Perf. 14x15***

597 A263 30c No. 1 *(442,548)* .90 .80
First day cover 1.25
Inscription block of 4 3.00 —
598 A263 40c No. 3 *(419,127)* 1.25 1.00
First day cover 1.50
First day cover, #597-598 2.00
Inscription block of 4 6.00 —
Panes of 25, #597-598 50.00

First day covers of Nos. 597-598 total 81,177 (New York), 58,501 (State College, PA).
See Offices in Geneva Nos. 207-208; Vienna Nos. 121-122.

Human Rights Type of 1989

Printed by Johann Enschede and Sons, the Netherlands. Panes of 12+12 se-tenant labels containing Articles 13 (30c) or 14 (50c) inscribed in English, French or German. Designed by Robert Stein, US.

Artwork: 30c, The Last of England, by Ford Madox Brown. 40c, The Emigration to the East, by Tito Salas.

1991, Nov. 20 **Litho.** ***Perf. 13½***

599 A250 30c **multicolored** *(1,261,198)* .50 .45
First day cover 1.25
Inscription block of 3 + 3 labels 2.10 —
600 A250 50c **multicolored** *(1,255,077)* 1.10 1.00
First day cover 1.75
First day cover, #599-600 2.25
Inscription block of 3 + 3 labels 4.00 —
Panes of 12, #599-600 16.00

First day covers of Nos. 599-600 total 136,605.
See Offices in Geneva Nos. 209-210; Vienna Nos. 123-124.

World Heritage Type of 1984

Printed by Cartor S.A., France. Panes of 50. Designed by Robert Stein, U.S.

Designs: 30c, Uluru Natl. Park, Australia. 50c, The Great Wall of China.

1992, Jan. 24 **Litho.** ***Perf. 13***

Size: 35x28mm

601 A215 30c **multicolored** *(337,717)* .70 .60
First day cover 2.00
Inscription block of 4 2.75 —
602 A215 50c **multicolored** *(358,000)* 1.10 1.00
First day cover 2.75
First day cover, #601-602 3.75
Inscription block of 4 6.50 —

First day covers of Nos. 601-602 total 62,733.
See Offices in Geneva Nos. 211-212; Vienna Nos. 125-126.

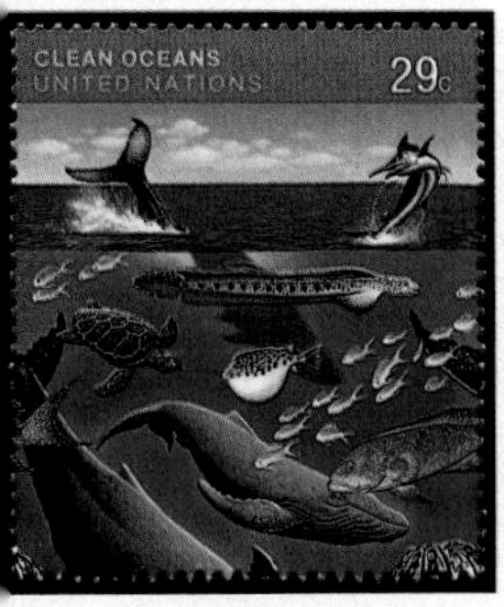

Clean Oceans — A264

Printed by The House of Questa, United Kingdom. Panes of 12. Designed by Braldt Bralds, Netherlands.

1992, Mar. 13 Litho. *Perf. 14*

603 A264 29c Ocean surface *(983,126)* .60 .55
604 A264 29c Ocean bottom *(983,126)* .60 .55
a. Pair, #603-604 1.25 1.10
First day cover, #604a 4.00
First day cover, #603-604, any single 1.75
Inscription block of 4, #603-604 4.00 —
Pane of 12, #603-604 8.50

First day covers of Nos. 603-604 total 75,511.
See Offices in Geneva Nos. 214-215, Vienna Nos. 127-128.

Earth Summit — A265

Printed by Helio Courvoisier S.A., Switzerland. Panes of 40. Designed by Peter Max, US.
Designs: No. 605, Globe at LR. No. 606, Globe at LL. No. 607, Globe at UR. No. 608, Globe at UL.

1992, May 22 Photo. *Perf. 11½*

605 A265 29c **multicolored** *(806,268)* .65 .60
606 A265 29c **multicolored** *(806,268)* .65 .60
607 A265 29c **multicolored** *(806,268)* .65 .60
608 A265 29c **multicolored** *(806,268)* .65 .60
a. Block of 4, #605-608 4.00 3.50
First day cover, #608a 3.50
First day cover, #605-608, each 2.50
Inscription block of 4, #608a 5.00 —
Pane of 40, #605-608 27.50

First day covers of Nos. 605-608a total 110,577.
See Offices in Geneva Nos. 216-219, Vienna Nos. 129-132.

Mission to Planet Earth — A266

Printed by Helio Courvoisier, S.A., Switzerland. Designed by Attilla Hejja, US.
Designs: No. 609, Satellites over city, sailboats, fishing boat. No. 610, Satellite over coast, passenger liner, dolphins, whale, volcano.

1992, Sept. 4 Photo. *Rouletted 8*
Granite Paper

609 A266 29c **multicolored** *(643,647)* 2.50 2.50
610 A266 29c **multicolored** *(643,647)* 2.50 2.50
a. Pair, #609-610 5.00 5.00
First day cover, #610a 3.00
First day cover, #609-610, each 4.50
Inscription block of 4 11.00 —
Pane of 10, #609-610 24.00

First day covers of Nos. 609-610a total 69,343.
See Offices in Geneva Nos. 220-221, Vienna Nos. 133-134.

Science and Technology for Development A267

Printed by Unicover Corp., US. Designed by Saul Mandel, US.
Design: 50c, Animal, man drinking.

1992, Oct. 2 Litho. *Perf. 14*

611 A267 29c **multicolored** *(453,365)* .50 .45
First day cover 1.75
Inscription block of 4 2.25 —
612 A267 50c **multicolored** *(377,377)* .90 .70
First day cover 2.00
First day cover, #611-612 5.75
Inscription block of 4 4.75

First day covers of Nos. 611-612 total 69,195.
See Offices in Geneva Nos. 222-223, Vienna Nos. 135-136.

UN University Building, Tokyo A268

UN Headquarters, New York — A269

Printed by Cartor SA, France (4c, 40c), Walsall Security Printers, Ltd., UK (29c). Designed by Banks and Miles, UK (4c, 40c), Robert Stein, US (29c).
Design: 40c, UN University Building, Tokyo, diff.

1992, Oct. 2 Litho. *Perf. 14, 13½x13 (29c)*

613 A268 4c **multicolored** *(1,500,000)+* .20 .20
First day cover 1.50
Inscription block of 4 .80 —
614 A269 29c **multicolored** *(1,750,000)+* .65 .50
First day cover 1.50
Inscription block of 4 2.75 —
615 A268 40c **multicolored** *(1,500,000)+* .85 .65
First day cover 1.50
First day cover, #613-615 2.00
Inscription block of 4 5.75 —
Nos. 613-615 (3) 1.70 1.35

First day covers of Nos. 613-615 total 62,697.

Human Rights Type of 1989

Printed by Johann Enschede and Sons, the Netherlands. Panes of 12+12 se-tenant labels containing Articles 19 (29c) and 20 (50c) inscribed in English, French or German. Designed by Robert Stein, US.
Artwork: 29c, Lady Writing a Letter with her Maid, by Vermeer. 50c, The Meeting, by Ester Almqvist.

1992, Nov. 20 Litho. *Perf. 13½*

616 A250 29c **multicolored,** *(1,184,531)* .70 .60
First day cover 1.50
Inscription block of 3 + 3 labels 2.25 —
617 A250 50c **multicolored,** *(1,107,044)* .90 .80
First day cover 2.00
First day cover, #616-617 3.50
Inscription block of 3 + 3 labels 3.25 —
Panes of 12, #616-617 14.00

First day covers of Nos. 616-617 total 104,470.
See Offices in Geneva Nos. 224-225; Vienna Nos. 139-140.

Aging With Dignity — A270

Printed by Cartor SA, France. Designed by C.M. Dudash, US.
Designs: 29c, Elderly couple, family. 52c, Old man, physician, woman holding fruit basket.

1993, Feb. 5 Litho. *Perf. 13*

618 A270 29c **multicolored** *(336,933)* .80 .70
First day cover 1.00
Inscription block of 4 3.50 —
619 A270 52c **multicolored** *(308,080)* 1.50 1.25
First day cover 1.75
First day cover, #618-619 2.75
Inscription block of 4 7.50 —

First day covers of Nos. 618-619 total 52,932.
See Offices in Geneva Nos. 226-227; Vienna Nos. 141-142.

Endangered Species A271

Printed by Johann Enschede and Sons, the Netherlands. Designed by Rocco J. Callari and Norman Adams, US.
Designs: No. 620, Hairy-nosed wombat. No. 621, Whooping crane. No. 622, Giant clam. No. 623, Giant sable antelope.

1993, Mar. 2 Litho. *Perf. 13x12½*

620 A271 29c **multicolored** *(1,200,000)+* .55 .50
621 A271 29c **multicolored** *(1,200,000)+* .55 .50
622 A271 29c **multicolored** *(1,200,000)+* .55 .50
623 A271 29c **multicolored** *(1,200,000)+* .55 .50
a. Block of 4, #620-623 2.25 2.25
First day cover, #623a 4.50
First day cover, #620-623, each 2.00
Inscription block of 4, #623a 2.40 —
Pane of 16, #620-623 11.00

First day covers of Nos. 620-623a total 64,794.
See Nos. 639-642, 657-660, 674-677, 700-703, 730-733, 757-760, 773-776; Offices in Geneva Nos. 228-231, 246-249, 264-267, 280-283, 298-301, 318-321, 336-339, 352-355; Vienna Nos. 143-146, 162-165, 180-183, 196-199, 214-217, 235-238, 253-256, 269-272.

Healthy Environment A272

Printed by Leigh-Mardon Pty. Limited, Australia. Designed by Milton Glaser, US.
Designs: 29c, Personal. 50c, Family.

1993, May 7 Litho. *Perf. 15x14½*

624 A272 29c Man *(430,463)* .80 .65
First day cover 1.25
Inscription block of 4 3.50 —
625 A272 50c Family *(326,692)* 1.10 1.00
First day cover 1.75
First day cover, #624-625 2.50
Inscription block of 4 4.75 —

WHO, 45th anniv. First day covers of Nos. 624-625 total 55,139.
See Offices in Geneva Nos. 232-233; Vienna Nos. 147-148.

A273

Printed by House of Questa, Ltd., United Kingdom. Designed by Salahattin Kanidinc, US.

1993, May 7 **Litho.** ***Perf. 15x14***

626 A273 5c **multicolored** *(1,500,000)+* .20 .20
First day cover *(23,452)* 1.00
Inscription block of 4 .70 —

Human Rights Type of 1989

Printed by Johann Enschede and Sons, the Netherlands. Panes of 12 + 12 se-tenant labels containing Articles 25 (29c) and 26 (35c) inscribed in English, French or German. Designed by Robert Stein, US.
Artwork: 29c, Shocking Corn, by Thomas Hart Benton. 35c, The Library, by Jacob Lawrence.

1993, June 11 **Litho.** ***Perf. 13½***

627 A250 29c **multicolored** *(1,049,134)* .50 .40
First day cover 1.25
Inscription block of 3 + 3 labels 3.00 —
628 A250 35c **multicolored** *(1,045,346)* .60 .45
First day cover 1.75
First day cover, #627-628 3.00
Inscription block of 3 + 3 labels 3.75 —
Panes of 12, #627-628 16.00

First day covers of Nos. 627-628 total 77,719.
See Offices in Geneva Nos. 234-235; Vienna Nos. 150-151.

Intl. Peace Day — A274

Printed by the PTT, Switzerland. Designed by Hans Erni, Switzerland.
Denomination at: #629, UL. #630, UR. #631, LL. #632, LR.

1993, Sept. 21 **Litho. & Engr.** ***Rouletted 12½***

629 A274 29c **blue & multi** *(298,367)* 1.75 1.75
630 A274 29c **blue & multi** *(298,367)* 1.75 1.75
631 A274 29c **blue & multi** *(298,367)* 1.75 1.75
632 A274 29c **blue & multi** *(298,367)* 1.75 1.75
a. Block of 4, #629-632 7.00 7.00
First day cover, #629-632, each 3.00
First day cover, #632a 5.00
Inscription block of 4, #632a 9.00 —
Pane of 40, #629-632 *80.00*

First day covers of Nos. 629-632a total 41,743.
See Offices in Geneva Nos. 236-239; Vienna Nos. 152-155.

Environment-Climate — A275

Printed by House of Questa, Ltd., United Kingdom. Designed by Braldt Bralds, Netherlands.
Designs: #633, Chameleon. #634, Palm trees, top of funnel cloud. #635, Bottom of funnel cloud, deer, antelope. #636, Bird of paradise.

1993, Oct. 29 **Litho.** ***Perf. 14½***

633 A275 29c **multicolored** *(383,434)* .75 .60
634 A275 29c **multicolored** *(383,434)* .75 .60
635 A275 29c **multicolored** *(383,434)* .75 .60
636 A275 29c **multicolored** *(383,434)* .75 .60
a. Strip of 4, #633-636 3.50 3.50
First day cover, #636a 3.75
First day cover, #633-636, each 3.00
Inscription block, 2 #636a 8.50 —
Pane of 24, #633-636 23.50

First day covers of Nos. 633-636a total 38,182.
See Offices in Geneva Nos. 240-243; Vienna Nos. 156-159.

Intl. Year of the Family — A276

Printed by Cartor S.A., France. Designed by Rocco J. Callari, US.
Designs: 29c, Mother holding child, two children, woman. 45c, People tending crops.

1994, Feb. 4 **Litho.** ***Perf. 13.1***

637 A276 29c **green & multi** *(590,000)+* 1.00 .90
First day cover 1.25
Inscription block of 4 4.50 —
638 A276 45c **blue & multi** *(540,000)+* 1.25 1.00
First day cover 1.75
First day cover, #637-638 2.00
Inscription block of 4 6.50 —

First day covers of Nos. 637-638 total 47,982. See Offices in Geneva Nos. 244-245; Vienna Nos. 160-161.

Endangered Species Type of 1993

Printed by Johann Enschede and Sons, the Netherlands. Designed by Rocco J. Callari, US (frame), and Kerrie Maddeford, Australia (stamps).
Designs: No. 639, Chimpanzee. No. 640, St. Lucia Amazon. No. 641, American crocodile. No. 642, Dama gazelle.

1994, Mar. 18 **Litho.** ***Perf. 12.7***

639 A271 29c **multicolored** *(1,200,000)+* .50 .50
640 A271 29c **multicolored** *(1,200,000)+* .50 .50
641 A271 29c **multicolored** *(1,200,000)+* .50 .50
642 A271 29c **multicolored** *(1,200,000)+* .50 .50
a. Block of 4, #639-642 2.00 2.00
First day cover, #642a 4.50
First day cover, #639-642, each 1.50
Inscription block of 4, #642a 2.50 —
Pane of 16, #639-642 10.00

First day covers of Nos. 639-642 total 79,599. See Offices in Geneva Nos. 246-249; Vienna Nos. 162-165.

Protection for Refugees — A277

Printed by Leigh-Mardon Pty. Limited, Australia. Designed by Francoise Peyroux, France.

1994, Apr. 29 **Litho.** ***Perf. 14.3x14.8***

643 A277 50c **multicolored** *(600,000)+* 1.00 .90
First day cover *(33,558)* 2.50
Inscription block of 4 5.25 —

See Offices in Geneva No. 250; Vienna No. 166.

Dove of Peace — A278

Sleeping Child, by Stanislaw Wyspianski — A279

Mourning Owl, by Vanessa Isitt — A280

Printed by Cartor S.A., France, and Norges Banks Seddeltrykkeri, Norway (#646).

1994, Apr. 29 **Litho.** ***Perf. 12.5***

644 A278 10c **multicolored** *(1,000,000)+* .20 .20
First day cover 1.25
Inscription block of 4 .80 —
645 A279 19c **multicolored** *(1,000,000)+* .40 .35
First day cover 2.00
Inscription block of 4 1.75 —

Engr.

Perf. 13.1

646 A280 $1 **red brown** *(1,000,000)+* 1.75 1.75
First day cover 4.00
Inscription block of 4 7.50 —
Nos. 644-646 (3) 2.35 2.30

First day covers of Nos. 644-646 total 48,946.

Intl. Decade for Natural Disaster Reduction — A281

Printed by The House of Questa, UK. Designed by Kenji Koga, Japan.
Earth seen from space, outline map of: #647, North America. #648, Eurasia. #649, South America, #650, Australia and South Asia.

1994, May 27 **Litho.** ***Perf. 13.9x14.2***

647 A281 29c **multicolored** *(630,000)+* 1.50 1.25
648 A281 29c **multicolored** *(630,000)+* 1.50 1.25
649 A281 29c **multicolored** *(630,000)+* 1.50 1.25
650 A281 29c **multicolored** *(630,000)+* 1.50 1.25
a. Block of 4, #647-650 8.00 8.00
First day cover, #650a 5.00
First day cover, #647-650, each 2.50
Inscription block of 4, #650a 9.00 —
Pane of 40, #647-650 77.50

First day covers of Nos. 647-650 total 37,135. See Offices in Geneva Nos. 251-254; Vienna Nos. 170-173.

Population and Development A282

Printed by Johann Enschede and Sons, the Netherlands. Designed by Jerry Smath, US.
Designs: 29c, Children playing. 52c, Family with house, car, other possessions.

1994, Sept. 1 **Litho.** ***Perf. 13.2x13.6***

651 A282 29c **multicolored** *(590,000)+* .50 .40
First day cover 1.25
Inscription block of 4 2.25 —
652 A282 52c **multicolored** *(540,000)+* 1.00 .90
First day cover 1.75
First day cover, #651-652 2.25
Inscription block of 4 4.25 —

First day covers of Nos. 651-652 total 45,256.
See Offices in Geneva Nos. 258-259; Vienna Nos. 174-175.

UNCTAD, 30th Anniv. — A283

Printed by Johann Enschede and Sons, the Netherlands. Designed by Luis Sarda, Spain.

1994, Oct. 28

653 A283 29c **multicolored** *(590,000)+* .50 .40
First day cover 1.25
Inscription block of 4 2.25 —
654 A283 50c **multi, diff.** *(540,000)+* 1.00 .70
First day cover 1.75
First day cover, #653-654 2.25
Inscription block of 4 4.25

First day covers of Nos. 653-654 total 42,763. See Offices in Geneva Nos. 260-261; Vienna Nos. 176-177.

UN, 50th Anniv. — A284

Printed by Swiss Postal Service. Designed by Rocco J. Callari, US.

1995, Jan. 1 Litho. & Engr. *Perf. 13.4*

655 A284 32c **multicolored** *(938,644)* 1.00 1.00
First day cover *(39,817)* 2.50
Inscription block of 4 4.25 —

See Offices in Geneva No. 262; Vienna No. 178.

Social Summit, Copenhagen — A285

1995, Feb. 3 Photo. & Engr. *Perf. 13.6x13.9*

Printed by Austrian Government Printing Office. Designed by Friedensreich Hundertwasser.

656 A285 50c **multicolored** *(495,388)* 1.00 .90
First day cover *(31,797)* 3.00
Inscription block of 4 4.00 —

See Offices in Geneva No. 263; Vienna No. 179.

Endangered Species Type of 1993

Printed by Johann Enschede and Sons, the Netherlands. Designed by Chris Calle, US.

Designs: No. 657, Giant armadillo. No. 658, American bald eagle. No. 659, Fijian/Tongan banded iguana. No. 660, Giant panda.

1995, Mar. 24 Litho. *Perf. 13x12½*

657 A271 32c **multicolored** *(756,000)+* .45 .45
658 A271 32c **multicolored** *(756,000)+* .45 .45
659 A271 32c **multicolored** *(756,000)+* .45 .45
660 A271 32c **multicolored** *(756,000)+* .45 .45
a. Block of 4, 657-660 2.25 2.25
First day cover, #660a 3.25
First day cover, #657-660, each 1.75
Inscription block of 4, #660a 2.50 —
Pane of 16, #657-660 11.00

First day covers of Nos. 657-660 total 67,311. See Offices in Geneva Nos. 264-267; Vienna Nos. 180-183.

Intl. Youth Year, 10th Anniv. — A286

Printed by The House of Questa (UK). Designed by Gottfried Kumpf, Austria.

Designs: 32c, Seated child. 55c, Children cycling.

1995, May 26 Litho. *Perf. 14.4x14.7*

661 A286 32c **multicolored** *(358,695)* .75 .60
First day cover 1.00
Inscription block of 4 3.25 —
662 A286 55c **multicolored** *(288,424)* 1.25 1.00
First day cover 1.50
First day cover, #661-662 2.25
Inscription block of 4 5.25 —

First day covers of Nos. 661-662 total 42,846. See Offices in Geneva Nos. 268-269; Vienna Nos. 184-185.

UN, 50th Anniv. — A287

Printed by Johann Enschede Security Printing, the Netherlands. Designed by Paul and Chris Calle, US.

Designs: 32c, Hand with pen signing UN Charter, flags. 50c, Veterans' War Memorial, Opera House, San Francisco.

1995, June 26 Engr. *Perf. 13.3x13.6*

663 A287 32c **black** *(501,961)* .75 .60
First day cover 1.50
Inscription block of 4 2.75 —
664 A287 50c **maroon** *(419,932)* 1.50 1.50
First day cover 2.00
First day cover, #663-664 3.75
Inscription block of 4 5.00 —

Souvenir Sheet

Litho. & Engr.

Imperf

665 Sheet of 2, #663-664 *(347,963)+* 2.75 2.50
a. A287 32c **black** 1.10 .95
b. A287 50c **maroon** 1.50 1.40
First day cover

First day covers of Nos. 663-665 total: New York, 69,263; San Francisco, 53,354.

No. 665 exists with gold China 1996 overprint. Value $15.

See Offices in Geneva Nos. 270-272; Vienna Nos. 186-188.

4th World Conference on Women, Beijing — A288

Printed by Postage Stamp Printing House, MPT, People's Republic of China. Designed by Ting Shao Kuang, People's Republic of China.

Designs: 32c, Mother and child. 40c, Seated woman, cranes flying above.

1995, Sept. 5 Photo. *Perf. 12*

666 A288 32c **multicolored** *(561,847)* .65 .50
First day cover 1.25
Inscription block of 4 2.75 —

Size: 28x50mm

667 A288 40c **multicolored** *(499,850)* 1.00 .90
First day cover 1.25
First day cover, #666-667 3.50
Inscription block of 4 4.25 —

First day covers of Nos. 666-667 total 103,963. See Offices in Geneva Nos. 273-274; Vienna Nos. 189-190.

UN Headquarters A289

Designed by John B. De Santis, Jr. US.

1995, Sept. 5 Litho. *Perf. 15*

668 A289 20c **multicolored** .40 .30
First day cover *(18,326)* 2.00
Inscription block of 4 2.00 —

Miniature Sheet

United Nations, 50th Anniv. — A290

Designed by Ben Verkaaik, Netherlands.
Printed by House of Questa, UK.

Designs: #669a-669 l, Various people in continuous design (2 blocks of six stamps with gutter between).

1995, Oct. 24 Litho. *Perf. 14*

669 Sheet of 12 *(214,639 sheets)* 12.00 10.00
First day cover 15.00
a.-l. A290 32c any single .80 .60
First day cover, #669a-669l, each 7.00
670 Souvenir booklet *(85,256 booklets)* 15.00
a. A290 32c Booklet pane of 3, vert. strip of 3 from UL of sheet 3.50 3.50
b. A290 32c Booklet pane of 3, vert. strip of 3 from UR of sheet 3.50 3.50
c. A290 32c Booklet pane of 3, vert. strip of 3 from LL of sheet 3.50 3.50
d. A290 32c Booklet pane of 3, vert. strip of 3 from LR of sheet 3.50 3.50
First day covers, #670a-670d, set booklet tab singles 140.00

First day covers of Nos. 669-670 total 47,632. See Offices in Geneva Nos. 275-276; Vienna Nos. 191-192.

WFUNA, 50th Anniv. — A291

Designed by Rudolf Mirer, Switzerland.
Printed by Johann Enschede and Sons, the Netherlands.

1996, Feb. 2 Litho. *Perf. 13x13½*

671 A291 32c **multicolored** *(580,000)+* .55 .45
First day cover 1.25
Inscription block of 4 2.25 —

See Offices in Geneva No. 277; Vienna No. 193.

Mural, by Fernand Leger — A292

Designed by Fernand Leger, France.
Printed by House of Questa, UK.

1996, Feb. 2 Litho. *Perf. 14½x15*

672 A292 32c **multicolored** *(780,000)+* .50 .40
First day cover 1.25
Inscription block of 4 2.25 —
673 A292 60c **multi, diff.** *(680,000)+* 1.00 .80
First day cover 1.75
First day cover, #672-673 2.25
Inscription block of 4 4.25 —

Endangered Species Type of 1993

Printed by Johann Enschede and Sons, the Netherlands. Designed by Diane Bruyninckx, Belgium.

Designs: No. 674, Masdevallia veitchiana. No. 675, Saguaro cactus. No. 676, West Australian pitcher plant. No. 677, Encephalartos horridus.

1996, Mar. 14 — Litho. — *Perf. 12½*

674	A271 32c **multicolored** *(640,000)+*		.50	.50
675	A271 32c **multicolored** *(640,000)+*		.50	.50
676	A271 32c **multicolored** *(640,000)+*		.50	.50
677	A271 32c **multicolored** *(640,000)+*		.50	.50
a.	Block of 4, #674-677		2.40	2.40
		First day cover, #677a		3.25
		First day cover, #674-677, each		1.75
		Inscription block of 4, #677a	3.00	—
		Pane of 16, #674-677	12.00	

See Offices in Geneva Nos. 280-283; Vienna Nos. 196-199.

City Summit (Habitat II) — A293

Printed by Johann Enschede and Sons, the Netherlands. Designed by Teresa Fasolino, US.

Designs: No. 678, Deer. No. 679, Man, child, dog sitting on hill, overlooking town. No. 680, People walking in park, city skyline. No. 681, Tropical park, Polynesian woman, boy. No. 682, Polynesian village, orchids, bird.

1996, June 3 — Litho. — *Perf. 14x13½*

678	A293 32c **multicolored** *(475,000)+*		.90	.75
679	A293 32c **multicolored** *(475,000)+*		.90	.75
680	A293 32c **multicolored** *(475,000)+*		.90	.75
681	A293 32c **multicolored** *(475,000)+*		.90	.75
682	A293 32c **multicolored** *(475,000)+*		.90	.75
a.	Strip of 5, #678-682		6.25	6.25
		First day cover, #682a		10.00
		First day cover, #678-682, each		3.50
		Inscription block of 10, 2 #682a	13.50	
		Sheet of 25	34.50	

See Offices in Geneva Nos. 284-288; Vienna Nos. 200-204.

Sport and the Environment — A294

Printed by The House of Questa, UK. Designed by LeRoy Neiman, US.

Designs: 32c, Men's basketball. 50c, Women's volleyball, horiz.

1996, July 19 — Litho. — *Perf. 14x14½, 14½x14*

683	A294 32c **multicolored** *(680,000)+*		.75	.60
		First day cover		1.25
		Inscription block of 4	3.25	—
684	A294 50c **multicolored** *(680,000)+*		1.50	1.50
		First day cover		1.50
		First day cover, #683-684		2.25
		Inscription block of 4	7.75	—

Souvenir Sheet

685	A294	Sheet of 2, #683-684 *(370,000)+*	2.50	2.50
		First day cover		3.50

See Offices in Geneva Nos. 289-291; Vienna Nos. 205-207.
1996 Summer Olympic Games, Atlanta, GA.

Plea for Peace — A295

Printed by House of Questa, UK.
Designed by: 32c, Peng Yue, China. 60c, Cao Chenyu, China.

Designs: 32c, Doves. 60c, Stylized dove.

1996, Sept. 17 — Litho. — *Perf. 14½x15*

686	A295 32c **multicolored** *(580,000)+*		.60	.45
		First day cover		1.25
		Inscription block of 4	2.75	—
687	A295 60c **multicolored** *(580,000)+*		1.10	.90
		First day cover		1.50
		First day cover, #686-687		2.25
		Inscription block of 4	4.75	—

See Offices in Geneva Nos. 292-293; Vienna Nos. 208-209.

UNICEF, 50th Anniv. — A296

Printed by The House of Questa, UK. Designed by The Walt Disney Co.

Fairy Tales: 32c, Yeh-Shen, China. 60c, The Ugly Duckling, by Hans Christian Andersen.

1996, Nov. 20 — Litho. — *Perf. 14½x15*

688	A296 32c **multicolored** *(1,000,000)+*		.50	.40
		First day cover		1.25
		Pane of 8 + label	4.50	
689	A296 60c **multicolored** *(1,000,000)+*		1.25	1.00
		First day cover		1.50
		First day cover, #688-689		2.50
		Pane of 8 + label	12.50	

See Offices in Geneva Nos. 294-295; Vienna Nos. 210-211.

Flag Type of 1980

Printed by Helio Courvoisier, S.A., Switzerland. Designed by Oliver Corwin,US, and Robert Stein, UN. Each pane contains 4 blocks of 4 (Nos. 690-693, 694-697). A se-tenant block of 4 designs centers each pane.

1997, Feb. 12 — Photo. — *Perf. 12*

Granite Paper

690	A185 32c Tadjikistan *(940,000)+*		1.00	.75
691	A185 32c Georgia *(940,000)+*		1.00	.75
692	A185 32c Armenia *(940,000)+*		1.00	.75
693	A185 32c Namibia *(940,000)+*		1.00	.75
a.	Block of 4, #690-693		5.00	4.00
694	A185 32c Liechtenstein *(940,000)+*		1.00	.75
695	A185 32c Republic of Korea *(940,000)+*		1.00	.75
696	A185 32c Kazakhstan *(940,000)+*		1.00	.75
697	A185 32c Latvia *(940,000)+*		1.00	.75
a.	Block of 4, #694-697		5.00	4.00
		First day cover, #690-697, each		3.00
		Set of 2 panes of 16	21.00	

First day covers of Nos. 690-697 total 136,114.

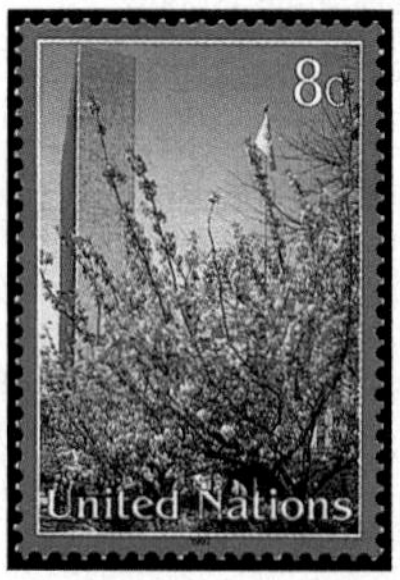

Cherry Blossoms, UN Headquarters — A297

Peace Rose — A298

Printed by The House of Questa, Ltd., UK.

1997, Feb. 12 — Litho. — *Perf. 14*

698	A297 8c **multicolored** *(700,000)+*		.20	.2
		First day cover		1.5
		Inscription block of 4	.90	–
699	A298 55c **multicolored** *(700,000)+*		1.10	1.0
		First day cover		1.5
		First day cover, #698-699		2.5
		Inscription block of 4	5.00	–

First day covers of Nos. 698-699 total 34,794.

Endangered Species Type of 1993

Printed by Johann Enschedé and Sons, the Netherland
Designed by Rocco J. Callari, US.
Designs: No. 700, African elephant. No. 701, Major Mitchell cockatoo. No. 702, Black-footed ferret. No. 703, Cougar.

1997, Mar. 13 — Litho. — *Perf. 12*

700	A271 32c **multicolored** *(532,000)+*		.45	.4
701	A271 32c **multicolored** *(532,000)+*		.45	.4
702	A271 32c **multicolored** *(532,000)+*		.45	.4
703	A271 32c **multicolored** *(532,000)+*		.45	.4
a.	Block of 4, #700-703		2.40	2.4
		First day cover, #703a		3.5
		First day cover, #700-703, each		2.0
		Inscription block of 4, #703a	2.75	
		Pane of 16	10.00	

First day covers of Nos. 700-703 total 66,863.
See Offices in Geneva Nos. 298-301; Vienna Nos. 214-21

Earth Summit, 5th Anniv. — A299

Printed by Helio Courvoisier SA, Switzerland. Designed b Peter Max, US.
Designs: No. 704, Sailboat. No. 705, Three sailboats. No 706, Two people watching sailboat, sun. No. 707, Person sailboat.
$1, Combined design similar to Nos. 704-707.

1997, May 30 — Photo. — *Perf. 11.*

Granite Paper

704	A299 32c **multicolored** *(328,566)*		.75	.7
705	A299 32c **multicolored** *(328,566)*		.75	.7
706	A299 32c **multicolored** *(328,566)*		.75	.7
707	A299 32c **multicolored** *(328,566)*		.75	.7
a.	Block of 4, #704-707		4.00	4.0
		First day cover, #707a		2.7
		First day cover, #704-707, each		2.0
		Inscription block of 4, #707a	4.50	

Souvenir Sheet

708	A299 $1 **multicolored** *(181,667)*		2.75	2.7
		First day cover		3.0
a.	Ovptd. in sheet margin *(154,435)*		*16.50*	*16.5*
		First day cover, #708a		16.5

First day covers of Nos. 704-708 total: New York, 52,528; Sa Francisco, 49,197.
See Offices in Geneva Nos. 302-306; Vienna Nos. 218-222
No. 708 contains one 60x43mm stamp. Overprint in shee margin of No. 708a reads "PACIFIC 97 / World Philatelic Exhib tion / San Francisco, California / 29 May - 8 June 1997".

Transportation — A300

Printed by The House of Questa, UK. Panes of 20.
Designed by Michael Cockcroft, UK.

Ships: No. 709, Clipper ship. No. 710, Paddle steamer. No. 711, Ocean liner. No. 712, Hovercraft. No. 713, Hydrofoil.

1997, Aug. 29 Litho. *Perf. 14x14½*

709 A300 32c **multicolored** *(303,767)* .50 .50
710 A300 32c **multicolored** *(303,767)* .50 .50
711 A300 32c **multicolored** *(303,767)* .50 .50
712 A300 32c **multicolored** *(303,767)* .50 .50
713 A300 32c **multicolored** *(303,767)* .50 .50
a. Strip of 5, #709-713 3.25 3.25
First day cover, #713a 5.00
First day cover, #709-713, each 3.00
Inscription block of 10, 2#713a 8.00
Sheet of 20 16.50

First day covers of Nos. 709-713 total 29,287.
See Offices in Geneva Nos. 307-311; Vienna Nos. 223-227.
No. 713a has continuous design.

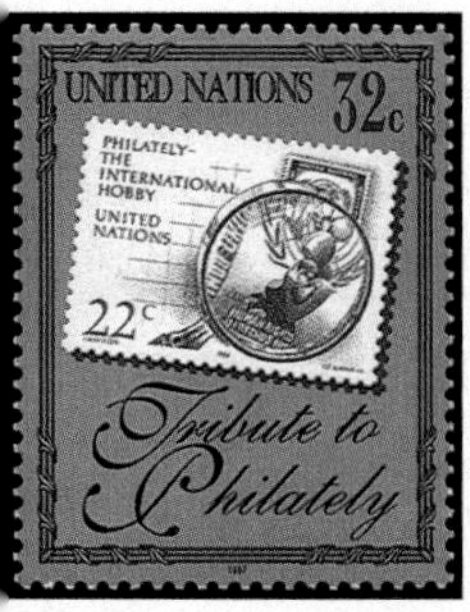

Philately — A301

Printed by Joh. Enschedé and Sons, the Netherlands. Panes of 20. Designed by Robert Stein, US.
Designs: 32c, No. 473. 50c, No. 474.

1997, Oct. 14 Litho. *Perf. 13½x14*

714 A301 32c **multicolored** *(363,237)* .75 .75
First day cover 1.25
Inscription block of 4 3.50 —
715 A301 50c **multicolored** *(294,967)* 1.75 1.75
First day cover 1.50
First day cover, #714-715 2.50
Inscription block of 4 9.50 —

First day covers of Nos. 714-715 total 43,684.
See Offices in Geneva Nos. 312-313; Vienna Nos. 228-229.

World Heritage Convention, 25th Anniv. — A302

Printed by Government Printing Office, Austria. Panes of 20. Designed by Robert Stein, US, based on photographs by Guo Youmin, People's Republic of China.
Terracotta warriors of Xian: 32c, Single warrior. 60c, Massed warriors. No. 718a, like #716. No. 718b, like #717. No. 718c, like Geneva #314. No. 718d, like Geneva #315. No. 718e, like Vienna #230. No. 718f, like Vienna #231.

1997, Nov. 19 Litho. *Perf. 13½*

716 A302 32c **multicolored** *(549,095)* .75 .60
First day cover 1.25
Inscription block of 4 3.25 —
717 A302 60c **multicolored** *(505,265)* 1.25 1.00
First day cover 1.75
First day cover, #716-717 2.75
Inscription block of 4 5.25 —
718 Souvenir booklet *(304,406 booklets)* 8.00
a.-f. A302 8c any single .30 .30
g. Booklet pane of 4 #718a .75 .50
h. Booklet pane of 4 #718b .75 .50
i. Booklet pane of 4 #718c .75 .50
j. Booklet pane of 4 #718d .75 .50
k. Booklet pane of 4 #718e .75 .50
l. Booklet pane of 4 #718f .75 .50

First day covers of Nos. 716-718 total 33,386.
See Offices in Geneva Nos. 314-316; Vienna Nos. 230-232.

Flag Type of 1980

Printed by Helio Courvoisier, S.A., Switzerland. Designed by Oliver Corwin, and Robert Stein, US. Each pane contains 4 blocks of 4 (Nos. 719-722, 723-726). A se-tenant block of 4 designs centers each pane.

1998, Feb. 13 Photo. *Perf. 12*
Granite Paper

719 A185 32c Micronesia *(718,000)+* .80 .50
720 A185 32c Slovakia *(718,000)+* .80 .50
721 A185 32c Democratic People's Republic of Korea *(718,000)+* .80 .50
722 A185 32c Azerbaijan *(718,000)+* .80 .50
a. Block of 4, #719-722 5.50 5.00
723 A185 32c Uzbekistan *(718,000)+* .80 .50
724 A185 32c Monaco *(718,000)+* .80 .50
725 A185 32c Czech Republic *(718,000)+* .80 .50
726 A185 32c Estonia *(718,000)+* .80 .50
a. Block of 4, #723-726 5.50 5.00
First day cover, #719-726, each 3.00
Set of 2 panes of 16 21.00
Nos. 719-726 (8) 6.40 4.00

A303

A304

A305

Printed by The House of Questa, UK. Designed by Zhang Le Lu, China (1c), Robert Stein, US (2c), Gregory Halili, Philippines (21c). Panes of 20.

1998, Feb. 13 Litho. *Perf. 14½x15, 15x14½*

727 A303 1c **multicolored** *(1,000,000)+* .20 .20
First day cover 1.00
Inscription block of 4 .20 —
728 A304 2c **multicolored** *(1,000,000)+* .20 .20
First day cover 1.00
Inscription block of 4 .20 —
729 A305 21c **multicolored** *(1,000,000)+* .40 .30
First day cover 1.00
First day cover, #727-729 3.00
Inscription block of 4 1.75 —
Nos. 727-729 (3) .80 .70

Endangered Species Type of 1993

Printed by Johann Enschedé and Sons, the Netherlands. Designed by Rocco J. Callari, US and Pat Medearis-Altman, New Zealand.
Designs: No. 730, Lesser galago. No. 731, Hawaiian goose. No. 732, Golden birdwing. No. 733, Sun bear.

1998, Mar. 13 Litho. *Perf. 12½*

730 A271 32c **multicolored** *(502,000)+* .50 .45
731 A271 32c **multicolored** *(502,000)+* .50 .45
732 A271 32c **multicolored** *(502,000)+* .50 .45
733 A271 32c **multicolored** *(502,000)+* .50 .45
a. Block of 4, #730-733 2.40 2.40
First day cover, #733a 3.50
First day cover, #730-733, each 2.50
Inscription block of 4, #733a 2.75 —
Pane of 16 11.00

See Offices in Geneva Nos. 318-321; Vienna Nos. 235-238.

Intl. Year of the Ocean — A306

Printed by Johann Enschedé and Sons, the Netherlands. Designed by Larry Taugher, US.

1998, May 20 Litho. *Perf. 13x13½*

734 A306 Sheet of 12 *(280,000)+* 8.75 8.50
First day cover 12.50
a.-l. 32c any single .65 .55
First day cover, #734a-734l, each 4.00

See Offices in Geneva No. 322; Vienna No. 239.

Rain Forests A307

Printed by Government Printing Bureau, Japan. Designed by Rick Garcia, US.

1998, June 19 Litho. *Perf. 13x13½*

735 A307 32c Jaguar *(570,000)+* .60 .60
First day cover 2.50
Inscription block of 4 2.75 —

Souvenir Sheet

736 A307 $2 like #735 *(280,000)+* 3.00 2.00
First day cover 3.00

See Offices in Geneva Nos. 323-324; Vienna Nos. 240-241.

U.N. Peacekeeping Forces, 50th Anniv. — A308

Printed by Helio Courvoisier, S.A. (Switzerland). Designed by Andrew Davidson, UK.
Designs: 33c, Commander with binoculars. 40c, Two soldiers on vehicle.

1998, Sept. 15 Photo. *Perf. 12*

737 A308 33c **multicolored** *(485,000)+* .50 .40
First day cover 1.25
Inscription block of 4 2.25 —
738 A308 40c **multicolored** *(445,000)+* .95 .85
First day cover 1.25
First day cover, #737-738 2.00
Inscription block of 4 4.25 —

See Offices in Geneva Nos. 325-326; Vienna Nos. 242-243.

Universal Declaration of Human Rights, 50th Anniv. — A309

Printed by Cartor Security Printing (France). Designed by Jean-Michel Folon, France.

Stylized people: 32c, Carrying flag. 55c, Carrying pens.

1998, Oct. 27 Litho. & Photo. *Perf. 13*

739 A309 32c **multicolored** *(485,000)+* .50 .40
First day cover 1.25
Inscription block of 4 2.25 —
740 A309 55c **multicolored** *(445,000)+* .95 .85
First day cover 1.50
First day cover, #739-740 2.50
Inscription block of 4 4.25 —

See Offices in Geneva Nos. 327-328; Vienna Nos. 244-245.

Schönbrunn Palace, Vienna — A310

Printed by the House of Questa, UK. Panes of 20. Designed by Robert Stein, US.

Designs: 33c, #743f, The Gloriette. 60c, #743b, Wall painting on fabric (detail), by Johann Wenzl Bergl, vert. No. 743a, Blue porcelain vase, vert. No. 743c, Porcelain stove, vert. No. 743d, Palace. No. 743e, Great Palm House (conservatory).

1998, Dec. 4 Litho. *Perf. 14*

741 A310 33c **multicolored** *(485,000)+* .60 .55
First day cover 1.25
Inscription block of 4 2.75 —
742 A310 60c **multicolored** *(445,000)+* 1.25 1.00
First day cover 1.50
First day cover, #741-742 2.50
Inscription block of 4 5.25 —

Souvenir Booklet

743 Booklet *(110,000)+* 10.50
a.-c. A310 11c any single .40 .40
d.-f. A310 15c any single .55 .55
g. Booklet pane of 4 #743d 2.20 2.20
h. Booklet pane of 3 #743a 1.25 1.25
i. Booklet pane of 3 #743b 1.25 1.25
j. Booklet pane of 3 #743c 1.25 1.25
k. Booklet pane of 4 #743e 2.20 2.20
l. Booklet pane of 4 #743f 2.20 2.20

See Offices in Geneva Nos. 329-331; Vienna Nos. 246-248.

Flag Type of 1980

Printed by Helio Courvoisier S.A., Switzerland. Designed by Oliver Corwin, Robert Stein and Blake Tarpley, US. Each pane contains 4 blocks of 4 (Nos. 744-747, 748-751). A se-tenant block of 4 designs centers each pane.

1999, Feb. 5 Photo. *Perf. 12*

744 A185 33c Lithuania *(524,000)+* .80 .60
745 A185 33c San Marino *(524,000)+* .80 .60
746 A185 33c Turkmenistan *(524,000)+* .80 .60
747 A185 33c Marshall Islands *(524,000)+* .80 .60
a. Block of 4, #744-747 6.00 5.00
748 A185 33c Moldova *(524,000)+* .80 .60
749 A185 33c Kyrgyzstan *(524,000)+* .80 .60
750 A185 33c Bosnia & Herzegovina *(524,000)+* .80 .60
751 A185 33c Eritrea *(524,000)+* .80 .60
a. Block of 4, #748-751 6.00 5.00
First day cover, #744-751, each 2.50
Set of 2 panes of 16 22.50
Nos. 744-751 (8) 6.40 4.80

First day covers of Nos. 744-751 total 102,040.

Flags and Globe — A311

Roses — A312

Designed by Blake Tarpley (#752), Rorie Katz, (#753), US.

Printed by Johann Enschedé and Sons, the Netherlands (#752), Helio Courvoisier SA, Switzerland (#753).

1999, Feb. 5 Litho. *Perf. 14x13½*

752 A311 33c **multicolored** *(960,000)+* .50 .40
First day cover 1.25
Inscription block of 4 2.25 —

Photo.

Granite Paper

Perf. 11½x12

753 A312 $5 **multicolored** *(420,000)+* 7.50 1.00
First day cover 7.50
First day cover, #752-753 8.25
Inscription block of 4 27.50 —

First day covers of Nos. 752-753 total 32,142.

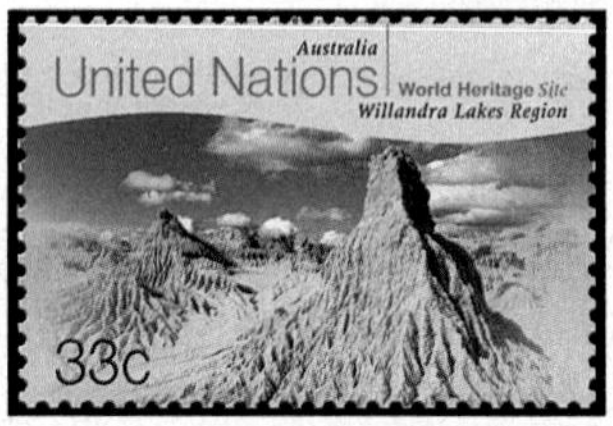

World Heritage Sites, Australia A313

Printed by House of Questa, UK. Panes of 20. Designed by Passmore Design, Australia.

Designs: 33c, #756f, Willandra Lakes region. 60c, #756b, Wet tropics of Queensland. No. 756a, Tasmanian wilderness. No. 756c, Great Barrier Reef. No. 756d, Uluru-Kata Tjuta Natl. Park. No. 756e, Kakadu Natl. Park.

1999, Mar. 19 Litho. *Perf. 13*

754 A313 33c **multicolored** *(480,000)+* .60 .75
First day cover 1.25
Inscription block of 4 3.00 —
755 A313 60c **multicolored** *(440,000)+* 1.25 1.50
First day cover 1.50
First day cover, #754-755 2.50
Inscription block of 4 6.00 —

Souvenir Booklet

756 Booklet *(97,000)+* 12.00
a.-c. A313 5c any single .20 .20
d.-f. A313 15c any single .60 .60
g. Booklet pane of 4, #756a .70 .70
h. Booklet pane of 4, #756d 2.50 2.50
i. Booklet pane of 4, #756b .70 .70
j. Booklet pane of 4, #756e 2.50 2.50
k. Booklet pane of 4, #756c .70 .70
l. Booklet pane of 4, #756f 2.50 2.50

First day covers of Nos. 754-756 total 42,385.

See Offices in Geneva Nos. 333-335; Vienna Nos. 250-252.

Endangered Species Type of 1993

Printed by Johann Enschedé and Sons, the Netherlands. Designed by Jimmy Wang, China.

Designs: No. 757, Tiger. No. 758, Secretary bird. No. 759, Green tree python. No. 760, Long-tailed chinchilla.

1999, Apr. 22 Litho. *Perf. 12½*

757 A271 33c **multicolored** *(494,000)+* .50 .40
758 A271 33c **multicolored** *(494,000)+* .50 .40
759 A271 33c **multicolored** *(494,000)+* .50 .40
760 A271 33c **multicolored** *(494,000)+* .50 .40
a. Block of 4, #757-760 2.50 2.50
First day cover, #760a 3.50
First day cover, #757-760, each 2.00
Inscription block of 4, #760a 2.75 —
Pane of 16 11.00

First day covers of Nos. 757-760 total 49,656.

See Offices in Geneva Nos. 336-339; Vienna Nos. 253-256.

UNISPACE III, Vienna — A314

Printed by Helio Courvoisier SA, Switzerland. Designed by Attila Hejja, US.

Designs: No. 761, Probe on planet's surface. No. 762, Planetary rover. No. 763, Composite of #761-762.

1999, July 7 Photo. *Rouletted 8*

761 A314 33c **multicolored** *(1,000,000)+* .50 .45
762 A314 33c **multicolored** *(1,000,000)+* .50 .45
a. Pair, #761-762 1.75 1.50
First day cover, #762a 2.00
First day cover, #761-762, each 1.25
Inscription block of 4 4.00 —
Pane of 10, #761-762 9.00 —

Souvenir Sheet

Perf. 14½

763 A314 $2 **multicolored** *(530,000)+* 4.00 2.50
First day cover 3.00
a. Ovptd. in sheet margin 14.00 10.00
First day cover 10.00

No. 763a was issued 7/7/00 and is overprinted in violet blue "WORLD STAMP EXPO 2000 / ANAHEIM, CALIFORNIA / U.S.A./ 7-16 JULY 2000."

First day covers of Nos. 761-763 total 48,190.

See Offices in Geneva #340-342; Vienna #257-259.

UPU, 125th Anniv. — A315

Printed by Helio Courvoisier S.A., Switzerland. Panes of 24. Designed by Mark Hess, US.

Various people, 19th century methods of mail transportation, denomination at: No. 764, UL. No. 765, UR. No. 766, LL. No. 767, LR.

1999, Aug. 23 Photo. *Perf. 11¾*

764 A315 33c **multicolored** *(378,000)+* .50 .45
765 A315 33c **multicolored** *(378,000)+* .50 .45
766 A315 33c **multicolored** *(378,000)+* .50 .45
767 A315 33c **multicolored** *(378,000)+* .50 .45
a. Block of 4, #764-767 2.75 2.75
Inscription block of 4 3.25 —
First day cover, #767a 4.25
First day cover, #764-767, each 1.50
Sheet of 20 17.00

First day covers of Nos. 764-767 total 25,294.

See Offices in Geneva Nos. 343-346; Vienna Nos. 260-263.

In Memoriam — A316

Printed by Walsall Security Printers, Ltd., United Kingdom. Panes of 20. Designed by Robert Stein, US.

Designs: 33c, $1, UN Headquarters. Size of $1 stamp 34x63mm.

1999, Sept. 21 Litho. *Perf. 14½x14*

768 A316 33c **multicolored** *(550,000)+* 1.25 1.25
Inscription block of 4 5.25 —
First day cover 1.25

Souvenir Sheet

Perf. 14

769 A316 $1 **multicolored** *(235,000)+* 2.50 1.75
First day cover 2.00

First day covers of Nos. 768-769 total 42,130.

See Offices in Geneva #347-348, Vienna #264-265.

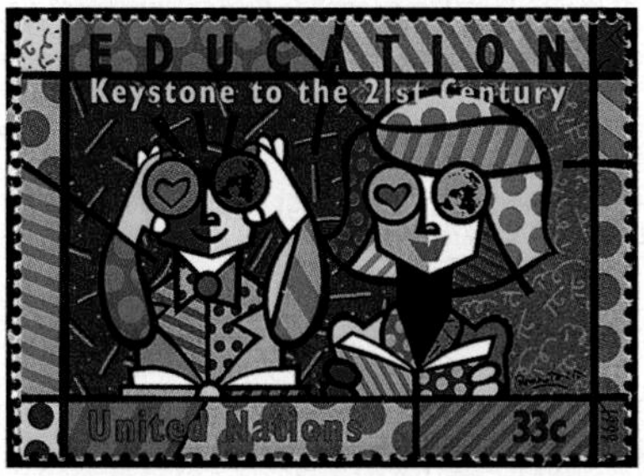

Education, Keystone to the 21st Century — A317

Printed by Government Printing Office, Austria. Panes of 20. Designed by Romero Britto, Brazil.

1999, Nov. 18 Litho. *Perf. 13½x13¾*

770 A317 33c Two readers *(450,000)+* .55 .30
First day cover 1.25
Inscription block of 4 2.40 —
771 A317 60c Heart *(430,000)+* 1.10 .60
First day cover 1.50
First day cover, #770-771 2.50
Inscription block of 4 4.75 —

First day covers of Nos. 770-771 total 34,679.

See Offices in Geneva Nos. 349-350, Vienna Nos. 266-267.

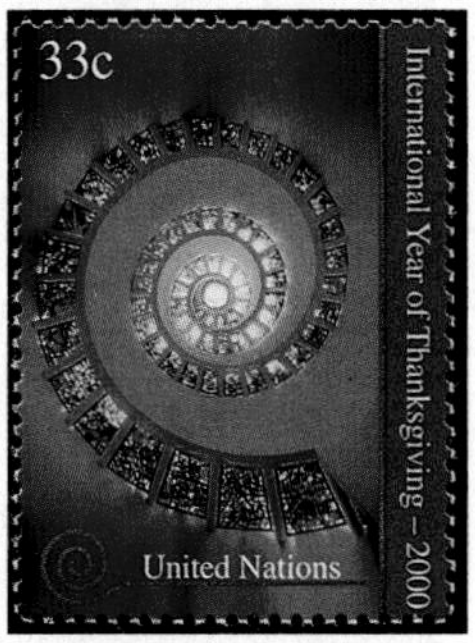

International Year of Thanksgiving — A318

Printed by Cartor Security Printing, France. Panes of 20. Designed by Rorie Katz, US.

2000, Jan. 1 Litho. *Perf. 13¼x13½*

772 A318 33c **multicolored** *(550,000)+* .65 .60
First day cover 1.25
Inscription block of 4 3.25 —

On No. 772 parts of the design were applied by a thermographic process producing a shiny, raised effect. See Offices in Geneva No. 351, Vienna No. 268.

Endangered Species Type of 1993

Printed by Johann Enschedé and Sons, the Netherlands. Designed by Suzanne Duranceau, Canada.

Designs: No. 773, Brown bear. No. 774, Black-bellied bustard. No. 775, Chinese crocodile lizard. No. 776, Pygmy chimpanzee.

2000, Apr. 6 Litho. *Perf. 12¾x12½*

773 A271 33c **multicolored** *(490,000)+* .50 .30
774 A271 33c **multicolored** *(490,000)+* .50 .30
775 A271 33c **multicolored** *(490,000)+* .50 .30
776 A271 33c **multicolored** *(490,000)+* .50 .30
a. Block of 4, #773-776 2.50 2.50
First day cover, #776a 3.50
First day cover, #773-776, each 1.75
Inscription block of 4, #776a 2.75 —
Pane of 16 10.50

See Offices in Geneva Nos. 352-355; Vienna Nos. 269-272.

Our World 2000 — A319

Printed by Cartor Security Printing, France. Panes of 20. Designed by Robert Stein, US.

Winning artwork in Millennium painting competition: 33c, Crawling Toward the Millennium, by Sam Yeates, US. 60c, Crossing, by Masakazu Takahata, Japan, vert.

2000, May 30 Litho. *Perf. 13x13½, 13½x13*

777 A319 33c **multicolored** *(400,000)+* .60 .30
First day cover 1.25
Inscription block of 4 2.50 —
778 A319 60c **multicolored** *(360,000)+* 1.00 .60
First day cover 1.50
First day cover, #777-778 2.50
Inscription block of 4 4.50 —

See Offices in Geneva No. 356-357, Vienna No. 273-274.

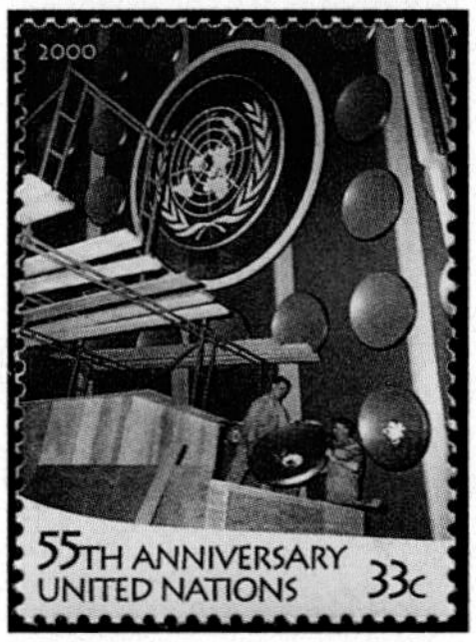

UN, 55th Anniv. — A320

Printed by Cartor Security Printing, France. Panes of 20. Designed by Rorie Katz, US.

Designs: 33c, Workmen removing decorative discs in General Assembly Hall, 1956. 55c, UN Building in 1951.

2000, July 7 Litho. *Perf. 13¼x13*

779 A320 33c **multicolored** *(400,000)+* .60 .30
First day cover 1.25
Inscription block of 4 2.50 —
780 A320 55c **multicolored** *(360,000)+* 1.00 .55
First day cover 1.50
First day cover, #779-780 2.25
Inscription block of 4 4.25 —

Souvenir Sheet

781 A320 Sheet of 2, #779-780 *(277,000)+* 2.50 2.50
First day cover 3.00

See Offices in Geneva No. 358-360, Vienna No. 275-277.

International Flag of Peace — A321

Printed by House of Questa, UK. Panes of 20. Designed by Mateja Prunk, Slovenia.

2000, Sept. 15 Litho. *Perf. 14½x14*

782 A321 33c **multicolored** *(400,000)+* .65 .30
First day cover 1.25
Inscription block of 4 2.60 —

The UN in the 21st Century — A322

Printed by Government Printing Office, Austria. Designed by Wilson McLean, UK.

No. 783: a, Farmers, animals in rice paddy. b, Vehicle chassis being lifted. c, People voting. d, Baby receiving inoculation. e, Woman, man at pump. f, Mason, construction workers.

2000, Sept. 15 Litho. *Perf. 14*

783 A322 Sheet of 6 *(274,000)+* 5.00 5.00
First day cover 7.50
a.-f. 33c any single .80 .30

See Offices in Geneva No. 361; Vienna No. 278.

World Heritage Sites, Spain — A323

Printed by House of Questa, UK. Panes of 20. Designed by Robert Stein, US.

Designs: Nos. 784, 786a, Alhambra, Generalife and Albayzin, Granada. Nos. 785, 786d, Amphitheater of Mérida. #786b, Walled Town of Cuenca. #786c, Aqueduct of Segovia. #786e, Toledo. #786f, Güell Park, Barcelona.

2000, Oct. 6 Litho. *Perf. 14¾x14½*

784 A323 33c **multicolored** *(400,000)+* .55 .30
First day cover 1.25
Inscription block of 4 2.60 —
785 A323 60c **multicolored** *(360,000)+* 1.10 .60
First day cover 1.50
First day cover, #784-785 2.50
Inscription block of 4 5.00 —

Souvenir Booklet

786 Booklet *(63,000)+* 7.00
a.-c. A323 5c any single .20 .20
d.-f. A323 15c any single .30 .30
g. Booklet pane of 4, #786a .50 .50
h. Booklet pane of 4, #786d 1.50 1.50
i. Booklet pane of 4, #786b .50 .50
j. Booklet pane of 4, #786e 1.50 1.50
k. Booklet pane of 4, #786c .50 .50
l. Booklet pane of 4, #786f 1.50 1.50

See Offices in Geneva Nos. 362-364, Vienna Nos. 279-281.

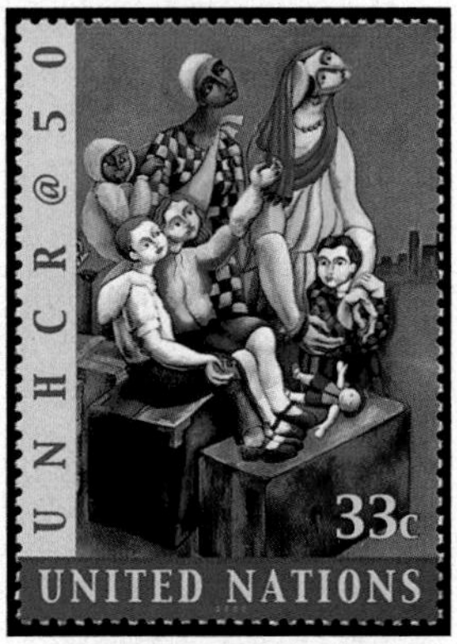

Respect for Refugees — A324

Printed by Johann Enschedé and Sons, the Netherlands. Panes of 20. Designed by Yuri Gevorgian, Armenia.

2000, Nov. 9 **Litho.** *Perf. 13¼x12¾*

787	A324	33c	**multicolored** *(540,000)+*	.65	.30
			First day cover		1.25
			Inscription block of 4	3.00	—

Souvenir Sheet

788	A324	$1	**multicolored** *(225,000)+*	2.00	1.50
			First day cover		2.00

See Offices in Geneva Nos. 365-366, Vienna Nos. 282-283.

Endangered Species Type of 1993

Printed by Johann Enschedé and Sons, the Netherlands. Designed by Grace DeVito, US.

Designs: No. 789, Common spotted cuscus. No. 790, Resplendent quetzal. No. 791, Gila monster. No. 792, Guereza.

2001, Feb. 1 **Litho.** *Perf. 12¾x12½*

789	A271	34c	**multicolored** *(430,000)+*	.50	.30
790	A271	34c	**multicolored** *(430,000)+*	.50	.30
791	A271	34c	**multicolored** *(430,000)+*	.50	.30
792	A271	34c	**multicolored** *(430,000)+*	.50	.30
a.			Block of 4, #789-792	2.60	2.50
			First day cover, #792a		3.50
			First day cover, #789-792 each		1.25
			Inscription block of 4, #792a	2.75	—
			Pane of 16	10.50	

See Offices in Geneva Nos. 367-370; Vienna Nos. 284-287.

Intl. Volunteers Year — A325

Printed by Johann Enschedé and Sons, the Netherlands. Panes of 20. Designed by Rorie Katz and Robert Stein, US.

Paintings by: 34c, Jose Zaragoza, Brazil. 80c, John Terry, Australia.

2001, Mar. 29 **Litho.** *Perf. 13¼*

793	A325	34c	**multicolored** *(390,000)+*	.65	.30
			First day cover		1.25
			Inscription block of 4	2.60	
794	A325	80c	**multicolored** *(360,000)+*	1.60	.80
			First day cover		2.40
			First day cover, #793-794		3.00
			Inscription block of 4	6.50	

See Offices in Geneva Nos. 371-372; Vienna Nos. 288-289.

Flag Type of 1980

Printed by Helio Courvoisier, Switzerland. Designed by Ole Hamann. Issued in panes of 16; each contains 4 blocks of 4 (Nos. 795-798, 799-802). A se-tenant block of 4 designs centers each pane.

2001, May 25 **Photo.** *Perf. 12*

Granite Paper

795	A185	34c	Slovenia *(460,000)+*	.80	.30
796	A185	34c	Palau *(460,000)+*	.80	.30
797	A185	34c	Tonga *(460,000)+*	.80	.30
798	A185	34c	Croatia *(460,000)+*	.80	.30
a.			Block of 4, #795-798	6.00	5.00
799	A185	34c	Former Yugoslav Republic of Macedonia *(460,000)+*	.80	.30
800	A185	34c	Kiribati *(460,000)+*	.80	.30
801	A185	34c	Andorra *(460,000)+*	.80	.30
802	A185	34c	Nauru *(460,000)+*	.80	.30
a.			Block of 4, #799-802	6.00	5.00
			First day cover, #795-802, each		1.25
			Set of 2 panes of 16	21.00	
			Nos. 795-802 (8)	6.40	2.40

Sunflower — A326

Rose — A327

Printed by Johann Enschedé and Sons, the Netherlands. Panes of 20. Designed by Rorie Katz, US.

2001, May 25 **Litho.** *Perf. 13¼x13¾*

803	A326	7c	**multicolored** *(550,000)+*	.20	.20
			First day cover		1.25
			Margin block of 4, inscription	.50	—
804	A327	34c	**multicolored** *(650,000)+*	.60	.30
			First day cover		1.25
			First day cover, #803-804		1.40
			Margin block of 4, inscription	3.00	—

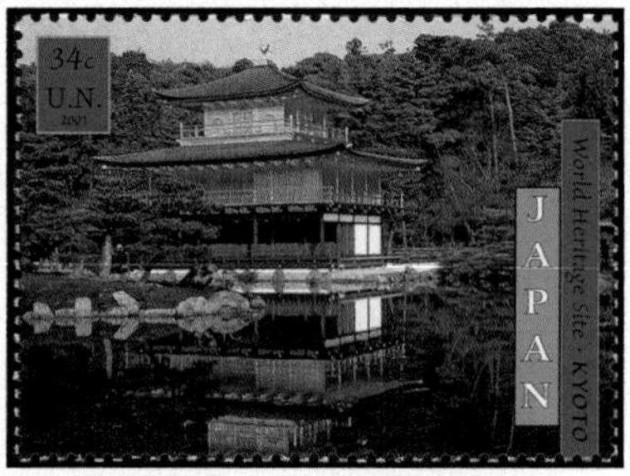

World Heritage Sites, Japan — A328

Printed by Johann Enschedé and Sons, the Netherlands. Panes of 20. Designed by Rorie Katz, US.

Designs: 34c, #807a, Kyoto. 70c, #807d, Shirakawa-Go and Gokayama. #807b, Nara. #807c, Himeji-Jo. #807e, Itsukushima Shinto Shrine. #807f, Nikko.

2001, Aug. 1 **Litho.** *Perf. 12¾x13¼*

805	A328	34c	**multicolored** *(380,000)+*	.60	.30
			First day cover		1.25
			Inscription block of 4	2.50	—
806	A328	70c	**multicolored** *(360,000)+*	1.25	.70
			First day cover		2.10
			First day cover, #805-806		2.75
			Inscription block of 4	5.50	—

Souvenir Booklet

807	Booklet *(51,000)+*	8.00	
a.-c.	A328 5c any single	.20	.20
d.-f.	A328 20c any single	.40	.40
g.	Booklet pane of 4, #807a	.40	.40
h.	Booklet pane of 4, #807d	1.75	1.75
i.	Booklet pane of 4, #807b	.40	.40
j.	Booklet pane of 4, #807e	1.75	1.75
k.	Booklet pane of 4, #807c	.40	.40
l.	Booklet pane of 4, #807f	1.75	1.75

See Offices in Geneva Nos. 373-375, Vienna Nos. 290-292.

Dag Hammarskjöld (1905-61), UN Secretary General — A329

Printed by Banknote Corporation of America, US. Panes of 20. Designed by Robert Stein, US.

2001, Sept. 18 **Engr.** *Perf. 11x11*

808	A329	80c	**blue** *(530,000)+*	1.50	.7
			First day cover		2.2
			Inscription block of 4	6.00	—

See Offices in Geneva No. 376, Vienna No. 293.

A330

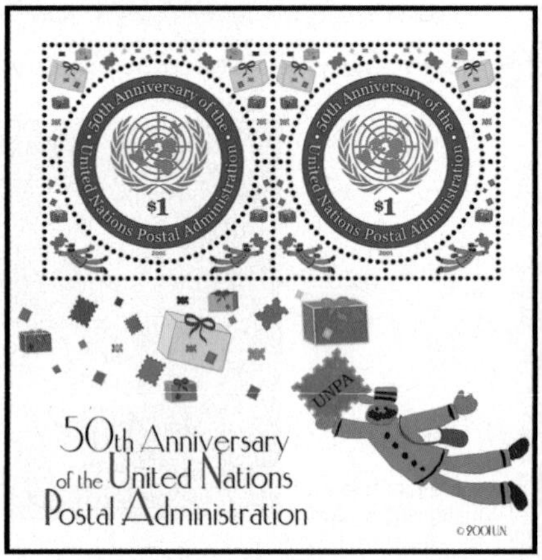

UN Postal Administration, 50th Anniv. — A331

Printed by Johann Enschedé and Sons, the Netherlands. Panes of 20. Designed by Rorie Katz, US.

2001, Oct. 18 **Litho.** *Perf. 13*

809	A330	34c	Stamps, streamers *(350,000)+*	.60	.5
			First day cover		1.2
			Inscription block of 4	3.00	—
810	A330	80c	Stamps, gifts *(310,000)+*	1.60	1.2
			First day cover		2.2
			First day cover, #809-810		3.0
			Inscription block of 4	7.00	—

Souvenir Sheet

811	A331		Sheet of 2 #811a *(180,000)+*	4.00	2.5
a.		$1	**blue & light blue,** 38mm diameter	2.00	1.2
			First day cover		12.0

See Offices in Geneva Nos. 377-379, Vienna Nos. 294-296.

Climate Change — A332

Printed by Walsall Security Printers Limited, UK. Panes of 24. Designed by Robert Giusti, US.

Designs: No. 812, Canada geese, greenhouses, butterfly, thistle. No. 813, Canada geese, iceberg, penguins, tomato plant. No. 814, Palm tree, solar collector. No. 815, Hand planting ginkgo cutting.

2001, Nov. 16 **Litho.** ***Perf. 13¼***

812 A332 34c **multicolored** *(70,500)+* .75 .45
813 A332 34c **multicolored** *(70,500)+* .75 .45
814 A332 34c **multicolored** *(70,500)+* .75 .45
815 A332 34c **multicolored** *(70,500)+* .75 .45
a. Horiz. strip, #812-815 3.00 3.00
Inscription block of 8 6.00 —
First day cover, #815a 3.50
Pane of 24 18.00 —

See Offices in Geneva Nos. 380-383, Vienna Nos. 297-300.

Awarding of Nobel Peace Prize to Secretary General Kofi Annan and UN — A333

Printed by Cartor S. A., France. Panes of 12. Designed by Robert Stein, US.

2001, Dec. 10 **Litho.** ***Perf. 13¼***

816 A333 34c **multicolored** *(840,000)+* .70 .60
Inscription block of 4 3.50 —
First day cover 1.25
Pane of 12 11.50 —

See Offices in Geneva Nos. 384, Vienna Nos. 301.

Children and Stamps — A334

Printed by Government Printing Office, Austria. Panes of 20. Designed by Jerry Smath, US.

2002, Mar. 1 **Litho.** ***Perf. 13¾***

817 A334 80c **multicolored** *(420,000)+* 1.40 .80
First day cover 2.25
Inscription block of 4 6.50 —

Endangered Species Type of 1993

Printed by Johann Enschedé and Sons, the Netherlands. Designed by Teresa Fasolino, US.

Designs: No. 818, Hoffmann's two-toed sloth. No. 819, Bighorn sheep. No. 820, Cheetah. No. 821, San Esteban Island chuckwalla.

2002, Apr. 4 **Litho.** ***Perf. 12¾x12½***

818 A271 34c **multicolored** *(414,000)+* .60 .40
819 A271 34c **multicolored** *(414,000)+* .60 .40
820 A271 34c **multicolored** *(414,000)+* .60 .40
821 A271 34c **multicolored** *(414,000)+* .60 .40
a. Block of 4, #818-821 3.00 2.75
First day cover, #821a 3.50
First day cover, #818-821 each 1.50
Inscription block of 4, #821a 3.25 —
Pane of 16 11.00 —

See Offices in Geneva Nos. 386-389; Vienna 308-311.

Independence of East Timor — A335

Printed by The House of Questa, UK. Designed by Karen Kelleher, US. Panes of 20

Designs: 34c, Wooden ritual mask. 57c, Decorative door panel.

2002, May 20 **Litho.** ***Perf. 14x14½***

822 A335 34c **multicolored** *(355,000)+* .70 .40
First day cover 1.25
Inscription block of 4 3.00 —
823 A335 57c **multicolored** *(325,000)+* 1.20 .70
First day cover 1.90
First day cover, #822-823 2.50
Inscription block of 4 5.00 —

See Offices in Geneva Nos. 390-391; Vienna Nos. 312-313.

Intl. Year of Mountains A336

Printed by Cartor Security Printing, France. Designed by Robert Stein and Rorie Katz, US.

Designs: No. 824, Khan Tengri, Kyrgyzstan. No. 825, Mt. Kilimanjaro, Tanzania. No. 826, Mt. Foraker, US. No. 827, Paine Grande, Chile.

2002, May 24 **Litho.** ***Perf. 13x13¼***

824 A336 34c **multicolored** *(1,362,000)+* .75 .40
First day cover 1.25
825 A336 34c **multicolored** *(1,362,000)+* .75 .40
First day cover 1.25
826 A336 80c **multicolored** *(1,362,000)+* 1.70 1.00
First day cover 2.25
First day cover, #824, 826 3.25
827 A336 80c **multicolored** *(1,362,000)+* 1.70 1.00
a. Vert. strip or block of four, #824-827 5.00 4.00
First day cover 2.25
First day cover, #825, 827 3.25
First day cover, #823-827 5.25
Pane of 12, 3 each #824-827 13.50 —

See Offices in Geneva Nos. 392-395; Vienna Nos. 314-317.

World Summit on Sustainable Development, Johannesburg A337

Printed by The House of Questa, UK. Designed by Peter Max, US.

Designs: No. 828, Sun, Earth, planets, stars. No. 829, Three women. No. 830, Sailboat. No. 831, Three faceless people.

2002, June 27 **Litho.** ***Perf. 14½x14***

828 A337 37c **multicolored** *(1,350,000)+* .75 .40
First day cover 1.25
829 A337 37c **multicolored** *(1,350,000)+* .75 .40
First day cover 1.25
830 A337 60c **multicolored** *(1,350,000)+* 1.50 .80
First day cover 2.00
First day cover, #828, 830 2.25
831 A337 60c **multicolored** *(1,350,000)+* 1.50 .80
a. Vert. strip or block of four, #828-831 4.50 3.50
First day cover 2.00
First day cover, #829, 831 2.25
First day cover, #828-831 4.50
Pane of 12, 3 each #828-831 12.00 —

See Offices in Geneva Nos. 396-399; Vienna Nos. 318-321.

World Heritage Sites, Italy — A338

Printed by Cartor Security Printing, France. Panes of 20. Designed by Rorie Katz, US.

Designs: 37c, #834d, Florence. 70c, #834a, Amalfi Coast. #834b, Aeolian Islands. #834c, Rome. #834e, Pisa. #834f, Pompeii.

2002, Aug. 30 **Litho.** ***Perf. 13½x13¼***

832 A338 37c **multicolored** *(365,000)+* .70 .40
First day cover 1.25
Inscription block of 4 3.00 —
833 A338 70c **multicolored** *(345,000)+* 1.40 .80
First day cover 2.40
First day cover, #832-833 3.00
Inscription block of 4 6.00 —

Souvenir Booklet

834 Booklet *(52,000)+* 7.00
a.-c. A338 5c any single .20 .20
d.-f. A338 15c any single .30 .30
g. Booklet pane of 4, #834d 1.25 1.25
h. Booklet pane of 4, #834a .40 .40
i. Booklet pane of 4, #834e 1.25 1.25
j. Booklet pane of 4, #834b .40 .40
k. Booklet pane of 4, #834f 1.25 1.25
l. Booklet pane of 4, #834c .40 .40

See Offices in Geneva Nos. 400-402, Vienna Nos. 322-324.
See Italy Nos. 2506-2507.

AIDS Awareness — A339

Printed by Walsall Security Printers Limited, UK. Panes of 20. Designed by Rorie Katz, US.

2002, Oct. 24 **Litho.** ***Perf. 13½***

835 A339 70c **multicolored** *(365,000)+* 1.40 .80
Inscription block of 4 5.75
First day cover, #835 2.10
Pane of 20 30.00

See No. B1, Offices in Geneva Nos. 403, B1, Vienna Nos. 325, B1.

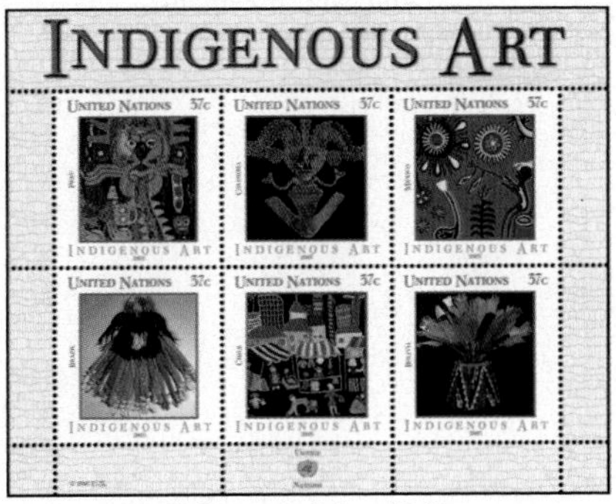

Indigenous Art — A340

Printed by House of Questa, UK.
Designed by Rorie Katz and Robert Stein, US.

No. 836: a, Detail of Paracas textile, Peru. b, Sinu culture anthropo-zoomorphic pendant, Colombia. c, Hicholi Indian embroidery, Mexico. d, Rigpaktsa back ornament, Brazil. e, Wool crafts, Chile. f, Huari feathered woven hat, Bolivia.

2003, Jan. 31 **Litho.** ***Perf. 14¼***

836	A340 Sheet of 6 *(165,000)+*	4.25	2.75
	First day cover		6.25
a.-f.	37c Any single	.60	.40

See Offies in Geneva No. 405; Vienna No. 326.

Clasped Hands — A341

UN Emblem — A342

UN Headquarters A343

Printed by House of Questa, UK (23c, 37c); Walsall Security Printers Ltd., UK (70c). Designed by Rorie Katz, US (23c, 37c), Robert Stein and Rorie Katz (70c). Panes of 20.

2003, Mar. 28 **Litho.** ***Perf. 14¼***

837	A341 23c **multicolored** *(870,000)+*	.45	.30
	First day cover		1.25
	Inscription block of 4	1.80	—

Litho. with Foil Application

838	A342 37c **gold & multicolored** *(870,000)+*	.75	.50
	First day cover		1.25
	Inscription block of 4	3.00	—

Litho. with Hologram

839	A343 70c **multicolored** *(910,000)+*	1.40	.90
	First day cover		2.50
	First day cover, #837-839		3.25
	Inscription block of 4	5.60	—

Powered Flight, Cent. — A344

Printed by Government Printing Office, Austria. Designed by Robert Stein, US. Panes of 16 (eight pairs).

2003, Mar. 28 **Litho.** ***Perf. 13½x13¾***

840	23c **multicolored** *(175,000)+*	.50	.35
841	70c **multicolored** *(175,000)+*	1.50	.90
a.	A344 Tete beche pair, #840-841	2.00	1.25
	First day cover, #841a		2.60
	Inscription block of 4	3.75	

Endangered Species Type of 1993

Printed by Johann Enschedé and Sons, the Netherlands. Designed by Joseph Hautman, US.

Designs: No. 842, Great hornbill. No. 843, Scarlet ibis. No. 844, Knob-billed goose. No. 845, White-faced whistling duck.

2003, Apr. 3 **Litho.** ***Perf. 12¾x12½***

842	A271 37c **multicolored** *(364,000)+*	.75	.40
843	A271 37c **multicolored** *(364,000)+*	.75	.40
844	A271 37c **multicolored** *(364,000)+*	.75	.40
845	A271 37c **multicolored** *(364,000)+*	.75	.40
a.	Block of 4, #842-845	3.00	2.50
	First day cover, #845a		3.75
	First day cover, #842-845 each		1.25
	Inscription block of 4, #845a	3.00	—
	Pane of 16	12.00	—

See Offices in Geneva Nos. 407-410; Vienna 329-332.

Intl. Year of Freshwater A345

Printed by De La Rue Global Services, United Kingdom. Panes of 20. Designed by Rick Garcia, US.

2003, June 20 **Litho.** ***Perf. 14¼x14½***

846	A345 23c Wildlife, garbage *(211,000)+*	.60	.35
847	A345 37c Trees, canoe *(211,000)+*	.90	.40
a.	Horiz. pair, #846-847	1.50	.75
	First day cover, #847a		3.00
	Inscription block of 4	2.50	—

See Offices in Geneva, Nos. 411-412; Vienna Nos. 333-334.

Ralph Bunche (1903-71), Diplomat — A346

Printed by Johann Enschedé and Sons, the Netherlands. Panes of 20. Designed by Rorie Katz, US.

Litho. With Foil Application

2003, Aug. 7 ***Perf. 13½x14***

848	A346 37c **blue & multicolored** *(405,000)+*	.75	.40
	First day cover		1.25
	Inscription block of 4	3.00	—
	Pane of 20	15.00	—

See Offices in Geneva No. 413; Vienna No. 336.

In Memoriam of Victims of Aug. 19 Bombing of UN Complex in Baghdad, Iraq — A347

Printed by Cartor Security Printing, France. Panes of 20. Designed by Jenny J. Karia and Robert Stein, US.

2003, Oct. 24 **Litho.** ***Perf. 13¼x13***

849	A347 60c **multicolored** *(850,000)+*	1.25	.75
	First day cover		1.90
	Inscription block of 4	5.00	—
	Pane of 20	25.00	—

See Offices in Geneva No. 414, Vienna No. 337.

World Heritage Sites, United States A348

Printed by De La Rue Global Services, United Kingdom. Panes of 20. Designed by Rorie Katz, US.

Designs: 37c, #852a, Yosemite National Park. 60c, #852d, Hawaii Volcanoes National Park. #852b, Great Smoky Mountains National Park. #852c, Olympic National Park. #852e, Everglades National Park. #852f, Yellowstone National Park.

2003, Oct. 24 **Litho.** ***Perf. 14½x14¼***

850	A348 37c **multicolored** *(303,000)+*	.90	.50
	First day cover		1.25
	Inscription block of 4	3.75	—
851	A348 60c **multicolored** *(193,000)+*	1.50	.90
	First day cover		2.10
	First day cover, #850-851		2.75
	Inscription block of 4	6.50	—

Souvenir Booklet

852	Booklet *(38,500)+*	9.00	
a.-c.	A348 10c any single	.25	.25
d.-f.	A348 20c any single	.50	.50
g.	Booklet pane of 4 #852a	1.00	1.00
h.	Booklet pane of 4 #852d	2.00	2.00
i.	Booklet pane of 4 #852b	1.00	1.00
j.	Booklet pane of 4 #852e	2.00	2.00
k.	Booklet pane of 4 #852c	1.00	1.00
l.	Booklet pane of 4 #852f	1.60	2.00

See Offices in Geneva Nos. 415-417, Vienna Nos. 338-340.

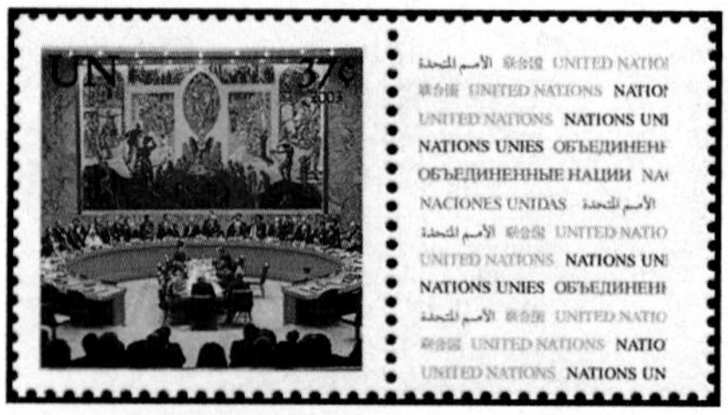

UN Security Council — A349

UN Emblem — A350

UN General Assembly — A351

Flags — A352

UN Headquarters — A353

2003, Nov. 26	Litho.	Perf. 13¼	
853 A349 37c **multicolored** + label		2.50	2.50
854 A350 37c **multicolored** + label		2.50	2.50
855 A351 37c **multicolored** + label		2.50	2.50
856 A352 37c **multicolored** + label		2.50	2.50
857 A353 37c **multicolored** + label		2.50	2.50
a. Vert. strip of 5, #853-857, + 5 labels		12.50	12.50
Sheet, 4 #857a		50.00	—
First day cover, #857a			—
First day cover, #853-857, each			3.75

The full sheet sold for $14.95 with or without personalized labels. The personalization of labels was available only at UN Headquarters, and not through mail order.

One thousand full sheets with sheet margins inscribed "Hong Kong Stamp Expo" were sold only at that venue. Value $110. Also exists with sheet margins inscribed "Essen." Value $55.

A sheet containing two strips of five stamps similar to Nos. 853-857 but dated "2005" and ten labels sold for $4.95. These sheets were only available canceled. An imperforate error of this sheet is known.

Endangered Species Type of 1993

Printed by Johann Enschedé and Sons, the Netherlands. Designed by Yuan Lee, U.S.

Designs: No. 858, American black bear. No. 859, Musk deer. No. 860, Golden snub-nosed monkey. No. 861, Wild yak.

2004, Jan. 29	Litho.	Perf. 12¾x12½	
858 A271 37c **multicolored** *(316,000)+*		.75	.35
859 A271 37c **multicolored** *(316,000)+*		.75	.35
860 A271 37c **multicolored** *(316,000)+*		.75	.35
861 A271 37c **multicolored** *(316,000)+*		.75	.35
a. Block of 4, #858-861		3.00	2.50
First day cover, #861a			3.75
First day cover, #858-861, each			1.25
Inscription block of 4, #861a		3.00	—
Pane of 16		12.00	—

See Offices in Geneva Nos. 418-421; Vienna Nos. 342-345.

Indigenous Art Type of 2003

Printed by Johann Enschedé and Sons, the Netherlands. Designed by Rorie Katz and Robert Stein, US.

No. 862: a, Viking wood carving depicting Saga of Sigurd Favnesbane, Norway. b, Stele, Italy. c, Detail of matador's suit, Spain. d, Amphora, Greece. e, Bronze figurine of bull, Czech Republic. f, Detail of lacquer box illustration depicting scene from "On the Seashore," by Alexander Pushkin, Russia.

2004, Mar. 4	Litho.	Perf. 13¼	
862 A340 Sheet of 6 *(134,000)+*		4.00	3.00
First day cover			6.25
a.-f. 37c Any single		.50	.35
First day cover, a.-f., each			3.00

See Offices in Geneva No. 422; Vienna No. 346.

Road Safety — A354

Printed by Cartor Security Printing. Panes of 20. Designed by Michel Granger, France.

Road map art with: 37c, Automobile with road signs, city skyline. 70c, Automobile, hand, vert.

2004, Apr. 7	Litho.	Perf. 13x13¼, 13¼x13	
863 A354 37c **multicolored** *(266,000)+*		.70	.35
First day cover			1.25
Inscription block of 4		2.75	—
864 A354 70c **multicolored** *(196,000)+*		1.25	.70
First day cover			2.40
First day cover, #863-864			3.00
Inscription block of 4		5.25	—

See Offices in Geneva Nos. 423-424, Vienna Nos. 347-348.

Japanese Peace Bell, 50th Anniv. — A355

Printed by Imprimerie des Timbres-Poste, France. Panes of 20. Designed by Martin Mörck, Norway.

2004, June 3	Litho. & Engr.	Perf. 13¼x13	
865 A355 80c **multicolored** *(376,000)+*		1.50	.80
First day cover			2.25
Inscription block of 4		6.25	—
Pane of 20		30.00	

See Offices in Geneva No. 425; Vienna No. 349.

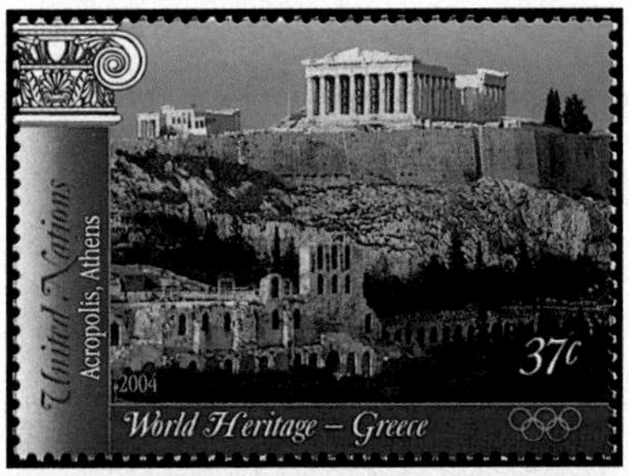

World Heritage Sites, Greece — A356

Printed by Johann Enschedé and Sons, the Netherlands. Panes of 20. Designed by Rorie Katz, US.

Designs: No. 866, Acropolis, Athens. Nos. 867, 868e, Delos. No. 868a, Delphi. No. 868b, Pythagoreion and Heraion of Samos. No. 868c, Olympia. No. 868d, Mycenae and Tiryns.

2004, Aug. 12	Litho.	Perf. 14x13¼	
866 A356 37c **multicolored** *(275,000)+*		.70	.35
First day cover			1.25
Inscription block of 4		2.75	—
a. Booklet pane of 4		3.00	—
867 A356 60c **multicolored** *(195,000)+*		1.10	.60
First day cover			2.10
First day cover, #866-867			2.75
Inscription block of 4		4.75	—

Souvenir Booklet

868 Booklet, #866a, 868f-868j *(31,000)+*		11.00	
a.-d. A356 23c any single		.50	.25
e. A356 37c multi		.80	.80
f. Booklet pane of 4 #868a		2.00	2.00
g. Booklet pane of 4 #868b		2.00	2.00
h. Booklet pane of 4 #868c		2.00	2.00
i. Booklet pane of 4 #868d		2.00	2.00
j. Booklet pane of 4 #868e		3.25	3.25

See Offices in Geneva Nos. 426-428, Vienna Nos. 350-352. No. 868 sold for $7.20.

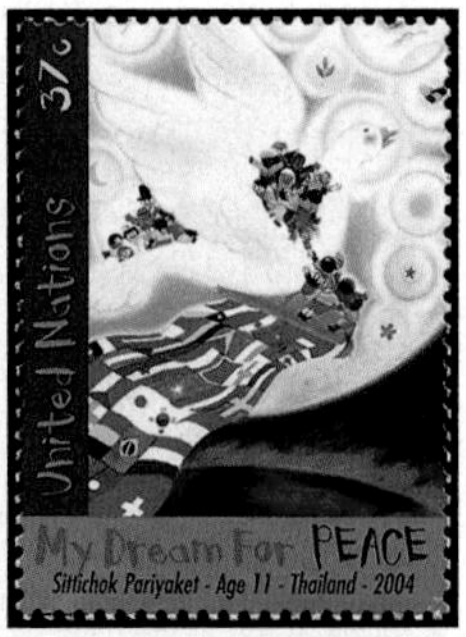

My Dream for Peace — A357

Printed by Government Printing Office, Austria. Panes of 20. Winning designs of Lions Club International children's global peace poster contest by: 37c, Sittichok Pariyaket, Thailand. 80c, Bayan Fais Abu Bial, Israel.

2004, Sept. 21	Litho.	Perf. 14	
869 A357 37c **multicolored** *(276,000)+*		.75	.35
First day cover			1.25
Inscription block of 4		3.00	—
Pane of 20		15.00	—
870 A357 80c **multicolored** *(206,000)+*		1.60	.80
First day cover			2.40
First day cover, #869-870			3.00
Inscription block of 4		6.50	—
Pane of 20		32.00	—

See Offices in Geneva Nos. 429-430, Vienna Nos. 353-354.

A358

Human Rights — A359

Printed by Banknote Corporation of America, US. Designed by Yuri Gervorgian, Armenia.

2004, Oct. 14	Litho.	Perf. 11¼	
871 A358 37c **multicolored** *(464,000)+*		.75	.75
First day cover			1.25
Pane of 8		6.00	—
872 A359 70c **multicolored** *(464,000)+*		1.40	1.40
First day cover			2.40
First day cover, #871-872			3.00
Pane of 8		11.50	—

See Offices in Geneva Nos. 431-432, Vienna Nos. 355-356.

Disarmament A360

Printed by Government Printing Office, Austria. Designed by Michel Granger, France.

2004, Oct. 15	**Litho.**	***Perf. 13¾***	
873 A360 37c **multicolored** *(270,000)+*		.70	.70
First day cover			1.25
Inscription block of 4		3.00	—
Pane of 20		15.00	—

The U.N. Postal Administration announced that it would begin offering canceled-to-order stamps at the same price as mint stamps, effective Feb. 4, 2005. It has been reliably reported that this did not happen.

United Nations, 60th Anniv. — A361

Printed by Banknote Corporation of America, US. Designed by Czeslaw Slania, Sweden.

2005, Feb. 4	**Litho. & Engr.**	***Perf. 11x11¼***	
874 A361 80c **multicolored** *(395,000)+*		1.60	1.60
First day cover			2.50
Inscription block of 4		6.50	—
Pane of 20		32.50	

Souvenir Sheet
Litho.
Imperf

875 A361 $1 **multicolored** *(135,000)+*	17.50	15.00
First day cover		3.25

See Offices in Geneva Nos. 434-435; Vienna Nos. 357-358.

Endangered Species Type of 1993

Printed by Johann Enschedé and Sons, the Netherlands. Designed by Boris Zlotsky, US.

Designs: No. 876, Blue orchid. No. 877, Swan orchid. No. 878, Christmas orchid. No. 879, Aerangis modesta.

2005, Mar. 3	**Litho.**	***Perf. 12¾x12½***	
876 A271 37c **multicolored** *(248,000)+*		.75	.75
877 A271 37c **multicolored** *(248,000)+*		.75	.75
878 A271 37c **multicolored** *(248,000)+*		.75	.75
879 A271 37c **multicolored** *(248,000)+*		.75	.75
a. Block of 4, #876-879		3.00	3.00
First day cover, #879a			4.25
First day cover, #876-879, each			1.75
Inscription block of 4, #879a		3.00	—
Pane of 16		11.00	

See Offices in Geneva Nos. 436-439; Vienna Nos. 360-363.

Non-Violence, Sculpture by Carl Fredrik Reuterswärd, New York — A362

Armillary Sphere, Sculpture by Paul Manship, Geneva — A363

Terra Cotta Warriors, Vienna — A364

Single Form, Sculpture by Barbara Hepworth, New York — A365

Sphere Within a Sphere, Sculpture by Arnaldo Pomodoro, New York — A366

2005, Mar. 3	**Litho.**	***Perf. 13¼***	
880 A362 80c **multicolored** + label		*12.00*	*12.00*
881 A363 80c **multicolored** + label		*12.00*	*12.00*
882 A364 80c **multicolored** + label		*12.00*	*12.00*
883 A365 80c **multicolored** + label		*12.00*	*12.00*
884 A366 80c **multicolored** + label		*12.00*	*12.00*
a. Vert. strip of 5, #880-884, + 5 labels		*60.00*	*60.00*
Sheet, 2 #884a		*125.00*	—
First day cover, #884a			—
First day cover, #880-884, each			4.00
b. Sheet of 10, both #884 37c (error)		—	

The full sheet sold for $14.95 with or without personalized labels. The personalization of labels was available only at UN Headquarters, and not through mail order.

The full sheet exists with sheet margins and labels commemorating the Riccione 2005 Philatelic Exhibition. This sheet went on sale 8/20/05 and was also sold for $14.95. Value $50.

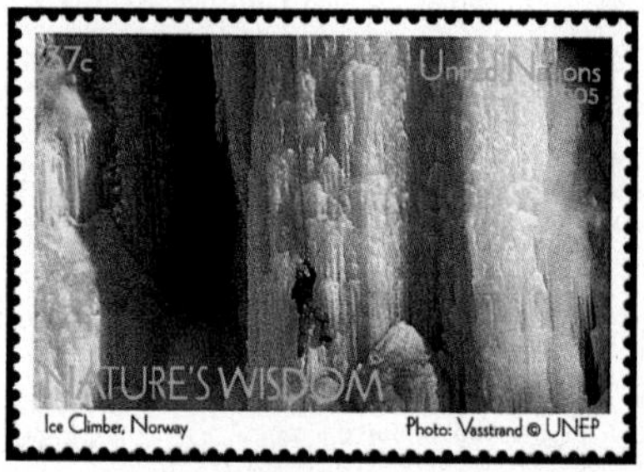

Nature's Wisdom — A367

Printed by Cartor Security Printing, France. Panes of 20. Designed by Robert Stein, US.

Designs: 37c, Ice climber, Norway. 80c, Egret, Japan.

2005, Apr. 21	**Litho.**	***Perf. 13½x13¼***	
885 A367 37c **multicolored** *(280,000)+*		.65	.65
First day cover			1.40
Inscription block of 4		2.75	—
Pane of 20		13.00	—
886 A367 80c **multicolored** *(200,000)+*		1.50	1.50
First day cover			3.00
First day cover, #885-886			3.50
Inscription block of 4		6.00	—
Pane of 20		30.00	—

See Offices in Geneva Nos. 440-441, Vienna Nos. 364-365.

Intl. Year of Sport — A368

Printed by Cartor Security Printing, France. Designed by Roland Hirter, Switzerland.

2005, June 3	**Litho.**	***Perf. 13x13¼***	
887 A368 37c Sailing *(255,000)+*		.65	.65
First day cover			1.50
Inscription block of 4		2.75	—
Pane of 20		13.00	—
888 A368 70c Running *(185,000)+*		1.25	1.25
First day cover			2.75
First day cover, #887-888			3.50
Inscription block of 4		5.25	—
Pane of 20		25.00	—

See Offices in Geneva Nos. 442-443; Vienna Nos. 366-367.

World Heritage Sites, Egypt — A369

Printed by Johann Enschedé and Sons, the Netherlands. Panes of 20. Designed by Rorie Katz, US.

Designs: Nos. 889, 891a, Memphis and its Necropolis. Nos. 890, 891d, Ancient Thebes. No. 891b, Philae. No. 891c, Abu Mena. No. 891e, Islamic Cairo. No. 891f, St. Catherine area.

2005, Aug. 4 Litho. *Perf. 14x13¼*

889 A369 37c **multicolored** *(275,000)+* .60 .60
First day cover 1.40
Inscription block of 4 2.75 —
890 A369 80c **multicolored** *(195,000)+* 1.40 1.40
First day cover 3.00
First day cover, #889-890 3.50
Inscription block of 4 6.00 —

Souvenir Booklet

891 Booklet, #891g-891l *(29,000)+* 12.00
a.-c. A369 23c any single .40 .40
d.-f. A369 37c any single .65 .65
g. Booklet pane of 4 #891a 1.75 —
h. Booklet pane of 4 #891b 1.75 —
i. Booklet pane of 4 #891c 1.75 —
j. Booklet pane of 4 #891d 2.50 —
k. Booklet pane of 4 #891e 2.50 —
l. Booklet pane of 4 #891e 2.50 —

See Offices in Geneva Nos. 444-446, Vienna Nos. 368-370.

My Dream for Peace Type of 2004

Printed by Government Printing Office, Austria. Panes of 20.

Winning designs of Lions Club International children's global peace poster contest by: 37c, Vittoria Sansebastiano, Italy. 80c, Jordan Harris, US.

2005, Sept. 21 Litho. *Perf. 14*

892 A357 37c **multicolored** *(270,000)+* .60 .60
First day cover 1.40
Inscription block of 4 2.75 —
Pane of 20 12.00 —
893 A357 80c **multicolored** *(200,000)+* 1.40 1.40
First day cover 3.00
First day cover, #892-893 3.50
Inscription block of 4 5.75 —
Pane of 20 28.00 —

See Offices in Geneva Nos. 447-448, Vienna Nos. 371-372.

Food for Life A370

Printed by Government Printing Office, Austria. Designed by Andrew Davidson, United Kingdom.

Designs: 37c, Oats, children and adults. 80c, Wheat, mothers breastfeeding babies.

2005, Oct. 20 Litho. *Perf. 13¾*

894 A370 37c **multicolored** *(245,000)+* .60 .60
First day cover 1.25
Inscription block of 4 2.75 —
Pane of 20 12.00 —
895 A370 80c **multicolored** *(185,000)+* 1.40 1.40
First day cover 2.75
First day cover, #894-895 3.25
Inscription block of 4 5.75 —
Pane of 20 28.00 —

See Offices in Geneva Nos. 449-450; Vienna Nos. 373-374.

Stylized Flags in Heart and Hands — A371

Printed by Cartor Security Printing, France. Panes of 20. Designed by Eliezer Weishoff, Israel.

2006, Feb. 3 Litho. *Perf. 13x13¼*

896 A371 25c **multicolored** *(670,000)+* .50 .50
First day cover 1.75
Inscription block of 4 2.00 —
Pane of 20 10.00 —

Indigenous Art Type of 2003

Printed by Johann Enschedé and Sons, the Netherlands. Designed by Robert Stein, US.

No. 897 — Musical instruments: a, Drum, Ivory Coast. b, Drum, Tunisia. c, Stringed instruments, Morocco. d, Drums, Sudan. e, Instruments, Cameroun. f, Harp, Congo.

2006, Feb. 3 Litho. *Perf. 13¼*

897 A340 Sheet of 6 *(88,000)+* 4.50 4.50
First day cover 6.25
a.-f. 37c Any single .75 .75

See Offices in Geneva No. 452; Vienna No. 375.

UN Symbols Type of 2003

2006, Mar. 6 Litho. *Perf. 13¼*

898 A349 39c **multicolored** + label 1.75 1.75
899 A350 39c **multicolored** + label 1.75 1.75
900 A351 39c **multicolored** + label 1.75 1.75
901 A352 39c **multicolored** + label 1.75 1.75
902 A353 39c **multicolored** + label 1.75 1.75
a. Vert. strip of 5, #898-902, + 5 labels 8.75 8.75
Sheet, 4 #902a 35.00 —

The full sheet sold for $14.95 with or without personalized labels. The personalization of labels was available only at UN Headquarters, and not through mail order.

Sculpture Type of 2005

2006, Mar. 6 Litho. *Perf. 13¼*

903 A362 84c **multicolored** + label 4.00 4.00
a. Perf. 14½x14 + label 10.00 10.00
904 A363 84c **multicolored** + label 4.00 4.00
a. Perf. 14½x14 + label 10.00 10.00
905 A364 84c **multicolored** + label 4.00 4.00
a. Perf. 14½x14 + label 10.00 10.00
906 A365 84c **multicolored** + label 4.00 4.00
a. Perf. 14½x14 + label 10.00 10.00
907 A366 84c **multicolored** + label 4.00 4.00
a. Vert. strip of 5, #903-907, + 5 labels *20.00 20.00*
Sheet, 2 #907a *40.00 40.00*
b. Perf. 14½x14 + label 10.00 10.00
c. Vert. strip of 5, #903a-906a, 907b, + 5 labels 50.00 50.00
Sheet, 2 #907c 110.00 110.00

The full sheet sold for $14.95 with or without personalized labels. The personalization of labels was available only at UN Headquarters, and not through mail order.

Nos. 903a-906a, 907b, issued 9/21/06. Nos. 903a-906a, 907a were from sheet for 2006 Berlin Stamp Show. The year "2006" is slightly larger on Nos. 903a-906a, 907b than on Nos. 903-907.

Full sheets with different margins were sold at the Washington 2006 World Philatelic Exhibition, where the labels could be personalized.

Endangered Species Type of 1993

Printed by Johann Enschedé and Sons, the Netherlands. Designed by John D. Dawson, US.

Designs: No. 908, Golden mantella. No. 909, Panther chameleon. No. 910, Peruvian rainbow boa. No. 911, Dyeing poison frog.

2006, Mar. 16 Litho. *Perf. 12¾x12½*

908 A271 39c **multicolored** *(212,000)+* .60 .60
909 A271 39c **multicolored** *(212,000)+* .60 .60
910 A271 39c **multicolored** *(212,000)+* .60 .60
911 A271 39c **multicolored** *(212,000)+* .60 .60
a. Block of 4, #908-911 2.75 2.75
First day cover, #911a 4.50
First day cover, #908-911, each 2.00
Inscription block of 4, #911a 3.00 —
Pane of 16 11.50 —

See Offices in Geneva Nos. 453-456; Vienna Nos. 376-379.

Dove Between War and Peace — A372

Designed by Armando Milani, Italy.

2006, Apr. 10 Litho. *Perf. 13¼*

912 A372 75c **multicolored** + label 2.75 2.75
Sheet of 10 + 10 labels 25.00 —

The full sheet sold for $14.95 with or without personalized labels. The personalization of labels was available only at UN Headquarters, and not through mail order.

Intl. Day of Families A373

Printed by Johann Enschedé and Sons, the Netherlands. Designed by Shelly Bartek, US.

Designs: 39c, Family harvesting grapes. 84c, Children playing with toy sailboats.

2006, May 27 Litho. *Perf. 14x13½*

913 A373 39c **multicolored** *(226,000)+* .70 .70
First day cover 1.50
Inscription block of 4 3.00 —
Pane of 20 14.00 —
914 A373 84c **multicolored** *(186,000)+* 1.50 1.50
First day cover 3.25
First day cover, #913-914 3.75
Inscription block of 4 6.25 —
Pane of 20 30.00 —

See Offices in Geneva Nos. 457-458; Vienna Nos. 380-381.

World Heritage Sites, France — A374

Printed by Cartor Security Printing, France. Panes of 20. Designed by Robert Stein, US.

Eiffel Tower and: Nos. 915, 917a, Banks of the Seine. Nos. 916, 917d, Roman Aqueduct. No. 917b, Provins. No. 917c, Carcasonne. No. 917e, Mont Saint-Michel. No. 917f, Chateau de Chambord.

Litho. & Embossed with Foil Application

2006, June 17 *Perf. 13½x13¼*

915 A374 39c **multicolored** *(260,000)+* .70 .70
First day cover 1.50
Inscription block of 4 3.00 —
916 A374 84c **multicolored** *(180,000)+* 1.50 1.50
First day cover 3.25
First day cover, #889-890 3.75
Inscription block of 4 6.25 —

Souvenir Booklet

917 Booklet, #917g-917l *(28,000)+* 14.00
a.-c. A374 24c any single .40 .40
d.-f. A374 39c any single .70 .70
g. Booklet pane of 4 #917a 1.60 —
h. Booklet pane of 4 #917b 1.60 —
i. Booklet pane of 4 #917c 1.60 —
j. Booklet pane of 4 #917d 3.00 —
k. Booklet pane of 4 #917e 3.00 —
l. Booklet pane of 4 #917f 3.00 —

See Offices in Geneva Nos. 459-461, Vienna Nos. 382-384.

My Dream for Peace Type of 2004

Printed by Cartor Security Printing, France. Panes of 20.

Winning designs of Lions Club International children's global peace poster contest by: 39c, Cheuk Tat Li, Hong Kong. 84c, Kosshapan Paitoon, Thailand.

2006, Sept. 21 **Litho.** ***Perf. 13½x13***

918 A357 39c **multicolored** *(246,000)+* .80 .80
First day cover 1.50
Inscription block of 4 3.20 —
Pane of 20 16.00 —
919 A357 84c **multicolored** *(186,000)+* 1.75 1.75
First day cover 3.25
First day cover, #918-919 3.75
Inscription block of 4 7.00 —
Pane of 20 35.00 —

See Offices in Geneva Nos. 462-463; Vienna Nos. 385-386.

Flags and Coins — A375

Printed by Cartor Security Printing, France. Designed by Rorie Katz, US.

No. 920 — Flag of: a, People's Republic of China, 1 yuan coin. b, Australia, 1 dollar coin. c, Ghana, 50 cedi coin. d, Israel, 10 agorot coin. e, Russia, 1 ruble coin. f, Mexico, 10 peso coin. g, Japan, 10 yen coin. h, Cambodia, 200 riel coin.

2006, Oct. 5 **Litho.** ***Perf. 13¼x13***

920 Sheet of 8 6.50 6.50
a.-h. A375 39c Any single .80 .80
First day cover 9.00

A column of rouletting in the middle of the sheet separates it into two parts. See Offices in Geneva No. 464; Vienna No. 387.

Flag Type of 1980

Printed by Government Printing Office, Austria. Designed by Rorie Katz, US. Issued in panes of 16; each pane contains 4 blocks of 4. A se-tenant block of 4 designs centers each pane.

2007, Feb. 2 **Litho.** ***Perf. 14***

921 A185 39c Tuvalu *(275,000)+* .80 .80
922 A185 39c Switzerland *(275,000)+* .80 .80
923 A185 39c Timor-Leste *(275,000)+* .80 .80
924 A185 39c Montenegro *(275,000)+* .80 .80
a. Block of 4, #921-924 3.20 3.20
First day cover, #921-924, each 1.90
Pane of 16 13.00
Nos. 921-924 (4) 3.20 3.20

Endangered Species Type of 1993

Printed by Johann Enschedé and Sons, the Netherlands. Designed by John Rowe, US.

Designs: No. 925, Drill. No. 926, Common squirrel monkey. No. 927, Ring-tailed lemur. No. 928, Collared mangabey.

2007, Mar. 15 **Litho.** ***Perf. 12¾x12½***

925 A271 39c **multicolored** *(212,000)+* .80 .80
926 A271 39c **multicolored** *(212,000)+* .80 .80
927 A271 39c **multicolored** *(212,000)+* .80 .80
928 A271 39c **multicolored** *(212,000)+* .80 .80
a. Block of 4, #925-928 3.20 3.20
First day cover, #928a 4.50
First day cover, #925-928, each 2.00
Inscription block of 4, #928a 3.20 —
Pane of 16 13.00 —

See Offices in Geneva Nos. 465-468; Vienna Nos. 388-391.

UN Emblem — A376

Designed by Robert Stein.

2007, Feb. 5 **Litho.** ***Perf. 14½x14***

929 A376 84c **dark blue** + label *3.00 3.00*
Sheet of 10 + 10 labels *30.00* —

The full sheet sold for $14.95. The sheet has two each of five different labels that could not be personalized. The sheet was distributed to members of the Japanese mission on Sept. 21, 2006, but it was not sold to the public until 2007. The sheet's availability to the public was not announced through press releases or on the UNPA website prior to the day of issue or afterward. It was sent to standing order customers in May 2007.

Compare with Type A377.

Flags and Coins Type of 2006

Printed by Cartor Security Printing, France. Designed by Rorie Katz, US.

No. 930 — Flag of: a, Brazil, 50 centavo coin. b, Thailand, 1 baht coin. c, Viet Nam, 5,000 dong coin. d, Ecuador, 10 centavo coin. e, India, 5 rupee coin. f, South Africa, 5 cent coin. g, Barbados, 25 cent coin. h, Republic of Korea, 500 won coin.

2007, May 3 **Litho.** ***Perf. 13¼x13***

930 Sheet of 8 *(125,000)+* 6.50 6.50
a.-h. A375 39c Any single .80 .80
First day cover 9.00

A column of rouletting in the middle of the sheet separates it into two parts. See Offices in Geneva No. 469; Vienna No. 392.

UN Emblem — A377

2007, June 1 **Litho.** ***Perf. 13¼***

931 A377 84c **blue** + label *3.00 3.00*
Sheet of 10 + 10 labels *30.00* —

The full sheet sold for $14.95. The sheet has two each of five different labels that could not be personalized.

Compare with Type A376.

Peaceful Visions — A378

Printed by Lowe-Martin Company, Canada. Designed by Slavka Kolesar, Canada. Panes of 20.

Designs: 39c, "Nest." 84c, "Sisters Weave the Olive Branch."

2007, June 1 **Litho.** ***Perf. 13x12½***

932 A378 39c **multicolored** *(264,000)+* .80 .80
First day cover 1.50
Inscription block of 4 3.20 —
Pane of 20 16.00 —
933 A378 84c **multicolored** *(214,000)+* 1.75 1.75
First day cover 3.25
First day cover, #932-933 3.75
Inscription block of 4 7.00 —
Pane of 20 35.00 —

See Offices in Geneva Nos. 470-471; Vienna Nos. 398-399.

UN Symbols Type of 2003

2007, May 14 **Litho.** ***Perf. 13¼***

934 A349 41c **multicolored** + label 1.50 1.50
935 A350 41c **multicolored** + label 1.50 1.50
936 A351 41c **multicolored** + label 1.50 1.50
937 A352 41c **multicolored** + label 1.50 1.50
938 A353 41c **multicolored** + label 1.50 1.50
a. Vert. strip of 5, #934-938, + 5 labels 7.50 7.50
Sheet, 4 #938a 30.00 —

The full sheet sold for $14.95 with or without personalized labels. The personalization of labels was available only at UN Headquarters, and not through mail order.

UN Flag — A379

2007, May 14 **Litho.** ***Perf. 13¼***

939 A379 90c **blue** + label *3.00 3.00*
Sheet of 10 + 10 labels *30.00* —

The full sheet sold for $14.95. The sheet has two each of five different labels that could not be personalized.

Helmet of UN Peacekeeper — A380

Printed by Lowe-Martin Group, Canada. Panes of 20.

2007, Aug. 9 **Litho.** ***Perf. 12½x13¼***

940 A380 90c **multicolored** *(550,000)+* 1.90 1.90
First day cover 3.00
Inscription block of 4 7.60 —
Pane of 20 38.00 —

World Heritage Sites, South America — A381

Printed by Lowe-Martin Group, Canada. Panes of 20. Designed by Rorie Katz, US.

Designs: No. 941, Galapagos Islands, Ecuador. Nos. 942, 943a, Rapa Nui, Chile. No. 943b, Cueva de las Manos, Argentina. No. 943c, Machu Picchu, Peru. No. 943d, Tiwanaku, Bolivia. No. 943e, Iguaçu National Park, Brazil.

2007, Aug. 9 **Litho.** ***Perf. 13¼x13***

941 A381 41c **multicolored** *(254,000)+* .85 .85
First day cover 1.50
Inscription block of 4 3.40 —
a. Booklet pane of 4 3.40 —
942 A381 90c **multicolored** *(254,000)+* 1.90 1.90
First day cover 3.25
First day cover, #941-942 4.00
Inscription block of 4 7.60 —

Souvenir Booklet

943 Booklet, #941a, 943f-943j *(26,500)+* 17.00
a.-c. A381 26c Any single .55 .55
d.-e. A381 41c Either single .85 .85
f. Booklet pane of 4 #943a 2.20 —
g. Booklet pane of 4 #943b 2.20 —
h. Booklet pane of 4 #943c 2.20 —
i. Booklet pane of 4 #943d 3.40 —
j. Booklet pane of 4 #943e 3.40 —

See Offices in Geneva Nos. 472-474, Vienna Nos. 400-402. No. 943 sold for $8.50.

Humanitarian Mail — A382

Printed by Lowe-Martin Group, Canada. Panes of 10.

2007, Sept. 6 **Litho.** ***Perf. 12½x13¼***
944 A382 90c **multicolored** *(288,000)+* 1.90 1.90
First day cover 3.00
Inscription block of 4 7.60 —
Pane of 10 19.00 —

See Offices in Geneva No. 475, Vienna No. 403, Switzerland No. 9021.

Space for Humanity A383

Printed by Johann Enschedé and Sons, the Netherlands. Panes of 6. Designed by Donato Giancola, US.
Designs: 41c, Space Shuttle. 90c, Astronauts spacewalking. $1, International Space Station.

2007, Oct. 25 **Litho.** ***Perf. 13½x14***
945 A383 41c **multicolored** *(264,000)+* .85 .85
First day cover 1.50
Inscription block of 4 3.40 —
Sheet of 6 5.10 —
946 A383 90c **multicolored** *(264,000)+* 1.90 1.90
First day cover 3.25
First day cover, #945-946 4.00
Inscription block of 4 7.60 —
Sheet of 6 11.40 —

Souvenir Sheet

947 A383 $1 **multicolored** *(110,000)+* 2.00 2.00
First day cover 3.25
a. With World Space Week emblem in margin *(110,000)+* 2.00 2.00
First day cover 3.25

See Offices in Geneva Nos. 476-478, Vienna Nos. 409-411.

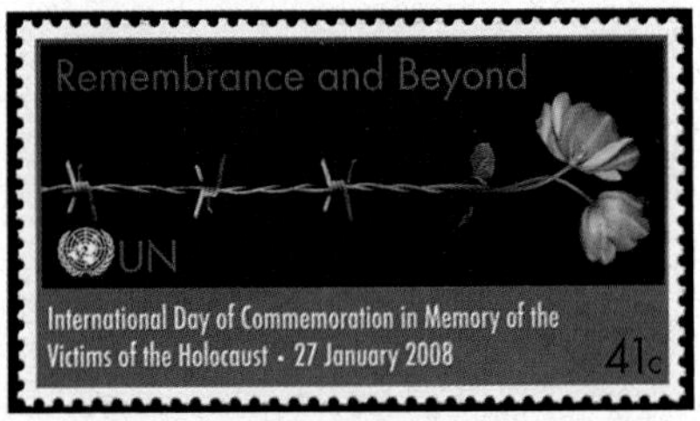

Intl. Holocaust Remembrance Day — A384

Printed by Lowe-Martin Company, Canada. Panes of 9. Designed by Matías Delfino, Argentina.

2008, Jan. 27 **Litho.** ***Perf. 13***
948 A384 41c **multicolored** *(495,000)+* .85 .85
First day cover 1.90
Sheet of 9 7.75 —

See Offices in Geneva No. 479, Vienna No. 412, Israel No. 1715.

Endangered Species Type of 1993

Printed by Johann Enschedé and Sons, the Netherlands. Designed by Suzanne Duranceau, Canada.
Designs: No. 949, South African fur seal. No. 950, Orange cup coral. No. 951, Longsnout seahorse. No. 952, Gray whale.

2008, Mar. 6 **Litho.** ***Perf. 12¾x12½***
949 A271 41c **multicolored** *(164,000)+* .85 .85
950 A271 41c **multicolored** *(164,000)+* .85 .85
941 A271 41c **multicolored** *(164,000)+* .85 .85
952 A271 41c **multicolored** *(164,000)+* .85 .85
a. Block of 4, #949-952 3.40 3.40
First day cover, #952a 4.75
First day cover, #949-952, each 2.00
Inscription block of 4, #952a 3.40 —
Pane of 16 14.00 —

See Offices in Geneva Nos. 480-483; Vienna Nos. 417-420.

Flags and Coins Type of 2006

Printed by Cartor Security Printing, France. Designed by Rorie Katz, US.
No. 953 - Flag of: a, United Kingdom, 2 pound coin. b, Singapore, 5 dollar coin. c, Colombia, 500 peso coin. d, Sri Lanka, 10 rupee coin. e, Philippines, 1 peso coin. f, Indonesia, 500 rupiah coin. g, United Arab Emirates, 1 dirham coin. h, Libya, 50 dinar coin.

2008, May 8 **Litho.** ***Perf. 13¼x13***
953 Sheet of 8 *(100,000)+* 7.00 7.00
a.-h. A375 41c Any single .85 .85
First day cover 9.25

A column of rouletting in the middle of the sheet separates it into two parts. See Offices in Geneva No. 484; Vienna No. 421.

Sculpture and Flags — A385

UN Flag — A386

UN General Assembly — A387

Flags — A388

UN Headquarters — A389

Designed by Rorie Katz, US.

2008, May 12 **Litho.** ***Perf. 13¼***
954 A385 42c **multicolored** + label *1.50 1.50*
955 A386 42c **multicolored** + label *1.50 1.50*
956 A387 42c **multicolored** + label *1.50 1.50*
957 A388 42c **multicolored** + label *1.50 1.50*
958 A389 42c **multicolored** + label *1.50 1.50*
a. Vert. strip of 5, #954-958, + 5 labels *7.50 7.50*
Sheet, 4 #958a *30.00* —

The full sheet sold for $14.95 with or without personalized labels. The personalization of labels was available only at UN Headquarters, and not through mail order.

UN Emblem — A390

Designed by Rorie Katz, US.

2008, May 12 **Litho.** ***Perf. 13¼***
959 A390 94c **blue** + label *3.00 3.00*
Sheet of 10 + 10 labels *30.00* —

The full sheet sold for $14.95 with or without labels that could be personalized. The personalization of labels was available only at UN Headquarters, and not through mail order.

2008 END-OF-YEAR ISSUES

The UNPA has announced that the following items will be released in late 2008. Dates and denominations are tentative.

Convention on the Rights of Disabled Persons, *June 6,* 42c, 94c stamps; Geneva 1fr, 1.80fr stamps; Vienna 55c, €1.40 stamps.

Sport for Peace / Beijing 2008 Olympic Games, *Aug. 9,* 42c, 94c, $1.25 souvenir sheet; Geneva 1fr, 1.80fr, 3fr souvenir sheet; Vienna 65c, €1.30, €3 souvenir sheet.

We Can End Poverty *Sept. 18,* 42c, 94c stamps; Geneva 1f, 1.80fr stamps; Vienna 65c, 75c stamps.

Personalized stamp / WIPA 2008 World Philatelic Exhibition, Vienna *Sept. 18,* Geneva, €1.40 with attached label.

International Year of Planet Earth / Climate Change *Oct. 30,* 42c, 94c booklet containing 27 and 42c stamps; Geneva 1.20fr, 1.80fr booklet containing 20c and 50c stamps; Vienna 65c, €1.60 booklet containing 30c and 35c stamps.

Listings as of 6PM, July 31, 2008.

SEMI-POSTAL STAMPS

Souvenir Sheet

AIDS Awareness — SP1

Printed by Walsall Security Printers Limited, UK. Designed by Rorie Katz, US.

2002, Oct. 24 **Litho.** ***Perf. 14½***

B1 SP1 37c + 6c **multicolored** *(175,000)+* 2.50 2.50
First day cover, #B1 3.00

See Offices in Geneva No. B1, Vienna No. B1.

AIR POST STAMPS

Plane and Gull — AP1

Swallows and UN Emblem AP2

Engraved and printed by Thomas De La Rue & Co., Ltd., London. Panes of 50. Designed by Ole Hamann (AP1) and Olav Mathiesen (AP2).

1951, Dec. 14 **Unwmk.** ***Perf. 14***

C1 AP1 6c **henna brown** *(2,500,000)* .20 .20
First day cover 2.00
Inscription block of 4 .25 —
C2 AP1 10c **bright blue green** *(2,750,000)* .30 .20
First day cover 2.00
Inscription block of 4 1.10 —
C3 AP2 15c **deep ultramarine** *(3,250,000)* .40 .25
First day cover 3.00
Inscription block of 4 1.60 —
a. 15c **Prussian blue** 75.00
C4 AP2 25c **gray black** *(2,250,000)* .85 .50
First day cover 7.50
First day cover, #C1-C4 30.00
Inscription block of 4 4.75 —
Nos. C1-C4 (4) 1.75 1.15

First day covers of Nos. 1-11 and C1-C4 total 1,113,216.

Early printings of Nos. C1-C4 have wide, imperforate sheet margins on three sides. Later printings were perforated through all margins.

Airplane Wing and Globe — AP3

Engraved and printed by Thomas De La Rue & Co., Ltd., London. Panes of 50. Designed by W. W. Wind.

1957, May 27 ***Perf. 12½x14***

C5 AP3 4c **maroon** *(5,000,000)* .20 .20
First day cover *(282,933)* 1.00
Inscription block of 4 .30 —

For 5c see No. C6.

Type of 1957 and

UN Flag and Plane — AP4

Engraved and printed by Waterlow & Sons, Ltd., London. Panes of 50. Designed by W. W. Wind (5c) and Olav Mathiesen (7c).

1959, Feb. 9 **Unwmk.** ***Perf. 12½x13½***

C6 AP3 5c **rose red** *(4,000,000)* .20 .20
First day cover 1.00
Inscription block of 4 .50 —

Perf. 13½x14

C7 AP4 7c **ultramarine** *(4,000,000)* .20 .20
First day cover 1.00
First day cover, #C6-C7 17.50
Inscription block of 4 .75 —

First day covers of Nos. C6 and C7 total 413,556.

Outer Space — AP5

UN Emblem — AP6

Bird of Laurel Leaves — AP7

Printed by Courvoisier S.A., La Chaux-de-Fonds, Switzerland. Panes of 50. Designed by Claude Bottiau (6c), George Hamori (8c) and Kurt Plowitz (13c).

1963, June 17 **Photo.** **Unwmk.** ***Perf. 11½***

C8 AP5 6c **black, blue & yellow green** *(4,000,000)* .20 .20
First day cover 1.00
Inscription block of 4 .45 —
C9 AP6 8c **yellow, olive green & red** *(4,000,000)* .20 .20
First day cover 1.00
Inscription block of 4 .60 —

Perf. 12½x12

C10 AP7 13c **ultra, aquamarine, gray & carmine** *(2,700,000)* .20 .20
First day cover 1.00
First day cover, #C8-C10 8.50
Inscription block of 4 .90 —

First day covers of Nos. C8-C10 total 535,824.

"Flight Across the Globe" — AP8

Jet Plane and Envelope — AP9

Printed by the Austrian Government Printing Office, Vienna, Austria. Panes of 50. Designed by Ole Hamann (15c) and George Hamori (25c).

Perf. 11½x12, 12x11½

1964, May 1 **Photo.** **Unwmk.**

C11 AP8 15c **violet, buff, gray & pale green** *(3,000,000)* .30 .20
First day cover 1.00
Inscription block of 4 1.40 —
a. Gray omitted —
C12 AP9 25c **yellow, orange, gray, blue & red** *(2,000,000)* .50 .30
First day cover 1.00
First day cover, #C11-C12 8.00
Inscription block of 4 2.50 —
Nos. C8-C12 (5) 1.40 1.10

First day covers of Nos. C11-C12 total 353,696.

For 75c in type AP8, see UN Offices in Geneva No. 8.

Jet Plane and UN Emblem — AP10

Printed by Setelipaino, Finland. Panes of 50. Designed by Ole Hamann.

1968, Apr. 18 **Litho.** ***Perf. 13***

C13 AP10 20c **multicolored** *(3,000,000)* .35 .25
First day cover *(225,378)* 1.00
Inscription block of 4 1.60 —

Wings, Envelopes and UN Emblem — AP11

Printed by Setelipaino, Finland. Panes of 50. Designed by Olav S. Mathiesen.

1969, Apr. 21 **Litho.** ***Perf. 13***

C14 AP11 10c **orange vermilion, orange, yellow & black** *(4,000,000)* .20 .20
First day cover *(132,686)* 1.00
Inscription block of 4 .75 —

UN Emblem and Stylized Wing — AP12

Birds in Flight — AP13

Clouds AP14

"UN" and Plane — AP15

Printed by Government Printing Bureau, Japan (9c); Heraclio Fournier, S. A., Spain (11c, 17c); Setelipaino, Finland (21c). Panes of 50. Designed by Lyell L. Dolan (9c), Arne Johnson (11c), British American Bank Note Co. (17c) and Asher Kalderon (21c).

1972, May 1 Litho. & Engr. *Perf. 13x13½*

C15	AP12	9c	**light blue, dark red & violet blue** *(3,000,000)+*	.20	.20
			First day cover		1.00
			Inscription block of 4	.50	—

Photo.

Perf. 14x13½

C16	AP13	11c	**blue & multicolored** *(3,000,000)+*	.20	.20
			First day cover		1.00
			Inscription block of 4	.75	—

Perf. 13½x14

C17	AP14	17c	**yellow, red & orange** *(3,000,000)+*	.25	.20
			First day cover		1.00
			Inscription block of 4	1.10	—

Perf. 13

C18	AP15	21c	**silver & multi** *(3,500,000)*	.25	.25
			First day cover		1.00
			First day cover, #C15-C18		3.50
			Inscription block of 4	1.25	—
			Nos. C15-C18 (4)	.90	.85

First day covers of Nos. C15-C18 total 553,535.

Globe and Jet — AP16

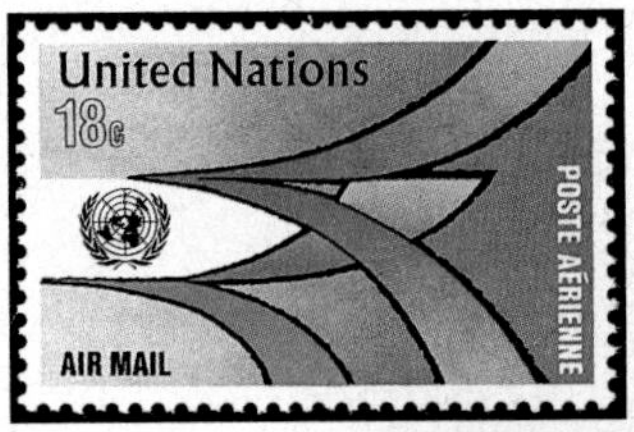

Pathways Radiating from UN Emblem AP17

Bird in Flight, UN Headquarters AP18

Printed by Setelipaino, Finland. Panes of 50. Designed by George Hamori (13c), Shamir Bros. (18c) and Olav S. Mathiesen (26c).

1974, Sept. 16 Litho. *Perf. 13, 12½x13 (18c)*

C19	AP16	13c	**multicolored** *(2,500,000)+*	.20	.20
			First day cover		1.00
			Inscription block of 4	.80	—
C20	AP17	18c	**gray olive & multicolored** *(2,000,000)*	.25	.20
			First day cover		1.00
			Inscription block of 4	1.10	—
C21	AP18	26c	**blue & multi** *(2,000,000)*	.35	.30
			First day cover		1.25
			First day cover, #C19-C21		2.50
			Inscription block of 4	1.60	—
			Nos. C19-C21 (3)	.80	.70

First day covers of Nos. C19-C21 total 309,610.

Winged Airmail Letter — AP19

Symbolic Globe and Plane — AP20

Printed by Heraclio Fournier, S.A. Panes of 50. Designed by Eliezer Weishoff (25c) and Alan L. Pollock (31c).

1977, June 27 Photo. *Perf. 14*

C22	AP19	25c	**greenish blue & multi** *(2,000,000)+*	.40	.25
			First day cover		1.25
			Inscription block of 4	1.75	—
C23	AP20	31c	**magenta** *(2,000,000)*	.45	.30
			First day cover		1.25
			First day cover, #C22-C23		1.50
			Inscription block of 4	2.10	—

First day covers of Nos. C22-C23 total 209,060.

ENVELOPES

Used values for all postal stationery are for non-philatelic contemporaneous usages.

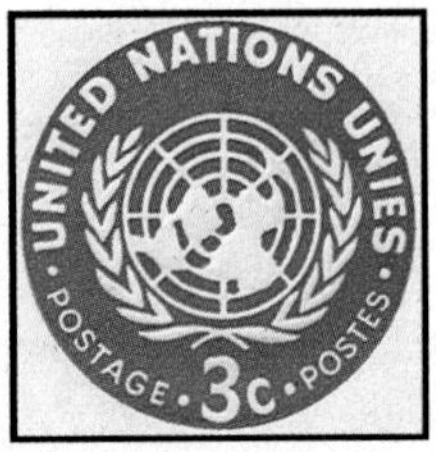

Emblem of United Nations — U1

Printed by the International Envelope Corp., Dayton, Ohio. Die engraved by the American Bank Note Co., New York.

1953, Sept. 15 Embossed

U1	U1	3c	**blue,** entire *(555,000)*	.40	.40
			Entire, first day cancel *(102,278)*		1.00

Printed by International Envelope Corp., Dayton, Ohio.

1958, Sept. 22 Embossed

U2	U1	4c	**ultramarine,** entire *(1,000,000)*	.40	.40
			Entire, first day cancel *(213,621)*		1.00

Stylized Globe and Weather Vane — U2

Printed by United States Envelope Co., Springfield, Mass. Designed by Hatim El Mekki.

1963, Apr. 26 Litho.

U3	U2	5c	**multicolored,** entire *(1,115,888)*	.25	.25
			Entire, first day cancel *(165,188)*		1.00

Printed by Setelipaino, Finland.

1969, Jan. 8 Litho.

U4	U2	6c	**black, blue, magenta & dull yellow,** entire *(850,000)*	.25	.25
			Entire, first day cancel *(152,593)*		1.00

Headquarters Type of Regular Issue, 1968

Printed by Eureka Co., a division of Litton Industries.

1973, Jan. 12 Litho.

U5	A99	8c	**sepia, blue & olive,** entire *(700,000)*	.50	.50
			Entire, first day cancel *(145,510)*		1.00

Headquarters Type of Regular Issue, 1974

Printed by United States Envelope Co., Springfield, Mass.

1975, Jan. 10 Litho.

U6	A138	10c	**blue, olive bister & multi,** entire *(547,500)*	.40	.40
			Entire, first day cancel *(122,000)*		1.00

Bouquet of Ribbons — U3

Printed by Carl Ueberreuter Druck and Verlag M. Salzer, Austria. Designed by George Hamori, Australia.

1985, May 10 Litho.

U7	U3	22c	**multicolored,** entire *(250,000)*	8.50	3.50
			Entire, first day cancel *(28,600)*		3.50

New York Headquarters U4

Printed by Mercury Walch, Australia. Designed by Rocco J. Callari, United States.

1989, Mar. 17 **Litho.**
U8 U4 25c **multicolored,** entire *(350,000)* 2.75 2.75
Entire, first day cancel *(28,567)* 6.00

For surcharge see No. U9A.

No. U8 Surcharged

1991, Apr. 15 **Litho.**
U9 U4 25c +4c **multicolored,** entire *(50,000)+* 2.75 4.00
Entire, first day cover 5.50

No. U8 Surcharged

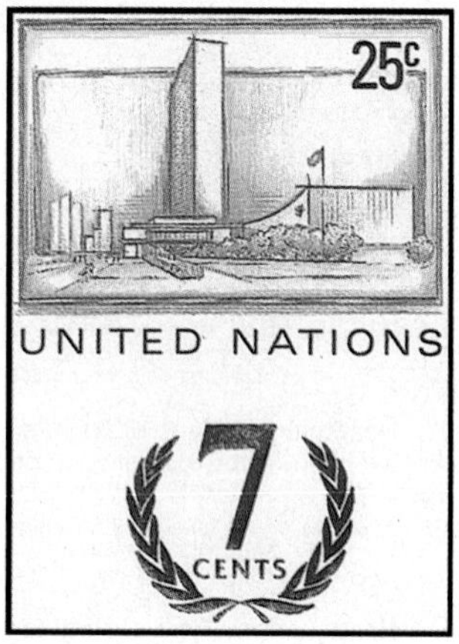

1995 **Litho.**
U9A U4 25c +7c **multicolored,** entire 3.00 4.50
Entire, first day cover 6.00

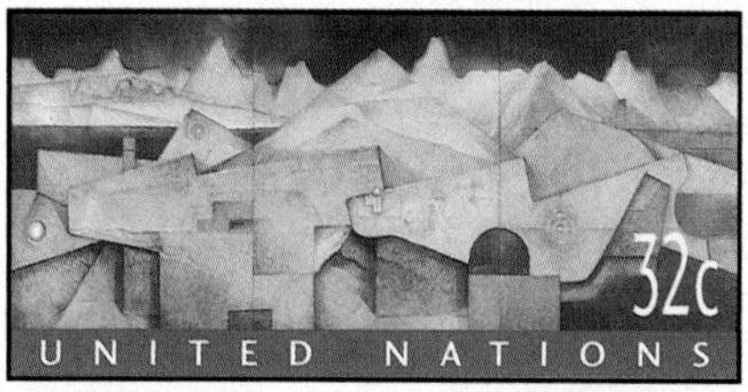

Cripticandina, by Alfredo La Placa — U5

Illustration reduced.
Design sizes: No. U10, 79x38mm. No. U11, 89x44mm.

1997, Feb. 12 **Litho.**
U10 U5 32c **multicolored,** #6¾, entire *(65,000)+* 3.00 2.00
Entire, first day cancel 5.50
U11 U5 32c **multicolored,** #10, entire *(80,000)+* 3.00 2.00
Entire, first day cancel 5.50

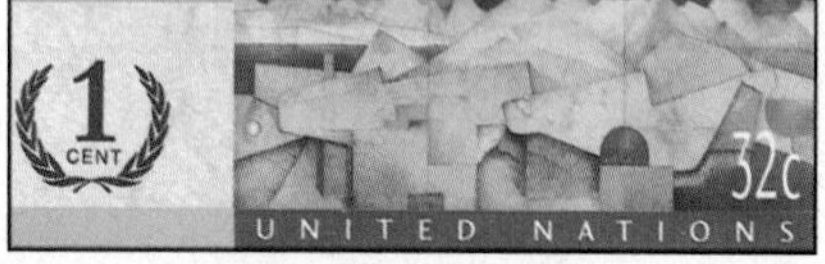

Nos. U10-U11 Surcharged

1999, Jan. 10 **Litho.**
U12 U5 32c +1c **multicolored,** on #U10, entire 2.00 2.00
First day cancel, entire 2.50
U13 U5 32c +1c **multicolored,** on #U11, entire 2.25 2.25
First day cancel, entire 2.50

New York Headquarters — U6

Design sizes: No. U14, 34x34mm. No. U15, 36x36mm.

2001, May 25 **Litho.**
U14 U6 34c **multicolored,** #6¾, entire .90 .90
Entire, first day cancel 1.25
U15 U6 34c **multicolored,** #10, entire .90 .90
Entire, first day cancel 1.25

Nos. U14-U15 Surcharged

2002, June 30 **Litho.**
U16 U6 34c +3c **multicolored,** entire (#U14) 1.75 1.75
Entire, first day cancel 2.00
U17 U6 34c +3c **multicolored,** entire (#U15) 1.75 1.75
Entire, first day cancel 2.00

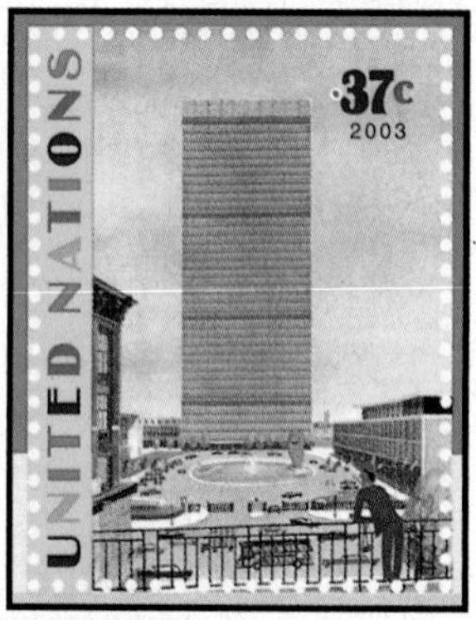

UN Headquarters U7

Printed by Australia Post Spintpak, Australia.
Design sizes: No. U18, 37x47mm. No. U19, 40x52mm.

2003, Mar. 28 **Litho.**
U18 U7 37c **multicolored,** #6¾, entire *(62,000)+* 1.00 .50
Entire, first day cancel 1.25
U19 U7 37c **multicolored,** #10, entire *(72,000)+* 1.00 .50
Entire, first day cancel 1.25

Nos. U18-U19 Surcharged

2006, Jan. 8 **Litho.**
U20 U7 37c +2c **multicolored,** entire (#U18) 1.50 1.75
Entire, first day cancel 1.25
U21 U7 37c +2c **multicolored,** entire (#U19) 1.50 1.75
Entire, first day cancel 1.25

Nos. U18-U19 Surcharged Like No. U20

2007, May 14 **Litho.**
U22 U7 37c +4c **multicolored,** entire (#U18) 1.10 1.10
Entire, first day cancel 2.10
U23 U7 37c +4c **multicolored,** entire (#U19) 1.10 1.10
Entire, first day cancel 2.10

United Nations Emblem — U8

Printed by Lowe-Martin Group, Canada. Designed by Robert Stein, US.
Design sizes: No. U24, 22x28mm. No. U25, 29x38mm.

2007, Aug. 9 **Litho.**
U24 U8 41c **multicolored,** #6¾, entire *(35,000)+* 1.10 1.10
Entire, first day cancel 2.10
U25 U8 41c **multicolored,** #10, entire *(35,000)+* 1.10 1.10
Entire, first day cancel 2.10

Nos. U24-U25 Surcharged Like No. U20

2008, May 12 **Litho.**
U26 U8 41c +1c **multicolored,** entire (#U24) 1.10 1.10
Entire, first day cancel 2.10
U27 U8 41c +1c **multicolored,** entire (#U25) 1.10 1.10
Entire, first day cancel 2.10

AIR POST ENVELOPES AND AIR LETTER SHEETS

Used values for all postal stationery are for non-philatelic contemporaneous usages.

Letter Sheet
Type of Air Post Stamp of 1951
Inscribed "Air Letter" at Left
Printed by Dennison & Sons, Long Island City, NY.

1952, Aug. 29 **Litho.**
UC1 AP2 10c **blue,** *bluish,* entire *(187,000)* 22.50 *20.00*
Entire, 1st day cancel *(57,274)* 2.50

Designed by C. Mutver.

Letter Sheet
Inscribed "Air Letter" and "Aerogramme" at Left

1954, Sept. 14 **Litho.**
UC2 AP2 10c **royal blue,** *bluish,* entire, *(207,000)* 9.50 5.00
Entire, 1st day cancel *200.00*
a. No white border, *1958 (148,800)* 7.00 *8.00*

No. UC2 was printed with a narrow white border (½ to 1mm wide) surrounding the stamp. On No. UC2a, this border has been partly or entirely eliminated.

UN Flag and Plane — UC1

(UN Emblem Emblossed)

Printed by International Envelope Corp., Dayton, O.
Die engraved by American Bank Note Co., New York.

1959, Sept. 21 **Embossed**
UC3 UC1 7c **blue,** entire *(550,000)* 1.00 *1.25*
Entire, 1st day cancel *(172,107)* 1.00

Letter Sheet
Type of Air Post Stamp of 1959
Printed by Thomas De La Rue & Co., Ltd., London

1960, Jan. 18 **Litho.**
UC4 AP4 10c **ultramarine,** *bluish,* entire *(405,000)* .65 .65
Entire, 1st day cancel *(122,425)* .50

Printed on protective tinted paper containing colorless inscription "United Nations" in the five official languages of the UN.

Letter Sheet
Type of Air Post Stamp of 1951
Inscribed "Correo Aereo" instead of "Poste Aerienne"
Printed by Thomas De La Rue & Co., Ltd., London

1961, June 26 **Litho.**

UC5 AP1 11c **ultramarine,** *bluish,* entire *(550,000)* .50 .50
Entire, 1st day cancel *(128,557)* .50
a. 11c **dark blue,** *green* entire, *July 16, 1965* *(419,000)* 1.25 1.25

Printed on protective tinted paper containing colorless inscription "United Nations" in the five official languages of the UN.

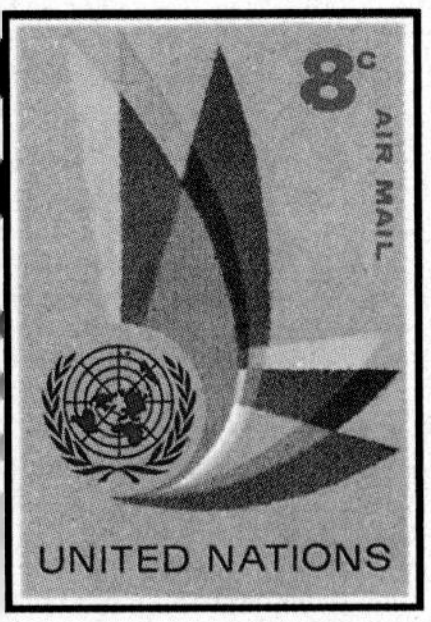

UN Emblem — UC2

Printed by United States Envelope Co., Springfield, Mass. Designed by George Hamori.

1963, Apr. 26 **Litho.**

UC6 UC2 8c **multicolored,** entire *(880,000)* .30 .30
Entire, 1st day cancel *(165,208)* 1.00

Letter Sheet

UN Emblem and Stylized Plane — UC3

Printed by Setelipaino, Finland. Designed by Robert Perrot.

1968, May 31 **Litho.**

UC7 UC3 13c **violet blue & light blue,** entire *(750,000)* .30 .30
Entire, 1st day cancel *(106,700)* .50

Type of 1963
Printed by Setelipaino, Finland.

1969, Jan. 8 **Litho.**

UC8 UC2 10c **pink, Prussian blue, orange & sepia,** entire *(750,000)* .35 .35
Entire, 1st day cancel *(153,472)* .50

Letter Sheet

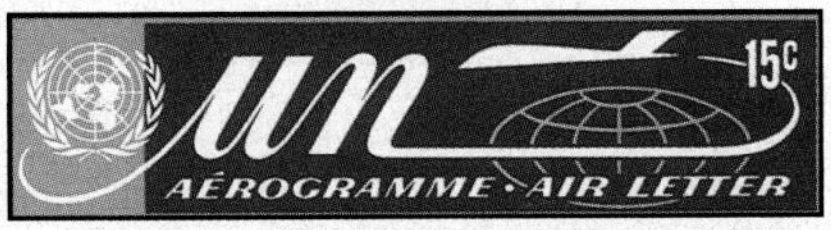

UN Emblem, "UN," Globe and Plane — UC4

Printed by Joh. Enschede and Sons. Designed by Edmondo Calivis, Egypt. Sheet surface printed in greenish blue.

1972, Oct. 16 **Litho.**

UC9 UC4 15c **violet blue & greenish blue,** entire *(500,000)* .60 .60
Entire, 1st day cancel *(85,500)* 1.00

Bird Type of Air Post Stamp, 1972
Printed by Eureka Co., a division of Litton Industries

1973, Jan. 12 **Litho.**

UC10 AP13 11c **blue & multicolored,** entire *(700,000)* .40 .40
Entire, 1st day cancel *(134,500)* 1.00

Globe and Jet Air Post Type of 1974
Printed by United States Envelope Co., Springfield, Mass.

1975, Jan. 10 **Litho.**

UC11 AP16 13c **blue & multicolored,** entire *(555,539)* .60 .60
Entire, 1st day cancel *(122,000)* 1.00

Letter Sheet
Headquarters Type of Regular Issue, 1971
Printed by Joh. Enschede and Sons, Netherlands

1975, Jan. 10 **Photo.**

UC12 A120 18c **blue & multicolored,** entire *(400,000)* .60 .60
Entire, 1st day cancel *(70,500)* 1.00

Letter Sheet

"UN" Emblem and Birds UC5

Printed by Joh. Enschede and Sons. Designed by Angel Medina Medina.

1977, June 27 **Litho.**

UC13 UC5 22c **multicolored,** entire *(400,000)* .65 .60
Entire, 1st day cancel *(70,000)* 1.00

Letter Sheet

Paper Airplane UC6

Printed by Joh. Enschede and Sons. Designed by Margaret-Ann Champion.

1982, Apr. 28 **Litho.**

UC14 UC6 30c **black,** *pale green,* entire *(400,000)* 1.50 1.50
Entire, 1st day cancel *(61,400)* 1.25

Letter Sheet No. UC14 Surcharged

1987, July 7 **Litho.**

UC15 UC6 30c + 6c **black,** *green,* entire *(43,000)* *45.00 45.00*
Entire, 1st day cancel 20.00

New York Headquarters UC7

Printed by Mercury Walch, Australia. Designed by Thomas Lee, China.

1989, Mar. 17 **Litho.**

UC16 UC7 39c **multicolored,** entire *(350,000)* 3.00 3.00
Entire, 1st day cancel *(14,798)* 9.50

No. UC16 Surcharged

1991, Feb. 12 **Litho.**

UC17 UC7 39c + 6c **multicolored,** entire *(35,563)* 16.00 25.00
Entire, first day cancel 8.50

UC8

Designed by Robert Stein. Printed by Mercury-Walch, Australia.

1992, Sept. 4 **Litho.**

UC18 UC8 45c **multicolored,** entire, *(185,000)+* 2.75 3.00
First day cancel 10.00

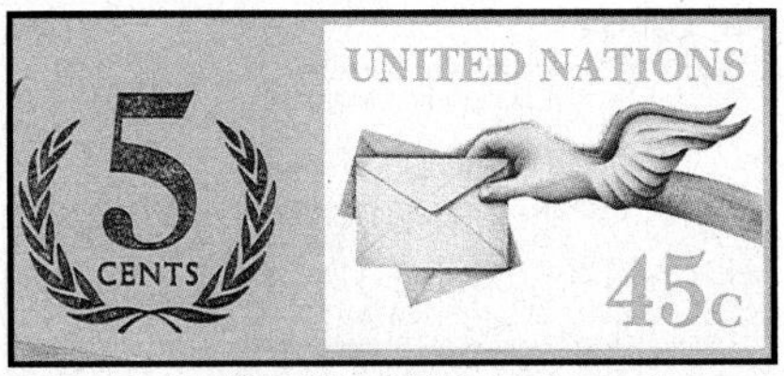

Letter Sheet No. UC18 Surcharged

1995, July 9 **Litho.**

UC19 UC8 45c +5c **multicolored,** entire 4.75 7.50
First day cover 9.00

Cherry Blossoms — UC9

1997, Mar. 13 **Litho.**

UC20 UC9 50c **multicolored,** entire *(115,000)+* 2.50 2.00
Entire, first day cancel 2.50

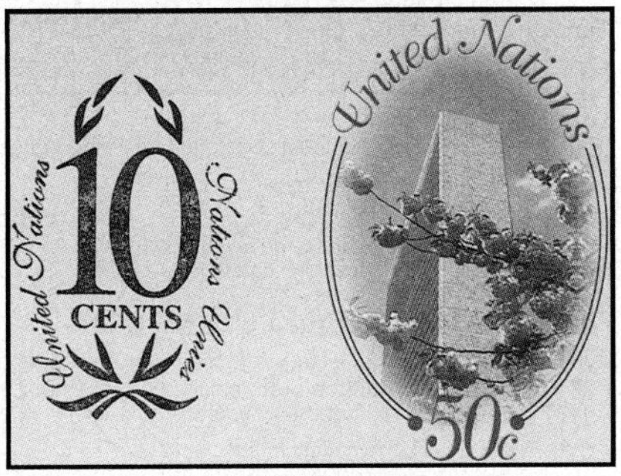

No. UC20 Surcharged

1999, Aug. 23 **Litho.**

UC21 UC9 50c +10c **multicolored,** entire 2.25 2.75
Entire, first day cancel 2.00

No. UC20 Surcharged

2001, Jan. 9 **Litho.**

UC22 UC9 50c +20c **multicolored,** entire 2.25 2.75
Entire, first day cancel 2.00

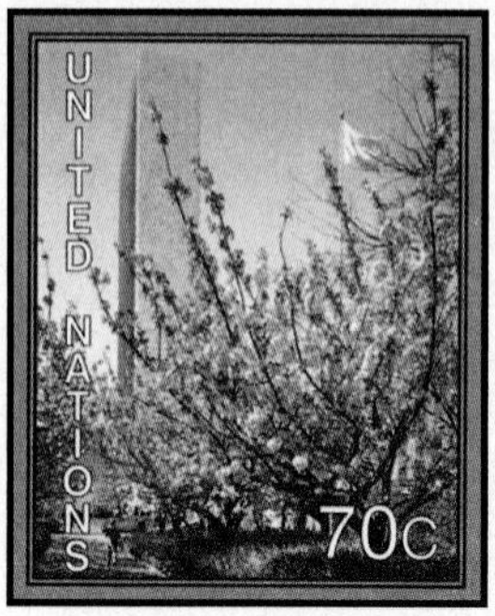

Cherry Blossoms at New York Headquarters
UC10

2001, May 25 **Litho.**
UC23 UC10 70c **multicolored,** entire 1.75 1.75
Entire, first day cancel 1.75

No. UC23 Surcharged

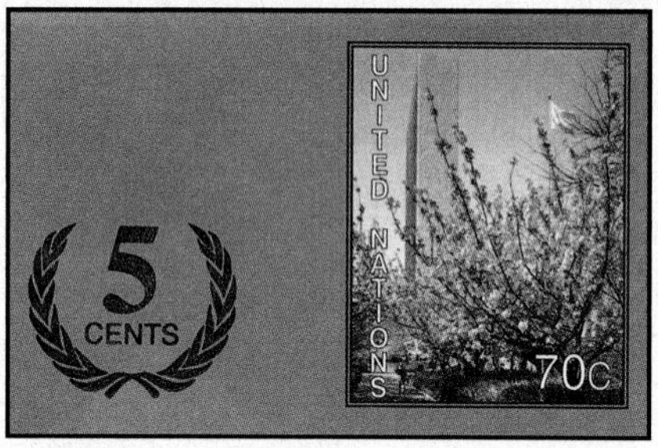

2006, Jan. 8 **Litho.**
UC24 UC10 70c +5c **multicolored,** entire 2.00 3.00
Entire, first day cancel 1.50

No. UC23 Surcharged Like No. UC24

2007, May 14 **Litho.**
UC25 UC10 70c +20c **multicolored,** entire 1.90 1.90
Entire, first day cancel 3.00

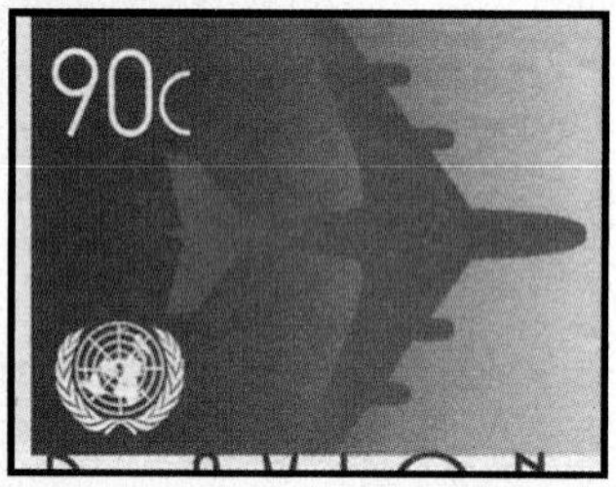

United Nations Emblem and Airplane
UC11

Printed by Sprintpak, Australia. Designed by Robert Stein, US.

2007, Aug. 9 **Litho.**
UC26 UC11 90c **multicolored,** entire *(40,000)+* 1.90 1.90
Entire, first day cancel 3.00

No. UC26 Surcharged Like No. UC24

2008, May 12 **Litho.**
UC27 UC11 90c +4c **multicolored,** entire 1.90 1.90
Entire, first day cancel 3.00

POSTAL CARDS

Values are for entire cards.

Type of Postage Issue of 1951

Printed by Dennison & Sons, Long Island City, N.Y.

1952, July 18 **Litho.**
UX1 A2 2c **blue,** *buff (899,415)* .20 .20
First day cancel *(116,023)* .50

Printed by British American Bank Note Co., Ltd., Ottawa, Canada

1958, Sept. 22 **Litho.**
UX2 A2 3c **gray olive,** *buff (575,000)* .20 .20
First day cancel *(145,557)* .50

World Map, Sinusoidal Projection — PC1

Printed by Eureka Specialty Printing Co., Scranton, Pa.

1963, Apr. 26 **Litho.**
UX3 PC1 4c **light blue, violet blue, orange & bright citron** *(784,000)* .25 .20
First day cancel *(112,280)* .50
a. Bright citron omitted —

UN Emblem and Post Horn — PC2

"UN" — PC3

Printed by Canadian Bank Note Co., Ltd., Ottawa. Designed by John Mason.

1969, Jan. 8 **Litho.**
UX4 PC2 5c **blue & black** *(500,000)* .25 .20
First day cancel *(95,975)* .50

1973, Jan. 12 **Litho.**

Printed by Government Printing Bureau, Tokyo. Designed by Asher Kalderon.

UX5 PC3 6c **gray & multicolored** *(500,000)* .20 .20
First day cancel *(84,500)* .50

Type of 1973

Printed by Setelipaino, Finland.

1975, Jan. 10 **Litho.**
UX6 PC3 8c **light green & multi** *(450,000)* .60 .60
First day cancel *(72,500)* .50

UN Emblem — PC4

Printed by Setelipaino, Finland. Designed by George Hamori.

1977, June 27 **Litho.**
UX7 PC4 9c **multicolored** *(350,000)* .60 .60
First day cancel *(70,000)* .50

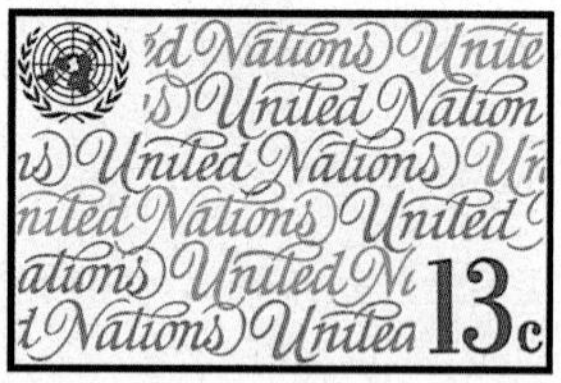

PC5

Printed by Courvoisier. Designed by Salahattin Kanidinc.

1982, Apr. 28 **Photo.**
UX8 PC5 13c **multicolored** *(350,000)* .50 .50
First day cancel *(59,200)* 1.00

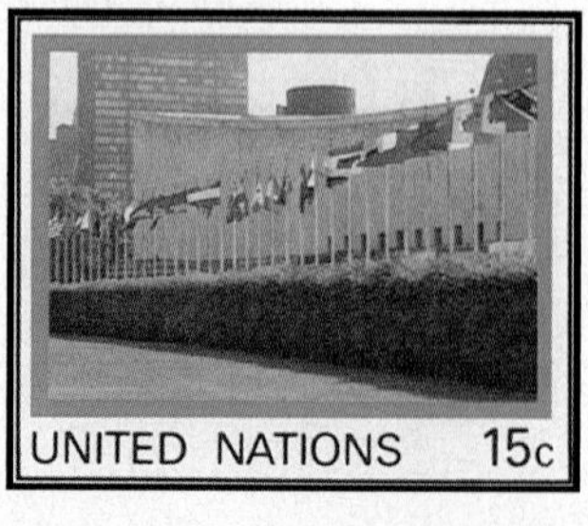

Views of New York Headquarters
PC6

Designs: No. UX9, Spring at U.N. Headquarters, vert. No. UX10, Cherry Blossoms, U.N. Gardens, vert. No. UXC11, Row of Flags of member states. No. UX12, U.N. General Assembly. No. UX13, River view, U.N. Headquarters. No. UX14, U.N. Headquarters, vert. No. UX15, Row of flags of member states, vert. No. UX16, Night view, U.N. Headquarters, vert. No. UX17, U.N. Security Council. No. UX18, U.N. Gardens.

Printed by Johann Enschede and Sons, the Netherlands. Designed by Thomas Lee, China, from photographs.

1989, Mar. 17 **Litho.**
UX9 PC6 15c **multicolored** *(120,000)+* .65 1.00
First day cancel 2.25
UX10 PC6 15c **multicolored** *(120,000)+* .65 1.00
First day cancel 2.25
UX11 PC6 15c **multicolored** *(120,000)+* .65 1.00
First day cancel 2.25
UX12 PC6 15c **multicolored** *(120,000)+* .65 1.00
First day cancel 2.25
UX13 PC6 15c **multicolored** *(120,000)+* .65 1.00
First day cancel 2.25
UX14 PC6 36c **multicolored** *(120,000)+* .90 1.50
First day cancel 2.50
UX15 PC6 36c **multicolored** *(120,000)+* .90 1.50
First day cancel 2.50
UX16 PC6 36c **multicolored** *(120,000)+* .90 1.50
First day cancel 2.50
UX17 PC6 36c **multicolored** *(120,000)+* .90 1.50
First day cancel 2.50
UX18 PC6 36c **multicolored** *(120,000)+* .90 1.50
First day cancel 2.50
Nos. UX9-UX18 (10) 7.75 12.50

Nos. UX9-UX13 and UX14-UX18 sold only in sets. Nos. UX9-UX13 sold for $2 and Nos. UX14-UX18 sold for $3.
First day cancels of Nos. UX9-UX18 total 125,526.

New York Headquarters Type of 1991

Printed by Mercury-Walch, Australia.

1992, Sept. 4 **Litho.**
UX19 A260 40c **blue** *(150,000)+* 3.50 4.00
First day cancel *(9,603)* 12.50

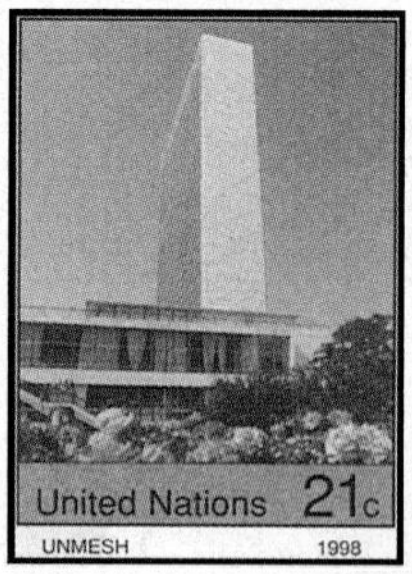

Secretariat Building, Roses — PC7

UN Complex — PC8

Printed by Mercury-Walsh, Australia.

1998, May 20 **Litho.**
UX20 PC7 21c **multicolored** *(150,000)+* 1.25 1.25
First day cancel 1.75
UX21 PC8 50c **multicolored** *(150,000)+* 2.00 2.00
First day cancel 2.25

Illustrations of the buildings and other scenes are shown on the back of each card.

New York Headquarters
PC9

2001, May 25 **Litho.**
UX22 PC9 70c **multicolored** 1.75 1.75
Entire, first day cancel 1.75

No. UX20 Surcharged

2002, June 30 **Litho.**
UX23 PC7 21c +2c **multicolored** 1.10 1.25
First day cancel 1.25

PC10

PC11

PC12

PC13

PC14

PC15

PC16

PC17

PC18

Illustrations from *This is the United Nations,* by M. Sasek — PC19

Printed by Banknote Corporation of America, US.

2003, Mar. 28 **Litho.**
UX24 PC10 23c **multicolored** *(61,500)+* .45 .45
Entire, first day cancel 1.00
UX25 PC11 23c **multicolored** *(61,500)+* .45 .45
Entire, first day cancel 1.00
UX26 PC12 23c **multicolored** *(61,500)+* .45 .45
Entire, first day cancel 1.00
UX27 PC13 23c **multicolored** *(61,500)+* .45 .45
Entire, first day cancel 1.00
UX28 PC14 23c **multicolored** *(61,500)+* .45 .45
Entire, first day cancel 1.00
UX29 PC15 70c **multicolored** *(86,500)+* 1.40 1.40
Entire, first day cancel 1.40
UX30 PC16 70c **multicolored** *(86,500)+* 1.40 1.40
Entire, first day cancel 1.40
UX31 PC17 70c **multicolored** *(86,500)+* 1.40 1.40
Entire, first day cancel 1.40
UX32 PC18 70c **multicolored** *(86,500)+* 1.40 1.40
Entire, first day cancel 1.40
UX33 PC19 70c **multicolored** *(86,500)+* 1.40 1.40
Entire, first day cancel 1.40
Nos. UX24-UX33 (10) 9.25 9.25

Nos. UX24-UX28 and UX29-UX33 were sold only in shrink-wrapped sets.

AIR POST POSTAL CARDS

Values are for entire cards.

Type of Air Post Stamp of 1957

Printed by British American Bank Note Co., Ltd., Ottawa.

1957, May 27 **Litho.**
UXC1 AP3 4c **maroon,** *buff (631,000)* .25 .30
First day cancel *(260,005)* 1.00

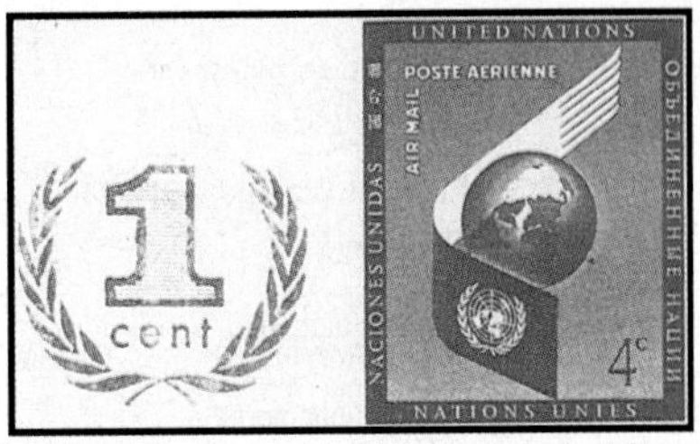

No. UXC1 Surcharged in Maroon at Left of Stamp

1959, June 5 **Litho.**
UXC2 AP3 4c + 1c **maroon,** *buff (1,119,000)* .30 .50
Cancel first day of public use, June 8 300.00
a. Double surcharge —
b. Inverted surcharge —
c. Double surcharge, one inverted —

This surcharge also exists on a No. U1 envelope. Status uncertain.

Type of Air Post Stamp, 1957

Printed by Eureka Specialty Printing Co., Scranton, Pa.

1959, Sept. 21 **Litho.**
UXC3 AP3 5c **crimson,** *buff (500,000)* .65 .65
First day cancel *(119,479)* .50

Outer Space — APC1

Printed by Eureka Specialty Printing Co., Scranton, Pa.

1963, Apr. 26 **Litho.**
UXC4 APC1 6c **black & blue** *(350,000)* .60 .60
First day cancel *(109,236)* .50

APC2

Printed by Eureka-Carlisle Co., Scranton, Pa. Designed by Olav S. Mathiesen.

1966, June 9 **Litho.**
UXC5 APC2 11c **dark red, rose, yellow & brown** *(764,500)* .30 .30
First day cancel *(162,588)* .50

1968, May 31 **Litho.**
UXC6 APC2 13c **dark green, bright green & yellow** *(829,000)* .40 .40
First day cancel *(106,500)* 1.00

UN Emblem and Stylized Planes — APC3

Printed by Canadian Bank Note Co., Ltd., Ottawa. Designed by Lawrence Kurtz.

1969, Jan. 8 **Litho.**
UXC7 APC3 8c **gray, dull yellow, lt blue, indigo & red** *(500,000)* .65 .65
First day cancel *(94,037)* .50

Type of Air Post Stamp of 1972

Printed by Government Printing Bureau, Tokyo. Designed by L. L. Dolan.

1972, Oct. 16 **Litho.**
UXC8 AP12 9c **orange, red, gray & green** *(500,000)* .45 .45
First day cancel *(85,600)* .50

Type of 1969

Printed by Government Printing Bureau, Tokyo

1972, Oct. 16 **Litho.**
UXC9 APC3 15c **lilac, light blue, pink & carmine** *(500,000)* .50 .50
First day cancel *(84,800)* .50

Types of Air Post Stamps, 1972-74

Printed by Setelipaino, Finland.

1975, Jan. 10 **Litho.**
UXC10 AP14 11c **greenish blue, blue & dark blue** *(250,000)* .50 .50
First day cancel *(70,500)* .50
UXC11 AP17 18c **gray & multicolored** *(250,000)* .50 .50
First day cancel *(70,500)* .50

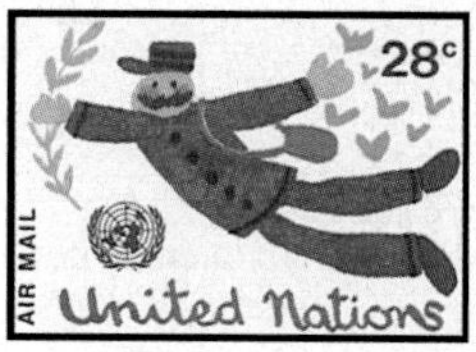

Flying Mailman — APC4

Printed by Courvoisier. Designed by Arieh Glaser.

1982, Apr. 28 **Photo.**
UXC12 APC4 28c **multicolored** *(350,000)* .45 .50
First day cancel *(58,700)* 1.40

OFFICES IN GENEVA, SWITZERLAND

For use only on mail posted at the Palais des Nations (UN European Office), Geneva. Inscribed in French unless otherwise stated.

100 Centimes = 1 Franc

Types of United Nations Issues 1961-69 and

United Nations European Office, Geneva — G1

Printed by Setelipaino, Finland (5c, 70c, 80c, 90c, 2fr, 10fr), Courvoisier, S.A., Switzerland (10c, 20c, 30c, 50c, 60c, 3fr). Government Printing Office, Austria (75c) and Government Printing Office, Federal Republic of Germany (1fr).

Panes of 50. 30c designed by Ole Hamann, others as before.

Designs: 5c, UN Headquarters, New York, and world map. 10c, UN flag. 20c, Three men united before globe. 50c, Opening words of UN Charter. 60c, UN emblem over globe. 70c, "un" and UN emblem. 75c, "Flight Across Globe." 80c, UN Headquarters and emblem. 90c, Abstract group of flags. 1fr, UN emblem. 2fr, Stylized globe and weather vane. 3fr, Statue by Henrik Starcke. 10fr, "Peace, Justice, Security."

The 20c, 80c and 90c are inscribed in French. The 75c and 10fr carry French inscription at top, English at bottom.

1969-70 Photo. Unwmk.

Perf. 13 (5c, 70c, 90c); 12½x12 (10c);

1 A88 5c **purple & multi,** *Oct. 4, 1969 (3,300,000)* .20 .20
First day cover 1.00
Inscription block of 4 .25 —
a. Green omitted —
2 A52 10c **salmon & multi,** *Oct. 4, 1969 (4,300,000)+* .20 .20
First day cover 1.00
Inscription block of 4 .25 —

Perf. 11½ (20c-60c, 3fr)

3 A66 20c **black & multi,** *Oct. 4, 1969 (4,500.000)* .20 .20
First day cover 1.00
Inscription block of 4 .45 —
4 G1 30c **dark blue & multi,** *Oct. 4, 1969 (3,000,000)* .20 .20
First day cover 1.00
Inscription block of 4 .60 —
5 A77 50c **ultra & multi,** *Oct. 4, 1969 (3,300,000)* .30 .30
First day cover 1.25
Inscription block of 4 .80 —
6 A54 60c **dark brown, salmon & gold,** *Apr. 17, 1970 (3,300,000)+* .35 .35
First day cover 1.00
Inscription block of 4 1.50 —
7 A104 70c **red, black & gold,** *Sept. 22, 1970 (3,300,000)+* .40 .40
First day cover 1.00
Inscription block of 4 1.75 —

Perf. 11½x12 (75c)

8 AP8 75c **carmine rose & multi,** *Oct. 4, 1969 (3,300,000)+* .45 .45
First day cover 1.00
Inscription block of 4 1.90 —

Perf. 13½x14 (80c)

9 A78 80c **blue green, red & yellow,** *Sept. 22, 1970 (3,300,000)* .45 .45
First day cover 1.00
Inscription block of 4 1.90 —
10 A45 90c **blue & multi,** *Sept. 22, 1970 (3,300,000)* .50 .50
First day cover 1.00
Inscription block of 4 2.10 —

Litho. & Embossed

Perf. 14 (1fr)

11 A79 1fr **light & dark green,** *Oct. 4, 1969 (3,000,000)* .55 .55
First day cover 1.00
Inscription block of 4 2.40 —

Photo.

Perf. 12x11½ (2fr)

12 A67 2fr **blue & multi,** *Sept. 22, 1970 (3,000,000)+* 1.10 1.10
First day cover 2.00
Inscription block of 4 4.50 —
13 A97 3fr **olive & multi,** *Oct. 4, 1969 (3,000,000)+* 1.75 1.75
First day cover 2.25
Inscription block of 4 7.50 —

Engr.

Perf. 12 (10fr)

14 A3 10fr **dark blue,** *Apr. 17, 1970 (2,250,000)+* 5.75 5.75
First day cover 8.50
Inscription block of 4 24.00 —
Nos. 1-14 (14) 12.40 12.40

+ Printing orders to June 1984.

First day covers of Nos. 1-5, 8, 11, 13 total 607,578; of Nos. 6 and 14, 148,055; of Nos. 7, 9-10 and 12, 226,000.

Sea Bed Type of UN

1971, Jan. 25 Photo. & Engr. *Perf. 13*

15 A114 30c **green & multi** *(1,935,871)* .20 .20
First day cover *(152,590)* 1.00
Inscription block of 4 .65 —

Refugee Type of UN

1971, Mar. 12 Litho. *Perf. 13x12½*

16 A115 50c **deep carmine, deep orange & black** *(1,820,114)* .25 .25
First day cover *(148,220)* 1.00
Inscription block of 4 1.05 —

World Food Program Type of UN

1971, Apr. 13 Photo. *Perf. 14*

17 A116 50c **dark violet & multi** *(1,824,170)* .25 .25
First day cover *(151,580)* 1.00
Inscription block of 4 1.05 —

UPU Headquarters Type of UN

1971, May 28 Photo. *Perf. 11½*

18 A117 75c **green & multi** *(1,821,878)* .35 .35
First day cover *(140,679)* 1.00
Inscription block of 4 1.60 —

Eliminate Racial Discrimination Types of UN

Designed by Daniel Gonzague (30c) and Ole Hamann (50c).

1971, Sept. 21 Photo. *Perf. 13½*

19 A118 30c **blue & multi** *(1,838,474)* .20 .20
First day cover 1.00
Inscription block of 4 .75 —
20 A119 50c **yellow green & multi** *(1,804,126)* .25 .25
First day cover 1.00
First day cover, #19-20 1.25
Inscription block of 4 1.10 —

First day covers of Nos. 19-20 total 308,420.

Picasso Type of UN

1971, Nov. 19 Photo. *Perf. 11½*

21 A122 1.10fr **multicolored** *(1,467,993)* .75 .75
First day cover *(195,215)* 1.25
Inscription block of 4 3.00 —

Palais des Nations, Geneva — G2

Printed by Courvoisier, S. A. Panes of 50. Designed by Ole Hamann.

1972, Jan. 5 Photo. *Perf. 11½*

22 G2 40c **olive, blue, salmon & dark green** *(3,500,000)+* .25 .25
First day cover *(152,300)* 1.00
Inscription block of 4 1.05 —

+ Initial printing order.

Nuclear Weapons Type of UN

1972, Feb. 14 Photo. *Perf. 13½x14*

23 A124 40c **yellow, green, black, rose & gray** *(1,567,305)* .25 .25
First day cover *(151,350)* 1.00
Inscription block of 4 1.25 —

World Health Day Type of UN

1972, Apr. 7 Litho. & Engr. *Perf. 13x13½*

24 A125 80c **black & multi** *(1,543,368)* .45 .45
First day cover *(192,600)* 1.00
Inscription block of 4 2.00 —

Human Environment Type of UN

Lithographed & Embossed

1972, June 5 *Perf. 12½x14*

25 A126 40c **olive, lemon, green & blue** *(1,594,089)* .25 .25
First day cover 1.00
Inscription block of 4 1.00 —
26 A126 80c **ultra, pink, green & blue** *(1,568,009)* .45 .45
First day cover 1.40
First day cover, #25-26 1.75
Inscription block of 4 1.80 —

First day covers of Nos. 25-26 total 296,700.

Economic Commission for Europe Type of UN

1972, Sept. 11 Litho. *Perf. 13x13½*

27 A127 1.10fr **red & multi** *(1,604,082)* 1.00 1.00
First day cover *(149,630)* 1.75
Inscription block of 4 4.25 —

Art at UN (Sert) Type of UN

1972, Nov. 17 Photo. *Perf. 12x12½*

28 A128 40c **gold, red & brown** *(1,932,428)* .30 .30
First day cover 1.00
Inscription block of 4 1.25 —
29 A128 80c **gold, brown & olive** *(1,759,600)* .60 .60
First day cover 1.25
First day cover, #28-29 1.75
Inscription block of 4 2.50 —

First day covers of Nos. 28-29 total 295,470.

Disarmament Decade Type of UN

1973, Mar. 9 Litho. *Perf. 13½x13*

30 A129 60c **violet & multi** *(1,586,845)* .40 .40
First day cover 1.00
Inscription block of 4 1.60 —
31 A129 1.10fr **olive & multi** *(1,408,169)* .85 .85
First day cover 1.40
First day cover, #30-31 1.75
Inscription block of 4 3.50 —

First day covers of Nos. 30-31 total 260,680.

Drug Abuse Type of UN

1973, Apr. 13 Photo. *Perf. 13½*

32 A130 60c **blue & multi** *(1,481,432)* .45 .45
First day cover *(144,760)* 1.00
Inscription block of 4 1.90 —

Volunteers Type of UN

1973, May 25 Photo. *Perf. 14*

33 A131 80c **gray green & multi** *(1,443,519)* .35 .35
First day cover *(143,430)* 1.10
Inscription block of 4 1.50 —

Namibia Type of UN

1973, Oct. 1 Photo. *Perf. 13½*

34 A132 60c **red & multi** *(1,673,898)* .35 .35
First day cover *(148,077)* 1.00
Inscription block of 4 1.50 —

Human Rights Type of UN

1973, Nov. 16 Photo. *Perf. 13½*

35 A133 40c **ultramarine & multi** *(1,480,791)* .30 .30
First day cover 1.00
Inscription block of 4 1.25 —
36 A133 80c **olive & multi** *(1,343,349)* .50 .50
First day cover 1.25
First day cover, #35-36 1.75
Inscription block of 4 2.10 —

First day covers of Nos. 35-36 total 438,260.

ILO Headquarters Type of UN

1974, Jan. 11 Photo. *Perf. 14*

37 A134 60c **violet & multi** *(1,212,703)* .45 .45
First day cover 1.00
Inscription block of 4 1.90 —
38 A134 80c **brown & multi** *(1,229,851)* .65 .65
First day cover 1.10
First day cover, #37-38 1.25
Inscription block of 4 2.75 —

First day covers of Nos. 37-38 total 240,660.

Centenary of UPU Type of UN

1974, Mar. 22 Litho. *Perf. 12½*

39 A135 30c **gold & multi** *(1,567,517)* .25 .25
First day cover 1.00
Inscription block of 4 1.25 —
40 A135 60c **gold & multi** *(1,430,839)* .60 .60
First day cover 1.25
First day cover, #39-40 1.50
Inscription block of 4 2.50 —

First day covers of Nos. 39-40 total 231,840.

Art at UN (Portinari) Type of UN

1974, May 6 Photo. *Perf. 14*

41 A136 60c **dark red & multi** *(1,202,357)* .40 .40
First day cover 1.00
Inscription block of 4 1.75 —
42 A136 1fr **green & multi** *(1,230,045)* .70 .70
First day cover 1.20
First day cover, #41-42 1.50
Inscription block of 4 3.00 —

First day covers of Nos. 41-42 total 249,130.

World Population Year Type of UN

1974, Oct. 18 Photo. *Perf. 14*

43 A140 60c **bright green & multi** *(1,292,954)* .50 .50
First day cover 1.00
Inscription block of 4 2.25 —
44 A140 80c **brown & multi** *(1,221,288)* .70 .70
First day cover 1.00
First day cover, #43-44 1.25
Inscription block of 4 3.25 —

First day covers of Nos. 43-44 total 189,597.

Law of the Sea Type of UN

1974, Nov. 22 Photo. *Perf. 14*

45 A141 1.30fr **blue & multicolored** *(1,266,270)* 1.00 1.00
First day cover *(181,000)* 1.25
Inscription block of 4 4.00 —

Outer Space Type of UN

1975, Mar. 14 Litho. *Perf. 13*

46 A142 60c **multicolored** *(1,339,704)* .50 .50
First day cover 1.00
Inscription block of 4 2.00 —
47 A142 90c **multicolored** *(1,383,888)* .75 .75
First day cover 1.00
First day cover, #46-47 1.50
Inscription block of 4 3.25 —

First day covers of Nos. 46-47 total 250,400.

International Women's Year Type of UN

1975, May 9 Litho. *Perf. 15*

48 A143 60c **multicolored** *(1,176,080)* .40 .40
First day cover 1.00
Inscription block of 4 1.90 —
49 A143 90c **multicolored** *(1,167,863)* .70 .70
First day cover 1.00
First day cover, #48-49 1.50
Inscription block of 4 3.25 —

First day covers of Nos. 48-49 total 250,660.

30th Anniversary Type of UN

1975, June 26 Litho. *Perf. 13*

50 A144 60c **green & multi** *(1,442,075)* .40 .40
First day cover 1.00
Inscription block of 4 2.00 —
51 A144 90c **violet & multi** *(1,612,411)* .70 .70
First day cover 1.00
First day cover, #50-51 1.25
Inscription block of 4 3.25 —

Souvenir Sheet

Imperf

52 Sheet of 2 *(1,210,148)* 1.00 1.00
a. A144 60c **green & multicolored** .30 .30
b. A144 90c **violet & multicolored** .60 .60
First day cover 1.25

No. 52 has blue and bister margin with inscription and UN emblem. Size: 92x70mm.
First day covers of Nos. 50-52 total 402,500.

Namibia Type of UN

1975, Sept. 22 Photo. *Perf. 13½*

53 A145 50c **multicolored** *(1,261,019)* .30 .30
First day cover 1.00
Inscription block of 4 1.25 —
54 A145 1.30fr **multicolored** *(1,241,990)* .85 .85
First day cover 1.10
First day cover, #53-54 1.25
Inscription block of 4 4.00 —

First day covers of Nos. 53-54 total 226,260.

Peace-keeping Operations Type of UN

1975, Nov. 21 Engr. *Perf. 12½*

55 A146 60c **greenish blue** *(1,249,305)* .35 .35
First day cover 1.00
Inscription block of 4 1.50 —
56 A146 70c **bright violet** *(1,249,935)* .65 .65
First day cover 1.00
First day cover, #55-56 1.25
Inscription block of 4 2.75 —

First day covers of Nos. 55-56 total 229,245.

WFUNA Type of UN

1976, Mar. 12 Photo. *Perf. 14*

57 A152 90c **multicolored** *(1,186,563)* .90 .90
First day cover 1.00
Inscription block of 4 4.00 —

First day covers of No. 57 total 121,645.

UNCTAD Type of UN

1976, Apr. 23 Photo. *Perf. 11½*

58 A153 1.10fr **sepia & multi** *(1,167,284)* .90 .90
First day cover *(107,030)* 1.25
Inscription block of 4 4.00 —

Habitat Type of UN

1976, May 28 Photo. *Perf. 14*

59 A154 40c **dull blue & multi** *(1,258,986)* .20 .20
First day cover 1.00
Inscription block of 4 1.00 —
60 A154 1.50fr **violet & multi** *(1,110,507)* .75 .75
First day cover 1.25
First day cover, #59-60 1.60
Inscription block of 4 3.50 —

First day covers of Nos. 59-60 total 242,530.

UN Emblem, Post Horn and Rainbow — G3

UN Postal Administration, 25th anniversary.
Printed by Courvoisier, S.A. Panes of 20 (5x4). Designed by Hector Viola.

1976, Oct. 8 Photo. *Perf. 11½*

61 G3 80c **tan & multicolored** *(1,794,009)* .50 .50
First day cover 2.00
Inscription block of 4 2.50 —
62 A3 1.10fr **light green & multi** *(1,751,178)* 1.60 1.60
First day cover 2.00
Inscription block of 4 8.00 —
First day cover, #61-62 3.00
Panes of 20, #61-62 37.50

Upper margin blocks are inscribed "XXVe ANNIVERSAIRE"; lower margin blocks "ADMINISTRATION POSTALE DES NATIONS UNIES."
First day covers of Nos. 61-62 total 152,450.

World Food Council Type of UN

1976, Nov. 19 Litho. *Perf. 14½*

63 A156 70c **multicolored** *(1,507,630)* .50 .50
First day cover *(170,540)* 1.00
Inscription block of 4 2.25 —

WIPO Type of UN

1977, Mar. 11 Photo. *Perf. 14*

64 A157 80c **red & multi** *(1,232,664)* .60 .60
First day cover *(212,470)* 1.00
Inscription block of 4 2.75 —

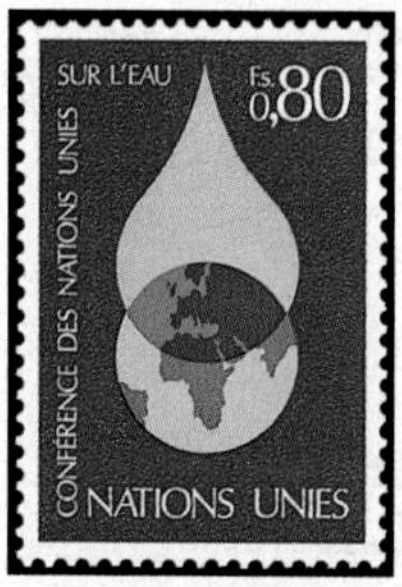

Drop of Water and Globe — G4

UN Water Conference, Mar del Plata, Argentina, Mar. 14-25.
Printed by Government Printing Bureau, Tokyo. Panes of 50. Designed by Eliezer Weishoff.

1977, Apr. 22 Photo. *Perf. 13½x13*

65 G4 80c **ultramarine & multi** *(1,146,650)* .50 .50
First day cover 1.00
Inscription block of 4 2.25 —
66 G4 1.10fr **dark carmine & multi** *(1,138,236)* .80 .80
First day cover 1.25
First day cover, #65-66 1.75
Inscription block of 4 3.50 —

First day covers of Nos. 65-66 total 289,836.

Hands Protecting UN Emblem — G5

UN Security Council.

Printed by Heraclio Fournier, S.A., Spain. Panes of 50. Designed by George Hamori.

1977, May 27 Photo. *Perf. 11*

67 G5 80c **blue & multi** *(1,096,030)* .50 .50
First day cover 1.00
Inscription block of 4 2.25 —
68 G5 1.10fr **emerald & multi** *(1,075,925)* .80 .80
First day cover 1.25
First day cover, #67-68 1.75
Inscription block of 4 3.50 —

First day covers of Nos. 67-68 total 305,349.

Colors of Five Races Spun into One Firm Rope — G6

Fight against racial discrimination.
Printed by Setelipaino, Finland. Panes of 50. Designed by M. A. Munnawar.

1977, Sept. 19 Litho. *Perf. 13½x13*

69 G6 40c **multicolored** *(1,218,834)* .25 .25
First day cover 1.00
Inscription block of 4 1.10 —
70 G6 1.10fr **multicolored** *(1,138,250)* .65 .65
First day cover 1.25
First day cover, #69-70 1.75
Inscription block of 4 2.75 —

First day covers of Nos. 69-70 total 308,722.

Atomic Energy Turning Partly into Olive Branch — G7

Peaceful uses of atomic energy.
Printed by Heraclio Fournier, S.A., Spain. Panes of 50. Designed by Witold Janowski and Marek Freudenreich.

1977, Nov. 18 Photo. *Perf. 14*

71 G7 80c **dark carmine & multi** *(1,147,787)* .55 .55
First day cover 1.00
Inscription block of 4 2.50 —
72 G7 1.10fr **Prussian blue & multi** *(1,121,209)* .75 .75
First day cover 1.20
First day cover, #71-72 1.50
Inscription block of 4 3.50 —

First day covers of Nos. 71-72 total 298,075.

"Tree" of Doves — G8

Printed by Questa Colour Security Printers, United Kingdom. Panes of 50. Designed by M. Hioki.

1978, Jan. 27 Litho. *Perf. 14½*

73 G8 35c **multicolored** *(3,000,000)*+ .20 .20
First day cover *(259,735)* 1.00
Inscription block of 4 .75 —

Globes with Smallpox Distribution — G9

Global eradication of smallpox.

Printed by Courvoisier, S.A. Panes of 50. Designed by Eliezer Weishoff.

1978, Mar. 31 Photo. *Perf. 12x11½*

74 G9 80c **yellow & multi** *(1,116,044)* .60 .60
First day cover 1.00
Inscription block of 4 2.50 —
75 G9 1.10fr **light green & multi** *(1,109,946)* .90 .90
First day cover 1.25
First day cover, #74-75 2.00
Inscription block of 4 3.75 —

First day covers of Nos. 74-75 total 254,700.

Namibia Type of UN

1978, May 5 Photo. *Perf. 12*

76 A166 80c **multicolored** *(1,183,208)* .85 .85
First day cover *(316,610)* 1.00
Inscription block of 4 3.50 —

Jets and Flight Patterns — G10

International Civil Aviation Organization for "Safety in the Air."
Printed by Heraclio Fournier, S.A., Spain. Panes of 50. Designed by Tomas Savrda.

1978, June 12 Photo. *Perf. 14*

77 G10 70c **multicolored** *(1,275,106)* .40 .40
First day cover 1.00
Inscription block of 4 1.75 —
78 G10 80c **multicolored** *(1,144,339)* .70 .70
First day cover 1.00
First day cover, #77-78 1.60
Inscription block of 4 3.00 —

First day covers of Nos. 77-78 total 255,700.

General Assembly, Flags and Globe — G11

Printed by Government Printing Bureau, Tokyo. Panes of 50. Designed by Henry Bencsath.

1978, Sept. 15 Photo. *Perf. 13½*

79 G11 70c **multicolored** *(1,204,441)* .45 .45
First day cover 1.00
Inscription block of 4 2.25 —
80 G11 1.10fr **multicolored** *(1,183,889)* .85 .85
First day cover 1.25
First day cover, #79-80 1.75
Inscription block of 4 3.75 —

First day covers of Nos. 79-80 total 245,600.

Technical Cooperation Type of UN

1978, Nov. 17 Photo. *Perf. 14*

81 A169 80c **multicolored** *(1,173,220)* .70 .70
First day cover *(264,700)* 1.00
Inscription block of 4 3.25 —

Seismograph Recording Earthquake — G12

Office of the UN Disaster Relief Coordinator (UNDRO).
Printed by Heraclio Fournier, S.A., Spain. Panes of 50. Designed by Michael Klutmann.

1979, Mar. 9 Photo. *Perf. 14*

82 G12 80c **multicolored** *(1,183,155)* .50 .50
First day cover 1.00
Inscription block of 4 2.00 —
83 G12 1.50fr **multicolored** *(1,168,121)* .80 .80
First day cover 1.40
First day cover, #82-83 1.90
Inscription block of 4 3.50 —

First day covers of Nos. 82-83 total 162,070.

Children and Rainbow — G13

International Year of the Child.
Printed by Heraclio Fournier, S.A., Spain. Panes of 20 (5x4). Designed by Arieh Glaser.

1979, May 4 Photo. *Perf. 14*

84 G13 80c **multicolored** *(2,251,623)* .35 .35
First day cover 1.25
Inscription block of 4 1.60 —
85 G13 1.10fr **multicolored** *(2,220,463)* .65 .65
First day cover 1.75
Inscription block of 4 2.75 —
First day cover, #84-85 1.25
Panes of 20, #84-85 20.00

First day covers of Nos. 84-85 total 176,120.

Namibia Type of UN

1979, Oct. 5 Litho. *Perf. 13½*

86 A176 1.10fr **multicolored** *(1,229,830)* .60 .60
First day cover *(134,160)* 1.25
Inscription block of 4 2.25 —

International Court of Justice, Scales — G14

International Court of Justice, The Hague, Netherlands.
Printed by Setelipaino, Finland. Panes of 50. Designed by Kyohei Maeno.

1979, Nov. 9 Litho. *Perf. 13x13½*

87 G14 80c **multicolored** *(1,123,193)* .40 .40
First day cover 1.00
Inscription block of 4 1.75 —
88 G14 1.10fr **multicolored** *(1,063,067)* .60 .60
First day cover 1.25
First day cover, #87-88 1.75
Inscription block of 4 2.75 —

First day covers of Nos. 87-88 total 158,170.

New Economic Order Type of UN

1980, Jan. 11 Litho. *Perf. 15x14½*

89 A179 80c **multicolored** *(1,315,918)* .85 .85
First day cover *(176,250)* 1.00
Inscription block of 4 3.50 —

Women's Year Emblem — G15

United Nations Decade for Women.
Printed by Questa Colour Security Printers, United Kingdom. Panes of 50. Designed by M.A. Munnawar.

1980, Mar. 7 Litho. *Perf. 14½x15*

90 G15 40c **multicolored** *(1,265,221)* .30 .30
First day cover 1.00
Inscription block of 4 1.40 —
91 G15 70c **multicolored** *(1,240,375)* .70 .70
First day cover 1.10
First day cover, #90-91 1.25
Inscription block of 4 3.50 —

First day covers of Nos. 90-91 total 204,350.

Peace-keeping Operations Type of UN

1980, May 16 Litho. *Perf. 14x13*

92 A181 1.10fr **blue & green** *(1,335,391)* .85 .85
First day cover *(184,700)* 1.00
Inscription block of 4 3.50 —

35th Anniversary Type of UN and Dove and "35" — G16

35th Anniversary of the United Nations.
Printed by Ashton-Potter Ltd., Canada. Panes of 50. Designed by Gidon Sagi (40c), Cemalattin Mutver (70c).

1980, June 26 Litho. *Perf. 13x13½*

93 G16 40c **blue green & black** *(1,462,005)* .35 .30
First day cover 1.00
Inscription block of 4 1.40 —
94 A183 70c **multicolored** *(1,444,639)* .65 .65
First day cover 1.00
First day cover, #93-94 1.50
Inscription block of 4 3.00 —

Souvenir Sheet

Imperf

95 Sheet of 2 *(1,235,200)* 1.10 1.10
a. G16 40c **blue green & black** .30 .30
b. A183 70c **multicolored** .80 .80
First day cover 1.00

First day covers of Nos. 93-95 total 379,800.

ECOSOC Type of UN and

Family Climbing Line Graph — G17

Printed by Ashton-Potter Ltd., Canada. Panes of 50. Designed by Eliezer Weishoff (40c), A. Medina Medina (70c).

1980, Nov. 21 Litho. *Perf. 13½x13*

96 A186 40c **multicolored** *(986,435)* .30 .30
First day cover 1.00
Inscription block of 4 1.25 —
97 G17 70c **multicolored** *(1,016,462)* .60 .60
First day cover 1.00
First day cover #96-97 1.50
Inscription block of 4 2.50 —

Economic and Social Council.
First day covers of Nos. 96-97 total 210,460.

Palestinian Rights

Printed by Courvoisier S.A., Switzerland. Panes of 50. Designed by David Dewhurst.

1981, Jan. 30 Photo. *Perf. 12x11½*

98 A188 80c **multicolored** *(1,031,737)* .55 .55
First day cover *(117,480)* 1.00
Inscription block of 4 2.75 —

International Year of the Disabled.

Printed by Heraclio Fournier S.A., Spain. Panes of 50. Designed by G.P. Van der Hyde (40c) and Sophia van Heeswijk (1.50fr).

1981, Mar. 6 Photo. *Perf. 14*

99 A190 40c **black & blue** *(1,057,909)* .25 .25
First day cover 1.00
Inscription block of 4 1.00 —
100 V4 1.50fr **black & red** *(994,748)* 1.00 1.00
First day cover 1.25
First day cover, #99-100 1.75
Inscription block of 4 4.00 —

First day covers of Nos. 99-100 total 202,853.

Art Type of UN

1981, Apr. 15 Photo. *Perf. 11½*

Granite Paper

101 A191 80c **multicolored** *(1,128,782)* .80 .80
First day cover *(121,383)* 1.00
Inscription block of 4 3.75 —

Energy Type of 1981

1981, May 29 **Litho.** *Perf. 13*

102 A192 1.10fr **multicolored** *(1,096,806)* .75 .75
First day cover *(113,700)* 1.25
Inscription block of 4 3.50 —

Volunteers Program Type and

Symbols of Science, Agriculture and Industry — G18

Printed by Walsall Security Printers, Ltd., United Kingdom. Panes of 50.
Designed by Gabriele Nussgen (40c), Bernd Mirbach (70c).

1981, Nov. 13 **Litho.**

103 A194 40c **multicolored** *(1,032,700)* .45 .45
First day cover 1.00
Inscription block of 4 2.25 —
104 G18 70c **multicolored** *(1,123,672)* .90 .90
First day cover 1.00
First day cover, #103-104 1.50
Inscription block of 4 4.25 —

First day covers of Nos. 103-104 total 190,667.

Fight against Apartheid — G19

Flower of Flags — G20

Printed by Courvoisier, S.A., Switzerland. Panes of 50. Designed by Tomas Savrda (30c); Dietmar Kowall (1fr).

1982, Jan. 22 *Perf. 11½x12*

105 G19 30c **multicolored** *(3,000,000)+* .25 .25
First day cover 1.00
Inscription block of 4 1.10 —
106 G20 1fr **multicolored** *(3,000,000)+* .80 .80
First day cover 1.00
First day cover, #105-106 1.25
Inscription block of 4 3.25 —

First day covers of Nos. 105-106 total 199,347.

Human Environment Type of UN and:

Sun and Leaves — G21

10th Anniversary of United Nations Environment Program.
Printed by Joh. Enschede en Zonen, Netherlands. Panes of 50. Designed by Sybille Brunner (40c); Philine Hartert (1.20fr).

1982, Mar. 19 **Litho.** *Perf. 13½x13*

107 G21 40c **multicolored** *(948,743)* .30 .30
First day cover 1.00
Inscription block of 4 1.50 —
108 A199 1.20fr **multicolored** *(901,096)* 1.10 1.25
First day cover 1.10
First day cover, #107-108 1.40
Inscription block of 4 5.25 —

First day covers of Nos. 107-108 total 190,155.

Outer Space Type of UN and:

Satellite, Applications of Space Technology G22

Exploration and Peaceful Uses of Outer Space.
Printed by Enschede. Panes of 50. Designed by Wiktor C. Nerwinski (80c) and George Hamori (1fr).

1982, June 11 **Litho.** *Perf. 13x13½*

109 A201 80c **multicolored** *(964,593)* .60 .60
First day cover 1.00
Inscription block of 4 3.00 —
110 G22 1fr **multicolored** *(898,367)* .80 .80
First day cover 1.25
First day cover, #109-110 1.50
Inscription block of 4 3.75 —

First day covers of Nos. 109-110 total 205,815.

Conservation & Protection of Nature

1982, Nov. 19 **Photo.** *Perf. 14*

111 A202 40c Bird *(928,143)* .45 .40
First day cover 1.00
Inscription block of 4 2.10 —
112 A202 1.50fr Reptile *(847,173)* 1.10 1.10
First day cover 1.25
First day cover, #111-112 1.75
Inscription block of 4 5.25 —

First day covers of Nos. 111-112 total 198,504.

World Communications Year

1983, Jan. 28 **Litho.** *Perf. 13*

113 A204 1.20fr **multicolored** *(894,025)* 1.25 1.25
First day cover *(131,075)* 1.25
Inscription block of 4 5.25 —

Safety at Sea Type of UN and

G23

Designed by Valentin Wurnitsch (A22).

1983, Mar. 18 **Litho.** *Perf. 14½*

114 A205 40c **multicolored** *(892,365)* .40 .40
First day cover 1.00
Inscription block of 4 1.75 —
115 G23 80c **multicolored** *(882,720)* .80 .80
First day cover 1.00
First day cover, #114-115 1.50
Inscription block of 4 3.50 —

First day covers of Nos. 114-115 total 219,592.

World Food Program

1983, Apr. 22 **Engr.** *Perf. 13½*

116 A207 1.50fr **blue** *(876,591)* 1.25 1.25
First day cover 1.25
Inscription block of 4 5.25 —

Trade Type of UN and

G24

Designed by Wladyslaw Brykczynski (A23).

1983, June 6 **Litho.** *Perf. 14*

117 A208 80c **multicolored** *(902,495)* .50 .50
First day cover 1.00
Inscription block of 4 2.50 —
118 G24 1.10fr **multicolored** *(921,424)* .90 .90
First day cover 1.00
First day cover, #117-118 1.40
Inscription block of 4 4.00 —

First day covers of Nos. 117-118 total 146,507.

Homo Humus Humanitas — G25

Right to Create — G26

35th Anniversary of the Universal Declaration of Human Rights.
Printed by Government Printing Office, Austria. Designed by Friedensreich Hundertwasser, Austria. Panes of 16 (4x4).

1983, Dec. 9 **Photo. & Engr.** *Perf. 13½*

119 G25 40c **multicolored** *(1,770,921)* .45 .45
First day cover 1.00
Inscription block of 4 2.00 —
120 G26 1.20fr **multicolored** *(1,746,735)* .95 .95
First day cover 1.10
Inscription block of 4 4.25 —
First day cover, #119-120 1.40
Panes of 16, #119-120 22.50

First day covers of Nos. 119-120 total 315,052.

International Conference on Population Type

1984, Feb. 3 **Litho.** *Perf. 14*

121 A212 1.20fr **multicolored** *(776,879)* .90 .90
First day cover *(105,377)* 1.00
Inscription block of 4 4.00 —

Fishing G27

Women Farm Workers, Africa — G28

World Food Day, Oct. 16
Printed by Walsall Security Printers, Ltd., United Kingdom. Panes of 50. Designed by Adth Vanooijen, Netherlands.

1984, Mar. 15 **Litho.** *Perf. 14½*

122 G27 50c **multicolored** *(744,506)* .30 .30
First day cover 1.00
Inscription block of 4 1.60 —
123 G28 80c **multicolored** *(784,047)* .60 .60

First day cover		1.25
First day cover, #122-123		1.75
Inscription block of 4	2.75	—

First day covers of Nos. 122-123 total 155,234.

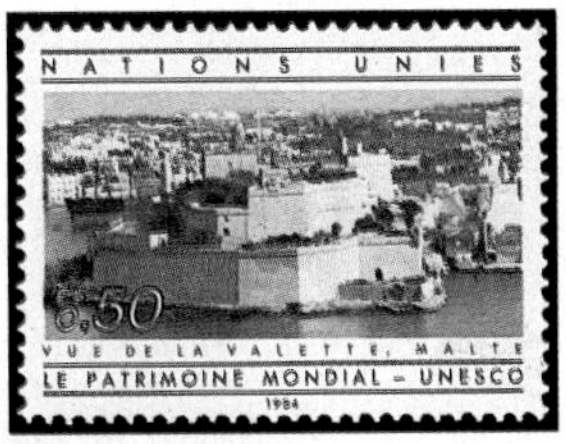

Valletta, Malta — G29

Los Glaciares National Park, Argentina — G30

World Heritage
Printed by Harrison and Sons, United Kingdom. Panes of 50. Designs adapted by Rocco J. Callari, US, and Thomas Lee, China.

1984, Apr. 18 Litho. *Perf. 14*

124	G29	50c	**multicolored** *(763,627)*	.60	.60
			First day cover		1.00
			Inscription block of 4	2.50	—
125	G30	70c	**multicolored** *(784,489)*	.85	.85
			First day cover		1.25
			First day cover, #124-125		1.75
			Inscription block of 4	4.50	—

First day covers of Nos. 124-125 total 164,498.

G31

G32

Future for Refugees
Printed by Courvoisier. Panes of 50. Designed by Hans Erni, Switzerland.

1984, May 29 Photo. *Perf. 11½*

126	G31	35c	**multicolored** *(880,762)*	.30	.30
			First day cover		1.00
			Inscription block of 4	1.50	—
127	G32	1.50fr	**multicolored** *(829,895)*	1.10	1.10
			First day cover		1.25
			First day cover, #126-127		1.75
			Inscription block of 4	5.00	—

First day covers of Nos. 126-127 total 170,306.

International Youth Year — G33

Printed by Waddingtons Ltd., United Kingdom. Panes of 50. Designed by Eliezer Weishoff, Israel.

1984, Nov. 15 Litho. *Perf. 13½*

128	G33	1.20fr	**multicolored** *(755,622)*	1.25	1.25
			First day cover *(96,680)*		1.00
			Inscription block of 4	5.50	—

ILO Type of UN and

ILO Turin Center — G34

Printed by the Government Printing Bureau, Japan. Panes of 50. Engraved by Mamoru Iwakuni and Hiroshi Ozaki, Japan (#129) and adapted from photographs by Rocco J. Callari, US, and Thomas Lee, China (#130).

1985, Feb. 1 Engr. *Perf. 13½*

129	A220	80c	**dull red** *(654,431)*	.70	.70
			First day cover		1.00
			Inscription block of 4	3.00	—
130	G34	1.20fr	U Thant Pavilion *(609,493)*	1.10	1.10
			First day cover		1.50
			First day cover, #129-130		2.25
			Inscription block of 4	4.75	—

First day covers of Nos. 129-130 total 118,467.

UN University Type

1985, Mar. 15 Photo. *Perf. 13½*

131	A221	50c	Pastoral scene, advanced communications *(625,087)*	.60	.60
			First day cover		1.00
			Inscription block of 4	2.75	—
132	A221	80c	like No. 131 *(712,674)*	1.00	1.00
			First day cover		1.25
			First day cover, #131-132		1.75
			Inscription block of 4	4.50	—

First day covers of Nos. 131-132 total 93,324.

Flying Postman — G35

Interlocked Peace Doves — G36

Printed by Carl Ueberreuter Druck and Verlag M. Salzer, Austria. Panes of 50. Designed by Arieh Glaser, Israel (#133), and Carol Sliwka, Poland (#134).

1985, May 10 Litho. *Perf. 14*

133	G35	20c	**multicolored** *(2,000,000)+*	.25	.25
			First day cover		1.00
			Inscription block of 4	1.25	—
134	G36	1.20fr	**multicolored** *(2,000,000)+*	1.25	1.25
			First day cover		1.50
			First day cover, #133-134		2.00
			Inscription block of 4	6.00	—

First day covers of Nos. 133-134 total 103,165.

40th Anniversary Type

Designed by Rocco J. Callari, U.S., and Thomas Lee, China (No. 137).

1985, June 26 Photo. *Perf. 12 x 11½*

135	A224	50c	**multicolored** *(764,924)*	.60	.60
			First day cover		1.00
			Inscription block of 4	2.50	—
136	A225	70c	**multicolored** *(779,074)*	.90	.90
			First day cover		1.25
			First day cover, #135-136		2.00
			Inscription block of 4	4.00	—

Souvenir Sheet

Imperf

137			Sheet of 2 *(498,041)*	2.25	2.25
a.	A224	50c	**multicolored**	.85	.85
b.	A225	70c	**multicolored**	1.10	1.10
			First day cover		1.25

First day covers of Nos. 135-137 total 252,418.

UNICEF Child Survival Campaign Type

Printed by the Government Printing Bureau, Japan. Panes of 50. Designed by Mel Harris, United Kingdom (#138) and Adth Vanooijen, Netherlands (#139).

1985, Nov. 22 Photo. & Engr. *Perf. 13½*

138	A226	50c	Three girls *(657,409)*	.40	.40
			First day cover		1.00
			Inscription block of 4	2.00	—
139	A226	1.20fr	Infant drinking *(593,568)*	1.10	1.10
			First day cover		1.25
			First day cover, #138-139		1.75
			Inscription block of 4	4.50	—

First day covers of Nos. 138-139 total 217,696.

Africa in Crisis Type

Printed by Helio Courvoisier, Switzerland. Panes of 50. Designed by Alemayehou Gabremedhiu, Ethiopia.

1986, Jan. 31 Photo. *Perf. 11½x12*

140	A227	1.40fr	Mother, hungry children *(590,576)*	1.25	1.25
			First day cover *(80,159)*		2.00
			Inscription block of 4	5.25	—

UN Development Program Type

Forestry. Printed by the Government Printing Bureau, Japan. Pane of 40, 2 blocks of 4 horizontal and 5 blocks of 4 vertical. Designed by Thomas Lee, China.

1986, Mar. 14 Photo. *Perf. 13½*

141	A228	35c	Erosion control *(547,567)*	1.75	1.75
142	A228	35c	Logging *(547,567)*	1.75	1.75
143	A228	35c	Lumber transport *(547,567)*	1.75	1.75
144	A228	35c	Nursery *(547,567)*	1.75	1.75
a.			Block of 4, #141-144	7.50	7.50
			First day cover, #144a		8.50
			First day cover, #141-144, each		2.50
			Inscription block of 4, #144a	8.50	—
			Pane of 40, #141-144	80.00	

No. 144a has a continuous design.
First day covers of Nos. 141-144 total 200,212.

Dove and Sun — G37

Printed by Questa Color Security Printers, Ltd., United Kingdom. Panes of 50. Designed by Ramon Alcantara Rodriguez, Mexico.

1986, Mar. 14 Litho. *Perf. 15x14½*

145	G37	5c	**multicolored** *(2,000,000)+*	.20	.20
			First day cover *(58,908)*		1.00
			Inscription block of 4	.50	—

Stamp Collecting Type

Designs: 50c, UN Human Rights stamp. 80c, UN stamps. Printed by the Swedish Post Office, Sweden. Panes of 50. Designed by Czeslaw Slania and Ingalill Axelsson, Sweden.

1986, May 22 Engr. *Perf. 12½*

146	A229	50c	**dark green & henna brown** *(722,015)*	.60	.60
			First day cover		1.50
			Inscription block of 4	2.50	—
147	A229	80c	**dark green & yellow orange** *(750,945)*	.90	.90
			First day cover		1.50
			First day cover, #146-147		1.75
			Inscription block of 4	3.75	—

First day covers of Nos. 146-147 total 137,653.

Flags and Globe as Dove — G38

Peace in French — G39

International Peace Year. Printed by the Government Printing Bureau, Japan. Panes of 50. Designed by Renato Ferrini, Italy (#148), and Salahattin Kanidinc, US (#149).

1986, June 20 Photo. & Embossed *Perf. 13½*

148 G38 45c **multicolored** *(620,978)* .60 .60
First day cover 1.00
Inscription block of 4 2.75 —
149 G39 1.40fr **multicolored** *(559,658)* 1.25 1.25
First day cover 1.60
First day cover, #148-149 3.00
Inscription block of 4 5.50 —

First day covers of Nos. 148-149 total 123,542.

WFUNA Anniversary Type
Souvenir Sheet

Printed by Johann Enschede and Sons, Netherlands. Designed by Rocco J. Callari, US.

Designs: 35c, Abstract by Benigno Gomez, Honduras. 45c, Abstract by Alexander Calder (1898-1976), US. 50c, Abstract by Joan Miro (b. 1893), Spain. 70c, Sextet with Dove, by Ole Hamann, Denmark.

1986, Nov. 14 Litho. *Perf. 13x13½*

150 Sheet of 4 *(478,833)* 3.75 3.75
a. A232 35c **multicolored** .50 .50
b. A232 45c **multicolored** .70 .70
c. A232 50c **multicolored** .90 .90
d. A232 70c **multicolored** 1.25 1.25
First day cover *(58,452)* 2.00

No. 150 has inscribed margin picturing UN and WFUNA emblems.

Trygve Lie Type

1987, Jan. 30 Photo. & Engr. *Perf. 13½*

151 A233 1.40fr **multicolored** *(516,605)* 1.10 1.10
First day cover *(76,152)* 1.50
Inscription block of 4 5.50 —

Sheaf of Colored Bands, by Georges Mathieu — G40

Armillary Sphere, Palais des Nations — G41

Printed by Helio Courvoisier, Switzerland (#152), and the Government Printing Bureau, Japan (#153). Panes of 50. Designed by Georges Mathieu (#152) and Rocco J. Callari (#153), US.

Photo., Photo. & Engr. (#153)

1987, Jan. 30 *Perf. 11½x12, 13½*

152 G40 90c **multicolored** *(1,600,000)+* .65 .65
First day cover 1.00
Inscription block of 4 3.00 —
153 G41 1.40fr **multicolored** *(1,600,000)+* 1.25 1.25
First day cover 1.00
First day cover, #152-153 2.00
Inscription block of 4 5.00 —

First day covers of Nos. 152-153 total 85,737.

Shelter for the Homeless Type

Designs: 50c, Cement-making and brick-making. 90c, Interior construction and decorating.

1987, Mar. 13 Litho. *Perf. 13½x12½*

154 A234 50c **multicolored** *(564,445)* .50 .50
First day cover 1.00
Inscription block of 4 2.50 —
155 A234 90c **multicolored** *(526,646)* 1.00 1.00
First day cover 1.10
First day cover, #154-155 2.00
Inscription block of 4 4.25 —

First day covers of Nos. 154-155 total 100,366.

Fight Drug Abuse Type

Designs: 80c, Mother and child. 1.20fr, Workers in rice paddy.

1987, June 12 Litho. *Perf. 14½x15*

156 A235 80c **multicolored** *(634,776)* .50 .50
First day cover 1.25
Inscription block of 4 3.00 —
157 A235 1.20fr **multicolored** *(609,475)* 1.00 1.00
First day cover 1.75
First day cover, #156-157 2.50
Inscription block of 4 4.75 —

First day covers of Nos. 156-157 total 95,247.

UN Day Type

Designed by Elisabeth von Janota-Bzowski (35c) and Fritz Oerter (50c).

Designs: Multinational people in various occupations.

1987, Oct. 23 Litho. *Perf. 14½x15*

158 A236 35c **multicolored** *(1,114,756)* .55 .55
First day cover 1.60
Inscription block of 4 2.50 —
159 A236 50c **multicolored** *(1,117,464)* .80 .80
First day cover 1.90
Inscription block of 4 3.50 —
First day cover, #158-159 2.50
Panes of 12, #158-159 15.00

Immunize Every Child Type

Designs: 90c, Whooping cough. 1.70fr, Tuberculosis.

1987, Nov. 20 Litho. *Perf. 15x14½*

160 A237 90c **multicolored** *(634,614)* 1.50 1.50
First day cover 1.00
Inscription block of 4 6.25 —
161 A237 1.70fr **multicolored** *(607,725)* 2.75 2.75
First day cover 1.25
First day cover, #160-161 2.50
Inscription block of 4 11.50 —

IFAD Type

Designs: 35c, Flocks, dairy products. 1.40fr, Fruit.

1988, Jan. 29 Litho. *Perf. 13½*

162 A238 35c **multicolored** *(524,817)* .35 .35
First day cover 1.00
Inscription block of 4 1.90 —
163 A238 1.40fr **multicolored** *(499,103)* 1.40 1.40
First day cover 1.50
First day cover, #162-163 2.00
Inscription block of 4 7.00 —

G42

Printed by Heraclio Fournier, S.A., Spain. Panes of 50. Designed by Bjorn Wiinblad, Denmark.

1988, Jan. 29 Photo. *Perf. 14*

164 G42 50c **multicolored** *(1,600,000)+* .80 .80
First day cover 2.00
Inscription block of 4 3.75 —

Survival of the Forests Type

Pine forest: 50c, Treetops, mountains. 1.10fr, Lake, tree trunks. Printed se-tenant in a continuous design.

1988, Mar. 18 Litho. *Perf. 14x15*

165 A240 50c **multicolored** *(728,569)* 1.25 1.25
First day cover 4.00
166 A240 1.10fr **multicolored** *(728,569)* 3.50 3.50
First day cover 6.00
a. Pair, #165-166 5.50 5.25
First day cover, #166a 10.00
Inscription block of 4, 2 #166a 12.50 —
Pane of 12, #165-166 30.00

Intl. Volunteer Day Type

Designed by Christopher Magadini, US.

Designs: 80c, Agriculture, vert. 90c, Veterinary medicine.

1988, May 6 Litho. *Perf. 13x14, 14x13*

167 A241 80c **multicolored** *(612,166)* .80 .80
First day cover 1.50
Inscription block of 4 4.00 —
168 A241 90c **multicolored** *(467,334)* 1.00 1.00
First day cover 1.75
First day cover, #167-168 3.50
Inscription block of 4 4.25 —

Health in Sports Type

Paintings by LeRoy Neiman, American sports artist: 50c, Soccer, vert. 1.40fr, Swimming.

1988, June 17 Litho. *Perf. 13½x13, 13x13½*

169 A242 50c **multicolored** *(541,421)* .40 .40
First day cover 1.25
Inscription block of 4 3.00 —
170 A242 1.40fr **multicolored** *(475,445)* 1.40 1.40
First day cover 2.40
First day cover, #169-170 3.00
Inscription block of 4 10.00 —

Universal Declaration of Human Rights 40th Anniv. Type

1988, Dec. 9 Photo. & Engr. *Perf. 12*

171 A243 90c **multicolored** *(745,508)* .70 .70
First day cover 2.50
Inscription block of 4 3.25 —

Souvenir Sheet

172 A243 2fr **multicolored** *(517,453)* 2.75 2.75
First day cover 4.00

World Bank Type

1989, Jan. 27 Litho. *Perf. 13x14*

173 A244 80c Telecommunications *(524,056)* 1.00 1.00
First day cover 1.50
Inscription block of 4 4.50 —
174 A244 1.40fr Industry *(488,058)* 2.00 2.00
First day cover 2.40
First day cover, #173-174 3.50
Inscription block of 4 9.00 —

First day covers of Nos. 173-174 total 111,004.

Peace-Keeping Force Type

1989, Mar. 17 *Perf. 14x13½*

175 A245 90c **multicolored** *(684,566)* 1.25 1.25
First day cover *(52,463)* 1.00
Inscription block of 4 6.75 —

World Weather Watch Type

Satellite photographs: 90c, Europe under the influence of Arctic air. 1.10fr, Surface temperatures of sea, ice and land surrounding the Kattegat between Denmark and Sweden.

1989, Apr. 21 Litho. *Perf. 13x14*

176 A247 90c **multicolored** *(864,409)* 1.25 1.25
First day cover 1.50
Inscription block of 4 5.50 —
177 A247 1.10fr **multicolored** *(853,556)* 2.00 2.00
First day cover 1.90
First day cover, #176-177 3.00
Inscription block of 4 9.00 —

First day covers of Nos. 176-177 total 83,343.

Offices in Geneva, 10th Anniv.
G43 G44

Printed by Government Printing Office, Austria. Panes of 25. Designed by Anton Lehmden (50c) and Arik Brauer (2fr), Austria.

Photo., Photo. & Engr. (2fr)

1989, Aug. 23 *Perf. 14*

178 G43 50c **multicolored** *(605,382)* 1.00 1.00
First day cover 1.25
Inscription block of 4 5.00 —

179 G44 2fr **multicolored** *(538,140)* 3.50 3.50
First day cover 2.75
Inscription block of 4 15.00 —
First day cover, #178-179 3.25
Panes of 25, #178-179 110.00

First day covers of Nos. 178-179 total 83,304.

Human Rights Type of 1989

Printed by Johann Enschede and Sons, the Netherlands. Panes of 12+12 se-tenant labels containing Articles 3 (35c) or 4 (80c) inscribed in English, French or German. Designed by Rocco J. Callari and Robert Stein, US.

Artwork: 35c, Young Mother Sewing, by Mary Cassatt. 80c, The Unknown Slave, sculpture by Albert Mangones.

1989, Nov. 17 Litho. *Perf. 13½*

180 A250 35c **multicolored** *(1,923,818)* .35 .35
First day cover 1.25
Inscription block of 3 + 3 labels 1.60 —
181 A250 80c **multicolored** *(1,917,953)* 1.00 1.00
First day cover 3.00
Inscription block of 3 + 3 labels 4.50 —
First day cover, #180-181 4.50
Panes of 12, #180-181 17.50

First day covers of Nos. 180-181 total 134,469.
See Nos. 193-194, 209-210, 234-235.

Intl. Trade Center Type

1990, Feb. 2 Litho. *Perf. 14½x15*

182 A251 1.50fr **multicolored** *(409,561)* 2.25 2.25
First day cover *(61,098)* 3.50
Inscription block of 4 11.00 —

G45

Printed by Heraclio Fournier, S.A., Spain. Designed by Guy Breniaux, France and Elizabeth White, US.

1990, Feb. 2 Photo. *Perf. 14x13½*

183 G45 5fr **multicolored** *(1,600,000)+* 4.75 4.75
First day cover *(54,462)* 7.00
Inscription block of 4 21.00 —

G46

Fight AIDS Worldwide — G46a

Fight AIDS Type

Designed by Jacek Tofil, Poland (50c) and Lee Keun Moon, Korea (80c).

Designs: 50c, "SIDA." 80c, Proportional drawing of man like the illustration by Leonardo da Vinci.

1990, Mar. 16 Litho. *Perf. 13½x12½*

184 G46 50c **multicolored** *(480,625)* 1.00 1.00
First day cover 1.25
Inscription block of 4 5.00 —
185 G46a 80c **multicolored** *(602,721)* 1.75 1.75
First day cover 1.50
First day cover, #184-185 2.00
Inscription block of 4 7.75 —

First day covers of Nos. 184-185 total 108,364.

Medicinal Plants Type

1990, May 4 Photo. Granite Paper *Perf. 11½*

186 A253 90c Plumeria rubra *(625,522)* 1.00 1.00
First day cover 1.40
Inscription block of 4 5.00 —
187 A253 1.40fr Cinchona officinalis *(648,619)* 2.00 2.00
First day cover 2.25
First day cover, #186-187 3.50
Inscription block of 4 9.50 —

First day covers of Nos. 186-187 total 114,062.

UN 45th Anniv. Type

Designed by Fritz Henry Oerter and Ruth Schmidthammer, Federal Republic of Germany (90c), Michiel Mertens, Belgium (1.10fr), Robert Stein, US (No. 190).

"45," emblem and: 90c, Symbols of clean environment, transportation and industry. 1.10fr, Dove in silhouette.

1990, June 26 Litho. *Perf. 14½x13*

188 A254 90c **multicolored** *(557,253)* 1.10 1.10
First day cover 1.40
Inscription block of 4 5.25 —
189 A254 1.10fr **multicolored** *(519,635)* 2.25 2.25
First day cover 2.00
First day cover, #188-189 3.00
Inscription block of 4 9.50 —

Souvenir Sheet

190 Sheet of 2, #188-189 *(401,027)* 6.00 6.00
First day cover 4.50

First day covers of Nos. 188-190 total 148,975.

Crime Prevention Type

1990, Sept. 13 Photo. *Perf. 14*

191 A255 50c Official corruption *(494,876)* 1.25 1.25
First day cover 1.40
Inscription block of 4 5.50 —
192 A255 2fr Environmental crime *(417,033)* 3.00 3.00
First day cover 3.25
First day cover, #191-192 4.50
Inscription block of 4 15.00 —

First day covers of Nos. 191-192 total 76,605.

Human Rights Type of 1989

Panes of 12+12 se-tenant labels containing Articles 9 (35c) or 10 (90c) inscribed in French, German or English.

Artwork: 35c, The Prison Courtyard by Vincent Van Gogh. 90c, Katho's Son Redeems the Evil Doer From Execution by Albrecht Durer.

1990, Nov. 16 Litho. *Perf. 13½*

193 A250 35c **multicolored** *(1,578,828)* .45 .45
First day cover 2.75
Inscription block of 3 + 3 labels 1.75 —
194 A250 90c **black & brown** *(1,540,200)* 1.25 1.25
First day cover 6.00
Inscription block of 3 + 3 labels 4.50 —
First day cover, #193-194 2.50
Panes of 12, #193-194 20.00

First day covers of Nos. 193-194 total 100,282.

Economic Commission for Europe Type

1991, Mar. 15 Litho. *Perf. 14*

195 A256 90c Owl, gull *(643,143)+* 1.25 1.25
First day cover 3.00
196 A256 90c Bittern, otter *(643,143)+* 1.25 1.25
First day cover 3.00
197 A256 90c Swan, lizard *(643,143)+* 1.25 1.25
First day cover 3.00
198 A256 90c Great crested grebe *(643,143)+* 1.25 1.25
First day cover 3.00
a. Block of 4, #195-198 5.00 5.00
First day cover, #198a 5.50
Inscription block of 4, #198a 6.50 —
Pane of 40, #195-198 52.50

First day covers of Nos. 195-198a total 75,759.

Namibian Independence Type

1991, May 10 Litho. *Perf. 14*

199 A257 70c Mountains *(328,014)* 1.25 1.25
First day cover 1.60
Inscription block of 4 5.50 —
200 A257 90c Baobab tree *(395,362)* 2.25 2.25
First day cover 2.25
First day cover, #199-200 5.00
Inscription block of 4 10.00 —

First day covers of Nos. 199-200 total 94,201.

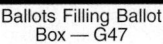

Ballots Filling Ballot Box — G47

UN Emblem — G48

Printed by House of Questa, United Kingdom. Designed by Ran Banda Mawilmada, Sri Lanka (80c), Maurice Gouju, France (1.50fr).

1991, May 10 Litho. *Perf. 15x14½*

201 G47 80c **multicolored** *(1,600,000)+* 1.00 1.00
First day cover 1.75
Inscription block of 4 4.50 —
202 G48 1.50fr **multicolored** *(1,600,000)+* 2.25 2.25
First day cover 3.25
First day cover, #201-202 3.75
Inscription block of 4 10.00 —

First day covers of Nos. 201-202 total 77,590.

G49

Rights of the Child — G50

Printed by The House of Questa. Panes of 50. Designed by Ryuta Nakajima, Japan (80c) and David Popper, Switzerland (1.10fr).

1991, June 14 Litho. *Perf. 14½*

203 G49 80c Hands holding infant *(469,962)* 1.25 1.25
First day cover 1.75
Inscription block of 4 6.25 —
204 G50 1.10fr Children, flowers *(494,382)* 2.00 2.00
First day cover 2.25
First day cover, #203-204 3.25
Inscription block of 4 9.50 —

First day covers of Nos. 203-204 total 97,732.

G51

Banning of Chemical Weapons G52

Printed by Heraclio Fournier S.A. Panes of 50. Designed by Oscar Asboth, Austria (80c), Michel Granger, France (1.40fr).

1991, Sept. 11 Litho. *Perf. 13½*

205 G51 80c **multicolored** *(345,658)* 2.25 2.25
First day cover 1.75
Inscription block of 4 9.50
206 G52 1.40fr **multicolored** *(366,076)* 3.75 3.75
First day cover 2.50
First day cover, #205-206 3.50
Inscription block of 4 16.50 —

First day covers of Nos. 205-206 total 91,887.

UN Postal Administration, 40th Anniv. Type

1991, Oct. 24 *Perf. 14x15*

207 A263 50c UN NY No. 7 *(506,839)* 1.00 1.00
First day cover 1.25
Inscription block of 4 4.50 —
208 A263 1.60fr UN NY No. 10 *(580,493)* 2.50 2.50
First day cover 3.00
Inscription block of 4 11.00 —
First day cover, #207-208 3.25
Panes of 25, #207-208 75.00

First day covers of Nos. 207-208 total 88,784.

Human Rights Type of 1989

Panes of 12+12 se-tenant labels containing Articles 15 (50c) or 16 (90c) inscribed in French, German or English.

Artwork: 50c, Early Morning in Rio...1925, by Paul Klee. 90c, Marriage of Giovanni (?) Arnolfini and Giovanna Cenami (?), by Jan Van Eyck.

1991, Nov. 20 Litho. *Perf. 13½*
209 A250 50c **multicolored** *(1,295,172)* .85 .85
First day cover 3.25
Inscription block of 3 + 3 labels 2.75 —
210 A250 90c **multicolored** *(1,324,091)* 1.50 1.50
First day cover 6.75
Inscription block of 3 + 3 labels 4.50 —
First day cover, #209-210 2.00
Panes of 12, #209-210 27.50

First day covers of Nos. 209-210 total 139,904.

World Heritage Type of 1984

Designs: 50c, Sagarmatha Natl. Park, Nepal. 1.10fr, Stonehenge, United Kingdom.

1992, Jan. 24 Litho. *Perf. 13*
Size: 35x28mm
211 G29 50c **multicolored** *(468,647)* 1.10 1.10
First day cover 1.25
Inscription block of 4 4.75 —
212 G29 1.10fr **multicolored** *(369,345)* 2.25 2.25
First day cover 2.25
First day cover, #211-212 3.00
Inscription block of 4 9.50 —

First day covers of Nos. 211-212 total 77,034.

G53

Printed by The House of Questa. Panes of 50. Designed by Nestor Jose Martin, Argentina.

1992, Jan. 24 Litho. *Perf. 15x14½*
213 G53 3fr **multicolored** *(1,600,000)+* 3.50 3.50
First day cover *(36,135)* 4.00
Inscription block of 4 14.00 —

Clean Oceans Type

1992, Mar. 13 Litho. *Perf. 14*
214 A264 80c Ocean surface, diff. *(850,699)* .90 .90
215 A264 80c Ocean bottom, diff. *(850,699)* .90 .90
a. Pair, #214-215 1.80 *2.00*
First day cover, #215a 2.75
First day cover, #214-215, each 1.75
Inscription block of 4, 2 #215a 5.00 —
Pane of 12, #214-215 11.00

First day covers of Nos. 214-215a total 90,725.

Earth Summit Type

Designs: No. 216, Rainbow. No. 217, Two clouds shaped as faces. No. 218, Two sailboats. No. 219, Woman with parasol, boat, flowers.

1992, May 22 Photo. *Perf. 11½*
216 A265 75c **multicolored** *(826,543)* 1.25 1.25
217 A265 75c **multicolored** *(826,543)* 1.25 1.25
218 A265 75c **multicolored** *(826,543)* 1.25 1.25
219 A265 75c **multicolored** *(826,543)* 1.25 1.25
a. Block of 4, #216-219 5.25 5.25
First day cover, #219a 4.00
First day cover, #216-219, each 2.50
Inscription block of 4, #216-219 5.75 —
Pane of 40, #216-219 55.00

First day covers of Nos. 216-219a total 74,629.

Mission to Planet Earth Type

Designs: No. 220, Space station. No. 221, Probes near Jupiter.

1992, Sept. 4 Photo. *Rouletted 8*
Granite Paper
220 A266 1.10fr **multicolored** *(668,241)* 2.50 2.50
221 A266 1.10fr **multicolored** *(668,241)* 2.50 2.50
a. Pair, #220-221 5.00 5.00
First day cover, #221a 5.00
First day cover, #220-221, each 5.50
Inscription block of 4, 2 #220-221 11.00 —
Pane of 10, #220-221 25.00

First day covers of Nos. 220-221 total 76,060.

Science and Technology Type of 1992

Designs: 90c, Doctor, nurse. 1.60fr, Graduate seated before computer.

1992, Oct. 2 Litho. *Perf. 14*
222 A267 90c **multicolored** *(438,943)* 1.50 1.50
First day cover 1.60
Inscription block of 4 6.00 —
223 A267 1.60fr **multicolored** *(400,701)* 3.50 3.50
First day cover 2.50
First day cover, #222-223 3.25
Inscription block of 4 14.00 —

First day covers of Nos. 222-223 total 75,882.

Human Rights Type of 1989

Panes of 12+12 se-tenant labels containing Articles 21 (50c) and 22 (90c) inscribed in French, German or English.
Artwork: 50c, The Oath of the Tennis Court, by Jacques Louis David. 90c, Rocking Chair I, by Henry Moore.

1992, Nov. 20 Litho. *Perf. 13½*
224 A250 50c **multicolored,** *(1,201,788)* .80 .80
First day cover 3.00
Inscription block of 3 + 3 labels 3.00 —
225 A250 90c **multicolored,** *(1,179,294)* 1.50 1.50
First day cover 6.00
Inscription block of 3 + 3 labels 5.00 —
First day cover, #224-225 1.75
Panes of 12, #224-225 26.00

First day covers of Nos. 224-225 total 104,491.

Aging With Dignity Type

Designs: 50c, Older man coaching soccer. 1.60fr, Older man working at computer terminal.

1993, Feb. 5 Litho. *Perf. 13*
226 A270 50c **multicolored** *(483,452)* .70 .70
First day cover 1.00
Inscription block of 4 3.50 —
227 A270 1.60fr **multicolored** *(331,008)* 2.25 2.25
First day cover 2.75
First day cover, #226-227 3.00
Inscription block of 4 10.50 —

First day covers of Nos. 226-227 total 61,361.

Endangered Species Type

Designed by Rocco J. Callari, US, and Betina Ogden, Australia.
Designs: No. 228, Pongidae (gorilla). No. 229, Falco peregrinus (peregrine falcon). No. 230, Trichechus inunguis (Amazonian manatee). No. 231, Panthera uncia (snow leopard).

1993, Mar. 2 Litho. *Perf. 13x12½*
228 A271 80c **multicolored** *(1,200,000)+* 1.10 1.10
229 A271 80c **multicolored** *(1,200,000)+* 1.10 1.10
230 A271 80c **multicolored** *(1,200,000)+* 1.10 1.10
231 A271 80c **multicolored** *(1,200,000)+* 1.10 1.10
a. Block of 4, #228-231 4.50 4.50
First day cover, #231a 5.00
First day cover, #228-231, each 2.00
Inscription block of 4, #228-231 4.50 —
Pane of 16, #228-231 19.00

First day covers of Nos. 228-231a total 75,363.

Healthy Environment Type

1993, May 7 Litho. *Perf. 15x14½*
232 A272 60c **Neighborhood** *(456,304)* 1.10 1.10
First day cover 1.25
Inscription block of 4 4.75 —
233 A272 1fr **Urban skyscrapers** *(392,015)* 2.25 2.25
First day cover 2.00
First day cover, #232-233 3.25
Inscription block of 4 9.50 —

First day covers of Nos. 232-233 total 59,790.

Human Rights Type of 1989

Printed in panes of 12 + 12 se-tenant labels containing Article 27 (50c) and 28 (90c) inscribed in French, German or English.
Artwork: 50c, Three Musicians, by Pablo Picasso. 90c, Voice of Space, by Rene Magritte.

1993, June 11 Litho. *Perf. 13½*
234 A250 50c **multicolored** *(1,166,286)* .85 .85
First day cover 2.50
Inscription block of 3 + 3 labels 2.75 —
235 A250 90c **multicolored** *(1,122,348)* 2.00 2.00
First day cover 4.50
Inscription block of 3 + 3 labels 6.25 —
First day cover, #234-235 2.00
Panes of 12, #234-235 26.00

First day covers of Nos. 234-235 total 83,432.

Intl. Peace Day Type

Denomination at: #236, UL. #237, UR. #238, LL. #239, LR.

1993, Sept. 21 Litho. & Engr. *Rouletted 12½*
236 A274 60c **purple & multi** *(357,760)* 2.00 2.00
237 A274 60c **purple & multi** *(357,760)* 2.00 2.00
238 A274 60c **purple & multi** *(357,760)* 2.00 2.00
239 A274 60c **purple & multi** *(357,760)* 2.00 2.00
a. Block of 4, #236-239 8.00 8.00
First day cover, #239a 5.50
First day cover, #236-239, each 3.00
Inscription block of 4, #239a 9.50 —
Pane of 40, #236-239 75.00

First day covers of Nos. 236-239a total 47,207.

Environment-Climate Type

1993, Oct. 29 Litho. *Perf. 14½*
240 A275 1.10fr Polar bears *(391,593)* 2.00 2.00
241 A275 1.10fr Whale sounding *(391,593)* 2.00 2.00
242 A275 1.10fr Elephant seal *(391,593)* 2.00 2.00
243 A275 1.10fr Penguins *(391,593)* 2.00 2.00
a. Strip of 4, #240-243 8.00 8.00
First day cover, #243a 7.25
First day cover, #240-243, each 6.00
Inscription block of 8, 2 #243a 22.50 —
Pane of 24, #240-243 52.50

First day covers of Nos. 240-243a total 41,819.

Intl. Year of the Family Type of 1993

Designs: 80c, Parents teaching child to walk. 1fr, Two women and child picking plants.

1994, Feb. 4 Litho. *Perf. 13.1*
244 A276 80c **rose violet & multi** *(535,000)+* 1.20 1.20
First day cover 1.75
Inscription block of 4 5.75 —
245 A276 1fr **brown & multi** *(535,000)+* 1.60 1.60
First day cover 2.00
First day cover, #244-245 3.25
Inscription block of 4 7.25 —

First day covers of Nos. 244-245 total 50,080.

Endangered Species Type of 1993

Designed by Rocco J. Callari (frame) and Leon Parson, US (stamps).
Designs: No. 246, Mexican prairie dog. No. 247, Jabiru. No. 248, Blue whale. No. 249, Golden lion tamarin.

1994, Mar. 18 Litho. *Perf. 12.7*
246 A271 80c **multicolored** *(1,200,000)+* 1.10 1.10
247 A271 80c **multicolored** *(1,200,000)+* 1.10 1.10
248 A271 80c **multicolored** *(1,200,000)+* 1.10 1.10
249 A271 80c **multicolored** *(1,200,000)+* 1.10 1.10
a. Block of 4, #246-249 4.50 4.50
First day cover, #249a 5.50
First day cover, #246-249, each 1.75
Inscription block of 4, #246-249 4.75 —
Pane of 16, #246-249 20.00

First day covers of Nos. 246-249a total 82,043.

Protection for Refugees Type of 1994

Design: 1.20fr, Hand lifting figure over chasm.

1994, Apr. 29 Litho. *Perf. 14.3x14.8*
250 A277 1.20fr **multicolored** *(550,000)+* 2.50 2.50
First day cover *(33,805)* 2.50
Inscription block of 4 11.00 —

Intl. Decade for Natural Disaster Reduction Type of 1994

Earth seen from space, outline map of: No. 251, North America. No. 252, Eurasia. No. 253, South America. No. 254, Australia and South Pacific region.

1994, May 27 Litho. *Perf. 13.9x14.2*
251 A281 60c **multicolored** *(570,000)+* 1.75 1.75
252 A281 60c **multicolored** *(570,000)+* 1.75 1.75
253 A281 60c **multicolored** *(570,000)+* 1.75 1.75
254 A281 60c **multicolored** *(570,000)+* 1.75 1.75
a. Block of 4, #251-254 7.00 7.00
First day cover, #254a 7.00
First day cover, #251-254, each 4.00
Inscription block of 4, #254a 9.50 —
Pane of 40, #251-254 75.00

First day covers of Nos. 251-254a total 37,595.

Palais des Nations, Geneva — G54

Creation of the World, by Oili Maki — G55

Printed by House of Questa, United Kingdom. Designed by Rocco J. Callari, US.

1994, Sept. 1 Litho. *Perf. 14.3x14.6*
255 G54 60c **multicolored** *(1,075,000)+* .75 .75
First day cover 1.10
Inscription block of 4 3.25 —
256 G55 80c **multicolored** *(1,075,000)+* 1.00 1.00
First day cover 1.50
Inscription block of 4 4.25 —
257 G54 1.80fr **multi, diff.** *(1,075,000)+* 2.25 2.25
First day cover 2.75
Inscription block of 4 9.50 —
First day cover, #255-257 4.50

First day covers of Nos. 255-257 total 51,637.

Population and Development Type of 1994

Designs: 60c, People shopping at open-air market. 80c, People on vacation crossing bridge.

1994, Sept. 1 Litho. *Perf. 13.2x13.6*

258 A282 60c **multicolored** *(535,000)+* 1.10 1.10
First day cover 1.25
Inscription block of 4 5.00 —
259 A282 80c **multicolored** *(535,000)+* 1.50 1.50
First day cover 1.75
Inscription block of 4 7.50 —
First day cover, #258-259 3.00

First day covers of Nos. 258-259 total 50,443.

UNCTAD Type of 1994

1994, Oct. 28

260 A283 80c **multi**, diff. *(535,000)+* 1.25 1.25
First day cover 1.75
Inscription block of 4 5.50 —
261 A283 1fr **multi**, diff. *(535,000)+* 1.75 1.75
First day cover 2.00
Inscription block of 4 7.75 —
First day cover, #260-261 3.50
a. Grayish green omitted —
Inscription block of 4 —

First day covers of Nos. 260-261 total 48,122.

UN 50th Anniv. Type of 1995

1995, Jan. 1 Litho. & Engr. *Perf. 13.4*

262 A284 80c **multicolored** *(823,827)* 1.25 1.25
First day cover *(38,988)* 3.00
Inscription block of 4 5.75 —

Social Summit Type of 1995

1995, Feb. 3 Photo. & Engr. *Perf. 13.6x13.9*

263 A285 1fr **multi**, diff. *(452,116)* 1.50 1.50
First day cover *(35,246)* 2.00
Inscription block of 4 7.00 —

Endangered Species Type of 1993

Designed by Sibylle Erni, Switzerland.
Designs: No. 264, Crowned lemur, Lemur coronatus. No. 265, Giant Scops owl, Otus gurneyi. No. 266, Zetek's frog, Atelopus varius zeteki. No. 267, Wood bison, Bison bison athabascae.

1995, Mar. 24 Litho. *Perf. 13x12½*

264 A271 80c **multicolored** *(730,000)+* 1.25 1.25
265 A271 80c **multicolored** *(730,000)+* 1.25 1.25
266 A271 80c **multicolored** *(730,000)+* 1.25 1.25
267 A271 80c **multicolored** *(730,000)+* 1.25 1.25
a. Block of 4, 264-267 5.00 5.00
First day cover, #267a 4.50
First day cover, #264-267, each 1.60
Inscription block of 4, #267a 5.75 —
Pane of 16, #264-267 19.00

First day covers of Nos. 264-267a total 71,907.

Intl. Youth Year Type of 1995

Designs: 80c, Farmer on tractor, fields at harvest time. 1fr, Couple standing by fields at night.

1995, May 26 Litho. *Perf. 14.4x14.7*

268 A286 80c **multicolored** *(294,987)* 1.60 1.60
First day cover 1.75
Inscription block of 4 7.00 —
269 A286 1fr **multicolored** *(264,823)* 2.75 2.75
First day cover 2.00
First day cover, #268-269 4.00
Inscription block of 4 12.00 —

First day covers of Nos. 268-269 total 45,665.

UN, 50th Anniv. Type of 1995

Designs: 60c, Like No. 663. 1.80fr, Like No. 664.

1995, June 26 Engr. *Perf. 13.3x13.6*

270 A287 60c **maroon** *(352,336)* 1.00 1.00
First day cover .90
Inscription block of 4 4.50 —
271 A287 1.80fr **green** *(377,391)* 3.25 3.25
First day cover 3.00
First day cover, #270-271 4.00
Inscription block of 4 14.00 —

Souvenir Sheet
Litho. & Engr.
Imperf

272 Sheet of 2, #270-271 *(251,272)* 4.25 4.25
a. A287 60c **maroon** 1.00 1.00
b. A287 1.80fr **green** 3.25 3.25
First day cover 8.00

First day covers of Nos. 270-272 total 72,666.

Conference on Women Type of 1995

Designs: 60c, Black woman, cranes flying above. 1fr, Women, dove.

1995, Sept. 5 Photo. *Perf. 12*

273 A288 60c **multicolored** *(342,336)* 1.40 1.40
First day cover 1.25
Inscription block of 4 6.00 —

Size: 28x50mm

274 A288 1fr **multicolored** *(345,489)* 2.50 2.00
First day cover 2.25
First day cover, #273-274 3.25
Inscription block of 4 11.00 —

First day covers of Nos. 273-274 total 57,542.

UN People, 50th Anniv. Type of 1995

1995, Oct. 24 Litho. *Perf. 14*

275 Sheet of 12 *(216,832 sheets)* 17.00 12.50
First day cover 20.00
a.-l. A290 30c each 1.30 1.25
First day cover, #275a-275l, each 5.00
276 Souvenir booklet, *(74,151 booklets)* 17.00
a. A290 30c Booklet pane of 3, vert. strip of 3 from UL of sheet 4.25 4.25
b. A290 30c Booklet pane of 3, vert. strip of 3 from UR of sheet 4.25 4.25
c. A290 30c Booklet pane of 3, vert. strip of 3 from LL of sheet 4.25 4.25
d. A290 30c Booklet pane of 3, vert. strip of 3 from LR of sheet 4.25 4.25

First day covers of Nos. 275-276d total 53,245.

WFUNA, 50th Anniv. Type

Design: 80c, Fishing boat, fish in net.

1996, Feb. 2 Litho. *Perf. 13x13½*

277 A291 80c **multicolored** *(550,000)+* 1.25 1.25
First day cover 2.00
Inscription block of 4 6.50 —

The Galloping Horse Treading on a Flying Swallow, Chinese Bronzework, Eastern Han Dynasty (25-220 A.D.) — G56

Palais des Nations, Geneva — G57

Printed by House of Questa, UK.

1996, Feb. 2 Litho. *Perf. 14½x15*

278 G56 40c **multicolored** *(1,125,000)+* .50 .50
First day cover 1.25
Inscription block of 4 2.50 —
279 G57 70c **multicolored** *(1,125,000+)* 1.10 1.10
First day cover 1.50
First day cover, #278-279 3.50
Inscription block of 4 4.75 —

Endangered Species Type of 1993

Designs: No. 280, Paphiopedilum delenatii. No. 281, Pachypodium baronii. No. 282, Sternbergia lutea. No. 283, Darlingtonia californica.

1996, Mar. 14 Litho. *Perf. 12½*

280 A271 80c **multicolored** *(680,000)+* 1.10 1.10
281 A271 80c **multicolored** *(680,000)+* 1.10 1.10
282 A271 80c **multicolored** *(680,000)+* 1.10 1.10
283 A271 80c **multicolored** *(680,000)+* 1.10 1.10
a. Block of 4, #280-283 4.50 4.50
First day cover, #280-283, each 2.00
First day cover, #283a 4.50
Inscription block of 4, #283a 4.75 —
Pane of 16, #280-283 18.00

City Summit Type of 1996

Designs: No. 284, Asian family. No. 285, Oriental garden. No. 286, Fruit, vegetable vendor, mosque. No. 287, Boys playing ball. No. 288, Couple reading newspaper.

1996, June 3 Litho. *Perf. 14x13½*

284 A293 70c **multicolored** *(420,000)+* 1.50 1.50
285 A293 70c **multicolored** *(420,000)+* 1.50 1.50
286 A293 70c **multicolored** *(420,000)+* 1.50 1.50
287 A293 70c **multicolored** *(420,000)+* 1.50 1.50
288 A293 70c **multicolored** *(420,000)+* 1.50 1.50
a. Strip of 5, #284-288 7.50 7.50
First day cover, #288a 11.00
First day cover, #284-288, each 5.00
Inscription block of 10, 2 #288a 20.00

Sport and the Environment Type

Designs: 70c, Cycling, vert. 1.10fr, Sprinters.

1996, July 19 Litho. *Perf. 14x14½, 14½x14*

289 A294 70c **multicolored** *(625,000)+* 1.25 1.25
First day cover 1.50
Inscription block of 4 5.75 —
290 A294 1.10fr **multicolored***(625,000)+* 1.75 1.75
First day cover 2.25
First day cover, #289-290 4.50
Inscription block of 4 8.75 —

Souvenir Sheet

291 A294 Sheet of 2, #289-290 *(345,000)+* 3.00 3.00
First day cover 12.00

Plea for Peace Type

Designed by: 90c, Chen Yu, China. 1.10fr, Zhou Jing, China.

Designs: 90c, Tree filled with birds, vert. 1.10fr, Bouquet of flowers in rocket tail vase, vert.

1996, Sept. 17 Litho. *Perf. 15x14½*

292 A295 90c **multicolored** *(550,000)+* 1.50 1.50
First day cover 1.50
Inscription block of 4 6.50 —
293 A295 1.10fr **multicolored** *(550,000)+* 2.00 2.00
First day cover 2.25
First day cover, #292-293 3.75
Inscription block of 4 10.00 —

UNICEF Type

Fairy Tales: 70c, The Sun and the Moon, South America. 1.80fr, Ananse, Africa.

1996, Nov. 20 Litho. *Perf. 14½x15*

294 A296 70c **multicolored** *(1,000,000)+* 1.00 1.00
First day cover 1.50
Pane of 8 + label 8.50
295 A296 1.80fr **multicolored** *(1,000,000)+* 2.40 2.40
First day cover 3.00
First day cover, #294-295 4.00
Pane of 8 + label 21.00

UN Flag — G58

Palais des Nations Under Construction by Massimo Campigli — G59

Printed by The House of Questa, Ltd., UK.

1997, Feb. 12 Litho. *Perf. 14½*

296 G58 10c **multicolored** *(600,000)+* .20 .20
First day cover 1.25
Inscription block of 4 .55 —
297 G59 1.10fr **multicolored** *(700,000)+* 1.50 1.50
First day cover 2.25
First day cover, #296-297 3.50
Inscription block of 4 6.00 —

First day covers of Nos. 296-297 total 41,186.

Endangered Species Type of 1993

Designs: No. 298, Ursus maritimus (polar bear). No. 299, Goura cristata (blue-crowned pigeon). No. 300, Amblyrhynchus cristatus (marine iguana). No. 301, Lama guanicoe (guanaco).

1997, Mar. 13 Litho. *Perf. 12½*

298 A271 80c **multicolored** *(620,000)+* 1.00 1.00
299 A271 80c **multicolored** *(620,000)+* 1.00 1.00
300 A271 80c **multicolored** *(620,000)+* 1.00 1.00
301 A271 80c **multicolored** *(620,000)+* 1.00 1.00
a. Block of 4, #298-301 4.00 4.00
First day cover, #301a 5.00
First day cover, #298-301, each 2.50
Inscription block of 4, #301a 4.50
Pane of 16 17.00

First day covers of Nos. 298-301 total 71,905.

Earth Summit Anniv. Type

Designs: No. 302, Person flying over mountain. No. 303, Mountain, person's face. No. 304, Person standing on mountain, sailboats. No. 305, Person, mountain, trees.
1.10fr, Combined design similar to Nos. 302-305.

1997, May 30 Photo. *Perf. 11½*

Granite Paper

302 A299 45c **multicolored** *(227,187)* 1.00 1.00
303 A299 45c **multicolored** *(227,187)* 1.00 1.00
304 A299 45c **multicolored** *(227,187)* 1.00 1.00
305 A299 45c **multicolored** *(227,187)* 1.00 1.00
a. Block of 4, #302-305 4.00 4.00
First day cover, #305a 8.00
First day cover, #302-305, each 3.50
Inscription block of 4, #305a 6.25

Souvenir Sheet

306 A299 1.10fr **multicolored** *(176,386)* 3.50 3.50
First day cover 9.00

First day covers of Nos. 302-306 total 55,389.

Transportation Type of 1997

Air transportation: No. 307, Zeppelin, Fokker tri-motor. No. 308, Boeing 314 Clipper, Lockheed Constellation. No. 309, DeHavilland Comet. No. 310, Boeing 747, Illyushin jet. No. 311, Concorde.

1997, Aug. 29 Litho. *Perf. 14x14½*

307 A300 70c **multicolored** *(271,575)* 1.00 1.00
308 A300 70c **multicolored** *(271,575)* 1.00 1.00
309 A300 70c **multicolored** *(271,575)* 1.00 1.00
310 A300 70c **multicolored** *(271,575)* 1.00 1.00
311 A300 70c **multicolored** *(271,575)* 1.00 1.00
a. Strip of 5, #307-311 5.00 5.00
First day cover, #311a 7.00
First day cover, #307-311, each 3.00
Margin block of 10, 2#311a 12.50

No. 311a has continuous design.
First day covers of Nos. 307-311 total 33,303.

Philately Type

Designs: 70c, No. 146. 1.10fr, No. 147.

1997, Oct. 14 Litho. *Perf. 13½x14*

312 A301 70c **multicolored** *(254,406)* 1.25 1.25
First day cover 1.75
Inscription block of 4 5.50 —
313 A301 1.10fr **multicolored** *(303,125)* 2.00 2.00
First day cover 2.25
First day cover, #312-313 6.00
Inscription block of 4 9.00 —

First day covers of Nos. 312-313 total 47,528.

World Heritage Convention Type

Terracotta warriors of Xian: 45c, Single warrior. 70c, Massed warriors. No. 316a, like #716. No. 316b, like #717. No. 316c, like Geneva #314. No. 316d, like Geneva #315. No. 316e, like Vienna #230. No. 316f, like Vienna #231.

1997, Nov. 19 Litho. *Perf. 13½*

314 A302 45c **multicolored** *(409,820)* 1.25 1.25
First day cover 1.40
Inscription block of 4 5.50 —
315 A302 70c **multicolored** *(414,059)* 2.25 2.25
First day cover 1.50
First day cover, #314-315 4.00
Inscription block of 4 9.50 —
316 Souvenir booklet *(275,114 booklets)* 8.50
a.-f. A302 10c any single .35 .35
g. Booklet pane of 4 #316a 1.40 1.40
h. Booklet pane of 4 #316b 1.40 1.40
i. Booklet pane of 4 #316c 1.40 1.40
j. Booklet pane of 4 #316d 1.40 1.40
k. Booklet pane of 4 #316e 1.40 1.40
l. Booklet pane of 4 #316f 1.40 1.40

First day covers of Nos. 314-316 total 40,366.

Palais des Nations, Geneva — G60

Printed by The House of Questa, UK. Designed by UN (2fr).

1998, Feb. 13 Litho. *Perf. 14½x15*

317 G60 2fr **multicolored** *(550,000)+* 2.50 2.50
First day cover 6.00
Inscription block of 4 11.00 —

Endangered Species Type of 1993

Designed by Rocco J. Callari, US and Suzanne Duranceau, Canada.
Designs: No. 318, Macaca thibetana (short-tailed Tibetan macaque). No. 319, Phoenicopterus ruber (Caribbean flamingo). No. 320, Ornithoptera alexandrae (Queen Alexandra's birdwing). No. 321, Dama mesopotamica (Persian fallow deer).

1998, Mar. 13 Litho. *Perf. 12½*

318 A271 80c **multicolored** *(560,000)+* 1.10 1.10
319 A271 80c **multicolored** *(560,000)+* 1.10 1.10
320 A271 80c **multicolored** *(560,000)+* 1.10 1.10
321 A271 80c **multicolored** *(560,000)+* 1.10 1.10
a. Block of 4, #318-321 4.50 4.50
First day cover, #321a 6.00
First day cover, #318-321, each 2.50
Inscription block of 4, #321a 4.75 —
Pane of 16 17.00

Intl. Year of the Ocean — G61

Designed by Jon Ellis, US.

1998, May 20 Litho. *Perf. 13x13½*

322 G61 Sheet of 12 *(270,000)+* 11.00 11.00
First day cover 14.50
a.-l. 45c any single .90 .90
First day cover, #322a-322l, each 2.00

Rain Forests Type

1998, June 19 *Perf. 13x13½*

323 A307 70c Orangutans *(430,000)+* .90 .90
First day cover 5.00
Inscription block of 4 4.00 —

Souvenir Sheet

324 A307 3fr like #323 *(250,000)+* 5.00 5.00
First day cover 10.00

Peacekeeping Type

Designs: 70c, Soldier with two children. 90c, Two soldiers, children.

1998, Sept. 15 Photo. *Perf. 12*

325 A308 70c **multicolored** *(400,000)+* 1.00 1.00
First day cover 1.50
Inscription block of 4 4.50 —
326 A308 90c **multicolored** *(390,000)+* 1.90 1.90
First day cover 4.00
First day cover, #325-326 5.00
Inscription block of 4 8.00 —

Declaration of Human Rights Type of 1998

Designs: 90c, Stylized birds. 1.80fr, Stylized birds flying from hand.

1998, Oct. 27 Litho. & Photo. *Perf. 13*

327 A309 90c **multicolored** *(400,000)+* 1.10 1.10
First day cover 2.00
Inscription block of 4 5.75 —
328 A309 1.80fr **multicolored** *(390,000)+* 2.75 2.75
First day cover 3.50
First day cover, #327-328 5.00
Inscription block of 4 12.00 —

Schönbrunn Palace Type

Designs: 70c, #331b, Great Palm House. 1.10fr, #331d, Blue porcelain vase, vert. No. 331a, Palace. No. 331c, The Gloriette (archway). No. 331e, Wall painting on fabric (detail), by Johann Wenzl Bergl, vert. No. 331f, Porcelain stove, vert.

1998, Dec. 4 Litho. *Perf. 14*

329 A310 70c **multicolored** *(375,000)+* 1.25 1.25
First day cover 1.50
Inscription block of 4 4.00 —
330 A310 1.10fr **multicolored** *(375,000)+* 1.50 1.50
First day cover 2.25
First day cover, #329-330 5.00
Inscription block of 4 6.00 —

Souvenir Booklet

331 Booklet *(100,000)+* 9.00
a.-c. A310 10c any single .25 .25
d.-f. A310 30c any single .75 .75
g. Booklet pane of 4 #331a .75 .75
h. Booklet pane of 3 #331d 2.25 2.25
i. Booklet pane of 3 #331e 2.25 2.25
j. Booklet pane of 3 #331f 2.25 2.25
k. Booklet pane of 4 #331b .75 .75
l. Booklet pane of 4 #331c .75 .75

Palais Wilson, Geneva — G62

Designed and printed by Helio Courvoisier, SA, Switzerland.

1999, Feb. 5 Photo. *Perf. 11½*

Granite Paper

332 G62 1.70fr **brown red** *(600,000)+* 2.25 2.25
First day cover *(25,568)* 3.50
Inscription block of 4 11.00 —

World Heritage, Australia Type

Designs: 90c, #335e, Kakadu Natl. Park. 1.10fr, #335c, Great Barrier Reef. No. 335a, Tasmanian Wilderness. No. 335b, Wet tropics of Queensland. No. 335d, Uluru-Kata Tjuta Natl. Park. No. 335f, Willandra Lakes region.

1999, Mar. 19 Litho. *Perf. 13*

333 A313 90c **multicolored** *(420,000)+* 1.40 1.40
First day cover 2.00
Inscription block of 4 5.75 —
334 A313 1.10fr **multicolored** *(420,000)+* 1.50 1.50
First day cover 2.25
First day cover, #333-334 4.50
Inscription block of 4 8.00 —

Souvenir Booklet

335 Booklet *(90,000)+* 8.00
a.-c. A313 10c any single .20 .20
d.-f. A313 20c any single .50 .50
g. Booklet pane of 4, #335a .65 .65
h. Booklet pane of 4, #335d 2.00 2.00
i. Booklet pane of 4, #335b .65 .65
j. Booklet pane of 4, #335e 2.00 2.00
k. Booklet pane of 4, #335c .65 .65
l. Booklet pane of 4, #335f 2.00 2.00

First day covers of Nos. 333-335 total 44,622.

Endangered Species Type of 1993

Designed by Tim Barrall, US.
Designs: No. 336, Equus hemionus (Asiatic wild ass). No. 337, Anodorhynchus hyacinthinus (hyacinth macaw). No. 338, Epicrates subflavus (Jamaican boa). No. 339, Dendrolagus bennettianus (Bennetts' tree kangaroo).

1999, Apr. 22 Litho. *Perf. 12½*

336 A271 90c **multicolored** *(488,000)+* 1.25 1.25
337 A271 90c **multicolored** *(488,000)+* 1.25 1.25
338 A271 90c **multicolored** *(488,000)+* 1.25 1.25
339 A271 90c **multicolored** *(488,000)+* 1.25 1.25
a. Block of 4, #336-339 5.00 5.00
First day cover, #339a 5.75
First day cover, #336-339, each 2.00
Inscription block of 4, #339a 6.00 —
Pane of 16 19.00

First day covers of Nos. 336-339 total 52,856.

UNISPACE III Type

Designs: No. 340, Farm, satellite dish. No. 341, City, satellite in orbit. No. 342, Composite of #340-341.

1999, July 7 Photo. *Rouletted 8*

340 A314 45c **multicolored** *(925,000)+* .90 .90
341 A314 45c **multicolored** *(925,000)+* .90 .90
a. Pair, #340-341 2.00 2.00
First day cover, #341a 2.25
First day cover, #340-341, each 3.00
Inscription block of 4 5.00 —
Pane of 10, #340-341 9.50 —

Souvenir Sheet

Perf. 14½

342 A314 2fr **multicolored** *(275,000)+* 4.50 4.50
First day cover 6.00
a. Ovptd. in sheet margin 9.50 9.50
First day cover 19.00

No. 342a is ovptd. in violet blue "PHILEXFRANCE 99 / LE MONDIAL DU TIMBRE / PARIS / 2 AU 11 JUILLET 1999.
First day covers of Nos. 340-342 total 63,412.

UPU Type

Various people, early 20th century methods of mail transportation, denomination at: No. 343, UL. No. 344, UR. No. 345, LL. No. 346, LR.

1999, Aug. 23 Photo. *Perf. 11¾*

343 A315 70c **multicolored** *(336,000)+* 1.00 1.00
344 A315 70c **multicolored** *(336,000)+* 1.00 1.00
345 A315 70c **multicolored** *(336,000)+* 1.00 1.00
346 A315 70c **multicolored** *(336,000)+* 1.00 1.00
a. Block of 4, #343-346 4.00 4.00
First day cover, #346a 3.50
First day cover, #343-346, each 1.50
Inscription block of 4, #346a 4.25 —

First day covers of Nos. 343-346 total 27,041.

In Memoriam Type

Designs: 1.10fr, 2fr, Armillary sphere, Palais de Nations. Size of 2fr stamp: 34x63mm.

1999, Sept. 21 Litho. *Perf. 14½x14*

347 A316 1.10fr **multicolored** *(400,000)+* 1.40 1.40
First day cover 3.00
Inscription block of 4 6.00 —

Souvenir Sheet

Perf. 14

348 A316 2fr **multicolored** *(225,000)+* 3.00 3.00
First day cover 3.50

First day covers of Nos. 347-348 total 46,527.

Education Type

1999, Nov. 18 Litho. *Perf. 13½x13¾*

349 A317 90c Rainbow over globe *(350,000)+* 1.25 1.25
First day cover 1.75
Inscription block of 4 5.50 —
350 A317 1.80fr Fish, tree, globe, book *(370,000)+* 2.25 2.25
First day cover 3.50
First day cover, #349-350 4.50
Inscription block of 4 10.00 —

First day covers of Nos. 349-350 total 37,925.

Intl. Year Of Thanksgiving Type

2000, Jan 1 Litho. *Perf. 13¼x13½*

351 A318 90c **multicolored** *(450,000)+* 1.25 1.25
First day cover 3.00
Inscription block of 4 5.50 —

On No. 351 portions of the design were applied by a thermographic process producing a shiny, raised effect.

Endangered Species Type of 1993

Designed by Robert Hynes, US.

Designs: No. 352, Hippopotamus amphibius (hippopotamus). No. 353, Coscoroba coscoroba (Coscoroba swan). No. 354, Varanus prasinus (emerald monitor). No. 355, Enhydra lutris (sea otter).

2000, Apr. 6 Litho. *Perf. 12¾x12½*

352 A271 90c **multicolored** *(488,000)+* 1.25 1.25
353 A271 90c **multicolored** *(488,000)+* 1.25 1.25
354 A271 90c **multicolored** *(488,000)+* 1.25 1.25
355 A271 90c **multicolored** *(488,000)+* 1.25 1.25
a. Block of 4, #352-355 5.00 5.00
First day cover, #355a 5.00
First day cover, #352-355, each 1.90
Inscription block of 4, #355a 5.25 —
Pane of 16 20.00

Our World 2000 Type

Winning artwork in Millennium painting competition: 90c, The Embrace, by Rita Adaimy, Lebanon. 1.10fr, Living Single, by Richard Kimanthi, Kenya, vert.

2000, May 30 Litho. *Perf. 13x13½, 13½x13*

356 A319 90c **multicolored** *(330,000)+* 1.25 1.25
First day cover 1.75
Inscription block of 4 5.00 —
357 A319 1.10fr **multicolored** *(330,000)+* 1.50 1.50
First day cover 2.25
First day cover, #356-357 3.50
Inscription block of 4 6.00 —

55th Anniversary Type

Designs: 90c, Trygve Lie, Harry S Truman, workers at cornerstone dedication ceremony, 1949. 1.40fr, Window cleaner on Secretariat Building, General Assembly Hall under construction, 1951.

2000, July 7 Litho. *Perf. 13¼x13*

358 A320 90c **multicolored** *(370,000)+* 1.25 1.25
First day cover 1.75
Inscription block of 4 5.00 —
359 A320 1.40fr **multicolored** *(370,000)+* 2.00 2.00
First day cover 2.60
First day cover, #358-359 3.75
Inscription block of 4 8.00 —

Souvenir Sheet

360 A320 Sheet of 2, #358-359 *(235,000)+* 3.25 3.25
First day cover 5.00

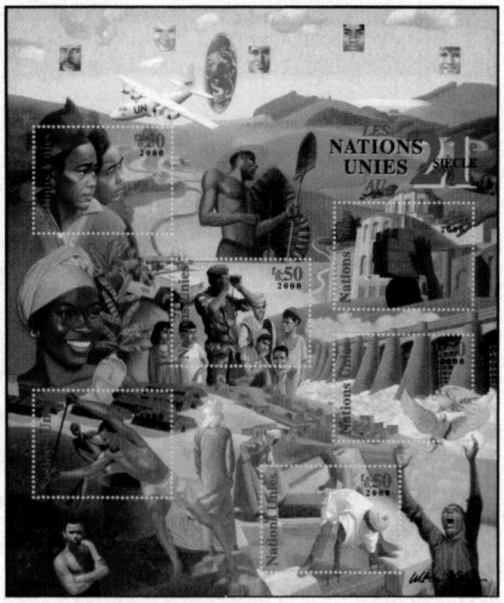

The UN in the 21st Century — G63

Printed by Government Printing Office, Austria. Designed by Wilson McLean, UK.

No. 361: a, Two people, terraced rice paddy. b, Man carrying bricks on head. c, UN Peacekeeper with binoculars. d, Dam, doves. e, Men with shovels. f, People working on irrigation system.

2000, Sept. 15 Litho. *Perf. 14*

361 G63 Sheet of 6 *(266,000)+* 7.50 7.50
First day cover 10.00
a.-f. 50c any single 1.25 1.25

World Heritage, Spain Type

Designs: Nos. 362, 364b, Walled Town of Cuenca. Nos. 363, 364e, Toledo. #364a, Alhambra, Generalife and Albayzin, Granada. #364c, Aqueduct of Segovia. #364d, Amphitheater of Mérida. #364f, Güell Park, Barcelona.

2000, Oct. 6 Litho. *Perf. 14¾x14½*

362 A323 1fr **multicolored** *(340,000)+* 1.40 1.40
First day cover 1.90
Inscription block of 4 5.75 —
363 A323 1.20fr **multicolored** *(340,000)+* 1.60 1.60
First day cover 2.25
First day cover, #362-363 3.50
Inscription block of 4 6.50 —

Souvenir Booklet

364 Booklet *(64,000)+* 5.50
a.-c. A323 10c any single .20 .20
d.-f. A323 20c any single .30 .30
g. Booklet pane of 4, #364a .55 .55
h. Booklet pane of 4, #364d 1.25 1.25
i. Booklet pane of 4, #364b .55 .55
j. Booklet pane of 4, #364e 1.25 1.25
k. Booklet pane of 4, #364c .55 .55
l. Booklet pane of 4, #364f 1.25 1.25

Respect for Refugees Type

Designs: 80c, 1.80fr, Refugee with cane, four other refugees.

2000, Nov. 9 Litho. *Perf. 13¼x12¾*

365 A324 80c **multicolored** *(400,000)+* 1.25 1.25
First day cover 1.75
Inscription block of 4 4.50 —

Souvenir Sheet

366 A324 1.80fr **multicolored** *(215,000)+* 2.50 2.50
First day cover 3.00

Endangered Species Type of 1993

Printed by Johann Enschedé and Sons, the Netherlands. Designed by Higgins Bond, US.

Designs: No. 367, Felis lynx canadensis (North American lynx). No. 368, Pavo muticus (green peafowl). No. 369, Geochelone elephantopus (Galapagos giant tortoise). No. 370, Lepilemur spp. (sportive lemur).

2001, Feb. 1 Litho. *Perf. 12¾x12½*

367 A271 90c **multicolored** *(448,000)+* 1.25 1.25
368 A271 90c **multicolored** *(448,000)+* 1.25 1.25
369 A271 90c **multicolored** *(448,000)+* 1.25 1.25
370 A271 90c **multicolored** *(448,000)+* 1.25 1.25
a. Block of 4, #367-370 5.00 5.00
First day cover, #370a 5.50
First day cover, #367-370 each 1.90
Inscription block of 4, #370a 5.25 —
Pane of 16 20.00

Intl. Volunteers Year — G64

Printed by Johann Enschedé and Sons, the Netherlands. Panes of 20. Designed by Rorie Katz and Robert Stein, US.

Paintings by: 90c, Ernest Pignon-Ernest, France. 1.30fr, Paul Siché, France.

2001, Mar. 29 Litho. *Perf. 13¼*

371 G64 90c **multicolored** *(350,000)+* 1.10 1.10
First day cover 1.75
Inscription block of 4 4.50
372 G64 1.30fr **multicolored** *(340,000)+* 1.60 1.60
First day cover 2.40
First day cover, #371-372 3.50
Inscription block of 4 6.50

World Heritage, Japan Type

Designs: 1.10fr, #375b, Nara. 1.30fr, #375e, Itsukushima Shinto Shrine. #375a, Kyoto. #375c, Himeji-Jo. #375d, Shirakawa-Go and Gokayama. #375f, Nikko.

2001, Aug. 1 Litho. *Perf. 12¾x13¼*

373 A328 1.10fr **multicolored** *(350,000)+* 1.30 1.30
First day cover 2.00
Inscription block of 4 5.75 —
374 A328 1.30fr **multicolored** *(350,000)+* 1.50 1.50
First day cover 2.40
First day cover, #373-374 3.75
Inscription block of 4 6.50 —

Souvenir Booklet

375 Booklet *(52,000)+* 7.50
a.-c. A328 10c any single .25 .25
d.-f. A328 30c any single .40 .40
g. Booklet pane of 4, #375a .75 .75
h. Booklet pane of 4, #375d 1.75 1.75
i. Booklet pane of 4, #375b .75 .75
j. Booklet pane of 4, #375e 1.75 1.75
k. Booklet pane of 4, #375c .75 .75
l. Booklet pane of 4, #375f 1.75 1.75

Dag Hammarskjöld Type

2001, Sept. 18 Engr. *Perf. 11x11¼*

376 A329 2fr **carmine lake** *(380,000)+* 2.50 2.50
First day cover 3.25
Inscription block of 4 10.00 —

UN Postal Administration, 50th Anniv. Types

2001, Oct. 18 Litho. *Perf. 13½*

377 A330 90c Stamps, globe *(310,000)+* 1.25 1.25
First day cover 1.60
Inscription block of 4 5.25 —
378 A330 1.30fr Stamps, horns *(310,000)+* 2.25 2.25
First day cover 2.40
First day cover, #377-378 3.50
Inscription block of 4 9.25 —

Souvenir Sheet

379 A331 Sheet of 2 *(175,000)+* 4.00 4.00
a. 1.30fr **red & light blue,** 38mm diameter 1.75 1.75
b. 1.80fr **red & light blue,** 38mm diameter 2.25 2.25
First day cover 4.50

Climate Change Type

Designs: No. 380, Lizard, flowers, shoreline. No. 381, Windmills, construction workers. No. 382, Non-polluting factory. No. 383, Solar oven, city, village, picnickers.

2001, Nov. 16 Litho. *Perf. 13¼*

380 A332 90c **multicolored** *(73,500)+* 1.10 1.10
381 A332 90c **multicolored** *(73,500)+* 1.10 1.10
382 A332 90c **multicolored** *(73,500)+* 1.10 1.10
383 A332 90c **multicolored** *(73,500)+* 1.10 1.10
a. Horiz. strip, #380-383 4.50 4.50
Inscription block of 8 9.00 —
First day cover, #383a 5.25
Pane of 24 25.00 —

Nobel Peace Prize Type

2001, Dec. 10 Litho. *Perf. 13¼*

384 A333 90c **multicolored** *(840,000)+* 1.10 1.10
Inscription block of 4 4.50 —
First day cover 1.75
Pane of 12 13.50 —

Palais des Nations — G65

Printed by Government Printing Office, Austria. Panes of 20. Designed by Robert Stein, US.

2002, Mar. 1 Litho. *Perf. 13¾*

385 G65 1.30fr **multicolored** *(630,000)+* 1.75 1.75
First day cover 2.25
Inscription block of 4 7.25 —

Endangered Species Type of 1993

Printed by Johann Enschedé and Sons, the Netherlands. Designed by Lori Anzalone, US.

Designs: No. 386, Cacajao calvus (white uakari). No. 387, Mellivora capensis (honey badger). No. 388, Otocolobus manul (manul). No. 389, Varanus exanthematicus (Bosc's monitor).

2002, Apr. 4 Litho. *Perf. 12¾x12½*

386 A271 90c **multicolored** *(420,000)+* 1.25 1.25
387 A271 90c **multicolored** *(420,000)+* 1.25 1.25
388 A271 90c **multicolored** *(420,000)+* 1.25 1.25
389 A271 90c **multicolored** *(420,000)+* 1.25 1.25
a. Block of 4, #386-389 5.00 5.00
First day cover, #389a 5.50
First day cover, #386-389 each 1.90
Inscription block of 4, #389a 5.25 —
Pane of 16 18.00 —

Independence of East Timor Type

Designs: 90c, Wooden statue of male figure. 1.30fr, Carved wooden container.

2002, May 20 Litho. *Perf. 14x14½*

390 A335 90c **multicolored** *(305,000)+* 1.25 1.25
First day cover 1.90
Inscription block of 4 5.00 —
391 A335 1.30fr **multicolored** *(295,000)+* 1.75 1.75
First day cover 2.60
First day cover, #390-391 3.75
Inscription block of 4 7.00 —

Intl. Year of Mountains Type

Designs: No. 392, Weisshorn, Switzerland. No. 393, Mt. Fuji, Japan. No. 394, Vinson Massif, Antarctica. No. 395, Mt. Kamet, India.

2002, May 24 Litho. *Perf. 13x13¼*

392 A336 70c **multicolored** *(1,230,000)+* .90 .90
First day cover 1.40
393 A336 70c **multicolored** *(1,230,000)+* .90 .90
First day cover 1.40
394 A336 1.20fr **multicolored** *(1,230,000)+* 1.60 1.60
First day cover 2.40
First day cover, #392, 394 3.25
395 A336 1.20fr **multicolored** *(1,230,000)+* 1.60 1.60
a. Vert. strip or block of four, #392-395 5.25 5.25
First day cover 2.40
First day cover, #392, 395 3.25
First day cover, #392-395 6.00
Pane of 12, 3 each #392-395 16.00 —

World Summit on Sustainable Development (Peter Max) Type

Designs: No. 396, Sun, birds, flowers, heart. No. 397, Three faceless people, diff. No. 398, Three women, diff. No. 399, Sailboat, mountain.

2002, June 27 Litho. *Perf. 14½x14*

396 A337 90c **multicolored** *(1,215,000)+* 1.25 1.25
First day cover 1.90
397 A337 90c **multicolored** *(1,215,000)+* 1.25 1.25
First day cover 1.90
398 A337 1.80fr **multicolored** *(1,215,000)+* 2.50 2.50
First day cover 3.50
First day cover, #396, 398 4.00
399 A337 1.80fr **multicolored** *(1,215,000)+* 2.50 2.50
a. Vert. strip or block of four, #396-399 7.75 7.75
First day cover 3.50
First day cover, #397, 399 4.00
First day cover, #396-399 8.00
Pane of 12, 3 each #396-399 23.50 —

World Heritage, Italy Type

Designs: 90c, #402e, Pisa. 1.30fr, #402b, Aeolian Islands. #402a, Amalfi Coast. #402c, Rome. #402d, Florence. #402f, Pompeii.

2002, Aug. 30 Litho. *Perf. 13½x13¼*

400 A338 90c **multicolored** *(355,000)+* 1.25 1.25
First day cover 1.90
Inscription block of 4 5.00 —
401 A338 1.30fr **multicolored** *(355,000)+* 2.00 2.00
First day cover 2.75
First day cover, #400-401 4.00
Inscription block of 4 8.25 —

Souvenir Booklet

402 Booklet *(51,000)+* 17.50
a.-c. A338 10c any single .35 .35
d.-f. A338 20c any single 1.00 1.00
g. Booklet pane of 4, #402d 4.00 4.00
h. Booklet pane of 4, #402a 1.50 1.50
i. Booklet pane of 4, #402e 4.00 4.00
j. Booklet pane of 4, #402b 1.50 1.50
k. Booklet pane of 4, #402f 4.00 4.00
l. Booklet pane of 4, #402c 1.50 1.50

AIDS Awareness Type

2002, Oct. 24 Litho. *Perf. 13½*

403 A339 1.30fr **multicolored** *(305,000)+* 2.00 2.00
Inscription block of 4 7.75 —
First day cover, #403 2.60
Pane of 20 40.00 —

Entry of Switzerland into United Nations — G66

Printed by House of Questa, UK. Panes of 20. Designed by Thierry Clauson, Switzerland.

2002, Oct. 24 Litho. *Perf. 14½x14¾*

404 G66 3fr **multicolored** *(580,000)+* 4.25 4.25
Inscription block of 4 17.00 —
First day cover, #404 5.00
Pane of 20 85.00 —

Indigenous Art — G67

Printed by House of Questa, UK.
Designed by Rorie Katz and Robert Stein, US.

No. 405: a, Detail of Inca poncho, Peru. b, Bahia culture seated figure, Brazil. c, Blanket, Ecuador. d, Mayan stone sculpture, Belize. e, Embroidered fabric, Guatemala. f, Colima terra-cotta dog sculpture, Mexico.

2003, Jan. 31 Litho. *Perf. 14¼*

405 G67 Sheet of 6 *(168,000)+* 7.75 7.75
First day cover 9.75
a.-f. 90c Any single 1.25 1.25
First day cover, a.-f., each 2.50

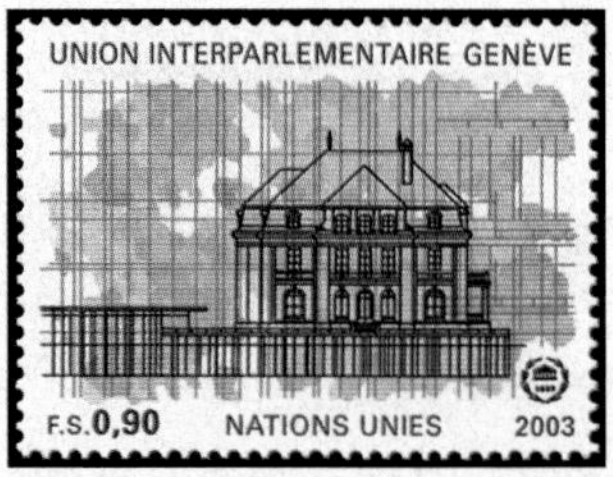

New Inter-Parliamentary Union Headquarters, Geneva — G68

Printed by House of Questa, UK. Panes of 20. Designed by Cyril Wursten, Switzerland.

2003, Feb. 20 Litho. *Perf. 14½x14*

406 G68 90c **multicolored** *(480,000)+* 1.75 1.75
Inscription block of 4 7.25 —
First day cover 2.00
Pane of 20 25.00 —

Endangered Species Type of 1993

Printed by Johann Enschedé and Sons, the Netherlands. Designed by James Hautman, US.

Designs: No. 407, Branta ruficollis (red-breasted goose). No. 408, Geronticus calvus (bald ibis). No. 409, Dendrocygna bicolor (fulvous whistling duck). No. 410, Ramphastos vitellinus (channel-billed toucan).

2003, Apr. 3 Litho. *Perf. 12¾x12½*

407 A271 90c **multicolored** *(368,000)+* 1.25 1.25
408 A271 90c **multicolored** *(368,000)+* 1.25 1.25
409 A271 90c **multicolored** *(368,000)+* 1.25 1.25
410 A271 90c **multicolored** *(368,000)+* 1.25 1.25
a. Block of 4, #407-410 5.00 5.00
First day cover, #410a 6.25
First day cover, #407-410 each 2.10
Inscription block of 4, #410a 5.60 —
Pane of 16 22.50 —

International Year of Freshwater Type of 2003

2003, June 20 Litho. *Perf. 14¼x14½*

411 A345 70c Waterfall *(255,000)+* 1.00 1.00
412 A345 1.30fr People, mountain *(255,000)+* 2.00 2.00
a. Horiz. pair, #411-412 3.00 3.00
First day cover, #412a 3.75
Inscription block of 4 6.00 —

Ralph Bunche Type

Litho. With Foil Application

2003, Aug. 7 *Perf. 13½x14*

413 A346 1.80fr **brown red & multicolored** *(300,000)+* 2.75 2.75
First day cover 3.50
Inscription block of 4 11.00
Pane of 20 55.00

In Memoriam Type of 2003

2003, Oct. 24 Litho. *Perf. 13¼x13*

414 A347 85c **multicolored** *(700,000)+* 1.50 1.50
First day cover 2.10
Inscription block of 4 6.00 —
Pane of 20 30.00 —

World Heritage Sites, United States Type

Designs: 90c, #417b, Great Smoky Mountains National Park. 1.30fr, #417f, Yellowstone National Park. #417a, Yosemite National Park. #417c, Olympic National Park. #417d, Hawaii Volcanoes National Park. #417e, Everglades National Park.

2003, Oct. 24 Litho. *Perf. 14½x14¼*

415 A348 90c **multicolored** *(205,000)+* 1.50 1.50
First day cover 2.10
Inscription block of 4 6.25 —
416 A348 1.30fr **multicolored** *(205,000)+* 2.25 2.25
First day cover 3.25
First day cover, #415-416 4.50
Inscription block of 4 9.25 —

Souvenir Booklet

417 Booklet *(39,000)+* 9.00
a.-c. A348 10c any single .20 .20
d.-f. A348 30c any single .55 .55
g. Booklet pane of 4 #417a .70 .70
h. Booklet pane of 4 #417d 2.25 2.25
i. Booklet pane of 4 #417b .70 .70
j. Booklet pane of 4 #417e 2.25 2.25
k. Booklet pane of 4 #417c .70 .70
l. Booklet pane of 4 #417f 2.25 2.25

Endangered Species Type of 1993

Printed by Johann Enschedé and Sons, the Netherlands. Designed by Yuan Lee, US.

Designs: No. 418, Ursus thibetanus (Asiatic black bear). No. 419, Hippocamelus antisensis (Northern Andean deer). No. 420, Macaca silenus (Lion-tailed macaque). No. 421, Bos gaurus (Gaur).

2004, Jan. 29 Litho. *Perf. 12¾x12½*

418 A271 1fr **multicolored** *(300,000)+* 1.40 1.40
419 A271 1fr **multicolored** *(300,000)+* 1.40 1.40
420 A271 1fr **multicolored** *(300,000)+* 1.40 1.40
421 A271 1fr **multicolored** *(300,000)+* 1.40 1.40
a. Block of 4, #418-421 5.75 5.75
First day cover, #421a 7.50
First day cover, #418-421, each 2.50
Inscription block of 4, #421a 6.25 —
Pane of 16 28.00 —

Indigenous Art Type of 2003

Printed by Johann Enschedé and Sons, the Netherlands. Designed by Rorie Katz and Robert Stein, US.

No. 422: a, Decoration for cows, Switzerland. b, Stone Age terra cotta sculpture of seated woman, Romania. c, Butter stamps, France. d, Detail of herald's tabard, United Kingdom. e, Woodcut print of medieval Cologne, Germany. f, Mesolithic era terra cotta sculpture of mother and child, Serbia and Montenegro.

2004, Mar. 4 Litho. *Perf. 13¼*

422 G67 Sheet of 6 *(102,000)+* 9.00 9.00
First day cover 12.00
a.-f. 1fr Any single 1.50 1.50

Road Safety Type

Road map art with: 85c, Man on hand. 1fr, Person, seat belt, vert.

2004, Apr. 7 Litho. *Perf. 13x13¼, 13¼x13*

423 A354 85c **multicolored** *(185,000)+* 1.40 1.40
First day cover 2.10
Inscription block of 4 6.00 —
424 A354 1fr **multicolored** *(185,000)+* 1.75 1.75
First day cover 2.50
First day cover, #423-424 4.00
Inscription block of 4 7.25 —

See France No. 3011.

Japanese Peace Bell, 50th Anniv. Type

2004, June 3 Litho. & Engr. *Perf. 13¼x13*

425 A355 1.30fr **multicolored** *(230,000)+* 2.00 2.00
First day cover 3.00
Inscription block of 4 8.50 —
Pane of 20 45.00

World Heritage Sites, Greece Type

Designs: 1fr, No. 428b, Delphi. 1.30fr, #428e, Pythagoreion and Heraion of Samos. No. 428a, Acropolis, Athens. No. 428c, Olympia. #428d, Delos. #428f, Mycenae and Tiryns.

2004, Aug. 12 Litho. *Perf. 14x13¼*

426 A356	1fr **multicolored** *(180,000)+*		1.50	1.50
	First day cover			2.25
	Inscription block of 4		6.50	—
427 A356	1.30fr **multicolored** *(180,000)+*		2.00	2.00
	First day cover			3.00
	First day cover, #426-427			4.50
	Inscription block of 4		8.50	—

Souvenir Booklet

428	Booklet *(33,000)+*	12.00	
a.-c.	A356 20c any single	.25	.25
d.-f.	A356 50c any single	.75	.75
g.	Booklet pane of 4 #428a	1.00	1.00
h.	Booklet pane of 4 #428b	1.00	1.00
i.	Booklet pane of 4 #428c	1.00	1.00
j.	Booklet pane of 4 #428d	3.00	3.00
k.	Booklet pane of 4 #428e	3.00	3.00
l.	Booklet pane of 4 #428f	3.00	3.00

My Dream for Peace Type

Winning designs of Lions Club International children's global peace poster contest by: 85c, Anggun Sita Rustinya, Indonesia. 1.20fr, Amanda Nunez, Belize.

2004, Sept. 21 Litho. *Perf. 14*

429 A357	85c **multicolored** *(195,000)+*	1.40	1.40
	First day cover		1.90
	Inscription block of 4	5.75	
	Pane of 20	28.00	
430 A357	1.20fr **multicolored** *(195,000)+*	2.00	2.00
	First day cover		2.75
	First day cover, #429-430		4.00
	Inscription block of 4	8.25	
	Pane of 20	40.00	

G69

Human Rights — G70

Printed by Banknote Corporation of America, US. Designed by Yuri Gervorgian, Armenia. Panes of 8.

2004, Oct. 14 Litho. *Perf. 11¼*

431 G69	85c **multicolored** *(408,000)+*	1.25	1.25
	First day cover		2.10
	Pane of 8	10.00	—
432 G70	1.30fr **multicolored** *(408,000)+*	2.25	2.25
	First day cover		3.25
	First day cover, #431-432		4.50
	Pane of 8	18.00	—

Sports — G71

Printed by Cartor Security Printing, France. Designed by Roland Hirter, Switzerland. Panes of 20.

2004, Nov. 23 Litho. *Perf. 13x13½*

433 G71	180c **multicolored** *(216,000)+*	3.25	3.25
	First day cover		4.00
	Inscription block of 4	13.00	—
	Pane of 20	65.00	—

See Switzerland No. 1196.

United Nations, 60th Anniv. Type of 2005

Printed by Banknote Corporation of America, US. Designed by Czeslaw Slania, Sweden.

2005, Feb. 4 Litho. & Engr. *Perf. 11x11¼*

434 A361	1.30fr **multicolored** *(270,000)+*	2.50	2.50
	First day cover		3.50
	Inscription block of 4	10.00	—
	Pane of 20	50.00	—

Souvenir Sheet

Litho.

Imperf

435 A361	3fr **multicolored** *(125,000)+*	5.00	5.00
	First day cover		6.75

Endangered Species Type of 1993

Printed by Johann Enschedé and Sons, the Netherlands. Designed by Boris Zlotsky, US.

Designs: No. 436, Laelia milleri. No. 437, Psygmorchis pusilla. No. 438, Dendrobium cruentum. No. 439, Orchis purpurea.

2005, Mar. 3 Litho. *Perf. 12¾x12½*

436 A271	1fr **multicolored** *(248,000)+*	1.75	1.75
437 A271	1fr **multicolored** *(248,000)+*	1.75	1.75
438 A271	1fr **multicolored** *(248,000)+*	1.75	1.75
439 A271	1fr **multicolored** *(248,000)+*	1.75	1.75
a.	Block of 4, #436-439	7.00	7.00
	First day cover, #439a		8.75
	First day cover, #436-439, each		3.00
	Inscription block of 4, #439a	7.75	—
	Pane of 16	27.50	

Nature's Wisdom — G72

Printed by Cartor Security Printing, France. Panes of 20. Designed by Robert Stein, US.

Designs: 1fr, Children collecting water, India. 80c, Ruby brittle star, Bahamas.

2005, Apr. 21 Litho. *Perf. 13½x13¼*

440 G72	1fr **multicolored** *(180,000)+*	1.75	1.75
	First day cover		2.75
	Inscription block of 4	7.25	—
	Pane of 20	35.00	—
441 G72	1.30fr **multicolored** *(180,000)+*	2.00	2.00
	First day cover		3.75
	First day cover, #440-441		5.50
	Inscription block of 4	9.25	—
	Pane of 20	40.00	—

Intl. Year of Sport Type

Printed by Cartor Security Printing, France. Designed by Roland Hirter, Switzerland.

2005, June 3 Litho. *Perf. 13x13¼*

442 A368	1fr Wheelchair racing *(185,000)+*	1.75	1.75
	First day cover		2.75
	Inscription block of 4	7.75	—
	Pane of 20	35.00	—
443 A368	1.30fr Cycling *(185,000)+*	2.25	2.25
	First day cover		3.75
	First day cover, #442-443		5.50
	Inscription block of 4	9.25	—
	Pane of 20	45.00	—

World Heritage Sites, Egypt Type

Printed by Johann Enschedé and Sons, the Netherlands. Panes of 20. Designed by Rorie Katz, US.

Designs: Nos. 444, 446b, Philae. Nos. 445, 446e, Islamic Cairo. No. 446a, Memphis and its Necropolis. No. 446c, Abu Mena. No. 446d, Ancient Thebes. No. 446f, St. Catherine area.

2005, Aug. 4 Litho. *Perf. 14x13¼*

444 A369	1fr **multicolored** *(180,000)+*	2.00	2.00
	First day cover		2.75
	Inscription block of 4	8.00	—
445 A369	1.30fr **multicolored** *(180,000)+*	2.50	2.50
	First day cover		3.75
	First day cover, #444-445		5.50
	Inscription block of 4	10.00	—

Souvenir Booklet

446	Booklet, #446g-446l *(31,000)+*	16.50	
a.-c.	A369 20c any single	.40	.40
d.-f.	A369 50c any single	.90	.90
g.	Booklet pane of 4 #446a	1.60	—
h.	Booklet pane of 4 #446b	1.60	—
i.	Booklet pane of 4 #446c	1.60	—
j.	Booklet pane of 4 #446d	3.75	—
k.	Booklet pane of 4 #446e	3.75	—
l.	Booklet pane of 4 #446f	3.75	—

My Dream for Peace Type

Winning designs of Lions Club International children's global peace poster contest by: 1fr, Marisa Harun, Indonesia. 1.30fr, Carlos Javier Parramón Teixidó, Spain.

2005, Sept. 21 Litho. *Perf. 14*

447 A357	1fr **multicolored** *(175,000)+*	1.75	1.75
	First day cover		2.60
	Inscription block of 4	7.25	
	Pane of 20	35.00	
448 A357	1.30fr **multicolored** *(175,000)+*	2.00	2.00
	First day cover		3.50
	First day cover, #447-448		5.00
	Inscription block of 4	8.25	
	Pane of 20	40.00	

Food for Life Type

Printed by Government Printing Office, Austria. Designed by Andrew Davidson, United Kingdom.

Designs: 1fr, Rye, airplane dropping parcels, camel caravan. 1.30fr, Sorghum, people carrying grain sacks, trucks.

2005, Oct. 20 Litho. *Perf. 13¾*

449 A370	1fr **multicolored** *(170,000)+*	1.90	1.90
	First day cover		2.60
	Inscription block of 4	7.75	—
	Pane of 20	38.00	—
450 A370	1.30fr **multicolored** *(170,000)+*	2.40	2.40
	First day cover		3.50
	First day cover, #449-450		5.00
	Inscription block of 4	9.75	—
	Pane of 20	48.00	—

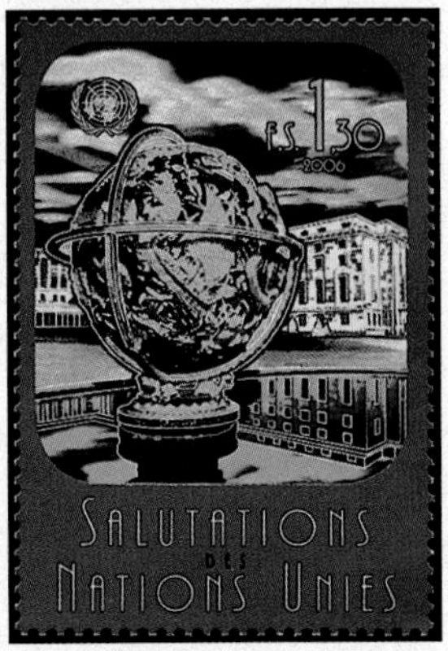

Armillary Sphere, Palais des Nations — G73

Printed by Cartor Security Printing, France. Panes of 20. Designed by Rorie Katz, United States.

Litho. with Hologram

2006, Feb. 3 *Perf. 13¼x13½*

451 G73	1.30fr **multicolored** *(280,000)+*	2.25	2.25
	First day cover		3.25
	Inscription block of 4	9.00	—
	Pane of 20	45.00	—

Indigenous Art Type of 2003

Printed by Johann Enschedé and Sons, the Netherlands. Designed by Robert Stein, US.

No. 452 — Musical instruments: a, Bell, Benin. b, Drum, Swaziland. c, Sanza, Congo. d, Stringed instruments, Cape Verde. e, Caixixi, Ghana. f, Bells, Central Africa.

2006, Feb. 3 Litho. *Perf. 13¼*

452 G67	Sheet of 6 *(91,000)+*	12.00	12.00
	First day cover		14.00
a.-f.	1.20fr Any single	2.00	2.00

Endangered Species Type of 1993

Printed by Johann Enschedé and Sons, the Netherlands. Designed by John D. Dawson, US.

Designs: No. 453, Dyscophus antongilii. No. 454, Chamaeleo dilepsis. No. 455, Corallus caninus. No. 456, Phyllobates vittatus.

2006, Mar. 16 Litho. *Perf. 12¾x12½*

453 A271 1fr **multicolored** *(228,000)+* 1.75 1.75
454 A271 1fr **multicolored** *(228,000)+* 1.75 1.75
455 A271 1fr **multicolored** *(228,000)+* 1.75 1.75
456 A271 1fr **multicolored** *(228,000)+* 1.75 1.75
a. Block of 4, #453-456 7.00 7.00
First day cover, #456a 7.75
First day cover, #453-456, each 2.60
Inscription block of 4, #456a 7.00 —
Pane of 16 28.00

Intl. Day of Families Type

Printed by Johann Enschedé and Sons, the Netherlands. Designed by Shelly Bartek, US.

Designs: 1fr, Family reading together. 1.30fr, Family on motorcycle.

2006, May 27 Litho. *Perf. 14x13½*

457 A373 1fr **multicolored** *(150,000)+* 1.75 1.75
First day cover 2.50
Inscription block of 4 7.00 —
Pane of 20 35.00 —
458 A373 1.30fr **multicolored** *(150,000)+* 2.25 2.25
First day cover 3.25
First day cover, #457-458 5.00
Inscription block of 4 7.00 —
Pane of 20 35.00 —

World Heritage Sites, France Type

Printed by Cartor Security Printing, France. Panes of 20. Designed by Robert Stein, US.

Eiffel Tower and: Nos. 459, 461b, Provins. Nos. 460, 461e, Mont Saint-Michel. No. 461a, Banks of the Seine. No. 461c, Carcasonne. No. 461d, Roman Aqueduct. No. 446f, Chateau de Chambord.

Litho. & Embossed with Foil Application

2006, June 17 *Perf. 13½x13¼*

459 A374 1fr **multicolored** *(280,000)+* 1.75 1.75
First day cover 2.50
Inscription block of 4 7.00 —
460 A374 1.30fr **multicolored** *(280,000)+* 2.25 2.25
First day cover 3.25
First day cover, #444-445 5.00
Inscription block of 4 9.00 —

Souvenir Booklet

461 Booklet, #461g-461l *(29,000)+* 15.00
a.-c. A374 20c any single .35 .35
d.-f. A374 50c any single .85 .85
g. Booklet pane of 4 #461a 1.40 —
h. Booklet pane of 4 #461b 1.40 —
i. Booklet pane of 4 #461c 1.40 —
j. Booklet pane of 4 #461d 3.50 —
k. Booklet pane of 4 #461e 3.50 —
l. Booklet pane of 4 #461f 3.50 —

See France Nos. 3219-3220.

My Dream for Peace Type of 2004

Printed by Cartor Security Printing, France. Panes of 20.

Winning designs of Lions Club International children's global peace poster contest by: 85c, Ariam Boaglio, Italy. 1.20fr, Sierra Spicer, US.

2006, Sept. 21 Litho. *Perf. 13½x13*

462 A357 85c **multicolored** *(160,000)+* 1.60 1.60
First day cover 2.40
Inscription block of 4 6.40 —
Pane of 20 32.00 —
463 A357 1.20fr **multicolored** *(160,000)+* 2.25 2.25
First day cover 3.25
First day cover, #462-463 4.75
Inscription block of 4 9.00 —
Pane of 20 45.00 —

Flags and Coins Type

Printed by Cartor Security Printing, France. Designed by Rorie Katz, US.

No. 464 - Flag of: a, Uganda, 500 shilling coin. b, Luxembourg, 1 euro coin. c, Cape Verde, 20 escudo coin. d, Belgium, 1 euro coin. e, Italy, 1 euro coin. f, New Zealand, 1 dollar coin. g, Switzerland, 2 franc coin. h, Lebanon, 500 pound coin.

2006, Oct. 5 Litho. *Perf. 13¼x13*

464 Sheet of 8 12.50 12.50
a.-h. A375 85c Any single 1.50 1.50
First day cover 14.50

A column of rouletting in the middle of the sheet separates it into two parts.

Endangered Species Type of 1993

Printed by Johann Enschedé and Sons, the Netherlands. Designed by John Rowe, US.

Designs: No. 465, Theropithecus gelada. No. 466, Cercopithecus neglectus. No. 467, Varecia variegata. No. 468, Hylobates moloch.

2007, Mar. 15 Litho. *Perf. 12¾x12½*

465 A271 1fr **multicolored** *(208,000)+* 1.75 1.75
466 A271 1fr **multicolored** *(208,000)+* 1.75 1.75
467 A271 1fr **multicolored** *(208,000)+* 1.75 1.75
468 A271 1fr **multicolored** *(208,000)+* 1.75 1.75
a. Block of 4, #465-468 7.00 7.00
First day cover, #468a 8.25
First day cover, #465-468, each 2.75
Inscription block of 4, #468a 7.00 —
Pane of 16 28.00 —

Flags and Coins Type of 2006

Printed by Cartor Security Printing, France. Designed by Rorie Katz, US.

No. 469 — Flag of: a, Burkina Faso, 500 franc coin. b, France, 50 cent coin. c, Moldova, 50 bani coin. d, Papua New Guinea, 1 kina coin. e, Bolivia, 1 boliviano coin. f, Myanmar, 100 kyat coin. g, Mali, 500 franc coin. h, Tunisia, 5 dinar coin.

2007, May 3 Litho. *Perf. 13¼x13*

469 Sheet of 8 *(125,000)+* 12.50 12.50
a.-h. A375 85c Any single 1.50 1.50
First day cover 14.50

A column of rouletting in the middle of the sheet separates it into two parts.

Peaceful Visions Type of 2007

Printed by Lowe-Martin Company, Canada. Designed by Slavka Kolesar, Canada. Panes of 20.

Designs: 1.20fr, "Harvest for All." 1.80fr, "This Dream Has Wings."

2007, June 1 Litho. *Perf. 13x12½*

470 A378 1.20fr **multicolored** *(156,000)+* 2.25 2.25
First day cover 3.00
Inscription block of 4 9.00 —
Pane of 20 45.00 —
471 A378 1.80fr **multicolored** *(156,000)+* 3.25 3.25
First day cover 4.50
First day cover, #470-471 6.50
Inscription block of 4 13.00 —
Pane of 20 65.00 —

World Heritage Sites, South America Type

Printed by Lowe-Martin Group, Canada. Panes of 20. Designed by Rorie Katz, US.

Designs: Nos. 472, 474a, Tiwanaku, Bolivia. Nos. 473, 474f, Machu Picchu, Peru. No. 474b, Iguaçu National Park, Brazil. No. 474c, Galapagos Islands, Ecuador. No. 474d, Rapa Nui, Chile. No. 474e, Cueva de las Manos, Argentina.

2007, Aug. 9 Litho. *Perf. 13¼x13*

472 A381 1fr **multicolored** *(150,000)+* 1.90 1.90
First day cover 2.50
Inscription block of 4 7.60 —
473 A381 1.80fr **multicolored** *(150,000)+* 3.25 3.25
First day cover 4.50
First day cover, #472-473 6.00
Inscription block of 4 13.00 —

Souvenir Booklet

474 Booklet, #474g-474l *(27,000)+* 15.50
a.-c. A381 20c Any single .35 .35
d.-f. A381 50c Any single .90 .90
g. Booklet pane of 4 #474a 1.40 —
h. Booklet pane of 4 #474b 1.40 —
i. Booklet pane of 4 #474c 1.40 —
j. Booklet pane of 4 #474d 3.60 —
k. Booklet pane of 4 #474e 3.60 —
l. Booklet pane of 4 #474f 3.60 —

Humanitarian Mail Type

Printed by Lowe-Martin Group, Canada. Panes of 10.

2007, Sept. 6 Litho. *Perf. 12½x13¼*

475 A382 1.80fr **multicolored** *(320,000)+* 3.25 3.25
First day cover 4.25
Inscription block of 4 13.00 —
Pane of 10 32.50 —

Space for Humanity Type

Printed by Johann Enschedé and Sons, the Netherlands. Panes of 6. Designed by Donato Giancola, US.

Designs: 1fr, Astronaut spacewalking. 1.80fr, International Space Station, space probe, Jupiter.

3fr, Astronauts spacewalking.

2007, Oct. 25 Litho. *Perf. 13½x14*

476 A383 1fr **multicolored** *(252,000)+* 1.90 1.90
First day cover 2.50
Inscription block of 4 7.60 —
Sheet of 6 11.40 —
477 A383 1.80fr **multicolored** *(252,000)+* 3.25 3.25
First day cover 4.50
First day cover, #476-477 6.00
Inscription block of 4 13.00 —
Sheet of 6 19.50 —

Souvenir Sheet

478 A383 3fr **multicolored** *(110,000)+* 5.50 5.50
First day cover 6.50

Intl. Holocaust Remembrance Day Type

Printed by Lowe-Martin Company, Canada. Panes of 9. Designed by Matías Delfino, Argentina.

2008, Jan. 27 Litho. *Perf. 13*

479 A384 85c **multicolored** *(495,000)+* 1.75 1.75
First day cover 2.75
Sheet of 9 16.00 —

Endangered Species Type of 1993

Printed by Johann Enschedé and Sons, the Netherlands. Designed by Suzanne Duranceau, Canada.

Designs: No. 480, Odobenus rosmarus. No. 481, Platygyra daedalea. No. 482, Hippocampus bargibanti. No. 483, Delphinapterus leucas.

2008, Mar. 6 Litho. *Perf. 12¾x12½*

480 A271 1fr **multicolored** *(172,000)+* 2.00 2.00
481 A271 1fr **multicolored** *(172,000)+* 2.00 2.00
482 A271 1fr **multicolored** *(172,000)+* 2.00 2.00
483 A271 1fr **multicolored** *(172,000)+* 2.00 2.00
a. Block of 4, #480-483 8.00 8.00
First day cover, #483a 9.00
First day cover, #480-483, each 3.00
Inscription block of 4, #483a 8.00 —
Pane of 16 32.00 —

Flags and Coins Type of 2006

Printed by Cartor Security Printing, France. Designed by Rorie Katz, US.

No. 484 — Flag of: a, Madagascar, 1 ariary coin. b, Rwanda, 50 franc coin. c, Benin, 10 franc coin. d, Iran, 500 rial coin. e, Namibia, 5 dollar coin. f, Maldives, 1 rufiyaa coin. g, Albania, 10 lek coin. h, Turkey, 1 lira coin.

2008, May 8 Litho. *Perf. 13¼x13*

484 Sheet of 8 *(100,000)+* 15.00 15.00
a.-h. A375 85c Any single 1.75 1.75
First day cover 17.00

A column of rouletting in the middle of the sheet separates it into two parts.

2008 END-OF-YEAR ISSUES

See end of New York postage listings.

SEMI-POSTAL STAMP

AIDS Awareness Semi-postal Type

Souvenir Sheet

2002, Oct. 24 Litho. *Perf. 14½*

B1 SP1 90c + 30c **multicolored** *(171,000)+* 2.50 2.50
First day cover, #B1 3.00

AIR LETTER SHEET

Used values for all postal stationery are for non-philatelic contemporaneous usages.

UN Type of 1968

Printed by Setelipaino, Finland. Designed by Robert Perrot.

1969, Oct. 4 Litho.

UC1 UC3 65c **ultra & light blue,** entire *(350,000)* .50 *1.50*
Entire, first day cancel *(52,000)* .75

POSTAL CARDS

UN Type of 1969 and Type of Air Post Postal Card, 1966

Printed by Courvoisier, S.A., Switzerland. Designed by John Mason (20c) and Olav S. Mathiesen (30c).

Wmk. Post Horn, Swiss Cross, "S" or "Z"

1969, Oct. 4 Litho.

UX1 PC2 20c **olive green & black,** *buff (415,000)* .25 .30
First day cancel *(51,500)* .50
UX2 APC2 30c **violet blue, blue, light & dark green,** *buff (275,000)* .25 .30
First day cancel *(49,000)* .50

No. UX2, although of design APC2, is not inscribed "Poste Aerienne" or "Air Mail."

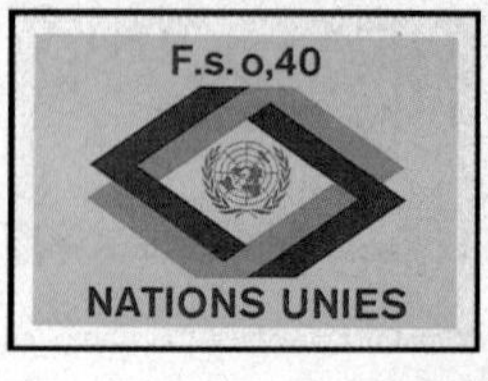

UN Emblem — GPC1

UN Emblem and Ribbons — GPC2

Printed by Setelipaino, Finland. Designed by Veronique Crombez (40c) and Lieve Baeten (70c).

1977, June 27 Litho.

UX3 GPC1 40c **multicolored** *(500,000)* .30 .30
First day cancel *(65,000)* 1.00
UX4 GPC2 70c **multicolored** *(300,000)* .40 .40
First day cancel *(65,000)* .50

A second printing of No. UX3 was made in 1984. It was released after the Swiss postal card rate had been increased to

50c so instructions were issued that all cards must have a 10c stamp affixed before being sold. A few were sold in NY without the added stamp. The card stock differs from the original printing.

Emblem of the United Nations — GPC3

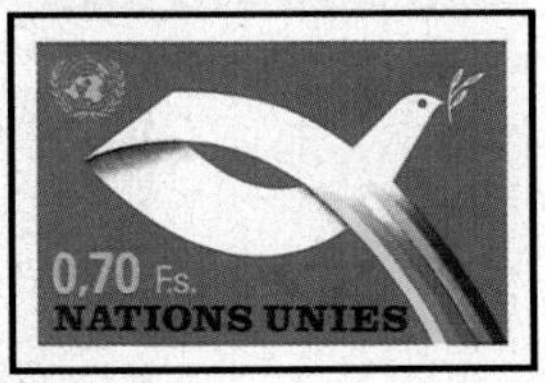

Peace Dove — GPC4

Printed by Johann Enschede en Zonen, Netherlands.
Designed by George Hamori, Australia (50c) and Ryszard Dudzicki, Poland (70c).

1985, May 10 **Litho.**
UX5 GPC3 50c **multicolored** *(300,000)* 1.00 3.50
First day cancel *(34,700)* 1.00
UX6 GPC4 70c **multicolored** *(300,000)* 3.25 3.25
First day cancel *(34,700)* 4.50

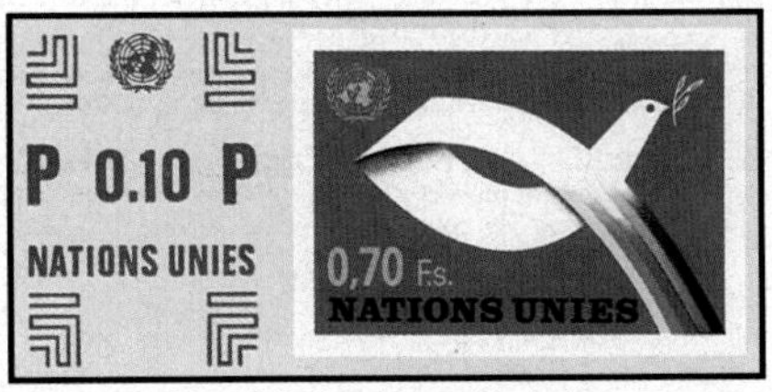

No. UX6 Surcharged in Lake

1986, Jan. 2 **Litho.**
UX7 GPC4 70c + 10c **multi** *(90,500)* 2.50 2.50
First day cancel *(8,000 est.)* 10.00

Type of 1990

Printed by Mercury-Walch, Australia.

1992, Sept. 4 **Litho.**
UX8 G45 90c **multicolored** *(150,000)+* 1.75 1.75
First day cancel *(12,385)* 6.00

No. UX5 Surcharged in Lake like No. UX7

1993, May 7 **Litho.**
UX9 GPC3 50c +10c **multicolored** *(47,000)+* 1.50 1.50
First day cancel 20.00

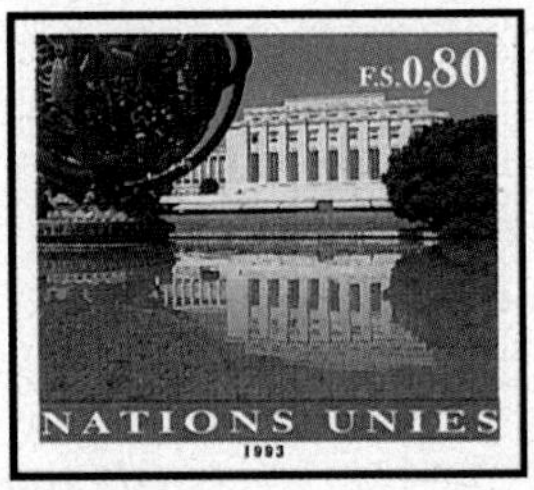

Palais des Nations — GPC5

Printed by Leigh Mardon Pty. Limited, Australia.

1993, May 7 **Litho.**
UX10 GPC5 80c **multicolored** *(200,000)+* 3.00 3.00
First day cancel 7.50

#UX5, UX10 Surcharged in Carmine like #UX7

1996, Mar. 22 **Litho.**
UX11 GPC3 50c +20c **multi** 3.00 3.00
First day cancel 4.00
UX12 GPC5 80c +30c **multi** 3.00 3.00
First day cancel 4.00

Assembly Hall — GPC6

Palais des Nations — GPC7

Printed by Mercury-Walsh, Australia.

1998, May 20 **Litho.**
UX13 GPC6 70c **multicolored** *(80,000)+* 2.00 2.00
First day cancel 3.00
UX14 GPC7 1.10fr **multicolored** *(80,000)+* 3.00 3.00
First day cancel 3.25

Illustrations of the buildings are shown on the back of each card.

Type of 2002

Printed by Johann Enschedé and Sons, the Netherlands.

2002, Mar. 1 **Litho.**
UX15 G65 1.30fr **multicolored** *(68,000)+* 1.75 1.75
First day cancel 2.00

Nos. UX8, UX13 and UX14 Surcharged Like No. UX7, But With Serifed Numerals

2004, Sept. 21 **Litho.**
UX16 GPC6 70c +15c **multicolored** 2.00 2.00
First day cancel 2.00
UX17 G45 90c +10c **multicolored** 2.10 2.10
First day cancel 2.10
UX18 GPC7 1.10fr +10c **multicolored** 2.25 2.25
First day cancel 2.25

OFFICES IN VIENNA, AUSTRIA

For use only on mail posted at the Vienna International Center for the UN and the International Atomic Energy Agency.

100 Groschen = 1 Schilling
100 Cents = 1 Euro (2002)

Type of Geneva, 1978, UN Types of 1961-72 and

Donaupark, Vienna — V1

Aerial View — V2

Printed by Helio Courvoisier S.A., Switzerland. Panes of 50. Designed by Henryk Chylinski (4s); Jozsef Vertel (6s).

1979, Aug. 24 **Photo.** ***Perf. 11½***
Granite Paper

1	G8	50g	**multicolored** *(3,500,000)+*	.20	.20
			First day cover		1.00
			Inscription block of 4	.20	—
2	A52	1s	**multicolored** *(3,800,000)+*	.20	.20
			First day cover		1.00
			Inscription block of 4	.40	—
3	V1	4s	**multicolored** *(3,500,000)+*	.25	.25
			First day cover		1.00
			Inscription block of 4	1.10	—
4	AP13	5s	**multicolored** *(3,500,000)+*	.30	.30
			First day cover		1.00
			Inscription block of 4	1.40	—
5	V2	6s	**multicolored** *(4,500,000)+*	.35	.35
			First day cover		1.25
			Inscription block of 4	1.75	—
6	A45	10s	**multicolored** *(3,500,000)+*	.60	.60
			First day cover		2.00
			Inscription block of 4	3.25	—
			Nos. 1-6 (6)	1.90	1.90

+ Printing orders to Mar. 1993.
No. 4 is not inscribed "Air Mail," No. 6 has no frame.
First day covers of Nos. 1-6 total 1,026,575.

New Economic Order Type of UN

1980, Jan. 11 **Litho.** ***Perf. 15x14½***
7 A178 4s **multicolored** *(1,418,418)* .60 .60
First day cover 1.25
Inscription block of 4 *9.00* —

Value for margin inscription block is for one from bottom of sheet. One from top is about twice the value shown.

Dove Type of UN

1980, Jan. 11 **Litho.** ***Perf. 14x13½***
8 A147 2.50s **multicolored** *(3,500,000)+* .25 .25
First day cover 1.00
Inscription block of 4 1.25 —

First day covers of Nos. 7-8 total 336,229.

Women's Year Emblem on World Map — V3

United Nations Decade for Women.

Printed by Questa Colour Security Printers, United Kingdom. Panes of 50. Designed by Gunnar Janssen.

1980, Mar. 7 **Litho.** ***Perf. 14½x15***
9 V3 4s **light green & dark green** *(1,569,080)* .40 .40
First day cover 1.00
Inscription block of 4 1.75 —
10 V3 6s **bister brown** *(1,556,016)* .75 .75
First day cover 1.25
First day cover, #9-10 1.50
Inscription block of 4 3.25 —

First day covers of Nos. 9-10 total 443,893.

Peace-keeping Operations Type of UN

1980, May 16 **Litho.** ***Perf. 14x13***
11 A182 6s **multicolored** *(1,719,852)* .40 .40
First day cover *(323,923)* 1.00
Inscription block of 4 2.00 —

35th Anniversary Types of Geneva and UN

1980, June 26 **Litho.** ***Perf. 13x13½***
12 G16 4s **carmine rose & black** *(1,626,582)* .35 .35
First day cover 1.00
Inscription block of 4 1.60 —
13 A184 6s **multicolored** *(1,625,400)* .60 .60
First day cover 1.25
Inscription block of 4 2.75 —

Souvenir Sheet

Imperf

14 Sheet of 2 *(1,675,191)* .90 .90
a. G16 4s carmine rose & black .25 .25
b. A184 6s multicolored .65 .65
First day cover 1.00

First day covers of Nos. 12-14 total 657,402.

ECOSOC Types of UN and Geneva

Printed by Ashton-Potter Ltd., Canada. Panes of 50. Designed by Dietman Kowall (4s), Angel Medina Medina (6s).

1980, Nov. 21 **Litho.** ***Perf. 13½x13***
15 A187 4s **multicolored** *(1,811,218)* .30 .30
First day cover 1.00
Inscription block of 4 1.50 —
16 G17 6s **multicolored** *(1,258,420)* .60 .60
First day cover 1.00
First day cover #15-16 1.25
Inscription block of 4 2.50 —

Economic and Social Council (ECOSOC).
First day covers of Nos. 15-16 total 224,631.

Palestinian Rights Type of UN

Printed by Courvoisier S.A., Switzerland. Panes of 50. Designed by David Dewhurst.

1981, Jan. 30 **Photo.** ***Perf. 12x11½***
17 A188 4s **multicolored** *(1,673,310)* .45 .45
First day cover *(208,812)* 1.00
Inscription block of 4 2.00 —

Disabled Type of UN and

Interlocking Stitches — V4

International Year of the Disabled.
Printed by Heraclio Fournier S.A., Spain. Panes of 50. Designed by Sophia van Heeswijk.

1981, Mar. 6 **Photo.** ***Perf. 14***
18 A189 4s **multicolored** *(1,508,719)* .40 .40
First day cover 1.00
Inscription block of 4 1.75 —
19 V4 6s **black & orange** *(1,569,385)* .60 .60
First day cover 1.00
First day cover, #18-19 1.25
Inscription block of 4 2.75 —

First day covers of Nos. 18-19 total 290,603.

Art Type of UN

1981, Apr. 15 **Photo.** ***Perf. 11½***

Granite Paper

20 A191 6s **multicolored** *(1,643,527)* .75 .75
First day cover *(196,916)* 1.00
Inscription block of 4 3.25 —

Energy Type of UN

1981, May 29 **Litho.** ***Perf. 13***
21 A193 7.50s **multicolored** *(1,611,130)* .70 .70
First day cover *(216,197)* 1.00
Inscription block of 4 3.00 —

Volunteers Program Types

1981, Nov. 13 **Litho.**
22 A195 5s **multicolored** *(1,582,780)* .40 .40
First day cover 1.00
Inscription block of 4 2.25 —
23 G18 7s **multicolored** *(1,516,139)* .90 .90
First day cover 1.00
First day cover, #22-23 1.00
Inscription block of 4 4.25 —

First day covers of Nos. 22-23 total 282,414.

"For a Better World" — V5

Printed by Courvoisier, S.A., Switzerland. Sheets of 50. Designed by Eliezer Weishoff.

1982, Jan. 22 ***Perf. 11½x12***
24 V5 3s **multicolored** *(3,300,000)+* .35 .35
First day cover *(203,872)* 1.00
Inscription block of 4 1.75

Human Environment Types of UN

10th Anniversary of United Nations Environment Program. Printed by Joh. Enschede en Zonen, Netherlands. Panes of 50. Designed by Peer-Ulrich Bremer (5s); Sybille Brunner (7s).

1982, Mar. 19 **Litho.** ***Perf. 13½x13***
25 A200 5s **multicolored** *(1,312,765)* .40 .40
First day cover 1.00
Inscription block of 4 1.90 —
26 G21 7s **multicolored** *(1,357,513)* .80 .80
First day cover 1.00
First day cover, #25-26 1.25
Inscription block of 4 3.75 —

First day covers of Nos. 25-26 total 248,576.

Outer Space Type of UN

Exploration and Peaceful Uses of Outer Space. Printed by Enschede. Panes of 50. Designed by George Hamori.

1982, June 11 **Litho.** ***Perf. 13x13½***
27 G22 5s **multicolored** *(1,339,038)* .60 .60
First day cover *(150,845)* 1.75
Inscription block of 4 3.00 —

Conservation & Protection of Nature Type

1982, Nov. 16 **Photo.** ***Perf. 14***
28 A202 5s Fish *(1,202,694)* .50 .50
First day cover 1.00
Inscription block of 4 2.50 —
29 A202 7s Animal *(1,194,403)* .70 .70
First day cover 1.00
First day cover, #28-29 1.40
Inscription block of 4 3.00 —

First day covers of Nos. 28-29 total 243,548.

World Communications Year Type

1983, Jan. 28 **Litho.** ***Perf. 13***
30 A203 4s **multicolored** *(1,517,443)* .40 .40
First day cover *(150,541)* 1.40
Inscription block of 4 2.10 —

Safety at Sea Type

1983, Mar. 18 **Litho.** ***Perf. 14½***
31 G23 4s **multicolored** *(1,506,052)* .40 .40
First day cover 1.00
Inscription block of 4 2.00 —
32 A206 6s **multicolored** *(1,527,990)* .65 .65
First day cover 1.00
First day cover, #31-32 2.25
Inscription block of 4 2.75 —

First day covers of Nos. 31-32 total 219,118.

World Food Program Type

1983, Apr. 22 **Engr.** ***Perf. 13½***
33 A207 5s **green** *(1,419,237)* .45 .45
First day cover 1.00
Inscription block of 4 2.25 —
34 A207 7s **brown** *(1,454,227)* .70 .70
First day cover 1.00
First day cover, #33-34 1.25
Inscription block of 4 2.75 —

First day covers of Nos. 33-34 total 212,267.

UN Conference on Trade and Development Type

1983, June 6 **Litho.** ***Perf. 14***
35 G24 4s **multicolored** *(1,544,973)* .30 .30
First day cover 1.00
Inscription block of 4 1.90 —
36 A209 8.50s **multicolored** *(1,423,172)* .75 .75
First day cover 1.00
First day cover, #35-36 1.25
Inscription block of 4 3.25 —

First day covers of Nos. 35-36 total 184,023.

The Second Skin — V6

Right to Think — V7

35th Anniversary of the Universal Declaration of Human Rights

Printed by Government Printing Office, Austria. Designed by Friedensreich Hundertwasser, Austria. Panes of 16 (4x4).

1983, Dec. 9 **Photo. & Engr.** ***Perf. 13½***
37 V6 5s **multicolored** *(2,163,419)* .45 .45
First day cover 1.25
Inscription block of 4 2.25
38 V7 7s **multicolored** *(2,163,542)* .70 .70
First day cover 1.25
First day cover, #37-38 2.25
Inscription block of 4 3.25
Panes of 16, #37-38 18.00

First day covers of Nos. 37-38 total 246,440.

International Conference on Population Type

Printed by Bundesdruckerei, Federal Republic of Germany. Panes of 50. Designed by Marina Langer-Rosa and Helmut Langer, Federal Republic of Germany.

1984, Feb. 3 **Litho.** ***Perf. 14***
39 A212 7s **multicolored** *(1,135,791)* .65 .65
First day cover *(80,570)* 1.50
Inscription block of 4 2.75 —

Field Irrigation V8

Harvesting Machines V9

World Food Day, Oct. 16

Printed by Walsall Security Printers, Ltd., United Kingdom. Panes of 50. Designed by Adth Vanooijen, Netherlands.

1984, Mar. 15 **Litho.** ***Perf. 14½***
40 V8 4.50s **multicolored** *(994,106)* .40 .40
First day cover 1.00
Inscription block of 4 2.00 —
41 V9 6s **multicolored** *(1,027,115)* .65 .65
First day cover 1.00
First day cover #40-41 2.25
Inscription block of 4 2.50 —

First day covers of Nos. 40-41 total 194,546.

Serengeti Park, Tanzania — V10

Ancient City of Shiban, People's Democratic Rep. of Yemen — V11

World Heritage

Printed by Harrison and Sons, United Kingdom. Panes of 50. Designs adapted by Rocco J. Callari, US, and Thomas Lee, China.

1984, Mar. 15 Litho. *Perf. 14*

42 V10 3.50s **multicolored** *(957,518)* .25 .25
First day cover 1.25
Inscription block of 4 1.25 —
43 V11 15s **multicolored** *(928,794)* 1.25 1.25
First day cover 1.75
First day cover, #42-43 2.50
Inscription block of 4 5.75 —

First day covers of Nos. 42-43 total 193,845.

V12

V13

Future for Refugees

Designed by Hans Erni, Switzerland.
Printed by Courvoisier. Panes of 50.

1984, Mar. 29 Photo. *Perf. 11½*

44 V12 4.50s **multicolored** *(1,086,393)* .45 .45
First day cover 1.25
Inscription block of 4 2.25 —
45 V13 8.50s **multicolored** *(1,109,865)* 1.25 1.25
First day cover 1.75
First day cover, #44-45 2.25
Inscription block of 4 5.75 —

First day covers of Nos. 44-45 total 185,349.

International Youth Year — V14

Printed by Waddingtons Ltd., United Kingdom. Panes of 50. Designed by Ruel A. Mayo, Phillipines.

1984, Nov. 15 Litho. *Perf. 13½*

46 V14 3.50s **multicolored** *(1,178,833)* .45 .45
First day cover 1.25
Inscription block of 4 2.10 —
47 V14 6.50s **multicolored** *(1,109,337)* .70 .70
First day cover 1.50
First day cover, #46-47 2.25
Inscription block of 4 3.25 —

First day covers of Nos. 46-47 total 165,762.

ILO Type of Geneva

Printed by the Government Printing Bureau, Japan. Panes of 50. Adapted from photographs by Rocco J. Callari, US, and Thomas Lee, China.

1985, Feb. 1 Engr. *Perf. 13½*

48 G34 7.50s U Thant Pavilion *(948,317)* .75 .75
First day cover *(115,916)* 1.75
Inscription block of 4 3.50 —

UN University Type

Printed by Helio Courvoisier, Switzerland. Panes of 50. Designed by Moshe Pereg, Israel, and Hinedi Geluda, Brazil.

1985, Mar. 15 Photo. *Perf. 13½*

49 A221 8.50s Rural scene, lab researcher *(863,673)* .75 .75
First day cover *(108,479)* 1.75
Inscription block of 4 3.75 —

Ship of Peace — V15

Shelter under UN Umbrella — V16

Printed by Carl Ueberreuter Druck and Verlag M. Salzer, Austria. Panes of 50. Designed by Ran Banda Mawilmada, Sri Lanka (4.50s), and Sophia van Heeswijk, Federal Republic of Germany (15s).

1985, May 10 Litho. *Perf. 14*

50 V15 4.50s **multicolored** *(2,000,000)+* .30 .30
First day cover .75
Inscription block of 4 1.50 —
51 V16 15s **multicolored** *(2,000,000)+* 2.00 2.00
First day cover 2.75
First day cover, #50-51 3.50
Inscription block of 4 9.50 —

First day covers of Nos. 50-51 total 142,687.

40th Anniversary Type

Designed by Rocco J. Callari, U.S., and Thomas Lee, China (No. 54).

1985, June 26 Photo. *Perf. 12 x 11½*

52 A224 6.50s **multicolored** *(984,820)* .90 .90
First day cover 1.25
Inscription block of 4 4.25 —
53 A225 8.50s **multicolored** *(914,347)* 1.40 1.40
First day cover 1.75
First day cover, #52-53 2.50
Inscription block of 4 6.25 —

Souvenir Sheet

Imperf

54 Sheet of 2 *(676,648)* 2.50 2.50
a. A224 6.50s **multi** 1.00 1.00
b. A225 8.50s **multi** 1.40 1.40
First day cover 2.50

First day covers of Nos. 52-54 total 317,652.

UNICEF Child Survival Campaign Type

Printed by the Government Printing Bureau, Japan. Panes of 50. Designed by Mel Harris, United Kingdom (No. 55) and Vreni Wyss-Fischer, Switzerland (No. 56).

1985, Nov. 22 Photo. & Engr. *Perf. 13½*

55 A226 4s Spoonfeeding children *(889,918)* .75 .75
First day cover 1.50
Inscription block of 4 3.50 —
56 A226 6s Mother hugging infant *(852,958)* 1.40 1.40
First day cover 1.50
First day cover, #55-56 2.50
Inscription block of 4 6.00 —

First day covers of Nos. 55-56 total 239,532.

Africa in Crisis Type

Printed by Helio Courvoisier, Switzerland. Panes of 50. Designed by Tesfaye Tessema, Ethiopia.

1986, Jan. 31 Photo. *Perf. 11½x12*

57 A227 8s **multicolored** *(809,854)* .80 .80
First day cover *(99,996)* 2.75
Inscription block of 4 3.50 —

UN Development Program Type

Agriculture. Printed by the Government Printing Bureau, Japan. Panes of 40, 2 blocks of 4 horizontal and 5 blocks of 4 vertical. Designed by Thomas Lee, China.

1986, Mar. 14 Photo. *Perf. 13½*

58 A228 4.50s Developing crop strains *(730,691)* 1.50 1.25
59 A228 4.50s Animal husbandry *(730,691)* 1.50 1.25
60 A228 4.50s Technical instruction *(730,691)* 1.50 1.25
61 A228 4.50s Nutrition education *(730,691)* 1.50 1.25
a. Block of 4, #58-61 6.25 5.50
First day cover, #61a 6.00
First day cover, #58-61, each 2.00
Inscription block of 4, #58-61 7.00 —
Pane of 40, #58-61 87.50

No. 61a has a continuous design.
First day covers of Nos. 58-61 total 227,664.

Stamp Collecting Type

Designs: 3.50s, UN stamps. 6.50s, Engraver. Printed by the Swedish Post Office, Sweden. Panes of 50. Designed by Czeslaw Slania and Ingalill Axelsson, Sweden.

1986, May 22 Engr. *Perf. 12½*

62 A229 3.50s **dk ultra & dk brown** *(874,119)* .40 .40
First day cover 1.50
Inscription block of 4 2.25 —
63 A229 6.50s **int blue & brt rose** *(877,284)* .90 .90
First day cover 1.50
First day cover, #62-63 2.25
Inscription block of 4 4.50 —

First day covers of Nos. 62-63 total 150,836.

Olive Branch, Rainbow, Earth — V17

International Peace Year. Printed by the Government Printing Bureau, Japan. Panes of 50. Designed by Milo Schor, Israel (No. 64), and Mohammad Sardar, Pakistan (No. 65).

Photogravure & Embossed

1986, June 20 *Perf. 13½*

64 V17 5s shown *(914,699)* .75 .75
First day cover 1.50
Inscription block of 4 3.75 —
65 V17 6s Doves, UN emblem *(818,386)* 1.00 1.00
First day cover 1.50
First day cover, #64-65 2.50
Inscription block of 4 4.50 —

First day covers of Nos. 64-65 total 169,551.

WFUNA Anniversary Type

Souvenir Sheet

Printed by Johann Enschede and Sons, Netherlands. Designed by Rocco J. Callari, US.

Designs: 4s, White stallion by Elisabeth von Janota-Bzowski, Germany. 5s, Surrealistic landscape by Ernst Fuchs, Austria. 6s, Geometric abstract by Victor Vasarely (b. 1908), France. 7s, Mythological abstract by Wolfgang Hutter (b. 1928), Austria.

1986, Nov. 14 Litho. *Perf. 13x13½*

66 Sheet of 4 *(668,264)* 4.00 4.00
a. A232 4s **multicolored** .75 .75
b. A232 5s **multicolored** .85 .85
c. A232 6s **multicolored** 1.00 1.00
d. A232 7s **multicolored** 1.25 1.25
First day cover *(121,852)* 4.00

No. 66 has inscribed margin picturing UN and WFUNA emblems.

Trygve Lie Type

Photogravure & Engraved

1987, Jan. 30 *Perf. 13½*

67 A233 8s **multicolored** *(778,010)* .70 .70
First day cover *(94,112)* 2.50
Inscription block of 4 3.50 —

Shelter for the Homeless Type

Designs: 4s, Family and homes. 9.50s, Family entering home.

1987, Mar. 13 Litho. *Perf. 13½x12½*

68 A234 4s **multicolored** *(704,922)* .50 .50
First day cover 1.25
Inscription block of 4 2.40 —
69 A234 9.50s **multicolored** *(671,200)* 1.10 1.10

First day cover 1.75
First day cover, #68-69 2.75
Inscription block of 4 4.75 —

First day covers of Nos. 68-69 total 117,941.

Fight Drug Abuse Type

Designs: 5s, Soccer players. 8s, Family.

1987, June 12 Litho. *Perf. 14½x15*

70 A235 5s **multicolored** *(869,875)* .40 .40
First day cover 1.40
Inscription block of 4 2.40 —
71 A235 8s **multicolored** *(797,889)* .90 .90
First day cover 1.75
First day cover, #70-71 2.75
Inscription block of 4 4.00 —

First day covers of Nos. 70-71 total 117,964.

Donaupark, Vienna — V18

Peace Embracing the Earth — V19

Printed by The House of Questa, United Kingdom. Panes of 50. Designed by Henry Bencsath, US (2s), and Eliezer Weishoff, Israel (17s).

1987, June 12 Litho. *Perf. 14½x15*

72 V18 2s **multicolored** *(2,000,000)+* .30 .30
First day cover 1.25
Inscription block of 4 1.40 —
73 V19 17s **multicolored** *(2,000,000)+* 1.60 1.60
First day cover 2.50
First day cover, #72-73 3.50
Inscription block of 4 7.00 —

First day covers of Nos. 72-73 total 111,153.

UN Day Type

Designed by Elisabeth von Janota-Bzowski (5s) and Fritz Henry Oerter (6s), Federal Republic of Germany.
Designs: Multinational people in various occupations.

1987, Oct. 23 Litho. *Perf. 14½x15*

74 A236 5s **multicolored** *(1,575,731)* .75 .75
First day cover 1.40
Inscription block of 4 3.75 —
75 A236 6s **multicolored** *(1,540,523)* .90 .90
First day cover 1.75
First day cover, #74-75 2.75
Inscription block of 4 4.25 —
Panes of 12, #74-75 22.00

Immunize Every Child Type

Designs: 4s, Poliomyelitis. 9.50s, Diphtheria.

1987, Nov. 20 Litho. *Perf. 15x14½*

76 A237 4s **multicolored** *(793,716)* .75 .75
First day cover 1.00
Inscription block of 4 4.00 —
77 A237 9.50s **multicolored** *(769,288)* 2.00 2.00
First day cover 1.90
First day cover, #76-77 2.75
Inscription block of 4 8.25 —

IFAD Type

Designs: 4s, Grains. 6s, Vegetables.

1988, Jan. 29 Litho. *Perf. 13½*

78 A238 4s **multicolored** *(697,307)* .40 .40
First day cover 1.25
Inscription block of 4 2.75 —
79 A238 6s **multicolored** *(701,521)* .90 .90
First day cover 1.75
First day cover, #78-79 2.75
Inscription block of 4 4.25 —

Survival of the Forests Type

Deciduous forest in fall: 4s, Treetops, hills and dales. 5s, Tree trunks. Printed se-tenant in a continuous design.

1988, Mar. 18 Litho. *Perf. 14x15*

80 A240 4s **multicolored** *(990,607)* 2.25 2.25
First day cover 4.50
81 A240 5s **multicolored** *(990,607)* 3.00 3.00
First day cover 5.50
a. Pair, #80-81 5.25 5.25
First day cover, #81a 9.00
Inscription block of 4, #80-81 12.00 —
Pane of 12, #80-81 30.00

Intl. Volunteer Day Type

Designed by George Fernandez, U.S.
Designs: 6s, Medical care, vert. 7.50s, Construction.

1988, May 6 Litho. *Perf. 13x14, 14x13*

82 A241 6s **multicolored** *(701,167)* .75 .75
First day cover 1.40
Inscription block of 4 4.00 —
83 A241 7.50s **multicolored** *(638,240)* 1.00 1.00
First day cover 1.60
First day cover, #82-83 3.00
Inscription block of 4 5.75 —

Health in Sports Type

Paintings by LeRoy Neiman, American Sports artist: 6s, Skiing, vert. 8s, Tennis.

1988, June 17 Litho. *Perf. 13½x13, 13x13½*

84 A242 6s **multicolored** *(668,902)* .90 .90
First day cover 1.40
Inscription block of 4 5.00 —
85 A242 8s **multicolored** *(647,915)* 1.40 1.40
First day cover 2.00
First day cover #84-85 4.00
Inscription block of 4 8.50 —

Universal Declaration of Human Rights 40th Anniv. Type

1988, Dec. 9 Photo. & Engr. *Perf. 11½*

86 A243 5s **multicolored** *(1,080,041)* .50 .50
First day cover 2.50
Inscription block of 4 3.00 —

Souvenir Sheet

87 A243 11s **multicolored** *(688,994)* 1.25 1.25
First day cover 4.75

No. 87 has multicolored decorative margin inscribed with preamble to the human rights declaration in German.

World Bank Type

1989, Jan. 27 Litho. *Perf. 13x14*

88 A244 5.50s Transportation *(682,124)* 1.10 1.10
First day cover 1.40
Inscription block of 4 5.25 —
89 A244 8s Health care, education *(628,649)* 1.75 1.75
First day cover 2.00
First day cover, #88-89 3.00
Inscription block of 4 8.25 —

First day covers of Nos. 88-89 total 135,964.

Peace-Keeping Force Type

1989, Mar. 17 *Perf. 14x13½*

90 A245 6s **multicolored** *(912,731)* .85 .85
First day cover *(81,837)* 2.00
Inscription block of 4 4.00 —

World Weather Watch Type

Satellite photograph and radar image: 4s, Helical cloud formation over Italy, the eastern Alps, and parts of Yugoslavia. 9.50s, Rainfall in Tokyo, Japan.

1989, Apr. 21 Litho. *Perf. 13x14*

91 A247 4s **multicolored** *(948,680)* 1.00 1.00
First day cover 1.40
Inscription block of 4 4.50 —
92 A247 9.50s **multicolored** *(880,138)* 2.10 2.10
First day cover 2.00
First day cover, #91-92 4.00
Inscription block of 4 10.50 —

First day covers of Nos. 91-92 total 116,846.

Offices in Vienna, 10th Anniv.
V20 V21

Printed by the Government Printing Office, Austria. Panes of 25. Designed by Gottfried Kumpf (5s) and Andre Heller (7.50s), Austria.

Photo. & Engr., Photo. (7.50s)

1989, Aug. 23 *Perf. 14*

93 V20 5s **multicolored** *(958,339)* 2.25 2.25
First day cover 1.25
Inscription block of 4 11.50 —
94 V21 7.50s **multicolored** *(785,517)* 2.25 2.25
First day cover 3.00
First day cover, #93-94 4.00
Inscription block of 4 11.50 —
Panes of 25, #93-94 *100.00*

First day covers of Nos. 93-94 total 210,746.

Human Rights Type of 1989

Panes of 12+12 se-tenant labels containing Articles 5 (4s) or 6 (6s) inscribed in German, English or French.
Paintings: 4s, The Prisoners, by Kathe Kollwitz. 6s, Justice, by Raphael.

1989, Nov. 17 Litho. *Perf. 13½*

95 A250 4s **multicolored** *(2,267,450)* .50 .50
First day cover 2.50
Inscription block of 3 + 3 labels 1.75 —
96 A250 6s **multicolored** *(2,264,876)* .75 .75
First day cover 3.50
First day cover, #95-96 3.00
Inscription block of 3 + 3 labels 2.50 —
Panes of 12, #95-96 15.00

First day covers of Nos. 95-96 total 183,199.
See Nos. 108-109, 123-124, 150-151.

Intl. Trade Center Type

1990, Feb. 2 Litho. *Perf. 14½x15*

97 A251 12s **multicolored** *(559,556)* 1.50 1.50
First day cover *(77,928)* 4.00
Inscription block of 4 6.75 —

Painting by Kurt Regschek V22

Printed by the National Postage Stamps and Fiduciary Printing Works, France. Designed by Robert J. Stein, US.

1990, Feb. 2 Litho. *Perf. 13x13½*

98 V22 1.50s **multicolored** *(1,000,000)+* .30 .30
First day cover *(64,622)* 2.50
Inscription block of 4 1.40 —

Fight AIDS Type

Designed by Jacek Tofil, Poland (5s), Orlando Pelaez, Colombia (11s).
Designs: 5s, "SIDA." 11s, Stylized figures, ink blot.

1990, Mar. 16 Litho. *Perf. 13½x12½*

99 A252 5s **multicolored** *(623,155)* 1.00 1.00
First day cover 1.50
Inscription block of 4 6.00 —
100 A252 11s **multicolored** *(588,742)* 2.25 2.25
First day cover 2.50
First day cover, #99-100 4.75
Inscription block of 4 11.50 —

First day covers of Nos. 99-100 total 123,657.

Medicinal Plants Type

1990, May 4 Photo. Granite Paper *Perf. 11½*

101 A253 4.50s Bixa orellana *(709,840)* 1.25 1.25
First day cover 1.50
Inscription block of 4 5.50 —
102 A253 9.50s Momordica charantia *(732,883)* 2.50 2.50
First day cover 2.50
First day cover, #101-102 4.75
Inscription block of 4 10.50 —

First day covers of Nos. 101-102 total 117,545.

UN 45th Anniv. Type

Designed by Talib Nauman, Pakistan (7s), Marleen Bosmans (9s), Robert Stein, US (No. 105).
Designs: 7s, 9s, "45" and emblem.

1990, June 26 Litho. *Perf. 14½x13*

103 A254 7s **multicolored** *(604,878)* 1.40 1.40
First day cover 1.75
Inscription block of 4 6.00 —
104 A254 9s **multicolored, diff.** *(550,902)* 2.40 2.40
First day cover 2.25
First day cover, #103-104 4.00
Inscription block of 4 10.50 —

Souvenir Sheet

105 Sheet of 2, #103-104 *(423,370)* 5.50 5.50
First day cover 5.00

First day covers of Nos. 103-105 total 181,174.

Crime Prevention Type

1990, Sept. 13 Photo. *Perf. 14*

106 A255 6s Domestic violence *(661,810)* 1.00 1.00
First day cover 1.50
Inscription block of 4 5.50 —
107 A255 8s Crimes against cultural heritage *(607,940)* 2.25 2.25

First day cover 2.25
First day cover, #106-107 3.00
Inscription block of 4 11.00 —

First day covers of Nos. 106-107 total 112,193.

Human Rights Type of 1989

Panes of 12+12 se-tenant labels containing Articles 11 (4.50s) or 12 (7s) inscribed in German, English or French.
Paintings: 4.50s, Before the Judge, by Sandor Bihari. 7s, Young Man Greeted by a Woman Writing a Poem, by Suzuki Harunobu.

1990, Nov. 16 Litho. *Perf. 13½*
108 A250 4.50s **multicolored** *(1,684,833)* .30 .30
First day cover 2.50
Inscription block of 3 + 3 labels 1.25 —
109 A250 7s **multicolored** *(1,541,022)* .90 .90
First day cover 3.50
First day cover, #108-109 2.50
Inscription block of 3 + 3 labels 4.25 —
Panes of 12, #108-109 20.00

First day covers of Nos. 108-109 total 168,831.

Economic Commission for Europe Type

1991, Mar. 15 Litho. *Perf. 14*
110 A256 5s Weasel, hoopoe *(727,436)* 1.10 1.10
111 A256 5s Warbler, swans *(727,436)* 1.10 1.10
112 A256 5s Badgers, squirrel *(727,436)* 1.10 1.10
113 A256 5s Fish *(727,436)* 1.10 1.10
a. Block of 4, #110-113 4.50 4.50
First day cover, No. 113a 5.00
First day cover, Nos. 110-113, each 3.25
Inscription block of 4, #110-113 5.50 —
Pane of 40, #110-113 50.00

First day covers of Nos. 110-113 total 81,624.

Namibian Independence Type

1991, May 10 Litho. *Perf. 14*
114 A257 6s Mountains, clouds *(531,789)* 1.25 1.50
First day cover 2.50
Inscription block of 4 5.25 —
115 A257 9.50s Dune, Namib Desert *(503,735)* 2.75 2.75
First day cover 3.75
First day cover, #114-115 4.50
Inscription block of 4 11.50 —

First day covers of Nos. 114-115 total 111,184.

V24

Printed by House of Questa, United Kingdom. Designed by Marina Langer-Rosa, Germany.

1991, May 10 Litho. *Perf. 15x14½*
116 V24 20s **multicolored** *(1,750,000)+* 3.50 3.50
First day cover *(60,843)* 4.00
Inscription block of 4 14.50 —

V25

Rights of the Child — V26

Printed by The House of Questa. Panes of 50. Designed by Anna Harmer, Austria (7s) and Emiko Takegawa, Japan (9s).

1991, June 14 Litho. *Perf. 14½*
117 V25 7s Stick drawings *(645,145)* 1.50 1.50
First day cover 1.75
Inscription block of 4 6.25 —
118 V26 9s Child, clock, fruit *(568,214)* 2.00 2.00
First day cover 2.25
First day cover, #117-118 3.50
Inscription block of 4 8.50 —

First day covers of Nos. 117-118 total 120,619.

V27

Banning of Chemical Weapons V28

Printed by Heraclio Fournier, S.A. Panes of 50. Designed by Oscar Asboth, Austria (5s), Michel Granger, France (10s).

1991, Sept. 11 Litho. *Perf. 13½*
119 V27 5s **multicolored** *(469,454)* 1.00 1.00
First day cover 1.40
Inscription block of 4 4.50 —
120 V28 10s **multicolored** *(525,704)* 2.25 2.25
First day cover 2.50
First day cover, #119-120 3.00
Inscription block of 4 10.00 —

First day covers of Nos. 119-120 total 116,862.

UN Postal Administration, 40th Anniv. Type

1991, Oct. 24 Litho. *Perf. 14x15*
121 A263 5s UN NY No. 8 *(564,450)* .75 .75
First day cover 1.40
Inscription block of 4 4.00 —
122 A263 8s UN NY No. 5 *(609,830)* 1.75 1.75
First day cover 2.10
First day cover, #121-122 3.25
Inscription block of 4 9.00 —
Panes of 25, #121-122 60.00

First day covers of Nos. 121-122 total 107,802.

Human Rights Type of 1989

Panes of 12+12 se-tenant labels containing Articles 17 (4.50s) or 18 (7s) inscribed in German, English or French.
Artwork: 4.50s, Pre-columbian Mexican pottery. 7s, Windows, by Robert Delaunay.

1991, Nov. 20 Litho. *Perf. 13½*
123 A250 4.50s **black & brown** *(1,717,097)* .50 .50
First day cover 2.75
Inscription block of 3 + 3 labels 3.00 —
124 A250 7s **multicolored** *(1,717,738)* .80 .80
First day cover 5.00
First day cover, #123-124 1.75
Inscription block of 3 + 3 labels 5.00 —
Panes of 12+12 labels, #123-124 25.00 25.00

First day covers of Nos. 123-124 total 204,854.

World Heritage Type of 1984

Designs: 5s, Iguacu Natl. Park, Brazil. 9s, Abu Simbel, Egypt.

1992, Jan. 24 Litho. *Perf. 13*
Size: 35x28mm
125 V10 5s **multicolored** *(586,738)* 1.25 1.25
First day cancel 1.50
Inscription block of 4 5.75 —
126 V10 9s **multicolored** *(476,965)* 2.25 2.25
First day cancel 2.75
First day cancel, #125-126 4.00
Inscription block of 4 9.00 —

First day covers of Nos. 125-126 total 93,016.

Clean Oceans Type

1992, Mar. 13 Litho. *Perf. 14*
127 A264 7s Ocean surface, diff. *(1,121,870)* 1.00 1.00
128 A264 7s Ocean bottom, diff. *(1,121,870)* 1.00 1.00
a. Pair, #127-128 2.25 2.25
First day cover, #128a 3.25
First day cover, #127-128, any single 2.00
Inscription block of 4, 2 each #127-128 5.00 —
Pane of 12, #127-128 14.00

First day covers of Nos. 127-128 total 128,478.

Earth Summit Type

1992, May 22 Photo. *Perf. 11½*
129 A265 5.50s Man in space *(784,197)* 1.30 1.30
130 A265 5.50s Sun *(784,197)* 1.30 1.30
131 A265 5.50s Man fishing *(784,197)* 1.30 1.30
132 A265 5.50s Sailboat *(784,197)* 1.30 1.30
a. Block of 4, #129-132 5.50 5.50
First day cover, #132a 6.00
First day cover, #129-132, any single 4.00
Inscription block of 4, #129-132 7.00 —
Pane of 40, #129-132 60.00

First day covers of Nos. 129-132a total 82,920.

Mission to Planet Earth Type

Designs: No. 133, Satellite, person's mouth. No. 134, Satellite, person's ear.

1992, Sept. 4 Photo. *Rouletted 8*
Granite Paper
133 A266 10s **multicolored** *(881,716)* 2.50 2.50
134 A266 10s **multicolored** *(881,716)* 2.50 2.50
a. Pair, #133-134 5.00 5.00
First day cover, #134a 4.50
First day cover, #133-134, any single 7.50
Inscription block of 4, #133-134 12.50 —
Pane of 10, #133-134 30.00

First day covers of Nos. 133-134 total 99,459.

Science and Technology Type of 1992

Designs: 5.50s, Woman emerging from computer screen. 7s, Green thumb growing flowers.

1992, Oct. 2 Litho. *Perf. 14*
135 A267 5.50s **multicolored** *(482,830)* .75 .75
First day cover 1.75
Inscription block of 4 3.75 —
136 A267 7s **multicolored** *(500,517)* 1.40 1.40
First day cover 2.00
First day cover, #135-136 4.00
Inscription block of 4 6.75 —

First day covers of Nos. 135-136 total 98,091.

V29

Intl. Center, Vienna — V30

Printed by Walsall Secruity Printers, Ltd., UK. Designed by Gundi Groh, Austria (5.50s), Rocco J. Callari, US (7s).

1992, Oct. 2 Litho. *Perf. 13x13½*
137 V29 5.50s **multicolored** *(2,100,000)+* .90 .90
First day cover 1.25
Inscription block of 4 4.25 —

Perf. 13½x13
138 V30 7s **multicolored** *(2,100,000)+* 1.25 1.25
First day cover 2.00
First day cover, #137-138 3.50
Inscription block of 4 6.00 —

First day covers of Nos. 137-138 total 151,788.

Human Rights Type of 1989

Panes of 12+12 se-tenant labels containing Articles 23 (6s) and 24 (10s) inscribed in German, English or French.
Artwork: 6s, Les Constructeurs, by Fernand Leger. 10s, Sunday Afternoon on the Island of Le Grande Jatte, by Georges Seurat.

1992, Nov. 20 Litho. *Perf. 13½*
139 A250 6s **multicolored,** *(1,536,516)* .75 .75
First day cover 3.50
Inscription block of 3 + 3 labels 3.00 —
140 A250 10s **multicolored,** *(1,527,861)* 1.25 1.25
First day cover 5.00
Inscription block of 3 + 3 labels 5.50 —
First day cover, #139-140 2.00
Panes of 12, #139-140 30.00 30.00

Aging With Dignity Type

Designs: 5.50s, Elderly couple, family working in garden. 7s, Older woman teaching.

1993, Feb. 5 **Litho.** ***Perf. 13***

141 A270 5.50s **multicolored** *(428,886)* .75 .75
First day cover 1.60
Inscription block of 4 4.50 —
142 A270 7s **multicolored** *(459,471)* 1.40 1.40
First day cover 2.00
First day cover, #141-142 3.00
Inscription block of 4 7.50 —

First day covers of Nos. 141-142 total 87,052.

Endangered Species Type

Designed by Rocco J. Callari and Steve Brennan, US.

Designs: No. 143, Equus grevyi (Grevy's zebra). No. 144, Spheniscus humboldti (Humboldt's penguins). No. 145, Varanus griseus (desert monitor). No. 146, Canis lupus (gray wolf).

1993, Mar. 2 **Litho.** ***Perf. 13x12½***

143 A271 7s **multicolored** *(1,200,000)+* 1.05 1.05
144 A271 7s **multicolored** *(1,200,000)+* 1.05 1.05
145 A271 7s **multicolored** *(1,200,000)+* 1.05 1.05
146 A271 7s **multicolored** *(1,200,000)+* 1.05 1.05
a. Block of 4, #143-146 4.25 4.25
First day cover, #146a 5.25
First day cover, #143-146, any single 1.75
Inscription block of 4, #146a 5.00 —
Pane of 16, #143-146 18.00

First day covers of Nos. 143-146a total 106,211.

Healthy Environment Type

1993, May 7 **Litho.** ***Perf. 15x14½***

147 A272 6s **Wave in ocean** *(517,433)* 1.25 1.25
First day cover 1.50
Inscription block of 4 5.25
148 A272 10s **Globe** *(453,123)* 2.00 2.00
First day cover 2.25
First day cover, #147-148 3.50
Inscription block of 4 8.75 —

First day covers of Nos. 147-148 total 79,773.

V31

Designed by Marek Kwiatkowski, Poland. Printed by Helio Courvoisier S.A., Switzerland.

1993, May 7 **Photo.** ***Perf. 11½***
Granite Paper

149 V31 13s **multicolored** *(1,500,000)+* 2.50 2.50
Inscription block of 4 10.50 —

Human Rights Type of 1989

Printed in sheets of 12 + 12 se-tenant labels containing Article 29 (5s) and 30 (6s) inscribed in German, English or French.

Artwork: 5s, Lower Austrian Peasants' Wedding, by Ferdinand G. Waldmuller. 6s, Outback, by Sally Morgan.

1993, June 11 **Litho.** ***Perf. 13½***

150 A250 5s **multicolored** *(1,532,531)* 1.00 1.00
First day cover 2.50
Inscription block of 3 + 3 labels 4.00 —
151 A250 6s **multicolored** *(1,542,716)* 1.25 1.25
First day cover 3.50
First day cover, #150-151 1.50
Inscription block of 3 + 3 labels 5.00 —
Panes of 12, #150-151 28.00 25.00

First day covers of Nos. 150-151 total 128,687.

Intl. Peace Day Type

Denomination at: No. 152, UL. No. 153, UR. No. 154, LL. No. 155, LR.

1993, Sept. 21 **Litho. & Engr.** ***Rouletted 12½***

152 A274 5.50s **green & multi** *(445,699)* 1.80 1.80
153 A274 5.50s **green & multi** *(445,699)* 1.80 1.80
154 A274 5.50s **green & multi** *(445,699)* 1.80 1.80
155 A274 5.50s **green & multi** *(445,699)* 1.80 1.80
a. Block of 4, #152-155 7.25 7.25
First day cover, #155a 4.00
First day cover, #152-155, any single 2.25
Inscription block of 4, #155a 8.75 —
Pane of 40, #152-155 80.00

First day covers of Nos. 152-155a total 67,075.

Environment-Climate Type

Designs: No. 156, Monkeys. No. 157, Bluebird, industrial pollution, volcano. No. 158, Volcano, nuclear power plant, tree stumps. No. 159, Cactus, tree stumps, owl.

1993, Oct. 29 **Litho.** ***Perf. 14½***

156 A275 7s **multicolored** *(484,517)* 2.00 2.00
157 A275 7s **multicolored** *(484,517)* 2.00 2.00
158 A275 7s **multicolored** *(484,517)* 2.00 2.00
159 A275 7s **multicolored** *(484,517)* 2.00 2.00
a. Strip of 4, #156-159 8.00 8.00
First day cover, #159a 9.50
First day cover, #156-159, any single 4.00
Inscription block of 8, 2 #159a 21.00 —
Pane of 24, #156-159 47.50

First day covers of Nos. 156-159a total 61,946.

Intl. Year of the Family Type of 1993

Designs: 5.50s, Adults, children holding hands. 8s, Two adults, child planting crops.

1994, Feb. 4 **Litho.** ***Perf. 13.1***

160 A276 5.50s **blue green & multi** *(650,000)+* 1.20 1.20
First day cover 1.60
Inscription block of 4 5.00 —
161 A276 8s **red & multi** *(650,000)+* 1.80 1.80
First day cover 2.25
First day cover, #160-161 3.00
Inscription block of 4 8.00 —

First day covers of Nos. 160-161 total 78,532.

Endangered Species Type of 1993

Designed by Rocco J. Callari, US (frame), and Paul Margocsy, Australia (stamps).

Designs: No. 162, Ocelot. No. 163, White-breasted silver-eye. No. 164, Mediterranean monk seal. No. 165, Asian elephant.

1994, Mar. 18 **Litho.** ***Perf. 12.7***

162 A271 7s **multicolored** *(1,200,000)+* 1.30 1.30
163 A271 7s **multicolored** *(1,200,000)+* 1.30 1.30
164 A271 7s **multicolored** *(1,200,000)+* 1.30 1.30
165 A271 7s **multicolored** *(1,200,000)+* 1.30 1.30
a. Block of 4, #162-165 5.25 5.25
First day cover, #165a 6.00
First day cover, #162-165, each 2.25
Inscription block of 4, #165a 5.75 —
Pane of 16, #162-165 21.00

First day covers of Nos. 162-165a total 104,478.

Protection for Refugees Type

Design: 12s, Protective hands surround group of refugees.

1994, Apr. 29 **Litho.** ***Perf. 14.3x14.8***

166 A277 12s **multicolored** *(650,000)+* 1.50 1.50
First day cover *(49,519)* 3.00
Inscription block of 4 8.00 —

V32

V33

V34

Designed by Masatoshi Hioki, Japan (#167), Ramon Alcantara Rodriguez, Mexico (#168), Eliezer Weishoff, Israel (#169).

Printed by Cartor, S.A., France.

1994, Apr. 29 **Litho.** ***Perf. 12.9***

167 V32 50g **multicolored** *(1,450,000)+* .20 .20
First day cover 1.25
Inscription block of 4 .40 —
168 V33 4s **multicolored** *(1,150,000)+* .50 .50
First day cover 1.25
Inscription block of 4 2.75 —
169 V34 30s **multicolored** *(560,000)+* 4.50 4.5
First day cover 5.0
Inscription block of 4 20.00 —

First day covers of Nos. 167-169 total 74,558.

Intl. Decade for Natural Disaster Reduction Type

Earth seen from space, outline map of: No. 170, North America. No. 171, Eurasia. No. 172, South America. No. 173, Australia and South Asia.

1994, May 27 **Litho.** ***Perf. 13.9x14.***

170 A281 6s **multicolored** *(690,000)+* 1.75 1.7
171 A281 6s **multicolored** *(690,000)+* 1.75 1.7
172 A281 6s **multicolored** *(690,000)+* 1.75 1.7
173 A281 6s **multicolored** *(690,000)+* 1.75 1.7
a. Block of 4, #170-173 7.00 7.0
First day cover, #173a 6.0
First day cover, #170-173, each 3.2
Inscription block of 4, #173a 8.50 —
Pane of 40, #170-173 82.50

First day covers of Nos. 170-173a total 52,502.

Population and Development Type

Designs: 5.50s, Women teaching, running machine tool, coming home to family. 7s, Family on tropical island.

1994, Sept. 1 **Litho.** ***Perf. 13.2x13.***

174 A282 5.50s **multicolored** *(650,000)+* 1.50 1.5
First day cover 2.0
Inscription block of 4 6.25 —
175 A282 7s **multicolored** *(650,000)+* 2.00 2.0
First day cover 2.0
First day cover, #174-175 5.0
Inscription block of 4 8.50 —

First day covers of Nos. 174-175 total 67,423.

UNCTAD Type

1994, Oct. 28

176 A283 6s **multi, diff.** *(650,000)+* 1.25 1.2
First day cover 1.2
Inscription block of 4 6.25 —
177 A283 7s **multi, diff.** *(650,000)+* 1.50 1.5
First day cover 1.7
First day cover, #176-177 3.0
Inscription block of 4 7.00 —

First day covers of Nos. 176-177 total 67,064.

UN 50th Anniv. Type

1995, Jan. 1 **Litho. & Engr.** ***Perf. 13.4***

178 A284 7s **multicolored** *(742,052)* 1.25 1.2
First day cover *(118,537)* 2.0
Inscription block of 4 5.50 —

Social Summit Type

1995, Feb. 3 **Photo. & Engr.** ***Perf. 13.6x13.***

179 A285 14s **multi, diff.** *(595,554)* 2.25 2.2
First day cover *(51,244)* 3.5
Inscription block of 4 11.00 —

Endangered Species Type of 1993

Designed by Salvatore Catalano, US.

Designs: No. 180, Black rhinoceros, Diceros bicornis. No. 181, Golden conure, Aratinga guarouba. No. 182, Douc langur, Pygathrix nemaeus. No. 183, Arabian oryx, Oryx leucoryx.

1995, Mar. 24 **Litho.** ***Perf. 13x12½***

180 A271 7s **multicolored** *(938,000)+* 1.00 1.0
181 A271 7s **multicolored** *(938,000)+* 1.00 1.0
182 A271 7s **multicolored** *(938,000)+* 1.00 1.0
183 A271 7s **multicolored** *(938,000)+* 1.00 1.0
a. Block of 4, 180-183 4.00 4.0
First day cover, #183a 4.5
First day cover, #180-183, each 2.0
Inscription block of 4, #183a 5.00 —
Pane of 16, #180-183 17.50

First day covers of Nos. 180-183a total 95,401.

Intl. Youth Year Type

Designs: 6s, Village in winter. 7s, Teepees.

1995, May 26 **Litho.** ***Perf. 14.4x14.***

184 A286 6s **multicolored** *(437,462)* 1.50 1.5
First day cover 1.5
Inscription block of 4 6.00 —
185 A286 7s **multicolored** *(409,449)* 1.75 1.7
First day cover 2.5
First day cover, #184-185 4.2
Inscription block of 4 7.50 —

First day covers of Nos. 184-185 total 60,979.

UN, 50th Anniv. Type

Designs: 7s, Like No. 663. 10s, Like No. 664.

1995, June 26 **Engr.** ***Perf. 13.3x13.***

186 A287 7s **green** *(433,922)* 1.25 1.2
First day cover 2.0
Inscription block of 4 5.50 —
187 A287 10s **black** *(471,198)* 2.00 2.0
First day cover 1.7
First day cover, #186-187 4.0
Inscription block of 4 9.00 —

Souvenir Sheet
Litho. & Engr.
Imperf

188 Sheet of 2, #186-187 *(367,773)* 4.50 4.50
a. A287 7s **green** 1.75 1.75
b. A287 10s **black** 2.50 2.50
First day cover 6.50

First day covers of Nos. 186-188b total 171,765.

Conference on Women Type

Designs: 5.50s, Women amid tropical plants. 6s, Woman reading, swans on lake.

1995, Sept. 5 Photo. *Perf. 12*
189 A288 5.50s **multicolored** *(549,951)* 1.25 1.25
First day cover 1.50
Inscription block of 4 5.25 —

Size: 28x50mm

190 A288 6s **multicolored** *(556,569)* 2.25 2.25
First day cover 1.50
First day cover, #189-190 3.50
Inscription block of 4 9.50 —

First day covers of Nos. 189-190 total 71,976.

UN People, 50th Anniv. Type

1995, Oct. 24 Litho. *Perf. 14*
191 Sheet of 12 *(280,528 sheets)* 16.00 16.00
First day cover 16.00
a.-l. A290 3s any single 1.30 1.30
First day cover, #191a-191 l, each 1.25
192 Souvenir booklet, *(95,449 booklets)* 19.00
a. A290 3s Booklet pane of 3, vert. strip of 3 from UL of sheet 4.75 4.75
b. A290 3s Booklet pane of 3, vert. strip of 3 from UR of sheet 4.75 4.75
c. A290 3s Booklet pane of 3, vert. strip of 3 from LL of sheet 4.75 4.75
d. A290 3s Booklet pane of 3, vert. strip of 3 from LR of sheet 4.75 4.75

First day covers of Nos. 191-192d total 107,436.

WFUNA, 50th Anniv. Type

Design: 7s, Harlequin holding dove.

1996, Feb. 2 Litho. *Perf. 13x13½*
193 A291 7s **multicolored** *(655,000)+* 1.25 1.25
First day cover 2.00
Inscription block of 4 6.00 —

UN Flag — V35

Abstract, by Karl Korab — V36

Printed by House of Questa, UK.

1996, Feb. 2 Litho. *Perf. 15x14½*
194 V35 1s **multicolored** *(1,180,000)+* .20 .20
First day cover 1.25
Inscription block of 4 .80 —
195 V36 10s **multicolored** *(880,000)+* 1.60 1.60
First day cover 2.75
First day cover, #194-195 4.50
Inscription block of 4 7.00 —

Endangered Species Type of 1993

Designs: No. 196, Cypripedium calceolus. No. 197, Aztekium ritteri. No. 198, Euphorbia cremersii. No. 199, Dracula bella.

1996, Mar. 14 Litho. *Perf. 12½*
196 A271 7s **multicolored** *(846,000)+* 1.00 1.00
197 A271 7s **multicolored** *(846,000)+* 1.00 1.00
198 A271 7s **multicolored** *(846,000)+* 1.00 1.00
199 A271 7s **multicolored** *(846,000)+* 1.00 1.00
a. Block of 4, #196-199 4.00 4.00
First day cover, #199a 4.50
First day cover, #196-199, each 2.00
Inscription block of 4, #199a 5.50 —
Pane of 16, #196-199 17.50

City Summit Type

Designs: No. 200, Arab family selling fruits, vegetables. No. 201, Women beside stream, camels. No. 202, Woman carrying bundle on head, city skyline. No. 203, Woman threshing grain, yoke of oxen in field. No. 204, Native village, elephant.

1996, June 3 Litho. *Perf. 14x13½*
200 A293 6s **multicolored** *(500,000)+* 1.50 1.50
201 A293 6s **multicolored** *(500,000)+* 1.50 1.50
202 A293 6s **multicolored** *(500,000)+* 1.50 1.50
203 A293 6s **multicolored** *(500,000)+* 1.50 1.50
204 A293 6s **multicolored** *(500,000)+* 1.50 1.50
a. Strip of 5, #200-204 7.50 7.50
First day cover, #204a 11.50
First day cover, #200-204, each 3.00
Inscription block of 10, 2 #204a 16.00

Sport and the Environment Type

6s, Men's parallel bars (gymnastics), vert. 7s, Hurdles.

1996, July 19 Litho. *Perf. 14x14½, 14½x14*
205 A294 6s **multicolored** *(730,000)+* 1.00 1.00
First day cover 2.75
Inscription block of 4 5.00 —
206 A294 7s **multicolored** *(730,000)+* 1.50 1.50
First day cover 3.00
First day cover, #205-206 6.00
Inscription block of 4 7.00 —

Souvenir Sheet

207 A294 Sheet of 2, #205-206 *(500,000)+* 2.50 2.50
First day cover 10.00

Plea for Peace Type

Designed by: 7s, Du Keqing, China. 10s, Xu Kangdeng, China.

Designs: 7s, Dove and butterflies. 10s, Stylized dove, diff.

1996, Sept. 17 Litho. *Perf. 14½x15*
208 A295 7s **multicolored** *(655,000)+* 1.00 1.00
First day cover 1.50
Inscription block of 4 4.75 —
209 A295 10s **multicolored** *(655,000)+* 2.00 2.00
First day cover 2.50
First day cover, #208-209 5.00
Inscription block of 4 9.00 —

UNICEF Type

Fairy Tales: 5.50s, Hansel and Gretel, by the Brothers Grimm. 8s, How Maui Stole Fire from the Gods, South Pacific.

1996, Nov. 20 Litho. *Perf. 14½x15*
210 A296 5.50s **multicolored** *(1,160,000)+* .90 .90
First day cover 1.25
Pane of 8 + label 8.00
211 A296 8s **multicolored** *(1,160,000)+* 1.40 1.40
First day cover 2.00
First day cover, #210-211 4.00
Pane of 8 + label 12.00

V37

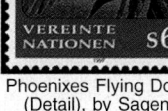

Phoenixes Flying Down (Detail), by Sagenji Yoshida — V38

Printed by The House of Questa, Ltd., UK.

1997, Feb. 12 Litho. *Perf. 14½*
212 V37 5s **multicolored** *(750,000)+* .80 .80
First day cover 1.25
Inscription block of 4 3.40 —
213 V38 6s **multicolored** *(1,050,000)+* .90 .90
First day cover 1.50
First day cover, #212-213 4.00
Inscription block of 4 4.00 —

First day covers of Nos. 212-213 total 156,021.

Endangered Species Type of 1993

Designs: No. 214, Macaca sylvanus (Barbary macaque). No. 215, Anthropoides paradisea (blue crane). No. 216, Equus przewalskii (Przewalski horse). No. 217, Myrmecophaga tridactyla (giant anteater).

1997, Mar. 13 Litho. *Perf. 12½*
214 A271 7s **multicolored** *(710,000)+* 1.10 1.10
215 A271 7s **multicolored** *(710,000)+* 1.10 1.10
216 A271 7s **multicolored** *(710,000)+* 1.10 1.10
217 A271 7s **multicolored** *(710,000)+* 1.10 1.10
a. Block of 4, #214-217 4.50 4.50
First day cover, #217a 6.00
First day cover, #214-217, each 2.50
Inscription block of 4, #217a 6.25
Pane of 16 25.00

First day covers of Nos. 214-217 total 86,406.

Earth Summit Anniv. Type

Designs: No. 218, Person running. No. 219, Hills, stream, trees. No. 220, Tree with orange leaves. No. 221, Tree with pink leaves.
11s, Combined design similar to Nos. 218-221.

1997, May 30 Photo. *Perf. 11.5*
Granite Paper
218 A299 3.50s **multicolored** *(282,016)* 1.25 1.25
219 A299 3.50s **multicolored** *(282,016)* 1.25 1.25
220 A299 3.50s **multicolored** *(282,016)* 1.25 1.25
221 A299 3.50s **multicolored** *(282,016)* 1.25 1.25
a. Block of 4, #218-221 5.00 5.00
First day cover, #221a 10.00
First day cover, #218-221, each 3.50
Inscription block of 4, #221a 6.00

Souvenir Sheet

222 A299 11s **multicolored** *(221,434)* 2.50 2.50
First day cover 12.00

First day covers of Nos. 218-222 total 62,390.

Transportation Type

Ground transportation: No. 223, 1829 Rocket, 1901 Darraque. No. 224, Steam engine from Vladikawska Railway, trolley. No. 225, Double-decker bus. No. 226, 1950s diesel locomotive, semi-trailer. No. 227, High-speed train, electric car.

1997, Aug. 29 Litho. *Perf. 14x14½*
223 A300 7s **multicolored** *(356,097)* 1.00 1.00
224 A300 7s **multicolored** *(356,097)* 1.00 1.00
225 A300 7s **multicolored** *(356,097)* 1.00 1.00
226 A300 7s **multicolored** *(356,097)* 1.00 1.00
227 A300 7s **multicolored** *(356,097)* 1.00 1.00
a. Strip of 5, #223-227 5.00 5.00
First day cover, #227a 16.00
First day cover, #223-227, each 4.75
Inscription block of 10, 2#227a 11.00

No. 227a has continuous design.
First day covers of Nos. 223-227 total 44,877.

Philately Type

Designs: 6.50s, No. 62. 7s, No. 63.

1997, Oct. 14 Litho. *Perf. 13½x14*
228 A301 6.50s **multicolored** *(379,767)* 1.00 1.00
First day cover 2.50
Inscription block of 4 5.25 —
229 A301 7s **multicolored** *(378,107)* 1.50 1.50
First day cover 3.50
First day cover, #228-229 6.00
Inscription block of 4 7.00 —

First day covers of Nos. 228-229 total 57,651.

World Heritage Convention Type

Terracotta warriors of Xian: 3s, Single warrior. 6s, Massed warriors. No. 232a, like #716. No. 232b, like #717. No. 232c, like Geneva #314. No. 232d, like Geneva #315. No. 232e, like Vienna #230. No. 232f, like Vienna #231.

1997, Nov. 19 Litho. *Perf. 13½*
230 A302 3s **multicolored** *(528,352)* 1.00 1.00
First day cover 1.50
Inscription block of 4 4.25 —
231 A302 6s **multicolored** *(530,947)* 2.00 2.00
First day cover 2.75
First day cover, #230-231 5.00
Inscription block of 4 9.00 —
232 Souvenir booklet *(298,055 booklets)* 8.00
a.-f. A302 1s any single .30 .30
g. Booklet pane of 4 #232a 1.25 1.25
h. Booklet pane of 4 #232b 1.25 1.25
i. Booklet pane of 4 #232c 1.25 1.25
j. Booklet pane of 4 #232d 1.25 1.25
k. Booklet pane of 4 #232e 1.25 1.25
l. Booklet pane of 4 #232f 1.25 1.25

First day covers of Nos. 230-232 total 71,708.

Japanese Peace Bell, Vienna — V39

Vienna Subway, Vienna Intl. Center — V40

Printed by The House of Questa, UK. Panes of 20.
Designed by Heinz Pfeifer, Austria (6.50s), Pigneter, Austria (9s).

1998, Feb. 13 Litho. *Perf. 15x14½*
233 V39 6.50s **multicolored** *(670,000)+* 1.00 1.00
First day cover 3.25
Inscription block of 4 4.50 —
234 V40 9s **multicolored** *(770,000)+* 1.50 1.50
First day cover 4.50
First day cover, #233-234 3.00
Inscription block of 4 6.25 —

Endangered Species Type of 1993

Designed by Rocco J. Callari, US and Robert Hynes, US.

Designs: No. 235, Chelonia mydas (green turtle). No. 236, Speotyto cunicularia (burrowing owl). No. 237, Trogonoptera brookiana (Rajah Brooke's birdwing). No. 238, Ailurus fulgens (lesser panda).

1998, Mar. 13 Litho. *Perf. 12½*

235 A271 7s **multicolored** *(620,000)+* 1.10 1.10
236 A271 7s **multicolored** *(620,000)+* 1.10 1.10
237 A271 7s **multicolored** *(620,000)+* 1.10 1.10
238 A271 7s **multicolored** *(620,000)+* 1.10 1.10
a. Block of 4, #235-238 4.50 4.50
First day cover, #238a 5.00
First day cover, #235-238, each 2.50
Inscription block of 4, #238a 5.00 —
Pane of 16 19.00

Intl. Year of the Ocean — V41

Designed by Yuan Lee, China.

1998, May 20 Litho. *Perf. 13x13½*

239 V41 Sheet of 12 *(345,000)+* 13.00 13.00
a.-l. 3.50s any single 1.10 1.10
First day cover, 3239 17.00
First day cover, #239a-239l, each 2.00

Rain Forests Type

1998, June 19 *Perf. 13x13½*

240 A307 6.50s Ocelot *(590,000)+* .90 .90
First day cover 4.00
Inscription block of 4 4.75 —

Souvenir Sheet

241 A307 22s like #240 *(340,000)+* 3.50 3.50
First day cover 5.25

Peacekeeping Type of 1998

Designs: 4s, Soldier passing out relief supplies. 7.50s, UN supervised voting.

1998, Sept. 15 Photo. *Perf. 12*

242 A308 4s multicolored *(555,000)+* .70 .70
First day cover 1.25
Inscription block of 4 2.80 —
243 A308 7.50s multicolored *(545,000)+* 1.25 1.25
First day cover 1.75
First day cover, #242-243 4.00
Inscription block of 4 5.25 —

Declaration of Human Rights Type

Designs: 4.50s, Stylized person. 7s, Gears.

1998, Oct. 27 Litho. & Photo. *Perf. 13*

244 A309 4.50s multicolored *(555,000)+* .80 .80
First day cover 1.50
Inscription block of 4 3.25 —
245 A309 7s multicolored *(545,000)+* 1.25 1.25
First day cover 2.75
First day cover, #244-245 4.00
Inscription block of 4 5.00 —

Schönbrunn Palace Type

Designs: 3.50s, #248d, Palace. 7s, #248c, Porcelain stove, vert. No. 248a, Blue porcelain vase, vert. No. 248b, Wall painting on fabric (detail), by Johann Wenzl Bergl, vert. No. 248e, Great Palm House (conservatory). No. 248f, The Gloriette (archway).

1998, Dec. 4 Litho. *Perf. 14*

246 A310 3.50s **multicolored** *(615,000)+* .60 .60
First day cover 2.00
Inscription block of 4 2.50 —
247 A310 7s **multicolored** *(615,000)+* 1.10 1.10
First day cover 2.75
First day cover, #246-247 4.00
Inscription block of 4 4.50 —

Souvenir Booklet

248 Booklet *(158,000)+* 9.00
a.-c. A310 1s any single .25 .25
d.-f. A310 2s any single .55 .55
g. Booklet pane of 4 #248d 2.20 2.20
h. Booklet pane of 3 #248a .75 .75
i. Booklet pane of 3 #248b .75 .75
j. Booklet pane of 3 #248c .75 .75
k. Booklet pane of 4 #248e 2.20 2.20
l. Booklet pane of 4 #248f 2.20 2.20

Volcanic Landscape — V42

Designed by Peter Pongratz, Austria. Printed by Johann Enschedé and Sons, the Netherlands.

1999, Feb. 5 Litho. *Perf. 13x13½*

249 V42 8s **multicolored** *(660,000)+* 1.50 1.50
First day cover *(33,022)* 4.00
Inscription block of 4 7.50 —

World Heritage, Australia Type

Designs: 4.50s, #252d, Uluru-Kata Tjuta Natl. Park. 6.50s, #252a, Tasmanian Wilderness. No. 252b, Wet tropics of Queensland. No. 252c, Great Barrier Reef. No. 252e, Kakadu Natl. Park. No. 252f, Willandra Lakes region.

1999, Mar. 19 Litho. *Perf. 13*

250 A313 4.50s **multicolored** *(540,000)+* .75 .75
First day cover 1.25
Inscription block of 4 3.00 —
251 A313 6.50s **multicolored** *(540,000)+* 1.10 1.10
First day cover 1.50
First day cover, #250-251 4.50
Inscription block of 4 4.50 —

Souvenir Booklet

252 Booklet *(116,000)+* 7.50
a.-c. A313 1s any single .20 .20
d.-f. A313 2s any single .40 .40
g. Booklet pane of 4, #252a .80 .80
h. Booklet pane of 4, #252d 1.60 1.60
i. Booklet pane of 4, #252b .80 .80
j. Booklet pane of 4, #252e 1.60 1.60
k. Booklet pane of 4, #252c .80 .80
l. Booklet pane of 4, #252f 1.60 1.60

First day covers of Nos. 250-252 total 65,123.

Endangered Species Type of 1993

Designed by Jeffrey Terreson, US.

Designs: No. 253, Pongo pygmaeus (oran-utan). No. 254, Pelecanus crispus (Dalmatian pelican). No. 255, Eunectes notaeus (yellow anaconda). No. 256, Caracal.

1999, Apr. 22 Litho. *Perf. 12½*

253 A271 7s **multicolored** *(552,000)+* 1.00 1.00
254 A271 7s **multicolored** *(552,000)+* 1.00 1.00
255 A271 7s **multicolored** *(552,000)+* 1.00 1.00
256 A271 7s **multicolored** *(552,000)+* 1.00 1.00
a. Block of 4, #253-256 4.00 4.00
First day cover, #256a 6.00
First day cover, #253-256, each 2.25
Inscription block of 4, #256a 4.75 —
Pane of 16 17.00

First day covers of Nos. 253-256 total 66,733.

UNISPACE III Type

Designs: No. 257, Satellite over ships. No. 258, Satellite up close. No. 259, Composite of #257-258.

1999, July 7 Photo. *Rouletted 8*

257 A314 3.50s **multicolored** *(1,200,000)+* .75 .75
258 A314 3.50s **multicolored** *(1,200,000)+* .75 .75
a. Pair, #257-258 1.60 1.60
First day cover, #258a 3.00
First day cover, #257-258, each 2.50
Inscription block of 4 6.50 —
Pane of 10, #257-258 9.00 —

Souvenir Sheet

Perf. 14½

259 A314 13s **multicolored** *(350,000)+* 4.50 4.50
First day cover 5.00

First day covers of Nos. 257-259 total 72,143.

UPU Type

Various people, late 20th century methods of mail transportation, denomination at: No. 260, UL. No. 261, UR. No. 262, LL. No. 263, LR.

1999, Aug. 23 Photo. *Perf. 11¾*

260 A315 6.50s **multicolored** *(417,000)+* 1.00 1.00
261 A315 6.50s **multicolored** *(417,000)+* 1.00 1.00
262 A315 6.50s **multicolored** *(417,000)+* 1.00 1.00
263 A315 6.50s **multicolored** *(417,000)+* 1.00 1.00
a. Block of 4, #260-263 4.00 4.00
First day cover, #263a 4.5
First day cover, #260-263, each 2.0
Inscription block of 4 4.50 —

First day covers of Nos. 260-263 total 38,453.

In Memoriam Type

Designs: 6.50s, 14s, Donaupark. Size of 14s stamp 34x63mm.

1999, Sept. 21 Litho. *Perf. 14½x14*

264 A316 6.50s **multicolored** *(530,000)+* .90 .9
First day cover 3.0
Inscription block of 4 4.50 —

Souvenir Sheet

Perf. 14

265 A316 14s **multicolored** *(338,000)+* 2.40 2.4
First day cover 4.0

First day covers of Nos. 264-265 total 61,089.

Education Type

1999, Nov. 18 Litho. *Perf. 13½x13¾*

266 A317 7s Boy, girl, book *(490,000)+* 1.00 1.0
First day cover 1.6
Inscription block of 4 4.25 —
267 A317 13s Group reading *(490,000)+* 2.00 2.0
First day cover 3.0
First day cover, #266-267 4.0
Inscription block of 4 8.50 —

First day covers of Nos. 266-267 total 48,590.

Intl. Year of Thanksgiving Type

2000, Jan. 1 Litho. *Perf. 13¼x13½*

268 A318 7s **multicolored** *(510,000)+* 1.00 1.0
First day cover 3.0
Inscription block of 4 4.75 —

On No. 268 parts of the design were applied by a thermographic process producing a shiny, raised effect.

Endangered Species Type of 1993

Designed by Lori Anzalone, US.

Designs: No. 269, Panthera pardus (leopard). No. 270, Platalea leucorodia (white spoonbill). No. 271, Hippocamelus bisulcus (huemal). No. 272, Orcinus orca (killer whale).

2000, Apr. 6 Litho. *Perf. 12¾x12½*

269 A271 7s **multicolored** *(548,000)+* 1.10 1.1
270 A271 7s **multicolored** *(548,000)+* 1.10 1.1
271 A271 7s **multicolored** *(548,000)+* 1.10 1.1
272 A271 7s **multicolored** *(548,000)+* 1.10 1.1
a. Block of 4, #269-272 4.50 4.5
First day cover, #272a 6.0
First day cover, #269-272, each 2.0
Inscription block of 4, #272a 4.75 —
Pane of 16 18.00

Our World 2000 Type

Winning artwork in Millennium painting competition: 7s, Tomorrow's Dream, by Voltaire Perez, Philippines. 8s, Remembrance, by Dimitris Nalbandis, Greece, vert.

2000, May 30 Litho. *Perf. 13x13½, 13½x13*

273 A319 7s **multicolored** *(430,000)+* 1.00 1.0
First day cover 1.7
Inscription block of 4 4.50 —
274 A319 8s **multicolored** *(430,000)+* 1.20 1.2
First day cover 2.0
First day cover, #273-274 3.0
Inscription block of 4 5.00 —

55th Anniversary Type

Designs: 7s, Secretariat Building, unfinished dome of General Assembly Hall, 1951. 9s, Trygve Lie and Headquarters Advisory Committee at topping-out ceremony, 1949.

2000, July 7 Litho. *Perf. 13¼x13*

275 A320 7s **multicolored** *(440,000)+* .90 .9
First day cover 1.7
Inscription block of 4 4.50 —
276 A320 9s **multicolored** *(440,000)+* 1.25 1.2
First day cover 2.2
First day cover, #275-276 3.0
Inscription block of 4 6.00 —

Souvenir Sheet

277 A320 Sheet of 2, #275-276 *(300,000)+* 2.75 2.7
First day cover 3.2

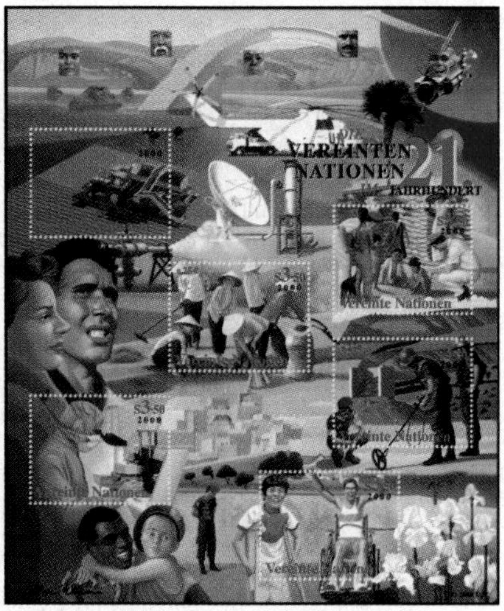

The UN in the 21st Century — V43

Printed by Government Printing Office, Austria. Designed by Wilson McLean, UK.

No. 278: a, Farm machinery. b, UN Peacekeepers and children. c, Oriental farm workers. d, Peacekeepers searching for mines. e, Medical research. f, Handicapped people.

2000, Sept. 15 Litho. *Perf. 14*

278 V43 Sheet of 6 *(330,000)+* 6.00 6.00
First day cover 3.75
a.-f. 3.50s any single 1.00 1.00

World Heritage, Spain Type

Designs: Nos. 279, 281c, Aqueduct of Segovia. Nos. 280, 281f, Güell Park, Barcelona. #281a, Alhambra, Generalife and Albayzin, Granada. #281b, Walled Town of Cuenca. #281d, Amphitheater of Mérida. #281e, Toledo.

2000, Oct. 6 Litho. *Perf. 14¾x14½*

279 A323 4.50s **multicolored** *(430,000)+* .80 .80
First day cover 1.25
Inscription block of 4 3.00 —
280 A323 6.50s **multicolored** *(430,000)+* 1.20 1.20
First day cover 1.75
First day cover, #279-280 2.40
Inscription block of 4 4.00 —

Souvenir Booklet

281 Booklet *(92,000)+* 7.00
a.-c. A323 1s any single .20 .20
d.-f. A323 2s any single .40 .40
g. Booklet pane of 4, #281a .65 .65
h. Booklet pane of 4, #281d 1.60 1.60
i. Booklet pane of 4, #281b .65 .65
j. Booklet pane of 4, #281e 1.60 1.60
k. Booklet pane of 4, #281c .65 .65
l. Booklet pane of 4, #281f 1.60 1.60

Respect for Refugees Type

Designs: 7s, 25s, Refugee with hat, three other refugees.

2000, Nov. 9 Litho. *Perf. 13¼x12¾*

282 A324 7s **multicolored** *(530,000)+* 1.10 1.10
First day cover 1.75
Inscription block of 4 4.50 —

Souvenir Sheet

283 A324 25s **multicolored** *(273,000)+* 3.75 3.75
First day cover 4.50

Endangered Species Type of 1993

Printed by Johann Enschedé and Sons, the Netherlands. Designed by Betina Ogden, Australia.

Designs: No. 284, Tremarctos ornatus (spectacled bear). No. 285, Anas laysanensis (Laysan duck). No. 286, Proteles cristatus (aardwolf). No. 287, Trachypithecus cristatus (silvered leaf monkey).

2001, Feb. 1 Litho. *Perf. 12¾x12½*

284 A271 7s **multicolored** *(540,000)+* 1.10 1.10
285 A271 7s **multicolored** *(540,000)+* 1.10 1.10
286 A271 7s **multicolored** *(540,000)+* 1.10 1.10
287 A271 7s **multicolored** *(540,000)+* 1.10 1.10
a. Block of 4, #284-287 4.50 4.50
First day cover, #287a 5.00
First day cover, #284-287 each 1.75
Inscription block of 4, #287a 4.25 —
Pane of 16 16.00

Intl. Volunteers Year — V44

Printed by Johann Enschedé and Sons, the Netherlands. Panes of 20. Designed by Rorie Katz and Robert Stein, US.

Paintings by: 10s, Nguyen Thanh Chuong, Viet Nam. 12s, Ikko Tanaka, Japan.

2001, Mar. 29 Litho. *Perf. 13¼*

288 V44 10s **multicolored** *(440,000)+* 1.40 1.40
First day cover 2.00
Inscription block of 4 5.75
289 V44 12s **multicolored** *(430,000)+* 1.75 1.75
First day cover 2.40
First day cover, #288-289 3.75
Inscription block of 4 7.00

World Heritage, Japan Type

Designs: 7s, #290c, Himeji-Jo. 15s, #291f, Nikko. #292a, Kyoto. #292b, Nara. #292d, Shirakawa-Go and Gokayama. #292e, Itsukushima Shinto Shrine.

2001, Aug. 1 Litho. *Perf. 12¾x13¼*

290 A328 7s **multicolored** *(440,000)+* 1.00 1.00
First day cover 1.40
Inscription block of 4 4.00 —
291 A328 15s **multicolored** *(440,000)+* 2.10 2.10
First day cover 3.00
First day cover, #290-291 3.75
Inscription block of 4 8.50 —

Souvenir Booklet

292 Booklet *(78,000)+* 6.00
a.-c. A328 1s any single .20 .20
d.-f. A328 2s any single .30 .30
g. Booklet pane of 4, #292a .60 .60
h. Booklet pane of 4, #292d 1.25 1.25
i. Booklet pane of 4, #292b .60 .60
j. Booklet pane of 4, #292e 1.25 1.25
k. Booklet pane of 4, #292c .60 .60
l. Booklet pane of 4, #292f 1.25 1.25

Dag Hammarskjöld Type

2001, Sept. 18 Engr. *Perf. 11x11¼*

293 A329 7s **green** *(480,000)+* 1.00 1.00
First day cover 1.60
Inscription block of 4 4.25 —

UN Postal Administration, 50th Anniv. Types

2001, Oct. 18 Litho. *Perf. 13½*

294 A330 7s Stamps, balloons *(380,000)+* 1.00 1.00
First day cover 1.60
Inscription block of 4 4.00 —
295 A330 8s Stamps, cake *(380,000)+* 1.10 1.10
First day cover 1.75
First day cover, #294-295 2.75
Inscription block of 4 4.50 —

Souvenir Sheet

296 A331 Sheet of 2 *(225,000)+* 4.00 4.00
a. 7s **green & light blue,** 38mm diameter 1.00 1.00
b. 21s **green & light blue,** 38mm diameter 3.00 3.00
First day cover 4.50

Climate Change Type

Designs: No. 297, Solar panels, automobile at pump. No. 298, Blimp, bicyclists, horse and rider. No. 299, Balloon, sailboat, lighthouse, train. No. 300, Bird, train, traffic signs.

2001, Nov. 16 Litho. *Perf. 13¼*

297 A332 7s **multicolored** *(87,000)+* 1.00 1.00
298 A332 7s **multicolored** *(87,000)+* 1.00 1.00
299 A332 7s **multicolored** *(87,000)+* 1.00 1.00
300 A332 7s **multicolored** *(87,000)+* 1.00 1.00
a. Horiz. strip, #297-300 4.00 4.00
Inscription block of 8 8.25 —
First day cover, #300a 4.50
Pane of 24 24.00 —

Nobel Peace Prize Type

2001, Dec. 10 Litho. *Perf. 13¼*

301 A333 7s **multicolored** *(1,260,000)+* 1.00 .50
Inscription block of 4 5.00 —
First day cover 1.60
Pane of 12 14.00 —

100 Cents = 1 Euro (€)

Austrian Tourist Attractions V45

Printed by House of Questa, UK. Panes of 20. Designed by Rorie Katz, US.

Designs: 7c, Semmering Railway. 51c, Pferdschwemme, Salzburg. 58c, Aggstein an der Donau Ruins. 73c, Hallstatt. 87c, Melk Abbey. €2.03, Kapitelschwemme, Salzburg.

2002, Mar. 1 Litho. *Perf. 14½x14*

302 V45 7c **multicolored** *(860,000)+* .20 .20
First day cover 1.25
Inscription block of 4 .65 —
303 V45 51c **multicolored** *(960,000)+* 1.10 1.10
First day cover 1.40
Inscription block of 4 4.50 —
304 V45 58c **multicolored** *(860,000)+* 1.25 1.25
First day cover 1.60
Inscription block of 4 5.25 —
305 V45 73c **multicolored** *(760,000)+* 1.50 1.50
First day cover 2.00
Inscription block of 4 6.75 —
306 V45 87c **multicolored** *(760,000)+* 2.00 2.00
First day cover 2.40
Inscription block of 4 8.25 —
307 V45 €2.03 **multicolored** *(710,000)+* 4.25 4.25
First day cover 5.50
First day cover, #288-289 10.50
Inscription block of 4 18.00 —
Nos. 302-307 (6) 10.30 10.30

Endangered Species Type of 1993

Printed by Johann Enschedé and Sons, the Netherlands. Designed by Tim Barrall, US.

Designs: No. 308, Hylobates syndactylus (siamang). No. 309, Spheniscus demersus (jackass penguin). No. 310, Prionodon linsang (banded linsang). No. 311, Bufo retiformis (Sonoran green toad).

2002, Apr. 4 Litho. *Perf. 12¾x12½*

308 A271 51c **multicolored** *(500,000)+* 1.25 1.25
309 A271 51c **multicolored** *(500,000)+* 1.25 1.25
310 A271 51c **multicolored** *(500,000)+* 1.25 1.25
311 A271 51c **multicolored** *(500,000)+* 1.25 1.25
a. Block of 4, #308-311 5.00 5.00
First day cover, #311a 4.75
First day cover, #308-311 each 1.75
Inscription block of 4, #311a 5.25 —
Pane of 16 18.00 —

Independence of East Timor Type

Designs: 51c, Deer horn container with carved wooden stopper. €1.09, Carved wooden tai weaving loom.

2002, May 20 Litho. *Perf. 14x14½*

312 A335 51c **multicolored** *(384,000)+* 1.00 1.00
First day cover 1.50
Inscription block of 4 4.50 —
313 A335 €1.09 **multicolored** *(374,000)+* 2.25 2.25
First day cover 3.25
First day cover, #312-313 4.00
Inscription block of 4 9.50 —

Intl. Year of Mountains Type

Designs: No. 314, Mt. Cook, New Zealand. No. 315, Mt. Robson, Canada. No. 316, Mt. Rakaposhi, Pakistan. No. 317, Mt. Everest (Sagarmatha), Nepal.

2002, May 24 Litho. *Perf. 13x13¼*

314 A336 22c **multicolored** *(1,335,000)+* .50 .50
First day cover 1.25
315 A336 22c **multicolored** *(1,335,000)+* .50 .50
First day cover 1.25
316 A336 51c **multicolored** *(1,335,000)+* 1.10 1.10
First day cover 1.50
First day cover, #314, 316 2.25
317 A336 51c **multicolored** *(1,335,000)+* 1.10 1.10
a. Vert. strip or block of four, #314-317 3.50 3.50
First day cover 1.50
First day cover, #315, 317 2.25
First day cover, #314-317 3.75
Pane of 12, 3 each #314-317 10.50 —

World Summit on Sustainable Development (Peter Max) Type

Designs: No. 318, Rainbow. No. 319, Three women, diff. No. 320, Three faceless people. No. 321, Birds, wave.

2002, June 27 Litho. *Perf. 14½x14*

318 A337 51c **multicolored** *(1,305,000)+* 1.10 1.10
First day cover 1.50
319 A337 51c **multicolored** *(1,305,000)+* 1.10 1.10
First day cover 1.50
320 A337 58c **multicolored** *(1,305,000)+* 1.25 1.25
First day cover 1.60
First day cover, #318, 320 2.50
321 A337 58c **multicolored** *(1,305,000)+* 1.25 1.25
a. Vert. strip or block of four, #318-321 4.75 4.75

First day cover 1.60
First day cover, #319, 321 2.50
First day cover, #318-321 3.75
Pane of 12, 3 each #318-321 14.50 —

World Heritage, Italy Type

Designs: 51c, #324f, Pompeii. 58c, #324c, Rome. #324a, Amalfi Coast. #324b, Aeolian Islands. #324d, Florence. #324e, Pisa.

2002, Aug. 30 Litho. ***Perf. 13½x13¼***

322 A338 51c **multicolored** *(400,000)+* 1.10 1.10
First day cover 1.75
Inscription block of 4 4.50 —
323 A338 58c **multicolored** *(400,000)+* 1.25 1.25
First day cover 2.00
First day cover, #322-323 3.00
Inscription block of 4 5.00 —

Souvenir Booklet

324 Booklet *(71,000)+* 7.00
a.-c. A338 7c any single .20 .20
d.-f. A338 15c any single .40 .40
g. Booklet pane of 4, #324d 1.60 1.60
h. Booklet pane of 4, #324a .65 .65
i. Booklet pane of 4, #324e 1.60 1.60
j. Booklet pane of 4, #324b .65 .65
k. Booklet pane of 4, #324f 1.60 1.60
l. Booklet pane of 4, #324c .65 .65

AIDS Awareness Type

2002, Oct. 24 Litho. ***Perf. 13½***

325 A339 €1.53 **multicolored** *(370,000)+* 3.50 3.75
Inscription block of 4 13.00
First day cover, #325 4.00
Pane of 20 65.00

Indigenous Art — V46

Printed by House of Questa, UK.
Designed by Rorie Katz and Robert Stein, US.

No. 326: a, Mola, Panama. b, Mochican llama-shaped spouted vessel, Peru. c, Tarabuco woven cloth, Bolivia. d, Masks, Cuba. e, Aztec priest's feather headdress, Mexico. f, Bird-shaped staff head, Colombia.

2003, Jan. 31 Litho. ***Perf. 14¼***

326 V46 Sheet of 6 *(212,000)+* 6.00 6.00
First day cover 8.25
a.-f. 51c Any single 1.00 1.00
First day cover, a.-f., each 2.75

Austrian Tourist Attractions Type of 2002

Printed by House of Quest, UK. Designed by Rorie Katz, US. Panes of 20.
Designs: 25c, Kunsthistorisches Museum, Vienna. €1, Belvedere Palace, Vienna.

2003, Mar. 28 Litho. ***Perf. 14½x14***

327 V45 25c **multicolored** *(650,000)+* .55 .55
First day cover 1.25
Inscription block of 4 2.25 —
328 V45 €1 **multicolored** *(650,000)+* 2.25 2.25
First day cover 3.25
First day cover, #327-328 3.50
Inscription block of 4 9.00 —

Endangered Species Type of 1993

Printed by Johann Enschedé and Sons, the Netherlands. Designed by Robert Hautman, US.
Designs: No. 329, Anas formosa (Baikal teal). No. 330, Bostrychia hagedash (Hadada ibis). No. 331, Ramphastos toco (toco toucan). No. 332, Alopochen aegyptiacus (Egyptian goose).

2003, Apr. 3 Litho. ***Perf. 12¾x12½***

329 A271 51c **multicolored** *(432,000)+* 1.00 1.00
330 A271 51c **multicolored** *(432,000)+* 1.00 1.00
331 A271 51c **multicolored** *(432,000)+* 1.00 1.00
332 A271 51c **multicolored** *(432,000)+* 1.00 1.00
a. Block of 4, #329-332 4.00 4.00
First day cover, #332a 5.25
First day cover, #329-332 each 1.90
Inscription block of 4, #332a 4.50 —
Pane of 16 18.00 —

International Year of Freshwater Type of 2003

2003, June 20 Litho. ***Perf. 14¼x14½***

333 A345 55c Bridge, bird *(316,000)+* 1.40 1.40
334 A345 75c Horse, empty river *(316,000)+* 1.90 1.90
a. Horiz. pair, #333-334 3.30 3.30
First day cover, #334a 3.75
Inscription block of 4 7.50 —

Austrian Tourist Attractions Type of 2002

Printed by Johann Enschedé and Sons, the Netherlands. Panes of 20. Designed by Rorie Katz, US.
Design: 4c, Schloss Eggenberg, Graz.

2003, Aug. 7 Litho. ***Perf. 14x13¼***

335 V45 4c **multicolored** *(650,000)+* .20 .20
First day cover 1.25
Inscription block of 4 .35
Pane of 20 1.60

Ralph Bunche Type

Litho. With Foil Application

2003, Aug. 7 ***Perf. 13½x14***

336 A346 €2.10 **olive green & multicolored** *(384,000)+* 4.50 4.50
First day cover 5.50
Inscription block of 4 19.00
Pane of 20 95.00

In Memoriam Type of 2003

2003, Oct. 24 Litho. ***Perf. 13¼x13***

337 A347 €2.10 **multicolored** *(670,000)+* 5.00 5.00
First day cover 6.25
Inscription block of 4 22.00 —
Pane of 20 110.00 —

World Heritage Sites, United States Type

Designs: 55c, #340c, Olympic National Park. 75c, #340e, Everglades National Park. #340a, Yosemite National Park. #340b, Great Smoky Mountains National Park. #340d, Hawaii Volcanoes National Park. #340f, Yellowstone National Park.

2003, Oct. 24 Litho. ***Perf. 14½x14¼***

338 A348 55c **multicolored** *(275,000)+* 1.50 .75
First day cover 2.10
Inscription block of 4 6.00 —
339 A348 75c **multicolored** *(275,000)+* 2.00 1.00
First day cover 2.75
First day cover, #338-339 4.25
Inscription block of 4 8.00 —

Souvenir Booklet

340 Booklet *(57,500)+* 9.00
a.-c. A348 15c any single .35 .35
d.-f. A348 20c any single .40 .40
g. Booklet pane of 4 #340a 1.40 1.40
h. Booklet pane of 4 #340d 1.60 1.60
i. Booklet pane of 4 #340b 1.40 1.40
j. Booklet pane of 4 #340e 1.60 1.60
k. Booklet pane of 4 #340c 1.40 1.40
l. Booklet pane of 4 #340f 1.60 1.60

Austrian Tourist Attractions Type of 2002

Printed by Imprimerie de Timbres-Poste, France.
Design: 55c, Schloss Schönbrunn, Vienna.

2004, Jan. 29 Litho. ***Perf. 13x13¼***

341 V45 55c **multicolored** *(740,000)+* 1.50 1.50
First day cover 2.10
Inscription block of 4 6.00 —
Pane of 20 30.00 —

Endangered Species Type of 1993

Printed by Johann Enschedé and Sons, the Netherlands. Designed by Yuan Lee, U.S.
Designs: No. 342, Melursus ursinus (Sloth bear). No. 343, Cervus eldi (Eld's deer). No. 344, Cercocebus torquatus (Cherry-crowned mangabey). No. 345, Bubalus arnee (Wild water buffalo).

2004, Jan. 29 Litho. ***Perf. 12¾x12½***

342 A271 55c **multicolored** *(376,000)+* 1.25 1.25
343 A271 55c **multicolored** *(376,000)+* 1.25 1.25
344 A271 55c **multicolored** *(376,000)+* 1.25 1.25
345 A271 55c **multicolored** *(376,000)+* 1.25 1.25
a. Block of 4, #342-345 5.00 5.00
First day cover, #345a 6.50
First day cover, #342-345, each 2.25
Inscription block of 4, #345a 6.00 —
Pane of 16 24.00 —

Indigenous Art Type of 2003

Printed by Johann Enschedé and Sons, the Netherlands. Designed by Rorie Katz and Robert Stein, US.

No. 346: a, Illuminated illustration from the Book of Kells, Ireland. b, Easter eggs, Ukraine. c, Venus of Willendorf, Paleolithic age limestone statue, Austria. d, Flatatunga panel, Iceland. e, Neolithic era idol, Hungary. f, Illuminated illustration from medical treatise, Portugal.

2004, Mar. 4 Litho. ***Perf. 13¼***

346 V46 Sheet of 6 *(133,000)+* 7.50 7.50
First day cover 10.50
a.-f. 55c Any single 1.25 1.25
First day cover, a.-f., each 2.75

Road Safety Type

Road map art with: 55c, Automobile, alcohol bottles. 75c, Road, clouds in traffic light colors, vert.

2004, Apr. 7 Litho. ***Perf. 13x13¼, 13¼x13***

347 A354 55c **multicolored** *(225,000)+* 1.25 1.25
First day cover 2.10
Inscription block of 4 6.00 —
348 A354 75c **multicolored** *(225,000)+* 1.75 1.75
First day cover 2.75
First day cover, #338-339 4.25
Inscription block of 4 8.00 —

Japanese Peace Bell, 50th Anniv. Type

2004, June 3 Litho. & Engr. ***Perf. 13¼x13***

349 A355 €2.10 **multicolored** *(280,000)+* 4.50 4.50
First day cover 6.25
Inscription block of 4 22.00 —
Pane of 20 110.00

World Heritage Sites, Greece Type

Designs: 55c, No. 352f, Mycenae and Tiryns. 75c, No. 352e, Olympia. No. 352a, Acropolis, Athens. No. 352b, Delos. No 352c, Delphi. No. 352d, Pythagoreion and Heraion of Samos.

2004, Aug. 12 Litho. ***Perf. 14x13¼***

350 A356 55c **multicolored** *(250,000)+* 1.40 1.40
First day cover 1.90
Inscription block of 4 5.75 —
351 A356 75c **multicolored** *(250,000)+* 1.90 1.90
First day cover 2.75
First day cover, #350-351 4.00
Inscription block of 4 7.75 —

Souvenir Booklet

352 Booklet *(49,000)+* 14.00
a.-d. A356 25c any single .55 .55
e.-f. A356 30c either single .70 .70
g. Booklet pane of 4 #352a 2.20 2.20
h. Booklet pane of 4 #352b 2.20 2.20
i. Booklet pane of 4 #352c 2.20 2.20
j. Booklet pane of 4 #352d 2.20 2.20
k. Booklet pane of 4 #352e 2.80 2.80
l. Booklet pane of 4 #352f 2.80 2.80

My Dream for Peace Type

Winning designs of Lions Club International children's global peace poster contest by: 55c, Henry Ulfe Renteria, Peru. €1, Michelle Fortaliza, Philippines.

2004, Sept. 21 Litho. ***Perf. 14***

353 A357 55c **multicolored** *(235,000)+* 1.40 1.40
First day cover 1.90
Inscription block of 4 5.75
Pane of 20 28.00
354 A357 €1 **multicolored** *(235,000)+* 2.50 2.50
First day cover 3.50
First day cover, #353-354 4.50
Inscription block of 4 10.00
Pane of 20 50.00

V47

Human Rights — V48

Printed by Banknote Corporation of America, US. Designed by Yuri Gervorgian, Armenia. Panes of 8.

2004, Oct. 14 Litho. ***Perf. 11¼***

355 V47 55c **multicolored** *(480,000)+* 1.00 1.00
First day cover 2.00
Pane of 8 12.00 —

56 V48 €1.25 **multicolored** *(480,000)+* 3.00 3.00
First day cover 4.50
First day cover, #355-356 5.75
Pane of 8 28.00 —

United Nations, 60th Anniv. Type of 2005

Printed by Banknote Corporation of America, US. Designed / Czeslaw Slania, Sweden.

005, Feb. 4 Litho. & Engr. ***Perf. 11x11¼***
57 A361 55c **multicolored** *(310,000)+* 1.60 1.60
First day cover 2.60
Inscription block of 4 6.50 —
Pane of 20 32.50 —

Souvenir Sheet

Litho.

Imperf

58 A361 €2.10 **multicolored** *(165,000)+* 5.50 5.50
First day cover 6.25

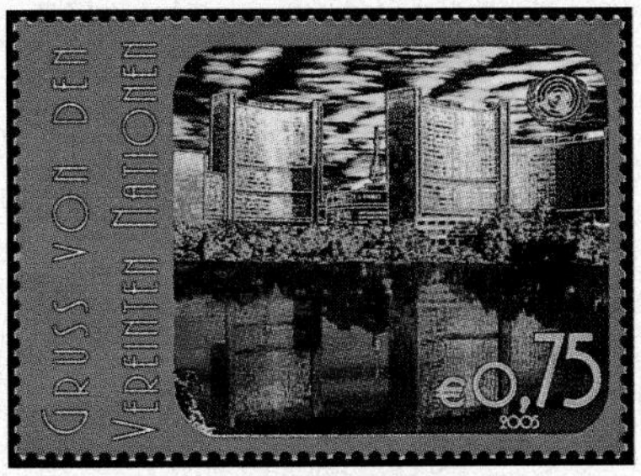

International Center, Vienna — V49

Printed by Cartor Security Printing, France.

Litho. with Hologram

005, Feb. 4 ***Perf. 13½x13¼***
59 V49 75c **multicolored** *(360,000)+* 2.25 2.25
First day cover 3.25
Inscription block of 4 9.00 —
Pane of 20 45.00 —

Endangered Species Type of 1993

Designs: No. 360, Ansellia africana. No. 361, Phragmipedium ovachii. No. 362, Cymbidium ensifolium. No. 363, Renanthera nschootiana.

005, Mar. 3 Litho. ***Perf. 12¾x12½***
60 A271 55c multicolored 1.40 1.40
61 A271 55c multicolored 1.40 1.40
62 A271 55c multicolored 1.40 1.40
63 A271 55c multicolored 1.40 1.40
a. Block of 4, #360-363 6.00 6.00
First day cover, #363a 7.00
First day cover, #360-363, each 2.25
Inscription block of 4, #363a 6.25 —
Pane of 16 19.00 —

Nature's Wisdom — V50

Printed by Cartor Security Printing, France. Panes of 20. Designed by Robert Stein, US.
Designs: 55c, Desert landscape, China. 80c, Cheetah family, Africa.

005, Apr. 21 Litho. ***Perf. 13½x13¼***
64 V50 55c **multicolored** *(230,000)+* 1.60 1.60
First day cover 2.40
Inscription block of 4 6.50 —
Pane of 20 32.50 —
65 V50 75c **multicolored** *(230,000)+* 2.25 2.25
First day cover 3.50
First day cover, #364-365 4.75
Inscription block of 4 9.00 —
Pane of 20 45.00 —

Intl. Year of Sport Type

Printed by Cartor Security Printing, France. Designed by Roland Hirter, Switzerland.

005, June 3 Litho. ***Perf. 13x13¼***
66 A368 55c Equestrian *(245,000)+* 1.60 1.60
First day cover 2.25
Inscription block of 4 6.50 —
Pane of 20 32.50 —
67 A368 €1.10 Soccer *(245,000)+* 3.25 3.25
First day cover 4.50
First day cover, #366-367 6.00
Inscription block of 4 13.00 —
Pane of 20 65.00 —

World Heritage Sites, Egypt Type

Printed by Johann Enschedé and Sons, the Netherlands. Panes of 20. Designed by Rorie Katz, US.
Designs: Nos. 368, 370c, Abu Mena. Nos. 369, 370f, St. Catherine area. No. 370a, Memphis and its Necropolis. No. 370b, Philae. No. 370d, Ancient Thebes. No. 370e, Islamic Cairo.

2005, Aug. 4 Litho. ***Perf. 14x13¼***
368 A369 55c **multicolored** *(250,000)+* 1.60 1.60
First day cover 2.40
Inscription block of 4 6.50 —
369 A369 75c **multicolored** *(250,000)+* 2.25 2.25
First day cover 3.25
First day cover, #368-369 4.75
Inscription block of 4 9.00 —

Souvenir Booklet

370 Booklet, #370g-370l *(45,000)+* 19.50
a.-c. A369 25c any single .75 .75
d.-f. A369 30c any single .85 .85
g. Booklet pane of 4 #370a 3.00 —
h. Booklet pane of 4 #370b 3.00 —
i. Booklet pane of 4 #370c 3.00 —
j. Booklet pane of 4 #370d 3.50 —
k. Booklet pane of 4 #370e 3.50 —
l. Booklet pane of 4 #370f 3.50 —

No. 370 sold for €6.80.

My Dream for Peace Type

Winning designs of Lions Club International children's global peace poster contest by: 55c, Lee Min Gi, Republic of Korea. €1, Natalie Chan, US.

2004, Sept. 21 Litho. ***Perf. 14***
371 A357 55c **multicolored** *(225,000)+* 1.60 1.60
First day cover 2.25
Inscription block of 4 6.50
Pane of 20 32.00
372 A357 €1 **multicolored** *(225,000)+* 2.75 2.75
First day cover 4.00
First day cover, #371-372 5.25
Inscription block of 4 11.00
Pane of 20 55.00

Food for Life Type

Printed by Government Printing Office, Austria. Designed by Andrew Davidson, United Kingdom.
Designs: 55c, Corn, people with food bowls, teacher and students. €1.25, Rice, helicopter dropping food, elephant caravan.

2005, Oct. 20 Litho. ***Perf. 13¾***
373 A370 55c **multicolored** *(210,000)+* 1.60 1.60
First day cover 2.10
Inscription block of 4 6.50 —
Pane of 20 32.00 —
374 A370 €1.25 **multicolored** *(210,000)+* 3.50 3.50
First day cover 4.75
First day cover, #373-374 6.00
Inscription block of 4 14.00 —
Pane of 20 70.00 —

Indigenous Art Type of 2003

Printed by Johann Enschedé and Sons, the Netherlands. Designed by Robert Stein, US.

No. 375 — Musical instruments: a, Drum, Guinea. b, Whistle, Congo. c, Horn, Botswana. d, Drums, Burundi. e, Harp, Gabon. f, Bell, Nigeria.

2006, Feb. 3 Litho. ***Perf. 13¼***
375 V46 Sheet of 6 *(117,000)+* 8.50 8.50
First day cover 10.50
a.-f. 55c Any single 1.40 1.40

Endangered Species Type of 1993

Printed by Johann Enschedé and Sons, the Netherlands. Designed by John D. Dawson, US.

Designs: No. 376, Dendrobates pumilio. No. 377, Furcifer lateralis. No. 378, Corallus hortulanus. No. 379, Dendrobates leucomelas.

2006, Mar. 16 Litho. ***Perf. 12¾x12½***
376 A271 55c **multicolored** *(260,000)+* 1.40 1.40
377 A271 55c **multicolored** *(260,000)+* 1.40 1.40
378 A271 55c **multicolored** *(260,000)+* 1.40 1.40
379 A271 55c **multicolored** *(260,000)+* 1.40 1.40
a. Block of 4, #376-379 5.75 5.75
First day cover, #379a 6.75
First day cover, #376-379, each 2.40
Inscription block of 4, #379a 5.75 —
Pane of 16 23.00 —

Intl. Day of Families Type

Printed by Johann Enschedé and Sons, the Netherlands. Designed by Shelly Bartek, US.
Designs: 55c, Family at water pump. €1.25, Family preparing food.

2006, May 27 Litho. ***Perf. 14x13½***
380 A373 55c **multicolored** *(190,000)+* 1.50 1.50
First day cover 2.00
Inscription block of 4 6.00 —
Pane of 20 30.00 —
381 A373 €1.25 **multicolored** *(190,000)+* 3.25 3.25
First day cover 4.50
First day cover, #380-381 5.75
Inscription block of 4 13.00 —
Pane of 20 65.00 —

World Heritage Sites, France Type

Printed by Cartor Security Printing, France. Panes of 20. Designed by Robert Stein, US.
Eiffel Tower and: Nos. 382, 384c, Carcasonne. Nos. 383, 384f, Chateau de Chambord. No. 384a, Banks of the Seine. No. 384b, Provins. No. 384d, Roman Aqueduct. No. 384e, Mont Saint-Michel.

Litho. & Embossed with Foil Application

2006, June 17 ***Perf. 13½x13¼***
382 A374 55c **multicolored** *(220,000)+* 1.50 1.50
First day cover 2.25
Inscription block of 4 6.00 —
383 A374 75c **multicolored** *(220,000)+* 2.00 2.00
First day cover 3.00
First day cover, #368-369 4.50
Inscription block of 4 8.00 —

Souvenir Booklet

384 Booklet, #384g-384l *(41,000)+* 18.00
a.-c. A374 25c any single .65 .65
d.-f. A374 30c any single .80 .80
g. Booklet pane of 4 #384a 2.60 —
h. Booklet pane of 4 #384b 2.60 —
i. Booklet pane of 4 #384c 2.60 —
j. Booklet pane of 4 #384d 3.25 —
k. Booklet pane of 4 #384e 3.25 —
l. Booklet pane of 4 #384f 3.25 —

No. 384 sold for €6.80.

My Dream for Peace Type of 2004

Printed by Cartor Security Printing, France. Panes of 20.
Winning designs of Lions Club International children's global peace poster contest by: 55c, Klara Thein, Germany. €1, Laurensia Levina, Indonesia.

2006, Sept. 21 Litho. ***Perf. 13½x13***
385 A357 55c **multicolored** *(200,000)+* 1.60 1.60
First day cover 2.25
Inscription block of 4 6.40 —
Pane of 20 32.00 —
386 A357 €1 **multicolored** *(200,000)+* 3.00 3.00
First day cover 4.00
First day cover, #385-386 5.50
Inscription block of 4 12.00 —
Pane of 20 60.00 —

Flags and Coins Type

Printed by Cartor Security Printing, France. Designed by Rorie Katz, US.
No. 387 — Flag of: a, Gambia, 1 dalasi coin. b, Pakistan, 1 rupee coin. c, Afghanistan, 2 afghani coin. d, Austria, 1 euro coin. e, Germany, 50 cent coin. f, Haiti, 50 centimes coin. g, Denmark, 20 krone coin. h, Netherlands, 1 euro coin.

2006, Oct. 5 Litho. ***Perf. 13¼x13***
387 Sheet of 8 12.50 12.50
a.-h. A375 55c Any single 1.50 1.50
First day cover 14.50

A column of rouletting in the middle of the sheet separates it into two parts.

Endangered Species Type of 1993

Printed by Johann Enschedé and Sons, the Netherlands. Designed by John Rowe, US.
Designs: No. 388, Chlorocebus aethiops. No. 389, Nasalis larvatus. No. 390, Papio hamadryas. No. 391, Erythrocebus patas.

2007, Mar. 15 Litho. ***Perf. 12¾x12½***
388 A271 55c **multicolored** *(256,000)+* 1.60 1.60
389 A271 55c **multicolored** *(256,000)+* 1.60 1.60
390 A271 55c **multicolored** *(256,000)+* 1.60 1.60
391 A271 55c **multicolored** *(256,000)+* 1.60 1.60
a. Block of 4, #388-391 6.40 6.40
First day cover, #391a 7.50
First day cover, #388-391, each 2.60
Inscription block of 4, #391a 6.40 —
Pane of 16 26.00 —

Flags and Coins Type of 2006

Printed by Cartor Security Printing, France. Designed by Rorie Katz, US.
No. 392 — Flag of: a, Trinidad and Tobago, 50 cent coin. b, Sierra Leone, 10 cent coin. c, Hungary, 100 forint coin. d, San Marino, 2 euro coin. e, Croatia, 1 kuna coin. f, Spain, 1 euro coin. g, Kazakhstan, 100 tenge coin. h, Ireland, 5 cent coin.

2007, May 3 Litho. ***Perf. 13¼x13***
392 Sheet of 8 *(155,000)+* 13.00 13.00
a.-h. A375 55c Any single 1.60 1.60
First day cover 15.00

A column of rouletting in the middle of the sheet separates it into two parts.

Vienna International Center — V51

Flags on Flagpoles, Vienna International Center — V52

Vienna International Center and Lake — V53

United Nations Flag — V54

Flags Hanging From Rotunda of Vienna International Center — V55

Designed by Robert Stein.

2007, May 3 **Litho.** ***Perf. 13¼***

393	V51	55c	**multicolored** + label	*3.00*	*3.00*
394	V52	55c	**multicolored** + label	*3.00*	*3.00*
395	V53	55c	**multicolored** + label	*3.00*	*3.00*
396	V54	55c	**blue** + label	*3.00*	*3.00*
397	V55	55c	**multicolored** + label	*3.00*	*3.00*
a.			Vert. strip of 5, #393-397, + 5 labels	*15.00*	*15.00*
			Sheet, 2 #397a	*30.00*	—

The full sheet sold for $14.95 from the New York office and €11 in Vienna. The sheet has two each of five different labels that could not be personalized.

Peaceful Visions Type of 2007

Printed by Lowe-Martin Company, Canada. Designed by Slavka Kolesar. Panes of 20.

Designs: 55c, "The Sowers." €1.25, "We All Thrive Under the Same Sky."

2007, June 1 **Litho.** ***Perf. 13x12½***

398	A378	55c	**multicolored** *(200,000)+*	1.60	1.60
			First day cover		2.25
			Inscription block of 4	6.40	—
			Pane of 20	32.00	—
399	A378	€1.25	**multicolored** *(200,000)+*	3.75	3.75
			First day cover		5.00
			First day cover, #398-399		6.25
			Inscription block of 4	15.00	—
			Pane of 20	75.00	—

World Heritage Sites, South America Type

Printed by Lowe-Martin Group, Canada. Panes of 20. Designed by Rorie Katz, US.

Designs: Nos. 400, 402e, Iguaçu National Park, Brazil. Nos. 401, 402b, Cueva de las Manos, Argentina. No. 402a, Rapa Nui, Chile. No. 402c, Machu Picchu, Peru. No. 402d, Tiwanaku, Bolivia. No. 474f, Galapagos Islands, Ecuador.

2007, Aug. 9 **Litho.** ***Perf. 13¼x13***

400	A381	55c	**multicolored** *(210,000)+*	1.75	1.75
			First day cover		2.50
			Inscription block of 4	7.00	—
401	A381	75c	**multicolored** *(210,000)+*	2.25	2.25
			First day cover		3.50
			First day cover, #400-401		5.00
			Inscription block of 4	9.00	—

Souvenir Booklet

402	Booklet, #402g-402l *(37,000)+*	20.00	
a.-c.	A381 25c Any single	.75	.75
d.-f.	A381 30c Any single	.90	.90
g.	Booklet pane of 4 #402a	3.00	—
h.	Booklet pane of 4 #402b	3.00	—
i.	Booklet pane of 4 #402c	3.00	—
j.	Booklet pane of 4 #402d	3.60	—
k.	Booklet pane of 4 #402e	3.60	—
l.	Booklet pane of 4 #402f	3.60	—

Humanitarian Mail Type

Printed by Lowe-Martin Group, Canada. Panes of 10.

2007, Sept. 6 **Litho.** ***Perf. 12½x13¼***

403	A382	75c	**multicolored** *(310,000)+*	2.25	2.25
			First day cover		3.25
			Inscription block of 4	9.00	—
			Pane of 10	22.50	—

International Space Station and Space Shuttle — V56

Astronaut — V57

Planets — V58

International Space Station — V59

Astronaut and Lunar Rover — V60

2007, Oct. 1 **Litho.** ***Perf. 13***

404	V56	65c	**multicolored** + label	*3.00*	*3.(*
405	V57	65c	**multicolored** + label	*3.00*	*3.(*
406	V58	65c	**multicolored** + label	*3.00*	*3.(*
407	V59	65c	**multicolored** + label	*3.00*	*3.(*
408	V60	65c	**multicolored** + label	*3.00*	*3.(*
a.			Vert. strip of 5, #404-408, + 5 labels	*15.00*	*15.(*
			Sheet, 2 #408a	*30.00*	

The full sheet sold for $14.95 from the New York office an €10.14 in Vienna. The sheet has ten labels that could not b personalized.

Space for Humanity Type

Printed by Johann Enschedé and Sons, the Netherlands Panes of 6. Designed by Donato Giancola, US.

Designs: 65c, Space stations. €1.15, Space Station. €2.10, Space probe, Jupiter.

2007, Oct. 25 **Litho.** ***Perf. 13½x1***

409	A383	65c	**multicolored** *(306,000)+*	2.00	2.0
			First day cover		2.6
			Inscription block of 4	8.00	
			Sheet of 6	12.00	
410	A383	€1.15	**multicolored** *(306,000)+*	3.50	3.5
			First day cover		4.7
			First day cover, #409-410		6.2
			Inscription block of 4	14.00	
			Sheet of 6	21.00	

Souvenir Sheet

411	A383	€2.10	**multicolored** *(130,000)+*	6.25	6.2
			First day cover		7.2

Intl. Holocaust Remembrance Day Type

Printed by Lowe-Martin Company, Canada. Panes of 9 Designed by Matías Delfino, Argentina.

2008, Jan. 27 **Litho.** ***Perf. 1***

412	A384	65c	**multicolored** *(540,000)+*	2.25	2.2
			First day cover		3.2
			Sheet of 9	21.00	

Johann Strauss Memorial, Vienna — V61

Pallas Athene Fountain, Vienna — V62

Pegasus Fountain, Salzburg V63

Statue, Belvedere Palace Gardens, Vienna — V64

Printed by Johann Enschedé and Sons, the Netherlands. anes of 20. Designed by Rorie Katz, US.

008, Jan. 28 **Litho.** ***Perf. 13½x14***

13 V61 10c **black** *(320,000)+* .35 .35
First day cover .50
Inscription block of 4 1.40 —
Pane of 20 7.00 —

Perf. 14x13½

14 V62 15c **black** *(320,000)+* .50 .50
First day cover .75
Inscription block of 4 2.00 —
Pane of 20 10.00 —
15 V63 65c **black** *(320,000)+* 2.25 2.25
First day cover 3.25
Inscription block of 4 9.00 —
Pane of 20 45.00 —
16 V64 €1.40 **black** *(320,000)+* 4.75 4.75
First day cover 7.00
Inscription block of 4 19.00 —
Pane of 20 95.00 —
Nos. 413-416 (4) 7.85 7.85

Endangered Species Type of 1993

Printed by Johann Enschedé and Sons, the Netherlands. esigned by Suzanne Duranceau, Canada.
Designs: No. 4170, Mirounga angustirostris. No. 418, Milleɔra alcicornis. No. 419, Hippocampus histrix. No. 420, hyseter catodon.

008, Mar. 6 **Litho.** ***Perf. 12¾x12½***

17 A271 65c **multicolored** *(212,000)+* 2.10 2.10
18 A271 65c **multicolored** *(212,000)+* 2.10 2.10
19 A271 65c **multicolored** *(212,000)+* 2.10 2.10
20 A271 65c **multicolored** *(212,000)+* 2.10 2.10
a. Block of 4, #417-420 8.40 8.40
First day cover, #420a 9.50
First day cover, #417-420, each 3.25
Inscription block of 4, #420a 8.40 —
Pane of 16 34.00 —

2008 END-OF-YEAR ISSUES

See end of New York postage listings.

SEMI-POSTAL STAMP

AIDS Awareness Semi-postal Type

Souvenir Sheet

002, Oct. 24 **Litho.** ***Perf. 14½***

1 SP1 51c + 25c **multicolored** *(220,000)+* 2.50 2.50
First day cover, #B1 3.00

ENVELOPES

Used values for all postal stationery are for nonhilatelic contemporaneous usages.

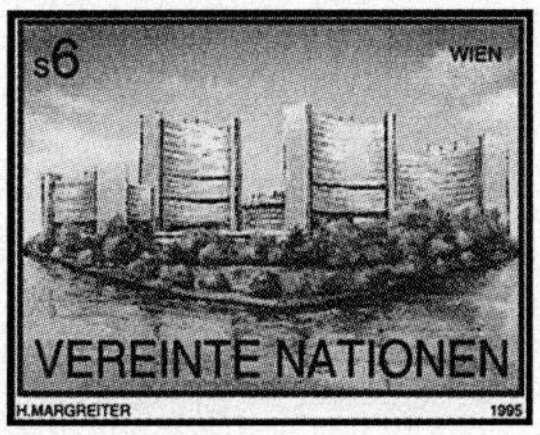

Donaupark, Vienna — VU1

Printed by Mercury-Walch Pty. Ltd. (Australia). Designed by annes Margreiter (Austria).
Design: 7s, Landscape. Design at lower left shows Vienna ndmarks (6s), river scene (7s).

995, Feb. 3 **Litho.**

1 VU1 6s **multicolored,** entire *(128,000)+* 2.00 2.00
First day cancel *(14,132)* 2.75
2 VU1 7s **multicolored,** entire *(128,000)+* 2.00 2.00
First day cancel *(9,684)* 3.50

VU2

Printed by Mercury-Walch Pty. Ltd. (Australia).

1998, Mar. 13 **Litho.**

U3 VU2 13s **multicolored,** entire *(87,000)+* 3.50 3.00
Entire, first day cancel 3.50

VU3

Vienna International Center — VU4

Printed by Australia Post Sprintpak (Australia). Designed by Robert Stein (US).

2002, June 27 **Litho.**

U4 VU3 51c **multicolored,** entire *(93,000)+* 1.50 1.50
Entire, first day cancel 2.00
U5 VU4 €1.09 **multicolored,** entire *(88,000)+* 2.60 2.60
Entire, first day cancel 3.25

Nos. U4-U5 Surcharged

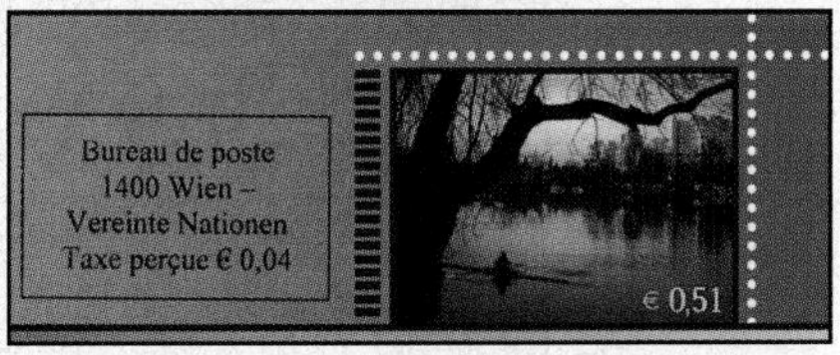

2003, June 2 **Litho.**

U6 VU3 51c +4c **multicolored,** entire 4.25 4.25
Entire, first day cancel 3.75
U7 VU4 €1.09 +16c **multicolored,** entire 5.75 5.75
Entire, first day cancel 4.75

UN Flag — VU5

Dove With Olive Branch — VU6

Printed by Government Printing Office, Austria. Designed by Rorie Katz, US.

2004, June 3 **Litho.**

U8 VU5 55c **multicolored,** entire *(53,000)+* 2.10 1.40
Entire, first day cancel 2.50
U9 VU6 €1.25 **multicolored,** entire *(48,000)+* 4.00 2.75
Entire, first day cancel 4.50

Nos. U8-U9 Surcharged Like No. U6

2007, Sept. 3 **Litho.**

U10 VU5 55c +10c **multicolored,** entire 3.00 3.00
Entire, first day cancel 3.75
U11 VU6 €1.25 +15c **multicolored,** entire 5.25 5.25
Entire, first day cancel 6.00

AIR LETTER SHEETS

VLS1

Printed by Joh. Enschede and Sons. Designed by Ingrid Ousland.

1982, Apr. 28 **Litho.**

UC1 VLS1 9s **multi,** *light green,* entire *(650,000)* 2.50 2.50
First day cancel *(120,650)* 3.00

No. UC1 Surcharged in Lake

1986, Feb. 3 **Litho.**

UC2 VLS1 9s +2s **multi,** *light green,* entire *(131,190)* 52.50 *60.00*
First day cancel *(18,500)* 26.00

Birds in Flight, UN Emblem VLS2

Printed by Mercury-Walch, Australia. Designed by Mieczyslaw Wasiliewski, Poland.

1987, Jan. 30 **Litho.**

UC3 VLS2 11s **bright blue,** entire *(414,000)* 3.00 3.00
First day cancel *(48,348)* 4.00

No. UC3 Surcharged

1992, Jan. 1 **Litho.**
UC4 VLS2 11s +1s **bright blue,** entire *(80,000)* 52.50 *60.00*
First day cancel 25.00

Donaupark, Vienna — VLS3

Designed by Rocco J. Callari. Printed by Mercury-Walch, Australia.

1992, Sept. 4 **Litho.**
UC5 VLS3 12s **multicolored,** entire *(200,000)+* 5.00 5.00
First day cancel *(16,261)* 27.50

POSTAL CARDS

Olive Branch — VPC1

Bird Carrying Olive Branch — VPC2

Printed by Courvoisier. Designed by Rolf Christianson (3s), M.A. Munnawar (5s).

1982, Apr. 28 **Photo.**
UX1 VPC1 3s **multicolored,** *cream (500,000)* 1.00 1.00
First day cancel *(93,010)* 1.65
UX2 VPC2 5s **multicolored** *(500,000)* .75 1.00
First day cancel *(89,502)* 1.65

Emblem of the United Nations — VPC3

Printed by Johann Enschede en Zonen, Netherlands. Designed by George Hamori, Australia.

1985, May 10 **Litho.**
UX3 VPC3 4s **multicolored** *(350,000)* 1.50 3.50
First day cancel *(53,450)* 3.00

No. UX2 Surcharged Like No. UC4

1992, Jan. 1 **Photo.**
UX4 VPC2 5s +1s **multicolored** *(71,700)* 19.00 19.00
First day cancel 17.00

Type of 1990

Printed by Mercury-Walch, Australia.

1992, Sept. 4 **Litho.**
UX5 V22 6s **multicolored** *(445,000)+* 2.00 3.00
First day cancel *(16,359)* 10.00

See No. UX9.

Type of 1985

Printed by Leigh Mardon Pty. Limited, Australia.

1993, May 7 **Litho.**
UX6 A222 5s **multicolored** *(450,000)* 16.00 16.00
First day cancel 10.00

Donaupark, Vienna — VPC4

Printed by Leigh Mardon Pty. Limited, Australia.

1993, May 7 **Litho.**
UX7 VPC4 6s **multicolored** *(450,000)+* 4.00 4.00
First day cancel 7.50

See No. UX10.

No. UX6 with design of Vienna No.1 Added

1994, Jan. 1 **Litho.**
UX8 A222+G8 5s +50g **multi** *(350,000)+* 2.50 4.00
First day cancel 4.00

No. UX5 with design of Vienna #167 Added

1997, July 1 **Litho.**
UX9 V22+V32 6s +50g **multi** 2.50 2.50
First day cancel 5.00

No. UX7 with design of Vienna #194 Added

UX10 VPC4+V35 6s +1s **multi** 3.00 3.00
First day cancel 5.00

VPC5

Designed by Günter Leidenfrost.

1998, May 20 **Litho.**
UX11 VPC5 6.50s **multicolored** *(137,000)+* 1.50 1.50
First day cancel 2.00

The Gloriette — VPC6

1999, Feb. 5 **Litho.**
UX12 VPC6 7s **multicolored** *(136,000)+* 2.00 2.00
First day cancel 2.50

Type of 1983

2000, June 2 **Litho.**
UX13 V7 7s **multicolored** 2.25 2.25
First day cancel 2.25

Clock Tower, Graz, Austria — VPC7

Printed by Johann Enschedé and Sons, the Netherlands. Designed by Robert Stein, US.

2002, Mar. 1 **Litho.**
UX14 VPC7 51c **multicolored** *(83,000)+* 1.00 1.00
First day cancel 1.25

No. UX14 Surcharged

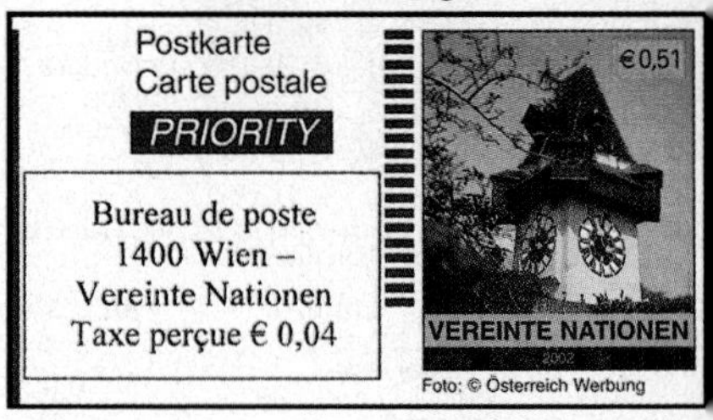

2003, June 2 **Litho.**
UX15 VPC7 51c +4c **multicolored** 2.75 2.75
First day cancel 2.75

Vienna International Center — VPC8

Printed by Government Printing Office, Austria. Designed by Rorie Katz, US.

2004, June 3 **Litho.**
UX16 VPC8 55c **multicolored** *(63,000)+* 2.60 1.25
First day cancel 3.00

No. UX16 Surcharged Like No. UX15

2007, Sept. 3 **Litho.**
UX17 VPC8 55c +10c **multicolored,** entire 3.75 3.75
Entire, first day cancel 4.50

U.N. SOUVENIR CARDS

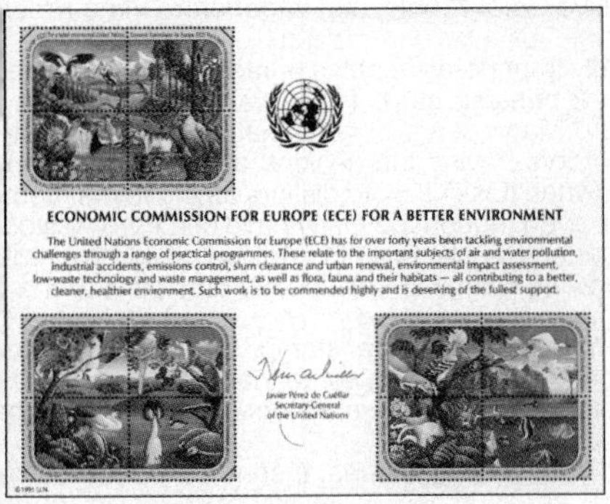

ECONOMIC COMMISSION FOR EUROPE (ECE) FOR A BETTER ENVIRONMENT
The United Nations Economic Commission for Europe (ECE) has for over forty years been tackling environmental challenges through a range of practical programmes. These relate to the important subjects of air and water pollution, industrial accidents, emissions control, slum clearance and urban renewal, environmental impact assessment, low-waste technology and waste management, as well as flora, fauna and their habitats — all contributing to a better, cleaner, healthier environment. Such work is to be commended highly and is deserving of the fullest support.
Javier Pérez de Cuéllar
Secretary-General
of the United Nations

No. 39

These cards were issued by the United Nations Postal Administration and were not valid for postage.

Each card bears reproductions of UN stamps and a statement by the Secretary-General in English.

Values are for mint cards without cancels.

SC1 World Health Day, Apr. 7, 1972. Card of 5: #43, 102, 156, 207, 228. .65

A second printing shows several minor differences.

SC2 Art on UN Stamps, Nov. 17, 1972. Card of 11: #170, 171, 173, 174, 180, 183, 201, 202, 203, 224, 232. #201, 202 form a simulated setenant pair .45

SC3 Disarmament Decade, Mar. 9, 1973. Card of 5: #133, 147, 177, 227, 234 .50

SC4 Declaration of Human Rights, 25th Anniversary, Nov. 16, 1973. Card of 10: #13, 22, 29, 39, 47, 58, 68, 121, 190, 242 .75

SC5 UPU centenary, Mar. 22, 1974. Card of 7: #17, 18, 219, 246; Geneva 18, 39, 40. .75

SC6 World Population Year, Oct. 18, 1974. Card of 7: #151, 152, 153, 252, 253; Geneva 43, 44. 4.00

SC7 Peaceful Uses of Outer Space, Mar. 14, 1975. Card of 6: #112, 113, 256, 257; Geneva 46, 47. 2.00

SC8 UN Peace Keeping Operations, Nov. 21, 1975. Card of 9: #52, 111, 118, 139, 160, 265, 266; Geneva 55, 56. 2.00

SC9 World Federation of United Nations Associations, Mar. 12, 1976. Card of 5: #154, 155, 272, 273; Geneva 57. 2.00

SC10 World Food Council, Nov. 19, 1976. Card of 6: #116, 117, 218, 280; Geneva 17, 63. 2.50

SC11 World Intellectual Property Organization (WIPO), Mar. 11, 1977. Card of 15: #17, 23, 25, 31, 33, 41, 43, 49, 59, 86, 90, 123, 281, 282; Geneva 64. 2.50

SC12 Combat Racism, Sept. 19, 1977. Card of 8: #220, 221, 287, 288; Geneva 19, 20, 69, 70. 2.50

SC13 Namibia, May 5, 1978. Card of 10: #240, 241, 263, 264, 296, 297; Geneva 34, 53, 54, 76. 1.00

SC14 Intl. Civil Aviation Organization, June 12, 1978. Card of 6: #31, 32, 298, 299; Geneva 77, 78. 2.50

SC15 Intl. Year of the Child, May 4, 1979. Card of 9: #5, 97, 161, 162, 163, 310, 311; Geneva 84, 85. .75

SC16 Intl. Court of Justice, Nov. 9, 1979. Card of 6: #88, 89, 314, 315; Geneva 87, 88. .75

SC17 UN Decade for Women, Mar. 7, 1980. Card of 4: #258, 318; Geneva 90; Vienna 9. 10.00

SC18 Economic and Social Council, Nov. 7, 1980. Card of 8: #65, 66, 341, 342; Geneva 96, 97; Vienna 15, 16. .75

SC19 Intl. Year of Disabled Persons, Mar. 6, 1981. Card of 6; #344, 345; Geneva 99, 100; Vienna 18, 19. .65

SC20 New and Renewable Sources of Energy, May 29, 1981. Card of 4; #348, 349; Geneva 102; Vienna 21. 1.00

SC21 Human Environment, Mar. 19, 1982. Card of 5: #230, 371; Geneva 26, 107; Vienna 25 .75

SC22 Exploration and Peaceful Uses of Outer Space, June 11, 1982. Card of 7: #112, 256, 373; Geneva 46, 109, 110; Vienna 27. 1.40

SC23 Safety at Sea, Mar. 18, 1983. Card of 8: #123, 124, 394, 395; Geneva 114, 115; Vienna 31, 32. 1.10

SC24 Trade and Development, June 6, 1983. Card of 11: #129, 130, 274, 275, 397, 398; Geneva 58, 117, 118; Vienna 31, 32. 1.50

SC25 Intl. Conference on Population, Feb. 3, 1984. Card of 10: #151, 153, 252, 253, 417, 418; Geneva 43, 44, 121; Vienna 39. 2.00

SC26 Intl. Youth Year, Nov. 15, 1984. Card of 5: #441, 442; Geneva 128; Vienna 46, 47. 3.00

SC27 ILO Turin Center, Feb. 1, 1985. Card of 8: #25, 200, 244, 443; Geneva 37, 129, 130; Vienna 48. 2.75

SC28 Child Survival Campaign, Nov. 22, 1985. Card of 6: #466, 467; Geneva 138, 139; Vienna 55, 56. 3.00

SC29 Stamp Collecting, May 22, 1986. Card of 5: #278, 473; Geneva 61, 147; Vienna 63. *8.25*

No. 29 with stitch marks has been removed from the Ameripex program. Value is one-half that of unstitched copy.

SC30 Intl. Peace Year, June 20, 1986. Card of 6: #475, 476; Geneva 148, 149; Vienna 64, 65. 4.00

SC31 Shelter for the Homeless, Mar. 13, 1987. Card of 6: #495, 496; Geneva 154, 155; Vienna 68, 69. 2.50

SC32 Immunize Every Child, Nov. 20, 1987. Card of 13: #44, 103, 157, 208, 294, 517, 518; Vienna 76, 77. 3.00

SC33 Intl. Volunteer Day, May 6, 1988. Card of 10; #239, 367, 524, 525; Geneva 103, 167, 168; Vienna 23, 82, 83. 4.00

SC34 Health in Sports, June 17, 1988. Card of 6; #526, 527; Geneva 169, 170; Vienna 84, 85. 5.00

SC35 World Bank, Jan. 27, 1989. Card of 8; #86-87, 546-547; Geneva 173-174; Vienna 88-89. 5.00

SC36 World Weather Watch, Apr. 21, 1989. Card of 10; #49-50, 188-189, 550-551; Geneva 176-177; Vienna 91-92. 5.00

SC37 Fight AIDS Worldwide, Mar. 16, 1990. Card of 6, #573-574; Geneva 184-185; Vienna 99-100 6.50

SC38 Crime Prevention, Sept. 13, 1990. Card of 6; #580-581; Geneva 191-192; Vienna 106-107. 6.00

SC39 Economic Commission for Europe, Mar. 15, 1991. Card of 12; #584-587; Geneva 195-198; Vienna 110-113. 6.00

SC40 Rights of the Child, June 14, 1991. Card of 6; #593-594; Geneva 203-204; Vienna 117-118. 7.00

SC41 Mission to Planet Earth, Sept. 4, 1992, Card of 6, #609-610; Geneva 220-221; Vienna 133-134 17.00

SC42 Science and Technology for Development, Oct. 2, 1992, Card of 6, #611-612; Geneva 222-223; Vienna 135-136 15.00

SC43 Healthy Environment, May 7, 1993, Card of 6, #624-625; Geneva #232-233; Vienna #147-148 17.50

SC44 Peace, Sept. 21, 1993, Card of 12, #629-632; Geneva #236-239; Vienna #152-155 16.00

No. 44 exists overprinted in gold with Hong Kong '94 emblem.

SC45 Intl. Year of the Family, Feb. 4, 1994, Card of 6, #637-638; Geneva #244-245; Vienna #160-161 13.50

SC46 Population & Development, 1994, Card of 9, #151, 651-652; Geneva #43, 258-259; Vienna #39, 174-175 12.50

SC47 World Summit for Social Development, 1995, Card of 3, #656; Geneva #263; Vienna #179 10.50

SC48 Intl. Youth Year, 1995, Card of 9, #441, 661-662; Geneva #128, 268-269; Vienna #46, 184-185 16.00

SC49 WFUNA, 1996, Card of 3, #671; Geneva #277; Vienna #193 14.00

SC50 UNICEF, 1996, Card of 6, #688-689; Geneva #294-295; Vienna #210-211 9.00

SC51 Philately, 1997, Card of 6, #714-715; Geneva #312-313; Vienna #228-229 12.50

SC52 Peacekeeping, #737-738; Geneva #325-326; Vienna #242-243 9.00

SC53 Universal Declaration of Human Rights, #739-740; Geneva #327-328; Vienna #244-245 9.00

SC54 UPU, #767a; Geneva #346a; Vienna #263a 5.00

SC55 Respect for Refugees, #787; Geneva #365; Vienna #282 6.00

SC56 Intl. Volunteers Year, #793-794; Geneva #371-372; Vienna #288-289 4.00

SC57 Johannesburg Summit on Sustainable Development, #828-831; Geneva #396-399; Vienna #318-321 5.00

SC58 International Year of Freshwater, #846-8471; Geneva #411-412; Vienna #333-334 4.00

SC59 Japanese Peace Bell, 50th Anniv., #865; Geneva #425; Vienna #349 4.00

SC60 Nature's Wisdom, #885-886; Geneva #440-441; Vienna #364-365 4.00

SC61 Intl. Day of Families, #913-914, Geneva #457-458, Vienna #380-381 4.00

SC62 As #SC61, with Washington 2006 World Philatelic Exhibition emblem and text *17.50*

No. SC62 was only sold canceled.

U.N. PROOFS

Proofs of United Nations stamps are known in four basic types: Die Proofs, Trial Color Proofs, Progressive Color Proofs, and Imperforate Plate Proof on gummed stamp paper.

Die Proofs (PD suffix) for United Nations stamps show the design of the issued stamp. They are usually imperforate singles printed on stamp pape that are either affixed to a backing paper that is a component of a printer's card, or affixed directly to a printer's card. These cards usually have handstamp denoting the status of the proof (approved, approved with corrections, not approved, etc.). Many cards have signatures of UN Posta Administration officials. Cards with an "approved" handstamp and/or signature do not always contain proofs having the designs of the actual stam produced for sale. As most proof cards have a handstamp, the listings mention specific handstamps only when it is critical to distinguishing items. Item not affixed to cards that are indistinguishable from imperforate singles of the issued stamps are not listed, even though they may have come from "stoc sheet style" proof cards that have approval handstamps. Items affixed to art boards available to the general public are not considered to be proof unless they are identified, usually by handstamps, that they are proofs. Die proofs of sheet layouts showing marginal inscriptions only exist, but ar beyond the scope of these listings.

Trial Color Proofs (TC suffix) show the design of the stamp, but with one or more colors differing from that of the actual stamp. Items will be liste as trial color proofs when they differ significantly from the issued color. As evidenced by printer's identification numbers on some trial color proof cards shades of individual items may differ slightly, but two similar yet discrete shades may fall under one color description. Trial colors can sometimes b found on cards with die proofs.

Progressive Color Proofs (PP suffix) are a set of color proofs containing the number of items stated in the listing. Values, therefore, are for the se of singles (unless otherwise mentioned in the description), not a single progressive color proof from that set. Numbers in parentheses represent th total number of complete sets that were created. Partial sets are not listed if complete sets are known.

Imperforate Plate Proofs (PI suffix) are usually found on gummed stamp paper. Any exceptions are noted in the listing description. Numbers i parentheses represent the total number of imperforate proof stamps created. Many items have inked fingerprints on the reverse as a security device Values are for pairs unless otherwise stated. Many gutter pairs will have creases. Some gutter pairs will have marginal inscriptions. These are wort more.

Organization of listings Listings have all of the New York, Geneva and Vienna stamps and souvenir cards for any set all together. The first part of a item's catalogue number is the same catalogue number as shown in the listings for stamps and postal stationery. The prefix "G" is before the catalogu number for items from Geneva; prefix "V" for items from Vienna. Items with prefix "SC" are souvenir cards, and catalogue numbers without prefix ar from New York. The suffix describing the type of proof follows the catalogue number. Die proofs (suffix PD) are the first proof category in the listings and will be followed by the other categories in the same order as listed above. Each proof category will list New York items first, followed by Genev items, Vienna items, and then souvenir cards.

Often cards of proofs will contain all of the items in an issued set. The catalogue numbers for cards that contain New York, Geneva and Vienna proof are organized by the highest New York catalogue number of the various die proof items in the set. If there are no New York items in the card, then th numbering will be organized by the highest Geneva or Vienna catalogue number in the card of die proofs. Cards that contain both die proofs and tria color proofs are catalogued under the die proofs.

Numbers in parentheses represent the total number of items created. The number of items coming in part or in total from printer's archives ar approximations. Listings for single proofs affixed to cards do not usually mention that they are affixed to a card. Cards containing more than one proo will have a minor letter following the PD suffix, and the listing will detail the component parts, as some cards may in the future be broken down b owners into individual proof items. Cutting up cards, however, may destroy their value, as listings are often based on the presence of the handstamp Removing proofs from the card will lower their value, as it may then be impossible to distinguish them from imperforate singles.

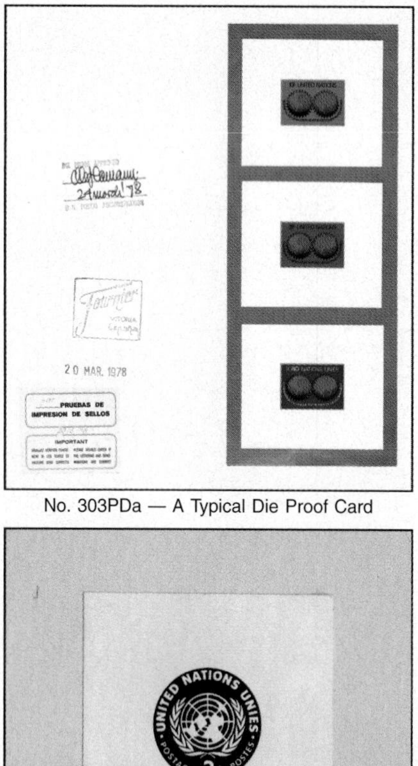

No. 303PDa — A Typical Die Proof Card

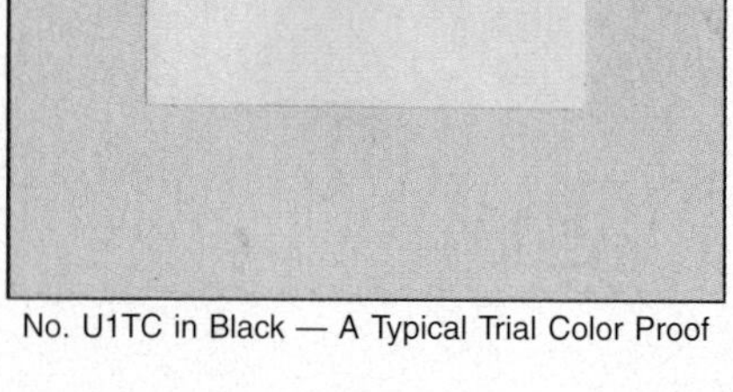

No. U1TC in Black — A Typical Trial Color Proof

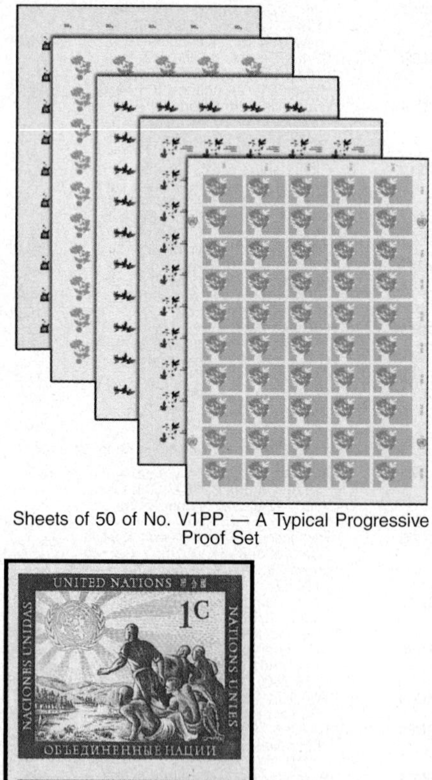

Sheets of 50 of No. V1PP — A Typical Progressive Proof Set

No. 1PI — A Typical Pair of Imperforate Plate Proofs

New York #1-11 Definitives

1951

1PD	(1)	600
2PD	(3)	500
3PD	(3)	450
3PDa	Card, #3PD, 3TC blue violet (1)	575
4PD	(1)	600
5PD	(1)	575
5PDa	Card, #5PD, 5TC dark blue violet	1,150
6PD	(1)	600
6PDa	Card, #1PD, 6PD (3)	3,100
7PD	(1)	600
8PD	(4)	300
9PD	(1)	600
9PDa	Card, #4PD, 7PD, 9PD, essays of #7, 9 (1)	1,850
9PDb	Card, #9PD, 9TC green (1)	825
10PD	(1)	500
11PD	(4)	475
2TC	indigo (1)	—
3TC	red violet (2)	
3TC	dark red (2)	350
3TC	red orange (1)	450
3TC	carmine (3)	—
3TC	orange red (3)	—
3TCa	Card, #3TC carmine, #3TC orange red (1)	700
5TC	orange red (1)	750
5TC	brown (1)	750
5TC	bright blue (1)	—
5TC	light blue (1)	—
5TC	dark blue (1)	—
5TC	black (1)	—
5TC	red orange (1)	—
5TCa	Card, #5TC black, 5TC brown (1)	925
10TC	black (1)	—
10TC	dark green (1)	—
10TCa	Card, #10TC blue green , #10TC yellow green (1)	—
11TC	dark red, 2 impressions side by side (1)	—
11TC	purple, 2 impressions side by side (1)	—
11TCa	dark blue (2 impressions side by side below two impressions of #5TC (1)	—
1PI	Pair (25)	1,000
2PI	Pair (5)	—
5PI	Pair (42)	350
	Vert. pair with horiz. gutter (8)	—
6PI	Pair (25)	375
8PI	Pair (50)	500
11PI	Pair (3)	800

Imperforate printer's waste has impression of No. 6 wit stamps of other countries.

New York #12
Signing of UN Charter, 7th Anniv.

1952

12PD	(3)	—
12TC	dark blue (2)	—
12TC	black (2)	—
12TC	green (2)	—
12TC	light blue (1)	—

New York #13-14
Universal Declaration of Human Rights, 4th Anniv.

1952

13PDa	Card, #13PD and two #13TC in slightly different shades (1)	975.
14PDa	Card, #14PD and two #14TC in slightly different shades (1)	975.
14PDb	Card, #13PD, 14PD (1)	—

New York #15-16
Protection for Refugees

1953

15PD	(1)	450.
16PD	(1)	450.
16PDa	Card, #15PD, 16PD (3)	775.
16PDb	Card, #15PD, 16PD, 16TC indigo (1)	875.
16PDc	Card, #16PDb and card, #15PD, 15TC, 16PD (some staining) (1)	575.
15PI	Pair (80)	400.
	Vert. pair with horiz. gutter (20)	—
16PI	Pair (80)	400.
	Vert. pair with horiz. gutter (20)	—

New York #17-18
Universal Postal Union

1953

17PDa	Card, #17PD, 17TC red brown, 17TC ultramarine, 17TC blue	2,000.
17PDb	Card, #17PD, 17TC violet brown (1)	—
18PDa	Card, #18PD, 18TC bright blue (1)	—
18PDb	Card, #17PDa, 18PDa (1)	—
17PI	Pair (82)	200.
	Horiz. pair with vert. gutter (8)	—
18PI	Pair (84)	200.
	Horiz. pair with vert. gutter (6)	—

Approximately half of PI items are stained and glued on cardboard. Imperforate printer's waste has No. 17 with No. 18 and impressions of other items on the reverse.

New York #19-20
Technical Assistance

1953

20PDa	Card, #19PD-20PD, #19TC-20TC in slightly different shades (2)	1,250.

New York #21-22
Human Rights Day

1953

22PDa	Card, #23PD-24PD, two #23TC, two #24TC in slightly different shades (2)	1,600.
21PI	Pair (40)	350.
	Vert. pair with horiz. gutter (10)	—
22PI	Pair (40)	350.
	Vert. pair with horiz. gutter (10)	—

New York #23-24
Food and Agricultural Organization

1954

24PDa	Card, #23PD-24PD, two #23TC-24TC in slightly different colors (2)	1,600.
23PI	Pair (40)	225.
	Vert. pair with horiz. gutter (10)	—
24PI	Pair (40)	225.
	Vert. pair with horiz. gutter (120)	—

New York #25-26
International Labor Organization

1954

25PDa	Card, #25PD, two #25TC in slightly different shades, three #26TC in purple shades (2)	2,400.
26PDa	Card, #25PD-26PD, #26TC in slightly different shade (2)	—
25PI	Pair (40)	350.
	Vert. pair with horiz. gutter (10)	—
26PI	Pair (40)	350.
	Vert. pair with horiz. gutter (10)	—

New York #27-28
United Nations Day

1954

27PI	Pair (40)	300.
	Horiz. pair with vert. gutter (10)	—
28PI	Pair (40)	300.
	Horiz. pair with vert. gutter (10)	—

New York #29-30
Human Rights Day

1954

29PD	(5)	350.
30PD	(5)	350.
29PI	Pair (40)	350.
	Vert. pair with horiz. gutter (10)	—
30PI	Pair (40)	—
	Vert. pair with horiz. gutter (10)	—

New York #31-32
International Civil Aviation Organization

1955

31PDa	Card, #31PD, two #31TC in different blue shades (3)	—
32PDa	Card, #32PD, three #32TC in different red shades (3)	1,400.
32PDb	Card, #31PD-32PD, #31TC-#32TC in different shades, three essays of #31-32 (1)	1,650.
31TC	black (1)	—
32TC	black (1)	—
31PI	Pair (171)	225.
	Horiz. pair with vert. gutter (26)	—
32PI	Pair (130)	225.
	Horiz. pair with vert. gutter (20)	—

No. 31PI exists with and without punch holes.

New York #33-34
UN Educational, Scientific and Cultural Organization

1955

33PD	(1)	—
33PDa	Card, #33PD, two #33TC in different shades (3)	700.
34PD	(1)	—
34PDa	Card, #34PD, two #34TC in different shades (3)	700.
33TC	black (1)	—
34TC	black (1)	—
33PI	Pair (128)	—
	Horiz. pair with vert. gutter (16)	—
34PI	Pair (90)	—
	Horiz. pair with vert. gutter (10)	—

No. 33PI exists with and without punch holes.

New York #35-38
UN, 10th Anniv.

1955

35PDa	Card, #35PD, two #35TC in different shades (2)	2,400.
35PDb	Card, #35PD, #35TC in lighter shade (1)	—
36PDa	Card, #36PD, two #36TC in different shades (3)	—
37PDa	Card, #37PD, two #37TC in different shades (3)	—
38PD	Sheet of #38 with security punches (2)	1,950.
38bPD	Watermarked sheet of nine #38b and nine #38c with security punches (1)	4,250.
38cPD	Watermarked sheet of nine #38c with security punches (1)	5,000.
35TC	carmine (1)	—
35TC	black (1)	—
36TC	black (1)	—
37TC	black (1)	—
38PP	4 items (9 souvenir sheets)	—
38PP	Retouch, 2 items (9 souvenir sheets)	—
35PI	Pair (130)	325.
	Horiz. pair with vert. gutter (20)	—
36PI	Pair (130)	325.
	Horiz. pair with vert. gutter (20)	—
37PI	Pair (180)	325.
	Horiz. pair with vert. gutter (30)	—
38PI	Pairs of souvenir sheets (16)	3,000.
	Single with sheet margin (4)	850.
38PI	Retouch Pairs of souvenir sheets (4)	—
	Retouch, single with sheet margin (1)	—

No. 37PI exists with and without punch holes.

New York #39-40
Human Rights Day

1955

39PDa	Card, #39PD, two #39TC in different shades (2)	850.
40PDa	Card, #40PD, two #40TC in different shades (2)	850.
39TC	black (1)	—
40TC	black (1)	—
40TCa	Card, #39TC in aquamarine, #40TC in dark green and two essays (1)	1,250.
39PI	Pair (180)	425.
	Vert. pair with horiz. gutter (20)	—
40PI	Pair (130)	425.
	Vert. pair with horiz. gutter (20)	—

No. 39PI exists with and without punch holes.

New York #41-42
International Telecommunication Union

1956

41PD	(2)	300.
42PD	(2)	300.
41PI	Pair (40)	350.
	Horiz. pair with vert. gutter (10)	—
42PI	Pair (40)	350.
	Horiz. pair with vert. gutter (10)	—

New York #43-44
World Health Organization

1956

43PD	(2)	225.
44PD	(2)	225.
43PI	Pair (40)	250.
	Vert. pair with horiz. gutter (10)	—
44PI	Pair (40)	250.
	Vert. pair with horiz. gutter (10)	—

Nos. 43PI-44PI have "Colour approved" handstamped in margin.

New York #45-46
General Assembly

1956

45PD	(7)	275.
46PD	(7)	275.
45PI	Pair (40)	350.
	Horiz. pair with vert. gutter (10)	—
46PI	Pair (40)	350.
	Horiz. pair with vert. gutter (10)	—

New York #47-48
Human Rights Day

1956

47PD	(2)	375.
48PD	(2)	375.
47TC	red (3)	400.
47TC	carmine (3)	—
48TC	blue (6)	400.
47PI	Pair (40)	300.
	Horiz. pair with vert. gutter (10)	—
48PI	Pair (40)	300.
	Horiz. pair with vert. gutter (10)	—

New York #49-50
World Meteorological Organization

1957

49PD	(2)	275.
50PD	(2)	275.
49TC	blue (3)	250.
50TC	carmine rose (3)	250.
49PI	Pair (40)	—
	Vert. pair with horiz. gutter (10)	—
50PI	Pair (40)	—
	Vert. pair with horiz. gutter (10)	—

Nos. 49PI-50PI have "Colour approved" handstamped in margin.

New York #51-52
UN Emergency Force

1957

51PD	(7)	275.
52PD	(7)	275.
51PI	Pair (40)	—
	Horiz. pair with vert. gutter (10)	—
52PI	Pair (40)	—
	Horiz. pair with vert. gutter (10)	—

New York #55-56
Security Council

1957

55PD	(6)	275.
56PD	(11)	275.
55TC	golden brown (6)	—
55TC	brown (5)	—
55PI	Pair (40)	—
	Vert. pair with horiz. gutter (10)	—
56PI	Pair (40)	—
	Vert. pair with horiz. gutter (10)	—

New York #57-58
Human Rights Day

1957

57PD	(12)	275.
58PD	(9)	275.
57TC	light red brown (1)	300.
58TC	dark blue (3)	—
58TC	gray green (6)	300.
57PI	Pair (50)	—
58PI	Pair (50)	—

Nos. 57TC-58TC have handstamps with "Approved" crossed out.

New York #59-60
International Atomic Energy Agency

1958

59PD	(12)	250.
60PD	(13)	250.
59TC	emerald (7)	—
59TC	black (7)	350.
60TC	black (8)	350.
59PI	With security punch (358 pairs)	—
	Cross gutter block, with security punch (4)	—
	Horiz. pair with vert. gutter, with security punch (52)	—
	Vert. pair with horiz. gutter, with security punch (32)	—
60PI	Pair with security punch (358)	—
	Cross gutter block, with security punch (4)	—

Horiz. pair with vert. gutter, with security punch (52) —
Vert. pair with horiz. gutter, with security punch (32) —

New York #61-62
Central Hall, Site of First General Assembly Meeting

1958

61PD	(8)	275.
62PD	(8)	275.
61TC	black (3)	275.
62TC	black (3)	275.
61PI	With security punch (358 pairs)	—
	Cross gutter block, with security punch (4)	—
	Horiz. pair with vert. gutter, with security punch (32)	—
	Vert. pair with horiz. gutter, with security punch (52)	—
62PI	Pair with security punch (358)	—
	Cross gutter block, with security punch (4)	—
	Horiz. pair with vert. gutter, with security punch (32)	—
	Vert. pair with horiz. gutter, with security punch (52)	—

New York #63-64
UN Emblem

1958

63PD	(21)	250.
64PD	(7)	250.
64PDa	Card, #64PD, #64TC Prussian blue, #64TC ultramarine (2)	975.
63TC	brown orange (3)	300.
64TC	light blue (1)	300.
64TC	ultramarine (1)	500.
63PI	Pair (80)	—
	Vert. pair with horiz. gutter (20)	—
64PI	Pair (80)	—
	Vert. pair with horiz. gutter (20)	—

No. 63TC is affixed to cards inscribed "D."

New York #65-66
Economic and Social Council

1958

65PD	(8)	250.
66PD	(7)	250.
65TC	black (2)	325.
65TC	orange brown (1)	—
65TC	green (1)	—
65TC	red orange (1)	—
66TC	black (2)	325.
65PI	Pair with security punch (358)	—
	Cross gutter block, with security punch (4)	—
	Horiz. pair with vert. gutter, with security punch (32)	—
	Vert. pair with horiz. gutter, with security punch (52)	—
66PI	Pair with security punch (358)	—
	Cross gutter block, with security punch (4)	—
	Horiz. pair with vert. gutter, with security punch (32)	—
	Vert. pair with horiz. gutter, with security punch (52)	—

New York #67-68
Human Rights Day

1958

67PD	(5)	300.
68PD	(5)	300.
67TC	black (2)	425.
68TC	black (1)	425.
67PI	Pair (358)	—
	Cross gutter block, with security punch and "SPECIMEN" ovpt. (4)	—
	Horiz. pair with vert. gutter, with security punch and "SPECIMEN" ovpt. (52)	—
	Vert. pair with horiz. gutter, with security punch and "SPECIMEN" ovpt. (32)	—
68PI	Pair (358)	—
	Cross gutter block, with security punch and "SPECIMEN" ovpt. (4)	—
	Horiz. pair with vert. gutter, with security punch and "SPECIMEN" ovpt. (52)	—
	Vert. pair with horiz. gutter, with security punch and "SPECIMEN" ovpt. (32)	—

Essays of Nos. 67 and 68 without denominations exist in issued colors and black.

New York #69-70
New York City Building, Flushing Meadows

1959

69PD	(7)	300.
70PD	(7)	300.
69PI	Pair (216)	—
	Cross gutter block (3)	—
	Horiz. pair with vert. gutter (54)	—
	Vert. pair with horiz. gutter (24)	—
70PI	Pair (216)	—
	Cross gutter block (3)	—
	Horiz. pair with vert. gutter (54)	—
	Vert. pair with horiz. gutter (24)	—

New York #71-72
Economic Commission for Europe

1959

71PD	(7)	275.
72PD	(7)	275.
71PI	Pair (216)	—
	Cross gutter block (3)	—
	Horiz. pair with vert. gutter (24)	—
	Vert. pair with horiz. gutter (54)	—
72PI	Pair (216)	—
	Cross gutter block (3)	—
	Horiz. pair with vert. gutter (24)	—
	Vert. pair with horiz. gutter (54)	—

New York #73-74
Trusteeship Council

1959

73PD	(5)	300.
74PD	(5)	300.
73TC	orange red (2)	—
73PI	Pair (216)	—
	Cross gutter block (3)	—
	Horiz. pair with vert. gutter (24)	—
	Vert. pair with horiz. gutter (54)	—
74PI	Pair (216)	—
	Cross gutter block (3)	—
	Horiz. pair with vert. gutter (24)	—
	Vert. pair with horiz. gutter (54)	—

No. 73TC has handstamps with words "Color and" crossed out.

New York #75-76
World Refugee Year

1959

75PD	(6)	300.
76PD	(5)	300.
75TC	purple & red (3)	—
76TC	olive & Prussian blue (2)	—
76TC	purple & green (3)	—
75PI	Pair (216)	—
	Cross gutter block (3)	—
	Horiz. pair with vert. gutter (54)	—
	Vert. pair with horiz. gutter (24)	—
76PI	Pair (216)	—
	Cross gutter block (3)	—
	Horiz. pair with vert. gutter (54)	—
	Vert. pair with horiz. gutter (24)	—

New York #77-78
Chaillot Palace

1960

77PD	(4)	250.
78PD	(4)	250.
78TC	brown & blue green(1)	325.
78TC	blue & red (1)	325.
78TCa	Card, #78TC brown & blue green, #78TC blue &red (1)	—
77PI	Pair (25)	—
78PI	Pair (25)	—

New York #79-80
Economic Commission for Asia and the Far East

1960

79PD	(1)	—
80PDa	Card, #79PD, #80PD (1)	—
80PDb	Card, two #79PD, two #80PD (1)	1,250.
79PI	Pair (50)	—
80PI	Pair (50)	—

New York #81-82
World Forestry Congress

1960

81PD	(2)	425.
82PDa	Card, #81PD-82PD (3)	350.
81PI	Pair (100)	—
82PI	Pair (100)	—

New York #83-85
UN, 15th Anniv.

1960

83PD	(5)	325.
84PD	(6)	325.
85PD	(2)	700.
83TC	black (1)	—
83TC	bright blue (2)	—
83PI	Pair (144)	—
	Cross gutter block (2)	—
	Horiz. pair with vert. gutter (36)	—
	Vert. pair with horiz. gutter (16)	—
84PI	Pair (119)	—
	Cross gutter block (2)	—
	Horiz. pair with vert. gutter (36)	—
	Vert. pair with horiz. gutter (16)	—
85PI	Pair (16)	—
	Cross gutter block (2)	—
	Horiz. pair with vert. gutter (8)	—
	Vert. pair with horiz. gutter (8)	—

An essay in blue has diagonal lines in background rather than cross-hatching.

New York #86-87
International Bank for Reconstruction and Development

1960

87PDa	Card, 2 #86PD, 2 #87PD (2)	1,15
87PDb	Card, #86PD-87PD with simulated perforations (1)	—
86PI	Pair (100)	—
87PI	Pair (100)	—

New York #88-89
International Court of Justice

1961

89PDa	Card, #88PD-89PD affixed, dated 10/31/61 (2)	45
89PDb	Card, 2 #88PD, 2 #89PD, disapproved (2)	—
88PI	Pair (100)	—
89PI	Pair (100)	—

New York #90-91
International Monetary Fund

1961

91PDa	Card with 2 #90PD, 2 #91PD in slightly different shades (1)	1,30
90PI	Pair (100)	—
91PI	Pair (50)	—

New York #92
Abstract Flags

1961

92PI	Pair (80)	—
	Horiz. pair with vert. gutter (20)	—

New York #93-94
Economic Commission for Latin America

1961

93PDa	Card, 2 #93PD, 2 essays of #94 (2)	—
94PDa	Card, 2 #94PD (1)	40

Essays of No. 94 lack serifs in "1's."

New York #95-96
Economic Commission for Africa

1961

96PDa	Card with #95PD-96PD affixed (8)	50
95PP	4 items (100)	—
96PP	8 items (100)	—
95PI	Pair (100)	—
96PI	Pair (100)	—

New York #97-99
UN Children's Fund (UNICEF)

1961

99PDa	Card, #97PD-99PD, with approval handstamp (3)	1,05
99PDb	Card, #97PD-99PD, no approval handstamp (5)	60
97PP	4 items (80)	—
	Vert. pair with horiz. gutter (10)	—
98PP	4 items (80)	—
	Vert. pair with horiz. gutter (10)	—
99PP	4 items (80)	—
	Vert. pair with horiz. gutter (10)	—
97PI	Pair (80)	—
	Vert. pair with horiz. gutter (20)	—
98PI	Pair (80)	—
	Vert. pair with horiz. gutter (20)	—
99PI	Pair (80)	—
	Vert. pair with horiz. gutter (20)	—

New York #100-101
Housing and Urban Development Program

1962

100PD	With approval handstamp (3)	20
101PD	With approval handstamp (3)	20
100PI	Pair with oval "Harrison's Photogravure Specimen" handstamp (25)	35
101PI	Pair with oval "Harrison's Photogravure Specimen" handstamp (25)	35

Three essays each of Nos. 100 and 101 have larger numerals than issued stamps are are on cards marked "disapproved."

New York #102-103
Malaria Eradication Campaign

1962

102PD	(5)	40
103PD	(5)	40

New York #104-107
Definitives

1962

104PD	(5)	40
105PD	(7)	42
106PD	With approval handstamp & signature (2)	40
107PD	(3)	50
104PI	Pair with oval "Harrison's Photogravure Specimen" handstamp (25)	25
105PI	Pair with oval "Harrison's Photogravure Specimen" handstamp (25)	25

07PI Pair with oval "Harrison's Photogravure Specimen" handstamp (25) 250.
Same, without handstamp (25) 400.

Three essays of No. 106 have indistinct line between "U" and N," and are on cards marked "disapproved."

New York #108-109
Death of Dag Hammarskjold, 1st Anniv.

962
08PDa Card, #108PD, essay of #109 (1) —
09PDa Card, #109PD, essay of #108 (1) —
09PDb Card, #108PD-#109PD (2) 600.
08PI Pair (80) —
Vert. pair with horiz. gutter (20) —
09PI Pair (80) —
Vert. pair with horiz. gutter (20) —

Essays of Nos 108-109 lack denomination.

New York #110-111
UN Operation in the Congo

1962
111PDa Card, 3 #110PD, 3 #111PD (1) 1,150.
111PDb Card, #111PD, essay of #110 (2) 550.
110PP 4 items (80) —
Horiz. pair with vert. gutter (10) —
11PP 4 items (80) —
Horiz. pair with vert. gutter (10) —
10PI Pair (80) —
Horiz. pair with vert. gutter (20) —
11PI Pair (80) —
Horiz. pair with vert. gutter (20) —

Essays of No. 110 have 5c denomination.

New York #112-113
Committee on Peaceful Uses of Outer Space

1962
112PD (2) —
113PD (1) —
113PDa Card, #112PD-113PD (3) 500.

Essays similar to Nos. 112PD-113PD have text in white panel below palm frond.

New York #114-115
UN Development Decade

1963
115PDa Card, #114PD, 2 #115PD (one in slightly different shade) with approval handstamp (3) 875.
115PDb Card, #114PD-115PD (3) 400.
114PP 4 items (80) —
Vert. pair with horiz. gutter (10) —
115PP 4 items (80) —
Vert. pair with horiz. gutter (10) —
114PI Pair (80) —
Vert. pair with horiz. gutter (20) —
115PI Pair (80) —
Vert. pair with horiz. gutter (20) —

New York #116-117
Freedom from Hunger Campaign

1963
116PD (1) —
117PD (1) —
117PDa Card, #116PD-117PD (5) 500.
116PP 3 items (80) —
Horiz. pair with vert. gutter (10) —
117PP 3 items (80) —
Horiz. pair with vert. gutter (10) —
116PI Pair (80) —
Horiz. pair with vert. gutter (20) —
117PI Pair (80) —
Horiz. pair with vert. gutter (20) —

Essays similar to Nos. 116PD-117PD have taller numerals and lettering.

New York #118
UN Temporary Executive Authority in West New Guinea

1963
118PD With approval handstamp (2) 400.
118PDa Card, #118PD (approved), #118TC (not approved) (3) 500.
118TCa Card, 2 #118TC (disapproved or with instructions to printer) (3) 500.
118PP 3 items (100) —
Horiz. pair with vert. gutter (10) —
118PI Pair (100) —
Horiz. pair with vert. gutter (20) —

No. 118TC has right side of map in a lighter shade of green.

New York #119-120
General Assembly Building, New York

1963
120PDa Card, #119PD-120PD (2) 400.

New York #121-122
Universal Declaration of Human Rights, 15th Anniv.

1963
121PD (2) 250.
122PD (2) 250.
121PI Pair (100) —
122PI Pair (100) —

Essays similar to Nos. 121PD-122PD have top line of frame text flush left rather than centered, and are on a disapproved card.

New York #123-124
Intergovernmental Maritime Consultative Organization

1964
124PDa Card, #123PD-124PD (3) 550.
123PP 4 items (80) —
Horiz. pair with vert. gutter (10) —
124PP 4 items (80) —
Horiz. pair with vert. gutter (10) —
123PI Pair (80) —
Horiz. pair with vert. gutter (20) —
124PI Pair (80) —
Horiz. pair with vert. gutter (20) —

New York #125-128
Definitives

1964
125PD (3) 275.
125PDa Card, #125 perforated with approval handstamp (1) —
126PD (3) 240.
127PDa Card, #126PD-127PD with approval handstamp (3) 550.
127PDb Card, #127PD (approved), #127PD (not approved, in slightly different shade, #126PD (disapproved in slightly different shade (3) 925.
128PD (3) 240.
125PP 3 items (100) —
126PI 3 items (80) —
Vert. pair with horiz. gutter (10) —
127PP 4 items (80) —
Horiz. pair with vert. gutter (10) —
128PP 4 items (80) —
Horiz. pair with vert. gutter (10) —
125PI Pair (65) —
Horiz. pair with vert. gutter (10) —
126PI Pair (80) —
Vert. pair with horiz. gutter (20) —
127PI Pair (80) —
Horiz. pair with vert. gutter (20) —
128PI Pair (80) —
Horiz. pair with vert. gutter (20) —

Essays similar to No. 125PD have larger numerals and blue text.

New York #129-130
UN Conference on Trade and Development

1964
129PD (6) 250.
130PD (6) 250.
129PI Pair (25) —
130PI Pair (25) —

New York #131-132
Narcotics Control

1964
131PD (2) 250.
132PD (2) 250.
132PDa Card, #131PD-132PD (3) 600.

New York #133
Nuclear Test Ban Treaty

1964
133TC dark red & black, perforated, litho. & engr. (1) 300.
133TC lilac, perforated, engr. (20) —
133TCa Card, 2 #133TC dark red & dark brown, litho. & vignette essay, litho. (1) —
133TCb Card, #133TC dark red & black, engr. & 5 vignette essays, engr. (1) —
133TCc Card, 11 #133TC in red, claret, brown rose, brown, dark brown, dull blue, blue, blue violet, gray, dark gray, black, engr. (1) —

New York #134-136
Education for Progress Campaign

1964
135PD (1) —
136PDa Card, #134PD-136PD, with approval stamp (3) —
136PDb Card, #134PD-136PD, without approval stamp (2) 300.
136PDc Card, #134PD, #136PD, without approval stamp (1) 450.
134PP 4 items (80) —
Horiz. pair with vert. gutter (10) —
135PP 4 items (80) —
Horiz. pair with vert. gutter (10) —
136PP 4 items (80) —
Horiz. pair with vert. gutter (10) —
134PI Pair (80) —
Horiz. pair with vert. gutter (20) —
135PI Pair (80) —
Horiz. pair with vert. gutter (20) —
136PI Pair (80) —
Horiz. pair with vert. gutter (20) —

New York #137-138
Special Fund Program

1965
137PD (2) 225.
138PD (2) 225.
138PDa Card, #137PD-138PD, with approval stamp (1) 500.
138PDb Card, #137PD-138PD, without approval stamp (1) —

New York #139-140
UN Peace-Keeping Force in Cyprus

1965
140PDa Card #139PD-140PD, with approval stamp (5) 500.
140PP 3 items (80) —
Vert. pair with horiz. gutter (10) —
139PI Pair (40) —
Vert. pair with horiz. gutter (10) —
140PI Pair (40) —
Vert. pair with horiz. gutter (10) —

Smaller-size essays (30x38mm) of Nos. 139-140 are in three cards with approval stamps.

New York #141-142
International Telecommunication Union

1965
142PDa Card, #141PD-142PD, with approval stamp (3) 500.
142PDb Card, #141PD-142PD, no approval stamp (3) 450.
142PDc Card, #141PD-142PD, #141TC dated "8.2.65" (3) 925.
141PP 4 items (80) —
Horiz. pair with vert. gutter (10) —
142PP 4 items (80) —
Horiz. pair with vert. gutter (10) —
141PI Pair (80) —
Horiz. pair with vert. gutter (20) —
142PI Pair (80) —
Horiz. pair with vert. gutter (20) —

No. 141TC has orange yellow lines instead of orange lines.

New York #143-145
UN, 20th Anniv. and International Cooperation Year

1965
143PD (3) 275.
143PDa Card, #143PD, 144TC orange red (3) 825.
144PD (3) 275.
144PDa Card, #143PD-144PD, with approval stamp (7) 500.
145PD Imperforate sheet with manuscript printer's instructions (4) —
Issued souvenir sheet, perforated (on printer's card) (1) 110.
145PDa #143PD, #144PD affixed to #145 souvenir sheet margin (5) 600.

New York #146-150
Definitives

1965-66
146PD (7) 200.
148PDa Block of 12 perforated stamps with approval handstamp in margin (2) 140.
148PDb Card, #147-148 perforated, with approval handstamp (3) 500.
149PD Perforated, with approval handstamp (2) 250.
149PDa Card, #149PD (2nd printing), #149PD, first printing, perforated, with approval handstamp (2) 600.
150PD (3) 240.
149TC Prussian blue & dark blue, perforated (1) —
150PP 3 items (80), affixed on cards —
Horiz. pair with vert. gutter (10) —
150PI Pair (161) 375.
Horiz. pair with vert. gutter (19) —

Two cards without approval handstamp have perforated essays of both Nos. 147 and 148. The essay of No. 147 has larger numerals and the essay of No. 148 has bright yellow text at bottom. No. 150PI has had extra glue applied.

New York #151-153
Population Trends and Development

1965
152PDa Card, #151PD-152PD, 153TC, perforated, with approval handstamp (2) 825.

No. 153TC has "Nations Unies" in black instead of gray.

New York #154-155
World Federation of United Nations Associations

1966
155PDa Card, #154-155PD with approval handstamp (3) 500.
154PP 4 items (80) —

Vert. pair with horiz. gutter (10) —
155PP 4 items (80) —
Vert. pair with horiz. gutter (10) —
154PI Pair (80) —
Vert. pair with horiz. gutter (20) —
155PI Pair (80) —
Vert. pair with horiz. gutter (20) —

New York #156-157
World Health Organization

1966

157TCa Card, #156TC-157TC, with approval handstamp (3) 500.
156PP 4 items (50) —
157PP 4 items (80) —
Horiz. pair with vert. gutter (10) —
156PI Pair (65) —
Horiz. pair with vert. gutter (10) —
157PI Pair (80) —
Horiz. pair with vert. gutter (20) —

Nos. 156TC and 157TC have side and front of building the same shade of blue.

New York #158-159
International Coffee Agreement of 1962

1966

159PDa Card, #158PD-159PD (3) 625.

New York #160
UN Observers

1964

160PD (2) on cards dated "3.2.1966" 125.
160PP 4 items (50) —
160PI Pair (65) —
Vert. pair with horiz. gutter (10) —

Two essays of No. 160 with white text lines larger and closer together are on cards dated "17.1.1966."

New York #161-163
UNICEF, 20th Anniv.

1966

161PD (3) 250.
162PD (3) 250.
163PD (3) 250.
161PI Pair (72) —
Cross gutter block (1) —
Horiz. pair with vert. gutter (18) —
Vert. pair with horiz. gutter (8) —
162PI Pair (72) —
Cross gutter block (1) —
Horiz. pair with vert. gutter (18) —
Vert. pair with horiz. gutter (8) —
163PI Pair (72) —
Cross gutter block (1) —
Horiz. pair with vert. gutter (18) —
Vert. pair with horiz. gutter (8) —

New York #164-165
UN Development Program

1967

165PDa Card, # 164PD-165PD, dated "6.9. 1966" (3) 725.
165PDb Card, #165PD, 2 #164PD, with approval handstamp, dated "4.10.66" (6) 925.
164PI Pair (40) —
Horiz. pair with vert. gutter (10) —
165PI Pair (40) —
Horiz. pair with vert. gutter (10) —

New York #166-167
Definitives

1967

166PD (6) 225.
166PDa Card, 2 #166PD (3) 575.
167PD (3) 200.
167TC With brown line separating "UN" in vignette, on card dated "27.4.1966" (3) 250.
166PP 4 items (80) —
Vert. pair with horiz. gutter (10) —
167PP 3 items (80) —
Horiz. pair with vert. gutter (10) —
166PI Pair (80) —
Vert. pair with horiz. gutter (20) —
167PI Pair (80) —
Horiz. pair with vert. gutter (20) —

New York #168-169
Independence

1967

168PD (2) 250.
169PD (3) 250.

New York #170-174
EXPO '67

1967

170PD (1) 300.
171PD (1) 300.
172PD (3) 300.
173PD (1) 300.
174PD (3) 300.
170PP 2 items (144) —
Cross gutter block (1) —
Horiz. pair with vert. gutter (8) —
Vert. pair with horiz. gutter (18) —
171PP 2 items (144) —
Cross gutter block (1) —
Horiz. pair with vert. gutter (8) —
Vert. pair with horiz. gutter (18) —
172PP 3 items (144) —
Cross gutter block (1) —
Horiz. pair with vert. gutter (18) —
Vert. pair with horiz. gutter (8) —
173PP 2 items (144) —
Cross gutter block (1) —
Horiz. pair with vert. gutter (8) —
Vert. pair with horiz. gutter (18) —
174PP 2 items (144) —
Cross gutter block (1) —
Horiz. pair with vert. gutter (8) —
Vert. pair with horiz. gutter (18) —
170PI Pair (72) —
Cross gutter block (1) —
Horiz. pair with vert. gutter (8) —
Vert. pair with horiz. gutter (18) —
171PI Pair (72) —
Cross gutter block (1) —
Horiz. pair with vert. gutter (8) —
Vert. pair with horiz. gutter (18) —
172PI Pair (72) —
Cross gutter block (1) —
Horiz. pair with vert. gutter (18) —
Vert. pair with horiz. gutter (8) —
173PI Pair (72) —
Cross gutter block (1) —
Horiz. pair with vert. gutter (8) —
Vert. pair with horiz. gutter (18) —
174PI Pair (72) —
Cross gutter block (1) —
Horiz. pair with vert. gutter (8) —
Vert. pair with horiz. gutter (18) —

New York #175-176
International Tourist Year

1967

176PDa #175-176, perforated, affixed to printer's card (2) 600.

New York #177-178
Towards Disarmament

1967

177PD (3) —
178PD (3) 200.
178TC Wall text in copper, gold lines in wall (1) 110.
178TC Wall text in copper, blue gray lines in wall (3) 110.
178TC Wall text in brown, silver lines in wall (1) 110.
178TC Wall text in brown, blue gray lines in wall (3) 110.

New York #179-180
Chagall Stained Glass Windows

1967

179PP 8 items (29) —
180PP 8 items (29) —
179PI Pair on card stock (24) 1,050.
180PI Pair on card stock (135) 650.
Horiz. pair with vert. gutter, on card stock (15) —
180PI Pair on stamp paper (75) 525.

Essays of Nos. 179-180 in 5c denomination exist.

New York #181-182
UN Secretariat

1968

181PD (1) 110.
182PD (1) 110.
182PDa Card, #181PD-182PD (1) —
181PP 5 items (160) —
Horiz. pair with vert. gutter (20) —
182PP 5 items (160) —
Horiz. pair with vert. gutter (20) —
181PI Pair (80) —
Horiz. pair with vert. gutter (20) —
182PI Pair (80) —
Horiz. pair with vert. gutter (20) —

New York #183-184
Art at the UN

1968

183PD (1) 250.
184PD (1) 250.
184PDa Card, #183PD-184PD, dated "5.12.67" (2) —
184TCa Card, #183TC-184TC, dated "10.XI.67" (3) 725.
183PP 5 items (80) —
Vert. pair with horiz. gutter (10) —
184PP 5 items (80) —
Vert. pair with horiz. gutter (10) —
183PI Pair (65) —
Vert. pair with horiz. gutter (10) —
184PI Pair (80) —
Vert. pair with horiz. gutter (20) —

No. 183TC has a bright blue frame; No. 184TC a birght red frame.

New York #185-186
UN Industrial Development Orgainzation

1968

185PD (4) 325.
186PD (3) 500.
186TC brown frame, deep blue "ONUDI" (2) —
185PP 4 items, affixed to cards (3) —
186PP 4 items, affixed to cards (3) —
185PI Pair with security punch (25) 250.
186PI Pair with security punch (25) 250.

New York #187
UN Headquarters

1964

187TC light gray roof in foreground, numbered 34 or 38, dated July 7, 1967 (2) 140.
187TC With wide curved white line under window of General Assembly building, numbered 397 or 404, dated 11.8.1967 (2) 125
187TC With halo around UN emblem, dated Feb. 12, 1968 (2) 240
187PP 11 items, on card with staple holes (3) —
187PI Pair with "Specimen" overprint (80) 250
Vert. pair with horiz. gutter, with "Specimen" overprint (20) —
187PI Pair without "Specimen" overprint (80) 375
Vert. pair with horiz. gutter, without "Specimen" overprint (20) —

New York #188-189
World Weather Watch

1968

189PDa Card, #188PD-189PD (1) 500
188PP 5 items (100) —
189PP 5 items (100) —

New York #190-191
International Human Rights Year

1968

190PD (6) 210
191PD (6) 210
190PP 4 items (100) —
191PP 4 items (100) —
190PI Pair (50) —
191PI Pair (50) —

New York #192-193
UN Institute for Training and Research

1969

193PDa Card, #192PD-193PD (2) 425
192PP 6 items (50) —
193PP 6 items (100) —
192PI Pair (15) 425
193PI Pair (15) 425

New York #194-195
Economic Commission for Latin America

1969

195PDa #194-195, perforated, affixed to printer's card (4) 425

New York #196
"UN" and Emblem

1969

196PD With approval handstamp (2) 250
196TC Card, #196PD, 196TC dark blue background (2) —
196PP 3 items (100) —

New York #197-198
UN International Law Commission

1969

198PDa Card, #197PD-198PD (9) 650
197PP 4 items (80) —
Horiz. pair with vert. gutter (10) —
198PP 4 items (80) —
Horiz. pair with vert. gutter (10) —
197PI (40 pairs) —
Horiz. pair with vert. gutter (10) —
198PI (40 pairs) —
Horiz. pair with vert. gutter (10) —

New York #199-200
Labor and Development

1969

199PD With approval handstamp (1) —
200PD (1) —
200PDa Card, #199PD-200PD, with approval handstamp (1) 425
199TC Men in dark blue, perforated (3) —
200TC Rose pink background, perforated (3) —
200PP 4 items (91) —

Geneva #1-14
Definitives

1969-70

G1PD (2) 200
G3PD (1) —
G3PDa Card, 2 #G3PD, with approval handstamp (2) —
G4PD (2) —

G5PD	(3)	325.
G7PD	(1)	250.
G8PD	Perforated, on card with approval handstamp (2)	275.
G8PDa	Perforated layout sheet proof with 4 #G8PD affixed (1)	—
G8PDb	Partial perforated layout sheet proof with 2 #G8PD affixed (1)	—
G9PD	(1)	275.
G10PD	(1)	200.
G11PD	(1)	—
G12PD	(1)	225.
G13PD	(4)	240.
G14PD	(3)	225.
G1TC	Black panel behind "UN" (1)	—
G6TCa	Card, #G6PD, #G6TC pewter emblem, dated "7.10.69" (3)	—
G6TCb	Card, #G6TC silver emblem, 2 #G6PD dated "17.9.69" (3)	—
G6TCc	Card, #G6PD, #G6TC orange denomination, dated "27.8.69" (3)	—
G12TC	gray background, on card marked "Rejected" (2)	325.
G1PP	3 items, perforated (100)	—
G2PP	5 items (160)	—
	Horiz. pair with vert. gutter (20)	—
G3PP	5 items (160)	—
	Horiz. pair with vert. gutter (20)	—
G4PP	5 items (151)	—
	Horiz. pair with vert. gutter (20)	—
G5PP	4 items (160)	—
	Vert. pair with horiz. gutter (20)	—
G6PP	3 items (160)	—
	Horiz. pair with vert. gutter (20)	—
G7PP	4 items (100)	—
G8PP	8 items (150)	—
G9PP	6 items (100)	—
G10PP	8 items (100)	—
G12PP	6 items (100)	—
G13PP	5 items (160)	—
	Vert. pair with horiz. gutter (20)	—
G2PI	Pair (80)	—
	Horiz. pair with vert. gutter (20)	—
G3PI	Pair (80)	—
	Horiz. pair with vert. gutter (20)	—
G4PI	Pair (73)	—
	Horiz. pair with vert. gutter (20)	—
G5PI	Pair (80)	—
	Vert. pair with horiz. gutter (20)	—
G6PI	Pair (80)	—
	Horiz. pair with vert. gutter (20)	—
G7PI	Pair (50)	—
G8PI	Pair (75)	—
G9PI	Pair (50)	—
G10PI	Pair (50)	—
G13PI	Pair (80)	—
	Vert. pair with horiz. gutter (20)	—

Four essays of No. G2 exist, having "0" below "F" jutting out to left. Two essays of No. G10 with small "F.S." are on rejected cards.

New York #201-202
Mosaic Art at the UN

1969

201PD	(3)	210.
202PD	(3)	210.
202PDa	Card, #201PD-202PD (2)	—
201PP	8 items (100)	—
202PP	8 items (100)	—
201PI	Pair (50)	—
202PI	Pair (50)	—

New York #203-204
Peace Bell

1970

204PDa	Card, 2 each #203PD-204PD (2)	1,300.
203PP	5 items (100)	—
204PP	5 items (100)	—

About half of Nos. 203PP and 204PP have faults.

New York #205-206
Lower Mekong Basin Development Project

1970

205PD	(2)	250.
206PD	(2)	250.
205PP	10 items (100)	—
206PP	10 items (100)	—
205PI	Pair (50)	—
206PI	Pair (50)	—

New York #207-208
Fight Cancer

1970

207PD	Perforated, non-glossy paper, on piece of printer's card (1)	—
208PD	Perforated, non-glossy paper, on piece of printer's card (1)	—
208PDa	Card, #207PD-208PD, perforated, non-glossy paper (1)	—
208PDb	Card, 2 #207PD-208PD, perforated, non-glossy paper, with approval handstamp (1)	1,050.
208PDc	#207-208, perforated, glossy paper, on printer's card (2)	—
207PP	2 items (50)	—
208PP	2 items (50)	—
207PI	Pair (50)	—
208PI	Pair (50)	—

New York #209-212
UN, 25th Anniv.

1970

209PD	(2)	—
210PD	(2)	—
211PD	On card (3)	—
211PDa	Card, #209PD-211PD (2)	750.
212PD	(1)	275.
212PDa	Card, #209PD-212PD (1)	—
209PP	4 items (180)	—
	Horiz. pair with vert. gutter (10)	—
210PP	5 items (180)	—
	Horiz. pair with vert. gutter (10)	—
211PP	3 items (180)	—
	Vert. pair with horiz. gutter (10)	—
212PP	5 items (22)	—
209PI	Pair (80)	—
	Horiz. pair with vert. gutter (20)	—
210PI	Pair (80)	—
	Horiz. pair with vert. gutter (20)	—
211PI	Pair (80)	—
	Vert. pair with horiz. gutter (20)	—
212PI	Pair (12)	—

New York #213-214
Peace, Justice and Progress

1970

214PDa	Card, #213PD-214PD (3)	600.
214PDb	Card, 2 each #213PD-214PD (2)	1,300.
213PP	4 items (50)	—
214PP	4 items (50)	—

New York #215, Geneva #15
Peaceful Uses of the Sea Bed

1971

215PD	(2)	200.
G15PD	(1)	—
215PP	6 items (100)	—
G15PP	6 items (100)	—
215PI	Pair (50)	—
G15PI	Pair (50)	—

New York #216-217, Geneva #16
International Support for Refugees

1971

217PDa	Card, #216PD-217PD, #G16PD (2)	775.
216PP	4 items (80)	—
	Horiz. pair with vert. gutter (10)	—
217PP	4 items (80)	—
	Horiz. pair with vert. gutter (10)	—
G16PP	4 items (160)	—
	Horiz. pair with vert. gutter (20)	—
216PI	Pair (80)	—
	Horiz. pair with vert. gutter (20)	—
217PI	Pair (80)	—
	Horiz. pair with vert. gutter (20)	—
G16PI	Pair (80)	—
	Horiz. pair with vert. gutter (20)	—

New York #218, Geneva #17
World Food Program

1971

218PD	(4)	225.
G17PD	(4)	225.
G17TC	(1)	375.
218PP	6 items (100)	—
G17PP	6 items (100)	—
218PI	Pair (50)	—
G17PI	Pair (50)	—

New York #219, Geneva #18
Universal Postal Union

1971

219PDa	Card, #219PD, #G18PD (3)	550.
219PP	5 items (130)	—
	Horiz. pair with vert. gutter (10)	—
G18PP	5 items (150)	—
219PI	Pair (80)	—
	Horiz. pair with vert. gutter (20)	—
G18PI	Pair (80)	—
	Horiz. pair with vert. gutter (20)	—

New York #220-221, Geneva #19-20
International Year Against Racial Discrimination

1971

221PDa	Card, #220PD-221PD, #G19PD-G20PD and 4 similar items with slightly different colors (1)	2,400.
221PDb	Card with affixed plastic sheet with #220PD-221PD, #G19PD-G20PD affixed (1)	600.
221PDc	Cut-up card, #220PD-221PD, G19PD-G20PD (1)	—
220PP	5 items (100)	—
221PP	5 items (75)	—
G19PP	5 items (100)	—
G20PP	5 items (100)	—

New York #222-223
UN Headquarters, New York

1971

222PD	(4)	275.
223PD	(2)	275.
222PP	8 items (91)	—
223PP	5 items (92)	—
222PI	Pair (175)	—

Two sheets of 50 of No. 222PI are "approved."

New York #224-225, Geneva #21
UN International School

1971

225PDa	Card, #224PD-225PD, G21PD, with approval stamp (2)	750.
225PDb	Card or sheet, #224PD-225PD, 1fr essay of #G21 (3)	925.
224PP	5 items (180)	—
	Vert. pair with horiz. gutter (10)	—
225PP	5 items (100)	—
	Vert. pair with horiz. gutter (10)	—
G21PP	5 items (180)	—
	Vert. pair with horiz. gutter (10)	—
224PI	Pair (80)	—
	Vert. pair with horiz. gutter (20)	—
225PI	Pair (80)	—
	Vert. pair with horiz. gutter (20)	—
G21PI	Pair (80)	—
	Vert. pair with horiz. gutter (20)	—

New York #226, Geneva #22
Definitives

1972

226PD	Perforated on printer's card (3)	225.
G22PD	(5)	225.
226PP	4 items (100)	—
G22PP	4 items (180)	—
	Horiz. pair with vert. gutter (10)	—
226PI	Pair (50)	—
G22PI	Pair (80)	—
	Horiz. pair with vert. gutter (20)	—

New York #227, Geneva #23
Non-proliferation of Nuclear Weapons

1972

227PD	(2)	200.
G23PD	(2)	225.
227PP	6 items (100)	—
G23PP	6 items (100)	—
227PI	Pair (50)	—
G23PI	Pair (50)	—

Two essays each of Nos. 227 and G23 lacking strong gray billowing in center of cloud exist on cards dated "22.Set.1971."

New York #228, Geneva #24, Souvenir Card #1
World Health Day

1972

228PDa	Card, #228PD, #G24PD with approval handstamp (1)	500.
G24PD	(1)	—
SC1PD	Card with stamps with simulated perforations and cancels (2)	600.
228PP	8 items (80)	—
	Vert. pair with horiz. gutter (10)	—
G24PP	8 items (160)	—
	Vert. pair with horiz. gutter (20)	—
G24PI	Pair (180)	—
	Vert. pair with horiz. gutter (20)	—

New York #229-230, Geneva #25-26
UN Conference on Human Environment

1972

229PD	(1)	—
230PDa	Card, #229PD-230PD, #G25PD-G26PD (3)	450.
230PDb	Card, #230PD, #G25PD-G26PD (1)	—
229PP	6 items (288)	—
	Cross gutter block (2)	—
	Horiz. pair with vert. gutter (16)	—
	Vert. pair with horiz. gutter (36)	—
230PP	6 items (288)	—
	Cross gutter block (2)	—
	Horiz. pair with vert. gutter (16)	—
	Vert. pair with horiz. gutter (36)	—
G25PP	6 items (288)	—
	Cross gutter block (2)	—
	Horiz. pair with vert. gutter (16)	—
	Vert. pair with horiz. gutter (36)	—
G26PP	6 items (288)	—
	Cross gutter block (2)	—
	Horiz. pair with vert. gutter (16)	—
	Vert. pair with horiz. gutter (36)	—
229PI	Pair (144)	—
	Cross gutter block (2)	—
	Horiz. pair with vert. gutter (16)	—
	Vert. pair with horiz. gutter (36)	—
230PI	Pair (144)	—
	Cross gutter block (2)	—
	Horiz. pair with vert. gutter (16)	—
	Vert. pair with horiz. gutter (36)	—
G25PI	Pair (144)	—
	Cross gutter block (2)	—
	Horiz. pair with vert. gutter (16)	—
	Vert. pair with horiz. gutter (36)	—
G26PI	Pair (144)	—
	Cross gutter block (2)	—
	Horiz. pair with vert. gutter (16)	—
	Vert. pair with horiz. gutter (36)	—

New York #231, Geneva #27
Economic Commission for Europe

1972

231PDa	Card, #231PD, #G27PD (4)	550.
231PP	8 items (100)	—
G27PP	8 items (50)	—

New York #232-233, Geneva #28-29, Souvenir Card #2
Art at the UN

1972

232PDa	Card, #232PD, #233TC text in dull blue green, #G28PD-G29PD (1)	975.
G28PD	(1)	—
G29PDa	Card, #G28PD-G29PD, #233TC text in dull blue green (1)	—
G29PDb	Card, #G29PD, #233TC text in dull blue green (1)	—
SC2PD	(25)	—
SC2PDa	Defaced card, with corrections marked in blue (8)	—
SC2TC	Untrimmed card, signature in light blue(3)	160.
G28PP	3 items (50)	—
G29PP	3 items (50)	—
232PI	Pair (80)	—
	Vert. pair with horiz. gutter (20)	—
233PI	Pair (80)	—
	Vert. pair with horiz. gutter (20)	—
G28PI	Pair (80)	—
	Vert. pair with horiz. gutter (20)	—
G29PI	Pair (80)	—
	Vert. pair with horiz. gutter (20)	—

New York #234-235, Geneva #30-31, Souvenir Card #3
Disarmament Decade

1973

235PDa	Card, #234PD-235PD, #G30PD-G31PD, with approval handstamp (1)	825.
SC3PD	With printer's stamp or approval handstamp (9)	110.
234PP	8 items (130)	—
	Horiz. pair with vert. gutter (20)	—
235PP	8 items (100)	—
G30PP	8 items (130)	—
	Horiz. pair with vert. gutter (20)	—
G31PP	8 items (100)	—
234PI	Pair (230)	—
	Horiz. pair with vert. gutter (20)	—
235PI	Pair (230)	—
	Horiz. pair with vert. gutter (20)	—
G30PI	Pair (205)	—
	Horiz. pair with vert. gutter (20)	—
G31PI	Pair (230)	—
	Horiz. pair with vert. gutter (20)	—

Two examples of #SC3PD are cut in half.

New York #236-237, Geneva #32
Fight Against Drug Abuse

1973

236PD	(1)	—
237PDa	Card, #236PD-237PD, #G32PD with approval handstamp (4)	725.
237PDb	Card, #237PD, #G32PD with approval handstamp (1)	—
237PDc	Card, #237PD, #G32PD, 9c essay of #236 (6)	—
236PP	8 items (75)	—
237PP	8 items (100)	—
G32PP	8 items (50)	—
236PI	Pair (50)	—
237PI	Pair (50)	—
G32PI	Pair (50)	—

New York #238-239, Geneva #33
UN Volunteer Program

1973

239PDa	Card, #238PD-239PD, #G33PD (9)	600.
238PP	8 items (80)	—
239PP	8 items (100)	—
G33PP	8 items (50)	—
238PI	Pair (50)	—
239PI	Pair (50)	—
G33PI	Pair (25)	—

New York #240-241, Geneva #34
Namibia

1973

241PDa	Card, #240PD-241PD, #G34PD (1)	—
241PDb	Card, #240PD-241PD, #G34PD, essays of #240-241, #G34 with Africa outlined in gold (3)	1,400.
240PP	8 items (100)	—
241PP	8 items (100)	—
G34PP	8 items (50)	—
240PI	Pair (50)	—
241PI	Pair (50)	—
G34PI	Pair (50)	—

Two cards containing only the essays exist.

New York #242-243, Geneva #35-36, Souvenir Card #4
Universal Declaration of Human Rights, 25th Anniv.

1973

242PD	(9)	275.
243PDa	Card, #242PD-243PD, #G35PD-G36PD (6)	1,300.
243PDb	Card, #242PD-243PD (9)	725.
243PDc	Card, #243PD, #G35PD-G36PD (1)	—
SC4PD	With approval handstamp (3)	—
242PP	5 items (100)	—
243PP	5 items (100)	—
G35PP	5 items (100)	—
G36PP	5 items (50)	—
SC4PP	2 items (1)	—
SC4PI	untrimmed card (1)	—

No. SC4PP may not be a complete set of progressive proofs.

New York #244-245, Geneva #37-38
New International Labor Organization Headquarters

1974

245PDa	Card, #245PD, #G37PD-G38PD, 8c essay of #244 (4)	1,200.
244PP	8 items (75)	—
245PP	8 items (75)	—
G37PP	8 items (50)	—
G38PP	8 items (50)	—
244PI	Pair (50)	—
245PI	Pair (50)	—
G37PI	Pair (50)	—
G38PI	Pair (50)	—

New York #246, Geneva #39-40, Souvenir Card #5
Universal Postal Union, Cent.

1974

246PD	(1)	—
246PDa	Card, #246PD, #G39PD-G40PD (7)	925.
G40PDa	Card, #G39PD-G40PD (1)	—
SC5PD	Affixed to card (5)	400.
SC5PDa	Card with printer instructions in ink (1)	—
SC5PDb	Progressive proof sheet with printer instructions in ink (1)	400.
246PP	6 items (100)	—
G39PP	5 items (50)	—
G40PP	5 items (50)	—
246PI	Pair (25)	—
G39PI	Pair (25)	—
G40PI	Pair (25)	—

New York #247-248, Geneva #41-42
Art at the UN

1974

247PDa	Card, #247PD, #G41PD-G42PD, 15c essay of #248 (5)	1,250.
248PDa	Card, #247PD-248PD, #G41PD-G42PD (3)	925.
247PP	8 items (100)	—
248PP	8 items (100)	—
G41PP	8 items (50)	—
G42PP	8 items (50)	—
247PI	Pair (50)	—
248PI	Pair (50)	—
G41PI	Pair (50)	—
G42PI	Pair (50)	—

New York #249-251
Definitives

1974

249PD	Affixed on perforated blank (1)	—
250PD	Affixed on perforated blank (1)	—
250PDa	Taped to card (1)	—
250PDb	Card, #250PD, 251TC with darker brown background, essay of #249 with flat top "S," with "21.DIC.1973" date and approval stamp (2)	—
251PD	Affixed on perforated blank (1)	125.
251PDa	Card, #249PD, #251PD, with "17.ENE.1974" date and approval stamp (3)	500.
251TCa	Darker brown background, on cards dated "21.DIC.1973" (3)	—
250PP	10 items (50)	—
251PP	8 items (35)	—
249PI	Pair (200)	—
250PI	Pair (50)	—
251PI	Pair (100)	—

New York #252-253, Geneva #43-44, Souvenir Card #6
World Population Year

1974

252PDa	Card, #252PD, #G44PD, 21c essay of #253, 40c essay of #G43 in se-tenant strip (5)	725.
253PDa	Card, #252PD-253PD, G44PD, 40c essay of #G43 in se-tenant strip (4)	800.
SC6PD	With approval handstamp (10)	—
252PP	10 items (50)	—
253PP	10 items (50)	—
G43PP	10 items (50)	—
G44PP	10 items (50)	—
252PI	Pair (50)	—
253PI	Pair (50)	—
G43PI	Pair (50)	—
G44PI	Pair (50)	—

All examples of No. SC6PD show the 40c essay.

New York #254-255, Geneva #45
Law of the Sea

1974

255PDa	Card, #254PD-255PD, #G45TC with blue green sky (3)	800.
254PP	10 items (50)	—
255PP	10 items (50)	—
G45PP	10 items (50)	—
254PI	Pair (50)	—
255PI	Pair (50)	—
G45PI	Pair (50)	—

New York #256-257, Geneva #46-47, Souvenir Card #7
Peaceful Uses of Outer Space

1975

256PDa	Card, #256PD, #G46PD-G47PD (1)	—
257PD	Cut from #256PDa (1)	—
257PDa	Card, #256PD-257PD, G46PD-G47PD (3)	825
SC7PD	with approval handstamp (4)	—
256PP	8 items (150)	—
257PP	8 items (150)	—
G46PP	8 items (50)	—
G47PP	8 items (50)	—
256PI	Pair (100)	—
257PI	Pair (100)	—
G46PI	Pair (50)	—
G47PI	Pair (50)	—

New York #258-259, Geneva #48-49
International Women's Year

1975

258PD	On card dated "16 Oct. 1974" (4)	250
259PD	(4)	250
G48PD	On card dated "16 Oct. 1974" (4)	325
G49PD	(4)	325
258TC	bright blue background (on cards dated "17 Sep. 1974") (4)	—
G48TC	red brown background (on cards dated "17 Sep. 1974") (4)	—
258PP	6 items (50)	—
259PP	6 items (50)	—
G48PP	6 items (50)	—
G49PP	6 items (50)	—
258PI	Pair (50)	—
259PI	Pair (50)	—
G48PI	Pair (50)	—
G49PI	Pair (50)	—

Six essays of the 18c stamp with "Nations Unies" inscription and six essays of the 90c stamp with "United Nations" inscription exist.

New York #260-262, Geneva #50-52
UN, 30th Anniv.

1975

261PDa	Card, #260PD-261PD, #G51PD, #G50TC in olive green, se-tenant (4)	1,200
262PD	(5)	500
G52PD	(1)	—
G52TC	With #G52aTC olive green (5)	700
260PP	6 items (50)	—
261PP	6 items (50)	—
262PP	10 items (6)	—
G50PP	6 items (50)	—
G51PP	6 items (50)	—
G52PP	10 items (6)	—
260PI	Pair (50)	—
261PI	Pair (50)	—
262PI	Pair of souvenir sheets (26)	—
G50PI	Pair (50)	—
G51PI	Pair (50)	—
G52PI	Pair of souvenir sheets (26)	—

New York #263-264, Geneva #53-54
Namibia

1975

264PDa	Card, #263PD-264PD, #G53PD-G54PD (9)	975
263PP	8 items (50)	—
264PP	8 items (50)	—
G53PP	8 items (50)	—
G54PP	7 items (50)	—
263PI	Pair (50)	—
264PI	Pair (50)	—
G53PI	Pair (50)	—
G54PI	Pair (50)	—

New York #265-266, Geneva #55-56, Souvenir Card #8
UN Peacekeeping Operations

1975

266PDa	Card, #265PD-266PD, #G55PD-G56PD (3)	1,300
266PDb	Card, #266PD, #G55PD-G56PD, 10c essay of #265 (5)	1,200
SC8PD	With approval handstamp (5)	—
265PI	Pair (25)	—
266PI	Pair (25)	—
G55PI	Pair (25)	—
G56PI	Pair (25)	—

New York #267-271
Definitives

1976

267PD	(4)	225
268PD	(3)	350
269PD	(5)	110
270PD	(8)	225
271PD	(4)	200
271TC	Dark green background (not approved cards dated "30 June 1975" (5)	—
267PP	10 items (25)	—
268PP	8 items (50)	—
269PP	3 items (50)	—
270PP	6 items (50)	—

271PP	10 items (25)	—
267PI	Pair (50)	—
268PI	Pair (50)	—
269PI	Pair (50)	—
270PI	Pair (50)	—
271PI	Pair (50)	—

New York #272-273, Geneva #57, Souvenir Card #9
World Federation of United Nations Associations

1976

273PDa	Card, #272PD-273PD, #G57PD (4)	825.
SC9PD	With approval handstamp dated "18 Sep 1975" (4)	—
SC9TC	With light blue denominations on 1966 stamp (not approved) (5)	—
272PP	6 items (50)	—
273PP	6 items (50)	—
G57PP	6 items (50)	—
272PI	Pair (50)	—
273PI	Pair (50)	—
G57PI	Pair (50)	—

New York #274-275, Geneva #58
UN Conference on Trade and Development

1976

G58PDa	Card, #G58PD, non-denominated essays of #274-275 (5)	725.
274PP	5 items (130)	—
	Vert. pair with horiz. gutter (10)	—
275PP	5 items (130)	—
	Vert. pair with horiz. gutter (10)	—
G58PP	5 items (150)	—
274PI	Pair (80)	—
	Vert. pair with horiz. gutter (20)	—
275PI	Pair (80)	—
	Vert. pair with horiz. gutter (20)	—
G58PI	Pair (80)	—
	Vert. pair with horiz. gutter (20)	—

New York #276-277, Geneva #59-60
UN Conference on Human Settlements

1976

277PDa	Card, #276PD-277PD, #G59PD-G60PD (4)	1,100.
276PP	12 items (50)	—
277PP	12 items (50)	—
G59PP	12 items (50)	—
G60PP	12 items (50)	—
276PI	Pair (50)	—
277PI	Pair (50)	—
G59PI	Pair (50)	—
G60PI	Pair (50)	—

New York #278-279, Geneva #61-62
UN Postal Administration, 25th Anniv.

1976

279PDa	Card, #278PD-279PD, #G61PD-G62PD (5)	700.
278PP	5 items (64)	—
	Horiz. pair with vert. gutter (4)	—
	Vert. pair with horiz. gutter (4)	—
279PP	5 items (64)	—
	Horiz. pair with vert. gutter (4)	—
	Vert. pair with horiz. gutter (4)	—
G61PP	5 items (72)	—
	Horiz. pair with vert. gutter (4)	—
G62PP	5 items (63)	—
	Horiz. pair with vert. gutter (4)	—
	Vert. pair with horiz. gutter (4)	—

New York #280, Geneva #63, Souvenir Card #10
World Food Council

1976

280PD	(5)	200.
G63PD	(5)	200.
SC10PD	With approval handstamp (12)	—
280PP	2 items (50)	—
G63PP	2 items (50)	—
280PI	Pair (50)	—
G63PI	Pair (50)	—

New York #281-282, Geneva #64, Souvenir Card #11
World Intellectual Property Organization

1977

282PDa	Card, #281PD-282PD, #G64PD (4)	650.
SC11PD	With approval handstamp (4)	—
281PP	8 items (50)	—
282PP	8 items (50)	—
G64PP	8 items (50)	—
281PI	Pair (50)	—
282PI	Pair (50)	—
G64PI	Pair (50)	—

New York #283-284, Geneva #65-66
UN Water Conference

1977

283PD	Cut out from #284PDb (1)	—
284PDa	Card, #283PD-284PD, #G65PD-G66PD (2)	925.
284PDb	Card, #284PD, #G65PD-G66PD (1)	—
284PDc	Card, #284PD, #G66PD (1)	—
283PP	6 items (50)	—
284PP	6 items (50)	—
G65PP	5 items (50)	—
G66PP	5 items (50)	—
283PI	Pair (50)	—
284PI	Pair (50)	—
G65PI	Pair (50)	—
G66PI	Pair (50)	—

New York #285-286, Geneva #67-68
UN Security Council

1977

286PDa	Card, #285PD-286PD, essays of #G67-G68 with small top Chinese character (4)	975.
G68PDa	Card, #G67PD-G68PD (large Chinese character) (4)	450.
286PP	8 items (50)	—
G67PP	8 items (50)	—
G68PP	8 items (50)	—
285PI	Pair (50)	—
286PI	Pair (50)	—
G67PI	Pair (50)	—
G68PI	Pair (50)	—

A card with the two essays only (a cutout of No. 286PDa) with "not approved" handstamp exists.

New York #287-288, Geneva #69-70, Souvenir Card #12
Combat Racism

1977

288PDa	Card, #287PD-288PD (4)	425.
G70PDa	Card, #G69PD-G70PD (4)	500.
SC12PD	With approval handstamp and specimen perfin (5)	—
287PP	3 items (50)	—
288PP	3 items (50)	—
G69PP	6 items (150)	—
G70PP	6 items (150)	—
287PI	Pair (175)	—
288PI	Pair (175)	—
G69PI	Pair (225)	—
G70PI	Pair (225)	—

New York #289-290, Geneva #71-72
Peaceful Uses of Atomic Energy

1977

290PDa	Card, #289PD-290PD, #G71PD-G72PD (4)	1,100.
290PDb	Card, #289PD-290PD, #G71PD, essay of #G72 with capital "F" in "Fins" (5)	975.
289PP	8 items (50)	—
290PP	8 items (50)	—
G71PP	6 items (50)	—
G72PP	6 items (50)	—
289PI	Pair (50)	—
290PI	Pair (50)	—
G71PI	Pair (50)	—
G72PI	Pair (50)	—

New York #291-293, Geneva #73
Definitives

1978

291PD	(4)	200.
292PD	(5)	225.
293PD	(4)	200.
G73PD	With approval handstamp (4)	225.
G73TC	Tree in deep brown (with "not approved" handstamp (6)	175.
G73PP	6 items (50)	—
291PI	Pair (50)	—
292PI	Pair (50)	—
293PI	Pair (75)	—
G73PI	Pair (50)	—

Six essays of No. 293 having "C" in Naciones not even with "A" exist on card with "not approved" handstamp.

New York #294-295, Geneva #74-75
Global Eradication of Smallpox

1978

295PDa	Card, #294PD-295PD, #G74PD-G75PD (5)	1,000.
294PP	2 items (50)	—
295PP	2 items (50)	—
G74PP	4 items (50)	—
G75PP	4 items (50)	—
294PI	Pair (50)	—
295PI	Pair (50)	—
G74PI	Pair (50)	—
G75PI	Pair (50)	—

New York #296-297, Geneva #76, Souvenir Card #13
Liberation, Justice and Cooperation for Namibia

1978

296PD	On perforated sheet layout (2)	—
297PD	On perforated sheet layout (1)	—
297PDa	Card, #296-297, #G76, perforated (4)	725.
297PDb	Card, #296-297 perforated, essay of #G76 ("F." and "S." same size, not approved) (5)	725.
G76PD	On perforated sheet layout (9)	—
SC13PD	With approval handstamp (5)	110.
296PP	6 items (50)	—
297PP	6 items (50)	—
G76PP	6 items (50)	—
296PI	Pair (50)	—
297PI	Pair (50)	—
G76PI	Pair (50)	—

The essay of No. G76 exists on a not approved perforated sheet layout.

New York #298-299, Geneva #77-78, Souvenir Card #14
Safety in the Air

1978

298PDa	Card, #298PD, #G77PD-G78PD (1)	—
299PD	Cut out from #298PDa (1)	—
299PDa	Card, #298PD-299PD, #G77PD-G78PD (3)	875.
SC14PD	With approval handstamp (4)	—
298PP	10 items (50)	—
299PP	10 items (50)	—
G77PP	6 items (50)	—
G78PP	6 items (50)	—
298PI	Pair (50)	—
299PI	Pair (50)	—
G77PI	Pair (50)	—
G78PI	Pair (50)	—

New York #300-301, Geneva #79-80
UN General Assembly

1978

301PDa	Card, #300PD-301PD, #G79PD-G80PD (4)	975.
300PP	4 items (50)	—
301PP	5 items (50)	—
G79PP	6 items (50)	—
G80PP	6 items (50)	—
300PI	Pair (25)	—
301PI	Pair (25)	—
G79PI	Pair (25)	—
G80PI	Pair (25)	—

New York #302-303, Geneva #81
Technical Cooperation Conference

1978

303PDa	Card, #302PD-303PD, #G81PD (3)	975.
302PP	10 items (50)	—
303PP	10 items (50)	—
G81PP	8 items (50)	—
302PI	Pair (50)	—
303PI	Pair (50)	—
G81PI	Pair (50)	—

Five not approved cards have essays of the set showing black behind closer cogwheels and text close to bottom frame. Value $725.

New York #304-307
Definitives

1979

304PD	(1)	—
304PDa	Card, #304PD-307PD (9)	—
304PDb	Card, #304PD, essays of #305, 306, 307 with inked-in corrections for printer (2)	875.
307PDa	Card, #305PD-307PD (3)	725.
304PP	8 items (50)	—
305PP	8 items (50)	—
306PP	6 items (50)	—
307PP	4 items (50)	—
304PI	Pair (50)	—
305PI	Pair (50)	—
306PI	Pair (75)	—
307PI	Pair (75)	—

Three cut-up not approved cards exist containing the three essays with inked-in corrections.

Nos. 306PI and 307PI include 25 pairs of reprints.

New York #308-309, Geneva #82-83
UN Disaster Relief Coordinator

1979

309PDa	Card, #308PD-309PD (4)	425.
G83PDa	Card, #G82PD-G83PD (1)	—
G83PDb	Card, #G82PD-G83PD, essays of #308-309 with inked-in corrections for printer (3)	875.
308PP	9 items (50)	—
309PP	9 items (50)	—
G82PP	4 items (50)	—
G83PP	4 items (50)	—
308PI	Pair (50)	—
309PI	Pair (50)	—
G82PI	Pair (50)	—
G83PI	Pair (50)	—

Two not approved cards contain the essays with inked-in corrections for printer.

New York #310-311, Geneva #84-85, Souvenir Card #15
International Year of the Child

1979

310PDa	Card, #310PD, essays of #G84-G85 (with IYC emblem above bottom of children's feet) (1)	—
311PD	Cut out from #310PDa (1)	—
311PDa	Card, #310PD-311PD, essays #G84-G85 (2)	1,350.
G85PDa	Card, #G84PD-G85PD (4)	625.
SC15PD	With manuscript approval (4)	—
310PP	9 items (20)	—
311PP	9 items (20)	—
G84PP	8 items (20)	—
G85PP	10 items (20)	—
310PI	Pair (40)	140.

311PI	Pair (40)	140.
G84PI	Pair (20)	140.
G85PI	Pair (20)	140.

One cut up not approved card contains the two essays. Five essays of No. SC15 marked "not approved" show the stamp essays.

Vienna #1-6
Definitives

1979

V6PDa	Card, #V1PD-V6PD (5)	2,000.
V1PP	5 items (50)	—
V2PP	5 items (150)	—
V3PP	5 items (50)	—
V4PP	5 items (50)	—
V5PP	5 items (50)	—
V6PP	5 items (50)	—
V1PI	Pair (50)	—
V2PI	Pair (150)	—
V3PI	Pair (50)	—
V4PI	Pair (50)	—
V5PI	Pair (50)	—
V6PI	Pair (50)	—

New York #312-313, Geneva #86
Namibia

1979

313PDa	Card, #312PD-313PD, #G86PD (4)	825.
312PP	8 items (50)	—
313PP	8 items (50)	—
G86PP	8 items (50)	—
312PI	Pair (50)	—
313PI	Pair (50)	—
G86PI	Pair (50)	—

One card of No. 313PDa is badly damaged.

New York #314-315, Geneva #87-88, Souvenir Card #16
International Court of Justice

1979

315PDa	Card, #314PD-315PD, #G87PD-G88PD 2 each (4)	1,650.
SC16PD	With "not approved" handstamp and "Specimen" perfin (5)	—
314PP	4 items (50)	—
315PP	4 items (50)	—
G87PP	6 items (50)	—
G88PP	7 items (50)	—
314PI	Pair (50)	—
315PI	Pair (50)	—
G87PI	Pair (50)	—
G88PI	Pair (50)	—

New York #316-317, Geneva #89, Vienna #7
New International Economic Order

1980

316PD	(11)	225.
317PD	(5)	200.
G89PD	With approval handstamp (5)	175.
V7PD	(5)	225.
316PP	4 items (50)	—
317PP	4 items (50)	—
G89PP	4 items (50)	—
V7PP	5 items (50)	—
316PI	Pair (50)	—
317PI	Pair (50)	—
G89PI	Pair (50)	—
V7PI	Pair (50)	—

Five cards of No. 316PD are marked "not approved" but there are no discernable differences between it and approved proofs. Six "not approved" cards have essays of No. G89 with text "Nouvel International Economique Ordre." Six "not approved" cards have essays of No. V7 with the same text.

Vienna #8
Definitive

1980

V8PD	(4)	200.
V8PP	11 items, perforated (250)	—
V8PI	Pair (25)	—

New York #318-319, Geneva #90-91, Vienna #9-10, Souvenir Card #17
Decade for Women

1980

318PD	(13)	225.
319PD	(11)	200.
G90PD	(13)	225.
G91PD	(5)	225.
V9PD	(5)	175.
V10PD	(5)	200.
SC17PD	With approval handstamp (5)	175.
318PP	4 items (50)	—
319PP	4 items (50)	—
G90PP	4 items (50)	—
G91PP	4 items (50)	—
V9PP	3 items (50)	—
V10PP	2 items (50)	—
318PI	Pair (50)	—
319PI	Pair (50)	—
G90PI	Pair (50)	—
G91PI	Pair (50)	—
V9PI	Pair (50)	—
V10PI	Pair (50)	—

New York #320-321, Geneva #92, Vienna #11
UN Peace-keeping Operations

1980

321PDa	Card, #320PD-321PD, #V11PD, essay of #G92 with "de" on top line (3)	975.
G92PD	(4)	240.
320PP	2 items (50)	—
321PP	8 items (50)	—
G92PP	4 items (50)	—
V11PP	12 items (50)	—
320PI	Pair (50)	—
321PI	Pair (50)	—
G92PI	Pair (50)	—
V11PI	Pair (50)	—

New York #322-324, Geneva #93-95, Vienna #12-14
UN, 35th Anniv.

1980

324PDa	Card, #324PD, #G95D, #V14PD (4)	1,050.
324PDb	Card, #322PD-324PD, #G93PD-G94PD, #V12PD-V14PD, essay of #G95 with incomplete marginal inscription (3)	1,050.
322PP	8 items (50)	—
323PP	8 items (50)	—
G93PP	6 items (300)	—
G94PP	13 items (650)	—
V12PP	3 items (50)	—
V13PP	8 items (50)	—
322PI	Pair (100)	—
323PI	Pair (100)	—
G93PI	Pair (100)	—
G94PI	Pair (100)	—
V12PI	Pair (175)	—
V13PI	Pair (100)	—

New York #325-340
Flags

1980

325PD	Cut from #340PDa (1)	—
332PD	Cut from #340PDa (1)	—
340PDa	Card, #325PD-340PD (4)	3,500.
340PDb	Card, #326PD-331PD, #333PD-340PD (1)	—
325-340PP	Set of 20 sheets (1)	—
325-340PI	Set of 4 sheets (2)	—

On Nos. 325-340PP, there are five progressive proof sheets per issued sheet.

New York #341-342, Geneva #96-97, Vienna #15-16, Souvenir Card #18
Economic and Social Council

1980

342PDa	Sheet, #341PD-342PD, #G96PD-G97PD, #V15PD-V16PD (4)	110.
G96PD	(4)	—
G97PD	(4)	—
V15PD	(4)	—
V16PD	(4)	—
SC18PD	(4)	—
341PP	6 items (50)	—
342PP	6 items (50)	—
G96PP	6 items (50)	—
G97PP	6 items (50)	—
V15PP	6 items (50)	—
V16PP	6 items (50)	—
341PI	Pair (50)	—
342PI	Pair (50)	—
G96PI	Pair (50)	—
G97PI	Pair (50)	—
V15PI	Pair (50)	—
V16PI	Pair (50)	—

An essay of No. SC18 with curved cancel on 4s stamp has "not approved" handstamp.

New York #343, Geneva #98, Vienna #17
Inalienable Rights of the Palestinian People

1981

343TCa	Card, #343TC blue, #G98PD, #V17PD (1)	625.
G98PD	(5)	—
V17PD	(5)	—
343PP	4 items (50)	—
G98PP	5 items (50)	—
V17PP	4 items (50)	—
343PI	Pair (50)	—
G98PI	Pair (50)	—
V17PI	Pair (50)	—

New York #344-345, Geneva #99-100, Vienna #18-19, Souvenir Card #19
Intl. Year of the Disabled

1980

344PD	Cut out from #G100PDa (1)	—
344PDa	Card, #344PD, #G99PD-G100PD, #V18PD-V19PD, 31c essay of #345 (4)	1,450.
344PDb	Card, #344PD, #G100PD, #V18PD-V19PD (4)	—
G100PDa	Card, #G100PD, #V18PD-V19PD (1)	—
SC19PD	With "not approved" handstamp (9)	110.
344PP	6 items (50)	—
345PP	2 items (50)	—
G99PP	2 items (50)	—
G100PP	2 items (50)	—
V18PP	6 items (50)	—
V19PP	2 items (50)	—
344PI	Pair (50)	—
345PI	Pair (50)	—
G99PI	Pair (50)	—
G100PI	Pair (50)	—
V18PI	Pair (50)	—
V19PI	Pair (50)	—

All die proof cards are stamped "not approved." One example of No. SC19PD has "35c" covering "31c."

New York #346-347, Geneva #101, Vienna #20
Art at the UN

1981

347PDa	Card, #346PD-347PD, #G101PD, #V20PD (1)	1,050.
347PDb	Card, #347PD, #G101PD, #V20PD, 15c essay of #346 (not approved) (6)	—
346PP	5 items (50)	—
347PP	5 items (50)	—
G101PP	5 items (50)	—
V20PP	5 items (50)	—
346PI	Pair (50)	—
347PI	Pair (50)	—
G101PI	Pair (50)	—
V20PI	Pair (50)	—

New York #348-349, Geneva #102, Vienna #21, Souvenir Card #20
Conference on New and Renewable Sources of Energy

1981

348PDa	Card, #348PD, #G102PD, #V21PD, 31c essay of #349 (3)	925.
SC20PD	With approval and specimen handstamps (4)	—
348PP	6 items (50)	—
349PP	4 items (50)	—
G102PP	6 items (50)	—
V21PP	4 items (50)	—
348PI	Pair (50)	—
349PI	Pair (50)	—
G102PI	Pair (50)	—
V21PI	Pair (50)	—

All examples of No. SC20PD have the 31c essay.

New York #350-365
Flags

1981

357PDa	Card, #350PD-357PD (5)	—
365PDa	Card, #358PD-365PD (5)	2,300.
350-365PP	Set of 19 sheets (1)	—
350-365PI	Set of 4 sheets (2)	4,600.

On Nos. 350-365PP, there are four progressive sheets for the issued sheet containing Nos. 354-357, and five progressive proof sheets per issued sheet for the issued sheets containing Nos. 350-353, 358-361 and 362-365. Two sets of imperforate sheets of Nos. 350-353 and two sets of imperforate sheets of Nos. 354-357 exist with 15c denominations are essays.

New York #366-367, Geneva #103-104, Vienna #22-23
Volunteers Program, 10th Anniv.

1981

367PDa	Card, #367PD, #G103PD-G104PD, #V22PD-V23PD, 20c essay of #366 (3)	1,450.
G103TC	white background (1)	—
V22TC	white background (1)	—
V23TC	white background (1)	—
366PI	Pair (50)	—
367PI	Pair (50)	—
G103PI	Pair (50)	—
G104PI	Pair (50)	—
V22PI	Pair (50)	—
V23PI	Pair (50)	—

New York #368-370, Geneva #105-106, Vienna #24
Definitives

1982

370PDa	Card, #368PD-370PD, #G106PD, #V24PD, essay of #G105 with no "l'" before "apartheid" (5)	1,450.
368PP	5 items (50)	—
369PP	5 items (50)	—
370PP	5 items (50)	—
G105PP	4 items (50)	—
G106PP	5 items (50)	—
V24PP	5 items (50)	—
368PI	Pair (50)	—
369PI	Pair (50)	—
370PI	Pair (50)	—
G105PI	Pair (50)	—
C106PI	Pair (50)	—
V24PI	Pair (50)	—

One example of No. 370PDa has all stamps canceled and #G105 altered.

New York #371-372, Geneva #107-108, Vienna #25-26, Souvenir Card #21
Environment Program, 10th Anniv.

1982

372PDa	Card, #371PD-372PD, #G107PD, #V25PD-V26PD, 1.30fr essay of #G108 (5)	1,600.
372PDb	Card, #372PD, #G107PD-G108PD, #V25PD-V26PD, 18c essay of #371 (4)	1,450.
SC21PD	(5)	—
371PP	8 items (50)	—
372PP	7 items (50)	—
G107PP	12 items (50)	—
G108PP	8 items (50)	—
V25PP	7 items (50)	—
V26PP	11 items (50)	—
371PI	Pair (50)	—
372PI	Pair (50)	—
G107PI	Pair (50)	—
G108PI	Pair (50)	—
V25PI	Pair (50)	—
V26PI	Pair (50)	—

One example of No. 372PDb has had some stamps defaced. Five essays of No. SC21PD show the 18c essay, with one altered to change 18c to 20c.

New York #373, Geneva #109-110, Vienna #27, Souvenir Card #22
Exploration and Peaceful Uses of Outer Space

1982

373PDa	Card, #373PD, #G109PD-G110PD, #V27PD (4)	925.
G109PD	(4)	—
G110PD	(4)	—
V27PD	(4)	—
SC22PD	(4)	—
373PP	6 items (50)	—
G109PP	6 items (50)	—
G110PP	14 items (50)	—
V27PP	14 items (50)	—
373PI	Pair (50)	—
G109PI	Pair (50)	—
G110PI	Pair (50)	—
V27PI	Pair (50)	—

New York #374-389
Flags

1982

381PDa	Card, #374PD-381PD (5)	2,000.
389PDa	Card, #382PD-389PD (4)	2,000.
374-389PP	Set of 20 sheets (1)	—
374-389PI	Set of 4 sheets (2)	5,250.

On Nos. 374-389PP, there are five progressive proof sheets per issued sheet.

New York #390-391, Geneva #111-112, Vienna #28-29
Conservation and Protection of Nature

1982

390PDa	Card, #390PD, #G111PD, #V29PD, essays of #G112 and #V28 (1)	—
391PD	(1)	—
391PDa	Card, #390PD-391PD, #G111PD, #V29PD, essays of #G112 and #V28 (3)	1,400.
G112PD	(3)	250.
V29PD	(3)	200.
390PP	10 items (50)	—
391PP	10 items (50)	—
G111PP	10 items (50)	—
G112PP	10 items (50)	—
V28PP	10 items (50)	—
V29PP	10 items (50)	—
390PI	Pair (50)	—
391PI	Pair (50)	—
G111PI	Pair (50)	—
G112PI	Pair (50)	—
V28PI	Pair (50)	—
V29PI	Pair (50)	—

Essays of No. G112 have snake with lighter stripes. Essays of No. V28 have umlaut missing one dot.

New York #392-393, Geneva #113, Vienna #30
World Communications Year

1983

392PD	(5)	225.
393PD	(4)	200.
G113PD	(4)	200.
V30PD	(5)	200.
392TC	Dark blue and green colors switched (4)	300.
V30TC	Dark blue and green colors switched (3)	325.
392PP	10 items (50)	—
393PP	15 items (50)	—
G113PP	15 items (50)	—
V30PP	10 items (50)	—
392PI	Pair (50)	—
393PI	Pair (50)	—
G113PI	Pair (50)	—
V30PI	Pair (50)	—

New York #394-395, Geneva #114-115, Vienna #31-32, Souvenir Card #23
Safety at Sea

1983

395PDa	Card, #394PD-395PD, #G114PD-G115PD, #V31PD-V32PD, #394TC-395TC, #G114TC (1)	—
395PDb	Card, #394PD-395PD, #G114PD (4)	750.
G115PDa	Card, #G115PD, #V31PD-V32PD, #394TC-395TC,#G114TC(10)	—
SC23PD	(5)	—
SC23TC	(6)	—
394PP	10 items (50)	—
395PP	8 items (50)	—
G114PP	11 items (50)	—
G115PP	5 items (50)	—
V31PP	5 items (50)	—
V32PP	8 items (50)	—
394PI	Pair (50)	—
395PI	Pair (50)	—
G114PI	Pair (50)	—
G115PI	Pair (50)	—
V31PI	Pair (50)	—
V32PI	Pair (50)	—

Nos. 394TC and G114TC have orange buoy lights instead of red, and No. 395TC has red violet line in ship instead of orange. These appear on No. SC23TC.

New York #396, Geneva #116, Vienna #33-34
World Food Program

1983

396PD	(3)	225.
G116PD	(3)	225.
V33PD	(3)	200.
V34PD	(3)	225.
396PI	Pair (25)	—
G116PI	Pair (25)	—
V33PI	Pair (25)	—
V34PI	Pair (25)	—

New York #397-398, Geneva #117-118, Vienna #35-36, Souvenir Card #24
UN Conference on Trade and Development

1983

398PDa	Card, #397PD-398PD, #G117PD-G118PD, #V35PD-V36PD, approval handstamp (4)	—
398PDb	Card, #397PD-398PD, #G117PD, #V36PD, essays of #G118 and #V35, (not approved, undated) (5)	1,300.
398PDc	As #398PDb, with red dot essays (not approved, dated) (5)	—
SC24PD	With approval handstamp (4)	—
SC24TC	With "not approved" handstamp (5)	—
397PP	5 items (50)	—
398PP	7 items (50)	—
G117PP	5 items (50)	—
G118PP	6 items (50)	—
V35PP	6 items (50)	—
V36PP	7 items (50)	—
397PI	Pair (50)	—
398PI	Pair (50)	—
G117PI	Pair (50)	—
G118PI	Pair (50)	—
V35PI	Pair (50)	—
V36PI	Pair (50)	—

Essays of Nos. G118 and V35 have blue rectangle instead of blue and yellow triangles on bottom row of flags, along with other differences. No. 398PDb has essays showing flag with green dot in 3rd row; No. 398PDc has red dot on this flag. No. SC24TC has Nos. G118 and V35 with lighter box bottom.

New York #399-414
Flags

1983

403PD	With approval handstamp (1)	240.
406PDa	Card, #399PD-402PD, 404PD-406PD, #403 essay (5)	1,600.
414PDa	Card, #407PD, 409PD-414PD, #408 essay (5)	2,100.
399-414PP	Set of 20 sheets (1)	—
399-414PI	Set of 4 sheets (2)	5,000.

The essay of No. 403 has fewer sun rays than on the issued stamp. The essay of No. 408 has incomplete ring above crest and thinner garlands at left and right. Nos. 413PD-414PD are marked "not approved" on No. 414PDa, but there is no appreciable difference between these and the issued stamps. On Nos. 399-414PP, there are five progressive proof sheets per issued sheet.

New York #415-416, Geneva #119-120, Vienna #37-38
Universal Declaration of Human Rights, 35th Anniv.

1983

415PD	mounted on presentation folder, perforated	450.
416PD	mounted on presentation folder, perforated	450.
G120PDa	Card, #G119PD-G120PD (10)	500.
V37PD	mounted on presentation folder, perforated	325.
V38PD	mounted on presentation folder, perforated	400.
415PP	7 items, with "Muster" overprint (32)	—
415PPa	6 items, without "Muster" overprint (24)	—
	Horiz. pair with vert. gutter, without "Muster" overprint (4)	—
416PP	7 items, with "Muster" overprint (24)	—
	Horiz. pair with vert. gutter, with "Muster" overprint (16)	—
416PPa	6 items, without "Muster" overprint (24)	—
	Horiz. pair with vert. gutter, without "Muster" overprint (4)	—
G119PP	7 items, with "Muster" overprint (24)	—
	Horiz. pair with vert. gutter, with "Muster" overprint (16)	—
G119PPa	6 items, without "Muster" overprint (24)	—
	Horiz. pair with vert. gutter, without "Muster" overprint (4)	—
G120PP	7 items, with "Muster" overprint (24)	—
	Horiz. pair with vert. gutter, with "Muster" overprint (16)	—
G120PPa	6 items, without "Muster" overprint (24)	—
	Horiz. pair with vert. gutter, without "Muster" overprint (4)	—
V37PP	7 items, with "Muster" overprint (24)	—
	Horiz. pair with vert. gutter, with "Muster" overprint (16)	—
V37PPa	6 items, without "Muster" overprint (24)	—
	Horiz. pair with vert. gutter, without "Muster" overprint (4)	—
V38PP	7 items, with "Muster" overprint (24)	—
	Horiz. pair with vert. gutter, with "Muster" overprint (16)	—
V38PPa	6 items, without "Muster" overprint (24)	—
	Horiz. pair with vert. gutter, without "Muster" overprint (4)	—
415PI	Pair (64)	—
	Horiz. pair with vert. gutter (16)	—
416PI	Pair (64)	—
	Horiz. pair with vert. gutter (16)	—
G119PI	Pair (64)	—
	Horiz. pair with vert. gutter (16)	—
G120PI	Pair (64)	—
	Horiz. pair with vert. gutter (16)	—
V37PI	Pair (64)	—
	Horiz. pair with vert. gutter (16)	—
V38PI	Pair (64)	—
	Horiz. pair with vert. gutter (16)	—

On Nos. 415PP-416PP, G119PP-G120PP, V37PP-V38PP, one of the items with "Muster" overprint is a finished imperforate.

New York #417-418, Geneva #121, Vienna #39, Souvenir Card #25
Intl. Conference on Population

1984

417PD	(4)	240.
418PD	(4)	250.
G121PD	(4)	250.
V39PD	(4)	250.
SC25PD	With "not approved" handstamp (9)	—
417PP	8 items (50)	—
418PP	7 items (50)	—
G121PP	8 items (50)	—
V39PP	8 items (50)	—
417PI	Pair (50)	—
418PI	Pair (50)	—
G121PI	Pair (50)	—
V39PI	Pair (50)	—

No. 418PP does not include the blue progressive proof found in No. 417PP.

New York #419-420, Geneva #122-123, Vienna #40-41
World Food Day

1984

419PD	(5)	—
420PDa	Card, #419PD-420PD, #G122PD-G123PD, #V40PD-V41PD with "not approved" handstamp (8)	1,500.
419PP	6 items (50)	—
420PP	6 items (50)	—
G122PP	6 items (50)	—
G123PP	6 items (50)	—
V40PP	6 items (50)	—
V41PP	6 items (50)	—
419PI	Pair (50)	—
420PI	Pair (50)	—
G122PI	Pair (50)	—
G123PI	Pair (50)	—
V40PI	Pair (50)	—
V41PI	Pair (50)	—

There is no appreciable difference between approved and not approved examples of No. 419PD.

New York #421-422, Geneva #124-125, Vienna #42-43
World Heritage Sites

1984

422PDa	Card, #421PD-422PD, with approval handstamp (4)	875.
G125PDa	Card, #G124PD-G125PD, with approval handstamp (4)	625.
V43PDa	Card, #V42PD-V43PD, with approval handstamp (4)	625.
V43TCa	Card, #V42PD (darker sky), V43PD prussian blue sky, "not approved" handstamp (8)	875.
421PP	6 items (80)	—
	Horiz. pair with vert. gutter (10)	—
422PP	6 items (80)	—
	Horiz. pair with vert. gutter (10)	—

G124PP	6 items (80)	—
	Horiz. pair with vert. gutter (10)	—
G125PP	6 items (80)	—
	Horiz. pair with vert. gutter (10)	—
V42PP	6 items (80)	—
	Horiz. pair with vert. gutter (10)	—
V43PP	6 items (80)	—
	Horiz. pair with vert. gutter (10)	—
421PI	Pair (80)	—
	Horiz. pair with vert. gutter (20)	—
422PI	Pair (80)	—
	Horiz. pair with vert. gutter (20)	—
G124PI	Pair (80)	—
	Horiz. pair with vert. gutter (20)	—
G125PI	Pair (80)	—
	Horiz. pair with vert. gutter (20)	—
V42PI	Pair (80)	—
	Horiz. pair with vert. gutter (20)	—
V43PI	Pair (80)	—
	Horiz. pair with vert. gutter (20)	—

Four cards like No. 422PDa with "not approved" handstamp contain essays with slightly different vignettes having taller sky area that is brighter blue and with less distinct designs. Four cards like No. G125PDa contain essays lacking "F.S." before denominations.

New York #423-424, Geneva #126-127, Vienna #44-45
Future for Refugees

1984

424PDa	Card, #423PD-424PD, #G126PD-G127PD, #V44PD-V45PD (2)	—
424PDb	Card, #423PD, #G127PD, 2 each #424PD, #G126PD, #V44PD-V45PD (3)	—
424PDc	Card, #423PD-424PD, #G126PD-G127PD, #V44PD-V45PD, #423TC-424TC, #G126TC-G127TC, V44TC-V45TC (5)	2,750.
424TCa	Card, #423TC-424TC, #G126TC-G127TC, #V44TC-V45TC (1)	—
423PP	2 items (50)	—
G126PP	2 items (50)	—
G127PP	2 items (50)	—
V44PP	2 items (50)	—
V45PP	2 items (50)	—
423PI	Pair (50)	—
424PI	Pair (25)	—
G126PI	Pair (50)	—
G127PI	Pair (50)	—
V44PI	Pair (50)	—
V45PI	Pair (50)	—

Trial color items have backgrounds in buff.

New York #425-440
Flags

1984

432PDa	Card, #429PD-432PD (1)	925.
432PDb	Card, 2 each #429PD-432PD (2)	—
436PDa	Card, #425PD, 427PD, 433PD-436PD, essays of #426, 428 (5)	1,850.
440PDa	Card, #437PD-440PD (1)	925.
440PDb	Card, 2 each #437PD-440PD (2)	—
425-440PP	Set of 21 sheets (1)	—
425-440PI	Set of 4 sheets (2)	4,250.

Essays of Nos. 426 and 428 have country name in smaller type. On Nos. 425-440PP, there are six progressive proof sheets for the issued sheet containing Nos. 429-432, and five progressive proof sheets for the issued sheets containing Nos. 425-428, 433-436 and 437-440.

New York #441-442, Geneva #128, Vienna #46-47, Souvenir Card #26
Intl. Youth Year

1984

441PD	With approval handstamp (4)	350.
442PD	With approval handstamp (3)	240.
G128PD	With approval handstamp (4)	300.
V46PD	(4)	250.
V47PD	(4)	300.
SC26PD	With approval handstamp (4)	—
G128TC	Greenish black strand in center (not approved) (5)	325.
SC26TC	With #G128TC "not approved" handstamp (5)	—
441PP	7 items (50)	—
442PP	9 items (50)	—
G128PP	9 items (50)	—
V46PP	7 items (50)	—
V47PP	7 items (50)	—
441PI	Pair (50)	—
442PI	Pair (50)	—
G128PI	Pair (50)	—
V46PI	Pair (50)	—
V47PI	Pair (50)	—

Five "not approved" essays of No. 441 and four of No. 442 have "N" in "Nations" not touching white frame at bottom. A card with a cutout version of the approved No. 442, but with a "not approved" handstamp, and a card with a cutout essay of No. 442 with an "approved" handstamp exist, probably in error.

New York #443, Geneva #129-130, Vienna #48, Souvenir Card #27
Intl. Labor Organization

1985

443PD	Card, imperforate sheet of 50 stamps (1)	—
443PDa	Card, #443PD (single), #G129PD (single) (4)	500.
G130PDa	Card, #G130PD (single), #V48PD (single) (4)	550.
V48PD	Card, imperforate sheet of 50 stamps (4)	—
SC27PD	With approval handstamp (4)	—
443PI	Pair (50)	—
G129PI	Pair (50)	—
G130PI	Pair (50)	—
V48PI	Pair (50)	—

Essays of No. SC27 exist which have the 1954 stamp with a buff background.

New York #444, Geneva #131-132, Vienna #49
UN University

1985

444PDa	Card, #444PD, #G131PD-G132PD, #V49PD, with approval handstamp (5)	1,150.
G132TC	Bright colors in background ("not approved" handstamp) (6)	400.
444PP	6 items (50)	—
G131PP	6 items (50)	—
G132PP	6 items (50)	—
V49PP	6 items (50)	—
444PI	Pair (50)	—
G131PI	Pair (50)	—
G132PI	Pair (50)	—
V49PI	Pair (50)	—

New York #445-446, Geneva #133-134, Vienna #50-51
Definitives

1985

445PDa	Card, #445PD, #G133PD-G134PD, #V50PD-V51PD, #446TC ("not approved handstamp") (4)	1,600.
446PDa	Card, #445PD-446PD, #G134PD (4)	775.
445PP	4 items (50)	—
446PP	5 items (50)	—
G133PP	7 items (50)	—
G134PP	3 items (50)	—
V50PP	5 items (50)	—
V51PP	5 items (50)	—
V50PI	Pair (50)	—
V51PI	Pair (50)	—

No. 446TC has a lighter blue emblem. Other items in No. 445PDa were declared "not approved," but do not have any appreciable difference from approved items.

New York #447-449, Geneva #135-137, Vienna #52-54
UN, 40th Anniv.

1985

447PDa	Card, 4 each #447PD, #G135PD, #V52PD (1)	—
448PDa	Card, 4 each #448PD, #G136PD, #V53PD (1)	—
449PDa	Card, #447PD-449PD, #G135PD-G137PD, #V52PD-V54PD (1)	1,850.
449PDb	Card, #449PD, #G137PD, #V54PD (4)	—
447PP	5 items (50)	—
448PP	5 items (50)	—
449PP	6 items (36)	—
G135PP	5 items (50)	—
G136PP	5 items (50)	—
G137PP	6 items (36)	—
V52PP	5 items (50)	—
V53PP	5 items (50)	—
V54PP	6 items (36)	—
447PI	Pair (50)	—
448PI	Pair (50)	—
449PI	Pair of souvenir sheets (27)	—
G135PI	Pair (50)	—
G136PI	Pair (50)	—
G137PI	Pair of souvenir sheets (27)	—
V52PI	Pair (50)	—
V53PI	Pair (50)	—
V54PI	Pair of souvenir sheets (27)	—

New York #450-465
Flags

1985

465PDa	Card, #450PD-455PD, 457PD-465PD, essay of #456 (5)	2,900.
450-465PP	Set of 24 sheets (1)	—
450-465PI	Set of 4 sheets (2)	4,000.

Essay of Nos. 456 has thin-lined star. On Nos. 425-440PP, there are six progressive proof sheets per issued sheet.

New York #466-467, Geneva #138-139, Vienna #55-56, Souvenir Card #28
UNICEF Child Survival Campaign

1985

466PD	(4)	300.
466PDa	Card, with cut-up pane of 50 (1)	—
467PD	(4)	—
467PDa	Card, with cut-up pane of 50 (1)	—
G138PD	(4)	300.
G138PDa	Card, with cut-up pane of 50 (1)	—
G139PD	(4)	225.
G139PDa	Card, with cut-up pane of 50 (1)	—
V55PD	(4)	300.
V55PDa	Card, with cut-up pane of 50 (1)	—
V56PD	(4)	250.
V56PDa	Card, with cut-up pane of 50 (1)	—
SC28PD	(4)	—
466PP	5 items (50)	—
467PP	5 items (50)	—
G138PP	5 items (50)	—
G139PP	5 items (50)	—
V55PP	5 items (50)	—
V56PP	5 items (50)	—
466PI	Pair (50)	—
467PI	Pair (50)	—
G138PI	Pair (50)	—
G139PI	Pair (50)	—
V55PI	Pair (50)	—
V56PI	Pair (50)	—

New York #468, Geneva #140, Vienna #57
Africa in Crisis

1986

468PDa	Card, #468PD, #G140PD, essay of #V57 (4)	—
468PP	5 items (50)	—
G140PP	4 items (50)	—
V57PP	4 items (50)	—
468PI	Pair (50)	—
G140PI	Pair (50)	—
V57PI	Pair (50)	—

One example of No. 468PDa has essay of No. V57 corrected to show small loop of "8" at top as in the issued stamp.

New York #472a, Geneva #144a, Vienna #61a
UN Development Program

1986

472aPD	(4)	825
472aPDa	Card, pane of 10 blocks (2)	—
G144aPD	(4)	825
G144aPDa	Card, pane of 10 blocks (2)	—
V61aPD	(4)	825
V61aPDa	Card, pane of 10 blocks (2)	—
472aPP	6 items (10 blocks)	—
G144aPP	6 items (10 blocks)	—
V61aPP	6 items (10 blocks)	—
472aPI	Pair (20)	—
G144aPI	Pair (20)	—
V61aPI	Pair (20)	—

Geneva #145
Definitive

1986

G145PD	(5)	—
G145PP	5 items (50)	—
G145PI	Pair (50)	—

New York #473-474, Geneva #146-147, Vienna #62-63, Souvenir Card #29
Philately

1986

473PDa	Partial pane of 39 with approval handstamp on reverse (1)	—
473PDb	Full pane of 50 with approval handstamp on reverse (3)	—
474PDa	Imperforate pane of 50 with approval handstamp on reverse (4)	—
G146PDa	Imperforate pane of 50 with approval handstamp on reverse (4)	—
G147PDa	Partial pane of 41 with approval handstamp on reverse (1)	—
G147PDb	Full pane of 50 with approval handstamp on reverse (3)	—
V62PDa	Imperforate pane of 50 with approval handstamp on reverse (4)	—
V63PDa	Partial pane of 41 with approval handstamp on reverse (1)	—
V63PDb	Full pane of 50 with approval handstamp on reverse (4)	—
SC29PD	(3)	—
473TC	greenish black (5)	725
474TC	purple (1)	725
474TC	blue (1)	725.
474TC	red brown (1)	725.
474TC	olive brown (1)	725
474TC	dark green (1)	725.
G146TC	purple (1)	725.
G146TC	blue (1)	725.
G146TC	reddish purple (1)	725.
G146TC	greenish black (1)	725.
G146TC	dark olive brown (1)	725.
G147TC	dark blue (5)	775.
V62TC	purple (1)	725.
V62TC	blue (1)	725.
V62TC	red brown (1)	725.
V62TC	greenish black (1)	725.
V62TC	dark olive brown (1)	725.
V63TC	greenish black (5)	775.

New York #475-476, Geneva #148-149, Vienna #64-65, Souvenir Card #30
International Peace Year

1986

475PD	(4)	300.
475PDa	Card, imperforate pane of 50 (1)	—
476PD	(4)	250.
476PDa	Card, imperforate pane of 50 (1)	—
G148PD	(4)	450.
G148PDa	Card, imperforate pane of 50 (1)	—
G149PD	(4)	250.
V64PD	(1)	300.
V65PD	(4)	—
V65PDa	Card, imperforate pane of 50 (1)	—
SC30PD	(4)	—
475PP	4 items (50)	—
476PP	4 items (50)	—
G148PP	4 items (50)	—
G149PP	4 items (50)	—
V64PP	4 items (50)	—

V65PP	3 items (50)	—
475PI	Pair (50)	—
476PI	Pair (50)	—
G148PI	Pair (50)	—
G149PI	Pair (50)	—
V64PI	Pair (50)	—
V65PI	Pair (50)	—

Essays of No. V64 with 7s denominations exist in three cards with singles and one card with an imperforate pane of 50.

New York #477-492 Flags

1986

492PDa	Card, #477PD-492PD (5)	3,250.
477-492PP	Set of 24 sheets (1)	—
477-492PI	Set of 4 sheets (2)	4,000.

On Nos. 477-492PP, there are six progressive proof sheets per issued sheet.

New York #493, Geneva #150, Vienna #66 World Federation of UN Associations, 40th Anniv.

1986

493PD	(3)	525.
493PDa	Imperforate souvenir sheet with cancel lines added (1)	—
G150PD	(3)	300.
G150PDa	Imperforate souvenir sheet with cancel lines added (1)	—
V66PD	(3)	400.
V66PDa	Imperforate souvenir sheet with cancel lines added (1)	—
493PP	8 items (16)	—
G150PP	11 items (16)	—
V66PP	6 items (16)	—
493PI	souvenir sheets (32)	—
G150PI	souvenir sheets (32)	—
V66PI	souvenir sheets (32)	—

New York #494, Geneva #151, Vienna #67 Trygve Lie

1987

494PD	On imperforate sheet layout (1)	—
494PDa	Card, #494PD, #G151PD, V67PD (4)	725.
G151PD	On imperforate sheet layout (1)	—
V67PD	On imperforate sheet layout (1)	—
494PP	10 items (50)	—
G151PP	10 items (50)	—
V67PP	10 items (50)	—
494PI	Pair (50)	—
G151PI	Pair (100)	—
V67PI	Pair (50)	—

Geneva #152-153 Definitives

1987

G152PD	(1)	375.
G153PD	(4)	—
G153TCa	Card, 2 #G153TC dark blue panel (5)	—
G153TCb	Card, imperforate pane of 50 #G153TC dark blue panel (2)	525.
G152PP	6 items (50)	—
G153PP	5 items (50)	—
G152PI	Pair (50)	—
G153PI	Pair (50)	—

Six essays of No. G152 with design 33mm high exist on cards marked "approved text only."

New York #495-496, Geneva #154-155, Vienna #68-69, Souvenir Card #31 International Year of Shelter for the Homeless

1987

496PDa	Card, #495PD-496PD, #G154PD-G155PD, #V68PD-V69PD (4)	1,350.
SC31PD	(3)	—
495PP	6 items (80)	—
	Horiz. pair with vert. gutter (10)	—
496PP	6 items (80)	—
	Horiz. pair with vert. gutter (10)	—
G154PP	6 items (80)	—
	Horiz. pair with vert. gutter (10)	—
G155PP	6 items (80)	—
	Horiz. pair with vert. gutter (10)	—
V68PP	6 items (80)	—
	Horiz. pair with vert. gutter (10)	—
V69PP	6 items (80)	—
	Horiz. pair with vert. gutter (10)	—
495PI	Pair (80)	—
	Horiz. pair with vert. gutter (20)	—
496PI	Pair (80)	—
	Horiz. pair with vert. gutter (20)	—
G154PI	Pair (80)	—
	Horiz. pair with vert. gutter (20)	—
G155PI	Pair (80)	—
	Horiz. pair with vert. gutter (20)	—
V68PI	Pair (80)	—
	Horiz. pair with vert. gutter (20)	—
V69PI	Pair (80)	—
	Horiz. pair with vert. gutter (20)	—

New York #497-498, Geneva #156-157, Vienna #70-71 Fight Drug Abuse

1987

498PDa	Card, #497PD-498PD, #G156PD-G157PD, #V70PD-V71PD with approval handstamp (5)	1,450.
497PP	8 items (50)	—
498PP	8 items (50)	—
G156PP	8 items (50)	—
G157PP	8 items (50)	—
V70PP	8 items (50)	—
V71PP	8 items (50)	—
497PI	Pair (100)	—
498PI	Pair (100)	—
G156PI	Pair (100)	—
G157PI	Pair (100)	—
V70PI	Pair (100)	—
V71PI	Pair (100)	—

Six "not approved" cards contain essays of the six stamps, each lacking the white line separating the halves of the vignette.

Vienna #72-73 Definitives

1987

V73PDa	Card, #V72PD-V73PD (5)	575.
V72PP	8 items (50)	—
V73PP	7 items (50)	—
V72PI	Pair (100)	—
V73PI	Pair (100)	—

New York #499-514 Flags

1987

511PDa	Card, #500PD, 501PD, 503PD, 507PD, 509PD, 511PD (1)	—
514PDa	Card, #499PD-514PD (5)	3,750.
514PDb	Card, #499PD, 500PD, 502PD, 504PD-506PD, 508PD, 510PD, 512PD-514PD (1)	—
499-514PP	Set of 24 sheets (1)	—
499-502PI	Sheet (2)	—
503-506PI	Sheet (2)	—

On Nos. 499-514PP, there are six progressive proof sheets per issued sheet.

New York #515-516, Geneva #158-159, Vienna #74-75 United Nations Day

1987

515PDa	Card, #515PD, #V74PD, essay of #G158 (1)	—
516PDa	Card, #516PD, #G159PD, #V75PD (1)	—
516PDb	Card, #515PD-516PD, #G159PD, #V74PD-V75PD, essay of #G158 (4)	1,250.
515PP	8 items (36)	—
	Cross gutter block (3)	—
	Horiz. pair with vert. gutter (6)	—
	Vert. pair with horiz. gutter (18)	—
516PP	8 items (36)	—
	Cross gutter block (3)	—
	Horiz. pair with vert. gutter (6)	—
	Vert. pair with horiz. gutter (18)	—
G158PP	8 items (36)	—
	Cross gutter block (3)	—
	Horiz. pair with vert. gutter (6)	—
	Vert. pair with horiz. gutter (18)	—
G159PP	8 items (36)	—
	Cross gutter block (3)	—
	Horiz. pair with vert. gutter (6)	—
	Vert. pair with horiz. gutter (18)	—
V74PP	8 items (36)	—
	Cross gutter block (3)	—
	Horiz. pair with vert. gutter (6)	—
	Vert. pair with horiz. gutter (18)	—
V75PP	8 items (36)	—
	Cross gutter block (3)	—
	Horiz. pair with vert. gutter (6)	—
	Vert. pair with horiz. gutter (18)	—
515PI	Pair (12)	—
516PI	Pair (12)	—
G158PI	Pair (28)	—
	Cross gutter block (3)	—
	Horiz. pair with vert. gutter (6)	—
	Vert. pair with horiz. gutter (18)	—
G159PI	Pair (28)	—
	Cross gutter block (3)	—
	Horiz. pair with vert. gutter (6)	—
	Vert. pair with horiz. gutter (18)	—
V74PI	Pair (28)	—
	Cross gutter block (3)	—
	Horiz. pair with vert. gutter (6)	—
	Vert. pair with horiz. gutter (18)	—
V75PI	Pair (28)	—
	Cross gutter block (3)	—
	Horiz. pair with vert. gutter (6)	—
	Vert. pair with horiz. gutter (18)	—

Essay of No. G158 lacks accent in "Journée."

New York #517-518, Geneva #160-161, Vienna #76-77, Souvenir Card #32 Immunize Every Child

1987

518PDa	Card, #517PD-518PD, #G161PD, #V76PD-V77PD, 35c essay of #G160 (11)	1,500.
SC32PD	(11)	—
517PP	11 items (50)	—
518PP	11 items (50)	—
G160PP	11 items (50)	—
G161PP	12 items (50)	—
V76PP	12 items (50)	—
V77PP	9 items (50)	—
5178PI	Pair (50)	—
518PI	Pair (50)	—
G160PI	Pair (75)	—
G161PI	Pair (75)	—
V76PI	Pair (75)	—
V77PI	Pair (75)	—

All examples of No. SC32PD have the essay of No. G160. There is no appreciable difference between approved and not approved examples of Nos. 518PDa or SC32PD.

New York #519-520, Geneva #162-163, Vienna #78-79 International Fund for Agricultural Development

1988

520PDa	Card, #519PD-520PD, #G162PD-G163PD, #V78PD-V79PD (4)	1,550.
519PP	8 items (50)	—
520PP	8 items (50)	—
G162PP	9 items (50)	—
G163PP	9 items (50)	—
V78PP	9 items (50)	—
V79PP	9 items (50)	—
519PI	Pair (50)	—
520PI	Pair (50)	—
G162PI	Pair (50)	—
G163PI	Pair (50)	—
V78PI	Pair (50)	—
V79PI	Pair (50)	—

New York #521, Geneva #164 Definitives

1988

521PD	(4)	575.
G164PD	(6)	300.
521PP	6 items (50)	—
G164PP	11 items (50)	—
521PI	Pair (50)	—
G164PI	Pair (50)	—

New York #523a, Geneva #166a, Vienna #81a Survival of the Forests

1988

523aPDa	Card, imperforate pane of 6 pairs with approval handstamp (6)	2,750.
523aPDb	Card, perforated pane of 6 pairs with approval handstamp (1)	—
G166aPDa	Card, imperforate pane of 6 pairs with approval handstamp (7)	2,400.
V81aPDa	Card, imperforate pane of 6 pairs with approval handstamp (7)	2,400.
523aPP	8 items (6 pairs)	—
G166aPP	8 items (6 pairs)	—
V81aPP	8 items (6 pairs)	—
523aPI	Pair (12)	—
G166aPI	Pair (24)	—
V81aPI	Pair (24)	—

Panes on Nos. 523aPDa, 523aPDb, G166aPDa, V81aPDa are not affixed to cards but are between stamp mounts.

New York #524-525, Geneva #167-168, Vienna #82-83, Souvenir Card #33 Intl. Volunteer Day

1988

524PDa	Card, #524PD, #G167PD-G168PD, #V82PD-V83PD with approval handstamp (4)	1,400.
525PDa	Card, #525PD, #G168PD, #V83PD, essays of #524, #G167, #V82 with "not approved" handstamp (4)	875.
SC33PD	(4)	—
SC33TC	light blue signature (4)	—
524PP	6 items (40)	—
525PP	6 items (40)	—
525PPa	Horiz. se-tenant pair with vert. gutter, #524PP-525PP (10)	—
G167PP	6 items (40)	—
G168PP	6 items (40)	—
G168PPa	Horiz. se-tenant pair with vert. gutter, #G167PP-G168PP (10)	—
V82PP	6 items (40)	—
V83PP	6 items (40)	—
V83PPa	Horiz. se-tenant pair with vert. gutter, #V82PP-V83PP (10)	—
524PI	Pair (70)	—
525PI	Pair (70)	—
G167PI	Pair (70)	—
G168PI	Pair (70)	—
V82PI	Pair (70)	—
V83PI	Pair (70)	—

Essays have incomplete dates at bottom.

New York #526-527, Geneva #169-170, Vienna #84-85, Souvenir Card #34 Health in Sports

1988

526PD	With approval handstamp(2)	250.
526PDa	Card, #526PD, #527TC (1)	—
526PDb	Card, imperforate pane of 50 #526PD (1)	—
527PD	(6)	150.
527PDa	Card, 2 #527PD (1)	—
527PDb	Card, imperforate pane of 50 #527PD (2)	—
G169PD	(6)	350.
G169PDa	Card, 2 #G169PD (1)	—
G169PDb	Card, imperforate pane of 50 #G169PD (2)	—

G170PD	With approval handstamp (2)	350.
G170PDa	Card, #G170PD, #G170TC (1)	—
G170PDb	Card, imperforate pane of 50 #G170PD (1)	—
V84PD	With approval handstamp (2)	450.
V84PDa	Card, #V84PD, #V84TC (1)	—
V84PDb	Card, imperforate pane of 50 #V84PD (1)	—
V85PD	(6)	450.
V85PDa	Card, 2 #V85PD (1)	—
V85PDb	Card, imperforate pane of 50 #V85PD (2)	—
SC34PD	With approval handstamp (5)	—
526TC	Card, darker brown in LL part of vignette (not approved) (4)	325.
526TCa	Card, imperforate pane of 50 #526TC (1)	—
G170TC	Card, black "F.S." (not approved) (4)	—
G170TCa	Card, imperforate pane of 50 #G170TC (1)	—
V84TC	Card, red splotches in UL of vignette (not approved) (4)	325.
V84TCa	Card, imperforate pane of 50 #V84TC (109)	—
SC34TC	With #526TC (not approved) (4)	—
526PP	4 items (50)	—
527PP	4 items (50)	—
G169PP	4 items (50)	—
G170PP	4 items (50)	—
V84PP	5 items (50)	—
V85PP	4 items (50)	—
526PI	Pair (50)	—
527PI	Pair (50)	—
G169PI	Pair (50)	—
G170PI	Pair (45)	—
V84PI	Pair (50)	—
V85PI	Pair (50)	—

There is no appreciable difference between approved and not approved examples of Nos. 527PD, G169PD and V85PD.

New York #528-543
Flags

1988

543PDa	Card, #540PD, 543PD (2)	425.
543PDb	Card, #540PD, 543PD, 22c essays of #528-539, 541-542 (2)	—
528-543PP	Set of 24 sheets (1)	—
528-543PI	Set of 4 sheets (2)	3,000.

Nine cards each containing 22c essays of Nos. 528-543 exist. Value $2,900 each. On Nos. 528-543PP, there are six progressive proof sheets per issued sheet.

New York #544-545, Geneva #171-172, Vienna #86-87
Universal Declaration of Human Rights, 40th Anniv.

1988

545PDa	Card, #544PD-545PD, #G171PD-G172PD, #V86PD-V87PD (5)	2,900.
G172PDa	Card, #172PD, 90c essay of #G172 (6)	775.
544PP	6 items (50)	—
545PP	6 items (1)	—
G171PP	6 items (50)	—
G172PP	6 items (1)	—
V86PP	6 items (50)	—
V87PP	6 items (1)	—
544PI	Pair (50)	—
545PI	souvenir sheets (2)	650.
G171PI	Pair (50)	—
G172PI	souvenir sheets (2)	975.
V86PI	Pair (50)	625.
V87PI	souvenir sheets (2)	—

New York #546-547, Geneva #173-174, Vienna #88-89, Souvenir Card #35
World Bank

1989

547PDa	Card, #546PD-547PD, #G173PD-G174PD, #V88PD-V89PD with approval handstamp (4)	1,250.
547PDb	Card, #547PD in slightly lighter colors, #V88PD, #G173TC, essays of #546, #G174, #V89 (5)	1,150.
SC35PD	With "29 Aug. 1988" handstamp on back (4)	—
546PP	6 items (40)	—
547PP	6 items (40)	—
547PPa	Vert. se-tenant pair with horiz. gutter, #546PP-547PP (10)	—
G173PP	6 items (40)	—
G174PP	6 items (40)	—
G174PPa	Vert. se-tenant pair with horiz. gutter, #G173PP-G174PP (10)	—
V88PP	6 items (40)	—
V89PP	6 items (40)	—
V89PPa	Vert. se-tenant pair with horiz. gutter, #V88PP-V89PP (10)	—
546PI	Pair (40)	—
547PI	Pair (40)	—
G173PI	Pair (70)	—
G174PI	Pair (70)	—
G174PIa	Vert. se-tenant pair with horiz. gutter, #G173PI-G174PI (10)	—
V88PI	Pair (50)	—
V89PI	Pair (50)	—

No. G173TC has lighter orange background. Essays of Nos. 546, G174, and V89 have incomplete years at bottom.

New York #548, Geneva #175, Vienna #90
UN Peace-keeping Force

1989

548PD	Imperforate pane of 50 with "not approved" handstamp (1)	—
548PDa	Card, #548PD, #G175PD, #V90PD (5)	—
G175PD	Imperforate pane of 50 with "not approved" handstamp (1)	—
V90PD	Imperforate pane of 50 with "not approved" handstamp (1)	—
548PP	6 items (90)	—
	Horiz. pair with vert. gutter (5)	—
G175PP	6 items (90)	—
	Horiz. pair with vert. gutter (5)	—
V90PP	6 items (90)	—
	Horiz. pair with vert. gutter (5)	—
548PI	Pair (70)	—
G175PI	Pair (138)	—
	Horiz. pair with vert. gutter (10)	—
V90PI	Pair (138)	—
	Horiz. pair with vert. gutter (10)	—

There is no appreciable difference between approved and not approved examples of No. 548PDa.

New York #549
Definitive

1989

549PD	(9)	—
549PP	6 items (64)	—
	Cross gutter block (1)	—
	Horiz. pair with vert. gutter (8)	—
	Vert. pair with horiz. gutter (8)	—
549PI	Pair (24)	—

There is no appreciable difference between approved and not approved examples of No. 549PD.

New York #550-551, Geneva #176-177, Vienna #91-92, Souvenir Card #36
World Weather Watch

1989

551PDa	Card, #550PD-551PD, #G176PD-G177PD, #V91PD-V92PD (9)	—
SC36PD	(4)	—
550PP	6 items (40)	—
551PP	6 items (40)	—
551PPa	Vert. se-tenant pair with horiz. gutter, #550PP-551PP (10)	—
G176PP	6 items (40)	—
G177PP	6 items (40)	—
G177PPa	Vert. se-tenant pair with horiz. gutter, #G176PP-G177PP (10)	—
V91PP	6 items (40)	—
V92PP	6 items (40)	—
V92PPa	Vert. se-tenant pair with horiz. gutter, #V91PP-V92PP (10)	—
550PI	(50 pairs)	—
551PI	(50 pairs)	—
G176PI	(70 pairs)	—
G177PI	(70 pairs)	—
G177PIa	Vert. se-tenant pair with horiz. gutter, #G176PI-G177PI (10)	—
V91PI	(50 pairs)	—
V92PI	(50 pairs)	—

There is no appreciable difference between approved and not approved examples of No. 551PDa.

New York #552-553, Geneva #178-179, Vienna #93-94
Offices in Vienna, 10th Anniv.

1989

552PD	With approval handstamp (4)	—
553PD	(4)	—
G178PD	(4)	—
G179PDa	Card, #G179PD, #G179TC orange background, #G179TC dull green background (4)	—
V93PD	(4)	—
V94PD	(9)	—
552PP	10 items (25)	—
553PP	12 items (25)	—
G178PP	10 items (25)	—
G179PP	10 items (25)	—
V93PP	10 items (25)	—
V94PP	10 items (25)	—
552PI	(24 pairs)	—
553PI	(24 pairs)	—
G178PI	(24 pairs)	—
G179PI	(24 pairs)	—
V93PI	(24 pairs)	—
V94PI	(24 pairs)	—

Five not approved essays of #552 have clearly defined cross-hatching in background. There is no appreciable difference between approved and not approved examples of No. V94PD. One item from No. G179PP and V93PP is blank as it is from progressive proof sheet showing only black sheet margins.

New York #554-569
Flags

1989

568PDa	Card, #558PD-561PD, 563PD, 564PD, 566PD-568PD (6)	—
569PDa	Card, #554PD-569PD (5)	—
554-569PP	Set of 24 sheets (1)	—
554-569PI	Set of 4 sheets (2)	—

On Nos. 554-569PP, there are six progressive proof sheets per issued sheet.

New York #570-571, Geneva #180-181, Vienna #95-96
Human Rights

1989

570PD	Strip of 3 + 3 labels (4)	—
571PD	Strip of 3 + 3 labels (4)	—
571PDa	Card, #570PD-571PD, #G180PD-G181PD, #V95PD-V96PD (5)	—
G180PD	3 singles or strip of 3 + 3 labels (4)	—
G181PD	Strip of 3 + 3 labels (4)	—
V95PD	Strip of 3 + 3 labels (4)	—
V96PD	3 singles or strip of 3 + 3 labels (4)	—
570PP	6 items (20)	—
	Cross gutter block (1)	—
	Horiz. pair with vert. gutter (2)	—
	Vert. pair with horiz. gutter (10)	—
571PP	6 items (20)	—
	Cross gutter block (1)	—
	Horiz. pair with vert. gutter (2)	—
	Vert. pair with horiz. gutter (10)	—
G180PP	6 items (20)	—
	Cross gutter block (1)	—
	Horiz. pair with vert. gutter (2)	—
	Vert. pair with horiz. gutter (10)	—
G181PP	6 items (20)	—
	Cross gutter block (1)	—
	Horiz. pair with vert. gutter (2)	—
	Vert. pair with horiz. gutter (10)	—
V95PP	6 items (48)	—
	Cross gutter block (1)	—
	Horiz. pair with vert. gutter (2)	—
	Vert. pair with horiz. gutter (10)	—
V96PP	6 items (48)	—
	Cross gutter block (1)	—
	Horiz. pair with vert. gutter (2)	—
	Vert. pair with horiz. gutter (10)	—
570PI	(12 pairs)	—
	Cross gutter block (1)	—
	Horiz. pair with vert. gutter (2)	—
	Vert. pair with horiz. gutter (10)	—
571PI	(12 pairs)	—
	Cross gutter block (1)	—
	Horiz. pair with vert. gutter (2)	—
	Vert. pair with horiz. gutter (10)	—
G180PI	(20 pairs)	—
	Cross gutter block (1)	—
	Horiz. pair with vert. gutter (2)	—
	Vert. pair with horiz. gutter (10)	—
G181PI	(20 pairs)	—
	Cross gutter block (1)	—
	Horiz. pair with vert. gutter (2)	—
	Vert. pair with horiz. gutter (10)	—
V95PI	(20 pairs)	—
	Cross gutter block (1)	—
	Horiz. pair with vert. gutter (2)	—
	Vert. pair with horiz. gutter (10)	—
V96PI	(20 pairs)	—
	Cross gutter block (1)	—
	Horiz. pair with vert. gutter (2)	—
	Vert. pair with horiz. gutter (10)	—

New York #572, Geneva #182, Vienna #97
International Trade Center

1990

572PDa	Card, #572PD, #G182PD, #V97PD with approval handstamp (5)	—
572TCa	Card, #572TC blue green ship, #G182TC red orange ship, #V97TC light pink building, with "not approved" handstamp (6)	—
572PP	9 items (50)	—
G182PP	7 items (50)	—
V97PP	8 items (50)	—
572PI	(50 pairs)	—
G182PI	(75 pairs)	—
V97PI	(50 pairs)	—

Geneva #183, Vienna #98
Definitives

1990

G183PD	(6)	—
V98PD	Proof on large sheet with approval or "not approved" handstamp, and set of 7 progressive proofs on large sheets (9)	—
G183PP	9 items (1)	—
V98PP	7 items (50)	—
G183PI	(50 pairs)	—
V98PI	(50 pairs)	—

The not approved proofs of No. V98PD are slightly lighter in color than the approved proofs.

New York #573-574, Geneva #184-185, Vienna #99-100, Souvenir Card #37
Fight AIDS Worldwide

1990

573PDa	Card, #573PD, #G184PD, #V99PD (4)	—
574PDa	Card, #574PD, #G185PD, #573TC white background, #G184TC white background, #V99TC white background, 10s essay of #V100 (4)	—
SC37PD	(4)	—
573PP	7 items (50)	—
574PP	6 items (50)	—
G184PP	7 items (50)	—
G185PP	7 items (50)	—
V99PP	7 items (50)	—
V100PP	6 items (50)	—
573PI	(50 pairs)	—
574PI	(50 pairs)	—

G184PI	(75 pairs)	—
G185PI	(75 pairs)	—
V99PI	(75 pairs)	—
V100PI	(75 pairs)	—

New York #575-576, Geneva #186-187, Vienna #101-102
Medicinal Plants

1990

576PDa	Card, #575PD-576PD, #G186PD-G187PD, #V101PD-V102PD (4)	—
G187PD	(4)	—
G186PP	6 items (50)	—
G187PP	6 items (50)	—
V101PP	6 items (50)	—
V102PP	6 items (50)	—
575PI	(50 pairs)	—
576PI	(50 pairs)	—
G186PI	(50 pairs)	—
G187PI	(50 pairs)	—
V101PI	(50 pairs)	—
V102PI	(50 pairs)	—

New York #577-579, Geneva #188-190, Vienna #103-105
United Nations, 45th Anniv.

1990

578PDa	Card, #577PD-578PD, #G188PD-G189PD, 6s essay of #V103, 8s essay of #V104 (4)	—
579PDa	Card, #579PD, #G190PD, #V105PD (4)	—
577PP	8 items (320)	—
	Horiz. pair with vert. gutter (40)	—
578PP	8 items (320)	—
	Horiz. pair with vert. gutter (40)	—
579PP	8 items (100)	—
G188PP	10 items (160)	—
	Horiz. pair with vert. gutter (20)	—
G189PP	8 items (320)	—
	Horiz. pair with vert. gutter (40)	—
G190PP	9 items (100)	—
V103PP	8 items (320)	—
	Horiz. pair with vert. gutter (40)	—
V104PP	8 items (320)	—
	Horiz. pair with vert. gutter (40)	—
V105PP	8 items (100)	—
577PI	(80 pairs)	—
	Horiz. pair with vert. gutter (10)	—
578PI	(80 pairs)	—
	Horiz. pair with vert. gutter (10)	—
579PI	(100 souvenir sheets)	—
G188PI	(260 pairs)	—
	Horiz. pair with vert. gutter (40)	—
G189PI	(260 pairs)	—
	Horiz. pair with vert. gutter (40)	—
G190PI	(100 souvenir sheets)	—
V103PI	(260 pairs)	—
	Horiz. pair with vert. gutter (40)	—
V104PI	(260 pairs)	—
	Horiz. pair with vert. gutter (40)	—
V105PI	(100 souvenir sheets)	—

New York #580-581, Geneva #191-192, Vienna #106-107, Souvenir Card #38
Crime Prevention

1990

581PDa	Card, #580PD-581PD, #G191PD-G192PD, #V106PD-V107PD, #SC38PD (5)	—
580PP	8 items (50)	—
581PP	8 items (50)	—
G191PP	8 items (50)	—
G192PP	8 items (50)	—
V106PP	8 items (100)	—
V107PP	8 items (100)	—
580PI	(50 pairs)	—
581PI	(50 pairs)	—
G191PI	(75 pairs)	—
G192PI	(75 pairs)	—
V106PI	(75 pairs)	—
V107PI	(75 pairs)	—

New York #582-583, Geneva #193-194, Vienna #108-109,
Human Rights

1990

582PDa	Strip of 3 + 3 labels (9)	—
583PDa	Strip of 3 + 3 labels with approval handstamp (4)	—
G193PDa	Strip of 3 + 3 labels (9)	—
G194PDa	Strip of 3 + 3 labels (9)	—
V108PDa	Strip of 3 + 3 labels (9)	—
V109PDa	Strip of 3 + 3 labels (9)	—
583TCa	Strip of 3 + 3 labels (chocolate panels) with "not approved" handstamp (5)	—
582PP	6 items (20)	—
	Cross gutter block (1)	—
	Horiz. pair with vert. gutter (2)	—
	Vert. pair with horiz. gutter (10)	—
583PP	6 items (20)	—
	Cross gutter block (1)	—
	Horiz. pair with vert. gutter (2)	—
	Vert. pair with horiz. gutter (10)	—
G193PP	6 items (20)	—
	Cross gutter block (1)	—
	Horiz. pair with vert. gutter (2)	—
	Vert. pair with horiz. gutter (10)	—
G194PP	8 items (20)	—
	Cross gutter block (1)	—
	Horiz. pair with vert. gutter (2)	—
	Vert. pair with horiz. gutter (10)	—
V108PP	6 items (20)	—
	Cross gutter block (1)	—
	Horiz. pair with vert. gutter (2)	—
	Vert. pair with horiz. gutter (10)	—
V109PP	6 items (20)	—
	Cross gutter block (1)	—
	Horiz. pair with vert. gutter (2)	—
	Vert. pair with horiz. gutter (10)	—
582PI	(20 pairs)	—
	Cross gutter block (1)	—
	Horiz. pair with vert. gutter (2)	—
	Vert. pair with horiz. gutter (10)	—
583PI	(20 pairs)	—
	Cross gutter block (1)	—
	Horiz. pair with vert. gutter (2)	—
	Vert. pair with horiz. gutter (10)	—
G193PI	(20 pairs)	—
	Cross gutter block (1)	—
	Horiz. pair with vert. gutter (2)	—
	Vert. pair with horiz. gutter (10)	—
G194PI	(20 pairs)	—
	Cross gutter block (1)	—
	Horiz. pair with vert. gutter (2)	—
	Vert. pair with horiz. gutter (10)	—
V108PI	(20 pairs)	—
	Cross gutter block (1)	—
	Horiz. pair with vert. gutter (2)	—
	Vert. pair with horiz. gutter (10)	—
V109PI	(20 pairs)	—
	Cross gutter block (1)	—
	Horiz. pair with vert. gutter (2)	—
	Vert. pair with horiz. gutter (10)	—

There is no appreciable difference between approved and not approved examples of Nos. 582PD, G193PD, G194PD, V108PD and V109PD.

New York #587a, Geneva #198a, Vienna #113a, Souvenir Card #39
Economic Council for Europe

1991

587aPDa	Card, #587aPD, #G198aPD, #V113aPD with printed perforations (2)	—
587aPDb	Card, #587aPDa, SC39PD (1)	—
SC39PD	(1)	—
587aPP	13 items (20 blocks)	—
G198aPP	13 items (20 blocks)	—
V113aPP	13 items (20 blocks)	—
587aPI	(40 blocks)	—
G198aPI	(40 blocks)	—
V113aPI	(40 blocks)	—

Second sets of blocks of Nos. 587aPP and G198aPP with 10 items, and No. V113aPP with 11 items (some items differing from the 13 item set) exist.

New York #588-589, Geneva #199-200, Vienna #114-115
Namibian Independence

1991

588PDa	Card, #588PD, #G199PD-G200PD, #V114PD-V115PD, 36c essay of #589 (8)	—
589PDa	Card, #588PD-589PD, #G199PD-G200PD, #V114PD-V115PD (1)	—
588PP	7 items (50)	—
589PP	7 items (50)	—
G199PP	8 items (50)	—
G200PP	8 items (50)	—
V114PP	6 items (50)	—
V115PP	6 items (50)	—
588PI	(100 pairs)	—
589PI	(100 pairs)	—
G199PI	(75 pairs)	—
G200PI	(75 pairs)	—
V114PI	(75 pairs)	—
V115PI	(75 pairs)	—

New York #590-592, Geneva #201-202, Vienna #116
Definitives

1991

590PD	With approval handstamp (4)	—
592PD	(4)	—
592PDa	Card, imperforate pane of 50 (1)	—
G201PD	(5)	—
G202PDa	Card, #G201PD-G202PD, #G213PD, #V116PD (4)	—
590TC	deep blue background (not approved) (5)	—
592TC	black (1)	—
590PP	8 items (80)	—
	Horiz. pair with vert. gutter (10)	—
591PP	4 items (150)	—
G201PP	8 items (50)	—
G202PP	7 items (50)	—
V116PP	7 items (50)	—
590PI	(90 pairs)	—
	Horiz. pair with vert. gutter (10)	—
591PI	(175 pairs)	—
592PI	(50 pairs)	—
G201PI	(75 pairs)	—
G202PI	(100 pairs)	—
V116PI	(75 pairs)	—

An essay of No. 592 with emblem in solid color exists.

New York #593-594, Geneva #203-204, Vienna #117-118, Souvenir Card #40
Rights of the Child

1991

593PDa	Card, #593PD, #G203PD-G204PD, #V117PD-V118PD, 90c essay of #594 (6)	—
594PDa	Card, #593PD-594PD, #G203PD-G204PD, #V117PD-V118PD (4)	—
594PDb	Card, #593PD-594PD (4)	—
SC40PD	(4)	—
593PP	9 items (50)	—
594PP	9 items (50)	—
G203PP	8 items (50)	—
G204PP	7 items (50)	—
V117PP	7 items (50)	—
V118PP	7 items (50)	—
SC40PP	15 items (1)	—
593PI	(75 pairs)	—
594PI	(75 pairs)	—
G203PI	(75 pairs)	—
G204PI	(75 pairs)	—
V117PI	(75 pairs)	—
V118PI	(75 pairs)	—

No. SC40PP may not be a complete set of progressive proofs. Five essays of No. SC40PD with the 90c essay of No. 594 exist; one is attached to No. 593PDa.

New York #595-596, Geneva #205-206, Vienna #119-120,
Banning of Chemical Weapons

1991

596PDa	Card, #595PD-596PD, #G205PD-G206PD, #V119PD-V120PD with approval handstamp (5)	—
596PDb	Card, #596PD, #G206PD, #V120PD, essays of #595, #G205, #V119 (each with gray panels taller than numerals) with "not approved" handstamp (4)	—
595PP	9 items (50)	—
596PP	9 items (50)	—
G205PP	9 items (100)	—
G206PP	9 items (100)	—
V119PP	8 items (50)	—
V120PP	8 items (50)	—
595PI	(125 pairs)	—
596PI	(125 pairs)	—
G205PI	(125 pairs)	—
G206PI	(125 pairs)	—
V119PI	(125 pairs)	—
V120PI	(125 pairs)	—

Second sets of six items of Nos. 595PP-596PP, G205PP-G206PP, and V119PP-V120PP exist. Some items differ from those found in the listed sets.

New York #597-598, Geneva #207-208, Vienna #121-122
UN Postal Administration, 40th Anniv.

1991

598PDa	Card, #597PD-598PD, #G207PD-G208PD, #V121PD-V122PD (4)	—
597TCa	Card, #597TC, #G207TC-G208TCD, #V121TC-V122TC (each with white background), 36c essay of #598 (6)	—
597PP	2 items (64)	—
	Cross gutter block (1)	—
	Horiz. pair with vert. gutter (8)	—
	Vert. pair with horiz. gutter (8)	—
598PP	2 items (64)	—
	Cross gutter block (1)	—
	Horiz. pair with vert. gutter (8)	—
	Vert. pair with horiz. gutter (8)	—
G207PP	2 items (64)	—
	Cross gutter block (1)	—
	Horiz. pair with vert. gutter (8)	—
	Vert. pair with horiz. gutter (8)	—
G208PP	2 items (64)	—
	Cross gutter block (1)	—
	Horiz. pair with vert. gutter (8)	—
	Vert. pair with horiz. gutter (8)	—
V121PP	2 items (64)	—
	Cross gutter block (1)	—
	Horiz. pair with vert. gutter (8)	—
	Vert. pair with horiz. gutter (8)	—
V122PP	2 items (64)	—
	Cross gutter block (1)	—
	Horiz. pair with vert. gutter (8)	—
	Vert. pair with horiz. gutter (8)	—
597PI	(120 pairs)	—
	Cross gutter block (3)	—
	Horiz. pair with vert. gutter (24)	—
	Vert. pair with horiz. gutter (24)	—
598PI	(120 pairs)	—
	Cross gutter block (3)	—
	Horiz. pair with vert. gutter (24)	—
	Vert. pair with horiz. gutter (24)	—
G207PI	(120 pairs)	—
	Cross gutter block (3)	—
	Horiz. pair with vert. gutter (24)	—
	Vert. pair with horiz. gutter (24)	—
G208PI	(120 pairs)	—
	Cross gutter block (3)	—
	Horiz. pair with vert. gutter (24)	—
	Vert. pair with horiz. gutter (24)	—
V121PI	(120 pairs)	—
	Cross gutter block (3)	—
	Horiz. pair with vert. gutter (24)	—
	Vert. pair with horiz. gutter (24)	—
V122PI	(120 pairs)	—

	Cross gutter block (3)	—
	Horiz. pair with vert. gutter (24)	—
	Vert. pair with horiz. gutter (24)	—

Four cross gutter blocks, 32 horizontal pairs with vertical gutters and 32 vertical pairs with horizontal gutters can be cut from four perforated sheets of Nos. 597PI-598PI, G207PI-G208PI, V119PI-V120PI. No. 598PI is difficult to distinguish from one item from No. 598PP.

New York #599-600, Geneva #209-210, Vienna #123-124, Human Rights

1991

599PDa	Strip of 3 + 3 labels with approval handstamp (4)	—
600PDa	Strip of 3 + 3 labels with approval handstamp (4)	—
G209PDa	Strip of 3 + 3 labels with approval handstamp (4)	—
G210PDa	Strip of 3 + 3 labels with approval handstamp (4)	—
V123PDa	Strip of 3 + 3 labels with approval handstamp (4)	—
V124PDa	Strip of 3 + 3 labels with approval handstamp (4)	—
599TC	Strip of 3 (dark gray background) + 3 labels with "not approved" handstamp (5)	—
600TC	Strip of 3 (dark green background) + 3 labels with "not approved" handstamp (5)	—
G209TC	Strip of 3 (light brown in painting) + 3 labels with "not approved" handstamp (5)	—
G210TC	Strip of 3 (dark green background) + 3 labels with "not approved" handstamp (5)	—
V124TC	Strip of 3 (black background) + 3 labels with "not approved" handstamp (5)	—
599PP	6 items (20)	—
	Cross gutter block (1)	—
	Horiz. pair with vert. gutter (2)	—
	Vert. pair with horiz. gutter (10)	—
600PP	6 items (20)	—
	Cross gutter block (1)	—
	Horiz. pair with vert. gutter (2)	—
	Vert. pair with horiz. gutter (10)	—
G209PP	6 items (20)	—
	Cross gutter block (1)	—
	Horiz. pair with vert. gutter (2)	—
	Vert. pair with horiz. gutter (10)	—
G210PP	6 items (20)	—
	Cross gutter block (1)	—
	Horiz. pair with vert. gutter (2)	—
	Vert. pair with horiz. gutter (10)	—
V123PP	6 items (20)	—
	Cross gutter block (1)	—
	Horiz. pair with vert. gutter (2)	—
	Vert. pair with horiz. gutter (10)	—
V124PP	6 items (20)	—
	Cross gutter block (1)	—
	Horiz. pair with vert. gutter (2)	—
	Vert. pair with horiz. gutter (10)	—
599PI	(56 pairs)	—
	Cross gutter block (1)	—
	Horiz. pair with vert. gutter (2)	—
	Vert. pair with horiz. gutter (10)	—
600PI	(56 pairs)	—
	Cross gutter block (1)	—
	Horiz. pair with vert. gutter (2)	—
	Vert. pair with horiz. gutter (10)	—
G209PI	(56 pairs)	—
	Cross gutter block (1)	—
	Horiz. pair with vert. gutter (2)	—
	Vert. pair with horiz. gutter (10)	—
G210PI	(56 pairs)	—
	Cross gutter block (1)	—
	Horiz. pair with vert. gutter (2)	—
	Vert. pair with horiz. gutter (10)	—
V123PI	(56 pairs)	—
	Cross gutter block (1)	—
	Horiz. pair with vert. gutter (2)	—
	Vert. pair with horiz. gutter (10)	—
V124PI	(56 pairs)	—
	Cross gutter block (1)	—
	Horiz. pair with vert. gutter (2)	—
	Vert. pair with horiz. gutter (10)	—

New York #601-602, Geneva #211-212, Vienna #125-126 World Heritage

1992

602PDa	Card, #601PD-602PD (5)	—
G212PDa	Card, #G211PD-G212PD (5)	—
V126PDa	Card, #V125PD-V126PD (5)	—
601PP	6 items (50)	—
602PP	6 items (50)	—
G211PP	6 items (50)	—
G212PP	6 items (50)	—
V125PP	6 items (50)	—
V126PP	6 items (50)	—
601PI	(50 pairs)	—
602PI	(50 pairs)	—
G211PI	(50 pairs)	—
G212PI	(50 pairs)	—
V125PI	(50 pairs)	—
V126PI	(50 pairs)	—

Geneva #213 Definitive

1992

G213PP	6 items (50)	—
G213PI	(75 pairs)	—

See No. G202PDa.

New York #604a, Geneva #215a, Vienna #128a Clean Oceans

1992

604aPDa	Card, imperforate pane of 6 #604aPD (2)	—
604aPDb	Card, as "a," with one pair removed (1)	—
G215aPDa	Card, imperforate pane of 6 #G215aPD (2)	—
G215aPDb	(Card, as "a," with one pair removed (1)	—
V128aPDa	Card, imperforate pane of 6 #V128aPD (2)	—
V128aPDb	Card, as "a," with one pair removed (1)	—
604aPP	8 items, vert. pair of pairs with narrow horiz. gutter (20)	—
	Cross gutter block (1)	—
	Horiz. pair of pairs with vert. gutter (4)	—
	Vert. pair of pairs with wide horiz. gutter (10)	—
G215aPP	8 items, vert. pair of pairs with narrow horiz. gutter (20)	—
	Cross gutter block (1)	—
	Horiz. pair of pairs with vert. gutter (4)	—
	Vert. pair of pairs with wide horiz. gutter (10)	—
V128aPP	8 items, vert. pair of pairs with narrow horiz. gutter (20)	—
	Cross gutter block (1)	—
	Horiz. pair of pairs with vert. gutter (4)	—
	Vert. pair of pairs with wide horiz. gutter (10)	—
604aPI	Vert. pair of pairs with narrow horiz. gutter (20)	—
	Cross gutter block (1)	—
	Horiz. pair of pairs with vert. gutter (4)	—
	Vert. pair of pairs with wide horiz. gutter (10)	—
G215aPI	Vert. pair of pairs with narrow horiz. gutter (20)	—
	Cross gutter block (1)	—
	Horiz. pair of pairs with vert. gutter (4)	—
	Vert. pair of pairs with wide horiz. gutter (10)	—
V128aPI	Vert. pair of pairs with narrow horiz. gutter (20)	—
	Cross gutter block (1)	—
	Horiz. pair of pairs with vert. gutter (4)	—
	Vert. pair of pairs with wide horiz. gutter (10)	—

New York #608a, Geneva #219a, Vienna #132a Earth Summit

1992

608aPDa	Card, #608aPD, #G219aPD, #V132aPD (5)	—
608aPP	4 items (10)	—
G219aPP	4 items (10)	—
V132aPP	4 items (10)	—
608aPI	(20 blocks)	—
G219aPI	(20 blocks)	—
V132aPI	(20 blocks)	—

New York #609-610, Geneva #220-221, Vienna #133-134 Mission to Planet Earth

1992

610PDa	Card, #610aPD, G221aPD, #V134aPD (3)	—
SC41PD	(3)	—
610aPP	6 items (5)	—
G221aPP	6 items (5)	—
V134aPP	6 items (5)	—
610aPI	(10 pairs)	—
G221aPI	(10 pairs)	—
V134aPI	(10 pairs)	—

One item in No. G221aPP is a blank from a sheet showing marginal inscriptions only.

New York #611-612, Geneva #222-223, Vienna #135-136, Souvenir Card #42 Science and Technology for Development

1992

611PDa	Card, 2 #611PD, 2 #V136PD (4)	—
612PDa	Card, #611PD-612PD, #G222PD-G223PD, #V135PD-V136PD (4)	—
SC42PD	(18)	—
611PP	6 items (50)	—
612PP	6 items (50)	—
G222PP	6 items (50)	—
G223PP	6 items (50)	—
V135PP	6 items (50)	—
V136PP	6 items (50)	—
611PI	(100 pairs)	—
612PI	(100 pairs)	—
G222PI	(100 pairs)	—
G223PI	(100 pairs)	—
V135PI	(100 pairs)	—
V136PI	(100 pairs)	—

There is no appreciable difference between approved and not approved die proofs.

New York #613-615, Vienna #137-138 Definitives

1992

614PDa	Card, #614PD, #V137PD-V138PD (4)	—
615PDa	Card, #613PD, #615PD (3)	—
613PP	6 items (50)	—
614PP	6 items (50)	—
615PP	6 items (50)	—
V137PP	6 items (50)	—
V138PP	6 items (50)	—
613PI	(50 pairs)	—
614PI	(269 pairs)	—
	Cross gutter block (2)	—
	Horiz. pair with vert. gutter (36)	—
	Vert. pair with horiz. gutter (16)	—
615PI	(50 pairs)	—
V137PI	(269 pairs)	—
	Cross gutter block (2)	—
	Horiz. pair with vert. gutter (16)	—
	Vert. pair with horiz. gutter (36)	—
V138PI	(269 pairs)	—
	Cross gutter block (2)	—
	Horiz. pair with vert. gutter (36)	—
	Vert. pair with horiz. gutter (16)	—

Three "not approved" cards containing essays of Nos. 613 and 615 lacking year date and designer inscriptions exist.

New York #616-617, Geneva #224-225, Vienna #139-140 Human Rights

1992

616PDa	Strip of 3 + 3 labels (4)	—
617PDa	Strip of 3 + 3 labels (4)	—
G224PDa	Strip of 3 + 3 labels (4)	—
G225PDa	Strip of 3 + 3 labels (4)	—
V139PDa	Strip of 3 + 3 labels (4)	—
V140PDa	Strip of 3 + 3 labels (4)	—
G225TCa	Strip of 3 (dark brown background under chair) + 3 labels (not approved) (5)	—
616PP	6 items (20)	—
	Cross gutter block (1)	—
	Horiz. pair with vert. gutter (2)	—
	Vert. pair with horiz. gutter (10)	—
617PP	6 items (20)	—
	Cross gutter block (1)	—
	Horiz. pair with vert. gutter (2)	—
	Vert. pair with horiz. gutter (10)	—
G224PP	6 items (20)	—
	Cross gutter block (1)	—
	Horiz. pair with vert. gutter (2)	—
	Vert. pair with horiz. gutter (10)	—
G225PP	6 items (20)	—
	Cross gutter block (1)	—
	Horiz. pair with vert. gutter (2)	—
	Vert. pair with horiz. gutter (10)	—
V139PP	6 items (20)	—
	Cross gutter block (1)	—
	Horiz. pair with vert. gutter (2)	—
	Vert. pair with horiz. gutter (10)	—
V140PP	6 items (20)	—
	Cross gutter block (1)	—
	Horiz. pair with vert. gutter (2)	—
	Vert. pair with horiz. gutter (10)	—
616PI	(32 pairs)	—
	Cross gutter block (4)	—
	Horiz. pair with vert. gutter (8)	—
	Vert. pair with horiz. gutter (40)	—
617PI	(32 pairs)	—
	Cross gutter block (4)	—
	Horiz. pair with vert. gutter (8)	—
	Vert. pair with horiz. gutter (40)	—
G224PI	(32 pairs)	—
	Cross gutter block (4)	—
	Horiz. pair with vert. gutter (8)	—
	Vert. pair with horiz. gutter (40)	—
G225PI	(32 pairs)	—
	Cross gutter block (4)	—
	Horiz. pair with vert. gutter (8)	—
	Vert. pair with horiz. gutter (40)	—
V139PI	(32 pairs)	—
	Cross gutter block (4)	—
	Horiz. pair with vert. gutter (8)	—
	Vert. pair with horiz. gutter (40)	—
V140PI	(32 pairs)	—
	Cross gutter block (4)	—
	Horiz. pair with vert. gutter (8)	—
	Vert. pair with horiz. gutter (40)	—

Five "not approved" cards contain 4.50s essays of No. V139, and five "not approved" cards contain 9.50s essays of No. V140.

New York #618-619, Geneva #226-227, Vienna #141-142 Aging With Dignity

1993

618PDa	Card, #618PD, #G226PD-G227PD, #V141PD-V142PD, #619TC yellow flowers (not approved) (5)	—
619PDa	Card, #618PD-619PD, #V141PD-V142PD, #G226TC pink denomination, #G227TC yellow denomination, with approval handstamp (4)	—

619TCb	Card, #618TC-619TC, #G226TC-G227TC, #V141TC-V142TC, each with white denominations (5)	—
618PP	7 items (50)	—
619PP	7 items (50)	—
G226PP	7 items (50)	—
G227PP	7 items (50)	—
V141PP	7 items (50)	—
V142PP	7 items (50)	—
618PI	(50 pairs)	—
619PI	(50 pairs)	—
G226PI	(50 pairs)	—
G227PI	(50 pairs)	—
V141PI	(50 pairs)	—
V142PI	(50 pairs)	—

New York #623a, Geneva #231a, Vienna #146a
Endangered Species

1993

623aPDa	Card, imperforate pane of 4 blocks of #623aPD (3)	—
G231aPDa	Card, imperforate pane of 4 blocks of #G231aPD (4)	—
V146aPDa	Card, imperforate pane of 4 blocks of #V146aPD (3)	—
G231aTCa	Card, imperforate pane of 4 blocks of #G231aTC black (1)	—
G231aPP	6 items (4 blocks)	—
	Cross gutter block (1)	—
	Horiz. pair with vert. gutter (2)	—
	Vert. pair with horiz. gutter (4)	—
V146aPP	6 items (4 blocks)	—
	Cross gutter block (1)	—
	Horiz. pair with vert. gutter (2)	—
	Vert. pair with horiz. gutter (4)	—
623aPI	(20 blocks)	—
	Cross gutter block (8)	—
	Horiz. pair with vert. gutter (8)	—
	Vert. pair with horiz. gutter (16)	—
G231aPI	(44 blocks)	—
	Cross gutter block (10)	—
	Horiz. pair with vert. gutter (10)	—
	Vert. pair with horiz. gutter (20)	—
V146aPI	(20 blocks)	—
	Cross gutter block (8)	—
	Horiz. pair with vert. gutter (8)	—
	Vert. pair with horiz. gutter (16)	—

New York #624-625, Geneva #232-233, Vienna #147-148, Souvenir Card #43
Healthy Environment

1993

625PDa	Card, #624PD-625PD, #V147PD-V148PD, 90c essay of #G232, 1.10fr essay of #G233 (4)	—
SC43PD	(4)	—
624PP	6 items (50)	—
625PP	6 items (50)	—
G232PP	6 items (50)	—
G233PP	6 items (50)	—
V147PP	6 items (50)	—
V148PP	6 items (50)	—
624PI	(50 pairs)	—
625PI	(50 pairs)	—
G232PI	(50 pairs)	—
G233PI	(50 pairs)	—
V147PI	(50 pairs)	—
V148PI	(50 pairs)	—

New York #626, Vienna #149
Definitives

1993

626PD	(5)	—
V149PD	(5)	—
626PP	8 items (144)	—
	Cross gutter block (1)	—
	Horiz. pair with vert. gutter (18)	—
	Vert. pair with horiz. gutter (8)	—
V149PP	5 items (50)	—
626PI	(194 pairs)	—
	Cross gutter block (2)	—
	Horiz. pair with vert. gutter (36)	—
	Vert. pair with horiz. gutter (16)	—
V149PI	(50 pairs)	—

New York #627-628, Geneva #234-235, Vienna #150-151
Human Rights

1993

627PDa	Strip of 3 + 3 labels (4)	—
628PDa	Strip of 3 + 3 labels (4)	—
G234PDa	Strip of 3 + 3 labels (4)	—
G235PDa	Strip of 3 + 3 labels (4)	—
V150PDa	Strip of 3 + 3 labels (3)	—
V151PDa	Strip of 3 + 3 labels (4)	—
627PP	6 items (20)	—
	Cross gutter block (1)	—
	Horiz. pair with vert. gutter (2)	—
	Vert. pair with horiz. gutter (10)	—
628PP	6 items (20)	—
	Cross gutter block (1)	—
	Horiz. pair with vert. gutter (2)	—
	Vert. pair with horiz. gutter (10)	—
G234PP	6 items (20)	—
	Cross gutter block (1)	—
	Horiz. pair with vert. gutter (2)	—
	Vert. pair with horiz. gutter (10)	—
G235PP	6 items (20)	—
	Cross gutter block (1)	—
	Horiz. pair with vert. gutter (2)	—
	Vert. pair with horiz. gutter (10)	—
627PI	(20 pairs)	—
	Cross gutter block (1)	—
	Horiz. pair with vert. gutter (2)	—
	Vert. pair with horiz. gutter (10)	—
628PI	(20 pairs)	—
	Cross gutter block (1)	—
	Horiz. pair with vert. gutter (2)	—
	Vert. pair with horiz. gutter (10)	—
G234PI	(20 pairs)	—
	Cross gutter block (1)	—
	Horiz. pair with vert. gutter (2)	—
	Vert. pair with horiz. gutter (10)	—
G235PI	(20 pairs)	—
	Cross gutter block (1)	—
	Horiz. pair with vert. gutter (2)	—
	Vert. pair with horiz. gutter (10)	—
V150PI	(6 pairs)	—
V151PI	(6 pairs)	—

New York #632a, Geneva #239a, Vienna #155a, Souvenir Card #44
International Peace Day

1993

632aPD	(4)	—
G239aPD	(4)	—
V155aPD	(4)	—
SC44PD	(4)	—
632aPP	7 items (10 blocks)	—
G239aPP	7 items (10 blocks)	—
V155aPP	7 items (10 blocks)	—
632aPI	(40 blocks)	—
G239aPI	(40 blocks)	—
V155aPI	(40 blocks)	—

New York #636a, Geneva #243a, Vienna #159a
Environment & Climate

1993

636aPDa	Card, #636aPD, #V159aPD (4)	—
G243aPD	(4)	—
636aPP	8 items (6 strips)	—
	Horiz. pair of strips with vert. gutter (6)	—
G243aPP	8 items (6 strips)	—
	Horiz. pair of strips with vert. gutter (6)	—
V155aPP	8 items (6 strips)	—
	Horiz. pair of strips with vert. gutter (6)	—
636aPI	(18 strips)	—
	Horiz. pair of strips with vert. gutter (18)	—
G243aPI	(18 strips)	—
	Horiz. pair of strips with vert. gutter (18)	—
V159aPI	(18 strips)	—
	Horiz. pair of strips with vert. gutter (18)	—

New York #637-638, Geneva #244-245, Vienna #160-161, Souvenir Card #45
International Year of the Family

1994

638PDa	Card, #637PD-638PD, #G244PD-G245PD, #V160PD-V161PD (4)	—
SC45PD	(4)	—
637PP	11 items (50)	—
638PP	11 items (50)	—
G244PP	10 items (50)	—
G245PP	10 items (50)	—
V160PP	11 items (50)	—
V161PP	11 items (50)	—
637PI	(100 pairs)	—
638PI	(100 pairs)	—
G244PI	(100 pairs)	—
G245PI	(100 pairs)	—
V160PI	(100 pairs)	—
V161PI	(100 pairs)	—

New York #642a, Geneva #249a, Vienna #165a
Endangered Species

1994

642aPDa	Card, imperforate pane of 4 #642aPD (9)	—
G249aPDa	Card, imperforate pane of 4 #G249aPD (4)	—
V165aPDa	Card, imperforate pane of 4 #V165aPD (4)	—
642aPP	6 items (4 blocks)	—
	Cross gutter block (2)	—
	Horiz. pair with vert. gutter (2)	—
	Vert. pair with horiz. gutter (4)	—
G249aPP	6 items (4 blocks)	—
	Cross gutter block (2)	—
	Horiz. pair with vert. gutter (2)	—
	Vert. pair with horiz. gutter (4)	—
V165aPP	6 items (4 blocks)	—
	Cross gutter block (2)	—
	Horiz. pair with vert. gutter (2)	—
	Vert. pair with horiz. gutter (4)	—
642aPI	(16 blocks)	—
	Cross gutter block (8)	—
	Horiz. pair with vert. gutter (8)	—
	Vert. pair with horiz. gutter (16)	—
G249aPI	(16 blocks)	—
	Cross gutter block (8)	—
	Horiz. pair with vert. gutter (8)	—
	Vert. pair with horiz. gutter (16)	—
V165aPI	(16 blocks)	—
	Cross gutter block (8)	—
	Horiz. pair with vert. gutter (8)	—
	Vert. pair with horiz. gutter (16)	—

There is no appreciable difference between appoved and not approved examples of No. 642aPD. Five cards with imperforate panes of 40c essays of No. G249a and five cards with imperforate panes of 5s essays of No. V165a exist.

New York #643, Geneva #250, Vienna #166
Protection for Refugees

1994

643PDa	Card, #643PD, #G250PD, #V166PD (4)	—
643PP	8 items (50)	—
G250PP	8 items (50)	—
V166PP	6 items (50)	—
643PI	(69 pairs)	—
	Horiz. pair with vert. gutter (8)	—
G250PI	(69 pairs)	—
	Horiz. pair with vert. gutter (8)	—
V166PI	(69 pairs)	—
	Horiz. pair with vert. gutter (8)	—

New York #644-646, Vienna #167-169
Definitives

1994

645PDa	Card, #644PD-645PD, #V167PD-V169PD (5)	—
646PD	(1)	—
644PP	6 items (50)	—
645PP	6 items (50)	—
V167PP	12 items (50)	—
V168PP	11 items (50)	—
V169PP	11 items (50)	—
644PI	(100 pairs)	—
645PI	(100 pairs)	—
646PI	(50 pairs)	—
V167PI	(100 pairs)	—
V168PI	(100 pairs)	—
V169PI	(100 pairs)	—

There is no appreciable difference between approved and not approved examples of No. 645PDa.

New York #650a, Geneva #254a, Vienna #173a
International Decade for Natural Disaster Reduction

1994

650aPDa	Card, #650aPD, #G254aPD, #V173aPD (5)	—
650aPP	6 items (16 blocks)	—
	Cross gutter block (1)	—
	Horiz. pair with vert. gutter (8)	—
	Vert. pair with horiz. gutter (2)	—
G254aPP	6 items (16 blocks)	—
	Cross gutter block (1)	—
	Horiz. pair with vert. gutter (8)	—
	Vert. pair with horiz. gutter (2)	—
V173aPP	6 items (16 blocks)	—
	Cross gutter block (1)	—
	Horiz. pair with vert. gutter (8)	—
	Vert. pair with horiz. gutter (2)	—
650aPI	(48 blocks)	—
	Cross gutter block (3)	—
	Horiz. pair with vert. gutter (24)	—
	Vert. pair with horiz. gutter (6)	—
G254aPI	(48 blocks)	—
	Cross gutter block (3)	—
	Horiz. pair with vert. gutter (24)	—
	Vert. pair with horiz. gutter (6)	—
V173aPI	(48 blocks)	—
	Cross gutter block (3)	—
	Horiz. pair with vert. gutter (24)	—
	Vert. pair with horiz. gutter (6)	—

Geneva #255-257
Definitives

1994

G257PDa	Card, #G255PD-G257PD (5)	—
G255PP	10 items (144)	—
	Cross gutter block (1)	—
	Horiz. pair with vert. gutter (18)	—
	Vert. pair with horiz. gutter (8)	—
G256PP	10 items (144)	—
	Cross gutter block (1)	—
	Horiz. pair with vert. gutter (18)	—
	Vert. pair with horiz. gutter (8)	—
G257PP	11 items (144)	—
	Cross gutter block (1)	—
	Horiz. pair with vert. gutter (18)	—
	Vert. pair with horiz. gutter (8)	—
G255PI	(288 pairs)	—
	Cross gutter block (4)	—
	Horiz. pair with vert. gutter (72)	—
	Vert. pair with horiz. gutter (32)	—
G256PI	(288 pairs)	—
	Cross gutter block (4)	—
	Horiz. pair with vert. gutter (72)	—
	Vert. pair with horiz. gutter (32)	—
G257PI	(288 pairs)	—
	Cross gutter block (4)	—
	Horiz. pair with vert. gutter (72)	—
	Vert. pair with horiz. gutter (32)	—

New York #651-652, Geneva #258-259, Vienna #174-175, Souvenir Card #46
Population and Development

1994

652PDa	Card, #651PD-652PD, #G258PD-G259PD, #V174PD-V175PD (4)	—
SC46PD	(4)	—
G258PP	6 items (40)	—
G259PP	6 items (40)	—
G259PPa	Horiz. se-tenant pair with vert. gutter, #G258PP-G259PP (10)	—
V174PP	6 items (40)	—
V175PP	6 items (40)	—
V175PPa	Horiz. se-tenant pair with vert. gutter, #V174PP-V175PP (10)	—
651PI	(50 pairs)	—

652PI	(50 pairs)	—
G258PI	(70 pairs)	—
G259PI	(70 pairs)	—
G259PIa	Horiz. se-tenant pair with vert. gutter, #G258PI-G259PI (10)	—
V174PI	(70 pairs)	—
V175PI	(70 pairs)	—
V175PIa	Horiz. se-tenant pair with vert. gutter, #V174PI-V175PI (10)	—

New York #653-654, Geneva #260-261, Vienna #176-177
UNCTAD, 30th Anniv.

1994

653PP	15 items (40)	—
654PP	15 items (40)	—
654PPa	Horiz. se-tenant pair with vert. gutter, #653PP-654PP (10)	—
G260PP	16 items (40)	—
G261PP	16 items (40)	—
G261PPa	Horiz. se-tenant pair with vert. gutter, #G260PP-G261PP (10)	—
V176PP	14 items (40)	—
V177PP	14 items (40)	—
V177PPa	Horiz. se-tenant pair with vert. gutter, #V176PP-V177PP (10)	—
653PI	(60 pairs)	—
654PI	(60 pairs)	—
654PIa	Horiz. se-tenant pair with vert. gutter, #653PI-654PI (30)	—
G260PI	(60 pairs)	—
G261PI	(60 pairs)	—
G261PIa	Horiz. se-tenant pair with vert. gutter, #G260PI-G261PI (30)	—
V176PI	(60 pairs)	—
V177PI	(60 pairs)	—
V177PIa	Horiz. se-tenant pair with vert. gutter, #V176PI-V177PI (30)	—

Two items from No. G260PP and one from No. V176PP are blank due to color arrangement on progressive proof sheet.

New York # 655, Geneva #262, Vienna #178
United Nations, 50th Anniv.

1995

655PD	(3)	—
G262PD	(3)	—
V178PD	(3)	—
655PP	8 items (50)	—
G262PP	8 items (50)	—
V178PP	8 items (50)	—
655PI	(100 pairs)	—
G262PI	(200 pairs)	—
V178PI	(200 pairs)	—

New York #656, Geneva #263, Vienna #179, Souvenir Card #47
World Summit for Social Development, Copenhagen

1995

656PDa	Card, #656PD, #G263PD, #V179PD (3)	—
SC47PD	Card, 4 #SC47PD (1)	—
656PP	12 items (25)	—
G263PP	8 items (25)	—
V179PP	8 items (25)	—
656PI	(24 pairs)	—
G263PI	(24 pairs)	—
V179PI	(24 pairs)	—

New York #660a, Geneva #267a, Vienna #183a
Endangered Species

1995

660aPDa	Card, imperforate pane of 4 blocks, #660aPD (5)	—
660aPDb	Card, broken imperforate pane of 4 blocks, #660aPD (1)	—
660aPDc	Card, 2 imperforate panes of 4 blocks, #660aPD (1)	—
G267aPDa	Card, imperforate pane of 4 blocks, #G267aPD (6)	—
G267aPDb	Card, 2 imperforate panes of 4 blocks, #G267aPD (1)	—
V183aPDa	Card, imperforate pane of 4 blocks, #V183aPD with "14. Okt. 1994" handstamp (approved) (3)	—
V183aTCa	Card, imperforate pane of 4 blocks, #V183aTC (violet blue sky on #181TC), not approved (3)	—
V183aTCb	Card, 2 imperforate pane of 4 blocks, #V183aTC, not approved (1)	—
660aPP	6 items (9 blocks)	—
	Cross gutter block (3)	—
	Horiz. pair with vert. gutter (4)	—
	Vert. pair with horiz. gutter (7)	—
G267aPP	6 items (12 blocks)	—
	Cross gutter block (3)	—
	Horiz. pair with vert. gutter (4)	—
	Vert. pair with horiz. gutter (6)	—
V183aPP	6 items (12 blocks)	—
	Cross gutter block (3)	—
	Horiz. pair with vert. gutter (4)	—
	Vert. pair with horiz. gutter (7)	—
660aPI	(11 blocks)	—
	Cross gutter block (3)	—
	Horiz. pair with vert. gutter (4)	—
	Vert. pair with horiz. gutter (7)	—
G267aPI	(16 blocks)	—
	Cross gutter block (3)	—
	Horiz. pair with vert. gutter (4)	—
	Vert. pair with horiz. gutter (6)	—
V183aPI	(11 blocks)	—
	Cross gutter block (3)	—
	Horiz. pair with vert. gutter (4)	—
	Vert. pair with horiz. gutter (7)	—

Three cross gutter blocks, four horizontal pairs with vertical gutters, seven vertical pairs with horizontal gutters and nine blocks with untrimmed margins can be cut from perforated sheets of Nos. V180PI-V183PI.

New York #661-662, Geneva #268-269, Vienna #184-185, Souvenir Card #48
International Youth Year

1995

662PDa	Card, #661PD-662PD, #G268PD-G269PD, #V184PD-V185PD (6)	—
SC48PD	(6)	—
661PP	5 items (160)	—
	Cross gutter block (5)	—
	Horiz. pair with vert. gutter (25)	—
	Vert. pair with horiz. gutter (44)	—
662PP	8 items (160)	—
	Cross gutter block (5)	—
	Horiz. pair with vert. gutter (25)	—
	Vert. pair with horiz. gutter (44)	—
G268PP	6 items (208)	—
	Cross gutter block (5)	—
	Horiz. pair with vert. gutter (25)	—
	Vert. pair with horiz. gutter (44)	—
G269PP	5 items (208)	—
	Cross gutter block (5)	—
	Horiz. pair with vert. gutter (25)	—
	Vert. pair with horiz. gutter (44)	—
V184PP	7 items (101)	—
	Cross gutter block (2)	—
	Horiz. pair with vert. gutter (11)	—
	Vert. pair with horiz. gutter (12)	—
V185PP	6 items (197)	—
	Cross gutter block (5)	—
	Horiz. pair with vert. gutter (25)	—
	Vert. pair with horiz. gutter (44)	—
661PI	(128 pairs)	—
	Cross gutter block (5)	—
	Horiz. pair with vert. gutter (25)	—
	Vert. pair with horiz. gutter (44)	—
662PI	(128 pairs)	—
	Cross gutter block (5)	—
	Horiz. pair with vert. gutter (25)	—
	Vert. pair with horiz. gutter (44)	—
G268PI	(128 pairs)	—
	Cross gutter block (5)	—
	Horiz. pair with vert. gutter (25)	—
	Vert. pair with horiz. gutter (44)	—
G269PI	(128 pairs)	—
	Cross gutter block (5)	—
	Horiz. pair with vert. gutter (25)	—
	Vert. pair with horiz. gutter (44)	—
V184PI	(128 pairs)	—
	Cross gutter block (5)	—
	Horiz. pair with vert. gutter (25)	—
	Vert. pair with horiz. gutter (44)	—
V185PI	(128 pairs)	—
	Cross gutter block (5)	—
	Horiz. pair with vert. gutter (25)	—
	Vert. pair with horiz. gutter (44)	—

New York #663-665, Geneva #270-272, Vienna #186-188
United Nations, 50th Anniv.

1995

664PDa	Card, # 664PD, #663TC maroon, #663TC dark blue, #663TC green, #664TC dark blue, #664TC green (3)	—
663PI	(80 pairs)	—
664PI	(80 pairs)	—
664PIa	Horiz. se-tenant pair with vert. gutter, #663PI-664PI (40)	—
665PI	(8 pairs of souvenir sheets)	—
G270PI	(80 pairs)	—
G271PI	(80 pairs)	—
G271PIa	Horiz. se-tenant pair with vert. gutter, #G270PI-G271PI (40)	—
G272PI	(8 pairs of souvenir sheets)	—
V186PI	(80 pairs)	—
V187PI	(80 pairs)	—
V187PIa	Horiz. se-tenant pair with vert. gutter, #V186PI-V187PI (40)	—
V188PI	(8 pairs of souvenir sheets)	—

Three cards with non-engraved essays of No. 665 in red violet exist.

New York #666-667, Geneva #273-274, Vienna #189-190
Fourth World Conference on Women

1995

666PP	10 items, perforated (275)	—
667PP	10 items, perforated (250)	—
G273PP	10 items, perforated (100)	—
G274PP	10 items, perforated (250)	—
V189PP	9 items, perforated (275)	—
V190PP	9 items, perforated (275)	—
666PI	(144 pairs)	—
667PI	(144 pairs)	—
G273PI	(108 pairs)	—
G274PI	(144 pairs)	—
V189PI	(132 pairs)	—
V190PI	(144 pairs)	—

On No. V189PP and V190PP, 125 sets have a red and multicolored item while the remaining 150 sets have a blue and multicolored item.

New York #668
UN Headquarters

1995

668PD	(5)	—
668PP	6 items (162)	—
	Horiz. pair with vert. gutter (9)	—
	Vert. pair with horiz. gutter (5)	—
668PI	(85 pairs)	—
	Horiz. pair with vert. gutter (9)	—
	Vert. pair with horiz. gutter (5)	—

New York #669-670, Geneva #275-276, Vienna #191-192
United Nations, 50th Anniversary

1995

669PD	(4)	—
G275PD	(4)	—
V191PD	(4)	—
669PP	6 items (6)	—
G275PP	8 items (6)	—
V191PP	7 items (6)	—
669PI	(2 full panes)	—
669PIa	(3 pairs of full panes)	—
670PI	(3 booklets)	—
G275PI	(2 full panes)	—
G275PIa	(3 pairs of full panes)	—
G276PI	(3 booklets)	—
V191PI	(2 full panes)	—
V191PIa	(4 pairs of full panes)	—
V192PI	(3 booklets)	—

New York #671, Geneva #277, Vienna #193, Souvenir Card #49
World Federation of United Nations Associations, 50th Anniv.

1996

671PDa	Card, #671PD, #G277PD, #V193PD (3)	—
SC49PD	(4)	—
671PP	6 items (150)	—
	Horiz. pair with vert. gutter (25)	—
G277PP	6 items (150)	—
	Horiz. pair with vert. gutter (25)	—
V193PP	6 items (305)	—
	Cross gutter block (5)	—
	Horiz. pair with vert. gutter (40)	—
	Vert. pair with horiz. gutter (30)	—
671PI	(155 pairs)	—
	Horiz. pair with vert. gutter (55)	—
G277PI	(155 pairs)	—
	Horiz. pair with vert. gutter (55)	—
V193PI	(264 pairs)	—
	Cross gutter block (11)	—
	Horiz. pair with vert. gutter (88)	—
	Vert. pair with horiz. gutter (63)	—

New York #672-673, Geneva #278-279, Vienna #194-195
Definitives

1996

673PDa	Card, #672PD-673PD, #G278PD-G279PD, #V194PD-V195PD with approval handstamp (4)	—
673PDb	Card, #673PD, #672TC gray in vignette, #G278TC-G279TC tan background in panel, essays of #V194PD-V195PD (larger frames) (not approved) (4)	—
673PDc	#673PDa and 673PDb stapled together (1)	—
672PP	8 items (144)	—
	Cross gutter block (1)	—
	Horiz. pair with vert. gutter (18)	—
	Vert. pair with horiz. gutter (8)	—
673PP	8 items (144)	—
	Cross gutter block (1)	—
	Horiz. pair with vert. gutter (18)	—
	Vert. pair with horiz. gutter (8)	—
G278PP	8 items (144)	—
	Cross gutter block (1)	—
	Horiz. pair with vert. gutter (18)	—
	Vert. pair with horiz. gutter (8)	—
G279PP	8 items (144)	—
	Cross gutter block (1)	—
	Horiz. pair with vert. gutter (18)	—
	Vert. pair with horiz. gutter (8)	—
V194PP	8 items (144)	—
	Cross gutter block (1)	—
	Horiz. pair with vert. gutter (18)	—
	Vert. pair with horiz. gutter (8)	—
V195PP	8 items (144)	—
	Cross gutter block (1)	—
	Horiz. pair with vert. gutter (18)	—
	Vert. pair with horiz. gutter (8)	—
672PI	(216 pairs)	—
	Cross gutter block (3)	—
	Horiz. pair with vert. gutter (54)	—
	Vert. pair with horiz. gutter (16)	—
673PI	(144 pairs)	—
	Cross gutter block (3)	—
	Horiz. pair with vert. gutter (54)	—
	Vert. pair with horiz. gutter (16)	—
G278PI	(216 pairs)	—
	Cross gutter block (3)	—
	Horiz. pair with vert. gutter (54)	—
	Vert. pair with horiz. gutter (24)	—
G279PI	(216 pairs)	—
	Cross gutter block (3)	—
	Horiz. pair with vert. gutter (54)	—
	Vert. pair with horiz. gutter (24)	—
V194PI	(216 pairs)	—
	Cross gutter block (3)	—
	Horiz. pair with vert. gutter (24)	—

	Vert. pair with horiz. gutter (36)	—
V195PI	(216 pairs)	—
	Cross gutter block (3)	—
	Horiz. pair with vert. gutter (24)	—
	Vert. pair with horiz. gutter (36)	—

New York #677a, Geneva #283a, Vienna #199a Endangered Species

1996

677aPDa	Card, imperforate pane of 4 blocks, #677aPD (3)	—
677aPDb	Card, broken imperforate pane of 4 blocks, #677aPD (1)	—
G283aPDa	Card, imperforate pane of 4 blocks, #G283aPD (3)	—
G283aPDb	Card, broken imperforate pane of 4 blocks, #G283aPD (1)	—
V199aPDa	Card, imperforate pane of 4 blocks, #V199aPD (3)	—
V199aPDb	Card, broken imperforate pane of 4 blocks, #V199aPD (1)	—
677aPP	6 items (14 blocks)	—
	Cross gutter block (5)	—
	Horiz. pair with vert. gutter (6)	—
	Vert. pair with horiz. gutter (11)	—
G283aPP	6 items (14 blocks)	—
	Cross gutter block (5)	—
	Horiz. pair with vert. gutter (6)	—
	Vert. pair with horiz. gutter (11)	—
V199aPP	6 items (14 blocks)	—
	Cross gutter block (5)	—
	Horiz. pair with vert. gutter (6)	—
	Vert. pair with horiz. gutter (11)	—
677aPI	(25 blocks)	—
	Cross gutter block (11)	—
	Horiz. pair with vert. gutter (12)	—
	Vert. pair with horiz. gutter (23)	—
G283aPI	(25 blocks)	—
	Cross gutter block (11)	—
	Horiz. pair with vert. gutter (12)	—
	Vert. pair with horiz. gutter (23)	—
V199aPI	(25 blocks)	—
	Cross gutter block (11)	—
	Horiz. pair with vert. gutter (12)	—
	Vert. pair with horiz. gutter (23)	—

New York #682a, Geneva #288a, Vienna #204a City Summit

1996

682aPDa	Card, imperforate pane of 5 strips, #682aPD (4)	—
G288aPDa	Card, imperforate pane of 5 strips, #G288aPD (4)	—
V204aPDa	Card, imperforate pane of 5 strips, #V204aPD (4)	—
682aPP	10 items (15 horiz. pairs of strips with vert. gutter)	—
G288aPP	10 items (24 horiz. pairs of strips with vert. gutter)	—
	Cross gutter block of strips (3)	—
V204aPP	10 items (15 horiz. pairs of strips with vert. gutter)	—
682aPI	(35 horiz. pairs of strips with vert. gutter)	—
G288aPI	(56 horiz. pairs of strips with vert. gutter)	—
	Cross gutter block of strips (7)	—
V204aPI	(35 horiz. pairs of strips with vert. gutter)	—

New York #683-685, Geneva #289-291, Vienna #205-207 Sport and the Environment

1996

684PDa	Card, #683PD-684PD (10)	—
685PD	(10)	—
G290PDa	Card, #G289PD-G290PD (10)	—
G291PD	(10)	—
V206PDa	Card, #V205PD-V206PD (10)	—
V207PD	(10)	—
683PP	8 items (88)	—
	Cross gutter block (2)	—
	Horiz. pair with vert. gutter (16)	—
	Vert. pair with horiz. gutter (11)	—
684PP	8 items (88)	—
	Cross gutter block (2)	—
	Horiz. pair with vert. gutter (11)	—
	Vert. pair with horiz. gutter (16)	—
685PP	12 items (25 souvenir sheets)	—
G289PP	8 items (88)	—
	Cross gutter block (2)	—
	Horiz. pair with vert. gutter (16)	—
	Vert. pair with horiz. gutter (11)	—
G290PP	8 items (88)	—
	Cross gutter block (2)	—
	Horiz. pair with vert. gutter (11)	—
	Vert. pair with horiz. gutter (16)	—
G291PP	10 items (25 souvenir sheets)	—
V205PP	8 items (88)	—
	Cross gutter block (2)	—
	Horiz. pair with vert. gutter (16)	—
	Vert. pair with horiz. gutter (11)	—
V206PP	8 items (88)	—
	Cross gutter block (2)	—
	Horiz. pair with vert. gutter (11)	—
	Vert. pair with horiz. gutter (16)	—
V207PP	11 items (25 souvenir sheets)	—
683PI	(44 pairs)	—
	Cross gutter block (2)	—
	Horiz. pair with vert. gutter (16)	—
	Vert. pair with horiz. gutter (11)	—
684PI	(44 pairs)	—
	Cross gutter block (2)	—
	Horiz. pair with vert. gutter (11)	—
	Vert. pair with horiz. gutter (16)	—
685PI	(75 souvenir sheets)	—
G289PI	(88 pairs)	—
	Cross gutter block (4)	—
	Horiz. pair with vert. gutter (32)	—
	Vert. pair with horiz. gutter (22)	—
G290PI	(88 pairs)	—
	Cross gutter block (4)	—
	Horiz. pair with vert. gutter (22)	—
	Vert. pair with horiz. gutter (32)	—
G291PI	(75 souvenir sheets)	—
V205PI	(132 pairs)	—
	Cross gutter block (6)	—
	Horiz. pair with vert. gutter (48)	—
	Vert. pair with horiz. gutter (33)	—
V206PI	(132 pairs)	—
	Cross gutter block (6)	—
	Horiz. pair with vert. gutter (33)	—
	Vert. pair with horiz. gutter (48)	—
V207PI	(75 souvenir sheets)	—

New York #686-687, Geneva #292-293, Vienna #208-209 Plea for Peace

1996

687PDa	Card, #686PD-687PD, #G292PD-G293PD, #V208PD-V209PD (4)	—
686PP	10 items (112)	—
	Cross gutter block (3)	—
	Horiz. pair with vert. gutter (14)	—
	Vert. pair with horiz. gutter (24)	—
687PP	10 items (112)	—
	Cross gutter block (3)	—
	Horiz. pair with vert. gutter (14)	—
	Vert. pair with horiz. gutter (24)	—
G292PP	10 items (112)	—
	Cross gutter block (3)	—
	Horiz. pair with vert. gutter (24)	—
	Vert. pair with horiz. gutter (14)	—
G293PP	10 items (112)	—
	Cross gutter block (2)	—
	Horiz. pair with vert. gutter (24)	—
	Vert. pair with horiz. gutter (14)	—
V208PP	10 items (112)	—
	Cross gutter block (3)	—
	Horiz. pair with vert. gutter (14)	—
	Vert. pair with horiz. gutter (24)	—
V209PP	10 items (112)	—
	Cross gutter block (3)	—
	Horiz. pair with vert. gutter (14)	—
	Vert. pair with horiz. gutter (24)	—
686PI	(104 pairs)	—
	Cross gutter block (3)	—
	Horiz. pair with vert. gutter (14)	—
	Vert. pair with horiz. gutter (24)	—
687PI	(104 pairs)	—
	Cross gutter block (3)	—
	Horiz. pair with vert. gutter (14)	—
	Vert. pair with horiz. gutter (24)	—
G292PI	(80 pairs)	—
	Cross gutter block (3)	—
	Horiz. pair with vert. gutter (24)	—
	Vert. pair with horiz. gutter (14)	—
G293PI	(80 pairs)	—
	Cross gutter block (3)	—
	Horiz. pair with vert. gutter (24)	—
	Vert. pair with horiz. gutter (14)	—
V208PI	(80 pairs)	—
	Cross gutter block (3)	—
	Horiz. pair with vert. gutter (14)	—
	Vert. pair with horiz. gutter (24)	—
V209PI	(80 pairs)	—
	Cross gutter block (3)	—
	Horiz. pair with vert. gutter (14)	—
	Vert. pair with horiz. gutter (24)	—

New York #688-689, Geneva #294-295, Vienna #210-211, Souvenir Card #50 UNICEF, 50th Anniv.

1996

689PDa	Imperforate pane, #689PD (4)	—
G294PDa	Imperforate pane, #G294PD (4)	—
G295PDa	Imperforate pane, #G295PD (6)	—
V210PDa	Imperforate pane, #V210PD (on photographic paper) (2)	—
V211PDa	Imperforate pane, #V211PD (4)	—
SC50PD	(1)	—
688PP	10 items (18)	—
	Cross gutter block (6)	—
	Horiz. pair with vert. gutter (12)	—
	Vert. pair with horiz. gutter (15)	—
689PP	11 items (18)	—
	Cross gutter block (6)	—
	Horiz. pair with vert. gutter (12)	—
	Vert. pair with horiz. gutter (15)	—
G294PP	9 items (18)	—
	Cross gutter block (6)	—
	Horiz. pair with vert. gutter (12)	—
	Vert. pair with horiz. gutter (15)	—
G295PP	9 items (18)	—
	Cross gutter block (6)	—
	Horiz. pair with vert. gutter (12)	—
	Vert. pair with horiz. gutter (15)	—
V210PP	9 items (18)	—
	Cross gutter block (6)	—
	Horiz. pair with vert. gutter (18)	—
	Vert. pair with horiz. gutter (14)	—
V211PP	9 items (18)	—
	Cross gutter block (6)	—
	Horiz. pair with vert. gutter (18)	—
	Vert. pair with horiz. gutter (14)	—
688PI	(12 pairs)	—
	Cross gutter block (18)	—
	Horiz. pair with vert. gutter (36)	—
	Vert. pair with horiz. gutter (45)	—
689PI	(12 pairs)	—
	Cross gutter block (18)	—
	Horiz. pair with vert. gutter (36)	—
	Vert. pair with horiz. gutter (45)	—
G294PI	(12 pairs)	—
	Cross gutter block (18)	—
	Horiz. pair with vert. gutter (36)	—
	Vert. pair with horiz. gutter (45)	—
G295PI	(12 pairs)	—
	Cross gutter block (18)	—
	Horiz. pair with vert. gutter (36)	—
	Vert. pair with horiz. gutter (45)	—
V210PI	(12 pairs)	—
	Cross gutter block (18)	—
	Horiz. pair with vert. gutter (36)	—
	Vert. pair with horiz. gutter (45)	—
V211PI	(12 pairs)	—
	Cross gutter block (18)	—
	Horiz. pair with vert. gutter (36)	—
	Vert. pair with horiz. gutter (45)	—

Two of the No. G295PDa items are on photographic paper. Four cards with imperforate panes of 32c Hansel & Gretel essays exist. Four cards with imperforate panes of 5.50s Yeh-Shen essays exist. Four essays of No. SC50 showing these two essay items exist.

New York #690-697 Flags

1997

690-697PP	Set of 20 sheets (1)	—
690-697PI	Set of 2 sheets (3)	—

On Nos. 690-697PP, there are ten progressive proof sheets per issued sheet.

New York #698-699, Geneva #296-297, Vienna #212-213 Definitives

1997

698PDa	Card, #698PD, #G296PD-G297PD, #V212PD-V213PD (1)	—
699PDa	Card, #698PD-699PD, #G296PD-G297PD, #V212PD-V213PD (4)	—
698PP	8 items (84)	—
	Cross gutter block (3)	—
	Horiz. pair with vert. gutter (18)	—
	Vert. pair with horiz. gutter (14)	—
699PP	8 items (84)	—
	Cross gutter block (3)	—
	Horiz. pair with vert. gutter (14)	—
	Vert. pair with horiz. gutter (18)	—
G296PP	8 items (84)	—
	Cross gutter block (3)	—
	Horiz. pair with vert. gutter (14)	—
	Vert. pair with horiz. gutter (18)	—
G297PP	8 items (84)	—
	Cross gutter block (3)	—
	Horiz. pair with vert. gutter (14)	—
	Vert. pair with horiz. gutter (18)	—
V212PP	10 items (84)	—
	Cross gutter block (3)	—
	Horiz. pair with vert. gutter (18)	—
	Vert. pair with horiz. gutter (14)	—
V213PP	10 items (84)	—
	Cross gutter block (3)	—
	Horiz. pair with vert. gutter (18)	—
	Vert. pair with horiz. gutter (14)	—
698PI	(60 pairs)	—
	Cross gutter block (3)	—
	Horiz. pair with vert. gutter (18)	—
	Vert. pair with horiz. gutter (14)	—
699PI	(60 pairs)	—
	Cross gutter block (3)	—
	Horiz. pair with vert. gutter (14)	—
	Vert. pair with horiz. gutter (18)	—
G296PI	(60 pairs)	—
	Cross gutter block (3)	—
	Horiz. pair with vert. gutter (14)	—
	Vert. pair with horiz. gutter (18)	—
G297PI	(60 pairs)	—
	Cross gutter block (3)	—
	Horiz. pair with vert. gutter (14)	—
	Vert. pair with horiz. gutter (18)	—
V212PI	(60 pairs)	—
	Cross gutter block (3)	—
	Horiz. pair with vert. gutter (18)	—
	Vert. pair with horiz. gutter (14)	—
V213PI	(60 pairs)	—
	Cross gutter block (3)	—
	Horiz. pair with vert. gutter (18)	—
	Vert. pair with horiz. gutter (14)	—

New York #703a, Geneva #301a, Vienna #217a Endangered Species

1997

703aPDa	Card, imperforate pane of 4 blocks #703aPD, imperforate pane of 4 blocks #G301aPD (4)	—
V217aPDa	Card, imperforate pane of 4 blocks #V217aPD (4)	—
703aPP	6 items (4 blocks)	—
	Cross gutter block (2)	—
	Horiz. pair with vert. gutter (2)	—
	Vert. pair with horiz. gutter (4)	—
G301aPP	6 items (4 blocks)	—
	Cross gutter block (2)	—
	Horiz. pair with vert. gutter (2)	—
	Vert. pair with horiz. gutter (4)	—
V217aPP	6 items (4 blocks)	—
	Cross gutter block (2)	—
	Horiz. pair with vert. gutter (2)	—
	Vert. pair with horiz. gutter (4)	—
703aPI	(12 blocks)	—
	Cross gutter block (6)	—
	Horiz. pair with vert. gutter (6)	—
	Vert. pair with horiz. gutter (12)	—

G301aPI	(12 blocks)	—
	Cross gutter block (6)	—
	Horiz. pair with vert. gutter (6)	—
	Vert. pair with horiz. gutter (12)	—
V217aPI	(12 blocks)	—
	Cross gutter block (6)	—
	Horiz. pair with vert. gutter (6)	—
	Vert. pair with horiz. gutter (12)	—

New York #707a, 708, Geneva #305a, 306, Vienna #221a, 222
Earth Summit

1997

707aPP	6 items (6 blocks)	—
708PP	6 items (1 souvenir sheet)	—
708aPP	6 items (1 souvenir sheet)	—
G305aPP	6 items (6 blocks)	—
V221aPP	6 items (6 blocks)	—
707aPI	(15 blocks)	—
708PI	(6 souvenir sheets)	—
708aPI	(6 souvenir sheets)	—
G305aPI	(15 blocks)	—
G306PI	(6 souvenir sheets)	—
V221aPI	(15 blocks)	—
V222PI	(6 souvenir sheets)	—

New York #713a, Geneva #311a, Vienna #227a
Transportation

1997

713aPDa	Imperforate pane, #713aPD (9)	—
G311aPDa	Imperforate pane, #G311aPD (9)	—
V227aPDa	Imperforate pane, #V227aPD (9)	—
713aPP	9 items (6 strips)	—
	Cross gutter block of strips (1)	—
	Horiz. pair of strips with vert. gutter (6)	—
	Vert. pair of strips with horiz. gutter (1)	—
G311aPP	10 items (6 strips)	—
	Cross gutter block of strips (1)	—
	Horiz. pair of strips with vert. gutter (6)	—
	Vert. pair of strips with horiz. gutter (1)	—
V227aPP	9 items (6 strips)	—
	Cross gutter block of strips (1)	—
	Horiz. pair of strips with vert. gutter (6)	—
	Vert. pair of strips with horiz. gutter (1)	—
713aPI	(14 strips)	—
	Cross gutter block of strips (1)	—
	Horiz. pair of strips with vert. gutter (6)	—
	Vert. pair of strips with horiz. gutter (1)	—
G311aPI	(14 strips)	—
	Cross gutter block of strips (1)	—
	Horiz. pair of strips with vert. gutter (6)	—
	Vert. pair of strips with horiz. gutter (1)	—
V227aPI	(14 strips)	—
	Cross gutter block of strips (1)	—
	Horiz. pair of strips with vert. gutter (6)	—
	Vert. pair of strips with horiz. gutter (1)	—

New York #714-715, Geneva #312-313, Vienna #228-229, Souvenir Card #51
Philately

1997

715TCa	Card, #714TC-715TC, #G312TC-G313TC, #V228TC-V229TC, all with white denominations (4)	—
715TCb	Card, #714TC-715TC, #G312TC-G313TC, #V228TC-V229TC, all with light blue green backgrounds (1)	—
SC51PD	(4)	—
714PP	11 items (33)	—
	Horiz. pair with vert. gutter (6)	—
715PP	11 items (33)	—
	Horiz. pair with vert. gutter (6)	—
715PPa	Cross gutter block, 2 each #714PP-715PP (2)	—
715PPb	Vert. pair with horiz. gutter, #714PP-715PP (11)	—
G312PP	11 items (33)	—
	Horiz. pair with vert. gutter (6)	—
G313PP	11 items (33)	—
	Horiz. pair with vert. gutter (6)	—
G313PPa	Cross gutter block, 2 each #G312PP-G313PP (2)	—
G313PPb	Vert. pair with horiz. gutter, #G312PP-G313PP (11)	—
V228PP	10 items (33)	—
	Horiz. pair with vert. gutter (6)	—
V229PP	10 items (33)	—
	Horiz. pair with vert. gutter (6)	—
V229PPa	Cross gutter block, 2 each #V228PP-V229PP (2)	—
V229PPb	Vert. pair with horiz. gutter, #V228PP-V229PP (11)	—
714PI	(48 pairs)	—
	Horiz. pair with vert. gutter (18)	—
715PI	(48 pairs)	—
	Horiz. pair with vert. gutter (18)	—
715PIa	Cross gutter block, 2 each #714PI-715PI (6)	—
715PIb	Vert. pair with horiz. gutter, #714PI-715PI (33)	—
G312PI	(48 pairs)	—
	Horiz. pair with vert. gutter (18)	—
G313PI	(48 pairs)	—
	Horiz. pair with vert. gutter (18)	—
G313PIa	Cross gutter block, 2 each #G312PI-G313PI (6)	—
G313PIb	Vert. pair with horiz. gutter, #G312PI-G313PI (33)	—
V228PI	(48 pairs)	—
	Horiz. pair with vert. gutter (18)	—
V229PI	(48 pairs)	—
	Horiz. pair with vert. gutter (18)	—
V229PIa	Cross gutter block, 2 each #V228PI-V229PI (6)	—
V229PIb	Vert. pair with horiz. gutter, #V228PI-V229PI (33)	—

On Nos. 714PP-715PP, G312PP-G313PP and V228PP-V229PP some progressive proof items are blank due to color arrangements on sheets.

New York #716-717, Geneva #314-315, Vienna #230-231
World Heritage

1997

717PDa	Stapled set of 6 layout sheets with #716PD-717PD, #G314PD-G315PD, #V230PD-V231PD affixed (3)	—
716PP	10 items (20)	—
717PP	10 items (20)	—
G314PP	10 items (20)	—
G315PP	10 items (20)	—
V230PP	10 items (20)	—
V231PP	10 items (20)	—
716PI	(30 pairs)	—
717PI	(30 pairs)	—
G314PI	(30 pairs)	—
G315PI	(30 pairs)	—
V230PI	(30 pairs)	—
V231PI	(30 pairs)	—

New York #719-726
Flags

1998

719-726PP	Set of 20 sheets (1)	—
719-726PI	Set of 2 sheets (3)	—

On Nos. 719-726PP, there are ten progressive proof sheets per issued sheet.

New York #727-729, Geneva #317, Vienna #233-234
Definitives

1998

727PDa	Card, #727PD, #G317TC black (1)	—
729PDa	Card, #727PD-729PD, #G317PD, #V233PD-V234PD (4)	—
727PP	10 items (84)	—
	Cross gutter block (3)	—
	Horiz. pair with vert. gutter (14)	—
	Vert. pair with horiz. gutter (18)	—
728PP	8 items (84)	—
	Cross gutter block (3)	—
	Horiz. pair with vert. gutter (14)	—
	Vert. pair with horiz. gutter (18)	—
729PP	9 items (84)	—
	Cross gutter block (3)	—
	Horiz. pair with vert. gutter (18)	—
	Vert. pair with horiz. gutter (14)	—
G317PP	10 items (84)	—
	Cross gutter block (3)	—
	Horiz. pair with vert. gutter (14)	—
	Vert. pair with horiz. gutter (18)	—
V233PP	8 items (84)	—
	Cross gutter block (3)	—
	Horiz. pair with vert. gutter (18)	—
	Vert. pair with horiz. gutter (14)	—
V234PP	10 items (84)	—
	Cross gutter block (3)	—
	Horiz. pair with vert. gutter (18)	—
	Vert. pair with horiz. gutter (14)	—
727PI	(60 pairs)	—
	Cross gutter block (3)	—
	Horiz. pair with vert. gutter (14)	—
	Vert. pair with horiz. gutter (18)	—
728PI	(60 pairs)	—
	Cross gutter block (3)	—
	Horiz. pair with vert. gutter (14)	—
	Vert. pair with horiz. gutter (18)	—
729PI	(60 pairs)	—
	Cross gutter block (3)	—
	Horiz. pair with vert. gutter (18)	—
	Vert. pair with horiz. gutter (14)	—
G317PI	(60 pairs)	—
	Cross gutter block (3)	—
	Horiz. pair with vert. gutter (14)	—
	Vert. pair with horiz. gutter (18)	—
V233PI	(60 pairs)	—
	Cross gutter block (3)	—
	Horiz. pair with vert. gutter (18)	—
	Vert. pair with horiz. gutter (14)	—
V234PI	(60 pairs)	—
	Cross gutter block (3)	—
	Horiz. pair with vert. gutter (18)	—
	Vert. pair with horiz. gutter (14)	—

New York #733a, Geneva #321a, Vienna #238a
Endangered Species

1998

733PDa	Card, imperforate pane of 4 blocks, #733aPD (1)	—
733PDb	Card, broken imperforate pane of 4 blocks, #733aPD (1)	—
G321PDa	Card, imperforate pane of 4 blocks, #G321aPD (1)	—
G321PDb	Card, broken imperforate pane of 4 blocks, #G321aPD (1)	—
V238PDa	Card, imperforate pane of 4 blocks, #V238aPD (1)	—
V238PDb	Card, broken imperforate pane of 4 blocks, #V238aPD (1)	—
733aPP	6 items (4 blocks)	—
	Cross gutter block (2)	—
	Horiz. pair with vert. gutter (2)	—
	Vert. pair with horiz. gutter (4)	—
G321aPP	4 items (4 blocks)	—
	Cross gutter block (2)	—
	Horiz. pair with vert. gutter (2)	—
	Vert. pair with horiz. gutter (4)	—
V238aPP	6 items (4 blocks)	—
	Cross gutter block (2)	—
	Horiz. pair with vert. gutter (2)	—
	Vert. pair with horiz. gutter (4)	—
733aPI	(12 blocks)	—
	Cross gutter block (2)	—
	Horiz. pair with vert. gutter (2)	—
	Vert. pair with horiz. gutter (4)	—
G321aPI	(12 blocks)	—
	Cross gutter block (2)	—
	Horiz. pair with vert. gutter (2)	—
	Vert. pair with horiz. gutter (4)	—
V238aPI	(12 blocks)	—
	Cross gutter block (2)	—
	Horiz. pair with vert. gutter (2)	—
	Vert. pair with horiz. gutter (4)	—

No. G321aPP is not a complete set, as there are no black only and cyan only items.

New York #734, Geneva #322, Vienna #239
International Year of the Ocean

1998

734PD	(not approved) (4)	—
G322PD	(4)	—
V239PD	(4)	—
734PP	6 items (6 panes)	—
G322PP	6 items (6 panes)	—
V239PP	6 items (6 panes)	—
734PI	(18 panes)	—
G322PI	(18 panes)	—
V239PI	(18 panes)	—

New York #735-736, Geneva #323-324, Vienna #240-241
Rain Forests

1998

735PDa	Card, imperforate pane of 20 #735PD (8)	—
736PDa	Card, #736PD, #G324PD, #V241PD (8)	—
G323PDa	Card, imperforate pane of 20 #G323PD (8)	—
V240PDa	Card, imperforate pane of 20 #V240PD (8)	—
735PP	6 items (see note)	—
G323PP	6 items (see note)	—
V240PP	6 items (see note)	—
735PI	(see note)	—
G323PI	(see note)	—
V240PI	(see note)	—

There are two types of Nos. 735PP and V240PP, one with cats lacking spots on the red item, the other with the cat with spots on the magenta item. There are 20 of each type.

There are two types of No. G323PP, one with orangutan with small dots in eyes on the cyan item, the other with large dots in eyes.

Similarly, there are two types of Nos. 735PI, G323PI and V240PI, one with a lighter background, the other with a bolder background. There are 20 pairs of each type.

New York #737-738, Geneva #325-326, Vienna #242-243, Souvenir Card #52
UN Peacekeeping Forces, 50th Anniv.

1998

737TC	Dark blue panel (on Cromalin paper) (5)	—
738TC	Dark blue panel (on Cromalin paper) (5)	—
G325TC	Dark blue panel (on Cromalin paper) (5)	—
G326TC	Dark blue panel (on Cromalin paper) (5)	—
V242TC	Dark blue panel (on Cromalin paper) (5)	—
V243TC	Dark blue panel (on Cromalin paper) (5)	—
SC52PD	(4)	—
737PP	10 items (20)	—
738PP	10 items (20)	—
G325PP	10 items (20)	—
G326PP	10 items (20)	—
V242PP	10 items (20)	—
V243PP	10 items (20)	—
737PI	(20 pairs)	—
738PI	(20 pairs)	—
G325PI	(20 pairs)	—
G326PI	(20 pairs)	—
V242PI	(20 pairs)	—
V243PI	(20 pairs)	—

New York #739-740, Geneva #327-328, Vienna #244-245, Souvenir Card #53
Universal Declaration of Human Rights, 50th Anniv.

1998

740PDa	Card, #739PD-740PD, #G327PD-G328PD, #V244PD-V245PD (4)	—
SC53PD	(4)	—
739PP	8 items (64)	—
	Cross gutter block (2)	—
	Horiz. pair with vert. gutter (8)	—
	Vert. pair with horiz. gutter (16)	—
740PP	8 items (64)	—
	Cross gutter block (2)	—
	Horiz. pair with vert. gutter (8)	—
	Vert. pair with horiz. gutter (16)	—
G327PP	8 items (64)	—
	Cross gutter block (2)	—
	Horiz. pair with vert. gutter (8)	—
	Vert. pair with horiz. gutter (16)	—
G328PP	8 items (64)	—
	Cross gutter block (2)	—
	Horiz. pair with vert. gutter (8)	—
	Vert. pair with horiz. gutter (16)	—
V244PP	8 items (64)	—
	Cross gutter block (2)	—
	Horiz. pair with vert. gutter (8)	—
	Vert. pair with horiz. gutter (16)	—
V245PP	8 items (64)	—
	Cross gutter block (2)	—
	Horiz. pair with vert. gutter (8)	—
	Vert. pair with horiz. gutter (16)	—
739PI	(52 pairs)	—
	Cross gutter block (2)	—
	Horiz. pair with vert. gutter (8)	—
	Vert. pair with horiz. gutter (16)	—
740PI	(52 pairs)	—
	Cross gutter block (2)	—
	Horiz. pair with vert. gutter (8)	—
	Vert. pair with horiz. gutter (16)	—
G327PI	(52 pairs)	—
	Cross gutter block (2)	—
	Horiz. pair with vert. gutter (8)	—
	Vert. pair with horiz. gutter (16)	—
G328PI	(52 pairs)	—
	Cross gutter block (2)	—
	Horiz. pair with vert. gutter (8)	—
	Vert. pair with horiz. gutter (16)	—
V244PI	(52 pairs)	—
	Cross gutter block (2)	—
	Horiz. pair with vert. gutter (8)	—
	Vert. pair with horiz. gutter (16)	—
V245PI	(52 pairs)	—
	Cross gutter block (2)	—
	Horiz. pair with vert. gutter (8)	—
	Vert. pair with horiz. gutter (16)	—

New York #741-743, Geneva #329-331, Vienna #246-248
Schönbrunn Palace

1998

742PDa	Card, blocks of 4, #741PD-742PD (3)	—
742PDb	Card, cut apart blocks of 4, #741PD-742PD (1)	—
G330PDa	Card, blocks of 4, #G329PD-G330PD (3)	—
G330PDb	Card, cut apart blocks of 4, #G329PD-G330PD (1)	—
V247PDa	Card, blocks of 4, #V246PD-V247PD (3)	—
V247PDb	Card, cut apart blocks of 4, #V246PD-V247PD (1)	—
742TCa	Card, block of 4 #742TC dark blue denomination (on photographic paper) (1)	—
743TCa	Card, strips of 3, #743aTC-743cTC bright red violet denomination (on photographic paper) (1)	—
743TCb	Card, blocks of 4, #743dTC-743fTC bright red violet denomination (on photographic paper) (1)	—
743TCc	Entire booklet (black & white, on photographic paper) (1)	—
G330TCa	Card, blocks of 4, #G329TC-G330TC bright red violet denominations (on photographic paper) (1)	—
G331TCa	Card, blocks of 4, #G331aTC-G331cTC bright red violet denomination (on photographic paper) (1)	—
G331TCb	Card, strips of 3, #G331dTC-G331fTC bright red violet denomination (on photographic paper) (1)	—
G331TCc	Entire booklet (black & white, on photographic paper) (1)	—
V247TCa	Card, block of 4 #V247TC bright green denomination (on photographic paper) (1)	—
V248TCa	Card, strips of 3, #V248aTC-V248cTC bright red violet denomination (on photographic paper) (1)	—
V248TCb	Card, blocks of 4, #V248dTC-V248fTC bright red violet denomination (on photographic paper) (1)	—
V248TCc	Entire booklet (black & white, on photographic paper) (1)	—
741PP	10 items (24)	—
	Vert. pair with horiz. gutter (3)	—
742PP	10 items (24)	—
	Horiz. pair with vert. gutter (3)	—
742PPa	Cross gutter block, 2 #741PP-742PP (1)	—
742PPb	Vert. pair with horiz. gutter, #741PP-742PP (8)	—
G329PP	10 items (24)	—
	Vert. pair with horiz. gutter (3)	—
G330PP	10 items (24)	—
	Horiz. pair with vert. gutter (3)	—
G330PPa	Cross gutter block, 2 #G329PP-G330PP (1)	—
G330PPb	Vert. pair with horiz. gutter, #G329PP-G330PP (8)	—
V246PP	10 items (24)	—
	Vert. pair with horiz. gutter (3)	—
V247PP	10 items (24)	—
	Horiz. pair with vert. gutter (3)	—
V247PPa	Cross gutter block, 2 #V246PP-V247PP (1)	—
V247PPb	Vert. pair with horiz. gutter, #V246PP-V247PP (8)	—
741PI	(32 pairs)	—
	Vert. pair with horiz. gutter (3)	—
742PI	(32 pairs)	—
	Horiz. pair with vert. gutter (3)	—
742PIa	Cross gutter block, 2 #741PI-742PI (1)	—
742PIb	Vert. pair with horiz. gutter, #741PI-742PI (8)	—
G329PI	(32 pairs)	—
	Vert. pair with horiz. gutter (3)	—
G330PI	(32 pairs)	—
	Horiz. pair with vert. gutter (3)	—
G330PIa	Cross gutter block, 2 #G329PI-G330PI (1)	—
G330PIb	Vert. pair with horiz. gutter, #G329PI-G330PI (8)	—
V246PI	(32 pairs)	—
	Vert. pair with horiz. gutter (3)	—
V247PI	(32 pairs)	—
	Horiz. pair with vert. gutter (3)	—
V247PIa	Cross gutter block, 2 #V246PI-V247PI (1)	—
V247PIb	Vert. pair with horiz. gutter, #V246PI-V247PI (8)	—

Five cards with blocks of four essays with gold frames over vignette exist for each of the New York, Geneva and Vienna pairings.

New York #744-751
Flags

1999

744-751PP	Set of 20 sheets (1)	—
744-751PI	Set of 2 sheets (4)	—

On Nos. 744-751PP, there are ten progressive proof sheets per issued sheet.

New York #752-753, Geneva #332, Vienna #249
Definitives

1999

752PDa	Card, #752PD, #V249PD (3)	—
752PDb	Card, #752PD, #V249PD, #753TC lacking gray in pink frame boxes (1)	—
753PDa	Card, block of 4, #753PD (2)	—
753TC	Lacking gray in pink frame boxes (3)	—
G332TC	red (4)	—
G332TC	brown (4)	—
752PP	9 items (48)	—
	Cross gutter block (1)	—
	Horiz. pair with vert. gutter (6)	—
	Vert. pair with horiz. gutter (8)	—
753PP	10 items (20)	—
V249PP	9 items (48)	—
	Cross gutter block (1)	—
	Horiz. pair with vert. gutter (6)	—
	Vert. pair with horiz. gutter (8)	—
752PI	(24 pairs)	—
	Cross gutter block (3)	—
	Horiz. pair with vert. gutter (18)	—
	Vert. pair with horiz. gutter (24)	—
753PI	(20 pairs)	—
G332PI	(20 pairs)	—
V249PI	(72 pairs)	—
	Cross gutter block (3)	—
	Horiz. pair with vert. gutter (18)	—
	Vert. pair with horiz. gutter (24)	—

New York #754-756, Geneva #333-335, Vienna #250-252
World Heritage

1999

755PDa	Card, pairs of #754PD-755PD, #G333PD-G334PD, #V250PD-V251PD (1)	—
756PDa	Card, pairs of #756aPD-756fPD (1)	—
756PDb	Sheet, pairs of #754PD-755PD, #756aPD-756fPD, #G333PD-G334PD, #G335aPD-G335fPD, #V250PD-V251PD, #V252aPD-V252fPD (2)	—
756PDc	Cut-up section of #756PDb with pairs of stamps issued in sheets (2)	—
756PDd	Cut-up section of #756PDb with pairs of stamps issued in booklets (2)	—
754TC	Black and white image on layout sheet of photographic paper (2)	—
755TC	Black and white image on layout sheet of photographic paper (2)	—
G333TC	Black and white image on layout sheet of photographic paper (2)	—
G334TC	Black and white image on layout sheet of photographic paper (2)	—
V250TCa	Black and white image on layout sheet of photographic paper (2)	—
V250TCb	2 pairs of black and white images on layout sheet of photographic paper, affixed to card (1)	—
V251TCa	Black and white image on layout sheet of photographic paper (2)	—
V251TCb	2 pairs of black and white images on layout sheet of photographic paper, affixed to card (1)	—
754PP	6 items (32)	—
	Horiz. pair with vert. gutter (8)	—
755PP	6 items (32)	—
	Horiz. pair with vert. gutter (8)	—
755PPa	Cross gutter block, 2 #754PP-755PP (2)	—
755PPb	Vert. pair with horiz. gutter, #754PP-755PP (8)	—
G333PP	6 items (32)	—
	Horiz. pair with vert. gutter (8)	—
G334PP	6 items (32)	—
	Horiz. pair with vert. gutter (8)	—
G334PPa	Cross gutter block, 2 #G333PP-G334PP (2)	—
G334PPb	Vert. pair with horiz. gutter, #G333PP-G334PP (8)	—
V250PP	6 items (32)	—
	Horiz. pair with vert. gutter (8)	—
V251PP	6 items (32)	—
	Horiz. pair with vert. gutter (8)	—
V251PPa	Cross gutter block, 2 #V250PP-V251PP (2)	—
V251PPb	Vert. pair with horiz. gutter, #V250PP-V251PP (8)	—
754PI	(52 pairs)	—
	Horiz. pair with vert. gutter (16)	—
755PI	(52 pairs)	—
	Horiz. pair with vert. gutter (16)	—
755PIa	Cross gutter block, 2 #754PI-755PI (4)	—
755PIb	Vert. pair with horiz. gutter, #754PI-755PI (16)	—
G333PI	(36 pairs)	—
	Horiz. pair with vert. gutter (8)	—
G334PI	(36 pairs)	—
	Horiz. pair with vert. gutter (8)	—
G334PIa	Cross gutter block, 2 #G333PI-G334PI (2)	—
G334PIb	Vert. pair with horiz. gutter, #G333PI-G334PI (8)	—
V250PI	(36 pairs)	—
	Horiz. pair with vert. gutter (8)	—
V251PI	(36 pairs)	—
	Horiz. pair with vert. gutter (8)	—
V251PIa	Cross gutter block, 2 #V250PI-V251PI (2)	—
V251PIb	Vert. pair with horiz. gutter, #V250PI-V251PI (8)	—

New York #760a, Geneva #339a, Vienna #256a
Endangered Species

1999

760aPDa	Card, imperf pane of 4 blocks, #760aPD (2)	—
760aPDb	Card, 2 each #757PD-760PD (1)	—
G339aPDa	Card, 2 each #G336PD-G339PD (on Cromalin paper), broken pane of 80c essays of #G336-G339 (1)	—
V256aPDa	Card, imperf pane of 4 blocks, #V256aPD (3)	—
V256aPDb	Card, 2 each #V253PD-V256PD (1)	—
760aPP	6 items (4 blocks)	—
	Cross gutter block (2)	—
	Horiz. pair with vert. gutter (2)	—
	Vert. pair with horiz. gutter (4)	—
G339aPP	6 items (4 blocks)	—
	Cross gutter block (2)	—
	Horiz. pair with vert. gutter (2)	—
	Vert. pair with horiz. gutter (4)	—
V256aPP	6 items (4 blocks)	—
	Cross gutter block (2)	—
	Horiz. pair with vert. gutter (2)	—
	Vert. pair with horiz. gutter (4)	—
760aPI	(12 blocks)	—
	Cross gutter block (2)	—
	Horiz. pair with vert. gutter (2)	—
	Vert. pair with horiz. gutter (4)	—
G339aPI	(12 blocks)	—
	Cross gutter block (2)	—
	Horiz. pair with vert. gutter (2)	—
	Vert. pair with horiz. gutter (4)	—
V256aPI	(12 blocks)	—
	Cross gutter block (2)	—
	Horiz. pair with vert. gutter (2)	—
	Vert. pair with horiz. gutter (4)	—

Three cards exist containing imperforate panes of four blocks of the 80c essays.

New York #762a, 763, Geneva #341a, 342, Vienna #258a, 259
UNISPACE III

1999

762aPDa	Card, imperforate pane of 5 pairs, #762aPD (3)	—
763PD	With printed perforations on overlay (3)	—
763aPD	With printed perforations on overlay (2)	—

G341aPDa	Card, imperforate pane of 5 pairs, #G341aPD (4)	—
G342PD	With printed perforations on overlay (2)	—
G342aPD	With printed perforations on overlay (2)	—
V258aPDa	Card, imperforate pane of 5 pairs, #V258aPD (4)	—
V259PD	With printed perforations on overlay (2)	—
762PP	8 items (5 pairs)	—
762aPP	8 items (1 souvenir sheet)	—
763PP	9 items (1 pair)	—
763aPP	10 items (1 souvenir sheet)	—
762aPI	(10 pairs)	—
763PI	(3 souvenir sheets)	—
763aPI	(4 souvenir sheets)	—
G341aPI	(10 pairs)	—
G342PI	(3 souvenir sheets)	—
V258aPI	(10 pairs)	—
V259PI	(3 souvenir sheets)	—

New York #767a, Geneva #346a, Vienna #263a, Souvenir Card #54
Universal Postal Union, 125th Anniv.

1999

767aPDa	Card, #767aPD, #G346aPD, #V263aPD with approval handstamp (4)	—
767aTCa	Card, #767aTC, #G346aTCD, #V263aTC (dark blue denominations, not approved (4)	—
SC54PD	(4)	—
767aPP	8 items (6 blocks)	—
G346aPP	8 items (6 blocks)	—
V263aPP	8 items (6 blocks)	—
767aPI	(12 blocks)	—
G346aPI	(12 blocks)	—
V263aPI	(12 blocks)	—

New York #768-769, Geneva #347-348, Vienna #264-265
In Memoriam

1999

769PDa	Card, #768PD-769PD (4)	—
G348PDa	Card, #G347PD-G348PD (4)	—
V265PDa	Card, #V264PD-V265PD (4)	—
768PP	10 items (66)	—
	Cross gutter block (2)	—
	Horiz. pair with vert. gutter (12)	—
	Vert. pair with horiz. gutter (11)	—
769PP	10 items (24 souvenir sheets)	—
G347PP	10 items (66)	—
	Cross gutter block (2)	—
	Horiz. pair with vert. gutter (12)	—
	Vert. pair with horiz. gutter (11)	—
G348PP	10 items (24 souvenir sheets)	—
V264PP	10 items (66)	—
	Cross gutter block (2)	—
	Horiz. pair with vert. gutter (12)	—
	Vert. pair with horiz. gutter (11)	—
V265PP	10 items (24 souvenir sheets)	—
768PI	(52 pairs)	—
	Cross gutter block (2)	—
	Horiz. pair with vert. gutter (12)	—
	Vert. pair with horiz. gutter (11)	—
769PI	(24 souvenir sheets)	—
G347PI	(52 pairs)	—
	Cross gutter block (2)	—
	Horiz. pair with vert. gutter (12)	—
	Vert. pair with horiz. gutter (11)	—
G348PI	(24 souvenir sheets)	—
V264PI	(52 pairs)	—
	Cross gutter block (2)	—
	Horiz. pair with vert. gutter (12)	—
	Vert. pair with horiz. gutter (11)	—
V265PI	(24 souvenir sheets)	—

New York #770-771, Geneva #349-350, Vienna #266-267
Education

1999

771PDa	Card, #770PD-771PD, #G349PD-G350PD, #V266PD-V267PD with approval handstamp (4)	—
771PDb	Card, #770PD, #G350PD, #V266PD-V267PD, #771TC red denomination, #G349TC red violet denomination with "approved with corrections" handstamp (4)	—
770PP	9 items (20)	—
771PP	8 items (20)	—
G349PP	7 items (20)	—
G350PP	7 items (20)	—
V266PP	7 items (20)	—
V267PP	8 items (20)	—
770PI	(20 pairs)	—
771PI	(20 pairs)	—
G349PI	(30 pairs)	—
G350PI	(30 pairs)	—
V266PI	(30 pairs)	—
V267PI	(30 pairs)	—

New York #772, Geneva #351, Vienna #268
International Year of Thanksgiving

2000

772PDa	Card, #772PD, #G351PD, #V268PD (4)	—
772TCa	Card, #772TC, #G351TC, #V268TC, all with black background (4)	—
772PP	12 items (32)	—
	Horiz. pair with vert. gutter (4)	—
G351PP	12 items (32)	—
	Horiz. pair with vert. gutter (4)	—
V268PP	12 items (32)	—
	Horiz. pair with vert. gutter (4)	—
772PI	(36 pairs)	—
	Horiz. pair with vert. gutter (4)	—
G351PI	(36 pairs)	—
	Horiz. pair with vert. gutter (4)	—
V268PI	(36 pairs)	—
	Horiz. pair with vert. gutter (4)	—

New York #776a, Geneva #355a, Vienna #272a
Endangered Species

2000

776aPDa	Card, imperforate pane of 4 blocks, #776aPD (3)	—
776aPDb	Card, 3 each #773PD-776PD (1)	—
G355aPDa	Card, imperforate pane of 4 blocks, #G355aPD, imperforate pane of 4 blocks, #V272aPD (3)	—
G355aPDb	Card, 3 each #G352PD-G355PD, #V269PD-V272PD (1)	—
776aPP	6 items (4 blocks)	—
	Cross gutter block (2)	—
	Horiz. pair with vert. gutter (2)	—
	Vert. pair with horiz. gutter (4)	—
G355aPP	6 items (4 blocks)	—
	Cross gutter block (2)	—
	Horiz. pair with vert. gutter (2)	—
	Vert. pair with horiz. gutter (4)	—
V272aPP	6 items (4 blocks)	—
	Cross gutter block (2)	—
	Horiz. pair with vert. gutter (2)	—
	Vert. pair with horiz. gutter (4)	—
776aPI	(12 blocks)	—
	Cross gutter block (2)	—
	Horiz. pair with vert. gutter (2)	—
	Vert. pair with horiz. gutter (4)	—
G355aPI	(12 blocks)	—
	Cross gutter block (2)	—
	Horiz. pair with vert. gutter (2)	—
	Vert. pair with horiz. gutter (4)	—
V272aPI	(12 blocks)	—
	Cross gutter block (2)	—
	Horiz. pair with vert. gutter (2)	—
	Vert. pair with horiz. gutter (4)	—

New York #777-778, Geneva #356-357, Vienna #273-274
Our World 2000

2000

778PDa	Card, #777PD-778PD, #G356PD-G357PD, #V273PD-V274PD (4)	—
778PDb	Card, #777PD-778PD, #G356PD-G357PD, #V274PD, #V273TC black denomination, with "not approved" handstamp (2)	—
777PP	8 items (64)	—
	Cross gutter block (2)	—
	Horiz. pair with vert. gutter (16)	—
	Vert. pair with horiz. gutter (8)	—
778PP	8 items (64)	—
	Cross gutter block (2)	—
	Horiz. pair with vert. gutter (8)	—
	Vert. pair with horiz. gutter (16)	—
G356PP	8 items (64)	—
	Cross gutter block (2)	—
	Horiz. pair with vert. gutter (8)	—
	Vert. pair with horiz. gutter (16)	—
G357PP	8 items (64)	—
	Cross gutter block (2)	—
	Horiz. pair with vert. gutter (16)	—
	Vert. pair with horiz. gutter (8)	—
V273PP	8 items (64)	—
	Cross gutter block (2)	—
	Horiz. pair with vert. gutter (16)	—
	Vert. pair with horiz. gutter (8)	—
V274PP	8 items (64)	—
	Cross gutter block (2)	—
	Horiz. pair with vert. gutter (8)	—
	Vert. pair with horiz. gutter (16)	—
777PI	(52 pairs)	—
	Cross gutter block (2)	—
	Horiz. pair with vert. gutter (16)	—
	Vert. pair with horiz. gutter (8)	—
778PI	(52 pairs)	—
	Cross gutter block (2)	—
	Horiz. pair with vert. gutter (8)	—
	Vert. pair with horiz. gutter (16)	—
G356PI	(52 pairs)	—
	Cross gutter block (2)	—
	Horiz. pair with vert. gutter (16)	—
	Vert. pair with horiz. gutter (8)	—
G357PI	(52 pairs)	—
	Cross gutter block (2)	—
	Horiz. pair with vert. gutter (8)	—
	Vert. pair with horiz. gutter (16)	—
V273PI	(52 pairs)	—
	Cross gutter block (2)	—
	Horiz. pair with vert. gutter (16)	—
	Vert. pair with horiz. gutter (8)	—
V274PI	(52 pairs)	—
	Cross gutter block (2)	—
	Horiz. pair with vert. gutter (8)	—
	Vert. pair with horiz. gutter (16)	—

New York #779-781, Geneva #358-360, Vienna #275-277
United Nations, 55th Anniv.

2000

780TCa	Card, #779TC-780TC, #G358TC-G359TC, #V275TC-V276TC (all with white denominations with colored outlines (4)	—
781TCa	Card, #781TC, #G360TC, #V277TC (all with white denominations with colored outlines (4)	—
781TCb	Card, #779TC-781TC ultramarine & silver (2)	—
781TCc	Card, #779TC-781TC blue & silver (2)	—
781TCd	Card, #781TC, #G360TC silver backgrounds, white denominations with colored outlines (5)	—
G359TCa	Card, #G358TC-G359TC brown red & silver (2)	—
G360TCa	Card, #G358TC-G360TC carmine & silver (2)	—
G360TCb	Card, #G358TC-G360TC cerise & silver (2)	—
V277TCa	Card, #V275TC-V277TC green & silver (2)	—
V277TCb	Card, #V275TC-V277TC dark green & silver (2)	—
V277TCc	Silver background, white denominations with green outlines (5)	—
779PP	7 items (128)	—
	Cross gutter block (4)	—
	Horiz. pair with vert. gutter (16)	—
	Vert. pair with horiz. gutter (32)	—
780PP	7 items (128)	—
	Cross gutter block (4)	—
	Horiz. pair with vert. gutter (16)	—
	Vert. pair with horiz. gutter (32)	—
781PP	6 items (60 souvenir sheets)	—
G358PP	9 items (128)	—
	Cross gutter block (4)	—
	Horiz. pair with vert. gutter (16)	—
	Vert. pair with horiz. gutter (32)	—
G359PP	9 items (128)	—
	Cross gutter block (4)	—
	Horiz. pair with vert. gutter (16)	—
	Vert. pair with horiz. gutter (32)	—
G360PP	9 items (60 souvenir sheets)	—
V275PP	10 items (128)	—
	Cross gutter block (4)	—
	Horiz. pair with vert. gutter (16)	—
	Vert. pair with horiz. gutter (32)	—
V276PP	10 items (128)	—
	Cross gutter block (4)	—
	Horiz. pair with vert. gutter (16)	—
	Vert. pair with horiz. gutter (32)	—
V277PP	10 items (60 souvenir sheets)	—
779PI	(84 pairs)	—
	Cross gutter block (4)	—
	Horiz. pair with vert. gutter (16)	—
	Vert. pair with horiz. gutter (32)	—
780PI	(84 pairs)	—
	Cross gutter block (4)	—
	Horiz. pair with vert. gutter (16)	—
	Vert. pair with horiz. gutter (32)	—
781PI	(60 souvenir sheets)	—
G358PI	(84 pairs)	—
	Cross gutter block (4)	—
	Horiz. pair with vert. gutter (16)	—
	Vert. pair with horiz. gutter (32)	—
G359PI	(84 pairs)	—
	Cross gutter block (4)	—
	Horiz. pair with vert. gutter (16)	—
	Vert. pair with horiz. gutter (32)	—
V275PI	(84 pairs)	—
	Cross gutter block (4)	—
	Horiz. pair with vert. gutter (16)	—
	Vert. pair with horiz. gutter (32)	—
V276PI	(84 pairs)	—
	Cross gutter block (4)	—
	Horiz. pair with vert. gutter (16)	—
	Vert. pair with horiz. gutter (32)	—
781PI	(60 souvenir sheets)	—

One item in Nos. G358PP and G359PP is blank, coming from sheet with marginal inscriptions only.

New York #782
International Flag of Peace

2000

782PD	With approval handstamp (4)	—
782TC	Black and white photocopy of layout of pane of 20, with approval handstamp and signature (1)	—
782PP	9 items (96)	—
	Cross gutter block (2)	—
	Horiz. pair with vert. gutter (16)	—
	Vert. pair with horiz. gutter (8)	—
782PI	(96 pairs)	—
	Cross gutter block (6)	—
	Horiz. pair with vert. gutter (48)	—
	Vert. pair with horiz. gutter (24)	—

An essay with "age 12" after artist's name exists in five cards and a black and white layout of the pane of 20 on photographic paper.

New York #783, Geneva #361, Vienna #278
UN in the 21st Century

2000

783PDa	Card, #783PD, #G361PD, #V278PD with approval handstamp (4)	—
783TCa	Card, #783TC, #G361TC, #V278TC all with washed-out colors, with "not approved" handstamp (5)	—
783PP	8 items (1)	—
G361PP	8 items (1)	—
V278PP	8 items (1)	—
783PI	(2 sheets)	—
G361PI	(2 sheets)	—
V278PI	(2 sheets)	—

New York #784-786, Geneva #362-364, Vienna #279-281
World Heritage

2000

785PDa	Card, #784PD-785PD, #G362PD-G364PD, #V279PD-V280PD (4)	—
784TC	Black and white image of pane of 20 on layout sheet on photographic paper (1)	—
785TC	Black and white image of pane of 20 on layout sheet on photographic paper (1)	—
G362TC	Black and white image of pane of 20 on layout sheet on photographic paper (1)	—
G363TC	Black and white image of pane of 20 on layout sheet on photographic paper (1)	—
V279TC	Black and white image of pane of 20 on layout sheet on photographic paper (1)	—
V280TC	Black and white image of pane of 20 on layout sheet on photographic paper (1)	—
784PP	9 items (24)	—
	Vert. pair with horiz. gutter (3)	—
785PP	9 items (24)	—
	Vert. pair with horiz. gutter (3)	—
785PPa	Cross gutter block, 2 #784PP-785PP (1)	—
785PPb	Horiz. pair with vert. gutter, #784PP-785PP (8)	—
786iPPa	9 items, Strip of #786gPP-786iPP, with vert. gutters between (4)	—
G362PP	9 items (24)	—
	Vert. pair with horiz. gutter (3)	—
G363PP	9 items (24)	—
	Vert. pair with horiz. gutter (3)	—
G363PPa	Cross gutter block, 2 #G362PP-G363PP (1)	—
G363PPb	Horiz. pair with vert. gutter, #G362PP-G363PP (8)	—
V279PP	7 items (24)	—
	Vert. pair with horiz. gutter (3)	—
V280PP	7 items (24)	—
	Vert. pair with horiz. gutter (3)	—
V280PPa	Cross gutter block, 2 #V279PP-V280PP (1)	—
V280PPb	Horiz. pair with vert. gutter, #V279PP-V280PP (8)	—
784PI	(32 pairs)	—
	Vert. pair with horiz. gutter (3)	—
785PI	(32 pairs)	—
	Vert. pair with horiz. gutter (3)	—
785PIa	Cross gutter block, 2 #784PI-785PI (1)	—
785PIb	Horiz. pair with vert. gutter, #784PI-785PI (8)	—
786gPI	(5 booklet panes)	—
786hPI	(5 booklet panes)	—
786iPI	(5 booklet panes)	—
786iPIa	Strip of #786gPI-786iPI, with vert. gutters between (4)	—
786jPI	(5 booklet panes)	—
786kPI	(5 booklet panes)	—
786lPI	(5 booklet panes)	—
G362PI	(32 pairs)	—
	Vert. pair with horiz. gutter (3)	—
G363PI	(32 pairs)	—
	Vert. pair with horiz. gutter (3)	—
G363PIa	Cross gutter block, 2 #G362PI-G363PI (1)	—
G363PIb	Horiz. pair with vert. gutter, #G362PI-G363PI (8)	—
G364gPI	(5 booklet panes)	—
G364hPI	(5 booklet panes)	—
G364iPI	(5 booklet panes)	—
G364jPI	(5 booklet panes)	—
G364kPI	(5 booklet panes)	—
G364lPI	(5 booklet panes)	—
V279PI	(82 pairs)	—
	Vert. pair with horiz. gutter (3)	—
V280PI	(32 pairs)	—
	Vert. pair with horiz. gutter (3)	—
V280PIa	Cross gutter block, 2 #V279PI-V280PI (1)	—
V280PIb	Horiz. pair with vert. gutter, #V279PI-V280PI (8)	—
V281gPI	(5 booklet panes)	—
V281hPI	(5 booklet panes)	—
V281iPI	(5 booklet panes)	—
V281jPI	(5 booklet panes)	—
V281kPI	(5 booklet panes)	—
V281lPI	(5 booklet panes)	—

Some pairs of No. V279PI are defaced with blue marker.

New York #787-788, Geneva #365-366, Vienna #282-283, Souvenir Card #55
Respect for Refugees

2000

787PDa	Card, #787PD, #G365PD, #V282PD (4)	—
788PDa	Card, #788PD, #G366PD, #V283PD (4)	—
SC55PD	(4)	—
787PP	6 items (32)	—
	Horiz. pair with vert. gutter (4)	—
788PP	6 items (20 souvenir sheets)	—
G365PP	6 items (32)	—
	Cross gutter block (1)	—
	Horiz. pair with vert. gutter (6)	—
	Vert. pair with horiz. gutter (8)	—
G366PP	6 items (20 souvenir sheets)	—
V282PP	6 items (32)	—
	Horiz. pair with vert. gutter (4)	—
V283PP	6 items (20 souvenir sheets)	—
787PI	(36 pairs)	—
	Horiz. pair with vert. gutter (4)	—
788PI	(20 souvenir sheets)	—
G365PI	(44 pairs)	—
	Cross gutter block (1)	—
	Horiz. pair with vert. gutter (6)	—
	Vert. pair with horiz. gutter (8)	—
G366PI	(20 souvenir sheets)	—
V282PI	(36 pairs)	—
	Horiz. pair with vert. gutter (4)	—
V283PI	(20 souvenir sheets)	—

AIR POST STAMPS
New York #C1-C4
Plane and Gull, Swallows and UN Emblem

1951

C1PD	(1)	—
C2PD	(1)	—
C3PD	(1)	—
C4PD	(1)	—
C1PI	(25 pairs)	—
C2PI	(25 pairs)	—
C3PI	(25 pairs)	—
C4PI	(25 pairs)	—

New York #C5
Airplane Wing and Globe

1957

C5PD	(4)	—
C5TC	brown (not approved) (5)	—
C5TC	indigo (5)	—
C5PI	(40 pairs)	—
	Vert. pair with horiz. gutter (10)	—

New York #C6-C7
Airplane Wing and Globe; UN Flag and Plane

1959

C6PD	(1)	—
C6PDa	Card, #C6PD, 2 #C6TC in slightly different shades (2)	—
C6PDb	Card, 2 #C6PD, 2 #C7TC Prussian blue (1)	—
C7PD	(1)	—
C7PDa	Card, #C7PD, #C7TC Prussian blue, #C7TC dark blue (2)	—
C6TC	black (1)	—
C7TC	black (1)	—
C6PI	(115 pairs)	—
	Vert. pair with horiz. gutter (10)	—
C7PI	(90 pairs)	—
	Horiz. pair with vert. gutter (10)	—

New York #C8-C10
Definitives

1963

C10PDa	Card, #C8PD-C10PD (3)	—
C10PDb	Card, #C8PD, #C10PD, 3 #C9PD (3)	—
C8PP	3 items (80)	—
	Horiz. pair with vert. gutter (10)	—
C9PP	4 items (80)	—
	Vert. pair with horiz. gutter (10)	—
C10PP	4 items (80)	—
	Horiz. pair with vert. gutter (10)	—
C8PI	(80 pairs)	—
	Horiz. pair with vert. gutter (20)	—
C9PI	(80 pairs)	—
	Vert. pair with horiz. gutter (20)	—
C10PI	(80 pairs)	—
	Horiz. pair with vert. gutter (20)	—

New York #C11-C12
Definitives

1964

C11PDa	Card, #C11PD, #C12TC peach and brown background (disapproved) (2)	—
C12PD	(2)	—
C12PDa	Card, #C11PD-C12PD (4)	—
C11PI	(25 pairs)	—
C12PI	(25 pairs)	—

New York #C13
Jet and UN Emblem

1968

C13PD	(3)	—
C13PDa	Card, #C13PD, 2 #C13TC with slightly different shades (2)	—
C13PP	9 items, perforated, mounted on card (1)	—

New York #C14
Wings, Envelopes and UN Emblem

1969

C14PD	(4)	—
C14PP	6 items, perforated (50)	—

New York #C15-C18
Definitives

1972

C15PD	(2)	—
C16PD	With approval handstamp (2)	—
C17PD	(2)	—
C18PD	(2)	—
C16TC	dark blue emblem (dated 16. Oct. 1971) (2)	—
C15PP	4 items (100)	—
C16PP	10 items (100)	—
C17PP	4 items (100)	—
C18PP	10 items (160)	—
	Horiz. pair with vert. gutter (20)	—
C16PI	(50 pairs)	—
C17PI	(50 pairs)	—

New York #C19-C21
Definitives

1974

C19PD	(3)	—
C20PD	(3)	—
C21PD	(3)	—
C19PP	8 items (50)	—
C21PP	5 items (50)	—
C19PI	(50 pairs)	—
C20PI	(50 pairs)	—
C21PI	(50 pairs)	—

Five cards with essays of No. C21 with incorrect Russian inscription exist.

New York #C22-C23
Definitives

1977

C22PD	With approval handstamp (4)	—
C22TC	Gray wings and envelope, with "not approved" handstamp (2)	—
C23PD	(1)	—
C23PDa	Card, #C23PD, #C22TC gray wings and envelope (3)	—
C22PP	6 items (50)	—
C22PI	(50 pairs)	—
C23PI	(50 pairs)	—

ENVELOPES
New York #U1
UN Emblem

1952

U1PD	(1)	—
U1TC	black (1)	—

New York #U2
UN Emblem

1958

U2PD	with manuscript approval (2)	—
U2TC	black, on card, with manuscript approval (1)	—

New York #U3
Stylized Globe and Weather Vane

1963

U3PD	(2)	—
U3PI	Indicia only on small piece of paper (1)	—

See No. UC6PI.

New York #U5
UN Headquarters

1973

U5PD	(41)	—
U5PP	6 items (5)	—
U5PI	Unfolded and uncut (2)	—

New York #U6
UN Headquarters

1975

U6PD	With approval handstamp (5)	—
U6PDa	Die cut and unfolded, without approval handstamp (4)	—

New York #U7
Bouquet of Ribbons

1985

U7PD	Indicia only, in folder (9)	—

Vienna #U1-U2
Donaupark

1995

VU1PD	On Cromalin paper (approved) (6)	—
VU1PDa	On AGFA paper (not approved) (5)	—
VU2PD	On Cromalin paper (approved) (6)	—
VU2PDa	On AGFA paper (not approved) (5)	—

New York #U10-U11
Cripticandina

1997

U10PD	On Cromalin paper (4)	—
U11PD	On Cromalin paper (4)	—

Vienna #U3
Landscape

1998

VU3PD	On Cromalin paper (4)	—

AIR POST ENVELOPES & AIR LETTER SHEETS
New York #UC1 Swallows and UN Emblem

1952

UC1PI	(32)	—
UC1PIa	On white paper (22)	—

New York #UC3
UN Flag and Plane Envelope

1959

UC3PD	(1)	—

New York #UC4
UN Flag and Plane Letter Sheet

1960

UC4PD	(1)	—

Two "not approved" essays exist with diagonal lines rather than bars around envelope.

New York #UC5 Plane and Gull

1961

UC5PD	With approval handstamp (1)	—
UC5aPD	With approval handstamp (3)	—

New York #UC6
UN Emblem

1963

UC6PDa	Sheet, #UC6PD, #U3PD, with approval handstamp (2)	—
UC6PI	(1)	—
UC6PIa	Sheet, #UC6PD (2 sizes), #U3PD (2 sizes) (6)	—
UC6PIb	As #UC6PIa with one #U3PI removed (1)	—

New York #UC7
UN Emblem and Stylized Plane

1968

UC7PD	With specimen perfin and approval handstamp (7)	—

New York #UC8
UN Emblem

1969

UC8PD	With specimen perfin at left (4)	—

Geneva #UC1
UN Emblem and Stylized Plane

1969

GUC1PD	With specimen perfin and approval handstamp (1)	—
GUC1TC	light blue (2)	—
GUC1TC	ultramarine (3)	—

New York #UC9
UN Emblem, "UN," Globe and Plane

1972

UC9PD	With approval handstamp (2)	—

New York #UC10
Birds in Flight

1973

UC10PDa	Small envelope, die cut and folded, with approval handstamp (1)	—
UC10PDb	Large envelope, partially folded, with approval handstamp (2)	—
UC10PPa	Uncut and unfolded, large and small envelopes (6 items)	—

Three sets of essays exist with blue UN inscriptions close.

New York #UC11
Globe and Jet

1975

UC11PD	With approval handstamp (5)	—
UC11PDa	Die cut and unfolded, without approval handstamp (1)	—

New York #UC12
UN Headquarters

1975

UC12PD	With approval handstamp (1)	—

New York #UC13
UN Emblem and Birds

1977

UC13PD	With approval handstamp (2)	—

Five "not approved" essays have design flaw at end of orange line.

New York #UC14, Vienna #UC1
Paper Airplane, Dove

1982

UC14PD	With approval handstamp (3)	—
UC14PDa	On thin card stock (1)	—
VUC1PD	With approval handstamp (3)	—
VUC1PDa	On thin card stock (1)	—

Vienna #UC3
Birds in Flight and UN Emblem

1987

VUC3PD	On plastic, with approval handstamp (4)	—

New York #UC16
UN Headquarters

1989

UC16PD	With approval handstamp (approved) (3)	—
UC16PDa	With approval handstamp (not approved) (10)	—

Vienna #UC5
Donaupark

1992

VUC5PD	On Cromalin paper (3)	—

New York #UC19
Winged Hand With Envelopes Surcharge

1995

UC19PD	On Cromalin paper (1)	—

New York #UC20
Cherry Blossoms

1997

UC20PD	(5)	—

POSTAL CARDS
New York #UX1
UN Headquarters

1952

UX1TC	olive brown, on white paper (1)	—
UX1PI	(4 pairs)	—

New York #UX2
UN Headquarters

1958

UX2PD	With approval handstamp (2)	—

New York #UX3
World Map

1963

UX3PD	(2)	—

New York #UX4
UN Emblem and Post Horn

1969

UX4PD	With approval handstamp on reverse (1)	—

Geneva #UX1-UX2
UN Emblem and Post Horn, Stylized Space View

1969

GUX1PD	With approval handstamp (3)	—
GUX1PI	(53 pairs)	—
GUX2PI	(52 pairs)	—

New York #UX5
"UN"

1973

UX5PD	(1)	—

Five "not approved" essays similar to #UX5 exist. Ten 7c essays exist, three with approval handstamp, the others lacking any handstamp.

New York #UX6
"UN"

1975

UX6PD	With specimen perfin and approval handstamp (4)	—

Five "not approved" essays have incorrect Russian inscription.

New York #UX7, Geneva #UX3-UX4
UN Emblem, UN Emblem in Rectangles, UN Emblem and Ribbons

1977

UX7PD	With specimen perfin at left (4)	—
GUX3PD	With specimen perfin (5)	—
GUX4PD	With specimen perfin at left (4)	—

New York #UX8, Vienna #UX1-UX2
"United Nations," Olive Branch, Bird Carrying Olive Branch

1982

UX8PD	(2)	—
VUX1PD	With approval handstamp on reverse (4)	—
VUX2PD	With approval handstamp on reverse (16)	—

Geneva #UX5-UX6, Vienna #UX3
Peace Dove, UN Emblem

1985

GUX5PD	(3)	—
GUX6PD	With approval handstamp on reverse (3)	—
VUX3PD	(3)	—

One example of No. GUX5PD has inked lines at left of card. One example of No. GUX6PD has inked lines around address lines.

New York #UX9-UX18
Views of UN Headquarters

1989

UX9PD	Message side (4)	—
UX9PDa	Picture side (4)	—
UX10PD	Message side (4)	—
UX10PDa	Picture side (4)	—
UX11PD	Message side (4)	—
UX11PDa	Picture side (4)	—
UX12PD	Message side (4)	—
UX12PDa	Picture side (4)	—
UX13PD	Message side (4)	—
UX13PDa	Picture side (4)	—
UX14PD	Message side (4)	—
UX14PDa	Picture side (4)	—
UX15PD	Message side (4)	—
UX15PDa	Picture side (4)	—
UX16PD	Message side (4)	—
UX16PDa	Picture side (4)	—
UX17PD	Message side (4)	—
UX17PDa	Picture side (4)	—
UX18PD	Message side (4)	—
UX18PDa	Picture side (4)	—

New York #UX19, Geneva #UX8, Vienna #UX5
UN Headquarters, Palais des Nations, Regschek Painting

1992

UX19PD	On Cromalin paper (4)	—
GUX8PD	On Cromalin paper (4)	—
VUX5PD	On Cromalin paper (4)	—
VUX5PDa	Sheet, #GUX8PD, #VUX5PD on Cromalin paper (1)	—
UX19TC	ultramarine (1)	—

Geneva #UX10, Vienna #UX6-UX7
Palais des Nations, Peoples of the World United, Donaupark

1993

GUX10PD	On Cromalin paper (4)	—
VUX6PD	On Cromalin paper (4)	—
VUX7PD	On Cromalin paper (4)	—

Vienna #UX12
The Gloriette

1999

VUX12TCa	Light blue text (4)	—

AIR POST POSTAL CARDS
New York #UXC1
UN Flag and Plane

1957

UXC1PD	With printer and approval handstamps (6)	—
UXC1PI	(30 pairs)	—

New York #UXC3
Airplane Wing and Globe

1959

UXC3PD	With approval handstamp (3)	—

Six essays of No. UXC3 lacking outlined letters on "Airmail" and "Poste Aerienne" exist.

New York #UXC4
Outer Space

1963

UXC4PD	(2)	—

New York #UXC6
Outer Space

1968

UXC6PD	With "Canceled" perfin (2)	—
UXC6PDa	Strip of 3 cards with 2 "Canceled" perfins (2)	—

New York #UXC7
UN Emblem and Stylized Planes

1969

UXC7PD	(1)	—
UXC7TC	black (2)	—

New York #UXC8
UN Emblem and Stylized Wing

1972

UXC8PDa	Folder with mounted #UXC8PD with approval handstamp, and #UXC8 (2)	—

New York #UXC9
UN Emblem and Stylized Planes

1972

UXC9PD	Folder with mounted #UXC9, with approval handstamp (2)	—

New York #UXC10-UXC11
Clouds; Pathways

1975

UXC10PD	With specimen perfin and approval handstamp (4)	—
UXC11PD	With specimen perfin and approval handstamp (4)	—

UXC10TC	With manuscript "Lighter as on sample," and approval handstamp (not approved) (5)	—

New York #UXC12
Flying Mailman

1982

UXC12PD	With approval handstamp on reverse (5)	—

U.N. TEMPORARY EXECUTIVE AUTHORITY, WEST NEW GUINEA

Located in the western half of New Guinea, southwest Pacific Ocean, the former Netherlands New Guinea became a territory under the administration of the United Nations Temporary Executive Authority on Oct. 1, 1962. The size was 151,789 sq. mi. and the population was estimated at 730,000 in 1958. The capital was Hollandia.

The territory came under Indonesian administration on May 1, 1963. For stamps issued by Indonesia see West Irian in Vol. 6.

100 Cents = 1 Gulden

Catalogue values for all unused stamps in this country are for Never Hinged items.

First Printing (Hollandia)

Netherlands New Guinea Stamps of 1950-60 Overprinted

Overprint size: 17x3½mm. Top of "N" is slightly lower than the "U," and the base of the "T" is straight, or nearly so.

Photo.; Litho. (#4, 6, 8)

1962 Unwmk. *Perf. 12½x12, 12½x13½*

1	A4	1c	**vermilion & yellow,** *Oct. 1*	.20	.20
2	A1	2c	**deep orange,** *Oct. 1*	.25	.25
3	A4	5c	**chocolate & yellow,** *Oct. 1*	.25	.25
4	A5	7c	**org red, bl & brn vio,** *Nov. 1*	.25	*.35*
5	A4	10c	**aqua & red brown,** *Oct. 1*	.25	*.35*
6	A5	12c	**green, bl & brn vio,** *Nov. 1*	.25	*.35*
7	A4	15c	**deep yel & red brn,** *Nov. 1*	.50	.50
8	A5	17c	**brown violet & blue,** *Oct. 1*	.60	*.75*
9	A4	20c	**lt bl grn & red brn,** *Nov. 1*	.60	*.75*
10	A6	25c	**red,** *Oct. 1*	.35	*.55*
11	A6	30c	**deep blue,** *Oct. 1*	.80	.80
12	A6	40c	**deep orange,** *Oct. 1*	.80	.80
13	A6	45c	**dark olive,** *Nov. 1*	1.40	*1.60*
14	A6	55c	**slate blue,** *Nov. 1*	*17.50*	1.25
15	A6	80c	**dull gray violet,** *Nov. 1*	5.75	5.75
16	A6	85c	**dark violet brown,** *Nov. 1*	3.00	3.00
17	A6	1g	**plum,** *Oct. 1*	9.75	3.00

Engr.

18	A3	2g	**reddish brown,** *Oct. 1*	9.75	22.50
19	A3	5g	**green,** *Oct. 1*	7.75	5.50
			Nos. 1-19 (19)	60.00	48.50

Overprinted locally and sold in West New Guinea. Stamps of the second printing were used to complete sets sold to collectors.

Second Printing (Haarlen, Netherlands)

Overprint size: 17x3½mm. Top of the "N" is slightly higher than the "U," and the base of the "T" is concave.

Photo.; Litho. (#4a, 6a, 8a)

1962 Unwmk. *Perf. 12½x12, 12½x13½*

1a	A4	1c	**vermilion & yellow**	.20	.20
2a	A1	2c	**deep orange**	.25	.20
3a	A4	5c	**chocolate & yellow**	.25	.20
4a	A5	7c	**org red, bl & brn vio**	.25	.20
5a	A4	10c	**aqua & red brown**	.25	.20
6a	A5	12c	**green, bl & brn vio**	.25	.20
7a	A4	15c	**deep yel & red brn**	.50	.25
8a	A5	17c	**brown violet & blue**	.60	.35
9a	A4	20c	**lt blue grn & red brn**	.60	.35
10a	A6	25c	**red**	.35	.30
11a	A6	30c	**deep blue**	.80	.35
12a	A6	40c	**deep orange**	.80	.35
13a	A6	45c	**dark olive**	1.40	.75
14a	A6	55c	**slate blue**	1.25	.55
15a	A6	80c	**dull gray violet**	5.75	5.75
16a	A6	85c	**dark violet brown**	3.00	3.00
17a	A6	1g	**plum**	3.50	1.90

Engr.

18a	A3	2g	**reddish brown**	9.75	13.00
19a	A3	5g	**green**	6.00	3.50
			Nos. 1a-19a (19)	35.75	31.60

Overprinted in the Netherlands and sold by the UN in New York.

Third Printing

Overprint 14mm long.

Photo.; Litho. (#4b, 6b, 8b)

1963, Mar. Photo. Unwmk. *Perf. 12½x12*

1b	A4	1c	**vermilion & yellow**	*4.25*	*2.00*
3b	A4	5c	**chocolate & yellow**	*4.75*	*3.00*
4b	A5	7c	**org red, bl & brn vio**	*20.00*	*20.00*
5b	A4	10c	**aqua & red brown**	*4.75*	*3.00*
6b	A5	12c	**green, bl & brn vio**	*30.00*	*30.00*
7b	A4	15c	**deep yel & red brn**	*97.50*	*105.00*
8b	A5	17c	**brown violet & blue**	*11.00*	*11.00*
9b	A4	20c	**lt blue grn & red brn**	*6.25*	*3.75*
			Nos. 1b-9b (8)	*178.50*	*177.75*

The third printing was applied in West New Guinea and it is doubtful whether it was regularly issued. Used values are for canceled to order stamps.

Fourth Printing

Overprint 19mm long.

Photogravure

1963, Mar. Unwmk. *Perf. 12½x12*

1c	A4	1c	**vermilion & yellow**	*45.00*	*45.00*
5c	A4	10c	**aqua & red brown**	*130.00*	*130.00*

The fourth printing was applied in West New Guinea and it is doubtful whether it was regularly issued. Used values are for canceled to order stamps.

U.N. INTERIM ADMINISTRATION IN KOSOVO

These stamps were issued by the United Nations Interim Administration Mission in Kosovo and the Post & Telecommunications of Kosovo. Service was local for the first two months, with international use starting in mid-May 2000.

Starting with No. 6, stamps were not made available to collectors through the United Nations Postal Administration.

100 pfennigs = 1 mark
100 cents = €1 (2002)

Catalogue values for all unused stamps in this country are for Never Hinged items.

Peace in Kosovo — A1

Printed by La Poste, France. Panes of 40. Designed by Shyqri Nimani, Kosovo.

Designs: 20pf, Mosaic depicting Orpheus, c. 5th-6th cent., Podujeve. 30pf, Dardinian idol, Museum of Kosovo. 50pf, Silver coin of Damastion from 4th cent. B.C. 1m, Statue of Mother Teresa, Prizren. 2m, Map of Kosovo.

Perf. 13½x13, 13½x13¼ (30pf)

2000, Mar. 14 **Litho.** **Unwmk.**

1	A1 20pf **multicolored**		.75	.75
	First day cover			1.50
2	A1 30pf **multicolored**		1.25	1.25
	First day cover			1.50
3	A1 50pf **multicolored**		2.00	2.00
	First day cover			1.75
4	A1 1m **multicolored**		4.00	4.00
	First day cover			4.00
5	A1 2m **multicolored**		8.00	8.00
	First day cover			7.00
	First day cover, #1-5			9.00
	Nos. 1-5 (5)		16.00	16.00

Peace in Kosovo — A2

Designs: 20pf, Bird. 30pf, Street musician. 50pf, Butterfly and pear. 1m, Children and stars. 2m, Globe and handprints.

2001, Nov. 12 **Litho.** ***Perf. 14***

6	A2 20pf **multicolored**	1.50	1.50
7	A2 30pf **multicolored**	2.00	2.00
8	A2 50pf **multicolored**	3.50	3.50
9	A2 1m **multicolored**	7.50	7.50
10	A2 2m **multicolored**	15.00	15.00
	Nos. 6-10 (5)	29.50	29.50

100 Cents = 1 Euro (€)

Peace in Kosovo Type of 2001 With Denominations in Euros Only

2002, May 2 **Litho.** ***Perf. 14***

11	A2 10c Like #6	1.75	1.75
12	A2 15c Like #7	2.50	2.50
13	A2 26c Like #8	3.75	3.75
14	A2 51c Like #9	7.50	7.50
15	A2 €1.02 Like #10	15.00	15.00
	Nos. 11-15 (5)	30.50	30.50

Christmas — A3

Designs: 50c, Candles and garland. €1, Stylized men.

2003, Dec. 20 **Litho.** ***Perf. 14***

16	A3 50c **multicolored**	*15.00*	*15.00*
17	A3 €1 **multicolored**	*24.00*	*24.00*

Return of Refugees — A4

Five Years of Peace — A5

2004, June 29 **Litho.** ***Perf. 13¼x13***

18	A4 €1 **multicolored**	*13.50*	*13.50*
19	A5 €2 **multicolored**	*16.50*	*16.50*

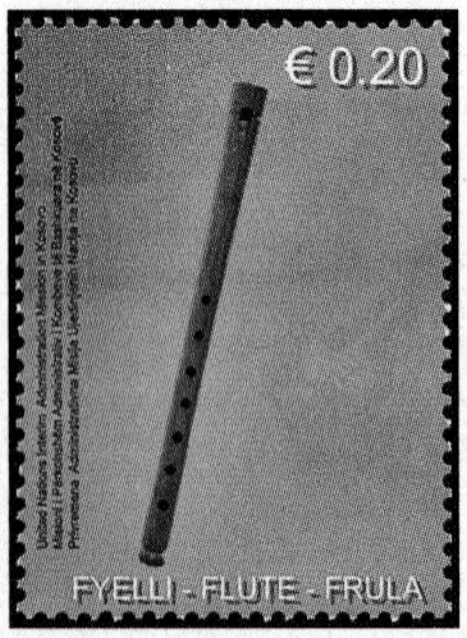

Musical Instruments — A6

2004, Aug. 31 **Litho.** ***Perf. 13¼x13***

20	A6 20c Flute	*7.00*	*7.00*
21	A6 30c Ocarina	*11.00*	*11.00*

Aprons — A7

Vests — A8

Designs: 20c, Apron from Prizren. 30c, Apron from Rugova. 50c, Three vests. €1, Two vests.

2004, Oct. 28 **Litho.** ***Perf. 13x13¼***

22	A7 20c **multicolored**	*7.00*	*7.00*
23	A7 30c **multicolored**	*10.00*	*10.00*
24	A8 50c **multicolored**	*16.00*	*16.00*
25	A8 €1 **multicolored**	*32.50*	*32.50*
	Nos. 22-25 (4)	*65.50*	*65.50*

Mirusha Waterfall — A9

2004, Nov. 26 **Litho.** ***Perf. 13x13¼***

26	A9 €2 **multicolored**	*14.00*	*14.00*

House — A10

2004, Dec. 14 **Litho.** ***Perf. 13x13¼***

27	A10 50c **multicolored**	*6.00*	*6.00*

Flowers — A11

2005, June 29 **Litho.** *Perf. 13½*

28	A11	15c Peony		3.00	3.00
29	A11	20c Poppies		4.00	4.00
30	A11	30c Gentian		6.00	6.00
		Nos. 28-30 (3)		13.00	13.00

A12

Handicrafts — A13

2005, July 20 *Perf. 13¼x13*

31	A12	20c shown	1.50	1.50
32	A12	30c Cradle	2.00	2.00
33	A13	50c shown	3.50	3.50
34	A12	€1 Necklace	7.50	7.50
		Nos. 31-34 (4)	14.50	14.50

Village — A14

Town — A15

City — A16

2005, Sept. 15 *Perf. 13x13½*

35	A14	20c **multicolored**	2.25	2.25
36	A15	50c **multicolored**	5.00	5.00
37	A16	€1 **multicolored**	9.00	9.00
		Nos. 35-37 (3)	16.25	16.25

Archaeological Artifacts — A17

2005, Nov. 2 *Perf. 13½x13*

38	A17	20c shown	1.25	1.25
39	A17	30c Statue	2.00	2.00
40	A17	50c Sculpture	4.00	4.00
41	A17	€1 Helmet	8.00	8.00
		Nos. 38-41 (4)	15.25	15.25

Minerals A18

2005, Dec. 10 *Perf. 13x13½*

42	A18	€2 **multicolored**	17.50	17.50

A19

Europa — A20

2006, July 20 *Perf. 13¼x13*

43	A19	50c **multicolored**	4.00	4.00
44	A20	€1 **multicolored**	8.00	8.00

Fauna A21

2006, May 23 **Litho.** *Perf. 13*

45	A21	15c Wolf	.90	.90
46	A21	20c Cow	1.25	1.25
47	A21	30c Pigeon	1.75	1.75
48	A21	50c Swan	2.50	2.50
49	A21	€1 Dog	5.00	5.00
a.		Souvenir sheet, #45-49, + label	12.50	12.50
		Nos. 45-49 (5)	11.40	11.40

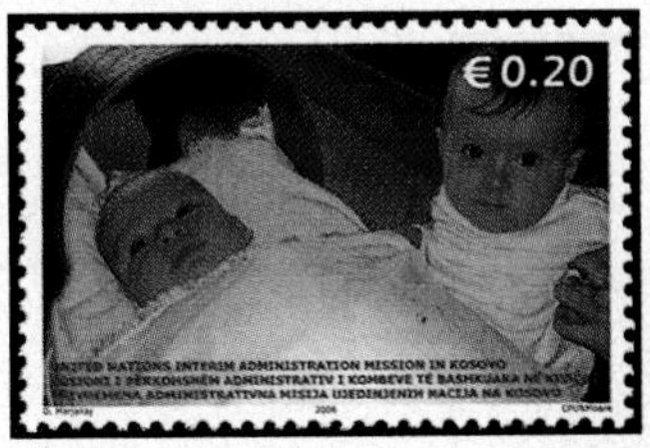

Children A22

Designs: 20c, Children in cradle. 30c, Children reading. 50c, Girls dancing. €1, Child in water.

2006, June 30 **Litho.** *Perf. 13*

50	A22	20c **multicolored**	.90	.90
51	A22	30c **multicolored**	1.25	1.25
52	A22	50c **multicolored**	2.25	2.25
53	A22	€1 **multicolored**	4.50	4.50
a.		Souvenir sheet, #50-53	8.50	8.50
		Nos. 50-53 (4)	8.90	8.90

A23

A24

A25

Tourist Attractions A26

2006, Sept. 1 **Litho.** *Perf. 13*

54	A23	20c **multicolored**	.90	.90
55	A24	30c **multicolored**	1.25	1.25
56	A25	50c **multicolored**	2.25	2.25
57	A26	€1 **multicolored**	4.50	4.50
a.		Souvenir sheet, #54-57	8.50	8.50
		Nos. 50-53 (4)	8.90	8.90

Intl. Peace Day — A27

2006, Sept. 21 **Litho.** ***Perf. 13***

58	A27	€2 **multicolored**	*7.50 7.50*

Ancient Coins — A28

Various coins.

2006, Nov. 1 **Litho.** ***Perf. 13***

59	A28	20c **multicolored**	*.75 .75*
60	A28	30c **multicolored**	*1.10 1.10*
61	A28	50c **multicolored**	*1.90 1.90*
62	A28	€1 **multicolored**	*3.75 3.75*
a.		Souvenir sheet, #59-62	*7.50 7.50*

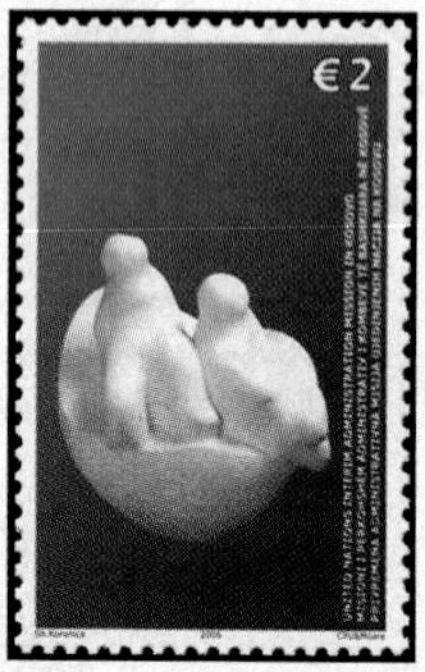

Sculpture — A29

2006, Dec. 1 **Litho.** ***Perf. 13***

63	A29	€2 **multicolored**	*7.50 7.50*
a.		Miniature sheet, #45-57, 59-63, + 2 labels	*40.00 40.00*

Convention on the Rights of Persons With Disabilities — A30

Emblems of handicaps and: 20c, Children and butterfly. 50c, Handicapped women. 70c, Map of Kosovo. €1, Stylized flower.

2007, Apr. 23 **Litho.** ***Perf. 14x14¼***

64	A30	20c **multicolored**	*.75 .75*
65	A30	50c **multicolored**	*2.00 2.00*
66	A30	70c **multicolored**	*2.75 2.75*
67	A30	€1 **multicolored**	*4.00 4.00*
a.		Souvenir sheet, #64-67	*9.50 9.50*
		Nos. 64-67 (4)	*9.50 9.50*

Scouting, Cent. — A31

Europa — A32

2007, May 12 **Litho.** ***Perf. 13¼***

68	A31	70c **multicolored**	*2.75 2.75*
69	A32	€1 **multicolored**	*4.00 4.00*
a.		Souvenir sheet, #68-69	*6.75 6.75*

A33

A34

A35

International Children's Day — A36

2007, June 1 **Litho.** ***Perf. 13¼***

70	A33	20c **multicolored**	*.75 .75*
71	A34	30c **multicolored**	*1.25 1.25*
72	A35	70c **multicolored**	*2.75 2.75*
73	A36	€1 **multicolored**	*4.00 4.00*
		Nos. 70-73 (4)	*8.75 8.75*

Native Costumes — A37

Designs: 20c, Serbian woman. 30c, Prizren Region woman. 50c, Sword dancer. 70c, Drenica Region woman. €1, Shepherd, Rugova.

2007, July 6 **Litho.** ***Perf. 13½x13¼***

74	A37	20c **multicolored**	*.65 .65*
75	A37	30c **multicolored**	*1.00 1.00*
76	A37	50c **multicolored**	*1.75 1.75*
77	A37	70c **multicolored**	*2.40 2.40*
78	A37	€1 **multicolored**	*3.50 3.50*
a.		Souvenir sheet, #74-78, + label	*9.50 9.50*
		Nos. 74-78 (5)	*9.30 9.30*

Masks — A38

Various masks.

2007, Sept. 11 **Litho.** ***Perf. 13½x13¼***

79	A38	15c **multicolored**	*.50 .50*
80	A38	30c **multicolored**	*1.00 1.00*
81	A38	50c **multicolored**	*1.60 1.60*
82	A38	€1 **multicolored**	*3.25 3.25*
		Nos. 79-82 (4)	*6.35 6.35*

Sports — A39

Designs: 20c, Soccer ball, basketball, two people standing, person in wheelchair. 50c, Wrestlers. €1, Symbols of 24 sports.

2007, Oct. 2 **Litho.** ***Perf. 13¼x13½***

83	A39	20c **multicolored**	*.70 .70*
84	A39	50c **multicolored**	*1.60 1.60*
85	A39	€1 **multicolored**	*3.25 3.25*
		Nos. 83-85 (3)	*5.55 5.55*

Architecture — A40

Designs: 30c, Stone bridge, Vushtrri. 50c, Hamam, Prizren. 70c, Tower. €1, Tower, diff.

2007, Nov. 6 **Litho.** ***Perf. 13¼***

86	A40	30c **multicolored**	*1.10 1.10*
87	A40	50c **multicolored**	*1.90 1.90*
88	A40	70c **multicolored**	*2.75 2.75*
89	A40	€1 **multicolored**	*3.75 3.75*
		Nos. 86-89 (4)	*9.50 9.50*

Locomotives
A41

Designs: €1, Diesel locomotive. €2, Steam locomotive

2007, Dec. 7 **Litho.** ***Perf. 13¼***

90 A41	€1 **multicolored**	*3.50*	*3.50*
91 A41	€2 **multicolored**	*6.50*	*6.50*

Skanderbeg (1405-68), Albanian National Hero — A42

2008, Jan. 17 **Litho.** ***Perf. 13¼***

92 A42	€2 **multicolored**	*6.25*	*6.25*

Kosovo declared its independence from Serbia on Feb. 17, 2008, ending the United Nations Interim Administration. Stamps issued after Feb. 17, 2008 by the Republic of Kosovo will be listed under Kosovo in the *Scott Standard Postage Stamp Catalogue.*

MINKUS
Album Series

The Minkus album line is now available through Amos Hobby Publishing.
The supplement schedule is listed below. Pages are punched to fit 2 or 3-ring binders.
Sold as page units only. Binders, slipcases and labels sold separately.
For more information album contents visit our web site at www.amosadvantage.com.

FEBRUARY
Global Part 1
Global Part 2
All American Regular & Commemoratives

MARCH
All American Part 3 United Nations
U.N Singles
U.N. Imprint Blocks
U.N. Postal Stationery

APRIL
All American Part 2 Postal Stationery
All American Part 4 Booklet Panes
All American Part 5 Sheetlets
All American Part 7 Postal Cards
U.S. Commemoratives
U.S. Plate Blocks
U.S. Regular Issues
U.S. Booklet Panes
U.S. Postal Stationery
U.S. Sheetlets

MAY
Albania
Austria
Bulgaria
Canada
Croatia
France
French Andorra
Germany
Gibraltar
Great Britain, Ireland
Guernsey, Jersey, Isle Of Man
Hong Kong
Ireland
Monaco
Romania
Serbia & Montenegro
Singapore
Slovenia

JUNE
Denmark
Egypt
Finland
Greece
Israel Singles
Israel Plate Blocks
Israel Tab Singles
Korea
Liechtenstein
Norway
Sweden
Switzerland

JULY
Bangladesh
India
Italy
Japan
Pakistan
People's Republic of China
Portugal/Azores/Maderia
San Marino
Spain
Sri Lanka
Thailand
Vatican City

AUGUST
Armenia
Azerbaijan
Belarus
Belgium
Czech Republic & Slovakia
Georgia
Hungary
Kazakhstan
Kyrgyzstan
Latvia, Lithuania, Estonia
Luxembourg
Moldova
Netherlands
Poland
Russia
Tajikistan
Turkmenistan
Ukraine
Uzbekistan

SEPTEMBER
Argentina
Australia
Brazil
Chile
Colombia
Dominican Republic
Haiti
Mexico
New Zealand
Venezuela

DECEMBER
All American Part 6 Plate No. Coils
U.S. Plate No. Coils

SCOTT®

AMOS
ADVANTAGE
911 Vandemark Road
Sidney OH 45365
1-800-572-6885
www.amosadvantage.com

INDEX TO ADVERTISERS – 2009 U.S. SPECIALIZED

2009
UNITED STATES SPECIALIZED
DEALER DIRECTORY
YELLOW PAGE LISTINGS

This section of your Scott Catalogue contains advertisements to help you conveniently find what you need, when you need it...!

Looking For A Dealer In Your Area? It's As Easy As 1-2-3

1. Go to: www.asdaonline.com

2. Click on Member Dealer Search

3. Enter Your State

IT'S THAT SIMPLE!

American Stamp Dealers Association, Inc.

516-759-7000

Established 1914

Just $19.95*

Buys you 10 Colorful Issues Of

or SAVE with a two year subscription at $29.95*

The American Stamp Dealer & Collector

Subscribe Online at www.americanstampdealer.com

OR Simply send your Name & Mailing Address with payment made out to the ASDA to:

The American Stamp Dealer & Collector Magazine

3 School Street, Suite 205, Glen Cove, NY 11542

*U.S. subscription. Check website for foreign rates.

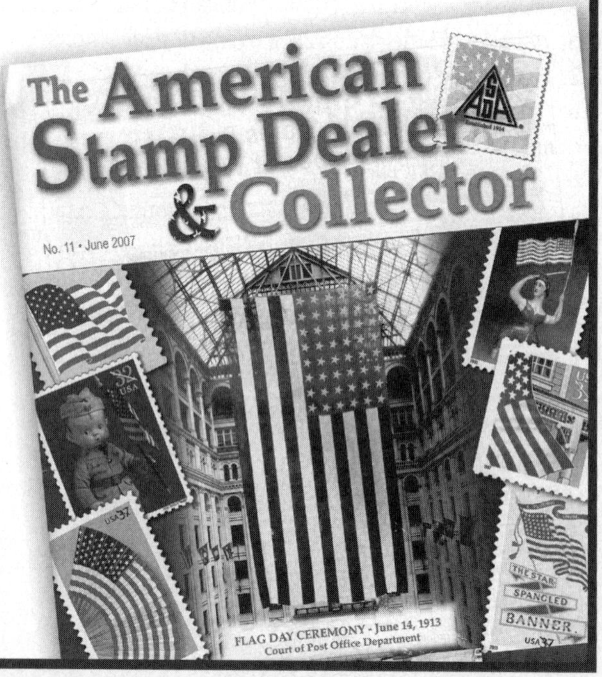

Accessories

BROOKLYN GALLERY COIN & STAMP, INC.
8725 4th Ave.
Brooklyn, NY 11209
PH: 718-745-5701
FAX: 718-745-2775
info@brooklyngallery.com
www.brooklyngallery.com

Appraisals

DALE ENTERPRISES, INC.
PO Box 539-C
Emmaus, PA 18049
PH: 610-433-3303
FAX: 610-965-6089
daleent@ptd.net
www.dalestamps.com

PHILIP WEISS AUCTIONS
1 Neil Court
Oceanside, NY 11572
PH: 516-594-0731
FAX: 516-594-9414

Asia

MICHAEL ROGERS, INC.
415 South Orlando Ave
Winter Park, FL 32789-3683
PH: 407-644-2290
PH: 800-843-3751
FAX: 407-645-4434
Stamps@michaelrogersinc.com
www.michaelrogersinc.com

Auctions

DANIEL F. KELLEHER CO., INC.
20 Walnut St.
Suite 213
Wellesley, MA 02481
PH: 781-235-0990
FAX: 781-235-0945

JACQUES C. SCHIFF, JR., INC.
195 Main St.
Ridgefield Park, NJ 07660
PH: 201-641-5566
FAX: 201-641-5705

MICHAEL ROGERS, INC.
415 South Orlando Ave
Winter Park, FL 32789-3683
PH: 407-644-2290
PH: 800-843-3751
FAX: 407-645-4434
Stamps@michaelrogersinc.com
www.michaelrogersinc.com

PHILIP WEISS AUCTIONS
1 Neil Court
Oceanside, NY 11572
PH: 516-594-0731
FAX: 516-594-9414

R. MARESCH & SON LTD.
5th Floor - 6075 Yonge St.
Toronto, ON M2M 3W2
CANADA
PH: 416-363-7777
FAX: 416-363-6511
www.maresch.com

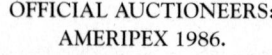

Auctions

Schiff Auctions

Buyers, Auctioneers & Appraisers of U.S. & Worldwide Stamps & Covers

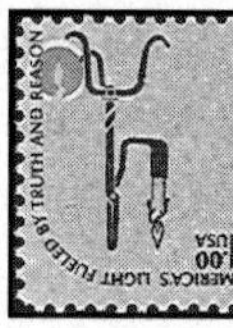

We have been catering to the individual buyer and seller since 1947. Let us put our over **60 years** of experience to work for you when selling your stamps, covers or your collection. Whether you prefer consigning to public auction or selling outright, call us first. Describe your material before sending. Please include your address and telephone numbers.

CATALOG SUBSCRIPTIONS	N. AMERICA	OVERSEAS
1 Year Catalogs & Prices Realized	$10.00	$18.00
1 Year Catalog Only	$7.50	$15.00
1 Catalog with Prices Realized	$1.50	$2.50
1 Catalog Only	$1.00	$1.50

Send a self-addressed, stamped envelope for our complimentary brochure "How to auction your stamps and covers".

JACQUES C. SCHIFF, JR., INC.

195 Main St., Ridgefield Park, NJ 07660 USA
Telephone 201-641-5566 FAX 201-641-5705

OFFICIAL AUCTIONEERS:
AMERIPEX 1986.
WORLD STAMP EXPO 1989.
WORLD COLUMBIAN STAMP EXPO 1992.
AMERICAN PHILATELIC SOCIETY 2000-2003

Qualified Auctioneer

Auctions

SAM HOUSTON PHILATELICS
PO Box 820087
Houston, TX 77282
PH: 281-493-6386
PH: 800-231-5926
FAX: 281-496-1445
shduck@aol.com
www.shpauctions.com

THE STAMP CENTER DUTCH COUNTRY AUCTIONS
4115 Concord Pike
Wilmington, DE 19803
PH: 302-478-8740
FAX: 302-478-8779
auctions@thestampcenter.com
www.thestampcenter.com

Auctions-Mail Bid

DALE ENTERPRISES, INC.
PO Box 539-C
Emmaus, PA 18049
PH: 610-433-3303
FAX: 610-965-6089
daleent@ptd.net
www.dalestamps.com

Auctions - Public

ALAN BLAIR STAMPS/ AUCTIONS
5405 Lakeside Ave.
Suite 1
Richmond, VA 23228
PH: 800-689-5602
FAX: 804-262-9307
alanblair@verizon.net
www.alanblairstamps.com

China

MICHAEL ROGERS, INC.
415 South Orlando Ave
Winter Park, FL 32789-3683
PH: 407-644-2290
PH: 800-843-3751
FAX: 407-645-4434
Stamps@michaelrogersinc.com
www.michaelrogersinc.com

Classics

GARY POSNER, INC.
1407 Ave. Z, PMB #535
Brooklyn, NY 11235
PH: 800-323-4279
CELL PH: 917-538-8133
FAX: 718-241-2801
garyposnerinc@aol.com
www. garyposnerinc.com
www.gemstamps.com

J. NALBANDIAN, INC.
PO Box 71
East Greenwich, RI 02818
PH: 401-885-5020
FAX: 401-885-3040
nalbandianj@earthlink.net
www.nalbandstamp.com

Confed. Stamps & Postal History

STANLEY M. PILLER & ASSOCIATES
(HOURS BY APPT. ONLY)
800 S. Broadway
Suite 201
Walnut Creek, CA 94596
PH: 925-938-8290
FAX: 925-938-8812
stmpdlr@aol.com
www.smpiller.com

SUN COAST STAMP CO.
8520 S. Tamiami Tr., Unit1
Sarasota, FL 34238
PH: 941-921-9761
PH: 800-927-3351
FAX: 941-921-1762
email@suncoaststamp.com

Covers-Zeppelins

HENRY GITNER PHILATELISTS, INC.
PO Box 3077-S
Middletown, NY 10940
PH: 845-343-5151
PH: 800-947-8267
FAX: 845-343-0068
hgitner@hgitner.com
www.hgitner.com

Cuba

R.D.C. STAMPS
R. del Campo
Museo Historico Cubano
3131 Coral Way
Miami, FL 33145
PH: 305-815-0577
PH: 305-567-3131
FAX: 305-567-1416
rdcstamps@aol.com

Ducks

MICHAEL JAFFE
PO Box 61484
Vancouver, WA 98666
PH: 360-695-6161
PH: 800-782-6770
FAX: 360-695-1616
mjaffe@brookmanstamps.com
www.brookmanstamps.com

SAM HOUSTON DUCK CO.
PO Box 820087
Houston, TX 77282
PH: 281-493-6386
PH: 800-231-5926
FAX: 281-496-1445
shduck@aol.com
www.shduck.com

Ducks

TRENTON STAMP & COIN CO./COASTAL BEND DUCK STAMP CO.
Thomas DeLuca
Mail: PO Box 8574
Trenton, NJ 08650
Store: Forest Glen Plaza
1804 Route 33
Hamilton Square, NJ 08690
PH: 800-446-8664
PH: 609-584-8100
FAX: 609-587-8664
TOMD4TSC@aol.com

Errors, Freaks & Oddities

J. NALBANDIAN, INC.
PO Box 71
East Greenwich, RI 02818
PH: 401-885-5020
FAX: 401-885-3040
nalbandianj@earthlink.net
www.nalbandstamp.com

SAM HOUSTON PHILATELICS
PO Box 820087
Houston, TX 77282
PH: 281-493-6386
PH: 800-231-5926
FAX: 281-496-1445
shduck@aol.com
www.shpauctions.com

Classics - U.S. Stamps & Covers

PETER MOSIONDZ, JR.
Serving Philately Since 1968
26 Cameron Circle
Laurel Springs, NJ 08021
(856) 627-6865
mosiondz@comcast.net

Pre-1940 United States Stamps
Accurately Graded & Competitively Priced
Request Your Free Price List Today
EXPERIENCE • INTEGRITY • TRUST

Auctions - Public

ALAN BLAIR PUBLIC AUCTIONS

1. REGULARLY SCHEDULED AUCTIONS
2. MOST LOTS $20 TO $500 VALUE
3. WRITE FOR CONSIGNMENT INFORMATION

5405 LAKESIDE AVENUE, SUITE 1
RICHMOND, VA 23228
Phone: 800-689-5602 Fax: 804-262-9307
E-mail: alanblair@verizon.net
www.alanblairstamps.com
APS
ASDA Qualified Auctioneer

Expertizing

EXPERTIZING ANY U.S. STAMP, COVER, CANCEL, PROOF, etc.

Only $10.00 plus cost of shipping. Paper certificate also available for $15.00. Why pay $30.-$40. or more only to find out the item isn't what you thought it was?

42 year APS member and 33 year *Linn's* Advertiser.

William R. Weiss, Jr.
P.O.B. 5358, Bethlehem, PA 18015
Ph: (610) 691-6857 Email: weissauction@rcn.com
APS USSS

Expertizing

STANLEY M. PILLER & ASSOCIATES
(HOURS BY APPT. ONLY)
800 S. Broadway
Suite 201
Walnut Creek, CA 94596
PH: 925-938-8290
FAX: 925-938-8812
stmpdlr@aol.com
www.smpiller.com

First Day Covers

HENRY GITNER PHILATELISTS, INC.
PO Box 3077-S
Middletown, NY 10940
PH: 845-343-5151
PH: 800-947-8267
FAX: 845-343-0068
hgitner@hgitner.com
www.hgitner.com

German Colonies

COLONIAL STAMP COMPANY
View our on-line price list at our website!
5757 Wilshire Blvd. PH #8
Los Angeles, CA 90036
PH: 323-933-9435
FAX: 323-939-9930
Toll Free in North America
PH: 877-272-6693
FAX: 877-272-6694
info@colonialstampcompany.com
www.colonialstampcompany.com

STANLEY M. PILLER & ASSOCIATES
(HOURS BY APPT. ONLY)
800 S. Broadway
Suite 201
Walnut Creek, CA 94596
PH: 925-938-8290
FAX: 925-938-8812
stmpdlr@aol.com
www.smpiller.com

Insurance

COLLECTIBLES INSURANCE SERVICES, LLC.
11350 McCormick Rd., Ste. 700
Hunt Valley, MD 21031
PH: 888-837-9537
www.collectinsure.com

Japan

MICHAEL ROGERS, INC.
415 South Orlando Ave
Winter Park, FL 32789-3683
PH: 407-644-2290
PH: 800-843-3751
FAX: 407-645-4434
Stamps@michaelrogersinc.com
www.michaelrogersinc.com

Korea

MICHAEL ROGERS, INC.
415 South Orlando Ave
Winter Park, FL 32789-3683
PH: 407-644-2290
PH: 800-843-3751
FAX: 407-645-4434
Stamps@michaelrogersinc.com
www.michaelrogersinc.com

Manchukuo

MICHAEL ROGERS, INC.
415 South Orlando Ave
Winter Park, FL 32789-3683
PH: 407-644-2290
PH: 800-843-3751
FAX: 407-645-4434
Stamps@michaelrogersinc.com
www.michaelrogersinc.com

Middle East-Arab

MICHAEL ROGERS, INC.
415 South Orlando Ave
Winter Park, FL 32789-3683
PH: 407-644-2290
PH: 800-843-3751
FAX: 407-645-4434
Stamps@michaelrogersinc.com
www.michaelrogersinc.com

New Issues

DAVIDSON'S STAMP SERVICE
PO Box 36355
Indianapolis, IN 46236-0355
PH: 317-826-2620
davidson@in.net
www.newstampissues.com

New Issues - Retail

BOMBAY PHILATELIC INC.
PO Box 90937
Raleigh, NC 27675
PH: 561-499-7990
FAX: 561-499-7553
sales@bombaystamps.com
www.bombaystamps.com

One of a Kind

DALE ENTERPRISES, INC.
PO Box 539-C
Emmaus, PA 18049
PH: 610-433-3303
FAX: 610-965-6089
daleent@ptd.net
www.dalestamps.com

Philatelic Literature

LEWIS KAUFMAN
PO Box 255
Kiamesha Lake, NY 12751
PH/FAX: 845-794-8013
PH/FAX: 800-491-5453
mamet1@aol.com

Postal History

STANLEY M. PILLER & ASSOCIATES
(HOURS BY APPT. ONLY)
800 S. Broadway
Suite 201
Walnut Creek, CA 94596
PH: 925-938-8290
FAX: 925-938-8812
stmpdlr@aol.com
www.smpiller.com

Proofs & Essays

HENRY GITNER PHILATELISTS, INC.
PO Box 3077-S
Middletown, NY 10940
PH: 845-343-5151
PH: 800-947-8267
FAX: 845-343-0068
hgitner@hgitner.com
www.hgitner.com

Publications-Collector

THE AMERICAN PHILATELIST
Dept. TZ
100 Match Factory Pl.
Bellefonte, PA 16823-1367
PH: 814-933-3803
FAX: 814-933-6128
apsinfo@stamps.org
www.stamps.org

Souvenir Cards

AALLSTAMPS
38 N. Main St.
PO Box 249
Milltown, NJ 08850
PH: 732-247-1093
FAX: 732-247-1094
mail@aallstamps.com
www.aallstamps.com

STAMP STORES

California

BROSIUS STAMP, COIN & SUPPLIES
2105 Main St.
Santa Monica, CA 90405
PH: 310-396-7480
FAX: 310-396-7455

COLONIAL STAMP CO./ BRITISH EMPIRE SPECIALIST
5757 Wilshire Blvd. PH #8
(by appt.)
Los Angeles, CA 90036
PH: 323-933-9435
FAX: 323-939-9930
Toll Free in North America
PH: 877-272-6693
FAX: 877-272-6694
info@colonialstampcompany.com
www.colonialstampcompany.com

FISCHER-WOLK PHILATELICS
22762 Aspan St.
Suite 211
Lake Forest, CA 92630
PH: 949-837-2932
fw@occoxmail.com

NATICK STAMPS & HOBBIES
411 E. Huntington Dr.
Suite 209
Arcadia, CA 91006
PH: 626-445-2185
natickco@att.net

STAMP STORES

Colorado

SHOWCASE STAMPS
3865 Wadsworth
Wheat Ridge, CO 80033
PH: 303-425-9252
kbeiner@colbi.net
www.showcasestamps.com

Connecticut

SILVER CITY COIN & STAMP
41 Colony St.
Meriden, CT 06451
PH: 203-235-7634
FAX: 203-237-4915

Florida

R.D.C. STAMPS
R. del Campo
Museo Historico Cubano
3131 Coral Way
Miami, FL 33145
PH: 305-815-0577
PH: 305-567-3131
FAX: 305-567-1416
rdcstamps@aol.com

Georgia

STAMPS UNLIMITED OF GEORGIA, INC.
100 Peachtree St.
Suite 1460
Atlanta, GA 30303
PH: 404-688-9161
tonyroozen@yahoo.com

Illinois

DR. ROBERT FRIEDMAN & SONS
2029 W. 75th St.
Woodridge, IL 60517
PH: 800-588-8100
FAX: 630-985-1588
drbobstamps@yahoo.com
www.drbobfriedmanstamps.com

SIDMORE STAMPS
145 E. Lincoln Hwy.
DeKalb, IL 60115
PH: 815-787-7000
sidmorestamps@verizon.net
Authorized APS Dealer

Stamp Shows

STAMP STORES

Indiana

KNIGHT STAMP & COIN CO.
237 Main St.
Hobart, IN 46342
PH: 219-942-4341
PH: 800-634-2646
knight@knightcoin.com
www.knightcoin.com

Massachusetts

KAPPY'S COINS & STAMPS
534 Washington St.
Norwood, MA 02062
PH: 781-762-5552
kappyscoins@aol.com

SUBURBAN STAMP INC.
176 Worthington St.
Springfield, MA 01103
PH: 413-785-5348
FAX: 413-746-3788
suburbanstamp@earthlink.net

Maryland

BULLDOG STAMP COMPANY
4641 Montgomery Ave.
Bethesda, MD 20814
PH: 301-654-1138

New Jersey

AALLSTAMPS
38 N. Main St.
PO Box 249
Milltown, NJ 08850
PH: 732-247-1093
FAX: 732-247-1094
mail@aallstamps.com
www.aallstamps.com

BERGEN STAMPS & COLLECTIBLES
306 Queen Anne Rd.
Teaneck, NJ 07666
PH: 201-836-8987

TRENTON STAMP & COIN CO.
Thomas DeLuca
Store: Forest Glen Plaza
1804 Route 33
Hamilton Square, NJ 08690
Mail: PO Box 8574
Trenton, NJ 08650
PH: 800-446-8664
PH: 609-584-8100
FAX: 609-587-8664
TOMD4TSC@aol.com

New York

CHAMPION STAMP CO., INC.
432 W. 54th St.
New York, NY 10019
PH: 212-489-8130
FAX: 212-581-8130
championstamp@aol.com
www.championstamp.com

MODLOW-ARVAI STAMPS & COLLECTIBLES
504 E. 118th St. Apt #2
New York, NY 10035
PH: 917-868-4850
FAX: 888-655-1655
Mastamps@aol.com
Visit our Free Auction site:
http://www.modlow-arvai.com

STAMP STORES

Ohio

HILLTOP STAMP SERVICE
Richard A. Peterson
PO Box 626
Wooster, OH 44691
PH: 330-262-8907
PH: 330-262-5378
hilltop@bright.net

THE LINK STAMP CO.
3461 E. Livingston Ave.
Columbus, OH 43227
PH/FAX: 614-237-4125
PH/FAX: 800-546-5726

Tennessee

HERRON HILL, INC.
5007 Black Rd.
Suite 140
Memphis, TN 38117
PH: 901-683-9644

Texas

SAM HOUSTON PHILATELICS
14780 Memorial Dr. #110
Houston, TX 77079
PH: 281-493-6386
PH: 800-231-5926
FAX: 281-496-1445
shduck@aol.com
www.shduck.com

Virginia

KENNEDY'S STAMPS & COINS, INC.
7059 Brookfield Plaza
Springfield, VA 22150
PH: 703-569-7300
FAX: 703-569-7644
j.w.kennedy@verizon.net

LATHEROW & CO., INC.
5054 Lee Hwy.
Arlington, VA 22207
PH: 703-538-2727
PH: 800-647-4624
FAX: 703-538-5210
latherow@filatco.com

Topicals-Columbus

MR. COLUMBUS
PO Box 1492
Fennville, MI 49408
PH: 269-543-4755
columbus@accn.org

United States

ACS STAMP COMPANY
10831 Chambers Way
Commerce City, CO 80022
PH: 303-841-8666
ACS@ACSStamp.com
www.acsstamp.com

B.J.'S STAMPS
Barbara J. Johnson
6342 W. Bell Rd.
Glendale, AZ 85308
PH: 623-878-2080
FAX: 623-412-3456
info@bjstamps.com
www.bjstamps.com

BROOKMAN STAMP CO.
PO Box 90
Vancouver, WA 98666
PH: 360-695-1391
PH: 800-545-4871
FAX: 360-695-1616
larry@brookmanstamps.com
www.brookmanstamps.com

United States

DALE ENTERPRISES, INC.
PO Box 539-C
Emmaus, PA 18049
PH: 610-433-3303
FAX: 610-965-6089
daleent@ptd.net
www.dalestamps.com

GARY POSNER, INC.
1407 Ave. Z, PMB #535
Brooklyn, NY 11235
PH: 800-323-4279
CELL PH: 917-538-8133
FAX: 718-241-2801
garyposnerinc@aol.com
www. garyposnerinc.com
www.gemstamps.com

SUBURBAN STAMP INC.
176 Worthington St.
Springfield, MA 01103
PH: 413-785-5348
FAX: 413-746-3788
suburbanstamp@earthlink.net

U.S.-Booklets

DALE ENTERPRISES, INC.
PO Box 539-C
Emmaus, PA 18049
PH: 610-433-3303
FAX: 610-965-6089
daleent@ptd.net
www.dalestamps.com

U.S.-Classics

DALE ENTERPRISES, INC.
PO Box 539-C
Emmaus, PA 18049
PH: 610-433-3303
FAX: 610-965-6089
daleent@ptd.net
www.dalestamps.com

J. NALBANDIAN, INC.
PO Box 71
East Greenwich, RI 02818
PH: 401-885-5020
FAX: 401-885-3040
nalbandianj@earthlink.net
www.nalbandstamp.com

STANLEY M. PILLER & ASSOCIATES
(HOURS BY APPT. ONLY)
800 S. Broadway
Suite 201
Walnut Creek, CA 94596
PH: 925-938-8290
FAX: 925-938-8812
stmpdlr@aol.com
www.smpiller.com

SUBURBAN STAMP INC.
176 Worthington St.
Springfield, MA 01103
PH: 413-785-5348
FAX: 413-746-3788
suburbanstamp@earthlink.net

United States

U.S.-Classics/Moderns

WULFF'S STAMPS
PO Box 661746
Sacramento, CA 95866
PH/FAX: 800-884-0656
PH/FAX: 916-489-0656
service@wulffstamps.com
www.wulffstamps.com

U.S.-Collections Wanted

DR. ROBERT FRIEDMAN & SONS
2029 W. 75th St.
Woodridge, IL 60517
PH: 800-588-8100
FAX: 630-985-1588
drbobstamps@yahoo.com
www.drbobfriedmanstamps.com

SUBURBAN STAMP INC.
176 Worthington St.
Springfield, MA 01103
PH: 413-785-5348
FAX: 413-746-3788
suburbanstamp@earthlink.net

THE STAMP CENTER DUTCH COUNTRY AUCTIONS
4115 Concord Pike
Wilmington, DE 19803
PH: 302-478-8740
FAX: 302-478-8779
auctions@thestampcenter.com
www.thestampcenter.com

U.S.-Errors, Freaks & Oddities

GARY POSNER, INC.
1407 Ave. Z, PMB #535
Brooklyn, NY 11235
PH: 800-323-4279
CELL PH: 917-538-8133
FAX: 718-241-2801
garyposnerinc@aol.com
www. garyposnerinc.com
www.gemstamps.com

SUBURBAN STAMP INC.
176 Worthington St.
Springfield, MA 01103
PH: 413-785-5348
FAX: 413-746-3788
suburbanstamp@earthlink.net

U.S.-Federal Duck Stamps

HENRY GITNER PHILATELISTS, INC.
PO Box 3077-S
Middletown, NY 10940
PH: 845-343-5151
PH: 800-947-8267
FAX: 845-343-0068
hgitner@hgitner.com
www.hgitner.com

SAM HOUSTON DUCK CO.
PO Box 820087
Houston, TX 77282
PH: 281-493-6386
PH: 800-231-5926
FAX: 281-496-1445
shduck@aol.com
www.shduck.com

U.S.-Mint Sheets

HENRY GITNER PHILATELISTS, INC.
PO Box 3077-S
Middletown, NY 10940
PH: 845-343-5151
PH: 800-947-8267
FAX: 845-343-0068
hgitner@hgitner.com
www.hgitner.com

U.S.-Plate Blocks

GARY POSNER, INC.
1407 Ave. Z, PMB #535
Brooklyn, NY 11235
PH: 800-323-4279
CELL PH: 917-538-8133
FAX: 718-241-2801
garyposnerinc@aol.com
www. garyposnerinc.com
www.gemstamps.com

U.S.-Postal History

SUN COAST STAMP CO.
8520 S. Tamiami Tr., Unit1
Sarasota, FL 34238
PH: 941-921-9761
PH: 800-927-3351
FAX: 941-921-1762
email@suncoaststamp.com

U.S.-Price Lists

DALE ENTERPRISES, INC.
PO Box 539-C
Emmaus, PA 18049
PH: 610-433-3303
FAX: 610-965-6089
daleent@ptd.net
www.dalestamps.com

U.S.-Proofs & Essays

J. NALBANDIAN, INC.
PO Box 71
East Greenwich, RI 02818
PH: 401-885-5020
FAX: 401-885-3040
nalbandianj@earthlink.net
www.nalbandstamp.com

SUBURBAN STAMP INC.
176 Worthington St.
Springfield, MA 01103
PH: 413-785-5348
FAX: 413-746-3788
suburbanstamp@earthlink.net

U.S.-Rare Stamps

GARY POSNER, INC.
1407 Ave. Z, PMB #535
Brooklyn, NY 11235
PH: 800-323-4279
CELL PH: 917-538-8133
FAX: 718-241-2801
garyposnerinc@aol.com
www. garyposnerinc.com
www.gemstamps.com

U.S. Revenues

WULFF'S STAMPS
PO Box 661746
Sacramento, CA 95866
PH/FAX: 800-884-0656
PH/FAX: 916-489-0656
service@wulffstamps.com
www.wulffstamps.com

U.S.-Trust Territories

HENRY GITNER PHILATELISTS, INC.
PO Box 3077-S
Middletown, NY 10940
PH: 845-343-5151
PH: 800-947-8267
FAX: 845-343-0068
hgitner@hgitner.com
www.hgitner.com

Want Lists

CHARLES P. SCHWARTZ
PO Box 165
Mora, MN 55051
PH: 320-679-4705
charlesp@ecenet.com

Want Lists-U.S.

GARY POSNER, INC.
1407 Ave. Z, PMB #535
Brooklyn, NY 11235
PH: 800-323-4279
CELL PH: 917-538-8133
FAX: 718-241-2801
garyposnerinc@aol.com
www. garyposnerinc.com
www.gemstamps.com

Wanted-Collections

DALE ENTERPRISES, INC.
PO Box 539-C
Emmaus, PA 18049
PH: 610-433-3303
FAX: 610-965-6089
daleent@ptd.net
www.dalestamps.com

Wanted-Estates

DALE ENTERPRISES, INC.
PO Box 539-C
Emmaus, PA 18049
PH: 610-433-3303
FAX: 610-965-6089
daleent@ptd.net
www.dalestamps.com

Wanted-U.S.

GARY POSNER, INC.
1407 Ave. Z, PMB #535
Brooklyn, NY 11235
PH: 800-323-4279
CELL PH: 917-538-8133
FAX: 718-241-2801
garyposnerinc@aol.com
www. garyposnerinc.com
www.gemstamps.com

SUBURBAN STAMP INC.
176 Worthington St.
Springfield, MA 01103
PH: 413-785-5348
FAX: 413-746-3788
suburbanstamp@earthlink.net

Wanted-U.S. Collections

BROOKMAN STAMP CO.
PO Box 90
Vancouver, WA 98666
PH: 360-695-1391
PH: 800-545-4871
FAX: 360-695-1616
larry@brookmanstamps.com
www.brookmanstamps.com

Wanted-Worldwide Collections

DANIEL F. KELLEHER CO., INC.
20 Walnut St.
Suite 213
Wellesley, MA 02481
PH: 781-235-0990
FAX: 781-235-0945

DR. ROBERT FRIEDMAN & SONS
2029 W. 75th St.
Woodridge, IL 60517
PH: 800-588-8100
FAX: 630-985-1588
drbobstamps@yahoo.com
www.drbobfriedmanstamps.com

SUBURBAN STAMP INC.
176 Worthington St.
Springfield, MA 01103
PH: 413-785-5348
FAX: 413-746-3788
suburbanstamp@earthlink.net

THE STAMP CENTER DUTCH COUNTRY AUCTIONS
4115 Concord Pike
Wilmington, DE 19803
PH: 302-478-8740
FAX: 302-478-8779
auctions@thestampcenter.com
www.thestampcenter.com

Websites

ACS STAMP COMPANY
10831 Chambers Way
Commerce City, CO 80022
PH: 303-841-8666
ACS@ACSStamp.com
www.acsstamp.com

J. NALBANDIAN, INC.
PO Box 71
East Greenwich, RI 02818
PH: 401-885-5020
FAX: 401-885-3040
nalbandianj@earthlink.net
www.nalbandstamp.com

Wholesale

HENRY GITNER PHILATELISTS, INC.
PO Box 3077-S
Middletown, NY 10940
PH: 845-343-5151
PH: 800-947-8267
FAX: 845-343-0068
hgitner@hgitner.com
www.hgitner.com

Wholesale-Dealers

GARY POSNER, INC.
1407 Ave. Z, PMB #535
Brooklyn, NY 11235
PH: 800-323-4279
CELL PH: 917-538-8133
FAX: 718-241-2801
garyposnerinc@aol.com
www. garyposnerinc.com
www.gemstamps.com

Wholesale-U.S.

GARY POSNER, INC.
1407 Ave. Z, PMB #535
Brooklyn, NY 11235
PH: 800-323-4279
CELL PH: 917-538-8133
FAX: 718-241-2801
garyposnerinc@aol.com
www. garyposnerinc.com
www.gemstamps.com